Raceform

FLAT ANNUAL FOR 1998

All The 1997 Returns

The BHB's Official Form Book

Complete record of all Flat Racing in Great Britain from November 12th, 1996 to November 8th, 1997

Published by Raceform Ltd,
Compton, Newbury, Berkshire, RG20 6NL
Tel: 01635-578080
Fax: 01635-578101
Editorial: 01635-578643
Web http://www.raceform.co.uk
Email: raceform.co.uk

Printed by BPC Wheatons, Hennick Road,
Exeter, Devon EX2 8RP
01392-420222

Typeset by Raceform

Edited by Ashley Rumney
Production Editor: Steven Clarke

ISBN 1 901100 55 3

£24.00

CONTENTS

How to Read Raceform..vi
Abbreviations and their meanings..xi
Raceform Top Rated..xv
How to use Raceform Ratings...xvi
Official table of Weight-For-Age...xvii
1996 Winter Racing..xix
1997 Racing...1
Index to Meetings...1690
Index to Horses...1691
Statistics...1807
Review of the Season..1809
Record Times..1825
Raceform Standard Times...1835
1997 Speed Figures...1838
Injuries and Suspensions...1861

Raceform, The Official Form Book, is updated weekly. Subscribers receive a binder, together with all the early racing. Weekly sections and a new index are threaded into the binder to keep it up to date.

The data contained in Raceform Annual for 1998 is available in paper form or on computer disk. The disk service contains the same data as Raceform, The Form Book, and operates on any PC within a 'Windows' environment. The database is designed to allow access to the information in a number of different ways, and is extremely quick and easy to use.

Full details of all Raceform services and publications are available from Raceform, Compton, Newbury, Berkshire RG20 6NL.
Tel: 01635 578080 Fax: 01635 578101.

Cover Photo: Alan Johnson
Dashing Blue wins the Napoleons Racing Handicap at York

- FIRST RACE NUMBER OF PREVIOUS MEETING ON THE COURSE
- POST TIME AND OFF TIME
- DISTANCE
- VALUE TO FIRST SIX
- RACE CLASSIFICATIONS
- CONDITIONS OF RACE FROM CLASS A – G
- POSITION OF STALLS
- RACEFORM GOING/GOING ALLOWANCE PER RACE
- THE RACE NUMBER TO WHICH THE INDEX REFERS
- RACEFORM RATING FOR THIS PERFORMANCE
- PREVIOUS RACE NUMBER PLUS FINISHING POSITION
- OFFICIAL HANDICAP RATING
- SPEED FIGURE
- TRAINER, AGE, WEIGHT, BLINKERS, JOCKEY, ALLOWANCE, OVERWEIGHT, DRAW
- TOTAL STARTING PRICE PERCENTAGE
- STEWARDS ENQUIRY AND SUSPENSIONS WHERE APPROPRIATE
- WINNING OWNER, TRAINER LOCATION (IN BRACKETS) AND BREEDER
- RACE TIME, SECONDS ABOVE/BELOW RACEFORM STANDARD TIME
- WEIGHT-FOR-AGE ALLOWANCE
- COMPUTER & TOTE DIVIDENDS
- STARTING PRICE WITH MARKET MOVES WHERE APPROPRIATE

3668-**YORK (L-H) (Good, Good to firm back st)**
Wednesday August 21st
WEATHER: fine & warm WIND: st half against

3688 ASTON UPTHORPE YORKSHIRE OAKS STKS (Gp1) (3-Y.O+ F & M) (Class A)
2-35 (2-37) **1m 3f 195y** £78,815.50 (£28,964.50: £13,732.25: £5,423.75: £1,961.88: £577.12) Stalls: Low GOING minus 0.33 sec per fur (GF)

			SP	RR	SF
2837a³ **Key Change (IRE)** (JOxx, Ireland) **3-8-8** JPMurtagh(1) (a.p: led over 6f out: styd on strly fnl f)	—	1	7/1	116	67
3231² **Papering (IRE) (103)** (LMCumani) **3-8-8** KDarley(6) (hld up: hdwy on ins over 3f out: styd on wl ins fnl f)	1¾	2	8/1	114	65
3231⁵ **Mezzogiorno (108)** (GWragg) **3-8-8** MHills(5) (hld up: effrt & drvn along 3f out: styd on fnl f: nvr able to chal: fin 4th, 3l: plcd 3rd)		3	16/1	109	60
2837a² **Shamadara (IRE)** (AdeRoyerDupre,France) **3-8-8** GMosse(8) (gd sort: hld up: outpcd & lost pl over 5f out: rdn & styd on fnl 2f: fin 5th, nk: plcd 4th)		4	2/1¹	109	60
3231⁴ **Whitewater Affair (105)** (MRStoute) **3-8-8** TQuinn(7) (trckd ldrs: rdn 3f out: sltly hmpd wl over 1f out: one pce: fin 6th, nk: plcd 5th)		5	14/1	108	59
395a² **Russian Snows (IRE)** (SbinSuroor) **4-9-4** LDettori(3) (led 1f: trckd ldrs: hrd drvn 2f out: edged lft & kpt on fnl f: fin 3rd, nk: disq & plcd 6th)		6	11/2³	113	74
2886* **Shemozzle (IRE) (107)** (JHMGosden) **3-8-8** PatEddery(4) (lw: led 7f out: sn hdd: rdn over 2f out: one pce)	1	7	15/2	107	58
1144² **Quota** (HRACecil) **3-8-8** WRyan(2) (led after 1f to 7f out: hung rt over 4f out: wknd over 2f out)	4	8	16/1	102	53
1949a* **Sil Sila (IRE) (115)** (BSmart) **3-8-8** RCochrane(9) (hld up: effrt 4f out: lost pl & eased wl over 2f out: t.o)	24	9	9/2²	69	20

(SP 120.7%) 9 Rn

2m 27.56 (-0.24) CSF £57.76 TOTE £11.50: £2.30 £2.80 £5.10 (£66.40) Trio £333.40 OWNER Lady Clague (CURRABEG) BRED Collinstown Stud Farm Ltd
WEIGHT FOR AGE 3yo-10lb
STEWARDS' ENQUIRY Dettori susp. 30-31/8 & 2-3/9/96 (irresponsible riding).

2837a Key Change (IRE) had it all to do to beat the favourite at levels, but she made sure that this was going to be a true test of stamina, and in the end, the ploy worked a treat (7/1)

3231 Papering (IRE) turned in a very pleasing display at this first attempt at the trip, staying on relentlessly inside the distance. There will be plenty more opportunities coming her way. (8/1)

3231 Mezzogiorno tried to come from behind to deliver a challenge, but could not step up her pace under strong driving and was always being comfortably held. (16/1)

2837a Shamadara (IRE) adopted the wrong tactics on such fast ground, and though she did try to get herself into the action, was fighting a lost cause from the turn into the straight. (2/1)

3231 Whitewater Affair, hard at work and making little impression, was squeezed for room entering the final quarter-mile and always feeling the pace. (14/1)

395a Russian Snows (IRE) produced fresh and well for her first run in this country, pushed the pace and was just beginning to stay on, when she edged left and tightened up a couple of rivals two furlongs out. After finishing third, she was demoted to sixth. In the past, she has found her best form in the autumn. (11/2)

THE NOTE-BOOK COMMENT: ILLUSTRATES IN DEPTH THE PERFORMANCE, AND INDICATES HOW THE HORSE CAN BE PLACED TO FUTURE ADVANTAGE

RACEFORM
The Official Form Book

RACEFORM, THE OFFICIAL FORM BOOK, records comprehensive race details of every domestic race, every major European Group race and every foreign event in which a British-trained runner participated. Extended notes are given to runners, during the turf season, worthy of a mention, including all placed horses and all favourites. Generally speaking, the higher the class of race, the greater the number of runners noted.

MEETING BACK REFERENCE NUMBER is the Raceform number of the last meeting run at the track and is shown to the left of the course name. Abandoned meetings are signified by a †.

THE OFFICIAL GOING, shown at the head of each meeting, is recorded as follows:

Turf:	Hard; Firm; Good to firm; Good; Good to soft; Soft; Heavy.
All-Weather:	Fast; Standard; Slow.

THE WEATHER is shown below to the date.

THE WIND is given as a strength and direction, classified as follows:

Strength:	gale; v.str; str; fresh; mod; slt; almost nil; nil.
Direction:	(half) against; (half) bhd; (half) across.

VISIBILITY is good unless otherwise stated.

RACEFORM GOING, which may differ from the Official Going, now appears against each race to allow for changing conditions of the ground. It takes into account the race times compared with the Raceform Standard Times, the wind and other elements, and is recorded in the following stages:

Turf:	**HD** (Hard); **F** (Firm); **GF** (Good to firm); **G** (Good); **GS** (Good to soft); **S** (Soft); **HY** (Heavy).
All-Weather:	**FST** (Fast); **STD** (Standard); **SLW** (Slow).

THE POSITION OF THE STARTING STALLS is shown against each race, in the form of: High (H), Centre (C) or Low (L). The actual position of the stalls can make a vital difference to a runner's chances and reference should be made to the *Effect of the Draw* summary when assessing a horse's performance.

THE RACE DISTANCE is given for all races, and is accompanied by (straight) for all races run on straight courses and (round) for courses where there is a round track of comparable distance. Tracks which are identified by a specific name i.e. (Rowley) (July) and (Jubilee) are also indicated. On All-Weather courses (Fibresand) or (Equitrack) indicates the nature of the artificial surface on which the race is run.

PRIZE MONEY shows penalty values down to sixth place (where applicable).

Competitive Racing Classifications are shown on a scale from Class A to Class G. All Pattern races are Class A.

Weight-For-Age allowances are given where applicable for mixed-age races.

Race Numbers for Foreign races carry the suffix 'a'.

In The Race Result, the figures to the left of each horse show the race number of its most recent listing in Raceform. A figure in *italics* indicates the previous performance was recorded on an All-Weather course. The superscript figures indicate its finishing position in that race and are coded as follows:

> * - winner;
> **2..40** - finishing positions second to fortieth;
> **b** - brought down; **c** - carried out; **f** - fell; **p** - pulled up;
> **r** - refused (to race); **ro** - ran out; **s** - slipped up; **u** - unseated rider;
> **v** - void race; **w** - withdrawn.

A figure to the left of the *Raceform Note-Book* comment is the last race in which the horse warranted an extended comment.

The Adjusted Official Rating is the figure in **bold type** directly after the horse's name in the race result. This figure indicates the Official BHB rating, at entry, after the following adjustments had been made:

(i) Overweight carried by the rider.
(ii) The number of pounds out of the handicap (if applicable).
(iii) Penalties incurred after the publication of the weights.

However, **no** adjustments have been made for:

(i) Weight-for-age.
(ii) Rider's claims.

The Trainer is shown in brackets for every runner.

The Horse's age is shown immediately before the weight carried.

Weights shown are actual weights carried. A figure next to the weight with ^{ow} is the amount of overweight put up by the jockey, e.g. ^{ow4}.
Allowances are shown between the weight and the jockey name, e.g. **8-10** $^{(3)}$ S. Copp.

Long Handicap Weights for runners allotted a lower-than-minimum weight at entry **(handicaps only)** are shown directly after the breeder of the winning horse in each race, and above the *Note-Book* comments.

Apprentice Allowances The holders of apprentice jockeys' licences under the provisions of Rule 60(iii) are permitted to claim the following allowances in Flat races:

7lb until they have won 20 Flat races run under the Rules of any recognised Turf Authority; thereafter 5lb until they have won 50 such Flat races; thereafter 3lb until they have won 95 such Flat races.
These allowances can be claimed in the Flat races set out below, with the exception of races confined to apprentice jockeys:

(a) All handicap and all selling races.
(b) All other races with guaranteed prize money of not more than £8000.

HEADGEAR is shown after the actual weight carried and expressed as: **b** (blinkers); **v** (visor); **h** (hood); **e** (eyeshield); **c** (eyecover).

THE DRAW for places at the start is shown after each jockey's name in brackets.

THE OFFICIAL DISTANCES between the first six horses are shown on the right-hand side immediately preceding their position at the finish. Distances beyond sixth place may be shown after inspection of race-finish photographs.

STARTING PRICES (SP) appear to the right of the finishing position in the race result. The favourite indicator appears to the right of the Starting Price, ^{1} for the favourite, ^{2} for the second-favourite and ^{3} for third-favourite.

RACEFORM RATINGS (RR), which record the level of performance attained in this race for each horse, are given to the right of the starting price. Reference to the *Raceform Ratings* page should be made for a full description of this feature.

SPEED FIGURES (SF) now appear for every horse that clocks a sufficiently fast time, and appear in the column to the right of the *Raceform Ratings*. The figures are adjusted to 9st, and calculations made for going, wind, and distance behind the winner. To apply Speed Figures to future races, add 1 point for each 1lb below 9st, and deduct 1 point for each 1lb above 9st. The highest resultant figure is best.

WITHDRAWN horses that fail to come under orders after the jockey has weighed out, are included in the index to past racing (with W after the race number); side reference, odds at the time of withdrawal and the reason for withdrawal (if known) are shown in the race comment for that horse.

RULE 4C TATTERSALL'S COMMITTEE RULES ON BETTING STATES:

In the case of bets made at a price on the day of the race before it has been officially notified that a horse has been withdrawn before coming under Starter's Orders or has been declared "not to have started", the liability of a layer against any horse remaining in the race, win or place, will be reduced in accordance with the following scale depending on the odds current against the withdrawn horse at the time of such official notification:

(a) if the current odds are 30/100 or longer odds on by 75p in the £
(b) if shorter odds on than 30/100 up to and including 2/5 by 70p in £
(c) if shorter odds on than 2/5 up to and including 8/15 by 65p in the £

(d) if shorter odds on than 8/15 up to and including 8/13 by 60p in the £
(e) if shorter odds on than 8/13 up to and including 4/5 by 55p in the £
(f) if shorter odds on than 4/5 up to and including 20/21 by 50p in the £
(g) if shorter odds on than 20/21 up to and including 6/5 by 45p in the £
(h) if over 6/5 up to and including 6/4 by 40p in the £
(i) if over 6/4 up to and including 7/4 by 35p in the £
(j) if over 7/4 up to and including 9/4 by 30p in the £
(k) if over 9/4 up to and including 3/1 by 25p in the £
(l) if over 3/1 up to and including 4/1 by 20p in the £
(m) if over 4/1 up to and including 11/2 by 15p in the £
(n) if over 11/2 up to and including 9/1 by 10p in the £
(o) if over 9/1 up to and including 14/1 by 5p in the £
(p) if over 14/1 the liability would be unchanged
(q) in the case of two or more horses being withdrawn, the total deduction shall not exceed 75p in the £

Ante-post bets are not affected and SP bets are also not affected, except in cases where insufficient time arises for a fresh market to be formed, when the above named scale reductions will apply.

STEWARDS' ENQUIRY, except in special circumstances, is included only if it concerns a prize winner. Objections by jockeys and Officials are included.

OFFICIAL EXPLANATIONS are included where the horse is deemed to have run well above or below expectation, unless the explanation is covered by the in-running or note book comment.

RACE TIMES in Great Britain, (except official times which are electronically recorded and shown to 100th of a second), are clocked by Raceform's own watch-holders. Figures in parentheses following the time show the number of seconds slower than the Raceform Standard Time for the course and distance.

RACEFORM STANDARD AND RECORD TIMES were originally compiled from times recorded on good to firm going after adjustments had been made for weights carried above or below a norm of 9st. Times equal to the standard are shown as (equals standard). Times under the standard are preceded by -, for instance, 1.8 seconds under the standard would be shown (-1.8). Record times are displayed either referring to the juvenile record (1.2 under 2y best) or to the overall record (1.2 under best).

STARTING PRICE PERCENTAGE is ranged right below the final finisher and gives the total SP percentage of all runners that competed.

TOTE prices include £1 stake. Dual Forecast dividends are shown in parentheses. The Computer Straight Forecast dividend is preceded by the letters CSF, Computer Tricast is preceded by CT and Tote Trio dividend is preceded by the word Trio. Jackpot, Placepot and Quadpot details appear at the end of the meeting to which they refer.

THE OWNER of the winner is shown immediately below the Tote returns together with the breeder, result of the auction for sellers, and details regarding any claimed horse. Friendly claims are not detailed.

Abbreviations and their meanings

Paddock comments

gd sort	- well made, above average on looks
h.d.w	- has done well, improved in looks
wl grwn	- well grown, has filled to its frame
lengthy	- longer than average for its height
tall	- tall
rangy	- lengthy and tall but in proportion, covers a deal of ground
scope	- scope for physical development
str	- strong, powerful looking
w'like	- workmanlike, ordinary in looks
lt-f	- light-framed, not much substance
neat	- smallish, well put together
leggy	- long legs compared to body
angular	- unfurnished behind the saddle, not filled to frame
unf	- unfurnished in the midriff, not filled to frame
narrow	- not as wide as side appearance would suggest
small	- lacks any physical scope
nt grwn	- not grown
lw	- looked fit and well
bkwd	- backward in condition
t	- tubed
swtg	- sweating
b.(off fore or nr fore)	- bandaged in front
b.hind (off or nr)	- bandaged behind

At the start

stdd s	0	- jockey purposely reins back the horse
dwlt	1	- missed the break and left for a short time
s.s	2	- slow to start, left longer than a horse that dwelt
s.i.s	2	- started on terms but took time to get going
ref to r		- either does not jump off, or travels a few yards and then stops
rel to r		- tries to pull itself up in mid-race

Position in the race

led	- in lead on its own
disp ld	- upsides the leader
w ldr	- almost upsides the leader
w ldrs	- in a line of three or more disputing the lead
prom	- on the heels of the leaders, in the front third of the field
trckd ldr(s)	- just in behind the leaders giving impression that it could lead if asked
chsd ldr	- horse in second place
chsd clr ldrs	- horse heads main body of field behind two clear leaders
chsd ldrs	- horse is in the first four or five but making more of an effort to stay close to the pace than if it were tracking the leaders.
in tch	- close enough to have a chance
hdwy	- making ground on the leader
gd hdwy	- making ground quickly on the leader, could be a deliberate move

sme hdwy	- making some ground but no real impact on the race
stdy hdwy	- gradually making ground
ev ch	- upsides the leaders when the race starts in earnest
rr	- last of main group but not detached
bhd	- detached from the main body of runners
hld up	- restrained as a deliberate tactical move
nt rcvr	- lost all chance after interference, mistake etc.
wknd	- stride shortened as it began to tire
lost tch	- had been in the main body but a gap appeared as it tired
lost pl	- remains in main body of runners but lost several positions quickly

Riding

effrt	- short-lived effort
pushed along	- received urgings with hands only, jockey not using legs
rdn	- received forceful urgings without use of whip, or jockey waving whip without making contact
drvn	- received forceful urgings, jockey putting in a lot of effort and using whip
hrd drvn	- jockey very animated, plenty of kicking, pushing and reminders

Finishing Comments

jst failed	- closing rapidly on the winner and probably would have led a stride after the line
r.o	- jockey's efforts usually involved to produce an increase in pace without finding an appreciable turn of speed
r.o wl	- jockey's efforts usually involved to produce an obvious increase in pace without finding an appreciable turn of speed
unable qckn	- not visibly tiring but does not possess a sufficient change of pace
one pce	- not tiring but does not find a turn of speed, from a position further out than unable qckn
nt r.o	- did not consent to respond to pressure
styd on	- going on well towards the end, utilising stamina
nvr plcd to chal	- never apparently given the chance to make a challenge
nvr able to chal	- unable to produce a challenge without a specific reason
nvr nr to chal	- unable to produce a challenge, normally due to a slow start, stumbling etc.
nrst fin	- nearer to the winner in distance beaten than at any time since the race had begun in earnest
nvr nrr	- nearer to the winner position wise than at any time since the race had begun in earnest
rallied	- responded to pressure to come back with a chance having lost its place
no ex	- unable to sustain its run due to lack of strength or effort from the saddle, enthusiasm etc.
bttr for r	- likely to improve for the run and experience
rn green	- inclined to wander and falter through inexperience
too much to do	- left with too much leeway to make up

Winning Comments

v.easily	- a great deal in hand
easily	- plenty in hand
comf	- something in hand, always holding the others

pushed out	- kept up to its work with hands and heels without jockey resorting to whip or kicking along and wins fairly comfortably
rdn out	- pushed and kicked out to the line
drvn out	- pushed and kicked out to the line, with the whip employed
all out	- nothing to spare, could not have found any more
jst hld on	- holding on to a rapidly diminishing lead, could not have found any more if passed
unchal	- must either make all or a majority of the running and not be challenged from an early stage

Complete list of abbreviations

a - always
a.p - always prominent
abt - about
appr - approaching
awrdd - awarded
b.b.v - broke blood-vessel
b.d - brought down
bdly - badly
bef - before
bhd - behind
bk - back
blkd - baulked
bmpd - bumped
bnd - bend
btn - beaten
bttr - better
c - came
ch - chance
chal - challenged
chsd - chased
circ - circuit
cl - close
clr - clear
comf - comfortably
cpld - coupled
crse - course
ct - caught
dismntd - dismounted
disp - disputed
dist - distance
div - division
drvn - driven
dwlt - dwelt
edgd - edged
effrt - effort
ent - entering
ev ch - every chance
ex - extra
f - furlong
fin - finished
fnd - found
fnl - final
fr - from
gd - good
gng - going
grad - gradually
grnd - ground
hd - head
hdd - headed
hdwy - headway
hld - held
hmpd - hampered
hrd rdn - hard ridden
imp - impression
ins - inside
j.b - jumped badly
jnd - joined
jst - just
kpt - kept
l - length
ld - lead
ldr - leader
lft - left
m - mile
m.n.s - made no show
mde - made
mid div - mid division
n.d - never dangerous
n.g.t - not go through
n.m.r - not much room
nk - neck
no ex - no extra
nr - near
nrr - nearer
nrst fin - nearest finish
nt - not
nvr - never
one pce - one pace
out - from finish
outpcd - outpaced
p.u - pulled up
pce - pace
pl - place
plcd - placed
plld - pulled
press - pressure
prog - progress
prom - prominent
qckly - quickly
qckn - quicken
r - race
racd - raced
rch - reach
rcvr - recover
rdn - ridden
rdr - rider
reard - reared
ref - refused
rn - ran
rnd - round
r.o - ran on
rr - rear
rspnse - response
rt - right
s - start
slt - slight
sme - some
sn - soon
spd - speed
st - straight
stdd - steadied
stdy - steady
styd - stayed
swtchd - switched
swvd - swerved
t.o - tailed off
tch - touch
thrght - throughout
trckd - tracked
u.p - under pressure
w - with
w.r.s - whipped round start
wd - wide
whn - when
wknd - weakened
wl - well
wnr - winner
wnt - went
½-wy - halfway

RACEFORM TOP RATED
THREE-YEAR-OLDS AND UPWARDS OF 1997

Peintre Celebre (USA)	141
Pilsudski (IRE)	140
Singspiel (IRE)	135
Swain (IRE)	135
Desert King	133
Helissio	133
Spinning World	132
Predappio (GB)	132
Oscar Schindler (IRE)	132
First Island (IRE)	131
Bosra Sham (USA)	131
Benny The Dip (USA)	130
Classic Cliche	130
Ali-Royal (IRE)	129
Shantou (USA)	129
Chief Bearhart (CAN)	129
Sandpit (BRA)	128
Air Express (IRE)	128
Starborough (GB)	128
Annus Mirabilis (FR)	128
Loup Sauvage (USA)	128
Persian Punch (IRE)	128
Caitano (GB)	128

RACEFORM TOP RATED
TWO-YEAR-OLDS OF 1997

Xaar	127
Second Empire (IRE)	116
Lend A Hand (GB)	115
Daggers Drawn (USA)	114
Kilimanjaro	114
Charge D'Affaires (GB)	113
Saratoga Springs (CAN)	113
Mudeer	113
Halmahera (IRE)	111
Central Park (IRE)	111
Tamarisk (IRE)	111
Mutamam	111
Lord Kintyre	110
Haami (USA)	110
Zelding (IRE)	109
Bintang (IRE)	109
Docksider (USA)	108
La-Faah (IRE)	108
King Of Kings	107
Alboostan (GB)	107
Teapot Row (IRE)	107
Sideman	106

RACEFORM RATINGS

Raceform Ratings for each horse are listed after the Starting Price and indicate the actual level of performance attained in that race. The figure in the back index represents the BEST public form that Raceform's Handicappers still believe the horse capable of reproducing.

To use the ratings constructively in determining those horses *best-in* in future events, the following procedure should be followed:

(i) In races where all runners are the same age and are set to carry the same weight, no calculations are necessary. The horse with the highest rating is *best-in.*

(ii) In races where all runners are the same age but are set to carry different weights, add one point to the Raceform Rating for every pound less than 10 stone to be carried; deduct one point for every pound more than 10 stone.

For example,

Horse	Age & Weight	Adjustment from 10st	RR base rating	Adjusted rating
Pecan Danish	3-10-1	-1	78	77
Arctic Roll	3-9-13	+1	80	81
Tiramisu	3-9-7	+7	71	78
Crepes Suzette	3-8-11	+17	60	77

Therefore Arctic Roll is top-rated (best-in)

(iii) In races concerning horses of different ages the procedure in example (ii) should again be followed, but reference must also be made to the Official Scale of Weight-For-Age.

For example,
12 furlongs July 20th

Horse	Age & Weight	Adjusted from 10st	RR base rating	Adjusted rating	W-F-A deduct	Final rating
Macca's Cracker	5-10-0	0	90	90	Nil	90
Tone Ales	4-9-9	+5	83	88	Nil	88
Ben O'Winky	3-9-4	+10	85	95	-12	83
Dick the Spuddler	4-8-7	+21	73	94	Nil	94

Therefore Dick the Spuddler is top-rated (best-in)

(A 4-y-o is deemed 12lb less mature than a 5-y-o or older horse on 20th January over 2m. Therefore, the deduction of 12 points is necessary.)

The following symbols are used in conjunction with the ratings:

++ almost certain to prove better
d disappointing (has run well below best recently)
t tentative rating based on race-time
\+ likely to prove better
? form hard to evaluate - rating may prove unreliable

Weight adjusted ratings for every race are published daily in Raceform Private Handicap. For subscription terms please contact the Subscription Department on (01635) 578080.

THE OFFICIAL SCALE OF WEIGHT, AGE & DISTANCE (Flat)

The following scale of weight-for-age should be used only in conjunction with the Official ratings published in this book. Use of any other scale will introduce errors into calculations. The allowances are expressed as the number of pounds that is deemed the average horse in each group falls short of maturity at different dates and distances.

		JAN		FEB		MARCH		APRIL		MAY		JUNE		JULY		AUGUST		SEPT		OCT		NOV		DEC	
Distance Furlongs	Age	1/15	16/31	1/14	15/28	1/15	16/31	1/15	16/30	1/15	16/31	1/15	16/30	1/15	16/31	1/15	16/31	1/15	16/30	1/15	16/31	1/15	16/30	1/15	16/31
5	2	–	–	–	–	–	47	44	41	38	36	34	32	30	28	26	24	22	20	19	18	17	17	16	16
	3	15	15	14	14	13	12	11	10	9	8	7	6	5	4	3	2	1	1	–	–	–	–	–	–
6	2	–	–	–	–	–	–	–	–	44	41	38	36	33	31	28	26	24	22	21	20	19	18	17	17
	3	16	16	15	15	14	13	12	11	10	9	8	7	6	5	4	3	2	2	1	1	–	–	–	–
7	2	–	–	–	–	–	–	–	–	–	–	–	–	38	35	32	30	27	25	23	22	21	20	19	19
	3	18	18	17	17	16	15	14	13	12	11	10	9	8	7	6	5	4	3	2	2	1	1	–	–
8	2	–	–	–	–	–	–	–	–	–	–	–	–	–	–	37	34	31	28	26	24	23	22	21	20
	3	20	20	19	19	18	17	15	14	13	12	11	10	9	8	7	6	5	4	3	3	2	2	1	1
9	3	22	22	21	21	20	19	17	15	14	13	12	11	10	9	8	7	6	5	4	4	3	3	2	2
	4	1	1	–	–	–	–	–	–	–	–	–	–	–	–	–	–	–	–	–	–	–	–	–	–
10	3	23	23	22	22	21	20	19	17	15	14	13	12	11	10	9	8	7	6	5	5	4	4	3	3
	4	2	2	1	1	–	–	–	–	–	–	–	–	–	–	–	–	–	–	–	–	–	–	–	–
11	3	24	24	23	23	22	21	20	19	17	15	14	13	12	11	10	9	8	7	6	6	5	5	4	4
	4	3	3	2	2	1	1	–	–	–	–	–	–	–	–	–	–	–	–	–	–	–	–	–	–
12	3	25	25	24	24	23	22	21	20	19	17	15	14	13	12	11	10	9	8	7	7	6	6	5	5
	4	4	4	3	3	2	2	1	1	–	–	–	–	–	–	–	–	–	–	–	–	–	–	–	–
13	3	26	26	25	25	24	23	22	21	20	19	17	15	14	13	12	11	10	9	8	8	7	7	6	6
	4	5	5	4	4	3	3	2	1	–	–	–	–	–	–	–	–	–	–	–	–	–	–	–	–
14	3	27	27	26	26	25	24	23	22	21	20	19	17	15	14	13	12	11	10	9	9	8	8	7	7
	4	6	6	5	5	4	4	3	2	1	–	–	–	–	–	–	–	–	–	–	–	–	–	–	–
15	3	28	28	27	27	26	25	24	23	22	21	20	19	17	15	14	13	12	11	10	9	8	8	7	7
	4	6	6	5	5	4	4	3	3	2	1	–	–	–	–	–	–	–	–	–	–	–	–	–	–
16	3	29	29	28	28	27	26	25	24	23	22	21	20	19	17	15	14	13	12	11	10	9	9	8	8
	4	7	7	6	6	5	5	4	4	3	2	1	–	–	–	–	–	–	–	–	–	–	–	–	–
18	3	31	31	30	30	29	28	27	26	25	24	23	22	21	20	18	16	14	13	12	11	10	10	9	9
	4	8	8	7	7	6	6	5	5	4	3	2	1	–	–	–	–	–	–	–	–	–	–	–	–
20	3	33	33	32	32	31	30	29	28	27	26	25	24	23	22	20	18	16	14	13	12	11	11	10	10
	4	9	9	8	8	7	7	6	6	5	4	3	2	1	–	–	–	–	–	–	–	–	–	–	–

Raceform

WINTER
RACING 1996

Complete record of Foreign Turf Racing and All-Weather from November 12th to December 31st, 1996

4996-**LINGFIELD** (L-H) (Standard)

Tuesday November 12th

WEATHER: raining WIND: almost nil

5079 PULLMAN FOODS H'CAP (0-70) (I) (3-Y.O+) (Class E)

12-30 (12-31) **1m (Equitrack)** £2,602.40 (£786.20: £382.60: £180.80) Stalls: Low GOING minus 0.48 sec per fur (FST)

				SP	RR	SF
4781*	**Thai Morning (69)** (PWHarris) **3-9-11** GDuffield(3) (hld up: led over 2f out: clr over 1f out: comf)	—	1	5/2[1]	82+	62
3516[7]	**Greatest (70)** (MissGayKelleway) **5-10-0** DHarrison(10) (b: b.hind: a.p: led over 3f out tl over 2f out: unable qckn)	3	2	8/1[3]	77	59
4497[5]	**Barbason (56)** (AMoore) **4-9-0** CandyMorris(8) (b.hind: hdwy over 3f out: hrd rdn over 2f out: r.o one pce)	1¼	3	16/1	61	43
4432[12]	**Sooty Tern (52)** (JMBradley) **9-8-10** LCharnock(4) (led 1f: led 4f out tl over 3f out: wknd over 1f out)	2	4	6/1[2]	53	35
4982[2]	**Ilandra (IRE) (43)** (RAkehurst) **4-8-1** SSanders(5) (rdn thrght: nvr nr to chal)	2	5	6/1[2]	40	22
4900[7]	**Mimosa (63)** (SDow) **3-9-5e** DaneO'Neill(9) (hdwy over 3f out: wknd wl over 1f out)	1¼	6	8/1[3]	57	37
4915[11]	**Czarna (IRE) (65)** (CEBrittain) **5-9-9** MRoberts(2) (prom over 4f)	10	7	10/1	39	21
4829[17]	**Richard House Lad (41)** (RHollinshead) **3-7-4**(7)ow1 RMullen(11) (a bhd)	1¾	8	16/1	12	—
4107[12]	**Medland (IRE) (45)** (BJMcMath) **6-8-3** DBiggs(1) (b: lw: led 7f out to 4f out: wknd over 3f out)	1¾	9	14/1	12	—
3831[5]	**Wingnut (IRE) (40)** (RIngram) **3-7-7**(3) DWright(7) (s.s: a wl bhd)	3½	10	16/1	—	—
3661[13]	**Hong Kong Dollar (38)** (BAPearce) **4-7-10v**[1] JQuinn(6) (prom over 5f)	7	11	50/1	—	—

(SP 114.7%) **11 Rn**

1m 38.08 (0.68) CSF £20.83 CT £242.90 TOTE £3.40: £1.40 £2.20 £3.70 (£36.10) Trio £85.70 OWNER The Thai Connection (BERKHAMSTED) BRED R. G. Percival

LONG HANDICAP Richard House Lad 7-6 Wingnut (IRE) 7-7 Hong Kong Dollar 7-9

WEIGHT FOR AGE 3yo-2lb

5080 NEWMARKET MAIDEN STKS (2-Y.O) (Class D)

1-00 (1-01) **5f (Equitrack)** £3,318.65 (£1,005.20: £491.10: £234.05) Stalls: Low GOING minus 0.48 sec per fur (FST)

				SP	RR	SF
4762[2]	**Hyde Park (IRE)** (SirMarkPrescott) **2-9-0** GDuffield(7) (chsd ldr: led over 2f out: all out)	—	1	6/4[1]	71	28
4796[3]	**Lady Shirl (IRE)** (PMitchell) **2-8-9** JQuinn(6) (a.p: chsd wnr over 1f out: hrd rdn & ev ch ins fnl f: r.o wl)	nk	2	14/1	65	22
4593[3]	**Splashed** (TDBarron) **2-8-9** DeanMcKeown(4) (a.p: rdn over 3f out: unable qckn)	4	3	11/2[3]	52	9
4782[13]	**Rock To The Top (IRE) (47)** (JJSheehan) **2-9-0** AMorris(10) (lw: outpcd: hdwy fnl f: r.o)	nk	4	100/1	56	13
5005[3]	**Enchantica (61)** (JBerry) **2-8-9v**[1] GCarter(1) (led over 2f: wknd over 1f out)	2	5	3/1[2]	45	2
4889[10]	**Snow Eagle (IRE)** (RHannon) **2-8-9** DaneO'Neill(2) (s.s: nvr nr to chal)	1¼	6	16/1	41	—
4786[11]	**College Princess** (CADwyer) **2-8-2**(7) JoHunnam(5) (bhd fnl 2f)	2	7	66/1	35	—
4593[5]	**Come Dancing** (MJohnston) **2-8-9** MRoberts(3) (a bhd)	5	8	12/1	19	—
3336[W]	**Miss Darling** (JAkehurst) **2-8-9** SSanders(9) (bhd fnl 2f)	1½	9	16/1	14	—
4887[12]	**Trevor Mitchell** (JJBridger) **2-8-2**(7) RMullen(8) (bhd fnl 2f)	nk	10	100/1	13	—

(SP 110.0%) **10 Rn**

59.69 secs (1.49) CSF £19.61 TOTE £2.30: £1.30 £3.80 £1.70 (£8.10) Trio £18.30 OWNER Mr Neil Greig (NEWMARKET) BRED Lodge Park Stud

IN-FOCUS: This field consisted of little rabbits with no scope whatsoever.

5081 MIDDLEHAM LIMITED STKS (0-55) (I) (3-Y.O+) (Class F)

1-30 (1-31) **1m 2f (Equitrack)** £2,048.00 (£573.00: £278.00) Stalls: High GOING minus 0.48 sec per fur (FST)

				SP	RR	SF
4894[7]	**Awesome Power (52)** (JWHills) **10-9-2** AClark(7) (hdwy over 4f out: led wl over 1f out: pushed out)	—	1	2/1[1]	58	36
4898[10]	**Sweet Amoret (46)** (PHowling) **3-8-9** FNorton(4) (b.off hind: lw:a.p: led 3f out tl wl over 1f out: unable qckn)	1½	2	14/1	53	27
4967[16]	**Bellateena (38)** (HJCollingridge) **4-8-13** JQuinn(3) (a.p: led 5f out to 3f out: one pce)	2½	3	11/1	49	27
4480[7]	**Rose Tint (IRE) (50)** (LordHuntingdon) **3-8-9** DHarrison(8) (rdn & no hdwy fnl 3f)	3½	4	4/1[2]	43	17
3860[8]	**Kirov Protege (IRE) (44)** (MrsLCJewell) **4-9-2** DaneO'Neill(5) (nvr nr to chal)	7	5	33/1	35	13
4900[W]	**Premier League (IRE) (53)** (JELong) **6-9-2** LeesaLong(1) (led 5f)	1½	6	9/2[3]	32	10
	Kissavos (36) (BJMeehan) **10-8-9e**(7) GHannon(2) (b.hind: bhd fnl 5f)	¾	7	16/1	31	9
	Kedwick (IRE) (54) (PRHedger) **7-9-2** AMcGlone(9) (b: b.hind: s.s: a bhd)	3	8	15/2	26	4
663[11]	**Be Satisfied (55)** (AMoore) **3-8-12** SSanders(6) (b.hind: bit bkwd: prom over 6f)	19	9	20/1	—	—

(SP 111.9%) **9 Rn**

2m 7.54 (3.24) CSF £25.72 TOTE £2.80: £1.20 £5.70 £1.50 (£27.90) Trio £41.50 OWNER Mr Garrett Freyne (LAMBOURN) BRED G. J. Freyne

WEIGHT FOR AGE 3yo-4lb

IN-FOCUS: This race was no better than selling class.

5082 PULLMAN FOODS H'CAP (0-70) (II) (3-Y.O+) (Class E)

2-00 (2-02) **1m (Equitrack)** £2,588.75 (£782.00: £380.50: £179.75) Stalls: Low GOING minus 0.48 sec per fur (FST)

				SP	RR	SF
4989[3]	**Zahran (IRE) (39)** (JMBradley) **5-7-11** LCharnock(6) (b: lw: a.p: led over 3f out: rdn out)	—	1	3/1[1]	50	32
4820[21]	**Hurtleberry (IRE) (65)** (LordHuntingdon) **3-9-7** DHarrison(9) (hdwy over 3f out: chsd wnr wl over 1f out: r.o)	½	2	5/1[3]	75	55
4915[5]	**Allinson's Mate (IRE) (60)** (TDBarron) **8-8-11b**(7) VictoriaAppleby(4) (lost pl over 3f out: rallied over 1f out: r.o)	3	3	7/2[2]	64	46
4921[6]	**Mono Lady (IRE) (55)** (DHaydnJones) **3-8-11** MFenton(3) (led over 4f: wknd wl over 1f out)	4	4	10/1	51	31
4921[9]	**Queen's Insignia (USA) (60)** (PFICole) **3-9-2** CRutter(11) (hdwy over 3f out: wknd over 2f out)	2½	5	7/1	51	31
4860[11]	**Fancy Design (IRE) (42)** (PMitchell) **3-7-12** JQuinn(10) (b.hind: hdwy over 3f out: sn wknd)	1¾	6	20/1	30	10
1460[9]	**Private Fixture (IRE) (50)** (DMarks) **5-8-8** GDuffield(2) (prom 4f)	2½	7	33/1	33	15
3698[12]	**Forgotten Dancer (IRE) (42)** (RIngram) **5-7-11**(3) DWright(7) (b: b.hind: a bhd)	1¾	8	25/1	21	3
4901[16]	**Show Faith (IRE) (68)** (RHannon) **6-9-12** DaneO'Neill(5) (lw: prom 5f)	½	9	10/1	46	28
·	**Norfolk Glory (38)** (DJGMurraySmith) **4-7-10** NAdams(8) (hdwy over 3f out: sn wknd)	8	10	33/1	—	—
4981[11]	**Incatinka (53)** (JLSpearing) **3-8-9b**[1] SDrowne(1) (prom over 4f)	19	11	33/1	—	—

(SP 112.0%) **11 Rn**

1m 38.42 (1.02) CSF £16.46 CT £48.89 TOTE £2.90: £1.60 £2.10 £1.80 (£11.80) Trio £6.00 OWNER Mr Smith (CHEPSTOW) BRED S.Niarchos

WEIGHT FOR AGE 3yo-2lb

5083 WANTAGE NURSERY H'CAP (0-85) (2-Y.O) (Class E)

2-30 (2-32) **6f (Equitrack)** £2,954.70 (£894.60: £436.80: £207.90) Stalls: High GOING minus 0.48 sec per fur (FST)

Form	Horse	Dist	Pos	SP	RR	SF
4715[15]	**Seretse's Nephew (53)** (SCWilliams) **2-7-7**(3) DWright(9) (a.p: led over 1f out: rdn out)	—	1	16/1	49	3
4803[12]	**Mon Bruce (75)** (WRMuir) **2-9-1**(3) FLynch(1) (lw: dwlt: hdwy over 3f out: rdn over 2f out: r.o wl ins fnl f)	¾	2	10/1	69	23
4786[7]	**Peter Perfect (58)** (GLewis) **2-8-1b[1]** JQuinn(3) (hld up: ev ch 1f out: unable qckn)	1¼	3	13/2[3]	49	3
4903[6]	**Soda (65)** (TDBarron) **2-8-8** DeanMcKeown(10) (s.s: hdwy over 1f out: nvr nrr)	5	4	9/1	42	—
4867[8]	**Barresbo (62)** (CWFairhurst) **2-8-0**(5) PFessey(4) (lost pl over 3f out: r.o one pce fnl 2f)	1	5	20/1	37	—
4976[2]	**Cee-N-K (IRE) (77)** (MJohnston) **2-9-6** MRoberts(6) (lw: a.p: led 3f out to 2f out: ev ch over 1f out: sn wknd)	¾	6	11/4[1]	50	4
4999[4]	**Suite Factors (66)** (KRBurke) **2-8-9v** SSanders(8) (led 3f: led 2f out tl over 1f out: sn wknd)	s.h	7	9/1	39	—
4586[4]	**Masterstroke (69)** (BJMeehan) **2-8-12** MTebbutt(2) (a.p: ev ch over 1f out: sn wknd)	¾	8	9/1	40	—
4787[9]	**Mystery (55)** (SDow) **2-7-5e**(7) RMullen(7) (lw: bhd fnl 5f)	hd	9	33/1	25	—
4878[8]	**Aegean Sound (78)** (RHannon) **2-9-7** DaneO'Neill(5) (a bhd)	s.h	10	6/1[2]	48	2
4902[8]	**Royal Emblem (58)** (AGFoster) **2-8-1**ow1 TSprake(11) (hld up: rdn over 3f out: wknd over 2f out)	½	11	14/1	27	—

(SP 113.6%) **11 Rn**

1m 13.34 (2.24) CSF £143.98 CT £1,067.47 TOTE £38.80: £5.20 £2.20 £1.80 (£160.40) Trio £220.20 OWNER Mr J. W. Lovitt (NEWMARKET) BRED P. J. C. Simmonite

LONG HANDICAP Seretse's Nephew 7-9

OFFICIAL EXPLANATION Cee-N-K (IRE): had coughed a few times after the race.

5084 LAMBOURN H'CAP (0-65) (3-Y.O+) (Class F)

3-00 (3-04) **2m (Equitrack)** £2,398.00 (£673.00: £328.00) Stalls: High GOING minus 0.48 sec per fur (FST)

Form	Horse	Dist	Pos	SP	RR	SF
4252[9]	**Guest Alliance (IRE) (55)** (AMoore) **4-9-13** CandyMorris(13) (b.hind: hdwy over 5f out: led over 1f out: r.o wl)	—	1	10/1[3]	69	49
4832[6]	**Coleridge (56)** (JJSheehan) **8-10-0b** AClark(7) (s.s: hdwy 13f out: lost pl over 4f out: rallied over 1f out: r.o)	3	2	6/1[2]	67	47
4892[2]	**Matthias Mystique (55)** (MissBSanders) **3-9-4** SSanders(14) (hld up: led over 2f out tl over 1f out: unable qckn)	s.h	3	4/1[1]	66	37
4892[3]	**Coh Sho No (53)** (SDow) **3-9-2e** DaneO'Neill(3) (rdn over 3f out: hdwy 2f out: r.o one pce)	2	4	6/1[2]	62	33
5008[14]	**Platinum Plus (45)** (CADwyer) **4-9-3** JStack(8) (b: lw: a.p: led over 3f out tl over 2f out: one pce)	¾	5	25/1	53	33
4832[9]	**Broughtons Formula (50)** (WJMusson) **6-9-8b** DRMcCabe(2) (lw: hdwy over 3f out: nvr nrr)	2½	6	4/1[1]	56	36
3104*	**Brighter Byfaah (IRE) (48)** (NAGraham) **3-8-11** MRoberts(6) (lost pl 9f out: no hdwy fnl 3f)	¾	7	6/1[2]	53	24
3466[6]	**Bursul Lady (33)** (MissBSanders) **3-7-10** JQuinn(9) (led over 4f: led over 5f out tl over 3f out: sn wknd)	4	8	66/1	34	5
4821[13]	**Mull House (44)** (GPEnright) **9-9-2v[1]** NAdams(12) (b: prom over 13f)	3½	9	33/1	41	21
1444[9]	**Ela-Ment (IRE) (35)** (BAPearce) **4-8-7** DeanMcKeown(1) (b: a bhd)	6	10	66/1	26	6
4252[13]	**Trapper Norman (32)** (RIngram) **4-8-4** AMcGlone(11) (hdwy to ld over 11f out: hdd over 5f out: sn wknd)	3½	11	66/1	20	—
	Sleeptite (FR) (54) (WGMTurner) **6-9-5**(7) DMcGaffin(5) (b: a bhd)	20	12	6/1[2]	22	2
4815[P]	**Quillwork (USA) (55)** (JPearce) **4-9-13** MWigham(4) (bhd fnl 14f)	3	13	25/1	20	—
4703[17]	**Haddit (35)** (AGNewcombe) **3-7-12**ow2 FNorton(10) (lw: prom 6f)	7	14	50/1	—	—

(SP 123.3%) **14 Rn**

3m 26.8 (5.80) CSF £65.49 CT £260.67 TOTE £15.80: £3.90 £2.30 £2.20 (£35.10) Trio £82.20 OWNER Ballard (1834) Ltd (BRIGHTON) BRED R. Kennedy

LONG HANDICAP Haddit 7-8

WEIGHT FOR AGE 3yo-9lb

5085 EPSOM MAIDEN STKS (3-Y.O) (Class D)

3-30 (3-33) **7f (Equitrack)** £3,566.25 (£1,080.00: £527.50: £251.25) Stalls: High GOING minus 0.48 sec per fur (FST)

Form	Horse	Dist	Pos	SP	RR	SF
4865[5]	**Gad Yakoun (67)** (MGMeagher) **3-9-0** JQuinn(3) (lw: hld up: led 2f out: r.o wl)	—	1	9/4[2]	75	32
4824[8]	**Mazurek** (PWChapple-Hyam) **3-9-0** DHarrison(2) (rdn over 4f out: lost pl over 2f out: rallied over 1f out: r.o)	1¾	2	3/1[3]	71	28
4997[2]	**Woodbury Lad (USA) (80)** (WRMuir) **3-9-0b[1]** DaneO'Neill(7) (b: lw: led 5f: wknd over 1f out)	6	3	Evens[1]	57	14
4785[13]	**Veronica Franco (43)** (BAPearce) **3-8-9b[1]** SSanders(6) (prom 4f)	3½	4	33/1	44	1
5001[7]	**Madison's Touch** (RMFlower) **3-8-9** SDrowne(5) (a bhd)	6	5	50/1	31	—
4997[8]	**First Gallery** (RMFlower) **3-8-9** DBiggs(4) (bhd fnl 5f)	15	6	50/1	—	—
2197[17]	**Wey River Mist** (JJBridger) **3-8-2**(7) RMullen(8) (a bhd)	24	7	50/1	—	—

(SP 114.6%) **7 Rn**

1m 26.23 (1.83) CSF £9.18 TOTE £3.70: £2.10 £2.30 (£4.80) OWNER Mr M. R. Johnson (ORMSKIRK) BRED Sheikh Ahmed Bin Rashid Al Maktoum

5086 MIDDLEHAM LIMITED STKS (0-55) (II) (3-Y.O+) (Class F)

4-00 (4-00) **1m 2f (Equitrack)** £2,048.00 (£573.00: £278.00) Stalls: High GOING minus 0.48 sec per fur (FST)

Form	Horse	Dist	Pos	SP	RR	SF
4900[4]	**Double Rush (IRE) (53)** (TGMills) **4-9-6** SSanders(7) (lw: stdy hdwy over 3f out: led 2f out: qcknd over 1f out: comf)	—	1	5/6[1]	65+	46
4573[4]	**Eastleigh (43)** (RHollinshead) **7-8-13**(3) FLynch(8) (a.p: rdn over 3f out: r.o one pce fnl 2f)	6	2	9/1	51	32
1893[15]	**Komodo (USA) (38)** (JELong) **4-8-9**(7) TField(2) (b: a.p: led over 3f out to 2f out: one pce)	2	3	33/1	48	29
4496[9]	**Smile Forever (USA) (54)** (MissGayKelleway) **3-8-9** DaneO'Neill(6) (b: b.hind: lw: rdn over 4f out: hdwy 2f out: nvr nrr)	2	4	6/1[3]	42	19
4497[3]	**Racing Telegraph (32)** (CNAllen) **6-8-9**(7) RMullen(3) (led over 6f)	3	5	16/1	40	21
353[11]	**Dia Georgy (35)** (CADwyer) **5-9-2** MWigham(5) (b: prom 5f)	9	6	20/1	26	7
4692[10]	**Chalky Dancer (32)** (HJCollingridge) **4-9-2** JQuinn(4) (hld up: rdn over 3f out: wknd over 2f out)	¾	7	20/1	25	6
*4986**	**No Submission (USA) (55)** (DWChapman) **10-9-4v** ACulhane(1) (a wl bhd)	10	8	100/30[2]	11	—

(SP 120.3%) **8 Rn**

2m 6.67 (2.37) CSF £9.45 TOTE £1.90: £1.00 £1.80 £9.50 (£7.30) OWNER Mr Tony Murray (EPSOM) BRED Dermot Finnegan

WEIGHT FOR AGE 3yo-4lb

T/Jkpt: £10,105.80 (0.09 Tckts); £12,952.52 to Worcester 13/11/96. T/Plpt: £200.30 (51.45 Tckts). T/Qdpt: £52.50 (16.22 Tckts). AK

5079-**LINGFIELD** (L-H) (Standard)
Thursday November 14th
WEATHER: sunny WIND: nil

5087 E.B.F. FAUCETS GROHE AQUA WATER MANAGEMENT CONTROL MAIDEN STKS (I) (2-Y.O) (Class D)
12-10 (12-11) **1m (Equitrack)** £2,933.85 (£886.80: £431.90: £204.45) Stalls: High GOING minus 0.49 sec per fur (FST)

				SP	RR	SF
4914[10]	**Miracle Kid (USA)** (JHMGosden) **2-9-0** WRyan(5) (mde virtually all: drvn out)	—	**1**	11/4[1]	75	34
4897[4]	**Protocol (IRE)** (JWHills) **2-9-0** DHolland(2) (a.p: chsd wnr fnl 2f: hrd rdn & ev ch ins fnl f: r.o)	nk	**2**	11/4[1]	74	33
5033[15]	**Chief Predator (USA)** (RHannon) **2-9-0** DaneO'Neill(9) (lw: a.p: rdn over 2f out: r.o one pce fnl f)	2½	**3**	33/1	69	28
4608[13]	**Old Colony** (PFICole) **2-8-2**(7) JBosley(1) (no hdwy fnl 3f)	8	**4**	10/1	48	7
4830[12]	**The Roundsills** (RFJohnsonHoughton) **2-9-0** AMcGlone(3) (hld up: rdn 4f out: wknd over 2f out)	6	**5**	7/1[2]	41	—
3964[6]	**Alimerjam (55)** (JWhite) **2-8-9** SDrowne(8) (bhd fnl 3f)	nk	**6**	33/1	36	—
4891[12]	**Oliver (IRE)** (RWArmstrong) **2-9-0** GCarter(6) (lw: s.i.s: a wl bhd)	¾	**7**	8/1[3]	39	—
4720[13]	**Oaken Wood (IRE)** (NACallaghan) **2-9-0** SWhitworth(7) (a bhd)	hd	**8**	25/1	39	—
4861[14]	**Dear Drue** (CEBrittain) **2-8-9** MRoberts(4) (prom over 3f)	5	**9**	12/1	24	—
				(SP 103.5%)		**9 Rn**

1m 39.73 (2.33) CSF £8.99 TOTE £3.70: £1.10 £1.10 £6.30 (£2.30) Trio £13.60 OWNER Mr Louis Lo (NEWMARKET) BRED Sally Nims

5088 FAUCETS GROHE WATER TECHNOLOGY H'CAP (0-70) (I) (3-Y.O+) (Class E)
12-40 (12-40) **1m 2f (Equitrack)** £2,547.80 (£769.40: £374.20: £176.60) Stalls: Low GOING minus 0.49 sec per fur (FST)

				SP	RR	SF
4598[12]	**Ambassadori (USA) (50)** (CEBrittain) **3-8-6** MRoberts(5) (mde all: clr 2f out: r.o wl)	—	**1**	7/1	62	40
4785[10]	**Rowlandsons Charm (IRE) (58)** (MissBSanders) **3-9-0v** SSanders(4) (lw: chsd wnr 9f out: rdn 4f out: unable qckn fnl 3f)	5	**2**	6/1[2]	62	40
3627[11]	**Philistar (69)** (JMPEustace) **3-9-11** TSprake(2) (hdwy 4f out: rdn over 3f out: r.o one pce fnl f)	nk	**3**	5/1[1]	73	51
3608[4]	**Mujtahida (IRE) (51)** (RWArmstrong) **3-8-7** GCarter(3) (hld up: rdn over 3f out: r.o one pce fnl f)	½	**4**	10/1	54	32
1102[13]	**Tribal Peace (IRE) (67)** (BGubby) **4-9-13** JStack(6) (a.p: rdn over 4f out: 4th & btn whn nt clr run 2f out)	3½	**5**	10/1	64	46
4769[19]	**Blaze of Song (67)** (RHannon) **4-9-13** DaneO'Neill(8) (b: hld up: rdn 4f out: wknd 3f out)	8	**6**	13/2[3]	51	33
4898[8]	**Alakhluki (40)** (GLewis) **3-7-10** NAdams(7) (bhd fnl 5f: lame)	4	**7**	5/1[1]	18	—
1996[3]	**Errant (65)** (DJSCosgrove) **4-9-11** JQuinn(1) (b: bit bkwd: bhd fnl 4f)	3	**8**	5/1[1]	38	20
				(SP 108.3%)		**8 Rn**

2m 5.69 (1.39) CSF £41.73 CT £183.94 TOTE £5.80: £3.20 £1.90 £2.10 (£11.70) OWNER Mr C. J. Rusbridge (NEWMARKET) BRED Donald MacRae
LONG HANDICAP Alakhluki 7-8
WEIGHT FOR AGE 3yo-4lb
OFFICIAL EXPLANATION Alakhluki: was lame.

5089 FAUCETS GROHEDAL WASHROOM & FLUSHING EQUIPMENT APPRENTICE H'CAP (0-75) (3-Y.O+) (Class G)
1-10 (1-12) **7f (Equitrack)** £2,221.00 (£631.00: £313.00) Stalls: Low GOING minus 0.49 sec per fur (FST)

				SP	RR	SF
*5001**	**Smithereens (67)** (PTWalwyn) **3-9-2**(5) 7x SCopp(5) (lw: mde all: clr over 2f out: hrd rdn over 1f out: r.o)	—	**1**	11/2[1]	72	46
5055[3]	**Statistician (60)** (JohnBerry) **4-8-8b**(7)ow1 AmyQuirk(6) (a.p: rdn fnl f: r.o)	1¼	**2**	10/1[3]	62	36
5010[12]	**Shontaine (60)** (MJohnston) **3-8-9**(5) KSked(11) (outpcd: gd hdwy over 1f out: r.o wl ins fnl f)	½	**3**	16/1	61	35
*4997**	**Lancashire Legend (67)** (SDow) **3-9-7e** 7x DaneO'Neill(1) (hld up: rdn over 2f out: unable qckn)	½	**4**	10/1[3]	67	41
4571[6]	**Speedy Classic (USA) (72)** (MJHeaton-Ellis) **7-9-13** SDrowne(7) (a.p: rdn 3f out: one pce)	¾	**5**	11/2[1]	70	45
5002[3]	**Perilous Plight (65)** (MrsLStubbs) **5-9-3**(3) PFessey(2) (b.hind: lw: hdwy over 1f out: nvr nrr)	3	**6**	6/1[2]	56	31
4256[7]	**Dark Menace (46)** (EAWheeler) **4-8-1** DRMcCabe(3) (nvr nr to chal)	s.h	**7**	25/1	37	12
4689[13]	**Faith Alone (65)** (CFWall) **3-8-12**(7) PClarke(9) (b: outpcd: nvr nrr)	nk	**8**	14/1	56	30
4915[12]	**Don Pepe (62)** (RBoss) **5-8-12**(5) RMullen(14) (outpcd: hdwy on ins wl over 1f out: sn wknd)	1¼	**9**	12/1	50	25
4784[2]	**Scathebury (54)** (KRBurke) **3-8-1v**(7) EmilyJoyce(12) (hdwy over 3f out: wknd over 2f out)	2½	**10**	14/1	36	10
4511[15]	**Mr Cube (IRE) (55)** (JMBradley) **6-8-7b**(3) SophieMitchell(8) (lw: a bhd)	¾	**11**	16/1	35	10
4428[4]	**Sapphire Son (IRE) (48)** (PCClarke) **4-7-10**(7)ow2 TField(10) (prom over 2f)	nk	**12**	14/1	28	1
4979[3]	**No Monkey Nuts (65)** (JBerry) **3-9-0**(5) IonaWands(4) (lw: bhd fnl 3f)	s.h	**13**	12/1	44	18
4996[10]	**Distant Dynasty (49)** (BAPearce) **6-7-11**(7) DSalt(13) (prom 4f)	5	**14**	33/1	17	—
				(SP 117.2%)		**14 Rn**

1m 25.48 (1.08) CSF £53.19 CT £777.64 TOTE £6.40: £1.60 £5.40 £6.20 (£67.50) Trio £153.20 OWNER Major & Mrs Kennard and Partners (LAMBOURN) BRED Mrs R. B. Kennard
WEIGHT FOR AGE 3yo-1lb
OFFICIAL EXPLANATION Sapphire Son (IRE): was struck into.

5090 E.B.F. FAUCETS GROHE AQUA WATER MANAGEMENT CONTROL MAIDEN STKS (II) (2-Y.O) (Class D)
1-40 (1-41) **1m (Equitrack)** £2,918.90 (£882.20: £429.60: £203.30) Stalls: High GOING minus 0.49 sec per fur (FST)

				SP	RR	SF
	Hayes Way (IRE) (TGMills) **2-9-0** SSanders(9) (b.hind: w'like: chsd ldr: led over 2f out: pushed out)	—	**1**	10/1	78	43
4818[W]	**Premier** (MJohnston) **2-9-0** DeanMcKeown(1) (led over 5f: unable qckn)	2½	**2**	6/4[1]	73	38
4570[10]	**Lochlass (IRE)** (SPCWoods) **2-8-9** DBiggs(2) (a.p: rdn over 2f out: one pce)	2½	**3**	16/1	63	28
4879[7]	**Serenade (IRE) (62)** (MJHaynes) **2-9-0** GDuffield(6) (b: b.hind: lost pl over 6f out: r.o one pce fnl 2f)	6	**4**	20/1	56	21
4884[9]	**Freedom Chance (IRE)** (JWHills) **2-9-0** DHolland(7) (lw: s.i.s: wl bhd 4f: nvr nr to chal)	hd	**5**	14/1	56	21
4825[17]	**Purchasing Power (IRE)** (NACallaghan) **2-9-0** SWhitworth(5) (prom 5f)	½	**6**	6/1[3]	55	20
4118[9]	**Palisander (IRE) (74)** (SDow) **2-9-0e** DaneO'Neill(8) (lw: prom 5f)	½	**7**	6/1[3]	54	19
4754[7]	**Il Principe (IRE)** (JohnBerry) **2-9-0** TWilliams(4) (bit bkwd: prom 3f)	20	**8**	50/1	14	—
4817[10]	**Macaroni Beach** (CEBrittain) **2-8-9** MRoberts(3) (s.s: a wl bhd)	3½	**9**	11/2[2]	2	—
				(SP 112.3%)		**9 Rn**

1m 38.88 (1.48) CSF £23.74 TOTE £6.10: £2.20 £1.10 £6.70 (£11.10) Trio £123.70 OWNER Mr Alan Ward (EPSOM) BRED L. K. McCreery

5091 FAUCETS GROHEART PERFECT WATER FITTINGS CONDITIONS STKS (3-Y.O+) (Class D)

2-10 (2-10) **1m 4f (Equitrack)** £3,485.00 (£1,055.00: £515.00: £245.00) Stalls: Low GOING minus 0.49 sec per fur (FST)

				SP	RR	SF
4615^{9}	**Steamroller Stanly (74)** (CACyzer) **3-8-10** GCarter(2) (a.p: rdn over 4f out: led 2f out: clr over 1f out: r.o wl)	—	1	14/1	90	50
4487^{8}	**Polar Champ (75)** (SPCWoods) **3-9-1b^{1}** WRyan(9) (led 10f: unable qckn)	3½	2	8/1	90	50
4675^{12}	**More Than You Know (IRE) (84)** (KRBurke) **3-8-5** JQuinn(4) (lw: hdwy over 3f out: rdn & one pce)	2½	3	20/1	77	37
4919^{12}	**Prince Kinsky (77)** (LordHuntingdon) **3-8-13** DHarrison(6) (lw: hld up: rdn over 6f out: wknd 4f out)	7	4	$7/1^{3}$	76	36
2002^{7}	**Opera Buff (IRE) (87)** (MissGayKelleway) **5-9-2** SSanders(8) (b: b.hind: stdy hdwy 7f out: rdn over 3f out: sn wknd)	5	5	$Evens^{1}$	66	32
4998^{*}	**Persian Conquest (IRE) (67)** (RIngram) **4-9-2b** AMcGlone(1) (w ldr over 7f)	1¾	6	14/1	64	30
4611^{*}	**Smilin N Wishin (USA) (80)** (PWChapple-Hyam) **3-8-10** GDuffield(7) (lw: prom over 8f)	2	7	$7/2^{2}$	61	21
3656^{13}	**Bigwig (IRE)** (AMoore) **3-8-10** CandyMorris(5) (b.hind: bit bkwd: a bhd)	18	8	100/1	37	—
5035^{5}	**Patiala (IRE)** (RWArmstrong) **3-8-5** JStack(3) (lw: bhd fnl 9f)	2½	9	33/1	29	—

(SP 117.9%) **9 Rn**

2m 30.68 (0.68) CSF £109.36 TOTE £24.70: £6.00 £3.60 £8.00 (£59.60) Trio £198.20 OWNER Mr R. M. Cyzer (HORSHAM) BRED R. D. Hubbard

WEIGHT FOR AGE 3yo-6lb

5092 FAUCETS FOR GROHE FROM STOCK WHEN YOU NEED IT CLAIMING STKS (2-Y.O) (Class F)

2-40 (2-43) **6f (Equitrack)** £2,588.40 (£727.40: £355.20) Stalls: Low GOING minus 0.49 sec per fur (FST)

				SP	RR	SF
4777^{2}	**Just Loui (69)** (WGMTurner) **2-8-9** TSprake(3) (mde all: clr over 3f out: rn wd bnd wl over 1f out: rdn out)	—	1	$7/2^{1}$	71	15
5061^{4}	**Silent Valley (48)** (BJMeehan) **2-7-10b** JQuinn(2) (s.s: outpcd: hdwy over 1f out: r.o)	5	2	16/1	45	—
5083^{8}	**Masterstroke (69)** (BJMeehan) **2-9-3** MTebbutt(7) (outpcd: hdwy over 2f out: unable qckn)	2½	3	11/1	59	3
4495^{15}	**Misty Cay (IRE) (64)** (SDow) **2-8-6e** SSanders(6) (outpcd: nvr nrr)	¾	4	12/1	46	—
4787^{3}	**Jilly Woo (51)** (DRCElsworth) **2-8-4b**ow2 DaneO'Neill(4) (outpcd: nvr nrr)	1½	5	$9/2^{2}$	40	—
4796^{7}	**Magyar Titok (IRE) (51)** (BobJones) **2-8-9** FNorton(9) (a.p: rdn 3f out: wknd wl over 1f out)	2	6	16/1	40	—
	She's Electric (JJBridger) **2-7-7**(7) RMullen(1) (unf: lw: bhd fnl 5f)	½	7	50/1	29	—
4999^{5}	**Come Too Mamma's (65)** (JBerry) **2-8-1**(5) PFessey(8) (b.hind: prom over 3f)	3	8	$6/1^{3}$	27	—
4966^{7}	**Last Chance (70)** (CNAllen) **2-8-11** GCarter(5) (lw: chsd wnr over 2f)	1½	9	$7/2^{1}$	28	—

(SP 106.7%) **9 Rn**

1m 13.28 (2.18) CSF £45.19 TOTE £3.60: £1.50 £2.40 £2.30 (£23.90) Trio £103.50 OWNER Mr A. Poole (SHERBORNE) BRED M. A. Poole

5093 FAUCETS GROHETEC PULSOMAT SURF RATING RELATED MAIDEN STKS (0-65) (3-Y.O+) (Class F)

3-10 (3-13) **6f (Equitrack)** £2,600.30 (£730.80: £356.90) Stalls: Low GOING minus 0.49 sec per fur (FST)

				SP	RR	SF
4983^{3}	**Madrina (62)** (JBerry) **3-8-6**(5) PFessey(5) (lw: mde all: clr wl over 1f out: r.o wl)	—	1	$5/2^{1}$	62	34
5058^{3}	**School Boy (64)** (TJNaughton) **3-9-0** DHolland(9) (a.p: chsd wnr over 1f out: unable qckn)	5	2	$5/1^{2}$	52	24
4336^{8}	**Rawi (55)** (MissGayKelleway) **3-9-0** GDuffield(1) (b: b.hind: lw: a.p: rdn over 2f out: one pce)	4	3	$5/1^{2}$	41	13
4996^{8}	**Mystery Matthias (48)** (MissBSanders) **3-8-11v** SSanders(10) (a.p: rdn over 2f out: one pce)	s.h	4	10/1	38	10
4428^{10}	**Time For Tea (IRE) (62)** (CACyzer) **3-8-11** GCarter(12) (outpcd: hdwy over 1f out: nvr nrr)	3	5	$5/1^{2}$	30	2
4987^{5}	**Lawsimina (48)** (MissJFCraze) **3-8-11** SDrowne(6) (prom over 3f)	s.h	6	20/1	30	2
4323^{16}	**Emei Shan (40)** (WGMTurner) **3-8-4**(7) DMcGaffin(7) (outpcd: nvr nrr)	1¾	7	40/1	25	—
4212^{9}	**Barbrallen (36)** (MrsLCJewell) **4-8-6**(5) SophieMitchell(2) (outpcd: nvr nrr)	hd	8	40/1	25	—
4229^{11}	**Avant Huit (45)** (MrsNMacauley) **4-8-8**(3) CTeague(3) (prom over 4f)	2	9	25/1	20	—
4130^{10}	**Logie Pert Lad (26)** (JJBridger) **4-8-7**(7) RMullen(8) (bhd fnl 2f)	3	10	50/1	15	—
4107^{14}	**Kellaire Girl (IRE) (44)** (AMoore) **4-8-8**(3) AWhelan(13) (b: b.hind: lw: bhd fnl 4f)	2	11	20/1	6	—
4888^{5}	**Maraschino (37)** (BJMeehan) **3-8-11** MTebbutt(11) (bhd fnl 4f)	¾	12	$6/1^{3}$	4	—
4978^{11}	**Inaminit (40)** (HJCollingridge) **3-9-0** JQuinn(4) (lw: ref to r: t.n.p)		R	33/1	—	—

(SP 125.1%) **13 Rn**

1m 11.99 (0.89) CSF £15.57 TOTE £3.40: £1.50 £1.50 £3.60 (£9.10) Trio £15.90 OWNER Mr J. Berry (COCKERHAM) BRED David John Brown

5094 FAUCETS GROHE WATER TECHNOLOGY H'CAP (0-70) (II) (3-Y.O+) (Class E)

3-40 (3-41) **1m 2f (Equitrack)** £2,547.80 (£769.40: £374.20: £176.60) Stalls: Low GOING minus 0.49 sec per fur (FST)

				SP	RR	SF
5003^{*}	**Arzani (USA) (51)** (DJSCosgrove) **5-8-4**(7) 6x RMullen(7) (lw: a gng wl: stdy hdwy over 4f out: shkn up over 1f out: led ins fnl f: r.o wl)	—	1	$6/5^{1}$	58	31
4906^{9}	**Paronomasia (36)** (JLHarris) **4-7-10** JQuinn(2) (a.p: led over 3f out tl ins fnl f: unable qckn)	1½	2	50/1	41	14
4967^{8}	**Alfayza (43)** (JDBethell) **3-7-13** TWilliams(4) (a.p: rdn over 3f out: wknd over 1f out)	7	3	$5/1^{2}$	36	5
4967^{13}	**Absolutelystunning (56)** (MrsBarbaraWaring) **3-8-12** WRyan(1) (b: b.hind: led over 6f: wknd over 1f out)	1¾	4	9/1	47	16
4793^{13}	**Tormount (USA) (69)** (LordHuntingdon) **3-9-11** DHarrison(5) (lw: a.p: rdn over 2f out: wknd over 1f out)	1½	5	$7/1^{3}$	57	26
4998^{4}	**Our Eddie (61)** (BGubby) **7-9-7v** DHolland(6) (bhd fnl 5f)	½	6	$5/1^{2}$	48	21
4968^{14}	**One In The Eye (46)** (JRPoulton) **3-8-2**ow1 SDrowne(3) (a bhd)	s.h	7	25/1	33	1
4702^{14}	**Renata's Prince (IRE) (63)** (KRBurke) **3-9-5** SSanders(8) (bhd fnl 5f)	1¼	8	20/1	48	17

(SP 111.9%) **8 Rn**

2m 7.41 (3.11) CSF £38.74 CT £208.59 TOTE £1.80: £1.00 £12.60 £1.40 (£15.00) OWNER Mr Derrick Yarwood (NEWMARKET) BRED Eaton and Thorne and Robert N. Clay

LONG HANDICAP Paronomasia 7-2

WEIGHT FOR AGE 3yo-4lb

T/Plpt: £210.50 (32.89 Tckts). T/Qdpt: £68.50 (11.23 Tckts). AK

5087-LINGFIELD (L-H) (Standard)
Friday November 15th
WEATHER: sunny WIND: nil

5095 SHOWFORCE CLAIMING STKS (I) (3-Y.O+) (Class F)
12-05 (12-05) **7f (Equitrack)** £2,297.90 (£644.40: £313.70) Stalls: Low GOING minus 0.43 sec per fur (FST)

Form	Horse / details	Dist	Pos	SP	RR	SF
4895[7]	**Apollo Red (58)** (AMoore) **7-8-10** CandyMorris(4) (b: mde all: rdn out)	—	1	6/1	65	37
4915[14]	**Soaking (70)** (PBurgoyne) **6-9-0** DRMcCabe(6) (nt clr run & lost pl over 4f out: rallied over 3f out: r.o wl ins fnl f)	nk	2	7/2[1]	68	40
4590[8]	**Ivor's Deed (52)** (CFWall) **3-9-1** SSanders(3) (w ldr: ev ch over 1f out: wknd fnl f)	4	3	16/1	61	32
4979[4]	**Bold Street (IRE) (60)** (ABailey) **6-9-0** DWright(5) (b: rdn over 3f out: hdwy over 1f out: nvr nrr)	¾	4	4/1[2]	58	30
4215[4]	**Lennox Lewis (74)** (APJarvis) **4-8-13**(7) CCarver(7) (a.p: rdn wl over 1f out: sn wknd)	3	5	9/2[3]	57	29
4888[10]	**Jareer Do (IRE) (55)** (BPalling) **4-8-7** TSprake(8) (a p: rdn over 3f out: wkng whn n.m.r over 2f out)	2	6	8/1	39	11
	Arcus (IRE) (WRMuir) **3-9-3** DaneO'Neill(10) (nvr nrr)	1½	7	10/1	47	18
4202[12]	**Justinianus (IRE) (34)** (JJBridger) **4-7-13**(7) RMullen(11) (bhd fnl 3f)	2½	8	50/1	29	1
4573[9]	**Dancing Lawyer (73)** (BJMeehan) **5-9-2** MTebbutt(9) (a bhd)	1¼	9	10/1	36	8
4829[13]	**Mystic Legend (IRE) (27)** (JJSheehan) **4-8-10** SDrowne(2) (lw: a bhd)	1¾	10	50/1	26	—
4768[17]	**Regal Fanfare (IRE) (53)** (MrsLStubbs) **4-8-7b** SWhitworth(1) (bhd fnl 3f)	1¾	11	12/1	19	—

(SP 121.5%) **11 Rn**

1m 25.85 (1.45) CSF £26.68 TOTE £6.60: £1.20 £1.60 £3.60 (£9.00) Trio £80.30 OWNER Mr A. Moore (BRIGHTON) BRED Crest Stud Ltd
WEIGHT FOR AGE 3yo-1lb

5096 CONFERENCE STAGING H'CAP (0-70) (I) (3-Y.O+) (Class E)
12-35 (12-35) **5f (Equitrack)** £2,547.80 (£769.40: £374.20: £176.60) Stalls: High GOING minus 0.43 sec per fur (FST)

Form	Horse / details	Dist	Pos	SP	RR	SF
4996[5]	**Kalar (61)** (DWChapman) **7-9-5b** ACulhane(5) (mde all: rdn out)	—	1	12/1	69	31
*4996**	**Ramsey Hope (72)** (CWFairhurst) **3-9-13v**(3) 7x FLynch(2) (lw: hld up: rdn over 2f out: r.o wl ins fnl f)	2	2	6/1[3]	74	36
4996[2]	**Another Batchworth (63)** (EAWheeler) **4-9-7b** MRoberts(6) (w wnr: ev ch ins fnl f: sn wknd)	¾	3	2/1[1]	62	24
4372[9]	**Tachycardia (40)** (RJO'Sullivan) **4-7-12** JQuinn(7) (hld up: rdn over 2f out: r.o one pce fnl f)	nk	4	20/1	38	—
4995[2]	**Friendly Brave (USA) (70)** (MissGayKelleway) **6-10-0** SSanders(3) (rdn over 3f out: hdwy over 1f out: nvr nrr)	¾	5	9/4[2]	66	28
4996[6]	**Bashful Brave (50)** (BPJBaugh) **5-8-8** RPerham(10) (a.p: rdn over 1f out: one pce)	½	6	25/1	44	6
4888[6]	**Scissor Ridge (65)** (JJBridger) **4-9-2**(7) RMullen(1) (nvr nr to chal)	½	7	10/1	58	20
4765[4]	**Silk Cottage (68)** (RMWhitaker) **4-9-12v** DeanMcKeown(4) (a bhd)	2½	8	16/1	53	15
5000[6]	**Lloc (55)** (CADwyer) **4-8-6**(7) 7x NicolaCole(8) (b: a bhd)	1½	9	25/1	35	—

(SP 113.5%) **9 Rn**

60.05 secs (1.85) CSF £73.68 CT £187.20 TOTE £14.70: £4.70 £2.30 £1.10 (£50.30) Trio £14.20 OWNER Mr J. M. Chapman (YORK) BRED C. C. and Mrs Pryor

5097 CONFERENCE STAGING H'CAP (0-70) (II) (3-Y.O+) (Class E)
1-05 (1-07) **5f (Equitrack)** £2,547.80 (£769.40: £374.20: £176.60) Stalls: High GOING minus 0.43 sec per fur (FST)

Form	Horse / details	Dist	Pos	SP	RR	SF
5039[16]	**Chemcast (63)** (JLEyre) **3-9-7** RLappin(10) (a.p: led 1f out: rdn out)	—	1	11/1	70	30
4996[3]	**Napier Star (57)** (MrsNMacauley) **3-8-12v**(3) CTeague(3) (led to 1f out: r.o)	nk	2	7/2[1]	63	23
4521[8]	**Sharp Pearl (70)** (JWhite) **3-10-0** RHughes(9) (lw: a.p: rdn over 2f out: unable qckn)	1¼	3	16/1	72	32
5000[3]	**Featherstone Lane (63)** (MissLCSiddall) **5-9-7v** DRMcCabe(5) (outpcd: gd hdwy fnl f: fin wl)	hd	4	6/1[3]	65	25
5093[6]	**Lawsimina (48)** (MissJFCraze) **3-8-6** SDrowne(2) (rdn over 3f out: hdwy over 1f out: r.o one pce)	1¾	5	33/1	44	4
4521[15]	**Mijas (66)** (LMontagueHall) **3-9-10** DaneO'Neill(6) (a.p: rdn over 2f out: sn wknd)	½	6	25/1	61	21
*5000**	**Mister Raider (55)** (EAWheeler) **4-8-8**(5) 7x DGriffiths(8) (outpcd: nvr nrr)	½	7	7/1	48	8
5000[4]	**Cheeky Chappy (61)** (DWChapman) **5-9-5b** ACulhane(4) (squeezed out & lost pl over 4f out: rdn over 3f out: sme hdwy over 1f out: eased whn btn fnl f)	2½	8	4/1[2]	46	6
5000[9]	**Gi La High (50)** (JBerry) **3-8-8** GCarter(7) (outpcd)	1	9	4/1[2]	32	—
5000[8]	**Midnight Cookie (51)** (BAPearce) **3-8-9** JQuinn(1) (prom 3f)	3	10	25/1	23	—

(SP 113.9%) **10 Rn**

60.2 secs (2.00) CSF £45.43 CT £577.35 TOTE £10.70: £2.50 £1.30 £3.60 (£31.10) Trio £132.00 OWNER Clayton Bigley Partnership Ltd (HAMBLETON) BRED C. R. and V. M. Withers

5098 CUTTING EDGE (S) STKS (2-Y.O) (Class G)
1-40 (1-46) **7f (Equitrack)** £2,284.50 (£642.00: £313.50) Stalls: Low GOING minus 0.43 sec per fur (FST)

Form	Horse / details	Dist	Pos	SP	RR	SF
4795[13]	**Rebuke (51)** (RFJohnsonHoughton) **2-8-11b** SSanders(4) (uns rdr & bolted bef s: a.p: rdn over 3f out: led over 1f out: r.o wl)	—	1	8/1	57	10
2750[5]	**Ekaterini Paritsi (44)** (WGMTurner) **2-8-6v[1]** TSprake(2) (a.p: led over 3f out tl over 1f out: unable qckn)	3	2	6/1	45	—
4988[2]	**Slightly Oliver (IRE)** (GLewis) **2-8-8b**(3) AWhelan(7) (s.s: t.o over 4f: gd hdwy over 1f out: fin wl)	3	3	9/4[1]	43+	—
5048[7]	**Battle Ground (IRE) (54)** (NACallaghan) **2-8-4b[1]**(7) RMullen(1) (led over 3f: wknd over 2f out)	s.h	4	3/1[2]	43	—
4715[18]	**Waterville Boy (IRE) (61)** (RHannon) **2-8-11** DaneO'Neill(6) (prom over 3f)	3	5	7/2[3]	36	—
4970[12]	**Santella Twinkle (IRE)** (DMorris) **2-8-6** StephenDavies(8) (bhd fnl 5f)	3	6	20/1	25	—
	Heavenly Hand (AMoore) **2-8-6** CandyMorris(3) (b.hind: str: bit bkwd: s.s: a wl bhd)	nk	7	25/1	24	—
4991[11]	**Panooras Lord (IRE)** (JSWainwright) **2-8-11** LCharnock(5) (bit bkwd: bhd fnl 5f)	6	8	25/1	15	—

(SP 115.8%) **8 Rn**

1m 28.27 (3.87) CSF £50.57 TOTE £14.10: £3.90 £1.60 £1.10 (£39.00) OWNER Mr R. F. JohnsonHoughton (DIDCOT) BRED Mrs E. Longton
No bid

5099 SHOWFORCE CLAIMING STKS (II) (3-Y.O+) (Class F)
2-15 (2-17) **7f (Equitrack)** £2,286.00 (£641.00: £312.00) Stalls: Low GOING minus 0.43 sec per fur (FST)

Form	Horse / details	Dist	Pos	SP	RR	SF
4788[W]	**Deeply Vale (IRE) (73)** (GLMoore) **5-8-11** SWhitworth(5) (b: hld up: led over 1f out: all out)	—	1	7/4[1]	68	37

			Pos	SP	RR	SF
	Barossa Valley (IRE) (70) (PButler) **5-9-2** SDrowne(12) (hdwy 4f out: chsd wnr fnl f: hrd rdn: r.o wl)	s.h	**2**	12/1	73	42
4979[10]	**Sharp 'n Smart (65)** (BSmart) **4-9-6** MTebbutt(11) (lw: a.p: rdn over 2f out: unable qckn)	5	**3**	13/2	66	35
5059[7]	**Ragazzo (IRE) (40)** (JSWainwright) **6-8-10b** LCharnock(7) (b.hind: a.p: led over 2f out tl over 1f out: wknd fnl f)	nk	**4**	16/1	55	24
4828[9]	**Standown (73)** (JBerry) **3-8-13** GCarter(1) (a.p: rdn over 2f out: sn wknd)	2	**5**	5/1[2]	54	22
4259[15]	**Samsolom (55)** (PHowling) **8-8-10** JQuinn(9) (b.hind: nvr nr to chal)	1½	**6**	12/1	47	16
4987[12]	**Into Debt (35)** (JRPoulton) **3-8-3**ow2 SSanders(3) (led over 4f)	½	**7**	50/1	40	6
4727[9]	**Saint Amigo (34)** (RMWhitaker) **4-8-4v** FNorton(8) (nvr nrr)	2½	**8**	25/1	34	3
4088[15]	**Xenophon of Cunaxa (IRE) (76)** (MJFetherston-Godley) **3-9-5** DHarrison(6) (s.s: hdwy 4f out: wknd over 3f out)	¾	**9**	6/1[3]	48	16
2285[7]	**Jovie King (IRE) (37)** (KMcAuliffe) **4-9-2v** RHughes(2) (lw: bhd fnl 4f)	½	**10**	20/1	43	12
4895[12]	**Agwa (56)** (RJO'Sullivan) **7-8-10b[1]** DBiggs(10) (prom over 3f)	hd	**11**	11/1	37	6
	Alicia Lea (IRE) (AMoore) **4-8-4**ow1 CandyMorris(4) (dwlt: a bhd)	16	**12**	33/1	—	—

(SP 123.8%) **12 Rn**

1m 25.87 (1.47) CSF £23.11 TOTE £2.80: £1.30 £4.20 £1.90 (£48.40) Trio £77.00 OWNER Mr Danny Bloor (BRIGHTON) BRED Biddestone Stud

WEIGHT FOR AGE 3yo-1lb

Deeply Vale (IRE) clmd N Clark £5,500

5100 MALAYA GATWICK NURSERY H'CAP (0-85) (2-Y.O) (Class E)

2-50 (2-51) **1m (Equitrack)** £2,941.05 (£890.40: £434.70: £206.85) Stalls: High GOING minus 0.43 sec per fur (FST)

			Pos	SP	RR	SF
4990[2]	**Double Espresso (IRE) (65)** (MJohnston) **2-8-6** MRoberts(3) (led over 6f out: rdn 2f out: clr over 1f out: r.o wl)	—	**1**	11/8[1]	75	40
4602[9]	**Noble Hero (66)** (JJSheehan) **2-8-7** SDrowne(9) (lw: a.p: rdn over 2f out: unable qckn)	4	**2**	14/1	68	33
5038[3]	**Kaiser Kache (IRE) (80)** (KMcAuliffe) **2-9-7** RHughes(8) (a.p: rdn over 2f out: one pce)	½	**3**	4/1[2]	81	46
4867*	**Broughtons Error (69)** (WJMusson) **2-8-10** JQuinn(6) (lw: s.i.s: hdwy over 1f out: nvr nrr)	5	**4**	6/1[3]	60	25
*4572**	**Davis Rock (74)** (WRMuir) **2-9-1** DaneO'Neill(5) (lw: a.p: rdn over 2f out: wknd fnl f)	¾	**5**	9/1	64	29
4970[5]	**Motcombs Club (64)** (NACallaghan) **2-7-12**(7) RMullen(1) (lw: hld up: rdn 3f out: wknd over 2f out)	1¼	**6**	10/1	51	16
4814[6]	**Irish Fiction (IRE) (65)** (DJSCosgrove) **2-8-6** GCarter(2) (a bhd)	12	**7**	20/1	28	—
4891[7]	**Cheval Roc (70)** (RHannon) **2-8-11** RPerham(7) (lw: led over 1f: wknd over 4f out)	5	**8**	14/1	23	—
3523[5]	**Aztec Traveller (62)** (GLMoore) **2-8-3**ow3 SSanders(4) (prom 5f)	3½	**9**	20/1	8	—

(SP 118.3%) **9 Rn**

1m 38.89 (1.49) CSF £19.88 CT £58.43 TOTE £2.00: £1.30 £3.20 £1.90 (£17.50) Trio £64.10 OWNER Mr R. W. Huggins (MIDDLEHAM) BRED Godolphin Management Co Ltd

5101 SOUTHRIVER TOOLS & FIXINGS MEDIAN AUCTION MAIDEN STKS (3-Y.O) (Class F)

3-25 (3-25) **1m 2f (Equitrack)** £2,517.00 (£707.00: £345.00) Stalls: Low GOING minus 0.43 sec per fur (FST)

			Pos	SP	RR	SF
4827[7]	**Persuasion** (LordHuntingdon) **3-8-9** DHarrison(2) (a.p: led over 4f out: clr over 2f out: easily)	—	**1**	9/4[2]	76+	32
	Go Too Moor (IRE) (GCBravery) **3-9-0** DRMcCabe(6) (b.hind: bit bkwd: rdn & hdwy over 2f out: chsd wnr ins fnl f: r.o one pce)	6	**2**	14/1	71	27
	Keen Companion (TJNaughton) **3-8-6**(3) JDSmith(5) (leggy: bit bkwd: rdn & hdwy over 4f out: chsd wnr over 3f out tl ins fnl f: one pce)	5	**3**	14/1	58	14
4824[10]	**Lavender Della (IRE) (63)** (MJFetherston-Godley) **3-8-9** DHolland(1) (a.p: led over 5f out tl over 4f out: wknd 3f out)	6	**4**	11/8[1]	49	5
2015[5]	**Bellaphento (45)** (JRinger) **3-8-2**(7) RMullen(8) (b: a.p: rdn over 4f out: wknd over 2f out)	2	**5**	25/1	46	2
4989[14]	**D J Cat (48)** (WRMuir) **3-9-0** DaneO'Neill(9) (lw: nvr nrr)	2½	**6**	33/1	47	3
5058[7]	**Stretching (IRE)** (ABailey) **3-9-0** DWright(4) (b: led over 4f: wknd over 4f out)	3	**7**	7/2[3]	42	—
	Dutch Dyane (GPEnright) **3-8-9** NAdams(7) (b: b.hind: str: bit bkwd: a bhd)	½	**8**	33/1	36	—
	Mad Alex (MJHaynes) **3-9-0** SSanders(3) (b.hind: w'like: bhd fnl 6f)	27	**9**	25/1	—	—

(SP 122.0%) **9 Rn**

2m 7.72 (3.42) CSF £31.48 TOTE £3.00: £1.90 £9.00 £4.90 (£66.60) Trio £196.10; £201.71 to Cheltenham 16/11/96 OWNER Countess of Lonsdale (WEST ILSLEY) BRED Lady Lonsdale

IN-FOCUS: This looked a desperate race if paddock appearance is anything to go by.

5102 SCENA H'CAP (0-70) (3-Y.O+) (Class E)

3-55 (3-55) **1m 4f (Equitrack)** £2,845.50 (£861.00: £420.00: £199.50) Stalls: Low GOING minus 0.43 sec per fur (FST)

			Pos	SP	RR	SF
*4892**	**Hoofprints (IRE) (62)** (MrsAJPerrett) **3-9-11** JQuinn(2) (lw: chsd ldr: led over 6f out: clr over 2f out: hrd rdn over 1f out: r.o wl)	—	**1**	3/1[1]	74	44
4868[3]	**Taniyar (FR) (35)** (RHollinshead) **4-8-1**(3) FLynch(3) (a.p: chsd wnr over 4f out: rdn over 3f out: unable qckn)	3	**2**	7/2[2]	43	19
5003[5]	**Our Main Man (50)** (RMWhitaker) **6-9-5** RHughes(5) (lost pl over 3f out: rallied fnl f: r.o)	1½	**3**	6/1[3]	56	32
4815[2]	**Rock The Barney (IRE) (40)** (PBurgoyne) **7-8-6v[1]**(3) PMcCabe(1) (s.s: hdwy 4f out: rdn over 3f out: one pce)	1¼	**4**	7/1	44	20
4984[2]	**Stalled (IRE) (58)** (PTWalwyn) **6-9-13** SSanders(7) (lw: hdwy over 8f out: rdn over 4f out: wknd over 3f out)	3½	**5**	3/1[1]	58	34
*2372**	**Flow Back (58)** (GPEnright) **4-9-6**(7) RMullen(6) (a bhd)	7	**6**	14/1	48	24
2953[7]	**Dolliver (USA) (59)** (SDow) **4-10-0e** DaneO'Neill(4) (bhd fnl 6f)	13	**7**	20/1	32	8
4986[15]	**Silver Hunter (USA) (52)** (GCBravery) **5-9-7** DRMcCabe(8) (lw: led over 5f: wknd over 4f out)	nk	**8**	20/1	25	1

(SP 115.2%) **8 Rn**

2m 34.54 (4.54) CSF £13.36 CT £51.51 TOTE £3.80: £1.30 £1.90 £1.50 (£10.20) OWNER Mr Selwyn Lewis (PULBOROUGH) BRED Eamon Freaney

WEIGHT FOR AGE 3yo-6lb

T/Plpt: £16.40 (545.87 Tckts). T/Qdpt: £6.40 (153.72 Tckts). AK

5055-WOLVERHAMPTON (L-H) (Standard)

Saturday November 16th

WEATHER: mist WIND: nil

5103 POPLAR MAIDEN STKS (2-Y.O) (Class D)

7-00 (7-00) **7f (Fibresand)** £2,840.00 (£860.00: £420.00: £200.00) Stalls: High GOING minus 0.04 sec per fur (STD)

Form	Horse / details	Dist	Pos	SP	RR	SF
4889^{3}	**Amaryllis (IRE)** (JHMGosden) **2-8-9** AMcGlone(3) (mde all: edgd lft over 1f out: rdn out)	—	1	$4/7^{1}$	68	25
4976^{3}	**Colins Choice (62)** (JLSpearing) **2-8-6**(3) FLynch(2) (w wnr: ev ch over 1f out: r.o one pce)	2½	2	12/1	62	19
4884^{10}	**Patina** (RHollinshead) **2-8-5**(5)ow1 DGriffiths(8) (hld up: hdwy ½-wy: styd on same pce fnl 2f)	5	3	50/1	52	8
4241^{5}	**Star Entry** (WJarvis) **2-8-9** SSanders(5) (sn pushed along: nvr able to chal)	1¼	4	$9/2^{2}$	48	5
4830^{8}	**Little Acorn** (SCWilliams) **2-9-0** DRMcCabe(6) (nvr trbld ldrs)	2½	5	20/1	47	4
4783^{11}	**Fleuve d'Or (IRE)** (DHaydnJones) **2-8-9** LCharnock(9) (hdwy 4f out: wknd over 2f out)	¾	6	40/1	41	—
4969^{14}	**Double Eight (IRE)** (BWHills) **2-8-6**(3) JDSmith(7) (a in rr)	1	7	$6/1^{3}$	38	—
	Rissaga (CWFairhurst) **2-8-9** DeanMcKeown(1) (s.i.s: a outpcd)	8	8	50/1	20	—
	First Man (BJLlewellyn) **2-9-0** TWilliams(4) (chsd ldrs tl wknd 3f out: t.o)	24	9	50/1	—	—
				(SP 116.9%)		**9 Rn**

1m 30.3 (5.60) CSF £8.50 TOTE £1.80: £1.10 £2.00 £6.00 (£4.00) Trio £38.50; £48.82 to 18/11/96 OWNER Mr George Strawbridge (NEWMARKET) BRED George Strawbridge

5104 ROWAN LIMITED STKS (0-65) (3-Y.O+) (Class F)

7-30 (7-30) **1m 4f (Fibresand)** £2,085.00 (£585.00: £285.00) Stalls: Low GOING minus 0.04 sec per fur (STD)

Form	Horse / details	Dist	Pos	SP	RR	SF
*5062**	**Hill Farm Dancer (53)** (WMBrisbourne) **5-8-8**(7) RMullen(1) (s.i.s: hld up: hdwy to ld over 2f out: sn clr)	—	1	$5/6^{1}$	76	44
4993^{2}	**Shaffishayes (63)** (MrsMReveley) **4-9-4** DeanMcKeown(4) (hld up in tch: nt clr run & lost pl 3f out: chsd wnr over 1f out: no imp)	5	2	$13/8^{2}$	72	40
4669^{13}	**Red Phantom (IRE) (64)** (SMellor) **4-9-4** MWigham(3) (prom 6f out: outpcd fnl 2f)	8	3	$9/1^{3}$	62	30
4609^{17}	**Classic Ballet (FR) (61)** (RHarris) **3-8-11** DBatteate(2) (led: rdn & hdd 4f out: wknd over 2f out)	6	4	12/1	53	15
5004^{13}	**Western Venture (IRE) (44)** (RMMcKellar) **3-8-12** TWilliams(5) (chsd ldr: plld hrd: led 4f out: rdn & hdd over 2f out: sn btn)	7	5	25/1	44	6
				(SP 114.2%)		**5 Rn**

2m 40.4 (7.90) CSF £2.65 TOTE £1.70: £1.10 £1.20 (£1.50) OWNER Mr M. E. Hughes (NESSCLIFFE) BRED D. Newton

WEIGHT FOR AGE 3yo-6lb

5105 S. J. DIXONS & SONS H'CAP (0-85) (3-Y.O+) (Class D)

8-00 (8-00) **6f (Fibresand)** £2,801.00 (£848.00: £414.00: £197.00) Stalls: Low GOING minus 0.04 sec per fur (STD)

Form	Horse / details	Dist	Pos	SP	RR	SF
4994^{10}	**Prima Silk (70)** (MJRyan) **5-9-0** AClark(4) (hld up in tch: led over 1f out: rdn out)	—	1	14/1	77	51
*4778**	**Imposing Time (71)** (MissGayKelleway) **5-9-1b** SSanders(3) (chsd ldrs: led over 3f out: rdn & hdd over 1f out: r.o one pce)	1¼	2	$11/2^{2}$	75	49
4994^{16}	**Garnock Valley (70)** (JBerry) **6-9-0b** GCarter(5) (mid div: hdwy ½-wy: nvr able to chal)	1¼	3	$4/1^{1}$	70	44
4687^{15}	**Portend (78)** (SRBowring) **4-9-5b**(3) CTeague(1) (bhd: hdwy over 2f out: styd on u.p)	s.h	4	10/1	78	52
4776^{2}	**Night Harmony (IRE) (56)** (MissSJWilton) **3-8-0** DRMcCabe(6) (chsd ldrs: led 4f out: sn hdd: no ex appr fnl f)	1	5	12/1	54	28
3790^{12}	**Steal 'Em (62)** (ABailey) **3-8-6** DWright(8) (bhd tl r.o appr fnl f: nrst fin)	nk	6	10/1	59	33
4994^{2}	**Tiler (IRE) (82)** (MJohnston) **4-9-12** DHolland(11) (led: hdd 4f out: r.o fnl 2f)	½	7	$4/1^{1}$	77	51
4994^{15}	**Castlerea Lad (62)** (RHollinshead) **7-8-3**(3) FLynch(12) (s.i.s: nvr rchd ldrs)	5	8	16/1	44	18
4811^{3}	**Ziggy's Dancer (USA) (84)** (EJAlston) **5-10-0** SDrowne(2) (chsd ldrs: rdn over 2f out: sn wknd)	2½	9	$6/1^{3}$	59	33
4971^{6}	**Naissant (73)** (RMMcKellar) **3-9-3** TWilliams(7) (trckd ldrs tl wknd 2f out)	1	10	20/1	46	20
4994^{19}	**Saddlehome (USA) (80)** (TDBarron) **7-9-10** DeanMcKeown(10) (outpcd fr ½-wy)	1¼	11	12/1	49	23
4312^{26}	**Tart and a Half (72)** (BJMeehan) **4-9-2** MTebbutt(13) (a in rr)	5	12	16/1	28	2
5000^{7}	**Dieci Anno (IRE) (63)** (BPalling) **3-8-7** TSprake(9) (chsd ldrs over 3f)	1¼	13	20/1	16	—
				(SP 131.2%)		**13 Rn**

1m 14.5 (3.30) CSF £90.42 CT £286.70 TOTE £18.30: £3.70 £2.30 £2.20 (£26.70) Trio £123.60 OWNER Norcroft Park Stud (NEWMARKET) BRED R. M. Scott

5106 ESSENCE OF TIME ANTIQUE CLOCKS (LICHFIELD) H'CAP (0-85) (3-Y.O+) (Class D)

8-30 (8-31) **1m 100y (Fibresand)** £2,814.00 (£852.00: £416.00: £198.00) Stalls: Low GOING minus 0.04 sec per fur (STD)

Form	Horse / details	Dist	Pos	SP	RR	SF
4432^{4}	**Duke Valentino (80)** (RHollinshead) **4-9-6**(5) DGriffiths(3) (a.p: rdn to ld ins fnl f: r.o)	—	1	16/1	87	69
4882^{7}	**Just Harry (75)** (MJRyan) **5-9-6** AClark(8) (mid div: hdwy over 2f out: nt clr run ins fnl f: r.o)	nk	2	20/1	81	63
4915^{13}	**Bentico (75)** (MrsNMacauley) **7-9-3**(3) CTeague(10) (prom: outpcd over 2f out: r.o wl ins fnl f)	s.h	3	14/1	81	63
4812^{2}	**Explosive Power (73)** (GCBravery) **5-9-4** DRMcCabe(4) (led: rdn & hdd ins fnl f: no ex)	½	4	$5/1^{3}$	78	60
5010*	**Absolute Magic (80)** (WJHaggas) **6-9-8**(3) FLynch(6) (hld up: hdwy over 3f out: ev ch ins fnl f: unable qckn)	1	5	$2/1^{1}$	84	66
5054^{16}	**North Reef (IRE) (76)** (JPearce) **5-9-7** MWigham(12) (sn pushed along: hdwy over 2f out: nt rch ldrs)	1	6	14/1	78	60
4885*	**Mashmoum (82)** (JHMGosden) **3-9-11** AMcGlone(11) (s.i.s: hld up: hdwy over 4f out: sn hung lft: n.d)	3	7	$9/2^{2}$	78	58
4812^{3}	**Super High (83)** (PHowling) **4-10-0b** DHolland(7) (chsd ldrs: rdn over 2f out: sn btn)	2½	8	7/1	74	56
4463^{18}	**Daryabad (IRE) (75)** (TJNaughton) **4-9-3**(3) JDSmith(13) (a in rr)	3	9	20/1	61	43
5042^{16}	**Maple Bay (IRE) (80)** (ABailey) **7-9-6**(5) GFaulkner(9) (mid div: effrt ½-wy: wknd over 3f out)	¾	10	14/1	64	46
4906^{8}	**Johnnie the Joker (73)** (JPLeigh) **5-9-4b** DeanMcKeown(1) (stumbled s: sn prom: wknd over 3f out)	1½	11	25/1	54	36
4909^{12}	**Ashgore (76)** (JLEyre) **6-9-7** TWilliams(5) (chsd ldr tl wknd over 3f out)	hd	12	16/1	57	39
2320^{7}	**So Amazing (74)** (JLEyre) **4-8-12**(7) SBuckley(2) (a in rr)	s.h	13	16/1	55	37
				(SP 131.7%)		**13 Rn**

1m 48.8 (3.80) CSF £276.65 CT £4,312.66 TOTE £17.60: £3.40 £4.00 £3.10 (£125.00) Trio £154.70; £152.54 to 18/11/96 OWNER Mr J. E. Bigg (UPPER LONGDON) BRED Shadwell Estate Company Limited

WEIGHT FOR AGE 3yo-2lb

5107 PLYVINE CATERING (S) STKS (2-Y.O) (Class G)
9-00 (9-02) **5f (Fibresand)** £2,085.00 (£585.00: £285.00) Stalls: Low GOING minus 0.04 sec per fur (STD)

			SP	RR	SF
4999^{6}	**Sparkling Edge (48)** (CADwyer) **2-8-11** DRMcCabe(10) (w ldrs: outpcd over 2f out: r.o wl to ld nr fin) ......—	**1**	10/1	61	18
5080^{5}	**Enchantica (67)** (JBerry) **2-8-6** GCarter(7) (led: hdd over 3f out: led again over 2f out: sn clr: rdn & hdd nr fin) ......½	**2**	5/2 ^{2}	54	11
4576^{6}	**Fit For The Job (IRE) (50)** (WGMTurner) **2-8-4**$^{(7)}$ DSweeney(5) (bhd tl r.o appr fnl f: nrst fin) 3½	**3**	14/1	48	5
4572^{9}	**Master Foley (50)** (NPLittmoden) **2-8-11** TGMcLaughlin(6) (hdwy over 2f out: nvr able to chal) ......nk	**4**	33/1	47	4
5005^{4}	**Tinker's Surprise (IRE) (64)** (JBalding) **2-9-2b** NCarlisle(1) (chsd ldrs: ev ch 2f out: sn outpcd) 1½	**5**	9/1 ^{3}	47	4
5005^{6}	**Le Shuttle (52)** (MHTompkins) **2-7-13**$^{(7)}$ RMullen(4) (hmpd s: nvr nrr) ......s.h	**6**	10/1	37	—
5037^{2}	**Figlia (65)** (CBBBooth) **2-8-6b** LCharnock(8) (s.i.s: nvr rchd ldrs) 2	**7**	11/8 ^{1}	31	—
5080^{9}	**Miss Darling** (JAkehurst) **2-8-6** SSanders(9) (led over 3f out: hdd over 2f out: sn rdn & btn) ......s.h	**8**	25/1	31	—
5061^{7}	**Municipal Girl (IRE) (48)** (BPalling) **2-8-6** TSprake(2) (sn pushed along: outpcd fr ½-wy) ......¾	**9**	33/1	28	—
5005^{11}	**Cantsaynowt (31)** (RMMcKellar) **2-8-6b** TWilliams(3) (hmpd s: a bhd: t.o) 30	**10**	20/1	—	—

(SP 120.0%) **10 Rn**

63.1 secs (4.20) CSF £34.49 TOTE £15.70: £3.50 £1.40 £4.10 (£32.00) Trio £120.40; £101.79 to 18/11/96 OWNER Mr S. I. Ross (NEWMARKET) BRED Benham Stud
No bid

5108 HAWTHORN H'CAP (0-65) (3-Y.O+) (Class F)
9-30 (9-30) **1m 6f 166y (Fibresand)** £2,085.00 (£585.00: £285.00) Stalls: High GOING minus 0.04 sec per fur (STD)

			SP	RR	SF
5062^{2}	**Sharp Command (48)** (PEccles) **3-8-12** DHolland(7) (trckd ldrs: led over 1f out: rdn out) ......—	**1**	2/1 ^{1}	54	32
4977^{10}	**Rose of Glenn (36)** (BPalling) **5-8-8** TSprake(2) (led & sn clr: hdd over 1f out: no ex) 1½	**2**	9/1	40	26
3928^{11}	**Code Red (57)** (WRMuir) **3-9-0**$^{(7)}$ JWilkinson(1) (chsd ldrs: rdn over 3f out: styd on same pce fnl 2f) 1¼	**3**	16/1	60	38
4919^{13}	**Backwoods (64)** (WMBrisbourne) **3-10-0** AGarth(5) (hld up: reminder 7f out: nvr nr ldrs) 11	**4**	7/2 ^{2}	55	33
5008^{12}	**Havana Heights (IRE) (45)** (JLEyre) **3-8-9** TWilliams(8) (prom: chsd ldr 7f out: rdn & wknd over 2f out) 1¾	**5**	14/1	34	12
4832^{8}	**Classic Affair (USA) (50)** (RHarris) **3-9-0** DBatteate(4) (hld up: hdwy 7f out: rdn & wknd over 3f out) 2½	**6**	5/1 ^{3}	37	15
4977^{9}	**Rousitto (42)** (RHollinshead) **8-8-9**$^{(5)}$ DGriffiths(9) (hld up: nvr rchd ldrs) ......½	**7**	14/1	28	14
4334^{3}	**Sommersby (IRE) (48)** (MrsNMacauley) **5-9-3**$^{(3)}$ CTeague(6) (hld up: hdwy over 5f out: wknd over 3f out: fin lame) 2	**8**	6/1	32	18
5008^{6}	**Highfield Fizz (43)** (CWFairhurst) **4-9-1** LCharnock(10) (a in rr: t.o) 14	**9**	12/1	12	—

(SP 123.4%) **9 Rn**

3m 18.9 (11.50) CSF £20.44 CT £219.61 TOTE £2.70: £1.20 £2.30 £5.30 (£14.20) Trio £117.30; £19.84 to 18/11/96 OWNER Mr A. P. Holland (LAMBOURN) BRED Coral'S Farm and Stud
WEIGHT FOR AGE 3yo-8lb

T/Plpt: £132.50 (79.65 Tckts). T/Qdpt: £254.50 (1.5 Tckts). CR

4982-SOUTHWELL (L-H) (Standard)
Monday November 18th
WEATHER: fine and sunny WIND: slt half bhd

5109 TOGO H'CAP (0-65) (I) (3-Y.O+ F & M) (Class F)
12-15 (12-18) **6f (Fibresand)** £2,048.00 (£573.00: £278.00) Stalls: Low GOING minus 0.15 sec per fur (FST)

			SP	RR	SF
4987^{4}	**Honeyhall (34)** (NBycroft) **3-7-13** JQuinn(2) (s.i.s: sn w ldrs: led ½-wy: hld on wl towards fin) ......—	**1**	8/1 ^{3}	39	5
4776^{3}	**Queens Check (63)** (MissJFCraze) **3-10-0b** SDWilliams(11) (b: a chsng ldrs: nt qckn wl ins fnl f) ......½	**2**	7/1 ^{2}	67	33
4975^{16}	**Ballard Lady (IRE) (43)** (JSWainwright) **4-8-1**$^{(7)}$ JBramhill(7) (lw: s.i.s: gd hdwy ½-wy: n.m.r 1f out: kpt on wl ins fnl f) ......s.h	**3**	8/1 ^{3}	47	13
4983^{6}	**Margaretrose Anna (38)** (BPJBaugh) **4-8-3** NAdams(8) (a chsng ldrs: nt qckn appr fnl f) 2	**4**	20/1	36	2
3761^{9}	**Florrie'm (32)** (JLHarris) **3-7-6**$^{(5)ow1}$ PFessey(4) (hld up: hdwy 2f out: hrd rdn & styd on ins fnl f) 2½	**5**	25/1	24	—
4983^{4}	**Miss Aragon (32)** (MissLCSiddall) **8-7-11** NCarlisle(13) (bhd: hdwy over 2f out: hung lft: nvr nr to chal) ......s.h	**6**	13/2 ^{1}	23	—
4805*	**Leading Princess (IRE) (50)** (MissLAPerratt) **5-9-1b** DHolland(1) (led to ½-wy: wknd over 1f out) 1¼	**7**	7/1 ^{2}	38	4
4473^{3}	**My Cherrywell (58)** (LRLloyd-James) **6-9-2v**$^{(7)}$ CWebb(10) (bhd: hdwy over 2f out: n.d) 1¾	**8**	8/1 ^{3}	41	7
4727^{11}	**Swifty Nifty (IRE) (34)** (WWHaigh) **3-7-13**^{ow1} FNorton(5) (nvr bttr than mid div) 1	**9**	20/1	15	—
4888^{14}	**Redskin Lady (52)** (RJO'Sullivan) **3-9-3** SSanders(16) (in tch: rdn & lost pl over 2f out) 2½	**10**	12/1	26	—
4981^{12}	**Lady Eclat (46)** (JAGlover) **3-8-11b** MBirch(15) (in tch: rdn over 2f out: sn wknd) 4	**11**	16/1	9	—
4692^{18}	**Lia Fail (IRE) (53)** (RHollinshead) **3-8-13**$^{(5)}$ DGriffiths(12) (s.i.s: a bhd) ......½	**12**	7/1 ^{2}	15	—
748^{14}	**Summer Princess (45)** (AStreeter) **3-8-10** DRMcCabe(6) (a rr div) 3	**13**	11/1	—	—
4333^{11}	**Klipspinger (63)** (BSRothwell) **3-10-0** JStack(3) (lw: a bhd) 6	**14**	14/1	1	—
5055^{12}	**Daffodil Express (IRE) (41)** (MJRyan) **3-8-6v**^{1} MRoberts(14) (a bhd: t.o) 27	**15**	14/1	—	—

(SP 132.8%) **15 Rn**

1m 18.5 (5.00) CSF £63.91 CT £452.06 TOTE £11.60: £3.80 £2.20 £2.40 (£21.70) Trio £77.10 OWNER Mr Steve McLaughlin (BRANDSBY) BRED S. J. and Mrs McLaughlin
LONG HANDICAP Florrie'm 7-6

5110 CHAD LIMITED STKS (0-55) (I) (3-Y.O+) (Class F)
12-45 (12-46) **1m (Fibresand)** £2,048.00 (£573.00: £278.00) Stalls: Low GOING minus 0.15 sec per fur (FST)

			SP	RR	SF
4975^{2}	**Indiahra (44)** (JLEyre) **5-8-11v** TWilliams(14) (sn chsng ldrs: led 2f out: styd on wl) ......—	**1**	9/4 ^{1}	65	35
4982^{8}	**Three Weeks (34)** (WRMuir) **3-8-12** DaneO'Neill(9) (lw: bhd: hrd rdn & styd on wl fnl 2f: nt rch wnr) 1¼	**2**	14/1	66	34
5060^{3}	**Sandmoor Denim (49)** (SRBowring) **9-9-3** DeanMcKeown(7) (b: a chsng ldrs: nt qckn appr fnl f) ......nk	**3**	5/1 ^{2}	68	38
4860^{19}	**Napoleon's Return (45)** (JLEyre) **3-8-12** RLappin(13) (mde most to 2f out: kpt on same pce) 2½	**4**	14/1	60	28
5055^{8}	**Have a Nightcap (40)** (NPLittmoden) **7-9-0b** TGMcLaughlin(8) (in tch: outpcd over 3f out: kpt on appr fnl f) 3	**5**	25/1	54	24
5055^{5}	**Loch Style (53)** (RHollinshead) **3-8-12**$^{(3)}$ FLynch(16) (s.i.s: gd hdwy ½-wy: styd on same pce fnl 2f) 1	**6**	5/1 ^{2}	55	23

Form	Horse / details	Dist	Pos	SP	RR	SF
5086[8]	**No Submission (USA) (56)** (DWChapman) **10-9-3b** ACulhane(6) (bhd: swtchd outside 5f out: kpt on fnl 2f: n.d)	hd	**7**	8/1[3]	55	25
4983[13]	**Havana Miss (32)** (BPalling) **4-8-11** TSprake(2) (w ldrs tl lost pl 2f out)	4	**8**	20/1	41	11
5093[8]	**Barbrallen (36)** (MrsLCJewell) **4-8-6**(5) SophieMitchell(15) (s.i.s: a wl bhd)	13	**9**	50/1	15	—
4503[9]	**Peacefull Reply (USA) (34)** (FHLee) **6-9-0** AMcGlone(4) (a in rr)	3	**10**	25/1	12	—
613[10]	**Captain Tandy (IRE) (29)** (CSmith) **7-9-0** AClark(5) (sn wl outpcd & bhd)	4	**11**	50/1	4	—
5086[5]	**Racing Telegraph (32)** (CNAllen) **6-9-0** MRoberts(12) (w ldrs tl lost pl over 3f out)	5	**12**	14/1	—	—
4045[20]	**Larrylukeathugh (41)** (JJO'Neill) **3-8-12** JQuinn(11) (sn bhd)	4	**13**	20/1	—	—
4905[11]	**Kanat Lee (IRE) (25)** (MrsVAAconley) **5-8-11** MDeering(1) (s.s: a wl bhd)	9	**14**	25/1	—	—
4982[3]	**Lady Silk (46)** (MissJFCraze) **5-9-0** SDWilliams(10) (lw: sn drvn along & bhd: eased fnl 2f)	12	**15**	9/1	—	—
				(SP 130.2%)	**15 Rn**	

1m 44.8 (5.80) CSF £34.58 TOTE £3.80: £1.20 £9.30 £1.70 (£50.70) Trio £178.80 OWNER Mr P. J. Lawton (HAMBLETON) BRED Glazeley Stud

WEIGHT FOR AGE 3yo-2lb

5111 MOZAMBIQUE MEDIAN AUCTION MAIDEN STKS (2-Y.O) (Class F)

1-15 (1-20) **6f (Fibresand)** £2,398.00 (£673.00: £328.00) Stalls: Low GOING minus 0.15 sec per fur (FST)

Form	Horse / details	Dist	Pos	SP	RR	SF
5034[10]	**Sally Green (IRE) (64)** (CFWall) **2-8-9** GDuffield(8) (lw: sn chsng ldrs: chal & hung lft 2f out: styd on wl to ld wl ins fnl f)	—	**1**	11/2	66	34
5083[6]	**Cee-N-K (IRE) (77)** (MJohnston) **2-9-0** MRoberts(2) (w ldr: chal & hung lft 2f out: led ins fnl f: sn hdd & nt qckn)	1¼	**2**	2/1[1]	68	36
4970[9]	**Double-O** (WJarvis) **2-9-0** SSanders(1) (lw: led tl ins fnl f)	nk	**3**	16/1	67	35
4751[5]	**Fearless Sioux** (CWThornton) **2-8-9** DeanMcKeown(5) (chsd ldrs: drvn along over 2f out: one pce)	5	**4**	9/1	49	17
4578[9]	**Amico** (CWThornton) **2-9-0** SDrowne(4) (sn bhd & pushed along: hdwy ½-wy: styd on appr fnl f)	½	**5**	25/1	52	20
4790[6]	**Chasetown Flyer (USA) (60)** (RHollinshead) **2-8-11**(3) FLynch(10) (a in tch: effrt ½-wy: nvr able to chal)	1¼	**6**	16/1	49	17
	Miami Moon (CWThornton) **2-8-9** JQuinn(13) (leggy: scope: s.i.s: bhd tl styd on ins fnl 2f)	s.h	**7**	14/1	44	12
2932[4]	**Music Express (IRE)** (JLEyre) **2-8-9** TWilliams(7) (a in tch: drvn along ½-wy: no imp)	1	**8**	5/1[3]	41	9
5034[7]	**Jay-Owe-Two (IRE)** (RMWhitaker) **2-9-0** ACulhane(9) (lw: s.s: sn wl bhd: hdwy over 2f out: nt rch ldrs)	¾	**9**	6/1	44+	12
683[F]	**Simply Times (USA)** (WAO'Gorman) **2-8-9** EmmaO'Gorman(11) (chsd ldrs: effrt over 2f out: wknd over 1f out)	6	**10**	4/1[2]	23	—
	Magic Fizz (TJEtherington) **2-9-0** MBirch(14) (sn bhd)	¾	**11**	25/1	26	—
	Kustom Kit Klassic (SRBowring) **2-8-11**(3) CTeague(15) (w'like: bit bkwd: a bhd)	1	**12**	25/1	23	—
4807[W]	**Hio Nod** (MJCamacho) **2-9-0** LCharnock(6) (w'like: scope: bit bkwd: a bhd)	3½	**13**	16/1	14	—
4715[27]	**Diamonds Are** (DTThom) **2-8-9** DBiggs(12) (hdwy on outside ½-wy: sn lost pl)	1¼	**14**	33/1	6	—
2413[8]	***Frandickbob*** (JohnHarris) **2-9-0** DRMcCabe(16) (Withdrawn not under Starter's orders: uns rdr & bolted bef s)		**W**	25/1	—	—
4962[6]	***Supreme Maimoon*** (MJPolglase) **2-9-0** TGMcLaughlin(3) (Withdrawn not under Starter's orders: unruly & burst out of stalls)		**W**	9/1	—	—
				(SP 162.3%)	**14 Rn**	

1m 17.0 (3.50) CSF £18.52 TOTE £5.40: £1.70 £1.50 £5.80 (£7.80) Trio £66.10 OWNER Mr K. V. Stenborg (NEWMARKET) BRED Mrs C. A. Moore

5112 TOGO H'CAP (0-65) (II) (3-Y.O+ F & M) (Class F)

1-45 (1-50) **6f (Fibresand)** £2,048.00 (£573.00: £278.00) Stalls: Low GOING minus 0.15 sec per fur (FST)

Form	Horse / details	Dist	Pos	SP	RR	SF
4805[13]	**Shashi (IRE) (55)** (WWHaigh) **4-9-7** RLappin(1) (chsd ldrs: styd on to ld ins fnl f: drvn out)	—	**1**	20/1	63	41
4981[5]	**Anita's Contessa (IRE) (52)** (BPalling) **4-9-4** TSprake(8) (mid div: hdwy over 2f out: styd on wl fnl f)	¾	**2**	7/1[3]	58	36
4989[13]	**Juba (35)** (DrJDScargill) **4-8-1** NCarlisle(2) (hdwy ½-wy: styd on wl fnl f)	1	**3**	16/1	38	16
5093*	**Madrina (65)** (JBerry) **3-9-12**(5) 7x PFessey(15) (trckd ldrs: led over 2f out tl hdd ins fnl f: wknd)	2	**4**	11/4[1]	63	41
4983[10]	**Bent Raiwand (USA) (41)** (DonEnricoIncisa) **3-8-7** KimTinkler(9) (w ldrs: led over 3f out tl over 2f out: wknd appr fnl f)	½	**5**	33/1	38	16
4981[9]	**Polar Refrain (47)** (CADwyer) **3-8-6**(7) JoHunnam(6) (s.i.s: bhd tl styd on fnl 2f)	3	**6**	9/1	36	14
4693[6]	**Lachesis (54)** (BRichmond) **3-9-3**(3) CTeague(4) (s.i.s: hdwy ½-wy: wknd 2f out:)	4	**7**	25/1	32	10
5059[2]	**Elite Hope (USA) (55)** (NTinkler) **4-9-7** LCharnock(13) (mid div: drvn along ½-wy: no imp)	½	**8**	5/1[2]	32	10
5001[3]	**Daisy Bates (IRE) (54)** (PWHarris) **3-9-6** GDuffield(5) (lw: chsd ldrs: drvn along over 2f out: sn wknd)	1¼	**9**	5/1[2]	27	5
1156[8]	**Lithe Spirit (IRE) (45)** (JohnHarris) **4-8-11** DeanMcKeown(11) (a rr div)	8	**10**	33/1	—	—
5010[9]	**Another Nightmare (IRE) (46)** (RMMcKellar) **4-8-12** TWilliams(3) (led over 2f: wknd over 2f out: eased)	nk	**11**	8/1	—	—
4356[19]	**Hickleton Miss (42)** (MrsVAAconley) **3-8-8** MDeering(14) (sn bhd)	5	**12**	33/1	—	—
5059[12]	**Penny's Wishing (40)** (CSmith) **4-8-6** AClark(12) (lw: a in rr)	3½	**13**	20/1	—	—
5059[10]	**Miss Carottene (48)** (MJRyan) **3-9-0v** MRoberts(10) (sn bhd)	2½	**14**	14/1	—	—
	Ann's Music (37) (JMJefferson) **3-8-3** JQuinn(7) (lw: a bhd)	5	**15**	20/1	—	—
				(SP 133.1%)	**15 Rn**	

1m 17.3 (3.80) CSF £154.00 CT £2,174.41 TOTE £16.90: £4.20 £1.90 £6.60 (£107.40) Trio £205.80; £202.94 to Wetherby 19/11/96 OWNER Mr B. Valentine (MALTON) BRED Sheikh Mohammed bin Rashid al Maktoum

5113 ANGOLA NURSERY H'CAP (2-Y.O) (Class E)

2-15 (2-18) **7f (Fibresand)** £3,048.00 (£924.00: £452.00: £216.00) Stalls: Low GOING minus 0.15 sec per fur (FST)

Form	Horse / details	Dist	Pos	SP	RR	SF
4867[4]	**Erosion (IRE) (77)** (MJohnston) **2-8-6** MRoberts(8) (cl up: led over 1f out: put hd in air: jst hld on)	—	**1**	5/1[2]	78	39
5043[10]	**Effervescence (77)** (RHannon) **2-8-6** DaneO'Neill(4) (chsd ldrs: kpt on wl fnl f: jst failed)	s.h	**2**	9/1	78	39
5037[5]	**Nomore Mr Niceguy (77)** (EJAlston) **2-8-6** GDuffield(9) (lw: sn chsng ldrs: kpt on u.p fnl f)	½	**3**	14/1	77	38
4880[4]	**Merciless Cop (68)** (BJMeehan) **2-7-11b** JQuinn(10) (led tl hdd appr fnl f: no ex)	2	**4**	6/1[3]	63	24
5048[3]	**Spaniard's Mount (67)** (MHTompkins) **2-7-10v** DWright(5) (lw: hld up: effrt 3f out: nvr able to chal)	3	**5**	6/1[3]	55	16
4883[16]	**Ninth Symphony (70)** (PCHaslam) **2-7-13** LCharnock(3) (in tch: drvn along thrght: no imp fr ½-wy)	1¾	**6**	16/1	54	15
4586[15]	**Danehill Princess (IRE) (69)** (RHollinshead) **2-7-12** NCarlisle(1) (s.i.s: nvr trbld ldrs)	6	**7**	16/1	40	1
5057[6]	**Our Kevin (67)** (KMcAuliffe) **2-7-5v**(5) PFessey(7) (lw: sn outpcd)	3	**8**	20/1	31	—
5043*	**Jeffrey Anotherred (92)** (KMcAuliffe) **2-9-7** RHughes(2) (trckd ldrs tl lost pl fnl 2f)	¾	**9**	2/1[1]	54	15
4694[7]	**Captain Flint (67)** (ASmith) **2-7-10** NAdams(6) (t.o ½-wy: n.d)	11	**10**	33/1	4	—

4806[5]	**Patrita Park (67)** (WWHaigh) **2-7-3**(7) JBramhill(11) (lw: unruly gng to s: in tch 4f: wknd)	¾	**11**	33/1	2	—
4896[2]	**Canton Ron (67)** (CADwyer) **2-7-7**(3) NVarley(12) (lw: racd wd: sn drvn along & bhd)	6	**12**	8/1	—	—

(SP 128.8%) **12 Rn**

1m 30.2 (3.70) CSF £49.44 CT £564.88 TOTE £6.20: £2.40 £2.40 £4.80 (£22.40) Trio £103.20 OWNER Sheikh Mohammed (MIDDLEHAM) BRED Sheikh Mohammed Bin Rashid Al Maktoum
LONG HANDICAP Our Kevin 7-8 Captain Flint 6-5 Patrita Park 6-13 Canton Ron 7-6
OFFICIAL EXPLANATION Jeffrey Anotherred: had choked.

5114 CHAD LIMITED STKS (0-55) (II) (3-Y.O+) (Class F)

2-45 (2-48) **1m (Fibresand)** £2,048.00 (£573.00: £278.00) Stalls: Low GOING minus 0.15 sec per fur (FST)

				SP	RR	SF
4989[2]	**Domino Flyer (60)** (MrsASwinbank) **3-8-12** DHolland(11) (lw: cl up: led over 2f out: rdn & r.o wl)	—	**1**	Evens[1]	68	48
5004[3]	**Desert Zone (USA) (54)** (JohnHarris) **7-9-3** SSanders(8) (b: trckd ldrs: effrt over 2f out: r.o: nt pce of wnr)	3	**2**	11/2[2]	65	47
4989[5]	**Ya Marhaba (37)** (JWPayne) **3-8-12** MRoberts(10) (in tch: hung lft & styd on fnl 3f)	4	**3**	12/1	54	34
4805[15]	**Principal Boy (IRE) (53)** (TJEtherington) **3-8-12** LCharnock(6) (sn chsng ldrs: kpt on one pce fnl 2f)	2½	**4**	9/1	49	29
5010[14]	**Raindeer Quest (43)** (JLEyre) **4-8-11** RLappin(5) (cl up tl outpcd fnl 2f)	6	**5**	8/1[3]	34	16
4983[8]	**Anaxagoras (32)** (SGollings) **6-9-0** JQuinn(4) (bit bkwd: led tl hdd & wknd over 2f out)	2	**6**	33/1	33	15
4989[4]	**Pleasure Trick (USA) (34)** (DonEnricoIncisa) **5-9-0** KimTinkler(1) (bhd tl styd on fnl 3f)	1¼	**7**	20/1	31	13
4895[9]	**Fresh Fruit Daily (53)** (PAKelleway) **4-8-11** MWigham(15) (drvn along ½-wy: n.d)	¾	**8**	10/1	26	8
5059[3]	**Dragonjoy (52)** (NPLittmoden) **3-9-4v** AMcGlone(12) (in tch: effrt 3f out: sn wknd)	½	**9**	8/1[3]	34	14
4968[19]	**Hadadabble (38)** (PatMitchell) **3-8-9** DaneO'Neill(9) (nvr bttr than mid div)	nk	**10**	20/1	24	4
4881[15]	**Mu-Arrik (33)** (GROldroyd) **8-8-7**(7) ClaireWest(14) (bhd: sme hdwy ½-wy: sn wknd)	6	**11**	33/1	15	—
5010[13]	**Northern Spark (47)** (MissLAPerratt) **8-9-0**(3) FLynch(13) (b: a outpcd & bhd)	11	**12**	10/1	—	—
3578[10]	**Wild Prospect (28)** (ABailey) **8-9-0** DWright(16) (bit bkwd: b: a bhd)	1¾	**13**	33/1	—	—
4978[8]	**Soul Sister (40)** (DHaydnJones) **3-8-9** AClark(3) (a bhd)	1¾	**14**	20/1	—	—
4828[11]	**Supreme Desire (28)** (MissJFCraze) **8-8-11** SDWilliams(7) (chsd ldrs to ½-wy: wknd qckly)	s.h	**15**	33/1	—	—

(SP 149.5%) **15 Rn**

1m 43.6 (4.60) CSF £9.51 TOTE £2.70: £1.30 £2.00 £2.60 (£4.00) Trio £23.50 OWNER Mr S. Smith (RICHMOND) BRED Mrs K. Livingstone
WEIGHT FOR AGE 3yo-2lb

5115 ZAMBIA (S) STKS (3, 4 & 5-Y.O) (Class G)

3-15 (3-16) **1m 3f (Fibresand)** £2,085.00 (£585.00: £285.00) Stalls: Low GOING minus 0.15 sec per fur (FST)

				SP	RR	SF
4986[3]	**Ihtimaam (FR) (54)** (MrsASwinbank) **4-9-7** DHolland(4) (led tl hdd 5f out: led 2f out: styd on)	—	**1**	7/2[2]	69	31
1082[7]	**Greenspan (IRE) (76)** (WRMuir) **4-9-7** DaneO'Neill(2) (chsd ldrs: led 5f out to 2f out: nt qckn)	1½	**2**	7/4[1]	67	29
4779[12]	**Forzair (60)** (JJO'Neill) **4-9-0**(7) DJewett(3) (lw: a.p: effrt 4f out: one pce)	5	**3**	11/1	60	22
4904[5]	**Elite Bliss (IRE) (38)** (MJCamacho) **4-8-11** LCharnock(14) (lw: sn outpcd: styd on fnl 3f: nrst fin)	¾	**4**	10/1	49	11
4921[5]	**Petite Heritiere (38)** (MJRyan) **3-8-6** MRoberts(13) (hdwy 7f out: styd on: no imp)	s.h	**5**	10/1	48	5
4882[4]	**Yuppy Girl (IRE) (49)** (CaptJWilson) **3-8-3**(3) FLynch(1) (bhd: hdwy 6f out: nvr able to chal)	5	**6**	12/1	41	—
5053[16]	**Petoskin (68)** (JPearce) **4-9-7** MWigham(12) (in tch: pushed along 7f out: no imp)	8	**7**	6/1[3]	40	2
5007[8]	**Hutchies Lady (32)** (RMMcKellar) **4-8-9**(7) JMcAuley(10) (b.hind: cl up tl wknd fnl 3½f)	10	**8**	20/1	20	—
3308[8]	**Toulston Lady (IRE) (46)** (JWharton) **4-8-11** JQuinn(16) (bhd: sme hdwy 4f out: nvr nr to chal)	5	**9**	12/1	8	—
4812[8]	**Bold Top (38)** (BSRothwell) **4-9-2b** JStack(7) (bhd: effrt 5f out: sn btn)	1¼	**10**	16/1	11	—
4982[9]	**Spanish Stripper (USA) (35)** (MCChapman) **5-8-13**(3) PMcCabe(8) (swtg: a rr div)	hd	**11**	20/1	11	—
4070[10]	**Mill Dancer (IRE) (37)** (EJAlston) **4-8-11** DWright(15) (prom 8f: wknd)	¾	**12**	20/1	5	—
4829[4]	**Absolute Ruler (IRE) (38)** (JLHarris) **5-9-2b** SSanders(9) (nvr wnt pce)	3	**13**	12/1	5	—
4815[15]	**Shedansar (IRE) (25)** (RCSpicer) **4-9-2b[1]** JO'Reilly(11) (chsd ldrs tl wknd 5f out)	12	**14**	33/1	—	—
4982[12]	**Maybank (IRE) (50)** (AStreeter) **4-9-2**(5) ADaly(5) (bhd fr ½-wy: t.o)	23	**15**	20/1	—	—
4997[9]	**Jendali Princess** (MJPolglase) **3-8-6** TGMcLaughlin(6) (prom tl rdn & wknd 7f out)	18	**16**	25/1	—	—

(SP 154.2%) **16 Rn**

2m 28.7 (8.70) CSF £12.26 TOTE £7.20: £2.10 £1.30 £10.90 (£7.00) Trio £13.20 OWNER Upex Electrical Distributors Ltd (RICHMOND) BRED Gainsborough Stud Management Ltd
WEIGHT FOR AGE 3yo-5lb
No bid

5116 SENEGAL H'CAP (0-70) (3-Y.O+) (Class E)

3-45 (3-47) **2m (Fibresand)** £2,853.00 (£864.00: £422.00: £201.00) Stalls: Low GOING minus 0.15 sec per fur (FST)

				SP	RR	SF
*4984**	**Onefourseven (52)** (JLEyre) **3-8-6** TWilliams(1) (lw: trckd ldrs: led on bit 2f out: edgd lft: rdn & styd on wl towards fin)	—	**1**	6/4[1]	64	—
5084[2]	**Coleridge (56)** (JJSheehan) **8-9-5b** AClark(2) (prom: chal 7f out: led 5f out to 2f out: swtchd & qcknd to disp ld wl ins fnl f: hung lft & no ex)	nk	**2**	6/1[3]	68	7
5008[13]	**Iota (48)** (JLHarris) **7-8-11** SSanders(11) (hld up: hdwy 4f out: styd on: nt pce to chal)	5	**3**	12/1	55	—
5052*	**No More Hassle (IRE) (42)** (MrsMReveley) **3-7-10** 4x DWright(9) (lw: hld up: stdy hdwy 7f out: effrt 3f out: one pce)	6	**4**	5/1[2]	43	—
5008[4]	**Arc of The Diver (IRE) (55)** (JBerry) **3-8-4b**(5) PRoberts(3) (in tch: effrt 4f out: one pce)	7	**5**	9/1	49	—
5008[3]	**Shakiyr (FR) (65)** (RHollinshead) **5-9-11**(3) FLynch(6) (hld up & bhd: effrt 5f out: rdn & no imp)	4	**6**	7/1	55	—
3130[5]	**Pickens (USA) (56)** (NTinkler) **4-9-5** KimTinkler(10) (a.p: effrt 4f out: wknd over 2f out)	8	**7**	20/1	38	—
5007[3]	**Moonlight Calypso (38)** (MartynWane) **5-8-1** LCharnock(5) (chsd ldrs tl wknd over 2f out)	2½	**8**	10/1	17	—
4794[8]	**Amiarge (50)** (MBrittain) **6-8-13** GCarter(7) (cl up: drvn along 6f out: wknd 4f out)	5	**9**	10/1	24	—
4899[6]	**Chik's Secret (50)** (BPalling) **3-8-4** TSprake(4) (led tl hdd 5f out: sn wknd)	¾	**10**	33/1	23	—
	Acerbus Dulcis (55) (MCChapman) **5-9-1**(3) PMcCabe(8) (chsd ldrs tl wknd rapidly ½-wy: wl t.o)	dist	**11**	50/1	—	—

(SP 129.0%) **11 Rn**

3m 44.2 (18.20) CSF £12.13 CT £82.69 TOTE £2.50: £1.90 £1.50 £3.60 (£8.10) Trio £45.90 OWNER Mr J. Roundtree (HAMBLETON) BRED Peter Storey
LONG HANDICAP No More Hassle (IRE) 7-2
WEIGHT FOR AGE 3yo-9lb

T/Plpt: £543.30 (15.14 Tckts). T/Qdpt: £200.10 (4.79 Tckts). WG

5095-LINGFIELD (L-H) (Standard)
Tuesday November 19th
Racing delayed 15 mins
WEATHER: rainy periods WIND: almost nil

5117 MARK MAIDEN STKS (I) (3-Y.O) (Class D)
12-20 (12-36) **1m (Equitrack)** £3,046.25 (£920.00: £447.50: £211.25) Stalls: High GOING minus 0.48 sec per fur (FST)

				SP	RR	SF
4813[3]	**Royal Action (73)** (JEBanks) **3-9-0** MWigham(4) (a.p: led 5f out: clr over 1f out: r.o wl)	—	**1**	5/1	79	53
5042[5]	**Catumbella (USA) (73)** (JHMGosden) **3-8-9** AMcGlone(6) (led 3f: ev ch over 2f out: unable qckn)	5	**2**	7/4[1]	64	38
5004[6]	**Kazimiera (IRE) (60)** (CWCElsey) **3-8-5**(5)ow1 GFaulkner(1) (hld up: rdn over 2f out: sn wknd)	8	**3**	7/1	49	22
3949[3]	**Scherma** (WJarvis) **3-8-9** DaneO'Neill(5) (a.p: rdn over 3f out: wknd over 2f out)	½	**4**	9/2[3]	47	21
4998[7]	**Efficacious (IRE) (40)** (AMoore) **3-8-9** CandyMorris(7) (b.hind: bhd fnl 5f)	1½	**5**	33/1	44	18
5082[6]	**Fancy Design (IRE) (42)** (PMitchell) **3-8-9** JQuinn(2) (dwlt: a bhd)	2½	**6**	33/1	39	13
4827[4]	**Lacandona (USA)** (PWChapple-Hyam) **3-8-9** DHolland(8) (prom over 4f)	19	**7**	7/2[2]	1	—
				(SP 111.8%)	**7 Rn**	

1m 37.96 (0.56) CSF £13.49 TOTE £51.30: £1.90 £2.10 (£7.80) OWNER Mr E. Carter (NEWMARKET) BRED D. J. and Mrs Deer
IN-FOCUS: **An inch and a half of rain fell on the course in the morning, leaving a lot of surface water on the track. Conditions were certainly very sloppy and the horses had to plough their way through.**

5118 PESETA H'CAP (0-65) (I) (3-Y.O+) (Class F)
12-50 (1-03) **1m 2f (Equitrack)** £2,048.00 (£573.00: £278.00) Stalls: Low GOING minus 0.48 sec per fur (FST)

				SP	RR	SF
*5086**	**Double Rush (IRE) (58)** (TGMills) **4-9-9** 5x SSanders(7) (a gng wl: hld up: nt clr run on ins over 1f out: led ins fnl f: hrd rdn: r.o wl)	—	**1**	11/4[1]	67	46
4793*	**Maradata (IRE) (57)** (RHollinshead) **4-9-8** MWigham(1) (hdwy over 3f out: ev ch ins fnl f: r.o)	½	**2**	5/1[3]	65	44
4815[12]	**Comedy River (50)** (NEBerry) **9-9-1** DaneO'Neill(13) (hdwy over 3f out: ev ch 1f out: sn wknd)	5	**3**	10/1	50	29
5079[6]	**Mimosa (63)** (SDow) **3-9-5e**(5) ADaly(6) (hld up: rdn over 4f out: r.o ins fnl f)	1¼	**4**	9/1	61	36
5060[2]	**Golden Touch (USA) (60)** (DJSCosgrove) **4-9-6**(5) GFaulkner(9) (a.p: led over 3f out: hrd rdn over 1f out: hdd ins fnl f: sn wknd)	hd	**5**	7/2[2]	58	37
5081[5]	**Kirov Protege (IRE) (44)** (MrsLCJewell) **4-8-2**(7) DarrenWilliams(5) (a.p: rdn over 3f out: wknd over 2f out)	2½	**6**	33/1	38	17
4968[6]	**Burning Flame (37)** (RMFlower) **3-7-12** FNorton(2) (nvr nrr)	3	**7**	12/1	26	1
670[13]	**Zahid (USA) (60)** (KRBurke) **5-9-11** JQuinn(10) (lw: nvr nrr)	6	**8**	10/1	40	19
4982[10]	**Return To Brighton (40)** (JMBradley) **4-8-5** SDrowne(4) (prom over 6f)	hd	**9**	20/1	20	—
5079[10]	**Wingnut (IRE) (37)** (RIngram) **3-7-12b** TWilliams(3) (led over 6f)	14	**10**	25/1	—	—
	Robin Island (50) (PRHedger) **4-9-1** AMcGlone(11) (b.hind: a bhd)	7	**11**	33/1	—	—
3965[R]	**Carwyn's Choice (35)** (PCClarke) **3-7-10** NAdams(8) (virtually ref to r: a t.o)	8	**12**	66/1	—	—
274[8]	**Callonescy (IRE) (41)** (DCO'Brien) **4-8-6**ow1 GCarter(12) (a wl bhd: t.o)	10	**13**	50/1	—	—
				(SP 119.4%)	**13 Rn**	

2m 7.06 (2.76) CSF £16.06 CT £111.37 TOTE £4.50: £2.10 £1.70 £1.50 (£9.00) Trio £13.00 OWNER Mr Tony Murray (EPSOM) BRED Dermot Finnegan
LONG HANDICAP Carwyn's Choice 7-7
WEIGHT FOR AGE 3yo-4lb

5119 GUILDER H'CAP (0-70) (3-Y.O+) (Class E)
1-20 (1-28) **1m 4f (Equitrack)** £2,900.10 (£877.80: £428.40: £203.70) Stalls: Low GOING minus 0.48 sec per fur (FST)

				SP	RR	SF
4986[6]	**Basood (USA) (47)** (SPCWoods) **3-8-1b**ow1 DBiggs(8) (a gng wl: hld up: chsd ldr over 4f out: led over 1f out: rdn: r.o wl)	—	**1**	14/1	57	30
5056[2]	**Master Millfield (IRE) (63)** (PDEvans) **4-9-9** ACulhane(3) (rdn 7f out: hdwy over 4f out: r.o one pce fnl f)	2	**2**	5/1[2]	70	50
*5102**	**Hoofprints (IRE) (67)** (MrsAJPerrett) **3-9-7** 5x AClark(5) (b: lw: chsd ldr: led over 7f out tl over 1f out: one pce)	nk	**3**	Evens[1]	74	48
4993[5]	**Your Most Welcome (66)** (DJSffrenchDavis) **5-9-7**(5) GParkin(2) (nvr gng wl: lost pl over 10f out: no hdwy fnl 3f)	6	**4**	6/1[3]	65	45
4899[3]	**Ceilidh Star (IRE) (65)** (BWHills) **3-9-5b** DHolland(7) (a.p: chsd ldr over 7f out tl over 4f out: wknd over 2f out)	¾	**5**	6/1[3]	63	37
4919[11]	**Johns Act (USA) (68)** (DHaydnJones) **6-10-0b**[1] GDuffield(1) (led over 4f)	26	**6**	14/1	31	11
5086[4]	**Smile Forever (USA) (54)** (MissGayKelleway) **3-8-8** DaneO'Neill(6) (b: b.hind: a bhd)	4	**7**	16/1	12	—
				(SP 114.5%)	**7 Rn**	

2m 32.55 (2.55) CSF £74.43 CT £122.78 TOTE £12.10: £5.80 £2.10 (£26.70) Trio £36.20 OWNER Mr Ian Deane (NEWMARKET) BRED Gainsborough Farm Inc.
WEIGHT FOR AGE 3yo-6lb

5120 FRANC CONDITIONS STKS (3-Y.O+) (Class D)
1-50 (1-58) **1m 2f (Equitrack)** £3,647.50 (£1,105.00: £540.00: £257.50) Stalls: Low GOING minus 0.48 sec per fur (FST)

				SP	RR	SF
*5079**	**Thai Morning (69)** (PWHarris) **3-8-10** GDuffield(8) (hld up: led over 3f out: clr over 2f out: rdn out)	—	**1**	5/2[1]	89	48
4874[11]	**Night Wink (USA) (81)** (GLMoore) **4-9-0** DaneO'Neill(13) (lw: hdwy over 2f out: chsd wnr over 1f out: r.o one pce)	2½	**2**	7/1[3]	85	48
4226[7]	**South Eastern Fred (80)** (HJCollingridge) **5-9-0** JQuinn(1) (b: a.p: chsd wnr over 3f out tl over 1f out: one pce)	3½	**3**	10/1	79	42
5045[6]	**Weet-A-Minute (IRE) (97)** (RHollinshead) **3-8-10** MWigham(12) (lw: hdwy over 1f out: r.o wl ins fnl f)	1½	**4**	4/1[2]	77	36
5022a[13]	**Cedez le Passage (FR) (90)** (KOCunningham-Brown) **5-9-0b** MRoberts(3) (led over 6f: wknd over 2f out)	½	**5**	10/1	76	39
4695[5]	**Filial (IRE) (78)** (BJMeehan) **3-9-1** MTebbutt(5) (a.p: rdn over 4f out: wknd 3f out)	¾	**6**	25/1	80	39
*4978**	**Two To Tango (IRE) (77)** (JHMGosden) **3-8-8** AMcGlone(9) (hld up: rdn over 3f out: sn wknd)	2	**7**	8/1	70	29
4769[25]	**Cool Fire (74)** (SPCWoods) **3-8-10** WRyan(7) (prom over 7f)	s.h	**8**	25/1	72	31
5091[5]	**Opera Buff (IRE) (87)** (MissGayKelleway) **5-9-0** SSanders(11) (b: b.hind: lw: rdn 7f out: sme hdwy wl over 1f out: sn wknd)	½	**9**	11/1	71	34

				SP	RR	SF
4819^{5}	**Sadler's Walk (70)** (GWragg) **5-9-0** AClark(2) (bhd fnl 4f)	23	**10**	14/1	34	—
1811^{10}	**Able Choice (IRE) (71)** (RWArmstrong) **6-9-0** GCarter(4) (chsd ldr over 5f: wknd over 4f out)	3	**11**	25/1	29	—
3113^{12}	**Kintwyn (70)** (WRMuir) **6-9-0** DHarrison(10) (b.hind: a bhd)	20	**12**	20/1	—	—

(SP 121.7%) **12 Rn**

2m 5.24 (0.94) CSF £19.92 TOTE £3.30: £1.50 £2.30 £2.40 (£27.00) Trio £73.50 OWNER The Thai Connection (BERKHAMSTED) BRED R. G. Percival
WEIGHT FOR AGE 3yo-4lb

5121 ARTHUR BRADLEY RETIREMENT MEDIAN AUCTION MAIDEN STKS (2-Y.O) (Class E)

2-20 (2-26) **7f (Equitrack)** £3,009.30 (£911.40: £445.20: £212.10) Stalls: Low GOING minus 0.48 sec per fur (FST)

				SP	RR	SF
4976^{11}	**Henley (USA)** (DRLoder) **2-9-0** DRMcCabe(5) (a.p: led 5f out: drvn out)	—	**1**	7/2^{2}	90	39
4328^{9}	**Millroy (USA) (87)** (PAKelleway) **2-9-0** MWigham(12) (b.nr hind: a.p: rdn over 4f out: chsd wnr over 1f out: r.o)	¾	**2**	7/1^{3}	88	37
4918^{9}	**Boater** (DMorley) **2-9-0** GCarter(6) (lw: led 2f: rdn over 2f out: unable qckn)	3	**3**	16/1	81	30
5034^{3}	**Wild Sky (IRE)** (MJHeaton-Ellis) **2-9-0** SDrowne(1) (a.p: rdn over 2f out: wknd over 1f out)	6	**4**	2/1^{1}	68	17
5083^{2}	**Mon Bruce (75)** (WRMuir) **2-9-0** GDuffield(4) (a.p: rdn over 2f out: wknd wl over 1f out)	¾	**5**	7/2^{2}	66	15
	Over The Moon (MJFetherston-Godley) **2-8-9** DHarrison(9) (unf: nvr nr to chal)	5	**6**	33/1	50	—
5050^{6}	**Lights of Home** (RHannon) **2-9-0** DaneO'Neill(13) (bit bkwd: s.i.s: rdn over 4f out: nvr nrr)	s.h	**7**	20/1	55	4
5040^{7}	**Fruitie O'Flarety (65)** (CEBrittain) **2-9-0** MRoberts(11) (rdn & hdwy over 3f out: wknd over 2f out)	nk	**8**	16/1	54	3
4891^{10}	**Zorro** (RMFlower) **2-9-0** DBiggs(2) (a bhd)	nk	**9**	66/1	53	2
5083^{9}	**Mystery (55)** (SDow) **2-8-4e**$^{(5)}$ ADaly(8) (lw: bhd fnl 5f)	s.h	**10**	33/1	48	—
3982^{19}	**Flower Hill Lad (IRE) (68)** (DJSCosgrove) **2-9-0** JQuinn(3) (a bhd)	1½	**11**	16/1	50	—
4902^{6}	**Myosotis (67)** (PJMakin) **2-9-0** SSanders(7) (a bhd)	7	**12**	20/1	34	—
5033^{18}	**Hever Golf Magic (IRE)** (MJohnston) **2-8-9** DHolland(10) (lw: bhd fnl 3f)	1½	**13**	16/1	25	—

(SP 130.7%) **13 Rn**

1m 25.6 (1.20) CSF £29.27 TOTE £5.50: £1.70 £1.80 £4.20 (£30.20) Trio £197.20; £177.83 to Hereford 20/11/96 OWNER Mrs Virginia Kraft Payson (NEWMARKET) BRED Jesse M. Henley Jr

5122 MARK MAIDEN STKS (II) (3-Y.O) (Class D)

2-50 (2-55) **1m (Equitrack)** £3,046.25 (£920.00: £447.50: £211.25) Stalls: High GOING minus 0.48 sec per fur (FST)

				SP	RR	SF
4582^{12}	**Tissue of Lies (USA) (76)** (MJohnston) **3-9-0** MRoberts(3) (led over 5f out: drvn out)	—	**1**	5/2^{1}	65	35
3800^{12}	**Passage Creeping (IRE) (70)** (SDow) **3-8-9e** SSanders(8) (hdwy over 3f out: chsd wnr over 2f out: ev ch fnl 2f: r.o)	nk	**2**	3/1^{2}	59	29
4997^{4}	**Questing Star (52)** (GWragg) **3-8-9** AClark(5) (hld up: rdn over 4f out: r.o wl ins fnl f)	1¼	**3**	9/2^{3}	57	27
3059^{11}	**Lahik (IRE) (35)** (KTIvory) **3-9-0** NAdams(1) (prom over 4f)	11	**4**	33/1	40	10
4997^{3}	**Balinsky (IRE) (55)** (JBerry) **3-8-9** GCarter(7) (hld up: rdn over 3f out: wknd over 2f out)	4	**5**	11/1	27	—
4968^{18}	**Commin' Up (62)** (JWHills) **3-8-9** DHolland(2) (led over 2f: rdn over 4f out: wknd 3f out)	5	**6**	6/1	17	—
5001^{2}	**The Fugative (55)** (PMitchell) **3-8-9** JQuinn(6) (b: bhd fnl 4f)	9	**7**	5/1	—	—
5058^{6}	**Daratown** (PDEvans) **3-9-0** ACulhane(4) (bhd fnl 5f)	12	**8**	33/1	—	—

(SP 116.9%) **8 Rn**

1m 39.73 (2.33) CSF £10.29 TOTE £2.90: £1.10 £1.10 £2.40 (£13.10) OWNER The No Hassle Partnership (MIDDLEHAM) BRED Margaux Stud Inc, Dr I. Mersack et al

5123 PESETA H'CAP (0-65) (II) (3-Y.O+) (Class F)

3-20 (3-22) **1m 2f (Equitrack)** £2,048.00 (£573.00: £278.00) Stalls: Low GOING minus 0.48 sec per fur (FST)

				SP	RR	SF
4812*	**Adamton (49)** (MrsJCecil) **4-9-0** MRoberts(6) (mde all: clr 2f out: eased ins fnl f)	—	**1**	7/2^{2}	62	44
5094^{2}	**Paronomasia (31)** (JLHarris) **4-7-10** JQuinn(7) (a.p: rdn over 4f out: chsd wnr over 3f out: no imp)	5	**2**	13/2^{3}	36	18
5003^{3}	**Father Dan (IRE) (58)** (MissGayKelleway) **7-9-9** SSanders(11) (b: b.hind: rdn & hdwy over 3f out: one pce)	1¾	**3**	13/2^{3}	60	42
4900^{15}	**Myfontaine (60)** (KTIvory) **9-9-11** DBiggs(3) (b: hdwy over 1f out: r.o)	1¾	**4**	14/1	59	41
4894^{8}	**By The Bay (40)** (SDow) **4-8-0e**$^{(5)}$ ADaly(5) (stdy hdwy 5f out: rdn over 3f out: wknd over 1f out)	nk	**5**	25/1	39	21
4789^{7}	**Hatta Sunshine (USA) (52)** (AMoore) **6-9-0**$^{(3)}$ AWhelan(4) (b.hind: nvr nr to chal)	3	**6**	14/1	46	28
*5094**	**Arzani (USA) (58)** (DJSCosgrove) **5-9-4**$^{(5)}$ 5x GFaulkner(10) (hld up: rdn 4f out: wknd over 2f out)	¾	**7**	100/30^{1}	51	33
5082^{5}	**Queen's Insignia (USA) (60)** (PFICole) **3-9-7** CRutter(8) (bhd fnl 3f)	3	**8**	16/1	48	26
5010^{8}	**Vanborough Lad (39)** (MJBolton) **7-8-4** GDuffield(1) (chsd wnr over 6f)	6	**9**	33/1	18	—
4499^{8}	**Rainy Day Song (52)** (LordHuntingdon) **3-8-13** DHarrison(9) (prom over 5f)	4	**10**	16/1	24	2
*5082**	**Zahran (IRE) (44)** (JMBradley) **5-8-9** 5x SDrowne(12) (b: lw: sme hdwy 4f out: wknd over 3f out)	¾	**11**	7/1	15	—

(SP 116.4%) **11 Rn**

2m 6.27 (1.97) CSF £24.53 CT £129.34 TOTE £5.00: £4.70 £1.50 £1.90 (£13.50) Trio £46.60 OWNER Mrs J. Cecil (NEWMARKET) BRED Lady Murless
LONG HANDICAP Paronomasia 7-7
WEIGHT FOR AGE 3yo-4lb

5124 LADBROKE ALL-WEATHER TROPHY (QUALIFIER) H'CAP (0-70) (3-Y.O+) (Class E)

3-50 (3-55) **7f (Equitrack)** £3,173.10 (£961.80: £347.55: £347.55) Stalls: Low GOING minus 0.48 sec per fur (FST)

				SP	RR	SF
*4895**	**Twin Creeks (65)** (VSoane) **5-9-9** CRutter(12) (a.p: rdn over 2f out: chsd ldr over 1f out: led wl ins fnl f: r.o wl)	—	**1**	9/1^{3}	73	47
*5089**	**Smithereens (65)** (PTWalwyn) **3-9-3**$^{(5)}$ SCopp(2) (lw: led over 5f out: clr 2f out: rdn over 1f out: hdd wl ins fnl f: unable qckn)	1¾	**2**	15/8^{1}	69	42
4768^{3}	**Utmost Zeal (USA) (64)** (PWHarris) **3-9-7** AMcGlone(14) (hld up: rdn over 2f out: r.o wl ins fnl f)	1¼	**3**	10/1	65	38
4781^{6}	**Hawaii Storm (FR) (50)** (DJSffrenchDavis) **8-8-5**$^{(3)}$ PMcCabe(3) (hdwy over 1f out: r.o wl ins fnl f)	d.h	**3**	16/1	51	25
5000^{5}	**Invocation (60)** (AMoore) **9-9-4** CandyMorris(5) (b.hind: lw: rdn & hdwy over 2f out: one pce)	½	**5**	7/1^{2}	60	34
*4983**	**Miss Offset (70)** (MJohnston) **3-9-13b** DHolland(11) (led over 1f: rdn over 4f out: wknd ins fnl f)	1½	**6**	10/1	67	40
5000^{10}	**Risking (47)** (GLewis) **3-8-1e**$^{(3)}$ow1 AWhelan(6) (b.nr fore: nvr nr to chal)	hd	**7**	33/1	43	15
4987^{9}	**Never Think Twice (60)** (KTIvory) **3-9-3b** DBiggs(1) (a mid div)	2½	**8**	16/1	51	24
4915^{15}	**Our Shadee (USA) (56)** (KTIvory) **6-9-0** GDuffield(7) (nvr nrr)	1½	**9**	14/1	43	17

				SP	RR	SF
4498[2]	**Sweet Wilhelmina (70)** (LordHuntingdon) **3-9-13** DHarrison(4) (a.p: rdn over 3f out: wknd fnl f)	nk	**10**	7/1[2]	57	30
5086[6]	**Dia Georgy (38)** (CADwyer) **5-7-10** JQuinn(10) (bhd fnl 3f)	8	**11**	33/1	6	—
4987[14]	**Sihafi (USA) (60)** (JMCarr) **3-9-3** AClark(8) (lw: a bhd)	1½	**12**	25/1	25	—
4701[13]	**Charming Bride (53)** (SCWilliams) **3-8-10b**[1] DRMcCabe(9) (a bhd)	7	**13**	25/1	2	—
				(SP 120.0%)		**13 Rn**

1m 25.63 (1.23) CSF £24.88 CT TC, S & UZ £83.43 TC, S & HS £128.89 TOTE £20.50: £4.80 £2.10 UZ £1.10 HS £0.80 (£18.90) Trio TC, S & UZ £10.40, TC, S & HS £52.90 OWNER The Armchair Jockeys-Four Seasons Racing (ASTON ROWANT) BRED Crest Stud Ltd
LONG HANDICAP Dia Georgy 7-7
WEIGHT FOR AGE 3yo-1lb

T/Plpt: £196.60 (38.7 Tckts). T/Qdpt: £46.60 (19.28 Tckts). AK

5071a-**EVRY (France)** (R-H) (Very Soft)
Tuesday November 12th

5125a PRIX SCARAMOUCHE (Listed) (3-Y.O+)
2-40 (2-36) **1m 7f** £18,445.00 (£6,324.00: £3,953.00: £2,055.00)

				SP	RR	SF
	Fairhonor (FR) (AFabre,France) **3-8-9** TJarnet	—	**1**		113	—
4959a[5]	**Always Earnest (USA)** (MmeMBollack-Badel,France) **8-9-3b** ABadel	2	**2**		111	—
1138a[7]	**Suave Tern (USA)** (JEHammond,France) **5-9-3** OPeslier	s.nk	**3**		111	—
4665a*	**Snow Princess (IRE)** (LordHuntingdon) **4-9-4** JReid	2½	**4**		109	—
4551[3]	**Ayunli** (SCWilliams) **5-9-0** AJunk		**7**		—	—
						7 Rn

3m 32.65 (22.35) P-M 8.80F: 2.40F 1.40F OWNER J-G Verdier (CHANTILLY) BRED Colonel Jean-Gerard Verdier
4665a* Snow Princess (IRE) stayed on at one pace in the very soft ground.
4551 Ayunli finished last after attempting to make all and she will now be retired

4034a-**BORDEAUX (France)** (R-H) (Very Soft)
Sunday November 17th

5126a GRAND PRIX DE BORDEAUX (3-Y.O+)
2-10 (2-11) **1m 4f** £26,350.00 (£9,486.00: £4,743.00: £2,372.00)

				SP	RR	SF
4856a[3]	**Rainbow Dancer (FR)** (PBary,France) **5-9-8** TJarnet	—	**1**		115	—
5030a[3]	**Peckinpah's Soul (FR)** (DSmaga,France) **4-8-12** FHead	3½	**2**		100	—
2668a[12]	**Bon Jovi (GER)** (HJentzsch,Germany) **3-9-2** PSchiergen	1	**3**		109	—
4465[12]	**Whitechapel (USA)** (LordHuntingdon) **8-8-10** DHarrison	2½	**4**		94	—
						8 Rn

0m P-M 2.60F: 1.10F 1.20F 1.30F (6.40F) OWNER Mr D. Tsui (CHANTILLY)
4327 Whitechapel (USA) was always racing in mid-division and, when asked to quicken two furlongs out, found little.

5073a-**CAPANNELLE (Rome, Italy)** (R-H) (Heavy)
Sunday November 17th

5127a PREMIO UMBRIA (Gp 3)
1-45 (1-55) **6f** £25,700.00 (£11,723.00: £6,516.00)

				SP	RR	SF
	Golden Oriental (USA) (GFratini,Italy) **2-8-5** OFrancera	—	**1**		111	—
1136a*	**Beat of Drums** (GBotti,Italy) **5-9-8** EBotti	nk	**2**		109	—
794a[14]	**Bella Michela (IRE)** (GCrivelli,Italy) **3-9-5** ACorrias	1½	**3**		102	—
4958a[4]	**Leap for Joy** (JHMGosden) **4-9-5** LDettori (btn approx 3½l)		**5**		—	—
						10 Rn

1m 10.3 TOTE 532L: 99L 26L 87L (1253L) OWNER Scuderia Golden Horse BRED Luis de Hechevarria
4958a Leap for Joy did not have the pace on the heavy ground to be a live contender. In touch for the first half-mile, when the pace quickened two furlongs from home she was left slightly one-paced and was unable to accelerate with the principals.

5128a PREMIO GUIDO BERARDELLI (Gp 2) (2-Y.O)
2-10 (2-28) **1m 1f** £30,309.00 (£13,922.00: £7,766.00: £3,883.00)

				SP	RR	SF
5028a*	**Golden Aventura (IRE)** (GFratini,Italy) **2-8-11** LDettori (mid div: gd hdwy fr 3f out: led appr fnl f: drvn out)	—	**1**		104	—
5031a*	**Yavlensky (IRE)** (JLDunlop) **2-8-11** MRoberts (trckd ldr: led wl over 1f out: hdd appr fnl f: styd on)	1½	**2**		101	—
	Madler (IRE) (VCaruso,Italy) **2-8-11** MEsposito (mid div: rdn to go 3rd 1½f out: styd on)	nk	**3**		101	—
4859a[7]	**Woods of Cisterna (IRE)** (LCamici,Italy) **2-8-11** MPasquale (cl up: 3rd st: ev ch over 1f out: wknd)	2	**4**		97	—
	Special Star (Italy) **2-8-11** ACorniani (set pce tl hdd wl over 1f out: wknd)	5	**5**		88	—
4666a[2]	**White Gulch** (Italy) **2-8-11** EBotti (in tch tl wknd over 1f out)	3	**6**		83	—
4023a[5]	**Quest Express** (Italy) **2-8-11** FJovine (a in rr)	1	**7**		81	—
	Big Erotavlas (ITY) (Italy) **2-8-11** MCangiano (a bhd)	1	**8**		80	—
						8 Rn

1m 54.7 TOTE 36L: 15L 14L 15L (46L) OWNER Scuderia Golden Horse
5031a* Yavlensky (IRE) put up a very good performance when stepping up in class here. Tracking the leader for the first part of the race, he entered the straight in a prominent position. After hitting the front well over a furlong and a half out, he was unable to hold off the final flurry of the winner, but battled gamely all the way to the line.

5109-SOUTHWELL (L-H) (Standard)

Friday November 22nd

WEATHER: overcast & cold WIND: slt half bhd

5129 RIVER IDLE CLAIMING STKS (I) (3-Y.O+) (Class F)

12-00 (12-02) **1m (Fibresand)** £2,048.00 (£573.00: £278.00) Stalls: Low GOING minus 0.14 sec per fur (FST)

Form	Horse	Btn	Pos	SP	RR	SF
5060^{4}	**Chadleigh Lane (USA) (62)** (RHollinshead) **4-8-6**(3) FLynch(1) (lw: hld up: hdwy over 2f out: styd on u.p to ld cl home)	—	**1**	7/4^{1}	69	39
4987^{2}	**Elton Ledger (IRE) (73)** (MrsNMacauley) **7-8-9v** EmmaO'Gorman(7) (lw: b: sn trckng ldrs: led over 1f out tl nr fin)	hd	**2**	7/2^{2}	69	39
5058^{5}	**Ruby Angel** (HCandy) **3-8-0** CRutter(6) (a chsng ldrs: one pce appr fnl f)	8	**3**	12/1	46	14
5079^{9}	**Medland (IRE) (45)** (BJMcMath) **6-8-5**ow2 DBiggs(5) (b: mde most tl over 1f out: grad wknd)	1½	**4**	16/1	46	14
4360^{9}	**Saxon Bay** (KOCunningham-Brown) **4-9-3** DRMcCabe(8) (sn outpcd & bhd: styd on fnl 2f: nrst fin)	hd	**5**	25/1	58	28
4901^{5}	**Mustn't Grumble (IRE) (53)** (MissSJWilton) **6-9-3v** MTebbutt(3) (trckd ldrs: ev ch tl edgd rt & wknd over 1f out)	½	**6**	6/1^{3}	57	27
5110^{8}	**Havana Miss (32)** (BPalling) **4-8-7**ow3 AClark(11) (chsd ldrs tl rdn & outpcd fnl 2f)	1	**7**	20/1	45	12
	Joseph's Wine (IRE) (DNicholls) **7-9-7** AlexGreaves(9) (bit bkwd: hld up: stdy hdwy 2f out: nvr rchd ldrs)	½	**8**	9/1	58	28
3901^{1}	**Blondane** (SRBowring) **3-8-5** DeanMcKeown(13) (b: racd wd: sn outpcd: bhd fnl 3f)	4	**9**	20/1	36	4
5095^{7}	**Arcus (IRE)** (WRMuir) **3-8-6**(7) JWilkinson(12) (in tch: drvn along ½-wy: sn lost pl)	1	**10**	14/1	42	10
3970^{8}	**Undawaterscubadiva (31)** (MPBielby) **4-8-13** ACulhane(10) (chsd ldrs: sn drvn along: lost pl 2f out)	2	**11**	50/1	36	6
5093^{7}	**Emei Shan (40)** (WGMTurner) **3-7-10** NAdams(4) (prom early: outpcd & bhd fr ½-wy)	4	**12**	50/1	13	—
5115^{14}	**Shedansar (IRE) (25)** (RCSpicer) **4-8-9b** JO'Reilly(14) (s.i.s: racd wd: sn drvn along: a bhd)	5	**13**	50/1	14	—

(SP 122.4%) **13 Rn**

1m 44.3 (5.30) CSF £8.30 TOTE £2.50: £1.10 £1.00 £3.50 (£3.90) Trio £20.60 OWNER Mr J. E. Bigg (UPPER LONGDON) BRED Windwoods Farm, Bruce Brown and Connie Brown

WEIGHT FOR AGE 3yo-2lb

OFFICIAL EXPLANATION Joseph's Wine (IRE): had blown up turning for home over what was an insufficient trip, and being mindful of his previous history of leg trouble, his jockey finished as close as she could without being unduly hard on him.

5130 FARMERS WEEKLY H'CAP (0-60) (I) (3-Y.O+) (Class F)

12-30 (12-31) **7f (Fibresand)** £2,048.00 (£573.00: £278.00) Stalls: Low GOING minus 0.14 sec per fur (FST)

Form	Horse	Btn	Pos	SP	RR	SF
5089^{3}	**Shontaine (60)** (MJohnston) **3-9-13** DHolland(8) (lw: trckd ldrs: led 3f out: sn clr: hung lft over 1f out: all out)	—	**1**	9/2^{2}	73	46
5058^{4}	**Surf City (57)** (WWHaigh) **3-9-10** JQuinn(9) (hld up: hdwy to chse wnr over 1f out: styd on towards fin)	nk	**2**	12/1	69	42
5042^{14}	**Ben Gunn (58)** (PTWalwyn) **4-9-7**(5) DGriffiths(5) (trckd ldrs: shkn up & kpt on wl fnl 2f)	3	**3**	10/1	64	38
4348^{13}	**Truly Bay (50)** (TDBarron) **3-8-10**(7) VictoriaAppleby(6) (lw: a in tch: effrt over 2f out: edgd lft & styd on one pce appr fnl f)	3	**4**	20/1	49	22
5110^{4}	**Napoleon's Return (45)** (JLEyre) **3-8-12** RLappin(14) (w ldrs: rdn & outpcd over 2f out: hung lft & kpt on fnl f)	½	**5**	4/1^{1}	43	16
2934^{8}	**Sheraz (IRE) (60)** (NTinkler) **4-10-0** CRutter(4) (sn wl bhd: styd on wl fnl 2f)	2	**6**	12/1	53	27
4785^{12}	**Reem Fever (IRE) (47)** (DWPArbuthnot) **3-9-0** AClark(10) (sn outpcd: kpt on fnl 2f: nvr rchd ldrs)	1¾	**7**	25/1	36	9
5089^{10}	**Scathebury (54)** (KRBurke) **3-9-7** DRMcCabe(16) (racd wd: prom: effrt 3f out: grad wknd)	1	**8**	12/1	41	14
5060^{8}	**Time Clash (50)** (BPalling) **3-9-3** RPerham(13) (sn outpcd: n.d)	5	**9**	16/1	25	—
4921^{17}	**Guy's Gamble (54)** (JWharton) **3-9-7** GDuffield(7) (chsd ldrs: drvn along over 3f out: sn lost pl)	2½	**10**	10/1	24	—
4432^{17}	**Nkapen Rocks (SPA) (53)** (CaptJWilson) **3-9-6** SDWilliams(15) (racd wd: prom: rdn & hung lft over 2f out: sn lost pl)	7	**11**	20/1	7	—
5056^{11}	**Eccentric Dancer (46)** (MPBielby) **3-8-10b**(3) PMcCabe(11) (b.off hind: sn rdn along & bhd)	nk	**12**	20/1	—	—
1716^{11}	**Rennyholme (56)** (JHetherton) **5-9-10** NAdams(12) (chsd ldrs tl lost pl 3f out)	5	**13**	16/1	—	—
5003^{11}	**Mapengo (48)** (JCullinan) **5-9-2** VSlattery(3) (w ldrs tl wknd over 2f out)	½	**14**	33/1	—	—
4996^{9}	**Dissentor (IRE) (50)** (JAGlover) **4-9-4v** GCarter(2) (mde most to 3f out: sn wknd)	nk	**15**	13/2^{3}	—	—
4484^{8}	**De-Veers Currie (IRE) (50)** (DMoffatt) **4-9-4** DeanMcKeown(1) (sn wl bhd)	¾	**16**	25/1	—	—

(SP 129.5%) **16 Rn**

1m 31.4 (4.90) CSF £56.36 CT £490.98 TOTE £4.00: £1.70 £3.20 £1.90 £7.70 (£26.10) Trio £44.70 OWNER Mr Paul Dean (MIDDLEHAM) BRED Mark Johnston Racing Ltd

WEIGHT FOR AGE 3yo-1lb

5131 TRENT APPRENTICE H'CAP (0-85) (3-Y.O+) (Class G)

1-00 (1-03) **5f (Fibresand)** £2,085.00 (£585.00: £285.00) Stalls: High GOING minus 0.14 sec per fur (FST)

Form	Horse	Btn	Pos	SP	RR	SF
5105^{4}	**Portend (78)** (SRBowring) **4-9-8** HBastiman(3) (a in tch: hdwy & swtchd 1f out: styd on to ld nr fin)	—	**1**	7/1^{2}	85	56
4995*	**Palacegate Jack (IRE) (80)** (CADwyer) **5-9-10** FLynch(4) (lw: w ldrs: led over 1f out tl nr fin)	1	**2**	7/1^{2}	84	55
4869^{5}	**Ansellman (84)** (JBerry) **6-10-0b** PRoberts(12) (a chsng ldrs: styd on wl ins fnl f)	s.h	**3**	12/1	88	59
5039^{13}	**Master of Passion (65)** (JMPEustace) **7-8-6**(3) DSweeney(8) (a chsng ldrs: kpt on same pce fnl 2f)	½	**4**	16/1	67	38
5105^{11}	**Saddlehome (USA) (80)** (TDBarron) **7-9-5**(5) VictoriaAppleby(6) (hld up: hdwy over 1f out: styd on towards fin)	¾	**5**	20/1	80	51
4809^{9}	**Amy Leigh (IRE) (54)** (CaptJWilson) **3-7-5b**(7)ow2 AngelaHartley(14) (hld up: effrt 2f out: styd on towards fin)	1	**6**	16/1	50	19
5039^{2}	**Chadwell Hall (80)** (SRBowring) **5-9-5**(5) JBramhill(17) (w ldr: led & hung lft 2f out: sn hdd & wknd)	1¼	**7**	9/1^{3}	72	43
4220^{8}	**Primula Bairn (64)** (DNicholls) **6-8-3b**(5)ow3 ClaireWest(13) (hld up: styd on appr fnl f: nvr nr to chal)	¾	**8**	25/1	54	22
5039^{14}	**Shadow Jury (75)** (DWChapman) **6-9-5b** PFessey(7) (chsd ldrs over 3f: sn wknd)	hd	**9**	10/1	65	36
4909^{18}	**Antonias Melody (70)** (SRBowring) **3-9-0b** CTeague(9) (lw: led 3f: sn wknd)	hd	**10**	5/1^{1}	59	30
1642^{20}	**Sir Tasker (52)** (JLHarris) **8-7-7**(3) IonaWands(11) (in tch to ½-wy: sn wknd)	2½	**11**	20/1	33	4
4995^{6}	**Wollstonecraft (IRE) (70)** (JHMGosden) **3-9-0** MartinDwyer(1) (nvr wnt pce)	½	**12**	14/1	50	21
4616^{3}	**Squire Corrie (66)** (DWChapman) **4-8-10** DWright(2) (hld up: a bhd)	s.h	**13**	12/1	46	17
5096^{8}	**Silk Cottage (68)** (RMWhitaker) **4-8-7**(5) PFredericks(10) (mid div: drvn along ½-wy: n.d)	1½	**14**	20/1	43	14
4996^{7}	**Windrush Boy (52)** (JRBosley) **6-7-5**(5) PDoe(16) (in tch: sddle slipped & lost pl ½-wy)	2	**15**	25/1	20	—
*5096**	**Kalar (66)** (DWChapman) **7-8-10b** 7x DRMcCabe(5) (hld up: sn bhd)	nk	**16**	9/1^{3}	34	5

				SP	RR	SF
5039^{17}	**Perfect Brave (70)** (JBalding) **5-8-11**(3) GFaulkner(15) (stumbled s: a wl bhd: virtually p.u)	20	**17**	14/1	—	—

(SP 133.2%) **17 Rn**

59.1 secs (2.10) CSF £55.68 CT £567.29 TOTE £9.10: £1.90 £2.40 £4.10 £2.60 (£28.50) Trio £76.90 OWNER Mr D. H. Bowring (EDWINSTOWE) BRED Hollow Hole Stud

LONG HANDICAP Windrush Boy 7-8 Sir Tasker 7-8 Amy Leigh (IRE) 7-3

5132 RIVER IDLE CLAIMING STKS (II) (3-Y.O+) (Class F)

1-30 (1-30) **1m (Fibresand)** £2,048.00 (£573.00: £278.00) Stalls: Low GOING minus 0.14 sec per fur (FST)

				SP	RR	SF
5055^{2}	**Best of All (IRE)** (JBerry) **4-9-2e** GCarter(13) (lw: trckd ldrs: led over 1f out: hung lft: drvn out)	—	**1**	9/4^{2}	67	41
4129^{10}	**Manabar (63)** (MJPolglase) **4-8-7** TGMcLaughlin(2) (trckd ldrs: effrt & ev ch over 1f out: styd on towards fin)	nk	**2**	12/1	57	31
	Genuine John (IRE) (JParkes) **3-9-0**(3) PMcCabe(12) (b: sn chsng ldrs: led 3f out tl over 1f out: kpt on same pce)	1½	**3**	5/1^{3}	66	38
4904^{10}	**Running Green** (DMoffatt) **5-8-2**(3) DarrenMoffatt(5) (b: s.i.s: sn in tch: hrd rdn & nt clr run over 2f out: kpt on wl fnl f)	1½	**4**	20/1	49	23
5055^{9}	**Galacia (IRE) (45)** (WGMTurner) **4-7-12** NAdams(9) (sn drvn along: a in tch: one pce fnl 2f)	2	**5**	25/1	38	12
1081^{5}	**Spencer's Revenge (73)** (NTinkler) **7-8-9b** CRutter(4) (sn outpcd & pushed along: sme hdwy on outside over 2f out: nvr nr ldrs)	hd	**6**	7/4^{1}	49	23
4865^{8}	**Oriel Lad (53)** (DonEnricoIncisa) **3-8-3** KimTinkler(10) (sn outpcd: kpt on fnl 2f: n.d)	hd	**7**	20/1	45	17
2082^{5}	**Hornpipe (55)** (JWharton) **4-8-10** SDWilliams(7) (b: chsd ldrs: rdn over 3f out: one pce)	½	**8**	11/1	49	23
1454^{8}	**Northern Chief (28)** (JCullinan) **6-8-9**ow2 VSlattery(8) (s.i.s: a bhd)	17	**9**	50/1	14	—
5114^{6}	**Anaxagoras (32)** (SGollings) **6-8-7b** JQuinn(6) (mde most to 3f out: wknd)	5	**10**	20/1	2	—
5093^{2}	**School Boy (60)** (TJNaughton) **3-9-5** DHolland(1) (w ldrs tl wknd 3f out)	10	**11**	7/1	—	—
	Auchinleck Judge (RMMcKellar) **3-8-11** MWigham(3) (leggy: b.hind: s.s: a wl bhd: t.o 3f out)	dist	**12**	33/1	—	—

(SP 135.4%) **12 Rn**

1m 44.8 (5.80) CSF £31.98 TOTE £4.20: £1.10 £4.90 £1.50 (£24.50) Trio £51.50 OWNER Mr Robert Aird (COCKERHAM) BRED Mrs D. Hutch

WEIGHT FOR AGE 3yo-2lb

5133 GRAND UNION NURSERY H'CAP (2-Y.O) (Class E)

2-00 (2-02) **6f (Fibresand)** £3,104.85 (£940.80: £459.90: £219.45) Stalls: Low GOING minus 0.14 sec per fur (FST)

				SP	RR	SF
4887*	**Arapi (IRE) (82)** (SirMarkPrescott) **2-9-5** GDuffield(9) (a.p: led over 1f out: styd on)	—	**1**	3/1^{1}	83	48
4916^{7}	**C-Harry (IRE) (67)** (RHollinshead) **2-8-1**(3) FLynch(10) (a.p: effrt & ev ch over 1f out: kpt on)	1¼	**2**	12/1	65	30
3625^{3}	**Siouxrouge (74)** (PCHaslam) **2-8-11** GCarter(4) (a.p: ev ch appr fnl f: kpt on)	nk	**3**	12/1	71	36
*5113**	**Erosion (IRE) (83)** (MJohnston) **2-9-6** 6x DHolland(11) (disp ld tl led over 2f out: hdd over 1f out: no ex)	2½	**4**	13/2^{2}	73	38
4918^{5}	**Secret Combe (IRE) (84)** (PJMakin) **2-9-0**(7) DSweeney(13) (hld up: effrt over 2f out: edgd lft & no imp)	2	**5**	16/1	69	34
4991^{6}	**Catria (IRE) (76)** (JHMGosden) **2-8-13** WRyan(2) (disp ld tl hdd over 2f out: grad wknd)	hd	**6**	3/1^{1}	61	26
2382^{4}	**Enchanting Eve (74)** (CNAllen) **2-8-6**(5) MartinDwyer(14) (lw: a.p: effrt over 2f out: edgd lft & nt qckn)	nk	**7**	10/1	58	23
4916^{9}	**Petite Danseuse (80)** (CADwyer) **2-9-3** CDwyer(8) (hld up: nvr nr to chal)	2	**8**	10/1	59	24
5043^{9}	**Manhattan Diamond (59)** (ABailey) **2-7-3**(7) IonaWands(1) (b.hind: nvr trbld ldrs)	4	**9**	33/1	27	—
5050^{4}	**Village Pub (FR) (70)** (KOCunningham-Brown) **2-8-7b** DRMcCabe(3) (dwlt: hdwy ½-wy: sn rdn & no imp)	1¼	**10**	25/1	35	—
4803*	**Strat's Quest (67)** (DWPArbuthnot) **2-8-4** JQuinn(7) (b: prom tl wknd fnl 2f)	2	**11**	8/1^{3}	26	—
5083^{5}	**Barresbo (62)** (CWFairhurst) **2-7-8**(5) PFessey(15) (outpcd & bhd fr ½-wy)	¾	**12**	33/1	19	—
2083^{3}	**Komasta (70)** (CaptJWilson) **2-8-0**(7) AngelaHartley(5) (outpcd fr ½-wy)	8	**13**	25/1	6	—
2245^{5}	**Kustom Kit Xpres (78)** (SRBowring) **2-9-1** SDWilliams(6) (outpcd fr ½-wy)	3	**14**	25/1	6	—
3467^{4}	**Sherzetto (73)** (DWChapman) **2-8-10** ACulhane(12) (outpcd & lost tch 4f out: sn t.o)	23	**15**	16/1	—	—

(SP 137.2%) **15 Rn**

1m 16.7 (3.20) CSF £41.56 CT £385.83 TOTE £4.50: £1.80 £4.20 £3.20 (£47.60) Trio £198.70 OWNER Hesmonds Stud (NEWMARKET) BRED Hesmonds Stud Ltd

OFFICIAL EXPLANATION **Petite Danseuse: turning for home the jockey said he was completely unsighted by the kick-back.**

5134 FARMERS WEEKLY H'CAP (0-60) (II) (3-Y.O+) (Class F)

2-30 (2-32) **7f (Fibresand)** £2,048.00 (£573.00: £278.00) Stalls: Low GOING minus 0.14 sec per fur (FST)

				SP	RR	SF
*5055**	**Leigh Crofter (53)** (PDCundell) **7-9-7b** 6x DHolland(13) (trckd ldrs: led 2f out: rdn & r.o appr fnl f)	—	**1**	6/1^{2}	63	45
4983^{2}	**The Barnsley Belle (IRE) (47)** (JLEyre) **3-9-0** RLappin(14) (w ldrs: led 3f out to 2f out: kpt on one pce)	2	**2**	3/1^{1}	52	33
5105^{5}	**Night Harmony (IRE) (56)** (MissSJWilton) **3-9-9** MTebbutt(10) (b: trckd ldrs: effrt & ch 2f out: rdn & no ex)	1	**3**	14/1	59	40
4982^{5}	**Legal Issue (IRE) (55)** (WWHaigh) **4-9-9** DRMcCabe(1) (lw: mid div: effrt over 2f out: sn chsng ldrs: nt qckn fnl f)	1½	**4**	13/2^{3}	55	37
2367^{10}	**Ebony Boy (47)** (JWharton) **3-8-11**(3) CTeague(8) (hld up & bhd: effrt over 2f out: nrst fin)	½	**5**	12/1	46	27
4805^{10}	**Craigie Boy (47)** (NBycroft) **6-9-1** JQuinn(16) (a.p: effrt 3f out: r.o one pce)	2½	**6**	14/1	40	22
4987^{10}	**Sagebrush Roller (60)** (JWWatts) **8-10-0** GDuffield(3) (lw: sn outpcd & bhd: styd on fnl 2f)	3	**7**	7/1	46	28
5089^{2}	**Statistician (59)** (JohnBerry) **4-9-13b** CDwyer(2) (w ldrs tl wknd fnl 2f)	31	**8**	7/1	—	—
4987^{15}	**Square Deal (FR) (58)** (SRBowring) **5-9-12** SDWilliams(12) (sn pushed along & bhd: n.d)	1½	**9**	16/1	—	—
5112^{10}	**Lithe Spirit (IRE) (45)** (JohnHarris) **4-8-13** DeanMcKeown(11) (hld up & bhd: n.d)	½	**10**	33/1	—	—
4979^{7}	**Encore M'Lady (IRE) (60)** (FHLee) **5-10-0** CRutter(7) (disp ld 4f: wknd)	3	**11**	20/1	—	—
	Rumpelstiltskin (50) (HSHowe) **4-9-1**(3) FLynch(9) (bit bkwd: disp ld 4f: wknd)	6	**12**	20/1	—	—
4915^{8}	**Rapier Point (IRE) (43)** (CMurray) **5-8-11** GCarter(4) (n.d)	¾	**13**	20/1	—	—
5124^{13}	**Charming Bride (53)** (SCWilliams) **3-9-6b** DWright(5) (b.nr hind: s.i.s: n.d)	½	**14**	20/1	—	—
404^{5}	**Welsh Melody (49)** (KRBurke) **3-9-2** AClark(15) (sn pushed along: bhd fr ½-wy)	9	**15**	20/1	—	—
5109^{13}	**Summer Princess (45)** (AStreeter) **3-8-12v^{1}** MWigham(6) (chsd ldrs tl rdn & wknd 3f out)	9	**16**	33/1	—	—

(SP 134.2%) **16 Rn**

1m 31.0 (4.50) CSF £25.16 CT £238.41 TOTE £6.10: £1.10 £1.70 £4.20 £1.70 (£12.50) Trio £41.30 OWNER Mr P. D. Cundell (NEWBURY) BRED Richard Castle

WEIGHT FOR AGE 3yo-1lb

5135 SEVERN (S) STKS (2-Y.O F & M) (Class F)

3-00 (3-02) **7f (Fibresand)** £2,398.00 (£673.00: £328.00) Stalls: Low GOING minus 0.14 sec per fur (FST)

				SP	RR	SF
4990^{18}	**Compact Disc (IRE) (50)** (MJohnston) **2-8-9** DHolland(2) (lw: mde all: kpt on wl fnl f)	—	1	8/1	58	11
4796^{5}	**Head Girl (IRE) (63)** (CWThornton) **2-8-9** DeanMcKeown(13) (trckd ldrs: effrt over 2f out: hung lft: kpt on towards fin)	1½	2	7/4^{1}	55	8
4988^{6}	**Cool Grey** (JJO'Neill) **2-8-9** JQuinn(7) (b.nr hind: a chsng ldrs: kpt on fnl 2f)	nk	3	16/1	54	7
4988^{8}	**Hopperetta (47)** (BPalling) **2-8-9** AClark(6) (sn outpcd: gd hdwy 2f out: nt qckn ins fnl f)	hd	4	20/1	54	7
4970^{8}	**Royal Roulette (56)** (SPCWoods) **2-8-9b^{1}** DBiggs(4) (chsd ldrs: effrt & ev ch 2f out: nt qckn)	3	5	3/1^{2}	47	—
	Showgirl (CaptJWilson) **2-8-9** SDWilliams(5) (leggy: unf: w ldrs tl rdn & btn appr fnl f)	½	6	12/1	46	—
4988^{4}	**Racing Carr (40)** (TJNaughton) **2-8-6**(3) JDSmith(15) (b.nr fore: bhd & drvn along: styd on fnl 2f)	1¾	7	12/1	42	—
4988^{5}	**Diamond Eyre** (JLEyre) **2-8-9** RLappin(12) (hld up & bhd: styd hdwy 2f out: nvr plcd to chal)	nk	8	14/1	41	—
5098^{2}	**Ekaterini Paritsi (44)** (WGMTurner) **2-8-2v**(7) DSweeney(10) (chsd ldrs tl wknd fnl 2f)	4	9	6/1^{3}	32	—
	Katherine (JRinger) **2-8-9** MWigham(8) (leggy: b: outpcd & bhd fr ½-wy)	4	10	20/1	23	—
5005^{10}	**Thewrightone (IRE) (40)** (GROldroyd) **2-8-9b** MMcAndrew(11) (outpcd fr ½-wy)	½	11	25/1	22	—
4970^{17}	**Mechilie** (JWPayne) **2-8-9** MTebbutt(9) (racd wd: a bhd)	2	12	20/1	17	—
5111^{14}	**Diamonds Are** (DTThom) **2-8-9v^{1}** DRMcCabe(14) (plld v.hrd: sn wl bhd: n.d)	5	13	33/1	6	—
4988^{10}	**Mustang Scally** (JMackie) **2-8-9** JFanning(1) (prom 4f: sn lost tch)	4	14	25/1	—	—
1842^{11}	**Miskin Heights (IRE)** (KRBurke) **2-8-9** GCarter(3) (outpcd after 2f: sn wl bhd: t.o)	22	15	12/1	—	—

(SP 147.3%) **15 Rn**

1m 33.1 (6.60) CSF £25.67 TOTE £15.60: £4.50 £1.70 £5.30 (£19.40) Trio £68.40 OWNER Mr R. C. Moules (MIDDLEHAM) BRED Lodge Park Stud

No bid

OFFICIAL EXPLANATION **Diamond Eyre: was found to have a blood disorder.**

5136 CUCKMERE H'CAP (0-65) (3-Y.O+) (Class F)

3-30 (3-33) **1m 6f (Fibresand)** £2,398.00 (£673.00: £328.00) Stalls: High GOING minus 0.14 sec per fur (FST)

				SP	RR	SF
5054^{2}	**Compass Pointer (57)** (JMPEustace) **3-9-1**(5) MartinDwyer(13) (hdwy ½-wy: led over 2f out: styd on wl)	—	1	9/4^{1}	69	30
5102^{3}	**Our Main Man (48)** (RMWhitaker) **6-9-5** ACulhane(12) (hdwy 8f out: sn prom: outpcd over 2f out: kpt on fnl f)	3	2	10/1	57	26
5008^{U}	**Mr Speculator (50)** (JEBanks) **3-8-8v**(5) GFaulkner(9) (cl up: led over 4f out tl over 2f out: sn btn)	7	3	12/1	51	12
5108^{3}	**Code Red (57)** (WRMuir) **3-8-13**(7) JWilkinson(10) (lw: in tch: hdwy & ev ch 6f out: one pce fnl 3f)	1¾	4	7/1^{3}	56	17
5060^{6}	**Classic Romance (65)** (RHarris) **3-10-0** DBatteate(8) (in tch: effrt 4f out: no imp)	8	5	14/1	54	15
4984^{7}	**Greek Night Out (IRE) (50)** (JLEyre) **5-9-0**(7) DSweeney(3) (bhd: effrt ½-wy: sme hdwy 4f out: n.d)	17	6	4/1^{2}	20	—
3116^{*}	**Tagatay (41)** (MJCamacho) **3-8-4**ow1 GCarter(7) (chsd ldrs tl outpcd 5f out: n.d after)	hd	7	8/1	11	—
5053^{6}	**Tablets of Stone (IRE) (38)** (JRBosley) **3-8-1e** DWright(5) (chsd ldrs: sn pushed along: no ch fr ½-wy)	10	8	20/1	—	—
2848^{10}	**Bold Joker (25)** (GROldroyd) **5-7-3**(7) IonaWands(4) (wl bhd fr ½-wy)	1	9	33/1	—	—
5062^{10}	**Drama King (42)** (SRBowring) **4-8-13** JQuinn(11) (hld up: effrt ½-wy: a bhd)	1	10	14/1	—	—
5007^{*}	**Peep O Day (41)** (JLEyre) **5-8-12** DHolland(6) (cl up: led 9f out to 4½f out: wknd qckly)	2	11	7/1^{3}	—	—
4993^{16}	**Blackpatch Hill (53)** (NTinkler) **7-9-10b** KimTinkler(2) (led tl hdd 9f out: wknd 6f out: t.o)	dist	12	20/1	—	—
787^{18}	**Appearance Money (IRE) (40)** (FMurphy) **5-8-4**(7)ow5 DHayden(1) (b: dwlt: a bhd: t.o)	1	13	20/1	—	—

(SP 134.2%) **13 Rn**

3m 10.3 (12.30) CSF £27.19 CT £228.92 TOTE £3.90: £1.40 £2.50 £4.40 (£16.40) Trio £221.10 OWNER Park Lane Racing (NEWMARKET) BRED The Hon. Miss Pearl Lawson Johnston

LONG HANDICAP Bold Joker 7-7

WEIGHT FOR AGE 3yo-8lb

T/Plpt: £44.20 (191.8 Tckts). T/Qdpt: £21.80 (43.82 Tckts). WG

5103-WOLVERHAMPTON (L-H) (Standard)

Monday November 25th

WEATHER: stormy WIND: almost nil

5137 GEORGE FISCHER-INSTAFLEX CLAIMING STKS (I) (3, 4 & 5-Y.O) (Class F)

12-50 (12-54) **1m 1f 79y (Fibresand)** £2,187.00 (£612.00: £297.00) Stalls: Low GOING minus 0.19 sec per fur (FST)

				SP	RR	SF
5120^{5}	**Cedez le Passage (FR) (90)** (KOCunningham-Brown) **5-9-5b**(3) MHenry(4) (a.p: led over 2f out: rdn & r.o wl)	—	1	8/1	76	40
5010^{7}	**Yeoman Oliver (70)** (BAMcMahon) **3-8-10b**(5) LNewton(3) (lw: led tl over 2f out: rallied u.p appr fnl f: no imp)	3½	2	3/1^{2}	66	27
5106^{2}	**Just Harry (77)** (MJRyan) **5-9-4** AClark(1) (hld up: hdwy 6f out: drvn along 3f out: kpt on one pce)	3½	3	6/4^{1}	60	24
1508^{16}	**Conwy** (SCWilliams) **3-8-6** GCarter(10) (s.s: wl bhd tl sme late hdwy)	10	4	33/1	34	—
5081^{4}	**Rose Tint (IRE) (40)** (LordHuntingdon) **3-8-6**ow2 MRoberts(5) (drvn along 6f out: sn lost tch)	8	5	16/1	20	—
	Kulepopsie (IRE) (ABMulholland) **3-9-6** DeanMcKeown(6) (lt-f: s.s: nvr nr ldrs: t.o)	10	6	33/1	17	—
5056^{7}	**Comeonup (36)** (JMBradley) **5-8-6** DaneO'Neill(2) (b: chsd ldrs: rdn along over 5f out: sn wknd: t.o)	1	7	33/1	—	—
5079^{8}	**Richard House Lad (31)** (RHollinshead) **3-8-2**(3) FLynch(7) (b: prom: rdn ½-wy: sn wknd: t.o)	nk	8	16/1	—	—
5109^{11}	**Lady Eclat (46)** (JAGlover) **3-7-10b** NCarlisle(9) (bhd fr ½-wy: t.o)	nk	9	20/1	—	—
5091^{3}	**More Than You Know (IRE) (77)** (KRBurke) **3-9-6** JQuinn(8) (a bhd: t.o)	½	10	5/1^{3}	14	—

(SP 118.1%) **10 Rn**

2m 1.9 (5.90) CSF £30.95 TOTE £7.50: £2.40 £1.10 £1.30 (£15.30) Trio £10.90 OWNER Mr A. J. Richards (STOCKBRIDGE) BRED Ewar Stud Farm in France

WEIGHT FOR AGE 3yo-3lb

Just Harry clmd CBjorling £10,000

5138 H & V NEWS H'CAP (0-70) (I) (3-Y.O+) (Class E)

1-20 (1-23) **6f (Fibresand)** £2,799.00 (£846.00: £412.00: £195.00) Stalls: Low GOING minus 0.19 sec per fur (FST)

Form	Horse	Dist	Pos	SP	RR	SF
4987*	**Naughty Pistol (USA) (59)** (PDEvans) **4-9-4v** JFEgan(6) (outpcd & rdn along ½-wy: hdwy & swtchd lft appr fnl f: r.o to ld cl home)	—	1	9/2[1]	62	43
5055[4]	**How's Yer Father (57)** (RJHodges) **10-8-11**(5) PPMurphy(12) (outpcd ½-wy: hdwy wl over 1f out: fin wl)	nk	2	11/2[2]	59	40
4828*	**Superbit (48)** (BAMcMahon) **4-8-7** SSanders(13) (lw: a.p: led over 2f out tl wl ins fnl f)	½	3	9/2[1]	49	30
1812[10]	**Lord Sky (65)** (ABailey) **5-9-3**(7) AngelaGallimore(2) (b: a.p: ev ch 1f out: unable qckn)	½	4	25/1	65	46
5097[8]	**Cheeky Chappy (62)** (DWChapman) **5-9-7b** ACulhane(9) (a.p: rdn along 3f out: ev ch over 1f out: one pce)	2	5	9/1	56	37
	Southern Rule (37) (KAMorgan) **9-7-10** NCarlisle(8) (bit bkwd: nvr nr to chal)	2½	6	33/1	25	6
4881[2]	**Beau Venture (USA) (64)** (BPalling) **8-9-9** TSprake(4) (led 4f out tl over 2f out: wknd ent fnl f)	1¾	7	7/1[3]	47	28
	Kajostar (37) (SWCampion) **6-7-10** JQuinn(1) (outpcd)	3	8	100/1	12	—
4860[6]	**Finisterre (IRE) (62)** (JJO'Neill) **3-9-7** DaneO'Neill(10) (lw: chsd ldrs over 3f out: sn outpcd)	1¼	9	14/1	34	15
4865[16]	**Niteowl Raider (IRE) (55)** (JohnHarris) **3-9-0** JO'Reilly(7) (b.hind: led 2f: prom tl wknd over 2f out)	s.h	10	12/1	26	7
4888[20]	**Rowlandsons Stud (IRE) (60)** (PBurgoyne) **3-8-12**(7) JBosley(5) (outpcd)	3	11	25/1	23	4
4987[6]	**Plum First (48)** (JLEyre) **6-8-7** RLappin(3) (sn drvn along: a outpcd)	s.h	12	12/1	11	—
2968[5]	**Dhes-C (51)** (RHollinshead) **3-8-7**(3) FLynch(11) (bkwd: prom 3f: sn rdn & outpcd: t.o)	13	13	16/1	—	—

(SP 113.8%) **13 Rn**

1m 14.5 (3.30) CSF £26.20 CT £109.54 TOTE £7.20: £2.80 £1.70 £2.30 (£23.50) Trio £16.90 OWNER Mr Colin Booth (WELSHPOOL) BRED Brereton C. Jones

LONG HANDICAP Kajostar 6-12 Southern Rule 7-5

5139 AMBI-RAD H'CAP (0-65) (3-Y.O+ F & M) (Class F)

1-50 (1-51) **1m 6f 166y (Fibresand)** £2,537.00 (£712.00: £347.00) Stalls: High GOING minus 0.19 sec per fur (FST)

Form	Horse	Dist	Pos	SP	RR	SF
4894[11]	**Arcady (55)** (PTWalwyn) **3-9-9** GDuffield(2) (mde virtually all: hrd rdn fnl f: r.o wl)	—	1	9/1	68	29
5007[9]	**Miss Prism (51)** (JLDunlop) **3-9-5** TSprake(10) (a.p: jnd wnr 2f out: hrd rdn & r.o)	s.h	2	11/1	64	25
5007[2]	**Rasayel (USA) (44)** (PDEvans) **6-9-6** JFEgan(7) (a.p: pushed along over 3f out: styd on same pce)	7	3	5/1[3]	49	18
5054[6]	**Shoshone (49)** (JHMGosden) **3-9-3** AClark(8) (b: b.hind: trckd ldrs: sn pushed along: no imp fnl 3f)	11	4	10/1	42	3
5116[3]	**Iota (48)** (JLHarris) **7-9-10** SSanders(5) (hmpd & lost pl after 1f: hdwy u.p over 5f out: nt rch ldrs)	3½	5	4/1[1]	38	7
5091[9]	**Patiala (IRE) (40)** (RWArmstrong) **3-8-5**(3) MHenry(9) (prom over 8f: sn drvn along & wknd: t.o)	19	6	20/1	9	—
4612[9]	**Dance Model (45)** (JJSheehan) **3-8-13** AMorris(4) (hdwy on ins 8f out: wknd over 4f out: t.o)	1½	7	66/1	12	—
5108[2]	**Rose of Glenn (38)** (BPalling) **5-9-0** CRutter(12) (prom tl wknd 5f out: t.o)	nk	8	13/2	5	—
5053*	**Lucy Tufty (42)** (JPearce) **5-9-4** FNorton(11) (mid div: rdn over 5f out: no imp: t.o)	15	9	9/1	—	—
5008[8]	**Arian Spirit (IRE) (43)** (JLEyre) **5-9-5** RLappin(1) (lost pl ½-wy: sn drvn along: t.o)	2½	10	9/2[2]	—	—
5115[9]	**Toulston Lady (IRE) (46)** (JWharton) **4-9-8** JQuinn(3) (rdn 7f out: a bhd: t.o)	¾	11	14/1	—	—
5062[11]	**Miss Pravda (40)** (BJLlewellyn) **3-8-1**(7) JBramhill(6) (b.hind: a bhd: t.o)	dist	12	33/1	—	—

(SP 121.5%) **12 Rn**

3m 19.3 (11.90) CSF £95.53 CT £509.28 TOTE £12.90: £3.10 £3.10 £2.00 (£20.60) Trio £58.10 OWNER Windsor House Racing (LAMBOURN) BRED A. D. G. Oldrey

WEIGHT FOR AGE 3yo-8lb

OFFICIAL EXPLANATION Arian Spirit (IRE): did not handle the surface.

5140 GEORGE FISCHER-INSTAFLEX CLAIMING STKS (II) (3, 4 & 5-Y.O) (Class F)

2-20 (2-20) **1m 1f 79y (Fibresand)** £2,187.00 (£612.00: £297.00) Stalls: Low GOING minus 0.19 sec per fur (FST)

Form	Horse	Dist	Pos	SP	RR	SF
4977[6]	**Honestly (64)** (BSmart) **3-8-6** SSanders(8) (in tch: hrd rdn over 3f out: styd on to ld cl home)	—	1	8/1[3]	59	13
5114[9]	**Dragonjoy (52)** (NPLittmoden) **3-8-5b**(5)ow1 DGriffiths(3) (lw: hld up: hdwy 4f out: led over 2f out: sn clr: eased & ct fnl strides)	hd	2	8/1[3]	63+	16
4617[2]	**Obelos (USA) (70)** (MissSJWilton) **5-9-8** MTebbutt(4) (lw: a.p: hrd rdn 3f out: one pce)	4	3	Evens[1]	65	22
3951[7]	**My Handsome Prince (29)** (PJBevan) **4-8-8** NCarlisle(6) (s.s: hdwy 6f out: kpt on one pce fnl 2f)	1¼	4	50/1	49	6
5094[5]	**Tormount (USA) (64)** (LordHuntingdon) **3-8-9** MRoberts(1) (lw: led over 6f out tl over 2f out: one pce)	½	5	9/2[2]	52	6
5056[5]	**Hand of Straw (IRE) (42)** (PGMurphy) **4-8-6v** CRutter(10) (rdn & hdwy over 4f out: wknd fnl 2f)	7	6	20/1	34	—
4882[9]	**Super Park (45)** (JPearce) **4-8-10** MWigham(9) (a in rr: t.o)	10	7	10/1	21	—
	Parellie (PDEvans) **3-8-3**ow5 JFEgan(7) (still unf: prom 5f: sn rdn & wknd: t.o)	1¾	8	50/1	14	—
5010[10]	**Harvest Reaper (35)** (JLHarris) **4-8-6** JQuinn(5) (led to 3f: wknd 4f out: t.o)	15	9	12/1	—	—
424[8]	**Komiamaite (49)** (DBurchell) **4-8-4** TWilson(2) (a t.o)	28	10	20/1	—	—

(SP 120.6%) **10 Rn**

2m 3.4 (7.40) CSF £65.89 TOTE £7.70: £2.30 £2.70 £1.10 (£27.00) Trio £22.20 OWNER Mr B. Hoggart (LAMBOURN) BRED Aston Park Stud

WEIGHT FOR AGE 3yo-3lb

STEWARDS' ENQUIRY Griffiths susp. 4,7,11 & 13-14/12/96 (failure to ensure best possible placing).

5141 ROOF UNITS NURSERY H'CAP (0-75) (2-Y.O) (Class E)

2-50 (2-50) **1m 100y (Fibresand)** £3,095.40 (£937.20: £457.60: £217.80) Stalls: Low GOING minus 0.19 sec per fur (FST)

Form	Horse	Dist	Pos	SP	RR	SF
5057*	**Hello Dolly (IRE) (65)** (KRBurke) **2-8-5**(7) DSweeney(9) (a.p: chsd ldr 2f out: led last strides)	—	1	11/2[3]	67	25
4897[13]	**Chaluz (50)** (MJohnston) **2-7-11** NAdams(7) (led: rdn over 1f out: hdd last strides)	hd	2	33/1	52	10
5100*	**Double Espresso (IRE) (74)** (MJohnston) **2-9-7** MRoberts(3) (lw: s.i.s: sn prom: rdn over 4f out: outpcd over 3f out: styd on fnl f)	3	3	6/4[1]	70	28
5006[2]	**Zorba (66)** (CWThornton) **2-8-13** DeanMcKeown(2) (a.p: hrd rdn & ev ch 2f out: edgd lft over 1f out: one pce)	½	4	7/1	61	19
5057[2]	**Skelton Sovereign (IRE) (60)** (RHollinshead) **2-8-4**(3) FLynch(4) (prom: outpcd over 3f out: styd on fnl f)	½	5	7/2[2]	54	12
5057[8]	**Ben's Ridge (72)** (PCHaslam) **2-9-5** GCarter(5) (lw: hdwy 3f out: eased whn btn fnl f)	8	6	7/1	51	9
4764[13]	**Sea Mist (IRE) (61)** (PWChapple-Hyam) **2-8-1**(7) RCody-Boutcher(6) (wl bhd fnl 5f)	10	7	25/1	21	—
4985[2]	**Ziggy's Viola (IRE) (64)** (MrsMReveley) **2-8-11** ACulhane(8) (wl bhd fnl 4f)	2	8	9/1	20	—

4790^{7}	**Real Fire (IRE) (49)** (MGMeagher) **2-7-10** JQuinn(1) (lw: hrd rdn 4f out: a bhd)	s.h	**9**	50/1	5	—
				(SP 121.4%)	**9 Rn**	

1m 51.0 (6.00) CSF £124.04 CT £374.13 TOTE £7.60: £2.30 £4.80 £1.10 (£125.70) Trio £92.80 OWNER Mr Nigel Shields (WANTAGE) BRED Rathasker Stud

LONG HANDICAP Real Fire (IRE) 7-9

5142 MICHAEL J. LONSDALE MAIDEN AUCTION STKS (2-Y.O F) (Class E)

3-20 (3-22) **7f (Fibresand)** £3,052.50 (£924.00: £451.00: £214.50) Stalls: High GOING minus 0.19 sec per fur (FST)

				SP	RR	SF
4783^{3}	**Rechullin** (DRLoder) **2-8-4** DRMcCabe(10) (a.p: led 4f out: pushed out)	—	**1**	$2/1^{1}$	82+	21
4605^{2}	**Superbelle** (MAJarvis) **2-8-4** EmmaO'Gorman(6) (a.p: chsd wnr over 2f out: rdn over 1f out: r.o one pce)	1¼	**2**	$2/1^{1}$	79	18
5103^{2}	**Colins Choice (62)** (JLSpearing) **2-7-13**$^{(3)ow2}$ FLynch(12) (chsd ldrs: hrd rdn 3f out: one pce)	10	**3**	$12/1^{3}$	54	—
3454^{10}	**Bestelina** (DJSCosgrove) **2-8-0** FNorton(8) (lost pl after 2f: sme hdwy fnl 2f)	2½	**4**	33/1	47	—
	Double Crest (IRE) (MJohnston) **2-8-2** JFanning(4) (leggy: lt-f: sn outpcd: sme late hdwy)	1¼	**5**	$12/1^{3}$	46	—
4790^{2}	**Phylida (70)** (PJMakin) **2-8-2** SSanders(7) (s.i.s: sn rdn: nvr trbld ldrs)	¾	**6**	$12/1^{3}$	44	—
4782^{3}	**Sidney The Kidney** (MJRyan) **2-7-7**$^{(7)}$ AMcCarthy(9) (prom 4f)	¾	**7**	14/1	40	—
5092^{5}	**Jilly Woo (48)** (DRCElsworth) **2-8-2b** NCarlisle(5) (outpcd)	½	**8**	25/1	41	—
	Saeko-Beauty (SirMarkPrescott) **2-8-7** GDuffield(3) (cmpt: bkwd: s.v.s: a wl bhd)	½	**9**	$12/1^{3}$	45	—
5051^{2}	**Khairun Nisaa** (MJPolglase) **2-8-0** JQuinn(2) (prom over 4f)	1	**10**	$8/1^{2}$	36	—
4795^{7}	**Circle of Magic (55)** (PJMakin) **2-8-4** AClark(11) (sn outpcd)	¾	**11**	33/1	38	—
4999^{7}	**Will To Win (60)** (PGMurphy) **2-7-12**$^{(3)ow1}$ MHenry(1) (b.hind: led 3f: wknd 3f out)	¾	**12**	33/1	33	—
				(SP 127.9%)	**12 Rn**	

1m 29.2 (4.50) CSF £6.77 TOTE £3.00: £1.40 £1.10 £2.30 (£3.80) Trio £18.50 OWNER Mrs P. D. Player (NEWMARKET) BRED P. D. Player and Mrs J. Shipway-Pratt

5143 SPECIFIERS GUIDE (S) STKS (3-Y.O+) (Class G)

3-50 (3-51) **1m 4f (Fibresand)** £2,259.00 (£634.00: £309.00) Stalls: Low GOING minus 0.19 sec per fur (FST)

				SP	RR	SF
5115^{2}	**Greenspan (IRE) (76)** (WRMuir) **4-9-8** DaneO'Neill(2) (hld up: hdwy over 4f out: led wl over 1f out: sn clr: comf)	—	**1**	$8/11^{1}$	66+	42
1893^{14}	**Kinnescash (IRE) (54)** (PBowen) **3-8-8**$^{(3)}$ FLynch(9) (w ldr: led over 5f out tl wl over 1f out: sn btn)	9	**2**	9/1	49	19
5115^{3}	**Forzair (60)** (JJO'Neill) **4-9-1**$^{(7)}$ DJewett(11) (trckd ldrs: r.o one pce fnl 3f)	½	**3**	10/1	53	29
4904^{3}	**Mcgillycuddy Reeks (IRE) (40)** (NTinkler) **5-8-12** GCarter(5) (s.i.s: sn prom: hrd rdn & wknd over 3f out)	5	**4**	$8/1^{3}$	37	13
5108^{7}	**Rousitto (38)** (RHollinshead) **8-8-12**$^{(5)}$ DGriffiths(7) (nvr trbld ldrs)	1¼	**5**	12/1	40	16
4977^{5}	**Mr Bean (56)** (KRBurke) **6-9-3** JQuinn(10) (bit bkwd: prom tl outpcd 3f out)	1¼	**6**	$9/2^{2}$	38	14
3066^{8}	**Stevie's Wonder (IRE) (55)** (BJLlewellyn) **6-9-1v**$^{(7)}$ JBramhill(8) (bkwd: bhd fnl 4f)	8	**7**	14/1	33	9
4998^{3}	**Proud Image (56)** (GMMcCourt) **4-9-8** CRutter(3) (led over 6f: wknd 4f out)	½	**8**	10/1	32	8
4604^{10}	**Acrow Line (35)** (DBurchell) **11-9-3** TWilson(12) (sn rdn along: wl bhd fnl 5f)	6	**9**	20/1	19	—
5110^{7}	**No Submission (USA) (56)** (DWChapman) **10-9-8v** ACulhane(1) (a bhd)	1½	**10**	$8/1^{3}$	22	—
3297^{11}	**Kismetim (32)** (DWChapman) **6-9-3** GDuffield(6) (bkwd: wl bhd fnl 5f: t.o)	12	**11**	33/1	1	—
	Star of Lugana (TTClement) **3-7-13**$^{(7)}$ CWebb(4) (b: unf: bkwd: s.i.s: a bhd: t.o: sddle slipped)	dist	**12**	33/1	—	—
				(SP 151.5%)	**12 Rn**	

2m 40.0 (7.50) CSF £12.13 TOTE £1.80: £1.40 £2.80 £2.30 (£13.70) Trio £58.00 OWNER Camelot Racing (LAMBOURN) BRED Dermot and Meta Cantillon

WEIGHT FOR AGE 3yo-6lb

Bt in 13,600 gns

5144 H & V NEWS H'CAP (0-70) (II) (3-Y.O+) (Class E)

4-20 (4-23) **6f (Fibresand)** £2,784.70 (£841.60: £409.80: £193.90) Stalls: Low GOING minus 0.19 sec per fur (FST)

				SP	RR	SF
3758^{8}	**Cim Bom Bom (IRE) (70)** (MBell) **4-9-9v**$^{(5)}$ GFaulkner(1) (lw: mde virtually all: clr over 2f out: drvn out)	—	**1**	10/1	83	61
5002^{7}	**Desert Invader (IRE) (68)** (DWChapman) **5-9-12** ACulhane(10) (chsd ldrs: hrd rdn & edgd lft fnl f: r.o)	7	**2**	10/1	62	40
5109^{6}	**Miss Aragon (38)** (MissLCSiddall) **8-7-10** NCarlisle(12) (a.p: chsd wnr over 2f out: no imp)	s.h	**3**	$4/1^{1}$	32	10
5105^{8}	**Castlerea Lad (56)** (RHollinshead) **7-8-11**$^{(3)}$ FLynch(11) (hdwy over 1f out: r.o)	2	**4**	$5/1^{2}$	45	23
5097^{5}	**Lawsimina (43)** (MissJFCraze) **3-8-1** FNorton(6) (hdwy 2f out: nt rch ldrs)	1¼	**5**	20/1	29	7
4981^{4}	**Delrob (54)** (DHaydnJones) **5-8-12b** AClark(4) (lw: nvr nr to chal)	¾	**6**	$8/1^{3}$	38	16
5085^{*}	**Gad Yakoun (67)** (MGMeagher) **3-9-11** JQuinn(13) (hdwy over 3f out: wknd wl over 1f out)	1¼	**7**	$4/1^{1}$	47	25
4979^{*}	**Jigsaw Boy (67)** (PGMurphy) **7-9-11** MRoberts(9) (outpcd)	d.h	**7**	$5/1^{2}$	51	29
4981^{6}	**Marino Street (49)** (PDEvans) **3-8-7v** JFEgan(5) (outpcd)	1¾	**9**	12/1	25	3
4881^{18}	**Halbert (42)** (PBurgoyne) **7-8-0**^{ow2} DRMcCabe(8) (prom over 4f)	2	**10**	33/1	12	—
4130^{4}	**Al Shaati (FR) (38)** (RJO'Sullivan) **6-7-10** NAdams(3) (prom: rdn 4f out: sn wknd)	3½	**11**	$4/1^{1}$	—	—
4727^{12}	**She's a Madam (38)** (LRLloyd-James) **5-7-3b**$^{1(7)}$ IonaWands(2) (bhd fnl 3f)	1¾	**12**	50/1	—	—
5131^{11}	**Sir Tasker (50)** (JLHarris) **8-8-8** SSanders(7) (bhd fnl 3f)	3	**13**	16/1	—	—
				(SP 145.9%)	**13 Rn**	

1m 13.9 (2.70) CSF £115.69 CT £459.65 TOTE £12.40: £5.10 £6.20 £2.60 (£44.30) Trio £255.80 OWNER Mr Yucel Birol (NEWMARKET) BRED Tarworth Bloodstock Investments Ltd and J.J. Melk

LONG HANDICAP Al Shaati (FR) 7-4 She's a Madam 7-5 Miss Aragon 7-4

T/Plpt: £8.90 (1,427.14 Tckts). T/Qdpt: £7.00 (166.25 Tckts). IM/KH

5117-LINGFIELD (L-H) (Standard)
Tuesday November 26th

Race 4: hand-timed
WEATHER: fine WIND: almost nil

5145 DANCING FLOOR (S) STKS (I) (3-Y.O+) (Class G)
11-50 (11-52) **1m 2f (Equitrack)** £1,388.00 (£388.00: £188.00) Stalls: Low GOING minus 0.47 sec per fur (FST)

				SP	RR	SF
4206[24]	**Angel Face (USA) (50)** (PDEvans) **3-8-9** ACulhane(3) (a.p: led 5f out: clr 2f out: r.o wl)	—	**1**	5/1[2]	62	40
4563[12]	**Soldier Cove (USA) (41)** (MartynMeade) **6-8-11**(7) TField(6) (a.p: chsd wnr over 4f out: rdn over 2f out: unable qckn)	8	**2**	14/1	54	36
5117[5]	**Efficacious (IRE) (40)** (AMoore) **3-8-9** DaneO'Neill(4) (lw: b.hind: a.p: rdn over 3f out: one pce)	4	**3**	20/1	43	21
5094[6]	**Our Eddie (60)** (BGubby) **7-9-9b** JQuinn(5) (a.p: rdn over 3f out: one pce)	1	**4**	5/1[2]	51	33
5081*	**Awesome Power (52)** (JWHills) **10-9-9** AClark(8) (a.p: rdn over 3f out: eased whn btn fnl f)	6	**5**	2/1[1]	42	24
5081[2]	**Sweet Amoret (46)** (PHowling) **3-9-0** FNorton(1) (b.off hind: prom over 5f)	2	**6**	6/1[3]	33	11
4202[14]	**Sarum (32)** (JELong) **10-9-9** LeesaLong(7) (b: a mid div)	1¼	**7**	33/1	36	18
3501[9]	**Oozlem (IRE) (41)** (LMontagueHall) **7-8-13b**(5) GFaulkner(9) (nvr nrr)	1½	**8**	14/1	29	11
5085[4]	**Veronica Franco (44)** (BAPearce) **3-8-9b** SSanders(14) (prom over 6f)	10	**9**	16/1	8	—
4515[W]	**Broughtons Champ** (WJMusson) **4-9-4** DRMcCabe(13) (a bhd)	nk	**10**	33/1	13	—
5095[10]	**Mystic Legend (IRE) (27)** (JJSheehan) **4-9-4** CRutter(11) (lw: a bhd)	hd	**11**	50/1	12	—
5122[4]	**Lahik (IRE) (35)** (KTIvory) **3-9-0** NAdams(12) (b: a bhd)	1¼	**12**	33/1	10	—
5082[8]	**Forgotten Dancer (IRE) (33)** (RIngram) **5-9-4** AMcGlone(2) (b: led 7f)	1½	**13**	33/1	8	—
4498[8]	**The Grey Weaver (28)** (RMFlower) **3-9-0b** DBiggs(10) (p.u 8f out: broke leg: dead)		**P**	50/1	—	—
				(SP 120.6%)	**14 Rn**	

2m 6.26 (1.96) CSF £66.26 TOTE £5.20: £3.50 £5.80 £4.90 (£22.90) Trio £171.30; £120.68 to Chepstow 27/11/96 OWNER Mrs E. J. Williams (WELSHPOOL) BRED Gainsborough Farm Inc.
WEIGHT FOR AGE 3yo-4lb
Bt in 6,200 gns

5146 FLEURETS NURSERY H'CAP (2-Y.O) (Class E)
12-20 (12-21) **5f (Equitrack)** £2,232.00 (£627.00: £306.00) Stalls: High GOING minus 0.47 sec per fur (FST)

				SP	RR	SF
4999[2]	**Kilcullen Lad (IRE) (61)** (PMooney) **2-8-2v** DRMcCabe(2) (lw: rdn & hdwy over 1f out: led ins fnl f: r.o wl)	—	**1**	9/2[1]	77	17
5092*	**Just Loui (75)** (WGMTurner) **2-8-9**(7) DSweeney(1) (lw: a.p: rdn over 1f out: r.o one pce)	3	**2**	5/1[2]	81	21
5083*	**Seretse's Nephew (58)** (SCWilliams) **2-7-13** DWright(6) (a.p: rdn 2f out: one pce fnl f)	¾	**3**	8/1	62	2
5061[2]	**Lightning Bolt (IRE) (59)** (MJohnston) **2-8-0** NAdams(3) (led over 1f: rdn over 2f out: led 1f out tl ins fnl f: sn wknd)	1¾	**4**	8/1	57	—
4916[12]	**Threeplay (IRE) (65)** (JAkehurst) **2-8-6** MTebbutt(7) (a.p: rdn over 2f out: one pce)	s.h	**5**	16/1	63	3
4546[11]	**Hever Golf Charger (IRE) (65)** (TJNaughton) **2-8-6** DHolland(8) (bmpd s: outpcd: hdwy fnl f: nvr nrr)	½	**6**	16/1	62	2
5080[4]	**Rock To The Top (IRE) (70)** (JJSheehan) **2-8-11** AMorris(5) (outpcd: nvr nrr)	1¾	**7**	20/1	61	1
4999*	**Fruitana (IRE) (80)** (JBerry) **2-9-2**(5) PRoberts(10) (a.p: led over 3f out to 1f out: sn wknd)	1¼	**8**	13/2[3]	67	7
4912*	**Dominant Air (74)** (SirMarkPrescott) **2-9-1** GDuffield(4) (a bhd)	½	**9**	5/1[2]	59	—
5037[13]	**Whisper Low (IRE) (64)** (RHollinshead) **2-8-2**(3) FLynch(9) (a bhd)	1¾	**10**	16/1	44	—
				(SP 109.5%)	**10 Rn**	

59.74 secs (1.54) CSF £23.87 CT £146.64 TOTE £4.90: £1.10 £2.20 £2.40 (£7.30) Trio £29.30 OWNER Mr George Tobitt (ASTON UPTHORPE) BRED S. W. D. McIlveen

5147 THIRTY NINE STEPS MEDIAN AUCTION MAIDEN STKS (2-Y.O) (Class E)
12-50 (12-51) **1m 2f (Equitrack)** £2,200.50 (£618.00: £301.50) Stalls: Low GOING minus 0.47 sec per fur (FST)

				SP	RR	SF
	Mersey Beat (GLMoore) **2-9-0** GDuffield(10) (w'like: s.s: stdy hdwy over 7f out: rdn over 3f out: led ins fnl f: r.o wl)	—	**1**	9/1	77+	26
4990[3]	**Castles Burning (USA) (55)** (CACyzer) **2-9-0** MRoberts(7) (a.p: rdn over 4f out: ev ch ins fnl f: unable qckn)	1	**2**	10/1	75	24
5100[2]	**Noble Hero (67)** (JJSheehan) **2-8-11**(3) FLynch(8) (a.p: rdn over 4f out: led 3f out tl ins fnl f: one pce)	1½	**3**	9/2[3]	73	22
5057[3]	**Greenwich Fore (69)** (TGMills) **2-9-0** SSanders(5) (a.p: led 4f out to 3f out: rdn: one pce)	1½	**4**	5/2[1]	71	20
5090[3]	**Lochlass (IRE) (65)** (SPCWoods) **2-8-9** DBiggs(2) (lw: lost pl over 4f out: r.o one pce fnl 2f)	1½	**5**	7/1	63	12
4970[2]	**Hallmark (IRE) (67)** (RHannon) **2-9-0** DaneO'Neill(1) (led 6f)	9	**6**	7/2[2]	54	3
5111[4]	**Fearless Sioux** (CWThornton) **2-8-9** DeanMcKeown(6) (hld up: rdn over 4f out: sn wknd)	s.h	**7**	20/1	49	—
5087[6]	**Alimerjam (49)** (JWhite) **2-8-9** DRMcCabe(3) (bhd fnl 8f)	3½	**8**	33/1	43	—
5090[4]	**Serenade (IRE) (62)** (MJHaynes) **2-9-0** AClark(4) (b: b.hind: a bhd)	15	**9**	20/1	24	—
5041[7]	**Ginger Rogers** (DWPArbuthnot) **2-8-9** CRutter(9) (bhd fnl 6f)	9	**10**	25/1	5	—
				(SP 116.9%)	**10 Rn**	

2m 8.62 (4.32) CSF £84.98 TOTE £10.70: £2.20 £1.70 £2.00 (£33.50) Trio £23.10 OWNER Mr K. Higson (BRIGHTON) BRED K. Higson

5148 RICHARD HANNAY H'CAP (0-70) (3-Y.O+) (Class E)
1-25 (1-26) **1m 5f (Equitrack)** £2,659.10 (£747.60: £365.30) Stalls: Low GOING minus 0.47 sec per fur (FST)

				SP	RR	SF
4779[2]	**Heighth of Fame (66)** (DBurchell) **5-9-9**(5) SCopp(15) (a.p: led over 7f out: hrd rdn over 2f out: r.o wl)	—	**1**	14/1	76	48
5119*	**Basood (USA) (51)** (SPCWoods) **3-8-6b** 5x DBiggs(16) (a.p: chsd wnr over 6f out: ev ch fnl 3f: hrd rdn ins fnl f: no rspnse)	½	**2**	4/1[1]	60	25
4993[3]	**Rex Mundi (61)** (PDEvans) **4-9-9** ACulhane(11) (rdn & hdwy over 4f out: one pce fnl 2f)	2	**3**	8/1[3]	68	40
5084[6]	**Broughtons Formula (48)** (WJMusson) **6-8-10b** DRMcCabe(1) (lw: wl bhd over 5f: gd hdwy fnl 3f: r.o wl)	3½	**4**	7/1[2]	51	23
5088[2]	**Rowlandsons Charm (IRE) (58)** (MissBSanders) **3-8-13v** SSanders(13) (lw: a.p: rdn over 4f out: wknd over 2f out)	2½	**5**	11/1	58	23
5084*	**Guest Alliance (IRE) (60)** (AMoore) **4-9-8** CandyMorris(10) (b.hind: nvr nr to chal)	3½	**6**	11/1	55	27
5102[4]	**Rock The Barney (IRE) (38)** (PBurgoyne) **7-8-0v** CRutter(5) (prom 7f)	2½	**7**	12/1	30	2
3870[5]	**Suitor (47)** (SDow) **3-7-11e**(5) ADaly(3) (lw: led over 10f out tl over 7f out: wknd over 3f out)	hd	**8**	7/1[2]	39	4
4789[6]	**Howqua River (52)** (PWChapple-Hyam) **4-8-7**(7) RCody-Boutcher(4) (b.hind: a mid div)	hd	**9**	20/1	44	16

				SP	RR	SF
4789^{9}	**Strat's Legacy (41)** (DWPArbuthnot) **9-8-3** JQuinn(6) (b.hind: a bhd)	4	**10**	20/1	28	—
4827^{3}	**Madame Steinlen (70)** (BWHills) **3-9-11** DHolland(7) (b: b.hind: led over 2f: rdn over 8f out: wknd over 5f out)	hd	**11**	12/1	57	22
5053^{8}	**Pat's Splendour (41)** (HJCollingridge) **5-7-10**$^{(7)ow7}$ JoHunnam(9) (a bhd)	s.h	**12**	25/1	28	—
	Euro Singer (47) (PRWebber) **4-8-9** RPerham(12) (bhd fnl 6f)	6	**13**	10/1	26	—
5102^{6}	**Flow Back (58)** (GPEnright) **4-9-6** NAdams(8) (a bhd)	4	**14**	25/1	33	5
5084^{11}	**Trapper Norman (34)** (RIngram) **4-7-10** DWright(2) (sme hdwy over 6f out: wknd over 5f out)	3	**15**	100/1	5	—
5053^{14}	**Moving Up (IRE) (41)** (TEPowell) **3-7-7**$^{(3)}$ MBaird(14) (bhd fnl 5f)	7	**16**	33/1	3	—

(SP 125.1%) **16 Rn**

2m 47.4 (5.40) CSF £66.11 CT £456.52 TOTE £15.60: £5.30 £2.20 £4.00 £1.90 (£16.40) Trio £39.50 OWNER Mr Simon Lewis (EBBW VALE) BRED Paul Mellon

LONG HANDICAP Pat's Splendour 7-9 Trapper Norman 7-3 Moving Up (IRE) 7-7

WEIGHT FOR AGE 3yo-7lb

OFFICIAL EXPLANATION Suitor: spread his near-fore plate.

5149 DANCING FLOOR (S) STKS (II) (3-Y.O+) (Class E)

2-00 (2-00) **1m 2f (Equitrack)** £1,388.00 (£388.00: £188.00) Stalls: Low GOING minus 0.47 sec per fur (FST)

				SP	RR	SF
5091^{6}	**Persian Conquest (IRE) (67)** (RIngram) **4-9-9b** AMcGlone(5) (led 6f: lost pl over 3f out: rallied fnl f: led nr fin)	—	**1**	$9/4^{2}$	66	37
1506^{6}	**Bagshot (77)** (GLMoore) **5-9-4** DaneO'Neill(7) (a.p: led 4f out: hrd rdn over 1f out: hdd nr fin)	½	**2**	$7/4^{1}$	60	31
5124^{9}	**Our Shadee (USA) (56)** (KTIvory) **6-9-9v** GDuffield(2) (b: a.p: rdn over 3f out: one pce)	1½	**3**	20/1	63	34
4882^{2}	**Arcatura (56)** (CJames) **4-8-11**$^{(7)}$ RCody-Boutcher(3) (hld up: rdn over 3f out: one pce)	2	**4**	12/1	55	26
5053^{9}	**Chilly Lad (52)** (MJRyan) **5-9-4b** AClark(9) (lw: nvr nr to chal)	7	**5**	25/1	43	14
5086^{2}	**Eastleigh (41)** (RHollinshead) **7-9-1**$^{(3)}$ FLynch(8) (prom over 5f)	1½	**6**	8/1	41	12
5123^{6}	**Hatta Sunshine (USA) (52)** (AMoore) **6-9-4** CandyMorris(13) (stdy hdwy over 7f out: wknd over 4f out)	4	**7**	$7/1^{3}$	35	6
5101^{8}	**Dutch Dyane** (GPEnright) **3-8-9** NAdams(10) (b: b.hind: dwlt: nvr nrr)	12	**8**	66/1	10	—
5085^{5}	**Madison's Touch (35)** (RMFlower) **3-8-9** DBiggs(12) (a bhd)	12	**9**	50/1	—	—
5093^{10}	**Logie Pert Lad (30)** (JJBridger) **4-9-4** DHarrison(11) (prom over 5f)	¾	**10**	66/1	—	—
2736^{4}	**Another Fiddle (IRE) (62)** (BAPearce) **6-9-4** SSanders(1) (b.hind: bhd fnl 3f)	s.h	**11**	12/1	—	—
5118^{11}	**Robin Island (50)** (PRHedger) **4-9-4e** JQuinn(6) (b.hind: dwlt: a bhd)	¾	**12**	33/1	—	—
5052^{10}	**Sussex Gorse (15)** (JELong) **5-9-4** LeesaLong(4) (b.nr hind: prom 5f)	15	**13**	66/1	—	—

(SP 124.1%) **13 Rn**

2m 8.24 (3.94) CSF £6.57 TOTE £3.10: £1.40 £1.40 £3.80 (£3.60) Trio £17.40 OWNER Mr C. G. Adams (EPSOM) BRED Louis A. Walshe

WEIGHT FOR AGE 3yo-4lb

No bid

OFFICIAL EXPLANATION Dutch Dyane: the rider reported that the filly was keen early on, but was unable to quicken when asked, and appeared moderate.

5150 MAURICE ROBERTSON BIRTHDAY H'CAP (0-85) (3-Y.O+) (Class D)

2-35 (2-38) **6f (Equitrack)** £3,598.75 (£1,090.00: £532.50: £253.75) Stalls: Low GOING minus 0.47 sec per fur (FST)

				SP	RR	SF
5096^{7}	**Scissor Ridge (61)** (JJBridger) **4-8-4**^{ow1} DHarrison(12) (mde all: rdn over 3f out: r.o wl)	—	**1**	10/1	71	27
5002^{2}	**Kings Harmony (IRE) (72)** (PJMakin) **3-9-1** DHolland(13) (chsd wnr: ev ch fnl 3f: unable qckn ins fnl f)	1½	**2**	$15/2^{3}$	78	35
5106^{*}	**Duke Valentino (82)** (RHollinshead) **4-9-6**$^{(5)}$ DGriffiths(9) (chsd ldrs: rdn over 4f out: r.o one pce fnl 2f)	3	**3**	10/1	80	37
4788^{*}	**Purple Fling (70)** (LGCottrell) **5-8-13** JQuinn(8) (a.p: rdn over 2f out: one pce)	s.h	**4**	9/1	68	25
5099^{*}	**Deeply Vale (IRE) (73)** (EAWheeler) **5-9-2** EmmaO'Gorman(3) (hld up: rdn over 1f out: r.o one pce)	s.h	**5**	8/1	71	28
5096^{5}	**Friendly Brave (USA) (69)** (MissGayKelleway) **6-8-7**$^{(5)}$ ADaly(5) (b: b.hind: a.p: rdn over 3f out: one pce)	nk	**6**	$7/1^{2}$	66	23
5124^{8}	**Never Think Twice (60)** (KTIvory) **3-8-3b** NAdams(2) (b: b.hind: hmpd s: outpcd: nvr nrr)	2	**7**	33/1	52	9
5105^{*}	**Prima Silk (77)** (MJRyan) **5-9-6** AClark(14) (outpcd: nvr nrr)	hd	**8**	12/1	68	25
5105^{2}	**Imposing Time (74)** (MissGayKelleway) **5-9-3b** SSanders(10) (b: b.hind: prom over 4f)	s.h	**9**	8/1	65	22
4994^{11}	**Double Blue (85)** (MJohnston) **7-10-0** MRoberts(11) (bhd fnl 4f)	2	**10**	$6/1^{1}$	71	28
5097^{6}	**Mijas (62)** (LMontagueHall) **3-8-5** DaneO'Neill(6) (bhd fnl 3f)	nk	**11**	25/1	47	4
4901^{10}	**Queenfisher (79)** (GLMoore) **4-9-8** GDuffield(7) (a bhd)	8	**12**	14/1	43	—
5105^{12}	**Tart and a Half (66)** (BJMeehan) **4-8-9b** MTebbutt(1) (bhd fnl 3f)	8	**13**	33/1	8	—
5097^{3}	**Sharp Pearl (70)** (JWhite) **3-8-13** DRMcCabe(4) (lw: prom over 2f)	3½	**14**	12/1	3	—

(SP 120.7%) **14 Rn**

1m 12.16 (1.06) CSF £76.76 CT £708.35 TOTE £21.20: £4.00 £3.00 £6.60 (£73.70) Trio £296.10 OWNER Mr Donald Smith (LIPHOOK) BRED J. K. Keegan

5151 LADBROKE ALL-WEATHER TROPHY (QUALIFIER) H'CAP (0-75) (I) (3-Y.O+) (Class D)

3-10 (3-11) **1m (Equitrack)** £2,616.05 (£790.40: £384.70: £181.85) Stalls: High GOING minus 0.47 sec per fur (FST)

				SP	RR	SF
5003^{4}	**Montone (IRE) (58)** (JRJenkins) **6-9-0v** DHarrison(8) (hdwy over 3f out: hrd rdn wl over 1f out: led last strides)	—	**1**	$6/1^{3}$	66	49
5079^{4}	**Sooty Tern (52)** (JMBradley) **9-8-5**$^{(3)}$ FLynch(3) (a.p: led over 1f out: rdn: hdd last strides)	s.h	**2**	10/1	60	43
3314^{4}	**Harlequin Walk (IRE) (49)** (RJO'Sullivan) **5-8-5** SSanders(12) (led tl over 1f out: hrd rdn & ev ch ins fnl f: r.o)	hd	**3**	8/1	57	40
5042^{3}	**Polly Peculiar (50)** (BSmart) **5-8-6** TSprake(2) (b.hind: hdwy over 6f out: hrd rdn over 1f out: one pce)	3	**4**	$4/1^{1}$	52	35
4894^{4}	**Sweet Supposin (IRE) (66)** (CADwyer) **5-9-8v** CDwyer(5) (nvr nr to chal)	4	**5**	11/1	60	43
5088^{8}	**Errant (62)** (DJSCosgrove) **4-9-4** JQuinn(7) (lw: nvr nrr)	4	**6**	14/1	48	31
4905^{5}	**Waft (USA) (61)** (BWHills) **3-9-1** DHolland(4) (b: b.hind: prom over 4f)	nk	**7**	9/1	46	27
5089^{12}	**Sapphire Son (IRE) (49)** (PCClarke) **4-8-5**^{ow3} DaneO'Neill(11) (lw: prom over 5f)	1	**8**	20/1	32	12
5124^{3}	**Utmost Zeal (USA) (64)** (PWHarris) **3-9-4** AMcGlone(9) (bhd fnl 4f)	5	**9**	$5/1^{2}$	37	18
5059^{6}	**Caddy's First (52)** (SMellor) **4-8-8v** MWigham(1) (bhd fnl 5f)	1	**10**	25/1	23	6
5095^{9}	**Dancing Lawyer (71)** (BJMeehan) **5-9-13** MTebbutt(10) (lw: bhd fnl 4f)	7	**11**	20/1	28	11
5093^{5}	**Time For Tea (IRE) (57)** (CACyzer) **3-8-11** MRoberts(6) (prom over 5f)	1	**12**	14/1	12	—

(SP 116.2%) **12 Rn**

1m 38.41 (1.01) CSF £57.68 CT £446.85 TOTE £7.40: £2.50 £1.60 £3.30 (£23.00) Trio £75.90 OWNER Mr B. Shirazi (ROYSTON) BRED Sean Gorman

WEIGHT FOR AGE 3yo-2lb

5152 LADBROKE ALL-WEATHER TROPHY (QUALIFIER) H'CAP (0-75) (II) (3-Y.O+) (Class D)

3-45 (3-45) **1m (Equitrack)** £2,602.40 (£786.20: £382.60: £180.80) Stalls: High GOING minus 0.47 sec per fur (FST)

Form	Horse	Btn	Pos	SP	RR	SF
5085^{2}	**Mazurek (63)** (PWChapple-Hyam) **3-9-3** DHolland(7) (b.hind: gd hdwy to chse ldr over 2f out: led ins fnl f: r.o wl)	—	**1**	6/1^{2}	76	53
5004^{5}	**Kingchip Boy (66)** (MJRyan) **7-9-8v** AClark(10) (a.p: led 5f out: rdn over 2f out: hdd ins fnl f: unableqckn)	2½	**2**	10/1	74	53
5123^{11}	**Zahran (IRE) (47)** (JMBradley) **5-8-0**$^{(3)ow2}$ FLynch(5) (rdn & hdwy over 3f out: r.o one pce fnl 2f)	4	**3**	12/1	47	24
5124^{3}	**Hawaii Storm (FR) (50)** (DJSffrenchDavis) **8-8-3**$^{(3)}$ PMcCabe(4) (s.i.s: wl bhd 4f: gd hdwy over 2f out: rdn over 1f out: one pce)	hd	**4**	7/1^{3}	50	29
5081^{8}	**Kedwick (IRE) (50)** (PRHedger) **7-8-6** AMcGlone(2) (b: b.hind: nvr nr to chal)	5	**5**	20/1	40	19
5079^{2}	**Greatest (72)** (MissGayKelleway) **5-10-0** SSanders(8) (b: b.hind: led 3f: rdn over 3f out: wknd over 1f out)	1½	**6**	7/2^{1}	59	38
4865^{12}	**Sweet Mate (59)** (MartynMeade) **4-8-8b**$^{(7)}$ DSweeney(9) (bhd fnl 4f)	4	**7**	25/1	38	17
4692*	**Present Situation (69)** (LordHuntingdon) **5-9-11** DHarrison(3) (bhd fnl 3f)	nk	**8**	7/2^{1}	47	26
*5059**	**Sis Garden (60)** (JCullinan) **3-8-9b**$^{(5)}$ MartinDwyer(12) (prom 6f)	½	**9**	12/1	37	14
5089^{8}	**Faith Alone (63)** (CFWall) **3-9-3** GDuffield(11) (b: prom 6f)	5	**10**	10/1	30	7
5089^{4}	**Lancashire Legend (66)** (SDow) **3-9-1e**$^{(5)}$ ADaly(1) (prom over 4f)	2	**11**	14/1	29	6
4186^{12}	**Mogin (52)** (TJNaughton) **3-8-3**$^{(3)}$ JDSmith(6) (swtg: bhd fnl 6f)	3	**12**	33/1	9	—
				(SP 123.0%)	**12 Rn**	

1m 38.31 (0.91) CSF £61.04 CT £659.16 TOTE £7.00: £2.70 £2.60 £2.90 (£30.10) Trio £319.40 OWNER Mr R. E. Sangster (MARLBOROUGH) BRED Miss K. Rausing and Calogo Bloodstock AG

WEIGHT FOR AGE 3yo-2lb

T/Plpt: £801.70 (9.91 Tckts). T/Qdpt: £24.70 (63.85 Tckts). AK

5125a-EVRY (France) (R-H) (Soft)

Monday November 18th

5153a PRIX SARACA (Listed) (2-Y.O F)

1-40 (1-40) **1m** £18,445.00 (£6,324.00: £3,953.00)

Form	Horse	Btn	Pos	SP	RR	SF
3566a^{3}	**Yxenery (IRE)** (MmeCHead,France) **2-9-0** ODoleuze	—	**1**		98	—
4670*	**Dances With Dreams** (PWChapple-Hyam) **2-9-0** JReid	1½	**2**		95	—
	Marethea (FR) (ADeMoussac,France) **2-9-0** SGuillot	2	**3**		91	—
						7 Rn

1m 46.12 (9.12) P-M 5.60F: 2.60F 2.20F (11.80F) OWNER Wertheimer Brothers (CHANTILLY)

4670* Dances With Dreams held a slight lead over a furlong out but was headed and could find no extra close home. She stayed well here and was only beaten by one better on the day.

5154a PRIX FILLE DE L'AIR (Gp 3) (3-Y.O+ F & M)

2-40 (2-42) **1m 2f 110y** £28,986.00 (£10,540.00: £5,270.00: £2,635.00)

Form	Horse	Btn	Pos	SP	RR	SF
4946a*	**Maroussie (FR)** (NClement,France) **3-8-8** J-MBreux	—	**1**		116	—
5025a*	**Dance Treat (USA)** (DSepulchre,France) **4-9-4b** CAsmussen	2½	**2**		118	—
3392a^{4}	**Restiv Star (FR)** (AFabre,France) **4-8-11** TJarnet	nk	**3**		111	—
5015a*	**Asmara (USA)** (JOxx,Ireland) **3-8-8** GMosse	1½	**4**		109	—
						11 Rn

2m 20.45 (10.45) P-M 10.50F: 2.20F 1.40F 1.50F (20.30F) OWNER Mr J. F. Malle (CHANTILLY) BRED Mme Frauke Schlaudecker Herbig & Bruce McNall

5015a* Asmara (USA) was always prominent and challenged two furlongs out. She was soon outpaced, but stayed on for the prize money.

5153a-EVRY (France) (R-H) (Very Soft)

Friday November 22nd

5155a PRIX CONTESSINA (Listed) (3-Y.O+)

2-10 (2-13) **6f**

Form	Horse	Btn	Pos	SP	RR	SF
5044*	**Astrac (IRE)** (MissGayKelleway) **5-9-2** SSanders	—	**1**		119	—
	Linoise (FR) (AFabre,France) **4-8-8** TJarnet	1	**2**		108	—
720a^{2}	**Rose Bourbon (USA)** (ELellouche,France) **3-8-8** SGuillot	1½	**3**		104	—
5044^{4}	**Carranita (IRE)** (BPalling) **6-8-12** TSprake	1½	**4**		104	—
5027a^{3}	**Branston Abby (IRE)** (MJohnston) **7-8-12** MRoberts (btn approx 4l)		**7**		—	—
4957a^{2}	**My Cadeaux** (RGuest) **4-8-8** DaneO'Neill (btn approx 11½l)		**10**		—	—
						10 Rn

1m 15.65 (5.65) P-M 5.10F: 2.10F 2.90F 3.70F (31.30F) OWNER L. Beecroft (WHITCOMBE) BRED Miss Aisling O'Connell

5044* Astrac (IRE), smartly away, was always in the leading group, and ran on really well to hold off the challenge of his two closest pursuers.

5044 Carranita (IRE) has had a busy campaign and finished just under two lengths behind the winner last time out. This was yet again another decent effort and this is her best trip.

5027a Branston Abby (IRE) never really had a race here. She will now be retired to stud at the end of the year after a quite remarkable career. She is however going to be entered for the Wulfrun Stakes, a listed event at Wolverhampton next month, where she will not be without a chance.

4957a My Cadeaux, who finished second beaten a neck by Branston Abby last time out, goes well fresh but was disappointing here.

1055a-CHURCHILL DOWNS (Louisville, USA) (L-H) (Firm)
Saturday November 23rd

5156a MRS REVERE STKS (Gp 3) (3-Y.O F)
9-32 (9-32) **1m 110y** £46,680.00 (£15,058.00: £7,529.00)

	Horse	Dist	Pos	SP	RR	SF
	Maxzene (USA) (TSkiffington,USA) **3-8-5** JulieKrone	—	1		112	—
	Fasta (USA) (WMott,USA) **3-8-5** BPeck	nk	2		111	—
	Turkappeal (USA) (TPletcher,USA) **3-8-7** DonnaBarton	¾	3		112	—
4718[4]	**Thrilling Day** (NAGraham) **3-8-7** HMcCauley (btn approx 11l)		9		—	—

12 Rn

1m 43.6 P-M 9.80: (1-2) 5.60 26.80 (1-2-3) 4.60 12.60 6.20 OWNER Ken-Mort Stable BRED M. Epstein
4718 Thrilling Day was slowly away and although she made some progress at halfway she seemed to be outpaced turning into the straight.

LE CROISE-LAROCHE (Lille, France) (L-H) (Very Soft)
Saturday November 23rd

5157a GRAND PRIX DU NORD (Listed) (3-Y.O+)
2-00 (2-00) **1m 2f 165y** £15,810.00 (£6,324.00: £2,635.00)

	Horse	Dist	Pos	SP	RR	SF
	Mistra (IRE) (MmeCHead,France) **3-8-8b[1]** ODoleuze	—	1		104	—
4445[9]	**Cabaret (IRE)** (PWChapple-Hyam) **3-8-8** SGuillot	nk	2		104	—
5070a[2]	**Grisellito (FR)** (TClout,France) **3-8-11** TThulliez	nk	3		106	—

10 Rn

0m P-M 7.60F: 2.00F 2.10F 1.70F (56.80F) OWNER Mr G. A. Oldham (CHANTILLY) BRED Citadel Stud Establishmant
3836 Cabaret (IRE) raced in a prominent position and stayed on well to the end, only just failing to take the honours.

5127a-CAPANNELLE (Rome, Italy) (R-H) (Heavy)
Sunday November 24th

5158a PREMIO ROMA VECCHIA H'CAP (3-Y.O+)
1-45 (2-00) **1m 6f** £40,600.00 (£17,864.00: £9,744.00)

	Horse	Dist	Pos	SP	RR	SF
5023a*	**Duke of Flight (USA)** (RRossini,Italy) **3-8-10** GForte	—	1		118	—
5023a[2]	**Lear White (USA)** (PAKelleway) **5-8-13** JReid	nk	2		113	—
1579a[5]	**Torrismondo (USA)** (GVerricelli,Italy) **5-8-2** MEsposito	1¼	3		100	—

11 Rn

3m 5.3 TOTE 83L: 21L 13L 26L (53L) OWNER Allevamento Cavallin Nero BRED David's Farm
5023a Lear White (USA) was 4lb better off with Duke of Flight for a recent length and a half beating. Hard driven to hit the front inside the final furlong, he was collared in the final fifty yards.

4668a-FUCHU (Tokyo, Japan) (L-H) (Firm)
Sunday November 24th

5159a JAPAN CUP (Gp 1) (3-Y.O+)
6-20 (6-20) **1m 4f** £1,093,662.00 (£436,466.00: £216,828.00: £216,828.00)

	Horse	Dist	Pos	SP	RR	SF
4955a[2]	**Singspiel (IRE)** (MRStoute) **4-8-13** LDettori (prom: led 2f out to 1½f out: rallied to ld cl home: all out)	—	1		130	—
	Fabulous La Fouine (FR) (HNagahama,Japan) **3-8-5** MMatsunaga (trckd ldrs: 3rd st: led 1½f out tl ct cl home)	nse	2		128	—
4747a[3]	**Strategic Choice (USA)** (PFICole) **5-8-13b[1]** TQuinn (racd in 4th: ev ch 2f out tl ins fnl f: r.o one pce)	1¼	3		128	—
4662a*	**Helissio (FR)** (ELellouche,France) **3-8-9** OPeslier (prom: 2nd & gng wl st: ev ch 2f out tl ins fnl f: r.o one pce)	d.h	3		130	—
4955a[9]	**Awad (USA)** (DDonk,USA) **6-8-13** CMcCarron (hld up: mid div st: styd on strly fnl 2f: nrst fin)	nk	5		128	—
	Taiki Fortune (USA) (YTakahashi,Japan) **3-8-9** YShibata (mid div: 5th st: one pce fnl 2f)	1½	6		128	—
	Hishi Natalie (USA) (MSayama,Japan) **3-8-5** KTsunoda (hld up in rr: 13th st: kpt on fnl 2f: nvr nrr)	nk	7		124	—
4662a[10]	**Pentire** (GWragg) **4-8-13** MHills (mid div: cl 8th on outside st: one pce fnl 2f)	hd	8		125	—
	Flag Down (CAN) (CClement,USA) **6-8-13** JSantos (mid div st: sn rdn & unable qckn)	2	9		123	—

15 Rn

2m 23.8 TOTE 760Y: 210Y 360Y SC 560Y HE 150Y (5100Y) OWNER Sheikh Mohammed (NEWMARKET) BRED Sheikh Mohammed bin Rashid al Maktoum
4955a Singspiel (IRE) put up an ultra-game performance considering he arrived in Japan with a temperature and had twice flown to Canada and back in the last nine weeks. A close sixth into the straight, he made good headway to take the lead passing the two-furlong pole. Marginally headed by the runner-up half a furlong later, he responded to Dettori's strong driving to regain the advantage close home.
Fabulous La Fouine (FR) ran brilliantly for a filly having only her sixth start. Always close up, she was touched off after an epic duel with Singspiel throughout the final furlong. The owner is toying with the idea of racing her in France next year.
4747a Strategic Choice (USA) raced keenly in the early stages in his first-time blinkers. Fourth into the straight, he briefly threatened a big upset but still kept on stoutly to land the biggest prize of his career.
4662a* Helissio (FR) was in the perfect position, in second place rounding the home turn, but failed to find his usual turn of foot. This was clearly not his true form and he may have gone over the top.
4662a Pentire was plenty close enough three furlongs out, but failed to quicken in the straight. Hills reported that he ran flat, just like the Arc, but he did pick up £49,454 for his efforts.

5129-SOUTHWELL (L-H) (Standard)

Friday November 29th

WEATHER: cold showers WIND: mod half bhd

5160 LILY (S) STKS (I) (2-Y.O) (Class G)

12-10 (12-11) **1m (Fibresand)** £1,735.00 (£485.00: £235.00) Stalls: Low GOING minus 0.29 sec per fur (FST)

Form	Horse	Dist	Pos	SP	RR	SF
5041[9]	**Pinchincha (FR)** (DMorris) **2-8-11** AClark(5) (s.i.s: sn chsng ldrs: shkn up & led 2f out: styd on strly u.p ins fnl f)	—	1	6/1	72	26
5057[7]	**Bonne Ville (62)** (BPalling) **2-8-11** TSprake(7) (chsd ldrs: rdn & outpcd 4f out: kpt on same pce fnl f)	2	2	3/1[2]	68	22
5111[6]	**Chasetown Flyer (USA) (60)** (RHollinshead) **2-8-8**(3) FLynch(1) (hld up: hdwy ½-wy: edgd lft & kpt on same pce appr fnl f)	4	3	6/1	60	14
*5135**	**Compact Disc (IRE) (50)** (MJohnston) **2-8-11** DHolland(6) (led early: led 5f out tl over 3f out: led over 2f out: sn hdd & wknd)	8	4	7/2[3]	44	—
4985[5]	**Macari** (BPJBaugh) **2-8-11** RPerham(4) (lw: sn led: hdd 5f out: led over 3f out tl over 2f out: wknd over 1f out)	2	5	33/1	40	—
5135[2]	**Head Girl (IRE) (63)** (CWThornton) **2-8-6** DeanMcKeown(2) (lw: trckd ldrs: effrt over 2f out: no rspnse)	1¼	6	7/4[1]	33	—
5113[10]	**Captain Flint (48)** (ASmith) **2-8-11** NAdams(8) (sn bhd & rdn along)	18	7	25/1	2	—
5103[9]	**First Man** (BJLlewellyn) **2-8-4**(7) JBramhill(9) (sn chsng ldrs: lost pl over 3f out)	8	8	50/1	—	—
4988[12]	**Woodland Dove (30)** (KGWingrove) **2-8-6** RLappin(3) (chsd ldrs over 2f: sn bhd)	9	9	50/1	—	—

(SP 122.9%) **9 Rn**

1m 44.7 (5.70) CSF £24.64 TOTE £5.70: £1.70 £1.40 £1.10 (£23.90) Trio £92.80 OWNER Mr T. J. Wells (NEWMARKET) BRED Fluorocarbon Bloodstock
Bt in 4,000 gns
OFFICIAL EXPLANATION **Head Girl (IRE): resented the kick-back.**

5161 DAFFODIL H'CAP (0-70) (I) (3-Y.O+) (Class E)

12-40 (12-41) **7f (Fibresand)** £2,657.00 (£803.00: £391.00: £185.00) Stalls: Low GOING minus 0.29 sec per fur (FST)

Form	Horse	Dist	Pos	SP	RR	SF
5114[7]	**Pleasure Trick (USA) (37)** (DonEnricoIncisa) **5-7-10b** KimTinkler(6) (sn bhd & drvn along: swtchd rt & hdwy over 2f out: str run to ld nr fin)	—	1	20/1	49	18
4915[9]	**First Gold (43)** (JWharton) **7-8-2b** FNorton(10) (hld up: stdy hdwy ½-wy: led over 1f out tl wl ins fnl f)	1¾	2	11/1	51	20
4820[19]	**Barrel of Hope (65)** (JLEyre) **4-9-10b** RLappin(9) (sn drvn along: hdwy on outside 2f out: hrd rdn & styd on)	1¾	3	12/1	69	38
5130[2]	**Surf City (53)** (WWHaigh) **3-8-11** JQuinn(11) (trckd ldrs: effrt & ev ch over 1f out: kpt on one pce)	½	4	2/1[1]	56	24
4979[2]	**Sea Spouse (64)** (MBlanshard) **5-9-2**(7) KerryBaker(5) (mde most tl over 1f out: sn wknd)	1¾	5	6/1[2]	63	32
5099[9]	**Xenophon of Cunaxa (IRE) (62)** (MJFetherston-Godley) **3-9-6** DaneO'Neill(12) (racd wd: trckd ldrs: effrt 2f out: styd on one pce)	nk	6	10/1[3]	60	28
4337[11]	**Best Kept Secret (52)** (LJBarratt) **5-8-4b**(7) CLowther(3) (sn outpcd & bhd: sme hdwy 2f out: n.d)	5	7	14/1	39	8
5095[6]	**Jareer Do (IRE) (49)** (BPalling) **4-8-8** TSprake(7) (lw: chsd ldrs tl wknd 2f out)	1¼	8	14/1	33	2
4906[5]	**Grey Kingdom (41)** (MBrittain) **5-8-0** NCarlisle(4) (w ldr tl wknd over 1f out)	3½	9	10/1[3]	17	—
3451[8]	**Elle Mac (38)** (MPBielby) **3-7-5v[1]**(5) PFessey(14) (racd wd: sn drvn along & bhd)	2½	10	33/1	8	—
5114[4]	**Principal Boy (IRE) (53)** (TJEtherington) **3-8-11** MBirch(1) (trckd ldrs: effrt over 2f out: sn wknd)	3½	11	6/1[2]	15	—
4805[14]	**Sharp Move (40)** (MrsJCecil) **4-7-8**(5)ow3 MartinDwyer(2) (in tch: drvn along ½-wy: rdn & lost pl over 2f ut)	1½	12	12/1	—	—
4202[17]	**Indian Wolf (41)** (BJLlewellyn) **3-7-6**(7)ow3 JBramhill(13) (in tch tl lost pl 3f out)	3	13	50/1	—	—
5138[5]	**Cheeky Chappy (62)** (DWChapman) **5-9-7b** ACulhane(8) (hld up: effrt over 2f out: sn lost pl)	11	14	10/1[3]	—	—

(SP 135.9%) **14 Rn**

1m 30.3 (3.80) CSF £223.58 CT £2,557.44 TOTE £37.80: £6.40 £5.20 £4.50 (£78.60) Trio £247.70; £87.25 to Newcastle 30/11/96 OWNER Don Enrico Incisa (MIDDLEHAM) BRED W. S. Farish
LONG HANDICAP Elle Mac 7-7 Sharp Move 7-9 Indian Wolf 6-12 Pleasure Trick (USA) 7-7
WEIGHT FOR AGE 3yo-1lb
OFFICIAL EXPLANATION **Cheeky Chappy: resented the kick-back.**
Pleasure Trick (USA): regarding the apparent improvement in form, the trainer reported that the application of blinkers for the first time on the Flat had motivated the gelding.

5162 ORCHID MAIDEN AUCTION STKS (2-Y.O) (Class F)

1-10 (1-12) **5f (Fibresand)** £2,398.00 (£673.00: £328.00) Stalls: High GOING minus 0.29 sec per fur (FST)

Form	Horse	Dist	Pos	SP	RR	SF
5034[2]	**Nor-Do-I** (JMPEustace) **2-8-4b**(5) MartinDwyer(10) (lw: sn trckng ldrs: led over 1f out: drvn out)	—	1	Evens[1]	68	35
4907[2]	**The Wyandotte Inn (65)** (RHollinshead) **2-8-3**(3) FLynch(5) (lw: chsd ldrs: rdn ½-wy: kpt on fnl f)	2	2	7/2[2]	59	26
5107[3]	**Fit For The Job (IRE) (50)** (WGMTurner) **2-8-3** TSprake(4) (w ldrs: kpt on same pce appr fnl f)	½	3	10/1	54	21
4343[2]	**Molly Music (59)** (GGMargarson) **2-7-8b[1]**(7) AMcCarthy(3) (lw: in tch: sn drvn along: styd on fnl 2f)	1½	4	9/1	47	14
5111[11]	**Magic Fizz** (TJEtherington) **2-8-9** MBirch(8) (shkn up & hdwy over 1f out: nvr nr to chal)	hd	5	25/1	55	22
	Harvey's Future (TTClement) **2-8-3**(5)ow2 GFaulkner(6) (cmpt: led tl over 1f out: sn wknd)	2	6	12/1	48	13
2076[6]	**Krystal Davey (IRE)** (TDBarron) **2-8-9** DeanMcKeown(11) (bit bkwd: dwlt: bhd tl kpt on fnl 2f: n.d)	½	7	8/1[3]	47	14
5107[2]	**Enchantica (60)** (JBerry) **2-8-4** GCarter(9) (prom: rdn ½-wy: sn wknd)	1½	8	8/1[3]	37	4
3508[6]	**Gymcrak Watermill (IRE)** (GHolmes) **2-7-12** JQuinn(1) (b.hind: chsd ldrs tl grad wknd fnl 2f)	2½	9	25/1	23	—
5050[7]	**Prix de Clermont (IRE)** (GLewis) **2-8-9** AClark(7) (sn outpcd: rdn & wnt lft 2f out: sn wknd)	2½	10	14/1	26	—
5111[W]	**Frandickbob** (JohnHarris) **2-8-6** RPerham(2) (unruly s: s.s: a bhd)	1¼	11	25/1	19	—

(SP 139.4%) **11 Rn**

58.9 secs (0.10 under 2y best) (1.90) CSF £6.41 TOTE £1.80: £1.10 £1.60 £3.10 (£3.30) Trio £15.70 OWNER The MacDougall Partnership (NEWMARKET) BRED R. E. A. Bott (Wigmore Street) Ltd

5163 CARNATION CLAIMING STKS (3, 4 & 5-Y.O) (Class F)

1-40 (1-42) **6f (Fibresand)** £2,398.00 (£673.00: £328.00) Stalls: Low GOING minus 0.29 sec per fur (FST)

Form	Horse	Dist	Pos	SP	RR	SF
5131[7]	**Chadwell Hall (80)** (SRBowring) **5-9-0**(3) CTeague(12) (b: mde all: styd on u.p fnl 2f: all out)	—	1	5/1[2]	76	45
5097[9]	**Gi La High (46)** (JBerry) **3-7-7**(5) PFessey(13) (b.hind: trckd ldrs: styd on u.p fnl f: nt qckn nr fin)	nk	2	25/1	56	25

Form	Horse / Details	Dist	Pos	SP	RR	SF
4987[3]	**Bold Aristocrat (IRE) (57)** (RHollinshead) **5-8-3**(3)ow1 FLynch(8) (trckd ldrs: effrt & ev ch 2f out: kpt on same pce)	1½	**3**	7/1	60	28
5134[3]	**Night Harmony (IRE) (55)** (MissSJWilton) **3-8-11** DeanMcKeown(5) (b: a in tch: effrt & ev ch 2f out: nt qckn fnl f)	½	**4**	10/1	64	33
5000[2]	**Step On Degas (62)** (MJFetherston-Godley) **3-7-13**(5) MartinDwyer(6) (a in tch: drvn along ½-wy: kpt on one pce)	¾	**5**	9/2[1]	55	24
*5112**	**Shashi (IRE) (55)** (WWHaigh) **4-8-10** RLappin(4) (trckd ldrs: ev ch 2f out: wknd over 1f out)	½	**6**	7/1	60	29
2425[8]	**Krystal Max (IRE) (86)** (TDBarron) **3-8-10**(7) VictoriaAppleby(9) (b.off fore: hld up: hdwy on outside 2f out: kpt on wl: nvr rchd ldrs)	hd	**7**	6/1[3]	66	35
4888[11]	**Prudent Princess (46)** (AHide) **4-7-9v[1]**(7)ow2 JoHunnam(16) (racd wd: chsd ldrs tl wknd over 1f out)	½	**8**	33/1	50	17
4860[3]	**Myttons Mistake (70)** (ABailey) **3-8-9** DWright(7) (hld up: styd on fnl 2f: nvr nr to chal)	1¾	**9**	6/1[3]	52	21
5099[5]	**Standown (73)** (JBerry) **3-8-6e**(7) CLowther(10) (b.hind: mid div: drvn along ½-wy: sn outpcd)	3½	**10**	10/1	47	16
4045[15]	**Boffy (IRE) (65)** (BPJBaugh) **3-8-9** RPerham(2) (mid div: drvn along ½-wy: n.d)	¾	**11**	20/1	41	10
5055[6]	**Sue Me (IRE) (51)** (WRMuir) **4-9-3** DaneO'Neill(3) (lw: hld up: effrt over 2f out: sn wknd)	2½	**12**	16/1	42	11
5144[9]	**Marino Street (49)** (PDEvans) **3-8-4b**ow2 GCarter(11) (b.off hind: sn bhd)	nk	**13**	16/1	29	—
	Seanchai (IRE) (PSFelgate) **3-8-8**(3) PMcCabe(15) (b: s.s: sn t.o)	3½	**14**	20/1	26	—
4589[13]	**The Frisky Farmer (60)** (WGMTurner) **3-8-9** AClark(14) (w ldrs tl wknd 2f out)	6	**15**	16/1	8	—
4898[19]	**Sarasota Ryde** (JEBanks) **3-8-4** JQuinn(1) (sn pushed along: outpcd fr ½-wy)	2½	**16**	50/1	—	—

(SP 142.5%) **16 Rn**

1m 15.9 (2.40) CSF £125.15 TOTE £6.40: £2.70 £4.40 £2.30 (£103.30) Trio £166.20; £74.94 to Newcastle 30/11/96 OWNER Mr D. H. Bowring (EDWINSTOWE) BRED J. C. and Mrs C. L. Owen

STEWARDS' ENQUIRY Teague susp. 11/12/96 + 1 day (excessive use of whip).

5164 TULIP NURSERY H'CAP (0-75) (2-Y.O) (Class E)

2-10 (2-10) **7f (Fibresand)** £2,968.35 (£898.80: £438.90: £208.95) Stalls: Low GOING minus 0.29 sec per fur (FST)

Form	Horse / Details	Dist	Pos	SP	RR	SF
5048*	**Return of Amin (70)** (JDBethell) **2-9-7** DHolland(9) (led after 2f: styd on wl fnl 2f)	—	**1**	11/4[1]	82	47
5133[2]	**C-Harry (IRE) (67)** (RHollinshead) **2-9-1**(3) FLynch(10) (lw: a.p: kpt on fnl f: no ch w wnr)	4	**2**	3/1[2]	70	35
4916[2]	**Sharp Return (62)** (MJRyan) **2-8-13** AClark(3) (lw: a.p: effrt over 2f out: styd on one pce)	1¾	**3**	9/2[3]	61	26
4990[11]	**Broctune Line (47)** (MrsMReveley) **2-7-12** DWright(2) (bhd tl styd on fnl 3f: nrst fin)	s.h	**4**	12/1	46	11
*5111**	**Sally Green (IRE) (71)** (CFWall) **2-9-8** 7x GDuffield(8) (lw: trckd ldrs: effrt over 2f out: grad wknd)	1¾	**5**	5/1	66	31
4250[8]	**Treasure Touch (IRE) (65)** (GMMoore) **2-9-2** ACulhane(1) (chsd ldrs tl wknd fnl 2f)	2	**6**	14/1	55	20
4795[10]	**Good Day (65)** (CWThornton) **2-9-2** DeanMcKeown(5) (outpcd & bhd ½-wy: n.d after)	nk	**7**	10/1	55	20
5133[9]	**Manhattan Diamond (59)** (ABailey) **2-8-10** GCarter(7) (b.hind: s.i.s: sme hdwy ½-wy: sn rdn & no imp)	nk	**8**	20/1	48	13
4903[11]	**Mirror Four Sport (57)** (MJohnston) **2-8-8** JFanning(4) (led 2f: cl up tl wknd over 2f out)	6	**9**	16/1	32	—
3950[7]	**Rock The Casbah (55)** (JHetherton) **2-8-6** JQuinn(6) (outpcd & bhd fr ½-wy)	3½	**10**	20/1	22	—

(SP 125.4%) **10 Rn**

1m 29.8 (3.30) CSF £11.95 CT £34.00 TOTE £3.80: £2.00 £1.40 £1.80 (£5.90) Trio £5.00 OWNER Sheikh Amin Dahlawi (MIDDLEHAM) BRED Al Dahlawi Stud Co Ltd

5165 DAFFODIL H'CAP (0-70) (II) (3-Y.O+) (Class E)

2-40 (2-46) **7f (Fibresand)** £2,657.00 (£803.00: £391.00: £185.00) Stalls: Low GOING minus 0.29 sec per fur (FST)

Form	Horse / Details	Dist	Pos	SP	RR	SF
5134[2]	**The Barnsley Belle (IRE) (47)** (JLEyre) **3-8-5** RLappin(3) (chsd ldrs: led appr fnl f: styd on)	—	**1**	11/2[3]	55	38
5004[7]	**Tael of Silver (40)** (ABailey) **4-7-13** DWright(4) (lw: in tch: hdwy to chse ldrs ½-wy: one pce fnl 2f)	3½	**2**	6/1	40	24
5056[3]	**Theatre Magic (60)** (SRBowring) **3-9-4b** DeanMcKeown(2) (lw: led: clr 3f out: hdd appr fnl f: sn btn)	hd	**3**	10/1	60	43
5144[2]	**Desert Invader (IRE) (68)** (DWChapman) **5-9-13b** ACulhane(10) (trckd ldrs: effrt over 2f out: hrd rdn & styd on one pce)	1¾	**4**	8/1	64	48
5134[4]	**Legal Issue (IRE) (55)** (WWHaigh) **4-9-0v[1]** DRMcCabe(8) (lw: s.i.s: n.m.r over 2f out: hrd rdn & r.o fnl f)	1	**5**	5/1[2]	49	33
5114[11]	**Mu-Arrik (37)** (GROldroyd) **8-7-3v**(7) IonaWands(7) (lw: hdwy over 2f out: styd on: no imp)	3½	**6**	33/1	23	7
5134[6]	**Craigie Boy (47)** (NBycroft) **6-8-6b** GDuffield(12) (chsd ldrs tl hung lft & grad wknd fnl 2½f)	5	**7**	16/1	21	5
4979[8]	**Jimmy the Skunk (IRE) (60)** (PDEvans) **5-9-5** GCarter(6) (chsd ldrs tl wknd fnl 2½f)	1½	**8**	10/1	31	15
5082[3]	**Allinson's Mate (IRE) (60)** (TDBarron) **8-8-12b**(7) VictoriaAppleby(1) (sn outpcd & bhd)	1¼	**9**	4/1[1]	28	12
5112[3]	**Juba (37)** (DrJDScargill) **4-7-10** NCarlisle(5) (chsd ldrs over 4f)	s.h	**10**	12/1	5	—
5117[3]	**Kazimiera (IRE) (60)** (CWCElsey) **3-8-13**(5) PFessey(9) (unruly s: outpcd & lost tch fnl 3f)	4	**11**	14/1	19	2
5109[5]	**Florrie'm (38)** (JohnHarris) **3-7-10** JQuinn(13) (prom tl wknd over 2f out)	4	**12**	33/1	—	—
3279[7]	**Three Arch Bridge (67)** (MJohnston) **4-9-12b** DHolland(11) (racd wd: sn bhd)	4	**13**	10/1	7	—

(SP 130.8%) **13 Rn**

1m 29.2 (2.70) CSF £39.48 CT £244.61 TOTE £5.20: £2.10 £1.40 £5.30 (£16.20) Trio £37.40 OWNER Mr K. Meynell (HAMBLETON) BRED Kim McCall

LONG HANDICAP Juba 7-8 Florrie'm 6-13 Mu-Arrik 7-6

WEIGHT FOR AGE 3yo-1lb

5166 LILY (S) STKS (II) (2-Y.O) (Class G)

3-10 (3-12) **1m (Fibresand)** £1,735.00 (£485.00: £235.00) Stalls: Low GOING minus 0.29 sec per fur (FST)

Form	Horse / Details	Dist	Pos	SP	RR	SF
4980[2]	**Bali-Pet (59)** (WGMTurner) **2-8-4b**(7) DSweeney(2) (lw: mde all: clr 3f out: styd on)	—	**1**	2/1[1]	56	8
4562[16]	**Senate Swings (61)** (WRMuir) **2-8-11** DaneO'Neill(1) (a.p: rdn ½-wy: kpt on fnl 2f: nvr able to chal)	2½	**2**	4/1[3]	51	3
4902[9]	**Aspecto Lad (IRE) (55)** (MJohnston) **2-8-11** DeanMcKeown(4) (lw: sn drvn along & wl bhd: r.o fnl 2f)	s.h	**3**	9/2	51	3
5135[13]	**Diamonds Are** (DTThom) **2-8-6** JQuinn(8) (in tch: rdn ½-wy: one pce)	3	**4**	33/1	40	—
5107[9]	**Municipal Girl (IRE) (38)** (BPalling) **2-8-6** TSprake(7) (chsd wnr after 2f tl wknd fnl 2½f)	4	**5**	25/1	32	—
4970[10]	**Beveled Mill** (PDEvans) **2-8-6** GCarter(6) (drvn along ½-wy: sn no ch)	10	**6**	9/2	12	—
4796[14]	**Gymcrak Jester** (GHolmes) **2-8-11** JFanning(3) (b: bit bkwd: chsd ldrs 4f: sn wknd)	12	**7**	16/1	—	—
5098[3]	**Slightly Oliver (IRE) (59)** (MrsNMacauley) **2-8-8v[1]**(3) CTeague(5) (lw: rel to s: swvd & uns rdr after s: rmntd & continued 4f bhd)	dist	**8**	3/1[2]	—	—

(SP 127.4%) **8 Rn**

1m 46.6 (7.60) CSF £11.45 TOTE £3.50: £1.10 £2.20 £1.20 (£5.80) OWNER H G Carnell & Son Ltd (SHERBORNE) BRED E. W. Carnell

No bid

STEWARDS' ENQUIRY O' Neill susp. 11 & 13/12/96 (excessive use of whip).

5167 IRIS AMATEUR H'CAP (0-75) (4-Y.O+) (Class G)

3-40 (3-42) **1m 6f (Fibresand)** £2,085.00 (£585.00: £285.00) Stalls: High GOING minus 0.29 sec per fur (FST)

Form	Horse / details	Dist	Pos	SP	RR	SF
5054[7]	**Golden Hadeer (44)** (MJRyan) **5-9-8**(3) MrSLavallin(1) (b: mde all: hld on wl)	—	1	8/1[3]	54	27
5136[2]	**Our Main Man (48)** (RMWhitaker) **6-10-1** MissPJones(7) (lw: hld up: n.m.r over 2f out: hdwy & ch 2f out: kpt on towards fin)	½	2	2/1[1]	57	30
5115[4]	**Elite Bliss (IRE) (40)** (MJCamacho) **4-9-7** MissDianaJones(9) (in tch: hdwy & ch 2f out: nt qckn wl ins fnl f)	nk	3	9/1	49	22
5047[4]	**Paradise Navy (70)** (CREgerton) **7-11-2b**(7) MissSDuckett(3) (lw: hld up: stdy hdwy 5f out: effrt & ch 2f out: r.o one pce)	1¼	4	4/1[2]	78	51
5102[5]	**Stalled (IRE) (58)** (PTWalwyn) **6-10-8**(3) MarchionessBlandford(10) (lw: prom: rdn 3f out: wknd over 1f out)	11	5	4/1[2]	53	26
4984[11]	**Gold Blade (67)** (JPearce) **7-11-6** MrsLPearce(2) (in tch: hdwy 4f out: wknd fnl 2f)	1¾	6	9/1	60	33
4984[10]	**Claque (55)** (DWChapman) **4-10-5b**(3) MissRClark(5) (cl up tl rdn & wknd over 2f out)	13	7	14/1	33	6
2717[9]	**Backview (75)** (BJLlewellyn) **4-11-11**(3) MrsCWilliams(8) (lw: chsd ldrs tl wknd 5f out: sn wl bhd)	21	8	14/1	29	2
	Kirkie Cross (43) (KGWingrove) **4-9-3**(7)ow3 MrAnthonyBrown(11) (rdn & wl bhd fnl 4f)	1½	9	33/1	—	—
	Burning Cost (45) (REPeacock) **6-9-5**(7)ow5 MrsCPeacock(6) (chsd ldrs 7f: sn t.o)	6	10	50/1	—	—

(SP 122.7%) **10 Rn**

3m 9.7 (11.70) CSF £24.52 CT £142.42 TOTE £14.80: £2.60 £1.30 £1.60 (£31.60) Trio £73.00 OWNER Four Jays Racing Partnership (NEWMARKET) BRED Stetchworth Park Stud Ltd

LONG HANDICAP Elite Bliss (IRE) 9-5 Kirkie Cross 8-13 Burning Cost 8-9

T/Plpt: £469.50 (17.42 Tckts). T/Qdpt: £8.10 (145.06 Tckts). WG

5137-WOLVERHAMPTON (L-H) (Standard)

Saturday November 30th

WEATHER: fine

5168 OHIO EXPRESS MAIDEN STKS (2-Y.O) (Class D)

7-00 (7-01) **1m 100y (Fibresand)** £2,827.00 (£856.00: £418.00: £199.00) Stalls: Low GOING minus 0.08 sec per fur (STD)

Form	Horse / details	Dist	Pos	SP	RR	SF
5090[2]	**Premier** (MJohnston) **2-9-0** DeanMcKeown(4) (led: hdd over 1f out: edgd rt u.p ins fnl f: rallied to regain ld cl home)	—	1	7/4[1]	73	38
4619[4]	**Selberry** (PCHaslam) **2-9-0** GCarter(2) (cl up: rdn & lost pl over 5f out: hdwy on ins to chal over 2f out: led over 1f out: edgd rt ins fnl f: hdd & no ex cl home)	nk	2	5/2[2]	72	37
5041[W]	**Move The Clouds** (JRFanshawe) **2-8-6**(3) NVarley(3) (plld hrd: chsd ldrs: rdn 3f out: sn swished tail: drvn & ev ch ent fnl f: sn hung rt: one pce fnl 100yds)	3½	3	12/1	61	26
5111[12]	**Kustom Kit Klassic** (SRBowring) **2-9-0** SDWilliams(6) (bit bkwd: bhd: rdn over 3f out: mod hdwy: no imp fnl 2f)	15	4	40/1	37	2
3848[11]	**Hoh Down (IRE)** (KMcAuliffe) **2-8-9** DaneO'Neill(7) (b.hind: bit bkwd: cl up: rdn over 4f out: wknd 3f out: eased whn btn ins fnl f)	1¾	5	33/1	29	—
	Dixie Eyes Blazing (USA) (RCharlton) **2-8-9** TSprake(1) (lt-f: prom tl rdn & wknd ½-wy)	hd	6	5/1	29	—
5009[6]	**Touch'n'go** (MJohnston) **2-9-0** JFanning(8) (bit bkwd: s.i.s: in tch: hdwy over 5f out: sn prom: wknd 3f out)	1¼	7	20/1	32	—
	Princess Sarara (USA) (SirMarkPrescott) **2-8-9** SSanders(5) (lt-f: hld up: effrt on ins ½-wy: sn btn)	4	8	7/2[3]	19	—
5040[9]	**Eternal Host (IRE)** (RHollinshead) **2-8-11**(3) FLynch(9) (bit bkwd: in tch: rdn over 3f out: wknd qckly: sn bhd: t.o)	18	9	25/1	—	—

(SP 125.5%) **9 Rn**

1m 50.6 (5.60) CSF £7.10 TOTE £3.00: £1.20 £1.10 £2.70 (£4.50) Trio £21.80 OWNER Roldvale Ltd (MIDDLEHAM) BRED Claredore Ltd

5169 OHIO EXPRESS CLAIMING STKS (3-Y.O+) (Class F)

7-30 (7-30) **1m 6f 166y (Fibresand)** £2,085.00 (£585.00: £285.00) Stalls: High GOING minus 0.08 sec per fur (STD)

Form	Horse / details	Dist	Pos	SP	RR	SF
5115[7]	**Petoskin (67)** (JPearce) **4-9-2** MWigham(7) (trckd ldrs: effrt to ld 2f out: styd on ins fnl f)	—	1	12/1[3]	73	37
*5104**	**Hill Farm Dancer (68)** (WMBrisbourne) **5-9-0**(5) MartinDwyer(5) (hld up: hdwy 4f out: ev ch 2f out: kpt on same pce fnl f)	1¾	2	13/8[2]	74	38
*4977**	**Pharly Dancer (68)** (WWHaigh) **7-9-1**(5) LNewton(8) (hld up in tch: trckd ldrs after 6f: led over 3f out: rdn & hdd 2 out: one pce fr over 1f out)	3½	3	5/6[1]	71	35
	Suleika Dancer (PDEvans) **3-8-7** GCarter(6) (bit bkwd: sn cl up: rdn over 3f out: sn wknd)	12	4	33/1	53	9
5136[10]	**Drama King (38)** (SRBowring) **4-8-10b** SDWilliams(2) (led: rdn & hdd over 3f out: wknd qckly)	14	5	20/1	33	—
4480[2]	**Jilly Beveled (39)** (RonaldThompson) **4-9-1** JQuinn(1) (plld hrd: trckd ldrs: lost pl ½-wy: bhd 5f out: t.o)	dist	6	25/1	—	—
1644[12]	**Action Replay** (RHollinshead) **3-8-3**(3) FLynch(4) (bkwd: sn bhd: lost tch ½-wy: t.o)	dist	7	50/1	—	—

(SP 113.8%) **7 Rn**

3m 18.0 (10.60) CSF £30.94 TOTE £8.30: £5.80 £2.00 (£14.50) OWNER Mr Jeff Pearce (NEWMARKET) BRED James Wigan

WEIGHT FOR AGE 3yo-8lb

5170 OHIO EXPRESS H'CAP (0-65) (3-Y.O+ F & M) (Class F)

8-00 (8-00) **7f (Fibresand)** £2,433.00 (£683.00: £333.00) Stalls: High GOING minus 0.08 sec per fur (STD)

Form	Horse / details	Dist	Pos	SP	RR	SF
5112[8]	**Elite Hope (USA) (52)** (NTinkler) **4-9-2** DeanMcKeown(5) (w ldr: led 3f out: drvn clr fnl f)	—	1	10/1	66	51
5134[11]	**Encore M'Lady (IRE) (57)** (FHLee) **5-9-7** RLappin(11) (in tch: hdwy u.p 3f out: kpt on ins fnl f: no imp on wnr)	7	2	16/1	55	40
5152[9]	**Sis Garden (60)** (JCullinan) **3-9-2**(7) DSweeney(7) (led: hdd 3f out: one pce)	hd	3	6/1[3]	58	42
4982[13]	**Holloway Melody (49)** (BAMcMahon) **3-8-12** GCarter(3) (chsd ldrs: rdn ½-wy: sn no imp)	nk	4	11/1	46	30
5112[2]	**Anita's Contessa (IRE) (54)** (BPalling) **4-9-4** TSprake(6) (in tch: rdn 5f out: no hdwy)	2½	5	11/2[2]	45	30
5059[4]	**Komlucky (45)** (ABMulholland) **4-8-9v** JQuinn(9) (dwlt: chsd ldrs: drvn over 2f out: wknd over 1f out)	hd	6	6/1[3]	36	21
5105[6]	**Steal 'Em (61)** (ABailey) **3-9-10** DWright(8) (b: prom: rdn 4f out: wknd ent fnl 2f)	2½	7	5/2[1]	46	30
4768[19]	**Chilibang Bang (65)** (JBerry) **3-9-7**(7) CLowther(4) (mid div early: bhd fr ½-wy)	7	8	20/1	34	18
5109[12]	**Lia Fail (IRE) (51)** (RHollinshead) **3-8-9**(5) DGriffiths(12) (a bhd: n.d)	2½	9	14/1	15	—
4692[11]	**Foreign Relation (IRE) (55)** (PRWebber) **3-9-4** DaneO'Neill(1) (in tch: effrt ½-wy: sn wknd)	nk	10	16/1	18	2
5144[6]	**Delrob (54)** (DHaydnJones) **5-9-4b** AClark(2) (a bhd)	14	11	9/1	—	—

				SP	RR	SF
5059[11]	**Skelton Countess (IRE) (55)** (RHollinshead) **3-9-1**(3) FLynch(10) (a bhd: lost tch 2f out: t.o)	10	**12**	33/1	—	—

(SP 126.1%) **12 Rn**

1m 28.3 (3.60) CSF £145.94 CT £985.49 TOTE £13.70: £2.90 £3.60 £1.90 (£55.70) Trio £120.10 OWNER Elite Racing Club (MALTON) BRED Barbara Hunter
WEIGHT FOR AGE 3yo-1lb

5171 ROYAL BRUNEI AIRLINES H'CAP (0-85) (3-Y.O) (Class D)

8-30 (8-31) **1m 4f (Fibresand)** £3,074.60 (£930.80: £454.40: £216.20) Stalls: Low GOING minus 0.08 sec per fur (STD)

				SP	RR	SF
4551[12]	**Nikita's Star (IRE) (73)** (DJGMurraySmith) **3-9-0** DaneO'Neill(1) (prom: chsd clr ldr 2f out: styd on strly to ld 50y out: edgd rt cl home)	—	**1**	10/1	81	47
4217*	**Tart (FR) (70)** (JPearce) **3-8-11** MWigham(6) (hld up: hdwy 2f out: styd on u.p wl ins fnl f)	¾	**2**	5/1 3	77	43
*5122**	**Tissue of Lies (USA) (70)** (MJohnston) **3-8-11** DeanMcKeown(4) (lw: cl up: outpcd 3f out: kpt on again ins fnl f: hung lft fnl 50 yds)	1¼	**3**	6/1	75	41
5008*	**Northern Motto (55)** (JSGoldie) **3-7-10** JQuinn(5) (in tch: effrt to chse ldrs 3f out: one pce u.p fnl 2f)	1½	**4**	6/1	58	24
5046[8]	**Heart (80)** (MRStoute) **3-9-4**(3) FLynch(7) (led: clr 2f out: drvn over 1f out: eased, hdd & wknd 50y out)	2	**5**	9/4 1	81	47
5088[3]	**Philistar (69)** (JMPEustace) **3-8-10** TSprake(2) (plld hrd: hld up: drvn 3f out: sn btn)	7	**6**	4/1 2	60	26
5108[4]	**Backwoods (64)** (WMBrisbourne) **3-8-5** AGarth(3) (hld up: drvn ½-wy: sn outpcd & no imp)	10	**7**	7/1	42	8

(SP 117.6%) **7 Rn**

2m 39.3 (6.80) CSF £55.14 TOTE £10.70: £3.40 £2.40 (£26.90) OWNER Nikita's Partners (LAMBOURN) BRED D. Twomey
LONG HANDICAP Northern Motto 7-7
STEWARDS' ENQUIRY Obj. to Nikita's Star by Wigham overruled.
OFFICIAL EXPLANATION **Heart: the rider confirmed that the filly was extremely tired and could not have finished fourth or better.**

5172 OHIO EXPRESS (S) STKS (2-Y.O F) (Class G)

9-00 (9-01) **6f (Fibresand)** £2,085.00 (£585.00: £285.00) Stalls: Low GOING minus 0.08 sec per fur (STD)

				SP	RR	SF
5135[6]	**Showgirl** (CaptJWilson) **2-8-9** SDWilliams(5) (b: cl up: drvn to chse ldr 2f out: r.o to ld ins fnl f)	—	**1**	15/2 3	63	18
5146[4]	**Lightning Bolt (IRE) (59)** (MJohnston) **2-8-9** DeanMcKeown(4) (led after ½f: qcknd 2f out: hdd & no ex ins fnl f)	1¾	**2**	4/6 1	58	13
5061[5]	**Chilling (40)** (PGMurphy) **2-8-9** SDrowne(2) (prom: rdn 2f out: btn over 1f out)	6	**3**	33/1	42	—
2595[8]	**Sweet Emmaline (74)** (WGMTurner) **2-9-0** TSprake(1) (bit bkwd: in tch: outpcd fr ½-wy: n.d)	1½	**4**	100/30 2	43	—
5005[5]	**Face It (37)** (WGMTurner) **2-8-4**(7)ow2 DMcGaffin(6) (bhd: rdn ½-wy: n.d)	nk	**5**	33/1	40	—
4093[5]	**Wedding Music (52)** (PCHaslam) **2-8-9** GCarter(3) (led for ½f: cl up tl rdn & wknd over 2f out: eased whn btn ins fnl f)	7	**6**	8/1	19	—

(SP 111.8%) **6 Rn**

1m 16.4 (5.20) CSF £12.78 TOTE £6.30: £2.00 £1.50 (£3.20) OWNER Andy Partnership (PRESTON) BRED John W. Campion
Bt in 6,000 gns

5173 OHIO EXPRESS H'CAP (0-60) (3-Y.O+) (Class F)

9-30 (9-31) **5f (Fibresand)** £2,085.00 (£585.00: £285.00) Stalls: Low GOING minus 0.08 sec per fur (STD)

				SP	RR	SF
5097[2]	**Napier Star (60)** (MrsNMacauley) **3-9-11v**(3) CTeague(6) (b.hind: a cl up: led ½-wy: r.o gamely)	—	**1**	6/1 2	67	47
4983[12]	**Aljaz (45)** (MissGayKelleway) **6-8-13** DaneO'Neill(13) (b: a cl up: ev ch over 1f out: r.o u.p)	½	**2**	8/1	50	30
4589[7]	**Hoh Majestic (IRE) (52)** (RonaldThompson) **3-9-6v** JQuinn(5) (in tch: hdwy & nt clr run 2f out: swtchd lft over 1f out: styd on)	1¼	**3**	8/1	53	33
5131[6]	**Amy Leigh (IRE) (50)** (CaptJWilson) **3-9-1**(3) FLynch(11) (in tch: drvn 2f out: kpt on one pce)	1½	**4**	6/1 2	47	27
5138[3]	**Superbit (48)** (BAMcMahon) **4-9-2** SSanders(1) (chsd ldrs: u.p over 1f out: sn no ex)	1¼	**5**	2/1 1	41	21
5096[9]	**Lloc (48)** (CADwyer) **4-8-9**(7) JoHunnam(8) (b: chsd ldrs: outpcd over 1f out)	2½	**6**	7/1 3	33	13
5105[13]	**Dieci Anno (IRE) (58)** (BPalling) **3-9-12** TSprake(10) (in tch: rdn & outpcd over 1f out)	hd	**7**	20/1	42	22
5097[7]	**Mister Raider (52)** (EAWheeler) **4-9-1b**(5) ADaly(3) (in tch: sn drvn along: nvr able to chal)	½	**8**	10/1	35	15
934[10]	**Gloria Imperator (IRE) (51)** (ABMulholland) **3-9-5** DeanMcKeown(7) (in rr: n.m.r 3f out: sn outpcd)	6	**9**	33/1	15	—
2940[14]	**General Equation (53)** (JBalding) **3-9-7** SDrowne(12) (led to ½-wy: wknd over 1f out)	1½	**10**	25/1	12	—
3661[11]	**Gracious Gretclo (50)** (PDEvans) **3-9-4** GCarter(9) (a bhd)	½	**11**	11/1	7	—
4372[15]	**La Belle Dominique (54)** (SGKnight) **4-9-8** VSlattery(2) (s.i.s: a outpcd)	9	**12**	20/1	—	—

(SP 130.4%) **12 Rn**

62.1 secs (3.20) CSF £54.04 CT £373.41 TOTE £5.60: £2.10 £1.80 £2.70 (£11.20) Trio £109.30 OWNER Mr P. M. Heaton (MELTON MOWBRAY) BRED P. M. Heaton

T/Plpt: £80.40 (138.47 Tckts). T/Qdpt: £28.40 (16.78 Tckts). DO

5160-SOUTHWELL (L-H) (Slow)

Tuesday December 3rd

WEATHER: raining WIND: str across

5174 HAMLET H'CAP (0-70) (I) (3-Y.O+) (Class E)

11-40 (11-41) **6f (Fibresand)** £2,629.70 (£794.60: £386.80: £182.90) Stalls: Low

				SP	RR	SF
5042[18]	**Mr Frosty (54)** (WJarvis) **4-9-3** SSanders(1) (mde virtually all: clr 2f out: rdn & hld on wl)	—	**1**	14/1	63	45
5163[3]	**Bold Aristocrat (IRE) (57)** (RHollinshead) **5-9-3**(3) FLynch(9) (hld up: swtchd lft & hdwy 2f out: r.o wl ins fnl f)	1½	**2**	4/1 2	62	44
5138[12]	**Plum First (48)** (JLEyre) **6-8-11b** RLappin(7) (hdwy on ins 2f out: n.m.r ent fnl f: r.o wl nr fin)	¾	**3**	8/1 3	51	33
*5134**	**Leigh Crofter (58)** (PDCundell) **7-9-7b** DeanMcKeown(12) (a.p: effrt 2f out: rdn & unable qckn fnl f)	nk	**4**	11/8 1	60	42
5165[10]	**Juba (35)** (DrJDScargill) **4-7-12** NCarlisle(2) (a.p: rdn wl over 1f out: one pce)	¾	**5**	16/1	35	17
5130[8]	**Scathebury (44)** (KRBurke) **3-8-7b** GCarter(3) (chsd ldrs: eased whn btn fnl f)	4	**6**	10/1	34	16
4987[7]	**Green Golightly (USA) (35)** (RMFlower) **5-7-12be** FNorton(6) (sn drvn along in rr: n.d)	1¼	**7**	14/1	21	3
5129[9]	**Blondane (37)** (SRBowring) **3-8-0** NAdams(10) (b: chsd ldrs 4f: sn rdn & wknd: t.o)	9	**8**	12/1	—	—
5165[6]	**Mu-Arrik (36)** (GROldroyd) **8-7-8v**(5)ow3 MartinDwyer(11) (chsd ldrs 4f: sn wknd)	nk	**9**	20/1	—	—

				SP	RR	SF
5130^{11}	**Nkapen Rocks (SPA) (49)** (CaptJWilson) **3-8-12** SDWilliams(13) (sn drvn along & chsd ldrs on outside: bhd fnl 2f: t.o)	3	**10**	20/1	2	—
	Blue Domain (49) (RCraggs) **5-8-9**(3) CTeague(14) (outpcd: t.o)	¾	**11**	33/1	—	—
5131^{13}	**Squire Corrie (61)** (DWChapman) **4-9-10** ACulhane(5) (stdd s: a bhd: t.o)	5	**12**	10/1	—	—
5079^{11}	**Hong Kong Dollar (40)** (BAPearce) **4-7-12b**(5)ow6 ADaly(8) (gd spd 3f: wknd qckly: t.o)	17	**13**	33/1	—	—
				(SP 133.7%)	**13 Rn**	

1m 18.2 (4.70) CSF £72.29 CT £476.62 TOTE £11.80: £3.80 £1.00 £3.10 (£39.30) Trio £59.00 OWNER Mr D. G. Wright (NEWMARKET) BRED D. G. and Miss C. M. Wright
LONG HANDICAP Mu-Arrik 7-2
IN-FOCUS: **After heavy overnight rain and another drenching in the morning, the track had to pass an inspection before racing. The going was described as slow, and the jockeys said it was extremely testing.**

5175 WIMPEY HOMES H'CAP (0-60) (I) (3-Y.O+) (Class F)
12-10 (12-12) **1m (Fibresand)** £2,048.00 (£573.00: £278.00) Stalls: Low

				SP	RR	SF
5110^{2}	**Three Weeks (48)** (WRMuir) **3-9-2** DaneO'Neill(8) (mid div: hdwy ent st: hung lft & str run to ld nr fin)	—	**1**	8/1	67	44
5145*	**Angel Face (USA) (56)** (PDEvans) **3-9-10** 6x ACulhane(13) (lw: a.p: led ent st: qcknd appr fnl f: ct cl home)	nk	**2**	4/1 2	74	51
5114*	**Domino Flyer (56)** (MrsASwinbank) **3-9-10** DHolland(4) (a.p: slt ld over 4f out: hdd over 2f out: rdn & one pce appr fnl f)	4	**3**	3/1 1	66	43
4921*	**Scenicris (IRE) (42)** (RHollinshead) **3-8-7**(3) FLynch(5) (trckd ldrs: effrt over 2f out: kpt on one pce)	1¾	**4**	8/1	49	26
5161^{2}	**First Gold (43)** (JWharton) **7-8-12b** FNorton(6) (hld up: hdwy over 3f out: sn hrd drvn: nt pce to chal)	1¾	**5**	9/1	46	24
4982^{6}	**North Ardar (50)** (TWall) **6-9-2**(3) PMcCabe(15) (lw: hld up: sme late hdwy: nvr nrr)	6	**6**	14/1	41	19
4080^{7}	**Zatopek (49)** (JCullinan) **4-9-4** DeanMcKeown(12) (led over 3f: rdn & wknd over 2f out)	¾	**7**	20/1	39	17
3866^{12}	**Efipetite (42)** (NBycroft) **3-8-5**(5) MartinDwyer(10) (nvr nr to chal)	5	**8**	33/1	22	—
5112^{7}	**Lachesis (50)** (BRichmond) **3-9-1**(3) CTeague(1) (s.i.s: sn chsng ldrs: rdn ent st: grad wknd)	1½	**9**	20/1	27	4
5165^{2}	**Tael of Silver (40)** (ABailey) **4-8-9** DWright(14) (chsd ldrs over 5f)	s.h	**10**	7/1 3	17	—
5140^{7}	**Super Park (45)** (JPearce) **4-9-0v1** MWigham(3) (w ldrs 5f: sn rdn & wknd)	8	**11**	25/1	6	—
5004^{12}	**Prudent Pet (42)** (CWFairhurst) **4-8-11** RLappin(16) (prom 5f: sn drvn along & wknd)	½	**12**	33/1	2	—
5123^{2}	**Paronomasia (37)** (JLHarris) **4-8-6** SSanders(2) (b: b.hind: lw: a in rr)	3½	**13**	10/1	—	—
	Rozel Bay (48) (NATwiston-Davies) **3-9-2** VSlattery(11) (a bhd)	1¼	**14**	20/1	—	—
5129^{4}	**Medland (IRE) (43)** (BJMcMath) **6-8-12** GCarter(7) (lw: lost pl ½-wy: sn bhd)	¾	**15**	12/1	—	—
3780^{17}	**Samorelle (50)** (MJRyan) **3-9-4** AClark(9) (a in rr: t.o)	8	**16**	16/1	—	—
				(SP 143.1%)	**16 Rn**	

1m 46.4 (7.40) CSF £43.88 CT £121.09 TOTE £11.20: £2.20 £1.20 £1.30 £1.80 (£42.00) Trio £73.50 OWNER Mr Duncan Wiltshire (LAMBOURN) BRED Mrs K. W. Sneath
WEIGHT FOR AGE 3yo-1lb

5176 JULIUS CAESAR NURSERY H'CAP (0-75) (2-Y.O) (Class E)
12-40 (12-43) **5f (Fibresand)** £2,954.70 (£894.60: £436.80: £207.90) Stalls: High

				SP	RR	SF
5146^{9}	**Dominant Air (74)** (SirMarkPrescott) **2-9-7** GDuffield(2) (lw: chsd ldrs: led wl over 1f out: rdn & edgd rt fnl f: r.o strly)	—	**1**	7/1 2	81	54
5146^{5}	**Threeplay (IRE) (65)** (JAkehurst) **2-8-12** MTebbutt(13) (led stands' side: rdn & edgd lft fnl f: r.o)	2	**2**	12/1	66	39
5162^{2}	**The Wyandotte Inn (65)** (RHollinshead) **2-8-9**(3) FLynch(7) (a.p: rdn ent fnl f: r.o cl home)	hd	**3**	5/1 1	65	38
5133^{7}	**Enchanting Eve (72)** (CNAllen) **2-9-0**(5) MartinDwyer(9) (chsd ldrs: rdn 2f out: kpt on fnl f)	¾	**4**	5/1 1	70	43
5107^{4}	**Master Foley (50)** (NPLittmoden) **2-7-11** NCarlisle(1) (in tch far side: kpt on wl ins fnl f)	½	**5**	20/1	46	19
5100^{5}	**Davis Rock (72)** (WRMuir) **2-9-5** DaneO'Neill(12) (lw: dwlt: sn chsng ldrs: rdn along ½-wy: kpt on)	hd	**6**	10/1	68	41
4999^{3}	**Melbourne Princess (57)** (RMWhitaker) **2-8-4** FNorton(5) (led far side over 3f: sn drvn along & lost pl)	2	**7**	10/1	47	20
5162^{4}	**Molly Music (59)** (GGMargarson) **2-8-6v** AClark(8) (lw: nvr trbld ldrs)	1¾	**8**	14/1	43	16
5107*	**Sparkling Edge (60)** (CADwyer) **2-8-7** DRMcCabe(15) (bit bkwd: racd stands' side: nvr gng pce)	nk	**9**	10/1	43	16
5083^{7}	**Suite Factors (57)** (KRBurke) **2-8-4**ow1 GCarter(14) (racd stands' side: sn drvn along: n.d)	2	**10**	9/1 3	34	6
5133^{12}	**Barresbo (53)** (CWFairhurst) **2-7-9b1**(5) PFessey(10) (chsd ldrs centre: pushed along & wknd wl over 1f out)	½	**11**	20/1	28	1
5083^{4}	**Soda (58)** (TDBarron) **2-8-5** DeanMcKeown(3) (s.s: sn pushed along: a outpcd)	2	**12**	7/1 2	27	—
5133^{14}	**Kustom Kit Xpres (72)** (SRBowring) **2-9-5b1** SDWilliams(11) (chsd ldrs stands' side to ½-wy: t.o)	6	**13**	20/1	21	—
4383^{12}	**True Perspective (49)** (JDBethell) **2-7-10b1** DWright(6) (stdd s: a bhd & outpcd)	nk	**14**	20/1	—	—
2317^{6}	**Calchou (68)** (CWFairhurst) **2-9-1** RLappin(4) (dwlt: sn drvn along to chse ldrs: wknd 2f out: t.o)	7	**15**	16/1	—	—
				(SP 134.9%)	**15 Rn**	

60.4 secs (3.40) CSF £86.38 CT £431.38 TOTE £9.90: £2.90 £3.90 £1.10 (£240.40) Trio £139.50; £176.84 to Catterick 4/12/96 OWNER Mr Neil Greig (NEWMARKET) BRED W. N. Greig
LONG HANDICAP True Perspective 7-9

5177 KING HENRY VI AMATEUR CLAIMING STKS (3-Y.O+) (Class G)
1-10 (1-13) **1m 6f (Fibresand)** £2,085.00 (£585.00: £285.00) Stalls: High

				SP	RR	SF
5169^{3}	**Pharly Dancer (68)** (WWHaigh) **7-11-3** MissDianaJones(6) (hld up & bhd: hdwy over 3f out: styd on to ld wl ins fnl f)	—	**1**	2/1 1	74	41
369^{2}	**El Nido** (MJCamacho) **8-10-11** MissRClark(2) (chsd ldrs: led 7f out: clr 2f out: rdn & hdd nr fin)	¾	**2**	9/1	67	34
5136^{4}	**Code Red (55)** (WRMuir) **3-10-3**(5) MrVLukaniuk(3) (hdwy ½-wy: rdn & wknd over 2f out)	9	**3**	13/2 3	61	21
4910*	**Cross Talk (IRE) (55)** (NTinkler) **4-10-11** MissPJones(1) (hdwy after 5f: chsd ldr 4f out tl wknd wl over 1f out)	11	**4**	11/2 2	44	11
4750^{8}	**Another Quarter (IRE) (57)** (MCChapman) **3-10-3** MrsSBosley(14) (trckd ldrs: rdn over 3f out: sn btn)	2	**5**	8/1	41	1
5084^{13}	**Quillwork (USA) (49)** (JPearce) **4-10-4** MrsLPearce(12) (nvr nr to chal)	24	**6**	14/1	8	—
603^{5}	**Baher (USA) (36)** (MrsASwinbank) **7-10-10b**(5) MrChrisWilson(8) (led to ½-wy: sn drvn along: wknd fnl 4f: t.o)	3	**7**	12/1	15	—
4221^{19}	**Wahab** (RFMarvin) **3-9-13**(7) MrGWoodward(7) (prom over 8f: sn rdn & wknd: t.o)	6	**8**	33/1	6	—
5143^{6}	**Mr Bean (56)** (KRBurke) **6-10-8**(5) MrAWintle(13) (chsd ldrs 8f: sn wknd: t.o)	2½	**9**	12/1	3	—
4753^{5}	**All On (52)** (JHetherton) **5-10-11**(7)ow2 MrJHetherton(4) (chsd ldrs 6f: sn lost tch: t.o)	1¾	**10**	9/1	6	—
	Hancock (JHetherton) **4-11-0**(7) MrJByrne(15) (a bhd: t.o)	5	**11**	50/1	4	—
4703^{13}	**Chancancook** (JLEyre) **3-9-6**(7) MissAArmitage(9) (s.s: a bhd: t.o)	½	**12**	16/1	—	—

5167^{10}	**Burning Cost (28)** (REPeacock) **6-9-11**(7) MrsCPeacock(11) (a bhd: t.o)	1¼	**13**	50/1	—	—
	Drimard (IRE) (KMcAuliffe) **5-11-1b** MissJAllison(10) (a bhd: t.o)	nk	**14**	25/1	—	—
	Trauma (IRE) (WGMTurner) **4-9-11**(7) MrsCPrice(5) (chsd ldrs to ½-wy: sn wknd: t.o)	dist	**15**	25/1	—	—
				(SP 135.7%)	**15 Rn**	

3m 15.9 (17.90) CSF £22.48 TOTE £3.30: £1.70 £2.80 £3.90 (£12.90) Trio £29.70 OWNER Mr A. Marucci (MALTON) BRED Stud-On-The-Chart
WEIGHT FOR AGE 3yo-7lb
Cross Talk (IRE) clmd JDewhurst £5,000

5178 HAMLET H'CAP (0-70) (II) (3-Y.O+) (Class E)

1-40 (1-42) **6f (Fibresand)** £2,616.05 (£790.40: £384.70: £181.85) Stalls: Low

				SP	RR	SF
4975^{17}	**Jibereen (67)** (PHowling) **4-10-0** DHolland(3) (hdwy ½-wy: rdn wl over 1f out: styd on to ld nr fin)	—	**1**	12/1	73	54
5131^{8}	**Primula Bairn (61)** (DNicholls) **6-9-8b** MBirch(1) (trckd ldrs: led over 2f out: rdn clr appr fnl f: ct nr fin)	nk	**2**	13/2 3	66	47
3420^{6}	**Monis (IRE) (53)** (JBalding) **5-8-11v**(3) CTeague(12) (bhd: hdwy over 2f out: kpt on wl fnl f: nrst fin)	4	**3**	16/1	48	29
4888^{2}	**Souperficial (58)** (NTinkler) **5-9-5v** KimTinkler(9) (s.s: bhd: rdn ent st: hung lft & styd on fnl 2f: nvr nrr)	4	**4**	5/1 2	42	23
3354^{7}	**Down The Yard (38)** (MCChapman) **3-7-13** FNorton(4) (hdwy appr st: hmpd 2f out: one pce fr over 1f out)	¾	**5**	16/1	20	1
4075^{22}	**Belinda Blue (42)** (RAFahey) **4-7-10**(7) RWinston(2) (lw: dwlt: sn in tch: nt clr run on ins & swtchd over 1f out: no imp after)	2½	**6**	20/1	17	—
5109^{*}	**Honeyhall (39)** (NBycroft) **3-7-9**(5) MartinDwyer(7) (led tl over 2f out: sn rdn & btn)	1½	**7**	5/1 2	10	—
4981^{7}	**Disco Boy (53)** (PDEvans) **6-9-0** GCarter(11) (lw: sn rdn along in rr: no imp)	1¼	**8**	9/2 1	21	2
5093^{9}	**Avant Huit (42)** (MrsNMacauley) **4-7-10b**(7)ow3 JoHunnam(8) (chsd ldr tl rdn & wknd wl over 2f out)	1¼	**9**	25/1	7	—
4776^{8}	**Tymeera (52)** (BPalling) **3-8-13** AClark(5) (chsd ldrs: rdn over 2f out: wkng whn hmpd wl over 1f out)	1½	**10**	12/1	13	—
5144^{5}	**Lawsimina (43)** (MissJFCraze) **3-8-4** SDrowne(10) (chsd ldrs: sn rdn along: wknd wl over 2f out)	1¾	**11**	9/1	—	—
5109^{14}	**Klipspinger (60)** (BSRothwell) **3-9-7** JStack(13) (lw: sn rdn along: a in rr)	9	**12**	12/1	—	—
5130^{15}	**Dissentor (IRE) (50)** (JAGlover) **4-8-11b** SSanders(6) (a bhd)	1½	**13**	10/1	—	—
				(SP 127.4%)	**13 Rn**	

1m 18.3 (4.80) CSF £86.38 CT £1,210.96 TOTE £12.30: £4.10 £2.80 £4.30 (£29.30) Trio £182.70; £82.37 to Catterick 4/12/96 OWNER Mr Peter Skelton (NEWMARKET) BRED Mrs J. Everitt

5179 WIMPEY HOMES H'CAP (0-60) (II) (3-Y.O+) (Class F)

2-10 (2-11) **1m (Fibresand)** £2,048.00 (£573.00: £278.00) Stalls: Low

				SP	RR	SF
5132^{4}	**Running Green (48)** (DMoffatt) **5-8-13**(3) DarrenMoffatt(2) (led after 3f: rdn clr 2f out: hld on wl cl home)	—	**1**	12/1	65	41
5114^{3}	**Ya Marhaba (41)** (JWPayne) **3-8-8** AMcGlone(9) (chsd ldrs: rdn along 3f out: hdwy 2f out: kpt on wl ins fnl f)	½	**2**	8/1 3	57	32
5114^{2}	**Desert Zone (USA) (50)** (JohnHarris) **7-9-4** SSanders(10) (b: a.p: rdn 3f out: styd on one pce fnl 2f)	3½	**3**	2/1 1	59	35
5134^{5}	**Ebony Boy (47)** (JWharton) **3-9-0** GDuffield(7) (hdwy 3f out: styd on sme pce fnl 2f: nvr nrr)	4	**4**	20/1	48	23
4989^{6}	**Fiaba (41)** (MrsNMacauley) **8-8-6v**(3)ow3 CTeague(13) (hdwy appr st: styd on sme pce fnl 2f: nt rch ldrs)	2	**5**	12/1	38	11
5112^{6}	**Polar Refrain (44)** (CADwyer) **3-8-4**(7) JoHunnam(1) (mid div: effrt appr st: sltly hmpd 2f out: nvr trbld ldrs)	2½	**6**	14/1	36	11
5130^{4}	**Truly Bay (42)** (TDBarron) **3-8-2**(7) VictoriaAppleby(12) (mid div: no imp fr over 2f out)	1½	**7**	10/1	31	6
5130^{6}	**Sheraz (IRE) (58)** (NTinkler) **4-9-12** GCarter(11) (nvr trbld ldrs)	½	**8**	9/1	46	22
5053^{5}	**Nautical Jewel (45)** (MDIUsher) **4-8-13** RPerham(5) (sn rdn along: outpcd in rr: sme late hdwy)	2½	**9**	10/1	28	4
4982^{4}	**Pc's Cruiser (IRE) (46)** (JLEyre) **4-9-0b** DHolland(8) (dwlt: sn pushed along & racd wd in rr: n.d)	4	**10**	7/1 2	21	—
5151^{8}	**Sapphire Son (IRE) (46)** (PCClarke) **4-9-0** DaneO'Neill(3) (cl up: led after 1f to 5f out: wknd over 2f out)	2½	**11**	20/1	16	—
4904^{8}	**Jimjareer (IRE) (49)** (CaptJWilson) **3-9-2** SDWilliams(15) (chsd ldrs to ½-wy: sn lost pl: t.o)	13	**12**	20/1	—	—
5056^{10}	**Giddy (44)** (JHetherton) **3-8-11** DeanMcKeown(14) (racd wd: chsd ldrs tl btn appr st: t.o)	9	**13**	11/1	—	—
	Rub Al Khali (41) (AStreeter) **5-8-9** SDrowne(16) (b: bit bkwd: led 1f: chsd ldrs tl wknd qckly fnl 2f: t.o: b.b.v)	24	**14**	33/1	—	—
4982^{15}	**Roar on Tour (60)** (MrsMReveley) **7-10-0b** ACulhane(4) (s.i.s: a bhd: t.o)	4	**15**	12/1	—	—
3481^{8}	**Forget Paris (IRE) (49)** (BSRothwell) **3-9-2v**1 JStack(6) (s.i.s: a in rr: t.o)	1¾	**16**	33/1	—	—
				(SP 143.4%)	**16 Rn**	

1m 46.7 (7.70) CSF £112.08 CT £271.97 TOTE £14.50: £2.10 £1.80 £1.90 £2.80 (£67.90) Trio £88.10 OWNER Die-Hard Racing Club (CARTMEL) BRED Mount Coote Stud
WEIGHT FOR AGE 3yo-1lb
OFFICIAL EXPLANATION Rub Al Khali: bled from the nose.

5180 ANTONY & CLEOPATRA (S) STKS (2-Y.O F) (Class G)

2-40 (2-41) **1m (Fibresand)** £2,085.00 (£585.00: £285.00) Stalls: Low

				SP	RR	SF
5160^{6}	**Head Girl (IRE) (54)** (CWThornton) **2-8-9** DeanMcKeown(4) (mde all: rdn & kpt on wl fnl 2f)	—	**1**	13/2 3	64	21
5135^{5}	**Royal Roulette (54)** (SPCWoods) **2-8-2b**(7) CWebb(7) (hld up: hdwy to chse wnr over 2f out: ev ch whn hung lft over 1f out: nt rcvr)	1½	**2**	10/1	61	18
5135^{4}	**Hopperetta (50)** (BPalling) **2-8-9** AClark(3) (chsd ldrs: rdn ent st: outpcd fnl 2f)	16	**3**	9/1	29	—
5135^{7}	**Racing Carr (40)** (TJNaughton) **2-8-6**(3) JDSmith(11) (in tch: rdn & outpcd appr st: n.d after)	3½	**4**	16/1	22	—
5103^{4}	**Star Entry** (WJarvis) **2-8-9** SSanders(1) (bit bkwd: dwlt: sn drvn along & prom: hrd rdn appr st: sn btn)	8	**5**	6/4 1	6	—
5092^{2}	**Silent Valley (48)** (DNicholls) **2-8-9** MBirch(8) (in tch: effrt over 3f out: sn btn)	5	**6**	7/1	—	—
5166^{4}	**Diamonds Are (30)** (DTThom) **2-8-9** GDuffield(5) (outpcd & bhd fr ½-wy: t.o)	18	**7**	14/1	—	—
5166^{6}	**Beveled Mill** (PDEvans) **2-8-9** GCarter(10) (s.i.s: a outpcd: t.o)	7	**8**	12/1	—	—
838^{8}	**Belle Dancer** (TWall) **2-8-6**(3) FLynch(6) (dwlt: a outpcd & bhd: t.o)	1½	**9**	33/1	—	—
	Noetic (GHolmes) **2-8-9** EmmaO'Gorman(2) (b.nr fore: b.nr hind: neat: bkwd: s.s: a wl bhd: t.o)	6	**10**	20/1	—	—
5160^{4}	**Compact Disc (IRE) (55)** (MJohnston) **2-9-0** DHolland(9) (chsd ldrs: rdn along ½-wy: wknd & eased fnl 2f: t.o)	17	**11**	7/2 2	—	—
				(SP 135.1%)	**11 Rn**	

1m 48.1 (9.10) CSF £71.87 TOTE £6.10: £2.00 £3.50 £2.30 (£62.40) Trio £192.20; £56.86 to Catterick 4/12/96 OWNER The Challengers (MIDDLEHAM) BRED Mrs Marian Maguire
Bt in 4,000 gns

5181 KING LEAR H'CAP (0-65) (4-Y.O+) (Class F)

3-10 (3-12) **1m 3f (Fibresand)** £2,398.00 (£673.00: £328.00) Stalls: Low

Form	Horse	Dist	Pos	SP	RR	SF
4894*	**Manful (62)** (CWCElsey) **4-9-13b** GDuffield(3) (hld up & wl bhd: effrt & hdwy appr st: styd on strly fnl 2f to ld wl ins fnl f)	—	**1**	7/1	74	30
5123*	**Adamton (61)** (MrsJCecil) **4-9-12** AClark(15) (lw: led after 2f: hrd rdn over 2f out: hdd & no ex wl ins fnl f)	1¼	**2**	100/30[1]	71	27
5115*	**Ihtimaam (FR) (59)** (MrsASwinbank) **4-9-10** DHolland(7) (chsd ldrs: hdwy to chse wnr & ev ch over 1f out: hung lft: no ex)	1¼	**3**	11/2[2]	67	23
5139[3]	**Rasayel (USA) (44)** (PDEvans) **6-8-9** GCarter(4) (hdwy over 6f out: kpt on same pce fnl 3f: nt rch ldrs)	8	**4**	7/1	41	—
5054[11]	**Wildfire (SWI) (50)** (RAkehurst) **5-9-1** SSanders(12) (b: in tch: rdn 6f out: wknd over 3f out)	16	**5**	6/1[3]	24	—
5132[8]	**Hornpipe (55)** (JWharton) **4-9-3**(3) CTeague(2) (b: bhd: drvn along over 6f out: no imp)	8	**6**	33/1	17	—
5148[14]	**Flow Back (58)** (GPEnright) **4-9-4**(5) ADaly(14) (in tch: rdn 7f out: btn over 4f out)	4	**7**	16/1	14	—
5149[5]	**Chilly Lad (52)** (MJRyan) **5-9-0b**(3) MBaird(1) (bhd: effrt ½-wy & sme hdwy: n.d)	s.h	**8**	20/1	8	—
5007[11]	**Carol Again (47)** (NBycroft) **4-8-7**(5) MartinDwyer(8) (nvr nr ldrs)	3½	**9**	20/1	—	—
5110[3]	**Sandmoor Denim (50)** (SRBowring) **9-9-1** SDWilliams(16) (b: sme hdwy on outside ½-wy: btn 4f out)	¾	**10**	12/1	—	—
4993[12]	**Brambles Way (50)** (MrsMReveley) **7-8-10b**(5) SCopp(9) (bhd fr ½-wy)	nk	**11**	7/1	—	—
5056[8]	**River Run (IRE) (56)** (RHollinshead) **4-9-4**(3) FLynch(6) (bhd fnl 7f)	1¾	**12**	33/1	3	—
5104[2]	**Shaffishayes (63)** (MrsMReveley) **4-10-0** ACulhane(13) (dwlt: bhd: hdwy in mid div over 6f out: btn over 3f out)	3	**13**	11/1	5	—
5116[11]	**Acerbus Dulcis (46)** (MCChapman) **5-8-11** FNorton(10) (sn bhd)	¾	**14**	50/1	—	—
5134[9]	**Square Deal (FR) (55)** (SRBowring) **5-9-6** DeanMcKeown(5) (in tch to ½-wy: sn lost pl)	1¾	**15**	33/1	—	—
4575[10]	**Chevalier (USA) (63)** (ICampbell) **4-10-0** MWigham(11) (led 2f: chsd ldr tl broke leg & fell over 6f out: dead)		**F**	14/1	—	—
				(SP 139.1%)	**16 Rn**	

2m 32.5 (12.50) CSF £32.72 CT £138.81 TOTE £7.10: £1.90 £3.00 £1.10 £1.90 (£26.60) Trio £14.90 OWNER Mr C. D. Barber-Lomax (MALTON) BRED John Rose

STEWARDS' ENQUIRY Clark susp. 13-14&19/12/96 (excessive use of whip).

IN-FOCUS: This turned out to have been the last winner of Bill Elsey's distinguished career.

T/Plpt: £286.40 (25.96 Tckts). T/Qdpt: £45.30 (20.24 Tckts). IM

5145-LINGFIELD (L-H) (Standard)

Thursday December 5th

WEATHER: sunny WIND: almost nil

5182 ROBROT JERSEY CONDITIONS STKS (I) (3-Y.O+) (Class D)

12-10 (12-11) **1m (Equitrack)** £3,062.50 (£925.00: £450.00: £212.50) Stalls: High GOING minus 0.44 sec per fur (FST)

Form	Horse	Dist	Pos	SP	RR	SF
4820[5]	**Tatika (84)** (GWragg) **6-8-5**(7) GMilligan(4) (lw: hld up in tch: led gng wl over 2f out: sn clr: easily)	—	**1**	6/4[1]	79	56
5106[3]	**Bentico (76)** (MrsNMacauley) **7-8-9v**(3) CTeague(10) (hld up: hdwy 3f out: chsd wnr fnl 2f: one pce)	5	**2**	15/2[3]	69	46
5150[10]	**Double Blue (85)** (MJohnston) **7-8-12** DeanMcKeown(8) (hld up: rdn over 2f out: one pce)	4	**3**	9/1	61	38
5079[3]	**Barbason (55)** (AMoore) **4-9-3** CandyMorris(6) (chsd ldrs: rdn over 1f out: one pce)	1¾	**4**	16/1	63	40
	Katatonic (IRE) (JARToller) **3-8-11** SSanders(1) (unf: bit bkwd: dwlt: sn rcvrd: led over 5f out tl over 2f out: sn wknd)	7	**5**	33/1	44	20
5145[7]	**Sarum (32)** (JELong) **10-8-12** LeesaLong(9) (b: prom 6f)	1½	**6**	66/1	41	18
	Dowdency (RJWeaver) **4-8-2**(5) ADaly(2) (led over 2f: sn wknd)	11	**7**	66/1	14	—
5070a[9]	**Henry The Fifth (104)** (CEBrittain) **3-8-11b[1]** MRoberts(5) (prom to ½-wy)	hd	**8**	7/4[2]	18	—
	Naphtali (JRArnold) **3-8-6** CRutter(7) (neat: a bhd: t.o fnl 5f)	28	**9**	50/1	—	—
4865[4]	**Perang Polly** (LordHuntingdon) **4-8-7** DHolland(3) (bhd fnl 5f: t.o whn p.u over 3f out: b.b.v)		**P**	16/1	—	—
				(SP 117.8%)	**10 Rn**	

1m 37.74 (0.34) CSF £12.92 TOTE £2.40: £1.60 £2.60 £2.20 (£6.20) Trio £18.10 OWNER Mr G. Wragg (NEWMARKET) BRED D. J. and Mrs Deer

WEIGHT FOR AGE 3yo-1lb

5183 EQUITY FINANCIAL COLLECTIONS H'CAP (0-60) (I) (3-Y.O+) (Class F)

12-40 (12-43) **6f (Equitrack)** £2,238.40 (£627.40: £305.20) Stalls: Low GOING minus 0.44 sec per fur (FST)

Form	Horse	Dist	Pos	SP	RR	SF
5124[12]	**Sihafi (USA) (50)** (JMCarr) **3-9-4** AClark(9) (hld up: hdwy 3f out: led 1f out: r.o)	—	**1**	16/1	57	14
5150[7]	**Never Think Twice (52)** (KTIvory) **3-9-6b** NAdams(7) (b.hind: outpcd in rr: hdwy over 1f out: styd on strly ins fnl f: fin wl)	nk	**2**	15/2[3]	58	15
5059[9]	**River Seine (FR) (40)** (SGKnight) **4-8-8** SSanders(12) (rr: hdwy over 2f out: styd on strly ins fnl f)	½	**3**	20/1	45	2
5149[10]	**Logie Pert Lad (30)** (JJBridger) **4-7-12** FNorton(1) (chsd ldrs: ev ch 1f out: one pce)	2	**4**	40/1	30	—
5144[3]	**Miss Aragon (31)** (MissLCSiddall) **8-7-13** DRMcCabe(13) (hld up: hdwy 3f out: ev ch 1f out: one pce)	1¼	**5**	11/4[2]	27	—
4860[8]	**Belbay Star (42)** (JLEyre) **3-8-10** RLappin(2) (chsd ldrs: rdn over 1f out: one pce)	½	**6**	14/1	37	—
5124[5]	**Invocation (60)** (AMoore) **9-10-0** DaneO'Neill(5) (b.hind: sn rdn along towards rr: nvr nrr)	¾	**7**	5/2[1]	53	10
5112[9]	**Daisy Bates (IRE) (49)** (PWHarris) **3-9-3** AMcGlone(10) (lw: prom: led ½-wy: hdd 1f out: sn btn)	hd	**8**	9/1	42	—
1992[8]	**Supreme Illusion (AUS) (30)** (JohnBerry) **3-7-9b**(3) NVarley(4) (a bhd)	hd	**9**	33/1	22	—
5118[6]	**Kirov Protege (IRE) (40)** (MrsLCJewell) **4-8-1**(7) DarrenWilliams(6) (a bhd)	hd	**10**	20/1	32	—
4828[13]	**Carnival of Light (36)** (JSMoore) **4-8-4**[ow1] DeanMcKeown(11) (bhd fnl 2f)	4	**11**	14/1	17	—
4075[8]	**Desert Skimmer (USA) (44)** (MBell) **3-8-7**(5) GFaulkner(8) (swtg: chsd ldrs to ½-wy)	s.h	**12**	8/1	25	—
5089[14]	**Distant Dynasty (39)** (BAPearce) **6-8-2b**(5) ADaly(3) (led to ½-wy: wknd qckly: t.o)	19	**13**	16/1	—	—
				(SP 128.1%)	**13 Rn**	

1m 14.28 (3.18) CSF £128.01 CT £2,242.13 TOTE £21.70: £7.40 £2.20 £8.90 (£46.20) Trio Not won; £229.05 to Hereford 6/12/96 OWNER Mr John Gilbertson (MALTON) BRED Shadwell Farm Inc

5184 EQUITABLE HOLDINGS PLC H'CAP (0-70) (3-Y.O+) (Class E)

1-10 (1-12) **5f (Equitrack)** £2,913.75 (£882.00: £430.50: £204.75) Stalls: High GOING minus 0.44 sec per fur (FST)

Form	Horse	Dist	Pos	SP	RR	SF
5150*	**Scissor Ridge (67)** (JJBridger) **4-9-11** 7x SSanders(4) (lw: chsd ldrs: rdn over 2f out: led wl ins fnl f: r.o)	—	**1**	5/1[2]	71	35
5131[16]	**Kalar (68)** (DWChapman) **7-9-12b** ACulhane(3) (sn led: hrd rdn over 1f out: hdd wl ins fnl f: no ex)	1	**2**	7/1	69	33
5173*	**Napier Star (67)** (MrsNMacauley) **3-9-8v**(3) 7x CTeague(8) (lw: sn outpcd towards rr: styd on ins fnl f: nrst fin)	1½	**3**	6/1	63	27
5097*	**Chemcast (68)** (JLEyre) **3-9-12** RLappin(5) (chsd ldrs: hrd rdn fnl 2f: one pce)	nk	**4**	9/2[1]	63	27
4690[7]	**Will Do (70)** (MartynMeade) **3-9-7**(7) DSweeney(1) (lw: rr: rdn over 1f out: styd on ins fnl f: nrst fin)	hd	**5**	15/2	65	29
5096[3]	**Another Batchworth (68)** (EAWheeler) **4-9-7b**(5) ADaly(10) (sn pushed along: chsd ldr 4f out: ev ch over 1f out: wknd ins fnl f)	hd	**6**	11/2[3]	62	26
5097[4]	**Featherstone Lane (64)** (MissLCSiddall) **5-9-8v** DRMcCabe(6) (lw: a outpcd)	4	**7**	5/1[2]	46	10
5131[15]	**Windrush Boy (50)** (JRBosley) **6-8-8** CRutter(2) (lw: chsd ldrs: rdn over 2f out: sn wknd)	1½	**8**	25/1	27	—
5173[12]	**La Belle Dominique (54)** (SGKnight) **4-8-12** SDrowne(7) (sn rdn along: bhd fr ½-wy)	5	**9**	33/1	15	—

(SP 112.2%) **9 Rn**

60.07 secs (1.87) CSF £35.29 CT £194.10 TOTE £7.30: £2.30 £3.20 £2.70 (£18.10) Trio £31.60 OWNER Mr Donald Smith (LIPHOOK) BRED J. K. Keegan

5185 EQUITY FINANCIAL COLLECTIONS LIMITED STKS (0-55) (3-Y.O+) (Class F)

1-40 (1-42) **2m (Equitrack)** £2,612.20 (£734.20: £358.60) Stalls: Low GOING minus 0.44 sec per fur (FST)

Form	Horse	Dist	Pos	SP	RR	SF
5084[3]	**Matthias Mystique (55)** (MissBSanders) **3-8-6** SSanders(5) (a.p: rdn 5f out: chsd ldr 3f out: led over 1f out: hrd rdn: r.o)	—	**1**	5/2[2]	67	28
5139[2]	**Miss Prism (51)** (JLDunlop) **3-8-6** TSprake(7) (a.p: led 10f out: rdn 2f out: hdd over 1f out: one pce)	6	**2**	2/1[1]	61	22
4048[6]	**Supreme Star (USA) (53)** (PRHedger) **5-9-3b** DaneO'Neill(10) (b: a.p: chsd ldr 10f out to 3f out: sn rdn: one pce)	7	**3**	7/1	57	26
5148[8]	**Suitor (47)** (SDow) **3-8-4**(5) ADaly(3) (hdwy 10f out: wknd over 2f out)	9	**4**	14/1	48	9
5084[9]	**Mull House (39)** (GPEnright) **9-9-3v** NAdams(9) (b: b.hind: sme hdwy & mod 5th 6f out: no imp)	7	**5**	50/1	41	10
3141[5]	**Labudd (USA) (53)** (RIngram) **6-9-3** AMcGlone(12) (b: a bhd: t.o)	26	**6**	10/1	15	—
4551[11]	**Ela Agapi Mou (USA) (49)** (AMoore) **3-8-9** CandyMorris(4) (b.hind: s.s: a bhd: t.o)	3	**7**	20/1	12	—
5091[8]	**Bigwig (IRE) (45)** (AMoore) **3-8-9** AClark(6) (b.hind: bhd fr ½-wy: t.o)	1¾	**8**	50/1	10	—
5101[5]	**Bellaphento (45)** (JRinger) **3-8-7**ow1 SDrowne(2) (b: bhd fr ½-wy: t.o)	17	**9**	50/1	—	—
5108*	**Sharp Command (53)** (PEccles) **3-8-11** DHolland(8) (bhd fr ½-wy: t.o)	22	**10**	9/2[3]	—	—
4669[6]	**Sam Rockett (40)** (PMooney) **3-8-6b**[1](5)ow2 GFaulkner(1) (led 6f: sn wknd: t.o)	2	**11**	16/1	—	—
	Peatsville (IRE) (32) (MRChannon) **4-8-12**(5) PPMurphy(11) (hdwy 12f out: wknd 8f out: t.o)	2½	**12**	50/1	—	—

(SP 126.8%) **12 Rn**

3m 27.65 (6.65) CSF £8.19 TOTE £3.60: £1.20 £1.20 £2.80 (£4.50) Trio £7.90 OWNER M C M & Mrs J Laycock (EPSOM) BRED P. Cook

WEIGHT FOR AGE 3yo-8lb

5186 ROBROT JERSEY CONDITIONS STKS (II) (3-Y.O+) (Class D)

2-10 (2-11) **1m (Equitrack)** £3,046.25 (£920.00: £447.50: £211.25) Stalls: High GOING minus 0.44 sec per fur (FST)

Form	Horse	Dist	Pos	SP	RR	SF
4560[10]	**Queen of All Birds (IRE) (83)** (RBoss) **5-8-2**(5) ADaly(3) (mde all: pushed clr ins fnl f)	—	**1**	11/4[2]	80	43
5120[2]	**Night Wink (USA) (85)** (GLMoore) **4-8-12** SWhitworth(6) (a.p: chsd wnr 4f out: rdn over 1f out: one pce)	5	**2**	Evens[1]	75	38
5099[2]	**Barossa Valley (IRE) (70)** (PButler) **5-8-12** SDrowne(7) (chsd ldrs: rdn & outpcd over 2f out: kpt on one pce ins fnl f)	3	**3**	10/1	69	32
5002[13]	**Blue Flyer (IRE) (79)** (RIngram) **3-9-7** AMcGlone(9) (hld up: hdwy 3f out: rdn 2f out: one pce)	1¾	**4**	14/1	76	38
4186[6]	**Mr Rough (53)** (DMorris) **5-8-7**(5) GFaulkner(8) (hld up: pushed along over 4f out: outpcd over 2f out: kpt on one pce ins fnl f)	s.h	**5**	16/1	65	28
5152[6]	**Greatest (72)** (MissGayKelleway) **5-8-12** DaneO'Neill(1) (chsd ldrs: rdn over 4f out: wknd over 2f out)	1¾	**6**	15/2[3]	62	25
1461[6]	**Peetsie (IRE)** (NATwiston-Davies) **4-8-4**(3) FLynch(2) (bhd fnl 5f)	1½	**7**	33/1	54	17
5086[3]	**Komodo (USA) (38)** (JELong) **4-8-5**(7) TField(4) (prom 5f)	15	**8**	50/1	29	—

(SP 115.0%) **8 Rn**

1m 38.6 (1.20) CSF £5.71 TOTE £4.50: £1.10 £1.30 £1.60 (£4.50) Trio £12.00 OWNER Mr John Arnou (NEWMARKET) BRED Brownstown Stud Farm

WEIGHT FOR AGE 3yo-1lb

5187 EQUITY FINANCIAL COLLECTIONS MAIDEN STKS (2-Y.O) (Class D)

2-40 (2-41) **6f (Equitrack)** £3,318.65 (£1,005.20: £491.10: £234.05) Stalls: Low GOING minus 0.44 sec per fur (FST)

Form	Horse	Dist	Pos	SP	RR	SF
4918[2]	**Ursa Major (87)** (PAKelleway) **2-9-0** MWigham(12) (lw: a.p: led over 2f out: r.o)	—	**1**	15/8[2]	70+	15
5034[6]	**Share Delight (IRE)** (BWHills) **2-8-11**(3) JDSmith(2) (b: b.hind: mid div: sn rdn along: n.m.r on ins over 3f out tl over 2f out: rdn over 1f out: styd on ins fnl f)	6	**2**	7/4[1]	54	—
5135[9]	**Ekaterini Paritsi (52)** (WGMTurner) **2-8-9v** TSprake(8) (led tl over 2f out: one pce)	1½	**3**	20/1	45	—
4697[4]	**Forgotten Times (USA)** (TMJones) **2-8-9** NCarlisle(7) (b: b.hind: chsd ldrs: rdn 2f out: one pce)	1¾	**4**	9/1	40	—
5033[17]	**Ewar Arrangement (60)** (CEBrittain) **2-9-0** MRoberts(1) (sn rdn along: bdly hmpd & lost pl 5f out: bhd tl sme hdwy & nt clr run over 1f out: styd on ins fnl f: nvr nrr)	2	**5**	16/1	40+	—
4897[15]	**Aquatic Queen** (RJWeaver) **2-8-4**(5) ADaly(9) (prom tl wknd 2f out)	1¼	**6**	50/1	32	—
3502[4]	**Incatime** (CJames) **2-9-0** CRutter(6) (chsd ldrs: n.m.r over 3f out: sn wknd)	2½	**7**	8/1[3]	30	—
	Master Bobby (RBoss) **2-8-9**(5) GFaulkner(4) (w'like: dwlt: a bhd)	½	**8**	10/1	29	—
5080[10]	**Trevor Mitchell** (JJBridger) **2-8-9** DaneO'Neill(5) (a bhd)	2	**9**	50/1	18	—
3581[6]	**Formidable Spirit** (MJHeaton-Ellis) **2-9-0** AClark(10) (chsd ldrs tl wknd over 2f out)	2½	**10**	25/1	17	—
5092[7]	**She's Electric** (JJBridger) **2-8-9** SSanders(3) (a bhd)	1½	**11**	50/1	8	—

(SP 121.7%) **11 Rn**

1m 13.91 (2.81) CSF £5.58 TOTE £2.70: £1.60 £1.20 £2.10 (£2.90) Trio £19.40 OWNER Mr Ken Blake (NEWMARKET) BRED K. Blake

5188 EQUITY FINANCIAL COLLECTIONS H'CAP (0-60) (II) (3-Y.O+) (Class F)
3-10 (3-13) **6f (Equitrack)** £2,238.40 (£627.40: £305.20) Stalls: Low GOING minus 0.44 sec per fur (FST)

				SP	RR	SF
5144[10]	**Halbert (40)** (PBurgoyne) **7-8-5v**(3) PMcCabe(2) (mde all: hrd rdn ins fnl f: r.o)	—	1	20/1	50	6
5093[4]	**Mystery Matthias (44)** (MissBSanders) **3-8-5v**(7) JoHunnam(8) (a.p: ev ch 2f out: rdn over 1f out: r.o)	½	2	6/1[2]	53	9
4881[12]	**Colston-C (48)** (PDEvans) **4-9-2** ACulhane(6) (chsd ldrs: n.m.r over 4f out: hrd rdn over 1f out: r.o)	hd	3	10/1	56	12
5099[6]	**Samsolom (50)** (PHowling) **8-9-4** DeanMcKeown(9) (mid div: rdn 2f out: styd on one pce ins fnl f)	1½	4	9/1	54	10
5089[7]	**Dark Menace (43)** (EAWheeler) **4-8-6b**(5) ADaly(7) (a.p: rdn over 1f out: wknd ins fnl f)	2	5	8/1	42	—
5138[6]	**Southern Rule (32)** (MissMERowland) **9-8-0b** NCarlisle(12) (mid div: rdn over 2f out: one pce)	¾	6	12/1	29	—
5096[4]	**Tachycardia (40)** (RJO'Sullivan) **4-8-8** SSanders(13) (prom: rdn over 2f out: wknd over 1f out)	3	7	100/30[1]	29	—
5081[9]	**Be Satisfied (50)** (AMoore) **3-9-4** AClark(4) (sn rdn along: bhd fnl 3f)	3	8	20/1	31	—
4598[19]	**Shermood (33)** (KTIvory) **3-8-1** NAdams(1) (bhd fnl 4f)	s.h	9	12/1	14	—
5123[10]	**Rainy Day Song (47)** (LordHuntingdon) **3-9-1** DHolland(11) (a bhd)	4	10	14/1	17	—
4068[11]	**Press Again (44)** (PHayward) **4-8-12** CRutter(5) (a bhd)	hd	11	33/1	14	—
2500[9]	**Dancing Jack (57)** (JJBridger) **3-9-11** DaneO'Neill(3) (a bhd)	10	12	14/1	—	—
5059[8]	**Miss Pickpocket (IRE) (42)** (MissGayKelleway) **3-8-10** MWigham(10) (Withdrawn not under Starter's orders: ref to ent stalls)		W	7/1[3]	—	—

(SP 121.2%) **12 Rn**

1m 14.18 (3.08) CSF £104.56 CT £880.70 TOTE £19.90: £3.10 £1.70 £3.50 (£110.90) Trio £120.20; £84.71 to Hereford 6/12/96 OWNER Mr B. Jenkins (LAMBOURN) BRED Mr and Mrs J. K. S. Cresswell

5189 THIRTY NINE STEPS AMATEUR H'CAP (0-80) (3-Y.O+) (Class G)
3-40 (3-41) **1m 4f (Equitrack)** £2,221.50 (£624.00: £304.50) Stalls: Low GOING minus 0.44 sec per fur (FST)

				SP	RR	SF
5120[6]	**Filial (IRE) (80)** (BJMeehan) **3-11-7** MissJAllison(9) (chsd ldrs: led 2f out: sn clr: r.o wl)	—	1	8/1	92	68
4793[9]	**General Haven (69)** (TJNaughton) **3-10-6**(4) MrsJNaughton(3) (hld up in mid div: rdn 2f out: wnt 2nd ins fnl f: one pce)	7	2	7/1	72	48
5003[6]	**Don't Drop Bombs (USA) (40)** (DTThom) **7-9-0v** MissJFeilden(6) (led 3f: led 5f out to 4f out: rdn 2f out: one pce)	3½	3	11/2[2]	38	19
4900[16]	**No Pattern (69)** (GLMoore) **4-11-1v** MrKGoble(8) (a.p: led 4f out: hdd 2f out: one pce)	s.h	4	8/1	67	48
5106[4]	**Explosive Power (73)** (GCBravery) **5-10-12**(7) MissALHutchinson(5) (hld up in tch: rdn 2f out: one pce)	1½	5	11/2[2]	69	50
5062[7]	**Colosse (47)** (JLEyre) **4-9-7** MissDianaJones(2) (chsd ldrs: lost pl 8f out: hrd rdn 3f out: no hdwy)	4	6	5/2[1]	38	19
5151[5]	**Sweet Supposin (IRE) (66)** (CADwyer) **5-10-5v**(7) MrsSDwyer(4) (lw: hld up: hdwy 4f out: wknd over 2f out)	1	7	13/2[3]	55	36
5145[3]	**Efficacious (IRE) (45)** (AMoore) **3-8-10**(4) MrsJMoore(7) (chsd ldrs tl wknd over 4f out: sddle slipped)	12	8	16/1	18	—
3944[9]	**Phanan (51)** (REPeacock) **10-9-4**(7)ow11 MrsCPeacock(1) (bit bkwd: led after 3f: hdd 5f out: sn wknd)	½	9	66/1	24	—

(SP 114.8%) **9 Rn**

2m 34.15 (4.15) CSF £56.57 CT £305.13 TOTE £11.20: £3.80 £2.10 £1.60 (£80.80) Trio £126.20 OWNER Miss J. Semple (UPPER LAMBOURN) BRED Juddmonte Farms
LONG HANDICAP Efficacious (IRE) 8-9 Phanan 8-7
WEIGHT FOR AGE 3yo-5lb

T/Plpt: £118.20 (67.19 Tckts). T/Qdpt: £4.30 (319.18 Tckts) SM

5077a-SAINT-CLOUD (France) (L-H) (Heavy)
Monday November 25th

5190a PRIX GRIS PERLE (2-Y.O C & G)
1-10 (1-07) **7f** £11,858.00 (£4,743.00)

				SP	RR	SF
	Such Charisma (CAN) (MmeCHead,France) **2-8-2**(7) BHercend	—	1		59	—
5050[2]	**Mr Paradise (IRE)** (TJNaughton) **2-9-0** DHolland	2½	2		65	—
	Napoleonic (France) **2-9-0** GMosse	s.h	3		65	—

8 Rn

1m 37.7 P-M 10.80F: 3.30F 1.60F 1.90F (22.50F) OWNER R. Romanet (CHANTILLY) BRED Ferme Du Bois Vert & Gainsborough Stud
5050 Mr Paradise (IRE) made the running and set a good pace but, headed in the straight, he could do little more than stay on for second place when ridden two furlongs out. He simply met one too good.

5155a-EVRY (France) (R-H) (Very Soft)
Tuesday November 26th

5191a PRIX SAINT-ROMAN (Gp 3) (2-Y.O)
1-55 (1-53) **1m 1f** £28,986.00 (£10,540.00: £5,270.00)

				SP	RR	SF
5024a[5]	**Voyagers Quest (USA)** (PWChapple-Hyam) **2-8-11** JReid	—	1		102	—
5024a[3]	**Sendoro (IRE)** (AdeRoyerDupre,France) **2-8-11** GMosse	½	2		101	—
	Rate Cut (USA) (PBary,France) **2-8-11** SGuillot	½	3		100	—

8 Rn

2m 1.98 (11.98) P-M 10.70F: 1.60F 1.10F 1.30F (7.00F) OWNER R. Kaster (MARLBOROUGH) BRED Gulf States Racing Stables II
5024a Voyagers Quest (USA) made every yard and stayed on well at the finish. He may stay a little further.

5192a PRIX ISOLA BELLA (Listed) (3-Y.O F)
2-25 (2-21) **1m** £18,445.00 (£6,324.00: £3,953.00)

				SP	RR	SF
5072a[3]	**Ecoute (USA)** (MmeCHead,France) **3-9-0** ODoleuze	—	1		104	—
5072a[2]	**Whenby (USA)** (MmeCHead,France) **3-9-0** FHead	2	2		100	—
	Pleaselookatmenow (USA) (DSmaga,France) **3-9-0** DBoeuf	1½	3		97	—
4946a[3]	**Tea Party (USA)** (KOCunningham-Brown) **3-9-0** FSanchez (btn approx 17¼l)		10		—	—

				SP	RR	SF
4971⁴	**Volley (IRE)** (JBerry) **3-9-0** GCarter (btn over 17¼l)		11		—	—

11 Rn

1m 47.66 (10.66) P-M 1.90F: 1.50F 1.60F 5.00F (5.20F) OWNER Wertheimer Brothers (CHANTILLY) BRED Wertheimer Frere
4946a Tea Party (USA), ridden for an effort two furlongs out, was soon outpaced.
4971 Volley (IRE) was ridden over a furlong out, but dropped away disappointingly.
DS

5158a-CAPANNELLE (Rome, Italy) (R-H) (Heavy)
Wednesday November 27th

5193a PREMIO WATERLOO (2-Y.O)
2-10 (2-28) **1m 110y** £8,120.00 (£3,573.00: £1,949.00)

				SP	RR	SF
	Mastro Cantore (IRE) (LCamici,Italy) **2-8-13** MPasquale	—	1		—	—
	Mister Copper (Italy) **2-8-13** BJovine	1½	2		—	—
	Kiratas (Italy) **2-8-13** SBietolini	7	3		—	—
	Not Forgotten (USA) (PAKelleway) **2-8-9** JacquelineFreda (btn over 9½l)		5		—	—

14 Rn

0m TOTE 71L: 24L 29L 84L (245L) OWNER Scuderia Blueberry BRED Razza Del Sole
Not Forgotten (USA) put in an average debut on what was very heavy ground. He raced in mid-division but was unable to quicken coming into the straight and was soon beaten.

5191a-EVRY (France) (R-H) (Good to soft)
Friday November 29th

5194a PRIX ZEDDAAN (Listed) (2-Y.O)
1-40 (1-39) **6f** £18,445.00 (£6,324.00: £3,953.00)

				SP	RR	SF
4723⁶	**Tomba** (BJMeehan) **2-8-11** MTebbutt	—	1		104	—
5071a⁴	**Heaven's Command** (NClement,France) **2-8-12** GMosse	½	2		104	—
	Sweetheart (USA) (MmeCHead,France) **2-8-8** FHead	5	3		86	—
5034*	**Soviet State (USA)** (PWChapple-Hyam) **2-8-11** JReid (btn over 8½l)		5		—	—

9 Rn

1m 16.53 (6.53) P-M 5.70F: 2.20F 1.70F 3.40F (7.70F) OWNER Mr J. R. Good (UPPER LAMBOURN) BRED Mrs P. Good
4723 Tomba provided his jockey with his first success in France. Racing in mid-division, he made up good ground three furlongs out and, taking the lead with a furlong left to race, ran on well to the end.
5034* Soviet State (USA) raced prominently for much of the way, but found little when ridden over a furlong out. He collects £1,107 for this effort.
DS

5193a-CAPANNELLE (Rome, Italy) (R-H) (Heavy)
Saturday November 30th

5195a PREMIO FOUQUET (2-Y.O)
12-55 (1-00) **7f** £8,120.00

				SP	RR	SF
4658a*	**Viscoumtess Brave (IRE)** (LordHuntingdon) **2-8-11** FJovine	—	1		—	—
	City Girl (ITY) (Italy) **2-8-11** LFicuciello	1½	2		—	—
	Stato King (Italy) **2-9-1** VMezzatesta	3	3		—	—

8 Rn

1m 31.3 TOTE 17L: 13L 15L 18L (48L) OWNER Scuderia San Pancrazio (WEST ILSLEY)
4658a* Viscoumtess Brave (IRE) continued her unbeaten record. Racing in mid-division, she made steady headway from halfway to take the lead inside the final furlong. She should stay further and is not troubled by heavy ground.

5196a PREMIO PLEBEN MAIDEN (2-Y.O)
1-20 (1-31) **1m 2f** £8,120.00

				SP	RR	SF
	Ribelle Umbro (ITY) (EMichelotti,Italy) **2-9-0** FSantella	—	1		—	—
	Aldo Piccolo (IRE) (Italy) **2-9-0** GBietolini	5	2		—	—
	Roman Winner (Italy) **2-9-0** OFancera	3	3		—	—
5193a⁵	**Not Forgotten (USA)** (PAKelleway) **2-9-0** FJovine (btn over 33l)		10		—	—

12 Rn

1m 31.3 TOTE 142L: 26L 15L 14L (285L) OWNER R & C Mariotti
5193a Not Forgotten (USA) put in a disappointing performance on this second run in four days. He was always behind and never in a position to challenge.

5197a PREMIO MARRACCI MAIDEN (2-Y.O F)
1-45 (1-57) **1m 2f** £8,120.00

				SP	RR	SF
	Mythical Creek (USA) (AColella,Italy) **2-8-13** GBietolini	—	1		—	—
2666a²	**Swith Water (IRE)** (Italy) **2-8-13** LFicuciello	2	2		—	—
	Lady Leprechaun (IRE) (Italy) **2-8-13** OFancera	4	3		—	—
	Swing And Brave (IRE) (LordHuntingdon) **2-8-9** FJovine (btn approx 15l)		6		—	—

11 Rn

2m 13.6 TOTE 168L: 47L 25L 28L (587L) OWNER D. Venturi BRED Dr & Mrs Smiser West at el
Swing And Brave (IRE) raced in mid-division. Running on at the one pace, he did not appear to act on the heavy going.

5190a-SAINT-CLOUD (France) (L-H) (Heavy)
Saturday November 30th

5198a PRIX PETITE ETOILE (Listed) (3-Y.O F)
1-10 (1-10) **1m 2f** £18,445.00 (£6,324.00: £3,953.00: £2,055.00)

	Horse	Dist	Pos	SP	RR	SF
5026a^2	**Truly Generous (IRE)** (RCollet,France) **3-8-12** GGuignard	—	1		108	—
	Stage Manner (JEHammond,France) **3-9-2** TThulliez	2	2		109	—
	Krissante (USA) (MmeCHead,France) **3-8-12** ODoleuze	2	3		102	—
5157a^2	**Cabaret (IRE)** (PWChapple-Hyam) **3-8-12** JReid	6	4		92	—
5154a^4	**Asmara (USA)** (JOxx,Ireland) **3-9-2** GMosse (btn approx 13l)		6		—	—
5025a^6	**Altamura (USA)** (JHMGosden) **3-9-2** WRyan (btn approx 38l)		9		—	—
						10 Rn

2m 25.1 (21.60) P-M 26.20F: 6.20F 2.70F 3.60F (121.90F) OWNER Mr R. C. Strauss (CHANTILLY) BRED Kilfrush Stud Ltd

5157a Cabaret (IRE), prominent for most of the way, took the lead three furlongs from home but was soon headed and could only keep on at the one pace.

5154a Asmara (USA) showed disappointingly little on this occasion.

5025a Altamura (USA), the one-time leader, weakened quickly and proved disappointing.

5199a PRIX DENISY (Listed) (3-Y.O+)
2-45 (2-43) **1m 6f** £18,445.00 (£6,324.00: £3,953.00)

	Horse	Dist	Pos	SP	RR	SF
4553^4	**Heron Island (IRE)** (PWChapple-Hyam) **3-8-9** JReid	—	1		117	—
5125a^2	**Always Earnest (USA)** (MmeMBollack-Badel,France) **8-9-2b** ABadel	2½	2		113	—
	Killgham (IRE) (ELeenders,France) **5-8-13** J-LChouteau	8	3		101	—
5125a^7	**Ayunli** (SCWilliams) **5-8-13** DRMcCabe (btn over 36l)		7		—	—
5035^2	**Poltarf (USA)** (JHMGosden) **5-9-2** WRyan (btn dist)		8		—	—
						9 Rn

3m 25.3 (27.30) P-M 6.60F: 2.30F 1.40F 2.80F (10.80F) OWNER Mr R. E. Sangster (MARLBOROUGH) BRED Barronstown Stud and Roncon Ltd

4553 Heron Island (IRE), up against a decent field, was sent on turning into the straight and, appreciating the ground, won comfortably. He may be a force in the top Cup races next season.

5125a Ayunli failed to make any impression.

5035 Poltarf (USA) made no show.

DS

5168-WOLVERHAMPTON (L-H) (Standard)
Saturday December 7th
Vis: poor race 6

WEATHER: foggy

5200 HOLIDAY INN GARDEN COURT WOLVERHAMPTON H'CAP (0-70) (I) (3-Y.O+) (Class E)
1-05 (1-05) **1m 1f 79y (Fibresand)** £2,849.70 (£861.60: £419.80: £198.90) Stalls: Low GOING minus 0.01 sec per fur (STD)

	Horse	Dist	Pos	SP	RR	SF
5179^3	**Desert Zone (USA) (50)** (JohnHarris) **7-8-10** SSanders(12) (b: a.p: led over 3f out: sn clr: easily)	—	1	5/1^2	67+	45
5118^5	**Golden Touch (USA) (62)** (DJSCosgrove) **4-9-8** MRoberts(9) (chsd ldrs: effrt to chse wnr over 2f out: no imp)	8	2	15/2	65	43
4993^6	**Leif the Lucky (USA) (59)** (MissSEHall) **7-9-5** DaneO'Neill(2) (led over 5f out tl over 3f out: kpt on one pce)	2	3	11/2^3	59	37
4779^4	**China Castle (68)** (PCHaslam) **3-9-12** SDrowne(11) (s.i.s: hdwy 3f out: styd on: nt rch ldrs)	3	4	12/1	63	39
5140^2	**Dragonjoy (64)** (NPLittmoden) **3-9-1b**(7) DSweeney(5) (hld up: hdwy over 2f out: nrst fin)	1¼	5	10/1	57	33
5042*	**Mels Baby (IRE) (53)** (JLEyre) **3-8-11** RLappin(1) (w ldrs: hrd drvn over 2f out: sn btn)	6	6	3/1^1	35	11
*5132**	**Best of All (IRE) (65)** (JBerry) **4-9-11e** GCarter(8) (lw: sn drvn along: n.d)	3	7	8/1	42	20
5165^{13}	**Three Arch Bridge (67)** (MJohnston) **4-9-13b** DeanMcKeown(3) (trckd ldrs: rdn along 3f out: sn btn)	2½	8	16/1	40	18
5120^{12}	**Kintwyn (68)** (WRMuir) **6-10-0** JReid(6) (b.hind: a in rr)	4	9	33/1	34	12
5189^7	**Sweet Supposin (IRE) (64)** (CADwyer) **5-9-10v** JStack(4) (lw: led after 2f tl over 5f out: rdn & wknd over 3f out)	½	10	14/1	29	7
5181^{12}	**River Run (IRE) (56)** (RHollinshead) **4-8-13**(3) FLynch(10) (led 2f: wknd over 4f out: t.o)	10	11	40/1	4	—
5102^7	**Dolliver (USA) (52)** (SDow) **4-8-7**(5) ADaly(13) (mid div tl rdn & wknd over 4f out: sn t.o)	5	12	40/1	—	—
5094^8	**Renata's Prince (IRE) (55)** (KRBurke) **3-8-13** DHolland(7) (a in rr: t.o fnl 4f)	dist	13	40/1	—	—
				(SP 119.5%)		**13 Rn**

2m 1.6 (5.60) CSF £39.30 CT £193.72 TOTE £6.70: £1.90 £3.70 £2.80 (£20.00) Trio £119.30 OWNER Lavender Hill Leisure Ltd (GRANTHAM) BRED Michael D. Baudhuin

WEIGHT FOR AGE 3yo-2lb

5201 BIRMINGHAM MAIDEN STKS (I) (2-Y.O) (Class D)
1-40 (1-40) **6f (Fibresand)** £2,965.00 (£895.00: £435.00: £205.00) Stalls: Low GOING minus 0.01 sec per fur (STD)

	Horse	Dist	Pos	SP	RR	SF
5162^3	**Fit For The Job (IRE) (50)** (WGMTurner) **2-9-0** TSprake(9) (broke smartly: mde all: drvn out)	—	1	10/1	55	32
5049^4	**E-Mail (IRE) (75)** (JMPEustace) **2-9-0** MTebbutt(7) (a.p: rdn 2f out: kpt on: nt pce to chal)	1¾	2	3/1^2	50	27
5111^7	**Miami Moon** (CWThornton) **2-8-9** DeanMcKeown(3) (bit bkwd: prom: rdn over 2f out: kpt on one pce)	3	3	8/1^3	37	14
5080^6	**Snow Eagle (IRE) (59)** (RHannon) **2-8-9** DaneO'Neill(2) (chsd ldrs: rdn along over 2f out: no imp)	2½	4	8/1^3	31	8
3502^7	**Green Boulevard (USA)** (JBerry) **2-8-9** GCarter(1) (b: b.hind: bit bkwd: prom: hrd rdn over 2f out: one pce)	s.h	5	9/4^1	31	8
4364^{11}	**Heathyards Pearl (USA) (69)** (RHollinshead) **2-8-6**(3) FLynch(4) (a in rr: t.o)	7	6	10/1	12	—
	Warp Drive (IRE) (WRMuir) **2-9-0** JReid(6) (w'like: scope: bkwd: sn pushed along: a outpcd: t.o)	¾	7	8/1^3	15	—
5133^{13}	**Komasta (68)** (CaptJWilson) **2-9-0** SDWilliams(5) (outpcd: t.o)	3½	8	16/1	6	—

5160^{8} **First Man** (BJLlewellyn) **2-9-0** AClark(8) (dwlt: a bhd: t.o) ....8 **9** 50/1 — —
(SP 115.1%) **9 Rn**
1m 16.1 (4.90) CSF £37.84 TOTE £6.80: £1.80 £1.20 £2.30 (£9.70) Trio £43.40 OWNER Mr O. J. Stokes (SHERBORNE) BRED Mrs R. Leonard

5202 RADCLIFFE FAMILY & FRIENDS (S) STKS (2-Y.O) (Class E)

2-15 (2-16) **7f (Fibresand)** £3,566.25 (£1,080.00: £527.50: £251.25) Stalls: High GOING minus 0.01 sec per fur (STD)

				SP	RR	SF
5172^{2}	**Lightning Bolt (IRE) (59)** (MJohnston) **2-8-6** DHolland(10) (lw: hdwy ½-wy: led over 1f out: r.o wl)	—	**1**	5/1^{3}	57	—
5166*	**Bali-Pet (59)** (WGMTurner) **2-8-4b**(7) DSweeney(3) (s.i.s: bhd tl gd hdwy wl over 1f out: fin wl)	2½	**2**	5/1^{3}	56	—
5166^{2}	**Senate Swings (61)** (WRMuir) **2-8-11** DaneO'Neill(11) (hdwy on outside 3f out: rdn & no ex ins fnl f)	nk	**3**	10/1	56	—
5135^{3}	**Cool Grey (50)** (JJO'Neill) **2-8-6** GDuffield(1) (lw: led over 4f out tl hdd & no ex appr fnl f)	s.h	**4**	11/2	51	—
5113^{11}	**Patrita Park (56)** (WWHaigh) **2-8-6** RLappin(7) (outpcd tl styd on appr fnl f)	3	**5**	25/1	44	—
5142^{4}	**Bestelina** (DJSCosgrove) **2-8-6** FNorton(2) (led 2f: rdn 3f out: sn btn)	9	**6**	8/1	23	—
4920^{12}	**T-N-T Express (50)** (EJAlston) **2-8-11** SSanders(9) (sn pushed along: a outpcd)	nk	**7**	33/1	27	—
4976^{10}	**Swynford Charmer** (JFBottomley) **2-8-11** GCarter(5) (b.hind: nvr gng pce)	3	**8**	16/1	21	—
2942^{6}	**Countless Times** (WRMuir) **2-8-11** JReid(8) (lw: w ldrs: rdn whn n.m.r 3f out: sn lost pl)	1¾	**9**	12/1	17	—
5160^{3}	**Chasetown Flyer (USA) (60)** (RHollinshead) **2-8-8**(3) FLynch(4) (led after 2f: sn hdd: wknd wl over 2f out)	3½	**10**	9/2^{2}	9	—
5147^{6}	**Hallmark (IRE) (67)** (RHannon) **2-8-11** RPerham(6) (prom: drvn along whn nt clr run 3f out: nt rcvr)	5	**11**	7/2^{1}	—	—

(SP 129.7%) **11 Rn**
1m 32.9 (8.20) CSF £31.42 TOTE £4.80: £1.50 £1.90 £2.30 (£7.70) Trio £12.70 OWNER Mr W. M. Roper (MIDDLEHAM) BRED D. Cornwall
No bid

5203 TOTE MOBILE TERMINAL H'CAP (0-95) (3-Y.O+) (Class C)

2-45 (2-47) **7f (Fibresand)** £13,940.00 (£4,220.00: £2,060.00: £980.00) Stalls: High GOING minus 0.01 sec per fur (STD)

				SP	RR	SF
5144*	**Cim Bom Bom (IRE) (85)** (MBell) **4-8-13v**(5) GFaulkner(7) (lw: mde all: clr appr fnl f: hld on)	—	**1**	11/2^{3}	95	52
4975^{4}	**Stoppes Brow (91)** (GLMoore) **4-9-10v** GDuffield(3) (lw: hdwy 3f out: r.o u.p ins fnl f: nt rch wnr)	1½	**2**	12/1	98	55
4378^{7}	**Chewit (93)** (AMoore) **4-9-12** CandyMorris(9) (b.hind: a.p: chsd wnr over 2f out: nt pce to chal)	nk	**3**	14/1	99	56
4688^{15}	**Rakis (IRE) (87)** (MrsLStubbs) **6-9-6** SWhitworth(2) (a.p: hrd rdn 2f out: kpt on)	2	**4**	5/1^{2}	88	45
4994*	**Cretan Gift (90)** (NPLittmoden) **5-9-9b** TGMcLaughlin(4) (a.p: hrd rdn wl over 1f out: one pce)	1¼	**5**	7/1	89	46
4791^{2}	**Sailormaite (88)** (SRBowring) **5-9-7** DeanMcKeown(1) (chsd ldrs: no hdwy fnl 2f)	4	**6**	14/1	77	34
4994^{9}	**Mr Bergerac (IRE) (89)** (BPalling) **5-9-8** TSprake(6) (prom tl outpcd wl over 1f out)	¾	**7**	14/1	77	34
4848a^{4}	**Anzio (IRE) (95)** (MissGayKelleway) **5-10-0b** JReid(5) (hld up: a bhd & outpcd)	2	**8**	3/1^{1}	78	35
5163^{7}	**Krystal Max (IRE) (85)** (TDBarron) **3-9-4** DHolland(10) (outpcd)	4	**9**	14/1	59	16
4823^{8}	**Hard to Figure (93)** (RJHodges) **10-9-12** SDrowne(12) (outpcd: a bhd)	1¼	**10**	40/1	64	21
4800^{5}	**Chickawicka (IRE) (85)** (BPalling) **5-9-4** GCarter(8) (spd over 4f)	1	**11**	14/1	54	11
4974^{13}	**Carburton (84)** (JAGlover) **3-9-3** SSanders(11) (b.hind: lw: sn chsng ldrs: rdn & wknd over 2f out)	s.h	**12**	8/1	53	10

(SP 124.1%) **12 Rn**
1m 28.8 (4.10) CSF £65.72 CT £831.43 TOTE £6.00: £2.60 £2.80 £3.50 (£48.50) Trio £382.70 OWNER Mr Yucel Birol (NEWMARKET) BRED Tarworth Bloodstock Investments Ltd and J.J. Melk
OFFICIAL EXPLANATION Anzio (IRE): did not stay.

5204 BASS WULFRUN STKS (Listed) (3-Y.O+) (Class A)

3-20 (3-20) **1m 1f 79y (Fibresand)** £31,898.00 (£11,882.00: £5,766.00: £2,430.00: £1,040.00: £484.00) Stalls: Low GOING minus 0.01 sec per fur (STD)

				SP	RR	SF
3912a^{9}	**Prince of Andros (USA) (110)** (CFWall) **6-8-13** JReid(7) (lw: stumbled s: hdwy over 3f out: rdn to ld fnl strides)	—	**1**	7/2^{2}	111	53
5078a^{2}	**Decorated Hero (117)** (JHMGosden) **4-9-1** AMcGlone(2) (lw: a.p: led over 1f out: sn clr: wknd & ct cl home)	hd	**2**	100/30^{1}	113	55
5078a^{4}	**Royal Philosopher (105)** (JWHills) **4-9-1** DHolland(1) (lw: chsd ldr: led over 4f out tl over 1f out: rallied u.p nr fin)	hd	**3**	14/1	113	55
5045^{9}	**Punishment (112)** (CEBrittain) **5-8-13** MRoberts(10) (hld up & bhd: hdwy over 3f out: kpt on u.p towards fin)	¾	**4**	25/1	109	51
5120*	**Thai Morning (90)** (PWHarris) **3-8-11** AClark(13) (hdwy u.p ½-wy: styd on wl ins fnl f)	½	**5**	7/1	109	49
	Loch Bering (USA) (ALund,Norway) **4-8-13** FJohansson(8) (lw: hld up: hdwy over 3f out: styd on ins fnl f)	2	**6**	25/1	105	47
4479^{4}	**Maralinga (IRE) (99)** (LadyHerries) **4-8-13** DeclanO'Shea(4) (trckd ldrs: rdn over 3f out: sn btn)	8	**7**	20/1	91	33
4972^{2}	**Nijo (108)** (DRLoder) **5-8-13** DRMcCabe(3) (lw: slt ld over 5f: rdn & wknd 2f out)	nk	**8**	11/2	91	33
4964^{8}	**General Academy (IRE) (100)** (PAKelleway) **3-8-11v**^{1} MWigham(11) (a in rr)	5	**9**	50/1	82	22
4757^{4}	**Blomberg (IRE) (103)** (JRFanshawe) **4-9-3** GDuffield(9) (trckd ldrs over 6f: sn rdn & wknd)	½	**10**	14/1	86	28
4874^{7}	**Rebel County (IRE) (89)** (ABailey) **3-8-6** DBiggs(6) (b: outpcd: a bhd)	6	**11**	33/1	66	6
4553^{2}	**Key to My Heart (IRE) (114)** (MissSEHall) **6-9-1** SSanders(12) (b: lw: chsd ldrs 6f: sn outpcd)	2	**12**	5/1^{3}	70	12
4972^{4}	**Celestial Key (USA) (103)** (MJohnston) **6-8-13** DeanMcKeown(5) (chsd ldrs: wknd qckly over 2f out: virtually p.u: t.o)	dist	**13**	16/1	—	—

(SP 126.4%) **13 Rn**
2m 1.0 (5.00) CSF £15.76 TOTE £4.20: £2.80 £1.90 £3.40 (£7.50) Trio £74.90 OWNER Dr Sinn Dung Wing (NEWMARKET) BRED Spendthrift Farm
WEIGHT FOR AGE 3yo-2lb

3912a Prince of Andros (USA) has now won both runnings of this prestigious event, but he had to do it the hard way this time over a trip short of his best. He is a real star. (7/2)
5078a Decorated Hero, always pulling double over his rivals, entered the final furlong with a two-length advantage, but his stamina gave out in the last 100 yards and he just failed to hold on. (100/30)
5078a Royal Philosopher ran a fine race in defeat and was coming back for more nearing the finish. He has not won beyond a mile, but he is a battler and deserves to win another decent prize. (14/1)
4856a Punishment, having his first run on Fibresand, ran extremely well over a trip short of his best, and he would not be hard pressed to win a similar race over twelve furlongs. (25/1)
5120* Thai Morning acts well on this surface, but this was a big step up in class and, though he lost a winning sequence, this was definitely his best performance yet. (7/1: op 12/1)
Loch Bering (USA), a challenger from abroad, took time to find his stride and, when he did, the race was all but over. Connections should have been pleased with this promising effort. (25/1)

5205 G.A.L. COMMUNICATIONS H'CAP (0-85) (3-Y.O+) (Class D)

3-55 (3-56) **1m 4f (Fibresand)** £3,863.90 (£1,170.20: £571.60: £272.30) Stalls: Low GOING minus 0.01 sec per fur (STD)

Form	Horse	Dist	Pos	SP	RR	SF
3876[4]	**Prince Danzig (IRE) (79)** (DJGMurraySmith) **5-9-8** GDuffield(6) (hld up: hdwy 3f out: rdn to ld ins fnl f: all out)	—	**1**	16/1	89	71
5047[11]	**Sea Victor (76)** (JLHarris) **4-9-5** DeanMcKeown(3) (led to 2f out: rallied & ev ch ins fnl f: r.o)	½	**2**	4/1[1]	85	67
5120[9]	**Opera Buff (IRE) (85)** (MissGayKelleway) **5-10-0** SSanders(11) (hld up in tch: led 2f out tl ins fnl f)	nk	**3**	11/1	94	76
5143*	**Greenspan (IRE) (75)** (WRMuir) **4-9-4** DaneO'Neill(7) (chsd ldrs: one pce fnl 2f)	7	**4**	7/1	75	57
5047[15]	**Noufari (FR) (75)** (RHollinshead) **5-9-1**(3) FLynch(10) (hld up & bhd: hdwy 3f out: styd on u.p)	nk	**5**	16/1	74	56
5140[3]	**Obelos (USA) (69)** (MissSJWilton) **5-8-12** SWhitworth(2) (prom: ev ch wl over 1f out: wknd qckly)	1¾	**6**	16/1	66	48
4967[6]	**Glow Forum (71)** (LMontagueHall) **5-8-9**(5) MartinDwyer(4) (b: prom: hrd rdn over 3f out: sn wknd)	1½	**7**	5/1[2]	66	48
5046[9]	**Far Ahead (77)** (JLEyre) **4-9-6** RLappin(12) (prom tl wknd over 2f out)	1	**8**	14/1	71	53
4900[5]	**Troubadour Song (72)** (WWHaigh) **4-8-12**(3) PMcCabe(8) (hld up: a in rr)	nk	**9**	6/1	65	47
3113[7]	**Premier Dance (74)** (DHaydnJones) **9-9-3** AClark(1) (bkwd: a bhd: t.o)	13	**10**	14/1	50	32
5167[8]	**Backview (73)** (BJLlewellyn) **4-9-2** MRoberts(9) (bhd fnl 4f: t.o)	13	**11**	16/1	32	14
4900[2]	**Renown (72)** (LordHuntingdon) **4-9-1** DHolland(5) (b.hind: swtg: trckd ldrs: rdn & wknd over 2f out: t.o)	10	**12**	11/2[3]	17	—
				(SP 124.0%)	**12 Rn**	

2m 37.6 (5.10) CSF £77.21 CT £697.27 TOTE £21.90: £4.20 £3.10 £2.60 (£36.90) Trio £92.80 OWNER Mr A. H. Ulrick (LAMBOURN) BRED J. N. McCaffrey in Ireland

5206 HOLIDAY INN GARDEN COURT WOLVERHAMPTON H'CAP (0-70) (II) (3-Y.O+) (Class E)

4-25 (4-25) **1m 1f 79y (Fibresand)** £2,835.40 (£857.20: £417.60: £197.80) Stalls: Low GOING minus 0.01 sec per fur (STD)

Form	Horse	Dist	Pos	SP	RR	SF
5161[3]	**Barrel of Hope (63)** (JLEyre) **4-9-6b**(3) OPears(12) (a.p: led wl over 3f out: hld on gamely nr fin)	—	**1**	12/1	70	44
5175[2]	**Angel Face (USA) (62)** (PDEvans) **3-9-6** ACulhane(1) (a.p: jnd wnr 3f out: rdn & unable qckn fnl f)	hd	**2**	6/4[1]	69	41
5118[2]	**Maradata (IRE) (63)** (RHollinshead) **4-9-6**(3) FLynch(9) (lw: hld up: hdwy over 2f out: styd on fnl f)	3½	**3**	7/1[3]	64	38
5140[5]	**Tormount (USA) (57)** (LordHuntingdon) **3-9-1** JReid(10) (lw: hld up: hdwy over 2f out: nrst fin)	½	**4**	14/1	57	29
5129[6]	**Mustn't Grumble (IRE) (53)** (MissSJWilton) **6-8-13** SWhitworth(5) (hld up: hdwy u.p 2f out: styd on)	1¾	**5**	14/1	50	24
5010[5]	**Gadge (51)** (ABailey) **5-8-11** DWright(13) (b: nvr nr to chal)	8	**6**	12/1	34	8
5137[2]	**Yeoman Oliver (70)** (BAMcMahon) **3-9-9**(5) LNewton(8) (lw: w ldr: rdn over 3f out: grad wknd)	¾	**7**	10/1	52	24
5079[7]	**Czarna (IRE) (52)** (CEBrittain) **5-8-12** MRoberts(6) (b.hind: led tl wl over 3f out: rdn & wknd fnl 2f)	1¼	**8**	14/1	32	6
4901[18]	**Gulf Shaadi (61)** (EJAlston) **4-9-7** SSanders(3) (chsd ldrs over 5f: sn rdn & wknd)	3½	**9**	33/1	35	9
416[8]	**Sarasi (67)** (MJCamacho) **4-9-13** GDuffield(7) (a in rr: t.o)	8	**10**	12/1	27	1
5056*	**Shahik (USA) (68)** (DHaydnJones) **6-10-0** AClark(2) (lw: chsd ldrs over 6f: sn lost tch: t.o)	hd	**11**	11/2[2]	28	2
2943[10]	**Callaloo (63)** (RHarris) **3-9-7** JMcLaughlin(11) (bit bkwd: a in rr: t.o)	7	**12**	33/1	11	—
5171[3]	**Tissue of Lies (USA) (70)** (MJohnston) **3-10-0** DHolland(4) (s.s: a bhd: t.o)	13	**13**	7/1[3]	—	—
				(SP 138.4%)	**13 Rn**	

2m 3.2 (7.20) CSF £33.33 CT £144.53 TOTE £13.60: £4.00 £2.10 £2.80 (£46.00) Trio £100.10 OWNER Mr Peter Watson (HAMBLETON) BRED Bolton Grange

WEIGHT FOR AGE 3yo-2lb

5207 BIRMINGHAM MAIDEN STKS (II) (2-Y.O) (Class D)

4-55 (4-55) **6f (Fibresand)** £2,948.75 (£890.00: £432.50: £203.75) Stalls: Low GOING minus 0.01 sec per fur (STD)

Form	Horse	Dist	Pos	SP	RR	SF
5111[3]	**Double-O (74)** (WJarvis) **2-9-0** SSanders(8) (lw: mde all: drvn clr wl over 1f out: r.o)	—	**1**	5/6[1]	78	52
5111[9]	**Jay-Owe-Two (IRE)** (RMWhitaker) **2-9-0** ACulhane(3) (lw: a.p: chsd wnr fnl 2f: no imp)	1¾	**2**	5/1[2]	73	47
5103[3]	**Patina** (RHollinshead) **2-8-6**(3) FLynch(7) (chsd ldrs: kpt on one pce fnl 2f)	7	**3**	8/1[3]	50	24
2734[5]	**Hever Golf Dancer (72)** (TJNaughton) **2-9-0** SWhitworth(5) (bkwd: hdwy over 2f out: nvr nrr)	8	**4**	9/1	33	7
5133[10]	**Village Pub (FR) (63)** (KOCunningham-Brown) **2-9-0b** JReid(2) (chsd wnr tl wknd qckly 2f out)	½	**5**	8/1[3]	32	6
2413[3]	**Chynna** (MHTompkins) **2-8-9** GDuffield(6) (a bhd & outpcd)	5	**6**	5/1[2]	14	—
	Front View (BJLlewellyn) **2-9-0** AClark(1) (lt-f: bit bkwd: sn wl bhd & outpcd: t.o)	7	**7**	40/1	—	—
2083[9]	**Pet Express** (PCHaslam) **2-8-7**(7) PGoode(4) (bkwd: sn pushed along: a bhd & outpcd: t.o)	3½	**8**	33/1	—	—
				(SP 125.5%)	**8 Rn**	

1m 14.6 (3.40) CSF £6.40 TOTE £2.00: £1.60 £1.20 £2.00 (£11.40) OWNER R K Bids Ltd (NEWMARKET) BRED R. K. Bids Ltd

T/Jkpt: £25,283.10 (0.1 Tckts); £32,049.05 to Ludlow 9/12/96. T/Plpt: £251.20 (65.26 Tckts). T/Qdpt: £65.80 (15.72 Tckts). IM

5182-LINGFIELD (L-H) (Standard)

Wednesday December 11th

Race 8: hand-timed & no official dists after 6th

WEATHER: dull WIND: almost nil

5208 TOINHA CLAIMING STKS (I) (3-Y.O+) (Class E)

12-10 (12-11) **1m (Equitrack)** £2,697.95 (£815.60: £397.30: £188.15) Stalls: High GOING minus 0.46 sec per fur (FST)

Form	Horse	Dist	Pos	SP	RR	SF
5002[12]	**Bon Secret (IRE) (64)** (TJNaughton) **4-8-7** DHolland(3) (hld up: rdn over 2f out: led ins fnl f: r.o wl)	—	**1**	12/1	65	30
3627[8]	**Waikiki Beach (USA) (77)** (GLMoore) **5-9-7** SWhitworth(6) (b: hdwy over 3f out: led over 1f out tl ins fnl f: unable qckn)	5	**2**	2/1[1]	69	34
5002[9]	**Slip Jig (IRE) (78)** (RHannon) **3-9-2** RPerham(8) (b.nr fore: led over 1f: led over 2f out tl over 1f out: one pce)	1	**3**	6/1	63	27
5132[6]	**Spencer's Revenge (73)** (NTinkler) **7-8-9b** DeanMcKeown(9) (s.i.s: rdn thrght: hdwy over 3f out: wknd over 1f out)	2½	**4**	7/2[2]	50	15
5149[3]	**Our Shadee (USA) (55)** (KTIvory) **6-8-7v** GDuffield(1) (b: b.hind: led 5f out tl over 2f out: wknd over 1f out)	½	**5**	5/1[3]	47	12
5123[9]	**Vanborough Lad (34)** (MJBolton) **7-8-5** JQuinn(2) (b: b.hind: a.p: rdn over 3f out: wknd over 2f out)	1½	**6**	50/1	42	7
5183[10]	**Kirov Protege (IRE) (40)** (MrsLCJewell) **4-8-2**(7) DarrenWilliams(7) (lost pl over 6f out: r.o one pce fnl f)	5	**7**	33/1	36	1
	Grasshopper (JLSpearing) **3-8-8b**[1] SDrowne(12) (lt-f: prom 7f)	7	**8**	66/1	22	—
5086[7]	**Chalky Dancer (29)** (HJCollingridge) **4-8-1**(3)ow1 FLynch(5) (led over 6f out to 5f out: wknd over 2f out)	3½	**9**	33/1	10	—
	Klosters (RJHodges) **4-7-13**(5) PPMurphy(11) (b.nr fore: a bhd)	nk	**10**	66/1	9	—

				SP	RR	SF
5101^{9}	**Mad Alex** (MJHaynes) **3-7-13**(5) ADaly(4) (a bhd)	7	**11**	66/1	—	—
566^{5}	**Airborne Harris (IRE)** (ABailey) **3-8-12** SSanders(10) (bit bkwd: prom over 6f)	½	**12**	25/1	3	—

(SP 110.4%) **12 Rn**

1m 39.73 (2.33) CSF £32.00 TOTE £23.00: £3.00 £1.60 £2.20 (£25.30) Trio £78.30 OWNER Mr F. R. Jackman (EPSOM) BRED Sean Mc Donnell in Ireland
WEIGHT FOR AGE 3yo-1lb

5209 LADBROKE ALL-WEATHER TROPHY (QUALIFIER) H'CAP (0-70) (I) (3-Y.O+) (Class E)

12-40 (12-41) **7f (Equitrack)** £2,643.35 (£798.80: £388.90: £183.95) Stalls: Low GOING minus 0.46 sec per fur (FST)

				SP	RR	SF
*5095**	**Apollo Red (58)** (AMoore) **7-9-2** CandyMorris(12) (b.hind: mde all: r.o wl)	—	**1**	7/1^{3}	68	35
3696^{4}	**Star Talent (USA) (70)** (MissGayKelleway) **5-10-0** DHolland(10) (hdwy over 3f out: chsd wnr over 2f out: rdn over 1f out: unable qckn)	2½	**2**	8/1	74	41
4573^{6}	**Bargash (42)** (PDEvans) **4-8-0** DWright(11) (stdy hdwy over 3f out: rdn 2f out: r.o wl: too much to do)	nk	**3**	16/1	46	13
5163^{15}	**The Frisky Farmer (55)** (WGMTurner) **3-8-13b^{1}** TSprake(8) (rdn over 3f out: lost pl over 2f out: r.o one pce fnl f)	4	**4**	25/1	50	17
5149^{2}	**Bagshot (67)** (GLMoore) **5-9-11** SWhitworth(6) (outpcd: hdwy over 1f out: nvr nrr)	1½	**5**	10/1	58	25
3955^{10}	**Oberons Boy (IRE) (62)** (SDow) **3-9-1**(5) ADaly(5) (outpcd: hdwy over 1f out: nvr nrr)	hd	**6**	7/1^{3}	53	20
5152^{2}	**Kingchip Boy (68)** (MJRyan) **7-9-12v** AClark(3) (a.p: rdn over 3f out: wknd over 1f out)	¾	**7**	11/2^{2}	57	24
5188^{4}	**Samsolom (50)** (PHowling) **8-8-8** DeanMcKeown(9) (b.hind: prom over 4f)	¾	**8**	10/1	37	4
5130^{3}	**Ben Gunn (54)** (PTWalwyn) **4-8-12** GDuffield(2) (bhd fnl 4f)	3½	**9**	7/1^{3}	33	—
4598^{5}	**Ivory's Grab Hire (56)** (KTIvory) **3-9-0b** DBiggs(7) (b: b.hind: chsd wnr over 4f)	3	**10**	14/1	29	—
*5110**	**Indiahra (47)** (JLEyre) **5-8-5v** RLappin(4) (prom over 2f)	4	**11**	4/1^{1}	10	—
5001^{4}	**Misky Bay (59)** (DJSCosgrove) **3-9-3** DRMcCabe(1) (virtually ref to r: a t.o)	30	**12**	20/1	—	—

(SP 123.3%) **12 Rn**

1m 26.23 (1.83) CSF £59.20 CT £574.85 TOTE £9.50: £2.80 £2.80 £4.30 (£48.70) Trio £271.50; £344.21 to Taunton 12/12/96 OWNER Mr A. Moore (BRIGHTON) BRED Crest Stud Ltd
OFFICIAL EXPLANATION Indiahra: was found to be in season after the race.

5210 MARIA AMATEUR H'CAP (0-75) (3-Y.O+) (Class G)

1-10 (1-11) **1m 2f (Equitrack)** £2,085.00 (£585.00: £285.00) Stalls: Low GOING minus 0.46 sec per fur (FST)

				SP	RR	SF
5206^{2}	**Angel Face (USA) (62)** (PDEvans) **3-10-10**(7) MrAEvans(8) (a.p: led 7f out: clr over 1f out: r.o wl)	—	**1**	4/1^{1}	75	53
*5151**	**Montone (IRE) (60)** (JRJenkins) **6-11-4v** DrMMannish(5) (hdwy over 3f out: chsd wnr fnl f: r.o one pce)	3	**2**	6/1^{3}	68	49
5189^{3}	**Don't Drop Bombs (USA) (40)** (DTThom) **7-9-12v** MissJFeilden(7) (lw: led 3f: chsd wnr over 2f out to 1f out: one pce)	5	**3**	9/1	40	21
5114^{5}	**Raindeer Quest (35)** (JLEyre) **4-9-7** MissDianaJones(9) (hld up: r.o one pce fnl 2f)	½	**4**	12/1	34	15
5167^{6}	**Gold Blade (65)** (JPearce) **7-11-9** MrsLPearce(3) (lw: nvr plcd to chal)	1¾	**5**	8/1	62	43
5056^{4}	**Queens Stroller (IRE) (38)** (REPeacock) **5-9-3**(7)ow3 MrsCPeacock(12) (lost pl over 2f out: r.o one pce)	hd	**6**	25/1	34	12
5123^{7}	**Arzani (USA) (55)** (DJSCosgrove) **5-10-13** MissEJohnsonHoughton(2) (nvr nrr)	nk	**7**	7/1	51	32
5181^{4}	**Rasayel (USA) (43)** (PDEvans) **6-9-11**(4) MrWMcLaughlin(1) (b.off fore: nvr nrr)	¾	**8**	14/1	38	19
3067^{9}	**Safety (USA) (38)** (JWhite) **9-9-3b**(7) MrJCrowley(6) (prom 5f)	½	**9**	33/1	32	13
5118^{4}	**Mimosa (60)** (SDow) **3-11-1** MissYHaynes(14) (a bhd)	1¼	**10**	11/1	52	30
4997^{5}	**Areish (IRE) (45)** (JFfitch-Heyes) **3-10-0b** MrPScott(13) (prom over 7f)	1¾	**11**	33/1	34	12
5119^{4}	**Your Most Welcome (65)** (DJSffrenchDavis) **5-11-9b** MissJAllison(4) (b.hind: hdwy over 7f out: wknd over 3f out)	9	**12**	14/1	40	21
5002^{11}	**Autumn Cover (70)** (PRHedger) **4-12-0** MrTMcCarthy(10) (lw: a.p: w wnr 7f out tl over 2f out: sn wknd)	15	**13**	11/2^{2}	21	2
5188^{12}	**Dancing Jack (57)** (JJBridger) **3-10-5**(7) MrDBridger(11) (lw: prom over 3f: t.o fnl 4f)	dist	**14**	25/1	—	—

(SP 126.2%) **14 Rn**

2m 8.88 (4.58) CSF £27.93 CT £192.45 TOTE £4.20: £1.70 £2.70 £2.90 (£12.50) Trio £19.60 OWNER Mrs E. J. Williams (WELSHPOOL) BRED Gainsborough Farm Inc.
WEIGHT FOR AGE 3yo-3lb
IN-FOCUS: This was rider Mr Anthony Evans' first winner

5211 TOINHA CLAIMING STKS (II) (3-Y.O+) (Class E)

1-40 (1-42) **1m (Equitrack)** £2,684.30 (£811.40: £395.20: £187.10) Stalls: High GOING minus 0.46 sec per fur (FST)

				SP	RR	SF
*5002**	**Mr Nevermind (IRE) (76)** (GLMoore) **6-9-7** SWhitworth(6) (lw: hld up: led 3f out: clr over 2f out: easily)	—	**1**	6/4^{1}	68+	36
5152^{12}	**Mogin (47)** (TJNaughton) **3-8-5** TSprake(10) (stdy hdwy over 3f out: rdn over 1f out: r.o one pce)	4	**2**	20/1	45	12
5001^{6}	**Zelaya (IRE)** (GLMoore) **3-7-12** FNorton(4) (b: a.p: rdn 2f out: chsd wnr over 1f out tl ins fnl f: one pce)	2	**3**	25/1	34	1
4221^{13}	**Mediate (IRE) (55)** (AHide) **4-7-10**(7) JoHunnam(1) (hdwy over 1f out: nvr nrr)	1½	**4**	14/1	35	3
5188^{9}	**Shermood (33)** (KTIvory) **3-7-9**(5)ow1 MartinDwyer(12) (b.hind: rdn & hdwy 4f out: one pce fnl 3f)	¾	**5**	33/1	32	—
3967*	**Jo Maximus (72)** (SDow) **4-8-8**(5) ADaly(9) (b.off hind: led over 1f: ev ch 3f out: rdn over 2f out: wknd over 1f out)	¾	**6**	7/2^{2}	42	10
5182^{6}	**Sarum (32)** (JELong) **10-8-5** LeesaLong(8) (b: led over 6f out to 5f out: led 4f out to 3f out: wknd 2f out)	1¾	**7**	50/1	31	—
5145^{12}	**Lahik (IRE) (35)** (KTIvory) **3-8-2** NAdams(11) (b: b.hind: bhd fnl 4f)	¾	**8**	40/1	27	—
3944^{6}	**Battleship Bruce (77)** (TCasey) **4-9-3** SSanders(2) (a.p: led 5f out to 4f out: wknd over 2f out)	¾	**9**	7/2^{2}	40	8
	A Million Watts (GMMcCourt) **5-8-9** AClark(5) (a bhd)	1½	**10**	13/2^{3}	29	—
5138^{8}	**Kajostar (25)** (SWCampion) **6-7-12** JQuinn(7) (lw: bhd fnl 3f)	1¾	**11**	66/1	14	—
	Broughtons Relish (WJMusson) **3-8-3** DRMcCabe(3) (w'like: bit bkwd: s.s: a wl bhd)	3	**12**	50/1	14	—

(SP 123.8%) **12 Rn**

1m 40.43 (3.03) CSF £30.96 TOTE £2.40: £1.20 £5.90 £4.40 (£28.50) Trio £254.20; £107.41 to Taunton 12/12/96 OWNER Pennine Partners (BRIGHTON) BRED Robert Corridan
WEIGHT FOR AGE 3yo-1lb

5212 SELIA NURSERY H'CAP (2-Y.O) (Class D)

2-10 (2-11) **1m (Equitrack)** £3,303.70 (£1,000.60: £488.80: £232.90) Stalls: High GOING minus 0.46 sec per fur (FST)

				SP	RR	SF
5111^{2}	**Cee-N-K (IRE) (73)** (MJohnston) **2-9-7** DHolland(3) (lw: led over 6f out: clr over 1f out: r.o wl)	—	**1**	5/1^{2}	76	27

				SP	RR	SF
5087^{3}	**Chief Predator (USA) (68)** (RHannon) **2-9-2** RPerham(4) (lost pl over 4f out: rallied fnl f: r.o wl)	1¼	**2**	13/2^{3}	69	20
5147^{4}	**Greenwich Fore (69)** (TGMills) **2-9-3v^{1}** SSanders(9) (lw: hld up: rdn over 2f out: r.o one pce)	½	**3**	5/1^{2}	69	20
5141*	**Hello Dolly (IRE) (70)** (KRBurke) **2-8-11**$^{(7)}$ DSweeney(5) (a.p: ev ch over 2f out: one pce)	½	**4**	9/2^{1}	69	20
5092^{3}	**Masterstroke (64)** (BJMeehan) **2-8-12** MTebbutt(10) (hdwy over 3f out: rdn & one pce)	1¾	**5**	15/2	59	10
5164^{10}	**Rock The Casbah (48)** (JHetherton) **2-7-10** NCarlisle(7) (lw: s.i.s: sme hdwy over 3f out: sn wknd)	5	**6**	33/1	33	—
3943^{6}	**Barnwood Crackers (60)** (MissGayKelleway) **2-8-8e** GDuffield(2) (b: b.hind: lw: bhd fnl 4f)	hd	**7**	9/2^{1}	45	—
5166^{3}	**Aspecto Lad (IRE) (55)** (MJohnston) **2-8-3** NAdams(1) (prom over 3f)	2	**8**	9/1	36	—
4980^{13}	**Neon Deion (IRE) (49)** (SCWilliams) **2-7-4v^{1}**$^{(7)}$ DarrenWilliams(6) (led over 1f: wknd 3f out)	8	**9**	33/1	14	—
5100^{6}	**Motcombs Club (58)** (NACallaghan) **2-8-6** JQuinn(8) (a bhd)	7	**10**	10/1	9	—
				(SP 119.8%)		**10 Rn**

1m 41.34 (3.94) CSF £35.62 CT £159.70 TOTE £5.50: £1.90 £1.30 £2.10 (£21.60) Trio £29.10 OWNER Cotterill & Kimberley (MIDDLEHAM) BRED Swettenham Stud

5213 COMMERCIAL CEILING FACTORS H'CAP (0-65) (3-Y.O+) (Class F)

2-40 (2-42) **2m** **(Equitrack)** £2,624.10 (£737.60: £360.30) Stalls: Low GOING minus 0.46 sec per fur (FST)

				SP	RR	SF
3514^{3}	**Wottashambles (40)** (LMontagueHall) **5-8-8** DHolland(8) (hdwy 10f out: led over 2f out: rdn & r.o wl)	—	**1**	11/1	51	26
5148^{4}	**Broughtons Formula (47)** (WJMusson) **6-9-1b** DRMcCabe(2) (s.s: wl bhd over 11f: rapid hdwy over 3f out: fin wl)	3½	**2**	3/1^{1}	55	30
5185*	**Matthias Mystique (60)** (MissBSanders) **3-9-6** ^{5x} SSanders(7) (a.p: led 5f out tl over 2f out: unable qckn)	1	**3**	6/1^{3}	67	34
5148^{10}	**Strat's Legacy (36)** (DWPArbuthnot) **9-8-4** JQuinn(9) (b: a.p: rdn over 4f out: one pce)	1¾	**4**	20/1	41	16
5148^{6}	**Guest Alliance (IRE) (60)** (AMoore) **4-10-0** CandyMorris(12) (b.hind: nvr nr to chal)	7	**5**	9/2^{2}	58	33
5116^{2}	**Coleridge (59)** (JJSheehan) **8-9-13b** AClark(1) (no hdwy fnl 3f)	½	**6**	10/1	56	31
4427^{10}	**Chocolate Ice (60)** (RJO'Sullivan) **3-9-6** GDuffield(10) (b: rdn over 6f out: hdwy over 4f out: wknd 3f out)	2½	**7**	33/1	55	22
5108^{5}	**Havana Heights (IRE) (42)** (JLEyre) **3-8-2** DWright(4) (led 6f: led 7f out to 5f out: sn wknd)	13	**8**	20/1	24	—
5052^{3}	**Aydigo (36)** (JPearce) **3-7-10** FNorton(6) (prom over 9f)	¾	**9**	25/1	17	—
5008^{2}	**Anglesey Sea View (56)** (ABailey) **7-9-5**$^{(5)}$ GFaulkner(5) (a.p: led 10f out to 7f out: wknd over 4f out)	4	**10**	6/1^{3}	33	8
5136^{6}	**Greek Night Out (IRE) (47)** (JLEyre) **5-9-1** RLappin(11) (bhd fnl 7f)	19	**11**	14/1	5	—
5136*	**Compass Pointer (65)** (JMPEustace) **3-9-6**$^{(5)}$ MartinDwyer(3) (hld up: rdn over 6f out: 8th & wkng whn stumbled & uns rdr over 3f out)		**U**	6/1^{3}	—	—
				(SP 126.4%)		**12 Rn**

3m 28.2 (7.20) CSF £44.31 CT £210.12 TOTE £16.00: £2.00 £1.70 £3.20 (£27.80) Trio £123.00 OWNER Dream On Racing Partnership (EPSOM) BRED Arthur Sims

LONG HANDICAP Aydigo 7-9

WEIGHT FOR AGE 3yo-8lb

5214 SELMA MEDIAN AUCTION MAIDEN STKS (2-Y.O) (Class F)

3-10 (3-13) **7f** **(Equitrack)** £2,588.40 (£727.40: £355.20) Stalls: Low GOING minus 0.46 sec per fur (FST)

				SP	RR	SF
5121^{2}	**Millroy (USA) (79)** (PAKelleway) **2-9-0** MWigham(4) (b.hind: lw: a.p: rdn over 3f out: led over 2f out: r.o wl)	—	**1**	10/11^{1}	83	23
4916^{10}	**Bold Spring (IRE) (74)** (RHannon) **2-9-0** RPerham(6) (led over 3f: ev ch over 2f out: unable qckn)	2	**2**	7/1	78	18
5147^{2}	**Castles Burning (USA) (67)** (CACyzer) **2-9-0** AClark(8) (s.s: hdwy over 5f out: led over 3f out tl over 2f out: one pce)	1½	**3**	6/1^{3}	75	15
4883^{13}	**Windborn (56)** (CNAllen) **2-8-9** JQuinn(1) (nt clr run 5f out: hdwy over 3f out: one pce)	8	**4**	20/1	52	—
5040^{10}	**Mogul** (NAGraham) **2-9-0** AMcGlone(3) (nvr nr to chal)	1½	**5**	20/1	53	—
5142^{9}	**Saeko-Beauty** (SirMarkPrescott) **2-8-9** GDuffield(2) (lw: hld up: rdn over 4f out: wknd over 3f out)	hd	**6**	7/2^{2}	48	—
4380^{13}	**Buzzby Babe** (AGFoster) **2-8-9** TSprake(5) (b: b.hind: a bhd)	2½	**7**	33/1	42	—
5187^{11}	**She's Electric** (JJBridger) **2-8-9** FNorton(7) (lw: prom over 2f)	9	**8**	50/1	22	—
				(SP 115.8%)		**8 Rn**

1m 27.14 (2.74) CSF £7.82 TOTE £1.80: £1.70 £1.70 £1.10 (£6.40) OWNER Exors of the late Mr R B Belderson (NEWMARKET) BRED Cilia Farm

5215 LADBROKE ALL-WEATHER TROPHY (QUALIFIER) H'CAP (0-70) (II) (3-Y.O+) (Class E)

3-40 (3-42) **7f** **(Equitrack)** £2,643.35 (£798.80: £388.90: £183.95) Stalls: Low GOING minus 0.46 sec per fur (FST)

				SP	RR	SF
5186^{6}	**Greatest (70)** (MissGayKelleway) **5-10-0b** DHolland(9) (b: b.hind: led 5f: rdn over 1f out: led ins fnl f: r.o wl)	—	**1**	5/1^{2}	77	49
5188^{5}	**Dark Menace (43)** (EAWheeler) **4-7-10b**$^{(5)}$ ADaly(8) (a.p: chsd ldr over 4f out: led 2f out tl ins fnl f: r.o l)	s.h	**2**	14/1	50	22
5152^{4}	**Hawaii Storm (FR) (50)** (DJSffrenchDavis) **8-8-5**$^{(3)}$ PMcCabe(12) (b.hind: rdn & hdwy over 3f out: r.o one pce)	8	**3**	6/1^{3}	39	11
4784^{5}	**Morning Surprise (46)** (APJarvis) **3-8-4** SDrowne(10) (hdwy over 3f out: rdn over 2f out: one pce)	3	**4**	12/1	28	—
4921^{13}	**Waypoint (70)** (RCharlton) **3-10-0** TSprake(2) (a.p: rdn over 3f out: wknd over 2f out)	2	**5**	5/1^{2}	47	19
5179^{6}	**Polar Refrain (45)** (CADwyer) **3-7-10**$^{(7)ow1}$ JoHunnam(5) (nvr nr to chal)	2	**6**	14/1	18	—
5165*	**The Barnsley Belle (IRE) (55)** (JLEyre) **3-8-13** RLappin(4) (lw: nvr nrr)	3½	**7**	9/2^{1}	20	—
4820^{11}	**Jaazim (47)** (MMadgwick) **6-8-5**^{ow1} AClark(7) (lw: prom 2f)	s.h	**8**	12/1	12	—
5144^{11}	**Al Shaati (FR) (38)** (RJO'Sullivan) **6-7-10** JQuinn(3) (prom 2f)	¾	**9**	9/1	1	—
5183^{4}	**Logie Pert Lad (38)** (JJBridger) **4-7-10** FNorton(11) (lw: prom over 4f)	4	**10**	33/1	—	—
5134^{8}	**Statistician (61)** (JohnBerry) **4-9-5b** GDuffield(6) (prom 3f)	1½	**11**	8/1	11	—
5089^{6}	**Perilous Plight (65)** (MrsLStubbs) **5-9-9** SWhitworth(1) (b.hind: lw: a bhd)	3	**12**	6/1^{3}	8	—
				(SP 132.9%)		**12 Rn**

1m 26.0 (1.60) CSF £72.64 CT £412.43 TOTE £6.10: £2.00 £9.90 £2.50 (£100.00) Trio £168.90 OWNER Invoshire Ltd (WHITCOMBE) BRED Bloomsbury Stud

LONG HANDICAP Logie Pert Lad 7-2 Al Shaati (FR) 7-4

T/Plpt: £130.30 (66.28 Tckts). T/Qdpt: £7.70 (147.95 Tckts). AK

5194a-EVRY (France) (R-H) (Holding)
Tuesday December 3rd

5216a PRIX EDELLIC (Listed) (4-Y.O+)
2-40 (2-37) **1m 2f** £18,445.00 (£6,324.00: £3,953.00)

				SP	RR	SF
4874*	**Wilcuma** (PJMakin) **5-8-11** JReid	—	1		115	—
5022a^{2}	**Le Conquet (FR)** (ADeMoussac,France) **8-8-11** CTellier	4	2		109	—
	Callisthene (FR) (J-PGauvin,France) **4-8-11** EAntoinat	5	3		101	—

9 Rn

2m 17.75 (14.75) P-M 3.50F: 2.10F 2.20F 3.00F (16.10F) OWNER Mr T. G. Warner (MARLBOROUGH) BRED Red House Stud
IN-FOCUS: **This was the final day's racing at Evry, which has been closed for financial reasons.**
4874* Wilcuma moved reasonably well on this holding ground and took the lead entering the final furlong. He quickened clear to win easily and, as he stays in training next year, he may well return to France for similar events.

0724a-SHA TIN (Hong Kong) (R-H) (Good to firm)
Sunday December 8th

5217a HONG KONG INTERNATIONAL VASE (Gp 2) (3-Y.O+)
6-40 (6-40) **1m 4f** £290,000.00 (£110,000.00: £50,000.00) GOING minus 0.44 sec per fur (F)

				SP	RR	SF
4413a^{4}	**Luso** (CEBrittain) **4-9-5** LDettori	—	1		130	99
	Royal Snack (AUS) (GHanlon,Australia) **8-9-2** DOliver	1½	2		125	94
724a^{3}	**Privilege (IRE)** (IAllan,HongKong) **5-9-0v^{1}** BMarcus	2¾	3		119	88
4747a^{2}	**Sacrament** (MRStoute) **5-9-2** GaryStevens (btn approx 7 3/4l)		8		—	—

14 Rn

2m 26.1 (-4.50) TOTE 31.00: 16.00 40.50 36.00 (247.00) OWNER Mr Saeed Manana (NEWMARKET) BRED Saeed Manana
4413a Luso won this in superb style. Never more than a couple of lengths off the pace, Dettori only needed to shake him up vigorously to see him draw clear approaching the final furlong. He loves fast ground and may remain in training next year.
4747a Sacrament made good headway to breath down the leader's neck with a mile to run, but found little when Stevens pressed the button in the straight. He is better with some cut in the ground.

5218a HONG KONG INTERNATIONAL BOWL (Gp 2) (3-Y.O+)
7-20 (7-20) **7f** £290,000.00 (£110,000.00: £50,000.00: £23,500.00) GOING minus 0.44 sec per fur (F)

				SP	RR	SF
	Monopolize (AUS) (GBegg,Australia) **6-9-2** DBeadman	—	1		121	86
	Dojima Muteki (JPN) (HMori,Japan) **6-9-0** YMuramoto	s.h	2		119	84
	Michael's Choice (USA) (PLBiancone,HongKong) **4-9-0** ELegrix	1	3		117	82
4857a^{5}	**Tagula (IRE)** (IABalding) **3-9-4** LDettori	nk	4		120	85

13 Rn

1m 22.0 (-1.80) TOTE 60.50: 21.00 33.00 17.00 (344.00) OWNER N Begg & Partners Syndicate
4857a Tagula (IRE) was drawn thirteen of fourteen and would have gone close with an inside berth. Allowed to drop out three lengths last at the start, he came with a strong run through the field to get to within a length of the lead inside the final furlong, before his effort petered out.

5219a HONG KONG INTERNATIONAL CUP (Gp 2) (3-Y.O+)
8-30 (8-30) **1m 1f** £314,617.00 (£119,167.00: £54,167.00) GOING minus 0.44 sec per fur (F)

				SP	RR	SF
4773^{5}	**First Island (IRE)** (GWragg) **4-9-5** MHills	—	1		126+	87
	Seascay (NZ) (PHayes,Australia) **6-9-5b^{1}** DOliver	¾	2		125	86
	Kingston Bay (NZ) (BWallace,NewZealand) **7-9-5b^{1}** PTims	½	3		124	85
5073a^{3}	**Needle Gun (IRE)** (CEBrittain) **6-9-2** LDettori (btn approx 4 3/4l)		7		—	—

12 Rn

1m 48.2 (-2.10) TOTE 28.00: 17.00 36.50 78.50 (135.00) OWNER Mollers Racing (NEWMARKET) BRED Citadel Stud
4773 First Island (IRE) came round the entire field and, despite edging right, produced a sparkling turn of foot to scoot more than two lengths clear soon after the furlong pole. Seascay cut into his lead in the final one hundred yards, but the winner may just have been idling. This was a wonderful training performance as he has been on the go since January. He is to race on in 1997.
5073a Needle Gun (IRE) always held a prominent pitch. Rousted along into the straight, he looked beaten when snatched up by Dettori a furlong and a half from home. He kept on again afterwards, but is better over a longer trip.

5208-LINGFIELD (L-H) (Standard)
Friday December 13th
WEATHER: cold & damp WIND: slt half against

5220 KERSTEN PROMOTIONS H'CAP (0-70) (I) (3-Y.O+) (Class E)
11-25 (11-25) **5f** **(Equitrack)** £2,534.15 (£765.20: £372.10: £175.55) Stalls: High GOING minus 0.26 sec per fur (FST)

				SP	RR	SF
5131^{4}	**Master of Passion (65)** (JMPEustace) **7-9-4**$^{(7)}$ DSweeney(10) (b.nr hind: led over 2f: led ins fnl f: rdn out)	—	1	7/2^{1}	70	28
4995^{7}	**Sally Slade (68)** (CACyzer) **4-10-0** DBiggs(6) (outpcd: gd hdwy over 2f out: r.o)	1¼	2	5/1^{3}	69	27
5183^{5}	**Miss Aragon (38)** (MissLCSiddall) **8-7-12** NCarlisle(1) (a.p: led over 2f out tl ins fnl f: unable qckn)	s.h	3	15/2	39	—
5161^{14}	**Cheeky Chappy (60)** (DWChapman) **5-9-6b** ACulhane(9) (rdn thrght: a.p: 4th & btn whn n.m.r ins fnl f)	2	4	5/1^{3}	54	12
5184^{8}	**Windrush Boy (50)** (JRBosley) **6-8-10** CRutter(5) (nvr nr to chal)	3	5	20/1	35	—
4372^{14}	**Ashkernazy (IRE) (50)** (NEBerry) **5-8-10** NAdams(4) (a.p: rdn over 2f out: wknd over 1f out)	¾	6	7/1	32	—
5144^{12}	**She's a Madam (37)** (LRLloyd-James) **5-7-11b**^{ow1} JQuinn(3) (a bhd)	2½	7	50/1	11	—
5183^{13}	**Distant Dynasty (39)** (BAPearce) **6-7-13b** DeclanO'Shea(2) (hdwy on ins wl over 1f out: sn wknd)	1¾	8	25/1	8	—
5096^{6}	**Bashful Brave (47)** (BPJBaugh) **5-8-7** RPerham(7) (prom 3f)	1	9	4/1^{2}	13	—

				SP	RR	SF
5178^{9}	**Avant Huit (42)** (MrsNMacauley) **4-7-9b**(7)ow3 JoHunnam(8) (lw: bhd fnl 2f)	1¾	**10**	33/1	2	—
				(SP 113.3%)	**10 Rn**	

61.39 secs (3.19) CSF £19.49 CT £112.77 TOTE £3.80: £1.10 £2.00 £1.50 (£11.30) Trio £11.60 OWNER Mr & Mrs Michael Kwee (NEWMARKET) BRED Stratford Place Stud
LONG HANDICAP She's a Madam 7-6
IN-FOCUS: This looked a poor race.

5221 LADBROKE ALL-WEATHER TROPHY (QUALIFIER) H'CAP (0-70) (I) (3-Y.O+) (Class E)
11-55 (11-56) **1m (Equitrack)** £2,616.05 (£790.40: £384.70: £181.85) Stalls: High GOING minus 0.26 sec per fur (FST)

				SP	RR	SF
4829^{7}	**Shanghai Lil (40)** (MJFetherston-Godley) **4-7-12** FNorton(12) (hld up: rdn over 2f out: led ins fnl f: r.o wl)	—	**1**	14/1	51	33
5206^{13}	**Tissue of Lies (USA) (70)** (MJohnston) **3-9-13** DeanMcKeown(8) (rdn thrght: hdwy over 4f out: r.o ins fnl f)	2	**2**	6/1^{3}	77	58
3583^{8}	**Royal Carlton (IRE) (51)** (GLMoore) **4-8-9**ow1 SWhitworth(11) (a.p: rdn 2f out: r.o ins fnl f)	nk	**3**	20/1	57	38
5182^{4}	**Barbason (55)** (AMoore) **4-8-13** CandyMorris(10) (b.hind: a.p: rdn over 1f out: unable qckn)	s.h	**4**	5/1^{2}	61	43
5002^{4}	**Ertlon (67)** (CEBrittain) **6-9-11** MRoberts(2) (lw: led tl ins fnl f: sn wknd)	2	**5**	2/1^{1}	69	51
5186^{5}	**Mr Rough (53)** (DMorris) **5-8-11** SSanders(1) (hld up: rdn over 4f out: wknd wl over 1f out)	1¼	**6**	6/1^{3}	53	35
4975^{18}	**Double March (65)** (PRWebber) **3-9-8** RPerham(9) (lw: a.p: rdn over 2f out: wknd wl over 1f out)	hd	**7**	25/1	65	46
5081^{6}	**Premier League (IRE) (40)** (JELong) **6-7-12**ow2 NCarlisle(7) (bhd fnl 6f)	1¼	**8**	16/1	37	17
5152^{3}	**Zahran (IRE) (45)** (JMBradley) **5-8-3** SDrowne(6) (b: lw: dwlt: rdn 5f out: sme hdwy over 3f out: wknd over 2f out)	2	**9**	15/2	38	20
	Jubilee Scholar (IRE) (70) (KMcAuliffe) **3-9-13** MTebbutt(5) (bhd fnl 4f)	10	**10**	20/1	43	24
5151^{12}	**Time For Tea (IRE) (52)** (CACyzer) **3-8-9** AMcGlone(3) (a bhd)	½	**11**	25/1	24	5
5188^{11}	**Press Again (44)** (PHayward) **4-8-2** CRutter(4) (bhd fnl 7f)	6	**12**	40/1	4	—
				(SP 122.5%)	**12 Rn**	

1m 40.2 (2.80) CSF £91.21 CT £1,559.91 TOTE £23.80: £4.00 £1.70 £8.70 (£73.00) Trio £180.60; £178.06 to Haydock 14/12/96 OWNER George & Dragon Racing (EAST ILSLEY) BRED Highfield Stud Ltd
LONG HANDICAP Premier League (IRE) 7-9
WEIGHT FOR AGE 3yo-1lb

5222 COLD AS CHARITY H'CAP (0-70) (3-Y.O+) (Class E)
12-25 (12-27) **1m 5f (Equitrack)** £2,927.40 (£886.20: £432.60: £205.80) Stalls: Low GOING minus 0.26 sec per fur (FST)

				SP	RR	SF
5088^{4}	**Mujtahida (IRE) (51)** (RWArmstrong) **3-8-6** MRoberts(6) (hdwy over 3f out: led over 2f out: sn clr: comf)	—	**1**	14/1	57+	31
5189^{2}	**General Haven (69)** (TJNaughton) **3-9-7**(3) FLynch(2) (lost pl over 8f out: rallied over 3f out: chsd wnr over 1f out: r.o)	3	**2**	11/2^{2}	71	45
5053^{2}	**Nothing Doing (IRE) (37)** (WJMusson) **7-7-12** DeclanO'Shea(9) (hdwy over 3f out: one pce fnl 2f)	5	**3**	10/1	33	13
5167^{7}	**Claque (51)** (DWChapman) **4-8-12b** ACulhane(1) (a.p: rdn over 4f out: one pce)	2½	**4**	12/1	44	24
4302^{11}	**Philmist (52)** (CWCElsey) **4-8-13b** NKennedy(7) (hld up: chsd wnr over 2f out tl over 1f out: sn wknd)	¾	**5**	20/1	44	24
5167^{2}	**Our Main Man (50)** (RMWhitaker) **6-8-11** DeanMcKeown(10) (lw: a.p: led 4f out tl over 2f out: sn wknd)	hd	**6**	6/1^{3}	42	22
5053^{17}	**Etoile du Nord (36)** (HJCollingridge) **4-7-11**ow1 JQuinn(12) (b: hdwy over 3f out: wknd over 2f out)	3½	**7**	50/1	24	3
5148^{5}	**Rowlandsons Charm (IRE) (58)** (MissBSanders) **3-8-13v** SSanders(5) (lw: led 9f)	½	**8**	16/1	45	19
5149^{*}	**Persian Conquest (IRE) (67)** (RIngram) **4-10-0b** AMcGlone(3) (lw: w ldr over 8f)	s.h	**9**	10/1	54	34
5185^{4}	**Suitor (47)** (SDow) **3-7-11**(5) ADaly(11) (prom over 10f)	s.h	**10**	14/1	34	8
5123^{4}	**Myfontaine (58)** (KTIvory) **9-9-5** CScally(4) (b: b.hind: a bhd)	5	**11**	9/1	39	19
5148^{2}	**Basood (USA) (54)** (SPCWoods) **3-8-9hb** DBiggs(8) (prom 10f)	11	**12**	4/1^{1}	21	—
1661^{7}	**Considerable Charm (43)** (AMoore) **4-8-4**ow2 CandyMorris(14) (b.hind: bhd fnl 5f)	10	**13**	33/1	—	—
1488^{7}	**Brave Spy (52)** (CACyzer) **5-8-13** SDrowne(13) (bhd fnl 5f)	1½	**14**	25/1	5	—
				(SP 118.3%)	**14 Rn**	

2m 49.62 (7.62) CSF £81.40 CT £746.57 TOTE £13.40: £3.20 £2.40 £4.50 (£29.00) Trio £190.10; £241.07 to Haydock 14/12/96 OWNER Mr K. Hsu (NEWMARKET) BRED Gay O'Callaghan
LONG HANDICAP Etoile du Nord 7-3
WEIGHT FOR AGE 3yo-6lb
OFFICIAL EXPLANATION Basood (USA): was reluctant to race when getting crowded.

5223 APPLE A DAY APPRENTICE LIMITED STKS (0-60) (3-Y.O+) (Class F)
1-00 (1-00) **1m 2f (Equitrack)** £2,398.00 (£673.00: £328.00) Stalls: Low GOING minus 0.26 sec per fur (FST)

				SP	RR	SF
5094^{4}	**Absolutelystunning (46)** (MrsBarbaraWaring) **3-8-1**(3) PPMurphy(4) (b: b.hind: a.p: led over 3f out: clr over 2f out: hrd rdn over 1f out: r.o wl)	—	**1**	7/1	59	27
5123^{3}	**Father Dan (IRE) (58)** (MissGayKelleway) **7-8-5**(5) DSweeney(14) (b: b.hind: lw: stdy hdwy over 3f out: chsd wnr fnl 2f: r.o wl)	hd	**2**	2/1^{1}	62	33
5118^{8}	**Zahid (USA) (59)** (KRBurke) **5-8-7**(3) RPainter(8) (lw: hdwy over 4f out: 5th whn nt clr run over 2f out: unable qckn)	8	**3**	7/2^{2}	49	20
5179^{8}	**Sheraz (IRE) (58)** (NTinkler) **4-8-5**(5) JoHunnam(3) (hdwy over 1f out: nvr nrr)	¾	**4**	16/1	48	19
5003^{7}	**Can Can Charlie (60)** (JPearce) **6-8-10** FLynch(9) (hld up: rdn 4f out: one pce)	½	**5**	11/2^{3}	47	18
5132^{2}	**Manabar (60)** (MJPolglase) **4-8-10** MBaird(10) (reluctant to r: wl bhd over 4f: gd hdwy over 3f out: wknd over 2f out)	½	**6**	11/2^{3}	46	17
5149^{6}	**Eastleigh (41)** (RHollinshead) **7-8-3**(7) LisaWatson(1) (lw: nvr nr to chal)	½	**7**	16/1	45	16
5122^{6}	**Commin' Up (55)** (JWHills) **3-7-11**(7) AMcCarthy(6) (a.p: chsd wnr over 3f out to 2f out: sn wknd)	4	**8**	14/1	36	4
4986^{10}	**Nawaji (USA) (43)** (WRMuir) **3-8-3**(5)ow4 JWilkinson(12) (prom 5f)	½	**9**	25/1	39	3
4422^{8}	**Queens Fancy (30)** (SDow) **3-7-11**(7) DSalt(2) (bhd fnl 8f)	½	**10**	50/1	34	2
5208^{7}	**Kirov Protege (IRE) (40)** (MrsLCJewell) **4-8-3**(7) DarrenWilliams(5) (bhd fnl 6f)	4	**11**	33/1	31	2
5003^{8}	**She Said No (46)** (AMoore) **4-8-0**(7) TField(7) (b.hind: bhd fnl 4f)	2½	**12**	25/1	24	—
5081^{7}	**Kissavos (34)** (BJMeehan) **10-8-5e**(7)ow2 GHannon(13) (b.hind: led over 7f out tl over 3f out: sn wknd)	s.h	**13**	33/1	29	—
5058^{9}	**Bianca Cappello (IRE) (30)** (PSFelgate) **3-8-4b** DWright(11) (led over 2f: wknd over 3f out)	13	**14**	33/1	3	—
				(SP 135.7%)	**14 Rn**	

2m 9.39 (5.09) CSF £22.82 TOTE £8.40: £2.20 £1.20 £2.00 (£12.50) Trio £25.80 OWNER Miss Simmons Andrews Gibbs (CHIPPENHAM) BRED Mrs A. Plummer
WEIGHT FOR AGE 3yo-3lb

5224 GIFT HORSE NURSERY H'CAP (0-75) (2-Y.O) (Class E)

1-35 (1-36) **6f (Equitrack)** £2,995.65 (£907.20: £443.10: £211.05) Stalls: Low GOING minus 0.26 sec per fur (FST)

Form	Horse	Dist	Pos	SP	RR	SF
*5146**	**Kilcullen Lad (IRE) (70)** (PMooney) **2-9-3v** DRMcCabe(2) (lw: hdwy wl over 1f out: hrd rdn: led ins fnl f: r.o wl)	—	1	7/2[1]	75	31
5176[3]	**The Wyandotte Inn (65)** (RHollinshead) **2-8-9**(3) FLynch(9) (outpcd: hdwy wl over 1f out: ev ch ins fnl f: r.o wl)	hd	2	14/1	70	26
5214[2]	**Bold Spring (IRE) (74)** (RHannon) **2-9-7** RPerham(8) (hld up: rdn 4f out: r.o ins fnl f)	1¼	3	9/1	75	31
5164[3]	**Sharp Return (60)** (MJRyan) **2-8-4**(3) MBaird(6) (led 5f out tl ins fnl f: unable qckn)	nk	4	13/2[3]	61	17
5113[4]	**Merciless Cop (66)** (BJMeehan) **2-8-13b** MTebbutt(1) (lw: outpcd: hdwy over 1f out: r.o)	1¼	5	11/2[2]	63	19
5176[2]	**Threeplay (IRE) (62)** (JAkehurst) **2-8-9** DBiggs(3) (b: a.p: rdn over 2f out: ev ch ins fnl f: sn wknd)	¾	6	13/2[3]	57	13
4762[11]	**Hever Golf Mover (63)** (TJNaughton) **2-8-10** TSprake(5) (b.nr hind: nvr nrr)	7	7	20/1	40	—
4786[12]	**Little Progress (52)** (TMJones) **2-7-13** NCarlisle(12) (a.p: rdn over 2f out: wkng whn hmpd wl over 1f out)	2	8	33/1	23	—
4803[11]	**Eager To Please (72)** (MissGayKelleway) **2-8-12**(7) BFord(4) (b: b.hind: lw: spd 4f)	¾	9	16/1	41	—
4425[5]	**Tear White (IRE) (73)** (TGMills) **2-9-6b** SSanders(11) (spd over 4f)	¾	10	20/1	40	—
5146[3]	**Seretse's Nephew (58)** (SCWilliams) **2-8-5** DWright(7) (led 1f: wkng whn hmpd wl over 1f out)	1	11	11/2[2]	23	—
4916[5]	**Heavenly Miss (IRE) (68)** (JJBridger) **2-9-1** MRoberts(10) (bhd fnl 5f: t.o fnl 4f)	8	12	14/1	11	—

(SP 121.3%) **12 Rn**

1m 14.04 (2.94) CSF £47.83 CT £386.90 TOTE £3.10: £1.50 £3.10 £2.80 (£29.60) Trio £50.60 OWNER Mr George Tobitt (ASTON UPTHORPE) BRED S. W. D. McIlveen

5225 KERSTEN PROMOTIONS H'CAP (0-70) (II) (3-Y.O+) (Class E)

2-10 (2-11) **5f (Equitrack)** £2,534.15 (£765.20: £372.10: £175.55) Stalls: High GOING minus 0.26 sec per fur (FST)

Form	Horse	Dist	Pos	SP	RR	SF
5150[11]	**Mijas (59)** (LMontagueHall) **3-9-5** MRoberts(1) (mde all: clr over 1f out: comf)	—	1	8/1	71+	38
5184[3]	**Napier Star (65)** (MrsNMacauley) **3-9-8v**(3) CTeague(9) (b.off hind: a.p: rdn over 2f out: chsd wnr ins fnl f: no imp)	4	2	11/4[2]	64	31
5184[7]	**Featherstone Lane (64)** (MissLCSiddall) **5-9-10v** DRMcCabe(10) (hdwy over 1f out: r.o wl ins fnl f)	s.h	3	7/1[3]	63	30
5184[2]	**Kalar (68)** (DWChapman) **7-10-0b** ACulhane(6) (s.s: hdwy over 2f out: rdn over 1f out: one pce)	2	4	9/4[1]	61	28
1971[4]	**Daaniera (IRE) (37)** (PHowling) **6-7-11v**ow1 JQuinn(8) (b.hind: lw: chsd wnr tl ins fnl f: sn wknd)	1	5	10/1	26	—
5173[10]	**General Equation (47)** (JBalding) **3-8-7** SDrowne(5) (a.p: hrd rdn over 1f out: wknd fnl f)	¾	6	25/1	34	1
5131[14]	**Silk Cottage (57)** (RMWhitaker) **4-9-3v** DeanMcKeown(2) (rdn thrght: prom 4f)	½	7	10/1	42	9
5130[13]	**Rennyholme (55)** (JHetherton) **5-9-1b** NAdams(4) (prom 3f)	hd	8	12/1	40	7
4610[19]	**Sotonian (HOL) (36)** (PSFelgate) **3-7-10b** DWright(7) (bhd fnl 2f)	2½	9	33/1	13	—
5210[14]	**Dancing Jack (57)** (JJBridger) **3-9-3** SSanders(3) (lw: a bhd)	11	10	20/1	—	—

(SP 118.5%) **10 Rn**

60.48 secs (2.28) CSF £29.22 CT £155.46 TOTE £8.50: £2.30 £1.50 £2.50 (£18.70) Trio £25.00 OWNER The Mijas Partnership (EPSOM) BRED Roldvale Ltd

LONG HANDICAP Daaniera (IRE) 7-8

OFFICIAL EXPLANATION **Mijas: regarding the apparent improvement in form, the trainer reported that the filly's rating had dropped and that he was surprised by the ease of the victory.**

5226 ANY PORT MAIDEN AUCTION STKS (2-Y.O) (Class F)

2-45 (2-46) **7f (Equitrack)** £2,398.00 (£673.00: £328.00) Stalls: Low GOING minus 0.26 sec per fur (FST)

Form	Horse	Dist	Pos	SP	RR	SF
5111[W]	**Supreme Maimoon** (MJPolglase) **2-8-6**ow3 TGMcLaughlin(1) (lw: hld up: rdn over 2f out: led over 1f out: r.o wl)	—	1	3/1[1]	73+	29
4777[8]	**Hever Golf Lover (IRE) (50)** (TJNaughton) **2-8-3**ow2 TSprake(8) (lw: a.p: led over 2f out tl over 1f out: unable qckn)	4	2	20/1	61	18
5202[11]	**Hallmark (IRE) (62)** (RHannon) **2-8-9** MRoberts(6) (w ldr: led over 3f out tl over 2f out: sn wknd)	4	3	7/2[3]	58	17
5142[7]	**Sidney The Kidney** (MJRyan) **2-7-5**(7) AMcCarthy(3) (nvr nr to chal)	3	4	100/30[2]	40	—
5168[5]	**Hoh Down (IRE)** (KMcAuliffe) **2-8-4**ow3 SSanders(2) (b.hind: led over 3f)	2½	5	20/1	40	—
5187[10]	**Formidable Spirit** (MJHeaton-Ellis) **2-8-6** SDrowne(5) (lw: bhd fnl 3f)	7	6	20/1	26	—
5180[2]	**Royal Roulette (54)** (SPCWoods) **2-7-12b** CRutter(7) (lw: rdn & sme hdwy over 3f out: sn wknd)	2	7	3/1[1]	14	—
4493[7]	**Dozen Roses (45)** (TMJones) **2-7-12b** NCarlisle(4) (bhd fnl 5f)	4	8	14/1	4	—

(SP 116.3%) **8 Rn**

1m 27.4 (3.00) CSF £48.34 TOTE £4.20: £1.30 £5.70 £2.00 (£36.00) OWNER Mr Nilesh Unadkat (NEWMARKET) BRED Godolphin Management Co Ltd

5227 LADBROKE ALL-WEATHER TROPHY (QUALIFIER) H'CAP (0-70) (II) (3-Y.O+) (Class E)

3-15 (3-15) **1m (Equitrack)** £2,602.40 (£786.20: £382.60: £180.80) Stalls: High GOING minus 0.26 sec per fur (FST)

Form	Horse	Dist	Pos	SP	RR	SF
5095[2]	**Soaking (66)** (PBurgoyne) **6-9-10** DRMcCabe(10) (hld up: led over 2f out: clr over 1f out: r.o wl)	—	1	5/1[3]	80	60
5186[3]	**Barossa Valley (IRE) (70)** (PButler) **5-9-7**(7) DSweeney(6) (a.p: led 4f out tl over 2f out: unable qckn)	5	2	13/2	74	54
5151[6]	**Errant (59)** (DJSCosgrove) **4-9-3** JQuinn(3) (b: gd hdwy over 1f out: r.o wl ins fnl f)	hd	3	10/1	63	43
4915[6]	**Sea Danzig (65)** (JJBridger) **3-9-8** SSanders(5) (lw: led over 6f out to 4f out: rdn over 3f out: wknd over 1f out)	3½	4	9/1	62	41
5151[2]	**Sooty Tern (53)** (JMBradley) **9-8-11** SDrowne(7) (led over 1f: rdn & ev ch over 2f out: sn wknd)	1¼	5	2/1[1]	47	27
*5130**	**Shontaine (62)** (MJohnston) **3-8-12**(7) KSked(11) (hdwy over 3f out: wknd 2f out)	s.h	6	4/1[2]	56	35
4898[11]	**Ajkuit (IRE) (47)** (JJSheehan) **3-8-4** AMorris(4) (b: a bhd)	2	7	33/1	37	16
1844[12]	**Little Pilgrim (42)** (TMJones) **3-7-13** NCarlisle(2) (lw: prom 4f)	10	8	50/1	12	—
	Brecon (67) (WRMuir) **3-9-7**(3) FLynch(9) (bhd fnl 5f)	6	9	8/1	25	4

(SP 118.4%) **9 Rn**

1m 39.93 (2.53) CSF £35.22 CT £290.93 TOTE £8.00: £2.10 £2.20 £3.20 (£16.00) Trio £31.00 OWNER Mr Philip Saunders (LAMBOURN) BRED David John Brown

WEIGHT FOR AGE 3yo-1lb

T/Plpt: £769.40 (11.88 Tckts). T/Qdpt: £22.80 (60.03 Tckts). AK

5200-WOLVERHAMPTON (L-H) (Standard)

Saturday December 14th

WEATHER: dry & cold WIND: nil

5228 MEASURE FOR MEASURE MAIDEN STKS (2-Y.O) (Class D)

7-00 (7-01) **1m 100y (Fibresand)** £2,892.00 (£876.00: £428.00: £204.00) Stalls: Low GOING: 0.43 sec per fur (SLW)

Form	Horse	Dist	Pos	SP	RR	SF
	No More Pressure (IRE) (NJHWalker) **2-9-0** JStack(1) (w'like: scope: mde all: hrd drvn fnl f: hld on gamely)	—	1	33/1	84	40
	Enlisted (IRE) (SirMarkPrescott) **2-8-9** GDuffield(3) (w'like: bit bkwd: trckd ldrs: effrt 2f out: rdn & r.o wl fnl f)	hd	2	8/1	79	35
5142[2]	**Superbelle (79)** (MAJarvis) **2-8-9** EmmaO'Gorman(9) (hld up in tch: effrt 3f out: rdn & swtchd lft fnl f: nt pce to chal)	2½	3	6/4[1]	74	30
5113[2]	**Effervescence (78)** (RHannon) **2-9-0** DBiggs(10) (hld up: gd hdwy over 3f out: ev ch wl over 1f out: rdn & one pce fnl f)	½	4	5/1[2]	78	34
5142[5]	**Double Crest (IRE)** (MJohnston) **2-8-9** JFanning(8) (a.p: ev ch wl over 1f out: no ex appr fnl f)	3	5	12/1	68	24
5201[4]	**Snow Eagle (IRE) (59)** (RHannon) **2-8-9** DaneO'Neill(4) (prom: rdn & ev ch 2f out: wknd qckly)	8	6	12/1	52	8
4261[11]	**Baaheth (USA)** (SCWilliams) **2-9-0** DWright(11) (bkwd: s.i.s: hdwy 5f out: sn hrd drvn: no imp)	3	7	10/1	52	8
4370[10]	**Bentnose** (DMorris) **2-9-0** SSanders(6) (bit bkwd: chsd ldrs over 5f)	2	8	13/2[3]	48	4
4072[4]	**Jack The Lad (IRE) (71)** (JHetherton) **2-9-0** SWhitworth(5) (bkwd: chsd ldrs over 4f: sn lost tch: t.o)	9	9	20/1	31	—
5168[9]	**Eternal Host (IRE)** (RHollinshead) **2-8-11**(3) FLynch(2) (drvn along & outpcd 5f out: sn bhd: t.o)	10	10	33/1	12	—
	Just Rachel (SEKettlewell) **2-8-2**(7) JennyBenson(7) (lt-f: bkwd: s.s: a bhd: t.o)	½	11	33/1	6	—
5090[9]	**Macaroni Beach** (CEBrittain) **2-8-9** CRutter(12) (a in rr: t.o fnl 3f)	nk	12	25/1	5	—
				(SP 123.0%)		**12 Rn**

1m 54.7 (9.70) CSF £257.81 TOTE £30.30: £8.40 £2.80 £3.40 (£140.90) Trio £53.00; £37.37 to 16/12/96 OWNER Mr Paul Green (BLEWBURY) BRED Paul Green

5229 WINTER'S TALE CONDITIONS STKS (2-Y.O) (Class D)

7-30 (7-30) **7f (Fibresand)** £2,788.00 (£844.00: £412.00: £196.00) Stalls: High GOING: 0.43 sec per fur (SLW)

Form	Horse	Dist	Pos	SP	RR	SF
5146[2]	**Just Loui (76)** (WGMTurner) **2-8-11** TSprake(2) (mde all: qcknd 2f out: wknd fnl f: jst hld on)	—	1	9/1[3]	84	23
4723[25]	**Foot Battalion (IRE) (88)** (RHollinshead) **2-8-11**(3) FLynch(5) (sn wl bhd & drvn along: rapid hdwy on outside appr fnl f: jst failed)	nk	2	16/1	86	25
5113[3]	**Nomore Mr Niceguy (78)** (EJAlston) **2-9-0** SSanders(4) (a.p: rdn & outpcd 2f out: rallied u.p fnl f)	1¼	3	10/1	84	23
*4976**	**Trailblazer (83)** (CWThornton) **2-9-0** JQuinn(3) (lw: prom: pushed along 2f out: unable qckn ins fnl f)	1	4	5/2[2]	81	20
*5133**	**Arapi (IRE) (85)** (SirMarkPrescott) **2-9-0** GDuffield(1) (chsd wnr: outpcd & pushed along over 2f out: sn lost tch: t.o)	12	5	4/5[1]	54	—
4494[10]	**State of Gold (IRE) (67)** (JHetherton) **2-8-11** SWhitworth(6) (s.i.s: sn drvn along: a bhd & outpcd: t.o)	10	6	50/1	28	—
				(SP 111.1%)		**6 Rn**

1m 33.9 (9.20) CSF £94.64 TOTE £6.80: £3.20 £4.10 (£47.70) OWNER Mr A. Poole (SHERBORNE) BRED M. A. Poole

OFFICIAL EXPLANATION **Arapi (IRE): was not travelling in the latter stages and may have been feeling her legs.**

5230 AS YOU LIKE IT H'CAP (0-70) (3-Y.O+) (Class E)

8-00 (8-01) **6f (Fibresand)** £2,671.00 (£751.00: £367.00) Stalls: Low GOING: 0.43 sec per fur (SLW)

Form	Horse	Dist	Pos	SP	RR	SF
*5174**	**Mr Frosty (60)** (WJarvis) **4-9-6** SSanders(6) (a.p: reminders ½-wy: led ins fnl f: r.o wl)	—	1	6/1[1]	68	50
5165[4]	**Desert Invader (IRE) (68)** (DWChapman) **5-10-0** ACulhane(2) (a chsng ldrs: effrt u.p appr fnl f: nt pce of wnr)	1½	2	12/1	72	54
5220[4]	**Cheeky Chappy (60)** (DWChapman) **5-9-6b** JQuinn(3) (b: a.p: hrd drvn over 1f out: kpt on wl fnl f)	1½	3	12/1	60	42
5165[3]	**Theatre Magic (60)** (SRBowring) **3-9-6b** SDWilliams(7) (lw: led tl hdd & no ex ins fnl f)	¾	4	7/1[3]	58	40
4439[6]	**Kid Ory (52)** (DWChapman) **5-8-12** GDuffield(1) (bit bkwd: hdwy on ins over 2f out: rdn & one pce appr fnl f)	4	5	20/1	39	21
5138[2]	**How's Yer Father (60)** (RJHodges) **10-9-6** SDrowne(9) (mid div: effrt 2f out: nvr nr to chal)	¾	6	6/1[1]	45	27
5144[4]	**Castlerea Lad (53)** (RHollinshead) **7-8-10**(3) FLynch(12) (hdwy on outside 2f out: nt rch ldrs)	s.h	7	6/1[1]	38	20
5178[8]	**Disco Boy (50)** (PDEvans) **6-8-3**(7) AnthonyBond(8) (chsd ldrs 4f: sn rdn & wknd)	2	8	14/1	30	12
5178[4]	**Souperficial (56)** (NTinkler) **5-9-2v** KimTinkler(10) (effrt ent st: nt rch ldrs)	s.h	9	8/1	36	18
5109[2]	**Queens Check (65)** (MissJFCraze) **3-9-8b**(3) OPears(13) (b: sn outpcd: a bhd)	1¾	10	9/1	40	22
5163[11]	**Boffy (IRE) (60)** (BPJBaugh) **3-9-6** RPerham(11) (lw: outpcd)	1¾	11	33/1	30	12
5138[4]	**Lord Sky (66)** (ABailey) **5-9-7**(5) PRoberts(4) (s.i.s: in rr most of wy: t.o)	6	12	13/2[2]	20	2
177[9]	**Dragon Green (54)** (JCullinan) **5-9-0** TSprake(5) (bkwd: sn drvn along: a outpcd: t.o)	6	13	33/1	—	—
				(SP 122.5%)		**13 Rn**

1m 17.8 (6.60) CSF £70.42 CT £770.70 TOTE £7.00: £2.70 £5.00 £2.90 (£42.50) Trio £140.00 OWNER Mr D. G. Wright (NEWMARKET) BRED D. G. and Miss C. M. Wright

5231 BENTLEY JENNISON H'CAP (0-85) (3-Y.O+) (Class D)

8-30 (8-30) **1m 1f 79y (Fibresand)** £2,853.00 (£864.00: £422.00: £201.00) Stalls: Low GOING: 0.43 sec per fur (SLW)

Form	Horse	Dist	Pos	SP	RR	SF
5120[3]	**South Eastern Fred (80)** (HJCollingridge) **5-9-9** JQuinn(4) (b: a.p & gng wl: led over 2f out: clr ent fnl f: comf)	—	1	6/1[2]	92	54
5106[6]	**North Reef (IRE) (75)** (JPearce) **5-9-4** MWigham(7) (lw: a.p: hrd rdn 2f out: kpt on: no ch w wnr)	2½	2	8/1[3]	83	45
4974[7]	**High Premium (80)** (RAFahey) **8-9-9** ACulhane(5) (sn pushed along in rr: hdwy 4f out: styd on fnl f)	3	3	5/1[1]	83	45
5206[11]	**Shahik (USA) (68)** (DHaydnJones) **6-8-11** SWhitworth(1) (hdwy ½-wy: styd on u.p fnl f)	½	4	10/1	70	32
5182[2]	**Bentico (76)** (MrsNMacauley) **7-9-2v**(3) CTeague(10) (hdwy 4f out: sn rdn: wknd appr fnl f)	3½	5	5/1[1]	72	34
*5137**	**Cedez le Passage (FR) (85)** (KOCunningham-Brown) **5-10-0b** DaneO'Neill(2) (lw: led tl over 2f out: sn hrd drvn: wknd appr fnl f)	5	6	12/1	72	34
4812[12]	**Rood Music (72)** (MGMeagher) **5-9-1** FNorton(6) (w ldrs tl wknd qckly wl over 1f out)	4	7	20/1	52	14
4901[12]	**Dee-Lady (68)** (WGMTurner) **4-8-11** TSprake(13) (b: b.hind: hdwy 5f out: wknd fnl 2f)	5	8	14/1	40	2
5189[5]	**Explosive Power (72)** (GCBravery) **5-9-1** LNewton(3) (prom tl rdn & wknd wl over 2f out)	4	9	6/1[2]	37	—

2121[4] **Loveyoumillions (IRE) (75)** (NTinkler) **4-9-4** KimTinkler(8) (effrt over 3f out: wknd fnl 2f) ....6 **10** 20/1 30 —
2400[5] **Worldwide Elsie (USA) (73)** (ICampbell) **3-9-0** DBiggs(9) (bkwd: chsd ldrs to ½-wy: sn lost tch: t.o)....30 **11** 20/1 — —
4603[16] **Racing Brenda (74)** (BCMorgan) **5-9-3** SSanders(11) (sn bustled along: a bhd: t.o) ....1½ **12** 14/1 — —
(SP 117.4%) **12 Rn**

2m 6.1 (10.10) CSF £48.65 CT £231.85 TOTE £6.20: £1.90 £3.30 £2.80 (£28.00) Trio £97.10 OWNER South Eastern Electrical Plc (EXNING) BRED L. Audus
WEIGHT FOR AGE 3yo-2lb

5232 PLYVINE CATERING (S) STKS (3,4,5 & 6-Y.O) (Class G)
9-00 (9-00) **1m 6f 166y (Fibresand)** £2,085.00 (£585.00: £285.00) Stalls: High GOING: 0.43 sec per fur (SLW)

SP RR SF
*5169** **Petoskin (68)** (JPearce) **4-9-7** MWigham(6) (a.p: led over 4f out: sn clr: pushed out) ....— **1** 4/6[1] 72 24
5130[14] **Mapengo (40)** (JCullinan) **5-9-3** VSlattery(3) (hld up: hdwy 5f out: chsd wnr fnl 3f: no imp) 18 **2** 33/1 49 1
3257[11] **Still Here (IRE) (53)** (PBowen) **3-8-10** AMcGlone(1) (chsd ldrs: led over 5f out tl over 4f out: wknd wl over 2f out) ....5 **3** 12/1 43 —
5143[3] **Forzair (57)** (JJO'Neill) **4-9-2**(7)ow2 DJewett(4) (hld up: hdwy 7f out: sn drvn along: wknd over 3f out)....2½ **4** 5/1[2] 46 —
5139[8] **Rose of Glenn (36)** (BPalling) **5-8-12** CRutter(5) (led after 2f tl over 5f out: sn lost tch) ....3½ **5** 10/1[3] 32 —
5169[4] **Suleika Dancer** (PDEvans) **3-8-5** SSanders(7) (led 2f: rdn & wknd ½-wy: t.o) ....30 **6** 14/1 — —
4910[6] **Zeliba (23)** (MrsNMacauley) **4-8-9**(7) JoHunnam(9) (chsd ldrs over 8f: sn wknd: t.o) ....11 **7** 11/1 — —
5177[13] **Burning Cost (28)** (REPeacock) **6-8-12** DBiggs(2) (a bhd: t.o fnl 6f) ....6 **8** 50/1 — —
5143[12] **Star of Lugana** (TTClement) **3-7-13**(7)ow1 CWebb(8) (b: a bhd: rdn ½-wy: sn t.o) ....dist **9** 33/1 — —
(SP 116.3%) **9 Rn**

3m 29.1 (21.70) CSF £21.16 TOTE £1.70: £1.80 £6.80 £3.40 (£83.10) Trio £76.40; £86.12 to 16/12/96 OWNER Mr Jeff Pearce (NEWMARKET)
BRED James Wigan
WEIGHT FOR AGE 3yo-7lb
Bt in 5,000 gns

5233 COMEDY OF ERRORS H'CAP (0-70) (3-Y.O+) (Class E)
9-30 (9-32) **1m 4f (Fibresand)** £2,316.00 (£651.00: £318.00) Stalls: Low GOING: 0.43 sec per fur (SLW)

SP RR SF
5136[3] **Mr Speculator (48)** (JEBanks) **3-8-2v** JQuinn(9) (a.p: led over 5f out: hrd rdn fnl f: hld on gamely) ....— **1** 11/1 55 29
*5181** **Manful (69)** (CWCElsey) **4-10-0b** GDuffield(10) (hld up: hdwy 6f out: hrd rdn fnl f: r.o wl) ....¾ **2** 9/2[1] 75 54
4977[2] **Mad Militant (IRE) (65)** (AStreeter) **7-9-10** TSprake(11) (b: lw: hld up: hdwy over 4f out: rdn & r.o wl ins fnl f) ....nk **3** 9/2[1] 71 50
5062[5] **In the Money (IRE) (51)** (RHollinshead) **7-8-7**(3) FLynch(6) (hld up: hdwy 4f out: hrd drvn over 2f out: no ex ins fnl f) ....1 **4** 7/1[3] 55 34
5169[2] **Hill Farm Dancer (68)** (WMBrisbourne) **5-9-6**(7) IonaWands(4) (hld up: hdwy over 5f out: hrd drvn ent st: one pce ins fnl f) ....nk **5** 6/1[2] 72 51
5205[6] **Obelos (USA) (66)** (MissSJWilton) **5-9-11** SWhitworth(7) (hld up: hdwy 5f out: rdn & wknd over 2f out: t.o) ...25 **6** 15/2 37 16
5062[8] **Charlie Bigtime (43)** (ICampbell) **6-8-2** DBiggs(12) (b.hind: a in rr: t.o) ....7 **7** 10/1 4 —
5186[7] **Peetsie (IRE) (48)** (NATwiston-Davies) **4-8-7** SSanders(2) (lw: chsd ldrs: rdn along ½-wy: sn lost tch: t.o)....2½ **8** 25/1 6 —
5101[4] **Lavender Della (IRE) (50)** (MJFetherston-Godley) **3-8-4** CRutter(5) (a in rr: t.o) ....2½ **9** 10/1 5 —
5137[4] **Conwy (50)** (SCWilliams) **3-8-4** AMcGlone(3) (trckd ldrs: rdn & wknd 4f out: t.o) ....½ **10** 20/1 4 —
5206[6] **Gadge (47)** (ABailey) **5-8-6** DWright(1) (b: led over 6f: wknd over 3f out: t.o) ....¾ **11** 16/1 — —
4740a* **Set the Fashion (67)** (DLWilliams) **7-9-12b**[1] JRaja(8) (chsd ldrs over 7f: sn wknd: t.o) ....1½ **12** 25/1 18 —
(SP 119.8%) **12 Rn**

2m 46.5 (14.00) CSF £56.61 CT £236.24 TOTE £14.60: £3.30 £1.60 £2.10 (£63.20) Trio £65.10 OWNER The Speculators (NEWMARKET)
BRED Fittocks Stud
WEIGHT FOR AGE 3yo-5lb
STEWARDS' ENQUIRY Duffield susp. 31/12/96 - 3/1/97 (excessive use of whip).

T/Plpt: £356.40 (40.04 Tckts). T/Qdpt: £18.80 (32.28 Tckts). IM

5228-WOLVERHAMPTON (L-H) (Standard)
Thursday December 19th
WEATHER: rain WIND: almost nil

5234 DUNSTON CLAIMING STKS (I) (3-Y.O+) (Class F)
1-00 (1-02) **6f (Fibresand)** £2,187.00 (£612.00: £297.00) Stalls: Low GOING: 0.01 sec per fur (STD)

SP RR SF
4577[7] **Marjorie Rose (IRE) (63)** (ABailey) **3-8-2** DWright(6) (b: hdwy ½-wy: led over 1f out: rdn out) ....— **1** 13/2[3] 59 25
5163[6] **Shashi (IRE) (59)** (WWHaigh) **4-8-4** RLappin(5) (lw: chsd ldrs: rdn over 1f out: r.o nr fin) ....1 **2** 11/2[2] 58 24
3953[8] **Ultra Beet (64)** (PCHaslam) **4-8-8**(7) PGoode(11) (bit bkwd: chsd ldrs: rdn & effrt 2f out: kpt on towards fin) .1¼ **3** 12/1 66 32
5178[2] **Primula Bairn (66)** (DNicholls) **6-8-8b** CRutter(7) (a.p: led wl over 1f out: sn hdd: rdn & one pce fnl f) ....½ **4** 9/4[1] 58 24
5163[10] **Standown (70)** (JBerry) **3-8-8**(5) PRoberts(13) (b.hind: in tch: rdn over 2f out: styd on appr fnl f)....2½ **5** 12/1 56 22
5110[10] **Peacefull Reply (USA) (28)** (FHLee) **6-8-5v**ow3 DaneO'Neill(8) (chsd ldrs: rdn & one pce appr fnl f) 1¼ **6** 33/1 45 8
Sally Armstrong (CWThornton) **3-9-4** SDrowne(1) (w'like: leggy: bkwd: s.s: wl bhd tl styd on appr fnl f)......1¼ **7** 25/1 54 20
5188[6] **Southern Rule (29)** (MissMERowland) **9-8-3** JoannaMorgan(10) (prom to ½-wy: sn rdn & wknd) ....6 **8** 25/1 23 —
5138[13] **Dhes-C (46)** (RHollinshead) **3-8-6** MWigham(9) (lw: outpcd: a in rr) ....hd **9** 16/1 26 —
5215[10] **Logie Pert Lad (26)** (JJBridger) **4-8-5** SSanders(3) (led 2f: prom tl rdn & wknd 2f out) ....½ **10** 25/1 24 —
5230[11] **Boffy (IRE) (60)** (BPJBaugh) **3-8-9b**[1] RPerham(4) (lw: chsd ldr: led 4f out tl hdd & wknd wl over 1f out) ....½ **11** 16/1 26 —
4898[17] **Dunmebrains (IRE)** (JSMoore) **3-8-3**(5) PPMurphy(12) (outpcd: a bhd) ....3 **12** 33/1 17 —
4308[12] **Cross of Valour (78)** (PHowling) **3-9-0** JQuinn(2) (bkwd: s.s: in rr most of wy) ....nk **13** 13/2[3] 23 —
(SP 117.4%) **13 Rn**

1m 15.9 (4.70) CSF £38.63 TOTE £6.80: £1.80 £2.50 £5.20 (£22.50) Trio £33.20 OWNER Sandybrow Stables Ltd (TARPORLEY) BRED R. Selby and Partners
Shashi (IRE) clmd Pat Mitchell £6000

IN-FOCUS: Due to the continuous heavy rain lying on the track, the ground was very sloppy and the horses were finishing tired. The times held up well though and only on a few occasions did conditions seem to have any actual effect on performances.

5235 BRIDGETOWN H'CAP (0-70) (3-Y.O) (Class E)

1-30 (1-35) **1m 100y (Fibresand)** £3,203.30 (£970.40: £474.20: £226.10) Stalls: Low GOING: 0.01 sec per fur (STD)

Form	Horse	Btn	Pos	SP	RR	SF
*5175**	**Three Weeks (53)** (WRMuir) **3-8-6** DaneO'Neill(3) (lw: hld up: hdwy 5f out: led over 3f out: styd on wl)	—	1	7/4[1]	67	29
5138[9]	**Finisterre (IRE) (52)** (JJO'Neill) **3-8-5** JQuinn(8) (lw: hld up: hdwy over 3f out: chsd wnr fnl 2f: one pce fnl f)	2½	2	20/1	61	23
5206[7]	**Yeoman Oliver (68)** (BAMcMahon) **3-9-7b** DBiggs(10) (a.p: rdn along over 2f out: kpt on one pce)	6	3	20/1	66	28
5221[7]	**Double March (65)** (PRWebber) **3-9-4** RPerham(12) (lw: hld up: hdwy 3f out: rdn wl over 1f out: nt rch ldrs)	1¼	4	16/1	61	23
4979[11]	**Silver Harrow (51)** (AGNewcombe) **3-8-4** SDrowne(2) (hld up: pushed along ½-wy: styd on appr fnl f: nvr nrr)	½	5	14/1	46	8
5082[4]	**Mono Lady (IRE) (53)** (DHaydnJones) **3-8-6** TWilliams(4) (chsd ldrs: slt ld 5f out tl over 3f out: wknd fnl 2f)	1½	6	14/1	45	7
4906[15]	**Vanadium Ore (53)** (JLEyre) **3-8-6v** RLappin(6) (a in rr)	6	7	14/1	33	—
5170[8]	**Chilibang Bang (63)** (JBerry) **3-8-11**(5) PRoberts(1) (prom tl wknd over 2f out)	2½	8	16/1	39	1
5132[3]	**Genuine John (IRE) (65)** (JParkes) **3-9-1**(3) PMcCabe(11) (a in rr)	2½	9	12/1	36	—
5131[10]	**Antonias Melody (67)** (SRBowring) **3-9-6** SDWilliams(13) (chsd ldrs to ½-wy: sn rdn & wknd)	2½	10	12/1	33	—
5200[5]	**Dragonjoy (62)** (NPLittmoden) **3-9-1v** TGMcLaughlin(5) (trckd ldrs: drvn along ½-wy: sn wknd)	4	11	6/1[2]	21	—
5117[4]	**Scherma (60)** (WJarvis) **3-8-13** WRyan(7) (led over 3f: sn rdn & wknd)	nk	12	7/1[3]	18	—
4971[8]	**Windrush Holly (65)** (JRBosley) **3-9-4** TSprake(9) (unruly s: chsd ldrs over 4f: sn lost tch)	3½	13	14/1	17	—
				(SP 126.5%)	**13 Rn**	

1m 51.6 (6.60) CSF £36.36 CT £544.59 TOTE £2.20: £1.20 £3.20 £4.40 (£43.90) Trio £208.90; £44.14 to Hereford 20/12/96 OWNER Mr Duncan Wiltshire (LAMBOURN) BRED Mrs K. W. Sneath

5236 DUNSTON CLAIMING STKS (II) (3-Y.O+) (Class F)

2-00 (2-06) **6f (Fibresand)** £2,187.00 (£612.00: £297.00) Stalls: Low GOING: 0.01 sec per fur (STD)

Form	Horse	Btn	Pos	SP	RR	SF
*5230**	**Mr Frosty (60)** (WJarvis) **4-9-9** SSanders(5) (chsd ldrs: hrd drvn ½-wy: styd on gamely to ld cl home)	—	1	11/2[3]	83	62
*5163**	**Chadwell Hall (75)** (SRBowring) **5-9-3** SDWilliams(4) (b: mde most: hrd rdn fnl f: ct nr fin)	hd	2	4/1[2]	77	56
4917[6]	**The Happy Fox (IRE) (72)** (BAMcMahon) **4-8-13b** TWilliams(12) (chsd ldrs: effrt 2f out: sn hrd rdn: unable qckn)	3	3	8/1	65	44
*5178**	**Jibereen (73)** (PHowling) **4-9-9** SWhitworth(3) (b: lw: hdwy over 2f out: remained far side: rdn & one pce appr fnl f)	¾	4	7/1	73	52
5144[13]	**Sir Tasker (44)** (JLHarris) **8-8-5** JQuinn(6) (w ldr tl wknd wl over 1f out)	6	5	25/1	39	18
5131[2]	**Palacegate Jack (IRE) (81)** (CADwyer) **5-9-9** RHughes(8) (prom: rdn 2f out: wknd appr fnl f)	s.h	6	2/1[1]	57	36
3579[6]	**Little Ibnr (72)** (PDEvans) **5-8-2**(7) AnthonyBond(11) (bkwd: prom tl rdn & wknd 2f out)	hd	7	11/1	42	21
5174[2]	**Bold Aristocrat (IRE) (59)** (RHollinshead) **5-8-7** MWigham(2) (chsd ldrs 4f)	hd	8	7/1	40	19
4691[18]	**Miss Charlie (38)** (ABailey) **6-7-12** DWright(1) (b.hind: s.s: a bhd & outpcd)	3½	9	20/1	22	1
5095[8]	**Justinianus (IRE) (31)** (JJBridger) **4-8-3** NCarlisle(9) (outpcd)	nk	10	33/1	26	5
5163[14]	**Seanchai (IRE)** (PSFelgate) **3-8-8**(3) PMcCabe(13) (outpcd)	s.h	11	33/1	34	13
5055[11]	**Present 'n Correct (33)** (CBBBooth) **3-8-13** ACulhane(7) (outpcd)	1¾	12	33/1	31	10
4829[16]	***Khattat (USA) (50)*** (JohnHarris) **6-8-7** SDrowne(10) (Withdrawn not under Starter's orders: ref to ent stalls)		W	25/1	—	—
				(SP 134.4%)	**12 Rn**	

1m 14.6 (3.40) CSF £28.98 TOTE £6.60: £3.60 £1.70 £1.50 (£20.60) Trio £58.90 OWNER Mr D. G. Wright (NEWMARKET) BRED D. G. and Miss C. M. Wright

5237 DUDLEY H'CAP (0-65) (I) (3-Y.O+) (Class F)

2-30 (2-32) **7f (Fibresand)** £2,187.00 (£612.00: £297.00) Stalls: High GOING: 0.01 sec per fur (STD)

Form	Horse	Btn	Pos	SP	RR	SF
5174[4]	**Leigh Crofter (58)** (PDCundell) **7-9-7b** RHughes(1) (led 1f: led over 2f out: hrd rdn fnl f: jst hld on)	—	1	7/4[1]	70	41
4430[7]	**Blushing Grenadier (IRE) (47)** (MJFetherston-Godley) **4-8-10** FNorton(4) (w ldrs: led 4f out tl over 2f out: rallied u.p towards fin)	nk	2	12/1	58	29
5206[9]	**Gulf Shaadi (55)** (EJAlston) **4-9-4** SSanders(6) (chsd ldrs: effrt & rdn 2f out: kpt on fnl f)	1½	3	25/1	63	34
5161[5]	**Sea Spouse (64)** (MBlanshard) **5-9-13** NAdams(9) (led after 1f to 4f out: rdn & wknd over 2f out)	6	4	13/2[3]	58	29
5144[7]	**Jigsaw Boy (65)** (PGMurphy) **7-10-0** SDrowne(8) (in tch: rdn over 2f out: nvr nr to chal)	2½	5	6/1[2]	54	25
4882[5]	**Cats Bottom (53)** (AGNewcombe) **4-9-2** JQuinn(12) (nvr gng pce)	½	6	7/1	40	11
3316[8]	**Flagstaff (USA) (49)** (KRBurke) **3-8-5**(7) PWright(2) (dwlt: sme late hdwy: n.d)	hd	7	12/1	36	7
5230[9]	**Souperficial (56)** (NTinkler) **5-9-5v** KimTinkler(5) (sn pushed along: a in rr)	1¼	8	13/2[3]	40	11
589[9]	**Bogart (50)** (CWFairhurst) **5-8-13** RLappin(3) (mid div tl wknd over 2f out)	hd	9	16/1	34	5
5129[10]	**Arcus (IRE) (50)** (WRMuir) **3-8-13b** DaneO'Neill(7) (outpcd: a bhd)	2½	10	20/1	28	—
3627[13]	**African-Pard (IRE) (57)** (DHaydnJones) **4-9-6** SWhitworth(11) (bit bkwd: outpcd)	1½	11	20/1	32	3
4820[16]	**Croagh Patrick (51)** (JCFox) **4-9-0** CRutter(10) (lw: outpcd: t.o)	9	12	25/1	5	—
				(SP 128.3%)	**12 Rn**	

1m 30.2 (5.50) CSF £24.17 CT £390.54 TOTE £2.40: £1.80 £3.90 £3.30 (£25.40) Trio £156.10; £96.74 to Hereford 20/12/96 OWNER Mr P. D. Cundell (NEWBURY) BRED Richard Castle

5238 CANNOCK NURSERY H'CAP (0-85) (2-Y.O) (Class D)

3-00 (3-03) **7f (Fibresand)** £3,598.75 (£1,090.00: £532.50: £253.75) Stalls: High GOING: 0.01 sec per fur (STD)

Form	Horse	Btn	Pos	SP	RR	SF
5229[3]	**Nomore Mr Niceguy (78)** (EJAlston) **2-9-6** ACulhane(5) (hld up gng wl: nt clr run ent st: led appr fnl f: rdn out)	—	1	10/1	84	43
5228[4]	**Effervescence (78)** (RHannon) **2-9-6** DaneO'Neill(3) (a.p: ev ch over 1f out: rdn & no ex fnl f)	2½	2	7/1[3]	78	37
*5214**	**Millroy (USA) (86)** (PAKelleway) **2-10-0** 7x MWigham(7) (lw: chsd ldrs: drvn over 2f out: styd on)	3	3	8/1	79	38
5164[2]	**C-Harry (IRE) (68)** (RHollinshead) **2-8-10** NCarlisle(1) (a.p: jnd ldr 3f out: rdn & wknd over 1f out)	1¼	4	13/2[2]	59	18
*5207**	**Double-O (72)** (WJarvis) **2-9-0** SSanders(2) (lw: mde most tl hdd & wknd appr fnl f)	nk	5	6/4[1]	62	21
5113[6]	**Ninth Symphony (65)** (PCHaslam) **2-8-7** SDrowne(10) (a bhd & outpcd)	3	6	12/1	48	7
4501[2]	**Going For Broke (65)** (PCHaslam) **2-8-7** TWilliams(9) (bit bkwd: trckd ldrs: effrt 3f out: wknd wl over 1f out)	¾	7	11/1	46	5
5187[5]	**Ewar Arrangement (60)** (CEBrittain) **2-8-2** JQuinn(8) (sn drvn along: a bhd)	3½	8	20/1	33	—
5176[6]	**Davis Rock (72)** (WRMuir) **2-9-0** WRyan(6) (lw: s.i.s: sn pushed along: a in rr)	4	9	10/1	36	—

				SP	RR	SF
5111^{5}	***Amico* (66)** (CWThornton) **2-8-8** FNorton(4) (Withdrawn not under Starter's orders: ref to ent stalls)		**W**	25/1	—	—

(SP 119.8%) **9 Rn**

1m 29.9 (5.20) CSF £70.72 CT £539.15 TOTE £11.20: £3.00 £1.60 £2.90 (£19.20) Trio £32.40 OWNER Mrs Carol McPhail (PRESTON) BRED Brick Kiln Stud and Lariston Apartments Ltd

5239 MORVILLE (S) STKS (2-Y.O) (Class G)

3-30 (3-34) **6f (Fibresand)** £2,259.00 (£634.00: £309.00) Stalls: Low GOING: 0.01 sec per fur (STD)

				SP	RR	SF
5176^{5}	**Master Foley (48)** (NPLittmoden) **2-8-11** TGMcLaughlin(13) (mde all: qcknd clr 2f out: unchal)	—	**1**	11/1	66	24
4887^{13}	**Terry's Rose (50)** (RHollinshead) **2-8-7**^{ow1} MWigham(12) (chsd ldrs: rdn & kpt on ins fnl f: no ch w wnr)	7	**2**	16/1	43	—
5142^{12}	**Will To Win (56)** (PGMurphy) **2-8-6** SDrowne(10) (b.hind: a.p: chsd wnr over 2f out: no imp)	¾	**3**	12/1	40	—
3498^{3}	**Broadgate Flyer (IRE) (68)** (MrsLStubbs) **2-8-11** SWhitworth(4) (s.i.s: rdn & hdwy 2f out: kpt on appr fnl f)	2½	**4**	5/1^{2}	39	—
	Faym (IRE) (JWharton) **2-8-6** FNorton(2) (leggy: unf: s.s: hdwy wl over 1f out: styd on towards fin)	nk	**5**	33/1	33	—
	Royal Cascade (IRE) (BAMcMahon) **2-8-11** NCarlisle(7) (unf: bkwd: hdwy ent st: styd on ent fnl f)	½	**6**	20/1	37	—
2575^{6}	**Lily Jaques** (RGuest) **2-8-6** DBiggs(8) (bit bkwd: trckd ldrs over 3f: sn lost tch)	5	**7**	14/1	18	—
3121^{8}	**Joyful Joy** (BPJBaugh) **2-8-6** RPerham(11) (outpcd: t.o)	6	**8**	33/1	2	—
4562^{20}	**Full Traceability (IRE) (53)** (JJO'Neill) **2-8-11** JQuinn(9) (lw: a bhd & outpcd: t.o)	1	**9**	10/1^{3}	5	—
5207^{8}	**Pet Express** (PCHaslam) **2-8-4**$^{(7)}$ PGoode(1) (dwlt: sn rcvrd: ev ch over 2f out: wknd qckly: t.o)	2	**10**	33/1	—	—
5202*	**Lightning Bolt (IRE) (57)** (MJohnston) **2-8-11** TWilliams(6) (prom: hrd drvn over 2f out: wknd qckly: t.o)	2½	**11**	Evens^{1}	—	—
2371^{10}	**Ditty Box** (MDIUsher) **2-8-6** AMcGlone(5) (bkwd: a bhd: t.o)	½	**12**	50/1	—	—
5162^{11}	**Frandickbob (45)** (JohnHarris) **2-8-11** SSanders(3) (s.s: a bhd: t.o)	nk	**13**	50/1	—	—

(SP 121.8%) **13 Rn**

1m 16.6 (5.40) CSF £155.80 TOTE £15.30: £3.50 £3.60 £3.00 (£144.50) Trio £247.70; £122.12 to Hereford 20/12/96 OWNER Mountview Ventures (WOLVERHAMPTON) BRED Miss Jennifer Wolstencroft
No bid

5240 HIMLEY AMATEUR H'CAP (0-60) (3-Y.O+) (Class F)

4-00 (4-02) **1m 4f (Fibresand)** £2,537.00 (£712.00: £347.00) Stalls: Low GOING: 0.01 sec per fur (STD)

				SP	RR	SF
5210^{8}	**Rasayel (USA) (41)** (PDEvans) **6-10-1**$^{(5)}$ MrWMcLaughlin(3) (s.s: hdwy 5f out: hmpd & lost pl over 2f out: str run appr fnl f: led last stride)	—	**1**	10/1	55	36
5189^{6}	**Colosse (45)** (JLEyre) **4-10-10v^{1}** MissDianaJones(4) (a.p: led & qcknd clr over 2f out: wknd & ct fnl stride)	hd	**2**	4/1^{1}	59	40
5167*	**Golden Hadeer (48)** (MJRyan) **5-10-8**$^{(5)}$ MrSLavallin(10) (b: hdwy ½-wy: kpt on one pce fnl 2f)	5	**3**	11/2^{3}	55	36
5181^{5}	**Wildfire (SWI) (47)** (RAkehurst) **5-10-12** MrTMcCarthy(8) (a.p: led over 6f out tl over 2f out: sn btn)	½	**4**	7/1	54	35
124^{6}	**Beauman (56)** (PDEvans) **6-11-2**$^{(5)}$ MrAEvans(9) (in tch: hdwy & hrd drvn over 2f out: nt pce to chal)	2½	**5**	5/1^{2}	59	40
5222^{4}	**Claque (51)** (DWChapman) **4-11-2b** MissRClark(12) (trckd ldrs: effrt 3f out: sn outpcd)	s.h	**6**	6/1	54	35
5175^{6}	**North Ardar (48)** (TWall) **6-10-8**$^{(5)}$ MissAAnderson(5) (chsd ldrs 9f: sn rdn & outpcd)	2½	**7**	8/1	48	29
5143^{2}	**Kinnescash (IRE) (54)** (PBowen) **3-11-0** MrsLPearce(11) (nvr nr to chal)	¾	**8**	4/1^{1}	53	29
3958^{5}	**Globe Runner (47)** (JJO'Neill) **3-10-2**$^{(5)}$ MissSKerswell(1) (led after 3f tl over 6f out: wknd 4f out: t.o)	11	**9**	14/1	31	7
5179^{9}	**Nautical Jewel (45)** (MDIUsher) **4-10-5**$^{(5)}$ MrsAUsher(7) (a in rr: t.o)	1¾	**10**	20/1	27	8
4789^{8}	**Smuggler's Point (USA) (51)** (JJBridger) **6-10-11**$^{(5)}$ MrDBridger(6) (a bhd: t.o)	nk	**11**	20/1	32	13
5175^{14}	**Rozel Bay (48)** (NATwiston-Davies) **3-10-3**$^{(5)}$ MrAWintle(2) (led 3f: wknd 5f out: t.o)	30	**12**	25/1	—	—

(SP 139.1%) **12 Rn**

2m 45.0 (12.50) CSF £54.70 CT £240.16 TOTE £10.10: £2.10 £1.10 £3.20 (£21.90) Trio £53.70 OWNER Pentons Haulage and Cold Storage Ltd (WELSHPOOL) BRED Gainsborough Farm
WEIGHT FOR AGE 3yo-5lb

5241 DUDLEY H'CAP (0-65) (II) (3-Y.O+) (Class F)

4-30 (4-31) **7f (Fibresand)** £2,187.00 (£612.00: £297.00) Stalls: High GOING: 0.01 sec per fur (STD)

				SP	RR	SF
3951^{3}	**Quinzii Martin (48)** (DHaydnJones) **8-8-11** SDrowne(3) (hld up: hdwy over 2f out: led appr fnl f: r.o wl)	—	**1**	12/1	50	13
5178^{3}	**Monis (IRE) (53)** (JBalding) **5-8-11v**$^{(5)}$ GFaulkner(2) (in tch: rdn & hdwy wl over 1f out: edgd lft & fin wl)	1¼	**2**	14/1	52	15
5227^{4}	**Sea Danzig (65)** (JJBridger) **3-10-0** SSanders(7) (a.p: hrd rdn over 1f out: kpt on towards fin)	hd	**3**	8/1	64	27
5170^{9}	**Lia Fail (IRE) (49)** (RHollinshead) **3-8-12** MWigham(1) (bhd & outpcd: hdwy ent st: kpt on ins fnl f)	3½	**4**	20/1	40	3
5170^{2}	**Encore M'Lady (IRE) (57)** (FHLee) **5-9-6** RLappin(8) (a.p: ev ch over 1f out: eased whn btn fnl f)	1¾	**5**	9/2^{2}	44	7
5200^{8}	**Three Arch Bridge (64)** (MJohnston) **4-9-13b** FNorton(12) (s.i.s: bhd tl r.o wl appr fnl f)	hd	**6**	20/1	51	14
4809^{11}	**Dictation (USA) (57)** (JJO'Neill) **4-9-6b^{1}** DaneO'Neill(4) (led tl hdd & wknd appr fnl f)	1½	**7**	16/1	40	3
5230^{3}	**Cheeky Chappy (60)** (DWChapman) **5-9-9b** ACulhane(6) (w ldr early: wknd over 2f out)	2½	**8**	13/2^{3}	38	1
5230^{6}	**How's Yer Father (60)** (RJHodges) **10-9-9** TSprake(11) (a in rr)	hd	**9**	8/1	37	—
5179*	**Running Green (53)** (DMoffatt) **5-9-2** JQuinn(9) (chsd ldrs: rdn 2f out: sn btn)	nk	**10**	9/4^{1}	30	—
5170^{4}	**Holloway Melody (49)** (BAMcMahon) **3-8-12** NAdams(10) (a bhd)	nk	**11**	12/1	25	—
5173^{4}	**Amy Leigh (IRE) (49)** (CaptJWilson) **3-8-5b**$^{(7)}$ AngelaHartley(5) (a bhd & outpcd)	6	**12**	12/1	11	—

(SP 129.7%) **12 Rn**

1m 32.0 (7.30) CSF £159.92 CT £1,334.67 TOTE £11.70: £2.20 £3.10 £3.70 (£41.70) Trio £67.70 OWNER Monolithic Refractories Ltd (PONTYPRIDD) BRED Lord Fairhaven
T/Plpt: £1,102.00 (8.98 Tckts). T/Qdpt: £220.50 (6.42 Tckts). IM

5220-LINGFIELD (L-H) (Standard)

Friday December 20th

Races 7 & 8 - hand-timed
WEATHER: drizzle WIND: almost nil

5242 ATROPOS H'CAP (0-60) (I) (3-Y.O+) (Class F)

11-45 (11-48) **1m 2f (Equitrack)** £1,179.00 (£329.00: £79.50: £79.50) Stalls: Low GOING minus 0.52 sec per fur (FST)

				SP	RR	SF
5152^{5}	**Kedwick (IRE) (48)** (PRHedger) **7-9-2b** AMcGlone(9) (b: b.hind: stdy hdwy over 4f out: led 1f out: rdn out)	—	**1**	5/1^{2}	55	20
5179^{11}	**Sapphire Son (IRE) (41)** (PCClarke) **4-8-9** DaneO'Neill(2) (led over 1f: rdn over 1f out: r.o ins fnl f)	3	**2**	20/1	43	8
4513^{5}	**Bakers Daughter (57)** (JRArnold) **4-9-11** AClark(12) (swtg: a.p: rdn over 2f out: r.o one pce fnl f)	1½	**3**	7/1^{3}	57	22

5223[6]	**Manabar (60)** (MJPolglase) **4-10-0** TGMcLaughlin(1) (a.p: led over 3f out to 1f out: unable qckn)	d.h	**3**	12/1	60	25
4829[9]	**Bold Habit (40)** (JPearce) **11-8-8** MWigham(13) (s.s: rdn & hdwy over 3f out: r.o ins fnl f)	s.h	**5**	20/1	40	5
5151[3]	**Harlequin Walk (IRE) (50)** (RJO'Sullivan) **5-9-4b** DBiggs(4) (led over 8f out tl over 3f out: wknd 2f out)	7	**6**	3/1[1]	39	4
5102[2]	**Taniyar (FR) (35)** (RHollinshead) **4-8-3** NCarlisle(10) (hdwy over 3f out: sn wknd)	2½	**7**	5/1[2]	20	—
5175[15]	**Medland (IRE) (43)** (BJMcMath) **6-8-11** WRyan(11) (lw: prom 8f)	10	**8**	12/1	12	—
5186[8]	**Komodo (USA) (38)** (JELong) **4-7-13**(7) TField(14) (lw: s.s: hdwy over 3f out: sn wknd)	1¾	**9**	20/1	4	—
2978[7]	**Boston Tea Party (46)** (AMoore) **3-8-11** CRutter(6) (bhd fnl 8f)	4	**10**	25/1	5	—
5060[7]	**Great Bear (35)** (DWChapman) **4-8-3** DWright(8) (a bhd)	4	**11**	20/1	—	—
5081[3]	**Bellateena (40)** (HJCollingridge) **4-8-8** JQuinn(7) (bhd fnl 7f)	2½	**12**	11/1	—	—
	Premier Star (41) (KGWingrove) **6-8-6**(3)ow11 PMcCabe(5) (a bhd)	4	**13**	100/1	—	—
5122[7]	**The Fugative (50)** (PMitchell) **3-9-1** SSanders(3) (prom over 5f)	5	**14**	20/1	—	—
				(SP 123.2%)	**14 Rn**	

2m 9.16 (4.86) CSF £90.68 CT K, SS & M £529.45; K, SS & BD £326.56 TOTE £6.00: £2.40 £14.90 M £1.30 BD £0.60 (£29.30) Trio K, SS & M £43.60; K, SS & BD not won; £107.50 to Uttoxeter 21/12/96 OWNER Mrs Joyce Griffiths (CHICHESTER) BRED D. Cordell-Lavarack
WEIGHT FOR AGE 3yo-3lb

5243 SARAH CHAPMAN 21ST BIRTHDAY MAIDEN STKS (I) (2-Y.O) (Class D)

12-15 (12-16) **1m (Equitrack)** £2,437.00 (£736.00: £358.00: £169.00) Stalls: High GOING minus 0.52 sec per fur (FST)

				SP	RR	SF
4050[10]	**Zimiri** (JARToller) **2-9-0** SSanders(5) (hld up: rdn over 1f out: swtchd rt ins fnl f: led nr fin)	—	**1**	5/1[2]	74	53
4969[10]	**Night Sceptre (IRE)** (RWArmstrong) **2-8-9** AMcGlone(10) (a.p: led over 1f out: rdn: hdd nr fin)	hd	**2**	4/6[1]	69	48
5224[7]	**Hever Golf Mover (63)** (TJNaughton) **2-8-9** DHolland(9) (led 1f: led 6f out to 5f out: led over 3f out tl over 1f out: one pce)	1½	**3**	11/2[3]	66	45
	Pastiche (TGMills) **2-8-9** WRyan(8) (lt-f: a.p: rdn & ev ch over 2f out: one pce)	2½	**4**	10/1	61	40
4494[12]	**Kingsdown Trix (IRE) (59)** (AMoore) **2-9-0** CRutter(4) (b.hind: a.p: rdn over 4f out: wknd 3f out)	8	**5**	25/1	50	29
5201[7]	**Warp Drive (IRE)** (WRMuir) **2-9-0** DaneO'Neill(2) (nvr nrr)	8	**6**	20/1	34	13
4368[9]	**Foxford Lad** (TMJones) **2-9-0** NCarlisle(7) (b.hind: bit bkwd: nvr nrr)	1¾	**7**	50/1	30	9
5168[8]	**Princess Sarara (USA)** (SirMarkPrescott) **2-8-9** CNutter(6) (a.p: led 5f out tl over 3f out: sn wknd)	1½	**8**	10/1	22	1
4200[9]	**Frost King (65)** (MissBSanders) **2-8-11**(3) AWhelan(1) (led 7f out to 6f out: wknd 5f out)	7	**9**	25/1	13	—
3795[7]	**Tirol's Treasure (IRE)** (KTIvory) **2-8-9** CScally(3) (b: b.hind: a bhd)	26	**10**	100/1	—	—
				(SP 125.6%)	**10 Rn**	

1m 37.59 (0.19) CSF £9.06 TOTE £6.50: £1.50 £1.30 £1.30 (£5.40) Trio £10.70 OWNER Forum Trustees Ltd A/C Rannerdale (WHITSBURY) BRED Rannerdale Trust

5244 HOTSPUR AMATEUR LIMITED STKS (0-60) (3-Y.O+) (Class G)

12-45 (12-46) **1m 4f (Equitrack)** £1,390.00 (£390.00: £190.00) Stalls: Low GOING minus 0.52 sec per fur (FST)

				SP	RR	SF
4548[6]	**Zuno Flyer (USA) (34)** (AMoore) **4-10-7** MrsAPerrett(6) (b.hind: a.p: led over 2f out: rdn out)	—	**1**	16/1	51	21
5167[5]	**Stalled (IRE) (55)** (PTWalwyn) **6-10-2**(5) MarchionessBlandford(7) (b: stdy hdwy over 2f out: str run fnl f: fin wl)	s.h	**2**	9/2[2]	51	21
5223[3]	**Zahid (USA) (59)** (KRBurke) **5-10-7** MrMRimell(8) (lw: hdwy 6f out: ev ch ins fnl f: unable qckn)	1	**3**	100/30[1]	50	20
5223[4]	**Sheraz (IRE) (56)** (NTinkler) **4-10-7** MissPJones(9) (a.p: led 5f out tl over 3f out: ev ch 2f out: one pce)	1¼	**4**	7/1	48	18
5189[8]	**Efficacious (IRE) (39)** (AMoore) **3-9-8**(5) MrsJMoore(11) (b.hind: hld up: led over 3f out tl over 2f out: one pce)	1¾	**5**	20/1	43	8
5177[4]	**Cross Talk (IRE) (50)** (RMStronge) **4-10-2**(7) MrJDewhurst(12) (nvr nr to chal)	2	**6**	12/1	45	15
5223[5]	**Can Can Charlie (60)** (JPearce) **6-10-7** MrsLPearce(1) (nvr nrr)	2	**7**	13/2[3]	40	10
349[6]	**Carrolls Marc (IRE) (47)** (CMurray) **8-10-7** MrTMcCarthy(2) (b: sme hdwy over 2f out: sn wknd)	7	**8**	9/1	31	1
4426[14]	**Chez Catalan (48)** (RAkehurst) **5-10-4b**(3) MrKGoble(10) (bhd fnl 4f)	¾	**9**	20/1	30	—
5189[9]	**Phanan (33)** (REPeacock) **10-10-0**(7) MrsCPeacock(4) (bhd fnl 4f)	2½	**10**	33/1	27	—
	Al Haal (USA) (60) (RJO'Sullivan) **7-10-0**(7) MrJGoldstein(3) (led 7f)	s.h	**11**	14/1	27	—
4448[16]	**Alisura (60)** (DTThom) **3-9-13** MissJFeilden(5) (prom over 3f)	3½	**12**	8/1	19	—
				(SP 120.9%)	**12 Rn**	

2m 38.51 (8.51) CSF £82.28 TOTE £32.30: £7.10 £1.40 £1.60 (£67.10) Trio £114.40 OWNER Mr A. Moore (BRIGHTON) BRED Fittocks Stud Ltd
WEIGHT FOR AGE 3yo-5lb

5245 WITCH OF ENDOR CLAIMING STKS (2-Y.O) (Class F)

1-15 (1-16) **5f (Equitrack)** £1,529.00 (£429.00: £209.00) Stalls: High GOING minus 0.52 sec per fur (FST)

				SP	RR	SF
5224[12]	**Heavenly Miss (IRE) (68)** (JJBridger) **2-8-12** SSanders(3) (hld up: led over 1f out: rdn out)	—	**1**	8/1	71	—
5176[7]	**Melbourne Princess (56)** (RMWhitaker) **2-7-10v1** FNorton(4) (led over 3f: unable qckn)	2	**2**	11/4[2]	49	—
5224[6]	**Threeplay (IRE) (66)** (JAkehurst) **2-9-3** DBiggs(1) (b: stumbled s: w ldr: rdn over 2f out: one pce)	1¾	**3**	9/4[1]	64	—
5224[9]	**Eager To Please (72)** (MissGayKelleway) **2-9-3** DHolland(5) (b.hind: lw: rdn over 3f out: lost pl over 2f out: rallied fnl f: r.o)	½	**4**	9/4[1]	62	—
5146[10]	**Whisper Low (IRE) (58)** (RHollinshead) **2-8-6** WRyan(6) (lw: bhd fnl 3f)	10	**5**	15/2[3]	19	—
				(SP 111.1%)	**5 Rn**	

61.52 secs (3.32) CSF £27.55 TOTE £5.80: £2.10 £1.70 (£18.80) OWNER Mr Trevor Mitchell (LIPHOOK) BRED Edward and Mrs S. Hannigan
OFFICIAL EXPLANATION **Heavenly Miss (IRE): accounting for her apparent improvement in form, her rider reported that on her last run, the filly lost her back legs coming out of the stalls and he thought she was going to go down, so from then on she was nursed home as he thought she might have sustained an injury to her back.**

5246 LE REVE H'CAP (0-85) (3-Y.O+) (Class D)

1-45 (1-46) **6f (Equitrack)** £2,801.00 (£848.00: £414.00: £197.00) Stalls: Low GOING minus 0.52 sec per fur (FST)

				SP	RR	SF
5068a[11]	**Bold Effort (FR) (82)** (KOCunningham-Brown) **4-9-13b** WRyan(2) (led 4f out: clr over 2f out: r.o wl)	—	**1**	10/1	95	23
5163[5]	**Step On Degas (61)** (MJFetherston-Godley) **3-8-1**(5) MartinDwyer(3) (lw: a.p: rdn over 2f out: chsd wnr fnl f: r.o wl)	1¼	**2**	11/1	71	—
4256[8]	**Sharp Imp (58)** (RMFlower) **6-8-3b** JQuinn(4) (hdwy over 1f out: r.o wl ins fnl f)	nk	**3**	20/1	67	—
*5184**	**Scissor Ridge (75)** (JJBridger) **4-9-6** SSanders(12) (hmpd & lost pl 5f out: rallied fnl f: r.o)	2½	**4**	13/2[3]	77	5

				SP	RR	SF
5150^{8}	**Prima Silk (77)** (MJRyan) **5-9-8** AClark(6) (hdwy over 1f out: nvr nrr)	1¼	**5**	14/1	76	4
5131^{9}	**Shadow Jury (72)** (DWChapman) **6-9-3b** ACulhane(8) (hmpd 5f out: rdn & no hdwy fnl 3f)	1¼	**6**	25/1	68	—
	Bold Frontier (66) (KTIvory) **4-8-11b** CScally(5) (b: b.hind: bit bkwd: rdn over 3f out: nvr nrr)	1¾	**7**	25/1	57	—
5112^{4}	**Madrina (65)** (JBerry) **3-8-5**(5) PFessey(13) (hdwy over 4f out: chsd wnr over 3f out to 1f out: sn wknd)	½	**8**	8/1	55	—
5211^{6}	**Jo Maximus (72)** (SDow) **4-9-3** DaneO'Neill(10) (b.off hind: hdwy on ins over 1f out: eased whn btn ins fnl f)	s.h	**9**	16/1	61	—
5138^{7}	**Beau Venture (USA) (60)** (BPalling) **8-8-5** TSprake(14) (lw: prom over 3f)	½	**10**	14/1	48	—
4996^{4}	**Lift Boy (USA) (68)** (AMoore) **7-8-13** CandyMorris(11) (b.hind: bhd fnl 5f)	s.h	**11**	20/1	56	—
5225*	**Mijas (66)** (LMontagueHall) **3-8-11** 7x AMcGlone(1) (led 2f: rdn over 3f out: wknd wl over 1f out)	1	**12**	4/1 1	51	—
5150^{2}	**Kings Harmony (IRE) (77)** (PJMakin) **3-9-8** DHolland(7) (prom over 2f)	3	**13**	5/1 2	54	—
3439^{10}	**Robo Magic (USA) (83)** (LMontagueHall) **4-10-0e** MWigham(9) (s.s: a wl bhd: t.o fnl 4f)	dist	**14**	25/1	—	—

(SP 118.8%) **14 Rn**

1m 13.73 (2.63) CSF £103.24 CT £1,220.12 TOTE £12.30: £4.20 £2.30 £3.20 (£42.40) Trio £128.60 OWNER Mr A. J. Richards (STOCKBRIDGE) BRED Ewar Stud Farm
STEWARDS' ENQUIRY Sprake susp. 31/12/96-1/1/97 (careless riding)

5247 ATROPOS H'CAP (0-60) (II) (3-Y.O+) (Class F)

2-15 (2-17) **1m 2f (Equitrack)** £1,179.00 (£329.00: £159.00) Stalls: Low GOING minus 0.52 sec per fur (FST)

				SP	RR	SF
5223^{2}	**Father Dan (IRE) (58)** (MissGayKelleway) **7-9-12** DHolland(2) (b: b.hind: hdwy over 3f out: hrd rdn over 1f out: led last strides)	—	**1**	4/1 2	64	35
5209^{9}	**Ben Gunn (54)** (PTWalwyn) **4-9-8** TSprake(9) (a.p: led over 3f out: hrd rdn over 1f out: hdd last strides)	hd	**2**	16/1	60	31
5221*	**Shanghai Lil (45)** (MJFetherston-Godley) **4-8-13** 5x FNorton(14) (hdwy over 3f out: rdn over 2f out: r.o wl ins fnl f)	1¼	**3**	8/1	49	20
5079^{5}	**Ilandra (IRE) (45)** (RAkehurst) **4-8-13** SSanders(10) (lw: hld up: rdn over 3f out: one pce)	1¾	**4**	7/1 3	46	17
5221^{8}	**Premier League (IRE) (37)** (JELong) **6-8-5** LeesaLong(5) (led over 6f: rdn: one pce)	nk	**5**	20/1	38	9
5210^{7}	**Arzani (USA) (55)** (DJSCosgrove) **5-9-9** JQuinn(12) (lw: hdwy over 3f out: sn wknd)	6	**6**	8/1	46	17
4882^{11}	**Adilov (40)** (JJBridger) **4-8-8** DaneO'Neill(1) (lw: nvr nr to chal)	1¾	**7**	20/1	28	—
5223*	**Absolutelystunning (46)** (MrsBarbaraWaring) **3-8-6**(5) PPMurphy(6) (b: b.hind: prom over 8f)	1¼	**8**	3/1 1	32	—
	Fair Ella (IRE) (38) (GLMoore) **4-8-3**(3)ow3 AWhelan(3) (prom 5f)	4	**9**	20/1	18	—
5175^{13}	**Paronomasia (35)** (JLHarris) **4-8-3** DBiggs(4) (b.hind: sme hdwy over 3f out: sn wknd)	1¾	**10**	8/1	12	—
5211^{8}	**Lahik (IRE) (35)** (KTIvory) **3-8-0** NAdams(7) (b: b.hind: a bhd)	17	**11**	33/1	—	—
2155^{13}	**Mega Tid (39)** (BAPearce) **4-8-7** DeclanO'Shea(8) (b: a bhd)	1	**12**	20/1	—	—
5130^{7}	**Reem Fever (IRE) (36)** (DWPArbuthnot) **3-8-1** CRutter(13) (b: b.hind: prom over 5f)	1	**13**	25/1	—	—
3358^{7}	**Prince Rudolf (IRE) (38)** (WGMTurner) **4-8-6** SDrowne(11) (b.hind: prom 5f: t.o)	dist	**14**	14/1	—	—

(SP 129.2%) **14 Rn**

2m 8.39 (4.09) CSF £64.52 CT £469.42 TOTE £3.50: £1.70 £3.30 £2.90 (£16.30) Trio £71.70 OWNER Father Dan Partnership (WHITCOMBE) BRED John Michael
WEIGHT FOR AGE 3yo-3lb

5248 SARAH CHAPMAN 21ST BIRTHDAY MAIDEN STKS (II) (2-Y.O) (Class D)

2-45 (2-46) **1m (Equitrack)** £2,450.00 (£740.00: £360.00: £170.00) Stalls: High GOING minus 0.52 sec per fur (FST)

				SP	RR	SF
	Feather Bed (IRE) (MAJarvis) **2-8-9** DRMcCabe(3) (neat: a.p: led over 2f out: rdn: r.o wl)	—	**1**	100/30 2	61	9
4383^{8}	**Around Fore Alliss (76)** (TGMills) **2-8-7**(7) JCornally(6) (hdwy over 5f out: ev ch ins fnl f: unable qckn)	1	**2**	8/1	64	12
5147^{5}	**Lochlass (IRE) (62)** (SPCWoods) **2-8-9** WRyan(4) (lw: hld up: rdn over 2f out: r.o one pce)	¾	**3**	5/1 3	58	6
4891^{15}	**Jolly Jackson** (RAkehurst) **2-9-0** SSanders(10) (hdwy over 1f out: r.o wl ins fnl f)	s.h	**4**	16/1	62	10
2714^{5}	**Troia (IRE)** (BSmart) **2-8-9** TSprake(9) (hdwy over 3f out: rdn over 2f out: one pce)	½	**5**	5/1 3	56	4
3129^{9}	**Soura (USA)** (PAKelleway) **2-8-9** MWigham(2) (led 7f out tl over 2f out: ev ch wl over 1f out: wknd fnl f)	2½	**6**	8/1	51	—
5051^{3}	**Roffey Spinney (IRE)** (RHannon) **2-9-0** DaneO'Neill(1) (prom over 4f)	6	**7**	5/2 1	44	—
5207^{6}	**Chynna** (MHTompkins) **2-8-9** AClark(8) (hdwy over 3f out: wknd over 2f out)	15	**8**	10/1	9	—
5187^{9}	**Trevor Mitchell (45)** (JJBridger) **2-8-9** NCarlisle(7) (led 1f: wknd over 4f out)	½	**9**	25/1	8	—
5098^{7}	**Heavenly Hand** (AMoore) **2-8-9** CandyMorris(5) (b.hind: a bhd)	2	**10**	25/1	4	—

(SP 129.9%) **10 Rn**

1m 41.6 (4.20) CSF £31.27 TOTE £3.90: £2.10 £3.20 £1.80 (£31.70) Trio £45.60 OWNER Lord Harrington (NEWMARKET) BRED Lord Harrington

5249 LADBROKE ALL-WEATHER TROPHY (QUALIFIER) H'CAP (0-80) (3-Y.O+) (Class D)

3-15 (3-17) **7f (Equitrack)** £3,036.60 (£919.80: £449.40: £214.20) Stalls: Low GOING minus 0.52 sec per fur (FST)

				SP	RR	SF
5089^{5}	**Speedy Classic (USA) (72)** (MJHeaton-Ellis) **7-9-9** AClark(11) (mde virtually all: clr 2f out: r.o wl)	—	**1**	12/1	86	42
5183^{2}	**Never Think Twice (55)** (KTIvory) **3-8-6b** NAdams(14) (b: b.hind: hdwy 4f out: chsd wnr over 2f out: no imp)	4	**2**	12/1	60	16
5221^{4}	**Barbason (55)** (AMoore) **4-8-6** CandyMorris(5) (b.hind: hdwy over 2f out: r.o ins fnl f)	½	**3**	16/1	59	15
3967^{7}	**Fort Knox (IRE) (60)** (RMFlower) **5-8-11b** DBiggs(2) (hdwy over 1f out: r.o)	3½	**4**	12/1	56	12
5209^{2}	**Star Talent (USA) (70)** (MissGayKelleway) **5-9-7** DaneO'Neill(4) (b: b.hind: hdwy over 1f out: r.o)	hd	**5**	5/1 1	66	22
5227^{6}	**Shontaine (62)** (MJohnston) **3-8-6**(7) KSked(13) (hdwy & nt clr run over 1f out: nvr nrr)	¾	**6**	14/1	56	12
5230^{7}	**Castlerea Lad (53)** (RHollinshead) **7-8-4** JQuinn(3) (nvr nr to chal)	s.h	**7**	10/1	47	3
5215*	**Greatest (76)** (MissGayKelleway) **5-9-8b**(5) 6x DSweeney(8) (b: b.hind: chsd wnr over 4f: wknd over 1f out)	nk	**8**	9/1 3	69	25
5170*	**Elite Hope (USA) (66)** (NTinkler) **4-8-10**(7) JoHunnam(9) (prom over 2f)	s.h	**9**	10/1	59	15
4865*	**Thordis (75)** (PJMakin) **3-9-12v** SSanders(16) (a.p: rn wd bnd over 4f out: wknd over 2f out)	½	**10**	12/1	67	23
5208^{5}	**Our Shadee (USA) (55)** (KTIvory) **6-8-6v** CScally(7) (b: b.hind: a bhd)	1¾	**11**	12/1	43	—
5002^{5}	**Milos (71)** (TJNaughton) **5-9-8** DHolland(6) (prom 3f)	2	**12**	5/1 1	54	10
5002^{14}	**Tom Morgan (75)** (PTWalwyn) **5-9-12** TSprake(10) (prom over 3f)	3	**13**	20/1	51	7
5186^{4}	**Blue Flyer (IRE) (77)** (RIngram) **3-10-0b** AMcGlone(15) (lw: a bhd)	hd	**14**	16/1	53	9
5150^{5}	**Deeply Vale (IRE) (72)** (EAWheeler) **5-9-9** CRutter(12) (hdwy 4f out: wknd over 2f out)	3	**15**	7/1 2	41	—

(SP 135.7%) **15 Rn**

1m 25.8 (1.40) CSF £148.25 CT £2,195.74 TOTE £19.50: £7.00 £4.60 £7.60 (£107.10) Trio Not won; £622.41 to Uttoxeter 21/12/96 OWNER South Wales Shower S Faucets (WROUGHTON) BRED Lagrange Chance Partnership & Overbrook Farm

IN-FOCUS: It was a pity that the most competitive event of the day had to be run in the dark, but it lived up to its billing.

T/Plpt: £336.10 (18.85 Tckts). T/Qdpt: £23.90 (30.89 Tckts). AK

5242-LINGFIELD (L-H) (Standard)
Thursday December 26th

All race times put back 10 mins.
WEATHER: sunny & cold WIND: almost nil

5250 EPIPHANY CLAIMING STKS (I) (3-Y.O+) (Class F)

12-50 (1-00) **1m 2f (Equitrack)** £2,540.80 (£713.80: £348.40) Stalls: Low GOING minus 0.31 sec per fur (FST)

Form	Horse	Dist	Pos	SP	RR	SF
5227[2]	**Barossa Valley (IRE) (70)** (PButler) **5-9-0**(5) DSweeney(2) (led 7f out: clr fr 4f out: rn wide home turn: r.o wl)	—	1	11/4[2]	85	59
5208[3]	**Slip Jig (IRE) (65)** (RHannon) **3-9-0** DaneO'Neill(6) (hld up: hdwy 7f out: chsd wnr over 4f out: hrd rdn over 2f out: no imp)	12	2	4/1[3]	64	35
5231[6]	**Cedez le Passage (FR) (79)** (KOCunningham-Brown) **5-9-9b** WRyan(1) (lw: sn led: hdd 7f out: wknd over 4f out)	11	3	11/10[1]	52	26
5149[7]	**Hatta Sunshine (USA) (48)** (AMoore) **6-8-9** CandyMorris(4) (b.hind: bhd fnl 5f)	10	4	14/1	22	—
3300[5]	**How Could-I (IRE) (33)** (MrsNMacauley) **3-7-13** JQuinn(3) (bhd fnl 7f)	7	5	14/1	4	—
5132[9]	**Northern Chief (28)** (JCullinan) **6-8-10**ow1 VSlattery(5) (a bhd: t.o)	23	6	66/1	—	—
				(SP 109.1%)	**6 Rn**	

2m 6.59 (2.29) CSF £12.72 TOTE £3.00: £1.50 £2.30 (£6.30) OWNER Mr Christopher Wilson (LEWES) BRED Swettenham Stud
WEIGHT FOR AGE 3yo-3lb

5251 MARY & JOSEPH NURSERY H'CAP (2-Y.O) (Class E)

1-20 (1-31) **6f (Equitrack)** £2,845.50 (£861.00: £420.00: £199.50) Stalls: Low GOING minus 0.31 sec per fur (FST)

Form	Horse	Dist	Pos	SP	RR	SF
4990[9]	**Island Prince (47)** (NACallaghan) **2-7-10** JQuinn(2) (chsd ldrs: led ins fnl f: hrd rdn: r.o)	—	1	9/2[3]	49	—
5224[2]	**The Wyandotte Inn (68)** (RHollinshead) **2-9-3** WRyan(6) (a.p: hrd rdn & ev ch wl ins fnl f: r.o)	s.h	2	6/4[1]	70	10
5202[9]	**Countless Times (57)** (WRMuir) **2-8-6** AClark(3) (a.p: led over 2f out: hrd rdn over 1f out: hdd ins fnl f: one pce)	1¾	3	14/1	54	—
5121[10]	**Mystery (50)** (SDow) **2-7-6**(7)ow3 DSalt(5) (rr: sn pushed along: hdwy over 1f out: kpt on one pce ins fnl f)	3½	4	16/1	38	—
5245*	**Heavenly Miss (IRE) (70)** (JJBridger) **2-9-5** 7x SSanders(1) (led: hdd over 2f out: wknd over 1f out)	10	5	5/2[2]	31	—
5087[8]	**Oaken Wood (IRE) (53)** (NACallaghan) **2-7-9b**[1](7)ow1 AngelaGallimore(4) (sn pushed along: a bhd)	2	6	33/1	9	—
4798[16]	**Royal Orchid (IRE) (72)** (RHannon) **2-9-7** DaneO'Neill(7) (chsd ldrs tl wknd wl over 1f out)	12	7	5/1	—	—
				(SP 118.9%)	**7 Rn**	

1m 15.52 (4.42) CSF £11.93 TOTE £6.60: £2.60 £1.10 (£5.20) OWNER J B R Leisure Ltd (NEWMARKET) BRED M. E. Wates
LONG HANDICAP Mystery 7-9

5252 THREE WISE MEN MEDIAN AUCTION MAIDEN STKS (2-Y.O) (Class E)

1-50 (2-00) **7f (Equitrack)** £2,845.50 (£861.00: £420.00: £199.50) Stalls: Low GOING minus 0.31 sec per fur (FST)

Form	Horse	Dist	Pos	SP	RR	SF
5238[2]	**Effervescence (78)** (RHannon) **2-9-0** DaneO'Neill(4) (lw: a gng wl: led over 2f out: sn clr: easily)	—	1	4/6[1]	77+	39
5239[7]	**Lily Jaques** (RGuest) **2-8-9** SSanders(2) (in tch: sn pushed along: hrd rdn fnl 2f: one pce)	11	2	33/1	47	9
5248[6]	**Soura (USA)** (PAKelleway) **2-8-9** MWigham(3) (prom: hrd rdn over 3f out: grad wknd)	3	3	4/1[3]	40	2
5243[3]	**Hever Golf Mover (55)** (TJNaughton) **2-8-9** DHolland(1) (led: hdd over 2f out: grad wknd)	s.h	4	9/4[2]	40	2
				(SP 113.7%)	**4 Rn**	

1m 26.84 (2.44) CSF £10.97 TOTE £1.80 (£4.80) OWNER The Gold Buster Syndicate (2) (MARLBOROUGH) BRED T. Umpleby

5253 SANTA CLAUS MAIDEN STKS (3-Y.O+) (Class D)

2-20 (2-32) **1m (Equitrack)** £3,468.75 (£1,050.00: £512.50: £243.75) Stalls: High GOING minus 0.31 sec per fur (FST)

Form	Horse	Dist	Pos	SP	RR	SF
5221[3]	**Royal Carlton (IRE) (51)** (GLMoore) **4-9-0** SWhitworth(8) (lw: hld up in tch: chsd ldr 4f out: led 2f out: clr over 1f out: rdn & flashed tail ins fnl f: r.o)	—	1	4/1[2]	65	43
5122[2]	**Passage Creeping (IRE) (65)** (SDow) **3-8-8** SSanders(4) (lw: chsd ldrs: sn pushed along: hrd rdn over 2f out: kpt on to go 2nd ins fnl f)	4	2	5/6[1]	52	29
4989[9]	**Hever Golf Eagle (49)** (TJNaughton) **3-8-13** DHolland(6) (lw: led 4f out: hdd 2f out: one pce)	1	3	11/1	55	32
5183[3]	**River Seine (FR) (41)** (SGKnight) **4-8-9** WRyan(2) (hld up: rdn over 3f out: no hdwy)	11	4	5/1[3]	28	6
5117[6]	**Fancy Design (IRE) (33)** (PMitchell) **3-8-8v**[1] JQuinn(7) (s.i.s: hdwy 4f out: rdn over 2f out: sn btn)	2	5	16/1	24	1
5227[8]	**Little Pilgrim (32)** (TMJones) **3-8-13** RPerham(3) (lw: led 4f: sn wknd)	14	6	66/1	1	—
672[10]	**Georgie Boy (USA) (50)** (MissGayKelleway) **3-8-6**(7) AngelaGallimore(9) (b: b.hind: in tch tl rdn & wknd 3f out)	2½	7	14/1	—	—
5211[12]	**Broughtons Relish** (WJMusson) **3-8-1**(7) DarrenWilliams(5) (a bhd)	hd	8	33/1	—	—
5188[8]	**Be Satisfied (44)** (AMoore) **3-8-13** AClark(1) (b.hind: bhd fnl 4f: t.o)	dist	9	20/1	—	—
				(SP 121.3%)	**9 Rn**	

1m 40.26 (2.86) CSF £7.85 TOTE £4.40: £1.90 £1.00 £2.80 (£3.40) Trio £7.40 OWNER Mrs Mary Doyle (BRIGHTON) BRED Des De Vere Hunt
WEIGHT FOR AGE 3yo-1lb

5254 EPIPHANY CLAIMING STKS (II) (3-Y.O+) (Class F)

2-50 (3-02) **1m 2f (Equitrack)** £2,528.90 (£710.40: £346.70) Stalls: Low GOING minus 0.31 sec per fur (FST)

Form	Horse	Dist	Pos	SP	RR	SF
5208[2]	**Waikiki Beach (USA) (75)** (GLMoore) **5-9-9** SWhitworth(2) (b: hld up: hdwy 3f out: led over 2f out: hrd rdn ins fnl f: all out)	—	1	2/1[2]	75	49
5211[4]	**Mediate (IRE) (50)** (AHide) **4-7-12**(7) GMilligan(9) (hld up: hdwy 3f out: ev ch fnl 2f: r.o)	s.h	2	10/1[3]	57	31
5208*	**Bon Secret (IRE) (67)** (TJNaughton) **4-8-13** DHolland(8) (hld up in tch: rdn over 2f out: one pce)	6	3	5/4[1]	55	29
5230[13]	**Dragon Green (51)** (JCullinan) **5-8-8**ow1 RPerham(4) (hld up in rr: hdwy 3f out: sn rdn: one pce)	2½	4	25/1	46	19
3965[12]	**Uoni (50)** (PButler) **3-8-1** JQuinn(7) (a.p: led 4f out: hdd over 2f out: wknd over 1f out)	3½	5	10/1[3]	37	8
5223[7]	**Eastleigh (41)** (RHollinshead) **7-8-2**(7) LisaWatson(5) (chsd ldrs tl wknd 3f out)	4	6	12/1	35	9

				SP	RR	SF
5244^{5}	**Efficacious (IRE) (39)** (AMoore) **3-7-11** FNorton(1) (chsd ldrs: rdn over 2f out: wknd over 1f out)	3½	**7**	14/1	21	—
4263^{18}	**Topup (50)** (JWHills) **3-8-6** NAdams(10) (bhd fnl 4f)	11	**8**	14/1	12	—
5236^{10}	**Justinianus (IRE) (31)** (JJBridger) **4-8-5** SSanders(3) (led 6f)	3½	**9**	33/1	3	—

(SP 123.8%) **9 Rn**

2m 8.33 (4.03) CSF £22.27 TOTE £3.10: £1.30 £2.20 £1.40 (£12.00) Trio £6.60 OWNER Pennine Partners (BRIGHTON) BRED Dan C. Pitts & Frank Ramos
WEIGHT FOR AGE 3yo-3lb

5255 REINDEER H'CAP (0-60) (3-Y.O+) (Class F)

3-20 (3-34) **2m (Equitrack)** £2,540.80 (£713.80: £348.40) Stalls: Low GOING minus 0.31 sec per fur (FST)

				SP	RR	SF
5213*	**Wottashambles (47)** (LMontagueHall) **5-9-2** DHolland(10) (hld up: hdwy ½-wy: chsd ldr 5f out: led 3f out: sn clr: eased ins fnl f)	—	**1**	9/4 1	58	39
5213^{5}	**Guest Alliance (IRE) (59)** (AMoore) **4-10-0** CandyMorris(4) (b.hind: a.p: rdn over 2f out: chsd wnr over 1f out: one pce)	5	**2**	4/1 3	65	46
5084^{4}	**Coh Sho No (52)** (SDow) **3-8-13** SSanders(8) (hld up: hdwy 7f out: rdn 4f out: kpt on one pce fnl 2f)	4	**3**	6/1	54	27
5222^{3}	**Nothing Doing (IRE) (35)** (WJMusson) **7-8-4** FNorton(3) (hld up in rr: hdwy 5f out: rdn over 1f out: styd on ins fnl f)	3	**4**	7/2 2	34	15
5247^{7}	**Adilov (40)** (JJBridger) **4-8-4**(5) DSweeney(2) (mid div: rdn over 3f out: one pce)	1¾	**5**	25/1	37	18
5232^{2}	**Mapengo (41)** (JCullinan) **5-8-10**ow1 VSlattery(9) (prom: led 5f out: hdd 3f out: wknd over 1f out)	4	**6**	20/1	34	14
5177^{3}	**Code Red (53)** (WRMuir) **3-9-0v1** AClark(6) (led 12f out: hdd 5f out: sn wknd)	13	**7**	8/1	33	6
	Cavina (46) (NAGraham) **6-9-1** DaneO'Neill(5) (lw: led 4f: wknd ½-wy)	9	**8**	11/2	17	—
5232^{7}	**Zeliba (32)** (MrsNMacauley) **4-7-8**(7)ow5 AngelaGallimore(7) (a bhd: t.o)	21	**9**	20/1	—	—
5222^{7}	**Etoile du Nord (28)** (HJCollingridge) **4-7-11** JQuinn(1) (b: bhd fr ½-wy: t.o)	hd	**10**	33/1	—	—

(SP 130.1%) **10 Rn**

3m 29.39 (8.39) CSF £12.85 CT £48.18 TOTE £2.60: £1.40 £1.90 £2.40 (£7.00) Trio £13.40 OWNER Dream On Racing Partnership (EPSOM) BRED Arthur Sims
LONG HANDICAP Zeliba 7-3
WEIGHT FOR AGE 3yo-8lb
OFFICIAL EXPLANATION **Nothing Doing (IRE): the rider reported that his instructions were to settle the gelding and kid him into the race, but the gelding was very difficult to settle and hung throughout. The trainer added that the gelding is a character who takes some riding.**

T/Plpt: £6.90 (2,038.36 Tckts). T/Qdpt: £2.30 (373.27 Tckts). SM

5174-SOUTHWELL (L-H) (Slow)
Friday December 27th

WEATHER: fine WIND: mod half bhd

5256 FRENCH HEN H'CAP (0-70) (I) (3-Y.O+) (Class E)

12-15 (12-20) **1m (Fibresand)** £2,575.10 (£777.80: £378.40: £178.70) Stalls: Low GOING: 0.24 sec per fur (SLW)

				SP	RR	SF
5237^{6}	**Cats Bottom (47)** (AGNewcombe) **4-8-6** JQuinn(4) (trckd ldrs: led over 2f out: sn clr: r.o wl)	—	**1**	6/1	57	30
5209^{11}	**Indiahra (47)** (JLEyre) **5-7-13v**(7) JBramhill(1) (mde most tl rn wd & hdd ent st: kpt on u.p)	2	**2**	4/1 2	53	26
5004^{14}	**In Good Faith (56)** (JJQuinn) **4-9-1** ACulhane(5) (lw: hld up in rr: gd hdwy 2f out: fin wl)	½	**3**	14/1	61	34
5241^{6}	**Three Arch Bridge (62)** (MJohnston) **4-9-7b** JWeaver(10) (lw: chsd ldrs: outpcd over 2f out: styd on wl ins fnl f)	¾	**4**	11/4 1	66	39
5215^{7}	**The Barnsley Belle (IRE) (55)** (JLEyre) **3-8-13** RLappin(9) (lw: w ldrs tl wknd wl over 1f out)	nk	**5**	11/2 3	58	30
5175^{8}	**Efipetite (42)** (NBycroft) **3-8-0** NKennedy(3) (s.i.s: sn rcvrd: rdn wl over 1f out: one pce)	nk	**6**	33/1	44	16
5161*	**Pleasure Trick (USA) (44)** (DonEnricoIncisa) **5-8-3b** KimTinkler(11) (chsd ldrs: rdn 2f out: nvr able to chal)	¾	**7**	7/1	45	18
5241^{11}	**Holloway Melody (46)** (BAMcMahon) **3-8-4** LNewton(8) (b: mid div: rdn 2f out: no imp)	5	**8**	20/1	37	9
4436^{13}	**Northern Grey (46)** (DrJDScargill) **4-8-5** SDrowne(2) (s.i.s: a in rr: t.o)	8	**9**	20/1	21	—
509^{3}	**Kingdom Princess (66)** (MJCamacho) **3-9-5**(5) GParkin(6) (bkwd: sn pushed along & bhd: t.o)	5	**10**	14/1	31	3
4587^{15}	**Irish Sea (USA) (54)** (RFMarvin) **3-8-12** TGMcLaughlin(7) (sn bhd & drvn along: t.o)	26	**11**	25/1	—	—

(SP 118.5%) **11 Rn**

1m 48.0 (9.00) CSF £28.69 CT £298.19 TOTE £5.90: £2.10 £2.30 £3.90 (£15.00) Trio £64.50 OWNER Mr A. G. Newcombe (BARNSTAPLE) BRED R. A. Speight
WEIGHT FOR AGE 3yo-1lb

5257 TURTLE DOVE MEDIAN AUCTION MAIDEN STKS (2-Y.O) (Class E)

12-45 (12-50) **6f (Fibresand)** £2,886.45 (£873.60: £426.30: £202.65) Stalls: Low GOING: 0.24 sec per fur (SLW)

				SP	RR	SF
5207^{2}	**Jay-Owe-Two (IRE) (68)** (RMWhitaker) **2-9-0** ACulhane(5) (lw: hld up: shkn up to ld over 1f out: sn clr)	—	**1**	7/4 1	79+	58
5239^{5}	**Faym (IRE)** (JWharton) **2-8-9** FNorton(7) (a.p: chal 2f out: kpt on: no ch w wnr)	3	**2**	8/1 3	66	45
5162^{5}	**Magic Fizz** (TJEtherington) **2-9-0** DaneO'Neill(4) (a.p: led over 2f out tl over 1f out: one pce)	6	**3**	9/1	55	34
4318^{9}	**Bailieborough Boy (IRE) (65)** (TDBarron) **2-9-0** JWeaver(8) (bit bkwd: hld up: outpcd over 2f out: styd on ins fnl f)	2	**4**	8/1 3	50	29
	Sliema Creek (TDBarron) **2-9-0** DHolland(1) (tall: unf: s.i.s: bhd: rn wd ent st: sme late hdwy: nvr nrr)	1	**5**	16/1	47	26
5187^{2}	**Share Delight (IRE) (75)** (BWHills) **2-8-11**(3) JDSmith(6) (trckd ldrs: pushed along over 2f out: sn lost tch)	¾	**6**	2/1 2	45	24
5162^{7}	**Krystal Davey (IRE)** (TDBarron) **2-8-7**(7) VictoriaAppleby(9) (chsd ldrs 4f: sn outpcd)	1½	**7**	10/1	41	20
	Kingdom Pearl (MJCamacho) **2-8-9** JQuinn(3) (leggy: scope: s.s: a bhd & outpcd: t.o)	12	**8**	25/1	4	—
5245^{5}	**Whisper Low (IRE) (53)** (RHollinshead) **2-8-9** WRyan(2) (led tl hdd over 2f out: wknd qckly: t.o)	9	**9**	25/1	—	—

(SP 124.6%) **9 Rn**

1m 17.9 (4.40) CSF £16.78 TOTE £2.20: £1.10 £2.40 £1.70 (£13.70) Trio £18.90 OWNER Mr R. M. Whitaker (LEEDS) BRED Thoroughbred Trust

5258 CALLING BIRD H'CAP (0-70) (3-Y.O+) (Class E)

1-15 (1-20) **6f (Fibresand)** £2,927.40 (£886.20: £432.60: £205.80) Stalls: Low GOING: 0.24 sec per fur (SLW)

				SP	RR	SF
5225^{4}	**Kalar (70)** (DWChapman) **7-10-0b** ACulhane(6) (mde all: clr over 2f out: rdn & edgd rt fnl f: all out)	—	**1**	13/2^{3}	75	59
5165^{7}	**Craigie Boy (39)** (NBycroft) **6-7-11b**^{ow1} JQuinn(4) (a.p: rdn over 1f out: kpt on wl towards fin)	1½	**2**	9/2^{2}	40	23
5236^{8}	**Bold Aristocrat (IRE) (59)** (RHollinshead) **5-9-3** WRyan(9) (sn bhd: hdwy 2f out: hung lft: r.o wl fnl f)	nk	**3**	7/2^{1}	59	43
3761^{8}	**Unspoken Prayer (40)** (JRArnold) **3-7-7**$^{(5)}$ MartinDwyer(2) (a chsng ldrs: sltly hmpd ins fnl f: r.o)	1¼	**4**	14/1	37	21
5234^{6}	**Peacefull Reply (USA) (39)** (FHLee) **6-7-11b**^{ow1} NKennedy(7) (lw: bhd: hdwy wl over 1f out: nvr nrr)	4	**5**	16/1	25	8
3453^{W}	**Sound the Trumpet (IRE) (51)** (RCSpicer) **4-8-9** JO'Reilly(8) (in tch: r.o one pce fnl 2f)	3	**6**	10/1	29	13
5241^{5}	**Encore M'Lady (IRE) (55)** (FHLee) **5-8-13v** RLappin(5) (chsd wnr: c wd ent st: sn rdn: grad wknd)	2	**7**	7/2^{1}	28	12
5174^{5}	**Juba (38)** (DrJDScargill) **4-7-7**$^{(3)}$ NVarley(1) (sn bhd & outpcd: t.o)	13	**8**	8/1	—	—
4768^{20}	**Craignairn (57)** (JLEyre) **3-9-1b** DHolland(3) (wl bhd fr ½-wy: t.o)	dist	**9**	10/1	—	—
				(SP 117.8%)	**9 Rn**	

1m 18.8 (5.30) CSF £34.12 CT £110.51 TOTE £5.30: £2.10 £1.30 £1.70 (£16.20) Trio £23.90 OWNER Mr J. M. Chapman (YORK) BRED C. C. and Mrs Pryor

LONG HANDICAP Peacefull Reply (USA) 7-8 Craigie Boy 7-9 Juba 7-6

5259 PARTRIDGE MAIDEN STKS (3-Y.O+) (Class D)

1-45 (1-50) **1m 4f (Fibresand)** £3,436.25 (£1,040.00: £507.50: £241.25) Stalls: High GOING: 0.24 sec per fur (SLW)

				SP	RR	SF
4872^{9}	**Albaha (USA) (70)** (JEBanks) **3-8-12** JQuinn(5) (led after 3f: clr 4f out: eased fnl f: canter)	—	**1**	5/4^{1}	75+	28
4345^{3}	**Royal Legend (56)** (JPearce) **4-9-3** MWigham(1) (bit bkwd: a.p: chsd wnr & rdn 3f out: no imp)	17	**2**	7/2^{2}	52	10
5181^{6}	**Hornpipe (50)** (JWharton) **4-9-0**$^{(3)}$ CTeague(3) (b: lw: led 3f: rdn 5f out: sn outpcd)	2½	**3**	10/1	49	7
	Golden Hanoof (USA) (DrJDScargill) **4-8-12** SDrowne(7) (bkwd: drvn along ½-wy: nvr nr ldrs)	9	**4**	20/1	32	—
4095^{13}	**Nordic Hero (IRE) (43)** (APJarvis) **3-8-12** DaneO'Neill(2) (chsd ldrs: drvn along 8f out: lost tch 5f out: t.o)	dist	**5**	20/1	—	—
5242^{7}	**Taniyar (FR) (35)** (RHollinshead) **4-9-3** WRyan(4) (lw: hld up & bhd: pushed along ½-wy: sn t.o)	1	**6**	6/1	—	—
2505^{9}	**Hever Golf Classic (60)** (TJNaughton) **3-8-12** DHolland(6) (bkwd: lost pl ½-wy: virtually p.u: t.o)	dist	**7**	5/1^{3}	—	—
				(SP 116.2%)	**7 Rn**	

2m 45.9 (12.90) CSF £6.15 TOTE £2.20: £1.10 £3.20 (£4.20) OWNER UK Packaging Supplies Ltd (NEWMARKET) BRED Shadwell Estate Co., Ltd. and Shadwell Farm Inc.

WEIGHT FOR AGE 3yo-5lb

OFFICIAL EXPLANATION **Hever Golf Classic: hung badly left throughout, making it impossible for his jockey to ride him to any effect.**

5260 GOLD RINGS H'CAP (0-60) (3-Y.O+) (Class F)

2-15 (2-21) **1m 3f (Fibresand)** £2,683.60 (£754.60: £368.80) Stalls: High GOING: 0.24 sec per fur (SLW)

				SP	RR	SF
5210^{4}	**Raindeer Quest (31)** (JLEyre) **4-7-6**$^{(7)}$ JBramhill(8) (lw: hdwy 8f out: led over 4f out: sn clr: v.easily)	—	**1**	7/1	47+	18
5181^{9}	**Carol Again (42)** (NBycroft) **4-8-10** JQuinn(6) (hld up: hdwy 5f out: chsd wnr fr 2f out: no imp)	12	**2**	16/1	41	12
3979^{6}	**Risky Tu (45)** (PAKelleway) **5-8-13** MWigham(12) (sn chsng ldrs: pushed along & one pce fnl 2f)	nk	**3**	10/1	43	14
5242^{5}	**Bold Habit (40)** (JPearce) **11-8-8** FNorton(13) (bhd: hdwy 6f out: one pce fnl 3f)	3	**4**	14/1	34	5
4785^{3}	**Quiet Arch (IRE) (60)** (WRMuir) **3-9-10** DaneO'Neill(3) (b: b.hind: hdwy to chse ldrs 5f out: wknd 2f out)	6	**5**	11/2^{2}	45	12
5244^{4}	**Sheraz (IRE) (51)** (NTinkler) **4-9-5** GCarter(5) (lost pl ½-wy: styd on again fnl 2f)	6	**6**	10/1	27	—
5143^{10}	**No Submission (USA) (52)** (DWChapman) **10-9-6** ACulhane(2) (sn bhd: sme hdwy 4f out: nvr nr ldrs)	1	**7**	10/1	27	—
5054*	**Tonka (40)** (PJMakin) **4-8-8** SSanders(1) (lw: hld up: effrt 4f out: eased whn btn fnl 2f)	4	**8**	7/2^{1}	9	—
5177^{12}	**Chancancook (32)** (JLEyre) **3-7-7**$^{(3)}$ NVarley(10) (s.i.s: a in rr)	¾	**9**	14/1	—	—
4810^{11}	**El Don (34)** (MJRyan) **4-7-9**$^{(7)}$ AMcCarthy(11) (bhd: hdwy u.p 5f out: nvr nr ldrs)	½	**10**	6/1^{3}	1	—
	Katy's Lad (52) (BAMcMahon) **9-9-6** LNewton(7) (b: trckd ldrs tl lost pl over 4f out)	½	**11**	16/1	19	—
2180^{20}	**Classic Daisy (35)** (RCSpicer) **3-7-13b** JO'Reilly(9) (led 7f out tl over 4f out: sn lost tch: t.o)	dist	**12**	33/1	—	—
5062^{12}	**Flowing Ocean (41)** (DWChapman) **6-8-9b**^{1} DHolland(4) (led 4f: wknd qckly: t.o fnl 3f)	dist	**13**	25/1	—	—
				(SP 123.6%)	**13 Rn**	

2m 31.9 (11.90) CSF £103.48 CT £1,035.88 TOTE £7.90: £2.10 £3.70 £3.30 (£35.50) Trio £200.40 OWNER Whitestonecliffe Racing Partnership (HAMBLETON) BRED Stetchworth Park Stud Ltd

LONG HANDICAP Chancancook 7-8

WEIGHT FOR AGE 3yo-4lb

OFFICIAL EXPLANATION **Tonka: did not stay on the testing All-Weather surface of that day.**

5261 GEESE (S) STKS (2-Y.O) (Class F)

2-45 (2-55) **7f (Fibresand)** £2,505.10 (£703.60: £343.30) Stalls: Low GOING: 0.24 sec per fur (SLW)

				SP	RR	SF
3324^{6}	**Fast Spin (53)** (TDBarron) **2-8-12** ACulhane(2) (lw: hld up: hdwy over 2f out: led wl over 1f out: sn clr)	—	**1**	5/2^{2}	65	41
5202^{10}	**Chasetown Flyer (USA) (58)** (RHollinshead) **2-8-12** WRyan(5) (led tl hdd wl over 1f out: sn rdn & outpcd)	5	**2**	11/2^{3}	54	30
5142^{6}	**Phylida (62)** (PJMakin) **2-8-7** SSanders(1) (chsd ldrs: rdn & one pce fnl 2f)	3	**3**	5/2^{2}	42	18
4251^{5}	**Hever Golf Stormer (IRE) (52)** (TJNaughton) **2-8-12** DHolland(4) (trckd ldrs: rdn over 2f out: wknd over 1f out)	hd	**4**	10/1	47	23
5202^{3}	**Senate Swings (56)** (WRMuir) **2-8-12** DaneO'Neill(3) (prom: rdn over 2f out: sn btn)	2	**5**	2/1^{1}	42	18
				(SP 115.0%)	**5 Rn**	

1m 33.3 (6.80) CSF £14.69 TOTE £3.70: £2.30 £1.10 (£10.60) OWNER Mr E. Buck (THIRSK) BRED Fares Stables Ltd

No bid

5262 FRENCH HEN H'CAP (0-70) (II) (3-Y.O+) (Class E)

3-15 (3-31) **1m (Fibresand)** £2,575.10 (£777.80: £378.40: £178.70) Stalls: Low GOING: 0.24 sec per fur (SLW)

				SP	RR	SF
5060*	**Slievenamon (44)** (JEBanks) **3-8-2** JQuinn(3) (a.p: led wl over 1f out: drvn clr)	—	**1**	5/2^{1}	58	39
5209^{7}	**Kingchip Boy (68)** (MJRyan) **7-9-6v**$^{(7)}$ AMcCarthy(11) (trckd ldrs: effrt 2f out: edgd lft appr fnl f: one pce)	5	**2**	100/30^{2}	72	54
5206*	**Barrel of Hope (69)** (JLEyre) **4-10-0b** RLappin(6) (lw: mde most tl hdd wl over 1f out: kpt on same pce)	2	**3**	6/1	69	51
5161^{11}	**Principal Boy (IRE) (49)** (TJEtherington) **3-8-7** DaneO'Neill(4) (a chsng ldrs: rdn & one pce appr fnl f)	s.h	**4**	16/1	49	30
5241^{2}	**Monis (IRE) (53)** (JBalding) **5-8-12** DHolland(8) (lw: hld up: hdwy ½-wy: kpt on: nt pce to chal)	1½	**5**	9/2^{3}	50	32
5235^{5}	**Silver Harrow (47)** (AGNewcombe) **3-8-5** SDrowne(2) (in tch: drvn along ½-wy: no imp)	5	**6**	6/1	34	15
5215^{4}	**Morning Surprise (47)** (APJarvis) **3-7-12**$^{(7)ow4}$ CCarver(9) (s.i.s: bhd tl sme late hdwy)	1¾	**7**	20/1	30	7

				SP	RR	SF
5178^{5}	**Down The Yard (39)** (MCChapman) **3-7-11**ow1 NKennedy(1) (s.i.s: a in rr)	3½	**8**	20/1	15	—
5129^{13}	**Shedansar (IRE) (37)** (RCSpicer) **4-7-10b** JO'Reilly(7) (s.s: a bhd: t.o)	3½	**9**	50/1	6	—
5200^{2}	**Golden Touch (USA) (63)** (DJSCosgrove) **4-9-8** SSanders(5) (mid div: drvn along over 3f out: sn lost tch: t.o)	3	**10**	13/2	26	8
4474^{10}	**Ballykissangel (38)** (NBycroft) **3-7-7**(3) NVarley(10) (in tch: pushed along 4f out: sn lost tch: t.o)	10	**11**	50/1	—	—

(SP 131.1%) **11 Rn**

1m 46.7 (7.70) CSF £12.33 CT £45.74 TOTE £5.30: £2.10 £1.20 £2.30 (£12.70) Trio £10.50 OWNER Mr P. Cunningham (NEWMARKET) BRED Mrs Celia Miller

LONG HANDICAP Down The Yard 7-7 Shedansar (IRE) 6-12 Ballykissangel 7-1

WEIGHT FOR AGE 3yo-1lb

T/Plpt: £332.00 (44.21 Tckts). T/Qdpt: £60.90 (21.79 Tckts). IM

0543a-SAN ROSSORE (Pisa, Italy) (R-H) (Very Heavy)
Saturday December 21st

5263a PREMIO CALAMBRONE (2-Y.O)
2-30 (2-36) **1m 2f** £6,090.00

				SP	RR	SF
	Last Frontier (IRE) (DCrisanti,Italy) **2-8-3** PAgus	—	1		—	—
	Take (ITY) (RMinisini,Italy) **2-8-8** LSorrentino	1¾	2		—	—
4171a^{2}	**Columella (ITY)** (PCaravati,Italy) **2-8-6** ACarboni	1¼	3		—	—
4286a^{4}	**Shareef Allah** (KMcAuliffe) **2-8-3** GPretta (btn just under 5l)		5		—	—

10 Rn

2m 15.0 TOTE 251L: 46L 19L 18L (671L) OWNER Scuderia A & M BRED Islanmore Stud

5234-WOLVERHAMPTON (L-H) (Standard)
Saturday December 28th
WEATHER: fine WIND: slt half against

5264 PEREGRINE H'CAP (0-70) (I) (3-Y.O+) (Class E)
12-50 (12-51) **7f (Fibresand)** £2,561.45 (£773.60: £376.30: £177.65) Stalls: High GOING: 0.06 sec per fur (STD)

				SP	RR	SF
4724^{8}	**Murray's Mazda (IRE) (43)** (JLEyre) **7-7-8**(7) JBramhill(1) (chsd ldrs: led over 2f out: clr fnl f)	—	**1**	10/1	52	29
5234*	**Marjorie Rose (IRE) (63)** (ABailey) **3-9-7** DWright(2) (b: b.hind: lw: hld up: hdwy on ins ent st: kpt on: no ch w wnr)	3½	**2**	10/1	64	41
5230^{2}	**Desert Invader (IRE) (70)** (DWChapman) **5-10-0** ACulhane(3) (led tl over 2f out: hrd rdn & one pce appr fnl f)	1½	**3**	3/1 1	68	45
5237*	**Leigh Crofter (64)** (PDCundell) **7-9-8b** DHolland(4) (s.i.s: sn drvn along: hdwy ½-wy: one pce fnl 2f)	1½	**4**	3/1 1	58	35
5170^{5}	**Anita's Contessa (IRE) (53)** (BPalling) **4-8-11** DaneO'Neill(6) (chsd ldr over 3f: sn rdn: wknd over 2f out)	11	**5**	14/1	22	—
4724^{9}	**Failed To Hit (68)** (NPLittmoden) **3-9-12v**1 TGMcLaughlin(5) (a bhd & outpcd)	4	**6**	33/1	28	5
4979^{6}	**Anonym (IRE) (62)** (DNicholls) **4-9-6b** AlexGreaves(8) (sn pushed along: a outpcd)	5	**7**	10/1	10	—
5241*	**Quinzii Martin (51)** (DHaydnJones) **8-8-9** SDrowne(10) (a bhd & outpcd)	s.h	**8**	6/1 2	—	—
5237^{5}	**Jigsaw Boy (64)** (PGMurphy) **7-9-8v** JWeaver(9) (in tch: effrt over 3f out: sn rdn & btn)	¾	**9**	8/1 3	11	—
5208^{9}	**Chalky Dancer (38)** (HJCollingridge) **4-7-10v**1 JQuinn(7) (sn pushed along: lost tch ½-wy: t.o)	18	**10**	40/1	—	—

(SP 114.7%) **10 Rn**

1m 30.0 (5.30) CSF £92.37 CT £289.22 TOTE £9.80: £2.30 £2.90 £1.50 (£42.30) Trio £71.90 OWNER Mr Murray Grubb (HAMBLETON) BRED Patrick Kennedy

LONG HANDICAP Chalky Dancer 6-11

5265 BUZZARD MAIDEN AUCTION STKS (2-Y.O) (Class E)
1-20 (1-21) **7f (Fibresand)** £2,900.10 (£877.80: £428.40: £203.70) Stalls: High GOING: 0.06 sec per fur (STD)

				SP	RR	SF
5201^{8}	**Komasta (60)** (CaptJWilson) **2-8-3** FNorton(2) (mde all: clr fr ½-wy: unchal)	—	**1**	10/1	56	10
5239^{6}	**Royal Cascade (IRE)** (BAMcMahon) **2-8-10** NCarlisle(6) (a chsng wnr: rdn wl over 1f out: no imp)	7	**2**	7/2 3	47	1
5113^{7}	**Danehill Princess (IRE) (64)** (RHollinshead) **2-8-5** JQuinn(3) (chsd ldng pair: hrd drvn 2f out: one pce)	¾	**3**	3/1 2	40	—
	French Kiss (IRE) (MRChannon) **2-8-7** RPerham(1) (lt-f: bit bkwd: s.s: hdwy to chse ldrs 5f out: rdn & outpcd 3f out)	12	**4**	5/2 1	15	—
568^{7}	**Weet A Bit (IRE)** (RHollinshead) **2-8-10** MWigham(4) (bkwd: dwlt: sn drvn along: a outpcd)	½	**5**	7/1	17	—
	Spargo Express (BWHills) **2-8-7**(3) JDSmith(5) (unf: scope: b.hind: sn outpcd: a bhd: t.o)	13	**6**	5/1	—	—

(SP 114.1%) **6 Rn**

1m 31.9 (7.20) CSF £41.58 TOTE £10.50: £3.20 £2.20 (£40.70) OWNER Mr F. Cunliffe (PRESTON) BRED Franklin Cunliffe

5266 PEREGRINE H'CAP (0-70) (II) (3-Y.O+) (Class E)
1-50 (1-51) **7f (Fibresand)** £2,534.15 (£765.20: £372.10: £175.55) Stalls: High GOING: 0.06 sec per fur (STD)

				SP	RR	SF
5249^{9}	**Elite Hope (USA) (64)** (NTinkler) **4-9-8** GCarter(4) (lw: w ldr: led over 2f out: drvn out)	—	**1**	7/2 1	72	46
5227^{5}	**Sooty Tern (53)** (JMBradley) **9-8-11** DHolland(2) (mde most over 4f: hrd rdn & rallied fnl f: r.o)	½	**2**	9/1	60	34
5163^{9}	**Myttons Mistake (70)** (ABailey) **3-9-7**(7) GMilligan(1) (lw: a.p: effrt & rdn 2f out: nt pce to chal)	2½	**3**	10/1	71	45
5237^{3}	**Gulf Shaadi (57)** (EJAlston) **4-9-1** SSanders(9) (dwlt: nvr nr to chal)	9	**4**	9/2 2	38	12
5106^{13}	**So Amazing (70)** (JLEyre) **4-10-0** RLappin(6) (trckd ldrs: rdn & outpcd over 2f out)	7	**5**	9/1	35	9
5230^{5}	**Kid Ory (49)** (DWChapman) **5-8-7** ACulhane(5) (chsd ldrs 4f: sn wknd)	4	**6**	7/1	4	—
4128^{12}	**Astral Invader (IRE) (48)** (MSSaunders) **4-8-6** SDrowne(8) (sn rdn along: a bhd: t.o)	7	**7**	33/1	—	—
5170^{3}	**Sis Garden (60)** (JCullinan) **3-8-13b**(5) DSweeney(3) (lw: chsd ldrs to ½-wy: sn lost tch: t.o)	4	**8**	5/1 3	—	—

Form	Horse	Dist	Pos	SP	RR	SF
5144[7]	**Gad Yakoun (65)** (MGMeagher) **3-9-9** JQuinn(7) (dwlt: sn rcvrd to chse ldrs: wknd 3f out: t.o)	5	9	7/1	—	—
				(SP 114.1%)		**9 Rn**

1m 30.2 (5.50) CSF £31.14 CT £260.02 TOTE £4.40: £1.30 £2.10 £4.40 (£10.40) Trio £53.90 OWNER Elite Racing Club (MALTON) BRED Barbara Hunter

5267 EAGLE MAIDEN STKS (3-Y.O+) (Class D)

2-20 (2-20) **1m 100y (Fibresand)** £3,468.75 (£1,050.00: £512.50: £243.75) Stalls: Low GOING: 0.06 sec per fur (STD)

Form	Horse	Dist	Pos	SP	RR	SF
703[4]	**Raheen (USA) (85)** (WGMTurner) **3-8-8b[1]**(5) DSweeney(8) (bit bkwd: chsd ldr: led over 4f out: clr fnl 2f: v.easily)	—	1	100/30[2]	87+	54
	Holders Hill (IRE) (MGMeagher) **4-9-0** JQuinn(5) (hdwy 4f out: styd on fnl f: no ch w wnr)	8	2	16/1	71	40
5058[2]	**Agent (70)** (JLEyre) **3-8-13** RLappin(4) (a chsng ldrs: hrd drvn over 2f out: one pce)	1	3	3/1[1]	69	37
5227[9]	**Brecon (67)** (WRMuir) **3-8-13** JWeaver(2) (lw: sn drvn along: hdwy over 3f out: nt rch ldrs)	4	4	6/1	61	29
4978[2]	**Sounds Legal** (PDEvans) **3-8-8** ACulhane(9) (trckd ldrs: rdn over 5f out: styd on appr fnl f)	¾	5	7/2[3]	55	23
5122[5]	**Balinsky (IRE) (51)** (JBerry) **3-8-3**(5) PFessey(7) (led 4f: rdn & wknd over 2f out)	6	6	16/1	43	12
	Stonecutter (MRChannon) **3-8-13v** RPerham(11) (s.s: nvr nrr)	1½	7	9/1	45	14
4428[12]	**Hazel (57)** (MissGayKelleway) **4-8-9** DaneO'Neill(1) (bit bkwd: sn pushed along: a outpcd)	nk	8	10/1	39	9
4704[5]	**Condition Red** (MSSaunders) **3-8-8** SDrowne(10) (bit bkwd: a bhd: t.o)	14	9	33/1	11	—
5183[9]	**Supreme Illusion (AUS) (26)** (JohnBerry) **3-8-5e**(3) NVarley(3) (prom early: sn lost tch: t.o)	½	10	33/1	10	—
3427[11]	**Braes'O'Shieldhill (30)** (ABailey) **3-8-8** WHollick(6) (b: bkwd: a bhd: t.o)	¾	11	25/1	8	—
				(SP 125.2%)		**11 Rn**

1m 50.1 (5.10) CSF £52.26 TOTE £3.80: £1.70 £3.90 £1.80 (£90.70) Trio £92.80 OWNER Mr Basheer Kielany (SHERBORNE) BRED Gainsborough Farm Inc.
WEIGHT FOR AGE 3yo-1lb

5268 FALCON H'CAP (0-65) (3-Y.O+) (Class F)

2-50 (2-54) **5f (Fibresand)** £2,588.40 (£727.40: £355.20) Stalls: Low GOING: 0.06 sec per fur (STD)

Form	Horse	Dist	Pos	SP	RR	SF
4219[4]	**Amington Lass (60)** (PDEvans) **3-9-11** SSanders(2) (chsd ldrs: rdn 2f out: r.o to ld nr fin)	—	1	16/1	62	41
5234[11]	**Boffy (IRE) (47)** (BPJBaugh) **3-8-12b** RPerham(3) (chsd ldrs: hdwy to ld ins fnl f: hdd cl home)	¾	2	33/1	47	26
5225[9]	**Sotonian (HOL) (32)** (PSFelgate) **3-7-11**ow1 DWright(4) (led tl hdd & no ex ins fnl f)	1½	3	33/1	27+	5
4791[14]	**Captain Carat (61)** (DNicholls) **5-9-12** AlexGreaves(9) (hdwy ½-wy: r.o ins fnl f: nvr nrr)	1	4	8/1	53	32
5173[2]	**Aljaz (49)** (MissGayKelleway) **6-9-0** DaneO'Neill(5) (spd over 3f)	5	5	7/2[1]	25	4
5241[12]	**Amy Leigh (IRE) (46)** (CaptJWilson) **3-8-11b** DHolland(6) (chsd ldrs: rdn & wknd over 1f out)	2½	6	8/1	14	—
3420[8]	**Elraas (USA) (32)** (RJO'Sullivan) **4-7-11b[1]**ow1 FNorton(13) (bkwd: nvr plcd to chal)	4	7	16/1	—	—
5225[8]	**Rennyholme (50)** (JHetherton) **5-9-1b** NAdams(7) (chsd ldrs 3f: sn rdn & wknd)	2	8	14/1	—	—
5241[8]	**Cheeky Chappy (59)** (DWChapman) **5-9-10b** ACulhane(11) (nvr gng pce of ldrs)	1	9	7/1	4	—
5225[3]	**Featherstone Lane (63)** (MissLCSiddall) **5-10-0v** JWeaver(12) (dwlt: outpcd)	1	10	6/1[3]	5	—
5246[8]	**Madrina (62)** (JBerry) **3-9-6**(7) CLowther(1) (s.i.s: sn drvn along: a outpcd)	1¼	11	9/2[2]	—	—
1761[W]	**Miletrian Refurb (IRE) (60)** (MRChannon) **3-9-11** CandyMorris(8) (bit bkwd: outpcd)	1½	12	14/1	—	—
5220[10]	**Avant Huit (32)** (MrsNMacauley) **4-7-11b** JQuinn(10) (lw: outpcd: t.o)	8	13	33/1	—	—
				(SP 123.3%)		**13 Rn**

63.1 secs (4.20) CSF £371.81 CT £7,735.95 TOTE £13.50: £4.60 £4.00 £17.50 (£67.00) Trio £474.70 OWNER Mr M. J. Higgins (WELSHPOOL) BRED M. Higgins
LONG HANDICAP Elraas (USA) 7-0 Sotonian (HOL) 7-7

5269 MERLIN CLAIMING STKS (3-Y.O+) (Class F)

3-20 (3-20) **1m 1f 79y (Fibresand)** £2,683.60 (£754.60: £368.80) Stalls: Low GOING: 0.06 sec per fur (STD)

Form	Horse	Dist	Pos	SP	RR	SF
5205[4]	**Greenspan (IRE) (73)** (WRMuir) **4-9-8** DaneO'Neill(2) (chsd ldrs: led on bit over 1f out: drvn clr fnl f)	—	1	5/1[2]	78	49
5233[6]	**Obelos (USA) (64)** (MissSJWilton) **5-9-4v[1]** SWhitworth(9) (chsd ldrs: effrt wl over 1f out: nt pce of wnr fnl f)	3	2	14/1	69	40
5140*	**Honestly (55)** (BSmart) **3-8-5** SSanders(7) (hld up: hdwy 5f out: led over 2f out tl over 1f out: one pce)	3	3	6/1[3]	53	22
5250[3]	**Cedez le Passage (FR) (79)** (KOCunningham-Brown) **5-9-8b** JWeaver(5) (trckd ldrs: kpt on u.p fnl 2f)	1½	4	5/1[2]	65	36
5241[4]	**Lia Fail (IRE) (45)** (RHollinshead) **3-8-1** JQuinn(12) (bhd: hdwy over 3f out: nvr nrr)	8	5	14/1	33	2
4573[11]	**Young Benson (61)** (TWall) **4-8-3v[1]**(5) DSweeney(4) (chsd ldrs: ev ch & rdn 2f out: wknd appr fnl f)	1½	6	14/1	35	6
5235[3]	**Yeoman Oliver (66)** (BAMcMahon) **3-9-2** LNewton(3) (lw: chsd ldr: led over 3f out tl over 2f out: wknd appr fnl f)	1½	7	12/1	42	11
1775[14]	**Il Trastevere (FR) (72)** (MissGayKelleway) **4-8-11**(7) AngelaGallimore(1) (led tl over 3f out: rdn & wknd over 1f out)	2	8	10/1	39	10
1338[6]	**Northern Spruce (IRE) (25)** (AGFoster) **4-8-8** RPerham(11) (b: a bhd: t.o)	30	9	16/1	—	—
3978[12]	**Dyanko (26)** (MSSaunders) **3-8-2** AMackay(8) (a in rr: t.o fnl 4f)	1½	10	50/1	—	—
5231[5]	**Bentico (75)** (MrsNMacauley) **7-9-1**(3) CTeague(10) (b: lw: stdd s: a wl bhd: t.o)	2	11	100/30[1]	—	—
4769[14]	**Rambo Waltzer (78)** (DNicholls) **4-9-4** AlexGreaves(13) (bit bkwd: prom to ½-wy: sn wknd: t.o)	14	12	6/1[3]	—	—
				(SP 129.6%)		**12 Rn**

2m 3.2 (7.20) CSF £70.94 TOTE £5.10: £1.80 £3.40 £2.50 (£55.30) Trio £57.30 OWNER Camelot Racing (LAMBOURN) BRED Dermot and Meta Cantillon
WEIGHT FOR AGE 3yo-2lb
OFFICIAL EXPLANATION **Bentico: the rider reported that the gelding kept changing his legs and was never travelling.**

5270 OWL H'CAP (0-70) (3-Y.O+) (Class E)

3-50 (3-50) **1m 4f (Fibresand)** £2,982.00 (£903.00: £441.00: £210.00) Stalls: Low GOING: 0.06 sec per fur (STD)

Form	Horse	Dist	Pos	SP	RR	SF
2628[6]	**Canary Falcon (52)** (RJO'Sullivan) **5-8-11b[1]** DHolland(2) (mde all: qcknd clr over 2f out: unchal)	—	1	9/1	69+	51
5233[4]	**In the Money (IRE) (51)** (RHollinshead) **7-8-10** MWigham(10) (dwlt: bhd tl hdwy over 3f out: kpt on appr fnl f)	10	2	8/1	55	37
5233[3]	**Mad Militant (IRE) (66)** (AStreeter) **7-9-11** JQuinn(9) (lw: hld up: hdwy ½-wy: rdn over 2f out: one pce)	1	3	5/1[3]	68	50
5231[4]	**Shahik (USA) (68)** (DHaydnJones) **6-9-13** SDrowne(7) (lw: hld up: hdwy 5f out: rdn over 3f out: nvr nr to chal)	2	4	14/1	68	50

Form	Horse / Trainer / Age-Wt / Jockey / Comment	Dist	Pos	SP	RR	SF
510^{5}	**Pharly Reef (38)** (DBurchell) **4-7-11** NCarlisle(3) (prom tl rdn & wknd over 2f out)	1¼	**5**	14/1	36	18
*5240**	**Rasayel (USA) (48)** (PDEvans) **6-8-7** ACulhane(8) (dwlt: chsd ldrs fr ½-wy: rdn 3f out: sn btn)	2	**6**	5/2^{1}	43	25
3980^{8}	**Fabulous Mtoto (40)** (MSSaunders) **6-7-13**ow1 AMackay(4) (b: nvr nr ldrs)	2	**7**	10/1	33	14
5240^{2}	**Colosse (51)** (JLEyre) **4-8-10v** RLappin(6) (lw: hld up gng wl: effrt & pushed along over 2f out: sn btn)	nk	**8**	4/1^{2}	43	25
75^{6}	**Kalamata (60)** (JAGlover) **4-9-5** GCarter(1) (bkwd: prom over 8f: eased whn btn fnl 2f: t.o)	26	**9**	14/1	18	—
5053^{10}	**Ewar Bold (51)** (KOCunningham-Brown) **3-8-5b**ow1 SSanders(12) (lost pl ½-wy: sn t.o)	18	**10**	33/1	—	—
5206^{5}	**Mustn't Grumble (IRE) (51)** (MissSJWilton) **6-8-10v** SWhitworth(11) (a bhd: t.o fnl 4f)	1	**11**	14/1	—	—
5119^{6}	**Johns Act (USA) (61)** (DHaydnJones) **6-9-6b** JWeaver(5) (chsd ldrs over 7f: sn wknd: t.o)	1¼	**12**	20/1	—	—

(SP 129.8%) **12 Rn**

2m 40.0 (7.50) CSF £78.98 CT £379.06 TOTE £10.80: £2.90 £2.60 £2.20 (£58.30) Trio £78.20 OWNER Mr L. Pipe (WHITCOMBE) BRED Gainsborough Stud Management Ltd

WEIGHT FOR AGE 3yo-5lb

T/Jkpt: Not won; £11,092.89 to Lingfield 30/12/96. T/Plpt: £10,739.60 (2.68 Tckts). T/Qdpt: £1,035.80 (3.21 Tckts). IM

5250-LINGFIELD (L-H) (Standard)
Monday December 30th

WEATHER: cold & cloudy WIND: almost nil

5271 MANNY BERNSTEIN TRADE BETTING (S) STKS (3-Y.O+) (Class F)

1-05 (1-06) **1m 2f (Equitrack)** £2,636.00 (£741.00: £362.00) Stalls: Low GOING minus 0.25 sec per fur (FST)

Form	Horse / Trainer / Age-Wt / Jockey / Comment	Dist	Pos	SP	RR	SF
5149^{4}	**Arcatura (50)** (CJames) **4-9-3** CRutter(14) (a.p: led over 1f out: drvn out)	—	**1**	15/2^{3}	49	36
5209^{5}	**Bagshot (60)** (GLMoore) **5-9-3** SWhitworth(9) (hdwy 4f out: ev ch 1f out: hrd rdn: r.o)	¾	**2**	15/8^{1}	48	35
5254^{3}	**Bon Secret (IRE) (67)** (TJNaughton) **4-9-8** DHolland(6) (hmpd bnd after 1f: rdn & hdwy 3f out: r.o wl fnl f)	2½	**3**	3/1^{2}	49	36
5145^{8}	**Oozlem (IRE) (39)** (LMontagueHall) **7-9-3v** DaneO'Neill(12) (s.s: bhd & rdn along: gd hdwy fnl 2f: fin wl)	½	**4**	16/1	43	30
4509^{18}	**Warspite (33)** (PMooney) **6-9-3** JQuinn(8) (hrd rdn & hdwy 3f out: styd on fnl 2f)	nk	**5**	33/1	43	30
5145^{6}	**Sweet Amoret (44)** (PHowling) **3-9-0** FNorton(2) (b.off hind: sn led: rdn & hdd over 1f out: wknd fnl f)	nk	**6**	12/1	42	26
5254^{6}	**Eastleigh (41)** (RHollinshead) **7-8-10**(7) LisaWatson(4) (prom 4f: styd on fnl f)	1½	**7**	14/1	40	27
5237^{7}	**Flagstaff (USA) (49)** (KRBurke) **3-8-7**(7) PWright(1) (no hdwy fnl 3f)	5	**8**	16/1	32	16
4898^{9}	**Red Rusty (USA) (50)** (PRHedger) **3-9-0** AClark(13) (lw: b: b.hind: a.p: hrd rdn & ev ch 2f out: wknd over 1f out)	2½	**9**	12/1	28	12
5254^{4}	**Dragon Green (51)** (JCullinan) **5-9-3** RPerham(10) (rdn & hdwy 5f out: wknd over 2f out)	1¼	**10**	16/1	26	13
5223^{12}	**She Said No (40)** (AMoore) **4-8-12** CandyMorris(5) (b.hind: sn bhd)	9	**11**	20/1	6	—
5242^{9}	**Komodo (USA) (33)** (JELong) **4-9-3** LeesaLong(7) (b: a bhd)	4	**12**	33/1	5	—
5145^{13}	**Forgotten Dancer (IRE) (27)** (RIngram) **5-9-3b** SSanders(3) (bhd fnl 4f: t.o)	19	**13**	50/1	—	—
5250^{6}	**Northern Chief (28)** (JCullinan) **6-9-3b**1 VSlattery(11) (prom 5f: t.o)	13	**14**	66/1	—	—

(SP 125.3%) **14 Rn**

2m 9.88 (5.58) CSF £21.54 TOTE £11.90: £2.80 £1.10 £1.40 (£11.60) Trio £7.20 OWNER Mrs Carol Welch (NEWBURY) BRED Benham Stud

WEIGHT FOR AGE 3yo-3lb

No bid

OFFICIAL EXPLANATION Bon Secret (IRE): the jockey reported that he was hampered on the first bend, was inconvenienced by the kick-back entering the straight, and that he was unable to ride the gelding out sufficiently because he was showing a tendency to hang to his left.

5272 MANNY BERNSTEIN CREDIT BETTING NURSERY H'CAP (2-Y.O) (Class E)

1-35 (1-35) **7f (Equitrack)** £2,831.85 (£856.80: £417.90: £198.45) Stalls: Low GOING minus 0.25 sec per fur (FST)

Form	Horse / Trainer / Age-Wt / Jockey / Comment	Dist	Pos	SP	RR	SF
*5252**	**Effervescence (84)** (RHannon) **2-9-11** 6x DaneO'Neill(1) (chsd ldr: led 3f out: drvn out)	—	**1**	7/4^{1}	91	43
5238^{3}	**Millroy (USA) (80)** (PAKelleway) **2-9-7** MWigham(4) (drvn along thrght: hdwy 5f out: r.o ins fnl f)	1¼	**2**	2/1^{2}	84	36
5187^{4}	**Forgotten Times (USA) (64)** (TMJones) **2-8-5** NCarlisle(5) (led 4f: hrd rdn 2f out: one pce)	2½	**3**	12/1	62	14
*5251**	**Island Prince (55)** (NACallaghan) **2-7-3**(7) 6x JBramhill(2) (outpcd: sme hdwy 3f out: nvr nr to chal)	3½	**4**	7/2^{3}	45	—
5048^{5}	**Run Lucy Run (59)** (MissGayKelleway) **2-7-7**(7)ow1 AngelaGallimore(3) (prom 2f: bhd fnl 3f)	1½	**5**	10/1	46	—

(SP 108.7%) **5 Rn**

1m 27.79 (3.39) CSF £5.33 TOTE £2.40: £1.20 £1.40 (£1.90) OWNER The Gold Buster Syndicate (2) (MARLBOROUGH) BRED T. Umpleby

LONG HANDICAP Island Prince 7-2

5273 MANNY BERNSTEIN NEW YEAR MAIDEN STKS (3-Y.O+) (Class D)

2-05 (2-05) **7f (Equitrack)** £3,387.50 (£1,025.00: £500.00: £237.50) Stalls: Low GOING minus 0.25 sec per fur (FST)

Form	Horse / Trainer / Age-Wt / Jockey / Comment	Dist	Pos	SP	RR	SF
5093^{3}	**Rawi (51)** (MissGayKelleway) **3-9-0** DHolland(3) (lw: b: b.hind: w ldr: led 3f out: drvn out)	—	**1**	7/4^{1}	56	32
5211^{3}	**Zelaya (IRE) (40)** (GLMoore) **3-8-9** FNorton(4) (a.p: hrd rdn & ev ch fnl f: r.o)	nk	**2**	3/1^{2}	50	26
5182^{5}	**Katatonic (IRE)** (JARToller) **3-9-0** SSanders(2) (led 4f: hrd rdn over 1f out: one pce)	3½	**3**	7/4^{1}	47	23
3665^{4}	**One Dream (60)** (BSmart) **3-9-0v**1 RPerham(5) (lw: s.s: outpcd: nvr nr to chal)	6	**4**	8/1^{3}	34	10
2893^{7}	**Extra Hour (IRE) (55)** (WRMuir) **3-9-0** DaneO'Neill(1) (bhd fnl 4f)	10	**5**	20/1	11	—

(SP 113.6%) **5 Rn**

1m 27.83 (3.43) CSF £7.21 TOTE £2.70: £1.10 £2.50 (£5.10) OWNER Mr Chris Wilkinson (WHITCOMBE) BRED D. G. Mason

5274 MANNY BERNSTEIN 20TH ANNIVERSARY H'CAP (0-70) (3-Y.O+) (Class E)

2-35 (2-35) **1m 2f (Equitrack)** £2,900.10 (£877.80: £428.40: £203.70) Stalls: Low GOING minus 0.25 sec per fur (FST)

Form	Horse / Trainer / Age-Wt / Jockey / Comment	Dist	Pos	SP	RR	SF
*5250**	**Barossa Valley (IRE) (75)** (PButler) **5-10-0**(5) 5x DSweeney(6) (lw: mde virtually all: sn clr: rdn out)	—	**1**	9/2^{3}	86	68
5250^{2}	**Slip Jig (IRE) (65)** (RHannon) **3-8-13**(7) GGallagher(4) (hld up: chsd wnr 3f out: unable qckn fnl f)	2	**2**	12/1	73	52
*5247**	**Father Dan (IRE) (62)** (MissGayKelleway) **7-9-6** DHolland(10) (b: b.hind: rdn & hdwy 4f out: one pce fnl 2f)	4	**3**	7/1	63	45
5189^{4}	**No Pattern (67)** (GLMoore) **4-9-11v** SWhitworth(11) (hdwy & hrd rdn 3f out: one pce fnl 2f)	nk	**4**	12/1	68	50
4974^{8}	**Master Beveled (68)** (PDEvans) **6-9-12** ACulhane(3) (s.s: bhd & rdn along: hdwy 3f out: nvr nrr)	1½	**5**	7/2^{1}	67	49
5244^{3}	**Zahid (USA) (53)** (KRBurke) **5-8-11v** JQuinn(9) (dwlt: hdwy 4f out: one pce fnl 2f)	¾	**6**	9/1	50	32

Form	Horse / details	Dist	Pos	SP	RR	SF
5242*	**Kedwick (IRE) (55)** (PRHedger) **7-8-13b** DaneO'Neill(2) (lw: b: b.hind: hdwy 7f out: chsd wnr 6f out to 3f out: wknd 2f out)	5	**7**	4/1^{2}	44	26
5206^{3}	**Maradata (IRE) (63)** (RHollinshead) **4-9-4**$^{(3)}$ FLynch(1) (lost pl 6f out: no hdwy fnl 3f)	3½	**8**	10/1	47	29
3301^{3}	**Princesse Lyphard (41)** (MJPolglase) **3-7-10** NCarlisle(7) (prom 5f: t.o)	23	**9**	33/1	—	—
5242^{3}	**Bakers Daughter (57)** (JRArnold) **4-9-1** AClark(5) (lw: chsd wnr 4f: wknd 5f out: t.o)	5	**10**	15/2	—	—
4831^{11}	**Apollono (67)** (RLee) **4-9-11** SSanders(8) (hmpd 6f out: a bhd: t.o)	1¼	**11**	14/1	4	—
				(SP 128.8%)		**11 Rn**

2m 7.76 (3.46) CSF £56.34 CT £356.55 TOTE £6.30: £1.60 £6.20 £2.30 (£20.70) Trio £53.70 OWNER Mr Christopher Wilson (LEWES) BRED Swettenham Stud
LONG HANDICAP Princesse Lyphard 7-7
WEIGHT FOR AGE 3yo-3lb

5275 MANNY BERNSTEIN DON'T BE DISQUALIFIED MAIDEN AUCTION STKS (2-Y.O) (Class F)

3-05 (3-06) **6f** **(Equitrack)** £2,457.50 (£690.00: £336.50) Stalls: Low GOING minus 0.25 sec per fur (FST)

Form	Horse / details	Dist	Pos	SP	RR	SF
5251^{2}	**The Wyandotte Inn (68)** (RHollinshead) **2-8-4**$^{(3)}$ FLynch(3) (led 1f: led wl over 1f out: sn clr: pushed out)	—	**1**	4/9^{1}	70	—
5142^{10}	**Khairun Nisaa** (MJPolglase) **2-7-13** JQuinn(1) (outpcd after 2f: wnt mod 2nd nr fin)	7	**2**	4/1^{2}	43	—
5214^{4}	**Windborn (54)** (CNAllen) **2-8-0b**$^{1(5)}$ MartinDwyer(2) (s.i.s: led after 1f: hdd wl over 1f out: wknd fnl f)	½	**3**	4/1^{2}	48	—
				(SP 109.2%)		**3 Rn**

1m 16.0 (4.90) CSF £2.41 TOTE £1.40 (£1.60) OWNER Mr G. A. Farndon (UPPER LONGDON) BRED N. W. Rimington

5276 MANNY BERNSTEIN CONDITIONAL/IN RUNNING H'CAP (0-70) (3-Y.O+) (Class E)

3-35 (3-35) **1m 4f** **(Equitrack)** £2,804.55 (£848.40: £413.70: £196.35) Stalls: Low GOING minus 0.25 sec per fur (FST)

Form	Horse / details	Dist	Pos	SP	RR	SF
5053^{15}	**Yet Again (41)** (MissGayKelleway) **4-8-4**^{ow1} SSanders(5) (b: b.hind: chsd ldr 5f out: led 3f out: pushed clr 2f out: easily)	—	**1**	10/11^{1}	56+	33
5185^{11}	**Sam Rockett (39)** (PMooney) **3-7-11b**^{ow1} JQuinn(7) (hdwy on bit 4f out: ev ch over 2f out: shkn up: no rspnse)	3½	**2**	9/1	49	21
5222^{9}	**Persian Conquest (IRE) (65)** (RIngram) **4-10-0b** DHolland(1) (lw: led: rdn & hdd 3f out: sn wknd)	8	**3**	4/1^{2}	65	43
	Whippers Delight (IRE) (34) (GFHCharles-Jones) **8-7-4**$^{(7)ow1}$ AMcCarthy(4) (bhd & rdn along: hdwy 2f out: nvr nrr)	8	**4**	33/1	23	—
5244*	**Zuno Flyer (USA) (54)** (AMoore) **4-9-3** CandyMorris(6) (b.hind: bhd fnl 5f)	4	**5**	11/2^{3}	38	16
3978^{10}	**Half An Inch (IRE) (49)** (TMJones) **3-8-7b** NCarlisle(2) (b: b.hind: chsd ldr 7f: wknd 4f out)	8	**6**	14/1	22	—
5110^{12}	**Racing Telegraph (35)** (CNAllen) **6-7-7**$^{(5)ow2}$ MartinDwyer(3) (prom 7f: t.o)	15	**7**	12/1	—	—
				(SP 115.1%)		**7 Rn**

2m 35.3 (5.30) CSF £9.38 TOTE £2.10: £1.70 £2.20 (£4.80) OWNER Mr A. P. Griffin (WHITCOMBE) BRED Aston Park Stud
LONG HANDICAP Whippers Delight (IRE) 7-2 Sam Rockett 7-5 Racing Telegraph 7-8
WEIGHT FOR AGE 3yo-5lb

T/Jkpt: £1,197.30 (17.33 Tckts). T/Plpt: £12.70 (1,831.22 Tckts). T/Qdpt: £11.50 (121.51 Tckts). LMc

5271-LINGFIELD (L-H) (Standard)
Tuesday December 31st

WEATHER: snow showers & v.cold WIND: fresh half bhd

5277 SEVASTOPOL APPRENTICE H'CAP (0-70) (3-Y.O+) (Class G)

12-55 (12-55) **1m 5f** **(Equitrack)** £1,738.00 (£488.00: £238.00) Stalls: Low GOING minus 0.06 sec per fur (STD)

Form	Horse / details	Dist	Pos	SP	RR	SF
5270^{6}	**Rasayel (USA) (48)** (PDEvans) **6-8-7**$^{(5)}$ AnthonyBond(8) (hld up in tch: chal gng wl 3f out: led over 1f out: rdn out)	—	**1**	4/1^{3}	52	26
5213^{2}	**Broughtons Formula (50)** (WJMusson) **6-8-7b**$^{(7)}$ DarrenWilliams(4) (hld up: rdn & outpcd 5f out: hdwy over 2f out: rdn over 1f out: r.o wl ins fnl f)	½	**2**	3/1^{1}	53	27
5137^{10}	**More Than You Know (IRE) (70)** (KRBurke) **3-9-9**$^{(5)}$ EmilyJoyce(1) (chsd ldrs: rdn 3f out: led 2f out: hdd over 1f out: one pce)	1¾	**3**	12/1	71	39
5255^{5}	**Adilov (36)** (JJBridger) **4-8-0** MartinDwyer(7) (a.p: led 4f out: hdd 2f out: one pce)	2½	**4**	8/1	34	8
5244^{11}	**Al Haal (USA) (50)** (RJO'Sullivan) **7-9-0** DGriffiths(6) (sn led: hdd 9f out: hrd rdn over 2f out: one pce)	2	**5**	16/1	46	20
5213^{3}	**Matthias Mystique (62)** (MissBSanders) **3-9-3**$^{(3)}$ JoHunnam(3) (hld up: hdwy over 2f out: sn rdn: one pce)	½	**6**	3/1^{1}	57	25
5223^{10}	**Queens Fancy (38)** (SDow) **3-7-3**$^{(7)}$ DSalt(5) (hld up: sme hdwy 5f out: wknd 3f out)	14	**7**	33/1	16	—
5255^{3}	**Coh Sho No (52)** (SDow) **3-8-10** ADaly(2) (led 9f out: hdd 4f out: sn wknd)	6	**8**	7/2^{2}	23	—
				(SP 119.8%)		**8 Rn**

2m 54.0 (12.00) CSF £16.44 CT £123.05 TOTE £5.40: £1.90 £1.30 £3.90 (£8.80) OWNER Pentons Haulage and Cold Storage Ltd (WELSHPOOL) BRED Gainsborough Farm
LONG HANDICAP Queens Fancy 7-4
WEIGHT FOR AGE 3yo-6lb
OFFICIAL EXPLANATION **Coh Sho No: her rider reported that the filly was hanging right throughout.**

5278 ALMA NURSERY H'CAP (2-Y.O) (Class E)

1-25 (1-25) **6f** **(Equitrack)** £2,179.50 (£612.00: £298.50) Stalls: Low GOING minus 0.06 sec per fur (STD)

Form	Horse / details	Dist	Pos	SP	RR	SF
5229*	**Just Loui (78)** (WGMTurner) **2-9-2**$^{(5)}$ DSweeney(2) (mde all: rdn over 1f out: edgd rt ins fnl f: r.o wl)	—	**1**	11/4^{2}	89	18
5146^{7}	**Rock To The Top (IRE) (65)** (JJSheehan) **2-8-8** AMorris(7) (a.p: chsd wnr ½-wy: hrd rdn & hung lft ins fnl f: unable qckn)	1½	**2**	13/2^{3}	72	1
5245^{4}	**Eager To Please (66)** (MissGayKelleway) **2-8-9** DaneO'Neill(4) (b: b.hind: chsd ldrs: hrd rdn 2f out: kpt on one pce ins fnl f)	1	**3**	10/1	70	—
5251^{5}	**Heavenly Miss (IRE) (70)** (JJBridger) **2-8-13** SSanders(3) (lw: sn rdn along in rr: lost tch 4f out: wl bhd tl styd on fnl f: nvr nrr)	4	**4**	10/1	64	—

				SP	RR	SF
5224*	**Kilcullen Lad (IRE) (70)** (PMooney) **2-8-13b[1]** JQuinn(1) (dwlt rr: hdwy over 2f out: sn rdn & btn)	4	**5**	6/5 1	53	—
3417[7]	**Advance Repro (66)** (JAkehurst) **2-8-9b** DHolland(6) (spd to ½-wy)	6	**6**	10/1	33	—
				(SP 112.7%)		**6 Rn**

1m 16.46 (5.36) CSF £18.39 TOTE £3.60: £2.80 £4.50 (£12.50) OWNER Mr A. Poole (SHERBORNE) BRED M. A. Poole

OFFICIAL EXPLANATION **Kilcullen Lad (IRE): rider reported that his goggles were cracked by a frozen piece of Equitrack kicked up by the leaders.**

5279 LIGHT BRIGADE MEDIAN AUCTION MAIDEN STKS (2-Y.O) (Class F)

1-55 (1-55) **5f (Equitrack)** £1,738.00 (£488.00: £238.00) Stalls: High GOING minus 0.06 sec per fur (STD)

				SP	RR	SF
5226[2]	**Hever Golf Lover (IRE) (58)** (TJNaughton) **2-8-9** DHolland(5) (led 1f: led 2f out: sn clr: pushed out)	—	**1**	5/2 1	58+	10
5251[3]	**Countless Times (57)** (WRMuir) **2-9-0** DaneO'Neill(2) (sn rdn along in rr: hdwy over 1f out: styd on ins fnl f)	4	**2**	6/1	50	2
5201[5]	**Green Boulevard (USA)** (JBerry) **2-8-4**(5) PRoberts(3) (b: b.hind: dwlt: sn pushed along: hdwy 2f out: kpt on one pce ins fnl f)	s.h	**3**	7/2 3	45	—
5187[3]	**Ekaterini Paritsi (57)** (WGMTurner) **2-8-4v**(5) DSweeney(6) (led 4f out: hdd 2f out: wknd ins fnl f)	1½	**4**	7/2 3	40	—
5187[7]	**Incatime (64)** (CJames) **2-9-0** CRutter(4) (chsd ldrs tl wknd over 2f out)	7	**5**	100/30 2	23	—
5214[8]	**She's Electric (35)** (JJBridger) **2-8-9** SWhitworth(1) (sn rdn along: in tch tl wknd 3f out)	3½	**6**	33/1	7	—
				(SP 113.3%)		**6 Rn**

62.63 secs (4.43) CSF £16.05 TOTE £4.10: £1.90 £1.80 (£9.00) OWNER Hever Racing Club I (EPSOM) BRED Dr Michael Smurfit

5280 INKERMAN H'CAP (0-60) (3-Y.O+) (Class F)

2-25 (2-26) **5f (Equitrack)** £1,738.00 (£488.00: £238.00) Stalls: High GOING minus 0.06 sec per fur (STD)

				SP	RR	SF
5173[8]	**Mister Raider (50)** (EAWheeler) **4-9-0b**(5) ADaly(10) (chsd ldrs: hrd rdn to ld ins fnl f: r.o)	—	**1**	7/1	57	27
5183*	**Sihafi (USA) (55)** (JMCarr) **3-9-10** AClark(7) (chsd ldrs: hrd rdn & ev ch ins fnl f: unable qckn)	¾	**2**	9/2 3	60	30
5174[12]	**Squire Corrie (59)** (DWChapman) **4-10-0** DHolland(8) (a.p: led over 2f out: hdd ins fnl f: unable qckn)	nk	**3**	6/1	63	33
5225[5]	**Daaniera (IRE) (34)** (PHowling) **6-8-3b** JQuinn(5) (b.hind: led: hdd over 2f out: wknd appr fnl f)	6	**4**	8/1	18	—
5220[5]	**Windrush Boy (45)** (JRBosley) **6-9-0** CRutter(4) (chsd ldrs: rdn over 1f out: grad wknd)	nk	**5**	16/1	29	—
762[7]	**Bright Paragon (IRE) (36)** (KTIvory) **7-8-0**(5) MartinDwyer(9) (b: sn rdn along & outpcd)	6	**6**	20/1	—	—
5188[3]	**Colston-C (50)** (PDEvans) **4-9-5** SSanders(2) (sn rdn along & outpcd)	s.h	**7**	4/1 2	14	—
5268[9]	**Cheeky Chappy (59)** (DWChapman) **5-10-0b** ACulhane(1) (bdly hmpd after 1f: nt rcvr)	6	**8**	7/2 1	4	—
5225[10]	**Dancing Jack (50)** (JJBridger) **3-9-5b[1]** SWhitworth(6) (sltly hmpd after 1f: a bhd)	3½	**9**	33/1	—	—
4215[12]	**Oscilights Gift (30)** (MarkCampion) **4-7-13** NAdams(3) (propped leaving stalls: uns rdr after 100y)		**U**	8/1	—	—
				(SP 123.0%)		**10 Rn**

62.13 secs (3.93) CSF £38.07 CT £163.28 TOTE £9.40: £2.60 £2.30 £2.80 (£36.30) Trio £60.30 OWNER Raiders Partnership (PANGBOURNE) BRED Alan Hogan

5281 CRIMEA H'CAP (0-70) (3-Y.O+) (Class E)

2-55 (2-57) **1m 2f (Equitrack)** £2,263.50 (£636.00: £310.50) Stalls: Low GOING minus 0.06 sec per fur (STD)

				SP	RR	SF
5181[2]	**Adamton (66)** (MrsJCecil) **4-9-7**(5) MartinDwyer(9) (led after 1f: clr over 1f out: rdn ins fnl f: r.o)	—	**1**	7/2 2	75	64
5222[10]	**Suitor (47)** (SDow) **3-7-13**(5)ow5 ADaly(6) (pushed along in rr: hdwy over 2f out: hrd rdn to chse wnr over 1f out: r.o)	1¾	**2**	14/1	53	34
4899[4]	**Kitty Kitty Cancan (63)** (LadyHerries) **3-9-6b** AClark(3) (a.p: chsd wnr 4f out tl over 1f out: one pce)	2½	**3**	8/1	65	51
5171[6]	**Philistar (68)** (JMPEustace) **3-9-6**(5) DSweeney(8) (stdd s: hld up: hdwy 3f out: hrd rdn 2f out: one pce)	5	**4**	10/1	62	48
5242[6]	**Harlequin Walk (IRE) (50)** (RJO'Sullivan) **5-8-10** DHolland(4) (led 1f: chsd wnr to 4f out: wknd over 2f out)	4	**5**	7/1 3	38	27
2898[3]	**Dance of Joy (38)** (JMCarr) **4-7-12** JQuinn(5) (a bhd)	5	**6**	16/1	18	7
5118*	**Double Rush (IRE) (65)** (TGMills) **4-9-11** SSanders(2) (chsd ldrs tl wknd over 2f out)	3	**7**	3/1 1	40	29
5242[11]	**Great Bear (37)** (DWChapman) **4-7-4b**(7)ow1 JBramhill(1) (chsd ldrs: sn pushed along: wknd 5f out: t.o)	31	**8**	33/1	—	—
5210*	**Angel Face (USA) (69)** (PDEvans) **3-9-12** ACulhane(7) (chsd ldrs tl wknd over 3f out: t.o)	24	**9**	3/1 1	—	—
				(SP 120.4%)		**9 Rn**

2m 9.31 (5.01) CSF £46.06 CT £342.13 TOTE £4.50: £1.40 £2.60 £3.70 (£31.10) Trio £166.10 OWNER Mrs J. Cecil (NEWMARKET) BRED Lady Murless

LONG HANDICAP Great Bear 7-5

WEIGHT FOR AGE 3yo-3lb

OFFICIAL EXPLANATION **Angel Face (USA): the trainer reported that the filly was over the top and needed a rest.**
Double Rush (IRE): the trainer reported that the gelding appeared to resent the unusually severe kickback.

5282 THIN RED LINE MAIDEN STKS (3-Y.O+) (Class D)

3-25 (3-25) **7f (Equitrack)** £2,788.00 (£844.00: £412.00: £196.00) Stalls: Low GOING minus 0.06 sec per fur (STD)

				SP	RR	SF
5253[4]	**River Seine (FR) (41)** (SGKnight) **4-8-9** SSanders(9) (chsd ldrs: rdn to ld appr fnl f: r.o)	—	**1**	9/2	52	21
1670[8]	**Gold Lance (USA)** (RJO'Sullivan) **3-9-0b** DHolland(4) (rn wd 4f out: wl bhd tl hdwy & edgd lft over 1f out: hung lft & styd on strly fnl f)	1½	**2**	11/4 2	54	23
	Magazine Gap (MrsJCecil) **3-8-9**(5) AmandaSanders(10) (unf: hld up in tch: led 2f out: hdd appr fnl f: unable qckn)	nk	**3**	4/1 3	53	22
4429[12]	**Evening In Paris** (MJohnston) **3-8-9** JWeaver(3) (lw: sn rdn along: rn wd 4f out: wl bhd tl hdwy over 1f out: styd on ins fnl f)	2½	**4**	5/2 1	42	11
5161[8]	**Jareer Do (IRE) (43)** (BPalling) **4-8-9** DaneO'Neill(7) (led: hdd 2f out: grad wknd)	4	**5**	9/1	33	2
4898[7]	**Square Mile Miss (IRE) (40)** (PHowling) **3-8-9** JQuinn(2) (chsd ldrs tl wknd wl over 1f out)	nk	**6**	12/1	32	1
5211[5]	**Shermood (27)** (KTIvory) **3-8-4**(5) MartinDwyer(8) (chsd ldrs tl wknd 2f out)	5	**7**	16/1	21	—
	Hightide (JRArnold) **4-8-9** AClark(1) (w'like: rn wd 4f out: a bhd)	3	**8**	12/1	14	—
5234[10]	**Logie Pert Lad (26)** (JJBridger) **4-9-0b[1]** SWhitworth(5) (chsd ldrs tl wknd 2f out)	3½	**9**	33/1	11	—
5173[11]	**Gracious Gretclo (46)** (PDEvans) **3-8-9** TGMcLaughlin(6) (plld hrd: prom tl wknd over 3f out)	20	**10**	12/1	—	—
				(SP 135.3%)		**10 Rn**

1m 29.71 (5.31) CSF £19.37 TOTE £4.80: £1.70 £1.30 £3.60 (£10.10) Trio £28.00 OWNER Mrs Ginny Withers (TAUNTON) BRED San Gabriel Inv. Inc.

T/Jkpt: Not won; £5,847.38 to Southwell 1/1/97. T/Plpt: £121.10 (219.23 Tckts). T/Qdpt: £34.20 (92.9 Tckts). SM

Raceform

TURF AND ALL-WEATHER FLAT RACING 1997

Complete record of Turf and All-Weather Racing from January 1st to November 8th, 1997

SOUTHWELL (L-H) (Standard)

Wednesday January 1st

WEATHER: cold with snow showers WIND: slt across

1 RESOLUTION CLAIMING STKS (I) (4-Y.O+) (Class F)

12-35 (12-37) **7f (Fibresand)** £1,944.00 (£544.00: £264.00) Stalls: Low GOING: 0.06 sec per fur (STD)

			SP	RR	SF
Anonym (IRE) (62) (DNicholls) **5-8-10b**(7) JBramhill(3) (effrt over 3f out: styd on wl u.p to ld ins fnl f)	—	1	16/1	77	54
Elton Ledger (IRE) (73) (MrsNMacauley) **8-8-13v** SSanders(9) (b: trckd ldrs: led over 1f out: hung lft: hdd ins fnl f)	1	2	5/2[2]	71	48
Sea Devil (67) (MJCamacho) **11-8-3** LCharnock(5) (trckd ldrs: chal 2f out: edgd rt & nt qckn ins fnl f)	½	3	12/1	60	37
Havana Miss (32) (BPalling) **5-7-11**(5) MartinDwyer(10) (chsd ldrs tl wknd over 1f out)	4	4	50/1	49	26
Rambo Waltzer (78) (DNicholls) **5-8-13** AlexGreaves(4) (w ldr: led over 3f out tl over 2f out: edgd rt & wknd fnl f)	2	5	8/1[3]	56	33
Little Ibnr (70) (PDEvans) **6-8-5** JQuinn(8) (trckd ldrs: led over 2f out tl over 1f out: grad wknd)	nk	6	11/1	47	24
Standown (66) (JBerry) **4-8-4v**[1](5) PRoberts(6) (sn outpcd & drvn along: sme hdwy 2f out: n.d)	7	7	14/1	35	12
Sally Armstrong (CWThornton) **4-9-2** DeanMcKeown(11) (s.s: outpcd ½-wy: n.d)	½	8	20/1	41	18
High Premium (80) (RAFahey) **9-9-7** ACulhane(7) (b: sn drvn along: hmpd after 1f: n.d after)	hd	9	6/4[1]	46	23
Santella Katie (70) (MrsLStubbs) **4-8-8** SWhitworth(1) (lw: s.s a in rr)	2	10	16/1	28	5
Dictation (USA) (54) (JJO'Neill) **5-8-11b** DaneO'Neill(2) (led tl over 3f out: wknd qckly over 2f out: t.o)	30	11	20/1	—	—
			(SP 125.6%)	**11 Rn**	

1m 31.0 (4.50) CSF £56.55 TOTE £20.40: £6.50 £1.10 £2.40 (£41.50) Trio £76.60 OWNER Wetherby Racing Bureau Ltd (THIRSK) BRED T. G. Mooney

OFFICIAL EXPLANATION **High Premium: finished distressed.**

2 ONE TOO MANY MEDIAN AUCTION MAIDEN APPRENTICE STKS (4, 5 & 6-Y.O) (Class F)

1-05 (1-05) **1m 3f (Fibresand)** £2,502.00 (£702.00: £342.00) Stalls: Low GOING: 0.06 sec per fur (STD)

			SP	RR	SF
Fresh Fruit Daily (43) (PAKelleway) **5-8-6**(5) AngelaGallimore(9) (hld up: smooth hdwy 6f out: led over 2f out: sn clr: wandered)	—	1	6/1[3]	58	25
Hever Golf Eagle (49) (TJNaughton) **4-8-10**(3) PFessey(1) (led to 8f out: sn outpcd: styd on fnl 3f: no ch w wnr)	12	2	4/1[2]	46	10
Taniyar (FR) (35) (RHollinshead) **5-8-13**(3) DGriffiths(7) (chsd ldrs: kpt on one pce fnl 3f)	2½	3	12/1	42	9
Emei Shan (30) (WGMTurner) **4-8-4**(7)ow3 DMcGaffin(6) (jnd ldrs 7f out: wknd over 1f out)	½	4	25/1	39	—
Prophets Honour (PCHaslam) **5-8-13**(3) MartinDwyer(4) (w ldrs: led 8f out tl over 2f out: sn btn)	¾	5	6/4[1]	40	7
Zatopek (44) (JCullinan) **5-8-9**(7) RWinston(2) (prom tl lost pl ½-wy: n.d after: hrd rdn over 1f out)	12	6	7/1	23	—
Dishy Diamond (WRMuir) **4-8-3**(5) JWilkinson(5) (dwlt: nvr nr ldrs)	d.h	6	7/1	18	—
The Oddfellow (NBycroft) **4-8-8**(5) JBramhill(3) (w ldrs: drvn along 7f out: lost pl over 3f out)	21	8	25/1	—	—
Alana's Ballad (IRE) (BPJBaugh) **4-8-5**(3) PRoberts(10) (bhd fnl 6f)	¾	9	33/1	—	—
Acerbus Dulcis (37) (MCChapman) **6-9-3**ow1 OPears(8) (bhd fr ½-wy)	6	10	50/1	—	—
			(SP 119.6%)	**10 Rn**	

2m 30.6 (10.60) CSF £29.22 TOTE £6.00: £2.20 £1.60 £1.60 (£11.50) Trio £21.50 OWNER Mr Kevin Hudson (NEWMARKET) BRED Worksop Manor Stud Farm

WEIGHT FOR AGE 4yo-3lb

STEWARDS' ENQUIRY Winston susp. 10-11/1/97 (excessive & improper use of whip).

3 RESOLUTION CLAIMING STKS (II) (4-Y.O+) (Class F)

1-35 (1-36) **7f (Fibresand)** £1,944.00 (£544.00: £264.00) Stalls: Low GOING: 0.06 sec per fur (STD)

			SP	RR	SF
Dahiyah (USA) (51) (BSmart) **6-8-7v** SSanders(1) (mde virtually all: drvn clr over 1f out)	—	1	7/1	58	25
Awesome Venture (74) (MCChapman) **7-9-4**(3) OPears(10) (hld up: smooth hdwy to track ldrs ½-wy: rdn over 1f out: kpt on same pce)	4	2	9/2[2]	63	30
Sweet Mate (56) (MartynMeade) **5-8-1b** NAdams(8) (s.i.s: sn drvn along: hdwy to chse ldrs ½-wy: one pce fnl 2f)	½	3	7/1	42	9
Paint It Black (58) (DNicholls) **4-9-3** AlexGreaves(11) (a in tch: sn drvn along: hdwy & hung lft over 2f out: nvr nr to chal)	¾	4	13/2[3]	56	23
Deeply Vale (IRE) (70) (EAWheeler) **6-9-2**(5) ADaly(7) (w ldrs: chal over 2f out: hrd rdn & wknd 1f out)	¾	5	11/4[1]	58	25
Kajostar (22) (SWCampion) **7-7-10** NCarlisle(4) (in tch: outpcd ½-wy: styd on appr fnl f)	1¾	6	40/1	29	—
Jilly Beveled (35) (RonaldThompson) **5-8-6**(3)ow1 CTeague(9) (s.s: bhd tl styd on appr fnl f)	s.h	7	25/1	42	8
Chilibang Bang (60) (JBerry) **4-8-1v**(5) PFessey(5) (w ldrs: rdn over 2f out: sn btn)	8	8	8/1	21	—
Warhurst (IRE) (58) (DNicholls) **6-8-7** AClark(2) (lw: reluctant to go to s: sn outpcd & drvn along)	7	9	10/1	6	—
Seanchai (IRE) (PSFelgate) **4-8-11** JStack(6) (chsd ldrs tl lost pl 3f out)	12	10	33/1	—	—
Parellie (PDEvans) **4-7-12b**[1] JQuinn(3) (sn bhd)	½	11	20/1	—	—
			(SP 117.4%)	**11 Rn**	

1m 32.7 (6.20) CSF £36.05 TOTE £9.50: £2.80 £2.10 £1.80 (£19.50) Trio £44.90 OWNER Mr W. Clifford (LAMBOURN) BRED Foxfield

4 EAST MIDLANDS ELECTRICITY (LINCOLN) H'CAP (0-70) (4-Y.O+ F & M) (Class E)

2-05 (2-12) **6f (Fibresand)** £2,765.25 (£837.00: £408.50: £194.25) Stalls: Low GOING: 0.06 sec per fur (STD)

			SP	RR	SF
Ballard Lady (IRE) (44) (JSWainwright) **5-7-13**(7) JBramhill(11) (lw: sn drvn along: hdwy over 2f out: styd on wl u.p to ld ins fnl f: jst hld on)	—	1	6/1[3]	50	34
Klipspinger (53) (BSRothwell) **4-9-1b** JStack(9) (trckd ldrs: ev ch ins fnl f: r.o wl towards fin)	hd	2	16/1	59	43
Gi La High (52) (MartynMeade) **4-8-9**(5) DSweeney(1) (b.hind: led: qcknd clr over 2f out: edgd rt: wknd & hdd ins fnl f)	1¾	3	5/2[1]	53	37
Belinda Blue (40) (RAFahey) **5-7-9**(7)ow3 RWinston(12) (trckd ldrs: effrt over 1f out: styd on same pce)	1	4	11/1	38	19
Anita's Contessa (IRE) (53) (BPalling) **5-9-1** DaneO'Neill(2) (s.i.s: bhd tl styd on fnl 2f)	3½	5	7/1	42	26
Time Clash (44) (BPalling) **4-8-6b**[1] AClark(10) (mid div: drvn along ½-wy: n.d)	8	6	16/1	12	—
Honeyhall (38) (NBycroft) **4-8-0** JQuinn(4) (trckd ldrs tl rdn & wknd over 1f out)	5	7	8/1	—	—

Maysimp (IRE) (40) (BPJBaugh) **4-8-2** NAdams(3) (b: s.i.s: a bhd)....2½ **8** 50/1 — —
Napier Star (66) (MrsNMacauley) **4-9-11v**(3) CTeague(8) (sn bhd: rn wd ent st: eased)....1½ **9** 5/1[2] 10 —
Juba (34) (DrJDScargill) **5-7-10** NCarlisle(7) (sn bhd)....15 **10** 14/1 — —
Shashi (IRE) (59) (PatMitchell) **5-9-2**(5) AmandaSanders(6) (Withdrawn not under Starter's orders: v.unruly & bolted full circ).... **W** 6/1[3] — —

(SP 126.1%) **10 Rn**

1m 18.0 (4.50) CSF £72.27 CT £212.46 TOTE £6.10: £2.00 £4.40 £1.10 (£30.90) Trio £51.20 OWNER Mrs P. Wake (MALTON) BRED Airlie Stud

5 THINKING & DRINKING H'CAP (0-70) (4-Y.O+) (Class E)

2-40 (2-40) **2m (Fibresand)** £2,726.25 (£825.00: £402.50: £191.25) Stalls: Low GOING: 0.06 sec per fur (STD)

SP RR SF

Golden Hadeer (48) (MJRyan) **6-8-13** AClark(9) (lw: led after 3f: clr 5f out: v.easily)....— **1** 7/2[1] 69+ —
Record Lover (IRE) (36) (MCChapman) **7-7-8**(7) IonaWands(8) (prom: pushed along & outpcd ½-wy: styd on fnl 3f: no ch w wnr)....17 **2** 11/1 40 —
Master Foodbroker (IRE) (51) (WJMusson) **9-9-2b** SWhitworth(2) (b: dwlt: hdwy 10f out: one pce fnl f)....½ **3** 10/1 55 —
White Willow (63) (TWall) **8-10-0** SSanders(3) (sn bhd & drvn along: sme hdwy 5f out: nvr nr ldrs)....11 **4** 4/1[2] 56 —
What Jim Wants (IRE) (39) (JJO'Neill) **4-7-11**ow1 JQuinn(6) (lw: outpcd & drvn along 10f out: kpt on fnl 3f: n.d)....nk **5** 7/1 31 —
Tee Tee Too (IRE) (60) (AWCarroll) **5-9-4**(7) GMilligan(1) (plld hrd: led 3f: lost pl ½-wy: t.o 3f out)....dist **6** 33/1 — —
Hunting Ground (35) (BPJBaugh) **9-8-0** FNorton(5) (b.hind: chsd ldrs tl wknd qckly over 2f out: t.o)....1 **7** 25/1 — —
Elite Bliss (IRE) (42) (MJCamacho) **5-8-7** LCharnock(7) (trckd ldrs tl rdn & wknd qckly 5f out: sn t.o)....1¼ **8** 9/2[3] — —
Sharp Command (53) (PEccles) **4-8-11** JWeaver(4) (prom: reminders & lost pl 9f out: t.o whn p.u 7f out).... **P** 4/1[2] — —

(SP 117.1%) **9 Rn**

3m 51.5 (25.50) CSF £37.35 CT £323.26 TOTE £3.50: £1.40 £2.90 £3.10 (£18.70) Trio £74.50 OWNER Four Jays Racing Partnership (NEWMARKET) BRED Stetchworth Park Stud Ltd
LONG HANDICAP What Jim Wants (IRE) 7-9
WEIGHT FOR AGE 4yo-7lb
OFFICIAL EXPLANATION **Sharp Command: gurgled and swallowed his tongue.**

6 MORNING CALL (QUALIFIER) (S) STKS (3-Y.O) (Class G)

3-10 (3-11) **1m (Fibresand)** £2,189.00 (£614.00: £299.00) Stalls: Low GOING: 0.06 sec per fur (STD)

SP RR SF

Royal Roulette (57) (SPCWoods) **3-8-0v**[1](7) CWebb(1) (hld up: hdwy over 2f out: rdn to ld jst ins fnl f: drvn out)....— **1** 7/1 64 2
Diamond Eyre (50) (JLEyre) **3-8-7** RLappin(10) (outpcd & drvn along 5f out: hdwy over 2f out: ev ch ins fnl f: kpt on)....1 **2** 3/1[1] 62 —
Head Girl (IRE) (60) (CWThornton) **3-8-12** DeanMcKeown(3) (led tl jst ins fnl f: wknd towards fin)....5 **3** 5/1[3] 57 —
Chasetown Flyer (USA) (58) (RHollinshead) **3-8-12** WRyan(9) (trckd ldrs: rdn over 1f out: one pce)....1¾ **4** 6/1 54 —
Bali-Pet (59) (WGMTurner) **3-8-12b**(5) DSweeney(6) (prom: rdn over 2f out: no imp)....¾ **5** 100/30[2] 57 —
State of Gold (IRE) (65) (JHetherton) **3-8-12** SWhitworth(7) (lw: chsd ldrs: drvn along 4f out: nt run on appr fnl f)....hd **6** 25/1 52 —
Indian Rapture (68) (RonaldThompson) **3-8-7** JQuinn(11) (s.i.s: bhd tl some hdwy fnl 2f)....1½ **7** 8/1 44 —
Bentnose (DMorris) **3-8-12** AClark(8) (chsd ldrs: ev ch over 2f out: wknd over 1f out)....3 **8** 7/1 43 —
Billycan (IRE) (35) (BPJBaugh) **3-8-12** RPerham(2) (sn bhd: t.o)....27 **9** 50/1 — —
Pamela's Boy (ASmith) **3-8-12** MWigham(5) (bit bkwd: s.i.s: bit slipped: a wl bhd: t.o ½-wy)....29 **10** 25/1 — —

(SP 124.8%) **10 Rn**

1m 48.6 (9.60) CSF £28.77 TOTE £10.30: £2.50 £1.60 £1.80 (£26.40) Trio £35.20 OWNER Mr W. J. P. Jackson (NEWMARKET) BRED Roldvale Ltd
No bid
OFFICIAL EXPLANATION **Pamela's Boy: the bit had pulled through his mouth at the start.**

7 NEW YEAR H'CAP (0-70) (3-Y.O) (Class E)

3-40 (3-40) **1m (Fibresand)** £2,752.25 (£833.00: £406.50: £193.25) Stalls: Low GOING: 0.06 sec per fur (STD)

SP RR SF

Going For Broke (62) (PCHaslam) **3-9-4** SSanders(5) (trckd ldrs: shkn up to ld over 2f out: drvn clr fnl f: readily)....— **1** 9/1 77+ 29
Pinchincha (FR) (65) (DMorris) **3-9-7** AClark(2) (trckd ldrs: led 3f out: sn hdd: no ch w wnr)....4 **2** 11/4[2] 72 24
Skelton Sovereign (IRE) (60) (RHollinshead) **3-8-11**(5) DGriffiths(6) (hld up: hdwy on outside 2f out: kpt on same pce)....3 **3** 6/1 61 13
Fast Spin (59) (TDBarron) **3-9-1** 6x ACulhane(4) (lw: effrt 3f out: sn rdn: wknd over 1f out)....7 **4** 13/8[1] 46 —
As-Is (65) (MJohnston) **3-9-7** JWeaver(3) (led to 3f out: lost pl over 1f out)....7 **5** 5/1[3] 38 —
Marsh Marigold (65) (MartynMeade) **3-9-2**(5) DSweeney(1) (plld hrd: hung bdly lft & lost pl over 2f out)....½ **6** 8/1 37 —

(SP 116.8%) **6 Rn**

1m 46.8 (7.80) CSF £32.94 TOTE £9.30: £1.80 £2.10 (£26.40) OWNER Dunnington & Smart (MIDDLEHAM) BRED Mrs John Trotter

T/Jkpt: Not won; £10,792.49 to Lingfield 2/1/97. T/Plpt: £93.70 (238.68 Tckts). T/Qdpt: £30.30 (85.96 Tckts). WG

LINGFIELD (L-H) (Standard)

Thursday January 2nd

WEATHER: freezing WIND: almost nil

8 STITCH IN TIME CLAIMING STKS (3-Y.O) (Class E)

1-20 (1-27) **1m (Equitrack)** £2,778.25 (£841.00: £410.50: £195.25) Stalls: High GOING minus 0.33 sec per fur (FST)

SP RR SF

Misty Cay (IRE) (57) (SDow) **3-8-0**(5) ADaly(7) (lw: rdn thrght: hdwy 4f out: led over 1f out: r.o wl)....— **1** 5/2[1] 62 24
Serenade (IRE) (58) (MJHaynes) **3-8-1** GBardwell(1) (s.i.s: rdn thrght: hdwy over 1f out: chsd wnr fnl f: r.o)....2 **2** 9/1 54 16
Lily Jaques (55) (RGuest) **3-7-11**ow1 JQuinn(6) (lw: rdn over 3f out: hdwy over 1f out: r.o)....2 **3** 5/1[2] 46 7

Horse / details	Dist	Pos	SP	RR	SF
Kingsdown Trix (IRE) (59) (AMoore) **3-8-5** CRutter(8) (b.hind: 4th whn squeezed out 5f out: 5th whn n.m.r over 2f out: r.o one pce)	s.h	**4**	8/1	54	16
Barnwood Crackers (55) (MissGayKelleway) **3-9-0** DHolland(9) (b: lw: a.p: chsd ldr 5f out to 2f out: wknd over 1f out)	2½	**5**	11/2 [3]	58	20
Mirror Four Sport (50) (MJohnston) **3-7-3**(7) NPollard(4) (prom 3f)	1½	**6**	20/1	37	—
Verinder's Gift (49) (DrJDScargill) **3-8-1** NCarlisle(3) (b.hind: prom over 6f)	¾	**7**	10/1	40	2
Compact Disc (IRE) (55) (MJohnston) **3-8-1** NAdams(5) (lw: led over 6f)	5	**8**	10/1	30	—
Racing Carr (40) (TJNaughton) **3-7-8**(5)ow3 MartinDwyer(2) (a bhd)	1¾	**9**	33/1	25	—

(SP 107.6%) **9 Rn**

1m 41.15 (3.75) CSF £21.29 TOTE £3.20: £1.30 £2.50 £2.10 (£15.90) Trio £26.20 OWNER Mrs A. M. Upsdell (EPSOM) BRED T. Ward

9 BAD PENNY MAIDEN STKS (4-Y.O+) (Class D)

1-50 (1-58) **1m 2f (Equitrack)** £3,517.50 (£1,065.00: £520.00: £247.50) Stalls: Low GOING minus 0.33 sec per fur (FST)

Horse / details	Dist	Pos	SP	RR	SF
Tawafek (USA) (69) (SDow) **4-8-12** RPerham(6) (rdn 3f out: gd hdwy over 1f out: led ins fnl f: r.o wl)	—	**1**	8/1	62	41
Nakhal (50) (DJGMurraySmith) **4-8-12** DHolland(8) (hld up: rdn over 4f out: led over 1f out tl ins fnl f: unable qckn)	1¾	**2**	5/1 [3]	59	38
Hazel (57) (MissGayKelleway) **5-8-9b**[1] DaneO'Neill(9) (a.p: chsd ldr over 4f out tl over 2f out: hrd rdn over 1f out: r.o one pce)	1¼	**3**	12/1	52	33
Ilandra (IRE) (44) (RAkehurst) **5-8-9** SSanders(2) (lw: w ldr: led over 7f out tl over 1f out: wknd ins fnl f)	2½	**4**	11/8 [1]	48	29
Nawaji (USA) (36) (WRMuir) **4-8-7** AClark(4) (rdn over 4f out: nvr nr to chal)	2	**5**	14/1	45	24
Nails Tails (SDow) **4-8-12** WRyan(7) (bit bkwd: hld up: rdn over 4f out: sn wknd)	8	**6**	9/2 [2]	37	16
New Technique (FR) (25) (KMcAuliffe) **4-8-7** JQuinn(5) (bhd fnl 8f: t.o)	dist	**7**	50/1	—	—
Supergold (IRE) (CMurray) **4-8-12** JWeaver(1) (b: led over 2f: wknd over 3f out: t.o)	2½	**8**	20/1	—	—
Mad Alex (MJHaynes) **4-8-7**(5) ADaly(11) (bhd fnl 4f: t.o)	nk	**9**	50/1	—	—
Callonescy (IRE) (35) (DCO'Brien) **5-9-0** GBardwell(3) (s.i.s: hdwy over 5f out: wknd over 4f out: t.o)	1½	**10**	50/1	—	—
Naphtali (JRArnold) **4-8-7** CRutter(10) (bhd fnl 5f: t.o fnl 4f)	dist	**11**	33/1	—	—

(SP 116.0%) **11 Rn**

2m 7.86 (3.56) CSF £43.96 TOTE £8.50: £1.60 £2.10 £1.60 (£27.20) Trio £26.20 OWNER Mr Terry Shepherd (EPSOM) BRED Jayeff B Stables
WEIGHT FOR AGE 4yo-2lb

10 MANY HANDS LIMITED STKS (0-60) (4-Y.O+) (Class F)

2-20 (2-25) **1m 2f (Equitrack)** £2,506.80 (£704.80: £344.40) Stalls: Low GOING minus 0.33 sec per fur (FST)

Horse / details	Dist	Pos	SP	RR	SF
Quiet Arch (IRE) (60) (WRMuir) **4-8-12** DaneO'Neill(5) (b: b.hind: hdwy 2f out: led 1f out: hrd rdn: r.o wl)	—	**1**	3/1 [2]	57	35
Awesome Power (51) (JWHills) **11-9-3** AClark(2) (led: rdn over 2f out: hdd 1f out: unable qckn)	1¼	**2**	12/1	58	38
Ben Gunn (57) (PTWalwyn) **5-9-0** TSprake(8) (lw: a.p: rdn over 2f out: ev ch over 1f out: one pce)	½	**3**	11/4 [1]	54	34
Arzani (USA) (53) (DJSCosgrove) **6-9-1**(5) MartinDwyer(3) (a.p: rdn over 3f out: ev ch 1f out: one pce)	nk	**4**	12/1	60	40
Double March (58) (PRWebber) **4-8-12** RPerham(6) (lw: hdwy over 4f out: rdn over 2f out: ev ch over 1f out: one pce)	¾	**5**	7/2 [3]	53	31
Manabar (60) (MJPolglase) **5-9-0** TGMcLaughlin(7) (a.p: rdn over 3f out: wknd over 2f out)	2	**6**	7/1	49	29
Our Eddie (57) (BGubby) **8-9-3v** JWeaver(4) (lw: prom over 5f)	1¼	**7**	9/1	50	30
Kedwick (IRE) (55) (PRHedger) **8-9-3b** DHolland(1) (b: b.hind: a bhd)	¾	**8**	7/1	49	29

(SP 124.3%) **8 Rn**

2m 8.66 (4.36) CSF £36.02 TOTE £4.10: £1.10 £2.40 £2.30 (£20.20) OWNER Mr John Davies (LAMBOURN) BRED E. and Mrs Flannery
WEIGHT FOR AGE 4yo-2lb

11 TOO MANY COOKS H'CAP (0-70) (4-Y.O+) (Class E)

2-50 (2-52) **6f (Equitrack)** £2,739.25 (£829.00: £404.50: £192.25) Stalls: Low GOING minus 0.33 sec per fur (FST)

Horse / details	Dist	Pos	SP	RR	SF
Ultra Beet (65) (PCHaslam) **5-9-9** JWeaver(9) (w ldr: led 3f out: clr over 1f out: rdn out)	—	**1**	4/1 [3]	74	45
Sharp Imp (59) (RMFlower) **7-9-3b** JQuinn(8) (outpcd: hdwy over 1f out: r.o wl ins fnl f)	1¼	**2**	7/2 [2]	65	36
Captain Carat (61) (DNicholls) **6-9-5** AlexGreaves(2) (lw: hld up: hrd rdn over 1f out: unable qckn)	1	**3**	100/30 [1]	64	35
Lift Boy (USA) (64) (AMoore) **8-9-8** CandyMorris(5) (b.hind: hld up: hrd rdn 3f out: one pce)	2	**4**	14/1	62	33
Will Do (70) (MartynMeade) **4-9-9**(5) DSweeney(6) (nvr nr to chal)	½	**5**	7/2 [2]	66	37
Miss Pickpocket (IRE) (42) (MissGayKelleway) **4-7-7**(7) AngelaGallimore(3) (n.m.r 5f out: hdwy 2f out: wknd 1f out)	2	**6**	12/1	33	4
Astral Invader (IRE) (48) (MSSaunders) **5-8-6** RPerham(1) (bhd fnl 4f)	3½	**7**	20/1	30	1
Tachycardia (38) (RJO'Sullivan) **5-7-10** NCarlisle(4) (led 3f: wknd over 1f out)	½	**8**	12/1	18	—
Rapier Point (IRE) (38) (CMurray) **6-7-10** NicolaHowarth(7) (a bhd)	2½	**9**	33/1	12	—

(SP 117.3%) **9 Rn**

1m 13.51 (2.41) CSF £17.75 CT £47.34 TOTE £4.40: £1.10 £1.40 £1.50 (£6.70) Trio £7.70 OWNER Pet Express (W&R) Ltd (MIDDLEHAM)
BRED Rockhouse Farms Ltd

12 BIRD IN THE HAND H'CAP (0-80) (3-Y.O) (Class D)

3-20 (3-20) **7f (Equitrack)** £3,403.75 (£1,030.00: £502.50: £238.75) Stalls: Low GOING minus 0.33 sec per fur (FST)

Horse / details	Dist	Pos	SP	RR	SF
Effervescence (84) (RHannon) **3-9-8**(5) 6x DGriffiths(2) (hld up: chsd ldr over 2f out: hrd rdn fnl f: led last stride)	—	**1**	4/5 [1]	91	52
Eager To Please (66) (MissGayKelleway) **3-8-9b** DHolland(5) (b: b.hind: lw: led: hrd drvn fnl 2f: hdd last stride)	s.h	**2**	11/2	73	34
Forgotten Times (USA) (64) (TMJones) **3-8-7** NCarlisle(1) (b.hind: lw: chsd ldr over 4f: wknd over 1f out)	6	**3**	16/1	57	18
Ben's Ridge (68) (PCHaslam) **3-8-6**(5) MartinDwyer(3) (hld up: rdn 2f out: wknd over 1f out)	½	**4**	5/1 [3]	60	21
Ultra Boy (78) (PCHaslam) **3-9-7** GCarter(4) (s.s: a bhd)	8	**5**	4/1 [2]	52	13

(SP 113.5%) **5 Rn**

1m 26.98 (2.58) CSF £5.56 TOTE £1.80: £1.10 £2.00 (£3.10) OWNER The Gold Buster Syndicate (2) (MARLBOROUGH) BRED T. Umpleby
STEWARDS' ENQUIRY Holland susp. 11 & 13/1/97 (excessive use of whip).

13

ROLLING STONE H'CAP (0-60) (4-Y.O+) (Class F)
3-50 (3-50) **1m 4f (Equitrack)** £2,596.40 (£730.40: £357.20) Stalls: Low GOING minus 0.33 sec per fur (FST)

			SP	RR	SF
Yet Again (45) (MissGayKelleway) **5-9-3** 5x DHolland(4) (b: b.hind: a.p: led on bit 3f out: clr over 1f out: easily)	—	**1**	1/2[1]	59+	45
Premier League (IRE) (35) (JELong) **7-8-7** LeesaLong(7) (a.p: hrd rdn over 1f out: chsd wnr fnl f: no imp)	5	**2**	16/1	42	28
Pair of Jacks (IRE) (27) (GLMoore) **7-7-13** JQuinn(11) (hdwy over 3f out: rdn over 2f out: one pce)	2½	**3**	14/1[3]	31	17
Colour Counsellor (45) (RMFlower) **4-8-13b** MWigham(2) (b: hdwy 3f out: one pce)	7	**4**	12/1[2]	40	22
Sapphire Son (IRE) (43) (PCClarke) **5-9-1** DaneO'Neill(8) (a.p: rdn over 2f out: sn wknd)	1½	**5**	12/1[2]	36	22
Chocolate Ice (57) (RJO'Sullivan) **4-9-6**(5) MartinDwyer(6) (hdwy over 6f out: wknd over 4f out)	2	**6**	14/1[3]	47	29
Cross Talk (IRE) (48) (RMStronge) **5-9-6** AClark(12) (b: hdwy over 4f out: wknd over 2f out)	3½	**7**	14/1[3]	33	19
Old Hush Wing (IRE) (49) (PCHaslam) **4-9-3** SDrowne(3) (bhd fnl 6f)	12	**8**	12/1[2]	18	—
Ela Agapi Mou (USA) (45) (AMoore) **4-8-13** CandyMorris(10) (b.hind: a bhd)	1¼	**9**	33/1	13	—
Brother Roy (60) (TGMills) **4-9-7**(7) JCornally(13) (a.p: led 6f out to 3f out: wknd qckly over 2f out)	1	**10**	33/1	26	8
Patiala (IRE) (37) (RWArmstrong) **4-8-5**ow2 SSanders(9) (prom over 8f)	1½	**11**	16/1	1	—
Mega Tid (36) (BAPearce) **5-8-8b**[1] GBardwell(14) (a bhd: t.o fnl 5f)	dist	**12**	14/1[3]	—	—
Flow Back (53) (GPEnright) **5-9-6v**(5) ADaly(1) (led 6f: wknd over 4f out: t.o: fin lame)	28	**13**	16/1	—	—

(SP 139.9%) **13 Rn**

2m 34.48 (4.48) CSF £13.67 CT £84.04 TOTE £1.70: £1.10 £3.80 £4.80 (£13.90) Trio £67.70 OWNER Mr A. P. Griffin (WHITCOMBE) BRED Aston Park Stud

WEIGHT FOR AGE 4yo-4lb

OFFICIAL EXPLANATION **Flow Back: was found to be lame behind after the race.**

T/Jkpt: £1,775.00 (9.08 Tckts). T/Plpt: £15.70 (1,693.11 Tckts). T/Qdpt: £1.90 (1,529.5 Tckts). AK

0001-SOUTHWELL (L-H) (Standard)

Friday January 3rd

WEATHER: cold with snowy showers WIND: mod across

14

LEICESTERSHIRE CLAIMING STKS (4-Y.O+) (Class F)
1-00 (1-00) **1m (Fibresand)** £2,294.00 (£644.00: £314.00) Stalls: Low GOING minus 0.43 sec per fur (FST)

			SP	RR	SF
Joseph's Wine (IRE) (75) (DNicholls) **8-9-7b** AlexGreaves(12) (lw: trckd ldrs: led ½-wy: clr over 2f out: eased ins fnl f)	—	**1**	7/1	72	19
Spencer's Revenge (69) (NTinkler) **8-8-9b** GBardwell(4) (lw: racd wd: sn wl bhd & drvn along: styd on wl fnl 2f: no ch w wnr)	3	**2**	8/1	54	1
Bernard Seven (IRE) (72) (MDods) **5-9-3b** AClark(8) (chsd ldrs: kpt on one pce fnl 2f)	1¾	**3**	5/1[3]	59	6
Giddy (42) (JHetherton) **4-8-2** NKennedy(3) (mid div: styd on fnl 2f: nvr nr to chal)	2	**4**	25/1	40	—
Afaan (IRE) (RFMarvin) **4-8-7** TGMcLaughlin(10) (s.s: racd wd: bhd tl styd on u.p fnl 2f)	1¼	**5**	50/1	42	—
Chadleigh Lane (USA) (62) (RHollinshead) **5-8-9** WRyan(14) (lw: mid div: effrt 3f out: nvr nr to chal)	10	**6**	7/2[2]	24	—
Absolute Magic (80) (WJHaggas) **7-9-2**(5) DGriffiths(9) (prom: drvn along & outpcd ½-wy: n.d after)	nk	**7**	11/8[1]	35	—
Ruby Angel (40) (HCandy) **4-8-0** CRutter(6) (w ldrs tl lost pl 2f out)	¾	**8**	25/1	13	—
Magication (KGWingrove) **7-7-12** NCarlisle(11) (b: s.s: racd wd: a bhd)	6	**9**	50/1	—	—
Spanish Stripper (USA) (35) (MCChapman) **6-8-7** FNorton(1) (s.i.s: sn led: hdd ½-wy: lost pl 2f out)	1¾	**10**	50/1	4	—
Shoja (MrsVAAconley) **4-8-0v**[1](7) GMilligan(7) (outpcd & bhd fr ½-wy)	1¼	**11**	100/1	2	—
Broughtons Relish (WJMusson) **4-7-11**(7) DarrenWilliams(5) (prom: outpcd & lost pl ½-wy)	1	**12**	50/1	—	—
Lady Eclat (34) (KGWingrove) **4-7-9**(3) NVarley(2) (led early: sn drvn along: lost pl ½-wy: sn bhd)	5	**13**	50/1	—	—

(SP 123.1%) **13 Rn**

1m 44.2 (5.20) CSF £58.85 TOTE £9.20: £2.60 £1.10 £2.50 (£20.10) Trio £35.80 OWNER Wetherby Racing Bureau Ltd (THIRSK) BRED Michael Fennessy

15

LINCOLNSHIRE AMATEUR H'CAP (0-75) (4-Y.O+) (Class F)
1-30 (1-30) **1m (Fibresand)** £2,294.00 (£644.00: £314.00) Stalls: Low GOING minus 0.43 sec per fur (FST)

			SP	RR	SF
Domino Flyer (58) (MrsASwinbank) **4-10-5** MrChrisWilson(7) (lw: led 1f: led over 2f out: hung lft & pushed out fnl f)	—	**1**	6/1[2]	62	36
Desert Invader (IRE) (70) (DWChapman) **6-11-3** MrRHale(6) (led after 1f tl over 2f out: kpt on same pce fnl f)	3	**2**	10/1	68	42
Cats Bottom (52) (AGNewcombe) **5-9-13** 5x MrTMcCarthy(10) (lw: hld up: hdwy to chal 2f out: sn rdn & nt qckn)	1¾	**3**	7/1	47	21
Montone (IRE) (62) (JRJenkins) **7-10-9v** DrMMannish(14) (sn outpcd: hdwy 3f out: hrd rdn & kpt on one pce)	5	**4**	13/2[3]	47	21
Royal Acclaim (39) (RDickin) **12-8-7**(7) MissRJPatman(8) (s.s: bhd tl r.o fnl 2f)	5	**5**	50/1	14	—
First Gold (44) (JWharton) **8-8-12**(7) MrCWatson(15) (s.i.s: bhd tl kpt on fnl 2f)	s.h	**6**	20/1	18	—
3[2] **Awesome Venture (74)** (MCChapman) **7-11-0**(7) MrKLoads(9) (trckd ldrs: effrt over 2f out: grad wknd)	s.h	**7**	12/1	48	22
Napoleon's Return (43) (JLEyre) **4-9-4b**[1] MissDianaJones(11) (chsd ldrs: outpcd over 2f out: n.d after)	hd	**8**	11/1	17	—
Fred's Delight (IRE) (59) (MrsVAAconley) **6-9-13v**(7)ow20 MrGMarkham(5) (prom: outpcd over 2f out: grad wknd)	¾	**9**	50/1	32	—
Globe Runner (51) (JJO'Neill) **4-9-5**(7)ow6 MissSKerswell(13) (chsd ldrs tl wknd over 2f out)	¾	**10**	33/1	22	—
Carol Again (42) (NBycroft) **5-8-13**(4) MrsCWilliams(12) (s.i.s: bhd: sme hdwy 3f out: sn wknd)	7	**11**	20/1	—	—
Dream Carrier (IRE) (51) (REPeacock) **9-9-5**(7)ow2 MrsCPeacock(4) (prom 3f: sn lost pl & bhd)	1	**12**	50/1	6	—
Ring the Chief (42) (MDIUsher) **5-8-13**(4)ow3 MrsAUsher(3) (sn bhd)	½	**13**	20/1	—	—
Kingchip Boy (68) (MJRyan) **8-10-11v**(4) MrSLavallin(1) (chsd ldrs tl lost pl over 2f out)	7	**14**	3/1[1]	8	—
Twin Creeks (70) (VSoane) **6-10-10**(7) MrFQuinlan(2) (chsd ldrs tl lost pl over 2f out)	3	**15**	8/1	4	—

(SP 124.5%) **15 Rn**

1m 43.5 (4.50) CSF £61.14 CT £397.56 TOTE £7.60: £3.20 £3.30 £2.00 (£35.10) Trio £122.60 OWNER Mr S. Smith (RICHMOND) BRED Mrs K. Livingstone

LONG HANDICAP Fred's Delight (IRE) 7-11 Ring the Chief 8-10 Royal Acclaim 8-7

16 DERBYSHIRE MAIDEN H'CAP (0-65) (4-Y.O+) (Class F)

2-00 (2-02) **1m 4f (Fibresand)** £2,710.00 (£760.00: £370.00) Stalls: Low GOING minus 0.43 sec per fur (FST)

	Horse	Dist	Pos	SP	RR	SF
	Parklife (IRE) (38) (PCHaslam) **5-8-6** SDrowne(14) (s.s: hdwy ½-wy: led jst ins fnl f: sn clr)	—	1	3/1[1]	45	20
	Raffles Rooster (56) (AGNewcombe) **5-9-5**(5) DGriffiths(11) (trckd ldrs: led over 2f out tl jst ins fnl f: no ch w wnr)	6	2	4/1[2]	55	30
	Shepherds Rest (IRE) (33) (SMellor) **5-8-1** JQuinn(5) (w ldrs: led over 3f out tl over 2f out: hung lft & wknd appr fnl f)	9	3	4/1[2]	20	—
	Swandale Flyer (33) (NBycroft) **5-7-8**(7) JBramhill(8) (w ldr: led 7f out tl over 3f out: one pce)	2½	4	16/1	17	—
	Mustang (40) (CWThornton) **4-8-4** LCharnock(10) (trckd ldrs: chal 4f out: rdn & wknd 2f out)	3½	5	12/1	19	—
	Burning Flame (34) (RMFlower) **4-7-12** FNorton(12) (bhd & drvn along ½-wy: sme hdwy 2f out: n.d)	1¼	6	10/1	11	—
	Calendula (60) (DMorley) **4-9-10** GCarter(2) (w ldrs tl wknd over 2f out)	2½	7	9/1[3]	34	5
	El Don (34) (MJRyan) **5-8-2v**[1] GBardwell(9) (chsd ldrs: drvn along ½-wy: hung lft & lost pl over 2f out)	¾	8	11/1	7	—
210	**Acerbus Dulcis (37)** (MCChapman) **6-7-12**(7) IonaWands(6) (mid div & sn drvn along: n.d)	hd	9	66/1	10	—
	Dispol Dancer (30) (MrsVAAconley) **6-7-12**ow2 NCarlisle(4) (led to 7f out: lost pl over 4f out)	2	10	33/1	—	—
	Turrill House (35) (WJMusson) **5-8-3** CRutter(15) (a bhd)	½	11	20/1	5	—
	Captain Tandy (IRE) (28) (CSmith) **8-7-7**(3) NVarley(13) (sn bhd & drvn along: sme hdwy 5f out: sn wknd)	9	12	33/1	—	—
	Elle Mac (34) (MPBielby) **4-7-7v**(5)ow2 PFessey(7) (hld up: bhd fr ½-wy)	4	13	50/1	—	—
	Ballet de Cour (48) (TJEtherington) **4-8-12** ACulhane(3) (prom: drvn along ½-wy: sn lost pl & bhd)	3½	14	20/1	—	—
	Nautical Jewel (42) (MDIUsher) **5-8-10v** MWigham(1) (a bhd: t.o 3f out)	24	15	16/1	—	—

(SP 130.7%) **15 Rn**

2m 38.8 (5.80) CSF £15.96 CT £48.26 TOTE £4.60: £1.50 £1.40 £1.40 (£9.50) Trio £8.40 OWNER Mr Keith Middleton (MIDDLEHAM) BRED Limestone Stud

LONG HANDICAP Dispol Dancer 7-6 Elle Mac 7-8

WEIGHT FOR AGE 4yo-4lb

17 NOTTINGHAMSHIRE H'CAP (0-75) (3-Y.O) (Class D)

2-30 (2-31) **6f (Fibresand)** £3,355.00 (£1,015.00: £495.00: £235.00) Stalls: Low GOING minus 0.43 sec per fur (FST)

Horse	Dist	Pos	SP	RR	SF
Brutal Fantasy (IRE) (65) (JLEyre) **3-8-12** RLappin(7) (mde all: edgd rt & styd on strly fnl f)	—	1	10/1	80	46
Siouxrouge (74) (PCHaslam) **3-9-7** GCarter(1) (sn chsng ldrs: ev ch 2f out: nt qckn ins fnl f)	2	2	6/1	84	50
Enchanting Eve (70) (CNAllen) **3-8-12**(5) GFaulkner(5) (a chsng ldrs: styd on same pce fnl 2f)	4	3	8/1	69	35
Master Foley (62) (NPLittmoden) **3-8-9** TGMcLaughlin(2) (chsd wnr: one pce fnl 2f)	hd	4	8/1	61	27
Sharp Return (59) (MJRyan) **3-8-6** AClark(3) (sn drvn along: sme hdwy 2f out: sn wknd)	7	5	11/2[3]	39	5
Double-O (72) (WJarvis) **3-9-5** SSanders(6) (lw: in tch: sn drvn along: lost pl over 3f out)	½	6	11/4[2]	51	17
Jay-Owe-Two (IRE) (75) (RMWhitaker) **3-9-8** 7x ACulhane(4) (lw: sn bhd & drvn along: sme hdwy 2f out: sn wknd)	nk	7	2/1[1]	53	19
C-Harry (IRE) (67) (RHollinshead) **3-8-9**(5) DGriffiths(8) (bhd fr ½-wy: eased)	9	8	10/1	21	—

(SP 130.1%) **8 Rn**

1m 14.6 (1.10) CSF £69.50 CT £483.47 TOTE £13.90: £4.00 £1.90 £3.80 (£49.90) OWNER Diamond Racing Ltd (HAMBLETON) BRED Michael G. O'Brien

18 YORKSHIRE (S) STKS (4, 5 & 6-Y.O) (Class G)

3-00 (3-00) **1m 3f (Fibresand)** £2,085.00 (£585.00: £285.00) Stalls: Low GOING minus 0.43 sec per fur (FST)

Horse	Dist	Pos	SP	RR	SF
Sarasi (67) (MJCamacho) **5-9-1** LCharnock(2) (lw: trckd ldrs: led over 4f out: edgd rt & kpt on fnl f)	—	1	5/1[2]	49	22
Forzair (55) (JJO'Neill) **5-9-1** WRyan(7) (lw: w ldr: led 6f out tl over 4f out: hung rt & nt qckn fnl f)	1	2	5/1[2]	48	21
Threesocks (BSmart) **4-8-7** RPerham(13) (lw: in tch: hdwy to chse ldrs 2f out: hung lft: styd on)	¾	3	16/1	42	12
Undawaterscubadiva (28) (MPBielby) **5-9-1** JWeaver(11) (bhd: hdwy over 4f out: nt qckn fnl 2f)	1¾	4	25/1	44	17
Calder King (70) (JLEyre) **6-9-1b** RLappin(14) (sn trckng ldrs: effrt & hung lft over 1f out: kpt on same pce)	1¾	5	8/11[1]	41	14
Al Helal (43) (JRJenkins) **5-9-1b** SSanders(3) (rel to r: sn drvn along: hdwy 4f out: kpt on fnl 2f: nvr rchd ldrs)	½	6	16/1	41	14
Bold Charlie (SMellor) **5-9-1v**[1] JQuinn(9) (bhd 7f out: sme hdwy over 3f out: sn wknd)	21	7	50/1	10	—
Blue Domain (43) (RCraggs) **6-8-10**(5) DSweeney(4) (led to 6f out: wknd 2f out)	s.h	8	50/1	10	—
Hornpipe (50) (JWharton) **5-8-12**(3) CTeague(10) (b: w ldrs tl lost pl 3f out)	2	9	14/1	7	—
Chilly Lad (47) (RTJuckes) **6-9-1v** ACulhane(1) (rel to r: sn drvn along: a bhd)	3	10	33/1	3	—
Flint And Steel (60) (BobJones) **4-8-12** MWigham(6) (chsd ldrs: drvn along 7f out: sn lost pl)	3	11	8/1[3]	—	—
Jeanne Cutrona (KGWingrove) **4-8-7** GBardwell(12) (b.hind: sn bhd: t.o 3f out)	9	12	33/1	—	—
Britannia Mills (MCChapman) **6-8-3**(7) IonaWands(5) (in tch 5f: sn bhd)	1¾	13	33/1	—	—
Fenian Court (IRE) (MissJBower) **6-8-10b**[1] SDWilliams(8) (t.o 3f out)	s.h	14	16/1	—	—

(SP 143.2%) **14 Rn**

2m 26.2 (6.20) CSF £34.07 TOTE £7.00: £2.00 £1.20 £5.00 (£17.10) Trio £125.20 OWNER The Blue Chip Group (MALTON) BRED C. J. R. Trotter

WEIGHT FOR AGE 4yo-3lb

No bid

19 RUTLAND H'CAP (0-65) (3-Y.O) (Class F)

3-30 (3-31) **7f (Fibresand)** £2,703.60 (£759.60: £370.80) Stalls: Low GOING minus 0.43 sec per fur (FST)

Horse	Dist	Pos	SP	RR	SF
Pet Express (39) (PCHaslam) **3-7-10** LCharnock(7) (trckd ldrs: led over 2f out: hung lft & hld on wl ins fnl f)	—	1	16/1	44	11
Patina (53) (RHollinshead) **3-8-10** WRyan(5) (trckd ldrs: ev ch fnl f: nt qckn towards fin)	½	2	13/8[1]	57	24
Hever Golf Dancer (64) (TJNaughton) **3-9-7** GCarter(4) (lw: prom: drvn along & lost pl over 4f out: styd on fnl 2f)	5	3	6/1	56	23
Silent Weapon (59) (KMcAuliffe) **3-9-2v**[1] SSanders(1) (chsd ldrs: drvn along 2f out: edgd rt & one pce)	1¼	4	8/1	49	16
Full Traceability (IRE) (48) (JJO'Neill) **3-8-5** JQuinn(6) (trckd ldrs: effrt 3f out: wknd 2f out)	2½	5	10/1	32	—
Lycius Touch (49) (AGNewcombe) **3-8-6** SDrowne(8) (sn chsng ldrs: drvn along 3f out: wknd over 1f out)	1	6	4/1[2]	31	—
Come Dancing (53) (MJohnston) **3-8-10** JWeaver(3) (led tl over 2f out: sn wknd)	4	7	5/1[3]	25	—

Amy (50) (CSmith) **3-8-7** AClark(2) (s.i.s: sn wl bhd: t.o fnl 2f) ....dist	8	33/1	—	—
		(SP 118.1%) **8 Rn**		

1m 29.6 (3.10) CSF £42.05 CT £169.40 TOTE £20.80: £4.80 £1.10 £1.10 (£46.20) OWNER Pet Express (W&R) Ltd (MIDDLEHAM) BRED A. J. Sexton
LONG HANDICAP Pet Express 7-1

T/Jkpt: Not won; £4,462.74 to Lingfield 4/1/97. T/Plpt: £119.80 (212.74 Tckts). T/Qdpt: £18.40 (204.12 Tckts). WG

0008-LINGFIELD (L-H) (Standard)
Saturday January 4th
WEATHER: overcast with snow showers & very cold WIND: fresh half against

20 LADBROKE ON COURSE BETTING SHOP H'CAP (0-60) (I) (3-Y.O+) (Class F)
12-15 (12-17) **6f (Equitrack)** £2,100.80 (£588.80: £286.40) Stalls: Low GOING minus 0.34 sec per fur (FST)

	Horse		SP	RR	SF
	Invocation (58) (AMoore) **10-9-13** AClark(5) (b.hind: chsd ldrs: pushed along ½-wy: led over 1f out: hrd rdn ins fnl: r.o) ....—	1	7/1	65	41
	Hoh Majestic (IRE) (51) (RonaldThompson) **4-9-6v** JWeaver(3) (lw: mde most tl hdd over 1f out: hrd rdn & ev ch ins fnl f: r.o) ....nk	2	4/1 1	57	33
	Aljaz (48) (MissGayKelleway) **7-9-3** SSanders(10) (b: hld up: rdn over 2f out: styd on ins fnl f) 1½	3	6/1 3	50	26
	Norling (IRE) (39) (KOCunningham-Brown) **7-8-8** CMunday(9) (chsd ldrs: outpcd 2f out: rdn over 1f out: kpt on one pce ins fnl f) 1¼	4	20/1	38	14
4³	**Gi La High (52)** (MartynMeade) **4-9-2**(5) DSweeney(2) (b.hind: w ldr: rdn over 1f out: wknd ins fnl f) 1¼	5	9/2 2	48	24
4ᵂ	**Shashi (IRE) (59)** (PatMitchell) **5-10-0** RLappin(7) (chsd ldrs: rdn over 2f out: wknd over 1f out) ....nk	6	7/1	54	30
	Our Shadee (USA) (53) (KTIvory) **7-9-8v** CScally(6) (b: b.hind: sn rdn along: outpcd in rr: sme hdwy ins fnl f: nvr nrr) 1½	7	9/1	44	20
	Viennese Dancer (30) (RJRWilliams) **4-7-10**(3) MBaird(4) (b.hind: dwlt: a bhd) 4	8	50/1	10	—
	Indian Wolf (27) (BJLlewellyn) **4-7-10** GBardwell(1) (a bhd) 7	9	50/1	—	—
	Miletrian Refurb (IRE) (56) (MRChannon) **4-9-11** CandyMorris(8) (bhd fnl 3f) 2½	10	14/1	11	—
	Colston-C (50) (PDEvans) **5-9-5** GCarter(11) (bhd fnl 3f) 3	11	13/2	—	—
			(SP 116.2%) **11 Rn**		

1m 14.03 (2.93) CSF £32.63 CT £165.20 TOTE £8.50: £2.90 £3.10 £1.70 (£20.70) Trio £42.10 OWNER Mr R. Kiernan (BRIGHTON) BRED Juddmonte Farms
LONG HANDICAP Indian Wolf 7-6

21 LADBROKE ALL-WEATHER TROPHY (QUALIFIER) H'CAP (0-70) (I) (4-Y.O+) (Class E)
12-45 (12-48) **7f (Equitrack)** £2,427.25 (£733.00: £356.50: £168.25) Stalls: Low GOING minus 0.34 sec per fur (FST)

Horse		SP	RR	SF
Royal Carlton (IRE) (60) (GLMoore) **5-9-4** SWhitworth(5) (lw: a.p: chsd ldr gng wl over 2f out: led over 1f out: pushed out) ....—	1	3/1 1	76	51
Never Think Twice (56) (KTIvory) **4-9-0b** NAdams(4) (b: b.hind: hld up: hdwy ½-wy: hrd rdn & ev ch 1f out: r.o) ....nk	2	13/2	71	46
Hawaii Storm (FR) (46) (DJSffrenchDavis) **9-8-1**(3) MBaird(3) (s.s: wl bhd tl styd on fnl 2f: nvr nrr) 4	3	11/2	52	27
Apollo Red (64) (AMoore) **8-9-8** CandyMorris(8) (b.hind: led tl ½-wy: hrd rdn fnl 2f: one pce) 1	4	7/2 2	68	43
Daryabad (IRE) (65) (TJNaughton) **5-9-6**(3) JDSmith(6) (wl bhd tl mod late hdwy: nvr nrr) 3½	5	10/1	61	36
Zamalek (USA) (46) (RMFlower) **5-8-4e** SDrowne(1) (sn outpcd) 2	6	25/1	37	12
Ki Chi Saga (USA) (70) (MMadgwick) **5-10-0** AClark(2) (bhd fnl 4f) ....¾	7	25/1	60	35
Dark Menace (47) (EAWheeler) **5-8-0b**(5) ADaly(9) (chsd ldr: led ½-wy: hdd over 1f out: sn wknd) ....½	8	5/1 3	36	11
Golden Silver (43) (JSMoore) **4-7-8**(7) KAxon(7) (s.s: a bhd) 13	9	25/1	2	—
		(SP 113.2%) **9 Rn**		

1m 26.32 (1.92) CSF £20.74 CT £90.64 TOTE £3.50: £1.10 £2.20 £1.80 (£9.40) Trio £22.90 OWNER Mrs Mary Doyle (BRIGHTON) BRED Des De Vere Hunt

22 LADBROKE APPRENTICE CLAIMING STKS (4-Y.O+) (Class F)
1-15 (1-15) **1m 4f (Equitrack)** £2,343.50 (£666.00: £330.50) Stalls: Low GOING minus 0.34 sec per fur (FST)

	Horse		SP	RR	SF
	Slip Jig (IRE) (65) (RHannon) **4-9-1**(7) GGallagher(4) (lw: a gng wl: hld up: hdwy ½-wy: led over 2f out: clr over 1f out: comf) ....—	1	8/11 1	78+	48
	Soldier Cove (USA) (50) (MartynMeade) **7-8-9**(5) TField(5) (t.k.h: a.p: led 5f out: hdd over 2f out: one pce) 9	2	5/1 2	54	28
	Il Trastevere (FR) (72) (MissGayKelleway) **5-9-12** AngelaGallimore(8) (led after 2f: hdd 5f out: hrd rdn: one pce) 7	3	20/1	57	31
	Captain Marmalade (44) (DTThom) **8-8-10**(7) DSalt(7) (bit bkwd: hld up: hdwy 6f out: rdn 3f out: one pce) 5	4	10/1 3	41	15
	Al Haal (USA) (50) (RJO'Sullivan) **8-8-8** DDenby(9) (dropped rr after 3f: sn wl bhd: styd on fnl 2f: nvr nrr) ....nk	5	14/1	32	6
13⁸	**Old Hush Wing (IRE) (49)** (PCHaslam) **4-9-1v**1(7) PGoode(10) (sn led: hdd 10f out: rdn 5f out: wknd 3f out) 5	6	16/1	43	13
	One In The Eye (41) (JRPoulton) **4-8-8**(5) RCody-Boutcher(2) (bhd fnl 5f) 7	7	20/1	25	—
	Haute Cuisine (43) (RJRWilliams) **4-8-10** CWebb(3) (b.hind: sme hdwy 6f out: wknd over 3f out: t.o) 15	8	20/1	2	—
	Stonecutter (MRChannon) **4-8-5v**(5) GHannon(6) (a bhd: t.o) 8	9	10/1 3	—	—
	Memory's Music (46) (MMadgwick) **5-9-1**(5) CCarver(1) (bhd fnl 6f: t.o) 11	10	33/1	—	—
			(SP 122.5%) **10 Rn**		

2m 34.5 (4.50) CSF £5.41 TOTE £1.80: £1.10 £1.50 £3.90 (£3.50) Trio £32.80 OWNER Mr John Horgan (MARLBOROUGH) BRED Scuderia Milano
WEIGHT FOR AGE 4yo-4lb
IN-FOCUS: Geoff Gallagher was riding his first winner.

23 LADBROKE H'CAP (0-80) (4-Y.O+) (Class D)

1-45 (1-48) **1m 4f** **(Equitrack)** £3,371.25 (£1,020.00: £497.50: £236.25) Stalls: Low GOING minus 0.34 sec per fur (FST)

	Horse	Dist	Pos	SP	RR	SF
	Steamroller Stanly (80) (CACyzer) **4-9-12** GCarter(2) (lw: a.p: led ½-wy: hdd 2f out: hrd rdn to ld wl ins fnl f: r.o)	—	1	9/2[1]	96	54
	General Haven (70) (TJNaughton) **4-9-2** JWeaver(8) (chsd ldrs: led 2f out: sn rdn: hdd wl ins fnl f: r.o)	hd	2	9/2[1]	86	44
	Glow Forum (70) (LMontagueHall) **6-9-6** WRyan(4) (a.p: rdn 3f out: one pce)	10	3	11/2[3]	73	35
	No Speeches (IRE) (64) (SDow) **6-8-9**(5) ADaly(7) (lw: hld up: hdwy 5f out: hrd rdn 3f out: one pce)	2	4	9/1	64	26
	Nikita's Star (IRE) (77) (DJGMurraySmith) **4-9-9** DaneO'Neill(5) (hld up: rdn over 3f out: one pce)	1¾	5	8/1	75	33
	Tart (FR) (72) (JPearce) **4-9-4** MWigham(6) (chsd ldrs: hrd rdn 4f out: wknd 2f out)	11	6	5/1[2]	55	13
	Set the Fashion (62) (DLWilliams) **8-8-12** DHarrison(10) (rr: sme hdwy 4f out: sn rdn & btn)	1¼	7	25/1	43	5
	Out on a Promise (IRE) (71) (NJHWalker) **5-9-7** JStack(9) (lw: a bhd)	6	8	6/1	44	6
	Bayrak (USA) (53) (PAKelleway) **7-8-3** GBardwell(1) (b: led to ½-wy: sn wknd: t.o)	30	9	25/1	—	—
	A Million Watts (70) (GMMcCourt) **6-9-6** AClark(3) (dwlt: sn rcvrd: in tch tl wknd 5f out: t.o)	6	10	25/1	—	—

(SP 115.4%) **10 Rn**

2m 34.17 (4.17) CSF £23.31 CT £101.19 TOTE £5.90: £1.90 £2.00 £1.90 (£10.50) Trio £28.40 OWNER Mr R. M. Cyzer (HORSHAM) BRED R. D. Hubbard

WEIGHT FOR AGE 4yo-4lb

OFFICIAL EXPLANATION **Out on a Promise (IRE): hung badly left throughout.**

24 LADBROKE ON COURSE BETTING SHOP H'CAP (0-60) (II) (3-Y.O+) (Class F)

2-15 (2-18) **6f** **(Equitrack)** £2,100.80 (£588.80: £286.40) Stalls: Low GOING minus 0.34 sec per fur (FST)

	Horse	Dist	Pos	SP	RR	SF
11[2]	**Sharp Imp (59)** (RMFlower) **7-10-0b** DaneO'Neill(10) (hld up in rr: pushed along early: hdwy 2f out: led ins fnl f: r.o wl)	—	1	5/2[1]	68	38
	Thick as Thieves (42) (RonaldThompson) **5-8-8**(3) CTeague(11) (racd wd: hld up: hdwy over 2f out: led over 1f out: hdd ins fnl f: unable qckn)	1	2	33/1	48	18
	Barbason (55) (AMoore) **5-9-10** CandyMorris(7) (b.hind: rr: rdn 4f out: hdwy 2f out: styd on one pce fnl f)	1¾	3	5/1[2]	57	27
	Mystery Matthias (46) (MissBSanders) **4-8-8v**(7) JoHunnam(6) (lw: a.p: ev ch over 1f out: one pce)	½	4	8/1	46	16
	Allstars Dancer (37) (TJNaughton) **4-7-13**(7) RachaelMoody(5) (chsd ldrs: rdn 2f out: one pce)	1½	5	25/1	33	3
	Mister Raider (57) (EAWheeler) **5-9-7b**(5) 7x ADaly(4) (mid div: hrd rdn 3f out: one pce)	3	6	11/2[3]	45	15
	Superlao (BEL) (41) (JJBridger) **5-8-5**(5) DSweeney(9) (a bhd)	2½	7	25/1	23	—
	Samsolom (45) (PHowling) **9-9-0** AClark(8) (a bhd)	¾	8	8/1	25	—
11[8]	**Tachycardia (38)** (RJO'Sullivan) **5-8-7** SSanders(3) (prom: led over 2f out: hdd over 1f out: sn wknd)	nk	9	14/1	17	—
	Into Debt (31) (JRPoulton) **4-8-0** GBardwell(1) (chsd ldrs tl wknd ½-wy)	1½	10	14/1	6	—
	Halbert (45) (PBurgoyne) **8-8-9v**(5) GFaulkner(2) (lw: sn led: hdd over 2f out: sn wknd)	4	11	7/1	9	—

(SP 119.3%) **11 Rn**

1m 14.27 (3.17) CSF £66.82 CT £363.12 TOTE £3.10: £1.10 £8.80 £2.90 (£47.30) Trio £267.90 OWNER Mrs G. M. Temmerman (JEVINGTON) BRED James Wigan

25 LADBROKE TELEBETTING H'CAP (0-80) (3-Y.O) (Class D)

2-45 (2-46) **5f** **(Equitrack)** £3,322.50 (£1,005.00: £490.00: £232.50) Stalls: High GOING minus 0.34 sec per fur (FST)

	Horse	Dist	Pos	SP	RR	SF
	Krystal Davey (IRE) (58) (TDBarron) **3-8-7** DHarrison(4) (chsd ldrs: hrd rdn 1f out: led ins fnl f: all out)	—	1	9/2[3]	62	2
	Heavenly Miss (IRE) (70) (JJBridger) **3-9-5** JWeaver(8) (lw: chsd ldrs: pushed along 3f out: hrd rdn ins fnl f: r.o)	s.h	2	10/1	74	14
	Tear White (IRE) (65) (TGMills) **3-9-0b** SSanders(7) (lw: sn led: hdd ins fnl f: no ex)	1½	3	3/1[2]	64	4
	Imperial Garden (IRE) (65) (PCHaslam) **3-9-0** SDrowne(5) (a.p: rdn appr fnl f: one pce)	s.h	4	11/2	64	4
	Nightingale Song (72) (MartynMeade) **3-9-2**(5) DSweeney(6) (dwlt: sn in tch: rdn over 1f out: kpt on one pce ins fnl f)	nk	5	8/1	70	10
	Enchantica (60) (JBerry) **3-8-4**(5) PFessey(3) (b.hind: a.p: rdn over 1f out: one pce)	1¼	6	7/1	54	—
	Countless Times (55) (WRMuir) **3-8-4** AClark(2) (sn outpcd)	2	7	11/4[1]	43	—
	Calchou (60) (CWFairhurst) **3-8-9** RLappin(1) (in tch tl wknd over 2f out: t.o)	18	8	16/1	—	—

(SP 123.8%) **8 Rn**

61.9 secs (3.70) CSF £45.43 CT £147.35 TOTE £5.50: £1.30 £2.20 £2.00 (£40.50) OWNER The Oakfield Nurseries Partnership (THIRSK) BRED David Barry

OFFICIAL EXPLANATION **Countless Times: the rider reported that the colt needs further and, after becoming outpaced, resented the kick-back.**

26 LADBROKE MEDIAN AUCTION MAIDEN STKS (3-Y.O) (Class E)

3-15 (3-16) **1m 2f** **(Equitrack)** £2,804.25 (£849.00: £414.50: £197.25) Stalls: Low GOING minus 0.34 sec per fur (FST)

	Horse	Dist	Pos	SP	RR	SF
	Superbelle (79) (MAJarvis) **3-8-9** SSanders(7) (lw: hld up in tch: led 3f out: clr over 1f out: easily)	—	1	8/11[1]	77	30
	Mogul (NAGraham) **3-9-0** DaneO'Neill(11) (racd wd in rr: hdwy 4f out: rdn over 3f out: styd on one pce fnl 2f)	6	2	20/1	72	25
	Lochlass (IRE) (67) (SPCWoods) **3-8-2**(7) CWebb(8) (lw: hld up: hdwy 5f out: rdn 3f out: one pce)	6	3	8/1	58	11
	My Legal Eagle (IRE) (JWHills) **3-9-0** AClark(1) (chsd ldrs: rdn over 2f out: one pce)	nk	4	10/1	62	15
	Love Me Do (USA) (69) (MJohnston) **3-9-0** JWeaver(3) (sn rdn along towards rr tl styd on one pce fnl 2f)	1¼	5	11/2[3]	60	13
	Alimerjam (49) (JWhite) **3-8-9b**[1] SDrowne(4) (sn led: hdd 3f out: grad wknd)	1¼	6	50/1	53	6
	Around Fore Alliss (76) (TGMills) **3-9-0** WRyan(5) (prom: rdn 2f out: sn wknd)	3	7	7/2[2]	54	7
	Leg Beforum (IRE) (LMontagueHall) **3-9-0** GCarter(10) (dwlt: a bhd)	9	8	33/1	39	—
	Buzzby Babe (AGFoster) **3-8-9** TSprake(2) (b: prom tl wknd 6f out)	5	9	50/1	26	—
	French Kiss (IRE) (MRChannon) **3-9-0** CandyMorris(12) (dwlt: sn in tch: wknd 5f out: t.o)	8	10	20/1	18	—
	Foxford Lad (TMJones) **3-8-9**(5) GFaulkner(6) (bhd fnl 5f: t.o)	hd	11	50/1	18	—
	Tirol's Treasure (IRE) (24) (KTIvory) **3-8-9** CScally(9) (b: b.hind: a bhd: t.o)	s.h	12	50/1	13	—

(SP 136.0%) **12 Rn**

2m 8.81 (4.51) CSF £19.65 TOTE £1.90: £1.50 £2.50 £1.80 (£16.00) Trio £47.50 OWNER Mr N. S. Yong (NEWMARKET) BRED N. S. Yong

27 LADBROKE ALL-WEATHER TROPHY (QUALIFIER) H'CAP (0-70) (II) (4-Y.O+) (Class E)
3-45 (3-46) **7f (Equitrack)** £2,401.25 (£725.00: £352.50: £166.25) Stalls: Low GOING minus 0.34 sec per fur (FST)

Horse	Dist	Pos	SP	RR	SF
Step On Degas (63) (MJFetherston-Godley) **4-9-3**(5) DGriffiths(5) (lw: a.p: led over 1f out: r.o)	—	**1**	5/1	69	45
Fort Knox (IRE) (60) (RMFlower) **6-9-5b** DaneO'Neill(2) (dwlt: sn rdn in rr: hdwy 2f out: swtchd rt over 1f out: styd on ins fnl f)	¾	**2**	7/2[2]	64	40
Jo Maximus (62) (SDow) **5-9-7** WRyan(8) (lw: a.p: rdn over 1f out: styd on one pce ins fnl f)	nk	**3**	9/2[3]	66	42
Bargash (44) (PDEvans) **5-8-3**ow2 GCarter(4) (a.p: rdn over 1f out: styd on one pce ins fnl f)	nk	**4**	11/4[1]	47	21
Mellors (IRE) (57) (MJHeaton-Ellis) **4-9-2** SDrowne(3) (led: hdd over 1f out: one pce)	s.h	**5**	9/1	60	36
Private Fixture (IRE) (45) (DMarks) **6-8-4** TSprake(6) (chsd ldrs: rdn & lost pl over 4f out: kpt on one pce ins fnl f)	1½	**6**	33/1	44	20
Unspoken Prayer (40) (JRArnold) **4-7-10**(3) MBaird(7) (lw: sn outpcd: racd wd: hdwy 2f out: rdn over 1f out: one pce)	hd	**7**	12/1	39	15
Sea Danzig (65) (JJBridger) **4-9-10** SSanders(1) (chsd ldr: sn rdn along: wknd over 2f out)	6	**8**	11/2	50	26

(SP 119.8%) **8 Rn**

1m 27.17 (2.77) CSF £22.60 CT £79.27 TOTE £6.00: £1.80 £1.50 £1.60 (£14.00) OWNER The Degas Partnership (EAST ILSLEY) BRED A. J. Poulton (Epping) Ltd

T/Jkpt: £7,100.00 (0.1 Tckts); £8,966.94 to Southwell 6/1/97. T/Plpt: £36.50 (747.21 Tckts). T/Qdpt: £13.50 (222.73 Tckts). SM

WOLVERHAMPTON (L-H) (Standard becoming Slow)

Saturday January 4th

30 min delay after race 2 while work was carried out on the track.
WEATHER: overcast

28 MANNY BERNSTEIN BOOKMAKERS MAIDEN STKS (4-Y.O+) (Class D)
1-00 (1-03) **1m 1f 79y (Fibresand)** £3,436.25 (£1,040.00: £507.50: £241.25) Stalls: Low

Horse	Dist	Pos	SP	RR	SF
Onefortheditch (USA) (65) (JRFanshawe) **4-8-5**(3) NVarley(4) (a.p: led over 3f out: sn clr)	—	**1**	4/1[2]	75	25
Holders Hill (IRE) (69) (MGMeagher) **5-9-0** JQuinn(9) (lw: hld up: hdwy over 4f out: rdn over 3f out: chsd wnr wl over 1f out: no imp)	5	**2**	7/2[1]	72	23
Tallulah Belle (37) (NPLittmoden) **4-8-8** TGMcLaughlin(11) (hld up & plld hrd: hdwy over 4f out: rdn over 3f out: one pce fnl 2f)	2½	**3**	12/1	62	12
Degree (72) (SCWilliams) **4-8-1**(7) DarrenWilliams(6) (bit bkwd: led tl rn wd bnd 7f out: one pce fnl 2f)	1¾	**4**	5/1[3]	59	9
1[8] **Sally Armstrong** (CWThornton) **4-8-8** DeanMcKeown(8) (a.p: no hdwy fnl 3f)	3½	**5**	20/1	53	3
Soviet King (IRE) (55) (PMitchell) **4-8-13** CRutter(13) (w bhd tl sme late hdwy)	11	**6**	8/1	39	—
One Dream (60) (BSmart) **4-8-13v** RPerham(1) (nvr nr ldrs)	3	**7**	10/1	34	—
Sounds Legal (PDEvans) **4-8-8** ACulhane(7) (prom: rdn 7f out: wknd 4f out)	1¾	**8**	8/1	26	—
Jubilee Scholar (IRE) (65) (KMcAuliffe) **4-8-10**(3) FLynch(5) (lw: led 7f out tl over 3f out: wknd over 2f out: eased whn btn over 1f out)	1¼	**9**	20/1	29	—
Northern Diamond (IRE) (MissMERowland) **4-8-13** NCarlisle(3) (a bhd)	9	**10**	33/1	14	—
Double Indemnity (IRE) (GCBravery) **4-8-13** DWright(2) (b.hind: s.s: a bhd)	2½	**11**	20/1	10	—
Eccentric Dancer (41) (MPBielby) **4-8-8b** JFanning(10) (a bhd)	8	**12**	25/1	—	—
Rupert Manners (30) (EJAlston) **4-8-13** SDWilliams(12) (bhd fnl 6f)	4	**13**	33/1	—	—

(SP 121.9%) **13 Rn**

2m 2.9 (6.90) CSF £17.79 TOTE £3.60: £1.90 £1.10 £3.30 (£17.00) Trio £29.20 OWNER Onefortheditch Partnership (NEWMARKET) BRED Linda L. Ramsey
WEIGHT FOR AGE 4yo-1lb

29 MANNY BERNSTEIN LEICESTER H'CAP (0-70) (I) (4-Y.O+) (Class E)
1-30 (1-31) **1m 1f 79y (Fibresand)** £2,453.25 (£741.00: £360.50: £170.25) Stalls: Low

Horse	Dist	Pos	SP	RR	SF
Forest Boy (70) (JRBosley) **4-9-13** CRutter(2) (a.p: led over 2f out tl wl over 1f out: hrd rdn to ld wl ins fnl f: r.o)	—	**1**	7/2[2]	76	40
15[3] **Cats Bottom (52)** (AGNewcombe) **5-8-10** JQuinn(8) (hld up: stdy hdwy over 4f out: led wl over 1f out: hrd rdn & hdd wl ins fnl f)	hd	**2**	7/4[1]	58	23
Court Nap (IRE) (62) (SMellor) **5-9-6** RPerham(3) (hdwy on ins 3f out: one pce fnl 2f)	6	**3**	6/1	58	23
Roussi (USA) (40) (DNicholls) **5-7-5**(7)ow2 JBramhill(6) (plld hrd: prom: rdn & wknd 3f out)	5	**4**	5/1[3]	27	—
Southern Rule (38) (MissMERowland) **10-7-3b**(7) DarrenWilliams(1) (led over 6f: sn wknd)	½	**5**	20/1	24	—
Red Tie Affair (USA) (51) (JMBradley) **4-8-5**(3) FLynch(5) (b: rdn over 5f out: a bhd)	1½	**6**	11/1	35	—
Dhes-C (40) (RHollinshead) **4-7-11**ow1 NCarlisle(4) (hld up: rdn over 3f out: sn wknd)	3	**7**	12/1	19	—
Desert Lore (50) (RMMcKellar) **6-8-8** DWright(7) (b: racd wd: prom over 4f: t.o)	28	**8**	10/1	—	—

(SP 119.4%) **8 Rn**

2m 3.2 (7.20) CSF £10.18 CT £32.68 TOTE £3.90: £1.30 £1.20 £2.60 (£4.10) OWNER Marks (Banbury) (WANTAGE) BRED J. B. H. Stevens
LONG HANDICAP Roussi (USA) 7-7 Dhes-C 7-9 Southern Rule 7-1
WEIGHT FOR AGE 4yo-1lb

30 MANNY BERNSTEIN COVENTRY H'CAP (0-65) (4-Y.O+) (Class F)
2-00 (2-32) **1m 6f 166y (Fibresand)** £2,495.60 (£701.60: £342.80) Stalls: High

Horse	Dist	Pos	SP	RR	SF
The Great Flood (53) (CADwyer) **4-8-10** ACulhane(4) (hld up: rdn & hdwy over 6f out: led wl over 2f out: r.o wl)	—	**1**	7/1	65	24
Mr Speculator (51) (JEBanks) **4-8-8v** JQuinn(1) (hld up: rdn 6f out: hdwy 3f out: hung lft over 1f out: styd on ins fnl f)	5	**2**	4/1[2]	58	17
Canary Falcon (60) (RJO'Sullivan) **6-9-9b** DBiggs(8) (led 12f: one pce)	½	**3**	3/1[1]	66	31
Philmist (52) (JHetherton) **5-9-1b** NKennedy(5) (a.p: wnt 2nd over 5f out: one pce fnl 3f)	½	**4**	10/1	58	23
Tremendisto (35) (CaptJWilson) **7-7-5**(7) AngelaHartley(3) (chsd ldr 9f: wknd over 4f out)	6	**5**	12/1	34	—

Evezio Rufo (56) (NPLittmoden) **5-9-5v** TGMcLaughlin(6) (rdn after 4f: sn lost pl: bhd whn rdn & rel to r 7f out)	1¾	**6**	20/1	53	18
In the Money (IRE) (51) (RHollinshead) **8-8-11**(3) FLynch(9) (s.i.s: sn prom: wknd over 4f out)	12	**7**	5/1	35	—
Red Raja (57) (PMitchell) **4-9-0** CRutter(7) (s.i.s: sn rcvrd: bhd fnl 6f)	2½	**8**	9/2 3	38	—
Red Phantom (IRE) (61) (SMellor) **5-9-10** RPerham(2) (a bhd)	1	**9**	14/1	41	6
			(SP 120.6%)		**9 Rn**

3m 19.3 (11.90) CSF £34.39 CT £95.29 TOTE £7.50: £1.50 £1.80 £1.90 (£38.30) Trio £34.50 OWNER Richard Flood Bloodstock Ltd (NEWMARKET) BRED Roldvale Ltd
WEIGHT FOR AGE 4yo-6lb

31 MANNY BERNSTEIN WEDNESBURY H'CAP (0-75) (I) (4-Y.O+) (Class D)
2-30 (3-00) **7f (Fibresand)** £2,900.00 (£875.00: £425.00: £200.00) Stalls: High

			SP	RR	SF
Leigh Crofter (62) (PDCundell) **8-9-5b** RPerham(2) (mde all: rdn over 1f out: r.o wl)	—	**1**	2/1 1	72	47
Sooty Tern (55) (JMBradley) **10-8-12** LCharnock(7) (lw: a.p: rdn over 3f out: chsd wnr over 2f out: r.o one pce fnl f)	2	**2**	3/1 2	60	35
16 **Little Ibnr (70)** (PDEvans) **6-9-6**(7) AnthonyBond(4) (lw: chsd wnr: rdn over 3f out: one pce fnl 2f)	3½	**3**	10/1	67	42
Gulf Shaadi (55) (EJAlston) **5-8-12** ACulhane(6) (s.i.s: rdn & hdwy over 4f out: one pce fnl 2f)	1	**4**	11/2 3	50	25
Gad Yakoun (65) (MGMeagher) **4-9-8** JQuinn(1) (no hdwy fnl 2f)	1¼	**5**	10/1	57	32
Gadge (43) (ABailey) **6-8-0** DWright(8) (b: bhd fnl 4f)	¾	**6**	10/1	34	9
The Fugative (45) (PMitchell) **4-8-2** CRutter(3) (bhd fnl 3f)	s.h	**7**	14/1	36	11
Dawalib (USA) (57) (DHaydnJones) **7-9-0** AMackay(5) (bhd: rdn over 4f out: eased whn no ch over 1f out)	dist	**8**	7/1	—	—
			(SP 120.2%)		**8 Rn**

1m 28.7 (4.00) CSF £8.67 CT £44.86 TOTE £2.90: £1.40 £1.30 £1.30 (£3.40) OWNER Mr P. D. Cundell (NEWBURY) BRED Richard Castle

32 MANNY BERNSTEIN BIRMINGHAM CLAIMING STKS (3-Y.O+) (Class E)
3-00 (3-31) **5f (Fibresand)** £2,752.25 (£833.00: £406.50: £193.25) Stalls: Low

			SP	RR	SF
Amy Leigh (IRE) (43) (CaptJWilson) **4-9-1b** FNorton(6) (mde all: all out)	—	**1**	25/1	47	38
Krystal Max (IRE) (83) (TDBarron) **4-8-13**(7) VictoriaAppleby(2) (a.p: ev ch fnl f: r.o)	nk	**2**	11/4 3	51	42
Boffy (IRE) (50) (BPJBaugh) **4-9-6b** RPerham(4) (hld up: hrd rdn over 1f out: hdwy fnl f: nt rch ldrs)	1	**3**	14/1	48	39
Amington Lass (66) (PDEvans) **4-9-5** ACulhane(3) (prom: sn rdn along: n.m.r over 3f out: one pce fnl 2f)	2	**4**	9/4 2	40	31
Sue Me (IRE) (48) (WRMuir) **5-8-9b**(7) JWilkinson(1) (sn chsng wnr: rdn & ev ch wl over 1f out: wknd fnl f)	hd	**5**	14/1	37	28
Primula Bairn (65) (DNicholls) **7-9-1b** AlexGreaves(8) (prom: hrd rdn & wknd over 1f out)	2½	**6**	2/1 1	28	19
Fancy Design (IRE) (33) (PMitchell) **4-9-1v** CRutter(7) (s.v.s: a wl bhd)	8	**7**	33/1	3	—
Warm Hearted (USA) (55) (AGNewcombe) **5-9-2** AMackay(5) (Withdrawn not under Starter's orders: jockey uns & inj)		**W**	25/1	—	—
			(SP 114.7%)		**7 Rn**

62.0 secs (3.10) CSF £85.28 TOTE £22.10: £3.30 £1.80 (£28.60) OWNER Mr J. P. Hacking (PRESTON) BRED S. W. D. McIlveen
OFFICIAL EXPLANATION **Amy Leigh (IRE): accounting for the filly's apparent improvement in form, connections reported she had been suffering from joint problems and a loss of confidence, and that this race had been run to suit her in that she had more racing room.**

33 MANNY BERNSTEIN WALSALL LIMITED STKS (0-60) (3-Y.O) (Class F)
3-30 (3-55) **1m 100y (Fibresand)** £2,406.00 (£676.00: £330.00) Stalls: Low

			SP	RR	SF
Globetrotter (IRE) (60) (MJohnston) **3-8-12** DeanMcKeown(3) (prom: rdn & sltly outpcd over 3f out: rallied over 1f out: hrd rdn & edgd lft ins fnl f: led nr fin)	—	**1**	6/1	67	33
Komasta (67) (CaptJWilson) **3-9-1** FNorton(1) (led: rdn 2f out: hdd nr fin)	¾	**2**	9/4 1	69	35
Senate Swings (55) (WRMuir) **3-8-12** JQuinn(2) (lw: chsd ldr: rdn over 3f out: wknd 1f out)	5	**3**	11/2 3	56	22
73 **Skelton Sovereign (IRE) (60)** (RHollinshead) **3-8-12**(3) FLynch(5) (sn wl bhd: hdwy 2f out: n.d)	½	**4**	9/4 1	58	24
74 **Fast Spin (64)** (TDBarron) **3-9-1b1** ACulhane(6) (hld up: stdy hdwy over 5f out: rdn over 3f out: wknd wl over 1f out)	7	**5**	9/2 2	45	11
Flood's Hot Stuff (53) (NPLittmoden) **3-8-9** TGMcLaughlin(4) (hld up: stdy hdwy over 5f out: wknd 4f out)	13	**6**	25/1	14	—
			(SP 113.2%)		**6 Rn**

1m 50.8 (5.80) CSF £19.11 TOTE £7.00: £6.90 £2.30 (£16.00) OWNER Brian Yeardley Continental Ltd (MIDDLEHAM) BRED Norelands Bloodstock

34 MANNY BERNSTEIN LEICESTER H'CAP (0-70) (II) (4-Y.O+) (Class E)
4-00 (4-20) **1m 1f 79y (Fibresand)** £2,453.25 (£741.00: £360.50: £170.25) Stalls: Low

			SP	RR	SF
Mono Lady (IRE) (48) (DHaydnJones) **4-8-5b1** CRutter(5) (hld up: hdwy over 3f out: led 2f out: r.o wl)	—	**1**	9/1 3	58	30
Three Weeks (61) (WRMuir) **4-9-1**(3) FLynch(4) (lw: hld up: rdn 3f out: r.o one pce fnl f)	3	**2**	4/5 1	66	38
Suga Hawk (IRE) (55) (EJAlston) **5-8-13** ACulhane(1) (plld hrd: a.p: led 5f out: hrd rdn & hdd 2f out: one pce)	nk	**3**	11/1	59	32
Beauman (54) (PDEvans) **7-8-5**(7) AnthonyBond(2) (lw: trckd ldrs: nt clr run on ins wl over 1f out: swtchd rt 1f out: one pce)	½	**4**	5/1 2	58	31
Princely Affair (44) (JMBradley) **4-8-1** LCharnock(8) (prom: rdn over 4f out: no hdwy fnl 2f)	3	**5**	20/1	42	14
Explosive Power (70) (GCBravery) **6-10-0** DWright(7) (lw: hld up & bhd: sme hdwy 3f out: nvr nr to chal)	s.h	**6**	5/1 2	68	41
Dia Georgy (39) (CADwyer) **6-7-11**ow1 FNorton(6) (b: led over 4f: wknd over 3f out)	9	**7**	20/1	22	—
			(SP 116.7%)		**7 Rn**

2m 2.0 (6.00) CSF £16.84 CT £74.22 TOTE £15.40: £5.00 £1.10 (£5.80) OWNER Monolithic Refractories Ltd (PONTYPRIDD) BRED Dr. Michael Smurfit
LONG HANDICAP Dia Georgy 6-10
WEIGHT FOR AGE 4yo-1lb

35 MANNY BERNSTEIN WEDNESBURY H'CAP (0-75) (II) (4-Y.O+) (Class D)
4-30 (4-45) **7f (Fibresand)** £2,883.75 (£870.00: £422.50: £198.75) Stalls: High

			SP	RR	SF
Elite Hope (USA) (67) (NTinkler) **5-9-7**(3) FLynch(8) (led over 5f out: clr 3f out: r.o wl)	—	**1**	15/8 2	77	59
Zahran (IRE) (43) (JMBradley) **6-8-0** LCharnock(6) (a.p: chsd wnr & edgd lft over 3f out: no imp)	5	**2**	8/1	42	24

	Horse	Dist	Pos	SP	RR	SF
	Lia Fail (IRE) (43) (RHollinshead) **4-8-0** JQuinn(5) (hld up: hdwy over 3f out: one pce fnl 2f)	4	**3**	8/1	32	14
	Live Project (IRE) (60) (MJohnston) **5-9-3** DeanMcKeown(3) (lw: led 6f out: sn hdd: bdly hmpd on ins over 3f out: nt rcvr)	2	**4**	11/2[3]	45	27
	Princesse Lyphard (39) (MJPolglase) **4-7-10** NCarlisle(1) (hdwy over 4f out: wknd 3f out)	5	**5**	20/1	12	—
	Marjorie Rose (IRE) (63) (ABailey) **4-9-6** DWright(4) (b: b.hind: stdd s: hdwy 4f out: wknd 3f out)	6	**6**	7/4[1]	23	5
	Justfortherecord (41) (BRMillman) **5-7-12** FNorton(2) (bkwd: led 1f: wknd 5f out)	6	**7**	20/1	—	—

(SP 118.3%) **7 Rn**

1m 28.1 (3.40) CSF £16.41 CT £87.53 TOTE £2.70: £1.70 £2.50 (£11.70) OWNER Elite Racing Club (MALTON) BRED Barbara Hunter
LONG HANDICAP Princesse Lyphard 7-9

T/Plpt: £63.70 (282.05 Tckts). T/Qdpt: £22.00 (68.06 Tckts). KH

0014-SOUTHWELL (L-H) (Standard)
Monday January 6th
WEATHER: overcast WIND: slt across

36 TIPPERARY APPRENTICE H'CAP (0-60) (I) (4-Y.O+) (Class F)
12-45 (12-45) **1m** **(Fibresand)** £1,955.00 (£555.00: £275.00) Stalls: Low GOING: 0.27 sec per fur (SLW)

	Horse	Dist	Pos	SP	RR	SF
	Broughton's Pride (IRE) (38) (JLEyre) **6-8-3**(5)ow2 SBuckley(7) (trckd ldrs: effrt over 2f out: led over 1f out: styd on u.p)	—	**1**	11/8[1]	49	25
	In Good Faith (56) (JJQuinn) **5-9-7**(5) RCody-Boutcher(4) (a.p: c wd st: ch over 1f out: nt qckn)	3	**2**	3/1[2]	61	39
	Supreme Illusion (AUS) (26) (JohnBerry) **4-7-3b**(7) DarrenWilliams(9) (led tl hdd over 1f out: no ex)	3½	**3**	25/1	24	2
	Lachesis (42) (BRichmond) **4-8-9**(3) CLowther(8) (chsd ldrs: ev ch over 2f out: btn appr fnl f)	7	**4**	11/2[3]	26	4
	Blue Lugana (28) (NBycroft) **5-7-7**(5) CCogan(3) (prom tl wknd over 2f out)	8	**5**	25/1	—	—
	Whitelock Quest (32) (NEBerry) **9-7-11**(5) KerryBaker(5) (a bhd: wl outpcd fnl 3f)	3	**6**	10/1	—	—
3[9]	**Warhurst (IRE) (58)** (DNicholls) **6-9-9b1**(5) TSiddall(6) (lw: s.s: wnt prom ½-wy: sn rdn & wknd)	4	**7**	7/1	12	—

(SP 111.8%) **7 Rn**

1m 47.9 (8.90) CSF £5.66 CT £55.64 TOTE £1.90: £1.10 £2.00 (£5.10) Trio £49.60 OWNER Mrs Janet Morris (HAMBLETON) BRED A. J. Poulton (Epping) Ltd

37 WATERFORD MEDIAN AUCTION MAIDEN STKS (4, 5 & 6-Y.O) (Class F)
1-15 (1-15) **1m 4f** **(Fibresand)** £2,294.00 (£644.00: £314.00) Stalls: Low GOING: 0.27 sec per fur (SLW)

	Horse	Dist	Pos	SP	RR	SF
	Nishamira (IRE) (TDBarron) **5-8-12** DeanMcKeown(4) (lw: mde most: pushed clr fnl 4f)	—	**1**	2/5[1]	64+	22
	Golden Hanoof (USA) (DrJDScargill) **5-8-12** NCarlisle(1) (in tch: effrt 6f out: styd on u.p: n.d)	24	**2**	14/1	32	—
18[9]	**Hornpipe (48)** (JWharton) **5-9-0b1**(3) CTeague(8) (b: cl up: led after 3f to 6f out: sn outpcd)	3	**3**	10/1[3]	33	—
9[8]	**Supergold (IRE)** (CMurray) **4-8-13** JWeaver(7) (bhd: styd on u.p fnl 3f: n.d)	2½	**4**	33/1	30	—
	Impending Danger (38) (KSBridgwater) **4-8-13** VSlattery(3) (outpcd ½-wy: a bhd)	11	**5**	20/1	15	—
2[3]	**Taniyar (FR) (35)** (RHollinshead) **5-8-12**(5) DGriffiths(6) (lw: outpcd ½-wy: n.d after)	5	**6**	10/1[3]	8	—
	Beau Matelot (54) (MissMKMilligan) **5-9-3** JQuinn(2) (hdwy ½-wy: sn chsng wnr: wknd over 2f out)	1½	**7**	10/1[3]	6	—
	Vendimia (KMcAuliffe) **4-8-8v1** SSanders(5) (cl up tl rdn & wknd 4f out)	4	**8**	8/1[2]	—	—

(SP 124.2%) **8 Rn**

2m 47.7 (14.70) CSF £8.49 TOTE £1.20: £1.10 £1.90 £1.10 (£9.10) OWNER M P Burke Developments Ltd (THIRSK) BRED His Highness the Aga Khans Studs S. C.
WEIGHT FOR AGE 4yo-4lb

38 LIMERICK CLAIMING STKS (3-Y.O) (Class F)
1-45 (1-47) **6f** **(Fibresand)** £2,294.00 (£644.00: £314.00) Stalls: Low GOING: 0.27 sec per fur (SLW)

	Horse	Dist	Pos	SP	RR	SF
	Dominant Air (74) (SirMarkPrescott) **3-9-5** SSanders(2) (lw: pushed along after 2f: hdwy 2f out: hung rt: led ins fnl f: styd on)	—	**1**	10/11[1]	78	39
	Figlia (58) (JLHarris) **3-8-2b** JQuinn(3) (lw: trckd ldrs: led over 2f out tl ins fnl f: no ex)	1½	**2**	11/2[3]	57	18
	Treasure Touch (IRE) (60) (GMMoore) **3-9-5** ACulhane(6) (a.p: ch 2f out: r.o one pce)	3	**3**	10/1	66	27
	Fit For The Job (IRE) (74) (TWall) **3-9-1** TSprake(5) (led tl hdd over 2f out: grad wknd)	2½	**4**	7/2[2]	55	16
	Jack Says (64) (DShaw) **3-8-12**(3) CTeague(1) (outpcd ½-wy: styd on fnl 2f: n.d)	1¾	**5**	12/1	51	12
	Joyful Joy (BPJBaugh) **3-8-4** DWright(4) (hld up: effrt ½-wy: sn btn)	13	**6**	33/1	5	—
	Bailieborough Boy (IRE) (62) (TDBarron) **3-9-1** DeanMcKeown(7) (s.i.s: drvn along: sn w ldr: wknd wl over 2f out)	s.h	**7**	10/1	16	—

(SP 118.8%) **7 Rn**

1m 19.8 (6.30) CSF £6.78 TOTE £2.00: £1.20 £2.10 (£4.80) OWNER Mr Neil Greig (NEWMARKET) BRED W. N. Greig

39 KILDARE H'CAP (0-80) (4-Y.O+) (Class D)
2-15 (2-16) **1m 3f** **(Fibresand)** £3,533.75 (£1,070.00: £522.50: £248.75) Stalls: Low GOING: 0.27 sec per fur (SLW)

	Horse	Dist	Pos	SP	RR	SF
	China Castle (67) (PCHaslam) **4-8-12** SDrowne(10) (lw: in tch: hdwy 4f out: rdn to ld 1½f out: styd on wl)	—	**1**	9/2[3]	83	47
	Albaha (USA) (74) (JEBanks) **4-9-5** JQuinn(7) (led tl hdd 1½f out: one pce)	5	**2**	5/2[1]	83	47
	Maftun (USA) (51) (GMMoore) **5-7-13** NKennedy(9) (chsd ldrs: effrt 4f out: one pce)	10	**3**	20/1	45	12
	Sea Victor (80) (JLHarris) **5-10-0** JWeaver(8) (a chsng ldrs: rdn over 3f out: r.o one pce)	3	**4**	7/1	70	37
	Sea God (48) (MCChapman) **6-7-10** GBardwell(6) (bhd: effrt 5f out: nvr rchd ldrs)	10	**5**	20/1	23	—
	Shahik (USA) (65) (DHaydnJones) **7-8-13** LCharnock(5) (effrt ½-wy: sn prom: drvn along 4f out: no imp)	5	**6**	10/1	33	—
14*	**Joseph's Wine (IRE) (80)** (DNicholls) **8-10-0b** 5x AlexGreaves(11) (lw: hld up: hdwy ½-wy: sn prom: wknd 3f out)	2	**7**	3/1[2]	45	12
	Greenspan (IRE) (74) (WRMuir) **5-9-8** DaneO'Neill(12) (in tch: outpcd 4f out: sn btn)	12	**8**	15/2	22	—
	Pistols At Dawn (USA) (59) (BJMeehan) **7-8-7**ow2 RPerham(1) (chsd ldrs tl outpcd 6f out: sn wknd)	8	**9**	20/1	—	—
	Noble Canonire (54) (DShaw) **5-8-2** JFanning(3) (a rr div)	2½	**10**	20/1	—	—

	Horse	Dist	Pos	SP	RR	SF
	Premier Dance (74) (DHaydnJones) **10-9-8** AClark(4) (nvr nr to chal)	16	**11**	16/1	—	—

(SP 130.0%) **11 Rn**

2m 29.9 (9.90) CSF £16.72 CT £184.72 TOTE £6.60: £2.00 £1.60 £5.30 (£10.00) Trio £374.00 OWNER Mr J. M. Davis (MIDDLEHAM) BRED Mrs Frances Cronin
LONG HANDICAP Sea God 7-9
WEIGHT FOR AGE 4yo-3lb

40 WICKLOW H'CAP (0-70) (4-Y.O+) (Class E)

2-45 (2-47) **7f (Fibresand)** £2,905.00 (£880.00: £430.00: £205.00) Stalls: Low GOING: 0.27 sec per fur (SLW)

	Horse	Dist	Pos	SP	RR	SF
	Pleasure Trick (USA) (42) (DonEnricoIncisa) **6-8-0b** KimTinkler(3) (s.i.s: hdwy over 2f out: rdn to ld over 1f out: sn clr)	—	**1**	10/1	52	34
	Plum First (49) (JLEyre) **7-8-7b** RLappin(7) (prom: hdwy over 2f out: hung lft: styd on)	4	**2**	$9/2^{2}$	50	32
	Craigie Boy (40) (NBycroft) **7-7-5b**$^{(7)}$ JBramhill(1) (chsd ldrs: led over 3f out tl appr fnl f: no ex)	½	**3**	8/1	40	22
15^{2}	**Desert Invader (IRE) (70)** (DWChapman) **6-10-0** ACulhane(12) (w ldrs: rdn 3f out: one pce)	1¼	**4**	$5/2^{1}$	67	49
	Green Golightly (USA) (39) (RMFlower) **6-7-11be**^{ow1} FNorton(2) (styd on wl fnl 3f: nrst fin)	1	**5**	25/1	34	15
	Surf City (58) (WWHaigh) **4-9-2** JQuinn(13) (in tch: effrt 3f out: no imp)	2	**6**	8/1	48	30
	Sense of Priority (70) (DNicholls) **8-10-0** MWigham(10) (mid div: hdwy to chse ldrs 2f out: wknd fnl f)	1½	**7**	20/1	57	39
3^{4}	**Paint It Black (58)** (DNicholls) **4-9-2** AlexGreaves(4) (prom tl wknd fnl 2½f)	1	**8**	$7/1^{3}$	42	24
11^{9}	**Rapier Point (IRE) (38)** (CMurray) **6-7-10** NicolaHowarth(11) (nvr trbld ldrs)	2	**9**	50/1	18	—
	Lady Silk (43) (MissJFCraze) **6-8-1** JFanning(5) (led tl hdd over 3f out: wknd)	3½	**10**	14/1	15	—
	Cheerful Groom (IRE) (41) (DShaw) **6-7-13** NKennedy(8) (a rr div)	2½	**11**	20/1	7	—
	Tajar (USA) (53) (MDods) **5-8-11** AClark(9) (lw: s.i.s: a bhd)	12	**12**	33/1	—	—
	Imp Express (IRE) (44) (GMMoore) **4-8-2** GBardwell(6) (chsd ldrs tl rdn & wknd 3f out)	16	**13**	20/1	—	—

(SP 120.3%) **13 Rn**

1m 32.8 (6.30) CSF £51.40 CT £364.77 TOTE £10.30: £2.80 £2.40 £1.90 (£39.30) Trio £117.40 OWNER Don Enrico Incisa (MIDDLEHAM) BRED W. S. Farish
LONG HANDICAP Green Golightly (USA) 7-3

41 KERRY (QUALIFIER) (S) STKS (3-Y.O) (Class G)

3-15 (3-19) **1m (Fibresand)** £2,085.00 (£585.00: £285.00) Stalls: Low GOING: 0.27 sec per fur (SLW)

	Horse	Dist	Pos	SP	RR	SF
	Aspecto Lad (IRE) (55) (MJohnston) **3-9-0** JWeaver(10) (hdwy to chse ldrs 5f out: led wl over 1f out: wandered u.p: drvn out)	—	**1**	$11/4^{2}$	64	2
6^{3}	**Head Girl (IRE) (60)** (CWThornton) **3-9-0** DeanMcKeown(6) (led 1f: led over 3f out tl wl over 1f out: kpt on towards fin)	nk	**2**	$9/4^{1}$	63	1
	Hoh Down (IRE) (KMcAuliffe) **3-8-9v**^{1} SSanders(3) (b.hind: lw: hdwy & prom after ½-wy: ev ch 2f out: nt qckn towards fin)	hd	**3**	5/1	58	—
6^{6}	**State of Gold (IRE) (65)** (JHetherton) **3-9-0** NKennedy(9) (in tch: hdwy over 3f out: sn chsng ldrs: wknd fnl f)	4	**4**	10/1	55	—
6^{5}	**Bali-Pet (59)** (WGMTurner) **3-9-0b**$^{(5)}$ DSweeney(4) (led after 1f tl over 3f out: sn btn)	16	**5**	$4/1^{3}$	28	—
6^{10}	**Pamela's Boy** (ASmith) **3-9-0** RLappin(2) (in tch: rdn ½-wy: no imp after)	4	**6**	20/1	15	—
19^{8}	**Amy (50)** (CSmith) **3-8-9** AClark(7) (prom: rdn after 2f: sn lost pl)	15	**7**	33/1	—	—
6^{9}	**Billycan (IRE) (35)** (BPJBaugh) **3-9-0b**^{1} RPerham(5) (sn drvn along: chsd ldrs tl wknd over 2f out)	¾	**8**	50/1	—	—
	Noetic (GHolmes) **3-8-9b**^{1} JQuinn(1) (b.nr fore: sn t.o)	17	**9**	33/1	—	—
	Love Over Gold (MCChapman) **3-8-9** FNorton(8) (bkwd: s.s: t.o)	s.h	**10**	20/1	—	—

(SP 120.6%) **10 Rn**

1m 50.9 (11.90) CSF £9.35 TOTE £3.00: £1.40 £1.60 £1.40 (£4.70) Trio £13.90 OWNER Aspecto Clothing Co Ltd (MIDDLEHAM) BRED Rathbarry Stud
No bid

42 TIPPERARY APPRENTICE H'CAP (0-60) (II) (4-Y.O+) (Class F)

3-45 (3-46) **1m (Fibresand)** £1,955.00 (£555.00: £275.00) Stalls: Low GOING: 0.27 sec per fur (SLW)

	Horse	Dist	Pos	SP	RR	SF
	Down The Yard (31) (MCChapman) **4-8-3**$^{(5)}$ RBrisland(2) (sn chsng ldrs: led wl over 2f out: styd on strly fnl f)	—	**1**	$5/1^{3}$	42	15
15^{5}	**Royal Acclaim (32)** (RDickin) **12-8-2v**$^{(7)}$ PMundy(3) (s.i.s: hdwy on outside ½-wy: ch 2f out: edgd lft & nt qckn)	7	**2**	$5/1^{3}$	29	2
	Efipetite (40) (NBycroft) **4-9-3** AngelaGallimore(7) (lw: cl up: rdn over 2f out: r.o one pce)	½	**3**	$5/2^{1}$	36	9
	Caddy's First (47) (SMellor) **5-9-10v** JDennis(4) (led after 1f tl wl over 2f out: wknd over 1f out)	3	**4**	$9/2^{2}$	37	10
29^{5}	**Southern Rule (29)** (MissMERowland) **10-7-13b**$^{(7)}$ DarrenWilliams(8) (chsd ldrs: one pce fnl 3f)	5	**5**	12/1	9	—
	Kissavos (30) (BJMeehan) **11-8-2**$^{(5)}$ GHannon(6) (b.hind: in tch: effrt 3f out: no imp)	6	**6**	6/1	—	—
	Dispol Conqueror (IRE) (36) (PCalver) **4-8-8**$^{(5)}$ PClarke(5) (b.nr hind: lw: led 1f: cl up tl wknd over 3f out)	9	**7**	14/1	—	—
	Trianna (42) (RBrotherton) **4-9-0b**$^{1(5)}$ JFowle(1) (sn wl bhd)	13	**8**	12/1	—	—

(SP 116.4%) **8 Rn**

1m 48.9 (9.90) CSF £28.38 CT £70.53 TOTE £4.30: £2.10 £3.70 £1.00 (£13.20) OWNER Mr Geoff Whiting (MARKET RASEN) BRED Fonthill Stud

T/Jkpt: £10,160.80 (1.09 Tckts). T/Plpt: £21.90 (816.59 Tckts). T/Qdpt: £16.00 (124.77 Tckts). AA

0020-LINGFIELD (L-H) (Standard)

Tuesday January 7th

Race 1 - hand-timed
WEATHER: v.cold WIND: almost nil

43 HOOD (S) H'CAP (0-60) (4-Y.O+) (Class G)

1-00 (1-01) **1m 5f (Equitrack)** £2,155.30 (£605.80: £295.90) Stalls: Low GOING minus 0.38 sec per fur (FST)

	Horse	Dist	Pos	SP	RR	SF
	Supreme Star (USA) (53) (PRHedger) **6-10-0b** DaneO'Neill(7) (b: lw: a.p: led over 3f out tl over 2f out: hrd rdn over 1f out: led ins fnl f: r.o wl)	—	1	11/4 ^{2}	63	22
	Nothing Doing (IRE) (33) (WJMusson) **8-8-8** JQuinn(8) (s.s: hdwy over 6f out: rdn 2f out: r.o ins fnl f)	1½	2	15/8 ^{1}	41	—
18^{6}	**Al Helal (43)** (JRJenkins) **5-9-4b** DHarrison(6) (a.p: led over 2f out: hrd rdn over 1f out: wknd & hdd ins fnl f)	2	3	10/1 ^{3}	49	8
	Persian Bud (IRE) (32) (JRBosley) **9-8-7e**ow1 RPerham(11) (rdn 8f out: no hdwy fnl 3f)	11	4	25/1	24	—
	Rose of Glenn (36) (BPalling) **6-8-11** CRutter(13) (led 8f out tl over 4f out: wknd over 3f out)	2½	5	11/1	25	—
	Mr Bean (47) (KRBurke) **7-9-8v** SSanders(1) (hdwy 8f out: wknd over 4f out)	7	6	12/1	28	—
	Efficacious (IRE) (40) (AMoore) **4-8-10** AClark(4) (b.hind: hld up: rdn over 5f out: sn wknd)	3½	7	12/1	16	—
	Sweet Amoret (44) (PHowling) **4-9-0** FNorton(9) (b.off hind: plld hrd: led 5f: led over 4f out tl over 3f out: sn wknd)	1	8	12/1	19	—
	Embroidered (28) (RMFlower) **4-7-9**(3)ow1 NVarley(2) (a bhd: t.o fnl 6f)	12	9	33/1	—	—
	Mapengo (40) (JCullinan) **6-9-1** VSlattery(3) (bhd fnl 13f: t.o fnl 3f)	dist	10	14/1	—	—
	Brave Spy (47) (CACyzer) **6-9-8** GCarter(5) (prom over 4f: t.o fnl 5f)	7	11	14/1	—	—
	Tennyson Bay (25) (JRPoulton) **5-8-0** GBardwell(12) (b: bhd fnl 12f: t.o fnl 6f)	dist	12	50/1	—	—

(SP 124.0%) **12 Rn**

2m 51.7 (9.70) CSF £8.37 CT £42.74 TOTE £3.10: £1.10 £1.10 £2.80 (£4.10) Trio £10.70 OWNER Mr J. J. Whelan (CHICHESTER) BRED Peter M. Brant
WEIGHT FOR AGE 4yo-5lb
No bid

44 RENOWN CLAIMING STKS (3-Y.O) (Class E)

1-30 (1-30) **7f (Equitrack)** £2,765.25 (£837.00: £408.50: £194.25) Stalls: Low GOING minus 0.38 sec per fur (FST)

	Horse	Dist	Pos	SP	RR	SF
8*	**Misty Cay (IRE) (57)** (SDow) **3-8-1**(5) ADaly(4) (lw: lost pl over 4f out: rallied over 3f out: led over 1f out: r.o: wl)	—	1	5/2 ^{2}	65	4
	Broadgate Flyer (IRE) (60) (MrsLStubbs) **3-8-9** SSanders(5) (hld up: led over 2f out tl over 1f out: unable qckn)	2	2	7/1	63	2
	Windborn (54) (CNAllen) **3-7-11**(3) MBaird(1) (dwlt: rdn over 2f out: hdwy fnl f: r.o)	1	3	14/1	52	—
	Masterstroke (63) (BJMeehan) **3-8-7** DaneO'Neill(2) (w ldr: led 4f out tl over 2f out: rdn: r.o one pce fnl f)	nk	4	Evens ^{1}	59	—
12^{4}	**Ben's Ridge (68)** (PCHaslam) **3-9-5b**1 GCarter(3) (led 3f: wknd over 2f out)	14	5	5/1 ^{3}	39	—

(SP 114.4%) **5 Rn**

1m 29.19 (4.79) CSF £16.96 TOTE £2.50: £1.10 £2.20 (£17.80) OWNER Mrs A. M. Upsdell (EPSOM) BRED T. Ward

45 VICTORY MEDIAN AUCTION MAIDEN STKS (3-Y.O) (Class F)

2-00 (2-00) **5f (Equitrack)** £2,406.00 (£676.00: £330.00) Stalls: High GOING: minus 0.38 sec per fur (FST)

	Horse	Dist	Pos	SP	RR	SF
	Green Boulevard (USA) (JBerry) **3-8-9** GCarter(5) (b: b.hind: hld up: rdn 2f out: led over 1f out: edgd lft ins fnl f: r.o wl)	—	1	5/1 ^{2}	55	—
	Harmony In Red (66) (CADwyer) **3-9-0** MWigham(2) (hld up: rdn over 1f out: unable qckn fnl f)	1¼	2	10/1 ^{3}	56	—
	Ekaterini Paritsi (57) (WGMTurner) **3-8-9v** TSprake(4) (led over 3f: one pce)	1¾	3	12/1	45	—
	Nopalea (73) (TJNaughton) **3-8-9** JWeaver(3) (lw: chsd ldr 3f: wknd over 1f out)	8	4	4/11 ^{1}	20	—
	Incatime (64) (CJames) **3-9-0b**1 CRutter(1) (prom over 2f)	2	5	20/1	18	—

(SP 111.5%) **5 Rn**

62.32 secs (4.12) CSF £37.94 TOTE £6.30: £1.20 £3.10 (£17.10) OWNER Mrs J. M. Ryan (COCKERHAM) BRED Clovelly Farms, Division of Gnl Agri Services
STEWARDS' ENQUIRY Obj. to Green Boulevard (USA) by Wigham overruled.

46 NELSON H'CAP (0-75) (3-Y.O) (Class D)

2-30 (2-30) **1m 2f (Equitrack)** £3,322.50 (£1,005.00: £490.00: £232.50) Stalls: Low GOING minus 0.38 sec per fur (FST)

	Horse	Dist	Pos	SP	RR	SF
	Chateauherault (IRE) (56) (PCHaslam) **3-8-3** SDrowne(5) (hdwy to chse ldr 2f out: rdn over 1f out: led nr fin)	—	1	14/1	67	13
	Double Espresso (IRE) (74) (MJohnston) **3-9-7** JWeaver(4) (led: clr over 2f out: rdn over 1f out: hdd nr fin)	¾	2	2/1 ^{1}	84	30
	Hello Dolly (IRE) (70) (KRBurke) **3-8-12**(5) DSweeney(6) (a.p: chsd ldr 5f out tl over 3f out: wknd 2f out)	8	3	15/2	67	13
8^{5}	**Barnwood Crackers (55)** (MissGayKelleway) **3-7-9**(7) AngelaGallimore(7) (b: hld up: rdn over 4f out: wknd over 2f out)	1	4	12/1	50	—
7*	**Going For Broke (67)** (PCHaslam) **3-9-0** 5x SSanders(2) (lw: hld up: chsd ldr over 3f out to 2f out: wknd 1f out)	¾	5	5/2 ^{2}	61	7
	Greenwich Fore (69) (TGMills) **3-9-2v** WRyan(3) (bhd fnl 5f)	2½	6	13/2	59	5
	Feather Bed (IRE) (72) (MAJarvis) **3-9-2**(3) FLynch(1) (chsd ldr 5f)	3	7	6/1 ^{3}	57	3

(SP 115.6%) **7 Rn**

2m 9.96 (5.66) CSF £41.25 TOTE £21.80: £5.30 £1.30 (£25.10) OWNER Mr Michael Cook (MIDDLEHAM) BRED E. O'Leary

47 WARSPITE H'CAP (0-65) (4-Y.O+) (Class F)

3-00 (3-01) **1m (Equitrack)** £2,506.80 (£704.80: £344.40) Stalls: High GOING minus 0.38 sec per fur (FST)

	Horse	Dist	Pos	SP	RR	SF
	Shanghai Lil (46) (MJFetherston-Godley) **5-8-9** FNorton(8) (hdwy 4f out: led over 1f out: rdn out)	—	1	7/2 ^{2}	57	35
	Oberons Boy (IRE) (58) (SDow) **4-9-7** WRyan(10) (rdn & hdwy over 2f out: r.o)	1½	2	12/1	66	44
31^{2}	**Sooty Tern (55)** (JMBradley) **10-9-4** JWeaver(7) (a.p: led 2f out tl over 1f out: unable qckn ins fnl f)	1¾	3	3/1 ^{1}	60	38
27^{6}	**Private Fixture (IRE) (45)** (DMarks) **6-8-8** TSprake(12) (rdn over 3f out: hdwy over 1f out: r.o)	1¼	4	14/1	47	25

				SP	RR	SF
	Rawi (57) (MissGayKelleway) **4-9-6** 6x DaneO'Neill(6) (b: lw: a.p: led 3f out to 2f out: ev ch to 1f out: wknd ins fnl f)	1	**5**	10/1	57	35
	Bagshot (60) (GLMoore) **6-9-9** CRutter(5) (hld up: rdn 2f out: one pce)	1½	**6**	$6/1^{3}$	57	35
	Mogin (44) (TJNaughton) **4-8-4**(3)ow2 JDSmith(9) (nvr nr to chal)	3	**7**	14/1	35	11
21^{6}	**Zamalek (USA) (46)** (RMFlower) **5-8-9e** SDrowne(3) (bhd fnl 5f)	2½	**8**	25/1	32	10
	Harlequin Walk (IRE) (50) (RJO'Sullivan) **6-8-13** SSanders(4) (w ldr: led 5f out to 3f out: wknd over 2f out)	1	**9**	$6/1^{3}$	34	12
35^{2}	**Zahran (IRE) (43)** (JMBradley) **6-8-6** LCharnock(2) (led 3f: wkng whn hmpd on ins over 2f out)	7	**10**	7/1	13	—
	Superior Force (62) (MissBSanders) **4-9-8**(3) AWhelan(11) (lw: bhd fnl 5f)	1¼	**11**	12/1	30	8
	Red Rusty (USA) (50) (PRHedger) **4-8-13** AClark(1) (lw: b: b.hind: prom 3f: t.o)	dist	**12**	16/1	—	—
				(SP 135.8%)	**12 Rn**	

1m 40.01 (2.61) CSF £47.46 CT £138.79 TOTE £4.30: £3.00 £3.80 £1.40 (£72.70) Trio £68.00 OWNER Mr M. J. Fetherston-Godley (EAST ILSLEY) BRED Highfield Stud Ltd

48 REPULSE H'CAP (0-80) (4-Y.O+) (Class D)

3-30 (3-31) **6f (Equitrack)** £3,306.25 (£1,000.00: £487.50: £231.25) Stalls: Low GOING minus 0.38 sec per fur (FST)

				SP	RR	SF
	Pageboy (73) (PCHaslam) **8-9-9** JWeaver(5) (hld up: led over 1f out: rdn out)	—	**1**	$4/1^{3}$	81	34
	Scissor Ridge (75) (JJBridger) **5-9-11** SSanders(6) (lw: chsd ldr 4f out: rdn & ev ch over 1f out: unable qckn fnl f)	2	**2**	$7/4^{1}$	78	31
27^{8}	**Sea Danzig (65)** (JJBridger) **4-9-1** DHarrison(2) (lw: chsd ldr 2f: lost pl 3f out: r.o one pce fnl f)	1¾	**3**	11/1	63	16
21^{4}	**Apollo Red (64)** (AMoore) **8-9-0** CandyMorris(4) (b.hind: led over 4f)	s.h	**4**	11/2	62	15
20^{6}	**Shashi (IRE) (59)** (PatMitchell) **5-8-9** RLappin(3) (bhd fnl 4f)	3½	**5**	11/1	48	1
	Sally Slade (69) (CACyzer) **5-9-5** GCarter(1) (bhd fnl 5f)	1	**6**	$11/4^{2}$	55	8
				(SP 115.1%)	**6 Rn**	

1m 13.99 (2.89) CSF £11.36 TOTE £3.70: £4.40 £1.30 (£5.80) OWNER Lord Scarsdale (MIDDLEHAM) BRED K. T. Ivory and Partners

T/Jkpt: Not won; £4,710.87 to Wolverhampton 8/1/97. T/Plpt: £83.60 (241.61 Tckts). T/Qdpt: £23.00 (93.14 Tckts). AK

0028-WOLVERHAMPTON (L-H) (Standard)

Wednesday January 8th

WEATHER: cloudy & dry WIND: slt half against

49 MALIBU MAIDEN STKS (I) (3-Y.O) (Class D)

12-30 (12-30) **7f (Fibresand)** £2,916.25 (£880.00: £427.50: £201.25) Stalls: Low GOING: 0.17 sec per fur (SLW)

				SP	RR	SF
	Flamboyance (USA) (JRFanshawe) **3-8-9** DHarrison(1) (unf: scope: chsd ldr: led over 4f out: sn clr: eased fnl f)	—	**1**	$11/2^{2}$	85+	26
	Selberry (PCHaslam) **3-9-0** GCarter(8) (trckd ldrs: rdn to chse wnr fnl 2f: no imp)	7	**2**	$8/11^{1}$	74	15
	Faym (IRE) (JWharton) **3-8-9** FNorton(9) (lw: a.p: rdn 2f out: kpt on same pce)	4	**3**	$7/1^{3}$	60	1
	Attribute (73) (RGuest) **3-8-9** DaneO'Neill(7) (effrt & rdn ½-wy: nt rch ldrs)	2½	**4**	8/1	54	—
	Supercharmer (71) (DNicholls) **3-9-0** AlexGreaves(2) (bit bkwd: slt ld over 2f: wknd wl over 1f out)	nk	**5**	8/1	59	—
	Weet And See (RHollinshead) **3-8-9**(5) DGriffiths(6) (lt-f: unf: dwlt: a bhd & outpcd)	¾	**6**	25/1	57	—
	Rose Burton (TDBarron) **3-8-9** DeanMcKeown(3) (leggy: lt-f: in tch to ½-wy: sn drvn along & wknd)	2	**7**	8/1	47	—
	Gymcrak Watermill (IRE) (GHolmes) **3-8-9** JQuinn(4) (prom 4f: sn rdn & wknd)	4	**8**	50/1	38	—
	Just Rachel (SEKettlewell) **3-8-2**(7) JennyBenson(5) (outpcd: a bhd: t.o)	17	**9**	50/1	—	—
				(SP 126.9%)	**9 Rn**	

1m 31.6 (6.90) CSF £10.57 TOTE £6.30: £1.80 £1.10 £1.60 (£4.70) Trio £12.10 OWNER Dr Catherine Wills (NEWMARKET) BRED Crescent Hill Farm

50 MALIBU MAIDEN STKS (II) (3-Y.O) (Class D)

1-00 (1-02) **7f (Fibresand)** £2,900.00 (£875.00: £425.00: £200.00) Stalls: Low GOING: 0.17 sec per fur (SLW)

				SP	RR	SF
	Cold Steel (WJarvis) **3-9-0** SSanders(2) (mde all: hrd drvn over 1f out: comf)	—	**1**	$5/1^{2}$	77+	25
	Sliema Creek (TDBarron) **3-9-0** ACulhane(3) (a.p: kpt on u.p fnl f: no ch w wnr)	2	**2**	12/1	72	20
17^{2}	**Siouxrouge (74)** (PCHaslam) **3-9-0** SDrowne(6) (hdwy over 3f out: rdn wl over 1f out: nt pce to chal)	1¼	**3**	$4/5^{1}$	70	18
	Hint of Victory (MBell) **3-8-9**(5) GFaulkner(1) (w'like: scope: bit bkwd: s.i.s: hdwy ½-wy: outpcd ent st: kpt on u.p fnl f)	1½	**4**	$7/1^{3}$	66	14
	Reeds (JRFanshawe) **3-9-0** DHarrison(4) (w'like: str: bkwd: trckd ldrs: rdn & lost tch over 2f out)	10	**5**	$7/1^{3}$	43	—
	Native Thatch (IRE) (WGMTurner) **3-8-9** TSprake(5) (scope: dwlt: a in rr: lost tch fnl 3f)	s.h	**6**	12/1	38	—
	Mendoza (57) (DJGMurraySmith) **3-9-0** JWeaver(7) (bit bkwd: chsd ldrs over 4f: sn rdn & outpcd)	3	**7**	16/1	36	—
	Heathyards Pearl (USA) (60) (RHollinshead) **3-8-6**(3) FLynch(8) (s.s: a in rr)	4	**8**	16/1	22	—
				(SP 124.4%)	**8 Rn**	

1m 32.1 (7.40) CSF £57.19 TOTE £4.50: £1.70 £2.40 £1.00 (£33.20) OWNER Mr A. A. Penney (NEWMARKET) BRED J. R. M. and Mrs P. Lewis

51 BAILEY CLAIMING STKS (3-Y.O+) (Class F)

1-30 (1-31) **6f (Fibresand)** £2,433.00 (£683.00: £333.00) Stalls: High GOING: 0.17 sec per fur (SLW)

				SP	RR	SF
11^{*}	**Ultra Beet (65)** (PCHaslam) **5-10-0** JWeaver(5) (led 1f: rdn to ld wl ins fnl f)	—	**1**	$2/1^{1}$	78	53
	Kalar (77) (DWChapman) **8-9-12b** ACulhane(8) (led after 1f tl hdd & no ex fnl 50y)	1½	**2**	$4/1^{3}$	72	47
32^{2}	**Krystal Max (IRE) (83)** (TDBarron) **4-9-5**(7) VictoriaAppleby(1) (mid div: effrt over 2f out: r.o wl ins fnl f)	½	**3**	$7/2^{2}$	71	46
	Chilling (40) (PGMurphy) **3-7-5**(7) JBramhill(3) (trckd ldrs: drvn along 3f out: nvr nr to chal)	6	**4**	20/1	43	2
31^{3}	**Little Ibnr (70)** (PDEvans) **6-9-6** JQuinn(9) (chsd ldrs: sn drvn along: nt pce to chal)	1¼	**5**	10/1	45	20
	Double Oscar (IRE) (52) (DNicholls) **4-9-10** MWigham(2) (bkwd: s.s: nvr nrr)	4	**6**	20/1	39	14
11^{3}	**Captain Carat (61)** (DNicholls) **6-10-0** AlexGreaves(12) (chsd ldrs: hrd drvn over 2f out: sn outpcd)	2½	**7**	6/1	36	11
32^{5}	**Sue Me (IRE) (48)** (WRMuir) **5-9-6b** DaneO'Neill(4) (sn chsng ldrs: rdn ½-wy: wknd wl over 1f out)	d.h	**7**	20/1	28	3
	She's a Madam (30) (LRLloyd-James) **6-8-6**(7) CLowther(7) (outpcd)	hd	**9**	50/1	21	—
	Will To Win (49) (PGMurphy) **3-8-3**ow1 SDrowne(6) (b.hind: rdn & outpcd fr ½-wy)	2	**10**	20/1	21	—
1^{4}	**Havana Miss (32)** (BPalling) **5-8-12**(5) DSweeney(11) (outpcd: a bhd)	¾	**11**	25/1	17	—

	Horse	Dist	Pos	SP	RR	SF
	Mrs McBadger (52) (BSmart) **4-9-1b** RPerham(10) (lw: s.i.s: a bhd: t.o)	5	**12**	33/1	2	—

(SP 126.7%) **12 Rn**

1m 16.4 (5.20) CSF £10.97 TOTE £3.20: £1.60 £2.40 £1.10 (£10.60) Trio £12.80 OWNER Pet Express (W&R) Ltd (MIDDLEHAM) BRED Rockhouse Farms Ltd
WEIGHT FOR AGE 3yo-16lb

52 JAFFA H'CAP (0-90) (I) (4-Y.O+) (Class C)

2-00 (2-00) **1m 1f 79y (Fibresand)** £5,251.00 (£1,588.00: £774.00: £367.00) Stalls: High GOING: 0.17 sec per fur (SLW)

	Horse	Dist	Pos	SP	RR	SF
	Royal Action (80) (JEBanks) **4-9-3** MWigham(5) (mde virtually all: drvn clr 3f out: r.o wl)	—	**1**	8/1	88	43
	Celestial Choir (87) (JLEyre) **7-9-8**(3) OPears(3) (hld up in rr: hdwy over 3f out: r.o wl ins fnl f)	2½	**2**	9/2[2]	91	47
	South Eastern Fred (90) (HJCollingridge) **6-10-0** JQuinn(8) (b: hdwy over 3f out: nvr nr to chal)	9	**3**	5/1[3]	78	34
	Montecristo (72) (RGuest) **4-8-2**(7) LucyBrown(2) (bkwd: sn wl bhd: effrt 3f out: nvr nrr)	4	**4**	12/1	54	9
	Queen of All Birds (IRE) (83) (RBoss) **6-9-2**(5) ADaly(4) (b: prom: hrd drvn 3f out: sn outpcd)	1¾	**5**	5/1[3]	62	18
	Raheen (USA) (88) (WGMTurner) **4-9-6b**(5) DSweeney(9) (w ldrs tl rdn & lost tch over 3f out)	nk	**6**	15/8[1]	66	21
	Doctor Bravious (IRE) (71) (MBell) **4-8-3v**(5)ow1 GFaulkner(6) (lw: prom 6f: sn rdn & lost tch)	3	**7**	12/1	44	—
	Tea Party (USA) (74) (KOCunningham-Brown) **4-8-11b**[1] TSprake(1) (chsd ldrs: rdn 3f out: grad wknd)	1¼	**8**	6/1	45	—

(SP 127.1%) **8 Rn**

2m 4.3 (8.30) CSF £44.83 CT £189.63 TOTE £10.40: £1.50 £2.90 £1.60 (£19.10) Trio £56.30 OWNER Mr E. Carter (NEWMARKET) BRED D. J. and Mrs Deer
WEIGHT FOR AGE 4yo-1lb
OFFICIAL EXPLANATION **Raheen (USA): was unable to dominate and resented the kick-back.**

53 HOLLAND FINNEY & ASSOCIATES H'CAP (0-75) (3-Y.O+) (Class D)

2-30 (2-30) **5f (Fibresand)** £3,420.00 (£1,035.00: £505.00: £240.00) Stalls: High GOING: 0.17 sec per fur (SLW)

	Horse	Dist	Pos	SP	RR	SF
	Sotonian (HOL) (44) (PSFelgate) **4-7-5**(7)ow2 JBramhill(4) (a.p: rdn to ld ins fnl f: all out)	—	**1**	20/1	50	18
	Chemcast (68) (JLEyre) **4-9-8b** RLappin(8) (led after 1f: clr ½-wy: hdd ins fnl f: rallied cl home)	½	**2**	6/1[3]	72	42
	Ramsey Hope (74) (CWFairhurst) **4-10-0v** NKennedy(3) (led 1f: kpt on u.p ins fnl f)	1¼	**3**	13/2	74	44
	Shadow Jury (69) (DWChapman) **7-9-9b** LCharnock(7) (s.i.s: hdwy wl over 1f out: nrst fin)	½	**4**	3/1[1]	68	38
	Dande Flyer (72) (DWPArbuthnot) **4-9-7**(5) DGriffiths(1) (b: bit bkwd: prom tl wknd appr fnl f)	hd	**5**	10/1	71	41
	Master of Passion (71) (JMPEustace) **8-9-6**(5) DSweeney(2) (outpcd & wl bhd tl sme late hdwy)	hd	**6**	3/1[1]	69	39
	Lord Sky (65) (ABailey) **6-9-5** GCarter(9) (b: chsd ldrs to ½-wy: sn outpcd: t.o)	8	**7**	10/1	38	8
32[4]	**Amington Lass (66)** (PDEvans) **4-9-6** SSanders(5) (outpcd: t.o)	2½	**8**	4/1[2]	31	1

(SP 120.6%) **8 Rn**

63.6 secs (4.70) CSF £126.06 CT £812.43 TOTE £24.80: £2.30 £1.50 £1.60 (£68.70) Trio £63.40 OWNER Mr Tim Dean (MELTON MOWBRAY) BRED Stal de Kraal
LONG HANDICAP Sotonian (HOL) 6-12

54 BASIL (S) STKS (4-Y.O+) (Class F)

3-00 (3-00) **1m 100y (Fibresand)** £2,433.00 (£683.00: £333.00) Stalls: High GOING: 0.17 sec per fur (SLW)

	Horse	Dist	Pos	SP	RR	SF
	Loch Style (53) (RHollinshead) **4-8-11**(3) FLynch(5) (a.p: led on bit over 3f out: sn clr: easily)	—	**1**	4/1[2]	59+	52
	Galapino (78) (GCBravery) **4-9-0** DWright(13) (bhd & drvn along ½-wy: hdwy over 2f out: kpt on wl fnl f)	2	**2**	3/1[1]	55	48
	Bon Secret (IRE) (65) (TJNaughton) **5-9-2**(3) JDSmith(3) (a.p: rdn over 2f out: r.o one pce)	3½	**3**	5/1[3]	54	47
	Miss Charlie (35) (ABailey) **7-8-9** GCarter(8) (b: b.hind: led 5f: rdn & wknd 2f out)	11	**4**	14/1	23	16
	Carmosa (USA) (55) (DNicholls) **4-8-9** MWigham(1) (bkwd: trckd ldrs: rdn 3f out: one pce)	1¼	**5**	10/1	20	13
2[4]	**Emei Shan (30)** (WGMTurner) **4-8-4**(7)ow2 DMcGaffin(9) (in tch: no hdwy fnl 3f)	s.h	**6**	50/1	22	13
	El Bardador (IRE) (50) (RJHodges) **4-9-0** SDrowne(4) (nvr nr ldrs)	4	**7**	16/1	18	11
	A S Jim (OO'Neill) **6-9-0** VSlattery(10) (mid div tl wknd over 3f out)	6	**8**	33/1	6	—
	Welsh Melody (49) (KRBurke) **4-8-9b** JQuinn(2) (prom over 4f: sn lost pl)	1	**9**	14/1	—	—
14[2]	**Spencer's Revenge (69)** (NTinkler) **8-9-0b** GBardwell(12) (sn bhd & rdn along: effrt 4f out: wknd 2f out)	½	**10**	3/1[1]	4	—
2[9]	**Alana's Ballad (IRE)** (BPJBaugh) **4-8-6**(5)ow2 DGriffiths(11) (a bhd)	2	**11**	50/1	—	—
	Fleet Cadet (MCPipe) **6-9-0b** DHarrison(7) (a bhd: t.o)	13	**12**	4/1[2]	—	—
29[8]	**Desert Lore (50)** (RMMcKellar) **6-9-0** ACulhane(6) (b: bit bkwd: hdwy 5f out: rdn & wknd over 3f out: sn t.o)	21	**13**	25/1	—	—

(SP 145.7%) **13 Rn**

1m 51.3 (6.30) CSF £19.36 TOTE £6.50: £2.10 £1.50 £2.20 (£37.70) Trio £44.90 OWNER Mr J. B. Wilcox (UPPER LONGDON) BRED Longdon Stud Ltd
No bid

55 JERICHO H'CAP (0-75) (4-Y.O+) (Class D)

3-30 (3-30) **1m 6f 166y (Fibresand)** £3,420.00 (£1,035.00: £505.00: £240.00) Stalls: Low GOING: 0.17 sec per fur (SLW)

	Horse	Dist	Pos	SP	RR	SF
5*	**Golden Hadeer (52)** (MJRyan) **6-8-7** 4x AClark(4) (led 9f out: clr fnl 2f: canter)	—	**1**	13/8[2]	69+	46
	Rood Music (68) (MGMeagher) **6-9-9** ACulhane(3) (led over 5f: rdn & ev ch 3f out: sn outpcd)	7	**2**	25/1	77	54
	Noufari (FR) (73) (RHollinshead) **6-9-11**(3) FLynch(2) (hld up: hdwy 5f out: nt rch ldrs)	10	**3**	13/2[3]	72	49
	Sterling Fellow (58) (DLWilliams) **4-8-7v** DHarrison(7) (in tch: rdn ½-wy: styd on ins fnl f)	2½	**4**	7/1	54	25
	Beaumont (IRE) (65) (JEBanks) **7-9-6** JQuinn(1) (lw: trckd ldrs: drvn along 5f out: sn lost tch)	½	**5**	6/5[1]	60	37
30[6]	**Evezio Rufo (56)** (NPLittmoden) **5-8-6**(5) DGriffiths(8) (chsd ldrs 10f: sn drvn & wknd: t.o)	11	**6**	16/1	39	16
	Scottish Wedding (43) (TWall) **7-7-5**(7)ow2 JBramhill(9) (lost tch 5f out: t.o)	7	**7**	50/1	19	—
30[9]	**Red Phantom (IRE) (61)** (SMellor) **5-9-2v**[1] MWigham(6) (a in rr: t.o)	¾	**8**	25/1	36	13
5[7]	**Hunting Ground (42)** (BPJBaugh) **9-7-11**ow1 FNorton(5) (b: b.hind: prom tl wknd qckly over 4f out: sn t.o)	dist	**9**	50/1	—	—

(SP 126.9%) **9 Rn**

3m 18.4 (11.00) CSF £38.09 CT £214.88 TOTE £2.40: £1.10 £5.70 £1.10 (£40.90) Trio £55.70 OWNER Four Jays Racing Partnership (NEWMARKET) BRED Stetchworth Park Stud Ltd
LONG HANDICAP Scottish Wedding 6-13 Hunting Ground 7-4
WEIGHT FOR AGE 4yo-6lb

56

JAFFA H'CAP (0-90) (II) (4-Y.O+) (Class C)
4-00 (4-00) **1m 1f 79y (Fibresand)** £5,251.00 (£1,588.00: £774.00: £367.00) Stalls: High GOING: 0.17 sec per fur (SLW)

	Horse	Dist	Pos	SP	RR	SF
	Second Colours (USA) (79) (MCPipe) **7-9-3** DHarrison(3) (bit bkwd: hld up: smooth hdwy 3f out: led appr fnl f: r.o wl)	—	1	6/1	90	66
	Super High (83) (PHowling) **5-9-7b** FNorton(1) (led tl over 1f out: rallied u.p fnl f)	¾	2	11/2 [3]	93	69
	Golden Touch (USA) (62) (DJSCosgrove) **5-8-0** GBardwell(6) (chsd ldrs: drvn along ½-wy: one pce fnl 3f)	8	3	6/1	58	34
	Barrel of Hope (69) (JLEyre) **5-8-0**(7) JBramhill(8) (chsd ldrs: rdn along over 2f out: sn outpcd)	3	4	3/1 [1]	60	36
	Duke Valentino (82) (RHollinshead) **5-9-1**(5) DGriffiths(4) (lw: prom: effrt 3f out: wknd wl over 1f out)	1¼	5	9/2 [2]	71	47
	Cedez le Passage (FR) (75) (KOCunningham-Brown) **6-8-13** TSprake(7) (lw: chsd ldrs: rdn & outpcd over 3f out: sn btn)	5	6	7/1	55	31
	Tom Morgan (65) (PTWalwyn) **6-8-3** JQuinn(9) (hld up in rr: effrt over 3f out: sn no imp: t.o)	17	7	12/1	16	—
	Rebel County (IRE) (89) (ABailey) **4-9-12** DBiggs(5) (b: s.i.s: a bhd: t.o)	19	8	7/1	8	—

(SP 119.8%) **8 Rn**

2m 1.6 (5.60) CSF £37.25 CT £191.92 TOTE £6.30: £2.20 £1.40 £2.30 (£18.50) Trio £64.80 OWNER Mr C. R. Fleet (WELLINGTON) BRED Dinnaken Farm in USA
WEIGHT FOR AGE 4yo-1lb

T/Jkpt: Not won; £9,424.43 to Lingfield 9/1/97. T/Plpt: £33.30 (576.24 Tckts). T/Qdpt: £22.10 (96.15 Tckts). IM

0043-LINGFIELD (L-H) (Standard)
Thursday January 9th
WEATHER: snowing WIND: almost nil

57

REDGAUNTLET (S) STKS (I) (4-Y.O+) (Class G)
12-30 (12-33) **7f (Equitrack)** £1,648.50 (£461.00: £223.50) Stalls: Low GOING minus 0.29 sec per fur (FST)

	Horse	Dist	Pos	SP	RR	SF
21[3]	**Hawaii Storm (FR) (46)** (DJSffrenchDavis) **9-8-9b**(3) MBaird(5) (s.i.s: hdwy over 3f out: hrd rdn over 1f out: led nr fin)	—	1	11/2 [3]	61	39
	Statistician (59) (JohnBerry) **5-8-12e** JQuinn(8) (a.p: rdn over 2f out: led ins fnl f: hdd nr fin)	hd	2	8/1	61	39
24[4]	**Mystery Matthias (46)** (MissBSanders) **4-8-7v** SSanders(11) (hld up: led over 2f out tl ins fnl f: one pce)	1½	3	11/2 [3]	52	30
	Shontaine (61) (MJohnston) **4-9-4** JWeaver(7) (hdwy over 3f out: rdn over 2f out: one pce)	2½	4	11/4 [1]	58	36
	Multan (47) (GLMoore) **5-8-9**(3) FLynch(10) (b: a.p: rdn over 3f out: one pce)	2	5	16/1	47	25
20[7]	**Our Shadee (USA) (53)** (KTIvory) **7-8-12v** CScally(2) (b: b.hind: nvr nr to chal)	1	6	11/1	45	23
	Trible Pet (BGubby) **4-8-7v**[1] DaneO'Neill(12) (nvr nrr)	2	7	25/1	35	13
1[10]	**Santella Katie (70)** (MrsLStubbs) **4-8-7** SDrowne(3) (b: bhd fnl 4f)	2½	8	7/1	30	8
	Lancashire Legend (65) (SDow) **4-8-13**(5) ADaly(6) (led over 5f out tl over 2f out: sn wknd)	nk	9	9/2 [2]	40	18
	Red Time (43) (MSSaunders) **4-8-12** RPerham(4) (bhd fnl 5f)	3½	10	25/1	26	4
	Dancing Jack (50) (JJBridger) **4-8-12** DHarrison(9) (lw: prom 3f)	16	11	33/1	—	—
	Al Shaati (FR) (32) (RJO'Sullivan) **7-8-7b** FNorton(1) (led over 1f: wknd over 3f out)	5	12	16/1	—	—

(SP 130.0%) **12 Rn**

1m 27.17 (2.77) CSF £49.64 TOTE £4.80: £1.70 £3.60 £3.70 (£19.70) Trio £42.00 OWNER Mr C. C. Capel (UPPER LAMBOURN) BRED Horse France
No bid
IN-FOCUS: **This was not a bad All-Weather seller, with most of these having been competing unsuccessfully of late in handicaps.**

58

GUY MANNERING CLAIMING STKS (4-Y.O+) (Class E)
1-00 (1-02) **5f (Equitrack)** £2,726.25 (£825.00: £402.50: £191.25) Stalls: High GOING minus 0.29 sec per fur (FST)

	Horse	Dist	Pos	SP	RR	SF
51[3]	**Krystal Max (IRE) (83)** (TDBarron) **4-8-4**(7) VictoriaAppleby(7) (a.p: chsd ldr over 2f out: led ins fnl f: r.o wl)	—	1	100/30 [2]	73	36
	Madrina (60) (JBerry) **4-8-3**(5) PFessey(8) (led tl ins fnl f: unable qckn)	1¼	2	11/2	66	29
11[4]	**Lift Boy (USA) (64)** (AMoore) **8-8-7** CandyMorris(4) (b.hind: chsd ldrs: rdn over 2f out: r.o ins fnl f)	2	3	4/1 [3]	59	22
	Palacegate Jack (IRE) (80) (CADwyer) **6-9-0**(3) FLynch(5) (hdwy over 1f out: r.o one pce)	¾	4	13/8 [1]	66	29
	Windrush Boy (45) (JRBosley) **7-8-3** CRutter(2) (nvr nr to chal)	6	5	25/1	33	—
24[7]	**Superlao (BEL) (41)** (JJBridger) **5-7-12** JQuinn(1) (a bhd)	nk	6	33/1	27	—
32[3]	**Boffy (IRE) (50)** (BPJBaugh) **4-8-11b** RPerham(3) (lw: chsd ldr over 2f: wknd over 1f out)	¾	7	9/1	38	1
	Logie Pert Lad (26) (JJBridger) **5-8-0**(5) ADaly(6) (bhd fnl 2f)	1¼	8	66/1	28	—

(SP 114.8%) **8 Rn**

60.21 secs (2.01) CSF £20.47 TOTE £4.60: £1.30 £7.00 £1.10 (£20.90) OWNER The Oakfield Nurseries Partnership (THIRSK) BRED Baronrath Stud
Krystal Max (IRE) clmd ASpargo £7,000

59

REDGAUNTLET (S) STKS (II) (4-Y.O+) (Class G)
1-30 (1-32) **7f (Equitrack)** £1,648.50 (£461.00: £223.50) Stalls: Low GOING minus 0.29 sec per fur (FST)

	Horse	Dist	Pos	SP	RR	SF
	Milos (67) (TJNaughton) **6-8-12** JWeaver(10) (hdwy over 4f out: led 3f out: rdn out)	—	1	4/5 [1]	63	41
21[7]	**Ki Chi Saga (USA) (70)** (MMadgwick) **5-8-12** DHarrison(6) (lw: hld up: rdn over 3f out: r.o ins fnl f)	2	2	8/1 [3]	58	36
	The Frisky Farmer (52) (WGMTurner) **4-8-12v**[1] TSprake(11) (a.p: led over 3f out: sn hdd: rdn over 2f out: unable qckn)	1¼	3	9/2 [2]	56	34
11[7]	**Astral Invader (IRE) (42)** (MSSaunders) **5-8-12** RPerham(5) (led over 3f: rdn over 2f out: one pce)	7	4	25/1	40	18
	Madonna da Rossi (38) (MDods) **4-8-7** AClark(12) (s.s: rdn & hdwy over 3f out: wknd wl over 1f out)	¾	5	14/1	33	11
	Grey Legend (50) (RMFlower) **4-8-12b** MWigham(4) (bit bkwd: prom over 3f)	2	6	14/1	33	11
	Forgotten Dancer (IRE) (27) (RIngram) **6-8-12b** SDrowne(8) (b: s.s: rdn over 4f out: nvr nr to chal)	4	7	50/1	24	2
32[7]	**Fancy Design (IRE) (33)** (PMitchell) **4-8-7** SSanders(7) (b.hind: s.s: nvr nrr)	½	8	33/1	18	—
	Ragazzo (IRE) (40) (JSWainwright) **7-8-12b** LCharnock(3) (b.hind: prom over 4f)	1	9	9/1	21	—
	Shermood (27) (KTIvory) **4-8-7** NAdams(9) (b: b.hind: bhd fnl 4f)	½	10	33/1	15	—
	Fair Ella (IRE) (33) (GLMoore) **5-8-7** JQuinn(2) (bhd fnl 5f)	2	11	20/1	10	—

21[9]	**Golden Silver (43)** (JSMoore) **4-8-0**(7) KAxon(1) (s.s: a bhd: t.o)	dist	**12**	25/1	—	—
				(SP 128.5%)	**12 Rn**	

1m 27.03 (2.63) CSF £9.10 TOTE £1.50: £1.10 £2.90 £4.30 (£6.20) Trio £11.50 OWNER Mr R. A. Popely (EPSOM) BRED R. A. and J. H. Popely
No bid
IN-FOCUS: This was by far the weaker of the two divisions of the seller.

60 QUENTIN DURWARD MAIDEN STKS (3-Y.O) (Class D)

2-00 (2-02) **1m (Equitrack)** £3,485.00 (£1,055.00: £515.00: £245.00) Stalls: High GOING minus 0.29 sec per fur (FST)

				SP	RR	SF
	Royal Aty (IRE) (PAKelleway) **3-9-0** MWigham(3) (scope: lw: mde virtually all: clr wl over 1f out: shkn up: r.o wl)	—	**1**	5/2 2	87	43
	Jolly Jackson (RAkehurst) **3-9-0** SSanders(5) (rdn over 3f out: hdwy over 2f out: r.o one pce)	10	**2**	12/1	67	23
	Enlisted (IRE) (SirMarkPrescott) **3-8-9** CNutter(6) (a.p: chsd wnr over 3f out: rdn: one pce)	½	**3**	5/6 1	61	17
	Double Crest (IRE) (MJohnston) **3-8-9** JWeaver(7) (lw: chsd ldrs: rdn over 4f out: one pce)	¾	**4**	13/2 3	60	16
8[2]	**Serenade (IRE) (58)** (MJHaynes) **3-9-0** GBardwell(1) (b.hind: outpcd)	1¼	**5**	33/1	62	18
	Troia (IRE) (BSmart) **3-8-9** TSprake(4) (lw: a bhd)	¾	**6**	16/1	56	12
19[2]	**Patina (53)** (RHollinshead) **3-8-6**(3) FLynch(2) (w wnr over 4f: wknd over 2f out)	21	**7**	20/1	14	—
				(SP 117.7%)	**7 Rn**	

1m 40.42 (3.02) CSF £28.04 TOTE £3.00: £1.10 £5.20 (£22.60) OWNER Gen Horse Advertising SRL (NEWMARKET) BRED Allevamento Annarosa Di V Schirone

61 TALISMAN H'CAP (0-65) (4-Y.O+) (Class F)

2-30 (2-32) **1m 2f (Equitrack)** £2,641.20 (£743.20: £363.60) Stalls: Low GOING minus 0.29 sec per fur (FST)

				SP	RR	SF
	Tribal Peace (IRE) (65) (BGubby) **5-9-7**(7) GGallagher(6) (hdwy over 1f out: led ins fnl f: pushed out)	—	**1**	25/1	76	46
	Can Can Charlie (52) (JPearce) **7-9-1** GBardwell(10) (rdn over 3f out: hdwy over 1f out: r.o wl ins fnl f)	nk	**2**	25/1	63	33
	Suitor (44) (SDow) **4-8-5**ow2 SSanders(7) (lw: hdwy over 3f out: led over 1f out tl ins fnl f: r.o)	s.h	**3**	4/1 1	54	20
	Sheraz (IRE) (48) (NTinkler) **5-8-11** CRutter(14) (rdn & hdwy over 3f out: rdn over 1f out: unable qckn)	3½	**4**	20/1	53	23
	Mediate (IRE) (52) (AHide) **5-8-8b**(7) GMilligan(11) (hdwy 2f out: one pce fnl f)	hd	**5**	8/1	57	27
10[5]	**Double March (58)** (PRWebber) **4-9-5** DaneO'Neill(13) (lw: rdn & hdwy over 1f out: one pce)	hd	**6**	14/1	63	31
	Dr Edgar (52) (MDods) **5-9-1b**[1] FNorton(5) (lw: a.p: rdn over 3f out: wknd fnl f)	1¾	**7**	14/1	54	24
9[2]	**Nakhal (50)** (DJGMurraySmith) **4-8-11** JWeaver(9) (a.p: led over 3f out tl over 1f out: wknd ins fnl f)	½	**8**	9/2 2	51	19
	Multi Franchise (56) (BGubby) **4-9-3** MWigham(12) (bit bkwd: hdwy 7f out: wknd over 4f out)	9	**9**	25/1	43	11
	Squire's Occasion (CAN) (65) (RAkehurst) **4-9-7**(5) ADaly(1) (lw: bhd fnl 4f)	hd	**10**	12/1	51	19
	Kitty Kitty Cancan (63) (LadyHerries) **4-9-10b** AClark(4) (led over 6f)	3½	**11**	9/2 2	44	12
28[9]	**Jubilee Scholar (IRE) (65)** (KMcAuliffe) **4-9-9**(3) FLynch(8) (hdwy over 6f out: rdn over 4f out: wknd wl over 1f out)	¾	**12**	50/1	45	13
	Racing Hawk (USA) (55) (MSSaunders) **5-9-4** RPerham(3) (prom over 3f)	17	**13**	33/1	7	—
	Daratown (40) (PDEvans) **4-8-1v**[1] JQuinn(2) (prom over 4f)	s.h	**14**	5/1 3	—	—
				(SP 126.4%)	**14 Rn**	

2m 9.55 (5.25) CSF £468.53 CT £2,758.76 TOTE £23.30: £10.60 £14.30 £1.10 (£226.80) Trio £428.60; £247.54 to Southwell 10/1/97 OWNER Brian Gubby Ltd (BAGSHOT) BRED Mrs P. H. Burns in Ireland
WEIGHT FOR AGE 4yo-2lb

62 WAVERLEY H'CAP (0-80) (3-Y.O) (Class D)

3-00 (3-00) **6f (Equitrack)** £3,387.50 (£1,025.00: £500.00: £237.50) Stalls: Low GOING minus 0.29 sec per fur (FST)

				SP	RR	SF
	Just Loui (85) (WGMTurner) **3-9-7**(5) 7x DSweeney(5) (mde all: rdn out)	—	**1**	5/2 2	89	36
12[3]	**Forgotten Times (USA) (64)** (TMJones) **3-8-5** NCarlisle(3) (b.hind: chsd wnr: rdn over 2f out: unable qckn fnl f)	1¼	**2**	10/1	65	12
	Petite Danseuse (80) (CADwyer) **3-9-0**(7) JoHunnam(6) (outpcd: hdwy fnl f: r.o)	1¼	**3**	6/1	77	24
	The Wyandotte Inn (76) (RHollinshead) **3-9-0**(3) 7x FLynch(2) (hld up: rdn over 2f out: one pce)	1	**4**	9/4 1	71	18
	La Dolce Vita (77) (TDBarron) **3-9-4** DHarrison(1) (lw: hld up: rdn 3f out: sn wknd)	10	**5**	7/2 3	45	—
	Taome (IRE) (60) (PDEvans) **3-8-1** JQuinn(4) (a bhd)	1¼	**6**	16/1	25	—
				(SP 110.8%)	**6 Rn**	

1m 14.64 (3.54) CSF £22.19 TOTE £4.10: £1.00 £6.00 (£13.30) OWNER Mr A. Poole (SHERBORNE) BRED M. A. Poole

63 IVANHOE H'CAP (0-60) (4-Y.O+) (Class F)

3-30 (3-30) **1m 5f (Equitrack)** £2,562.80 (£720.80: £352.40) Stalls: Low GOING minus 0.29 sec per fur (FST)

				SP	RR	SF
13*	**Yet Again (45)** (MissGayKelleway) **5-9-5** 5x SSanders(1) (b: hdwy over 4f out: led ins fnl f: rdn out)	—	**1**	8/15 1	58	19
	Rasayel (USA) (48) (PDEvans) **7-9-1**(7) JoHunnam(8) (a.p: rdn over 1f out: r.o wl ins fnl f)	½	**2**	12/1	60	21
	Sassiver (USA) (30) (PAKelleway) **7-8-4** DWright(3) (hdwy over 8f out: led 3f out tl ins fnl f: unable qckn)	1	**3**	20/1	41	2
	Etoile du Nord (23) (HJCollingridge) **5-7-11** NAdams(11) (b: hdwy over 4f out: ev ch over 1f out: one pce)	1¼	**4**	100/1	33	—
13[5]	**Sapphire Son (IRE) (43)** (PCClarke) **5-9-3** DaneO'Neill(9) (a.p: led over 3f out: sn hdd: wknd over 1f out)	4	**5**	33/1	48	9
	Broughtons Formula (50) (WJMusson) **7-9-10b** GCarter(5) (lw: nvr nrr)	10	**6**	5/1 2	42	3
	Fabulous Mtoto (35) (MSSaunders) **7-8-9** RPerham(7) (led 11f out tl over 3f out: sn wknd)	6	**7**	16/1	20	—
	Sam Rockett (33) (PMooney) **4-8-2b** JQuinn(2) (stdy hdwy over 4f out: wknd 3f out)	nk	**8**	8/1 3	18	—
	Whippers Delight (IRE) (25) (GFHCharles-Jones) **9-7-6**(7) AMcCarthy(10) (lw: hdwy 11f out: wknd over 6f out)	¾	**9**	66/1	9	—
	City Run (USA) (30) (DJSCosgrove) **5-8-4** FNorton(4) (bhd fnl 7f: t.o)	dist	**10**	100/1	—	—
	Lucy Tufty (36) (JPearce) **6-8-10** GBardwell(6) (led 2f: wknd over 5f out: t.o)	7	**11**	33/1	—	—
				(SP 120.7%)	**11 Rn**	

2m 51.94 (9.94) CSF £8.54 CT £67.76 TOTE £1.50: £1.00 £4.10 £5.80 (£8.40) Trio £40.20 OWNER Mr A. P. Griffin (WHITCOMBE) BRED Aston Park Stud
WEIGHT FOR AGE 4yo-5lb

T/Jkpt: £13,077.30 (0.09 Tckts); £16,761.15 to Southwell 10/1/97. T/Plpt: £177.80 (100.28 Tckts). T/Qdpt: £65.10 (36.41 Tckts). AK

SAN ROSSORE (Pisa, Italy) (R-H) (Heavy)
Sunday January 5th

64a PREMIO UNIONE INDUSTRIALE PISANA H'CAP (3-Y.O)
3-05 (3-05) **1m 2f** £6,090.00

Horse	Dist	Pos	SP	RR	SF
Charsy (IRE) (EPistoletti,Italy) **3-7-10** CCocca	—	**1**		57	—
Cayo Guillermo (IRE) (GBotti,Italy) **3-7-11** ROpazo	3¼	**2**		53	—
Sopran Bistop (ITY) (FGnesi,Italy) **3-7-13** MDemuro	½	**3**		54	—
Shareef Allah (KMcAuliffe) **3-7-12** BCook (btn over 10l)		**9**		—	—
					10 Rn

2m 16.6 TOTE 287L: 70L 51L 35L (1249L) OWNER E. Pistoletti BRED A. F. O'Callaghan
Shareef Allah raced in a prominent position until losing her place over four furlongs out, and made no progress in the straight.

0036-SOUTHWELL (L-H) (Standard)
Friday January 10th
WEATHER: overcast WIND: almost nil
Other race under Rules of National Hunt Racing

65 RYEGRASS H'CAP (0-65) (I) (3-Y.O+) (Class F)
12-05 (12-06) **6f (Fibresand)** £1,944.00 (£544.00: £264.00) Stalls: Low GOING: 0.32 sec per fur (SLW)

Form	Horse	Dist	Pos	SP	RR	SF
4^{5}	**Anita's Contessa (IRE) (51)** (BPalling) **5-9-0** TSprake(6) (sn bhd: hdwy & hmpd 2f out: styd on strly u.p to ld last 30y)	—	**1**	8/1	58	40
24^{2}	**Thick as Thieves (42)** (RonaldThompson) **5-8-0**(5) PFessey(8) (w ldr: led over 2f out tl nr fin)	nk	**2**	5/1 3	48	30
	Dissentor (IRE) (43) (JAGlover) **5-8-6v** GCarter(1) (sn trckng ldrs: ev ch over 1f out: wknd ins fnl f)	2½	**3**	12/1	43	25
31^{*}	**Leigh Crofter (69)** (PDCundell) **8-10-4b** 7x RPerham(4) (lw: sltly hmpd s: sn drvn along & chsng ldrs: nt qckn fnl 2f)	nk	**4**	7/2 2	68	50
	Bold Aristocrat (IRE) (60) (RHollinshead) **6-9-6**(3) FLynch(2) (trckd ldrs: rdn & hung bdly rt 2f out: sn tn)	6	**5**	11/4 1	43	25
	Oscilights Gift (33) (MarkCampion) **5-7-10** NAdams(3) (swvd rt s: led tl over 2f out: wknd over 1f out)	1	**6**	14/1	13	—
	Balinsky (IRE) (49) (JBerry) **4-8-7v**1(5) PRoberts(11) (outpcd ½-wy: kpt on appr fnl f)	½	**7**	16/1	28	10
	Sound the Trumpet (IRE) (48) (RCSpicer) **5-8-11** DeanMcKeown(10) (outpcd ½-wy: n.d after)	nk	**8**	14/1	26	8
	River Seine (FR) (48) (SGKnight) **5-8-11** 7x DHarrison(5) (in tch: outpcd ½-wy: sn lost pl)	6	**9**	10/1	10	—
	Serape (58) (MrsLStubbs) **4-9-7** SDrowne(9) (sn outpcd & bhd)	5	**10**	20/1	7	—
	Ballykissangel (33) (NBycroft) **4-7-10b** GBardwell(7) (s.i.s: a bhd)	1¼	**11**	50/1	—	—
				(SP 119.4%)		**11 Rn**

1m 19.7 (6.20) CSF £45.24 CT £450.12 TOTE £6.20: £2.80 £1.90 £1.40 (£22.90) Trio £82.20 OWNER Mrs Anita Quinn (COWBRIDGE) BRED Mrs Anita Quinn
LONG HANDICAP Oscilights Gift 7-7 Ballykissangel 7-3

66 BUTTERCUP AMATEUR H'CAP (0-65) (I) (4-Y.O+) (Class G)
12-30 (12-31) **1m 3f (Fibresand)** £1,735.00 (£485.00: £235.00) Stalls: Low GOING: 0.32 sec per fur (SLW)

Form	Horse	Dist	Pos	SP	RR	SF
42^{2}	**Royal Acclaim (32)** (RDickin) **12-9-0v**(5) MissRJPatman(1) (s.i.s: bhd tl hdwy 3f out: styd on to ld nr fin)	—	**1**	10/1	42	9
39^{5}	**Sea God (49)** (MCChapman) **6-10-3**(5)ow2 MrKLoads(6) (trckd ldrs: led 3f out tl nr fin)	nk	**2**	10/1	59	24
30^{2}	**Mr Speculator (51)** (JEBanks) **4-10-7v** MrTMcCarthy(3) (w ldr: led over 4f out: hrd rdn & hdd 3f out: nt qckn fnl f)	2½	**3**	3/1 2	57	21
2^{*}	**Fresh Fruit Daily (43)** (PAKelleway) **5-10-2** MissPJones(7) (chsd ldrs: rdn 3f out: styd on one pce)	3	**4**	7/4 1	45	12
	Phanan (37) (REPeacock) **11-9-5**(5)ow4 MrsCPeacock(4) (prom tl lost pl 7f out: kpt on wl fnl 3f)	1¼	**5**	50/1	37	—
	Forget Paris (IRE) (49) (BSRothwell) **4-10-5** MrRThornton(5) (chsd ldrs: drvn along 5f out: one pce fnl 3f)	¾	**6**	33/1	48	12
	Rumpelstiltskin (50) (HSHowe) **5-10-4**(5) MrRWidger(2) (led tl over 4f out: wknd 2f out)	16	**7**	50/1	25	—
	Ihtimaam (FR) (62) (MrsASwinbank) **5-11-7** MrChrisWilson(8) (lw: in tch tl lost pl over 4f out: eased)	6	**8**	7/2 3	29	—
	Spitfire Bridge (IRE) (56) (GMMcCourt) **5-10-10**(5)ow1 MrAWintle(12) (in tch: pushed along ½-wy: sn lost pl)	hd	**9**	14/1	23	—
	Nord Lys (IRE) (27) (BJLlewellyn) **6-8-9**(5) MissEJJones(9) (sn in tch: lost pl 5f out)	10	**10**	20/1	—	—
	Fly by North (USA) (37) (DNicholson) **9-9-5**(5) MissEWilliams(10) (t.o ½-wy: p.u over 2f out: dead)		**P**	20/1	—	—
				(SP 124.8%)		**11 Rn**

2m 37.0 (17.00) CSF £100.18 CT £346.97 TOTE £12.30: £4.60 £2.40 £2.00 (£32.90) Trio £27.90 OWNER Mr David Foster (STRATFORD) BRED Miss V. K. Hermon-Hodge
LONG HANDICAP Nord Lys (IRE) 8-9 WEIGHT FOR AGE 4yo-3lb
OFFICIAL EXPLANATION Ihtimaam (FR): his rider reported that the gelding was never travelling well and did not respond to pressure. The trainer added that the gelding is inconsistent and needs his own way.

67 BUTTERCUP AMATEUR H'CAP (0-65) (II) (4-Y.O+) (Class G)
1-20 (1-21) **1m 3f (Fibresand)** £1,735.00 (£485.00: £235.00) Stalls: Low GOING: 0.32 sec per fur (SLW)

Form	Horse	Dist	Pos	SP	RR	SF
18^{4}	**Undawaterscubadiva (28)** (MPBielby) **5-9-5**(5) MrsCWilliams(4) (lw: sn trckng ldrs: led over 3f out: sn clr: pushed out)	—	**1**	6/1 2	44	21
	Raindeer Quest (45) (JLEyre) **5-10-13** MissDianaJones(9) (sn trckng ldrs: wnt 2nd over 2f out: sn rdn & no imp)	4	**2**	6/4 1	55	32
	Kilnamartyra Girl (41) (JParkes) **7-10-9** MrsDKettlewell(5) (in tch: drvn along & lost pl 6f out: styd on fnl 2f)	4	**3**	7/1 3	45	22
	Kinnescash (IRE) (52) (PBowen) **4-11-3** MrRThornton(10) (trckd ldrs: led 7f out tl over 3f out: wknd 2f out)	4	**4**	7/1 3	51	25
	Warspite (33) (PMooney) **7-9-10**(5) MrFQuinlan(2) (in tch: drvn along & outpcd 5f out: kpt on fnl 3f)	2½	**5**	8/1	28	5
	North Ardar (45) (TWall) **7-10-8**(5) MissAAnderson(6) (sn drvn along: hdwy to chse ldrs 7f out: lost pl over 3f out)	15	**6**	7/1 3	18	—
	Stevie's Wonder (IRE) (53) (BJLlewellyn) **7-11-7** MrJLLlewellyn(7) (chsd ldrs tl lost pl over 5f out)	1½	**7**	14/1	24	1
	Lebedinski (IRE) (38) (MrsPSly) **4-9-12**(5) MissLAllan(8) (a in tch: drvn along over 3f out: grad wknd)	nk	**8**	20/1	9	—
14^{9}	**Magication (37)** (KGWingrove) **7-10-0**(5) MrABrown(3) (led 4f: lost pl over 4f out)	2½	**9**	33/1	4	—

	Horse	Dist	Pos	SP	RR	SF
	King's Shilling (USA) (44) (HOliver) **10-10-7**(5) MrHJOliver(11) (in tch: rdn over 5f out: sn lost pl)	4	**10**	12/1	5	—
	Rimouski (36) (BRCambidge) **9-9-13**(5)ow5 MrsHNoonan(1) (reluctant to r: a wl bhd: t.o ½-wy)	15	**11**	33/1	—	—
	Classic Daisy (30) (RCSpicer) **4-9-4b**(5) MrSRutherford(12) (s.s: a bhd: t.o)	20	**12**	50/1	—	—

(SP 129.9%) **12 Rn**

2m 35.8 (15.80) CSF £16.12 CT £65.97 TOTE £6.20: £1.80 £1.10 £4.40 (£5.30) Trio £26.40 OWNER Mr J. F. Coupland (GRIMSBY) BRED Hollow Hole Stud

WEIGHT FOR AGE 4yo-3lb

68 DAISY CLAIMING STKS (4-Y.O+) (Class F)

1-55 (1-56) **2m (Fibresand)** £2,294.00 (£644.00: £314.00) Stalls: Low GOING: 0.32 sec per fur (SLW)

	Horse	Dist	Pos	SP	RR	SF
	El Nido (56) (MJCamacho) **9-8-13** LCharnock(11) (lw: trckd ldrs gng wl: led on bit over 5f out: sn wl clr)	—	**1**	7/4 [1]	60	—
	Tirmizi (USA) (MrsASwinbank) **6-9-3** JWeaver(14) (lw: bhd: gd hdwy ½-wy: kpt on fnl 2f: no ch w wnr)	12	**2**	11/2	52	—
	Shakiyr (FR) (61) (RHollinshead) **6-9-4**(3) FLynch(16) (hdwy u.p 9f out: sn chsng ldrs: one pce fnl 3f)	8	**3**	9/2 [2]	48	—
	Shuttlecock (37) (MrsNMacauley) **6-8-12**(3) CTeague(1) (led to 7f out: one pce fnl 3f)	1	**4**	20/1	41	—
	Strike-a-Pose (BJLlewellyn) **7-8-1**(7) JBramhill(15) (hdwy ½-wy: sn chsng ldrs: lost pl over 3f out)	10	**5**	33/1	24	—
	Gunmaker (39) (BJLlewellyn) **8-9-1** TWilliams(3) (chsd ldrs: led 7f out tl over 5f out: sn wknd)	¾	**6**	14/1	30	—
5^{2}	**Record Lover (IRE) (36)** (MCChapman) **7-9-0**(7) IonaWands(2) (chsd ldrs: rdn 6f out: sn lost pl)	hd	**7**	14/1	36	—
	Daily Sport Girl (40) (BJLlewellyn) **8-9-0** VSlattery(8) (chsd ldrs 10f: sn lost pl)	17	**8**	20/1	12	—
	Young Tess (PBowen) **7-8-8** SDrowne(10) (sn bhd & drvn along)	2	**9**	16/1	4	—
	Joyrider (MissMKMilligan) **6-8-6**(5) PFessey(4) (chsd ldrs to ½-wy: sn lost pl)	¾	**10**	33/1	6	—
5^{4}	**White Willow (63)** (TWall) **8-9-7v** DHarrison(13) (bhd: sme hdwy ½-wy: outpcd 6f out: sn lost pl)	¾	**11**	5/1 [3]	16	—
	Sakbah (USA) (JAPickering) **8-8-6** NCarlisle(7) (mid div: drvn along 10f out: sn bhd: t.o)	30	**12**	50/1	—	—
	Daring Hen (IRE) (RTJuckes) **7-8-8v1** ACulhane(5) (s.i.s: sn drvn along & a wl bhd: t.o)	6	**13**	50/1	—	—
	Tristan's Comet (JLHarris) **10-9-1b** DeanMcKeown(6) (bhd & drvn along 10f out: t.o)	2½	**14**	33/1	—	—
18^{14}	**Fenian Court (IRE)** (MissJBower) **6-8-8b** SDWilliams(9) (chsd ldrs tl lost pl 7f out: wl t.o)	17	**15**	33/1	—	—
	Credit Call (IRE) (RGBrazington) **9-8-13** JQuinn(12) (prom to ½-wy: sn bhd: wl t.o)	10	**16**	66/1	—	—

(SP 132.5%) **16 Rn**

3m 53.1 (27.10) CSF £12.77 TOTE £2.90: £1.40 £2.80 £2.40 (£10.10) Trio £23.70 OWNER Mrs S. Camacho (MALTON) BRED M. J. Camacho

69 RYEGRASS H'CAP (0-65) (II) (3-Y.O+) (Class F)

2-25 (2-27) **6f (Fibresand)** £1,944.00 (£544.00: £264.00) Stalls: Low GOING: 0.32 sec per fur (SLW)

	Horse	Dist	Pos	SP	RR	SF
40^{10}	**Lady Silk (43)** (MissJFCraze) **6-8-6** JFanning(5) (lw: sn chsng ldrs: led over 1f out: r.o wl: eased nr fin)	—	**1**	12/1	51+	29
36^{5}	**Blue Lugana (35)** (NBycroft) **5-7-5**(7)ow2 JBramhill(2) (chsd ldr: led 3f out tl over 1f out: no ch w wnr)	3½	**2**	16/1	34	10
	Blushing Grenadier (IRE) (50) (PDCundell) **5-8-13b** DHarrison(6) (lw: a chsng ldrs: styd on same pce fnl 2f)	1	**3**	3/1 [3]	46	24
	Sir Tasker (40) (JLHarris) **9-8-3** LCharnock(9) (hdwy ½-wy: kpt on one pce fnl 2f)	¾	**4**	10/1	34	12
4^{2}	**Klipspinger (53)** (BSRothwell) **4-9-2b** JStack(10) (racd wd: sn bhd & drvn along: kpt on fnl 2f: nvr nr ldrs)	2	**5**	5/2 [1]	42	20
40^{11}	**Cheerful Groom (IRE) (41)** (DShaw) **6-8-4** NKennedy(8) (sn outpcd & bhd: kpt on fnl 2f: n.d)	1½	**6**	20/1	26	4
	Featherstone Lane (61) (MissLCSiddall) **6-9-3v**(7) TSiddall(3) (trckd ldrs tl wknd over 1f out)	1	**7**	10/1	43	21
40^{3}	**Craigie Boy (40)** (NBycroft) **7-8-3b** JQuinn(7) (s.i.s: bhd & drvn along: sme hdwy 2f out: n.d)	hd	**8**	11/4 [2]	22	—
20^{9}	**Indian Wolf (33)** (BJLlewellyn) **4-7-3**(7) IonaWands(4) (prom tl lost pl ½-wy)	3½	**9**	50/1	5	—
51^{9}	**She's a Madam (35)** (LRLloyd-James) **6-7-7**(5)ow2 PFessey(1) (lw: led to 3f out: wknd qckly over 1f out)	12	**10**	33/1	—	—

(SP 121.7%) **10 Rn**

1m 20.0 (6.50) CSF £163.20 CT £667.45 TOTE £10.30: £3.60 £4.00 £1.20 (£67.90) Trio £247.70; £13.96 to Leopardstown 11/1/97 OWNER Mr K. C. West (YORK) BRED Hesmonds Stud Ltd

LONG HANDICAP Blue Lugana 7-5 Indian Wolf 7-0 She's a Madam 7-7

70 COWSLIP LIMITED STKS (0-75) (4-Y.O+) (Class D)

2-55 (2-55) **1m 4f (Fibresand)** £3,387.50 (£1,025.00: £500.00: £237.50) Stalls: Low GOING: 0.32 sec per fur (SLW)

	Horse	Dist	Pos	SP	RR	SF
39^{2}	**Albaha (USA) (74)** (JEBanks) **4-8-13** JQuinn(3) (mde all: clr over 4f out: drvn along over 1f out: all out)	—	**1**	2/5 [1]	79	47
	Circled (USA) (69) (JohnHarris) **4-8-8** DeanMcKeown(7) (hdwy to chse ldrs 8f out: wnt 2nd over 3f out: styd on u.p: nt rch wnr)	½	**2**	10/1	73	41
	Gulliver (75) (NJHWalker) **4-8-11** GCarter(1) (trckd ldrs tl wknd 3f out)	19	**3**	13/2 [2]	51	19
	Far Ahead (74) (JLEyre) **5-9-3**(3)ow1 OPears(2) (chsd ldrs: drvn along & outpcd 4f out: n.d after)	4	**4**	8/1 [3]	51	22
39^{11}	**Premier Dance (74)** (DHaydnJones) **10-9-1** AClark(6) (in tch tl lost pl 5f out)	nk	**5**	20/1	45	17
	Still Here (IRE) (50) (PBowen) **4-8-11** SDrowne(4) (chsd ldrs: sn drvn along: lost pl over 5f out)	22	**6**	33/1	16	—
	Dancing Cavalier (71) (RHollinshead) **4-8-6**(5) DGriffiths(5) (sn bhd & drvn along)	¾	**7**	12/1	15	—

(SP 120.4%) **7 Rn**

2m 44.5 (11.50) CSF £6.04 TOTE £1.40: £1.10 £3.30 (£8.90) OWNER UK Packaging Supplies Ltd (NEWMARKET) BRED Shadwell Estate Co., Ltd. and Shadwell Farm Inc.

WEIGHT FOR AGE 4yo-4lb

71 BLUEBELL (S) STKS (4-Y.O+) (Class G)

3-25 (3-27) **7f (Fibresand)** £2,085.00 (£585.00: £285.00) Stalls: Low GOING: 0.32 sec per fur (SLW)

	Horse	Dist	Pos	SP	RR	SF
40^{7}	**Sense of Priority (70)** (DNicholls) **8-8-12** AlexGreaves(1) (led after 1f: clr 2f out: rdn fnl f: jst hld on)	—	**1**	5/1 [2]	76	48
1^{2}	**Elton Ledger (IRE) (73)** (MrsNMacauley) **8-8-12v** JWeaver(6) (lw: b: trckd ldrs: effrt over 2f out: hung lft: styd on ins fnl f)	½	**2**	11/10 [1]	75	47
1^{3}	**Sea Devil (67)** (MJCamacho) **11-8-12** LCharnock(5) (in tch: effrt over 2f out: kpt on same pce: nvr nr to chal)	6	**3**	9/1 [3]	61	33
	Guy's Gamble (50) (JWharton) **4-8-12** JFanning(7) (lw: a chsng ldrs: one pce fnl 2f)	6	**4**	25/1	47	19
15^{6}	**First Gold (44)** (JWharton) **8-8-12v1** JQuinn(12) (unruly in stalls: s.i.s: bhd tl styd on fnl 2f)	¾	**5**	9/1 [3]	46	18
	Soaked (64) (DWChapman) **4-8-12** ACulhane(4) (s.i.s: hdwy ½-wy: kpt on fnl 2f: nvr rchd ldrs)	½	**6**	20/1	45	17
3^{6}	**Kajostar (22)** (SWCampion) **7-8-7** DeanMcKeown(9) (in tch: sn drvn along: outpcd fr ½-wy)	4	**7**	66/1	30	2
	Visimotion (USA) (62) (MissMERowland) **7-8-12** NCarlisle(2) (chsd ldrs tl outpcd fnl 3f)	1¼	**8**	33/1	33	5
	Major Mouse (WWHaigh) **9-8-12** VHalliday(14) (bit bkwd: sn outpcd & drvn along: kpt on fnl 2f: n.d)	s.h	**9**	20/1	33	5
	Awafeh (44) (SMellor) **4-8-12v** MWigham(3) (nvr bttr than mid div)	1	**10**	33/1	30	2
51^{11}	**Havana Miss (32)** (BPalling) **5-8-7** AClark(11) (a bhd)	½	**11**	33/1	24	—

				SP	RR	SF
54^{4}	**Miss Charlie (35)** (ABailey) **7-8-7** GCarter(8) (b: b.hind: s.i.s: a in rr)	½	**12**	20/1	23	—
	Jareer Do (IRE) (43) (BPalling) **5-8-7** TSprake(13) (led 1f: lost pl ½-wy)	2	**13**	33/1	18	—
54^{5}	**Carmosa (USA) (55)** (DNicholls) **4-8-0**$^{(7)}$ JBramhill(16) (s.i.s: a in rr)	1½	**14**	20/1	15	—
4^{8}	**Maysimp (IRE) (40)** (BPJBaugh) **4-8-7** RPerham(15) (chsd ldrs tl lost pl ½-wy: sn bhd)	3	**15**	66/1	8	—
3^{7}	**Jilly Beveled (35)** (RonaldThompson) **5-8-2**$^{(5)}$ PFessey(10) (hld up: p.u over 2f out: struck into)		**P**	20/1	—	—

(SP 126.7%) **16 Rn**

1m 32.9 (6.40) CSF £10.57 TOTE £5.50: £2.00 £1.70 £2.40 (£5.30) Trio £3.60 OWNER Mr M. A. Scaife (THIRSK) BRED Cheveley Park Stud Ltd
No bid

72 PRIMROSE H'CAP (0-70) (4-Y.O+) (Class E)

3-55 (3-55) **1m (Fibresand)** £3,289.10 (£996.80: £487.40: £232.70) Stalls: Low GOING: 0.32 sec per fur (SLW)

				SP	RR	SF
31^{4}	**Gulf Shaadi (55)** (EJAlston) **5-8-13** SDrowne(3) (lw: s.s: hdwy ½-wy: led jst ins fnl f: r.o strly)	—	**1**	12/1	66	33
	Nordic Breeze (IRE) (69) (MCPipe) **5-9-13** DHarrison(12) (lw: chsd ldrs: rdn & outpcd over 2f out: styd on fnl f)	2½	**2**	8/1	75	42
15^{*}	**Domino Flyer (64)** (MrsASwinbank) **4-9-8** 6x JQuinn(9) (sn trckng ldrs: led over 1f out tl jst ins fnl f: nt qckn)	½	**3**	2/1 ^{1}	69	36
	Three Arch Bridge (62) (MJohnston) **5-9-6b** JWeaver(8) (sn trckng ldr: led over 2f out tl over 1f out: grad wknd)	2½	**4**	6/1 ^{2}	62	29
14^{10}	**Spanish Stripper (USA) (38)** (MCChapman) **6-7-10** GBardwell(10) (chsd ldrs: sn drvn along: one pce fnl 2f)	1	**5**	33/1	36	3
	Perpetual Light (65) (JJQuinn) **4-9-4**$^{(5)}$ GParkin(6) (sn outpcd: styd on fnl 3f: nvr nr to chal)	s.h	**6**	8/1	63	30
31^{8}	**Dawalib (USA) (57)** (DHaydnJones) **7-9-1** LCharnock(11) (hld up: hdwy ½-wy: nvr rchd ldrs)	3½	**7**	16/1	48	15
	Principal Boy (IRE) (46) (TJEtherington) **4-8-4** CRutter(1) (sn trckng ldrs: effrt over 2f out: wknd over 1f out)	2½	**8**	8/1	32	—
	Obelos (USA) (64) (MissSJWilton) **6-9-8v** DeanMcKeown(5) (sn outpcd & drvn along)	15	**9**	7/1 ^{3}	20	—
	Oneoftheoldones (63) (JNorton) **5-9-4**$^{(3)}$ OPears(2) (sn bhd & reminders: hmpd over 2f out: eased)	15	**10**	25/1	—	—
	African-Pard (IRE) (55) (DHaydnJones) **5-8-13** AClark(7) (outpcd & bhd fr ½-wy: eased)	5	**11**	25/1	—	—
	So Amazing (68) (JLEyre) **5-9-12** TWilliams(4) (led: hdd over 2f out: sn collapsed & fell: dead)		**F**	7/1 ^{3}	—	—

(SP 130.2%) **12 Rn**

1m 47.9 (8.90) CSF £104.10 CT £259.92 TOTE £10.90: £6.70 £2.90 £1.10 (£17.00) Trio £107.10 OWNER The Bibby Halliday Partnership (PRESTON) BRED Sheikh Mohammed bin Rashid al Maktoum
LONG HANDICAP Spanish Stripper (USA) 7-7

T/Jkpt: Not won; £23,409.76 to Wolverhampton 11/1/97. T/Plpt: £282.00 (46.53 Tckts). T/Qdpt: £32.20 (42.3 Tckts). WG

0057-LINGFIELD (L-H) (Standard)
Saturday January 11th

Vis: poor race 6
WEATHER: mist & drizzle WIND: almost nil

73 TYRONE MAIDEN STKS (4-Y.O+) (Class D)

12-50 (12-51) **1m 5f (Equitrack)** £3,582.50 (£1,085.00: £530.00: £252.50) Stalls: High GOING minus 0.32 sec per fur (FST)

				SP	RR	SF
	Classy Chief (66) (JWhite) **4-9-0** CRutter(13) (lw: dwlt: sn in tch: led over 2f out: clr over 1f out: r.o wl)	—	**1**	20/1	62	27
9^{5}	**Nawaji (USA) (36)** (WRMuir) **4-8-9** AClark(11) (rr: hdwy 4f out: rdn over 2f out: styd on strly to go 2nd ins fnl f)	3½	**2**	16/1	53	18
28^{6}	**Soviet King (IRE) (50)** (PMitchell) **4-9-0** WRyan(8) (rr: sme hdwy 6f out: rdn 3f out: styd on one pce fnl 2f)	1½	**3**	20/1	56	21
	River Captain (USA) (DJGMurraySmith) **4-9-0** GCarter(10) (prom: chsd wnr over 2f out to 1f out: no ex ins fnl f)	2½	**4**	12/1	53	18
	Random Kindness (74) (RIngram) **4-9-0** JStack(6) (bit bkwd: led 7f out: hdd over 2f out: wknd over 1f out)	2½	**5**	15/2 ^{3}	50	15
	Dutch Dyane (GPEnright) **4-8-9** NAdams(7) (b: b.hind: nvr nrr)	7	**6**	50/1	36	1
	Adilov (36) (JJBridger) **5-9-0**$^{(5)}$ ADaly(12) (lw: prom tl wknd over 3f out)	½	**7**	20/1	41	11
	Hayling-Billy (PRHedger) **4-9-0** DBiggs(3) (a bhd)	9	**8**	50/1	29	—
	Turia (65) (NAGraham) **4-8-9** DHarrison(9) (bhd fnl 5f)	nk	**9**	10/1	24	—
	Perfect Pal (IRE) (MissGayKelleway) **6-9-5** SSanders(4) (b: prom: rdn 6f out: wknd 4f out)	4	**10**	5/6 ^{1}	24	—
	Slippery Fin (46) (WGMTurner) **5-9-0b** TSprake(5) (bhd fnl 8f: t.o)	dist	**11**	20/1	—	—
	Warning Reef (80) (CLPopham) **4-9-0** SDWilliams(2) (lw: led 6f: sn wknd: t.o)	25	**12**	4/1 ^{2}	—	—
28^{11}	**Double Indemnity (IRE)** (GCBravery) **4-9-0** DWright(1) (b.nr hind: prom 4f: sn wknd: t.o)	dist	**13**	50/1	—	—

(SP 133.9%) **13 Rn**

2m 49.42 (7.42) CSF £291.60 TOTE £44.90: £3.90 £3.10 £3.30 (£398.50) Trio £263.20 OWNER Mr Keith Sturgis (ASTON ROWANT) BRED The Lavington Stud
WEIGHT FOR AGE 4yo-5lb
OFFICIAL EXPLANATION Perfect Pal (IRE): suffered a cut on his off-fore.

74 ARMAGH H'CAP (0-70) (4-Y.O+) (Class E)

1-25 (1-25) **1m 4f (Equitrack)** £2,869.25 (£869.00: £424.50: £202.25) Stalls: Low GOING minus 0.32 sec per fur (FST)

				SP	RR	SF
23^{2}	**General Haven (74)** (TJNaughton) **4-10-0** TSprake(7) (hld up in tch: led over 3f out: hrd rdn over 1f out: r.o wl)	—	**1**	9/4 ^{1}	85	40
47^{9}	**Harlequin Walk (IRE) (48)** (RJO'Sullivan) **6-8-6** DHarrison(4) (chsd ldr: led 5f out: hdd over 3f out: one pce)	3½	**2**	7/1	54	13
	Seattle Alley (USA) (68) (PRWebber) **4-9-8** WRyan(5) (hld up: hdwy over 3f out: sn rdn: one pce)	2½	**3**	9/1	71	26
	Father Dan (IRE) (61) (MissGayKelleway) **8-9-5** SSanders(6) (lw: hld up: rdn 5f out: kpt on one pce fnl 2f)	s.h	**4**	11/4 ^{2}	64	23
	Rehaab (66) (DMorris) **4-9-1**$^{(5)}$ GFaulkner(8) (prom: rdn 3f out: wknd over 1f out)	4	**5**	10/1	64	19
	State Approval (62) (PEccles) **4-9-2** GCarter(2) (led: hdd 5f out: sn wknd)	15	**6**	9/2 ^{3}	40	—
	Bakers Daughter (55) (JRArnold) **5-8-13** AClark(3) (hld up: rdn over 4f out: wknd 3f out)	4	**7**	14/1	27	—

(SP 113.9%) **7 Rn**

2m 36.9 (6.90) CSF £16.75 CT £107.02 TOTE £3.70: £1.90 £2.90 (£7.90) OWNER Mr A. Callard (EPSOM) BRED Stetchworth Park Stud Ltd
WEIGHT FOR AGE 4yo-4lb

75 ANTRIM LIMITED STKS (0-60) (3-Y.O) (Class F)

1-55 (1-55) **5f (Equitrack)** £2,394.80 (£672.80: £328.40) Stalls: Low GOING minus 0.32 sec per fur (FST)

				SP	RR	SF
	Hever Golf Lover (IRE) (59) (TJNaughton) **3-8-11** GCarter(2) (lw: mde all: rdn ins fnl f: r.o)	—	**1**	8/13[1]	63	12
	Come Too Mamma's (60) (JBerry) **3-8-6**(5) PFessey(3) (lw: dwlt: sn pushed along: hdwy 3f out: chsd wnr 2f out: rdn over 1f out: unable qckn)	1	**2**	4/1[3]	60	9
	Seretse's Nephew (56) (SCWilliams) **3-9-0** SSanders(1) (w wnr 2f: wknd wl over 1f out)	7	**3**	100/30[2]	40	—
25[8]	**Calchou (55)** (CWFairhurst) **3-8-8** RLappin(4) (in tch to ½-wy)	9	**4**	25/1	6	—

(SP 108.8%) **4 Rn**

61.56 secs (3.36) CSF £3.29 TOTE £1.30 (£2.00) OWNER Hever Racing Club (EPSOM) BRED Dr Michael Smurfit

76 DOWN CLAIMING STKS (4-Y.O+) (Class E)

2-30 (2-32) **1m 2f (Equitrack)** £2,908.25 (£881.00: £430.50: £205.25) Stalls: Low GOING minus 0.32 sec per fur (FST)

				SP	RR	SF
	Arcatura (56) (CJames) **5-8-12** CRutter(13) (hld up: hdwy ½-wy: led 3f out: r.o wl)	—	**1**	5/1[3]	68	30
54[3]	**Bon Secret (IRE) (65)** (TJNaughton) **5-8-9**(3) JDSmith(7) (chsd ldrs: rdn over 2f out: styd on one pce ins fnl f)	3½	**2**	4/1[1]	62	24
	Zacaroon (45) (JFfitch-Heyes) **6-8-4** DBiggs(10) (b.hind: a.p: rdn over 2f: one pce)	1	**3**	33/1	53	15
	Media Express (43) (MrsLStubbs) **5-8-6b[1]** TSprake(2) (dwlt: hdwy 4f out: rdn over 2f out: styd on one pce)	hd	**4**	50/1	55	17
10[7]	**Our Eddie (50)** (BGubby) **8-7-12v**(5) PFessey(9) (hld up: hdwy 5f out: rdn over 3f out: kpt on one pce fnl 2f)	nk	**5**	9/2[2]	51	13
	Honestly (51) (BSmart) **4-8-8** SSanders(5) (in tch: rdn & outpcd 4f out: kpt on one pce fnl 2f)	2½	**6**	11/2	54	14
22[3]	**Il Trastevere (FR) (65)** (MissGayKelleway) **5-9-2**(5) GFaulkner(6) (b: b.hind: led: hdd 3f out: wknd over 1f out)	1¾	**7**	10/1	62	24
	Areish (IRE) (40) (JFfitch-Heyes) **4-7-10b** NAdams(1) (dwlt: nvr nrr)	4	**8**	33/1	33	—
22[10]	**Memory's Music (46)** (MMadgwick) **5-8-12** AClark(11) (prom 6f)	¾	**9**	50/1	46	8
	Te Amo (IRE) (60) (MCPipe) **5-8-12** DHarrison(14) (lw: in tch to ½-wy)	1¼	**10**	4/1[1]	44	6
	Little Pilgrim (32) (TMJones) **4-8-2**(5) ADaly(12) (dwlt: a bhd)	1	**11**	50/1	39	—
	Bath Knight (47) (DJSffrenchDavis) **4-8-4** GCarter(8) (b.hind: prom to ½-wy)	9	**12**	12/1	22	—
	Kentavrus Way (IRE) (35) (AMoore) **6-8-9** CandyMorris(4) (prom over 3f)	1¾	**13**	25/1	22	—
	Fiery Footsteps (34) (CLPopham) **5-7-12** DWright(3) (a bhd)	½	**14**	50/1	10	—

(SP 124.6%) **14 Rn**

2m 9.41 (5.11) CSF £24.59 TOTE £6.60: £1.90 £1.40 £9.70 (£13.50) Trio £311.50; £350.99 to 13/1/97 OWNER Mrs Carol Welch (NEWBURY) BRED Benham Stud

WEIGHT FOR AGE 4yo-2lb

77 LONDONDERRY H'CAP (0-60) (3-Y.O F) (Class F)

3-00 (3-01) **7f (Equitrack)** £2,428.40 (£682.40: £333.20) Stalls: Low GOING minus 0.32 sec per fur (FST)

				SP	RR	SF
	Mystery (44) (SDow) **3-8-6**(5) ADaly(5) (a.p: led gng wl over 3f out: clr 2f out: easily)	—	**1**	3/1[1]	57+	21
8[3]	**Lily Jaques (54)** (RGuest) **3-9-7** DBiggs(4) (hld up: hdwy to chse wnr over 2f out: sn rdn: no imp)	6	**2**	7/2[2]	53	17
44[3]	**Windborn (54)** (CNAllen) **3-9-2**(5) GFaulkner(2) (in tch: rdn 5f out: one pce fnl 3f)	6	**3**	7/2[2]	40	4
	Wedding Music (48) (PCHaslam) **3-9-1** GCarter(3) (led 5f out: hdd over 3f out: wknd over 2f out)	10	**4**	9/2[3]	11	—
	Run Lucy Run (52) (MissGayKelleway) **3-9-5b[1]** SSanders(1) (led 2f: wknd over 3f out)	1¾	**5**	7/2[2]	11	—

(SP 109.8%) **5 Rn**

1m 28.49 (4.09) CSF £12.47 TOTE £4.70: £1.40 £1.90 (£4.80) OWNER Mrs G. R. Smith (EPSOM) BRED G. R. Smith (Thriplow) Ltd

78 FERMANAGH AMATEUR H'CAP (0-70) (4-Y.O+) (Class E)

3-30 (3-37) **2m (Equitrack)** £2,804.25 (£849.00: £414.50: £197.25) Stalls: Low GOING minus 0.32 sec per fur (FST)

				SP	RR	SF
	Hattaafeh (IRE) (54) (MissBSanders) **6-10-9**(7) MissLSheen(1) (hld up: hdwy 5f out: led 1f out: pushed out)	—	**1**	5/1[3]	66	34
	Pedaltothemetal (IRE) (44) (PMitchell) **5-10-6** MrRThornton(9) (hld up: rdn 5f out: hdwy 3f out: led over 2f out: hdd 1f out: r.o)	½	**2**	11/2	56	24
	Guest Alliance (IRE) (59) (AMoore) **5-11-2**(5) MrsJMoore(3) (hld up: hdwy on outside 3f out: sn rdn: styd on ins fnl f)	1½	**3**	4/1[2]	69	37
	Ela Man Howa (50) (ABailey) **6-10-5**(7) MissALHutchinson(6) (mid div: rdn over 3f out: kpt on one pce ins fnl f)	1	**4**	12/1	59	27
43[4]	**Persian Bud (IRE) (31)** (JRBosley) **9-9-4e**(3) MrsSBosley(5) (chsd ldrs: led over 3f out: hdd over 2f out: wknd over 1f out)	3½	**5**	16/1	37	5
	Code Red (53) (WRMuir) **4-10-1b[1]**(7) MissSNewby-Vincent(2) (mid div: rdn over 4f out: one pce)	5	**6**	14/1	54	15
22[5]	**Al Haal (USA) (46)** (RJO'Sullivan) **8-10-1**(7) MrJGoldstein(11) (led after 3f: hdd over 3f out: sn wknd)	6	**7**	12/1	41	9
	Stalled (IRE) (54) (PTWalwyn) **7-10-11**(5) MarchionessBlandford(8) (a bhd)	15	**8**	15/8[1]	34	2
	Zuno Flyer (USA) (50) (AMoore) **5-10-12** MrsAPerrett(10) (b.hind: led 3f: wknd 7f out)	10	**9**	10/1	20	—
	Little Luke (IRE) (38) (PButler) **6-9-7**(7) MrIMongan(4) (bhd from ½-wy: t.o)	dist	**10**	33/1	—	—
	Ismeno (48) (SDow) **6-10-5**(5) MrSFetherstonhaugh(7) (Withdrawn not under Starter's orders: broke out of stalls)		**W**	11/2	—	—

(SP 142.2%) **10 Rn**

3m 34.65 (13.65) CSF £33.20 CT £115.11 TOTE £7.00: £2.40 £2.20 £2.40 (£16.10) Trio £32.30 OWNER Mrs P. J. Sheen (EPSOM) BRED Sheikh Ahmed bin Rashid al Maktoum in Ireland

WEIGHT FOR AGE 4yo-7lb

IN-FOCUS: The winning rider Laura Sheen was having her first ride in public.

T/Plpt: £453.70 (31.15 Tckts). T/Qdpt: £19.50 (79 Tckts). SM

0049-WOLVERHAMPTON (L-H) (Standard)
Saturday January 11th
WEATHER: drizzle WIND: mod half bhd

79 JUPITER H'CAP (0-65) (3-Y.O+) (Class F)
1-20 (1-27) **5f (Fibresand)** £2,484.40 (£698.40: £341.20) Stalls: Low GOING minus 0.24 sec per fur (FST)

				SP	RR	SF
53^{*}	**Sotonian (HOL) (37)** (PSFelgate) **4-7-7**(7) 7x JBramhill(4) (lw: mde all: reminder ½-wy: r.o wl)	—	1	$3/1^{1}$	50	24
20^{3}	**Aljaz (48)** (MissGayKelleway) **7-8-8**(3) FLynch(1) (a.p: effrt u.p appr fnl f: nt pce to chal)	2	2	$9/2^{2}$	55	29
4^{4}	**Belinda Blue (37)** (RAFahey) **5-8-0** FNorton(3) (a.p: hrd drvn wl over 1f out: nvr able to chal)	3½	3	$6/1^{3}$	32	6
58^{7}	**Boffy (IRE) (55)** (BPJBaugh) **4-9-4b** RPerham(5) (chsd wnr over 3f: sn rdn: one pce)	2	4	7/1	44	18
69^{4}	**Sir Tasker (40)** (JLHarris) **9-8-3** LCharnock(6) (chsd ldrs: rdn 2f out: nvr nr to chal)	½	5	20/1	27	1
	Hurgill Times (63) (DShaw) **3-8-11** JFanning(2) (nvr nr to chal)	2½	6	33/1	42	1
31^{5}	**Gad Yakoun (60)** (MGMeagher) **4-9-9** MWigham(10) (s.s: a outpcd)	1¾	7	20/1	34	8
	Walk the Beat (65) (MartynMeade) **7-9-9**(5) DSweeney(9) (bit bkwd: trckd ldrs: drvn along ½-wy: no imp)	1	8	16/1	36	10
	Suite Factors (54) (KRBurke) **3-8-2** SDrowne(7) (outpcd: t.o)	6	9	20/1	5	—
	Victoria Sioux (40) (JAPickering) **4-8-3** NCarlisle(8) (bit bkwd: outpcd: t.o)	¾	10	33/1	—	—
25^{6}	**Enchantica (58)** (JBerry) **3-7-13**(7) CLowther(13) (b.hind: outpcd: t.o)	6	11	16/1	—	—
	Cheeky Chappy (57) (DWChapman) **6-9-6b** ACulhane(11) (sn outpcd: a bhd: t.o)	5	12	10/1	—	—
4^{7}	***Honeyhall* (36)** (NBycroft) **4-7-13** JQuinn(12) (Withdrawn not under Starter's orders: broke out of stall)		W	25/1	—	—

(SP 114.8%) **12 Rn**

61.3 secs (2.40) CSF £14.84 CT £63.01 TOTE £3.70: £1.80 £2.10 £1.30 (£6.00) Trio £15.50 OWNER Mr Tim Dean (MELTON MOWBRAY) BRED Stal de Kraal
WEIGHT FOR AGE 3yo-15lb

80 RUSSELL BALDWIN & BRIGHT DUNSTALL PARK BREEZE-UP SALE CLAIMING STKS (4-Y.O+) (Class E)
1-50 (1-55) **1m 6f 166y (Fibresand)** £2,765.25 (£837.00: £408.50: £194.25) Stalls: High GOING minus 0.24 sec per fur (FST)

				SP	RR	SF
22^{9}	**Stonecutter** (MRChannon) **4-8-10v** RPerham(1) (mde all: drvn clr 3f out: hld on wl fnl f)	—	1	14/1	62	17
	Royal Citizen (IRE) (58) (JFBottomley) **8-9-8** LCharnock(2) (b: hld up in tch: hdwy 4f out: chsd wnr over 2f out: styd on)	1½	2	9/1	66	27
30^{7}	**In the Money (IRE) (51)** (RHollinshead) **8-9-3**(3) FLynch(3) (prom: drvn along over 3f out: sn btn)	15	3	$4/1^{3}$	48	9
18^{3}	**Threesocks (42)** (BSmart) **4-8-5** JQuinn(7) (lw: hld up: hdwy over 6f out: nt rch ldrs)	2	4	$7/2^{2}$	37	—
	Biya (IRE) (DMcCain) **5-9-4** VSlattery(5) (lw: hld up: effrt 4f out: one pce fnl 3f)	6	5	33/1	37	—
22^{2}	**Soldier Cove (USA) (50)** (MartynMeade) **7-8-9**(7) TField(8) (trckd ldrs: rdn 4f out: sn wknd)	6	6	5/1	29	—
	Astral Invasion (USA) (GMMcCourt) **6-8-7b**(7) RStudholme(9) (lost pl ½-wy: sn t.o)	15	7	16/1	11	—
	Eulogy (FR) (64) (KRBurke) **10-9-4** SDrowne(10) (dropped rr after 5f: sn rdn: no imp: t.o)	16	8	$5/2^{1}$	—	—
18^{10}	**Chilly Lad (41)** (RTJuckes) **6-8-12** ACulhane(12) (bit bkwd: a in rr: t.o)	22	9	20/1	—	—
	Garlandhayes (MissKMGeorge) **5-8-2**(7) JBramhill(6) (bkwd: s.i.s: a bhd: t.o)	17	10	50/1	—	—

(SP 119.7%) **10 Rn**

3m 18.6 (11.20) CSF £121.92 TOTE £12.90: £2.60 £3.10 £1.50 (£22.60) Trio £109.70 OWNER Miss S. Deburiatte (UPPER LAMBOURN) BRED Worksop Manor Stud Farm
WEIGHT FOR AGE 4yo-6lb

81 TOTE ALL-WEATHER LIMITED STKS (0-70) (4-Y.O+) (Class E)
2-20 (2-20) **7f (Fibresand)** £2,726.25 (£825.00: £402.50: £191.25) Stalls: High GOING minus 0.24 sec per fur (FST)

				SP	RR	SF
51^{5}	**Little Ibnr (66)** (PDEvans) **6-8-5**(7) AnthonyBond(3) (a.p: led over 4f out tl over 2f out: r.o strly to ld fnl 50y)	—	1	10/1	69	20
35^{*}	**Elite Hope (USA) (75)** (NTinkler) **5-9-1**(3) FLynch(8) (a.p: led over 2f out tl hdd & no ex wl ins fnl f)	nk	2	$6/4^{1}$	74	25
40^{4}	**Desert Invader (IRE) (70)** (DWChapman) **6-8-12** ACulhane(2) (prom: drvn along & outpcd ½-wy: rallied fnl f)	hd	3	$4/1^{3}$	68	19
10^{6}	**Manabar (58)** (MJPolglase) **5-8-12** TGMcLaughlin(5) (chsd ldrs: rdn wl over 1f out: one pce)	2½	4	20/1	62	13
23^{7}	**Set the Fashion (57)** (DLWilliams) **8-8-13v**(5) DGriffiths(4) (hld up: hdwy 2f out: nt pce to chal)	¾	5	20/1	67	18
	Myttons Mistake (67) (ABailey) **4-8-5**(7) IonaWands(7) (hld up: hdwy over 3f out: sn rdn: nt rch ldrs)	2	6	9/2	56	7
	Failed To Hit (65) (NPLittmoden) **4-8-10v**(5) DSweeney(6) (dwlt: a bhd & outpcd)	2½	7	33/1	53	4
	Miss Offset (70) (MJohnston) **4-8-12b** JWeaver(1) (lw: led over 2f: rdn & wknd ent st: t.o)	dist	8	$100/30^{2}$	—	—

(SP 122.8%) **8 Rn**

1m 29.6 (4.90) CSF £26.35 TOTE £9.20: £1.20 £1.30 £1.40 (£7.90) OWNER Swinnerton Transport Ltd (WELSHPOOL) BRED R. E. Waugh

82 PERTEMPS H'CAP (0-90) (4-Y.O+) (Class C)
2-50 (2-51) **1m 100y (Fibresand)** £5,181.25 (£1,570.00: £767.50: £366.25) Stalls: Low GOING minus 0.24 sec per fur (FST)

				SP	RR	SF
1^{*}	**Anonym (IRE) (63)** (DNicholls) **5-7-8b**(7) JBramhill(4) (hld up gng wl: stdy hdwy 3f out: led appr fnl f: pushed out)	—	1	$11/2^{2}$	74	39
	Sabot (90) (CWThornton) **4-10-0** DeanMcKeown(7) (chsd ldrs: effrt 3f out: ev ch 1f out: unable qckn)	2	2	20/1	97	62
	Punkah (USA) (75) (GMMcCourt) **4-8-6**(7)ow2 RStudholme(5) (bit bkwd: a.p: led 4f out tl appr fnl f: one pce)	1½	3	16/1	79	42
	Star Talent (USA) (69) (MissGayKelleway) **6-8-0**(7) AngelaGallimore(9) (hld up: gd hdwy over 3f out: nrst fin)	1¾	4	8/1	70	35
34^{2}	**Three Weeks (61)** (WRMuir) **4-7-13** JQuinn(3) (lw: chsd ldrs: rdn over 2f out: one pce)	1½	5	$9/2^{1}$	59	24
	Pater Noster (USA) (90) (JohnHarris) **8-10-0** SDrowne(6) (b: bkwd: prom tl wknd wl over 1f out)	s.h	6	8/1	88	53
56^{5}	**Duke Valentino (82)** (RHollinshead) **5-9-1**(5) DGriffiths(10) (hld up: hdwy 5f out: rdn & wknd over 2f out)	1¼	7	10/1	78	43
	Nashaat (USA) (78) (KRBurke) **9-8-11**(5) RPainter(2) (nvr nr to chal)	2½	8	14/1	69	34
56^{2}	**Super High (83)** (PHowling) **5-9-7b** FNorton(12) (a in rr: hrd drvn 3f out: no imp)	½	9	$6/1^{3}$	73	38
	Amber Valley (USA) (58) (DLWilliams) **6-7-10** LCharnock(8) (a in rr)	3	10	50/1	42	7
34^{4}	**Beauman (58)** (PDEvans) **7-7-7**(3) MBaird(11) (a in rr: t.o)	6	11	10/1	31	—
34^{3}	**Suga Hawk (IRE) (58)** (EJAlston) **5-7-7**(3) NVarley(1) (led over 4f: sn rdn & wknd: t.o)	9	12	10/1	14	—

35[4] **Live Project (IRE) (60)** (MJohnston) **5-7-12** TWilliams(13) (hdwy ½-wy: eased whn btn over 2f out: t.o) .... **13** 12/1 — —
(SP 124.3%) **13 Rn**

1m 47.9 (2.90) CSF £99.33 CT £1,537.57 TOTE £8.00: £2.90 £5.30 £2.70 (£465.20) Trio £392.70; £331.89 to 11/1/97 OWNER Wetherby Racing Bureau Ltd (THIRSK) BRED T. G. Mooney
LONG HANDICAP Beauman 7-6 Suga Hawk (IRE) 7-7 Amber Valley (USA) 7-9

83 WEATHERBYS GROUP MAIDEN STKS (3-Y.O+) (Class D)

3-20 (3-24) **1m 1f 79y (Fibresand)** £3,468.75 (£1,050.00: £512.50: £243.75) Stalls: Low GOING minus 0.24 sec per fur (FST)

Form	Horse / details	Dist	Pos	SP	RR	SF
28[3]	**Tallulah Belle (46)** (NPLittmoden) **4-9-7** TGMcLaughlin(9) (chsd ldrs: hdwy to ld wl over 1f out: drvn clr)	—	**1**	10/1	62	46
2[5]	**Prophets Honour (67)** (PCHaslam) **5-9-13** SDrowne(6) (led 4f: rdn & outpcd ent st: styd on u.p fnl f)	4	**2**	9/2[3]	60	45
9[3]	**Hazel (46)** (MissGayKelleway) **5-9-8v[1]** JWeaver(3) (trckd ldrs: effrt & rdn over 2f out: r.o one pce)	1¾	**3**	9/2[3]	52	37
	Touch'n'go (MJohnston) **3-8-5** TWilliams(7) (w ldr: led over 5f out tl over 1f out: hrd rdn: sn btn)	nk	**4**	20/1	57	20
	Move The Clouds (JRFanshawe) **3-7-11**(3) NVarley(8) (prom: ev ch whn rdn & swished tail over 2f out: nt run on)	7	**5**	3/1[1]	40	3
	Flagstaff (USA) (42) (KRBurke) **4-9-12** ACulhane(10) (lw: nvr nr to chal)	1¼	**6**	33/1	43	27
28[2]	**Holders Hill (IRE) (65)** (MGMeagher) **5-9-13** JQuinn(11) (hld up: hdwy 5f out: rdn & wknd over 3f out: t.o)	6	**7**	7/2[2]	32	17
	Tango Man (IRE) (RJPrice) **5-9-13** FNorton(1) (s.s: a in rr: t.o)	1	**8**	50/1	31	16
	Name of Our Father (USA) (60) (PBowen) **4-9-12**) RJohnson(4) (trckd ldrs mid div: hrd drvn ½-wy: sn lost tch: t.o)	1	**9**	13/2	29	13
	Kulepopsie (IRE) (ABMulholland) **4-9-7** VHalliday(5) (a bhd: t.o)	12	**10**	50/1	3	—
	Pridewood Picker (RJPrice) **10-9-13** RPerham(2) (a in rr: t.o)	5	**11**	20/1	—	—

(SP 122.4%) **11 Rn**

2m 0.6 (4.60) CSF £53.11 TOTE £13.90: £1.70 £2.00 £1.40 (£39.40) Trio £29.80 OWNER Trojan Racing (WOLVERHAMPTON) BRED Bowler (Presswork) Services Ltd
WEIGHT FOR AGE 3yo-22lb, 4yo-1lb

84 CORAL H'CAP (0-80) (3-Y.O) (Class D)

3-50 (3-50) **1m 1f 79y (Fibresand)** £3,355.00 (£1,015.00: £495.00: £235.00) Stalls: Low GOING minus 0.24 sec per fur (FST)

Form	Horse / details	Dist	Pos	SP	RR	SF
	Millroy (USA) (80) (PAKelleway) **3-9-7v[1]** MWigham(7) (a.p: led over 3f out: sn clr: drvn out)	—	**1**	3/1[2]	91	44
46*	**Chateauherault (IRE) (61)** (PCHaslam) **3-8-2** 5x SDrowne(5) (sn pushed along & bhd: hdwy 4f out: chsd wnr fnl 2f: no imp)	4	**2**	5/4[1]	65	18
	Silent Valley (55) (DNicholls) **3-7-3b**(7) JBramhill(1) (a chsng ldrs: rdn & one pce fnl 2f)	3½	**3**	8/1	53	6
33[4]	**Skelton Sovereign (IRE) (58)** (RHollinshead) **3-7-13** NCarlisle(3) (nvr trbld ldrs)	nk	**4**	6/1[3]	56	9
	Mutahadeth (62) (DShaw) **3-8-3** JFanning(2) (hld up: hdwy over 4f out: rdn & wknd wl over 2f out)	1	**5**	16/1	58	11
41[4]	**State of Gold (IRE) (56)** (JHetherton) **3-7-11b[1]** NKennedy(4) (mde most tl hdd & wknd over 3f out: t.o)	7	**6**	20/1	40	—
	Danehill Princess (IRE) (57) (RHollinshead) **3-7-12b[1]** JQuinn(6) (s.s: sn rcvrd to press ldrs: rdn & lost pl ½-wy: t.o)	hd	**7**	14/1	41	—

(SP 112.2%) **7 Rn**

2m 0.8 (4.80) CSF £6.87 TOTE £4.80: £1.60 £1.80 (£2.70) OWNER Exors of the late Mr R B Belderson (NEWMARKET) BRED Cilia Farm
LONG HANDICAP Silent Valley 7-3

T/Jkpt: Not won; £38,941.68 to Southwell 11/1/97. T/Plpt: £414.10 (71.07 Tckts). T/Qdpt: £55.50 (41.33 Tckts). IM

0065-SOUTHWELL (L-H) (Standard)
Monday January 13th

WEATHER: fine but cloudy WIND: mod across

85 FAIR ISLE H'CAP (0-65) (I) (4-Y.O+) (Class F)

12-55 (12-57) **1m (Fibresand)** £1,944.00 (£544.00: £264.00) Stalls: Low GOING: 0.35 sec per fur (SLW)

Form	Horse / details	Dist	Pos	SP	RR	SF
14[6]	**Chadleigh Lane (USA) (59)** (RHollinshead) **5-9-7**(3) FLynch(6) (in tch: effrt 3 out: led 1½f out: styd on wl)	—	**1**	6/1[2]	72	49
9[4]	**Ilandra (IRE) (43)** (RAkehurst) **5-8-8** SSanders(9) (mde most tl hdd 1½f out: no ex)	5	**2**	11/4[1]	46	23
	The Barnsley Belle (IRE) (55) (JLEyre) **4-9-6** TWilliams(3) (lw: outpcd & lost tch ½-wy: swtchd wd 2f out: styd on towards fin)	1	**3**	6/1[2]	56	33
	Shanoora (IRE) (37) (MrsNMacauley) **4-8-2** JQuinn(10) (hdwy 2f out: styd on: no imp)	s.h	**4**	25/1	38	15
47[10]	**Zahran (IRE) (43)** (JMBradley) **6-8-8** LCharnock(4) (in tch: pushed along most of wy: no imp fnl 3f)	3½	**5**	10/1[3]	37	14
42*	**Down The Yard (34)** (MCChapman) **4-7-6**(7)ow3 RBrisland(1) (lw: disp ld 3f: chsd ldrs tl wknd fnl 2f)	s.h	**6**	11/4[1]	28	2
54[11]	**Alana's Ballad (IRE) (33)** (BPJBaugh) **4-7-5**(7)ow2 JBramhill(8) (s.i.s: hdwy to chal over 3f out: wknd wl over 1f out)	1¾	**7**	50/1	23	—
4[6]	**Time Clash (41)** (BPalling) **4-8-6**ow3 AClark(7) (bhd: effrt over 3f out: n.d)	5	**8**	16/1	21	—
15[13]	**Ring the Chief (35)** (MDIUsher) **5-8-0** NCarlisle(5) (hld up: effrt over 2f out: nvr nr to chal)	3	**9**	12/1	9	—
42[3]	**Efipetite (40)** (NBycroft) **4-8-5** GBardwell(2) (s.i.s: hdwy & prom ½-wy: wknd over 2f out)	8	**10**	12/1	—	—

(SP 118.1%) **10 Rn**

1m 47.6 (8.60) CSF £22.02 CT £98.04 TOTE £6.50: £1.50 £1.10 £2.70 (£14.80) Trio £29.30 OWNER Mr J. E. Bigg (UPPER LONGDON) BRED Windwoods Farm, Bruce Brown and Connie Brown
LONG HANDICAP Alana's Ballad (IRE) 7-6
OFFICIAL EXPLANATION **Chadleigh Lane (USA): had been halted in his preparation for his previous run, due to the poor weather.**

86 BARRA MAIDEN APPRENTICE H'CAP (0-60) (4-Y.O+) (Class F)

1-25 (1-26) **1m 4f (Fibresand)** £2,294.00 (£644.00: £314.00) Stalls: Low GOING: 0.35 sec per fur (SLW)

Form	Horse / details	Dist	Pos	SP	RR	SF
16[2]	**Raffles Rooster (56)** (AGNewcombe) **5-9-10** JoHunnam(8) (hld up: stdy hdwy 3f out: qcknd to ld ins fnl f)	—	**1**	5/2[1]	66	33
16[9]	**Acerbus Dulcis (32)** (MCChapman) **6-8-0** IonaWands(7) (hdwy ½-wy: led 4f out tl ins fnl f: no ex)	1¼	**2**	66/1	40	7
	Toulston Lady (IRE) (38) (JWharton) **5-8-3v[1]**(3) VictoriaAppleby(14) (hdwy to chse ldrs ½-wy: ev ch 4f out: one pce)	4	**3**	16/1	41	8

				SP	RR	SF
16^{5}	**Mustang (35)** (CWThornton) **4-7-8**(5) AMcCarthy(12) (a chsng ldrs: one pce fnl 2f)	1	**4**	12/1	37	—
	Sheemore (IRE) (40) (MDHammond) **4-7-13**(5) CLowther(2) (a chsng ldrs: one pce fnl 4f)	hd	**5**	14/1	42	5
	Theme Arena (47) (MCPipe) **4-8-8**(3) CWebb(3) (bhd: hdwy over 3f out: nrst fin)	hd	**6**	9/2^{2}	48	11
29^{6}	**Red Tie Affair (USA) (43)** (JMBradley) **4-8-2**(5) AnthonyBond(4) (b: nvr trbld ldrs)	13	**7**	16/1	27	—
16^{4}	**Swandale Flyer (30)** (NBycroft) **5-7-12** JBramhill(6) (lw: in tch: rdn 6f out: no imp)	1¼	**8**	16/1	12	—
	Kaye's Secret (32) (JLHarris) **4-7-5**(5) JFowle(16) (sn bhd: sme hdwy fnl 3f: n.d)	¾	**9**	66/1	13	—
	Executive Officer (33) (RMFlower) **4-7-6**(5)ow1 RBrisland(13) (n.d)	s.h	**10**	20/1	14	—
2^{2}	**Hever Golf Eagle (49)** (TJNaughton) **4-8-13** GMilligan(11) (chsd clr ldrs: ev ch 4f out: wknd fnl 2½f)	s.h	**11**	8/1^{3}	30	—
	Amazing Sail (IRE) (53) (MissMKMilligan) **4-9-3** KSked(10) (in tch tl outpcd fnl 4f)	nk	**12**	33/1	34	—
37^{5}	**Impending Danger (38)** (KSBridgwater) **4-7-11**(5) RCody-Boutcher(5) (chsd ldrs tl wknd fnl 4f)	½	**13**	33/1	18	—
22^{6}	**Old Hush Wing (IRE) (45)** (PCHaslam) **4-8-2**(7) PGoode(9) (a bhd)	1	**14**	16/1	24	—
	Intrepid Fort (28) (BWMurray) **8-7-5b**(5) TFinn(15) (wnt prom after 4f: rdn 6f out: wknd over 3f out)	¾	**15**	16/1	6	—
	Miss Prism (55) (JLDunlop) **4-9-5b**1 DSweeney(17) (set str pce tl hdd & wknd qckly 4f out)	17	**16**	9/2^{2}	10	—
37^{3}	**Hornpipe (45)** (JWharton) **5-8-8b**(5) GGallagher(1) (b: disp ld tl wknd qckly over 4f out)	4	**17**	14/1	—	—
				(SP 140.1%)	**17 Rn**	

2m 48.7 (15.70) CSF £143.92 CT £2,227.05 TOTE £5.10: £1.10 £26.30 £8.20 £3.70 (£442.10) Trio £1,134.70; £319.64 to Leicester 14/1/97
OWNER Mr Mark Leatham (BARNSTAPLE) BRED G. Strawbridge & London Thoroughbred Services Ltd
LONG HANDICAP Intrepid Fort 7-6 Executive Officer 7-8 Kaye's Secret 7-6
WEIGHT FOR AGE 4yo-4lb

87 ISLE OF SKYE CLAIMING STKS (4-Y.O+) (Class F)

1-55 (1-55) **7f (Fibresand)** £2,294.00 (£644.00: £314.00) Stalls: Low GOING: 0.35 sec per fur (SLW)

				SP	RR	SF
	Jibereen (72) (PHowling) **5-9-7** DHarrison(8) (b: lw: trckd ldrs: led over 2f out: rdn & r.o)	—	**1**	5/2^{1}	79	63
14^{5}	**Afaan (IRE)** (RFMarvin) **4-8-13** TGMcLaughlin(7) (b: trckd ldrs: effrt over 2f out: styd on: nt pce of wnr)	5	**2**	14/1	60	44
65^{5}	**Bold Aristocrat (IRE) (60)** (RHollinshead) **6-8-4**(3) FLynch(9) (trckd ldrs: effrt over 2f out: styd on: nvr able to chal)	nk	**3**	7/1	53	37
71^{3}	**Sea Devil (67)** (MJCamacho) **11-8-3** LCharnock(4) (chsd ldrs: rdn 3f out: r.o one pce)	½	**4**	100/30^{2}	48	32
3*	**Dahiyah (USA) (57)** (BSmart) **6-9-0v** SSanders(5) (lw: cl up tl outpcd fnl 2f)	4	**5**	7/2^{3}	50	34
	Answers-To-Thomas (52) (JMJefferson) **4-8-11** DeanMcKeown(3) (led tl hdd over 2f out: grad wknd)	4	**6**	33/1	38	22
	Time To Fly (34) (BWMurray) **4-8-7**ow1 VHalliday(1) (hld up: effrt 4f out: no imp)	8	**7**	50/1	15	—
	Sonya Marie (JGFitzGerald) **4-8-0** NKennedy(6) (s.i.s: rdn ½-wy: n.d)	8	**8**	20/1	—	—
51^{6}	**Double Oscar (IRE) (52)** (DNicholls) **4-8-6** MWigham(2) (sn pushed along & bhd)	16	**9**	8/1	—	—
				(SP 113.8%)	**9 Rn**	

1m 32.5 (6.00) CSF £32.07 TOTE £3.10: £1.30 £1.90 £1.50 (£12.40) Trio £48.90 OWNER Mr Peter Skelton (NEWMARKET) BRED Mrs J. Everitt

88 MULL H'CAP (0-70) (4-Y.O+) (Class E)

2-25 (2-26) **1m 3f (Fibresand)** £2,957.00 (£896.00: £438.00: £209.00) Stalls: Low GOING: 0.35 sec per fur (SLW)

				SP	RR	SF
39*	**China Castle (72)** (PCHaslam) **4-9-13** 5x SDrowne(11) (lw: a.p: led 1½f out: shkn up & r.o wl)	—	**1**	13/8^{1}	93	62
39^{3}	**Maftun (USA) (51)** (GMMoore) **5-8-9** ACulhane(8) (lw: cl up: led after 3f to 1½f out: no ch w wnr)	9	**2**	8/1	59	31
	Wildfire (SWI) (46) (RAkehurst) **6-8-4** SSanders(3) (b: a chsng ldrs: one pce fnl 3f)	10	**3**	7/1^{3}	39	11
	Manful (70) (JHetherton) **5-10-0b** GCarter(5) (bhd: styd on fnl 4f: n.d)	3½	**4**	5/1^{2}	58	30
15^{11}	**Carol Again (42)** (NBycroft) **5-8-0** JQuinn(1) (hdwy ½-wy: rdn to chse ldrs 3f out: sn wknd)	7	**5**	16/1	20	—
82^{11}	**Beauman (54)** (PDEvans) **7-8-5**(7) AnthonyBond(14) (in tch: hdwy 4f out: outpcd fnl 2f)	nk	**6**	16/1	32	4
34^{5}	**Princely Affair (42)** (JMBradley) **4-7-11**ow1 LCharnock(10) (nvr trbld ldrs)	5	**7**	20/1	12	—
	Sarawat (69) (DNicholls) **9-9-13** AlexGreaves(9) (chsd ldr tl wknd fnl 3f)	½	**8**	9/1	39	11
	Nijmegen (65) (JGFitzGerald) **9-9-4**(5) GParkin(4) (b: bit bkwd: bhd: sme hdwy 3f out: n.d)	3½	**9**	16/1	30	2
16^{6}	**Burning Flame (42)** (RMFlower) **4-7-11**ow1 FNorton(13) (drvn along ½-wy: n.d)	1¼	**10**	25/1	5	—
	Total Rach (IRE) (49) (AGNewcombe) **5-8-4**(3) NVarley(6) (b: bhd: hdwy 5f out: wknd over 2f out)	12	**11**	20/1	—	—
	Pharly Reef (38) (DBurchell) **5-7-10** NCarlisle(12) (bhd fr ½-wy)	nk	**12**	14/1	—	—
39^{10}	**Noble Canonire (54)** (DShaw) **5-8-12** JFanning(2) (prom: pushed along after 2f: wknd 6f out)	15	**13**	25/1	—	—
	Ann's Music (43) (JMJefferson) **4-7-7**(5)ow2 PFessey(7) (led 3f: cl up tl wknd qckly 4f out)	hd	**14**	66/1	—	—
				(SP 131.4%)	**14 Rn**	

2m 30.6 (10.60) CSF £16.46 CT £76.37 TOTE £2.00: £1.40 £2.50 £2.70 (£9.50) Trio £24.50 OWNER Mr J. M. Davis (MIDDLEHAM) BRED Mrs Frances Cronin
LONG HANDICAP Burning Flame 6-13 Ann's Music 6-13
WEIGHT FOR AGE 4yo-3lb

89 LUNDY H'CAP (0-80) (3-Y.O+) (Class D)

2-55 (2-57) **6f (Fibresand)** £3,517.50 (£1,065.00: £520.00: £247.50) Stalls: Low GOING: 0.35 sec per fur (SLW)

				SP	RR	SF
71^{2}	**Elton Ledger (IRE) (70)** (MrsNMacauley) **8-9-4v** JWeaver(3) (b: hld up: stdy hdwy 2f out: led ins fnl f: drvn out)	—	**1**	4/1^{1}	75	57
15^{7}	**Awesome Venture (70)** (MCChapman) **7-9-4** SDrowne(6) (a cl up: disp ld 2f out: hdd ins fnl f: kpt on wl)	nk	**2**	14/1	74	56
81*	**Little Ibnr (73)** (PDEvans) **6-9-0**(7) 7x AnthonyBond(11) (a chsng ldrs: kpt on fnl f)	2½	**3**	10/1	71	53
	Chadwell Hall (73) (SRBowring) **6-9-7** SDWilliams(10) (led 2f: cl up: disp ld 2f out: no ex fnl f)	1	**4**	6/1^{3}	68	50
17*	**Brutal Fantasy (IRE) (74)** (JLEyre) **3-8-6** RLappin(4) (lw: cl up: led after 2f tl disp ld 2f out: wknd ins fnl f)	3	**5**	5/1^{2}	61	27
	Mr Frosty (80) (WJarvis) **5-10-0** SSanders(5) (lw: chsd ldrs: rdn & ch 2f out: wknd fnl f)	2½	**6**	5/1^{2}	60	42
	Ashgore (74) (JLEyre) **7-9-8** TWilliams(7) (sn outpcd & bhd: sme late hdwy)	2½	**7**	14/1	48	30
	Prima Silk (75) (MJRyan) **6-9-9** AClark(9) (sn pushed along & bhd: n.d)	2½	**8**	5/1^{2}	42	24
53^{4}	**Shadow Jury (69)** (DWChapman) **7-9-3b** LCharnock(2) (sn drvn along: chsd ldrs after 2f: wknd appr fnl f)	2	**9**	9/1	31	13
69^{5}	**Klipspinger (57)** (BSRothwell) **4-7-12b**(7) JBramhill(1) (nvr wnt pce)	3	**10**	12/1	11	—
	Broadstairs Beauty (IRE) (80) (DShaw) **7-9-11**(3) CTeague(8) (b: b.hind: bit bkwd: prom: hmpd after 2f: wknd over 2f out)	9	**11**	33/1	10	—
				(SP 127.3%)	**11 Rn**	

1m 18.9 (5.40) CSF £56.48 CT £506.31 TOTE £5.10: £1.50 £3.00 £4.70 (£54.90) Trio £214.10 OWNER The Posse (MELTON MOWBRAY) BRED Thomas Doherty
WEIGHT FOR AGE 3yo-16lb

90 SHETLAND (QUALIFIER) (S) STKS (3-Y.O) (Class G)

3-25 (3-25) **1m (Fibresand)** £2,085.00 (£585.00: £285.00) Stalls: Low GOING: 0.35 sec per fur (SLW)

				SP	RR	SF
	Mardrew (DJSffrenchDavis) **3-9-0** JQuinn(11) (neat: s.i.s: sn chsng ldrs: led wl over 1f out: r.o u.p)	—	**1**	$5/1^{2}$	75	37
41^{*}	**Aspecto Lad (IRE) (53)** (MJohnston) **3-9-5** JWeaver(6) (lw: in tch: hdwy 2f out: hung lft: nt pce to chal)	4	**2**	$5/1^{2}$	72	34
6^{2}	**Diamond Eyre (56)** (JLEyre) **3-8-9** RLappin(5) (outpcd ½-wy: hdwy u.p 2f out: nvr able to chal)	6	**3**	$6/4^{1}$	50	12
41^{3}	**Hoh Down (IRE) (48)** (KMcAuliffe) **3-8-9b¹** SSanders(8) (b.hind: hld up: effrt 3f out: rdn & no ex appr fnl f)	4	**4**	6/1	42	4
6^{4}	**Chasetown Flyer (USA) (56)** (RHollinshead) **3-8-11**(3) FLynch(2) (cl up: led after 3f tl wl over 1f out: wknd)	3	**5**	12/1	41	3
41^{2}	**Head Girl (IRE) (60)** (CWThornton) **3-9-0** DeanMcKeown(7) (led 3f: chsd ldrs: no imp fnl 2f)	s.h	**6**	$11/2^{3}$	41	3
6^{7}	**Indian Rapture (56)** (RonaldThompson) **3-8-6**(3) CTeague(1) (sn outpcd & bhd: n.d)	9	**7**	7/1	18	—
	Belushi (DMorley) **3-8-9** GCarter(12) (neat: chsd ldrs tl wknd fnl 2f)	¾	**8**	10/1	16	—
	Patrick (DBurchell) **3-9-0** NCarlisle(9) (leggy: s.i.s: sn prom: wknd fnl 2½f)	nk	**9**	25/1	21	—
	Lord High Emperor (DShaw) **3-9-0** SDWilliams(3) (leggy: unf: s.i.s: n.d)	5	**10**	33/1	11	—
	T-N-T Express (45) (EJAlston) **3-9-0** SDrowne(4) (prom tl outpcd after 3f: sn wknd)	6	**11**	33/1	—	—
41^{6}	**Pamela's Boy** (ASmith) **3-9-0** MWigham(10) (spd 3f: sn wknd)	26	**12**	66/1	—	—
				(SP 143.5%)	**12 Rn**	

1m 47.9 (8.90) CSF £34.67 TOTE £5.20: £1.30 £3.10 £1.50 (£22.50) Trio £44.00 OWNER Mrs Mary Moloney (UPPER LAMBOURN) BRED Cleaboy Farms Co
Bt in 9,200 gns

91 FAIR ISLE H'CAP (0-65) (II) (4-Y.O+) (Class F)

3-55 (3-56) **1m (Fibresand)** £1,944.00 (£544.00: £264.00) Stalls: Low GOING: 0.35 sec per fur (SLW)

				SP	RR	SF
72^{*}	**Gulf Shaadi (57)** (EJAlston) **5-9-6** 6x SDrowne(7) (lw: s.i.s: stdy hdwy ½-wy: led over 1f out: r.o)	—	**1**	$9/4^{2}$	73	55
36^{*}	**Broughton's Pride (IRE) (36)** (JLEyre) **6-7-13** TWilliams(2) (lw: led early: cl up: led 5f out tl appr fnl f: one pce)	3	**2**	$6/5^{1}$	46	28
72^{5}	**Spanish Stripper (USA) (33)** (MCChapman) **6-7-10** GBardwell(3) (swtg: chsd ldrs: rdn ½-wy: kpt on fnl 2f)	6	**3**	20/1	31	13
	Scenicris (IRE) (45) (RHollinshead) **4-8-5**(3) FLynch(9) (sn wl bhd: c wd st: r.o: nrst fin)	½	**4**	$5/1^{3}$	42	24
72^{10}	**Oneoftheoldones (63)** (JNorton) **5-9-9**(3) OPears(8) (chsd ldrs: outpcd ½-wy: no imp after)	4	**5**	50/1	52	34
	Mislemani (IRE) (50) (AGNewcombe) **7-8-8**(5) DGriffiths(6) (a chsng ldrs: one pce fnl 3f)	1½	**6**	12/1	36	18
36^{3}	**Supreme Illusion (AUS) (33)** (JohnBerry) **4-7-3b**(7) DarrenWilliams(5) (sn led: hdd 5f out: ev ch tl wknd over 2f out)	9	**7**	20/1	1	—
	Duffertoes (58) (MJRyan) **5-9-7** AClark(4) (chsd ldrs over 5f: wknd)	12	**8**	16/1	2	—
2^{8}	**The Oddfellow (35)** (NBycroft) **4-7-5**(7)ow2 JBramhill(10) (b.hind: outpcd ½-wy: sn bhd)	1	**9**	25/1	—	—
	Our Tom (54) (JWharton) **5-9-3b** JQuinn(1) (b: lw: outpcd & bhd fr ½-wy)	1½	**10**	12/1	—	—
				(SP 129.5%)	**10 Rn**	

1m 46.6 (7.60) CSF £5.83 CT £43.47 TOTE £3.90: £2.60 £1.10 £2.40 (£3.60) Trio £11.00 OWNER The Bibby Halliday Partnership (PRESTON) BRED Sheikh Mohammed bin Rashid al Maktoum
LONG HANDICAP Spanish Stripper (USA) 7-7 The Oddfellow 7-9 Supreme Illusion (AUS) 7-3

T/Jkpt: Not won; £58,629.63 to Carlisle 14/1/97. T/Plpt: £61.30 (342.75 Tckts). T/Qdpt: £14.60 (143.04 Tckts) AA

0073-LINGFIELD (L-H) (Standard)
Tuesday January 14th

WEATHER: sunny & misty WIND: almost nil

92 NEWPORT APPRENTICE H'CAP (0-70) (4-Y.O+) (Class F)

1-20 (1-21) **1m 2f (Equitrack)** £2,495.60 (£701.60: £342.80) Stalls: Low GOING minus 0.27 sec per fur (FST)

				SP	RR	SF
47^{8}	**Zamalek (USA) (41)** (RMFlower) **5-7-12e**(3)ow3 GMilligan(7) (hdwy over 6f out: led over 3f out: hrd rdn fnl f: r.o wl)	—	**1**	20/1	50	28
10^{*}	**Quiet Arch (IRE) (57)** (WRMuir) **4-8-10**(5) JWilkinson(6) (b: b.hind: hdwy over 6f out: ev ch fnl 4f: r.o)	nk	**2**	$15/8^{1}$	66	45
	Master Beveled (67) (PDEvans) **7-9-8**(5) AnthonyBond(1) (lw: a.p: hrd rdn over 2f out: unable qckn)	2½	**3**	$2/1^{2}$	72	53
	In Cahoots (46) (AGNewcombe) **4-8-1**(3) JBramhill(5) (b: hld up: rdn over 4f out: wknd 3f out)	7	**4**	20/1	39	18
	Silver Harrow (44) (AGNewcombe) **4-7-13**(3) IonaWands(4) (b: lw: plld hrd: bhd fnl 5f)	5	**5**	20/1	29	8
47^{4}	**Private Fixture (IRE) (42)** (DMarks) **6-7-11**(5) KerryBaker(3) (a.p: led over 4f out tl over 3f out: wknd over 2f out)	½	**6**	$100/30^{3}$	27	8
43^{8}	**Sweet Amoret (41)** (PHowling) **4-7-13** ADaly(2) (b.off hind: led over 5f)	13	**7**	10/1	5	—
				(SP 114.6%)	**7 Rn**	

2m 8.78 (4.48) CSF £55.82 TOTE £24.00: £4.40 £1.10 (£32.40) OWNER Miss Victoria Markowiak (JEVINGTON) BRED Buckram Oak Farm
WEIGHT FOR AGE 4yo-2lb
OFFICIAL EXPLANATION Zamalek (USA): was suited by the longer trip and keeping away from the kick-back.

93 YARMOUTH CLAIMING STKS (4-Y.O+) (Class E)

1-50 (1-50) **1m 5f (Equitrack)** £2,739.25 (£829.00: £404.50: £192.25) Stalls: Low GOING minus 0.27 sec per fur (FST)

				SP	RR	SF
	Persian Conquest (IRE) (65) (RIngram) **5-9-4b** JWeaver(1) (hdwy 7f out: led over 4f out: clr wl over 1f out: comf)	—	**1**	$1/2^{1}$	58+	30
	Chez Catalan (44) (RAkehurst) **6-9-4b** SSanders(2) (lw: hdwy 4f out: chsd wnr over 3f out: unable qckn)	10	**2**	14/1	46	18
	Tamandu (43) (CJames) **7-8-9** CRutter(5) (chsd ldr 10f out: led over 7f out tl over 4f out: wknd over 3f out)	8	**3**	16/1	27	—
13^{2}	**Premier League (IRE) (35)** (JELong) **7-9-6** LeesaLong(3) (chsd ldr 3f: wknd over 3f out)	hd	**4**	$4/1^{2}$	38	10
76^{4}	**Media Express (43)** (MrsLStubbs) **5-8-12b** TSprake(4) (hdwy 7f out: wknd over 3f out)	5	**5**	$7/1^{3}$	24	—
	Derisbay (IRE) (JJBridger) **9-8-5b**(5) ADaly(6) (b.off hind: led over 5f: t.o fnl 4f)	18	**6**	100/1	—	—
				(SP 112.7%)	**6 Rn**	

2m 50.14 (8.14) CSF £7.78 TOTE £1.50: £1.10 £4.80 (£4.00) OWNER Mr C. G. Adams (EPSOM) BRED Louis A. Walshe

94 VENTNOR (S) STKS (3-Y.O) (Class G)

2-20 (2-20) **7f (Equitrack)** £2,076.90 (£583.40: £284.70) Stalls: Low GOING minus 0.27 sec per fur (FST)

				SP	RR	SF
44^{4}	**Masterstroke (63)** (BJMeehan) **3-9-7** JWeaver(5) (mde all: clr 2f out: hrd rdn over 1f out: r.o wl)	—	1	3/1[2]	74	27
44^{2}	**Broadgate Flyer (IRE) (60)** (MrsLStubbs) **3-8-11** SSanders(4) (lw: hld up: chsd wnr fnl 4f: rdn 3f out: unable qckn)	8	2	Evens[1]	46	—
62^{6}	**Taome (IRE) (60)** (PDEvans) **3-7-13**(7) AnthonyBond(1) (wl bhd over 5f: hdwy fnl f: r.o)	1½	3	12/1	37	—
	Stakis Casinos Lad (IRE) (60) (MJohnston) **3-8-4**(7) KSked(3) (lw: prom 3f)	5	4	4/1[3]	31	—
	Zanabay (61) (MartynMeade) **3-8-6** NAdams(2) (chsd wnr 3f)	19	5	10/1	—	—

(SP 111.8%) **5 Rn**

1m 29.12 (4.72) CSF £6.35 TOTE £4.30: £2.70 £1.10 (£2.10) OWNER Mr N. B. Attenborough (UPPER LAMBOURN) BRED G. C. Morley
Bt in 3,800 gns
OFFICIAL EXPLANATION **Masterstroke: accounting for the gelding's apparent improvement in form, his jockey reported that his instructions had been to ride the horse in an aggressive and forceful manner from the start. He added that Masterstroke had blown up last time and needed the race.**

95 RYDE H'CAP (0-70) (4-Y.O+) (Class E)

2-50 (2-55) **5f (Equitrack)** £2,739.25 (£829.00: £404.50: £192.25) Stalls: High GOING minus 0.27 sec per fur (FST)

				SP	RR	SF
48^{6}	**Sally Slade (69)** (CACyzer) **5-9-13** DBiggs(1) (dwlt: hdwy 4f out: rdn over 2f out: r.o ins fnl f: fin 2nd, 2½l: awrdd r)	—	1	7/1	68	45
4^{9}	**Napier Star (65)** (MrsNMacauley) **4-9-6v**(3) CTeague(7) (b.off hind: s.i.s: hdwy over 1f out: r.o: fin 3rd, 3/4l: plcd 2nd)	¾	2	6/1[3]	62	39
	Daaniera (IRE) (38) (PHowling) **7-7-10b** JQuinn(8) (b.hind: lw: a.p: rdn 2f out: unable qckn: fin 4th, 1l: plcd 3rd)	1	3	16/1	31	8
	The Institute Boy (64) (MissJFCraze) **7-9-8** JWeaver(3) (b: bit bkwd: chsd ldr tl ins fnl f: sn wknd: fin 5th, 1¼l: plcd 4th)	1¼	4	6/1[3]	53	30
	Sihafi (USA) (57) (JMCarr) **4-9-1** AClark(4) (nvr nr to chal: fin 6th, 3½l: plcd 5th)	3½	5	100/30[1]	35	12
	Distant Dynasty (38) (BAPearce) **7-7-3v**[1](7) DSalt(5) (b.hind: bhd fnl 2f: fin 7th, 1 3/4l: plcd 6th)	1¾	6	33/1	11	—
	Sharp Pearl (69) (JWhite) **4-9-13b** CRutter(2) (lw: dwlt: bhd fnl 2f: fin 8th, 1½l: plcd 7th)	1½	7	13/2	37	14
24^{6}	**Mister Raider (55)** (EAWheeler) **5-8-8b**(5) ADaly(6) (bhd fnl 4f: fin 9th, nk: plcd 8th)	nk	8	11/2[2]	22	—
	Mijas (70) (LMontagueHall) **4-9-11**(3) FLynch(9) (lw: mde all: clr wl over 1f out: pushed out: fin 1st: disq: plcd last)		D	7/1	77	54

(SP 114.2%) **9 Rn**

60.16 secs (1.96) CSF £44.06 CT £592.72 TOTE £8.80: £2.80 £2.50 £2.60 (£21.70) OWNER Mr R. M. Cyzer (HORSHAM) BRED C. A. Cyzer
LONG HANDICAP Daaniera (IRE) 7-4 Distant Dynasty 7-2
STEWARDS' ENQUIRY Lynch referred to Portman Square, later susp. 28-30/1/97 & 3-17/2/97+ 5 days (irresponsible riding).

96 SHANKLIN H'CAP (0-75) (3-Y.O) (Class D)

3-20 (3-30) **1m (Equitrack)** £3,322.50 (£1,005.00: £490.00: £232.50) Stalls: High GOING minus 0.27 sec per fur (FST)

				SP	RR	SF
33*	**Globetrotter (IRE) (65)** (MJohnston) **3-9-0** JWeaver(7) (lw: stumbled s: led 7f out tl over 5f out: led 3f out: clr over 1f out: rdn out)	—	1	13/8[1]	69	30
	Baaheth (USA) (72) (SCWilliams) **3-9-7** GCarter(5) (lw: a.p: rdn 4f out: chsd wnr fnl 2f: r.o)	1½	2	9/1	73	34
	Rochea (66) (WJHaggas) **3-8-12**(3) FLynch(2) (s.s: rdn 4f out: hdwy fnl f: nvr nrr)	6	3	6/1	55	16
8^{7}	**Verinder's Gift (47)** (DrJDScargill) **3-7-10** NCarlisle(4) (stdy hdwy 3f out: wknd over 1f out)	¾	4	10/1	35	—
44*	**Misty Cay (IRE) (68)** (SDow) **3-8-12**(5) 6x ADaly(3) (led 1f: rdn over 4f out: wknd wl over 1f out)	¾	5	100/30[2]	54	15
8^{4}	**Kingsdown Trix (IRE) (55)** (AMoore) **3-8-4** CRutter(1) (led over 5f out to 3f out: wknd 2f out)	5	6	5/1[3]	31	—
	Nattie (49) (AGNewcombe) **3-7-12** JQuinn(6) (b: plld hrd: bhd fnl 5f)	15	7	20/1	—	—

(SP 116.0%) **7 Rn**

1m 41.96 (4.56) CSF £15.43 TOTE £2.30: £1.40 £2.50 (£12.20) OWNER Brian Yeardley Continental Ltd (MIDDLEHAM) BRED Norelands Bloodstock
IN-FOCUS: **Kingsdown Trix (IRE): was trainer Charlie Moore's last runner.**

97 COWES MAIDEN STKS (3-Y.O+) (Class D)

3-50 (3-56) **6f (Equitrack)** £3,338.75 (£1,010.00: £492.50: £233.75) Stalls: Low GOING minus 0.27 sec per fur (FST)

				SP	RR	SF
62^{2}	**Forgotten Times (USA) (61)** (TMJones) **3-8-0** NCarlisle(3) (b.hind: lw: chsd ldr: led over 3f out: clr over 1f out: comf)	—	1	5/4[1]	65	18
57^{3}	**Mystery Matthias (44)** (MissBSanders) **4-9-2v** SSanders(2) (a.p: chsd wnr fnl 3f: rdn 2f out: unable qckn)	5	2	11/4[3]	52	21
19^{4}	**Silent Weapon (56)** (KMcAuliffe) **3-8-5be** DHarrison(4) (s.i.s: hdwy & nt clr run over 2f out: rdn wl over 1f out: wknd fnl f)	10	3	9/4[2]	30	—
19^{7}	**Come Dancing (47)** (MJohnston) **3-8-0** TWilliams(5) (lw: hdwy over 2f out: sn wknd)	4	4	14/1	14	—
58^{8}	**Logie Pert Lad (23)** (JJBridger) **5-9-2v**[1](5) ADaly(6) (hld up: rdn over 2f out: sn wknd)	3½	5	50/1	10	—
	Avant Huit (24) (MrsNMacauley) **5-8-13v**(3) CTeague(1) (led over 2f: wknd over 2f out)	7	6	33/1	—	—

(SP 113.4%) **6 Rn**

1m 14.26 (3.16) CSF £5.07 TOTE £1.80: £1.10 £1.30 (£2.20) OWNER Mr John Crook (GUILDFORD) BRED Gainsborough Farm Inc
WEIGHT FOR AGE 3yo-16lb

T/Plpt: £44.30 (204.04 Tckts). T/Qdpt: £11.80 (76.09 Tckts). AK

0079-WOLVERHAMPTON (L-H) (Standard)
Wednesday January 15th
Vis: poor
WEATHER: foggy WIND: almost nil

98 NETHERTON MAIDEN STKS (4-Y.O+) (Class D)
1-40 (1-42) **1m 100y (Fibresand)** £3,322.50 (£1,005.00: £490.00: £232.50) Stalls: Low GOING: 0.50 sec per fur (SLW)

	Horse	Dist	Pos	SP	RR	SF
	Priolo Prima (SirMarkPrescott) **4-9-0** SSanders(7) (bit bkwd: a.p: led wl over 1f out: sn clr)	—	1	7/4[1]	60+	17
	Evening In Paris (MJohnston) **4-8-9** JWeaver(1) (lw: hld up: effrt & rdn over 2f out: r.o strly towards fin)	2½	2	5/2[2]	50	7
	Gold Lance (USA) (44) (RJO'Sullivan) **4-9-0b** DHarrison(3) (led tl rdn & hdd wl over 1f out: sn btn)	1¾	3	7/1[3]	52	9
	Tauten (IRE) (38) (PBurgoyne) **7-8-9v** DRMcCabe(5) (bit bkwd: s.s: bhd: rdn over 2f out: nvr nrr)	9	4	12/1	30	—
	Woodbury Lad (USA) (60) (WRMuir) **4-9-0** AClark(2) (bit bkwd: chsd ldrs: hrd drvn & outpcd 3f out: sn btn)	1¼	5	5/2[2]	33	—
83[8]	**Tango Man (IRE)** (RJPrice) **5-8-7**(7) AnthonyBond(6) (a in rr)	4	6	33/1	25	—
	Little Murray (FMurphy) **4-9-0** JFanning(8) (bkwd: prom to ½-wy: sn lost tch: t.o)	30	7	16/1	—	—
2[6]	**Dishy Diamond** (WRMuir) **4-8-9** RPerham(4) (unruly stalls: a bhd: t.o)	2½	8	25/1	—	—

(SP 126.4%) **8 Rn**

1m 57.9 (12.90) CSF £7.26 TOTE £2.60: £1.10 £1.10 £3.00 (£6.10) OWNER Petra Bloodstock (NEWMARKET) BRED P. D. and Mrs Player
IN-FOCUS: **Visibility was very poor and, with television cameras not ideally sited down the back straight, it was almost impossible to record everything.**

99 TIPTON CLAIMING STKS (4-Y.O+) (Class E)
2-10 (2-11) **1m 4f (Fibresand)** £2,843.25 (£861.00: £420.50: £200.25) Stalls: Low GOING: 0.50 sec per fur (SLW)

	Horse	Dist	Pos	SP	RR	SF
54[2]	**Galapino (78)** (GCBravery) **4-8-13** MRimmer(7) (hld up in tch: hdwy to ld ent fnl f: drvn clr)	—	1	11/4[2]	72	23
	Eurolink the Lad (DBurchell) **10-8-6** FNorton(5) (bit bkwd: hld up: hdwy 4f out: led over 2f out: hrd rdn & hdd ent fnl f: no ex)	5	2	20/1	54	9
	Zahid (USA) (51) (KRBurke) **6-9-6** JQuinn(2) (hld up: hdwy & rdn 3f out: nt rch ldrs)	6	3	10/1	60	15
39[8]	**Greenspan (IRE) (74)** (WRMuir) **5-9-10** JWeaver(1) (lw: a.p: led over 3f out tl over 2f out: sn rdn: btn appr fnl f)	2	4	5/4[1]	62	17
	Thorntoun Estate (IRE) (60) (MartinTodhunter) **4-8-6b** DeanMcKeown(8) (led: hrd rdn 4f out: sn hdd: wknd fnl 2f)	13	5	12/1	30	—
	Wadada (34) (DBurchell) **6-8-10** SDrowne(6) (chsd ldrs: rdn 3f out: sn btn)	3½	6	20/1	26	—
39[9]	**Pistols At Dawn (USA) (57)** (BJMeehan) **7-7-13**(7) GHannon(3) (a in rr)	nk	7	7/1[3]	21	—
	High Low (USA) (WJenks) **9-9-6** VSlattery(10) (bkwd: trckd ldrs 7f: sn lost tch: t.o)	8	8	20/1	25	—
	Appearance Money (IRE) (31) (FMurphy) **6-8-7** JFanning(9) (lw: s.s: a bhd: t.o)	25	9	33/1	—	—
	Miss The Beat (30) (SMellor) **5-7-8**(7) JBramhill(4) (lost tch ½-wy: t.o)	dist	10	33/1	—	—

(SP 120.6%) **10 Rn**

2m 49.9 (17.40) CSF £49.54 TOTE £4.70: £1.40 £3.50 £2.20 (£46.20) Trio £98.00 OWNER Mrs F. E. Bravery (NEWMARKET) BRED Dayspring Co Ltd
WEIGHT FOR AGE 4yo-4lb

100 MANCHESTER H'CAP (0-90) (4-Y.O+) (Class C)
2-40 (2-41) **1m 4f (Fibresand)** £5,146.45 (£1,558.60: £761.30: £362.65) Stalls: Low GOING: 0.50 sec per fur (SLW)

	Horse	Dist	Pos	SP	RR	SF
	Opera Buff (IRE) (89) (MissGayKelleway) **6-9-11**(3) AWhelan(10) (hld up & bhd: hdwy 3f out: led ins fnl f: r.o wl)	—	1	6/1[2]	99	50
	Star Rage (IRE) (78) (JLHarris) **7-9-3** JWeaver(9) (bit bkwd: hld up in rr: hdwy 4f out: led wl over 1f out tl ins fnl f)	1	2	12/1	87	38
	Infamous (USA) (79) (RJO'Sullivan) **4-9-0** JQuinn(8) (bit bkwd: hld up: hdwy 4f out: ev ch over 2f out: sn rdn & outpcd)	10	3	14/1	74	21
23[5]	**Nikita's Star (IRE) (77)** (DJGMurraySmith) **4-8-12** SSanders(5) (chsd ldrs: led over 3f out tl wl over 1f out: sn rdn & wknd)	7	4	14/1	63	10
	Prince Danzig (IRE) (85) (DJGMurraySmith) **6-9-10** DHarrison(7) (hld up: hdwy 5f out: rdn over 2f out: sn wknd)	5	5	6/1[2]	64	15
52[2]	**Celestial Choir (87)** (JLEyre) **7-9-9**(3) OPears(6) (hld up in rr: effrt & rdn 3f out: no imp: t.o)	22	6	6/4[1]	37	—
23[8]	**Out on a Promise (IRE) (71)** (NJHWalker) **5-8-7**(3) FLynch(4) (led after 4f: rdn & hdd over 3f out: sn wknd: t.o)	s.h	7	8/1[3]	21	—
74[6]	**State Approval (62)** (PEccles) **4-7-4**(7) JBramhill(3) (chsd ldrs 7f: sn rdn & lost tch: t.o: fin lame)	25	8	16/1	—	—
83[2]	**Prophets Honour (67)** (PCHaslam) **5-8-6** SDrowne(2) (led 4f: wknd 5f out: t.o)	21	9	6/1[2]	—	—
	At Liberty (IRE) (77) (RHannon) **5-9-2** RPerham(1) (chsd ldrs to ½-wy: sn wknd: t.o)	27	10	14/1	—	—

(SP 127.5%) **10 Rn**

2m 47.8 (15.30) CSF £72.21 CT £908.44 TOTE £6.90: £2.40 £3.30 £5.10 (£46.70) Trio £30.10 OWNER Mr B. Tregurtha (WHITCOMBE) BRED Juddmonte Farms
WEIGHT FOR AGE 4yo-4lb
OFFICIAL EXPLANATION **State Approval: was lame on his near-fore.**

101 DUDLEY H'CAP (0-75) (4-Y.O+) (Class D)
3-10 (3-10) **2m 46y (Fibresand)** £3,436.25 (£1,040.00: £507.50: £241.25) Stalls: High GOING: 0.50 sec per fur (SLW)

	Horse	Dist	Pos	SP	RR	SF
55*	**Golden Hadeer (58)** (MJRyan) **6-8-13** 4x AClark(7) (led 10f out: drew clr ent st: comf)	—	1	4/7[1]	72+	—
55[3]	**Noufari (FR) (73)** (RHollinshead) **6-9-11**(3) FLynch(9) (hld up & wl bhd: hdwy 4f out: chsd wnr fnl 2f: no imp)	8	2	7/1[3]	79	—
	Anglesey Sea View (51) (ABailey) **8-7-13**(7) IonaWands(1) (hld up: effrt & pushed along ½-wy: ev ch 3f out: sn rdn & outpcd)	3½	3	14/1	54	—
	Classic Account (41) (JLEyre) **9-7-7**(3) NVarley(6) (bkwd: prom tl drvn along & lost tch 4f out)	2½	4	33/1	41	—
5[P]	**Sharp Command (53)** (PEccles) **4-7-8**(7) JBramhill(8) (lw: chsd ldrs: rdn 7f out: wknd over 3f out)	14	5	12/1	39	—
16*	**Parklife (IRE) (47)** (PCHaslam) **5-8-2** SDrowne(2) (s.i.s: hdwy ½-wy: rdn & wknd over 3f out)	1¾	6	7/2[2]	32	—
78[7]	**Al Haal (USA) (46)** (RJO'Sullivan) **8-8-1** FNorton(3) (a wl bhd)	2	7	33/1	29	—

				SP	RR	SF
55^{2}	**Rood Music (68)** (MGMeagher) **6-9-9** ACulhane(4) (led 6f: sn pushed along: wknd 5f out: t.o)	dist	**8**	10/1	—	—

(SP 127.7%) **8 Rn**

3m 57.9 (30.90) CSF £6.49 CT £32.76 TOTE £1.90: £1.30 £1.20 £1.80 (£7.90) Trio £15.40 OWNER Four Jays Racing Partnership (NEWMARKET) BRED Stetchworth Park Stud Ltd
LONG HANDICAP Classic Account 7-4
WEIGHT FOR AGE 4yo-7lb

102 BILSTON (S) STKS (3-Y.O) (Class F)
3-40 (3-40) **5f** **(Fibresand)** £2,675.00 (£750.00: £365.00) Stalls: Low GOING: 0.50 sec per fur (SLW)

				SP	RR	SF
38^{2}	**Figlia (58)** (JLHarris) **3-8-7v¹** JQuinn(2) (sn pushed along & bhd: hdwy 2f out: rdn to ld wl ins fnl f)	—	**1**	$5/2^{1}$	57	24
25^{4}	**Imperial Garden (IRE) (64)** (PCHaslam) **3-9-5** SDrowne(7) (w ldr: led wl over 1f out tl hdd & no ex nr fin)	1¼	**2**	$3/1^{2}$	65	32
	My Girl (53) (RHollinshead) **3-8-4**$^{(3)}$ FLynch(6) (bit bkwd: sn bhd & outpcd: r.o appr fnl f: nrst fin)	3	**3**	16/1	43	10
38^{4}	**Fit For The Job (IRE) (74)** (TWall) **3-8-12**$^{(7)}$ JBramhill(5) (led over 3f: sn hrd drvn: btn appr fnl f)	hd	**4**	$4/1^{3}$	55	22
	Le Shuttle (45) (MHTompkins) **3-8-7** GCarter(4) (bhd & outpcd tl sme late hdwy)	1½	**5**	12/1	38	5
45^{3}	**Ekaterini Paritsi (52)** (WGMTurner) **3-8-7v** TSprake(3) (chsd ldrs: rdn along ½-wy: nvr able to chal)	1	**6**	12/1	35	2
33^{6}	**Flood's Hot Stuff (45)** (NPLittmoden) **3-8-2**$^{(5)}$ ADaly(8) (outpcd)	5	**7**	25/1	19	—
75^{2}	**Come Too Mamma's (60)** (JBerry) **3-8-9**$^{(5)}$ PFessey(1) (chsd ldrs: hrd rdn 2f out: sn wknd)	hd	**8**	$5/2^{1}$	26	—

(SP 127.3%) **8 Rn**

65.4 secs (6.50) CSF £11.39 TOTE £4.60: £1.80 £1.30 £8.30 (£8.00) OWNER Mr R. Atkinson (MELTON MOWBRAY) BRED Victor Wade
No bid

103 BIRMINGHAM H'CAP (0-85) (3-Y.O) (Class D)
4-10 (4-11) **7f** **(Fibresand)** £3,387.50 (£1,025.00: £500.00: £237.50) Stalls: High GOING: 0.50 sec per fur (SLW)

				SP	RR	SF
	Foot Battalion (IRE) (83) (RHollinshead) **3-9-3**$^{(3)}$ FLynch(3) (bhd: rdn 3f out: gd hdwy to ld fnl 100y: sn clr)	—	**1**	4/1	92	36
12^{5}	**Ultra Boy (75)** (PCHaslam) **3-8-12** GCarter(6) (hdwy 3f out: hrd drvn 2f out: ev ch ins fnl f: unable qckn)	2½	**2**	10/1	78	22
17^{3}	**Enchanting Eve (70)** (CNAllen) **3-8-0**$^{(7)}$ JBramhill(7) (lw: a.p: led over 2f out tl hdd & wknd ins fnl f)	5	**3**	6/1	62	6
	Nomore Mr Niceguy (84) (EJAlston) **3-9-7** ACulhane(5) (lw: dwlt: hdwy 3f out: rdn over 1f out: sn btn)	3½	**4**	$11/4^{1}$	68	12
12^{2}	**Eager To Please (69)** (MissGayKelleway) **3-8-6b** SSanders(2) (lw: prom: led ½-wy tl over 2f out: sn rdn & outpcd)	6	**5**	$7/2^{3}$	39	—
	Advance Repro (61) (JAkehurst) **3-7-12b** JQuinn(4) (chsd ldr: chal 3f out: sn hrd drvn & wknd)	6	**6**	20/1	17	—
33^{2}	**Komasta (67)** (CaptJWilson) **3-8-4** FNorton(1) (led to ½-wy: wknd qckly over 2f out: t.o)	9	**7**	$3/1^{2}$	3	—

(SP 122.0%) **7 Rn**

1m 34.0 (9.30) CSF £38.95 TOTE £5.30: £1.90 £3.20 (£20.50) OWNER Mr A. S. Hill (UPPER LONGDON) BRED Ennistown Stud

T/Plpt: £209.70 (101.49 Tckts). T/Qdpt: £24.20 (80.77 Tckts). IM

0092-LINGFIELD (L-H) (Standard)
Thursday January 16th
WEATHER: sunny & misty WIND: almost nil

104 LITTLE ACORNS (S) H'CAP (0-60) (4-Y.O+) (Class G)
1-30 (1-31) **1m 4f** **(Equitrack)** £2,223.90 (£625.40: £305.70) Stalls: Low GOING minus 0.33 sec per fur (FST)

				SP	RR	SF
76^{3}	**Zacaroon (45)** (JFfitch-Heyes) **6-9-3** DBiggs(6) (b.hind: a.p: led 3f out: all out)	—	**1**	12/1	56	32
	Labudd (USA) (52) (RIngram) **7-9-10** JStack(8) (b: hdwy 2f out: hrd rdn fnl f: r.o wl)	s.h	**2**	9/1	63	39
	Oozlem (IRE) (39) (LMontagueHall) **8-8-8v**$^{(3)}$ FLynch(3) (hdwy 2f out: hrd rdn over 1f out: unable qckn)	1¾	**3**	$9/2^{2}$	48	24
43^{3}	**Al Helal (43)** (JRJenkins) **5-9-1b** DHarrison(10) (hld up: chsd wnr 2f out tl ins fnl f: one pce)	1¾	**4**	$8/1^{3}$	49	25
	Eastleigh (38) (RHollinshead) **8-8-3**$^{(7)}$ LisaWatson(12) (b.nr hind: a.p: ev ch over 2f out: one pce)	2½	**5**	14/1	41	17
67^{5}	**Warspite (38)** (PMooney) **7-8-10** JQuinn(2) (nvr nr to chal)	10	**6**	12/1	28	4
14^{12}	**Broughtons Relish (28)** (WJMusson) **4-7-10** DeclanO'Shea(4) (nvr nrr)	2	**7**	33/1	15	—
	Colosse (51) (JLEyre) **5-9-2v**$^{(7)}$ SBuckley(13) (s.s: hdwy 10f out: wknd 4f out)	1½	**8**	$9/2^{2}$	36	12
63^{5}	**Sapphire Son (IRE) (41)** (PCClarke) **5-8-13** NAdams(7) (led over 4f: wknd 4f out)	13	**9**	12/1	9	—
9^{10}	**Callonescy (IRE) (30)** (DCO'Brien) **5-8-2** GBardwell(9) (lw: hdwy over 10f out: led over 7f out to 3f out: sn wknd)	¾	**10**	33/1	—	—
43^{7}	**Efficacious (IRE) (40)** (GLMoore) **4-8-8** RPerham(5) (bhd fnl 4f)	½	**11**	25/1	6	—
	Carrolls Marc (IRE) (45) (CMurray) **9-9-3** JWeaver(1) (a bhd)	s.h	**12**	$100/30^{1}$	11	—
	Extremely Friendly (45) (BobJones) **4-8-13** MWigham(11) (prom 8f)	1¾	**13**	$8/1^{3}$	9	—

(SP 131.1%) **13 Rn**

2m 36.51 (6.51) CSF £113.90 CT £525.79 TOTE £15.80: £4.80 £4.90 £2.70 (£87.40) Trio £201.50 OWNER Mr C. Harradine (LEWES) BRED Juddmonte Farms
LONG HANDICAP Broughtons Relish 7-5
WEIGHT FOR AGE 4yo-4lb
No bid
OFFICIAL EXPLANATION Carrolls Marc (IRE): the jockey thought the gelding had gone lame during the race, but it was sound on pulling up.

105 PENNY WISE CLAIMING STKS (4-Y.O+) (Class E)
2-00 (2-02) **1m** **(Equitrack)** £2,986.25 (£905.00: £442.50: £211.25) Stalls: High GOING minus 0.33 sec per fur (FST)

				SP	RR	SF
	Soaking (79) (PBurgoyne) **7-9-2** DRMcCabe(6) (hdwy over 2f out: led over 1f out: comf)	—	**1**	$2/1^{2}$	70	52
59^{*}	**Milos (67)** (TJNaughton) **6-8-8** JWeaver(10) (a.p: led over 2f out tl over 1f out: unable qckn)	4	**2**	$5/1^{3}$	54	36
57^{6}	**Our Shadee (USA) (51)** (KTIvory) **7-8-6v** CScally(11) (b: b.hind: hld up: ev ch over 1f out: one pce)	1¼	**3**	20/1	50	32
	Lahik (IRE) (30) (KTIvory) **4-8-2** DBiggs(1) (b: hdwy over 1f out: r.o)	3½	**4**	100/1	39	21
	Waikiki Beach (USA) (74) (GLMoore) **6-9-8** CandyMorris(5) (b: nvr gng wl: no hdwy fnl 2f)	2½	**5**	8/1	54	36
	Rachel's Rock (GLMoore) **4-8-1** CRutter(7) (nvr nr to chal)	1½	**6**	66/1	30	12
61^{9}	**Multi Franchise (56)** (BGubby) **4-8-4** JTate(2) (prom over 5f)	3½	**7**	25/1	26	8

56* **Second Colours (USA) (79)** (MCPipe) **7-9-12** DHarrison(4) (a bhd) ....¾ **8** 6/4[1] 46 28
Medland (IRE) (40) (BJMcMath) **7-8-2b[1]** GBardwell(8) (b: led over 5f)....4 **9** 40/1 14 —
40[9] **Rapier Point (IRE) (30)** (CMurray) **6-8-2b** NicolaHowarth(9) (prom 4f)....1 **10** 66/1 12 —
22[7] **One In The Eye (38)** (JRPoulton) **4-8-6b** SDrowne(3) (a bhd) ....1½ **11** 100/1 13 —
(SP 117.1%) **11 Rn**

1m 39.41 (2.01) CSF £10.76 TOTE £2.70: £1.10 £1.50 £3.50 (£8.30) Trio £21.00 OWNER Mr Philip Saunders (LAMBOURN) BRED David John Brown
Milos clmd DBloor £6,000

106 CAVEAT EMPTOR H'CAP (0-65) (4-Y.O+) (Class F)

2-30 (2-32) **2m (Equitrack)** £2,518.00 (£708.00: £346.00) Stalls: Low GOING minus 0.33 sec per fur (FST)

SP RR SF

78* **Hattaafeh (IRE) (58)** (MissBSanders) **6-9-13** 4x SSanders(3) (lw: hld up: rdn over 3f out: led wl ins fnl f: r.o wl)....— **1** 5/2[2] 70 41
Wottashambles (54) (LMontagueHall) **6-9-9** JWeaver(7) (hdwy 6f out: led 5f out tl over 4f out: led 3f out tl wl ins fnl f: unable qckn)....¾ **2** 9/4[1] 65 36
43* **Supreme Star (USA) (57)** (PRHedger) **6-9-9b**(3) 4x NVarley(9) (b: a.p: led over 4f out to 3f out: ev ch ins fnl f: one pce)....nk **3** 10/1 68 39
80[3] **In the Money (IRE) (51)** (RHollinshead) **8-9-3**(3) FLynch(5) (lw: hdwy 2f out: r.o wl ins fnl f)....1 **4** 20/1 61 32
63[3] **Sassiver (USA) (30)** (PAKelleway) **7-7-13** DWright(6) (hdwy 6f out: rdn over 3f out: wknd 2f out)....7 **5** 6/1[3] 33 4
78[3] **Guest Alliance (IRE) (59)** (GLMoore) **5-10-0** CandyMorris(4) (a.p: rdn over 3f out: wknd over 2f out)....2½ **6** 8/1 59 30
16[11] **Turrill House (30)** (WJMusson) **5-7-13** CRutter(10) (hdwy 6f out: rdn over 3f out: wknd over 2f out)....1¾ **7** 50/1 29 —
Khatir (CAN) (50) (MCPipe) **6-9-5b** TSprake(8) (prom 11f)....16 **8** 16/1 33 4
Stoney Valley (50) (JRJenkins) **7-9-5e** DHarrison(1) (b.hind: bhd fnl 6f: t.o)....25 **9** 16/1 8 —
13[4] **Colour Counsellor (41)** (RMFlower) **4-8-3b** JQuinn(2) (b: led 11f: t.o)....8 **10** 20/1 — —
(SP 117.1%) **10 Rn**

3m 29.78 (8.78) CSF £7.59 CT £42.44 TOTE £3.90: £1.50 £2.00 £2.20 (£3.10) Trio £7.80 OWNER Mrs P. J. Sheen (EPSOM) BRED Sheikh Ahmed bin Rashid al Maktoum in Ireland
WEIGHT FOR AGE 4yo-7lb

107 APPLE A DAY H'CAP (0-70) (3-Y.O+) (Class E)

3-00 (3-03) **6f (Equitrack)** £2,791.25 (£845.00: £412.50: £196.25) Stalls: Low GOING minus 0.33 sec per fur (FST)

SP RR SF

27[5] **Mellors (IRE) (57)** (MJHeaton-Ellis) **4-9-7** SDrowne(5) (lw: a.p: led over 1f out: drvn out)....— **1** 9/2[3] 66 29
95[4] **The Institute Boy (64)** (MissJFCraze) **7-10-0** JWeaver(2) (rdn 2f out: gd hdwy fnl f: fin wl)....1 **2** 6/1 70 33
Rock To The Top (IRE) (68) (JJSheehan) **3-9-2** AMorris(7) (lw: hdwy over 1f out: hrd rdn: r.o ins fnl f)....¾ **3** 10/1 72 19
24[9] **Tachycardia (33)** (RJO'Sullivan) **5-7-11** FNorton(10) (rdn 2f out: hdwy over 1f out: r.o ins fnl f)....nk **4** 20/1 37 —
58[6] **Superlao (BEL) (39)** (JJBridger) **5-7-12**(5)ow2 ADaly(9) (b.hind: a.p: rdn over 2f out: unable qckn)....1¾ **5** 33/1 38 —
79[2] **Aljaz (48)** (MissGayKelleway) **7-8-12** SSanders(6) (b: b.hind: hdwy 2f out: hrd rdn over 1f out: wknd ins fnl f)....1¼ **6** 7/2[2] 44 7
24* **Sharp Imp (63)** (RMFlower) **7-9-13b** JQuinn(3) (nvr nrr)....2½ **7** 100/30[1] 52 15
Bright Paragon (IRE) (33) (KTIvory) **8-7-11** NAdams(8) (b: b.hind: chsd ldr: led over 2f out tl over 1f out: eased whn btn ins fnl f)....½ **8** 33/1 21 —
20* **Invocation (63)** (GLMoore) **10-9-13** AClark(4) (b.nr hind: lw: bhd fnl 2f)....½ **9** 13/2 49 12
24[11] **Halbert (43)** (PBurgoyne) **8-8-7v** DRMcCabe(1) (led over 3f: wknd over 1f out)....4 **10** 10/1 19 —
(SP 119.9%) **10 Rn**

1m 14.56 (3.46) CSF £29.10 CT £241.31 TOTE £4.50: £1.30 £2.60 £2.70 (£18.10) Trio £110.20 OWNER Mr M. Heaton-Ellis (WROUGHTON) BRED Jimmy Coogan
WEIGHT FOR AGE 3yo-16lb

108 DOCKLANDS CARS & COURIERS MAIDEN STKS (4-Y.O+) (Class D)

3-30 (3-32) **1m 2f (Equitrack)** £3,403.75 (£1,030.00: £502.50: £238.75) Stalls: Low GOING minus 0.33 sec per fur (FST)

SP RR SF

Dances With Hooves (77) (DJSffrenchDavis) **5-9-2** JWeaver(5) (lw: s.s: stdy hdwy 4f out: chsd ldr 3f out: hrd rdn over 1f out: led ins fnl f: r.o wl)....— **1** 13/8[1] 63 39
61[8] **Nakhal (53)** (DJGMurraySmith) **4-8-11**(3) FLynch(11) (rdn over 4f out: hdwy over 2f out: r.o wl ins fnl f)....1 **2** 9/1 61 35
Passage Creeping (IRE) (62) (SDow) **4-8-9e** SSanders(10) (hdwy over 7f out: led over 3f out: hrd rdn over 1f out: hdd ins fnl f: unable qckn)....1 **3** 9/4[2] 55 29
9[6] **Nails Tails** (SDow) **4-8-9**(5) ADaly(9) (rdn over 3f out: hdwy over 1f out: nvr nrr)....9 **4** 20/1 45 19
Regal Splendour (CAN) (67) (RJO'Sullivan) **4-9-0** DHarrison(1) (led over 1f: rdn over 3f out: wknd over 2f out)....3½ **5** 6/1[3] 40 14
Square Mile Miss (IRE) (35) (PHowling) **4-8-9** JQuinn(2) (hld up: rdn over 3f out: sn wknd)....7 **6** 25/1 24 —
Docklands Courier (46) (BJMcMath) **5-9-2** GBardwell(4) (lw: bhd fnl 5f)....7 **7** 10/1 17 —
13[10] **Brother Roy (55)** (TGMills) **4-8-7**(7) JCornally(6) (led over 8f out: clr 7f out: hdd over 3f out: sn wknd)....3 **8** 33/1 13 —
Trapper Norman (27) (RIngram) **5-9-2** JStack(3) (b.hind: prom 6f)....3 **9** 25/1 8 —
54[6] **Emei Shan (30)** (WGMTurner) **4-8-3**(7)ow1 DMcGaffin(7) (bhd fnl 5f)....½ **10** 66/1 3 —
Hightide (JRArnold) **5-8-11** AClark(8) (a bhd)....3½ **11** 66/1 — —
(SP 120.6%) **11 Rn**

2m 8.56 (4.26) CSF £15.07 TOTE £2.50: £1.90 £2.90 £1.50 (£14.00) Trio £8.40 OWNER Mr V. Squeglia (UPPER LAMBOURN) BRED Theakston Stud
WEIGHT FOR AGE 4yo-2lb

109 FRIEND IN NEED H'CAP (0-70) (4-Y.O+) (Class E)

4-00 (4-03) **7f (Equitrack)** £2,830.25 (£857.00: £418.50: £199.25) Stalls: Low GOING minus 0.33 sec per fur (FST)

SP RR SF

48[3] **Sea Danzig (63)** (JJBridger) **4-9-8** DHarrison(9) (lw: led 5f: hrd rdn over 1f out: led wl ins fnl f: r.o wl)....— **1** 5/1[3] 64 56
82[4] **Star Talent (USA) (69)** (MissGayKelleway) **6-10-0** JWeaver(4) (b: b.hind: rdn & hdwy over 1f out: r.o wl ins fnl f)....hd **2** 3/1[1] 70 62
57[9] **Lancashire Legend (65)** (SDow) **4-9-5**(5) ADaly(10) (hdwy over 3f out: led 2f out tl wl ins fnl f: unable qckn)..½ **3** 20/1 65 57

				SP	RR	SF
24[3]	**Barbason (55)** (GLMoore) **5-9-0** CandyMorris(7) (hdwy over 3f out: rdn 2f out: one pce)	2½	**4**	4/1[2]	49	41
59[3]	**The Frisky Farmer (52)** (WGMTurner) **4-8-11** TSprake(11) (lw: a.p: rdn 3f out: wknd over 1f out)	3½	**5**	12/1	38	30
	Sharp 'n Smart (65) (BSmart) **5-9-10** SSanders(8) (hld up: rdn 3f out: wknd 2f out)	1½	**6**	6/1	48	40
40[2]	**Plum First (49)** (JLEyre) **7-8-8b** RLappin(6) (s.s: nvr nrr)	5	**7**	7/1	20	12
	Shaynes Domain (38) (RMFlower) **6-7-11b**ow1 FNorton(3) (prom 3f)	3	**8**	33/1	2	—
24[10]	**Into Debt (37)** (JRPoulton) **4-7-10e** GBardwell(5) (lw: prom 4f)	2	**9**	66/1	—	—
61[12]	**Jubilee Scholar (IRE) (55)** (KMcAuliffe) **4-8-11be**(3) FLynch(2) (bhd fnl 5f)	1	**10**	14/1	12	4
	Tymeera (46) (BPalling) **4-8-5** SDrowne(1) (prom 3f)	15	**11**	14/1	—	—

(SP 118.7%) **11 Rn**

1m 26.24 (1.84) CSF £18.39 CT £260.02 TOTE £6.80: £3.20 £1.50 £4.80 (£7.70) Trio £50.40 OWNER Mr P. Cook (LIPHOOK) BRED Theobalds Stud

LONG HANDICAP Into Debt 7-3 Shaynes Domain 7-7

T/Jkpt: Not won; £3,778.21 to Kempton 17/1/97. T/Plpt: £133.50 (116.53 Tckts). T/Qdpt: £11.20 (124.74 Tckts). AK

0085-SOUTHWELL (L-H) (Standard)

Friday January 17th

12-45 - run under National Hunt rules.

WEATHER: overcast & misty WIND: almost nil

110 SHARK H'CAP (0-70) (3-Y.O) (Class E)

1-15 (1-17) **6f (Fibresand)** £2,801.00 (£848.00: £414.00: £197.00) Stalls: Low GOING: 0.34 sec per fur (SLW)

				SP	RR	SF
19*	**Pet Express (44)** (PCHaslam) **3-8-1** LCharnock(3) (lw: mde all: drvn along & styd on wl fnl 2f)	—	**1**	5/2[1]	54	27
38[3]	**Treasure Touch (IRE) (60)** (GMMoore) **3-9-3** ACulhane(7) (sn trckng ldrs: chsd wnr fnl 2f: styd on towards fin)	1	**2**	5/2[1]	67	40
8[6]	**Mirror Four Sport (46)** (MJohnston) **3-8-3** TWilliams(6) (chsd ldrs: sn drvn along: one pce fnl 2f)	7	**3**	12/1	35	8
38[5]	**Jack Says (64)** (DShaw) **3-9-4b**(3) CTeague(4) (hdwy & outside ½-wy: rdn & hung rt 2f out: sn wknd)	1¼	**4**	12/1	49	22
	Contravene (IRE) (64) (JBerry) **3-9-7** GCarter(1) (chsd ldrs tl wknd 2f out)	5	**5**	8/1[3]	36	9
17[5]	**Sharp Return (57)** (MJRyan) **3-8-11**(3) MBaird(5) (s.s: sn trckng ldrs: rdn & lost pl over 2f out)	4	**6**	3/1[2]	18	—
50[8]	**Heathyards Pearl (USA) (60)** (RHollinshead) **3-9-0**(3) FLynch(2) (s.s: a last)	12	**7**	14/1	—	—

(SP 115.3%) **7 Rn**

1m 19.9 (6.40) CSF £8.31 TOTE £3.60: £1.80 £1.50 (£2.80) OWNER Pet Express (W&R) Ltd (MIDDLEHAM) BRED A. J. Sexton

111 HALIBUT APPRENTICE CLAIMING STKS (4-Y.O+) (Class G)

1-50 (1-52) **1m (Fibresand)** £2,085.00 (£585.00: £285.00) Stalls: Low GOING: 0.34 sec per fur (SLW)

				SP	RR	SF
1[5]	**Rambo Waltzer (65)** (DNicholls) **5-9-2**(3) JBramhill(11) (trckd ldrs: led over 3f out: sn clr: v.easily)	—	**1**	5/2[2]	87+	48
85*	**Chadleigh Lane (USA) (59)** (RHollinshead) **5-8-10** DGriffiths(5) (lw: unruly s: hdwy ½-wy: sn drvn along & chsng ldrs: edgd lft 2f out: no ch w wnr)	8	**2**	11/8[1]	62	23
	Sandmoor Denim (50) (SRBowring) **10-8-4** ADaly(13) (b: trckd ldrs: kpt on same pce fnl 2f)	1¼	**3**	13/2[3]	54	15
	Le Sport (70) (DNicholls) **4-9-0**(5) TSiddall(12) (in tch: rdn & outpcd ½-wy: kpt on fnl f)	3	**4**	16/1	63	24
	Appeal Again (IRE) (49) (DBurchell) **4-8-1**(3) KSked(10) (hmpd & lost pl after 1f: racd wd & sn bhd: styd on fnl 2f)	3½	**5**	20/1	41	2
87[8]	**Sonya Marie (46)** (JGFitzGerald) **4-7-8**(5) RBrisland(9) (sn bhd & drvn along: n.d)	13	**6**	25/1	10	—
14[13]	**Lady Eclat (29)** (KGWingrove) **4-7-8b**(5) AMcCarthy(2) (w ldrs: lost pl over 2f out)	2½	**7**	50/1	5	—
	Buddy's Friend (IRE) (43) (RJRWilliams) **9-8-1**(3) GMilligan(3) (a in rr)	1	**8**	16/1	8	—
28[12]	**Eccentric Dancer (36)** (MPBielby) **4-8-2** PFessey(6) (s.i.s: chsd ldrs tl outpcd fnl 3f)	2	**9**	33/1	2	—
	Nantgarw (DBurchell) **4-7-8**(5) CCogan(4) (b.nr hind: w ldrs to ½-wy: hung lft & sn lost pl)	½	**10**	50/1	—	—
3[3]	**Sweet Mate (54)** (MartynMeade) **5-8-1b**(3)ow3 DSweeney(8) (mde most tl over 3f out: wknd over 2f out)	2½	**11**	7/1	—	—
18[13]	**Britannia Mills (24)** (MCChapman) **6-7-10**(3) IonaWands(7) (w ldrs 3f: sn bhd)	13	**12**	50/1	—	—

(SP 125.7%) **12 Rn**

1m 47.1 (8.10) CSF £5.75 TOTE £3.00: £1.80 £1.50 £2.00 (£2.50) Trio £6.10 OWNER Mr W. G. Swiers (THIRSK) BRED Triangle Thoroughbreds Ltd

Chadleigh Lane (USA) clmd Glory of Darley Racing Partnership £5,000

112 OYSTER MEDIAN AUCTION MAIDEN STKS (4, 5 & 6-Y.O) (Class F)

2-20 (2-21) **7f (Fibresand)** £2,294.00 (£644.00: £314.00) Stalls: Low GOING: 0.34 sec per fur (SLW)

				SP	RR	SF
	Truly Bay (42) (TDBarron) **4-9-0** DHarrison(4) (chsd ldrs: rdn to ld 2f out: styd on)	—	**1**	11/4[3]	52	13
71[6]	**Soaked (64)** (DWChapman) **4-9-0** ACulhane(3) (hld up: smooth hdwy to chal over 1f out: sn rdn & fnd nil)	3	**2**	9/4[1]	45	6
27[7]	**Unspoken Prayer (38)** (JRArnold) **4-8-9b[1]** SSanders(2) (w ldrs: led over 2f out: sn hdd: one pce)	5	**3**	5/2[2]	29	—
83[10]	**Kulepopsie (IRE)** (ABMulholland) **4-8-9** DeanMcKeown(1) (mde most tl over 2f out: sn wknd)	9	**4**	25/1	8	—
	Our Robert (JGFitzGerald) **5-9-0** NKennedy(5) (bit bkwd: chsd ldrs: drvn along ½-wy: sn wl outpcd)	1¾	**5**	7/2	9	—

(SP 112.1%) **5 Rn**

1m 36.4 (9.90) CSF £8.67 TOTE £3.80: £1.90 £1.50 (£4.80) OWNER The Oakfield Nurseries Partnership (THIRSK) BRED Doverlodge Stud

113 WHALE H'CAP (0-70) (3-Y.O+) (Class E)

2-50 (2-52) **7f (Fibresand)** £3,231.90 (£979.20: £478.60: £228.30) Stalls: Low GOING: 0.34 sec per fur (SLW)

				SP	RR	SF
15[14]	**Kingchip Boy (68)** (MJRyan) **8-9-12v** AClark(5) (lw: mde virtually all: hrd rdn fnl f: jst hld on)	—	**1**	10/1	74	41
87[3]	**Bold Aristocrat (IRE) (60)** (RHollinshead) **6-9-1**(3) FLynch(4) (hdwy on outside 2f out: hung lft & kpt on fnl f)	½	**2**	11/1	65	32
40*	**Pleasure Trick (USA) (48)** (DonEnricoIncisa) **6-8-6b** 6x KimTinkler(6) (sn outpcd & bhd: hdwy on outside 2f out: fin wl)	¾	**3**	11/2[2]	51	18
65*	**Anita's Contessa (IRE) (56)** (BPalling) **5-9-0** 6x TSprake(9) (hld up & bhd: hdwy on outside 2f out: styd on wl ins fnl f)	1¼	**4**	9/1	56	23

				SP	RR	SF
72[7]	**Dawalib (USA) (57)** (DHaydnJones) **7-9-1** LCharnock(14) (sn trckng ldrs: effrt over 1f out: wknd & eased ins fnl f)	2½	**5**	16/1	52	19
81[4]	**Manabar (58)** (MJPolglase) **5-9-2b[1]** TGMcLaughlin(3) (a chsng ldrs: drvn along ½-wy: one pce fnl 2f)	s.h	**6**	12/1	53	20
40[5]	**Green Golightly (USA) (39)** (RMFlower) **6-7-11be**ow1 FNorton(1) (s.i.s: bhd tl styd on fnl 2f)	½	**7**	12/1	32	—
69[8]	**Craigie Boy (40)** (NBycroft) **7-7-5b**(7) JBramhill(8) (w ldrs tl wknd fnl f)	6	**8**	14/1	20	—
65[4]	**Leigh Crofter (66)** (PDCundell) **8-9-10b** RPerham(11) (w ldrs tl wknd over 1f out)	1½	**9**	6/1[3]	42	9
71[7]	**Kajostar (41)** (SWCampion) **7-7-8**(5)ow3 PFessey(7) (trckd ldrs to ½-wy: sn lost pl)	2	**10**	50/1	13	—
89[2]	**Awesome Venture (70)** (MCChapman) **7-10-0** SDrowne(12) (chsd ldrs: outpcd & lost pl ½-wy)	½	**11**	5/1[1]	41	8
69[6]	**Cheerful Groom (IRE) (41)** (DShaw) **6-7-13** NKennedy(2) (sn reminders: sn chsng ldrs: wknd over 2f out)	hd	**12**	16/1	11	—
	Napoleon Star (IRE) (54) (SRBowring) **6-8-12b** SDWilliams(13) (chsd ldrs tl wknd over 2f out)	3½	**13**	14/1	16	—
	Murray's Mazda (IRE) (50) (JLEyre) **8-8-8** RLappin(10) (b.nr hind: chsd ldrs to ½-wy: sn lost pl: virtually p.u)	16	**14**	6/1[3]	—	—

(SP 130.5%) **14 Rn**

1m 34.8 (8.30) CSF £114.13 CT £627.27 TOTE £11.00: £3.10 £3.90 £4.30 (£41.00) Trio £153.70 OWNER Four Jays Racing Partnership (NEWMARKET) BRED R. M. Scott
LONG HANDICAP Kajostar 6-8 Green Golightly (USA) 7-3
OFFICIAL EXPLANATION Dawalib (USA): rider reported that the gelding had gurgled

114 LOBSTER (S) STKS (4-Y.O+) (Class G)

3-20 (3-20) **1m 3f (Fibresand)** £2,085.00 (£585.00: £285.00) Stalls: Low GOING: 0.34 sec per fur (SLW)

				SP	RR	SF
18[5]	**Calder King (65)** (JLEyre) **6-9-2b** RLappin(11) (chsd ldrs: led over 3f out: hrd rdn fnl f: all out)	—	**1**	7/2[3]	68	29
18[2]	**Forzair (53)** (JJO'Neill) **5-9-2** JQuinn(8) (lw: trckd ldrs: chal over 2f out: edgd rt u.p: styd on towards fin)	nk	**2**	100/30[2]	68	29
	Mad Militant (IRE) (66) (AStreeter) **8-9-2** TSprake(2) (lw: trckd ldrs: effrt 2f out: rdn & hung lft u.p: nt qckn)	4	**3**	5/4[1]	62	23
80[6]	**Soldier Cove (USA) (50)** (MartynMeade) **7-8-11**(5) DSweeney(5) (a.p: rdn 3f out: sn wl outpcd)	8	**4**	14/1	50	11
67[8]	**Lebedinski (IRE) (38)** (MrsPSly) **4-8-8** ACulhane(1) (led tl over 3f out: one pce)	13	**5**	50/1	26	—
	Summer Villa (40) (KGWingrove) **5-8-4**(7) AMcCarthy(3) (b.nr hind: sn bhd: sme hdwy 3f out: n.d)	3	**6**	20/1	22	—
85[4]	**Shanoora (IRE) (37)** (MrsNMacauley) **4-8-5**(3) CTeague(10) (hld up: a in rr)	8	**7**	10/1	10	—
54[8]	**A S Jim** (OO'Neill) **6-9-2b[1]** VSlattery(6) (chsd ldrs tl rdn & lost pl 6f out: sn bhd: t.o 3f out)	dist	**8**	33/1	—	—
54[10]	**Spencer's Revenge (62)** (NTinkler) **8-9-2b** GBardwell(7) (b.nr hind: sn drvn along: hdwy 8f out: sn chsng ldrs: lost pl over 2f out: eased: t.o)	5	**9**	7/1	—	—
	Harlestone Heath (MDods) **4-8-8** AClark(9) (s.i.s: t.o 4f out)	dist	**10**	16/1	—	—
	Double Vintage (IRE) (25) (MCChapman) **4-8-6**(7) IonaWands(4) (hld up & plld hrd: drvn along 7f out: nt keen: t.o)	nk	**11**	50/1	—	—

(SP 135.5%) **11 Rn**

2m 33.7 (13.70) CSF £16.37 TOTE £7.00: £2.10 £2.40 £1.10 (£14.20) Trio £5.30 OWNER Mr D. Clarkson (HAMBLETON) BRED Bellmor Stud
WEIGHT FOR AGE 4yo-3lb
No bid
STEWARDS' ENQUIRY Lappin fined £100 (failure to ride to draw).

115 OCTOPUS H'CAP (0-70) (4-Y.O+) (Class E)

3-55 (3-56) **1m 4f (Fibresand)** £2,801.00 (£848.00: £414.00: £197.00) Stalls: Low GOING: 0.34 sec per fur (SLW)

				SP	RR	SF
88*	**China Castle (72)** (PCHaslam) **4-10-5** 5x SDrowne(1) (lw: chsd ldrs: shkn up over 5f out: led on bit over 1f out: readily)	—	**1**	10/11[1]	88+	58
	Qualitair Pride (37) (JFBottomley) **5-8-2** NCarlisle(2) (led tl over 1f out: kpt on: no ch w wnr)	4	**2**	50/1	48	22
101*	**Golden Hadeer (59)** (MJRyan) **6-9-10** 5x AClark(9) (lw: sn pushed along: a chsng ldrs: nt qckn appr fnl f)	½	**3**	3/1[2]	69	43
86[4]	**Mustang (36)** (CWThornton) **4-7-11**ow1 LCharnock(7) (a chsng ldrs: drvn along 3f out: kpt on same pce)	¾	**4**	11/1	45	14
16[7]	**Calendula (55)** (DMorley) **4-9-2** GCarter(6) (hld up: smooth hdwy 5f out: ev ch over 2f out: sn wknd & eased)	29	**5**	25/1	25	—
43[2]	**Nothing Doing (IRE) (33)** (WJMusson) **8-7-12** JQuinn(8) (unruly: hld up: effrt 5f out: no rspnse)	9	**6**	7/1[3]	—	—
30[4]	**Philmist (50)** (JHetherton) **5-9-1b** NKennedy(5) (sn bhd & drvn along: sme hdwy 6f out: lost pl over 3f out)	½	**7**	20/1	8	—
88[5]	**Carol Again (42)** (NBycroft) **5-8-0**(7) JBramhill(3) (chsd ldrs: sn pushed along: lost pl over 4f out)	hd	**8**	20/1	—	—
66[2]	**Sea God (47)** (MCChapman) **6-8-12** GBardwell(4) (chsd ldrs: drvn along & lost pl 7f out)	¾	**9**	14/1	4	—

(SP 120.2%) **9 Rn**

2m 45.9 (12.90) CSF £73.02 CT £109.55 TOTE £1.90: £1.10 £13.20 £1.20 (£225.20) Trio £71.60 OWNER Mr J. M. Davis (MIDDLEHAM) BRED Mrs Frances Cronin
WEIGHT FOR AGE 4yo-4lb

T/Plpt: £15.40 (472.45 Tckts). T/Qdpt: £6.10 (125.13 Tckts). WG

0104-LINGFIELD (L-H) (Standard)
Saturday January 18th

WEATHER: drizzling WIND: almost nil

116 STUBBS AMATEUR H'CAP (0-65) (4-Y.O+) (Class F)

1-25 (1-27) **1m 4f (Equitrack)** £2,484.40 (£698.40: £341.20) Stalls: Low GOING minus 0.36 sec per fur (FST)

				SP	RR	SF
61[10]	**Squire's Occasion (CAN) (60)** (RAkehurst) **4-10-10**(5) MrJTizzard(11) (hld up: hdwy 4f out: led over 1f out: r.o)	—	**1**	20/1	70	52
63[2]	**Rasayel (USA) (52)** (PDEvans) **7-10-6**(5) MrWMcLaughlin(2) (hld up: hdwy 4f out: rdn 2f out: r.o wl ins fnl f)	1¼	**2**	9/4[1]	60	46
	Soojama (IRE) (41) (RMFlower) **7-10-0b**ow1 MrTMcCarthy(12) (chsd ldrs: led over 2f out: hdd over 1f out: one pce)	nk	**3**	5/2[2]	49	34
78[4]	**Ela Man Howa (49)** (ABailey) **6-10-3**(5) MissALHutchinson(1) (b: hld up: hdwy 3f out: rdn 2f out: kpt on one pce ins fnl f)	3	**4**	15/2	53	39
15[4]	**Montone (IRE) (62)** (JRJenkins) **7-11-7v** DrMMannish(7) (hld up: hdwy 4f out: rdn over 2f out: one pce)	1¼	**5**	7/1[3]	64	50

Form	Horse / details	Dist	Pos	SP	RR	SF
22^{4}	**Captain Marmalade (44)** (DTThom) **8-10-3** MissDianaJones(10) (hld up: hdwy 4f out: rdn over 2f out: wknd over 1f out)	3	**6**	16/1	42	28
	Don't Drop Bombs (USA) (38) (DTThom) **8-9-11v** MissJFeilden(9) (prom: led 5f out: hdd over 2f out: sn wknd)	3	**7**	7/1 3	32	18
	Outstayed Welcome (50) (MJHaynes) **5-10-9** MissYHaynes(8) (b.off hind: led after 1f: hdd 5f out: wknd over 3f out)	9	**8**	14/1	32	18
	Sarum (38) (JELong) **11-9-6**(5)ow6 MrTWaters(3) (b: bhd fr ½-wy)	12	**9**	40/1	4	—
	Chieftain's Crown (USA) (37) (THind) **6-9-10b** MissPJones(6) (bit bkwd: plld hrd: chsd ldrs tl over 4f out)	3½	**10**	14/1	—	—
	Thorniwama (49) (JJBridger) **6-10-3**(5)ow8 MrDBridger(5) (a bhd)	4	**11**	33/1	5	—
	Alosaili (35) (JCullinan) **10-9-3**(5) MissEmmaGarley(4) (led 1f: bhd fnl 7f)	2	**12**	40/1	—	—

(SP 127.9%) **12 Rn**

2m 36.66 (6.66) CSF £62.14 CT £149.83 TOTE £29.10: £6.20 £1.10 £1.70 (£59.20) Trio £115.80 OWNER Chelgate Public Relations Ltd (EPSOM) BRED Spring Farm & Associates
WEIGHT FOR AGE 4yo-4lb
OFFICIAL EXPLANATION **Squire's Occasion (CAN): the trainer reported that the gelding had been slowly away and was never travelling last time, and benefited from the longer trip here.**

117 HARRINGTON BIRD CLAIMING STKS (4-Y.O+) (Class E)

1-55 (1-56) **6f (Equitrack)** £2,817.25 (£853.00: £416.50: £198.25) Stalls: Low GOING minus 0.36 sec per fur (FST)

Form	Horse / details	Dist	Pos	SP	RR	SF
53^{7}	**Lord Sky (62)** (ABailey) **6-8-9** SSanders(9) (mde all: rdn out)	—	**1**	12/1	67	20
107^{9}	**Invocation (63)** (GLMoore) **10-8-7** AClark(1) (rr: sn rdn along: hdwy 2f out: styd on strly ins fnl f)	hd	**2**	6/1 3	65	18
11^{6}	**Miss Pickpocket (IRE) (39)** (MissGayKelleway) **4-7-8**(7)ow1 AngelaGallimore(8) (dwlt: rdn ½-wy: styd on ins fnl f)	1	**3**	25/1	56	8
20^{4}	**Norling (IRE) (38)** (KOCunningham-Brown) **7-8-9** CMunday(6) (in tch: outpcd ½-wy: styd on ins fnl f)	1	**4**	25/1	61	14
58^{*}	**Krystal Max (IRE) (76)** (JCullinan) **4-8-8**(5) DSweeney(3) (lw: prom: rdn over 2f out: wknd 1f out)	¾	**5**	5/4 1	63	16
	Robo Magic (USA) (80) (LMontagueHall) **5-9-4**(3) FLynch(4) (lw: prom: ev ch 2f out: wknd ins fnl f)	1¼	**6**	9/2 2	68	21
109^{5}	**The Frisky Farmer (52)** (WGMTurner) **4-8-11** TSprake(5) (lw: sn outpcd)	1	**7**	16/1	55	8
58^{3}	**Lift Boy (USA) (61)** (GLMoore) **8-8-7** CandyMorris(2) (prom early: sn outpcd)	nk	**8**	6/1 3	51	4
	Silent Symphony (MrsSDWilliams) **5-8-3**ow1 SDrowne(7) (w'like: bit bkwd: dwlt: a bhd)	7	**9**	33/1	28	—

(SP 115.4%) **9 Rn**

1m 14.22 (3.12) CSF £72.73 TOTE £14.80: £3.20 £1.50 £4.50 (£37.70) Trio £175.30; £222.32 to Newton Abbot 20/1/97 OWNER Mr Ray Bailey (TARPORLEY) BRED R. Barber

118 SNAFFLES MEDIAN AUCTION MAIDEN STKS (3-Y.O) (Class E)

2-25 (2-26) **6f (Equitrack)** £2,700.25 (£817.00: £398.50: £189.25) Stalls: Low GOING minus 0.36 sec per fur (FST)

Form	Horse / details	Dist	Pos	SP	RR	SF
25^{7}	**Countless Times (55)** (WRMuir) **3-9-0** AClark(5) (chsd ldrs: pushed along after 2f: hrd rdn over 2f out: rn wd home turn: led ins fnl f: r.o wl)	—	**1**	14/1	75	14
	Blues Magic (IRE) (MBell) **3-8-9**(5) GFaulkner(6) (w'like: bit bkwd: dwlt: sn rcvrd to jn ldrs: led ½-wy: hdd ins fnl f: no ex)	4	**2**	4/5 1	64	3
	She's Dawan (IRE) (PMitchell) **3-8-6**(3) AWhelan(1) (outpcd & bhd tl styd on ins fnl f: r.o wl)	hd	**3**	16/1	59	—
45^{2}	**Harmony In Red (66)** (CADwyer) **3-9-0** MWigham(2) (outpcd in rr tl styd on ins fnl f: r.o)	1	**4**	5/1 3	61	—
	Hever Golf Charger (IRE) (62) (TJNaughton) **3-9-0** JWeaver(4) (led to ½-wy: wknd 1f out)	1¾	**5**	7/2 2	57	—
	Eliza (LordHuntingdon) **3-8-9** DHarrison(3) (bhd fr ½-wy)	20	**6**	8/1	—	—

(SP 118.1%) **6 Rn**

1m 15.03 (3.93) CSF £25.24 TOTE £17.70: £4.40 £1.10 (£17.30) OWNER The Pri Way Racing Partnership (LAMBOURN) BRED Hellwood Stud Farm

119 MUNNINGS LIMITED STKS (0-65) (3-Y.O) (Class F)

2-55 (2-55) **1m 2f (Equitrack)** £2,383.60 (£669.60: £326.80) Stalls: Low GOING minus 0.36 sec per fur (FST)

Form	Horse / details	Dist	Pos	SP	RR	SF
96^{*}	**Globetrotter (IRE) (65)** (MJohnston) **3-9-1** 2x JWeaver(4) (lw: hld up in tch: chsd ldr over 3f out: led over 2f out: sn clr: comf)	—	**1**	4/9 1	76+	24
	Spaniard's Mount (65) (MHTompkins) **3-8-13v** SSanders(3) (keen hold: hld up in tch: led 4f out: hdd over 2f out: sn btn)	9	**2**	11/4 2	60	8
	Lawn Lothario (65) (MJohnston) **3-8-11** DeanMcKeown(2) (led: hdd & outpcd 4f out: kpt on one pce ins fnl f)	½	**3**	10/1 3	57	5
60^{5}	**Serenade (IRE) (56)** (MJHaynes) **3-8-11** SDrowne(1) (w ldr tl wknd 5f out)	13	**4**	12/1	36	—

(SP 112.7%) **4 Rn**

2m 10.11 (5.81) CSF £1.94 TOTE £1.30 (£1.50) OWNER Brian Yeardley Continental Ltd (MIDDLEHAM) BRED Norelands Bloodstock

120 CECIL ALDIN H'CAP (0-80) (4-Y.O+) (Class D)

3-25 (3-26) **1m (Equitrack)** £3,436.25 (£1,040.00: £507.50: £241.25) Stalls: High GOING minus 0.36 sec per fur (FST)

Form	Horse / details	Dist	Pos	SP	RR	SF
	Mr Nevermind (IRE) (76) (GLMoore) **7-10-0** SWhitworth(9) (hld up: hdwy over 3f out: led over 1f out: r.o wl)	—	**1**	11/4 2	86	58
	Robellion (68) (DWPArbuthnot) **6-9-6v** DHarrison(2) (hld up: hdwy over 2f out: rdn over 1f out: styd on to go 2nd wl ins fnl f)	2	**2**	12/1	74	46
47^{3}	**Sooty Tern (55)** (JMBradley) **10-8-7** SDrowne(5) (led: hdd over 1f out: one pce)	nk	**3**	7/1	60	32
47^{11}	**Superior Force (62)** (MissBSanders) **4-8-11**(3) AWhelan(10) (hld up: hdwy 3f out: rdn 2f out: r.o one pce ins fnl f)	½	**4**	20/1	66	38
61^{6}	**Double March (56)** (PRWebber) **4-8-8** RPerham(7) (mid div: rdn & lost pl 3f out: kpt on one pce ins fnl f)	1¼	**5**	10/1	58	30
47^{2}	**Oberons Boy (IRE) (62)** (SDow) **4-9-0** SSanders(1) (dwlt: rdn thrght: nvr on terms)	1¼	**6**	5/2 1	61	33
113^{6}	**Manabar (58)** (MJPolglase) **5-8-10b** TGMcLaughlin(8) (prom: rdn 2f out: sn wknd)	½	**7**	16/1	56	28
98^{3}	**Gold Lance (USA) (44)** (RJO'Sullivan) **4-7-10b** JQuinn(3) (chsd ldrs tl wknd over 3f out)	4	**8**	7/2 3	34	6
	Queenfisher (74) (GLMoore) **5-9-9**(3) FLynch(4) (chsd ldr 5f: sn wknd)	3	**9**	25/1	58	30

(SP 121.2%) **9 Rn**

1m 39.65 (2.25) CSF £34.40 CT £198.87 TOTE £3.90: £1.20 £2.70 £2.00 (£26.00) Trio £24.00 OWNER Pennine Partners (BRIGHTON) BRED Robert Corridan

121 LADBROKE ALL-WEATHER TROPHY (FINAL) H'CAP (4-Y.O+) (Class B)

3-55 (3-57) **7f (Equitrack)** £9,061.00 (£2,743.00: £1,339.00: £637.00) Stalls: Low GOING minus 0.36 sec per fur (FST)

			SP	RR	SF
	Blue Flyer (IRE) (74) (RIngram) **4-9-7b** JWeaver(9) (lw: rr: gd hdwy over 2f out: led wl over 1f out: r.o wl)....—	1	20/1	83	64
109^{*}	**Sea Danzig (67)** (JJBridger) **4-9-0** 4x DHarrison(11) (a.p: ev ch over 1f out: one pce)....2½	2	15/2	70	51
48^{4}	**Apollo Red (62)** (GLMoore) **8-8-9** CandyMorris(7) (a.p: rdn & sltly outpcd 2f out: styd on one pce ins fnl f)...1½	3	20/1	62	43
21^{*}	**Royal Carlton (IRE) (66)** (GLMoore) **5-8-13** SWhitworth(6) (nvr nrr)....3	4	$5/2^{1}$	59	40
15^{15}	**Twin Creeks (70)** (VSoane) **6-9-3** CRutter(8) (chsd ldr: rdn over 2f out: wknd over 1f out)....2	5	12/1	58	39
27^{2}	**Fort Knox (IRE) (61)** (RMFlower) **6-8-8b** MWigham(10) (nvr nrr)....s.h	6	15/2	49	30
57^{4}	**Shontaine (60)** (MJohnston) **4-8-7** DeanMcKeown(2) (nvr nrr)....2	7	20/1	44	25
	Speedy Classic (USA) (81) (MJHeaton-Ellis) **8-10-0** AClark(13) (led 5f out: hdd wl over 1f out: sn wknd).....s.h	8	$13/2^{3}$	65	46
27^{*}	**Step On Degas (66)** (MJFetherston-Godley) **4-8-8**(5) DGriffiths(4) (lw: mid div: rdn 5f out: wknd over 2f out).s.h	9	9/1	50	31
57^{*}	**Hawaii Storm (FR) (50)** (DJSffrenchDavis) **9-7-8b**(3) MBaird(1) (a bhd)....3	10	8/1	27	8
27^{3}	**Jo Maximus (62)** (SDow) **5-8-4**(5) ADaly(5) (bhd fnl 4f)....2	11	$6/1^{2}$	34	15
	Greatest (75) (MissGayKelleway) **6-9-8b** SSanders(3) (b: led: hdd 5f out: wknd over 3f out: t.o)....16	12	20/1	11	—

(SP 127.6%) **12 Rn**

1m 25.33 (0.93) CSF £151.23 CT £2,773.72 TOTE £20.40: £3.90 £3.20 £3.40 (£88.70) Trio £455.40; £468.23 to Newton Abbot 20/1/97
OWNER Mr B. Scott (EPSOM) BRED Matt Carr

OFFICIAL EXPLANATION **Blue Flyer (IRE): accounting for the horse's apparent improvement in form, the trainer stated that his stable had been below par before Christmas, but after blood tests and treatment they have regained their form.**

T/Plpt: £2,103.80 (4.87 Tckts). T/Qdpt: £110.90 (7.66 Tckts). SM

0110-SOUTHWELL (L-H) (Standard)
Monday January 20th

WEATHER: fine WIND: slt bhd

122 JADE JEWEL MEDIAN AUCTION MAIDEN STKS (4, 5 & 6-Y.O) (Class F)

1-45 (1-46) **1m 4f (Fibresand)** £2,294.00 (£644.00: £314.00) Stalls: Low GOING: 0.19 sec per fur (SLW)

			SP	RR	SF
73^{3}	**Soviet King (IRE) (50)** (PMitchell) **4-8-12** SSanders(4) (lw: hld up: stdy hdwy to ld wl over 1f out: comf)....—	1	$7/4^{1}$	39+	25
86^{8}	**Swandale Flyer (30)** (NBycroft) **5-8-9**(7) JBramhill(1) (mde most tl hdd wl over 1f out: no ch w wnr)....1¾	2	16/1	37	27
86^{3}	**Toulston Lady (IRE) (38)** (JWharton) **5-8-11b**[1] JQuinn(5) (lw: prom: hdwy 4f out: sn ev ch: outpcd fnl 2f).....10	3	$7/2^{3}$	18	8
80^{4}	**Threesocks (42)** (BSmart) **4-8-7** RPerham(3) (disp ld 8f: rdn & btn over 2f out)....6	4	$9/4^{2}$	10	—
86^{2}	**Acerbus Dulcis (32)** (MCChapman) **6-8-9**(7) IonaWands(8) (cl up tl outpcd 4f out: sn btn)....22	5	6/1	—	—
	Bold Joker (21) (GROldroyd) **6-8-13**(3) CTeague(2) (a outpcd & bhd)....13	6	50/1	—	—
	Northern Spruce (IRE) (25) (AGFoster) **5-9-2** TSprake(6) (effrt 5f out: sme hdwy 3f out: sn btn)....nk	7	50/1	—	—
16^{14}	**Ballet de Cour (45)** (TJEtherington) **4-8-12** ACulhane(7) (chsd ldrs: drvn along 6f out: sn wknd: t.o)....dist	8	33/1	—	—

(SP 116.4%) **8 Rn**

2m 46.3 (13.30) CSF £28.54 TOTE £2.50: £1.10 £3.00 £1.80 (£12.90) OWNER Mrs Patricia Mitchell (EPSOM) BRED Frank Lucey
WEIGHT FOR AGE 4yo-4lb

123 BLUE VELVET H'CAP (0-70) (4-Y.O+) (Class E)

2-15 (2-16) **1m 3f (Fibresand)** £2,830.25 (£857.00: £418.50: £199.25) Stalls: Low GOING: 0.19 sec per fur (SLW)

			SP	RR	SF
86^{*}	**Raffles Rooster (56)** (AGNewcombe) **5-9-0**(7) JoHunnam(2) (sn trckng ldrs: qcknd to ld cl home)....—	1	$11/4^{2}$	66	36
88^{2}	**Maftun (USA) (51)** (GMMoore) **5-9-2** ACulhane(7) (led: hrd rdn fnl f: hdd & nt qckn towards fin)....1¼	2	$9/4^{1}$	59	29
67^{3}	**Kilnamartyra Girl (41)** (JParkes) **7-8-6** DHarrison(10) (lw: prom: ev ch 3f out: sn rdn & one pce)....5	3	$9/1^{3}$	42	12
	Risky Tu (45) (PAKelleway) **6-8-10** MWigham(5) (lw: chsd ldrs: drvn along thrght: kpt on fnl f)....s.h	4	$9/1^{3}$	46	16
2^{6}	**Zatopek (41)** (JCullinan) **5-8-6** JQuinn(8) (chsd ldrs: hrd rdn over 2f out: sn btn)....8	5	33/1	30	—
	Ambidextrous (IRE) (49) (EJAlston) **5-9-0** DWright(6) (bhd: pushed along ½-wy: styd on: n.d)....5	6	11/1	31	1
	Genuine John (IRE) (65) (JParkes) **4-9-6**(7) JBramhill(4) (lw: bhd: effrt 4f out: rdn & no imp)....3	7	20/1	43	10
91^{3}	**Spanish Stripper (USA) (32)** (MCChapman) **6-7-4**(7) IonaWands(12) (hdwy 6f out: sn prom: wknd over 2f out)¾	8	20/1	9	—
88^{3}	**Wildfire (SWI) (46)** (RAkehurst) **6-8-11** SSanders(1) (b: chsd ldrs: rdn 4f out: wknd 3f out)....10	9	$9/1^{3}$	8	—
39^{6}	**Shahik (USA) (63)** (DHaydnJones) **7-10-0** LCharnock(9) (a bhd)....5	10	14/1	18	—
	Pc's Cruiser (IRE) (42) (JLEyre) **5-8-7b** DRMcCabe(13) (hdwy 8f out: sn prom: rdn 6f out: sn lost tch)....nk	11	12/1	—	—
74^{5}	**Rehaab (61)** (DMorris) **4-9-4**(5) GFaulkner(11) (bhd fnl 5f)....18	12	14/1	—	—
23^{10}	**A Million Watts (62)** (GMMcCourt) **6-9-13** AClark(3) (rdn & lost tch 5f out: wl t.o)....dist	13	25/1	—	—

(SP 133.1%) **13 Rn**

2m 31.7 (11.70) CSF £9.19 CT £50.41 TOTE £2.70: £1.10 £1.50 £3.20 (£5.10) Trio £13.90 OWNER Mr Mark Leatham (BARNSTAPLE) BRED G. Strawbridge & London Thoroughbred Services Ltd
WEIGHT FOR AGE 4yo-3lb

124 MARTIN WAIN 38TH BIRTHDAY H'CAP (0-60) (3-Y.O) (Class F)

2-45 (2-52) **1m (Fibresand)** £2,294.00 (£644.00: £314.00) Stalls: Low GOING: 0.19 sec per fur (SLW)

			SP	RR	SF
	Broctune Line (45) (MrsMReveley) **3-8-6** ACulhane(12) (bhd: hdwy 3f out: led wl over 1f out: comf)....—	1	$5/1^{2}$	52	13
90^{2}	**Aspecto Lad (IRE) (58)** (MJohnston) **3-9-5** JWeaver(7) (lw: s.i.s: racd wd: gd hdwy over 2f out: r.o: nt pce to chal)....2½	2	$2/1^{1}$	60	21
	Neon Deion (IRE) (42) (SCWilliams) **3-7-10v**(7) DarrenWilliams(13) (chsd ldrs: kpt on one pce fnl 2f)....4	3	33/1	36	—
33^{3}	**Senate Swings (55)** (WRMuir) **3-9-2** AClark(4) (led tl hdd wl over 1f out: sn outpcd)....½	4	11/1	48	9
	Samspet (47) (RAFahey) **3-8-1**(7) RWinston(15) (w ldrs tl wknd 2f out)....2	5	33/1	36	—
77^{3}	**Windborn (52)** (CNAllen) **3-8-6**(7) JBramhill(8) (in tch: rdn 3f out: one pce)....3½	6	12/1	34	—
	Rock Fantasy (56) (CMurray) **3-8-12**(5) GFaulkner(11) (nvr trbld ldrs)....1¼	7	25/1	36	—
84^{6}	**State of Gold (IRE) (52)** (JHetherton) **3-8-13b** SWhitworth(3) (lw: in tch tl wknd fnl 3f)....1	8	25/1	30	—
26^{9}	**Buzzby Babe (48)** (AGFoster) **3-8-9** TSprake(14) (b: broke wl: lost pl after 2f)....1¼	9	33/1	23	—

				SP	RR	SF
84[3]	**Silent Valley (50)** (DNicholls) **3-8-11b** AlexGreaves(9) (lw: s.s: nt rcvr)	4	**10**	15/2[3]	17	—
90[11]	**T-N-T Express (45)** (EJAlston) **3-8-6** SSanders(6) (n.d fr ½-wy)	5	**11**	33/1	2	—
	Eternal Host (IRE) (46) (RHollinshead) **3-8-4**(3) FLynch(5) (n.d)	½	**12**	16/1	2	—
77[2]	**Lily Jaques (54)** (RGuest) **3-9-1** DBiggs(1) (nvr wnt pce)	16	**13**	11/1	—	—
19[6]	**Lycius Touch (49)** (AGNewcombe) **3-8-10** FNorton(10) (unruly gng to s: n.d)	¾	**14**	11/1	—	—
96[7]	**Nattie (49)** (AGNewcombe) **3-8-10** JQuinn(16) (cl up tl wknd over 3f out)	5	**15**	33/1	—	—
83[5]	**Move The Clouds (60)** (JRFanshawe) **3-9-4**(3) NVarley(2) (chsd ldrs tl rdn & fnd nil over 3f out)	½	**16**	8/1	—	—

(SP 133.8%) **16 Rn**

1m 48.3 (9.30) CSF £14.34 CT £283.63 TOTE £5.20: £1.50 £1.10 £12.50 £1.70 (£9.00) Trio Not won; £284.34 to Market Rasen 21/1/97
OWNER Mr D. Playforth (SALTBURN) BRED Ronald Wilkie

125 CHAMPAGNE GOLD H'CAP (0-70) (4-Y.O+ F & M) (Class E)

3-15 (3-18) **1m (Fibresand)** £2,817.25 (£853.00: £416.50: £198.25) Stalls: Low GOING: 0.19 sec per fur (SLW)

				SP	RR	SF
34*	**Mono Lady (IRE) (54)** (DHaydnJones) **4-9-3b** CRutter(11) (in tch: effrt over 2f out: r.o wl fnl f to ld cl home)	—	**1**	8/1	64	25
72[4]	**Three Arch Bridge (60)** (MJohnston) **5-9-9b** JWeaver(6) (w ldrs: led over 2f out tl ct cl home)	½	**2**	9/2[2]	69	30
14[4]	**Giddy (42)** (JHetherton) **4-8-5** NKennedy(1) (cl up: chal over 2f out: one pce appr fnl f)	2½	**3**	14/1	46	7
85[2]	**Ilandra (IRE) (43)** (RAkehurst) **5-8-6** SSanders(4) (lw: chsd ldrs: rdn ½-wy: kpt on one pce)	1	**4**	7/1	45	6
85[10]	**Efipetite (40)** (NBycroft) **4-8-3** GBardwell(8) (s.i.s: c wd st: sme late hdwy)	3	**5**	20/1	36	—
	Palacegate Jo (IRE) (33) (DWChapman) **6-7-10** DWright(10) (bit bkwd: s.i.s: hdwy over 2f out: nvr nr to chal)	nk	**6**	25/1	28	—
91[4]	**Scenicris (IRE) (45)** (RHollinshead) **4-8-5**(3) FLynch(9) (bhd: c wd st: hdwy 2f out: nvr rchd ldrs)	½	**7**	7/1	39	—
29[2]	**Cats Bottom (52)** (AGNewcombe) **5-9-1** JQuinn(15) (in tch: hdwy u.p 2f out: wknd fnl f)	¾	**8**	4/1[1]	45	6
85[6]	**Down The Yard (40)** (MCChapman) **4-7-10**(7) IonaWands(7) (lw: nvr wnt pce)	7	**9**	14/1	19	—
91[2]	**Broughton's Pride (IRE) (48)** (JLEyre) **6-8-11** TWilliams(2) (lw: led tl hdd over 2f out: grad wknd)	nk	**10**	5/1[3]	26	—
	Blue Jumbo (IRE) (45) (WJMusson) **4-8-8** DRMcCabe(13) (s.i.s: a bhd)	6	**11**	14/1	11	—
	Kingdom Princess (64) (MJCamacho) **4-9-13** LCharnock(5) (w ldrs tl wknd fnl 2f)	3½	**12**	14/1	23	—
88[14]	**Ann's Music (34)** (JMJefferson) **4-7-4**(7)ow1 JBramhill(12) (cl up tl wknd fnl 3f)	½	**13**	50/1	—	—
71[14]	**Carmosa (USA) (50)** (DNicholls) **4-8-13** AlexGreaves(3) (prom tl wknd 3f out)	nk	**14**	14/1	8	—

(SP 134.9%) **14 Rn**

1m 48.1 (9.10) CSF £44.14 CT £495.62 TOTE £9.60: £3.50 £3.00 £4.70 (£21.20) Trio £218.40; £279.96 to Market Rasen 21/1/97 OWNER Monolithic Refractories Ltd (PONTYPRIDD) BRED Dr. Michael Smurfit
LONG HANDICAP Palacegate Jo (IRE) 7-7 Ann's Music 7-7
STEWARDS' ENQUIRY Weaver susp. 29-30/1 & Kennedy susp. 29-31/1/97 (excessive use of whip)

126 SILVER ICE (S) STKS (3-Y.O+) (Class F)

3-45 (3-45) **6f (Fibresand)** £2,294.00 (£644.00: £314.00) Stalls: Low GOING: 0.19 sec per fur (SLW)

				SP	RR	SF
71*	**Sense of Priority (70)** (DNicholls) **8-9-12** AlexGreaves(4) (trckd ldrs: effrt 2f out: hrd rdn to ld wl ins fnl f)	—	**1**	6/4[1]	64	49
51[2]	**Kalar (76)** (DWChapman) **8-9-12b** ACulhane(2) (rdn to ld after 1f: ct wl ins fnl f)	3	**2**	2/1[2]	56	41
	Fiaba (36) (MrsNMacauley) **9-8-13v**(3) CTeague(6) (sn outpcd: styd on wl fnl f: nrst fin)	2	**3**	14/1	41	26
89[3]	**Little Ibnr (69)** (PDEvans) **6-9-5**(7) AnthonyBond(9) (lw: cl up: rdn over 2f out: r.o one pce)	¾	**4**	11/4[3]	49	34
59[9]	**Ragazzo (IRE) (34)** (JSWainwright) **7-9-7b** LCharnock(3) (b.hind: led 1f: cl up tl outpcd ½-wy: n.d after)	s.h	**5**	20/1	44	29
	Nukud (USA) (35) (GROldroyd) **5-9-0**(7) DMernagh(5) (nvr wnt pce)	2	**6**	50/1	38	23
	Lights of Home (MissCJohnsey) **3-8-5** NAdams(1) (sn outpcd & bhd)	9	**7**	40/1	14	—
79[10]	**Victoria Sioux (35)** (JAPickering) **4-9-2v[1]** NCarlisle(7) (nvr wnt pce)	17	**8**	33/1	—	—

(SP 118.8%) **8 Rn**

1m 19.1 (5.60) CSF £4.41 TOTE £2.80: £1.10 £1.10 £6.10 (£2.10) Trio £31.90 OWNER Mr M. A. Scaife (THIRSK) BRED Cheveley Park Stud Ltd
WEIGHT FOR AGE 3yo-16lb
No bid

127 PURPLE IRIS H'CAP (0-70) (4-Y.O+) (Class E)

4-15 (4-20) **6f (Fibresand)** £2,804.25 (£849.00: £414.50: £197.25) Stalls: Low GOING: 0.19 sec per fur (SLW)

				SP	RR	SF
79[8]	**Walk the Beat (65)** (MartynMeade) **7-9-4**(5) DSweeney(5) (mde most: r.o wl fnl 2f)	—	**1**	10/1	74	46
69[2]	**Blue Lugana (38)** (NBycroft) **5-7-3**(7) JBramhill(13) (racd wd: hdwy over 2f out: hung lft: nrst fin)	2	**2**	12/1	42	14
81[3]	**Desert Invader (IRE) (68)** (DWChapman) **6-9-12** ACulhane(11) (in tch: sn drvn along: hmpd over 1f out: kpt on wl fnl f)	½	**3**	8/1[3]	70	42
51[7]	**Captain Carat (62)** (DNicholls) **6-9-6** AlexGreaves(1) (a.p: effrt over 2f out: nt qckn fnl f)	½	**4**	5/1[1]	63	35
87[6]	**Answers-To-Thomas (52)** (JMJefferson) **4-8-10** DeanMcKeown(4) (drvn along & sn disp ld: hrd rdn 2f out: wknd fnl f)	s.h	**5**	16/1	53	25
113[11]	**Awesome Venture (70)** (MCChapman) **7-10-0** DRMcCabe(3) (chsd ldrs: n.m.r over 1f out: kpt on)	nk	**6**	8/1[3]	70	42
48[5]	**Shashi (IRE) (57)** (PatMitchell) **5-9-1** RLappin(12) (lw: chsd ldrs tl outpcd ½-wy: kpt on wl fnl f)	hd	**7**	10/1	57	29
89*	**Elton Ledger (IRE) (77)** (MrsNMacauley) **8-10-7v** 7x JWeaver(6) (b: lw: bhd: hdwy 2f out: n.m.r 1f out: n.d)	1	**8**	8/1[3]	74	46
69[7]	**Featherstone Lane (58)** (MissLCSiddall) **6-9-2v** DHarrison(7) (prom tl outpcd fnl 2f)	¾	**9**	16/1	53	25
72[8]	**Principal Boy (IRE) (46)** (TJEtherington) **4-8-4v[1]** CRutter(10) (n.d)	¾	**10**	14/1	39	11
69*	**Lady Silk (52)** (MissJFCraze) **6-8-10** JFanning(14) (lw: nvr wnt pce)	4	**11**	10/1	35	7
65[3]	**Dissentor (IRE) (41)** (JAGlover) **5-7-13v** JQuinn(2) (prom over 3f: wknd)	13	**12**	11/2[2]	—	—
71[15]	**Maysimp (IRE) (38)** (BPJBaugh) **4-7-3b[1]**(7) IonaWands(9) (a bhd)	5	**13**	50/1	—	—
40[13]	**Imp Express (IRE) (40)** (GMMoore) **4-7-12** GBardwell(8) (a outpcd & bhd)	1¾	**14**	33/1	—	—

(SP 123.7%) **14 Rn**

1m 19.1 (5.60) CSF £116.66 CT £953.65 TOTE £10.90: £4.20 £4.90 £2.70 (£116.90) Trio £325.00; £283.81 to Market Rasen 21/1/97 OWNER The Country Life Partnership (MALMESBURY) BRED R. B. Warren
LONG HANDICAP Blue Lugana 7-6 Maysimp (IRE) 7-2
STEWARDS' ENQUIRY Bramhill susp. 29-30/1/97 (careless riding) Culhane susp. 29/1-1/2 & 3/2/97 (improper riding)

T/Plpt: £87.00 (124.21 Tckts). T/Qdpt: £29.40 (32.12 Tckts). AA

0116-LINGFIELD (L-H) (Standard)
Tuesday January 21st
WEATHER: sunny WIND: almost nil

128 HUNGERFORD APPRENTICE H'CAP (0-60) (I) (4-Y.O+) (Class F)
1-20 (1-22) **7f (Equitrack)** £2,067.20 (£579.20: £281.60) Stalls: Low GOING minus 0.35 sec per fur (FST)

			SP	RR	SF
47[5]	**Rawi (53)** (MissGayKelleway) **4-9-3**(5) AngelaGallimore(9) (b: b.hind: hdwy over 2f out: led over 1f out: r.o wl) —	**1**	4/1 3	62	35
24[5]	**Allstars Dancer (35)** (TJNaughton) **4-8-1**(3) PFessey(10) (a.p: led over 3f out tl over 1f out: unable qckn) 4	**2**	9/1	35	8
59[5]	**Madonna da Rossi (35)** (MDods) **4-7-13**(5) JBramhill(8) (hdwy over 3f out: ev ch over 1f out: one pce) 1½	**3**	8/1	31	4
	Justinianus (IRE) (29) (JJBridger) **5-7-5**(7) RBrisland(7) (a.p: rdn over 3f out: ev ch wl over 1f out: one pce) ¾	**4**	33/1	24	—
9[9]	**Mad Alex (27)** (MJHaynes) **4-7-10** DWright(4) (b.hind: dwlt: wl bhd over 4f: hdwy over 1f out: nvr nrr) 1	**5**	40/1	19	—
97[2]	**Mystery Matthias (41)** (MissBSanders) **4-8-5v**(5) JoHunnam(2) (lost pl over 3f out: no hdwy fnl 2f) 1½	**6**	7/2 2	30	3
109[4]	**Barbason (55)** (GLMoore) **5-9-7**(3) GFaulkner(5) (a.p: rdn over 3f out: wknd over 1f out) 3½	**7**	100/30 1	36	9
34[7]	**Dia Georgy (27)** (CADwyer) **6-7-10** NVarley(6) (b: bhd fnl 6f) 1	**8**	20/1	6	—
91[7]	**Supreme Illusion (AUS) (27)** (JohnBerry) **4-7-3b**(7) DarrenWilliams(1) (a bhd) 2	**9**	25/1	1	—
95[6]	**Distant Dynasty (33)** (BAPearce) **7-7-13**(3)ow3 ADaly(11) (b.hind: prom over 4f) 2½	**10**	20/1	1	—
69[3]	**Blushing Grenadier (IRE) (49)** (MJFetherston-Godley) **5-9-4** FLynch(3) (led over 3f: wkng whn n.m.r on ins over 2f out) 13	**11**	4/1 3	—	—

(SP 125.2%) **11 Rn**

1m 27.96 (3.56) CSF £35.76 CT £215.87 TOTE £6.90: £2.00 £3.40 £1.60 (£61.90) Trio £39.60 OWNER Mr Chris Wilkinson (WHITCOMBE) BRED D. G. Mason
LONG HANDICAP Supreme Illusion (AUS) 7-7 Mad Alex 7-8 Dia Georgy 7-7
Rawi clmd N Dearman £10,000

129 WESTMINSTER CLAIMING STKS (4-Y.O+) (Class E)
1-50 (1-50) **1m 4f (Equitrack)** £2,700.25 (£817.00: £398.50: £189.25) Stalls: Low GOING minus 0.35 sec per fur (FST)

			SP	RR	SF
93*	**Persian Conquest (IRE) (65)** (RIngram) **5-9-3b** JWeaver(6) (lw: hdwy to chse ldr 4f out: led over 2f out: clr over 1f out: rdn out) —	**1**	13/8 2	68	37
99*	**Galapino (70)** (GCBravery) **4-9-3** MRimmer(3) (b: hdwy over 4f out: chsd wnr over 1f out: hrd rdn: r.o wl) 1	**2**	Evens 1	71	36
99[3]	**Zahid (USA) (51)** (KRBurke) **6-9-3v** JQuinn(2) (lw: rdn 5f out: hdwy over 3f out: wknd wl over 1f out) 6	**3**	12/1	59	28
	English Invader (82) (RAkehurst) **6-9-3** SSanders(5) (lw: a.p: led over 4f out tl over 2f out: wknd wl over 1f out) nk	**4**	8/1 3	58	27
76[12]	**Bath Knight (40)** (DJSffrenchDavis) **4-8-5** GCarter(4) (chsd ldr 8f) 20	**5**	20/1	24	—
	Topup (43) (JWHills) **4-8-5b**1 NAdams(1) (led over 7f: t.o) 27	**6**	33/1	—	—

(SP 114.6%) **6 Rn**

2m 35.43 (5.43) CSF £3.37 TOTE £2.30: £1.50 £1.20 (£1.60) OWNER Mr B. Scott (EPSOM) BRED Louis A. Walshe
WEIGHT FOR AGE 4yo-4lb
Galapino clmd N Dearman £10,000

130 VAUXHALL (S) STKS (3-Y.O) (Class G)
2-20 (2-20) **1m (Equitrack)** £2,144.10 (£594.60: £290.30) Stalls: High GOING minus 0.35 sec per fur (FST)

			SP	RR	SF
7[5]	**As-Is (60)** (MJohnston) **3-8-11** JWeaver(6) (hld up: led over 3f out: hrd rdn & edgd lft over 1f out: r.o wl) —	**1**	3/1 3	64	14
	Our Kevin (53) (KMcAuliffe) **3-8-11be** DRMcCabe(2) (led 3f: led 4f out tl over 3f out: ev ch 2f out: unable qckn) 5	**2**	100/30	54	4
94[3]	**Taome (IRE) (53)** (PDEvans) **3-8-6** SSanders(3) (rdn over 5f out: no hdwy fnl 3f) 6	**3**	11/4 2	37	—
7[6]	**Marsh Marigold (60)** (MartynMeade) **3-8-6** NAdams(1) (a.p: led 5f out to 4f out: wknd over 3f out) 5	**4**	2/1 1	27	—
	Ditty Box (30) (MDIUsher) **3-8-8**ow2 MWigham(5) (a bhd) 29	**5**	33/1	—	—

(SP 111.0%) **5 Rn**

1m 42.61 (5.21) CSF £12.06 TOTE £4.50: £2.60 £2.00 (£4.30) OWNER Mr Robinson (Wigan) (MIDDLEHAM) BRED Roldvale Ltd
Bt in 3,700 gns

131 ALBERT H'CAP (0-85) (4-Y.O+) (Class D)
2-50 (2-51) **1m 2f (Equitrack)** £3,485.00 (£1,055.00: £515.00: £245.00) Stalls: Low GOING minus 0.35 sec per fur (FST)

			SP	RR	SF
92[2]	**Quiet Arch (IRE) (57)** (WRMuir) **4-7-5**(7) JBramhill(10) (b: b.hind: lw: hdwy 4f out: chsd ldr over 2f out: led over 1f out: r.o wl) —	**1**	4/1 1	73	31
23*	**Steamroller Stanly (85)** (CACyzer) **4-9-12** GCarter(7) (a.p: led over 3f out tl over 1f out: unable qckn) 3	**2**	9/2 2	96	54
	Sweet Supposin (IRE) (61) (CADwyer) **6-8-4v** JStack(4) (hdwy 4f out: rdn over 3f out: one pce) 11	**3**	16/1	55	15
	Soviet Bride (IRE) (72) (SDow) **5-8-10**(5) ADaly(5) (rdn & hdwy 3f out: one pce) 1	**4**	6/1	64	24
10[3]	**Ben Gunn (56)** (PTWalwyn) **5-7-13v**1 DWright(6) (chsd ldr over 6f) 1¾	**5**	9/1	45	5
	Barossa Valley (IRE) (82) (PButler) **6-9-6**(5) DGriffiths(2) (led over 6f) 6	**6**	5/1 3	62	22
	No Pattern (66) (GLMoore) **5-8-9v** JQuinn(9) (lw: a bhd) 11	**7**	11/1	28	—
	Mutadarra (IRE) (79) (WJMusson) **4-9-6** DRMcCabe(8) (bhd fnl 3f) 1	**8**	33/1	39	—
120[2]	**Robellion (68)** (DWPArbuthnot) **6-8-11v** DHarrison(1) (b: b.hind: hld up: rdn over 3f out: sn wknd) 3½	**9**	5/1 3	23	—
	Law Dancer (IRE) (77) (TGMills) **4-9-4** SSanders(3) (prom over 5f) 12	**10**	16/1	13	—

(SP 118.8%) **10 Rn**

2m 7.28 (2.98) CSF £20.38 CT £239.91 TOTE £4.70: £1.20 £2.50 £2.80 (£8.60) Trio £88.60 OWNER Mr John Davies (LAMBOURN) BRED E. and Mrs Flannery
WEIGHT FOR AGE 4yo-2lb

132 CHELSEA H'CAP (0-60) (3-Y.O) (Class F)
3-20 (3-21) **6f (Equitrack)** £2,450.80 (£688.80: £336.40) Stalls: Low GOING minus 0.35 sec per fur (FST)

			SP	RR	SF
118*	**Countless Times (62)** (WRMuir) **3-9-5**(7) 7x JWilkinson(5) (outpcd: gd hdwy to ld 1f out: r.o wl) —	**1**	3/1 1	78	9

Form	Horse	Dist	Pos	SP	RR	SF
110[3]	**Mirror Four Sport (46)** (MJohnston) **3-8-3**(7) KSked(1) (outpcd: hdwy fnl f: r.o)	6	**2**	9/1	46	—
	Sparkling Edge (57) (CADwyer) **3-9-7** DRMcCabe(8) (hld up: rdn over 2f out: led over 1f out: sn hdd: unable qckn)	1¼	**3**	13/2[3]	54	—
	Formidable Spirit (36) (MJHeaton-Ellis) **3-8-0v[1]** DWright(9) (lw: hdwy over 3f out: rdn over 2f out: one pce)	¾	**4**	16/1	31	—
	Hever Golf Stormer (IRE) (50) (TJNaughton) **3-9-0** DHolland(3) (bmpd s: a.p: led 4f out tl over 1f out: one pce)	s.h	**5**	8/1	45	—
90[5]	**Chasetown Flyer (USA) (56)** (RHollinshead) **3-9-3**(3) FLynch(7) (nvr nr to chal)	nk	**6**	7/1	50	—
	Magyar Titok (IRE) (51) (BobJones) **3-9-1** MRimmer(2) (bmpd s: bhd fnl 4f)	1¼	**7**	8/1	41	—
97[3]	**Silent Weapon (56)** (KMcAuliffe) **3-9-6** SSanders(6) (lw: led 1f: rdn over 2f out: 3rd whn hmpd over 1f out: sn wknd)	½	**8**	10/1	45	—
75[3]	**Seretse's Nephew (54)** (SCWilliams) **3-9-4b[1]** JTate(4) (led 5f out to 4f out: wknd over 2f out)	17	**9**	100/30[2]	—	—

(SP 121.1%) **9 Rn**

1m 16.33 (5.23) CSF £29.48 CT £155.11 TOTE £3.00: £2.20 £3.60 £2.60 (£24.70) Trio £65.00 OWNER The Pri Way Racing Partnership (LAMBOURN) BRED Hellwood Stud Farm

133 TOWER H'CAP (0-80) (4-Y.O+) (Class D)

3-50 (3-51) **2m** **(Equitrack)** £3,338.75 (£1,010.00: £492.50: £233.75) Stalls: Low GOING minus 0.35 sec per fur (FST)

Form	Horse	Dist	Pos	SP	RR	SF
63[6]	**Broughtons Formula (53)** (WJMusson) **7-8-1b** DRMcCabe(1) (lw: hdwy over 11f out: rdn over 4f out: led ins fnl f: r.o wl)	—	**1**	10/1	66	1
73[5]	**Random Kindness (65)** (RIngram) **4-8-6** JStack(7) (hdwy to ld 3f out: hrd rdn over 1f out: hdd ins fnl f: unable qckn)	1	**2**	7/1	77	5
100[2]	**Star Rage (IRE) (78)** (JLHarris) **7-9-12** JWeaver(4) (rdn over 3f out: hdwy over 1f out: r.o one pce)	5	**3**	9/4[1]	85	20
74*	**General Haven (75)** (TJNaughton) **4-9-2** DHolland(5) (lw: a.p: rdn over 4f out: wknd fnl f)	½	**4**	100/30[3]	82	10
30*	**The Great Flood (60)** (CADwyer) **4-8-1** JQuinn(6) (chsd ldr: led over 4f out to 3f out: wknd 2f out)	4	**5**	11/4[2]	63	—
	Matthias Mystique (58) (MissBSanders) **4-7-13** GBardwell(3) (led over 11f)	6	**6**	6/1	55	—
	Coleridge (58) (JJSheehan) **9-8-6b** AClark(2) (bhd fnl 5f)	1¼	**7**	20/1	53	—

(SP 121.2%) **7 Rn**

3m 32.82 (11.82) CSF £73.86 TOTE £12.30: £3.40 £4.60 (£73.70) OWNER Crawford Gray & Aylett (NEWMARKET) BRED The Lavington Stud
WEIGHT FOR AGE 4yo-7lb

134 HUNGERFORD APPRENTICE H'CAP (0-60) (II) (4-Y.O+) (Class F)

4-20 (4-20) **7f** **(Equitrack)** £2,078.40 (£582.40: £283.20) Stalls: Low GOING minus 0.35 sec per fur (FST)

Form	Horse	Dist	Pos	SP	RR	SF
109[9]	**Into Debt (30)** (JRPoulton) **4-7-5e**(7) AMcCarthy(10) (hdwy 4f out: led over 3f out: r.o wl)	—	**1**	33/1	40	22
121[10]	**Hawaii Storm (FR) (50)** (DJSffrenchDavis) **9-8-11**(7) KerryBaker(11) (hdwy 4f out: ev ch fnl 3f: r.o wl)	s.h	**2**	100/30[1]	60	42
65[9]	**River Seine (FR) (47)** (SGKnight) **5-8-8**(7) GHannon(8) (hrd rdn & hdwy over 1f out: r.o)	3½	**3**	9/1	49	31
59[8]	**Fancy Design (IRE) (29)** (PMitchell) **4-7-8**(3) PFessey(7) (b.hind: rdn & hdwy 2f out: r.o one pce)	½	**4**	12/1	30	12
36[4]	**Lachesis (38)** (BRichmond) **4-8-6**ow1 CTeague(6) (led over 1f: rdn 2f out: wknd fnl f)	2½	**5**	14/1	33	14
109[8]	**Shaynes Domain (34)** (RMFlower) **6-7-11b**(5) GMilligan(5) (a.p: rdn over 1f out: sn wknd)	1½	**6**	8/1	26	8
57[2]	**Statistician (57)** (JohnBerry) **5-9-4e**(7) AmyQuirk(2) (led over 5f out tl over 3f out: sn wknd)	1½	**7**	11/2[3]	45	27
	Panther (IRE) (48) (PDEvans) **7-8-9v**(7) AnthonyBond(4) (prom over 4f)	1¼	**8**	4/1[2]	33	15
	Absolutelystunning (50) (MrsBarbaraWaring) **4-9-4** NVarley(9) (b: b.hind: bhd fnl 3f)	hd	**9**	15/2	35	17
71[12]	**Miss Charlie (30)** (ABailey) **7-7-12** DWright(3) (b.hind: dwlt: hdwy over 5f out: wknd over 3f out)	4	**10**	10/1	6	—
	Respectable Jones (45) (RHollinshead) **11-8-6**(7) LisaWatson(1) (lw: dwlt: a bhd)	1¾	**11**	33/1	17	—

(SP 120.7%) **11 Rn**

1m 27.15 (2.75) CSF £131.47 CT £790.05 TOTE £62.20: £10.30 £1.10 £3.40 (£142.90) Trio £83.60 OWNER Mrs J. Druce (LEWES) BRED Mrs J. B. Druce

T/Plpt: £557.00 (16.25 Tckts). T/Qdpt: £98.20 (9.24 Tckts) AK

0098-WOLVERHAMPTON (L-H) (Standard)

Wednesday January 22nd

WEATHER: overcast WIND: almost nil

135 HADDOCK MAIDEN STKS (3-Y.O+) (Class D)

1-50 (2-01) **6f** **(Fibresand)** £3,420.00 (£1,035.00: £505.00: £240.00) Stalls: Low GOING: 0.27 sec per fur (SLW)

Form	Horse	Dist	Pos	SP	RR	SF
50[3]	**Siouxrouge (74)** (PCHaslam) **3-8-8** JWeaver(6) (a.p: led over 3f out: clr over 1f out: pushed out)	—	**1**	5/4[1]	84	50
87[2]	**Afaan (IRE)** (RFMarvin) **4-9-10** TGMcLaughlin(3) (s.i.s: sn rcvrd: chsd wnr fnl 3f: no imp)	10	**2**	7/1[3]	57	39
	Julia's Relative (RGuest) **3-8-3** JQuinn(10) (b: a.p: one pce fnl 2f)	3	**3**	14/1	44	10
	Beau Bruno (76) (MBell) **4-9-5**(5) GFaulkner(9) (bit bkwd: no hdwy fnl 2f)	2½	**4**	2/1[2]	43	25
49[7]	**Rose Burton** (TDBarron) **3-8-3** LCharnock(1) (sn rdn along: bhd fnl 3f)	7	**5**	16/1	19	—
	Cindy Kate (IRE) (52) (WRMuir) **4-9-5** CRutter(7) (bhd fnl 3f)	1¾	**6**	16/1	14	—
65[6]	**Oscilights Gift (29)** (MarkCampion) **5-9-5** NAdams(5) (led over 4f out tl over 3f out: wknd over 2f out: t.o)	9	**7**	33/1	—	—
	Palacegate Chief (28) (NPLittmoden) **4-9-5b[1]**(5) ADaly(8) (wl bhd fnl 3f: t.o)	1½	**8**	50/1	—	—
	Ho Mei Surprise (34) (BPreece) **5-9-10v[1]** VSlattery(2) (led over 1f: wknd 3f out: t.o)	12	**9**	50/1	—	—

(SP 115.6%) **9 Rn**

1m 15.8 (4.60) CSF £9.92 TOTE £2.00: £1.10 £2.50 £4.10 (£6.10) Trio £10.90 OWNER Les Buckley & Middleham Park Racing V (MIDDLEHAM)
WEIGHT FOR AGE 3yo-16lb

136 MACKEREL CLAIMING STKS (4-Y.O+) (Class F)

2-20 (2-25) **7f** **(Fibresand)** £2,580.00 (£780.00: £380.00: £180.00) Stalls: High GOING: 0.27 sec per fur (SLW)

Form	Horse	Dist	Pos	SP	RR	SF
87*	**Jibereen (72)** (PHowling) **5-9-5** SWhitworth(1) (b: plld hrd: w ldr: led over 3f out: rdn over 1f out: r.o wl)	—	**1**	13/8[2]	79	36
82*	**Anonym (IRE) (70)** (DNicholls) **5-8-12b**(7) JBramhill(3) (hld up: hdwy over 2f out: ev ch over 1f out: rdn & r.o)	nk	**2**	6/4[1]	78	35

				SP	RR	SF
	Bogart (48) (CWFairhurst) **6-8-3** RLappin(8) (hld up: hdwy over 3f out: hung rt & wknd over 1f out)	8	**3**	25/1	44	1
	Jigsaw Boy (64) (PGMurphy) **8-8-7** SDrowne(5) (a.p: rdn over 2f out: wknd over 1f out)	1½	**4**	$6/1^{3}$	45	2
29^{7}	**Dhes-C (35)** (RHollinshead) **4-8-1**(3) FLynch(4) (hld up: wknd wl over 1f out)	2	**5**	33/1	37	—
126^{4}	**Little Ibnr (69)** (PDEvans) **6-8-0**(7) AnthonyBond(7) (led over 3f: rdn & wknd 2f out)	1½	**6**	$6/1^{3}$	37	—
121^{7}	**Shontaine (60)** (MJohnston) **4-8-5** JFanning(6) (prom tl rdn & wknd 3f out)	1½	**7**	8/1	31	—
99^{8}	**High Low (USA)** (WJenks) **9-9-1** VSlattery(2) (sn outpcd: t.o)	13	**8**	33/1	12	—

(SP 127.5%) **8 Rn**

1m 32.3 (7.60) CSF £4.61 TOTE £2.80: £1.40 £1.10 £5.50 (£2.50) OWNER Mr Peter Skelton (NEWMARKET) BRED Mrs J. Everitt

137 COD H'CAP (0-75) (3-Y.O+) (Class D)

2-50 (2-56) **5f (Fibresand)** £3,436.25 (£1,040.00: £507.50: £241.25) Stalls: Low GOING: 0.27 sec per fur (SLW)

				SP	RR	SF
20^{5}	**Gi La High (51)** (MartynMeade) **4-8-5** NAdams(12) (b.hind: hrd rdn over 2f out: gd hdwy over 1f out: led wl ins fnl f: r.o)	—	**1**	14/1	58	28
53^{2}	**Chemcast (70)** (JLEyre) **4-9-7b**(3) OPears(13) (a.p: led ins fnl f: sn hdd: nt qckn)	1¼	**2**	10/1	73	43
95^{2}	**Napier Star (65)** (MrsNMacauley) **4-9-2v**(3) CTeague(9) (b.off hind: gd hdwy over 1f out: r.o)	1	**3**	10/1	65	35
53^{3}	**Ramsey Hope (74)** (CWFairhurst) **4-10-0v** NKennedy(8) (a.p: r.o one pce fnl 2f)	hd	**4**	$5/1^{2}$	74	44
	Bold Frontier (64) (KTIvory) **5-9-4b** CScally(10) (b: b.hind: s.i.s: hdwy & swtchd rt 1f out: nvr nrr)	1½	**5**	25/1	59	29
79^{4}	**Boffy (IRE) (53)** (BPJBaugh) **4-8-7** RPerham(11) (hdwy over 1f out: nvr nr to chal)	hd	**6**	16/1	47	17
	Rennyholme (46) (JHetherton) **6-8-0b** LCharnock(6) (b.off fore: no hdwy fnl 2f)	1½	**7**	33/1	36	6
	Squire Corrie (60) (DWChapman) **5-9-0** ACulhane(2) (a.p: led 3f out tl ins fnl f)	½	**8**	10/1	48	18
	Lucky Revenge (57) (DNicholls) **4-8-4**(7) IonaWands(1) (no hdwy fnl 2f)	¾	**9**	16/1	43	13
79*	**Sotonian (HOL) (48)** (PSFelgate) **4-7-9**(7) JBramhill(7) (lw: w ldrs over 3f)	1	**10**	$4/1^{1}$	30	—
79^{3}	**Belinda Blue (43)** (RAFahey) **5-7-11**ow1 JQuinn(3) (prom 3f)	2½	**11**	$13/2^{3}$	17	—
89^{4}	**Chadwell Hall (73)** (SRBowring) **6-9-13b** SDWilliams(5) (led 2f: wknd over 1f out)	3	**12**	$5/1^{2}$	38	8
32^{6}	**Primula Bairn (63)** (DNicholls) **7-9-3b** AlexGreaves(4) (outpcd)	1½	**13**	10/1	23	—

(SP 128.2%) **13 Rn**

63.9 secs (5.00) CSF £143.63 CT £902.90 TOTE £16.10: £1.80 £1.50 £2.60 (£100.80) Trio £134.40 OWNER Ladyswood Racing Club (MALMESBURY) BRED J. H. Heath

LONG HANDICAP Belinda Blue 7-4

138 TROUT H'CAP (0-90) (3-Y.O) (Class C)

3-20 (3-27) **1m 100y (Fibresand)** £4,940.70 (£1,494.60: £728.80: £345.90) Stalls: Low GOING: 0.27 sec per fur (SLW)

				SP	RR	SF
49^{2}	**Selberry (77)** (PCHaslam) **3-8-11** SDrowne(8) (hld up: hdwy over 2f out: led ins fnl f: r.o wl)	—	**1**	$5/1^{3}$	84	45
84*	**Millroy (USA) (87)** (PAKelleway) **3-9-7v** MWigham(4) (led: rdn over 2f out: hdd ins fnl f)	1¼	**2**	$3/1^{2}$	92	53
103^{4}	**Nomore Mr Niceguy (84)** (EJAlston) **3-9-4** ACulhane(2) (lw: s.i.s: hld up & bhd: hdwy over 2f out: hrd rdn & r.o ins fnl f)	2½	**3**	7/1	84	45
	Time Can Tell (70) (CMurray) **3-8-4** NicolaHowarth(7) (chsd ldr over 6f: one pce)	s.h	**4**	16/1	70	31
	Plan For Profit (IRE) (77) (MJohnston) **3-8-11** JWeaver(1) (a.p: no hdwy fnl 2f)	1½	**5**	8/1	74	35
103^{3}	**Enchanting Eve (70)** (CNAllen) **3-7-11**(7) JBramhill(6) (lost pl 3f out: no hdwy fnl 2f)	1½	**6**	16/1	64	25
103*	**Foot Battalion (IRE) (88)** (RHollinshead) **3-9-5**(3) 5x FLynch(3) (lw: hld up: rdn over 2f out: sn bhd)	3½	**7**	$11/4^{1}$	76	37
46^{3}	**Hello Dolly (IRE) (69)** (KRBurke) **3-8-3** DRMcCabe(5) (prom over 4f: eased whn no ch wl over 1f out)	7	**8**	13/2	43	4

(SP 117.0%) **8 Rn**

1m 52.5 (7.50) CSF £19.07 CT £97.32 TOTE £5.50: £1.50 £1.40 £2.00 (£10.40) OWNER Middleham Park Racing VI (MIDDLEHAM) BRED Bjorn Neilson

139 BREAM (S) STKS (4-Y.O+) (Class F)

3-50 (3-55) **1m 6f 166y (Fibresand)** £2,580.00 (£780.00: £380.00: £180.00) Stalls: High GOING: 0.27 sec per fur (SLW)

				SP	RR	SF
68^{3}	**Shakiyr (FR) (52)** (RHollinshead) **6-9-0b**1(3) FLynch(4) (hld up: hdwy to ld 5f out: hrd rdn fnl 3f: all out)	—	**1**	$3/1^{2}$	65	16
99^{5}	**Thorntoun Estate (IRE) (60)** (MartinTodhunter) **4-8-11b** DeanMcKeown(6) (hld up: hdwy on ins 6f out: chsd wnr 4f out: outpcd over 2f out: hrd rdn over 1f out: rallied ins fnl f: styd on)	¾	**2**	$20/1^{3}$	64	9
	Petoskin (68) (JPearce) **5-9-8** MWigham(9) (prom tl wknd over 3f out)	11	**3**	Evens^{1}	57	8
99^{6}	**Wadada (34)** (DBurchell) **6-9-3** SDrowne(7) (lost pl 6f out: styd on fnl 2f: n.d)	3	**4**	25/1	49	—
68*	**El Nido (58)** (DWChapman) **9-9-8** LCharnock(5) (hld up & plld hrd: wknd over 4f out)	1½	**5**	$3/1^{2}$	52	3
68^{4}	**Shuttlecock (40)** (MrsNMacauley) **6-9-0**(3) CTeague(3) (led over 6f: wknd over 4f out)	10	**6**	33/1	37	—
78^{5}	**Persian Bud (IRE) (27)** (JRBosley) **9-9-3e** CRutter(10) (prom 13f)	6	**7**	33/1	30	—
	Awestruck (32) (BPreece) **7-9-3b** JWeaver(1) (wl bhd fnl 7f: t.o)	17	**8**	33/1	12	—
98^{6}	**Tango Man (IRE)** (RJPrice) **5-8-10**(7) AnthonyBond(8) (hld up: hdwy to ld 8f out: hdd 5f out: sn wknd: t.o)	2	**9**	33/1	9	—
	Edward Seymour (USA) (WJenks) **10-9-3** VSlattery(2) (bit bkwd: wl bhd fnl 7f: t.o)	dist	**10**	33/1	—	—

(SP 123.3%) **10 Rn**

3m 27.5 (20.10) CSF £56.27 TOTE £3.70: £1.90 £3.30 £1.70 (£15.30) Trio £80.80 OWNER L & R Roadlines (UPPER LONGDON) BRED S. A. Aga Khan in France

WEIGHT FOR AGE 4yo-6lb

Bt in 4,400 gns

STEWARDS' ENQUIRY Lynch susp. 31/1-1/2/97 (excessive use of whip)

140 SALMON H'CAP (0-80) (4-Y.O+) (Class D)

4-20 (4-25) **1m 1f 79y (Fibresand)** £3,436.25 (£1,040.00: £507.50: £241.25) Stalls: Low GOING: 0.27 sec per fur (SLW)

				SP	RR	SF
28*	**Oneforthedditch (USA) (65)** (JRFanshawe) **4-9-5**(3) NVarley(4) (a.p: led over 3f out: r.o wl)	—	**1**	$5/2^{1}$	76	43
	Maradata (IRE) (63) (RHollinshead) **5-9-4**(3) FLynch(9) (hld up & bhd: hdwy over 2f out: r.o ins fnl f: nt trble wnr)	1½	**2**	15/2	71	39
14^{3}	**Bernard Seven (IRE) (67)** (MDods) **5-9-11b** AClark(8) (a.p: led over 4f out tl over 3f out: one pce fnl 2f)	1¾	**3**	8/1	72	40
10^{4}	**Arzani (USA) (53)** (DJSCosgrove) **6-8-11** MRimmer(7) (lw: hdwy 4f out: one pce fnl 2f)	1¾	**4**	8/1	56	24
	Seventh Edition (52) (DBurchell) **4-8-9** SDrowne(10) (no hdwy fnl 4f)	11	**5**	33/1	36	3
56^{3}	**Golden Touch (USA) (60)** (DJSCosgrove) **5-8-13**(5) ADaly(5) (lw: prom over 5f)	nk	**6**	10/1	43	11
81^{7}	**Failed To Hit (60)** (NPLittmoden) **4-9-3v** TGMcLaughlin(2) (bhd fnl 4f)	6	**7**	11/1	33	—

				SP	RR	SF
72^{11}	**African-Pard (IRE) (48)** (DHaydnJones) **5-8-6** TWilliams(3) (led over 1f: wknd 4f out)	nk	**8**	33/1	20	—
29^{*}	**Forest Boy (71)** (JRBosley) **4-10-0** CRutter(6) (rdn 5f out: bhd fnl 4f)	s.h	**9**	$4/1^{2}$	43	10
82^{5}	**Three Weeks (60)** (WRMuir) **4-9-3** JWeaver(1) (led 7f out tl over 4f out: sn wknd: t.o)	24	**10**	$6/1^{3}$	—	—
				(SP 120.2%)	**10 Rn**	

2m 5.8 (9.80) CSF £20.69 CT £120.80 TOTE £3.30: £1.80 £3.30 £2.60 (£38.90) Trio £52.80 OWNER Onefortheditch Partnership (NEWMARKET) BRED Linda L. Ramsey
WEIGHT FOR AGE 4yo-1lb

T/Plpt: £43.70 (334.33 Tckts). T/Qdpt: £34.10 (34.67 Tckts) KH

0128-LINGFIELD (L-H) (Standard)
Thursday January 23rd
Race 3: hand-timed
WEATHER: fine WIND: almost nil

141 WILSON H'CAP (0-60) (I) (4-Y.O+) (Class F)
1-10 (1-10) **1m 2f** **(Equitrack)** £2,145.60 (£601.60: £292.80) Stalls: Low GOING minus 0.34 sec per fur (FST)

				SP	RR	SF
	Bold Habit (38) (JPearce) **12-8-6** GBardwell(4) (hld up: hdwy 4f out: chsd ldr 3f out: led over 1f out: hrd rdn: r.o)	—	**1**	14/1	50	16
108^{2}	**Nakhal (51)** (DJGMurraySmith) **4-9-3** JWeaver(2) (hld up in rr: hdwy over 2f out: hrd rdn over 1f out: styd on strly ins fnl f)	1	**2**	$2/1^{1}$	61	25
83^{*}	**Tallulah Belle (56)** (NPLittmoden) **4-9-8** TGMcLaughlin(1) (hld up in tch: led 3f out: hdd over 1f out: unable qckn)	hd	**3**	11/2	66	30
61^{3}	**Suitor (47)** (SDow) **4-8-13** SSanders(5) (lw: a.p: rdn over 2f out: one pce)	3	**4**	$3/1^{2}$	52	16
	Bajan (IRE) (60) (LadyHerries) **6-10-0** AClark(9) (lw: led: hdd 3f out: sn wknd)	6	**5**	$4/1^{3}$	56	22
	Cuban Reef (36) (WJMusson) **5-8-4** DRMcCabe(8) (prom: rdn 3f out: sn wknd)	nk	**6**	7/1	31	—
	Lord Ellangowan (IRE) (45) (RIngram) **4-8-11b** JStack(6) (b: prom 6f)	8	**7**	20/1	28	—
				(SP 117.6%)	**7 Rn**	

2m 10.34 (6.04) CSF £40.28 CT £165.63 TOTE £27.00: £8.30 £1.10 (£35.10) Trio £28.30 OWNER Mr Jeff Pearce (NEWMARKET) BRED R. Butters
WEIGHT FOR AGE 4yo-2lb

142 MACMILLAN H'CAP (0-70) (3-Y.O) (Class E)
1-40 (1-41) **5f** **(Equitrack)** £2,713.25 (£821.00: £400.50: £190.25) Stalls: High GOING minus 0.34 sec per fur (FST)

				SP	RR	SF
132^{3}	**Sparkling Edge (57)** (CADwyer) **3-9-0** DRMcCabe(4) (chsd ldrs: sn pushed along: hrd rdn 2f out: styd on strly to ld wl ins fnl f)	—	**1**	5/1	63	30
25^{3}	**Tear White (IRE) (64)** (TGMills) **3-9-7b** SSanders(3) (led: clr over 1f out: hdd wl ins fnl f: no ex)	¾	**2**	$100/30^{3}$	68	35
102^{2}	**Imperial Garden (IRE) (64)** (PCHaslam) **3-9-7** JWeaver(2) (a.p: rdn 2f out: styd on one pce ins fnl f)	½	**3**	$9/4^{1}$	66	33
79^{9}	**Suite Factors (50)** (KRBurke) **3-8-0**(7) JBramhill(6) (a.p: rdn 2f out: one pce)	1¾	**4**	7/1	46	13
	Lucy of Arabia (IRE) (64) (JJSheehan) **3-9-7** AMorris(5) (s.s: wl bhd tl sme hdwy fnl f: nvr nrr)	nk	**5**	40/1	59	26
45^{*}	**Green Boulevard (USA) (61)** (JBerry) **3-9-4** GCarter(1) (b: b.hind: s.i.s: a bhd)	2½	**6**	$3/1^{2}$	48	15
				(SP 110.5%)	**6 Rn**	

60.5 secs (2.30) CSF £19.18 TOTE £9.30: £2.60 £1.50 (£22.80) OWNER Mr S. I. Ross (NEWMARKET) BRED Benham Stud

143 GLADSTONE CLAIMING STKS (4-Y.O+) (Class E)
2-10 (2-10) **1m** **(Equitrack)** £2,791.25 (£845.00: £412.50: £196.25) Stalls: High GOING minus 0.34 sec per fur (FST)

				SP	RR	SF
	Hatta Sunshine (USA) (48) (GLMoore) **7-8-4**(3) AWhelan(9) (a.p: led 2f out: sn clr: r.o wl)	—	**1**	$6/1^{3}$	64	36
82^{8}	**Nashaat (USA) (76)** (KRBurke) **9-9-1** DRMcCabe(4) (hld up: hdwy 3f out: hrd rdn 2f out: styd on to go 2nd ins fnl f)	3½	**2**	$7/4^{1}$	65	37
	Whatever's Right (IRE) (65) (MDIUsher) **8-9-3** JWeaver(6) (bit bkwd: chsd ldr: led over 3f out: hdd 2f out: one pce)	1½	**3**	$5/2^{2}$	64	36
	Commin' Up (45) (JWHills) **4-8-2** NAdams(10) (hld up: hdwy 5f out: rdn over 2f out: one pce)	hd	**4**	16/1	49	21
93^{5}	**Media Express (45)** (MrsLStubbs) **5-8-7b** TSprake(8) (hld up: hdwy over 4f out: rdn over 2f out: kpt on one pce)	1½	**5**	8/1	51	23
57^{7}	**Trible Pet (40)** (BGubby) **4-7-11v**ow1 JQuinn(7) (mid div: rdn 5f out: no hdwy)	3½	**6**	14/1	34	5
134^{10}	**Miss Charlie (30)** (ABailey) **7-7-12** DWright(1) (b: b.hind: led: hdd over 3f out: sn wknd)	10	**7**	14/1	15	—
104^{10}	**Callonescy (IRE) (30)** (DCO'Brien) **5-8-1** GBardwell(3) (s.i.s: a bhd)	1¾	**8**	33/1	14	—
128^{3}	**Madonna da Rossi (35)** (MDods) **4-8-4** AClark(5) (mid div: rdn 4f out: wknd over 2f out)	3	**9**	15/2	11	—
				(SP 124.3%)	**9 Rn**	

1m 40.1 (2.70) CSF £16.66 TOTE £7.60: £1.80 £1.50 £3.40 (£9.30) Trio £5.80 OWNER Mr R. Kiernan (BRIGHTON) BRED Daniel M. Galbreath

144 WILSON H'CAP (0-60) (II) (4-Y.O+) (Class F)
2-40 (2-42) **1m 2f** **(Equitrack)** £2,134.40 (£598.40: £291.20) Stalls: Low GOING minus 0.34 sec per fur (FST)

				SP	RR	SF
63^{7}	**Fabulous Mtoto (30)** (MSSaunders) **7-7-12** NCarlisle(7) (stdd s: hld up in rr: hdwy 2f out: rdn to ld ins fnl f: r.o wl)	—	**1**	9/2	40	18
61^{4}	**Sheraz (IRE) (46)** (NTinkler) **5-9-0b**[1] CRutter(3) (chsd ldr 8f out: led over 2f out: hdd ins fnl f: unable qckn)	¾	**2**	$5/2^{1}$	55	33
61^{7}	**Dr Edgar (50)** (MDods) **5-9-4** JWeaver(5) (led: hdd over 2f out: rdn & ev ch ins fnl f: unable qckn)	nk	**3**	$4/1^{3}$	58	36
71^{11}	**Havana Miss (36)** (BPalling) **5-8-4**ow1 AClark(6) (hld up in tch: rdn 3f out: kpt on one pce fnl 2f)	¾	**4**	16/1	43	20
105^{4}	**Lahik (IRE) (35)** (KTIvory) **4-8-1**ow5 DBiggs(8) (b: hld up: hdwy 5f out: rdn over 2f out: one pce)	1¾	**5**	7/1	39	10
	Misky Bay (59) (DJSCosgrove) **4-9-11** MRimmer(4) (dwlt: sn in tch: rdn 4f out: sn wknd)	9	**6**	14/1	49	25
83^{6}	**Flagstaff (USA) (42)** (KRBurke) **4-8-8** ACulhane(1) (hld up: rdn over 3f out: sn btn)	6	**7**	$3/1^{2}$	22	—

				SP	RR	SF
66^{7}	**Rumpelstiltskin (45)** (HSHowe) **5-8-10**(3) FLynch(2) (tk keen hold: chsd ldr 2f: rdn over 4f out: grad wknd)	2½	8	25/1	21	—
				(SP 120.6%)		**8 Rn**

2m 9.03 (4.73) CSF £15.66 CT £45.56 TOTE £4.10: £1.10 £1.50 £2.60 (£30.30) OWNER Mr N. R. Pike (WELLS)
WEIGHT FOR AGE 4yo-2lb

145 DISRAELI MAIDEN STKS (3-Y.O) (Class D)
3-10 (3-10) **7f (Equitrack)** £3,322.50 (£1,005.00: £490.00: £232.50) Stalls: Low GOING minus 0.34 sec per fur (FST)

				SP	RR	SF
	Galibis (FR) (PAKelleway) **3-9-0** MWigham(4) (lw: in tch: hrd rdn over 4f out: hdwy over 1f out: str run to ld ins fnl f: r.o wl)	—	1	5/4^{1}	66+	28
	Alvilde (72) (DJSCosgrove) **3-8-9** MRimmer(7) (s.s: hdwy over 4f out: ev ch ins fnl f: unable qckn)	2½	2	9/1^{3}	55	17
	Roffey Spinney (IRE) (RHannon) **3-9-0** RPerham(8) (led: rdn over 1f out: hdd ins fnl f: unable qckn)	nk	3	10/1	60	22
	Dixie Eyes Blazing (USA) (RCharlton) **3-8-9** TSprake(5) (lw: hld up: rdn 3f out: kpt on one pce fnl 2f)	3½	4	10/1	47	9
	Talisman (IRE) (60) (SDow) **3-8-9**(5) ADaly(1) (bit bkwd: prom: rdn over 2f out: sn wknd)	2½	5	10/1	46	8
50^{6}	**Native Thatch (IRE)** (WGMTurner) **3-8-9** AClark(6) (a.p: ev ch 2f out: wknd over 1f out)	1¼	6	16/1	38	—
49^{4}	**Attribute (65)** (RGuest) **3-8-9** JQuinn(3) (chsd ldrs: rdn over 3f out: sn btn)	2½	7	3/1^{2}	32	—
	Princess Sarara (USA) (SirMarkPrescott) **3-8-9** SSanders(2) (bhd fnl 3f)	2½	8	10/1	27	—
				(SP 121.7%)		**8 Rn**

1m 27.94 (3.54) CSF £13.83 TOTE £2.30: £1.10 £4.80 £3.30 (£11.30) OWNER International Racing Services Ltd (NEWMARKET) BRED Francois Geffroy
STEWARDS' ENQUIRY Perham fined £100 (failure to ride to draw)

146 LLOYD GEORGE H'CAP (0-80) (4-Y.O+) (Class D)
3-40 (3-41) **7f (Equitrack)** £3,306.25 (£1,000.00: £487.50: £231.25) Stalls: Low GOING minus 0.34 sec per fur (FST)

				SP	RR	SF
121^{5}	**Twin Creeks (70)** (VSoane) **6-9-4** CRutter(2) (lw: hld up: hdwy ½-wy: led ins fnl f: r.o wl)	—	1	10/1	79	55
82^{7}	**Duke Valentino (80)** (RHollinshead) **5-9-9**(5) DGriffiths(8) (lw: a.p: rdn 2f out: r.o ins fnl f)	1¼	2	7/2^{2}	86	62
109^{2}	**Star Talent (USA) (69)** (MissGayKelleway) **6-9-3** DHolland(4) (b: b.hind: hld up: hdwy ½-wy: led over 2f out: hdd ins fnl f: one pce)	2½	3	9/4^{1}	69	45
48^{2}	**Scissor Ridge (76)** (JJBridger) **5-9-10** SSanders(6) (led: rdn 3f out: sn hdd: styd on one pce ins fnl f)	s.h	4	5/1^{3}	76	52
109^{3}	**Lancashire Legend (62)** (SDow) **4-8-5**(5) ADaly(7) (a.p: n.m.r & lost pl over 1f out: kpt on one pce ins fnl f)	1	5	7/1	60	36
	Perilous Plight (63) (MrsLStubbs) **6-8-11** JWeaver(3) (chsd ldrs: rdn 2f out: wknd over 1f out)	3	6	9/1	54	30
121^{6}	**Fort Knox (IRE) (61)** (RMFlower) **6-8-9b** MWigham(1) (dwlt: a bhd)	3	7	7/1	45	21
56^{7}	**Tom Morgan (58)** (PTWalwyn) **6-8-6v** TSprake(5) (prom to ½-wy)	4	8	25/1	33	9
				(SP 117.6%)		**8 Rn**

1m 25.99 (1.59) CSF £42.14 CT £99.87 TOTE £15.50: £2.60 £1.50 £1.30 (£26.40) OWNER The Armchair Jockeys-Four Seasons Racing (ASTON ROWANT) BRED Crest Stud Ltd

147 THATCHER LIMITED STKS (0-50) (4-Y.O+) (Class F)
4-10 (4-13) **1m 4f (Equitrack)** £2,585.20 (£727.20: £355.60) Stalls: Low GOING minus 0.34 sec per fur (FST)

				SP	RR	SF
106^{4}	**In the Money (IRE) (50)** (RHollinshead) **8-8-11**(3) FLynch(10) (lw: hld up: hdwy over 4f out: chsd ldr 3f out: led over 1f out: r.o wl)	—	1	5/1^{2}	50	38
104^{4}	**Al Helal (43)** (JRJenkins) **5-9-0** SWhitworth(13) (lw: dwlt: hld up: hdwy 4f out: rdn 2f out: styd on to go 2nd ins fnl f)	2	2	14/1	47	35
104^{9}	**Sapphire Son (IRE) (39)** (PCClarke) **5-9-0** NAdams(12) (chsd ldrs: led 4f out: hdd over 1f out: one pce)	3	3	25/1	43	31
73^{2}	**Nawaji (USA) (45)** (WRMuir) **4-8-7** AClark(6) (rr: rdn & hdwy over 2f out: styd on ins fnl f)	1¾	4	7/1^{3}	38	22
	Blue And Royal (IRE) (47) (VSoane) **5-9-0** CRutter(11) (chsd ldrs: rdn & lost pl 4f out: rallied over 1f out: styd on ins fnl f)	¾	5	33/1	40	28
122*	**Soviet King (IRE) (50)** (PMitchell) **4-8-12** 2x SSanders(8) (prom: rdn 3f out: wknd wl over 1f out)	5	6	3/1^{1}	35	19
116^{3}	**Soojama (IRE) (40)** (RMFlower) **7-9-0b** MWigham(5) (dwlt: nvr nrr)	2	7	7/1^{3}	31	19
116^{6}	**Captain Marmalade (44)** (DTThom) **8-9-0** JTate(9) (bhd fnl 3f)	¾	8	16/1	30	18
83^{3}	**Hazel (46)** (MissGayKelleway) **5-8-11** DHolland(2) (b: b.hind: chsd ldrs tl wknd over 3f out)	2½	9	5/1^{2}	23	11
	Dolliver (USA) (45) (CADwyer) **5-8-7e**(7) JoHunnam(4) (lw: bhd fnl 3f)	nk	10	33/1	26	14
	Royal Circus (42) (PRWebber) **8-8-7**(7) JBramhill(1) (led: hdd 4f out: sn wknd)	¾	11	12/1	25	13
92^{4}	**In Cahoots (46)** (AGNewcombe) **4-8-12** JQuinn(7) (b: tk keen hold: chsd ldr tl 3f out: sn wknd)	1	12	16/1	26	10
63^{4}	**Etoile du Nord (23)** (HJCollingridge) **5-9-0** MRimmer(14) (b: a bhd)	5	13	20/1	17	5
98^{4}	**Tauten (IRE) (38)** (PBurgoyne) **7-8-11** DRMcCabe(3) (a bhd)	½	14	25/1	13	1
				(SP 127.8%)		**14 Rn**

2m 34.99 (4.99) CSF £66.22 TOTE £7.60: £2.80 £9.10 £11.80 (£40.70) Trio £263.00; £296.42 to Folkestone 24/1/97 OWNER Mr J. E. Bigg (UPPER LONGDON) BRED Cheveley Park Stud Ltd
WEIGHT FOR AGE 4yo-4lb

T/Plpt: £62.20 (130.71 Tckts). T/Qdpt: £6.30 (107.31 Tckts). SM

CAGNES-SUR-MER (Nice, France) (L-H) (Holding)
Friday January 17th

148a PRIX DU DOCTEUR GAZAGNAIRE (4-Y.O+)
2-10 (2-10) **1m 2f** £6,172.00 (£3,086.00: £1,852.00)

				SP	RR	SF
	Philanthrop (FR) (J-PGallorini,France) **5-8-11** SHureau	—	1		73	—
	L'Affranchi (FR) (JForesi,France) **4-8-7** GLemius	3	2		66	—
	Bybus (FR) (MmeARossio,France) **6-9-2** MCesandri	1	3		72	—
23^{4}	**No Speeches (IRE)** (SDow) **6-8-7** FSanchez		6		—	—
						11 Rn

2m 6.5 P-M 3.10F: 1.40F 4.30F 1.30F (77.50F) OWNER J. Menuisier BRED S. Niarchos
23 No Speeches (IRE) raced with the leaders during the early part of the race, but was beaten as the field entered the straight.

0148a-CAGNES-SUR-MER (Nice, France) (L-H) (Holding)
Sunday January 19th

149a PRIX CHARLES DU BREIL GENTLEMEN'S (4-Y.O+)
1m £3,367.00 (£1,684.00: £1,010.00)

				SP	RR	SF
	Roi Hoi (FR) (J-CRouget,France) **6-10-0** MrJ-PBoisgont	—	**1**		68	—
	Confronter (SDow) **8-10-4** MrTMcCarthy	dist	**2**		—	—
	Bricviste (FR) (MmeARossio,France) **5-10-8** MrJ-CMonnin	1	**3**		—	—
						10 Rn

1m 50.8 P-M 1.90F: 1.20F 1.80F 2.10F (5.60F) OWNER Mme M de Chambure (PAU) BRED Henri Rouillere & Mme Therese Louveau
Confronter close up and with every chance from two furlongs out, stayed on well but did not have the pace of the winner. The official winning margin was a distance but this would equate to six lengths in British terms. He is due to run again in the Prix des Peupliers on Friday.

0122-SOUTHWELL (L-H) (Standard)
Friday January 24th
WEATHER: fine WIND: slt across

150 NEWARK H'CAP (0-65) (I) (4-Y.O+) (Class F)
12-20 (12-22) **1m (Fibresand)** £2,463.50 (£691.00: £336.50) Stalls: Low GOING: 0.09 sec per fur (STD)

				SP	RR	SF
	Yeoman Oliver (64) (BAMcMahon) **4-9-13b** LNewton(3) (trckd ldrs: led ins fnl f: rdn & hung lft: hld on towards fin)	—	**1**	12/1[3]	73	50
111*	**Rambo Waltzer (65)** (DNicholls) **5-10-0** AlexGreaves(2) (lw: chsd ldrs: pushed along ½-wy: ev ch ins fnl f: bmpd: no ex)	nk	**2**	2/5[1]	73	50
123[7]	**Genuine John (IRE) (65)** (JParkes) **4-10-0** DHarrison(10) (led tl ins fnl f: nt qckn)	3	**3**	20/1	67	44
82[12]	**Suga Hawk (IRE) (54)** (EJAlston) **5-9-3** SDrowne(1) (chsd ldrs: outpcd 3f out: edgd lft & kpt on appr fnl f)	7	**4**	10/1[2]	42	19
126[6]	**Nukud (USA) (35)** (GROldroyd) **5-7-5(7)** DMernagh(5) (sn wl bhd: hdwy 2f out: nvr nr to chal)	½	**5**	40/1	22	—
36[6]	**Whitelock Quest (34)** (NEBerry) **9-7-11[ow1]** NCarlisle(8) (lw: bhd tl kpt on fnl 2f)	nk	**6**	16/1	21	—
	Quinzii Martin (50) (DHaydnJones) **9-8-13** CRutter(9) (sme hdwy ½-wy: n.d)	6	**7**	10/1[2]	25	2
	Kass Alhawa (40) (DWChapman) **4-8-3** LCharnock(11) (sn chsng ldrs: wknd 2f out)	6	**8**	10/1[2]	3	—
111[8]	**Buddy's Friend (IRE) (43)** (RJRWilliams) **9-8-6** DBiggs(7) (a in rr)	7	**9**	14/1	—	—
42[6]	**Kissavos (34)** (BJMeehan) **11-7-11b[ow1]** JQuinn(4) (b.hind: s.i.s: sn chsng ldrs: lost pl over 2f out)	5	**10**	33/1	—	—
85[7]	**Alana's Ballad (IRE) (33)** (BPJBaugh) **4-7-3(7)** JBramhill(6) (hmpd after 1f: bhd: sme hdwy on outside ½-wy: sn wknd)	1	**11**	40/1	—	—
				(SP 131.5%)		**11 Rn**

1m 45.7 (6.70) CSF £17.14 CT £128.46 TOTE £24.50: £2.60 £1.10 £4.60 (£4.20) Trio £27.10 OWNER Mr Michael Stokes (TAMWORTH) BRED M. G. T. Stokes
LONG HANDICAP Whitelock Quest 7-5 Kissavos 7-2 Alana's Ballad (IRE) 7-1

151 BALDERTON AMATEUR H'CAP (0-60) (I) (4-Y.O+) (Class G)
12-50 (12-51) **1m 4f (Fibresand)** £1,735.00 (£485.00: £235.00) Stalls: Low GOING: 0.09 sec per fur (STD)

				SP	RR	SF
123[3]	**Kilnamartyra Girl (41)** (JParkes) **7-11-0** MrCBonner(7) (sn pushed along: hdwy ½-wy: styd on fnl 2f: led ins fnl f: jst hld on)	—	**1**	5/2[1]	51	30
115[9]	**Sea God (49)** (MCChapman) **6-11-3(5)** MrKLoads(2) (led tl ins fnl f: rallied)	hd	**2**	8/1[3]	59	38
	Mr Moriarty (IRE) (36) (SRBowring) **6-10-9** MrsMMorris(4) (lw: b: chsd ldrs: one pce appr fnl f)	6	**3**	5/2[1]	38	17
68[5]	**Strike-a-Pose (30)** (BJLlewellyn) **7-10-3** MissEJJones(5) (chsd ldrs tl outpcd fnl 3f)	6	**4**	20/1	24	3
15[9]	**Fred's Delight (IRE) (28)** (MrsVAAconley) **6-9-10v(5)ow6** MrGMarkham(9) (hld up: hdwy ½-wy: sn prom: grad wknd fnl 2f)	hd	**5**	40/1	22	—
68[8]	**Daily Sport Girl (38)** (BJLlewellyn) **8-10-11** MrJLLlewellyn(8) (in tch: pushed along over 3f out: sn outpcd)	2½	**6**	12/1	28	7
99[7]	**Pistols At Dawn (USA) (55)** (BJMeehan) **7-12-0** MissJAllison(1) (in tch: drvn along 3f out: sn outpcd)	3	**7**	14/1	41	20
66[5]	**Phanan (33)** (REPeacock) **11-10-1(5)** MrsCPeacock(6) (hld up: sme hdwy on outside ½-wy: lost pl 4f out)	6	**8**	20/1	11	—
	Spa Lane (58) (MPBielby) **4-11-13** MrAWintle(3) (lw: in tch tl lost pl 3f out)	9	**9**	4/1[2]	24	—
				(SP 114.6%)		**9 Rn**

2m 48.8 (15.80) CSF £20.72 CT £49.22 TOTE £3.40: £1.10 £1.90 £1.30 (£11.90) Trio £11.50 OWNER Mr P. J. Cronin (MALTON) BRED F. R. Colley
WEIGHT FOR AGE 4yo-4lb

152 ANNESLEY LIMITED STKS (0-55) (4-Y.O+) (Class F)
1-20 (1-24) **6f (Fibresand)** £2,294.00 (£644.00: £314.00) Stalls: Low GOING: 0.09 sec per fur (STD)

				SP	RR	SF
	Mansab (USA) (54) (PGMurphy) **4-8-11** SDrowne(1) (trckd ldrs gng wl: led appr fnl f: rdn clr)	—	**1**	13/8[1]	68	48
20[2]	**Hoh Majestic (IRE) (55)** (RonaldThompson) **4-8-8(3)** CTeague(4) (sn drvn along: chsd ldrs: led over 1f out: sn hdd: no ch w wnr)	3½	**2**	4/1[2]	59	39
127[11]	**Lady Silk (52)** (MissJFCraze) **6-8-11** JFanning(7) (lw: sn drvn along: bhd tl styd on fnl 2f)	3½	**3**	12/1	49	29
32*	**Amy Leigh (IRE) (55)** (CaptJWilson) **4-8-11** DHolland(10) (lw: led 2f: kpt on same pce appr fnl f)	1½	**4**	11/1	45	25
4*	**Ballard Lady (IRE) (50)** (JSWainwright) **5-8-7(7)** JBramhill(16) (rr div: hdwy & hung lft 2f out: nvr rchd ldrs)	¾	**5**	12/1	46	26
127[14]	**Imp Express (IRE) (40)** (GMMoore) **4-8-11b** GBardwell(11) (led after 2f tl over 1f out: sn wknd)	4	**6**	33/1	33	13
82[13]	**Live Project (IRE) (55)** (MJohnston) **5-8-11** JWeaver(2) (nvr nr to chal)	d.h	**6**	10/1[3]	33	13
107[10]	**Halbert (43)** (PBurgoyne) **8-9-0** DRMcCabe(5) (bhd tl styd on fnl 2f)	s.h	**8**	33/1	36	16
113[13]	**Napoleon Star (IRE) (54)** (SRBowring) **6-8-11b** SDWilliams(9) (mid div: hdwy ½-wy: wkng whn n.m.r over 1f out)	½	**9**	20/1	31	11
65[8]	**Sound the Trumpet (IRE) (43)** (RCSpicer) **5-8-11** DeanMcKeown(8) (a in rr)	¾	**10**	33/1	29	9
	Southern Dominion (47) (MissJFCraze) **5-8-11** NAdams(14) (in tch: hung lft & wknd over 1f out)	2	**11**	25/1	24	4
127[10]	**Principal Boy (IRE) (46)** (TJEtherington) **4-8-11** CRutter(6) (s.i.s: hdwy ½-wy: sn lost pl)	2½	**12**	14/1	17	—

Playmaker (49) (DNicholls) **4-8-11b** AlexGreaves(3) (s.i.s: sn in tch: lost pl over 2f out)....10 **13** 14/1 — —
Hershebar (47) (MrsVAAconley) **7-8-11** MDeering(12) (swtg: sn wl bhd)....¾ **14** 50/1 — —
Monis (IRE) (53) (JBalding) **6-8-6v**(5) GFaulkner(15) (s.i.s: a bhd)....3 **15** 11/1 — —
Newington Butts (IRE) (54) (KMcAuliffe) **7-8-8e** JQuinn(13) (chsd ldrs tl lost pl 2f out)....1¼ **16** 11/1 — —
(SP 140.3%) **16 Rn**

1m 17.5 (4.00) CSF £7.42 TOTE £2.70: £1.60 £1.30 £3.80 (£6.20) Trio £27.50 OWNER Mrs Louise Murphy (BRISTOL) BRED Jonabell, J Bell, B Williams, J Nicholson and J Be

153 NEWARK H'CAP (0-65) (II) (4-Y.O+) (Class F)

1-55 (1-55) **1m (Fibresand)** £2,450.90 (£687.40: £334.70) Stalls: Low GOING: 0.09 sec per fur (STD)

SP RR SF

29[4] **Roussi (USA) (33)** (DNicholls) **5-7-3**(7) JBramhill(8) (lw: chsd ldrs: rdn over 2f out: led over 1f out: edgd rt: drew clr: fin 1st: disq)....— **1d** 11/2[3] 50 19
Sea Spouse (61) (MBlanshard) **6-9-10** NAdams(2) (lw: led tl over 1f out: kpt on same pce: 2nd, 3l, awrdd r).— **1** 8/1 72 41
111[3] **Sandmoor Denim (50)** (SRBowring) **10-8-13** SDWilliams(5) (b: bhd: hdwy 2f out: edgd lft: nrst fin: fin 3rd, 3l & 2l: plcd 2nd)....5 **2** 11/1 57 26
112* **Truly Bay (48)** (TDBarron) **4-8-11b**[1] 6x DHarrison(4) (chsd ldrs: rdn & hung rt 2f out: one pce: plcd 3rd)....5 **3** 7/1 45 14
31[6] **Gadge (38)** (ABailey) **6-8-1** DWright(10) (b: chsd ldrs: rdn over 2f out: one pce: plcd 4th)....3½ **4** 4/1[2] 28 —
113[3] **Pleasure Trick (USA) (50)** (DonEnricoIncisa) **6-8-13b** KimTinkler(7) (bhd: sme hdwy 2f out: nvr nr ldrs: 5th)1½ **5** 6/1 37 6
Gilling Dancer (IRE) (57) (PCalver) **4-9-6** ACulhane(9) (bhd: sme hdwy over 2f out: n.d: plcd 6th)....1¾ **6** 20/1 41 10
Running Green (53) (DMoffatt) **6-9-2** JQuinn(6) (b: chsd ldrs tl wknd fnl 2f: plcd 7th)....1¼ **7** 7/1 34 3
91* **Gulf Shaadi (68)** (EJAlston) **5-10-3** 6x SDrowne(1) (hld up: in tch tl outpcd ½-wy: n.d: plcd 8th)....s.h **8** 7/2[1] 49 18
71[9] **Major Mouse (65)** (WWHaigh) **9-10-0** VHalliday(3) (bit bkwd: hld up: a in rr: plcd 9th)....1¼ **9** 25/1 43 12
(SP 124.9%) **10 Rn**

1m 45.9 (6.90) CSF £48.07 CT £448.72 TOTE £7.00: £1.30 £3.60 £3.70 (£40.30) Trio £138.60; £27.35 to Doncaster 25/1/97 OWNER A A Bloodstock Ltd (THIRSK) BRED Gainsborough Farm Inc

LONG HANDICAP Roussi (USA) 7-9

SUBSEQUENT STEWARDS' ENQUIRY: Roussi disq. (prohibited substances (theobromine, theophylline and caffeine) in urine). Nicholls fined £200.

154 DANETHORPE MEDIAN AUCTION MAIDEN STKS (3-Y.O) (Class E)

2-25 (2-25) **1m (Fibresand)** £2,791.25 (£845.00: £412.50: £196.25) Stalls: Low GOING: 0.09 sec per fur (STD)

SP RR SF

Projectvision (IRE) (WRMuir) **3-9-0** AClark(5) (tall: s.i.s: sn trckng ldrs: led 2f out: drvn out)....— **1** 9/2[3] 75 20
50[2] **Sliema Creek** (TDBarron) **3-9-0** DHarrison(1) (chsd ldrs: sn pushed along: rdn & hdwy 2f out: kpt on: no imp)....3½ **2** 6/4[1] 68 13
26[5] **Love Me Do (USA) (67)** (MJohnston) **3-9-0** JWeaver(8) (trckd ldrs: effrt 2f out: r.o same pce)....¾ **3** 9/4[2] 67 12
96[3] **Rochea (66)** (WJHaggas) **3-8-6**(3) FLynch(2) (lw: prom tl outpcd ½-wy: sme hdwy over 1f out: n.d)....3½ **4** 8/1 55 —
Kingdom Pearl (MJCamacho) **3-8-9** LCharnock(7) (s.i.s: sn trckng ldrs: led over 4f out to 2f out: wknd appr fnl f)....3½ **5** 25/1 48 —
Euroquest (DNicholls) **3-9-0** AlexGreaves(4) (hld up: outpcd ½-wy: sn bhd)....29 **6** 25/1 — —
Kustom Kit Xpres (65) (SRBowring) **3-8-9b** SDWilliams(6) (plld hrd: w ldrs tl lost pl over 3f out: sn bhd)....5 **7** 25/1 — —
19[3] **Hever Golf Dancer (63)** (TJNaughton) **3-9-0** DHolland(3) (mde most tl over 4f out: wknd over 2f out: eased)..5 **8** 13/2 — —
(SP 124.9%) **8 Rn**

1m 47.6 (8.60) CSF £11.54 TOTE £13.70: £3.40 £1.10 £1.90 (£9.30) OWNER Camelot Racing (LAMBOURN) BRED B. Kennedy

OFFICIAL EXPLANATION Hever Golf Dancer: finished distressed.

155 CARLTON-ON-TRENT H'CAP (0-80) (3-Y.O) (Class D)

2-55 (2-56) **7f (Fibresand)** £3,403.75 (£1,030.00: £502.50: £238.75) Stalls: Low GOING: 0.09 sec per fur (STD)

SP RR SF

119* **Globetrotter (IRE) (71)** (MJohnston) **3-9-3** 6x JWeaver(7) (trckd ldrs: shkn up to ld over 1f out: drvn out)....— **1** 9/4[2] 77 38
62[4] **The Wyandotte Inn (72)** (RHollinshead) **3-9-1**(3) FLynch(1) (hdwy ½-wy: rdn to chal over 1f out: kpt on same pce)....1½ **2** 6/1[3] 75 36
62[5] **La Dolce Vita (75)** (TDBarron) **3-9-7** DHarrison(4) (lw: hld up: effrt over 2f out: sn rdn & outpcd: styd on ins fnl f)....2 **3** 9/1 73 34
49[5] **Supercharmer (70)** (DNicholls) **3-9-2** AlexGreaves(5) (plld hrd: led tl over 1f out: grad wknd)....5 **4** 12/1 57 18
103[2] **Ultra Boy (75)** (PCHaslam) **3-9-7** SDrowne(8) (racd wd: hld up: effrt 3f out: sn rdn: nvr nr ldrs)....2 **5** 13/8[1] 57 18
Hever Golf Mover (63) (TJNaughton) **3-8-9** DHolland(3) (bit bkwd: bhd fr ½-wy)....17 **6** 12/1 6 —
Swynford Charmer (50) (JFBottomley) **3-7-10b**[1] LCharnock(6) (chsd ldrs: rdn over 2f out: sn wknd)....½ **7** 16/1 — —
Sherzetto (68) (DWChapman) **3-9-0** ACulhane(2) (prom early: outpcd & bhd fr ½-wy: virtually p.u)....dist **8** 16/1 — —
(SP 120.3%) **8 Rn**

1m 32.6 (6.10) CSF £15.84 CT £97.00 TOTE £2.60: £2.10 £1.30 £2.40 (£5.90) OWNER Brian Yeardley Continental Ltd (MIDDLEHAM) BRED Norelands Bloodstock

LONG HANDICAP Swynford Charmer 7-2

156 FACKLEY (S) STKS (3-Y.O) (Class G)

3-30 (3-31) **7f (Fibresand)** £2,085.00 (£585.00: £285.00) Stalls: Low GOING: 0.09 sec per fur (STD)

SP RR SF

33[5] **Fast Spin (60)** (TDBarron) **3-9-4** ACulhane(4) (chsd ldrs: led over 2f out: hld on wl towards fin)....— **1** 9/4[2] 59 22
38[7] **Bailieborough Boy (IRE) (58)** (TDBarron) **3-8-12** DeanMcKeown(5) (trckd ldrs: effrt over 2f out: hung lft: ev ch & rdn over 1f out: nt qckn)....¾ **2** 11/8[1] 51 14
90[8] **Belushi** (DMorley) **3-8-7** GCarter(1) (plld hrd: w ldrs tl outpcd ½-wy: styd on appr fnl f)....6 **3** 11/2 33 —
90[4] **Hoh Down (IRE) (52)** (KMcAuliffe) **3-8-7v** JQuinn(6) (b.hind: led tl over 2f out: one pce)....2 **4** 7/2[3] 28 —
90[10] **Lord High Emperor** (DShaw) **3-8-12** SDWilliams(2) (bit bkwd: w ldrs: drvn along ½-wy: sn wknd)....7 **5** 20/1 17 —
41[10] **Love Over Gold** (MCChapman) **3-8-7** DRMcCabe(3) (swtg: bolted gng to s: s.s: racd wd: t.o ½-wy)....dist **6** 33/1 — —
(SP 118.2%) **6 Rn**

1m 34.1 (7.60) CSF £5.62 TOTE £2.90: £1.30 £1.70 (£2.60) OWNER Mr E. Buck (THIRSK) BRED Fares Stables Ltd

No bid

OFFICIAL EXPLANATION Love Over Gold: the rider reported that the filly was very free going to the start and that the bit had pulled through.

157 BALDERTON AMATEUR H'CAP (0-60) (II) (4-Y.O+) (Class G)
4-00 (4-00) **1m 4f (Fibresand)** £1,735.00 (£485.00: £235.00) Stalls: Low GOING: 0.09 sec per fur (STD)

				SP	RR	SF
115[2]	**Qualitair Pride (37)** (JFBottomley) **5-10-7** MrsLPearce(6) (mde all: drew clr over 1f out: unchal)	—	**1**	11/8[1]	53	34
67[2]	**Raindeer Quest (48)** (JLEyre) **5-11-4** MissDianaJones(3) (chsd ldrs: wnt 2nd 3f out: no imp)	9	**2**	5/2[2]	52	33
80[5]	**Biya (IRE) (45)** (DMcCain) **5-10-10**(5) MrGLake(4) (sn trckng ldrs: rdn 4f out: one pce)	4	**3**	25/1	44	25
139[5]	**El Nido (58)** (DWChapman) **9-12-0** MissRClark(8) (chsd ldrs: pushed along 5f out: btn over 3f out)	1¾	**4**	3/1[3]	54	35
67[7]	**Stevie's Wonder (IRE) (49)** (BJLlewellyn) **7-11-5v** MrJLLlewellyn(2) (chsd ldrs: drvn along & lost pl 7f out: sme hdwy 3f out: n.d)	3	**5**	25/1	41	22
101[5]	**Sharp Command (53)** (PEccles) **4-11-5b¹** MrTMcCarthy(7) (chsd ldrs: rdn ½-wy: lost pl over 3f out)	2	**6**	10/1	43	20
	Al Jinn (29) (MartynWane) **6-9-13**ow4 MrRDGreen(5) (b: bhd fnl 7f)	7	**7**	33/1	9	—
	Shedansar (IRE) (23) (RCSpicer) **5-9-7** MrSRutherford(1) (sn bhd)	½	**8**	40/1	3	—

(SP 117.8%) **8 Rn**

2m 47.0 (14.00) CSF £4.57 CT £50.58 TOTE £2.30: £1.00 £1.70 £4.70 (£3.90) Trio £30.50 OWNER Qualitair Holdings Ltd (MALTON) BRED Qualitair Stud Ltd
LONG HANDICAP Shedansar (IRE) 9-4
WEIGHT FOR AGE 4yo-4lb

T/Plpt: £35.00 (160.15 Tckts). T/Qdpt: £22.90 (21.46 Tckts). WG

0141-LINGFIELD (L-H) (Standard)
Saturday January 25th
WEATHER: sunny & mild WIND: almost nil

158 CRUSADER CLAIMING STKS (3-Y.O) (Class F)
1-10 (1-10) **5f (Equitrack)** £2,417.20 (£679.20: £331.60) Stalls: High GOING minus 0.29 sec per fur (FST)

				SP	RR	SF
142[3]	**Imperial Garden (IRE) (64)** (PCHaslam) **3-8-9** JWeaver(4) (b.off hind: lw: a.p: hrd rdn over 1f out: led wl ins fnl f: r.o wl)	—	**1**	11/8[1]	65	6
	Lunar Music (73) (MartynMeade) **3-8-8** NAdams(5) (a.p: hrd rdn over 1f out: ev ch ins fnl f: r.o)	nk	**2**	5/2[2]	63	4
79[11]	**Enchantica (55)** (JBerry) **3-8-5**(5) TEDurcan(6) (b.hind: led: hrd rdn over 1f out: hdd wl ins fnl f: unable qckn)	¾	**3**	20/1	63	4
	Whizz Kid (57) (JJBridger) **3-7-12**(5)ow1 ADaly(2) (rdn over 3f out: sme hdwy over 2f out: sn wknd)	6	**4**	11/1	36	—
102[8]	**Come Too Mamma's (58)** (JBerry) **3-7-13**(5) PFessey(3) (sme hdwy over 2f out: sn wknd)	1½	**5**	9/2[3]	33	—
102[6]	**Ekaterini Paritsi (53)** (WGMTurner) **3-7-12v** JQuinn(1) (bhd fnl 3f)	¾	**6**	14/1	24	—

(SP 108.6%) **6 Rn**

61.94 secs (3.74) CSF £4.18 TOTE £1.90: £1.20 £2.30 (£3.50) OWNER Mr D. P. Ruttledge (MIDDLEHAM) BRED Mrs C. L. Weld

159 MARGARET JONES BIRTHDAY H'CAP (0-70) (4-Y.O+) (Class E)
1-45 (1-47) **6f (Equitrack)** £2,765.25 (£837.00: £408.50: £194.25) Stalls: Low GOING minus 0.29 sec per fur (FST)

				SP	RR	SF
107[4]	**Tachycardia (35)** (RJO'Sullivan) **5-7-7**(3) NVarley(8) (hld up: chsd ldrs over 2f out: led 2f out: clr over 1f out: pushed out)	—	**1**	4/1[2]	44	15
	Xenophon of Cunaxa (IRE) (58) (MJFetherston-Godley) **4-9-5b¹** ACulhane(5) (hdwy 2f out: hrd rdn over 1f out: r.o)	3	**2**	12/1	59	30
107[2]	**The Institute Boy (67)** (MissJFCraze) **7-10-0** JWeaver(7) (stdy hdwy over 2f out: chsd wnr over 1f out: unable qckn)	nk	**3**	11/8[1]	67	38
113[12]	**Cheerful Groom (IRE) (35)** (DShaw) **6-7-3**(7) JBramhill(4) (lw: lost pl over 4f out: r.o one pce fnl 2f)	3	**4**	25/1	27	—
	Ivory's Grab Hire (46) (KTIvory) **4-8-7b** DBiggs(6) (b: b.hind: led: clr over 4f out: hdd 2f out: wknd over 1f out)	1	**5**	12/1	36	7
107[5]	**Superlao (BEL) (35)** (JJBridger) **5-7-10** JQuinn(9) (chsd ldrs 4f out tl over 2f out: wknd over 1f out)	2½	**6**	9/1	18	—
107[8]	**Bright Paragon (IRE) (35)** (KTIvory) **8-7-10** NAdams(3) (b: b.hind: a wl bhd)	2½	**7**	10/1	11	—
134[8]	**Panther (IRE) (48)** (PDEvans) **7-8-9v** SSanders(1) (lw: chsd ldrs 2f: wknd 3f out)	3	**8**	11/2[3]	16	—

(SP 115.8%) **8 Rn**

1m 14.1 (3.00) CSF £46.08 CT £88.41 TOTE £6.80: £1.70 £2.90 £1.10 (£41.30) Trio £21.50 OWNER Mr Christopher Lane (WHITCOMBE) BRED Patrick Eddery Ltd
LONG HANDICAP Tachycardia 7-9 Cheerful Groom (IRE) 7-8 Bright Paragon (IRE) 7-4

160 AWESOME POWER CLAIMING STKS (4-Y.O+) (Class E)
2-20 (2-20) **1m 2f (Equitrack)** £2,843.25 (£861.00: £420.50: £200.25) Stalls: Low GOING minus 0.29 sec per fur (FST)

				SP	RR	SF
47[6]	**Bagshot (53)** (GLMoore) **6-9-1** SWhitworth(2) (hdwy over 4f out: led ins fnl f: rdn out)	—	**1**	5/2[2]	72	39
10[2]	**Awesome Power (52)** (JWHills) **11-8-6** AClark(6) (hld up: rdn over 4f out: led over 1f out tl ins fnl f: unable qckn)	¾	**2**	9/4[1]	62	29
76[6]	**Honestly (48)** (BSmart) **4-8-5** SSanders(8) (lw: a.p: led over 5f out tl over 1f out: wknd fnl f)	5	**3**	7/1	55	20
76[5]	**Our Eddie (47)** (BGubby) **8-8-3v** JQuinn(5) (lw: hdwy 8f out: rdn over 4f out: wknd over 2f out)	2½	**4**	5/1[3]	47	14
56[6]	**Cedez le Passage (FR) (70)** (KOCunningham-Brown) **6-9-7b** JWeaver(9) (led 7f out tl over 5f out: wknd 2f out)	5	**5**	7/1	57	24
	Young Frederick (IRE) (60) (KRBurke) **4-8-7** ACulhane(1) (lw: hdwy over 3f out: sn wknd)	8	**6**	12/1	32	—
76[11]	**Little Pilgrim (32)** (TMJones) **4-8-2**(5) ADaly(4) (lost pl 7f out: rallied over 4f out: wknd over 3f out)	1	**7**	66/1	30	—
	Half An Inch (IRE) (44) (TMJones) **4-8-7b** RPerham(7) (b.hind: led 3f: wknd over 4f out)	hd	**8**	25/1	30	—
116[11]	**Thorniwama (41)** (JJBridger) **6-7-12b** NCarlisle(3) (a bhd)	2	**9**	33/1	16	—

(SP 117.0%) **9 Rn**

2m 8.88 (4.58) CSF £7.79 TOTE £3.60: £1.50 £1.10 £2.30 (£2.90) Trio £11.70 OWNER Mr Danny Bloor (BRIGHTON) BRED Newgate Stud Co
WEIGHT FOR AGE 4yo-2lb

161 CHIEFTAIN MEDIAN AUCTION MAIDEN STKS (3-Y.O) (Class E)
2-55 (2-56) **1m (Equitrack)** £2,765.25 (£837.00: £408.50: £194.25) Stalls: High GOING minus 0.29 sec per fur (FST)

Form	Horse	Dist	Pos	SP	RR	SF
50^{4}	**Hint of Victory** (MBell) **3-8-9**(5) GFaulkner(2) (lw: hld up: chsd ldr 6f out: led 3f out: hrd rdn 2f out: clr over 1f out: r.o wl)	—	1	Evens ^{1}	67	22
118^{4}	**Harmony In Red (64)** (CADwyer) **3-9-0e** DRMcCabe(3) (wl bhd 4f: hdwy 3f out: chsd wnr fnl 2f: unable qckn)	3	2	5/1 ^{3}	61	16
	Twin Time (MJHeaton-Ellis) **3-8-9** SDrowne(5) (w'like: chsd ldrs 2f: wknd wl over 1f out)	7	3	20/1	42	—
26^{8}	**Leg Beforum (IRE)** (LMontagueHall) **3-9-0** JWeaver(6) (nvr nr to chal)	3½	4	33/1	40	—
60^{2}	**Jolly Jackson (70)** (RAkehurst) **3-9-0** SSanders(4) (bhd fnl 4f)	4	5	9/4 ^{2}	32	—
	Polgwynne (BSmart) **3-8-9** RPerham(1) (w'like: bit bkwd: led: sn clr: hdd 3f out: sn wknd)	6	6	14/1	15	—

(SP 111.8%) **6 Rn**

1m 42.53 (5.13) CSF £5.96 TOTE £1.70: £1.10 £2.00 (£4.40) OWNER Sir Thomas Pilkington (NEWMARKET) BRED Sir T. H. Pilkington and I. D. Cameron

162 CHALLENGER H'CAP (0-80) (3-Y.O) (Class D)
3-30 (3-30) **1m (Equitrack)** £3,290.00 (£995.00: £485.00: £230.00) Stalls: High GOING minus 0.29 sec per fur (FST)

Form	Horse	Dist	Pos	SP	RR	SF
50^{7}	**Mendoza (55)** (DJGMurraySmith) **3-7-10**(7) JBramhill(3) (lw: hld up: rdn 2f out: led ins fnl f: r.o wl)	—	1	14/1	59	20
130^{*}	**As-Is (66)** (MJohnston) **3-9-0** 6x JWeaver(1) (chsd ldr: led 2f out tl ins fnl f: r.o)	½	2	5/4 ^{1}	69	30
138^{4}	**Time Can Tell (70)** (CMurray) **3-8-13**(5) GFaulkner(4) (led 6f: ev ch 1f out: unable qckn ins fnl f)	1½	3	6/4 ^{2}	70	31
25^{2}	**Heavenly Miss (IRE) (73)** (JJBridger) **3-9-7** DHarrison(2) (bhd fnl 3f)	25	4	9/2 ^{3}	23	—

(SP 109.3%) **4 Rn**

1m 41.69 (4.29) CSF £29.40 TOTE £11.00: (£11.60) OWNER Bid Defence Partnership (LAMBOURN) BRED Noel Winstanley

163 CENTURION H'CAP (0-70) (4-Y.O+ F & M) (Class E)
4-00 (4-00) **1m 4f (Equitrack)** £2,700.25 (£817.00: £398.50: £189.25) Stalls: Low GOING minus 0.29 sec per fur (FST)

Form	Horse	Dist	Pos	SP	RR	SF
	Persuasion (68) (LordHuntingdon) **4-9-8** DHarrison(6) (a.p: led 2f out: rdn out)	—	1	9/2 ^{2}	80	41
23^{3}	**Glow Forum (70)** (LMontagueHall) **6-9-11**(3) FLynch(1) (b: hdwy over 1f out: r.o wl ins fnl f)	1¼	2	7/1 ^{3}	80	45
	More Than You Know (IRE) (64) (KRBurke) **4-8-11**(7) JBramhill(4) (hld up: rdn over 3f out: r.o one pce fnl f)	1¾	3	3/1 ^{1}	72	33
74^{2}	**Harlequin Walk (IRE) (46)** (RJO'Sullivan) **6-8-4**ow1 SSanders(5) (lw: plld hrd: led 10f: hrd rdn: wknd ins fnl f)	1	4	9/2 ^{2}	53	17
116^{2}	**Rasayel (USA) (53)** (PDEvans) **7-8-4**(7) AnthonyBond(7) (hld up: rdn over 2f out: sn wknd)	1¼	5	9/2 ^{2}	58	23
86^{16}	**Miss Prism (52)** (JLDunlop) **4-8-6b** TSprake(2) (hld up: rdn over 3f out: ev ch over 1f out: wknd fnl f)	½	6	9/1	56	17
28^{4}	**Degree (65)** (SCWilliams) **4-9-5** JTate(3) (w ldr over 7f: wknd over 3f out: t.o)	dist	7	8/1	—	—

(SP 113.2%) **7 Rn**

2m 36.29 (6.29) CSF £31.30 TOTE £4.50: £2.90 £2.50 (£11.80) OWNER Countess of Lonsdale (WEST ILSLEY) BRED Lady Lonsdale
WEIGHT FOR AGE 4yo-4lb

T/Plpt: £360.70 (23.39 Tckts). T/Qdpt: £298.90 (1.62 Tckts). AK

0150-SOUTHWELL (L-H) (Standard)
Monday January 27th
WEATHER: misty with drizzle WIND: slt half bhd

164 FERMANAGH MEDIAN AUCTION MAIDEN STKS (3, 4 & 5-Y.O) (Class F)
1-50 (1-51) **7f (Fibresand)** £2,294.00 (£644.00: £314.00) Stalls: Low GOING: 0.20 sec per fur (SLW)

Form	Horse	Dist	Pos	SP	RR	SF
	State of Caution (78) (DShaw) **4-9-10b** JFanning(13) (lw: trckd ldr: led over 2f out: pushed clr fnl f)	—	1	3/1 ^{1}	77+	56
	Zorba (64) (CWThornton) **3-8-6** DeanMcKeown(8) (chsd ldrs: chal over 2f out: nt qckn appr fnl f)	4	2	4/1 ^{2}	68	29
49^{6}	**Weet And See** (RHollinshead) **3-8-3**(3) FLynch(12) (bhd tl styd on fnl 3f)	7	3	12/1	52	13
40^{6}	**Surf City (58)** (WWHaigh) **4-9-10** SWhitworth(7) (hld up: effrt over 2f out: kpt on same pce)	s.h	4	5/1 ^{3}	52	31
50^{5}	**Reeds** (JRFanshawe) **3-8-6** DHarrison(1) (lw: chsd ldrs: sn drvn along: kpt on one pce fnl 3f)	nk	5	4/1 ^{2}	51	12
71^{P}	**Jilly Beveled (35)** (RonaldThompson) **5-9-2**(3) CTeague(6) (led tl over 2f out: wknd fnl f)	3½	6	14/1	38	17
	Sebastian Duke (FR) (JCullinan) **5-9-10** TWilliams(3) (s.i.s: a in rr)	4	7	33/1	34	13
	Needwood Nutkin (BCMorgan) **4-9-5** GCarter(2) (outpcd & drvn along ½-wy: n.d)	2	8	20/1	24	3
	Lost In The Post (IRE) (CWThornton) **4-9-10** SDrowne(11) (cl up: outpcd & lost pl ½-wy)	1	9	10/1	27	6
	Prince Emar (TDEasterby) **3-8-6** JQuinn(9) (small: bit bkwd: s.i.s: sme hdwy ½-wy: sn wknd)	17	10	14/1	—	—
	Nashalong (IRE) (JJQuinn) **4-9-10** ACulhane(5) (mid div: sn drvn along: bhd fr ½-wy)	2	11	16/1	—	—
	Gloria Imperator (IRE) (46) (ABMulholland) **4-9-10** VHalliday(4) (plld hrd: cl up tl lost pl over 2f out)	1¼	12	33/1	—	—
	Lady Komaite (TTBill) **4-9-5** NCarlisle(10) (s.s: hung bdly rt thrght: sn t.o)	dist	13	33/1	—	—

(SP 131.3%) **13 Rn**

1m 32.3 (5.80) CSF £14.29 TOTE £6.40: £2.70 £1.80 £2.40 (£10.10) Trio £14.60 OWNER Mr J. C. Fretwell (NEWARK) BRED C. Wiggins
WEIGHT FOR AGE 3yo-18lb

165 DOWN CLAIMING STKS (4-Y.O+) (Class F)
2-20 (2-20) **6f (Fibresand)** £2,310.00 (£644.00: £314.00) Stalls: Low GOING: 0.20 sec per fur (SLW)

Form	Horse	Dist	Pos	SP	RR	SF
126^{*}	**Sense of Priority (70)** (DNicholls) **8-8-9** AlexGreaves(4) (lw: trckd ldr: plld hrd: led over 3f out: rdn out)	—	1	4/6 ^{1}	76	48
81^{6}	**Myttons Mistake (67)** (ABailey) **4-8-7** DWright(2) (trckd ldrs: r.o fnl f: nt rch wnr)	2	2	5/2 ^{2}	69	41
87^{4}	**Sea Devil (56)** (MJCamacho) **11-8-3** LCharnock(3) (chsd ldrs: wnt 2nd 2f out: one pce)	3½	3	9/2 ^{3}	55	27
123^{8}	**Spanish Stripper (USA) (32)** (MCChapman) **6-8-3** DRMcCabe(5) (led tl over 3f out: outpcd & swtchd rt 2f out: no imp)	1¼	4	20/1	42 t	24

(SP 111.5%) **4 Rn**

1m 18.0 (4.50) CSF £2.51 TOTE £1.70 (£2.00) OWNER Mr M. A. Scaife (THIRSK) BRED Cheveley Park Stud Ltd

166 ARMAGH H'CAP (0-80) (4-Y.O+) (Class D)

2-50 (2-51) **6f** **(Fibresand)** £3,387.50 (£1,025.00: £500.00: £237.50) Stalls: Low GOING: 0.20 sec per fur (SLW)

Form	Horse	Dist	Pl	SP	RR	SF
89[8]	**Prima Silk (73)** (MJRyan) **6-9-11** AClark(4) (chsd ldrs: styd on to ld ins fnl f)	—	1	6/1	81	61
89[11]	**Broadstairs Beauty (IRE) (75)** (DShaw) **7-9-10**(3) CTeague(1) (b: b.hind: sn led: clr ½-wy: hdd & no ex ins fnl f)	1	2	16/1	80	60
	Naughty Pistol (USA) (63) (PDEvans) **5-9-1v** SSanders(8) (hdwy ½-wy: sn rdn: styd on fnl f)	¾	3	9/2[3]	66	46
40[8]	**Paint It Black (52)** (DNicholls) **4-7-13**(5) JBramhill(5) (chsd ldrs: styd on same pce appr fnl f)	1¼	4	8/1	52	32
137[9]	**Lucky Revenge (57)** (DNicholls) **4-8-9** AlexGreaves(6) (hld up: trckd ldrs & plld hrd: effrt 2f out: kpt on one pce)	1	5	4/1[2]	54	34
127[7]	**Shashi (IRE) (57)** (PatMitchell) **5-8-9** RLappin(7) (led early: drvn along & outpcd ½-wy: n.d)	nk	6	7/1	54	34
127[3]	**Desert Invader (IRE) (68)** (DWChapman) **6-9-6** ACulhane(3) (chsd ldrs: drvn along & outpcd ½-wy: kpt on fnl 2f)	1	7	3/1[1]	62	42
127[8]	**Elton Ledger (IRE) (76)** (MrsNMacauley) **8-10-0v** JWeaver(2) (b: lw: hld up: effrt 2f out: n.d)	¾	8	11/2	68	48

(SP 122.3%) **8 Rn**

1m 18.2 (4.70) CSF £90.28 CT £440.62 TOTE £5.60: £1.70 £1.90 £2.30 (£154.50) OWNER Norcroft Park Stud (NEWMARKET) BRED R. M. Scott

167 ANTRIM H'CAP (0-70) (4-Y.O+) (Class E)

3-20 (3-20) **2m** **(Fibresand)** £2,892.00 (£876.00: £428.00: £204.00) Stalls: Low GOING: 0.20 sec per fur (SLW)

Form	Horse	Dist	Pl	SP	RR	SF
	Sudden Spin (61) (JNorton) **7-10-0** JWeaver(9) (hld up: wnt prom 10f out: wnt 2nd over 2f out: styd on to ld jst ins fnl f: jst hld on)	—	1	9/1	73	11
5[3]	**Master Foodbroker (IRE) (47)** (WJMusson) **9-9-0b** DRMcCabe(8) (bhd: gd hdwy 3f out: styd on wl ins fnl f)	nk	2	12/1	59	—
43[10]	**Mapengo (33)** (JCullinan) **6-8-0** LCharnock(4) (led: clr over 4f out: hdd jst ins fnl f: wknd)	11	3	33/1	34	—
101[3]	**Anglesey Sea View (48)** (ABailey) **8-9-1** GCarter(5) (prom tl outpcd ½-wy: kpt on fnl 2f)	1¼	4	5/1[1]	47	—
101[4]	**Classic Account (35)** (JLEyre) **9-8-2** TWilliams(11) (trckd ldrs: drvn along 6f out: grad wknd)	3½	5	8/1	31	—
101[6]	**Parklife (IRE) (47)** (PCHaslam) **5-9-0** SDrowne(13) (bhd: sme hdwy 5f out: sn hrd drvn & wknd)	3	6	6/1[2]	40	—
122[2]	**Swandale Flyer (29)** (NBycroft) **5-7-5**(5) JBramhill(1) (chsd ldrs tl wknd 3f out)	s.h	7	13/2[3]	22	—
80*	**Stonecutter (57)** (MRChannon) **4-9-3v** RPerham(7) (chsd ldr tl wknd 4f out)	19	8	5/1[1]	31	—
68[7]	**Record Lover (IRE) (32)** (MCChapman) **7-7-8**(5) PFessey(12) (chsd ldrs tl lost pl 5f out)	2½	9	14/1	3	—
	Top Prize (31) (MBrittain) **9-7-12v** GBardwell(2) (s.s: a bhd: sn drvn along: t.o fnl 5f)	30	10	14/1	—	—
86[5]	**Sheemore (IRE) (37)** (MDHammond) **4-7-11**ow1 JQuinn(10) (lw: hdwy to chse ldrs ½-wy: wknd 5f out: t.o)	14	11	10/1	—	—
78[2]	**Pedaltothemetal (IRE) (46)** (PMitchell) **5-8-13** SSanders(6) (lw: t.o 5f out)	hd	12	6/1[2]	—	—
86[12]	**Amazing Sail (IRE) (49)** (MissMKMilligan) **4-8-9** ACulhane(3) (sn drvn along: bhd fr ½-wy: t.o)	1	13	33/1	—	—

(SP 132.3%) **13 Rn**

3m 50.4 (24.40) CSF £113.62 CT £3,143.77 TOTE £11.80: £3.00 £3.60 £12.60 (£55.90) Trio £182.40; £208.16 to Warwick 28/1/97 OWNER Mr Billy Parker (BARNSLEY) BRED The Arrow Farm and Stud

WEIGHT FOR AGE 4yo-7lb

168 TYRONE (QUALIFIER) (S) H'CAP (0-60) (3-Y.O) (Class G)

3-50 (3-51) **1m** **(Fibresand)** £2,085.00 (£585.00: £285.00) Stalls: Low GOING: 0.20 sec per fur (SLW)

Form	Horse	Dist	Pl	SP	RR	SF
132[2]	**Mirror Four Sport (43)** (MJohnston) **3-7-12**(7) NPollard(4) (led tl over 3f out: led over 1f out: kpt on towards fin)	—	1	15/2	52	7
156[2]	**Bailieborough Boy (IRE) (58)** (TDBarron) **3-9-6** DeanMcKeown(5) (trckd ldrs: hdwy to chal 1f out: hung lft: nt r.o towards fin)	nk	2	11/2[3]	66	21
110[4]	**Jack Says (59)** (DShaw) **3-9-4b**(3) CTeague(2) (trckd ldrs: led over 3f out: sn clr: hdd over 1f out: sn wknd)	8	3	5/1[2]	51	6
130[2]	**Our Kevin (53)** (KMcAuliffe) **3-9-1be** DRMcCabe(9) (racd wd: gd hdwy ½-wy: sn chsng ldrs: one pce fnl 2f)	3	4	8/1	39	—
124[3]	**Neon Deion (IRE) (42)** (SCWilliams) **3-7-11v**(7) DarrenWilliams(10) (racd wd: hdwy ½-wy: sn rdn: hung lft & grad wknd)	2½	5	4/1[1]	23	—
124[9]	**Buzzby Babe (48)** (AGFoster) **3-8-10** TSprake(7) (b: in tch: drvn along ½-wy: n.d)	nk	6	33/1	29	—
94[4]	**Stakis Casinos Lad (IRE) (55)** (MJohnston) **3-8-10**(7) KSked(1) (w ldrs tl wknd over 2f out)	hd	7	8/1	36	—
124[7]	**Rock Fantasy (56)** (CMurray) **3-8-13**(5) GFaulkner(6) (in tch: drvn along ½-wy: sn btn)	hd	8	20/1	36	—
124[4]	**Senate Swings (55)** (WRMuir) **3-9-3b[1]** AClark(11) (racd wd: hdwy ½-wy: sn rdn & wknd)	4	9	6/1	27	—
124[10]	**Silent Valley (50)** (DNicholls) **3-8-12b** AlexGreaves(3) (s.s: sn chsng ldrs: lost pl ½-wy)	8	10	8/1	6	—
	Common Rock (IRE) (54) (JNorton) **3-8-11v**(5) JBramhill(8) (chsd ldrs: sn drvn along: lost pl 3f out)	14	11	16/1	—	—

(SP 125.0%) **11 Rn**

1m 48.9 (9.90) CSF £47.07 CT £213.73 TOTE £7.20: £3.60 £1.10 £1.90 (£18.80) Trio £39.30 OWNER Mark Johnston Racing Ltd (MIDDLEHAM) BRED T. Young

No bid

IN-FOCUS: This was a first winner for young Neil Pollard.

169 LONDONDERRY H'CAP (0-65) (4-Y.O+ F & M) (Class F)

4-20 (4-21) **1m** **(Fibresand)** £2,294.00 (£644.00: £314.00) Stalls: Low GOING: 0.20 sec per fur (SLW)

Form	Horse	Dist	Pl	SP	RR	SF
125[2]	**Three Arch Bridge (60)** (MJohnston) **5-9-11b** JWeaver(7) (s.i.s: hdwy ½-wy: led 2f out: styd on strly fnl f)	—	1	13/8[1]	72	45
	Queens Stroller (IRE) (32) (REPeacock) **6-7-6**(5) JBramhill(9) (sn drvn along: in tch: hdwy & ev ch 2f out: hrd rdn & kpt on same pce)	4	2	12/1	36	9
125*	**Mono Lady (IRE) (60)** (DHaydnJones) **4-9-11b** 6x CRutter(6) (trckd ldrs: chal 2f out: nt qckn appr fnl f)	3	3	7/2[2]	58	31
125[9]	**Down The Yard (40)** (MCChapman) **4-8-5** DRMcCabe(8) (racd wd: hdwy over 2f out: kpt on fnl f)	2	4	16/1	34	7
3[8]	**Chilibang Bang (56)** (JBerry) **4-9-2**(5) PRoberts(5) (lw: w ldrs: led over 2f out: sn hdd: edgd rt & grad wknd)	4	5	20/1	42	15
125[5]	**Efipetite (37)** (NBycroft) **4-8-2** GBardwell(12) (sn chsng ldrs: wknd 2f out)	2	6	14/1	19	—
125[6]	**Palacegate Jo (IRE) (31)** (DWChapman) **6-7-10** DWright(10) (uns rdr gng to s: led after 2f tl over 2f out: sn outpcd)	¾	7	8/1[3]	12	—
	Image Maker (IRE) (42) (PDEvans) **4-8-7** SSanders(1) (chsd ldrs tl lost pl 3f out)	3½	8	33/1	16	—
	Harry's Treat (50) (JLEyre) **5-9-1** RLappin(11) (w ldrs tl lost pl over 3f out)	13	9	10/1	—	—
114[7]	**Shanoora (IRE) (37)** (MrsNMacauley) **4-8-2** JQuinn(4) (sn bhd)	½	10	14/1	—	—

	Horse	Dist	Pos	SP	RR	SF
	Amnesty Bay (39) (MDIUsher) **5-8-4**ow1 SDrowne(2) (sn drvn along & bhd)	4	**11**	25/1	—	—
134^{4}	**Fancy Design (IRE) (31)** (PMitchell) **4-7-5**(5) PFessey(3) (b.hind: led 2f: lost pl 3f out)	¾	**12**	12/1	—	—
				(SP 126.7%)	**12 Rn**	

1m 46.9 (7.90) CSF £22.72 CT £62.38 TOTE £3.00: £1.20 £2.10 £1.50 (£42.10) Trio £12.30 OWNER Mr R. N. Pennell (MIDDLEHAM) BRED R. Taylor

LONG HANDICAP Palacegate Jo (IRE) 7-9 Fancy Design (IRE) 7-8

T/Plpt: £226.30 (41.17 Tckts). T/Qdpt: £123.70 (6.69 Tckts) WG

0158-LINGFIELD (L-H) (Standard)

Tuesday January 28th

Race 1 - hand-timed

WEATHER: overcast WIND: almost nil

170 LANDAU H'CAP (0-80) (3-Y.O+) (Class D)

1-30 (1-30) **5f** **(Equitrack)** £3,322.50 (£1,005.00: £490.00: £232.50: £25.00: £25.00) Stalls: High GOING minus 0.34 sec per fur (FST)

	Horse	Dist	Pos	SP	RR	SF
95*	**Sally Slade (69)** (CACyzer) **5-9-3** DBiggs(4) (outpcd: gd hdwy fnl f: str run to ld last strides)	—	**1**	13/2	75	33
117*	**Lord Sky (63)** (ABailey) **6-8-11** SSanders(6) (b: lw: hld up: rdn 2f out: led ins fnl f: hdd last strides)	hd	**2**	7/1	69	27
146^{4}	**Scissor Ridge (76)** (JJBridger) **5-9-10** DHarrison(3) (outpcd: hdwy over 1f out: r.o wl ins fnl f)	1½	**3**	15/2	77	35
58^{2}	**Madrina (65)** (JBerry) **4-8-8**(5) PFessey(5) (led: clr over 1f out: hdd ins fnl f: one pce)	s.h	**4**	12/1	66	24
159^{3}	**The Institute Boy (67)** (MissJFCraze) **7-9-1** JWeaver(7) (outpcd: hdwy fnl f: r.o wl)	¾	**5**	6/1 3	65	23
137^{2}	**Chemcast (70)** (JLEyre) **4-9-4b** RLappin(2) (a.p: rdn over 2f out: wknd ins fnl f)	2½	**6**	5/1 2	60	18
95^{D}	**Mijas (76)** (LMontagueHall) **4-9-10** DHolland(1) (lw: spd 3f)	5	**7**	13/8 1	50	8
				(SP 114.3%)	**7 Rn**	

60.5 secs (2.30) CSF £45.50 TOTE £9.70: £3.50 £3.50 (£28.60) OWNER Mr R. M. Cyzer (HORSHAM) BRED C. A. Cyzer

OFFICIAL EXPLANATION **Mijas: missed the break and was unable to dominate as a result.**

171 DOG CART CLAIMING STKS (4-Y.O+) (Class E)

2-00 (2-01) **1m** **(Equitrack)** £2,817.25 (£853.00: £416.50: £198.25) Stalls: High GOING minus 0.34 sec per fur (FST)

	Horse	Dist	Pos	SP	RR	SF
117^{2}	**Invocation (63)** (GLMoore) **10-8-9** AClark(8) (b.nr hind: lw: rdn & hdwy over 2f out: led ins fnl f: edgd lft: r.o wl)	—	**1**	13/2 2	70	44
114^{9}	**Spencer's Revenge (56)** (NTinkler) **8-8-5b** GBardwell(7) (lw: outpcd: hdwy over 1f out: r.o wl ins fnl f)	1	**2**	12/1	64	38
105*	**Soaking (79)** (PBurgoyne) **7-9-5** DRMcCabe(1) (s.i.s: chsd ldrs: rdn 2f out: 3rd & btn whn n.m.r wl ins fnl f)	nk	**3**	8/11 1	77	51
121^{12}	**Greatest (75)** (MissGayKelleway) **6-9-5** DHolland(5) (b: b.hind: led 1f: led over 3f out: hrd rdn over 1f out: hdd ins fnl f: one pce)	s.h	**4**	8/1 3	77	51
109^{6}	**Sharp 'n Smart (65)** (BSmart) **5-8-13** SSanders(3) (lw: led 7f out tl over 3f out: wknd over 1f out)	3	**5**	8/1 3	65	39
143^{2}	**Nashaat (USA) (76)** (KRBurke) **9-8-10**(7) KSked(4) (bhd fnl 3f)	6	**6**	13/2 2	57	31
	Uoni (45) (PButler) **4-7-13**(5) JBramhill(2) (prom 3f)	3	**7**	25/1	38	12
	Mr Hacker (32) (GThorner) **4-8-5b**1 CRutter(6) (bhd fnl 5f)	12	**8**	66/1	15	—
				(SP 119.8%)	**8 Rn**	

1m 39.44 (2.04) CSF £75.50 TOTE £10.50: £2.30 £1.10 £1.40 (£26.60) OWNER Mr R. Kiernan (BRIGHTON) BRED Juddmonte Farms

Spencer's Revenge clmd Mrs E Lucy Butler £3,000.

172 PHAETON H'CAP (0-65) (4-Y.O+) (Class F)

2-30 (2-30) **6f** **(Equitrack)** £2,428.40 (£682.40: £333.20: £16.00: £16.00: £16.00) Stalls: Low GOING minus 0.34 sec per fur (FST)

	Horse	Dist	Pos	SP	RR	SF
159*	**Tachycardia (41)** (RJO'Sullivan) **5-8-1**(3) 7x NVarley(5) (hld up: rdn over 2f out: led over 1f out: r.o wl)	—	**1**	3/1 2	47	7
107*	**Mellors (IRE) (64)** (MJHeaton-Ellis) **4-9-13** SDrowne(6) (a.p: rdn over 2f out: r.o ins fnl f)	1¼	**2**	9/4 1	67	27
127^{2}	**Blue Lugana (34)** (NBycroft) **5-7-6**(5) JBramhill(2) (w ldr: led over 2f out tl over 1f out: unable qckn fnl f)	nk	**3**	5/1 3	36	—
128^{2}	**Allstars Dancer (35)** (TJNaughton) **4-7-7**(5) PFessey(1) (led over 3f: rdn: one pce fnl f)	nk	**4**	8/1	36	—
117^{4}	**Norling (IRE) (47)** (KOCunningham-Brown) **7-8-10** CMunday(8) (rdn 3f out: hdwy fnl f: r.o)	1¼	**5**	5/1 3	45	5
114^{4}	**Soldier Cove (USA) (48)** (MartynMeade) **7-8-11** NAdams(7) (lw: bhd fnl 5f)	4	**6**	20/1	35	—
	Efficacy (57) (APJarvis) **6-9-6** WRyan(3) (bit bkwd: prom over 3f)	3	**7**	14/1	36	—
	Daydream Island (35) (RJBaker) **4-7-12** JQuinn(4) (bhd fnl 4f: t.o)	dist	**8**	66/1	—	—
				(SP 113.1%)	**8 Rn**	

1m 14.96 (3.86) CSF £9.05 CT £28.24 TOTE £3.40: £1.40 £1.40 £1.50 (£4.30) OWNER Mr Christopher Lane (WHITCOMBE) BRED Patrick Eddery Ltd

173 SULKY MAIDEN STKS (3-Y.O+) (Class D)

3-00 (3-03) **1m 2f** **(Equitrack)** £3,371.25 (£1,020.00: £497.50: £236.25: £25.00: £25.00) Stalls: Low GOING minus 0.34 sec per fur (FST)

	Horse	Dist	Pos	SP	RR	SF
	Alarico (FR) (IPWilliams) **4-9-10** DHolland(7) (w ldr: led over 7f out: clr over 2f out: rdn out)	—	**1**	25/1	80	48
108^{3}	**Passage Creeping (IRE) (56)** (SDow) **4-9-5e** SSanders(8) (hdwy 4f out: chsd wnr over 3f out: rdn over 2f out: unable qckn)	11	**2**	4/1 2	57	25
96^{2}	**Baaheth (USA) (77)** (SCWilliams) **3-8-3** GCarter(4) (hld up: rdn over 4f out: wknd over 2f out)	4	**3**	5/6 1	56	3
60^{4}	**Double Crest (IRE) (65)** (MJohnston) **3-7-12** NAdams(1) (led over 2f: wknd over 3f out)	11	**4**	11/2 3	33	—
	On The Piste (RAFahey) **4-9-5** ACulhane(2) (prom 6f)	1½	**5**	11/2 3	31	—
	On The Green (AHide) **4-9-5** JStack(5) (bkwd: a bhd: t.o)	20	**6**	25/1	—	—
	Currer Bell (CMurray) **4-9-5** NicolaHowarth(6) (bhd fnl 6f: t.o)	9	**7**	25/1	—	—
	Plenty of Sunshine (ICampbell) **4-9-5** AClark(3) (bit bkwd: bhd fnl 4f: t.o)	dist	**8**	33/1	—	—
				(SP 119.8%)	**8 Rn**	

2m 8.28 (3.98) CSF £111.77 TOTE £67.60: £6.60 £1.10 £1.60 (£41.90) OWNER Mr & Mrs John Poynton (ALVECHURCH) BRED Mrs Claude Aubree

WEIGHT FOR AGE 3yo-23lb, 4yo-2lb
IN-FOCUS: This looked a dreadful maiden consisting of either one-paced or talentless individuals.

174 BROUGHAM H'CAP (0-70) (3-Y.O) (Class E)

3-30 (3-31) **1m 2f (Equitrack)** £2,687.25 (£813.00: £396.50: £188.25) Stalls: Low GOING minus 0.34 sec per fur (FST)

				SP	RR	SF
119³	**Lawn Lothario (60)** (MJohnston) **3-8-11** JWeaver(2) (lw: led over 2f: led over 4f out: clr over 3f out: r.o wl)	—	**1**	4/1 ³	70	31
162³	**Time Can Tell (70)** (CMurray) **3-9-7** MTebbutt(4) (w wnr: led over 7f out tl over 4f out: rdn: unable qckn)	7	**2**	7/2 ²	69	30
84²	**Chateauherault (IRE) (62)** (PCHaslam) **3-8-13** SDrowne(3) (nvr gng wl: no hdwy fnl 3f)	5	**3**	5/4 ¹	53	14
162*	**Mendoza (60)** (DJGMurraySmith) **3-8-6**(5) 5x JBramhill(1) (bhd fnl 4f)	26	**4**	7/2 ²	9	—
				(SP 108.9%)		**4 Rn**

2m 8.89 (4.59) CSF £15.27 TOTE £3.90 (£9.50) OWNER Mr J. S. Morrison (MIDDLEHAM) BRED Snailwell Stud Co Ltd
OFFICIAL EXPLANATION Chateauherault (IRE): was never going.

175 HANSOM LIMITED STKS (0-70) (3-Y.O+) (Class E)

4-00 (4-00) **7f (Equitrack)** £2,700.25 (£817.00: £398.50: £189.25: £20.00: £20.00) Stalls: Low GOING minus 0.34 sec per fur (FST)

				SP	RR	SF
	Hurtleberry (IRE) (68) (LordHuntingdon) **4-9-4** DHarrison(5) (hld up: rdn over 2f out: led over 1f out: r.o wl)	—	**1**	5/2 ²	77	54
56⁴	**Barrel of Hope (67)** (JLEyre) **5-9-7b**(3) OPears(3) (a.p: led 4f out tl over 1f out: unable qckn)	4	**2**	6/1	74	51
90*	**Mardrew (70)** (DJSffrenchDavis) **3-8-6** JQuinn(7) (lw: stdy hdwy over 2f out: rdn wl over 1f out: r.o one pce)	1½	**3**	4/1 ³	70	29
146³	**Star Talent (USA) (70)** (MissGayKelleway) **6-9-7** DHolland(4) (b: b.hind: stdy hdwy over 2f out: wknd over 1f out)	5	**4**	13/8 ¹	56	33
	Worldwide Elsie (USA) (70) (ICampbell) **4-9-4** DBatteate(1) (lw: led 3f: wknd over 2f out)	1¼	**5**	20/1	50	27
	Cross of Valour (70) (PHowling) **4-9-7** SWhitworth(2) (prom over 3f)	12	**6**	12/1	26	3
				(SP 113.4%)		**6 Rn**

1m 26.05 (1.65) CSF £16.20 TOTE £3.60: £1.50 £2.40 (£5.80) OWNER Mrs Ian Pilkington (WEST ILSLEY) BRED D. Maher
WEIGHT FOR AGE 3yo-18lb

T/Plpt: £203.50 (44.68 Tckts). T/Qdpt: £25.60 (25.17 Tckts) AK

0135-WOLVERHAMPTON (L-H) (Standard)
Wednesday January 29th

WEATHER: overcast WIND: almost nil

176 ROSEMARY H'CAP (0-90) (I) (4-Y.O+) (Class C)

1-20 (1-21) **1m 1f 79y (Fibresand)** £4,557.85 (£1,376.80: £669.90: £316.45) Stalls: Low GOING: 0.28 sec per fur (SLW)

				SP	RR	SF
52³	**South Eastern Fred (88)** (HJCollingridge) **6-9-13** MRimmer(9) (lw: a gng wl: led over 4f out: clr over 1f out: easily)	—	**1**	6/1	97+	58
22*	**Slip Jig (IRE) (68)** (KRBurke) **4-7-13**(7) KSked(7) (hld up: hdwy over 1f out: hung lft ins fnl f: fin wl)	3½	**2**	4/1 ¹	71	31
	Bardon Hill Boy (IRE) (87) (BHanbury) **5-9-12** JStack(10) (a.p: one pce fnl 2f)	1¾	**3**	8/1	87	48
153⁹	**Gulf Shaadi (67)** (EJAlston) **5-8-6** SDrowne(6) (hld up & bhd: hdwy over 2f out: one pce)	nk	**4**	11/2	67	28
39⁷	**Joseph's Wine (IRE) (80)** (DNicholls) **8-9-5b** AlexGreaves(1) (nvr nr to chal)	2½	**5**	5/1 ³	75	36
100³	**Infamous (USA) (78)** (RJO'Sullivan) **4-9-2** DHolland(5) (lw: plld hrd: prom: hrd rdn over 3f out: wknd wl over 1f out)	1½	**6**	9/2 ²	71	31
105⁵	**Waikiki Beach (USA) (71)** (GLMoore) **6-8-10** SWhitworth(4) (sme hdwy over 2f out: n.d)	9	**7**	9/1	48	9
141³	**Tallulah Belle (58)** (NPLittmoden) **4-7-10** NCarlisle(3) (prom over 6f)	6	**8**	7/1	25	—
136³	**Bogart (58)** (CWFairhurst) **6-7-11**ow1 LCharnock(8) (lw: bhd fnl 3f)	1¼	**9**	14/1	23	—
	Loveyoumillions (IRE) (75) (NTinkler) **5-9-0** GCarter(2) (led 5f: wknd 3f out)	4	**10**	16/1	33	—
				(SP 130.7%)		**10 Rn**

2m 4.7 (8.70) CSF £31.17 CT £188.16 TOTE £7.60: £2.80 £2.10 £2.00 (£19.80) Trio £81.30 OWNER South Eastern Electrical Plc (EXNING) BRED L. Audus
LONG HANDICAP Tallulah Belle 7-8 Bogart 7-1
WEIGHT FOR AGE 4yo-1lb

177 CHIVE MAIDEN H'CAP (0-70) (4-Y.O+) (Class E)

1-50 (1-51) **7f (Fibresand)** £2,804.25 (£849.00: £414.50: £197.25) Stalls: High GOING: 0.28 sec per fur (SLW)

				SP	RR	SF
	What A Fuss (64) (BHanbury) **4-10-0** JStack(4) (prom: outpcd over 2f out: str run ins fnl f: led nr fin)	—	**1**	4/1 ¹	73	36
86¹⁷	**Hornpipe (33)** (JWharton) **5-7-11b**ow1 JQuinn(7) (b: w ldrs: ev ch fnl f: r.o)	1¼	**2**	12/1	39	1
	Gold Lining (IRE) (32) (EJAlston) **4-7-7**(3) NVarley(2) (a.p: hrd rdn to ld over 2f out: hdd nr fin)	nk	**3**	20/1	38	1
	Dino's Mistral (37) (FHLee) **4-8-1** CRutter(5) (chsd ldrs: r.o one pce fnl 2f)	2½	**4**	16/1	37	—
85⁹	**Ring the Chief (32)** (MDIUsher) **5-7-10** NCarlisle(10) (hdwy over 2f out: one pce fnl f)	¾	**5**	13/2	30	—
	Elraas (USA) (32) (RJO'Sullivan) **5-7-10v** FNorton(6) (led over 4f: eased whn btn over 1f out)	6	**6**	10/1	16	—
	Zelaya (IRE) (50) (GLMoore) **4-9-0** SWhitworth(9) (chsd ldrs over 4f)	¾	**7**	4/1 ¹	33	—
3¹⁰	**Seanchai (IRE) (34)** (PSFelgate) **4-7-12** DWright(1) (lw: chsd ldrs over 4f)	1	**8**	16/1	14	—
	Ocean Stream (IRE) (59) (JLEyre) **4-9-9** DeanMcKeown(8) (rdn over 5f out: sn bhd)	1¾	**9**	11/2 ²	35	—
	Grand Crack (IRE) (37) (CADwyer) **5-8-1** DRMcCabe(12) (a bhd)	¾	**10**	10/1	12	—
112²	**Soaked (43)** (DWChapman) **4-8-7** LCharnock(3) (a bhd)	6	**11**	6/1 ³	4	—
125¹⁴	**Carmosa (USA) (50)** (DNicholls) **4-9-0b¹** MWigham(11) (a bhd)	4	**12**	11/1	2	—
				(SP 133.7%)		**12 Rn**

1m 33.1 (8.40) CSF £56.52 CT £842.76 TOTE £6.90: £2.70 £1.40 £13.50 (£11.60) Trio £83.20; £93.82 to Towcester 30/1/97 OWNER Mr B. Hanbury (NEWMARKET) BRED Gainsborough Stud Management Ltd
LONG HANDICAP Elraas (USA) 7-2 Gold Lining (IRE) 7-8

178 SAGE CLAIMING STKS (3-Y.O+) (Class F)

2-20 (2-24) **5f (Fibresand)** £2,294.00 (£644.00: £314.00) Stalls: Low GOING: 0.28 sec per fur (SLW)

				SP	RR	SF
126[2]	**Kalar (76)** (DWChapman) **8-9-10b** LCharnock(6) (mde all: rdn wl over 1f out: r.o wl)	—	**1**	10/11[1]	66	51
87[9]	**Double Oscar (IRE) (45)** (DNicholls) **4-9-2b** AlexGreaves(4) (chsd wnr: hrd rdn over 1f out: nt qckn)	1¾	**2**	16/1	52	37
127[9]	**Featherstone Lane (58)** (MissLCSiddall) **6-9-1v**(7) TSiddall(1) (hdwy over 1f out: nt rch ldrs)	3½	**3**	14/1	47	32
137[6]	**Boffy (IRE) (53)** (BPJBaugh) **4-9-8** RPerham(5) (a.p: one pce fnl 2f)	¾	**4**	9/1[3]	45	30
58[4]	**Palacegate Jack (IRE) (77)** (CADwyer) **6-10-0** DRMcCabe(2) (hld up: btn whn hung rt over 1f out)	3½	**5**	6/4[2]	40	25
87[7]	**Time To Fly (31)** (BWMurray) **4-9-2** VHalliday(3) (no hdwy fnl 2f)	s.h	**6**	50/1	27	12

(SP 116.9%) **6 Rn**

63.6 secs (4.70) CSF £16.66 TOTE £2.00: £1.10 £5.50 (£11.70) OWNER Mr J. M. Chapman (YORK) BRED C. C. and Mrs Pryor

179 ROSEMARY H'CAP (0-90) (II) (4-Y.O+) (Class C)

2-50 (2-50) **1m 1f 79y (Fibresand)** £4,509.75 (£1,362.00: £662.50: £312.75) Stalls: High GOING: 0.28 sec per fur (SLW)

				SP	RR	SF
146[2]	**Duke Valentino (80)** (RHollinshead) **5-9-0**(5) DGriffiths(8) (hld up: hdwy 3f out: rdn to ld over 1f out: r.o wl)	—	**1**	9/2[3]	88	34
105[8]	**Second Colours (USA) (82)** (MCPipe) **7-9-7** DHarrison(9) (hld up: hdwy over 2f out: r.o wl ins fnl f: nt trble wnr)	2½	**2**	5/2[1]	86	32
82[6]	**Pater Noster (USA) (89)** (JohnHarris) **8-10-0** SSanders(6) (chsd ldr: led over 5f out tl over 1f out: one pce)	1¾	**3**	11/2	90	36
131[10]	**Law Dancer (IRE) (77)** (TGMills) **4-9-1** TWilliams(7) (hld up: stdy hdwy over 4f out: rdn & ev ch 2f out: wknd over 1f out)	3½	**4**	16/1	72	17
140[9]	**Forest Boy (71)** (JRBosley) **4-8-9** CRutter(5) (prom: rdn over 2f out: wknd over 1f out)	3	**5**	8/1	61	6
111[4]	**Le Sport (67)** (DNicholls) **4-8-5** DWright(3) (s.i.s: rdn & sme hdwy over 3f out: wknd over 2f out)	2½	**6**	14/1	52	—
52[8]	**Tea Party (USA) (72)** (KOCunningham-Brown) **4-8-10** WRyan(1) (bhd fnl 2f)	hd	**7**	14/1	57	2
	Northern Fan (IRE) (87) (NTinkler) **5-9-12** SWhitworth(2) (s.s: a bhd: t.o)	21	**8**	8/1	36	—
136[2]	**Anonym (IRE) (70)** (DNicholls) **5-8-9b** AlexGreaves(4) (plld hrd: led 4f out: wknd 3f out: t.o)	5	**9**	11/4[2]	11	—

(SP 130.2%) **9 Rn**

2m 6.6 (10.60) CSF £16.87 CT £62.79 TOTE £7.00: £1.90 £2.20 £2.70 (£10.60) Trio £10.60 OWNER Mr J. E. Bigg (UPPER LONGDON) BRED Shadwell Estate Company Limited

WEIGHT FOR AGE 4yo-1lb

OFFICIAL EXPLANATION Anonym (IRE): ran too freely.

180 OREGANO H'CAP (0-90) (3-Y.O) (Class C)

3-20 (3-21) **6f (Fibresand)** £5,012.85 (£1,516.80: £739.90: £351.45: £37.00: £37.00) Stalls: Low GOING: 0.28 sec per fur (SLW)

				SP	RR	SF
155[2]	**The Wyandotte Inn (72)** (RHollinshead) **3-8-3** JQuinn(8) (lw: hdwy over 2f out: led over 1f out: r.o wl)	—	**1**	6/1	79	38
138[3]	**Nomore Mr Niceguy (84)** (EJAlston) **3-9-1** KFallon(7) (lw: rdn & hdwy 2f out: r.o ins fnl f)	2½	**2**	13/2	84	43
38*	**Dominant Air (80)** (SirMarkPrescott) **3-8-11** GDuffield(5) (a.p: chsd wnr over 1f out: no imp)	s.h	**3**	3/1[1]	80	39
62*	**Just Loui (90)** (WGMTurner) **3-9-0**(7) DMcGaffin(4) (w ldr: led over 4f out tl over 1f out: wknd fnl f)	4	**4**	5/1[3]	80	39
135*	**Siouxrouge (81)** (PCHaslam) **3-8-5**(7) 7x PGoode(3) (no hdwy fnl 2f)	s.h	**5**	100/30[2]	70	29
17[4]	**Master Foley (65)** (NPLittmoden) **3-7-10** NCarlisle(6) (lw: led over 1f: wknd over 1f out)	5	**6**	14/1	41	—
	A Breeze (78) (DMorris) **3-8-9** NDay(1) (prom over 3f)	9	**7**	20/1	30	—
155[3]	**La Dolce Vita (75)** (TDBarron) **3-8-6** DHarrison(2) (s.i.s: eased whn btn wl over 1f out)	5	**8**	14/1	14	—

(SP 110.5%) **8 Rn**

1m 16.4 (5.20) CSF £37.53 CT £119.65 TOTE £4.10: £1.30 £2.10 £1.40 (£7.30) OWNER Mr G. A. Farndon (UPPER LONGDON) BRED N. W. Rimington

LONG HANDICAP Master Foley 7-7

STEWARDS' ENQUIRY McGaffin susp. 7-8/2/97 (excessive use of whip).

181 MARJORAM (S) STKS (3-Y.O) (Class G)

3-50 (3-51) **6f (Fibresand)** £2,085.00 (£585.00: £285.00) Stalls: Low GOING: 0.28 sec per fur (SLW)

				SP	RR	SF
51[4]	**Chilling (46)** (PGMurphy) **3-8-0**(7) KSked(10) (chsd ldr: led over 3f out: clr wl over 1f out: r.o wl)	—	**1**	6/1[3]	63	24
	Pretty Sally (IRE) (54) (DJGMurraySmith) **3-8-7** DHarrison(5) (hdwy over 2f out: chsd wnr wl over 1f out: sn hung lft: r.o ins fnl f)	1¾	**2**	16/1	58	19
158*	**Imperial Garden (IRE) (64)** (PCHaslam) **3-9-3** SDrowne(12) (a.p: rdn over 2f out: r.o one pce)	1½	**3**	2/1[1]	64	25
132[6]	**Chasetown Flyer (USA) (53)** (RHollinshead) **3-8-12** WRyan(7) (hdwy over 1f out: r.o)	3½	**4**	12/1	50	11
	Terry's Rose (50) (RHollinshead) **3-8-8**ow1 MWigham(3) (hdwy fnl f: nrst fin)	1¼	**5**	16/1	43	3
102[4]	**Fit For The Job (IRE) (67)** (TWall) **3-9-3** SSanders(6) (chsd ldrs: no hdwy fnl 2f)	s.h	**6**	11/2[2]	52	13
103[6]	**Advance Repro (54)** (JAkehurst) **3-8-12b** MTebbutt(13) (led over 2f: wknd over 1f out)	s.h	**7**	6/1[3]	46	7
94[2]	**Broadgate Flyer (IRE) (62)** (MrsLStubbs) **3-8-12** SWhitworth(11) (nvr trbld ldrs)	4	**8**	7/1	36	—
126[7]	**Lights of Home** (MissCJohnsey) **3-8-12** NAdams(4) (lw: outpcd)	4	**9**	25/1	25	—
155[8]	**Sherzetto (68)** (DWChapman) **3-8-12** LCharnock(8) (outpcd)	1½	**10**	12/1	21	—
38[6]	**Joyful Joy (35)** (BPJBaugh) **3-8-7** RPerham(9) (chsd ldrs over 3f)	1¼	**11**	33/1	13	—
132[9]	**Seretse's Nephew (54)** (SCWilliams) **3-9-3** KFallon(2) (chsd ldrs over 3f)	½	**12**	16/1	21	—
102[7]	**Flood's Hot Stuff (37)** (NPLittmoden) **3-8-2**(5) ADaly(1) (outpcd)	5	**13**	33/1	—	—

(SP 132.5%) **13 Rn**

1m 17.7 (6.50) CSF £97.89 TOTE £7.30: £2.70 £6.10 £1.10 (£53.40) Trio £141.00 OWNER Miss A. Amey (BRISTOL) BRED D. J. Simpson

Sold W Jones 5,000 gns

182 THYME H'CAP (0-80) (4-Y.O+) (Class D)

4-20 (4-22) **1m 4f (Fibresand)** £3,452.50 (£1,045.00: £510.00: £242.50) Stalls: Low GOING: 0.28 sec per fur (SLW)

				SP	RR	SF
	Hill Farm Dancer (68) (WMBrisbourne) **6-9-3**(7) AnthonyBond(4) (s.s: gd hdwy to ld over 4f out: sn clr: pushed out)	—	**1**	8/1[3]	82	47
100[4]	**Nikita's Star (IRE) (75)** (DJGMurraySmith) **4-9-13** DHarrison(2) (hld up: hdwy to chse wnr over 2f out: no imp)	9	**2**	8/1[3]	77	38
	Studio Thirty (41) (RDickin) **5-7-11**ow1 JQuinn(6) (rdn & hdwy over 3f out: one pce fnl 2f)	2	**3**	20/1	40	4

70^{5} **Premier Dance (69)** (DHaydnJones) **10-9-11** AClark(10) (hld up: stdy hdwy over 5f out: styd on fnl f)...........2½ **4** 14/1 65 30
70^{7} **Dancing Cavalier (69)** (RHollinshead) **4-9-2**(5) DGriffiths(7) (nvr nr to chal)...........4 **5** 14/1 60 21
70^{4} **Far Ahead (72)** (JLEyre) **5-9-11**(3) OPears(11) (nvr nr ldrs)...........1¼ **6** 14/1 61 26
70^{2} **Circled (USA) (72)** (JohnHarris) **4-9-10** DeanMcKeown(5) (prom: rdn 6f out: wknd over 4f out)...........½ **7** 11/4 1 60 21
160^{5} **Cedez le Passage (FR) (70)** (KOCunningham-Brown) **6-9-12b** SSanders(8) (lw: hld up: hdwy over 5f out: wknd 3f out)...........hd **8** 16/1 58 23
23^{6} **Tart (FR) (70)** (JPearce) **4-9-8** MWigham(1) (bhd fnl 3f)...........4 **9** 9/1 53 14
52^{4} **Montecristo (72)** (RGuest) **4-9-3**(7) LucyBrown(12) (prom over 8f)...........7 **10** 8/1 3 46 7
Eagle Canyon (IRE) (75) (BHanbury) **4-9-13** MRimmer(3) (lw: prom tl wknd over 2f out)...........nk **11** 16/1 48 9
30^{3} **Canary Falcon (60)** (RJO'Sullivan) **6-9-2** DHolland(9) (led over 7f: sn wknd: t.o)...........9 **12** 4/1 2 21 —
(SP 126.5%) **12 Rn**

2m 45.1 (12.60) CSF £68.82 CT £1,156.63 TOTE £18.80: £3.20 £2.90 £6.00 (£52.00) Trio £163.90; £207.78 to Towcester 30/1/97 OWNER Mr M. E. Hughes (NESSCLIFFE) BRED D. Newton
LONG HANDICAP Studio Thirty 7-6
WEIGHT FOR AGE 4yo-4lb

T/Plpt: £38.90 (242.43 Tckts). T/Qdpt: £10.30 (87.77 Tckts) KH

0170-LINGFIELD (L-H) (Standard)
Thursday January 30th

Races 2 & 3: hand timed.
WEATHER: overcast WIND: mod half across

183 ALBERTA (S) H'CAP (0-60) (4-Y.O+) (Class G)
1-50 (1-56) **1m 5f (Equitrack)** £2,194.50 (£617.00: £301.50) Stalls: Low GOING minus 0.39 sec per fur (FST)

SP RR SF

106^{3} **Supreme Star (USA) (59)** (PRHedger) **6-9-11b**(3) NVarley(8) (a.p: led over 3f out: r.o wl)...........— **1** 9/2 2 75 40
147^{2} **Al Helal (40)** (JRJenkins) **5-8-9** SWhitworth(2) (hld up: hdwy 4f out: chsd wnr over 2f out: r.o one pce ins fnl f)...........3 **2** 5/1 3 52 17
Illegally Yours (44) (LMontagueHall) **4-8-8** WRyan(13) (rr tl gd hdwy fnl 2f: fin wl)...........¾ **3** 20/1 55 15
147^{3} **Sapphire Son (IRE) (36)** (PCClarke) **5-8-5** NAdams(15) (hld up: hdwy 6f out: rdn over 2f out: one pce)...........3½ **4** 10/1 43 8
Sharp Thrill (34) (BSmart) **6-8-3b** SDrowne(11) (chsd ldrs: rdn over 2f out: one pce)...........¾ **5** 20/1 40 5
101^{7} **Al Haal (USA) (40)** (RJO'Sullivan) **8-8-9** DBiggs(5) (nvr nrr)...........3½ **6** 25/1 42 7
116^{4} **Ela Man Howa (48)** (ABailey) **6-9-3** SSanders(7) (prom: rdn over 2f out: sn wknd)...........5 **7** 7/2 1 44 9
Storm Wind (IRE) (45) (KRBurke) **4-8-2v**1(7)ow5 JMMaguire(6) (led: hdd 5f out: grad wknd)...........1¼ **8** 33/1 39 —
104^{7} **Broughtons Relish (32)** (WJMusson) **4-7-7**(3) MBaird(10) (in tch: rdn 5f out: wknd 3f out)...........1¼ **9** 25/1 25 —
93^{3} **Tamandu (30)** (CJames) **7-7-13v**1ow3 CRutter(12) (chsd ldrs tl wknd over 3f out)...........7 **10** 16/1 14 —
129^{5} **Bath Knight (40)** (DJSffrenchDavis) **4-8-4** GCarter(14) (led 5f out: hdd over 3f out: sn wknd)...........¾ **11** 20/1 23 —
104^{3} **Oozlem (IRE) (39)** (LMontagueHall) **8-8-8v** DHolland(4) (a bhd)...........7 **12** 11/2 14 —
78^{9} **Zuno Flyer (USA) (50)** (GLMoore) **5-9-5** CandyMorris(1) (bhd fnl 9f: t.o fnl 5f)...........8 **13** 14/1 15 —
111^{6} **Sonya Marie (34)** (JGFitzGerald) **4-7-5**(7) RBrisland(9) (bhd fnl 7f: t.o fnl 5f)...........14 **14** 20/1 — —
147^{13} **Etoile du Nord (28)** (HJCollingridge) **5-7-11**ow1 JQuinn(3) (bhd fnl 9f: t.o fnl 5f)...........15 **15** 20/1 — —
(SP 128.5%) **15 Rn**

2m 48.53 (6.53) CSF £22.70 CT £393.88 TOTE £5.00: £2.30 £1.70 £3.40 (£10.90) Trio £215.70; £151.92 to Lingfield 31/1/97 OWNER Mr J. J. Whelan (CHICHESTER) BRED Peter M. Brant
LONG HANDICAP Broughtons Relish 7-1 Tamandu 7-7 Etoile du Nord 7-6
WEIGHT FOR AGE 4yo-5lb
Bt in 6000 gns
OFFICIAL EXPLANATION **Oozlem (IRE): the rider's instructions on the gelding were to sit and kid him along, but he never picked up the bit, and was unable to improve his position. The trainer added that the gelding never runs two races alike, and does not respond to vigorous riding.**

184 BRITISH COLUMBIA CLAIMING STKS (4-Y.O+) (Class F)
2-20 (2-25) **6f (Equitrack)** £2,394.80 (£672.80: £328.40) Stalls: Low GOING minus 0.39 sec per fur (FST)

SP RR SF

117^{6} **Robo Magic (USA) (75)** (LMontagueHall) **5-9-3** DHolland(1) (blind off-eye: led: rdn, edgd rt & hdd briefly ins fnl f: r.o)...........— **1** 5/2 2 72 23
51^{*} **Ultra Beet (80)** (PCHaslam) **5-9-4** SDrowne(5) (a.p: led ins fnl f: sn hdd: r.o)...........hd **2** 4/9 1 73 24
117^{7} **The Frisky Farmer (50)** (WGMTurner) **4-8-7** TSprake(2) (w ldr: ev ch over 1f out: one pce)...........2 **3** 12/1 3 56 7
128^{4} **Justinianus (IRE) (29)** (JJBridger) **5-8-5**ow2 DHarrison(3) (prom: rdn 3f out: sn wknd)...........6 **4** 33/1 7 t —
X-Ray (IRE) (JRJenkins) **4-8-7** SSanders(4) (w'like: sn outpcd & wl bhd: t.o)...........dist **5** 100/1 — —
(SP 109.4%) **5 Rn**

1m 14.4 (3.30) CSF £3.56 TOTE £3.90: £1.50 £1.10 (£1.60) OWNER Mr A D Green and Partners (EPSOM) BRED Curtis C. Green

185 QUEBEC MAIDEN STKS (3-Y.O) (Class D)
2-50 (2-56) **1m (Equitrack)** £3,290.00 (£995.00: £485.00: £230.00) Stalls: High GOING minus 0.39 sec per fur (FST)

SP RR SF

Pastiche (TGMills) **3-8-9** WRyan(3) (lw: a.p: chsd ldr 3f out: led over 1f out: pushed clr ins fnl f: comf)...........— **1** 13/8 2 59+ 24
145^{2} **Alvilde (72)** (DJSCosgrove) **3-8-9** MRimmer(2) (lw: sn chsng ldr: led over 3f out: hdd over 1f out: one pce)...........4 **2** Evens 1 51 16
Kayzee (IRE) (SDow) **3-8-4**(5) ADaly(4) (chsd ldrs: rdn over 2f out: one pce)...........1¼ **3** 14/1 49 14
161^{4} **Leg Beforum (IRE)** (LMontagueHall) **3-9-0** GCarter(5) (hld up: rdn over 2f out: styd on ins fnl f)...........s.h **4** 25/1 53 18
Krosno (SCWilliams) **3-9-0** JTate(1) (w'like: led: hdd over 3f out: sn wknd)...........5 **5** 7/1 3 43 8
(SP 111.1%) **5 Rn**

1m 41.1 (3.70) CSF £3.31 TOTE £2.40: £2.80 £1.10 (£1.40) OWNER Mrs Val Morgan (EPSOM) BRED Mrs V. Morgan

186 TONY STAFFORD 25 YEARS AT THE TELEGRAPH H'CAP (0-70) (4-Y.O+) (Class E)
3-20 (3-26) **1m (Equitrack)** £2,765.25 (£837.00: £408.50: £194.25) Stalls: High GOING minus 0.39 sec per fur (FST)

Form	Horse	Dist	Pos	SP	RR	SF
121[4]	**Royal Carlton (IRE) (65)** (GLMoore) **5-9-11** SWhitworth(4) (a.p: gng wl: led over 1f out: pushed out ins fnl f)	—	1	9/4[1]	74	47
47*	**Shanghai Lil (53)** (MJFetherston-Godley) **5-8-13** FNorton(7) (lw: hld up: hdwy 4f out: rdn 2f out: styd on to go 2nd ins fnl f)	¾	2	100/30[2]	61	34
120[3]	**Sooty Tern (55)** (JMBradley) **10-9-1** DHolland(3) (a.p: led 3f out: hdd over 1f out: one pce)	1¼	3	7/1	60	33
121[2]	**Sea Danzig (67)** (JJBridger) **4-9-13** DHarrison(2) (sn led: hdd 3f out: wknd 2f out)	5	4	9/2[3]	62	35
134[9]	**Absolutelystunning (50)** (MrsBarbaraWaring) **4-8-10** WRyan(5) (b: b.hind: bhd fnl 5f)	5	5	16/1	35	8
120[4]	**Superior Force (61)** (MissBSanders) **4-9-4**(3) AWhelan(6) (in tch: rdn 4f out: wknd 3f out)	1¼	6	11/2	44	17
134[3]	**River Seine (FR) (47)** (SGKnight) **5-8-7** SSanders(1) (in tch: rdn 4f out: sn wknd)	9	7	16/1	12	—

(SP 111.7%) **7 Rn**

1m 40.3 (2.90) CSF £8.52 TOTE £3.10: £2.20 £1.60 (£5.40) OWNER Mrs Mary Doyle (BRIGHTON) BRED Des De Vere Hunt

187 MANITOBA H'CAP (0-80) (4-Y.O+) (Class D)
3-50 (3-56) **1m 4f (Equitrack)** £3,290.00 (£995.00: £485.00: £230.00) Stalls: Low GOING minus 0.39 sec per fur (FST)

Form	Horse	Dist	Pos	SP	RR	SF
163[2]	**Glow Forum (70)** (LMontagueHall) **6-10-0** WRyan(4) (b: trckd ldrs: pushed along 4f out: chsd ldr 2f out: sn hrd rdn: led cl home)	—	1	11/8[1]	80	40
	Always Happy (70) (MissGayKelleway) **4-9-10** DHolland(3) (b: b.hind: led: hrd rdn over 1f out: hdd cl home)	nk	2	11/4[2]	80	36
163[3]	**More Than You Know (IRE) (64)** (KRBurke) **4-8-11**(7) JMMaguire(2) (dwlt: sn rcvrd: chsd ldr 4f out to 2f out: wknd over 1f out)	7	3	5/1	64	20
140[4]	**Arzani (USA) (53)** (DJSCosgrove) **6-8-11** MRimmer(1) (chsd ldr 8f: wknd 3f out)	14	4	7/2[3]	35	—

(SP 107.7%) **4 Rn**

2m 36.07 (6.07) CSF £4.83 TOTE £2.30: (£3.00) OWNER Mr Andy Smith (EPSOM) BRED Forum Bloodstock Ltd
WEIGHT FOR AGE 4yo-4lb

188 NEWFOUNDLAND AMATEUR H'CAP (0-65) (4-Y.O+) (Class F)
4-20 (4-26) **1m 2f (Equitrack)** £2,518.00 (£708.00: £346.00) Stalls: Low GOING minus 0.39 sec per fur (FST)

Form	Horse	Dist	Pos	SP	RR	SF
157[3]	**Biya (IRE) (45)** (DMcCain) **5-10-6**(5) MrGLake(8) (a.p: led over 3f out: hrd rdn ins fnl f: all out)	—	1	20/1	54	35
144[2]	**Sheraz (IRE) (46)** (NTinkler) **5-10-12b** MissJAllison(10) (hld up: hdwy 6f out: hrd rdn & ev ch ins fnl f: r.o)	hd	2	11/2	55	36
92*	**Zamalek (USA) (43)** (RMFlower) **5-10-9e** MrTMcCarthy(1) (lw: hld up: hdwy 5f out: ev ch ins fnl f: r.o)	hd	3	11/4[1]	52	33
147[8]	**Captain Marmalade (40)** (DTThom) **8-10-6v** MissDianaJones(4) (chsd ldrs: rdn over 2f out: kpt on one pce ins fnl f)	2½	4	14/1	45	26
141[2]	**Nakhal (53)** (DJGMurraySmith) **4-10-12**(5) MissSBrown(7) (lw: bhd tl styd on fnl 2f: nvr nrr)	1½	5	13/2	55	34
116[7]	**Don't Drop Bombs (USA) (35)** (DTThom) **8-10-1v** MissJFeilden(3) (led: hdd over 3f out: wknd wl over 1f out)	2	6	9/2[2]	34	15
153[5]	**Gadge (38)** (ABailey) **6-9-13**(5) MissALHutchinson(9) (b: mid div tl wknd 3f out)	½	7	16/1	36	17
61[2]	**Can Can Charlie (55)** (JPearce) **7-11-7** MrsLPearce(6) (prom tl wknd over 2f out)	1½	8	5/1[3]	51	32
66*	**Royal Acclaim (34)** (RDickin) **12-10-0v** MissRJPatman(5) (s.s: a bhd)	4	9	9/1	24	5
143[6]	**Trible Pet (40)** (BGubby) **4-10-4** MrsMTingey(2) (prom tl wknd over 2f out)	4	10	20/1	23	2

(SP 122.3%) **10 Rn**

2m 11.27 (6.97) CSF £120.47 CT £369.80 TOTE £28.70: £5.00 £2.30 £1.70 (£44.00) Trio £112.60 OWNER Mr D. McCain (CHOLMONDELEY) BRED Kirtlington Stud Ltd
WEIGHT FOR AGE 4yo-2lb
T/Plpt: £17.40 (468.22 Tckts). T/Qdpt: £5.80 (74.73 Tckts) SM

0149a-CAGNES-SUR-MER (Nice, France) (L-H) (Holding)
Friday January 24th

189a PRIX DES PEUPLIERS H'CAP (4-Y.O+)
2-31 (2-31) **1m** £8,418.00

Form	Horse	Dist	Pos	SP	RR	SF
	Flashnight (FR) (CScandella,France) **5-8-4** PCourty	—	1		75	—
	Ipoh (FR) (J-CRouget,France) **5-8-13** PDumortier	½	2		83	—
	Bakio (FR) (JForesi,France) **6-8-6** GElorriaga-Santos	nk	3		75	—
149a[2]	**Confronter** (SDow) **8-8-9** FSanchez (btn 11 3/4l)		7		—	—

18 Rn

1m 47.3 P-M 8.80F: 2.70F 2.00F 2.10F (17.40F) OWNER R. Sorrentino BRED Jean Lecourtiller
149a Confronter raced in a prominent position until weakening over two furlongs out. The ground was extremely testing which may not have been totally to his liking.

0189a-CAGNES-SUR-MER (Nice, France) (L-H) (Holding)
Sunday January 26th

190a PRIX DUFY (4-Y.O+)
1m 2f £4,489.00

Form	Horse	Dist	Pos	SP	RR	SF
	Mr Keating (FR) (CBoutin,France) **7-8-11b[1]** SCoffigny	—	1		66	—
	Sharkhan (BSchutz,Germany) **5-8-11** SGuillot	1	2		64	—
	Soldiers Bay (JForesi,France) **7-8-11** GElorriaga-Santos	s.h	3		64	—
148a[6]	**No Speeches (IRE)** (SDow) **6-8-11** DBoeuf (btn 6½l)		8		—	—
	Ela-Yie-Mou (IRE) (SDow) **4-8-11** FSanchez (btn a dist)		14		—	—

18 Rn

2m 11.4 P-M 56.60F: 11.50F 11.90F 4.10F (1000.00F)
OWNER C. Boutin BRED Guy Ebely

0164-SOUTHWELL (L-H) (Standard)
Friday January 31st
WEATHER: Fine but misty WIND: almost nil

191 OLD CLIPSTONE MEDIAN AUCTION MAIDEN STKS (3-Y.O) (Class F)
1-50 (1-51) **1m 3f (Fibresand)** £2,294.00 (£644.00: £314.00) Stalls: Low GOING: 0.20 sec per fur (SLW)

				SP	RR	SF
	Head Gardener (IRE) (75) (NPLittmoden) **3-9-0** TGMcLaughlin(3) (trckd ldrs: led over 1f out: all out)	—	1	7/2[2]	77	21
154[3]	**Love Me Do (USA) (67)** (MJohnston) **3-9-0** DHolland(1) (lw: led tl over 1f out: styd on towards fin)	½	2	8/11[1]	76	20
124[8]	**State of Gold (IRE) (51)** (JHetherton) **3-9-0b** SWhitworth(7) (lw: trckd ldrs: drvn along over 3f out: hung lft & sn wknd)	18	3	20/1	50	—
168[8]	**Rock Fantasy (56)** (CMurray) **3-8-9** MTebbutt(9) (hdwy 7f out: sn chsng ldrs: one pce fnl 3f)	½	4	20/1	44	—
	Good Day (62) (CWThornton) **3-9-0** DeanMcKeown(2) (in tch: drvn along & outpcd 6f out: n.d after)	½	5	9/2[3]	49	—
124[11]	**T-N-T Express (40)** (EJAlston) **3-9-0v[1]** SDrowne(6) (w ldrs tl wknd over 4f out)	2½	6	33/1	45	—
90[7]	**Indian Rapture (48)** (RonaldThompson) **3-8-6**(3) CTeague(5) (racd wd: bhd: sme hdwy 5f out: sn wknd: t.o 3f out)	17	7	20/1	15	—
	Melodic Squaw (MPBielby) **3-8-9** TWilliams(4) (leggy: scope: bit bkwd: s.s: a bhd: t.o 3f out)	4	8	20/1	10	—
156[5]	**Lord High Emperor** (DShaw) **3-9-0** SDWilliams(8) (in tch: drvn along & outpcd 6f out: sn lost pl: t.o 3f out)	4	9	50/1	9	—
				(SP 122.2%)	**9 Rn**	

2m 33.1 (13.10) CSF £5.73 TOTE £7.70: £2.30 £1.10 £2.40 (£2.50) Trio £10.00 OWNER The Gardening Partnership (WOLVERHAMPTON) BRED Nicholas M. H. Jones

192 LANGFORD APPRENTICE CLAIMING STKS (4-Y.O+) (Class G)
2-20 (2-21) **7f (Fibresand)** £2,095.00 (£595.00: £295.00) Stalls: Low GOING: 0.20 sec per fur (SLW)

				SP	RR	SF
150[2]	**Rambo Waltzer (75)** (DNicholls) **5-9-2**(5) TSiddall(6) (lw: trckd ldrs: led 3f out: pushed clr fnl f: eased nr fin)	—	1	11/10[1]	76+	39
99[2]	**Eurolink the Lad (50)** (DBurchell) **10-7-12**(5) CCogan(9) (rdn, rn wd & lost pl over 4f out: hdwy 2f out: styd on wl towards fin)	1	2	13/2[3]	56	19
153[3]	**Sandmoor Denim (47)** (SRBowring) **10-8-0**(3) AnthonyBond(4) (b: in tch: sn pushed along: styd on ins fnl f)	½	3	7/1	55	18
171[6]	**Nashaat (USA) (76)** (KRBurke) **9-9-7** JMMaguire(10) (swtg: unruly s: chsd ldrs: chal 3f out: hrd rdn & one pce appr fnl f)	2	4	7/1	68	31
113[2]	**Bold Aristocrat (IRE) (62)** (RHollinshead) **6-8-5**(7) DHayden(1) (plld hrd: led after 2f to 3f out: one pce appr fnl f)	¾	5	7/2[2]	57	20
165[4]	**Spanish Stripper (USA) (32)** (MCChapman) **6-7-12**(5) JFowle(8) (swtg: racd wd: outpcd ½-wy: edgd lft & styd on fnl f)	3	6	20/1	41	4
	So Natural (IRE) (45) (WStorey) **5-7-12** AngelaGallimore(5) (led 2f: chsd ldrs tl grad wknd fnl 2f: eased nr fin)	3	7	20/1	30	—
	Recessions Over (NPLittmoden) **6-8-1**(5) RCody-Boutcher(7) (dwlt s: sn in tch: outpcd fnl 2f)	2	8	40/1	33	—
	Mu-Arrik (25) (GROldroyd) **9-7-13v**(7) DMernagh(2) (s.i.s: hdwy ½-wy: sn prom: wknd 2f out)	nk	9	50/1	32	—
111[9]	**Eccentric Dancer (30)** (MPBielby) **4-8-1** DDenby(3) (s.s: a wl bhd)	13	10	40/1	—	—
				(SP 124.5%)	**10 Rn**	

1m 33.6 (7.10) CSF £8.45 TOTE £2.40: £1.40 £2.30 £1.40 (£12.80) Trio £20.40 OWNER Mr W. G. Swiers (THIRSK) BRED Triangle Thoroughbreds Ltd

193 HALHAM H'CAP (0-70) (3-Y.O) (Class E)
2-50 (2-51) **6f (Fibresand)** £2,778.25 (£841.00: £410.50: £195.25) Stalls: Low GOING: 0.20 sec per fur (SLW)

				SP	RR	SF
110*	**Pet Express (52)** (PCHaslam) **3-8-3** LCharnock(7) (lw: trckd ldrs: led 3f out: qcknd clr over 1f out: eased ins fnl f)	—	1	11/8[1]	62+	23
180[6]	**Master Foley (62)** (NPLittmoden) **3-8-13** TGMcLaughlin(6) (sn chsng ldrs: hrd rdn: styd on fnl 2f: edgd lft & no ch w wnr)	3	2	6/1[3]	64	25
155[4]	**Supercharmer (70)** (DNicholls) **3-9-7** AlexGreaves(8) (trckd ldrs: rdn & outpcd over 2f out: styd on appr fnl f)	1½	3	6/1[3]	68	29
	Bon Guest (IRE) (64) (TJNaughton) **3-8-12**(3) JDSmith(4) (sn outpcd & bhd: styd on fnl 2f)	2½	4	12/1	55	16
25*	**Krystal Davey (IRE) (62)** (TDBarron) **3-8-13** DHarrison(1) (led 3f: wknd over 1f out)	4	5	5/1[2]	43	4
	Magic Fizz (64) (TJEtherington) **3-9-1** GCarter(3) (bit bkwd: hld up: outpcd ½-wy: sme hdwy 2f out: n.d)	3	6	8/1	37	—
102[5]	**Le Shuttle (45)** (MHTompkins) **3-7-10** GBardwell(5) (chsd ldrs tl lost pl after 2f: sn bhd)	3	7	8/1	10	—
49[8]	**Gymcrak Watermill (IRE) (46)** (GHolmes) **3-7-11**ow1 JQuinn(2) (chsd ldrs: outpcd ½-wy: sn lost pl)	7	8	25/1	—	—
				(SP 121.1%)	**8 Rn**	

1m 19.5 (6.00) CSF £10.01 CT £36.91 TOTE £2.20: £1.10 £1.50 £2.70 (£6.50) OWNER Pet Express (W&R) Ltd (MIDDLEHAM) BRED A. J. Sexton

194 KELHAM H'CAP (0-70) (3-Y.O+) (Class E)
3-20 (3-21) **1m (Fibresand)** £3,223.75 (£976.00: £476.50: £226.75) Stalls: Low GOING: 0.20 sec per fur (SLW)

				SP	RR	SF
153[2]	**Sea Spouse (61)** (MBlanshard) **6-9-7** NAdams(7) (lw: led: qcknd over 4f out: sn clr: hld on wl)	—	1	11/1	72	45
153*	**Roussi (USA) (38)** (DNicholls) **5-7-7**(5) 6x JBramhill(2) (lw: chsd ldrs: rdn over 2f out: n.m.r 1f out: styd on wl)	¾	2	5/1[2]	48	21
	Captain's Day (40) (HJCollingridge) **5-7-11**(3) MBaird(1) (sn chsng ldrs: edgd lft 1f out: styd on same pce)	½	3	7/1[3]	49	22
179[6]	**Le Sport (67)** (DNicholls) **4-9-6b**(7) TSiddall(8) (hld up & bhd: stdy hdwy on ins 2f out: swtchd and styd on wl ins fnl f)	hd	4	25/1	75	48
169*	**Three Arch Bridge (66)** (MJohnston) **5-9-12b** 6x TWilliams(3) (s.i.s: hdwy u.p ½-wy: no imp)	8	5	5/1[2]	58	31
175[2]	**Barrel of Hope (67)** (JLEyre) **5-9-10v[1]**(3) OPears(11) (lw: racd wd: lost pl over 3f out: n.d)	3½	6	12/1	52	25
153[10]	**Major Mouse (65)** (WWHaigh) **9-9-11** VHalliday(6) (bit bkwd: a in rr)	s.h	7	25/1	50	23
91[6]	**Mislemani (IRE) (47)** (AGNewcombe) **7-8-7** SDrowne(5) (chsd ldrs tl drvn along & lost pl over 3f out)	1¾	8	25/1	29	2
88[11]	**Total Rach (IRE) (47)** (AGNewcombe) **5-8-4**(3) NVarley(10) (b: racd wd: prom early: bhd fr ½-wy)	1	9	25/1	27	—
54*	**Loch Style (60)** (RHollinshead) **4-9-1**(5) DGriffiths(9) (trckd ldrs: effrt 3f out: wknd over 1f out)	1	10	10/1	38	11

				SP	RR	SF
98*	**Priolo Prima (68)** (SirMarkPrescott) **4-10-0** GDuffield(4) (s.i.s: sn trckng ldrs: rdn & lost pl over 2f out)	¾	**11**	6/5 1	44	17

(SP 131.8%) **11 Rn**

1m 46.5 (7.50) CSF £63.99 CT £391.13 TOTE £15.00: £3.40 £3.10 £1.10 (£23.90) Trio £145.60 OWNER Seven Seas Racing (UPPER LAMBOURN) BRED Cheveley Park Stud Ltd

195 NEW BALDERTON (S) STKS (4-Y.O+) (Class G)

3-50 (3-50) **1m 3f (Fibresand)** £2,085.00 (£585.00: £285.00) Stalls: Low GOING: 0.20 sec per fur (SLW)

				SP	RR	SF
114*	**Calder King (63)** (JLEyre) **6-9-5b** RLappin(5) (trckd ldrs: led 3f out: rdn & wl clr over 1f out: eased towards fin)	—	**1**	5/2 1	71+	24
88 8	**Sarawat (67)** (DNicholls) **9-9-0** AlexGreaves(3) (mde most to 3f out: kpt on: no ch w wnr)	7	**2**	5/2 1	56	9
	Myfontaine (58) (KTIvory) **10-9-0** GBardwell(4) (b: b.hind: bhd: hdwy 7f out: chal 3f out: sn rdn & one pce)	1	**3**	7/2 2	54	7
104 5	**Eastleigh (36)** (RHollinshead) **8-8-7**(7) LisaWatson(6) (b.nr hind: chsd ldrs: disp ld 7f out to 5f out: outpcd fnl 3f)	7	**4**	33/1	44	—
80 8	**Eulogy (FR) (60)** (KRBurke) **10-8-7b**1(7) JMMaguire(8) (racd wd: chsd ldrs: sn drvn along: rdn & lost pl fnl 5f out)	10	**5**	10/1	30	—
111 5	**Appeal Again (IRE) (49)** (DBurchell) **4-8-4**(7) KSked(1) (sn bhd: hdwy 7f out: sn chsng ldrs: rdn & lost pl over 5f out)	21	**6**	4/1 3	—	—
	Friendly Coast (DTThom) **11-9-0** JQuinn(7) (bit bkwd: sn bhd: t.o 3f out)	19	**7**	33/1	—	—
	New Regime (IRE) (19) (PTDalton) **4-8-6** LCharnock(2) (chsd ldrs: sn drvn along: lost pl 7f out: wl t.o 4f out)	dist	**8**	50/1	—	—

(SP 116.3%) **8 Rn**

2m 33.4 (13.40) CSF £8.16 TOTE £3.30: £2.00 £1.30 £2.00 (£6.10) OWNER Mr D. Clarkson (HAMBLETON) BRED Bellmor Stud
WEIGHT FOR AGE 4yo-3lb
Sold Laurel Leisure 8,600 gns
OFFICIAL EXPLANATION **Sarawat: finished sore.**

196 MANSFIELD H'CAP (0-70) (4-Y.O+) (Class E)

4-20 (4-21) **1m 4f (Fibresand)** £2,778.25 (£841.00: £410.50: £195.25) Stalls: Low GOING: 0.20 sec per fur (SLW)

				SP	RR	SF
115 5	**Calendula (50)** (DMorley) **4-8-4** GCarter(7) (trckd ldrs: led over 2f out: styd on wl)	—	**1**	7/1 3	61	12
115 8	**Carol Again (39)** (NBycroft) **5-7-11**ow1 JQuinn(1) (chsd ldrs: drvn along & outpcd ½-wy: hdwy & ev ch 2f out: nt qckn)	2	**2**	20/1	47	1
151 2	**Sea God (49)** (MCChapman) **6-8-7** DRMcCabe(3) (led to 6f out: sn lost pl: hdwy on outside 2f out: styd on wl ins fnl f)	1½	**3**	7/1 3	55	10
	Kalamata (57) (JAGlover) **5-9-1** NDay(4) (trckd ldrs: outpcd over 4f out: hung lft & swtchd rt over 1f out: kpt on)	5	**4**	8/1	57	12
157*	**Qualitair Pride (39)** (JFBottomley) **5-7-11** 5x NCarlisle(6) (b.off hind: w ldr: led 6f out tl over 2f out: grad wknd)	nk	**5**	4/5 1	38	—
	Pharly Dancer (65) (WWHaigh) **8-9-9** VHalliday(2) (lw: sn bhd & pushed along: hdwy ½-wy: rdn & outpcd over 3f out: kpt on fnl 2f)	1	**6**	8/1	63	18
88 4	**Manful (70)** (JHetherton) **5-10-0b** GDuffield(8) (sn pushed along: hdwy to chse ldr 7f out: outpcd over 3f out: n.d after)	3½	**7**	5/1 2	63	18

(SP 124.2%) **7 Rn**

2m 47.4 (14.40) CSF £120.15 CT £942.45 TOTE £10.30: £2.10 £4.00 (£88.00) OWNER Mr Christopher Spence (NEWMARKET) BRED Chieveley Manor Enterprises
LONG HANDICAP Carol Again 7-7
WEIGHT FOR AGE 4yo-4lb
OFFICIAL EXPLANATION **Calendula: had been held up by the weather prior to her previous start.**
T/Plpt: £119.80 (71 Tckts). T/Qdpt: £100.80 (6.22 Tckts) WG

0183-LINGFIELD (L-H) (Standard)

Saturday February 1st

Race 1 - hand-timed.
WEATHER: Cloudy WIND: almost nil

197 PELLEW APPRENTICE H'CAP (0-60) (4-Y.O+) (Class G)

1-30 (1-37) **1m (Equitrack)** £2,145.50 (£603.00: £294.50) Stalls: High GOING minus 0.29 sec per fur (FST)

				SP	RR	SF
134 2	**Hawaii Storm (FR) (52)** (DJSffrenchDavis) **9-9-1**(5) KerryBaker(3) (hld up: hdwy over 3f out: led over 2f out: r.o)	—	**1**	9/2 2	61	37
105 3	**Our Shadee (USA) (46)** (KTIvory) **7-8-9v**(5) AnthonyBond(5) (b: b.hind: hld up: hdwy 3f out: chsd wnr over 1f out: r.o ins fnl f)	nk	**2**	5/1 3	54	30
61 5	**Mediate (IRE) (50)** (AHide) **5-9-4v**1 JoHunnam(8) (hld up mid div: rdn to improve over 1f out: styd on ins fnl f)	2½	**3**	7/1	53	29
	Spectacle Jim (44) (BAPearce) **8-8-7**(5) GGallagher(7) (plld hrd: sn led: hdd over 4f out: rdn 3f out: one pce)	3½	**4**	50/1	40	16
128*	**Rawi (60)** (MissGayKelleway) **4-9-11**(3) AngelaGallimore(6) (b: b.hind: lw: chsd ldrs: rdn 2f out: wknd appr fnl f)	1¼	**5**	7/2 1	54	30
143*	**Hatta Sunshine (USA) (60)** (GLMoore) **7-9-9**(5) MBatchelor(4) (lw: dwlt: sn rcvrd to chse ldrs: led over 3f out: hdd over 2f out: wknd appr fnl f)	½	**6**	13/2	53	29
113 7	**Green Golightly (USA) (31)** (RMFlower) **6-7-13be** GMilligan(1) (plld hrd: bhd fnl 5f)	nk	**7**	7/1	23	—
128 5	**Mad Alex (28)** (MJHaynes) **4-7-5**(5) JFowle(9) (b: b.hind: bhd fnl 4f)	hd	**8**	25/1	20	—
134*	**Into Debt (33)** (JRPoulton) **4-7-10e**(5) AMcCarthy(2) (a.p: led over 4f out: hdd over 3f out: wknd over 2f out)	5	**9**	7/1	15	—

(SP 113.7%) **9 Rn**

1m 41.6 (4.20) CSF £24.39 CT £141.01 TOTE £5.70: £1.80 £1.50 £2.20 (£6.00) Trio £19.20 OWNER Mr C. C. Capel (UPPER LAMBOURN) BRED Horse France
LONG HANDICAP Mad Alex 7-6

198 BLACKWOOD CLAIMING STKS (3-Y.O+) (Class E)

2-00 (2-01) **5f (Equitrack)** £2,739.25 (£829.00: £404.50: £192.25) Stalls: High GOING minus 0.29 sec per fur (FST)

				SP	RR	SF
178*	**Kalar (74)** (DWChapman) **8-9-9b** LCharnock(1) (sn led: clr appr fnl f: r.o wl)	—	1	6/4[1]	73	40
158[3]	**Enchantica (55)** (JBerry) **3-7-5**(5) PFessey(6) (a.p: rdn over 1f out: styd on ins fnl f: no imp on wnr)	4	2	4/1[3]	47	—
152[6]	**Imp Express (IRE) (35)** (GMMoore) **4-9-7b** GBardwell(4) (dwlt: sn pushed along: hdwy to chse wnr over 2f out tl ins fnl f: one pce)	1¼	3	16/1	54	21
	Ma Vielle Pouque (IRE) (WGMTurner) **3-8-4** TSprake(5) (chsd ldrs: rdn over 1f out: one pce)	hd	4	14/1	51	4
152[2]	**Hoh Majestic (IRE) (55)** (RonaldThompson) **4-9-0**(3) CTeague(3) (chsd ldrs: sn pushed along: n.m.r over 1f out: swtchd rt: kpt on one pce ins fnl f)	¾	5	3/1[2]	48	15
162[4]	**Heavenly Miss (IRE) (73)** (JJBridger) **3-8-8** DHarrison(2) (broke wl: spd 3f)	1¾	6	11/2	47	—

(SP 112.9%) **6 Rn**

60.61 secs (2.41) CSF £7.25 TOTE £1.90: £1.10 £3.50 (£4.50) OWNER Mr J. M. Chapman (YORK) BRED C. C. and Mrs Pryor
WEIGHT FOR AGE 3yo-14lb

199 COCHRANE LIMITED STKS (0-50) (3-Y.O+) (Class F)

2-35 (2-37) **6f (Equitrack)** £2,495.60 (£701.60: £342.80) Stalls: Low GOING minus 0.29 sec per fur (FST)

				SP	RR	SF
79[5]	**Sir Tasker (37)** (JLHarris) **9-9-5** DHolland(9) (a.p: led 3f out: hrd rdn ins fnl f: r.o)	—	1	9/2[3]	48	19
159[5]	**Ivory's Grab Hire (43)** (KTIvory) **4-9-5b** DBiggs(7) (hld up: hdwy 2f out: chsd wnr 1f out: r.o)	½	2	6/1	47	18
152[11]	**Southern Dominion (44)** (MissJFCraze) **5-9-5** SWebster(4) (lw: led 3f: rdn 2f out: one pce)	3	3	16/1	39	10
159[6]	**Superlao (BEL) (33)** (JJBridger) **5-9-2** JQuinn(3) (rr: rdn over 2f out: styd on ins fnl f)	1¼	4	12/1	32	3
159[7]	**Bright Paragon (IRE) (27)** (KTIvory) **8-9-5** CScally(6) (b: b.hind: chsd ldrs: rdn & outpcd 4f out: kpt on one pce ins fnl f)	2½	5	33/1	29	—
97[5]	**Logie Pert Lad (23)** (JJBridger) **5-9-5** FNorton(5) (prom: rdn 3f out: wknd over 1f out)	1	6	50/1	26	—
21[8]	**Dark Menace (47)** (EAWheeler) **5-9-0b**(5) ADaly(8) (lw: chsd ldrs tl wknd 2f out)	2½	7	11/4[2]	19	—
65[2]	**Thick as Thieves (44)** (RonaldThompson) **5-9-2**(3) CTeague(2) (bhd fnl 4f)	hd	8	15/8[1]	19	—
	Veesey (50) (JohnBerry) **4-9-2e** DHarrison(1) (sn rdn along: bhd fnl 4f: t.o)	20	9	20/1	—	—

(SP 117.2%) **9 Rn**

1m 15.41 (4.31) CSF £28.58 TOTE £5.50: £1.60 £1.20 £4.50 (£15.50) Trio £63.20 OWNER Mr J. F. Coupland (MELTON MOWBRAY) BRED W. H. Joyce
OFFICIAL EXPLANATION **Thick as Thieves: missed the break, was tightened up soon after the start and from then on, was never able to get into the race.**

200 DICKIE WILLMOTT MAIDEN STKS (4-Y.O+) (Class D)

3-10 (3-11) **1m (Equitrack)** £3,355.00 (£1,015.00: £495.00: £235.00) Stalls: High GOING minus 0.29 sec per fur (FST)

				SP	RR	SF
	Zurs (IRE) (80) (MissGayKelleway) **4-9-0** DHolland(5) (b: b.hind: mde all: clr 3f out: easily)	—	1	2/7[1]	62+	28
144[6]	**Misky Bay (53)** (DJSCosgrove) **4-9-0** MRimmer(4) (v.slowly away: rel to r: wl bhd tl styd on fnl 2f: wnt 2nd wl ins fnl f)	8	2	12/1[3]	46	12
22[8]	**Haute Cuisine (40)** (RJRWilliams) **4-9-0** DBiggs(1) (b.hind: chsd ldrs: rdn 4f out: wnt mod 2nd over 1f out tl wl ins fnl f)	¾	3	25/1	45	11
	Rudolphine (IRE) (BobJones) **6-9-0** MWigham(2) (b: chsd wnr: rdn over 3f out: wknd over 1f out)	2	4	8/1[2]	41	7
105[6]	**Rachel's Rock** (GLMoore) **4-8-9** SWhitworth(3) (chsd ldrs: rdn 4f out: wknd over 1f out)	3	5	8/1[2]	30	—

(SP 111.5%) **5 Rn**

1m 41.99 (4.59) CSF £4.59 TOTE £1.50: £1.10 £2.20 (£4.80) OWNER Mr Nigel Dearman (WHITCOMBE) BRED Mrs A. Whitehead

201 JERVIS H'CAP (0-80) (4-Y.O+) (Class D)

3-40 (3-40) **7f (Equitrack)** £3,371.25 (£1,020.00: £497.50: £236.25) Stalls: Low GOING minus 0.29 sec per fur (FST)

				SP	RR	SF
120*	**Mr Nevermind (IRE) (80)** (GLMoore) **7-10-0** SWhitworth(3) (hld up: rdn & hdwy on ins over 2f out: led ent fnl f: r.o)	—	1	5/2[1]	89	57
166[3]	**Naughty Pistol (USA) (63)** (PDEvans) **5-8-11v** SSanders(7) (rr: sn pushed along: hdwy over 1f out: styd on strly ins fnl f)	½	2	6/1[3]	71	39
121[8]	**Speedy Classic (USA) (80)** (MJHeaton-Ellis) **8-10-0** AClark(2) (lw: sn led: hdd ent fnl f: one pce)	1¾	3	7/1	84	52
146[6]	**Perilous Plight (60)** (MrsLStubbs) **6-8-8** TSprake(4) (chsd ldrs: rdn over 1f out: one pce)	1¼	4	8/1	61	29
89[6]	**Mr Frosty (78)** (WJarvis) **5-9-12** DHolland(5) (broke wl: sn stdd: effrt over 1f out: sn btn)	1½	5	8/1	76	44
121[11]	**Jo Maximus (62)** (SDow) **5-8-5**(5) ADaly(6) (chsd ldrs: rdn 3f out: wknd wl over 1f out)	½	6	7/1	58	26
117[5]	**Krystal Max (IRE) (73)** (JCullinan) **4-9-0**(7) VictoriaAppleby(8) (chsd ldrs tl wknd over 1f out)	1	7	14/1	67	35
146*	**Twin Creeks (75)** (VSoane) **6-9-9** CRutter(1) (chsd ldrs: wkng whn hmpd 2f out)	4	8	9/2[2]	60	28

(SP 114.9%) **8 Rn**

1m 26.95 (2.55) CSF £16.26 CT £84.51 TOTE £3.00: £1.10 £2.30 £2.60 (£7.40) OWNER Pennine Partners (BRIGHTON) BRED Robert Corridan

202 AYLISH FANE-SAUNDERS H'CAP (0-70) (4-Y.O+) (Class E)

4-15 (4-15) **1m 5f (Equitrack)** £2,804.25 (£849.00: £414.50: £197.25) Stalls: Low GOING minus 0.29 sec per fur (FST)

				SP	RR	SF
106[2]	**Wottashambles (57)** (LMontagueHall) **6-9-9** DHolland(4) (hld up: hdwy 5f out: led 3f out: clr over 1f out: comf)	—	1	9/4[1]	69	47
133[2]	**Random Kindness (66)** (RIngram) **4-10-0** JStack(3) (hld up: hdwy over 3f out: chsd wnr 2f out: rdn over 1f out: one pce)	4	2	6/1[3]	73	47
147[11]	**Royal Circus (40)** (PRWebber) **8-8-6** DHarrison(9) (w ldr: led over 3f out: sn hdd: hrd rdn over 1f out: one pce)	nk	3	16/1	47	25
115[4]	**Mustang (34)** (CWThornton) **4-7-3**(7) AMcCarthy(7) (a.p: rdn over 2f out: wknd over 1f out)	10	4	8/1	28	2
93[2]	**Chez Catalan (41)** (RAkehurst) **6-8-7b** SSanders(2) (chsd ldrs: rdn over 6f out: wknd over 2f out)	3	5	10/1	32	10
73*	**Classy Chief (60)** (JWhite) **4-9-8** CRutter(1) (dwlt: hld up: hdwy 6f out: wknd 4f out)	2	6	11/4[2]	48	22
125[4]	**Ilandra (IRE) (43)** (RAkehurst) **5-8-4**(5) JBramhill(8) (plld hrd: sn led: hdd over 3f out: sn wknd)	4	7	14/1	26	4
	Children's Choice (IRE) (56) (WJMusson) **6-9-8** GCarter(5) (a bhd)	5	8	14/1	33	11

37[6]	**Taniyar (FR) (35)** (RHollinshead) **5-8-1b[1]** JQuinn(6) (prom 8f: t.o fnl 3f) 30	**9**	14/1	—	—
				(SP 117.8%)	**9 Rn**	

2m 47.96 (5.96) CSF £15.17 CT £160.48 TOTE £3.50: £1.10 £1.90 £5.20 (£9.20) Trio £102.00 OWNER Dream On Racing Partnership (EPSOM) BRED Arthur Sims
LONG HANDICAP Mustang 7-7
WEIGHT FOR AGE 4yo-4lb

T/Plpt: £42.80 (202.02 Tckts). T/Qdpt: £19.70 (31.51 Tckts). SM

0191-SOUTHWELL (L-H) (Standard)
Monday February 3rd
WEATHER: bright WIND: fresh across

203 MACKENZIE H'CAP (0-60) (I) (4-Y.O+) (Class F)
1-30 (1-35) **7f (Fibresand)** £1,944.00 (£544.00: £264.00) Stalls: Low GOING: 0.34 sec per fur (SLW)

			SP	RR	SF
113[5]	**Dawalib (USA) (50)** (DHaydnJones) **7-9-8** CRutter(4) (led after 1f: kpt on wl fnl 2f) .....—	**1**	4/1 [1]	60	42
153[4]	**Truly Bay (46)** (TDBarron) **4-9-4b** DHarrison(14) (lw: a cl up: effrt over 2f out: kpt on) .....¾	**2**	7/1 [2]	54	36
92[6]	**Private Fixture (IRE) (42)** (DMarks) **6-9-0** SSanders(12) (lw: outpcd: c wd st: styd on wl fnl 2f: nrst fin) 2	**3**	9/1	46	28
192[6]	**Spanish Stripper (USA) (30)** (MCChapman) **6-8-2** DRMcCabe(1) (chsd ldrs: effrt & stly hmpd over 2f out: kpt on) .....nk	**4**	7/1 [2]	33	15
152[5]	**Ballard Lady (IRE) (50)** (JSWainwright) **5-9-3(5)** JBramhill(9) (lw: bhd: hdwy 3f out: sn chsng ldrs & rdn: no ex fnl f) .....½	**5**	4/1 [1]	52	34
152[3]	**Lady Silk (52)** (MissJFCraze) **6-9-10** SWebster(3) (outpcd: swtchd & hdwy over 2f out: no imp fnl f) .....nk	**6**	8/1 [3]	53	35
	Barbara's Jewel (48) (ABailey) **5-9-6** DWright(10) (outpcd tl hdwy over 2f out: no imp) 5	**7**	16/1	38	20
159[4]	**Cheerful Groom (IRE) (31)** (DShaw) **6-8-3** NKennedy(13) (cl up tl wknd fnl 2f) .....nk	**8**	10/1	20	2
	Arcus (IRE) (40) (WRMuir) **4-8-5b(7)** JWilkinson(8) (a outpcd & bhd) 5	**9**	20/1	18	—
152[9]	**Napoleon Star (IRE) (46)** (SRBowring) **6-9-4b** SDWilliams(6) (cl up tl wknd fnl 2f) .....½	**10**	20/1	23	5
152[15]	**Monis (IRE) (49)** (JBalding) **6-9-7v** SDrowne(7) (led 1f: cl up tl wknd fnl 2f) 1	**11**	11/1	23	5
169[10]	**Shanoora (IRE) (37)** (MrsNMacauley) **4-8-6b(3)** CTeague(2) (a outpcd & bhd) 8	**12**	20/1	—	—
152[14]	**Hershebar (44)** (MrsVAAconley) **7-9-2** MDeering(5) (stumbled s: hdwy after 1f: wknd 1f out) 6	**13**	33/1	—	—
	Wali (USA) (50) (JLEyre) **7-9-8** TWilliams(11) (bit bkwd: cl up 4f: sn wknd) 15	**14**	16/1	—	—
			(SP 132.5%)	**14 Rn**	

1m 34.4 (7.90) CSF £30.12 CT £238.47 TOTE £4.70: £2.80 £2.10 £3.10 (£18.90) Trio £86.40 OWNER Jack Brown (Bookmaker) Ltd (PONTYPRIDD) BRED Hilary J. Boone Jnr
OFFICIAL EXPLANATION Wali (USA): swallowed his tongue. He had been declared to wear a tongue-strap, but it became loose at the start and could not be re-fitted.

204 MISSOURI MEDIAN AUCTION MAIDEN STKS (3-Y.O) (Class F)
2-00 (2-02) **6f (Fibresand)** £2,294.00 (£644.00: £314.00) Stalls: Low GOING: 0.34 sec per fur (SLW)

			SP	RR	SF
110[2]	**Treasure Touch (IRE) (65)** (GMMoore) **3-9-0** DHolland(4) (lw: cl up: led over 1f out: qcknd: comf) .....—	**1**	4/7 [1]	75+	45
	Mangus (IRE) (70) (KOCunningham-Brown) **3-9-0** CMunday(5) (led tl hdd over 1f out: sn btn) 6	**2**	7/1 [3]	59	29
	Castle Ashby Jack (72) (PHowling) **3-9-0** JQuinn(6) (a chsng ldrs: one pce fnl 3f) 8	**3**	6/1 [2]	38	8
	Crackerbox (HAkbary) **3-8-9** WRyan(2) (b: s.i.s: rdn & hdwy ½-wy: no imp) .....hd	**4**	8/1	32	2
	Impish (IRE) (40) (TJEtherington) **3-9-0** LCharnock(3) (s.s: n.d) 6	**5**	50/1	21	—
	Weet A Bit (IRE) (RHollinshead) **3-8-9(5)** DGriffiths(7) (lw: sn outpcd & bhd) 5	**6**	12/1	8	—
154[7]	**Kustom Kit Xpres (55)** (SRBowring) **3-8-9** SDWilliams(8) (chsd ldrs over 3f: sn btn) 5	**7**	25/1	—	—
	Sodelk (JHetherton) **3-8-9** MTebbutt(1) (unruly gng to s: sn drvn along: bhd fr ½-wy) 1½	**8**	16/1	—	—
			(SP 120.9%)	**8 Rn**	

1m 19.4 (5.90) CSF £5.41 TOTE £1.40: £1.40 £2.90 £1.40 (£5.10) OWNER Mr N. Honeyman (MIDDLEHAM) BRED St Simon Foundation

205 NILE AMATEUR H'CAP (0-80) (4-Y.O+) (Class F)
2-30 (2-33) **2m (Fibresand)** £2,294.00 (£644.00: £314.00) Stalls: Low GOING: 0.34 sec per fur (SLW)

			SP	RR	SF
157[4]	**El Nido (58)** (DWChapman) **9-9-12(3)** MissRClark(3) (cl up: led 7f out tl over 2f out: styd on to ld wl ins fnl f) .....—	**1**	10/1	67	—
115[3]	**Golden Hadeer (65)** (MJRyan) **6-10-5(3)** MrSLavallin(7) (chsd ldrs: chal 6f out: led over 2f out: no ex towards fin) 1	**2**	2/1 [1]	73	—
133[7]	**Coleridge (53)** (JJSheehan) **9-9-3b(7)** MissCHannaford(14) (bhd: hdwy 7f out: styd on fnl 3f: nvr able chal) 4	**3**	8/1	57	—
78[8]	**Stalled (IRE) (54)** (PTWalwyn) **7-9-8(3)** MarchionessBlandford(12) (b: hld up: effrt ½-wy: nvr rchd ldrs) 2½	**4**	6/1 [3]	56	—
167*	**Sudden Spin (65)** (JNorton) **7-10-8** 4x MrMHNaughton(11) (mid div: effrt 7f out: styd on: n.d) 7	**5**	5/1 [2]	60	—
196[3]	**Sea God (47)** (MCChapman) **6-9-1(3)** MrsSBosley(1) (led tl hdd 7f out: wknd fnl 4f) 18	**6**	10/1	24	—
	Open Affair (54) (HAkbary) **4-9-2(3)** MissIFoustok(13) (b: in tch tl outpcd ½-wy: n.d after) 12	**7**	25/1	19	—
	Glide Path (USA) (78) (JRJenkins) **8-11-4(3)** DrMMannish(2) (dwlt: sn trckng ldrs: wknd fnl 4f) 11	**8**	20/1	32	—
	Charter (72) (TJNaughton) **6-10-12(3)** MrsJNaughton(10) (outpcd ½-wy: n.d) 4	**9**	14/1	22	—
	Hard Love (51) (JLEyre) **5-9-5(3)** MrsCWilliams(9) (prom to ½-wy: sn lost pl) .....hd	**10**	14/1	—	—
139[3]	**Petoskin (65)** (JPearce) **5-10-8** MrsLPearce(5) (chsd ldrs tl rdn & wknd fnl 7f) 2	**11**	6/1 [3]	12	—
188[9]	**Royal Acclaim (43)** (RDickin) **12-8-11v(3)** MissRJPatman(6) (a rr div) 10	**12**	20/1	—	—
	Eurolink Shadow (55) (DMcCain) **5-9-9(3)** MrGLake(4) (prom to ½-wy: sn bhd) 7	**13**	25/1	—	—
	Daru (USA) (64) (RHollinshead) **8-10-7ow4** MrMRimell(8) (a bhd) 5	**14**	20/1	—	—
			(SP 143.2%)	**14 Rn**	

3m 56.7 (30.70) CSF £30.72 CT £175.57 TOTE £14.20: £4.30 £1.50 £1.60 (£35.10) Trio £55.50 OWNER Mr David Chapman (YORK) BRED M. J. Camacho
LONG HANDICAP Royal Acclaim 8-5
WEIGHT FOR AGE 4yo-6lb

206 AMAZON H'CAP (0-70) (4-Y.O+) (Class E)

3-00 (3-01) **1m 3f (Fibresand)** £2,804.25 (£849.00: £414.50: £197.25) Stalls: Low GOING: 0.34 sec per fur (SLW)

	Horse / details	Dist	Pos	SP	RR	SF
123^{9}	**Wildfire (SWI) (42)** (RAkehurst) **6-8-10** SSanders(8) (b: cl up: led over 2f out: styd on wl)	—	**1**	10/1	56	25
123^{2}	**Maftun (USA) (54)** (GMMoore) **5-9-8** DHolland(5) (led tl hdd over 2f out: one pce)	4	**2**	$11/10^{1}$	62	31
151*	**Kilnamartyra Girl (40)** (JParkes) **7-8-8** DHarrison(4) (lw: chsd ldrs: outpcd over 3f out: n.d after)	6	**3**	$7/2^{2}$	40	9
67*	**Undawaterscubadiva (38)** (MPBielby) **5-8-6** TWilliams(2) (b.nr hind: a chsng ldrs: one pce fnl 3f)	2	**4**	$6/1^{3}$	35	4
91^{5}	**Oneoftheoldones (56)** (JNorton) **5-9-10** GCarter(9) (outpcd after 3f: n.d after)	3	**5**	33/1	48	17
151^{5}	**Fred's Delight (IRE) (32)** (MrsVAAconley) **6-8-0v**^{ow4} MDeering(7) (bhd: sme hdwy ½-wy: sn rdn & no imp)	1¼	**6**	33/1	22	—
169^{4}	**Down The Yard (38)** (MCChapman) **4-8-4** DRMcCabe(3) (sn pushed along: n.d)	s.h	**7**	14/1	28	—
	Fiasco (43) (MJCamacho) **4-8-9** LCharnock(6) (b.nr fore: chsd ldrs: pushed along 8f out: wknd over 2f out)	6	**8**	16/1	25	—
169^{7}	**Palacegate Jo (IRE) (30)** (DWChapman) **6-7-12** DWright(1) (unruly gng to s: dwlt: hdwy u.p ½-wy: sn wknd)	14	**9**	7/1	—	—

(SP 124.1%) **9 Rn**

2m 33.6 (13.60) CSF £21.04 CT £46.56 TOTE £9.30: £2.80 £1.50 £1.30 (£10.60) Trio £11.50 OWNER Mr R. F. Kilby (EPSOM) BRED J. P. Jackson

LONG HANDICAP Fred's Delight (IRE) 7-4

WEIGHT FOR AGE 4yo-2lb

OFFICIAL EXPLANATION Wildfire (SWI): accounting for the gelding's apparently improved form, his jockey reported him to be something of a character who does not always give of his best.

207 ORINOCO H'CAP (0-80) (3-Y.O+) (Class D)

3-30 (3-30) **1m (Fibresand)** £3,517.50 (£1,065.00: £520.00: £247.50) Stalls: Low GOING: 0.34 sec per fur (SLW)

	Horse / details	Dist	Pos	SP	RR	SF
113*	**Kingchip Boy (71)** (MJRyan) **8-9-6** AClark(3) (mde all: qcknd over 2f out: r.o wl)	—	**1**	$11/2^{2}$	81	48
150*	**Yeoman Oliver (70)** (BAMcMahon) **4-9-5b** LNewton(6) (hld up: effrt 2f out: hung lft & nt pce to chal)	6	**2**	$7/1^{3}$	68	35
176^{4}	**Gulf Shaadi (67)** (EJAlston) **5-9-2** SDrowne(10) (lw: s.i.s: stdy hdwy 3f out: hung lft & no imp fnl 2f)	6	**3**	9/1	53	20
136*	**Jibereen (72)** (PHowling) **5-9-7** SWhitworth(1) (b: lw: hld up: effrt ½-wy: sn chsng ldrs: rdn & btn wl over 1f out)	nk	**4**	$11/4^{1}$	57	24
150^{3}	**Genuine John (IRE) (65)** (JParkes) **4-9-0** DHarrison(2) (chsd ldrs: effrt 4f out: r.o one pce)	2½	**5**	9/1	45	12
72^{3}	**Domino Flyer (66)** (MrsASwinbank) **4-9-1** DHolland(5) (lw: cl up tl lost pl fnl 2f)	7	**6**	$11/4^{1}$	32	—
176^{10}	**Loveyoumillions (IRE) (75)** (NTinkler) **5-9-10** KimTinkler(9) (cl up tl wknd fnl 3f)	8	**7**	33/1	25	—
	Up in Flames (IRE) (69) (SRBowring) **6-9-4** SDWilliams(8) (chsd ldrs: outpcd ½-wy: sn bhd)	6	**8**	9/1	7	—
182^{8}	**Cedez le Passage (FR) (65)** (KOCunningham-Brown) **6-9-0b** SSanders(4) (broke wl: sn drvn along: lost tch after 3f)	2	**9**	12/1	—	—

(SP 121.9%) **9 Rn**

1m 47.2 (8.20) CSF £42.05 CT £320.31 TOTE £5.30: £1.80 £5.90 £3.30 (£22.30) Trio £10.60 OWNER Four Jays Racing Partnership (NEWMARKET) BRED R. M. Scott

208 RIO GRANDE (S) STKS (3-Y.O+) (Class G)

4-00 (4-00) **6f (Fibresand)** £2,085.00 (£585.00: £285.00) Stalls: Low GOING: 0.34 sec per fur (SLW)

	Horse / details	Dist	Pos	SP	RR	SF
166^{8}	**Elton Ledger (IRE) (75)** (MrsNMacauley) **8-9-13v** SSanders(4) (b: cl up: led ½-wy: r.o fnl f: lame)	—	**1**	$13/8^{2}$	77	42
165^{2}	**Myttons Mistake (67)** (ABailey) **4-9-9** DWright(3) (b: chsd ldrs: hmpd ½-wy: hdwy 2f out: nt pce of wnr)	2½	**2**	$11/4^{3}$	66	31
165*	**Sense of Priority (75)** (DNicholls) **8-9-13** AlexGreaves(5) (cl up: chal ½-wy: btn appr fnl f)	2	**3**	$6/4^{1}$	65	30
	Takhlid (USA) (73) (DWChapman) **6-9-9** LCharnock(6) (sn chsng ldrs: effrt ½-wy: kpt on: nvr able chal)	1¾	**4**	12/1	56	21
	Tutu Sixtysix (24) (DonEnricoIncisa) **6-9-4** KimTinkler(7) (sn drvn along: bhd fr ½-wy)	19	**5**	50/1	1	—
	Waverley Star (18) (JSWainwright) **12-9-9b** DeanMcKeown(2) (sn outpcd & bhd)	5	**6**	66/1	—	—
111^{10}	**Nantgarw** (DBurchell) **4-8-11**(7) KSked(1) (led to ½-wy: wknd qckly)	9	**7**	66/1	—	—

(SP 117.4%) **7 Rn**

1m 20.6 (7.10) CSF £6.28 TOTE £2.80: £1.50 £1.90 (£5.00) OWNER The Posse (MELTON MOWBRAY) BRED Thomas Doherty

No bid

209 MACKENZIE H'CAP (0-60) (II) (4-Y.O+) (Class F)

4-30 (4-31) **7f (Fibresand)** £1,944.00 (£544.00: £264.00) Stalls: Low GOING: 0.34 sec per fur (SLW)

	Horse / details	Dist	Pos	SP	RR	SF
152^{6}	**Live Project (IRE) (50)** (MJohnston) **5-9-4** DHolland(14) (a.p: led 2f out: r.o u.p)	—	**1**	$4/1^{1}$	60	33
153^{6}	**Pleasure Trick (USA) (48)** (DonEnricoIncisa) **6-9-2b** KimTinkler(8) (outpcd & bhd: gd hdwy on outside 2f out: chsng wnr ins fnl f: nt qckn)	1¾	**2**	$6/1^{2}$	54	27
113^{4}	**Anita's Contessa (IRE) (55)** (BPalling) **5-9-9** TSprake(12) (hdwy 3f out: sn chsng ldrs: one pce fnl f)	2	**3**	$13/2^{3}$	56	29
126^{3}	**Fiaba (41)** (MrsNMacauley) **9-8-6v**(3)^{ow2} CTeague(5) (lw: outpcd & bhd: c wd st: r.o fnl 2f)	¾	**4**	$13/2^{3}$	41	12
166^{6}	**Shashi (IRE) (56)** (PatMitchell) **5-9-10** RLappin(3) (swtchd rt & hdwy over 2f out: styd on: no imp)	2	**5**	8/1	51	24
126^{5}	**Ragazzo (IRE) (40)** (JSWainwright) **7-8-8b** LCharnock(7) (b.hind: led 2f: cl up tl wknd fnl 2½f)	3½	**6**	8/1	27	—
	Orange And Blue (39) (MissJFCraze) **4-8-4c**(3) NVarley(1) (chsd ldrs tl wknd fnl 2f)	½	**7**	25/1	25	—
91^{8}	**Duffertoes (50)** (MJRyan) **5-9-4** AClark(9) (led after 2f to 2f out: grad wknd)	6	**8**	7/1	22	—
143^{9}	**Madonna da Rossi (33)** (MDods) **4-7-10**(5) JBramhill(6) (in tch: sn drvn along: no imp fnl 3f)	hd	**9**	16/1	5	—
135^{6}	**Cindy Kate (IRE) (47)** (WRMuir) **4-9-1** CRutter(11) (sn outpcd & bhd)	1	**10**	20/1	17	—
128^{9}	**Supreme Illusion (AUS) (28)** (JohnBerry) **4-7-10b** NAdams(2) (s.i.s: a outpcd & bhd)	nk	**11**	33/1	—	—
71^{4}	**Guy's Gamble (46)** (JWharton) **4-9-0** JFanning(4) (lw: sn drvn along: n.d)	nk	**12**	10/1	14	—
	Kid Ory (45) (DWChapman) **6-8-13** JQuinn(10) (chsd ldrs 5f: eased whn btn)	1¼	**13**	12/1	11	—
	Roseate Lodge (44) (SEKettlewell) **11-8-5**(7) JennyBenson(13) (s.i.s: n.d)	1½	**14**	20/1	6	—

(SP 134.7%) **14 Rn**

1m 34.9 (8.40) CSF £26.62 CT £155.18 TOTE £4.90: £1.80 £3.30 £2.70 (£19.50) Trio £38.40 OWNER Mrs Gillian Quinn (MIDDLEHAM) BRED Una Bolger

LONG HANDICAP Supreme Illusion (AUS) 7-3

T/Plpt: £49.70 (187.03 Tckts). T/Qdpt: £15.40 (58.74 Tckts) AA

0197-LINGFIELD (L-H) (Standard)
Tuesday February 4th
Race 7: hand-timed
WEATHER: rain WIND: almost nil

210 PEACH AMATEUR H'CAP (0-70) (I) (4-Y.O+) (Class E)
1-20 (1-21) **1m (Equitrack)** £2,427.25 (£733.00: £356.50: £168.25) Stalls: High GOING minus 0.41 sec per fur (FST)

				SP	RR	SF
116^{5}	**Montone (IRE) (60)** (JRJenkins) **7-12-0v** DrMMannish(3) (a.p: led over 3f out: rdn out)	—	1	$11/4^{1}$	72	46
141^{*}	**Bold Habit (41)** (JPearce) **12-10-9** MrsLPearce(8) (hld up: hdwy 3f out: chsd wnr over 1f out: nt qckn)	1½	2	$4/1^{2}$	50	24
188^{6}	**Don't Drop Bombs (USA) (35)** (DTThom) **8-10-3** MissJFeilden(2) (lw: a.p: ev ch over 2f out: one pce)	8	3	$4/1^{2}$	28	2
116^{9}	**Sarum (30)** (JELong) **11-9-6**(6) MrTWaters(1) (b: led 5f out tl over 3f out: wknd over 2f out)	19	4	16/1	—	—
197^{4}	**Spectacle Jim (44)** (BAPearce) **8-10-6**(6) MrsSColville(7) (led 3f: wknd 4f out)	3½	5	16/1	—	—
	Rapid Liner (41) (RJBaker) **4-10-3**(6) MissLPope(6) (prom over 3f)	3½	6	50/1	—	—
76^{2}	**Bon Secret (IRE) (60)** (TJNaughton) **5-11-10**(4) MrsJNaughton(4) (in tch whn bmpd 5f out: nt rcvr)	1½	7	$11/4^{1}$	—	—
105^{7}	**Multi Franchise (48)** (BGubby) **4-10-12v**(4) MrGLake(5) (in tch whn bmpd 5f out: bhd fnl 4f)	5	8	$12/1^{3}$	—	—

(SP 114.8%) **8 Rn**

1m 43.08 (5.68) CSF £12.79 CT £39.18 TOTE £3.70: £1.70 £1.60 £1.10 (£9.10) OWNER Mr B. Shirazi (ROYSTON) BRED Sean Gorman

211 PEACH AMATEUR H'CAP (0-70) (II) (4-Y.O+) (Class E)
1-50 (1-51) **1m (Equitrack)** £2,427.25 (£733.00: £356.50: £168.25) Stalls: High GOING minus 0.41 sec per fur (FST)

				SP	RR	SF
108^{5}	**Regal Splendour (CAN) (60)** (RJO'Sullivan) **4-11-0**(6) MrDBridger(3) (chsd ldr: led over 1f out: rdn out)	—	1	$13/2^{3}$	68	50
131^{9}	**Robellion (68)** (DWPArbuthnot) **6-12-0v** MrsDArbuthnot(4) (chsd ldrs: ev ch fnl f: r.o)	½	2	$3/1^{1}$	75	57
188^{7}	**Gadge (44)** (ABailey) **6-9-12**(6)ow10 MissALHutchinson(8) (b: rdn & hdwy 4f out: r.o ins fnl f)	5	3	10/1	41	13
146^{7}	**Fort Knox (IRE) (60)** (RMFlower) **6-11-6b** MrTMcCarthy(5) (hrd rdn over 1f out: nvr nr to chal)	3	4	$100/30^{2}$	51	33
15^{12}	**Dream Carrier (IRE) (44)** (REPeacock) **9-9-12**(6) MrsCPeacock(7) (bhd: rdn 4f out: nrst fin)	s.h	5	33/1	35	17
195^{4}	**Eastleigh (43)** (RHollinshead) **8-9-11**(6)ow7 MrDDickenson(2) (chsd ldrs 4f)	2	6	9/1	30	5
171^{2}	**Spencer's Revenge (56)** (PButler) **8-10-10b**(6) MrJGoldstein(6) (led: sn clr: hdd over 1f out: sn hrd rdn & wknd)	3½	7	$3/1^{1}$	36	18
	Bellas Gate Boy (50) (JPearce) **5-10-10** MrsLPearce(1) (bhd fnl 4f)	3½	8	8/1	23	5

(SP 119.6%) **8 Rn**

1m 41.97 (4.57) CSF £25.16 CT £183.02 TOTE £8.20: £1.40 £1.60 £2.60 (£24.20) OWNER Miss Sarah Jones (WHITCOMBE) BRED Pedigree Farms Ltd
STEWARDS' ENQUIRY Goldstein susp. 13-15 & 17/2/97 (excessive use of whip).
IN-FOCUS: This was rider David Bridger's first winner.

212 DAMSON (S) STKS (3-Y.O) (Class G)
2-20 (2-20) **6f (Equitrack)** £2,057.30 (£577.80: £281.90) Stalls: Low GOING minus 0.41 sec per fur (FST)

				SP	RR	SF
103^{5}	**Eager To Please (69)** (MissGayKelleway) **3-9-5b** DHolland(2) (b: b.hind: mde all: rdn out)	—	1	$4/6^{1}$	69	9
118^{5}	**Hever Golf Charger (IRE) (60)** (TJNaughton) **3-8-12** SSanders(1) (w wnr: rdn 3f out: one pce fnl 2f)	2½	2	$2/1^{2}$	55	—
181^{7}	**Advance Repro (54)** (JAkehurst) **3-9-0** MTebbutt(3) (prom over 2f: hrd rdn & styd on fnl f)	3	3	$11/1^{3}$	49	—
158^{4}	**Whizz Kid (50)** (JJBridger) **3-9-0** DHarrison(5) (sn outpcd: hrd rdn & hdwy 2f out: wknd over 1f out)	2½	4	12/1	43	—
158^{6}	**Ekaterini Paritsi (50)** (WGMTurner) **3-8-2v**(5) JBramhill(4) (lw: rdn along: prom 4f)	3½	5	12/1	26	—

(SP 117.1%) **5 Rn**

1m 15.43 (4.33) CSF £2.27 TOTE £1.40: £1.10 £1.40 (£2.40) OWNER Miss Jo Crowley (WHITCOMBE) BRED Mrs Sara Hood
No bid

213 PLUM CLAIMING STKS (4-Y.O+) (Class E)
2-50 (2-50) **1m 2f (Equitrack)** £2,778.25 (£841.00: £410.50: £195.25) Stalls: Low GOING minus 0.41 sec per fur (FST)

				SP	RR	SF
176^{5}	**Joseph's Wine (IRE) (80)** (DNicholls) **8-9-6b** AlexGreaves(6) (a gng wl: qcknd & led over 2f out: sn clr: easily)	—	1	$6/4^{1}$	86+	26
171^{*}	**Invocation (63)** (GLMoore) **10-8-6** AClark(5) (b.nr hind: lw: s.s: rdn & hdwy 5f out: chsd wnr fnl f: no imp)	7	2	$11/4^{2}$	61	1
140^{3}	**Bernard Seven (IRE) (66)** (MDods) **5-9-6b** DHolland(7) (a.p: led 5f out tl over 3f out: one pce)	2½	3	$6/1^{3}$	71	11
	Bold Faith (WJMusson) **4-8-7**(3) MBaird(9) (s.i.s: hdwy 8f out: led over 3f out tl over 2f out: wknd over 1f out)	nk	4	16/1	61	—
160^{4}	**Our Eddie (44)** (BGubby) **8-8-2v** JQuinn(8) (lw: led 8f out to 5f out: wknd 3f out)	2	5	12/1	49	—
	Water Hazard (IRE) (55) (SDow) **5-7-12**(5)ow1 ADaly(1) (sn drvn along: rr after 3f: sme hdwy fnl 2f)	3	6	20/1	45	—
150^{9}	**Buddy's Friend (IRE) (35)** (RJRWilliams) **9-8-2** DBiggs(4) (rdn 5f out: nvr nr to chal)	6	7	33/1	35	—
144^{4}	**Havana Miss (34)** (BPalling) **5-8-3** TSprake(2) (led 1f: bhd fnl 5f)	s.h	8	16/1	36	—
177^{10}	**Grand Crack (IRE) (37)** (CADwyer) **5-8-6** DRMcCabe(3) (led after 1f: hdd 8f out: wknd 5f out)	3	9	25/1	34	—

(SP 112.0%) **9 Rn**

2m 9.93 (5.63) CSF £4.65 TOTE £2.20: £1.50 £1.70 £1.60 (£2.40) Trio £2.60 OWNER Wetherby Racing Bureau Ltd (THIRSK) BRED Michael Fennessy
WEIGHT FOR AGE 4yo-1lb

214 GREENGAGE H'CAP (0-75) (3-Y.O+) (Class D)
3-20 (3-21) **6f (Equitrack)** £3,420.00 (£1,035.00: £505.00: £240.00) Stalls: Low GOING minus 0.41 sec per fur (FST)

				SP	RR	SF
121^{3}	**Apollo Red (60)** (GLMoore) **8-8-13** CandyMorris(6) (chsd ldr: led 3f out: rdn out)	—	1	$6/1^{3}$	71	36
97^{*}	**Forgotten Times (USA) (65)** (TMJones) **3-8-3** NCarlisle(9) (b.hind: hdwy 3f out: chsd wnr 2f out: hrd rdn fnl f: r.o)	1¾	2	$4/1^{2}$	71	21
59^{4}	**Astral Invader (IRE) (44)** (MSSaunders) **5-7-11**ow1 JQuinn(8) (hld up: hdwy fnl 2f: nvr nrr)	6	3	33/1	34	—
95^{7}	**Sharp Pearl (65)** (JWhite) **4-9-4b** DHolland(4) (b.off hind: lw: a.p: one pce fnl 2f)	4	4	14/1	45	10
53^{5}	**Dande Flyer (71)** (DWPArbuthnot) **4-9-5**(5) PPMurphy(2) (b: hdwy 4f out: one pce fnl 2f)	1½	5	14/1	47	12
166^{5}	**Lucky Revenge (55)** (DNicholls) **4-8-8** AClark(10) (sn rdn along: no hdwy fnl 3f)	½	6	$6/1^{3}$	29	—

178^{2} **Double Oscar (IRE) (45)** (DNicholls) **4-7-7b**$^{(5)}$ JBramhill(1) (sn led: hdd 3f out: wknd 2f out) ....2 **7** 4/1^{2} 14 —
170^{5} **The Institute Boy (67)** (MissJFCraze) **7-9-6** SWebster(3) (a bhd) ....3 **8** 9/1 28 —
170^{2} **Lord Sky (63)** (ABailey) **6-9-2** SSanders(5) (b: lw: bhd fnl 3f) ....1½ **9** 100/30^{1} 20 —
(SP 117.9%) **9 Rn**

1m 13.04 (1.94) CSF £28.15 CT £672.99 TOTE £6.80: £1.20 £2.40 £7.30 (£23.50) Trio £148.10 OWNER Mr A. Moore (BRIGHTON) BRED Crest Stud Ltd
LONG HANDICAP Astral Invader (IRE) 7-8
WEIGHT FOR AGE 3yo-15lb
OFFICIAL EXPLANATION Lord Sky: lost a shoe.

215 NECTARINE MAIDEN STKS (3-Y.O+) (Class D)
3-50 (3-52) **7f (Equitrack)** £3,322.50 (£1,005.00: £490.00: £232.50) Stalls: Low GOING minus 0.41 sec per fur (FST)

				SP	RR	SF
	First Chance (IRE) (DRCElsworth) **3-8-2** SDrowne(7) (rdn 5f out: hdwy 3f out: r.o to ld nr fin)	—	1	5/2^{1}	64	9
	Perang Polly (LordHuntingdon) **5-9-5** DHarrison(9) (hdwy 4f out: led wl over 1f out: ct nr fin)	nk	2	10/1	63	25
11^{5}	**Will Do (69)** (MartynMeade) **4-9-10** NAdams(6) (chsd ldr: led over 3f out: hrd rdn & hdd wl over 1f out: one pce)	9	3	3/1^{2}	48	10
185^{2}	**Alvilde (67)** (DJSCosgrove) **3-8-2** JQuinn(1) (rdn & hdwy 3f out: one pce fnl 2f)	3½	4	100/30^{3}	35	—
	Magazine Gap (PatMitchell) **4-9-5**$^{(5)}$ AmandaSanders(3) (lw: bhd: hdwy over 1f out: nvr nrr)	2	5	16/1	35	—
	Missed May (BPJBaugh) **3-8-2** FNorton(2) (unf: bhd: sme hdwy over 1f out: nvr nr to chal)	1¾	6	33/1	26	—
135^{4}	**Beau Bruno (71)** (MBell) **4-9-5v**$^{1(5)}$ GFaulkner(8) (s.i.s: hdwy 6f out: wknd over 2f out)	6	7	7/2	18	—
	Scboo (REPeacock) **8-9-5**$^{(5)}$ ADaly(4) (sn rdn along: led over 3f)	2½	8	50/1	12	—
117^{9}	**Silent Symphony** (MrsSDWilliams) **5-9-0**$^{(5)}$ JBramhill(5) (lw: bhd fnl 3f)	2½	9	25/1	1	—

(SP 122.6%) **9 Rn**

1m 28.25 (3.85) CSF £27.69 TOTE £2.90: £2.20 £1.70 £2.30 (£9.80) Trio £46.70 OWNER Michael Jackson Bloodstock Ltd (WHITCOMBE)
BRED Rathbarry Stud
WEIGHT FOR AGE 3yo-17lb

216 CHERRY H'CAP (0-70) (4-Y.O+) (Class E)
4-20 (4-21) **1m 4f (Equitrack)** £2,804.25 (£849.00: £414.50: £197.25) Stalls: Low GOING minus 0.41 sec per fur (FST)

				SP	RR	SF
147^{*}	**In the Money (IRE) (51)** (RHollinshead) **8-8-9**$^{(5)}$ DGriffiths(13) (a.p: hrd rdn 2f out: r.o to ld last stride)	—	1	7/2^{1}	62	28
144^{3}	**Dr Edgar (49)** (MDods) **5-8-12** AClark(11) (a.p: led 2f out: hrd rdn: hdd last stride)	s.h	2	10/1	60	26
171^{7}	**Uoni (45)** (PButler) **4-8-0**$^{(5)}$ JBramhill(7) (hdwy 5f out: hrd rdn over 2f out: one pce)	3	3	25/1	52	15
163^{4}	**Harlequin Walk (IRE) (46)** (RJO'Sullivan) **6-8-9** DHarrison(10) (lw: led after 2f tl over 2f out: one pce)	2½	4	6/1^{3}	50	16
144^{*}	**Fabulous Mtoto (33)** (MSSaunders) **7-7-10** NCarlisle(9) (s.s: plld hrd: hdwy 3f out: rdn 2f out: styd on)	hd	5	6/1^{3}	37	3
108^{4}	**Nails Tails (43)** (SDow) **4-7-12**$^{(5)ow3}$ ADaly(5) (a.p: hrd rdn & led over 2f out: sn hdd: one pce)	nk	6	6/1^{3}	46	6
74^{4}	**Father Dan (IRE) (61)** (MissGayKelleway) **8-9-10** DHolland(4) (b: b.hind: lw: hld up: hdwy 5f out: nvr nr to chal)	2½	7	8/1	61	27
98^{2}	**Evening In Paris (44)** (MJohnston) **4-8-4** DeanMcKeown(8) (prom 6f: wkng whn bmpd over 4f out)	1¾	8	4/1^{2}	41	4
	Real Madrid (43) (GPEnright) **6-8-6v** NAdams(6) (hld up: hdwy 5f out: rdn & wknd 3f out)	8	9	16/1	30	—
	Pyrrhic Dance (35) (MJHaynes) **7-7-12** GBardwell(2) (b: led 2f: bhd fnl 6f)	4	10	33/1	16	—
128^{8}	**Dia Georgy (33)** (CADwyer) **6-7-7**$^{(3)}$ NVarley(3) (b: bhd fnl 7f)	½	11	33/1	14	—
	Western Playboy (62) (RJBaker) **5-9-11** JQuinn(12) (hdwy 7f out: wknd 5f out: t.o)	16	12	25/1	21	—
183^{2}	**Al Helal (41)** (JRJenkins) **5-8-4** SSanders(1) (broke leg & p.u after 3f: dead)		P	7/1	—	—

(SP 137.2%) **13 Rn**

2m 35.7 (5.70) CSF £40.78 CT £746.44 TOTE £4.40: £1.70 £5.20 £9.10 (£14.90) Trio £698.40 OWNER Mr J. E. Bigg (UPPER LONGDON)
BRED Cheveley Park Stud Ltd
LONG HANDICAP Dia Georgy 6-13 Fabulous Mtoto 7-9
WEIGHT FOR AGE 4yo-3lb

T/Plpt: £53.50 (167.68 Tckts). T/Qdpt: £13.40 (47.31 Tckts) AK/LMc

0176-WOLVERHAMPTON (L-H) (Standard)
Wednesday February 5th
WEATHER: fine & dry WIND: mod half bhd

217 AVON H'CAP (0-75) (3-Y.O) (Class D)
1-50 (1-50) **7f (Fibresand)** £3,306.25 (£1,000.00: £487.50: £231.25) Stalls: High GOING: 0.37 sec per fur (SLW)

				SP	RR	SF
17^{8}	**C-Harry (IRE) (64)** (RHollinshead) **3-8-11** MWigham(1) (trckd ldrs: nt clr run & swtchd rt ent st: led ins fnl f: jst hld on)	—	1	11/2	70	23
138^{5}	**Plan For Profit (IRE) (74)** (MJohnston) **3-9-7** DHolland(2) (led: hrd drvn over 1f out: hdd ins fnl f: rallied cl home)	s.h	2	13/8^{1}	80	33
49^{3}	**Faym (IRE) (66)** (JWharton) **3-8-13** FNorton(3) (lw: hld up in rr: effrt & outpcd over 2f out: styd on appr fnl f: nvr nrr)	3	3	6/1	65	18
164^{2}	**Zorba (64)** (CWThornton) **3-8-11** DeanMcKeown(5) (w ldr: hrd drvn 2f out: outpcd appr fnl f)	nk	4	5/2^{2}	62	15
138^{6}	**Enchanting Eve (65)** (CNAllen) **3-8-7**$^{(5)}$ MartinDwyer(4) (bhd: rdn & hdwy 3f out: wknd wl over 1f out)	13	5	5/1^{3}	34	—

(SP 113.0%) **5 Rn**

1m 33.5 (8.80) CSF £13.99 TOTE £10.60: £2.90 £1.60 (£28.20) OWNER Mr D. Coppenhall (UPPER LONGDON) BRED Dan O'Loughlin
OFFICIAL EXPLANATION **C-Harry (IRE): hung so badly last time that the jockey had been unable to ride him properly.**

218 NENE MEDIAN AUCTION MAIDEN STKS (4, 5 & 6-Y.O) (Class E)
2-20 (2-22) **1m 4f (Fibresand)** £2,713.25 (£821.00: £400.50: £190.25) Stalls: Low GOING: 0.37 sec per fur (SLW)

				SP	RR	SF
	Cashaplenty (NPLittmoden) **4-8-13** TGMcLaughlin(6) (swtg: led 2f: led over 4f out: sn clr: v.easily)	—	1	11/2^{3}	50+	13
123^{5}	**Zatopek (37)** (JCullinan) **5-9-2** JQuinn(4) (chsd ldrs: rdn 3f out: r.o one pce)	9	2	8/1	38	4
	Zine Lane (JGMO'Shea) **5-9-2v**^{1} DHolland(2) (led after 2f tl over 4f out: sn rdn: styd on same pce)	2½	3	9/2^{1}	35	1

				SP	RR	SF
37^{2}	**Golden Hanoof (USA)** (DrJDScargill) **5-8-11** NCarlisle(7) (swtg: rr tl styd on fnl 3f)	7	**4**	7/1	20	—
	Reno's Treasure (USA) (35) (JohnHarris) **4-8-8** DeanMcKeown(9) (trckd ldrs: rdn 4f out: sn lost tch)	10	**5**	20/1	7	—
200^{3}	**Haute Cuisine (40)** (RJRWilliams) **4-8-13** DBiggs(8) (nvr nr to chal)	10	**6**	7/1	—	—
164^{7}	**Sebastian Duke (FR)** (JCullinan) **5-9-2** TWilliams(1) (lw: hld up: hdwy 5f out: rdn & wknd over 2f out: t.o)	4	**7**	$5/1^{2}$	—	—
	Deux Carr (USA) (BobJones) **4-8-13** MWigham(3) (bit bkwd: chsd ldrs: rdn along 5f out: sn wknd: t.o)	dist	**8**	7/1	—	—
167^{7}	**Swandale Flyer (33)** (NBycroft) **5-8-11**(5) JBramhill(5) (lost pl after 4f: sn t.o: p.u 3f out)		**P**	$5/1^{2}$	—	—

(SP 120.3%) **9 Rn**

2m 50.0 (17.50) CSF £46.34 TOTE £5.60: £1.60 £2.50 £3.00 (£28.10) Trio £44.70 OWNER Mr John Bell (WOLVERHAMPTON) BRED Brig Andrew Parker Bowles
WEIGHT FOR AGE 4yo-3lb

219 THAMES H'CAP (0-80) (4-Y.O+) (Class D)

2-50 (2-50) **1m 4f (Fibresand)** £3,387.50 (£1,025.00: £500.00: £237.50) Stalls: Low GOING: 0.37 sec per fur (SLW)

				SP	RR	SF
66^{3}	**Mr Speculator (51)** (JEBanks) **4-8-6b¹** JQuinn(3) (racd wd: mde all: hrd rdn over 1f out: r.o wl)	—	**1**	$2/1^{2}$	58	21
129^{*}	**Persian Conquest (IRE) (65)** (RIngram) **5-9-9b** SSanders(2) (lw: a.p: jnd wnr 2f out: hrd rdn & one pce appr fnl f)	2½	**2**	$3/1^{3}$	69	35
182^{4}	**Premier Dance (69)** (DHaydnJones) **10-9-13** AClark(5) (hld up: effrt & hrd drvn over 3f out: no imp)	8	**3**	$3/1^{3}$	62	28
140^{2}	**Maradata (IRE) (64)** (RHollinshead) **5-9-8** LDettori(1) (s.i.s: hld up in rr: hdwy 4f out: sn rdn: wknd & eased wl over 1f out: t.o)	19	**4**	$15/8^{1}$	32	—
	Allez Cyrano (IRE) (70) (OO'Neill) **6-10-0** VSlattery(4) (bkwd: plld hrd: chsd wnr 7f: sn wknd: t.o)	10	**5**	25/1	24	—

(SP 122.0%) **5 Rn**

2m 47.7 (15.20) CSF £8.65 TOTE £4.00: £1.60 £1.60 (£4.40) OWNER The Speculators (NEWMARKET) BRED Fittocks Stud
WEIGHT FOR AGE 4yo-3lb

220 TYNE H'CAP (0-100) (3-Y.O+) (Class C)

3-25 (3-25) **1m 100y (Fibresand)** £5,198.75 (£1,574.00: £768.50: £365.75) Stalls: Low GOING: 0.37 sec per fur (SLW)

				SP	RR	SF
52^{*}	**Royal Action (88)** (JEBanks) **4-9-10** MWigham(9) (lw: led over 2f: rdn to ld over 1f out: r.o wl)	—	**1**	$3/1^{2}$	96	48
82^{2}	**Sabot (92)** (CWThornton) **4-10-0** DeanMcKeown(8) (lw: chsd ldrs: hdwy over 2f out: ev ch appr fnl f: no ex)	1¼	**2**	6/1	98	50
176^{*}	**South Eastern Fred (94)** (HJCollingridge) **6-10-2** 6x MRimmer(1) (a.p: pushed along over 3f out: rdn & unable qckn appr fnl f)	1¾	**3**	$5/1^{3}$	96	48
179^{3}	**Pater Noster (USA) (89)** (JohnHarris) **8-9-11** SSanders(6) (b: chsd ldrs: rdn & outpcd over 2f out: rallied ins fnl f)	½	**4**	7/1	90	42
113^{9}	**Leigh Crofter (66)** (PDCundell) **8-8-2b** SDrowne(5) (led 6f out tl hdd & outpcd appr fnl f)	1¾	**5**	20/1	64	16
179^{*}	**Duke Valentino (88)** (RHollinshead) **5-9-5**(5) 6x DGriffiths(2) (lw: rdn along ½-wy: nvr nr ldrs: t.o)	15	**6**	9/1	58	10
	Whispering Dawn (65) (CPEBrooks) **4-8-1** JQuinn(7) (b.hind: a in rr: t.o)	1¾	**7**	16/1	31	—
82^{3}	**Punkah (USA) (75)** (GMMcCourt) **4-8-11** LDettori(3) (hld up in rr: effrt & hrd drvn 3f out: no imp: t.o)	2½	**8**	$11/4^{1}$	37	—
179^{8}	**Northern Fan (IRE) (87)** (NTinkler) **5-9-9** GCarter(4) (bit bkwd: a bhd: t.o)	hd	**9**	33/1	48	—

(SP 118.7%) **9 Rn**

1m 54.4 (9.40) CSF £20.21 CT £80.95 TOTE £3.90: £2.00 £1.80 £1.90 (£30.10) Trio £23.80 OWNER Mr E. Carter (NEWMARKET) BRED D. J. and Mrs Deer

221 WELLAND (S) STKS (3-Y.O) (Class F)

3-55 (3-56) **5f (Fibresand)** £2,580.00 (£780.00: £380.00: £180.00) Stalls: Low GOING: 0.37 sec per fur (SLW)

				SP	RR	SF
51^{10}	**Will To Win (45)** (PGMurphy) **3-8-7** SDrowne(4) (b.off hind: trckd ldrs: hrd drvn 2f out: str run to ld fnl strides)	—	**1**	12/1	60	11
	Threeplay (IRE) (66) (JAkehurst) **3-8-12** MTebbutt(5) (bit bkwd: a.p: rdn to ld wl ins fnl f: ct post)	nk	**2**	$11/8^{1}$	64	15
198^{4}	**Ma Vielle Pouque (IRE) (1)** (WGMTurner) **3-8-7** TSprake(6) (b.nr fore: a.p: led over 1f out tl wl ins fnl f)	s.h	**3**	$5/1^{3}$	59	10
142^{2}	**Tear White (IRE) (64)** (TGMills) **3-9-5b** TWilliams(3) (smartly away: led tl hdd & wknd over 1f out)	5	**4**	$6/4^{2}$	55	6
	Ballerina's Dream (1) (MartynMeade) **3-8-7** NAdams(2) (unf: swtg: s.i.s: a wl bhd & outpcd)	4	**5**	14/1	30	—
	Whisper Low (IRE) (47) (RHollinshead) **3-8-7** LDettori(1) (sn outpcd: a bhd)	10	**6**	9/1	—	—

(SP 123.1%) **6 Rn**

65.6 secs (6.70) CSF £29.42 TOTE £18.30: £5.30 £1.20 (£12.10) OWNER Mrs Pat Wyatt (BRISTOL) BRED Red House Stud
No bid

222 SEVERN H'CAP (0-70) (3-Y.O+) (Class E)

4-25 (4-26) **5f (Fibresand)** £2,765.25 (£837.00: £408.50: £194.25) Stalls: Low GOING: 0.37 sec per fur (SLW)

				SP	RR	SF
137^{8}	**Squire Corrie (58)** (DWChapman) **5-9-9** ACulhane(7) (hdwy to ld ½-wy: clr appr fnl f)	—	**1**	$11/4^{1}$	69	51
137^{*}	**Gi La High (59)** (MartynMeade) **4-9-10** NAdams(9) (chsd ldrs: rdn 2f out: kpt on fnl f: no ch w wnr)	4	**2**	$5/1^{2}$	57	39
178^{3}	**Featherstone Lane (56)** (MissLCSiddall) **6-9-0v**(7) TSiddall(1) (bhd & outpcd: gd hdwy 2f out: rdn & r.o wl towards fin)	1¼	**3**	11/1	50	32
79^{W}	**Honeyhall (36)** (NBycroft) **4-8-1v¹** JQuinn(6) (a.p: led 3f out: sn hdd: rdn & one pce appr fnl f)	hd	**4**	16/1	30	12
178^{4}	**Boffy (IRE) (51)** (BPJBaugh) **4-8-11b**(5) PRoberts(10) (hdwy over 2f out: sn rdn: nvr able to chal)	¾	**5**	$5/1^{2}$	43	25
152^{13}	**Playmaker (46)** (DNicholls) **4-8-11b** AClark(8) (bit bkwd: trckd ldrs: swtchd ins over 1f out: r.o)	1½	**6**	8/1	33	15
137^{7}	**Rennyholme (43)** (JHetherton) **6-8-8b** SSanders(5) (spd 3f)	½	**7**	11/1	28	10
152^{4}	**Amy Leigh (IRE) (54)** (CaptJWilson) **4-9-5b** GCarter(4) (prom 3f: sn drvn along & outpcd)	5	**8**	9/1	23	5
137^{10}	**Sotonian (HOL) (48)** (PSFelgate) **4-8-8**(5) JBramhill(3) (chsd ldrs ½-wy: sn outpcd: t.o)	12	**9**	$6/1^{3}$	—	—
75^{4}	**Calchou (47)** (CWFairhurst) **3-7-12v¹** LCharnock(2) (broke wl: led 2f: sn rdn & wknd: t.o)	½	**10**	20/1	—	—

(SP 122.7%) **10 Rn**

64.1 secs (5.20) CSF £15.68 CT £126.49 TOTE £3.60: £1.30 £1.20 £3.40 (£8.10) Trio £37.80 OWNER Miss N. F. Thesiger (YORK) BRED Whitsbury Manor Stud
WEIGHT FOR AGE 3yo-14lb

T/Plpt: £78.90 (104.69 Tckts). T/Qdpt: £16.70 (42.31 Tckts) IM

0210-LINGFIELD (L-H) (Standard)
Thursday February 6th
WEATHER: overcast WIND: mod half bhd

223
PRIMROSE H'CAP (0-60) (3-Y.O+) (Class F)
1-55 (1-56) **5f (Equitrack)** £2,484.40 (£698.40: £341.20) Stalls: High GOING minus 0.39 sec per fur (FST)

				SP	RR	SF
199[2]	**Ivory's Grab Hire (43)** (KTIvory) **4-8-12b** DBiggs(6) (hrd rdn & hdwy over 1f out: str run fnl f: led last stride)	—	**1**	5/1[2]	50	32
172[4]	**Allstars Dancer (35)** (TJNaughton) **4-8-4** SSanders(4) (a.p: rdn over 2f out: led wl ins fnl f: hdd last stride)	hd	**2**	8/1	42	24
199[8]	**Thick as Thieves (44)** (RonaldThompson) **5-8-13** JFanning(5) (a.p: rdn over 3f out: ev ch wl ins fnl f: r.o wl)	hd	**3**	8/1	50	32
214[7]	**Double Oscar (IRE) (45)** (DNicholls) **4-9-0b** LDettori(1) (lw: a.p: rdn 2f out: led over 1f out: hrd rdn fnl f: hdd nr fin)	hd	**4**	11/2[3]	51	33
199[6]	**Logie Pert Lad (27)** (JJBridger) **5-7-10** FNorton(8) (nt clr run 2f out: hdwy fnl f: r.o)	1½	**5**	25/1	28	10
198[3]	**Imp Express (IRE) (35)** (GMMoore) **4-8-4b** GBardwell(2) (dwlt: rdn over 3f out: hdwy over 1f out: r.o)	1	**6**	3/1[1]	33	15
142[4]	**Suite Factors (46)** (KRBurke) **3-7-8b[1](7)** CCogan(7) (prom 3f)	3½	**7**	9/1	33	1
214[6]	**Lucky Revenge (55)** (DNicholls) **4-9-3b[1](7)** IonaWands(9) (bhd fnl 2f)	1¾	**8**	11/1	36	18
95[3]	**Daaniera (IRE) (34)** (PHowling) **7-8-3b** TWilliams(3) (b.hind: lw: led over 3f)	2	**9**	6/1	9	—

(SP 115.7%) **9 Rn**

60.01 secs (1.81) CSF £40.57 CT £287.37 TOTE £5.40: £1.70 £2.30 £3.80 (£13.00) Trio £34.30 OWNER Mr Dean Ivory (RADLETT) BRED Japan Bloodstock Ltd
LONG HANDICAP Logie Pert Lad 7-6
WEIGHT FOR AGE 3yo-14lb

224
WISTERIA CLAIMING STKS (4-Y.O+) (Class F)
2-25 (2-25) **7f (Equitrack)** £2,518.00 (£708.00: £346.00) Stalls: Low GOING minus 0.39 sec per fur (FST)

				SP	RR	SF
171[4]	**Greatest (75)** (MissGayKelleway) **6-9-1b** DHolland(9) (b: b.hind: a.p: led over 3f out: hrd rdn over 1f out: r.o wl)	—	**1**	2/1[1]	72	36
105[2]	**Milos (62)** (GLMoore) **6-9-2** SWhitworth(5) (b: lw: dwlt: hdwy over 3f out: chsd wnr fnl f: unable qckn)	1½	**2**	3/1[2]	70	34
117[8]	**Lift Boy (USA) (60)** (GLMoore) **8-8-9** CandyMorris(2) (led over 3f: one pce)	¾	**3**	10/1[3]	61	25
	Piquant (LordHuntingdon) **10-8-12**(7) CCogan(4) (bkwd: wl bhd over 5f: hdwy fnl f: nvr plcd to chal)	3½	**4**	20/1	63	27
184[2]	**Ultra Beet (80)** (PCHaslam) **5-9-5** LDettori(6) (lw: hdwy over 3f out: wknd over 2f out)	2½	**5**	2/1[1]	57	21
160[7]	**Little Pilgrim (32)** (TMJones) **4-8-0**(5) ADaly(7) (prom over 3f)	5	**6**	66/1	32	—
	Masruf (IRE) (52) (KCBailey) **5-8-7** SSanders(8) (s.s: bhd fnl 4f)	1¼	**7**	66/1	31	—
172[5]	**Norling (IRE) (47)** (KOCunningham-Brown) **7-8-9** LCharnock(1) (prom 3f)	19	**8**	12/1	—	—
	Prince Rudolf (IRE) (33) (WGMTurner) **5-8-3b** TSprake(3) (bhd fnl 4f)	5	**9**	66/1	—	—

(SP 117.7%) **9 Rn**

1m 27.04 (2.64) CSF £7.58 TOTE £2.70: £1.50 £1.80 £2.50 (£7.30) Trio £15.50 OWNER Invoshire Ltd (WHITCOMBE) BRED Bloomsbury Stud

225
JAPONICA H'CAP (0-70) (3-Y.O) (Class E)
2-55 (2-56) **7f (Equitrack)** £2,778.25 (£841.00: £410.50: £195.25) Stalls: Low GOING minus 0.39 sec per fur (FST)

				SP	RR	SF
119[2]	**Spaniard's Mount (63)** (MHTompkins) **3-9-7v** DHolland(6) (mde all: clr over 1f out: hrd rdn: r.o wl)	—	**1**	11/2[3]	72	39
161[2]	**Harmony In Red (62)** (CADwyer) **3-9-6v[1]** DRMcCabe(5) (plld hrd: stdy hdwy over 2f out: chsd wnr ins fnl f: r.o)	3	**2**	10/1	64	31
*193**	**Pet Express (58)** (PCHaslam) **3-9-2** 6x LCharnock(7) (lw: a.p: chsd wnr 3f out tl ins fnl f: sn wknd)	5	**3**	13/8[1]	49	16
	Abstone Queen (59) (PDEvans) **3-9-3v** SSanders(9) (hld up: rdn over 2f out: sn wknd)	5	**4**	9/1	38	5
	Puzzlement (57) (CEBrittain) **3-9-1** LDettori(2) (prom over 4f)	2½	**5**	6/1	31	—
	Be True (60) (GLMoore) **3-9-4** CandyMorris(8) (a bhd)	½	**6**	20/1	32	—
96[4]	**Verinder's Gift (44)** (DrJDScargill) **3-8-2** NCarlisle(4) (bhd fnl 3f)	hd	**7**	20/1	16	—
145[5]	**Talisman (IRE) (60)** (SDow) **3-8-13**(5) ADaly(3) (a bhd)	2½	**8**	20/1	27	—
	Island Prince (49) (NACallaghan) **3-8-2**(5) JBramhill(1) (prom over 3f)	6	**9**	4/1[2]	2	—

(SP 121.1%) **9 Rn**

1m 27.22 (2.82) CSF £53.91 CT £115.10 TOTE £9.90: £1.20 £2.70 £1.60 (£14.00) Trio £10.90 OWNER Mr B. Schmidt-Bodner (NEWMARKET) BRED Whitsbury Manor Stud

226
CLEMATIS H'CAP (0-80) (4-Y.O+) (Class D)
3-25 (3-26) **1m 2f (Equitrack)** £3,436.25 (£1,040.00: £507.50: £241.25) Stalls: Low GOING minus 0.39 sec per fur (FST)

				SP	RR	SF
131[3]	**Sweet Supposin (IRE) (60)** (CADwyer) **6-8-10v** LDettori(9) (b: lw: hld up: rdn to ld ins fnl f: r.o wl)	—	**1**	11/2	68	30
	Renown (72) (LordHuntingdon) **5-9-8** DHarrison(6) (hld up: led 2f out tl ins fnl f: unable qckn)	1	**2**	9/2[2]	78	40
*131**	**Quiet Arch (IRE) (65)** (WRMuir) **4-8-9**(5) JBramhill(1) (hld up: rdn over 1f out: r.o one pce)	2½	**3**	3/1[1]	67	28
*9**	**Tawafek (USA) (65)** (SDow) **4-9-0** RPerham(4) (hld up: rdn over 3f out: one pce fnl 2f)	s.h	**4**	13/2	67	28
179[4]	**Law Dancer (IRE) (75)** (TGMills) **4-9-10** TWilliams(7) (stdy hdwy over 5f out: ev ch wl over 1f out: wknd fnl f)	5	**5**	25/1	69	30
187[2]	**Always Happy (70)** (MissGayKelleway) **4-9-5** DHolland(8) (b: b.hind: prom over 7f)	1¾	**6**	9/2[2]	62	23
*108**	**Dances With Hooves (72)** (DJSffrenchDavis) **5-9-8** DRMcCabe(5) (led over 7f out to 2f out: wknd over 1f out)	8	**7**	5/1[3]	51	13
	Rival Bid (USA) (60) (MrsNMacauley) **9-8-7**(3) CTeague(3) (b: s.s: a bhd)	14	**8**	14/1	16	—
	Paronomasia (47) (JLHarris) **5-7-11**ow1 LCharnock(2) (b: b.hind: led over 2f: wknd over 4f out)	2	**9**	66/1	—	—

(SP 118.8%) **9 Rn**

2m 8.49 (4.19) CSF £28.59 CT £81.23 TOTE £5.20: £1.90 £1.20 £2.10 (£14.00) Trio £17.90 OWNER Mr G. Middlemiss (NEWMARKET) BRED Ballylinch Stud Ltd
LONG HANDICAP Paronomasia 6-11
WEIGHT FOR AGE 4yo-1lb

227 FORSYTHIA CONDITIONS STKS (3-Y.O) (Class D)
3-55 (3-56) **1m (Equitrack)** £3,273.75 (£990.00: £482.50: £228.75) Stalls: High GOING minus 0.39 sec per fur (FST)

				SP	RR	SF
	Hayes Way (IRE) (TGMills) **3-9-2** WRyan(5) (lw: plld hrd: hld up: chsd ldr over 3f out: rdn over 1f out: led ins fnl f: edgd lft: drvn out)	—	1	2/1[2]	93	36
138[2]	**Millroy (USA) (90)** (PAKelleway) **3-9-2v** MWigham(4) (led 1f: led over 3f out: rdn over 2f out: hdd ins fnl f: r.o)	½	2	7/4[1]	92	35
	Supreme Maimoon (70) (MJPolglase) **3-8-11** TGMcLaughlin(2) (hld up: rdn over 2f out: unable qckn)	4	3	6/1[3]	79	22
132*	**Countless Times (75)** (WRMuir) **3-9-0** AClark(3) (plld hrd: bhd fnl 5f)	9	4	6/1[3]	64	7
	Bonnie Lassie (79) (CWThornton) **3-8-6** DeanMcKeown(1) (led 7f out tl over 3f out: sn wknd)	3	5	6/1[3]	50	—

(SP 112.6%) **5 Rn**

1m 40.57 (3.17) CSF £5.54 TOTE £2.50: £1.10 £1.10 (£1.90) OWNER Mr Alan Ward (EPSOM) BRED L. K. McCreery

228 BUDDLEIA MAIDEN STKS (3-Y.O+) (Class D)
4-25 (4-25) **1m 4f (Equitrack)** £3,257.50 (£985.00: £480.00: £227.50) Stalls: Low GOING minus 0.39 sec per fur (FST)

				SP	RR	SF
	Illuminate (67) (DCO'Brien) **4-9-10** GBardwell(4) (lw: hld up: chsd ldr 7f out: rdn over 4f out: led 3f out: r.o)	—	1	7/1[3]	70	31
188[5]	**Nakhal (53)** (DJGMurraySmith) **4-9-10** DHolland(2) (hld up: chsd wnr over 2f out: unable qckn)	4	2	6/5[2]	65	26
191[2]	**Love Me Do (USA) (67)** (MJohnston) **3-8-3** JFanning(5) (lw: chsd ldr: led 8f out to 3f out: rdn: one pce)	1½	3	Evens[1]	63	3
26[11]	**Foxford Lad (42)** (TMJones) **3-8-3** NCarlisle(1) (plld hrd: bhd fnl 7f)	13	4	50/1	45	—
49[9]	**Just Rachel** (SEKettlewell) **3-7-12** LCharnock(3) (b.hind: led 4f: t.o fnl 5f)	dist	5	25/1	—	—

(SP 113.8%) **5 Rn**

2m 36.9 (6.90) CSF £15.14 TOTE £7.10: £2.40 £1.50 (£4.60) OWNER Mr D. C. O'Brien (TONBRIDGE)
WEIGHT FOR AGE 3yo-24lb, 4yo-3lb
IN-FOCUS: **This was an extremely bad maiden which featured just plodders.**

T/Plpt: £31.60 (270.69 Tckts). T/Qdpt: £7.30 (94.37 Tckts) AK

SAINT-MORITZ (Switzerland) (R-H) (Snow)
Sunday February 2nd

229a CHRISTOFFEL BAU TROPHY (4-Y.O+)
1m 1f £5,053.00 (£2,021.00: £1,516.00)

			SP	RR	SF
Sentosa Star (IRE) (MHourigan,Ireland) **6-9-13** PGHourigan	—	1		100	—
Shturm (RUS) (MWeiss,Switzerland) **4-9-10** RKaderli	2	2		93	—
Celestial Key (USA) (MJohnston) **7-9-2** DHolland	½	3		85	—

15 Rn

1m 59.7 6.40SF: 2.80SF 1.90SF 1.70SF (50.90SF) OWNER Peter Piller (PATRICKSWELL)
Celestial Key (USA) put up a brave performance and tried to make every post a winning one. Unfortunately he was unable to do so, and was collared approaching the final furlong, losing second close home. He will have another race at this track next weekend.

0203-SOUTHWELL (L-H) (Standard)
Friday February 7th
WEATHER: fine & sunny WIND: mod half bhd

230 FLYING DRAGON MAIDEN STKS (3-Y.O+) (Class D)
2-15 (2-17) **7f (Fibresand)** £3,969.20 (£1,202.60: £587.80: £280.40) Stalls: Low GOING: 0.25 sec per fur (SLW)

				SP	RR	SF
	Knotty Hill (73) (RCraggs) **5-9-10** DHolland(4) (lw: mde all: qcknd clr 3f out: easily)	—	1	6/4[1]	85+	65
	Amico (66) (CWThornton) **3-8-7** DeanMcKeown(10) (sn in tch: drvn along & outpcd 3f out: styd on fnl f: no ch w wnr)	10	2	15/2[3]	62	25
154[2]	**Sliema Creek (72)** (TDBarron) **3-8-7** DHarrison(9) (a.p: drvn along over 2f out: kpt on one pce)	¾	3	2/1[2]	60	23
	Only Josh (IRE) (MrsJRRamsden) **3-8-7** MDeering(11) (leggy: unf: hdwy ½-wy: sn chsng ldrs: kpt on same pce fnl 2f)	hd	4	12/1	60	23
144[5]	**Lahik (IRE) (30)** (KTIvory) **4-9-5**(5) DSweeney(2) (hld up & bhd: sme hdwy 2f out: nvr nr ldrs)	9	5	20/1	40	20
164[9]	**Lost In The Post (IRE)** (CWThornton) **4-9-10** SDrowne(6) (sn outpcd & bhd: kpt on fnl 2f: n.d)	s.h	6	25/1	40	20
154[5]	**Kingdom Pearl** (MJCamacho) **3-8-2** LCharnock(1) (bit bkwd: chsd ldrs tl wknd over 2f out)	2½	7	9/1	29	—
	Barwell Boy (JLHarris) **3-8-2**(5) JBramhill(5) (cmpt: unruly s: chsd ldrs tl wknd over 2f out)	3	8	25/1	27	—
90[9]	**Patrick** (DBurchell) **3-8-7** NCarlisle(7) (chsd ldrs tl wknd over 2f out)	4	9	33/1	18	—
164[8]	**Needwood Nutkin** (BCMorgan) **4-9-5** GCarter(3) (s.i.s: a wl bhd)	2	10	25/1	8	—
215[6]	**Missed May** (BPJBaugh) **3-8-2** FNorton(8) (a bhd)	4	11	20/1	—	—
35[7]	**Justfortherecord (41)** (BRMillman) **5-9-5** SSanders(12) (racd wd: chsd ldrs tl lost pl over 4f out: sn wl bhd: t.o)	dist	12	33/1	—	—

(SP 129.7%) **12 Rn**

1m 31.9 (5.40) CSF £12.67 TOTE £2.60: £1.10 £3.30 £1.10 (£9.80) Trio £6.50 OWNER Knotty Hill Golf Centre (SEDGEFIELD) BRED R. and Mrs Parker
WEIGHT FOR AGE 3yo-17lb

231 SEA GOAT CLAIMING STKS (4-Y.O+) (Class F)
2-45 (2-46) **1m 4f (Fibresand)** £2,294.00 (£644.00: £314.00) Stalls: Low GOING: 0.25 sec per fur (SLW)

				SP	RR	SF
99[4]	**Greenspan (IRE) (70)** (WRMuir) **5-9-8** AClark(6) (lw: trckd ldrs: led 2f out: pushed clr: readily)	—	1	7/2[2]	77+	37
139[6]	**Shuttlecock (36)** (MrsNMacauley) **6-8-7**(3) CTeague(1) (sn drvn along: led to 3f out: kpt on wl u.p: no ch w wnr)	3½	2	33/1	60	20
205*	**El Nido (58)** (DWChapman) **9-8-12** LCharnock(8) (sn trckng ldrs: drvn along 5f out: kpt on one pce fnl 2f)	2	3	5/1	60	20

				SP	RR	SF
114[2]	**Forzair (58)** (JJO'Neill) **5-9-4** WRyan(7) (trckd ldrs: effrt & outpcd over 2f out: kpt on one pce)	2	**4**	6/1	63	23
195[2]	**Sarawat (67)** (DNicholls) **9-9-0** AlexGreaves(2) (lw: trckd ldrs: chal 3f out: rdn & lost pl 2f out)	9	**5d**	6/4[1]	47	7
66[8]	**Ihtimaam (FR) (62)** (MrsASwinbank) **5-9-0** DHolland(3) (w ldrs: led 3f out to 2f out: hung lft & sn wknd)	5	**6**	4/1[3]	40	—
157[5]	**Stevie's Wonder (IRE) (42)** (BJLlewellyn) **7-8-2**(5) JBramhill(5) (sn outpcd & drvn along: a bhd)	16	**7**	20/1	12	—
	Past Master (USA) (SGollings) **9-9-0e** DHarrison(4) (sn bhd: t.o 4f out)	27	**8**	11/1	—	—
				(SP 129.2%)	**8 Rn**	

2m 46.6 (13.60) CSF £102.56 TOTE £4.90: £1.90 £3.30 £2.60 (£117.70) OWNER Camelot Racing (LAMBOURN) BRED Dermot and Meta Cantillon

OFFICIAL EXPLANATION **Sarawat: lost his action in the straight and was eased when beaten. Ihtimaam (FR): felt flat and seemed lifeless.**

SUBSEQUENT STEWARDS' ENQUIRY: Sarawat disq. (prohibited substance (procaine) in urine). Nicholls fined £450.

232 MILKY WAY H'CAP (0-65) (4-Y.O+) (Class F)

3-15 (3-16) **2m (Fibresand)** £2,294.00 (£644.00: £314.00) Stalls: Low GOING: 0.25 sec per fur (SLW)

				SP	RR	SF
205[2]	**Golden Hadeer (65)** (MJRyan) **6-10-0** AClark(3) (mde all: clr 7f out: drvn out fnl f: unchal)	—	**1**	5/4[1]	83	16
167[2]	**Master Foodbroker (IRE) (47)** (WJMusson) **9-8-10b** DRMcCabe(2) (b: dwlt s: racd wd: wl bhd: gd hdwy 6f out: wnt 2nd over 4f out: kpt on fnl f: no imp)	2	**2**	4/1[2]	63	—
68[6]	**Gunmaker (39)** (BJLlewellyn) **8-8-2** TWilliams(8) (in tch: hdwy 6f out: one pce fnl 4f)	29	**3**	12/1	26	—
205[5]	**Sudden Spin (65)** (JNorton) **7-10-0** 4x GCarter(5) (chsd ldrs: pushed along 6f out: wknd over 4f out)	8	**4**	15/2	44	—
147[4]	**Nawaji (USA) (45)** (WRMuir) **4-7-11**(5) JBramhill(9) (hld up: effrt u.p ½-wy: wknd over 5f out)	dist	**5**	11/2[3]	—	—
122[5]	**Acerbus Dulcis (33)** (MCChapman) **6-7-10** GBardwell(7) (chsd ldrs: drvn along ½-wy: lost pl 5f out)	dist	**6**	16/1	—	—
	Ship's Dancer (39) (DonEnricoIncisa) **4-7-10** KimTinkler(10) (sn bhd & pushed along: t.o 3f out)	2	**7**	33/1	—	—
5[8]	**Elite Bliss (IRE) (42)** (MJCamacho) **5-8-5** LCharnock(1) (b: s.i.s: sn trckng ldrs: drvn along 10f out: lost pl 6f out: t.o 3f out)	6	**8**	9/1	—	—
205[10]	**Hard Love (51)** (JLEyre) **5-9-0** RLappin(4) (in tch: pushed along 10f out: sn bhd: t.o 5f out)	27	**9**	16/1	—	—
				(SP 124.0%)	**9 Rn**	

3m 50.1 (24.10) CSF £6.33 CT £41.00 TOTE £2.50: £1.40 £1.30 £3.60 (£3.10) Trio £24.30 OWNER Four Jays Racing Partnership (NEWMARKET) BRED Stetchworth Park Stud Ltd

LONG HANDICAP Sudden Spin 10-0 Ship's Dancer 7-9 Acerbus Dulcis 7-9

WEIGHT FOR AGE 4yo-6lb

233 NORTH STAR H'CAP (0-70) (3-Y.O+) (Class E)

3-45 (3-48) **6f (Fibresand)** £3,047.00 (£923.00: £451.00: £215.00) Stalls: Low GOING: 0.25 sec per fur (SLW)

				SP	RR	SF
152*	**Mansab (USA) (66)** (PGMurphy) **4-9-11** SDrowne(10) (lw: trckd ldrs gng wl: led on bit over 1f out: shkn up & pulled clr: readily)	—	**1**	5/4[1]	83+	65
137[5]	**Bold Frontier (62)** (KTIvory) **5-9-7b** CScally(11) (b: b.hind: racd wd: in tch: hdwy over 2f out: kpt on wl: no ch w wnr)	1¾	**2**	8/1[2]	74	56
89[9]	**Shadow Jury (66)** (DWChapman) **7-9-11b** LCharnock(9) (w ldrs: nt qckn fnl 2f)	5	**3**	14/1	65	47
113[8]	**Craigie Boy (38)** (NBycroft) **7-7-6b**(5) JBramhill(7) (w ldrs: one pce fnl 2f)	nk	**4**	14/1	36	18
166[4]	**Paint It Black (52)** (DNicholls) **4-8-4**(7) IonaWands(8) (bhd: hdwy over 2f out: nvr nr ldrs)	2½	**5**	10/1[3]	44	26
111[11]	**Sweet Mate (49)** (SRBowring) **5-8-8** SDWilliams(6) (b.hind: s.i.s: bhd tl styd on fnl 2f)	¾	**6**	10/1[3]	39	21
127[4]	**Captain Carat (61)** (DNicholls) **6-9-6** AlexGreaves(2) (in tch: effrt over 2f out: no imp)	2½	**7**	8/1[2]	44	26
	Delrob (51) (DHaydnJones) **6-8-10** CRutter(12) (racd wd: bhd tl sme hdwy fnl 2f)	½	**8**	14/1	33	15
209[7]	**Orange And Blue (39)** (MissJFCraze) **4-7-9c**(3) NVarley(1) (mde most tl over 1f out: sn wknd)	nk	**9**	25/1	20	2
192[5]	**Bold Aristocrat (IRE) (62)** (RHollinshead) **6-9-0**(7) DHayden(4) (s.i.s: a in rr)	½	**10**	12/1	41	23
208[5]	**Tutu Sixtysix (37)** (DonEnricoIncisa) **6-7-10** KimTinkler(5) (a bhd)	2	**11**	50/1	11	—
136[6]	**Little Ibnr (69)** (PDEvans) **6-9-7**(7) AnthonyBond(3) (chsd ldrs tl lost pl 2f out)	nk	**12**	12/1	42	24
	Great Chief (55) (BobJones) **4-9-0** MWigham(13) (b.hind: s.i.s: a bhd)	11	**13**	11/1	—	—
				(SP 134.4%)	**13 Rn**	

1m 18.2 (4.70) CSF £12.45 CT £108.46 TOTE £2.40: £1.80 £4.00 £6.00 (£19.60) Trio £252.40; £124.45 to Newbury 8/2/97 OWNER Mrs Louise Murphy (BRISTOL) BRED Jonabell, J Bell, B Williams, J Nicholson and J Be

LONG HANDICAP Tutu Sixtysix 6-11

234 PEACOCK (S) STKS (3-Y.O) (Class F)

4-15 (4-17) **7f (Fibresand)** £2,294.00 (£644.00: £314.00) Stalls: Low GOING: 0.25 sec per fur (SLW)

				SP	RR	SF
168[2]	**Bailieborough Boy (IRE) (55)** (TDBarron) **3-8-11b[1]** DeanMcKeown(3) (trckd ldrs: shkn up to ld 2f out: hung lft: drvn clr ins fnl f)	—	**1**	6/4[1]	63	8
	Warp Drive (IRE) (WRMuir) **3-8-11** AClark(6) (a chsng ldrs: kpt on same pce fnl 2f)	5	**2**	8/1	52	—
168[3]	**Jack Says (59)** (DShaw) **3-8-8b**(3) CTeague(5) (trckd ldrs: led 3f to 2f out: one pce)	¾	**3**	7/4[2]	50	—
168*	**Mirror Four Sport (48)** (MJohnston) **3-8-5**(7) NPollard(4) (lw: led to 3f out: one pce)	½	**4**	7/1	50	—
	Merryhill Mariner (40) (JLHarris) **3-8-11** SSanders(1) (uns rdr gng to s: sn chsng ldrs: lost pl over 3f out: sn bhd)	18	**5**	20/1	8	—
156[3]	**Belushi** (DMorley) **3-8-6** GCarter(2) (chsd ldrs: drvn along over 3f out: sn lost pl & bhd)	23	**6**	6/1[3]	—	—
				(SP 119.0%)	**6 Rn**	

1m 36.0 (9.50) CSF £13.94 TOTE £2.40: £1.10 £6.60 (£7.00) OWNER M P Burke Developments Ltd (THIRSK) BRED John Purfield

Bt in 4,000 gns

235 GREAT BEAR H'CAP (0-65) (3-Y.O+) (Class F)

4-45 (4-46) **1m (Fibresand)** £2,294.00 (£644.00: £314.00) Stalls: Low GOING: 0.25 sec per fur (SLW)

				SP	RR	SF
84[5]	**Mutahadeth (58)** (DShaw) **3-8-7** JFanning(13) (s.i.s: racd wd: hld up: stdy hdwy 2f out: qcknd clr nr fin: cleverly)	—	**1**	7/1[3]	66+	13
192[3]	**Sandmoor Denim (47)** (SRBowring) **10-8-10**(5) ADaly(4) (b: mid div: hdwy 2f out: styd on to ld ins fn f: hdd nr fin)	½	**2**	4/1[1]	54	20
177[5]	**Ring the Chief (32)** (MDIUsher) **5-8-0** NCarlisle(3) (trckd ldrs: led over 1f out tl ins fnl f)	1¾	**3**	10/1	36	2
203[10]	**Napoleon Star (IRE) (46)** (SRBowring) **6-9-0** SDWilliams(8) (w ldrs: drvn along & outpcd ½-wy: styd on same pce fnl 2f)	¾	**4**	16/1	48	14

Form	Horse	Dist	Pos	SP	RR	SF
169^{2}	**Queens Stroller (IRE) (32)** (REPeacock) **6-7-9**(5) JBramhill(6) (a chsng ldrs: rdn over 2f out: one pce)	½	5	$5/1^{2}$	33	—
150^{7}	**Quinzii Martin (50)** (DHaydnJones) **9-9-4b** CRutter(12) (a in tch: hdwy & ev ch 2f out: grad wknd)	4	6	$7/1^{3}$	43	9
209^{2}	**Pleasure Trick (USA) (48)** (DonEnricoIncisa) **6-9-2b** KimTinkler(15) (w ldrs: led over 4f out to 3f out: wknd over 1f out)	2	7	$5/1^{2}$	37	3
169^{8}	**Image Maker (IRE) (42)** (PDEvans) **4-8-10v**¹ SSanders(5) (mid div: hdwy u.p 2f out: wknd ins fnl f: eased)	¾	8	14/1	30	—
153^{7}	**Gilling Dancer (IRE) (53)** (PCalver) **4-9-7** ACulhane(14) (led tl over 4f out: led 3f out tl over 1f out: sn wknd: eased nr fin)	hd	9	14/1	40	6
206^{5}	**Oneoftheoldones (56)** (JNorton) **5-9-10** GCarter(9) (bhd: sme hdwy 2f out: n.d)	5	10	14/1	33	—
63^{10}	**City Run (USA) (28)** (DJSCosgrove) **5-7-10** FNorton(7) (sn bhd)	3	11	16/1	—	—
	Father Eddie (62) (JJO'Neill) **3-8-11** WRyan(11) (bit bkwd: racd wd: sn bhd)	4	12	12/1	25	—
	Alpheton Prince (40) (JohnHarris) **4-8-8** DeanMcKeown(10) (racd wd: a bhd)	7	13	25/1	—	—
	Reverse Charge (39) (DNicholls) **5-8-0**(7) IonaWands(1) (a bhd)	2½	14	25/1	—	—
	Sweet Ciseaux (IRE) (55) (BJLlewellyn) **4-9-9** AClark(2) (bit bkwd: in tch: drvn along ½-wy: sn lost pl: t.o)	28	15	16/1	—	—

(SP 140.5%) **15 Rn**

1m 48.9 (9.90) CSF £37.17 CT £281.56 TOTE £8.00: £2.50 £2.40 £2.80 (£19.30) Trio £96.50 OWNER Mr J. C. Fretwell (NEWARK) BRED Cheveley Park Stud Ltd
LONG HANDICAP City Run (USA) 7-2
WEIGHT FOR AGE 3yo-19lb

T/Plpt: £13.60 (659.34 Tckts). T/Qdpt: £6.20 (95.89 Tckts) WG

0223-LINGFIELD (L-H) (Standard)
Saturday February 8th
WEATHER: gloomy WIND: almost nil

236 AGATHA CHRISTIE (S) H'CAP (0-60) (4-Y.O+) (Class G)
2-15 (2-16) **1m 5f (Equitrack)** £2,145.50 (£603.00: £294.50) Stalls: Low GOING minus 0.40 sec per fur (FST)

Form	Horse	Dist	Pos	SP	RR	SF
129^{4}	**English Invader (48)** (RAkehurst) **6-9-7** SSanders(1) (lw: hdwy 7f out: led over 3f out: clr over 2f out: rdn out)	—	1	$4/1^{2}$	56	31
104^{8}	**Colosse (51)** (JLEyre) **5-9-3**(7) RFfrench(4) (lost pl 9f out: rallied 4f out: chsd wnr over 1f out: r.o)	3½	2	$5/1^{3}$	55	30
183^{5}	**Sharp Thrill (30)** (BSmart) **6-7-12b**(5) ADaly(7) (hdwy 7f out: chsd wnr over 3f out tl over 1f out: unable qckn)	3½	3	13/2	29	4
183^{12}	**Oozlem (IRE) (39)** (LMontagueHall) **8-8-7v**(5) MartinDwyer(9) (hdwy 10f out: rdn 7f out: one pce fnl 3f)	3½	4	7/1	34	9
183^{7}	**Ela Man Howa (44)** (ABailey) **6-9-3** LDettori(3) (b: led over 6f: led over 4f out tl over 3f out: sn wknd)	17	5	$11/4^{1}$	18	—
125^{11}	**Blue Jumbo (IRE) (40)** (WJMusson) **4-8-6**(3) MBaird(5) (lw: a bhd)	7	6	$5/1^{3}$	6	—
	Komodo (USA) (33) (JELong) **5-8-6** LeesaLong(8) (b: plld hrd: hdwy 10f out: wknd over 3f out)	2½	7	50/1	—	—
	Royal Legend (53) (JPearce) **5-9-12** MWigham(6) (b: plld hrd: a.p: led over 6f out tl over 4f out: wknd over 3f out)	5	8	9/1	9	—
	Prince Zizim (37) (RCSpicer) **4-8-1**(5) JBramhill(2) (bhd fnl 7f: t.o)	dist	9	25/1	—	—

(SP 121.6%) **9 Rn**

2m 48.89 (6.89) CSF £23.54 CT £119.46 TOTE £4.00: £2.40 £2.50 £3.60 (£16.80) Trio £46.80 OWNER Mr Michael Blackburn (EPSOM) BRED Bloodstock Management Int Pty Ltd
WEIGHT FOR AGE 4yo-4lb
Sold J Purcell 4,200 gns

237 GEORGETTE HEYER CLAIMING STKS (3-Y.O) (Class F)
2-45 (2-45) **7f (Equitrack)** £2,383.60 (£669.60: £326.80) Stalls: Low GOING minus 0.40 sec per fur (FST)

Form	Horse	Dist	Pos	SP	RR	SF
217^{5}	**Enchanting Eve (65)** (CNAllen) **3-8-6**(5) MartinDwyer(4) (lw: w ldr: led over 1f out: rdn out)	—	1	$2/1^{2}$	73	25
212*	**Eager To Please (69)** (MissGayKelleway) **3-8-12b** DHolland(1) (lw: b: b.hind: led over 5f: rdn: r.o)	½	2	$15/8^{1}$	73	25
96^{5}	**Misty Cay (IRE) (64)** (SDow) **3-7-12**(5) ADaly(3) (wl bhd 5f: hdwy fnl f: r.o)	3½	3	$9/4^{3}$	56	8
	Red Embers (75) (RCSpicer) **3-8-3**(5) JBramhill(2) (bhd fnl 4f: t.o)	dist	4	9/1	—	—

(SP 108.9%) **4 Rn**

1m 27.6 (3.20) CSF £5.57 TOTE £4.10 (£5.60) OWNER Newmarket Connections (NEWMARKET) BRED P. Young
OFFICIAL EXPLANATION **Enchanting Eve: had been unsuited by being held up last time.**

238 EVELYN ANTHONY H'CAP (0-85) (3-Y.O+) (Class D)
3-15 (3-15) **1m (Equitrack)** £3,290.00 (£995.00: £485.00: £230.00) Stalls: High GOING minus 0.40 sec per fur (FST)

Form	Horse	Dist	Pos	SP	RR	SF
	Present Situation (67) (LordHuntingdon) **6-8-10** LDettori(1) (hld up: rdn 2f out: led ins fnl f: r.o wl)	—	1	$11/4^{2}$	76	46
211^{2}	**Robellion (68)** (DWPArbuthnot) **6-8-11v** DHarrison(2) (b.hind: hdwy over 3f out: ev ch ins fnl f: unable qckn)	1¼	2	$4/1^{3}$	75	45
201*	**Mr Nevermind (IRE) (85)** (GLMoore) **7-10-0** SWhitworth(5) (hld up: led over 2f out tl ins fnl f: one pce)	2	3	5/1	88	58
	La Modiste (73) (SDow) **4-9-2** WRyan(7) (bit bkwd: hdwy over 3f out: wknd over 2f out)	4	4	25/1	68	38
197^{2}	**Our Shadee (USA) (53)** (KTIvory) **7-7-5v**(5) JBramhill(3) (b: b.hind: prom 6f)	¾	5	9/1	46	16
121*	**Blue Flyer (IRE) (81)** (RIngram) **4-9-10b** DHolland(4) (a.p: led over 3f out tl over 2f out: wknd fnl f)	hd	6	$5/2^{1}$	74	44
52^{5}	**Queen of All Birds (IRE) (82)** (RBoss) **6-9-6**(5) ADaly(6) (b: led over 4f: wkng whn n.m.r on ins over 2f out)	1¾	7	7/1	71	41

(SP 118.3%) **7 Rn**

1m 38.92 (1.52) CSF £13.65 TOTE £3.10: £1.40 £2.50 (£11.10) OWNER Mr Chris van Hoorn (WEST ILSLEY) BRED The Queen
LONG HANDICAP Our Shadee (USA) 7-5

239 HELEN MCINNES MEDIAN AUCTION MAIDEN STKS (3-Y.O) (Class E)
3-45 (3-46) **1m 2f (Equitrack)** £2,700.25 (£817.00: £398.50: £189.25) Stalls: Low GOING minus 0.40 sec per fur (FST)

Form	Horse	Dist	Pos	SP	RR	SF
	Belle Bijou (MJohnston) **3-8-9** LDettori(3) (hld up: chsd ldr over 3f out: led over 2f out to 1f out: ev ch whn carried rt fnl f: r.o wl: fin 2nd, s.h: awrdd r)	—	1	$7/4^{2}$	67	18

				SP	RR	SF
26^{2}	**Mogul (75)** (NAGraham) **3-9-0** DHolland(4) (chsd ldr: led over 4f out tl over 2f out: led 1f out: edgd rt: all out: fin 1st: disq: plcd 2nd)		**2**	$8/11^{1}$	72	23
	Sixties Melody (RBoss) **3-9-0** MTebbutt(6) (bit bkwd: dwlt: hdwy over 4f out: wknd over 3f out)	24	**3**	$12/1^{3}$	34	—
26^{6}	**Alimerjam (49)** (JWhite) **3-8-4b**(5) PPMurphy(1) (lt-f: led over 5f)	1¾	**4**	25/1	26	—
	Katherine (JRinger) **3-8-9** SDrowne(5) (b: lw: bhd fnl 4f)	10	**5**	25/1	10	—
	Mambo Music (FR) (DJSCosgrove) **3-8-9** MRimmer(2) (dwlt: bhd fnl 5f)	½	**6**	$12/1^{3}$	9	—

(SP 117.3%) **6 Rn**

2m 9.7 (5.40) CSF £3.24 TOTE £2.50: £1.10 £1.10 (£1.60) OWNER J S Morrison and J W Armstrong (MIDDLEHAM) BRED Whitsbury Manor Stud

240 MARGERY ALLINGHAM H'CAP (0-65) (3-Y.O) (Class F)

4-15 (4-15) **1m 2f (Equitrack)** £2,383.60 (£669.60: £326.80) Stalls: Low GOING minus 0.40 sec per fur (FST)

				SP	RR	SF
96^{6}	**Kingsdown Trix (IRE) (54)** (GLMoore) **3-8-13** RPerham(2) (rdn over 3f out: outpcd 2f out: str run fnl f: led last stride)	—	**1**	7/1	61	11
174^{4}	**Mendoza (56)** (DJGMurraySmith) **3-8-10**(5) JBramhill(3) (chsd ldr: led over 2f out: clr over 1f out: hdd last stride)	s.h	**2**	$5/1^{3}$	63	13
124^{2}	**Aspecto Lad (IRE) (62)** (MJohnston) **3-9-7** LDettori(4) (lw: led over 7f: rdn: r.o wl ins fnl f)	½	**3**	$4/6^{1}$	68	18
90^{3}	**Diamond Eyre (54)** (JLEyre) **3-8-13** RLappin(1) (hld up: rdn over 2f out: sn wknd)	7	**4**	$9/2^{2}$	49	—
130^{3}	**Taome (IRE) (43)** (PDEvans) **3-7-9**(7) RFfrench(5) (hld up: rdn over 2f out: sn wknd)	1	**5**	8/1	36	—

(SP 118.5%) **5 Rn**

2m 11.17 (6.87) CSF £37.78 TOTE £12.40: £4.10 £2.80 (£17.80) OWNER Mr David Allen (BRIGHTON) BRED Owen Bourke

OFFICIAL EXPLANATION **Mendoza: accounting for the horse's apparent improvement in form, his trainer explained that his previous run had probably come too soon after his win on 25th January.**

241 DOROTHY L SAYERS H'CAP (0-70) (4-Y.O+) (Class E)

4-45 (4-48) **7f (Equitrack)** £2,843.25 (£861.00: £420.50: £200.25) Stalls: Low GOING minus 0.40 sec per fur (FST)

				SP	RR	SF
203*	**Dawalib (USA) (56)** (DHaydnJones) **7-9-3** 6x AClark(12) (lw: a.p: led over 2f out: drvn out)	—	**1**	$9/2^{2}$	63	45
	Ertlon (67) (CEBrittain) **7-10-0** LDettori(11) (lw: hdwy over 3f out: chsd wnr over 1f out: r.o wl ins fnl f)	s.h	**2**	$5/1^{3}$	74	56
146^{5}	**Lancashire Legend (65)** (SDow) **4-9-7**(5) ADaly(7) (hld up: rdn 2f out: r.o one pce)	1¾	**3**	10/1	68	50
197^{9}	**Into Debt (37)** (JRPoulton) **4-7-5e**(7)ow2 AMcCarthy(5) (s.s: swtchd rt & racd wd: rdn & hdwy 2f out: r.o one pce)	3	**4**	20/1	33	13
3^{5}	**Deeply Vale (IRE) (67)** (PButler) **6-10-0** SWhitworth(4) (b.off fore: nt clr run over 3f out: hrd rdn over 1f out: gd hdwy fnl f: r.o wl)	¾	**5**	9/1	61	43
172^{2}	**Mellors (IRE) (65)** (MJHeaton-Ellis) **4-9-12** SDrowne(10) (a.p: led over 3f out tl over 2f out: wknd over 1f out)	½	**6**	8/1	58	40
134^{7}	**Statistician (52)** (JohnBerry) **5-8-13e** DHarrison(8) (nvr nr to chal)	½	**7**	10/1	44	26
203^{8}	**Cheerful Groom (IRE) (35)** (DShaw) **6-7-10** DWright(6) (nvr nrr)	hd	**8**	20/1	27	9
152^{10}	**Sound the Trumpet (IRE) (38)** (RCSpicer) **5-7-8**(5) JBramhill(3) (bhd fnl 3f)	2	**9**	33/1	25	7
171^{5}	**Sharp 'n Smart (66)** (BSmart) **5-9-8**(5) DGriffiths(9) (lw: prom over 4f)	1½	**10**	12/1	50	32
120^{8}	**Gold Lance (USA) (45)** (RJO'Sullivan) **4-8-6b**ow1 DHolland(2) (lw: led over 3f: wknd over 2f out)	1½	**11**	12/1	25	6
21^{5}	**Daryabad (IRE) (60)** (TJNaughton) **5-9-4b**(3) JDSmith(1) (chsd ldrs: rdn over 4f out: wknd 3f out)	19	**12**	$9/4^{1}$	—	—

(SP 132.8%) **12 Rn**

1m 26.32 (1.92) CSF £27.56 CT £211.98 TOTE £5.60: £2.60 £2.00 £2.50 (£16.70) Trio £42.60 OWNER Jack Brown (Bookmaker) Ltd (PONTYPRIDD) BRED Hilary J. Boone Jnr

LONG HANDICAP Cheerful Groom (IRE) 7-6 Into Debt 7-8

T/Plpt: £555.30 (13.54 Tckts). T/Qdpt: £52.90 (12.46 Tckts) AK

0230-SOUTHWELL (L-H) (Standard)

Monday February 10th

WEATHER: cloudy and windy WIND: str half bhd

242 NEVADA LIMITED STKS (0-60) (4-Y.O+) (Class F)

2-10 (2-16) **1m 4f (Fibresand)** £2,294.00 (£644.00: £314.00) Stalls: Low GOING: 0.40 sec per fur (SLW)

				SP	RR	SF
196^{4}	**Kalamata (50)** (JAGlover) **5-9-0** NDay(3) (lw: led tl hdd 4f out: styd on to ld appr fnl f)	—	**1**	$3/1^{2}$	65	39
	Dancing-Alone (35) (RJRWilliams) **5-8-9**(5) GFaulkner(6) (b: cl up: led 4f out to 1f out: no ex)	5	**2**	33/1	58	32
206^{2}	**Maftun (USA) (54)** (GMMoore) **5-9-0** ACulhane(5) (lw: chsd ldrs: chal 5f out: sn hrd drvn: wl outpcd fnl 3f)	8	**3**	$Evens^{1}$	48	22
231^{3}	**El Nido (58)** (DWChapman) **9-9-4** LCharnock(4) (chsd ldrs tl lost tch 6f out: n.d after)	¾	**4**	$3/1^{2}$	51	25
206^{4}	**Undawaterscubadiva (38)** (MPBielby) **5-9-2** DeanMcKeown(1) (lw: sn outpcd & bhd)	9	**5**	20/1	37	11
	Evan 'elp Us (57) (JLEyre) **5-9-0b** TWilliams(2) (sn drvn along & bhd)	dist	**6**	$14/1^{3}$	—	—

(SP 114.4%) **6 Rn**

2m 46.8 (13.80) CSF £66.54 TOTE £3.90: £1.60 £8.00 (£75.90) OWNER Mr B. H. Farr (WORKSOP) BRED Worksop Manor Stud Farm

243 SYRIAN DESERT CLAIMING STKS (4-Y.O+) (Class F)

2-40 (2-45) **7f (Fibresand)** £2,294.00 (£644.00: £314.00) Stalls: Low GOING: 0.40 sec per fur (SLW)

				SP	RR	SF
165^{3}	**Sea Devil (53)** (MJCamacho) **11-8-3** LCharnock(10) (lw: chsd ldrs: effrt over 2f out: styd on to ld ins fnl f)	—	**1**	8/1	61	35
192*	**Rambo Waltzer (73)** (DNicholls) **5-9-1** AlexGreaves(5) (disp ld: outpcd 2f out: kpt on fnl f)	1¾	**2**	$7/4^{1}$	69	43
87^{5}	**Dahiyah (USA) (55)** (BSmart) **6-8-7v** SSanders(8) (lw: disp ld tl led 2f out: hdd & wknd ins fnl f)	1½	**3**	15/2	58	32
	Bentico (73) (MrsNMacauley) **8-8-11v**(3) CTeague(13) (b: s.i.s: sn drvn along: styd on wl fnl 2f: nrst fin)	nk	**4**	$7/1^{3}$	64	38
220^{9}	**Northern Fan (IRE) (82)** (NTinkler) **5-8-9** DeanMcKeown(1) (shkn up after s: sn chsng ldrs: nt qckn fnl 2f)	2	**5**	9/1	54	28
166^{7}	**Desert Invader (IRE) (67)** (DWChapman) **6-8-10** ACulhane(4) (disp ld tl wknd fnl 2f)	1¼	**6**	$11/4^{2}$	53	27
203^{4}	**Spanish Stripper (USA) (38)** (MCChapman) **6-8-7** GBardwell(6) (in tch: sn pushed along: no imp fnl 3f)	nk	**7**	25/1	49	23
192^{7}	**So Natural (IRE) (45)** (WStorey) **5-7-3**(7) IonaWands(7) (prom 5f: grad wknd)	nk	**8**	20/1	37	11
235^{6}	**Quinzii Martin (50)** (DHaydnJones) **9-8-9b** SWhitworth(14) (lw: effrt ½-wy: no imp)	1¾	**9**	10/1	46	20
203^{11}	**Monis (IRE) (49)** (JBalding) **6-8-3v** SDrowne(12) (disp ld 4f: wknd)	4	**10**	20/1	31	5

192^{9}	**Mu-Arrik (25)** (GROldroyd) **9-8-3v** MMcAndrew(9) (s.i.s: n.d)	1¾	**11**	50/1	27	1
	Airborne Harris (IRE) (ABailey) **4-8-9** DWright(3) (sn outpcd & wl bhd)	19	**12**	33/1	—	—
	Natal Ridge (55) (DHaydnJones) **4-8-5** AClark(2) (hld up & a bhd)	1¼	**13**	25/1	—	—
122^{6}	**Bold Joker (21)** (GROldroyd) **6-8-5b¹** TWilliams(11) (Withdrawn not under Starter's orders: veterinary advice)		**W**	50/1	—	—

(SP 141.6%) **13 Rn**

1m 33.9 (7.40) CSF £22.33 TOTE £10.90: £3.50 £1.50 £2.60 (£8.80) Trio £12.50 OWNER Mr A. N. Goacher (MALTON) BRED A. L. Goacher and E. G. Noble

244 KALAHARI H'CAP (0-85) (4-Y.O+) (Class D)

3-10 (3-10) **1m 3f (Fibresand)** £3,688.40 (£1,116.20: £544.60: £258.80) Stalls: Low GOING: 0.40 sec per fur (SLW)

				SP	RR	SF
82^{9}	**Super High (83)** (PHowling) **5-10-0b** FNorton(2) (lw: mde all: jst hld on)	—	**1**	7/1	87	51
115^{*}	**China Castle (85)** (PCHaslam) **4-9-9**(5) MartinDwyer(1) (lw: hdwy ½-wy: rdn over 2f out: chal over 1f out: styd on wl towards fin)	s.h	**2**	$4/5^{1}$	89	51
182^{5}	**Dancing Cavalier (67)** (RHollinshead) **4-8-5**(5) DGriffiths(5) (bhd: hdwy ½-wy: prom over 2f out: sn rdn & no imp)	17	**3**	$6/1^{3}$	46	8
72^{6}	**Perpetual Light (65)** (JJQuinn) **4-8-8** DHolland(6) (lw: hdwy ½-wy: chsng ldrs 3f out: sn btn)	8	**4**	$5/1^{2}$	33	—
205^{6}	**Sea God (51)** (MCChapman) **6-7-3**(7) IonaWands(4) (chsd ldrs tl rdn & wknd 3f out)	4	**5**	15/2	13	—
	Dont Shoot Fairies (70) (JPearce) **5-9-1** MWigham(3) (cl up tl outpcd 6f out: sn wknd)	6	**6**	$6/1^{3}$	23	—

(SP 125.1%) **6 Rn**

2m 32.8 (12.80) CSF £13.58 TOTE £13.50: £2.50 £1.40 (£6.60) OWNER Mr C. Hammond (NEWMARKET) BRED Nam Seng Yong
LONG HANDICAP Sea God 7-6
WEIGHT FOR AGE 4yo-2lb

245 JOHN SHILHAM 50TH BIRTHDAY H'CAP (0-70) (4-Y.O+ F & M) (Class E)

3-40 (3-40) **1m (Fibresand)** £2,924.15 (£885.20: £432.10: £205.55) Stalls: Low GOING: 0.40 sec per fur (SLW)

				SP	RR	SF
194^{5}	**Three Arch Bridge (66)** (MJohnston) **5-10-0b** DeanMcKeown(6) (lw: sn cl up: led 4f out: kpt on wl fnl f)	—	**1**	$11/4^{1}$	75	48
125^{10}	**Broughton's Pride (IRE) (44)** (JLEyre) **6-8-6** TWilliams(2) (a chsng ldrs: ev ch over 1f out: nt qckn)	1¾	**2**	$4/1^{3}$	50	23
169^{6}	**Efipetite (37)** (NBycroft) **4-7-8v¹**(5) JBramhill(7) (a chsng ldrs: one pce fnl 3f)	8	**3**	8/1	27	—
74^{7}	**Bakers Daughter (52)** (JRArnold) **5-9-0** AClark(5) (chsd ldrs: effrt 3f out: r.o one pce)	1¼	**4**	6/1	39	12
206^{7}	**Down The Yard (38)** (MCChapman) **4-8-0** GBardwell(4) (bhd: effrt appr st: no imp)	1¼	**5**	12/1	23	—
209^{4}	**Fiaba (46)** (MrsNMacauley) **9-8-5v**(3)ow7 CTeague(1) (lw: prom early: outpcd & lost tch after 3f: c wd st: n.d after)	1¾	**6**	$100/30^{2}$	27	—
206^{9}	**Palacegate Jo (IRE) (34)** (DWChapman) **6-7-10b¹** DWright(3) (s.s: hdwy & in tch after 3f: wknd fnl 2f)	5	**7**	14/1	5	—
163^{7}	**Degree (58)** (SCWilliams) **4-9-6** JTate(8) (led 4f: wknd over 2f out)	9	**8**	7/1	11	—

(SP 122.0%) **8 Rn**

1m 48.5 (9.50) CSF £13.79 CT £74.39 TOTE £3.70: £1.70 £1.20 £2.00 (£5.20) OWNER Mr R. N. Pennell (MIDDLEHAM) BRED R. Taylor
LONG HANDICAP Palacegate Jo (IRE) 7-4

246 NUBIAN (S) STKS (3-Y.O F) (Class F)

4-10 (4-10) **1m (Fibresand)** £1,469.00 (£1,469.00: £314.00) Stalls: Low GOING: 0.40 sec per fur (SLW)

				SP	RR	SF
135^{5}	**Rose Burton** (TDBarron) **3-8-12** LCharnock(4) (trckd ldrs: effrt over 2f out: chal ins fnl f: kpt on to jn ldr line)	—	**1**	13/2	60	15
90^{6}	**Head Girl (IRE) (55)** (CWThornton) **3-9-4** DeanMcKeown(3) (lw: led: qcknd over 2f out: kpt on u.p & jnd on line)	—	**1**	$3/1^{3}$	66	21
154^{4}	**Rochea (61)** (WJHaggas) **3-8-12be** DHolland(2) (lw: trckd ldr: effrt over 2f out: put hd in air & nt run on)	2½	**3**	$10/11^{1}$	55	10
181^{5}	**Terry's Rose (48)** (RHollinshead) **3-8-12** MWigham(1) (hld up: effrt ½-wy: wl outpcd fnl 3f)	15	**4**	$5/2^{2}$	25	—

(SP 119.3%) **4 Rn**

1m 50.3 (11.30) CSF HG & RB £9.15 RB & HG £11.93 TOTE HG £2.30 RB £4.20 (£11.90) OWNER Mr R. M. West (THIRSK)/The Challengers (MIDDLEHAM) BRED R. M. West/Mrs Marian Maguire
No bid for either dead-heater

247 SAHARA H'CAP (0-65) (3-Y.O) (Class F)

4-40 (4-40) **6f (Fibresand)** £2,294.00 (£644.00: £314.00) Stalls: Low GOING: 0.40 sec per fur (SLW)

				SP	RR	SF
	V I P Charlie (60) (JRJenkins) **3-9-2** SSanders(5) (lw: trckd ldrs: led on bit 2f out: r.o wl: easily)	—	**1**	$7/4^{1}$	80+	42
225^{3}	**Pet Express (65)** (PCHaslam) **3-9-2**(5) MartinDwyer(3) (lw: disp ld tl led ½-wy: hdd 2f out: no ch w wnr)	11	**2**	$2/1^{2}$	56	18
124^{6}	**Windborn (49)** (CNAllen) **3-8-2**(3) PMcCabe(4) (outpcd tl styd on fnl 2f: n.d)	½	**3**	8/1	38	—
158^{2}	**Lunar Music (63)** (MartynMeade) **3-9-5** NAdams(1) (cl up tl outpcd ½-wy: sn btn)	9	**4**	$3/1^{3}$	28	—
181^{*}	**Chilling (60)** (NTinkler) **3-8-9**(7) KSked(2) (lw: sn disp ld: hdd ½-wy: wknd 2f out)	1½	**5**	6/1	21	—
204^{5}	**Impish (IRE) (40)** (TJEtherington) **3-7-5**(5) JBramhill(6) (prom over 3f: wknd)	3½	**6**	25/1	—	—
	Aquatic Queen (49) (RJWeaver) **3-8-0**(5) ADaly(7) (a outpcd & bhd)	1¾	**7**	25/1	—	—

(SP 127.8%) **7 Rn**

1m 20.2 (6.70) CSF £5.97 TOTE £2.90: £1.60 £1.80 (£6.50) OWNER Mr Andy Taylor (ROYSTON) BRED T. F. Parrett

T/Plpt: £222.00 (41.35 Tckts). T/Qdpt: £14.10 (49.18 Tckts) AA

0236-LINGFIELD (L-H) (Standard)
Tuesday February 11th
WEATHER: raining WIND: mod half bhd

248 HURST POINT LIMITED STKS (0-65) (4-Y.O+) (Class F)
1-50 (1-54) **1m (Equitrack)** £2,462.00 (£692.00: £338.00) Stalls: High GOING minus 0.29 sec per fur (FST)

Form	Horse / Details	Dist	Pos	SP	RR	SF
	Sweet Wilhelmina (63) (LordHuntingdon) **4-8-9** DHarrison(9) (a gng wl: stdy hdwy over 3f out: chsd ldr over 1f out: led ins fnl f: comf)	—	1	3/1^{1}	67+	44
194^{4}	**Le Sport (64)** (DNicholls) **4-8-5b**$^{(7)}$ IonaWands(7) (led: hrd rdn over 1f out: hdd ins fnl f: unable qckn)	1¼	2	5/1	68	45
216^{7}	**Father Dan (IRE) (61)** (MissGayKelleway) **8-9-1** DHolland(8) (b: b.hind: hld up: rdn over 3f out: r.o ins fnl f)	1½	3	11/1	68	45
211^{7}	**Spencer's Revenge (56)** (PButler) **8-8-12** GBardwell(5) (lw: lost pl over 3f out: rallied wl over 1f out: r.o ins fnl f)	nk	4	10/1	64	41
224^{2}	**Milos (62)** (GLMoore) **6-9-1** SWhitworth(1) (b: a.p: rdn over 4f out: chsd ldr over 3f out tl over 1f out: sn wknd)	2	5	100/30^{2}	63	40
143^{3}	**Whatever's Right (IRE) (63)** (MDIUsher) **8-8-12** SSanders(6) (rdn over 4f out: bhd fnl 3f)	4	6	7/2^{3}	52	29
59^{2}	**Ki Chi Saga (USA) (55)** (MMadgwick) **5-8-12** AClark(3) (hdwy 7f out: chsd ldr over 6f out tl over 3f out: sn wknd)	7	7	10/1	38	15
	Whitley Grange Boy (64) (JLEyre) **4-8-5**$^{(7)}$ SBuckley(4) (bhd fnl 5f)	10	8	33/1	18	—
111^{2}	**Chadleigh Lane (USA) (65)** (ABMulholland) **5-8-13**$^{(5)}$ DSweeney(2) (Withdrawn not under Starter's orders: ref to ent stalls)		W	14/1	—	—

(SP 123.1%) **8 Rn**

1m 39.88 (2.48) CSF £16.45 TOTE £4.20: £1.20 £2.40 £3.60 (£17.90) Trio £47.20 OWNER Mr Chris van Hoorn (WEST ILSLEY) BRED D. Walker

249 DUNGENESS POINT CLAIMING STKS (3-Y.O) (Class E)
2-20 (2-20) **1m 2f (Equitrack)** £2,700.25 (£817.00: £398.50: £189.25) Stalls: Low GOING minus 0.29 sec per fur (FST)

Form	Horse / Details	Dist	Pos	SP	RR	SF
162^{2}	**As-Is (65)** (MJohnston) **3-8-9** DHolland(3) (mde virtually all: hrd rdn over 1f out: edgd rt ins fnl f: r.o wl)	—	1	4/7^{1}	57	14
185^{4}	**Leg Beforum (IRE) (55)** (LMontagueHall) **3-8-9** WRyan(2) (s.s: hdwy to chse wnr 3f out: ev ch fnl 2f: carried rt ins fnl f: r.o)	½	2	9/2^{3}	56	13
174^{3}	**Chateauherault (IRE) (62)** (PCHaslam) **3-9-3v**^{1} SDrowne(4) (lw: w wnr 7f: wknd over 2f out)	3½	3	7/2^{2}	59	16
	Saxonbury (GLMoore) **3-9-3** SSanders(1) (bit bkwd: hld up: rdn over 4f out: wknd over 2f out)	5	4	8/1	51?	8

(SP 115.2%) **4 Rn**

2m 11.44 (7.14) CSF £3.64 TOTE £1.50 (£3.20) OWNER Mr Robinson (Wigan) (MIDDLEHAM) BRED Roldvale Ltd

250 BISHOPS ROCK CONDITIONS STKS (3-Y.O+) (Class D)
2-50 (2-51) **1m 2f (Equitrack)** £3,306.25 (£1,000.00: £487.50: £231.25) Stalls: Low GOING minus 0.29 sec per fur (FST)

Form	Horse / Details	Dist	Pos	SP	RR	SF
131^{2}	**Steamroller Stanly (87)** (CACyzer) **4-10-1** DBiggs(4) (hld up: led over 2f out: rdn out)	—	1	9/4^{1}	96	66
	Brilliant Red (95) (PRHedger) **4-9-7** MRichards(1) (a.p: led 5f out tl over 2f out: rdn: r.o ins fnl f)	¾	2	11/4^{2}	87	57
173^{*}	**Alarico (FR) (75)** (IPWilliams) **4-9-12** DHolland(3) (led 5f: wknd 3f out)	14	3	100/30^{3}	69	39
	Dark Age (IRE) (RAkehurst) **4-9-12** SSanders(5) (lw: prom over 5f)	12	4	16/1	50	20
46^{2}	**Double Espresso (IRE) (79)** (MJohnston) **3-8-2** TWilliams(2) (prom over 6f: virtually p.u fnl 3f: t.o)	24	5	11/4^{2}	9	—

(SP 113.1%) **5 Rn**

2m 7.14 (2.84) CSF £8.22 TOTE £3.10: £1.30 £1.20 (£7.90) OWNER Mr R. M. Cyzer (HORSHAM) BRED R. D. Hubbard
WEIGHT FOR AGE 3yo-22lb, 4yo-1lb

251 DURLSTON HEAD MEDIAN AUCTION MAIDEN STKS (3-Y.O) (Class F)
3-20 (3-21) **6f (Equitrack)** £2,394.80 (£672.80: £328.40) Stalls: Low GOING minus 0.29 sec per fur (FST)

Form	Horse / Details	Dist	Pos	SP	RR	SF
145^{3}	**Roffey Spinney (IRE) (70)** (RHannon) **3-9-0** RPerham(4) (lw: a.p: led over 2f out: hrd rdn over 1f out: r.o wl)	—	1	7/2^{2}	69	22
204^{3}	**Castle Ashby Jack (72)** (PHowling) **3-9-0b** FNorton(3) (bmpd s: hdwy over 4f out: chsd wnr wl over 1f out: hrd rdn: unable qckn)	1½	2	11/1	65	18
193^{4}	**Bon Guest (IRE) (61)** (TJNaughton) **3-9-0** DHolland(5) (lw: a.p: led over 3f out tl over 2f out: wknd over 1f out)	2½	3	11/1	58	11
118^{2}	**Blues Magic (IRE)** (MBell) **3-8-9**$^{(5)}$ GFaulkner(2) (lw: bhd fnl 4f)	1¼	4	4/6^{1}	55	8
142^{5}	**Lucy of Arabia (IRE) (62)** (JJSheehan) **3-8-4**$^{(5)}$ ADaly(1) (led over 2f: wknd over 2f out)	3	5	9/2^{3}	42	—

(SP 117.1%) **5 Rn**

1m 14.87 (3.77) CSF £33.37 TOTE £5.30: £2.30 £1.90 (£7.00) OWNER Mrs D. F. Cock (MARLBOROUGH) BRED P. Henley
OFFICIAL EXPLANATION **Blues Magic (IRE): returned wth abrasions on his left fore-leg, his trainer added that the gelding might have swallowed his tongue and did not apppreciate the kick-back.**

252 EDDYSTONE H'CAP (0-65) (4-Y.O+) (Class F)
3-50 (3-50) **2m (Equitrack)** £2,417.20 (£679.20: £331.60) Stalls: Low GOING minus 0.29 sec per fur (FST)

Form	Horse / Details	Dist	Pos	SP	RR	SF
133^{*}	**Broughtons Formula (56)** (WJMusson) **7-9-5b** DRMcCabe(6) (lw: wl bhd 11f: hdwy over 3f out: str run fnl f: led nr fin)	—	1	4/1^{2}	67	44
106^{6}	**Guest Alliance (IRE) (59)** (GLMoore) **5-9-8** CandyMorris(4) (lw: hdwy 14f out: led 4f out tl over 3f out: led 1f out: shkn up: hdd nr fin)	½	2	7/1	70	47
202^{*}	**Wottashambles (64)** (LMontagueHall) **6-9-13** DHolland(8) (hdwy over 6f out: led over 3f out to 1f out: one pce)	1¼	3	15/8^{1}	73	50
147^{5}	**Blue And Royal (IRE) (36)** (VSoane) **5-7-13** NAdams(3) (hdwy 14f out: led over 5f out to 4f out: sn wknd)	15	4	10/1	30	7
167^{5}	**Classic Account (36)** (JLEyre) **9-7-6**$^{(7)ow3}$ RFfrench(5) (led over 10f)	1¾	5	12/1	29	3
205^{3}	**Coleridge (53)** (JJSheehan) **9-9-2b** AClark(1) (rel to r 9f out: bhd fnl 8f: t.o fnl 7f)	dist	6	10/1	—	—
216^{10}	**Pyrrhic Dance (35)** (MJHaynes) **7-7-12** GBardwell(7) (b: prom 10f: t.o)	10	7	66/1	—	—

183* **Supreme Star (USA) (65)** (PRHedger) **6-9-11b**(3) NVarley(2) (b: lw: bhd fnl 6f: t.o whn p.u nr fin: lame)............ **P** 11/2[3] — —
(SP 110.0%) **8 Rn**

3m 28.08 (7.08) CSF £26.71 CT £57.21 TOTE £6.20: £1.20 £1.60 £1.20 (£12.20) OWNER Crawford Gray & Aylett (NEWMARKET) BRED The Lavington Stud

LONG HANDICAP Classic Account 7-8

253 NEEDLES H'CAP (0-85) (4-Y.O+) (Class D)

4-20 (4-20) **6f (Equitrack)** £3,322.50 (£1,005.00: £490.00: £232.50) Stalls: Low GOING minus 0.29 sec per fur (FST)

Form	Horse	Pos	SP	RR	SF
	Princely Sound (75) (MBell) **4-9-9** WRyan(3) (mde all: hrd rdn fnl f: r.o wl)........................—	1	11/4[1]	82	57
184*	**Robo Magic (USA) (78)** (LMontagueHall) **5-9-12** DHolland(7) (hdwy over 3f out: chsd wnr fnl 2f: unable qckn)1½	2	8/1	81	56
214*	**Apollo Red (67)** (GLMoore) **8-9-1** 7x CandyMorris(6) (a.p: one pce fnl 2f)........................½	3	6/1	69	44
170[3]	**Scissor Ridge (75)** (JJBridger) **5-9-9** DHarrison(5) (rdn 5f out: lost pl over 2f out: one pce)........................3	4	11/2[3]	69	44
222*	**Squire Corrie (65)** (DWChapman) **5-8-13** 7x ACulhane(4) (lw: hld up: rdn 2f out: wknd fnl f)........................3	5	7/2[2]	51	26
48*	**Pageboy (80)** (PCHaslam) **8-10-0** SDrowne(1) (prom 2f)........................1½	6	7/1	62	37
201[5]	**Mr Frosty (77)** (WJarvis) **5-9-11** SSanders(8) (a bhd)........................nk	7	8/1	58	33
201[7]	**Krystal Max (IRE) (70)** (JCullinan) **4-8-11**(7) VictoriaAppleby(2) (a bhd)........................½	8	16/1	50	25

(SP 119.2%) **8 Rn**

1m 12.88 (1.78) CSF £24.30 CT £114.87 TOTE £5.20: £1.30 £2.30 £2.30 (£40.00) OWNER Mr G. W. Byrne (NEWMARKET) BRED James William Mitchell and Simon Edward Mitchell

T/Plpt: £104.20 (71.76 Tckts). T/Qdpt: £21.10 (27.4 Tckts) AK

0217-WOLVERHAMPTON (L-H) (Standard)
Wednesday February 12th

WEATHER: overcast & rain WIND: mod half bhd

254 IRIS H'CAP (0-90) (I) (4-Y.O+) (Class C)

1-50 (1-51) **7f (Fibresand)** £4,965.00 (£1,500.00: £730.00: £345.00) Stalls: High GOING: 0.25 sec per fur (SLW)

Form	Horse	Pos	SP	RR	SF
233*	**Mansab (USA) (72)** (PGMurphy) **4-8-10** 6x SDrowne(3) (hld up: pushed along ½-wy: str run to ld nr fin)........—	1	2/1[1]	80	46
	Bold Effort (FR) (90) (KOCunningham-Brown) **5-10-0v** WRyan(5) (a.p: led on bit wl over 1f out: hrd drvn fnl f: ct cl home)........................¾	2	8/1	96	62
81[2]	**Elite Hope (USA) (74)** (NTinkler) **5-8-12** DeanMcKeown(6) (led tl wl over 1f out: kpt on u.p fnl f)........................1¼	3	6/1[3]	77	43
220[6]	**Duke Valentino (85)** (RHollinshead) **5-9-4**(5) DGriffiths(2) (a.p: rdn & outpcd wl over 1f out: sn btn)........................2½	4	10/1	83	49
201[2]	**Naughty Pistol (USA) (67)** (PDEvans) **5-8-5v** SSanders(7) (trckd ldrs: rdn & outpcd over 2f out)........................3½	5	11/4[2]	57	23
194[6]	**Barrel of Hope (66)** (JLEyre) **5-8-4b** DWright(8) (dwlt: nvr nr to chal)........................5	6	12/1	44	10
219[5]	**Allez Cyrano (IRE) (71)** (OO'Neill) **6-8-9**ow1 VSlattery(4) (mid div: drvn along over 3f out: no imp)........................2	7	25/1	45	10
	King Rat (IRE) (70) (JGMO'Shea) **6-8-8v** ACulhane(1) (lw: a wl bhd: t.o)........................12	8	12/1	16	—
192[4]	***Nashaat* (USA) (65)** (KRBurke) **9-7-10**(7) RFfrench(9) (Withdrawn not under Starter's orders: ref to ent stalls)...	W	20/1	—	—

(SP 118.5%) **8 Rn**

1m 30.5 (5.80) CSF £16.94 CT £74.04 TOTE £4.20: £2.40 £3.80 £1.30 (£21.50) Trio £23.80 OWNER Mrs Louise Murphy (BRISTOL) BRED Jonabell, J Bell, B Williams, J Nicholson and J Be

255 DAFFODIL MAIDEN STKS (3-Y.O) (Class D)

2-20 (2-21) **1m 1f 79y (Fibresand)** £3,485.00 (£1,055.00: £515.00: £245.00) Stalls: Low GOING: 0.25 sec per fur (SLW)

Form	Horse	Pos	SP	RR	SF
	Don Sebastian (78) (WJHaggas) **3-9-0** DHolland(7) (h.d.w: hld up: hdwy 3f out: led ins fnl f: comf)........................—	1	11/10[1]	78+	47
	Pennywell (RFJohnsonHoughton) **3-8-9** SSanders(5) (unf: scope: dwlt: sn chsng ldrs: led 4f out tl ins fnl f)...2	2	4/1[2]	70	39
	Venture Connect (CPEBrooks) **3-9-0** DHarrison(11) (w'like: str: bkwd: chsd ldrs: rdn over 1f out: one pce)...2	3	9/2[3]	71	40
217[3]	**Faym (IRE) (66)** (JWharton) **3-8-9** FNorton(1) (prom: drvn along 4f out: wknd over 2f out)........................6	4	6/1	56	25
	Woodland Nymph (DJGMurraySmith) **3-8-9** DRMcCabe(10) (chsd ldrs: rdn 3f out: sn lost tch)........................1½	5	14/1	53	22
164[3]	**Weet And See** (RHollinshead) **3-8-9**(5) DGriffiths(6) (hld up: hdwy 4f out: rdn & wknd 2f out)........................5	6	14/1	50	19
185[5]	**Krosno** (SCWilliams) **3-9-0** JTate(2) (w'like: bkwd: led over 5f: sn rdn & wknd: t.o)........................9	7	14/1	34	3
	Triple Challenge (KRBurke) **3-8-9** ACulhane(8) (neat: a in rr: t.o)........................5	8	20/1	21	—
	Sir Alidaf (OO'Neill) **3-9-0** VSlattery(4) (a in rr: t.o)........................18	9	33/1	—	—
	Front View (BJLlewellyn) **3-9-0** TWilliams(9) (bit bkwd: s.s: sn pushed along: a bhd: t.o)........................4	10	50/1	—	—
	Little Tucker (BPreece) **3-9-0** RPerham(3) (a bhd: t.o)........................20	11	50/1	—	—

(SP 131.7%) **11 Rn**

2m 4.3 (8.30) CSF £5.82 TOTE £2.10: £1.10 £3.60 £2.40 (£6.60) Trio £14.60 OWNER Khanmaher (NEWMARKET) BRED R. G. Percival and Red House Stud

256 TULIP CLAIMING STKS (4-Y.O+) (Class F)

2-50 (2-52) **1m 6f 166y (Fibresand)** £2,580.00 (£780.00: £380.00: £180.00) Stalls: High GOING: 0.25 sec per fur (SLW)

Form	Horse	Pos	SP	RR	SF
205[11]	**Petoskin (65)** (JPearce) **5-9-0** MWigham(2) (chsd ldrs: rdn & outpcd 3f out: plld wd & styd on to ld ins fnl f) .—	1	4/1[2]	74	34
	Heighth of Fame (71) (DBurchell) **6-8-3**(7) KSked(6) (bit bkwd: chsd ldr: led over 5f out: hrd rdn & hdd ins fnl f)........................1¼	2	9/4[1]	69	29
115[7]	**Philmist (50)** (JHetherton) **5-8-7b** NKennedy(3) (hld up: hdwy 6f out: rdn ent st: no imp)........................6	3	16/1	59	19
	Cutthroat Kid (IRE) (66) (MrsMReveley) **7-9-6b** ACulhane(4) (bkwd: hld up: effrt & drvn along 4f out: nvr nrr)........................18	4	11/2[3]	53	13
139*	**Shakiyr (FR) (60)** (RHollinshead) **6-8-9b**(5) DGriffiths(5) (sn wl bhd: rdn along 5f out: no real imp)........................11	5	9/4[1]	35	—
183[8]	**Storm Wind (IRE) (40)** (KRBurke) **4-7-12v**(7)ow2 PWright(11) (lw: trckd ldrs over 8f: sn lost tch)........................hd	6	33/1	31	—
231[7]	**Stevie's Wonder (IRE) (42)** (BJLlewellyn) **7-8-6v** TWilliams(9) (reminders after 6f: a bhd: t.o)........................7	7	25/1	19	—
104[11]	**Efficacious (IRE) (31)** (PEccles) **4-7-5**(5) JBramhill(1) (a in rr: t.o)........................nk	8	33/1	14	—
167[3]	**Mapengo (31)** (JCullinan) **6-8-10** LCharnock(8) (lw: set str pce over 9f: sn wknd t.o)........................dist	9	16/1	—	—

				SP	RR	SF
	Thorntoun House (IRE) (JSGoldie) **4-8-5** DeanMcKeown(7) (bit bkwd: s.i.s: a wl bhd: t.o)	23	**10**	33/1	—	—
				(SP 121.4%)		**10 Rn**

3m 23.1 (15.70) CSF £12.36 TOTE £4.40: £1.60 £1.70 £2.80 (£13.50) Trio £35.30 OWNER Mrs Jean Routledge (NEWMARKET) BRED James Wigan
WEIGHT FOR AGE 4yo-5lb
Heighth of Fame clmd J Byrne £5,000
OFFICIAL EXPLANATION **Petoskin: the gelding had been held up prior to his last run and, having had a history of breaking blood-vessels, may have bled internally. The jockey added that the race was run to suit his mount. Shakiyr (FR): appeared to resent the kickback.**

257 IRIS H'CAP (0-90) (II) (4-Y.O+) (Class C)

3-20 (3-21) **7f (Fibresand)** £4,965.00 (£1,500.00: £730.00: £345.00) Stalls: High GOING: 0.25 sec per fur (SLW)

				SP	RR	SF
	Rakis (IRE) (87) (MrsLStubbs) **7-9-11** DHolland(5) (hld up & bhd: gd hdwy over 2f out: rdn to ld nr fin)	—	**1**	9/1	93	62
	Cim Bom Bom (IRE) (90) (MBell) **5-9-9v**(5) GFaulkner(4) (lw: led: clr 2f out: hrd rdn & ct fnl stride)	nk	**2**	100/30 [1]	95	64
207[2]	**Yeoman Oliver (70)** (BAMcMahon) **4-8-8b** LNewton(8) (lw: a.p: rdn over 1f out: kpt on one pce)	2½	**3**	10/1	70	39
207[3]	**Gulf Shaadi (66)** (EJAlston) **5-8-4** SDrowne(2) (hdwy 2f out: rdn & r.o wl ins fnl f)	s.h	**4**	12/1	66	35
*186**	**Royal Carlton (IRE) (71)** (GLMoore) **5-8-9** SWhitworth(6) (sn drvn along: a outpcd)	1½	**5**	4/1 [3]	67	36
*241**	**Dawalib (USA) (58)** (DHaydnJones) **7-7-10** [6x] LCharnock(3) (chsd ldrs tl rdn & outpcd fnl 2f)	nk	**6**	7/2 [2]	53	22
220[5]	**Leigh Crofter (66)** (PDCundell) **8-8-4b** DHarrison(1) (lw: chsd ldr over 5f: wknd qckly: t.o)	14	**7**	11/1	29	—
*166**	**Prima Silk (79)** (MJRyan) **6-9-3** AClark(7) (sn pushed along: nvr gng pce of ldrs: t.o)	1½	**8**	7/1	39	8
				(SP 112.9%)		**8 Rn**

1m 30.4 (5.70) CSF £34.69 CT £281.65 TOTE £12.60: £1.50 £2.80 £2.80 (£18.00) OWNER Mr P. G. Shorrock (WARTHILL) BRED The Mount Coote Partnership
LONG HANDICAP Dawalib (USA) 7-2

258 FREESIA H'CAP (0-80) (3-Y.O) (Class D)

3-50 (3-51) **5f (Fibresand)** £3,273.75 (£990.00: £482.50: £228.75) Stalls: Low GOING: 0.25 sec per fur (SLW)

				SP	RR	SF
89[5]	**Brutal Fantasy (IRE) (72)** (JLEyre) **3-9-2** RLappin(6) (chsd ldrs tl ld wl over 1f out: drvn out)	—	**1**	3/1 [1]	78	45
204[2]	**Mangus (IRE) (70)** (KOCunningham-Brown) **3-9-0** CMunday(5) (s.i.s: hdwy 2f out: r.o wl ins fnl f)	1½	**2**	5/1 [3]	71	38
25[5]	**Nightingale Song (71)** (MartynMeade) **3-8-10**(5) DSweeney(2) (led tl wl over 1f out: kpt on u.p)	½	**3**	5/1 [3]	71	38
*142**	**Sparkling Edge (61)** (CADwyer) **3-8-5** DRMcCabe(3) (drvn along & outpcd ½-wy: kpt on ins fnl f: nvr nrr)	1	**4**	4/1 [2]	57	24
193[2]	**Master Foley (62)** (NPLittmoden) **3-8-1**(5) ADaly(4) (chsd ldr 3f: sn rdn & one pce)	1¼	**5**	13/2	54	21
180[5]	**Siouxrouge (77)** (PCHaslam) **3-9-7** SDrowne(1) (trckd ldrs: rdn & outpcd fnl 2f)	1¾	**6**	3/1 [1]	64	31
				(SP 116.7%)		**6 Rn**

63.4 secs (4.50) CSF £17.40 TOTE £3.30: £1.70 £4.90 (£11.50) OWNER Diamond Racing Ltd (HAMBLETON) BRED Michael G. O'Brien

259 LILY (S) STKS (3-Y.O) (Class F)

4-20 (4-21) **6f (Fibresand)** £2,580.00 (£780.00: £380.00: £180.00) Stalls: Low GOING: 0.25 sec per fur (SLW)

				SP	RR	SF
	Royal Cascade (IRE) (BAMcMahon) **3-8-11** LNewton(1) (mde all: hrd drvn appr fnl f: r.o gamely)	—	**1**	9/2	62	31
212[2]	**Hever Golf Charger (IRE) (60)** (TJNaughton) **3-8-11** SSanders(2) (hld up: hdwy ½-wy: ev ch appr fnl f: unable qckn)	¾	**2**	3/1 [1]	60	29
181[2]	**Pretty Sally (IRE) (56)** (DJGMurraySmith) **3-8-6** DHarrison(4) (hld up: hdwy 2f out: rdn & swished tail ins fnl f: nt qckn)	nk	**3**	4/1 [3]	54	23
*221**	**Will To Win (45)** (PGMurphy) **3-8-13** SDrowne(8) (b.hind: chsd ldrs: rdn & outpcd appr fnl f)	7	**4**	7/2 [2]	43	12
110[5]	**Contravene (IRE) (60)** (JBerry) **3-8-8**(5) TEDurcan(9) (hld up: effrt & rdn over 2f out: no imp)	3	**5**	6/1	35	4
221[5]	**Bailerina's Dream** (MartynMeade) **3-8-6** NAdams(5) (s.i.s: a bhd & outpcd)	½	**6**	25/1	26	—
164[10]	**Prince Emar** (TDEasterby) **3-8-11** LCharnock(7) (a bhd & outpcd)	1¼	**7**	14/1	28	—
181[11]	**Joyful Joy (32)** (BPJBaugh) **3-7-13**(7) IonaWands(3) (lost tch ½-wy: t.o)	10	**8**	40/1	—	—
102[3]	**My Girl (49)** (RHollinshead) **3-8-6** WRyan(6) (prom over 3f: sn lost tch: t.o)	s.h	**9**	6/1	—	—
				(SP 126.9%)		**9 Rn**

1m 17.3 (6.10) CSF £18.66 TOTE £7.60: £2.30 £1.60 £1.70 (£60.50) Trio £11.40 OWNER Mr R. L. Bedding (TAMWORTH) BRED Philip Mahon
No Bid

260 ROSE APPRENTICE H'CAP (0-70) (4-Y.O+) (Class E)

4-50 (4-51) **1m 4f (Fibresand)** £2,814.00 (£852.00: £416.00: £198.00) Stalls: Low GOING: 0.25 sec per fur (SLW)

				SP	RR	SF
	Northern Motto (52) (JSGoldie) **4-8-10** DGriffiths(7) (a.p: slt ld over 3f out: qcknd appr fnl f: sn clr)	—	**1**	5/1 [3]	63	42
182[3]	**Studio Thirty (40)** (RDickin) **5-7-12**(3)ow1 AEddery(4) (a.p: led after 4f tl over 3f out: one pce appr fnl f)	4	**2**	12/1	46	27
123[6]	**Ambidextrous (IRE) (46)** (EJAlston) **5-8-7** DSweeney(9) (hld up: hdwy over 4f out: nt rch ldrs)	1¼	**3**	10/1	50	32
147[6]	**Soviet King (IRE) (50)** (PMitchell) **4-8-8** TEDurcan(5) (chsd ldrs: rdn 3f out: kpt on same pce)	½	**4**	8/1	53	32
188[2]	**Sheraz (IRE) (47)** (NTinkler) **5-8-5b**(3) JoHunnam(10) (hld up: hdwy 5f out: rdn & wknd over 2f out)	7	**5**	5/1 [3]	41	23
157[2]	**Raindeer Quest (46)** (JLEyre) **5-8-2**(5) SBuckley(6) (chsd ldrs: rdn & wknd over 2f out)	1¾	**6**	4/1 [2]	38	20
176[2]	**Slip Jig (IRE) (70)** (KRBurke) **4-9-11**(3) RFfrench(8) (hld up: a in rr)	6	**7**	6/4 [1]	54	33
63[8]	**Sam Rockett (38)** (PMooney) **4-7-5b**(5) AMcCarthy(3) (a bhd: t.o)	17	**8**	16/1	—	—
169[11]	**Amnesty Bay (35)** (MDIUsher) **5-7-5**(5) RBrisland(2) (led 4f: wknd 5f out: t.o)	dist	**9**	33/1	—	—
				(SP 130.1%)		**9 Rn**

2m 43.5 (11.00) CSF £64.68 CT £551.60 TOTE £9.80: £1.40 £1.90 £1.90 (£31.60) Trio £35.60 OWNER Mr D. Callaghan (GLASGOW) BRED Exors of the late Sir Robin McAlpine
LONG HANDICAP Sam Rockett 7-2 Amnesty Bay 7-8
WEIGHT FOR AGE 4yo-3lb
OFFICIAL EXPLANATION **Slip Jig (IRE): was found to be lame upon returning home.**

T/Plpt: £45.40 (209.65 Tckts). T/Qdpt: £13.00 (50.32 Tckts) IM

0248-LINGFIELD (L-H) (Standard)
Thursday February 13th
WEATHER: fine WIND: str across

261 ST VALENTINES AMATEUR H'CAP (0-70) (4-Y.O+) (Class E)
1-55 (1-55) **1m 5f (Equitrack)** £2,778.25 (£841.00: £410.50: £195.25) Stalls: Low GOING minus 0.39 sec per fur (FST)

				SP	RR	SF
106^{*}	**Hattaafeh (IRE) (68)** (MissBSanders) **6-11-3**(4) MissLSheen(7) (lw: a.p: led 2f out: hrd rdn ins fnl f: r.o)	—	**1**	$5/2^{1}$	78	52
196^{*}	**Calendula (50)** (DMorley) **4-9-13** MissDianaJones(3) (lw: hld up: hdwy 4f out: hrd rdn & ev ch ins fnl f: unable qckn)	1	**2**	$3/1^{2}$	59	29
202^{6}	**Classy Chief (60)** (JWhite) **4-10-2**(7) MrJCrowley(2) (chsd ldrs: led over 3f out: hdd 2f out: one pce)	7	**3**	12/1	60	30
210^{3}	**Don't Drop Bombs (USA) (33)** (DTThom) **8-9-0v** MissJFeilden(4) (chsd ldrs: rdn 2f out: wknd over 1f out)	2½	**4**	10/1	30	4
232^{*}	**Golden Hadeer (70)** (MJRyan) **6-11-5**(4) 5x MrSLavallin(6) (prom: led 7f out: hdd over 3f out: grad wknd)	3	**5**	$9/2^{3}$	63	37
13^{7}	**Cross Talk (IRE) (54)** (RMStronge) **5-10-0**(7)ow10 MrJDewhurst(5) (a bhd)	13	**6**	25/1	31	—
216^{3}	**Uoni (40)** (PButler) **4-9-3** MrsAPerrett(1) (bhd fnl 5f)	½	**7**	7/1	17	—
196^{5}	**Qualitair Pride (44)** (JFBottomley) **5-9-11** MrsLPearce(8) (b.off hind: led: hdd 7f out: sn wknd: t.o)	28	**8**	6/1	—	—

(SP 119.2%) **8 Rn**

2m 49.8 (7.80) CSF £9.74 CT £69.29 TOTE £3.70: £2.10 £1.30 £4.60 (£10.00) OWNER Mrs P. J. Sheen (EPSOM) BRED Sheikh Ahmed bin Rashid al Maktoum in Ireland
WEIGHT FOR AGE 4yo-4lb

262 YOUNG LOVE (S) H'CAP (0-60) (4-Y.O+) (Class G)
2-25 (2-25) **2m (Equitrack)** £2,076.90 (£583.40: £284.70) Stalls: Low GOING minus 0.39 sec per fur (FST)

				SP	RR	SF
133^{6}	**Matthias Mystique (52)** (MissBSanders) **4-9-12** SSanders(5) (a.p: led over 3f out: clr over 1f out: comf)	—	**1**	$6/4^{1}$	67	39
86^{14}	**Old Hush Wing (IRE) (41)** (PCHaslam) **4-9-1** SDrowne(7) (lw: chsd ldrs: rdn 3f out: styd on to go 2nd ins fnl f)	3	**2**	$14/1^{3}$	53	25
183^{3}	**Illegally Yours (44)** (LMontagueHall) **4-9-4** WRyan(6) (hld up: hdwy 9f out: chsd wnr over 3f out tl ins fnl f: one pce)	nk	**3**	$6/4^{1}$	56	28
236^{5}	**Ela Man Howa (44)** (ABailey) **6-9-10** RHughes(4) (led 8f out: hdd over 3f out: sn wknd)	23	**4**	$6/1^{2}$	33	11
139^{7}	**Persian Bud (IRE) (27)** (MRBosley) **9-8-2e**(5) JBramhill(3) (chsd ldrs tl wknd over 3f out)	2	**5**	16/1	14	—
183^{9}	**Broughtons Relish (23)** (WJMusson) **4-7-8**(3) MBaird(2) (hld up: hdwy 9f out: wknd 4f out)	nk	**6**	20/1	9	—
	Kalakate (26) (JJBridger) **12-8-1**(5) ADaly(1) (b: sn led: hdd 8f out: wknd 5f out)	12	**7**	25/1	—	—

(SP 115.4%) **7 Rn**

3m 29.05 (8.05) CSF £24.34 TOTE £2.30: £1.30 £2.00 (£11.10) OWNER Mrs J. M. Laycock (EPSOM) BRED P. Cook
WEIGHT FOR AGE 4yo-6lb
No bid

263 CASANOVA H'CAP (0-60) (3-Y.O+) (Class F)
3-00 (3-02) **6f (Equitrack)** £2,495.60 (£701.60: £342.80) Stalls: Low GOING minus 0.39 sec per fur (FST)

				SP	RR	SF
95^{5}	**Sihafi (USA) (56)** (JMCarr) **4-9-12** AClark(8) (chsd ldrs: rdn over 1f out: styd on to ld cl home)	—	**1**	$7/1^{3}$	63	45
253^{5}	**Squire Corrie (65)** (DWChapman) **5-10-7** 7x ACulhane(12) (a.p: led 2f out: hdd cl home)	¾	**2**	8/1	70	52
199^{4}	**Superlao (BEL) (33)** (JJBridger) **5-7-12**(5) ADaly(9) (a.p: ev ch 1f out: unable qckn)	¾	**3**	12/1	36	18
223^{4}	**Double Oscar (IRE) (54)** (DNicholls) **4-9-10b** AlexGreaves(2) (hdwy 2f out: rdn over 1f out: r.o one pce ins fnl f)	1¼	**4**	10/1	54	36
223^{*}	**Ivory's Grab Hire (51)** (KTIvory) **4-9-7b** 7x DBiggs(7) (mid div: sltly hmpd over 4f out: hrd rdn over 1f out: kpt on one pce ins fnl f)	¾	**5**	$5/1^{2}$	49	31
222^{3}	**Featherstone Lane (53)** (MissLCSiddall) **6-9-2v**(7) TSiddall(13) (mid div: rdn over 2f out: kpt on one pce fnl f)	1½	**6**	12/1	47	29
223^{3}	**Thick as Thieves (44)** (RonaldThompson) **5-9-0** JFanning(4) (led: hdd 2f out: wknd over 1f out)	1¼	**7**	9/1	34	16
172^{*}	**Tachycardia (48)** (RJO'Sullivan) **5-9-1**(3) NVarley(14) (nvr nrr)	1½	**8**	15/2	34	16
199^{*}	**Sir Tasker (46)** (JLHarris) **9-9-2** SSanders(5) (rr: effrt over 2f out: sn btn)	s.h	**9**	$9/2^{1}$	32	14
199^{3}	**Southern Dominion (41)** (MissJFCraze) **5-8-11** SWebster(1) (prom 2f)	2½	**10**	14/1	21	3
184^{3}	**The Frisky Farmer (55)** (WGMTurner) **4-9-4v**(7) DMcGaffin(6) (a bhd)	s.h	**11**	14/1	34	16
	Lochon (53) (MrsNMacauley) **6-9-6**(3) CTeague(10) (b: chsd ldrs tl wknd 2f out)	½	**12**	33/1	31	13
159^{2}	**Xenophon of Cunaxa (IRE) (58)** (MJFetherston-Godley) **4-10-0b** WRyan(3) (a bhd)	2	**13**	$5/1^{2}$	31	13

(SP 137.6%) **13 Rn**

1m 13.35 (2.25) CSF £65.61 CT £639.17 TOTE £10.60: £3.00 £4.10 £5.00 (£71.20) Trio £368.20; £368.21 to Newcastle 14/2/97 OWNER Mr John Gilbertson (MALTON) BRED Shadwell Farm Inc
OFFICIAL EXPLANATION **Xenophon of Cunaxa (IRE): failed to face the kickback.**

264 SEALED WITH A LOVING KISS H'CAP (0-70) (3-Y.O) (Class E)
3-35 (3-35) **1m (Equitrack)** £2,700.25 (£817.00: £398.50: £189.25) Stalls: High GOING minus 0.39 sec per fur (FST)

				SP	RR	SF
225^{5}	**Puzzlement (57)** (CEBrittain) **3-8-9** DHolland(3) (set modest pce: qcknd over 2f out: r.o wl)	—	**1**	$11/2^{3}$	65	24
	Swift (60) (MJPolglase) **3-8-12** MRimmer(2) (chsd ldr: rdn & ev ch over 1f out: one pce)	3½	**2**	11/1	61	20
161^{*}	**Hint of Victory (69)** (MBell) **3-9-2**(5) GFaulkner(4) (trckd ldrs: rdn over 2f out: one pce)	2	**3**	$6/4^{2}$	66	25
185^{*}	**Pastiche (69)** (TGMills) **3-9-7** WRyan(1) (plld hrd: hld up: rdn over 2f out: sn btn)	4	**4**	$11/10^{1}$	58	17

(SP 111.3%) **4 Rn**

1m 41.09 (3.69) CSF £39.11 TOTE £6.10 (£29.40) OWNER Mrs C. E. Brittain (NEWMARKET) BRED Mrs C. E. Brittain
OFFICIAL EXPLANATION **Puzzlement: the colt had blown up on his previous start, his first for three months, and was suited by the running of this race. Hint of Victory: was unable to quicken when asked in the straight. Pastiche: the rider reported that the filly was unsuited by the slow early pace, failed to settle early on and did not quicken thereafter.**

265 CUPID MEDIAN AUCTION MAIDEN STKS (3-Y.O F) (Class F)

4-10 (4-10) **7f (Equitrack)** £2,372.40 (£666.40: £325.20) Stalls: Low GOING minus 0.39 sec per fur (FST)

	Horse	Dist	Pos	SP	RR	SF
	Shalstayholy (IRE) (66) (GLMoore) **3-8-11** SWhitworth(6) (hld up gng wl: led appr fnl f: r.o wl)	—	**1**	11/10[1]	63	32
118[3]	**She's Dawan (IRE)** (PMitchell) **3-8-8**(3) AWhelan(2) (a.p: led over 2f out: hdd appr fnl f: unable qckn)	5	**2**	11/4[2]	52	21
135[3]	**Julia's Relative** (RGuest) **3-8-11** PBloomfield(5) (b: prom: rdn & outpcd over 2f out: kpt on one pce ins fnl f)	3½	**3**	5/1[3]	44	13
	Miss Barcelona (IRE) (52) (MJPolglase) **3-8-11** TGMcLaughlin(4) (bit bkwd: prom: ev ch over 2f out: wknd over 1f out)	2	**4**	11/1	39	8
145[6]	**Native Thatch (IRE)** (WGMTurner) **3-8-6**(5) DSweeney(1) (led: hdd over 2f out: sn wknd)	16	**5**	13/2	2	—
	She's Electric (35) (JJBridger) **3-8-6**(5) ADaly(3) (bhd fnl 5f)	3½	**6**	50/1	—	—
				(SP 114.6%)	**6 Rn**	

1m 27.03 (2.63) CSF £4.11 TOTE £2.00: £1.40 £2.20 (£3.60) OWNER J B R Leisure Ltd (BRIGHTON) BRED Mrs P. Grubb

266 SAY IT WITH ROSES MAIDEN STKS (3-Y.O+) (Class D)

4-40 (4-40) **1m 4f (Equitrack)** £3,306.25 (£1,000.00: £487.50: £231.25) Stalls: Low GOING minus 0.39 sec per fur (FST)

	Horse	Dist	Pos	SP	RR	SF
	Ramike (IRE) (MJohnston) **3-8-3** JFanning(4) (trckd ldrs: pushed along 4f out: hrd rdn over 1f out: led cl home)	—	**1**	7/2[2]	59	—
202[2]	**Random Kindness (67)** (RIngram) **4-9-10** SSanders(2) (w ldr: led 4f out: hrd rdn over 1f out: hdd cl home)	1	**2**	8/15[1]	58	6
	Happy Medium (IRE) (GPEnright) **4-9-5**(5) ADaly(3) (led: hdd 4f out: hrd rdn over 1f out: unable qckn)	1¼	**3**	9/1	56	4
228[2]	**Nakhal (53)** (DJGMurraySmith) **4-9-10b** DHolland(1) (hld up: rdn over 3f out: virtually p.u over 2f out)	dist	**4**	4/1[3]	—	—
				(SP 117.4%)	**4 Rn**	

2m 41.1 (11.10) CSF £5.91 TOTE £5.20 (£3.50) OWNER Miss Belinda Lee (MIDDLEHAM) BRED Dene Investments N V
WEIGHT FOR AGE 3yo-24lb, 4yo-3lb
OFFICIAL EXPLANATION **Nakhal: The rider reported that the gelding had lost his action approaching the final bend.**

T/Plpt: £2,871.70 (2.36 Tckts). T/Qdpt: £468.10 (0.69 Tckts); £196.12 SM

0190a-CAGNES-SUR-MER (Nice, France) (L-H) (Good to soft)
Wednesday February 5th

267a PRIX WILLIAM ALEXANDRE RUINAT (4-Y.O+)

2-44 (2-45) **1m 5f** £6,734.00

	Horse	Dist	Pos	SP	RR	SF
	Peckinpah's Soul (FR) (DSmaga,France) **5-9-2** DBoeuf	—	**1**		111	—
	Pibarnon (FR) (CMaillard,France) **7-9-2** SGuillot	5½	**2**		104	—
	Mon Domino (RCollet,France) **8-9-7** GGuignard	hd	**3**		109	—
	Whitechapel (USA) (LordHuntingdon) **9-8-7** GElorriaga-Santos (btn approx 12½l)		**7**		—	—
190a[14]	**Ela-Yie-Mou (IRE)** (SDow) **4-8-7** WRyan (btn approx 14½l)		**8**		—	—
						15 Rn

2m 54.9 P-M 1.70F: 1.10F 1.90F 1.30F (11.10F) OWNER A. Lequeux (LAMORLAYE) BRED Manita Investment Corporation
Whitechapel (USA) had every chance two furlongs out having been close up for most of the way. However, he was unable to go with the leaders when the tempo quickened and came home at one pace.
190a Ela-Yie-Mou (IRE) disappointed connections once again. Held up in the rear, he stayed on at the one pace for the final two furlongs. He is likely to return home with his stable-companions.

268a PRIX DU LOGIS DU PIN (3-Y.O C & G)

3-12 (3-13) **1m 110y** £4,489.00

	Horse	Dist	Pos	SP	RR	SF
	Mister Valentin (FR) (MPimbonnet,France) **3-9-2** FBlondel	—	**1**		80?	—
	Valet De Coeur (USA) (RCollet,France) **3-9-2** DBoeuf	2½	**2**		75	—
	Royal Groom (FR) (J-CNapoli,France) **3-9-2** HGineux	1½	**3**		73	—
	Palisander (IRE) (SDow) **3-9-2** WRyan (btn over 8l)		**9**		—	—
						15 Rn

1m 52.5 P-M 19.40F: 4.80F 2.30F 5.20F (43.40F) OWNER Jacques Romero BRED Rene Goin
Palisander (IRE) made the running, but ran out of steam two and a half furlongs out and soon weakened.

269a PRIX D'AVIGNON H'CAP (4-Y.O+)

3-40 (3-41) **1m** £8,418.00

	Horse	Dist	Pos	SP	RR	SF
	Fun Harbour (FR) (J-CRouget,France) **7-8-8** J-RDubosc	—	**1**		82	—
	Super Bely (FR) (GBlanco,France) **4-8-10** SHureau	hd	**2**		84	—
189a[3]	**Bakio (FR)** (JForesi,France) **6-8-5** GElorriaga-Santos	½	**3**		78	—
189a[7]	**Confronter** (SDow) **8-8-7** WRyan (btn over 2½l)		**12**		—	—
						18 Rn

1m 40.1 R-M 11.60F: 4.70F 4.80F 2.80F (90.60F) OWNER A. Lapoterie (PAU) BRED Mme Francois-Plessis
189a Confronter ran a rather lack-lustre race. Always towards the rear, he never got into a challenging position.

0267a-CAGNES-SUR-MER (Nice, France) (L-H) (Good to soft)
Sunday February 9th

270a PRIX GENERAL DE SAINT-DIDIER AMATEUR (4-Y.O+)

1-30 (1-31) **1m 3f** £3,928.00

	Horse	Dist	Pos	SP	RR	SF
	Lighted Rainbow (FR) (Jean-MarcCapitte,Belgium) **8-9-13** MrLMaynard	—	**1**		72?	—
	Mr Peillon (USA) (JRossi,France) **5-10-4** MrsJRossi	1	**2**		76	—

Hazama (CBauer,France) **7-10-0** MissSGryson ....nk **3** 71 —
190a8 **No Speeches (IRE)** (SDow) **6-10-4** MrTDoumen (btn over 11l) .... **12** — —
17 Rn

2m 27.0 P-M 1.60F: 1.20F 1.80F 3.40F (6.80F) OWNER Mr Y. Fayt BRED Petra Bloodstock Ltd. in France
190a No Speeches (IRE) rounded off a disappointing spell for Simon Dow at Cagnes-Sur-Mer. Held up towards the rear of the pack, he made some progress at halfway but was unable to make any impression.

0229a-SAINT-MORITZ (Switzerland) (R-H) (Snow)
Sunday February 9th

271a GRAND PRIX MOVENPICK (3-Y.O+)
2-45 (3-03) **1m** £5,053.00 (£2,021.00)

SP RR SF

Henderson (GER) (KSchafflutzel,Switzerland) **7-9-7** GHuber ....— **1** — —
229a3 **Celestial Key (USA)** (MJohnston) **7-9-2** DHolland ....nk **2** — —
King of Heights (GER) (MWeber,Germany) **5-9-8** TMundry ....3 **3** — —
9 Rn

1m 45.7 TOTE 23.50SF: 3.10SF 1.40SF 2.00SF (44.00SF) OWNER A. Krauliger BRED Gestut Hof Ittlingen
229a Celestial Key (USA) ran a big race and went down narrowly. Chasing the leaders, he made his move two furlongs from home and looked to be cruising approaching the final furlong, but when asked the big question, he was unable to quicken.

0242-SOUTHWELL (L-H) (Standard)
Friday February 14th
WEATHER: fine WIND: mod half bhd

272 LAXTON H'CAP (0-60) (4-Y.O+) (Class F)
2-10 (2-10) **2m** **(Fibresand)** £2,345.50 (£658.00: £320.50) Stalls: Low GOING: 0.08 sec per fur (STD)

SP RR SF

2322 **Master Foodbroker (IRE) (51)** (WJMusson) **9-9-7b** DRMcCabe(3) (lw: dwlt s: sn wl bhd: hdwy 6f out: styd on strly u.p fnl f: led post) ....— **1** 7/4 1 64 8
La Menorquina (USA) (43) (DMarks) **7-8-13** SSanders(6) (trckd ldrs: smooth hdwy to ld 2f out: jst ct) ....s.h **2** 6/1 3 56 —
2569 **Mapengo (31)** (JCullinan) **6-8-1** JQuinn(1) (led to 2f out: grad wknd) ....14 **3** 11/1 30 —
2068 **Fiasco (43)** (MJCamacho) **4-8-7** LCharnock(8) (in tch: pushed along 10f out: lost pl over 3f out) ....5 **4** 20/1 37 —
1676 **Parklife (IRE) (44)** (PCHaslam) **5-8-7**(7) PGoode(7) (s.i.s: sn pushed along: sme hdwy 6f out: lost pl over 4f out) ....1½ **5** 10/1 36 —
World Without End (USA) (34) (MESowersby) **8-7-13b**(5) PFessey(5) (chsd ldrs: ev ch tl wknd over 2f out) ...4 **6** 33/1 22 —
2424 **El Nido (62)** (DWChapman) **9-9-13**(5) 4x HBastiman(4) (w ldr: rdn & lost pl over 4f out: sn bhd) ....25 **7** 3/1 2 25 —
2063 **Kilnamartyra Girl (40)** (JParkes) **7-8-10** DHarrison(9) (sn pushed along: sme hdwy 6f out: rdn & lost pl over 4f out) ....6 **8** 6/1 3 — —
Swynford Supreme (40) (JFBottomley) **4-8-4** NCarlisle(2) (chsd ldrs: drvn along 6f out: sn lost pl: t.o) ....25 **9** 20/1 — —
(SP 119.8%) **9 Rn**

3m 47.7 (21.70) CSF £11.89 CT £84.50 TOTE £2.70: £1.10 £2.30 £3.30 (£6.40) Trio £48.10 OWNER Broughton Thermal Insulation (NEWMARKET) BRED Limestone Stud
WEIGHT FOR AGE 4yo-6lb

273 HARDWICK CLAIMING STKS (4-Y.O+) (Class F)
2-45 (2-46) **1m** **(Fibresand)** £2,294.00 (£644.00: £157.00: £157.00) Stalls: Low GOING: 0.08 sec per fur (STD)

SP RR SF

*18** **Sarasi (65)** (MJCamacho) **5-8-9** LCharnock(14) (lw: b.nr fore: racd wd: trckd ldrs: styd on to ld wl ins fnl f) ...— **1** 7/1 62 28
2432 **Rambo Waltzer (73)** (DNicholls) **5-8-8**(7) IonaWands(13) (lw: chsd ldrs: drvn along over 4f out: led over 1f out tl nr fin) ....½ **2** 4/1 3 67 33
2435 **Northern Fan (IRE) (82)** (NTinkler) **5-8-9** DHolland(8) (mde most tl over 1f out: kpt on same pce) ....d.h **3** 14/1 54 20
Whothehellisharry (62) (JBerry) **4-8-6**(7) CLowther(5) (sn bhd & pushed along: hdwy 2f out: styd on wl ins fnl f) 3½ **3** 33/1 58 24
1345 **Lachesis (34)** (DNicholls) **4-7-13**(5) JBramhill(3) (trckd ldrs: chal 2f out: wknd fnl f) 2 **5** 33/1 45 11
1947 **Major Mouse (56)** (WWHaigh) **9-8-5** RLappin(10) (racd wd: outpcd ½-wy: hdwy u.p 2f out: nvr rchd ldrs) 3 **6** 16/1 40 6
*213** **Joseph's Wine (IRE) (78)** (DNicholls) **8-9-7b** AlexGreaves(2) (lw: sn bhd: effrt u.p 2f out: nvr nr to chal) 3 **7** 2/1 1 50 16
1434 **Commin' Up (42)** (JWHills) **4-8-2** NAdams(6) (trckd ldrs tl wknd over 1f out) ....1¾ **8** 20/1 28 —
2306 **Lost In The Post (IRE)** (CWThornton) **4-8-13** DeanMcKeown(12) (sn outpcd & bhd) 1¾ **9** 33/1 35 1
1253 **Giddy (42)** (JHetherton) **4-8-2** NKennedy(7) (mid div: drvn along & outpcd ½-wy) ....1¼ **10** 16/1 22 —
367 **Warhurst (IRE) (54)** (DNicholls) **6-8-0**(7) CarolynBales(4) (s.s: bhd: stdy hdwy over 2f out: eased whn no ch appr fnl f) ....1¼ **11** 33/1 24 —
147 **Absolute Magic (78)** (WJHaggas) **7-9-7** WRyan(1) (s.s: a in rr) ....¾ **12** 100/30 2 37 3
Lady Westbury (IRE) (PCRitchens) **6-8-4**ow2 SDrowne(11) (chsd ldrs tl wknd over 2f out) ....10 **13** 40/1 — —
Golden Tyke (IRE) (MissMKMilligan) **4-8-1** JQuinn(9) (prom tl lost pl 3f out: sn bhd) ....14 **14** 40/1 — —
(SP 128.7%) **14 Rn**

1m 46.2 (7.20) CSF £32.23 TOTE £9.70: £2.50 £1.40 W £5.70 NF £2.20 (£22.80) Trio S, RW & W £90.70 S, RW & NF £12.60 OWNER The Blue Chip Group (MALTON) BRED C. J. R. Trotter
OFFICIAL EXPLANATION Joseph's Wine (IRE): was never racing with his usual enthusiasm.

274 RAINWORTH H'CAP (0-85) (3-Y.O+) (Class D)
3-20 (3-20) **1m** **(Fibresand)** £4,143.00 (£1,254.00: £612.00: £291.00) Stalls: Low GOING: 0.08 sec per fur (STD)

SP RR SF

*207** **Kingchip Boy (76)** (MJRyan) **8-9-11** 5x AClark(2) (lw: led 2f: sn drvn along: squeezed through & bmpd over 1f out: led ins fnl f: r.o strly) ....— **1** 3/1 1 85 48
2482 **Le Sport (64)** (DNicholls) **4-8-6b**(7) IonaWands(1) (trckd ldrs: effrt on ins & hung lft 2f out: swtchd & styd on wl ins fnl f) ....½ **2** 5/1 3 72 35

			SP	RR	SF
164*	**State of Caution (75)** (DShaw) **4-9-10b** JFanning(3) (lw: b: trckd ldrs: chal & edgd lft over 1f out: bmpd: nt qckn ins fnl f) ....hd	**3**	4/1[2]	83	46
194*	**Sea Spouse (66)** (MBlanshard) **6-9-1** NAdams(7) (chsd ldr: led after 2f tl ins fnl f: wknd towards fin) 2½	**4**	8/1	69	32
257[4]	**Gulf Shaadi (66)** (EJAlston) **5-9-1** SDrowne(6) (dwlt s: bhd tl kpt on wl fnl 2f) 1¼	**5**	12/1	66	29
243[6]	**Desert Invader (IRE) (67)** (DWChapman) **6-9-2** ACulhane(8) (chsd ldrs tl wknd over 1f out) 4	**6**	16/1	59	22
209*	**Live Project (IRE) (55)** (MJohnston) **5-8-4** 5x DHolland(10) (sn bhd: effrt on outside ½-wy: nvr rchd ldrs) ....hd	**7**	5/1[3]	47	10
195[3]	**Myfontaine (56)** (KTIvory) **10-8-5** GBardwell(9) (lw: b: b.hind: sn outpcd & bhd: sme hdwy over 1f out: n.d)..s.h	**8**	20/1	48	11
243[4]	**Bentico (73)** (MrsNMacauley) **8-9-5v**(3) CTeague(5) (in tch: rdn & outpcd 2f out: n.d) 1¼	**9**	8/1	63	26
127[6]	**Awesome Venture (73)** (MCChapman) **7-9-8** DRMcCabe(4) (hld up & plld hrd: bhd fr ½-wy: t.o) ....dist	**10**	16/1	—	—
			(SP 124.8%)	**10 Rn**	

1m 45.6 (6.60) CSF £17.82 CT £58.15 TOTE £3.50: £1.40 £2.10 £1.70 (£16.60) Trio £36.90 OWNER Four Jays Racing Partnership (NEWMARKET) BRED R. M. Scott

275 KIRKBY-IN-ASHFIELD H'CAP (0-70) (3-Y.O+ F & M) (Class E)

3-55 (3-55) **6f (Fibresand)** £2,752.25 (£833.00: £406.50: £193.25) Stalls: Low GOING: 0.08 sec per fur (STD)

			SP	RR	SF
	Antonias Melody (64) (SRBowring) **4-10-0** SWebster(1) (mde all: drvn clr 2f out: unchal) ....—	**1**	10/1	82	63
233[8]	**Delrob (51)** (DHaydnJones) **6-9-1b** AClark(3) (chsd ldrs: styd on fnl 2f: no imp) 5	**2**	7/2[2]	56	37
209[3]	**Anita's Contessa (IRE) (55)** (BPalling) **5-9-5** TSprake(6) (sn outpcd & bhd: sn pushed along: hdwy 2f out: styd on ins fnl f) 1¼	**3**	2/1[1]	56	37
65[7]	**Balinsky (IRE) (45)** (JBerry) **4-8-4b**[1](5) PRoberts(5) (s.i.s: bhd tl styd on u.p fnl 2f: nt rch ldrs) 2½	**4**	10/1	40	21
35[6]	**Marjorie Rose (IRE) (63)** (ABailey) **4-9-13** DWright(4) (sn pushed along: hdwy ½-wy: nvr nr to chal) 1	**5**	4/1[3]	55	36
222[4]	**Honeyhall (36)** (NBycroft) **4-8-0v** JQuinn(9) (trckd ldrs: effrt over 2f out: wknd over 1f out) 3½	**6**	6/1	19	—
136[5]	**Dhes-C (35)** (RHollinshead) **4-7-13** NCarlisle(8) (chsd ldrs tl lost pl 2f out) 8	**7**	12/1	—	—
	Carnival of Light (33) (JSMoore) **5-7-11**ow1 NAdams(2) (w ldrs: sn pushed along: lost pl over 2f out) 4	**8**	20/1	—	—
	Gormire (51) (JHetherton) **4-9-1** MTebbutt(7) (racd wd: sn bhd) 6	**9**	25/1	—	—
			(SP 124.3%)	**9 Rn**	

1m 17.5 (4.00) CSF £44.21 CT £94.41 TOTE £13.90: £3.10 £1.10 £1.20 (£24.90) Trio £19.30 OWNER Mrs B. D. Georgiou (EDWINSTOWE) BRED B. D. Georgiou

276 MAPLEBECK (S) STKS (4-Y.O+) (Class G)

4-25 (4-25) **1m 4f (Fibresand)** £2,085.00 (£585.00: £285.00) Stalls: Low GOING: 0.08 sec per fur (STD)

			SP	RR	SF
231[4]	**Forzair (58)** (JJO'Neill) **5-9-0** WRyan(3) (lw: hld up: effrt over 4f out: sn rdn: styd on u.p on outside to ld wl ins fnl f) ....—	**1**	7/4[1]	62	13
231[2]	**Shuttlecock (36)** (DWChapman) **6-8-11**(3) CTeague(5) (led: sn drvn along: clr 5f out: hdd & no ex ins fnl f).....2	**2**	9/2	59	10
	Sharp Gazelle (50) (BSmart) **7-8-9** SSanders(1) (sn trckng ldr: effrt 2f out: sn rdn: one pce) 1½	**3**	2/1[2]	52	3
	Another Quarter (IRE) (54) (MCChapman) **4-8-6** DRMcCabe(4) (drvn along & outpcd 7f out: hrd rdn & kpt on fnl 3f: n.d) 10	**4**	4/1[3]	39	—
	Song For Jess (IRE) (FJordan) **4-8-6** AClark(2) (drvn along & outpcd 7f out: bhd fnl 4f: t.o) ....dist	**5**	20/1	—	—
			(SP 112.6%)	**5 Rn**	

2m 47.2 (14.20) CSF £9.27 TOTE £1.80: £1.10 £1.90 (£3.90) OWNER Clayton Bigley Partnership Ltd (PENRITH) BRED J. G. Charlton
WEIGHT FOR AGE 4yo-3lb
No bid

277 GIRTON H'CAP (0-60) (3-Y.O) (Class F)

5-00 (5-00) **1m 3f (Fibresand)** £2,294.00 (£644.00: £314.00) Stalls: Low GOING: 0.08 sec per fur (STD)

			SP	RR	SF
191[3]	**State of Gold (IRE) (47)** (JHetherton) **3-8-10** MTebbutt(5) (sn trckng ldrs: led 8f out: pushed clr over 2f out: unchal) ....—	**1**	10/1[3]	56	5
235*	**Mutahadeth (63)** (DShaw) **3-9-12** 5x JFanning(4) (lw: hld up: effrt on outside over 2f out: sn rdn & hung lft: kpt on: no imp) 5	**2**	8/11[1]	65	14
84[4]	**Skelton Sovereign (IRE) (56)** (RHollinshead) **3-9-0**(5) DGriffiths(6) (hld up: hdwy 7f out: edgd lft & styd on same pce fnl 2f) 2½	**3**	11/4[2]	54	3
168[6]	**Buzzby Babe (41)** (AGFoster) **3-8-4** TSprake(7) (hld up: effrt 4f out: one pce) ....nk	**4**	14/1	39	—
168[5]	**Neon Deion (IRE) (40)** (SCWilliams) **3-7-10v**(7) DarrenWilliams(3) (trckd ldrs: effrt over 2f out: sn outpcd) 4	**5**	10/1[3]	32	—
	Apiculate (IRE) (40) (SRBowring) **3-7-12**(5)ow1 ADaly(2) (chsd ldrs: lost pl 6f out: n.d) 7	**6**	20/1	22	—
8[9]	**Racing Carr (40)** (TJNaughton) **3-8-3** JQuinn(1) (led tl 8f out: wknd 2f out) 5	**7**	20/1	14	—
			(SP 118.9%)	**7 Rn**	

2m 33.7 (13.70) CSF £17.17 TOTE £11.60: £4.30 £1.10 (£4.50) OWNER Keith West Partnership (MALTON) BRED Ali K. Al Jafleh

T/Plpt: £16.60 (547.05 Tckts). T/Qdpt: £4.20 (161.88 Tckts) WG

0261-LINGFIELD (L-H) (Standard)

Saturday February 15th

WEATHER: sunny WIND: almost nil

278 RED ROSE APPRENTICE H'CAP (0-70) (4-Y.O+) (Class E)

2-10 (2-11) **7f (Equitrack)** £2,843.25 (£861.00: £420.50: £200.25) Stalls: Low GOING minus 0.39 sec per fur (FST)

			SP	RR	SF
224[3]	**Lift Boy (USA) (58)** (GLMoore) **8-9-1**(5) MBatchelor(7) (mde most tl over 2f out: led over 1f out: rdn out) ....—	**1**	4/1[2]	66	42
186[7]	**River Seine (FR) (42)** (SGKnight) **5-8-4** GFaulkner(8) (hdwy 3f out: hrd rdn & ev ch fnl f: r.o) ....hd	**2**	11/1	50	26
241[4]	**Into Debt (34)** (JRPoulton) **4-7-5e**(5) AMcCarthy(6) (s.s: racd wd: hdwy 4f out: ev ch 2f out: unable qckn) 2	**3**	7/1	37	13
241[3]	**Lancashire Legend (65)** (SDow) **4-9-13** ADaly(3) (w ldrs: led over 2f out tl over 1f out: one pce) ....nk	**4**	9/2[3]	68	44
197*	**Hawaii Storm (FR) (55)** (DJSffrenchDavis) **9-8-12**(5) KerryBaker(10) (racd wd: hdwy over 3f out: styd on fnl f) ....hd	**5**	7/2[1]	57	33
203[3]	**Private Fixture (IRE) (42)** (DMarks) **6-8-1**(3) RMullen(5) (a.p: one pce fnl 2f) ....hd	**6**	5/1	44	20
	Tuigamala (60) (RIngram) **6-9-8** DSweeney(2) (in tch tl dropped rr over 4f out: hdwy over 1f out: styd on) ....hd	**7**	9/1	62	38

Form	Horse	Dist	Pos	SP	RR	SF
214[3]	**Astral Invader (IRE) (40)** (MSSaunders) **5-8-2**ow1 PPMurphy(9) (prom tl wknd over 1f out)	1¼	**8**	10/1	39	14
224[7]	**Masruf (IRE) (45)** (KCBailey) **5-8-7** SophieMitchell(4) (prom 4f)	5	**9**	33/1	33	9
	Vera's First (IRE) (54) (MissGayKelleway) **4-8-11**(5) AngelaGallimore(1) (b: b.hind: s.i.s: bhd fnl 4f)	8	**10**	25/1	23	—
				(SP 123.8%)	**10 Rn**	

1m 26.88 (2.48) CSF £46.23 CT £282.03 TOTE £6.00: £2.40 £2.60 £2.70 (£49.00) Trio £86.40 OWNER Mr A. Moore (BRIGHTON) BRED Paul & Arnold Bryant in USA
LONG HANDICAP Into Debt 7-8
STEWARDS' ENQUIRY Faulkner susp. 24-25/2/97 (excessive use of whip). Knight fined £80 under Rule 150(i) (saddling in stables).

279 ROMEO CLAIMING STKS (3-Y.O) (Class F)

2-40 (2-40) **7f (Equitrack)** £2,439.60 (£685.60: £334.80) Stalls: Low GOING minus 0.39 sec per fur (FST)

Form	Horse	Dist	Pos	SP	RR	SF
259[2]	**Hever Golf Charger (IRE) (60)** (TJNaughton) **3-8-6** DHolland(1) (b: mde all: clr fnl 2f: easily)	—	**1**	11/8 1	69+	34
154[8]	**Hever Golf Dancer (60)** (TJNaughton) **3-8-11** TSprake(3) (rdn 5f out: hdwy over 2f out: chsd wnr wl over 1f out: no imp)	9	**2**	8/1	53	18
198[6]	**Heavenly Miss (IRE) (70)** (JJBridger) **3-7-11**(5) RMullen(2) (chsd wnr: one pce fnl 3f)	½	**3**	9/4 2	43	8
181[8]	**Broadgate Flyer (IRE) (60)** (MrsLStubbs) **3-8-6b1** SWhitworth(4) (rdn 5f out: bhd fnl 2f)	8	**4**	3/1 3	29	—
				(SP 109.0%)	**4 Rn**	

1m 26.47 (2.07) CSF £10.30 TOTE £2.10 (£3.50) OWNER Hever Racing Club (EPSOM) BRED Mull Enterprises Ltd

280 JULIET (S) STKS (4-Y.O+) (Class G)

3-10 (3-10) **1m (Equitrack)** £2,174.90 (£611.40: £298.70) Stalls: High GOING minus 0.39 sec per fur (FST)

Form	Horse	Dist	Pos	SP	RR	SF
160*	**Bagshot (63)** (GLMoore) **6-9-5** SWhitworth(4) (hld up: led on bit over 1f out: comf)	—	**1**	8/11 1	62	38
241[7]	**Statistician (52)** (JohnBerry) **5-8-13e** JQuinn(2) (plld hrd in rr: hdwy 3f out: rdn 2f out: styd on fnl f)	2	**2**	7/2 2	52	28
211[5]	**Dream Carrier (IRE) (44)** (REPeacock) **9-8-8**(5) ADaly(1) (led 1f: rdn & lost pl 4f out: rallied & r.o ins fnl f)	½	**3**	16/1	51	27
197[6]	**Hatta Sunshine (USA) (56)** (GLMoore) **7-9-2**(3) AWhelan(6) (lw: plld hrd: led over 3f out tl over 1f out: one pce)	1	**4**	4/1 3	55	31
160[6]	**Young Frederick (IRE) (57)** (KRBurke) **4-8-13** ACulhane(5) (hld up: ev ch 3f out: hrd rdn & wknd 2f out)	7	**5**	20/1	35	11
	Callaloo (56) (RHarris) **4-8-13** DBiggs(3) (s.i.s: plld hrd: led after 1f: hdd & wknd over 3f out)	4	**6**	20/1	27?	3
				(SP 115.5%)	**6 Rn**	

1m 40.6 (3.20) CSF £3.47 TOTE £1.50: £1.10 £1.70 (£2.80) OWNER Mr Danny Bloor (BRIGHTON) BRED Newgate Stud Co
No bid

281 JACK & GILL COLE H'CAP (0-90) (3-Y.O) (Class C)

3-45 (3-45) **1m 2f (Equitrack)** £5,006.05 (£1,515.40: £739.70: £351.85) Stalls: Low GOING minus 0.39 sec per fur (FST)

Form	Horse	Dist	Pos	SP	RR	SF
174*	**Lawn Lothario (67)** (MJohnston) **3-7-13** TWilliams(6) (lw: mde all: clr 3f out: rdn out)	—	**1**	3/1 1	77	35
7[2]	**Pinchincha (FR) (65)** (DMorris) **3-7-11** GBardwell(2) (hdwy 5f out: chsd wnr fnl 3f: unable qckn)	5	**2**	14/1	67	25
155*	**Globetrotter (IRE) (78)** (MJohnston) **3-8-10** DeanMcKeown(3) (lw: rr & rdn 6f out: hdwy over 1f out: nvr nrr)	1¼	**3**	3/1 1	78	36
26*	**Superbelle (79)** (MAJarvis) **3-8-11** EmmaO'Gorman(5) (no hdwy fnl 3f)	¾	**4**	7/2 2	78	36
174[2]	**Time Can Tell (68)** (CMurray) **3-8-0** JQuinn(1) (prom 7f)	6	**5**	8/1 3	57	15
227[2]	**Millroy (USA) (89)** (PAKelleway) **3-9-7v** MWigham(4) (w wnr 6f)	9	**6**	7/2 2	64	22
				(SP 112.2%)	**6 Rn**	

2m 6.45 (2.15) CSF £37.56 TOTE £4.20: £1.40 £4.10 (£93.10) OWNER Mr J. S. Morrison (MIDDLEHAM) BRED Snailwell Stud Co Ltd

282 DEMPSTERS DIARY MAIDEN STKS (3-Y.O+) (Class D)

4-20 (4-21) **5f (Equitrack)** £3,306.25 (£1,000.00: £487.50: £231.25) Stalls: High GOING minus 0.39 sec per fur (FST)

Form	Horse	Dist	Pos	SP	RR	SF
	Rififi (60) (RIngram) **4-9-10** SWhitworth(4) (lw: hdwy 3f out: led 1f out: rdn out)	—	**1**	5/2 1	72	42
251[4]	**Blues Magic (IRE)** (MBell) **3-8-5**(5) GFaulkner(2) (lw: led after 1f: hrd rdn & hdd 1f out: unable qckn)	2½	**2**	5/2 1	64	20
221[3]	**Ma Vielle Pouque (IRE)** (WGMTurner) **3-8-5** TSprake(5) (led 1f: one pce fnl 2f)	2½	**3**	4/1 2	51	7
45[4]	**Nopalea (73)** (TJNaughton) **3-8-5** DHolland(3) (b: prom tl wknd wl over 1f out)	1	**4**	5/2 1	48	4
223[5]	**Logie Pert Lad (25)** (JJBridger) **5-9-10** FNorton(1) (bhd fnl 3f)	3½	**5**	14/1 3	42	12
	Emma's Risk (38) (RHarris) **3-8-5** DBiggs(6) (a bhd)	5	**6**	33/1	21	—
				(SP 115.3%)	**6 Rn**	

60.05 secs (1.85) CSF £8.52 TOTE £3.10: £2.80 £2.10 (£10.40) OWNER Brooknight Guarding Ltd (EPSOM) BRED Milton Park Stud Partnership
WEIGHT FOR AGE 3yo-14lb

283 SWEETHEART H'CAP (0-75) (4-Y.O+ F & M) (Class D)

4-55 (4-56) **1m 4f (Equitrack)** £3,306.25 (£1,000.00: £487.50: £231.25) Stalls: Low GOING minus 0.39 sec per fur (FST)

Form	Horse	Dist	Pos	SP	RR	SF
216[4]	**Harlequin Walk (IRE) (43)** (RJO'Sullivan) **6-7-12** JQuinn(2) (hdwy 2f out: led 1f out: rdn out)	—	**1**	11/4 3	55	2
187*	**Glow Forum (73)** (LMontagueHall) **6-9-11**(3) MartinDwyer(4) (led 11f: hrd rdn: unable qckn)	1½	**2**	5/2 2	83	30
232[5]	**Nawaji (USA) (44)** (WRMuir) **4-7-5**(5) JBramhill(1) (a.p: one pce fnl 2f)	1¾	**3**	12/1	52	—
163*	**Persuasion (74)** (LordHuntingdon) **4-9-12** DHarrison(3) (trckd ldr: rdn & ev ch 2f out: wknd 1f out)	1¾	**4**	10/11 1	79	23
				(SP 115.3%)	**4 Rn**	

2m 37.7 (7.70) CSF £9.39 TOTE £4.20 (£8.30) OWNER Mrs R. J. Doorgachurn (WHITCOMBE) BRED Ronnie Boland in Ireland
LONG HANDICAP Nawaji (USA) 7-2
WEIGHT FOR AGE 4yo-3lb

T/Plpt: £634.70 (13.28 Tckts). T/Qdpt: £106.20 (4.93 Tckts) LMc

0272-SOUTHWELL (L-H) (Standard)
Monday February 17th
WEATHER: wet and windy WIND: str across

284 BERING H'CAP (0-65) (4-Y.O+) (Class F)
2-30 (2-30) **1m 3f (Fibresand)** £2,294.00 (£644.00: £314.00) Stalls: Low GOING: 0.28 sec per fur (SLW)

	Horse	Dist	Pos	SP	RR	SF
196[2]	**Carol Again (39)** (NBycroft) **5-8-10** JQuinn(15) (trckd ldrs: stdy hdwy 3f out: led wl over 1f out: drvn out)	—	1	13/2[3]	49	34
140[8]	**African-Pard (IRE) (40)** (DHaydnJones) **5-8-11** AClark(14) (a.p: led over 2f out: hdd wl over 1f out: kpt n)	¾	2	33/1	49	34
150[4]	**Suga Hawk (IRE) (53)** (EJAlston) **5-9-10** DHolland(13) (lw: w ldrs: rdn 3f out: styd on one pce)	¾	3	9/1	61	46
276[2]	**Shuttlecock (40)** (DWChapman) **6-8-8**(3) CTeague(6) (led tl hdd 2f out: one pce)	½	4	7/2[1]	47	32
	Road Racer (IRE) (53) (MrsJRRamsden) **4-9-8** TSprake(10) (mid div: styd on fnl 2f: nvr rchd ldrs)	4	5	8/1	54	37
	No Submission (USA) (48) (DWChapman) **11-9-5b** ACulhane(1) (bhd: styd on fnl 2f: nvr nrr)	1	6	16/1	48	33
242[5]	**Undawaterscubadiva (35)** (MPBielby) **5-8-6** DeanMcKeown(3) (chsd ldrs tl wknd fnl 3f)	5	7	11/1	28	13
202[4]	**Mustang (31)** (CWThornton) **4-8-0** LCharnock(8) (w ldr: rdn 3f out: wknd 2f out)	1¼	8	6/1[2]	22	5
66[4]	**Fresh Fruit Daily (50)** (PAKelleway) **5-9-7** MWigham(4) (cl up tl outpcd over 3f out: sn wknd)	17	9	13/2[3]	16	1
235[10]	**Oneoftheoldones (48)** (JNorton) **5-9-5** GCarter(9) (a rr div)	2½	10	20/1	10	—
236[9]	**Prince Zizim (30)** (RCSpicer) **4-7-8v[1]**(5) JBramhill(11) (in tch tl wknd 5f out)	2	11	33/1	—	—
	The Fullbangladesh (41) (JLEyre) **4-8-10** RLappin(7) (prom tl rdn & wknd 5f out)	1¾	12	16/1	—	—
140[5]	**Seventh Edition (47)** (DBurchell) **4-9-2** SDrowne(5) (bhd fnl 6f)	10	13	16/1	—	—
	Cohiba (52) (BJCurley) **4-9-7** WRyan(2) (drvn along 5f out: a bhd)	1¼	14	6/1[2]	—	—
232[6]	**Acerbus Dulcis (30)** (MCChapman) **6-8-1b[1]** GBardwell(12) (sn pushed along: bhd: hdwy after 3f: wknd 5f out)	1½	15	16/1	—	—

(SP 141.1%) **15 Rn**

2m 31.6 (11.60) CSF £215.21 CT £1,828.73 TOTE £7.80: £2.40 £8.80 £2.20 (£160.60) Trio £184.20; £134.97 to Market Rasen 18/2/97
OWNER Mr J. G. Lumsden (BRANDSBY) BRED Clive Tomkins WEIGHT FOR AGE 4yo-2lb

285 BALTIC CLAIMING STKS (4-Y.O+) (Class F)
3-00 (3-01) **1m 4f (Fibresand)** £2,294.00 (£644.00: £314.00) Stalls: Low GOING: 0.28 sec per fur (SLW)

	Horse	Dist	Pos	SP	RR	SF
	Once More for Luck (IRE) (65) (MrsMReveley) **6-9-5** ACulhane(4) (lw: bhd: hdwy 5f out: chal over 1f out: rdn to ld cl home; fin 1st: disq: plcd last)	—	1d	11/4[2]	68	43
231*	**Greenspan (IRE) (70)** (WRMuir) **5-9-7** AClark(5) (trckd ldrs: led & qcknd over 2f out: rdn wl ins fnl f: hdd & no ex towards fin: fin 2nd, nk: awrdd r)	—	1	10/11[1]	70	45
236*	**English Invader (58)** (CADwyer) **6-8-10**(7) JoHunnam(1) (lw: chsd ldrs tl outpcd ½-wy: styd on fnl 2f: no imp: fin 3rd, nk & 7l: plcd 2nd)	7¼	2	3/1[3]	56	31
218[2]	**Zatopek (40)** (JCullinan) **5-8-11** JQuinn(3) (lw: chsd ldrs tl outpcd fnl 2½f: fin 4th: plcd 3rd)	3	3	14/1	46	21
	Presuming Ed (IRE) (NJHWalker) **4-8-10** CRutter(6) (cl up: led over 3f out tl over 2f out: sn wknd: fin 5th: plcd 4th)	9	4	40/1	36	8
244[5]	**Sea God (46)** (MCChapman) **6-9-7** MWigham(8) (led tl hdd over 3f out: sn outpcd: fin 6th plcd 5th)	nk	5	14/1	44	19
	Doctor's Remedy (23) (MrsJJordan) **11-8-2**(7) JennyMurphy(2) (bit bkwd: wl t.o: fin 7th: plcd 6th)	dist	6	40/1	—	—
	Cerbera (40) (JPSmith) **8-8-9** DRMcCabe(7) (bit bkwd: wl t.o: fin 8th: plcd 7th)	4	7	40/1	—	—

(SP 124.7%) **8 Rn**

2m 45.5 (12.50) CSF £5.62 TOTE £3.40: £1.80 £1.00 £1.10 (£1.60) OWNER The Mary Reveley Racing Club (SALTBURN) BRED Kerr and Co Ltd
SUBSEQUENT STEWARDS' ENQUIRY: Once More for Luck (IRE) disq. (prohibited substance (procaine) in urine. Reveley fined £400.
WEIGHT FOR AGE 4yo-3lb

286 CASPIAN H'CAP (0-70) (3-Y.O+ F & M) (Class E)
3-30 (3-31) **7f (Fibresand)** £2,937.80 (£889.40: £434.20: £206.60) Stalls: Low GOING: 0.28 sec per fur (SLW)

	Horse	Dist	Pos	SP	RR	SF
275*	**Antonias Melody (70)** (SRBowring) **4-10-4** 6x SWebster(3) (mde all: pushed along & r.o wl fnl 2f)	—	1	5/4[1]	83	58
237*	**Enchanting Eve (69)** (CNAllen) **3-8-11**(3) MartinDwyer(5) (chsd ldrs: chal ½-wy: sn rdn: btn over 1f out)	4	2	5/1[2]	73	31
177[3]	**Gold Lining (IRE) (34)** (EJAlston) **4-7-3**(7) JFowle(2) (cl up tl outpcd ½-wy: styd on fnl f)	nk	3	10/1	37	12
209[5]	**Shashi (IRE) (53)** (PatMitchell) **5-9-1** RLappin(6) (chsd ldrs: rdn ½-wy: no imp after)	2½	4	5/1[2]	51	26
245[3]	**Efipetite (37)** (NBycroft) **4-7-8v**(5) JBramhill(8) (prom: hdwy to chal ½-wy: rdn & wknd fnl 2½f)	2	5	7/1[3]	30	5
243[8]	**So Natural (IRE) (45)** (WStorey) **5-8-0**(7) IonaWands(4) (lw: chsd ldrs tl outpcd fnl 2f)	1	6	12/1	36	11
	Funky (44) (DNicholls) **4-7-13**(7) CarolynBales(7) (a bhd)	10	7	14/1	12	—
199[9]	**Veesey (42)** (JohnBerry) **4-8-4e** TWilliams(1) (sn pushed along: wl bhd fr ½-wy)	27	8	33/1	—	—

(SP 116.7%) **8 Rn**

1m 33.4 (6.90) CSF £7.25 CT £39.83 TOTE £2.80: £1.10 £2.20 £2.20 (£4.70) OWNER Mrs B. D. Georgiou (EDWINSTOWE) BRED B. D. Georgiou
LONG HANDICAP Gold Lining (IRE) 7-7 WEIGHT FOR AGE 3yo-17lb

287 HUDSON BAY MAIDEN STKS (3-Y.O+) (Class D)
4-00 (4-00) **6f (Fibresand)** £3,723.50 (£1,127.00: £550.00: £261.50) Stalls: Low GOING: 0.28 sec per fur (SLW)

	Horse	Dist	Pos	SP	RR	SF
154[6]	**Euroquest** (DNicholls) **3-8-2**(7) IonaWands(7) (hdwy ½-wy: led over 1f out: styd on wl)	—	1	20/1	49	13
172[3]	**Blue Lugana (37)** (NBycroft) **5-9-10** DHolland(4) (prom: hdwy 3f out: styd on fnl f: nt pce to chal)	1½	2	8/1	45	24
	Captain Carparts (JLEyre) **3-8-9** TWilliams(6) (cl up: disp ld 2f out tl over 1f out: one pce)	1¾	3	7/1[3]	40	4
230[8]	**Barwell Boy** (JLHarris) **3-8-4**(5) JBramhill(2) (cl up: lft in ld ½-wy: disp ld 2f out: grad wknd fnl f)	1¾	4	10/1	36	—
	Glimmering Hope (IRE) (MissJFCraze) **3-8-9** SWebster(5) (cl up: carried wide ½-wy: wknd over 1f out)	1¾	5	16/1	31	—
193[3]	**Supercharmer (67)** (DNicholls) **3-8-10**ow1 AlexGreaves(1) (lw: plld hrd: led: hung bdly rt & hdd 3f out: wknd wl over 1f out)	5	6	4/6[1]	19	—
	Buena Vista (CWThornton) **3-8-5**ow1 DeanMcKeown(8) (cmpt: bkwd: dwlt: nvr rchd ldrs)	2	7	6/1[2]	8	—
	Bustingoutallover (USA) (CWThornton) **3-8-4** LCharnock(3) (neat: bit bkwd: s.s: a bhd)	20	8	12/1	—	—

(SP 125.3%) **8 Rn**

1m 21.2 (7.70) CSF £166.31 TOTE £52.50: £5.20 £1.80 £2.30 (£21.80) OWNER Mr W. G. Swiers (THIRSK) BRED Ahmed M. Foustok
WEIGHT FOR AGE 3yo-15lb

STEWARDS' ENQUIRY Wands susp. 26-27/2/97 (incorrect use of whip). Nicholls fined £230 (failure to inform rdr of horse's hyper-sensitive skin).
OFFICIAL EXPLANATION Supercharmer: the rider reported that the gelding had hung violently to the right throughout the race.

288 PERSIAN GULF (S) STKS (3-Y.O+) (Class G)

4-30 (4-31) **6f (Fibresand)** £2,085.00 (£585.00: £285.00) Stalls: Low GOING: 0.28 sec per fur (SLW)

				SP	RR	SF
208^{3}	**Sense of Priority (70)** (DNicholls) **8-9-12** AlexGreaves(4) (trckd ldrs: stdy hdwy to chal 2f out: styd on to ld cl home)	—	1	$3/1^{2}$	65	44
208^{*}	**Elton Ledger (IRE) (75)** (MrsNMacauley) **8-9-12v** SSanders(7) (b: cl up: led 2f out: sn rdn: hdd & no ex towards fin)	nk	2	$6/4^{1}$	64	43
274^{6}	**Desert Invader (IRE) (67)** (DWChapman) **6-9-7** ACulhane(5) (chsd ldrs: kpt on fnl 2f: nt pce to chal)	3½	3	$5/1^{3}$	50	29
243^{13}	**Natal Ridge (55)** (DHaydnJones) **4-9-7** AClark(8) (in tch: kpt on fnl 2f: nvr able to chal)	½	4	12/1	49	28
	Margaretrose Anna (36) (BPJBaugh) **5-9-2** NAdams(9) (b: bhd: hdwy 2f out: n.m.r & nvr trbld ldrs)	¾	5	25/1	42	21
127^{5}	**Answers-To-Thomas (51)** (JMJefferson) **4-9-7** DeanMcKeown(2) (lw: led 4f: wknd)	4	6	14/1	36	15
	Chinour (IRE) (EJAlston) **9-9-7** DHolland(1) (s.s: a bhd)	5	7	14/1	23	2
243^{7}	**Spanish Stripper (USA) (34)** (MCChapman) **6-9-2b^{1}**(5) TEDurcan(6) (cl up 4f: wknd)	¾	8	20/1	21	—
	Baptismal Rock (IRE) (BJCurley) **3-8-6** WRyan(3) (cl up 4f: wknd qckly)	1½	9	$5/1^{3}$	17	—

(SP 128.0%) **9 Rn**

1m 20.0 (6.50) CSF £8.11 TOTE £3.90: £1.10 £1.10 £2.50 (£2.30) Trio £4.00 OWNER Mr M. A. Scaife (THIRSK) BRED Cheveley Park Stud Ltd
WEIGHT FOR AGE 3yo-15lb
No bid

289 ADRIATIC MAIDEN H'CAP (0-60) (3-Y.O) (Class F)

5-00 (5-01) **1m (Fibresand)** £2,294.00 (£644.00: £314.00) Stalls: Low GOING: 0.28 sec per fur (SLW)

				SP	RR	SF
83^{4}	**Touch'n'go (51)** (MJohnston) **3-9-0** DHolland(2) (lw: mde all: styd on strly fnl f)	—	1	$10/11^{1}$	61	14
	Fearless Sioux (58) (CWThornton) **3-9-7** DeanMcKeown(1) (trckd ldrs tl lost pl over 3f out: hdwy 2f out: edgd rt & no ch w wnr)	8	2	$5/1^{3}$	52	5
234^{3}	**Jack Says (55)** (DShaw) **3-9-4** JFanning(3) (lw: chsd ldrs: effrt over 2f out: rdn & no ex)	s.h	3	$11/4^{2}$	49	2
181^{9}	**Lights of Home (43)** (MissCJohnsey) **3-8-6** NAdams(4) (chsd wnr: chal 3f out: wknd wl over 1f out)	½	4	25/1	36	—
	Petula Boy (45) (SRBowring) **3-8-3**(5) ADaly(5) (cl up tl outpcd fnl 3f)	½	5	13/2	37	—

(SP 112.9%) **5 Rn**

1m 49.7 (10.70) CSF £5.67 TOTE £1.90: £2.20 £2.00 (£3.60) OWNER Greenland Park Ltd (MIDDLEHAM) BRED Laharna Ltd

T/Plpt: £40.00 (230.71 Tckts). T/Qdpt: £7.80 (95.84 Tckts) AA

0278-LINGFIELD (L-H) (Standard)

Tuesday February 18th

WEATHER: windy WIND: v.str half bhd

290 SEINE CLAIMING STKS (4-Y.O+) (Class E)

2-20 (2-21) **1m 2f (Equitrack)** £2,817.25 (£853.00: £416.50: £198.25) Stalls: Low GOING minus 0.44 sec per fur (FST)

				SP	RR	SF
248^{4}	**Spencer's Revenge (56)** (PButler) **8-8-10** GBardwell(3) (lw: hdwy over 4f out: led over 1f out: rdn out)	—	1	$6/1^{3}$	64	30
	Stellar Line (USA) (72) (DRCElsworth) **4-9-0**(5) DGriffiths(11) (lw: hdwy 5f out: led over 3f out tl over 1f out: unable qckn)	1¼	2	13/2	72	37
230^{5}	**Lahik (IRE) (30)** (KTIvory) **4-8-3** DBiggs(8) (rdn & hdwy 3f out: r.o)	2½	3	14/1	52	17
160^{2}	**Awesome Power (52)** (JWHills) **11-8-8** AClark(6) (a.p: rdn over 4f out: one pce)	2	4	$2/1^{1}$	53	19
160^{3}	**Honestly (47)** (BSmart) **4-8-4** SSanders(5) (led over 6f: wknd over 1f out)	2	5	15/2	47	12
197^{3}	**Mediate (IRE) (48)** (AHide) **5-8-2v**(7)ow1 JoHunnam(9) (nvr nr to chal)	½	6	$4/1^{2}$	50	15
211^{6}	**Eastleigh (35)** (RHollinshead) **8-8-3**(7) LisaWatson(1) (b.nr hind: bhd fnl 6f)	7	7	25/1	40	6
	Tomal (35) (RIngram) **5-8-10** TWilliams(2) (b.hind: bhd fnl 2f)	6	8	9/1	30	—
236^{7}	**Komodo (USA) (29)** (JELong) **5-8-5** LeesaLong(7) (b: lw: prom over 5f)	22	9	50/1	—	—
	Elite Force (IRE) (67) (MMadgwick) **4-8-11** DHarrison(4) (chsd ldr over 5f)	13	10	16/1	—	—
150^{11}	**Alana's Ballad (IRE) (24)** (BPJBaugh) **4-7-7**(5) JBramhill(10) (bhd fnl 5f)	8	11	50/1	—	—

(SP 123.0%) **11 Rn**

2m 7.95 (3.65) CSF £42.28 TOTE £8.00: £3.00 £3.80 £5.80 (£29.20) Trio Not won; £363.62 to Folkestone 19/2/97 OWNER Mrs Janet Coleman (LEWES) BRED Lord Crawshaw
WEIGHT FOR AGE 4yo-1lb

291 AISNE H'CAP (0-85) (4-Y.O+) (Class D)

2-50 (2-51) **1m 2f (Equitrack)** £3,355.00 (£1,015.00: £495.00: £235.00) Stalls: Low GOING minus 0.44 sec per fur (FST)

				SP	RR	SF
220^{8}	**Punkah (USA) (74)** (GMMcCourt) **4-8-10**(7) RStudholme(3) (a.p: led over 1f out: pushed out)	—	1	10/1	82	44
	Secret Aly (CAN) (80) (CEBrittain) **7-9-10** DHolland(9) (bit bkwd: chsd ldr: led over 3f out tl over 1f out: r.o)	¾	2	10/1	87	50
226^{3}	**Quiet Arch (IRE) (65)** (WRMuir) **4-8-3**(5) JBramhill(4) (b.hind: hld up: rdn 3f out: r.o)	½	3	$7/2^{2}$	71	33
	Night Wink (USA) (84) (GLMoore) **5-10-0** SWhitworth(5) (lw: hld up: rdn over 2f out: unable qckn)	4	4	$4/1^{3}$	84	47
74^{3}	**Seattle Alley (USA) (63)** (PRWebber) **4-7-13**(7) RFfrench(8) (hdwy over 2f out: one pce)	nk	5	11/2	62	24
	Digpast (IRE) (71) (MMadgwick) **7-9-1** SSanders(1) (lost pl over 3f out: n.m.r 2f out: rallied 1f out: sn wknd)	3½	6	20/1	65	28
226^{*}	**Sweet Supposin (IRE) (65)** (CADwyer) **6-8-9v** KFallon(7) (b: lw: rdn over 4f out: bhd whn nt clr run over 2f out)	½	7	$5/2^{1}$	58	21
226^{5}	**Law Dancer (IRE) (73)** (TGMills) **4-9-2** TWilliams(6) (a bhd)	1¼	8	14/1	64	26
238^{4}	**La Modiste (71)** (SDow) **4-9-0** WRyan(10) (bhd fnl 2f)	2	9	9/1	59	21
	Baranov (IRE) (61) (DJGMurraySmith) **4-8-4**ow1 DHarrison(2) (led over 6f)	½	10	16/1	48	9

(SP 131.7%) **10 Rn**

2m 7.01 (2.71) CSF £108.25 CT £396.80 TOTE £15.80: £3.30 £3.80 £2.20 (£62.10) Trio £59.20 OWNER McCourt Fine Meats Ltd & D J Rushen (WANTAGE) BRED The Queen

WEIGHT FOR AGE 4yo-1lb
OFFICIAL EXPLANATION **Punkah (USA): was dropped out and had resented the kickback last time.**

292 DORDOGNE MEDIAN AUCTION MAIDEN STKS (3-Y.O) (Class F)
3-20 (3-21) **1m (Equitrack)** £2,394.80 (£672.80: £328.40) Stalls: High GOING minus 0.44 sec per fur (FST)

				SP	RR	SF
230^{2}	**Amico (62)** (CWThornton) **3-9-0** DeanMcKeown(4) (a.p: rdn 3f out: led 2f out: r.o wl)	—	**1**	$7/2^{3}$	66	30
	Isis Honda (IRE) (CEBrittain) **3-8-9** DHolland(3) (b.hind: unf: lw: a.p: led over 2f out: sn hdd: hrd rdn over 1f out: r.o)	¾	**2**	$11/10^{1}$	60	24
225^{8}	**Talisman (IRE) (53)** (SDow) **3-9-0** WRyan(5) (led over 1f: lost pl over 4f out: rallied over 2f out: unable qckn)	2½	**3**	10/1	60	24
26^{7}	**Around Fore Alliss (71)** (TGMills) **3-8-7**(7) JCornally(2) (led over 6f out tl over 2f out: sn wknd)	3	**4**	$2/1^{2}$	54	18
230^{11}	**Missed May** (BPJBaugh) 3-8-9 FNorton(1) (a bhd)	24	**5**	50/1	1	—
				(SP 114.2%)	**5 Rn**	

1m 40.54 (3.14) CSF £7.45 TOTE £4.50: £2.30 £1.10 (£3.30) OWNER Mr Guy Reed (MIDDLEHAM) BRED M. J. Paver

293 LOIRE H'CAP (0-70) (3-Y.O) (Class E)
3-50 (3-50) **6f (Equitrack)** £2,817.25 (£853.00: £416.50: £198.25) Stalls: Low GOING minus 0.44 sec per fur (FST)

				SP	RR	SF
247*	**V I P Charlie (67)** (JRJenkins) **3-9-4** 7x SSanders(2) (lw: a.p: led on bit 1f out: easily)	—	**1**	$10/11^{1}$	77+	32
214^{2}	**Forgotten Times (USA) (69)** (TMJones) **3-9-6** NCarlisle(1) (b: b.hind: lw: led to 1f out: unable qckn)	3	**2**	$5/2^{2}$	71	26
247^{3}	**Windborn (49)** (CNAllen) **3-7-11**(3) MartinDwyer(5) (outpcd: hdwy fnl f: r.o)	nk	**3**	20/1	50	5
181^{6}	**Fit For The Job (IRE) (63)** (TWall) **3-8-9**(5) JBramhill(4) (a.p: rdn over 2f out: one pce)	1¼	**4**	25/1	61	16
215*	**First Chance (IRE) (70)** (DRCElsworth) **3-9-7** SDrowne(3) (lw: lost pl 2f out: r.o one pce fnl f)	1½	**5**	$3/1^{3}$	64	19
				(SP 114.6%)	**5 Rn**	

1m 13.43 (2.33) CSF £3.39 TOTE £1.70: £1.00 £2.60 (£2.60) OWNER Mr Andy Taylor (ROYSTON) BRED T. F. Parrett

294 RHONE H'CAP (0-70) (4-Y.O+) (Class E)
4-20 (4-21) **1m (Equitrack)** £2,843.25 (£861.00: £420.50: £200.25) Stalls: High GOING minus 0.44 sec per fur (FST)

				SP	RR	SF
213^{2}	**Invocation (63)** (GLMoore) **10-9-7** CandyMorris(11) (b.nr hind: hld up: rdn over 1f out: led ins fnl f: r.o wl)	—	**1**	14/1	70	52
241^{2}	**Ertlon (70)** (CEBrittain) **7-10-0** DHolland(3) (led 7f out tl ins fnl f: unable qckn)	½	**2**	$100/30^{1}$	76	58
238^{2}	**Robellion (69)** (DWPArbuthnot) **6-9-13v** SWhitworth(10) (b.hind: stdy hdwy 3f out: rdn over 1f out: one pce ins fnl f)	hd	**3**	$5/1^{2}$	75	57
	Desert Calm (IRE) (48) (PDEvans) **8-7-13**(7)ow6 AnthonyBond(5) (lost pl 7f out: hdwy over 1f out: str run fnl f: fin wl)	s.h	**4**	25/1	54	30
216^{6}	**Nails Tails (40)** (SDow) **4-7-12** JQuinn(9) (hld up: rdn over 2f out: one pce)	3	**5**	12/1	40	22
194^{3}	**Captain's Day (43)** (HJCollingridge) **5-7-10**(5) RMullen(2) (a.p: rdn over 3f out: wknd over 2f out)	1½	**6**	$13/2^{3}$	40	22
213^{3}	**Bernard Seven (IRE) (65)** (MDods) **5-9-9b** AClark(4) (a.p: rdn over 3f out: wknd over 1f out)	nk	**7**	14/1	61	43
211*	**Regal Splendour (CAN) (62)** (RJO'Sullivan) **4-9-6** SSanders(1) (lw: prom over 6f)	4	**8**	$5/1^{2}$	50	32
	Nordinex (IRE) (67) (DRCElsworth) **5-9-6**(5) DGriffiths(6) (b: lw: led 1f: wknd 4f out)	1½	**9**	7/1	52	34
194^{10}	**Loch Style (57)** (RHollinshead) **4-8-12**(3) FLynch(8) (bhd fnl 5f)	nk	**10**	12/1	42	24
210*	**Montone (IRE) (64)** (JRJenkins) **7-9-8v** DHarrison(7) (bhd fnl 4f)	25	**11**	9/1	—	—
				(SP 124.8%)	**11 Rn**	

1m 39.03 (1.63) CSF £58.35 CT £259.25 TOTE £12.60: £5.60 £2.50 £3.90 (£14.30) Trio £40.00 OWNER Mr R. Kiernan (BRIGHTON) BRED Juddmonte Farms

295 GIRONDE H'CAP (0-60) (4-Y.O+) (Class F)
4-50 (4-51) **1m 4f (Equitrack)** £2,585.20 (£727.20: £355.60) Stalls: Low GOING minus 0.44 sec per fur (FST)

				SP	RR	SF
147^{7}	**Soojama (IRE) (41)** (RMFlower) **7-8-11b** MWigham(16) (s.s: rdn & hdwy over 2f out: led wl ins fnl f: r.o wl)	—	**1**	7/1	50	35
216^{5}	**Fabulous Mtoto (32)** (MSSaunders) **7-8-2** NCarlisle(8) (hdwy over 4f out: rdn 2f out: led ins fnl f: sn hdd: unable qckn)	2½	**2**	13/2	38	23
216*	**In the Money (IRE) (57)** (RHollinshead) **8-9-8**(5) DGriffiths(12) (stdy hdwy 6f out: rdn over 3f out: r.o one pce)	1¾	**3**	$9/2^{1}$	60	45
	Czarna (IRE) (43) (CEBrittain) **6-8-13** DHolland(10) (led: rdn over 2f out: hdd ins fnl f: sn wknd)	nk	**4**	$5/1^{2}$	46	31
216^{2}	**Dr Edgar (54)** (MDods) **5-9-10** AClark(2) (lw: a.p: rdn over 4f out: one pce)	2	**5**	$6/1^{3}$	54	39
216^{9}	**Real Madrid (38)** (GPEnright) **6-8-3v**(5) ADaly(11) (a.p: rdn over 3f out: one pce)	s.h	**6**	14/1	38	23
93^{4}	**Premier League (IRE) (35)** (JELong) **7-8-5** LeesaLong(14) (a.p: rdn over 3f out: one pce)	nk	**7**	12/1	35	20
141^{6}	**Cuban Reef (33)** (WJMusson) **5-8-0**(3) MBaird(13) (nvr nr to chal)	9	**8**	12/1	21	6
104^{12}	**Carrolls Marc (IRE) (40)** (CMurray) **9-8-10** MTebbutt(5) (hdwy over 3f out: wknd over 2f out)	1¼	**9**	12/1	26	11
260^{2}	**Studio Thirty (39)** (RDickin) **5-8-9** JQuinn(1) (a mid div)	2	**10**	8/1	23	8
261^{7}	**Uoni (45)** (PButler) **4-8-7**(5) JBramhill(15) (prom 8f)	nk	**11**	14/1	28	10
	High Five (IRE) (26) (RIngram) **7-7-10** GBardwell(6) (b: s.s: a bhd)	¾	**12**	33/1	8	—
141^{7}	**Lord Ellangowan (IRE) (40)** (RIngram) **4-8-7b** TWilliams(7) (b: lw: bhd fnl 4f)	10	**13**	25/1	9	—
43^{9}	**Embroidered (29)** (RMFlower) **4-7-10e** FNorton(3) (bhd fnl 9f)	¾	**14**	50/1	—	—
67^{6}	**North Ardar (43)** (TWall) **7-8-13** DHarrison(9) (prom 7f)	1	**15**	14/1	9	—
	Petros Pride (40) (MJBolton) **4-8-7b1** SSanders(4) (b: b.hind: lw: prom 5f: t.o fnl 4f)	dist	**16**	50/1	—	—
				(SP 139.9%)	**16 Rn**	

2m 33.76 (3.76) CSF £53.48 CT £221.67 TOTE £8.40: £2.00 £2.30 £1.90 £2.20 (£30.10) Trio £34.20 OWNER Mr M. G. Rogers (JEVINGTON) BRED E. and Mrs Hanley
LONG HANDICAP Embroidered 7-1 High Five (IRE) 7-4
WEIGHT FOR AGE 4yo-3lb

T/Plpt: £120.40 (108.97 Tckts). T/Qdpt: £6.20 (218.36 Tckts) AK

0254-WOLVERHAMPTON (L-H) (Standard)
Wednesday February 19th
WEATHER: unsettled WIND: str half bhd

296 GROUSE MEDIAN AUCTION MAIDEN STKS (3, 4 & 5-Y.O) (Class E)
2-00 (2-02) **7f (Fibresand)** £2,804.25 (£849.00: £414.50: £197.25) Stalls: High GOING: 0.21 sec per fur (SLW)

				SP	RR	SF
	Mysterium (NPLittmoden) **3-8-7** TGMcLaughlin(6) (hld up: hdwy over 3f out: rdn over 2f out: r.o to ld nr fin)	—	**1**	25/1	65	18
	Sharpo Wassl (WJHaggas) **3-8-7** DHolland(8) (lt-f: s.i.s: sn prom: led over 2f out: edgd lft over 1f out: hdd nr fin)	nk	**2**	8/13[1]	64	17
	Qualitair Silver (JFBottomley) **3-8-2** LCharnock(1) (w'like: bkwd: led tl rdn & hdd over 2f out: ev ch over 1f out: one pce)	2½	**3**	14/1	54	7
169[9]	**Harry's Treat (45)** (JLEyre) **5-9-5** RLappin(10) (a.p: one pce fnl 2f)	2	**4**	14/1	49	19
234[2]	**Warp Drive (IRE) (55)** (WRMuir) **3-8-7** AClark(4) (prom tl wknd wl over 1f out)	1½	**5**	10/1[2]	51	4
	Who's That Man (SCWilliams) **3-8-7** JTate(11) (lengthy: bkwd: wl bhd 4f out: nrst fin)	4	**6**	11/1[3]	42	—
	Ron's Round (KOCunningham-Brown) **3-8-7** CMunday(7) (s.i.s: nvr nrr)	½	**7**	25/1	40	—
173[8]	**Plenty of Sunshine** (ICampbell) **4-9-5** SWhitworth(9) (prom over 4f)	1	**8**	33/1	33	3
	Solar Dawn (MJohnston) **3-8-2** JFanning(3) (neat: bit bkwd: s.i.s: bhd fnl 3f)	4	**9**	12/1	24	—
	Sweet Seventeen (40) (HJCollingridge) **4-9-5** MRimmer(2) (bkwd: prom over 3f)	2½	**10**	20/1	18	—
	Heathyard's Flight (RHollinshead) **3-8-4**(3) FLynch(5) (lt-f: a bhd: t.o)	dist	**11**	10/1[2]	—	—

(SP 124.8%) **11 Rn**

1m 32.5 (7.80) CSF £38.25 TOTE £33.70: £4.30 £1.50 £6.60 (£37.20) Trio £140.20; £144.18 to Wincanton 20/2/97 OWNER Mrs G. L. Taylor (WOLVERHAMPTON) BRED Stetchworth Park Stud Ltd
WEIGHT FOR AGE 3yo-17lb
IN-FOCUS: **The close proximity of the apparently unfit third raises a few question marks about this form.**

297 PARTRIDGE CLAIMING STKS (4-Y.O+) (Class F)
2-30 (2-30) **7f (Fibresand)** £2,580.00 (£780.00: £380.00: £180.00) Stalls: High GOING: 0.21 sec per fur (SLW)

				SP	RR	SF
254[4]	**Duke Valentino (85)** (RHollinshead) **5-8-13**(5) DGriffiths(4) (lw: led 1f: led over 2f out: clr over 1f out: r.o wl)	—	**1**	10/11[1]	71	53
136[4]	**Jigsaw Boy (62)** (PGMurphy) **8-8-8** SDrowne(5) (hld up: hdwy over 2f out: rdn over 1f out: no imp)	3½	**2**	9/2[2]	53	35
176[9]	**Bogart (45)** (CWFairhurst) **6-8-10v** KFallon(6) (hld up: rdn over 2f out: hdwy over 1f out: one pce fnl f)	2½	**3**	14/1	49	31
243*	**Sea Devil (53)** (MJCamacho) **11-8-6** LCharnock(3) (hld up: hdwy over 3f out: rdn over 2f out: wknd fnl f)	2½	**4**	5/1[3]	40	22
274[9]	**Bentico (73)** (MrsNMacauley) **8-8-9**(3) CTeague(2) (no hdwy fnl 2f)	½	**5**	6/1	44	26
	Miletrian City (56) (JBerry) **4-8-4b**(5) PRoberts(8) (s.i.s: nvr trbld ldrs)	nk	**6**	9/1	41	23
213[4]	**Bold Faith** (WJMusson) **4-8-7**(3) MBaird(1) (s.i.s: led 6f out tl over 2f out: sn wknd)	8	**7**	8/1	24	6
	Peacefull Reply (USA) (31) (FHLee) **7-8-6v** CRutter(7) (rdn 3f out: sn bhd: t.o)	8	**8**	33/1	1	—

(SP 132.2%) **8 Rn**

1m 30.3 (5.60) CSF £6.23 TOTE £2.30: £1.10 £2.10 £3.10 (£6.70) OWNER Mr J. E. Bigg (UPPER LONGDON) BRED Shadwell Estate Company Limited

298 SNIPE H'CAP (0-80) (3-Y.O) (Class D)
3-00 (3-00) **1m 1f 79y (Fibresand)** £3,387.50 (£1,025.00: £500.00: £237.50) Stalls: Low GOING: 0.21 sec per fur (SLW)

				SP	RR	SF
264*	**Puzzlement (57)** (CEBrittain) **3-8-0** 5x DaleGibson(5) (lw: mde virtually all: rdn & wnt lft wl over 1f out: rdn out)	—	**1**	7/2[3]	66	43
281[3]	**Globetrotter (IRE) (78)** (MJohnston) **3-9-7** DHolland(4) (lw: w wnr: hrd rdn over 2f out: ev ch whn bmpd wl over 1f out: one pce)	2½	**2**	9/2	83	60
281[2]	**Pinchincha (FR) (65)** (DMorris) **3-8-8** NDay(6) (hld up: hdwy over 4f out: rdn over 3f out: one pce fnl 2f)	3	**3**	100/30[2]	65	42
281[5]	**Time Can Tell (68)** (CMurray) **3-8-11** NicolaHowarth(7) (hld up: hdwy over 4f out: rdn over 3f out: hung lft over 1f out: one pce)	½	**4**	14/1	67	44
124*	**Broctune Line (55)** (MrsMReveley) **3-7-12** DWright(1) (s.s: hdwy over 4f out: wknd 3f out)	1	**5**	4/1	52	29
175[3]	**Mardrew (64)** (DJSffrenchDavis) **3-8-4**(3) PMcCabe(3) (w ldrs tl wknd over 4f out: t.o)	14	**6**	3/1[1]	37	14
240[3]	**Aspecto Lad (IRE) (62)** (MJohnston) **3-8-5b**[1] JFanning(2) (a bhd: t.o)	hd	**7**	15/2	35	12

(SP 126.9%) **7 Rn**

2m 2.8 (6.80) CSF £20.31 TOTE £3.80: £2.00 £2.20 (£5.80) OWNER Mrs C. E. Brittain (NEWMARKET) BRED Mrs C. E. Brittain
OFFICIAL EXPLANATION **Mardrew: no explanation offered.**
IN-FOCUS: **Dale Gibson was making his comeback after five months out through injury.**

299 WOODCOCK H'CAP (0-90) (4-Y.O+) (Class C)
3-30 (3-30) **1m 4f (Fibresand)** £5,446.00 (£1,648.00: £804.00: £382.00) Stalls: Low GOING: 0.21 sec per fur (SLW)

				SP	RR	SF
	Leading Spirit (IRE) (71) (CFWall) **5-8-12** DHolland(4) (a.p: led over 5f out: clr 2f out: easily)	—	**1**	13/8[1]	85+	66
182[2]	**Nikita's Star (IRE) (75)** (DJGMurraySmith) **4-8-13** DHarrison(8) (hld up: hdwy over 4f out: sn rdn: chsd wnr over 3f out: no imp)	6	**2**	4/1[2]	81	59
179[2]	**Second Colours (USA) (83)** (MCPipe) **7-9-10** KFallon(9) (hld up: hdwy over 3f out: one pce fnl 2f)	nk	**3**	8/1	89	70
244[2]	**China Castle (85)** (PCHaslam) **4-9-9** SDrowne(6) (hld up: hdwy over 3f out: hrd rdn over 2f out: one pce)	1	**4**	5/1[3]	89	67
100[5]	**Prince Danzig (IRE) (85)** (DJGMurraySmith) **6-9-7**(5) JBramhill(5) (hld up: hdwy over 3f out: wknd wl over 1f out)	4	**5**	10/1	84	65
176[3]	**Bardon Hill Boy (IRE) (87)** (BHanbury) **5-10-0** JStack(2) (bhd fnl 3f)	15	**6**	8/1	66	47
72[9]	**Obelos (USA) (62)** (MissSJWilton) **6-8-0**(3) MartinDwyer(1) (prom over 6f)	6	**7**	25/1	33	14
244[3]	**Dancing Cavalier (67)** (RHollinshead) **4-8-2**(3) FLynch(3) (sn wl bhd: t.o)	21	**8**	14/1	10	—
244*	**Super High (88)** (PHowling) **5-10-1b** 5x FNorton(7) (led over 6f: rdn & wknd over 4f out: t.o)	20	**9**	8/1	4	—

(SP 127.7%) **9 Rn**

2m 39.6 (7.10) CSF £8.44 CT £41.11 TOTE £2.90: £1.10 £1.40 £3.40 (£7.90) Trio £29.30 OWNER Induna Racing Partners Two (NEWMARKET) BRED Sir Peter Nugent and Ascot Stables
WEIGHT FOR AGE 4yo-3lb

300 PHEASANT (S) STKS (3-Y.O) (Class F)

4-00 (4-00) **1m 100y (Fibresand)** £2,640.00 (£740.00: £360.00) Stalls: Low GOING: 0.21 sec per fur (SLW)

				SP	RR	SF
234^{*}	**Bailieborough Boy (IRE) (63)** (TDBarron) **3-9-3b** DHarrison(5) (hld up: hdwy over 3f out: led ins fnl f: pushed out)	—	1	$3/1^{2}$	71	33
217^{4}	**Zorba (61)** (CWThornton) **3-8-12** KFallon(4) (plld hrd: led: wandered & hdd ins fnl f: hrd rdn: r.o)	hd	2	Evens ^{1}	66	28
	Riscatto (USA) (66) (WRMuir) **3-8-12** AClark(6) (a.p: ev ch wl over 1f out: one pce)	2½	3	$5/1^{3}$	61	23
	Ejeer (IRE) (MRChannon) **3-8-7**$^{(5)}$ PPMurphy(3) (dwlt: hdwy over 2f out: wknd over 1f out)	2½	4	$3/1^{2}$	56	18
259^{5}	**Contravene (IRE) (60)** (JBerry) **3-8-7b**$^{1(5)}$ TEDurcan(1) (prom: sddle slipped over 5f out: wknd over 2f out)	10	5	9/1	37	—
240^{5}	**Taome (IRE) (39)** (PDEvans) **3-8-5**$^{(7)}$ AnthonyBond(2) (chsd ldr: wknd over 2f out)	1¾	6	16/1	34	—
				(SP 132.5%)	**6 Rn**	

1m 54.0 (9.00) CSF £7.17 TOTE £3.60: £1.90 £1.20 (£2.40) OWNER M P Burke Developments Ltd (THIRSK) BRED John Purfield
Bt in 4,200 gns

301 JAY H'CAP (0-80) (3-Y.O+) (Class D)

4-30 (4-32) **5f (Fibresand)** £3,468.75 (£1,050.00: £512.50: £243.75) Stalls: Low GOING: 0.21 sec per fur (SLW)

				SP	RR	SF
	The Happy Fox (IRE) (70) (BAMcMahon) **5-9-7b** LNewton(12) (a.p: led wl over 1f out: r.o wl)	—	1	16/1	79	51
170^{4}	**Madrina (64)** (JBerry) **4-8-10**$^{(5)}$ PFessey(13) (s.i.s: hdwy on outside 3f out: ev ch over 1f out: r.o)	¾	2	14/1	71	43
	Sing With the Band (76) (BAMcMahon) **6-9-6**$^{(7)}$ SRighton(10) (hdwy over 1f out: r.o)	¾	3	20/1	80	52
166^{2}	**Broadstairs Beauty (IRE) (77)** (DShaw) **7-9-11b**$^{(3)}$ CTeague(7) (led over 3f out tl wl over 1f out: sn hung rt: nt qckn)	nk	4	$6/1^{2}$	80	52
137^{12}	**Chadwell Hall (70)** (SRBowring) **6-9-2b**$^{(5)}$ ADaly(6) (a.p: ev ch over 1f out: one pce)	1¾	5	12/1	68	40
222^{2}	**Gi La High (60)** (MartynMeade) **4-8-6**$^{(5)}$ DSweeney(4) (led 1f: wknd over 1f out)	1	6	$6/1^{2}$	54	26
222^{9}	**Sotonian (HOL) (47)** (PSFelgate) **4-7-7**$^{(5)}$ JBramhill(11) (prom over 3f)	1¼	7	16/1	37	9
286^{*}	**Antonias Melody (71)** (SRBowring) **4-9-8** ^{7x} SWebster(8) (prom 3f)	1¾	8	$4/1^{1}$	56	28
214^{5}	**Dande Flyer (68)** (DWPArbuthnot) **4-9-5** DHolland(1) (b: outpcd)	nk	9	$6/1^{2}$	52	24
	Night Harmony (IRE) (58) (MissSJWilton) **4-8-9** SWhitworth(3) (prom over 3f)	1	10	20/1	39	11
170^{6}	**Chemcast (70)** (JLEyre) **4-9-4b**$^{(3)}$ OPears(9) (nvr trbld ldrs)	1½	11	8/1	46	18
137^{4}	**Ramsey Hope (73)** (CWFairhurst) **4-9-10v** KFallon(5) (led after 1f: sn hdd: eased whn btn fnl f)	s.h	12	$7/1^{3}$	49	21
137^{3}	**Napier Star (64)** (MrsNMacauley) **4-9-1v** SSanders(2) (b.off hind: outpcd)	s.h	13	8/1	40	12
				(SP 133.2%)	**13 Rn**	

63.1 secs (4.20) CSF £225.08 CT £2,414.37 TOTE £12.70: £3.00 £4.20 £9.50 (£115.80) Trio £515.70; £523.00 to Wincanton 20/2/97 OWNER Mr G. Whitaker (TAMWORTH) BRED Abbey Lodge Stud

T/Plpt: £770.40 (17.18 Tckts). T/Qdpt: £196.30 (5.01 Tckts) KH

0290-LINGFIELD (L-H) (Standard)

Thursday February 20th

1st race hand-timed
WEATHER: overcast & damp WIND: str half bhd

302 BARNABY RUDGE CLAIMING STKS (4-Y.O+) (Class F)

2-15 (2-16) **1m 4f (Equitrack)** £2,417.20 (£679.20: £331.60) Stalls: Low GOING minus 0.37 sec per fur (FST)

				SP	RR	SF
219^{2}	**Persian Conquest (IRE) (65)** (RIngram) **5-9-3b** SSanders(2) (chsd ldr 4f: chsd ldr 5f out: led over 2f out: drvn out)	—	1	$8/11^{1}$	69	31
236^{2}	**Colosse (55)** (JLEyre) **5-7-11**$^{(7)}$ RFfrench(4) (led over 9f: hrd rdn over 1f out: r.o)	½	2	$7/4^{2}$	55	17
	Bedouin Prince (USA) (13) (MrsLStubbs) **10-8-9** ACulhane(5) (b: a.p: chsd ldr 8f out to 5f out: wknd over 3f out)	10	3	40/1	47	9
295^{9}	**Carrolls Marc (IRE) (40)** (CMurray) **9-8-11** MTebbutt(3) (bhd fnl 4f)	6	4	$10/1^{3}$	41	3
252^{7}	**Pyrrhic Dance (30)** (MJHaynes) **7-8-11** GBardwell(6) (b: bhd fnl 4f)	hd	5	100/1	41	3
	Yellow Dragon (IRE) (46) (BAPearce) **4-8-5**$^{(7)}$ GGallagher(1) (b: s.s: bhd fnl 4f)	8	6	14/1	34	—
				(SP 113.4%)	**6 Rn**	

2m 36.2 (6.20) CSF £2.06 TOTE £1.50: £1.10 £1.10 (£1.50) OWNER Mr B. Scott (EPSOM) BRED Louis A. Walshe
WEIGHT FOR AGE 4yo-3lb
Colosse clmd M S Anderson £4,000

303 BLEAK HOUSE (S) STKS (3-Y.O+) (Class G)

2-45 (2-46) **6f (Equitrack)** £2,106.30 (£591.80: £288.90) Stalls: Low GOING minus 0.37 sec per fur (FST)

				SP	RR	SF
184^{4}	**Justinianus (IRE) (33)** (JJBridger) **5-9-2**$^{(5)}$ ADaly(2) (w ldr: rdn over 2f out: led ins fnl f: drvn out)	—	1	50/1	50	37
152^{16}	**Newington Butts (IRE) (50)** (KMcAuliffe) **7-9-2e** DHolland(6) (led tl ins fnl f: unable qckn)	1¼	2	$7/1^{3}$	42	29
263^{4}	**Double Oscar (IRE) (47)** (DNicholls) **4-9-7b** AlexGreaves(3) (hld up: rdn over 2f out: r.o ins fnl f)	½	3	$7/4^{2}$	45	32
208^{2}	**Myttons Mistake (64)** (ABailey) **4-9-7** SSanders(7) (lw: hdwy over 3f out: rdn over 2f out: one pce)	1½	4	$5/4^{1}$	41	28
169^{12}	**Fancy Design (IRE) (25)** (PMitchell) **4-9-2** AClark(1) (b.hind: rdn over 4f out: bhd fnl 2f)	3	5	20/1	28	15
263^{6}	**Featherstone Lane (54)** (MissLCSiddall) **6-9-0v**$^{(7)}$ TSiddall(5) (a bhd)	nk	6	$7/1^{3}$	33	20
134^{11}	**Respectable Jones (40)** (RHollinshead) **11-9-2b**$^{(5)}$ DGriffiths(4) (dwlt: a bhd)	2	7	20/1	27	14
				(SP 117.3%)	**7 Rn**	

1m 13.69 (2.59) CSF £328.47 TOTE £39.80: £6.70 £3.20 (£98.40) OWNER Mr J. J. Bridger (LIPHOOK) BRED W. H. E. Lagro
No bid

304 GREAT EXPECTATIONS H'CAP (0-70) (4-Y.O+) (Class E)

3-15 (3-15) **5f (Equitrack)** £2,752.25 (£833.00: £406.50: £193.25) Stalls: High GOING minus 0.37 sec per fur (FST)

				SP	RR	SF
282^{*}	**Rififi (67)** (RIngram) **4-9-11** ^{7x} SWhitworth(9) (dwlt: hdwy over 2f out: hrd rdn over 1f out: led ins fnl f: r.o wl)	—	1	$9/4^{1}$	72	56
263^{5}	**Ivory's Grab Hire (47)** (KTIvory) **4-8-5b** DBiggs(5) (rdn over 2f out: hdwy over 1f out: r.o wl ins fnl f)	¾	2	$11/2^{3}$	50	34

				SP	RR	SF
263[3]	**Superlao (BEL) (38)** (JJBridger) **5-7-5**(5) RMullen(3) (b.nr hind: lost pl 3f out: rallied fnl f: fin wl)	1½	3	12/1	36	20
	Bowcliffe Grange (IRE) (50) (DWChapman) **5-8-8** ACulhane(6) (led tl ins fnl f: sn wknd)	1	4	14/1	45	29
222[7]	**Rennyholme (39)** (JHetherton) **6-7-11b** NAdams(1) (a.p: rdn over 1f out: one pce)	1	5	20/1	30	14
214[9]	**Lord Sky (66)** (ABailey) **6-9-10** SSanders(2) (lost pl over 2f out: one pce)	1	6	9/2[2]	54	38
223[2]	**Allstars Dancer (38)** (TJNaughton) **4-7-10** GBardwell(8) (a bhd)	2½	7	11/2[3]	18	2
282[5]	**Logie Pert Lad (39)** (JJBridger) **5-7-11**ow1 FNorton(7) (s.i.s: a bhd)	¾	8	20/1	17	—
223[6]	**Imp Express (IRE) (40)** (GMMoore) **4-7-12b** NCarlisle(10) (spd over 3f)	s.h	9	8/1	18	2

(SP 114.7%) **9 Rn**

59.34 secs (1.14) CSF £13.23 CT £106.99 TOTE £2.80: £1.70 £1.50 £2.40 (£9.00) Trio £42.00 OWNER Brooknight Guarding Ltd (EPSOM) BRED Milton Park Stud Partnership

LONG HANDICAP Allstars Dancer 7-9 Logie Pert Lad 6-11 Superlao (BEL) 7-5

305 DAVID COPPERFIELD H'CAP (0-70) (4-Y.O+ F & M) (Class E)

3-45 (3-46) **1m 2f (Equitrack)** £2,830.25 (£857.00: £418.50: £199.25) Stalls: Low GOING minus 0.37 sec per fur (FST)

				SP	RR	SF
176[8]	**Tallulah Belle (57)** (NPLittmoden) **4-9-2** TGMcLaughlin(4) (hld up: led over 3f out: clr over 2f out: rdn out)	—	1	9/1	72	41
186[2]	**Shanghai Lil (55)** (MJFetherston-Godley) **5-9-1** FNorton(7) (hdwy over 3f out: chsd wnr over 2f out: no imp)	6	2	9/4[1]	60	30
235[5]	**Queens Stroller (IRE) (36)** (REPeacock) **6-7-5**(5) JBramhill(5) (rdn over 3f out: hdwy over 1f out: r.o one pce)	5	3	10/1	33	3
	Mimosa (60) (SDow) **4-9-0**(5) ADaly(10) (s.s: rdn over 4f out: hdwy over 1f out: nvr nrr)	1¼	4	16/1	55	24
179[7]	**Tea Party (USA) (69)** (KOCunningham-Brown) **4-10-0** DHolland(6) (hdwy over 5f out: wknd over 2f out)	8	5	10/1	52	21
194[9]	**Total Rach (IRE) (40)** (AGNewcombe) **5-7-11b**(3) NVarley(1) (b: a.p: led over 4f out tl over 3f out: wknd over 2f out)	1¾	6	8/1	20	—
186[5]	**Absolutelystunning (46)** (MrsBarbaraWaring) **4-8-5** WRyan(8) (b: b.hind: prom over 5f)	2	7	14/1	23	—
173[2]	**Passage Creeping (IRE) (56)** (SDow) **4-9-1e** SSanders(9) (prom over 6f)	1½	8	9/2[2]	30	—
28[5]	**Sally Armstrong (45)** (CWThornton) **4-8-4** SDrowne(3) (bhd fnl 6f)	7	9	12/1	8	—
47[7]	**Mogin (40)** (TJNaughton) **4-7-13** GBardwell(2) (led over 5f: wknd over 3f out)	1½	10	15/2[3]	1	—

(SP 120.3%) **10 Rn**

2m 8.0 (3.70) CSF £27.78 CT £197.00 TOTE £8.00: £2.30 £1.10 £5.70 (£18.20) Trio £33.00 OWNER Trojan Racing (WOLVERHAMPTON)
BRED Bowler (Presswork) Services Ltd

LONG HANDICAP Queens Stroller (IRE) 7-4

WEIGHT FOR AGE 4yo-1lb

OFFICIAL EXPLANATION **Tallulah Belle: regarding the apparent improvement in form, the trainer stated that he could not account for the filly's disappointing run last time, but that it may have come too quickly after her three previous starts.**

306 HARD TIMES MAIDEN STKS (3-Y.O+) (Class D)

4-15 (4-16) **7f (Equitrack)** £3,273.75 (£990.00: £482.50: £228.75) Stalls: Low GOING minus 0.37 sec per fur (FST)

				SP	RR	SF
	Agent (67) (JLEyre) **4-9-10** DeanMcKeown(2) (led 6f out: rdn out)	—	1	5/2[2]	65	32
177[7]	**Zelaya (IRE) (50)** (GLMoore) **4-9-5** FNorton(4) (a.p: chsd wnr fnl 2f: unable qckn)	2	2	7/1[3]	55	22
215[2]	**Perang Polly** (LordHuntingdon) **5-9-5** DHarrison(1) (b.hind: led 1f: rdn over 4f out: one pce)	1¾	3	4/6[1]	51	18
215[5]	**Magazine Gap** (PatMitchell) **4-9-5**(5) AmandaSanders(5) (hld up: chsd wnr over 4f out to 2f out: one pce)	s.h	4	33/1	56	23
273[13]	**Lady Westbury (IRE)** (PCRitchens) **6-9-5** SDrowne(6) (bhd fnl 5f)	10	5	100/1	29	—
	Alagna (SCWilliams) **3-8-2** JTate(3) (leggy: bhd fnl 4f)	2½	6	16/1	23	—

(SP 110.9%) **6 Rn**

1m 28.32 (3.92) CSF £17.43 TOTE £3.40: £1.10 £1.80 (£8.00) OWNER Mr M. Gleason (HAMBLETON) BRED Carlton Consultants Ltd

WEIGHT FOR AGE 3yo-17lb

307 NICHOLAS NICKLEBY H'CAP (0-80) (3-Y.O) (Class D)

4-45 (4-46) **7f (Equitrack)** £3,387.50 (£1,025.00: £500.00: £237.50) Stalls: Low GOING minus 0.37 sec per fur (FST)

				SP	RR	SF
180*	**The Wyandotte Inn (77)** (RHollinshead) **3-9-4**(3) FLynch(8) (hdwy over 3f out: led over 1f out: rdn out)	—	1	4/1[2]	85	40
217[2]	**Plan For Profit (IRE) (77)** (MJohnston) **3-9-7** DHolland(6) (rdn & hdwy over 3f out: edgd lft ins fnl f: r.o wl)	nk	2	11/4[1]	84	39
264[2]	**Swift (60)** (MJPolglase) **3-7-11**(7) RFfrench(3) (chsd ldr 6f out: led over 3f out: rn wd bnd wl over 1f out: sn hdd: 3rd & btn whn bmpd ins fnl f)	1¼	3	4/1[2]	65	20
	Noble Hero (67) (JJSheehan) **3-8-11** SDrowne(2) (hdwy over 1f out: nvr nrr)	3	4	12/1	65	20
227[4]	**Countless Times (77)** (WRMuir) **3-9-0**(7) JWilkinson(4) (led over 3f: wknd over 2f out)	3½	5	10/1	67	22
225[4]	**Abstone Queen (54)** (PDEvans) **3-7-12v** DWright(1) (bhd fnl 2f)	s.h	6	8/1[3]	44	—
185[3]	**Kayzee (IRE) (52)** (SDow) **3-7-5**(5) RMullen(7) (lw: a bhd)	9	7	12/1	21	—
180[7]	**A Breeze (73)** (DMorris) **3-9-3** NDay(5) (prom over 3f)	1¾	8	8/1[3]	38	—

(SP 113.4%) **8 Rn**

1m 27.33 (2.93) CSF £13.79 CT £41.57 TOTE £3.00: £2.60 £1.30 £1.40 (£5.30) OWNER Mr G. A. Farndon (UPPER LONGDON) BRED N. W. Rimington

LONG HANDICAP Kayzee (IRE) 7-8

T/Plpt: £379.20 (24.63 Tckts). T/Qdpt: £11.60 (70.47 Tckts) AK

ABU DHABI (UAE) (L-H) (Firm)
Friday January 31st

308a H. H. THE PRESIDENT'S CUP (3-Y.O+)

7f (Turf) £14,539.57 (£7,269.78: £4,361.87: £2,907.91)

			SP	RR	SF
Kassbaan (USA) (SbinSuroor,UAE) **7-9-3** JCarroll	—	1		105	—
Numbered Account (SSeemar,UAE) **6-9-2** RHills	1	2		102	—
Airport (USA) (DJSelvaratnam,UAE) **6-9-2** BDoyle	¾	3		100	—
Ikaab (USA) (KPMcLaughlin,UAE) **5-9-3** JCArias	2¼	4		96	—
Takkatamm (USA) (SbinSuroor,UAE) **5-9-2** JCarroll	nk	5		94	—

Kahir Almaydan (IRE) (DJSelvaratnam,UAE) **4-9-2** WSupple	2	6		90	—
Dancing Zena (IRE) (PLRudkin,UAE) **7-9-3** PaulEddery	¾	7		89	—
					7 Rn

1m 22.12 OWNER Sh Rashid bin Maktoum Al Maktoum BRED Gainsborough Farm Inc
Kassbaan (USA), whose trainer won this last year with Diffident, made it two out of two for the season. Tracking the leaders on the inside, he challenged over a furlong out and, soon asserting himself, ran on well.
Numbered Account, who finished half-a-length behind Dancing Zena last time out, reversed that form here. He has come close on a number of occasions this term and met an in-form rival in the winner.

NAD AL SHEBA (Dubai, UAE) (L-H) (Fast)
Thursday February 13th

309a H. H. SHEIKH MAKTOUM BIN RASHID AL MAKTOUM CHALLENGE (Listed) (4-Y.O+)
5-00 (5-08) **1m (Dirt)** £8,078.00 (£4,039.00: £2,423.00: £1,616.00)

				SP	RR	SF
	Kammtarra (USA) (SbinSuroor,UAE) **4-8-11** LDettori	—	1		113	—
308a*	**Kassbaan (USA)** (SbinSuroor,UAE) **7-8-11** JCarroll	4½	2		104	—
	Wathik (USA) (PLRudkin,UAE) **7-8-11b** PaulEddery	5	3		94	—
	Gothenberg (IRE) (MJohnston) **4-8-11** JWeaver	4½	4		85	—
						11 Rn

1m 35.62 OWNER Mr Saeed Maktoum Al Maktoum BRED Gainsborough Farm Inc.
Kammtarra (USA) took it up over two furlongs out and won in very good style. Though he is highly unlikely to reach the heights of his unbeaten half-brother, Lammtarra, he is still improving and looks well worth a place in the field for the Dubai World Cup.
Gothenberg (IRE) disappointed connections with a lacklustre display, racing in second place but only plugging on at the same pace when Kammtarra swept past. This was his first try on dirt, and he was some way off full fitness.

0270a-CAGNES-SUR-MER (Nice, France) (L-H) (Good)
Sunday February 16th

310a GRAND PRIX DU CONSEIL GENERAL DES ALPES MARITIMES (Listed) (4-Y.O+)
3-05 (3-06) **1m 5f** £28,058.00 (£10,325.00: £6,453.00)

				SP	RR	SF
267a*	**Peckinpah's Soul (FR)** (DSmaga,France) **5-8-9** DBoeuf	—	1		104	—
148a*	**Philanthrop (FR)** (J-PGallorini,France) **5-8-7** ODoleuze	½	2		101	—
	Kariver (FR) (XPuleo,France) **6-9-0** FCheyer	½	3		108	—
267a7	**Whitechapel (USA)** (LordHuntingdon) **9-8-7** DHarrison (btn approx 6½l)		7		—	—
	Major Change (MissGayKelleway) **5-8-7** DHolland (btn over 8l)		10		—	—
	Twilight Sleep (USA) (LordHuntingdon) **5-8-7** AJunk (btn wl over 8l)		13		—	—
						13 Rn

2m 48.1 P-M 1.70F: 1.10F 2.00F 2.20F (6.00F) OWNER A. Lequeux (LAMORLAYE) BRED Manita Investment Corporation
267a Whitechapel (USA) was never far off the pace and led briefly at the two-furlong pole, but could not quicken up thereafter. He needs softer ground.
Major Change, having his first run since being sold out of Richard Hannon's yard, moved up to be a close fifth turning into the straight, but lack of a recent run took its toll in the final quarter mile.
Twilight Sleep (USA) was prominent until beginning to weaken three furlongs out.

0271a-SAINT-MORITZ (Switzerland) (R-H) (Good (Snow))
Sunday February 16th

311a GROSSER PREIS VON ST MORITZ (Listed) (4-Y.O+)
2-45 (2-45) **1m 2f** £23,148.00 (£9,259.00: £6,944.00)

				SP	RR	SF
	Diamond Pro (ALowe,Germany) **6-9-6** KMarks	—	1		98	—
229a2	**Shturm (RUS)** (MWeiss,Switzerland) **4-9-9** RKaderli	5½	2		93	—
229a*	**Sentosa Star (IRE)** (MHourigan,Ireland) **6-9-12** PGHourigan	¾	3		94	—
271a2	**Celestial Key (USA)** (MJohnston) **7-9-0** DeanMcKeown (btn over 16l)		7		—	—
						17 Rn

2m 11.0 TOTE 16.80SF: 3.40SF 1.70SF 1.80SF (96.00SF) OWNER Mr J. Lamote BRED Lariston Bloodstock
271a Celestial Key (USA) tracked the leaders before moving into second rounding the home turn. He began to weaken a furlong and a half out, and clearly did not stay the trip.

0296-WOLVERHAMPTON (L-H) (Standard)
Friday February 21st
WEATHER: fine WIND: str across

312 FARNSFIELD MAIDEN APPRENTICE H'CAP (0-60) (I) (4-Y.O+) (Class G)
1-55 (1-55) **1m 100y (Fibresand)** £1,745.00 (£495.00: £245.00) Stalls: Low GOING minus 0.13 sec per fur (FST)

				SP	RR	SF
*164*6	**Jilly Beveled (35)** (RonaldThompson) **5-8-6** DDenby(8) (hld up: hdwy 4f out: led over 1f out: rdn out)	—	1	10/1	37	14
*150*5	**Nukud (USA) (37)** (GROldroyd) **5-8-3v**(5)ow2 SBuckley(11) (hdwy 5f out: led wl over 1f out: sn hdd: r.o ins fnl f)	½	2	6/1	38	13
*122*8	**Ballet de Cour (35)** (TJEtherington) **4-8-3**(3) CLowther(10) (dwlt: racd wd: gd hdwy fnl 2f: nrst fin)	1¼	3	33/1	34	11
*192*8	**Recessions Over (38)** (NPLittmoden) **6-8-4**(5) RCody-Boutcher(1) (w ldr tl lost pl over 3f out: plld out 2f out: kpt on)	1¾	4	11/4 1	33	10
*202*9	**Taniyar (FR) (34)** (RHollinshead) **5-7-12**(7)ow4 DHayden(3) (in tch: lost pl 4f out: plld out & r.o wl appr fnl f)	s.h	5	8/1	29	2

Form	Horse (details)	Dist	Pos	SP	RR	SF
	Happy Brave (35) (PDCundell) **5-8-6** PDoe(9) (lw: prom: rdn 2f out: sn btn)	s.h	**6**	14/1	30	7
284^{8}	**Mustang (31)** (CWThornton) **4-7-11**(5) AMcCarthy(7) (hld up: hdwy 6f out: led 3f out tl wl over 1f out: sn btn)	s.h	**7**	$4/1^{3}$	26	3
177^{2}	**Hornpipe (33)** (JWharton) **5-8-4b** AnthonyBond(6) (b: trckd ldrs: rdn over 2f out: nt run on)	1	**8**	$3/1^{2}$	26	3
209^{11}	**Supreme Illusion (AUS) (25)** (JohnBerry) **4-7-3e**(7) DarrenWilliams(4) (led tl hdd & wknd 3f out)	5	**9**	20/1	9	—
280^{5}	**Young Frederick (IRE) (57)** (KRBurke) **4-9-7b**^{1}(7) PWright(2) (prom 5f)	6	**10**	20/1	29	6
192^{10}	**Eccentric Dancer (25)** (MPBielby) **4-7-5b**(5) RBrisland(5) (s.i.s: hdwy after 2f: wknd 3f out)	22	**11**	33/1	—	—

(SP 128.2%) **11 Rn**

1m 52.1 (7.10) CSF £65.51 CT £1,228.32 TOTE £9.60: £2.00 £1.70 £9.10 (£23.30) Trio £116.10; £130.83 to Kempton 22/2/97 OWNER P D Q Express Security Services (DONCASTER) BRED W. J. Kelly

LONG HANDICAP Supreme Illusion (AUS) 7-5

IN-FOCUS: **The inside of the course appeared to be riding particularly slow, having a considerable effect on most of the results.**

313 FARNSFIELD MAIDEN APPRENTICE H'CAP (0-60) (II) (4-Y.O+) (Class G)

2-25 (2-25) **1m 100y (Fibresand)** £1,745.00 (£495.00: £245.00) Stalls: Low GOING minus 0.13 sec per fur (FST)

Form	Horse (details)	Dist	Pos	SP	RR	SF
286^{3}	**Gold Lining (IRE) (31)** (EJAlston) **4-8-10**(5) JFowle(7) (trckd ldrs: led over 1f out: pushed out)	—	**1**	$3/1^{1}$	43	28
144^{7}	**Flagstaff (USA) (36)** (KRBurke) **4-8-13**(7) PWright(9) (hdwy over 3f out: kpt on wl fnl f)	1¼	**2**	$6/1^{3}$	46	31
235^{3}	**Ring the Chief (30)** (MDIUsher) **5-8-9**(5) RBrisland(8) (lw: led: clr over 4f out: hdd over 1f out: sn btn)	5	**3**	$3/1^{1}$	30	15
177^{4}	**Dino's Mistral (32)** (FHLee) **4-8-11**(5) RCody-Boutcher(6) (hdwy 5f out: rdn over 2f out: sn btn)	1¼	**4**	$7/2^{2}$	30	15
	Seconds Away (22) (JSGoldie) **6-8-1**(5) JMcAuley(10) (chsd ldrs 5f)	1¾	**5**	10/1	17	2
256^{8}	**Efficacious (IRE) (31)** (PEccles) **4-9-1** PDoe(5) (chsd ldr over 4f)	1	**6**	20/1	24	9
	Mr Titch (23) (WMcKeown) **4-8-4**(3) CLowther(4) (bit bkwd: in tch: effrt 4f out: no imp)	4	**7**	20/1	8	—
230^{10}	**Needwood Nutkin (40)** (BCMorgan) **4-9-3**(7) DHayden(2) (hmpd after 1f: in tch for 5f)	7	**8**	25/1	12	—
	Jackson's Panther (IRE) (33) (CADwyer) **5-8-12**(5) AMcCarthy(3) (sn bhd)	1¼	**9**	10/1	2	—
243^{W}	**Bold Joker (21)** (GROldroyd) **6-7-12b**(7) DMernagh(11) (s.s: sn rdn along: nvr nr ldrs)	2	**10**	33/1	—	—
	Bad News (28) (JMBradley) **5-8-12** AnthonyBond(1) (chsd ldrs: rdn over 3f out: sn wknd)	14	**11**	25/1	—	—

(SP 124.8%) **11 Rn**

1m 51.4 (6.40) CSF £19.31 CT £55.85 TOTE £4.00: £1.90 £3.10 £1.70 (£12.00) Trio £28.40 OWNER Mr Peter Onslow (PRESTON) BRED Consultores Asociados S A

314 BEESTHORPE CLAIMING STKS (3-Y.O) (Class F)

2-55 (2-56) **1m 4f (Fibresand)** £2,294.00 (£644.00: £314.00) Stalls: Low GOING minus 0.13 sec per fur (FST)

Form	Horse (details)	Dist	Pos	SP	RR	SF
277^{*}	**State of Gold (IRE) (47)** (JHetherton) **3-8-9** MTebbutt(9) (lw: trckd ldrs: led wl over 1f out: pushed out)	—	**1**	$7/1^{3}$	64	22
249^{*}	**As-Is (66)** (MJohnston) **3-8-11** DHolland(8) (prom: led over 4f out tl wl over 1f out: r.o)	2	**2**	$4/1^{2}$	63	21
277^{3}	**Skelton Sovereign (IRE) (56)** (RHollinshead) **3-8-5**(3) FLynch(7) (hdwy 5f out: ev ch 2f out: one pce appr fnl f)	1¼	**3**	10/1	59	17
240^{*}	**Kingsdown Trix (IRE) (56)** (GLMoore) **3-8-8** CRutter(5) (hld up: hdwy over 4f out: rdn over 2f out: no imp)	3	**4**	10/1	55	13
191^{*}	**Head Gardener (IRE) (70)** (NPLittmoden) **3-9-1** TGMcLaughlin(2) (hld up: rdn 4f out: nvr trbld ldrs)	1	**5**	$8/11^{1}$	60	18
234^{4}	**Mirror Four Sport (51)** (MJohnston) **3-7-6**(7) NPollard(1) (led 1f: wknd over 4f out)	2	**6**	14/1	42	—
191^{7}	**Indian Rapture (44)** (RonaldThompson) **3-7-12v**^{1} DWright(6) (chsd ldrs tl wknd 6f out)	14	**7**	25/1	22	—
191^{8}	**Melodic Squaw** (MPBielby) **3-8-3** TWilliams(10) (bit bkwd: led after 1f tl after 2f: wknd 4f out)	19	**8**	33/1	2	—
191^{4}	**Rock Fantasy (48)** (CMurray) **3-8-0** NicolaHowarth(3) (led after 2f: hdd over 4f out: sn wknd)	½	**9**	33/1	—	—
19^{5}	**Full Traceability (IRE) (40)** (JJO'Neill) **3-8-0** JQuinn(4) (a bhd)	nk	**10**	20/1	—	—

(SP 129.7%) **10 Rn**

2m 41.9 (9.40) CSF £34.48 TOTE £12.60: £3.10 £3.10 £2.30 (£15.60) Trio £32.30 OWNER Keith West Partnership (MALTON) BRED Ali K. Al Jafleh

315 ADELPHI FOR CNC MACHINING H'CAP (0-70) (4-Y.O+) (Class E)

3-25 (3-26) **1m 4f (Fibresand)** £2,843.25 (£861.00: £420.50: £200.25) Stalls: Low GOING minus 0.13 sec per fur (FST)

Form	Horse (details)	Dist	Pos	SP	RR	SF
295^{3}	**In the Money (IRE) (57)** (RHollinshead) **8-8-10**(5) DGriffiths(6) (lw: hdwy 5f out: chal over 1f out: sn rdn: led wl ins fnl f)	—	**1**	6/1	62	34
260^{3}	**Ambidextrous (IRE) (46)** (EJAlston) **5-8-1**(3) FLynch(9) (lw: hdwy 4f out: led over 2f out: sn rdn: hdd & no ex wl ins fnl f)	¾	**2**	$4/1^{3}$	50	22
252^{5}	**Classic Account (40)** (JLEyre) **9-7-5**(7)ow2 RFfrench(7) (chsd ldrs: effrt 3f out: r.o wl ins fnl f)	1½	**3**	25/1	42	12
219^{3}	**Premier Dance (64)** (DHaydnJones) **10-9-8** AClark(11) (lw: dwlt: racd wd: hdwy 5f out: no imp appr fnl f)	nk	**4**	6/1	66	38
	Backview (70) (BJLlewellyn) **5-10-0** TWilliams(10) (lw: chsd ldrs: led 4f out to 3f out: wknd 2f out)	10	**5**	20/1	58	30
207^{8}	**Up in Flames (IRE) (66)** (SRBowring) **6-9-10** SWebster(3) (prom: rdn 4f out: wknd over 2f out)	¾	**6**	14/1	53	25
260^{*}	**Northern Motto (52)** (JSGoldie) **4-8-7** DeanMcKeown(2) (led 4f: led 5f out to 4f out: sn btn)	1¾	**7**	$2/1^{1}$	37	6
276^{*}	**Forzair (60)** (JJO'Neill) **5-9-4** 5x WRyan(8) (prom: lost pl 7f out: n.d after)	2½	**8**	10/1	42	14
219^{*}	**Mr Speculator (55)** (JEBanks) **4-8-10b** JQuinn(5) (w ldr: led 8f out to 5f out: led 3f out: sn hdd & wknd)	3	**9**	$11/4^{2}$	33	2
	Missed the Boat (IRE) (38) (AGNewcombe) **7-7-7**(3) NVarley(1) (bit bkwd: rdn 7f out: a bhd)	30	**10**	20/1	—	—
205^{9}	**Charter (65)** (TJNaughton) **6-9-9** DHolland(12) (prom 5f: sn wl bhd)	dist	**11**	16/1	—	—

(SP 143.6%) **11 Rn**

2m 40.9 (8.40) CSF £33.36 CT £565.78 TOTE £6.10: £2.70 £1.80 £3.00 (£9.60) Trio £69.30 OWNER Mr J. E. Bigg (UPPER LONGDON) BRED Cheveley Park Stud Ltd

LONG HANDICAP Missed the Boat (IRE) 7-3 Classic Account 7-3

WEIGHT FOR AGE 4yo-3lb

OFFICIAL EXPLANATION **Northern Mtoto: the rider reported that the gelding was never travelling well and was leading off the wrong leg. The veterinary officer also reported that the gelding was stiff behind.**

316 EAST MIDLANDS ELECTRICITY (LINCOLN) H'CAP (0-85) (3-Y.O+) (Class D)

3-55 (3-56) **7f (Fibresand)** £3,713.75 (£1,124.00: £548.50: £260.75) Stalls: Low GOING minus 0.13 sec per fur (FST)

Form	Horse (details)	Dist	Pos	SP	RR	SF
238^{3}	**Mr Nevermind (IRE) (85)** (GLMoore) **7-10-0** SWhitworth(9) (lw: in tch: hdwy over 2f out: rdn to ld nr fin)	—	**1**	$11/2^{3}$	91	49
257^{7}	**Leigh Crofter (65)** (PDCundell) **8-8-8b** DHolland(8) (w ldr: led over 3f out tl ct nr fin)	hd	**2**	10/1	71	29

				SP	RR	SF
257[6]	**Dawalib (USA) (61)** (DHaydnJones) **7-8-4** AClark(10) (hld up: hdwy 3f out: ev ch over 1f out: unable qckn nr fin)	hd	**3**	4/1[1]	67	25
254[3]	**Elite Hope (USA) (74)** (NTinkler) **5-9-3** GCarter(1) (led over 3f: kpt on fnl f)	nk	**4**	4/1[1]	79	37
	Kira (74) (JLEyre) **7-9-3** KFallon(5) (prom tl rdn & wknd 2f out)	3	**5**	8/1	72	30
274[5]	**Gulf Shaadi (65)** (EJAlston) **5-8-8** SDrowne(3) (lw: in tch 4f)	2	**6**	8/1	58	16
294[10]	**Loch Style (57)** (RHollinshead) **4-8-0** NCarlisle(2) (lw: prom over 3f)	s.h	**7**	10/1	50	8
	Safio (68) (ABailey) **4-8-11** DWright(6) (hld up & plld hrd: hdwy whn nt clr run 3f out: no ch after)	3	**8**	10/1	55	13
245*	**Three Arch Bridge (72)** (MJohnston) **5-9-1b** 6x DeanMcKeown(4) (in tch 4f)	¾	**9**	5/1[2]	57	15
	Pengamon (80) (HJCollingridge) **5-9-9** JQuinn(7) (b: bit bkwd: hld up: hdwy over 2f out: sn rdn & wknd)	¾	**10**	8/1	63	21
				(SP 132.7%)	**10 Rn**	

1m 29.1 (4.40) CSF £61.91 CT £201.54 TOTE £8.70: £2.20 £3.50 £2.60 (£39.30) Trio £32.20 OWNER Pennine Partners (BRIGHTON) BRED Robert Corridan

317 WELLOW (QUALIFIER) (S) STKS (3-Y.O) (Class F)

4-25 (4-25) **7f** **(Fibresand)** £2,294.00 (£644.00: £314.00) Stalls: Low GOING minus 0.13 sec per fur (FST)

				SP	RR	SF
240[4]	**Diamond Eyre (50)** (JLEyre) **3-8-6** RLappin(6) (hld up: hdwy 3f out: led ins fnl f: comf)	—	**1**	11/4[2]	53	—
265[3]	**Julia's Relative** (RGuest) **3-8-1**(5) JBramhill(4) (b: lw: w ldrs: led 2f out: hdd & unable qckn ins fnl f)	2½	**2**	5/1[3]	47	—
156*	**Fast Spin (62)** (TDBarron) **3-9-4** ACulhane(8) (chsd ldrs: rdn & no ex fnl f)	3½	**3**	6/4[1]	51	—
300[5]	**Contravene (IRE) (60)** (JBerry) **3-8-8b**(5) TEDurcan(2) (lw: led after 1f: hdd 2f out: sn rdn & btn)	3½	**4**	12/1	38	—
246[4]	**Terry's Rose (48)** (RHollinshead) **3-8-3**(3) FLynch(3) (lw: bhd: rdn 3f out: nvr rchd ldrs)	4	**5**	12/1	22	—
	Jack The Lad (IRE) (68) (JHetherton) **3-8-11** MTebbutt(5) (led 1f: wknd over 2f out)	¾	**6**	5/1[3]	25	—
259[3]	**Pretty Sally (IRE) (56)** (DJGMurraySmith) **3-8-6b**[1] DHarrison(1) (hld up: hdwy 4f out: wknd over 2f out)	3½	**7**	5/1[3]	12	—
259[7]	**Prince Emar** (TDEasterby) **3-8-11** LCharnock(7) (rdn over 3f out: a bhd)	½	**8**	25/1	16	—
204[8]	**Sodelk (40)** (JHetherton) **3-8-6** CRutter(9) (chsd ldrs over 3f)	1¾	**9**	25/1	7	—
				(SP 139.7%)	**9 Rn**	

1m 31.7 (7.00) CSF £19.55 TOTE £4.20: £1.50 £2.10 £1.70 (£16.10) Trio £45.90 OWNER Diamond Racing Ltd (HAMBLETON) BRED Mrs M. Chaworth Musters
No bid

318 FARNDON H'CAP (0-70) (3-Y.O+) (Class E)

4-55 (4-58) **6f** **(Fibresand)** £2,843.25 (£861.00: £420.50: £200.25) Stalls: Low GOING minus 0.13 sec per fur (FST)

				SP	RR	SF
	Needle Match (53) (JJO'Neill) **4-9-1** WRyan(10) (hdwy 2f out: led ins fnl f: rdn out)	—	**1**	25/1	62	31
263[9]	**Sir Tasker (46)** (JLHarris) **9-8-8** SSanders(11) (lw: led: clr over 2f out: hdd ins fnl f: unable qckn)	1¾	**2**	8/1[3]	50	19
233[2]	**Bold Frontier (62)** (KTIvory) **5-9-10b** CScally(6) (b: b.hind: plld hrd: trckd ldrs: rdn 2f out: r.o wl ins f)	hd	**3**	7/4[1]	66	35
275[5]	**Marjorie Rose (IRE) (63)** (ABailey) **4-9-11** DWright(9) (chsd ldrs: one pce appr fnl f)	1¼	**4**	10/1	64	33
198[5]	**Hoh Majestic (IRE) (55)** (RonaldThompson) **4-9-3** JQuinn(7) (chsd ldr 4f)	nk	**5**	8/1[3]	55	24
107[6]	**Aljaz (50)** (MissGayKelleway) **7-8-12** DHolland(2) (bit bkwd: bhd: plld out wl over 1f out: r.o)	1	**6**	6/1[2]	47	16
235[4]	**Napoleon Star (IRE) (43)** (SRBowring) **6-8-5** NAdams(13) (hdwy 3f out: no imp appr fnl f)	1½	**7**	8/1[3]	36	5
208[4]	**Takhlid (USA) (66)** (DWChapman) **6-10-0** ACulhane(5) (effrt 2f out: nvr rchd ldrs)	1½	**8**	20/1	55	24
287[2]	**Blue Lugana (37)** (NBycroft) **5-7-8**(5) JBramhill(4) (prom over 3f)	hd	**9**	8/1[3]	26	—
275[2]	**Delrob (49)** (DHaydnJones) **6-8-11b** AClark(1) (s.i.s: nvr nr ldrs)	s.h	**10**	6/1[2]	38	7
288[6]	**Answers-To-Thomas (51)** (JMJefferson) **4-8-13** DeanMcKeown(3) (nvr nr to chal)	hd	**11**	25/1	40	9
	Stephensons Rocket (50) (RAFahey) **6-8-12** FNorton(12) (bit bkwd: chsd ldrs tl wknd over 2f out)	2½	**12**	25/1	32	1
	Speedy Snaps Pride (38) (PDCundell) **5-7-11b**(3) MartinDwyer(8) (in tch 3f)	¾	**13**	25/1	18	—
				(SP 138.6%)	**13 Rn**	

1m 15.3 (4.10) CSF £210.58 CT £499.98 TOTE £56.00: £18.10 £2.90 £1.80 (£57.90) Trio £285.00; £321.15 to Kempton 22/2/97 OWNER Clayton Bigley Partnership Ltd (PENRITH) BRED Tarworth Bloodstock Investments Ltd

T/Plpt: £215.50 (40 Tckts). T/Qdpt: £18.60 (41.01 Tckts) Dk

0302-**LINGFIELD (L-H) (Standard)**
Saturday February 22nd

WEATHER: fine WIND: slt bhd

319 MERLIN (S) H'CAP (0-60) (I) (4-Y.O+) (Class F)

1-50 (1-51) **1m** **(Equitrack)** £2,134.40 (£598.40: £291.20) Stalls: High GOING minus 0.35 sec per fur (FST)

				SP	RR	SF
172[6]	**Soldier Cove (USA) (46)** (MartynMeade) **7-8-9**(5) DSweeney(2) (chsd ldrs: rdn over 2f out: styd on ins fnl f: led last stride)	—	**1**	16/1	56	30
128[11]	**Blushing Grenadier (IRE) (49)** (MJFetherston-Godley) **5-9-3v** DHolland(5) (led: clr over 1f out: rdn ins fnl f: hdd last stride)	s.h	**2**	10/1	59	33
210[2]	**Bold Habit (43)** (JPearce) **12-8-11** GBardwell(1) (rr: hdwy over 1f out: r.o)	2½	**3**	7/1	48	22
278[5]	**Hawaii Storm (FR) (55)** (DJSffrenchDavis) **9-9-2**(7) KerryBaker(11) (rr: hdwy over 1f out: r.o ins fnl f)	hd	**4**	7/2[1]	60	34
303*	**Justinianus (IRE) (38)** (JJBridger) **5-8-1**(5) 5x ADaly(7) (prom: rdn over 1f out: wknd ins fnl f)	2½	**5**	13/2[3]	38	12
	Ajkuit (IRE) (40) (JJSheehan) **4-8-8** AClark(10) (nvr nrr)	2½	**6**	11/1	35	9
273[5]	**Lachesis (38)** (DNicholls) **4-7-13**(7) IonaWands(6) (prom: rdn 2f out: wknd 1f out)	2	**7**	4/1[2]	29	3
120[7]	**Manabar (56)** (MJPolglase) **5-9-10b** TGMcLaughlin(8) (a bhd)	5	**8**	10/1	37	11
199[5]	**Bright Paragon (IRE) (28)** (KTIvory) **8-7-10** NAdams(12) (hdwy 5f out: wknd over 2f out)	2	**9**	20/1	5	—
92[7]	**Sweet Amoret (37)** (PHowling) **4-8-5** FNorton(4) (prom to ½-wy)	hd	**10**	25/1	14	—
134[6]	**Shaynes Domain (30)** (RMFlower) **6-7-12b** JQuinn(3) (bhd fr ½-wy)	11	**11**	8/1	—	—
				(SP 120.2%)	**11 Rn**	

1m 41.23 (3.83) CSF £154.92 CT £1,126.90 TOTE £24.20: £2.60 £2.40 £1.80 (£43.30) Trio £55.60 OWNER Ladyswood Racing Club (MALMESBURY) BRED Weststar Bloodstock
LONG HANDICAP Bright Paragon (IRE) 7-9
No bid

320 BUZZARD H'CAP (0-80) (3-Y.O) (Class D)

2-20 (2-20) **5f (Equitrack)** £3,322.50 (£1,005.00: £490.00: £232.50) Stalls: High GOING minus 0.35 sec per fur (FST)

				SP	RR	SF
251^{*}	**Roffey Spinney (IRE) (66)** (RHannon) **3-9-3** SSanders(8) (a.p: chsd ldr 2f out: led over 1f out: r.o wl)	—	**1**	$4/1^{2}$	75	43
251^{2}	**Castle Ashby Jack (62)** (PHowling) **3-8-13b** FNorton(6) (a.p: rdn 2f out: kpt on one pce ins fnl f)	3	**2**	13/2	61	29
282^{2}	**Blues Magic (IRE) (65)** (MBell) **3-8-11v1**(5) GFaulkner(2) (b.off hind: led 3f out: hdd over 1f out: one pce)	nk	**3**	$5/1^{3}$	63	31
258^{4}	**Sparkling Edge (60)** (CADwyer) **3-8-11** DRMcCabe(5) (outpcd in rr: hdwy over 1f out: r.o)	1¾	**4**	7/1	53	21
75^{*}	**Hever Golf Lover (IRE) (62)** (TJNaughton) **3-8-13** DHolland(7) (b.nr hind: chsd ldrs: rdn 2f out: one pce)	1½	**5**	$9/4^{1}$	50	18
258^{3}	**Nightingale Song (70)** (MartynMeade) **3-9-2**(5) DSweeney(1) (led 2f: grad wknd)	1¾	**6**	$5/1^{3}$	52	20
251^{5}	**Lucy of Arabia (IRE) (59)** (JJSheehan) **3-8-10** SDrowne(3) (a bhd)	1¾	**7**	20/1	36	4
212^{4}	**Whizz Kid (47)** (JJBridger) **3-7-7**(5) RMullen(4) (chsd ldrs to ½-wy)	¾	**8**	20/1	21	—

(SP 119.5%) **8 Rn**

59.81 secs (1.61) CSF £28.70 CT £120.43 TOTE £5.20: £1.90 £1.50 £1.80 (£21.60) OWNER Mrs D. F. Cock (MARLBOROUGH) BRED P. Henley

321 MERLIN (S) H'CAP (0-60) (II) (4-Y.O+) (Class F)

2-50 (2-51) **1m (Equitrack)** £2,134.40 (£598.40: £291.20) Stalls: High GOING minus 0.35 sec per fur (FST)

				SP	RR	SF
211^{3}	**Gadge (40)** (ABailey) **6-8-8** SSanders(5) (led 6f out: rdn over 1f out: r.o)	—	**1**	$5/1^{2}$	50	25
274^{7}	**Live Project (IRE) (55)** (MJohnston) **5-9-9** DHolland(1) (chsd ldrs: rdn 2f out: styd on ins fnl f)	1¼	**2**	$5/1^{2}$	63	38
280^{2}	**Statistician (45)** (JohnBerry) **5-8-13e** JQuinn(11) (hld up: hdwy ½-wy: rdn over 1f out: r.o one pce)	nk	**3**	$11/2^{3}$	52	27
241^{11}	**Gold Lance (USA) (42)** (RJO'Sullivan) **4-8-10b** DHarrison(6) (a.p: rdn over 1f out: one pce)	1	**4**	14/1	47	22
238^{5}	**Our Shadee (USA) (48)** (KTIvory) **7-9-2v** CScally(12) (b: b.nr hind: rr: hdwy over 2f out: rdn over 1f out: one pce)	1¼	**5**	$3/1^{1}$	50	25
241^{9}	**Sound the Trumpet (IRE) (35)** (RCSpicer) **5-7-12**(5) JBramhill(10) (hdwy over 3f out: rdn 2f out: one pce)	1¼	**6**	33/1	35	10
71^{10}	**Awafeh (40)** (SMellor) **4-8-8v** NAdams(4) (bhd fr ½-wy)	12	**7**	33/1	16	—
210^{5}	**Spectacle Jim (40)** (BAPearce) **8-8-1**(7) GGallagher(3) (b: rr: sme hdwy 6f out: wknd 3f out)	½	**8**	25/1	15	—
	Wingnut (IRE) (30) (RIngram) **4-7-7b**(5) RMullen(7) (a bhd)	2½	**9**	14/1	—	—
	Roman Reel (USA) (57) (GLMoore) **6-9-11** SWhitworth(9) (led 2f: sn wknd)	1	**10**	13/2	25	—
209^{9}	**Madonna da Rossi (30)** (MDods) **4-7-12** DaleGibson(8) (prom 3f)	1¼	**11**	25/1	—	—
59^{6}	**Grey Legend (40)** (RMFlower) **4-8-8b** MWigham(2) (dwlt: a bhd: t.o)	12	**12**	12/1	—	—

(SP 121.7%) **12 Rn**

1m 41.26 (3.86) CSF £27.17 CT £133.17 TOTE £6.60: £2.10 £2.90 £2.40 (£21.60) Trio £18.70 OWNER Mr J. B. Wilcox (TARPORLEY) BRED Snowdrop Stud Co Ltd

No bid

322 BARN OWL MAIDEN STKS (4-Y.O+) (Class D)

3-25 (3-26) **1m (Equitrack)** £3,338.75 (£1,010.00: £492.50: £233.75) Stalls: High GOING minus 0.35 sec per fur (FST)

				SP	RR	SF
	Besweetome (JPearce) **4-8-9** MWigham(9) (led after 1f: clr 2f out: pushed out ins fnl f)	—	**1**	$7/4^{1}$	76	36
207^{5}	**Genuine John (IRE) (63)** (JParkes) **4-8-9**(5) JBramhill(5) (a.p: chsd wnr over 3f out: rdn 2f out: no imp)	7	**2**	$4/1^{3}$	67	27
218^{6}	**Haute Cuisine (40)** (RJRWilliams) **4-9-0b1** DBiggs(8) (b.hind: s.i.s: sn rcvrd to chse wnr tl over 3f out: grad wknd)	12	**3**	33/1	43	3
108^{6}	**Square Mile Miss (IRE) (30)** (PHowling) **4-8-9** JQuinn(1) (led 1f: wknd 3f out)	3	**4**	40/1	32	—
	Rash Gift (67) (LordHuntingdon) **4-8-9** DHarrison(3) (in tch tl wknd over 3f out)	7	**5**	$15/8^{2}$	18	—
	Lovely Morning (55) (DJGMurraySmith) **4-8-9** GCarter(4) (a bhd: t.o)	10	**6**	20/1	—	—
	Camphar (RMFlower) **4-8-9** SDrowne(2) (b: dwlt: a bhd: t.o)	15	**7**	50/1	—	—
	Be Satisfied (37) (GLMoore) **4-9-0** AClark(6) (in tch tl wknd 5f out: t.o)	18	**8**	50/1	—	—
200^{2}	**Misky Bay (53)** (DJSCosgrove) **4-9-0b1** MRimmer(7) (ref to r: t.n.p)		**R**	6/1	—	—

(SP 119.5%) **9 Rn**

1m 40.17 (2.77) CSF £8.37 TOTE £2.70: £1.90 £1.10 £2.20 (£8.20) Trio £73.50 OWNER Hon Robert Acton (NEWMARKET) BRED R. P. Acton

323 SPARROWHAWK H'CAP (0-90) (3-Y.O+) (Class C)

3-55 (3-56) **6f (Equitrack)** £5,052.85 (£1,529.80: £746.90: £355.45) Stalls: Low GOING minus 0.35 sec per fur (FST)

				SP	RR	SF
263^{2}	**Squire Corrie (68)** (DWChapman) **5-8-8** ACulhane(6) (chsd ldr: led wl over 1f out: hrd rdn & edgd lft ins fnl f: all out)	—	**1**	$6/1^{3}$	75	40
253^{3}	**Apollo Red (68)** (GLMoore) **8-8-8** CandyMorris(2) (a.p: rdn & ev ch wl ins fnl f: r.o)	s.h	**2**	9/1	75	40
304^{6}	**Lord Sky (66)** (ABailey) **6-8-6** SSanders(5) (a.p: ev ch ins fnl f: r.o)	nk	**3**	12/1	72	37
	Stand Tall (81) (LadyHerries) **5-9-7** DeanMcKeown(8) (b.hind: bit bkwd: dwlt: outpcd & bhd: hdwy over 1f out: r.o ins fnl f)	4	**4**	7/1	76	41
253^{4}	**Scissor Ridge (74)** (JJBridger) **5-8-9**(5) RMullen(1) (prom: rdn & outpcd over 3f out: rallied ins fnl f: r.o)	s.h	**5**	12/1	69	34
253^{2}	**Robo Magic (USA) (80)** (LMontagueHall) **5-9-6** DHolland(7) (b: hdwy 3f out: rdn 2f out: wknd over 1f out)	2	**6**	$9/2^{2}$	70	35
253^{*}	**Princely Sound (84)** (MBell) **4-9-5**(5) GFaulkner(3) (led: hdd wl over 1f out: wkng whn hmpd ins fnl f)	½	**7**	$9/4^{1}$	73	38
238^{6}	**Blue Flyer (IRE) (80)** (RIngram) **4-9-6b** SWhitworth(4) (sn outpcd: a bhd)	1	**8**	$9/2^{2}$	66	31
253^{8}	**Krystal Max (IRE) (66)** (JCullinan) **4-8-6** JQuinn(9) (hdwy 3f out: wknd 2f out)	3	**9**	25/1	44	9

(SP 123.1%) **9 Rn**

1m 12.73 (1.63) CSF £56.98 CT £588.89 TOTE £6.60: £2.70 £1.80 £2.20 (£19.60) Trio £63.40 OWNER Miss N. F. Thesiger (YORK) BRED Whitsbury Manor Stud

324 OSPREY H'CAP (0-70) (4-Y.O+) (Class E)

4-30 (4-30) **2m (Equitrack)** £2,843.25 (£861.00: £420.50: £200.25) Stalls: Low GOING minus 0.35 sec per fur (FST)

				SP	RR	SF
252^{6}	**Coleridge (51)** (JJSheehan) **9-8-9b** AClark(6) (a.p: led over 4f out: hdd 2f out: rallied to ld 1f out: r.o)	—	**1**	25/1	61	38
256^{*}	**Petoskin (68)** (JPearce) **5-9-12** MWigham(3) (a.p: led 2f out: hdd 1f out: r.o)	¾	**2**	10/1	77	54
261^{*}	**Hattaafeh (IRE) (73)** (MissBSanders) **6-10-3** SSanders(9) (hld up: rdn to improve 3f out: sn hrd rdn: one ce)	7	**3**	$5/4^{1}$	75	52
285^{3}	**English Invader (58)** (CADwyer) **6-9-2** DRMcCabe(4) (hld up: hdwy 4f out: rdn over 2f out: one pce)	nk	**4**	12/1	60	37
252^{2}	**Guest Alliance (IRE) (61)** (GLMoore) **5-9-5** CandyMorris(7) (sn led: hdd after 4f: wknd over 3f out)	7	**5**	$7/2^{2}$	56	33
202^{5}	**Chez Catalan (39)** (RAkehurst) **6-7-11b**ow1 JQuinn(8) (keen hold: prom tl wknd over 2f out)	8	**6**	16/1	26	2

205^{4} **Stalled (IRE) (51)** (PTWalwyn) **7-8-9** WRyan(1) (led after 4f: hdd over 4f out: sn wknd: t.o) ....15 **7** 5/1^{3} 23 —
228* **Illuminate (65)** (DCO'Brien) **4-9-3** GBardwell(5) (bhd fnl 5f: t.o) ....30 **8** 10/1 7 —
(SP 118.9%) **8 Rn**

3m 26.53 (5.53) CSF £233.52 CT £504.15 TOTE £17.10: £1.60 £3.80 £1.10 (£66.80) Trio £57.70 OWNER Mr P. J. Sheehan (FINDON) BRED W. and R. Barnett Ltd
WEIGHT FOR AGE 4yo-6lb

325 HARRIER LIMITED STKS (0-65) (3-Y.O+) (Class F)
5-00 (5-00) **7f (Equitrack)** £2,450.80 (£688.80: £336.40) Stalls: Low GOING minus 0.35 sec per fur (FST)

			SP	RR	SF
248*	**Sweet Wilhelmina (66)** (LordHuntingdon) **4-9-5** DHarrison(7) (hld up: hdwy over 2f out: led over 1f out: pushed out) .... —	**1**	4/6^{1}	72+	47
278^{4}	**Lancashire Legend (65)** (SDow) **4-9-3**(5) ADaly(1) (led: hdd over 1f out: one pce) 1¼	**2**	11/1	72	47
121^{9}	**Step On Degas (65)** (MJFetherston-Godley) **4-9-0**(5) DGriffiths(2) (chsd ldr over 3f: rdn & outpcd over 2f out: rallied ins fnl f: r.o) ....hd	**3**	7/1	69	44
241^{5}	**Deeply Vale (IRE) (65)** (PButler) **6-9-8** SWhitworth(3) (chsd ldr over 3f out tl over 1f out: sn rdn: one pce)....2½	**4**	5/1^{3}	66	41
274^{2}	**Le Sport (67)** (DNicholls) **4-8-13b**(7) IonaWands(5) (sn outpcd: bhd tl sme late hdwy) 1½	**5**	9/2^{2}	61	36
168^{4}	**Our Kevin (52)** (BAPearce) **3-8-3** DRMcCabe(4) (in tch tl wknd ½-wy: t.o) 23	**6**	33/1	8	—
107^{7}	**Sharp Imp (63)** (RMFlower) **7-9-8b** MWigham(6) (Withdrawn not under Starters' orders: rdr ill in paddock)	**W**	10/1	—	—

(SP 127.7%) **6 Rn**

1m 26.67 (2.27) CSF £9.63 TOTE £1.50: £1.30 £2.30 (£5.60) OWNER Mr Chris van Hoorn (WEST ILSLEY) BRED D. Walker
WEIGHT FOR AGE 3yo-17lb

T/Plpt: £144.60 (76.06 Tckts). T/Qdpt: £20.80 (36.31 Tckts) SM

0284-SOUTHWELL (L-H) (Standard)
Monday February 24th
WEATHER: overcast with heavy showers WIND: str half bhd

326 APENNINES (S) H'CAP (0-60) (I) (3-Y.O+) (Class F)
1-25 (1-25) **6f (Fibresand)** £2,083.00 (£583.00: £283.00) Stalls: Low GOING: 0.02 sec per fur (STD)

			SP	RR	SF
318^{7}	**Napoleon Star (IRE) (43)** (SRBowring) **6-8-11** SWebster(7) (sn bhd & drvn along: hdwy 2f out: styd on wl u.p to ld last 50y) .... —	**1**	7/1^{3}	49	31
297^{4}	**Sea Devil (58)** (MJCamacho) **11-9-12** MTebbutt(6) (trckd ldr: led 2f out tl wl ins fnl f) 1	**2**	9/2^{1}	61	43
1^{11}	**Dictation (USA) (47)** (JJO'Neill) **5-9-1** WRyan(8) (hdwy on outside 2f out: styd on ins fnl f) ....hd	**3**	13/2^{2}	50	32
288^{5}	**Margaretrose Anna (36)** (BPJBaugh) **5-8-4** NAdams(3) (hld up: effrt ½-wy: hrd rdn: edgd rt & styd on fnl f) ...½	**4**	13/2^{2}	38	20
178^{6}	**Time To Fly (34)** (BWMurray) **4-8-2b^{1}** JQuinn(5) (led: hung lft & hdd 2f out: wknd appr fnl f) 3½	**5**	7/1^{3}	26	8
245^{6}	**Fiaba (41)** (MrsNMacauley) **9-8-6v**(3)ow2 CTeague(4) (sn bhd: rn wd ent st: edgd lft & styd on appr fnl f)....2½	**6**	7/1^{3}	27	7
286^{4}	**Shashi (IRE) (53)** (PatMitchell) **5-9-7v^{1}** RLappin(1) (in tch: effrt & wandered 2f out: grad wknd) 1	**7**	13/2^{2}	36	18
	Young Ben (IRE) (29) (JSWainwright) **5-7-6v**(5) JBramhill(9) (b.hind: s.i.s: sn chsng ldrs: outpcd fnl 2f) ....nk	**8**	20/1	11	—
	Niteowl Raider (IRE) (46) (JohnHarris) **4-9-0** JO'Reilly(12) (sn chsng ldrs: wknd over 2f out) 2½	**9**	16/1	22	4
	Silent System (IRE) (28) (DWChapman) **4-7-10** DWright(11) (racd wd: a bhd) 1½	**10**	33/1	—	—
203^{14}	**Wali (USA) (50)** (JLEyre) **7-9-4** TWilliams(2) (mid div: rdn & outpcd ½-wy: n.d) 6	**11**	13/2^{2}	6	—
233^{9}	**Orange And Blue (35)** (MissJFCraze) **4-8-0c**(3) NVarley(10) (racd wd: mid div: rdn & hung lft ½-wy: sn bhd)1½	**12**	20/1	—	—

(SP 127.4%) **12 Rn**

1m 18.4 (4.90) CSF £36.93 CT £205.39 TOTE £10.60: £4.70 £1.30 £4.10 (£33.30) Trio £46.00 OWNER Mr Roland Wheatley (EDWINSTOWE)
BRED Eamon O'Mahony
LONG HANDICAP Silent System (IRE) 7-7
No bid

327 CAUCASUS AMATEUR H'CAP (0-60) (I) (4-Y.O+) (Class F)
1-55 (1-55) **7f (Fibresand)** £2,083.00 (£583.00: £283.00) Stalls: Low GOING: 0.02 sec per fur (STD)

			SP	RR	SF
313^{3}	**Ring the Chief (30)** (MDIUsher) **5-9-5**(4) MrsAUsher(1) (mde all: clr 3f out: unchal) .... —	**1**	11/2^{3}	40	30
278^{6}	**Private Fixture (IRE) (40)** (DMarks) **6-10-5b^{1}** MrTMcCarthy(6) (sn chsng ldrs: styd on same pce fnl 2f) 1¼	**2**	5/2^{2}	47	37
280^{3}	**Dream Carrier (IRE) (40)** (REPeacock) **9-9-12**(7) MrsCPeacock(3) (a chsng ldrs: kpt on one pce fnl 2f) ....nk	**3**	8/1	47	37
	Mels Baby (IRE) (51) (JLEyre) **4-11-2** MissDianaJones(5) (lw: hld up & bhd: effrt 2f out: hung lft: kpt on: nvr rchd ldrs) 4	**4**	9/4^{1}	48	38
177^{11}	**Soaked (40)** (DWChapman) **4-10-5** MissRClark(8) (sn trckng ldrs: effrt 2f out: wknd ins fnl f) ....hd	**5**	9/1	37	27
	Karinska (56) (MCChapman) **7-11-0**(7) MrKLoads(4) (s.i.s: sn chsng ldrs: lost pl over 2f out) 14	**6**	12/1	21	11
203^{13}	**Hershebar (41)** (MrsVAAconley) **7-9-13**(7)ow7 MrGMarkham(2) (chsd ldrs tl lost pl over 2f out) 9	**7**	33/1	—	—
209^{14}	**Roseate Lodge (44)** (SEKettlewell) **11-10-5**(4) MrsCWilliams(10) (racd wd: a bhd) 5	**8**	12/1	—	—
164^{12}	**Gloria Imperator (IRE) (36)** (ABMulholland) **4-10-1** MrMHNaughton(7) (b.off hind: swvd rt st: a bhd & sn drvn along) 5	**9**	25/1	—	—
	Ticka Ticka Timing (40) (BWMurray) **4-10-5v** MissPRobson(9) (racd wd: plld hrd: w ldrs tl lost pl 4f out: sn bhd) 3½	**10**	33/1	—	—

(SP 120.9%) **10 Rn**

1m 33.4 (6.90) CSF £18.29 CT £105.02 TOTE £6.40: £1.30 £1.40 £2.90 (£9.10) Trio £17.50 OWNER Mr G. A. Summers (WANTAGE) BRED Mrs Trisha Dunbar

328 SIERRA MADRE MEDIAN AUCTION MAIDEN STKS (3, 4 & 5-Y.O) (Class E)
2-25 (2-25) **1m 4f (Fibresand)** £3,046.00 (£922.00: £450.00: £214.00) Stalls: Low GOING: 0.02 sec per fur (STD)

			SP	RR	SF
228^{3}	**Love Me Do (USA) (65)** (MJohnston) **3-8-3** JFanning(6) (lw: w ldrs: led over 5f out: rdn over 2f out: edgd rt: hld on towards fin) .... —	**1**	8/11^{1}	61	12
285^{4}	**Zatopek (40)** (JCullinan) **5-9-8**(5) DSweeney(5) (sn drvn along: hdwy to chal over 2f out: nt qckn wl ins fnl f)..nk	**2**	12/1	61	36

	Moonraking (55) (TJEtherington) **4-9-3**(7) CLowther(1) (sn wl bhd: hdwy 5f out: chsd ldrs over 2f out: no imp fnl f)	1¾	**3**	11/2 2	58	30
218 3	**Zine Lane (37)** (JGMO'Shea) **5-9-8v**(5) GLee(8) (chsd ldrs: one pce fnl 3f)	3½	**4**	12/1	54	29
191 5	**Good Day (57)** (CWThornton) **3-8-3** JQuinn(2) (chsd ldrs: drvn along 4f out: wknd over 1f out: eased)	21	**5**	13/2 3	26	—
256 6	**Storm Wind (IRE) (40)** (KRBurke) **4-9-10b**1 ACulhane(4) (led 8f out tl over 5f out: wknd 4f out)	14	**6**	40/1	7	—
	African Sun (IRE) (43) (MCChapman) **4-9-10** DHolland(3) (plld hrd: led to 8f out: wknd qckly 5f out: sn t.o: virtually p.u)	29	**7**	14/1	—	—
286 8	**Veesey (42)** (JohnBerry) **4-9-5e** TWilliams(7) (w ldrs tl lost pl 7f out: t.o 3f out: virtually p.u)	1¾	**8**	33/1	—	—

(SP 114.0%) **8 Rn**

2m 45.0 (12.00) CSF £10.08 TOTE £1.70: £1.10 £1.80 £1.90 (£5.70) OWNER Mr M. Doyle (MIDDLEHAM) BRED Robert S. West Jr.
WEIGHT FOR AGE 3yo-24lb, 4yo-3lb

329 ROCKY CLAIMING STKS (3-Y.O) (Class F)

2-55 (2-58) **1m (Fibresand)** £2,433.00 (£683.00: £333.00) Stalls: Low GOING: 0.02 sec per fur (STD)

				SP	RR	SF
300*	**Bailieborough Boy (IRE) (63)** (TDBarron) **3-8-9b** DHarrison(3) (trckd ldrs: shkn up to ld over 1f out: drvn clr)	—	**1**	13/8 2	73	25
227 5	**Bonnie Lassie (77)** (CWThornton) **3-9-0** DeanMcKeown(1) (chsd ldr: led 5f out tl over 1f out: no ch w wnr)	4	**2**	8/11 1	70	22
193 7	**Le Shuttle (42)** (MHTompkins) **3-7-12** DaleGibson(4) (sn outpcd & drvn along: edgd rt & kpt on fnl f: nvr nr to chal)	5	**3**	16/1	44	—
300 4	**Ejeer (IRE)** (MRChannon) **3-8-6**(5) PPMurphy(2) (dwlt: sn trckng ldrs: effrt over 2f out: wknd over 1f out)	½	**4**	10/1 3	56	8
	What's That Amy (CSmith) **3-8-4** AClark(5) (plld hrd: led to 5f out: wknd over 3f out: sn t.o: virtually p.u)	dist	**5**	50/1	—	—

(SP 112.9%) **5 Rn**

1m 46.0 (7.00) CSF £2.95 TOTE £2.60: £2.20 £1.00 (£1.10) OWNER M P Burke Developments Ltd (THIRSK) BRED John Purfield

330 ALPS H'CAP (0-85) (3-Y.O+) (Class D)

3-25 (3-27) **1m (Fibresand)** £4,484.20 (£1,357.60: £662.80: £315.40) Stalls: Low GOING: 0.02 sec per fur (STD)

				SP	RR	SF
235 7	**Pleasure Trick (USA) (52)** (DonEnricoIncisa) **6-7-10b** KimTinkler(9) (s.i.s: racd wd: hdwy 3f out: hrd rdn & edgd lft: styd on to ld last 50y)	—	**1**	14/1	62	25
273 2	**Rambo Waltzer (70)** (DNicholls) **5-8-7**(7) IonaWands(7) (lw: trckd ldrs: chal ins fnl f: r.o)	nk	**2**	10/1	79	42
274 4	**Sea Spouse (65)** (MBlanshard) **6-8-9** NAdams(2) (lw: trckd ldrs: led over 3f out tl wl ins fnl f)	1¾	**3**	11/2 3	71	34
294 2	**Ertlon (70)** (CEBrittain) **7-9-0** DHolland(1) (sn trckng ldrs: effrt 2f out: wknd appr fnl f)	3½	**4**	9/4 1	69	32
177*	**What A Fuss (67)** (BHanbury) **4-8-11** JStack(5) (trckd ldrs: rdn & outpcd over 3f out: n.d)	13	**5**	6/1	40	3
	Iamus (82) (TDBarron) **4-9-12** DeanMcKeown(4) (mde most tl over 3f out: lost pl 2f out)	1¾	**6**	7/1	51	14
	Mazurek (71) (MGMeagher) **4-9-1** JQuinn(6) (lw: racd wd: outpcd over 4f out: sn bhd)	1¾	**7**	6/1	37	—
274*	**Kingchip Boy (80)** (MJRyan) **8-9-10** AClark(8) (w ldr: wknd over 1f out: eased)	2	**8**	9/2 2	42	5
	Sherqy (IRE) (79) (SEKettlewell) **5-9-2**(7) JennyBenson(3) (hmpd s: a in rr)	18	**9**	33/1	5	—

(SP 124.1%) **9 Rn**

1m 44.7 (5.70) CSF £140.86 CT £807.00 TOTE £17.50: £3.30 £2.40 £1.90 (£44.40) Trio £71.70 OWNER Don Enrico Incisa (MIDDLEHAM)
BRED W. S. Farish
LONG HANDICAP Pleasure Trick (USA) 7-7
STEWARDS' ENQUIRY Holland susp. 5,8 & 13-14/3/97 (irresponsible riding).

331 PYRENEES H'CAP (0-95) (3-Y.O) (Class C)

3-55 (3-55) **1m 3f (Fibresand)** £5,342.00 (£1,616.00: £788.00: £374.00) Stalls: Low GOING: 0.02 sec per fur (STD)

				SP	RR	SF
281*	**Lawn Lothario (75)** (MJohnston) **3-8-9** TWilliams(1) (lw: led: qcknd over 4f out: clr 2f out: drvn along & styd on strly)	—	**1**	11/8 1	86	29
281 6	**Millroy (USA) (87)** (PAKelleway) **3-9-0**(7) AngelaGallimore(5) (hld up: rdn & wnt 2nd 2f out: kpt on: no imp)	7	**2**	7/1	88	31
46 5	**Going For Broke (68)** (PCHaslam) **3-7-13**(3) MartinDwyer(3) (hld up: effrt & swtchd rt over 2f out: hung lft & kpt on u.p: nvr nr to chal)	½	**3**	7/1	68	11
298 4	**Time Can Tell (66)** (CMurray) **3-8-0** NicolaHowarth(2) (trckd ldrs: outpcd 3f out: n.d)	7	**4**	6/1 3	56	—
298*	**Puzzlement (67)** (CEBrittain) **3-8-1** 5x DaleGibson(4) (lw: trckd ldrs: rdn & hung lft 2f out: sn wknd)	8	**5**	9/4 2	45	—

(SP 112.2%) **5 Rn**

2m 29.3 (9.30) CSF £10.52 TOTE £2.70: £1.10 £2.40 (£9.40) OWNER Mr J. S. Morrison (MIDDLEHAM) BRED Snailwell Stud Co Ltd

332 APENNINES (S) H'CAP (0-60) (II) (3-Y.O+) (Class F)

4-25 (4-26) **6f (Fibresand)** £2,083.00 (£583.00: £283.00) Stalls: Low GOING: 0.02 sec per fur (STD)

				SP	RR	SF
233 10	**Bold Aristocrat (IRE) (60)** (RHollinshead) **6-9-11**(3) FLynch(8) (hld up: hdwy on outside 2f out: edgd lft: styd on to ld last 50y)	—	**1**	9/2 2	66	46
318 5	**Hoh Majestic (IRE) (55)** (RonaldThompson) **4-9-9v** JQuinn(11) (lw: racd wd: sn trckng ldrs: styd on fnl f)	¾	**2**	4/1 1	59	39
233 11	**Tutu Sixtysix (28)** (DonEnricoIncisa) **6-7-10** KimTinkler(3) (sn prom: styd on appr fnl f)	hd	**3**	33/1	32	12
233 6	**Sweet Mate (49)** (SRBowring) **5-9-3b** SWebster(6) (b.hind: sn outpcd & drvn along: hdwy & hung lft 2f out: styd on fnl f)	1½	**4**	5/1 3	49	29
89 10	**Klipspinger (55)** (BSRothwell) **4-9-9b** JStack(2) (led to 3f out: led over 1f out tl wl ins fnl f)	s.h	**5**	9/1	55	35
241 8	**Cheerful Groom (IRE) (28)** (DShaw) **6-7-10** NKennedy(4) (s.i.s: bhd tl kpt on fnl 2f)	nk	**6**	12/1	27	7
209 12	**Guy's Gamble (43)** (JWharton) **4-8-11** JFanning(10) (lw: racd wd: bhd: kpt on fnl 2f: nvr nr to chal)	s.h	**7**	16/1	42	22
233 4	**Craigie Boy (35)** (NBycroft) **7-7-12b**(5) JBramhill(1) (chsd ldrs: effrt on ins 2f out: nt clr run: wknd ins fnl f)	1¼	**8**	5/1 3	30	10
127 13	**Maysimp (IRE) (30)** (BPJBaugh) **4-7-12** NAdams(7) (w ldrs: led 3f out tl over 1f out: sn wknd)	2½	**9**	50/1	19	—
209 6	**Ragazzo (IRE) (35)** (JSWainwright) **7-8-0**(3) NVarley(5) (b.hind: s.s: a bhd)	2	**10**	8/1	18	—
20 10	**Miletrian Refurb (IRE) (50)** (MRChannon) **4-9-4** CandyMorris(9) (racd wd: sn chsng ldrs: lost pl 2f out)	1¼	**11**	16/1	30	10

(SP 117.0%) **11 Rn**

1m 18.4 (4.90) CSF £20.67 CT £491.25 TOTE £4.90: £2.10 £2.10 £5.00 (£9.90) Trio £149.60 OWNER Mrs J. Hughes (UPPER LONGDON)
BRED Scarteen Stud
LONG HANDICAP Tutu Sixtysix 7-2
No bid

333 CAUCASUS AMATEUR H'CAP (0-60) (II) (4-Y.O+) (Class F)

4-55 (4-55) **7f (Fibresand)** £2,083.00 (£583.00: £283.00) Stalls: Low GOING: 0.02 sec per fur (STD)

Form	Horse / details	Dist	Pos	SP	RR	SF
245^{2}	**Broughton's Pride (IRE) (48)** (JLEyre) **6-10-9** MissDianaJones(3) (trckd ldrs: styd on appr fnl f: led last 30y)	—	1	$7/2^{2}$	59	40
203^{2}	**Truly Bay (48)** (TDBarron) **4-10-5b**(4) MissMKeuthen(8) (trckd ldrs: led 2f out tl wl ins fnl f)	1	2	$11/4^{1}$	57	38
319^{3}	**Bold Habit (43)** (JPearce) **12-10-4** MrsLPearce(9) (s.i.s: bhd: hdwy over 2f out: kpt on wl fnl f)	1¾	3	$4/1^{3}$	48	29
205^{12}	**Royal Acclaim (33)** (CFCJackson) **12-9-4v**(4) MissRJPatman(7) (bhd tl styd on fnl 2f: nvr nr to chal)	4	4	14/1	29	10
209^{13}	**Kid Ory (40)** (DWChapman) **6-10-1** MissRClark(4) (prom: rdn & outpcd 2f out: edgd lft & kpt on)	1	5	10/1	33	14
288^{8}	**Spanish Stripper (USA) (38)** (MCChapman) **6-9-6**(7) MrCWatson(1) (mde most to 2f out: wknd over 1f out)	nk	6	11/1	31	12
	David James' Girl (52) (ABailey) **5-10-6**(7) MissALHutchinson(6) (sn bhd: sme hdwy 2f out: styd on: nvr nr ldrs)	s.h	7	10/1	45	26
	Dancing Sioux (60) (RGuest) **5-11-0**(7) MissZBurkett(5) (b: chsd ldrs tl wknd over 1f out: eased)	7	8	9/1	37	18
	Just Flamenco (38) (MJRyan) **6-9-13**ow3 MrRVanderKraats(2) (lw: in tch: sn drvn along: outpcd ½-wy: sn bhd)	13	9	25/1	—	—
	Sussex Gorse (39) (JELong) **6-9-7**(7)ow14 MrTWaters(10) (racd wd: in tch tl lost pl 3f out)	8	10	50/1	—	—
				(SP 117.9%)	**10 Rn**	

1m 33.6 (7.10) CSF £12.49 CT £37.22 TOTE £4.60: £1.20 £1.10 £1.90 (£5.10) Trio £6.30 OWNER Mrs Janet Morris (HAMBLETON) BRED A. J. Poulton (Epping) Ltd
LONG HANDICAP Sussex Gorse 8-4

T/Plpt: £24.70 (396.91 Tckts). T/Qdpt: £8.20 (120.65 Tckts) WG

0319-LINGFIELD (L-H) (Standard)
Tuesday February 25th

Race 5: hand timed.
WEATHER: fine with rain later WIND: str half bhd

334 MARCO POLO APPRENTICE H'CAP (0-70) (4-Y.O+) (Class F)

2-00 (2-00) **1m 4f (Equitrack)** £2,333.00 (£663.00: £329.00) Stalls: Low GOING minus 0.40 sec per fur (FST)

Form	Horse / details	Dist	Pos	SP	RR	SF
	Amadour (IRE) (65) (PMitchell) **4-9-9**(5) AMcCarthy(4) (hld up: led over 3f out: rdn out)	—	1	$7/2^{3}$	72	51
295*	**Soojama (IRE) (46)** (RMFlower) **7-8-12b** 5x JWilkinson(1) (hdwy to chse wnr 2f out: unable qckn)	1¼	2	$6/5^{1}$	51	33
116*	**Squire's Occasion (CAN) (63)** (RAkehurst) **4-9-12** DDenby(5) (lw: chsd ldr: rdn over 2f out: wknd over 1f out)	4	3	$11/4^{2}$	63	42
	In The Band (59) (LordHuntingdon) **4-9-3v**(5) CCogan(2) (hld up: rdn over 2f out: sn wknd)	7	4	7/1	50	29
	Kirov Protege (IRE) (34) (MrsLCJewell) **5-7-7**(7) DarrenWilliams(3) (led over 8f: wknd over 2f out)	s.h	5	33/1	25	7
				(SP 109.8%)	**5 Rn**	

2m 34.24 (4.24) CSF £7.41 TOTE £5.80: £5.80 £1.00 (£6.00) OWNER Mr Derek Crowson (EPSOM) BRED Pierce Molony
WEIGHT FOR AGE 4yo-3lb

335 COLUMBUS CLAIMING STKS (4-Y.O+) (Class F)

2-30 (2-30) **7f (Equitrack)** £2,394.80 (£672.80: £328.40) Stalls: Low GOING minus 0.40 sec per fur (FST)

Form	Horse / details	Dist	Pos	SP	RR	SF
224*	**Greatest (70)** (MissGayKelleway) **6-9-4b** DHolland(5) (b: b.hind: mde all: drvn out)	—	1	$5/4^{1}$	80	55
278*	**Lift Boy (USA) (63)** (GLMoore) **8-8-8** CandyMorris(4) (w wnr: hrd rdn over 1f out: ev ch ins fnl f: unable qckn)	2	2	$11/4^{2}$	65	40
291^{9}	**La Modiste (71)** (SDow) **4-7-13**(5)ow1 ADaly(3) (rdn over 3f out: lost pl over 2f out: r.o one pce fnl f)	3	3	$3/1^{3}$	55	29
210^{7}	**Bon Secret (IRE) (60)** (TJNaughton) **5-8-10** SSanders(2) (hld up: rdn over 3f out: sn wknd)	4	4	13/2	51	26
278^{8}	**Astral Invader (IRE) (35)** (MSSaunders) **5-8-10** JQuinn(1) (hld up: rdn over 3f out: sn wknd)	1½	5	33/1	41 t	23
				(SP 112.4%)	**5 Rn**	

1m 25.5 (1.10) CSF £4.68 TOTE £1.70: £1.40 £1.10 (£2.80) OWNER Invoshire Ltd (WHITCOMBE) BRED Bloomsbury Stud
La Modiste clmd J Purcell £5,000

336 VASCO DA GAMA MAIDEN STKS (3-Y.O+) (Class D)

3-00 (3-01) **1m 2f (Equitrack)** £3,306.25 (£1,000.00: £487.50: £231.25) Stalls: Low GOING minus 0.40 sec per fur (FST)

Form	Horse / details	Dist	Pos	SP	RR	SF
	Effectual (MissGayKelleway) **4-9-10** DHolland(2) (b: b.hind: bit bkwd: chsd ldr: led over 2f out: clr over 1f out: easily)	—	1	$4/6^{1}$	78+	51
290^{2}	**Stellar Line (USA) (72)** (DRCElsworth) **4-9-5**(5) DGriffiths(4) (lw: led over 7f: unable qckn)	9	2	$13/8^{2}$	64	37
28^{8}	**Sounds Legal (63)** (PDEvans) **4-9-5** ACulhane(1) (hld up: rdn over 4f out: wknd 3f out)	15	3	$10/1^{3}$	35	8
65^{10}	**Serape (53)** (MrsLStubbs) **4-9-5** KFallon(5) (b: hld up: rdn over 4f out: wknd over 3f out)	13	4	14/1	14	—
	Rosalee Royale (JELong) **5-9-6** LeesaLong(3) (lw: a in rr)	14	5	50/1	—	—
				(SP 115.8%)	**5 Rn**	

2m 7.36 (3.06) CSF £1.99 TOTE £2.00: £1.10 £1.40 (£1.40) OWNER Blandford Thoroughbreds (WHITCOMBE) BRED Miss Sarah Hollinshead
WEIGHT FOR AGE 4yo-1lb

337 LIVINGSTONE H'CAP (0-80) (3-Y.O) (Class D)

3-30 (3-32) **1m (Equitrack)** £3,562.50 (£1,000.00: £487.50) Stalls: High GOING minus 0.40 sec per fur (FST)

Form	Horse / details	Dist	Pos	SP	RR	SF
	Top Shelf (66) (CEBrittain) **3-8-9** DHolland(2) (rdn & hdwy 4f out: jnd ldr over 3f out: hrd rdn over 1f out: led ins fnl f: r.o wl)	—	1	$100/30^{3}$	76	21
279*	**Hever Golf Charger (IRE) (61)** (TJNaughton) **3-8-4** SSanders(1) (chsd ldr: led over 3f out: rdn over 2f out: hdd ins fnl f: r.o)	nk	2	$11/8^{2}$	70	15
	Premier (78) (MJohnston) **3-9-7** DeanMcKeown(3) (led over 4f)	17	3	$6/5^{1}$	53	—
				(SP 110.6%)	**3 Rn**	

1m 41.31 (3.91) CSF £7.32 TOTE £3.90 (£6.10) OWNER Kings Bloodstock Ltd (NEWMARKET) BRED Kings Bloodstock Ltd
STEWARDS' ENQUIRY McKeown fined £200 (not riding to his draw)
OFFICIAL EXPLANATION Premier: no explanation offered.

338 COOK LIMITED STKS (0-50) (I) (4-Y.O+) (Class F)

4-00 (4-03) **1m 2f (Equitrack)** £2,100.80 (£588.80: £286.40) Stalls: Low GOING minus 0.40 sec per fur (FST)

				SP	RR	SF
86^{11}	**Hever Golf Eagle (45)** (TJNaughton) **4-8-11** SSanders(3) (lw: a.p: led over 3f out: drvn out)	—	**1**	12/1	60	34
129^{3}	**Zahid (USA) (48)** (KRBurke) **6-8-12v** JQuinn(7) (lw: a.p: chsd wnr over 3f out: hrd rdn over 2f out: unable qckn)	1¼	**2**	$4/1^{3}$	58	33
	Claque (49) (DWChapman) **5-8-12b** ACulhane(10) (rdn thrght: hdwy over 3f out: one pce)	4	**3**	14/1	52	27
290^{3}	**Lahik (IRE) (30)** (KTIvory) **4-8-11** DBiggs(9) (rdn over 5f out: hdwy 3f out: r.o one pce)	1¼	**4**	12/1	50	24
294^{4}	**Desert Calm (IRE) (42)** (PDEvans) **8-8-5**$^{(7)}$ AnthonyBond(8) (rdn over 4f out: hdwy over 3f out: one pce)	½	**5**	$3/1^{2}$	49	24
319^{10}	**Sweet Amoret (37)** (PHowling) **4-8-8** FNorton(1) (b.hind: prom tl nt clr run on ins & wknd over 4f out)	18	**6**	25/1	17	—
143^{5}	**Media Express (45)** (MrsLStubbs) **5-8-12b** KFallon(6) (bhd fnl 3f)	1½	**7**	9/1	18	—
290^{9}	**Komodo (USA) (29)** (JELong) **5-8-12** LeesaLong(2) (b: led 3f: wkng whn n.m.r over 4f out)	4	**8**	100/1	11	—
321^{12}	**Grey Legend (40)** (RMFlower) **4-8-11b** DRMcCabe(5) (a bhd)	4	**9**	33/1	5	—
295^{4}	**Czarna (IRE) (43)** (CEBrittain) **6-8-12** DHolland(4) (led 7f out tl over 3f out: sn wknd)	½	**10**	$2/1^{1}$	4	—

(SP 118.2%) **10 Rn**

2m 8.0 (3.70) CSF £54.40 TOTE £12.70: £5.80 £1.20 £2.20 (£22.60) Trio £45.40 OWNER Hever Racing Club (EPSOM) BRED Mrs L. Popely
WEIGHT FOR AGE 4yo-1lb
OFFICIAL EXPLANATION Czarna (IRE): gurgled.

339 WALTER RALEIGH H'CAP (0-70) (3-Y.O+ F & M) (Class E)

4-30 (4-32) **6f (Equitrack)** £2,739.25 (£829.00: £404.50: £192.25) Stalls: Low GOING minus 0.40 sec per fur (FST)

				SP	RR	SF
293^{2}	**Forgotten Times (USA) (69)** (TMJones) **3-9-10** NCarlisle(5) (b: b.hind: lw: hdwy to ld over 2f out: clr over 1f out: rdn out)	—	**1**	$2/1^{1}$	77	43
128^{6}	**Mystery Matthias (43)** (MissBSanders) **4-8-13v** SSanders(6) (a.p: chsd wnr over 1f out: r.o wl ins fnl f)	¾	**2**	$5/1^{2}$	49	30
263^{8}	**Tachycardia (48)** (RJO'Sullivan) **5-9-1**$^{(3)}$ NVarley(3) (rdn over 4f out: hdwy over 1f out: r.o)	2½	**3**	$5/1^{2}$	47	28
282^{4}	**Nopalea (58)** (TJNaughton) **3-8-13** DHolland(4) (led over 3f: wknd over 1f out)	1¾	**4**	$11/2^{3}$	53	19
275^{6}	**Honeyhall (34)** (NBycroft) **4-8-4** JQuinn(2) (chsd ldr 3f: wknd over 1f out)	¾	**5**	16/1	27	8
304^{7}	**Allstars Dancer (37)** (TJNaughton) **4-8-0**$^{(7)}$ RFfrench(1) (bhd fnl 4f)	3½	**6**	$5/1^{2}$	20	1

(SP 104.6%) **6 Rn**

1m 13.28 (2.18) CSF £9.40 TOTE £2.30: £1.20 £2.40 (£4.30) OWNER Mr John Crook (GUILDFORD) BRED Gainsborough Farm Inc
WEIGHT FOR AGE 3yo-15lb

340 COOK LIMITED STKS (0-50) (II) (4-Y.O+) (Class F)

5-00 (5-00) **1m 2f (Equitrack)** £2,089.60 (£585.60: £284.80) Stalls: Low GOING minus 0.40 sec per fur (FST)

				SP	RR	SF
294^{6}	**Captain's Day (41)** (HJCollingridge) **5-8-7**$^{(5)}$ RMullen(2) (hld up: led wl over 1f out: rdn out)	—	**1**	10/1	56	43
245^{4}	**Bakers Daughter (49)** (JRArnold) **5-8-6**$^{(3)}$ MartinDwyer(4) (a.p: led 4f out tl wl over 1f out: unable qckn)	6	**2**	$5/1^{2}$	43	30
290^{5}	**Honestly (47)** (BSmart) **4-8-11** SSanders(7) (hld up: rdn over 3f out: wknd over 1f out)	2	**3**	10/1	43	29
260^{5}	**Sheraz (IRE) (47)** (NTinkler) **5-8-12b** CRutter(9) (lw: hdwy over 3f out: wknd over 2f out)	1¼	**4**	$4/1^{1}$	41	28
295^{6}	**Real Madrid (38)** (GPEnright) **6-8-7v**$^{(5)}$ ADaly(3) (led 1f: wknd over 3f out)	2½	**5**	$5/1^{2}$	37	24
295^{2}	**Fabulous Mtoto (32)** (MSSaunders) **7-9-1** NCarlisle(8) (lw: dwlt: hdwy, nt clr run on ins & lost pl over 4f out: nvr nr to chal)	10	**6**	$4/1^{1}$	24	11
	Persian Butterfly (50) (RMStronge) **5-8-9v** DRMcCabe(1) (led 9f out to 4f out: sn wknd)	½	**7**	20/1	17	4
	Lila Pedigo (IRE) (50) (MissJFCraze) **4-8-8** SWebster(5) (prom 5f)	2	**8**	$6/1^{3}$	14	—
290^{6}	**Mediate (IRE) (48)** (AHide) **5-8-5b**$^{(7)}$ JoHunnam(6) (bhd fnl 4f)	3	**9**	8/1	12	—
	Realms of Glory (IRE) (48) (PMitchell) **4-8-11** AClark(10) (hdwy 4f out: wknd over 3f out)	10	**10**	20/1	—	—

(SP 126.4%) **10 Rn**

2m 6.92 (2.62) CSF £58.76 TOTE £8.50: £3.90 £2.00 £2.70 (£52.30) Trio £127.90 OWNER Mr D. Burke (EXNING) BRED R. Hutt
WEIGHT FOR AGE 4yo-1lb

T/Plpt: £81.40 (89.23 Tckts). T/Qdpt: £16.20 (28.87 Tckts) AK

0312-WOLVERHAMPTON (L-H) (Standard)

Wednesday February 26th

WEATHER: unsettled WIND: str half bhd

341 CAPRICORN MAIDEN STKS (3-Y.O) (Class D)

2-10 (2-11) **1m 100y (Fibresand)** £3,371.25 (£1,020.00: £497.50: £236.25) Stalls: Low GOING minus 0.19 sec per fur (FST)

				SP	RR	SF
255^{2}	**Pennywell** (RFJohnsonHoughton) **3-8-9** TSprake(7) (a.p: r.o u.p to ld wl ins fnl f)	—	**1**	$6/4^{1}$	64	30
161^{5}	**Jolly Jackson (63)** (RAkehurst) **3-9-0** SSanders(3) (chsd ldrs: rdn to ld over 1f out: hdd wl ins fnl f: no ex nr fin)	½	**2**	12/1	68	34
	Big Bang (MBlanshard) **3-9-0** JQuinn(5) (bit bkwd: mid div: hdwy over 2f out: r.o ins fnl f)	1¼	**3**	33/1	66	32
	Daring Flight (USA) (75) (LordHuntingdon) **3-9-0** DHarrison(10) (bit bkwd: hld up: hdwy 4f out: rdn over 2f out: r.o one pce)	1	**4**	$3/1^{2}$	64	30
	Allied Academy (SCWilliams) **3-9-0** JTate(1) (b: led 7f out: rdn & hdd over 1f out: unable qckn)	2½	**5**	12/1	59	25
	Ocean Light (ABailey) **3-8-9** DWright(2) (bkwd: in rr: sn pushed along: nvr nr ldrs)	½	**6**	33/1	53	19
292^{2}	**Isis Honda (IRE)** (CEBrittain) **3-8-9** DHolland(4) (b.hind: led: hdd 7f out: wknd wl over 1f out)	3	**7**	15/2	47	13
296^{7}	**Ron's Round** (KOCunningham-Brown) **3-9-0** CMunday(6) (s.i.s: sn prom: wknd over 2f out)	5	**8**	33/1	43	9
230^{4}	**Only Josh (IRE)** (MrsJRRamsden) **3-9-0** MDeering(8) (hld up: a in rr)	s.h	**9**	16/1	43	9
255^{3}	**Venture Connect** (CPEBrooks) **3-9-0** CRutter(9) (trckd ldrs: rdn over 3f out: sn lost pl)	½	**10**	$5/1^{3}$	42	8

(SP 123.5%) **10 Rn**

1m 50.1 (5.10) CSF £21.42 TOTE £3.00: £1.50 £2.10 £6.10 (£9.90) Trio £109.00; £125.98 to Ludlow 27/2/97 OWNER Lady Rothschild (DIDCOT) BRED Lord Rothschild

342 ARIES CLAIMING STKS (4-Y.O+) (Class F)

2-40 (2-40) **7f (Fibresand)** £2,293.00 (£643.00: £313.00) Stalls: High GOING minus 0.19 sec per fur (FST)

	Horse	Dist	Pos	SP	RR	SF
*288**	**Sense of Priority (70)** (DNicholls) **8-8-11** AlexGreaves(6) (led: hdd over 2f out: sn rdn & hung lft: styd on u.p to ld nr fin)	—	**1**	Evens[1]	58	22
	Dragonjoy (58) (NPLittmoden) **4-8-11v**(5) DGriffiths(1) (b.off hind: trckd ldrs: rdn to ld over 2f out: hdd nr fin)	hd	**2**	7/1[3]	63	27
297[2]	**Jigsaw Boy (62)** (PGMurphy) **8-8-9** SDrowne(7) (hld up: hdwy ½-wy: r.o)	1¼	**3**	7/4[2]	53	17
243[9]	**Quinzii Martin (44)** (DHaydnJones) **9-8-2b**(7) GMilligan(2) (lw: trckd ldrs: rdn over 2f out: r.o one pce)	2½	**4**	9/1	47	11
143[7]	**Miss Charlie (25)** (ABailey) **7-8-2b**[1ow2] RLappin(4) (chsd ldr: rdn 3f out: styd on same pce fnl 2f)	2	**5**	25/1	36	—
	Scott's Risk (32) (LJBarratt) **7-8-5** NCarlisle(3) (bkwd: s.i.s: sn pushed along: outpcd fr ½-wy: t.o)	20	**6**	33/1	—	—

(SP 115.7%) **6 Rn**

1m 29.6 (4.90) CSF £8.60 TOTE £1.50: £1.70 £3.10 (£5.60) OWNER Mr M. A. Scaife (THIRSK) BRED Cheveley Park Stud Ltd

343 TAURUS CONDITIONS STKS (3-Y.O+) (Class C)

3-10 (3-10) **7f (Fibresand)** £5,088.83 (£1,646.78: £805.39) Stalls: High GOING minus 0.19 sec per fur (FST)

	Horse	Dist	Pos	SP	RR	SF
257[2]	**Cim Bom Bom (IRE) (95)** (MBell) **5-8-13v**(5) GFaulkner(2) (lw: mde all: clr ½-wy: rdn out)	—	**1**	8/15[1]	95	47
	Defined Feature (IRE) (90) (DrJDScargill) **4-8-13** DHolland(1) (bit bkwd: chsd wnr: outpcd ½-wy: r.o ins fnl f)	nk	**2**	7/2[2]	89	41
138[7]	**Foot Battalion (IRE) (90)** (RHollinshead) **3-8-2**(3)ow4 FLynch(3) (outpcd: nvr able to chal)	3	**3**	7/2[2]	92	23

(SP 109.7%) **3 Rn**

1m 28.0 (3.30) CSF £2.53 TOTE £1.30: (£2.50) OWNER Mr Yucel Birol (NEWMARKET) BRED Tarworth Bloodstock Investments Ltd and J.J. Melk

WEIGHT FOR AGE 3yo-17lb

344 LEO H'CAP (0-100) (4-Y.O+) (Class C)

3-40 (3-40) **1m 1f 79y (Fibresand)** £4,959.25 (£1,501.00: £732.50: £348.25) Stalls: Low GOING minus 0.19 sec per fur (FST)

	Horse	Dist	Pos	SP	RR	SF
	New Century (USA) (92) (DNicholls) **5-9-13** AlexGreaves(6) (a.p: led over 3f out: pushed out)	—	**1**	4/1[1]	100	68
220[4]	**Pater Noster (USA) (87)** (JohnHarris) **8-9-8** SSanders(2) (b: a.p: chsd wnr over 1f out: r.o)	1	**2**	6/1[3]	93	61
*182**	**Hill Farm Dancer (79)** (WMBrisbourne) **6-8-9**(5) RMullen(7) (dwlt: hld up: hdwy over 2f out: r.o)	½	**3**	9/1	84	52
316[9]	**Three Arch Bridge (73)** (MJohnston) **5-8-8b** DeanMcKeown(8) (lw: trckd ldrs: ev ch 2f out: no ex fnl f)	1½	**4**	10/1	76	44
299[3]	**Second Colours (USA) (83)** (MCPipe) **7-9-4** DHarrison(3) (hld up: nvr rchd ldrs)	1¾	**5**	9/2[2]	83	51
291[2]	**Secret Aly (CAN) (80)** (CEBrittain) **7-9-1** DHolland(4) (w ldr: rdn over 2f out: r.o one pce)	2	**6**	4/1[1]	77	45
220[3]	**South Eastern Fred (93)** (HJCollingridge) **6-10-0** MRimmer(5) (b: chsd ldrs: led over 4f out: hdd over 3f out: wknd wl over 1f out)	2½	**7**	9/2[2]	85	53
	Bend Wavy (IRE) (84) (THCaldwell) **5-9-5** ACulhane(1) (led: hdd over 4f out: sn lost pl: t.o)	dist	**8**	16/1	—	—

(SP 115.6%) **8 Rn**

1m 59.1 (3.10) CSF £25.95 CT £185.16 TOTE £4.30: £1.90 £2.00 £2.20 (£20.30) OWNER A A Bloodstock Ltd (THIRSK) BRED Sterlingbrook Farm

OFFICIAL EXPLANATION **South Eastern Fred: the trainer reported that the horse was found to be lame behind immediately after the race.**

345 AQUARIUS (S) H'CAP (0-60) (3-Y.O) (Class G)

4-10 (4-10) **5f (Fibresand)** £2,085.00 (£585.00: £285.00) Stalls: Low GOING minus 0.19 sec per fur (FST)

	Horse	Dist	Pos	SP	RR	SF
247[5]	**Chilling (60)** (NTinkler) **3-9-0**(7) KSked(1) (led over 3f out: rdn out)	—	**1**	9/2	65	33
259[4]	**Will To Win (59)** (PGMurphy) **3-9-6** SDrowne(4) (b.hind: chsd ldrs: rdn 2f out: r.o)	1¼	**2**	7/2[2]	60	28
	College Princess (54) (CADwyer) **3-8-8**(7) JoHunnam(5) (prom: outpcd ½-wy: r.o ins fnl f)	1	**3**	10/1	52	20
181[12]	**Seretse's Nephew (50)** (SCWilliams) **3-8-11** JTate(3) (led: hdd over 3f out: no ex fnl f)	¾	**4**	6/1	45	13
282[3]	**Ma Vielle Pouque (IRE) (58)** (WGMTurner) **3-8-12**(7) DMcGaffin(2) (a.p: rdn over 2f out: r.o one pce fnl f)	hd	**5**	4/1[3]	53	21
198[2]	**Enchantica (60)** (JBerry) **3-9-2**(5) TEDurcan(6) (b.hind: prom: rdn ½-wy: sn outpcd)	3½	**6**	3/1[1]	44	12
221[6]	**Whisper Low (IRE) (44)** (RHollinshead) **3-8-2**(3)ow2 FLynch(7) (outpcd fr ½-wy)	6	**7**	12/1	9	—

(SP 116.5%) **7 Rn**

62.2 secs (3.30) CSF £19.37 TOTE £4.30: £2.50 £2.50 (£6.90) OWNER Speedlith Group (MALTON) BRED D. J. Simpson

No bid

346 GEMINI H'CAP (0-70) (4-Y.O+ F & M) (Class E)

4-40 (4-40) **1m 4f (Fibresand)** £2,700.25 (£817.00: £398.50: £189.25) Stalls: Low GOING minus 0.19 sec per fur (FST)

	Horse	Dist	Pos	SP	RR	SF
261[2]	**Calendula (53)** (DMorley) **4-8-13** GCarter(1) (mde all: rdn out)	—	**1**	6/4[1]	65	36
169[3]	**Mono Lady (IRE) (59)** (DHaydnJones) **4-9-5b** CRutter(6) (b.off hind: hld up: hdwy to chse wnr over 2f out: sn ev ch: r.o)	s.h	**2**	6/1[3]	70	41
*104**	**Zacaroon (48)** (JFfitch-Heyes) **6-8-11** DBiggs(4) (chsd wnr: rdn 2f out: styd on same pce)	9	**3**	6/1[3]	47	21
182[9]	**Tart (FR) (68)** (JPearce) **4-10-0** GBardwell(5) (chsd ldrs: rdn over 2f out: sn outpcd)	½	**4**	8/1	67	38
*283**	**Harlequin Walk (IRE) (46)** (RJO'Sullivan) **6-8-9** JQuinn(3) (hld up: hdwy over 3f out: wknd 2f out)	6	**5**	11/4[2]	37	11
125[7]	**Scenicris (IRE) (45)** (RHollinshead) **4-8-2**(3)ow3 FLynch(2) (plld hrd: hld up: rdn & wknd 3f out)	1¾	**6**	10/1	33	1

(SP 115.4%) **6 Rn**

2m 39.6 (7.10) CSF £10.55 TOTE £2.10: £1.60 £2.90 (£4.10) OWNER Mr Christopher Spence (NEWMARKET) BRED Chieveley Manor Enterprises

WEIGHT FOR AGE 4yo-3lb

T/Plpt: £87.60 (91.14 Tckts). T/Qdpt: £27.10 (19.33 Tckts) CR

0334-LINGFIELD (L-H) (Standard)
Thursday February 27th
WEATHER: fine WIND: almost nil

347 SUMTER APPRENTICE CLAIMING STKS (3-Y.O) (Class E)
2-25 (2-25) **1m 4f (Equitrack)** £2,687.25 (£813.00: £396.50: £188.25) Stalls: Low GOING minus 0.43 sec per fur (FST)

Form	Horse / details	Dist	Pos	SP	RR	SF
314^{2}	**As-Is (66)** (MJohnston) **3-9-1** KSked(4) (lost pl 9f out: rallied to ld 4f out: rn wd bnd wl over 1f out: edgd lft ins fnl f: rdn out)	—	**1**	$5/2^{2}$	69	30
314^{*}	**State of Gold (IRE) (53)** (JHetherton) **3-9-3** JBramhill(1) (lw: hld up: ev ch fnl 4f: rn wd bnd wl over 1f out: unable qckn ins fnl f)	2	**2**	$11/4^{3}$	68	29
277^{5}	**Neon Deion (IRE) (36)** (SCWilliams) **3-7-9**(7) DarrenWilliams(5) (a.p: led 7f out to 4f out: wknd over 3f out)	5	**3**	20/1	47	8
249^{2}	**Leg Beforum (IRE) (58)** (LMontagueHall) **3-8-13** GMilligan(3) (hld up: rdn 4f out: wknd over 3f out)	1½	**4**	$15/8^{1}$	56	17
228^{4}	**Foxford Lad (38)** (TMJones) **3-8-4**(3) DDenby(2) (led 5f: wknd over 4f out)	11	**5**	66/1	35	—
249^{4}	**Saxonbury** (GLMoore) **3-8-12v**1(5) MBatchelor(6) (sddle slipped s: hdwy 10f out: wknd over 4f out)	4	**6**	5/1	40	1

(SP 112.9%) **6 Rn**

2m 35.33 (5.33) CSF £9.05 TOTE £2.90: £1.30 £1.40 (£3.00) OWNER Mr Robinson (Wigan) (MIDDLEHAM) BRED Roldvale Ltd

348 CHATTANOOGA H'CAP (0-80) (3-Y.O+) (Class D)
2-55 (2-55) **5f (Equitrack)** £3,338.75 (£1,010.00: £492.50: £233.75) Stalls: High GOING minus 0.43 sec per fur (FST)

Form	Horse / details	Dist	Pos	SP	RR	SF
301^{12}	**Ramsey Hope (73)** (CWFairhurst) **4-9-12v** KFallon(7) (chsd ldrs: rdn over 3f out: led wl ins fnl f: r.o wl)	—	**1**	10/1	80	53
323^{3}	**Lord Sky (66)** (ABailey) **6-9-5** SSanders(3) (lw: led over 1f: rdn over 2f out: r.o ins fnl f: n.m.r nr fin)	1½	**2**	$11/2^{3}$	68	41
318^{2}	**Sir Tasker (46)** (JLHarris) **9-7-8**(5) RMullen(2) (rdn over 2f out: hdwy fnl f: r.o wl)	s.h	**3**	13/2	48	21
304^{4}	**Bowcliffe Grange (IRE) (50)** (DWChapman) **5-8-3** JQuinn(5) (lw: dwlt: hdwy to ld over 3f out: clr over 1f out: wknd & hdd wl ins fnl f)	s.h	**4**	$11/4^{1}$	52	25
304^{2}	**Ivory's Grab Hire (47)** (KTIvory) **4-7-11b**(3) MartinDwyer(1) (rdn over 2f out: hdwy wl over 1f out: r.o)	½	**5**	$11/2^{3}$	47	20
170^{*}	**Sally Slade (74)** (CACyzer) **5-9-13** DBiggs(6) (outpcd: hdwy over 2f out: one pce)	1½	**6**	$9/2^{2}$	70	43
170^{7}	**Mijas (75)** (LMontagueHall) **4-10-0b**1 DHolland(4) (spd over 2f)	21	**7**	6/1	3	—

(SP 112.3%) **7 Rn**

59.3 secs (1.10) CSF £55.20 TOTE £12.50: £3.40 £1.80 (£15.00) OWNER Mr C. D. Barber-Lomax (MIDDLEHAM) BRED Norton Grove Stud Ltd

OFFICIAL EXPLANATION **Ramsey Hope: the gelding had taken on the front-runners last time, and had run himself out after three furlongs. He had not liked the wind and rain when being saddled on that occasion, and also prefers the Equitrack. Mijas: had bolted to post, which contributed to her poor performance.**

349 H.E.A.T. H'CAP (0-70) (3-Y.O+) (Class E)
3-25 (3-26) **7f (Equitrack)** £2,791.25 (£845.00: £412.50: £196.25) Stalls: Low GOING minus 0.43 sec per fur (FST)

Form	Horse / details	Dist	Pos	SP	RR	SF
128^{7}	**Barbason (53)** (GLMoore) **5-8-12** CandyMorris(2) (hdwy over 1f out: led wl ins fnl f: r.o wl)	—	**1**	$11/2^{3}$	62	35
316^{3}	**Dawalib (USA) (60)** (DHaydnJones) **7-9-5** AClark(6) (lw: hdwy over 3f out: led over 1f out tl wl ins fnl f: unable qckn)	1¼	**2**	$7/4^{1}$	66	39
275^{3}	**Anita's Contessa (IRE) (54)** (BPalling) **5-8-13** TSprake(4) (led over 4f: rdn: ev ch ins fnl f: one pce)	nk	**3**	8/1	60	33
278^{2}	**River Seine (FR) (46)** (SGKnight) **5-7-12**(7) RFfrench(1) (lw: lost pl over 3f out: rn wd bnd wl over 1f out: rallied fnl f: r.o wl)	½	**4**	7/1	50	23
241^{6}	**Mellors (IRE) (65)** (MJHeaton-Ellis) **4-9-10** SDrowne(5) (a.p: led over 2f out tl over 1f out: wknd ins fnl f)	2	**5**	6/1	65	38
297^{3}	**Bogart (46)** (CWFairhurst) **6-8-5v**ow1 SSanders(7) (a.p: rdn over 3f out: wknd over 1f out)	2½	**6**	$5/1^{2}$	40	12
263^{12}	**Lochon (51)** (MrsNMacauley) **6-8-7**(3) CTeague(8) (b: hdwy over 3f out: wknd over 2f out)	nk	**7**	16/1	44	17
321^{5}	**Our Shadee (USA) (48)** (KTIvory) **7-8-7b** CScally(3) (b: b.hind: prom over 4f)	1¾	**8**	12/1	37	10

(SP 119.9%) **8 Rn**

1m 26.59 (2.19) CSF £14.93 CT £72.91 TOTE £7.00: £2.00 £1.50 £2.10 (£7.00) Trio £27.50 OWNER Mr F. L. Hill (BRIGHTON) BRED Sheikh Mohammed bin Rashid al Maktoum

350 ATLANTA MAIDEN STKS (3-Y.O) (Class D)
3-55 (3-56) **1m 2f (Equitrack)** £3,322.50 (£1,005.00: £490.00: £232.50) Stalls: Low GOING minus 0.43 sec per fur (FST)

Form	Horse / details	Dist	Pos	SP	RR	SF
	Running Stag (USA) (PMitchell) **3-9-0** AClark(5) (w'like: a gng wl: hld up: led 3f out: qcknd wl over 1f out: easily)	—	**1**	$8/11^{1}$	65++	37
292^{4}	**Around Fore Alliss (71)** (TGMills) **3-9-0** SSanders(2) (plld hrd: hld up: rdn over 3f out: chsd wnr over 1f out: no imp)	7	**2**	16/1	54	26
296^{9}	**Solar Dawn** (MJohnston) **3-8-9** DeanMcKeown(4) (chsd ldr: led over 4f out to 3f out: rdn over 2f out: one pce)	2	**3**	14/1	46	18
	Bogan (IRE) (LordHuntingdon) **3-9-0** DHarrison(1) (unf: hld up: rdn over 4f out: wknd over 3f out)	8	**4**	$5/2^{2}$	38	10
124^{13}	**Lily Jaques (52)** (RGuest) **3-8-9** DBiggs(6) (prom over 6f)	1¾	**5**	20/1	30	2
	Not Forgotten (USA) (PAKelleway) **3-9-0** MWigham(3) (w'like: bit bkwd: led over 5f)	12	**6**	$5/1^{3}$	16	—

(SP 120.4%) **6 Rn**

2m 7.6 (3.30) CSF £15.32 TOTE £1.40: £1.10 £3.10 (£8.20) OWNER Mr Derek Crowson (EPSOM) BRED Juddmonte Farms

351 H.E.A.T. CONTRACTORS H'CAP (0-60) (4-Y.O+) (Class F)
4-25 (4-25) **2m (Equitrack)** £2,383.60 (£669.60: £326.80) Stalls: Low GOING minus 0.43 sec per fur (FST)

Form	Horse / details	Dist	Pos	SP	RR	SF
334^{2}	**Soojama (IRE) (45)** (RMFlower) **7-9-0b** 4x SDrowne(4) (a.p: chsd ldr over 1f out: led ins fnl f: pushed out)	—	**1**	$9/4^{1}$	59	17
295^{12}	**High Five (IRE) (27)** (RIngram) **7-7-10** GBardwell(2) (b: hdwy over 9f out: led 4f out: rdn over 3f out: hdd ins fnl f: unable qckn)	1	**2**	11/2	40	—
262^{*}	**Matthias Mystique (58)** (MissBSanders) **4-9-7** SSanders(5) (chsd ldr: rdn over 3f out: wknd fnl f)	6	**3**	$4/1^{2}$	65	17
260^{4}	**Soviet King (IRE) (48)** (PMitchell) **4-8-11** AClark(6) (led 12f)	7	**4**	10/1	48	—
262^{3}	**Illegally Yours (44)** (LMontagueHall) **4-8-7** WRyan(3) (a bhd)	9	**5**	$5/1^{3}$	35	—

				SP	RR	SF
252*	**Broughtons Formula (59)** (WJMusson) **7-9-11b**(3) MBaird(7) (lw: bhd fnl 12f)	4	**6**	4/1 2	46	4
				(SP 111.9%)		**6 Rn**

3m 30.76 (9.76) CSF £13.50 TOTE £3.00: £1.30 £2.60 (£7.90) OWNER Mr M. G. Rogers (JEVINGTON) BRED E. and Mrs Hanley
LONG HANDICAP High Five (IRE) 7-3
WEIGHT FOR AGE 4yo-6lb

352 VICKSBURGH H'CAP (0-65) (3-Y.O+) (Class F)
4-55 (4-56) **1m (Equitrack)** £2,518.00 (£708.00: £346.00) Stalls: High GOING minus 0.43 sec per fur (FST)

				SP	RR	SF
290 7	**Eastleigh (35)** (RHollinshead) **8-7-13** JQuinn(9) (b.nr hind: chsd ldr: led over 3f out: clr over 1f out: rdn out)	—	**1**	16/1	49	26
280*	**Bagshot (63)** (GLMoore) **6-9-13** SWhitworth(4) (b: lw: hld up: chsd wnr over 3f out: rdn over 2f out: unable qckn)	4	**2**	11/4 2	69	46
278 7	**Tuigamala (60)** (RIngram) **6-9-10** AMcGlone(2) (lw: hdwy 3f out: one pce)	3½	**3**	9/4 1	59	36
224 4	**Piquant (64)** (LordHuntingdon) **10-9-7**(7) CCogan(8) (hdwy over 1f out: r.o)	nk	**4**	5/1 3	62	39
226 9	**Paronomasia (33)** (JLHarris) **5-7-6**(5) RMullen(7) (b: b.hind: lost pl over 5f out: one pce fnl 3f)	hd	**5**	20/1	31	8
278 3	**Into Debt (34)** (JRPoulton) **4-7-5e**(7) AMcCarthy(6) (s.s: hdwy over 6f out: rdn over 2f out: one pce)	1	**6**	10/1	30	7
248 6	**Whatever's Right (IRE) (56)** (MDIUsher) **8-9-6** KFallon(5) (led over 4f)	hd	**7**	5/1 3	52	29
303 5	**Fancy Design (IRE) (32)** (PMitchell) **4-7-5**(5) PFessey(1) (b.hind: bhd fnl 7f)	3½	**8**	20/1	21	—
				(SP 115.3%)		**8 Rn**

1m 39.63 (2.23) CSF £55.08 CT £127.57 TOTE £12.70: £3.20 £1.10 £2.50 (£13.40) Trio £23.10 OWNER Mr J. E. Bigg (UPPER LONGDON)
BRED Hever Castle Stud
LONG HANDICAP Fancy Design (IRE) 7-3

T/Plpt: £93.90 (96.6 Tckts). T/Qdpt: £8.40 (90.61 Tckts) AK

SAINT-MORITZ (Switzerland) (R-H) (Good (Snow))
Sunday February 2nd

353a GRAND PRIX BADRUTT'S PALACE HOTEL, DUBAI CUP
5f 110y

				SP	RR	SF
	One Man Band (IRE) (TStack,Ireland) **6-9-5** PGHourigan	—	**1**		61	—
	Satisfied Prince (Switzerland) **5-9-7** OFrei	2½	**2**		56	—
	Rooftop Flyer (IRE) (Switzerland) **6-9-5** GHuber	2	**3**		48	—
						11 Rn

61.6 secs TOTE 5.70SF: 2.10SF 2.10SF 2.80SF OWNER Peter Piller (CASHEL)

0271a-SAINT-MORITZ (Switzerland) (R-H) (Good (Snow))
Sunday February 16th

354a GROSSER PREIS CASHMERE HOUSE LAMM (4-Y.O+)
12-30 (12-38) **5f 110y** £6,316.00 (£2,526.00: £1,895.00)

				SP	RR	SF
	Le Rastaquouere (USA) (ALowe,Germany) **6-9-11** KMarks	—	**1**		85	—
	Roseate Wood (FR) (Switzerland) **4-9-2** MissSeverineBottani	2¼	**2**		70	—
353a*	**One Man Band (IRE)** (TStack,Ireland) **6-9-7** PGHourigan	4½	**3**		61	—
						11 Rn

65.5 secs TOTE 5.10SF: 2.00SF 2.10SF 1.50SF OWNER Mr J. Lamote BRED Kinghaven Farms Ltd

0326-SOUTHWELL (L-H) (Standard)
Friday February 28th
WEATHER: Fine WIND: str half bhd

355 SKEGBY MAIDEN STKS (3-Y.O) (Class D)
2-15 (2-15) **1m 4f (Fibresand)** £3,371.25 (£1,020.00: £497.50: £236.25) Stalls: Low GOING: 0.19 sec per fur (SLW)

				SP	RR	SF
	Maradi (IRE) (74) (MBell) **3-8-9**(5) RMullen(7) (lw: trckd ldrs gng wl: led on bit 3f out: v.easily)	—	**1**	4/9 1	59++	14
328 5	**Good Day (57)** (CWThornton) **3-9-0** DeanMcKeown(4) (hld up: hdwy over 4f out: chal 2f out: kpt on same pce: no ch w wnr)	3½	**2**	12/1	54	9
255 5	**Woodland Nymph (58)** (DJGMurraySmith) **3-8-9** DRMcCabe(2) (hdwy over 4f out: chal 2f out: kpt on one pce)	nk	**3**	5/1 2	49	4
	Tracks of My Tears (51) (WGMTurner) **3-8-9** TSprake(3) (trckd ldrs: led over 3f out: sn hdd: wknd over 1f out)	14	**4**	8/1 3	30	—
277 6	**Apiculate (IRE) (35)** (SRBowring) **3-9-0** SWebster(1) (mde most tl over 3f out: hung lft & lost pl over 2f out)	hd	**5**	25/1	35	—
255 9	**Sir Alidaf** (OO'Neill) **3-8-9**(5) JBramhill(6) (plld hrd: trckd ldrs tl wknd 2f out)	13	**6**	50/1	18	—
	Kissandy (MrsVAAconley) **3-8-9** MDeering(5) (tall: bkwd: dwlt: bhd: outpcd 7f out: t.o 3f out)	10	**7**	33/1	—	—
				(SP 113.4%)		**7 Rn**

2m 48.3 (15.30) CSF £6.35 TOTE £1.30: £1.10 £7.90 (£5.20) OWNER Mrs Daphne Kilgour (NEWMARKET) BRED A. Malone

356 NORMANTON CLAIMING STKS (4-Y.O+) (Class E)
2-45 (2-45) **1m 6f (Fibresand)** £2,788.00 (£844.00: £412.00: £196.00) Stalls: High GOING: 0.19 sec per fur (SLW)

				SP	RR	SF
	Grand Cru (MrsMReveley) **6-8-10** ACulhane(3) (lw: pushed along & hdwy 8f out: led over 4f out: sn rdn: styd on appr fnl f)	—	**1**	9/2 2	45	23
284 7	**Undawaterscubadiva (31)** (MPBielby) **5-8-7**(5) DSweeney(9) (hld up: hdwy 7f out: chal 3f out: nt qckn appr fnl f)	2½	**2**	8/1 3	44	22

272[6] **World Without End (USA) (30)** (MESowersby) **8-8-5b**(5) PFessey(7) (a chsng ldrs: rdn over 3f out: one pce) 11 **3** 8/1[3] 30 8
272[7] **El Nido (60)** (DWChapman) **9-8-11** KFallon(1) (led tl over 4f out: grad wknd) 4 **4** 6/4[1] 26 4
Culrain (35) (THCaldwell) **6-8-8** WRyan(4) (sn bhd: t.o 8f out: sme hdwy 4f out: sn wknd) 20 **5** 25/1 — —
Anistop (60) (JLEyre) **5-8-10** TWilliams(8) (b: chsd ldrs tl lost pl 3f out: eased) 6 **6** 9/2[2] — —
73[6] **Dutch Dyane (33)** (GPEnright) **4-7-12**(5)ow5 ADaly(2) (b: b.hind: trckd ldrs: rdn & lost pl ½-wy: sn bhd) 2 **7** 14/1 — —
232[7] **Ship's Dancer (30)** (DonEnricoIncisa) **4-8-2b** KimTinkler(6) (in tch: pushed along & outpcd over 4f out: sn wknd) 2 **8** 33/1 — —
I Don't Think So (THind) **6-7-12**(3) DarrenMoffatt(5) (chsd ldrs: sn pushed along: lost pl 7f out: sn bhd) ½ **9** 33/1 — —
(SP 115.0%) **9 Rn**

3m 13.4 (15.40) CSF £35.41 TOTE £6.40: £2.50 £1.70 £2.30 (£20.80) Trio £35.50 OWNER Dr Glyn Meredith (SALTBURN) BRED A. Dimmock
WEIGHT FOR AGE 4yo-5lb
OFFICIAL EXPLANATION **El Nido: might be feeling the effects of a hard winter campaign.**

357 MARKHAM MOOR H'CAP (0-95) (3-Y.O+) (Class C)

3-15 (3-17) **6f (Fibresand)** £5,246.85 (£1,588.80: £775.90: £369.45) Stalls: Low GOING: 0.19 sec per fur (SLW)

SP RR SF

Cretan Gift (90) (NPLittmoden) **6-9-9v** TGMcLaughlin(12) (lw: racd wd: hld up: stdy hdwy 2f out: edgd lft & led wl ins fnl f: r.o wl) — **1** 12/1 103 86
318[3] **Bold Frontier (63)** (KTIvory) **5-7-10b** JQuinn(2) (b: b.hind: trckd ldrs: led 2f out: edgd rt: hdd & nt qckn wl ins fnl f) 1¼ **2** 6/1[2] 73 56
301[4] **Broadstairs Beauty (IRE) (77)** (DShaw) **7-8-7**(3) CTeague(7) (b: b.hind: sn drvn along: led to 2f out: sn outpcd: kpt on ins fnl f) 6 **3** 12/1 71 54
257[8] **Prima Silk (79)** (MJRyan) **6-8-12** AClark(10) (in tch: styd on fnl 2f: nvr rchd ldrs) ½ **4** 14/1 71 54
Daawe (USA) (70) (MrsVAAconley) **6-8-3** MDeering(8) (outpcd ½-wy: hrd rdn & edgd lft 1f out: kpt on: nvr nr to chal) nk **5** 9/1[3] 62 45
254[2] **Bold Effort (FR) (90)** (KOCunningham-Brown) **5-9-9v** WRyan(6) (chsd ldrs: styd on same pce fnl 2f) s.h **6** 4/1[1] 81 64
253[7] **Mr Frosty (73)** (WJarvis) **5-8-6** SSanders(4) (chsd ldrs: rdn over 2f out: wkng whn hmpd jst ins fnl f) 1½ **7** 20/1 60 43
53[6] **Master of Passion (70)** (JMPEustace) **8-8-0**(3) MartinDwyer(5) (w ldrs tl wknd 2f out) 2 **8** 9/1[3] 52 35
301[5] **Chadwell Hall (70)** (SRBowring) **6-7-12**(5) ADaly(11) (racd wd: in tch: outpcd ½-wy: n.d after) ½ **9** 14/1 51 34
254[5] **Naughty Pistol (USA) (66)** (PDEvans) **5-7-13v** DWright(3) (sn wl bhd) 1¼ **10** 10/1 43 26
Stoppes Brow (93) (GLMoore) **5-9-12v** GDuffield(13) (lw: racd wd: bhd fr ½-wy) 1¼ **11** 4/1[1] 67 50
Sailormaite (85) (SRBowring) **6-9-4** SWebster(1) (ref to r: virtually t.n.p) **R** 16/1 — —
(SP 122.7%) **12 Rn**

1m 16.2 (2.70) CSF £77.66 CT £836.64 TOTE £17.40: £5.30 £2.60 £4.80 (£64.60) Trio £216.00 OWNER Mr T. Clarke (WOLVERHAMPTON) BRED Hesmonds Stud Ltd
LONG HANDICAP Bold Frontier 7-9

358 RETFORD H'CAP (0-80) (3-Y.O+) (Class D)

3-45 (3-49) **1m (Fibresand)** £3,566.25 (£1,080.00: £527.50: £251.25) Stalls: Low GOING: 0.19 sec per fur (SLW)

SP RR SF

330[2] **Rambo Waltzer (70)** (DNicholls) **5-8-11**(7) IonaWands(8) (chsd ldrs: rdn over 2f out: led over 1f out: styd on wl) — **1** 6/1[3] 82 54
322[2] **Genuine John (IRE) (63)** (JParkes) **4-8-6**(5) JBramhill(11) (chsd ldrs: led 2f out: sn hdd: nt qckn fnl f) 3½ **2** 14/1 68 40
248[W] **Chadleigh Lane (USA) (65)** (ABMulholland) **5-8-13** DeanMcKeown(4) (b.off fore: unruly s: a.p: styd on one pce fnl 2f) 2 **3** 16/1 66 38
330[8] **Kingchip Boy (80)** (MJRyan) **8-10-0b** AClark(5) (lw: chsd ldr: led 4f out to 2f out: one pce) 3 **4** 12/1 75 47
330* **Pleasure Trick (USA) (55)** (DonEnricoIncisa) **6-8-3b** 6x KimTinkler(7) (sn outpcd & bhd: styd on fnl 2f: nvr nr to chal) 3 **5** 9/1 44 16
257[5] **Royal Carlton (IRE) (69)** (GLMoore) **5-9-3** SWhitworth(12) (lw: chsd ldrs: rdn & outpcd over 2f out: kpt on) 1¾ **6** 9/2[2] 55 27
230* **Knotty Hill (77)** (RCraggs) **5-9-11** DHolland(13) (led to 4f out: wknd & eased over 1f out) 1½ **7** 9/4[1] 60 32
327[6] **Karinska (56)** (MCChapman) **7-8-4** DRMcCabe(1) (s.i.s: bhd tl sme hdwy fnl 2f) 2 **8** 25/1 35 7
Roar on Tour (58) (MrsMReveley) **8-8-6v** ACulhane(10) (lw: unruly s: racd wd: bhd: sme hdwy 2f out: n.d) ¾ **9** 16/1 35 7
Johnnie the Joker (73) (JPLeigh) **6-9-2**(5) PFessey(3) (s.i.s: bhd: sme hdwy 2f out: n.d) ½ **10** 33/1 49 21
305[5] **Tea Party (USA) (69)** (KOCunningham-Brown) **4-9-3** WRyan(2) (sn bhd) 2 **11** 33/1 41 13
Carburton (75) (JAGlover) **4-9-9** GCarter(6) (lw: chsd ldrs tl lost pl over 4f out: sn bhd) 8 **12** 13/2 31 3
330[7] **Mazurek (71)** (MGMeagher) **4-9-5** JQuinn(14) (b: racd wd: bhd fr ½-wy) 2 **13** 12/1 23 —
(SP 130.1%) **13 Rn**

1m 45.2 (6.20) CSF £85.36 CT £1,234.18 TOTE £5.40: £1.60 £3.40 £4.70 (£46.70) Trio £133.10 OWNER Mr W. G. Swiers (THIRSK) BRED Triangle Thoroughbreds Ltd
OFFICIAL EXPLANATION **Knotty Hill: rider reported that the gelding seemed lifeless, and that he felt it prudent to hold him together when he tired.**

359 RUFFORD (S) STKS (4-Y.O+) (Class E)

4-15 (4-15) **1m (Fibresand)** £3,095.40 (£937.20: £457.60: £217.80) Stalls: Low GOING: 0.19 sec per fur (SLW)

SP RR SF

273[3] **Northern Fan (IRE) (70)** (NTinkler) **5-8-12** DeanMcKeown(4) (led tl over 2f out: led jst ins fnl f: hld on towards fin) — **1** 3/1[2] 63 32
Flag Fen (USA) (58) (JParkes) **6-8-7**(5) JBramhill(5) (s.i.s: sn chsng ldrs: led over 2f out tl jst ins fnl f: no ex) nk **2** 12/1 62 31
288[3] **Desert Invader (IRE) (65)** (DWChapman) **6-8-12** ACulhane(3) (trckd ldrs: rdn & hung lft over 1f out: kpt on one pce) 3 **3** 11/2[3] 56 25
235[2] **Sandmoor Denim (48)** (SRBowring) **10-8-7**(5) ADaly(6) (b: racd wd: chsd ldrs: outpcd ½-wy: kpt on appr fnl f) 1 **4** 7/1 54 23
273[6] **Major Mouse (54)** (WWHaigh) **9-8-12** RLappin(1) (sn outpcd: hdwy over 2f out: sn rdn & no imp) ½ **5** 20/1 53 22
254[7] **Allez Cyrano (IRE) (60)** (OO'Neill) **6-8-7**(5) PRoberts(7) (sn w ldrs: rdn over 2f out: sn wl outpcd) 3½ **6** 20/1 46 15
273* **Sarasi (60)** (MJCamacho) **5-9-4** JQuinn(2) (lw: b.nr fore: chsd ldrs: pushed along over 3f out: rdn over 2f out: no rspnse: eased) 17 **7** 11/8[1] 18 —
(SP 112.2%) **7 Rn**

1m 46.9 (7.90) CSF £32.42 TOTE £3.10: £1.90 £8.90 (£14.70) OWNER Speedlith Group (MALTON) BRED Mrs Max Morris
Bt in 4,000 gns

OFFICIAL EXPLANATION Sarasi: the gelding likes to race up with the pace and, unable to do so here, resented the kickback.

360 TUXFORD H'CAP (0-65) (4-Y.O+) (Class F)

4-45 (4-45) **1m 4f (Fibresand)** £2,433.00 (£683.00: £333.00) Stalls: Low GOING: 0.19 sec per fur (SLW)

				SP	RR	SF
242[3]	**Maftun (USA) (54)** (GMMoore) **5-9-3** DHolland(4) (mde virtually all: hld on wl towards fin)	—	**1**	11/1	68	38
272[8]	**Kilnamartyra Girl (34)** (JParkes) **7-7-6**(5) JBramhill(10) (sn outpcd & bhd: hdwy ½-wy: styd on wl fnl f)	1	**2**	10/1	47	17
284[2]	**African-Pard (IRE) (40)** (DHaydnJones) **5-8-3** CRutter(9) (lw: hdwy ½-wy: sn chsng ldrs: ev ch over 1f out: nt qckn)	nk	**3**	9/1	52	22
284*	**Carol Again (44)** (NBycroft) **5-8-7** 5x JQuinn(12) (a.p: rdn 5f out: styd on same pce fnl 2f)	1¼	**4**	8/1[3]	55	25
242*	**Kalamata (50)** (JAGlover) **5-8-13** NDay(1) (lw: trckd ldrs: chal over 3f out: one pce appr fnl f)	½	**5**	2/1[1]	60	30
333[4]	**Royal Acclaim (34)** (CFCJackson) **12-7-11v**ow1 DaleGibson(2) (s.i.s: bhd: hdwy 4f out: kpt on fnl f)	1½	**6**	14/1	42	11
151[3]	**Mr Moriarty (IRE) (33)** (SRBowring) **6-7-5**(5) PFessey(11) (b: chsd ldrs: drvn along 5f out: one pce fnl 3f)	1¼	**7**	8/1[3]	39	9
260[6]	**Raindeer Quest (45)** (JLEyre) **5-8-1**(7)ow3 SBuckley(13) (trckd ldrs tl wknd 2f out)	7	**8**	10/1	42	9
	Royrace (33) (WMBrisbourne) **5-7-5b**[1](5) RMullen(8) (b: trckd ldrs: rdn over 3f out: lost pl 2f out)	9	**9**	33/1	18	—
	Compass Pointer (65) (JMPEustace) **4-9-8**(3) MartinDwyer(5) (sn outpcd & bhd: sme hdwy over 2f out: sn wknd)	11	**10**	6/1[2]	35	2
276[4]	**Another Quarter (IRE) (50)** (MCChapman) **4-8-10** DRMcCabe(3) (chsd ldrs tl lost pl 5f out: sn bhd)	d.h	**10**	20/1	20	—
284[6]	**No Submission (USA) (48)** (DWChapman) **11-8-11b** ACulhane(7) (s.i.s: racd wd: a wl bhd)	nk	**12**	20/1	18	—
	Inovar (33) (CBBBooth) **7-7-10** NKennedy(6) (bit bkwd: prom 4f: bhd fr ½-wy: t.o)	dist	**13**	33/1	—	—

(SP 128.4%) **13 Rn**

2m 45.0 (12.00) CSF £108.98 CT £960.72 TOTE £8.60: £4.60 £3.10 £2.90 (£43.90) Trio £228.30; £3.22 to Newbury 1/3/97 OWNER Anmaf Partnership (MIDDLEHAM) BRED Steeple Stone Bloodstock Co

LONG HANDICAP Carol Again 8-0 Mr Moriarty (IRE) 7-7 Royrace 7-7 Inovar 7-8

WEIGHT FOR AGE 4yo-3lb

OFFICIAL EXPLANATION Maftun (USA): had bitten his tongue quite badly last time.

T/Plpt: £1,926.90 (4.75 Tckts). T/Qdpt: £119.30 (6.93 Tckts) WG

0347-LINGFIELD (L-H) (Standard)

Saturday March 1st

WEATHER: Overcast WIND: fresh bhd

361 PISCES MEDIAN AUCTION MAIDEN STKS (3-Y.O) (Class F)

2-20 (2-20) **7f (Equitrack)** £2,372.40 (£666.40: £325.20) Stalls: Low GOING minus 0.43 sec per fur (FST)

				SP	RR	SF
161[6]	**Polgwynne** (BSmart) **3-8-9** MTebbutt(7) (lw: hdwy 5f out: chsd ldr 3f out: drvn to ld ins fnl f)	—	**1**	7/1	55	5
	Cheval Roc (66) (RHannon) **3-9-0** RPerham(3) (a.p: led 3f out: hdd ins fnl f: one pce)	1	**2**	4/1[2]	58	8
292[3]	**Talisman (IRE) (53)** (SDow) **3-9-0** WRyan(4) (hld up: rdn 3f out: r.o ins fnl f)	s.h	**3**	6/1	58	8
293[3]	**Windborn (46)** (CNAllen) **3-8-6**(3) MartinDwyer(2) (a.p: led ½-wy: sn hdd: hrd rdn over 1f out: one pce)	hd	**4**	9/2[3]	52	2
204[4]	**Crackerbox** (HAkbary) **3-8-9** OUrbina(6) (hld up: rdn 4f out: kpt on one pce fnl 2f)	3½	**5**	7/1	44	—
251[3]	**Bon Guest (IRE) (58)** (TJNaughton) **3-9-0** SSanders(1) (led to ½-wy: wknd 2f out)	2	**6**	15/8[1]	45	—
282[6]	**Emma's Risk (38)** (RHarris) **3-8-9** DBiggs(5) (bhd fnl 5f: t.o)	24	**7**	33/1	—	—

(SP 115.2%) **7 Rn**

1m 29.03 (4.63) CSF £32.20 TOTE £8.70: £2.30 £2.50 (£21.70) OWNER The Tregavethan Partners (LAMBOURN) BRED Mrs P. A. Clark

362 TAURUS CLAIMING STKS (3-Y.O) (Class F)

2-55 (2-55) **1m (Equitrack)** £2,417.20 (£679.20: £331.60) Stalls: High GOING minus 0.43 sec per fur (FST)

				SP	RR	SF
286[2]	**Enchanting Eve (69)** (CNAllen) **3-8-9**(3) MartinDwyer(6) (mde all: jst hld on)	—	**1**	6/4[1]	73	22
	Major Twist (IRE) (RHannon) **3-8-13** RPerham(3) (lw: a.p: chsd wnr 5f out: hrd rdn over 1f out: r.o wl ins fnl f)	s.h	**2**	16/1	74	23
329*	**Bailieborough Boy (IRE) (63)** (TDBarron) **3-9-1b** DeanMcKeown(2) (hld up: hdwy 3f out: n.m.r over 2f out: swtchd rt over 1f out: r.o one pce ins fnl f)	1¼	**3**	9/4[2]	73	22
237[3]	**Misty Cay (IRE) (61)** (SDow) **3-7-12**(5)ow1 ADaly(1) (prom tl lost pl 5f out: rallied 3f out: kpt on one pce fnl 2f)	1¾	**4**	3/1[3]	58	6
325[6]	**Our Kevin (52)** (BAPearce) **3-8-3b** DRMcCabe(5) (sn prom: wknd over 2f out)	10	**5**	20/1	38	—
225[6]	**Be True (54)** (GLMoore) **3-8-9** CandyMorris(4) (prom tl wknd over 3f out)	1	**6**	9/1	42?	—

(SP 116.4%) **6 Rn**

1m 41.26 (3.86) CSF £24.62 TOTE £2.40: £1.10 £3.50 (£33.10) OWNER Newmarket Connections (NEWMARKET) BRED P. Young

363 LODESTONE PATIENT CARE H'CAP (0-95) (4-Y.O+) (Class C)

3-30 (3-30) **1m (Equitrack)** £4,982.65 (£1,508.20: £736.10: £350.05) Stalls: High GOING minus 0.43 sec per fur (FST)

				SP	RR	SF
	Tatika (84) (GWragg) **7-8-11**(7) GMilligan(5) (chsd ldrs: led 3f out: rdn out)	—	**1**	3/1[1]	90	60
	Chewit (94) (GLMoore) **5-10-0** CandyMorris(4) (hld up: hdwy gng wl 2f out: drvn to chal ins fnl f: r.o)	½	**2**	3/1[1]	99	69
175*	**Hurtleberry (IRE) (72)** (LordHuntingdon) **4-8-6** DHarrison(1) (b.hind: a.p: rdn & ev ch over 1f out: unable qckn)	¾	**3**	4/1[2]	76	46
290*	**Spencer's Revenge (62)** (PButler) **8-7-5**(5) JBramhill(6) (hld up: hdwy over 3f out: ev ch over 1f out: one pce)	1¾	**4**	20/1	62	32
257*	**Rakis (IRE) (93)** (MrsLStubbs) **7-9-13** DHolland(8) (hld up: hdwy 3f out: rdn 2f out: one pce)	3	**5**	4/1[2]	87	57
297*	**Duke Valentino (84)** (RHollinshead) **5-8-13**(5) DGriffiths(2) (chsd ldr: rdn over 2f out: grad wknd)	1¾	**6**	12/1	75	45
226[7]	**Dances With Hooves (67)** (DJSffrenchDavis) **5-8-1** DRMcCabe(9) (lw: outpcd & wl bhd tl mod late hdwy: nrst fin)	1½	**7**	20/1	55	25

				SP	RR	SF
323[8]	**Blue Flyer (IRE) (80)** (RIngram) **4-9-0b** SWhitworth(7) (lw: hld up: hdwy over 3f out: wknd over 2f out)	8	**8**	9/1[3]	52	22
	Banzhaf (USA) (80) (GLMoore) **4-9-0** GDuffield(3) (led: hdd 3f out: sn wknd)	¾	**9**	20/1	50	20
				(SP 122.0%)	**9 Rn**	

1m 37.99 (0.59) CSF £11.25 CT £31.67 TOTE £4.00: £2.10 £1.10 £1.40 (£20.40) Trio £21.60 OWNER Mr G. Wragg (NEWMARKET) BRED D. J. and Mrs Deer
LONG HANDICAP Spencer's Revenge 7-5

364 KELVIN MACKENZIE HALF CENTURY H'CAP (0-80) (4-Y.O+) (Class D)

4-00 (4-00) **6f (Equitrack)** £3,290.00 (£995.00: £485.00: £230.00) Stalls: Low GOING minus 0.43 sec per fur (FST)

				SP	RR	SF
201[3]	**Speedy Classic (USA) (80)** (MJHeaton-Ellis) **8-10-0** AClark(2) (lw: hdwy over 2f out: rdn & str run ins fnl f: led nr fin)	—	**1**	4/1[2]	85	55
323*	**Squire Corrie (73)** (DWChapman) **5-9-7** ACulhane(4) (sn led: hrd rdn ins fnl f: hdd nr fin)	nk	**2**	6/1	77	47
323[2]	**Apollo Red (72)** (GLMoore) **8-9-6** CandyMorris(7) (a.p: ev ch ins fnl f: r.o)	nk	**3**	7/1	75	45
325[W]	**Sharp Imp (63)** (RMFlower) **7-8-11b** DHarrison(3) (outpcd & bhd tl gd hdwy ins fnl f: fin wl)	2	**4**	7/1	61	31
304*	**Rififi (73)** (RIngram) **4-9-7** SWhitworth(5) (hld up: hdwy 3f out: rdn over 1f out: wknd ins fnl f: fin me)	1¾	**5**	11/4[1]	66	36
127*	**Walk the Beat (73)** (MartynMeade) **7-9-2**(5) DSweeney(1) (prom tl wknd over 3f out)	2½	**6**	12/1	60	30
348[2]	**Lord Sky (70)** (ABailey) **6-9-4** SSanders(6) (lw: prom tl wknd over 2f out)	2	**7**	5/1[3]	51	21
				(SP 110.3%)	**7 Rn**	

1m 12.49 (1.39) CSF £23.44 TOTE £3.20: £2.40 £3.00 (£25.00) OWNER South Wales Shower S Faucets (WROUGHTON) BRED Lagrange Chance Partnership & Overbrook Farm

365 RAPPORTEUR CONDITIONS STKS (3-Y.O+) (Class D)

4-30 (4-30) **1m 2f (Equitrack)** £3,306.25 (£1,000.00: £487.50: £231.25) Stalls: Low GOING minus 0.43 sec per fur (FST)

				SP	RR	SF
220*	**Royal Action (93)** (JEBanks) **4-9-10** MWigham(4) (lw: mde all: all out)	—	**1**	8/11[1]	94	53
	Mersey Beat (GLMoore) **3-8-2**ow1 GDuffield(2) (hld up in tch: chsd wnr over 1f out: hrd rdn ins fnl f: r.o)	hd	**2**	11/4[2]	93	30
299[5]	**Prince Danzig (IRE) (83)** (DJGMurraySmith) **6-9-7** DHarrison(3) (lw: chsd ldrs: rdn 4f out: styd on ins fnl f)	1¼	**3**	7/1[3]	89	48
100[10]	**At Liberty (IRE) (72)** (RHannon) **5-9-10** RHughes(5) (lw: chsd wnr tl over 1f out: one pce)	½	**4**	20/1	91	50
291[4]	**Night Wink (USA) (82)** (GLMoore) **5-9-7** SWhitworth(1) (chsd ldrs tl wknd over 2f out)	7	**5**	7/1[3]	77	36
	Summerville Wood (62) (PMooney) **3-8-1** DRMcCabe(6) (hld up: rdn 4f out: wknd 3f out: t.o)	20	**6**	50/1	46?	—
				(SP 116.3%)	**6 Rn**	

2m 6.8 (2.50) CSF £2.90 TOTE £1.80: £1.20 £1.30 (£3.40) OWNER Mr E. Carter (NEWMARKET) BRED D. J. and Mrs Deer
WEIGHT FOR AGE 3yo-21lb
STEWARDS' ENQUIRY Duffield susp. 13-14/3/97 (improper use of whip).

366 LEO H'CAP (0-70) (3-Y.O) (Class E)

5-00 (5-01) **1m 2f (Equitrack)** £2,752.25 (£833.00: £406.50: £193.25) Stalls: Low GOING minus 0.43 sec per fur (FST)

				SP	RR	SF
289*	**Touch'n'go (60)** (MJohnston) **3-9-0** DHolland(5) (sn led: r.o wl)	—	**1**	7/2[2]	76	36
292*	**Amico (62)** (CWThornton) **3-9-2** DeanMcKeown(6) (hld up: hdwy 4f out: chsd wnr over 2f out: rdn over 1f out: one pce)	3	**2**	6/1	73	33
347[4]	**Leg Beforum (IRE) (58)** (LMontagueHall) **3-8-12** GCarter(3) (s.i.s: hld up: rdn over 3f out: kpt on one pce fnl 2f)	3½	**3**	10/1	64	24
240[2]	**Mendoza (57)** (DJGMurraySmith) **3-8-6**(5) JBramhill(2) (a.p: chsd wnr 5f out tl over 2f out: wknd ins fnl f)	s.h	**4**	9/1	63	23
347[2]	**State of Gold (IRE) (61)** (JHetherton) **3-9-1** MTebbutt(8) (chsd ldrs: rdn over 3f out: wknd over 2f out)	10	**5**	5/1[3]	51	11
246*	**Rose Burton (52)** (TDBarron) **3-8-6** DHarrison(7) (hld up in rr: rdn 4f out: sn btn)	2½	**6**	11/1	38	—
307[4]	**Noble Hero (65)** (JJSheehan) **3-9-5b[1]** GDuffield(9) (hld up in rr: rdn 4f out: sn btn)	1½	**7**	11/4[1]	48	8
	Interdream (67) (RHannon) **3-9-7** RHughes(4) (bit bkwd: w wnr tl wknd over 5f out: virtually p.u over 1f out)	dist	**8**	14/1	—	—
				(SP 113.9%)	**8 Rn**	

2m 7.7 (3.40) CSF £22.33 CT £172.37 TOTE £4.20: £2.10 £1.90 £1.80 (£12.00) Trio £55.70 OWNER Greenland Park Ltd (MIDDLEHAM) BRED Laharna Ltd
OFFICIAL EXPLANATION Noble Hero: the trainer's representavive stated that the colt had been disappointing recently and may not have faced the blinkers.

T/Plpt: £203.90 (47.12 Tckts). T/Qdpt: £15.40 (55.6 Tckts) SM

0341-WOLVERHAMPTON (L-H) (Standard)
Saturday March 1st
WEATHER: Unsettled

367 MARYLAND MAIDEN H'CAP (0-65) (3-Y.O+) (Class F)

7-00 (7-01) **7f (Fibresand)** £2,433.00 (£683.00: £333.00) Stalls: High GOING: 0.08 sec per fur (STD)

				SP	RR	SF
312[7]	**Mustang (27)** (CWThornton) **4-7-12b[1]** DaleGibson(10) (lw: plld hrd: led 4f out: qcknd clr ent fnl f: comf)	—	**1**	7/1	38	17
312[4]	**Recessions Over (34)** (NPLittmoden) **6-8-5** TGMcLaughlin(11) (a.p: rdn to chal over 1f out: nt pce of wnr fnl f)	3	**2**	9/2[1]	38	17
203[7]	**Barbara's Jewel (44)** (ABailey) **5-9-1** DWright(8) (bit bkwd: led after 2f to 4f out: rdn & one pce appr fnl f)	4	**3**	6/1[3]	39	18
312[6]	**Happy Brave (35)** (PDCundell) **5-8-3**(3) FLynch(4) (b: a.p: rdn over 2f out: kpt on same pce)	2½	**4**	8/1	24	3
312[8]	**Hornpipe (33)** (JWharton) **5-8-4b** FNorton(5) (b: lw: effrt & rdn ½-wy: edgd lft & styd on fnl f)	3½	**5**	6/1[3]	14	—
	Loxley's Girl (IRE) (45) (HAkbary) **3-7-7**(7) RFfrench(12) (b.hind: bkwd: prom on outside over 4f)	3½	**6**	20/1	18	—
312[10]	**Young Frederick (IRE) (47)** (KRBurke) **4-9-4v[1]** ACulhane(1) (drvn along ½-wy: effrt on outside over 2f out: no imp)	1½	**7**	20/1	17	—
288[4]	**Natal Ridge (55)** (DHaydnJones) **4-9-12** AClark(9) (chsd ldrs 4f: sn rdn & outpcd)	½	**8**	11/2[2]	24	3
312[3]	**Ballet de Cour (35)** (TJEtherington) **4-7-13**(7) CLowther(6) (led 2f: wknd 3f out)	¾	**9**	7/1	2	—
288[9]	**Baptismal Rock (IRE) (65)** (BJCurley) **3-9-6** WRyan(2) (a in rr: t.o fnl 3f)	16	**10**	8/1	—	—

				SP	RR	SF
	Members Welcome (IRE) (40) (WGMTurner) **4-8-11v** TSprake(7) (bit bkwd: virtually ref to r: a t.o)	22	**11**	8/1	—	—
				(SP 130.0%)		**11 Rn**

1m 30.9 (6.20) CSF £39.04 CT £190.33 TOTE £7.20: £2.30 £2.50 £1.90 (£18.60) Trio £76.20 OWNER Mr Guy Reed (MIDDLEHAM) BRED G. Reed

WEIGHT FOR AGE 3yo-16lb

368 IRISH ROW LIMITED STKS (0-60) (3-Y.O) (Class F)

7-30 (7-30) **1m 100y (Fibresand)** £2,363.00 (£663.00: £323.00) Stalls: Low GOING: 0.08 sec per fur (STD)

				SP	RR	SF
307^{3}	**Swift (60)** (MJPolglase) **3-9-1** MRimmer(5) (lw: mde all: drvn clr 3f out: unchal)	—	**1**	9/2	67	31
289^{2}	**Fearless Sioux (57)** (CWThornton) **3-8-9** KFallon(3) (sn pushed along in rr: styd on fnl 2f: nvr nrr)	5	**2**	11/2	52	16
314^{3}	**Skelton Sovereign (IRE) (55)** (RHollinshead) **3-8-12**(3) FLynch(2) (dwlt: sn chsng wnr: rdn over 2f out: one pce)	nk	**3**	7/2 3	57	21
215^{4}	**Alvilde (60)** (DJSCosgrove) **3-8-4**(5) RMullen(4) (hld up: hdwy to chse wnr over 2f out: wknd appr fnl f)	3	**4**	100/30 2	45	9
296^{*}	**Mysterium (60)** (NPLittmoden) **3-9-1** TGMcLaughlin(1) (lw: prom tl rdn & lost tch over 2f out: t.o)	21	**5**	5/2 1	12	—
				(SP 107.4%)		**5 Rn**

1m 52.9 (7.90) CSF £23.60 TOTE £3.90: £1.90 £1.80 (£11.10) OWNER Gen Sir Geoffrey Howlett (NEWMARKET) BRED Mrs Amschel Rothschild

OFFICIAL EXPLANATION **Mysterium: was unsuited by the slow early pace.**

369 MIAMI H'CAP (0-70) (4-Y.O+) (Class E)

8-00 (8-00) **1m 1f 79y (Fibresand)** £2,814.00 (£852.00: £416.00: £198.00) Stalls: Low GOING: 0.08 sec per fur (STD)

				SP	RR	SF
284^{3}	**Suga Hawk (IRE) (54)** (EJAlston) **5-8-12** KFallon(6) (a.p: led appr fnl f: pushed clr)	—	**1**	11/2 2	66	34
220^{7}	**Whispering Dawn (62)** (CPEBrooks) **4-9-1**(5) PPMurphy(8) (b.hind: hld up: hdwy ½-wy: r.o ins fnl f: no ch w wnr)	3½	**2**	6/1 3	68	36
342^{2}	**Dragonjoy (58)** (NPLittmoden) **4-8-11v**(5) DGriffiths(11) (hld up: hdwy 3f out: led over 1f out: sn hdd: no ex fnl f)	1¼	**3**	3/1 1	62	30
226^{8}	**Rival Bid (USA) (58)** (MrsNMacauley) **9-8-13v¹**(3) CTeague(13) (lw: hld up & bhd: hdwy over 2f out: nt rch ldrs)	1¾	**4**	10/1	59	27
305^{*}	**Tallulah Belle (68)** (NPLittmoden) **4-9-12** TGMcLaughlin(4) (a.p: led over 4f out tl over 1f out: sn rdn & wknd)	½	**5**	11/2 2	68	36
	Rajah (49) (CWThornton) **4-8-7** DeanMcKeown(10) (lw: prom: hrd drvn over 2f out: one pce)	¾	**6**	10/1	48	16
274^{8}	**Myfontaine (53)** (KTIvory) **10-8-11** GBardwell(2) (b: b.hind: trckd ldrs: rdn 3f out: no imp)	nk	**7**	10/1	51	19
284^{14}	**Cohiba (49)** (BJCurley) **4-8-7** WRyan(9) (nvr plcd to chal)	1½	**8**	12/1	45	13
	River Run (IRE) (49) (RHollinshead) **5-8-4**(3) FLynch(5) (bit bkwd: dropped rr ½-wy: sn bhd)	3½	**9**	20/1	39	7
140^{10}	**Three Weeks (60)** (WRMuir) **4-9-4** AClark(1) (lw: chsd ldrs 6f: sn lost tch)	½	**10**	7/1	49	17
	Decision Maker (IRE) (65) (KRBurke) **4-9-9v** ACulhane(3) (led 5f: sn drvn along: lost tch)	s.h	**11**	25/1	54	22
	Panto Queen (49) (CRBarwell) **6-8-7** TSprake(12) (b.hind: hld up & bhd: effrt 5f out: wknd 3f out)	2½	**12**	40/1	34	2
				(SP 128.6%)		**12 Rn**

2m 4.0 (8.00) CSF £37.53 CT £112.10 TOTE £5.70: £1.70 £1.30 £1.50 (£50.70) Trio £52.10 OWNER Mr John Patrick Barry (PRESTON) BRED Countess A. De Laubespin

370 TABLE MOUNTAIN H'CAP (0-85) (3-Y.O) (Class D)

8-30 (8-31) **1m 4f (Fibresand)** £4,809.20 (£1,351.20: £659.60) Stalls: Low GOING: 0.08 sec per fur (STD)

				SP	RR	SF
331^{*}	**Lawn Lothario (80)** (MJohnston) **3-9-12** 5x TWilliams(1) (lw: mde all: clr 3f out: unchal)	—	**1**	1/3 1	94	41
298^{7}	**Aspecto Lad (IRE) (62)** (MJohnston) **3-8-8b** DeanMcKeown(2) (sn nudged along in rr: wnt 2nd over 1f out: no ch w wnr)	6	**2**	7/1 3	68	15
314^{5}	**Head Gardener (IRE) (70)** (NPLittmoden) **3-8-11**(5) ADaly(3) (chsd wnr: rdn over 4f out: sn btn)	10	**3**	4/1 2	63	10
				(SP 107.5%)		**3 Rn**

2m 43.9 (11.40) CSF £2.76 TOTE £1.40 (£1.70) OWNER Mr J. S. Morrison (MIDDLEHAM) BRED Snailwell Stud Co Ltd

371 VENICE (S) STKS (4-Y.O+) (Class F)

9-00 (9-01) **5f (Fibresand)** £2,580.00 (£780.00: £380.00: £180.00) Stalls: Low GOING: 0.08 sec per fur (STD)

				SP	RR	SF
233^{12}	**Little Ibnr (68)** (PDEvans) **6-9-4** KFallon(6) (chsd ldrs: rdn to ld ins fnl f: drvn out)	—	**1**	4/1 3	64	36
303^{6}	**Featherstone Lane (52)** (MissLCSiddall) **6-8-11v** DRMcCabe(1) (sn bhd & outpcd: rapid hdwy appr fnl f: fin wl)	1¾	**2**	6/1	51	23
303^{4}	**Myttons Mistake (63)** (ABailey) **4-8-11** DWright(5) (a.p: ev ch 1f out: unable qckn)	½	**3**	100/30 2	50	22
222^{5}	**Boffy (IRE) (48)** (BPJBaugh) **4-8-4b**(7) IonaWands(3) (a.p: led wl over 1f out tl ins fnl f)	1½	**4**	6/1	45	17
304^{5}	**Rennyholme (36)** (JHetherton) **6-8-6b**(5) JBramhill(2) (prom: slt ld 2f out: sn hdd: rdn & wknd appr fnl f)	3½	**5**	10/1	34	6
	Super Rocky (65) (RBastiman) **8-8-11b** DaleGibson(4) (led 3f: rdn & wknd appr fnl f)	¾	**6**	2/1 1	31	3
				(SP 114.1%)		**6 Rn**

63.2 secs (4.30) CSF £25.33 TOTE £4.70: £2.10 £3.00 (£10.60) OWNER Swinnerton Transport Ltd (WELSHPOOL) BRED R. E. Waugh

No bid

372 CHRISTIENSTED H'CAP (0-70) (3-Y.O) (Class E)

9-30 (9-30) **6f (Fibresand)** £2,762.00 (£836.00: £408.00: £194.00) Stalls: Low GOING: 0.08 sec per fur (STD)

				SP	RR	SF
217^{*}	**C-Harry (IRE) (68)** (RHollinshead) **3-9-4**(3) FLynch(5) (hld up: hdwy to ld over 1f out: rdn & hung rt & lft: hld on)	—	**1**	100/30 2	73	27
258^{5}	**Master Foley (60)** (NPLittmoden) **3-8-13** TGMcLaughlin(4) (lw: chsd ldr: led ½-wy: rdn & hdd over 1f out: rallied cl home)	nk	**2**	11/2 3	64	18
193^{6}	**Magic Fizz (61)** (TJEtherington) **3-9-0** MTebbutt(3) (bhd: effrt 2f out: no imp fnl f)	5	**3**	16/1	52	6
	Splashed (66) (TDBarron) **3-9-5** RLappin(7) (bit bkwd: hdwy 2f out: kpt on ins fnl f: nvr nrr)	nk	**4**	11/2 3	56	10
307^{6}	**Abstone Queen (49)** (PDEvans) **3-7-11b**(5) RMullen(1) (sn bhd & outpcd: sme hdwy fnl 2f: nvr nrr)	nk	**5**	6/1	38	—
247^{2}	**Pet Express (61)** (PCHaslam) **3-8-11**(3) MartinDwyer(2) (lw: led to ½-wy: rdn & wknd wl over 1f out)	3	**6**	2/1 1	42	—

			SP	RR	SF
293^{4}	**Fit For The Job (IRE) (58)** (TWall) **3-8-8**$^{(3)}$ PMcCabe(6) (plld hrd: prom over 3f: sn wknd: t.o)........................10	**7**	9/1	13	—
			(SP 117.3%)		**7 Rn**

1m 17.3 (6.10) CSF £20.73 TOTE £4.30: £1.90 £3.20 (£11.50) OWNER Mr D. Coppenhall (UPPER LONGDON) BRED Dan O'Loughlin

T/Plpt: £169.00 (58.15 Tckts). T/Qdpt: £25.90 (11.91 Tckts) IM

0355-SOUTHWELL (L-H) (Standard)
Monday March 3rd
WEATHER: fine WIND: almost nil

373 HOOPLA MAIDEN STKS (3 & 4-Y.O) (Class D)
2-10 (2-16) **1m 3f (Fibresand)** £3,582.50 (£1,085.00: £530.00: £252.50) Stalls: Low

			SP	RR	SF
73^{4}	**River Captain (USA)** (DJGMurraySmith) **4-9-12** SSanders(4) (chsd ldrs: led 2f out: hung lft: kpt on wl)........—	**1**	10/1	68	42
	Stretching (IRE) (44) (ABailey) **4-9-12** DWright(11) (hld up: stdy hdwy 6f out: styd on fnl f)...........................2½	**2**	25/1	64	38
	Terdad (USA) (TDBarron) **4-9-12** DHarrison(3) (led after 1f out to 2f out: one pce)...¾	**3**	$5/4^{1}$	63	37
266^{3}	**Happy Medium (IRE)** (GPEnright) **4-9-7**$^{(5)}$ ADaly(2) (hdwy u.p 5f out: kpt on: nvr rchd ldrs)............................5	**4**	$7/1^{3}$	56	30
	Mountaineer (IRE) (MBell) **3-8-5** DBiggs(8) (rangy: hdwy 8f out: sn pushed along: rn green: styd on fnl f) ...s.h	**5**	$7/2^{2}$	56	9
	Picard (IRE) (FMurphy) **4-9-12** JFanning(7) (chsd ldrs tl outpcd fnl 3f)..2½	**6**	14/1	52	26
	Warrlin (64) (CWFairhurst) **3-8-5** LCharnock(6) (led 1f: sn drvn along: wknd 3f out)..10	**7**	12/1	38	—
289^{5}	**Petula Boy (42)** (SRBowring) **3-8-5** DeanMcKeown(10) (hdwy u.p 6f out: sn wknd)...4	**8**	33/1	32	—
314^{8}	**Melodic Squaw** (MPBielby) **3-8-0** TWilliams(12) (rdn ½-wy: sn wl bhd)..5	**9**	50/1	20	—
	Masrrah (IRE) (RWArmstrong) **3-8-5** GCarter(5) (bit bkwd: s.i.s: a bhd & sn drvn along).................................2	**10**	8/1	22	—
328^{7}	**African Sun (IRE) (43)** (MCChapman) **4-9-12** DRMcCabe(1) (bhd & rdn ½-wy)...5	**11**	50/1	15	—
235^{12}	**Father Eddie (58)** (JJO'Neill) **3-8-5** JStack(13) (bhd fr ½-wy: t.o 3f out)..14	**12**	20/1	—	—
	Romantic Warrior (KSBridgwater) **4-9-12** VSlattery(9) (rn wd bnd after 1f: sn bhd: t.o 5f out)........................12	**13**	33/1	—	—
			(SP 132.1%)		**13 Rn**

2m 30.6 (10.60) CSF £230.93 TOTE £15.90: £2.40 £11.00 £1.40 (£455.20) Trio £168.70; £2.38 to Leicester 4/3/97 OWNER Ms Diana Wilder (LAMBOURN) BRED Juddmonte Farms
WEIGHT FOR AGE 3yo-22lb, 4yo-1lb

374 CONKERS CLAIMING STKS (4-Y.O+) (Class E)
2-40 (2-41) **1m 4f (Fibresand)** £3,282.00 (£922.00: £450.00) Stalls: Low

			SP	RR	SF
285^{2}	**Greenspan (IRE) (69)** (WRMuir) **5-9-9** AClark(3) (lw: hld up gng wl: led on bit over 2f out: v.easily)..............—	**1**	$8/11^{1}$	74+	34
299^{8}	**Dancing Cavalier (60)** (RHollinshead) **4-8-8b**$^{1(3)}$ FLynch(2) (trckd ldrs: led over 4f out tl over 2f out: no ch w wnr)..8	**2**	$7/2^{3}$	53	11
	Soldier Mak (59) (AHide) **4-8-7** GBardwell(4) (w ldr: led 6f out tl over 4f out: sn drvn along & wl outpcd)..........3	**3**	$3/1^{2}$	45	3
285^{6}	**Sea God (45)** (MCChapman) **6-9-1** DRMcCabe(1) (led to 6f out: p.u over 4f out: lame)......................................	**P**	16/1	—	—
			(SP 111.0%)		**4 Rn**

2m 45.3 (12.30) CSF £3.43 TOTE £1.70 (£2.30) OWNER Camelot Racing (LAMBOURN) BRED Dermot and Meta Cantillon
WEIGHT FOR AGE 4yo-2lb

375 MARBLES H'CAP (0-65) (4-Y.O+) (Class F)
3-15 (3-15) **2m (Fibresand)** £2,433.00 (£683.00: £333.00) Stalls: Low

			SP	RR	SF
284^{5}	**Road Racer (IRE) (51)** (MrsJRRamsden) **4-9-1** KFallon(8) (hld up: shkn up & hdwy ½-wy: styd on to ld over 1f out: drvn out)........................—	**1**	$6/1^{2}$	64	4
324^{*}	**Coleridge (54)** (JJSheehan) **9-9-9b** AClark(1) (sn pushed along: chsd ldrs: led over 2f out tl over 1f out: nt qckn)...........................1¾	**2**	$6/1^{2}$	65	10
272^{2}	**La Menorquina (USA) (43)** (DMarks) **7-8-12** SSanders(7) (hld up: hdwy on outside 5f out: sn chsng ldrs: edgd lft & nt qckn appr fnl f)...........................¾	**3**	$7/4^{1}$	54	—
315^{8}	**Forzair (55)** (JJO'Neill) **5-9-10** WRyan(11) (hld up: hdwy 7f out: sn chsng ldrs: wknd over 1f out).........................6	**4**	14/1	60	5
	Vishnu (USA) (45) (JLEyre) **7-9-0** RLappin(9) (a chsng ldrs: sn pushed along: one pce fnl 3f)..........................9	**5**	16/1	41	—
356^{3}	**World Without End (USA) (30)** (MESowersby) **8-7-8b**$^{(5)}$ PFessey(10) (w ldrs gng wl: led 6f out tl over 2f out: wknd over 1f out)...........................4	**6**	16/1	22	—
252^{4}	**Blue And Royal (IRE) (30)** (VSoane) **5-7-13** CRutter(5) (b.off hind: s.i.s: sn drvn along: hdwy 6f out: hung lft & one pce fnl 3f)...........................¾	**7**	10/1	21	—
	Sujud (IRE) (49) (MDHammond) **5-8-11**$^{(7)}$ SBuckley(4) (mid div: sn pushed along: hrd rdn 5f out: sn lost pl) 3½	**8**	$8/1^{3}$	36	—
167^{9}	**Record Lover (IRE) (28)** (MCChapman) **7-7-11** GBardwell(6) (prom: sn pushed along: lost pl 6f out) 11	**9**	16/1	4	—
	Skram (45) (RDickin) **4-8-9** ACulhane(3) (led to 6f out: lost pl over 4f out)..¾	**10**	16/1	21	—
261^{8}	**Qualitair Pride (40)** (JFBottomley) **5-8-9** NCarlisle(12) (trckd ldrs: chal 6f out: wknd over 2f out)..........................3	**11**	10/1	13	—
	Distant Storm (46) (BJLlewellyn) **4-8-10v** TWilliams(13) (lw: hld up: racd wd: rdn ½-wy: sn chsng ldrs: wknd over 4f out)...........................10	**12**	20/1	9	—
			(SP 129.2%)		**12 Rn**

3m 47.6 (21.60) CSF £41.88 CT £84.92 TOTE £5.50: £2.60 £1.40 £1.60 (£20.00) Trio £12.40 OWNER Mr J. E. Swiers (THIRSK) BRED Michael M. Byrne
WEIGHT FOR AGE 4yo-5lb
STEWARDS' ENQUIRY Buckley susp. 13-15 & 17/3/97 (excessive use of whip).

376 HMS INTERNATIONAL H'CAP (0-95) (3-Y.O+) (Class C)
3-45 (3-45) **7f (Fibresand)** £5,602.00 (£1,696.00: £828.00: £394.00) Stalls: Low

			SP	RR	SF
274^{3}	**State of Caution (77)** (DShaw) **4-9-2b** JFanning(1) (b: lw: trckd ldrs: styd on to ld ins fnl f: drvn out) ....—	**1**	$5/1^{2}$	86	69
358^{7}	**Knotty Hill (77)** (RCraggs) **5-9-2** DHolland(5) (sn drvn along: led tl ins fnl f: no ex)...¾	**2**	7/1	84	67
323^{4}	**Stand Tall (80)** (LadyHerries) **5-8-12**$^{(7)}$ PDoe(9) (b.hind: hld up: effrt ½-wy: styd on appr fnl f)........................3½	**3**	15/2	79	62
	Iblis (IRE) (85) (GWragg) **5-9-3**$^{(7)}$ GMilligan(4) (hld up: effrt & n.m.r over 2f out: kpt on: nvr nr to chal)...........hd	**4**	$9/4^{1}$	84	67
207^{4}	**Jibereen (70)** (PHowling) **5-8-9** SWhitworth(11) (b: racd wd: bhd tl kpt on appr fnl f) 3½	**5**	$11/2^{3}$	61	44

Form	Horse	Btn	Pl	SP	RR	SF
330[3]	**Sea Spouse (65)** (MBlanshard) **6-8-4** AClark(2) (trckd ldrs: rdn & wnt lft over 2f out: grad wknd)	1¾	6	7/1	52	35
344[4]	**Three Arch Bridge (73)** (MJohnston) **5-8-12b** DeanMcKeown(3) (s.i.s: bhd: kpt on wl fnl 2f: nvr nr to chal)	½	7	12/1	59	42
330[6]	**Iamus (82)** (TDBarron) **4-9-7** DHarrison(6) (in tch: drvn along ½-wy: sn wl outpcd)	nk	8	14/1	67	50
	Cashmere Lady (82) (JLEyre) **5-9-7** RLappin(7) (racd wd: a in rr)	6	9	12/1	54	37
	First Maite (80) (SRBowring) **4-9-5** SWebster(10) (racd wd: chsd ldrs tl lost pl 3f out)	¾	10	25/1	50	33
	Intiaash (IRE) (75) (DHaydnJones) **5-9-0** TWilliams(8) (chsd ldrs: hung lft & wknd over 2f out)	3	11	20/1	38	21
				(SP 130.2%)	**11 Rn**	

1m 29.9 (3.40) CSF £40.75 CT £254.25 TOTE £7.90: £2.40 £1.90 £3.80 (£33.30) Trio £103.80 OWNER Mr J. C. Fretwell (NEWARK) BRED C. Wiggins

377 JACKS (S) STKS (3-Y.O) (Class E)

4-20 (4-23) **7f (Fibresand)** £3,060.30 (£926.40: £452.20: £215.10) Stalls: Low

Form	Horse	Btn	Pl	SP	RR	SF
180[8]	**La Dolce Vita (73)** (TDBarron) **3-8-5**(7) VictoriaAppleby(2) (lw: mde all: clr over 4f out: unchal: eased towards fin)	—	1	6/4[1]	77+	43
317[6]	**Jack The Lad (IRE) (58)** (JHetherton) **3-8-12** MTebbutt(5) (lw: sn bhd: styd on fnl 2f: no ch w wnr)	9	2	11/1	56	22
237[4]	**Red Embers (66)** (CADwyer) **3-8-12** DRMcCabe(6) (swtg: trckd ldrs: drvn along over 4f out: kpt on appr fnl f)	hd	3	10/1	56	22
	Polarize (TDBarron) **3-8-12** DHarrison(1) (bit bkwd: s.i.s: bhd: kpt on fnl 2f: nvr nr to chal)	2½	4	10/1	51	17
314[6]	**Mirror Four Sport (51)** (MJohnston) **3-8-5**(7) NPollard(9) (chsd ldrs: sn drvn along: outpcd fr ½-wy)	1¼	5	9/1[3]	48	14
296[3]	**Qualitair Silver** (JFBottomley) **3-8-7** LCharnock(4) (chsd wnr: drvn along 4f out: wknd fnl f)	s.h	6	7/2[2]	43	9
	See You Soon (CWThornton) **3-8-12** DeanMcKeown(7) (sn bhd & pushed along: sme hdwy over 1f out: n.d)	6	7	20/1	34	—
156[6]	**Love Over Gold** (MCChapman) **3-8-7** GBardwell(3) (dwlt s: sn chsng ldrs: wknd 2f out)	16	8	50/1	—	—
	Unknown Territory (IRE) (62) (RonaldThompson) **3-8-12v** KFallon(10) (racd wd: a bhd)	24	9	10/1	—	—
	Zafarelli (SCWilliams) **3-8-5**(7) DarrenWilliams(8) (Withdrawn not under Starter's orders: v.unruly at s: ref to ent stalls)		W	20/1	—	—
				(SP 119.3%)	**9 Rn**	

1m 31.8 (5.30) CSF £17.86 TOTE £2.30: £1.20 £2.10 £2.80 (£11.00) Trio £44.90 OWNER Mr Stephen Woodall (THIRSK) BRED D. R. Botterill
Bt in 5,200 gns

378 SKITTLES H'CAP (0-60) (3-Y.O) (Class F)

4-50 (4-50) **6f (Fibresand)** £2,433.00 (£683.00: £333.00) Stalls: Low

Form	Horse	Btn	Pl	SP	RR	SF
	Gresatre (54) (CADwyer) **3-8-11**(7) JoHunnam(9) (hld up: hdwy on outside over 2f out: sn rdn: led over 1f out: r.o)	—	1	9/1	68	49
287[3]	**Captain Carparts (38)** (JLEyre) **3-8-2** TWilliams(5) (chsd ldr: led 2f out: sn hdd: nt qckn ins fnl f)	2	2	9/2[3]	47	28
	Soda (55) (TDBarron) **3-9-5b**[1] DHarrison(1) (led to 2f out: wknd fnl f)	2	3	7/4[1]	58	39
320[7]	**Lucy of Arabia (IRE) (55)** (JJSheehan) **3-9-5** KFallon(2) (sltly hmpd s: hdwy over 2f out: hung lft: kpt on fnl f)	1	4	14/1	56	37
345[4]	**Seretse's Nephew (50)** (SCWilliams) **3-8-7**(7) DarrenWilliams(6) (chsd ldrs: outpcd over 2f out: kpt on fnl f)	2½	5	10/1	44	25
317[2]	**Julia's Relative (51)** (RGuest) **3-8-10**(5) DGriffiths(3) (b: hld up: nt clr run on ins 3f out: sn rdn & wknd)	9	6	7/2[2]	21	2
246[3]	**Rochea (57)** (MrsNMacauley) **3-9-7v**[1] AClark(7) (sn drvn along & bhd)	½	7	16/1	26	7
265[4]	**Miss Barcelona (IRE) (50)** (MJPolglase) **3-9-0** TGMcLaughlin(8) (swtg: w ldrs: rdn ½-wy: sn lost pl)	2	8	10/1	13	—
132[5]	**Hever Golf Stormer (IRE) (48)** (TJNaughton) **3-8-12** SSanders(4) (chsd ldrs: rdn over 4f out: wknd 2f out)	1½	9	10/1	7	—
				(SP 126.6%)	**9 Rn**	

1m 18.0 (4.50) CSF £49.27 CT £98.98 TOTE £9.50: £1.90 £1.10 £1.60 (£21.40) Trio £156.00; £79.14 to Leicester 4/3/97 OWNER Mr E. R. Kettenacker (NEWMARKET) BRED E. Kettenacker

T/Plpt: £49.00 (184.07 Tckts). T/Qdpt: £9.30 (80.23 Tckts) WG

0361-LINGFIELD (L-H) (Standard)

Tuesday March 4th

WEATHER: overcast WIND: almost nil

379 TENNYSON CLAIMING STKS (3-Y.O) (Class E)

2-10 (2-10) **5f (Equitrack)** £2,739.25 (£829.00: £404.50: £192.25) Stalls: High GOING minus 0.51 sec per fur (FST)

Form	Horse	Btn	Pl	SP	RR	SF
237[2]	**Eager To Please (69)** (MissGayKelleway) **3-8-11b** DHolland(1) (b: b.hind: lw: mde all: rdn out)	—	1	100/30[1]	75	31
320[3]	**Blues Magic (IRE) (65)** (MBell) **3-8-2**(5) GFaulkner(8) (a.p: chsd wnr 2f out tl over 1f out: unable qckn)	1¼	2	7/2[2]	67	23
320[4]	**Sparkling Edge (59)** (CADwyer) **3-8-2** DRMcCabe(3) (hld up: rdn over 2f out: chsd wnr over 1f out: one pce)	nk	3	11/2[3]	61	17
247[4]	**Lunar Music (61)** (MartynMeade) **3-8-5**(5) DSweeney(2) (chsd wnr 3f: one pce)	2½	4	10/1	61	17
221[2]	**Threeplay (IRE) (61)** (JAkehurst) **3-8-0**(5) JBramhill(5) (b: rdn over 3f out: hdwy on ins over 2f out: one pce)	1½	5	11/2[3]	51	7
193[5]	**Krystal Davey (IRE) (61)** (TDBarron) **3-8-11** DHarrison(9) (rdn 3f out: nvr nr to chal)	1¼	6	7/1	53	9
345[5]	**Ma Vielle Pouque (IRE) (56)** (WGMTurner) **3-7-10** NCarlisle(6) (bhd fnl 4f)	½	7	8/1	37	—
	Not Out Lad (PButler) **3-8-7** SDrowne(4) (b: b.nr hind: dwlt: a bhd)	10	8	50/1	16	—
				(SP 110.7%)	**8 Rn**	

59.42 secs (1.22) CSF £12.91 TOTE £3.60: £1.10 £2.10 £1.70 (£7.70) Trio £10.90 OWNER Miss Jo Crowley (WHITCOMBE) BRED Mrs Sara Hood
Blues Magic (IRE) clmd RIngram £6,000

380 KEATS H'CAP (0-80) (4-Y.O+) (Class D)

2-40 (2-41) **1m 2f (Equitrack)** £3,355.00 (£1,015.00: £495.00: £235.00) Stalls: Low GOING minus 0.51 sec per fur (FST)

Form	Horse	Btn	Pl	SP	RR	SF
340*	**Captain's Day (45)** (HJCollingridge) **5-7-7**(5) 5x RMullen(2) (a.p: led 2f out: hrd rdn over 1f out: r.o wl)	—	1	5/4[1]	54	30
291[6]	**Digpast (IRE) (69)** (MMadgwick) **7-9-8** DHarrison(8) (hdwy 6f out: led over 3f out to 2f out: unable qckn)	2½	2	16/1	74	50
305[4]	**Mimosa (57)** (SDow) **4-8-10** WRyan(1) (rdn over 3f out: hdwy over 2f out: one pce)	1½	3	16/1	60	36
	Fairy Knight (71) (RHannon) **5-9-10** RHughes(4) (rdn & hdwy over 3f out: wknd over 2f out)	5	4	5/1[2]	66	42
291[7]	**Sweet Supposin (IRE) (65)** (CADwyer) **6-9-4v** JStack(7) (b: lw: rdn & hdwy over 3f out: wknd over 2f out)	s.h	5	9/1	60	36
123[12]	**Rehaab (56)** (DMorris) **4-8-4**(5) GFaulkner(5) (chsd ldrs: led over 4f out tl over 3f out: sn wknd)	3	6	14/1	46	22

Form	Horse	Dist	Pos	SP	RR	SF
340^{2}	**Bakers Daughter (49)** (JRArnold) **5-7-13**(3) MartinDwyer(3) (swtg: led over 5f)	6	**7**	12/1	29	5
	Prizefighter (70) (JLEyre) **6-9-6**(3) OPears(6) (prom 5f)	13	**8**	6/1^{3}	29	5

(SP 111.5%) **8 Rn**

2m 5.75 (1.45) CSF £20.64 CT £192.68 TOTE £2.50: £1.10 £3.80 £3.40 (£15.20) OWNER Mr D. Burke (EXNING) BRED R. Hutt

OFFICIAL EXPLANATION **Prizefighter: the jockey reported that his instructions were to sit second or third in the early stages but that he was soon having to niggle and felt there was somethig amiss. The vet reported that during examination after the race the horse was found to be coughing.**

381 SPIRIT OF CHAMPIONS H'CAP (0-60) (4-Y.O+) (Class F)

3-10 (3-10) **2m (Equitrack)** £2,428.40 (£682.40: £333.20) Stalls: Low GOING minus 0.51 sec per fur (FST)

Form	Horse	Dist	Pos	SP	RR	SF
351^{2}	**High Five (IRE) (26)** (RIngram) **7-7-10** GBardwell(9) (b: hdwy over 4f out: led over 3f out: rdn over 2f out: eased wl ins fnl f)	—	**1**	9/4^{1}	40	14
116^{8}	**Outstayed Welcome (45)** (MJHaynes) **5-9-1** DHarrison(7) (b.hind: led over 14f out tl over 3f out: unable qckn)	3½	**2**	16/1	56	30
375^{2}	**Coleridge (54)** (JJSheehan) **9-9-10b** AClark(1) (s.s: hld up: rdn over 4f out: r.o one pce fnl f)	s.h	**3**	7/2^{2}	64	38
302^{3}	**Bedouin Prince (USA) (41)** (MrsLStubbs) **10-8-11** KFallon(5) (b: a.p: rdn over 4f out: one pce)	5	**4**	9/1	46	20
334^{5}	**Kirov Protege (IRE) (34)** (MrsLCJewell) **5-7-11**(7) DarrenWilliams(2) (led over 1f: bhd fnl 7f)	9	**5**	33/1	30	4
351^{3}	**Matthias Mystique (59)** (MissBSanders) **4-9-7**(3) AWhelan(6) (a.p: rdn over 4f out: sn wknd)	½	**6**	5/1^{3}	55	24
188^{4}	**Captain Marmalade (37)** (DTThom) **8-8-7v** JTate(10) (bhd fnl 4f)	1½	**7**	7/1	31	5
295^{11}	**Uoni (44)** (PButler) **4-8-4b**(5) JBramhill(8) (s.s: hdwy 15f out: rdn over 4f out: wknd over 3f out)	4	**8**	16/1	34	3
	Allez Pablo (26) (RRowe) **7-7-10** NCarlisle(3) (a bhd: t.o fnl 4f)	dist	**9**	50/1	—	—

(SP 108.8%) **9 Rn**

3m 26.53 (5.53) CSF £33.51 CT £98.70 TOTE £3.40: £1.50 £1.60 £1.50 (£23.10) Trio £33.80 OWNER Mr D. A. Wilson (EPSOM) BRED Rosemount House Stud

LONG HANDICAP High Five (IRE) 7-4 Allez Pablo 7-9

WEIGHT FOR AGE 4yo-5lb

382 COLERIDGE H'CAP (0-75) (4-Y.O+) (Class D)

3-40 (3-42) **1m (Equitrack)** £3,306.25 (£1,000.00: £487.50: £231.25) Stalls: High GOING minus 0.51 sec per fur (FST)

Form	Horse	Dist	Pos	SP	RR	SF
321^{2}	**Live Project (IRE) (55)** (MJohnston) **5-8-11** DHolland(6) (led over 1f: led over 3f out: rdn out)	—	**1**	11/4^{2}	63	45
358^{6}	**Royal Carlton (IRE) (69)** (GLMoore) **5-9-11** SWhitworth(7) (a.p: chsd wnr over 2f out: ev ch fnl 2f: r.o)	nk	**2**	5/2^{1}	76	58
294^{3}	**Robellion (70)** (DWPArbuthnot) **6-9-12v** DHarrison(1) (b.hind: hdwy over 3f out: rdn over 2f out: wknd over 1f out)	5	**3**	3/1^{3}	67	49
	Ethbaat (USA) (67) (MJHeaton-Ellis) **6-9-9** AClark(4) (hdwy over 3f out: one pce fnl 2f)	nk	**4**	12/1	64	46
325^{4}	**Deeply Vale (IRE) (63)** (PButler) **6-9-5** SDrowne(3) (b: rdn & hdwy over 2f out: sn wknd)	5	**5**	10/1	50	32
	Allinson's Mate (IRE) (60) (TDBarron) **9-8-9**(7) VictoriaAppleby(2) (bit bkwd: a bhd)	nk	**6**	10/1	46	28
175^{5}	**Worldwide Elsie (USA) (60)** (ICampbell) **4-9-2** TGMcLaughlin(5) (led over 6f out tl over 3f out: sn wknd)	7	**7**	9/1	32	14

(SP 116.1%) **7 Rn**

1m 38.25 (0.85) CSF £9.49 TOTE £4.00: £2.00 £1.40 (£4.10) OWNER Mrs Gillian Quinn (MIDDLEHAM) BRED Una Bolger

383 WORDSWORTH LIMITED STKS (0-60) (3-Y.O+) (Class F)

4-10 (4-11) **1m (Equitrack)** £2,473.20 (£695.20: £339.60) Stalls: High GOING minus 0.51 sec per fur (FST)

Form	Horse	Dist	Pos	SP	RR	SF
248^{7}	**Ki Chi Saga (USA) (52)** (MMadgwick) **5-9-6** RHughes(6) (lw: a.p: led over 3f out: rdn out)	—	**1**	16/1	67	44
352^{3}	**Tuigamala (60)** (RIngram) **6-9-6** AMcGlone(5) (lw: a.p: chsd wnr over 2f out: unable qckn)	2½	**2**	3/1^{1}	62	39
201^{4}	**Perilous Plight (58)** (MrsLStubbs) **6-9-6** KFallon(4) (rdn & hdwy over 2f out: one pce)	s.h	**3**	100/30^{2}	62	39
197^{5}	**Rawi (60)** (MissGayKelleway) **4-9-8** DHolland(3) (b: b.hind: lw: chsd ldrs: rdn over 4f out: one pce fnl 2f)	3½	**4**	3/1^{1}	57	34
186^{6}	**Superior Force (60)** (MissBSanders) **4-9-5**(3) AWhelan(1) (led over 4f)	1½	**5**	5/1^{3}	54	31
321^{3}	**Statistician (44)** (JohnBerry) **5-8-13e**(7) AmyQuirk(2) (chsd ldrs: shkn up over 2f out: wknd over 1f out)	2	**6**	14/1	48	25
	La Perruche (IRE) (47) (LordHuntingdon) **4-9-3** DHarrison(8) (prom 3f)	8	**7**	16/1	29	6
177^{9}	**Ocean Stream (IRE) (57)** (JLEyre) **4-9-6** DeanMcKeown(7) (a bhd)	2½	**8**	8/1	27	4

(SP 119.3%) **8 Rn**

1m 39.16 (1.76) CSF £60.60 TOTE £25.90: £3.20 £1.90 £1.10 (£36.40) OWNER Mr D. Knight (DENMEAD) BRED Green Island Properties Ltd

OFFICIAL EXPLANATION **Rawi: suffered an overreach on his near-fore.**

Ki Chi Saga (USA): after an enquiry into improvement, the trainer reported that the gelding had coughed and had a temperature after his last run.

384 SHAKESPEARE AMATEUR H'CAP (0-70) (4-Y.O+) (Class E)

4-40 (4-40) **1m 5f (Equitrack)** £2,804.25 (£849.00: £414.50: £197.25) Stalls: Low GOING minus 0.51 sec per fur (FST)

Form	Horse	Dist	Pos	SP	RR	SF
324^{4}	**English Invader (54)** (CADwyer) **6-10-5** MrTMcCarthy(8) (hdwy over 4f out: led over 1f out: comf)	—	**1**	5/1^{3}	65+	51
261^{4}	**Don't Drop Bombs (USA) (35)** (DTThom) **8-9-0v** MissJFeilden(5) (lw: chsd ldr: led over 2f out tl over 1f out: unable qckn)	4	**2**	16/1	41	27
256^{2}	**Heighth of Fame (70)** (JHetherton) **6-11-0**(7) MrJByrne(1) (led over 10f: one pce)	3	**3**	7/1	72	58
	Gold Blade (63) (JPearce) **8-11-0** MrsLPearce(7) (lw: hdwy over 4f out: one pce)	4	**4**	13/2	61	47
315^{3}	**Classic Account (36)** (JLEyre) **9-8-11**(4) MrsCWilliams(10) (prom over 10f)	¾	**5**	6/1	33	19
324^{7}	**Stalled (IRE) (51)** (PTWalwyn) **7-9-12**(4) MarchionessBlandford(9) (b: nvr nr to chal)	nk	**6**	12/1	47	33
324^{3}	**Hattaafeh (IRE) (70)** (MissBSanders) **6-11-3**(4) MissLSheen(3) (bhd fnl 5f)	3	**7**	4/1^{2}	63	49
	Swinging Sixties (IRE) (57) (GLMoore) **6-10-4**(4) MrsJMoore(2) (b: bhd fnl 4f)	2½	**8**	10/1	46	32
	Loki (IRE) (60) (GLewis) **9-10-11** MrMArmytage(6) (b.hind: bit bkwd: a bhd)	14	**9**	3/1^{1}	32	18
	Ray River (49) (KGWingrove) **5-9-10**(4)ow5 MrsHNoonan(4) (a bhd)	3	**10**	50/1	18	—

(SP 126.4%) **10 Rn**

2m 45.88 (3.88) CSF £80.54 CT £528.26 TOTE £7.00: £2.30 £1.80 £1.80 (£79.80) Trio £84.40 OWNER Mr John Purcell (NEWMARKET) BRED Bloodstock Management Int Pty Ltd

LONG HANDICAP Don't Drop Bombs (USA) 8-12

OFFICIAL EXPLANATION **Loki (IRE): no explanation offered.**

T/Plpt: £38.30 (286.56 Tckts). T/Qdpt: £21.90 (27.27 Tckts) AK

0367-WOLVERHAMPTON (L-H) (Standard)

Wednesday March 5th

WEATHER: overcast

385 SANDSTORM AMATEUR H'CAP (0-70) (I) (4-Y.O+) (Class G)

1-50 (1-50) **6f (Fibresand)** £1,648.50 (£461.00: £223.50) Stalls: Low GOING minus 0.03 sec per fur (STD)

				SP	RR	SF
	Another Nightmare (IRE) (41) (RMMcKellar) **5-9-6**(4) MrsCWilliams(2) (b.hind: mde all: rdn out)	—	1	20/1	48	30
335[5]	**Astral Invader (IRE) (35)** (MSSaunders) **5-9-4** MrKGoble(6) (a.p: rdn 2f out: r.o one pce fnl f)	1¼	2	14/1	39	21
327*	**Ring the Chief (37)** (MDIUsher) **5-9-2**(4) 7x MrsAUsher(1) (a.p: chsd wnr over 3f out: one pce fnl f)	hd	3	9/2[2]	40	22
359[3]	**Desert Invader (IRE) (61)** (DWChapman) **6-11-2** MissRClark(3) (lw: a.p: one pce fnl f)	nk	4	10/1	64	46
333[3]	**Bold Habit (43)** (JPearce) **12-9-12** MrsLPearce(9) (outpcd tl hdwy over 1f out: fin wl)	nk	5	8/1	45	27
326[4]	**Margaretrose Anna (42)** (BPJBaugh) **5-9-11** MissDianaJones(10) (b: no hdwy fnl 2f)	¾	6	15/2	42	24
	Steal 'Em (59) (ABailey) **4-10-7b**[1](7) MissALHutchinson(4) (bit bkwd: rdn over 3f out: no hdwy fnl 2f)	¾	7	6/1	57	39
243[3]	**Dahiyah (USA) (55)** (BSmart) **6-10-6v**(4) MissVMarshall(8) (lw: sn outpcd)	2½	8	11/2[3]	46	28
316[2]	**Leigh Crofter (66)** (PDCundell) **8-11-7b** MrTMcCarthy(5) (prom: rdn over 2f out: eased whn btn ins fnl f)	2½	9	9/4[1]	51	33
305[9]	**Sally Armstrong (40)** (CWThornton) **4-9-5**(4) MrVLukaniuk(7) (outpcd)	6	10	20/1	9	—
				(SP 126.8%)	**10 Rn**	

1m 16.6 (5.40) CSF £265.63 CT £1,396.15 TOTE £13.90: £2.60 £3.10 £4.50 (£135.90) Trio £160.30; £180.70 to Wincanton 6/3/97 OWNER GM Engineering (LESMAHAGOW) BRED John J. Ryan

386 SANDSTORM AMATEUR H'CAP (0-70) (II) (4-Y.O+) (Class G)

2-20 (2-20) **6f (Fibresand)** £1,648.50 (£461.00: £223.50) Stalls: Low GOING minus 0.03 sec per fur (STD)

				SP	RR	SF
318[8]	**Takhlid (USA) (61)** (DWChapman) **6-11-0** MissRClark(8) (lw: racd wd: hld up: hdwy over 1f out: led wl ins fnl f: r.o)	—	1	14/1	65	40
333[8]	**Dancing Sioux (60)** (RGuest) **5-10-6**(7) MissZBurkett(4) (b: outpcd: hdwy 2f out: ev ch ins fnl f: r.o)	1	2	10/1	61	36
349[7]	**Lochon (51)** (MrsNMacauley) **6-10-4v** MissDianaJones(6) (b: a.p: ev ch ins fnl f: r.o)	hd	3	16/1	52	27
327[3]	**Dream Carrier (IRE) (45)** (REPeacock) **9-9-5**(7)ow5 MrsCPeacock(1) (sn outpcd: gd hdwy fnl f: fin wl)	1½	4	7/1	42	12
263[10]	**Southern Dominion (43)** (MissJFCraze) **5-9-3**(7)ow5 MrWWenyon(7) (b.hind: prom: rdn over 3f out: led 1f out: edgd lft & hdd wl ins fnl f)	½	5	14/1	39	9
367*	**Mustang (34)** (CWThornton) **4-9-1b** 7x MrsLPearce(2) (led over 4f out to 1f out: wknd)	2	6	6/4[1]	24	—
371*	**Little Ibnr (75)** (PDEvans) **6-11-10**(4) 7x MrAEvans(3) (prom: rdn over 3f out: wknd wl over 1f out)	1¼	7	11/2[3]	62	37
	Chief's Lady (43) (JMBradley) **5-9-6**(4) MissEJJones(9) (s.i.s: sn prom: rdn, hung lft & wknd over 1f out)	2	8	40/1	25	—
318[4]	**Marjorie Rose (IRE) (61)** (ABailey) **4-10-10**(4) MissBridgetGatehouse(10) (outpcd tl hdwy on ins & nt clr run over 2f out: sn wknd)	3½	9	9/2[2]	33	8
	Naissant (67) (RMMcKellar) **4-11-2**(4) MrsCWilliams(5) (led over 1f: wknd over 2f out)	1	10	11/1	37	12
				(SP 125.1%)	**10 Rn**	

1m 17.1 (5.90) CSF £142.10 CT £2,087.22 TOTE £18.50: £4.70 £2.60 £4.20 (£74.20) Trio Not won; £236.90 to Wincanton 6/3/97 OWNER Miss N. F. Thesiger (YORK) BRED Cheveley Park Stud Ltd

STEWARDS' ENQUIRY Evans susp. 14-15 & 17/3/97 (careless riding).

387 TEMPEST MAIDEN STKS (3-Y.O+) (Class D)

2-50 (2-51) **1m 100y (Fibresand)** £3,403.75 (£1,030.00: £502.50: £238.75) Stalls: Low GOING minus 0.03 sec per fur (STD)

				SP	RR	SF
	Sword Arm (77) (RCharlton) **3-8-6** TSprake(7) (lw: a.p: shkn up over 3f out: led on bit over 1f out: easily)	—	1	Evens[1]	68+	31
	Little Acorn (SCWilliams) **3-8-6** JTate(8) (bit bkwd: rdn & hdwy over 2f out: r.o ins fnl f: no ch w wnr)	1	2	12/1[3]	66	29
341[9]	**Only Josh (IRE)** (MrsJRRamsden) **3-8-6** JFanning(9) (led: hdd over 1f out: one pce)	3	3	14/1	60	23
	Venice Beach (69) (CPEBrooks) **5-9-7**(3) JDSmith(5) (s.i.s: rdn & hdwy over 4f out: styd on fnl f)	2	4	14/1	57	38
255[7]	**Krosno** (SCWilliams) **3-7-13**(7) DarrenWilliams(6) (lw: plld hrd: prom tl wknd over 2f out)	3½	5	33/1	50	13
	Perfect Poppy (JRFanshawe) **3-8-3**ow2 DHarrison(1) (bit bkwd: sn chsng ldr: rdn over 2f out: sn wknd)	2½	6	7/4[2]	42	3
	Condition Red (MSSaunders) **4-9-5** SDrowne(4) (lw: bhd fnl 3f: t.o)	17	7	33/1	8	—
	Bout (RMMcKellar) **3-8-1** TWilliams(2) (b.hind: hdwy over 4f out: wknd over 3f out: t.o)	17	8	16/1	—	—
	Rinus Magic (EJAlston) **4-9-10** KFallon(3) (bkwd: s.i.s: a bhd: t.o fnl 4f)	½	9	33/1	—	—
				(SP 122.1%)	**9 Rn**	

1m 51.0 (6.00) CSF £14.89 TOTE £1.60: £1.10 £3.20 £1.60 (£21.00) Trio £20.80 OWNER Mr A. E. Oppenheimer (BECKHAMPTON) BRED Hascombe and Valiant Studs

WEIGHT FOR AGE 3yo-18lb

388 CYCLONE H'CAP (0-90) (3-Y.O) (Class C)

3-20 (3-20) **1m 100y (Fibresand)** £5,368.00 (£1,624.00: £792.00: £376.00) Stalls: Low GOING minus 0.03 sec per fur (STD)

				SP	RR	SF
298[2]	**Globetrotter (IRE) (79)** (MJohnston) **3-8-10** DeanMcKeown(8) (lw: a.p: rdn over 3f out: led over 2f out: r.o wl)	—	1	3/1[2]	86	42
343[3]	**Foot Battalion (IRE) (90)** (RHollinshead) **3-9-4**(3) FLynch(6) (lw: hld up: hdwy wl over 1f out: r.o ins fnl f)	2½	2	9/1	92	48
331[2]	**Millroy (USA) (87)** (PAKelleway) **3-9-4v** MWigham(5) (hld up: rdn & outpcd over 3f out: rallied over 2f out: r.o one pce fnl f)	¾	3	15/2	88	44
255*	**Don Sebastian (80)** (WJHaggas) **3-8-11** KFallon(2) (lw: a.p: one pce fnl 2f)	s.h	4	5/4[1]	81	37
277[2]	**Mutahadeth (65)** (DShaw) **3-7-5**(5) PFessey(4) (nvr nr to chal)	3	5	13/2[3]	60	16
	Tinkerbell (65) (WRMuir) **3-7-5v**(5) JBramhill(3) (a.p: led over 3f out tl over 2f out: wknd over 1f out)	¾	6	12/1	59	15
	I Can't Remember (80) (PDEvans) **3-8-11** DWright(7) (prom 5f)	1¾	7	12/1	70	26
	Cee-N-K (IRE) (78) (MJohnston) **3-8-9** JFanning(1) (lw: led 5f: wknd 2f out)	7	8	10/1	55	11
				(SP 129.0%)	**8 Rn**	

1m 50.2 (5.20) CSF £31.32 CT £181.63 TOTE £5.10: £1.80 £1.70 £1.90 (£10.00) OWNER Brian Yeardley Continental Ltd (MIDDLEHAM) BRED Norelands Bloodstock

LONG HANDICAP Mutahadeth 7-9

389 B.S.D. H'CAP (0-100) (4-Y.O+) (Class C)

3-50 (3-50) **1m 4f (Fibresand)** £5,472.00 (£1,656.00: £808.00: £384.00) Stalls: Low GOING minus 0.03 sec per fur (STD)

				SP	RR	SF
70^{*}	**Albaha (USA) (80)** (JEBanks) **4-8-1**$^{(5)}$ RMullen(4) (mde all: pushed out)	—	1	$2/1^{1}$	88	49
$310a^{10}$	**Major Change (88)** (MissGayKelleway) **5-9-2** KFallon(9) (b: b.hind: hld up: chsd wnr over 3f out: rdn & ev ch 2f out: r.o one pce)	¾	2	9/2	95	58
299^{4}	**China Castle (87)** (PCHaslam) **4-8-6**$^{(7)}$ PGoode(2) (chsd wnr over 6f: lost pl over 3f out: styd on same pce fnl 2f)	7	3	10/1	85	46
344^{3}	**Hill Farm Dancer (79)** (WMBrisbourne) **6-8-0**$^{(7)}$ AnthonyBond(1) (s.i.s: hld up: stdy hdwy over 6f out: one pce fnl 3f)	1	4	$7/2^{2}$	75	38
182^{10}	**Montecristo (70)** (RGuest) **4-7-5**$^{(5)}$ JBramhill(3) (bhd fnl 3f)	7	5	12/1	57	18
344^{5}	**Second Colours (USA) (83)** (MCPipe) **7-8-8**$^{(3)}$ MartinDwyer(6) (prom: chsd wnr over 5f out tl over 3f out: sn wknd)	2	6	7/1	67	30
299^{2}	**Nikita's Star (IRE) (77)** (DJGMurraySmith) **4-7-12**$^{(5)ow2}$ ADaly(5) (prom over 8f)	¾	7	$4/1^{3}$	60	19
	Leonato (FR) (100) (PDEvans) **5-9-9**$^{(5)}$ DGriffiths(7) (bit bkwd: a bhd: t.o fnl 4f)	dist	8	10/1	—	—

(SP 132.1%) **8 Rn**

2m 38.5 (6.00) CSF £12.50 CT £75.32 TOTE £3.00: £1.20 £2.30 £1.90 (£7.70) Trio £43.10 OWNER UK Packaging Supplies Ltd (NEWMARKET) BRED Shadwell Estate Co., Ltd. and Shadwell Farm Inc.
WEIGHT FOR AGE 4yo-2lb

390 BLIZZARD (S) STKS (4-Y.O+) (Class G)

4-20 (4-20) **1m 1f 79y (Fibresand)** £1,998.50 (£561.00: £273.50) Stalls: Low GOING minus 0.03 sec per fur (STD)

				SP	RR	SF
319^{*}	**Soldier Cove (USA) (52)** (MartynMeade) **7-8-13**$^{(5)}$ DSweeney(10) (mde all: r.o wl)	—	1	13/2	62	41
359^{*}	**Northern Fan (IRE) (70)** (NTinkler) **5-9-4** DeanMcKeown(6) (lw: a.p: sltly outpcd over 1f out: rallied & hung lft wl ins fnl f: r.o)	2½	2	$11/4^{2}$	58	37
333^{7}	**David James' Girl (52)** (ABailey) **5-8-2**$^{(5)}$ GFaulkner(7) (a.p: chsd wnr over 3f out: one pce fnl f)	½	3	$3/1^{3}$	46	25
313^{2}	**Flagstaff (USA) (37)** (KRBurke) **4-8-12** ACulhane(2) (no hdwy fnl 3f)	12	4	8/1	30	9
313^{6}	**Efficacious (IRE) (26)** (PEccles) **4-8-2b**$^{1(5)}$ JBramhill(8) (w wnr tl wknd over 3f out)	8	5	25/1	12	—
295^{15}	**North Ardar (40)** (TWall) **7-8-9v**$^{1(3)}$ PMcCabe(5) (hld up: hdwy over 4f out: wknd over 3f out)	7	6	16/1	5	—
359^{7}	**Sarasi (60)** (MJCamacho) **5-9-4** LCharnock(1) (prom 5f)	nk	7	$2/1^{1}$	10	—
260^{9}	**Amnesty Bay (25)** (MDIUsher) **5-8-7** CRutter(4) (t.o fnl 5f)	11	8	25/1	—	—
108^{10}	**Emei Shan (30)** (WGMTurner) **4-8-7** TSprake(3) (a bhd: t.o fnl 5f)	11	9	33/1	—	—

(SP 126.0%) **9 Rn**

2m 2.8 (6.80) CSF £24.30 TOTE £9.40: £2.10 £1.10 £1.20 (£7.50) Trio £6.90 OWNER Ladyswood Racing Club (MALMESBURY) BRED Weststar Bloodstock
No bid

391 MONSOON H'CAP (0-65) (3-Y.O+) (Class F)

4-50 (4-50) **5f (Fibresand)** £2,531.00 (£711.00: £347.00) Stalls: Low GOING minus 0.03 sec per fur (STD)

				SP	RR	SF
301^{6}	**Gi La High (59)** (MartynMeade) **4-9-3**$^{(5)}$ DSweeney(10) (lw: chsd ldrs: r.o to ld wl ins fnl f)	—	1	$5/1^{2}$	68	49
318^{6}	**Aljaz (48)** (MissGayKelleway) **7-8-11** KFallon(6) (a.p: led ins fnl f: sn hdd: r.o)	½	2	$5/1^{2}$	55	36
318^{*}	**Needle Match (60)** (JJO'Neill) **4-9-9** WRyan(11) (hdwy wl over 1f out: r.o one pce fnl f)	2	3	$11/2^{3}$	61	42
263^{7}	**Thick as Thieves (44)** (RonaldThompson) **5-8-0**$^{(7)}$ DDenby(7) (a.p: one pce fnl 2f)	nk	4	14/1	44	25
301^{7}	**Sotonian (HOL) (46)** (PSFelgate) **4-8-4**$^{(5)}$ JBramhill(5) (lw: chsd ldr: one pce fnl f)	½	5	16/1	44	25
301^{2}	**Madrina (65)** (JBerry) **4-9-9**$^{(5)}$ PFessey(9) (lw: stumbled & bmpd s: hdwy over 3f out: one pce fnl 2f)	2½	6	$9/2^{1}$	55	36
348^{4}	**Bowcliffe Grange (IRE) (50)** (DWChapman) **5-8-13** ACulhane(12) (led tl wknd & hdd ins fnl f)	1½	7	7/1	36	17
371^{2}	**Featherstone Lane (52)** (MissLCSiddall) **6-9-1v** DRMcCabe(1) (nvr trbld ldrs)	hd	8	8/1	37	18
233^{3}	**Shadow Jury (63)** (DWChapman) **7-9-12b** LCharnock(4) (chsd ldrs over 2f)	1¼	9	$5/1^{2}$	44	25
371^{4}	**Boffy (IRE) (48)** (BPJBaugh) **4-8-4b**$^{(7)}$ IonaWands(8) (lw: stdd s: a bhd)	3	10	14/1	20	1
	Songsheet (62) (MSSaunders) **4-9-11** RPerham(2) (prom over 2f)	½	11	25/1	32	13
332^{9}	**Maysimp (IRE) (34)** (BPJBaugh) **4-7-11**^{ow1} DaleGibson(13) (a bhd)	½	12	50/1	3	—
	Deardaw (40) (MissLCSiddall) **5-7-12**$^{(5)ow7}$ ADaly(3) (a bhd)	2½	13	40/1	1	—

(SP 134.6%) **13 Rn**

62.1 secs (3.20) CSF £31.04 CT £140.29 TOTE £5.70: £2.30 £2.00 £2.30 (£20.90) Trio £182.10 OWNER Ladyswood Racing Club (MALMESBURY) BRED J. H. Heath
LONG HANDICAP Maysimp (IRE) 7-7 Deardaw 7-9

T/Plpt: £1,026.60 (9.19 Tckts). T/Qdpt: £10.50 (88.72 Tckts) KH

JEBEL ALI (Dubai, UAE) (L-H) (Fast)
Friday February 21st

392a GROSVENOR CLUBS JEBEL ALI SPRINT (Listed) (4-Y.O+)

6f (Dirt) £12,116.31 (£6,058.15: £3,634.89)

			SP	RR	SF
Try Prospect (USA) (DJSelvaratnam,UAE) **5-8-10b**^{1} BDoyle	—	1		106	—
Yazaly (USA) (WDMather,UAE) **8-8-9v** PBrette	½	2		104	—
Dyhim (USA) (PLRudkin,UAE) **6-8-9** PaulEddery	s.h	3		104	—

5 Rn

1m 11.43 OWNER Sheikh Ahmed bin Rashid al Maktoum BRED Fourbros Stable,USA

Try Prospect (USA), unbeaten so far this season, was left clear two furlongs out after setting the pace, but his early exertions took their toll as he began to weaken rapidly inside the final furlong, only just keeping in front at the line.

Yazaly (USA), outpaced early on, was being ridden at halfway and finished with a strong challenge to be nearest at the line.

Dyhim (USA), a winner over this distance last time out, found a mile slightly too far on his seasonal debut. He put in a strong challenge close home and would appear to favour this distance.

SANTA ANITA (Los Angeles, USA) (L-H) (Fast)
Sunday March 2nd

393a SANTA ANITA H'CAP (Gp 1)
1m 2f £357,143.00 (£119,048.00: £71,429.00)

Horse	Dist	Pos	SP	RR	SF
Siphon (BRA) (RMandella,USA) **6-8-8** DFlores	—	**1**		126	—
Sandpit (BRA) (RMandella,USA) **8-8-9** CNakatani	3	**2**		122	—
Gentlemen (ARG) (RMandella,USA) **5-8-11** GaryStevens	s.h	**3**		124	—
					11 Rn

2m 0.23 P-M £12.20: (1-2) £6.20 £7.80 (1-2-3) £3.60 £4.60 £3.20 (£29.20) OWNER Rio Claro Thoroughbreds BRED Haras Sao Jose E Expedictus

IN-FOCUS: **Richard Mandella entered the history books here, as his three contenders filled the first three places, winning a total of $920,000 for his owners.**

Siphon (BRA) should, along with the other two placed Mandella contenders, now be in line for an invitation for the Dubai World Cup. Setting the pace, he disputed the lead with stablemate Gentlemen until the furlong marker, and soon quickened clear from that rival. This was an incredible victory as he had been sidelined for five months last year with injury.

Sandpit (BRA) finished fast and late on the outside to demote Gentlemen to third place.

Gentlemen (ARG) could not justify favouritism here, but is highly regarded and should play a major role in the Dubai World Cup if all goes well.

0385- WOLVERHAMPTON (L-H) (Standard)
Saturday March 8th
WEATHER: overcast WIND: mod across

394 MANNY BERNSTEIN BOOKMAKERS H'CAP (0-100) (I) (3-Y.O+) (Class C)
2-10 (2-11) **5f (Fibresand)** £4,480.85 (£1,353.80: £658.90: £311.45) Stalls: Low GOING: 0.16 sec per fur (SLW)

Form	Horse	Dist	Pos	SP	RR	SF
357^{2}	**Bold Frontier (67)** (KTIvory) **5-7-12b**(3) MartinDwyer(5) (b: b.hind: hdwy ½-wy: led over 1f out: sn clr)	—	**1**	$5/1^{3}$	79	60
357^{6}	**Bold Effort (FR) (90)** (KOCunningham-Brown) **5-9-10v** TQuinn(8) (hdwy 2f out: r.o wl ins fnl f: nt rch wnr)	3	**2**	$9/2^{2}$	92	73
316^{5}	**Kira (74)** (JLEyre) **7-8-8** RLappin(3) (b.off hind: chsd ldrs: rdn & one pce fnl f)	1¾	**3**	6/1	71	52
198*	**Kalar (75)** (DWChapman) **8-8-9b** ACulhane(6) (led tl hdd over 1f out: sn rdn & outpcd)	nk	**4**	13/2	71	52
301^{3}	**Sing With the Band (76)** (BAMcMahon) **6-8-10** LNewton(9) (prom: ev ch over 1f out: one pce fnl f)	¾	**5**	$3/1^{1}$	69	50
316^{8}	**Safio (66)** (ABailey) **4-8-0** DWright(2) (bit bkwd: effrt & rdn over 1f out: no imp)	1¼	**6**	16/1	55	36
	So Intrepid (IRE) (67) (JMBradley) **7-8-1** LCharnock(1) (bit bkwd: w ldr over 2f: eased whn btn appr fnl f)	6	**7**	8/1	37	18
348*	**Ramsey Hope (79)** (CWFairhurst) **4-8-13v** KFallon(7) (lw: outpcd)	¾	**8**	13/2	47	28
371^{5}	**Rennyholme (62)** (JHetherton) **6-7-5v**1(5) JBramhill(4) (outpcd)	8	**9**	50/1	4	—
				(SP 119.8%)		**9 Rn**

61.2 secs (2.30) CSF £26.32 CT £128.79 TOTE £6.70: £2.50 £2.10 £2.00 (£14.70) Trio £61.00 OWNER Mr K. T. Ivory (RADLETT) BRED J. Weinfeld

LONG HANDICAP Rennyholme 5-12

395 MANNY BERNSTEIN BOOKMAKERS MAIDEN STKS (3-Y.O) (Class D)
2-40 (2-41) **1m 100y (Fibresand)** £3,420.00 (£1,035.00: £505.00: £240.00) Stalls: Low GOING: 0.16 sec per fur (SLW)

Form	Horse	Dist	Pos	SP	RR	SF
	Cyrian (IRE) (PFICole) **3-9-0** TQuinn(6) (w'like: leggy: bit bkwd: a w ldrs: rdn wl over 1f out: led appr fnl f: pushed clr)	—	**1**	$8/11^{1}$	72	43
255^{6}	**Weet And See (55)** (RHollinshead) **3-8-9**(5) DGriffiths(8) (hld up: hdwy 3f out: ev ch 1f out: nt pce of wnr)	3	**2**	14/1	66	37
	Baby Jane (67) (RGuest) **3-8-9** MWigham(9) (still unf: hld up: hdwy to ld over 2f out: hdd appr fnl f: one pce)	1¼	**3**	$7/1^{3}$	59	30
	Tayovullin (IRE) (HMorrison) **3-8-9** CRutter(3) (b.hind: chsd ldrs: effrt over 2f out: wknd appr fnl f)	4	**4**	9/1	51	22
	Manhattan Diamond (52) (ABailey) **3-8-9** DWright(7) (led tl over 2f out: rdn over 1f out: one pce)	1¾	**5**	25/1	48	19
350^{3}	**Solar Dawn** (MJohnston) **3-8-9** DeanMcKeown(4) (hld up in tch: effrt & nt clr run over 3f out: wknd fnl 2f)	7	**6**	$11/2^{2}$	35	6
306^{6}	**Alagna** (SCWilliams) **3-8-9** KFallon(1) (prom: rdn wl over 1f out: sn outpcd)	nk	**7**	14/1	34	5
	Swiss Coast (IRE) (73) (NTinkler) **3-9-0** KimTinkler(5) (bit bkwd: a bhd: t.o)	10	**8**	$7/1^{3}$	20	—
	Master Bobby (RBoss) **3-9-0** MTebbutt(2) (s.i.s: sn chsng ldrs: rdn & wknd over 2f out: t.o)	8	**9**	8/1	5	—
				(SP 136.6%)		**9 Rn**

1m 52.1 (7.10) CSF £16.67 TOTE £1.60: £1.10 £3.20 £2.40 (£7.40) Trio £15.10 OWNER Lord Donoughmore (WHATCOMBE) BRED Cahalane O'Hanlon

396 MANNY BERNSTEIN BOOKMAKERS CONDITIONS STKS (3-Y.O+) (Class D)
3-15 (3-15) **1m 100y (Fibresand)** £3,338.75 (£1,010.00: £492.50: £233.75) Stalls: Low GOING: 0.16 sec per fur (SLW)

Form	Horse	Dist	Pos	SP	RR	SF
388^{2}	**Foot Battalion (IRE) (90)** (RHollinshead) **3-8-1**(3) FLynch(5) (hld up & bhd: hdwy over 3f out: led over 1f out: comf)	—	**1**	$3/1^{2}$	97	43
220^{2}	**Sabot (94)** (CWThornton) **4-9-10** DeanMcKeown(4) (lw: a.p: slt ld 2f out: sn hdd: kpt on u.p fnl f)	½	**2**	$6/4^{1}$	98	62
344^{2}	**Pater Noster (USA) (89)** (JohnHarris) **8-9-5** TQuinn(1) (b: a.p: ev ch wl over 1f out: unable qckn fnl f)	1¼	**3**	$100/30^{3}$	91	55
200*	**Zurs (IRE) (80)** (MissGayKelleway) **4-9-10** KFallon(3) (mde most over 6f: rdn & wknd over 1f out)	7	**4**	$3/1^{2}$	82	46
	Suez Tornado (IRE) (75) (EJAlston) **4-9-10** SDrowne(6) (bkwd: chsd ldrs: rdn along 3f out: sn lost tch)	s.h	**5**	33/1	82	46
	Billaddie (RBoss) **4-9-5** MTebbutt(2) (bit bkwd: hld up in tch tl rdn & wknd over 3f out: sn t.o)	12	**6**	33/1	55	19
				(SP 119.0%)		**6 Rn**

1m 51.1 (6.10) CSF £7.80 TOTE £3.60: £1.40 £1.40 (£3.10) OWNER Mr J. E. Bigg (UPPER LONGDON) BRED Ennistown Stud

WEIGHT FOR AGE 3yo-18lb

397 MANNY BERNSTEIN H'CAP (0-100) (II) (3-Y.O+) (Class C)
3-45 (3-45) **5f (Fibresand)** £4,457.45 (£1,346.60: £655.30: £309.65) Stalls: Low GOING: 0.16 sec per fur (SLW)

				SP	RR	SF
301^{*}	**The Happy Fox (IRE) (75)** (BAMcMahon) **5-7-11**(7) SRighton(7) (hld up: hdwy over 1f out: r.o to ld wl ins fnl f)	—	**1**	3/1 1	82	43
357^{*}	**Cretan Gift (99)** (NPLittmoden) **6-10-0v** TGMcLaughlin(1) (s.i.s: sn bhd & outpcd: sltly hmpd ½-wy: hdwy on outside over 1f out: fin wl)	1¼	**2**	3/1 1	102+	63
323^{6}	**Robo Magic (USA) (78)** (LMontagueHall) **5-8-4**(3) FLynch(6) (b: w ldrs: led over 2f out tl over 1f out: no ex wl ins fnl f)	1	**3**	6/1	78	39
	Ansellman (85) (JBerry) **7-9-0** GCarter(5) (bkwd: led over 2f: ev ch ins fnl f: unable qckn)	s.h	**4**	13/2	85	46
301^{11}	**Chemcast (69)** (JLEyre) **4-7-12b** TWilliams(8) (a.p: slt ld over 1f out: hdd & one pce fnl 100y)	1¼	**5**	11/2 3	65	26
357^{3}	**Broadstairs Beauty (IRE) (75)** (DShaw) **7-8-4** JFanning(2) (b: b.hind: trckd ldrs: effrt & rdn over 1f out: nt pce to chal)	1¼	**6**	5/1 2	67	28
391^{9}	**Shadow Jury (67)** (DWChapman) **7-7-10b** NKennedy(3) (a outpcd)	3	**7**	12/1	49	10

(SP 117.4%) **7 Rn**

62.4 secs (3.50) CSF £11.35 CT £46.03 TOTE £3.40: £2.70 £2.10 (£11.60) OWNER Mr G. Whitaker (TAMWORTH) BRED Abbey Lodge Stud
LONG HANDICAP Shadow Jury 7-6

398 MANNY BERNSTEIN BOOKMAKERS LINCOLN TRIAL H'CAP (0-105) (4-Y.O+) (Class B)
4-15 (4-15) **1m 100y (Fibresand)** £14,135.00 (£4,280.00: £2,090.00: £995.00) Stalls: Low GOING: 0.16 sec per fur (SLW)

				SP	RR	SF
358^{*}	**Rambo Waltzer (78)** (DNicholls) **5-7-13**(7) IonaWands(12) (hld up: hdwy 3f out: shkn up to ld fnl f: r.o wl)	—	**1**	11/1	84	63
344^{*}	**New Century (USA) (97)** (DNicholls) **5-9-11** AlexGreaves(9) (a.p: led over 2f out tl ins fnl f: nt qckn)	1	**2**	11/4 1	101	80
	Thai Morning (100) (PWHarris) **4-10-0** GDuffield(10) (bit bkwd: a.p: led 5f out tl over 2f out: rdn & hung lft appr fnl f: no ex)	1	**3**	9/2 2	102	81
	Kuala Lipis (USA) (86) (PFICole) **4-9-0** TQuinn(11) (bit bkwd: hld up: hdwy 2f out: nrst fin)	nk	**4**	8/1	88	67
	Shinerolla (87) (CParker) **5-9-1** DRMcCabe(13) (hld up: hdwy 3f out: one pce appr fnl f)	1	**5**	20/1	87	66
	Caudillo (IRE) (80) (MrsPNDutfield) **4-8-8** SDrowne(4) (trckd ldrs tl lost pl ½-wy: styd on again fnl 2f)	11	**6**	33/1	59	38
376^{*}	**State of Caution (81)** (DShaw) **4-8-9b** 4x JFanning(6) (b: chsd ldrs: rdn & wknd over 2f out)	1½	**7**	13/2 3	57	36
363^{6}	**Duke Valentino (82)** (RHollinshead) **5-8-5**(5) DGriffiths(1) (nvr plcd to chal)	1	**8**	20/1	56	35
365^{*}	**Royal Action (93)** (JEBanks) **4-9-7** MWigham(5) (lw: prom tl wknd over 2f out)	1½	**9**	7/1	64	43
	Amber Fort (70) (DRCElsworth) **4-7-12v** CRutter(2) (bit bkwd: a bhd: t.o)	10	**10**	9/1	22	1
	World Premier (95) (CEBrittain) **4-9-9** KFallon(7) (bit bkwd: hld up: effrt & drvn along 3f out: sn wknd: t.o)	2½	**11**	14/1	43	22
179^{9}	**Anonym (IRE) (70)** (JLEyre) **5-7-12b** TWilliams(3) (a in rr: t.o)	1½	**12**	14/1	15	—
	Persian Fayre (85) (JBerry) **5-8-8**(5) TEDurcan(8) (bkwd: sddle slipped: led over 3f: wknd 3f out: t.o)	dist	**13**	16/1	—	—

(SP 131.8%) **13 Rn**

1m 49.2 (4.20) CSF £40.60 CT £144.72 TOTE £16.00: £3.10 £2.40 £1.60 (£17.20) Trio £14.00 OWNER Mr W. G. Swiers (THIRSK) BRED Triangle Thoroughbreds Ltd

399 MANNY BERNSTEIN BOOKMAKERS WOLVERHAMPTON (S) STKS (3-Y.O) (Class E)
4-50 (4-51) **6f (Fibresand)** £4,084.50 (£1,236.00: £603.00: £286.50) Stalls: Low GOING: 0.16 sec per fur (SLW)

				SP	RR	SF
345^{2}	**Will To Win (57)** (PGMurphy) **3-8-7** SDrowne(8) (b.hind: chsd ldrs: rdn 2f out: styd on strly to ld wl ins fnl f)	—	**1**	5/2 1	64	32
378^{6}	**Julia's Relative (51)** (RGuest) **3-8-7b**1 PBloomfield(6) (b: s.i.s: sn pushed along: hdwy to ld wl over 1f out: hdd wl ins fnl f)	1½	**2**	8/1 3	60	28
377^{6}	**Qualitair Silver** (JFBottomley) **3-8-7** LCharnock(9) (hld up: hdwy 3f out: kpt on: nt pce to chal)	1¾	**3**	13/2 2	55	23
212^{3}	**Advance Repro (50)** (JAkehurst) **3-8-7b** MTebbutt(1) (a.p: rdn & outpcd over 2f out: kpt on fnl f)	4	**4**	14/1	45	13
345^{*}	**Chilling (63)** (NTinkler) **3-8-0**(7) KSked(7) (prom: pushed along over 2f out: outpcd appr fnl f)	¾	**5**	5/2 1	43	11
317^{4}	**Contravene (IRE) (51)** (JBerry) **3-8-8**(5) PRoberts(2) (nvr gng pce of ldrs)	2½	**6**	12/1	42	10
345^{3}	**College Princess (52)** (CADwyer) **3-8-0**(7) JoHunnam(5) (outpcd: a in rr)	½	**7**	13/2 2	35	3
259^{9}	**My Girl (45)** (RHollinshead) **3-8-4**(3) FLynch(4) (s.s: a outpcd)	nk	**8**	25/1	34	2
317^{7}	**Pretty Sally (IRE) (55)** (DJGMurraySmith) **3-8-7** GDuffield(3) (led: rdn & hdd wl over 1f out: wknd qckly)	5	**9**	8/1 3	21	—

(SP 124.2%) **9 Rn**

1m 16.4 (5.20) CSF £23.99 TOTE £4.30: £2.20 £1.60 £3.20 (£45.40) Trio £44.30 OWNER Mrs Pat Wyatt (BRISTOL) BRED Red House Stud
Bt in 5600 gns

400 MANNY BERNSTEIN BOOKMAKERS H'CAP (0-80) (4-Y.O+) (Class D)
5-25 (5-25) **1m 6f 166y (Fibresand)** £3,371.25 (£1,020.00: £497.50: £236.25) Stalls: High GOING: 0.16 sec per fur (SLW)

				SP	RR	SF
315^{4}	**Premier Dance (60)** (DHaydnJones) **10-9-0** TQuinn(4) (hld up & bhd: hdwy over 3f out: led appr fnl f: r.o wl)	—	**1**	5/2 2	68	29
256^{5}	**Shakiyr (FR) (60)** (RHollinshead) **6-8-11b**(3) FLynch(5) (a.p: rdn 2f out: styd on wl towards fin)	1¼	**2**	7/1	67	28
346^{*}	**Calendula (57)** (DMorley) **4-8-7** GCarter(6) (a.p: led 2f out: sn hdd: kpt on u.p ins fnl f)	1	**3**	13/8 1	63	20
	Onefourseven (57) (JLEyre) **4-8-7** TWilliams(3) (hld up: hdwy 5f out: slt ld wl over 1f out: sn hdd: no ex nr fin)	1	**4**	6/1	62	19
	Aztec Flyer (USA) (49) (CEBrittain) **4-7-13** DaleGibson(7) (bit bkwd: led after 3f tl over 7f out: wknd over 3f out: t.o)	15	**5**	9/1	37	—
324^{2}	**Petoskin (70)** (JPearce) **5-9-10** GBardwell(1) (swtg: led 3f: led over 7f out to 2f out: sn rdn & wknd: t.o)	1¼	**6**	100/30 3	57	18

(SP 126.5%) **6 Rn**

3m 22.9 (15.50) CSF £20.70 TOTE £3.70: £2.60 £2.50 (£7.60) OWNER J S Fox and Sons (PONTYPRIDD) BRED Brick Kiln Stud Farm
WEIGHT FOR AGE 4yo-4lb

324 Petoskin has had a couple of hard races inside the last month, and the way he dropped out here after being headed, would suggest a break could be needed. (100/30: 9/4-7/2)

T/Plpt: £45.50 (249.12 Tckts). T/Qdpt: £16.40 (40.07 Tckts) IM

0379-LINGFIELD (L-H) (Standard)
Thursday March 13th
WEATHER: sunny WIND: almost nil

401 REID MINTY LITIGATORS AMATEUR H'CAP (0-60) (I) (4-Y.O+) (Class F)
2-15 (2-16) **1m (Equitrack)** £2,089.60 (£585.60: £284.80) Stalls: High GOING minus 0.54 sec per fur (FST)

	Horse	Dist	Pos	SP	RR	SF
321[10]	**Roman Reel (USA) (54)** (GLMoore) **6-11-2**(5) MrsJMoore(5) (a.p: led 4f out: clr 3f out: r.o wl)	—	1	13/2	64	56
386[4]	**Dream Carrier (IRE) (40)** (REPeacock) **9-10-0**(7) MrsCPeacock(11) (hdwy to chse wnr over 3f out: no imp)	4	2	9/2[2]	42	34
	Love Legend (40) (DWPArbuthnot) **12-10-7** MrsDArbuthnot(2) (hld up: one pce fnl 3f)	3	3	20/1	36	28
188*	**Biya (IRE) (47)** (DMcCain) **5-10-9**(5) MrGLake(9) (lw: rdn over 4f out: hdwy over 2f out: one pce)	3½	4	4/1[1]	36	28
211[8]	**Bellas Gate Boy (48)** (JPearce) **5-11-1** MrsLPearce(6) (lw: hdwy over 1f out: nvr nrr)	hd	5	12/1	37	29
273[11]	**Warhurst (IRE) (51)** (DNicholls) **6-11-1**(3) MissRClark(10) (nvr nr to chal)	3½	6	5/1[3]	33	25
88[7]	**Princely Affair (37)** (JMBradley) **4-9-13**(5) MissEJJones(8) (lw: lost pl over 4f out: sme hdwy over 2f out: sn wknd)	1½	7	16/1	16	8
319[6]	**Ajkuit (IRE) (35)** (JJSheehan) **4-9-9**(7) MissCHannaford(4) (lw: led 1f: wknd over 3f out)	3½	8	12/1	7	—
338[10]	**Czarna (IRE) (43)** (CEBrittain) **6-10-5**(5) MrsCWilliams(1) (hdwy 7f out: wknd over 3f out)	1¾	9	9/2[2]	11	3
321[8]	**Spectacle Jim (35)** (BAPearce) **8-9-9b**(7) MrsKHills(3) (led 7f out to 4f out: wknd over 3f out)	5	10	33/1	—	—
				(SP 115.3%)		**10 Rn**

1m 40.39 (2.99) CSF £32.25 CT £516.75 TOTE £9.50: £2.80 £1.10 £3.90 (£12.60) Trio £24.90 OWNER Mr K. Higson (BRIGHTON) BRED Dorothy Price, Jackie W. Ramos & Ken Hickson

402 REID MINTY SOLICITORS H'CAP (0-80) (4-Y.O+) (Class D)
2-45 (2-45) **1m 4f (Equitrack)** £3,355.00 (£1,015.00: £495.00: £235.00) Stalls: Low GOING minus 0.54 sec per fur (FST)

	Horse	Dist	Pos	SP	RR	SF
315*	**In the Money (IRE) (57)** (RHollinshead) **8-8-6**(5) DGriffiths(4) (chsd ldr: led over 5f out: hrd rdn over 1f out: r.o wl)	—	1	7/4[1]	65	15
340[6]	**Fabulous Mtoto (43)** (MSSaunders) **7-7-4**(7)ow1 RFfrench(7) (lw: hdwy over 4f out: rdn over 2f out: chsd wnr fnl f: r.o)	¾	2	9/2[2]	50	—
	Mister Aspecto (IRE) (72) (MJohnston) **4-9-10v** DeanMcKeown(2) (led over 6f: rdn: unable qckn fnl 2f)	3½	3	5/1[3]	74	22
384[9]	**Loki (IRE) (60)** (GLewis) **9-8-11b**(3) AWhelan(3) (b.hind: bhd fnl 4f)	4	4	12/1	57	7
252[3]	**Wottashambles (65)** (LMontagueHall) **6-9-5** WRyan(6) (hdwy over 3f out: wknd wl over 1f out)	s.h	5	9/2[2]	62	12
	One Off the Rail (USA) (74) (GLMoore) **7-10-0** SWhitworth(5) (b: hdwy over 6f out: wknd over 3f out)	27	6	10/1	35	—
346[3]	**Zacaroon (48)** (JFfitch-Heyes) **6-8-2** DBiggs(1) (a.p: chsd wnr 5f out to 1f out: 3rd & btn whn broke leg and fell wl ins fnl f: dead)		F	7/1	—	—
				(SP 118.7%)		**7 Rn**

2m 35.69 (5.69) CSF £9.57 TOTE £2.30: £1.20 £3.70 (£4.30) OWNER Mr J. E. Bigg (UPPER LONGDON) BRED Cheveley Park Stud Ltd
LONG HANDICAP Fabulous Mtoto 7-3
WEIGHT FOR AGE 4yo-2lb

403 REID MINTY LIBEL & SLANDER CLAIMING STKS (3-Y.O+) (Class E)
3-20 (3-26) **7f (Equitrack)** £2,869.25 (£869.00: £424.50: £202.25) Stalls: Low GOING minus 0.54 sec per fur (FST)

	Horse	Dist	Pos	SP	RR	SF
330[4]	**Ertlon (71)** (CEBrittain) **7-9-12** WRyan(9) (a.p: led 3f out: clr 2f out: r.o wl)	—	1	5/2[1]	82	48
335*	**Greatest (76)** (MissGayKelleway) **6-9-11b** KFallon(2) (b: b.hind: led 4f: rdn: unable qckn)	3½	2	7/2[3]	73	39
363[4]	**Spencer's Revenge (59)** (PButler) **8-9-6** GBardwell(10) (lw: rdn over 3f out: hdwy over 1f out: r.o)	¾	3	10/1	66	32
	Purple Fling (70) (LGCottrell) **6-9-10** RCochrane(5) (lw: hld up: rdn over 3f out: one pce)	¾	4	11/2	69	35
171[3]	**Soaking (77)** (NEBerry) **7-9-10** DRMcCabe(4) (hld up: rdn over 3f out: wknd over 2f out)	1¾	5	100/30[2]	65	31
294[9]	**Nordinex (IRE) (67)** (DRCElsworth) **5-9-9**(5) ADaly(7) (chsd ldr 4f: wknd wl over 1f out)	3½	6	16/1	61	27
294*	**Invocation (65)** (GLMoore) **10-9-7** AClark(3) (hld up: rdn over 3f out: wknd fnl f)	1½	7	13/2	50	16
342[4]	**Quinzii Martin (44)** (DHaydnJones) **9-8-12**(7) JoeleneRichards(1) (a bhd)	2½	8	33/1	42	8
322[7]	**Camphar** (RMFlower) **4-9-9** SDrowne(6) (b: bhd fnl 5f: t.o)	dist	9	100/1	—	—
				(SP 121.5%)		**9 Rn**

1m 25.77 (1.37) CSF £11.05 TOTE £3.00: £1.90 £1.50 £1.90 (£12.10) Trio £64.30 OWNER Mr C. E. Brittain (NEWMARKET) BRED Hadi Al Tajir

404 COST AUDITING CLAIMING STKS (3-Y.O+) (Class F)
3-50 (3-51) **6f (Equitrack)** £2,484.40 (£698.40: £341.20) Stalls: Low GOING minus 0.54 sec per fur (FST)

	Horse	Dist	Pos	SP	RR	SF
136[7]	**Shontaine (55)** (MJohnston) **4-9-6** DeanMcKeown(4) (rdn over 4f out: hdwy over 2f out: led nr fin)	—	1	11/2[3]	58	16
349[5]	**Mellors (IRE) (64)** (MJHeaton-Ellis) **4-10-0** SDrowne(1) (lw: a.p: rdn over 2f out: led ins fnl f: hdd nr fin)	½	2	11/8[1]	65	23
319[5]	**Justinianus (IRE) (42)** (JJBridger) **5-8-10**(5) ADaly(6) (lw: led 2f: rdn over 3f out: led over 2f out tl ins fnl f: unable qckn)	¾	3	7/1	50	8
224[8]	**Norling (IRE) (42)** (KOCunningham-Brown) **7-9-4** CMunday(7) (a.p: led 4f out tl over 2f out: ev ch over 1f out: one pce)	1	4	16/1	50	8
306[2]	**Zelaya (IRE) (50)** (GLMoore) **4-8-11** FNorton(8) (lw: hld up: rdn over 2f out: wknd over 1f out)	6	5	7/2[2]	27	—
	Runs in the Family (48) (GMMcCourt) **5-8-12**(7) RStudholme(3) (a bhd)	6	6	10/1	19	—
367[11]	**Members Welcome (IRE) (40)** (WGMTurner) **4-9-4** TSprake(5) (spd over 3f)	2	7	20/1	13	—
20[8]	**Viennese Dancer (26)** (RJRWilliams) **4-8-10** RCochrane(2) (a bhd)	¾	8	33/1	3	—
				(SP 114.9%)		**8 Rn**

1m 14.23 (3.13) CSF £12.34 TOTE £6.90: £1.90 £1.10 £2.00 (£4.40) OWNER Mr Paul Dean (MIDDLEHAM) BRED Mark Johnston Racing Ltd

405 REID MINTY 17TH ANNIVERSARY H'CAP (0-95) (4-Y.O+) (Class C)
4-20 (4-21) **1m 2f (Equitrack)** £5,052.85 (£1,529.80: £746.90: £355.45) Stalls: Low GOING minus 0.54 sec per fur (FST)

	Horse	Dist	Pos	SP	RR	SF
344[6]	**Secret Aly (CAN) (81)** (CEBrittain) **7-9-2** WRyan(7) (lw: rdn over 2f out: hdwy over 1f out: str run fnl f: led nr fin)	—	1	8/1	88	28
365[3]	**Prince Danzig (IRE) (83)** (DJGMurraySmith) **6-9-4** DaneO'Neill(10) (lw: rdn over 4f out: hdwy over 3f out: led wl ins fnl f: hdd nr fin)	nk	2	12/1	90	30

				SP	RR	SF
369^{5}	**Tallulah Belle (67)** (NPLittmoden) **4-8-2** JQuinn(5) (hld up: rdn over 2f out: led ins fnl f: sn hdd: unable qckn)	1¼	**3**	15/2	72	12
299^{6}	**Bardon Hill Boy (IRE) (85)** (BHanbury) **5-9-6** MRimmer(8) (a.p: led over 3f out tl over 2f out: one pce fnl f)	1	**4**	12/1	88	28
226^{2}	**Renown (75)** (LordHuntingdon) **5-8-5**(5) AimeeCook(6) (b.hind: led over 2f: led over 2f out tl ins fnl f: sn wknd)	½	**5**	4/1^{1}	77	17
382^{3}	**Robellion (70)** (DWPArbuthnot) **6-8-5v** SWhitworth(1) (b.hind: hdwy over 3f out: lost pl over 2f out: rallied fnl f: r.o wl)	nk	**6**	12/1	72	12
344^{7}	**South Eastern Fred (93)** (HJCollingridge) **6-9-9**(5) RMullen(12) (b: a.p: led over 6f out tl over 3f out: wknd over 2f out)	3	**7**	10/1	90	30
291^{3}	**Quiet Arch (IRE) (65)** (WRMuir) **4-7-9**(5) JBramhill(3) (b: b.hind: hdwy over 3f out: wknd over 2f out)	¾	**8**	7/1^{3}	61	1
380^{2}	**Digpast (IRE) (69)** (MMadgwick) **7-8-1**(3) MartinDwyer(4) (lw: bhd fnl 4f)	5	**9**	7/1^{3}	57	—
	Ocean Park (85) (LadyHerries) **6-9-6** AClark(11) (b: a bhd)	4	**10**	11/2^{2}	66	6
330^{9}	**Sherqy (IRE) (70)** (SEKettlewell) **5-7-12**(7) JennyBenson(9) (led over 7f out tl over 6f out: wknd over 4f out)	11	**11**	50/1	34	—
291^{*}	**Punkah (USA) (78)** (GMMcCourt) **4-8-6**(7) RStudholme(2) (prom over 6f)	21	**12**	11/2^{2}	8	—

(SP 132.8%) **12 Rn**

2m 7.87 (3.57) CSF £102.47 CT £708.99 TOTE £10.30: £3.70 £2.90 £4.70 (£46.40) Trio £311.30; £43.86 to Southwell 14/3/97 OWNER Mr B. H. Voak (NEWMARKET) BRED Northern Equine Thoroughbred Productions

406 REID MINTY COMMERCIAL PROPERTY SOLUTIONS H'CAP (0-85) (3-Y.O+) (Class D)

4-50 (4-51) **5f (Equitrack)** £3,273.75 (£990.00: £482.50: £228.75) Stalls: High GOING minus 0.54 sec per fur (FST)

				SP	RR	SF
348^{5}	**Ivory's Grab Hire (48)** (KTIvory) **4-7-9b**(3) MartinDwyer(7) (hld up: rdn over 2f out: led ins fnl f: drvn out)	—	**1**	3/1^{2}	51	12
348^{6}	**Sally Slade (74)** (CACyzer) **5-9-10** KFallon(2) (outpcd: hdwy fnl f: r.o wl)	nk	**2**	6/1	76	37
391^{*}	**Gi La High (66)** (MartynMeade) **4-8-11**(5) 7x DSweeney(4) (outpcd: gd hdwy fnl f: r.o wl)	hd	**3**	4/1^{3}	68	29
348^{7}	**Mijas (75)** (LMontagueHall) **4-9-11** DaneO'Neill(5) (chsd ldr: led over 1f out tl ins fnl f: unable qckn)	½	**4**	15/2	75	36
397^{3}	**Robo Magic (USA) (78)** (LMontagueHall) **5-9-11**(3) FLynch(1) (outpcd: hdwy on ins over 1f out: r.o)	½	**5**	11/2	77	38
376^{11}	**Intiaash (IRE) (75)** (DHaydnJones) **5-9-11** TWilliams(6) (bhd fnl 2f)	1½	**6**	20/1	69	30
391^{7}	**Bowcliffe Grange (IRE) (51)** (DWChapman) **5-8-1** JQuinn(3) (lw: led over 3f)	5	**7**	2/1^{1}	29	—

(SP 124.5%) **7 Rn**

59.72 secs (1.52) CSF £21.56 TOTE £4.30: £1.50 £3.30 (£16.90) OWNER Mr Dean Ivory (RADLETT) BRED Japan Bloodstock Ltd

407 REID MINTY LITIGATORS AMATEUR H'CAP (0-60) (II) (4-Y.O+) (Class F)

5-25 (5-27) **1m (Equitrack)** £2,089.60 (£585.60: £284.80) Stalls: High GOING minus 0.54 sec per fur (FST)

				SP	RR	SF
384^{2}	**Don't Drop Bombs (USA) (33)** (DTThom) **8-10-0v** MissJFeilden(10) (lw: a.p: led over 1f out: r.o wl)	—	**1**	7/2^{1}	45	27
352^{*}	**Eastleigh (46)** (RHollinshead) **8-10-10**(3) MrKGoble(5) (b.nr hind: a.p: rdn 4f out: chsd wnr ins fnl f: r.o one pce)	1¾	**2**	5/1	55	37
321^{*}	**Gadge (43)** (ABailey) **6-10-3**(7) MissALHutchinson(8) (led 1f: led over 4f out tl over 1f out: one pce)	2½	**3**	11/1	47	29
383^{*}	**Ki Chi Saga (USA) (57)** (MMadgwick) **5-11-3**(7) 5x MrPMiddleton(7) (lw: hdwy over 1f out: nvr nrr)	1	**4**	4/1^{2}	59	41
383^{6}	**Statistician (44)** (JohnBerry) **5-10-4e**(7) MrCJMcEntee(2) (no hdwy fnl 4f)	1¼	**5**	12/1	43	25
280^{4}	**Hatta Sunshine (USA) (54)** (GLMoore) **7-11-2**(5) MrsJMoore(4) (lw: hdwy over 3f out: wknd over 1f out)	1½	**6**	11/1	50	32
	Return To Brighton (35) (JMBradley) **5-9-11**(5) MissEJJones(6) (bit bkwd: nvr nr to chal)	3	**7**	33/1	25	7
385^{5}	**Bold Habit (43)** (JPearce) **12-10-10** MrsLPearce(3) (lw: dwlt: a bhd)	½	**8**	6/1	32	14
327^{2}	**Private Fixture (IRE) (40)** (DMarks) **6-10-7** MrTMcCarthy(1) (lw: led 7f out tl over 4f out: wknd over 3f out)	12	**9**	9/2^{3}	5	—
333^{10}	**Sussex Gorse (31)** (JELong) **6-9-5**(7)ow12 MrTWaters(9) (bhd fnl 5f)	4	**10**	150/1	—	—

(SP 119.3%) **10 Rn**

1m 41.42 (4.02) CSF £19.80 CT £164.92 TOTE £2.80: £1.80 £3.60 £3.10 (£11.20) Trio £21.70 OWNER Miss J. Feilden (NEWMARKET) BRED Hurstland Farm Incorporated
LONG HANDICAP Sussex Gorse 8-10

T/Plpt: £154.60 (54.65 Tckts). T/Qdpt: £46.50 (11.67 Tckts) AK

0309a-NAD AL SHEBA (Dubai, UAE) (L-H) (Fast)
Thursday February 27th

408a HH SHEIKH MAKTOUM BIN RASHID AL MAKTOUM CHALLENGE (RND 2) (Listed) (4-Y.O+)

4-30 (4-32) **1m 1f (Dirt)** £12,116.00 (£6,058.00: £3,635.00)

				SP	RR	SF
	Tropicool (USA) (DJSelvaratnam,UAE) **4-8-11b**^{1} BDoyle	—	**1**		125	—
	Tamayaz (CAN) (SbinSuroor,UAE) **5-8-11** LDettori	¾	**2**		124	—
309a^{4}	**Gothenberg (IRE)** (MJohnston) **4-8-11** JWeaver	6	**3**		113	—

5 Rn

1m 50.34 OWNER Sheikh Ahmed Al Maktoum BRED Stone Ridge Partnership
Tropicool (USA) was disappointing in the first round of this challenge, but made amends here.
Tamayaz (CAN), a well-travelled sort last year, won rounds one and three of this event last season. He gave connections something to think about here after a performance that was slightly disappointing. Racing in third he was asked the question soon after entering the straight. He did close the gap on the leaders, but was not quite able to go through with his effort.
309a Gothenberg (IRE), who finished over seven lengths in front of this winner in round one, could not repeat that form here. He pulled hard and tracked the leader in the early part of the race, and with four furlongs left to run, lost his position and could only keep on at one pace.

0408a-NAD AL SHEBA (Dubai, UAE) (L-H) (Fast)
Sunday March 9th

409a AL FUTTAIM (4-Y.O+)
3-30 (3-31) **1m 1f (Dirt)** £4,847.00 (£1,454.00: £872.00: £582.00)

Horse		Pos	SP	RR	SF
Doreg (IRE) (DJSelvaratnam,UAE) **7-8-6** BDoyle	—	1		123	—
Hammerstein (SbinSuroor,UAE) **4-8-6** LDettori	7½	2		110	—
Key of Luck (USA) (KPMcLaughlin,UAE) **6-8-9** JCArias	1¾	3		110	—
Bijou d'Inde (MJohnston) **4-9-2** JWeaver	1¾	4		113	—
					4 Rn

1m 51.63 OWNER Sheikh Ahmed Al Maktoum BRED Patrick Headon
Doreg (IRE) caused something of an upset here. Looming up to the leaders, he went comfortably to the front and scored well.
Hammerstein, raced in third, made some headway to go second entering the straight. He had every chance over a furlong out, but had no answer to the finishing pace of the winner.
Key of Luck (USA) must have disappointed connections with this run, but he should have come on from this. He set a slow pace and when headed over a furlong out, he could not quicken up and was left in the wake of the winner.
Bijou d'Inde put up a disappointing display for a horse of his class. However, this was his first race on the dirt and may be excused this performance, but his trainer has to ask some questions - whether something was wrong with him, or if the preparation was inadequate. He now has to decide if the colt should take his place in the Dubai World Cup.

0373-SOUTHWELL (L-H) (Standard)
Friday March 14th
WEATHER: overcast WIND: slt bhd

410 ZEUS APPRENTICE H'CAP (0-70) (3-Y.O+) (Class F)
2-20 (2-20) **1m 4f (Fibresand)** £2,671.00 (£751.00: £367.00) Stalls: Low GOING: 0.13 sec per fur (SLW)

Form	Horse		Pos	SP	RR	SF
328³	**Moonraking (50)** (TJEtherington) **4-8-6** GParkin(7) (in tch: stdy hdwy to ld over 2f out: styd on wl)	—	1	9/1	62	20
360²	**Kilnamartyra Girl (39)** (JParkes) **7-7-8**(3) JBramhill(11) (hdwy 7f out: wnt prom 2f out: kpt on fnl f)	1	2	7/1 3	50	10
	Dirab (70) (TDBarron) **4-9-9**(3) KimberleyHart(17) (bhd: hdwy 4f out: styd on wl fnl 2f)	nk	3	7/1 3	80	38
	Hasta la Vista (39) (MWEasterby) **7-7-8b**(3) RMullen(8) (a cl up: chal over 2f out: no ex fnl f)	2½	4	8/1	46	6
360⁴	**Carol Again (47)** (NBycroft) **5-8-2**(3) JoHunnam(16) (in tch: effrt 3f out: sn chsng ldrs: one pce fnl 2f)	1½	5	10/1	52	12
	Northern Charmer (38) (EJAlston) **5-7-5**(5) JFowle(15) (in tch: effrt 3f out: r.o one pce)	3	6	50/1	39	—
346²	**Mono Lady (IRE) (63)** (DHaydnJones) **4-8-12**(7) JoeleneRichards(14) (b.off hind: chsd ldrs tl wknd fnl 2f)	¾	7	12/1	63	21
358¹³	**Mazurek (68)** (MGMeagher) **4-9-10** GLee(2) (bhd: effrt ½-wy: no imp)	hd	8	20/1	68	26
	May King Mayhem (40) (MrsALMKing) **4-7-5**(5) PDoe(6) (nvr bttr than mid div)	¾	9	33/1	39	—
88¹³	**Noble Canonire (47)** (DShaw) **5-8-0b**1(5) SRighton(10) (swtg: bhd: hdwy & in tch 3f out: sn btn)	s.h	10	20/1	46	6
328²	**Zatopek (52)** (JCullinan) **5-8-10** DSweeney(3) (a rr div)	2	11	16/1	48	8
360*	**Maftun (USA) (60)** (GMMoore) **5-9-1**(3) GMilligan(13) (cl up: slt ld 6f out: hdd over 2f out: wknd)	3½	12	6/1 2	51	11
358¹⁰	**Johnnie the Joker (69)** (JPLeigh) **6-9-13** PFessey(5) (bhd fnl 6f)	1	13	20/1	59	19
	I'm a Dreamer (IRE) (51) (MissMERowland) **7-8-2**(7) DarrenWilliams(12) (n.d)	2	14	20/1	38	—
384³	**Heighth of Fame (70)** (JHetherton) **6-10-0** HBastiman(4) (led tl hdd 6f out: wknd qckly over 2f out)	3½	15	6/1 2	53	13
206*	**Wildfire (SWI) (48)** (RAkehurst) **6-8-1**(5) DDenby(9) (b: cl up tl outpcd 4f out: sn wknd)	3	16	5/1 1	27	—
				(SP 138.0%)		**16 Rn**

2m 45.4 (12.40) CSF £66.82 CT £450.94 TOTE £17.90: £3.50 £2.40 £3.10 £2.80 (£90.00) Trio £334.20; £65.91 to Hereford 15/3/97 OWNER Mr Richard Hoiles (MALTON) BRED Mrs R. D. Peacock
LONG HANDICAP May King Mayhem 7-7 Northern Charmer 7-0
WEIGHT FOR AGE 4yo-2lb

411 APHRODITE CLAIMING LIMITED STKS (0-60) (I) (3-Y.O+) (Class E)
2-50 (2-50) **1m (Fibresand)** £2,528.00 (£764.00: £372.00: £176.00) Stalls: Low GOING: 0.13 sec per fur (SLW)

Form	Horse		Pos	SP	RR	SF
390*	**Soldier Cove (USA) (52)** (MartynMeade) **7-8-12**(5) DSweeney(8) (lw: hld up: smooth hdwy over 3f out: led wl over 2f out: r.o wl)	—	1	3/1 3	61	25
71⁵	**First Gold (44)** (JWharton) **8-9-6** KFallon(4) (sn wl bhd: hdwy over 3f out: ev ch 1f out: no ex)	2½	2	20/1	59	23
382*	**Live Project (IRE) (55)** (MJohnston) **5-9-6** DeanMcKeown(1) (led tl hdd wl over 2f out: rdn & one pce)	2½	3	9/4 1	54	18
390³	**David James' Girl (50)** (ABailey) **5-8-7**(7) AngelaGallimore(6) (s.i.s: outpcd & bhd: hdwy 3f out: chsng ldrs over 1f out: no ex)	1½	4	12/1	45	9
359²	**Flag Fen (USA) (58)** (JParkes) **6-9-2**(5) JBramhill(2) (b: lw: cl up tl wknd fnl 2½f)	7	5	5/2 2	38	2
359⁴	**Sandmoor Denim (50)** (SRBowring) **10-9-3** SWebster(9) (b: in tch: outpcd 4f out: n.d after)	nk	6	9/1	33	—
390⁷	**Sarasi (60)** (MJCamacho) **5-9-7b**1 LCharnock(7) (chsd ldrs: pushed along ½-wy: grad wknd)	1½	7	8/1	34	—
360⁶	**Royal Acclaim (33)** (CFCJackson) **12-9-3v** DaleGibson(5) (s.i.s: a outpcd & bhd)	8	8	33/1	14	—
367⁸	**Natal Ridge (50)** (DHaydnJones) **4-9-3** AClark(3) (prom tl wknd fnl 4f)	7	9	20/1	—	—
	Classic Victory (47) (ICampbell) **4-9-5hv** TGMcLaughlin(10) (cl up tl wknd 3f out)	23	10	33/1	—	—
				(SP 128.6%)		**10 Rn**

1m 47.6 (8.60) CSF £63.67 TOTE £5.80: £2.10 £3.00 £1.30 (£37.50) Trio £15.10 OWNER Ladyswood Racing Club (MALMESBURY) BRED Weststar Bloodstock

412 APOLLO MEDIAN AUCTION MAIDEN STKS (3-Y.O) (Class F)
3-20 (3-21) **6f (Fibresand)** £2,294.00 (£644.00: £314.00) Stalls: Low GOING: 0.13 sec per fur (SLW)

Form	Horse		Pos	SP	RR	SF
	Bonyalua Mill (AStreeter) **3-8-8**(3)ow2 RHavlin(6) (leggy: trckd ldrs: led over 2f out: styd on wl)	—	1	20/1	37	20
287⁴	**Barwell Boy** (JLHarris) **3-9-0** KFallon(1) (disp ld tl hdd over 2f out: kpt on u.p)	1½	2	8/1	36	21
247⁶	**Impish (IRE) (34)** (TJEtherington) **3-9-0** DaneO'Neill(9) (cl up: chal over 2f out: nt qckn appr fnl f)	1½	3	33/1	32	17
	K S Sunshine (USA) (WJHaggas) **3-8-9** RCochrane(7) (b.hind: neat: unf: a chsng ldrs: effrt over 2f out: t.o one pce)	nk	4	3/1 2	26	11

	Horse	Btn	Pos	SP	RR	SF
	Risk Me Too (PWHarris) **3-9-0** AClark(2) (cmpt: in tch: effrt over 2f out: btn over 1f out)	3½	**5**	6/1[3]	22	7
	Superapparos (SRBowring) **3-9-0** DeanMcKeown(4) (w'like: outpcd appr st: styd on fnl 2f: no imp)	nk	**6**	12/1	21	6
296[11]	**Heathyard's Flight** (RHollinshead) **3-9-0** WRyan(5) (in tch: effrt 3f out: r.o one pce)	½	**7**	8/1	20	5
	Saratoga Red (USA) (75) (WAO'Gorman) **3-9-0** EmmaO'Gorman(8) (bit bkwd: hld up: hdwy on outside to chal 3f out: wknd fnl 2f)	1	**8**	4/5[1]	17	2
287[5]	**Glimmering Hope (IRE)** (MissJFCraze) **3-9-0** SWebster(3) (disp ld tl hdd over 2f out: wknd)	6	**9**	25/1	1	—
				(SP 136.3%)		**9 Rn**

1m 19.9 (6.40) CSF £177.05 TOTE £54.20: £9.10 £1.20 £7.80 (£98.70) Trio £170.80; £125.11 to Hereford 15/3/97 OWNER Mrs Brenda Jeffery (UTTOXETER) BRED Mrs B. Jeffery

413 ACHILLES H'CAP (0-95) (3-Y.O) (Class C)

3-50 (3-50) **6f (Fibresand)** £4,889.05 (£1,479.40: £721.70: £342.85) Stalls: Low GOING: 0.13 sec per fur (SLW)

	Horse	Btn	Pos	SP	RR	SF
17[6]	**Double-O (70)** (WJarvis) **3-8-9** KFallon(1) (lw: mde all: r.o wl fnl 2f)	—	**1**	5/1	79	47
*307**	**The Wyandotte Inn (81)** (RHollinshead) **3-9-3**(3) FLynch(3) (a cl up: rdn 2f out: nt qckn)	6	**2**	4/1[2]	74	42
*293**	**V I P Charlie (82)** (JRJenkins) **3-9-7** SWhitworth(4) (lw: hld up: hdwy over 2f out: rdn over 1f out: sn btn)	1½	**3**	4/5[1]	71	39
307[2]	**Plan For Profit (IRE) (80)** (MJohnston) **3-9-5** DeanMcKeown(2) (lw: sn cl up: outpcd over 2f out: no imp after)	4	**4**	9/2[3]	58	26
				(SP 110.4%)		**4 Rn**

1m 17.7 (4.20) CSF £20.58 TOTE £4.80 (£5.30) OWNER R K Bids Ltd (NEWMARKET) BRED R. K. Bids Ltd

414 SOUTHWELL SERIES (FINAL) (S) H'CAP (3-Y.O) (Class E)

4-20 (4-23) **1m (Fibresand)** £4,026.00 (£1,218.00: £594.00: £282.00) Stalls: Low GOING: 0.13 sec per fur (SLW)

	Horse	Btn	Pos	SP	RR	SF
377[5]	**Mirror Four Sport (51)** (MJohnston) **3-7-11**(7) KSked(7) (chsd ldrs: led over 2f out: styd on wl)	—	**1**	10/1	60	17
370[2]	**Aspecto Lad (IRE) (60)** (MJohnston) **3-8-10**(3) MHenry(5) (chsd ldrs: pushed along after 2½f: hdwy 2f out: nt pce of wnr)	3	**2**	11/4[2]	63	20
298[6]	**Mardrew (64)** (DJSffrenchDavis) **3-9-3** JQuinn(2) (trckd ldrs: chal 3f out: rdn 2f out: not qckn)	4	**3**	2/1[1]	59	16
*246**	**Head Girl (IRE) (56)** (CWThornton) **3-8-9** DeanMcKeown(4) (led tl hdd over 2f out: one pce)	nk	**4**	8/1	50	7
378[7]	**Rochea (57)** (MrsNMacauley) **3-8-10v** AClark(3) (lw: pushed along early: qcknd to jn ldrs after 3f: rdn & fnd nil over 2f out)	¾	**5**	14/1	50	7
362[3]	**Bailieborough Boy (IRE) (68)** (TDBarron) **3-9-7b** DHarrison(1) (plld hrd: hdwy & ch 2½f out: sn btn)	10	**6**	3/1[3]	41	—
296[5]	**Warp Drive (IRE) (54)** (WRMuir) **3-8-7b[1]** DaneO'Neill(6) (b: hld up: effrt over 2f out: no rspnse)	nk	**7**	9/1	26	—
				(SP 121.9%)		**7 Rn**

1m 47.2 (8.20) CSF £37.07 TOTE £11.90: £4.20 £1.90 (£23.60) OWNER Mark Johnston Racing Ltd (MIDDLEHAM) BRED T. Young
No bid
OFFICIAL EXPLANATION **Bailieborough Boy (IRE): the trainer reported that the gelding was over the top.**

415 APHRODITE CLAIMING LIMITED STKS (0-60) (II) (3-Y.O+) (Class E)

4-50 (4-51) **1m (Fibresand)** £2,528.00 (£764.00: £372.00: £176.00) Stalls: Low GOING: 0.13 sec per fur (SLW)

	Horse	Btn	Pos	SP	RR	SF
	Square Deal (FR) (52) (SRBowring) **6-9-5** SWebster(5) (hld up: hdwy on outside over 2f out: hung bdly lft: rdn to ld wl ins fnl f)	—	**1**	12/1	57	29
359[5]	**Major Mouse (49)** (WWHaigh) **9-9-3** SWhitworth(10) (hld up & bhd: stdy hdwy ½-wy: rdn to ld 1f out: hdd & nt qckn towards fin)	1¼	**2**	8/1	53	25
385[4]	**Desert Invader (IRE) (58)** (DWChapman) **6-9-5** LCharnock(6) (lw: cl up: led over 2f out: sn hdd & nt qckn)	1¾	**3**	100/30[2]	51	23
377[2]	**Jack The Lad (IRE) (58)** (JHetherton) **3-8-8** MTebbutt(8) (lw: w ldrs: led 2f out to 1f out: wknd)	¾	**4**	5/1[3]	57	11
390[2]	**Northern Fan (IRE) (59)** (NTinkler) **5-9-6** DeanMcKeown(3) (led tl hdd over 2f out: one pce)	¾	**5**	3/1[1]	49	21
	Lordan Velvet (IRE) (60) (MrsWBAllen,Norway) **5-9-3** LNewton(7) (prom tl outpcd fnl 2½f)	8	**6**	14/1	30	2
192[2]	**Eurolink the Lad (48)** (DBurchell) **10-9-4** SDrowne(2) (bhd: hdwy ½-wy: sn chsng ldrs: rdn & wknd over 2f out)	4	**7**	100/30[2]	23	—
326[6]	**Fiaba (38)** (MrsNMacauley) **9-8-7v**(7) IonaWands(9) (b: outpcd & bhd fr ½-wy)	nk	**8**	20/1	18	—
	Born A Lady (47) (MrsVAAconley) **4-9-2** JQuinn(4) (prom to ½-wy: sn wknd)	10	**9**	16/1	—	—
				(SP 123.9%)		**9 Rn**

1m 47.4 (8.40) CSF £101.10 TOTE £14.00: £4.00 £1.80 £1.50 (£34.10) Trio £129.10 OWNER Mr Padraig Flanagan (EDWINSTOWE) BRED Crest Stud Ltd
WEIGHT FOR AGE 3yo-18lb

416 NEPTUNE MAIDEN H'CAP (0-80) (3-Y.O+) (Class D)

5-20 (5-20) **7f (Fibresand)** £3,371.25 (£1,020.00: £497.50: £236.25) Stalls: Low GOING: 0.13 sec per fur (SLW)

	Horse	Btn	Pos	SP	RR	SF
358[2]	**Genuine John (IRE) (65)** (JParkes) **4-9-4**(5) JBramhill(4) (lw: mde all: rdn & kpt on wl fnl 2f)	—	**1**	11/8[1]	70	30
216[8]	**Evening In Paris (44)** (MJohnston) **4-8-2** NAdams(1) (outpcd after 2f: hdwy 2f out: styd on towards fin)	1½	**2**	4/1[3]	46	6
215[3]	**Will Do (66)** (MartynMeade) **4-9-5**(5) DSweeney(5) (chsd ldrs: effrt over 1f out: nt run on)	1¼	**3**	5/1	65	25
372[4]	**Splashed (63)** (TDBarron) **3-8-5** RLappin(6) (a.p: effrt 2f out: no imp)	2	**4**	7/2[2]	57	1
248[8]	**Whitley Grange Boy (58)** (JLEyre) **4-9-2** TWilliams(3) (cl up tl wknd fnl 2f)	5	**5**	20/1	41	1
322[R]	**Misky Bay (53)** (DJSCosgrove) **4-8-11** MRimmer(2) (lw: reluctant to s: a t.o)	17	**6**	8/1	—	—
				(SP 116.9%)		**6 Rn**

1m 34.1 (7.60) CSF £7.02 TOTE £2.20: £2.60 £4.00 (£4.60) OWNER Mrs G. M. Z. Spink (MALTON) BRED Kilcarn Stud
WEIGHT FOR AGE 3yo-16lb

T/Plpt: £4,767.10 (2.19 Tckts). T/Qdpt: £608.20 (0.68 Tckts); £263.01 to Uttoxeter 15/3/97. AA

0394-WOLVERHAMPTON (L-H) (Standard)
Saturday March 15th

WEATHER: fine WIND: almost nil

IN-FOCUS: **At this meeting, the draw did not play quite the part it sometimes does but the outside still appeared to be riding fastest. A number of horses ruined their chances by sticking to the inside rails, although one winner, Random Kindness, did use the tactic successfully.**

417 BURNS MEDIAN AUCTION MAIDEN STKS (3, 4 & 5-Y.O) (Class E)
7-00 (7-00) **1m 1f 79y (Fibresand)** £2,580.00 (£780.00: £380.00: £180.00) Stalls: Low GOING: 0.21 sec per fur (SLW)

Form	Horse	Dist	Pos	SP	RR	SF
341[3]	**Big Bang (66)** (MBlanshard) **3-8-5** JQuinn(4) (lw: hld up: hdwy 4f out: chal over 1f out: led ins fnl f: rdn out)	—	1	5/4[1]	69	31
300[2]	**Zorba (61)** (CWThornton) **3-8-5** DeanMcKeown(2) (led tl hdd & unable qckn ins fnl f)	¾	2	11/4[2]	68	30
361[4]	**Windborn (46)** (CNAllen) **3-7-11**(3) MartinDwyer(8) (prom: swtchd ins & wknd over 1f out)	10	3	12/1	46	8
336[3]	**Sounds Legal (54)** (PDEvans) **4-9-5** JFEgan(5) (in tch: rdn 3f out: no imp)	5	4	9/1	36	18
387[9]	**Rinus Magic** (EJAlston) **4-9-10** KFallon(3) (bhd fnl 6f)	11	5	33/1	22	4
147[9]	**Hazel (46)** (MissGayKelleway) **5-9-5b** DHolland(6) (b.hind: prom tl rdn & wknd over 2f out)	1	6	7/2[3]	16	—

(SP 114.0%) **6 Rn**

2m 4.8 (8.80) CSF £4.61 TOTE £2.20: £1.60 £1.90 (£3.10) OWNER Mr Gregory West (UPPER LAMBOURN) BRED J. Hamilton
WEIGHT FOR AGE 3yo-20lb

418 CHORISTER CLAIMING LIMITED STKS (0-55) (4-Y.O+) (Class F)
7-30 (7-30) **1m 4f (Fibresand)** £2,580.00 (£780.00: £380.00: £180.00) Stalls: Low GOING: 0.21 sec per fur (SLW)

Form	Horse	Dist	Pos	SP	RR	SF
384*	**English Invader (59)** (CADwyer) **6-9-0** KFallon(3) (in tch: lost pl 6f out: plld out & hdwy over 2f out: led over 1f out: rdn out)	—	1	6/5[1]	63	40
340[3]	**Honestly (45)** (BSmart) **4-8-5** RPerham(2) (hld up: hdwy 5f out: r.o appr fnl f: nt trble wnr)	2	2	6/1[2]	53	28
295[5]	**Dr Edgar (52)** (MDods) **5-9-4** AClark(1) (a.p: one pce fnl 3f)	½	3	6/1[2]	64	41
284[9]	**Fresh Fruit Daily (47)** (PAKelleway) **5-8-8**(7) AngelaGallimore(9) (lw: trckd ldrs: no ex fnl 2f)	2½	4	8/1[3]	57	34
334[4]	**In The Band (53)** (LordHuntingdon) **4-8-3v** DaleGibson(10) (plld hrd: trckd ldr: rdn over 2f out: sn btn)	3	5	6/1[2]	43	18
338[4]	**Lahik (IRE) (38)** (KTIvory) **4-8-1**(3) MartinDwyer(6) (led over 5f: wknd 3f out)	3	6	10/1	40	15
	Elly Fleetfoot (IRE) (38) (GLMoore) **5-8-8** SWhitworth(4) (lw: trckd ldrs tl rdn and btn 4f out)	s.h	7	20/1	42	19
390[5]	**Efficacious (IRE) (22)** (PEccles) **4-7-8b**(5) JBramhill(8) (chsd ldr: led over 6f out: clr 3f out: hdd & wknd over 1f out)	½	8	40/1	35	10
302[4]	**Carrolls Marc (IRE) (35)** (CMurray) **9-8-6**(3)ow1 PMcCabe(7) (b.hind: s.i.s: hdwy 3f out: nvr nr ldrs)	1½	9	20/1	41	17

(SP 120.5%) **9 Rn**

2m 43.9 (11.40) CSF £8.26 TOTE £1.90: £1.10 £1.70 £2.10 (£4.20) Trio £11.70 OWNER Mr John Purcell (NEWMARKET) BRED Bloodstock Management Int Pty Ltd
WEIGHT FOR AGE 4yo-2lb

419 HARTSHORNE MOTOR COMPANY LIMITED STKS (0-70) (4-Y.O+) (Class E)
8-00 (8-00) **2m 46y (Fibresand)** £2,580.00 (£780.00: £380.00: £180.00) Stalls: Low GOING: 0.21 sec per fur (SLW)

Form	Horse	Dist	Pos	SP	RR	SF
266[2]	**Random Kindness (67)** (RIngram) **4-8-11** SWhitworth(3) (led 2f: led 4f out: rdn & r.o wl)	—	1	7/2[2]	83	15
101[2]	**Noufari (FR) (68)** (RHollinshead) **6-8-13**(3) FLynch(6) (hld up: hdwy 3f out: no imp appr fnl f)	4	2	9/4[1]	79	16
	Secret Service (IRE) (70) (CWThornton) **5-9-2** DeanMcKeown(5) (lw: chsd ldrs: lost pl 4f out: rallied 2f out: r.o)	1¼	3	9/4[1]	78	15
	Paradise Navy (70) (CREgerton) **8-8-11b**(5) SophieMitchell(4) (in tch: no hdwy fnl 3f)	2½	4	5/1[3]	75	12
100[8]	**State Approval (57)** (PEccles) **4-8-6**(5) JBramhill(2) (bit bkwd: plld hrd: led after 2f: hdd 4f out: wknd over 2f out)	10	5	25/1	66	—
389[5]	**Montecristo (65)** (RGuest) **4-8-11** DaneO'Neill(1) (wl bhd fnl 9f)	23	6	10/1	43	—

(SP 113.4%) **6 Rn**

3m 47.2 (20.20) CSF £10.95 TOTE £3.80: £1.60 £1.60 (£3.70) OWNER 949 Racing (EPSOM) BRED Pendley Farm
WEIGHT FOR AGE 4yo-5lb

420 CHESTERS H'CAP (0-85) (3-Y.O) (Class D)
8-30 (8-34) **7f (Fibresand)** £3,483.00 (£1,053.00: £513.00: £243.00) Stalls: High GOING: 0.21 sec per fur (SLW)

Form	Horse	Dist	Pos	SP	RR	SF
388[6]	**Tinkerbell (63)** (WRMuir) **3-8-6v** DaneO'Neill(4) (prom: led 3f out to 1f out: rdn to ld again ins fnl f)	—	1	3/1[2]	69	15
103[7]	**Komasta (65)** (CaptJWilson) **3-8-8** KFallon(5) (hld up: hdwy over 2f out: led 1f out tl hdd & unable qckn ins fnl f)	nk	2	9/1	70	16
60[7]	**Patina (55)** (RHollinshead) **3-7-12** JQuinn(6) (hdwy 3f out: one pce appr fnl f)	2	3	5/1[3]	56	2
388[8]	**Cee-N-K (IRE) (78)** (MJohnston) **3-9-7** DHolland(2) (lw: w ldr: led 5f out to 4f out: btn over 2f out)	1½	4	10/1	75	21
362*	**Enchanting Eve (70)** (CNAllen) **3-8-10**(3) MartinDwyer(3) (w ldrs: led 4f to 3f out: wknd appr fnl f)	1¾	5	11/1	63	9
337[2]	**Hever Golf Charger (IRE) (61)** (TJNaughton) **3-8-4** TSprake(1) (lw: led 2f: wknd 2f out)	1¼	6	15/2	52	—
50*	**Cold Steel (77)** (WJarvis) **3-9-6** WRyan(7) (lw: sn wl bhd: hdwy over 2f out: eased whn btn fnl f)	6	7	2/1[1]	54	—

(SP 114.2%) **7 Rn**

1m 32.7 (8.00) CSF £26.63 TOTE £3.60: £1.90 £3.80 (£26.50) OWNER Mr J. Jannaway (LAMBOURN) BRED Highclere Stud Ltd

421 WHITE HEAD (S) H'CAP (3-Y.O+) (Class F)
9-00 (9-02) **6f (Fibresand)** £2,580.00 (£780.00: £380.00: £180.00) Stalls: Low GOING: 0.21 sec per fur (SLW)

Form	Horse	Dist	Pos	SP	RR	SF
222[8]	**Amy Leigh (IRE) (51)** (CaptJWilson) **4-7-13b**(7) AngelaHartley(11) (lw: trckd ldrs: led over 1f out: comf)	—	1	20/1	56	31
332[2]	**Hoh Majestic (IRE) (55)** (RonaldThompson) **4-8-5v**(5) JBramhill(13) (hdwy over 2f out: ev ch whn edgd lft over 1f out: unable qckn fnl f)	1¼	2	3/1[1]	57	32
386[7]	**Little Ibnr (69)** (PDEvans) **6-9-10** JFEgan(6) (lw: chsd ldrs: kpt on fnl f)	1	3	14/1	68	43
391[8]	**Featherstone Lane (53)** (MissLCSiddall) **6-8-8v** DRMcCabe(5) (lw: hdwy over 1f out: fin wl)	1¼	4	7/1[3]	49	24
	Hannah's Usher (67) (CMurray) **5-9-8** NicolaHowarth(12) (chsd ldrs: led 2f out: hdd over 1f out: sn btn)	½	5	14/1	61	36
332*	**Bold Aristocrat (IRE) (63)** (RHollinshead) **6-9-1**(3) FLynch(7) (hdwy 2f out: one pce fnl f)	1½	6	7/1[3]	53	28

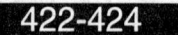

301^{10} **Night Harmony (IRE) (58)** (MissSJWilton) **4-8-13v¹** SWhitworth(2) (stdd s: hdwy over 2f out: wknd appr fnl f)........¾ **7** 8/1 46 21
386^{3} **Lochon (50)** (MrsNMacauley) **6-7-12v**(7) JoHunnam(10) (b: prom: led over 2f out: sn hdd & wknd)........¾ **8** 9/1 36 11
195^{6} **Appeal Again (IRE) (42)** (DBurchell) **4-7-11** NCarlisle(8) (sn outpcd)........¾ **9** 25/1 26 1
404* **Shontaine (61)** (MJohnston) **4-9-2** 6x DHolland(4) (w ldrs 4f)........½ **10** 11/2 2 44 19
326^{3} **Dictation (USA) (48)** (JJO'Neill) **5-8-3** JQuinn(1) (nvr trbld ldrs)........3½ **11** 8/1 22 —
385^{6} **Margaretrose Anna (43)** (BPJBaugh) **5-7-12**ow2 DaleGibson(9) (b: led over 3f: wknd)........3 **12** 20/1 9 —
326^{9} **Niteowl Raider (IRE) (41)** (JohnHarris) **4-7-10** JO'Reilly(3) (sn w ldrs: wknd over 2f out)........8 **13** 25/1 — —
(SP 128.2%) **13 Rn**

1m 16.7 (5.50) CSF £74.10 CT £858.58 TOTE £21.80: £5.60 £2.30 £2.50 (£82.00) Trio £73.80 OWNER Mr J. P. Hacking (PRESTON) BRED S. W. D. McIlveen
LONG HANDICAP Margaretrose Anna 7-5
Bt in 4,000 gns
IN-FOCUS: **This was the rider's first winner.**

422 TOMS H'CAP (0-70) (4-Y.O+) (Class E)

9-30 (9-32) **1m 1f 79y (Fibresand)** £2,580.00 (£780.00: £380.00: £180.00) Stalls: Low GOING: 0.21 sec per fur (SLW)

SP RR SF

Angel Face (USA) (69) (PDEvans) **4-10-0** JFEgan(7) (chsd ldrs: led over 4f out: clr over 1f out: rdn out)......— **1** 10/1 79 57
358^{3} **Chadleigh Lane (USA) (65)** (ABMulholland) **5-9-10** DeanMcKeown(13) (b.hind: hdwy 6f out: rdn over 2f out: r.o wl fnl f)........1¼ **2** 10/1 73 51
382^{4} **Ethbaat (USA) (67)** (MJHeaton-Ellis) **6-9-12** AClark(11) (prom: ev ch 3f out: kpt on fnl f)........1¼ **3** 12/1 73 51
380^{5} **Sweet Supposin (IRE) (64)** (CADwyer) **6-9-2v**(7) JoHunnam(6) (dwlt: hdwy 3f out: no imp appr fnl f)........3 **4** 11/1 65 43
316^{7} **Loch Style (53)** (RHollinshead) **4-8-9**(3) FLynch(10) (hdwy 4f out: no ex appr fnl f)........1¾ **5** 8/1 51 29
387^{4} **Venice Beach (65)** (CPEBrooks) **5-9-7**(3) JDSmith(12) (prom tl rdn & wknd over 2f out)........10 **6** 10/1 46 24
369^{3} **Dragonjoy (58)** (NPLittmoden) **4-8-12v**(5) DGriffiths(5) (s.i.s: hdwy over 3f out: eased ins fnl f)........¾ **7** 13/2 3 37 15
299^{7} **Obelos (USA) (58)** (MissSJWilton) **6-9-3v** SWhitworth(1) (nvr trbld ldrs)........13 **8** 20/1 15 —
369^{4} **Rival Bid (USA) (56)** (MrsNMacauley) **9-9-1v** JQuinn(9) (bhd: effrt 3f out: nvr nr ldrs)........nk **9** 6/1 2 13 —
338* **Hever Golf Eagle (50)** (TJNaughton) **4-8-9** DaneO'Neill(2) (lw: led 5f: wknd over 2f out)........½ **10** 10/1 6 —
369* **Suga Hawk (IRE) (62)** (EJAlston) **5-9-7** KFallon(8) (in tch: rdn 5f out: eased whn btn fnl 2f)........6 **11** 4/1 1 7 —
Backhander (IRE) (47) (RTPhillips) **5-8-6** SDrowne(4) (lw: prom 4f: sn bhd)........9 **12** 40/1 — —
140^{6} **Golden Touch (USA) (58)** (DJSCosgrove) **5-9-3** MRimmer(3) (prom over 4f)........1¾ **13** 12/1 — —
(SP 126.0%) **13 Rn**

2m 4.2 (8.20) CSF £102.14 CT £1,129.46 TOTE £8.40: £2.30 £2.30 £3.30 (£46.70) Trio £138.90 OWNER Mrs E. J. Williams (WELSHPOOL) BRED Gainsborough Farm Inc.
STEWARDS' ENQUIRY Egan susp. 24-25/3/97 (incorrect use of whip).

T/Plpt: £151.00 (94.74 Tckts). T/Qdpt: £114.60 (4.33 Tckts) Dk

0410-SOUTHWELL (L-H) (Standard)

Monday March 17th

WEATHER: fine & sunny WIND: almost nil

423 ST ANDREWS H'CAP (0-65) (I) (3-Y.O+) (Class F)

2-20 (2-27) **6f (Fibresand)** £1,944.00 (£544.00: £264.00) Stalls: Low GOING: 0.12 sec per fur (SLW)

SP RR SF

391^{3} **Needle Match (60)** (JJO'Neill) **4-9-10** WRyan(5) (hld up: hdwy over 2f out: rdn & edgd lft 1f out: led nr fin) ...— **1** 4/1 1 67 53
135^{2} **Afaan (IRE) (56)** (RFMarvin) **4-9-6** TGMcLaughlin(1) (a.p: led 4f out to nr fin)........nk **2** 10/1 62 48
332^{6} **Cheerful Groom (IRE) (32)** (DShaw) **6-7-3**(7) RFfrench(15) (lw: hdwy on outside 2f out: r.o one pce fnl f)........3 **3** 11/1 30 16
385^{3} **Ring the Chief (35)** (MDIUsher) **5-7-13** NCarlisle(7) (a.p: ev ch 2f out: wknd fnl f)........1¾ **4** 7/1 3 29 15
326* **Napoleon Star (IRE) (48)** (SRBowring) **6-8-12b** SWebster(3) (hld up: hdwy on ins 2f out: nt rch ldrs)........1½ **5** 9/1 38 24
327^{5} **Soaked (38)** (DWChapman) **4-8-2** LCharnock(14) (dwlt: hdwy over 2f out: edgd lft over 1f out: nvr nr to chal)..3 **6** 10/1 20 6
177^{8} **Seanchai (IRE) (32)** (PSFelgate) **4-7-3**(7) JFowle(11) (no hdwy fnl 3f)........3½ **7** 25/1 4 —
385* **Another Nightmare (IRE) (45)** (RMMcKellar) **5-8-2**(7) JMcAuley(13) (b: led tl rn wd 4f out: wknd over 2f out)1¼ **8** 6/1 2 14 —
Katie Komaite (36) (CaptJWilson) **4-7-7**(7) AngelaHartley(12) (bit bkwd: bhd fnl 2f)........1 **9** 20/1 2 —
203^{5} **Ballard Lady (IRE) (50)** (JSWainwright) **5-8-9**(5) JBramhill(2) (dwlt: a bhd)........1¾ **10** 8/1 12 —
Komlucky (47) (ABMulholland) **5-8-6**(5)ow5 GFaulkner(6) (bkwd: prom tl wknd over 2f out)........3½ **11** 20/1 — —
332^{3} **Tutu Sixtysix (32)** (DonEnricoIncisa) **6-7-10** KimTinkler(8) (swtg: a bhd)........1½ **12** 16/1 — —
327^{7} **Hershebar (36)** (MrsVAAconley) **7-8-0b**ow4 MDeering(9) (prom over 3f)........nk **13** 50/1 — —
Ginas Girl (39) (DShaw) **4-8-3** JFanning(10) (bit bkwd: a bhd)........2 **14** 20/1 — —
(SP 120.4%) **14 Rn**

1m 18.2 (4.70) CSF £36.83 CT £387.99 TOTE £5.70: £1.40 £3.00 £3.20 (£18.30) Trio £242.40 OWNER Clayton Bigley Partnership Ltd (PENRITH) BRED Tarworth Bloodstock Investments Ltd
LONG HANDICAP Cheerful Groom (IRE) 7-3 Tutu Sixtysix 7-6 Hershebar 7-9 Seanchai (IRE) 7-4

424 CARNOUSTIE CLAIMING STKS (3-Y.O+) (Class F)

2-50 (2-53) **7f (Fibresand)** £2,398.00 (£673.00: £328.00) Stalls: Low GOING: 0.12 sec per fur (SLW)

SP RR SF

364^{6} **Walk the Beat (71)** (MartynMeade) **7-9-1**(5) DSweeney(1) (lw: a.p: led over 4f out: rdn out)........— **1** 9/2 2 71 44
376^{5} **Jibereen (70)** (PHowling) **5-9-12** SWhitworth(15) (b: hld up: hdwy 3f out: chsd wnr & hung lft over 1f out: nt qckn ins fnl f)........1¼ **2** 5/2 1 74 47
317^{3} **Fast Spin (62)** (TDBarron) **3-7-11**(7) JoHunnam(14) (a.p: r.o one pce fnl f)........2½ **3** 7/1 61 19
109^{10} **Jubilee Scholar (IRE) (45)** (KMcAuliffe) **4-9-7b** JFEgan(13) (lw: prom tl wknd wl over 1f out)........7 **4** 33/1 47 20
403^{8} **Quinzii Martin (44)** (DHaydnJones) **9-9-4** SDrowne(7) (hld up: nt clr run 4f out: hdwy on outside over 2f out: n.d)........1¼ **5** 16/1 42 15
Be Warned (82) (MDods) **6-9-8v¹** AClark(10) (rdn over 4f out: no hdwy fnl 2f)........¾ **6** 13/2 3 44 17
326^{2} **Sea Devil (59)** (MJCamacho) **11-9-2** LCharnock(3) (prom tl wknd 2f out)........2½ **7** 13/2 3 32 5
415^{5} **Northern Fan (IRE) (59)** (NTinkler) **5-9-6** DeanMcKeown(12) (led over 2f: hung lft & wknd over 2f out)........2½ **8** 10/1 30 3

				SP	RR	SF
	Nobby Barnes (37) (DonEnricoIncisa) **8-9-8** KimTinkler(8) (bit bkwd: dwlt: a bhd)	10	**9**	33/1	10	—
	Persian Sunset (IRE) (MissJBower) **5-9-3** NCarlisle(2) (bhd fnl 4f)	2½	**10**	33/1	—	—
349^{6}	**Bogart (44)** (CWFairhurst) **6-9-4v** RCochrane(4) (a bhd)	2½	**11**	16/1	—	—
	Risky Lover (DShaw) **4-9-2** JFanning(6) (unf: swtg: a bhd)	2	**12**	20/1	—	—
	Dellen Walker (IRE) (JSWainwright) **4-8-12**(5) JBramhill(5) (lw: sn bhd)	4	**13**	16/1	—	—
	Wahab (RFMarvin) **4-9-5** TGMcLaughlin(9) (bit bkwd: bhd fnl 4f)	½	**14**	33/1	—	—

(SP 129.2%) **14 Rn**

1m 32.5 (6.00) CSF £14.97 TOTE £6.10: £2.80 £1.40 £2.10 (£10.70) Trio £39.00 OWNER Ladyswood Racing Club (MALMESBURY) BRED R. B. Warren
WEIGHT FOR AGE 3yo-15lb

425 MUIRFIELD MAIDEN STKS (3-Y.O) (Class D)

3-20 (3-21) **1m (Fibresand)** £3,566.25 (£1,080.00: £527.50: £251.25) Stalls: Low GOING: 0.12 sec per fur (SLW)

				SP	RR	SF
	Captain Scott (IRE) (JAGlover) **3-9-0** GCarter(9) (unf: hld up: hdwy after 3f out: led 2f out: rdn out)	—	**1**	$11/2^{3}$	76+	35
	Italian Symphony (IRE) (70) (MJohnston) **3-9-0** KDarley(3) (lw: led 6f: hrd rdn: one pce)	4	**2**	$5/1^{2}$	68	27
	Deep Water (USA) (PFICole) **3-9-0** TQuinn(1) (lw: prom: ev ch 3f out: hrd rdn & wknd over 2f out)	10	**3**	$1/2^{1}$	48	7
373^{7}	**Warrlin (55)** (CWFairhurst) **3-9-0** RCochrane(2) (lw: sn wl bhd: hdwy on ins 2f out: n.d)	6	**4**	14/1	36	—
	Robbo (CWThornton) **3-9-0** LCharnock(10) (lt-f: no hdwy fnl 3f)	1½	**5**	20/1	33	—
	Lightning Rebel (70) (CWThornton) **3-9-0** DeanMcKeown(5) (prom over 4f)	8	**6**	10/1	17	—
	Maremma (49) (DonEnricoIncisa) **3-8-9** KimTinkler(8) (wl bhd fnl 4f)	nk	**7**	50/1	11	—
	Sibor Star (DBurchell) **3-9-0** SDrowne(7) (bhd fnl 3f)	5	**8**	40/1	6	—
230^{9}	**Patrick** (DBurchell) **3-9-0** NCarlisle(6) (a bhd)	2½	**9**	25/1	1	—
387^{8}	**Bout (60)** (RMMcKellar) **3-8-9** TWilliams(4) (w ldr 3f: wknd qckly: virtually p.u fnl 2f)	dist	**10**	50/1	—	—

(SP 129.4%) **10 Rn**

1m 46.2 (7.20) CSF £32.05 TOTE £10.80: £1.90 £1.40 £1.10 (£18.90) Trio £9.50 OWNER The Write State Partnership (WORKSOP) BRED P. D. and Mrs Player

426 GLENEAGLES H'CAP (0-100) (4-Y.O+) (Class C)

3-55 (3-55) **1m 4f (Fibresand)** £6,097.50 (£1,845.00: £900.00: £427.50) Stalls: Low GOING: 0.12 sec per fur (SLW)

				SP	RR	SF
	River Keen (IRE) (96) (RWArmstrong) **5-10-0** GCarter(1) (lw: set slow pce: qcknd over 3f out: shkn up & clr over 1f out: easily)	—	**1**	$11/2^{2}$	110+	62
195^{*}	**Calder King (68)** (MrsMReveley) **6-7-9b**(5) PFessey(5) (hld up in rr: hdwy to chse wnr over 3f out: hrd rdn: sn outpcd)	8	**2**	10/1	71	23
374^{*}	**Greenspan (IRE) (74)** (WRMuir) **5-8-6** AClark(6) (lw: hld up: hdwy 5f out: r.o one pce fnl 3f)	2	**3**	13/2	75	27
299^{*}	**Leading Spirit (IRE) (85)** (CFWall) **5-8-10**(7) PClarke(7) (w wnr tl wknd over 3f out)	12	**4**	$5/4^{1}$	70	22
389^{3}	**China Castle (85)** (PCHaslam) **4-8-8**(7) PGoode(4) (lw: hld up: hdwy 8f out: wknd over 3f out)	1¼	**5**	$6/1^{3}$	68	18
389^{7}	**Nikita's Star (IRE) (76)** (DJGMurraySmith) **4-8-6**ow1 DHarrison(8) (prom: rdn over 5f out: wknd over 3f out)	8	**6**	10/1	48	—
	Swan Hunter (71) (DJSCosgrove) **4-8-1** JQuinn(3) (lw: hld up: rdn 4f out: sn wknd)	nk	**7**	20/1	43	—
182^{11}	**Eagle Canyon (IRE) (73)** (BHanbury) **4-7-12**(5) ADaly(2) (lw: bhd fnl 5f)	3	**8**	14/1	41	—

(SP 117.1%) **8 Rn**

2m 41.9 (8.90) CSF £54.15 CT £334.74 TOTE £6.20: £2.50 £1.70 £1.30 (£17.70) OWNER Dr Meou Tsen Geoffrey Yeh (NEWMARKET) BRED Ballylinch Stud Ltd
WEIGHT FOR AGE 4yo-2lb
OFFICIAL EXPLANATION **Leading Spirit (IRE): trainer reported that the gelding was never travelling from halfway down the back straight.**

427 SANDWICH (S) STKS (3-Y.O) (Class F)

4-25 (4-26) **5f (Fibresand)** £2,537.00 (£712.00: £347.00) Stalls: High GOING: 0.12 sec per fur (SLW)

				SP	RR	SF
379^{7}	**Ma Vielle Pouque (IRE) (53)** (WGMTurner) **3-8-7** TSprake(6) (a.p: led over 1f out: drvn out)	—	**1**	6/1	59	12
181^{3}	**Imperial Garden (IRE) (63)** (PCHaslam) **3-9-4** JFortune(5) (b.off hind: a.p: hrd rdn & ev ch fnl f: r.o)	hd	**2**	$7/2^{2}$	70	23
379^{4}	**Lunar Music (60)** (MartynMeade) **3-8-8**(5) DSweeney(3) (w ldrs: rdn over 2f out: ev ch over 1f out: r.o)	nk	**3**	$7/2^{2}$	64	17
399^{5}	**Chilling (63)** (NTinkler) **3-8-6**(7) KSked(7) (s.i.s: outpcd tl gd hdwy over 1f out: r.o)	½	**4**	$9/2^{3}$	62	15
329^{4}	**Ejeer (IRE) (54)** (MRChannon) **3-8-12** RPerham(8) (lw: a.p: ev ch 2f out: r.o one pce)	hd	**5**	10/1	61	14
379^{5}	**Threeplay (IRE) (59)** (JAkehurst) **3-8-12** MTebbutt(2) (lw: a.p: led 3f out tl over 1f out: one pce)	1¼	**6**	$5/2^{1}$	57	10
329^{5}	**What's That Amy (30)** (CSmith) **3-8-0**(7) JoHunnam(4) (bhd fnl 3f)	5	**7**	33/1	36	—
378^{9}	**Hever Golf Stormer (IRE) (46)** (TJNaughton) **3-8-12** DHarrison(9) (led 2f: eased whn btn ins fnl f)	1¾	**8**	20/1	35	—
	Nefertiti (30) (RFMarvin) **3-8-7** TGMcLaughlin(1) (lw: prom over 2f: t.o)	16	**9**	25/1	—	—

(SP 126.1%) **9 Rn**

62.2 secs (5.20) CSF £26.76 TOTE £4.60: £1.90 £1.90 £2.20 (£11.60) Trio £19.90 OWNER The Jersey Syndicate (SHERBORNE) BRED A. F. O'Callaghan
No bid

428 TROON APPRENTICE H'CAP (0-70) (4-Y.O+ F & M) (Class E)

4-55 (4-55) **1m (Fibresand)** £3,293.75 (£1,010.00: £502.50: £248.75) Stalls: Low GOING: 0.12 sec per fur (SLW)

				SP	RR	SF
125^{8}	**Cats Bottom (52)** (AGNewcombe) **5-9-10** MBatchelor(8) (hld up: hdwy on ins over 2f out: led 1f out: r.o wl)	—	**1**	$9/2^{1}$	65	29
305^{3}	**Queens Stroller (IRE) (30)** (REPeacock) **6-8-2** RBrisland(1) (led: hung rt 2f out: hdd 1f out: one pce)	1¼	**2**	10/1	41	5
313^{*}	**Gold Lining (IRE) (34)** (EJAlston) **4-8-6** JFowle(11) (stdd s: hdwy over 2f out: styd on ins fnl f)	2½	**3**	$5/1^{2}$	40	4
333^{*}	**Broughton's Pride (IRE) (52)** (JLEyre) **6-9-5**(5) GWright(9) (a.p: r.o one pce fnl 2f)	½	**4**	$5/1^{2}$	57	21
411^{4}	**David James' Girl (45)** (ABailey) **5-9-3** RStudholme(3) (hld up & bhd: rdn over 4f out: hdwy over 2f out: one pce fnl f)	s.h	**5**	$9/2^{1}$	49	13
286^{5}	**Efipetite (31)** (NBycroft) **4-8-3** AMcCarthy(2) (s.i.s: plld hrd: sn prom: wknd over 1f out)	¾	**6**	16/1	34	—
273^{10}	**Giddy (42)** (JHetherton) **4-9-0** CLowther(4) (prom 6f)	10	**7**	$9/1^{3}$	25	—
312^{*}	**Jilly Beveled (36)** (RonaldThompson) **5-8-8** RCody-Boutcher(7) (hld up & plld hrd: bhd fnl 2f)	1½	**8**	$9/1^{3}$	16	—
	Nicola's Princess (51) (BAMcMahon) **4-9-9** SRighton(5) (hld up & plld hrd: bhd fnl 4f)	7	**9**	$9/1^{3}$	17	—
	Yuppy Girl (IRE) (43) (CaptJWilson) **4-8-10**(5) AngelaHartley(6) (prom over 5f)	4	**10**	14/1	1	—

				SP	RR	SF
	Lomond Lassie (USA) (32) (TKersey) **4-8-4** PClarke(10) (b: a bhd)	2	**11**	33/1	—	—

(SP 124.3%) **11 Rn**

1m 47.8 (8.80) CSF £48.34 CT £223.09 TOTE £4.00: £1.50 £3.40 £3.00 (£15.00) Trio £55.50 OWNER Advanced Marketing Services Ltd (BARNSTAPLE) BRED R. A. Speight

429 ST ANDREWS H'CAP (0-65) (II) (3-Y.O+) (Class F)

5-25 (5-31) **6f (Fibresand)** £1,944.00 (£544.00: £264.00) Stalls: Low GOING: 0.12 sec per fur (SLW)

				SP	RR	SF
421[2]	**Hoh Majestic (IRE) (55)** (RonaldThompson) **4-8-12v**(7) GMilligan(8) (led after 1f: r.o wl)	—	**1**	6/1[2]	60	39
421[6]	**Bold Aristocrat (IRE) (63)** (RHollinshead) **6-9-10**(3) FLynch(7) (hld up: hdwy 2f out: ev ch ins fnl f: r.o)	nk	**2**	13/2[3]	67	46
332[4]	**Sweet Mate (46)** (SRBowring) **5-8-10b** SWebster(1) (b.hind: a.p: ev ch over 1f out: one pce)	3	**3**	5/1[1]	42	21
386[6]	**Mustang (34)** (CWThornton) **4-7-12b** DaleGibson(14) (chsd ldrs on outside: styd on one pce fnl f)	½	**4**	9/1	29	8
318[10]	**Delrob (51)** (DHaydnJones) **6-9-1b** AClark(2) (prom: ev ch over 1f out: one pce)	1½	**5**	10/1	42	21
318[11]	**Answers-To-Thomas (49)** (JMJefferson) **4-8-13** DeanMcKeown(4) (a.p: one pce fnl 2f)	s.h	**6**	14/1	40	19
386*	**Takhlid (USA) (64)** (DWChapman) **6-10-0** ACulhane(9) (prom tl hrd rdn & wknd over 1f out)	1¾	**7**	7/1	50	29
318[9]	**Blue Lugana (38)** (NBycroft) **5-8-2** JQuinn(3) (s.s: nvr nrr)	3½	**8**	20/1	15	—
385[2]	**Astral Invader (IRE) (33)** (MSSaunders) **5-7-4**(7) RFfrench(15) (spd on outside 3f)	2	**9**	12/1	4	—
243[10]	**Monis (IRE) (41)** (JBalding) **6-8-5v** SDrowne(12) (n.d)	¾	**10**	14/1	10	—
326[8]	**Young Ben (IRE) (32)** (JSWainwright) **5-7-5b**(5) JBramhill(13) (led 1f: hrd rdn & wknd 3f out)	nk	**11**	20/1	1	—
	Rymer's Rascal (56) (EJAlston) **5-9-6** JFortune(5) (prom over 3f)	1½	**12**	33/1	21	—
225[9]	**Island Prince (49)** (NACallaghan) **3-8-0b[1]** CRutter(11) (b.off hind: sn bhd)	1	**13**	7/1	11	—
	Dashing Dancer (IRE) (40) (DShaw) **6-8-4** JFanning(10) (rdn over 3f out: sn bhd)	3½	**14**	20/1	—	—
327[9]	**Gloria Imperator (IRE) (34)** (ABMulholland) **4-7-12**ow2 NAdams(6) (a bhd)	4	**15**	33/1	—	—

(SP 129.6%) **15 Rn**

1m 18.9 (5.40) CSF £40.59 CT £202.75 TOTE £7.60: £1.70 £3.50 £2.20 (£12.60) Trio £41.60 OWNER Mrs Ronnie Hague (DONCASTER) BRED Ballinacurra Stud

LONG HANDICAP Young Ben (IRE) 7-4 Gloria Imperator (IRE) 7-4

WEIGHT FOR AGE 3yo-13lb

T/Jkpt: Not won; £11,249.18 to Uttoxeter 18/3/97. T/Plpt: £78.40 (178.12 Tckts). T/Qdpt: £15.50 (54.88 Tckts) KH

DONCASTER (L-H) (Good to firm, Good patches)

Thursday March 20th

WEATHER: overcast WIND: mod half bhd

430 RACING CHANNEL APPRENTICE H'CAP (0-80) (4-Y.O+) (Class F)

1-30 (1-36) **1m 4f** £2,878.00 (£808.00: £394.00) Stalls: Low GOING minus 0.14 sec per fur (G)

				SP	RR	SF
129[2]	**Galapino (48)** (MissGayKelleway) **4-7-6**(5) RMullen(21) (trckd ldr: led 2f out: styd on wl fnl f)	—	**1**	13/2[1]	59	37
123*	**Raffles Rooster (59)** (AGNewcombe) **5-8-5**(5) JoHunnam(15) (hld up: hdwy 3f out: nt qckn ins fnl f)	1	**2**	8/1[2]	69	49
	Urgent Swift (70) (APJarvis) **4-8-12**(7) CCarver(24) (lw: hld up: stdy hdwy over 3f out: styd on same pce fnl f)	¾	**3**	20/1	79	57
374[2]	**Dancing Cavalier (58)** (RHollinshead) **4-8-7** FLynch(22) (hld up: gd hdwy on outside 3f out: hung lft: nt qckn fnl f)	1¼	**4**	20/1	65	43
	Chabrol (CAN) (62) (TTClement) **4-8-11** RHavlin(16) (lw: mid div: hdwy & hung lft 3f out: nvr rchd ldrs)	3	**5**	16/1	65	43
	Parrot's Hill (IRE) (47) (MHTompkins) **4-7-10** MHenry(8) (bhd: styd on fnl 3f: nt rch ldrs)	2½	**6**	14/1	47	25
402[2]	**Fabulous Mtoto (54)** (MSSaunders) **7-8-0**(5) RFfrench(17) (lw: led to 2f out: sn wknd)	1¼	**7**	16/1	52	32
	He's Got Wings (IRE) (58) (MrsJRRamsden) **4-8-7** MartinDwyer(6) (b.nr hind: mid div: effrt 3f out: kpt on: nvr rchd ldrs)	¾	**8**	12/1	55	33
410[2]	**Kilnamartyra Girl (45)** (JParkes) **7-7-5**(5) JBramhill(4) (lw: b.hind: bhd: drvn along ½-wy: sme hdwy 3f out: n.d)	5	**9**	25/1	35	15
100*	**Opera Buff (IRE) (73)** (MissGayKelleway) **6-9-10** AWhelan(2) (lw: hld up: nvr nr ldrs)	½	**10**	13/2[1]	63	43
400[6]	**Petoskin (54)** (JPearce) **5-8-5** CTeague(20) (sn bhd: sme hdwy 3f out: n.d)	1½	**11**	20/1	42	22
	General Glow (60) (PDEvans) **4-8-9** PMcCabe(23) (chsd ldrs tl wknd 3f out)	hd	**12**	20/1	48	26
	Midyan Blue (IRE) (73) (JMPEustace) **7-9-3**(7) SHoughton(12) (mid div: effrt u.p over 4f out: sn wknd)	s.h	**13**	25/1	61	41
369[11]	**Decision Maker (IRE) (65)** (KRBurke) **4-8-11b**(3) DGriffiths(19) (chsd ldrs tl lost pl 3f out)	1¼	**14**	50/1	51	29
	Pay Homage (70) (IABalding) **9-9-0**(7) RFowley(13) (mid div: effrt over 3f out: sn wknd)	hd	**15**	20/1	56	36
	Almuhtaram (68) (GLewis) **5-9-0**(5) JDennis(11) (bhd: sme hdwy over 3f out: sn wknd)	1	**16**	16/1	52	32
334*	**Amadour (IRE) (65)** (PMitchell) **4-8-7**(7) AMcCarthy(3) (bhd: hdwy u.p 3f out: n.d)	1¼	**17**	9/1[3]	48	26
380[4]	**Fairy Knight (71)** (RHannon) **5-9-1**(7) GGallagher(1) (sn wl bhd)	1¼	**18**	12/1	52	32
	Cois Na Farraige (IRE) (70) (MissLAPerratt) **4-9-0**(5) KSked(18) (bit bkwd: in tch: rdn over 3f out: sn wknd)	5	**19**	33/1	44	22
360[5]	**Kalamata (53)** (JAGlover) **5-8-1**(3)ow1 TEDurcan(5) (in tch: effrt u.p 3f out: sn wknd)	½	**20**	16/1	27	6
	Nosey Native (67) (JPearce) **4-8-9**(7) LisaMoncrieff(10) (sn wl bhd: t.o 7f out)	nk	**21**	16/1	40	18
	Tonnerre (65) (BAMcMahon) **5-8-9**(7) SRighton(9) (hld up in tch: effrt over 3f out: sn lost pl)	7	**22**	33/1	29	9
	Slasher Jack (IRE) (73) (DNicholls) **6-9-5**(5) IonaWands(7) (bit bkwd: a bhd)	1¾	**23**	20/1	35	15
	Reservation Rock (IRE) (55) (THind) **6-7-13**(7) SamanthaMcGinn(14) (a bhd)	2	**24**	50/1	14	—

(SP 145.3%) **24 Rn**

2m 35.11 (5.11) CSF £47.51 CT £964.57 TOTE £7.30: £2.00 £2.60 £7.00 £5.50 (£27.40) Trio £1367.00; £673.89 to Doncaster 21/3/97 OWNER Mr Nigel Dearman (WHITCOMBE) BRED Dayspring Co Ltd

LONG HANDICAP Kilnamartyra Girl 7-5

WEIGHT FOR AGE 4yo-2lb

129 Galapino, who lacks size, has slipped right down the weights over the last eleven months. Idling in front, he always looked to have the situation under control. (13/2)

123* Raffles Rooster, on his toes in the paddock, was ridden round by the jockey. He has to come late and lead near the line, but the winner was always going to contain him. (8/1)

Urgent Swift seemed to be ridden with the main aim of staying the trip. (20/1)

374 Dancing Cavalier, well in at the weights compared with the All-Weather, had the blinkers left off this time. (20/1)

Chabrol (CAN), fit from hurdling, raced with a tongue-strap. (16/1)

Parrot's Hill (IRE) either wants further or easier ground, probably both. (14/1)
100* Opera Buff (IRE), very fit after an All-Weather campaign, was 16lb lower here on Turf compared with the artificial surfaces, but possibly found the ground too fast. (13/2)
334* Amadour (IRE) (9/1: 8/1-12/1)

431 'BACK A WINNER BY TRAIN' H'CAP (0-85) (3-Y.O) (Class D)

2-05 (2-10) **1m 2f 60y** £3,882.50 (£1,160.00: £555.00: £252.50) Stalls: Low GOING minus 0.14 sec per fur (G)

	Horse	Dist	Pos	SP	RR	SF
	Miracle Kid (USA) (74) (JHMGosden) **3-8-10** LDettori(2) (lw: s.i.s: sn trckng ldrs: led 2f out: sn clr: easily)	—	1	9/2 2	87++	43
	Love Has No Pride (USA) (85) (RHannon) **3-9-7** DaneO'Neill(5) (bit bkwd: hld up: hdwy on ins 3f out: kpt on appr fnl f: no ch w wnr)	3	2	12/1	93	49
	The Deejay (IRE) (66) (MrsMerritaJones) **3-8-2**ow1 JFEgan(16) (lw: bhd & pushed along: styd on wl fnl 3f)	¾	3	16/1	73	28
138*	**Selberry (82)** (PCHaslam) **3-9-4** JFortune(12) (sn bhd & drvn along: styd on fnl 3f: nt rch ldrs)	1¼	4	10/1	87	43
331 4	**Time Can Tell (68)** (CMurray) **3-8-4** JStack(1) (sn bhd: hdwy on ins whn hmpd over 3f out: styd on fnl f)	6	5	16/1	64	20
347*	**As-Is (60)** (MJohnston) **3-7-10** NAdams(3) (led tl over 2f out: n.m.r & grad wknd)	hd	6	10/1	56	12
	Lady Godiva (70) (MJPolglase) **3-8-6** TGMcLaughlin(4) (chsd ldr: led over 2f out: sn hdd & grad wknd)	¾	7	7/1 3	65	21
	Baubigny (USA) (77) (MRChannon) **3-8-13** PaulEddery(8) (h.d.w: in tch: hdwy & ev ch over 2f out: hung lft & grad wknd)	2	8	25/1	68	24
239 2	**Mogul (75)** (NAGraham) **3-8-11** AMcGlone(6) (chsd ldrs: drvn along over 3f out: sn outpcd)	½	9	16/1	66	22
370 3	**Head Gardener (IRE) (70)** (NPLittmoden) **3-8-1**(5) ADaly(10) (sn bhd & pushed along)	nk	10	25/1	60	16
387*	**Sword Arm (77)** (RCharlton) **3-8-13** TSprake(13) (in tch: effrt over 2f out: hung lft & sn wknd)	½	11	3/1 1	66	22
341*	**Pennywell (66)** (RFJohnsonHoughton) **3-8-2** SSanders(9) (prom: rdn over 2f out: sn lost pl)	2	12	10/1	52	8
	Native Princess (IRE) (65) (BWHills) **3-8-1** GCarter(14) (mid div & sn drvn along: eased whn no ch 2f out)	3½	13	16/1	46	2
	Madison Welcome (IRE) (63) (MrsJRRamsden) **3-7-8**(5) RMullen(11) (bit bkwd: hld up & bhd: drvn along 5f out: n.d)	¾	14	12/1	43	—
281 4	**Superbelle (79)** (MAJarvis) **3-9-1** EmmaO'Gorman(7) (plld hrd: sn trckng ldrs: rdn 4f out: sn lost pl)	2	15	14/1	56	12
	Watercolour (IRE) (60) (NMBabbage) **3-7-3b1**(7) RFfrench(15) (a bhd)	¾	16	33/1	35	—
				(SP 139.2%)		**16 Rn**

2m 12.89 (5.09) CSF £59.88 CT £779.22 TOTE £6.20: £1.90 £3.40 £3.80 £3.10 (£39.70) Trio £424.10 OWNER Mr Louis Lo (NEWMARKET) BRED Sally Nims
LONG HANDICAP Watercolour (IRE) 6-13
Miracle Kid (USA) who holds Classic entries, took this in smart style and can hold his own in much better company. (9/2)
Love Has No Pride (USA), who looked on the burly side, proved well suited by the step-up in trip. Significantly, he seemed to show improvement on his final two starts as a juvenile. (12/1)
The Deejay (IRE), who has slipped down the weights, was having his first outing for his new trainer. Finding this hard work, the way he was staying on at the finish suggests he will be suited by a step up to one-and-a-half miles. (16/1)
138* Selberry, 5lb higher than when winning on the All-Weather at Wolverhampton, came from way off the pace and will be suited by further.(10/1)
331 Time Can Tell, fit from an All-Weather campaign, was staying on when it was all over. (16/1)
347* As-Is, who showed little on the Turf at two, has enjoyed a rewarding All-Weather campaign. (10/1)
Baubigny (USA) has improved physically from two to three, but he showed a poor action going down. Tending to hang, he should be suited by easier ground. (25/1)
387* Sword Arm gave his jockey problems and is clearly not a straightforward ride. (3/1)

87+ 77+ 74 66 (76)

432 TOTE BENVENUTO BROCKLESBY CONDITIONS STKS (2-Y.O) (Class C)

2-35 (2-37) **5f** £4,923.80 (£1,824.20: £877.10: £360.50: £145.25: £59.15) Stalls: High GOING minus 0.14 sec per fur (G)

Horse	Dist	Pos	SP	RR	SF
Blueridge Dancer (IRE) (BJMeehan) **2-8-11** MTebbutt(10) (leggy: scope: w ldrs: led 1f out: edgd rt: r.o wl)	—	1	7/1 3	88	28
Mister Bankes (WGMTurner) **2-8-11** TSprake(1) (w'like: lw: led: hung lft & hdd 1f out: r.o)	1½	2	15/2	83	23
Stately Princess (MRChannon) **2-8-6** TQuinn(15) (w'like: chsd ldrs: rn green & hung lft ½-wy: kpt on same pce appr fnl f)	3	3	4/1 1	69	9
Out Like Magic (PDEvans) **2-8-6** JFEgan(3) (lt-f: chsd ldrs: rdn 2f out: kpt on same pce)	nk	4	16/1	68	8
Days of Grace (MartynMeade) **2-8-1**(5) DSweeney(12) (cmpt: hdwy & swtchd rt ½-wy: kpt on: nvr rchd ldrs)	¾	5	20/1	65	5
Wrekin Pilot (RHannon) **2-8-11** PatEddery(14) (w'like: s.i.s: hdwy ½-wy: styd on fnl f)	s.h	6	9/2 2	70	10
Miquelon (RHollinshead) **2-8-11** KDarley(4) (cmpt: scope: bit bkwd: s.i.s: outpcd ½-wy: r.o fnl f)	3½	7	14/1	59	—
Yorkies Boy (BAMcMahon) **2-8-11** LNewton(13) (leggy: scope: bit bkwd: trckd ldrs: effrt 2f out: grad wknd)	1½	8	9/1	54	—
Filey Brigg (WTKemp) **2-8-6** JQuinn(9) (leggy: unf: a outpcd)	nk	9	25/1	48	—
Suggest (MissGayKelleway) **2-8-11** DHolland(5) (cmpt: lw: chsd ldrs: rdn ½-wy: sn btn: eased fnl f)	s.h	10	4/1 1	53	—
Five of Spades (IRE) (DNicholls) **2-8-11** AlexGreaves(7) (cmpt: bit bkwd: w ldrs tl wknd qckly 2f out)	3	11	16/1	43	—
Prince Nicholas (KWHogg) **2-8-11** DeanMcKeown(2) (cmpt: s.s: a bhd)	nk	12	33/1	42	—
Somosierra (IRE) (JBerry) **2-8-6**(5) TEDurcan(6) (w'like: leggy: scope: chsd ldrs 3f: sn wknd)	1¾	13	4/1 1	37	—
The Other Risk (DANolan) **2-8-11** GDuffield(11) (leggy: scope: s.s: hung bdly lft & wl bhd)	6	14	20/1	18	—
Far-So-La (TMJones) **2-8-11** RPerham(8) (cmpt: s.i.s: a outpcd & bhd)	s.h	15	25/1	17	—
			(SP 151.0%)		**15 Rn**

61.65 secs (3.25) CSF £63.42 TOTE £13.00: £3.30 £2.80 £1.90 (£37.90) Trio £139.10 OWNER Mr Alan Cunliffe (UPPER LAMBOURN) BRED K. Molloy
Blueridge Dancer (IRE), who is on the leg, took this in good style in the end. Only foaled on 30th April, he can do nothing but improve.(7/1)
Mister Bankes who was very fit, should soon go one better. (15/2)
Stately Princess showed definite signs of inexperience and will come on considerably for the outing. (4/1)
Out Like Magic lacks substance. (16/1)
Days of Grace is a close-coupled type. (20/1)
Wrekin Pilot showed promise after missing the break. (9/2: 3/1-5/1)
Miquelon, who needed the outing, was staying on when it was all over and probably needs six furlongs already. (14/1: 10/1-16/1)
Yorkies Boy travelled strongly only to fade. He does not lack speed and the outing should have brought him on. (9/1)
Suggest who looked very fit, was a 17th May foal and, with all chance gone, was eased up. He had apparently been showing plenty at home. (4/1: op 5/2)
Somosierra (IRE) who is on the leg, is one of the first crop of Paris House. (4/1: 3/1-9/2)

433 SPORTING LIFE DONCASTER MILE STKS (Listed) (4-Y.O+) (Class A)

3-10 (3-10) **1m (straight)** £11,453.50 (£3,412.00: £1,625.00: £731.50) Stalls: High GOING minus 0.14 sec per fur (G)

	Horse	Dist	Pos	SP	RR	SF
	Canyon Creek (IRE) (JHMGosden) **4-8-12** LDettori(2) (trckd ldrs: shkn up to ld over 1f out: edgd rt & sn qckndclr)	—	1	7/2[3]	107+	42
	Yeast (109) (WJHaggas) **5-9-1** RCochrane(5) (led: shkn up & qcknd over 3f out: hdd over 1f out: no ch w wnr)	4	2	Evens[1]	102	37
	Band on the Run (86) (BAMcMahon) **10-8-12** TQuinn(6) (chsd ldrs: rdn & outpcd over 3f out: kpt on wl ins fnl f)	nk	3	20/1	98	33
	Amrak Ajeeb (IRE) (108) (BHanbury) **5-8-12** MRimmer(1) (lw: trckd ldrs: outpcd over 2f out: styd on fnl f)	nk	4	100/30[2]	98	33
52[6]	**Raheen (USA) (86)** (WGMTurner) **4-8-12b** TSprake(4) (trckd ldrs: effrt 2f out: kpt on same pce)	nk	5	50/1	97	32
	Lonely Leader (IRE) (103) (RHannon) **4-8-12** PatEddery(3) (swtg: chsd ldrs: drvn along 3f out: sn outpcd)	¾	6	10/1	96	31

(SP 111.1%) **6 Rn**

1m 41.31 (4.11) CSF £6.61 TOTE £3.40: £1.60 £1.40 (£2.60) OWNER Sheikh Mohammed (NEWMARKET) BRED Sheikh Mohammed bin Rashid al Maktoum

IN-FOCUS: **This race developed into a three-and-a-half furlong sprint, and the efforts of Band on the Run and Raheen should be treated with caution.**

Canyon Creek (IRE), winner of a maiden at Pontefract in October on his only previous outing, took this in tremendous style. He might be even better suited by some give underfoot, and is clearly very useful. (7/2)

Yeast, who looked big and well, was allowed to set his own pace. Quickening it up at halfway, he was left for dead once the winner made his move. (Evens)

Band on the Run staged something of a revival and would have been meeting the favourite on 12lb better terms in a handicap. (20/1)

Amrak Ajeeb (IRE), who took a keen grip, was tapped for foot when the pace quickened. Staying on when it was all over, he is better suited by a bigger field and stronger gallop. (100/30)

52 Raheen (USA), who took some settling, belied his odds, and would have been meeting the favourite on 2st better terms in a handicap. The race was really only a three-furlong sprint and this effort should be treated with some caution. (50/1)

Lonely Leader (IRE) was warm beforehand and, once the taps were turned on, he was left for dead. (10/1)

434 MITSUBISHI DIAMOND VISION H'CAP (0-85) (3-Y.O) (Class D)

3-40 (3-41) **5f** £4,464.00 (£1,332.00: £636.00: £288.00) Stalls: High GOING: Not Established

	Horse	Dist	Pos	SP	RR	SF
258*	**Brutal Fantasy (IRE) (72)** (JLEyre) **3-8-10** RLappin(9) (chsd ldrs: led ½-wy: hld on towards fin)	—	1	13/2[2]	84	27
	Ellens Lad (IRE) (80) (RHannon) **3-9-4** PatEddery(10) (hdwy ½-wy: chal 1f out: nt qckn nr fin)	nk	2	4/1[1]	91	34
	Bishops Court (80) (MrsJRRamsden) **3-9-4** JFortune(12) (hld up & bhd: smooth hdwy 2f out: kpt on strly fnl f: improve)	2	3	4/1[1]	85++	28
	Swino (83) (PDEvans) **3-9-7** JFEgan(1) (led to ½-wy: nt qckn appr fnl f)	nk	4	10/1	87	30
	Ballymote (77) (JBerry) **3-9-1** KDarley(8) (chsd ldrs tl wknd over 1f out)	6	5	10/1	62	5
427[3]	**Lunar Music (67)** (MartynMeade) **3-8-0**(5)ow1 DSweeney(4) (a.p: rdn 2f out: no imp)	2	6	14/1	45	—
	Divide And Rule (83) (RHollinshead) **3-9-4**(3) DGriffiths(2) (lw: hld up: hdwy on outside ½-wy: kpt on: nvr rchd ldrs)	s.h	7	20/1	61	4
379*	**Eager To Please (70)** (MissGayKelleway) **3-8-8b** DHolland(3) (chsd ldrs tl wknd over 1f out)	nk	8	8/1[3]	47	—
320[2]	**Castle Ashby Jack (73)** (PHowling) **3-8-11b** PaulEddery(11) (lw: sn outpcd: sme hdwy u.p 2f out: n.d)	½	9	12/1	48	—
	Jedi Knight (75) (MWEasterby) **3-8-13** DaleGibson(6) (hmpd over 3f out: n.d)	¾	10	16/1	48	—
	Gunners Glory (79) (BJMeehan) **3-9-3** LDettori(7) (hmpd & lost pl over 3f out: n.d after)	1¾	11	8/1[3]	46	—
	Weet Ees Girl (IRE) (80) (PDEvans) **3-9-4** KFallon(13) (a outpcd & bhd)	1¼	12	20/1	43	—

(SP 123.5%) **12 Rn**

61.68 secs (3.28) CSF £31.03 CT £108.90 TOTE £7.50: £2.40 £2.00 £2.00 (£26.00) Trio £27.90 OWNER Diamond Racing Ltd (HAMBLETON) BRED Michael G. O'Brien

258* Brutal Fantasy (IRE), fit from the All-Weather, showed real determination in a tight finish. (13/2)

Ellens Lad (IRE), a progressive two-year-old, ran a fine first race. (4/1)

Bishops Court, an impressive winner of a maiden at Hamilton on his second and final outing at two, is a grand sprint type. Dropped in at the start, he took a keen hold. Moving up on the bridle shortly after halfway, he looked as though he could take the race at any time, but his rider elected to stay in behind horses, never picked up his whip and asked the horse to do just enough to secure third spot near the line. There is no doubt that, with a more aggressive ride and more positive tactics, he would have won this. (4/1)

Swino, a confirmed five-furlong performer, was nibbled at at long odds. (10/1: op 20/1)

Ballymote has started his second campaign on a fair handicap mark. (10/1)

435 FAUCETS FOR MIRA/RADA DOMESTIC & COMMERCIAL SHOWER EQUIPMENT LADIES' H'CAP (0-80) (4-Y.O+) (Class G)

4-10 (4-13) **1m 2f 60y** £2,402.00 (£672.00: £326.00) Stalls: Low GOING minus 0.14 sec per fur (G)

	Horse	Dist	Pos	SP	RR	SF
	Break the Rules (73) (MCPipe) **5-11-2** MrsAPerrett(3) (hld up: hdwy 3f out: led over 1f out: all out)	—	1	7/2[1]	88	73
327[4]	**Mels Baby (IRE) (65)** (JLEyre) **4-10-8** MissDianaJones(2) (hld up: gd hdwy over 3f out: chal over 1f out: nt qckn nr fin)	nk	2	7/1[2]	80	65
	Desert Fighter (68) (MrsMReveley) **6-10-11** MissPJones(5) (mde most tl over 1f out: grad wknd)	6	3	11/1	73	58
196[7]	**Manful (68)** (MissLAPerratt) **5-10-11b** MrsSBosley(13) (hdwy on outside 4f out: edgd lft: kpt on same pce fnl 2f)	1¾	4	9/1[3]	71	56
	Fourdaned (IRE) (65) (PWHarris) **4-10-8** MissAElsey(9) (in tch: rdn 3f out: one pce)	3	5	12/1	63	48
207[7]	**Loveyoumillions (IRE) (68)** (NTinkler) **5-10-11** MissJAllison(8) (s.s: hdwy 4f out: nvr nr to chal)	4	6	20/1	60	45
384[4]	**Gold Blade (69)** (JPearce) **8-10-12** MrsLPearce(20) (racd wd: hdwy 4f out: nvr rchd ldrs)	½	7	10/1	60	45
248[3]	**Father Dan (IRE) (56)** (MissGayKelleway) **8-9-8**(5) MissLKerr(12) (bhd: styd on fnl 2f: nvr nr ldrs)	s.h	8	12/1	47	32
	Squared Away (53) (JWPayne) **5-9-5b**(5)ow6 MissCLake(11) (s.i.s: wl bhd tl sme hdwy fnl 2f)	1¼	9	16/1	42	21
	Rising Dough (IRE) (68) (GLMoore) **5-10-11** MrsJMoore(7) (bhd: sme hdwy 2f out: n.d)	s.h	10	14/1	57	42
194[2]	**Roussi (USA) (50)** (DNicholls) **5-9-7** MissRClark(4) (chsd ldrs: hrd rdn over 2f out: grad wknd)	1¼	11	10/1	37	22
226[4]	**Tawafek (USA) (65)** (SDow) **4-10-8** MrsMCowdrey(6) (bhd: sme hdwy on outside 4f out: n.d)	nk	12	9/1[3]	51	36
	Flash In The Pan (IRE) (51) (JSMoore) **4-9-3**(5) MrsSMoore(17) (t.o 4f out: sme late hdwy)	s.h	13	16/1	37	22
	Forest Robin (78) (MrsJRRamsden) **4-11-2**(5) MissERamsden(15) (in tch tl wknd 3f out)	s.h	14	12/1	64	49
422*	**Angel Face (USA) (72)** (PDEvans) **4-10-10**(5) 5x MrsCFord(19) (v.unruly: chsd ldrs tl lost pl over 3f out)	2½	15	11/1	54	39

369[8]	Cohiba (52) (BJCurley) 4-9-4(5) MissABroderick(16) (hld up: a bhd) ...1	16	16/1	33	18
205[7]	Open Affair (54) (HAkbary) 4-9-6(5) MissIFoustok(18) (chsd ldrs tl lost pl 3f out) ...2½	17	25/1	31	16
	Nirvana Prince (65) (BPreece) 8-10-3(5) MissLBoswell(14) (a bhd) ...9	18	25/1	28	13
	Mybotye (75) (RBastiman) 4-10-13(5) MissRBastiman(10) (a in rr) ...1¾	19	16/1	35	20
	Take Notice (75) (RMMcKellar) 4-10-13(5) MrsCWilliams(1) (w ldr tl wknd qckly 4f out: t.o) ...30	20	25/1	—	—
			(SP 159.1%)	20 Rn	

2m 13.18 (5.38) CSF £29.32 CT £258.14 TOTE £4.00: £1.30 £1.60 £3.20 £2.20 (£11.40) Trio £42.30 OWNER Mr A. J. Lomas (WELLINGTON) BRED Cleaboy Farms Co

Break the Rules, twice a recent winner over hurdles, was given a fine ride by his highly-able pilot. (7/2)
327 Mels Baby (IRE), ridden to get the trip, was never doing quite enough to peg back the winner. (7/1)
Desert Fighter, fit from hurdling, tried to steal it early in the straight, but was left for dead by the first two in the final furlong.(11/1)
88 Manful, attempting to repeat his win in this race last year, came off a true line under pressure and will appreciate easier ground. (9/1)
Fourdaned (IRE), who lost his way at three, lacked nothing in assistance from the saddle. (12/1)
422* Angel Face (USA) (11/1: op 6/1)

436 MELTON WOOD MAIDEN STKS (3-Y.O) (Class D)

4-40 (4-41) **1m (straight)** £3,850.00 (£1,150.00: £550.00: £250.00) Stalls: High GOING minus 0.14 sec per fur (G)

		SP	RR	SF
Fly To The Stars (MJohnston) **3-9-0** JWeaver(2) (lw: trckd ldrs: shkn up to ld over 2f out: styd on strly appr fnl f: sn clr) ...—	**1**	5/6 [1]	98+	41
River's Source (USA) (BWHills) **3-9-0** MHills(6) (lw: trckd ldrs: effrt over 2f out: kpt on: no ch w wnr) ...7	**2**	3/1 [2]	84	27
Burning Truth (USA) (RCharlton) **3-9-0** TSprake(4) (bit bkwd: hld up: shkn up over 1f out: styd on wl ins fnl f: improve) ...2½	**3**	10/1	79	22
Get The Point (87) (RHollinshead) **3-9-0** LDettori(3) (w ldr: led wl over 2f out: sn hdd & grad wknd) ...nk	**4**	6/1 [3]	78	21
Toi Toi (IRE) (DWPArbuthnot) **3-8-9** SWhitworth(8) (chsd ldrs: effrt over 2f out: hung lft: one pce) ...3	**5**	11/1	67	10
Arboreal (USA) (MrsLStubbs) **3-8-9** KFallon(1) (w'like: chsd ldrs: outpcd over 2f out: sn wknd) ...10	**6**	20/1	47	—
Khayal (USA) (BWHills) **3-8-11**(3) JDSmith(5) (w'like: bit bkwd: s.s: rn green: a outpcd & bhd) ...1	**7**	14/1	50	—
April Jackson (PTDalton) **3-8-4**(5) JBramhill(7) (b.off hind: led: rdn over 3f out: hdd wl over 2f out: sn lost pl) ...4	**8**	50/1	37	—
		(SP 124.6%)	**8 Rn**	

1m 41.64 (4.44) CSF £3.66 TOTE £1.70: £1.10 £1.40 £2.40 (£2.30) OWNER Mr P. D. Savill (MIDDLEHAM) BRED Bishop's Down Farm
Fly To The Stars, noisy in the paddock, took this race, which developed into a sprint over the final three furlongs, in impressive fashion. Highly thought of, he is clearly very useful. (5/6)
River's Source (USA) met a tartar and should be a ready-made winner of a run-of-the-mill maiden. (3/1)
Burning Truth (USA), who looked burly, is still learning the ropes. Sticking on in promising fashion at the finish, he needs one more outing to qualify for a handicap mark. (10/1: op 6/1)
Get The Point, a pottery mover, probably needs further. (6/1: op 4/1)
Toi Toi (IRE) (11/1: 7/1-12/1)

T/Jkpt: Not won; £3,977.35 to Doncaster 21/3/97. T/Plpt: £52.40 (594.13 Tckts). T/Qdpt: £5.40 (348.11 Tckts) WG

FLEMINGTON (Melbourne, Australia) (L-H) (Good)
Monday March 10th

437a AUSTRALIAN CUP (Gp 1) (3-Y.O+)

1m 2f £382,009.00

		SP	RR	SF
Octagonal (NZ) (JHawkes,Australia) **5-9-0** SDye ...—	**1**		115	—
Gold City (NZ) (RAJohnson,Australia) **6-8-13** SKing ...hd	**2**		114	—
Juggler (AUS) (MrsGWaterhouse,Australia) **5-9-2** GBoss ...s.h	**3**		117	—
Istidaad (USA) (PHayes,Australia) **5-9-2** BThomson ...hd	**4**		117	—
				10 Rn

2m 1.0 OWNER Woodlands Stud Syndicate BRED Mrs J. A. and Mr P. Hogan
Juggler (AUS) did not enhance his credentials for the Dubai World Cup with this performance.

0409a-NAD AL SHEBA (Dubai, UAE) (L-H) (Fast)
Thursday March 13th

438a HH SHEIKH MAKTOUM BIN RASHID AL MAKTOUM CHALLENGE (RND 3) (Listed) (4-Y.O+)

4-30 (4-40) **1m 2f (Dirt)** £16,155.00 (£8,077.00: £4,846.00: £3,231.00)

			SP	RR	SF
309a*	**Kammtarra (USA)** (SbinSuroor,UAE) **4-8-11** LDettori ...—	**1**		112	—
	Tamhid (USA) (KPMcLaughlin,UAE) **4-8-11** RHills ...1½	**2**		110	—
	Learmont (USA) (ECharpy,UAE) **7-8-11b[1]** WJSupple ...7	**3**		98	—
408a[3]	**Gothenberg (IRE)** (MJohnston) **4-8-11** JWeaver ...1	**4**		97	—
					5 Rn

2m 3.83 OWNER Mr Saeed Maktoum Al Maktoum BRED Gainsborough Farm Inc.
309a* Kammtarra (USA) put up yet another useful performance to enhance his chances of making it into the line-up for the Dubai World Cup. Racing in fourth, he made progress to go second over two furlongs out and was then ridden out to lead inside the final furlong.
408a Gothenberg (IRE) tried to make it a fast pace. He was headed three furlongs out and looked to be weakening, but he stayed on again close home.

SAINT-CLOUD (France) (L-H) (Soft)
Saturday March 15th

439a PRIX EXBURY (Gp 3) (4-Y.O+)
2-50 (2-51) **1m 2f** £24,691.00 (£8,979.00: £4,489.00)

Horse	Dist	Pos	SP	RR	SF
Nero Zilzal (USA) (ELellouche,France) **4-8-9** OPeslier	—	1		114	—
Le Destin (FR) (PDemercastel,France) **4-8-11** TGillet	½	2		115	—
Thames (FR) (LAudon,France) **6-8-9** PCostanzo	s.nk	3		113	—
Prince of My Heart (BWHills) **4-8-11** MHills (btn nearly 3l)		7		—	—

9 Rn

2m 11.5 (8.00) P-M 2.80F: 1.40F 2.30F 2.30F (13.80F) OWNER Mr Osvaldo Pedroni BRED Foxfield
Nero Zilzal (USA) was ridden to perfection here. Striking the front inside the final one hundred yards, he kept on well from the fast finishing runner-up.
Prince of My Heart, attempting to make all the running, tired on this soft ground in the straight, but put up a good performance with this effort.

COLOGNE (Germany) (R-H) (Heavy)
Sunday March 16th

440a TNT EXPRESS-AUFGALOPP (Listed) (4-Y.O+)
4-00 (4-04) **1m 3f** £12,500.00 (£5,303.00: £3,220.00) GOING: Not Established

Horse	Dist	Pos	SP	RR	SF
Leconte (GER) (MWeber,Germany) **6-9-2** TMundry	—	1		104	—
Ocean Sea (USA) (BSchutz,Germany) **4-9-2** AStarke	½	2		104	—
Try Again (GER) (AWohler,Germany) **6-9-0** ABoschert	hd	3		101	—
Woodren (USA) (RGuest) **4-8-5** PBloomfield (btn 16¼l)		7		—	—

9 Rn

2m 25.7 (15.70) CSF 1314DM TOTE 276DM: 41DM 23DM 21DM OWNER Frau C & H Segieth BRED Gestut Etzean
Woodren (USA), having her first run for Rae Guest after moving from John Oxx's yard, raced in mid-division and was fourth entering the straight. Unfortunately, she was unable to go with the pace on the heavy going.

0430-DONCASTER (L-H) (Good to firm)
Friday March 21st
Race 3 hand timed
WEATHER: Sunny periods WIND: alm nil

58+ 52 57 55

441 BAWTRY MAIDEN (S) STKS (2-Y.O) (Class F) (55)
1-30 (1-32) **5f** £2,511.00 (£696.00: £333.00) Stalls: High GOING minus 0.36 sec per fur (F)

Horse	Dist	Pos	SP	RR	SF
Jackerin (IRE) (BSRothwell) **2-9-0** MFenton(9) (lengthy: dwlt: led after 1f: rdn & jst hld on)	—	1	6/1	63	11
Lord Smith (WGMTurner) **2-9-0** TSprake(5) (leggy: unf: a.p: sustained chal ins fnl f: jst failed)	hd	2	7/4 1	63	11
Pink Ticket (PDEvans) **2-8-9** JFEgan(1) (small: lt-f: led 1f: ev ch tl unable qckn fnl f)	1¾	3	9/1	52	—
Hopefully (MRChannon) **2-8-9** TQuinn(3) (small: prom: ev ch over 1f out: one pce)	2	4	7/1	46	—
Who Nose (IRE) (BJMeehan) **2-9-0** MTebbutt(6) (leggy: unf: chsd ldrs: no hdwy fnl 2f)	2	5	7/2 2	44	—
I'm Not Sure (JBerry) **2-8-9** GCarter(4) (cmpt: bit bkwd: unruly s: s.i.s: sn prom: wknd qckly over 1f out: t.o)	6	6	5/1 3	20	—
Sipping Soda (KTIvory) **2-8-6**(3) MartinDwyer(7) (lt-f: unf: s.s: a outpcd: t.o)	3½	7	20/1	9	—
Valslastchance (NTinkler) **2-9-0** KimTinkler(2) (cmpt: bit bkwd: s.i.s: a outpcd: t.o)	2	8	20/1	8	—
Racing Surveyor (MWEasterby) **2-8-9** DaleGibson(8) (neat: sn wl outpcd: a bhd: t.o)	4	9	25/1	—	—

(SP 125.4%) **9 Rn**

61.82 secs (3.42) CSF £16.43 TOTE £8.40: £1.70 £1.10 £2.70 (£7.90) Trio £20.10 OWNER Mr J. B. Young (MALTON) BRED Golden Vale Stud
Bt in 10,000 gns
Jackerin (IRE), a half-brother to winning stayer Bean King, looks the type to improve as he strengthens up, and the fact that he proved costly to retain would suggest other people also think along those lines. (6/1: 10/1-5/1)
Lord Smith, who is almost a month short of his second birthday, answered his jockey's every call and only just failed to peg back the winner. He will win in this company, but it may be wise not to over-do him at this early stage of his career. (7/4)
Pink Ticket, a very lean-looking filly, who has still to reach her second birthday, showed plenty of speed and had every chance until failing to quicken late on. (9/1: 8/1-12/1)
Hopefully, a small lightly-made filly, who was a late foal, pressed the principals until failing to find anything extra when the dash to the line developed. (7/1: 4/1-8/1)
Who Nose (IRE) looks to need time, and as he is still five weeks short of his second birthday will come into his own later on. (7/2)
I'm Not Sure comes from a good winning family, but she proved a real handful both before the start and also in the stalls, and weakened quickly after racing prominently for over three furlongs. (5/1: op 3/1)

442 TOWN MOOR H'CAP (0-90) (4-Y.O+) (Class C)
2-05 (2-08) **2m 2f** £5,352.55 (£1,596.40: £761.70: £344.35) Stalls: High GOING minus 0.36 sec per fur (F)

Prev	Horse	Dist	Pos	SP	RR	SF
400⁴	**Onefourseven (57)** (JLEyre) **4-7-11** TWilliams(3) (hld up: hdwy ½-wy: led over 1f out: sn hdd: rallied to ld wl ins fnl f)	—	1	9/2 2	71	30
419²	**Noufari (FR) (68)** (RHollinshead) **6-8-11**(3) FLynch(1) (lw: a.p: led 1f out: sn rdn: hdd fnl 100y)	1¼	2	11/2 3	81	46
272*	**Master Foodbroker (IRE) (51)** (WJMusson) **9-7-11b** JQuinn(4) (s.s: wl bhd tl styd on wl fnl 3f)	8	3	8/1	57	22
	Upper Mount Clair (71) (CEBrittain) **7-9-3** MRoberts(5) (led: qcknd over 3f out: hdd & wknd over 1f out)	¾	4	11/1	76	41
	Invest Wisely (75) (MDHammond) **5-9-7** JFortune(8) (chsd ldrs: rdn 8f out: lost pl 4f out)	8	5	10/1	73	38
	Inchcailloch (IRE) (78) (JSKing) **8-9-7**(3) RHavlin(2) (bit bkwd: hld up: hdwy ent st: wknd over 2f out)	4	6	8/1	72	37
	Brumon (IRE) (57) (DMoffatt) **6-8-0v**(3) DarrenMoffatt(10) (b: hld up & bhd: effrt 7f out: wknd 4f out)	½	7	16/1	51	16
55⁶	**Evezio Rufo (57)** (NPLittmoden) **5-7-12**(5)ow1 ADaly(7) (chsd ldrs: drvn along ½-wy: wknd 5f out)	1¼	8	33/1	50	14

Magic Combination (IRE) (85) (BJCurley) **4-9-11** LDettori(6) (hld up: smooth hdwy to chse ldr over 3f out: rdn & wknd over 2f out) ....s.h **9** 11/4[1] 78 37
Thaljanah (IRE) (82) (BSmart) **5-10-0** RCochrane(9) (bit bkwd: plld hrd: prom tl wknd over 3f out) 4 **10** 20/1 71 36
(SP 113.5%) **10 Rn**

3m 57.66 (5.66) CSF £26.05 CT £173.02 TOTE £5.40: £1.80 £1.60 £2.20 (£10.80) Trio £32.00 OWNER Mr J. Roundtree (HAMBLETON) BRED Peter Storey
WEIGHT FOR AGE 4yo-6lb

400 Onefourseven, sharpened up with a run on the All-Weather earlier in the month, was able to take advantage of his substantial weight advantage to shake off the persistent runner-up in the final hundred yards. (9/2)
419 Noufari (FR) has only ever won on the All-Weather, but he gave his all here and was maybe a shade unfortunate to be worried out of it nearing the line. (11/2)
272* Master Foodbroker (IRE) has a habit of trying to do it the hard way, but on ground as lively as this to win from where he was entering the straight would have been something of a miracle. (8/1)
Upper Mount Clair, winner of this event two years ago, did not look fully wound up, but she made sure it would be a true test of stamina, and was only forced to give best inside the distance. This should put an edge on her. (11/1)
Invest Wisely, successful over hurdles in December, was being bustled along a mile out and she began to drop away entering the straight. (10/1)
Inchcailloch (IRE), turned out looking a picture but carrying condition after a three-month break, was inclined to run in snatches, but had had enough halfway up the straight. There is no doubting he will be back. (8/1: op 5/1)
Magic Combination (IRE), fit from hurdling, acts well on this ground but he has not yet won at two miles, and although he was cantering when cruising up to deliver his challenge, he went out like a light when pressure was applied. (11/4)

443 MANELINE-SOLOCOMB H'CAP (0-90) (3-Y.O+) (Class C)

2-35 (2-39) **6f** £6,301.55 (£1,888.40: £907.70: £417.35) Stalls: High GOING minus 0.36 sec per fur (F)

SP RR SF

394[3] **Kira (66)** (JLEyre) **7-8-4** RLappin(10) (b: b.hind: racd centre: led ½-wy: qcknd clr 1f out: eased nr fin) ....— **1** 12/1[3] 80+ 41
394[6] **Safio (66)** (ABailey) **4-8-4** DWright(13) (a.p stands' side: kpt on fnl f: no ch w wnr) 2½ **2** 33/1 73 34
Sea-Deer (81) (CADwyer) **8-9-5** RCochrane(17) (lw: racd stands' side: gd hdwy appr fnl f: fin wl) ....nk **3** 6/1[1] 88 49
394[7] **So Intrepid (IRE) (75)** (JMBradley) **7-8-13** PatEddery(9) (lw: hdwy wl over 1f out: hrd rdn: r.o) ....hd **4** 12/1[3] 81 42
357[5] **Daawe (USA) (75)** (MrsVAAconley) **6-8-13** MDeering(8) (s.i.s: hdwy over 1f out: kpt on wl towards fin) 1½ **5** 14/1 77 38
394[2] **Bold Effort (FR) (89)** (KOCunningham-Brown) **5-9-13v** TQuinn(12) (racd centre: chsd ldrs: rdn & one pce fnl f) ....hd **6** 14/1 91 52
Garnock Valley (82) (JBerry) **7-9-6** GCarter(16) (racd stands' side: r.o fnl 2f: nvr nrr) 1¼ **7** 14/1 81 42
397[2] **Cretan Gift (85)** (NPLittmoden) **6-9-9v** TGMcLaughlin(7) (hdwy 2f out: hrd rdn: nt pce to chal) ....¾ **8** 9/1[2] 82 43
Barato (68) (MrsJRRamsden) **6-8-6** JFortune(11) (lw: b.hind: racd centre: sn chsng ldrs: wknd over 1f out) ..1¼ **9** 16/1 61 22
Jo Mell (84) (TDEasterby) **4-9-8** MBirch(15) (racd stands' side: in tch 4f) ....s.h **10** 25/1 77 38
254* **Mansab (USA) (68)** (PGMurphy) **4-8-6** SDrowne(22) (racd stands' side: w ldrs over 3f) ....hd **11** 6/1[1] 61 22
Miss Waterline (66) (PDEvans) **4-8-4** JFEgan(18) (s.i.s: outpcd) 1 **12** 25/1 56 17
Mindrace (66) (KTIvory) **4-8-1**(3) MartinDwyer(14) (w ldrs stands' side 4f) ....nk **13** 33/1 56 17
Sir Joey (USA) (85) (PGMurphy) **8-9-9** DHarrison(19) (racd stands' side: chsd ldrs 4f) ....nk **14** 20/1 74 35
Charlie Sillett (84) (BWHills) **5-9-8** MHills(6) (racd far side: nvr nr to chal) ....s.h **15** 20/1 73 34
Lord High Admiral (CAN) (90) (MJHeaton-Ellis) **9-10-0** MRoberts(4) (led to ½-wy: wknd & eased over 1f out)2 **16** 25/1 73 34
342* **Sense of Priority (61)** (DNicholls) **8-7-6**(7) IonaWands(1) (w ldrs far side over 3f) ....hd **17** 16/1 44 5
Weetman's Weigh (IRE) (76) (RHollinshead) **4-9-0** LDettori(3) (lw: outpcd) ....s.h **18** 14/1 59 20
Lennox Lewis (74) (APJarvis) **5-8-12** WJO'Connor(20) (spd stands' side over 3f) ....nk **19** 25/1 56 17
Kildee Lad (80) (APJones) **7-9-4** TSprake(2) (nvr gng pce of ldrs) ....nk **20** 20/1 61 22
Attarikh (IRE) (72) (MrsALMKing) **4-8-7**(3) FLynch(5) (prom far side tl ½-wy) 1 **21** 33/1 51 12
Tiler (IRE) (82) (MJohnston) **5-9-6** JWeaver(21) (racd stands' side: prom over 3f) ....½ **22** 14/1 59 20
(SP 137.5%) **22 Rn**

1m 12.2 (1.20) CSF £348.78 CT £2,435.13 TOTE £13.70: £3.00 £28.90 £1.70 £3.30 (£385.50) Trio £1,816.80 OWNER Mr J. E. Wilson (HAMBLETON) BRED J. S. Bell

394 Kira, winner of six races last season, won this competitive event in a common canter, and on this showing she is some way ahead of the Handicapper. (12/1)
394 Safio gave notice that he is returning to form with his best performance for quite a long time, and although he is flattered to finish as close as he did to the winner, a repeat could see him going one better. (33/1)
Sea-Deer, the gamble of the race, invariably runs best when fresh, but did not find top gear until far too late. On the strength of this good effort, he should not have too much trouble in recovering losses. (6/1)
So Intrepid (IRE), given the full Eddery treatment, did not fail for the want of trying, and on easier ground will soon show that he retains all of his ability. (12/1)
357 Daawe (USA), usually at his best in the first part of the year, was doing some sterling work in the closing stages, and he will soon make his mark. (14/1)
394 Bold Effort (FR), much better suited to an easier surface nowadays, performed with credit under a welter burden, and he is ready to strike when conditions come in his favour. (14/1)
Garnock Valley comes to hand early, but he found things happening to quickly for him this time, and he was only finding his stride when it was all over. (14/1)

444 WORTHINGTON SPRING MILE H'CAP (4-Y.O+) (Class B)

3-10 (3-12) **1m (straight)** £15,790.00 (£4,720.00: £2,260.00: £1,030.00) Stalls: Low GOING minus 0.36 sec per fur (F)

SP RR SF

Artful Dane (IRE) (72) (MJHeaton-Ellis) **5-9-1v** MRoberts(6) (lw: racd centre: chsd ldrs: led wl over 1f out: all out) ....— **1** 10/1[2] 85 53
398[5] **Shinerolla (77)** (CParker) **5-9-6** DRMcCabe(14) (hld up: hdwy centre 2f out: rdn & r.o wl cl home) ....¾ **2** 8/1[1] 89 57
Sharp Shuffle (IRE) (71) (RHannon) **4-9-0** PatEddery(5) (swtg: hld up in tch: hdwy to chal wl over 1f out: hrd rdn: r.o) ....hd **3** 10/1[2] 82 50
Sandmoor Chambray (81) (TDEasterby) **6-9-10** MBirch(17) (racd stands' side: hdwy 2f out: hrd rdn fnl f: nt pce to chal) 1¼ **4** 14/1 90 58
1[9] **High Premium (81)** (RAFahey) **9-9-10** ACulhane(9) (led centre to ½-wy: one pce appr fnl f) 3½ **5** 12/1 83 51
Night Dance (80) (KAMorgan) **5-9-2**(7) RFfrench(7) (w ldrs centre: led ½-wy tl wl over 1f out) 1¼ **6** 20/1 79 47
Smarter Charter (75) (MrsLStubbs) **4-9-4** KFallon(8) (chsd ldrs centre over 6f) 1¼ **7** 14/1 72 40

Form	Horse	Dist	Pos	SP	RR	SF
365^{5}	**Night Wink (USA) (81)** (GLMoore) **5-9-7**(3) MartinDwyer(23) (led stands' side over 5f: wknd appr fnl f)	½	**8**	20/1	77	45
254^{6}	**Barrel of Hope (73)** (JLEyre) **5-9-2b** TWilliams(13) (racd stands' side tl wknd wl over 1f out)	¾	**9**	20/1	67	35
376^{9}	**Cashmere Lady (70)** (JLEyre) **5-8-13** RLappin(11) (chsd ldrs centre over 6f)	hd	**10**	20/1	64	32
396^{5}	**Suez Tornado (IRE) (75)** (EJAlston) **4-9-4** JFortune(10) (hrd rdn & styd on fnl 2f: nvr nrr)	¾	**11**	10/1^{2}	68	36
	Therhea (IRE) (78) (BRMillman) **4-9-7** TSprake(3) (chsd ldrs far side 5f)	nk	**12**	25/1	70	38
	La Volta (72) (JGFitzGerald) **4-9-1** JWeaver(4) (chsd ldrs far side 6f)	½	**13**	16/1	63	31
396^{4}	**Zurs (IRE) (80)** (MissGayKelleway) **4-9-9** DHolland(12) (swtg: racd centre: w ldrs over 5f)	1¼	**14**	11/1^{3}	69	37
365^{4}	**At Liberty (IRE) (77)** (RHannon) **5-9-6** DaneO'Neill(2) (nvr trbld ldrs)	2	**15**	25/1	62	30
	Royal Result (USA) (80) (TDBarron) **4-9-9** DHarrison(20) (chsd ldrs stands' side tl wknd wl over 1f out)	1¼	**16**	14/1	62	30
	Maple Bay (IRE) (72) (BEllison) **8-8-10**(5) PRoberts(1) (racd far side: n.d)	nk	**17**	33/1	53	21
	Proud Monk (73) (GLMoore) **4-9-2** SWhitworth(22) (racd stands' side: a in rr)	1¾	**18**	25/1	51	19
398^{6}	**Caudillo (IRE) (80)** (MrsPNDutfield) **4-9-9** AProcter(19) (outpcd)	nk	**19**	33/1	57	25
	Knobbleeneeze (65) (MRChannon) **7-8-8v** LDettori(21) (lw: racd stands' side: n.d)	1	**20**	14/1	40	8
398^{8}	**Duke Valentino (58)** (RHollinshead) **5-8-1** JQuinn(15) (swtg: racd stands' side: a bhd)	4	**21**	16/1	25	—
369^{10}	**Three Weeks (60)** (WRMuir) **4-7-12**(5) JBramhill(16) (racd stands' side: a bhd)	5	**22**	33/1	17	—
	Crystal Heights (FR) (70) (RJO'Sullivan) **9-8-13** SSanders(18) (b: s.s: racd stands' side: a bhd)	4	**23**	20/1	19	—

(SP 137.0%) **23 Rn**

1m 38.76 (1.56) CSF £71.78 CT £786.48 TOTE £13.70: £3.90 £2.60 £2.20 £4.50 (£37.00) Trio £111.20 OWNER S P Lansdown Racing (WROUGHTON) BRED R. A. Keogh

Artful Dane (IRE) had to work to strike the front just inside the quarter-mile marker but, once there, he was always getting the better of the hard-ridden Sharp Shuffle, and also had too much pace for the strong-finishing favourite. He now goes for the Newbury Spring Cup. (10/1)

398 Shinerolla has only ever won over the stiff mile at Pontefract, and on a track as flat as this, he could never quicken enough to throw down a serious challenge. (8/1)

Sharp Shuffle (IRE) appeared to get tapped for toe when about to deliver his challenge entering the final quarter mile, but he renewed his effort once switched, only to find the winner in no mood to give best. He should not be long in making amends. (10/1)

Sandmoor Chambray stuck on willingly under a very strong ride, but just lacked that bit extra to get to terms. This was a very promising start to the season, and he should soon be paying his way. (14/1)

1 High Premium, in the action all the way, is not quite so effective when the ground rides so fast, and younger rivals had the legs of him when the battle really got under way. He is no back number yet. (12/1)

Night Dance, a winner over hurdles in January, had more use made of him here, and was only shaken off inside the distance. (20/1)

Smarter Charter, sure to strip fitter for the run, only began to feel the strain below the distance, and he should be worth keeping in mind from now on. (14/1)

445 P & J FOODS MAIDEN STKS (3-Y.O) (Class D)

3-40 (3-42) **1m 2f 60y** £3,687.50 (£1,100.00: £525.00: £237.50) Stalls: Low GOING minus 0.36 sec per fur (F)

Horse	Dist	Pos	SP	RR	SF
Mithak (USA) (BWHills) **3-9-0** MHills(5) (lw: chsd ldrs: shkn up 3f out: led ins fnl f: sn clr)	—	**1**	11/4^{2}	83+	52
Nambucca (MrsJCecil) **3-8-9** KDarley(6) (leggy: unf: scope: chsd ldr: led over 3f out tl hdd & no ex ins fnl f)	4	**2**	11/1	72	41
Heritage (JHMGosden) **3-9-0** LDettori(3) (w'like: leggy: chsd ldrs: rdn to chal 2f out: one pce appr fnl f)	2½	**3**	8/13^{1}	73	42
One For Baileys (MJohnston) **3-9-0** JWeaver(8) (led tl over 3f out: sn rdn: wknd)	1	**4**	8/1^{3}	71	40
Swiftway (KWHogg) **3-9-0** DeanMcKeown(2) (chsd ldrs tl outpcd ent st: kpt on appr fnl f)	1¾	**5**	33/1	69	38
Rare Talent (MRChannon) **3-9-0** PaulEddery(1) (w'like: s.s: hld up: sme hdwy fnl 2f: nvr nrr)	½	**6**	20/1	68	37
Manileno (JHetherton) **3-9-0** NKennedy(4) (hld up: bhd fnl 4f: t.o)	dist	**7**	50/1	—	—
Ile de Librate (RJO'Sullivan) **3-9-0** AProcter(7) (lengthy: unf: hld up: a in rr: t.o fnl 3f)	1½	**8**	33/1	—	—

(SP 120.6%) **8 Rn**

2m 9.99 (2.19) CSF £28.58 TOTE £3.40: £1.10 £1.70 £1.10 (£13.80) OWNER Mr Hamdan Al Maktoum (LAMBOURN) BRED Dr Louis Aitken and J. L. Mamakes

Mithak (USA) was highly tried on both his outings as a juvenile, but he ran with promise and, readily outpacing his rivals in the latter stages on this occasion, will now take his chance in the Group Three Chester Vase. (11/4)

Nambucca, a scopey half-sister to a couple of middle-distance winners, who ran with her tongue tied, could not match the winner for pace inside the final furlong, but she gave notice that she will be one to beat now that she has had this airing. (11/1)

Heritage threw down a determined challenge entering the final quarter-mile, but could not get the better of Nambucca, and had shot his bolt inside the distance. This run should put an edge on him. (8/13)

One For Baileys, settled down in the lead, was forced to give best soon after straightening up, and from then on he was fighting a lost cause. (8/1)

Swiftway looked certain to drop away when outpaced on the home turn, but he was coming back for more at the finish. If lowered in class there could be a race in him. (33/1)

Rare Talent, flat-footed as the stalls opened, was out with the washing until staying on steadily inside the last quarter-mile. (20/1)

446 MEXBOROUGH MAIDEN STKS (3-Y.O) (Class D)

4-10 (4-11) **7f** £3,720.00 (£1,110.00: £530.00: £240.00) Stalls: High GOING minus 0.36 sec per fur (F)

Horse	Dist	Pos	SP	RR	SF
Zaretski (82) (CEBrittain) **3-9-0** MRoberts(2) (mde all: hung lft fr ½-wy: r.o)	—	**1**	7/2^{3}	85	45
Titta Ruffo (BJMeehan) **3-9-0** MTebbutt(6) (s.i.s: bhd: hdwy over 2f out: r.o wl fnl f)	¾	**2**	5/2^{1}	83	43
Honourable (JWWatts) **3-9-0** WRyan(5) (w'like: leggy: scope: s.s: hdwy over 2f out: r.o wl fnl f)	1½	**3**	12/1	80	40
Highly Respected (IRE) (ABailey) **3-8-9** SSanders(3) (leggy: unf: bkwd: chsd ldrs: pushed along ½-wy: no imp fnl 2f)	1½	**4**	33/1	71	31
Compatibility (IRE) (JHMGosden) **3-9-0** LDettori(1) (bit bkwd: trckd wnr over 5f: sn wknd)	1½	**5**	4/1	73	33
Zaahir (IRE) (BWHills) **3-9-0** MHills(7) (b.hind: chsd ldrs: rdn 3f out: sn btn)	nk	**6**	3/1^{2}	72	32
Just Grand (IRE) (MJohnston) **3-9-0** JWeaver(4) (prom tl rdn & wknd over 2f out)	nk	**7**	7/1	72	32
Dorado Beach (BWHills) **3-8-6**(3) JDSmith(8) (hld up: plld hrd: lost tch ½-wy: t.o)	13	**8**	33/1	37	—

(SP 121.9%) **8 Rn**

1m 26.46 (1.96) CSF £12.47 TOTE £5.40: £1.50 £1.30 £2.70 (£9.70) OWNER Mr B. H. Voak (NEWMARKET) BRED West Lodge Stud

Zaretski, the most experienced member of the field, was allowed to take his chance in the Middle Park last term. He hung badly left in the closing stages, but was able to lengthen up to draw clear approaching the final furlong, and won this with a bit in hand. (7/2: op 6/1)

Titta Ruffo confirmed the promise shown on his only appearance in his first season, but may have trouble finding an opening until stepped up to a mile. (5/2)

Honourable, a half-brother to three winners, who has been gelded, is still hanging on to his winter coat. Last to exit from the stalls, he was beginning to realise what was required in the latter stages, and should certainly win races. (12/1: op 8/1)

Highly Respected (IRE), an unfurnished filly who moved badly to post, was off the bridle at halfway, but she stuck to her task, and will be all the wiser for the experience. (33/1)
Compatibility (IRE), put away after failing in a hot maiden at the Newmarket July meeting, has done well in the interim, but he looked to be carrying condition, and was not knocked about when he had blown up. He has plenty of time on his side. (4/1: 3/1-9/2)
Zaahir (IRE), who can be made fitter, was being nudged along soon after halfway and, failing to pick up, proved most disappointing. (3/1: op 7/4)
Just Grand (IRE) has not grown since last season, and he dropped away tamely from some way out. He might in time need a stiffer test, but as yet he is a disappointment. (7/1: 5/1-8/1)

T/Jkpt: Not won; £8,707.00 to Doncaster 22/3/97. T/Plpt: £135.90 (214.15 Tckts). T/Qdpt: £16.20 (148.66 Tckts) IM

0441-DONCASTER (L-H) (Good to firm)
Saturday March 22nd

WEATHER: Sunny WIND: mod half against

447 GREY FRIARS MAIDEN AUCTION STKS (2-Y.O) (Class D)
2-00 (2-02) **5f** £3,483.25 (£1,042.00: £499.50: £228.25) Stalls: High GOING minus 0.08 sec per fur (G)

Horse	Dist	Pos	SP	RR	SF
Rising of The Moon (IRE) (RHannon) **2-8-5** PatEddery(10) (unf: scope: a w ldrs: led 2f out: jst hld on)	—	**1**	7/2[1]	81	24
Classy Cleo (IRE) (RHannon) **2-8-3**ow2 DaneO'Neill(5) (cmpt: unf: a.p: hdwy over 1f out: r.o towards fin)	s.h	**2**	10/1	79	20
O' Higgins (IRE) (RBoss) **2-8-7** LDettori(11) (cmpt: cl up: effrt 2f out: kpt on)	2½	**3**	11/2[2]	75	18
Jim Dore (IRE) (APJarvis) **2-8-5** WRyan(13) (w'like: bit bkwd: chsd ldrs: outpcd 2f out: kpt on wl towards fin)	1¾	**4**	10/1	67	10
Oriel Girl (PDEvans) **2-8-1**ow3 JFEgan(9) (small: unf: b.nr fore: chsd ldrs: effrt 2f out: r.o one pce)	hd	**5**	9/1	63	3
Carol Grimes (JSMoore) **2-7-6**(7) RFfrench(6) (unf: led after 1f to 2f out: grad wknd)	2½	**6**	25/1	53	—
Captain Brady (IRE) (WGMTurner) **2-8-4**(5) DSweeney(4) (cmpt: unf: led 1f: chsd ldrs tl wknd appr fnl f)	¾	**7**	8/1	61	4
Banningham Blade (KTIvory) **2-7-9**(3) MartinDwyer(3) (unf: s.i.s: hdwy ½-wy: n.d)	1½	**8**	33/1	45	—
Livingstone (CADwyer) **2-8-4** DRMcCabe(2) (tall: sn drvn along: hdwy ½-wy: wknd over 1f out)	¾	**9**	11/2[2]	48	—
Satis (IRE) (MRChannon) **2-8-4** PaulEddery(8) (leggy: unf: s.i.s: sn in tch: wknd fnl 2f)	3	**10**	7/1[3]	39	—
Donna's Double (NTinkler) **2-8-7** KimTinkler(12) (w'like: leggy: dwlt: hdwy ½-wy: hung lft & sn wknd)	¾	**11**	33/1	39	—
Noble Saja (TDEasterby) **2-8-3** JQuinn(14) (lt-f: spd to ½-wy: wknd)	7	**12**	20/1	13	—
Mr Fund Switch (DNicholls) **2-7-10**(7) IonaWands(7) (neat: s.i.s: sn wl bhd)	6	**13**	25/1	—	—
Margaret's Dancer (CSmith) **2-8-4**ow1 AClark(1) (cmpt: unf: bit bkwd: s.s: a outpcd & wl bhd)	7	**14**	20/1	—	—
			(SP 127.9%)	**14 Rn**	

61.86 secs (3.46) CSF £34.91 TOTE £4.10: £2.30 £3.40 £2.10 (£15.80) Trio £23.70 OWNER Miss L. Regis (MARLBOROUGH) BRED Mrs M. L. Davis

Rising of The Moon (IRE), said to be in season, needed plenty of courage to hold on and will obviously improve for the experience. (7/2)
Classy Cleo (IRE), stable-companion of the winner, would have won in another stride. She will be all the better for this. (10/1)
O' Higgins (IRE), a sharp sort, had his chances but was short of toe late on. He may do better over further. (11/2: op 3/1)
Jim Dore (IRE), caused a few problems in the paddock, but gave plenty of encouragement in the race and looks one to side with. (10/1)
Oriel Girl is knee-high to the proverbial grasshopper, but she can go and a sharp track would suit. (9/1: 5/1-10/1)
Carol Grimes showed plenty of speed and should improve for this experience. (25/1)
Captain Brady (IRE) (8/1: op 5/1)
Livingstone, a very big colt to be out at this time of year, showed some ability. (11/2: 10/1-5/1)
Satis (IRE) (7/1: op 4/1)

448 MARCH H'CAP (0-85) (3-Y.O) (Class D)
2-30 (2-33) **7f** £4,110.00 (£1,230.00: £590.00: £270.00) Stalls: High GOING minus 0.08 sec per fur (G)

Last run	Horse	Dist	Pos	SP	RR	SF
	Share Delight (IRE) (70) (BWHills) **3-8-6** MHills(15) (hld up & bhd: hdwy 2f out: rdn to ld ins fnl f)	—	**1**	14/1	85	50
17[7]	**Jay-Owe-Two (IRE) (73)** (RMWhitaker) **3-8-9** PatEddery(3) (cl up: led over 1f out tl ins fnl f: nt qckn)	3	**2**	14/1	81	46
180[2]	**Nomore Mr Niceguy (80)** (EJAlston) **3-9-2** KFallon(1) (lw: a cl up: led 3f out tl over 1f out: kpt on)	¾	**3**	10/1	86	51
	Bollin Terry (67) (TDEasterby) **3-8-3** JCarroll(14) (sn pushed along: hdwy 2f out: styd on wl towards fin)	1½	**4**	16/1	70	35
	Sandbaggedagain (75) (MWEasterby) **3-8-11** TQuinn(22) (in tch: hdwy 2f out: kpt on)	hd	**5**	11/1	78	43
388[7]	**I Can't Remember (80)** (PDEvans) **3-9-2** JFEgan(6) (a chsng ldrs: kpt on same pce fnl 2f)	nk	**6**	14/1	82	47
307[8]	**A Breeze (76)** (DMorris) **3-8-12** NDay(20) (effrt ½-wy: styd on: nvr able to chal)	¾	**7**	25/1	76	41
	Mujova (IRE) (85) (RHollinshead) **3-9-4**(3) FLynch(11) (outpcd tl sme hdwy fnl 2f)	1¾	**8**	25/1	81	46
	Mungo Park (70) (MrsJRRamsden) **3-8-6** JFortune(5) (s.i.s: hdwy ½-wy: sn prom: wknd over 1f out)	hd	**9**	6/1[2]	66	31
	Rum Lad (67) (JJQuinn) **3-8-3** JQuinn(7) (mid div: effrt u.p 2½f out: no imp)	hd	**10**	25/1	63	28
	Jack Flush (IRE) (68) (BSRothwell) **3-8-4** MFenton(16) (outpcd & bhd ½-wy: n.d after)	nk	**11**	25/1	63	28
	Rude Awakening (82) (CWFairhurst) **3-9-4** RCochrane(13) (lw: hld up & bhd: hdwy over 2f out: nvr rchd ldrs)	s.h	**12**	20/1	77	42
	Rainbow Rain (USA) (80) (MJohnston) **3-9-2** JWeaver(8) (swtg: bhd: hdwy over 2f out: sn rdn: no imp)	½	**13**	11/2[1]	74	39
	Ivory Dawn (66) (KTIvory) **3-7-13**(3) MartinDwyer(12) (chsd ldrs 5f: wknd)	nk	**14**	33/1	59	24
	Fullopep (73) (MrsMReveley) **3-8-9** KDarley(9) (bit bkwd: hld up & bhd: shkn up over 2f out: n.d)	2½	**15**	20/1	61	26
	Levelled (72) (MRChannon) **3-8-8** RPerham(18) (chsd ldrs tl wknd fnl 2f)	1½	**16**	20/1	56	21
420*	**Tinkerbell (75)** (WRMuir) **3-8-11v** JReid(19) (a chsng ldrs: effrt over 2f out: r.o one pce)	1½	**17**	14/1	56	21
155[5]	**Ultra Boy (78)** (PCHaslam) **3-9-0** SDrowne(21) (dwlt: racd alone stands' side: n.d)	hd	**18**	20/1	59	24
	Double Gold (77) (BJMeehan) **3-8-13** MTebbutt(10) (prom 4f: grad lost pl)	1½	**19**	20/1	54	19
12*	**Effervescence (83)** (RHannon) **3-9-5** DaneO'Neill(4) (lw: outpcd fnl 3f)	1½	**20**	7/1[3]	57	22
377*	**La Dolce Vita (73)** (TDBarron) **3-8-2**(7) KimberleyHart(17) (led 4f: sn wknd)	½	**21**	14/1	46	11
	Blazing Castle (81) (WGMTurner) **3-8-10**(7) DMcGaffin(2) (nt grwn: w ldrs 5f: wknd qckly)	3	**22**	25/1	47	12
				(SP 144.8%)	**22 Rn**	

1m 27.35 (2.85) CSF £173.54 CT £1,949.67 TOTE £23.00: £4.90 £2.90 £1.80 £12.60 (£141.70) Trio £1,011.50 OWNER Mr A. L. R. Morton (LAMBOURN) BRED Mrs Josephine McAuley

Share Delight (IRE) had his tongue tied down for the first time and, despite carrying his head at an angle, he produced a useful turn of foot to settle it. (14/1)
17 Jay-Owe-Two (IRE), who had beaten the winner out of sight on the All-Weather surface, tried hard again but was well second best. (14/1)
180 Nomore Mr Niceguy has been running consistently well on the All-Weather and put up another decent show, only to be tapped for speed late on. (10/1)

Bollin Terry is obviously learning and took time to get going, but there was plenty to like about the way he finished. (16/1)
Sandbaggedagain proved frustrating last season. He ran well here and, if the key can be found, he certainly has the ability. (11/1)
I Can't Remember was extremely busy last season, running nineteen times and winning four. By the look of things he is as enthusiastic as ever, and may well need a bit further than this. (14/1)
A Breeze, at his second attempt at this trip, was keeping on well at the end to suggest that he gets it. (25/1)
Mungo Park, looking likely to be all the better for this, came from behind, only to blow up approaching the last furlong. (6/1)
Rainbow Rain (USA), who sweated badly beforehand, proved disappointing in the race. (11/2)

449 GAINSBOROUGH SPRING CONDITIONS STKS (3-Y.O) (Class C)

3-00 (3-03) **1m (straight)** £5,840.20 (£2,171.80: £1,050.90: £439.50: £184.75: £82.85) Stalls: High GOING minus 0.08 sec per fur (G)

				SP	RR	SF
	Musalsal (IRE) (BWHills) **3-8-13** MHills(2) (lw: plld hrd early: bhd: hdwy to disp ld 1½f out: r.o wl u.p)	—	**1**	13/2[3]	110	62
	Handsome Ridge (JHMGosden) **3-8-13** LDettori(10) (trckd ldrs: hdwy to disp ld 1½f out: rdn & r.o wl)	s.h	**2**	4/1[1]	110	62
	Craigievar (95) (JRFanshawe) **3-8-11** DHarrison(1) (lw: a.p: led 2f out: sn hdd: r.o)	5	**3**	9/2[2]	98	50
227*	**Hayes Way (IRE)** (TGMills) **3-9-1** SSanders(8) (lw: in tch: rdn over 2f out: kpt on wl)	nk	**4**	20/1	101	53
	Poseidon (MRChannon) **3-9-3** PaulEddery(11) (w'like: scope: in tch: hdwy & ch over 2f out: nt qckn)	s.h	**5**	16/1	103	55
	Pelham (IRE) (97) (RHannon) **3-9-3** DaneO'Neill(5) (prom: effrt over 2f out: kpt on one pce)	1	**6**	16/1	101	53
396*	**Foot Battalion (IRE) (90)** (RHollinshead) **3-8-10**(3) FLynch(12) (bhd: hdwy 3f out: no imp fnl 2f)	2½	**7**	20/1	92	44
388[3]	**Millroy (USA) (86)** (PAKelleway) **3-8-11** KFallon(7) (outpcd & bhd: hdwy 3f out: nvr rchd ldrs)	1¾	**8**	25/1	87	39
	Polar Flight (90) (MJohnston) **3-8-11** JWeaver(6) (lw: cl up tl wknd fnl 2f)	1¼	**9**	7/1	84	36
	Indian Spark (WGMTurner) **3-9-1** TSprake(3) (w ldrs: led 3f out to 2f out: grad wknd)	2½	**10**	10/1	83	35
	Jeffrey Anotherred (92) (KMcAuliffe) **3-8-11** JFEgan(4) (w ldrs tl outpcd fnl 2f)	3	**11**	20/1	73	25
	Danetime (IRE) (97) (NACallaghan) **3-8-13** PatEddery(9) (led 5f: grad lost pl fnl 2½f)	½	**12**	4/1[1]	74	26
				(SP 123.0%)	**12 Rn**	

1m 40.0 (2.80) CSF £29.11 TOTE £8.00: £3.00 £1.40 £2.00 (£13.10) Trio £18.00 OWNER Maktoum Al Maktoum (LAMBOURN) BRED Gainsborough Stud Management Ltd

Musalsal (IRE) did really well here considering how hard he pulled early on. There is obviously plenty of improvement in him. (13/2)
Handsome Ridge travelled well, and showed a good attitude under pressure which will bring its rewards. (4/1: 3/1-9/2)
Craigievar had his chances and kept answering his rider's calls, but probably met two useful opponents here. (9/2)
227* Hayes Way (IRE), a dual winner on the All-Weather at Lingfield, ran as though he is going to need a bit further than this on grass. (20/1)
Poseidon, a winner in Italy last year, ran pretty well and is likely to benefit from the outing. (16/1)
Pelham (IRE) was a good consistent sort last season, and looks to have trained on. (16/1)
Danetime (IRE) showed plenty of early speed and was then given an easy time when beaten. He should benefit from the kindness in due course. (4/1)

450 WORTHINGTON LINCOLN H'CAP (4-Y.O+) (Class B)

3-40 (3-41) **1m (straight)** £42,955.00 (£12,940.00: £6,270.00: £2,935.00) Stalls: High GOING minus 0.08 sec per fur (G)

				SP	RR	SF
398[4]	**Kuala Lipis (USA) (86)** (PFICole) **4-8-6** TQuinn(21) (prom: chal over 2f out: outpcd over 1f out: r.o wl to ld wl ins fnl f)	—	**1**	11/1[3]	99	66
	Hawksley Hill (IRE) (89) (MrsJRRamsden) **4-8-9** JFortune(6) (lw: hld up: hdwy 3f out: hrd rdn to chal wl ins fnl f: swvd rt: r.o)	s.h	**2**	7/1[1]	102	69
	Tumbleweed Ridge (85) (BJMeehan) **4-8-5b** MTebbutt(4) (lw: trckd ldrs gng wl: led over 2f out: qcknd clr over 1f out: hung lft: ct wl ins fnl f)	1	**3**	7/1[1]	96	63
376[8]	**Iamus (83)** (TDBarron) **4-8-3**[ow1] DHarrison(10) (bhd: hdwy over 2f out: styd on wl fnl f)	2½	**4**	50/1	89	55
	Kala Sunrise (86) (CSmith) **4-8-6** JFEgan(18) (a chsng ldrs: effrt over 2f out: kpt on wl fnl f)	¾	**5**	16/1	90	57
	Alamein (USA) (86) (WJHaggas) **4-8-6b**[ow1] KFallon(13) (lw: in tch: effrt & ch 2f out: nt qckn)	hd	**6**	12/1	90	56
	Sky Dome (IRE) (87) (MHTompkins) **4-8-4**(3) MHenry(23) (hld up: effrt 3f out: styd on: no imp)	hd	**7**	12/1	91	58
	Roving Minstrel (91) (BAMcMahon) **6-8-11** RCochrane(15) (lw: plld hrd: bhd: hdwy 3f out: sn chsng ldrs: nt qckn appr fnl f)	s.h	**8**	10/1[2]	95	62
	Hunters of Brora (IRE) (87) (JDBethell) **7-8-7**[ow1] JReid(17) (s.i.s: hdwy over 2f out: nvr rchd ldrs)	1½	**9**	25/1	88	54
396[2]	**Sabot (90)** (CWThornton) **4-8-10** DeanMcKeown(16) (hld up: n.m.r over 3f out: styd on: n.d)	¾	**10**	25/1	89	56
	Hazard a Guess (IRE) (84) (DNicholls) **7-7-11**(7) IonaWands(14) (lw: dwlt: hld up & bhd tl sme late hdwy)	hd	**11**	50/1	83	50
398[2]	**New Century (USA) (92)** (DNicholls) **5-8-12** AlexGreaves(9) (lw: trckd ldrs: effrt over 2f out: grad wknd)	½	**12**	11/1[3]	90	57
	Stone Ridge (IRE) (89) (RHannon) **5-8-9** DaneO'Neill(7) (trckd ldrs tl wknd fnl 2f)	¾	**13**	25/1	86	53
	La Petite Fusee (81) (RJO'Sullivan) **6-7-10**(5) JBramhill(3) (hld up: effrt ½-wy: n.d)	3	**14**	50/1	72	39
	Grand Musica (93) (IABalding) **4-8-13** LDettori(22) (hld up: effrt 3f out: nvr trbld ldrs)	2	**15**	12/1	80	47
	Whittle Rock (86) (MrsMReveley) **4-8-6** KDarley(8) (hld up: effrt 3f out: n.d)	hd	**16**	20/1	73	40
358[12]	**Carburton (82)** (JAGlover) **4-8-2b**[1] GCarter(5) (mde most tl hdd & wknd over 2f out)	1¾	**17**	20/1	65	32
	Russian Music (104) (MissGayKelleway) **4-9-10** DHolland(11) (hld up: effrt 3f out: n.d)	½	**18**	16/1	86	53
	Pusey Street Girl (85) (MRBosley) **4-8-5** RPerham(24) (prom stands' side tl wknd fnl 3f)	3½	**19**	50/1	60	27
	Neuwest (USA) (83) (NJHWalker) **5-8-3** CRutter(2) (lw: chsd ldrs: rdn 3f out: sn wknd)	d.h	**19**	25/1	58	25
131[6]	**Barossa Valley (IRE) (85)** (PButler) **6-8-0**(5)[ow3] DSweeney(12) (disp ld 2f: wknd qckly ½-wy)	2½	**21**	33/1	55	19
	Rockforce (85) (MRChannon) **5-8-5** PatEddery(20) (cl up 4f: wknd qckly & sn wl bhd)	6	**22**	20/1	43	10
343[2]	**Defined Feature (IRE) (90)** (DrJDScargill) **4-8-10** MHills(1) (outpcd & bhd fnl 3f)	5	**23**	33/1	38	5
396[3]	**Pater Noster (USA) (89)** (JohnHarris) **8-8-9** SSanders(19) (b: prom 5f)	4	**24**	40/1	29	—
				(SP 131.4%)	**24 Rn**	

1m 39.02 (1.82) CSF £66.75 CT £548.32 TOTE £11.90: £2.40 £2.80 £2.20 £15.00 (£52.90) Trio £82.30 OWNER H R H Sultan Ahmad Shah (WHATCOMBE) BRED Gallaghers Stud

398 Kuala Lipis (USA) is certainly a hard ride but he does respond to pressure and, although he has never won beyond a mile, he gives the impression that he should appreciate at least another furlong. (11/1)
Hawksley Hill (IRE) looks better than ever this season, but he showed again that he is a bit of a character by hanging badly into the whip. Had he won, he may well have lost this in the Stewards' room. (7/1)
Tumbleweed Ridge was stretching his stamina at this trip. He probably went for home too soon and did not help matters by hanging left, but is obviously in tremendous form and should soon find compensation. (7/1)
Iamus has changed stables and been gelded since last season and, judging by the way he finished, he has improved and may well need a bit further. (50/1)
Kala Sunrise looks in top form at present and, after getting outpaced at a vital stage, was keeping on really well at the end. (16/1)

Alamein (USA) had his chances but just failed to pick up at the business end and, although he looked well enough, he might well be all the better for this. (12/1)
Sky Dome (IRE) seems at his best when allowed to make it, and these tactics were not employed this time. (12/1)
Roving Minstrel did not help his cause by pulling hard early on, and in the circumstances ran quite well. (10/1)
Hunters of Brora (IRE) stays further than this, and was not helped by the steady early pace. (25/1)
396 Sabot, who is a bit of a character, got messed about here and, once he saw daylight, it was always too late. (25/1)
Hazard a Guess (IRE) never got into this, but ran really well and now looks likely to do better, especially over further. (50/1)

451 MIDLAND COPYING DONCASTER SHIELD CONDITIONS STKS (4-Y.O+) (Class B)

4-15 (4-15) **1m 4f** £7,309.00 (£2,701.00: £1,293.00: £525.00: £205.00: £77.00) Stalls: Low GOING minus 0.08 sec per fur (G)

				SP	RR	SF
	Sheer Danzig (IRE) (102) (RWArmstrong) **5-8-12** LDettori(4) (lw: trckd ldrs: hdwy to ld over 2f out: sn rdn clr & eased)	—	**1**	7/4 2	108+	76
	Wilawander (107) (BWHills) **4-8-10** MHills(6) (lw: b: trckd ldrs: led 3f out: sn hdd & no ch w wnr)	6	**2**	13/8 1	100	66
389[2]	**Major Change (88)** (MissGayKelleway) **5-8-12** DHolland(3) (cl up: led 6f out to 3f out: one pce)	3½	**3**	13/2 3	95	63
	Northern Drums (NMBabbage) **4-8-10** TSprake(5) (hld up: effrt 5f out: styd on: no imp)	¾	**4**	50/1	80 t	60
	Chai-Yo (JABOld) **7-8-12** GDuffield(1) (hld up: effrt over 4f out: sn btn)	5	**5**	10/1	74 t	56
	Desert Mountain (IRE) (90) (NACallaghan) **4-8-10** PatEddery(7) (led tl hdd 6f out: sn rdn & wknd)	8	**6**	8/1	63 t	43
				(SP 110.0%)		**6 Rn**

2m 32.14 (2.14) CSF £4.31 TOTE £2.30: £1.60 £1.40 (£2.00) OWNER Mr R. J. Arculli (NEWMARKET) BRED Mrs Max Morris
WEIGHT FOR AGE 4yo-2lb
Sheer Danzig (IRE) looked useful here and, the further they went, the better he got. (7/4)
Wilawander was a shade disappointing, getting well beaten after looking to be going strongly early in the straight. (13/8)
389 Major Change had plenty on here, but was fit from two runs already this year and ran as well as could be expected. (13/2)
Northern Drums looked to have an impossible task, but ran really well and probably spoilt a really good handicap mark. (50/1)
Chai-Yo raced too freely and then failed to pick up when asked a question. (10/1: 8/1-12/1)
Desert Mountain (IRE), who has taken well to hurdling, had little chance in this company. (8/1: 6/1-9/1)

452 CAMMIDGE TROPHY STKS (Listed) (3-Y.O+) (Class A)

4-45 (4-45) **6f** £12,274.50 (£3,666.00: £1,753.00: £796.50) Stalls: High GOING minus 0.08 sec per fur (G)

			SP	RR	SF
Royal Applause (108) (BWHills) **4-9-2** MHills(7) (lw: mde most: rdn & r.o wl fnl f)	—	**1**	6/4 1	115	65
Easy Dollar (106) (BGubby) **5-9-2b** AClark(4) (a chsng ldrs: kpt on fnl 2f: nt pce of wnr)	2	**2**	11/1	110	60
King of Peru (99) (APJarvis) **4-9-2** WJO'Connor(2) (in tch: hdwy 2f out: nt pce to chal)	1¾	**3**	25/1	105	55
Patsy Grimes (90) (JSMoore) **7-8-11** LDettori(5) (hld up: hdwy ½-wy: rdn & nt qckn appr fnl f)	s.h	**4**	20/1	100	50
Venture Capitalist (112) (DNicholls) **8-9-7** AlexGreaves(6) (hld up: effrt over 1f out: nt qckn)	1¾	**5**	6/1	105	55
Passion For Life (112) (GLewis) **4-9-7** PatEddery(1) (disp ld 4f: grad wknd)	¾	**6**	3/1 2	103	53
Warning Time (99) (BJMeehan) **4-9-2** MTebbutt(3) (lw: disp ld over 3f: wknd qckly)	11	**7**	20/1	69	19
Astrac (IRE) (106) (MissGayKelleway) **6-9-5** DHolland(8) (lw: chsd wnr: outpcd ½-wy: n.d after)	nk	**8**	11/2 3	71	21
			(SP 116.4%)		**8 Rn**

1m 13.01 (2.01) CSF £17.64 TOTE £2.30: £1.40 £2.40 £5.10 (£8.50) OWNER Maktoum Al Maktoum (LAMBOURN) BRED Gainsborough Stud Management Ltd
Royal Applause is obviously in good heart this year and won well, but there is plenty more needed if he is going to recapture his two-year-old form. (6/4)
Easy Dollar likes this fast ground, and kept responding to pressure, but just lacks a change of gear at that vital stage. (11/1: 8/1-12/1)
King of Peru may just find this trip too sharp for him these days, as he was putting his best work when it was all over. (25/1)
Patsy Grimes looked to have a lot to do in this company and in the circumstances ran pretty well. (20/1)
Venture Capitalist needs things to go just right, but he was always seeing too much daylight and that final kick was never there. (6/1)
Passion For Life was most disappointing here, dropping out tamely in the closing stages. (3/1: op 7/4)
Astrac (IRE) likes easier ground than this but it was still a poor effort. He has obviously not come to himself as yet. (11/2)

453 SELBY MAIDEN STKS (3-Y.O) (Class D)

5-15 (5-16) **6f** £3,525.00 (£1,050.00: £500.00: £225.00) Stalls: High GOING minus 0.08 sec per fur (G)

				SP	RR	SF
	Cadeaux Cher (79) (BWHills) **3-9-0** MHills(8) (trckd ldrs: smooth hdwy to ld 1f out: r.o)	—	**1**	5/1 2	82	41
	Mile High (MRChannon) **3-9-0** PatEddery(7) (lw: unruly s: disp ld tl hdd 1f out: kpt on u.p)	1¼	**2**	8/13 1	79	38
	Silent Miracle (IRE) (MBell) **3-8-9** MFenton(3) (bit bkwd: disp ld tl hdd 1f out: no ex)	nk	**3**	10/1	73	32
	Wild Sky (IRE) (MJHeaton-Ellis) **3-9-0** SDrowne(4) (a.p: one pce fnl 2f)	4	**4**	15/2 3	67	26
	Colway Ritz (JWWatts) **3-9-0** GDuffield(5) (w'like: b: dwlt: styd on fnl 2f: n.d)	1¼	**5**	14/1	64	23
	The Gay Fox (82) (BAMcMahon) **3-9-0** RCochrane(6) (chsd ldrs tl wknd over 1f out)	1½	**6**	15/2 3	60	19
	Prominent (MrsJRRamsden) **3-9-0** JFortune(2) (w'like: leggy: chsd ldrs: rn green & hung lft ½-wy: sn wknd)	8	**7**	12/1	39	—
412[7]	**Heathyard's Flight** (RHollinshead) **3-9-0** WRyan(1) (a bhd)	nk	**8**	50/1	38	—
				(SP 127.5%)		**8 Rn**

1m 14.56 (3.56) CSF £8.66 TOTE £4.90: £1.60 £1.10 £2.90 (£3.30) OWNER Mr N. N. Browne (LAMBOURN) BRED D. J. and Mrs Deer
Cadeaux Cher looked a bit of a monkey last season, but he did everything right here and won a shade cosily. (5/1: op 11/4)
Mile High gave problems before the start but still ran well, and gave the impression that he should appreciate further. (8/13)
Silent Miracle (IRE) looked likely to be all the better for this, but ran really well and would appear to be on the upgrade. (10/1)
Wild Sky (IRE), wearing a tongue-strap, was always handily placed, but looked short of a turn of foot when pressure was applied. (15/2)
Colway Ritz, clueless early on, showed ability as the race progressed and seems to have plenty scope for improvement. (14/1: 10/1-16/1)
The Gay Fox, with plenty of experience from last year, obviously needed this and failed to make any real impression. (15/2)
Prominent, a green and backward sort, just needs time. (12/1)

T/Jkpt: £11,387.40 (1 Tckts). T/Plpt: £93.20 (469.15 Tckts). T/Qdpt: £11.80 (254.86 Tckts) AA

0401-LINGFIELD (L-H) (Standard)
Monday March 24th
WEATHER: overcast WIND: almost nil

454 CAMDEN ROAD (S) H'CAP (0-60) (3-Y.O) (Class G)
2-20 (2-20) **1m 4f (Equitrack)** £1,984.50 (£547.00: £259.50) Stalls: Low GOING minus 0.52 sec per fur (FST)

				SP	RR	SF
314^{4}	**Kingsdown Trix (IRE) (55)** (GLMoore) **3-9-5** RPerham(3) (lw: led 8f out: clr over 2f out: easily)	—	1	5/6 1	63+	—
355^{4}	**Tracks of My Tears (49)** (WGMTurner) **3-8-13** TSprake(2) (hld up: chsd wnr over 4f out: rdn over 3f out: unable qckn)	3½	2	7/2 3	52	—
414^{*}	**Mirror Four Sport (57)** (MJohnston) **3-9-0**(7) KSked(1) (plld hrd: led 4f: one pce fnl 4f)	1¼	3	2/1 2	59	—

(SP 110.1%) **3 Rn**

2m 44.66 (14.66) CSF £3.58 TOTE £1.50 (£2.50) OWNER Mr David Allen (BRIGHTON) BRED Owen Bourke
No bid
314 Kingsdown Trix (IRE) was happier for the return to Equitrack, and had little more than an afternoon stroll, as he quickened up the tempo running down the hill and forged clear. He was eased down in the closing stages and was value for at least seven lengths. (5/6)
Tracks of My Tears moved into second place over half-a-mile from home, but had no hope with the winner in the last three furlongs. (7/2: op 9/4)
414* Mirror Four Sport failed to stay this trip last month, and took a ferocious hold as no-one wanted to lead and the three runners crawled. The reluctant leader, she was headed a mile out and could only plod on at one pace in the last four furlongs. There is still a big question mark as to whether she stays the trip as this race told us nothing. (2/1)

455 ST PIERS MEDIAN AUCTION MAIDEN STKS (3-Y.O) (Class F)
2-50 (2-51) **1m (Equitrack)** £2,277.00 (£627.00: £297.00) Stalls: High GOING minus 0.52 sec per fur (FST)

				SP	RR	SF
	Assume (USA) (JWHills) **3-9-0** DHolland(5) (lw: plld hrd: mde all: clr over 2f out: easily)	—	1	8/11 1	82+	32
	Here's To Howie (USA) (79) (RHannon) **3-9-0** DaneO'Neill(2) (chsd wnr: rdn 4f out: unable qckn)	7	2	2/1 2	68	18
	Farley Mount (LordHuntingdon) **3-9-0** DHarrison(4) (neat: s.s: outpcd: nvr nr to chal)	2½	3	100/30 3	63	13
395^{9}	**Master Bobby** (RBoss) **3-9-0** MTebbutt(1) (bhd fnl 6f: t.o)	30	4	16/1	3	—

(SP 120.2%) **4 Rn**

1m 39.76 (2.36) CSF £2.71 TOTE £1.50 (£1.40) OWNER Mr William Patterson (LAMBOURN) BRED Dr John A. Chandler
Assume (USA), who took a fierce hold on the way to the start, tanked off in front in the race itself with Holland trying his best to restrain him. However, he proved far superior to his rivals and scooted in. (8/11: 1/2-10/11)
Here's To Howie (USA), having his first run in four-and-a-half months, was the only danger to the winner, but he was easily brushed aside in the last three furlongs. (2/1)
Farley Mount, a small, chunky colt, lost ground at the start and, totally taken off his feet, could never get remotely near the winner. (100/30)

456 LINCOLNS MEAD H'CAP (0-70) (3-Y.O) (Class E)
3-20 (3-20) **1m (Equitrack)** £2,862.25 (£853.00: £406.50: £183.25) Stalls: High GOING minus 0.52 sec per fur (FST)

				SP	RR	SF
	Castles Burning (USA) (69) (CACyzer) **3-9-7** LDettori(1) (led over 5f out: rdn out)	—	1	3/1 2	84	49
366^{4}	**Mendoza (56)** (DJGMurraySmith) **3-8-3**(5) JBramhill(4) (lw: hdwy 6f out: ev ch fnl 2f: r.o)	½	2	5/1 3	70	35
368^{3}	**Skelton Sovereign (IRE) (55)** (RHollinshead) **3-8-4**(3) FLynch(2) (dwlt: rdn over 2f out: hdwy over 1f out: r.o one pce)	10	3	8/1	49	14
361^{3}	**Talisman (IRE) (55)** (SDow) **3-8-2**(5) ADaly(8) (rdn & hdwy over 4f out: wknd over 2f out)	2	4	12/1	45	10
368^{4}	**Alvilde (53)** (DJSCosgrove) **3-8-5** JQuinn(5) (lw: hdwy over 3f out: wknd over 2f out)	1¾	5	12/1	40	5
395^{3}	**Baby Jane (60)** (RGuest) **3-8-12** DHolland(3) (led 7f out tl over 5f out: wknd 3f out)	17	6	5/2 1	13	—
395^{6}	**Solar Dawn (54)** (MJohnston) **3-8-6** TWilliams(6) (lw: led 1f: rdn over 4f out: wknd 3f out)	8	7	5/1 3	—	—
	Highland Pass (IRE) (56) (GThorner) **3-8-8** DaneO'Neill(7) (bhd fnl 5f)	7	8	20/1	—	—

(SP 118.2%) **8 Rn**

1m 38.65 (1.25) CSF £17.47 CT £100.29 TOTE £4.80: £1.50 £1.90 £1.80 (£5.40) OWNER Mr R. M. Cyzer (HORSHAM) BRED Robert S. West Jr.
OFFICIAL EXPLANATION **Baby Jane: no explanation offered.**
Castles Burning (USA), beaten off a mark of 55 when last seen in a handicap on Turf, was racing off 69 here, his first run in three-and-a-half months. Soon at the head of affairs, he had a tremendous tussle with the runner-up in the straight, but just managed to prevail, losing his maiden tag at the twelfth attempt. (3/1)
240 Mendoza launched his challenge in the straight, and looked as if he would get past the winner. However, that rival proved to be a real tartar and, despite doing little wrong, he was unable to get his head in front. (5/1)
368 Skelton Sovereign (IRE) is very exposed, and one win now from twenty-one starts says it all. He stayed on when it was all over and maybe a mile-and-a-quarter is his trip. (8/1: 6/1-9/1)
361 Talisman (IRE) is a poor performer and had been seen off approaching the final quarter-mile. (12/1)
368 Alvilde made an effort running down the hill, but had shot her bolt over two furlongs from home. (12/1: 6/1-14/1)
395 Baby Jane ran no race at all, and had been seen off three furlongs from home. Her only other All-Weather run was on the Fibresand, and maybe that surface suits her better than the Equitrack. (5/2)
395 Solar Dawn (5/1: 6/1-4/1)

457 HAPPY BIRTHDAY DENISE H'CAP (0-80) (3-Y.O+) (Class D)
3-50 (3-52) **1m 2f (Equitrack)** £4,269.00 (£1,272.00: £606.00: £273.00) Stalls: Low GOING minus 0.52 sec per fur (FST)

				SP	RR	SF
422^{4}	**Sweet Supposin (IRE) (62)** (CADwyer) **6-8-12v** LDettori(10) (lw: hdwy on bit over 3f out: led ins fnl f: rdn & r.o wl)	—	1	9/4 1	70	36
$270a^{12}$	**No Speeches (IRE) (64)** (SDow) **6-8-9**(5) ADaly(5) (a.p: rdn over 4f out: ev ch ins fnl f: r.o)	½	2	9/1	71	37
405^{3}	**Tallulah Belle (67)** (NPLittmoden) **4-9-3** TGMcLaughlin(1) (lw: n.m.r on ins & lost pl over 3f out: rallied to ld over 2f out: hdd ins fnl f: r.o)	s.h	3	11/2 3	74	40
405^{8}	**Quiet Arch (IRE) (65)** (WRMuir) **4-9-1** DaneO'Neill(3) (b: b.hind: hdwy over 1f out: r.o one pce)	5	4	9/1	64	30
	Kriscliffe (78) (GLewis) **4-10-0** PaulEddery(8) (lw: hld up: led 4f out tl over 2f out: sn wknd)	½	5	12/1	76	42
401^{*}	**Roman Reel (USA) (60)** (GLMoore) **6-8-10** SWhitworth(2) (hld up: rdn over 5f out: wknd over 2f out)	1½	6	7/2 2	56	22
422^{3}	**Ethbaat (USA) (66)** (MJHeaton-Ellis) **6-9-2** AClark(7) (hdwy over 6f out: wknd over 2f out)	19	7	6/1	32	—
405^{6}	**Robellion (69)** (DWPArbuthnot) **6-9-5v** DHarrison(9) (b.hind: hdwy over 6f out: wknd over 2f out)	2	8	7/1	31	—

				SP	RR	SF
	Battle Spark (USA) (70) (CACyzer) **4-9-6** GCarter(4) (b: led 6f)	18	**9**	33/1	4	—
369[9]	**River Run (IRE) (55)** (RHollinshead) **5-8-2b**(3)ow9 FLynch(6) (lw: prom over 5f)	1½	**10**	20/1	—	—
				(SP 130.6%)	**10 Rn**	

2m 6.63 (2.33) CSF £25.12 CT £101.01 TOTE £3.00: £1.50 £4.20 £1.70 (£14.80) Trio £223.40 OWNER Mr G. Middlemiss (NEWMARKET) BRED Ballylinch Stud Ltd

LONG HANDICAP River Run (IRE) 7-8

422 Sweet Supposin (IRE) looked superb in the preliminaries, but was reluctant to come out of the paddock. However, Dettori knows how to ride him to perfection and he cruised into the action on the bridle over three furlongs from home. He always looked the winner in the straight although, once he struck the front inside the final furlong, he did not find as much as first looked likely. The booking of Dettori has now become very significant on him as Frankie has yet to be beaten in five races on this quirky character. (9/4: 3/1-7/4)

270a No Speeches (IRE), returning from an unsuccessful trip to Cagnes-Sur-Mer, was one of three almost in line inside the final furlong before finding the winner too good. (9/1)

405 Tallulah Belle, 10lb higher than when scoring here last month, was bustled into the lead over a quarter-of-a-mile from home, but was unable to hold on inside the final furlong. She remains in good form. (11/2)

291 Quiet Arch (IRE) stayed on from below the distance, but by then it was all over bar the shouting. (9/1)

Kriscliffe, who has changed stables since his last run nearly six months ago, looked in good heart beforehand and moved to the front half-a-mile from home. Collared approaching the final quarter-mile, he soon had bellows to mend. (12/1)

458 HARE LANE LIMITED STKS (0-60) (3-Y.O+) (Class F)

4-20 (4-20) **7f (Equitrack)** £2,277.00 (£627.00: £297.00) Stalls: Low GOING minus 0.52 sec per fur (FST)

				SP	RR	SF
*349**	**Barbason (57)** (GLMoore) **5-9-8** CandyMorris(3) (s.s: hdwy 5f out: chsd ldr over 2f out: led wl ins fnl f: r.o wl)	—	**1**	4/1 3	66	37
181[4]	**Chasetown Flyer (USA) (52)** (NEBerry) **3-8-5** RPerham(5) (led over 5f out: rdn over 1f out: hdd wl ins fnl f: r.o)	hd	**2**	20/1	64	20
403[3]	**Spencer's Revenge (60)** (PButler) **8-9-8** GBardwell(8) (lw: hld up: rdn over 4f out: r.o ins fnl f)	1½	**3**	3/1 1	62	33
361[2]	**Cheval Roc (58)** (RHannon) **3-8-5** DaneO'Neill(2) (a.p: rdn over 2f out: wknd over 1f out)	5	**4**	4/1 3	49	5
319[4]	**Hawaii Storm (FR) (55)** (DJSffrenchDavis) **9-9-1**(7) KerryBaker(6) (b.hind: s.s: nvr nr to chal)	hd	**5**	8/1	51	22
396[6]	**Billaddie (58)** (RBoss) **4-9-6** MTebbutt(9) (a.p: rdn over 2f out: sn wknd)	1¾	**6**	10/1	45	16
383[4]	**Rawi (60)** (MissGayKelleway) **4-9-5**(3) AWhelan(1) (b: b.hind: lw: bhd fnl 4f)	2½	**7**	7/2 2	41	12
	Jobie (52) (RTPhillips) **7-9-6** LDettori(7) (led over 1f: wknd over 3f out)	15	**8**	7/1	5	—
				(SP 124.7%)	**8 Rn**	

1m 26.57 (2.17) CSF £75.71 TOTE £4.90: £1.70 £2.60 £1.10 (£64.80) Trio £182.50; £115.73 to Newcastle 25/3/97 OWNER Mr F. L. Hill (BRIGHTON) BRED Sheikh Mohammed bin Rashid al Maktoum

WEIGHT FOR AGE 3yo-15lb

349* Barbason followed up last month's victory. Throwing down his challenge in the straight, he managed to get on top in the closing stages. All three of his victories to date have come here. (4/1)

90 Chasetown Flyer (USA) nearly caused an upset. Soon at the head of affairs, he was challenged by the winner in the straight, but was only passed in the closing stages. (20/1)

403 Spencer's Revenge again found this trip too sharp and, although running on inside the final furlong, found the line always beating him. A return to a mile-and-a-quarter is needed. (3/1)

361 Cheval Roc played an active role until coming to the end of his tether approaching the final furlong. (4/1: 5/2-9/2)

319 Hawaii Storm (FR) (8/1: op 5/1)

459 HOLLOW LANE H'CAP (0-75) (3-Y.O+) (Class D)

4-50 (4-51) **6f (Equitrack)** £3,518.20 (£1,048.60: £499.80: £225.40) Stalls: Low GOING minus 0.52 sec per fur (FST)

				SP	RR	SF
	Waypoint (62) (RCharlton) **4-9-2** TSprake(6) (hld up: hrd rdn over 1f out: led ins fnl f: drvn out)	—	**1**	9/1	70	34
364[3]	**Apollo Red (72)** (GLMoore) **8-9-12** CandyMorris(9) (hld up: rdn over 1f out: ev ch ins fnl f: r.o)	nk	**2**	9/1	79	43
*320**	**Roffey Spinney (IRE) (75)** (RHannon) **3-9-2** DaneO'Neill(5) (lw: led: hrd rdn over 1f out: hdd ins fnl f: unable qckn)	1¼	**3**	9/2 2	79	30
*406**	**Ivory's Grab Hire (51)** (KTIvory) **4-8-2b**(3) MartinDwyer(3) (outpcd: hdwy fnl f: r.o)	1	**4**	11/1	52	16
364[4]	**Sharp Imp (62)** (RMFlower) **7-9-2b** LDettori(8) (outpcd: gd hdwy over 1f out: one pce ins fnl f)	s.h	**5**	9/4 1	63	27
406[6]	**Intiaash (IRE) (70)** (DHaydnJones) **5-9-10** TWilliams(7) (a.p: hrd rdn over 1f out: sn wknd)	3	**6**	5/1 3	63	27
391[2]	**Aljaz (52)** (MissGayKelleway) **7-8-6** DHolland(11) (b: b.hind: hld up: rdn over 2f out: wknd wl over 1f out)	1	**7**	12/1	42	6
404[3]	**Justinianus (IRE) (50)** (JJBridger) **5-7-13**(5)ow8 ADaly(2) (lw: prom over 2f)	2	**8**	12/1	35	—
416[3]	**Will Do (65)** (MartynMeade) **4-9-0**(5) DSweeney(4) (bhd fnl 5f)	2½	**9**	9/1	43	7
364[2]	**Squire Corrie (74)** (DWChapman) **5-10-0** ACulhane(10) (spd over 4f)	8	**10**	11/2	31	—
				(SP 134.7%)	**10 Rn**	

1m 12.67 (1.57) CSF £91.71 CT £393.74 TOTE £8.90: £2.90 £4.40 £1.30 (£75.40) Trio £260.60; £80.75 to Newcastle 25/3/97 OWNER Mr Ray Richards (BECKHAMPTON) BRED Berkshire Equestrian Services Ltd

WEIGHT FOR AGE 3yo-13lb

Waypoint, having her first run in three-and-a-half months, goes well fresh and managed to get on top inside the final furlong. (9/1: 9/2-10/1)

364 Apollo Red has been a model of consistency this winter, and ran a first-class race, having every chance inside the final furlong and keeping on well to the line. (9/1: 6/1-10/1)

320* Roffey Spinney (IRE) was bustled into the lead. Coming under pressure in the straight, he carried his head rather high and was collared inside the final furlong. (9/2: 5/2-5/1)

406* Ivory's Grab Hire, unable to go the early pace, was putting in all his best work in the final furlong. (11/1: op 7/1)

364 Sharp Imp soon got himself well detached, but made giant strides early in the straight before that run came to an end inside the final furlong. (9/4)

Intiaash (IRE) played an active role until coming to the end of his tether entering the final furlong. (5/1)

391 Aljaz (12/1: op 8/1)

T/Plpt: £47.90 (185.57 Tckts). T/Qdpt: £12.50 (73.49 Tckts) AK

NEWCASTLE (L-H) (Good)
Tuesday March 25th
Races 2 & 4: hand timed
WEATHER: raining; sunny periods WIND: fresh half against

60+ 62+ 61

460 E.B.F. BACKWORTH MAIDEN STKS (2-Y.O) (Class D) (61)
2-35 (2-35) **5f** £3,355.00 (£1,015.00: £495.00: £235.00) Stalls: High GOING: Not Established

				SP	RR	SF
432[7]	**Miquelon** (RHollinshead) **2-9-0** KDarley(7) (disp ld tl led over 1f out: r.o u.p)	—	1	5/2[1]	73	16
	Flower O'Cannie (IRE) (MWEasterby) **2-8-9** LDettori(1) (leggy: lw: trckd ldrs: rn green ½-wy: hdwy over 1f out: r.o towards fin)	nk	2	11/4[2]	67	10
	Theatre of Dreams (PDEvans) **2-8-9** JFortune(5) (leggy: unf: disp ld tl rdn & grad wknd appr fnl f)	1	3	4/1[3]	64	7
	Last Knight (IRE) (MRChannon) **2-9-0** TQuinn(2) (cmpt: in tch: outpcd ½-wy: styd on u.p: no imp)	3½	4	11/4[2]	58	1
	Mill End Quest (MWEasterby) **2-8-9** DaleGibson(4) (neat: bit bkwd: prom tl outpcd fnl 2f)	1¾	5	25/1	47	—
	Anka Lady (DMoffatt) **2-8-6**(3) DarrenMoffatt(3) (leggy: prom tl outpcd fr ½-wy)	1½	6	12/1	42	—

(SP 113.4%) **6 Rn**

64.74 secs (6.34) CSF £9.02 TOTE £3.00: £1.30 £2.20 (£4.30) OWNER Mr P. D. Savill (UPPER LONGDON) BRED David Mathias

432 Miquelon, who had the best draw, put his experience to full use but he still tended to edge left. (5/2)
Flower O'Cannie (IRE) looked ultra-fit, but her undoing was probably her number one draw as she had to race on the outside and always tended to hang left. This run should have taught her plenty. (11/4)
Theatre of Dreams, a tall, lightly-made sort, ran well and plenty more will be seen of her. (4/1: 3/1-5/1)
Last Knight (IRE) could never go the pace here. He will appreciate further and will certainly be better for the run. (11/4: op 7/4)
Mill End Quest needed this and showed a little. (25/1)
Anka Lady, from a yard that often does well with first-time-out two-year-olds, proved a shade disappointing. (12/1: op 6/1)

461 CULLERCOATS H'CAP (0-70) (3-Y.O+) (Class E)
3-10 (3-12) **1m 2f 32y** £2,869.25 (£869.00: £424.50: £202.25) Stalls: Low GOING minus 0.03 sec per fur (G)

				SP	RR	SF
207[6]	**Domino Flyer (66)** (MrsASwinbank) **4-10-0** JSupple(7) (mde most: hld on wl)	—	1	14/1	78	60
	Sing And Dance (39) (EWeymes) **4-8-1** JQuinn(8) (trckd ldrs: smooth hdwy to chal 2f out: sn rdn: nt qckn towards fin)	½	2	14/1	50	32
	Pendolino (IRE) (37) (MBrittain) **6-7-13** GBardwell(14) (chsd ldrs: outpcd over 2f out: kpt on fnl f)	3½	3	14/1	43	25
422[11]	**Suga Hawk (IRE) (58)** (EJAlston) **5-9-6** KFallon(4) (in tch: styd on u.p fnl 2f: nvr able chal)	½	4	10/1[2]	63	45
	Shamokin (35) (FWatson) **5-7-11**ow1 FNorton(3) (cl up tl grad wknd fnl 2f)	1½	5	33/1	38	19
416[5]	**Whitley Grange Boy (58)** (JLEyre) **4-9-3**(3) OPears(13) (hld up & bhd: stdy hdwy 2f out: nvr plcd to chal)	nk	6	25/1	60	42
424[9]	**Nobby Barnes (37)** (DonEnricoIncisa) **8-7-13** KimTinkler(15) (dwlt: hdwy 3f out: nvr able chal)	1¼	7	25/1	37	19
411[5]	**Flag Fen (USA) (58)** (JParkes) **6-9-1**(5) JBramhill(10) (lw: in tch: hdwy u.p over 2f out: wknd over 1f out)	1	8	12/1[3]	57	39
405[11]	**Sherqy (IRE) (63)** (SEKettlewell) **5-9-11** OUrbina(16) (bit bkwd: bhd: hdwy on outside 3f out: nvr rchd ldrs)	1¾	9	12/1[3]	59	41
	Spanish Verdict (60) (DenysSmith) **10-9-8** JCarroll(9) (in tch: effrt over 3f out: no imp)	1	10	20/1	54	36
312[5]	**Taniyar (FR) (48)** (RHollinshead) **5-8-7**(3) FLynch(6) (n.d)	3	11	16/1	37	19
	Fatehalkhair (IRE) (37) (BEllison) **5-7-13** NKennedy(17) (chsd ldrs tl wknd fnl 2½f)	½	12	25/1	26	8
373[6]	**Picard (IRE) (43)** (FMurphy) **4-8-5** JFanning(5) (bhd: effrt 3f out: n.d)	1½	13	16/1	29	11
	Giftbox (USA) (52) (NBycroft) **5-9-0** LCharnock(2) (a rr div)	hd	14	14/1	38	20
435[11]	**Roussi (USA) (50)** (DNicholls) **5-8-5**(7) IonaWands(1) (lw: in tch tl wknd 3f out)	¾	15	10/1[2]	35	17
	Action Jackson (53) (BJMcMath) **5-9-1** KDarley(11) (chsd ldrs tl wknd fnl 3½f)	6	16	10/1[2]	29	11
422[2]	**Chadleigh Lane (USA) (56)** (ABMulholland) **5-9-4** DeanMcKeown(12) (b: bhd: rdn ent st: n.d)	5	17	4/1[1]	24	6
	Newbridge Boy (52) (MGMeagher) **4-9-0** JFortune(18) (in tch tl st: sn wknd)	4	18	10/1[2]	13	—

(SP 129.4%) **18 Rn**

2m 12.9 (6.20) CSF £175.82 CT £2,572.52 TOTE £29.10: £7.20 £3.60 £3.20 £2.90 (£284.90) Trio Not won; £2,181.47 to Folkestone 26/3/97 OWNER Mr S. Smith (RICHMOND) BRED Mrs K. Livingstone

OFFICIAL EXPLANATION **Whitley Grange Boy: hung left in the latter stages. Roussi (USA): finished lame behind. Chadleigh Lane (USA): no explanation offered.**

207 Domino Flyer, attempting this trip for the first time, obviously had no fears and got it really well. (14/1)
Sing And Dance has been promising to win a race for some time, and looked to be going really well early in the straight here but failed to find quite enough under pressure. To give her the benefit, she probably just needed it. (14/1: op 8/1)
Pendolino (IRE) looks well in, but lacks a change of gear and would seem to need a bit further. (14/1)
369* Suga Hawk (IRE) shaped as though longer trips should bring improvement. (10/1)
Shamokin put in a reasonable first effort of the season and is likely to benefit from it. (33/1)
416 Whitley Grange Boy looks very lean and tended to hang left in the race, but he showed plenty and was not over-punished. He finished to some purpose and is one to watch. (25/1)
Sherqy (IRE) (12/1: op 8/1)
Giftbox (USA) (14/1: op 8/1)
194 Roussi (USA) (10/1: 7/1-11/1)
422 Chadleigh Lane (USA) has only ever won on the All-Weather and, although well backed here, never gave supporters the slightest glimmer of hope. (4/1)

462 KILLINGWORTH (S) STKS (3-Y.O) (Class G)
3-40 (3-41) **6f** £2,134.00 (£599.00: £292.00) Stalls: High GOING: 0.29 sec per fur (G)

				SP	RR	SF
	Without Friends (IRE) (76) (WStorey) **3-9-0** SWhitworth(7) (a.p: slt ld ins fnl f: all out)	—	1	7/4[1]	62	31
	Skyers Flyer (IRE) (66) (RonaldThompson) **3-8-4**(5) JBramhill(6) (led tl hdd ins fnl f: rallied)	s.h	2	7/2[2]	57	26
453[7]	**Prominent** (MrsJRRamsden) **3-9-0** JFortune(1) (stdd s: bhd tl hdwy u.p 2f out: styd on wl towards fin)	1¼	3	9/2[3]	59	28
124[16]	**Move The Clouds** (DNicholls) **3-8-9** JCarroll(8) (hdwy ½-wy: chal over 1f out: no ex ins fnl f)	s.h	4	10/1	53	22
	Crosby Nod (45) (EWeymes) **3-9-0** KDarley(3) (bit bkwd: bhd: rdn over 2f out: styd on: no imp)	1½	5	33/1	54	23
427[5]	**Ejeer (IRE) (54)** (MRChannon) **3-9-0** TQuinn(9) (cl up tl rdn & grad wknd fnl 2f)	½	6	7/2[2]	53	22
	Bellarula (MDods) **3-8-9** SWebster(4) (leggy: unf: bit bkwd: bhd: hdwy u.p 2f out: n.d)	¾	7	20/1	46	15
	Interaction (RCraggs) **3-9-0** LCharnock(5) (unf: cl up over 3f: sn wknd)	8	8	16/1	30	—

				SP	RR	SF
427[4]	**Chilling (58)** (NTinkler) **3-8-6**(7) KSked(2) (cl up tl wknd appr fnl f)	4	9	11/2	18	—

(SP 137.1%) **9 Rn**

1m 18.05 (6.55) CSF £9.20 TOTE £2.30: £1.20 £1.40 £1.70 (£4.70) Trio £17.30 OWNER Mr W. Storey (CONSETT) BRED Churchtown House Stud

Bt in 3,400 gns

Without Friends (IRE) travelled well, but did nothing when in front and only just scraped home. (7/4)

Skyers Flyer (IRE) won twice over the minimum trip last season, but she stayed particularly well here and should find a suitable event before long. (7/2: op 2/1)

453 Prominent, dropped out early on, was wound up from halfway and was really getting the hang of things as the line approached. He is obviously learning fast. (9/2)

83 Move The Clouds, having her first run for her new yard, showed a bit more enthusiasm and if she can be persuaded, she certainly has plenty more ability. (10/1: 8/1-12/1)

Crosby Nod put in his best effort to date and should appreciate further. (33/1)

427 Ejeer (IRE) contested the lead, but was always inclined to edge left and was going nowhere in the last couple of furlongs. (7/2)

463 HOLYSTONE MAIDEN STKS (3-Y.O+) (Class D)

4-15 (4-17) **1m (round)** £3,338.75 (£1,010.00: £492.50: £233.75) Stalls: Low GOING minus 0.03 sec per fur (G)

				SP	RR	SF
	Maftool (82) (JHMGosden) **3-8-9** LDettori(5) (lw: trckd ldr: led on bit ins fnl f: hrd hld)	—	1	2/5[1]	71+	14
373[3]	**Terdad (USA)** (TDBarron) **4-9-12** DHarrison(4) (led tl hdd ins fnl f: no ch w wnr)	¾	2	5/1[2]	70	30
	Indigo Dawn (MJohnston) **3-8-4** DeanMcKeown(3) (w'like: chsd ldrs: outpcd & rn green 3f out: styd on wl fnl f)	2	3	8/1[3]	61	4
	Noirie (MBrittain) **3-8-9** JCarroll(2) (chsd ldrs tl outpcd fnl 3f)	2½	4	9/1	61	4
	Golden Thunderbolt (FR) (73) (NTinkler) **4-9-12** KimTinkler(1) (hld up: effrt 3f out: n.d)	3½	5	12/1	54	14
424[10]	**Persian Sunset (IRE)** (MissJBower) **5-9-7** LNewton(6) (dwlt: a bhd)	5	6	100/1	39	—
	Born On The Wild (SEKettlewell) **4-9-0**(7) JennyBenson(7) (hld up & bhd: rdn 3f out: n.d)	3½	7	100/1	32	—

(SP 118.9%) **7 Rn**

1m 46.7 (7.70) CSF £2.99 TOTE £1.30: £1.20 £1.70 (£2.60) OWNER Mr Hamdan Al Maktoum (NEWMARKET) BRED Shadwell Estate Company Limited

WEIGHT FOR AGE 3yo-17lb

Maftool probably did not beat much here, but the way he did it had to impress and he would seem to be improving. (2/5)

373 Terdad (USA) made this a true gallop, but he was completely outclassed by the winner and greatly flattered by his proximity at the finish. (5/1: 3/1-11/2)

Indigo Dawn needed this both fitness and experience-wise, and was picking up towards the finish. Time will see improvement. (8/1: op 5/1)

Noirie had a nice pipe-opener here, and should improve a little for it. (9/1)

Golden Thunderbolt (FR) came from the same stable as last year's winner, and this free-runner showed little this time, but probably needed it. (12/1: 8/1-14/1)

464 MONKSEATON SPRINT H'CAP (0-85) (3-Y.O+) (Class D)

4-50 (4-53) **5f** £3,436.25 (£1,040.00: £507.50: £241.25) Stalls: High GOING: 0.29 sec per fur (G)

				SP	RR	SF
	Amron (57) (JBerry) **10-8-7** NCarlisle(1) (in tch far side: hdwy to ld ins fnl f: r.o wl)	—	1	10/1	69	38
394[4]	**Kalar (57)** (DWChapman) **8-8-7b** ACulhane(3) (lw: chsd ldrs: led far side 2f out tl ins fnl f: no ex)	3½	2	7/1[2]	58	27
	Surprise Mission (71) (MrsJRRamsden) **5-9-7** JFortune(11) (trckd ldrs: led stands' side over 1f out: rdn & r.o: nvr able chal)	s.h	3	3/1[1]	72	41
233[7]	**Captain Carat (61)** (DNicholls) **6-8-11** JCarroll(13) (dwlt: racd stands' side: hld up & bhd: hdwy over 1f out: r.o wl)	1¼	4	10/1	58	27
	Present 'n Correct (51) (CBBBooth) **4-8-1** LCharnock(12) (prom stands' side: kpt on one pce fnl 2f)	½	5	16/1	46	15
318[12]	**Stephensons Rocket (54)** (RAFahey) **6-8-4** FNorton(8) (chsd ldrs stands' side: nt qckn fnl 2f)	1	6	14/1	46	15
	Sweet Magic (78) (PHowling) **6-10-0** PaulEddery(2) (chsd ldrs far side tl outpcd fnl 2f)	1¼	7	10/1	66	35
	Blessingindisguise (65) (MWEasterby) **4-9-1** KDarley(9) (s.i.s: racd stands' side & effrt ½-wy: nvr rchd ldrs)	nk	8	9/1[3]	52	21
	Able Sheriff (60) (MWEasterby) **5-8-10b** DaleGibson(14) (bit bkwd: hld up stands' side: sme late hdwy)	s.h	9	7/1[2]	47	16
	Express Girl (73) (DMoffatt) **3-8-8**(3) DarrenMoffatt(4) (chsd ldrs far side 3f: wknd)	½	10	12/1	58	15
	Insider Trader (73) (MrsJRRamsden) **6-9-2**(7) ClaireWest(6) (hld up stands' side: effrt ½-wy: no imp)	s.h	11	16/1	58	27
	Magic Lake (47) (EJAlston) **4-7-4v**(7)ow1 RFfrench(7) (lw: s.i.s: hdwy & prom centre ½-wy: sn rdn & btn)	1½	12	20/1	27	—
	Cross The Border (72) (DNicholls) **4-9-8** AlexGreaves(10) (bit bkwd: led stands' side tl hdd & wknd qckly over 1f out)	3	13	12/1	43	12
	Grand Chapeau (IRE) (56) (DNicholls) **5-7-13**(7) IonaWands(5) (bit bkwd: led far side 3f: sn wknd)	2	14	20/1	20	—

(SP 130.6%) **14 Rn**

63.0 secs (4.60) CSF £77.52 CT £251.23 TOTE £10.60: £3.20 £2.50 £2.10 (£18.70) Trio £65.40 OWNER Mr Roy Peebles (COCKERHAM) BRED Llety Stud

LONG HANDICAP Magic Lake 7-8

WEIGHT FOR AGE 3yo-12lb

Amron, well drawn here and certainly well handicapped, gained his first win for three years and did it in useful style. (10/1)

394 Kalar has been running his heart out on the All-Weather and tried hard here, but this stiff track just found him out. (7/1)

Surprise Mission spent most of the race on the bridle, and then won the race up the stands' side, but the draw proved to be the crucial factor and the far side always had the edge. (3/1)

127 Captain Carat ran well up the unfavoured stands' side and looks to be coming back to form. (10/1)

Present 'n Correct ran a fair race but failed to pick up in the closing stages. (16/1)

Stephensons Rocket has not won for three years and had subsequently slipped down the handicap, but if his new stable can persuade him he certainly still has ability. (14/1)

Able Sheriff looked likely to benefit from this, and showed enough without offering a threat. (7/1: 9/2-8/1)

Magic Lake, over too sharp a trip, picked the worst place to race, but she did look particularly well and is likely to do better before long. (20/1)

465 EARSDON H'CAP (0-70) (4-Y.O+) (Class E)

5-20 (5-23) **2m 19y** £2,856.25 (£865.00: £422.50: £201.25) Stalls: High GOING minus 0.03 sec per fur (G)

				SP	RR	SF
	Kinoko (35) (KWHogg) **9-7-5**(5) JBramhill(3) (trckd ldrs: led over 3f out: r.o wl)	—	1	33/1	46	18

Form	Horse / details	Dist	Pos	SP	RR	SF
	La Brief (57) (MJRyan) **5-9-4** GBardwell(1) (drvn along & hdwy 9f out: hrd rdn ent st: styd on: nt pce to chal)	3½	**2**	$7/1^{3}$	65	37
	All On (39) (JHetherton) **6-8-0** NKennedy(6) (outpcd ½-wy: hdwy u.p appr st: styd on: nrst fin)	¾	**3**	$6/1^{2}$	46	18
375*	**Road Racer (IRE) (53)** (MrsJRRamsden) **4-8-9** JFortune(11) (lw: hld up: stdy hdwy appr st: effrt & prom 2f out: hrd drvn & one pce)	½	**4**	$5/2^{1}$	59	26
	Romalito (35) (MBlanshard) **7-7-10** JQuinn(9) (mid div: effrt 6f out: styd on u.p: nvr able chal)	3½	**5**	20/1	38	10
232^{8}	**Elite Bliss (IRE) (38)** (MJCamacho) **5-7-13** LCharnock(16) (sn chsng ldrs: led 5f out tl over 3f out: grad wknd)	6	**6**	20/1	35	7
167^{10}	**Top Prize (35)** (MBrittain) **9-7-10v** NCarlisle(12) (lw: led & sn clr: hdd 5f out: sn outpcd)	3	**7**	25/1	29	1
	Opaque (67) (WStorey) **5-10-0** SWhitworth(10) (bhd tl sme hdwy fnl 3f)	4	**8**	12/1	57	29
356^{8}	**Ship's Dancer (40)** (DonEnricoIncisa) **4-7-10b** KimTinkler(7) (hld up & bhd: sme hdwy fnl 3f: n.d)	2	**9**	50/1	28	—
	Turgenev (IRE) (66) (RBastiman) **8-9-8b(5)** HBastiman(4) (hld up & bhd: effrt 3f out: n.d)	¾	**10**	11/1	53	25
232^{9}	**Hard Love (60)** (JLEyre) **5-9-7** TWilliams(13) (lw: chsd ldrs tl wknd 3f out)	1	**11**	20/1	46	18
400^{2}	**Shakiyr (FR) (46)** (RHollinshead) **6-8-4b(3)** FLynch(15) (outpcd 7f out: n.d after)	2	**12**	$6/1^{2}$	30	2
381^{7}	**Captain Marmalade (42)** (DTThom) **8-8-3v** PaulEddery(14) (chsd ldrs tl outpcd fnl 4f)	6	**13**	20/1	20	—
	Double Dash (IRE) (67) (DMoffatt) **4-9-6v(3)** DarrenMoffatt(8) (drvn along & lost tch ½-wy: n.d after)	2	**14**	25/1	43	10
	Lostris (IRE) (36) (MDods) **6-7-11**ow1 DaleGibson(2) (chsd ldrs tl wknd 7f out)	1¾	**15**	11/1	10	—
80^{2}	**Royal Citizen (IRE) (58)** (JFBottomley) **8-9-5** JLowe(5) (s.i.s: effrt ½-wy: sn wknd)	nk	**16**	12/1	32	4

(SP 133.3%) **16 Rn**

3m 38.03 (12.53) CSF £226.93 CT £1,485.53 TOTE £56.30: £8.80 £2.10 £1.70 £1.30 (£170.50) Trio £494.40; £564.11 to Folkestone 26/3/97
OWNER Mr Anthony White (ISLE OF MAN) BRED Auldyn Stud Ltd
LONG HANDICAP Ship's Dancer 7-8 Kinoko 7-5 Romalito 7-9 Top Prize 7-5
WEIGHT FOR AGE 4yo-5lb

Kinoko, who never impresses on looks, travelled well and, picking up immediately when asked a question, saw it out in splendid style. (33/1)
La Brief was off the bit before halfway and kept struggling on, but was never fast enough to trouble the winner. (7/1)
All On is slow but sure and, after getting left behind halfway through the race, she stayed on stoutly at the finish. (6/1)
375* Road Racer (IRE) went well for a long way but, when the button was pressed two furlongs out, he failed to pick up and was not given too hard a time. (5/2)
Romalito just stays and was never doing things fast enough to have a chance here. (20/1)
Elite Bliss (IRE) ran her best race for a while, but probably found this trip beyond her. (20/1)
Opaque (12/1: op 7/1)
80 Royal Citizen (IRE) (12/1: op 8/1)

T/Jkpt: Not won; £6,359.71 to Folkestone 26/3/97. T/Plpt: £47.00 (388.33 Tckts). T/Qdpt: £4.40 (247.15 Tckts) AA

CATTERICK (L-H) (Good, Good to soft patches)
Wednesday March 26th
WEATHER: overcast WIND: v.str across

466 SPRINGTIME LIMITED STKS (0-60) (3-Y.O) (Class F)
2-20 (2-20) **5f** £2,511.00 (£696.00: £333.00) Stalls: Low GOING: 0.77 sec per fur (S)

Form	Horse / details	Dist	Pos	SP	RR	SF
	Loch-Hurn Lady (58) (KWHogg) **3-8-8** KDarley(6) (chsd ldrs: led over 1f out: styd on wl)	—	**1**	$7/2^{2}$	72	34
378^{3}	**Soda (60)** (TDBarron) **3-8-11b** RLappin(7) (in tch: hdwy 2f out: styd on towards fin)	3	**2**	11/2	65	27
	Gold Edge (55) (MRChannon) **3-8-8** RPerham(4) (lw: led over 3f: grad wknd)	1½	**3**	7/1	58	20
412*	**Bonyalua Mill (60)** (AStreeter) **3-8-8(3)** RHavlin(8) (chsd ldrs: outpcd ½-wy: kpt on fnl f)	1¾	**4**	12/1	55	17
372^{2}	**Master Foley (57)** (NPLittmoden) **3-9-0** TGMcLaughlin(3) (lw: chsd ldrs tl rdn & btn over 1f out)	3	**5**	$4/1^{3}$	48	10
	Molly Music (59) (GGMargarson) **3-8-8b** GCarter(5) (bit bkwd: sn outpcd: n.d)	7	**6**	6/1	20	—
	William's Well (56) (MWEasterby) **3-8-11** DaleGibson(2) (bit bkwd: outpcd fr ½-wy)	8	**7**	20/1	—	—
	Keen To Please (60) (DenysSmith) **3-8-8** JCarroll(1) (lw: chsd ldrs to ½-wy: wknd)	1	**8**	$3/1^{1}$	—	—

(SP 121.8%) **8 Rn**

64.7 secs (7.00) CSF £22.60 TOTE £4.20: £1.20 £1.10 £2.20 (£20.70) OWNER Hurn Racing Club (ISLE OF MAN) BRED J. Hindmarch
IN-FOCUS: Due to a very strong headwind for the first three races, the runners were being blown right across the track.
Loch-Hurn Lady was dropping back in trip. Her stamina proved important in these extremely windy conditions and she saw it out most determinedly. (7/2)
378 Soda had blinkers on for the second time, and finished well, suggesting that further may well suit. (11/2)
Gold Edge, whose yard is not really firing at the moment, showed plenty of speed but just failed to see it out. (7/1)
412* Bonyalua Mill was always finding this trip a bit too sharp, but stayed on well to suggest that winning on this surface is not beyond her. (12/1: 8/1-14/1)
372 Master Foley has won over further than this on the All-Weather, and was always flat to the boards to keep up here. Keen to please, he was always getting the full force of the wind and was left behind from halfway. (4/1)

467 FORCETT PARK (S) STKS (3-Y.O+) (Class G)
2-50 (2-53) **7f** £2,374.00 (£664.00: £322.00) Stalls: Low GOING minus 0.03 sec per fur (G)

Form	Horse / details	Dist	Pos	SP	RR	SF
372^{5}	**Abstone Queen (63)** (PDEvans) **3-8-4v** JFEgan(2) (hld up: stdy hdwy to ld ins fnl f: r.o)	—	**1**	$7/2^{1}$	62	19
422^{5}	**Loch Style (46)** (RHollinshead) **4-9-3(3)** FLynch(5) (chsd ldrs: led wl over 1f out tl ins fnl f: kpt on)	¾	**2**	15/2	61	33
	Soviet Lady (IRE) (60) (JLEyre) **3-8-0** TWilliams(13) (lw: hdwy ½-wy: hmpd over 1f out: styd on wl)	1¼	**3**	$11/2^{3}$	53	10
421^{11}	**Dictation (USA) (50)** (JJO'Neill) **5-9-6** JFortune(3) (lw: trckd ldrs: n.m.r over 1f out: styd on towards fin)	hd	**4**	11/1	58	30
	Sir Silver Sox (USA) (NTinkler) **5-9-6** KimTinkler(9) (unruly gng to s: cl up: outpcd over 2f out: kpt on fnl f)	¾	**5**	$7/2^{1}$	57	29
443^{17}	**Sense of Priority (61)** (DNicholls) **8-9-10** AlexGreaves(7) (lw: plld hrd: led tl hdd wl over 1f out: hmpd & sn btn)	1½	**6**	$9/2^{2}$	61	33
	Hanby (JSGoldie) **5-9-6** JCarroll(10) (in tch: kpt on fnl 2f)	d.h	**6**	20/1	53	25
429^{14}	**Dashing Dancer (IRE) (55)** (DShaw) **6-9-6** JFanning(11) (chsd ldrs tl hmpd & wknd wl over 1f out)	1½	**8**	33/1	50	22
150^{8}	**Kass Alhawa (55)** (DWChapman) **4-9-6** ACulhane(4) (nvr nr ldrs)	½	**9**	16/1	49	21
288^{7}	**Chinour (IRE)** (EJAlston) **9-9-6** SDrowne(1) (hld up: effrt 2f out: n.d)	1¾	**10**	14/1	45	17
297^{6}	**Miletrian City (54)** (JBerry) **4-9-10b** KDarley(12) (bhd: hdwy after 2f: chsng ldrs ent st: wknd over 1f out)	s.h	**11**	12/1	48	20
	Incantrice (WStorey) **4-8-10(5)** PFessey(6) (bkwd: dwlt: a bhd)	5	**12**	100/1	28	—

Form	Horse	Dist	Pos	SP	RR	SF
	Kickonsun (IRE) (RAFahey) **3-7-12**$^{(7)}$ RWinston(14) (s.i.s a bhd)	hd	**13**	25/1	33	—
				(SP 130.9%)		**13 Rn**

1m 29.3 (5.70) CSF £29.68 TOTE £5.00: £1.60 £3.40 £2.10 (£24.70) Trio £39.00 OWNER Mr J. E. Abbey (WELSHPOOL) BRED Ridgebarn Farm

WEIGHT FOR AGE 3yo-15lb

No bid

372 Abstone Queen, having the twenty-sixth run of her short career, is amazingly game and consistent, and won her fifth race, coming from well off the pace. (7/2)

422 Loch Style clearly needs further than this, and was just tapped for speed in the closing stages. (15/2)

Soviet Lady (IRE) found trouble during the race as the runners were blown across the track, but she finished well, suggesting that she should stay further. (11/2)

326 Dictation (USA) has never been tried over further than this but, by the way he was keeping on, it looks likely that he will stay. (11/1)

Sir Silver Sox (USA) had the form to win this going backwards, but looked a real handful beforehand, and was never doing enough in the race. (7/2: op 6/4)

342* Sense of Priority raced too freely for his own good and then got messed about, but still showed enough to suggest that a win on turf is not beyond him. (9/2: op 3/1)

Hanby, from a yard whose runners have been going quite well over jumps recently, showed ability and should benefit from this. (20/1)

468 GODS SOLUTION H'CAP (0-80) (3-Y.O+) (Class D)

3-25 (3-28) **7f** £3,769.00 (£1,132.00: £546.00: £253.00) Stalls: Low GOING minus 0.03 sec per fur (G)

Form	Horse	Dist	Pos	SP	RR	SF
	Foist (47) (MWEasterby) **5-7-10** LCharnock(7) (a.p: rdn to ld 1½f out: styd on wl)	—	**1**	$3/1^{1}$	56	38
316^{6}	**Gulf Shaadi (58)** (EJAlston) **5-8-7** SDrowne(13) (chsd ldrs: kpt on fnl 2f: nt pce to chal)	1	**2**	33/1	65	47
398*	**Rambo Waltzer (65)** (DNicholls) **5-8-7**$^{(7)}$ IonaWands(1) (lw: a.p: kpt on fnl 2f: nvr able to chal)	½	**3**	$6/1^{3}$	71	53
416*	**Genuine John (IRE) (67)** (JParkes) **4-8-11**$^{(5)}$ JBramhill(18) (w ldrs: led 2f out: sn hdd & one pce)	hd	**4**	16/1	72	54
382^{6}	**Allinson's Mate (IRE) (62)** (TDBarron) **9-8-4b**$^{(7)}$ VictoriaAppleby(17) (cl up: wandered over 1f out: kpt on fnl f)	2	**5**	16/1	63	45
376^{7}	**Three Arch Bridge (64)** (MJohnston) **5-8-13b** MRoberts(19) (bhd tl styd on fnl 2f)	3	**6**	14/1	58	40
357^{10}	**Naughty Pistol (USA) (59)** (PDEvans) **5-8-8v** JFEgan(2) (sn drvn along: styd on fnl 2f: nvr nrr)	nk	**7**	16/1	52	34
	Fame Again (59) (MrsJRRamsden) **5-8-8** JFortune(8) (lw: hld up & bhd: sme late hdwy)	1½	**8**	9/1	49	31
	Cee-Jay-Ay (54) (JBerry) **10-7-12**$^{(5)}$ PFessey(14) (dwlt: styd on fnl 2f: n.d)	½	**9**	20/1	43	25
	Heathyards Lady (USA) (57) (RHollinshead) **6-8-3**$^{(3)}$ FLynch(12) (b: rdn ½-wy: n.d)	¾	**10**	25/1	44	26
	Bollin Dorothy (55) (TDEasterby) **4-8-4**^{ow1} JCarroll(15) (led tl hdd & wknd 2f out)	1	**11**	16/1	40	21
	Queens Consul (IRE) (76) (BSRothwell) **7-9-11** MFenton(5) (hld up: sme hdwy 2f out: nvr trbld ldrs)	½	**12**	16/1	60	42
423^{3}	**Cheerful Groom (IRE) (48)** (DShaw) **6-7-4**$^{(7)ow1}$ RFfrench(10) (lw: nvr trbld ldrs)	hd	**13**	25/1	31	12
263*	**Sihafi (USA) (60)** (JMCarr) **4-8-9** ACulhane(9) (nvr bttr than mid div)	1¼	**14**	11/1	40	22
363*	**Tatika (73)** (GWragg) **7-9-3**$^{(5)}$ GMilligan(6) (b: rdr lost iron leaving stalls: a rr div)	3½	**15**	$5/1^{2}$	45	27
	Trafalgar Lady (USA) (79) (JAGlover) **4-9-7**$^{(7)}$ TPengkerego(16) (bit bkwd: s.i.s: gd hdwy after 1f: wknd over 2f out)	2½	**16**	25/1	46	28
233^{5}	**Paint It Black (55)** (DNicholls) **4-7-11**$^{(7)}$ CarolynBales(3) (hld up & a bhd)	3	**17**	33/1	15	—
	Keston Pond (IRE) (74) (MrsVAAconley) **7-9-9** MDeering(4) (dwlt: a bhd)	6	**18**	25/1	20	2
	No Cliches (73) (DNicholls) **4-9-8** AlexGreaves(11) (bit bkwd: chsd ldrs 4f: wknd)	4	**19**	20/1	10	—
				(SP 141.2%)		**19 Rn**

1m 27.0 (3.40) CSF £121.51 CT £576.98 TOTE £4.40: £1.40 £8.10 £2.10 £5.50 (£166.40) Trio £504.60; £227.47 to Musselburgh 27/3/97

OWNER Mr D. F. Spence (SHERIFF HUTTON) BRED W. Cormack

LONG HANDICAP Cheerful Groom (IRE) 7-6 Foist 7-9

OFFICIAL EXPLANATION **Tatika: the rider reported that he lost a stirrup in the early stages of the race.**

Foist looked well handicapped and was certainly heavily supported in the market. He did the business well and should find further success. (3/1)

316 Gulf Shaadi, who has been running his socks off on the All-Weather, put in another decent effort here but the trip was just too short. (33/1)

398* Rambo Waltzer, after a brilliant All-Weather season, showed he handles this surface just as well and will appreciate a little further. (6/1)

416* Genuine John (IRE) runs consistently well but does not win that often, and he was tapped for speed here in the last furlong-and-a-half. (16/1)

Allinson's Mate (IRE) is a funny old customer these days but he did run really well here. (16/1)

376 Three Arch Bridge likes a bit further and needs to be out in front, but never got going until too late on this occasion. (14/1)

Fame Again, given plenty to do, made some late headway without offering a threat. (9/1: 6/1-10/1)

469 TOYTOP MAIDEN STKS (3-Y.O+) (Class D)

3-55 (3-56) **5f 212y** £3,431.00 (£1,028.00: £494.00: £227.00) Stalls: High GOING minus 0.03 sec per fur (G)

Form	Horse	Dist	Pos	SP	RR	SF
	Three For A Pound (JAGlover) **3-8-11** GCarter(1) (lw: cl up: led 2f out: rn green: rdn & r.o)	—	**1**	$7/2^{2}$	80	31
	Marylebone (IRE) (71) (JBerry) **3-8-11** KDarley(7) (lw: a cl up: effrt over 2f out: one pce appr fnl f)	2½	**2**	$7/4^{1}$	73	24
	Merrily (54) (MissSEHall) **4-9-5** JFortune(8) (trckd ldrs: effrt 2f out: rdn & no ex fnl f)	2	**3**	$4/1^{3}$	63	27
416^{4}	**Splashed (66)** (TDBarron) **3-8-6** RLappin(5) (hld up: effrt over 2f out: hmpd wl over 1f out: no imp)	2	**4**	9/2	58	9
412^{2}	**Barwell Boy** (JLHarris) **3-8-11** LCharnock(9) (s.i.s: plld hrd & hdwy ½-wy: btn over 1f out)	½	**5**	9/1	43 t	12
429^{8}	**Blue Lugana (26)** (NBycroft) **5-9-5**$^{(5)}$ JBramhill(2) (chsd ldrs: effrt over 2f out: one pce)	hd	**6**	40/1	43 t	25
424^{12}	**Risky Lover** (DShaw) **4-9-5** JFanning(3) (led 4f: wknd)	2½	**7**	25/1	31 t	13
391^{13}	**Deardaw (32)** (MissLCSiddall) **5-8-12**$^{(7)}$ TSiddall(4) (outpcd fr ½-wy)	s.h	**8**	50/1	31 t	13
	Impetuosity (IRE) (CWThornton) **3-8-6** DeanMcKeown(6) (unf: bkwd: s.i.s: sn outpcd & t.o: sme late hdwy)	6	**9**	12/1	15 t	—
				(SP 122.7%)		**9 Rn**

1m 15.3 (4.40) CSF £9.69 TOTE £6.40: £1.80 £2.00 £2.20 (£7.80) Trio £19.40 OWNER Hyde Sporting Promotions Ltd (WORKSOP) BRED Roldvale Ltd

WEIGHT FOR AGE 3yo-13lb

Three For A Pound, despite running green, won well, and further improvement looks likely. (7/2)

Marylebone (IRE) had his chances but found the winner far too strong in the closing stages. (7/4)

Merrily travelled well but, when an effort was required in the last two furlongs, she again disappointed. (4/1)

416 Splashed was tapped for speed and short of room early on. She never looked likely to get into it and may need further. (9/2: op 3/1)

412 Barwell Boy was having his first race on turf, and raced too freely for his own good. (9/1)

Impetuosity (IRE) (12/1: 6/1-14/1)

470 YARM H'CAP (0-80) (4-Y.O+) (Class D)

4-30 (4-31) **1m 5f 175y** £3,743.00 (£1,124.00: £542.00: £251.00) Stalls: Low GOING minus 0.03 sec per fur (G)

				SP	RR	SF
430^{4}	**Dancing Cavalier (59)** (RHollinshead) **4-8-2**(3)ow1 FLynch(6) (lw: hld up: hdwy 5f out: led 2f out: sn clr)	—	1	5/1 ^{1}	75	24
	Summerhill Special (IRE) (52) (DWBarker) **6-7-13**(3) DarrenMoffatt(3) (a chsng ldrs: ev ch 2f out: nt pce of wnr)	1½	2	33/1	66	20
	Embryonic (IRE) (74) (MartinTodhunter) **5-9-10** JCarroll(9) (hld up & bhd: hdwy 6f out: prom & rdn appr st: kpt on)	3½	3	8/1 ^{3}	84	38
410^{4}	**Hasta la Vista (46)** (MWEasterby) **7-7-10b** LCharnock(1) (cl up: led 5f out to 2f out: sn outpcd)	1½	4	6/1 ^{2}	55	9
	Field of Vision (IRE) (70) (MrsASwinbank) **7-9-6** JSupple(5) (a.p: effrt 4f out: one pce)	2	5	6/1 ^{2}	76	30
410^{3}	**Dirab (75)** (TDBarron) **4-9-7** RLappin(4) (hld up & bhd: kpt on fnl 3f)	½	6	8/1 ^{3}	81	31
	Anchorena (49) (DWBarker) **5-7-13** TWilliams(10) (drvn along 6f out: nvr trbld ldrs)	1¾	7	25/1	53	7
	Royal Expression (72) (MrsMReveley) **5-9-8** KDarley(11) (lw: hld up & bhd: n.d)	2½	8	16/1	73	27
315^{7}	**Northern Motto (52)** (JSGoldie) **4-7-12** DaleGibson(13) (lw: hdwy ½-wy: rdn appr st: sn wknd)	1¼	9	8/1 ^{3}	51	1
	Welsh Mill (IRE) (78) (MrsMReveley) **8-10-0** ACulhane(2) (prom tl outpcd over 4f out: sn wknd)	3½	10	14/1	73	27
	Karisma (IRE) (60) (DenysSmith) **4-8-6** JFortune(7) (bit bkwd: cl up: led 8f out to 5f out: wknd qckly 3f out)	3½	11	8/1 ^{3}	51	1
402^{3}	**Mister Aspecto (IRE) (69)** (MJohnston) **4-9-1v** MRoberts(8) (lw: led tl hdd 8f out: sn drvn along: wknd 4f out)	2½	12	6/1 ^{2}	57	7
415^{9}	**Born A Lady (50)** (MrsVAAconley) **4-7-10b** MDeering(12) (wl t.o fnl 5f)	dist	13	50/1	—	—
				(SP 125.3%)	**13 Rn**	

3m 6.7 (10.70) CSF £169.33 CT £1,214.03 TOTE £6.90: £1.90 £9.50 £1.60 (£122.80) Trio £353.10; £203.92 to Musselburgh 27/3/97 OWNER The Three R's (UPPER LONGDON) BRED A. P. Hume

LONG HANDICAP Born A Lady 7-7

WEIGHT FOR AGE 4yo-4lb

430 Dancing Cavalier is a funny customer but he was well suited by the strong pace and, obviously on good terms with himself, won in most convincing style. (5/1)

Summerhill Special (IRE) has been disappointing since her initial run over hurdles and this was more encouraging. (33/1)

Embryonic (IRE), whose stable is in really good form at the moment, ran well and should be all the better for it. (8/1: 14/1-7/1)

410 Hasta la Vista was never allowed his own way here and was tapped for speed in the home straight. (6/1: 3/1-7/1)

Field of Vision (IRE), trying his longest trip to date, was left struggling in the last half-mile. (6/1: op 4/1)

410 Dirab showed enough to suggest that there are races to be won again this season. (8/1)

Royal Expression looked pretty well but never got into this. Nevertheless he showed enough to suggest that better is now likely. (16/1)

Welsh Mill (IRE) (14/1: 10/1-16/1)

471 WHORLTON H'CAP (0-75) (3-Y.O) (Class D)

5-05 (5-07) **1m 3f 214y** £3,457.00 (£1,036.00: £498.00: £229.00) Stalls: Low GOING minus 0.03 sec per fur (G)

				SP	RR	SF
387^{2}	**Little Acorn (65)** (SCWilliams) **3-9-2** KDarley(4) (trckd ldr gng wl: led appr st: drvn clr over 1f out)	—	1	9/4 ^{1}	72	18
230^{7}	**Kingdom Pearl (47)** (MJCamacho) **3-7-12** LCharnock(1) (lw: chsd ldrs: effrt 4f out: styd on: nt pce of wnr)	6	2	20/1	46	—
366^{2}	**Amico (65)** (CWThornton) **3-9-2** DeanMcKeown(8) (in tch: hdwy u.p 4f out: one pce fnl 2f)	2	3	6/1	61	7
298^{5}	**Broctune Line (47)** (MrsMReveley) **3-7-12** DWright(6) (lw: bhd: rdn 7f out: hrd drvn 5f out: styd on: no imp)	4	4	5/2 ^{2}	38	—
	Pupil Master (IRE) (54) (DenysSmith) **3-8-2**(3)ow4 FLynch(2) (unruly s: nvr trbld ldrs)	5	5	33/1	38	—
328*	**Love Me Do (USA) (67)** (MJohnston) **3-9-4** MRoberts(3) (led tl hdd appr st: sn wknd)	6	6	11/2 ^{3}	43	—
	Wildmoor (60) (JDBethell) **3-8-11** SDrowne(5) (bit bkwd: chsd ldrs tl outpcd 4f out: n.d after)	2	7	9/1	34	—
431^{10}	**Head Gardener (IRE) (70)** (NPLittmoden) **3-9-7** TGMcLaughlin(7) (hld up & a bhd)	nk	8	11/1	43	—
				(SP 115.0%)	**8 Rn**	

2m 43.7 (12.30) CSF £43.25 CT £219.95 TOTE £3.10: £2.40 £3.80 £1.10 (£31.10) OWNER Mr Alasdair Simpson (NEWMARKET) BRED Alasdair J. Simpson

387 Little Acorn, suited by the step up in trip, travelled well and, although swishing his tail dramatically when asked a question, he did all that was required. (9/4)

154 Kingdom Pearl, taking a big step-up in distance, stayed on most determinedly but was always second best. (20/1)

366 Amico looked very one-paced when the pressure was on in the last half-mile. (6/1)

124* Broctune Line never looked happy at any stage despite making a little late headway. (5/2)

Pupil Master (IRE) gave problems before the start and showed little in the race. (33/1)

328* Love Me Do (USA) needed driving along to make it early on, and soon threw in the towel when tackled approaching the straight. (11/2: 4/1-6/1)

370 Head Gardener (IRE) (11/1: 6/1-12/1)

T/Plpt: £716.20 (15.9 Tckts). T/Qdpt: £17.90 (46.3 Tckts) AA

FOLKESTONE (R-H) (Rnd crse Good to firm, St crse Good, Good to firm ptchs)
Wednesday March 26th

WEATHER: overcast WIND: mod across

65+ 62 53

472 HEADCORN MAIDEN AUCTION STKS (2-Y.O F) (Class F) (60)

2-10 (2-12) **5f** £2,277.00 (£627.00: £297.00) Stalls: Low GOING minus 0.18 sec per fur (GF)

				SP	RR	SF
	Lady Moll (RBoss) **2-8-6** LDettori(10) (neat: mde virtually all: r.o wl ins fnl f)	—	1	2/1 ^{1}	73	20
	Conectis (IRE) (DJSCosgrove) **2-8-5** JQuinn(5) (w'like: bit bkwd: dwlt: sn in tch: rdn 2f out: styd on ins fnl f)	3	2	7/1	62	9
447^{6}	**Carol Grimes** (JSMoore) **2-8-2**(5) PPMurphy(3) (a.p: ev ch over 1f out: one pce)	1½	3	6/1 ^{3}	60	7
	Solway Lass (IRE) (PEccles) **2-8-6** CRutter(2) (leggy: dwlt: nvr nrr)	3	4	5/1 ^{2}	49	—
	Jack-N-Jilly (IRE) (JSMoore) **2-8-0**(3) MHenry(8) (neat: mid div: rdn over 2f out: kpt on one pce ins fnl f)	s.h	5	25/1	46	—
	Bliss (IRE) (MrsPNDutfield) **2-8-4** TSprake(9) (neat: bit bkwd: hdwy 3f out: sn rdn: one pce)	hd	6	16/1	47	—
	Shannon (IRE) (CADwyer) **2-8-6** JStack(1) (leggy: chsd ldrs tl wknd over 2f out)	1	7	7/1	45	—
	Miss Skye (IRE) (TJNaughton) **2-8-7** PaulEddery(4) (leggy: bit bkwd: prom tl wknd over 2f out)	1½	8	13/2	42	—
	Swanmore Lady (IRE) (SCWilliams) **2-8-4** DRMcCabe(6) (w'like: bit bkwd: a bhd)	7	9	14/1	16	—

Casa Rosa (RHannon) **2-8-7** DaneO'Neill(11) (w'like: bit bkwd: s.s: a bhd)	1	**10**	5/1[2]	16	—
			(SP 135.7%)		**10 Rn**

60.8 secs (3.20) CSF £18.63 TOTE £3.40: £1.10 £2.60 £2.50 (£36.30) Trio £36.70 OWNER Ms Lynn Bell (NEWMARKET) BRED Longdon Stud Ltd

Lady Moll is not very big, but she certainly knew what was required of her, making all the running and drawing clear in the final furlong for a decisive victory. (2/1)

Conectis (IRE) did not look fully wound up but, soon racing in touch, strode out well in the final furlong for second place, although having no hope with the winner. (7/1)

447 Carol Grimes, the only runner with experience on her side, had every chance below the distance before tapped for toe. (6/1)

Solway Lass (IRE), quite a tall individual, was well supported in the market but she lost ground at the start and, although staying on, never looked like getting into it. (5/1: op 10/1)

Jack-N-Jilly (IRE), who cost a mere IR2,100 guineas, raced in the middle of the pack but never looked like finding the required turn of foot. (25/1)

Bliss (IRE), carrying some condition, could only go up and down in the same place in the second half of the race. (16/1)

Shannon (IRE) (7/1: op 4/1)

Miss Skye (IRE) (13/2: 3/1-7/1)

Casa Rosa (5/1: 7/4-11/2)

473 ROCHESTER H'CAP (0-70) (3-Y.O+) (Class E)

2-40 (2-41) **5f** £3,122.25 (£933.00: £446.50: £203.25) Stalls: Low GOING minus 0.18 sec per fur (GF)

				SP	RR	SF
	Malibu Man (65) (EAWheeler) **5-9-9** TSprake(6) (lw: mde all: clr ½-wy: comf) —	**1**		9/4[1]	80+	56
301[9]	**Dande Flyer (70)** (DWPArbuthnot) **4-10-0** SWhitworth(7) (b: dwlt: hdwy 2f out: styd on to go 2nd ins fnl f) 3	**2**		6/1[3]	75	51
	College Night (IRE) (43) (CADwyer) **5-8-1** NVarley(1) (bit bkwd: a.p: rdn over 1f out: one pce) 1¼	**3**		8/1	44	20
332[11]	**Miletrian Refurb (IRE) (60)** (MRChannon) **4-9-4** TQuinn(10) (racd centre: prom: rdn over 1f out: one pce) ½	**4**		14/1	60	36
	Arnie (IRE) (40) (JRPoulton) **5-7-9**(3)ow2 MartinDwyer(4) (chsd ldrs: rdn 2f out: one pce) hd	**5**		33/1	40	14
	Barranak (IRE) (61) (GMMcCourt) **5-8-12**(7) RStudholme(2) (prom tl wknd ins fnl f) s.h	**6**		12/1	60	36
304[3]	**Superlao (BEL) (38)** (JJBridger) **5-7-5**(5) RMullen(3) (b.nr hind: mid div: rdn over 2f out: no hdwy) 1¼	**7**		11/2[2]	33	9
	Penlop (70) (BJMeehan) **3-9-2** MTebbutt(5) (dwlt: nvr nrr) hd	**8**		10/1	65	29
	Meranti (49) (JMBradley) **4-8-7** DHolland(8) (lw: racd centre: prom tl wknd over 1f out) 1½	**9**		10/1	39	15
223[7]	**Suite Factors (60)** (KRBurke) **3-8-6** PaulEddery(9) (racd centre: in tch tl wknd over 1f out) 2	**10**		14/1	44	8
	Keen Waters (60) (JRArnold) **3-8-6** SSanders(12) (lw: racd centre: prom to ½-wy) 4	**11**		12/1	31	—
	Mister Sean (IRE) (38) (JMBradley) **4-7-10** NCarlisle(11) (b.hind: bit bkwd: racd centre: a bhd) 8	**12**		33/1	—	—
				(SP 124.3%)		**12 Rn**

59.6 secs (2.00) CSF £14.57 CT £88.89 TOTE £3.00: £1.50 £2.10 £2.30 (£14.50) Trio £32.90 OWNER Church Racing Partnership (PANGBOURNE) BRED Mrs M. Chubb

LONG HANDICAP Superlao (BEL) 7-9 Arnie (IRE) 7-5 Mister Sean (IRE) 7-0

WEIGHT FOR AGE 3yo-12lb

Malibu Man, who was gelded in the winter, loves to front-run and, showing a great deal of pace from the front, was clear by halfway and never looked like being caught. He needs it firm. (9/4)

214 Dande Flyer, who has been running poorly on the All-Weather, appreciated the return to grass but, although staying on to take second prize inside the final furlong, had no hope of catching the winner. All three of his wins to date came way back in October 1995. (6/1)

College Night (IRE) did not look fully wound-up for this first run in six months, but was never far away, if failing to quicken in the second half of the race. She needs further and remains a maiden after twenty-three attempts. (8/1)

Miletrian Refurb (IRE), well beaten in three runs on the sand, ran better here if failing to quicken in the final quarter-mile. His two wins to date have both come in sellers and a drop in class would help. (14/1)

Arnie (IRE), off the course since November 1995, hunted up the leaders but could only go up and down in the same place in the final quarter-mile. (33/1)

Barranak (IRE) was close up and was still disputing second place entering the final furlong before tiring. He has only one win to his name. (12/1)

304 Superlao (BEL) (11/2: 4/1-6/1)

474 SHORNECLIFFE MEDIAN AUCTION MAIDEN STKS (3-Y.O) (Class F)

3-15 (3-17) **6f** £2,277.00 (£627.00: £297.00) Stalls: Low GOING minus 0.18 sec per fur (GF)

		SP	RR	SF
Wee Dram (74) (RHannon) **3-8-9** DaneO'Neill(7) (lw: a.p: led 2f out: r.o wl) —	**1**	6/1[3]	79+	35
John Emms (IRE) (MBell) **3-9-0** PatEddery(2) (lw: led: hdd 2f out: hrd rdn 1f out: one pce) 2½	**2**	5/6[1]	77+	33
Moon Song (APJarvis) **3-8-9** WJO'Connor(1) (w'like: bit bkwd: sn pushed along: hdwy 2f out: styd on one pce ins fnl f) 3½	**3**	12/1	63	19
Lamarita (84) (JMPEustace) **3-8-9** RCochrane(4) (chsd ldrs: rdn over 1f out: one pce) nk	**4**	7/2[2]	62	18
Prince Zando (CAHorgan) **3-9-0** PaulEddery(8) (unf: dwlt: rr tl styd on ins fnl f: nvr nrr) nk	**5**	16/1	66	22
Littlestone Rocket (45) (WRMuir) **3-9-0** JReid(6) (prom tl wknd over 1f out) s.h	**6**	33/1	66	22
Jukebox Jive (CADwyer) **3-8-2**(7) JoHunnam(11) (in tch tl wknd over 1f out) 2½	**7**	33/1	55	11
Junie (IRE) (70) (TGMills) **3-8-9** SSanders(5) (in tch tl wknd 2f out) 8	**8**	14/1	33	—
Nampara Bay (GCBravery) **3-8-9** MRimmer(3) (chsd ldrs tl wknd 2f out) 1¼	**9**	33/1	30	—
Batsman (WJMusson) **3-8-11**(3) MBaird(10) (a bhd) 9	**10**	12/1	11	—
Muara Bay (GLewis) **3-8-11**(3) AWhelan(9) (bit bkwd: prom to ½-wy) s.h	**11**	20/1	11	—
		(SP 132.6%)		**11 Rn**

1m 13.2 (3.00) CSF £11.38 TOTE £6.20: £1.50 £1.10 £2.50 (£5.70) Trio £32.50 OWNER Bloomsbury Stud (MARLBOROUGH) BRED Mrs D. Whittingham

Wee Dram looked in tremendous shape beforehand and, leading a quarter-of-a-mile from home, proved too strong for the runner-up.(6/1: 4/1-13/2)

John Emms (IRE) has done well physically from last year, and looked in good shape for this reappearance. Setting the pace, he was collared by the winner two furlongs out and, although unable to match that rival, finished clear of the remainder. He should be able to pick up a small race. (5/6)

Moon Song, not looking fully wound up for this racecourse debut, was being bustled along virtually throughout, but did struggle on to take third prize. (12/1: 8/1-14/1)

Lamarita, who looked dull in her coat for this reappearance, hunted up the principals but could only go up and down in the same place in the final quarter-mile. (7/2)

Prince Zando, an unfurnished gelding, was given an extremely tender introduction. With his jockey sitting as quiet as a church mouse at the back of the field, the combination made eye-catching progress from below the distance, as his jockey moved his arms a bit to finish a promising fifth. Sure to have learnt a lot from this, improvement can be expected. (16/1)
Junie (IRE) (14/1: op 5/1)
Batsman (12/1: 8/1-14/1)

475 ALDINGTON MEDIAN AUCTION MAIDEN STKS (3-Y.O) (Class F)

3-45 (3-47) **6f 189y** £2,277.00 (£627.00: £297.00) Stalls: High GOING minus 0.30 sec per fur (GF)

				SP	RR	SF
296²	**Sharpo Wassl** (WJHaggas) **3-9-0** MHills(14) (lw: hld up: led over 1f out: rdn out)	—	**1**	5/1 3	72	32
	Masterpiece (RHannon) **3-9-0** PatEddery(7) (leggy: scope: a.p: rdn over 2f out: ev ch fnl f: r.o)	½	**2**	9/2 2	71	31
	Sharp Temper (BWHills) **3-8-11**(3) JDSmith(10) (cmpt: bit bkwd: lost pl over 4f out: rallied over 1f out: r.o)	1½	**3**	4/5 1	67	27
	Nervous Rex (63) (WRMuir) **3-9-0** JReid(13) (bit bkwd: a.p: led over 2f out tl over 1f out: one pce)	1¾	**4**	16/1	63	23
	Eastern Eagle (IRE) (JMPEustace) **3-9-0** RCochrane(1) (bit bkwd: hdwy over 1f out: nvr nrr)	1½	**5**	14/1	60	20
	Bathe In Light (USA) (LordHuntingdon) **3-8-9** DHarrison(3) (lw: rdn & hdwy over 1f out: nvr nrr)	1¼	**6**	9/1	52	12
	Hajat (NAGraham) **3-8-9** DHolland(9) (led over 4f: wknd over 1f out)	½	**7**	10/1	51	11
296⁶	**Who's That Man** (SCWilliams) **3-9-0** KFallon(4) (nvr nrr)	1¾	**8**	33/1	52	12
265⁵	**Native Thatch (IRE)** (WGMTurner) **3-8-9** TSprake(6) (hld up: rdn over 2f out: wknd over 1f out)	hd	**9**	33/1	46	6
	Kierans Maiden (APJarvis) **3-8-9** WJO'Connor(11) (lt-f: a bhd)	½	**10**	20/1	45	5
	Regal Reprimand (GLewis) **3-9-0** PaulEddery(5) (bit bkwd: a bhd)	½	**11**	16/1	49	9
436⁶	**Arboreal (USA)** (MrsLStubbs) **3-8-9** SSanders(8) (bhd fnl 2f)	1½	**12**	33/1	41	1
	Hippios (SDow) **3-9-0** TQuinn(12) (bkwd: bhd fnl 2f)	hd	**13**	33/1	45	5
265²	**She's Dawan (IRE) (62)** (PMitchell) **3-8-9** LDettori(2) (mid div over 5f)	1¾	**14**	8/1	36	—
				(SP 155.6%)	**14 Rn**	

1m 25.0 (3.60) CSF £32.09 TOTE £6.40: £2.60 £2.20 £1.50 (£29.90) Trio £16.70 OWNER Mr Ali K Al Jafleh (NEWMARKET) BRED Ali K. Al Jafleh

296 Sharpo Wassl, just touched off on the Wolverhampton Fibresand on his debut in February, made no mistake this time, leading below the distance and being ridden along to keep the very persistent runner-up at bay. A June foal, he will be put away until the middle of the summer to mature. (5/1: op 5/2)
Masterpiece, quite a tall individual with some substance, made a very pleasing debut. Looking the possible winner as he threw down his challenge in the short straight, he had a good battle with Sharpo Wassl in the final furlong and only just lost out. He should not take long in opening his account. (9/2: 6/1-7/2)
Sharp Temper, a sturdy individual who is a half-brother to the useful juvenile hurdler Kerawi, was very well supported in the market. He rather lost his pitch running down the hill but, rousted along in the straight, picked up nicely. His jockey was easy on him in the closing stages when he realised he could not overhaul the front two in time, but the colt kept on in pleasing style. He is sure to come on for this and should be able to find a small race. (4/5: op 5/2)
Nervous Rex, who has been gelded since last year, did not look fully fit but still moved to the front turning for home. Headed below the distance, he could then only go up and down in the same place. (16/1)
Eastern Eagle (IRE), with something left to work on, was at the back of the field until staying on from below the distance. He ran a similar race over this trip here last year on his only start as a two-year-old, and certainly needs further. (14/1: op 8/1)
Bathe In Light (USA) was at the back of the field until making late headway. She will do better over further. (9/1: 5/1-10/1)
Hajat (10/1: op 6/1)

476 ALKHAM H'CAP (0-70) (4-Y.O+) (Class E)

4-20 (4-22) **1m 1f 149y** £3,226.25 (£965.00: £462.50: £211.25) Stalls: High GOING minus 0.30 sec per fur (GF)

				SP	RR	SF
10⁸	**Kedwick (IRE) (53)** (PRHedger) **8-9-1b** TQuinn(4) (b: stdy hdwy on ins over 4f out: led 1f out: r.o wl)	—	**1**	9/1	70	5
	Eurobox Boy (56) (APJarvis) **4-9-4** WJO'Connor(12) (led to 1f out: unable qckn)	5	**2**	11/1	65	—
405⁷	**South Eastern Fred (49)** (HJCollingridge) **6-8-11** JQuinn(7) (hld up: rdn & ev ch over 1f out: one pce)	1¼	**3**	9/2 3	56	—
187⁴	**Arzani (USA) (51)** (DJSCosgrove) **6-8-13** MRimmer(15) (lost pl over 3f out: r.o one pce fnl 2f)	2½	**4**	12/1	54	—
	Proud Brigadier (IRE) (45) (MRBosley) **9-8-7** CRutter(9) (b: dwlt: rdn & hdwy 2f out: one pce)	1¼	**5**	25/1	46	—
435⁸	**Father Dan (IRE) (56)** (MissGayKelleway) **8-9-4** DHolland(13) (nvr nr to chal)	1¾	**6**	11/1	54	—
	Country Thatch (55) (CAHorgan) **4-9-3** PaulEddery(11) (prom 8f)	½	**7**	20/1	52	—
290⁸	**Tomal (42)** (RIngram) **5-8-4** AMcGlone(6) (nvr nrr)	½	**8**	20/1	38	—
105¹¹	**One In The Eye (41)** (JRPoulton) **4-8-0**(3) MartinDwyer(14) (nvr nrr)	s.h	**9**	16/1	37	—
	Kristal Breeze (56) (WRMuir) **5-9-4** JReid(10) (bit bkwd: nvr nrr)	1¾	**10**	10/1	49	—
*380**	**Captain's Day (50)** (HJCollingridge) **5-8-7**(5) RMullen(1) (plld hrd: prom 8f)	1	**11**	7/2 1	41	—
380³	**Mimosa (63)** (SDow) **4-9-6**(5) ADaly(2) (plld hrd: prom 7f)	2	**12**	11/1	51	—
	Scottish Hero (55) (LadyHerries) **4-8-10**(7) PDoe(3) (lw: a bhd)	1½	**13**	12/1	41	—
	Challenger (IRE) (44) (JJSheehan) **4-8-6** AClark(8) (bit bkwd: hld up: rdn over 3f out: wknd over 2f out)	1½	**14**	25/1	27	—
352²	**Bagshot (53)** (GLMoore) **6-9-1** SWhitworth(5) (lw: hdwy over 3f out: wknd over 2f out)	4	**15**	4/1 2	29	—
				(SP 143.0%)	**15 Rn**	

2m 6.2 (8.50) CSF £107.36 CT £482.66 TOTE £13.00: £5.30 £3.00 £3.10 (£124.00) Trio £209.20 OWNER Mrs Joyce Griffiths (CHICHESTER) BRED D. Cordell-Lavarack

Kedwick (IRE) bounced back to form. Travelling well throughout the race, he was rousted along to lead a furlong from home and soon put the issue beyond doubt. He needs three weeks between his races according to his trainer. (9/1)
Eurobox Boy made a pleasing return, and set the pace until put in his place by the winner a furlong from home. (11/1: 7/1-12/1)
220 South Eastern Fred is better on the All-Weather - he has gained eight of his nine victories on the sand - but still gave a good account of himself, having every chance early in the short straight before tapped for toe. (9/2)
140 Arzani (USA) was outpaced as the race began in earnest running downhill, but struggled on again in the short straight to finish a moderate fourth. (12/1)
Proud Brigadier (IRE) began to pick up ground from the back of the field early in the straight, but could then only go up and down in the same place. (25/1)
248 Father Dan (IRE) (11/1: 8/1-12/1)
380 Mimosa (11/1: 8/1-12/1)

477 LEVY BOARD H'CAP (0-70) (3-Y.O+) (Class E)

4-55 (4-58) **6f 189y** £3,304.25 (£989.00: £474.50: £217.25) Stalls: High GOING minus 0.30 sec per fur (GF)

Form	Horse	Dist	Pos	SP	RR	SF
241^{10}	**Sharp 'n Smart (64)** (BSmart) **5-9-5**(5) ADaly(13) (lw: a.p: led 1f out: rdn out)	—	**1**	14/1	75	58
	Victory Team (IRE) (68) (GBBalding) **5-10-0** TQuinn(3) (a.p: hrd rdn over 1f out: r.o)	1½	**2**	$6/1^{2}$	76	59
	Scathebury (55) (KRBurke) **4-9-1** KFallon(11) (lw: hdwy on ins over 1f out: r.o ins fnl f)	1¾	**3**	14/1	58	41
321^{6}	**Sound the Trumpet (IRE) (53)** (RCSpicer) **5-8-13** TSprake(5) (a.p: led over 3f out to 1f out: unable qckn)	hd	**4**	33/1	56	39
	Sis Garden (45) (JCullinan) **4-8-5b** JQuinn(14) (hld up: rdn over 2f out: r.o one pce)	½	**5**	14/1	47	30
	Flying Harold (45) (MRChannon) **4-8-0**(5)ow3 PPMurphy(4) (led over 3f: rdn over 2f out: one pce)	s.h	**6**	25/1	47	27
	Aybeegirl (63) (MrsJCecil) **3-8-5**(3) MartinDwyer(9) (prom over 5f)	1¾	**7**	9/1	61	29
383^{3}	**Perilous Plight (62)** (MrsLStubbs) **6-9-8** JReid(15) (nvr nr to chal)	s.h	**8**	10/1	60	43
	Ameer Alfayaafi (IRE) (50) (BJMeehan) **4-8-10** MTebbutt(8) (a mid div)	5	**9**	9/1	36	19
403^{2}	**Greatest (66)** (MissGayKelleway) **6-9-12b** DHolland(1) (prom tl rn wd bnd & wknd over 2f out)	¾	**10**	$2/1^{1}$	50	33
382^{2}	**Royal Carlton (IRE) (65)** (GLMoore) **5-9-11** SWhitworth(2) (bhd fnl 4f)	1½	**11**	$8/1^{3}$	46	29
	Utmost Zeal (USA) (64) (PWHarris) **4-9-10** AMcGlone(10) (bhd fnl 2f)	s.h	**12**	$8/1^{3}$	45	28
120^{6}	**Oberons Boy (IRE) (62)** (SDow) **4-9-8** WRyan(7) (lw: s.i.s: a bhd)	½	**13**	16/1	42	25
	Generous Present (55) (JWPayne) **4-9-1** RCochrane(6) (a bhd)	1½	**14**	10/1	31	14
	Irish Fiction (IRE) (64) (DJSCosgrove) **3-8-9** MRimmer(12) (a bhd)	1½	**15**	25/1	37	5
362^{5}	**Our Kevin (59)** (BAPearce) **3-8-4b** DRMcCabe(16) (a bhd)	2½	**16**	25/1	26	—

(SP 148.4%) **16 Rn**

1m 23.6 (2.20) CSF £102.27 CT £1,205.71 TOTE £19.00: £5.80 £2.80 £4.30 £6.20 (£113.30) Trio £877.40 OWNER Mr K. H. Burks (LAMBOURN) BRED Aston Park Stud

WEIGHT FOR AGE 3yo-15lb

171 Sharp 'n Smart bounced back to form on this return to grass, leading a furlong from home and being rousted along to score. (14/1)

Victory Team (IRE) made a pleasing return under top weight. Never far away, he kept on well for second prize but never looked like overhauling the winner. Both his wins to date have come on the Equitrack. (6/1)

Scathebury, well beaten in a novice claiming hurdle at Wincanton at the end of January, made giant strides along the inside rail early in the straight and kept on well for third prize. (14/1)

Sound the Trumpet (IRE) moved to the front running down the hill but, collared a furlong from home, could only complete in his own time. He has won just once from twenty-nine starts and that victory came three years ago. (33/1)

Sis Garden chased the leaders but could only struggle on at one pace in the last three furlongs. (14/1)

Flying Harold, in front to halfway, could then only go up and down in the same place. He remains a maiden. (25/1)

382 Royal Carlton (IRE) (8/1: 6/1-9/1)

478 KINGSNORTH H'CAP (0-70) (3-Y.O) (Class E)

5-25 (5-26) **1m 4f** £2,940.25 (£877.00: £418.50: £189.25) Stalls: High GOING minus 0.30 sec per fur (GF)

Form	Horse	Dist	Pos	SP	RR	SF
	Tasik Chini (USA) (70) (PFICole) **3-9-7** TQuinn(6) (lw: mde all: rdn out)	—	**1**	$9/4^{1}$	78	—
	Herbshan Dancer (56) (BRMillman) **3-8-7** TSprake(4) (plld hrd: hdwy over 3f out: ev ch over 1f out: unable qckn)	1½	**2**	15/2	62	—
	Classic Mystery (IRE) (64) (BJMeehan) **3-9-1** MTebbutt(5) (chsd wnr over 3f: lost pl 4f out: rallied over 1f out: one pce ins fnl f)	¾	**3**	$9/2^{2}$	69	—
	Oliver (IRE) (50) (RWArmstrong) **3-8-1** JQuinn(3) (bit bkwd: rdn over 3f out: no hdwy fnl 2f)	3	**4**	$9/4^{1}$	51	—
	Warrior King (IRE) (55) (MrsPNDutfield) **3-8-6** DHolland(2) (w'like: bit bkwd: hdwy 6f out: chsd wnr over 4f out: ev ch over 1f out: sn wknd)	2½	**5**	14/1	53	—
366^{3}	**Leg Beforum (IRE) (55)** (LMontagueHall) **3-8-6** DaneO'Neill(1) (chsd wnr over 8f out tl over 4f out: wknd 3f out)	5	**6**	$6/1^{3}$	46	—

(SP 112.4%) **6 Rn**

2m 45.1 (13.90) CSF £18.05 TOTE £2.50: £2.00 £3.70 (£6.90) OWNER H R H Sultan Ahmad Shah (WHATCOMBE) BRED Oak Cliff Thoroughbred Bloodstock Ltd 1985

Tasik Chini (USA), who has been gelded over the winter, looked in great shape for this seasonal debut and made every post a winning one, showing real battling qualities to keep his persistent rivals at bay. (9/4)

Herbshan Dancer looked a serious threat to the winner in the straight, but that rival produced something extra in the final furlong. (15/2: 7/2-8/1)

Classic Mystery (IRE), who was outpaced as the race began in earnest in the last half-mile, tried to get back into it below the distance but was making no further impression in the last one hundred yards. (9/2)

Oliver (IRE) looked big and well for this reappearance, but was making little impression on the principals in the short home straight.(9/4: 3/1-2/1)

Warrior King (IRE), an ex-Irish gelding, did not look fully tuned up and so it proved, for after having every chance below the distance, he soon tired as lack of a recent run took its toll. (14/1: 6/1-16/1)

366 Leg Beforum (IRE) again demonstrated he does not stay this trip, and had shot his bolt three furlongs from home. (6/1)

T/Jkpt: Not won; £10,287.32 to Leicester 27/3/97. T/Plpt: £438.30 (29.08 Tckts). T/Qdpt: £264.60 (2.47 Tckts) AK

LEICESTER (R-H) (Good to firm, Good patches)

Thursday March 27th

WEATHER: sunny periods WIND: str bhd

479 BESCABY MAIDEN STKS (3-Y.O) (Class D)

2-10 (2-11) **1m 8y** £3,645.60 (£1,087.80: £519.40: £235.20) Stalls: High GOING minus 0.50 sec per fur (F)

Form	Horse	Dist	Pos	SP	RR	SF
	Sir Talbot (RHannon) **3-9-0** PatEddery(5) (lw: mde all: shkn up over 2f out: r.o wl)	—	**1**	10/1	85	35
446^{2}	**Titta Ruffo** (BJMeehan) **3-9-0** MTebbutt(2) (a.p: hdwy to chal over 1f out: rdn & no ex nr fin)	1¼	**2**	$7/4^{1}$	83	33
	Majesty (IRE) (PFICole) **3-9-0** TQuinn(8) (leggy: unf: hld up: hdwy over 3f out: hrd rdn wl over 1f out: nt pce to chal)	¾	**3**	$9/2^{3}$	81	31
	Bubbly (JLDunlop) **3-9-0** KDarley(7) (bit bkwd: chsd ldrs: ev ch 2f out: sn rdn: one pce)	2½	**4**	12/1	76	26
	Moonshiner (USA) (86) (GWragg) **3-9-0** MHills(1) (bit bkwd: plld hrd: hdwy over 2f out: rdn & edgd rt over 1f out: eased whn btn fnl f)	7	**5**	$9/4^{2}$	62	12
	Pen Friend (WJHaggas) **3-9-0** RCochrane(6) (lengthy: scope: bit bkwd: s.s: rdn along ½-wy: a in rr)	4	**6**	14/1	54	4

Form	Horse	Btn	Pos	SP	RR	SF
425^{8}	**Sibor Star** (DBurchell) **3-9-0** SDrowne(4) (rdn over 3f out: a bhd)	4	**7**	100/1	46	—
	Solar Storm (MBell) **3-9-0** MFenton(3) (unf: w wnr to ½-wy: rdn & wknd over 2f out: t.o)	10	**8**	14/1	26	—
				(SP 116.4%)	**8 Rn**	

1m 37.0 (2.00) CSF £25.96 TOTE £11.20: £2.60 £1.10 £1.40 (£22.80) OWNER Mrs F. Percy-Davis (MARLBOROUGH) BRED Mrs W. H. Gibson Fleming

Sir Talbot showed promise in a couple of outings in the autumn and, appreciating these more forceful tactics, won readily. (10/1: 8/1-12/1)
446 Titta Ruffo had the longer trip that he needs but he had been given insufficient time to recover from his pleasing seasonal debut just less than a week ago and the winner was always comfortably holding his sustained late challenge. (7/4)
Majesty (IRE), a lightly-made half-brother to two winners, has a lot of white about him and did not look particularly happy on this lively ground. Asked for his effort inside the distance, he did keep battling away but lacked the speed to mount a challenge. (9/2)
Bubbly, very much in need of this pipe-opener, showed up with the pace until finding demands too great inside the distance. (12/1: op 6/1)
Moonshiner (USA), a son of prolific race-mare Marling, will strip fitter with this run under his belt and may well do better if returning to sprinting. (9/4)
Pen Friend has plenty of stamina in his breeding but he lost ground at the start and was always being taken along much faster than he wished. (14/1: op 8/1)

480 BILLESDON (S) STKS (I) (3-Y.O+) (Class G)

2-40 (2-42) **7f 9y** £2,077.00 (£421.50: £421.50) Stalls: High GOING minus 0.50 sec per fur (F)

Form	Horse	Btn	Pos	SP	RR	SF
411^{2}	**First Gold (47)** (JWharton) **8-9-7** KFallon(10) (b: bhd: rdn over 4f out: hdwy 2f out: r.o strly to ld wl ins fnl f)	—	**1**	$5/2^{1}$	43	38
422^{12}	**Backhander (IRE) (41)** (RTPhillips) **5-9-7b** MTebbutt(5) (led: rdn & hung rt over 1f out: hdd wl ins fnl f)	½	**2**	25/1	42	37
424^{8}	**Northern Fan (IRE) (57)** (NTinkler) **5-9-12** KDarley(7) (lw: chsd ldrs: rdn & lost pl over 3f out: rallied appr fnl f: fin wl)	d.h	**2**	$4/1^{2}$	47	42
	Bag And A Bit (50) (NMBabbage) **4-9-2** WRyan(1) (a.p: ev ch over 1f out: rdn & unable qckn fnl f)	2½	**4**	$5/2^{1}$	31	26
	Rafter-J (JohnHarris) **6-9-7b¹** TQuinn(9) (b: lw: hdwy 3f out: sn rdn: btn whn eased ins fnl f)	4	**5**	14/1	27	22
425^{9}	**Patrick** (DBurchell) **3-8-1**$^{(5)}$ GMilligan(12) (chsd ldrs over 5f)	1¾	**6**	20/1	23	3
425^{5}	**Southern Rule** (PMooney) **10-9-0b**$^{(7)}$ DHayes(11) (prom: ev ch 2f out: wknd appr fnl f)	nk	**7**	12/1	22	17
275^{7}	**Dhes-C (46)** (RHollinshead) **4-8-13**$^{(3)}$ FLynch(2) (hld up: hdwy over 2f out: sn rdn: wknd appr fnl f)	6	**8**	$8/1^{3}$	4	—
	River Ensign (WMBrisbourne) **4-8-11**$^{(5)}$ RMullen(6) (small: lt-f: sn drvn along: nvr trbld ldrs: t.o)	9	**9**	50/1	—	—
285^{8}	**Cerbera (40)** (JPSmith) **8-9-7** DeclanO'Shea(8) (bhd fr ½-wy: t.o)	9	**10**	33/1	—	—
195^{8}	**New Regime (IRE) (19)** (PTDalton) **4-8-13**$^{(3)}$ PMcCabe(4) (s.s: a wl bhd: t.o)	s.h	**11**	50/1	—	—
164^{13}	**Lady Komaite** (TTBill) **4-9-2** SDrowne(3) (hung rt: a bhd: t.o fnl 3f)	13	**12**	50/1	—	—
				(SP 120.0%)	**12 Rn**	

1m 25.1 (2.50) CSF FG&NF £5.38 FG&B £35.44 TOTE £3.40: £1.40 NF £1.80 B £5.90 (FG&NF £3.40 FG&B £18.00) Trio £16.10 OWNER Mr K. D. Standen (MELTON MOWBRAY) BRED Messinger Stud Ltd
WEIGHT FOR AGE 3yo-15lb
No bid
STEWARDS' ENQUIRY Hayes susp. 5&7/4/97 (improper & incorrect use of whip).

411 First Gold, kept busy on the All-Weather and over hurdles, did not find top gear until late on but he produced a storming run when he did find his stride and gained command nearing the finish. (5/2)
Backhander (IRE) did his best to gallop his rivals into the ground and it was only inside the final fifty yards that he was finally forced to give best. This is his class and there is a prize in store. (25/1)
390 Northern Fan (IRE) has done all his winning at a mile and his strong, late challenge just failed to materialise. (4/1: 3/1-9/2)
Bag And A Bit, like a matchstick with the wood shaved off, pushed the pace and had every chance until failing to quicken in the last two hundred yards. (5/2)
Rafter-J wore blinkers for the first time and looked likely to make his presence felt entering the last quarter-mile but he did not find a lot when put to the test and the position was accepted. (14/1)
Southern Rule (12/1: op 8/1)

481 KINGFISHER H'CAP (0-70) (4-Y.O+) (Class E)

3-10 (3-11) **1m 3f 183y** £3,343.55 (£1,000.40: £479.70: £219.35) Stalls: High GOING minus 0.50 sec per fur (F)

Form	Horse	Btn	Pos	SP	RR	SF
402*	**In the Money (IRE) (47)** (RHollinshead) **8-8-5**$^{(3)}$ FLynch(5) (lw: hld up in tch: shkn up to ld over 2f out: r.o wl)	—	**1**	$5/2^{1}$	60	31
430^{7}	**Fabulous Mtoto (54)** (MSSaunders) **7-9-1** NCarlisle(7) (lw: s.s: plld hrd: hdwy ent st: hrd rdn over 1f out: kpt on wl towards fin)	¾	**2**	10/1	66	37
405^{2}	**Prince Danzig (IRE) (63)** (DJGMurraySmith) **6-9-10** MHills(2) (hld up mid div: rdn over 3f out: hdwy fnl 2f: nvr nrr)	6	**3**	$3/1^{2}$	67	38
	Reaganesque (USA) (54) (PGMurphy) **5-9-1** SDrowne(8) (lw: w ldr: led over 3f out tl over 2f out: rdn & outpcd appr fnl f)	½	**4**	$9/2^{3}$	57	28
410^{9}	**May King Mayhem (37)** (MrsALMKing) **4-7-10** DeclanO'Shea(10) (lost pl 6f out: hdwy on ins 3f out: hrd rdn over 2f out: wknd appr fnl f)	nk	**5**	20/1	40	9
	Kashan (IRE) (35) (PHayward) **9-7-3**$^{(7)}$ IonaWands(9) (hld up: effrt over 3f out: nt rch ldrs)	1¼	**6**	33/1	36	7
	Lucky Blue (48) (SEarle) **10-8-9** RPerham(12) (led tl hdd & wknd over 3f out)	8	**7**	25/1	38	9
	On The Wildside (50) (MRChannon) **4-8-9** TQuinn(11) (hld up: hdwy 5f out: wknd over 2f out)	nk	**8**	10/1	40	9
373^{13}	**Romantic Warrior (45)** (KSBridgwater) **4-8-4** TSprake(4) (prom to ½-wy: sn lost tch: t.o)	10	**9**	33/1	21	—
	Jump The Lights (60) (SPCWoods) **4-9-5** WRyan(6) (plld hrd: a bhd: t.o)	1½	**10**	10/1	34	3
	Contrarie (37) (MJRyan) **4-7-10** GBardwell(1) (chsd ldrs: rdn 5f out: wknd over 3f out: t.o)	4	**11**	12/1	6	—
				(SP 121.2%)	**11 Rn**	

2m 32.3 (3.80) CSF £25.74 CT £72.42 TOTE £3.20: £1.20 £2.10 £2.20 (£12.00) Trio £7.80 OWNER Mr J. E. Bigg (UPPER LONGDON) BRED Cheveley Park Stud Ltd
LONG HANDICAP Kashan (IRE) 7-5 Contrarie 7-7
WEIGHT FOR AGE 4yo-2lb

402* In the Money (IRE), a previous winner here, is at the top of his form at present and this comfortably-gained success enabled him to complete his hat-trick. (5/2)
402 Fabulous Mtoto has had a couple of head-to-heads with the winner on the All-Weather recently but on this altered handicapping on the Turf, had little or no chance of gaining his revenge. (10/1)

405 Prince Danzig (IRE) has not enjoyed much success on the All-Weather since the turn of the year, and he did not get going this time until it was far too late. (3/1: 5/2-4/1)
Reaganesque (USA), fit from a successful hurdling campaign, had everything in his favour but he had to do battle to get to the front and that had its effect when the principals delivered their bids. (9/2)
May King Mayhem has cut no ice up until now but this was a run full of promise and, with his attractive handicap mark, he could start earning his keep in the near future. (20/1)
Kashan (IRE), having his first outing on the level since June 1994 but fit from hurdling, was never able to prove troublesome despite sticking on. (33/1)

482 GREYHOUND H'CAP (0-80) (4-Y.O+) (Class D)

3-40 (3-40) **1m 1f 218y** £3,741.15 (£1,117.20: £534.10: £242.55) Stalls: High GOING minus 0.50 sec per fur (F)

				SP	RR	SF
422[8]	**Obelos (USA) (70)** (MissSJWilton) **6-9-6** MTebbutt(4) (a.p: led over 2f out: hrd rdn: all out)	—	**1**	14/1	80	39
	Shalateeno (65) (BRMillman) **4-9-1** KDarley(7) (b: led after 2f tl over 2f out: kpt on u.p fnl f)	¾	**2**	13/2[3]	74	33
	Danegold (IRE) (71) (MRChannon) **5-9-7v** TQuinn(3) (hld up: effrt u.p over 3f out: styd on wl fnl f)	1	**3**	7/2[1]	78	37
389[4]	**Hill Farm Dancer (59)** (WMBrisbourne) **6-8-4**(5) RMullen(8) (s.s: hdwy 5f out: rdn & one pce fnl 2f)	1¾	**4**	13/2[3]	63	22
	Zidac (74) (PJMakin) **5-9-10** PatEddery(9) (b: led 2f: hrd rdn over 1f out: one pce)	2	**5**	7/2[1]	75	34
131[4]	**Soviet Bride (IRE) (72)** (SDow) **5-9-8** WRyan(1) (plld hrd early: hld up: rdn over 2f out: eased whn btn fnl f)	3½	**6**	9/2[2]	68	27
346[6]	**Scenicris (IRE) (65)** (RHollinshead) **4-8-12**(3) FLynch(6) (hld up: effrt & rdn 3f out: no imp)	4	**7**	10/1	54	13
	Indian Nectar (55) (GBBalding) **4-8-5v[1]** SDrowne(5) (swtg: prom: rdn over 3f out: grad wknd)	1¼	**8**	14/1	42	1
	Haroldon (IRE) (72) (BPalling) **8-9-8** TSprake(2) (b: bkwd: rdn over 3f out: a bhd)	2½	**9**	16/1	55	14
				(SP 117.6%)	**9 Rn**	

2m 6.8 (3.10) CSF £94.17 CT £360.13 TOTE £15.20: £4.60 £2.30 £1.70 (£45.00) Trio £120.20 OWNER Gilberts Animal Feed Products (STOKE-ON-TRENT) BRED Lord Howard de Walden
OFFICIAL EXPLANATION **Obelos (USA): the gelding had a virus in January and subsequently resented the kick-back. He would be unlikely to run on the All-Weather again.**
Obelos (USA) would have put his most fervent fan off with his action to post but he did the business on the return journey and there was no fluke about it. (14/1)
Shalateeno, taken to post early, showed her true battling qualities after being headed and made the winner fight all the way to the line. She should not have much trouble in adding to her score. (13/2)
Danegold (IRE), a winner over hurdles in December, has plenty of ability when he cares to put it to good use but he did not put his best foot forward until far too late. (7/2)
389 Hill Farm Dancer can be a bit of a madam but she did look the possible winner entering the final quarter-mile only to be tapped for toe in an all-out battle to the post. She is a desperate mover on this sort of ground. (13/2)
Zidac runs his best races when fresh and he remained in the action with every chance until being eased when his measure had been taken. (7/2)

483 GADSBY H'CAP (0-90) (3-Y.O) (Class C)

4-10 (4-11) **7f 9y** £5,775.00 (£1,725.00: £825.00: £375.00) Stalls: High GOING minus 0.50 sec per fur (F)

				SP	RR	SF
	Plaisir d'Amour (IRE) (74) (NACallaghan) **3-8-5** PatEddery(4) (a.p: led over 1f out: rdn & hung rt fnl f: comf)	—	**1**	7/2[1]	87+	41
	Last Chance (67) (DJSCosgrove) **3-7-12** NCarlisle(8) (lt-f: unf: led tl hdd over 1f out: kpt on u.p)	1½	**2**	12/1	77	31
	Zaima (IRE) (84) (JLDunlop) **3-9-1** KDarley(2) (hld up mid div: rdn & hdwy over 2f out: kpt on towards fin)	1¼	**3**	9/2[2]	91	45
	Return of Amin (67) (JDBethell) **3-7-9**(3) MHenry(10) (a.p: ev ch over 1f out: one pce)	1½	**4**	5/1[3]	70	24
413[2]	**The Wyandotte Inn (73)** (RHollinshead) **3-8-1**(3) FLynch(6) (lw: plld hrd: trckd ldrs: kpt on one pce fnl f)	1¼	**5**	8/1	74	28
	Baritone (78) (JWWatts) **3-8-9** KFallon(3) (lw: hld up in rr: hdwy appr fnl f: nvr nrr)	1¼	**6**	8/1	76	30
	Kewarra (75) (BRMillman) **3-8-6** TSprake(9) (bkwd: plld hrd: hld up mid div: no hdwy fnl 2f)	½	**7**	20/1	72	26
	Trading Aces (68) (MBell) **3-7-8**(5) RMullen(11) (bkwd: prom: rdn over 3f out: wknd wl over 1f out)	s.h	**8**	14/1	64	18
	Always Alight (66) (KRBurke) **3-7-11**ow1 FNorton(5) (bit bkwd: a bhd: rdn ½-wy: no imp)	5	**9**	25/1	51	4
	Tycoon Girl (IRE) (81) (BJMeehan) **3-8-12** MTebbutt(7) (bkwd: hld up: a bhd)	2	**10**	8/1	62	16
	Doc Ryan's (78) (MJRyan) **3-8-9** GCarter(1) (bkwd: a bhd)	1½	**11**	12/1	55	9
				(SP 121.1%)	**11 Rn**	

1m 23.5 (0.90) CSF £44.25 CT £182.56 TOTE £3.50: £1.20 £2.50 £2.40 (£31.70) Trio £58.00 OWNER Mr M. Tabor (NEWMARKET) BRED L. K. and K. McCreery
Plaisir d'Amour (IRE), a full-sister to the high-class Danehill Dancer, put plenty of value to her name with this success and there should be more glory to follow. (7/2)
Last Chance produced his best form early on last year and this first run for his new stable would suggest now is the time to catch him. (12/1)
Zaima (IRE) is not really robust enough to carry weight and, finding this trip plenty short enough, was never really close enough to pose a threat. (9/2)
Return of Amin came good on easier ground in the autumn and, though he gave a good account of himself, was short of pace when the tempo picked up approaching the final furlong. (5/1)
413 The Wyandotte Inn did not impress to post and he was always struggling in an attempt to deliver his challenge. (8/1)
Baritone gave the impression that more yielding ground is needed and it was only late on that he began to stretch out. (8/1: 6/1-9/1)
Tycoon Girl (IRE) (8/1: op 9/2)
Doc Ryan's (12/1: 8/1-14/1)

484 BILLESDON (S) STKS (II) (3-Y.O+) (Class G)

4-40 (4-41) **7f 9y** £2,077.00 (£572.00: £271.00) Stalls: High GOING minus 0.50 sec per fur (F)

				SP	RR	SF
429[9]	**Astral Invader (IRE) (48)** (MSSaunders) **5-9-7v** RPerham(2) (mde all: edgd rt nr fin: r.o wl)	—	**1**	20/1	61	45
	Broughtons Turmoil (77) (WJMusson) **8-9-7** PatEddery(10) (stdd s: hdwy over 2f out: hung rt over 1f out: n.m.r nr fin)	1¼	**2**	5/6[1]	58	42
365[6]	**Summerville Wood (62)** (PMooney) **3-8-3b**(3) FLynch(12) (lw: a.p: rdn over 2f out: hung lft 1f out: r.o)	nk	**3**	9/2[2]	58	27
	Mubariz (IRE) (59) (CSmith) **5-9-7** WJO'Connor(8) (hld up: hdwy 3f out: sn rdn: one pce fnl 2f)	2½	**4**	33/1	52	36
385[8]	**Dahiyah (USA) (63)** (BSmart) **6-9-12v** RCochrane(7) (lw: hld up: hdwy 2f out: one pce appr fnl f)	hd	**5**	13/2[3]	57	41
421[10]	**Shontaine (58)** (MJohnston) **4-9-12** MHills(9) (lw: prom: hrd rdn over 2f out: eased whn btn fnl f)	½	**6**	13/2[3]	55	39
	Control Freak (52) (AGFoster) **3-8-1** TSprake(4) (hdwy ½-wy: wknd over 2f out: t.o)	15	**7**	25/1	11	—
404[5]	**Zelaya (IRE)** (GLMoore) **4-8-12**(7)ow3 MBatchelor(6) (plld hrd: prom over 4f: t.o)	3½	**8**	14/1	6	—
	Auchinleck Judge (JLHarris) **4-9-7** FNorton(3) (a bhd: t.o)	4	**9**	66/1	—	—
352[8]	**Fancy Design (IRE) (38)** (PMitchell) **4-8-13**(3) MHenry(1) (b.hind: bhd fnl 3f: t.o)	1	**10**	50/1	—	—

Dispol Prince (GROldroyd) **4-9-7** GCarter(11) (lt-f: unf: bkwd: s.s: a bhd: t.o) 1¼	**11**	33/1	—	—
76[14] **Fiery Footsteps (31)** (CLPopham) **5-8-13**(3) RHavlin(5) (prom tl rdn & wknd 3f out: t.o) 5	**12**	50/1	—	—

(SP 126.0%) **12 Rn**

1m 24.4 (1.80) CSF £34.66 TOTE £17.10: £2.80 £1.10 £1.90 (£36.80) Trio £28.00 OWNER Mr M. S. Saunders (WELLS) BRED J. C. Fagan
WEIGHT FOR AGE 3yo-15lb
No bid. Broughtons Turmoil clmd RMillman £6,000

385 Astral Invader (IRE) had the edge in fitness and, adopting more forceful tactics, was always finding enough to repel the determined late effort of the favourite. (20/1)

Broughtons Turmoil should have had the beating of these rivals but he was making hard work of it when hanging right at the distance and it is possible the ground was faster than he cared for. (5/6: 4/7-evens)

Summerville Wood, stepping back to a more suitable trip, ploughed a lone furrow up the far rail until edging left under pressure and tightening up the favourite nearing the finish. A race of this description is there for the taking. (9/2: op 7/1)

Mubariz (IRE), who may need another furlong, ran well in this first seller and he should not be hard to place if kept in this company. (33/1)

243 Dahiyah (USA), making progress from off the pace in the latter stages, is certainly capable of improving on this. (13/2: op 4/1)

404* Shontaine, struggling to hold his pitch entering the last quarter-mile, could do little more that stay on at the one pace. (13/2: op 4/1)

485 KEYTHORPE MAIDEN STKS (3-Y.O F) (Class D)

5-10 (5-13) **7f 9y** £3,645.60 (£1,087.80: £519.40: £235.20) Stalls: High GOING minus 0.50 sec per fur (F)

		SP	RR	SF
Dust Dancer (JLDunlop) **3-8-11** PatEddery(4) (still unf: mde virtually all: edgd rt u.p fnl f: hld on) ....—	**1**	10/11[1]	76	47
Heavenly Ray (USA) (JRFanshawe) **3-8-11** KFallon(8) (still unf: a.p: rdn over 2f out: jnd wnr & edgd rt 1f out: r.o) ....¾	**2**	5/2[2]	74	45
Tabasco Jazz (BJMeehan) **3-8-11** MTebbutt(1) (w'like: plld hrd: outpcd over 2f out: styd on fnl f) 4	**3**	12/1	65	36
Perlethorpe (MBell) **3-8-11** MFenton(10) (w'like: str: bkwd: nvr gng pce of ldrs) 8	**4**	14/1	47	18
Pretty Sharp (64) (NMBabbage) **3-8-11** TSprake(2) (plld hrd: prom: rdn over 2f out: wknd qckly over 1f out) ...6	**5**	7/1[3]	33	4
Victoria House (IRE) (MJHeaton-Ellis) **3-8-11** SDrowne(7) (leggy: lt-f: b: rdn 3f out: a bhd: t.o) 3½	**6**	16/1	25	—
247[7] **Aquatic Queen (42)** (RJWeaver) **3-8-4**(7) VictoriaAppleby(3) (outpcd: t.o) ....¾	**7**	66/1	24	—
Kay-Jay (MissSJWilton) **3-8-8**(3) RHavlin(6) (w'like: bit bkwd: dwlt: rdn 4f out: a bhd: t.o) 7	**8**	50/1	8	—

(SP 117.1%) **8 Rn**

1m 23.5 (0.90) CSF £3.09 TOTE £1.70: £1.10 £1.10 £2.20 (£1.60) Trio £9.90 OWNER Hesmonds Stud (ARUNDEL) BRED Hesmonds Stud Ltd

Dust Dancer, very free to post, was allowed to dictate from the break but she had to get serious to hold on towards the finish. She did edge off a true line in the closing stages and could have been feeling the ground. (10/11: 4/5-5/4)

Heavenly Ray (USA), a late May foal who will get further, responded to pressure and may have poked her head in front briefly but the favourite, under a strong ride, refused to give best. She does look a ready-made winner. (5/2)

Tabasco Jazz, a sister to a couple of winners, showed signs of greenness on this debut and is capable of better. (12/1: op 5/1)

Perlethorpe, a strongly-made debutante with plenty left to work on, was never able to get herself within striking range of the principals. (14/1: op 6/1)

Pretty Sharp, keen to get on with it, went with the pace until fading under pressure below the distance. She was probably a bit out of her class. (7/1)

T/Jkpt: Not won; £19,097.63 to 29/3/97. T/Plpt: £26.80 (707.6 Tckts). T/Qdpt: £13.20 (73.96 Tckts) IM

0454-LINGFIELD (L-H) (Standard)
Thursday March 27th

Race 5: hand timed
WEATHER: sunny WIND: fresh half bhd

486 COLD AS CHARITY CLAIMING STKS (4-Y.O+) (Class F)

2-30 (2-30) **1m 4f (Equitrack)** £2,277.00 (£627.00: £297.00) Stalls: Low GOING minus 0.43 sec per fur (FST)

		SP	RR	SF
444[15] **At Liberty (IRE) (77)** (RHannon) **5-9-10** DaneO'Neill(6) (lw: chsd ldr over 7f out: led over 3f out: rdn out) .....—	**1**	Evens[1]	81	51
402[6] **One Off the Rail (USA) (70)** (GLMoore) **7-9-0** SWhitworth(1) (b: lw: hld up: jnd wnr over 3f out: ev ch fnl 3f: unable qckn ins fnl f) 2½	**2**	11/8[2]	68	38
381[4] **Bedouin Prince (USA) (36)** (MrsLStubbs) **10-8-10** DHolland(2) (b: chsd ldr: led 8f out tl over 3f out: sn wknd) 11	**3**	11/1[3]	49	19
418[6] **Lahik (IRE) (38)** (KTIvory) **4-8-1**(3) MartinDwyer(3) (bhd fnl 3f) ....¾	**4**	12/1	44	12
321[9] **Wingnut (IRE) (27)** (RIngram) **4-8-2b**ow1 AMcGlone(5) (lw: bhd fnl 5f: t.o) ....dist	**5**	33/1	—	—
336[5] **Rosalee Royale** (JELong) **5-7-13b**[1] LeesaLong(7) (b.hind: lw: led 4f: wknd over 6f out: t.o) 20	**6**	66/1	—	—

(SP 112.6%) **6 Rn**

2m 33.3 (3.30) CSF £2.38 TOTE £2.40: £1.10 £1.10 (£1.10) OWNER Mr Bruce Adams (MARLBOROUGH) BRED Pegasus Farm
WEIGHT FOR AGE 4yo-2lb

At Liberty (IRE) had a tremendous battle with the runner-up and the two forged clear of the rest of the field from over three furlongs out. Rousted along, he managed to get the better of his rival inside the final furlong to gain his first All-Weather victory and his first over this trip. (Evens)

One Off the Rail (USA), taking a drop in class, joined the winner over three furlongs from home and had a tremendous battle with that rival. It looked as if he might gain the day but inside the final furlong he had to accept defeat. A real sand specialist, he has gained nine of his ten victories here, and although the All-Weather season is now all but over, there is one more meeting here next week and the odd All-Weather race here and there on the Turf cards. His shrewd trainer should be able to find a race with him. (11/8)

381 Bedouin Prince (USA), 27lb behind the winner on official adjusted ratings, is a poor performer and, when headed over three furlongs from home, was soon left for dead. (11/1: 8/1-12/1)

418 Lahik (IRE) is a very moderate and exposed animal who remains a maiden now after twenty-four attempts. (12/1: 8/1-14/1)

487 APPLE A DAY (S) STKS (4-Y.O+) (Class G)

3-00 (3-00) **1m 2f (Equitrack)** £1,984.50 (£547.00: £129.75: £129.75) Stalls: Low GOING minus 0.43 sec per fur (FST)

		SP	RR	SF
290[4] **Awesome Power (50)** (JWHills) **11-9-4** AClark(6) (a.p: led 4f out: rdn out) ....—	**1**	2/1[1]	51	20
407[6] **Hatta Sunshine (USA) (51)** (GLMoore) **7-9-1**(3) AWhelan(5) (lw: s.s: hdwy over 4f out: chsd wnr over 2f out: ev ch wl over 1f out: wknd ins fnl f) 2½	**2**	11/4[2]	47	16

418^{8}	**Efficacious (IRE) (22)** (PEccles) **4-8-7** CRutter(7) (a.p: ev ch over 2f out: one pce)	nk	**3**	25/1	36	5
	Duncombe Hall (38) (CACyzer) **4-8-12** DBiggs(8) (bit bkwd: lost pl over 4f out: r.o one pce fnl 2f)	d.h	**3**	$8/1^{3}$	41	10
380^{6}	**Rehaab (52)** (DMorris) **4-8-3**$^{(5)ow1}$ GFaulkner(1) (lost pl over 3f out: r.o one pce fnl 2f)	¾	**5**	$11/4^{2}$	35	3
	Wicklow Boy (IRE) (MrsLCJewell) **6-8-7**$^{(5)}$ SophieMitchell(3) (b: bit bkwd: a bhd)	6	**6**	40/1	30	—
	Circus Colours (JRJenkins) **7-8-12** SWhitworth(2) (lw: a bhd: lame)	6	**7**	10/1	20	—
338^{8}	**Komodo (USA) (24)** (JELong) **5-8-12b** LeesaLong(4) (b: led 6f)	1½	**8**	66/1	18	—

(SP 114.6%) **8 Rn**

2m 10.38 (6.08) CSF £6.95 TOTE £1.90: £1.70 £1.50 DH £0.60 E £1.20 (£4.40) OWNER Mr Garrett Freyne (LAMBOURN) BRED G. J. Freyne
No bid

290 Awesome Power knows every inch of this course - he rarely runs anywhere else - and thoroughly enjoyed himself as he led half a mile from home, and was ridden along to assert his authority in the straight to record his tenth course and distance victory - all with Clark aboard. He is yet to win anywhere else since coming over from Ireland many years ago. (2/1)
407 Hatta Sunshine (USA) gave chase to the winner over a quarter of a mile from home and looked a big danger as he sneaked upside the winner's inner turning for home. However, he had little left in the tank inside the final furlong. He won over this trip as a four-year-old but is probably best at a mile. (11/4)
418 Efficacious (IRE) is a very exposed, poor plater but she did not run badly here, having every chance over a quarter of a mile from home before tapped for toe. However, she remains a maiden after twenty-nine attempts, which says it all. (25/1)
Duncombe Hall, who looked dull in his coat and just in need of this first run in nearly six months, got outpaced as the tempo increased from halfway, but did plod on in the straight to force a dead-heat for third prize. He remains a maiden. (8/1)
Rehaab found the drop in class no help and, after getting slightly outpaced over three furlongs from home, could only keep on in her own time. She is yet to show any form on the All-Weather. (11/4)
Circus Colours (10/1: op 4/1)

488 ALL'S FAIR H'CAP (0-90) (3-Y.O+) (Class C)

3-30 (3-31) **5f (Equitrack)** £5,162.75 (£1,538.00: £732.50: £329.75) Stalls: High GOING minus 0.43 sec per fur (FST)

				SP	RR	SF
364^{7}	**Lord Sky (68)** (ABailey) **6-8-7** SSanders(4) (mde all: drvn out)	—	**1**	6/1	71	45
406^{4}	**Mijas (75)** (LMontagueHall) **4-9-0** DaneO'Neill(5) (lw: chsd wnr: rdn over 1f out: unable qckn)	¾	**2**	$5/1^{3}$	76	50
459^{4}	**Ivory's Grab Hire (59)** (KTIvory) **4-7-9b**$^{(3)ow2}$ MartinDwyer(7) (hdwy over 3f out: rdn over 1f out: one pce)	1¼	**3**	7/1	56	28
	Spender (89) (PWHarris) **8-10-0** JStack(3) (bit bkwd: outpcd: hdwy fnl f: r.o)	½	**4**	8/1	84	58
	Tuscan Dawn (75) (JBerry) **7-8-9**$^{(5)}$ PRoberts(2) (hld up: rdn over 2f out: wknd fnl f)	2	**5**	$4/1^{1}$	64	38
406^{2}	**Sally Slade (75)** (CACyzer) **5-9-0** DBiggs(1) (a bhd)	s.h	**6**	$4/1^{1}$	63	37
323^{7}	**Princely Sound (82)** (MBell) **4-9-2**$^{(5)}$ GFaulkner(6) (prom over 2f)	3	**7**	$9/2^{2}$	61	35

(SP 112.7%) **7 Rn**

58.76 secs (0.56) CSF £31.45 TOTE £6.30: £2.10 £4.70 (£17.70) OWNER Mr Ray Bailey (TARPORLEY) BRED R. Barber
LONG HANDICAP Ivory's Grab Hire 7-4

348 Lord Sky made every post a winning one and, responding to pressure, managed to keep his rivals at bay. (6/1)
406 Mijas needs to dominate to show her best, and although not at the front, she had a clear view racing on the outside of the winner. Bustled along in the straight, she could never find that vital turn of foot. (5/1)
459 Ivory's Grab Hire, making a quick reappearance, was carrying 5lb more than his long handicap weight and failed to pick up in the straight. (7/1)
Spender is too high in the handicap at present - 7lb higher than he has ever won off - and looked in need of this first run in four and a half months. Taken off his feet for much of the race, he was doing all his best work in the final furlong. He needs to come down in the weights. (8/1: op 5/1)
Tuscan Dawn, making his All-Weather debut, chased the leaders but was a spent force from below the distance. (4/1)
406 Sally Slade was disappointing and was always struggling. (4/1)

489 BARRY DENNIS BOOKMAKERS H'CAP (0-75) (3-Y.O) (Class D)

4-00 (4-01) **7f (Equitrack)** £3,390.80 (£1,009.40: £480.20: £215.60) Stalls: Low GOING minus 0.43 sec per fur (FST)

				SP	RR	SF
434^{8}	**Eager To Please (74)** (MissGayKelleway) **3-9-7b** DHolland(5) (b: b.hind: lw: hld up: jnd ldr over 3f out: led over 1f out: all out)	—	**1**	$11/4^{2}$	80	32
420^{5}	**Enchanting Eve (70)** (CNAllen) **3-9-0**$^{(3)}$ MartinDwyer(2) (rdn over 4f out: hdwy fnl f: r.o wl)	nk	**2**	$11/4^{2}$	75	27
	Gopi (67) (RHannon) **3-9-0** DaneO'Neill(4) (b: a.p: led over 3f out tl over 1f out: ev ch fnl f: r.o)	hd	**3**	$11/2^{3}$	72	24
420^{6}	**Hever Golf Charger (IRE) (61)** (TJNaughton) **3-8-8** SSanders(3) (w ldr: led over 4f out tl over 3f out: wknd over 2f out)	5	**4**	$9/4^{1}$	55	7
	Prix de Clermont (IRE) (56) (GLewis) **3-8-0**$^{(3)ow1}$ AWhelan(1) (b.off fore: led over 2f)	14	**5**	6/1	18	—

(SP 113.8%) **5 Rn**

1m 27.53 (3.13) CSF £10.05 TOTE £4.20: £1.80 £2.00 (£5.70) OWNER Miss Jo Crowley (WHITCOMBE) BRED Mrs Sara Hood

379* Eager To Please looked in tremendous shape beforehand and put up a really gutsy display to land his first handicap and his first race over seven furlongs. Managing to get in front below the distance, he had a real fight on his hands and, with the runner-up really finishing with a flourish, he found the line only just saving him. (11/4)
420 Enchanting Eve only just failed to land her first handicap. Only finding her stride in the final furlong, she finished in tremendous style and would surely have prevailed in another couple of strides. (11/4)
Gopi made a very pleasing debut on the All-Weather and showed in front at halfway. Collared below the distance, she refused to give way without a fight and only just lost out. (11/2: 9/4-13/2)
420 Hever Golf Charger (IRE) was already sending out distress signals over a quarter of a mile from home. (9/4)
Prix de Clermont (IRE), who showed little as a two-year-old, was very heavily supported for this handicap debut, but punters knew their fate before halfway. (6/1: op 12/1)

490 GIFT HORSE H'CAP (0-65) (3-Y.O+) (Class F)

4-30 (4-32) **1m (Equitrack)** £2,277.00 (£627.00: £297.00) Stalls: High GOING minus 0.43 sec per fur (FST)

				SP	RR	SF
458^{*}	**Barbason (62)** (GLMoore) **5-9-11** ^{5x} CandyMorris(5) (stdy hdwy over 3f out: led ins fnl f: pushed out)	—	**1**	$9/2^{2}$	74	51
407^{4}	**Ki Chi Saga (USA) (63)** (MMadgwick) **5-9-12** DHolland(3) (lw: a.p: led over 4f out to 2f out: hrd rdn & ev ch ins fnl f: unable qckn)	2½	**2**	$7/2^{1}$	70	47
407^{3}	**Gadge (43)** (ABailey) **6-8-6** SSanders(6) (b: led over 3f: led 2f out tl ins fnl f: one pce)	1	**3**	9/1	48	25
401^{2}	**Dream Carrier (IRE) (40)** (REPeacock) **9-8-3** DaneO'Neill(1) (a.p: rdn over 4f out: one pce fnl 2f)	1¾	**4**	9/1	42	19
403^{7}	**Invocation (65)** (GLMoore) **10-10-0** AClark(8) (lw: rdn over 5f out: hdwy over 3f out: one pce)	5	**5**	10/1	57	34

	Rocky Waters (USA) (50) (MDIUsher) **8-8-13** DRMcCabe(12) (b.hind: nvr nr to chal)	¾	**6**	10/1	40	17
349[4]	**River Seine (FR) (46)** (SGKnight) **5-8-4**(5) GFaulkner(4) (lw: a.p: rdn 3f out: wknd over 2f out)	½	**7**	8/1	35	12
407[2]	**Eastleigh (48)** (RHollinshead) **8-8-8**(3) DGriffiths(10) (b.nr hind: bhd fnl 2f)	1¼	**8**	7/1	35	12
458[5]	**Hawaii Storm (FR) (55)** (DJSffrenchDavis) **9-9-4** DHarrison(2) (hld up: rdn over 3f out: sn wknd)	5	**9**	6/1[3]	32	9
319[8]	**Manabar (53)** (MJPolglase) **5-9-2b** TGMcLaughlin(9) (a bhd)	1	**10**	16/1	28	5
367[9]	**Ballet de Cour (35)** (TJEtherington) **4-7-9**(3) MartinDwyer(11) (a bhd)	9	**11**	25/1	—	—
	Our Emma (36) (RJO'Sullivan) **8-7-13** JLowe(7) (bhd fnl 5f)	16	**12**	33/1	—	—

(SP 129.2%) **12 Rn**

1m 39.5 (2.10) CSF £20.65 CT £132.90 TOTE £5.50: £2.90 £3.00 £3.00 (£20.80) Trio £80.80 OWNER Mr F. L. Hill (BRIGHTON) BRED Sheikh Mohammed bin Rashid al Maktoum

458* Barbason has hit a rich vein at present, and followed up Monday's success here to complete the hat-trick, travelling well throughout the race and needing only to be nudged along to get on top inside the final furlong. (9/2)

407 Ki Chi Saga (USA), very well supported in the betting, moved to the front just before halfway. Collared a quarter of a mile out, he refused to give way and still had every chance inside the final furlong before the winner asserted. (7/2: op 6/1)

407 Gadge regained the advantage turning for home, but he was collared inside the final furlong and failed to find another gear. (9/1: 6/1-10/1)

401 Dream Carrier (IRE) has been running consistently of late but he is on a very long losing run and has not won for over two years. (9/1)

294* Invocation disappointed last time out and again ran poorly having won three times earlier in the year. (10/1)

491 ANY PORT MAIDEN STKS (3-Y.O+) (Class D)

5-00 (5-00) **1m 2f (Equitrack)** £3,454.50 (£1,029.00: £490.00: £220.50) Stalls: Low GOING minus 0.43 sec per fur (FST)

				SP	RR	SF
	Motet (GWragg) **3-8-4** AClark(3) (h.d.w: a.p: led 5f out: shkn up over 1f out: qcknd ins fnl f: easily)	—	**1**	6/5[1]	72+	10
	Western Sonata (IRE) (LordHuntingdon) **4-9-5** DHarrison(2) (hld up: chsd wnr over 1f out: unable qckn)	5	**2**	7/1[2]	59	17
	Chief Predator (USA) (68) (RHannon) **3-8-4** DaneO'Neill(1) (a.p: rdn over 3f out: eased whn btn ins fnl f)	1¾	**3**	6/5[1]	61	—
373[10]	**Masrrah (IRE)** (RWArmstrong) **3-8-4** AMcGlone(4) (bit bkwd: led 5f: wknd over 3f out)	7	**4**	20/1[3]	50?	—

(SP 108.2%) **4 Rn**

2m 9.99 (5.69) CSF £8.69 TOTE £1.60 (£4.80) OWNER Mr A. E. Oppenheimer (NEWMARKET) BRED Hascombe and Valiant Studs

WEIGHT FOR AGE 3yo-20lb

Motet, an attractive, deep-girthed colt who looked the part in the paddock, had little more than a workout, easing his way to the front at halfway, and needing only to be shaken up in the straight to quicken right away to win doing handsprings. He was certainly value for ten lengths. His jockey described him as still a big baby and this experience will surely have done him no end of good. (6/5: op 4/6)

Western Sonata (IRE), off the course for thirteen months, managed to struggle into second place below the distance, but had no hope with the winner. (7/1: 4/1-9/1)

Chief Predator (USA) was a leading player from the outset, but he was put in his place in the straight, and was eased when all chance had gone inside the final furlong. (6/5: 5/4-evens)

373 Masrrah (IRE), looking big and well in the paddock, had a whisker in front to halfway, but the writing was already on the wall approaching the last three furlongs. (20/1)

T/Plpt: £76.60 (135.67 Tckts). T/Qdpt: £49.70 (9.77 Tckts) AK

MUSSELBURGH (R-H) (Soft)

Thursday March 27th

WEATHER: overcast & raining WIND: mod across

65+ 63+ 68+

492 CARLYLE PLACE MAIDEN AUCTION STKS (2-Y.O) (Class F)

2-20 (2-21) **5f** £2,565.00 (£715.00: £345.00) Stalls: High GOING: 0.18 sec per fur (G)

				SP	RR	SF
	Salamanca (JBerry) **2-7-9**(5) PFessey(6) (leggy: mde all: r.o wl fnl f)	—	**1**	9/4[2]	77	7
	Heavenly Abstone (PDEvans) **2-8-1**[ow1] JFEgan(2) (neat: scope: s.i.s: sn trckng ldrs: effrt over 1f out: nt qckn)	2	**2**	6/4[1]	72	1
432[9]	**Filey Brigg** (WTKemp) **2-7-12** JQuinn(7) (cl up tl rdn & btn over 1f out)	5	**3**	9/1	53	—
	Captain Bliss (NTinkler) **2-8-10** JCarroll(1) (cmpt: scope: outpcd after 2f: hdwy over 1f out: nvr rchd ldrs)	1¼	**4**	6/1[3]	61	—
	Inchalong (MBrittain) **2-8-2** LCharnock(5) (small: lt-f: sn drvn along: nvr wnt pce)	6	**5**	10/1	33	—
	Good For You (SEKettlewell) **2-8-10** JFortune(3) (unf: outpcd & bhd after 2f)	13	**6**	12/1	—	—
	Sunshine Pet (IRE) (JJO'Neill) **2-8-2** JFanning(4) (neat: unf: s.s: a wl bhd)	4	**7**	9/1	—	—

(SP 121.8%) **7 Rn**

63.2 secs (5.50) CSF £6.03 TOTE £2.60: £2.60 £1.40 (£2.00) OWNER Mrs Chris Deuters (COCKERHAM) BRED Bearstone Stud

Salamanca, a very lean and leggy filly, she certainly knew her job. Flying out of the stalls, she got the favoured stands rails and was never going to stop. (9/4)

Heavenly Abstone just missed the kick but still travelled well, only failing to pick up when asked a question. She will no doubt be all the better for this. (6/4)

Filey Brigg, well beaten in the Brocklesby, made the experience tell here, showing plenty of speed, but this weak looking individual was beaten over a furlong out. (9/1: 6/1-10/1)

Captain Bliss, the best looker of the field, just needed it and should improve for the experience. (6/1: 5/1-8/1)

Inchalong has nothing to recommend her on looks and her performance left plenty to be desired. (10/1: op 20/1)

Good For You is not very big and, as yet, is not very good. (12/1: op 6/1)

Sunshine Pet (IRE) (9/1: 5/1-10/1)

493 PINKIE H'CAP (0-65) (4-Y.O+) (Class F)

2-50 (2-52) **2m** £2,775.00 (£775.00: £375.00) Stalls: High GOING: 0.00 sec per fur (G)

				SP	RR	SF
	Here Comes Herbie (37) (WStorey) **5-8-7** NKennedy(9) (hld up & bhd: hdwy on bit 6f out: led over 2f out: drvn clr)	—	**1**	6/4[1]	60?	—
261[5]	**Golden Hadeer (34)** (MJRyan) **6-8-4** JQuinn(13) (lw: chsd ldrs: led 6f out: qcknd ent st: hdd over 2f out: no ch w wnr)	21	**2**	13/8[2]	36	—
	Tancred Mischief (31) (DWBarker) **6-7-12**(3) DarrenMoffatt(7) (bhd: hdwy 5f out: styd on wl fnl 2f)	3	**3**	50/1	30	—
	Lord Advocate (39) (DANolan) **9-8-9b** NVarley(11) (chsd ldrs: rdn 6f out: r.o one pce)	14	**4**	20/1	24	—
	Bruz (31) (LLungo) **6-8-1** DaleGibson(14) (bhd tl styd on fnl 4f: nrst fin)	5	**5**	50/1	11	—

139[2]	**Thorntoun Estate (IRE) (52)** (MartinTodhunter) **4-9-3** DeanMcKeown(6) (bhd tl styd on fnl 3f: n.d)................10	**6**	14/1	22	—
256[10]	**Thorntoun House (IRE) (34)** (JSGoldie) **4-7-6v[1]**(7)ow3 JMcAuley(10) (in tch tl outpcd appr st: n.d after)..........8	**7**	100/1	—	—
430[11]	**Petoskin (54)** (JPearce) **5-9-10** MWigham(4) (lw: in tch: effrt ½-wy: sn outpcd)..½	**8**	12/1[3]	16	—
	Tagatay (40) (MJCamacho) **4-8-5** LCharnock(12) (cl up: led 7f out to 6f out: wknd over 3f out)........................6	**9**	16/1	—	—
	Rapid Mover (28) (DANolan) **10-7-7b**(5) PFessey(8) (led 6f: lost pl ½-wy) ....½	**10**	50/1	—	—
	Longcroft (40) (SEKettlewell) **5-8-10** JFortune(3) (in tch: effrt & prom appr st: sn wknd)..........................2½	**11**	20/1	—	—
	Finestatetobein (37) (FWatson) **4-7-11**(5) JBramhill(5) (prom to ½-wy)..hd	**12**	50/1	—	—
	Simafar (IRE) (53) (RAllan) **6-9-9** JFanning(1) (b: a bhd: fin lame) ....½	**13**	25/1	5	—
	Stingray City (USA) (38) (RMMcKellar) **8-8-8** TWilliams(2) (b: prom tl wknd over 3f out) ....s.h	**14**	66/1	—	—
	Nordisk Legend (27) (MrsDThomson) **5-7-11** DWright(15) (cl up: led after 6f to 7f out: sn wknd) 8	**15**	100/1	—	—
			(SP 123.0%)	**15 Rn**	

3m 38.1 CSF £3.41 CT £73.70 TOTE £2.80: £1.40 £1.20 £10.80 (£1.70) Trio £49.30 OWNER Mr H. S. Hutchinson (CONSETT) BRED H. Hutchinson

LONG HANDICAP Thorntoun House (IRE) 7-9

WEIGHT FOR AGE 4yo-5lb

OFFICIAL EXPLANATION Simafar (IRE): the trainer reported that the gelding hung right-handed turning into the straight, and was found to be lame on pulling up.

Here Comes Herbie has improved no end over hurdles and has obviously carried this on. Hopefully connections bought the distances on the spread as the Handicapper will no doubt wreak his revenge. (6/4)

232* Golden Hadeer has been in tremendous form all winter, and without the winner would have trotted up here, but once beaten he was wisely eased. (13/8)

Tancred Mischief obviously likes this soft ground and stays really well, but only ran when it was all over and was flattered by her proximity to the second. (50/1)

Lord Advocate needed this and should improve as a result. (20/1)

Bruz, having his first run for his new stable, showed a little but there was plenty needed. (50/1)

139 Thorntoun Estate (IRE) looks to have more than his fair share of weight and never looked likely to get anywhere near. (14/1: 10/1-16/1)

400 Petoskin (12/1: op 8/1)

494 BRUNTON HALL H'CAP (0-70) (3-Y.O+) (Class E)

3-20 (3-24) **5f** £3,168.00 (£954.00: £462.00: £216.00) Stalls: High GOING: 0.18 sec per fur (G)

			SP	RR	SF
397[5]	**Chemcast (68)** (JLEyre) **4-10-0b** RLappin(1) (lw: racd stands' side: mde all: all out) ....—	**1**	6/1[2]	74?	19
406[3]	**Gi La High (60)** (MartynMeade) **4-9-1**(5) DSweeney(12) (hdwy far side ½-wy: r.o fnl f: nrst fin) ....½	**2**	7/1[3]	64	9
	Tropical Beach (63) (JBerry) **4-9-2**(7) CLowther(3) (dwlt: hdwy & edgd rt over 1f out: r.o) 1¼	**3**	7/1[3]	63	8
	Goretski (IRE) (59) (NTinkler) **4-9-5** JCarroll(13) (cl up far side: ev ch ½-wy: no ex fnl f)..........................1¼	**4**	9/2[1]	55	—
	Queens Check (49) (MissJFCraze) **4-8-9b** SWebster(8) (b: sme hdwy 2f out: nvr rchd ldrs).............................6	**5**	10/1	26	—
	Johayro (54) (JSGoldie) **4-9-0** ACulhane(6) (cl up stands' side tl wknd wl over 1f out)..............................3½	**6**	10/1	20	—
423[8]	**Another Nightmare (IRE) (48)** (RMMcKellar) **5-8-8** TWilliams(14) (lw: led far side to ½-wy: sn outpcd) ....½	**7**	12/1	12	—
	Leading Princess (IRE) (50) (MissLAPerratt) **6-8-5b**(5) JBramhill(11) (racd far side: n.d).............................½	**8**	20/1	13	—
	Red Romance (60) (DenysSmith) **3-8-8** LCharnock(5) (sn outpcd) 1½	**9**	20/1	18	—
	Lunch Party (53) (DNicholls) **5-8-13** DaleGibson(9) (dwlt: a bhd)...1	**10**	16/1	8	—
	Sunset Harbour (IRE) (47) (SEKettlewell) **4-8-7** JFortune(7) (racd far side: n.d) ....nk	**11**	16/1	1	—
	Sarabi (64) (JPearce) **3-8-9**(3) CTeague(4) (chsd ldrs stands' side 3f: wknd)...hd	**12**	16/1	18	—
	Zain Dancer (55) (DNicholls) **5-9-1** AlexGreaves(10) (sn outpcd)...3	**13**	16/1	—	—
	Swan At Whalley (65) (RAFahey) **5-9-4**(7) RWinston(2) (Withdrawn not under Starter's orders: ref to ent stalls)	**W**	14/1	—	—
			(SP 123.1%)	**13 Rn**	

64.0 secs (6.30) CSF £40.41 CT £243.36 TOTE £6.80: £2.40 £2.30 £3.60 (£13.30) Trio £68.60 OWNER Clayton Bigley Partnership Ltd (HAMBLETON) BRED C. R. and V. M. Withers

WEIGHT FOR AGE 3yo-12lb

397 Chemcast had the best draw and stuck to the stands rails like glue, which made all the difference. (6/1)

406 Gi La High ran a smashing race from a poor draw, and would surely have won had she been up the stands side. (7/1: op 9/2)

Tropical Beach missed the break and did well to finish so close but did not help matters by hanging right. (7/1)

Goretski (IRE) showed speed a plenty from his poor draw but could never get all the way over to the stands side and his early efforts sapped reserves late on. (9/2)

Queens Check looked pretty straight for her first run of the season and made fair late headway. (10/1: 8/1-12/1)

Johayro showed bags of speed up the stands side but he probably needed this and dropped away in the last furlong and a half. (10/1: 8/1-16/1)

495 STONEYBANK MEDIAN AUCTION MAIDEN STKS (3 & 4-Y.O) (Class F)

3-50 (3-50) **1m 4f 31y** £2,512.50 (£700.00: £337.50) Stalls: High GOING: 0.18 sec per fur (G)

			SP	RR	SF
	Kathryn's Pet (61) (MrsMReveley) **4-9-8** ACulhane(3) (hld up: smooth hdwy appr st: led 2f out: rdn & r.o towards fin)...—	**1**	7/4[1]	62	35
373[5]	**Mountaineer (IRE)** (MBell) **3-8-7** JTate(2) (bit bkwd: prom: pushed along appr st: hrd rdn & r.o fnl 2f: nrst fin) 1¼	**2**	11/4[3]	65	18
	Abajany (MRChannon) **3-8-7** JFEgan(6) (trckd ldrs: smooth hdwy to ld 3f out: hdd 2f out: one pce) 3	**3**	9/2	61	14
461[13]	**Picard (IRE) (43)** (FMurphy) **4-9-13** JFanning(7) (led tl hdd & wknd 3f out) 9	**4**	50/1	50	23
	Think Again (IRE) (RCraggs) **3-8-7** LCharnock(1) (leggy: plld hrd: bhd: effrt ent st: n.d) 23	**5**	50/1	19	—
373[2]	**Stretching (IRE) (55)** (ABailey) **4-9-13** DWright(4) (lw: plld hrd: bhd: effrt 6f out: n.d) 4	**6**	5/2[2]	14	—
	Nordic Gift (DEN) (35) (MrsDThomson) **4-9-10**(3) OPears(5) (swtg: cl up: rdn 5f out: wknd over 3f out) 13	**7**	100/1	—	—
			(SP 114.7%)	**7 Rn**	

2m 46.1 (12.60) CSF £6.36 TOTE £2.90: £1.30 £2.30 (£4.60) OWNER Mr Bill Brown (SALTBURN) BRED N. J. Dent

WEIGHT FOR AGE 3yo-22lb, 4yo-2lb

STEWARDS' ENQUIRY Tate susp. 5 & 7/4/97 (excessive use of whip).

Kathryn's Pet always looked to be going best. She had the pace to get the stands' rails early in the straight and the race was always hers from then on. (7/4)

373 Mountaineer (IRE) still did not look fully wound up and took an age to get into his stride, but he certainly finished well and will obviously improve with experience and probably over further. (11/4)

Abajany went really well here on the bridle but failed to see it out, which at the moment can probably be put down to lack of experience. (9/2: 3/1-5/1)
Picard (IRE) made the running and was made to look very one-paced when tackled. (50/1)
Think Again (IRE) needs to learn to settle and has a lot of improving to do. (50/1)
373 Stretching (IRE) raced too freely and ran poorly. (5/2)

496 MAYFIELD (S) H'CAP (0-60) (3-Y.O+) (Class G)

4-20 (4-21) **1m 16y** £2,416.00 (£676.00: £328.00) Stalls: High GOING: 0.18 sec per fur (G)

				SP	RR	SF
411^{*}	**Soldier Cove (USA) (42)** (MartynMeade) **7-8-9**(5) DSweeney(9) (lw: a.p: led over 2f out: rdn & r.o fnl f)	—	1	11/4 1	56	45
153^{8}	**Running Green (52)** (DMoffatt) **6-9-7**(3) DarrenMoffatt(11) (b: mid div: hdwy 3f out: chal ins fnl f: nt qckn towards fin)	½	2	12/1	65	54
296^{4}	**Harry's Treat (45)** (JLEyre) **5-9-3** RLappin(2) (lw: a.p: effrt 3f out: one pce appr fnl f)	7	3	100/30 2	44	33
	Knave (49) (PMonteith) **4-9-0v**(7) KSked(7) (lw: a chsng ldrs: rdn & one pce fnl 3f)	2½	4	10/1	43	32
40^{12}	**Tajar (USA) (46)** (MDods) **5-9-4b¹** DaleGibson(10) (bhd tl styd on fnl 3f: n.d)	2	5	50/1	36	25
417^{4}	**Sounds Legal (49)** (PDEvans) **4-9-7b¹** JFEgan(5) (bhd: hdwy 3f out: nvr rchd ldrs)	2	6	20/1	35	24
	Termon (49) (MissLAPerratt) **4-9-7** JFortune(6) (cl up tl wknd fnl 3f)	1	7	10/1	33	22
	Rattle (43) (DANolan) **4-8-10**(5) PFessey(13) (chsd ldrs tl wknd over 3f out)	2½	8	20/1	22	11
286^{7}	**Funky (42)** (DNicholls) **4-9-0** AlexGreaves(8) (nvr trbld ldrs)	2½	9	10/1	16	5
327^{8}	**Roseate Lodge (44)** (SEKettlewell) **11-8-9**(7) JennyBenson(14) (a bhd)	3	10	25/1	12	1
416^{2}	**Evening In Paris (45)** (MJohnston) **4-9-3** DeanMcKeown(4) (outpcd ent st: n.d after)	1	11	13/2 3	11	—
	Western Venture (IRE) (44) (RMMcKellar) **4-9-2** TWilliams(1) (led tl hdd over 2f out: sn btn: eased fnl f)	1½	12	33/1	8	—
	Diet (46) (MissLAPerratt) **11-9-4v** JCarroll(12) (bkwd: early spd: sn outpcd & bhd)	25	13	25/1	—	—
				(SP 120.2%)		**13 Rn**

1m 45.3 (6.30) CSF £30.33 CT £110.68 TOTE £3.60: £1.40 £6.10 £1.30 (£45.20) Trio £45.20 OWNER Ladyswood Racing Club (MALMESBURY) BRED Weststar Bloodstock
Bt in 6,500 gns
411* Soldier Cove (USA) has improved on the All-Weather and has obviously carried that on here. He showed fine determination and will stay further. (11/4: op 6/4)
Running Green likes the soft ground but when the chips were down he just found one too determined. (12/1)
Harry's Treat had her chances but lacks any turn of foot to take them. (100/30: op 5/1)
Knave took the eye in the paddock and had his chances but lacked any change of gear. (10/1)
Tajar (USA), in blinkers for the first time, made up a lot of ground and has the ability if he can be persuaded. (50/1)
417 Sounds Legal had the blinkers but was never doing enough when ridden. (20/1)
Termon (10/1: op 5/1)
Funky (10/1: op 6/1)

497 STONEYHILL MAIDEN H'CAP (0-70) (3-Y.O) (Class E)

4-50 (4-51) **1m 16y** £2,895.00 (£870.00: £420.00: £195.00) Stalls: High GOING: 0.18 sec per fur (G)

				SP	RR	SF
377^{4}	**Polarize (51)** (TDBarron) **3-8-2** LCharnock(4) (lw: chsd ldrs: outpcd over 3f out: styd on to ld ins fnl f: eased nr fin)	—	1	9/1	59	12
387^{5}	**Krosno (55)** (SCWilliams) **3-8-6** JQuinn(6) (lw: hld up: hdwy to ld 2½f out: sn rdn: hdd ins fnl f: kpt on)	½	2	11/4 2	62	15
	Champagne On Ice (51) (PDEvans) **3-8-2**ow2 JFEgan(2) (hld up: hdwy 3f out: sn rdn & chsng ldrs: nt pce to chal)	2½	3	20/1	53	4
395^{5}	**Manhattan Diamond (54)** (ABailey) **3-8-5** DWright(5) (led tl hdd 2½f out: one pce)	8	4	9/2 3	40	—
	Silver Button (55) (SEKettlewell) **3-8-6**ow1 JFortune(3) (in tch tl outpcd fnl 3f)	5	5	9/2 3	31	—
425^{2}	**Italian Symphony (IRE) (70)** (MJohnston) **3-9-7** JCarroll(1) (w ldr tl wknd wl over 2f out)	12	6	5/2 1	23	—
				(SP 106.4%)		**6 Rn**

1m 47.5 (8.50) CSF £27.59 TOTE £9.80: £4.40 £1.10 (£15.20) OWNER Mr J. Baggott (THIRSK) BRED Exors of the late D. Macrae
OFFICIAL EXPLANATION **Italian Symphony (IRE): no explanation offered.**
377 Polarize looked in trouble turning for home but he responded well to driving and was nicely on top by the finish. (9/1: 6/1-10/1)
Krosno, the paddock pick by a mile, looked in command two furlongs out, but was worried out of it and may be happier on faster ground. (11/4: op 5/1)
Champagne On Ice almost got into it entering the last two furlongs but the soft ground proved against her. (20/1)
395 Manhattan Diamond went off in front but this trip on this ground seemed to find her out. (9/2)
Silver Button never made any impression on the race but looks the sort to improve as a result. (9/2)
425 Italian Symphony (IRE) has his own ideas about the game and probably needs the blinkers back on. (5/2)

T/Plpt: £37.10 (300.43 Tckts). T/Qdpt: £33.30 (20.84 Tckts) AA

HAYDOCK (L-H) (Soft)

Saturday March 29th

WEATHER: overcast WIND: mod against

498 DAIHATSU CONDITIONS STKS (4-Y.O+) (Class B)

1-15 (1-15) **2m 45y** £7,454.85 (£2,718.60: £1,329.30: £571.50: £255.75) Stalls: Centre GOING: 0.77 sec per fur (S)

			SP	RR	SF
Sweetness Herself (84) (MJRyan) **4-8-4** GCarter(5) (swtg: chsd ldrs: wnt 2nd 10f out: led over 3f out: styd on wl)	—	1	4/1 2	101?	39
Old Rouvel (USA) (101) (DJGMurraySmith) **6-9-0** KFallon(2) (lw: hld up in rr: shkn up 3f out: hdwy over 2f out: styd on one pce ins fnl f)	1¼	2	4/1 2	105	48
Orchestra Stall (104) (JLDunlop) **5-9-8** KDarley(1) (bit bkwd: racd keenly: chsd ldr over 6f: rdn over 2f out: no imp)	2½	3	5/6 1	110	53
Collier Bay (JABOld) **7-9-0** JReid(3) (led: sn clr: hdd over 3f out: rdn wl over 1f out: sn btn)	nk	4	15/2 3	63 t	45
Bellara (58) (NMBabbage) **5-8-9** TSprake(4) (bit bkwd: hld up in tch: effrt & rdn over 2f out: grad wknd)	2½	5	20/1	56 t	38
			(SP 111.1%)		**5 Rn**

3m 49.9 (22.70) CSF £17.94 TOTE £3.30: £1.40 £1.70 (£8.50) OWNER Mrs M. J. Lavell (NEWMARKET) BRED Stud-On-The-Chart

WEIGHT FOR AGE 4yo-5lb
Sweetness Herself started the season the way she finished the previous one, in the winner's enclosure, and as long as the ground remains in her favour, she will always be the one to beat. (4/1)
Old Rouvel (USA), filling the runner-up spot in this event for the third successive year, does not win as often as he should, and has yet to succeed on ground as testing as this. (4/1)
Orchestra Stall needed a run to put an edge on him last season, and though he ran too freely for his own good in the early stages, was struggling to hold on inside the final quarter-mile. (5/6: 4/5-evens)
Collier Bay, having his first run on the Flat for three years, adopted more forceful tactics, and held the call for over twelve furlongs, before having to admit himself short of the necessary acceleration. If the going is suitable, he will return to the winter game for the Grade One Martell Aintree Hurdle over two-and-a-half miles on Grand National day. (15/2)
Bellara acts well on the ground, but she was out of her depth here, and her measure had been taken from some way out. (20/1)

499 DAIHATSU H'CAP (0-95) (4-Y.O+) (Class C)
1-45 (1-46) **1m 3f 200y** £5,218.50 (£1,578.00: £769.00: £364.50) Stalls: High GOING: 0.77 sec per fur (S)

				SP	RR	SF
	Sugar Mill (77) (MrsMReveley) **7-8-13** ACulhane(10) (hld up: hdwy 3f out: led 2f out: drvn out)	—	**1**	5/1^{2}	91	73
	Eskimo Nel (IRE) (70) (JLSpearing) **6-8-3**$^{(3)ow4}$ FLynch(4) (hld up: hdwy 3f out: chsd wnr over 1f out: no imp)	1¾	**2**	13/2	82	60
430^{13}	**Midyan Blue (IRE) (70)** (JMPEustace) **7-8-6** JTate(3) (trckd ldrs: outpcd 3f out: styd on u.p fnl f)	5	**3**	10/1	75	57
	Al's Alibi (76) (WRMuir) **4-8-10** JReid(6) (bit bkwd: a.p: rdn & wknd appr fnl f)	3	**4**	9/1	77	57
	Song Of The Sword (90) (JABOld) **4-9-10** KDarley(9) (bit bkwd: hld up: effrt & rdn over 3f out: wknd fnl 2f)	10	**5**	14/1	78	58
	Myrtle Quest (78) (RCharlton) **5-9-0** TSprake(5) (bit bkwd: led 9f: rdn over 2f out: wknd)	5	**6**	7/1	59	41
451^{3}	**Major Change (88)** (MissGayKelleway) **5-9-10** KFallon(8) (lw: hld up: gd hdwy 5f out: wknd over 2f out)	7	**7**	11/2^{3}	59	41
*426**	**River Keen (IRE) (88)** (RWArmstrong) **5-9-10** GCarter(1) (chsd ldr: rdn over 3f out: sn wknd: t.o)	25	**8**	9/4^{1}	26	8
	Prospector's Cove (90) (JPearce) **4-9-10** GBardwell(7) (s.s: a bhd: t.o)	nk	**9**	11/1	27	7

(SP 122.7%) **9 Rn**

2m 42.2 (12.80) CSF £36.40 CT £293.74 TOTE £5.30: £1.60 £1.70 £2.60 (£15.10) Trio £21.80 OWNER Mr C. C. Buckley (SALTBURN) BRED Snailwell Stud Co Ltd
WEIGHT FOR AGE 4yo-2lb
OFFICIAL EXPLANATION **River Keen (IRE): no explanation offered other than the horse seemed unable to reproduce his All-Weather form.**
Sugar Mill, produced fresh and well for this seasonal debut, kicked on entering the final quarter-mile, and was always finding far too much for the very willing runner-up. (5/1)
Eskimo Nel (IRE) had the edge in fitness and the ground in her favour, but she allowed the winner to get first run, and was always fighting a lost cause. (13/2)
Midyan Blue (IRE) needs a stiffer test of stamina than he had here, but gave notice that he will be ready to strike when the opportunity arises.(10/1)
Al's Alibi, returning after over ten months out of action, had a summer bloom on his coat, but he still needed this race, and was beginning to feel the pinch from below the distance. He will not be hard-pressed to win a race if he gets the cut he requires. (9/1)
Song Of The Sword, an ex-Irish gelding having his first run in this country, was too backward to do himself justice, but he performed with credit and will soon improve on this. (14/1: 10/1-16/1)
Myrtle Quest, a very lightly-raced individual tackling a longer trip, only dropped away in the latter stages, and will be all the sharper with this spin under his belt. (7/1)
426* River Keen (IRE) repeated his form of twelve months ago, with an impressive win on the All-Weather, and then proving most disappointing when returning to the turf. Punters have only themselves to blame for throwing good money after bad. (9/4)
Prospector's Cove (11/1: 8/1-12/1)

66 63 82 64

500 DAIHATSU MAIDEN AUCTION STKS (2-Y.O) (Class E)
2-15 (2-18) **5f** £2,883.75 (£870.00: £422.50: £198.75) Stalls: High GOING: 0.77 sec per fur (S)

				SP	RR	SF
	Risky Whisky (JBerry) **2-8-3** GCarter(8) (lt-f: unf: chsd ldrs: reminders 2f out: r.o to ld wl ins fnl f)	—	**1**	5/1^{3}	76	22
	Pacifica (RBoss) **2-7-12** JQuinn(6) (lt-f: unf: led tl hdd over 1f out: rallied & ev ch wl ins fnl f: no ex nr fin)	1¼	**2**	9/2^{2}	67	13
447^{2}	**Classy Cleo (IRE)** (RHannon) **2-8-3**^{ow1} JCarroll(9) (a.p: led over 1f out tl wl ins fnl f)	¾	**3**	7/4^{1}	70	15
432^{8}	**Yorkies Boy** (BAMcMahon) **2-8-7** LNewton(5) (prom tl wknd qckly 1f out)	6	**4**	16/1	54	—
	Percy-P (WRMuir) **2-8-7** JReid(7) (w'like: lw: chsd ldrs: no hdwy appr fnl f)	3	**5**	5/1^{3}	45	—
	Marske Machine (NTinkler) **2-7-12** KimTinkler(3) (w'like: scope: s.s: swtchd rt ½-wy: kpt on wl ins fnl f)	¾	**6**	33/1	33	—
	My Bet (MWEasterby) **2-7-12** LCharnock(10) (lt-f: effrt & drvn along 2f out: rn green: no imp)	2	**7**	16/1	27	—
	Young Ibnr (IRE) (PDEvans) **2-8-7** JFEgan(1) (small: lt-f: swvd lft s: chsd ldrs 3f)	2	**8**	12/1	30	—
	Premium Pursuit (RAFahey) **2-8-10** ACulhane(4) (cmpt: bkwd: outpcd: a bhd)	4	**9**	12/1	20	—
	Killernan Kilmaine (IRE) (ABailey) **2-8-7** KFallon(2) (lengthy: lt-f: hdwy ½-wy: sn rdn: eased whn btn appr fnl f)	1	**10**	14/1	14	—
	Latin Bay (PWHarris) **2-8-3** MFenton(11) (lt-f: unf: a outpcd)	2½	**11**	10/1	2	—

(SP 133.7%) **11 Rn**

66.96 secs (7.46) CSF £29.18 TOTE £4.90: £1.90 £2.00 £1.30 (£20.60) Trio £9.30 OWNER Mr J. Berry (COCKERHAM) BRED Roldvale Ltd
Risky Whisky has plenty of filling-out to do, but he knew what was required on this racecourse debut, and proved the stronger in the battle to the post. (5/1: 4/1-6/1)
Pacifica, who proved quite a handful to load, did not look the type to handle soft ground, but she showed she has plenty of ability and the experience will not be lost. (9/2)
447 Classy Cleo (IRE) failed by the narrowest margin to make a winning debut a week ago, and she did her best to make amends this time but, on ground which may prove too testing, was forced to give best in the final hundred yards. (7/4)
432 Yorkies Boy has failed to get home in both his races to date having shown plenty of pace, and is probably doing too much too soon. (16/1)
Percy-P, a brother to Lennox Lewis, will need a much sounder surface to produce his true form. (5/1: op 8/1)
Marske Machine ran much better than her finishing position would suggest, after losing ground at the start, and she should be given the opportunity to show what she is made of. (33/1)

501 DAIHATSU FIELD MARSHAL STKS (Listed) (3-Y.O) (Class A)
2-45 (2-48) **5f** £12,136.50 (£3,672.00: £1,791.00: £850.50) Stalls: High GOING: 0.77 sec per fur (S)

			SP	RR	SF
Superior Premium (100) (RAFahey) **3-8-11** ACulhane(3) (lw: a.p gng wl: led over 1f out: drvn out)	—	**1**	11/2	106	41

	Myrmidon (87) (MrsLStubbs) **3-8-11** KFallon(4) (lt-f: bit bkwd: dwlt: hld up: hdwy 2f out: hrd rdn & ev ch ins fnl f: unable qckn)....1¾	**2**	20/1	100	35
	Rudi's Pet (IRE) (96) (RHannon) **3-8-11** JReid(1) (bit bkwd: hdwy ½-wy: outpcd over 1f out: kpt on u.p towards fin)....2½	**3**	8/1	92	27
434[4]	**Swino (83)** (PDEvans) **3-8-11** JFEgan(7) (led tl rdn & hdd over 1f out: one pce)....nk	**4**	16/1	91	26
	Vasari (IRE) (100) (MRChannon) **3-8-11** KDarley(8) (w ldr tl rdn & wknd over 1f out)....5	**5**	4/1 3	75	10
	Deep Finesse (113) (MAJarvis) **3-9-4** RCochrane(5) (h.d.w: bkwd: chsd ldrs: nt clr run ½-wy: rdn & wknd appr fnl f)....1¾	**6**	5/2 1	77	12
	Jennelle (100) (CADwyer) **3-8-6** JoHunnam(6) (hld up: effrt & nt clr run wl over 1f out: nt rcvr)....1½	**7**	7/2 2	60	—
	Largesse (90) (JohnBerry) **3-8-11** MFenton(2) (bit bkwd: outpcd: a bhd)....½	**8**	33/1	63	—

(SP 110.9%) **8 Rn**

66.26 secs (6.76) CSF £87.80 TOTE £6.70: £1.90 £4.20 £1.40 (£51.60) OWNER Mr J. C. Parsons (MALTON) BRED Giles W. Pritchard-Gordon

Superior Premium, a winner on his debut last year, had the ground in his favour, and only needed to be kept up to his work to add this listed prize to his collection. He looks the sort to go on improving. (11/2)

Myrmidon gave the impression the run was needed, and a tardy start certainly did not help his cause, but he delivered a sustained last-furlong challenge and he is one to keep in mind. (20/1)

Rudi's Pet (IRE) finished behind the winner when they clashed in the autumn, and he looked to be treading ground when ridden below the distance, but he was coming back for more towards the finish and a sixth furlong could be the answer. (8/1)

434 Swino has plenty of speed, but he was taking a step-up in class here, and he had given his best by the time they had reached the final furlong. (16/1)

Vasari (IRE), beaten less than a length by the winner when they met over course and distance in October, was unable to take advantage of his 3lb pull in the weights, and he may well have been more in need of the race than was apparent. (4/1)

Deep Finesse showed last year that he can handle all types of ground, but he looked far from fully wound up and, failing to get any sort of a run when poised to challenge, had had enough passing the furlong marker. (5/2)

Jennelle had a nightmare run up the inside rail, and was never able to get into the race, but whether she would have had the speed to muster a challenge with a clear passage only time will tell. (7/2)

502 DAIHATSU RATED STKS H'CAP (0-95) (3-Y.O) (Class C)

3-20 (3-21) **1m 2f 120y** £5,223.70 (£1,579.60: £769.80: £364.90) Stalls: High GOING: 0.77 sec per fur (S)

			SP	RR	SF
	Mister Pink (90) (RFJohnsonHoughton) **3-9-2** JReid(3) (hld up: hdwy over 2f out: hrd rdn to ld wl ins fnl f) ...—	**1**	13/2	91	54
	Mr Bombastique (IRE) (85) (BWHills) **3-8-11** KFallon(7) (bit bkwd: a.p: led over 3f out: hrd rdn & hdd nr fin).nk	**2**	11/4 1	86	49
	Iechyd-Da (IRE) (91) (MBell) **3-9-3** MFenton(1) (bit bkwd: chsd ldrs: rdn & outpcd over 2f out: rallied fnl f)....1¾	**3**	11/1	89	52
	Heart of Armor (81) (PFICole) **3-8-7** RCochrane(6) (bit bkwd: sn led: rdn & hdd over 3f out: wknd appr fnl f)2½	**4**	9/2 3	75	38
	Mardi Gras (IRE) (89) (JLDunlop) **3-9-1** KDarley(2) (small: unf: trckd ldrs: rdn over 2f out: one pce)....4	**5**	9/2 3	77	40
436[4]	**Get The Point (81)** (RHollinshead) **3-8-4**(3) FLynch(4) (lw: hld up: effrt & rdn 3f out: no imp)....3	**6**	4/1 2	65	28
	Braveheart (IRE) (95) (MRChannon) **3-9-2**(5) PPMurphy(5) (w'like: swtg: s.s: a bhd: t.o fnl 2f)....16	**7**	12/1	54	17

(SP 112.4%) **7 Rn**

2m 25.67 (14.17) CSF £21.70 TOTE £7.70: £2.80 £1.80 (£6.40) OWNER Mr C. W. Sumner (DIDCOT) BRED Southcourt Stud

LONG HANDICAP Get The Point 8-6

Mister Pink, still hanging on to his winter coat, wore blinkers when tackling this trip in his first season, but he showed he does not need them with a very gutsy performance under strong pressure to land the spoils in the dying strides. (13/2)

Mr Bombastique (IRE) struck the front early in the straight, and looked all over the winner entering the final furlong, but lack of peak fitness caught him out and he was touched off nearing the line. (11/4)

Iechyd-Da (IRE) still has plenty left to work on, but it is proving difficult to know exactly what trip he may require, for he was staying on best of all after getting his second wind, and we have not seen the best of him yet. (11/1)

Heart of Armor tried to make this a true test of stamina, and he stuck to his work after being collared, but he was getting legless approaching the final furlong and the position had to be accepted. (9/2)

Mardi Gras (IRE) has not filled out since his two-year-old days and, made to work over two furlongs out, was unable to make his presence felt. (9/2)

503 DAIHATSU MAIDEN STKS (3-Y.O) (Class D)

3-50 (3-52) **7f 30y** £3,436.25 (£1,040.00: £507.50: £241.25) Stalls: Low GOING: 0.77 sec per fur (S)

		SP	RR	SF
Romanov (IRE) (PWChapple-Hyam) **3-9-0** JReid(2) (gd sort: lw: hld up: nt clr run & swtchd rt over 1f out: led ent fnl f: drvn out)....—	**1**	1/2 1	86	53
Musharak (JLDunlop) **3-9-0** KDarley(6) (plld hrd: hld up: hdwy & nt clr run 2f out: str chal fnl f: r.o)....nk	**2**	13/2 3	85	52
Banbury (USA) (JWWatts) **3-9-0** JCarroll(4) (lt-f: unf: bit bkwd: stdd s: hld up: nt clr run over 1f out: swtchd rt & rapid hdwy appr fnl f: fin fast)....nk	**3**	20/1	85	52
Compromise (IRE) (BWHills) **3-9-0** KFallon(9) (w'like: scope: bit bkwd: hld up in rr: hdwy over 2f out: ev ch appr fnl f: sn outpcd)....6	**4**	6/1 2	71	38
Flirtation (RCharlton) **3-8-9** TSprake(3) (leggy: scope: bit bkwd: chsd ldr: led over 2f out tl wl over 1f out: sn outpcd)....6	**5**	10/1	53	20
Gablesea (64) (BPJBaugh) **3-9-0** WLord(7) (hdwy ½-wy: led wl over 1f out tl hdd & outpcd ent fnl f)....1	**6**	66/1	56	23
Midyan Call (MBell) **3-9-0** MFenton(8) (gd sort: lw: chsd ldrs: rdn 2f out: ev ch tl outpcd appr fnl f)....nk	**7**	20/1	55	22
Falls O'Moness (IRE) (70) (KRBurke) **3-8-9** DRMcCabe(1) (lt-f: led & sn clr: hdd over 2f out: sn rdn & wknd) .7	**8**	25/1	34	1
Hermanus (MAJarvis) **3-9-0** PBloomfield(5) (bkwd: a in rr: t.o fnl 3f)....18	**9**	33/1	—	—

(SP 121.2%) **9 Rn**

1m 36.94 (8.94) CSF £3.84 TOTE £1.50: £1.20 £2.00 £3.10 (£3.70) Trio £112.40 OWNER Mr R. E. Sangster (MARLBOROUGH) BRED Swettenham Stud

Romanov (IRE), whose racecourse appearance was delayed last season after he split a hind pastern, did not enjoy a trouble-free passage when poised to challenge, but he picked up well once switched and did just enough to make a winning debut. Sure to benefit from the experience, he holds a 2,000 Guineas entry, but could have another run before a decision is made about his participation. (1/2)

Musharak, forced to sit and suffer when denied a clear run below the distance, had the gap he needed entering the final furlong and, producing a determined challenge, found the highly-rated winner in no mood to give best. This was a display full of promise, and he should make amends before too long. (13/2)

Banbury (USA), an unfurnished colt who is bred to need much further, was trapped on the inside rails with nowhere to go approaching the final furlong but, after being switched to make his effort on the outside, fairly flew, and was without doubt a very unlucky loser. His future looks bright. (20/1)

Compromise (IRE), a newcomer with plenty of scope, was fighting for the lead approaching the final furlong, before finding the quickening tempo much more than he could cope with. (6/1)
Flirtation, a tall filly who has obviously needed time, helped force the pace until fitter rivals took her measure inside the distance. She should have little trouble paying her way. (10/1)
Gablesea did not show a lot in his first season, and looked out of his depth here, but he poked his nose in front below the distance before the big guns pounced and left him for dead. An ordinary run-of-the-mill maiden could be his for the taking. (66/1)
Midyan Call, an attractive colt related to a couple of winners, should not take long to find an opening if this very promising debut is anything to go by. (20/1)

T/Plpt: £78.60 (254.79 Tckts). T/Qdpt: £18.10 (47.01 Tckts) IM

KEMPTON (R-H) (Good, Good to firm patches)
Saturday March 29th
WEATHER: sunny WIND: almost nil

80 72+ 76 65+

504 E.B.F. WATFORD MAIDEN STKS (2-Y.O) (Class D)
1-40 (1-42) **5f** £3,338.75 (£1,010.00: £492.50: £233.75) Stalls: High GOING minus 0.26 sec per fur (GF)

				SP	RR	SF
432[6]	**Wrekin Pilot** (RHannon) **2-9-0** DaneO'Neill(3) (s.i.s: rdn over 2f out: hdwy over 1f out: led ins fnl f: r.o wl)	—	**1**	7/2[2]	70	7
	Bernardo Bellotto (IRE) (MBell) **2-9-0** MRoberts(8) (cmpt: bit bkwd: led over 2f: ev ch over 1f out: unable qckn fnl f)	1¾	**2**	5/1	64	1
	Tippitt Boy (KMcAuliffe) **2-9-0** WJO'Connor(4) (w'like: bit bkwd: a.p: led over 1f out tl ins fnl f: one pce)	¾	**3**	13/2	62	—
	Halmahera (IRE) (IABalding) **2-8-11**(3) MartinDwyer(7) (leggy: bit bkwd: w ldr: led over 2f out tl over 1f out: one pce)	¾	**4**	15/8[1]	60	—
	Mantles Pride (GLewis) **2-9-0** PatEddery(2) (neat: prom over 2f)	4	**5**	9/2[3]	47	—
	Royal Interview (IRE) (MRChannon) **2-9-0** TQuinn(6) (unf: scope: bkwd: j.path over 3f out: bhd fnl 3f)	1	**6**	8/1	44	—
				(SP 116.3%)	**6 Rn**	

62.35 secs (4.15) CSF £19.88 TOTE £3.60: £2.20 £2.30 (£7.00) OWNER The Winning Team (MARLBOROUGH) BRED Mrs R. D. Peacock
432 Wrekin Pilot may have looked rather rough in the paddock, and drifted badly in the betting, but he put his experience to good use, coming with a real rattle to storm into the lead inside the furlong. (7/2: op 5/4)
Bernardo Bellotto (IRE), quite an attractive, close-coupled newcomer, looked as though the run would benefit him, but still showed plenty of promise. In front to halfway, he was battling for the advantage approaching the final furlong before tapped for toe. He should not be difficult to win with. (5/1)
Tippitt Boy, a May foal who looked as though the run would help him, managed to get to the front below the distance, but was firmly put in his place when collared by the winner inside the final furlong. (13/2)
Halmahera (IRE), quite a tall, plain individual, raced in the front rank until going on at halfway. Collared below the distance, he could then only go up and down in the same place. (15/8)
Mantles Pride, a plain individual, who is not that big and still had his winter coat, is a half-brother to Stewards' Cup winner Very Adjacent and old campaigner Strat's Legacy. Undoubtedly the fittest in the paddock, he nevertheless drifted badly in the market, and was a spent force at halfway. (9/2: 5/2-5/1)
Royal Interview (IRE), a sturdy newcomer, who needs time to develop fully, was without doubt the fattest in the paddock and, after jumping the path over three furlongs from home, was soon left behind. (8/1: 5/1-10/1)

505 STANMORE CONDITIONS STKS (3-Y.O) (Class C)
2-10 (2-11) **1m 2f (Jubilee)** £4,642.65 (£1,691.40: £825.70: £353.50: £156.75) Stalls: High GOING minus 0.26 sec per fur (GF)

				SP	RR	SF
	Palio Sky (JLDunlop) **3-8-10** PatEddery(1) (hld up: chsd ldr 6f out: rdn over 2f out: led over 1f out: r.o wl)	—	**1**	10/11[1]	97	44
*350**	**Running Stag (USA)** (PMitchell) **3-8-13** AClark(3) (plld hrd: hld up: led over 2f out tl over 1f out: unable qckn fnl f)	1¾	**2**	3/1[2]	97	44
	Drive Assured (80) (CEBrittain) **3-8-10** MRoberts(2) (bit bkwd: led over 7f)	9	**3**	12/1	80	27
	Happy Go Lucky (85) (RJO'Sullivan) **3-8-8** DHolland(5) (swtg: a bhd)	1	**4**	7/1	76	23
*145**	**Galibis (FR) (80)** (PAKelleway) **3-8-13** MWigham(4) (chsd ldr 4f: wknd over 3f out)	2	**5**	13/2[3]	78	25
				(SP 110.9%)	**5 Rn**	

2m 7.11 (3.61) CSF £3.56 TOTE £1.70: £1.20 £1.60 (£2.20) OWNER Mr J. E. Nash (ARUNDEL) BRED Montealto Stud Establishment
Palio Sky made a pleasing reappearance. He did not appear to be going as well as Running Stag early in the straight, but Eddery managed to get him to the front approaching the final furlong and, ridden along, he asserted in the last one hundred and fifty yards. A mile and a half should suit him even better. (10/11)
350* Running Stag (USA), very impressive against weak opposition on the Equitrack last month, is very highly-regarded, but connections have had to shelve plans for the Kentucky Derby because of quarantine problems. Taking a keen hold early on, he appeared to be going better than the winner as he cruised into the lead early in the straight, but he was unable to shake off his rival and, headed approaching the final furlong, was then tapped for toe. Connections are now hoping to run him in the Belmont Stakes, and will give him an outing on a left-handed track before making the trip to America. (3/1: 2/1-100/3)
Drive Assured, carrying some condition for this seasonal bow, took the field along but, collared over a quarter-of-a-mile from home, was soon a spent force. He may be better suited by a shorter trip. (12/1: op 7/1)
Happy Go Lucky looked very fit, but was always at the back of the field. (7/1)
145* Galibis (FR), taking a step-up in distance, was not up to this class, and had shot his bolt turning for home. (13/2)

506 RUISLIP H'CAP (0-90) (3-Y.O) (Class C)
2-40 (2-42) **6f** £5,283.50 (£1,598.00: £779.00: £369.50) Stalls: High GOING: Not Established

				SP	RR	SF
	Supercal (89) (DRCElsworth) **3-9-4**(3) DGriffiths(4) (bit bkwd: dwlt: gd hdwy over 1f out: led wl ins fnl f: edgd rt: r.o wl)	—	**1**	16/1	94	46
448[14]	**Ivory Dawn (66)** (KTIvory) **3-7-9**(3)ow2 MartinDwyer(6) (dwlt: rdn over 2f out: hdwy over 1f out: r.o)	1¼	**2**	33/1	68	18
	Style Dancer (IRE) (75) (RMWhitaker) **3-8-7** DeanMcKeown(7) (hld up: rdn over 2f out: r.o ins fnl f)	nk	**3**	13/2	76	28
	Refuse To Lose (77) (JMPEustace) **3-8-9** MHills(3) (a.p: rdn over 2f out: ev ch over 1f out: 3rd & btn whn n.m.r nr fin)	s.h	**4**	4/1[1]	78+	30
	Bilko (85) (GLewis) **3-9-3** PatEddery(1) (bit bkwd: stdd s: plld hrd: hdwy over 2f out: led over 1f out tl wl ins fnl f: one pce)	hd	**5**	5/1[2]	86	38

			Pos	SP	RR	SF
	Papita (IRE) (78) (SDow) 3-8-10 MRoberts(8) (hdwy over 2f out: n.m.r wl over 1f out: eased whn btn fnl f)	3½	6	12/1	69	21
	Big Ben (89) (RHannon) 3-9-7 DaneO'Neill(2) (bit bkwd: nvr nr to chal)	7	7	12/1	62	14
	Loving And Giving (85) (HCandy) 3-9-3 CRutter(10) (spd over 4f)	1	8	11/2 3	55	7
434 11	Gunners Glory (77) (BJMeehan) 3-8-9 MTebbutt(9) (prom over 2f)	½	9	10/1	46	—
339*	Forgotten Times (USA) (73) (TMJones) 3-8-5 NCarlisle(11) (b: led over 4f)	2	10	13/2	36	—
279 3	Heavenly Miss (IRE) (72) (JJBridger) 3-8-4ow2 DHarrison(5) (spd over 4f)	10	11	16/1	9	—

(SP 117.9%) **11 Rn**

1m 13.9 (2.70) CSF £405.33 CT £3,405.41 TOTE £17.20: £3.30 £5.50 £2.00 (£348.70) Trio £711.70; £220.54 to Kempton 31/3/97 OWNER The Caledonian Racing Society (WHITCOMBE) BRED Stetchworth Park Stud Ltd

LONG HANDICAP Ivory Dawn 7-8

STEWARDS' ENQUIRY Griffiths susp. 7&8/4/97 (careless riding).

Supercal, off the course since Royal Ascot last year, belied her paddock appearance. Although last of all two furlongs from home, she came with a sweeping run to lead in the closing stages, despite edging slightly to her right. Her jockey was later suspended for two days for careless riding. (16/1)

Ivory Dawn, who has done most of her racing at seven furlongs, found this trip too sharp and, although running on strongly from below the distance, found the line always beating her. (33/1)

Style Dancer (IRE) chased the leaders, but appeared to be going nowhere over a quarter-of-a-mile from home. However, he got his second wind inside the final furlong, and kept on nicely. (13/2)

Refuse To Lose made a pleasing reappearance, having every chance below the distance before tapped for toe. (4/1)

Bilko had been off the course since the beginning of last May, and not surprisingly looked as though this run would do him good. Nevertheless he showed plenty of promise, despite being badly drawn and taking a very strong hold early on. Eddery took him over to the far rails, and came with a nice run through the pack to lead below the distance. It looked as if he would prevail early inside the final furlong, but he was overhauled in the closing stages. He should not take long to find a race. (5/1)

Papita (IRE), who looked dry in her coat, won a Goodwood maiden last year, but was well-beaten on her other five starts. Given very sympathetic handling on this reappearance, she moved through the pack and was only a length-and-a-half down early in the final furlong, when her jockey decided to take things easy. She looks one to keep an eye on. (12/1)

Big Ben (12/1: 8/1-14/1)

339* Forgotten Times (USA) (13/2: 9/2-7/1)

507 MILCARS MASAKA STKS (Listed) (3-Y.O F) (Class A)

3-10 (3-10) **1m (Jubilee)** £10,950.50 (£3,314.00: £1,617.00: £768.50) Stalls: High GOING minus 0.26 sec per fur (GF)

			Pos	SP	RR	SF
	Calypso Grant (IRE) (90) (PWHarris) 3-8-8 PatEddery(2) (lw: hdwy over 2f out: led over 1f out: pushed out)	—	1	5/2 1	102	41
	Lycility (IRE) (87) (CEBrittain) 3-8-8 MRoberts(3) (hdwy to chse wnr over 1f out: r.o one pce)	1½	2	12/1	99	38
	Raindancing (IRE) (102) (RHannon) 3-8-8 DaneO'Neill(9) (lw: lost pl over 3f out: rallied over 1f out: one pce)	4	3	7/2 3	91	30
	Stone Flower (USA) (86) (PWChapple-Hyam) 3-8-8 WRyan(8) (chsd ldr: led 4f out tl over 2f out: wknd over 1f out)	nk	4	12/1	90	29
	Miss Golden Sands (GWragg) 3-8-8 MHills(6) (bit bkwd: led 4f: led over 2f out tl over 1f out: sn wknd)	3½	5	9/1	83	22
	Blane Water (USA) (99) (JRFanshawe) 3-8-8 DHarrison(7) (prom over 6f)	3½	6	3/1 2	76	15
	Carati (92) (RBoss) 3-8-8 MTebbutt(5) (prom over 6f)	2½	7	10/1	71	10
	Lady Diesis (USA) (92) (BWHills) 3-8-8 DHolland(4) (bhd whn rn v.wd bnd over 3f out: virtually p.u fnl 3f)	8	8	7/1	55	—

(SP 122.8%) **8 Rn**

1m 40.16 (2.46) CSF £33.17 TOTE £3.10: £1.40 £3.90 £1.20 (£32.20) Trio £19.80 OWNER Mrs P. W. Harris (BERKHAMSTED) BRED Pendley Farm

OFFICIAL EXPLANATION **Lady Diesis (USA): rider reported that the filly hung badly left throughout and he could not ride her out.**

Calypso Grant (IRE), a full-sister to the very useful Poppy Carew, made a very pleasing return, coming through to lead below the distance and needing only to be nudged along to quickly assert. She will do even better over further, and could turn out to be pretty useful. (5/2)

Lycility (IRE) came through to take second place below the distance and, although unable to get on terms with the winner, still finished well clear of the remainder. She may well be suited by further. (12/1)

Raindancing (IRE) was outpaced as the race began in earnest turning for home and, although getting back into it below the distance, had nothing in reserve. (7/2)

Stone Flower (USA) went on at halfway but, collared early in the straight, was soon in trouble. (12/1)

Miss Golden Sands, who looked just in need of this reappearance, made the vast majority of the running until overhauled below the distance. (9/1)

Blane Water (USA) has not grown much since last year, and was very uneasy in the betting. The market proved right, as she was in trouble early in the straight. (3/1: op 7/4)

508 MILCARS EASTER STKS (Listed) (3-Y.O C & G) (Class A)

3-40 (3-41) **1m (Jubilee)** £10,950.50 (£3,314.00: £1,617.00: £768.50) Stalls: High GOING minus 0.26 sec per fur (GF)

			Pos	SP	RR	SF
449 6	Pelham (IRE) (97) (RHannon) 3-8-8 DaneO'Neill(3) (hld up: led over 1f out: pushed out)	—	1	6/1	105	49
	Groom's Gordon (FR) (104) (JLDunlop) 3-8-8 TQuinn(1) (bit bkwd: chsd ldr: ev ch over 1f out: unable qckn)	4	2	4/1 3	97	41
	Papua (108) (IABalding) 3-8-8 PatEddery(6) (lw: a.p: rdn over 3f out: r.o one pce fnl 2f)	1¼	3	3/1 1	95	39
446*	Zaretski (82) (CEBrittain) 3-8-8 MRoberts(2) (led over 6f)	nk	4	10/1	94	38
	Crystal Hearted (HCandy) 3-8-8 AMcGlone(4) (bkwd: plld hrd: hdwy 5f out: wknd over 2f out)	2½	5	100/30 2	89	33
60*	Royal Aty (IRE) (PAKelleway) 3-8-8 SSanders(7) (lw: bhd fnl 3f)	1	6	9/2	87	31
	Red Guard (81) (GWragg) 3-8-8 MHills(5) (bit bkwd: swtg: plld hrd: a bhd)	2½	7	16/1	82	26

(SP 115.5%) **7 Rn**

1m 39.3 (1.60) CSF £27.89 TOTE £9.10: £2.60 £2.60 (£23.50) OWNER Mr D. A. Lucie-Smith (MARLBOROUGH) BRED Golden Vale Stud

449 Pelham (IRE) comes from a stable that has dominated this race in the last few years. Fit from a run at Doncaster last week, he stormed into the lead below the distance, and needed only to be nudged along to give Richard Hannon his fifth win in this race in the last six runnings. (6/1)

Groom's Gordon (FR), looking big and well for this reappearance, had just poked a nostril in front over a furlong out, when the winner came sailing by. This should have put him nicely straight for a crack at the Italian 2,000 Guineas. (4/1: 3/1-9/2)

Papua, a leggy individual who showed good form as a two-year-old, looked fit, but drifted markedly in the betting. Pushed along turning for home, he stayed on well without looking likely to find that vital turn of foot. He is crying out for further and, over a more suitable trip, should not be difficult to win with. (3/1: 6/4-7/2)

446* Zaretski took the field along but, collared below the distance, had nothing more to offer. (10/1)

Crystal Hearted was well-supported in the market, which was rather surprising considering he looked pretty fat in the paddock. That opinion was certainly confirmed in the race itself for, after taking a keen hold, was a spent force early in the straight. He will come on a lot for this. (100/30: 5/1-3/1)
60* Royal Aty (IRE), who trotted up in a weak race on the Equitrack in January, found this a completely different kettle of fish, and was left behind in the straight. (9/2)

509 MILCARS TEMPLE FORTUNE H'CAP (0-85) (3-Y.O) (Class D)

4-10 (4-12) **1m 1f (round)** £4,599.50 (£1,391.00: £678.00: £321.50) Stalls: High GOING minus 0.26 sec per fur (GF)

Form	Horse	Dist	Pos	SP	RR	SF
	Northern Sun (79) (TGMills) **3-9-1** TQuinn(3) (hdwy over 2f out: hrd rdn & hung rt 1f out: led ins fnl f: r.o wl)	—	**1**	$9/1^{3}$	91	54
331^{5}	**Puzzlement (62)** (CEBrittain) **3-7-12** JLowe(2) (a.p: led 3f out: hrd rdn over 1f out: hdd ins fnl f: r.o)	¾	**2**	$7/1^{1}$	73	36
431^{11}	**Sword Arm (75)** (RCharlton) **3-8-11** DHarrison(8) (a.p: hrd rdn over 2f out: one pce)	3½	**3**	$8/1^{2}$	79	42
	Mantles Prince (79) (GLewis) **3-9-1** PatEddery(13) (rdn & hdwy over 2f out: r.o one pce)	¾	**4**	$7/1^{1}$	82	45
	Kaiser Kache (IRE) (80) (KMcAuliffe) **3-8-9**(7) TField(4) (a.p: hrd rdn over 1f out: wknd fnl f)	1¼	**5**	$9/1^{3}$	81	44
298^{3}	**Pinchincha (FR) (67)** (DMorris) **3-8-3**ow2 NDay(1) (hdwy over 1f out: nvr nrr)	1¼	**6**	16/1	66	27
	Bold Oriental (IRE) (80) (NACallaghan) **3-9-2** SDrowne(11) (bit bkwd: nt clr run on ins over 2f out: nvr nrr)	1¼	**7**	$9/1^{3}$	76	39
388^{4}	**Don Sebastian (78)** (WJHaggas) **3-9-0** MHills(6) (led over 7f out to 3f out: wknd over 1f out)	nk	**8**	$7/1^{1}$	74	37
	Contentment (IRE) (74) (JWHills) **3-8-7**(3) MHenry(9) (bit bkwd: rdn over 3f out: hdwy over 2f out: wknd over 1f out)	s.h	**9**	$7/1^{1}$	70	33
	Hoh Flyer (USA) (69) (MBell) **3-8-5** MRoberts(14) (prom 6f)	2	**10**	$7/1^{1}$	61	24
	Manikato (USA) (72) (DJSCosgrove) **3-8-8** MRimmer(5) (lw: hdwy 2f out: wknd over 1f out)	2	**11**	16/1	61	24
	Sudest (IRE) (68) (IABalding) **3-8-1**(3) MartinDwyer(12) (a bhd)	3	**12**	25/1	51	14
	Linden's Lad (IRE) (67) (JRJenkins) **3-7-12**(5)ow1 ADaly(7) (led over 1f: wknd over 2f out)	1	**13**	33/1	49	11
				(SP 122.2%)		**13 Rn**

1m 53.22 (2.62) CSF £65.87 CT £504.62 TOTE £9.40: £2.60 £2.00 £2.90 (£28.90) Trio £147.90 OWNER Mr T. G. Mills (EPSOM) BRED Broughton Bloodstock

Northern Sun began his run in the straight and, despite hanging right under pressure, managed to get on top inside the final furlong.(9/1)
331 Puzzlement, who failed to stay one mile three furlongs last time out, appreciated the return to a shorter trip and went on three furlongs from home. Eventually overhauled inside the last two hundred yards, he nevertheless finished well clear of the remainder. (7/1)
431 Sword Arm was never far away but, despite all his jockey's efforts in the straight, the gelding could only go up and down in the same place. (8/1: 6/1-9/1)
Mantles Prince, who raced mainly at six furlongs last year, coped with this longer trip and stayed on to take fourth prize. (7/1: 5/1-15/2)
Kaiser Kache (IRE) was never far away, but he was under pressure below the distance and had soon run out of gas. The drop back to a mile may help. (9/1: 12/1-8/1)
298 Pinchincha (FR), fit from an All-Weather campaign, stayed on in the closing stages without ever posing a threat. (16/1)
Bold Oriental (IRE) (9/1: 6/1-10/1)

510 MILCARS QUEEN'S PRIZE H'CAP (0-95) (4-Y.O+) (Class C)

4-45 (4-45) **2m** £5,628.00 (£1,704.00: £832.00: £396.00) Stalls: High GOING minus 0.26 sec per fur (GF)

Form	Horse	Dist	Pos	SP	RR	SF
442^{6}	**Inchcailloch (IRE) (78)** (JSKing) **8-8-9**(7) RFfrench(9) (rdn 6f out: hdwy over 2f out: led 1f out: r.o wl)	—	**1**	$11/2^{2}$	91	61
	Siege Perilous (IRE) (66) (SCWilliams) **4-7-10**(3) MartinDwyer(8) (hld up: rdn over 2f out: led over 1f out: sn hdd: unable qckn)	1¼	**2**	$5/1^{1}$	78	43
	Shining Dancer (60) (SDow) **5-7-12** NCarlisle(10) (plld hrd: hdwy over 2f out: rdn over 1f out: r.o one pce)	1¾	**3**	12/1	70	40
384^{7}	**Hattaafeh (IRE) (60)** (MissBSanders) **6-7-7**(5) RMullen(7) (hld up: rdn over 1f out: one pce)	nk	**4**	$13/2^{3}$	70	40
	Sea Freedom (58) (GBBalding) **6-7-10v** NVarley(5) (a.p: rdn over 6f out: one pce fnl 2f)	nk	**5**	8/1	67	37
	Frozen Sea (USA) (65) (GPEnright) **6-7-12**(5)ow1 ADaly(2) (lw: plld hrd: hld up: rdn over 2f out: ev ch over 1f out: wknd fnl f)	3	**6**	10/1	71	40
	Unchanged (72) (CEBrittain) **5-8-10** MRoberts(4) (led tl over 1f out: sn wknd)	3	**7**	$11/2^{2}$	75	45
	Salty Girl (IRE) (63) (JSMoore) **4-7-10** NAdams(11) (prom 8f: t.o)	27	**8**	25/1	39	4
430^{17}	**Amadour (IRE) (65)** (PMitchell) **4-7-9**(3)ow2 MHenry(3) (prom 11f: t.o)	4	**9**	14/1	37	—
*419**	**Random Kindness (70)** (RIngram) **4-8-3** SWhitworth(6) (lw: dwlt: hdwy 12f out: wknd qckly over 3f out: t.o)	4	**10**	$5/1^{1}$	38	3
				(SP 115.8%)		**10 Rn**

3m 28.45 (3.85) CSF £29.97 CT £289.05 TOTE £5.20: £2.10 £2.20 £2.60 (£10.60) Trio £54.00 OWNER Mr F. J. Carter (SWINDON) BRED Hascombe and Valiant Studs
LONG HANDICAP Salty Girl (IRE) 7-7 Amadour (IRE) 7-8
WEIGHT FOR AGE 4yo-5lb

442 Inchcailloch (IRE) is such a versatile performer - he won last year's Cesarewitch and then three steeplechases in a row - and returned to the winner's enclosure here. However the signs did not look good in the back straight as he was being niggled along fully threequarters-of-a-mile from home. However, he got into the action early in the straight and, moving to the front a furlong from home, soon had the race nicely sown-up. This ground suits him well. (11/2)
Siege Perilous (IRE) had just poked a nostril in front below the distance, when the winner came by and tapped him for toe. (5/1)
Shining Dancer is not an easy ride. Jumping as she left the stalls, she took a ferocious hold, and Carlisle had real difficulties trying to settle her. However, despite her earlier antics, she stayed on well to finish a respectable third. (12/1)
324 Hattaafeh (IRE), who has gained all four of her victories on the Lingfield Equitrack - three of them coming this year - appeared to be cruising in the straight. However, once let down below the distance, she did not find what was required. (13/2)
Sea Freedom has plenty of ability, but is a very tricky customer. A leading light from the off, he was being bustled along for the last threequarters-of-a-mile, and could only keep on at one pace in the last two furlongs. He remains a maiden after thirty attempts, and should be left well alone. (8/1)
Frozen Sea (USA), given a recent pipe-opener over hurdles, took a keen hold. Chasing the leaders, he was certainly close enough if good enough below the distance, before tiring in the final furlong. (10/1)

T/Jkpt: £23,197.70 (0.3 Tckts); £22,870.99 to Kempton 31/3/97. T/Plpt: £329.30 (87.35 Tckts). T/Qdpt: £136.30 (10.88 Tckts) AK

0417-WOLVERHAMPTON (L-H) (Standard)
Saturday March 29th
WEATHER: fine

511 CODSALL MAIDEN STKS (3-Y.O+) (Class D)
7-00 (7-00) **1m 1f 79y (Fibresand)** £3,581.90 (£1,068.20: £509.60: £230.30) Stalls: Low GOING: 0.12 sec per fur (SLW)

				SP	RR	SF
367^{3}	**Barbara's Jewel (41)** (ABailey) **5-9-12** SSanders(7) (hdwy 3f out: led over 1f out: drvn out)	—	**1**	$7/2^{2}$	67	32
	Canadian Fantasy (82) (MJohnston) **3-8-7** DHolland(6) (led: rdn & hdd over 4f out: styd on)	1	**2**	$11/8^{1}$	65	11
422^{6}	**Venice Beach (59)** (CPEBrooks) **5-9-9**(3) JDSmith(5) (chsd ldr: led over 4f out tl over 1f out: nt qckn)	1¼	**3**	8/1	63	28
	Classic Jenny (IRE) (ICampbell) **4-9-7** RPrice(4) (a.p: r.o one pce fnl 2f)	nk	**4**	12/1	58	23
	Wafa (IRE) (WJHaggas) **3-8-0**(3)ow1 FLynch(3) (plld hrd: hdwy 3f out: ev ch 2f out: sn wknd)	5	**5**	$5/1^{3}$	50	—
463^{6}	**Persian Sunset (IRE)** (MissJBower) **5-9-2**(5) JBramhill(2) (prom tl wknd 3f out)	8	**6**	50/1	35	—
	Badrinath (IRE) (HJCollingridge) **3-8-7** JTate(1) (hld up in rr: effrt & rdn 3f out: sn wknd)	¾	**7**	20/1	39	—
				(SP 106.5%)	**7 Rn**	

2m 6.2 (10.20) CSF £6.78 TOTE £4.40: £1.70 £1.90 (£3.10) OWNER Mrs Barbara Higgins (TARPORLEY) BRED L. J. Barratt
WEIGHT FOR AGE 3yo-19lb

367 Barbara's Jewel, patiently ridden, came storming through to lead approaching the final furlong and won readily. (7/2: op 8/1)
Canadian Fantasy looked fit despite an absence of almost six months. He tried to make all the running but was struggling when headed. He kept on though, and should appreciate a longer trip. (11/8: op 10/11)
422 Venice Beach took a narrow lead over four furlongs out and fought back well when headed approaching the final furlong. (8/1: tchd 12/1)
Classic Jenny (IRE) made a very satisfactory Flat debut, always hunting up the leaders and keeping on, though running very green when pressure was applied in the closing stages. (12/1)
Wafa (IRE) broke fast and pulled hard in the early stages before being steadied to the back of the field. She moved up to be at the leaders' quarters at the two-furlong marker before weakening. (5/1: op 5/2)

512 OAKEN CLAIMING STKS (4-Y.O+) (Class F)
7-30 (7-32) **6f (Fibresand)** £2,277.00 (£627.00: £297.00) Stalls: Low GOING: 0.12 sec per fur (SLW)

				SP	RR	SF
424*	**Walk the Beat (71)** (MartynMeade) **7-8-10**(5) DSweeney(6) (mde all: all out)	—	**1**	$4/1^{1}$	62	30
421^{5}	**Hannah's Usher (65)** (CMurray) **5-8-7** NicolaHowarth(4) (a.p: r.o wl ins fnl f)	hd	**2**	$5/1^{3}$	54	22
172^{7}	**Efficacy (54)** (APJarvis) **6-8-0**(7)ow7 CCarver(5) (w wnr: ev ch 1f out: r.o)	1¼	**3**	20/1	50	11
429^{2}	**Bold Aristocrat (IRE) (65)** (RHollinshead) **6-8-6**(3) FLynch(11) (styd on fnl 2f: nt rch ldrs)	1½	**4**	$9/2^{2}$	48	16
424^{4}	**Jubilee Scholar (IRE) (45)** (KMcAuliffe) **4-8-12b** JFEgan(8) (wl bhd tl gd hdwy over 1f out: nrst fin)	¾	**5**	50/1	49	17
335^{2}	**Lift Boy (USA) (63)** (GLMoore) **8-8-9** CandyMorris(7) (chsd ldrs: rdn & no hdwy fnl 2f)	1¼	**6**	8/1	43	11
224^{5}	**Ultra Beet (79)** (PCHaslam) **5-9-5** JFortune(2) (rdn along: prom tl wknd over 2f out)	½	**7**	$9/2^{2}$	52	20
306^{5}	**Lady Westbury (IRE) (33)** (PCRitchens) **6-7-12** NAdams(9) (prom tl wknd over 2f out)	2½	**8**	50/1	24	—
422^{7}	**Dragonjoy (57)** (NPLittmoden) **4-8-9v**(3) DGriffiths(1) (bhd fnl 2f)	4	**9**	10/1	27	—
404^{2}	**Mellors (IRE) (61)** (MJHeaton-Ellis) **4-9-3** SDrowne(3) (hmpd s: a wl bhd)	1¼	**10**	11/1	29	—
	Smart Guest (DShaw) **5-9-3b**¹ JFanning(10) (prom tl wknd over 2f out)	2½	**11**	16/1	22	—
				(SP 116.1%)	**11 Rn**	

1m 16.9 (5.70) CSF £21.08 TOTE £4.60: £1.40 £2.60 £4.90 (£20.80) Trio £89.00 OWNER Ladyswood Racing Club (MALMESBURY) BRED R. B. Warren

424* Walk the Beat made all the running. He shook off Efficacy entering the final furlong, but had to fight hard to hold the sustained challenge of the runner-up. (4/1)
421 Hannah's Usher, always chasing the leaders, looked held a furlong out, but found a strong burst in the final one hundred yards. (5/1)
Efficacy, carrying 7lb overweight, ran a blinder. She raced with the winner but, after having every chance, could find no extra inside the last furlong. (20/1)
429 Bold Aristocrat (IRE), struggling in the middle to rear for much of the way, stayed on in the last furlong. (9/2)
Jubilee Scholar (IRE) was virtually tailed off approaching the short straight, and did extremely well to reach his final position. (50/1)
335 Lift Boy (USA), always hunting up the leaders, could make no headway under pressure in the last two furlongs. (8/1)
404 Mellors (IRE) appeared to be badly hampered at the start, and was well behind two out. This run can be ignored. (11/1)

513 BLAKENHALL H'CAP (0-65) (3-Y.O) (Class F)
8-00 (8-01) **1m 100y (Fibresand)** £2,277.00 (£627.00: £297.00) Stalls: Low GOING: 0.12 sec per fur (SLW)

				SP	RR	SF
395^{2}	**Weet And See (63)** (RHollinshead) **3-9-2**(3) DGriffiths(9) (hdwy 3f out: led over 1f out: r.o wl)	—	**1**	$3/1^{1}$	70	25
388^{5}	**Mutahadeth (65)** (DShaw) **3-9-7** JFanning(6) (hdwy 4f out: ev ch fnl 2f: r.o)	1¼	**2**	10/1	70	25
377^{3}	**Red Embers (55)** (CADwyer) **3-8-11** RCochrane(5) (bhd tl r.o fnl 2f: nrst fin)	1½	**3**	$7/1^{3}$	57	12
367^{6}	**Loxley's Girl (IRE) (42)** (HAkbary) **3-7-5**(7)ow2 RFfrench(7) (a.p: r.o one pce fnl 2f)	s.h	**4**	40/1	44	—
454^{3}	**Mirror Four Sport (57)** (MJohnston) **3-8-6**(7) KSked(4) (a.p: rdn after 2f: one pce fnl 2f)	2½	**5**	9/1	54	9
	Scarrots (62) (SCWilliams) **3-9-4** KDarley(1) (chsd ldrs: ev ch & hrd rdn 2f out: one pce)	2	**6**	$7/2^{2}$	55	10
	Sheraton Girl (46) (NPLittmoden) **3-8-2** JQuinn(2) (led after 1f: hdd & wknd over 1f out)	½	**7**	12/1	38	—
415^{4}	**Jack The Lad (IRE) (55)** (JHetherton) **3-8-11** MTebbutt(3) (bhd fnl 3f)	10	**8**	$7/1^{3}$	28	—
259^{6}	**Ballerina's Dream (45)** (MartynMeade) **3-8-1** NAdams(10) (bhd fnl 3f)	2	**9**	14/1	15	—
	Skippy Was A Kiwi (IRE) (57) (APJarvis) **3-8-13** WJO'Connor(8) (led 1f: prom tl wknd 3f out)	¾	**10**	10/1	25	—
				(SP 117.2%)	**10 Rn**	

1m 54.3 (9.30) CSF £31.01 CT £178.57 TOTE £4.10: £2.00 £1.90 £2.20 (£10.60) Trio £40.80 OWNER Ed Weetman (Haulage & Storage) Ltd (UPPER LONGDON) BRED Longdon Stud Ltd
LONG HANDICAP Loxley's Girl (IRE) 7-8

395 Weet And See, running in a handicap for the first time, was settled towards the rear of the field until coming with a steady run from the three-furlong marker. Once he had struck the front approaching the final furlong, he was always in command. (3/1)
277 Mutahadeth moved up at halfway but, though having every chance entering the short straight, he could not quicken with the winner. (10/1: 8/1-12/1)
377 Red Embers was well behind for much of the way. She still had plenty to do at the two-furlong marker, but finished strongly to snatch third place on the line. (7/1)
367 Loxley's Girl (IRE), always hunting up the leaders, was slightly outpaced at the two-furlong marker but stayed on again at the finish. (40/1)

454 Mirror Four Sport, close up from the start, was soon being chased along to hold her place and, though she stayed on, she never held out much hope of winning. (9/1)
Scarrots looked a big danger approaching the straight, but then came under maximum pressure and could find no extra in the last furlong. (7/2: op 6/1)
Ballerina's Dream (14/1: 10/1-16/1)
Skippy Was A Kiwi (IRE) (10/1: op 6/1)

514 WEDNESBURY H'CAP (0-100) (3-Y.O+) (Class C)

8-45 (8-46) **7f (Fibresand)** £5,352.55 (£1,596.40: £761.70: £344.35) Stalls: High GOING: 0.12 sec per fur (SLW)

				SP	RR	SF
448^{3}	**Nomore Mr Niceguy (85)** (EJAlston) **3-8-2**^{ow1} JFEgan(2) (led 1f: a.p: led ins fnl f: r.o wl)	—	**1**	8/1	94	35
363^{2}	**Chewit (96)** (GLMoore) **5-10-0** CandyMorris(3) (hld up: qcknd & led over 2f out: hdd ins fnl f: r.o)	½	**2**	6/1^{3}	104	61
398^{7}	**State of Caution (82)** (DShaw) **4-9-0b** JFanning(1) (chsd ldrs: hrd rdn 2f out: r.o one pce)	3½	**3**	12/1	82	39
349^{2}	**Dawalib (USA) (66)** (DHaydnJones) **7-7-12**^{ow2} CRutter(4) (dwlt: nrst fin)	2	**4**	14/1	61	16
443^{18}	**Weetman's Weigh (IRE) (79)** (RHollinshead) **4-8-8**$^{(3)}$ FLynch(9) (bhd tl r.o fnl 2f)	s.h	**5**	20/1	74	31
450^{3}	**Tumbleweed Ridge (89)** (BJMeehan) **4-9-7b** MTebbutt(6) (a.p: jnd ldrs & ev ch over 2f out: hrd rdn & wknd over 1f out)	2	**6**	6/5^{1}	80	37
363^{5}	**Rakis (IRE) (93)** (MrsLStubbs) **7-9-11** RCochrane(8) (hld up: effrt & rdn over 2f out: sn wknd)	3	**7**	9/2^{2}	77	34
257^{3}	**Yeoman Oliver (70)** (BAMcMahon) **4-8-2b** LNewton(5) (led after 1f: hdd & wknd over 2f out)	2	**8**	12/1	49	6
	Classic Leader (79) (ICampbell) **4-8-11** RPrice(7) (w ldr tl wknd qckly 2f out)	2	**9**	20/1	54	11
				(SP 120.6%)	**9 Rn**	

1m 29.9 (5.20) CSF £52.58 CT £400.55 TOTE £7.10: £1.60 £2.10 £2.30 (£19.40) Trio £21.50 OWNER Mrs Carol McPhail (PRESTON) BRED Brick Kiln Stud and Lariston Apartments Ltd
LONG HANDICAP Dawalib (USA) 7-7
WEIGHT FOR AGE 3yo-15lb
OFFICIAL EXPLANATION **Tumbleweed Ridge: rider reported that the colt lost his action and finished lame, although he was reported sound later.**
448 Nomore Mr Niceguy ran rather too freely, but was always close up. He ran on well under pressure in the last furlong and gained the upper hand in the final one hundred yards. (8/1)
363 Chewit looked certain to win when bursting through to quicken clear just over two furlongs from home. He could not hold the winner but should soon find compensation. (6/1)
376* State of Caution, being chased along behind the leaders for much of the way, ran on at one pace under pressure in the last two furlongs. (12/1: op 8/1)
349 Dawalib (USA) missed the break and was never nearer than at the finish. (14/1)
Weetman's Weigh (IRE) failed to go the pace, but was staying on in the closing stages. (20/1)
450 Tumbleweed Ridge possibly ran a shade freely but had no real excuse. He still appeared to be travelling strongly on the outside at the two-furlong marker but, when let down, found nothing. (6/5)

515 BOWMER AND KIRKLAND (LONDON) (S) STKS (3,4,5 & 6-Y.O) (Class F)

9-15 (9-18) **5f (Fibresand)** £2,277.00 (£627.00: £297.00) Stalls: Low GOING: 0.12 sec per fur (SLW)

				SP	RR	SF
	Silk Cottage (54) (RMWhitaker) **5-9-11** DeanMcKeown(1) (mde all: drvn out)	—	**1**	10/1	54	36
421^{4}	**Featherstone Lane (51)** (MissLCSiddall) **6-9-4v**$^{(7)}$ TSiddall(4) (a.p: ev ch fnl f: nt qckn)	1	**2**	11/2^{3}	51	33
421^{3}	**Little Ibnr (68)** (PDEvans) **6-9-11** JFEgan(5) (a.p: hrd rdn fnl 2f: one pce)	2	**3**	4/5^{1}	44	26
394^{9}	**Rennyholme (36)** (JHetherton) **6-9-11b** RCochrane(6) (s.s: nrst fin)	1¼	**4**	12/1	40	22
	Perfect Brave (70) (JBalding) **6-9-5** SDrowne(2) (jinked & nrly uns rdr s: sn in tch: rdn & wknd 2f out)	2½	**5**	4/1^{2}	26	8
469^{8}	**Deardaw (26)** (MissLCSiddall) **5-9-0** SSanders(3) (w wnr tl hrd rdn & wknd over 2f out)	5	**6**	33/1	5	—
				(SP 110.7%)	**6 Rn**	

63.8 secs (4.90) CSF £54.36 TOTE £7.10: £2.70 £2.40 (£18.60) OWNER Mr Christopher Cooke (LEEDS) BRED G. G. Senior D. Lodge and L. Carver
Bt in 6,000 gns
Silk Cottage made all the running, and held on under strong driving in the last furlong. (10/1: 7/1-11/1)
421 Featherstone Lane lay much closer than usual. He had every chance in the last furlong but seemed disinclined to pass his rival. (11/2)
421 Little Ibnr had no excuse. Always well-placed on the outside, he failed to respond to hard driving in the last two furlongs. (4/5)
371 Rennyholme missed the break and, last for a long way, was never nearer than at the finish. (12/1: op 8/1)
Perfect Brave jinked at the start and almost lost his rider. Soon recovering, he was on the heels of the leaders until weakening two furlongs from home. (4/1: op 9/4)

516 WILLENHALL H'CAP (0-65) (3-Y.O+) (Class F)

9-45 (9-46) **1m 4f (Fibresand)** £2,715.90 (£752.40: £359.70) Stalls: Low GOING: 0.12 sec per fur (SLW)

				SP	RR	SF
419^{5}	**State Approval (57)** (PEccles) **4-9-5** CRutter(10) (hdwy 4f out: led over 1f out: r.o wl)	—	**1**	8/1	68	39
*400**	**Premier Dance (64)** (DHaydnJones) **10-9-9**$^{(5)}$ PPMurphy(12) (hld up in rr: stdy hdwy 3f out: ev ch 1f out: nt qckn)	2½	**2**	10/1	72	45
315^{9}	**Mr Speculator (52)** (JEBanks) **4-9-0v** JQuinn(5) (w ldr: led 5f out tl 1f out: one pce)	1¼	**3**	7/1	58	29
*418**	**English Invader (58)** (CADwyer) **6-9-8** RCochrane(7) (hld up: hdwy 4f out: ev ch over 2f out: one pce)	2	**4**	7/2^{2}	61	34
315^{2}	**Ambidextrous (IRE) (50)** (EJAlston) **5-8-9**$^{(5)}$ DSweeney(4) (mid div tl bdly hmpd & lost pl over 3f out: gd hdwy over 1f out: nvr nr to chal)	hd	**5**	3/1^{1}	53	26
	Golden Fawn (51) (NMBabbage) **4-8-13** VSlattery(8) (no hdwy fnl 3f)	8	**6**	20/1	44	15
410^{10}	**Noble Canonire (44)** (DShaw) **5-8-8b** JFanning(6) (prom tl wknd 3f out)	2½	**7**	25/1	33	6
418^{9}	**Carrolls Marc (IRE) (32)** (CMurray) **9-7-10** NicolaHowarth(9) (bhd fnl 5f)	3	**8**	20/1	17	—
*218**	**Cashaplenty (54)** (NPLittmoden) **4-9-2** TGMcLaughlin(2) (prom tl wknd 3f out)	1¾	**9**	5/1^{3}	37	8
	Bailiwick (53) (NAGraham) **4-9-1** MFenton(3) (led 3f: wknd 5f out)	18	**10**	33/1	12	—
	Mr Lowry (40) (LJBarratt) **5-8-4** NCarlisle(11) (dropped rr & hrd rdn 6f out: no rspnse)	5	**11**	50/1	—	—
*373**	**River Captain (USA) (60)** (DJGMurraySmith) **4-9-8** SSanders(1) (led after 3f to 5f out: sn wknd)	6	**12**	8/1	4	—
				(SP 126.0%)	**12 Rn**	

2m 43.7 (11.20) CSF £76.89 CT £550.21 TOTE £17.90: £3.60 £3.80 £1.60 (£206.40) Trio £149.70; £84.38 to Kempton 31/3/97 OWNER The Claddagh Ring Partnership (LAMBOURN) BRED Collin Stud and The Pharly Syndicate
LONG HANDICAP Carrolls Marc (IRE) 7-8

WEIGHT FOR AGE 4yo-2lb
419 State Approval moved up four furlongs out. After striking the front below the distance, he was strongly challenged but was going away again at the finish. (8/1: tchd 12/1)
400* Premier Dance, held up in last place, threaded his way through the field to challenge entering the final furlong, but could find no extra in the last one hundred yards. (10/1)
219* Mr Speculator led five furlongs out but was already under pressure. He hung on until approaching the final furlong, but could find no more. (7/1)
418* English Invader crept onto the heels of the leaders three furlongs out but, after looking dangerous, proved one-paced in the final quarter-mile. (7/2)
315 Ambidextrous (IRE) was hampered on the inside over three furlongs from home and dropped back to the rear. In the circumstances, he did extremely well to reach his final position. (3/1: op 5/1)

T/Plpt: £477.20 (25.56 Tckts). T/Qdpt: £74.80 (5.96 Tckts) Hn

0504-KEMPTON (R-H) (Good to firm)
Monday March 31st
WEATHER: fine, sunny & warm

517 STARK MAIDEN STKS (I) (3-Y.O+) (Class D)
1-40 (1-40) **7f (Jubilee)** £2,981.25 (£900.00: £437.50: £206.25) Stalls: High GOING minus 0.23 sec per fur (GF)

Runner	Dist	Pos	SP	RR	SF
Strathmore Clear (GLewis) **3-8-11** PatEddery(6) (led tl ins fnl f: hrd rdn: led last strides)	—	**1**	11/2[3]	77	36
Mr Majica (BJMeehan) **3-8-11** BDoyle(3) (gd hdwy over 1f out: led ins fnl f: hrd rdn: hdd last strides)	hd	**2**	16/1	77	36
Ijtinab (RAkehurst) **3-8-11** SSanders(2) (bit bkwd: chsd wnr: rdn over 2f out: ev ch ins fnl f: one pce)	hd	**3**	40/1	77	36
Beyond Calculation (USA) (PWHarris) **3-8-11** GDuffield(5) (lw: plld hrd: a.p: rdn over 2f out: ev ch ins fnl f: one pce)	nk	**4**	7/4[1]	76	35
Regal Patrol (MRStoute) **3-8-11** JReid(4) (hld up: rdn over 1f out: r.o ins fnl f)	nk	**5**	5/1[2]	75	34
Neronian (IRE) (BWHills) **3-8-11** DHolland(9) (unf: scope: a.p: rdn over 2f out: one pce)	1¼	**6**	7/1	72	31
Speculator (IRE) (WJHaggas) **3-8-11** RCochrane(10) (str: scope: plld hrd. hld up: rdn over 2f out: wknd fnl f)	½	**7**	10/1	71	30
Burundi (IRE) (PWChapple-Hyam) **3-8-11** SWhitworth(1) (swvd lft st: nvr nr to chal)	½	**8**	11/2[3]	70	29
Dandy Regent (CACyzer) **3-8-11** TQuinn(7) (hld up: rdn over 2f out: wknd over 1f out)	½	**9**	40/1	69	28
Gain Line (USA) (BobJones) **4-9-12** AMcGlone(8) (a bhd)	2½	**10**	40/1	63	37
			(SP 118.6%)	**10 Rn**	

1m 27.9 (3.40) CSF £80.39 TOTE £8.20: £2.10 £2.60 £8.30 (£40.90) Trio £380.80; £429.09 to Uttoxeter 1/4/97 OWNER Food Brokers Ltd (EPSOM) BRED Hyde Stud
WEIGHT FOR AGE 3yo-15lb
IN-FOCUS: This race was run at a sedate pace and basically turned into a sprint from the home turn, hence the runners finished on top of each other.
Strathmore Clear put up a gutsy display after a nine-month absence. Setting only a moderate pace, he quickened things up in the straight but looked set for second place when collared inside the final furlong. However, he showed a tremendous never-say-die attitude and got back up in the last few strides. (11/2)
Mr Majica made significant headway through the field below the distance despite his rider getting his reins in a bit of a twist. Striking the front inside the final furlong, he looked set for victory, but he had not bargained on such a tenacious winner and was worried out of it in the last couple of strides. He should soon go one better. (16/1)
Ijtinab, a round-bodied colt who was sold out of Peter Walwyn's stable for a mere 2,500 guineas after beating just one home on his sole start as a two-year-old, was gleaming in his coat but did appear to be carrying quite a lot of condition. However, he ran a very promising race, throwing down his challenge in the straight and still having every chance inside the final furlong before just tapped for toe. Sure to strip a lot fitter for this, he should soon be winning. (40/1)
Beyond Calculation (USA) looked in fine shape for this reappearance but took a keen hold in a race where there was no early pace. He looked a serious threat as he mounted his challenge in the straight but was just tapped for toe in the last half-furlong. He should not take long to find a race. (7/4)
Regal Patrol, who has been gelded since last year, has not grown much and looked dull in his coat. Chasing the leaders, he took a while to get going but did stay on nicely inside the final furlong. He was disappointing and unco-operative last season and, whilst his operation may well have helped, he still has it to prove. (5/1: op 3/1)
Neronian (IRE), quite a lengthy colt who still needs time to develop, was never far away but lacked that vital turn of foot in the final quarter-mile. (7/1: 5/1-8/1)
Speculator (IRE) (10/1: op 6/1)
Burundi (IRE) (11/2: 7/2-6/1)

518 STARK MAIDEN STKS (II) (3-Y.O+) (Class D)
2-10 (2-11) **7f (Jubilee)** £2,965.00 (£895.00: £435.00: £205.00) Stalls: High GOING minus 0.23 sec per fur (GF)

Runner	Dist	Pos	SP	RR	SF
Greenaway Bay (USA) (GWragg) **3-8-11** MHills(7) (w'like: scope: s.s: plld out over 2f out: hdwy over 1f out: led ins fnl f: ran green)	—	**1**	7/2[2]	86+	38
The Negotiator (MJHeaton-Ellis) **3-8-11** AClark(1) (leggy: hld up: rdn over 2f out: unable qckn fnl f)	3½	**2**	20/1	78	30
Foreign Rule (IRE) (PWChapple-Hyam) **3-8-11** JReid(4) (scope: dwlt: rdn over 3f out: hdwy over 1f out: r.o: rn green)	½	**3**	7/1	77	29
Blue Goblin (USA) (90) (LMCumani) **3-8-11** PatEddery(2) (led: clr over 2f out: hdd ins fnl f: sn wknd)	nk	**4**	2/1[1]	76	28
Rotor Man (IRE) (66) (JDBethell) **3-8-11** DHolland(9) (a.p: rdn over 2f out: one pce)	1	**5**	33/1	74	26
Out Line (65) (MMadgwick) **5-9-7** NVarley(5) (a.p: rdn over 3f out: chsd ldr over 2f out tl over 1f out: wknd fnl f)	1¾	**6**	33/1	65	32
Muhassil (IRE) (MajorWRHern) **4-9-12** SWhitworth(6) (lw: s.s: hdwy on ins over 1f out: eased whn btn fnl f: bttr for race)	1¼	**7**	7/1	67+	34
Wira (IRE) (PFICole) **3-8-11** TQuinn(3) (leggy: chsd ldr over 4f)	4	**8**	9/2[3]	58	10

				SP	RR	SF
	Teraab (JHMGosden) **3-8-11** AMcGlone(8) (bit bkwd: dwlt: bhd fnl 2f)	9	**9**	14/1	37	—
				(SP 116.0%)	**9 Rn**	

1m 27.74 (3.24) CSF £64.81 TOTE £5.10: £1.80 £3.30 £2.10 (£99.90) Trio £243.70 OWNER Mollers Racing (NEWMARKET) BRED Mike G. Rutherford

WEIGHT FOR AGE 3yo-15lb

Greenaway Bay (USA), who cost $110,000 as a yearling, was extremely green on this racecourse debut. Losing several lengths at the start, his jockey was quickly bustling him along in an attempt to get back to his rivals. He eventually managed to do so and came back on the bridle turning for home. Picking up ground in the straight, he came smoothly through to lead early inside the final furlong and quickly put daylight between himself and his rivals. Sure to have learnt a great deal, he can only improve and has a very bright future if this run is anything to go by. He can win again. (7/2)

The Negotiator, a tall gelding who still had his winter coat, chased the leaders. Only about a length or so down entering the final furlong, he then failed to find another gear. (20/1)

Foreign Rule (IRE), an angular gelding who is a half-brother to Italian Oaks winner Germignana, proved very green on this racecourse debut and, after losing ground at the start, was being bustled along at halfway. However, he grasped what was required of him in the last furlong and a half and ran on nicely. Sure to be a lot wiser for this, he should find a race in due course. (7/1: 5/1-8/1)

Blue Goblin (USA) certainly had the best form on offer and merrily bowled along in front. Forging clear in the straight, it looked as if victory was his but, when caught inside the final furlong, he found disappointingly little. Just as he showed on several occasions last year, he does not seem to save much for the closing stages of his races. (2/1)

Rotor Man (IRE) ran much better on this seasonal debut and was a leading player if failing to quicken in the straight. (33/1)

Out Line, the most exposed and experienced runner in the field, moved into second place over a quarter of a mile from home but she was collared for that position below the distance and soon done with. A drop in class is certainly required. (33/1)

Teraab (14/1: 10/1-16/1)

519 CITY INDUSTRIAL SUPPLIES CONDITIONS STKS (3-Y.O+) (Class C)

2-40 (2-43) **6f** £5,087.20 (£1,904.80: £932.40: £402.00: £181.00: £92.60) Stalls: High GOING minus 0.23 sec per fur (GF)

				SP	RR	SF
	Monaassib (107) (EALDunlop) **6-9-4**(3) DO'Donohoe(11) (chsd ldrs: led 2f out: pushed out)	—	**1**	11/2[2]	116	78
	Oh Nellie (USA) (NACallaghan) **3-8-3**(7) RFfrench(9) (unf: scope: led 4f: rdn & r.o ins fnl f)	¾	**2**	13/2[3]	116	65
398[11]	**World Premier (95)** (CEBrittain) **4-9-2** BDoyle(3) (hld up: rdn over 2f out: unable qckn)	4	**3**	14/1	98	60
	Loch Patrick (101) (MMadgwick) **7-9-7** JReid(6) (a.p: rdn over 2f out: one pce)	nk	**4**	14/1	103	65
	Tomba (106) (BJMeehan) **3-9-1** MRoberts(5) (hdwy over 1f out: nvr nrr)	1¼	**5**	7/1	106	55
452[4]	**Patsy Grimes (95)** (JSMoore) **7-8-11** DaneO'Neill(8) (nvr nr to chal)	1¼	**6**	11/2[2]	86	48
	Sea Dane (101) (PWHarris) **4-9-9** GDuffield(7) (b: bit bkwd: prom over 3f)	1¾	**7**	8/1	93	55
	Montendre (96) (RJHodges) **10-9-2** TQuinn(4) (sme hdwy 1f out: sn wknd)	1	**8**	10/1	84	46
	Sayyaramix (FR) (JVanLandschoot,Belgium) **4-9-2** RCochrane(1) (wnt rt s: bhd fnl 2f)	1½	**9**	33/1	80	42
	Watch Me (IRE) (105) (RHannon) **4-9-0** PatEddery(2) (hld up: rdn over 3f out: wknd over 2f out)	5	**10**	11/4[1]	64	26
	Funchal Way (NMBabbage) **5-9-2** AClark(10) (a bhd)	3	**11**	100/1	58	20
				(SP 120.7%)	**11 Rn**	

1m 11.86 (0.66) CSF £38.59 TOTE £6.20: £2.40 £1.90 £5.20 (£25.80) Trio £154.30 OWNER Maktoum Al Maktoum (NEWMARKET) BRED Side Hill Stud in Ireland

WEIGHT FOR AGE 3yo-13lb

OFFICIAL EXPLANATION **Watch Me (IRE): no explanation offered.**

IN-FOCUS: **Leading Irish apprentice Daragh O'Donohoe, who has ridden winners in Ireland and Australia, scored here for his first win in this country.**

Monaassib, still wearing his winter coat and looking dry, nevertheless goes well fresh and, striking the front a quarter of a mile from home, needed only to be nudged along to quickly assert. This is his ground. (11/2)

Oh Nellie (USA), winner of her first three races in Canada last year before finishing fourth of five at Belmont Park where she possibly failed to stay a mile, made a very promising English debut. Setting the pace, she was collared a quarter of a mile out and, although no match for the winner. ran on in pleasing style inside the final furlong to finish well clear of the remainder. She looks useful and there are certainly races to be won with her this year. (13/2: 10/1-5/1)

World Premier, one of only two in the field with a recent run under his belt, chased the leaders but failed to quicken in the final quarter-mile. (14/1)

Loch Patrick was never far away but lacked that vital turn of foot in the last two furlongs. He is not easy to place as he is high in the handicap but not up to winning in Listed company. (14/1: 10/1-16/1)

Tomba had no easy task under a 12lb penalty but did stay on in the latter stages to be nearest at the line. Two of his three wins to date have come with some cut and a few drops of rain would clearly be in his favour. (7/1)

Montendre (10/1: 7/1-11/1)

Watch Me (IRE) (11/4: op 6/4)

520 TEAL H'CAP (0-85) (4-Y.O+) (Class D)

3-10 (3-14) **6f** £3,550.00 (£1,075.00: £525.00: £250.00) Stalls: High GOING minus 0.23 sec per fur (GF)

				SP	RR	SF
	Eastern Prophets (79) (GLewis) **4-9-9** AClark(17) (racd far side: mde all: clr over 2f out: all out)	—	**1**	20/1	88	61
443[3]	**Sea-Deer (81)** (CADwyer) **8-9-11** RCochrane(8) (rdn & hdwy over 1f out: r.o wl ins fnl f)	½	**2**	5/1[1]	89	62
	Denbrae (IRE) (69) (DJGMurraySmith) **5-8-13** TQuinn(12) (hdwy 2f out: hrd rdn over 1f out: r.o ins fnl f)	hd	**3**	12/1	76	49
*343**	**Cim Bom Bom (IRE) (75)** (MBell) **5-9-0v**(5) GFaulkner(4) (a.p: rdn over 2f out: unable qckn)	1¼	**4**	7/1[3]	79	52
	Pointer (58) (MrsPNDutfield) **5-8-2** CRutter(18) (racd far side: a.p: rdn over 2f out: r.o one pce)	hd	**5**	16/1	62	35
	Erupt (66) (GBBalding) **4-8-10** MHills(10) (rdn over 2f out: hdwy over 1f out: r.o)	nk	**6**	33/1	69	42
	Time For Tea (IRE) (55) (CACyzer) **4-7-13** DeclanO'Shea(9) (prom over 3f)	s.h	**7**	33/1	58	31
	Delta Soleil (USA) (84) (PWHarris) **5-10-0** GDuffield(5) (bit bkwd: nvr nrr)	nk	**8**	12/1	86	59
	Bayin (USA) (75) (MDIUsher) **8-9-5** RStreet(15) (b: racd far side: hdwy over 1f out: nvr nrr)	1¼	**9**	14/1	74	47
443[14]	**Sir Joey (USA) (84)** (PGMurphy) **8-10-0** SSanders(16) (racd far side: prom 4f)	hd	**10**	14/1	83	56
443[4]	**So Intrepid (IRE) (75)** (JMBradley) **7-9-5** PatEddery(11) (lw: nvr nrr)	1¼	**11**	11/2[2]	70	43
325[3]	**Step On Degas (60)** (MJFetherston-Godley) **4-7-11**(7) RFfrench(3) (prom over 3f)	¾	**12**	20/1	53	26
	Newlands Corner (60) (JAkehurst) **4-8-4b** MRoberts(14) (racd far side: bhd fnl 3f)	¾	**13**	9/1	51	24
	Efra (65) (RHannon) **8-8-9** DaneO'Neill(1) (bkwd: prom over 3f)	2½	**14**	14/1	50	23
443[19]	**Lennox Lewis (72)** (APJarvis) **5-9-2** JTate(13) (racd far side: bhd fnl 4f)	3	**15**	16/1	49	22
	Friendly Brave (USA) (79) (MissGayKelleway) **7-9-9** DHolland(7) (b.hind: prom over 3f)	1½	**16**	20/1	52	25
	Longwick Lad (77) (WRMuir) **4-9-7** JReid(6) (prom 4f)	½	**17**	14/1	48	21

Form	Horse	Dist	Pos	SP	RR	SF
	General Sir Peter (IRE) (72) (NACallaghan) **5-8-13**(3) DO'Donohoe(2) (s.s: a bhd)	hd	**18**	33/1	43	16

(SP 131.5%) **18 Rn**

1m 13.17 (1.97) CSF £105.38 CT £1,214.26 TOTE £21.40: £4.90 £1.70 £3.80 £2.30 (£83.80) Trio £1,121.80 OWNER Mrs J. M. Purches (EPSOM) BRED Miss K. Zavon

Eastern Prophets, who has changed stables following a very poor season last year, has subsequently tumbled in the handicap. One of six who elected to race on the favoured far rails, he made all the running and had a clear advantage from halfway. That certainly stood him in good stead for with the rest of the pack closing on him in the final furlong, he found the line only just saving him. (20/1)

443 Sea-Deer once again did not really have the luck of the draw and ran a similar to that at Doncaster, running on really strongly in the last furlong and a half if unable to get there in time. He deserves a change of luck. (5/1)

Denbrae (IRE) picked up ground a quarter of a mile from home but, despite running on under pressure, was never going to get there in time. An exposed individual, he has won just once in the last two years. (12/1)

343* Cim Bom Bom (IRE) has been in tremendous form on the All-Weather this winter, winning three of his four races and ending up with a rating of 95. However, for this return to grass he was racing off a mere 75. Leading the stands' side group, he was unable to peg back the winner racing on the opposite side of the track and was overhauled inside the final furlong. (7/1)

Pointer, who chased the winner on the far side, stayed on without looking likely to peg back his rival in time. (16/1)

Efra (14/1: 10/1-16/1)

521 CORAL ROSEBERY H'CAP (0-95) (4-Y.O+) (Class C)

3-40 (3-44) **1m 2f (Jubilee)** £13,066.00 (£4,894.00: £2,397.00: £1,035.00: £467.50: £240.50) Stalls: High GOING minus 0.23 sec per fur (GF)

Form	Horse	Dist	Pos	SP	RR	SF
	Romios (IRE) (86) (PFICole) **5-9-7** TQuinn(10) (hdwy over 2f out: rdn over 1f out: led nr fin)	—	**1**	14/1	97	80
*405**	**Secret Aly (CAN) (82)** (CEBrittain) **7-9-3** BDoyle(3) (lw: hld up: led over 1f out: hrd rdn: hdd nr fin)	nk	**2**	12/1	93	76
	Dreams End (75) (PBowen) **9-8-10** MHills(6) (hdwy over 2f out: r.o ins fnl f)	1¼	**3**	8/1	84	67
450[11]	**Hazard a Guess (IRE) (83)** (DNicholls) **7-9-4** AlexGreaves(11) (hrd rdn & hdwy over 1f out: r.o)	½	**4**	7/1[3]	91	74
	Hardy Dancer (74) (GLMoore) **5-8-9** SWhitworth(8) (a.p: led over 2f out tl over 1f out: one pce)	½	**5**	5/1[1]	81	64
	Silver Groom (IRE) (78) (RAkehurst) **7-8-13** SSanders(7) (rdn & hdwy over 2f out: one pce)	1½	**6**	9/1	83	66
	Lookingforarainbow (IRE) (69) (BobJones) **9-8-4** AMcGlone(4) (hld up: rdn over 2f out: wknd fnl f)	1¾	**7**	25/1	71	54
	Remaadi Sun (80) (MDIUsher) **5-9-1** RStreet(9) (lw: hdwy over 4f out: wknd over 1f out)	1½	**8**	20/1	79	62
	Royal Seaton (84) (MrsPNDutfield) **8-9-5** AProcter(15) (bit bkwd: nvr nrr)	2½	**9**	33/1	79	62
405[5]	**Renown (69)** (LordHuntingdon) **5-7-13**(5) AimeeCook(13) (nvr nrr)	hd	**10**	14/1	64	47
444[16]	**Royal Result (USA) (80)** (TDBarron) **4-9-1** JReid(14) (swtg: mid div whn nt clr run over 2f out)	3	**11**	12/1	70	53
	Bowled Over (71) (CACyzer) **4-8-6** MRoberts(16) (hld up: rdn over 3f out: nt clr run on ins over 2f out: eased whn btn fnl 2f)	1¼	**12**	20/1	59	42
	Zermatt (IRE) (70) (MDIUsher) **7-8-5** DaneO'Neill(12) (hdwy over 2f out: wknd over 1f out)	1¼	**13**	25/1	56	39
	Hoh Express (93) (IABalding) **5-10-0** PatEddery(17) (mid div whn nt clr run on ins over 2f out: sn wknd)	1½	**14**	12/1	77	60
444[19]	**Caudillo (IRE) (75)** (MrsPNDutfield) **4-8-10** CRutter(2) (a bhd)	1¼	**15**	66/1	57	40
	Chairmans Choice (63) (APJarvis) **7-7-12** NVarley(19) (chsd ldr: led over 3f out tl over 2f out: sn wknd)	12	**16**	33/1	26	9
	Docklands Limo (82) (BJMcMath) **4-9-3** RCochrane(1) (prom over 6f)	nk	**17**	33/1	44	27
398[3]	**Thai Morning (74)** (PWHarris) **4-8-9** GDuffield(20) (prom over 7f)	1	**18**	13/2[2]	35	18
	Serendipity (FR) (82) (BRMillman) **4-9-3** FNorton(5) (led over 6f: wknd over 2f out)	1¾	**19**	20/1	40	23
	Sofyaan (USA) (84) (LadyHerries) **4-9-5** AClark(18) (s.s: a bhd)	14	**20**	20/1	20	3

(SP 137.1%) **20 Rn**

2m 4.32 (0.82) CSF £151.86 CT £1,348.97 TOTE £18.00: £3.90 £3.10 £2.50 £2.40 (£115.70) Trio £503.40 OWNER Mr C. Shiacolas (WHATCOMBE) BRED Gay O'Callaghan in Ireland

Romios (IRE), who failed to win last year, was given a daring ride by Quinn. Still towards the back of the field half a mile from home, he managed to weave his way through the pack early in the straight and, responding to pressure, got up near the line. (14/1)

405* Secret Aly (CAN) made his bid for glory below the distance but, despite doing little wrong, was worried out of it in the shadow of the post. This was fine effort but he is not very consistent. (12/1)

Dreams End, winner of two races over hurdles this winter including the Grade Two Kingwell Hurdle at Wincanton, may be nine years old but he can still run well on the Flat as he demonstrated here, staying on really well to take third prize. (8/1)

450 Hazard a Guess (IRE), who found a mile too sharp last time out, won this race last year off a mark of 76 but had 7lb more to carry this time. Responding to pressure, he stayed on well in the final quarter-mile, but was never going to get there in time. This is his trip. (7/1: 6/1-15/1)

Hardy Dancer, who ran badly in the second half of last season, fell in the handicap and consequently was racing off a 12lb lower mark than when third in this race last year. Unfortunately, his jockey may well have made his move too early, for after striking the front early in the straight, he was collared below the distance and tapped for toe. He seems best at this time of the year. (5/1)

Silver Groom (IRE), fit from hurdling this winter where he managed to win one race, lacks acceleration on the Flat and has now won just three times from forty-one starts. (9/1)

522 MAGNOLIA STKS (Listed) (4-Y.O+) (Class A)

4-15 (4-16) **1m 2f (Jubilee)** £11,210.50 (£3,394.00: £1,657.00: £788.50) Stalls: High GOING minus 0.23 sec per fur (GF)

Form	Horse	Dist	Pos	SP	RR	SF
	Dr Massini (IRE) (MRStoute) **4-8-11** JReid(5) (lw: stdy hdwy 2f out: led 1f out: pushed out)	—	**1**	11/10[1]	116+	49
	Germano (GWragg) **4-8-11** MHills(2) (chsd ldr: led over 1f out: sn hdd: unable qckn)	2½	**2**	16/1	112	45
	Proper Blue (USA) (103) (TGMills) **4-9-0** SSanders(4) (bit bkwd: s.s: rdn over 2f out: hdwy on ins over 1f out: one pce)	2	**3**	100/30[2]	112	45
	Captain Horatius (IRE) (110) (JLDunlop) **8-9-0** TQuinn(3) (hld up: rdn over 2f out: one pce)	hd	**4**	9/2[3]	112	45
439a[7]	**Prince of My Heart (103)** (BWHills) **4-8-11** PatEddery(1) (lw: led over 8f)	1	**5**	11/2	107	40

(SP 110.1%) **5 Rn**

2m 6.83 (3.33) CSF £16.90 TOTE £2.00: £1.40 £3.20 (£16.30) OWNER Mr M Tabor & Mrs John Magnier (NEWMARKET) BRED Mount Coote Partnership

Dr Massini (IRE) is very highly regarded and was ante-post favourite for last year's Derby after two impressive wins, but he had to be withdrawn a few days before because of a leg problem, and flopped in the Irish Derby on his only subsequent outing. Looking in fine form for his return, he gave clear indication that he is going to be a serious force to be reckoned with this season, following a very impressive display here, cruising into the lead a furlong out and needing only to be nudged along to quickly assert. He should not take long to win his first Group race, and the Group Three Gordon Richards Stakes at Sandown at the end of April looks ideal for him. (11/10)

Germano chased the leader until moving into a narrow advantage below the distance. However, he did not remain there for long as the winner soon swept by and put him in his place. (16/1)

Proper Blue (USA), who showed useful form last Autumn, looked big and well for this return. Picking up ground along the inside rail below the distance, he was then tapped for toe. He will come on for this. (100/30)
Captain Horatius (IRE) is a standing fixture in this race, having won it in 1993, finished second in 1994, won it in 1995 and finished third last year. Unfortunately the ground was too fast for him and, against rivals half his age, he never looked like quickening up in the straight. (9/2)
439a Prince of My Heart did a sound job of pacemaking but, once collared below the distance, was soon done with. (11/2)

523 FIFIELD MAIDEN STKS (3-Y.O) (Class D)

4-45 (4-45) **1m 3f 30y** £3,338.75 (£1,010.00: £492.50: £233.75) Stalls: High GOING minus 0.23 sec per fur (GF)

Horse	Dist	Pos	SP	RR	SF
Single Empire (IRE) (PWChapple-Hyam) **3-9-0** JReid(3) (scope: lw: hld up: n.m.r over 2f out: rdn over 1f out: led ins fnl f: all out)	—	1	3/1[2]	89	54
Prairie Falcon (IRE) (BWHills) **3-9-0** MHills(4) (hdwy over 2f out: led over 1f out tl ins fnl f: hrd rdn: r.o wl)	s.h	2	6/1	89	54
London Lights (PFICole) **3-9-0** TQuinn(2) (w'like: scope: hdwy 6f out: led 2f out tl over 1f out: unable qckn fnl f)	3½	3	7/4[1]	84	49
Pennys From Heaven (83) (HCandy) **3-9-0** CRutter(5) (chsd ldrs: led 3f out to 2f out: wknd over 1f out)	3	4	7/2[3]	80	45
Seattle Swing (JHMGosden) **3-8-9** GDuffield(6) (bit bkwd: led to 3f out: wknd over 2f out)	8	5	7/1	63	28
Mac's Delight (NMBabbage) **3-9-0** DaneO'Neill(1) (bhd fnl 4f)	9	6	33/1	55	20

(SP 113.3%) **6 Rn**

2m 22.36 (3.56) CSF £19.18 TOTE £4.10: £2.10 £2.30 (£11.40) OWNER Mr A. K. Collins (MARLBOROUGH) BRED Swettenham Stud
Single Empire (IRE), a medium-sized colt, looked in good shape beforehand but was green in both the paddock and the race itself. However, bustled along from below the distance, he managed to force his way into a narrow lead inside the final furlong, but with the runner-up fighting back really strongly, he found the line only just saving him. (3/1: 9/4-7/2)
Prairie Falcon (IRE) eased his way into the lead below the distance and looked likely to succeed. Collared inside the final furlong, he refused to give way, and would surely have got back up in another stride. Losses are only lent. (6/1: 7/2-13/2)
London Lights, a good-sized individual who cost 125,000 guineas looks rather green but, nevertheless, managed to get to the front a quarter of a mile from home. Headed below the distance, he was left for dead by the front two. Sure to have learnt a lot from this, he should soon find a suitable opportunity. (7/4: 5/4-15/8)
Pennys From Heaven went on three furlongs from home but, collared a quarter of a mile out, was done with. (7/2: 5/2-4/1)
Seattle Swing did not look fully wound up. Setting the pace, she was collared three furlongs from home, and was in trouble early in the straight. (7/1: op 4/1)
Mac's Delight, sold out of Ed Dunlop's stable for a mere 1,600gs, was out-classed in the paddock and in the race itself when things started to hot up. (33/1)

T/Jkpt: Not won; £34,143.70 to Uttoxeter 1/4/97. T/Plpt: £3,928.20 (7.39 Tckts). T/Qdpt: £25.90 (108.04 Tckts) AK

0460-NEWCASTLE (L-H) (Good to firm)

Monday March 31st

Races 1&3: hand timed
WEATHER: sunny WIND: mod against

524 NATIONAL FIRE SERVICE BENEVOLENT FUND MAIDEN STKS (3-Y.O) (Class D)

2-25 (2-27) **1m (round)** £3,420.00 (£1,035.00: £505.00: £240.00) Stalls: Low GOING minus 0.53 sec per fur (F)

	Horse	Dist	Pos	SP	RR	SF
	Minersville (USA) (JHMGosden) **3-9-0** LDettori(4) (h.d.w: trckd ldrs: outpcd over 2f out: hdwy over 1f out: r.o wl to ld nr fin)	—	1	8/11[1]	87+	20
	Tigrello (82) (GLewis) **3-9-0** NDay(5) (w ldr: led 3f out: qcknd: rdn ins fnl f: jst ct)	hd	2	10/1	87	20
	Final Trial (IRE) (GWragg) **3-9-0** KDarley(3) (hld up: effrt 3f out: styd on fnl f: nrst fin)	2	3	10/1	83	16
	Flirting Around (USA) (88) (MRStoute) **3-9-0** JFortune(9) (lw: chsd clr ldrs: kpt on fnl 2f: no imp)	hd	4	8/1[3]	83	16
	Sioux (CWThornton) **3-8-9** DeanMcKeown(6) (s.i.s: bhd tl styd on fnl 2f)	4	5	12/1	70	3
	Two On The Bridge (DenysSmith) **3-9-0** LCharnock(2) (led tl hdd 3f out: rdn & grad wknd)	nk	6	33/1	74	7
	Zibak (USA) (DMorley) **3-9-0** GCarter(7) (w'like: scope: hld up: effrt over 3f out: n.d)	3	7	9/2[2]	68	1
	Monarch's Pursuit (TDEasterby) **3-9-0** MBirch(8) (bit bkwd: hld up & bhd: n.d)	14	8	25/1	40	—
	Cochiti (CWThornton) **3-8-9** DaleGibson(10) (lt-f: unf: s.i.s: a bhd)	1¼	9	100/1	33	—
425[10]	**Bout (60)** (RMMcKellar) **3-8-9** TWilliams(1) (a bhd)	1½	10	66/1	30	—

(SP 122.3%) **10 Rn**

1m 42.6 (3.60) CSF £9.12 TOTE £1.70: £1.40 £1.50 £2.80 (£4.60) Trio £21.40 OWNER Sheikh Mohammed (NEWMARKET) BRED Loblolly Stable
Minersville (USA) has made up into a particularly nice sort and, given plenty to do here, quickened up in useful style to get there. He is obviously going to improve no end, especially over further. (8/11)
Tigrello tried to pinch this by kicking clear halfway up the straight and it looked to have worked until the final couple of strides. He is very well indeed and should find a race before long. (10/1)
Final Trial (IRE) is still learning what the game is all about and, judging by the way finished, it will not be long before he does a deal better. He will be suited by further. (10/1)
Flirting Around (USA) was never far away and kept staying on but was certainly not knocked about and the kindness will be repaid. (8/1: op 5/1)
Sioux, very green early on, picked up in pleasing style in the closing stages and looks one to keep an eye on. (12/1)
Two On The Bridge had a nice pipe-opener and should improve as a result. (33/1)
Zibak (USA) is a useful-looking sort but his action left something to be desired, and he ran as though this was needed. (9/2)

70+ 67+ 81 50

525 E.B.F. CAP HEATON MAIDEN STKS (2-Y.O F) (Class D)

2-55 (2-56) **5f** £3,241.25 (£980.00: £477.50: £226.25) Stalls: High GOING minus 0.07 sec per fur (G)

	Horse	Dist	Pos	SP	RR	SF
432[3]	**Stately Princess** (MRChannon) **2-8-11** LDettori(1) (mde all: edgd lft most of wy: drvn out)	—	1	5/4[2]	71	8
	Carambo (JLEyre) **2-8-11** RLappin(3) (w'like: bit bkwd: hld up: hdwy over 1f out: r.o)	¾	2	12/1	69	6
460[2]	**Flower O'Cannie (IRE)** (MWEasterby) **2-8-11** LCharnock(4) (chsd ldrs tl outpcd 2f out: kpt on fnl f)	½	3	11/2[3]	67	4

				SP	RR	SF
	Antonia's Double (JBerry) **2-8-11** KDarley(2) (w'like: scope: sn w ldr: effrt 2f out: wknd fnl f)	1¾	**4**	11/10[1]	61	—
				(SP 115.1%)	**4 Rn**	

63.25 secs (4.85) CSF £12.48 TOTE £2.30 (£7.10) OWNER Mr Stephen Crown (UPPER LAMBOURN) BRED S. Crown

432 Stately Princess gave her rider problems by continually going to her left but she still showed fine battling qualities to hold on. (5/4: op evens)

Carambo, needing this, ran a cracker and will not be long in going one better. She looks quite a useful sort. (12/1: 8/1-14/1)

460 Flower O'Cannie (IRE) ran as though another furlong would not go amiss. (11/2: op 3/1)

Antonia's Double, a fair sort, raced too freely for her own good and there is obviously better to come once she realises what is required. (11/10: op 7/4)

526 ANGERTON APPRENTICE (S) H'CAP (0-60) (3-Y.O+) (Class G)

3-30 (3-31) **1m 3y (straight)** £2,116.00 (£601.00: £298.00) Stalls: High GOING minus 0.07 sec per fur (G)

				SP	RR	SF
490[3]	**Gadge (50)** (ABailey) **6-9-1**(5) TSiddall(17) (lw: b: made all stands' side: clr fnl 2f: pushed out)	—	**1**	7/2[1]	65	38
411[6]	**Sandmoor Denim (45)** (SRBowring) **10-8-5**(10) FBoyle(18) (hdwy stands' side 2f out: r.o wl)	3	**2**	14/1	54	27
313[5]	**Seconds Away (26)** (JSGoldie) **6-7-5**(5) JMcAuley(16) (racd stands' side: styd on fnl 2f: nrst fin)	hd	**3**	16/1	35	8
340[4]	**Sheraz (IRE) (50)** (NTinkler) **5-9-3b**(3) RStudholme(15) (prom stands' side early: lost tch ½-wy: r.o fnl 2f)	3	**4**	10/1	53	26
467[11]	**Miletrian City (54)** (JBerry) **4-9-0b**(10) PBradley(12) (in tch stands' side: hdwy over 3f out: one pce fnl 2f)	1½	**5**	14/1	54	27
407[7]	**Return To Brighton (40)** (JMBradley) **5-8-10** VictoriaAppleby(19) (prom stands' side: one pce fnl 2f)	2	**6**	10/1	36	9
333[5]	**Kid Ory (50)** (DWChapman) **6-8-13**(7) CarolynBales(4) (led far side: no imp fnl 2f)	2	**7**	10/1	42	15
86[15]	**Intrepid Fort (33)** (BWMurray) **8-7-10b**(7)ow7 PMundy(6) (in tch far side: no imp fnl 2f)	hd	**8**	33/1	25	—
411[3]	**Live Project (IRE) (58)** (MJohnston) **5-9-6**(8) NPollard(7) (lw: chsd ldrs far side: no imp fnl 3f)	½	**9**	5/1[2]	49	22
15[8]	**Napoleon's Return (45)** (JLEyre) **4-8-10b**(5) JennyBenson(11) (outpcd fr ½-wy)	3½	**10**	12/1	29	2
	Dispol Diamond (56) (GROldroyd) **4-9-2**(10) RFarmer(13) (chsd ldrs stands' side over 5f)	¾	**11**	14/1	38	11
	Bedazzle (36) (MBrittain) **6-7-10**(10) DMernagh(2) (b.off hind: cl up far side 6f)	hd	**12**	14/1	18	—
	Ohnonotagain (31) (LRLloyd-James) **5-7-8**(7)ow5 DYoung(9) (racd centre: spd 5f)	½	**13**	20/1	12	—
496[5]	**Tajar (USA) (46)** (MDods) **5-8-11**(5) PFredericks(10) (lw: hdwy far side ½-wy: sn hrd rdn: wknd fnl 2f)	1	**14**	25/1	25	—
	Chalky Dancer (34) (HJCollingridge) **5-8-1**(3) CLowther(14) (cl up stands' side 5f)	¾	**15**	9/1	12	—
428[6]	**Efipetite (35)** (NBycroft) **4-8-0**(5)ow6 ClaireWest(1) (sn outpcd & bhd far side)	½	**16**	14/1	12	—
326[10]	**Silent System (IRE) (36)** (DWChapman) **4-7-13**(7)ow10 DHayden(20) (hung lft ½-wy & sn bhd)	¾	**17**	25/1	11	—
428[3]	**Gold Lining (IRE) (30)** (EJAlston) **4-7-9**(5) JFowle(3) (spd far side 5f)	1½	**18**	11/2[3]	2	—
428[8]	**Jilly Beveled (39)** (RonaldThompson) **5-8-9** DDenby(5) (racd far side: bhd fr ½-wy)	10	**19**	12/1	—	—
	Bridlington Bay (35) (BEllison) **4-7-12**(7) RWinston(8) (racd centre: bhd fr ½-wy)	¾	**20**	33/1	—	—
				(SP 164.5%)	**20 Rn**	

1m 44.5 (5.90) CSF £63.92 CT £538.98 TOTE £5.10: £1.80 £3.90 £7.10 £2.30 (£55.00) Trio £322.00 OWNER Mr J. B. Wilcox (TARPORLEY) BRED Snowdrop Stud Co Ltd

LONG HANDICAP Seconds Away 7-9 Intrepid Fort 7-8 Silent System (IRE) 7-9

Bt in 4,000 gns

OFFICIAL EXPLANATION **Gold Lining (IRE): the filly did not act on the turf and will revert to the All-Weather.**

490 Gadge is in top form just now and, after leading the stands'-side group, he turned it into a procession in the last two furlongs. (7/2)

359 Sandmoor Denim has ability and runs when in the mood, and was fairly co-operative here, although making no further impression on the winner in the closing stages. (14/1)

313 Seconds Away has yet to win a race after thirty-four attempts but yet again he showed he has ability. (16/1)

340 Sheraz (IRE) seemed to find this trip too sharp and finished well, albeit far too late. (10/1)

Miletrian City wins when things go his way and that was never the case here. (14/1)

Return To Brighton has lost her dash of late but she did give some signs of hope here. (10/1)

333 Kid Ory won the race on the far side to show he is not a lost cause. (10/1)

527 PATTERSON FORD 'MAGNIFICENT SEVEN' H'CAP (0-80) (3-Y.O+) (Class D)

4-00 (4-02) **5f** £3,452.50 (£1,045.00: £510.00: £242.50) Stalls: High GOING minus 0.07 sec per fur (G)

				SP	RR	SF
464[3]	**Surprise Mission (71)** (MrsJRRamsden) **5-9-13** JFortune(6) (hld up: hmpd after s & ½-wy: hdwy over 1f out: r.o wl to ld cl home)	—	**1**	15/8[1]	82+	39
397[6]	**Broadstairs Beauty (IRE) (70)** (DShaw) **7-9-9b**(3) CTeague(9) (b: b.hind: led: hung lft after s: ct cl home)	nk	**2**	16/1	80	37
	Maiteamia (72) (SRBowring) **4-10-0b** LDettori(8) (w ldr: disp ld over 1f out: wknd wl ins fnl f)	¾	**3**	9/1	80	37
	Camionneur (IRE) (50) (TDEasterby) **4-8-6** MBirch(4) (hld up & bhd: hmpd ½-wy: nt clr run over 1f out: r.o towards fin)	2	**4**	20/1	51	8
464[4]	**Captain Carat (61)** (DNicholls) **6-9-3** DaleGibson(10) (lw: trckd ldrs: effrt over 1f out: r.o one pce)	s.h	**5**	7/1	62	19
464*	**Amron (64)** (JBerry) **10-9-6** 7x NCarlisle(2) (outpcd ½-wy: n.m.r over 1f out: styd on fnl f)	2½	**6**	5/1[2]	57	14
464[2]	**Kalar (57)** (DWChapman) **8-8-13b** ACulhane(11) (lw: chsd ldrs: n.m.r 2f out: nt qckn)	½	**7**	13/2[3]	49	6
464[14]	**Grand Chapeau (IRE) (56)** (DNicholls) **5-8-5**(7) IonaWands(7) (nvr nr to chal)	1¼	**8**	33/1	44	1
	Stolen Kiss (IRE) (71) (MWEasterby) **5-9-13b** KDarley(3) (prom: effrt ½-wy: wknd 1f out)	1¼	**9**	10/1	55	12
443[9]	**Barato (67)** (MrsJRRamsden) **6-9-9** MDeering(5) (b.hind: s.i.s: hdwy ½-wy: sn wknd)	2	**10**	14/1	44	1
332[8]	**Craigie Boy (46)** (NBycroft) **7-8-2b** TWilliams(1) (drvn along ½-wy: sn outpcd)	2½	**11**	33/1	15	—
				(SP 119.6%)	**11 Rn**	

62.21 secs (3.81) CSF £33.13 CT £203.14 TOTE £2.60: £1.50 £2.40 £2.00 (£41.10) Trio £61.30 OWNER Mr D. R. Brotherton (THIRSK) BRED D. R. Brotherton

OFFICIAL EXPLANATION **Captain Carat: the jockey reported that the gelding had spread a plate during the race.**

464 Surprise Mission, hampered twice before halfway, put up an amazing performance to win this. (15/8)

397 Broadstairs Beauty (IRE), who stays further, didn't quite go fast enough soon enough and was just touched off, but this grand sort is obviously in tremendous form. (16/1)

Maiteamia ran a super race after a lengthy lay-off and looks one to keep in mind. (9/1)

Camionneur (IRE) is a funny customer who has plenty of ability and, after getting messed about no end here, he showed that if things go his way there are races to be won. (20/1)

464 Captain Carat travelled well but lost a shoe during the race and may well have been struck into. He is obviously in good heart. (7/1)

464* Amron never had things going his way this time and, short of room, he failed to get into it. (5/1)

528 JAMMY DODGER MAIDEN STKS (3-Y.O+) (Class D)

4-35 (4-35) **1m 4f 93y** £3,420.00 (£1,035.00: £505.00: £240.00) Stalls: Low GOING minus 0.53 sec per fur (F)

	Horse	Dist	Pos	SP	RR	SF
	Perfect Paradigm (IRE) (84) (JHMGosden) **3-8-7** LDettori(4) (lw: trckd ldrs: led ent st: r.o wl)	—	1	5/2[2]	88+	48
	Dark Green (USA) (PFICole) **3-8-7** KDarley(8) (trckd ldrs: smooth hdwy to disp ld ent st: r.o: nt pce of wnr fnl 2f)	1¼	2	11/10[1]	86	46
	Lawahik (DMorley) **3-8-7** GCarter(7) (w'like: hld up: hdwy appr st: effrt & ch over 2f out: r.o one pce)	1¾	3	5/2[2]	84	44
	Duraid (IRE) (DenysSmith) **5-9-13** ACulhane(5) (hld up: stdy hdwy appr st: nt qckn fnl 2f)	10	4	14/1[3]	69	51
355[7]	**Kissandy** (MrsVAAconley) **3-8-2** MDeering(6) (a bhd: t.o)	dist	5	150/1	—	—
	Arisaig (IRE) (PCalver) **3-8-7** MBirch(2) (a bhd: t.o)	1	6	100/1	—	—
	Most Respectful (DenysSmith) **4-9-13** LCharnock(3) (led tl hdd & wknd qckly ent st: t.o)	24	7	100/1	—	—
	Bright Desert (RMMcKellar) **4-9-13** TWilliams(1) (bit bkwd: b.hind: jnd ldr 7f out tl wknd qckly 4f out: p.u 3f out)		P	100/1	—	—
				(SP 115.1%)	**8 Rn**	

2m 37.8 (0.30) CSF £5.21 TOTE £3.00: £1.40 £1.10 £1.10 (£1.60) OWNER Sheikh Mohammed (NEWMARKET) BRED Airlie Stud

WEIGHT FOR AGE 3yo-22lb, 4yo-2lb

OFFICIAL EXPLANATION **Bright Desert: was distressed.**

Perfect Paradigm (IRE) looked superb and, appreciating this trip, won most convincingly. (5/2: 7/4-11/4)

Dark Green (USA) looked ultra-fit and kept tabs on the winner but lacked a change of gear at the business end. (11/10: 8/11-early/1)

Lawahik is a decent sort who ran well and will obviously benefit from the experience. (5/2)

Duraid (IRE), a very useful bumper winner, showed here he is going to make his mark at this game. (14/1: op 8/1)

529 NICE PRODUCTIONS H'CAP (0-85) (3-Y.O+) (Class D)

5-05 (5-08) **7f** £4,279.50 (£1,296.00: £633.00: £301.50) Stalls: High GOING minus 0.07 sec per fur (G)

	Horse	Dist	Pos	SP	RR	SF
468[6]	**Three Arch Bridge (64)** (MJohnston) **5-8-7b** DeanMcKeown(4) (bhd far side: rdn to ld ins fnl f: r.o wl)	—	1	14/1	72	54
	Impulsive Air (IRE) (65) (EWeymes) **5-8-8** LDettori(9) (racd stands' side: hdwy over 2f out: led over 1f out tl ins fnl f: r.o)	¾	2	7/1	71	53
468*	**Foist (53)** (MWEasterby) **5-7-10** 6x LCharnock(14) (hld up stands' side: effrt over 2f out: r.o towards fin)	s.h	3	11/4[1]	59	41
424[6]	**Be Warned (60)** (MDods) **6-8-3b** GCarter(18) (racd stands' side: hdwy & wnt lft 2f out: ev ch over 1f out: kpt on)	2	4	20/1	62	44
	Don't Care (IRE) (78) (MissLAPerratt) **6-9-0**(7) AEddery(7) (racd far side: hdwy over 2f out: hung rt 1f out: kpt on)	¾	5	33/1	78	60
	Sagebrush Roller (60) (JWWatts) **9-8-3** NCarlisle(15) (racd stands' side: bhd tl r.o appr fnl f)	d.h	5	14/1	60	42
444[7]	**Smarter Charter (75)** (MrsLStubbs) **4-9-4** JFortune(11) (lw: racd stands' side: nvr nr to chal)	nk	7	10/1	74	56
443[10]	**Jo Mell (83)** (TDEasterby) **4-9-12** MBirch(13) (lw: racd stands' side: effrt & hung lft over 2f out: n.d)	1¾	8	10/1	78	60
	Somerton Boy (IRE) (68) (PCalver) **7-8-8**(3) CTeague(8) (racd stands' side: effrt & wnt lft over 2f out: n.d)	½	9	16/1	62	44
468[18]	**Keston Pond (IRE) (74)** (MrsVAAconley) **7-9-3** MDeering(5) (racd far side: n.d)	nk	10	16/1	67	49
376[2]	**Knotty Hill (80)** (RCraggs) **5-9-9** VHalliday(3) (led far side tl hdd 2f out: btn whn hmpd ins fnl f)	¾	11	14/1	72	54
	Magic Mill (IRE) (85) (JLEyre) **4-10-0** TWilliams(1) (chsd ldr far side: led 2f out: hung rt & hdd ins fnl f: eased whn btn)	nk	12	5/1[2]	76	58
	Birchwood Sun (55) (MDods) **7-7-12** DaleGibson(17) (chsd ldrs stands' side 5f)	2	13	33/1	41	23
	Bold Brief (68) (DenysSmith) **3-7-3**(7) IonaWands(16) (led stands' side 3f: wknd 3f out)	1	14	33/1	52	19
398[13]	**Persian Fayre (85)** (JBerry) **5-10-0** KDarley(12) (cl up stands' side: led after 3f out tl over 1f out: wknd)	8	15	6/1[3]	51	33
	Mercury (IRE) (65) (JAGlover) **4-8-8** NDay(6) (racd far side: bhd fnl 3f)	1½	16	20/1	27	9
	Willie Miles (65) (DWChapman) **4-8-8** ACulhane(2) (racd far side: chsd ldrs 5f)	½	17	33/1	26	8
	Ziggy's Dancer (USA) (83) (EJAlston) **6-9-12** RLappin(10) (stumbled s: racd stands' side: cl up over 5f)	6	18	20/1	31	13
				(SP 146.1%)	**18 Rn**	

1m 27.18 (2.68) CSF £108.88 CT £342.91 TOTE £15.70: £3.60 £2.00 £1.60 £5.40 (£55.70) Trio £103.30 OWNER Mr R. N. Pennell (MIDDLEHAM) BRED R. Taylor

LONG HANDICAP Bold Brief 7-9 Foist 7-3

WEIGHT FOR AGE 3yo-15lb

468 Three Arch Bridge looked in trouble here until suddenly picking up approaching the final furlong, to show an amazing turn of foot to settle it. (14/1)

Impulsive Air (IRE) ran well and is obviously on good terms with himself at the moment. (7/1)

468* Foist was sticking on determinedly in the closing stages and should certainly not be written off yet. (11/4)

Be Warned still has a ability but looks a bit of a character. (20/1)

Don't Care (IRE) is beginning to slip down the handicap and this was a better effort. (33/1)

Sagebrush Roller knows too much about the game, but has plenty of ability and, after getting in all sorts of trouble, finished well but always too late. (14/1)

T/Plpt: £17.30 (556.38 Tckts). T/Qdpt: £8.80 (46.98 Tckts) AA

NOTTINGHAM (L-H) (Good to firm)

Monday March 31st

WEATHER: fine & sunny WIND: fresh half against

530 EASTER EGG (S) STKS (2-Y.O) (Class G)

2-20 (2-23) **5f 13y** £1,984.50 (£547.00: £259.50) Stalls: High GOING: 0.05 sec per fur (G)

	Horse	Dist	Pos	SP	RR	SF
441[2]	**Lord Smith** (WGMTurner) **2-8-6**(5) DSweeney(5) (a.p: led 2f out: pushed out)	—	1	11/10[1]	50+	22
441[5]	**Who Nose (IRE)** (BJMeehan) **2-8-11** MTebbutt(7) (a.p: pushed along ½-wy: ev ch 2f out: one pce)	2	2	8/1[3]	44	16
441[3]	**Pink Ticket** (PDEvans) **2-8-6** JFEgan(6) (led to 2f out: kpt on u.p fnl f)	s.h	3	6/1[2]	39	11
	Sandy Shore (JWharton) **2-8-6** JCarroll(8) (swtg: lt-f: unf: hdwy ½-wy: hung bdly lft fnl 2f: nt pce to chal)	s.h	4	14/1	38	10
472[10]	**Casa Rosa** (RHannon) **2-8-6** RPerham(4) (s.i.s: nvr gng pce of ldrs)	2½	5	10/1	31	3
	The Hobby Lobby (IRE) (MRChannon) **2-8-11** PaulEddery(2) (neat: dwlt: sn chsng ldrs: rdn & hung lft over 1f out: sn wknd)	nk	6	6/1[2]	35	7

				SP	RR	SF
	Wilfred Sherman (IRE) (JBerry) **2-8-6**$^{(5)}$ TEDurcan(3) (lt-f: unf: s.s: effrt & rdn 2f out: no imp)	2½	**7**	6/1^{2}	27	—
	Astrolfell (IRE) (JSMoore) **2-8-1**$^{(5)}$ PPMurphy(1) (lt-f: swvd lft s: a bhd & outpcd: t.o)	16	**8**	20/1	—	—

(SP 122.1%) **8 Rn**

63.2 secs (4.30) CSF £10.97 TOTE £2.10: £1.40 £2.20 £1.90 (£10.60) OWNER Mrs M. S. Teversham (SHERBORNE) BRED Mrs M. S. Teversham
Bt in 8,400 gns

441 Lord Smith made amends for a narrow defeat on his debut with a very comfortable success but he proved quite costly to retain, though at this stage of his career, it could be money well spent. (11/10)
441 Who Nose (IRE) moved very feelingly to post but he came back much better and he is gradually grasping what is required. (8/1)
441 Pink Ticket finished ahead of the runner-up on her racecourse debut but, after leading the way, had nothing more to give inside the final furlong. (6/1: op 7/2)
Sandy Shore, a lightly-made half-sister to three winners, would have made the frame had she kept straight in the latter stages but she did in fact finish out in the centre of the track after being drawn under the stands' rails. (14/1: op 8/1)
Casa Rosa, still to shed her winter coat, again lost ground at the start and was taken off her legs all the way. (10/1: 7/1-11/1)
The Hobby Lobby (IRE) shows plenty of knee-action and, after missing a beat at the start, did recover to press the leaders, but he was carried left approaching the final furlong and his chance quickly disappeared. (6/1: op 4/1)

531 ROBIN HOOD MEDIAN AUCTION MAIDEN STKS (3-Y.O) (Class E)

2-50 (2-52) **5f 13y** £2,862.25 (£853.00: £406.50: £183.25) Stalls: High GOING: 0.05 sec per fur (G)

				SP	RR	SF
453^{2}	**Mile High (85)** (MRChannon) **3-9-0** PaulEddery(3) (lw: made virtually all: rdn & r.o wl fnl f)	—	**1**	11/8^{2}	92	63
	Cathedral (IRE) (BJMeehan) **3-9-0** MTebbutt(7) (w wnr: ev ch 1f out: unable qckn)	2	**2**	10/11^{1}	86	57
	Bold Gayle (MrsJRRamsden) **3-8-9** JFanning(4) (lw: dwlt: rn green & outpcd tl kpt on ins fnl f)	7	**3**	16/1	59	30
	Corinchili (GGMargarson) **3-8-9** PBloomfield(6) (bit bkwd: plld hrd: chsd ldrs: rdn over 1f out: sn outpcd)	1	**4**	20/1	55	26
434^{9}	**Castle Ashby Jack (68)** (PHowling) **3-9-0b** MRimmer(2) (dwlt: sn trckng ldrs: hung lft fnl 2f: sn outpcd)	2	**5**	14/1	54	25
	Geordie Lad (60) (JABennett) **3-9-0** JCarroll(5) (legy: lt-f: outpcd: t.o fnl 2f)	13	**6**	33/1	13	—
	Astral Crown (IRE) (JBerry) **3-8-4**$^{(5)}$ TEDurcan(1) (unf: scope: b.hind: s.i.s: sn chsg ldrs: rdn & outpcd fnl 2f: t.o)	2	**7**	10/1^{3}	2	—

(SP 123.8%) **7 Rn**

60.9 secs (2.00) CSF £3.03 TOTE £2.00: £1.10 £1.40 (£1.10) OWNER Maygain Ltd (UPPER LAMBOURN) BRED G. A. Bosley

453 Mile High, a costly failure over an extra furlong at Doncaster, showed his true worth with an all the way success and, with the runner-up, could be set to go a long way. (11/8: 4/5-7/4)
Cathedral (IRE), who has been gelded since last term, looked well wound up and, though he was unable to match strides with the race-fit winner, will soon be paying his way. (10/11)
Bold Gayle had a couple of runs in her first year but she gave the impression she was seeing a racecourse for the first time and, running green after a sluggish start, was never nearer than at the finish. (16/1)
Corinchili will benefit from the run but she raced in pursuit of the leading pair until calling enough entering the final furlong. (20/1)
320 Castle Ashby Jack, flat-footed as the stalls opened, was always finding the tempo too strong and he was never a serious contender. (14/1: 8/1-16/1)
Astral Crown (IRE) (10/1: op 4/1)

532 'FAMILY DAY OUT' H'CAP (0-70) (3-Y.O) (Class E)

3-20 (3-23) **6f 15y** £3,174.25 (£949.00: £454.50: £207.25) Stalls: High GOING: 0.05 sec per fur (G)

				SP	RR	SF
*204**	**Treasure Touch (IRE) (63)** (DNicholls) **3-9-0** JCarroll(8) (mde all: qcknd clr over 1f out: comf)	—	**1**	7/1^{3}	77+	40
466^{5}	**Master Foley (57)** (NPLittmoden) **3-8-8** TGMcLaughlin(9) (swtg: a.p: rdn wl over 1f out: no ch w wnr)	3½	**2**	14/1	62	25
	Mike's Double (IRE) (52) (GLewis) **3-8-3b** PaulEddery(11) (chsd ldrs: rdn & wandered 2f out: kpt on)	¾	**3**	6/1^{2}	55	18
	Distinctive Dream (IRE) (47) (KTIvory) **3-7-12b^{1}** GBardwell(5) (dwlt: hdwy 3f out: rdn & r.o wl ins fnl f)	hd	**4**	25/1	50	13
	Jupiter (IRE) (70) (GCBravery) **3-9-7** MRimmer(12) (bit bkwd: hld up: hdwy 2f out: kpt on wl fnl f)	1	**5**	6/1^{2}	70	33
*372**	**C-Harry (IRE) (70)** (RHollinshead) **3-9-7** MWigham(2) (trckd ldrs far side: rdn wl over 1f out: one pce)	1¼	**6**	8/1	67	30
473^{8}	**Penlop (70)** (BJMeehan) **3-9-7** MTebbutt(15) (bhd: effrt over 2f out: sn hrd rdn: nt rch ldrs)	¾	**7**	7/2^{1}	65	28
	Chingachgook (62) (PWHarris) **3-8-13** MFenton(4) (bit bkwd: chsd ldrs: hrd drvn over 1f out: one pce)	s.h	**8**	12/1	57	20
420^{2}	**Komasta (65)** (CaptJWilson) **3-8-9v^{1}**$^{(7)}$ AngelaHartley(10) (hdwy 4f out: rdn & wknd appr fnl f)	nk	**9**	11/1	59	22
	Rockaroundtheclock (62) (PDEvans) **3-8-13v^{1}** JFEgan(3) (bkwd: chsd ldrs far side 4f)	1½	**10**	25/1	52	15
	Docklands Carriage (IRE) (65) (NTinkler) **3-9-2** KimTinkler(16) (nvr nr to chal)	1¼	**11**	20/1	51	14
	Biba (IRE) (54) (RBoss) **3-8-0**$^{(5)ow2}$ PPMurphy(14) (swtg: prom 4f)	nk	**12**	16/1	40	1
412^{9}	**Glimmering Hope (IRE) (48)** (DShaw) **3-7-6**$^{(7)ow3}$ AMcCarthy(13) (swtg; a in rr)	½	**13**	25/1	32	—
466^{2}	**Soda (60)** (TDBarron) **3-8-11b** WRyan(18) (swtg: a bhd)	nk	**14**	6/1^{2}	44	7
399^{3}	**Qualitair Silver (49)** (JFBottomley) **3-8-0** JLowe(7) (nvr nr ldrs)	1½	**15**	20/1	29	—
204^{7}	**Kustom Kit Xpres (62)** (SRBowring) **3-8-13** SWebster(17) (prom stands' side to ½-wy)	3½	**16**	25/1	32	—
	Strat's Quest (65) (DWPArbuthnot) **3-9-2** RPerham(1) (nt grwn: prom far side over 3f)	2	**17**	12/1	30	—
	Khairun Nisaa (60) (MJPolglase) **3-8-11** JWeaver(6) (still unf: swtg: outpcd: a bhd)	1½	**18**	10/1	21	—

(SP 159.0%) **18 Rn**

1m 14.9 (3.40) CSF £110.19 CT £606.32 TOTE £6.70: £1.80 £3.30 £1.60 £8.00 (£109.30) Trio £231.20; £260.58 to Uttoxeter 1/4/97 OWNER Mr N. Honeyman (THIRSK) BRED St Simon Foundation
LONG HANDICAP Glimmering Hope (IRE) 6-8

204* Treasure Touch (IRE) has changed stables since his most recent success but he landed quite a touch with the minimum of fuss and is capable of being stepped up in class. (7/1)
466 Master Foley has done the majority of his racing on the All-Weather but he handled this much faster ground well and, without the presence of the winner, would have opened his account on the Turf. (14/1)
Mike's Double (IRE), far from fluent striding to post, ran about a bit when getting down to work but he did keep running and he will be all the better for the spin. (6/1)
Distinctive Dream (IRE) turned in by far his best effort yet with the help of first-time blinkers, and once he masters the art of trapping should have little trouble making his mark. (25/1)
Jupiter (IRE) produced the goods at the first time of asking last season but he has not yet followed up that form on Turf. Running on pleasingly inside the last quarter-mile, there is certainly another race in him. (6/1)
372* C-Harry (IRE) finds this lively ground a bit of a problem and could never muster the pace to mount his challenge despite being in the right place from the break. (8/1)

Penlop was a maiden carrying top weight in a handicap, which usually means another pay day for the layers, and punters' hopes of collecting here were never on. (7/2)

533 EASTER BONNET H'CAP (0-80) (3-Y.O) (Class D)

3-50 (3-55) **1m 1f 213y** £3,773.00 (£1,127.00: £539.00: £245.00) Stalls: Low GOING minus 0.33 sec per fur (GF)

Form	Horse	Dist	Pos	SP	RR	SF
	Ikatania (77) (JLDunlop) **3-9-4** MRimmer(1) (lt-f: unf: b.hind: a.p: led over 1f out: hrd drvn: all out)	—	**1**	$6/1^{3}$	88	31
431^{5}	**Time Can Tell (65)** (CMurray) **3-8-6** JStack(5) (hld up: hdwy over 3f out: ev ch 1f out: sn rdn & no ex)	1½	**2**	$5/1^{2}$	74	17
431^{14}	**Madison Welcome (IRE) (61)** (MrsJRRamsden) **3-8-2** JFanning(11) (lw: hld up: hdwy 3f out: styd on u.p fnl f)	¾	**3**	16/1	68	11
	Agony Aunt (77) (MrsJCecil) **3-9-4** WRyan(3) (h.d.w: hld up in rr: hdwy over 2f out: sn rdn: nvr able to chal)	½	**4**	$4/1^{1}$	84	27
366^{8}	**Interdream (64)** (RHannon) **3-8-5**^{ow2} RPerham(7) (w ldr: led 4f out tl hdd & wknd over 1f out)	5	**5**	16/1	63	4
431^{8}	**Baubigny (USA) (74)** (MRChannon) **3-9-1** PaulEddery(2) (bit bkwd: prom: rdn over 2f out: sn btn)	1¾	**6**	10/1	70	13
	Sad Mad Bad (USA) (79) (MJohnston) **3-9-6** JWeaver(10) (swtg: bit bkwd: led to 4f out: rdn & wknd over 2f out)	2½	**7**	7/1	71	14
	Hurgill Dancer (68) (JWWatts) **3-8-9** JCarroll(8) (b: swtg: prom over 7f: sn lost pl & eased: t.o)	19	**8**	12/1	29	—
445^{5}	**Swiftway (69)** (KWHogg) **3-8-5**$^{(5)}$ DSweeney(6) (a in rr: hrd rdn over 3f out: sn t.o)	¾	**9**	7/1	29	—
173^{3}	**Baaheth (USA) (72)** (SCWilliams) **3-8-13** DRMcCabe(4) (a bhd: t.o fnl 4f)	1¾	**10**	$6/1^{3}$	29	—
	Kalinini (USA) (80) (LMCumani) **3-9-7** OUrbina(9) (bit bkwd: chsd ldrs 7f: sn wknd: t.o)	1½	**11**	$5/1^{2}$	35	—

(SP 135.5%) **11 Rn**

2m 8.0 (5.50) CSF £38.29 CT £447.31 TOTE £7.00: £1.80 £2.00 £5.60 (£26.30) Trio £173.70; £83.21 to Uttoxeter 1/4/97 OWNER Mr Derek Crowson (ARUNDEL) BRED Fares Stables Ltd

Ikatania showed plenty of promise without winning in his first season and this well-deserved success was not coming out of turn. (6/1)

431 Time Can Tell, a winner here in the Autumn, delivered a determined challenge entering the final furlong but the winner had got there first and was in no mood to give best. He can be kept in mind in the early part of the season. (5/1)

Madison Welcome (IRE) looks the type to benefit from easier ground but he finished much closer to the runner-up than he did earlier in the month and he could be coming into his own given a slightly stiffer test of stamina. (16/1)

Agony Aunt had worked her way onto the heels of the principals below the distance but, hard as she tried, could not summon the pace to get to terms. This was the fastest ground she had tackled yet and is more than likely not quite what she requires. (4/1)

Interdream had a run on the All-Weather at the beginning of the month and he did appear to be travelling extremely well when leading in the straight, but he tied up quickly once the winner took his measure. Paddock inspection would suggest he will improve in leaps and bounds when the warmer weather really arrives. (16/1)

Hurgill Dancer (12/1: op 8/1)

Kalinini (USA), an attractive colt not at all happy on this ground, did look as though he would strip fitter for the run and that opinion was confirmed. (5/1)

534 EASTER BUNNY H'CAP (0-70) (3-Y.O) (Class E)

4-20 (4-21) **1m 6f 15y** £2,862.25 (£853.00: £406.50: £183.25) Stalls: Low GOING minus 0.33 sec per fur (GF)

Form	Horse	Dist	Pos	SP	RR	SF
*266**	**Ramike (IRE) (68)** (MJohnston) **3-9-7** JWeaver(6) (lw: hld up: led over 3f out: sn rdn clr: hung lft wl over 1f out: drvn out)	—	**1**	$6/4^{1}$	78	36
355^{3}	**Woodland Nymph (58)** (DJGMurraySmith) **3-8-11** DRMcCabe(1) (hld up: hdwy 4f out: styd on fnl 2f: no ch w wnr)	7	**2**	6/1	60	18
425^{7}	**Maremma (49)** (DonEnricoIncisa) **3-8-2** KimTinkler(4) (hld up & bhd: hdwy 3f out: styd on u.p fnl f)	1¼	**3**	25/1	50	8
347^{5}	**Foxford Lad (44)** (TMJones) **3-7-8**$^{(3)ow1}$ DarrenMoffatt(5) (a.p: rdn to chal whn carried lft wl over 1f out: sn lost pl)	1¼	**4**	33/1	43	—
425^{4}	**Warrlin (62)** (CWFairhurst) **3-9-1** MFenton(3) (lw: lost pl 8f out: hdwy 4f out: rdn & one pce fnl 2f)	1¼	**5**	12/1	60	18
	Yangtze (IRE) (52) (BRMillman) **3-8-5** JLowe(8) (lt-f: bit bkwd: hld up: a in rr)	4	**6**	10/1	45	3
431^{13}	**Native Princess (IRE) (61)** (BWHills) **3-9-0** WRyan(2) (lw: led: clr 10f out: wknd & hdd over 3f out: t.o)	18	**7**	$3/1^{2}$	34	—
478^{4}	**Oliver (IRE) (52)** (RWArmstrong) **3-8-5**^{ow2} OUrbina(7) (bhd: hrd rdn ent st: no imp: t.o)	dist	**8**	$7/2^{3}$	—	—

(SP 125.1%) **8 Rn**

3m 6.2 (7.70) CSF £11.72 CT £159.31 TOTE £2.30: £1.40 £1.50 £7.00 (£6.90) OWNER Miss Belinda Lee (MIDDLEHAM) BRED Dene Investments N V

LONG HANDICAP Foxford Lad 7-2

OFFICIAL EXPLANATION **Oliver (IRE): was found to be distressed.**

266* Ramike (IRE) made light of top weight over a trip that suited him down to the ground and he has now found his way. (6/4)

355 Woodland Nymph is coming into her own now that she is tackling a more suitable trip and that initial success is not far away. (6/1)

Maremma, a small filly, was set quite a task on this first attempt at this extended trip but she battled on relentlessly inside the distance and this would seem to be her game. (25/1)

Foxford Lad was staying on strongly but already flat out when the winner carried him left below the distance and, forced to check, could never really recover his momentum. It could prove costly to think that he was in any way unlucky. (33/1)

Warrlin (12/1: op 8/1)

478 Oliver (IRE) (7/2: op 9/4)

535 EASTER MONDAY H'CAP (0-70) (3-Y.O) (Class E)

4-50 (4-53) **1m 54y** £3,304.25 (£989.00: £474.50: £217.25) Stalls: Low GOING minus 0.33 sec per fur (GF)

Form	Horse	Dist	Pos	SP	RR	SF
	Freedom Chance (IRE) (66) (JWHills) **3-9-0**$^{(3)}$ MHenry(2) (hld up in tch: hdwy over 2f out: rdn to ld wl ins fnl f)	—	**1**	8/1	75	38
431^{12}	**Pennywell (63)** (RFJohnsonHoughton) **3-9-0** JWeaver(5) (chsd ldrs: led over 3f out: hrd rdn over 1f out: hdd nr fin)	1	**2**	10/1	70	33
293^{5}	**First Chance (IRE) (67)** (DRCElsworth) **3-9-1**$^{(3)}$ DGriffiths(1) (hld up: hdwy 2f out: r.o wl ins fnl f)	¾	**3**	10/1	73	36
	Barresbo (59) (CWFairhurst) **3-8-10** JStack(12) (hld up & bhd: hdwy on outside 3f out: styd on wl fnl f)	2½	**4**	33/1	60	23
	Shaded (IRE) (66) (JWWatts) **3-9-3** JCarroll(16) (hld up: hdwy over 2f out: nrst fin)	3	**5**	12/1	61	24
341^{5}	**Allied Academy (70)** (SCWilliams) **3-9-7** DRMcCabe(11) (dwlt: hdwy over 2f out: swtchd lft & kpt on wl fnl f)	¾	**6**	12/1	64	27
	Carlton (IRE) (60) (GLewis) **3-8-11** PaulEddery(7) (bkwd: trckd ldrs: hrd rdn over 2f out: sn btn)	1¾	**7**	$5/1^{2}$	50	13
	Poker Princess (54) (MBell) **3-8-5** MFenton(6) (nt grwn: led 2f: wknd over 2f out)	1¼	**8**	10/1	42	5
*368**	**Swift (60)** (MJPolglase) **3-8-11** MRimmer(18) (prom: rdn 3f out: grad wknd)	3	**9**	10/1	42	5
414^{5}	**Rochea (60)** (MrsNMacauley) **3-8-11** SWebster(10) (nvr trbld ldrs)	1	**10**	25/1	40	3
	Swan Island (68) (BPalling) **3-9-0**$^{(5)}$ DSweeney(8) (bit bkwd: led after 2f tl over 3f out: rdn & wknd 2f out)	1¾	**11**	12/1	45	8

				SP	RR	SF
	King Uno (55) (MrsJRRamsden) **3-8-6** OUrbina(14) (s.i.s: a bhd)	½	**12**	12/1	31	—
	Feel A Line (70) (BJMeehan) **3-9-7** MTebbutt(3) (bit bkwd: a bhd)	1	**13**	20/1	44	7
	Hadawah (USA) (68) (JLDunlop) **3-9-5** WRyan(9) (nt grwn: chsd ldrs over 5f: sn wknd)	s.h	**14**	$7/1^3$	42	5
362^2	**Major Twist (IRE) (60)** (RHannon) **3-8-11** RPerham(15) (a bhd)	½	**15**	$7/2^1$	33	—
467*	**Abstone Queen (68)** (PDEvans) **3-9-5v** 5x JFEgan(17) (prom: rdn & outpcd 2f out: eased whn btn)	nk	**16**	11/1	40	3
	Folly Foot Fred (58) (BRMillman) **3-8-9** JLowe(13) (still unf: nvr trbld ldrs)	1	**17**	20/1	28	—
387^3	**Only Josh (IRE) (60)** (MrsJRRamsden) **3-8-11** JFanning(4) (a in rr)	1½	**18**	9/1	27	—

(SP 164.3%) **18 Rn**

1m 45.0 (3.70) CSF £100.14 CT £543.31 TOTE £20.60: £4.80 £2.40 £3.80 £7.20 (£82.50) Trio £331.50; £46.70 to Uttoxeter 1/4/97 OWNER Mr J Hawkes And Partners (LAMBOURN) BRED Mrs S. O'Riordan

OFFICIAL EXPLANATION **Major Twist: was unsuited by the firm going.**

Freedom Chance (IRE) had a comparatively light first season but he did not look well tuned up for this return to action and, in the end, did it well. He should continue to progress. (8/1)

341* Pennywell cut no ice on the Turf at Doncaster, but she had won on the All-Weather and she lost no caste in defeat here, only being forced to give best inside the last fifty yards. (10/1)

293 First Chance (IRE), fit from the All-Weather, weaved her way through in the latter stages and was still pegging back her rivals at the finish but the line was always going to arrive too soon. (10/1)

Barresbo has only ever raced at sprint distances but, ridden with restraint, she was staying on relentlessly in the closing stages and all is not lost yet. (33/1)

Shaded (IRE) only began to stay on in the latter stages and it is possible he is capable of stepping up on this. (12/1)

Allied Academy adopted more patient tactics on this return to the Turf and was only finding top gear when the race was all but over. (12/1)

Carlton (IRE), a well-made colt with room for improvement, was hard at work early in the straight and his measure had soon been taken. He should not be written off just yet . (5/1: op 10/1)

362 Major Twist (IRE), only beaten on the nod in a claimer at the start of the month, did not relish this lively ground and was always nearer last than first. (7/2)

467* Abstone Queen (11/1: 7/1-12/1)

387 Only Josh (IRE) (9/1: 6/1-10/1)

T/Plpt: £164.80 (40.93 Tckts). T/Qdpt: £136.50 (1.79 Tckts) IM

WARWICK (L-H) (Good to firm)

Monday March 31st

WEATHER: fine WIND: almost nil

A 77+ 74+ 68+ 68

536 LIONS CLUB INTERNATIONAL MEDIAN AUCTION MAIDEN STKS (2-Y.O F) (Class E) (72)

2-30 (2-33) **5f** £3,044.25 (£909.00: £434.50: £197.25) Stalls: Low GOING minus 0.53 sec per fur (F)

				SP	RR	SF
	Vax Rapide (JLSpearing) **2-8-11** SDrowne(13) (leggy: lt-f: w ldr: led over 1f out: r.o wl)	—	**1**	8/1	80	25
	Mugello (APJarvis) **2-8-11** WJO'Connor(7) (neat: led over 3f: r.o one pce)	1½	**2**	12/1	75	21
	Always Lucky (JBerry) **2-8-6**(5) PFessey(9) (lengthy: unf: chsd ldrs: rdn and hdd over 1f out: r.o ins fnl f)	nk	**3**	$5/1^2$	74	20
460^3	**Theatre of Dreams** (PDEvans) **2-8-11** KFallon(10) (a.p: ev ch 2f out: one pce)	1¾	**4**	$5/2^1$	69	15
	Going Places (KTIvory) **2-8-8**(3) MartinDwyer(5) (neat: a.p: no hdwy fnl 2f)	hd	**5**	16/1	68	14
	Island Girl (IRE) (DWPArbuthnot) **2-8-11** RPrice(11) (lt-f: a.p: ev ch 2f out: wknd ins fnl f)	1½	**6**	20/1	64	10
	Miss Scooter (APJones) **2-8-11** TSprake(6) (lt-f: prom over 3f)	2	**7**	14/1	57	4
	Supreme Angel (MPMuggeridge) **2-8-8**(3) MHenry(8) (small: unf: bkwd: s.s: nvr nrr)	½	**8**	8/1	56	3
	Swift Time (MRBosley) **2-8-11** DWright(1) (small: nvr nr ldrs)	2½	**9**	33/1	48	—
	Flirtina (PDEvans) **2-8-8**(3) PMcCabe(3) (leggy: lt-f: a bhd)	2	**10**	25/1	41	—
	Fey Rouge (IRE) (RHollinshead) **2-8-8**(3) FLynch(2) (neat: bit bkwd: bhd fnl 2f)	hd	**11**	12/1	41	—
	The Beat Rolls On (IRE) (MartynMeade) **2-8-11** NAdams(14) (small: bkwd: s.i.s: sn prom: wknd 2f out)	2½	**12**	33/1	33	—
	Grosvenor Miss (IRE) (PWChapple-Hyam) **2-8-8**(3) RHavlin(12) (lt-f: bit bkwd: prom over 2f)	2	**13**	$13/2^3$	26	—
	Gypsy Hill (DHaydnJones) **2-8-11** JQuinn(4) (leggy: s.s & swvd rt: a t.o)	15	**14**	25/1	—	—

(SP 127.1%) **14 Rn**

59.5 secs (1.50) CSF £90.28 TOTE £10.60: £2.70 £3.60 £1.70 (£71.10) Trio £45.90 OWNER Vax Ltd (ALCESTER) BRED A. Brazier

Vax Rapide, a half-sister to last season's dual juvenile winner Vax Star, was nibbled at in the ring having apparently been beating older horses at home. (8/1)

Mugello, a half-sister to Proud Image, was very green in the paddock. However, it quickly became obvious she had been taught her job once the race began, but one can't help thinking she will be better for the experience. (12/1: op 8/1)

Always Lucky, a sister to Paris House, had more substance than most of these and will not have to improve much to get off the mark. (5/1)

460 Theatre of Dreams lacks substance and connections will be keen to strike before things get more competitive later on. (5/2)

Going Places made a promising enough start to her career. (16/1)

Island Girl (IRE), a half-sister to Noosa and Bold Oriental, did not quite see out the trip on her debut. (20/1)

Supreme Angel (8/1: op 25/1)

Grosvenor Miss (IRE) (13/2: op 4/1)

537 SPRING H'CAP (0-70) (3-Y.O) (Class E)

3-00 (3-07) **1m 2f 169y** £3,122.25 (£933.00: £446.50: £203.25) Stalls: Low GOING minus 0.53 sec per fur (F)

				SP	RR	SF
	Count Tony (66) (SPCWoods) **3-9-3** DBiggs(2) (swtg: s.i.s: hld up mid div: gd hdwy over 3f out: led ins fnl f: drvn out)	—	**1**	25/1	75	24
	Tango King (67) (JLDunlop) **3-9-4** TSprake(6) (hld up & plld hrd: gd hdwy over 3f out: ev ch ins fnl f: r.o)	½	**2**	$11/2^1$	75	24
	Mystic Quest (IRE) (63) (KMcAuliffe) **3-8-7**(7) TField(10) (lw: a.p: led over 1f out tl ins fnl f)	1¾	**3**	12/1	69	18
456^3	**Skelton Sovereign (IRE) (58)** (RHollinshead) **3-8-6**(3) FLynch(7) (hld up & bhd: gd hdwy over 2f out: ev ch 1f out: one pce)	nk	**4**	7/1	63	12
	Nile Valley (IRE) (70) (PWChapple-Hyam) **3-9-4**(3) RHavlin(12) (hld up: hdwy over 1f out: r.o)	3	**5**	$13/2^3$	71	20
	Right Man (60) (GLewis) **3-8-8**(3) AWhelan(1) (no hdwy fnl 3f)	2	**6**	8/1	58	7
	Certain Magic (66) (WRMuir) **3-9-3** KFallon(5) (nvr nr to chal)	s.h	**7**	$6/1^2$	64	13
491^3	**Chief Predator (USA) (64)** (RHannon) **3-9-1** WJO'Connor(9) (w ldr: led over 4f out tl over 2f out: wknd over 1f out)	1¼	**8**	$6/1^2$	60	9

				SP	RR	SF
366^{7}	**Noble Hero (65)** (JJSheehan) **3-9-2** SDrowne(11) (lw: a.p: led over 2f out tl over 1f out: wknd fnl f)	2½	**9**	20/1	57	6
417^{*}	**Big Bang (66)** (MBlanshard) **3-9-3** JQuinn(8) (trckd ldrs: wknd 2f out)	1½	**10**	6/1^{2}	56	5
	Spondulicks (IRE) (57) (BPJBaugh) **3-8-8** RPrice(4) (plld hrd: prom 7f)	hd	**11**	16/1	47	—
	Willskip (USA) (53) (JBerry) **3-7-13**$^{(5)}$ PFessey(3) (led 6f: wknd over 2f out)	2	**12**	25/1	40	—
				(SP 121.2%)	**12 Rn**	

2m 18.8 (4.80) CSF £143.40 CT £1,604.02 TOTE £27.60: £5.90 £2.80 £4.00 (£110.60) Trio £227.00; £73.55 to Uttoxeter 1/4/97 OWNER One Dream Partnership (NEWMARKET) BRED Woodsway Stud

Count Tony, who threw his jockey in the paddock, appreciated this longer trip having not shown much in three outings last season. (25/1)
Tango King is bred to appreciate this sort of distance but met one too good in the winner. (11/2: 4/1-6/1)
Mystic Quest (IRE), who needed a visor to get off the mark at Wolverhampton last September, was 12lb lower than when running in a handicap next time. (12/1)
456 Skelton Sovereign (IRE), who has been kept busy on the All-Weather, is nothing if not consistent. (7/1)
Nile Valley (IRE) is certainly bred for this sort of trip and should not be inconvenienced by further. (13/2)
Right Man did not really prove he lasted the distance. (8/1)

538 HIGH TENSILE BOLTS H'CAP (0-80) (4-Y.O+) (Class D)

3-35 (3-35) **1m 2f 169y** £3,964.10 (£1,185.80: £568.40: £259.70) Stalls: Low GOING minus 0.53 sec per fur (F)

				SP	RR	SF
114^{3}	**Mad Militant (IRE) (52)** (AStreeter) **8-8-3** TSprake(7) (hld up: swtchd rt & gd hdwy over 1f out: led ins fnl f: r.o)	—	**1**	8/1	61	8
	Vola Via (USA) (78) (IABalding) **4-9-11**$^{(3)}$ MartinDwyer(10) (hld up: hdwy over 1f out: ev ch ins fnl f: r.o)	¾	**2**	12/1	86	32
410^{7}	**Mono Lady (IRE) (55)** (DHaydnJones) **4-8-5b** SDrowne(4) (hld up: gd hdwy over 1f out: nt clr run ins fnl f: r.o wl towards fin)	1½	**3**	10/1	61	7
92^{3}	**Master Beveled (72)** (PDEvans) **7-9-9** KFallon(13) (hld up: rdn 3f out: hdwy over 1f out: one pce fnl f)	1¼	**4**	4/1^{2}	76	23
235^{15}	**Sweet Ciseaux (IRE) (47)** (BJLlewellyn) **4-7-6**$^{(5)}$ JBramhill(1) (a.p: led 1f out tl ins fnl f)	1½	**5**	33/1	49	—
63^{*}	**Yet Again (45)** (MissGayKelleway) **5-7-5**$^{(5)}$ RMullen(5) (s.s: hdwy 8f out: rdn 3f out: one pce fnl 2f)	nk	**6**	5/2^{1}	46	—
422^{13}	**Golden Touch (USA) (57)** (DJSCosgrove) **5-8-5**$^{(3)}$ PMcCabe(8) (prom: led over 1f out: sn hdd & wknd)	1¾	**7**	16/1	56	3
430^{18}	**Fairy Knight (70)** (RHannon) **5-9-7** DBiggs(6) (hld up: rdn over 2f out: styng on whn nt clr run ins fnl f)	nk	**8**	9/1	68	15
430^{3}	**Urgent Swift (75)** (APJarvis) **4-9-11** WJO'Connor(2) (plld hrd: led over 1f: wknd 2f out)	3½	**9**	9/2^{3}	68	14
	Severn Mill (45) (JMBradley) **6-7-10** NAdams(3) (s.s: a bhd)	¾	**10**	50/1	37	—
	Whispered Melody (56) (RAkehurst) **4-8-6** JQuinn(12) (plld hrd: led 9f out tl over 1f out: sn wknd)	4	**11**	8/1	42	—
	Talk Back (IRE) (70) (GLewis) **5-9-4**$^{(3)}$ AWhelan(11) (s.s: a bhd)	2	**12**	20/1	53	—
401^{7}	**Princely Affair (46)** (JMBradley) **4-7-5**$^{(5)}$ PFessey(9) (bhd fnl 4f)	3½	**13**	33/1	24	—
				(SP 134.2%)	**13 Rn**	

2m 19.2 (5.20) CSF £99.51 CT £918.81 TOTE £7.00: £1.40 £3.10 £3.30 (£36.70) Trio £89.90 OWNER Mr K. Nicholls (UTTOXETER) BRED Cloghran Stud Farm Co in Ireland
LONG HANDICAP Severn Mill 6-13 Yet Again 7-5
WEIGHT FOR AGE 4yo-1lb

114 Mad Militant (IRE), rated a stone lower than on the sand, was 13lb lower than when last winning on turf back in May 1994. (8/1)
Vola Via (USA) was 6lb lower than when finishing a good third at Epsom on Oaks day last year. (12/1)
346 Mono Lady (IRE) was probably a shade unlucky and this was a good effort on ground plenty lively enough for her. (10/1)
92 Master Beveled, 5lb higher than his last run on the sand, could never make his presence felt. (4/1)
Sweet Ciseaux (IRE), a seven-furlong winner at Tipperary for Dermot Weld, ran much better than on his All-Weather debut in this country, but may have been stretching his stamina to the limit. (33/1)
63* Yet Again could not translate some good hurdle and sand form back to the grass on this occasion. (5/2)

539 WARWICK CARNIVAL CLAIMING STKS (3-Y.O) (Class E)

4-05 (4-06) **1m 4f 115y** £2,784.25 (£829.00: £394.50: £177.25) Stalls: Low GOING minus 0.53 sec per fur (F)

				SP	RR	SF
	Dominant Duchess (JWHills) **3-9-1** KFallon(2) (leggy: hld up: hdwy over 3f out: rdn to ld over 2f out: clr fnl f: eased nr fin)	—	**1**	5/2^{2}	67+	10
431^{6}	**As-Is (57)** (MJohnston) **3-8-9**$^{(7)}$ KSked(3) (hld up: hdwy over 1f out: r.o ins fnl f: nt trble wnr)	1¾	**2**	4/5^{1}	66	9
	Ronquista d'Or (GAHam) **3-8-12** SDrowne(1) (hld up: rdn 5f out: hdwy 3f out: one pce fnl 2f)	6	**3**	40/1	54	—
239^{4}	**Alimerjam (50)** (JWhite) **3-8-11b** DBiggs(4) (led: hdd wl over 2f out: wknd over 1f out)	3½	**4**	10/1	49	—
	Mazara (IRE) (AGFoster) **3-9-1** TSprake(5) (bit bkwd: prom tl wknd 2f out)	3½	**5**	7/1^{3}	48	—
292^{5}	**Missed May** (BPJBaugh) **3-8-2**$^{(5)}$ JBramhill(6) (plld hrd: chsd ldr: led wl over 2f out: sn hdd: wknd over 1f out)	2	**6**	16/1	38	—
				(SP 114.0%)	**6 Rn**	

2m 47.2 (9.70) CSF £4.54 TOTE £3.30: £1.70 £1.40 (£2.00) OWNER Mr C. R. Nelson (LAMBOURN) BRED L. Godfrey

Dominant Duchess, a half-sister to Artic Tracker, proved too sharp for this opposition. (5/2)
431 As-Is, an uneasy favourite, is flattered by his proximity to the winner. (4/5: 4/7-10/11)
Ronquista d'Or had been tailed off in both starts as a juvenile. (40/1)
Mazara (IRE) (7/1: op 14/1)

540 WEST MIDLANDS CONDITIONS STKS (4-Y.O+) (Class C)

4-40 (4-43) **7f** £4,810.60 (£1,779.40: £853.20: £348.00: £137.50: £53.30) Stalls: Low GOING minus 0.53 sec per fur (F)

				SP	RR	SF
450^{18}	**Russian Music (103)** (MissGayKelleway) **4-9-2b^{1}** KFallon(9) (mde all: rdn 2f out: drvn out)	—	**1**	11/4^{1}	114	70
	Carranita (IRE) (107) (BPalling) **7-9-7** TSprake(8) (a.p: chsd wnr over 2f out: rdn over 1f out: no imp)	3½	**2**	6/1^{2}	111	67
452^{3}	**King of Peru (100)** (APJarvis) **4-8-12** WJO'Connor(2) (lw: plld hrd early: hld up: rdn 2f out: r.o one pce)	3	**3**	11/4^{1}	95	51
	My Best Valentine (94) (JWhite) **7-8-12** DBiggs(1) (bit bkwd: hld up: hdwy over 3f out: one pce fnl 2f)	¾	**4**	15/2	93	49
	Marl (86) (RAkehurst) **4-8-7** JQuinn(6) (bit bkwd: no hdwy fnl 2f)	1¾	**5**	7/1^{3}	84	40
	Royal South (IRE) (PSFelgate) **4-8-9**$^{(3)}$ PMcCabe(3) (bit bkwd: s.s: a bhd)	8	**6**	33/1	71	27
	Varnishing Day (IRE) (PWChapple-Hyam) **5-8-5**$^{(7)}$ RCody-Boutcher(5) (bit bkwd: prom over 4f)	1¼	**7**	10/1	68	24
	Taoiste (RWArmstrong) **4-9-6** RPrice(7) (bit bkwd: plld hrd: chsd wnr over 4f: sn wknd)	6	**8**	8/1	63	19
				(SP 115.0%)	**8 Rn**	

1m 23.5 (0.30 under best) (-1.10) CSF £18.13 TOTE £3.90: £1.40 £2.30 £1.60 (£10.10) Trio £7.80 OWNER The Seventh Heaven Partnership (WHITCOMBE) BRED Mrs N. F. M. Sampson

Russian Music, blinkered for the first time, had disappointed under a welter burden in the Lincoln, following some consistently good efforts in some big handicaps last season. (11/4)
Carranita (IRE) gave the impression she may not have been really stretching on this fast ground when the chips were down. (6/1)
452 King of Peru, well backed over this longer trip, looked the part in the paddock, but never threatened to do the business. (11/4)
My Best Valentine should come on a little for the outing. (15/2)
Marl looked short of peak fitness. (7/1)
Varnishing Day (IRE) (10/1: op 6/1)

541 EASTER H'CAP (0-70) (3-Y.O+) (Class E)

5-10 (5-13) **5f** £3,096.25 (£925.00: £442.50: £201.25) Stalls: Low GOING minus 0.53 sec per fur (F)

				SP	RR	SF
423[5]	**Napoleon Star (IRE) (43)** (SRBowring) **6-8-2b** NAdams(4) (rdn & hdwy on ins over 2f out: r.o to ld nr fin)	—	**1**	12/1	55	38
391[5]	**Sotonian (HOL) (40)** (PSFelgate) **4-7-13** DWright(1) (led: qcknd clr over 1f out: ct nr fin)	½	**2**	16/1	50	33
494[2]	**Gi La High (60)** (MartynMeade) **4-9-5** KFallon(2) (lw: s.s: swtchd rt & hdwy over 1f out: fin wl)	1¼	**3**	5/2[1]	66	49
	Petraco (IRE) (57) (NASmith) **9-8-11**(5) JBramhill(6) (bit bkwd: sn pushed along: hdwy over 2f out: r.o one pce fnl f)	nk	**4**	14/1	62	45
95[8]	**Mister Raider (48)** (EAWheeler) **5-8-2b**(5) ADaly(3) (w ldr: one pce fnl 2f)	1½	**5**	12/1	49	32
421[7]	**Night Harmony (IRE) (53)** (MissSJWilton) **4-8-9**(3) RHavlin(8) (b: no hdwy fnl 2f)	nk	**6**	12/1	53	36
	Polly Golightly (61) (MBlanshard) **4-9-6** JQuinn(12) (bit bkwd: prom tl wknd fnl f)	3	**7**	7/1[3]	51	34
394[5]	**Sing With the Band (60)** (BAMcMahon) **6-8-12**(7) SRighton(9) (bhd fnl 2f)	½	**8**	3/1[2]	49	32
443[13]	**Mindrace (65)** (KTIvory) **4-9-7**(3) MartinDwyer(5) (prom: sn pushed along: btn whn n.m.r over 1f out)	nk	**9**	10/1	53	36
	Rockcracker (IRE) (57) (GGMargarson) **5-9-2** DBiggs(13) (bit bkwd: prom over 2f)	1½	**10**	14/1	40	23
69[9]	**Indian Wolf (37)** (BJLlewellyn) **4-7-5**(5) RMullen(11) (prom over 2f)	1½	**11**	50/1	15	—
	Secret Miss (47) (APJones) **5-8-6** TSprake(10) (s.i.s: a bhd)	1¼	**12**	16/1	21	4
	Nakami (61) (AJChamberlain) **5-9-1**(5) GMilligan(7) (bkwd: a bhd: t.o)	16	**13**	25/1	—	—

(SP 129.1%) **13 Rn**

58.2 secs (0.20) CSF £186.81 CT £489.46 TOTE £15.90: £3.00 £3.90 £1.70 (£103.30) Trio £79.80 OWNER Mr Roland Wheatley (EDWINSTOWE) BRED Eamon O'Mahony
LONG HANDICAP Indian Wolf 6-10
423 Napoleon Star (IRE), on the same mark as when winning a seller over six furlongs on the sand at Southwell in February, needed every yard of this trip. (12/1)
137 Sotonian (HOL), 6lb lower than on the sand, returned to the form which showed him twice win at Wolverhampton at the beginning of the year. (16/1)
494 Gi La High could not quite overcome a tardy start and is knocking at the door. (5/2)
Petraco (IRE) showed he still retains plenty of ability but is probably better suited to six furlongs these days. (14/1)
Mister Raider, lightly-raced on grass last year, showed plenty of speed until past halfway. (12/1: op 8/1)
Night Harmony (IRE) remains a maiden after fifteen attempts. (12/1)
Polly Golightly (7/1: op 12/1)
394 Sing With the Band (3/1: 4/1-5/2)

T/Plpt: £413.00 (18.49 Tckts). T/Qdpt: £19.00 (17.05 Tckts) KH

0423-SOUTHWELL (L-H) (Standard)
Tuesday April 1st
WEATHER: fine WIND: slt half bhd

542 APRIL FOOL APPRENTICE H'CAP (0-65) (4-Y.O+) (Class F)

2-00 (2-00) **1m 6f (Fibresand)** £2,305.00 (£655.00: £325.00) Stalls: Low GOING: 0.12 sec per fur (SLW)

				SP	RR	SF
	Sedbergh (USA) (64) (MrsMReveley) **4-9-6**(4) PFredericks(6) (w ldrs: led 3f out: jst hld on)	—	**1**	6/1	78	37
430[2]	**Raffles Rooster (63)** (AGNewcombe) **5-9-6**(6) FBoyle(4) (lw: hld up: rn wd bnd 9f out: stdy hdwy on outside over 2f out: r.o wl towards fin)	nk	**2**	3/1[1]	77	39
375[4]	**Forzair (50)** (JJO'Neill) **5-8-9**(4) CLowther(5) (chsd ldrs: pushed along 7f out: one pce fnl 3f)	8	**3**	14/1	55	17
470*	**Dancing Cavalier (57)** (RHollinshead) **4-8-11**(6) 5x DHayden(3) (hld up & bhd: hdwy on outside over 4f out: kpt on same pce fnl 2f)	1	**4**	7/2[2]	60	19
356[2]	**Undawaterscubadiva (33)** (MPBielby) **5-7-6**(4) JFowle(7) (trckd ldrs: effrt over 3f out: wknd 2f out)	4	**5**	13/2	32	—
55[5]	**Beaumont (IRE) (62)** (JEBanks) **7-9-11** DDenby(9) (hld up: sn trckng ldrs: hung lft & lost pl 2f out)	½	**6**	11/2[3]	60	22
465[3]	**All On (52)** (JHetherton) **6-8-11**(4) TSiddall(1) (mde most to 3f out: wknd over 1f out)	5	**7**	7/1	45	7
481[5]	**May King Mayhem (36)** (MrsALMKing) **4-7-10** PDoe(2) (w ldr tl lost pl over 2f out)	nk	**8**	20/1	28	—
	Fair and Fancy (FR) (37) (MissMKMilligan) **6-7-10**(4)ow3 RCody-Boutcher(8) (sn outpcd & bhd: hdwy on ins 6f out: wnt prom 3f out: sn lost pl)	8	**9**	20/1	20	—

(SP 118.9%) **9 Rn**

3m 12.3 (14.30) CSF £22.89 CT £219.12 TOTE £7.20: £1.70 £1.50 £3.50 (£10.20) Trio £18.60 OWNER Mr P. D. Savill (SALTBURN) BRED Mulholland Brothers
LONG HANDICAP May King Mayhem 7-9
WEIGHT FOR AGE 4yo-3lb
Sedbergh (USA), who won two successive claimers but did not reappear after mid-July at three, looked to have grown and done well physically over the winter. Sent for home off the bend, he just lasted out. (6/1)
430 Raffles Rooster, ridden by a substitute jockey who has yet to ride a winner, he lost a couple of lengths by running wide on the paddock bend. Travelling strongly on the outer turning in, he stayed on strongly towards the finish and, with a rider who knew him better, he must have prevailed. (3/1)
375 Forzair, who has run over a variety of trips, seems to have lost what he once possessed in the way of finishing speed. (14/1)
470* Dancing Cavalier was not suited by the modest pace. (7/2)
356 Undawaterscubadiva (13/2: op 10/1)

543 SWAN CLAIMING STKS (4-Y.O+) (Class F)

2-30 (2-30) **2m (Fibresand)** £2,277.00 (£627.00: £297.00) Stalls: Low GOING: 0.12 sec per fur (SLW)

				SP	RR	SF
430[20]	**Kalamata (52)** (JAGlover) **5-9-0** NDay(1) (trckd ldr: led over 4f out: hrd rdn fnl f: all out)	—	**1**	9/4[1]	59	—
465[7]	**Top Prize (28)** (MBrittain) **9-8-9v** GBardwell(3) (sn pushed along: hdwy to chse ldrs 10f out: styd on ins fnl f: jst failed)	½	**2**	12/1[3]	54	—
465[12]	**Shakiyr (FR) (62)** (RHollinshead) **6-8-13b**(3) FLynch(2) (hld up & bhd: hdwy on outside 6f out: sn rdn: one pce fnl 4f)	21	**3**	9/4[1]	40	—
356[4]	**El Nido (55)** (DWChapman) **9-9-0** LCharnock(6) (led tl over 4f out: wknd over 2f out)	½	**4**	7/2[2]	37	—
375[6]	**World Without End (USA) (25)** (MESowersby) **8-8-5b**(3) RHavlin(5) (sn wl bhd & pushed along: sme hdwy 4f out: n.d)	12	**5**	14/1	19	—
	Saint Keyne (DLWilliams) **7-9-5**(3) DGriffiths(8) (chsd ldrs: drvn along 9f out: sn bhd: t.o 3f out)	13	**6**	16/1	20	—
415[6]	**Lordan Velvet (IRE) (55)** (MrsWBAllen,Norway) **5-8-10** LNewton(4) (chsd ldrs: rdn 6f out: wknd over 4f out)	½	**7**	20/1	8	—
295[7]	**Premier League (IRE) (32)** (JELong) **7-9-4** LeesaLong(7) (chsd ldrs tl wknd 6f out: sn bhd)	9	**8**	12/1[3]	7	—

(SP 116.5%) **8 Rn**

3m 51.0 (25.00) CSF £29.20 TOTE £2.90: £1.20 £2.30 £1.70 (£14.00) OWNER Mr B. H. Farr (WORKSOP) BRED Worksop Manor Stud Farm

360 Kalamata, stepping up in trip, took a decisive advantage once in line for home but in the end his stamina only just lasted out. (9/4)

Top Prize proved dogged under pressure and in the end just failed to get there. He would have been meeting the winner on 19lb better terms in a handicap. (12/1)

400 Shakiyr (FR) is running half-heartedly at present. (9/4)

356 El Nido, freshened up after a thirty-two day rest, set a good pace and raced with plenty of enthusiasm. (7/2)

544 HERON MAIDEN H'CAP (0-70) (3-Y.O+) (Class E)

3-00 (3-03) **1m 3f (Fibresand)** £3,070.25 (£917.00: £438.50: £199.25) Stalls: Low GOING: 0.12 sec per fur (SLW)

				SP	RR	SF
367[4]	**Happy Brave (31)** (PDCundell) **5-7-10** JLowe(4) (b: chsd ldrs: led 1f out: hld on towards fin)	—	**1**	12/1	43	9
	Monte Cavo (31) (MBrittain) **6-7-10** GBardwell(14) (trckd ldr: led over 2f out: hdd 1f out: kpt on wl fnl f)	nk	**2**	12/1	43	9
	Evaporate (31) (MJHeaton-Ellis) **5-7-3**(7) JFowle(1) (b: hld up & bhd: hdwy over 3f out: kpt on same pce)	5	**3**	33/1	35	1
410[11]	**Zatopek (52)** (JCullinan) **5-9-3** JQuinn(3) (hdwy 6f out: sn in tch: drvn along & one pce fnl 4f)	1½	**4**	10/1	54	20
284[15]	**Acerbus Dulcis (31)** (MCChapman) **6-7-3**(7) IonaWands(2) (swtg: hdwy 6f out: sn chsng ldrs: one pce fnl 4f)	1¼	**5**	33/1	31	—
367[5]	**Hornpipe (31)** (JWharton) **5-7-10b** FNorton(8) (b: a chsng ldrs: drvn along 5f out: sn outpcd)	4	**6**	12/1	26	—
	Madam Lucy (51) (WWHaigh) **3-7-5**(5) JBramhill(6) (bit bkwd: hdwy 6f out: sn chsng ldrs: wknd 3f out)	4	**7**	20/1	40	—
435[5]	**Fourdaned (IRE) (63)** (PWHarris) **4-10-0** GDuffield(11) (lw: chsd ldrs: drvn along over 3f out: wknd 2f out)	2½	**8**	5/2[1]	48	14
417[2]	**Zorba (63)** (CWThornton) **3-8-8** DeanMcKeown(7) (led tl over 2f out: sn lost pl)	12	**9**	5/1[2]	31	—
	Gulf of Siam (55) (JMackie) **4-9-6** MBirch(9) (trckd ldrs: effrt 3f out: sn wknd)	4	**10**	9/1	17	—
	Moorbird (IRE) (62) (MJohnston) **3-8-7** JWeaver(12) (bit bkwd: w ldrs: drvn along & lost pl 6f out: sn bhd: t.o 3f out)	4	**11**	11/2[3]	18	—
355[6]	**Sir Alidaf (51)** (OO'Neill) **3-7-5**(5) PFessey(5) (unruly s: chsd ldrs tl lost pl 7f out: t.o 3f out)	1	**12**	50/1	6	—
	Melomania (USA) (40) (SRBowring) **5-8-5** NAdams(13) (chsd ldrs tl lost pl 6f out: t.o 3f out)	dist	**13**	20/1	—	—
	Formidable Flame (55) (WJMusson) **4-9-6** GCarter(10) (Withdrawn not Starter's orders: burst out of stalls)		**W**	9/1	—	—

(SP 130.2%) **13 Rn**

2m 31.5 (11.50) CSF £114.06 CT £3,109.39 TOTE £15.50: £3.20 £4.90 £11.50 (£76.60) Trio Not won; £210.71 to Worcester 2/4/97 OWNER Miss M. C. Fraser (NEWBURY) BRED Mrs K. R. Ensten

LONG HANDICAP Acerbus Dulcis 7-4 Monte Cavo 7-8 Evaporate 7-7 Sir Alidaf 6-8 Madam Lucy 7-6

WEIGHT FOR AGE 3yo-20lb

367 Happy Brave, taking a big step up in distance, did just enough. (12/1)

Monte Cavo, having his first outing for 178 days, fought back all the way to the line. (12/1)

Evaporate, having her first outing for two seasons and her first for her new stable, was happy to sit off the pace. Keeping on up the straight, she should be capable of some improvement. (33/1)

435 Fourdaned (IRE) looked different class in the paddock but, in trouble on the home turn, dropped away two furlongs out and possibly does not stay this far. (5/2)

Moorbird (IRE) (11/2: 4/1-6/1)

545 DAVID ARMES H'CAP (0-70) (4-Y.O+) (Class E)

3-30 (3-33) **5f (Fibresand)** £3,044.25 (£909.00: £434.50: £197.25) Stalls: Low GOING minus 0.05 sec per fur (STD)

				SP	RR	SF
443[5]	**Daawe (USA) (70)** (MrsVAAconley) **6-10-0** MDeering(9) (chsd ldrs: hrd rdn & styd on to ld ins fnl f: jst hld on)	—	**1**	5/2[1]	81	65
357[9]	**Chadwell Hall (68)** (SRBowring) **6-9-5b**(7) KSked(7) (led: clr ½-wy: hdd ins fnl f: kpt on wl towards fin)	nk	**2**	12/1	78	62
423[2]	**Afaan (IRE) (60)** (RFMarvin) **4-9-4** TGMcLaughlin(12) (b: a in tch: styd on same pce fnl 2f)	4	**3**	7/1[3]	57	41
127[12]	**Dissentor (IRE) (40)** (JAGlover) **5-7-12b**ow1 LCharnock(13) (chsd ldrs: kpt on same pce fnl 2f)	1	**4**	14/1	34	17
*429**	**Hoh Majestic (IRE) (59)** (RonaldThompson) **4-8-12v**(5) JBramhill(14) (hdwy ½-wy: kpt on fnl 2f: nvr rchd ldrs)	½	**5**	7/1[3]	51	35
178[5]	**Palacegate Jack (IRE) (70)** (CADwyer) **6-10-0** LDettori(6) (chsd ldrs: hung rt & nt qckn fnl 2f)	3½	**6**	3/1[2]	51	35
421[8]	**Lochon (50)** (MrsNMacauley) **6-8-5v**(3) CTeague(11) (s.i.s: bhd: kpt on appr fnl f: n.d)	½	**7**	20/1	30	14
	Al Reet (IRE) (65) (SRBowring) **6-9-2**(7) FBoyle(3) (sn bhd: sme hdwy 2f out: n.d)	¾	**8**	14/1	42	26
423[12]	**Tutu Sixtysix (38)** (DonEnricoIncisa) **6-7-10b** KimTinkler(4) (chsd ldrs to ½-wy: sn outpcd)	¾	**9**	50/1	13	—
494[5]	**Queens Check (64)** (MissJFCraze) **4-9-8** SWebster(2) (sn outpcd & rdn along: n.d)	¾	**10**	17/2	36	20
79[12]	**Cheeky Chappy (55)** (DWChapman) **6-8-13b** ACulhane(5) (sltly hmpd s: a bhd)	¾	**11**	14/1	25	9
404[6]	**Runs in the Family (47)** (GMMcCourt) **5-8-5** GCarter(10) (chsd ldrs: rdn ½-wy: sn outpcd)	nk	**12**	14/1	16	—
423[14]	**Ginas Girl (39)** (DShaw) **4-7-11**ow1 NKennedy(8) (unruly s: s.i.s: a in rr)	2	**13**	50/1	2	—
512[11]	**Smart Guest (67)** (DShaw) **5-9-11b** JFanning(1) (b: sn outpcd & bhd)	6	**14**	7/1[3]	11	—

(SP 144.6%) **14 Rn**

59.4 secs (2.40) CSF £38.76 CT £197.38 TOTE £4.50: £2.10 £3.90 £2.40 (£31.00) Trio £93.50 OWNER Mrs Andrea Mallinson (WESTOW) BRED Gainsborough Farm W.C.

LONG HANDICAP Tutu Sixtysix 7-0 Ginas Girl 7-3

443 Daawe (USA) stuck on under strong pressure to scrape home by the skin of his teeth. (5/2)

89 Chadwell Hall, who has slipped down the weights, showed all his old dash. In a clear lead at halfway, he battled on when collared. (12/1)

423 Afaan (IRE) was racing from a 4lb higher mark. Six furlongs should suit him better. (7/1)

65 Dissentor (IRE) was having his first race for seventy-one days. (14/1)
Al Reet (IRE) (14/1: op 33/1)
Smart Guest (7/1: op 16/1)

546 JAY (S) STKS (3-Y.O) (Class G)
4-00 (4-02) **6f (Fibresand)** £1,984.50 (£547.00: £259.50) Stalls: Low GOING: 0.12 sec per fur (SLW)

				SP	RR	SF
399[4]	**Advance Repro (48)** (JAkehurst) **3-8-11b** MTebbutt(8) (trckd ldrs: led over 2f out: drvn clr fnl f: eased towards fin)	—	**1**	12/1	67	37
399[2]	**Julia's Relative (53)** (RGuest) **3-8-6b** LDettori(2) (sltly hmpd s: sn trckng ldrs: effrt & ev ch over 1f out: wknd towards fin)	5	**2**	7/4 [1]	49	19
*427**	**Ma Vielle Pouque (IRE) (54)** (WGMTurner) **3-8-11** TSprake(4) (unruly in stalls: led over 1f: one pce fnl 2f)	1¼	**3**	4/1 [2]	50	20
289[3]	**Jack Says (52)** (DShaw) **3-8-11b** JFanning(1) (sn trckng ldrs: effrt & swtchd over 2f out: no imp)	3	**4**	5/1 [3]	42	12
453[8]	**Heathyard's Flight (52)** (RHollinshead) **3-8-11** WRyan(6) (sn outpcd: effrt on outside over 2f out: hung lft: eased fnl f)	20	**5**	8/1	—	—
377[9]	**Unknown Territory (IRE) (50)** (RonaldThompson) **3-8-11b[1]** TWilliams(3) (sn hrd rdn: hdwy to ld over 4f out: hdd over 2f out: sn wknd)	3½	**6**	25/1	—	—
	Antares (50) (NTinkler) **3-8-11** KimTinkler(5) (w ldrs: hung lft & lost pl 2f out)	3½	**7**	25/1	—	—
	Carrie's Fantasy (AGNewcombe) **3-8-6** JMarshall(9) (small: bit bkwd: s.i.s: sn wl bhd: t.o 3f out)	7	**8**	12/1	—	—
	Coscoroba (IRE) (JBerry) **3-8-1**(5) PFessey(7) (Withdrawn not under Starter's orders: unruly s & ref to ent stalls)		**W**	4/1 [2]	—	—

(SP 127.2%) **8 Rn**

1m 18.5 (5.00) CSF £24.01 TOTE £17.20: £2.90 £1.10 £1.50 (£10.20) Trio £6.50 OWNER Mrs S. K. McLean (LAMBOURN) BRED Roldvale Ltd
No bid
399 Advance Repro, a keen-going sort, took this poor event in decisive fashion. (12/1)
399 Julia's Relative, a very narrow type, was driven up to challenge but was never doing anything like enough to trouble the winner. (7/4)
427* Ma Vielle Pouque (IRE) gave trouble in the stalls. (4/1)
289 Jack Says was dropped back in distance but showed no improvement whatsoever. (5/1)
Carrie's Fantasy (12/1: op 4/1)

547 PEACOCK H'CAP (0-65) (3-Y.O) (Class F)
4-30 (4-30) **7f (Fibresand)** £2,277.00 (£627.00: £297.00) Stalls: Low GOING: 0.12 sec per fur (SLW)

				SP	RR	SF
395[4]	**Tayovullin (IRE) (56)** (HMorrison) **3-9-1** CRutter(6) (b.hind: trckd ldrs: led over 1f out: swvd rt ins fnl f: hld on wl)	—	**1**	8/1 [3]	69	34
*378**	**Gresatre (62)** (CADwyer) **3-9-0**(7) JoHunnam(7) (trckd ldrs: hdwy to chal over 1f out: hmpd wl ins fnl f: no ex)	nk	**2**	2/1 [1]	74	39
489[4]	**Hever Golf Charger (IRE) (61)** (TJNaughton) **3-9-6** DHolland(4) (w ldrs: rdn & edgd rt over 1f out: kpt on one pce)	4	**3**	5/1 [2]	64	29
414[7]	**Warp Drive (IRE) (48)** (WRMuir) **3-8-7** DaneO'Neill(5) (sn drvn along: hdwy ½-wy: kpt on same pce fnl 2f)	¾	**4**	14/1	50	15
420[3]	**Patina (53)** (RHollinshead) **3-8-12** LDettori(2) (mde most tl 3f out: hung lft: wknd over 1f out)	1¾	**5**	2/1 [1]	51	16
355[5]	**Apiculate (IRE) (37)** (SRBowring) **3-7-5**(5) PFessey(1) (trckd ldrs: led 3f out tl over 1f out: sn wknd)	¾	**6**	12/1	33	—
	Al Ava Consonant (60) (JDBethell) **3-9-5** JWeaver(3) (s.i.s: hdwy u.p ½-wy: hung lft & lost pl over 2f out: eased)	16	**7**	8/1 [3]	19	—

(SP 119.9%) **7 Rn**

1m 33.0 (6.50) CSF £23.72 TOTE £14.10: £5.20 £1.50 (£18.50) OWNER The Beach Club (EAST ILSLEY) BRED Irelandia Holdings Ltd
LONG HANDICAP Apiculate (IRE) 7-8
IN-FOCUS: **This was Hughie Morrison's first winner as a trainer. His family have been involved in racing for a long time, and his father bred and raced Oaks winner Juliette Marny. Morrison had been acting as assistant to Paul Cole for the last eighteeen months, prior to taking out a licence in February to train from Simon Sherwood's old yard in East Ilsley.**
395 Tayovullin (IRE), dropped back to seven, just held the upper hand when she swerved violently right under pressure well inside the last. (8/1: 6/1-9/1)
378* Gresatre, from an 8lb higher mark, was just getting the worse of the argument when pushed sideways inside the last one hundred yards. The result was in no way affected. (2/1)
489 Hever Golf Charger (IRE), a keen-going sort, was taken to post early. (5/1)
234 Warp Drive (IRE), with the blinkers left off, took a deal of driving before he got into top gear. (14/1)
420 Patina hung under pressure and found precious little. (2/1)

T/Plpt: £565.10 (21.58 Tckts). T/Qdpt: £35.40 (23.48 Tckts) WG

HAMILTON (R-H) (Soft, Good to soft patches)
Wednesday April 2nd
WEATHER: overcast WIND: mod across

77+ 53 64 63

548 JIMMY CRAIG (QUALIFIER) MAIDEN AUCTION STKS (2-Y.O) (Class E) (64)
2-10 (2-11) **5f 4y** £2,853.00 (£864.00: £422.00: £201.00) Stalls: High GOING: Not Established

				SP	RR	SF
432[2]	**Mister Bankes** (WGMTurner) **2-8-7** TSprake(3) (lw: mde all: pushed along & r.o wl appr fnl f)	—	**1**	1/3 [1]	83	24
	Mamma's Boy (JBerry) **2-8-8** KDarley(4) (w'like: str: bit bkwd: chsd ldrs: sn pushed along: kpt on fnl f: no ch w wnr)	2½	**2**	4/1 [2]	76	17
492[3]	**Filey Brigg** (WTKemp) **2-7-13** JQuinn(1) (hld up: effrt 2f out: styd on towards fin)	¾	**3**	33/1	65	6
447[5]	**Oriel Girl** (PDEvans) **2-8-1**ow1 JFEgan(2) (b.nr fore: w wnr: rdn ½-wy: wknd 1f out)	1¼	**4**	8/1 [3]	63	3

(SP 109.1%) **4 Rn**

63.0 secs (4.70) CSF £1.87 TOTE £1.20 (£1.40) OWNER Mr T. Lightbowne (SHERBORNE) BRED Ardview Farm
432 Mister Bankes is doing well physically and looked superb. Being by Risk Me, he was virtually guaranteed to go in the soft and won emphatically. (1/3: op 1/2)
Mamma's Boy, a really sturdy individual, showed plenty here and there is more to come. (4/1: op 5/2)

492 Filey Brigg, given a patient ride this time, took a while to find her stride but she certainly finished well, and this sparely-made individual can pick up a race. (33/1)
447 Oriel Girl spoiled her chances of a place by taking the winner on, and looks the type for a sharper track. (8/1)

549 TALKING PAGES H'CAP (0-60) (3-Y.O) (Class F)
2-40 (2-41) **6f 5y** £2,542.00 (£712.00: £346.00) Stalls: High GOING: 0.14 sec per fur (G)

				SP	RR	SF
	I'm Still Here (59) (JBerry) **3-9-6** KDarley(6) (b.nr fore: chsd ldrs: styd on to ld wl ins fnl f)	—	**1**	5/2[1]	64	36
475[9]	**Native Thatch (IRE) (43)** (WGMTurner) **3-8-4** TSprake(7) (chsd ldr: led 2f out & sn hrd drvn: hdd & nt qckn towards fin)	nk	**2**	5/1[3]	47	19
412[3]	**Impish (IRE) (35)** (TJEtherington) **3-7-10** DaleGibson(1) (dwlt: hdwy over 1f out: ev ch wl ins fnl f: nt qckn)	hd	**3**	8/1	39	11
	Murray Grey (54) (EWeymes) **3-9-1** JQuinn(4) (h.d.w: bit bkwd: trckd ldrs: effrt 2f out: sn wknd)	5	**4**	11/1	45	17
	Northern Sal (60) (MissLAPerratt) **3-9-7** JCarroll(3) (led 4f: wknd)	hd	**5**	8/1	50	22
	Why O Six (59) (RAFahey) **3-9-6** ACulhane(5) (drvn along thrght: sme hdwy ½-wy: sn btn)	1¼	**6**	11/4[2]	46	18

(SP 102.5%) **6 Rn**

1m 15.6 (5.60) CSF £11.24 TOTE £2.50: £1.10 £3.00 (£7.40) OWNER Mr J. K. M. Oliver (COCKERHAM) BRED T. K. Knox
LONG HANDICAP Impish (IRE) 7-9
STEWARDS' ENQUIRY Sprake susp. 11-12/4/97 (excessive use of whip).
I'm Still Here acted well on this course and similar ground early last season, and showed fine determination to just get the edge here. (5/2)
Native Thatch (IRE) has nothing much to recommend her on looks, but she does act in this ground and, although under pressure a long way out, kept battling on. (5/1)
412 Impish (IRE) did not impress on looks, but ran reasonably after a poor start, although the quality of this event has to be questioned. (8/1)
Murray Grey has made up into a nice sort, but needed this and blew up. (11/1: 8/1-12/1)
Northern Sal goes in the soft and has blistering early pace, and is probably better at the minimum trip. (8/1: op 4/1)
Why O Six was most disappointing, never going the pace at any stage. (11/4)

550 WESTCARS SAAB TRAINERS' CHALLENGE LAUNCH CLAIMING STKS (3-Y.O+) (Class F)
3-10 (3-10) **1m 1f 36y** £2,626.00 (£736.00: £358.00) Stalls: High GOING: 0.14 sec per fur (G)

				SP	RR	SF
444[5]	**High Premium (80)** (RAFahey) **9-9-13** ACulhane(5) (mid div: hdwy u.p 3f out: swtchd & styd on to ld wl ins fnl f)	—	**1**	2/1[1]	72	44
	Sun Mark (IRE) (MrsASwinbank) **6-9-8** GDuffield(4) (led: rdn 2f out: r.o: ct wl ins fnl f)	½	**2**	33/1	66	38
426[2]	**Calder King (62)** (MrsMReveley) **6-9-7b**(5) SCopp(10) (rr div: hdwy on ins 3f out: n.m.r 1f out: swtchd & styd on)	½	**3**	9/4[2]	69	41
	Leif the Lucky (USA) (59) (MissSEHall) **8-9-12** KDarley(6) (lw: trckd ldrs: ev ch 4f out: rdn 3f out: r.o one pce)	1¾	**4**	4/1[3]	66	38
467[6]	**Hanby** (JSGoldie) **5-9-11** TWilliams(1) (lw: trckd ldrs: hdwy & ev ch 2f out: wknd 1f out)	7	**5**	12/1	53	25
	Ten Past Six (72) (MartynWane) **5-9-6** JCarroll(3) (lw: chsd ldr tl wknd fnl 2½f)	9	**6**	10/1	32	4
377[7]	**See You Soon** (CWThornton) **3-8-6** DeanMcKeown(11) (b.hind: bhd tl sme late hdwy)	4	**7**	50/1	28	—
	Men Of Wickenby (RMMcKellar) **3-8-11** NVarley(12) (cmpt: bit bkwd: nvr nr ldrs)	2	**8**	25/1	30	—
	Amany (IRE) (DBurchell) **5-8-13** SDrowne(9) (nvr bttr than mid div)	1¾	**9**	14/1	12	—
467[12]	**Incantrice** (WStorey) **4-9-0** JFanning(8) (hld up & a bhd)	16	**10**	100/1	—	—
	Shmoozy (JSGoldie) **8-8-10**(5) PRoberts(7) (trckd ldrs tl wknd fnl 4f)	2½	**11**	66/1	—	—
	Samstotry (MissLAPerratt) **7-9-7** JQuinn(2) (hld up & a bhd)	1	**12**	50/1	—	—

(SP 120.7%) **12 Rn**

2m 3.2 (8.90) CSF £75.45 TOTE £3.40: £1.80 £4.20 £1.30 (£57.40) Trio £54.30 OWNER Mr J. C. Parsons (MALTON) BRED M.E Wates
WEIGHT FOR AGE 3yo-17lb
444 High Premium had not previously won on soft ground and, although looking in trouble for a long way, his class carried him through. (2/1: op 5/4)
Sun Mark (IRE), from a yard that has had a terrific season over jumps, ran a smashing race here and kept battling back. (33/1)
426 Calder King probably just found this trip a bit on the sharp side and, despite staying on, could never make it. (9/4)
Leif the Lucky (USA) travelled really well until an effort was required, then failed to run on. (4/1)
467 Hanby ran well again, and may just have found this trip beyond him. (12/1)
Ten Past Six, fit from hurdling, proved disappointing when the pressure was on. (10/1: 8/1-12/1)
Amany (IRE) (14/1: 33/1-66/1)

551 HAMILTON (S) STKS (3-Y.O) (Class G)
3-40 (3-42) **1m 65y** £2,220.00 (£620.00: £300.00) Stalls: High GOING: 0.14 sec per fur (G)

				SP	RR	SF
	Rock Island Line (IRE) (JBerry) **3-8-6**(5) PRoberts(5) (w'like: unf: a gng wl: led wl over 2f out: edgd lft & r.o wl)	—	**1**	5/1[3]	59	23
	Tycoon Tina (55) (WMBrisbourne) **3-8-1**(5) RMullen(2) (b: bhd: hdwy on outside 4f out: ev ch 3f out: one pce)	8	**2**	16/1	39	3
445[7]	**Manileno (42)** (JHetherton) **3-8-11** NKennedy(7) (chsd ldr: ev ch 3f out: one pce)	1¾	**3**	12/1	40	4
395[8]	**Swiss Coast (IRE) (70)** (NTinkler) **3-8-11b[1]** KDarley(6) (hld up: effrt 4f out: little rspnse)	¾	**4**	2/1[2]	39	3
	Murron Wallace (56) (RMWhitaker) **3-8-6** LCharnock(3) (chsd ldrs: led over 3f out tl wl over 2f out: wknd)	1½	**5**	7/4[1]	31	—
	Sweet Note (IRE) (MissLAPerratt) **3-8-6** JCarroll(1) (neat: bkwd: in tch tl outpcd fnl 3f)	3	**6**	12/1	25	—
	Eurolink Windsong (IRE) (RMMcKellar) **3-8-6** TWilliams(4) (led tl hdd & wknd over 3f out)	10	**7**	12/1	6	—

(SP 115.3%) **7 Rn**

1m 52.9 (8.80) CSF £69.32 TOTE £4.90: £4.80 £4.00 (£51.60) OWNER Mr J. Berry (COCKERHAM) BRED Drumconrath Stud
Bt in 6,200 gns
Rock Island Line (IRE), confidently ridden, travelled on the bridle and, despite going to his left when in front, there were never any doubts about the result. (5/1)
Tycoon Tina came wide on the slowest ground in the straight, and had no chance with the winner once the pace increased. (16/1)
Manileno had his chances but looked very one-paced when ridden. (12/1)
Swiss Coast (IRE) had blinkers on for the first time, but did not look in love with the game when ridden early in the straight. (2/1)
Murron Wallace looked fit, but she proved disappointing when pressure was applied. (7/4)
Sweet Note (IRE), well in need of this, dropped away in the last three furlongs. (12/1)
Eurolink Windsong (IRE) (12/1: 5/1-14/1)

552 YELLOW PAGES H'CAP (0-75) (3-Y.O+) (Class D)

4-10 (4-10) **1m 3f 16y** £3,899.00 (£1,181.00: £577.00: £275.00) Stalls: High GOING: 0.14 sec per fur (G)

Form	Horse	Dist	Pos	SP	RR	SF
435^{4}	**Manful (68)** (MissLAPerratt) **5-9-7b** NKennedy(7) (a.p: chal over 1f out: styd on to ld wl ins fnl f)	—	1	8/1	79	53
493^{4}	**Lord Advocate (43)** (DANolan) **9-7-10b** NVarley(3) (chsd ldr: led 5f out tl wl ins fnl f: kpt on)	nk	2	33/1	54	28
*410**	**Moonraking (49)** (TJEtherington) **4-8-2** DaleGibson(12) (outpcd & bhd tl styd on wl fnl 2f)	5	3	12/1	52	26
461^{4}	**Suga Hawk (IRE) (58)** (EJAlston) **5-8-11** JFEgan(11) (lw: a chsng ldrs: one pce fnl 3f)	s.h	4	14/1	61	35
493^{10}	**Rapid Mover (44)** (DANolan) **10-7-6b**$^{(5)ow1}$ PFessey(1) (led tl hdd 5f out: grad wknd fnl 2f)	10	5	100/1	33	6
	Express Gift (57) (MrsMReveley) **8-8-10** ACulhane(14) (lw: hdwy appr st: c wd & sn rdn: styd on fnl f: no imp)	½	6	9/4^{1}	45	19
461^{2}	**Sing And Dance (43)** (EWeymes) **4-7-10** JQuinn(8) (lw: sn pushed along: styd on fnl 3f: nvr rchd ldrs)	2½	7	7/1	28	2
	Lord Hastie (USA) (60) (CWThornton) **9-8-13** DeanMcKeown(13) (mid div: effrt 4f out: styd on one pce)	1	8	10/1	43	17
461^{14}	**Giftbox (USA) (52)** (NBycroft) **5-8-5** LCharnock(10) (rr div: effrt 4f out: n.d)	1¾	9	33/1	33	7
	Veridian (75) (PWHarris) **4-10-0** GDuffield(4) (in tch: effrt 4f out: edgd rt & no imp)	1	10	13/2^{3}	54	28
444^{11}	**Suez Tornado (IRE) (73)** (EJAlston) **4-9-12** SDrowne(6) (bhd: c wd st: hdwy 5f out: wknd over 2f out)	½	11	14/1	51	25
	Breydon (48) (PMonteith) **4-7-8**$^{(7)}$ KSked(15) (prom tl hmpd & lost pl over 3f out)	1¼	12	25/1	25	—
461*	**Domino Flyer (72)** (MrsASwinbank) **4-9-11** ^{6x} JSupple(9) (a outpcd & bhd)	10	13	6/1^{2}	34	8
	Hutchies Lady (43) (RMMcKellar) **5-7-3**$^{(7)}$ JennyBenson(5) (b.hind: wl bhd fnl 5f)	nk	14	66/1	5	—

(SP 124.3%) **14 Rn**

2m 28.1 (8.70) CSF £240.40 CT £2,876.47 TOTE £8.10: £2.40 £3.30 £3.40 (£40.50) Trio £355.40; £150.18 to Aintree 3/4/97 OWNER Mr C. D. Barber-Lomax (AYR) BRED John Rose

LONG HANDICAP Lord Advocate 7-6 Rapid Mover 6-9 Sing And Dance 7-6 Hutchies Lady 7-1

OFFICIAL EXPLANATION **Express Gift: rider reported that eleven furlongs was not far enough.**

Domino Flyer: no explanation offered.

435 Manful, on the ground he likes, responded well to pressure to get the better of a very determined runner-up. (8/1)

493 Lord Advocate, 4lb out of the handicap, ran his heart out to show he is coming right back to his best. (33/1)

410* Moonraking, an All-Weather winner, gave the impression that longer trips will see improvement at this game. (12/1: op 8/1)

461 Suga Hawk (IRE) again had his chances, but is woefully short of a turn of foot to take the opportunity. (14/1: 10/1-16/1)

Rapid Mover ran really well from 15lb out of the handicap. (100/1)

Express Gift has been in good form over hurdles and goes in the soft but, for some reason, he was never happy on this occasion. (9/4)

461 Sing And Dance was always struggling with the pace, and seems to like things to go her own way. She probably prefers faster ground. (7/1: 5/1-8/1)

461* Domino Flyer for some reason could never go the pace this time, and was always behind and struggling. (6/1)

553 LANARKSHIRE H'CAP (0-60) (3-Y.O+) (Class F)

4-40 (4-40) **1m 4f 17y** £2,808.00 (£788.00: £384.00) Stalls: High GOING: 0.14 sec per fur (G)

Form	Horse	Dist	Pos	SP	RR	SF
15^{10}	**Globe Runner (47)** (JJO'Neill) **4-9-0** KDarley(2) (lw: hld up: hdwy 4f out: led over 1f out: rdn & r.o)	—	1	20/1	61	26
493*	**Here Comes Herbie (42)** (WStorey) **5-8-10** ^{5x} NKennedy(3) (lw: hld up & bhd: stdy hdwy 5f out: ev ch over 1f out: nt qckn)	1½	2	4/7^{1}	54	20
256^{3}	**Philmist (45)** (MissLAPerratt) **5-8-13b** JCarroll(1) (cl up: led 3f out tl over 1f out: no ex)	2½	3	16/1	54	20
	Thrower (32) (WMBrisbourne) **6-7-9**$^{(5)}$ RMullen(7) (b: hdwy on outside 4f out: styd on: nvr trbld ldrs)	8	4	20/1	30	—
410^{5}	**Carol Again (37)** (NBycroft) **5-8-5** JQuinn(8) (a.p: effrt 4f out: one pce)	1½	5	20/1	33	—
	Passing Strangers (USA) (58) (PWHarris) **4-9-11** GDuffield(10) (in tch: rdn 4f out: no imp)	6	6	6/1^{2}	46	11
	Doubling Dice (34) (RAllan) **6-8-2**^{ow2} JFEgan(12) (b.hind: hdwy & prom appr st: rdn 3f out: grad wknd)	1½	7	50/1	20	—
	Rossel (USA) (60) (PMonteith) **4-9-6**$^{(7)}$ KSked(13) (lw: hdwy & prom 6f out: c wd: wknd fnl 3f)	¾	8	14/1	45	10
493^{14}	**Stingray City (USA) (38)** (RMMcKellar) **8-7-13**$^{(7)}$ JMcAuley(5) (b: trckd ldrs tl wknd fnl 2½f)	1	9	100/1	22	—
	Eurotwist (40) (SEKettlewell) **8-8-8** JFortune(9) (bhd & outpcd 5f out: n.d)	hd	10	10/1^{3}	24	—
375^{11}	**Qualitair Pride (37)** (JFBottomley) **5-8-5** NCarlisle(4) (led tl hdd 3f out: sn wknd)	7	11	25/1	12	—
360^{12}	**No Submission (USA) (34)** (DWChapman) **11-8-2b** LCharnock(14) (outpcd & bhd fnl 6f)	½	12	66/1	8	—
	Winnebago (53) (CWThornton) **4-9-6** DeanMcKeown(6) (prom: rdn 5f out: sn wknd)	½	13	12/1	26	—
	Jabaroot (IRE) (28) (RMMcKellar) **6-7-10** NVarley(11) (b: s.s: a bhd)	13	14	33/1	—	—

(SP 132.8%) **14 Rn**

2m 44.7 (12.70) CSF £30.08 CT £238.46 TOTE £30.50: £6.30 £1.10 £1.50 (£20.20) Trio £35.40 OWNER G & P Barker Ltd/Globe Engineering (PENRITH) BRED Badger Hill Stud

LONG HANDICAP Jabaroot (IRE) 7-6

WEIGHT FOR AGE 4yo-1lb

Globe Runner both looked and travelled well and, when it came down to a fight, he always had the edge. He seems to be improving. (20/1)

493* Here Comes Herbie, dropped back half-a-mile in trip, still looked likely to win but was worried out of it late on. (4/7: op 10/11)

256 Philmist keeps running well on Turf without winning, and deserves to pick up a race. (16/1)

Thrower came up the worse ground in the straight on the outside of the field and, in the circumstances, ran reasonably. (20/1)

360 Carol Again was always close enough if good enough, but she lacked any turn of foot. (20/1)

Passing Strangers (USA) never looked all that happy in this ground and, inclined to hang, was treading water fully three furlongs out. (6/1)

Rossel (USA) looks superb but seems better on a faster surface, and racing wide in the slower ground in the home straight gave him no chance. (14/1: 10/1-16/1)

Eurotwist (10/1: 7/1-12/1)

Winnebago (12/1: 7/1-16/1)

T/Plpt: £130.50 (82.33 Tckts). T/Qdpt: £28.30 (24.6 Tckts) AA

0479-LEICESTER (R-H) (Firm)
Thursday April 3rd
WEATHER: sunny spells WIND: fresh across

554 HARBOROUGH H'CAP (0-80) (4-Y.O+ F & M) (Class D)
2-25 (2-25) **1m 8y** £3,486.35 (£1,038.80: £494.90: £222.95) Stalls: High GOING minus 0.31 sec per fur (GF)

				SP	RR	SF
	Sylvan Princess (67) (DJSCosgrove) **4-9-5** MRimmer(3) (lw: hld up: nt clr run over 2f out: qcknd to ld over 1f out: rdn out)	—	**1**	5/2 1	75	20
476 12	**Mimosa (63)** (SDow) **4-9-1** WRyan(4) (hld up: hdwy 2f out: r.o fnl f)	1½	**2**	9/2	68	13
	Charlton Imp (USA) (54) (RJHodges) **4-8-6** SDrowne(5) (bit bkwd: set stdy pce over 3f: ev ch over 1f out: one pce)	2	**3**	7/2 3	55	—
468 10	**Heathyards Lady (USA) (57)** (RHollinshead) **6-8-6**(3) FLynch(2) (in tch: rdn over 2f out: no imp)	½	**4**	3/1 2	57	2
358 11	**Tea Party (USA) (72)** (KOCunningham-Brown) **4-9-10b** TSprake(7) (lw: plld hrd: prom tl led over 4f out: hdd over 1f out: sn btn)	1¾	**5**	10/1	69	14
	With The Tempo (IRE) (45) (DrJDScargill) **4-7-11** JQuinn(6) (w ldrs: ev ch over 2f out: sn rdn & btn)	1½	**6**	14/1	39	—
				(SP 109.7%)		**6 Rn**

1m 40.5 (5.50) CSF £12.12 TOTE £3.00: £1.30 £2.80 (£5.10) OWNER Camelot Racing (NEWMARKET) BRED K S P Leisure
Sylvan Princess looked in tremendous shape and has clearly suffered no ill effects from a busy campaign last season. (5/2)
380 Mimosa proved a little easier to settle over this shorter trip but, by the time she was on the move, the winner was away. (9/2)
Charlton Imp (USA) looked just in need of this, but moved better to post than she was doing towards the end of last season and shaped well. (7/2)
Heathyards Lady (USA), 6lb higher than her last turf success eighteen months ago, could make little impact once the chips were down. (3/1)
305 Tea Party (USA) was in fine form last October, but has lost her way since and was below par despite looking well. (10/1: op 3/1)
With The Tempo (IRE) was rather fresh both going down and early in the race, and paid the penalty in the last couple of furlongs. (14/1)

555 LODDINGTON CONDITIONS STKS (3-Y.O) (Class C)
2-55 (2-56) **5f 218y** £5,058.00 (£1,872.00: £898.50: £367.50: £146.25: £57.75) Stalls: High GOING minus 0.31 sec per fur (GF)

				SP	RR	SF
	Grand Lad (IRE) (106) (RWArmstrong) **3-9-0** MRoberts(3) (mde all: pushed clr appr fnl f: comf)	—	**1**	5/6 1	108	56
449 10	**Indian Spark (98)** (WGMTurner) **3-9-2** TSprake(5) (w wnr: ev ch over 2f out: no ex appr fnl f)	2½	**2**	5/1 3	103	51
	Irish Accord (USA) (MrsJRRamsden) **3-9-0** JFortune(6) (lw: s.i.s: hld up: hdwy over 1f out: r.o)	1	**3**	3/1 2	99	47
	Dancethenightaway (86) (BJMeehan) **3-8-9** PatEddery(2) (w ldrs: rdn 3f out: btn & edgd rt fnl f)	5	**4**	9/1	80	28
	Nant Y Gamer (FR) (83) (JBerry) **3-9-0** KDarley(4) (lw: chsd ldrs 4f)	1½	**5**	16/1	81	29
434 7	**Divide And Rule (79)** (RHollinshead) **3-8-9**(3) DGriffiths(1) (sn outpcd)	3½	**6**	25/1	70	18
				(SP 115.9%)		**6 Rn**

1m 11.1 (1.10) CSF £5.39 TOTE £1.50: £1.10 £1.80 (£2.70) OWNER Mr Hugh Hart (NEWMARKET) BRED Mrs A. Whitehead
Grand Lad (IRE), third in a pretty hot-looking Cornwallis at the end of last season, has not grown much but is a sprinter all over, and was far too good for these. (5/6)
Indian Spark tried to take the winner on at halfway and might have nosed ahead for a stride or two, but was well and truly put in his place approaching the final furlong. (5/1: op 3/1)
Irish Accord (USA) is quite heavy-topped, but shone in the paddock. Losing ground at the start, he raced on a much more even keel on this straight course, having given steering problems at two. He was not unduly knocked about and is well worth keeping an eye on. (3/1)
Dancethenightaway looked fit, and raced keenly close to the leaders. However, once let down, all she seemed to want to do was hang right. (9/1: op 6/1)
Nant Y Gamer (FR) looked fit and well but was outclassed. (16/1)
Divide And Rule looked out of his depth from an early stage. (25/1)

556 BURTON OVERY (S) STKS (3-Y.O) (Class G)
3-30 (3-30) **5f 218y** £2,469.00 (£684.00: £327.00) Stalls: High GOING minus 0.31 sec per fur (GF)

				SP	RR	SF
	Brave Envoy (MJHeaton-Ellis) **3-9-0v1** SDrowne(10) (s.i.s: sn pushed along & bhd: stumbled over 2f out: rapid hdwy to ld wl ins fnl f)	—	**1**	7/1 3	62	32
317 5	**Terry's Rose (53)** (RHollinshead) **3-8-9** KDarley(9) (prom: led over 2f out: clr 1f out: hdd & unable qckn wl ins fnl f)	1½	**2**	16/1	53	23
462 7	**Bellarula** (MDods) **3-8-9** SWebster(7) (bhd: rdn & hdwy 3f out: no ex fnl f)	nk	**3**	16/1	52	22
462*	**Without Friends (IRE) (76)** (WStorey) **3-9-5** SWhitworth(11) (lw: hdwy 3f out: rdn over 1f out: no imp)	1	**4**	11/4 1	60	30
	Battle Ground (IRE) (52) (NACallaghan) **3-9-0** PatEddery(5) (lw: led 2f: wknd over 1f out)	3	**5**	5/1 2	47	17
279 4	**Broadgate Flyer (IRE) (64)** (MrsLStubbs) **3-9-0** KFallon(6) (in tch: rdn 2f out: kpt on)	1½	**6**	11/1	43	13
	Charlton Spring (IRE) (75) (RJHodges) **3-9-0** TQuinn(4) (w ldrs 4f)	2½	**7**	11/4 1	36	6
372 7	**Fit For The Job (IRE) (55)** (TWall) **3-9-2**(3) DGriffiths(8) (w ldr: led 4f out tl over 2f out: wknd appr fnl f)	hd	**8**	16/1	41	11
367 10	**Baptismal Rock (IRE) (65)** (BJCurley) **3-9-0** WRyan(2) (spd over 3f)	9	**9**	7/1 3	12	—
	Seamus (CJHill) **3-9-0** JQuinn(3) (trckd ldrs 4f)	½	**10**	16/1	10	—
314 9	**Rock Fantasy (50)** (CMurray) **3-8-9b** NicolaHowarth(1) (lw: a bhd)	3	**11**	33/1	—	—
				(SP 129.8%)		**11 Rn**

1m 12.8 (2.80) CSF £113.54 TOTE £11.70: £3.20 £3.40 £7.80 (£99.90) Trio Not won; £331.52 to Aintree 4/4/97 OWNER Mr M. Heaton-Ellis (WROUGHTON) BRED Robert Courtney
Bt in 10,500 gns
Brave Envoy did not seem at home in the first-time visor, and was looking less than fully enthusiastic at the back of the field at halfway. With the action concentrated on the far rail, he was pulled out to the stands' side of the track and, suddenly taking hold of his bridle, shot past his rivals as if they were nailed to the ground. He clearly has ability, but getting him to use it to best advantage will be the trick. (7/1)
317 Terry's Rose may have had the best of the ground, making her move against the far rails, but could not make it count. (16/1)
Bellarula stuck to the far side, but looked out of it by halfway. Making her move from that point, she never quite looked like winning. (16/1)
462* Without Friends (IRE), still there with a chance at the distance, could then find no more. He would have been much worse off with the runner-up in a handicap. (11/4)
Battle Ground (IRE) broke well, but was left behind in the closing stages. He may do better over further. (5/1)
279 Broadgate Flyer (IRE) kept plugging away to the end without landing a blow. (11/1: 8/1-12/1)
Baptismal Rock (IRE) (7/1: 5/1-10/1)

Seamus raced up the centre of the track where the ground seemed at its slowest, but still travelled well for half-a-mile. He may well have the ability to find a small race. (16/1)

75 – 77 70+ 68

557 KNIGHTON MEDIAN AUCTION MAIDEN STKS (2-Y.O) (Class F)

4-05 (4-06) **5f 2y** £2,715.90 (£752.40: £359.70) Stalls: High GOING minus 0.31 sec per fur (GF)

				SP	RR	SF
	Prince Foley (WGMTurner) **2-8-7**(7) DMcGaffin(6) (leggy: s.i.s: rn green & sn wl bhd: gd hdwy to ld ins fnl f: rdn out)	—	**1**	16/1	79	25
	Arian Da (BPalling) **2-8-9** TSprake(7) (str: scope: bit bkwd: a.p: led over 1f out: hdd & unable qckn ins fnl f)	2	**2**	16/1	68	14
	Sea Imp (IRE) (MartynMeade) **2-8-9** JReid(4) (unf: bkwd: led 3f: carried lft: r.o ins fnl f)	1½	**3**	25/1	63	9
	Rejected (RHannon) **2-9-0** PatEddery(9) (leggy: scope: bit bkwd: chsd ldrs: led 2f out: hung lft: sn hdd & btn)	¾	**4**	13/8 1	65	11
	Smooth Sailing (KMcAuliffe) **2-9-0** JFEgan(5) (leggy: unf: chsd ldrs: no hdwy fnl 2f)	½	**5**	12/1	64	10
	Arm And A Leg (IRE) (CADwyer) **2-9-0** JStack(8) (leggy: bit bkwd: in tch: effrt 2f out: wknd fnl f)	1	**6**	16/1	61	7
	Rusty Babe (IRE) (JJQuinn) **2-9-0** JQuinn(3) (str: s.s: gd hdwy 2f out: eased whn btn ins fnl f)	s.h	**7**	11/1	61	7
	Dawn Patrol (KWHogg) **2-8-9** DeanMcKeown(10) (lengthy: unf: bit bkwd: s.s: hdwy over 1f out: r.o)	1	**8**	16/1	52	—
	Seventh Heaven (JBerry) **2-9-0** KDarley(2) (cmpt: prom over 2f)	7	**9**	7/1 3	35	—
447 3	**O' Higgins (IRE)** (RBoss) **2-9-0** WRyan(1) (spd 3f)	2	**10**	11/4 2	29	—
				(SP 120.7%)		**10 Rn**

61.3 secs (2.80) CSF £229.88 TOTE £35.20: £4.80 £6.00 £4.10 (£83.90) Trio £218.70 OWNER Foley Steelstock (SHERBORNE) BRED Ian Slocock

IN-FOCUS: **Eighteen-year-old Scot Derek McGaffin was riding his first winner here.**

Prince Foley is not very big and rather on the leg, but moved down well. Very green early on, he was soon at least eight lengths off the pace but, with the penny suddenly dropping, he showed an excellent burst of speed to win in good style. He should certainly stay six furlongs. (16/1)

Arian Da did not look quite as forward as some of her rivals, but knew her job and was staying on at the line. The stable have introduced some useful juveniles here in the past, notably Carranita. (16/1)

Sea Imp (IRE) is not very tall but has speed, and led until carried towards the stands' rail by the fourth. She should have finished a little closer. (25/1)

Rejected, well touted but easy to back, wore boots in front and never looked entirely happy. Once let down he hung markedly towards the stands' rail, ending his chance. He has a strange pedigree, his dam being an out-and-out stayer, and he may need further and more cut in the ground. (13/8: 4/5-2/1)

Smooth Sailing, on the heels of the leaders with two furlongs left, could make no further impression and the situation was accepted. (12/1)

Arm And A Leg (IRE) tried to get to the leaders below the distance, but the effort soon petered out. (16/1)

Rusty Babe (IRE), strongly-made and cheaply bought, lost all chance at the start, but did a lot of good running in the second half of the race before being eased in the last hundred yards. He has ability and should find a race or two. (11/1: 12/1-20/1)

Dawn Patrol, another to fall out of the stalls, had only just got going as the race finished. (16/1)

Seventh Heaven (7/1: op 9/2)

558 LANGHAM MAIDEN STKS (3 & 4-Y.O) (Class D)

4-40 (4-42) **1m 3f 183y** £3,677.45 (£1,097.60: £524.30: £237.65) Stalls: High GOING minus 0.20 sec per fur (GF)

			SP	RR	SF
Kota (JWharton) **4-9-12** KFallon(6) (tall: trckd ldrs: led over 1f out: rdn out)	—	**1**	9/1 3	74	47
Night Mirage (USA) (MJohnston) **3-8-1** JFanning(1) (led: hdd over 1f out: edgd lft ins fnl f: r.o nr fin)	nk	**2**	1/3 1	69	22
Three Cheers (IRE) (JHMGosden) **3-8-6b1** JCarroll(2) (a.p: ev ch over 3f out: btn 2f out)	7	**3**	7/2 2	64	17
Get A Life (JohnHarris) **4-9-2**(5) JBramhill(4) (unf: bkwd: hld up & plld hrd: hdwy over 4f out: wknd 2f out)	4	**4**	50/1	54	27
Wellcome Inn (JohnHarris) **3-8-6** JO'Reilly(5) (bit bkwd: dwlt: hdwy 5f out: wknd over 2f out)	¾	**5**	50/1	58	11
Owdy (MrsNMacauley) **3-8-6** SSanders(3) (leggy: unf: chsd ldr tl rdn & wknd over 3f out)	dist	**6**	33/1	—	—
			(SP 114.1%)		**6 Rn**

2m 35.5 (7.00) CSF £11.93 TOTE £7.50: £1.50 £1.40 (£5.40) OWNER Mr P. W. Lambert (MELTON MOWBRAY) BRED Mrs M. Burrell

WEIGHT FOR AGE 3yo-21lb, 4yo-1lb

Kota finished sixth in a bumper less than a month ago, but found a dreadful maiden, and won it in courageous style. (9/1: 5/1-10/1)

Night Mirage (USA), the clear form choice, looked to have an easy task but appears something of a handful. Tricky to load, she edged off the rail to let the winner through and then drifted again in a tight finish. (1/3: op 4/6)

Three Cheers (IRE), blinkered and gelded after showing nothing on his debut, was easily brushed aside once an effort was required. (7/2: op 5/4)

Get A Life looked badly in need of the run and refused to settle, not doing too badly in the circumstances. (50/1)

Wellcome Inn made a move on the outside turning for home, but could not sustain it for long. (50/1)

559 SIMON DE MONTFORT MAIDEN STKS (3-Y.O+) (Class D)

5-10 (5-10) **1m 1f 218y** £4,123.35 (£1,234.80: £592.90: £271.95) Stalls: High GOING minus 0.20 sec per fur (GF)

			SP	RR	SF
Stanton Harcourt (USA) (89) (JLDunlop) **3-8-7** PatEddery(7) (lw: hld up & plld hrd: smooth hdwy to ld over 1f out: sn clr: easily)	—	**1**	1/2 1	77++	40
Surtsey (MJohnston) **3-8-7** MHills(3) (w'like: unf: led: shkn up & rn green over 4f out: hdd over 1f out: r.o)	2½	**2**	7/2 2	73	36
London's Heart (USA) (PFICole) **3-8-2** CRutter(4) (unf: hld up & plld hrd: hdwy 4f out: ev ch over 2f out: kpt on same pce)	¾	**3**	6/1 3	67	30
Mukhlles (USA) (BobJones) **4-9-12** NDay(5) (bkwd: bhd: pushed along 5f out: nvr nrr)	3	**4**	14/1	67	49
Charnwood Jack (USA) (60) (ICampbell) **4-9-12** RPrice(9) (bit bkwd: prom: rdn over 3f out: ev ch over 2f out: sn btn)	¾	**5**	33/1	66	48
Taswib (USA) (DMorley) **4-9-12** RCochrane(1) (leggy: bit bkwd: prom: rdn & ev ch 3f out: sn wknd)	¾	**6**	6/1 3	65	47
			(SP 127.1%)		**6 Rn**

2m 8.1 (4.40) CSF £3.14 TOTE £1.30: £1.20 £2.40 (£2.90) Trio £5.20 OWNER Mr Cyril Humphris (ARUNDEL) BRED Pamela H. Firman

WEIGHT FOR AGE 3yo-19lb

Stanton Harcourt (USA) looked a shade keen last season, and could not be settled over this longer trip. Winning with his head in his chest like this should do wonders for his confidence, but he will need to relax if he is to realise his full potential. (1/2)

Surtsey looked inexperienced, wandering around off the home turn, but stuck to his task, although the winner was laughing at him. (7/2)

London's Heart (USA), a good mover, proved rather keen and, having moved into a challenging position halfway up the straight, could only stay on at the one pace. (6/1: op 4/1)
Mukhlles (USA) finished third to Nash House at around this time last year, but had not run since and has changed hands cheaply in the interim. Looking far from fully fit and moving poorly, he never got into the race. (14/1: op 8/1)
Charnwood Jack (USA) shaped well for a mile and is not yet a lost cause. (33/1)
Taswib (USA), already gelded for his debut effort, did not show much promise. (6/1: op 4/1)

560 KIBWORTH H'CAP (0-85) (3-Y.O+) (Class D)
5-40 (5-40) **7f 9y** £3,868.55 (£1,156.40: £553.70: £252.35) Stalls: High GOING minus 0.31 sec per fur (GF)

				SP	RR	SF
483*	**Plaisir d'Amour (IRE) (79)** (NACallaghan) **3-8-9** 5x PatEddery(5) (lw: hld up: qcknd to ld 2f out: edgd rt over 1f out: hrd rdn fnl f: jst hld on)	—	**1**	4/6[1]	88	36
	Arterxerxes (80) (MJHeaton-Ellis) **4-9-10** AClark(1) (led tl hdd 2f out: r.o fnl f: jst failed)	s.h	**2**	12/1	89	51
448[8]	**Mujova (IRE) (83)** (RHollinshead) **3-8-10**(3) FLynch(3) (hdwy 3f out: rdn & ev ch 2f out: unable qckn ins fnl f)	nk	**3**	14/1	91	39
	Master M-E-N (IRE) (56) (NMBabbage) **5-7-9v**(5) RMullen(9) (in tch: rdn 3f out: kpt on wl fnl f)	nk	**4**	14/1	64	26
477[2]	**Victory Team (IRE) (68)** (GBBalding) **5-8-12** TQuinn(7) (hld up: hdwy 3f out: ev ch 2f out: btn whn n.m.r nr fin)	½	**5**	5/1[2]	74	36
	Safey Ana (USA) (59) (BHanbury) **6-8-0**(3) DO'Donohoe(6) (b: prom: wkng whn hmpd over 1f out: eased fnl f)	8	**6**	7/1[3]	47	9
443[21]	**Attarikh (IRE) (69)** (MrsALMKing) **4-8-13** MRoberts(2) (a bhd)	7	**7**	20/1	41	3
	Time of Night (USA) (67) (RGuest) **4-8-8**(3) DGriffiths(4) (w ldrs 4f)	14	**8**	14/1	8	—

(SP 121.6%) **8 Rn**

1m 25.2 (2.60) CSF £10.69 CT £67.36 TOTE £1.80: £1.10 £2.30 £1.30 (£11.10) Trio £32.10 OWNER Mr M. Tabor (NEWMARKET) BRED L. K. and K. McCreery
WEIGHT FOR AGE 3yo-14lb
483* Plaisir d'Amour (IRE) may have found this race coming too quickly, for she had to pull out all the stops. (4/6)
Arterxerxes made the running as usual, but battled back well in the final furlong and has certainly trained on. (12/1: op 6/1)
Mujova (IRE) did his best to challenge from the furlong pole, but may have edged fractionally off a true line as Victory Team was tightened up. (14/1: op 8/1)
Master M-E-N (IRE) has never been an easy horse to place, but likes this ground and looked a big danger entering the final furlong. (14/1)
477 Victory Team (IRE), one of five with a chance inside the final furlong, was probably going least well but certainly had least room. (5/1: 3/1-11/2)
Safey Ana (USA) showed speed on the far rails, but was fading when the winner took his ground. After that, he was eased down. (7/1)
Time of Night (USA) (14/1: 10/1-16/1)

T/Plpt: £1,219.40 (7.52 Tckts). T/Qdpt: £647.80 (1 Tckts) Dk

0561a - 0563a : (Irish Racing) - See Computer Raceform

0486-LINGFIELD (L-H) (Turf Firm, AW Standard)
Friday April 4th
WEATHER: fine WIND: fresh across

68 66+ 70 ~~65?~~ 62 (66)

564 E.B.F. TANDRIDGE MAIDEN STKS (2-Y.O) (Class D)
2-20 (2-22) **5f** £3,231.70 (£964.60: £460.80: £208.90) Stalls: High GOING: Not Established

				SP	RR	SF
447[8]	**Banningham Blade** (KTIvory) **2-8-6**(3) MartinDwyer(7) (s.i.s: swtchd lft sn after s: rdn 3f out: hdwy over 2f out: led wl ins fnl f: r.o)	—	**1**	33/1	68	34
	Loch Laird (MMadgwick) **2-9-0** DHarrison(3) (unf: s.i.s: sn rdn along: hdwy over 2f out: ev ch wl ins fnl f: r.o)	hd	**2**	33/1	73	39
	Flaming Ember (IRE) (BJMeehan) **2-9-0** MTebbutt(8) (w'like: bit bkwd: stdd s: hld up: hdwy 2f out: rdn & ev ch wl ins fnl f: r.o)	hd	**3**	5/1[3]	72	38
432[5]	**Days of Grace** (MartynMeade) **2-8-9** JReid(5) (led: hdd wl ins fnl f: unable qckn)	¾	**4**	11/8[1]	65	31
	Sacchetti (IRE) (MRChannon) **2-9-0** TQuinn(4) (cmpt: chsd ldrs: ev ch whn rdn & edgd lft over 1f out: eased whn btn ins fnl f)	8	**5**	5/1[3]	44	10
432[10]	**Suggest** (MissGayKelleway) **2-9-0** DHolland(6) (lw: chsd ldr: rdn & hung lft over 2f out: ev ch over 1f out: wknd appr fnl f)	3	**6**	9/4[2]	35	1
	Keyser Soze (DHaydnJones) **2-9-0** CRutter(2) (leggy: bit bkwd: a outpcd)	7	**7**	33/1	12	—

(SP 115.0%) **7 Rn**

59.37 secs (2.37) CSF £628.19 TOTE £30.00: £3.30 £5.40 (£69.20) OWNER Crown Select (RADLETT) BRED K. T. Ivory
Banningham Blade showed here the benefit that can be derived from a previous run. (33/1)
Loch Laird was ridden from the start. He forced his way into contention approaching the final furlong and just lost out in a driving finish. (33/1)
Flaming Ember (IRE) travelled well here and looked like scoring entering the final furlong, but lack of condition told late on. (5/1: 2/1-11/2)
432 Days of Grace put her previous experience to good use and showed the way until challenged approaching the final furlong. To her credit, she battled on gamely enough, but found a quickening touch beyond her. (11/8: 4/5-6/4)
Sacchetti (IRE) looked ill at ease on the ground when let down. (5/1: 7/4-11/2)
432 Suggest appeared to find this ground much too firm. (9/4)

565 BAKERS LANE MAIDEN STKS (3-Y.O+) (Class D)
2-55 (2-55) **6f** £3,677.45 (£1,097.60: £524.30: £237.65) Stalls: High GOING minus 0.21 sec per fur (GF)

				SP	RR	SF
	Intisab (RWArmstrong) **4-9-5** GCarter(4) (lw: chsd ldrs: pushed along 3f out: led over 2f out: rn green over 1f out: rdn ins fnl f: r.o wl)	—	**1**	4/7[1]	78	44
	Malabi (USA) (JLDunlop) **3-8-12** LDettori(6) (unf: lw: plld hrd: chsd ldrs: rdn 3f out: swtchd lft over 1f out: str chal ins fnl f: unable qckn nr fin)	½	**2**	5/1[2]	82	36
425[3]	**Deep Water (USA)** (PFICole) **3-8-12** TQuinn(3) (lw: plld hrd: led: hdd over 3f out: rdn & outpcd over 1f out: kpt on one pce ins fnl f)	4	**3**	13/2[3]	71	25

Cambridge Blue (USA) (GLewis) **3-8-9**(3) AWhelan(2) (leggy: w ldr: led over 3f out: hdd over 2f out: wknd ins fnl f)........nk **4** 13/2 3 70 24
William Wallace (77) (DHaydnJones) **3-8-12** CRutter(5) (dwlt: a outpcd)........8 **5** 20/1 49 3
Little Annie (GLMoore) **3-8-7** SWhitworth(1) (w'like: in tch tl wknd over 3f out)........7 **6** 50/1 25 —
(SP 113.7%) **6 Rn**

1m 11.83 (2.83) CSF £3.68 TOTE £1.80: £1.10 £2.40 (£4.10) OWNER Mr Hamdan Al Maktoum (NEWMARKET) BRED Shadwell Estate Company Limited
WEIGHT FOR AGE 3yo-12lb
OFFICIAL EXPLANATION **William Wallace: regarding the apparent tender handling, the colt was unsuited by the ground, had suffered from muscle problems, and needed further.**
Intisab had reportedly been working well at home and was backed accordingly, and she won this a shade more comfortably than the winning margin suggests. She found the ground plenty fast enough and ran green when sent about her business, but the runner-up's challenge spurred her into action in the final furlong and she was well on top at the finish. (4/7: evens-11/10)
Malabi (USA) ran well and looked dangerous when challenging inside the final furlong but, at the finish, was definitely second best. Nevertheless a race can be found. (5/1: 9/4-11/2)
425 Deep Water (USA) found this six furlongs too sharp. (13/2: op 3/1)
Cambridge Blue (USA) showed plenty of speed and can improve. (13/2: 3/1-7/1)

566 WEATHERBYS BULLETIN MAGAZINE H'CAP (0-70) (3-Y.O+) (Class E)
3-30 (3-32) **1m 2f (Equitrack)** £2,914.25 (£869.00: £414.50: £187.25) Stalls: Low GOING minus 0.35 sec per fur (FST)

SP RR SF

Anak-Ku (69) (MissGayKelleway) **4-9-7**(7) AngelaGallimore(1) (b: b.hind: mde all: drvn out)........— **1** 14/1 80 52
352[5] **Paronomasia (40)** (JLHarris) **5-7-6**(7)ow3 RFfrench(3) (lw: chsd wnr 2f out: in tch & rdn 6f out: styd on to go 2nd again ins fnl f)........½ **2** 33/1 50 19
305[2] **Shanghai Lil (55)** (MJFetherston-Godley) **5-9-0** FNorton(5) (chsd ldrs: rdn & lost pl 5f out: rallied over 1f out: styd on wl ins fnl f)........1¼ **3** 8/1 63 35
346[5] **Harlequin Walk (IRE) (45)** (RJO'Sullivan) **6-8-4** JQuinn(4) (hld up in tch: chsd wnr over 1f out tl ins fnl f: one pce)........½ **4** 14/1 52 24
457* **Sweet Supposin (IRE) (67)** (CADwyer) **6-9-12v** 5x LDettori(7) (lw: hld up: sme hdwy 3f out: rdn 2f out: one pce)........1¼ **5** 15/8 1 72 44
457[3] **Tallulah Belle (67)** (NPLittmoden) **4-9-12** TGMcLaughlin(8) (lw: hld up: hdwy 5f out: hrd rdn 3f out: staying on whn n.m.r ins fnl f: nt rcvr)........hd **6** 4/1 2 72 44
400[3] **Calendula (58)** (DMorley) **4-9-3** GCarter(2) (chsd wnr 8f out tl over 1f out: wknd ins fnl f)........½ **7** 13/2 3 62 34
405[9] **Digpast (IRE) (69)** (MMadgwick) **7-10-0b** DHarrison(6) (hld up in tch: rdn over 2f out: wknd over 1f out: eased ins fnl f)........6 **8** 12/1 64 36
487* **Awesome Power (55)** (JWHills) **11-9-0** 5x AClark(9) (a bhd)........9 **9** 12/1 35 7
383[2] **Tuigamala (58)** (RIngram) **6-9-3** AMcGlone(10) (lw: a bhd)........2 **10** 12/1 35 7
(SP 118.6%) **10 Rn**

2m 8.2 (3.90) CSF £355.83 CT £3,553.44 TOTE £19.60: £5.40 £6.30 £1.10 (£154.50) Trio £350.50; £123.44 to Aintree 5/4/97 OWNER H R H Sultan Ahmad Shah (WHITCOMBE) BRED John Rose
LONG HANDICAP Paronomasia 7-4
OFFICIAL EXPLANATION **Sweet Supposin (IRE): no explanation offered.**
Anak-Ku made all under a fine ride. (14/1: 8/1-16/1)
352 Paronomasia was ridden throughout the final half of the race and, to his credit, kept staying on. (33/1)
305 Shanghai Lil lost a prominent position at halfway and, though staying on gamely in the final furlong, could never make up the lost ground. (8/1: 6/1-9/1)
283* Harlequin Walk (IRE) looked dangerous turning for home, but could not find a change of gear. (14/1)
457* Sweet Supposin (IRE) was making heavy weather of it in the final two furlongs. (15/8)
457 Tallulah Belle was staying on under pressure when short of room inside the last, and would have fought out the minor places. (4/1)

567 LIGHTWEIGHT PLASTERING H'CAP (0-80) (3-Y.O+) (Class D)
4-05 (4-06) **7f** £3,964.10 (£1,185.80: £568.40: £259.70) Stalls: High GOING minus 0.21 sec per fur (GF)

SP RR SF

490* **Barbason (56)** (GLMoore) **5-8-6** 6x CandyMorris(6) (lw: plld hrd: a.p: rdn to ld ins fnl f: r.o wl)........— **1** 4/1 2 68 52
403* **Ertlon (70)** (CEBrittain) **7-9-6** MRoberts(3) (lw: led: hdd ins fnl f: unable qckn)........1½ **2** 7/2 1 79 63
514[7] **Rakis (IRE) (78)** (MrsLStubbs) **7-10-0** LDettori(8) (hld up: rdn 2f out: r.o ins fnl f)........s.h **3** 7/2 1 87 71
Statoyork (65) (BWHills) **4-9-1** MHills(7) (lw: hld up: n.m.r over 2f out: hdwy over 1f out: kpt on one pce ins fnl f)........¾ **4** 7/2 1 72 56
Natural Key (71) (DHaydnJones) **4-9-7** CRutter(4) (bit bkwd: chsd ldr: rdn 1f out: wknd ins fnl f)........1 **5** 12/1 76 60
Saltando (IRE) (58) (PatMitchell) **6-8-5**(3) MartinDwyer(2) (rdn thrght: in tch tl wknd over 2f out)........7 **6** 20/1 47 31
363[9] **Banzhaf (USA) (72)** (GLMoore) **4-9-8** GDuffield(1) (lw: plld hrd: chsd ldrs: rdn 3f out: wknd 2f out)........1¼ **7** 9/2 3 58 42
(SP 117.3%) **7 Rn**

1m 22.92 (1.72) CSF £17.44 CT £48.91 TOTE £5.50: £2.60 £1.40 (£6.70) OWNER Mr F. L. Hill (BRIGHTON) BRED Sheikh Mohammed bin Rashid al Maktoum
490* Barbason, well treated on his All-Weather form, showed himself just as good on the Turf and ran out a ready winner. (4/1: 5/2-9/2)
403* Ertlon tried to make all but could not keep the well-handicapped winner at bay. (7/2: op 2/1)
257* Rakis (IRE) stayed on under pressure in the final furlong. (7/2)
Statoyork was put to sleep at the back. He had no room to manoeuvre when wanting to improve over two furlongs out but, once he found daylight, he could only stay on at the one speed. (7/2)
Natural Key showed up for six furlongs and the race should have brought her on. (12/1: 8/1-14/1)

568 HEVER MEDIAN AUCTION MAIDEN STKS (3-Y.O) (Class F)
4-40 (4-41) **1m 2f (Equitrack)** £2,277.00 (£627.00: £297.00) Stalls: Low GOING minus 0.35 sec per fur (FST)

SP RR SF

Davoski (BWHills) **3-9-0** MHills(7) (b.hind: hld up in tch: led over 1f out: pushed clr ins fnl f: comf)........— **1** 5/2 2 77+ 40
Protocol (IRE) (73) (JWHills) **3-9-0** DHolland(5) (led: rdn over 2f out: hdd over 1f out: one pce)........1¾ **2** 11/8 1 74 37
350[2] **Around Fore Alliss (65)** (TGMills) **3-9-0** SSanders(1) (s.i.s: sn in tch: rdn & ev ch over 1f out: one pce)........nk **3** 10/1 74 37
455[3] **Farley Mount** (LordHuntingdon) **3-9-0** DHarrison(3) (lw: chsd ldrs: rdn & outpcd over 4f out: rallied over 1f out: styd on ins fnl f)........1¼ **4** 7/1 72 35

	Horse / details	Dist	Pos	SP	RR	SF
	Eileen's Lady (GGMargarson) **3-8-9** GCarter(4) (leggy: hld up: hdwy 5f out: rdn 3f out: wknd 2f out)	6	**5**	9/2[3]	57	20
	Flashtalkin' Flood (CADwyer) **3-9-0** JStack(6) (w'like: in tch tl wknd over 3f out: t.o)	20	**6**	25/1	30	—
	Heavenly Hand (GLMoore) **3-8-9** CandyMorris(2) (prom 4f: sn wknd: t.o)	25	**7**	33/1	—	—

(SP 117.2%) **7 Rn**

2m 8.05 (3.75) CSF £6.02 TOTE £2.60: £1.40 £2.10 (£2.60) OWNER Mr Robert Ogden (LAMBOURN) BRED Sir Eric Parker
Davoski, despite drifting in the betting, won this readily. (5/2: op 4/5)
Protocol (IRE) made a brave effort to make all, but was comfortably put in his place by the winner. (11/8)
350 Around Fore Alliss missed the kick, but this made no difference and, after having every chance early in the straight, he was readily put in his place by the winner. (10/1: 5/1-14/1)
455 Farley Mount ran here as though further would suit. (7/1: 5/1-8/1)
Eileen's Lady (9/2: 8/1-12/1)

569 LINGFIELD APRIL SPRINT H'CAP (0-80) (3-Y.O+) (Class D)

5-10 (5-12) **6f (Equitrack)** £3,677.45 (£1,097.60: £524.30: £237.65) Stalls: Low GOING minus 0.35 sec per fur (FST)

	Horse / details	Dist	Pos	SP	RR	SF
459[2]	**Apollo Red (72)** (GLMoore) **8-9-8** CandyMorris(9) (a.p: led 3f out: clr over 1f out: r.o wl)	—	**1**	6/1	85	51
406[5]	**Robo Magic (USA) (77)** (LMontagueHall) **5-9-10**(3) FLynch(10) (rr: hdwy 3f out: rdn 2f out: styd on to go 2nd ins fnl f)	2½	**2**	6/1	83	49
459[6]	**Intiaash (IRE) (70)** (DHaydnJones) **5-8-13**(7) JoeleneRichards(5) (rr: hdwy 2f out: styd on ins fnl f)	¾	**3**	25/1	74	40
520[16]	**Friendly Brave (USA) (68)** (MissGayKelleway) **7-9-4** DHolland(1) (b: b.hind: lw: led 1f: rdn & outpcd over 2f out: rallied ins fnl f: r.o)	½	**4**	6/1	71	37
459[5]	**Sharp Imp (62)** (RMFlower) **7-8-12b** LDettori(4) (sn pushed along in mid div: hdwy to go 2nd 1f out: hrd rdn ins fnl f: one pce)	hd	**5**	7/2[2]	65	31
403[4]	**Purple Fling (66)** (LGCottrell) **6-9-2** RCochrane(11) (rr: sn rdn along: hdwy 2f out: n.m.r over 1f out: kpt on one pce ins fnl f: eased cl home)	2	**6**	3/1[1]	63	29
443[20]	**Kildee Lad (78)** (APJones) **7-10-0** TSprake(12) (nvr nrr)	2½	**7**	25/1	69	35
488[3]	**Ivory's Grab Hire (51)** (KTIvory) **4-7-12b**(3) MartinDwyer(8) (spd 3f: wknd over 1f out)	1	**8**	5/1[3]	39	5
348[3]	**Sir Tasker (47)** (JLHarris) **9-7-11** JQuinn(2) (lw: led after 1f: hdd 3f out: wknd over 1f out)	1½	**9**	10/1	31	—
448[22]	**Blazing Castle (78)** (WGMTurner) **3-8-9**(7) DMcGaffin(3) (bhd fnl 4f)	2½	**10**	16/1	55	9
320[6]	**Nightingale Song (69)** (MartynMeade) **3-8-7** JReid(6) (prom over 2f)	2½	**11**	12/1	40	—
339[3]	**Tachycardia (46)** (RJO'Sullivan) **5-7-10** NVarley(7) (sn rdn along in mid div: wknd over 3f out)	1	**12**	16/1	14	—

(SP 143.0%) **12 Rn**

1m 12.88 (1.78) CSF £46.69 CT £829.76 TOTE £5.00: £1.30 £4.00 £9.00 (£18.60) Trio £157.20 OWNER Mr A. Moore (BRIGHTON) BRED Crest Stud Ltd
WEIGHT FOR AGE 3yo-12lb
459 Apollo Red continued his trainer's rich vein of form with an emphatic success. (6/1)
406 Robo Magic (USA) struggled with the early pace, but kept on well up the straight to grab second. (6/1)
459 Intiaash (IRE) was another to do her best work in the closing stages. (25/1)
459 Sharp Imp was ridden throughout and, after briefly going second below the distance, found any further effort beyond him. (7/2: 5/1-3/1)
403 Purple Fling (3/1: op 6/1)
348 Sir Tasker (10/1: 8/1-12/1)

T/Plpt: £10,649.70 (0.6 Tckts); £5,835.49 to Aintree 5/4/97. T/Qdpt: £27.00 (42.21 Tckts) SM

BEVERLEY (R-H) (Good to firm)

Saturday April 5th

WEATHER: overcast WIND: str half against

570 VALENTINES (S) STKS (4-Y.O+) (Class G)

2-00 (2-00) **1m 3f 216y** £2,337.50 (£650.00: £312.50) Stalls: High GOING minus 0.33 sec per fur (GF)

	Horse / details	Dist	Pos	SP	RR	SF
	Champagne Warrior (IRE) (46) (MJCamacho) **4-8-7** LCharnock(6) (blind off eye: chsd ldrs: led over 2f out: hld on wl towards fin)	—	**1**	11/2	45	30
486[3]	**Bedouin Prince (USA) (36)** (MrsLStubbs) **10-8-13** KFallon(1) (b.nr fore: drvn along 7f out: hdwy over 3f out: chal over 1f out: nt qckn towards fin)	hd	**2**	16/1	50	36
	Portite Sophie (25) (MBrittain) **6-8-6**(7) DMernagh(9) (trckd ldrs: ev ch over 1f out: kpt on same pce)	1¾	**3**	40/1	48	34
	Risky Rose (42) (RHollinshead) **5-8-10**(3) DGriffiths(10) (lw: mid div: hdwy over 3f out: nt qckn appr fnl f)	nk	**4**	14/1	47	33
	Charity Crusader (MrsMReveley) **6-8-13** ACulhane(4) (hld up: hdwy on outside over 3f out: edgd rt over 1f out: nvr rchd ldrs)	1¼	**5**	4/1[3]	46	32
	Jackmanii (40) (JBerry) **5-8-13** NCarlisle(5) (bkwd: hld up: styd on fnl 3f: nvr nr to chal)	3½	**6**	14/1	41	27
465[9]	**Ship's Dancer (37)** (DonEnricoIncisa) **4-8-7b** KimTinkler(12) (lw: s.i.s: bhd: hrd rdn over 2f out: kpt on: nvr rchd ldrs)	1¼	**7**	50/1	34	19
	Brodessa (62) (MrsMReveley) **11-9-4** KDarley(2) (bit bkwd: in tch: effrt over 3f out: sn chsng ldrs: wknd over 1f out)	4	**8**	2/1[1]	39	25
	Philgem (20) (CWFairhurst) **4-8-7** NKennedy(7) (bit bkwd: dwlt: hdwy over 3f out: lost pl over 1f out)	5	**9**	33/1	22	7
	Ttyfran (32) (BPJBaugh) **7-8-13** RPerham(3) (b: w ldrs tl wknd over 3f out)	3	**10**	33/1	23	9
435[6]	**Loveyoumillions (IRE) (65)** (NTinkler) **5-8-13** PatEddery(11) (lw: led tl over 2f out: wknd & eased: b.b.v)	15	**11**	3/1[2]	3	—
	The Black Dubh (IRE) (33) (JJQuinn) **4-8-12** JQuinn(8) (w ldrs tl lost pl over 3f out)	16	**12**	25/1	—	—

(SP 127.1%) **12 Rn**

2m 38.5 (5.50) CSF £82.43 TOTE £8.60: £1.90 £3.20 £5.60 (£84.10) Trio £219.40; £71.10 to Southwell 7/4/97 OWNER M K Slinger & A Stuart (MALTON) BRED Dr Peter C. Yorke
WEIGHT FOR AGE 4yo-1lb
No bid
OFFICIAL EXPLANATION Loveyoumillions (IRE): bled from the nose.
Champagne Warrior (IRE) who has no right eye, held on bravely. (11/2)
486 Bedouin Prince (USA), fit from the sand, was only just denied. (16/1)
Portite Sophie, who has won just one of her thirty-four starts, ran as well as could be expected. She would have been 20lb better off with the winner in a handicap. (40/1)

Risky Rose, who has two ways of running, is better over further. (14/1)
Charity Crusader, absent since being narrowly beaten in a novice handicap hurdle at Hexham a year ago, was turned out in good trim. Edging right under pressure, this will have done his handicap mark no harm and he ought to be capable of better. (4/1: op 5/2)
Jackmanii (14/1: 10/1-16/1)
Brodessa looked and ran as if need of the outing. (2/1)
Loveyoumillions (IRE) went out like a light, and it transpired that he had broken a blood-vessel. (3/1: 2/1-100/30)

571 BECHERS BROOK H'CAP (0-70) (3-Y.O+) (Class E)

2-30 (2-32) **7f 100y** £3,286.50 (£987.00: £476.00: £220.50) Stalls: High GOING minus 0.33 sec per fur (GF)

				SP	RR	SF
468^{2}	**Gulf Shaadi (59)** (EJAlston) **5-9-3** SDrowne(16) (lw: trckd ldrs: led wl over 1f out: jst hld on)	—	1	$8/1^{3}$	68	51
468^{3}	**Rambo Waltzer (65)** (DNicholls) **5-9-2**(7) IonaWands(14) (lw: mid div: hdwy 2f out: styd on wl fnl f: jst failed)	s.h	2	$100/30^{2}$	74	57
468^{4}	**Genuine John (IRE) (67)** (JParkes) **4-9-11** RCochrane(4) (lw: hld up: gd hdwy over 2f out: kpt on same pce appr fnl f)	2	3	14/1	72	55
	Power Game (60) (JBerry) **4-9-4b** KDarley(10) (hld up: styd on fnl 2f: nt rch ldrs)	2	4	10/1	60	43
482^{7}	**Scenicris (IRE) (65)** (RHollinshead) **4-9-6**(3) FLynch(3) (lw: mid div: kpt on fnl 2f: nvr rchd ldrs)	1¼	5	20/1	63	46
319^{7}	**Lachesis (50)** (DShaw) **4-8-5b¹**(3) CTeague(2) (hld up & bhd: styd on wl fnl 2f: nvr nr to chal)	2½	6	25/1	42	25
477^{8}	**Perilous Plight (59)** (MrsLStubbs) **6-9-3** KFallon(15) (mid div: kpt on fnl 2f: nvr rchd ldrs)	nk	7	14/1	51	34
	Edgar Kirby (53) (PWHarris) **6-8-11** PatEddery(17) (led tl wl over 1f out: sn wknd)	s.h	8	12/1	45	28
435^{19}	**Mybotye (70)** (RBastiman) **4-9-9**(5) HBastiman(11) (hld up: sme hdwy 2f out: nvr nr to chal)	1¾	9	20/1	58	41
444^{13}	**La Volta (69)** (JGFitzGerald) **4-9-13** JFortune(13) (in tch: effrt over 2f out: grad wknd)	¾	10	10/1	55	38
529*	**Three Arch Bridge (67)** (MJohnston) **5-9-11b** 6x JWeaver(9) (s.i.s: a in rr)	2½	11	$3/1^{1}$	48	31
	Euro Sceptic (IRE) (56) (TDEasterby) **5-8-11b**(3) RHavlin(12) (bit bkwd: chsd ldrs tl wknd 2f out)	1½	12	12/1	34	17
	Godmersham Park (66) (PSFelgate) **5-9-10** GDuffield(5) (s.i.s: a bhd)	½	13	20/1	43	26
	Thatched (IRE) (51) (REBarr) **7-8-2**(7) KSked(7) (bit bkwd: sme hdwy on outside over 2f out: sn wknd)	s.h	14	14/1	27	10
336^{4}	**Serape (58)** (MrsLStubbs) **4-9-2** JFEgan(8) (b: chsd ldrs tl wknd over 2f out)	4	15	33/1	26	9
	Tinklers Folly (64) (RMWhitaker) **5-9-8** DeanMcKeown(6) (bit bkwd: chsd ldrs tl lost pl over 2f out)	½	16	20/1	31	14
	Superpride (60) (MrsMReveley) **5-9-4** ACulhane(1) (racd wd: chsd ldrs tl lost pl 3f out)	s.h	17	14/1	27	10

(SP 145.3%) **17 Rn**

1m 34.2 (2.20) CSF £34.19 CT £386.39 TOTE £8.50: £1.60 £1.20 £2.40 £2.20 (£15.20) Trio £16.20 OWNER The Bibby Halliday Partnership (PRESTON) BRED Sheikh Mohammed bin Rashid al Maktoum
OFFICIAL EXPLANATION **Three Arch Bridge: the mare started slowly, was unable to get into the race early on due to lack of luck in running, but stayed on in the closing stages.**
468 Gulf Shaadi is running really well at present, but the post came just in time. (8/1)
468 Rambo Waltzer was reeling in the winner all the way through the last furlong, but needed one more stride. (100/30)
468 Genuine John (IRE), badly drawn here, is running really well at present. (14/1)
Power Game ran a satisfactory first race. (10/1)
273 Lachesis, tried in blinkers for the first time, took a keen grip before running on nicely at the finish under a quiet ride. She is not without ability. (25/1)
Edgar Kirby (12/1: op 8/1)
Mybotye was not knocked about at any stage. (20/1)
529* Three Arch Bridge missed the break slightly and never gave her supporters any hope. (3/1: op 5/1)
Euro Sceptic (IRE) (12/1: op 7/1)
80 61 73

572 CHAIR MAIDEN AUCTION STKS (2-Y.O F) (Class F)

3-00 (3-00) **5f** £2,742.00 (£762.00: £366.00) Stalls: High GOING minus 0.33 sec per fur (GF)

				SP	RR	SF
500^{3}	**Classy Cleo (IRE)** (RHannon) **2-8-9** PatEddery(1) (swtg: chsd ldrs: styd on appr fnl f: led towards fin)	—	1	$6/4^{1}$	79	—
492^{2}	**Heavenly Abstone** (PDEvans) **2-8-2v¹** JFEgan(10) (lw: led: clr over 1f out: hdd towards fin)	¾	2	$13/8^{2}$	70	—
492^{5}	**Inchalong** (MBrittain) **2-8-4** GBardwell(7) (sn outpcd & drvn along: hdwy & hrd rdn 2f out: edgd lft: nvr nr to chal)	7	3	16/1	49	—
	Summerseat (CWFairhurst) **2-8-3** DeanMcKeown(4) (leggy: s.i.s: sn chsng ldrs: wknd over 1f out)	2	4	11/1	42	—
	Ellenbrook (IRE) (JBerry) **2-8-5** KDarley(2) (leggy: scope: chsd ldrs: outpcd ½-wy: n.d after)	1¼	5	$4/1^{3}$	40	—
	Blitz (MWEasterby) **2-8-1** DaleGibson(6) (w'like: scope: bit bkwd: rn green & sn bhd: sme hdwy over 1f out: nvr nr ldrs)	nk	6	14/1	35	—
	Daynabee (NTinkler) **2-8-1** KimTinkler(9) (unf: w ldrs: hung lft & lost pl ½-wy)	4	7	20/1	22	—
	Skippool Creek (IRE) (TDEasterby) **2-8-5** MBirch(5) (w'like: bit bkwd: s.i.s: a bhd)	4	8	11/1	13	—
	Companys Gamble (BPJBaugh) **2-8-5**ow3 ACulhane(8) (leggy: scope: bit bkwd: hld up & plld hrd: stumbled after 100y: sn lost pl)	3	9	33/1	4	—

(SP 135.0%) **9 Rn**

67.0 secs (5.20) CSF £4.74 TOTE £2.10: £1.10 £1.50 £3.10 (£3.00) Trio £10.50 OWNER Mrs A. Kane (MARLBOROUGH) BRED Rathasker Stud
500 Classy Cleo (IRE), the most experienced in the field, was warm beforehand. Sticking on under pressure, she got up near the line and will appreciate a step-up to six furlongs. (6/4)
492 Heavenly Abstone, tried in a visor, showed in a clear lead over a furlong out. Racing into a strong headwind, she was worn down near the line. (13/8: 9/4-6/4)
492 Inchalong, who was well beaten first time, was given a hard race here. (16/1)
Summerseat, who is on the leg, missed the break slightly and became tired in the final furlong. (11/1: 7/1-12/1)
Ellenbrook (IRE) was run off her legs at halfway. (4/1)
Blitz, a backward-looking newcomer, did not shape too badly. (14/1)
Skippool Creek (IRE) (11/1: 6/1-12/1)

573 EAST RIDING CONDITIONS STKS (3-Y.O+) (Class C)

3-30 (3-30) **5f** £4,648.00 (£1,732.00: £841.00: £355.00: £152.50: £71.50) Stalls: High GOING minus 0.33 sec per fur (GF)

				SP	RR	SF
	Bolshoi (IRE) (99) (JBerry) **5-9-2b** EmmaO'Gorman(2) (sn outpcd: hdwy ½-wy: led 1f out: rdn clr)	—	1	$9/4^{2}$	108	45
443^{8}	**Cretan Gift (83)** (NPLittmoden) **6-9-2b** TGMcLaughlin(5) (sn outpcd & drvn along: styd on wl appr fnl f: no ch w wnr)	5	2	14/1	92	29

	Brave Edge (106) (RHannon) **6-9-10** PatEddery(4) (sn drvn along: hdwy & swtchd lft over 1f out: nvr nr to chal) 1¾	3	2/1 1	94	31
	Westcourt Magic (101) (MWEasterby) **4-9-10** KDarley(6) (lw: led over 1f: led over 1f out: sn hdd & wknd) ....½	4	4/1 3	93	30
	Ya Malak (97) (DNicholls) **6-9-2** AlexGreaves(3) (bit bkwd: plld hrd: led over 3f out tl over 1f out: wknd) 2½	5	7/1	77	14
	Anotheranniversary (GLewis) **4-8-11** PaulEddery(1) (bit bkwd: b.off hind: trckd ldrs: effrt & hung rt over 1f out: sn wknd) 2½	6	7/1	64	1
			(SP 115.8%)	**6 Rn**	

63.6 secs (1.80) CSF £29.01 TOTE £3.40: £1.80 £4.10 (£12.20) OWNER Mrs David Brown (COCKERHAM) BRED David John Brown
Bolshoi (IRE), who likes to come from off the pace, took this in fine style. (9/4)
397 Cretan Gift would have been meeting the winner on 16lb better terms in a handicap. Putting in his best work at the finish, he is definitely better over six furlongs. (14/1: 10/1-16/1)
Brave Edge looked backward in his coat and will come on for the outing. (2/1)
Westcourt Magic, who looked very fit, usually runs well first time. He showed all his old speed here. (4/1)
Ya Malak, having his first outing for his new trainer, looked on the burly side. Racing really keenly, he faded coming to the final furlong but, when connections get him sorted out, no doubt there is a nice race to be won with him. (7/1)
Anotheranniversary, who did not run at three, has an awkward head carriage and ran here as if needing the outing, dropping right out coming to the final furlong. (7/1: 9/2-8/1)

574 MELLING ROAD H'CAP (0-60) (3-Y.O+) (Class F)
4-15 (4-16) **1m 1f 207y** £3,162.00 (£882.00: £426.00) Stalls: High GOING minus 0.33 sec per fur (GF)

			SP	RR	SF
	Brambles Way (50) (MrsMReveley) **8-8-13**(5) SCopp(5) (lw: mde all: clr 2f out: hld on towards fin) ....—	1	7/1 2	60	39
	Jean Pierre (53) (JPearce) **4-9-7** LDettori(7) (lw: bhd: hdwy 2f out: styd on wl fnl f: nt rch wnr) ....½	2	15/2 3	62	41
	Petit Flora (38) (GHolmes) **5-8-6** JFortune(11) (b.off hind: mid div: styd on wl fnl 2f: nt rch ldrs) 1¾	3	50/1	44	23
	Augustan (53) (SGollings) **6-9-7** PatEddery(9) (in tch: effrt over 2f out: kpt on wl fnl f) ....½	4	7/1 2	59	38
	Flyaway Blues (43) (MrsMReveley) **5-8-11** ACulhane(16) (lw: hld up & bhd: effrt & nt clr run over 2f out: styd on wl fnl f) 1¼	5	12/1	47	26
	Clued Up (47) (PDEvans) **4-9-1v** JFEgan(13) (a in tch: kpt on same pce fnl 2f) ....½	6	14/1	50	29
*18*8	**Blue Domain (40)** (RCraggs) **6-8-8** LCharnock(6) (in tch: effrt 2f out: kpt on one pce) ....hd	7	33/1	43	22
*516*5	**Ambidextrous (IRE) (49)** (EJAlston) **5-9-3** KFallon(15) (lw: sn bhd: hdwy on outside over 2f out: edgd rt: nvr nr ldrs) 1½	8	5/2 1	49	28
	Sandblaster (50) (JLEyre) **4-9-4** TWilliams(19) (s.i.s: hld up & plld hrd: hdwy over 2f out: edgd rt & stumbled over 1f out) ....hd	9	16/1	50	29
*356*6	**Anistop (45)** (JLEyre) **5-8-13** RLappin(14) (trckd ldrs tl wknd fnl 2f) ....nk	10	12/1	45	24
	Stolen Music (IRE) (52) (REBarr) **4-9-6** DeanMcKeown(8) (s.s: sme hdwy over 2f out: edgd rt ins fnl f: n.d) 1	11	33/1	50	29
430 9	**Kilnamartyra Girl (40)** (JParkes) **7-8-3**(5) JBramhill(3) (b.hind: mid div: hdwy u.p over 2f out: sltly hmpd ins fnl f: n.d) 1	12	10/1	36	15
*295*8	**Cuban Reef (44)** (WJMusson) **5-8-12** JLMartinez(2) (nvr nr to chal) ....½	13	11/1	40	19
*424*11	**Bogart (43)** (CWFairhurst) **6-8-11** RCochrane(1) (bhd: sme hdwy on outside 2f out: n.d) ....½	14	20/1	38	17
*340*8	**Lila Pedigo (IRE) (60)** (MissJFCraze) **4-10-0** SWebster(12) (trckd ldrs: n.m.r & lost pl 2f out) ....½	15	20/1	54	33
	Snowy Mantle (45) (JDBethell) **4-8-13** SDrowne(4) (racd wd: in tch: effrt over 2f out: sn wknd) 3	16	14/1	34	13
	Summer Princess (40) (GFierro) **4-8-8** GDuffield(10) (chsd ldrs tl lost pl over 2f out) 2	17	25/1	26	5
	Cottage Prince (IRE) (41) (JJQuinn) **4-8-9** JQuinn(17) (bhd: sme hdwy whn hmpd & stumbled over 1f out: eased) 14	18	14/1	4	—
	Khabar (58) (RBastiman) **4-9-7**(5) HBastiman(18) (unruly gng to s: a in rr: eased fnl f) 12	19	20/1	2	—
			(SP 150.0%)	**19 Rn**	

2m 7.6 (4.50) CSF £60.35 CT £2,385.59 TOTE £10.60: £2.20 £3.30 £20.20 £2.90 (£56.90) Trio Not won; £541.00 to Southwell 7/4/97 OWNER Mr Nigel Jones (SALTBURN) BRED W. P. S. Johnson
Brambles Way, much improved over hurdles winning three times in blinkers and usually coming from behind, set a strong gallop and, despite wandering in the strong headwind, was never going to be overhauled. (7/1: 5/1-8/1)
Jean Pierre, who ran badly on his final three outings last time, made significant ground on the wide outside, but was never going to quite overhaul the winner. (15/2)
Petit Flora, a National Hunt Flat race winner, will be suited by a step-up in distance. (50/1)
Augustan, putting in his best work at the finish, is better suited by a mile-and-a-half. (7/1)
Flyaway Blues, still a maiden on the Flat, has shown improvement over hurdles this winter. Having no run at all, he would not have been far away with better luck, and it is only a question of time before he opens his account on the level. (12/1: op 8/1)
516 Ambidextrous (IRE) looked really well but, getting well behind, had to make his effort on the wide outside and, edging right in the strong wind, he was never going to take a hand. Though he did not have the run of the race, a mile-and-a-quarter is probably on the sharp side for him. (5/2: op 9/2)
Snowy Mantle (14/1: 10/1-16/1)

575 GRAND NATIONAL DAY H'CAP (0-85) (3-Y.O) (Class D)
4-45 (4-49) **1m 100y** £3,769.00 (£1,132.00: £546.00: £253.00) Stalls: High GOING minus 0.33 sec per fur (GF)

			SP	RR	SF
	Blooming Amazing (72) (JLEyre) **3-8-9** TWilliams(14) (bit bkwd: mde all: styd on wl fnl 2f: unchal) ....—	1	16/1	82	31
509 5	**Kaiser Kache (IRE) (80)** (KMcAuliffe) **3-9-3** JFEgan(5) (swtg: sn chsng wnr: kpt on fnl f: nvr able to chal) 1¾	2	12/1	87	36
448 5	**Sandbaggedagain (75)** (MWEasterby) **3-8-7**(5) GParkin(10) (lw: hld up: hdwy ½-wy: rdn over 2f out: styd on ins fnl f) 1½	3	8/1	79	28
502 6	**Get The Point (78)** (RHollinshead) **3-9-1** KFallon(12) (lw: chsd ldrs: effrt & hung lft over 1f out: kpt on same pce) 1¾	4	11/1	79	28
	High Spirits (IRE) (63) (TDEasterby) **3-8-0** LCharnock(11) (bit bkwd: s.i.s: bhd: styd on fnl 2f: nvr nrr) 6	5	16/1	52	1
*513*8	**Jack The Lad (IRE) (63)** (JHetherton) **3-8-0** NKennedy(3) (sn bhd: sme hdwy 2f out: nvr nr ldrs) ....½	6	20/1	51	—
*388**	**Globetrotter (IRE) (76)** (MJohnston) **3-8-13** JWeaver(4) (lw: in tch: effrt over 2f out: no imp) ....hd	7	9/2 2	64	13
448 9	**Mungo Park (68)** (MrsJRRamsden) **3-8-5** JFortune(9) (lw: bhd: drvn along 3f out: kpt on appr fnl f: n.d) ....½	8	6/1 3	55	4
462 4	**Move The Clouds (59)** (DNicholls) **3-7-3**(7) IonaWands(1) (plld hrd: w ldrs: edgd rt & wknd 2f out) ....½	9	20/1	45	—
448 10	**Rum Lad (65)** (JJQuinn) **3-8-2** JQuinn(6) (in tch: effrt over 2f out: sn lost pl) 2	10	20/1	47	—
*513*2	**Mutahadeth (66)** (DShaw) **3-8-3** JFanning(2) (lw: b: in tch: effrt on outside over 2f out: sn wknd) 3½	11	10/1	42	—
448 15	**Fullopep (69)** (MrsMReveley) **3-8-6** KDarley(8) (in tch: effrt over 2f out: sn wknd) 3	12	16/1	39	—

				SP	RR	SF
	Kafaf (USA) (82) (JHMGosden) **3-9-5** LDettori(7) (Withdrawn not under Starter's orders: v.unruly bef s & ref to ent stalls)		**W**	13/8[1]	—	—

(SP 138.7%) **12 Rn**

1m 47.8 (3.80) CSF £96.15 CT £451.68 TOTE £14.00: £4.20 £3.50 £2.10 (£67.90) Trio £55.80 OWNER C H & D W Stephenson Ltd (HAMBLETON) BRED A. Surgay

LONG HANDICAP Move The Clouds 7-6

Blooming Amazing, despite looking on the burly side, made every post a winning one. Those who raced away from the running rail could make no impression whatsoever in the strong headwind. (16/1)

509 Kaiser Kache (IRE), in the first three throughout, seemed to appreciate the drop back in distance. (12/1: op 8/1)

448 Sandbaggedagain, under pressure some way from home, was staying on when it was all over and is worth a try over a mile-and-a-half. (8/1: op 5/1)

436 Get The Point ducked and dived under pressure. (11/1: 8/1-12/1)

High Spirits (IRE), who looked in need of the outing, stayed on late in the day. (16/1)

T/Plpt: £563.70 (27.13 Tckts). T/Qdpt: £35.60 (24.44 Tckts) WG

0542-SOUTHWELL (L-H) (Standard)

Monday April 7th

WEATHER: fine & sunny WIND: almost nil

576 KING ARTHUR MEDIAN AUCTION MAIDEN STKS (3-Y.O) (Class F)

2-15 (2-17) **7f (Fibresand)** £2,277.00 (£627.00: £297.00) Stalls: Low GOING: Not Established

				SP	RR	SF
	Water Garden (GWragg) **3-9-0** MHills(7) (dwlt: hdwy on outside ½-wy: chal 2f out: edgd lft & led ins fnl f: jst hld on)	—	**1**	7/2[2]	61	29
	Mr Paradise (IRE) (69) (TJNaughton) **3-9-0** DHolland(2) (lw: led tl ins fnl f: hrd rdn & r.o wl)	s.h	**2**	5/1	61	29
446[3]	**Honourable** (JWWatts) **3-9-0** JCarroll(1) (chsd ldrs: chal 2f out: kpt on same pce appr fnl f)	1½	**3**	7/4[1]	58	26
	Bison Belting (JAGlover) **3-9-0** GCarter(6) (leggy: scope: chsd ldrs: effrt over 2f out: n.m.r & wknd over 1f out)	5	**4**	4/1[3]	46	14
	Agent Mulder (PDCundell) **3-9-0** JLowe(9) (lost pl over 3f out: n.d after)	7	**5**	50/1	30	—
469[9]	**Impetuosity (IRE)** (CWThornton) **3-8-9** DeanMcKeown(8) (bit bkwd: s.i.s: some hdwy 2f out: n.d)	½	**6**	33/1	24	—
412[6]	**Superapparos** (SRBowring) **3-9-0** SWebster(4) (prom early: outpcd & wandered 3f out: sn bhd)	hd	**7**	14/1	29	—
511[7]	**Badrinath (IRE)** (HJCollingridge) **3-9-0** MFenton(3) (chsd ldrs tl wknd wl over 1f out)	5	**8**	25/1	17	—
503[9]	**Hermanus** (MAJarvis) **3-9-0b[1]** PBloomfield(5) (sn drvn along: reminders after 1f: nt run on)	13	**9**	14/1	—	—

(SP 117.3%) **9 Rn**

1m 32.1 (5.60) CSF £19.49 TOTE £4.70: £1.10 £3.00 £1.10 (£19.80) Trio £5.70 OWNER Mr A. E. Oppenheimer (NEWMARKET) BRED Hascombe and Valiant Studs

STEWARDS' ENQUIRY Holland susp. 16-17/4/97 (improper use of whip).

Water Garden has plenty of size and scope but is a scratchy mover. Recovering from a sluggish break, there was nothing to spare at the line. He looked as though he would need the outing. (7/2: 2/1-4/1)

Mr Paradise (IRE), lacking nothing in assistance from the saddle, looked very fit and battled back strongly. (5/1: op 3/1)

446 Honourable, racing on the inside, did not look to relish the kick-back. After having every chance, he could find no more in the final furlong. He might be happier back on Turf. (7/4)

Bison Belting, who is on the leg, came in for market support but, running a shade green, he was on the retreat when tightened up coming to the final furlong. (4/1)

Hermanus (14/1: op 7/1)

577 GALAHAD MAIDEN CLAIMING STKS (3-Y.O+) (Class F)

2-45 (2-46) **5f (Fibresand)** £2,277.00 (£627.00: £297.00) Stalls: Low GOING minus 0.07 sec per fur (STD)

				SP	RR	SF
546[2]	**Julia's Relative (53)** (RGuest) **3-7-6**(7) RFfrench(5) (b: w ldrs: edgd lft & ld over 1f out: pushed out)	—	**1**	11/10[1]	47	6
361[6]	**Bon Guest (IRE) (58)** (TJNaughton) **3-9-1** DHolland(8) (led tl over 1f out: hung lft & nt qckn)	1¾	**2**	7/2[3]	57	16
	Sharp Holly (IRE) (41) (JABennett) **5-8-13** TSprake(4) (w ldrs: rdn & outpcd ½-wy: kpt on fnl f)	4	**3**	20/1	32	2
429[15]	**Gloria Imperator (IRE) (24)** (ABMulholland) **4-9-6b[1]** MBirch(7) (s.i.s: sn outpcd: rdn & hung lft ½-wy: nvr nr to chal)	2	**4**	25/1	32	2
469[7]	**Risky Lover** (DShaw) **4-9-3** JFanning(3) (b: chsd ldrs: rdn & outpcd ½-wy: sn wknd)	s.h	**5**	3/1[2]	29	—
59[10]	**Shermood (27)** (KTIvory) **4-8-11** GBardwell(6) (b.hind: sltly hmpd s: sn bhd & drvn along: kpt on fnl f: n.d)	2½	**6**	14/1	15	—
427[7]	**What's That Amy (30)** (CSmith) **3-8-4** JFEgan(2) (unruly s: chsd ldrs: rdn & hung lft 2f out: sn wknd)	6	**7**	20/1	—	—
	Redspet (SRBowring) **3-8-4** DeanMcKeown(1) (w ldrs tl wknd over 1f out)	2	**8**	20/1	—	—

(SP 119.6%) **8 Rn**

61.2 secs (4.20) CSF £4.68 TOTE £1.90: £1.00 £2.10 £5.90 (£3.60) OWNER Dorwinion Syndicate (NEWMARKET) BRED P. and Mrs Homewood

WEIGHT FOR AGE 3yo-11lb

Julia's Relative clmd DChapman £2,500

546 Julia's Relative, runner-up on her two previous outings, found this step back to five furlongs no problem in what was a very poor event. (11/10)

361 Bon Guest (IRE), who was inclined to swish his tail in the paddock, was dropped back in distance. Showing plenty of dash, he hung left under pressure and, with the winner, ended up towards the far-side rail. (7/2: 5/2-4/1)

Sharp Holly (IRE) was run off her feet at the halfway mark. (20/1)

Gloria Imperator (IRE) wore a tongue-strap and wanted to do nothing but hang left. (25/1)

Risky Lover, well supported in a weak market, was flat out and getting nowhere at halfway. (3/1)

Shermood (14/1: op 8/1)

578 EXCALIBUR H'CAP (0-70) (3-Y.O+) (Class E)

3-15 (3-16) **1m (Fibresand)** £3,096.25 (£925.00: £442.50: £201.25) Stalls: High GOING minus 0.07 sec per fur (STD)

				SP	RR	SF
424[2]	**Jibereen (70)** (PHowling) **5-10-0** SWhitworth(10) (b: a in tch: styd on appr fnl f: led nr fin)	—	**1**	12/1	81	37
	Young Annabel (USA) (67) (CADwyer) **4-9-11** DRMcCabe(12) (b: led: clr over 2f out: jst ct)	nk	**2**	11/1	77	33

				SP	RR	SF
476[15]	**Bagshot (66)** (GLMoore) **6-9-10** CandyMorris(15) (b: a in tch: effrt over 2f out: nt qckn appr fnl f)	3	**3**	9/1[3]	70	26
516[7]	**Noble Canonire (40)** (DShaw) **5-7-5b**(7) RFfrench(16) (a chsng ldrs: styd on one pce fnl 2f)	s.h	**4**	20/1	44	—
*415**	**Square Deal (FR) (58)** (SRBowring) **6-9-2** SWebster(7) (trckd ldrs: effrt 2f out: kpt on one pce)	¾	**5**	7/1[1]	61	17
297[5]	**Bentico (65)** (MrsNMacauley) **8-9-9** JWeaver(6) (lw: bhd: hdwy on outside 2f out: nvr nr ldrs)	2	**6**	8/1[2]	64	20
428[4]	**Broughton's Pride (IRE) (52)** (JLEyre) **6-8-10** KFallon(13) (lw: s.i.s: sn bhd: hdwy 2f out: edgd lft: nvr nr to chal)	1¾	**7**	8/1[2]	47	3
*511**	**Barbara's Jewel (55)** (ABailey) **5-8-13** SSanders(4) (mid div: effrt u.p over 2f out: nvr rchd ldrs)	¾	**8**	9/1[3]	49	5
415[2]	**Major Mouse (52)** (WWHaigh) **9-8-10** JFortune(8) (mid div: drvn along & outpcd over 2f out: n.d)	1¼	**9**	8/1[2]	43	—
461[17]	**Chadleigh Lane (USA) (66)** (ABMulholland) **5-9-10** MBirch(14) (b: chsd ldrs tl lost pl 2f out)	hd	**10**	9/1[3]	57	13
410[13]	**Johnnie the Joker (64)** (JPLeigh) **6-9-8** DeanMcKeown(1) (chsd ldrs tl lost pl 2f out)	1¾	**11**	20/1	52	8
385[9]	**Leigh Crofter (65)** (PDCundell) **8-9-9b** DHolland(2) (hdwy on ins over 2f out: wknd over 1f out: eased)	7	**12**	12/1	39	—
92[5]	**Silver Harrow (40)** (AGNewcombe) **4-7-12** JQuinn(3) (plld hrd: trckd ldrs tl lost pl over 3f out)	nk	**13**	14/1	13	—
	Winston (63) (JDBethell) **4-9-7** SDrowne(9) (racd wd: a rr div)	1¾	**14**	12/1	33	—
358[5]	**Pleasure Trick (USA) (56)** (DonEnricoIncisa) **6-9-0b** KimTinkler(5) (s.i.s: a bhd)	s.h	**15**	12/1	25	—
284[10]	**Oneoftheoldones (45)** (JNorton) **5-8-3**ow3 GCarter(11) (racd wd: a bhd)	9	**16**	25/1	—	—
				(SP 135.0%)		**16 Rn**

1m 45.9 (6.90) CSF £135.27 CT £1,171.47 TOTE £14.90: £3.20 £3.10 £4.20 £2.50 (£61.60) Trio £366.70 OWNER Mr Liam Sheridan (NEWMARKET) BRED Mrs J. Everitt

424 Jibereen responded to pressure to get up on the line, and certainly stayed the mile alright here. (12/1)
Young Annabel (USA), who landed something of a gamble in a seven-furlong race here last July, ran poorly on her four subsequent outings. Showing in a clear lead once in line for home, she was just caught. (11/1)
352 Bagshot was back on his favourite surface. (9/1)
Noble Canonire ran her best race so far this year. (20/1)
243 Bentico ran perhaps his best race so far this year. (8/1)
316 Leigh Crofter (12/1: op 8/1)

579 LANCELOT LIMITED STKS (0-55) (3-Y.O+) (Class F)

3-45 (3-46) **7f (Fibresand)** £2,277.00 (£627.00: £297.00) Stalls: Low GOING minus 0.07 sec per fur (STD)

				SP	RR	SF
85[3]	**The Barnsley Belle (IRE) (55)** (JLEyre) **4-9-3**(3) OPears(11) (mde virtually all: clr over 2f out: hrd rdn & styd on wl fnl f: unchal)	—	**1**	7/1[2]	69	27
415[3]	**Desert Invader (IRE) (55)** (DWChapman) **6-9-7** ACulhane(6) (a chsng ldrs: kpt on u.p fnl 2f: no imp)	4	**2**	6/1[1]	61	19
*428**	**Cats Bottom (55)** (AGNewcombe) **5-9-6** JQuinn(10) (a chsng ldrs: effrt over 2f out: styd on same pce)	2½	**3**	7/1[2]	54	12
342[3]	**Jigsaw Boy (55)** (PGMurphy) **8-9-9** SDrowne(13) (hld up & bhd: hdwy on outside over 2f out: kpt on fnl f: nt rch ldrs)	¾	**4**	9/1	55	13
480[2]	**Northern Fan (IRE) (55)** (NTinkler) **5-9-9** DeanMcKeown(1) (s.i.s: bhd: hdwy on outside 2f out: edgd lft: nvr nr to chal)	¾	**5**	8/1	54	12
140[7]	**Failed To Hit (53)** (NPLittmoden) **4-9-7v** TGMcLaughlin(16) (w ldrs: rdn & edgd lft 2f out: grad wknd)	3	**6**	20/1	45	3
526[19]	**Jilly Beveled (36)** (RonaldThompson) **5-8-13**(5) JBramhill(2) (bhd: hdwy over 2f out: nvr nr ldrs)	1¼	**7**	20/1	39	—
480*	**First Gold (53)** (JWharton) **8-9-9** KFallon(14) (racd wd: bhd tl some hdwy 2f out: n.d)	2½	**8**	15/2[3]	38	—
526[2]	**Sandmoor Denim (48)** (SRBowring) **10-9-0**(7) FBoyle(7) (lw: nvr bttr than mid div)	2½	**9**	12/1	31	—
164[4]	**Surf City (52)** (WWHaigh) **4-9-7** SWhitworth(12) (s.i.s: some hdwy ½-wy: n.d)	2½	**10**	12/1	25	—
	Oriole (38) (DonEnricoIncisa) **4-9-7** KimTinkler(5) (bhd: hrd rdn & sme hdwy over 2f out: n.d)	3	**11**	33/1	18	—
477[16]	**Our Kevin (46)** (BAPearce) **3-8-7be** GBardwell(15) (racd wd: a in rr)	3	**12**	25/1	11	—
	Octavia Hill (55) (PWHarris) **4-9-4** AMcGlone(3) (b.nr hind: hld up: effrt 3f out: sn lost pl)	2½	**13**	14/1	2	—
512[5]	**Jubilee Scholar (IRE) (45)** (KMcAuliffe) **4-9-7v**[1] JFEgan(4) (lw: chsd ldrs tl lost pl over 2f out: sn bhd)	8	**14**	12/1	—	—
423[11]	**Komlucky (40)** (ABMulholland) **5-9-4v** MBirch(9) (w ldrs tl lost pl 3f out)	5	**15**	25/1	—	—
				(SP 122.1%)		**15 Rn**

1m 32.8 (6.30) CSF £41.08 TOTE £5.40: £1.90 £2.60 £1.30 (£30.00) Trio £37.00 OWNER Mr K. Meynell (HAMBLETON) BRED Kim McCall
WEIGHT FOR AGE 3yo-14lb

85 The Barnsley Belle (IRE), joint top on official figures, was having her first outing for 84 days but she goes best when fresh. Her rider left nothing to chance and if the rain ever comes she will revert to the Turf. (7/1)
415 Desert Invader (IRE) could never find sufficient to get in a serious blow. (6/1)
428* Cats Bottom found this trip on the sharp side. (7/1)
342 Jigsaw Boy probably ran up to his best. (9/1)
480 Northern Fan (IRE) showed a pronounced tendency to edge to his left. (8/1)

580 HOLY GRAIL APPRENTICE (S) STKS (4-Y.O+) (Class G)

4-15 (4-15) **1m 4f (Fibresand)** £2,095.00 (£595.00: £295.00) Stalls: Low GOING minus 0.07 sec per fur (STD)

				SP	RR	SF
*356**	**Grand Cru** (RCraggs) **6-9-5** DDenby(10) (hld up: hdwy over 4f out: rdn & hung lft over 2f out: styd on to ld ins fnl f: hld on wl)	—	**1**	15/2	73	4
196[6]	**Pharly Dancer (65)** (WWHaigh) **8-9-0**(5) TSiddall(1) (sn bhd: hdwy over 4f out: styd on fnl f: nvr able to chal)	1¼	**2**	9/4[1]	71	2
486[2]	**One Off the Rail (USA) (68)** (GLMoore) **7-8-10**(3) MBatchelor(2) (swtg: trckd ldrs: led 4f out tl ins fnl f: nt qckn)	1¾	**3**	3/1[2]	63	—
543[5]	**World Without End (USA) (25)** (MESowersby) **8-8-13v** VictoriaAppleby(4) (hdwy over 5f out: chal 3f out: one pce)	1½	**4**	25/1	61	—
516[10]	**Bailiwick (48)** (NAGraham) **4-8-7b**(5) TField(6) (w ldrs: led 6f out to 4f out: wknd 2f out)	10	**5**	20/1	48	—
543[4]	**El Nido (55)** (DWChapman) **9-8-12**(7) DHayden(3) (led to 6f out: wknd over 2f out)	5	**6**	10/1	47	—
553[12]	**No Submission (USA) (44)** (DWChapman) **11-9-0b**(5) CCogan(8) (s.i.s: sn wl bhd)	5	**7**	14/1	40	—
	Durgams First (IRE) (MrsMReveley) **5-8-8**(5) PFredericks(11) (chsd ldrs: drvn along 6f out: lost pl over 3f out)	¾	**8**	13/2[3]	33?	—
273[3]	**Whothehellisharry (57)** (PTDalton) **4-8-9**(3) CLowther(5) (sn bhd & drvn along)	hd	**9**	9/1	33	—
360[10]	**Another Quarter (IRE) (45)** (MCChapman) **4-8-0**(7) PBradley(7) (chsd ldrs 5f: sn lost pl)	¾	**10**	16/1	27	—
				(SP 121.1%)		**10 Rn**

2m 47.8 (14.80) CSF £23.41 TOTE £10.00: £2.30 £1.10 £2.30 (£9.20) Trio £9.40 OWNER Mr Ray Craggs (SEDGEFIELD) BRED A. Dimmock
WEIGHT FOR AGE 4yo-1lb
No bid

356* Grand Cru proved well suited by the strong pace and, despite a tendency to hang left, stuck on to lead inside the last. This trip is probably his bare minimum. (15/2: 5/1-8/1)
196 Pharly Dancer, dropped into a seller, was within two lengths of the winner three furlongs out. Staying on inside the last, he could never summon the speed to get in a real blow. (9/4)
486 One Off the Rail (USA), a winner nine times on the Equitrack at Lingfield, was run out of it inside the last. (3/1: op 7/4)
356 World Without End (USA) probably has more ability than he cares to show. (25/1)
Bailiwick seemed to run out of stamina after helping set a strong pace. (20/1)
543 El Nido seems to be off the boil at present. (10/1)
Durgams First (IRE), absent since September 1995, has had his fore-legs fired. (13/2)

581 PERCEVAL H'CAP (0-70) (3-Y.O) (Class E)
4-45 (4-45) **1m 3f (Fibresand)** £2,914.25 (£869.00: £414.50: £187.25) Stalls: Low GOING minus 0.07 sec per fur (STD)

Form	Horse	Dist	Pos	SP	RR	SF
471^{4}	**Broctune Line (55)** (MrsMReveley) **3-8-9** ACulhane(7) (lw: hld up: hdwy 7f out: led over 1f out: hld on towards fin)	—	1	$11/2^{2}$	64	6
*366**	**Touch'n'go (67)** (MJohnston) **3-9-7** JWeaver(11) (led after 2f tl over 1f out: kpt on wl)	nk	2	$7/4^{1}$	76	18
	Bonne Ville (62) (BPalling) **3-9-2** TSprake(8) (trckd ldrs: effrt over 3f out: kpt on same pce)	3	3	11/1	66	8
	Sam Peeb (46) (RAFahey) **3-7-7**(7)ow4 RWinston(1) (led 2f: chsd ldrs: one pce fnl 3f)	7	4	33/1	40	—
513^{3}	**Red Embers (55)** (CADwyer) **3-8-9** RCochrane(4) (hld up & plld hrd: a in rr)	25	5	$6/1^{3}$	13	—
*454**	**Kingsdown Trix (IRE) (62)** (GLMoore) **3-9-2** RPerham(9) (trckd ldrs: pushed along over 4f out: wknd over 2f out)	1¾	6	9/1	17	—
547^{2}	**Gresatre (62)** (CADwyer) **3-9-2** KFallon(2) (hld up: hdwy over 4f out: sn chsng ldrs: rdn & wknd over 2f out)	nk	7	$11/2^{2}$	17	—
537^{4}	**Skelton Sovereign (IRE) (53)** (RHollinshead) **3-8-4**(3) FLynch(10) (hld up & bhd: effrt over 3f out: sn wknd)	4	8	10/1	2	—
	Push A Venture (64) (SPCWoods) **3-8-11**(7) CWebb(6) (trckd ldrs: drvn along over 3f out: sn wknd)	3	9	14/1	9	—
534^{3}	**Maremma (46)** (DonEnricoIncisa) **3-8-0** KimTinkler(5) (a in rr)	7	10	25/1	—	—
	Propellant (60) (CWThornton) **3-9-0** DeanMcKeown(3) (bit bkwd: unruly in stalls: bhd: sn bhd: drvn along over 5f out)	1¾	11	16/1	—	—

(SP 128.2%) **11 Rn**

2m 31.8 (11.80) CSF £15.45 CT £102.38 TOTE £8.10: £1.80 £1.60 £2.70 (£11.70) Trio £151.60 OWNER Mr D. Playforth (SALTBURN) BRED Ronald Wilkie
LONG HANDICAP Sam Peeb 7-8
471 Broctune Line, on good terms with himself beforehand, did absolutely nothing wrong on this occasion. (11/2: 4/1-6/1)
366* Touch'n'go, 7lb higher compared with Lingfield, made a valiant attempt and battled on all the way to the line. (7/4)
Bonne Ville, a tall filly, looked as though the outing might do her good. (11/1: op 7/1)
Sam Peeb, making his All-Weather debut, showed his first glimmer of form. (33/1)
513 Red Embers, who looked very fit, never settled. (6/1)
454* Kingsdown Trix (IRE) (9/1: 6/1-10/1)
547 Gresatre, stepping up half a mile in trip, was under pressure and dropping out once in line for home. (11/2)

T/Jkpt: Not won; £21,484.67 to Nottingham 8/4/97. T/Plpt: £17.20 (948.25 Tckts). T/Qdpt: £19.30 (40.51 Tckts) WG

0530-NOTTINGHAM (L-H) (Good to firm)
Tuesday April 8th
WEATHER: fine but cloudy WIND: mod half against

582 LANGWITH (S) H'CAP (0-60) (3-Y.O) (Class G)
2-00 (2-05) **1m 1f 213y** £1,984.50 (£547.00: £259.50) Stalls: Low GOING minus 0.21 sec per fur (GF)

Form	Horse	Dist	Pos	SP	RR	SF
300^{3}	**Riscatto (USA) (48)** (WRMuir) **3-8-9** JReid(8) (lw: a.p: led 3f out: drvn out)	—	1	$7/2^{1}$	52	19
	Sidney The Kidney (55) (MJRyan) **3-9-2** GCarter(7) (hld up mid div: hdwy over 3f out: swtchd rt 1f out: no imp)	1¾	2	$11/2^{3}$	56	23
535^{10}	**Rochea (60)** (MrsNMacauley) **3-9-7** MFenton(1) (lw: hld up: hdwy 3f out: styd on fnl f)	2	3	14/1	58	25
537^{11}	**Spondulicks (IRE) (57)** (BPJBaugh) **3-9-4** RPrice(10) (lw: a.p: one pce fnl 2f)	1½	4	7/1	53	20
378^{8}	**Miss Barcelona (IRE) (50)** (MJPolglase) **3-8-11** TGMcLaughlin(6) (swtg: hdwy 3f out: one pce fnl 2f)	s.h	5	$5/1^{2}$	46	13
467^{13}	**Kickonsun (IRE) (36)** (RAFahey) **3-7-11**ow1 FNorton(11) (s.i.s: sme hdwy 3f out: nvr nr to chal)	3	6	16/1	27	—
	Mechilie (35) (JWPayne) **3-7-10** GBardwell(4) (nt grwn: s.i.s: bhd whn rdn 6f out: nvr nrr)	5	7	33/1	18	—
	Captain Flint (44) (ASmith) **3-8-5** MBirch(12) (rdn 6f out: no hdwy fnl 3f)	s.h	8	25/1	27	—
480^{6}	**Patrick (35)** (DBurchell) **3-7-3**(7) CCogan(2) (plld hrd: hung rt thrght: led 7f: sn wknd)	nk	9	14/1	17	—
513^{5}	**Mirror Four Sport (50)** (MJohnston) **3-8-4**(7) NPollard(5) (nvr bttr than mid div)	1	10	6/1	31	—
	Foolish Flutter (IRE) (40) (RBastiman) **3-8-1** DaleGibson(14) (prom over 7f)	1¾	11	16/1	18	—
	Top Titfer (36) (AGFoster) **3-7-4**(7) RFfrench(13) (bhd fnl 4f)	3½	12	33/1	8	—
484^{7}	**Control Freak (44)** (AGFoster) **3-8-5** TSprake(3) (prom over 6f)	hd	13	20/1	16	—
	Hello There (50) (NTinkler) **3-8-11** KimTinkler(15) (s.s: a bhd: t.o)	dist	14	14/1	—	—
6^{8}	**Bentnose (54)** (DMorris) **3-9-1b**1 DBiggs(9) (plld hrd: chsd ldr: carried wd 7f out: wknd over 3f out: t.o)	6	15	8/1	—	—

(SP 138.4%) **15 Rn**

2m 9.7 (7.20) CSF £22.36 CT £240.84 TOTE £6.70: £2.40 £2.90 £5.30 (£12.30) Trio £85.40 OWNER Mr F. Hope (LAMBOURN) BRED Joanna W. Beresford
LONG HANDICAP Mechilie 7-5 Patrick 7-1
Bt in 5,000 gns
300 Riscatto (USA), well-backed, finished last off a mark of 67 at Newbury last August. He dropped to 58 when only beating one home in a selling nursery at Sandown next time, and was another 10lb lower here. (7/2)
Sidney The Kidney subsequently disappointed on two runs on the sand after a promising-enough debut at Folkestone in October.(11/2: 4/1-6/1)
414 Rochea did not seem to mind this step up in distance. (14/1)
Spondulicks (IRE) was 3lb lower than when finishing third over a mile at Leicester in September. (7/1)
Miss Barcelona (IRE), a springer in the market, was trying a longer trip off a rating 11lb lower than her final run on grass last season. (5/1)
Kickonsun (IRE) was stepping up from 7f. (16/1)
513 Mirror Four Sport (6/1: op 4/1)

74+ — 73+

583 E.B.F. CINDERHILL MAIDEN STKS (2-Y.O) (Class D)

2-30 (2-31) **5f 13y** £3,203.75 (£956.00: £456.50: £206.75) Stalls: High GOING minus 0.21 sec per fur (GF)

				SP	RR	SF
	Blushing Victoria (MartynMeade) **2-8-4**(5) DSweeney(6) (w'like: unf: scope: hld up: hdwy 2f out: led wl ins fnl f: pushed out)	—	**1**	14/1	74	14
504[2]	**Bernardo Bellotto (IRE)** (MBell) **2-9-0** PatEddery(5) (led: edgd lft & hdd wl ins fnl f)	1½	**2**	Evens[1]	74	14
	Blakeset (RHannon) **2-9-0** RHughes(10) (w'like: leggy: scope: a.p: ev ch whn hung lft over 1f out: r.o one pce)	¾	**3**	9/1	72	12
557[8]	**Dawn Patrol** (KWHogg) **2-8-9** KDarley(7) (trckd ldrs: rdn & swtchd rt 2f out: styd on fnl f)	3½	**4**	25/1	56	—
	Magical Dancer (IRE) (MrsPNDutfield) **2-8-9** DHolland(3) (leggy: bit bkwd: dwlt: nvr nr to chal)	1¾	**5**	16/1	50	—
	Mishraak (IRE) (RWArmstrong) **2-9-0** RHills(8) (str: cmpt: bit bkwd: w ldrs: ev ch whn hung lft over 1f out: wknd ins fnl f)	½	**6**	3/1[2]	54	—
	Means Business (IRE) (BJMeehan) **2-9-0** MTebbutt(1) (leggy: unf: dwlt: a bhd)	1¾	**7**	10/1	48	—
504[3]	**Tippitt Boy** (KMcAuliffe) **2-9-0** WJO'Connor(2) (unruly stalls: prom over 3f: eased whn btn fnl f)	½	**8**	4/1[3]	47	—
	Miss All Alone (JAGlover) **2-8-9** GCarter(9) (w'like: leggy: scope: bit bkwd: w ldrs 3f: eased whn btn)	16	**9**	7/1	—	—

(SP 143.0%) **9 Rn**

62.6 secs (3.70) CSF £32.30 TOTE £29.70: £5.90 £1.10 £1.80 (£48.50) Trio £47.20 OWNER Mr Paul Dixon (MALMESBURY) BRED Miss R. A. Myatt

Blushing Victoria had apparently been working well at home despite not having come in her coat, and she was well on top at the end. (14/1)
504 Bernardo Bellotto (IRE) was well out-pointed towards the finish. (Evens)
Blakeset, a half-brother to hurdler Fleur de Tal, should be better for the experience. (9/1: 5/1-10/1)
557 Dawn Patrol broke on level terms this time. (25/1)
Magical Dancer (IRE), a half-sister to several winners, should be sharper for this. (16/1)
Mishraak (IRE), a half-brother to a juvenile winner in Italy, looked green when the race began in earnest and ran better than his finishing position suggests. (3/1)
504 Tippitt Boy (4/1: 5/2-9/2)
Miss All Alone (7/1: op 12/1)

584 FLYING HORSE MAIDEN STKS (3-Y.O F) (Class D)

3-00 (3-01) **5f 13y** £3,358.95 (£999.60: £475.30: £213.15) Stalls: High GOING minus 0.21 sec per fur (GF)

				SP	RR	SF
	Mouche (MrsJRRamsden) **3-8-11** JFortune(2) (lengthy: unf: hld up & bhd: hdwy 2f out: r.o wl to ld last stride)	—	**1**	7/1	73	32
474[4]	**Lamarita (78)** (JMPEustace) **3-8-11** RCochrane(1) (a.p: led over 1f out: edgd lft: hdd last stride)	s.h	**2**	11/2[3]	73	32
453[3]	**Silent Miracle (IRE)** (MBell) **3-8-11** MFenton(5) (w ldr: led 2f out tl over 1f out: ev ch ins fnl f: r.o)	s.h	**3**	Evens[1]	73	32
	Tajrebah (USA) (76) (PTWalwyn) **3-8-11** RHills(7) (a.p: one pce fnl f)	2½	**4**	5/1[2]	65	24
	Sang d'Antibes (FR) (DJSCosgrove) **3-8-11** MRimmer(3) (bit bkwd: no hdwy fnl 2f)	2½	**5**	14/1	57	16
485[7]	**Aquatic Queen (42)** (RJWeaver) **3-8-11** MWigham(4) (swtg: sn outpcd: nvr nrr)	1¾	**6**	50/1	51	10
531[4]	**Corinchili** (GGMargarson) **3-8-11** GCarter(6) (led 3f)	5	**7**	7/1	36	—

(SP 115.7%) **7 Rn**

61.6 secs (2.70) CSF £41.42 TOTE £10.40: £3.40 £2.70 (£18.90) OWNER Mr M. J. Simmonds (THIRSK) BRED M. J. Simmonds

Mouche, apparently always well regarded at home, missed last season because of a niggling cough. Bred to need further, she was dropped out at the start and needed every yard of this minimum trip. (7/1: op 3/1)
474 Lamarita stepped up on her reappearance and would have prevailed had she not edged over to the less-favoured far rail. (11/2)
453 Silent Miracle (IRE) was campaigned over six furlongs and seven furlongs last season. (Evens)
Tajrebah (USA) was also having her first run over the minimum trip. (5/1: op 3/1)
Sang d'Antibes (FR) was yet another dropping back to five furlongs for the first time. (14/1)
531 Corinchili (7/1: op 12/1)

585 BAGTHORPE H'CAP (0-70) (3-Y.O+) (Class E)

3-30 (3-34) **6f 15y** £3,382.25 (£1,013.00: £486.50: £223.25) Stalls: High GOING minus 0.21 sec per fur (GF)

				SP	RR	SF
473[9]	**Meranti (43)** (JMBradley) **4-7-8**(7) RFfrench(1) (a chsng ldrs: edgd rt & rdn to ld over 1f out: r.o wl)	—	**1**	12/1	63	46
	Beau Venture (USA) (64) (BPalling) **9-9-8** TSprake(11) (swtg: a.p: led wl over 1f out: sn hdd: one pce)	4	**2**	16/1	74	57
	Grey Kingdom (41) (MBrittain) **6-7-6**(7) DMernagh(10) (bit bkwd: a.p: r.o one pce fnl f)	2	**3**	20/1	45	28
520[5]	**Pointer (58)** (MrsPNDutfield) **5-9-2** DHolland(9) (lw: a chsng ldrs: one pce fnl f)	2½	**4**	4/1[1]	56	39
545[2]	**Chadwell Hall (68)** (SRBowring) **6-9-5v**[1](7) KSked(6) (lw: led over 4f: one pce)	½	**5**	7/1[2]	64	47
477[4]	**Sound the Trumpet (IRE) (53)** (RCSpicer) **5-8-8**(3) RHavlin(15) (hdwy over 1f out: r.o)	½	**6**	16/1	48	31
459[9]	**Will Do (70)** (MartynMeade) **4-10-0** JReid(5) (no hdwy fnl 2f)	s.h	**7**	16/1	65	48
468[8]	**Fame Again (56)** (MrsJRRamsden) **5-9-0** JFortune(4) (nvr nrr)	2	**8**	4/1[1]	46	29
541[8]	**Sing With the Band (60)** (BAMcMahon) **6-9-4** KDarley(18) (chsd ldrs over 3f)	nk	**9**	9/1[3]	49	32
	Gay Breeze (44) (PSFelgate) **4-8-2**ow1 GHind(16) (no hdwy fnl 2f)	¾	**10**	25/1	31	13
306[4]	**Magazine Gap (51)** (PatMitchell) **4-8-4**(5) AmandaSanders(19) (hung lft 3f out: n.d)	1	**11**	25/1	35	18
467[8]	**Dashing Dancer (IRE) (52)** (DShaw) **6-8-10** GCarter(14) (n.d)	¾	**12**	33/1	34	17
494[4]	**Goretski (IRE) (58)** (NTinkler) **4-9-2** KimTinkler(3) (swtg: nvr nr ldrs)	2	**13**	12/1	35	18
	Fairy Prince (IRE) (62) (MrsALMKing) **4-9-6** KFallon(20) (nvr rchd ldrs)	nk	**14**	12/1	38	21
473[3]	**College Night (IRE) (42)** (CADwyer) **5-8-0** NVarley(8) (chsd ldrs over 3f)	¾	**15**	12/1	16	—
352[6]	**Into Debt (40)** (JRPoulton) **4-7-5**(7)ow2 AMcCarthy(22) (swtg: sn bhd)	nk	**16**	33/1	13	—
421[12]	**Margaretrose Anna (38)** (BPJBaugh) **5-7-5**(5) JBramhill(17) (b: a bhd)	½	**17**	20/1	10	—
464[13]	**Cross The Border (68)** (DNicholls) **4-9-12** AlexGreaves(2) (lw: bhd fnl 3f)	¾	**18**	16/1	38	21
	Magic Melody (52) (JLSpearing) **4-8-10** JWeaver(13) (a bhd)	nk	**19**	33/1	21	4
494[13]	**Zain Dancer (53)** (DNicholls) **5-8-11** DaleGibson(12) (a bhd)	4	**20**	20/1	12	—
391[12]	**Maysimp (IRE) (46)** (BPJBaugh) **4-7-11**(7)ow6 PClarke(21) (a bhd: t.o)	12	**21**	33/1	—	—
	Miss Carottene (39) (MJRyan) **4-7-11** GBardwell(7) (a bhd: t.o)	1½	**22**	33/1	—	—

(SP 153.5%) **22 Rn**

1m 13.1 (1.60) CSF £189.42 CT £3,568.44 TOTE £16.20: £5.10 £6.90 £5.80 £1.40 (£229.70) Trio £1.877.30 OWNER Mr John Wallis (CHEPSTOW) BRED K. Birkinshaw

LONG HANDICAP Into Debt 7-7

OFFICIAL EXPLANATION **Fame Again: no explanation offered.**

IN-FOCUS: **Despite the large field, only a handful ever got into the race.**

Meranti, dropped 6lb, was 15lb lower than when finishing fifth in this race last year. Ending up on the favoured stands rail despite the number one draw, he fairly flew once getting there. (12/1: op 8/1)

Beau Venture (USA), 3lb higher than when runner-up at Leicester last October, had scored off this mark at Bath in June. (16/1)

Grey Kingdom ran very well over a trip short of his best and will be sharper for the outing. (20/1)

520 Pointer, well supported in the ring, was 7lb higher than the highest rating off which he has won. (4/1: op 8/1)

545 Chadwell Hall, tried in a visor, has yet to score beyond five furlongs on grass. (7/1)

477 Sound the Trumpet (IRE), who apparently gave trouble at the start, seemed to find this shorter distance inadequate. (16/1)

468 Fame Again was never in the hunt and connections could not offer the stewards any explanation. (4/1)

494 Goretski (IRE) (12/1: op 7/1)

586 LOWDHAM MAIDEN STKS (3-Y.O) (Class D)

4-00 (4-07) **1m 54y** £4,218.90 (£1,264.20: £607.60: £279.30) Stalls: Low GOING minus 0.21 sec per fur (GF)

				SP	RR	SF
	Latalomne (USA) (EALDunlop) **3-8-11**(3) DO'Donohoe(17) (rangy: sn trckng ldr: c wd st: led over 3f out: hung lft fnl 2f: r.o wl)	—	**1**	7/1 [3]	94	61
	Shawm (DRLoder) **3-9-0** KDarley(12) (lw: hld up: chal 2f out: nt qckn ins fnl f)	2	**2**	4/6 [1]	90	57
	Shaheen (USA) (HRACecil) **3-9-0** KFallon(1) (w'like: cmpt: hld up: hdwy 4f out: ev ch 2f out: one pce)	1½	**3**	7/2 [2]	87	54
	Epworth (JAGlover) **3-8-9** GCarter(2) (a.p: one pce fnl 3f)	8	**4**	20/1	67	34
	Mumaris (USA) (ACStewart) **3-9-0** MRoberts(9) (wl grwn: hld up: styd on fnl 3f: nt rch ldrs)	¾	**5**	25/1	70	37
	Final Warning (JEBanks) **3-9-0** MWigham(16) (leggy: bit bkwd: s.i.s: bhd tl sme hdwy fnl 2f: nvr nrr)	3½	**6**	33/1	63	30
	Muhawwil (RWArmstrong) **3-9-0** RHills(18) (lengthy: unf: bkwd: hld up mid div: no hdwy fnl 3f)	1½	**7**	12/1	61	28
	Select Choice (IRE) (80) (APJarvis) **3-9-0** WJO'Connor(6) (prom over 4f)	1½	**8**	20/1	58	25
	March Crusader (BHanbury) **3-9-0** WRyan(8) (w'like: str: bkwd: nvr plcd to chal)	½	**9**	16/1	57	24
	Top Jem (MJRyan) **3-8-9** GBardwell(3) (leggy: unf: s.s: nvr nr ldrs)	hd	**10**	50/1	52	19
	Nobel Lad (JLDunlop) **3-9-0** TSprake(7) (leggy: unf: a bhd)	hd	**11**	20/1	56	23
	Occam (IRE) (GWragg) **3-9-0** MHills(4) (mid div: rdn 3f out: sn bhd)	s.h	**12**	14/1	56	23
	Spy Knoll (MRStoute) **3-9-0** WRSwinburn(14) (nvr nr ldrs)	1¼	**13**	10/1	54	21
	Silver Jubilee (BPalling) **3-8-9** DHolland(13) (unruly s: led over 4f: sn wknd)	7	**14**	100/1	35	2
479[6]	**Pen Friend** (WJHaggas) **3-9-0** RCochrane(11) (bit bkwd: s.i.s: a bhd)	s.h	**15**	33/1	40	7
	Wild City (USA) (BHanbury) **3-9-0** MRimmer(10) (bit bkwd: prom: hrd rdn & wknd 3f out: t.o)	6	**16**	33/1	28	—
	Gold Clipper (MJRyan) **3-9-0** NDay(5) (a bhd: t.o)	7	**17**	50/1	15	—
	Reckless (JEBanks) **3-8-9** JStack(15) (lengthy: unf: prom over 4f: t.o)	5	**18**	33/1	—	—
				(SP 158.9%)	**18 Rn**	

1m 43.4 (2.10) CSF £12.90 TOTE £12.80: £2.60 £1.50 £1.10 (£7.20) Trio £15.50 OWNER Maktoum Al Maktoum (NEWMARKET) BRED Gainsborough Farm Inc

Latalomne (USA), a half-brother to amongst others Sheikh Albadou and Captain Jack, was considered too big and backward to run as a juvenile. He proved too good for the hot favourite despite running green, and seems sure to go on from here. (7/1)

Shawm, a Dante entry, could not take advantage of the winner's inexperience, and it remains to be seen if he caught a real tartar. (4/6)

Shaheen (USA), a well-bred $385,000 colt, did more than enough to suggest he will soon get off the mark. (7/2)

Epworth lacked the acceleration to go with the major players and should do better over a longer trip. (20/1)

Mumaris (USA), a half-brother to Ta Awun and Fakih, is out of a mare who won over both fourteen furlongs and fifteen furlongs. He certainly shaped like one who needs further. (25/1)

Final Warning, a half-brother to Vindaloo, is another with stamina on the dam's side. (33/1)

Muhawwil, a brother to Gabr and half-brother to Kutta and Intisab, is out of a mare who won over twelve furlongs. (12/1: 8/1-14/1)

March Crusader, out of a dual mile winner in Ireland, was given a much needed pipe-opener and will do better in due course. (16/1)

Occam (IRE) (14/1: op 8/1)

587 LANGWORTH APPRENTICE H'CAP (0-70) (3-Y.O+) (Class G)

4-30 (4-33) **1m 54y** £2,007.50 (£570.00: £282.50) Stalls: Low GOING minus 0.21 sec per fur (GF)

				SP	RR	SF
476[2]	**Eurobox Boy (56)** (APJarvis) **4-9-2** CCarver(2) (lw: a gng wl: led over 1f out: rdn out)	—	**1**	3/1 [1]	68	45
526[12]	**Bedazzle (36)** (MBrittain) **6-7-5**(5) DMernagh(17) (hld up: hdwy over 3f out: ev ch 1f out: nt qckn)	2	**2**	20/1	44	21
526[6]	**Return To Brighton (40)** (JMBradley) **5-8-0** JFowle(13) (s.i.s: hdwy over 2f out: r.o)	1½	**3**	20/1	45	22
428[2]	**Queens Stroller (IRE) (38)** (REPeacock) **6-7-12** RBrisland(14) (bhd: hdwy 2f out: r.o wl ins fnl f)	¾	**4**	10/1 [3]	42	19
	Richard House Lad (44) (RHollinshead) **4-7-13**(5) DHayden(12) (hdwy over 3f out: one pce fnl f)	1¾	**5**	16/1	44	21
476[9]	**One In The Eye (38)** (JRPoulton) **4-7-12** AMcCarthy(9) (unruly stalls: s.s: wl bhd tl hdwy fnl 3f: nrst fin)	hd	**6**	25/1	38	15
477[12]	**Utmost Zeal (USA) (64)** (PWHarris) **4-9-10** CLowther(10) (hld up: hdwy over 2f out: nvr nr to chal)	s.h	**7**	14/1	64	41
	Shouldbegrey (44) (WRMuir) **4-8-4** CCogan(11) (chsd ldrs: no hdwy fnl 3f)	1¼	**8**	11/1	42	19
407[8]	**Bold Habit (37)** (JPearce) **12-7-6**(5) LisaMoncrieff(4) (bhd: hmpd & swtchd rt over 2f out: n.d)	¾	**9**	12/1	33	10
	Cinnamon Stick (IRE) (36) (PSFelgate) **4-7-5**(5) DarrenWilliams(16) (n.d)	½	**10**	33/1	31	8
	Legend of Aragon (70) (JAGlover) **3-8-10**(5) TPengkerego(6) (b.hind: sn wl bhd: nvr nrr)	½	**11**	14/1	64	26
	Mezzoramio (48) (KAMorgan) **5-8-3**(5) RWinston(8) (b: led 5f out: rdn over 2f out: hdd over 1f out: sn wknd)	½	**12**	11/1	41	18
476[4]	**Arzani (USA) (48)** (DJSCosgrove) **6-8-8** PClarke(1) (hld up & plld hrd: bhd fnl 3f)	½	**13**	7/1 [2]	40	17
	Kevasingo (50) (JLSpearing) **5-8-10b** SRighton(7) (led 3f: wknd qckly over 3f out)	8	**14**	10/1 [3]	27	4
477[9]	**Ameer Alfayaafi (IRE) (44)** (BJMeehan) **4-8-4b** GHannon(3) (bhd fnl 4f)	1¾	**15**	14/1	17	—
480[5]	**Rafter-J (40)** (JohnHarris) **6-7-9b**(5) PBradley(15) (b: plld hrd: prom over 5f)	3	**16**	20/1	8	—
	Okay Baby (IRE) (36) (JMBradley) **5-7-10** RCody-Boutcher(5) (bhd fnl 3f)	½	**17**	33/1	3	—
484[6]	**Shontaine (55)** (MJohnston) **4-9-1** NPollard(18) (w ldrs tl wknd 3f out)	1¼	**18**	12/1	19	—
				(SP 137.6%)	**18 Rn**	

1m 45.2 (3.90) CSF £70.80 CT £1,037.93 TOTE £4.10: £1.70 £2.30 £5.30 £2.30 (£79.80) Trio £329.40; £241.32 to Ripon 9/4/97 OWNER Mr N. Coverdale (ASTON UPTHORPE) BRED G. Revitt

LONG HANDICAP Okay Baby (IRE) 7-4

WEIGHT FOR AGE 3yo-15lb

476 Eurobox Boy did not mind this return to one mile and probably had less to do than when runner-up off the same mark at Folkestone last time. (3/1)

Bedazzle won a seller at Musselburgh a year ago off a 2lb lower rating. (20/1)

526 Return To Brighton was 5lb lower than when winning an apprentices' seller at Ripon last June. (20/1)

428 Queens Stroller (IRE), 8lb higher than when second on the sand last month, finds a mile on Turf on the short side. (10/1)
Richard House Lad was 3lb higher than when taking a seller at Bath in September. (16/1)
One In The Eye had finished nearly eight lengths behind the winner at Folkestone off a 3lb higher mark. (25/1)

T/Jkpt: Not won; £28,618.60 to Ripon 9/4/97. T/Plpt: £236.90 (78.92 Tckts). T/Qdpt: £88.60 (11.78 Tckts) KH

0511-WOLVERHAMPTON (L-H) (Standard)
Tuesday April 8th
WEATHER: fine WIND: slt half bhd

588 JARVIS MEDIAN AUCTION MAIDEN STKS (3-Y.O) (Class F)
2-15 (2-15) **6f (Fibresand)** £2,277.00 (£627.00: £297.00) Stalls: Low GOING: 0.28 sec per fur (SLW)

				SP	RR	SF
	Mon Bruce (76) (WRMuir) **3-9-0** DaneO'Neill(3) (chsd ldr: led over 3f out: sn clr: hld on wl cl home)	—	**1**	13/8[1]	59	27
	Don't Worry Mike (57) (FHLee) **3-9-0** ACulhane(10) (bit bkwd: chsd ldrs: rdn over 2f out: sustained chal fnl f)	hd	**2**	12/1	59	27
412[4]	**K S Sunshine (USA)** (WJHaggas) **3-8-6**(3) FLynch(9) (hdwy 2f out: swtchd lft over 1f out: fin strly)	nk	**3**	4/1[2]	53	21
	Concer Arall (SCWilliams) **3-9-0** SDrowne(6) (neat: unf: bkwd: hdwy ½-wy: kpt on one pce fnl f)	3½	**4**	10/1	49	17
469[5]	**Barwell Boy (42)** (JLHarris) **3-9-0** LCharnock(5) (led over 2f: rdn wl over 1f out: sn btn)	1	**5**	5/1[3]	46	14
532[10]	**Rockaroundtheclock (62)** (PDEvans) **3-9-0** JFEgan(8) (s.s: a in rr)	5	**6**	20/1	33	1
	Dancing Mystery (EAWheeler) **3-8-9**(5) ADaly(4) (bit bkwd: s.s: a outpcd)	3	**7**	20/1	25	—
	Hever Golf Charmer (TJNaughton) **3-9-0** SSanders(2) (gd sort: bkwd: outpcd fr ½-wy)	½	**8**	10/1	23	—
	Thewrightone (IRE) (35) (GROldroyd) **3-8-9b** MMcAndrew(1) (outpcd: a bhd: t.o)	21	**9**	33/1	—	—
				(SP 113.1%)		**9 Rn**

1m 18.0 (6.80) CSF £19.87 TOTE £2.00: £1.10 £1.10 £2.10 (£13.70) Trio £24.10 OWNER Miss Monique Van Bakel (LAMBOURN) BRED E. A. Badger

Mon Bruce, well tuned up for this first outing since the autumn, looked set to score easily entering the final furlong but he tied up badly close home and only just held on. This was his first success but definitely not his last. (13/8)
Don't Worry Mike, taking a step down in trip on this seasonal debut, was hard at work before reaching the straight, but he kept his head down and was only a stride adrift at the line. (12/1)
412 K S Sunshine (USA), taken to post early, had the advantage of a recent run but did not find top gear until the race was all but over. She should be able to pick up a small race. (4/1)
Concer Arall, a small half-brother to Concer Un, was unable to match strides in the latter stages but he will come on for the run and should be capable of winning. (10/1)
469 Barwell Boy was unable to confirm the form with K S Sunshine on 3lb worse terms, but he remained in the action until tapped for speed inside the distance. (5/1: op 3/1)

589 PHOENIX LIMITED STKS (0-60) (3-Y.O+) (Class F)
2-45 (2-46) **1m 100y (Fibresand)** £2,277.00 (£627.00: £297.00) Stalls: Low GOING: 0.28 sec per fur (SLW)

				SP	RR	SF
512[9]	**Dragonjoy (56)** (NPLittmoden) **4-9-7b** RLappin(13) (hld up: hdwy 4f out: led over 2f out: sn clr: wknd fnl f: jst hld on)	—	**1**	5/1[2]	63	45
578[5]	**Square Deal (FR) (58)** (SRBowring) **6-9-9** SWebster(2) (a.p: outpcd over 2f out: rdn & r.o wl fnl f)	½	**2**	8/1	64	46
	Shaffishayes (60) (MrsMReveley) **5-9-7** DeanMcKeown(3) (prom: pushed along & outpcd 3f out: rallied u.p fnl f: r.o)	½	**3**	5/1[2]	61	43
	Premier Generation (IRE) (58) (DWPArbuthnot) **4-9-7** SWhitworth(8) (bit bkwd: trckd ldrs: styd on u.p appr fnl f)	3½	**4**	16/1	55	37
468[12]	**Queens Consul (IRE) (58)** (BSRothwell) **7-9-1**(3) FLynch(10) (a.p: rdn & outpcd over 2f out: kpt on towards fin)	1½	**5**	6/1[3]	49	31
	Theatre Magic (59) (DShaw) **4-9-4**(3) CTeague(4) (b: bkwd: bhd: hdwy over 2f out: nvr nrr)	½	**6**	14/1	51	33
150[6]	**Whitelock Quest (28)** (NEBerry) **9-9-7** RPerham(12) (hld up: hdwy 4f out: sn hrd rdn & no imp)	½	**7**	16/1	50	32
	Princess Efisio (58) (BAMcMahon) **4-9-4** LNewton(5) (bkwd: chsd ldrs over 5f: sn lost tch)	½	**8**	7/1	46	28
401[4]	**Biya (IRE) (47)** (DMcCain) **5-9-9** VSlattery(9) (lw: hld up: hdwy & rdn 3f out: nt pce to chal)	hd	**9**	14/1	51	33
578[8]	**Barbara's Jewel (55)** (ABailey) **5-9-9** SSanders(11) (hld up: effrt u.p 3f out: no imp)	nk	**10**	4/1[1]	50	32
	People Direct (58) (KMcAuliffe) **4-8-11**(7) TField(1) (led tl hdd & wknd over 2f out)	2	**11**	10/1	41	23
	Ath Cheannaithe (FR) (55) (JNeville) **5-9-7v** SDrowne(6) (outpcd: a bhd: t.o)	dist	**12**	14/1	—	—
				(SP 132.1%)		**12 Rn**

1m 53.7 (8.70) CSF £46.00 TOTE £9.40: £3.00 £3.40 £1.60 (£80.20) Trio £72.20 OWNER Foley Steelstock (WOLVERHAMPTON) BRED T. H. Barma

369 Dragonjoy, back over his correct trip, pinched the race when quickening clear below the distance and, though he was being reeled in with every stride late on, the post was always going to arrive in time. (5/1)
415* Square Deal (FR), never far away, was one of many who was struggling to hold on rounding the home turn, but he ran on particularly well inside the last furlong and should soon return to form. (8/1: 6/1-9/1)
Shaffishayes has not yet won on artificial surfaces but he does come to hand early and, though he was never going to win here, this run will at least put an edge on him. (5/1)
Premier Generation (IRE) tried hard to get himself into the action in the closing stages but, despite staying on, lacked the pace to make much impression. (16/1)
Queens Consul (IRE) fared better than she did on her seasonal debut, but she was always finding the tempo just too much for her and failed to land a blow. (6/1)
Theatre Magic, held up on this return to a longer trip, was doing all his best work when it was all too late. He is a truly desperate mover. (14/1)
511* Barbara's Jewel, unplaced at Southwell the previous day, did not impress to post and, never going at any stage, once again proved racehorses are not machines. (4/1)

590 STARBUCK H'CAP (0-75) (3-Y.O F) (Class D)
3-15 (3-15) **7f (Fibresand)** £3,390.80 (£1,009.40: £480.20: £215.60) Stalls: High GOING: 0.28 sec per fur (SLW)

				SP	RR	SF
483[8]	**Trading Aces (68)** (MBell) **3-9-2**(5) RMullen(6) (s.i.s: hdwy over 4f out: hung lft appr fnl f: r.o to ld post)	—	**1**	4/1[2]	77	42
255[4]	**Faym (IRE) (63)** (JWharton) **3-9-2** JQuinn(1) (led: rdn over 1f out: ct last stride)	s.h	**2**	4/1[2]	72	37

				SP	RR	SF
547*	**Tayovullin (IRE) (62)** (HMorrison) **3-9-1** 6x CRutter(7) (b.hind: chsd ldrs: rdn to chal over 1f out: one pce fnl f)	2½	**3**	7/2[1]	65	30
547[5]	**Patina (53)** (RHollinshead) **3-8-3**(3) FLynch(5) (trckd ldrs: effrt over 2f out: nt pce to chal)	3½	**4**	5/1[3]	48	13
	Janglynyve (55) (SPCWoods) **3-8-8** AClark(4) (hld up: effrt & pushed along 2f out: outpcd wl over 1f out)	9	**5**	4/1[2]	30	—
	Dayrella (57) (WRMuir) **3-8-10** DaneO'Neill(2) (bit bkwd: prom: hrd drvn over 2f out: sn outpcd)	1½	**6**	16/1	28	—
532[15]	**Qualitair Silver (49)** (JFBottomley) **3-8-2** LCharnock(3) (chsd ldr tl rdn & wknd 2f out)	2	**7**	8/1	16	—

(SP 115.9%) **7 Rn**

1m 32.0 (7.30) CSF £19.00 TOTE £4.30: £2.90 £2.50 (£7.90) OWNER Mr R. P. B. Michaelson (NEWMARKET) BRED Limestone Stud

Trading Aces made her first appearance on the sand a winning one, with a last gasp effort that enabled her to poke her head in front right on the line. (4/1: 3/1-9/2)

255 Faym (IRE) attempted to make every post a winning one, and for most of the time appeared in control, but the determined late challenge of the winner proved just too much. She is still striving for that initial success. (4/1)

547* Tayovullin (IRE), waiting to pounce, came to win her race approaching the final furlong but the leader just would not give best, and the 6lb penalty was taking its toll in the last two hundred yards. (7/2: op 2/1)

547 Patina began to stay on entering the straight, but failed to maintain the effort and as yet she is not quite seeing the trip out. (5/1)

Janglynyve was produced fit and well for this All-Weather debut and she attracted plenty of support in the ring, but failed to cut any ice and was well outpaced once in line for home. (4/1)

591 TONGAREVA H'CAP (0-100) (3-Y.O+) (Class C)

3-45 (3-46) **1m 4f (Fibresand)** £5,210.20 (£1,552.60: £739.80: £333.40) Stalls: Low GOING: 0.28 sec per fur (SLW)

				SP	RR	SF
542[2]	**Raffles Rooster (65)** (AGNewcombe) **5-7-3**(7) IonaWands(9) (hld up: hdwy over 4f out: led on bit ins fnl f: pushed clr)	—	**1**	4/1[2]	79+	39
542*	**Sedbergh (USA) (66)** (MrsMReveley) **4-7-10** JQuinn(3) (a.p: led over 3f out tl hdd & no ex ins fnl f)	2½	**2**	5/1[3]	77	36
	Etterby Park (USA) (69) (MJohnston) **4-7-13** JFanning(6) (led tl over 3f out: rdn over 1f out: one pce)	2	**3**	7/1	77	36
426[3]	**Greenspan (IRE) (73)** (WRMuir) **5-8-4** AClark(2) (lw: hld up: hdwy over 4f out: rdn 2f out: styd on)	¾	**4**	12/1	80	40
	Cotteir Chief (IRE) (97) (JNeville) **6-10-0** SDrowne(1) (b: chsd ldrs: rdn & outpcd 3f out: styd on ins fnl f)	¾	**5**	25/1	103	63
482[4]	**Hill Farm Dancer (80)** (WMBrisbourne) **6-8-6**(5) RMullen(8) (s.s: hdwy over 3f out: sn rdn: no imp)	11	**6**	8/1	71	31
426[7]	**Swan Hunter (69)** (DJSCosgrove) **4-7-13** CRutter(7) (chsd ldrs: rdn along over 3f out: sn btn)	nk	**7**	20/1	60	19
481*	**In the Money (IRE) (68)** (RHollinshead) **8-7-10**(3)ow3 MHenry(4) (hld up: hdwy 4f out: sn hrd drvn & wknd)	1¼	**8**	9/1	57	14
	Trojan Risk (72) (GLewis) **4-8-2** PaulEddery(10) (b: b.hind: bkwd: s.i.s: effrt 4f out: rdn & wknd over 2f out)	6	**9**	7/2[1]	53	12
430[10]	**Opera Buff (IRE) (93)** (MissGayKelleway) **6-9-7**(3) AWhelan(5) (lw: hld up: hdwy on ins 5f out: rdn over 3f out: sn btn)	nk	**10**	7/1	74	34

(SP 121.3%) **10 Rn**

2m 42.3 (9.80) CSF £23.24 CT £127.19 TOTE £5.70: £2.00 £2.00 £1.80 (£13.20) Trio £22.60 OWNER Mr Mark Leatham (BARNSTAPLE) BRED G. Strawbridge & London Thoroughbred Services Ltd

LONG HANDICAP In the Money (IRE) 7-5 Raffles Rooster 7-8 Sedbergh (USA) 7-8

WEIGHT FOR AGE 4yo-1lb

542 Raffles Rooster was able to turn the tables on the runner-up on 7lb better terms, but he won so easily under a supremely confident ride that he would appear to be still some way ahead of the Handicapper. (4/1)

542* Sedbergh (USA) has not yet won over a trip as short as this, but he did make the best of his way home before the winner appeared and spoilt the party. (5/1)

Etterby Park (USA) has run well when fresh in the past and, though he was being held entering the final furlong, there was plenty to like about his commitment to the task in hand. (7/1)

426 Greenspan (IRE) has been performing consistently well since the turn of the year, and he did his best to make his presence felt here. With the tempo never slackening, he was unable to mount a challenge. (12/1)

Cotteir Chief (IRE), fit from hurdling, stayed on pleasingly in the closing stages after getting tapped for toe on the home turn. (25/1)

481* In the Money (IRE), weak in the market, ran very flat indeed and he may have had enough for the time being. (9/1)

Trojan Risk, having his first run in six months, was without doubt the most backward animal performing at this venue today. It seems some punters are blind to paddock inspection and they quite rightly were made to pay. (7/2)

430 Opera Buff (IRE), well behind the winner on his previous outing, was flat to the boards at the end of the back straight and supporters soon knew their fate. (7/1)

52-55-56

592 FIJI (S) STKS (2-Y.O) (Class F)

4-15 (4-17) **5f (Fibresand)** £2,277.00 (£627.00: £297.00) Stalls: Low GOING: 0.28 sec per fur (SLW)

				SP	RR	SF
	Sage (WGMTurner) **2-8-6**(5) DSweeney(4) (neat: cmpt: led 1f: led 3f out: hrd drvn fnl f: hld on gamely)	—	**1**	5/1[3]	58	5
	Rosewood Lady (IRE) (KRBurke) **2-8-6** ACulhane(1) (lt-f: unf: outpcd: hdwy appr fnl f: fin fast)	½	**2**	12/1	51	—
530[2]	**Who Nose (IRE)** (BJMeehan) **2-8-11b[1]** MTebbutt(3) (prom: rdn & ev ch 1f out: unable qckn)	hd	**3**	9/4[2]	56	3
530[3]	**Pink Ticket** (PDEvans) **2-8-6** JFEgan(6) (led after 1f to 3f out: one pce fnl f)	½	**4**	2/1[1]	50	—
530[7]	**Wilfred Sherman (IRE)** (JBerry) **2-8-6**(5) TEDurcan(7) (lw: s.i.s: sn rcvrd: ev ch 1f out: wknd fnl f)	¾	**5**	7/1	52	—
472[5]	**Jack-N-Jilly (IRE)** (JSMoore) **2-8-3**(3) MHenry(5) (outpcd: a bhd)	3	**6**	10/1	38	—
530[6]	**The Hobby Lobby (IRE)** (MRChannon) **2-8-11** PaulEddery(2) (s.i.s: a bhd & outpcd)	1¾	**7**	8/1	37	—

(SP 121.2%) **7 Rn**

65.8 secs (6.90) CSF £58.37 TOTE £5.10: £1.60 £8.50 (£24.10) OWNER Major R. P. Thorman (SHERBORNE) BRED Major R. P. Thorman and P. P. Thorman

Sold CBjorling 4,600 gns

Sage, a neatly-turned, stocky colt from a yard that has been in form, held on grimly in the closing stages after seeming to be a sitting duck. He was sold to race in Sweden. (5/1)

Rosewood Lady (IRE), a mediocre mover making her racecourse debut, could not handle the early pace but she was fairly flying at the finish and would have made it in another stride. (12/1)

530 Who Nose (IRE), trying his luck on the sand and equipped with blinkers for the first time, had his chance throughout the final furlong but, hard as he tried, just could not peg back the winner. (9/4: op 6/4)

530 Pink Ticket, in the firing line from the break, kept plugging away but a turn of finishing speed was missing when it was most required. (2/1)

Wilfred Sherman (IRE) again missed the break but he soon recovered to press the leaders until weakening inside the final furlong. (7/1)

593 JOHNSTON H'CAP (0-60) (3-Y.O+) (Class F)

4-45 (4-47) **5f** **(Fibresand)** £2,277.00 (£627.00: £297.00) Stalls: Low GOING: 0.28 sec per fur (SLW)

				SP	RR	SF
326[5]	**Time To Fly (34)** (BWMurray) **4-8-2b**[ow2] JFEgan(6) (a.p: led wl over 1f out: qcknd clr ent fnl f)	—	**1**	25/1	49	31
*515**	**Silk Cottage (54)** (RMWhitaker) **5-9-8** DeanMcKeown(9) (a.p: effrt & hung lft over 1f out: kpt on: no ch w wnr)	4	**2**	4/1[1]	56	40
464[6]	**Stephensons Rocket (44)** (RAFahey) **6-8-12** ACulhane(10) (chsd ldrs: sn hrd drvn: r.o wl fnl f)	½	**3**	7/1[3]	45	29
391[10]	**Boffy (IRE) (46)** (BPJBaugh) **4-9-0b** RPerham(8) (lw: hdwy over 2f out: nt clr run appr fnl f: nt rcvr)	1¾	**4**	20/1	41	25
541[2]	**Sotonian (HOL) (46)** (PSFelgate) **4-9-0** DWright(3) (w ldrs: slt ld ½-wy tl wl over 1f out: one pce)	1	**5**	6/1[2]	38	22
545[7]	**Lochon (50)** (MrsNMacauley) **6-9-1b**(3) CTeague(11) (b: outpcd: rdn over 2f out: sme late hdwy)	hd	**6**	20/1	42	26
386[5]	**Southern Dominion (39)** (MissJFCraze) **5-8-7**[ow1] SWebster(4) (b.hind: led to ½-wy: rdn & outpcd over 1f out)	1¾	**7**	14/1	25	8
545[3]	**Afaan (IRE) (60)** (RFMarvin) **4-10-0** TGMcLaughlin(12) (lw: a outpcd)	s.h	**8**	8/1	46	30
515[2]	**Featherstone Lane (51)** (MissLCSiddall) **6-8-12v**(7) TSiddall(5) (outpcd)	½	**9**	6/1[2]	35	19
459[7]	**Aljaz (51)** (MissGayKelleway) **7-8-12**(7) RSmith(7) (outpcd)	1¼	**10**	15/2	31	15
223[9]	**Daaniera (IRE) (34)** (PHowling) **7-8-2b** JQuinn(1) (sn drvn along: a outpcd)	1	**11**	25/1	11	—
512[3]	**Efficacy (58)** (APJarvis) **6-9-5**(7) CDavies(13) (b.nr fore: outpcd)	6	**12**	7/1[3]	16	—
464[12]	**Magic Lake (46)** (EJAlston) **4-9-0** SDrowne(2) (bit bkwd: a bhd & outpcd)	2½	**13**	12/1	—	—
				(SP 128.0%)	**13 Rn**	

63.6 secs (4.70) CSF £114.39 CT £738.33 TOTE £37.10: £7.40 £1.50 £3.50 (£149.40) Trio £365.80; £309.17 to Ripon 9/4/97 OWNER Mr B. Murray (MALTON) BRED Miss N. A. Harrod

326 Time To Fly came good from the bottom of the handicap with a clear cut success, and one would wonder why it has taken so long for him to show what he is really capable of. (25/1)

515* Silk Cottage prevented Boffy from getting through when he hung badly left approaching the final furlong, and was fortunate not to get slung out. (4/1)

464 Stephensons Rocket, still to succeed on the All-Weather, stuck on well under strong pressure towards the finish and he could be returning to form. (7/1)

371 Boffy (IRE) may not have been able to trouble the winner, but he would almost certainly have been runner-up but for getting stopped in his tracks entering the final furlong. (20/1)

541 Sotonian (HOL) was unable to get away after showing ahead at halfway and the Handicapper has his measure on the All-Weather. (6/1:4/1-13/2)

386 Lochon does not seem to have the speed to win at this trip on a flat track, and he was only finding top gear when the outcome was as good as decided. (20/1)

T/Plpt: £336.00 (39.33 Tckts). T/Qdpt: £181.30 (4.83 Tckts) IM

RIPON (R-H) (Good to firm)

Wednesday April 9th

WEATHER: sunny & warm WIND: almost nil

75+ 79 73+ 67+

594 E.B.F. SPA WELTER MAIDEN STKS (2-Y.O) (Class D)

2-10 (2-12) **5f** £3,203.30 (£970.40: £474.20: £226.10) Stalls: Low GOING minus 0.51 sec per fur (F)

				SP	RR	SF
432[4]	**Out Like Magic** (PDEvans) **2-8-9** JFEgan(5) (chsd ldr: led 1½f out: r.o)	—	**1**	5/2[1]	74	17
	Happy Days (DMoffatt) **2-8-11**(3) DarrenMoffatt(10) (cmpt: unf: a in tch: hdwy over 1f out: r.o towards fin)	¾	**2**	20/1	77	20
	Quiz Master (EWeymes) **2-9-0** KFallon(11) (leggy: scope: in tch: hdwy over 1f out: styd on)	1¾	**3**	10/1	71	14
	Penniless (IRE) (NTinkler) **2-8-9** KimTinkler(6) (leggy: bit bkwd: chsd ldrs: nt qckn appr fnl f)	2½	**4**	5/1[2]	58	1
572[3]	**Inchalong** (MBrittain) **2-8-9** GBardwell(9) (in tch: kpt on same pce fnl 2f)	1½	**5**	14/1	53	—
432[11]	**Five of Spades (IRE)** (DNicholls) **2-9-0** AlexGreaves(3) (hdwy 2f out: nvr nr to chal)	nk	**6**	6/1[3]	57	—
	Durham Flyer (TDEasterby) **2-9-0** MBirch(12) (cmpt: bkwd: nvr bttr than mid div)	1½	**7**	16/1	52	—
	Laurel Pleasure (JBerry) **2-8-4**(5) TEDurcan(4) (lt-f: led over 3f: wknd)	1½	**8**	13/2	43	—
	Burnt Yates (IRE) (MWEasterby) **2-8-9**(5) GParkin(14) (cmpt: s.i.s: hdwy 2f out: hung lft: n.d)	¾	**9**	16/1	45	—
432[12]	**Prince Nicholas** (KWHogg) **2-9-0** DeanMcKeown(2) (dwlt: a bhd)	1¼	**10**	14/1	41	—
460[4]	**Last Knight (IRE)** (MRChannon) **2-8-9**(5) PPMurphy(13) (in tch tl ½-wy)	hd	**11**	10/1	41	—
	Diamond Steve (PDEvans) **2-9-0** RLappin(8) (leggy: unf: outpcd & bhd fr ½-wy)	2½	**12**	33/1	33	—
	Vet's Deceit (IRE) (RonaldThompson) **2-9-0** TWilliams(7) (lt-f: dwlt: a bhd)	5	**13**	33/1	17	—
	Burnden Days (IRE) (JHetherton) **2-9-0** SWebster(1) (str: cmpt: bit bkwd: s.i.s: a bhd)	8	**14**	9/1	—	—
				(SP 136.8%)	**14 Rn**	

59.7 secs (1.90) CSF £63.42 TOTE £3.20: £1.70 £5.70 £3.00 (£71.80) Trio £231.50; £169.57 to Hamilton 10/4/97 OWNER Mrs E. A. Dawson (WELSHPOOL) BRED M. C. Collins and N. Bycroft

432 Out Like Magic came out of what is turning out to be a red-hot Brocklesby Stakes. She made her experience tell here and won in determined style. (5/2)

Happy Days got better as the race progressed, and finished in good style, suggesting that she should no more about it next time. Another furlong would also help. (20/1)

Quiz Master ran well, and was sticking on at the end suggesting that the experience will improve him. (10/1: op 5/1)

Penniless (IRE) is not much to look at but she has plenty of toe and should be all the better for this. (5/1)

572 Inchalong ran her heart out here but it was always in vain. (14/1)

Five of Spades (IRE) has improved physically since Doncaster, and ran really well here suggesting that better is now likely. (6/1)

Laurel Pleasure is nothing special to look at, but she does possess bags of speed and probably needs time to strengthen. (13/2: 4/1-7/1)

460 Last Knight (IRE) spent most of his energy pulling far too hard on the way to post and ran no sort of race. (10/1)

595 MARKINGTON (S) H'CAP (0-60) (4-Y.O+) (Class F)

2-40 (2-41) **1m 4f 60y** £2,825.70 (£795.20: £389.10) Stalls: Low GOING minus 0.51 sec per fur (F)

				SP	RR	SF
461[3]	**Pendolino (IRE) (37)** (MBrittain) **6-8-11** GBardwell(14) (a chsng ldrs: led over 2f out: all out)	—	**1**	6/1[3]	45	21
	Totally Yours (IRE) (45) (MRChannon) **4-9-4** CandyMorris(10) (trckd ldrs: ev ch over 2f out: kpt on)	hd	**2**	9/1	53	28
493[8]	**Petoskin (50)** (JPearce) **5-9-7**(3) CTeague(6) (lw: hdwy 8f out: sn chsng ldrs: ev ch over 2f out: nt qckn towards fin)	s.h	**3**	14/1	58	34

435[17]	**Open Affair (49)** (HAkbary) **4-9-8** OUrbina(2) (mid div: hdwy 3f out: styd on ins fnl f) 1¼	**4**	14/1	55	30
542[3]	**Forzair (51)** (JJO'Neill) **5-9-11** WRyan(7) (lw: bhd: hdwy 4f out: edgd rt over 1f out: styd on towards fin) ......nk	**5**	12/1	57	33
570*	**Champagne Warrior (IRE) (51)** (MJCamacho) **4-9-10** 5x LCharnock(18) (chsd ldrs: effrt 3f out: r.o one pce) .nk	**6**	11/2 [2]	56	31
	Slapy Dam (47) (CASmith) **5-9-0**(7) IonaWands(16) (b.hind: hld up & bhd: styd on wl fnl 2f: nvr able chal) ......½	**7**	11/1	52	28
	Watch Me Go (IRE) (37) (BobJones) **8-8-11** MRimmer(20) (b: in tch: outpcd 4f out: hdwy over 1f out: nvr rchd ldrs) ......nk	**8**	4/1 [1]	41	17
465[6]	**Elite Bliss (IRE) (35)** (MJCamacho) **5-8-9** JQuinn(19) (bhd: sme hdwy 4f out: n.d) 1¼	**9**	10/1	38	14
553[10]	**Eurotwist (40)** (SEKettlewell) **8-9-0b**[1] JFortune(9) (hdwy 4f out: styd on: nvr able to chal) 1	**10**	25/1	41	17
273[9]	**Lost In The Post (IRE) (39)** (CWThornton) **4-8-12** DeanMcKeown(15) (lw: hld up: n.d) 1	**11**	25/1	39	14
313[4]	**Dino's Mistral (35)** (FHLee) **4-8-8** KFallon(5) (stdd s: n.d) 1¼	**12**	12/1	34	9
570[7]	**Ship's Dancer (37)** (DonEnricoIncisa) **4-8-10b** KimTinkler(4) (s.i.s: n.d) 1½	**13**	25/1	34	9
	Irish Oasis (IRE) (40) (BSRothwell) **4-8-13** MFenton(12) (led 2f: chsd ldr: wknd wl over 2f out) 1¼	**14**	20/1	35	10
	Antartictern (USA) (35) (GROldroyd) **7-8-9v** MMcAndrew(13) (dwlt: n.d) 7	**15**	33/1	21	—
	Smile Forever (USA) (55) (MissGayKelleway) **4-10-0** RCochrane(17) (lw: b: b.hind: mid div: effrt 4f out: n.d)nk	**16**	20/1	40	15
493[9]	**Tagatay (40)** (MJCamacho) **4-8-13b**[1] JCarroll(8) (swtg: plld hrd: led after 2f: sn clr: hdd & wknd over 2f out) ......½	**17**	14/1	25	—
	Cashmirie (35) (JLEyre) **5-8-9** RLappin(11) (chsd ldrs tl wknd fnl 4f) 6	**18**	16/1	12	—
495[4]	**Picard (IRE) (40)** (FMurphy) **4-8-13** JFanning(1) (sn chsng ldrs: wknd fnl 4f) ......nk	**19**	20/1	17	—
	Windyedge (USA) (55) (MrsAMNaughton) **4-10-0** JSupple(3) (b.nr fore: in tch tl wknd over 5f out) 5	**20**	14/1	25	—
			(SP 153.8%)		**20 Rn**

2m 38.9 (5.40) CSF £61.49 CT £726.30 TOTE £7.40: £1.70 £2.10 £3.50 £8.30 (£38.60) Trio £203.40 OWNER Mr Ian Booth (WARTHILL) BRED Mrs A. Whitehead
WEIGHT FOR AGE 4yo-1lb
No bid
Totally Yours (IRE) clmd JPearce £6,000
461 Pendolino (IRE), appreciating this trip, was given an aggressive ride and proved most resolute. (6/1)
Totally Yours (IRE) had her chances but could never quite overhaul a very determined winner. She should nevertheless find her chances in this company. (9/1: op 6/1)
400 Petoskin has been in really good form on the All-Weather and ran a useful race here. Judging from the way he struggled on, perhaps a bit further would help. (14/1)
Open Affair, trying a longer trip here, was staying on well and looks likely to do better in due course. (14/1)
542 Forzair, whose actions suggest that easier ground might well help, was inclined to hang when ridden but was staying on. (12/1)
570* Champagne Warrior (IRE) had her chances but her penalty probably just made the difference. (11/2)
Slapy Dam is happier on slightly easier ground and, by the way he finished here, he is in good heart. (11/1)
Watch Me Go (IRE) got messed about early in the straight and lacked the pace to fully recover. (4/1: op 6/1)

596 FOUNTAINS H'CAP (0-95) (3-Y.O+) (Class C)
3-10 (3-14) **6f** £5,373.60 (£1,627.80: £795.40: £379.20) Stalls: Low GOING minus 0.51 sec per fur (F)

			SP	RR	SF
	French Grit (IRE) (72) (MDods) **5-8-7** AClark(2) (trckd ldrs: hdwy 2f out: r.o to ld ins fnl f) ......—	**1**	10/1	84	43
443*	**Kira (75)** (JLEyre) **7-8-10** RLappin(12) (b: b.hind: led tl hdd & no ex ins fnl f) 1¾	**2**	2/1 [1]	82	41
527[3]	**Maiteamia (72)** (SRBowring) **4-8-0b**(7) KSked(1) (lw: w ldrs: outpcd over 2f out: kpt on fnl 2f) 1	**3**	11/2 [2]	77	36
	Bollin Harry (73) (TDEasterby) **5-8-8** MBirch(15) (lw: chsd ldrs: kpt on wl fnl 2f) ......¾	**4**	12/1	76	35
*397**	**The Happy Fox (IRE) (79)** (BAMcMahon) **5-9-0b** RCochrane(14) (hld up: swtchd & hdwy over 1f out: r.o) 1	**5**	11/1	79	38
443[22]	**Tiler (IRE) (82)** (MJohnston) **5-9-3** JWeaver(7) (lw: chsd ldrs: nt qckn fnl 2f) ......s.h	**6**	20/1	82	41
	Time To Tango (69) (GMMoore) **4-8-4** JFEgan(18) (w ldr 4f: grad wknd) ......hd	**7**	20/1	69	28
	Palacegate Touch (81) (JBerry) **7-8-11v**(5) PRoberts(3) (cl up 4f: grad wknd) ......hd	**8**	8/1 [3]	80	39
	The Lambton Worm (86) (DenysSmith) **3-8-9** KFallon(4) (nvr bttr than mid div) ......½	**9**	33/1	84	31
	Lago Di Varano (87) (RMWhitaker) **5-9-8** DeanMcKeown(11) (prom tl outpcd fnl 2f) ......s.h	**10**	25/1	85	44
	Highborn (IRE) (91) (PSFelgate) **8-9-12** KDarley(6) (s.i.s: nvr rchd ldrs) ......nk	**11**	14/1	88	47
450[17]	**Carburton (75)** (JAGlover) **4-8-10v**[1] GCarter(8) (lw: s.i.s: n.d) ......hd	**12**	9/1	72	31
	Halmanerror (61) (MrsJRRamsden) **7-7-5**(5) JBramhill(16) (nvr nr ldrs) ......¾	**13**	16/1	56	15
	Double Action (92) (TDEasterby) **3-9-1** ACulhane(13) (hld up: swtchd lft 2f out: nvr plcd to chal) ......½	**14**	33/1	86	33
	Benzoe (IRE) (73) (MrsJRRamsden) **7-8-8** JFortune(10) (s.i.s: a bhd) ......½	**15**	14/1	65	24
	Rich Glow (61) (NBycroft) **6-7-10** JQuinn(17) (bit bkwd: n.d) 5	**16**	33/1	40	—
467[5]	**Sir Silver Sox (USA) (80)** (NTinkler) **5-9-1** KimTinkler(9) (swtg: unruly s: a bhd) 1	**17**	50/1	56	15
	Mr Oscar (93) (WMcKeown) **5-10-0** JCarroll(5) (lost tch fr ½-wy) 6	**18**	50/1	53	12
			(SP 140.3%)		**18 Rn**

1m 10.9 (0.40) CSF £28.75 CT £129.85 TOTE £15.00: £2.60 £1.30 £1.70 £2.70 (£20.20) Trio £39.70 OWNER Mr Michael Wilson (DARLINGTON) BRED Miss Aisling O'Connell
LONG HANDICAP Rich Glow 7-6 Halmanerror 7-9
WEIGHT FOR AGE 3yo-12lb
French Grit (IRE), suited by the strong pace, was produced to settle it in tremendous style late on. (10/1)
443* Kira ran well up the unfavoured centre of the track, but just set the race up for the winner. (2/1)
527 Maiteamia, who has always looked better over the minimum trip previously, ran as though he got this well, and is in good heart. (11/2: 4/1-6/1)
Bollin Harry both looked and ran well, and better will be seen of him before long. (12/1)
397* The Happy Fox (IRE) ran really well from a poor draw and by the looks of things he can win at this trip. (11/1: 8/1-12/1)
Tiler (IRE) put in a fair effort but was always finding this opposition just too quick. Nevertheless the run should have brought him on. (20/1)
Time To Tango showed speed aplenty from a bad draw and should be all the better for this. (20/1)
Palacegate Touch showed he retains plenty of speed and, when things go his way, he will find plenty of opportunities. (8/1)
Double Action never got into this race but showed enough to suggest that he is well worth keeping an eye on. (33/1)

597 GALPHAY CONDITIONS STKS (3-Y.O) (Class C)
3-40 (3-44) **1m 1f** £4,426.09 (£1,655.90: £809.45: £347.75: £155.38: £78.43) Stalls: High GOING minus 0.51 sec per fur (F)

			SP	RR	SF
	Bold Words (CAN) (93) (EALDunlop) **3-9-2** KFallon(7) (lw: chsd ldrs: led 3f out: edgd lft: hld on wl towards fin) ......—	**1**	8/1	106	63

				SP	RR	SF
449[2]	**Handsome Ridge** (JHMGosden) **3-9-2** JCarroll(1) (lw: bhd: carried wd appr st: hdwy u.p 3f out: qcknd to chal ins fnl f: no ex towards fin)	nk	**2**	1/2[1]	106	63
502[3]	**Iechyd-Da (IRE) (91)** (MBell) **3-8-7**(5) GFaulkner(5) (rn wd appr st: hdwy 4f out: sn prom: nt qckn appr fnl f)	6	**3**	14/1	91	48
	Waiting Game (IRE) (DRLoder) **3-9-2** KDarley(2) (a chsng ldrs: effrt over 3f out: outpcd fnl 2f)	nk	**4**	11/2[2]	94	51
	Atlantic Desire (IRE) (90) (MJohnston) **3-8-11** JWeaver(3) (led tl hdd 5f out: wknd fnl 3f)	5	**5**	6/1[3]	80	37
449[7]	**Foot Battalion (IRE) (88)** (RHollinshead) **3-8-13**(3) FLynch(8) (bhd: rdn over 3f out: nvr rchd ldrs)	3½	**6**	50/1	79	36
449[8]	**Millroy (USA) (84)** (PAKelleway) **3-8-5v**(7) AngelaGallimore(6) (w ldr: led 5f out to 3f out: wknd)	8	**7**	66/1	61	18
	Rehearsal (IRE) (82) (CACyzer) **3-8-12** DeanMcKeown(4) (bhd whn p.u lame over 4f out)		**P**	25/1	—	—
				(SP 121.4%)	**8 Rn**	

1m 50.5 (0.30 under best) (-0.50) CSF £12.05 TOTE £10.30: £2.00 £1.10 £1.90 (£4.40) OWNER Maktoum Al Maktoum (NEWMARKET) BRED Crow's Nest & Hermitage Farm

Bold Words (CAN) proved yet again that he is a tough customer and refused to give in when challenged. That won him the day and this was a particularly good performance. (8/1)

449 Handsome Ridge got messed about on the home turn and then got outpaced, but he picked up a tremendous amount of ground halfway up thestraight to challenge inside the final furlong, only then to run out of fuel. He deserves a change of luck. (1/2)

502 Iechyd-Da (IRE) did not handle the bend at all well but he showed he has ability when he gets it fully together. (14/1)

Waiting Game (IRE) ran particularly well in this fast-run event and should be all the better for it. (11/2: 4/1-6/1)

Atlantic Desire (IRE) helped force the tremendous pace here but had run herself into the ground in the last couple of furlongs. (6/1)

396* Foot Battalion (IRE) always found things happening too quickly in this useful event. (50/1)

598 STUDLEY ROYAL H'CAP (0-70) (3-Y.O+) (Class E)

4-10 (4-11) **1m 4f 60y** £2,960.25 (£897.00: £438.50: £209.25) Stalls: Low GOING minus 0.51 sec per fur (F)

				SP	RR	SF
470[2]	**Summerhill Special (IRE) (55)** (DWBarker) **6-8-13** KDarley(5) (trckd ldrs: chal over 4f out: led over 2f out: r.o)	—	**1**	10/1	65	44
461[9]	**Sherqy (IRE) (60)** (SEKettlewell) **5-9-4** JFortune(12) (hdwy 4f out: sn chsng ldrs: kpt on u.p fnl f: nrst fin)	3½	**2**	25/1	65	44
410[12]	**Maftun (USA) (51)** (GMMoore) **5-8-9** DHolland(11) (lw: led early: cl up: led over 4f out tl over 2f out: r.o one pce)	¾	**3**	8/1[3]	56	35
430*	**Galapino (55)** (MissGayKelleway) **4-8-7**(5) RMullen(7) (hld up: hdwy & carried wd st: effrt over 3f out: chsng ldrs over 1f out: nt qckn)	s.h	**4**	6/4[1]	59	37
544[2]	**Monte Cavo (38)** (MBrittain) **6-7-10** GBardwell(15) (chsd ldrs: effrt over 4f out: wknd fnl 2½f)	12	**5**	20/1	27	6
461[6]	**Whitley Grange Boy (56)** (JLEyre) **4-8-13** TWilliams(2) (sn chsng ldrs: carried wd st: outpcd fnl 3f)	nk	**6**	6/1[2]	44	22
430[16]	**Almuhtaram (66)** (GLewis) **5-9-7b**(3) AWhelan(6) (effrt & carried wd appr st: outpcd fnl 3f)	¾	**7**	6/1[2]	53	32
430[23]	**Slasher Jack (IRE) (70)** (DNicholls) **6-10-0** AlexGreaves(3) (hld up: nvr nr to chal)	½	**8**	20/1	57	36
	Dashing Invader (USA) (43) (PWHarris) **4-8-0** GCarter(4) (hld up & bhd: sme hdwy fnl 3f: n.d)	½	**9**	14/1	29	7
418[3]	**Dr Edgar (52)** (MDods) **5-8-10** AClark(8) (nvr trbld ldrs)	7	**10**	9/1	29	8
	Morning Sir (48) (AStreeter) **4-8-5** TSprake(1) (sn led tl rn wd ent st: sn lost pl)	8	**11**	33/1	15	—
553[5]	**Carol Again (38)** (NBycroft) **5-7-10** JQuinn(9) (hld up: effrt 5f out: sn btn)	hd	**12**	20/1	4	—
	Meltemison (68) (MDHammond) **4-9-11** KFallon(10) (a in rr)	8	**13**	12/1	24	2
233[13]	**Great Chief (55)** (BobJones) **4-8-12** NDay(13) (b.hind: in tch tl wknd fnl 4f)	16	**14**	20/1	—	—
				(SP 139.0%)	**14 Rn**	

2m 35.5 (2.00) CSF £237.21 CT £1,960.74 TOTE £10.20: £2.30 £5.80 £3.70 (£65.00) Trio £166.50 OWNER Alba Racing Syndicate (RICHMOND) BRED Miss Audrey F. Thompson

LONG HANDICAP Carol Again 7-9 Monte Cavo 7-1

WEIGHT FOR AGE 4yo-1lb

470 Summerhill Special (IRE) always held a good position in this messy event and, given a good ride, got first run on several rivals. (10/1)

Sherqy (IRE) proved a game sort, responding to pressure in the last three furlongs, and needs either further or a stronger pace than was set here. (25/1)

360* Maftun (USA), a moderate-actioned individual, ran well but was basically short of toe late on. (8/1)

430* Galapino, held up in this slowly-run event, had an impossible task. (6/4)

544 Monte Cavo, from 9lb out of the handicap, raced with every chance but was getting completely outpaced in the last quarter-mile. (20/1)

461 Whitley Grange Boy, wearing a brush pricker to stop him hanging, was a shade disappointing in this messy event. (6/1)

599 GRANTLEY MAIDEN STKS (3-Y.O+) (Class D)

4-40 (4-44) **1m** £3,647.50 (£1,105.00: £540.00: £257.50) Stalls: High GOING minus 0.51 sec per fur (F)

				SP	RR	SF
	Green Card (USA) (SPCWoods) **3-8-12** WRyan(7) (lw: trckd ldrs: led wl over 1f out: r.o wl)	—	**1**	2/1[1]	87+	44
	Crystal Gold (MRStoute) **3-8-12** DeanMcKeown(18) (bit bkwd: cl up: led wl over 2f out tl wl over 1f out: nt qckn)	4	**2**	11/1	79	36
436[3]	**Burning Truth (USA)** (RCharlton) **3-8-12** TSprake(14) (lw: in tch: styd on wl fnl 2f: nrst fin)	¾	**3**	3/1[2]	78	35
	Fooled You (USA) (EALDunlop) **3-8-9**(3) DO'Donohoe(11) (lengthy: unf: s.i.s: bhd tl brought wd & hdwy over 3f out: chsng ldrs 2f out: nt qckn fnl f)	1¾	**4**	6/1[3]	74	31
	Yours In Sport (JWWatts) **3-8-12** WRSwinburn(17) (unf: scope: bkwd: bhd: hdwy on ins 4f out: swtchd 2f out: styd on wl towards fin)	nk	**5**	20/1	73	30
	Dispol Gem (60) (PCalver) **4-9-8** KDarley(16) (a chsng ldrs: one pce fnl 3f)	nk	**6**	50/1	68	40
528[4]	**Duraid (IRE)** (DenysSmith) **5-9-13** ACulhane(8) (hld up & bhd: sme late hdwy)	¾	**7**	11/1	71	43
	Premier Eclipse (PWHarris) **3-8-12** GHind(4) (w'like: bkwd: s.i.s: hdwy appr st: outpcd 3f out: n.d)	6	**8**	25/1	59	16
528[7]	**Most Respectful** (DenysSmith) **4-9-13** KFallon(2) (led tl hdd wl over 2f out: wknd)	½	**9**	200/1	58	30
	Quezon City (MJCamacho) **3-8-12** NKennedy(15) (chsd ldrs tl wknd fnl 3½f)	1¾	**10**	200/1	55	12
	American Whisper (PWHarris) **3-8-12** PatEddery(3) (in tch: hung rt over 2f out: sn btn & eased)	1	**11**	6/1[3]	53	10
	Zagros (IRE) (TDEasterby) **3-8-12** MBirch(9) (bit bkwd: hld up & bhd: n.d)	½	**12**	50/1	52	9
	Welcome Home (PTDalton) **3-8-7** JFEgan(10) (bit bkwd: lost tch fr ½-wy)	1¼	**13**	500/1	44	1
	Burlesque (JDBethell) **3-8-12** SDrowne(13) (n.d)	1¼	**14**	50/1	47	4
550[12]	**Samstotry** (MissLAPerratt) **7-9-13** JQuinn(12) (bit bkwd: chsd ldrs tl wknd over 3f out)	13	**15**	400/1	21	—
	Action Stations (CACyzer) **3-8-12** DBiggs(5) (wl grwn: bkwd: plld hrd early: sn bhd: t.o)	dist	**16**	25/1	—	—
	Makati (MJCamacho) **3-8-12** LCharnock(6) (Withdrawn not under Starter's orders: ref to ent stalls)		**W**	50/1	—	—
				(SP 125.3%)	**16 Rn**	

1m 39.3 (1.10) CSF £22.97 TOTE £2.90: £1.90 £3.50 £1.70 (£26.60) Trio £33.60 OWNER Mr P. K. L. Chu (NEWMARKET) BRED Pin Oak Stud

WEIGHT FOR AGE 3yo-15lb
Green Card (USA) took the eye on the way to post and won in useful style, and looks likely to be even better over further. (2/1)
Crystal Gold, just needing this, ran really well and is now qualified for handicaps. (11/1: 7/1-12/1)
436 Burning Truth (USA) was staying on splendidly in the last two furlongs suggesting that longer trips will bring plenty of improvement. (3/1)
Fooled You (USA) was a long way behind entering the straight and then showed an amazing turn of foot to almost get into it. He has not got the best of actions, but there is obviously plenty of ability when he gets it fully together. (6/1: 5/2-7/1)
Yours In Sport took time to get the hang of things but the way he finished suggested that he will do a deal better over longer distances. (20/1)
Dispol Gem ran a fair race and might well be on the upgrade. (50/1)
528 Duraid (IRE) never got into this but showed enough to suggest that when he is handicapped he will make his mark. (11/1: 33/1-50/1)
Premier Eclipse, needing this, looks the type to improve with experience. (25/1)

600 SAWLEY H'CAP (0-70) (3-Y.O) (Class E)

5-10 (5-13) **1m 2f** £2,882.25 (£873.00: £426.50: £203.25) Stalls: High GOING minus 0.51 sec per fur (F)

Form	Horse	Dist	Pl	SP	RR	SF
	Ibin St James (67) (JDBethell) **3-9-4** DHolland(4) (chsd ldrs: rdn to ld over 1f out: hld on wl)	—	**1**	8/1[3]	75	46
	Kingdom Emperor (47) (MJCamacho) **3-7-12** LCharnock(1) (hld up & bhd: hdwy 4f out: chal over 1f out: styd on towards fin)	hd	**2**	9/1	55	26
	Chaluz (50) (KRBurke) **3-8-1** JQuinn(6) (lw: led: clr 4f out: hdd & wknd appr fnl f)	6	**3**	14/1	48	19
*456**	**Castles Burning (USA) (65)** (CACyzer) **3-9-2** KFallon(12) (lw: outpcd & bhd appr st: hdwy 3f out: nvr rchd ldrs)	8	**4**	11/8[1]	50	21
373[8]	**Petula Boy (45)** (SRBowring) **3-7-5**(5) PFessey(2) (chsd ldrs tl outpcd fnl 3f)	6	**5**	33/1	21	—
	Floating Devon (56) (TDEasterby) **3-8-7** MBirch(5) (plld hrd: bhd: sme hdwy over 2f out: n.d)	2½	**6**	8/1[3]	28	—
*239**	**Belle Bijou (67)** (MJohnston) **3-9-4** JWeaver(8) (lw: chsd ldrs tl rdn & wknd fnl 3½f)	2	**7**	11/2[2]	36	7
497[5]	**Silver Button (48)** (SEKettlewell) **3-7-6**(7) JennyBenson(13) (effrt 4f out: nvr bttr than mid div)	1	**8**	12/1	15	—
463[4]	**Noirie (70)** (MBrittain) **3-9-7** JCarroll(11) (hld up & bhd: n.d)	2	**9**	8/1[3]	34	5
	Not A Lot (53) (MWEasterby) **3-8-4** TLucas(7) (bit bkwd: hld up & a bhd)	1¼	**10**	20/1	15	—
41[5]	**Bali-Pet (55)** (JParkes) **3-8-1**(5) JBramhill(3) (prom tl wknd fnl 3f)	s.h	**11**	33/1	17	—

(SP 125.8%) **11 Rn**

2m 5.3 (1.80) CSF £74.46 CT £921.00 TOTE £10.50: £2.70 £5.60 £2.70 (£195.70) Trio £132.90 OWNER Sheikh Amin Dahlawi (MIDDLEHAM) BRED Al Dahlawi Stud Co Ltd
Ibin St James had to work hard for this and showed a fine attitude late on. (8/1)
Kingdom Emperor raced too freely early on, and then showed signs of inexperience when in there with a chance. He should improve for the run. (9/1: 6/1-10/1)
Chaluz put up a decent effort here and seems to be improving. (14/1)
456* Castles Burning (USA) got completely outpaced on the turn and, although staying on, never had a chance. (11/8)
289 Petula Boy looked onepaced when the pressure was on in the last four furlongs. (33/1)
Floating Devon needs to learn to settle. (8/1)
239* Belle Bijou (11/2: 3/1-6/1)

T/Jkpt: £27,215.60 (0.5 Tckts); £19,165.94 to Hamilton 10/4/97. T/Plpt: £102.80 (185.64 Tckts). T/Qdpt: £15.50 (73.82 Tckts) AA

0472-FOLKESTONE (R-H) (St crse Good to firm, Firm ptchs, Rnd crse Firm, Good to firm ptchs)
Thursday April 10th

WEATHER: fine & sunny WIND: almost nil

601 LEVY BOARD APPRENTICE H'CAP (0-60) (3-Y.O+) (Class G)

2-00 (2-03) **6f** £2,116.00 (£601.00: £298.00) Stalls: Low GOING minus 0.12 sec per fur (G)

Form	Horse	Dist	Pl	SP	RR	SF
484[3]	**Summerville Wood (58)** (PMooney) **3-8-9b**(5) PFitzsimons(2) (dwlt: hdwy 3f out: led 2f out: rdn ins fnl f: r.o)	—	**1**	5/1[1]	70	23
477[3]	**Scathebury (55)** (KRBurke) **4-9-1**(8) PWright(7) (lw: stdd s: gd hdwy over 1f out: ev ch wl ins fnl f: unable qckn)	½	**2**	10/1	66	31
	Don't Forget Mikie (IRE) (56) (AlexVanderhaeghen,Belgium) **4-9-10** RCody-Boutcher(5) (mid div: hdwy 2f out: rdn over 1f out: one pce)	3½	**3**	25/1	57	22
	Velvet Jones (50) (GFHCharles-Jones) **4-8-10**(8) CharlotteCox(16) (bit bkwd: bhd: gd hdwy fnl f: r.o)	nk	**4**	20/1	51	16
569[9]	**Sir Tasker (48)** (JLHarris) **9-9-2** JFowle(4) (led: hdd 2f out: wknd ins fnl f)	¾	**5**	11/1	47	12
401[10]	**Spectacle Jim (44)** (BAPearce) **8-8-12v** GGallagher(6) (mid div: rdn 2f out: styd on one pce ins fnl f)	¾	**6**	33/1	41	6
541[5]	**Mister Raider (48)** (EAWheeler) **5-9-2b** KerryBaker(1) (spd over 4f)	1½	**7**	10/1	41	6
490[7]	**River Seine (FR) (49)** (SGKnight) **5-8-12**(5) DarrenWilliams(9) (lw: hdwy 3f out: rdn 2f out: one pce)	1	**8**	16/1	39	4
484*	**Astral Invader (IRE) (55)** (MSSaunders) **5-9-9v** AMcCarthy(3) (spd 4f)	1½	**9**	13/2[3]	41	6
	Nellie North (56) (GMMcCourt) **4-9-7b[1]**(3) RStudholme(12) (lw: spd on outside 4f)	1¼	**10**	10/1	39	4
	Ed's Folly (IRE) (56) (SDow) **4-9-2**(8) DSalt(8) (chsd ldrs tl wknd over 2f out)	2½	**11**	12/1	32	—
520[7]	**Time For Tea (IRE) (55)** (CACyzer) **4-9-1**(8) RSawyer(13) (chsd ldrs 4f)	1¼	**12**	16/1	28	—
335[4]	**Bon Secret (IRE) (56)** (TJNaughton) **5-9-2**(8) RachaelMoody(14) (a bhd)	½	**13**	12/1	27	—
	Pharaoh's Joy (59) (JWPayne) **4-9-5**(8) JacquelineCoppard(10) (prom to ½-wy)	s.h	**14**	11/1	30	—
458[8]	**Jobie (48)** (RTPhillips) **7-9-2v[1]** LJames(11) (prom to ½-wy)	¾	**15**	20/1	17	—
	Vax New Way (59) (AlexVanderhaeghen,Belgium) **4-9-13b** RBrisland(15) (bhd fr ½-wy)	4	**16**	11/2[2]	17	—

(SP 132.8%) **16 Rn**

1m 14.8 (4.60) CSF £51.68 CT £1,093.84 TOTE £6.80: £1.80 £2.70 £5.80 £3.20 (£27.80) Trio £347.70; £391.88 to Nottingham 11/4/97
OWNER Likely Lads Partnership (ASTON UPTHORPE) BRED Sean Kelly Bloodstock
WEIGHT FOR AGE 3yo-12lb
IN-FOCUS: Winning jockey Paul Fitzsimons was having his first ride.
484 Summerville Wood looked seriously threatened when the runner-up challenged inside the final furlong, but he found plenty and was well on top at the finish. (5/1)
477 Scathebury is a hard horse to win with. The jockey appeared to time this to perfection but the winner was not for passing. (10/1: op 11/2)
Don't Forget Mikie (IRE) kept on under pressure in the final two furlongs. (25/1)
Velvet Jones was right out the back door until making good late headway. He is best over further. (20/1)

348 Sir Tasker showed his usual early dash. (11/1: 8/1-12/1)
Spectacle Jim kept on in the final furlong without looking likely to get involved. (33/1)
335 Bon Secret (IRE) (12/1: op 8/1)
Pharaoh's Joy (11/1: 8/1-12/1)
Vax New Way (11/2: 8/1-5/1)

602 CHATHAM CLAIMING STKS (3-Y.O) (Class F)

2-30 (2-30) **5f** £2,277.00 (£627.00: £297.00) Stalls: Low GOING minus 0.12 sec per fur (G)

	Horse	Dist	Pos	SP	RR	SF
448^{16}	**Levelled (70)** (MRChannon) **3-8-10**(5) PPMurphy(7) (a.p: led 2f out: drvn out)	—	1	$3/1^{1}$	71	20
473^{10}	**Suite Factors (54)** (KRBurke) **3-8-13** RPerham(5) (a.p: ev ch over 1f out: hrd rdn ins fnl f: unable qckn)	½	2	11/1	67	16
427^{8}	**Hever Golf Stormer (IRE) (58)** (TJNaughton) **3-8-7** PaulEddery(2) (hdwy 2f out: sn rdn: r.o ins fnl f)	½	3	20/1	60	9
474^{7}	**Jukebox Jive (55)** (CADwyer) **3-7-7**(7) AMcCarthy(10) (outpcd in rr: gd hdwy fnl f: fin wl)	nk	4	$9/2^{2}$	52	1
320^{8}	**Whizz Kid (51)** (JJBridger) **3-7-9**(5) RMullen(4) (mid div: rdn 2f out: r.o one pce ins fnl f)	hd	5	12/1	52	1
506^{11}	**Heavenly Miss (IRE) (68)** (JJBridger) **3-8-1b**1(5) ADaly(1) (led: hdd 2f out: no ex ins fnl f)	¾	6	$5/1^{3}$	55	4
474^{6}	**Littlestone Rocket (62)** (WRMuir) **3-8-13** JReid(9) (prom: ev ch over 1f out: wknd ins fnl f)	1	7	$9/2^{2}$	59	8
	Village Pub (FR) (63) (KOCunningham-Brown) **3-9-3b** MRoberts(8) (sn outpcd)	3½	8	8/1	52	1
399^{7}	**College Princess (52)** (CADwyer) **3-8-0** JQuinn(6) (sn outpcd)	1¾	9	14/1	29	—
	Super Saint (AlexVanderhaeghen,Belgium) **3-8-13** MServranckx(3) (a bhd)	4	10	9/1	29	—

(SP 126.6%) **10 Rn**

61.6 secs (4.00) CSF £38.06 TOTE £4.40: £2.40 £6.50 £4.10 (£88.70) Trio £135.80; £61.22 to Nottingham 11/4/97 OWNER Maygain Ltd (UPPER LAMBOURN) BRED J. F. Watson
Levelled led going well two furlongs out, and though his rider had to get serious inside the final furlong, he was always holding his rivals at bay. (3/1)
Suite Factors was always to the fore but just got done for a turn of foot. (11/1: 8/1-12/1)
132 Hever Golf Stormer (IRE) stayed on in the final furlong without looking like reaching the principals, which was a better run than of late. (20/1)
Jukebox Jive was totally out-paced until staying on strongly in the final furlong. She needs further. (9/2: 8/1-4/1)
212 Whizz Kid kept on for pressure inside the final two furlongs. (12/1: op 8/1)
279 Heavenly Miss (IRE) didn't look keen under pressure. (5/1)
Super Saint (9/1: 6/1-10/1)

603 GRAVESEND H'CAP (0-70) (4-Y.O+) (Class E)

3-00 (3-02) **1m 7f 92y** £2,888.25 (£861.00: £410.50: £185.25) Stalls: Low GOING minus 0.12 sec per fur (G)

	Horse	Dist	Pos	SP	RR	SF
	Coh Sho No (54) (SDow) **4-9-1** TQuinn(7) (lw: a.p: chsd ldr 10f out: led over 1f out: hrd rdn ins fnl f: r.o)	—	1	$7/1^{3}$	68	46
*351**	**Soojama (IRE) (50)** (RMFlower) **7-9-0b** MRoberts(5) (hld up: hdwy 6f out: rdn over 1f out: unable qckn)	1½	2	$4/5^{1}$	62	43
	Ginka (35) (JWMullins) **6-7-13** FNorton(6) (chsd ldrs: rdn & outpcd 6f out: styd on one pce fnl 2f)	1¾	3	10/1	46	27
167^{8}	**Stonecutter (52)** (MRChannon) **4-8-13v** RPerham(4) (lw: led: hdd over 1f out: one pce)	1¼	4	$6/1^{2}$	61	39
	Ewar Bold (50) (KOCunningham-Brown) **4-8-11b** TSprake(3) (lw: bhd fr ½-wy)	15	5	20/1	44	22
381^{5}	**Kirov Protege (IRE) (32)** (MrsLCJewell) **5-7-3**(7) DarrenWilliams(2) (bhd fr ½-wy)	nk	6	33/1	26	7
	Hanbitooh (USA) (63) (MrsAJPerrett) **4-9-10** JReid(1) (lw: a bhd)	½	7	$6/1^{2}$	56	34

(SP 113.4%) **7 Rn**

3m 26.6 (8.60) CSF £11.71 TOTE £10.00: £3.10 £1.20 (£5.00) OWNER Mr Harold Nass (EPSOM) BRED Baron F. von Oppenheim
LONG HANDICAP Kirov Protege (IRE) 7-4
WEIGHT FOR AGE 4yo-3lb
Coh Sho No gave her trainer his first winner since January. (7/1)
351* Soojama (IRE) moved up threateningly below the distance, but never looked like reeling the winner in. (4/5: evens-11/10)
Ginka stayed on well up the straight having been out-paced after halfway. All she does is stay and soft ground would help slow her rivals down. (10/1: op 6/1)
80* Stonecutter set a fair pace but had no more to give once headed. (6/1)
Hanbitooh (USA) (6/1: op 4/1)

604 GILLINGHAM LIMITED STKS (0-65) (4-Y.O+) (Class F)

3-30 (3-30) **5f** £2,277.00 (£627.00: £297.00) Stalls: Low GOING minus 0.12 sec per fur (G)

	Horse	Dist	Pos	SP	RR	SF
585^{2}	**Beau Venture (USA) (64)** (BPalling) **9-8-11** TSprake(4) (mde all: hrd rdn ins fnl f: r.o wl)	—	1	$2/1^{1}$	73	52
391^{11}	**Songsheet (65)** (MSSaunders) **4-8-8** RPerham(5) (chsd ldrs: rdn over 2f out: styd on one pce ins fnl f)	1¾	2	8/1	64	43
	Hever Golf Star (65) (TJNaughton) **5-8-11** PaulEddery(3) (hld up: hdwy over 2f out: ev ch ent fnl f: no ex nr fin)	1½	3	$5/2^{2}$	63	42
	Village Native (FR) (59) (KOCunningham-Brown) **4-8-11** MRoberts(1) (a.p: ev ch 2f out: hrd rdn over 1f out: one pce)	nk	4	11/1	62	41
541^{7}	**Polly Golightly (61)** (MBlanshard) **4-8-8b** JQuinn(7) (prom: ev ch 2f out: wknd over 1f out)	3	5	$5/1^{3}$	49	28
	Myasha (USA) (65) (AlexVanderhaeghen,Belgium) **8-8-11** MServranckx(2) (spd to ½-wy)	1¾	6	9/1	46	25
569^{8}	**Ivory's Grab Hire (56)** (KTIvory) **4-9-0b**(3) MartinDwyer(6) (a outpcd)	2	7	11/1	46	25

(SP 116.3%) **7 Rn**

59.5 secs (1.90) CSF £17.63 TOTE £2.20: £1.50 £4.60 (£14.40) OWNER Mrs A. L. Stacey (COWBRIDGE) BRED Mrs C. Oliver Iselin III
STEWARDS' ENQUIRY Roberts susp. 19 & 21/4/97 (incorrect use of whip).
585 Beau Venture (USA), who ran really well only two days ago, was turned out again looking fresh and well and, after a sharp tussle entering the final furlong, won this going away. (2/1)
Songsheet was always just struggling to go the pace and, although keeping on, never looked like troubling the winner. (8/1)
Hever Golf Star moved up dangerously below the distance but had no more to give inside the last. He had not run for over a year and this run should bring him on. (5/2: 7/2-9/4)
Village Native (FR) was tapped for foot in the final two furlongs. (11/1: 8/1-12/1)
488 Ivory's Grab Hire (11/1: op 6/1)

605 DARTFORD MAIDEN STKS (3-Y.O+) (Class D)

4-00 (4-01) **1m 4f** £3,804.85 (£1,136.80: £543.90: £247.45) Stalls: Low GOING minus 0.12 sec per fur (G)

	Horse	Dist	Pos	SP	RR	SF
	Premier Night (70) (SDow) **4-9-7** TQuinn(5) (chsd ldr: led 2f out: drvn out)	—	1	$7/2^{2}$	76	39

				SP	RR	SF
502[5]	**Mardi Gras (IRE) (87)** (JLDunlop) **3-8-6** PatEddery(7) (lw: hdwy 8f out: chsd wnr 2f out: hrd rdn over 1f out: unable qckn)	2	**2**	Evens[1]	78	21
445[6]	**Rare Talent** (MRChannon) **3-8-6** PaulEddery(2) (hld up: pushed along 6f out: rdn 2f out: one pce)	3	**3**	9/2[3]	74	17
	Urgent Reply (USA) (CADwyer) **4-9-9**(3) JDSmith(8) (unf: hld up: outpcd 5f out: sme hdwy 3f out: rdn 2f out: one pce)	5	**4**	16/1	68	31
	Laurel Seeker (USA) (MrsAJPerrett) **3-8-7**ow1 JReid(3) (unf: scope: mid div: outpcd 5f out: sme hdwy 3f out: rdn 2f out: one pce)	hd	**5**	15/2	69	11
	Leatherneck (IRE) (PMooney) **4-9-9**(3) PMcCabe(6) (w'like: bit bkwd: s.s: rr: hdwy 3f out: wknd 2f out)	4	**6**	40/1	62	25
	Suleika Dancer (SGKnight) **4-9-2**(5) GFaulkner(4) (led: hdd 2f out: sn wknd)	3	**7**	50/1	53	16
	Mystical Island (CACyzer) **3-8-1** DBiggs(9) (bhd fr ½-wy)	3	**8**	33/1	49	—
	Victor Blum (USA) (CAHorgan) **4-9-12** MFenton(1) (w'like: bit bkwd: a bhd)	nk	**9**	33/1	54	17

(SP 118.3%) **9 Rn**

2m 39.8 (8.60) CSF £6.75 TOTE £6.90: £1.90 £1.10 £1.20 (£3.10) Trio £3.60 OWNER Mr D. G. Churston (EPSOM) BRED Sheikh Mohammed Bin Rashid Al Maktoum

WEIGHT FOR AGE 3yo-21lb, 4yo-1lb

Premier Night tracked the leader until going on early in the straight. She flashed her tail under pressure but ran on well enough to give her trainer a welcome double. (7/2: 9/4-4/1)

502 Mardi Gras (IRE) is badly handicapped on the strength of his debut and, dropped to moderate maiden company here, still couldn't score. (Evens)

445 Rare Talent kept on gamely enough up the straight, having been pushed along from halfway. (9/2)

Urgent Reply (USA) made some headway before the home turn but just plugged on up the straight. (16/1)

Laurel Seeker (USA) has the make and shape of a hurdler. (15/2: 6/1-10/1)

606 'PRIVY COUNCILLOR' MAIDEN STKS (3-Y.O) (Class D)

4-30 (4-30) **6f 189y** £3,868.55 (£1,156.40: £553.70: £252.35) Stalls: Low GOING minus 0.12 sec per fur (G)

				SP	RR	SF
479[4]	**Bubbly** (JLDunlop) **3-9-0** PatEddery(4) (lw: mde all: pushed clr over 1f out: comf)	—	**1**	8/13[1]	61+	38
	E Sharp (USA) (WJHaggas) **3-8-9** RCochrane(2) (plld hrd: chsd wnr fnl 6f: rdn over 1f out: unable qckn)	2	**2**	3/1[2]	51	28
	Wing of A Prayer (WJarvis) **3-9-0** JReid(6) (trckd ldng pair: rdn along over 1f out: one pce)	3	**3**	13/2[3]	49	26
395[7]	**Alagna** (SCWilliams) **3-8-2**(7) DarrenWilliams(5) (chsd wnr 1f: styd prom: rdn 2f out: one pce)	1½	**4**	20/1	41	18
474[11]	**Muara Bay** (GLewis) **3-8-7**(7) JDennis(1) (a bhd)	4	**5**	33/1	37	14
	Purple Maize (JAkehurst) **3-9-0** TQuinn(3) (w'like: bit bkwd: rr: effrt 3f out: sn btn)	1¼	**6**	16/1	34	11

(SP 113.8%) **6 Rn**

1m 25.7 (4.30) CSF £2.56 TOTE £1.60: £1.10 £1.90 (£1.50) OWNER Lord Swaythling (ARUNDEL) BRED Cheveley Park Stud Ltd

479 Bubbly made all the running and outclassed his rivals. (8/13)

E Sharp (USA), an odds-on failure in her only start last year for David Loder, didn't help herself by pulling hard, but she nevertheless ran well and will improve when learning to settle. (3/1)

Wing of A Prayer wasn't knocked about in third and is interesting now he is qualified for handicaps. (13/2)

Alagna was out-paced in the final two furlongs. (20/1)

607 BOLLINGER CHAMPAGNE CHALLENGE SERIES GENTLEMEN'S H'CAP (0-70) (4-Y.O+) (Class E)

5-00 (5-01) **1m 1f 149y** £3,148.25 (£941.00: £450.50: £205.25) Stalls: Low GOING minus 0.12 sec per fur (G)

				SP	RR	SF
418[4]	**Fresh Fruit Daily (63)** (PAKelleway) **5-11-3**(4) MrMSpillane(7) (lw: conf rdn: hld up: gd hdwy over 2f out: led over 1f out: qcknd clr ins fnl f: readily)	—	**1**	16/1	77	53
	Dauphin (IRE) (40) (WJMusson) **4-9-12** MrTMcCarthy(9) (b: a.p: ev ch over 1f out: unable qckn)	3	**2**	9/2[2]	49	25
294[5]	**Nails Tails (36)** (SDow) **4-9-4**(4) MrJGoldstein(12) (hld up in tch: rdn over 1f out: kpt on one pce ins fnl f)	½	**3**	5/1[3]	44	20
496*	**Soldier Cove (USA) (46)** (MartynMeade) **7-10-4** MrCBonner(11) (led: hdd over 1f out: wknd ins fnl f)	4	**4**	2/1[1]	48	24
	Lalindi (IRE) (70) (ACStewart) **6-11-10**(4) MrCRanson(5) (bit bkwd: dwlt: nvr nrr)	2	**5**	16/1	68	44
457[6]	**Roman Reel (USA) (64)** (GLMoore) **6-11-4**(4) MrIMongan(10) (chsd ldrs: c wd home turn: sn rdn: one pce)	nk	**6**	10/1	62	38
	Allstars Express (63) (KCBailey) **4-11-7** MrRWakley(3) (prom tl wknd over 2f out)	nk	**7**	6/1	60	36
261[3]	**Classy Chief (66)** (JWhite) **4-11-6**(4) MrJCrowley(13) (dwlt: sn rcvrd to chse ldrs: pushed wd home turn: sn wknd)	5	**8**	14/1	55	31
294[11]	**Montone (IRE) (65)** (JRJenkins) **7-11-9** DrMMannish(6) (hld up: hdwy 3 out: c wd home turn: sn rdn & wknd)	10	**9**	11/2	38	14
	Bataan (USA) (66) (AlexVanderhaeghen,Belgium) **6-11-6**(4) MrVLukaniuk(1) (b: prom tl wknd over 2f out)	2	**10**	20/1	35	11
	Friar's Oak (35) (PButler) **5-9-3**(4) MrOMcPhail(8) (bit bkwd: a bhd)	4	**11**	33/1	—	—
	Arcady (62) (JLHarris) **4-11-2**(4) MrJHenderson(4) (b: a bhd)	13	**12**	12/1	3	—
407[10]	**Sussex Gorse (37)** (JELong) **6-9-5**(4)ow2 MrTWaters(2) (a bhd)	15	**13**	100/1	—	—

(SP 141.8%) **13 Rn**

2m 5.7 (8.00) CSF £92.39 CT £405.35 TOTE £18.70: £4.90 £1.10 £1.40 (£39.60) Trio £186.70 OWNER Mr Kevin Hudson (NEWMARKET) BRED Worksop Manor Stud Farm

LONG HANDICAP Friar's Oak 9-6 Sussex Gorse 8-1

418 Fresh Fruit Daily won this under a very confident ride from Spillane, partnering his first winner. Held up, she made smooth headway before the home turn, and she got a lovely run as some of her rivals swung out. She took it up below the distance and soon came clear to score comfortably. (16/1)

Dauphin (IRE) was given a very competent ride here saving ground by running close to the rail throughout. He had every chance below the distance but couldn't match the winner's turn of foot. (9/2)

294 Nails Tails kept on well enough for pressure in the final two furlongs despite flashing his tail. (5/1)

496* Soldier Cove (USA) had every chance. He made a lot of the running but was left behind from below the distance. (2/1)

401* Roman Reel (USA) (10/1: 8/1-12/1)

261 Classy Chief (14/1: 10/1-16/1)

T/Plpt: £17.90 (562.14 Tckts). T/Qdpt: £2.00 (334.09 Tckts) SM

0548-HAMILTON (R-H) (Good to soft, Good patches)
Thursday April 10th
WEATHER: fine and sunny WIND: moderate, half against

608 CALDER APPRENTICE SERIES H'CAP (0-70) (3-Y.O+) (Class E)
2-20 (2-21) **1m 65y** £2,682.75 (£822.00: £408.50: £201.75) Stalls: High GOING minus 0.12 sec per fur (G)

Form	Horse	Dist	Pos	SP	RR	SF
571[2]	**Rambo Waltzer (65)** (DNicholls) **5-9-4**(5) CarolynBales(14) (lw: in tch: n.m.r 2f out: hdwy over 1f out: r.o wl to ld post)	—	**1**	9/2[1]	77	47
526*	**Gadge (55)** (ABailey) **6-8-10**(3) 5x TSiddall(5) (b: chsd ldr: led 4f out: clr over 1f out: ct last stride)	s.h	**2**	11/2[2]	67	37
435[2]	**Mels Baby (IRE) (70)** (JLEyre) **4-9-11**(3) SBuckley(4) (bhd: hdwy ent st: styd on strly fnl f: nrst fin)	s.h	**3**	7/1	82	52
570[3]	**Portite Sophie (38)** (MBrittain) **6-7-5**(5) DMernagh(12) (swtg: led tl hdd 4f out: cl up tl wknd fnl 2f)	4	**4**	16/1	42	12
461[12]	**Fatehalkhair (IRE) (40)** (BEllison) **5-7-7**(5)ow2 RWinston(7) (cl up: outpcd over 3f out: wknd over 1f out)	¾	**5**	20/1	43	11
	Best of All (IRE) (62) (JBerry) **5-9-3b**(3) CLowther(13) (styd on fnl 4f: nrst fin)	hd	**6**	7/1	65	35
496[2]	**Running Green (55)** (DMoffatt) **6-8-13** PDoe(10) (b: effrt ½-wy: outpcd fnl 2f)	6	**7**	7/1	46	16
526[9]	**Live Project (IRE) (58)** (MJohnston) **5-8-13**(3) NPollard(11) (swtg: chsd ldrs tl outpcd fnl 3½f)	2½	**8**	20/1	44	14
	Teejay'n'aitch (IRE) (38) (JSGoldie) **5-7-5**(5) PBradley(6) (lw: prom tl outpcd fnl 4f)	1¾	**9**	16/1	21	—
	Ca'd'oro (55) (GBBalding) **4-8-8**(5) FTynan(15) (a bhd)	½	**10**	6/1[3]	37	7
552[14]	**Hutchies Lady (38)** (RMMcKellar) **5-7-7**(3) JennyBenson(8) (b.hind: bhd: c wd st: n.d)	4	**11**	33/1	12	—
524[10]	**Bout (63)** (RMMcKellar) **3-8-1**(5)ow3 FionaBrown(3) (b.nr hind: a bhd)	2	**12**	100/1	33	—
552[9]	**Giftbox (USA) (49)** (NBycroft) **5-8-7** AnthonyBond(9) (lw: c wd st: n.d)	3½	**13**	20/1	12	—
435[20]	**Take Notice (68)** (RMMcKellar) **4-9-9**(3) JMcAuley(1) (b.hind: c wd st: n.d)	8	**14**	50/1	16	—
496[8]	**Rattle (39)** (DANolan) **4-7-8b**(3) AngelaHartley(2) (a bhd: rn wd st)	s.h	**15**	33/1	—	—
328[8]	**Veesey (45)** (JohnBerry) **4-8-0**(3)ow3 RSmith(16) (bhd & swtchd wd over 3f out: n.d)	2½	**16**	33/1	—	—

(SP 123.2%) **16 Rn**

1m 49.3 (5.20) CSF £23.38 CT £167.26 TOTE £5.60: £1.70 £2.00 £1.30 £2.80 (£9.50) Trio £5.70 OWNER Mr W. G. Swiers (THIRSK) BRED Triangle Thoroughbreds Ltd

LONG HANDICAP Portite Sophie 6-11 Fatehalkhair (IRE) 7-5 Teejay'n'aitch (IRE) 7-7 Hutchies Lady 7-6

WEIGHT FOR AGE 3yo-15lb

OFFICIAL EXPLANATION **Ca'd'oro: rider reported that his instructions were to settle the gelding early and make the best of his way home without using the stick so as not to unbalance his mount or himself, this being only his sixth ride. The trainer's representative added that she was happy with the ride.**

IN-FOCUS: **This was Bales' first winner.**

571 Rambo Waltzer is a super-consistent sort who goes well for inexperienced riders and produced a terrific burst to take this. (9/2)

526* Gadge looked to have this sewn up but is inclined to idle in front inside the final furlong and just failed to hang on. He is in tremendous heart. (11/2)

435 Mels Baby (IRE) did a lot of running from the home turn and was still finishing well to show he keeps his enthusiasm. (7/1)

570 Portite Sophie ran a fine race from 13lb out of the handicap, and she could well break her duck on Turf this season. (16/1)

Fatehalkhair (IRE) has ability but just found the struggle beyond him when the pressure was really on. (20/1)

Best of All (IRE) ran well, making headway up the slower ground in the straight and is worth keeping an eye on. (7/1)

Ca'd'oro never looked likely to get into this and with an experienced rider on board was certainly not given a hard time. (6/1)

609 SPRINGFIELD RATING RELATED MAIDEN STKS (0-60) (3-Y.O) (Class F)
2-50 (2-51) **1m 65y** £2,472.00 (£692.00: £336.00) Stalls: High GOING minus 0.12 sec per fur (G)

Form	Horse	Dist	Pos	SP	RR	SF
	Purchasing Power (IRE) (60) (NACallaghan) **3-9-0** SDrowne(5) (mde all: pushed along & r.o wl fnl 2f)	—	**1**	7/4[1]	60	27
	Step N Go (IRE) (60) (MrsJRRamsden) **3-8-11** JFortune(4) (lw: trckd ldrs: effrt & n.m.r 3f out: hdwy & ch ins fnl f: r.o u.p)	1¼	**2**	7/4[1]	55	22
535[4]	**Barresbo (59)** (CWFairhurst) **3-9-0** KFallon(3) (in tch: hdwy 4f out: sn chsng wnr: nt qckn appr fnl f)	3	**3**	7/1[2]	52	19
551[2]	**Tycoon Tina (55)** (WMBrisbourne) **3-8-11** KDarley(7) (s.s: hdwy 4f out: styd on: nvr able to chal)	3½	**4**	20/1	42	9
373[12]	**Father Eddie (55)** (JJO'Neill) **3-9-0** GDuffield(8) (chsd ldrs: pushed along after 2f: outpcd fnl 3f)	5	**5**	25/1	35	2
368[2]	**Fearless Sioux (55)** (CWThornton) **3-8-11** DeanMcKeown(2) (lw: in tch: hdwy ½-wy: sn chsng ldrs: wknd fnl 2f)	4	**6**	10/1[3]	25	—
537[12]	**Willskip (USA) (53)** (JBerry) **3-9-0** GCarter(6) (nvr trbld ldrs)	3	**7**	33/1	22	—
	My Saltarello (IRE) (60) (ABMulholland) **3-9-0** MBirch(1) (chsd wnr tl wknd over 3f out)	6	**8**	25/1	10	—

(SP 109.7%) **8 Rn**

1m 50.6 (6.50) CSF £3.76 TOTE £4.20: £1.80 £1.20 £1.40 (£3.50) OWNER Mr M. Tabor (NEWMARKET) BRED Barronstown Stud and Roncon Ltd

Purchasing Power (IRE), a powerful individual, won this really well and looks likely to go on from here. (7/4)

Step N Go (IRE) looked magnificent. She found trouble in running but this made no difference to the result as the winner was always far too good for her. She will find plenty of other opportunities. (7/4)

535 Barresbo ran well until finding this company too hot when the pace was really stepped up in the last couple of furlongs. (7/1)

551 Tycoon Tina threw all chances away with a slow start and then ran pretty well. (20/1)

Father Eddie, despite having been out on the All-Weather, gave the impression that he would still be all the better for this. (25/1)

368 Fearless Sioux disappointed here, stopping quickly in the last two furlongs after looking dangerous. (10/1)

610 DAVIE COOPER MEMORIAL H'CAP (0-75) (3-Y.O+) (Class D)
3-20 (3-23) **6f 5y** £3,712.50 (£1,125.00: £550.00: £262.50) Stalls: High GOING minus 0.12 sec per fur (G)

Form	Horse	Dist	Pos	SP	RR	SF
529[3]	**Foist (51)** (MWEasterby) **5-8-6**ow1 KFallon(16) (racd far side: sn drvn along: hdwy to ld ent fnl f: r.o wl)	—	**1**	5/2[1]	70	37
483[4]	**Return of Amin (67)** (JDBethell) **3-8-10** DHolland(12) (lw: racd far side: led tl hdd ent fnl f: kpt on)	2½	**2**	11/2[2]	79	35
494[3]	**Tropical Beach (63)** (JBerry) **4-8-11**(7) CLowther(14) (chsd ldrs far side: ev ch over 1f out: nt qckn)	7	**3**	8/1[3]	57	25
529[4]	**Be Warned (60)** (MDods) **6-9-1b** GCarter(18) (racd far side: styd on fnl 2f: nrst fin)	1¾	**4**	8/1[3]	49	17
	Stylish Ways (IRE) (73) (JPearce) **5-10-0** GBardwell(17) (lw: w ldrs far side tl rdn & btn over 1f out)	nk	**5**	10/1	61	29
*423**	**Needle Match (59)** (JJO'Neill) **4-9-0** KDarley(13) (chsd ldrs far side: nt qckn fnl 2f)	nk	**6**	8/1[3]	47	15
443[2]	**Safio (66)** (ABailey) **4-9-7** DWright(5) (lw: chsd ldrs: led stands' side 2f out: no ch w far side)	nk	**7**	9/1	53+	21
494[10]	**Lunch Party (51)** (DNicholls) **5-8-6** DaleGibson(15) (swtg: racd far side: nvr nrr)	2½	**8**	14/1	31	—
468[14]	**Sihafi (USA) (55)** (JMCarr) **4-8-10** AClark(10) (swtchd far side: nvr nr to chal)	nk	**9**	14/1	34	2

Prev	Horse / details	Dist	Pos	SP	RR	SF
	Mister Westsound (57) (MissLAPerratt) **5-8-12b** JCarroll(6) (bit bkwd: dwlt: racd stands' side: n.d)	3	**10**	20/1	28	—
	Precious Girl (70) (DMoffatt) **4-9-8**(3) DarrenMoffatt(4) (racd stands' side: n.d)	nk	**11**	25/1	41	9
*386*10	**Naissant (73)** (RMMcKellar) **4-9-7**(7) JMcAuley(11) (racd far side: a bhd)	2	**12**	66/1	38	6
	Bold Street (IRE) (62) (GMMoore) **7-9-3** ACulhane(2) (chsd ldrs stands' side tl wknd fnl 2f)	1¼	**13**	50/1	24	—
468 19	**No Cliches (73)** (DNicholls) **4-10-0** AlexGreaves(7) (racd stands' side: n.d)	2½	**14**	66/1	28	—
	Smokey From Caplaw (69) (JJO'Neill) **3-8-12** GDuffield(9) (hld up & bhd stands' side: n.d)	¾	**15**	66/1	22	—
*512*7	**Ultra Beet (70)** (PCHaslam) **5-9-11b** JWeaver(8) (lw: disp ld stands' side 4f: wknd qckly)	1½	**16**	25/1	19	—
*429*12	**Rymer's Rascal (58)** (EJAlston) **5-8-13** JFortune(1) (racd stands' side: n.d)	hd	**17**	100/1	7	—
	Six for Luck (51) (DANolan) **5-8-1**(5) PFessey(3) (disp ld stands' side 4f: wknd qckly)	½	**18**	100/1	—	—

(SP 130.6%) **18 Rn**

1m 13.0 (3.00) CSF £13.69 CT £95.94 TOTE £3.40: £1.40 £1.60 £1.70 £2.70 (£9.10) Trio £25.80 OWNER Mr D. F. Spence (SHERIFF HUTTON) BRED W. Cormack
WEIGHT FOR AGE 3yo-12lb

529 Foist needed to work hard to keep in touch at this shorter trip but, once he found his stride two furlongs out, the race was soon emphatically his. (5/2)
483 Return of Amin likes cut in the ground, had a good draw and beat all but the winner in style. No doubt the Handicapper will punish him for this defeat. (11/2)
494 Tropical Beach normally likes to come from off the pace but on this occasion he was well placed throughout, and that finishing kick was never forthcoming. (8/1)
529 Be Warned showed again he still has the ability and finished pretty well. (8/1)
Stylish Ways (IRE) made full use of his good draw but was struggling throughout the last two furlongs. (10/1)
423* Needle Match had plenty going for him here but, as it turned out, he just wasn't good enough. (8/1)
443 Safio won the race up the stands side and, in the circumstances, this was not a bad effort. (9/1)
Lunch Party, very edgy beforehand, got a long way behind until finishing quite well and this trip would seem to be on the short side. (14/1)
263* Sihafi (USA) never showed in the race but he left the impression that he can do a deal better. (14/1)

611 DUNWAN (QUALIFIER) MEDIAN AUCTION NOVICE STKS (2-Y.O) (Class F)
3-50 (3-56) **5f 4y** £2,556.00 (£716.00: £348.00) Stalls: High GOING minus 0.12 sec per fur (G)

Prev	Horse / details	Dist	Pos	SP	RR	SF
548 3	**Filey Brigg** (WTKemp) **2-8-7** KFallon(5) (bhd: hdwy 2f out: led ins fnl f: styd on strly)	—	**1**	10/1	65	12
500*	**Risky Whisky** (JBerry) **2-9-4** GCarter(3) (lw: cl up: led ½-wy tl ins fnl f: no ex)	2½	**2**	8/11 1	68	15
460 6	**Anka Lady** (DMoffatt) **2-8-4**(3) DarrenMoffatt(4) (chsd ldrs: outpcd ½-wy: styd on fnl f)	5	**3**	16/1	41	—
447 7	**Captain Brady (IRE)** (WGMTurner) **2-8-7**(5) DSweeney(2) (lw: unruly s: led to ½-wy: grad wknd)	hd	**4**	100/30 2	46	—
472 4	**Solway Lass (IRE)** (PEccles) **2-8-7** CRutter(6) (lw: cl up tl edgd lft & wknd appr fnl f)	7	**5**	9/1 3	18	—
447 13	**Mr Fund Switch** (DNicholls) **2-8-12** AlexGreaves(1) (bit bkwd: unruly gng to s: sn outpcd & bhd)	7	**6**	50/1	1	—

(SP 107.9%) **6 Rn**

62.4 secs (4.10) CSF £15.12 TOTE £11.10: £3.70 £1.20 (£3.60) OWNER Drakemyre Racing (DUNS) BRED L. T. and M. Foster

548 Filey Brigg again came from off the pace and won really well, suggesting that longer trips will see more improvement. (10/1)
500* Risky Whisky tried to make his experience tell but was well out-pointed in the closing stages. (8/11)
460 Anka Lady gives the impression that longer distances are needed. (16/1)
Captain Brady (IRE) led early on but was always finding things happening too quickly and was left behind from halfway. (100/30)
472 Solway Lass (IRE) has plenty of early speed but ran out of fuel in dramatic style approaching the final furlong. (9/1: 6/1-10/1)

612 GLEN LIMITED STKS (0-65) (4-Y.O+) (Class F)
4-20 (4-20) **1m 4f 17y** £2,458.00 (£688.00: £334.00) Stalls: High GOING minus 0.12 sec per fur (G)

Prev	Horse / details	Dist	Pos	SP	RR	SF
	Turnpole (IRE) (65) (MrsMReveley) **6-8-13** ACulhane(2) (trckd ldrs: led wl over 1f out: rdn & r.o fnl f)	—	**1**	6/4 1	75	36
	Blenheim Terrace (62) (CBBBooth) **4-8-12** LCharnock(6) (hld up: swtchd over 1f out: qcknd: no ex ins fnl f)	3	**2**	8/1	71	31
550 2	**Sun Mark (IRE) (58)** (MrsASwinbank) **6-8-13** GDuffield(5) (lw: cl up: led over 4f out tl wl over 1f out: one pce)	3½	**3**	5/1 3	66	27
*37**	**Nishamira (IRE) (65)** (TDBarron) **5-8-12** KDarley(4) (trckd ldrs: chal 3f out: sn rdn: outpcd fnl 2f)	nk	**4**	5/1 3	65	26
	Sharaf (IRE) (64) (WRMuir) **4-8-12** JWeaver(1) (lw: led tl hdd over 4f out: sn outpcd)	3½	**5**	4/1 2	61	21
*516**	**State Approval (60)** (PEccles) **4-9-0** CRutter(3) (in tch tl outpcd fnl 4f)	11	**6**	9/1	49	9
	French Project (IRE) (65) (MrsSCBradburne) **5-8-10** DeanMcKeown(7) (lost tch 6f out: t.o)	dist	**7**	50/1	—	—

(SP 116.4%) **7 Rn**

2m 39.8 (7.80) CSF £13.90 TOTE £2.70: £1.40 £3.70 (£30.00) OWNER Mr W. J. Williams (SALTBURN) BRED Old Meadow Stud
WEIGHT FOR AGE 4yo-1lb

Turnpole (IRE) is an edgy individual but he responded well to pressure here and won nicely. (6/4)
Blenheim Terrace looked likely to take a real hand in things when switched for a clear run approaching the final furlong but, yet again, he failed to go through with it when the pressure was on. (8/1)
550 Sun Mark (IRE) again ran well but probably just found this trip too far. (5/1)
37* Nishamira (IRE) had her chances only to find this company too hot in the last quarter-mile. (5/1)
Sharaf (IRE) looked fit enough for his first run this season but he proved disappointing when ridden. (4/1)

613 CHATELHERAULT H'CAP (0-70) (4-Y.O+) (Class E)
4-50 (4-51) **1m 5f 9y** £3,317.70 (£1,005.60: £491.80: £234.90) Stalls: High GOING minus 0.12 sec per fur (G)

Prev	Horse / details	Dist	Pos	SP	RR	SF
510 5	**Sea Freedom (58)** (GBBalding) **6-9-6v** SDrowne(8) (lw: sn prom: led 2f out: r.o wl)	—	**1**	5/1 1	72	53
470 11	**Karisma (IRE) (56)** (DenysSmith) **4-9-2** KFallon(7) (hdwy appr st: sn prom: ev ch over 2f out: hrd rdn & nt qckn appr fnl f)	4	**2**	8/1 3	65	44
430 8	**He's Got Wings (IRE) (56)** (MrsJRRamsden) **4-9-2** JFortune(16) (b.nr hind: mid div: effrt ent st: chsng ldrs appr fnl f: kpt on one pce)	3½	**3**	10/1	61	40
470 9	**Northern Motto (50)** (JSGoldie) **4-8-10** DeanMcKeown(5) (prom early: effrt 4f out: styd on: nvr able to chal)	1¾	**4**	16/1	53	32
*410*15	**Heighth of Fame (50)** (JHetherton) **6-8-12** KDarley(14) (prom: outpcd 3f out: styd on fnl f)	hd	**5**	14/1	53	34
552 8	**Lord Hastie (USA) (60)** (CWThornton) **9-9-5**(3) OPears(17) (sn wl bhd: hdwy 3f out: nvr plcd to chal)	4	**6**	9/1	58	39
*360*10	**Compass Pointer (60)** (JMPEustace) **4-9-1**(5) DSweeney(13) (hld up & bhd: hdwy on outside 4f out: hung rt & no imp)	hd	**7**	12/1	58	37
553 8	**Rossel (USA) (60)** (PMonteith) **4-9-1**(5) JBramhill(3) (hdwy 4f out: nvr trbld ldrs)	1¾	**8**	25/1	55	34
	Trilby (65) (GRichards) **4-9-11** ACulhane(10) (in tch: effrt 4f out: wknd fnl 2f)	nk	**9**	10/1	60	39

465[10]	**Turgenev (IRE) (65)** (RBastiman) **8-9-8b**(5) HBastiman(4) (bit bkwd: nvr rchd ldrs) 2½ **10**	12/1	57	38
493[6]	**Thorntoun Estate (IRE) (47)** (MartinTodhunter) **4-8-7** DaleGibson(11) (n.d) 1 **11**	25/1	38	17
442[7]	**Brumon (IRE) (57)** (DMoffatt) **6-9-2v**(3) DarrenMoffatt(9) (b: s.i.s: n.d) 3½ **12**	20/1	43	24
553[3]	**Philmist (45)** (MissLAPerratt) **5-8-7b** NKennedy(1) (cl up: led 4f out to 2f out: wknd qckly) ....½ **13**	6/1[2]	31	12
470[12]	**Mister Aspecto (IRE) (68)** (MJohnston) **4-10-0v** JWeaver(18) (led tl hdd 4f out: wknd over 2f out) 1½ **14**	16/1	52	31
430[19]	**Cois Na Farraige (IRE) (68)** (MissLAPerratt) **4-10-0** JCarroll(2) (hdwy & in tch 6f out: wknd 4f out) 1 **15**	33/1	51	30
167[11]	**Sheemore (IRE) (45)** (MDHammond) **4-8-5** GDuffield(12) (chsd ldrs tl wknd fnl 4f) 5 **16**	33/1	22	1
465[11]	**Hard Love (57)** (JLEyre) **5-9-5** RLappin(6) (lw: prom tl rdn & wknd over 4f out) 1½ **17**	20/1	32	13
157[6]	**Sharp Command (53)** (PEccles) **4-8-13** CRutter(15) (a rr div) 15 **18**	16/1	9	—
		(SP 133.0%)	**18 Rn**	

2m 52.5 (6.80) CSF £38.94 CT £369.97 TOTE £4.60: £1.10 £2.80 £4.10 £4.10 (£29.50) Trio £197.00 OWNER Miss B. Swire (ANDOVER)
BRED Stetchworth Park Stud Ltd
WEIGHT FOR AGE 4yo-2lb
OFFICIAL EXPLANATION Lord Hastie (USA): has had joint troubles in the past, and did not like the drying ground.
510 Sea Freedom broke his duck here at the thirty-first attempt and did it particularly well. (5/1)
Karisma (IRE) ran his best race for a while but he was comprehensively out-battled in the last couple of furlongs. (8/1)
He's Got Wings (IRE) ran well but just found this trip a bit on the sharp side. (10/1: op 6/1)
260* Northern Motto ran as though longer trips are what he needs. (16/1)
384 Heighth of Fame, fit from the All-Weather, looked very one-paced here. (14/1)
Lord Hastie (USA) got completely detached early on and was then given a most sympathetic ride, and finished in eye-catching style. (9/1)
Compass Pointer raced in the slower ground up the straight and did not help his cause by hanging badly. (12/1)
553 Rossel (USA) looks in good trim and is worth keeping in mind especially if put back over hurdles. (25/1)

T/Jkpt: £18,426.40 (0.3 Tckts); £18,166.94 to Nottingham 11/4/97. T/Plpt: £17.30 (953.8 Tckts). T/Qdpt: £12.70 (67.5 Tckts) AA

0614a - 0623a : (Irish Racing) - See Computer Raceform

LES LANDES (Jersey) (L-H) (Good)
Monday March 31st

624a ROBERT LEECH MEMORIAL SPRINT (3-Y.O+)
3-40 (3-40) **5f 100y** £1,200.00 (£500.00) GOING: Not Established

		SP	RR	SF
	Jimmy the Skunk (IRE) (MissAVibert,Jersey) **6-10-7** TWilliams ....— **1**		44	—
407[5]	**Statistician** (JohnBerry) **5-10-7** AMcCabe ....½ **2**		43	—
	Catawampus (MissAVibert,Jersey) **6-10-7** RSmith 3 **3**		34	—
				6 Rn

69.0 secs TOTE £8.60: £4.60 £4.80 (£2.00) OWNER Mr & Mrs T Gallienne BRED Martyn J. McEnery

LONGCHAMP (Paris, France) (R-H) (Good to firm)
Monday March 31st

625a PRIX D'HARCOURT (Gp 2) (4-Y.O+)
3-25 (3-25) **1m 2f** £33,670.00 (£13,468.00: £6,734.00: £3,367.00) GOING: Not Established

		SP	RR	SF
	River Bay (USA) (JEHammond,France) **4-8-12** TJarnet (a cl up: hdwy & led over 1f out: r.o wl: comf) ....— **1**		120+	—
439a*	**Nero Zilzal (USA)** (ELellouche,France) **4-8-12** OPeslier (mid div: rdn & hdwy 2f out: nt rch wnr) 2½ **2**		116	—
	Baroud d'Honneur (FR) (JBernard,France) **4-8-12** FBlondel (trckd ldr: hdwy to ld 2f out: hdd over 1f out: styd on one pce) ....hd **3**		116	—
	Steward (FR) (DSepulchre,France) **4-8-12** CAsmussen (mid div st: nvr able to chal) 3 **4**		111	—
439a[3]	**Thames (FR)** (LAudon,France) **6-8-12** FHead (in rr: one pce fr 1f out) ....nse **5**		111	—
	Arbatax (IRE) (PBary,France) **4-9-1** SGuillot (a in rr) 3 **6**		109	—
	Legal Right (USA) (PWChapple-Hyam) **4-8-12** DHarrison (led to 2f out: rdn & sn wknd) 1½ **7**		104	—
				7 Rn

2m 3.2 (3.20) P-M 2.40F: 1.70F 1.70F OWNER Mr H. Chalhoub (CHANTILLY) BRED Rosemont Farm Inc.
River Bay (USA) won this race in faultless style. Cruising into the lead just over a furlong out, he won unchallenged, and this colt could be something rather special in the making. A fine-looking animal, he was not fully wound up and would have possibly preferred the ground a little softer. His time was just 1.1 seconds outside the track record, and his trainer believes he will stay up to twelve furlongs. He now goes for the Prix Ganay where he will come against the Arc de Triomphe hero Helissio, and it promises to be a fascinating race.
439a* Nero Zilzal (USA) was held up and put his best work in at the finish. He did not come down the hill too well, but made rapid progress to steal second place close home and was just beaten by a better horse on the day.
Baroud d'Honneur (FR) raced in second place for much of the race. He led for a short time and then shortened his stride close home, but will definitely have benefited from the outing and will improve. He might even be suited by softer ground. He will be allowed to take his chance in the Ganay but might find the company a little hot.
Steward (FR) was never seen with a real chance of finishing in the first three. He stayed on one paced in the straight and battled well to hold fourth place by a nose. He may not be totally suited to the undulations of Longchamp.
Legal Right (USA) led soon after the stalls opened, but was a spent force after entering the straight. He wasn't up to the task on this occasion and looks to need a longer distance. Connections think a visor might have a positive effect.

0438a-NAD AL SHEBA (Dubai, UAE) (L-H) (Fast)
Thursday April 3rd

626a DUBAI PORTS AUTHORITY & JEBEL ALI FREE ZONE PORTS AUTHORITY H'CAP (4-Y.O+)
1-50 BST(1-53) **1m 4f (Dirt)** £8,078.00

	SP	RR	SF
Clever Cliche (SbinSuroor,UAE) **4-9-6** LDettori ....— **1**		112	—

	Horse	Dist	Pos	SP	RR	SF
	Battle Green (KPMcLaughlin,UAE) **4-8-4** JCArias	nk	2		96	—
	Sulb (USA) (ECharpy,UAE) **5-9-0** RHills	3½	3		100	—
	Time for Action (IRE) (MHTompkins) **5-8-6** PBrette (btn 10½l)		5		83	—

10 Rn

2m 31.89 OWNER Sheikh Ahmed bin Mohammed Al Maktoum BRED Cheveley Park Stud Ltd
Time for Action (IRE) ran a creditable-enough race on his first attempt on sand. In eighth place turning into the long straight, he kept on reasonably well and the jockey reported he could have been fourth, but for some interference two furlongs out.

627a DUBAI DUTY FREE (4-Y.O+)

3-50 (3-53) **1m 2f (Dirt)** £148,810.00 (£74,405.00: £44,643.00: £29,762.00)

	Horse	Dist	Pos	SP	RR	SF
408a²	**Tamayaz (CAN)** (SbinSuroor,UAE) **5-9-0v¹** LDettori (prom: rdn 3f out: led 2½f out: r.o wl)	—	1		124	—
	Needle Gun (IRE) (CEBrittain) **7-9-0** MJKinane (trckd ldrs: rdn 2f out: kpt on wl)	1	2		122	—
	Magellan (USA) (PLRudkin,UAE) **4-9-0** PaulEddery (in rr: 5th st: kpt on wl cl home)	1½	3		120	—
*409a**	**Doreg (IRE)** (DJSelvaratnam,UAE) **7-9-0** CNakatani (racd in rr: hdwy over 1f out: fin wl)	nk	4		120	—
	Desert Shot (KPMcLaughlin,UAE) **7-9-0** JCArias (hld up: styd on one pce)	7	5		108	—
438a⁴	**Gothenberg (IRE)** (MJohnston) **4-9-0** JWeaver (in rr: rdn & wnt wd st: styd on one pce)	3	6		104	—
*408a**	**Tropicool (USA)** (DJSelvaratnam,UAE) **4-9-0b** BDoyle (mid div: no hdwy)	1¾	7		101	—
	Kalabo (USA) (SbinSuroor,UAE) **5-9-0** JBravo (in rr: sn btn)	2½	8		97	—
438a²	**Tamhid (USA)** (KPMcLaughlin,UAE) **4-9-0** RHills (mid div: wknd qckly over 2f out)	½	9		96	—
	Fatefully (USA) (SbinSuroor,UAE) **4-8-11** JBailey (mid div: btn st)	½	10		92	—
	Balal (GR) (MCharalambous,Greece) **4-9-0** FBarimoglou (trckd ldr to 4f out: sn wknd)	9	11		81	—
438a³	**Learmont (USA)** (ECharpy,UAE) **7-9-0b** WJSupple (set gd pce: hdd & wknd 2½f out)	2¼	12		77	—
	Carling (FR) (MmePBarbe,France) **5-8-11** TThulliez (in rr: mde slt prog st: wknd qckly 1f out)	1	13		73	—

13 Rn

2m 2.2 OWNER Godolphin BRED Windfields Farm
408a Tamayaz (CAN) finished fifth in the World Cup last year so was entitled to win this. Never far off the pace, he took it up early in the straight, but had to be driven right out to hold the persistent challenge of the runner-up.
Needle Gun (IRE) seemed to handle the surface much better than when seventh in last year's World Cup. Always close up, he kept on most resolutely in the final quarter-mile.
438a Gothenberg (IRE) ran probably the best race of his four starts over here. Held up some way off the fast pace, he was brought wide into the straight and momentarily looked like he might claim a share of the minor place money.

628a DUBAI WORLD CUP (Listed) (4-Y.O+)

4-35 (4-40) **1m 2f (Dirt)** £1,428,571.00 (£476,190.00: £238,095.00: £119,048.00: £71,429.00: £47,619.00) GOING: Not Established

	Horse	Dist	Pos	SP	RR	SF
	Singspiel (IRE) (MRStoute) **5-9-0** JBailey (a cl up: jnd ldr over 2f out: hrd rdn to ld 1f out: r.o wl)	—	1		132	—
393a*	**Siphon (BRA)** (RMandella,USA) **6-9-0** DFlores (led tl hdd 1f out: r.o one pce)	1¼	2		130	—
393a²	**Sandpit (BRA)** (RMandella,USA) **8-9-0** CNakatani (cl up ½-wy: ev ch 2f out: kpt on one pce)	1½	3		128	—
409a³	**Key of Luck (USA)** (KPMcLaughlin,UAE) **6-9-0** JCArias (a cl up: one pce fnl f)	2½	4		124	—
	Formal Gold (CAN) (WPerry,USA) **4-9-0** JBravo (trckd ldr: ev ch over 1f out: sn wknd)	1½	5		121	—
437a³	**Juggler (AUS)** (MrsGWaterhouse,Australia) **5-9-0b¹** GBoss (outpcd & drvn along early: hdwy u.p 2f out: nvr nrr)	2½	6		117	—
	Even Top (IRE) (MHTompkins) **4-9-0** RHills (prom: cl up st: sn btn)	2½	7		113	—
*438a**	**Kammtarra (USA)** (SbinSuroor,UAE) **4-9-0** LDettori (hld up: drvn along st: wknd 2f out)	5½	8		104	—
	Luso (CEBrittain) **5-9-0** MJKinane (bhd fnl f)	2½	9		100	—
	Flemensfirth (USA) (JHMGosden) **5-9-0** GHind (a in rr)	nk	10		100	—
409a⁴	**Bijou d'Inde** (MJohnston) **4-9-0** JWeaver (in rr: b.d appr st)		B		—	—
	Hokuto Vega (JPN) (TNakano,Japan) **7-8-11** NYokoyama (in rr: fell appr st: dead)		F		—	—

12 Rn

2m 1.91 OWNER Sheikh Mohammed (NEWMARKET) BRED Sheikh Mohammed bin Rashid al Maktoum
IN-FOCUS: Torrential rain caused the postponement of this meeting from the previous Saturday.
Singspiel (IRE) must now be regarded as the best horse in the world. He has a dirt side to his pedigree - his dam is a half-sister to 1993 US juvenile champion Devil's Bag - and he took to the surface well. Always prominent, he joined the leader approaching the two-furlong pole and had begun to get the upper hand a furlong later. It world be fitting if he were aimed at the Breeders' Cup Classic in an attempt to win the world's three richest international races.
Even Top (IRE) raced in seventh and was still very much in touch when turning into the straight. He was swiftly left behind in the final quarter-mile.
438a* Kammtarra (USA) failed to live up to the pre-race hype and was already in trouble making the final turn. He should not, however, be difficult to place in Britain in the coming season.
Luso failed to handle this alien surface.
Flemensfirth (USA) was always in the rear and did not look like he was enjoying himself.
409a Bijou d'Inde seems to hate the sand and was well behind when brought down by the prostrate Hokuto Vega entering the straight. He suffered a crashing fall, and was later found to have injured a tendon.

0625a-LONGCHAMP (Paris, France) (R-H) (Good)
Sunday April 6th

629a PRIX NOAILLES (Gp 2) (3-Y.O C & F)

3-10 (3-11) **1m 3f** £32,938.00 (£13,175.00: £6,588.00: £3,294.00) GOING minus 0.08 sec per fur (G)

	Horse	Dist	Pos	SP	RR	SF
	Fragrant Mix (FR) (AFabre,France) **3-9-2** TJarnet (a cl up: led st: wnt clr: impressive)	—	1		112	75
	Sendoro (IRE) (AdeRoyerDupre,France) **3-9-2** GMosse (last early st: prog 2f out: r.o wl)	3	2		108	71
	Shaka (J-CRouget,France) **3-9-2** J-RDubosc (cl up: outpcd early st: r.o one pce cl home)	½	3		107	70
	Keroub (FR) (PBary,France) **3-9-2** SGuillot (a mid div: u.p 2f out: one pce)	1	4		106	69
	Barings (FR) (ELellouche,France) **3-9-2** TThulliez (mid div: slt effrt 2f out: one pce fnl f)	1½	5		103	66
	Napoli Express (FR) (AFabre,France) **3-9-2** OPeslier (led tl st: dropped out qckly)	6	6		95	58

6 Rn

2m 16.5 (2.50) P-M 3.50F: 1.90F 1.80F OWNER Mr J-L Lagardere (CHANTILLY) BRED J. L. Lagardere

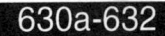

Fragrant Mix (FR) won the race in good style but had several things in his favour. He had already had two previous outings and acted better on the firm ground than several of his rivals. He burst clear early in the straight and had this race wrapped up shortly after. He will now probably go straight for the Prix du Jockey-Club and he looks as if he will stay the extra furlong. Things were in his favour on this occasion but he nevertheless is a smart performer.
Sendoro (IRE) was given a fairly tender race and he ran on well in the final stages. He would have preferred a softer surface and the outing will have done him good. The Prix Hocquart looks likely to be his next engagement.
Shaka looked superb in the paddock but he was carrying a lot of condition and will strip much fitter next time out in the Prix Hocquart. He was given every chance by his provincial jockey but was not fit enough on this occasion to show his best. There is also a strong possibility that he would appreciate softer ground. He is sure to improve from the outing.
Keroub (FR) ran an honest sort of race without ever looking likely to finish in the first three. He too will improve and a decent race should come his way.

630a PRIX LORD SEYMOUR (Listed) (4-Y.O+)
4-10 (4-06) **1m 4f** £15,713.00 (£5,387.00: £4,040.00: £2,694.00) GOING minus 0.08 sec per fur (G)

				SP	RR	SF
	Flyway (FR) (ELellouche,France) **4-9-2** OPeslier	—	1		111	31
	Prussian Blue (USA) (France) **5-9-2** GDoleuze	nk	2		110	31
	Altor (France) **5-8-12** FSanchez	nk	3		105	26
451*	**Sheer Danzig (IRE)** (RWArmstrong) **5-8-12** CAsmussen	¾	4		104	25
						5 Rn

2m 35.2 (9.20) P-M 5.00F: 2.60F 2.80F OWNER Mr B. Clin BRED Petra Bloodstock Agency Ltd
451* Sheer Danzig (IRE) was rather disappointing on this occasion. He raced in second place for much of the race but was outpaced in the straight. He was hampered by the winner which might have cost him a place, but it seemed his jockey did not make enough use of him. This race is probably best forgotten.

0570-BEVERLEY (R-H) (Good to firm)
Friday April 11th
WEATHER: sunny periods WIND: fresh across

48 52 63+ 45

631 SCARBOROUGH (S) STKS (2-Y.O) (Class F)
2-20 (2-21) **5f** £2,595.00 (£720.00: £345.00) Stalls: High GOING minus 0.35 sec per fur (F)

				SP	RR	SF
536[12]	**The Beat Rolls On (IRE)** (MartynMeade) **2-8-1**(5) DSweeney(8) (a cl up: rdn to ld wl ins fnl f: styd on)	—	1	11/1	59	15
441[4]	**Hopefully** (MRChannon) **2-8-6** JWeaver(10) (led tl hdd wl ins fnl f: kpt on)	nk	2	3/1[3]	58	14
492[4]	**Captain Bliss** (NTinkler) **2-8-11** JCarroll(2) (lw: a chsng ldrs: rdn & m green over 1f out: kpt on)	¾	3	9/4[1]	61	17
500[7]	**My Bet** (MWEasterby) **2-8-1**(5) GParkin(3) (chsd ldrs: hdwy wl in n.m.r & swtchd ins fnl f: nt rcvr)	¾	4	16/1	53	9
	Shindium (CADwyer) **2-8-3**(3) DO'Donohoe(4) (neat: scope: lw: s.i.s: shkn up ½-wy: nvr nr to chal)	2	5	5/2[2]	47	3
592[3]	**Who Nose (IRE)** (BJMeehan) **2-8-4b**(7) GHannon(1) (wnt lft s: hdwy & prom ½-wy: sn rdn & no imp)	4	6	13/2	39	—
	Just Nobby (NTinkler) **2-8-11** KimTinkler(6) (cmpt: nvr wnt pce)	1¼	7	25/1	35	—
	Miss Beveled (MBrittain) **2-8-6** GDuffield(9) (lt-f: sn outpcd)	1¾	8	16/1	24	—
	General Joey (MDods) **2-8-11** DaleGibson(5) (cmpt: bit bkwd: dwlt: n.d)	7	9	16/1	7	—
441[9]	**Racing Surveyor** (MWEasterby) **2-8-6** TLucas(7) (sn outpcd & bhd)	5	10	25/1	—	—
				(SP 131.3%)		**10 Rn**

64.8 secs (3.00) CSF £45.37 TOTE £19.10: £3.20 £1.10 £1.70 (£29.40) Trio £95.20 OWNER The Country Life Partnership (MALMESBURY) BRED Lydon Beese
Sold Claes Bjorling 6,600gns
The Beat Rolls On (IRE) obviously benefited from her previous outing and a drop in class, and she saw out this stiff five furlongs really well. (11/1)
441 Hopefully, although very small, can certainly motor and, when headed, kept fighting back. (3/1)
492 Captain Bliss looked particularly well, but threw his chances away by running green and should pick up a similar event before long. (9/4: op 7/2)
My Bet went well and, but for being short of room entering the final furlong, she would have been in the shake-up. (16/1)
Shindium looked fit enough, but it was her inexperience early on that made the difference. She should be a different proposition next time. (5/2)
592 Who Nose (IRE) spoiled any chance he had by diving left as the stalls opened, and he looks a bit of a character. (13/2)

632 BRIDLINGTON BAY H'CAP (0-70) (4-Y.O+) (Class E)
2-50 (2-50) **2m 35y** £3,104.50 (£931.00: £448.00: £206.50) Stalls: High GOING minus 0.35 sec per fur (F)

				SP	RR	SF
465*	**Kinoko (41)** (KWHogg) **9-8-0** LCharnock(9) (cl up: slt ld 3f out: r.o)	—	1	11/4[1]	51	7
	Shirley Sue (69) (MJohnston) **4-9-10** JWeaver(6) (led tl hdd 3f out: kpt on wl)	1	2	6/1[3]	78	30
465[5]	**Romalito (38)** (MBlanshard) **7-7-4**(7)ow1 RFfrench(5) (hld up: styd on wl fnl 3f: nrst fin)	¾	3	11/1	46	1
470[7]	**Anchorena (46)** (DWBarker) **5-8-5** TWilliams(2) (lw: plld hrd: hdwy 9f out: ev ch 2f out: r.o one pce)	nk	4	8/1	54	10
	Regal Eagle (65) (MDHammond) **4-9-6** GDuffield(7) (hld up: hdwy over 2f out: nvr able to chal)	1¼	5	16/1	72	24
	Alcian Blue (40) (MDHammond) **6-7-13** DaleGibson(3) (prom tl lost pl 6f out: n.d after)	2½	6	20/1	44	—
	Our Kris (62) (MESowersby) **5-9-7b** JCarroll(8) (chsd ldrs tl outpcd fnl 2f)	6	7	20/1	60	16
232[4]	**Sudden Spin (44)** (JNorton) **7-8-3** JFanning(10) (hld up: hdwy & prom 3f out: wknd over 1f out)	3	8	7/2[2]	39	—
	Lucky Hoof (62) (KAMorgan) **4-9-3v[1]** OUrbina(11) (chsd ldrs tl wknd fnl 3f)	6	9	25/1	51	3
543[2]	**Top Prize (39)** (MBrittain) **9-7-5v**(7)ow2 DMernagh(4) (b: chsd ldrs tl wknd 3f out)	1½	10	12/1	27	—
	French Ivy (USA) (69) (FMurphy) **10-10-0** RCochrane(1) (b: hld up & bhd: n.d)	15	11	8/1	42	—
				(SP 120.7%)		**11 Rn**

3m 41.5 (11.00) CSF £17.64 CT £147.44 TOTE £3.50: £1.10 £2.60 £2.60 (£11.40) Trio £66.80 OWNER Mr Anthony White (ISLE OF MAN) BRED Auldyn Stud Ltd
LONG HANDICAP Top Prize 7-3 Romalito 7-6
WEIGHT FOR AGE 4yo-4lb
465* Kinoko is in tremendous form at present, and was in command in the last two furlongs without being subjected to strong pressure. (11/4)
Shirley Sue showed that she retains her enthusiasm, and will soon be winning. (6/1)
465 Romalito, with plenty to do on the home turn, finished well, albeit too late. He is in good form at present. (11/1: 8/1-12/1)
Anchorena did not help matters by racing too freely and might have just found this trip too far, but is worth keeping in mind. (8/1)
Regal Eagle ran quite well and will obviously be better for this his first run of the season. He could well improve for his new stable. (16/1)

232 Sudden Spin won this event last year, but he is not the most reliable of characters and threw in the towel early in the straight this time. (7/2)

633 WELCOME TO THE PRESS H'CAP (0-85) (4-Y.O+) (Class D)

3-20 (3-20) **1m 1f 207y** £3,626.00 (£1,088.00: £524.00: £242.00) Stalls: High GOING minus 0.35 sec per fur (F)

	Horse	Dist	Pos	SP	RR	SF
	Gymcrak Premiere (73) (GHolmes) **9-9-4** NConnorton(11) (b.hind: hld up: hdwy 3f out: led 1½f out: edgd rt: r.o)	—	**1**	14/1	85	46
	Philistar (66) (JMPEustace) **4-8-11b^{1}** RCochrane(10) (prom: hdwy over 3f out: sltly hmpd 1f out: kpt on)	½	**2**	10/1	77	38
	Night of Glass (59) (JLEyre) **4-8-4**ow1 GHind(8) (lw: in tch: hdwy & ch over 1f out: no ex)	4	**3**	11/2^{1}	64	24
	Champagne Prince (83) (PWHarris) **4-10-0** GDuffield(3) (led tl hdd 1½f out: grad wknd)	2½	**4**	8/1	84	45
	Lucky Bea (53) (MWEasterby) **4-7-12** DaleGibson(2) (bhd: hdwy u.p over 2f out: nvr rchd ldrs)	1¾	**5**	10/1	51	12
482*	**Obelos (USA) (74)** (MissSJWilton) **6-9-5** DeanMcKeown(9) (cl up tl rdn & wknd fnl 2f)	2½	**6**	6/1^{2}	68	29
463^{5}	**Golden Thunderbolt (FR) (70)** (NTinkler) **4-9-1** JCarroll(1) (a bhd: eased ins fnl f)	18	**7**	16/1	35	—
	Celebration Cake (IRE) (75) (MissLAPerratt) **5-9-6** JWeaver(7) (bit bkwd: prom 7f: eased whn btn ins fnl f)	3	**8**	10/1	35	—
	Lapu-Lapu (55) (MJCamacho) **4-8-0** LCharnock(6) (cl up tl wknd wl over 2f out: eased fnl f)	2	**9**	15/2	12	—
463^{2}	**Terdad (USA) (77)** (TDBarron) **4-9-8** RLappin(4) (hld up & bhd: eased no ch ins fnl f)	7	**10**	7/1^{3}	23	—
	Polar Champ (75) (SPCWoods) **4-9-6v** DBiggs(5) (lw: chsd ldrs tl rdn & wknd 3f out: eased fnl f)	3	**11**	6/1^{2}	16	—

(SP 119.2%) **11 Rn**

2m 6.5 (3.40) CSF £135.13 CT £796.44 TOTE £16.70: £2.80 £3.20 £1.70 (£100.50) Trio £271.10; £118.39 to Warwick 12/4/97 OWNER The Gymcrak Thoroughbred Racing Club (PICKERING) BRED Cheveley Park Stud Ltd

Gymcrak Premiere last won two seasons ago and has now slipped down the handicap. He did this well, scoring at his longest trip to date. (14/1)
Philistar had blinkers on for the first time and saw the trip out well, but was short of room at a vital stage and never quite looked likely to peg back the winner. (10/1)
Night of Glass looked fit, but probably just found this trip too far and is certainly worth another chance. (11/2)
Champagne Prince just needed this and ran well until blowing up late on. (8/1)
Lucky Bea, stepping up in distance here, could never offer a threat despite struggling on. (10/1)
482* Obelos (USA) had his chances, but dropped tamely away in the last quarter-mile. (6/1)

634 WITHERNSEA H'CAP (0-80) (3-Y.O) (Class D)

3-50 (3-50) **7f 100y** £3,743.00 (£1,124.00: £542.00: £251.00) Stalls: High GOING minus 0.35 sec per fur (F)

	Horse	Dist	Pos	SP	RR	SF
448^{2}	**Jay-Owe-Two (IRE) (75)** (RMWhitaker) **3-9-2** DeanMcKeown(6) (in tch: hdwy 2f out: hrd rdn to ld wl ins fnl f)	—	**1**	5/2^{2}	87	43
483^{5}	**The Wyandotte Inn (70)** (RHollinshead) **3-8-8**(3) FLynch(9) (trckd ldrs: chal over 1f out: kpt on)	¾	**2**	7/1^{3}	80	36
	Wagga Moon (IRE) (67) (JJO'Neill) **3-8-8** GDuffield(8) (led tl hdd & wknd wl ins fnl f)	2	**3**	20/1	73	29
420^{4}	**Cee-N-K (IRE) (76)** (MJohnston) **3-9-3** JWeaver(3) (chsd ldrs: effrt ent st: one pce fnl 2f)	½	**4**	8/1	81	37
532^{11}	**Docklands Carriage (IRE) (65)** (NTinkler) **3-8-6** KimTinkler(7) (cl up tl wknd over 1f out)	3	**5**	16/1	64	20
475*	**Sharpo Wassl (71)** (WJHaggas) **3-8-9**(3) DO'Donohoe(1) (lw: hld up & bhd: rn wd st: hdwy over 2f out: no imp)	s.h	**6**	9/4^{1}	70	26
	In Good Nick (63) (MWEasterby) **3-8-4b** TLucas(2) (hld up: effrt on ins over 2f out: rdn & btn over 1f out)	2½	**7**	10/1	56	12
	Dawam Allail (80) (MAJarvis) **3-9-7** RCochrane(5) (hld up: effrt over 3f out: rdn & btn over 1f out)	7	**8**	8/1	58	14
	Eastern Firedragon (IRE) (56) (DNicholls) **3-7-11** DaleGibson(4) (bit bkwd: wl bhd fnl 4f)	30	**9**	25/1	—	—

(SP 117.6%) **9 Rn**

1m 34.6 (2.60) CSF £19.15 CT £263.42 TOTE £3.20: £1.40 £2.40 £4.30 (£14.30) Trio £157.20 OWNER Mr R. M. Whitaker (LEEDS) BRED Thoroughbred Trust

448 Jay-Owe-Two (IRE), trying a slightly longer trip and on a stiffer track, needed every yard of it to come out on top. (5/2)
483 The Wyandotte Inn, trying his longest trip to date, got it well enough but just lacked a change of gear. (7/1)
Wagga Moon (IRE) looks to be coming to hand and this was a fair effort. (20/1)
420 Cee-N-K (IRE) has been successful over a mile on the All-Weather and may need at least that distance on grass. (8/1)
Docklands Carriage (IRE) won twice last season when fitted with blinkers and may well need them back on again this year. (16/1)
475* Sharpo Wassl took a strong hold at the back of the field and then failed to handle this awkward bend, and his chance was gone. (9/4)

635 LECONFIELD LIMITED STKS (0-85) (3-Y.O+) (Class D)

4-20 (4-21) **7f 100y** £3,379.00 (£1,012.00: £486.00: £223.00) Stalls: High GOING minus 0.35 sec per fur (F)

	Horse	Dist	Pos	SP	RR	SF
444^{6}	**Night Dance (78)** (KAMorgan) **5-8-13**(7) RFfrench(4) (mde all: hld on wl ins fnl f)	—	**1**	11/2	84	67
	No More Pressure (IRE) (85) (NJHWalker) **3-8-9** CRutter(6) (lw: hld up: hdwy over 2f out: ev ch ins fnl f: r.o)	½	**2**	7/1	86	55
529^{7}	**Smarter Charter (75)** (MrsLStubbs) **4-9-6** RCochrane(5) (hld up: nt clr run 2f out: hdwy over 1f out: hung lft: hrd rdn & r.o towards fin)	hd	**3**	5/1^{3}	83	66
560^{3}	**Mujova (IRE) (83)** (RHollinshead) **3-8-3**(3) FLynch(7) (trckd ldrs: effrt over 2f out: wknd ins fnl f)	5	**4**	7/2^{2}	72	41
550^{6}	**Ten Past Six (72)** (MartynWane) **5-9-6b^{1}** JCarroll(3) (cl up tl wknd over 1f out)	5	**5**	16/1	61	44
529^{12}	**Magic Mill (IRE) (85)** (JLEyre) **4-9-6** TWilliams(1) (hld up: effrt over 3f out: sn btn)	2½	**6**	7/4^{1}	56	39
540^{6}	**Royal South (IRE) (75)** (PSFelgate) **4-9-6** GDuffield(2) (chsd ldrs tl rdn & wknd 1f out)	1¼	**7**	12/1	53	36

(SP 116.7%) **7 Rn**

1m 32.8 (0.80) CSF £40.12 TOTE £6.00: £2.20 £3.60 (£20.20) OWNER Racecourse Medical Officers Association (MELTON MOWBRAY) BRED Miss J. A. Challen

WEIGHT FOR AGE 3yo-14lb

444 Night Dance, given a most positive ride, showed fine determination to hold on. (11/2)
No More Pressure (IRE), an All-Weather winner, put up a decent performance here and gave the impression that a bit further would have seen him with the advantage. (7/1)
444 Smarter Charter should have won this, but he found trouble at a vital stage and then hung left when he found a clear passage. In the end he had a hard race for nothing. (5/1)
560 Mujova (IRE) had his chances but just found this stiff track beyond him. (7/2)
550 Ten Past Six, in blinkers for the first time, cried enough once put under pressure. (16/1)
Magic Mill (IRE) did not impress on looks and ran most disappointingly (7/4)

636 HUTTON CRANSWICK MAIDEN STKS (3-Y.O+) (Class D)

4-50 (4-51) **5f** £3,639.00 (£1,092.00: £526.00: £243.00) Stalls: High GOING minus 0.35 sec per fur (F)

	Horse	Dist	Pos	SP	RR	SF
	Prince Dome (IRE) (77) (MartynWane) **3-8-12** JCarroll(10) (mde all: all out)	—	**1**	5/1	76	47

			SP	RR	SF
469[2]	**Marylebone (IRE) (68)** (JBerry) **3-8-12** GCarter(7) (a chsng ldr: hrd rdn appr fnl f: styd on towards fin) ....nk	**2**	4/1 3	75	46
	Archello (IRE) (GROldroyd) **3-8-7** RCochrane(5) (cl up: rdn 2f out: nt qckn) 3½	**3**	7/2 2	59	30
453[6]	**The Gay Fox (77)** (BAMcMahon) **3-8-12** LNewton(4) (b: a chsng ldrs: rdn 2f out: kpt on one pce) 1¼	**4**	11/4 1	60	31
453[5]	**Colway Ritz** (JWWatts) **3-8-12** GDuffield(3) (b: hdwy after 2f: edgd rt: nvr nr to chal) 2	**5**	4/1 3	53	24
	Star of The Road (JMCarr) **3-8-12** ACulhane(6) (nvr wnt pce) 6	**6**	25/1	34	5
475[8]	**Who's That Man** (SCWilliams) **3-8-9b1**(3) FLynch(9) (outpcd: swtchd 2f out: n.d) 1	**7**	16/1	31	2
	Maydoro (MDods) **4-9-4** RLappin(1) (dwlt: a bhd) 1	**8**	33/1	23	5
	Celia's Rainbow (RMWhitaker) **4-9-4** DeanMcKeown(8) (dwlt: a bhd) 6	**9**	33/1	4	—

(SP 121.2%) **9 Rn**

63.1 secs (1.30) CSF £23.87 TOTE £5.20: £1.20 £1.20 £1.80 (£10.70) Trio £9.90 OWNER Mr G. W. Jones (RICHMOND) BRED Airlie Stud
WEIGHT FOR AGE 3yo-11lb
Prince Dome (IRE) proved to be the sharpest of this bunch, and the line came just in time. (5/1)
469 Marylebone (IRE) needed a bit further as he does not do anything quickly, but he does respond to pressure. (4/1)
Archello (IRE) had her chances but failed to pick up when ridden. (7/2)
453 The Gay Fox found this trip on the sharp side and was fighting a lost cause in the last couple of furlongs. (11/4)
453 Colway Ritz ran as though longer trips are needed, and he did tend to hang right. (4/1: op 5/2)

T/Plpt: £498.10 (25.71 Tckts). T/Qdpt: £88.10 (10.34 Tckts) AA

BRIGHTON (L-H) (Firm)
Friday April 11th
WEATHER: overcast WIND: mod half against

76 63+ 63+ 68

637 E.B.F. SOUTHWICK MEDIAN AUCTION NOVICE STKS (2-Y.O) (Class F)
2-00 (2-01) **5f 59y** £2,415.60 (£666.60: £316.80) Stalls: High GOING: Not Established

			SP	RR	SF
564*	**Banningham Blade** (KTIvory) **2-8-12**(3) MartinDwyer(3) (chsd ldr: hrd rdn over 1f out: led wl ins fnl f: all out)—	**1**	5/2 2	78	37
557*	**Prince Foley** (WGMTurner) **2-8-9**(7) DMcGaffin(2) (lw: led: hrd rdn over 1f out: hdd wl ins fnl f: r.o wl)..........s.h	**2**	8/11 1	79	38
	Soft Touch (IRE) (MissGayKelleway) **2-8-7** SSanders(1) (b: leggy: bit bkwd: s.s: hld up: rdn & ev ch over 1f out: wknd fnl f) 5	**3**	4/1 3	55	14

(SP 106.5%) **3 Rn**

61.0 secs (1.00) CSF £4.33 TOTE £3.50 (£1.60) OWNER Crown Select (RADLETT) BRED K. T. Ivory
STEWARDS' ENQUIRY McGaffin susp 21-24/4/97 (excessive & improper use of whip).
564* Banningham Blade is getting the hang of things at the start and for the first time broke on level terms. Engaged in a tremendous tussle with the runner-up in the final quarter-mile, she managed to have a whisker in front where it mattered most, but had nothing in reserve. (5/2: 2/1-3/1)
557* Prince Foley set the pace but looked all at sea on this very tricky switchback track. Despite wandering about, he fought hard as he came under severe pressure inside the distance. With his inexperienced rider going totally over the top and hitting the colt no less than eleven times, it was only on the nod that he just lost out. It came as no surprise that McGaffin was suspended for four days for his use of the whip. (8/11)
Soft Touch (IRE) looked as though the run would bring her on and so it proved. She is sure to come on for this. (4/1: 2/1-9/2)

638 ELM GROVE CLAIMING STKS (4-Y.O+) (Class F)
2-30 (2-30) **5f 213y** £2,277.00 (£627.00: £297.00) Stalls: High GOING minus 0.52 sec per fur (F)

			SP	RR	SF
	Sizzling (59) (RHannon) **5-8-12** DaneO'Neill(1) (w ldr: led over 2f out: rdn: r.o wl) ....—	**1**	7/2 2	62	40
459[8]	**Justinianus (IRE) (31)** (JJBridger) **5-8-10** DHarrison(3) (lw: led over 3f: hrd rdn over 1f out: unable qckn)....2½	**2**	16/1	53	31
201[6]	**Jo Maximus (72)** (SDow) **5-8-11**(5) ADaly(10) (a.p: rdn over 2f out: r.o one pce) ....¾	**3**	9/4 1	57	35
214[4]	**Sharp Pearl (70)** (JWhite) **4-9-8b** WJO'Connor(11) (lw: rdn & hdwy over 2f out: one pce)....................hd	**4**	7/1	63	41
	Pearl Dawn (IRE) (55) (PCClarke) **7-8-11** NAdams(4) (a.p: rdn over 2f out: one pce)....................3	**5**	16/1	44	22
152[8]	**Halbert (41)** (MDIUsher) **8-8-9v**(3) PMcCabe(7) (s.i.s: rdn over 2f out: hdwy fnl f: nvr nrr)....................½	**6**	20/1	44	22
512[10]	**Mellors (IRE) (64)** (MJHeaton-Ellis) **4-9-6** SDrowne(12) (prom over 3f)....................s.h	**7**	13/2 3	52	30
480[2]	**Backhander (IRE) (41)** (RTPhillips) **5-8-10b** JReid(8) (hdwy over 2f out: wknd over 1f out) ....½	**8**	9/1	40	18
512[6]	**Lift Boy (USA) (48)** (GLMoore) **8-8-12** CandyMorris(5) (mid div & wkng whn hmpd 3f out) 4	**9**	10/1	31	9
512[8]	**Lady Westbury (IRE)** (PCRitchens) **6-8-1** JLowe(6) (a bhd)....................2	**10**	33/1	15	—
	Cadford Jewel (WGMTurner) **4-8-3**(7) DMcGaffin(9) (prom over 2f) 13	**11**	33/1	—	—
	Maraeinca (PRHedger) **4-8-11** RPrice(2) (s.s: hdwy 5f out: wknd 3f out)....................1½	**12**	33/1	—	—

(SP 123.3%) **12 Rn**

1m 7.9 (0.70) CSF £52.96 TOTE £4.90: £2.00 £4.70 £1.40 (£45.00) Trio £80.00 OWNER Mrs P. Jubert (MARLBOROUGH) BRED Lord Victor Matthews
Sizzling, carrying some condition for this first run since last July, went on over a quarter-of-a-mile from home and was never going to be caught. (7/2)
404 Justinianus (IRE), who has been busy on the All-Weather so far this year, took the field along but was soon put in his place (16/1)
27 Jo Maximus, whose three victories to date have all come here, was 8lb clear on official ratings, but never posed a serious threat. (9/4)
214 Sharp Pearl, who did Lift Boy no favours at halfway, could only plod on at one pace in the final quarter-mile. He is a very moderate performer with just one victory to his name. (7/1: 5/1-8/1)
Pearl Dawn (IRE), who has changed stables since last season, was never far away but failed to quicken. (16/1)
Halbert, who has changed stables since his last run, made late headway but never threatened the principals. (20/1)
512 Mellors (IRE) (13/2: 9/2-7/1)
512 Lift Boy (USA) (10/1: 8/1-12/1)

639 HOLLINGBURY LIMITED STKS (0-75) (3-Y.O+) (Class D)
3-00 (3-00) **7f 214y** £3,550.05 (£1,058.40: £504.70: £227.85) Stalls: High GOING minus 0.52 sec per fur (F)

			SP	RR	SF
444[3]	**Sharp Shuffle (IRE) (74)** (RHannon) **4-9-8** DaneO'Neill(1) (b.off fore: swtg: hld up: nt clr run on ins & swtchd rt over 2f out: swtchd rt over 1f out: str run fnl f: led nr fin)....................—	**1**	10/11 1	80	28
336[2]	**Stellar Line (USA) (69)** (DRCElsworth) **4-9-5**(3) DGriffiths(5) (lw: led: hrd rdn over 1f out: hdd nr fin) ....nk	**2**	10/1	79	27
70[3]	**Gulliver (75)** (NJHWalker) **4-9-1**(7) BarrySmith(2) (b: lw: a.p: rdn over 2f out: one pce)....................1¼	**3**	7/1 3	77	25
	Scarlet Crescent (74) (PTWalwyn) **3-8-4** SSanders(4) (a.p: hrd rdn over 1f out: one pce) 1¼	**4**	3/1 2	71	4

Balance of Power (68) (SDow) **5-9-3**(5) ADaly(3) (bit bkwd: no hdwy fnl 2f)........1¼ **5** 7/1[3] 72 20

(SP 111.5%) **5 Rn**

1m 34.3 (3.00) CSF £9.96 TOTE £1.70: £1.20 £3.10 (£3.60) OWNER Mrs H. F. Prendergast (MARLBOROUGH) BRED W. Tierney
WEIGHT FOR AGE 3yo-15lb

444 Sharp Shuffle (IRE) confirmed the promise shown at Doncaster recently despite not having a trouble-free passage. (10/11)
336 Stellar Line (USA), as usual looked extremely well, and dictated matters from the front. Responding well to pressure from below the distance, he was only worried out of it near the line. His turn is surely not far away and he may be helped by a drop into claiming company. (10/1: 6/1-10/1)
70 Gulliver, twice pulled up over hurdles since his last Flat run, was always close up but failed to quicken in the final quarter-mile. (7/1: 6/1-9/1)
Scarlet Crescent was never far away but could only go up and down in the same place in the last two furlongs. (3/1)
Balance of Power, formerly with Reg Akehurst, was carrying some condition. Held up at the back of the field, he could never get on terms. (7/1: 5/1-15/2)

640 SHEEPCOTE VALLEY H'CAP (0-60) (3-Y.O+) (Class F)

3-30 (3-33) **1m 3f 196y** £2,277.00 (£627.00: £297.00) Stalls: Low GOING minus 0.52 sec per fur (F)

Form	Horse	Btn	Pos	SP	RR	SF
538[6]	**Yet Again (40)** (MissGayKelleway) **5-8-9** SSanders(7) (hld up: rdn over 3f out: led over 1f out: r.o wl)	—	**1**	11/10[1]	56	28
487[3]	**Duncombe Hall (36)** (CACyzer) **4-8-4** AClark(6) (a.p: led over 3f out tl over 1f out: r.o)	1	**2**	8/1[3]	51	22
183[4]	**Sapphire Son (IRE) (49)** (PCClarke) **5-9-4** NAdams(3) (chsd ldr over 6f: unable qckn fnl 4f)	9	**3**	20/1	52	24
	Clifton Game (45) (MRChannon) **7-8-9**(5) PPMurphy(5) (b.hind: hld up: one pce fnl 4f)	1¼	**4**	5/1[2]	46	18
106[10]	**Colour Counsellor (46)** (RMFlower) **4-9-0b** DaneO'Neill(8) (b: led 7f: wknd over 2f out)	2	**5**	16/1	44	15
481[2]	**Fabulous Mtoto (59)** (MSSaunders) **7-10-0** RPrice(1) (lw: plld hrd: a.p: led 5f out tl over 3f out: wknd 2f out: b.b.v)	nk	**6**	5/1[2]	57	29
63[11]	**Lucy Tufty (42)** (JPearce) **6-8-8**(3) CTeague(9) (a bhd)	16	**7**	25/1	18	—
478[5]	**Warrior King (IRE) (54)** (MrsPNDutfield) **3-8-2**[ow2] SDrowne(2) (lw: bhd fnl 10f)	2	**8**	33/1	28	—
	Yeath (IRE) (43) (SDow) **5-8-7**(5) ADaly(4) (a bhd)	nk	**9**	25/1	16	—

(SP 113.3%) **9 Rn**

2m 31.2 (3.60) CSF £8.76 CT £100.88 TOTE £1.80: £1.50 £1.40 £2.50 (£5.70) Trio £26.70 OWNER Mr A. P. Griffin (WHITCOMBE) BRED Aston Park Stud
WEIGHT FOR AGE 3yo-21lb, 4yo-1lb
OFFICIAL EXPLANATION **Fabulous Mtoto: bled from the nose.**

538 Yet Again has been in sparkling form on the All-Weather, and bounced back from his recent Turf disappointment, striking the front below the distance and keeping on well. (11/10)
487 Duncombe Hall made his bid for glory over three furlongs from home and, although collared below the distance, stuck on well to the line. (8/1: 6/1-10/1)
147 Sapphire Son (IRE), in second place in the first half of the race, was made to look very pedestrian in the last half-mile. (20/1)
Clifton Game was made to look very one-paced in the last four furlongs. (5/1)
13 Colour Counsellor, who took the field along until the top of the hill, had shot his bolt over two furlongs from home. (16/1)
481 Fabulous Mtoto gained a narrow lead at the top of the hill but he was collared over three furlongs from home and soon in trouble. It later transpired he had broken a blood vessel. He could do with dropping a few pounds in the handicap. (5/1: 3/1-11/2)

641 VARNDEAN MEDIAN AUCTION MAIDEN STKS (3-Y.O) (Class F)

4-00 (4-03) **1m 1f 209y** £2,277.00 (£627.00: £297.00) Stalls: Low GOING minus 0.52 sec per fur (F)

Form	Horse	Btn	Pos	SP	RR	SF
455[2]	**Here's To Howie (USA) (76)** (RHannon) **3-9-0** WJO'Connor(7) (chsd ldr: led over 1f out: hrd rdn: r.o wl)	—	**1**	3/1[2]	69	32
	High On Life (ACStewart) **3-9-0** DHarrison(4) (a.p: rdn over 2f out: r.o wl ins fnl f)	nk	**2**	15/8[1]	69	32
	Kalimat (73) (WJarvis) **3-8-9** DaneO'Neill(2) (b.nr hind: hld up: n.m.r over 2f out: rdn over 1f out: unable qckn ins fnl f)	1¼	**3**	15/8[1]	62	25
582[5]	**Miss Barcelona (IRE) (50)** (MJPolglase) **3-8-9** SSanders(1) (led over 8f: one pce)	nk	**4**	20/1	61	24
	The Green Grey (64) (WRMuir) **3-9-0** JReid(5) (bit bkwd: hld up: rdn over 3f out: sn wknd)	8	**5**	8/1[3]	53	16
	Northern Touch (SCWilliams) **3-8-6**(3) PMcCabe(3) (s.s: a wl bhd)	1¼	**6**	33/1	46	9
	Rock It Rosie (DrJDScargill) **3-8-9** MFenton(6) (w'like: a bhd)	12	**7**	20/1	27	—

(SP 118.1%) **7 Rn**

2m 1.0 (2.70) CSF £8.48 TOTE £3.80: £1.80 £1.20 (£3.70) OWNER The Breeze Uppers (MARLBOROUGH) BRED Holton Grigsby Ingram and Mr and Mrs T. Kuster

455 Here's To Howie (USA), racing in second place, struck the front below the distance and, responding to pressure, just managed to hold off the late flourish of the runner-up. (3/1: tchd 5/1)
High On Life put in some sterling work inside the final furlong, but the line was always going to beat him. (15/8)
Kalimat began a run inside the final furlong, but was tapped for toe inside the last hundred yards. (15/8: 11/10-2/1)
582 Miss Barcelona (IRE) took the field along but, collared below the distance, could only keep on at one pace. (20/1)
The Green Grey (8/1: 6/1-10/1)

642 CHURCHILL SQUARE H'CAP (0-70) (3-Y.O) (Class E)

4-30 (4-31) **7f 214y** £3,044.25 (£909.00: £434.50: £197.25) Stalls: High GOING minus 0.52 sec per fur (F)

Form	Horse	Btn	Pos	SP	RR	SF
	Boater (69) (DMorley) **3-9-7** MFenton(9) (mde all: all out)	—	**1**	3/1[1]	77	33
535[3]	**First Chance (IRE) (67)** (DRCElsworth) **3-9-5** WJO'Connor(5) (lw: chsd wnr: ev ch fnl 3f: r.o wl)	s.h	**2**	3/1[1]	75	31
533[5]	**Interdream (62)** (RHannon) **3-9-0** DaneO'Neill(1) (hld up: rdn over 2f out: unable qckn)	2½	**3**	6/1[3]	65	21
456[2]	**Mendoza (60)** (DJGMurraySmith) **3-8-12** DHarrison(8) (lw: a.p: rdn over 2f out: one pce)	nk	**4**	5/1[2]	62	18
475[4]	**Nervous Rex (63)** (WRMuir) **3-9-1** JReid(7) (a.p: rdn over 2f out: wknd over 1f out)	6	**5**	5/1[2]	53	9
474[8]	**Junie (IRE) (68)** (TGMills) **3-8-13**(7) JCornally(2) (lw: a bhd)	2	**6**	33/1	54	10
	Mister Jay (54) (PTWalwyn) **3-8-6** SSanders(3) (lw: prom tl nt clr run & lost pl 5f out: bhd fnl 3f)	nk	**7**	14/1	40	—
477[15]	**Irish Fiction (IRE) (61)** (DJSCosgrove) **3-8-13** JStack(4) (a bhd)	½	**8**	14/1	46	2
456[4]	**Talisman (IRE) (50)** (SDow) **3-7-11**(5) ADaly(6) (a bhd)	¾	**9**	14/1	33	—

(SP 120.6%) **9 Rn**

1m 33.7 (2.40) CSF £11.15 CT £47.52 TOTE £6.30: £2.30 £1.30 £1.90 (£5.50) Trio £54.30 OWNER Lord Hartington (NEWMARKET) BRED Side Hill Stud

Boater made every post a winning one and, in a tremendous battle in the last three furlongs, prevailed with not an ounce to spare. (3/1)

535 First Chance (IRE) had a titanic struggle with the winner in the last three furlongs and failed by only a whisker. (3/1)
533 Interdream chased the leaders, but failed to quicken in the last two furlongs. (6/1: op 3/1)
456 Mendoza was never far away but could make no impression in the final quarter-mile. (5/1: op 5/2)
475 Nervous Rex was close up until calling it a day below the distance. (5/1)
Mister Jay (14/1: op 7/1)
Irish Fiction (IRE) (14/1: op 6/1)
456 Talisman (IRE) (14/1: op 8/1)

643 BRIGHTON SPRING H'CAP (0-80) (3-Y.O+) (Class D)

5-00 (5-00) **5f 213y** £3,645.60 (£1,087.80: £519.40: £235.20) Stalls: High GOING minus 0.52 sec per fur (F)

			SP	RR	SF
488[4]	**Spender (74)** (PWHarris) **8-9-9** JReid(3) (lw: a.p: led over 1f out: drvn out)—	**1**	3/1[2]	83	48
*569**	**Apollo Red (67)** (GLMoore) **8-9-2** 7x CandyMorris(9) (led over 4f: r.o)½	**2**	11/4[1]	75	40
556[4]	**Without Friends (IRE) (75)** (JFfitch-Heyes) **3-8-12** SWhitworth(4) (hld up: rdn over 2f out: r.o one pce)1½	**3**	16/1	79	32
569[5]	**Sharp Imp (58)** (RMFlower) **7-8-7b** SSanders(8) (hld up: rdn over 2f out: one pce)1	**4**	11/2[3]	59	24
	Willow Dale (IRE) (73) (DRCElsworth) **4-9-8** MFenton(1) (a.p: rdn over 2f out: wknd fnl f)¾	**5**	12/1	72	37
444[23]	**Crystal Heights (FR) (70)** (RJO'Sullivan) **9-9-5** DHarrison(5) (b: nvr nr to chal)¾	**6**	6/1	67	32
520[9]	**Bayin (USA) (75)** (MDIUsher) **8-9-10** RStreet(2) (b: s.s: a bhd)½	**7**	13/2	71	36
569[4]	**Friendly Brave (USA) (79)** (MissGayKelleway) **7-10-0** WJO'Connor(6) (b: b.hind: lw: nvr plcd to chal)s.h	**8**	10/1	75	40
520[14]	**Efra (65)** (RHannon) **8-9-0** DaneO'Neill(7) (bhd fnl 3f)1	**9**	10/1	58	23
			(SP 126.4%)	**9 Rn**	

1m 8.0 (0.80) CSF £11.90 CT £110.38 TOTE £3.60: £1.50 £1.10 £3.00 (£5.90) Trio £29.90 OWNER The Entrepreneurs (BERKHAMSTED) BRED The Mount Coote Partnership
WEIGHT FOR AGE 3yo-12lb
488 Spender moved to the front below the distance, but found the line coming just in time. (3/1)
569* Apollo Red took the field along until collared below the distance, but got his second wind inside the last and was clawing back the advantage all the way to the line. (11/4: op 7/4)
556 Without Friends (IRE) struggled on to take third prize. (16/1)
569 Sharp Imp chased the leaders but failed to quicken inside the final quarter-mile. (11/2)
Willow Dale (IRE), a leading player from the outset, tired in the final furlong as lack of a recent run took its toll. (12/1)
Bayin (USA) (13/2: 4/1-7/1)
Friendly Brave (USA) was given a very quiet ride. Steadied back through the field after breaking well, his jockey gave him a smack a furlong from home but that was about it. High in the handicap at present, he will hopefully come down a few pounds. (10/1: op 6/1)
Efra (10/1: 7/1-11/1)

T/Plpt: £48.20 (173.41 Tckts). T/Qdpt: £6.40 (127.15 Tckts) AK

0582-NOTTINGHAM (L-H) (Good to firm)

Friday April 11th

WEATHER: cloudy WIND: mod behind

644 WATNALL (S) STKS (3-Y.O) (Class G)

2-10 (2-12) **1m 54y** £1,984.50 (£547.00: £259.50) Stalls: Low GOING: 0.07 sec per fur (G)

			SP	RR	SF
	Princess of Hearts (60) (BJMeehan) **3-8-11b** BDoyle(4) (dwlt: hld up: hdwy over 2f out: led ins fnl f: r.o wl).—	**1**	4/1[2]	70	36
	Aficionado (IRE) (65) (RJHodges) **3-9-2** TQuinn(8) (lw: hld up: hdwy 4f out: slt ld over 1f out: rdn & hdd ins fnl f)1½	**2**	2/1[1]	72	38
414[3]	**Mardrew** (DJSffrenchDavis) **3-9-2** JQuinn(5) (plld hrd: chsd ldrs: ev ch over 1f out: unable qckn fnl f)¾	**3**	6/1	71	37
582[9]	**Patrick (26)** (DBurchell) **3-8-12** PaulEddery(9) (hld up: hdwy fnl 2f: nrst fin)2½	**4**	20/1	62	28
497[3]	**Champagne On Ice (49)** (PDEvans) **3-8-7** JFEgan(11) (hld up & bhd: hdwy fnl 2f: nt rch ldrs)2½	**5**	5/1[3]	52	18
456[5]	**Alvilde (62)** (DJSCosgrove) **3-8-7** MRimmer(12) (stdd s: hdwy 5f out: led over 3f out tl over 1f out: sn wknd) ..6	**6**	10/1	40	6
259[8]	**Joyful Joy (40)** (BPJBaugh) **3-8-0**(7) IonaWands(10) (nvr plcd to chal)2	**7**	33/1	36	2
	Don't Forget Shoka (IRE) (40) (JSMoore) **3-8-6**(5) AimeeCook(3) (bit bkwd: hld up & plld hrd: no imp fnl 3f)...6	**8**	16/1	29	—
556[9]	**Baptismal Rock (IRE) (65)** (BJCurley) **3-8-12** WRyan(1) (led over 4f: sn rdn & wknd: t.o)9	**9**	10/1	12	—
	Heavenly Dancer (59) (MrsNMacauley) **3-8-7** RHills(2) (prom 5f: eased whn btn 2f out: t.o)½	**10**	16/1	6	—
475[10]	**Kierans Maiden** (APJarvis) **3-8-0**(7) CCarver(6) (lw: plld hrd: prom tl wknd 3f out: t.o)9	**11**	33/1	—	—
	Tom Pladdey (56) (RBastiman) **3-8-12** DHolland(7) (bkwd: chsd ldr over 4f: sn wknd: t.o)9	**12**	16/1	—	—
			(SP 130.8%)	**12 Rn**	

1m 47.9 (6.60) CSF £12.33 TOTE £4.60: £4.40 £1.10 £3.30 (£7.60) Trio £12.70 OWNER Mr A. S. Reid (UPPER LAMBOURN) BRED Cheveley Park Stud Ltd
Sold M Pipe for 5,000gns: Mardrew clmd TConnors £5,750
Princess of Hearts failed to impress with her action to post, but she fared much better once in action, and displayed her courage to out-battle the favourite inside the final furlong. (4/1)
Aficionado (IRE), turned out looking a picture, got the better of the long, drawn-out duel to forge ahead approaching the last furlong, but the winner soon appeared on the scene and he was outpointed near the finish. (2/1: tchd 3/1)
414 Mardrew, fit from the All-Weather, raced freely and posed a live threat below the distance, but the required finishing speed was not forthcoming. (6/1)
Patrick, making a quick reappearance, turned in his best performance yet. He seems to be grasping what is needed. (20/1)
497 Champagne On Ice made her move under the stands' rail in the final quarter-mile but, on ground far too lively, could not quicken sufficiently to make her presence felt. (5/1)
456 Alvilde struck the front early in the straight, but she failed to sustain the effort and was brushed aside with ease once the battle to the finish developed. (10/1: op 6/1)
Baptismal Rock (IRE) (10/1: op 5/1)

645 BASSINGFIELD MAIDEN STKS (3-Y.O) (Class D)

2-40 (2-42) **1m 54y** £4,441.85 (£1,332.80: £641.90: £296.45) Stalls: Low GOING: 0.07 sec per fur (G)

			SP	RR	SF
	China Red (USA) (90) (JWHills) **3-9-0** MHills(5) (lw: mde all: rdn over 1f out: r.o wl)—	**1**	3/1[1]	91	52

				SP	RR	SF
	Barrier Ridge (HRACecil) **3-9-0** KFallon(8) (cmpt: scope: lw: a.p: rdn over 2f out: ev ch whn edgd rt over 1f out: r.o wl towards fin)	½	**2**	4/1[2]	90	51
517[7]	**Speculator (IRE)** (WJHaggas) **3-9-0** TQuinn(10) (bit bkwd: chsd ldrs: ev ch over 1f out: one pce fnl f)	2	**3**	13/2[3]	86	47
	Madison Mist (MrsJRRamsden) **3-8-9** JFortune(4) (unf: scope: bkwd: hld up & bhd: hdwy 2f out: nt rch ldrs)	6	**4**	20/1	70	31
	Green Power (JRFanshawe) **3-9-0** NVarley(11) (bkwd: hld up in rr: stdy hdwy fnl 2f: nvr nrr)	hd	**5**	12/1	74+	35
	Irsal (ACStewart) **3-9-0** RHills(13) (hld up: hdwy 3f out: wknd over 1f out)	3	**6**	3/1[1]	69	30
	Travelmate (JRFanshawe) **3-9-0** NDay(12) (bit bkwd: nvr plcd to chal)	¾	**7**	20/1	67	28
	Kristopher (JWHills) **3-9-0** LDettori(9) (h.d.w: bit bkwd: prom tl wknd over 2f out)	1	**8**	20/1	65	26
	Viva Verdi (IRE) (JLDunlop) **3-8-9** PatEddery(1) (bkwd: trckd ldrs tl wknd 3f out)	6	**9**	8/1	49	10
	Misterton (JAGlover) **3-8-7**(7) TPengkerego(3) (w'like: str: bkwd: s.s: a in rr)	½	**10**	33/1	53	14
	Hulal (ACStewart) **3-9-0** MRoberts(2) (bkwd: a bhd)	hd	**11**	16/1	52	13
	Spanish Warrior (JWHills) **3-8-11**(3) MHenry(7) (bkwd: a in rr: rdn over 2f out: t.o)	5	**12**	25/1	43	4
	Craven Hill (IRE) (NAGraham) **3-9-0** DHolland(6) (still unf: bit bkwd: prom over 4f: sn wknd: t.o)	8	**13**	20/1	27	—

(SP 133.9%) **13 Rn**

1m 46.5 (5.20) CSF £13.77 TOTE £3.60: £1.70 £1.50 £2.50 (£6.00) Trio £23.90 OWNER Mr N N Browne And Partners (LAMBOURN) BRED Robert Masterson

STEWARDS' ENQUIRY Fanshawe fined £1,400 under Rule 151(ii) (schooling in public).Varley susp 21-26/4/97 (schooling in public).Green Power susp 30 days.

China Red (USA) appreciated these more forceful tactics, and stuck to his task willingly to record a well-deserved first success. (3/1)

Barrier Ridge, an attractive colt who is obviously a bit of a handful, was very weak in the market. Close up from the break, he was staying on really strongly towards the finish and should soon go one better. (4/1: 2/1-9/2)

Speculator (IRE) had a run at the end of last month but he still looked to need this, and this much-improved performance should put him spot on for next time. (13/2)

Madison Mist, a filly with plenty of scope, was finding her stride in the closing stages and s sure to strip fitter for the run. (20/1)

Green Power, bred to need further, looked too backward to do himself justice, but he caught the eyes of the Stewards, staying on steadily in the latter stages, and it proved a costly re-introduction. (12/1: op 8/1)

Irsal, did not enjoy the best of runs on his racecourse debut in the autumn, but had every chance here if he had been able to take it. (3/1)

Viva Verdi (IRE) has hardly shed any of her winter coat yet and, until she does, it is unlikely she will show her true form. (8/1)

646 LEVY BOARD CONDITIONS STKS (3-Y.O) (Class C)

3-10 (3-18) **1m 54y** £5,234.00 (£1,940.00: £933.50: £384.50: £155.75: £64.25) Stalls: Low GOING: 0.07 sec per fur (G)

				SP	RR	SF
	Sekari (DRLoder) **3-9-0** LDettori(1) (h.d.w: hld up: rdn & hdwy over 2f out: led wl ins fnl f)	—	**1**	11/8[1]	104	64
508[5]	**Crystal Hearted (92)** (HCandy) **3-9-0** AMcGlone(7) (led: rdn over 2f out: hdd wl ins fnl f)	½	**2**	5/1	103	63
	Sandstone (IRE) (104) (JLDunlop) **3-9-0** KDarley(6) (chsd ldrs: hrd drvn over 2f out: kpt on wl ins fnl f)	1¼	**3**	5/2[2]	101	61
	Bali Paradise (USA) (97) (PFICole) **3-9-0** TQuinn(8) (a.p: ev ch over 1f out: sn rdn: one pce)	1½	**4**	12/1	98	58
	Courtship (85) (HRACecil) **3-9-0** KFallon(4) (lw: hld up: rdn along ½-wy: no imp)	7	**5**	4/1[3]	84	44
	Speedball (IRE) (96) (IABalding) **3-9-0** PatEddery(3) (lw: prom tl wknd 2f out: eased whn btn: t.o)	11	**6**	8/1	63	23
	Ginzbourg (JLDunlop) **3-8-11** MHills(2) (still unf: bkwd: s.v.s: a wl bhd: t.o)	17	**7**	20/1	27	—
	Premier Bay (103) (PWHarris) **3-9-0** WRSwinburn(5) (Withdrawn not under Starter's orders: unruly in stalls & injured jockey)		**W**	8/1	—	—

(SP 142.0%) **7 Rn**

1m 45.3 (4.00) CSF £10.02 TOTE £2.20: £1.80 £2.30 (£8.80) OWNER Sheikh Mohammed (NEWMARKET) BRED Sheikh Mohammed Bin Rashid Al Maktoum

Sekari created a good impression when successful on his only previous outing in the autumn, and he stayed on resolutely to gain command in the final one hundred yards. (11/8)

508 Crystal Hearted had the edge in fitness over his rivals and attempted to put that to good use, but he was shadowed all the way, and courage alone was not enough inside the final furlong. (5/1)

Sandstone (IRE), a winner first time out as a two-year-old, was also narrowly beaten over this trip. He turned in a sound performance here, but looks to need a stiffer test of stamina. (5/2)

Bali Paradise (USA) failed to hold his own in a Group Three event in the autumn, but he showed plenty of ability in his previous races. Looking to have done his fair share of work for this seasonal debut, he was only tapped for toe inside the last furlong and will soon be paying his way again. (12/1)

Courtship looked on good terms with himself in the preliminaries, but he ran very flat and needs to prove he has trained on. (4/1)

647 ACER COMPUTERS H'CAP (0-80) (3-Y.O+) (Class D)

3-40 (3-46) **1m 1f 213y** £4,123.35 (£1,234.80: £592.90: £271.95) Stalls: Low GOING: 0.07 sec per fur (G)

				SP	RR	SF
	White Plains (IRE) (75) (MCPipe) **4-9-6**(5) RMullen(8) (hld up & bhd: hdwy over 2f out: r.o to ld last strides)	—	**1**	15/2	86	56
305[7]	**Absolutelystunning (56)** (MrsBarbaraWaring) **4-8-6** WRyan(6) (hld up & bhd: gd hdwy 2f out: led ins fnl f: hdd nr fin)	½	**2**	33/1	66	36
	Peppers (IRE) (65) (KRBurke) **4-9-1** KFallon(7) (bhd: hmpd 8f out: hdwy over 2f out: rdn to ld over 1f out: hdd & no ex ins fnl f)	1½	**3**	10/1	73	43
538[4]	**Master Beveled (72)** (PDEvans) **7-9-8** JFEgan(9) (hld up: hdwy 3f out: ev ch appr fnl f: hrd rdn: one pce)	¾	**4**	12/1	79	49
	Fern's Governor (58) (WJMusson) **5-8-8** DRMcCabe(2) (hld up & bhd: hdwy u.p fnl 2f: nvr nrr)	¾	**5**	10/1	63	33
	Atlantic Mist (56) (BRMillman) **4-8-6** BDoyle(15) (b.off hind: bit bkwd: dwlt: hdwy 3f out: ev ch over 1f out: wknd ins fnl f)	1	**6**	25/1	60	30
	Alfredo Alfredo (USA) (67) (JLDunlop) **5-9-3** TQuinn(11) (b: hld up mid div: nvr nr to chal)	1½	**7**	8/1	68+	38
	Nigel's Lad (IRE) (72) (PCHaslam) **5-9-8** LDettori(14) (chsd ldrs: no hdwy fnl 3f)	1¼	**8**	7/2[1]	71	41
487[5]	**Rehaab (60)** (DMorris) **4-8-5**(5) GFaulkner(13) (nvr nr ldrs)	1	**9**	33/1	58	28
405[12]	**Punkah (USA) (78)** (GMMcCourt) **4-9-7**(7) RStudholme(1) (trckd ldrs: led over 2f out tl over 1f out: sn wknd)	½	**10**	20/1	75	45
	Jalb (IRE) (76) (ACStewart) **3-8-7** RHills(12) (swtg: chsd ldrs over 7f)	2	**11**	4/1[2]	70	21
538[7]	**Golden Touch (USA) (57)** (DJSCosgrove) **5-8-7** MRoberts(17) (prom: led 5f out tl over 2f out: sn rdn & wknd)	1¾	**13**	25/1	37	7
435[14]	**Forest Robin (74)** (MrsJRRamsden) **4-9-10** JFortune(16) (b: prom 7f)	7	**13**	12/1	57	27
482[5]	**Zidac (73)** (PJMakin) **5-9-9** PatEddery(4) (plld hrd: bhd fnl 3f: t.o)	7	**14**	7/1[3]	42	12
457[5]	**Kriscliffe (78)** (GLewis) **4-10-0** PaulEddery(10) (prom tl wknd over 2f out)	2½	**15**	20/1	43	13
	Classic Dame (FR) (65) (ICampbell) **4-9-1** DBatteate(5) (bkwd: prom: led over 5f out: sn hdd: wknd 3f out: t.o)	16	**16**	25/1	4	—

	Buffalo River (57) (KAMorgan) **7-8-4**$^{(3)}$ RHavlin(3) (b: bit bkwd: bolted gng to s: led over 4f: wknd qckly: t.o)	dist	**17**	50/1	—	—
				(SP 140.1%)		**17 Rn**

2m 9.6 (7.10) CSF £236.87 CT £2,336.30 TOTE £11.00: £3.80 £4.90 £3.00 £1.90 (£147.70) Trio £570.40; £731.18 to Warwick 12/4/97
OWNER Phil Lake, Huw Lake (WELLINGTON) BRED Howard Kaskel
WEIGHT FOR AGE 3yo-19lb

White Plains (IRE) failed to win over hurdles, but he enjoyed a rewarding season on the Flat last year and, reunited with the apprentice who partnered him then, was produced to perfection to nose ahead when it mattered. (15/2)
Absolutelystunning delivered her challenge and poked her head in front two hundred yards out, but the determined late flourish of the winner proved too much. (33/1)
Peppers (IRE) has shown signs of ability in the past, but she is still to open her account. This very promising effort would suggest her turn is near at hand. (10/1)
538 Master Beveled lacks a turn of finishing speed when the ground rides so lively, but he did not fail for the want of trying and is no back number yet. (12/1)
Fern's Governor needs a run to put an edge on her, so this promising effort could be a sign that she is more forward this term. (10/1)
Atlantic Mist is not so effective over this shorter trip, but he gave notice that he has retained his ability and an early success will come as no surprise. (25/1)
Nigel's Lad (IRE), who has had an extremely good season over hurdles, tracked the leaders but was hard at work three furlongs out and could make no further progress. (7/2)
Jalb (IRE) looked ill-at-ease cantering to post and dropped away tamely after pushing the pace for seven furlongs. (4/1)
Forest Robin (12/1: op 8/1)

648 TROWELL MAIDEN AUCTION STKS (2-Y.O) (Class F)

4-10 (4-13) **5f 13y** £2,277.00 (£627.00: £297.00) Stalls: High GOING minus 0.17 sec per fur (GF)

				SP	RR	SF
	Dim Ots (BPalling) **2-8-0** JQuinn(3) (lt-f: unf: a.p: led ½-wy: rdn & edgd rt ins fnl f: hld on)	—	**1**	11/2^{2}	72	23
536^{4}	**Theatre of Dreams** (PDEvans) **2-8-1**^{ow1} JFEgan(5) (a.p: ev ch ins fnl f: unable qckn)	½	**2**	6/1^{3}	71	21
557^{3}	**Sea Imp (IRE)** (MartynMeade) **2-8-2** BDoyle(6) (a.p: ev ch over 1f out: one pce)	3	**3**	8/1	63	14
	Eleventh Duke (IRE) (RHannon) **2-8-10** PatEddery(11) (cmpt: lw: hdwy over 1f out: r.o wl fnl f)	1¾	**4**	9/2^{1}	65	16
472^{2}	**Conectis (IRE)** (DJSCosgrove) **2-8-2** NCarlisle(2) (dwlt: sn chsng ldrs: one pce fnl 2f)	2	**5**	9/2^{1}	51	2
	Fayrana (IRE) (JWHills) **2-8-5** RHills(13) (w'like: hld up: hdwy appr fnl f: nrst fin)	1½	**6**	6/1^{3}	49	—
472^{6}	**Bliss (IRE)** (MrsPNDutfield) **2-8-0** FNorton(1) (chsd ldrs over 3f)	½	**7**	25/1	43	—
	Dorton Grange (JLSpearing) **2-7-5**$^{(7)}$ JBosley(7) (leggy: lt-f: chsd ldrs 3f)	2½	**8**	25/1	33	—
	Thecomebackking (SCWilliams) **2-8-10** KDarley(8) (w'like: bit bkwd: outpcd)	hd	**9**	12/1	45	—
	Bellow (IRE) (HMorrison) **2-8-10** DHolland(4) (gd sort: nvr gng pce of ldrs)	2½	**10**	12/1	37	—
	After Dawn (IRE) (MrsPNDutfield) **2-8-3**^{ow1} MRoberts(9) (leggy: lt-f: s.s: a bhd: t.o)	1½	**11**	20/1	25	—
	Red Risk (PWHarris) **2-8-10** LDettori(12) (lt-f: a bhd)	hd	**12**	11/2^{2}	32	—
432^{15}	**Far-So-La** (TMJones) **2-8-7** RPerham(10) (led to ½-wy: sn lost tch)	½	**13**	33/1	27	—
	Ivory's Joy (KTIvory) **2-8-0** GBardwell(14) (w'like: bit bkwd: s.s: a bhd & outpcd: t.o)	dist	**14**	16/1	—	—
				(SP 143.5%)		**14 Rn**

61.7 secs (2.80) CSF £40.81 TOTE £9.60: £3.30 £1.90 £1.70 (£33.90) Trio £189.60; £138.91 to Warwick 12/4/97 OWNER Mrs D. J. Hughes (COWBRIDGE) BRED R. Bowers

Dim Ots, a lightly-made half-sister to three winning sprinters, had been taught the job well and, despite showing signs of greenness in the closing stages, held on courageously to the end. (11/2)
536 Theatre of Dreams, with a couple of runs already under her belt, tried hard to cash in on her experience inside the distance, but the winner just would not be denied, (6/1)
557 Sea Imp (IRE) probably found this race coming too quickly, but she gave it her best shot and is gaining experience all the time. (8/1)
Eleventh Duke (IRE) was only into his stride inside the final furlong and, when faced with a slightly stiffer test of stamina, will soon leave this form behind. (9/2: op 3/1)
472 Conectis (IRE) has not yet mastered the art of trapping, but when she does she will be the one to beat. (9/2)
Fayrana (IRE) took time to realise what was required, and was only getting down to some serious work when the race was over. (6/1)

649 NEW BASFORD H'CAP (0-70) (3-Y.O) (Class E)

4-40 (4-42) **6f 15y** £3,356.25 (£1,005.00: £482.50: £221.25) Stalls: High GOING minus 0.17 sec per fur (GF)

				SP	RR	SF
532*	**Treasure Touch (IRE) (70)** (DNicholls) **3-9-0**$^{(7)}$ ^{7x} IonaWands(5) (a.p: led 2f out: clr fnl f)	—	**1**	100/30^{1}	84+	57
483^{9}	**Always Alight (60)** (KRBurke) **3-8-11** RPainter(3) (chsd ldrs: rdn 2f out: kpt on fnl f: no ch w wnr)	3½	**2**	33/1	65	38
532^{2}	**Master Foley (55)** (NPLittmoden) **3-8-6** TGMcLaughlin(2) (led 4f: rdn & one pce appr fnl f)	hd	**3**	10/1	60	33
532^{5}	**Jupiter (IRE) (70)** (GCBravery) **3-9-7** MRimmer(17) (lw: chsd ldrs stands' side: rdn 2f out: one pce)	¾	**4**	5/1^{2}	73	46
532^{3}	**Mike's Double (IRE) (52)** (GLewis) **3-8-3b** PaulEddery(1) (trckd ldrs: hrd rdn appr fnl f: eased whn btn cl home)	¾	**5**	7/1^{3}	53	26
458^{2}	**Chasetown Flyer (USA) (55)** (NEBerry) **3-8-6** RPerham(7) (w ldrs: rdn & lost pl over 2f out: rallied u.p fnl f)	¾	**6**	16/1	54	27
532^{4}	**Distinctive Dream (IRE) (47)** (KTIvory) **3-7-12b** GBardwell(6) (hdwy 2f out: sn hrd rdn: nt rch ldrs)	3	**7**	14/1	38	11
	Cairn Dhu (55) (MrsJRRamsden) **3-8-6b**^{1} JFortune(12) (wnt lft s: nvr nrr)	nk	**8**	14/1	45	18
466^{7}	**William's Well (52)** (MWEasterby) **3-8-3** JFEgan(13) (bit bkwd: nvr nr to chal)	hd	**9**	16/1	42	15
*489**	**Eager To Please (67)** (MissGayKelleway) **3-9-4b** DHolland(11) (spd over 4f)	hd	**10**	10/1	56	29
287^{6}	**Supercharmer (67)** (DNicholls) **3-9-4** FNorton(4) (a in rr)	nk	**11**	10/1	56	29
546^{4}	**Jack Says (50)** (DShaw) **3-8-1** DWright(15) (outpcd)	1½	**12**	33/1	35	8
506^{10}	**Forgotten Times (USA) (69)** (TMJones) **3-9-6** NCarlisle(16) (b: prom over 3f)	1½	**13**	14/1	50	23
	Ludo (67) (RHannon) **3-9-4** PatEddery(14) (bit bkwd: a bhd)	½	**14**	9/1	46	19
	Fan of Vent-Axia (54) (DJSCosgrove) **3-8-2**$^{(3)}$ MBaird(8) (bkwd: outpcd)	4	**15**	20/1	23	—
473^{11}	**Keen Waters (58)** (JRArnold) **3-8-9** MRoberts(10) (bit bkwd: outpcd)	1¾	**16**	25/1	22	—
	Parijazz (IRE) (70) (MartynMeade) **3-9-4**$^{(3)}$ RHavlin(9) (bit bkwd: s.s: a bhd: t.o)	11	**17**	14/1	5	—
				(SP 142.4%)		**17 Rn**

1m 13.9 (2.40) CSF £135.06 CT £737.83 TOTE £3.80: £1.20 £15.40 £3.70 £1.60 (£147.70) Trio £705.60 OWNER Mr N. Honeyman (THIRSK) BRED St Simon Foundation

532* Treasure Touch (IRE), with a competent apprentice to off-load a 7lb penalty for a success over course and distance last month, again demolished the opposition, and he is certainly on a high since he arrived at this yard. (100/30)
Always Alight did not begin to pick up until far too late, but he finished well and that initial success cannot be far away. (33/1)

532 Master Foley again had to settle for a rear view of the winner in the latter stages, but he never stopped trying and deserves a change of fortune. (10/1)
532 Jupiter (IRE) had little chance of turning the tables on the winner on identical terms, and he finished exactly the same distance behind as he had done last month. (5/1: op 8/1)
532 Mike's Double (IRE), hard at work from below the distance, could not summon the speed to land a blow and the position was accepted nearing the finish. (7/1)
458 Chasetown Flyer (USA) appears to find this trip inadequate, but he kept battling away and deserves to pick up a race. (16/1)
532 Distinctive Dream (IRE) is crying out for a slightly longer trip and, once he gets that and a slight lowering in grade, he should start to pay dividends. (14/1)

650 SHIPLEY COMMON H'CAP (0-70) (4-Y.O+) (Class E)
5-10 (5-11) **1m 6f 15y** £3,382.25 (£1,013.00: £486.50: £223.25) Stalls: Low GOING: 0.07 sec per fur (G)

				SP	RR	SF
542⁴	**Dancing Cavalier (65)** (RHollinshead) **4-9-8** PatEddery(11) (hld up: hdwy to ld over 3f out: sn clr: comf)	—	1	5/1 2	80+	59
465⁴	**Road Racer (IRE) (53)** (MrsJRRamsden) **4-8-10** JFortune(3) (hld up: hdwy over 3f out: chsd wnr over 2f out: no imp)	4	2	3/1 1	64	43
430⁵	**Chabrol (CAN) (60)** (TTClement) **4-9-0(3)** RHavlin(5) (lw: a.p: rdn 2f out: kpt on one pce)	nk	3	6/1 3	70	49
	Lawful Love (IRE) (37) (TWDonnelly) **7-7-6(5)ow1** PFessey(8) (bit bkwd: hld up & bhd: gd hdwy 5f out: one pce fnl 2f)	5	4	33/1	41	22
	Forgie (IRE) (63) (PCalver) **4-9-6** WRSwinburn(2) (bit bkwd: led 2f: led 8f out tl over 3f out: one pce fnl 2f)	½	5	11/1	67	46
	Norsong (50) (RAkehurst) **5-8-10** TQuinn(10) (bkwd: hld up: hdwy 5f out: wknd over 2f out)	10	6	7/1	43	25
	Sweet Glow (FR) (60) (MCPipe) **10-9-6** MRoberts(4) (wl bhd tl sme late hdwy)	1¾	7	14/1	51	33
	Chris's Lad (68) (BJMeehan) **6-10-0b** BDoyle(1) (bkwd: hld up: hdwy over 4f out: wknd over 2f out)	½	8	10/1	58	40
435¹⁶	**Cohiba (47)** (BJCurley) **4-8-4** JQuinn(12) (plld hrd: prom tl wknd over 2f out)	nk	9	16/1	37	16
430¹²	**General Glow (58)** (PDEvans) **4-9-1** JFEgan(6) (chsd ldrs: rdn over 4f: eased whn btn fnl 2f: t.o)	12	10	12/1	34	13
	Brighter Byfaah (IRE) (48) (NAGraham) **4-8-5** DHolland(7) (bkwd: led after 2f to 8f out: wknd over 3f out: t.o)	23	11	14/1	—	—
	Requested (53) (RIngram) **10-8-13** DRMcCabe(9) (b: bit bkwd: s.i.s: a bhd: t.o fr ½-wy)	14	12	10/1	—	—

(SP 124.8%) **12 Rn**

3m 7.8 (9.30) CSF £19.57 CT £88.22 TOTE £5.10: £2.40 £1.10 £2.40 (£9.40) Trio £16.60 OWNER The Three R's (UPPER LONGDON) BRED A. P. Hume
LONG HANDICAP Lawful Love (IRE) 7-4
WEIGHT FOR AGE 4yo-3lb
542 Dancing Cavalier turned a competitive event into a cake-walk and provided Pat Eddery with a rare winner for this stable. (5/1)
465 Road Racer (IRE), stepping back from two miles, made his move at the same time as the winner, but he was always playing second fiddle in the last quarter-mile (3/1)
430 Chabrol (CAN) was meeting the winner on 12lb better terms for a beating of three lengths, but that was over a shorter trip and, hard as he tried, he was unable to redress the balance (6/1)
Lawful Love (IRE) has been lightly-raced of late, and this effort would suggest that he is capable of finding a small race over a distance of ground. (33/1)
Forgie (IRE) left the impression he will be better for the run and, after helping to force the pace, had shot his bolt two furlongs out. (11/1)
Norsong waited on the leaders, but did not find a lot when asked for his effort as lack of peak condition caught him out. (7/1)
Sweet Glow (FR), one of two tailed-off at halfway, stayed on steadily past beaten rivals in the last half-mile, and will be a different proposition over marathon trips, even at his advanced age. (14/1)

T/Jkpt: Not won; £24,002.19 to Warwick 12/4/97. T/Plpt: £54.40 (312.07 Tckts). T/Qdpt: £25.50 (36.84 Tckts) IM

0536-**WARWICK** (L-H) (Good to firm, Firm patches)
Saturday April 12th
WEATHER: Fine WIND: nil
82 57+ 78+

651 E.B.F. HATTON NOVICE STKS (2-Y.O) (Class D)
1-50 (1-54) **5f** £3,151.50 (£942.00: £451.00: £205.50) Stalls: Low GOING: Not Established

				SP	RR	SF
447*	**Rising of The Moon (IRE)** (RHannon) **2-8-13** PatEddery(3) (chsd ldr: rdn over 2f out: r.o to ld cl home)	—	1	8/11 1	82	25
492*	**Salamanca** (JBerry) **2-8-4(5)** PFessey(1) (lw: led: clr over 2f out: rdn & wknd ins fnl f: ct cl home)	nk	2	6/4 2	77	20
	Mai Tai (IRE) (MrsPNDutfield) **2-8-7** DHolland(2) (leggy: w'like: bit bkwd: outpcd tl gd hdwy over 1f out: r.o)	3½	3	33/1	64	7
583⁴	**Dawn Patrol** (KWHogg) **2-8-7** DeanMcKeown(5) (a.p: no hdwy fnl 2f)	3	4	20/1	54	—
	Fleet Lady (IRE) (MrsPNDutfield) **2-8-7** SDrowne(4) (w'like: bit bkwd: s.s: a wl bhd)	7	5	66/1	32	—
	Frundin (MrsWBAllen,Norway) **2-8-7** LNewton(7) (lt-f: swvd bdly rt s: a wl bhd)	1¾	6	66/1	26	—
	Zielana Gora (SCWilliams) **2-8-7** KDarley(6) (unf: prom over 3f)	nk	7	8/1 3	25	—

(SP 119.7%) **7 Rn**

60.6 secs (2.60) CSF £2.00 TOTE £1.70: £1.10 £1.40 (£1.30) OWNER Miss L. Regis (MARLBOROUGH) BRED Mrs M. L. Davis
447* Rising of The Moon (IRE), unable to go with the leader at halfway, was said by Eddery to have appreciated the cut in the home straight. A sixth furlong should not be a problem. (8/11)
492* Salamanca looked to have run the favourite ragged until tying up in the closing stages. She will now go for the Lily Agnes at Chester and could take some catching around there. (6/4)
Mai Tai (IRE), a half-sister to a couple of juvenile winners in Ireland, seems sure to know more next time. (33/1)
583 Dawn Patrol was finding it a bit of a struggle from halfway. (20/1)
Zielana Gora (8/1: 6/1-9/1)

652 WARWICK SPRING H'CAP (0-70) (3-Y.O) (Class E)
2-25 (2-31) **5f** £2,940.25 (£877.00: £418.50: £189.25) Stalls: Low GOING minus 0.33 sec per fur (GF)

				SP	RR	SF
258²	**Mangus (IRE) (70)** (KOCunningham-Brown) **3-9-7** TQuinn(1) (a.p: swtchd rt over 1f out: led ins fnl f: rdn out)	—	1	15/2 3	78	50
602²	**Suite Factors (54)** (KRBurke) **3-8-5** JFEgan(2) (led tl ins fnl f: r.o)	nk	2	6/1 2	61	33
549³	**Impish (IRE) (45)** (TJEtherington) **3-7-5(5)** JBramhill(9) (rdn & hdwy 2f out: r.o one pce fnl f)	2½	3	14/1	44	16

				SP	RR	SF
	Anokato (66) (KTIvory) **3-9-0b**(3) MartinDwyer(4) (prom tl wknd over 1f out)	4	**4**	9/2[1]	52	24
532[6]	**C-Harry (IRE) (67)** (RHollinshead) **3-9-4** MWigham(7) (lw: s.s: hdwy over 1f out: nt rch ldrs)	nk	**5**	8/1	52	24
	Royal Emblem (58) (AGFoster) **3-8-9** RPerham(8) (swtg: bit bkwd: nvr trbld ldrs)	4	**6**	20/1	31	3
	Bramble Bear (66) (MBlanshard) **3-9-3** JQuinn(10) (hld up: hdwy over 2f out: wknd over 1f out)	¾	**7**	14/1	36	8
466*	**Loch-Hurn Lady (67)** (KWHogg) **3-9-4** KDarley(11) (prom 3f)	1½	**8**	9/2[1]	32	4
494[12]	**Sarabi (62)** (JPearce) **3-8-10**(3) CTeague(6) (prom 3f)	1½	**9**	12/1	23	—
	Wild Nettle (53) (JCFox) **3-8-4**ow1 AClark(12) (swtg: bit bkwd: a bhd)	¾	**10**	25/1	11	—
	Hype Energy (70) (GLewis) **3-9-7** PaulEddery(5) (bit bkwd: stdd s: a bhd)	1	**11**	8/1	25	—
	Little Progress (45) (TMJones) **3-7-10** NCarlisle(3) (outpcd)	¾	**12**	50/1	—	—
				(SP 116.2%)	**12 Rn**	

59.5 secs (1.50) CSF £45.38 CT £572.33 TOTE £7.30: £2.40 £1.60 £4.70 (£11.70) Trio £56.90 OWNER Danebury Racing Stables Ltd (STOCKBRIDGE) BRED S. W. D. McIlveen

LONG HANDICAP Impish (IRE) 7-5 Little Progress 7-7

OFFICIAL EXPLANATION **Hype Energy: the jockey reported that the filly has suffered from joint problems and, on this good to firm ground, his instructions were to settle the filly early on. He added that at halfway the filly stumbled and, fearing she may have injured herself, he felt it prudent to keep her balanced throughout the remainder of the race. The trainer's representative stated that the filly would appear to need softer ground to produce her best.**

258 Mangus (IRE), very headstrong when coming on to the racecourse, was eventually trotted down to the start. This is his best trip. (15/2)

602 Suite Factors, 6lb lower than on his reappearance on Turf, is likely to be reassessed after two seconds in quick succession. (6/1)

549 Impish (IRE) ran well from 5lb out of the handicap, but may need a return to six with possibly more give in the ground. (14/1)

Anokato was 4lb lower than when third at Newmarket on his final outing last season. (9/2: 6/1-4/1)

532 C-Harry (IRE), dropped 3lb, was coming back to the minimum trip on ground plenty fast enough for him, and made matters worse with a tardy start. (8/1)

Hype Energy did not look particularly well-weighted on this handicap debut and caught the eye of the Stewards. A long-winded explanation which included the fact that the filly needs softer ground was recorded. (8/1: 6/1-9/1)

653 DUNSMORE CLAIMING STKS (4-Y.O+) (Class F)

3-00 (3-05) **1m** £2,994.00 (£834.00: £402.00) Stalls: Low GOING minus 0.33 sec per fur (GF)

				SP	RR	SF
175[4]	**Star Talent (USA) (82)** (MissGayKelleway) **6-9-7** RCochrane(2) (b: lw: stdd s: hdwy on ins 3f out: nt clr run 2f out: swtchd rt to ld 1f out: shkn up & qcknd clr: easily)	—	**1**	2/1[1]	81+	62
574[6]	**Clued Up (47)** (PDEvans) **4-8-2v**ow2 JFEgan(4) (a.p: rdn & ev ch 1f out: sn outpcd)	4	**2**	10/1	54	33
	King Athelstan (USA) (68) (BAMcMahon) **9-8-13** TQuinn(3) (b: led 6f out: rdn over 2f out: hdd 1f out: one pce)	2	**3**	14/1	61	42
467[10]	**Chinour (IRE) (61)** (EJAlston) **9-8-8**ow1 KFallon(14) (hdwy over 1f out: r.o one pce fnl f)	nk	**4**	33/1	55	35
571[4]	**Power Game (60)** (JBerry) **4-9-1b** KDarley(5) (s.s: rdn & hdwy over 1f out: nt rch ldrs)	1½	**5**	9/4[2]	59	40
526[15]	**Chalky Dancer (34)** (HJCollingridge) **5-8-3** JQuinn(6) (prom: rdn over 2f out: wknd over 1f out)	2½	**6**	50/1	42	23
457[7]	**Ethbaat (USA) (60)** (MJHeaton-Ellis) **6-9-7** AClark(7) (no hdwy fnl 3f)	3	**7**	9/1	54	35
543[7]	**Lordan Velvet (IRE)** (MrsWBAllen,Norway) **5-8-5** LNewton(10) (n.d)	½	**8**	33/1	37	18
490[10]	**Manabar (43)** (MJPolglase) **5-8-9** TGMcLaughlin(8) (prom: rdn 5f out: wknd 3f out)	nk	**9**	33/1	41	22
	Prove The Point (IRE) (MrsPNDutfield) **4-8-4** SDrowne(1) (a bhd: t.o)	11	**10**	50/1	14	—
484[2]	**Broughtons Turmoil (74)** (BRMillman) **8-9-7** WJO'Connor(13) (b.nr hind: led 2f: wknd qckly over 1f out: t.o)	¾	**11**	7/2[3]	29	10
	Kings Vision (WJenks) **5-8-5** DaneO'Neill(11) (bkwd: a bhd: t.o)	1	**12**	50/1	11	—
480[9]	**River Ensign** (WMBrisbourne) **4-7-7**(5) RMullen(9) (s.i.s: sn rcvrd: wknd over 3f out: t.o)	s.h	**13**	50/1	4	—
	Courting Newmarket (38) (MissKMGeorge) **9-7-12**(5) JBramhill(12) (bit bkwd: led 2f: wknd over 2f out: t.o)	7	**14**	50/1	—	—
				(SP 130.7%)	**14 Rn**	

1m 37.9 (1.50) CSF £22.52 TOTE £3.00: £1.20 £2.00 £2.20 (£19.20) Trio £110.30 OWNER Miss Gay Kelleway (WHITCOMBE) BRED Mrs Afaf A. Al Essa

Star Talent (USA) clmd David Allport £12,000

175 Star Talent (USA) described as badly-handicapped by his trainer, won this claimer easily and now goes to Ian Balding. (2/1: 5/4-9/4)

Clued Up, dropping back to a mile, did her best but had no chance with the winner. (10/1)

King Athelstan (USA) found the winner galloping all over him coming to the final furlong. (14/1)

Chinour (IRE), back to a mile, was stepping up from selling company. (33/1)

571 Power Game had plenty to do at the weights and made matters worse with a poor start. (9/4)

654 WELLESBOURNE H'CAP (0-95) (3-Y.O) (Class C)

3-30 (3-38) **1m** £7,457.50 (£2,260.00: £1,105.00: £527.50) Stalls: Low GOING minus 0.33 sec per fur (GF)

				SP	RR	SF
517*	**Strathmore Clear (78)** (GLewis) **3-8-11** PaulEddery(2) (lw: a.p: rdn over 2f out: led over 1f out: r.o wl)	—	**1**	7/2[1]	89	56
448[4]	**Bollin Terry (67)** (TDEasterby) **3-8-0** LCharnock(7) (lw: hld up: hdwy over 3f: nt clr run on ins over 1f out: squeezed thro ins fnl f: r.o)	1½	**2**	15/2[3]	75	42
	Cosmic Prince (IRE) (86) (MAJarvis) **3-9-5** RCochrane(3) (led 1f: led 3f out tl over 1f out: one pce)	1¼	**3**	8/1	92	59
483[3]	**Zaima (IRE) (84)** (JLDunlop) **3-9-3** KDarley(10) (lw: hdwy & c wd 3f out: r.o one pce fnl 2f)	4	**4**	7/2[1]	82	49
453[4]	**Wild Sky (IRE) (77)** (MJHeaton-Ellis) **3-8-10** SDrowne(6) (lw: hld up: hdwy over 3f out: one pce fnl 2f)	½	**5**	10/1	74	41
448[6]	**I Can't Remember (80)** (PDEvans) **3-8-13** JFEgan(13) (nvr trbld ldrs)	nk	**6**	12/1	76	43
	Halowing (USA) (88) (JGSmyth-Osbourne) **3-9-7** SSanders(9) (bit bkwd: prom over 4f)	2	**7**	25/1	80	47
509[2]	**Puzzlement (67)** (CEBrittain) **3-8-0** JLowe(11) (lw: bhd fnl 3f)	4	**8**	7/1[2]	51	18
448[19]	**Double Gold (77)** (BJMeehan) **3-8-3b**1(7) GHannon(1) (led after 1f: hdd 3f out: wknd wl over 1f out)	1¾	**9**	25/1	57	24
	Brandon Jack (85) (IABalding) **3-9-4** TQuinn(8) (lw: a bhd)	2½	**10**	8/1	60	27
	My Beloved (IRE) (82) (RHannon) **3-9-1** DaneO'Neill(5) (bit bkwd: a bhd)	s.h	**11**	14/1	57	24
483[2]	**Last Chance (70)** (DJSCosgrove) **3-8-3** NCarlisle(12) (prom over 4f: t.o)	12	**12**	11/1	21	—
				(SP 130.4%)	**12 Rn**	

1m 37.5 (1.10) CSF £30.43 CT £188.75 TOTE £5.20: £1.70 £2.70 £2.40 (£20.10) Trio £141.70 OWNER Food Brokers Ltd (EPSOM) BRED Hyde Stud

517* Strathmore Clear, nibbled at in the morning exchanges, is the type who needs plenty of rousting and benefited from the runner-up getting boxed-in. He should stay even further. (7/2)

448 Bollin Terry got hemmed in on the inside and looked an unlucky loser. Not inconvenienced by this return to a mile, he is bred to stay further and will soon make amends. (15/2)

Cosmic Prince (IRE) likes to force the pace, and made a satisfactory reappearance. (8/1)

483 Zaima (IRE) appreciated this return to a mile, but may be better suited by a more galloping course. (7/2: 3/1-9/2)
453 Wild Sky (IRE) stepping up to a mile, appears to need some give underfoot to show his best. (10/1)
448 I Can't Remember had finished only a length behind the runner-up at Doncaster on the same terms over seven furlongs. (12/1)
483 Last Chance (11/1: op 7/1)

655 MARTON H'CAP (0-95) (4-Y.O+) (Class C)

4-00 (4-02) **1m 6f 194y** £5,038.00 (£1,519.00: £737.00: £346.00) Stalls: Low GOING minus 0.33 sec per fur (GF)

				SP	RR	SF
	Bowcliffe Court (IRE) (72) (RAkehurst) **5-9-2** TQuinn(3) (trckd ldr: led wl over 1f out: rdn out)	—	1	$9/2^{2}$	84	46
470^{3}	**Embryonic (IRE) (74)** (MartinTodhunter) **5-9-4** JCarroll(6) (lw: hld up: hdwy over 4f out: nt clr run on ins 2f out: swtchd rt over 1f out: r.o ins fnl f)	¾	2	$100/30^{1}$	85	47
591^{3}	**Etterby Park (USA) (73)** (MJohnston) **4-9-0** JWeaver(4) (led tl hdd wl over 1f out: r.o one pce)	1¾	3	$100/30^{1}$	82	41
442^{10}	**Thaljanah (IRE) (80)** (BSmart) **5-9-10** RCochrane(5) (swtg: bit bkwd: s.i.s: plld hrd in rr: hdwy 4f out: rdn & ev ch 2f out: one pce)	¾	4	8/1	89	51
442^{4}	**Upper Mount Clair (71)** (CEBrittain) **7-9-1** BDoyle(1) (hld up: rdn & no hdwy fnl 2f)	nk	5	$5/1^{3}$	79	41
	Palamon (USA) (82) (JWhite) **4-9-9** WJO'Connor(2) (hld up: bhd fnl 3f)	6	6	10/1	84	43
133^{3}	**Star Rage (IRE) (78)** (JLHarris) **7-9-8** KFallon(7) (lw: hld up mid div: rdn & lost pl over 3f out: eased whn no ch fnl f)	1	7	$5/1^{3}$	79	41

(SP 117.9%) **7 Rn**

3m 15.3 (5.30) CSF £18.94 TOTE £5.60: £3.30 £1.70 (£16.20) OWNER Mr A. D. Spence (EPSOM) BRED Crest Stud Ltd
WEIGHT FOR AGE 4yo-3lb

Bowcliffe Court (IRE), a stone higher than when winning at Newbury last October, did not seem to mind this fast ground and was given a nice lead by the third. (9/2: op 3/1)
470 Embryonic (IRE) would almost certainly have given the winner more to think about with a trouble-free run. (100/30)
591 Etterby Park (USA) rated 4lb higher than on the sand, was also 4lb above the mark off which he won at Ayr last September. (100/30)
Thaljanah (IRE) was probably slow to pick up leaving the stalls by design, given the way he pulled. (8/1)
442 Upper Mount Clair, 10lb higher than when winning at Pontefract a year ago, even finds this trip on the short side. (5/1)

656 OLD MILVERTON MAIDEN STKS (3-Y.O+) (Class D)

4-35 (4-36) **5f** £3,461.75 (£1,034.00: £494.50: £224.75) Stalls: Low GOING minus 0.33 sec per fur (GF)

			SP	RR	SF
Darb Alola (USA) (99) (MRStoute) **3-8-10** JReid(1) (lw: a gng wl: led on bit over 1f out: v.easily)	—	1	$2/9^{1}$	84++	40
Captain Sinbad (KSBridgwater) **5-9-7b**^{1} SDrowne(2) (led over 3f: no ch w wnr)	5	2	100/1	68	35
Hoh Dancer (73) (IABalding) **3-8-5** TQuinn(6) (lw: w ldr over 2f: wknd over 1f out)	6	3	$6/1^{2}$	44	—
La Chatelaine (GLewis) **3-8-5** PaulEddery(3) (bkwd: chsd ldrs 2f)	1¼	4	33/1	40	—
Changed To Baileys (IRE) (64) (JBerry) **3-8-10** GCarter(5) (s.i.s: a bhd)	½	5	$10/1^{3}$	43	—
Sovereign (MPMuggeridge) **3-8-2**(3) MHenry(4) (w'like: bkwd: s.s: a wl bhd: t.o)	12	6	66/1	—	—

(SP 110.6%) **6 Rn**

59.5 secs (1.50) CSF £39.91 TOTE £1.20: £1.10 £9.10 (£45.90) OWNER Sheikh Ahmed Al Maktoum (NEWMARKET) BRED Heronwood Farm Inc. and Flaxman Holdings Ltd.
WEIGHT FOR AGE 3yo-11lb

Darb Alola (USA) had some useful form to his name last year and, proving different class to these, won hard held. (2/9)
Captain Sinbad looked straight enough despite not having been out since August 1995, and it remains to be seen if the first-time blinkers will work again. (100/1)
Hoh Dancer proved no match for the 100/1 runner-up let alone the long odds-on favourite. (6/1: op 3/1)
Changed To Baileys (IRE) (10/1: 6/1-12/1)

657 KINETON H'CAP (0-85) (4-Y.O+) (Class D)

5-05 (5-06) **1m 2f 169y** £3,666.50 (£1,097.00: £526.00: £240.50) Stalls: Low GOING minus 0.33 sec per fur (GF)

				SP	RR	SF
435^{15}	**Angel Face (USA) (70)** (PDEvans) **4-9-0** JFEgan(3) (plld hrd: sn chsng ldr: led 2f out: drvn out)	—	1	$13/2^{3}$	82	56
538^{2}	**Vola Via (USA) (80)** (IABalding) **4-9-7**(3) MartinDwyer(2) (lw: hld up: hdwy 5f out: swtchd lft & r.o ins fnl f)	1¼	2	$5/1^{2}$	90	64
430^{15}	**Pay Homage (68)** (IABalding) **9-8-5**(7) RFowley(9) (hld up & plld hrd: hdwy over 4f out: outpcd 2f out: styd on fnl f)	2½	3	14/1	74	48
482^{2}	**Shalateeno (67)** (BRMillman) **4-8-11** KDarley(5) (led: hdd 2f out: one pce)	1¼	4	$13/2^{3}$	72	46
	Bookcase (63) (DRCElsworth) **10-8-7** RCochrane(4) (bit bkwd: nvr nr to chal)	3	5	20/1	63	37
405^{10}	**Ocean Park (74)** (LadyHerries) **6-9-4** AClark(1) (hld up mid div: no hdwy fnl 2f)	hd	6	8/1	74	48
	Askern (62) (DHaydnJones) **6-8-6** CRutter(8) (bhd tl sme hdwy on outside over 3f out: one pce fnl 2f)	¾	7	9/1	61	35
430^{21}	**Nosey Native (65)** (JPearce) **4-8-9** MWigham(11) (a bhd)	2½	8	16/1	60	34
552^{11}	**Suez Tornado (IRE) (70)** (EJAlston) **4-9-0** SDrowne(7) (hld up: hdwy 4f out: c wd st: wknd 2f out)	s.h	9	12/1	65	39
476*	**Kedwick (IRE) (61)** (PRHedger) **8-8-5b** TQuinn(10) (b: lw: s.s: hdwy over 5f out: hmpd over 3f out: sn lost pl)	¾	10	$3/1^{1}$	55	29
591^{6}	**Hill Farm Dancer (58)** (WMBrisbourne) **6-7-11**(5) RMullen(6) (s.i.s: hdwy over 3f out: c wd st: wknd 2f out)	1	11	10/1	51	25
	Carol's Dream (USA) (72) (JWHills) **5-8-13**(3) MHenry(12) (prom over 7f)	3	12	11/1	60	34

(SP 131.9%) **12 Rn**

2m 16.0 (2.00) CSF £39.80 CT £425.59 TOTE £10.10: £2.70 £2.20 £3.70 (£31.00) Trio £258.70 OWNER Mrs E. J. Williams (WELSHPOOL) BRED Gainsborough Farm Inc.

422* Angel Face (USA), who played up badly in the preliminaries before the Ladies' race at Doncaster, was taken down to the start early and transferred her All-Weather form to grass. (13/2)
538 Vola Via (USA), raised 2lb, did not have the best of runs, but was close enough if good enough. (5/1)
Pay Homage, again the mount of an inexperienced pilot, was tried over a mile-and-a-half last time and one could see why. (14/1)
482 Shalateeno, raised 2lb, was 11lb higher than when scoring at Chepstow last August. (13/2)
Bookcase had not seen a racecourse since falling in the 1996 Tote Gold Trophy. (20/1)
Ocean Park, 11lb higher than when successful at Leicester a year ago, was still 11lb lower than his All-Weather rating. (8/1)

T/Jkpt: £1,801.30 (21.3 Tckts). T/Plpt: £33.80 (596.23 Tckts). T/Qdpt: £19.00 (42.19 Tckts) KH

0588-WOLVERHAMPTON (L-H) (Standard)
Saturday April 12th
WEATHER: Fine WIND: slt half bhd

658 TRESCOTT MAIDEN STKS (3-Y.O) (Class D)
7-00 (7-01) **1m 4f (Fibresand)** £3,645.60 (£1,087.80: £519.40: £235.20) Stalls: Low GOING: 0.17 sec per fur (SLW)

Form	Horse	Dist	Pos	SP	RR	SF
	Brand New Dance (DWPArbuthnot) **3-9-0** TQuinn(6) (bit bkwd: hld up: hdwy 4f out: led wl over 1f out: rdn out)	—	1	$7/4^{1}$	71	37
	Polyphony (USA) (RCharlton) **3-9-0** SSanders(4) (leggy: lt-f: chsd ldrs: rdn 7f out: effrt u.p over 2f out: styd on)	2½	2	$7/2^{2}$	68	34
491^{4}	**Masrrah (IRE)** (RWArmstrong) **3-9-0** RPrice(2) (lw: a.p: led over 3f out tl wl over 1f out: sn rdn & btn)	3½	3	25/1	63	29
495^{2}	**Mountaineer (IRE)** (MBell) **3-9-0b¹** MFenton(5) (lw: plld hrd: led after 4f tl over 3f out: sn rdn & wknd)	8	4	$7/4^{1}$	52	18
544^{11}	**Moorbird (IRE) (56)** (JLHarris) **3-9-0** DHolland(3) (bit bkwd: a in rr)	7	5	25/1	43	9
550^{8}	**Men Of Wickenby** (RMMcKellar) **3-9-0** NVarley(1) (led 4f: wknd 6f out: sn t.o)	dist	6	33/1	—	—
	Neville The Devil (NPLittmoden) **3-9-0** DaleGibson(7) (small: lt-f: bit bkwd: s.s: a bhd: t.o)	14	7	$20/1^{3}$	—	—
				(SP 110.3%)		**7 Rn**

2m 43.8 (11.30) CSF £6.81 TOTE £3.70: £2.90 £1.60 (£4.10) OWNER Mr J. S. Gutkin (COMPTON) BRED R. Barber

Brand New Dance, a late foal who has been given time to strengthen, won this poor race despite looking in need of the run, and there could be more improvement to follow. (7/4)

Polyphony (USA), a lightly-made colt who could hardly be made fitter, struggled on after being off the bridle all the way, and if he is to make the grade it is possible it will have to be on Turf. (7/2)

491 Masrrah (IRE) had less use made of him here, but he did show ahead in to the straight only to be swept aside with ease. (25/1)

495 Mountaineer (IRE) ran a bit too free in his first-time blinkers, and was down to a walk soon after losing the advantage at the end of the back straight. (7/4)

659 PERTON CLAIMING STKS (3-Y.O+) (Class F)
7-30 (7-31) **5f (Fibresand)** £2,070.00 (£570.00: £270.00) Stalls: Low GOING: 0.17 sec per fur (SLW)

Form	Horse	Dist	Pos	SP	RR	SF
520^{18}	**General Sir Peter (IRE) (69)** (NACallaghan) **5-9-6** SDrowne(1) (bit bkwd: chsd ldr: led over 1f out: r.o wl)	—	1	8/1	79	42
515^{5}	**Perfect Brave (65)** (JBalding) **6-9-2** RLappin(3) (led tl hdd over 1f out: rdn & no ex fnl f)	1¾	2	$6/1^{2}$	69	32
512^{2}	**Hannah's Usher (62)** (CMurray) **5-9-0** JWeaver(6) (trckd ldrs: rdn & outpcd 2f out: rallied ins fnl f)	1	3	$11/8^{1}$	64	27
577^{2}	**Bon Guest (IRE) (58)** (TJNaughton) **3-8-2**(7) RFfrench(8) (lw: chsd ldrs: outpcd ½-wy: n.d afterwards)	3½	4	$7/1^{3}$	59	11
462^{9}	**Chilling (62)** (NTinkler) **3-7-10**(7)ow3 KSked(2) (sn drvn along: a outpcd)	3	5	$7/1^{3}$	43	—
391^{4}	**Thick as Thieves (44)** (RonaldThompson) **5-8-11**(5) JBramhill(4) (hdwy ½-wy: rdn 2f out: sn btn)	1	6	10/1	42	5
	Little Papoose (BAMcMahon) **4-8-9** TQuinn(7) (lt-f: s.i.s: a bhd & outpcd)	1	7	40/1	32	—
515^{4}	**Rennyholme (41)** (JHetherton) **6-8-12b** NAdams(5) (lw: spd 3f: sn rdn & btn)	5	8	$6/1^{2}$	19	—
				(SP 118.3%)		**8 Rn**

63.4 secs (4.50) CSF £51.76 TOTE £9.20: £2.60 £2.40 £1.40 (£37.60) OWNER Mr N. A. Callaghan (NEWMARKET) BRED Hamilton Bloodstock (UK) Ltd

WEIGHT FOR AGE 3yo-11lb

General Sir Peter (IRE) finished last on his seasonal debut last month, and still looked to have something left to work on but, back over his ideal trip, he had too much pace for his pursuers. (8/1: op 5/1)

515 Perfect Brave tried hard to make it all, but he could still have needed this and was well outpointed inside the distance. (6/1: op 4/1)

512 Hannah's Usher could never quite overcome this step down in distance, and was only finding top gear when it was all but decided. (11/8)

577 Bon Guest (IRE) has been performing well enough to win a race of this description, but he was tapped for speed at a crucial time, and was never going to get back. (7/1)

427 Chilling (7/1: 9/2-8/1)

660 HAPPY BIRTHDAY JULIE H'CAP (0-65) (4-Y.O+) (Class F)
8-00 (8-02) **2m 46y (Fibresand)** £2,070.00 (£570.00: £270.00) Stalls: Low GOING: 0.17 sec per fur (SLW)

Form	Horse	Dist	Pos	SP	RR	SF
375^{3}	**La Menorquina (USA) (44)** (DMarks) **7-8-7** JFortune(4) (hld up in rr: hdwy over 4f out: led ins fnl f: all out)	—	1	$5/1^{1}$	57	9
	Cuban Nights (USA) (65) (BJLlewellyn) **5-9-9**(5) JBramhill(2) (hld up: hdwy over 2f out: str chal fnl f: r.o)	1¼	2	25/1	77	29
543*	**Kalamata (52)** (JAGlover) **5-9-1** GCarter(3) (hld up: hdwy 6f out: led over 1f out tl ins fnl f: r.o)	s.h	3	$5/1^{1}$	64	16
	Tiaphena (43) (JMackie) **6-8-6** JQuinn(5) (b: bkwd: led over 12f: ev ch wl over 1f out: hrd rdn: wknd fnl f)	6	4	14/1	49	1
381^{3}	**Coleridge (56)** (JJSheehan) **9-9-5b** AClark(13) (a.p: led over 3f out tl over 1f out: sn wknd)	d.h	4	$5/1^{1}$	62	14
612^{6}	**State Approval (63)** (PEccles) **4-9-8** CRutter(8) (hld up: hdwy over 3f out: hrd rdn 2f out: nt pce to chal)	½	6	$7/1^{3}$	68	16
465^{16}	**Royal Citizen (IRE) (60)** (JFBottomley) **8-9-9** LCharnock(11) (lw: trckd ldrs: effrt 5f out: rdn & outpcd over 2f out)	3½	7	16/1	62	14
	Castle Secret (50) (DBurchell) **11-8-6**(7) KSked(1) (hld up: hdwy 9f out: wknd over 2f out)	½	8	$7/1^{3}$	51	3
	Bridie's Pride (40) (GAHam) **6-8-3** SDrowne(7) (hld up: hdwy 5f out: rdn & outpcd over 3f out)	nk	9	50/1	41	—
543^{3}	**Shakiyr (FR) (62)** (RHollinshead) **6-9-8b**(3) FLynch(6) (a bhd: rdn over 3f out: no rspnse)	4	10	12/1	59	11
	Sally's Twins (52) (JSMoore) **4-8-11** JFEgan(9) (trckd ldrs over 12f: sn rdn & wknd)	s.h	11	20/1	49	—
498^{5}	**Bellara (62)** (NMBabbage) **5-9-11** DaneO'Neill(12) (lw: chsd ldrs: rdn & outpcd 7f out)	2½	12	$11/2^{2}$	57	9
	Subtle Touch (IRE) (49) (TTClement) **6-8-7**(5) GFaulkner(10) (bkwd: prom tl wknd over 3f out: sn eased: t.o)	dist	13	40/1	—	—
				(SP 123.6%)		**13 Rn**

3m 47.1 (20.10) CSF £126.37 CT £612.88 TOTE £5.20: £1.50 £6.50 £3.20 (£180.10) Trio £155.40; £21.90 to Musselburgh 14/4/97 OWNER Mr Joe Arden (UPPER LAMBOURN) BRED R. L. Elam

WEIGHT FOR AGE 4yo-4lb

STEWARDS' ENQUIRY Carter susp. 21-25/04/97 (failing to ensure best possible placing)

375 La Menorquina (USA), given a very patient ride, produced a telling burst of speed to take command a hundred yards out and win her third race at this trip. (5/1)

Cuban Nights (USA), fit from hurdling but trying this extended trip for the first time, came very late on the scene, and he should have little trouble in winning at this trip. (25/1)

543* Kalamata kicked on once in line for home and briefly looked to have stolen a march, but the challenges were coming in thick and fast, and he was forced to give best late on. (5/1)

Tiaphena, off the track for ten months, ran a fine race in defeat and, with this outing to put an edge on her, it will come as a surprise if she cannot take advantage in the coming months. (14/1)
381 Coleridge was unable to confirm the form with the winner, fading rather quickly after losing his lead early in the straight. (5/1)
516* State Approval did not last home when tried over this trip before, and he was hard at work and galloping on the spot from the turn for home. (7/1)

661 PENNY JOYCE 21ST BIRTHDAY H'CAP (0-100) (3-Y.O+) (Class C)

8-30 (8-30) **1m 100y (Fibresand)** £5,400.00 (£1,611.00: £769.00: £348.00) Stalls: Low GOING: 0.17 sec per fur (SLW)

	Horse	Dist	Pos	SP	RR	SF
	Hal's Pal (98) (DRLoder) **4-9-12** KDarley(7) (lw: a.p: led over 3f out: clr wl over 1f out: hdd & edgd rt ins fnl f: rallied to ld cl home)	—	1	9/4[1]	103	77
450[12]	**New Century (USA) (99)** (DNicholls) **5-9-13** AlexGreaves(5) (lw: hld up: hdwy 3f out: led ins fnl f: hrd rdn: hdd nr fin)	hd	2	5/1[3]	104	78
*336**	**Effectual (82)** (MissGayKelleway) **4-8-10** DHolland(11) (b: b.hind: trckd ldrs: hdwy & ev ch over 2f out: rdn & one pce appr fnl f)	4	3	7/2[2]	79	53
	Duello (74) (MBlanshard) **6-8-2**ow1 MRoberts(8) (bit bkwd: bhd: effrt 4f out: hrd drvn 2f out: nt rch ldrs)	7	4	10/1	58	31
	Polar Eclipse (80) (MJohnston) **4-8-8** JWeaver(9) (led tl hdd over 3f out: wknd fnl 2f)	6	5	9/1	53	27
444[21]	**Duke Valentino (81)** (RHollinshead) **5-8-6**(3) DGriffiths(10) (bhd: effrt & rdn 3f out: no real imp)	7	6	20/1	40	14
316[10]	**Pengamon (80)** (HJCollingridge) **5-8-8** JQuinn(1) (b.hind: bit bkwd: hld up: hdwy 4f out: rdn & wknd fnl 2f: t.o)	11	7	20/1	19	—
468[15]	**Tatika (87)** (GWragg) **7-8-10**(5) GMilligan(6) (lw: a in rr: t.o)	1¼	8	5/1[3]	23	—
	Zuhair (100) (DMcCain) **4-10-0** VSlattery(2) (b: bkwd: prom 5f: sn rdn & wknd: t.o)	6	9	50/1	25	—
	Van Gurp (90) (BAMcMahon) **4-9-4** TQuinn(3) (bit bkwd: chsd ldrs over 4f: sn rdn & wknd: t.o)	¾	10	12/1	13	—
514[9]	**Classic Leader (75)** (ICampbell) **4-8-3** RPrice(4) (a bhd: rdn ½-wy: t.o)	nk	11	33/1	—	—

(SP 127.5%) **11 Rn**

1m 49.8 (4.80) CSF £13.21 CT £38.90 TOTE £3.70: £2.20 £1.80 £1.80 (£8.20) Trio £43.80 OWNER Mr Wafic Said (NEWMARKET) BRED Cheveley Park Stud Ltd

Hal's Pal, carrying a summer bloom on his coat and looking trained to the minute, kept up his impressive winning sequence here over this slightly shorter trip with a tip-top performance that was a joy to watch. (9/4: op 7/2)
398 New Century (USA) had the edge in race fitness, and possibly ran the race of his life in running this Group-class winner so close, and he is a credit to connections. Although he emerged the loser in the photo no-one could have given him a better ride than he received from Alex Greaves. (5/1)
336* Effectual is not quite up to this class yet, but he turned in by far his best performance yet and he is a very progressive individual. (7/2)
Duello failed to land a blow on this introduction to the All-Weather, but he was certainly not disgraced in this class. (10/1)
Polar Eclipse had finished a long way behind the winner when they clashed in the autumn and, even on these altered terms, was struggling to hold on from the turn for home. (9/1)

662 EDGSON (S) STKS (3-Y.O) (Class G)

9-00 (9-00) **1m 1f 79y (Fibresand)** £2,070.00 (£570.00: £270.00) Stalls: Low GOING: 0.17 sec per fur (SLW)

	Horse	Dist	Pos	SP	RR	SF
582[10]	**Mirror Four Sport (57)** (MJohnston) **3-8-11** JWeaver(8) (chsd ldrs: hdwy 4f out: led over 1f out: r.o wl)	—	1	7/2[2]	65	8
456[6]	**Baby Jane (55)** (RGuest) **3-8-6** AMcGlone(3) (chsd ldrs: effrt over 1f out: r.o u.p towards fin)	1	2	3/1[1]	58	1
582[4]	**Spondulicks (IRE) (57)** (BPJBaugh) **3-8-11v** RPrice(4) (a.p: led 3f out tl over 1f out: rdn & one pce ins l f)	3½	3	9/2[3]	57	—
478[6]	**Leg Beforum (IRE) (56)** (LMontagueHall) **3-8-11** DaneO'Neill(1) (hld up: hdwy on ins over 3f out: rdn over 2f out: kpt on one pce)	3	4	7/1	52	—
556[5]	**Battle Ground (IRE) (50)** (NACallaghan) **3-8-11** SDrowne(6) (b.nr fore: hld up: effrt over 3f out: nvr nr to chal)	7	5	8/1	40	—
513[7]	**Sheraton Girl (43)** (NPLittmoden) **3-8-6** JQuinn(2) (led over 6f: wknd u.p wl over 1f out: t.o)	7	6	8/1	23	—
	Our Future (IRE) (69) (RonaldThompson) **3-8-11** TWilliams(5) (bkwd: prom: pushed along 4f out: sn lost tch: t.o)	21	7	8/1	—	—
	Our Drowsy Maggie (WMBrisbourne) **3-7-13**(7) IonaWands(7) (b: leggy: s.s: a in rr: t.o fnl 3f)	28	8	20/1	—	—

(SP 116.0%) **8 Rn**

2m 8.0 (12.00) CSF £13.39 TOTE £4.10: £1.40 £1.70 £1.60 (£7.90) OWNER Mark Johnston Racing Ltd (MIDDLEHAM) BRED T. Young
No bid

513 Mirror Four Sport reserves her best for this surface and, once she had nosed ahead, there was only going to be one winner. (7/2)
456 Baby Jane takes time to warm up, and it would certainly be worth giving her a try over twelve furlongs plus. (3/1: op 2/1)
582 Spondulicks (IRE) finished way ahead of the winner on 14lb worse terms four days ago, but that was on the Turf, and this surface suits some better than others. (9/2)
478 Leg Beforum (IRE), a poor mover, struggled over this shorter trip and was well held from the turn for home. (7/1)
556 Battle Ground (IRE) (8/1: 6/1-9/1)

663 PORTOBELLO H'CAP (0-70) (3-Y.O+) (Class E)

9-30 (9-31) **6f (Fibresand)** £2,976.00 (£888.00: £424.00: £192.00) Stalls: Low GOING: 0.17 sec per fur (SLW)

	Horse	Dist	Pos	SP	RR	SF
	Barrack Yard (62) (ACStewart) **4-9-7** SWhitworth(10) (hld up: hdwy 2f out: led & drifted lft ins fnl f: r.o)	—	1	6/1[2]	73	39
*459**	**Waypoint (66)** (RCharlton) **4-9-11** TQuinn(8) (lw: hdwy over 2f out: chal whn n.m.r & swtchd ins fnl f: nt rcvr)	1	2	5/2[1]	74+	40
	Nineacres (55) (NMBabbage) **6-8-7v**(7) RFfrench(11) (lw: a.p: led over 2f out tl ins fnl f)	2½	3	6/1[2]	57	23
529[16]	**Mercury (IRE) (60)** (JAGlover) **4-9-5** GCarter(4) (hdwy wl over 1f out: kpt on u.p fnl f)	1	4	20/1	59	25
610[17]	**Rymer's Rascal (51)** (EJAlston) **5-8-10** JFortune(6) (lw: outpcd: hdwy appr fnl f: nrst fin)	3	5	25/1	42	8
494[7]	**Another Nightmare (IRE) (44)** (RMMcKellar) **5-7-10**(7) KSked(2) (led over 3f: rdn & wknd wl over 1f out)	¾	6	12/1	33	—
429[5]	**Delrob (49)** (DHaydnJones) **6-8-1b**(7) JoeleneRichards(9) (s.i.s: effrt 2f out: nt pce to chal)	nk	7	20/1	37	3
545[5]	**Hoh Majestic (IRE) (59)** (RonaldThompson) **4-9-4v** TWilliams(7) (gd spd over 3f)	2½	8	6/1[2]	41	7
301[13]	**Napier Star (63)** (MrsNMacauley) **4-9-5b**1(3) CTeague(3) (b.off hind: chsd ldrs: ev ch on ins wl over 1f out: sn rdn & wknd)	hd	9	14/1	44	10
515[3]	**Little Ibnr (67)** (PDEvans) **6-9-12** JFEgan(5) (lw: spd over 3f)	nk	10	9/1[3]	48	14
578[12]	**Leigh Crofter (65)** (PDCundell) **8-9-10b** DHolland(1) (dwlt: a bhd: outpcd: t.o)	15	11	9/1[3]	6	—

(SP 119.2%) **11 Rn**

1m 16.9 (5.70) CSF £19.10 CT £85.61 TOTE £7.10: £2.50 £2.20 £1.60 (£7.30) Trio £15.50 OWNER R George And P Saunders (NEWMARKET) BRED Britton House Stud

Barrack Yard, trying his luck at sprinting, came with a well-timed challenge to lead just inside the final furlong, but he veered badly left under pressure and, though he won readily, the rules had been contravened, and he was very fortunate to be allowed to keep the prize. (6/1)
459* Waypoint worked hard to deliver her challenge entering the final furlong, but she was the meat in the sandwich and, forced to take a pull and switch when the winner took her ground, should have been awarded the race. (5/2: 3/1-2/1)
Nineacres has not won a race for over two years, but he performed with credit here, and it would seem his turn is near at hand. (6/1)
Mercury (IRE) having his first try at a sprint distance, only got going as they straightened up for home, and the line was always going to arrive far too soon. (20/1)
Rymer's Rascal may well need a stiffer test than he had here, for he was always at full stretch and going nowhere until it was too late. (25/1)
385* Another Nightmare (IRE) was able to make all on her previous outing over course and distance, and she attempted to give a repeat performance but was forced to give best soon after turning out of the back straight. (12/1)

T/Plpt: £14.40 (1,013.23 Tckts). T/Qdpt: £6.10 (85.69 Tckts) IM

0492-MUSSELBURGH (R-H) (Good to firm, Firm patches bk st)

Monday April 14th

WEATHER: fine WIND: mod half bhd

65+ 55? 56 61

664 BELFRY MAIDEN AUCTION STKS (2-Y.O) (Class F)

2-20 (2-21) **5f** £2,600.00 (£725.00: £350.00) Stalls: High GOING minus 0.43 sec per fur (F)

				SP	RR	SF
572[2]	**Heavenly Abstone** (PDEvans) **2-8-2v**ow2 JFEgan(4) (cl up: led after 2f: r.o wl appr fnl f)	—	1	4/9[1]	72	8
	Moss Side Monkey (JBerry) **2-8-7** KDarley(2) (w'like: bit bkwd: hdwy ½-wy: kpt on fnl f: no ch w wnr)	6	2	16/1	58	—
	Rock From The Sun (WGMTurner) **2-8-0** TSprake(1) (leggy: lw: a chsng ldrs: kpt on one pce appr fnl f)	s.h	3	9/2[2]	51	—
	Three Star Rated (IRE) (CWFairhurst) **2-8-5** JCarroll(5) (w'like: leggy: led 2f: cl up tl wknd fnl f)	1¼	4	8/1[3]	52	—
	Snappy Times (MDods) **2-8-10** RLappin(3) (cmpt: early spd: outpcd & lost tch fr ½-wy)	5	5	20/1	41	—

(SP 109.2%) **5 Rn**

60.2 secs (2.50) CSF £7.98 TOTE £1.30: £1.10 £2.40 (£3.30) OWNER Mr J. E. Abbey (WELSHPOOL) BRED Ridgebarn Farm
572 Heavenly Abstone, with the visor on for the second time, made no mistake on this occasion and won most emphatically. (4/9)
Moss Side Monkey, a fair sort, needed this and was gradually getting the hang of things as the race progressed. She will obviously improve.(16/1)
Rock From The Sun, a wiry type, looked very fit but she failed to pick up when ridden from halfway and may well have needed the experience. (9/2)
Three Star Rated (IRE) looks the type to do better later on as she strengthens. (8/1)
Snappy Times, a sharp sort, gave a few problems leaving the paddock and was soon left struggling once the race began from halfway. (20/1)

665 PINKIE PILLARS H'CAP (0-70) (3-Y.O) (Class E)

2-50 (2-50) **1m 4f 31y** £2,856.00 (£858.00: £414.00: £192.00) Stalls: High GOING minus 0.43 sec per fur (F)

				SP	RR	SF
539[2]	**As-Is (60)** (MJohnston) **3-9-2** JWeaver(2) (lw: cl up: rdn to ld 3f out: r.o wl)	—	1	11/10[1]	68	22
138[8]	**Hello Dolly (IRE) (65)** (KRBurke) **3-9-7** KFallon(6) (hld up: effrt 3f out: hung lft: sn chsng wnr: nt qckn fnl f)	2½	2	10/1	70	24
581[4]	**Sam Peeb (42)** (RAFahey) **3-7-5**(7)ow2 RWinston(1) (trckd ldrs: effrt 4f out: r.o one pce)	6	3	16/1	39	—
471[2]	**Kingdom Pearl (47)** (MJCamacho) **3-8-3** LCharnock(5) (led tl hdd 3f out: sn outpcd)	2½	4	9/4[2]	41	—
	Jucinda (60) (JPearce) **3-8-13**(3) CTeague(3) (wnt prom after 3f: outpcd fnl 3½f)	hd	5	4/1[3]	53	7
539[6]	**Missed May (40)** (BPJBaugh) **3-7-5**(5) JBramhill(4) (hld up & bhd: effrt over 4f out: sn btn)	13	6	50/1	16	—

(SP 115.3%) **6 Rn**

2m 40.4 (6.90) CSF £12.79 TOTE £1.80: £1.10 £2.80 (£4.30) OWNER Mr Robinson (Wigan) (MIDDLEHAM) BRED Roldvale Ltd
LONG HANDICAP Missed May 7-4
539 As-Is found a moderate race here and, leaving nothing to chance, went for home a long way out and quickly made it his. (11/10)
46 Hello Dolly (IRE) has not much of an action, and this edgy individual hung all the way across the track towards the stands' side when ridden in the straight, and found the favourite too strong. (10/1: op 5/1)
581 Sam Peeb showed a little here, but looked very one-paced when the pressure was applied. (16/1)
471 Kingdom Pearl was disappointing, dropping out tamely once tackled early in the straight. (9/4)
Jucinda, having her first run in a handicap here, has yet to show anything positive. (4/1)

666 FORTH FM TOLBOOTH LIMITED STKS (0-65) (3-Y.O+) (Class F)

3-20 (3-20) **5f** £2,582.50 (£720.00: £347.50) Stalls: High GOING minus 0.43 sec per fur (F)

				SP	RR	SF
494[6]	**Johayro (51)** (JSGoldie) **4-9-4** ACulhane(4) (mde all: edgd rt fnl f: all out)	—	1	5/1[3]	65	37
464[9]	**Able Sheriff (60)** (MWEasterby) **5-8-13b**(5) GParkin(1) (hld up: effrt ½-wy: ev ch & hrd drvn ins fnl f: btn whn bmpd towards fin: fin 3rd; ½l & nk: plcd 2nd)	½	2	11/10[1]	62	34
397[7]	**Shadow Jury (62)** (DWChapman) **7-9-4b** LCharnock(5) (lw: cl up: rdn ½-wy: btn whn bdly hmpd wl ins fnl f: fin 4th; ½l, nk & 13/4l: plcd 3rd)	nk	3	5/1[3]	57	29
	Manolo (FR) (62) (JBerry) **4-9-4b** KDarley(2) (trckd ldrs: nt clr run over 1f out: swtchd & pushed thro ins fnl f: nrst fin: fin 2nd; ½l: disq: plcd 4th)	1¾	4	7/2[2]	63	35
494[8]	**Leading Princess (IRE) (49)** (MissLAPerratt) **6-9-4b** JWeaver(6) (in tch: rdn ½-wy: sn btn)	4	5	12/1	44	16
	Sunday Mail Too (IRE) (38) (MissLAPerratt) **5-9-1** JCarroll(3) (prom tl outpcd fr ½-wy)	½	6	50/1	39	11

(SP 112.8%) **6 Rn**

59.3 secs (1.60) CSF £10.12 TOTE £9.50: £2.60 £1.70 (£5.00) OWNER Mr Frank Brady (GLASGOW) BRED R. M. Whitaker
STEWARDS' ENQUIRY Darley Susp. 23-26 & 28-29/4/97 (irresponsible riding).
494 Johayro had the speed to get the stands' rails and, despite going to his right in the closing stages, he proved very determined under pressure. (5/1)
464 Able Sheriff did not look fully wound up and was not plated up behind and, in the circumstances, ran well enough. (11/10)
233 Shadow Jury could never get his nose in front, and was beaten when almost getting knocked over late on. (5/1)
Manolo (FR) would probably have won this with a clear run, but in the end his rider tried to push his way through. With the winner hanging into him, it made matters worse, and the Stewards had no option but to demote him. (7/2)
Leading Princess (IRE) had little chance at these weights, but is gradually coming to herself looks-wise. (12/1: 8/1-14/1)
Sunday Mail Too (IRE) had far too much on here. (50/1)

667 INVERESK RATING RELATED MAIDEN LIMITED STKS (0-60) (3-Y.O) (Class F)

3-50 (3-51) **1m 16y** £2,512.50 (£700.00: £337.50) Stalls: High GOING minus 0.43 sec per fur (F)

	Horse	Dist	Pos	SP	RR	SF
497^{2}	**Krosno (55)** (SCWilliams) **3-9-0** KDarley(3) (lw: cl up: led ent st: rdn & r.o wl fnl 2f)	—	1	$11/8^{1}$	62	23
549^{4}	**Murray Grey (52)** (EWeymes) **3-8-11** KFallon(4) (b: trckd ldrs: effrt 3f out: kpt on: no imp)	3½	2	$6/1^{3}$	52	13
	Music Express (IRE) (59) (JLEyre) **3-8-11** RLappin(2) (prom: effrt 3f out: r.o one pce fnl 2f)	1¼	3	$5/1^{2}$	50	11
549^{6}	**Why O Six (56)** (RAFahey) **3-9-0** ACulhane(6) (prom: effrt 3f out: sn rdn & nt pce to chal)	1½	4	$6/1^{3}$	50	11
551^{5}	**Murron Wallace (51)** (RMWhitaker) **3-8-11** LCharnock(1) (dwlt: effrt ent st: sn btn)	2½	5	$5/1^{2}$	42	3
	Presentiment (58) (MartynWane) **3-9-0** JCarroll(5) (led tl rn wd ent st: ev ch tl wknd fnl 2f)	4	6	20/1	37	—

(SP 108.8%) **6 Rn**

1m 43.1 (4.10) CSF £8.50 TOTE £1.80: £1.40 £1.30 (£4.90) OWNER The Cherry Pickers Syndicate (NEWMARKET) BRED Sheikh Mohammed Bin Rashid Al Maktoum

497 Krosno left nothing to chance this time and, responding to pressure, got stronger as the race went on. He should certainly stay further. (11/8)
549 Murray Grey, who has had all sorts of problems in the past, is running well and deserves to pick up a race. (6/1: op 4/1)
Music Express (IRE) put up a reasonable first effort of the season here, and looks likely to improve as a result. (5/1)
549 Why O Six ran better on this faster ground but there is still plenty more needed. (6/1: op 4/1)
551 Murron Wallace looks to have her own ideas about the game. (5/1)
Presentiment had steering problems here. (20/1)

668 ESKMILL (S) H'CAP (0-60) (3-Y.O+) (Class G)

4-20 (4-21) **1m 16y** £2,360.00 (£660.00: £320.00) Stalls: High GOING minus 0.43 sec per fur (F)

	Horse	Dist	Pos	SP	RR	SF
601^{2}	**Scathebury (55)** (KRBurke) **4-10-0** KFallon(10) (lw: hld up: hdwy 2f out: rdn to ld wl ins fnl f)	—	1	$5/1^{2}$	66	48
587^{2}	**Bedazzle (34)** (MBrittain) **6-8-0**(7) DMernagh(4) (b.off fore: hdwy 4f out: edgd lft 2f out: sn ev ch: nt qckn towards fin)	½	2	$4/1^{1}$	44	26
467^{9}	**Kass Alhawa (51)** (DWChapman) **4-9-10** ACulhane(3) (hld up & bhd: gd hdwy to ld 2f out: hdd wl ins fnl f: kpt on u.p)	nk	3	$6/1^{3}$	60	42
587^{9}	**Bold Habit (37)** (JPearce) **12-8-7**(3) CTeague(13) (styd on fnl 3f: nvr able to chal)	5	4	7/1	37	19
496^{12}	**Western Venture (IRE) (38)** (RMMcKellar) **4-8-11** JCarroll(12) (b: lw: in tch: rdn 3f out: one pce)	1¾	5	16/1	34	16
496^{9}	**Funky (37)** (DNicholls) **4-8-3**(7) IonaWands(6) (lw: in tch: effrt 3f out: no imp)	1	6	9/1	31	13
	True Ballad (53) (JSGoldie) **5-9-9**(3) DGriffiths(1) (trckd ldrs: hdwy & ev ch over 2f out: sn rdn & btn)	1¾	7	14/1	44	26
608^{15}	**Rattle (39)** (DANolan) **4-8-7**(5) PFessey(5) (nvr trbld ldrs)	s.h	8	33/1	30	12
496^{13}	**Diet (44)** (MissLAPerratt) **11-9-3v** JWeaver(8) (cl up: led over 3f out to 2f out: wknd)	9	9	16/1	17	—
526^{10}	**Napoleon's Return (40)** (JLEyre) **4-8-13** TWilliams(11) (led: racd far side: hdd over 3f out: outpcd fnl 2½f)	½	10	$6/1^{3}$	12	—
	Ragtime Cowgirl (37) (DANolan) **4-8-10** NVarley(9) (chsd ldrs tl wknd fnl 3f)	9	11	14/1	—	—
	Office Hours (47) (WGMTurner) **5-9-6b** TSprake(7) (prom tl wknd fnl 3f)	s.h	12	9/1	1	—
496^{4}	**Knave (46)** (PMonteith) **4-9-0v**(5) JBramhill(14) (chsd ldrs tl wknd 3f out)	¾	13	9/1	—	—
312^{2}	**Nukud (USA) (37)** (GROldroyd) **5-8-5v**(5) GParkin(2) (bhd fr ½-wy)	7	14	14/1	—	—

(SP 142.4%) **14 Rn**

1m 41.8 (2.80) CSF £27.66 CT £127.74 TOTE £5.80: £2.00 £2.30 £1.90 (£6.90) Trio £84.60 OWNER Mr Nigel Shields (WANTAGE) BRED The Duke Of Marlborough
Bt in 5,100 gns
OFFICIAL EXPLANATION **Nukud (USA): the trainer reported that the gelding had choked turing into the straight.**

601 Scathebury, a funny customer, was given a perfect ride and swooped to conquer late on. (5/1: 3/1-11/2)
587 Bedazzle is in top form at present and deserves to pick up a race. (4/1)
Kass Alhawa has a turn of foot that will win him races, but he probably needs a more patient ride. (6/1)
385 Bold Habit was always finding things happening too quickly on this sharp track, but he finished with some purpose. (7/1)
Western Venture (IRE) looks in good condition and ran his best race for a while. (16/1)
Funky lacked any turn of foot to make an impression. (9/1)
True Ballad ran well after over eighteen months off, and should be all the better for it. (14/1)
312 Nukud (USA) (14/1: op 9/1)

669 FORTH FM MUSSELBURGH SPRING H'CAP (0-70) (3-Y.O+) (Class E)

4-50 (4-50) **2m** £3,012.00 (£906.00: £438.00: £204.00) Stalls: High GOING: 0.00 sec per fur (G)

	Horse	Dist	Pos	SP	RR	SF
493^{3}	**Tancred Mischief (28)** (DWBarker) **6-7-8**(3) DarrenMoffatt(5) (lw: hld up & bhd: effrt ent st: styd on wl to ld wl ins fnl f)	—	1	8/1	36	—
632^{4}	**Anchorena (46)** (DWBarker) **5-9-1** KDarley(4) (lw: trckd ldrs: led 3f out tl wl ins fnl f: hrd rdn & kpt on)	½	2	$4/1^{2}$	54	—
552^{12}	**Breydon (48)** (PMonteith) **4-8-8**(5) JBramhill(2) (in tch: hdwy appr st: ev ch 2f out: nt qckn)	6	3	14/1	50	—
553^{2}	**Here Comes Herbie (55)** (WStorey) **5-9-10** NKennedy(3) (hld up & bhd: gd hdwy 4f out: ev ch 2f out: rdn & no ex)	2½	4	$10/11^{1}$	54	—
570^{10}	**Ttyfran (30)** (BPJBaugh) **7-7-13** LCharnock(9) (b: prom tl outpcd fnl 3½f)	12	5	25/1	17	—
55^{9}	**Hunting Ground (35)** (BPJBaugh) **9-7-11**(7) IonaWands(6) (b.hind: cl up: led 7f out to 3f out: wknd)	1¾	6	50/1	20	—
552^{2}	**Lord Advocate (48)** (DANolan) **9-9-3b** NVarley(1) (lw: led after 4f to 7f out: wknd fnl 4f)	3	7	$7/1^{3}$	30	—
	King of the Horse (IRE) (27) (WStorey) **6-7-5**(5) PFessey(8) (led 4f: lost tch 9f out: n.d after)	1	8	100/1	8	—
	Imperial Bid (FR) (48) (FMurphy) **9-9-3** KFallon(7) (bhd most of wy)	30	9	16/1	—	—

(SP 115.3%) **9 Rn**

3m 35.6 CSF £36.04 CT £404.65 TOTE £8.70: £2.40 £1.60 £5.80 (£13.90) Trio £35.80 OWNER Mr D. W. Barker (RICHMOND) BRED W. G. Barker
LONG HANDICAP King of the Horse (IRE) 7-4
WEIGHT FOR AGE 4yo-4lb

493 Tancred Mischief, likes to come from off a fast pace, and this little mare made up a lot of ground in the straight to gain her first win on the level. (8/1)
632 Anchorena settled better and stayed well this time, but she found her stable-companion too tough late on. (4/1)
Breydon, trying his longest trip to date, ran quite well but was out-battled in the last furlong-and-a-half. He seems to be coming back to form. (14/1)
553 Here Comes Herbie, who did not impress on looks, came with every chance early in the straight but failed to pick up. His 18lb rise in the weights seems to have steadied him at the moment. (10/11: evens-5/4)

Ttyfran looked very one-paced. (25/1)
552 Lord Advocate (7/1: op 4/1)

T/Plpt: £65.20 (172.26 Tckts). T/Qdpt: £37.40 (15.02 Tckts) AA

NEWMARKET (R-H) (Good)
Tuesday April 15th
WEATHER: unsettled, sunny periods WIND: mod across

670 APRIL MAIDEN STKS (3-Y.O) (Class D)
2-05 (2-06) **1m 4f (Rowley)** £4,464.00 (£1,332.00: £636.00: £288.00) Stalls: High GOING minus 0.12 sec per fur (G)

				SP	RR	SF
	Street General (HRACecil) **3-9-0** KFallon(5) (lw: trckd ldrs: led over 2f out: shkn up & r.o wl)	—	**1**	$9/4^{1}$	88	57
	Salamah (RCharlton) **3-9-0** PatEddery(6) (gd sort: bit bkwd: a.p: outpcd over 2f out: kpt on ins fnl f)	2	**2**	$5/2^{2}$	85	54
	Assured Gamble (CEBrittain) **3-9-0** BDoyle(4) (str: scope: trckd ldr: led wl over 3f out tl over 2f out: r.o one pce)	s.h	**3**	12/1	85	54
350^{6}	**Not Forgotten (USA)** (PAKelleway) **3-9-0v¹** KDarley(8) (trckd ldrs: effrt over 3f out: no imp)	7	**4**	50/1	76	45
523^{2}	**Prairie Falcon (IRE) (89)** (BWHills) **3-9-0** MHills(1) (lw: hld up: stdy hdwy over 3f out: effrt over 2f out: fnd nil)	4	**5**	$5/2^{2}$	71	40
	Autumn Time (IRE) (PWChapple-Hyam) **3-8-9** JReid(9) (leggy: scope: lw: hld up & bhd: effrt 4f out: nvr trbld ldrs)	1¾	**6**	$11/1^{3}$	63	32
	Bisquet-de-Bouche (RDickin) **3-8-2(7)** PMundy(3) (unf: racd wd: a bhd)	17	**7**	100/1	41	10
	Pertemps Mission (72) (JPearce) **3-9-0** MWigham(2) (bhd: effrt 4f out: n.d)	8	**8**	33/1	35	4
568^{6}	**Flashtalkin' Flood** (CADwyer) **3-9-0** JStack(7) (led tl hdd & wknd wl over 3f out)	13	**9**	100/1	18	—

(SP 110.8%) **9 Rn**

2m 35.22 (4.72) CSF £6.86 TOTE £2.70: £1.40 £1.20 £2.40 (£4.50) Trio £28.90 OWNER Mr Luciano Gaucci (NEWMARKET) BRED Newgate Stud Co

Street General appreciated this trip and, the further they went, the better he got. There looks to be plenty more to come. (9/4: 11/8-5/2)
Salamah, a useful type, needed this and ran a fine race. Plenty more will be seen of him. (5/2)
Assured Gamble, an angular individual, showed plenty of promise here and looks likely to appreciate further. (12/1)
Not Forgotten (USA), in a visor for the first time, was never doing enough to make his presence felt. (50/1)
523 Prairie Falcon (IRE) travelled well but, when the button was pressed approaching the last two furlongs, his response was very disappointing. Unless connections come up with a valid excuse, he looks one to be wary of. (5/2)
Autumn Time (IRE) is nothing special to look at and showed little in the race. (11/1: 7/1-12/1)

671 SCOTTISH EQUITABLE/JOCKEYS ASSOCIATION ABERNANT STKS (Listed) (3-Y.O+) (Class A)
2-35 (2-37) **6f (Rowley)** £10,657.00 (£3,943.00: £1,891.50: £772.50: £306.25: £119.75) Stalls: Low GOING minus 0.12 sec per fur (G)

				SP	RR	SF
519*	**Monaassib (107)** (EALDunlop) **6-9-2** DO'Donohoe(3) (cl up: led 1½f out: edgd lft: r.o u.p)	—	**1**	$9/4^{1}$	116	97
452^{2}	**Easy Dollar (106)** (BGubby) **5-9-2b** AClark(2) (led tl hdd 1½f out: rallied: n.m.r wl ins fnl f)	½	**2**	8/1	115	96
	Sylva Paradise (IRE) (110) (CEBrittain) **4-9-2** MRoberts(7) (cl up: effrt 2f out: nt qckn fnl f)	1¼	**3**	12/1	111	92
540^{2}	**Carranita (IRE) (107)** (BPalling) **7-9-1** TSprake(5) (lw: chsd ldrs: rdn ½-wy: styd on: nt pce to chal)	nk	**4**	$5/1^{3}$	110	91
	Cayman Kai (IRE) (116) (RHannon) **4-9-6** PatEddery(1) (trckd ldrs: effrt & n.m.r 2f out: r.o one pce)	1¼	**5**	$3/1^{2}$	111	92
	Rambling Bear (112) (MBlanshard) **4-9-8** RCochrane(8) (hld up: hdwy ½-wy: sn rdn & no imp)	nk	**6**	10/1	112	93
	My Melody Parkes (100) (JBerry) **4-8-11** KDarley(6) (cl up over 4f: wknd)	4	**7**	12/1	91	72
	Wildwood Flower (99) (RHannon) **4-8-11** DaneO'Neill(4) (outpcd ½-wy: n.d after)	¾	**8**	9/1	89	70

(SP 118.0%) **8 Rn**

1m 11.42 (-0.38) CSF £19.95 TOTE £2.70: £1.60 £3.10 £1.80 (£19.00) OWNER Maktoum Al Maktoum (NEWMARKET) BRED Side Hill Stud in Ireland

STEWARDS' ENQUIRY Obj to Monaassib by Clark overruled.
519* Monaassib was always going best but, when in front, he did not find as much as looked likely, and was also inclined to hang into the runner-up. (9/4)
452 Easy Dollar is running his heart out at present, and gave the impression that another furlong would help his cause. (8/1)
Sylva Paradise (IRE) ran well, to show he is in really good form at the moment. (12/1)
540 Carranita (IRE) was always in behind the leaders, never had much room in which to manoeuvre, and failed to offer a threat. She looks particularly well just now. (5/1)
Cayman Kai (IRE), who looked big and well for this first run of the season, was never seeing enough daylight to make an impression. (3/1)
Rambling Bear never got into this, but he gave the impression that he should improve for the run. (10/1)
Wildwood Flower (9/1: 6/1-10/1)

672 SHADWELL STUD NELL GWYN STKS (Gp 3) (3-Y.O F) (Class A)
3-10 (3-11) **7f (Rowley)** £19,188.00 (£7,092.00: £3,396.00: £1,380.00: £540.00: £204.00) Stalls: Low GOING minus 0.12 sec per fur (G)

				SP	RR	SF
	Reunion (IRE) (JWHills) **3-8-9** RHills(4) (h.d.w: hld up & bhd: smooth hdwy 2f out: led ins fnl f: r.o wl)	—	**1**	8/1	119	74
519^{2}	**Oh Nellie (USA)** (NACallaghan) **3-8-9** PatEddery(8) (lw: led tl hdd ins fnl f: kpt on wl)	1	**2**	$9/4^{1}$	117	72
	Elegant Warning (IRE) (110) (BWHills) **3-8-9** MHills(9) (b.nr hind: hld up: hdwy on bit over 2f out: chal 1f out: rdn & nt run on)	1½	**3**	$7/2^{2}$	113	68
	Miss Sancerre (GWragg) **3-8-9** LDettori(6) (cl up tl rdn & btn over 1f out)	3	**4**	8/1	106	61
	Imperial Scholar (IRE) (JMPEustace) **3-8-9** RCochrane(1) (bhd: outpcd 3f out: rdn & hung rt: styd on u.p towards fin)	nk	**5**	25/1	106	61
	Baked Alaska (ACStewart) **3-8-9** MRoberts(3) (hld up: rdn 3f out: nvr trbld ldrs)	2½	**6**	$15/2^{3}$	100	55
	Connemara (IRE) (107) (CADwyer) **3-8-9** JReid(7) (chsd ldrs: effrt over 2f out: wknd over 1f out)	1½	**7**	25/1	97	52
	Dame Laura (IRE) (106) (HMorrison) **3-8-9** TQuinn(2) (unf: chsd ldrs: outpcd 3f out: sn btn)	6	**8**	10/1	83	38
	Open Credit (101) (HRACecil) **3-8-9** KFallon(10) (lw: prom tl wknd qckly 2f out)	1¼	**9**	$15/2^{3}$	80	35

	Horse	Dist	Pos	SP	RR	SF
	Caerfilly Dancer (94) (RAkehurst) **3-8-9** SSanders(5) (lw: chsd ldrs tl wknd fnl 2f)	¾	**10**	25/1	78	33
				(SP 119.4%)		**10 Rn**

1m 25.28 (0.78) CSF £24.05 TOTE £10.60: £2.40 £1.50 £2.00 (£19.20) Trio £31.40 OWNER Highclere Thoroughbred Racing Ltd (LAMBOURN) BRED Dr Michael Smurfit

Reunion (IRE) did this in useful style, travelling on the bridle and then quickening well. The time of this event was much faster than the three other races over the trip, and she will quite rightly take her chance in the Guineas. (8/1: 6/1-9/1)

519 Oh Nellie (USA), looking particularly fit, ran a sound race and looks as though at least another furlong is needed to bring out the best in her. (9/4)

Elegant Warning (IRE), an edgy individual, went well for much of the trip but, after coming through to challenge on the bridle, she then failed to respond to pressure. (7/2: 9/4-4/1)

Miss Sancerre, a lengthy individual, has a decent action, but probably just needed this and ran out of fuel approaching the final furlong. (8/1)

Imperial Scholar (IRE) needed this and proved clueless for a long way but, given a determined ride, she was picking up in good style at the finish, suggesting that longer trips will see plenty of improvement. (25/1)

Baked Alaska, needing the run, failed to make any impression and would seem to need a bit more time. (15/2)

Connemara (IRE), who got a shade warm beforehand, ran well until finding this trip beyond her. (25/1)

Dame Laura (IRE) looked edgy and light and ran no sort of race. (10/1)

Open Credit looked well enough but was most disappointing, dropping tamely away in the last two furlongs. Something must have gone wrong with her. (15/2)

Caerfilly Dancer did not impress with her action and, with plenty on here, she dropped out tamely in the last couple of furlongs. (25/1)

673 NGK SPARK PLUGS CONDITIONS STKS (3-Y.O) (Class C)

3-45 (3-46) **7f (Rowley)** £4,789.12 (£1,723.50: £824.25: £333.75: £129.38) Stalls: High GOING minus 0.12 sec per fur (G)

	Horse	Dist	Pos	SP	RR	SF
	Poteen (USA) (LMCumani) **3-9-1** PatEddery(4) (bit bkwd: trckd ldrs: effrt 2f out: rdn to ld wl ins fnl f)	—	**1**	1/3[1]	105	57
	Za-Im (BWHills) **3-9-1** RHills(1) (cl up: led & qcknd 2f out: hdd wl ins fnl f: r.o)	nk	**2**	100/30[2]	104	56
	Sugarfoot (NTinkler) **3-9-1** KDarley(5) (h.d.w: trckd ldrs: kpt on fnl f: no ch w ldrs)	5	**3**	20/1[3]	93?	45
	Space Race (CACyzer) **3-8-11** LDettori(2) (w'like: scope: dwlt: sn in tch: outpcd fnl 2½f)	2½	**4**	25/1	67 t	35
	Churchill's Shadow (IRE) (BAPearce) **3-8-11** KFallon(3) (cmpt: led 5f: sn wknd)	3½	**5**	100/1	59 t	27
				(SP 107.7%)		**5 Rn**

1m 27.18 (2.68) CSF £1.40 TOTE £1.30: £1.10 £1.20 (£1.30) OWNER Lord Vestey (NEWMARKET) BRED Dr and Mrs E. A. Neuman

Poteen (USA) looked likely to benefit a good deal from this, but he did what was required and had a real test in doing so, which should bring him on no end. (1/3)

Za-Im is doing really well physically and ran a super race here. He looks to be on the upgrade. (100/30)

Sugarfoot found the early pace too slow and raced too freely, but he still ran really well without offering a threat. (20/1)

Space Race needed the experience and had no chance in this useful event, but time will no doubt see better. (25/1)

Churchill's Shadow (IRE), a cheap purchase last year, ran as well as could be expected in this company. (100/1)

674 ALEX SCOTT MAIDEN STKS (3-Y.O C & G) (Class D)

4-15 (4-16) **7f (Rowley)** £4,659.00 (£1,392.00: £666.00: £303.00) Stalls: High GOING: Not Established

	Horse	Dist	Pos	SP	RR	SF
	Shawaf (USA) (JLDunlop) **3-8-11** RHills(6) (h.d.w: sn in tch: hdwy 2f out: led 1f out: r.o)	—	**1**	9/4[2]	98	52
	Komi (MRStoute) **3-8-11** WRSwinburn(12) (gd sort: bit bkwd: hld up: effrt over 2f out: r.o wl fnl f: nrst fin)	nk	**2**	16/1	97	51
	Darnaway (HRACecil) **3-8-11** KFallon(10) (a cl up: led 3f out tl hdd 1f out: no ex)	2	**3**	7/4[1]	93	47
479[8]	**Solar Storm** (MBell) **3-8-11** MFenton(3) (hdwy 3f out: styd on u.p: nrst fin)	2	**4**	66/1	88	42
	Broad River (USA) (EALDunlop) **3-8-8(3)** DO'Donohoe(9) (lw: trckd ldrs: effrt over 2f out: r.o one pce)	s.h	**5**	33/1	88	42
479[5]	**Moonshiner (USA) (86)** (GWragg) **3-8-11** MHills(5) (cl up: disp ld over 2f out tl wknd appr fnl f)	nk	**6**	14/1	87	41
	Judicial Supremacy (JRFanshawe) **3-8-11** PatEddery(7) (lw: hld up: effrt over 2f out: nvr rchd ldrs)	2½	**7**	14/1	82	36
	Wasp Ranger (USA) (92) (PFICole) **3-8-11** TQuinn(2) (in tch: effrt 3f out: sn outpcd)	nk	**8**	6/1[3]	81	35
	Regal Thunder (USA) (MRStoute) **3-8-11** KDarley(1) (hld up & bhd: nvr plcd to chal)	3	**9**	14/1	74	28
517[4]	**Beyond Calculation (USA)** (PWHarris) **3-8-11** JReid(4) (lw: b: in tch tl wknd fnl 2f)	1¾	**10**	16/1	70	24
	Chakra (SDow) **3-8-11** MRoberts(11) (led 4f: eased whn btn)	4	**11**	66/1	61?	15
	Satin Stone (USA) (JHMGosden) **3-8-11** LDettori(8) (cmpt: scope: hld up: outpcd ½-wy: n.d after)	nk	**12**	12/1	60?	14
				(SP 126.8%)		**12 Rn**

1m 27.31 (2.81) CSF £38.17 TOTE £3.10: £1.50 £3.30 £1.40 (£60.20) Trio £21.40 OWNER Mr Hamdan Al Maktoum (ARUNDEL) BRED Shadwell Farm Inc

Shawaf (USA) did the job required but, in the end, he was fast being caught and will need to improve for this. (9/4)

Komi, a real strong individual, had a cumbersome action going down but there was plenty to like about the way he came back and, over further, he is going to win some really nice races. (16/1)

Darnaway looked fit enough and had his chances but, in the end, proved a shade disappointing. (7/4)

Solar Storm, who showed nothing last time, has a terrible action but ran really well which, until proven otherwise, would seem to cast doubts on the form. (66/1)

Broad River (USA) is as yet a green individual who should do better as he gains experience. (33/1)

479 Moonshiner (USA) was up with the pace until crying off entering the final furlong, and looks to have stamina problems. (14/1: 8/1-16/1)

Judicial Supremacy (14/1: 8/1-16/1)

Wasp Ranger (USA) looks too big for his own good and showed little here. (6/1: 5/1-8/1)

Regal Thunder (USA), who needs one more run for handicaps, never showed here but left a distinctive impression that in time, he will leave this form well behind. (14/1)

Satin Stone (USA) (12/1: 7/1-14/1)

675 EQUITY FINANCIAL COLLECTIONS H'CAP (0-95) (3-Y.O) (Class C)

4-45 (4-47) **7f (Rowley)** £6,408.75 (£1,920.00: £922.50: £423.75) Stalls: High GOING minus 0.12 sec per fur (G)

	Horse	Dist	Pos	SP	RR	SF
	Summer Queen (72) (SPCWoods) **3-8-3** AClark(14) (hld up & bhd: hdwy over 2f out: led 1f out: r.o wl)	—	**1**	40/1	85	43
	Just Nick (76) (WRMuir) **3-8-7** PatEddery(4) (a.p: ev ch 2f out: nt qckn ins fnl f)	1½	**2**	14/1	86	44
518[4]	**Blue Goblin (USA) (87)** (LMCumani) **3-9-4b**[1] LDettori(18) (trckd ldrs tl lost pl ½-wy: nt clr run 2f out: r.o wl fnl f)	½	**3**	8/1[2]	95	53
	Sleepless (78) (NAGraham) **3-8-9** DHolland(16) (w ldrs: led 3f out to 1f out: no ex)	2	**4**	8/1[2]	82	40
	Sharp Hat (84) (RHannon) **3-9-1** RHughes(8) (hld up: stdy hdwy 3f out: rdn 2f out: swtchd rt & styd on one pce)	nk	**5**	12/1	87	45

				SP	RR	SF
509^{10}	**Hoh Flyer (USA) (69)** (MBell) **3-7-9**(5) RMullen(13) (lw: in tch: effrt over 2f out: nt qckn)	s.h	**6**	16/1	72	30
	Redwing (90) (JLDunlop) **3-9-7** KDarley(9) (h.d.w: s.i.s: stdy hdwy over 2f out: styd on wl)	nk	**7**	20/1	92	50
474*	**Wee Dram (76)** (RHannon) **3-8-7** DaneO'Neill(7) (lw: cl up: ev ch 2f out: wknd 1f out)	½	**8**	$10/1^{3}$	77	35
507^{4}	**Stone Flower (USA) (86)** (PWChapple-Hyam) **3-9-3** JReid(11) (prom tl grad wknd fnl 2f)	nk	**9**	$10/1^{3}$	87	45
	Al Masroor (USA) (75) (JWPayne) **3-8-6** AMcGlone(6) (in tch: n.m.r 2f out: wknd fnl f)	2½	**10**	16/1	70	28
	Great Child (77) (MRStoute) **3-8-8** KFallon(15) (bkwd: hld up & bhd: stdy hdwy fnl 2f: nvr plcd to chal)	hd	**11**	$10/1^{3}$	72	30
413^{4}	**Plan For Profit (IRE) (75)** (MJohnston) **3-8-6** JWeaver(5) (in tch: rdn 3f out: sn wknd)	1½	**12**	20/1	66	24
448*	**Share Delight (IRE) (79)** (BWHills) **3-8-10** MHills(10) (hld up: effrt on outside 2½f out: hung bdly rt: sn btn & eased)	nk	**13**	$5/1^{1}$	70	28
509^{13}	**Linden's Lad (IRE) (65)** (JRJenkins) **3-7-10** NCarlisle(17) (prom 4f)	s.h	**14**	50/1	55	13
	Topatori (IRE) (77) (MHTompkins) **3-8-5**(3) MHenry(20) (led 4f: wknd)	1¼	**15**	25/1	65	23
	Smart Boy (IRE) (74) (PFICole) **3-8-5** TQuinn(3) (a outpcd & bhd)	2½	**16**	14/1	56	14
412^{8}	**Saratoga Red (USA) (70)** (WAO'Gorman) **3-8-1** EmmaO'Gorman(2) (lw: dwlt: swtchd rt after s: a bhd)	1½	**17**	40/1	48	6
	Passiflora (80) (JLDunlop) **3-8-11** GDuffield(1) (a rr div)	1¾	**18**	20/1	54	12
	Royal Blackbird (65) (JEBanks) **3-7-10** JQuinn(19) (chsd ldrs over 4f: wknd)	6	**19**	11/1	26	—
	Shalaal (USA) (82) (EALDunlop) **3-8-10**(3) DO'Donohoe(12) (h.d.w: chsd ldrs tl rdn & wknd 3f out)	5	**20**	$8/1^{2}$	31	—
				(SP 143.4%)	**20 Rn**	

1m 27.45 (2.95) CSF £514.20 CT £4,581.20 TOTE £186.50: £33.60 £3.60 £2.00 £1.70 (£266.30) Trio £3,364.30; £1,516.31 to Newmarket 16/4/97 OWNER Mr Arashan Ali (NEWMARKET) BRED Arashan Ali

LONG HANDICAP Linden's Lad (IRE) 7-9

Summer Queen looked quite useful here, quickening from off the pace to win going away. (40/1)

Just Nick, from a yard in good form, ran well from a moderate draw and deserves a change of luck. (14/1: 10/1-16/1)

518 Blue Goblin (USA), in blinkers for the first time, looks a real handful, but if he gets it fully together he certainly has plenty of ability. (8/1)

Sleepless ran pretty well and should be all the sharper for this. (8/1)

Sharp Hat, as usual, took a strong hold going to post and in the race, but then failed to pick up when asked a question. (12/1)

Hoh Flyer (USA) is running quite well and gave the impression that over further she should improve. (16/1)

Redwing, one of the last away, caught the eye finishing to some purpose and is one to keep in mind, especially over longer trips. (20/1)

474* Wee Dram (10/1: 8/1-12/1)

Great Child needed this and never got into the race, but was certainly not knocked about and is one to bear in mind. (10/1)

448* Share Delight (IRE) looked a funny customer here and just wanted to hang right, giving his rider all sorts of problems. (5/1)

Shalaal (USA) (8/1: 6/1-9/1)

676 MUSEUM MAIDEN STKS (3-Y.O) (Class D)

5-20 (5-22) **1m 2f (Rowley)** £4,854.00 (£1,452.00: £696.00: £318.00) Stalls: High GOING minus 0.12 sec per fur (G)

				SP	RR	SF
	Kingfisher Mill (USA) (MrsJCecil) **3-9-0** PatEddery(7) (hld up: hdwy on outside to ld 2f out: r.o v.wl)	—	**1**	$3/1^{1}$	97+	63
	Purist (MRStoute) **3-9-0** LDettori(18) (lw: led tl hdd 4f out: kpt on wl: no ch w wnr)	5	**2**	$6/1^{3}$	89	55
	Monitor (HRACecil) **3-9-0** KFallon(9) (gd sort: in tch: effrt 3f out: styd on wl: nrst fin)	½	**3**	$6/1^{3}$	88	54
	Garuda (IRE) (JLDunlop) **3-9-0** TQuinn(17) (w'like: plld hrd: trckd ldrs: ev ch 2f out: wknd ins fnl f)	1½	**4**	$7/2^{2}$	86	52
	Natural Eight (IRE) (BWHills) **3-9-0** RHills(3) (hld up: hdwy over 2f out: styd on towards fin)	2	**5**	8/1	83	49
	Maid of Camelot (RCharlton) **3-8-9** TSprake(11) (leggy: scope: hld up: hdwy 2f out: nvr plcd to chal)	s.h	**6**	40/1	78	44
	Recourse (USA) (HRACecil) **3-9-0** WRyan(12) (lw: hdwy 4f out: sn prom: outpcd fnl 2f)	2	**7**	14/1	79	45
	Bedouin Honda (CEBrittain) **3-9-0** BDoyle(14) (sn cl up: led 4f out to 2f out: wknd)	hd	**8**	40/1	79	45
	Slipstream (RGuest) **3-9-0** GDuffield(8) (neat: hmpd 5f out: hdwy 2f out: nvr nr to chal)	1½	**9**	33/1	77	43
	Nichol Fifty (MHTompkins) **3-9-0** DBiggs(15) (hld up: effrt 3f out: no imp)	nk	**10**	50/1	76	42
	Groucho (USA) (RCharlton) **3-9-0** KDarley(16) (cmpt: bkwd: bhd: sme hdwy 2f out: n.d)	1½	**11**	20/1	74	40
	Party Romance (USA) (87) (BHanbury) **3-9-0** JStack(10) (plld hrd: cl up tl wknd fnl 3f)	nk	**12**	9/1	73	39
	Fabled Light (IRE) (GWragg) **3-9-0** MHills(5) (h.d.w: swtchd lft 5f out: n.d)	1½	**13**	25/1	71	37
	Final Stage (IRE) (PWChapple-Hyam) **3-9-0** JReid(13) (cmpt: a bhd)	1½	**14**	25/1	69	35
	Shadiann (IRE) (LMCumani) **3-9-0** OUrbina(1) (w'like: scope: bhd fr ½-wy)	5	**15**	20/1	61	27
446^{4}	**Highly Respected (IRE)** (ABailey) **3-8-9** DWright(6) (chsd ldrs 7f)	1¾	**16**	25/1	53	19
	Padauk (82) (MJHaynes) **3-9-0** GCarter(2) (w'like: in tch tl wknd fnl 3f)	2	**17**	50/1	55	21
	Keenest Reluctance (JRFanshawe) **3-8-9** DHarrison(4) (leggy: scope: bhd & hmpd 5f out: n.d)	7	**18**	40/1	38	4
				(SP 138.8%)	**18 Rn**	

2m 7.9 (3.20) CSF £19.26 TOTE £4.30: £1.70 £2.50 £3.00 (£20.70) Trio £41.70 OWNER Lord Howard de Walden (NEWMARKET) BRED Lord Howard de Walden

Kingfisher Mill (USA) looked particularly useful and, coming down what appeared the unfavoured outside of the field, won going right away and looks one to follow. (3/1)

Purist did a lot of the donkey work and kept staying on, suggesting that longer trips will bring improvement. (6/1)

Monitor, a really useful sort, was gradually learning as the race progressed and finished in pleasing style, and there would seem to be better to come. (6/1: 3/1-13/2)

Garuda (IRE) raced too freely for his own good and must learn to settle. (7/2)

Natural Eight (IRE) was putting in his best work at the end, suggesting that longer trips are what he needs. (8/1: 4/1-9/1)

Maid of Camelot ran pretty well, putting in his best work at the finish, and looks likely to come on for the experience. (40/1)

Slipstream has plenty to learn but, by the way he finished, there is more ability there. (33/1)

Party Romance (USA) (9/1: 5/1-10/1)

T/Jkpt: Not won; £10,231.44 to Newmarket 16/4/97. T/Plpt: £35.00 (940.8 Tckts). T/Qdpt: £13.20 (106.43 Tckts) AA

0670-NEWMARKET (R-H) (Good)

Wednesday April 16th

WEATHER: fine WIND: mod across

677 RACING & FOOTBALL OUTLOOK RATED STKS H'CAP (0-105) (4-Y.O+) (Class B)

2-05 (2-06) **7f (Rowley)** £7,976.00 (£2,954.00: £1,419.50: £582.50: £233.75: £94.25) Stalls: High GOING: Not Established

				SP	RR	SF
	Chickawicka (IRE) (85) (BPalling) **6-8-6** TSprake(11) (led far side tl wl over 1f out: rallied to ld cl home)	—	**1**	33/1	98	68
	Tregaron (USA) (90) (RAkehurst) **6-8-11** TQuinn(16) (a.p far side: led 1f out tl wknd & ct cl home)	½	**2**	$4/1^{1}$	102	72

				SP	RR	SF
	Emerging Market (99) (JLDunlop) **5-9-6** KDarley(6) (in tch stands' side: styd on fnl f: nrst fin)	1¾	**3**	14/1	107	77
	How Long (98) (LMCumani) **4-9-5** LDettori(15) (bkwd: w ldrs far side: led wl over 1f out to 1f out: no ex)	s.h	**4**	$7/1^{2}$	106	76
	Concer Un (96) (SCWilliams) **5-9-3** WRSwinburn(1) (b: a chsng ldrs stands' side: kpt on fnl f)	nk	**5**	12/1	103	73
	Cyrano's Lad (IRE) (98) (CADwyer) **8-9-5** KFallon(5) (chsd ldrs: led stands' side over 2f out: no imp appr fnl f)	s.h	**6**	16/1	105	75
596^{11}	**Highborn (IRE) (91)** (PSFelgate) **8-8-12** RCochrane(17) (lw: chsd ldrs far side: effrt 3f out: btn wl over 1f out)	1¼	**7**	10/1	95	65
444^{14}	**Zurs (IRE) (83)** (MissGayKelleway) **4-7-11**(7) AngelaGallimore(2) (racd stands' side: styd on fnl 2f: nvr rr)	1	**8**	33/1	85	55
661^{7}	**Pengamon (83)** (HJCollingridge) **5-8-4** JQuinn(7) (racd stands' side: nvr trbld ldrs)	½	**9**	33/1	84	54
661^{2}	**New Century (USA) (92)** (DNicholls) **5-8-13** AlexGreaves(3) (lw: chsd ldrs stands' side tl grad wknd fnl 2f)	nk	**10**	11/1	92	62
	Madly Sharp (100) (JWWatts) **6-9-7** PatEddery(13) (hld up far side: effrt over 2f out: no imp)	¾	**11**	$8/1^{3}$	98	68
	Saseedo (USA) (90) (WAO'Gorman) **7-8-11** EmmaO'Gorman(18) (wl bhd far side tl sme late hdwy)	1½	**12**	16/1	85	55
	Wild Rice (89) (GWragg) **5-8-10** MHills(4) (bkwd: led stands' side tl hdd & wknd over 2f out)	nk	**13**	10/1	83	53
540^{3}	**King of Peru (100)** (APJarvis) **4-9-7** WJO'Connor(10) (racd far side: n.d)	¾	**14**	14/1	92	62
	Babsy Babe (90) (JJQuinn) **4-8-11** MJKinane(9) (b.off hind: racd far side: bhd fnl 4f)	6	**15**	20/1	69	39
450^{19}	**Pusey Street Girl (85)** (MRBosley) **4-8-1**(5) AimeeCook(14) (chsd ldrs far side tl wknd over 2f out)	3½	**16**	33/1	56	26
450^{23}	**Defined Feature (IRE) (88)** (DrJDScargill) **4-8-9** MRoberts(12) (swtg: racd far side: spd 4f)	2	**17**	33/1	54	24
	Prends Ca (IRE) (91) (WRMuir) **4-8-12** DaneO'Neill(8) (racd far side: bhd fr ½-wy)	nk	**18**	16/1	57	27

(SP 128.3%) **18 Rn**

1m 25.55 (1.05) CSF £144.37 CT £1,843.61 TOTE £52.70: £8.10 £1.80 £5.30 £1.70 (£152.10) Trio £635.40 OWNER Merthyr Motor Auctions (COWBRIDGE) BRED Charlton Down Stud

LONG HANDICAP Zurs (IRE) 7-13 Pengamon 8-1

Chickawicka (IRE), fit from hurdling, did his usual and made it. He proved determined when headed and got back up near the line. (33/1)

Tregaron (USA), well suited by the strong pace, looked in command entering the final furlong, but this was his first run of the season, which just made the difference late on. (4/1)

Emerging Market took a fierce hold going to post and then produced his customary late run to win the race on the stands' side, but this group were always second best. (14/1)

How Long looked in tremendous condition and ran well, but still probably needed it and ran out of fuel late on. (7/1)

Concer Un was in brilliant form last season and looks to have carried that on this year. He will do even better over further. (12/1)

Cyrano's Lad (IRE) ran a useful race and looks likely to be all the better for it. (16/1)

Highborn (IRE) was always well enough placed, but never really fired. He has not yet come to himself but this should certainly help bring him on. (10/1)

396 Zurs (IRE) ran a fair race from 5lb out of the handicap and was picking up ground nicely at the end. (33/1)

661 New Century (USA) (11/1: op 7/1)

678 EARL OF SEFTON STKS (Gp 3) (4-Y.O+) (Class A)

2-35 (2-40) **1m 1f (Rowley)** £19,188.00 (£7,092.00: £3,396.00: £1,380.00: £540.00: £204.00) Stalls: Low GOING minus 0.12 sec per fur (G)

				SP	RR	SF
	Ali-Royal (IRE) (112) (HRACecil) **4-8-10** KFallon(6) (hld up: smooth hdwy to ld 1½f out: shkn up & r.o wl)	—	**1**	$11/4^{1}$	115	86
	Wixim (USA) (RCharlton) **4-8-10** PatEddery(4) (hld up: stdy hdwy to chal over 1f out: rdn & nt pce of wnr)	2	**2**	9/1	111	82
433^{4}	**Amrak Ajeeb (IRE) (108)** (BHanbury) **5-8-10** MRimmer(10) (bit bkwd: s.s: hld up & bhd: hdwy over 2f out: r.o)	nk	**3**	12/1	111	82
	Behaviour (105) (MrsJCecil) **5-8-10** JReid(5) (lw: in tch: hdwy over 2f out: kpt on one pce fnl f)	1¼	**4**	25/1	109	80
	Acharne (110) (CEBrittain) **4-8-10** BDoyle(8) (a.p: led 2f out: sn hdd: grad wknd)	nk	**5**	20/1	108	79
521^{3}	**Dreams End (76)** (PBowen) **9-8-10** RCochrane(11) (hld up: effrt 3f out: styd on: no imp)	1¼	**6**	50/1	106	77
	Farasan (IRE) (114) (HRACecil) **4-8-10** MJKinane(3) (lw: hld up: hdwy over 2f out: sn rdn & nvr able chal)	hd	**7**	$13/2^{3}$	106	77
	Restructure (IRE) (114) (MrsJCecil) **5-8-13** PaulEddery(7) (lw: in tch tl outpcd fnl 2 1/2f)	1¼	**8**	$13/2^{3}$	107	78
	Prince Babar (100) (JEBanks) **6-8-10** JStack(2) (led tl hdd 2f out: wknd)	¾	**9**	20/1	102	73
	Rocky Oasis (USA) (MRStoute) **4-8-10** TQuinn(1) (h.d.w: w ldr tl rdn & btn over 2f out)	11	**10**	$4/1^{2}$	83	54
540*	**Russian Music (106)** (MissGayKelleway) **4-8-10b** LDettori(9) (racd alone centre: slt ld 5f: sn wknd)	18	**11**	11/1	51	22

(SP 114.7%) **11 Rn**

1m 50.46 (-0.04) CSF £23.53 TOTE £2.90: £1.50 £3.00 £4.00 (£11.70) Trio £113.10 OWNER Greenbay Stables Ltd (NEWMARKET) BRED C. H. WACKER III

Ali-Royal (IRE), trying his longest trip to date, really appreciated it and won with some authority. He seems on the upgrade. (11/4)

Wixim (USA) travelled well but failed to match the winner in the closing stages. This was his first outing for ten months and he should be all the sharper for it. (9/1: 6/1-10/1)

433 Amrak Ajeeb (IRE) is a real character, and he decided to run late on to show what he can do if things go his way. (12/1: 8/1-14/1)

Behaviour had his chances, but his lack of pace was well exposed in the last furlong-and-a-half. (25/1)

Acharne ran quite well, but was found wanting for speed and probably needs further. (20/1)

521 Dreams End ran a cracker in this company and is obviously in top form and, should he try again over hurdles, he should be kept in mind. (50/1)

Farasan (IRE) looked pretty useful at times last year, but this was a shade disappointing. (13/2)

Restructure (IRE) (13/2: 9/2-7/1)

540* Russian Music (11/1: 7/1-12/1)

679 NGK SPARK PLUGS EUROPEAN H'CAP (Listed) (3-Y.O) (Class A)

3-05 (3-07) **7f (Rowley)** £16,280.00 (£6,020.00: £2,885.00: £1,175.00: £462.50: £177.50) Stalls: Low GOING: Not Established

				SP	RR	SF
	Hidden Meadow (108) (IABalding) **3-9-3** LDettori(3) (h.d.w: set stdy pce: qcknd 3f out: r.o v.wl fnl f: impressive)	—	**1**	$5/1^{1}$	117+	78
	Granny's Pet (105) (PFICole) **3-9-0** TQuinn(4) (hld up & bhd: hdwy 2f out: styd on wl: no ch w wnr)	5	**2**	12/1	103	64
	Rich Ground (108) (JDBethell) **3-9-3** JReid(2) (plld hrd: bhd: effrt 3f out: styd on wl)	¾	**3**	33/1	104	65
	Andreyev (IRE) (109) (RHannon) **3-9-4** MJKinane(7) (hld up & bhd: hdwy 3f out: kpt on: nvr able chal)	½	**4**	$6/1^{2}$	104	65
508^{2}	**Groom's Gordon (FR) (104)** (JLDunlop) **3-8-13** PatEddery(10) (cl up: rdn over 2f out: one pce)	¾	**5**	$13/2^{3}$	97	58
	Referendum (IRE) (112) (GLewis) **3-9-7** PaulEddery(6) (lw: trckd ldrs: effrt over 2f out: nt qckn)	½	**6**	$5/1^{1}$	104	65
	Nigrasine (105) (JLEyre) **3-9-0** DeanMcKeown(1) (hld up: rdn 3f out: nt pce to chal)	nk	**7**	$13/2^{3}$	96	57
	Proud Native (IRE) (112) (APJarvis) **3-9-7** WJO'Connor(5) (h.d.w: hld up & bhd: effrt 3f out: rdn & no imp)	nk	**8**	9/1	103	64
	Mukaddar (USA) (107) (CJBenstead) **3-9-2** RCochrane(11) (chsd ldrs tl wknd fnl 2f)	2½	**9**	12/1	92	53

				SP	RR	SF
	Juwwi (107) (MajorWRHern) **3-9-2** RHills(8) (chsd ldrs: rdn 3f out: wknd 2f out)	nk	**10**	8/1	91	52
	Omaha City (IRE) (107) (BGubby) **3-9-2** AClark(9) (hld up: effrt 3f out: n.d)	2½	**11**	20/1	85	46
				(SP 118.5%)		**11 Rn**

1m 25.6 (1.10) CSF £60.32 CT £1,142.43 TOTE £6.50: £2.50 £3.60 £5.30 (£54.40) Trio £369.80 OWNER Mr George Strawbridge (KINGSCLERE) BRED I. A. Balding

Hidden Meadow looked magnificent and did the job required with the minimum of fuss. He appears to have improved tremendously and is without doubt one to seriously consider for the 2,000 Guineas. (5/1)

Granny's Pet did well coming from off the pace, but never had a hope of getting near of the winner. Nevertheless, he is obviously in good form again this season. (12/1)

Rich Ground took a deal of settling and, in the end, did well to finish so close. A stronger early pace would have suited him. (33/1)

Andreyev (IRE) produced a useful-looking run approaching the final furlong but, soon under pressure, his limitations were quickly exposed. (6/1)

508 Groom's Gordon (FR) either needs further or a stronger pace than was set here. (13/2)

Referendum (IRE) looked in superb condition but he was disappointing, failing to pick up when the pace was really on in the last three furlongs. (5/1)

Nigrasine, who looked fit, needed more use made of him as there was no real pace on here. (13/2)

Proud Native (IRE) (9/1: 5/1-10/1)

680 GREENE KING H'CAP (0-95) (4-Y.O+) (Class C)

3-40 (3-43) **1m 4f (Rowley)** £6,116.25 (£1,830.00: £877.50: £401.25) Stalls: High GOING minus 0.12 sec per fur (G)

				SP	RR	SF
	Angus-G (82) (MrsMReveley) **5-9-6** KDarley(14) (lw: a gng wl: stdy hdwy to ld ins fnl f: r.o)	—	**1**	4/1[1]	93	73
598[4]	**Galapino (59)** (MissGayKelleway) **4-7-10** GBardwell(5) (cl up: led 5f out tl ins fnl f: kpt on)	1½	**2**	10/1[3]	68	47
521[4]	**Hazard a Guess (IRE) (83)** (DNicholls) **7-9-7** AlexGreaves(10) (in tch: hdwy 3f out: chsng ldrs over 1f out: kpt on)	½	**3**	8/1[2]	91	71
521[12]	**Bowled Over (69)** (CACyzer) **4-8-6** MRoberts(13) (a chsng ldrs: ev ch over 2f out: r.o one pce)	1¾	**4**	14/1	75	54
481[3]	**Prince Danzig (IRE) (62)** (DJGMurraySmith) **6-7-9**(5) RFfrench(17) (hdwy 4f out: styd on wl: nrst fin)	1¾	**5**	20/1	66	46
435[12]	**Tawafek (USA) (62)** (SDow) **4-7-13** JQuinn(18) (a chsng ldrs: effrt 4f out: one pce fnl 2½f)	s.h	**6**	25/1	66	45
521[8]	**Remaadi Sun (78)** (MDIUsher) **5-9-2** RStreet(7) (hld up & bhd: effrt over 3f out: too much to do)	1¼	**7**	8/1[2]	80	60
499[4]	**Al's Alibi (76)** (WRMuir) **4-8-13** JReid(9) (led tl hdd 5f out: grad wknd)	1½	**8**	16/1	76	55
	Classic Find (USA) (85) (ICampbell) **4-9-8** RPrice(15) (b: b.nr hind: bhd: effrt 4f out: nvr rchd ldrs)	4	**9**	33/1	80	59
	Traceability (81) (SCWilliams) **4-9-4** KFallon(12) (cl up tl rdn & wknd 2f out)	½	**10**	14/1	75	54
*486**	**At Liberty (IRE) (75)** (RHannon) **5-8-13** DaneO'Neill(6) (stdy hdwy 5f out: sn in tch: rdn & wknd over 2f out)	1¼	**11**	16/1	67	47
	Reimei (68) (RAkehurst) **8-8-6** TQuinn(3) (chsd ldrs tl wknd fnl 3f)	5	**12**	16/1	54	34
499[5]	**Song Of The Sword (88)** (JABOld) **4-9-11** WRSwinburn(16) (hld up & bhd: effrt over 3f out: n.d)	s.h	**13**	33/1	74	53
516[4]	**English Invader (75)** (CADwyer) **6-8-13** LDettori(4) (lost tch 5f out: n.d afterwards)	nk	**14**	20/1	60	40
	Florentino (IRE) (72) (BWHills) **4-8-9** MHills(2) (lw: bhd: effrt 5f out: n.d)	hd	**15**	8/1[2]	57	36
	Totem Dancer (79) (JLEyre) **4-9-2** RLappin(1) (a bhd)	10	**16**	14/1	51	30
559[4]	**Mukhlles (USA) (79)** (BobJones) **4-9-2** NDay(11) (n.d)	1½	**17**	33/1	49	28
*389**	**Albaha (USA) (79)** (JEBanks) **4-8-11**(5) RMullen(8) (a bhd)	5	**18**	10/1[3]	42	21
				(SP 131.4%)		**18 Rn**

2m 33.69 (3.19) CSF £37.81 CT £290.46 TOTE £4.40: £1.80 £3.20 £2.50 £3.30 (£37.30) Trio £156.10 OWNER Mr W. Ginzel (SALTBURN) BRED W. Ginzel

LONG HANDICAP Galapino 7-6

WEIGHT FOR AGE 4yo-1lb

Angus-G, who looked in brilliant condition, was stepping up in trip here and, appreciating every yard of it, was never going to be beaten. He is improving. (4/1)

598 Galapino, although 4lb out of the handicap, was given a more positive ride this time and ran really well only to find a very useful opponent. (10/1)

521 Hazard a Guess (IRE) won at this trip four seasons ago and ran well here, but just was not good enough in the end. (8/1)

Bowled Over looks quite well-in at the moment and is a persistent sort who deserves to find a race. (14/1)

481 Prince Danzig (IRE) was sticking gamely to his task in the last three furlongs and gives the impression that a bit further may well help. (20/1)

226 Tawafek (USA), trying his longest trip to date, had his chances but was short of toe in the last three furlongs. (25/1)

Remaadi Sun, dropped out as usual, had an impossible task in the last half-mile and was wisely not over-punished and hardly knew he was in a race. He is worth keeping in mind. (8/1)

Classic Find (USA) looked a fair horse last year but obviously has problems, although he still showed a little here and should be all the better for this. (33/1)

681 GEOFFREY BARLING MAIDEN STKS (3-Y.O F) (Class D)

4-15 (4-16) **7f (Rowley)** £4,581.00 (£1,368.00: £654.00: £297.00) Stalls: High GOING minus 0.12 sec per fur (G)

				SP	RR	SF
	Rebecca Sharp (GWragg) **3-8-11** MHills(7) (hld up: smooth hdwy over 2f out: led 1f out: r.o wl)	—	**1**	4/6[1]	86+	55
	Delilah (IRE) (MRStoute) **3-8-11** WRSwinburn(10) (h.d.w: hld up: effrt over 2f out: r.o wl towards fin)	3½	**2**	6/1[3]	78	47
	Change For A Buck (USA) (HRACecil) **3-8-11** KFallon(2) (gd sort: hmpd s: sn prom: led over 3f out to 1f out: no ex)	1	**3**	9/2[2]	76	45
	Sharkiyah (IRE) (RWArmstrong) **3-8-11** RHills(12) (chsd ldrs: effrt over 2f out: r.o one pce)	1¾	**4**	14/1	72	41
	Kaziranga (USA) (LMCumani) **3-8-6**(5) RFfrench(11) (cmpt: bkwd: disp ld to ½-wy: chsd ldrs: one pce appr fnl f)	1¼	**5**	33/1	69	38
	Gingersnap (HRACecil) **3-8-11** AMcGlone(9) (lw: mid div: sme hdwy over 2f out: nvr rchd ldrs)	4	**6**	16/1	60	29
	Misty Rain (BWHills) **3-8-8**(3) JDSmith(1) (wnt rt s: bhd tl styd on fnl 3f)	nk	**7**	33/1	59	28
	Dellua (IRE) (RGuest) **3-8-11** JReid(5) (cmpt: bkwd: nvr trbld ldrs)	2	**8**	33/1	55	24
	Fonteyn (ACStewart) **3-8-11** MRoberts(3) (cmpt: leggy: s.s: n.d)	2	**9**	25/1	50	19
485[4]	**Perlethorpe** (MBell) **3-8-11** LDettori(4) (outpcd after 3f: n.d afterwards)	1¼	**10**	33/1	47	16
	Going Green (JRFanshawe) **3-8-11** PatEddery(8) (neat: scope: b.hind: a in rr)	hd	**11**	20/1	47	16
	Soura (USA) (55) (PAKelleway) **3-8-4**(7) AngelaGallimore(6) (disp ld to ½-wy: wknd)	3½	**12**	100/1	39	8
				(SP 126.4%)		**12 Rn**

1m 27.05 (2.55) CSF £4.67 TOTE £1.60: £1.20 £1.80 £1.90 (£3.60) Trio £3.50 OWNER Mr A. E. Oppenheimer (NEWMARKET) BRED Hascombe and Valiant Studs

Rebecca Sharp went really well during the race and settled it with a useful turn of foot in the final furlong. How good the form is only time will tell. (4/6)
Delilah (IRE), from a yard whose horses are just coming to form, she showed plenty in finishing strongly. She will obviously improve and should appreciate a little further. (6/1)
Change For A Buck (USA) is a most attractive, albeit flashy-looking individual, but she obviously has an engine and will improve for this. (9/2: 2/1-5/1)
Sharkiyah (IRE) showed up well, but was tapped for foot in the last three furlongs and may well need further. (14/1: 8/1-16/1)
Kaziranga (USA), well in need of this, showed enough to suggest that in time she will do better. (33/1)
Gingersnap never got into this, but left the impression that with experience there is certainly more to come. (16/1)
Misty Rain, clueless early on, was gradually getting the hang of things as the race progressed. Over further and in due course, better will be seen. (33/1)

82 89 82 81

682 NGK SPARK PLUGS BARTLOW MAIDEN STKS (2-Y.O F) (Class D)

4-45 (4-47) **5f (Rowley)** £4,269.00 (£1,272.00: £606.00: £273.00) Stalls: High GOING minus 0.12 sec per fur (G)

				SP	RR	SF
500[2]	**Pacifica** (RBoss) **2-8-11** LDettori(5) (lw: mde most: r.o wl fnl f)	—	**1**	5/1[3]	76	47
	Kilcora (IRE) (CADwyer) **2-8-11** KFallon(8) (neat: scope: in tch: hdwy 2f out: ev ch jst ins fnl f: kpt on)	2½	**2**	5/1[3]	68	39
536[5]	**Going Places** (KTIvory) **2-8-8**(3) MartinDwyer(2) (a cl up: chal 2f out: nt qckn fnl f)	hd	**3**	20/1	68	39
564[4]	**Days of Grace** (MartynMeade) **2-8-11** JReid(1) (chsd ldrs: outpcd 2f out: kpt on towards fin)	2½	**4**	14/1	60	31
	Jewel (IRE) (RHannon) **2-8-11** PatEddery(3) (small: unf: s.i.s: jnd ldrs after 1½f: wknd ins fnl f)	s.h	**5**	3/1[2]	60	31
	Composition (MAJarvis) **2-8-11** RCochrane(6) (neat: scope: chsd ldrs: hung rt most of wy: hmpd over 1f out: nt qckn)	nk	**6**	2/1[1]	59	30
	Cloudberry (BJMeehan) **2-8-11** BDoyle(4) (cmpt: bkwd: dwlt: nvr trbld ldrs)	2½	**7**	16/1	51	22
	Summer Day Blues (IRE) (CMurray) **2-8-11** DeanMcKeown(9) (w'like: spd to ½-wy: wknd)	8	**8**	66/1	25	—
	Tinos Island (IRE) (MHTompkins) **2-8-11** WRSwinburn(7) (neat: sn outpcd & bhd)	6	**9**	20/1	6	—

(SP 115.2%) **9 Rn**

60.9 secs (2.20) CSF £26.71 TOTE £3.70: £1.10 £1.60 £3.80 (£18.80) Trio £84.10 OWNER Mr T. J. Wells (NEWMARKET) BRED Mrs Caroline Berry

500 Pacifica, happier on this faster surface, left nothing to chance and won in fine style. (5/1)
Kilcora (IRE), from a yard that can really get one ready, put in a useful performance, but the winner's experience gained the day. She should not be hard to place. (5/1)
536 Going Places is obviously improving and, judging from this, she will not be long in picking up a race. (20/1)
564 Days of Grace was always struggling for pace, but she stuck on well suggesting that further may help. (14/1: 7/1-16/1)
Jewel (IRE) made her task more difficult with a poor start, but she possesses plenty of speed and will find opportunities. (3/1: op 2/1)
Composition spoiled her chance by hanging right, and being hampered made little to no difference. (2/1)
Cloudberry looks the sort to improve with experience. (16/1)

683 WOOD DITTON MAIDEN STKS (UNRACED 3-Y.O) (Class D)

5-20 (5-23) **1m (Rowley)** £4,932.00 (£1,476.00: £708.00: £324.00) Stalls: High GOING minus 0.12 sec per fur (G)

			SP	RR	SF
Dokos (USA) (HRACecil) **3-9-0** KFallon(1) (cmpt: scope: mde most: shkn up over 2f out: styd on strly)	—	**1**	9/2[2]	95	50
Reggie Buck (USA) (LMCumani) **3-8-9**(5) RFfrench(10) (neat: a cl up: effrt over 2f out: r.o one pce)	3	**2**	33/1	89	44
Lord Eurolink (IRE) (JLDunlop) **3-9-0** TQuinn(9) (w'like: mid div: hdwy over 2f out: styd on wl towards fin)	nk	**3**	16/1	88	43
The Prince (GWragg) **3-9-0** MHills(12) (gd sort: s.i.s: sn in tch: hdwy over 3f out: ev ch over 2f out: no ex fnl f)	s.h	**4**	100/30[1]	88	43
Warningford (JRFanshawe) **3-9-0** DHarrison(4) (w'like: scope: mid div: hdwy 3f out: styd on wl)	1	**5**	25/1	86	41
Patriot Games (IRE) (MRStoute) **3-9-0** JReid(17) (w'like: scope: hld up far side: stdy hdwy 2f out: nrst fin)	2	**6**	20/1	82	37
Darcy (MRStoute) **3-9-0** WRSwinburn(15) (gd sort: outpcd after 2f: bhd: hdwy 3f out: styd on)	1	**7**	8/1	80	35
Coble (BWHills) **3-9-0** RHills(14) (w'like: scope: lw: hdwy far side 3f out: nvr rchd ldrs)	½	**8**	14/1	79	34
Big Target (IRE) (MRStoute) **3-9-0** KBradshaw(7) (w'like: scope: bhd tl styd on fnl 2f)	1	**9**	50/1	77	32
Lighten Up (CEBrittain) **3-8-9** BDoyle(8) (w'like: scope: in tch: effrt 3f out: grad wknd fnl 2f)	nk	**10**	25/1	72	27
Georgia Venture (SPCWoods) **3-8-2**(7) CWebb(13) (neat: nvr nr to chal)	1½	**11**	50/1	69	24
Water Flower (JRFanshawe) **3-8-9** PatEddery(2) (w'like: b.hind: dwlt: hdwy ½-wy: wknd fnl 2f)	s.h	**12**	20/1	69	24
Alfannan (JHMGosden) **3-9-0** LDettori(5) (wl grwn: bkwd: in tch: effrt 3f out: wknd fnl 2f)	3	**13**	11/2[3]	68	23
Butrinto (MajorWRHern) **3-9-0** TSprake(18) (tall: leggy: led far side: drifted lft 3f out: wknd 2f out)	nk	**14**	20/1	67	22
Go Hence (WJarvis) **3-9-0** RCochrane(19) (gd sort: bit bkwd: chsd ldrs far side tl outpcd fnl 3f)	nk	**15**	20/1	66	21
Prince of Bhutan (IRE) (RHannon) **3-9-0** DaneO'Neill(3) (str: cmpt: cl up tl wknd over 2f out)	nk	**16**	25/1	66	21
Grand Hotel (IRE) (PWHarris) **3-9-0** AClark(11) (w'like: scope: shkn up after 3f: hdwy 4f out: wknd over 2f out)	1¾	**17**	33/1	62	17
Sequoia Prince (CAN) (MBell) **3-9-0** PaulEddery(16) (leggy: scope: lw: in tch far side over 4f)	7	**18**	25/1	48	3
Ratb (SDow) **3-9-0** MRoberts(6) (cmpt: bkwd: plld hrd early: wl bhd fr ½-wy)	9	**19**	50/1	30	—
Behind The Scenes (CACyzer) **3-9-0** DeanMcKeown(20) (gd sort: str: chsd ldrs far side tl hung lft & wknd fnl 4f)	½	**20**	10/1	29	—

(SP 135.6%) **20 Rn**

1m 41.05 (3.75) CSF £144.30 TOTE £5.10: £2.10 £5.00 £3.50 (£127.20) Trio £403.00 OWNER Niarchos Family (NEWMARKET) BRED Flaxman Holdings Ltd

Dokos (USA), a brother to Miesque, looked about the only one fit enough to win this. He showed a superb action going to post and did the business particularly well, the only drawback with him being that he was rather coltish in the paddock and needed two handlers. (9/2: 3/1-5/1)
Reggie Buck (USA) needed this and also looks slightly on the weak side, but he ran particularly well and time is the key with him. (33/1)
Lord Eurolink (IRE) needed this quite badly and was noted picking up in terrific style at the business end. There is plenty to work on. (16/1)
The Prince, built like a tank, does not do anything quickly but he can gallop, and will improve a fair deal for the run. (100/30: 2/1-7/2)
Warningford was picking up in fine style in the closing stages, and looks likely to improve a fair amount for the outing. (25/1)
Patriot Games (IRE) raced up what appeared to be the unfavoured far side and showed bags of promise under a tender ride, and is one to watch. (20/1)
Darcy, very green early on, was gradually getting the hang of things at the end and will obviously improve with time. (8/1: 5/1-9/1)
Coble was getting going in the latter half of the contest and, over further, there is plenty more to come from him. (14/1: 8/1-16/1)
Big Target (IRE) never showed in the race until finishing quite well, and is one to keep an eye on. (50/1)
Georgia Venture ran well enough to suggest that she will pay her way in due course. (50/1)
Alfannan (11/2: 2/1-6/1)

T/Jkpt: Not won; £17,409.25 to Newmarket 17/4/97. T/Plpt: £82.40 (470.51 Tckts). T/Qdpt: £22.20 (65.13 Tckts) AA

PONTEFRACT (L-H) (Good to firm, Firm patches)
Wednesday April 16th
WEATHER: fine WIND: slt half against

73 68 72 74

684 STRAWBERRY HILL MEDIAN AUCTION MAIDEN STKS (2-Y.O) (Class E)
2-45 (2-46) **5f** £2,879.00 (£872.00: £426.00: £203.00) Stalls: Low GOING minus 0.51 sec per fur (F)

				SP	RR	SF
500^{8}	**Young Ibnr (IRE)** (PDEvans) **2-9-0** JFEgan(2) (w ldrs: led ½-wy: jst hld on)	—	1	16/1	82	23
	The Boy John (USA) (RHannon) **2-9-0** RHughes(10) (lengthy: unf: lw: trckd ldrs: chal over 1f out: r.o wl towards fin)	s.h	2	4/1 ^{3}	82	23
548^{2}	**Mamma's Boy** (JBerry) **2-9-0** GCarter(1) (s.i.s: bhd tl hdwy 2f out: r.o wl fnl f)	1¾	3	5/2 ^{1}	76	17
583^{2}	**Bernardo Bellotto (IRE)** (MBell) **2-9-0** MFenton(7) (lw: w ldrs: rdn & outpcd ½-wy: kpt on wl fnl f)	¾	4	5/2 ^{1}	74	15
594^{9}	**Burnt Yates (IRE)** (MWEasterby) **2-9-0** TLucas(3) (bit bkwd: s.i.s: outpcd & bhd: shkn up over 1f out: styd on wl: nvr plcd to chal)	½	5	11/1	72	13
525^{2}	**Carambo** (JLEyre) **2-8-9** TWilliams(4) (w ldrs tl wknd over 1f out)	3½	6	7/2 ^{2}	56	—
500^{4}	**Yorkies Boy** (BAMcMahon) **2-9-0** LNewton(6) (led to ½-wy: wknd over 1f out)	1¾	7	25/1	55	—
447^{11}	**Donna's Double** (NTinkler) **2-9-0** KimTinkler(11) (chsd ldrs to ½-wy: sn lost pl)	1½	8	50/1	51	—
	Candy Twist (RonaldThompson) **2-8-4**(5) JBramhill(8) (unf: sn wl bhd)	13	9	100/1	4	—
	Collacar (MrsNMacauley) **2-8-11**(3) CTeague(9) (leggy: scope: bit bkwd: s.s: a bhd)	6	10	100/1	—	—
				(SP 121.4%)	**10 Rn**	

63.9 secs (2.20) CSF £74.15 TOTE £26.20: £2.60 £1.30 £1.60 (£61.30) Trio £36.80 OWNER Mrs C. A. Torkington (WELSHPOOL) BRED Anamoine Ltd

OFFICIAL EXPLANATION **Burnt Yates (IRE): rider reported that his instructions were to keep the colt balanced and running straight without using the whip, as he had hung last time. He added that the colt only ran on once on the level ground in the straight, but even then did not stride out entirely freely. The trainer, happy with the ride, stated that the colt may have been suffering from sore shins and that his next race would be over six furlongs with cut in the ground.**

Young Ibnr (IRE), who lacks substance, held on by the skin of his teeth. (16/1)

The Boy John (USA) looked very fit on his debut and showed a good action going down. After moving upsides over a furlong out, he only really found his stride near the line and needed a few more yards. The outing wil have taught him plenty and he will soon go one better. (4/1: 3/1-9/2)

548 Mamma's Boy, who showed a pronounced knee action going down, lost several lengths at the start. Picking up ground on the bend, he finished in most determined fashion and, with a level break, must have prevailed. (5/2)

583 Bernardo Bellotto (IRE), a very scratchy mover, struggled to keep up at halfway and needs six furlongs already. (5/2)

Burnt Yates (IRE), who looked as though the outing would do him good, showed a good action going down. Handled with, to say the least, sympathy, the way he was running on at the finish suggests he can do much better in due course. In mitigation, the trainer told the stewards that the horse would not run again until the six-furlong races come along and there is some cut in the ground. (11/1)

525 Carambo had two handlers in the paddock and dropped tamely away. (7/2)

685 RACING CHANNEL H'CAP (0-80) (3-Y.O F) (Class D)
3-20 (3-22) **6f** £5,390.00 (£1,610.00: £770.00: £350.00) Stalls: Low GOING minus 0.51 sec per fur (F)

				SP	RR	SF
	Dayville (USA) (77) (JBerry) **3-9-7** JWeaver(2) (mde all: clr over 1f out: unchal)	—	1	10/1	89	46
	Song Mist (IRE) (75) (PFICole) **3-8-12**(7) DavidO'Neill(7) (swvd rt s: sn chsng ldrs: styd on appr fnl f: no ch w wnr)	3	2	11/2 ^{2}	79	36
503^{8}	**Falls O'Moness (IRE) (70)** (KRBurke) **3-9-0** DRMcCabe(5) (sn chsng ldrs: kpt on same pce fnl 2f)	¾	3	12/1	72	29
489^{3}	**Gopi (67)** (RHannon) **3-8-11** RHughes(6) (trckd wnr tl wknd fnl f)	1	4	9/1	66	23
448^{21}	**La Dolce Vita (70)** (TDBarron) **3-8-7**(7) VictoriaAppleby(3) (unruly s: s.i.s: bhd: hdwy 2f out: styng on on ins whn hmpd ins fnl f)	½	5	25/1	68	25
549^{2}	**Native Thatch (IRE) (52)** (WGMTurner) **3-7-5**(5) JBramhill(11) (sltly hmpd s: sn drvn along: hdwy ½-wy: nvr rchd ldrs)	nk	6	25/1	49	6
464^{10}	**Express Girl (71)** (DMoffatt) **3-8-12**(3) DarrenMoffatt(12) (sltly hmpd s: sn chsng ldrs: one pce whn n.m.r ins fnl f)	s.h	7	25/1	68	25
531^{3}	**Bold Gayle (61)** (MrsJRRamsden) **3-8-5**ow1 JFortune(13) (lw: hld up & bhd: effrt on outside 2f out: styd on ins fnl f)	1½	8	2/1 ^{1}	54	10
506^{2}	**Ivory Dawn (67)** (KTIvory) **3-8-11** GDuffield(10) (b: hmpd s: n.d)	¾	9	7/1 ^{3}	58	15
	Midnight Shift (IRE) (75) (RGuest) **3-9-5** PBloomfield(8) (hmpd s: sn drvn along & a bhd)	2½	10	12/1	59	16
	Oneknight With You (72) (MJFetherston-Godley) **3-9-2** ACulhane(4) (s.i.s: hld up & a bhd)	2½	11	8/1	50	7
467^{3}	**Soviet Lady (IRE) (60)** (JLEyre) **3-8-4** TWilliams(1) (chsd ldrs tl wknd 2f out: eased)	13	12	14/1	3	—
	Morning Star (72) (WMcKeown) **3-9-2** JCarroll(9) (hmpd s: sn chsng ldrs: lost pl 2f out: eased)	1½	13	50/1	11	—
				(SP 127.0%)	**13 Rn**	

1m 16.4 (1.40) CSF £60.02 CT £631.82 TOTE £7.70: £2.60 £2.60 £4.20 (£26.20) Trio £475.20; £301.23 to Newmarket 17/4/97 OWNER Mr T G & Mrs M E Holdcroft (COCKERHAM) BRED Juddmonte Farms

LONG HANDICAP Native Thatch (IRE) 7-6

Dayville (USA) was very keen going to post. She showed her rivals a clean pair of heels on the way back. (10/1)

Song Mist (IRE), taken very quietly to post, dived right coming out of the stalls causing interference to four of her rivals on her outside. (11/2)

Falls O'Moness (IRE) settled much better with this faster pace over a furlong shorter trip. (12/1)

489 Gopi showed a very scratchy action going down and is better suited by the All-Weather. (9/1: op 6/1)

377* La Dolce Vita gave trouble at the start. She was staying on in her own time when running out of room in the last one hundred yards. (25/1)

531 Bold Gayle looked outstanding in the paddock. Taken quietly to post, from her outside draw, she was dropped in. With nowhere to go on the inner, she was pulled wide off the bend. Staying on at the finish, she is almost certainly capable of better especially over seven furlongs. (2/1: op 7/2)

686 LADY BALK MAIDEN STKS (3-Y.O+) (Class D)

3-50 (3-51) **1m 2f 6y** £3,745.00 (£1,135.00: £555.00: £265.00) Stalls: Low GOING minus 0.51 sec per fur (F)

				SP	RR	SF
	Kyle Rhea (HRACecil) **3-8-5** WRyan(10) (lw: trckd ldrs: led 3f out: hld on towards fin)	—	**1**	Evens[1]	88	40
	Jaunty Jack (LMCumani) **3-8-10** OUrbina(7) (lw: sn trckng ldrs: rdn to chal over 1f out: nt qckn nr fin)	nk	**2**	2/1[2]	93	45
508[7]	**Red Guard (81)** (GWragg) **3-8-11**[ow1] RHughes(5) (swtg: sn trckng ldrs: kpt on same pce fnl 2f)	9	**3**	6/1[3]	79	30
	Nordic Crest (IRE) (PWHarris) **3-8-10** GDuffield(6) (trckd ldrs: led 4f out to 3f out: sn outpcd: kpt on appr fnl f)	3½	**4**	10/1	73	25
599[7]	**Duraid (IRE)** (DenysSmith) **5-9-13** ACulhane(9) (hld up: hdwy 3f out: kpt on: nvr nr ldrs)	3½	**5**	25/1	67	36
	Mr Montague (IRE) (TWDonnelly) **5-9-13** JFanning(2) (b: s.i.s: bhd tl sme hdwy fnl 2f: n.d)	5	**6**	100/1	59	28
	Needwood Legend (BCMorgan) **4-9-13** SWhitworth(3) (bit bkwd: sn trckng ldrs: lost pl over 3f out: n.d)	2	**7**	100/1	56	25
559[3]	**London's Heart (USA)** (PFICole) **3-8-5** CRutter(1) (led tl 4f out: wknd over 2f out)	3	**8**	20/1	46	—
	Dario's Girl (DMoffatt) **4-9-5**[(3)] DarrenMoffatt(4) (sn chsng ldrs: lost pl over 3f out)	8	**9**	100/1	33	2
173[6]	**On The Green** (AHide) **4-9-8** DBiggs(8) (hld up: hdwy on outside 5f out: lost pl over 2f out)	2	**10**	100/1	30	—

(SP 119.3%) **10 Rn**

2m 11.0 (1.40) CSF £2.84 TOTE £1.90: £1.10 £1.10 £1.60 (£2.40) Trio £3.00 OWNER Sir David Wills (NEWMARKET) BRED Sir David Wills
WEIGHT FOR AGE 3yo-17lb

Kyle Rhea, runner-up on her only outing at two, proved very willing and always just had the upper hand. She showed plenty of knee action going down and will be better for the run. (Evens)
Jaunty Jack, who looked very fit, never gave up trying but was always going to come off just second best. Runner-up on all his four outings to date, his turn is surely only delayed. (2/1)
Red Guard, warm beforehand, raced keenly. He was only asked to do just enough to secure third spot when it was clear the first two were in a different league. (6/1)
Nordic Crest (IRE), who has plenty of size and scope, is now qualified for a handicap mark. He will probably be better suited by a mile and a half. (10/1)
599 Duraid (IRE) was having his third run. It will be interesting to see what mark the Handicapper gives him. (25/1)

687 OSSETT (S) H'CAP (0-60) (3-Y.O+) (Class G)

4-25 (4-26) **1m 4y** £2,805.00 (£780.00: £375.00) Stalls: Low GOING minus 0.51 sec per fur (F)

				SP	RR	SF
321[4]	**Gold Lance (USA) (45)** (RJO'Sullivan) **4-8-13** RHughes(4) (trckd ldrs on ins: swtchd rt over 1f out: qcknd to ld 1f out: hld on towards fin)	—	**1**	11/1	59	36
322[4]	**Square Mile Miss (IRE) (40)** (PHowling) **4-8-8** FNorton(6) (hld up: hdwy over 3f out: ev ch fnl f: nt qckn nr fin)	nk	**2**	20/1	53	30
467[4]	**Dictation (USA) (50)** (JJO'Neill) **5-9-4** WRyan(2) (hld up & bhd: gd hdwy 2f out: styd on ins fnl f)	2½	**3**	10/1	58	35
429[10]	**Monis (IRE) (43)** (RonaldThompson) **6-8-6**[(5)] JBramhill(7) (mid div & sn drvn along: styd on fnl 3f: nt rch ldrs)	1¼	**4**	33/1	49	26
587[16]	**Rafter-J (40)** (JohnHarris) **6-8-8** TGMcLaughlin(17) (s.i.s: bhd tl kpt on fnl 2f: nvr nr to chal)	1¼	**5**	20/1	43	20
428[10]	**Yuppy Girl (IRE) (43)** (CaptJWilson) **4-8-11v[1]** JWeaver(15) (bhd: hdwy 2f out: styd on ins fnl f)	1¼	**6**	16/1	44	21
	Dannistar (52) (PDEvans) **5-9-6** JFEgan(16) (chsd ldrs: ev ch tl wknd over 1f out)	1½	**7**	6/1[2]	50	27
467[2]	**Loch Style (50)** (RHollinshead) **4-9-1**[(3)] FLynch(14) (chsd ldrs: pushed along over 3f out: sn outpcd)	s.h	**8**	3/1[1]	48	25
	Java Red (IRE) (47) (JGFitzGerald) **5-9-1** JFortune(19) (b: sn bhd & drvn along: sme hdwy 2f out: n.d)	1¼	**9**	8/1[3]	42	19
526[4]	**Sheraz (IRE) (48)** (NTinkler) **5-9-2b** KimTinkler(12) (mde most tl 3f out: sn wknd)	s.h	**10**	14/1	43	20
	Asterix (42) (JMBradley) **9-8-10b** LCharnock(11) (b: bit bkwd: chsd ldrs: led 3f out to 1f out: wknd)	1¾	**11**	16/1	34	11
496[3]	**Harry's Treat (45)** (JLEyre) **5-8-13** TWilliams(9) (chsd ldrs tl wknd over 2f out)	5	**12**	8/1[3]	27	4
578[9]	**Major Mouse (50)** (WWHaigh) **9-9-4** SWhitworth(8) (racd wd: a in rr)	5	**13**	16/1	22	—
529[17]	**Willie Miles (57)** (DWChapman) **4-9-11** NConnorton(3) (hld up: sme hdwy over 2f out: sn wknd)	2	**14**	16/1	25	2
484[4]	**Mubariz (IRE) (54)** (CSmith) **5-9-5**[(3)] DO'Donohoe(1) (s.s: a wl bhd)	2	**15**	12/1	18	—
490[11]	**Ballet de Cour (48)** (TJEtherington) **4-8-11**[(5)] GParkin(20) (racd wd: outpcd & drvn along 5f: n.d)	1¾	**16**	100/1	8	—
428[5]	**David James' Girl (40)** (ABailey) **5-8-8** DWright(13) (b: racd wd: drvn along over 3f out: sn bhd)	½	**17**	10/1	—	—
	Saturiba (USA) (47) (JohnHarris) **4-9-1** JCarroll(10) (b: w ldrs tl lost pl 3f out)	4	**18**	25/1	—	—

(SP 143.2%) **18 Rn**

1m 44.6 (2.20) CSF £218.54 CT £1,275.02 TOTE £14.30: £2.80 £9.70 £2.90 £10.30 (£300.60) Trio £212.00 OWNER Mrs Barbara Marchant (WHITCOMBE) BRED Societe Aland
No bid

98 Gold Lance (USA), who had been given a good chance at the weights, had to search for an opening. A step up to a mile and a quarter will be no problem. (11/1: 8/1-12/1)
Square Mile Miss (IRE), out of form on the All-Weather, was just denied. (20/1)
467 Dictation (USA), taken to post early, was putting in all his best work at the finish and certainly stayed the mile alright. (10/1)
Monis (IRE), who was having his first run for his new trainer, has only won once from forty-three starts but his new connections will have been encouraged by this. (33/1)
480 Rafter-J, who has slipped down the weights, had the headgear left off. (20/1)
Yuppy Girl (IRE), in a visor for the first time, was running on when it was all over. (16/1)
Dannistar, who runs well when fresh, came in for plenty of market support. (6/1)
467 Loch Style, heavily backed, was in trouble almost half a mile from home and never gave his supporters much hope. (3/1)
484 Mubariz (IRE) (12/1: 8/1-14/1)

688 WEFT GATE LIMITED STKS (0-85) (3-Y.O) (Class D)

5-00 (5-01) **1m 4y** £3,582.50 (£1,085.00: £530.00: £252.50) Stalls: Low GOING minus 0.51 sec per fur (F)

				SP	RR	SF
	Future Perfect (85) (PFICole) **3-8-11** CRutter(6) (hld up & bhd: gd hdwy 2f out: swtchd & styd on wl to ld wl ins fnl f)	—	**1**	16/1	96	55
	Rapier (84) (RHannon) **3-8-11** RHughes(3) (trckd ldrs: led jst ins fnl f: hdd nr fin)	½	**2**	7/1[3]	95	54
*425**	**Captain Scott (IRE) (80)** (JAGlover) **3-8-13** GCarter(1) (lw: hdwy over 2f out: sn chsng ldrs: kpt on wl fnl f)	3	**3**	12/1	91	50
	Vagabond Chanteuse (85) (TJEtherington) **3-8-8** LCharnock(5) (bit bkwd: hld up: outpcd & lost pl over 2f out: styd on ins fnl f)	3	**4**	14/1	80	39
	Rechullin (82) (DRLoder) **3-8-10** DRMcCabe(2) (lw: led: qcknd over 2f out: hdd jst ins fnl f: sn wknd)	¾	**5**	7/1[3]	81	40
	Telemania (IRE) (84) (WJHaggas) **3-8-8** JCarroll(4) (trckd ldrs: effrt over 2f out: wknd over 1f out)	4	**6**	9/1	71	30

	Over To You (USA) (84) (EALDunlop) **3-8-10**(3) DO'Donohoe(11) (lw: trckd ldrs: effrt 3f out: lost pl over 1f out)	½	**7**	2/1 1	75	34
	Brave Kris (IRE) (84) (LMCumani) **3-8-8** OUrbina(7) (hld up: effrt on outside over 3f out: sn lost pl)	1¾	**8**	100/30 2	66	25
635 4	**Mujova (IRE) (84)** (RHollinshead) **3-8-8**(3) FLynch(10) (hdwy on outside ½-wy: sn drvn along lost pl over 2f out)	½	**9**	25/1	68	27
654 6	**I Can't Remember (80)** (PDEvans) **3-8-13** JFEgan(9) (chsd ldrs: drvn along over 3f out: sn lost pl)	hd	**10**	25/1	70	29
	Indian Blaze (83) (PWHarris) **3-8-11** GDuffield(8) (bit bkwd: trckd ldrs: hung lft & lost pl over 2f out: sn bhd)	9	**11**	12/1	50	9
				(SP 127.0%)		**11 Rn**

1m 42.5 (0.10) CSF £121.54 TOTE £18.60: £3.40 £2.90 £5.80 (£36.40) Trio £116.30 OWNER R O M Racing (WHATCOMBE) BRED Mrs E. C. York

Future Perfect, who won his only outing at two over seven furlongs in soft ground at Haydock in October, handled this totally different surface well. Coming from off the pace, he stuck on strongly to get up near the line and a mile and a quarter could suit him even better. (16/1)
Rapier was worn down in the final strides and a mile is probably the limit of his stamina. (7/1)
425* Captain Scott (IRE), winner of his only previous outing, on the All-Weather at Southwell last month, showed signs of inexperience. He ran really well but this will not have done his handicap mark any good. (12/1)
Vagabond Chanteuse, a progressive juvenile, looked on the burly side. Sticking on at the finish after getting badly outpaced on the home turn, a step up in distance should see further improvement from her. (14/1)
Rechullin looked really well. Trying to pinch the race from the front, this is probably as good as she is. (7/1)
Telemania (IRE) might be suited by a drop back to seven. (9/1)
Over To You (USA), from a stable which has made a sparkling start to the turf Flat, showed signs of inexperience and was by no means knocked about when his chance had gone. (2/1)
Brave Kris (IRE), who wore a cross-noseband, was taken to post early. She showed next to nothing in the race. (100/30)

689 GARFORTH H'CAP (0-70) (3-Y.O+) (Class E)

5-30 (5-31) **1m 2f 6y** £3,145.00 (£940.00: £450.00: £205.00) Stalls: Low GOING minus 0.51 sec per fur (F)

				SP	RR	SF
595*	**Pendolino (IRE) (42)** (MBrittain) **6-8-4** 5x GCarter(4) (lw: trckd ldrs: n.m.r on ins 2f out: r.o wl to ld jst ins fnl f: hld on towards fin)	—	**1**	9/1	54	36
476 6	**Father Dan (IRE) (53)** (MissGayKelleway) **8-9-1** GDuffield(6) (trckd ldrs: n.m.r over 1f out: kpt on strly ins fnl f)	½	**2**	7/1	64	46
574 2	**Jean Pierre (56)** (JPearce) **4-9-4** JWeaver(2) (lw: hld up: hdwy over 3f out: swtchd outside & kpt on wl fnl f)	2½	**3**	4/1 2	63	45
495*	**Kathryn's Pet (61)** (MrsMReveley) **4-9-9** ACulhane(1) (lw: hld up: hdwy ½-wy: drvn along over 2f out: styd on same pce fnl f)	1½	**4**	7/2 1	66	48
566 6	**Tallulah Belle (57)** (NPLittmoden) **4-9-5** TGMcLaughlin(8) (lw: a chsng ldrs: drvn along 3f out: one pce)	¾	**5**	11/2 3	61	43
550 4	**Leif the Lucky (USA) (59)** (MissSEHall) **8-9-7** JFortune(10) (plld hrd: trckd ldrs tl wknd appr fnl f)	1¾	**6**	13/2	60	42
461 7	**Nobby Barnes (34)** (DonEnricoIncisa) **8-7-10** KimTinkler(13) (bhd: hdwy 7f out: led over 2f out: hung lft & hdd jst ins fnl f: sn wknd)	nk	**7**	20/1	34	16
	Bold Top (38) (BSRothwell) **5-7-9b**(5) JBramhill(9) (led tl over 2f out: wknd appr fnl f)	1½	**8**	33/1	36	18
461 5	**Shamokin (35)** (FWatson) **5-7-11**ow1 FNorton(3) (chsd ldrs: effrt over 2f out: wknd over 1f out: eased)	1¼	**9**	16/1	31	12
542 8	**May King Mayhem (35)** (MrsALMKing) **4-7-11** NAdams(11) (chsd ldrs: drvn along 4f out: lost pl over 2f out)	3	**10**	20/1	26	8
	Zingibar (59) (JMBradley) **5-9-2**(5) DSweeney(5) (a bhd)	5	**11**	16/1	42	24
417 5	**Rinus Magic (35)** (EJAlston) **4-7-11** LCharnock(12) (hld up & plld hrd: a in rr)	1½	**12**	66/1	16	—
571 5	**Scenicris (IRE) (65)** (RHollinshead) **4-9-10**(3) FLynch(7) (lw: a in rr)	2½	**13**	16/1	42	24
				(SP 125.0%)		**13 Rn**

2m 11.4 (1.80) CSF £64.88 CT £274.29 TOTE £9.10: £2.10 £2.00 £2.20 (£37.60) Trio £109.40 OWNER Mr Ian Booth (WARTHILL) BRED Mrs A. Whitehead

LONG HANDICAP Shamokin 7-9

595* Pendolino (IRE), dropping back two furlongs in trip, made light of his 5lb penalty having overcome difficulties in running. (9/1)
248 Father Dan (IRE) was pegging back the winner all the way to the line after being short of room. He seems equally effective on Turf as the All-Weather. (7/1)
574 Jean Pierre ran another good race and finished strongly after being given plenty to do. (4/1)
495* Kathryn's Pet did not look happy on this fast ground. (7/2)
566 Tallulah Belle was racing on a mark 10lb lower than she would have done on the All-Weather. (11/2)
550 Leif the Lucky (USA) raced far too keenly and, as usual, found nothing at the business end. (13/2)
Nobby Barnes is on a losing run of forty-eight. Ridden with more enterprise than usual, after hitting the front on the wide outside he hung left and ended up on the far rail. (20/1)
461 Shamokin was not knocked about when his chance had gone and there should be a selling handicap in him. (16/1)

T/Plpt: £382.40 (37.69 Tckts). T/Qdpt: £51.30 (19.09 Tckts) WG

0677-NEWMARKET (R-H) (Good to Firm)

Thursday April 17th

WEATHER: sunny periods WIND: slt across

690 NGK SPARK PLUGS H'CAP (0-95) (3-Y.O) (Class C)

2-00 (2-04) **1m 2f (Rowley)** £6,067.50 (£1,815.00: £870.00: £397.50) Stalls: Low GOING minus 0.15 sec per fur (GF)

				SP	RR	SF
436 2	**River's Source (USA) (82)** (BWHills) **3-8-9** PatEddery(4) (hld up in tch: hdwy over 2f out: led ins fnl f: jst hld on)	—	**1**	9/1	84	49
	Generous Gift (88) (EALDunlop) **3-8-12**(3) DO'Donohoe(10) (lw: plld hrd: a.p: led stands' side over 3f out: hdd ins fnl f: r.o wl)	s.h	**2**	13/2 1	90	55
	Ihtiyati (USA) (91) (JLDunlop) **3-9-4** RHills(18) (hdwy over 2f out: led ins fnl f: sn hdd: r.o)	s.h	**3**	8/1 3	93	58
	Sausalito Bay (85) (IABalding) **3-8-12** LDettori(6) (hld up: hdwy over 1f out: hrd drvn & r.o wl cl home)	s.h	**4**	12/1	87	52
	Blue River (IRE) (88) (TGMills) **3-9-1** BDoyle(20) (h.d.w: hld up & plld hrd: hdwy over 1f out: swtchd rt & r.o wl fnl f)	s.h	**5**	16/1	90	55
509 4	**Mantles Prince (79)** (GLewis) **3-8-6** PaulEddery(13) (led far side: clr over 2f out: hdd, rdn & no ex fnl f)	1	**6**	14/1	79	44

	Princess Topaz (71) (CACyzer) **3-7-12** JQuinn(1) (hld up: hdwy over 1f out: r.o wl fnl f)	s.h	**7**	33/1	71	36
509⁷	**Bold Oriental (IRE) (80)** (NACallaghan) **3-8-7** SDrowne(16) (bkwd: chsd ldrs far side tl rdn & one pce appr fnl f)	¾	**8**	16/1	79	44
*355**	**Maradi (IRE) (74)** (MBell) **3-7-10**(5) RMullen(5) (hld up centre: hdwy over 2f out: sn ev ch: wknd fnl f)	½	**9**	10/1	72	37
	Fantail (70) (MHTompkins) **3-7-11**ow1 DaleGibson(17) (hld up: rdn & hdwy 3f out: one pce fnl f)	nk	**10**	25/1	68	32
	City Gambler (75) (GCBravery) **3-8-2** DRMcCabe(15) (chsd ldrs far side: no hdwy fnl 2f)	1½	**11**	33/1	70	35
502*	**Mister Pink (94)** (RFJohnsonHoughton) **3-9-7** JReid(19) (chsd ldrs far side 7f: eased whn btn)	nk	**12**	16/1	89	54
449⁹	**Polar Flight (90)** (MJohnston) **3-9-3** MRoberts(8) (lw: led stands' side over 6f: wknd & eased over 1f out)	1¾	**13**	16/1	82	47
479*	**Sir Talbot (83)** (RHannon) **3-8-10** RHughes(11) (chsd ldrs: rdn & wknd 2f out)	¾	**14**	15/2 2	74	39
502⁴	**Heart of Armor (81)** (PFICole) **3-8-8** TQuinn(12) (a in rr)	7	**15**	20/1	60	25
	Sheer Face (90) (WRMuir) **3-9-3** MJKinane(7) (h.d.w: hld up: nvr nr ldrs)	¾	**16**	25/1	68	33
431²	**Love Has No Pride (USA) (88)** (RHannon) **3-9-1** DaneO'Neill(14) (chsd ldrs far side: wknd over 2f out)	1¼	**17**	12/1	64	29
*337**	**Top Shelf (69)** (CEBrittain) **3-7-10** JLowe(3) (prom to ½-wy: sn lost pl)	½	**18**	20/1	44	9
	Supreme Sound (82) (PWHarris) **3-8-9** KFallon(2) (bkwd: hld up & plld hrd: rdn 4f out: sn bhd)	1¼	**19**	16/1	55	20
581⁵	***Red Embers* (69)** (CADwyer) **3-7-3**(7) IonaWands(9) (Withdrawn not under Starter's orders: bolted bef s)		**W**	20/1	—	—
				(SP 134.6%)		**19 Rn**

2m 8.72 (4.02) CSF £57.28 CT £460.74 TOTE £9.40: £2.50 £1.80 £3.00 £2.60 (£23.00) Trio £45.90 OWNER Mr K. Abdulla (LAMBOURN) BRED Juddmonte Farms
LONG HANDICAP Fantail 7-9 Top Shelf 7-8 Red Embers 7-7

436 River's Source (USA), with the added benefit of a previous run this season, just scrambled home in a race that was a credit to the Handicapper. (9/1)
Generous Gift, with his stable in good form, was all the rage here. Pulling his way to the front some way out, he only just failed to hold on in a thrilling battle to the finish. (13/2)
Ihtiyati (USA) looked as though he would benefit from the run but he produced a good burst of speed to lead inside the final furlong and then rallied bravely, only to fail narrowly. (8/1)
Sausalito Bay took time to find top gear on ground plenty fast enough for him but he finished best of all and has certainly trained on. (12/1)
Blue River (IRE), an attractive colt who is sure to benefit from this outing, really found his stride when he was switched to the far rail two hundred yards out, and was still gaining at the line. (16/1)
509 Mantles Prince led the gallop on the far side and was probably the overall leader until finding an extra effort beyond him nearing the finish. He will not remain a maiden for long. (14/1)
Princess Topaz, set alight running into the Dip, finished with quite a flourish, and given a stiffer test of stamina can soon find an opening. (33/1)
355* Maradi (IRE) (10/1: 8/1-12/1)

691 GREENE KING FEILDEN STKS (Listed) (3-Y.O) (Class A)

2-30 (2-32) **1m 1f (Rowley)** £10,193.00 (£3,767.00: £1,803.50: £732.50: £286.25: £107.75) Stalls: Low GOING minus 0.15 sec per fur (GF)

				SP	RR	SF
	Fahris (IRE) (BHanbury) **3-8-11** RHills(3) (b: a.p: led over 2f out: drvn clr fnl f)	—	**1**	7/1	115	83
	Panama City (USA) (PWChapple-Hyam) **3-8-11** JReid(4) (h.d.w: hld up: hdwy over 2f out: ev ch whn bmpd over 1f out: nt pce of wnr)	3	**2**	10/1	110	78
	Crimson Tide (IRE) (JWHills) **3-8-11** MHills(1) (hld up: hdwy over 2f out: ev ch 1f out: hung lft & nt qckn)	1	**3**	5/4 1	108	76
	Barnum Sands (103) (JLDunlop) **3-8-11** PatEddery(2) (lw: hld up: hdwy 3f out: sn hrd drvn: outpcd fnl 2f)	4	**4**	6/1 3	101	69
597*	**Bold Words (CAN) (93)** (EALDunlop) **3-8-11** KFallon(6) (lw: prom: led 4f out tl over 2f out: sn rdn & outpcd)	1¼	**5**	4/1 2	99	67
	Shock Value (IRE) (102) (MRStoute) **3-8-11** TQuinn(7) (bit bkwd: stdd s: swtchd lft: nvr nr to chal)	1½	**6**	12/1	96	64
	Recondite (IRE) (108) (MRChannon) **3-9-0** LDettori(5) (led 5f: sn rdn & wknd: t.o)	27	**7**	16/1	51	19
				(SP 113.9%)		**7 Rn**

1m 50.57 (0.07) CSF £64.29 TOTE £7.70: £3.40 £3.10 (£28.80) OWNER Mr Hamdan Al Maktoum (NEWMARKET) BRED Shadwell Estate Company Limited

Fahris (IRE), having his first run for his present stable, landed this prize with a very polished runaway success, and will now be aimed at the Derby for which his price has been reduced by half. (7/1)
Panama City (USA), reportedly needed the run. He was continually being impeded by the hanging Crimson Tide inside the distance, but he turned in a very pleasing performance and his long term objective is also the Derby. (10/1: op 6/1)
Crimson Tide (IRE) made smooth headway from the Bushes and was almost on terms with the winner in the Dip, but he hung left when asked to quicken and his measure was soon taken. He is a progressive sort and more will be heard of him. (5/4)
Barnum Sands, a son of an Oaks winner, needs more of a test of stamina now and he could not muster the pace to deliver a challenge. (6/1: 7/2-7/1)
597* Bold Words (CAN), successful at this trip in his previous outing this season, could not handle the increasing tempo in the closing stages in this much hotter contest, but he was far from disgraced and can soon get back to winning ways. (4/1)
Shock Value (IRE), switched in behind his rivals on leaving the stalls, just could not pick up when popped the question and was more than a shade disappointing. (12/1: op 6/1)

692 CITY INDEX CRAVEN STKS (Gp 3) (3-Y.O C & G) (Class A)

3-00 (3-03) **1m (Rowley)** £19,188.00 (£7,092.00: £3,396.00: £1,380.00: £540.00: £204.00) Stalls: Low GOING: Not Established

				SP	RR	SF
	Desert Story (IRE) (111) (MRStoute) **3-8-12** MJKinane(4) (h.d.w: hld up: hdwy over 1f out: led ins fnl f: rdn out)	—	**1**	5/2 1	116	76
	Grapeshot (USA) (110) (LMCumani) **3-8-9** PatEddery(8) (lw: led tl ins fnl f: hrd rdn & kpt on wl)	¾	**2**	7/2 2	112	72
	Cape Cross (IRE) (JHMGosden) **3-8-9** LDettori(2) (h.d.w: bkwd: b.hind: stdd s: plld hrd: hld up: hdwy over 2f out: ev ch ins fnl f: unable qckn)	hd	**3**	4/1 3	111	71
	Air Express (IRE) (116) (CEBrittain) **3-8-9** BDoyle(6) (bit bkwd: hld up: plld hrd: hdwy 2f out: one pce fnl f)	1½	**4**	8/1	108	68
505²	**Running Stag (USA)** (PMitchell) **3-8-9** KFallon(3) (stdd s: pushed along in rr ½-wy: r.o wl fnl f: nvr nr to chal)	½	**5**	33/1	107	67
508*	**Pelham (IRE) (100)** (RHannon) **3-8-9** DaneO'Neill(7) (hld up in tch: effrt 2f out: sn hrd rdn: one pce)	½	**6**	10/1	106	66
	Shii-Take (101) (RAkehurst) **3-8-9** SSanders(5) (chsd ldr: rdn 3f out: wknd wl over 1f out)	½	**7**	16/1	105?	65

				SP	RR	SF
	Monza (USA) (PWChapple-Hyam) **3-8-9** JReid(1) (lw: hld up: effrt & nt clr run over 1f out: put hd in air: no imp)	nk	**8**	11/2	105?	65

(SP 115.2%) **8 Rn**

1m 38.08 (0.78) CSF £10.41 TOTE £3.40: £1.30 £1.40 £1.60 (£4.20) OWNER Maktoum Al Maktoum (NEWMARKET) BRED Gainsborough Stud Management Ltd

Desert Story (IRE), in a race that his stable have farmed over the years, did not win as convincingly as he promised to, but he could be called the winner from some way out and he is now being quoted as low as 12/1 for the 2,000 Guineas. A most attractive colt, he has in the past produced his best form when there has been cut in the ground. (5/2)

Grapeshot (USA) stepped up on what he has achieved so far with a very encouraging effort, and he could be all the rage by the time the Derby comes around. (7/2)

Cape Cross (IRE) did not stride out with any freedom on the way to post, but there was no faulting his commitment on the way back and, with only a maiden success to his name in his first season, he has improved out of all recognition. (4/1)

Air Express (IRE) finished adrift of the winner over this trip in the autumn, and he did look as though he still had something left to work on so this good performance could be the start of better things to come. (8/1: 6/1-9/1)

505 Running Stag (USA) was thrown in at the deep end over a trip which could be inadequate, but he was staying on to some effect in the closing stages and he has not yet produced his true potential. (33/1)

508* Pelham (IRE) sat in behind the leaders traveling well, but once the principals showed their class up the hill he was left floundering. (10/1: 8/1-12/1)

Shii-Take, off the bridle to hold his pitch three furlong out, had to admit the task beyond him running into the Dip. (16/1)

Monza (USA), restrained in the rear under the stands' rail, was always being squeezed for room when attempting to improve, but his head went up when a gap did appear so this performance must go down as most disappointing. (11/2: 4/1-6/1)

693 BRITISH HORSE SOCIETY GOLDEN JUBILEE MAIDEN STKS (3-Y.O) (Class D)

3-30 (3-36) **6f (Rowley)** £4,503.00 (£1,344.00: £642.00: £291.00) Stalls: High GOING minus 0.15 sec per fur (GF)

				SP	RR	SF
	Captain Collins (IRE) (PWChapple-Hyam) **3-9-0** JReid(4) (lw: hld up: hdwy to ld wl over 1f out: edgd lft wl ins fnl f: drvn out)	—	**1**	$4/7^{1}$	88	58
503^{7}	**Midyan Call** (MBell) **3-9-0** MRoberts(2) (h.d.w: hld up in rr: hdwy 2f out: jnd wnr 1f out: edgd lft ins fnl f: no ex nr fin)	1	**2**	$8/1^{3}$	85	55
	Shadoof (WRMuir) **3-9-0** DaneO'Neill(7) (w'like: leggy: bhd: rdn 2f out: r.o wl fnl f)	5	**3**	25/1	72	42
	Bintang Timor (USA) (PFICole) **3-9-0** TQuinn(11) (lw: prom: ev ch 2f out: rdn & outpcd appr fnl f)	½	**4**	$11/2^{2}$	71	41
475^{2}	**Masterpiece** (RHannon) **3-9-0** PatEddery(5) (prom: hrd rdn over 2f out: sn btn)	nk	**5**	$8/1^{3}$	70	40
	Blood Orange (GGMargarson) **3-9-0** NDay(9) (led to ½-wy: wknd fnl 2f)	3½	**6**	50/1	61	31
517^{9}	**Dandy Regent** (CACyzer) **3-9-0** KFallon(10) (sn prom: rdn & wknd wl over 1f out)	1	**7**	50/1	58	28
	Soviet Leader (RGuest) **3-9-0** GDuffield(1) (cmpt: bkwd: prom: led 3f out tl wl over 1f out: sn wknd)	1	**8**	25/1	55	25
	Hype Superior (IRE) (ABailey) **3-9-0** PaulEddery(3) (w'like: scope: a bhd & outpcd)	1¼	**9**	50/1	52	22
	Pat Said No (IRE) (DJSCosgrove) **3-8-9** JStack(8) (prom over 3f: sn outpcd)	1½	**10**	50/1	43	13
	Joli's Prince (CMurray) **3-9-0** KDarley(12) (rdn ½-wy: sn bhd)	hd	**11**	50/1	48	18
	Wonderboy (IRE) (RAkehurst) **3-9-0** SSanders(6) (lw: b.hind: lost pl after 2f: sn t.o)	6	**12**	50/1	32	2

(SP 120.7%) **12 Rn**

1m 13.77 (1.97) CSF £5.00 TOTE £1.60: £1.10 £2.10 £3.90 (£5.00) Trio £50.10 OWNER Mr R. E. Sangster (MARLBOROUGH) BRED Swettenham Stud

Captain Collins (IRE) rather surprisingly had the speed to win on this first attempt at sprinting, but he was not impressive, and it could not be said that any questions were answered here. (4/7)

503 Midyan Call blew up on his racecourse debut over a slightly longer trip last month, but he performed with credit under this more patient ride and he should have no trouble in winning a similar event. (8/1)

Shadoof did well to reach his final placing after being off the bridle for most of the way and the experience is sure to prove beneficial. (25/1)

Bintang Timor (USA), returning to sprinting, had his chance running into the Dip, but once the leading pair quickened he was left in their wake. (11/2: 7/2-6/1)

475 Masterpiece pushed the pace, but he was under pressure passing the Bushes and his chance had soon gone. (8/1)

Blood Orange showed plenty of speed but failed to respond when the principals came at him and he was galloping on the spot in the final quarter-mile. (50/1)

694 EQUITY FINANCIAL COLLECTIONS H'CAP (0-90) (3-Y.O) (Class C)

4-05 (4-08) **6f (Rowley)** £6,360.00 (£1,905.00: £915.00: £420.00) Stalls: High GOING minus 0.15 sec per fur (GF)

				SP	RR	SF
649*	**Treasure Touch (IRE) (79)** (DNicholls) **3-8-4**(7) 7x IonaWands(10) (lw: a.p: led over 2f out: r.o wl)	—	**1**	$5/1^{1}$	92	51
506^{4}	**Refuse To Lose (77)** (JMPEustace) **3-8-9** RCochrane(20) (racd alone far side: hdwy 2f out: kpt on wl fnl f)	1	**2**	$5/1^{1}$	87+	46
474^{2}	**John Emms (IRE) (71)** (MBell) **3-8-3** MRoberts(4) (prom: ev ch wl over 1f out: kpt on u.p)	nk	**3**	$9/1^{3}$	81	40
560*	**Plaisir d'Amour (IRE) (82)** (NACallaghan) **3-9-0** PatEddery(5) (chsd ldrs: rdn & hung rt over 1f out: one pce)	1¼	**4**	$13/2^{2}$	88	47
434^{2}	**Ellens Lad (IRE) (85)** (RHannon) **3-9-3** DaneO'Neill(6) (hld up: hdwy over 1f out: nrst fin)	½	**5**	$9/1^{3}$	90	49
	Arruhan (IRE) (86) (PTWalwyn) **3-9-4** RHills(18) (hld up: hdwy 2f out: rdn & wknd appr fnl f)	hd	**6**	25/1	91	50
448^{7}	**A Breeze (74)** (DMorris) **3-8-6** NDay(16) (hld up: hdwy over 1f out: nt rch ldrs)	1	**7**	14/1	76	35
506^{6}	**Papita (IRE) (76)** (SDow) **3-8-8** WRyan(19) (nvr rchd ldrs)	¾	**8**	14/1	76	35
	Marsad (IRE) (76) (RAkehurst) **3-8-8** TQuinn(9) (lw: hld up: hdwy whn n.m.r over 1f out: nt rcvr)	1¾	**9**	10/1	71	30
	Cherry Blossom (IRE) (85) (RHannon) **3-9-3** RHughes(15) (prom 4f)	1½	**10**	12/1	76	35
448^{12}	**Rude Awakening (79)** (CWFairhurst) **3-8-11** LDettori(7) (nvr bttr than mid div)	1½	**11**	14/1	66	25
	Yorkie George (89) (LMCumani) **3-9-2**(5) RFfrench(12) (bkwd: nvr plcd to chal)	¾	**12**	14/1	74	33
506^{3}	**Style Dancer (IRE) (75)** (RMWhitaker) **3-8-7** KFallon(3) (nvr plcd to chal)	½	**13**	10/1	59	18
	Aegean Sound (78) (HAkbary) **3-8-10** GHind(1) (outpcd)	2	**14**	25/1	57	16
	Saltimbanco (72) (RAkehurst) **3-8-4** SSanders(11) (bhd fnl 3f)	nk	**15**	20/1	50	9
	Signs And Wonders (66) (CACyzer) **3-7-12** JQuinn(13) (eased whn btn over 1f out: virtually p.u)	nk	**16**	25/1	43	2
474^{10}	**Batsman (64)** (WJMusson) **3-7-10** DeclanO'Shea(8) (s.s: a bhd: t.o)	9	**17**	33/1	17	—
489^{2}	**Enchanting Eve (66)** (CNAllen) **3-7-9**(3)ow1 MartinDwyer(17) (lw: bhd fr ½-wy: t.o)	10	**18**	20/1	—	—
	Ice Age (85) (RJRWilliams) **3-9-3** KDarley(2) (bkwd: led tl hdd & wknd over 2f out: t.o)	12	**19**	20/1	—	—

(SP 148.0%) **19 Rn**

1m 14.08 (2.28) CSF £28.00 CT £229.44 TOTE £5.30: £1.70 £1.70 £2.50 £2.10 (£13.80) Trio £41.00 OWNER Mr N. Honeyman (THIRSK) BRED St Simon Foundation

LONG HANDICAP Batsman 7-9

OFFICIAL EXPLANATION **Yorkie George: regarding the apparent tender ride, the rider reported that his orders were to settle his mount in midfield and ask him for an effort three furlongs out, but that the colt was never travelling, became unbalanced and hung right. The vet added that the colt had returned with a wound on a hind leg.**

649* Treasure Touch (IRE) maintained his winning run with his most important success yet and he is simply flying this season. (5/1)

506 Refuse To Lose appeared to be on the slower ground on his own under the far rail but he really picked up on meeting the rising ground, and it could be third-time lucky this term. (5/1)

474 John Emms (IRE) ran by far his best race yet and his days as a maiden are certainly numbered. (9/1)

560* Plaisir d'Amour (IRE) did not help her cause by continually hanging badly right inside the final quarter-mile, and when in this mood virtually cannot be ridden. (13/2)

434 Ellens Lad (IRE), ridden with restraint on this return to six furlongs, was only finding top gear when it was all too late. One to keep in mind. (9/1)

Arruhan (IRE), a winner on her initial outing as a juvenile, again gave it her best shot and her measure was only taken in the last two hundred yards. (25/1)

Marsad (IRE) carries condition but he was beginning to close when denied any sort of run approaching the final furlong and the position had to be accepted. (10/1)

78+ 81+ 79 77

695 E.B.F. STUNTNEY MAIDEN STKS (2-Y.O C & G) (Class D)

4-35 (4-36) **5f (Rowley)** £4,347.00 (£1,296.00: £618.00: £279.00) Stalls: High GOING minus 0.15 sec per fur (GF)

				SP	RR	SF
583[3]	**Blakeset** (RHannon) **2-8-11** RHughes(4) (chsd ldr: led on bit 2f out: sn rdn: r.o wl)	—	1	5/2 1	76	15
	Timekeeper (USA) (MBell) **2-8-11** MFenton(5) (cmpt: scope: bit bkwd: s.i.s: sn prom: ev ch ins fnl f: unable qckn)	½	2	11/4 2	74	13
	Mamora Bay (IRE) (MHTompkins) **2-8-11** RHills(7) (w'like: bkwd: hld up: hdwy over 1f out: r.o)	1½	3	10/1	70	9
	Opposition Leader (BWHills) **2-8-11** MHills(3) (neat: s.s: bhd: hdwy over 1f out: nt rch ldrs)	s.h	4	5/1 3	69	8
	Emperor Naheem (IRE) (BJMeehan) **2-8-11** PatEddery(6) (cmpt: leggy: led 3f: eased whn btn ins fnl f)	2½	5	5/1 3	61	—
	Henry The Proud (IRE) (JBerry) **2-8-11** KDarley(1) (neat: lw: chsd ldrs: rdn 2f out: edgd rt ins fnl f: sn wknd)	½	6	5/1 3	60	—
				(SP 114.3%)	**6 Rn**	

62.72 secs (4.02) CSF £9.07 TOTE £3.00: £1.50 £2.10 (£3.70) OWNER Mrs Caroline Parker (MARLBOROUGH) BRED Bolton Grange

583 Blakeset put his previous experience to good use and held on grimly after looking to have it sewn up in the Dip. (5/2: 4/1-9/4)

Timekeeper (USA), edgy in the stalls and flat-footed as they opened, was a most unfortunate loser and losses are merely lent. (11/4: 7/4-3/1)

Mamora Bay (IRE), looking far from fully wound up, was really into his stride coming up the hill and he could find his way when tackling six furlongs. (10/1)

Opposition Leader, a good mover but very green, gave away all chance with a tardy start, but the experience will not be lost. (5/1: 3/1-11/2)

Emperor Naheem (IRE) broke best to set the pace but he was in trouble running into the Dip and was allowed to complete in his own time. (5/1: 7/2-11/2)

Henry The Proud (IRE), bustled a long two furlongs out, swerved badly right just inside the final furlong and with his chance gone was not persevered with. (5/1: 7/2-11/2)

78+ 86+ 83 96?

696 CITY INDEX POLITICAL BETTING CONDITIONS STKS (2-Y.O) (Class C)

5-05 (5-06) **5f (Rowley)** £4,213.13 (£1,555.26: £743.13: £300.15: £115.58: £41.75) Stalls: High GOING minus 0.15 sec per fur (GF)

				SP	RR	SF
	Second Wind (PFICole) **2-8-9** TQuinn(5) (leggy: scope: a.p: led wl over 1f out: hrd drvn: jst hld on)	—	1	11/2 3	79	3
	Arpeggio (RHannon) **2-8-9** LDettori(3) (w'like: scope: b: dwlt: rdn 2f out: str chal fnl f: jst failed)	s.h	2	7/1	79	3
460*	**Miquelon** (RHollinshead) **2-9-4** KDarley(1) (lw: a chsng ldrs: effrt & hrd drvn appr fnl f: r.o wl cl home)	s.h	3	16/1	88	12
	Chieftain (IRE) (NACallaghan) **2-8-9** PatEddery(2) (gd sort: lw: hld up & plld hrd: hdwy 2f out: shkn up to chal ins fnl f: btn whn n.m.r nr fin)	2	4	4/6 1	72	—
	Anvil (USA) (GLewis) **2-8-9** PaulEddery(4) (cmpt: scope: bit bkwd: s.s: bhd: rdn 2f out: r.o one pce fnl f)	s.h	5	9/2 2	72	—
611[2]	**Risky Whisky** (JBerry) **2-8-11**(5) TEDurcan(6) (led over 3f: eased whn btn ins fnl f)	5	6	14/1	63	—
				(SP 118.6%)	**6 Rn**	

63.42 secs (4.72) CSF £40.00 TOTE £7.00: £3.10 £2.40 (£16.30) OWNER Mr David Simpson (WHATCOMBE) BRED P. T. Tellwright

Second Wind, with the pace from the start, put his stamp on proceedings entering the final furlong but he was tying up badly close home and the line arrived not a stride too soon. He can still be improved. (11/2: 7/2-7/1)

Arpeggio forfeited ground with a slow break and looked to be labouring two furlongs out, but he found his stride up the hill and only just failed to get up. (7/1: 6/1-14/1)

460* Miquelon made all when successful at Newcastle but he found the pace hotter here and did not really find his feet until it was far too late. (16/1)

Chieftain (IRE), not the most fluent of movers, did look the likely winner when putting in his challenge two hundred yards out, but the winner kept pulling out extra and he called enough before reaching the line. (4/6)

Anvil (USA) did not fair badly after losing ground at the start and with the race and the experience behind him should be able to go on from here. (9/2)

611 Risky Whisky set the pace but was a bit out of his depth in the latter stages and was eased when beaten. (14/1: 8/1-16/1)

T/Jkpt: £19,783.70 (0.09 Tckts); £25,356.70 to Newbury 18/4/97. T/Plpt: £67.40 (555.05 Tckts). T/Qdpt: £2.80 (747.02 Tckts) IM\

0594-RIPON (R-H) (Good to Firm)

Thursday April 17th

WEATHER: overcast WIND: almost nil

77+ 75+ 63 66

697 E.B.F. SHAROW MAIDEN STKS (2-Y.O) (Class D)

2-10 (2-10) **5f** £3,131.80 (£948.40: £463.20: £220.60) Stalls: Low GOING minus 0.27 sec per fur (GF)

				SP	RR	SF
	Occhi Verdi (IRE) (MJohnston) **2-8-9** JWeaver(1) (leggy: bit bkwd: mde all: shkn up & r.o strly appr fnl f: readily)	—	1	15/8 1	86	31
	Hirst Bridge (IRE) (MWEasterby) **2-9-0** TLucas(4) (neat: chsd ldrs: hung rt fnl 2f: kpt on: no ch w wnr)	5	2	11/1	75	20
	Prose (IRE) (RHannon) **2-9-0** RPerham(5) (unf: scope: chsd ldrs: nt qckn whn sltly hmpd 1f out)	1	3	4/1 2	72	17

	Erro Codigo (MrsJRRamsden) **2-9-0** JFortune(6) (w'like: str: bit bkwd: swvd rt s: hdwy ½-wy: kpt on wl fnl f)	2½	**4**	10/1	64	9
432[13]	**Somosierra (IRE)** (JBerry) **2-9-0** GCarter(8) (chsd ldrs: wkng whn rt over 1f out)	nk	**5**	5/1[3]	63	8
	Winsome George (CWFairhurst) **2-9-0** NKennedy(2) (w'like: bit bkwd: s.i.s: sn outpcd & bhd: kpt on fnl f: nvr nr to chal)	3	**6**	20/1	53	—
	Castle Friend (PCHaslam) **2-9-0** TWilliams(3) (w'like: leggy: scope: bit bkwd: sn wl outpcd & bhd)	5	**7**	10/1	37	—
	Statorhythm (TDBarron) **2-9-0** RLappin(7) (cmpt: bit bkwd: outpcd fr ½-wy)	¾	**8**	8/1	35	—
	Imbackagain (IRE) (PCHaslam) **2-9-0** LCharnock(9) (tall: sn outpcd: bhd fr ½-wy)	9	**9**	14/1	6	—

(SP 120.5%) **9 Rn**

60.1 secs (2.30) CSF £23.60 TOTE £2.70: £1.10 £4.30 £1.60 (£28.70) Trio £31.40 OWNER Mr Grant Mitchell (MIDDLEHAM) BRED J. F. Tutthill and Mrs A. Whitehead

Occhi Verdi (IRE), who has plenty of size and scope, did this in good style and is clearly useful. She was her trainer's first two-year-old runner this time and he has sixty-five juveniles in his care. (15/8: 3/1-7/4)

Hirst Bridge (IRE), very keen going to post, took some settling and showed a marked tendency to hang right. He should be even better suited by six. (11/1)

Prose (IRE), a narrow type, looked one of the fittest in the paddock. (4/1)

Erro Codigo, a heavy-topped colt, is not a good mover. After swerving at the start, he was handled with kid-gloves and would have finished upsides the second with a harder race. (10/1)

432 Somosierra (IRE) does not look to have progressed much since Doncaster. (5/1)

Winsome George, who showed a fair bit of knee-action going down, should come on considerably for the outing. (20/1)

698 COPT HEWICK CLAIMING STKS (3-Y.O+) (Class F)

2-40 (2-40) **5f** £2,563.90 (£720.40: £351.70) Stalls: Low GOING minus 0.27 sec per fur (GF)

				SP	RR	SF
397[4]	**Ansellman (83)** (JBerry) **7-9-7b** GCarter(9) (b.off hind: w ldr: led over 1f out: jst hld on)	—	**1**	2/1[1]	83	50
	Gone Savage (75) (WJMusson) **9-9-7** OUrbina(7) (lw: trckd ldrs: rdn to chal 1f out: r.o)	s.h	**2**	9/2[3]	83	50
596[8]	**Palacegate Touch (81)** (JBerry) **7-9-4b**(5) PRoberts(5) (w ldrs to ½-wy: nt clr run & swtchd rt over 1f out: kpt on wl towards fin)	2½	**3**	3/1[2]	77	44
	Antithesis (IRE) (JSHaldane) **4-8-12** JCarroll(2) (trckd ldrs: kpt on wl appr fnl f)	nk	**4**	11/1	65	32
376[10]	**First Maite (74)** (SRBowring) **4-9-9b** SWebster(1) (led tl over 1f out: wknd towards fin)	1	**5**	11/1	73	40
	John O'Dreams (50) (MrsALMKing) **12-9-3** JFortune(4) (b: s.i.s: sn drvn along: sme hdwy ½-wy: nvr nr ldrs)	4	**6**	20/1	54	21
636[8]	**Maydoro** (MDods) **4-8-13** RLappin(6) (sn outpcd & bhd: sme hdwy over 1f out: n.d)	3½	**7**	50/1	39	6
	The Wad (68) (DNicholls) **4-9-3** AlexGreaves(3) (reard s: sn chsng ldrs: lost pl ½-wy)	2½	**8**	8/1	35	2
550[11]	**Shmoozy** (JSGoldie) **8-8-11** ACulhane(8) (sn wl outpcd & bhd)	12	**9**	100/1	—	—

(SP 112.0%) **9 Rn**

59.6 secs (1.80) CSF £9.69 TOTE £2.70: £1.50 £1.40 £1.50 (£5.30) Trio £3.70 OWNER Ansells of Watford (COCKERHAM) BRED W. L. Caley

397 Ansellman, with the headgear back on, did just enough. (2/1: op 5/4)

Gone Savage, who looked fit for his first outing, would have been meeting the winner on 8lb better terms in a handicap. Despite the ground being firmer than he likes he pushed the winner all the way to the line. (9/2)

596 Palacegate Touch would have been 5lb better off with the winner in a handicap. Dropping back at halfway, he tried for an ambitious run up First Maite's inside and, forced to switch, he was staying on in good style at the end. There are surely more races of this type to be won with him. (3/1)

Antithesis (IRE) would have been 13lb better off with the winner in a handicap. A winner of a five-furlong handicap at Tipperary on easy ground last summer, it will be interesting to what the Handicapper does to her after this. (11/1)

First Maite made the running and considering he would have been 11lb better off with the winner in a handicap he probably ran right up to his best. (11/1)

699 COCKED HAT 'COCK O'THE NORTH' H'CAP (0-90) (3-Y.O) (Class C)

3-10 (3-10) **1m** £5,205.25 (£1,576.00: £769.50: £366.25) Stalls: High GOING minus 0.27 sec per fur (GF)

				SP	RR	SF
	Hen Harrier (82) (JLDunlop) **3-9-5** JWeaver(1) (trckd ldrs: shkn up 4f out: hdwy to ld 1f out: hung rt: sn clr)	—	**1**	9/1	94	62
483[6]	**Baritone (75)** (JWWatts) **3-8-12** JCarroll(10) (lw: trckd ldrs: led over 1f out: sn hdd: nt pce of wnr)	3½	**2**	9/1	80	48
575*	**Blooming Amazing (77)** (JLEyre) **3-9-0** TWilliams(6) (led tl over 1f out: no ex)	¾	**3**	7/2[1]	81	49
575[4]	**Get The Point (76)** (RHollinshead) **3-8-10**(3) FLynch(4) (lw: a chsng ldrs: kpt on same pce fnl 2f)	nk	**4**	12/1	79	47
575[5]	**High Spirits (IRE) (63)** (TDEasterby) **3-8-0** LCharnock(3) (sn chsng ldrs: effrt 3f out: wandered: grad wknd)	2½	**5**	10/1	61	29
688[10]	**I Can't Remember (80)** (PDEvans) **3-9-3** JFEgan(5) (chsd ldrs tl wknd 2f out)	nk	**6**	14/1	77	45
634*	**Jay-Owe-Two (IRE) (81)** (RMWhitaker) **3-9-4** 6x DeanMcKeown(11) (hld up: effrt over 3f out: nvr nr ldrs)	2½	**7**	5/1[2]	73	41
	Foxes Tail (78) (MissSEHall) **3-9-1** JFortune(9) (bit bkwd: hld up: shkn up & sme hdwy over 3f out: n.d)	3	**8**	14/1	64	32
	Pension Fund (80) (MWEasterby) **3-9-3** TLucas(8) (h.d.w: hld up & plld hrd: nvr plcd to chal)	hd	**9**	10/1	66	34
518[5]	**Rotor Man (IRE) (66)** (JDBethell) **3-8-0**(3) MHenry(7) (lw: hld up & plld hrd: rn wd ent st: sn bhd)	8	**10**	7/1	36	4
	Right Tune (84) (BHanbury) **3-9-7** MRimmer(2) (bit bkwd: trckd ldrs tl lost pl over 2f out: eased)	6	**11**	6/1[3]	42	10

(SP 124.9%) **11 Rn**

1m 40.0 (1.80) CSF £84.62 CT £321.53 TOTE £10.20: £2.70 £3.80 £1.60 (£34.50) Trio £131.60 OWNER Sir Thomas Pilkington (ARUNDEL) BRED Mrs Rebecca Philipps

OFFICIAL EXPLANATION **Jay-Owe-Two (IRE): the trainer reported that the gelding was later found to be coughing and to have a dirty nose.**

Hen Harrier, who has yet to come in her coat, again showed a tendency to hang but showed a good turn of foot to shoot clear inside the last.(9/1)

483 Baritone looked really well in the paddock. After getting his head in front coming to the final furlong, he was soon left for dead by the winner. A mile is likely to prove the limit of his stamina. (9/1)

575* Blooming Amazing, from a 5lb higher mark, set just a modest pace. Quickening it up halfway up the straight, he could not match the first two coming to the final furlong. (7/2)

575 Get The Point looked well but the Handicapper seems to have him to the pound. (12/1)

575 High Spirits (IRE) tended to wander under pressure. Not without ability, he will be better suited by a flatter, more galloping track. (10/1)

654 I Can't Remember was having his second outing in two days. (14/1)

634* Jay-Owe-Two (IRE), settled in the early stages under a 6lb penalty, never looked like taking a hand. (5/1)

Pension Fund has done really well from two to three. Taking a keen grip in the rear, he was never asked to improve. There is no doubt he is capable of much better and connections will be hoping for a little mercy from the Handicapper. (10/1)

Right Tune has gone the right way from two to three but needed the outing badly and was eased up. (6/1)

700 FARM FED CHICKEN H'CAP (0-85) (3-Y.O) (Class D)

3-40 (3-41) **1m 4f 60y** £3,371.25 (£1,020.00: £497.50: £236.25) Stalls: High GOING minus 0.27 sec per fur (GF)

Form	Horse	Dist	Pos	SP	RR	SF
533[8]	**Hurgill Dancer (65)** (JWWatts) **3-8-1** LCharnock(2) (hld up: hdwy on ins over 3f out: swtchd lft & led 2f out: drvn clr: eased ins fnl f)	—	**1**	16/1	74	16
533*	**Ikatania (85)** (JLDunlop) **3-9-7** MRimmer(5) (b: hld up & bhd: drvn along ½-wy: hdwy & hung rt 4f out: styd on fnl 2f: no ch w wnr)	5	**2**	9/4[1]	88	30
	Mutabari (USA) (78) (DMorley) **3-9-0** GCarter(3) (hld up & bhd: hdwy over 3f out: kpt on same pce fnl 2f)	nk	**3**	7/1[3]	80	22
533[2]	**Time Can Tell (69)** (CMurray) **3-8-5** DeanMcKeown(7) (sn trckng ldrs: one pce fnl 2f)	1½	**4**	9/1	69	11
533[7]	**Sad Mad Bad (USA) (77)** (MJohnston) **3-8-13** JWeaver(8) (chsd ldrs: reminders 9f out: hung rt & lost pl over 2f out: kpt on appr fnl f)	1	**5**	10/1	76	18
641[4]	**Miss Barcelona (IRE) (60)** (MJPolglase) **3-7-3**(7) JFowle(9) (set str pce: hdd 2f out: grad wknd)	2	**6**	33/1	56	—
	Noble Investment (77) (JMPEustace) **3-8-13** JTate(4) (bit bkwd: s.i.s: hdwy 7f out: sn chsng ldrs: lost pl over 2f out: eased: t.o)	dist	**7**	7/1[3]	—	—
	Michael Venture (84) (SPCWoods) **3-9-6** AClark(6) (bit bkwd: s.i.s: bhd: effrt 4f out: edgd rt & sn wknd: eased: t.o)	3½	**8**	3/1[2]	—	—
478[3]	**Classic Mystery (IRE) (63)** (BJMeehan) **3-7-13** TWilliams(1) (swtg: trckd ldrs: lost pl & p.u over 3f out)		**P**	7/1[3]	—	—

(SP 121.2%) **9 Rn**

2m 41.0 (7.50) CSF £49.93 CT £266.67 TOTE £22.70: £3.40 £1.30 £2.90 (£27.20) Trio £26.60 OWNER Mr Gerald Cooper (RICHMOND) BRED A. Vickers

LONG HANDICAP Miss Barcelona (IRE) 7-0

OFFICIAL EXPLANATION **Classic Mystery (IRE): was found to be suffering from respiratory distress.**

Hurgill Dancer, tailed off behind the runner-up on his reappearance, is an excitable type and had two handlers in the paddock. Wisely wanting nothing to do with the break-neck pace, after hitting the front he was soon many lengths clear and was able to win easing up. The pace was suicidal and the form must be treated with caution. (16/1)

533* Ikatania, from an 8lb higher mark, wore bandages and, under pressure, wanted to do nothing but hang right. (9/4)

Mutabari (USA), who carried plenty of condition, appreciated every yard of the trip. (7/1)

533 Time Can Tell was 4lb better off with Ikatania compared with Nottingham. (9/1: op 6/1)

Sad Mad Bad (USA) gave his rider problems throughout and is clearly a difficult ride. (10/1)

641 Miss Barcelona (IRE), a handful on the way to the start, set off as if this was a five-furlong sprint. (33/1)

Michael Venture, who carried plenty of condition, on breeding should have been suited by the step up in distance but he was in trouble once in line for home. With all chance gone, he was eased off. (3/1)

701 ELANDERS UK MAIDEN STKS (3-Y.O) (Class D)

4-15 (4-15) **1m** £3,550.00 (£1,075.00: £525.00: £250.00) Stalls: High GOING minus 0.27 sec per fur (GF)

Form	Horse	Dist	Pos	SP	RR	SF
	Silverani (IRE) (LMCumani) **3-9-0** OUrbina(4) (hld up: hdwy on bit to ld 2f out: pushed out)	—	**1**	1/10[1]	88+	30
	No Grousing (IRE) (PCHaslam) **3-9-0** JFortune(2) (rangy: bit bkwd: hld up: hdwy 3f out: styd on fnl f: no ch w wnr)	2½	**2**	33/1	83	25
	Zoom Up (IRE) (MJHeaton-Ellis) **3-9-0** JCarroll(8) (w'like: lengthy: trckd ldrs: chal 3f out: kpt on same pce)	½	**3**	12/1[2]	82	24
	Heart of Gold (IRE) (MissSEHall) **3-9-0** MBirch(3) (trckd ldrs: shkn up over 2f out: hung lft & no imp)	6	**4**	20/1[3]	70	12
	Fauna (IRE) (NAGraham) **3-8-9** DHarrison(6) (plld hrd: led after 1f to 2f out: edgd lft & grad wknd)	3½	**5**	20/1[3]	58	—
462[3]	**Prominent** (MrsVAAconley) **3-9-0** MDeering(5) (hld up & plld hrd: shkn up over 2f out: n.d)	2½	**6**	20/1[3]	58	—
	The Tig (LRLloyd-James) **3-9-0** TWilliams(7) (stdd s: hld up: sme hdwy on outside over 3f out: hung rt & sn wknd)	3	**7**	100/1	52?	—
	Hever Golf Angel (IRE) (PCHaslam) **3-8-9** JWeaver(1) (unf: scope: led 1f: chsd ldrs tl lost pl 3f out: sn bhd)	3½	**8**	20/1[3]	40?	—

(SP 121.6%) **8 Rn**

1m 42.8 (4.60) CSF £11.92 TOTE £1.10: £1.00 £10.10 £2.20 (£13.10) OWNER Mr Paul Silver (NEWMARKET) BRED J. Bowdren

OFFICIAL EXPLANATION **Prominent: the trainer reported that the colt was found to be coughing after the race and was off-colour the following day.**

Silverani (IRE), who showed very useful form when runner-up on both his outings at two, has not grown at all during the winter and is barely bigger than a pony but on the other hand he is well put together. Backed as if defeat was out of the question in this moderate contest, he won without knowing he had been in a race. Presumably his future lies in the hands of the Handicapper and he cannot expect any mercy. (1/10: op 2/9)

No Grousing (IRE), who has plenty of size and scope, showed ability. (33/1)

Zoom Up (IRE) ran with credit on his debut but it is hard to know what the race is worth. (12/1)

Heart of Gold (IRE), a full brother to Key To My Heart, is a keen going type. Hanging left and carrying his head high, he was possibly feeling the ground. This was his third outing and he now qualifies for a handicap mark. (20/1)

Fauna (IRE), a keen-going sort, was not knocked about and she too is now qualified for handicaps. (20/1)

462 Prominent is another who was having his third run. (20/1)

702 NEWBY APPRENTICE H'CAP (0-70) (4-Y.O+) (Class E)

4-45 (4-46) **5f** £2,705.50 (£829.00: £412.00: £203.50) Stalls: Low GOING minus 0.27 sec per fur (GF)

Form	Horse	Dist	Pos	SP	RR	SF
666*	**Johayro (58)** (JSGoldie) **4-8-11**(5) 7x JMcAuley(1) (lw: mde most stands' side: edgd rt & r.o fnl f)	—	**1**	7/1[2]	67	29
	River Tern (62) (JMBradley) **4-9-1**(5) JFowle(4) (s.s: wl bhd stands' side: sddle slipped: gd hdwy over 1f out: r.o wl: nt rch wnr)	1	**2**	20/1	68	30
585[5]	**Chadwell Hall (68)** (SRBowring) **6-9-2v**(10) FBoyle(6) (w ldr stands' side: edgd rt & kpt on wl fnl f)	½	**3**	9/1	72	34
585*	**Meranti (50)** (JMBradley) **4-8-8** 7x VictoriaAppleby(11) (lw: swvd rt s: sn chsng ldrs centre: kpt on wl fnl f)	½	**4**	4/1[1]	53	15
527[7]	**Kalar (56)** (DWChapman) **8-8-9b**(5) TSiddall(16) (led far side: nt qckn appr fnl f)	nk	**5**	12/1	58	20
610[3]	**Tropical Beach (63)** (JBerry) **4-8-11**(10) PBradley(9) (bhd stands' side: r.o wl fnl f)	hd	**6**	8/1[3]	64	26
394[8]	**Ramsey Hope (65)** (CWFairhurst) **4-9-9v** JDennis(18) (in tch centre: styd on fnl f)	hd	**7**	14/1	66	28
545[4]	**Dissentor (IRE) (40)** (JAGlover) **5-7-7v**(5) RBrisland(5) (a in tch stands' side: kpt on same pce appr fnl f)	1½	**8**	20/1	36	—
303[3]	**Double Oscar (IRE) (52)** (DNicholls) **4-8-0**(10) JoanneDavies(13) (bhd centre: styd on fnl f)	½	**9**	25/1	47	9
593[2]	**Silk Cottage (54)** (RMWhitaker) **5-8-12** PDoe(8) (chsd ldr centre over 3f)	½	**10**	10/1	47	9
	Lady Sheriff (68) (MWEasterby) **6-9-9b**(3) CLowther(19) (w ldr far side tl wknd over 1f out)	nk	**11**	16/1	60	22
527[10]	**Barato (64)** (MrsJRRamsden) **6-9-0**(8) ClaireWest(3) (b.hind: dwlt: a in rr)	s.h	**12**	10/1	56	18

				SP	RR	SF
494[11]	**Sunset Harbour (IRE) (45)** (SEKettlewell) **4-7-9**(8) JennyBenson(7) (in tch stands' side 3f: sn wknd)	nk	**13**	25/1	34	—
	Ned's Bonanza (60) (MDods) **8-8-13**(5) PFredericks(2) (w ldr stands' side tl wknd over 1f out)	d.h	**13**	14/1	51	13
585[9]	**Sing With the Band (59)** (BAMcMahon) **6-8-9**(8) SRighton(14) (lw: w ldr centre over 3f: wknd)	½	**15**	14/1	47	9
596[16]	**Rich Glow (57)** (NBycroft) **6-8-12**(3) AMcCarthy(10) (bhd centre & sn drvn along: n.d)	1¾	**16**	20/1	39	1
	Gagajulu (48) (PDEvans) **4-8-3**(3) AnthonyBond(17) (racd far side: sn outpcd & drvn along)	nk	**17**	20/1	29	—
473[6]	**Barranak (IRE) (58)** (GMMcCourt) **5-8-10**(6) RStudholme(12) (sltly hmpd s: a bhd centre)	1¼	**18**	12/1	35	—
	Dominelle (55) (TDEasterby) **5-8-8**(5) CarolynBales(15) (prom far side 3f: sn lost pl)	1¾	**19**	12/1	27	—
				(SP 147.5%)	**19 Rn**	

60.6 secs (2.80) CSF £145.98 CT £795.63 TOTE £7.40: £2.60 £13.60 £1.80 £1.80 (£124.70) Trio £330.10 OWNER Mr Frank Brady (GLASGOW) BRED R. M. Whitaker

666* Johayro made it two wins in four days. From a small stable in cracking form both on the Flat and over jumps at present, he again showed a tendency to edge right. (7/1)

River Tern, who showed his best form at three when fitted with a visor, did remarkably well in the circumstances, losing at least four lengths at the start and handicapped by a slipped saddle. He was overhauling the winner hand over fist in the final furlong. (20/1)

585 Chadwell Hall, who was suited by the drop back to the minimum trip, took this event a year ago from an 8lb lower mark. (9/1)

585* Meranti found the drop back to five against him. (4/1)

464 Kalar is about a 20lb better horse on the All-Weather. (12/1)

610 Tropical Beach needs every inch of six furlongs nowadays. (8/1)

T/Plpt: £10.20 (973.08 Tckts). T/Qdpt: £8.30 (74.63 Tckts) WG

0703a - 0712a & 0714a - 0715a: (Irish Racing) - See Computer Raceform

0617a-CURRAGH (Newbridge, Ireland) (R-H) (Good)
Saturday April 12th

713a GLADNESS STKS (Gp 3) (3-Y.O+)
4-15 (4-15) **7f** IR £19,500.00 (IR £5,700.00: IR £2,700.00: IR £900.00) GOING: 0.03 sec per fur (G)

			SP	RR	SF
Cool Edge (IRE) (MHTompkins) **6-9-7** NDay (mde all: rdn clr over 3f out: kpt on wl)	—	**1**	6/1[3]	112	64
Desert King (IRE) (APO'Brien,Ireland) **3-9-0** CRoche (sn chsng ldr: no imp on wnr 3f out: shkn up 1½f out: kpt on)	2½	**2**	3/1[2]	113	51
Mosconi (IRE) (JSBolger,Ireland) **3-8-7b** WJSupple (hld up: last over 2f out: r.o. ins fnl f: 3rd cl home)	5½	**3**	12/1	94	32
My Branch (BWHills) **4-9-4** MHills (hld up in tch: 3rd over 2f out: sn rdn: btn wl over 1f out)	hd	**4**	11/8[1]	91	43
Act Of Defiance (IRE) (DKWeld,Ireland) **3-8-4** MJKinane (hld up: 4th over 2f out: no imp last 1½f)	s.h	**5**	8/1	90	28
Raiyoun (IRE) (JOxx,Ireland) **4-9-7** JPMurtagh (hld up: 5th over 2f out: sn no imp: kpt on)	¾	**6**	8/1	92	44
			(SP 111.3%)	**6 Rn**	

1m 25.8 (2.80) OWNER Henry Chan (NEWMARKET) BRED Hollybank Breeders

Cool Edge (IRE), looking pretty straight, bounced out in front and was never headed. He was well clear at halfway and there was never any possibility of him being caught under a particularly good ride. (6/1: op 4/1)

Desert King (IRE), looking burly and with his tongue tied down as usual, was weak in the market. Soon in second place, he found himself totally outpaced by the winner's tactics and got only a hand ride, admittedly a vigorous enough one, by Roche. It wasn't a bad performance in the circumstances, as he was meeting the winner on 7lb worse terms than weight-for-age and he will certainly come on for this outing. He definitely needs a mile and remains a potential Classic colt. (3/1: op 2/1)

Mosconi (IRE), last of all with two furlongs to race, found his fitness taking him past beaten rivals. (12/1: op 8/1)

My Branch didn't impress in the paddock and could never get in a blow from her position on the outside. (11/8)

Act Of Defiance (IRE) never threatened. (8/1)

Raiyoun (IRE) was patently in need of the outing. (8/1)

0439a-SAINT-CLOUD (France) (L-H) (Good)
Wednesday April 9th

716a PRIX EDMOND BLANC (Gp 3) (4-Y.O+)
3-25 (3-25) **1m** £24,691.00 (£8,979.00: £4,489.00)

				SP	RR	SF
	Simon du Desert (FR) (RCollet,France) **4-8-11** CHanotel	—	**1**		116	—
	Precious Ring (USA) (MmeCHead,France) **4-8-11** FHead	¾	**2**		115	—
	Trojan Sea (USA) (DSmaga,France) **6-8-11** DBoeuf	s.nk	**3**		114	—
433*	**Canyon Creek (IRE)** (JHMGosden) **4-8-11** LDettori (btn approx 8¼l)		**8**		—	—
						8 Rn

1m 39.0 (0.50) P-M 8.30F: 2.00F 2.40F 1.70F (29.00F) OWNER Mr Arne Larsson (CHANTILLY) BRED M-3 Elevage

Simon du Desert (FR) thoroughly deserved his first victory in a Group race as he has been knocking on the door for some time. He was ridden with great confidence by young Christian Hanotel, who brought the colt to challenge on the rail inside the final furlong. He showed a good turn of foot, is getting better with age and will be allowed to take his chance in the Prix du Muguet.

Precious Ring (USA) looked all over the winner at the furlong marker but he only stayed on at one pace in the final stages. He may be suited by a slightly longer distance.

Trojan Sea (USA) did not have the best of luck in running and was switched before making his challenge. His effort was slightly disappointing as he was 5lb better off with the winner on this occasion.

433* Canyon Creek (IRE) was a great disappointment and never really took a hand, always being towards the tail of the field. His effort in the straight fizzled out quickly, and Dettori reported that the ground was too firm for the colt.

MAISONS-LAFFITTE (France) (Good to soft)
Friday April 11th

717a PRIX DJEBEL (Listed) (3-Y.O C & G)
2-25 (2-22) **7f** £15,713.00 (£5,387.00: £4,040.00: £2,697.00)

				SP	RR	SF
	Fantastic Fellow (USA) (CEBrittain) **3-9-3** OPeslier	—	1		114	—
	Nombre Premier (AdeRoyerDupre,France) **3-9-2** GMosse	¾	2		111	—
	Inkatha (FR) (FDoumen,France) **3-9-2** DBoeuf	2	3		107	—
519^{5}	**Tomba** (BJMeehan) **3-9-2** RHughes	3	4		100	—

6 Rn

1m 26.8 (4.50) P-M 3.20F: 1.90F 1.80F OWNER The Thoroughbred Corporation (NEWMARKET) BRED Mrs J. G. Jones

Fantastic Fellow (USA) still looked a little backward in the paddock. He was never far from the front and led a full two furlongs out. He idled, but found a second gear when challenged by the runner-up, and won with a little in hand. He looks sure to improve considerably for the race and will do even better over a longer distance. He will either be aimed at the English or French 2,000 Guineas, with the latter being the favourite at the moment, and looks a horse to keep in mind.

Nombre Premier looked extremely dangerous when he challenged approaching the final furlong but he was held in the final stages. His trainer considered that the track had been over-watered which did not help his colt who has a 'daisy-cutting' action. He has done well during the winter and will probably go for the Poulains, although he is more likely to find his ground at Newmarket.

Inkatha (FR) put in a decent effort, and was running on at the finish without ever being really dangerous. He may pick up a listed race over a longer distance.

519 Tomba was never going well and ran below expectations. This may have been due to travel problems, and this race is best forgotten.

718a PRIX IMPRUDENCE (Listed) (3-Y.O F)
2-55 (2-51) **7f** £15,713.00 (£5,387.00: £4,040.00) GOING: Not Established

			SP	RR	SF
Pas De Reponse (USA) (MmeCHead,France) **3-9-0** FHead	—	1		—	—
Barnata (FR) (PBary,France) **3-9-0** SGuillot	2½	2		—	—
Psylla (FR) (JEPease,France) **3-9-0** OPeslier	3	3		—	—

3 Rn

1m 30.9 (8.60) P-M 1.30F OWNER Wertheimer Brothers (CHANTILLY) BRED Wertheimer & Frere

Pas De Reponse (USA) has done extremely well during the winter. She had no option but to make all the running, and was asked to stretch out with a furlong and a half left to run, dominating the final stages. She totally out-classed her two rivals and this race was no more than a training spin. Indeed, her jockey continued to ride her after the finish to ensure that she had some decent work. She blew a little after the race and her connections were totally satisfied. She will strip much fitter for the 1,000 Guineas and there seems to be little worry about her staying the Rowley mile as she is such a relaxed individual. She will be very difficult to beat at Newmarket.

Barnata (FR) attempted to go with Pas De Reponse, but never managed to get on terms. She is not in the same class and may even be suited by a shorter distance.

Psylla (FR) was very slowly into her stride but it did not matter as the early pace was slow. She remained last throughout the race but collected a nice prize for turning up.

GELSENKIRCHEN-HORST (Gelsenkirchen, Germany) (R-H) (Good to soft)
Sunday April 13th

719a GROSSER PREIS DER GELSENKIRCHENER WIRTSCHAFT-BUCHMACHER LINDNER (Gp 3) (4-Y.O+)
3-40 (3-41) **1m 2f** £22,727.00 (£9,091.00: £4,545.00)

				SP	RR	SF
	Oxalagu (GER) (BSchutz,Germany) **5-9-2** AStarke	—	1		118	—
440a^{3}	**Try Again (GER)** (AWohler,Germany) **6-8-12** ABoschert	1½	2		112	—
	Zero Problemo (IRE) (BSchutz,Germany) **4-9-0** WNewnes	hd	3		113	—

12 Rn

2m 6.0 TOTE 41DM: 16DM 36DM 29DM OWNER Gestut Rietberg

Oxalagu (GER) repeated his success of last year and looks one to side with this season. Connections believe that he has Group One potential and he may be aimed at the Premio Presidente Della Repubblica at Capannelle in May.

SHA TIN (New Territories, Hong Kong) (R-H) (Good to firm)
Sunday April 13th

TF120

720a QUEEN ELIZABETH II CUP (Gp 1) (3-Y.O+)
8-10 (8-10) **1m 2f** £222,563.00 (£84,421.00: £38,373.00)

			SP	RR	SF
London News (SAF) (AlecLaird,SouthAfrica) **4-9-2** DJWhyte	—	1		123	—
Privilege (IRE) (IAllan,HongKong) **6-9-0** AMarcus	½	2		120	—
Annus Mirabilis (FR) (SbinSuroor,UAE) **5-9-0** LDettori	½	3		119	—

14 Rn

2m 0.3 TOTE £61.00: £14.50 £27.00 £11.50 (£1,297.50) OWNER Mr & Mrs L Jaffee BRED Koster Brothers

London News (SAF) did this well and is a credit to his trainer. It is said that he will be competing in Britain after accomplishing everything in South Africa, and he is sure to hold his own.

Privilege (IRE) is a tough individual to say the least. Finally challenged by the eventual winner in the closing stages, he kept fighting back but had to concede to one simply too good.

Annus Mirabilis (FR) ran well without quickening but it was later found that he had returned with a nasal discharge.

AYR (L-H) (Good)
Friday April 18th
Other races under Rules of National Hunt racing.
WEATHER: Fine

721
BRITISH FIELD SPORTS SOCIETY IN SCOTLAND AMATEUR H'CAP (0-60) (3-Y.O+) (Class G)
5-00 (5-01) **1m 2f** £2,085.00 (£585.00: £285.00) GOING: 0.09 sec per fur (G)

				SP	RR	SF
	Supertop (50) (LLungo) **9-11-0**(5) MrBGibson(5) (trckd ldrs: led wl over 1f out & qcknd clr: drvn out)	—	**1**	20/1	60	—
465[13]	**Captain Marmalade (41)** (DTThom) **8-10-5**(5)ow2 MrMSpillane(6) (bhd tl styd on wl fnl 3f: nrst fin)	1¾	**2**	25/1	48	—
595[5]	**Forzair (51)** (JJO'Neill) **5-11-6** MrPCraggs(13) (mid div: styd on fnl 3f: nrst fin)	hd	**3**	12/1	58	—
	Hand of Straw (IRE) (47) (MissZAGreen) **5-11-2** MrRHale(19) (mid div: hdwy 3f out: styd on wl fnl f)	1½	**4**	100/1	52	—
653[2]	**Clued Up (46)** (PDEvans) **4-10-10v**(5) MrAEvans(7) (chsd ldrs: r.o one pce fnl 3f)	5	**5**	5/1[2]	43	—
476[5]	**Proud Brigadier (IRE) (42)** (MRBosley) **9-10-6**(5) MrSJEdwards(12) (s.s: hdwy u.p 3f out: nrst fin)	2½	**6**	20/1	35	—
613[2]	**Karisma (IRE) (56)** (DenysSmith) **4-11-11** MrRThornton(11) (led after 2f tl wl over 1f out: sn btn)	hd	**7**	6/1[3]	49	—
136[8]	**High Low (USA) (52)** (MDHammond) **9-11-7** MrCBonner(18) (bhd tl styd on wl fnl 3f)	nk	**8**	25/1	44	—
608[2]	**Gadge (58)** (ABailey) **6-11-8**(5) MissALHutchinson(16) (lw: hld up: hmpd ent st: styd on: n.d)	nk	**9**	7/1	50	—
552[7]	**Sing And Dance (43)** (EWeymes) **4-10-7**(5) MrJWeymes(4) (mid div: hdwy on ins 3f out: no imp)	1	**10**	9/1	33	—
668[5]	**Western Venture (IRE) (38)** (RMMcKellar) **4-10-2**(5) MrCDunbar(9) (nvr trbld ldrs)	½	**11**	50/1	27	—
574[5]	**Flyaway Blues (43)** (MrsMReveley) **5-10-12b** MrSSwiers(14) (bhd: n.m.r ent st: styd on: n.d)	s.h	**12**	9/2[1]	32	—
	Tibbi Blues (42) (JSGoldie) **10-10-6**(5) MissBSpittal(8) (s.s: hdwy & c wd st: nvr rchd ldrs)	2½	**13**	12/1	27	—
613[13]	**Philmist (45)** (MissLAPerratt) **5-10-9b**(5) MrTJBarry(2) (cl up: chal 4f out: sn wknd fnl 2f)	2	**14**	14/1	27	—
544[4]	**Zatopek (48)** (JCullinan) **5-10-12**(5) MrBDGrant(17) (n.d)	¾	**15**	20/1	29	—
574[10]	**Anistop (43)** (JLEyre) **5-10-12** MissDianaJones(3) (led 2f: chsd ldrs tl wknd 4f out)	8	**16**	12/1	11	—
	The Boozing Brief (USA) (59) (CParker) **4-12-0b** MrAParker(1) (chsd ldrs tl wknd fnl 2f)	2½	**17**	20/1	23	—
	Fairelaine (43) (KCBailey) **5-10-7**(5) MrOMcPhail(15) (n.d)	10	**18**	20/1	—	—
338[3]	**Claque (40)** (DWChapman) **5-10-9b** MissRClark(20) (lw: mid div: rdn 4f out: n.d)	1¼	**19**	16/1	—	—
668[13]	**Knave (46)** (PMonteith) **4-10-10**(5) MissCHawe(10) (chsd ldrs tl wknd 3f out)	13	**20**	50/1	—	—
				(SP 143.7%)	**20 Rn**	

2m 18.4 (12.60) CSF £427.90 CT £5,639.23 TOTE £61.90: £7.10 £6.10 £3.00 £20.90 (£1,374.80) Trio Not won; £545.10 to Newbury 19/4/97
OWNER Mr G. A. Arthur (CARRUTHERSTOWN) BRED Limestone Stud

Supertop, given a good ride, travelled well and showed a useful turn of foot to settle it approaching the final furlong. (20/1)
188 Captain Marmalade produced his usual late burst, but on this occasion it was not soon enough. (25/1)
595 Forzair is in good heart after a busy All-Weather campaign. Well suited by the strong pace, he finished strongly and may well have preferred further. (12/1)
Hand of Straw (IRE), having his first run for his new stable, showed ability, making late headway. (100/1)
653 Clued Up was always well enough placed but lacked a change of gear. (5/1)
476 Proud Brigadier (IRE) gave the rest a start and then did well to finish so close. (20/1)
613 Karisma (IRE), made plenty of use of, finally threw in the towel approaching the last furlong. (6/1)
574 Flyaway Blues was made favourite here despite being a maiden after twenty-five attempts, and he never gave his supporters much hope. (9/2)

T/Plpt: £130.60 (143.09 Tckts). T/Qdpt: £61.10 (15.27 Tckts) AA

NEWBURY (L-H) (Good to firm)
Friday April 18th
WEATHER: Fine but cloudy WIND: slt bhd

82+ 89+ 84+ 92?

722
E.B.F. BECKHAMPTON NOVICE STKS (2-Y.O) (Class D)
2-10 (2-10) **5f 34y** £3,817.50 (£1,140.00: £545.00: £247.50) Stalls: Centre GOING minus 0.02 sec per fur (G)

				SP	RR	SF
	Mijana (IRE) (JHMGosden) **2-8-12** LDettori(6) (neat: a.p: led wl over 1f out: pushed out)	—	**1**	9/2[3]	82	26
	Kennet (PDCundell) **2-8-12** RPerham(7) (neat: hld up: rdn 3f out: r.o one pce fnl f)	2½	**2**	50/1	74	18
	Chips (IRE) (DRCElsworth) **2-8-12** OPeslier(8) (leggy: scope: lw: s.i.s: hdwy over 2f out: ev ch wl over 1f out: rn green: nt qckn ins fnl f)	hd	**3**	9/4[1]	74	18
504*	**Wrekin Pilot** (RHannon) **2-9-4** DaneO'Neill(3) (a.p: ev ch 2f out: one pce)	1½	**4**	9/2[3]	75	19
	Chunito (PWChapple-Hyam) **2-8-12** JReid(2) (leggy: lt-f: prom: ev ch 2f out: wknd fnl f)	4	**5**	5/2[2]	57	1
504[6]	**Royal Interview (IRE)** (MRChannon) **2-8-12** TQuinn(4) (led over 3f)	2½	**6**	16/1	49	—
	Distinctly Lillie (IRE) (JSMoore) **2-8-4**(3) MHenry(1) (leggy: wnt lft s: bhd fnl 2f)	s.h	**7**	50/1	44	—
	King Darius (IRE) (RHannon) **2-8-12** RHughes(9) (neat: bit bkwd: s.s: hld up: hdwy 3f out: wknd wl over 1f out)	4	**8**	10/1	37	—
				(SP 114.6%)	**8 Rn**	

64.36 secs (4.16) CSF £155.13 TOTE £4.40: £1.70 £6.00 £1.10 (£81.90) Trio £176.80; £201.79 to Newbury 19/4/97 OWNER Mr Nabil Mourad (NEWMARKET) BRED Churchtown House Stud

Mijana (IRE), a half-brother to Old Hickory, is by first-season sire Tenby. A rare April juvenile runner for his stable, he looked a typical early-season sort who can score again. (9/2: op 5/2)
Kennet kept on to secure the runner-up spot near the line, and already appears ready to tackle further. (50/1)
Chips (IRE), reported to have been working well at home, will be better for the experience and seems sure to improve. (9/4)
504* Wrekin Pilot, carrying a penalty, probably had more to do here than when winning at Kempton. (9/2: op 3/1)
Chunito is an angular half-brother to Bedazzle and juvenile winner A Breeze. (5/2: op 6/4)
504 Royal Interview (IRE) had finished just over eight lengths behind Wrekin Pilot at Kempton. (16/1)
King Darius (IRE) (10/1: op 6/1)

723 STROUD GREEN RATED STKS H'CAP (0-95) (3-Y.O) (Class C)

2-40 (2-42) **1m (straight)** £5,601.24 (£2,081.16: £1,005.58: £418.90: £174.45: £76.67) Stalls: Centre GOING: Not Established

	Runner	Dist	Pos	SP	RR	SF
	Amid Albadu (USA) (90) (JLDunlop) **3-9-4** LDettori(16) (lw: a.p: hrd rdn to ld wl ins fnl f: r.o)	—	1	9/1	104	67
	Peartree House (IRE) (86) (WRMuir) **3-9-0** JReid(7) (a.p: led over 2f out tl wl ins fnl f)	¾	2	20/1	99	62
509[3]	**Sword Arm (76)** (RCharlton) **3-8-4v[1]** TSprake(10) (hld up: hdwy 3f out: ev ch 2f out: wknd fnl f)	10	3	20/1	69	32
	Noble Dane (IRE) (80) (PWHarris) **3-8-8** PatEddery(14) (lw: s.s: hdwy over 1f out: r.o)	hd	4	13/2[2]	72	35
524[2]	**Tigrello (84)** (GLewis) **3-8-12** RHughes(17) (hld up: hdwy 3f out: wknd over 1f out)	3	5	10/1	70	33
	Test The Water (IRE) (93) (RHannon) **3-9-7** DaneO'Neill(6) (lw: hdwy 2f out: nvr nr to chal)	3½	6	20/1	72	35
	Sound Appeal (76) (AGFoster) **3-8-4b** RPerham(4) (led over 5f)	1¼	7	40/1	53	16
463*	**Maftool (85)** (JHMGosden) **3-8-13** RHills(8) (lw: prom: ev ch over 2f out: wknd over 1f out)	1½	8	4/1[1]	59	22
509[9]	**Contentment (IRE) (76)** (JWHills) **3-8-1**(3) MHenry(15) (hld up mid div: rdn over 2f out: wknd over 1f out)	1¼	9	20/1	47	10
	Faringdon Future (82) (BWHills) **3-8-10** MHills(13) (nvr nr ldrs)	s.h	10	25/1	53	16
	Mayflower (78) (IABalding) **3-8-6** KDarley(11) (bhd fnl 3f)	8	11	20/1	33	—
	Golden Fact (USA) (83) (RHannon) **3-8-11** DHarrison(9) (n.d)	nk	12	33/1	38	1
502[7]	**Braveheart (IRE) (90)** (MRChannon) **3-8-13**(5) PPMurphy(2) (prom over 5f)	nk	13	33/1	44	7
	Our Way (76) (CEBrittain) **3-7-11**(7) KParkin(5) (racd alone centre: bhd fnl 3f)	1¼	14	40/1	28	—
	Maladerie (IRE) (90) (MRChannon) **3-9-4** PaulEddery(18) (a bhd)	2	15	33/1	38	1
	Sturgeon (IRE) (87) (PFICole) **3-9-1** TQuinn(1) (lw: racd alone far side: prom over 4f: eased whn no ch over 1f out)	nk	16	13/2[2]	34	—
	Shoumatara (USA) (86) (MRStoute) **3-9-0** KFallon(3) (lw: bhd fnl 3f)	1½	17	16/1	30	—
	Maylane (90) (ACStewart) **3-9-4** MRoberts(12) (swvd lft & uns rdr s)		U	7/1[3]	—	—

(SP 125.5%) **18 Rn**

1m 41.23 (3.23) CSF £163.58 CT £3,275.93 TOTE £6.20: £1.60 £3.70 £4.00 £1.60 (£130.30) Trio £871.50 OWNER Mr Hamdan Al Maktoum (ARUNDEL) BRED Airlie Stud

LONG HANDICAP Our Way 8-0 Sound Appeal 7-9 Sword Arm 8-3 Contentment (IRE) 8-2

Amid Albadu (USA) continued where he left off last season, and gained the upper hand in the final one hundred yards. (9/1)
Peartree House (IRE), who has changed stables, likes this sort of ground and was 3lb lower than when beaten on his final start last season.(20/1)
509 **Sword Arm**, already due to go down a pound, was tried in a visor on this return to a mile. (20/1)
Noble Dane (IRE) may need further on ground as fast as this. (13/2)
524 **Tigrello** found this race a lot more competitive than his seasonal reappearance at Newcastle. (10/1)
Test The Water (IRE) was 8lb higher than when successful in an Ascot nursery last October. (20/1)

724 DUBAI DUTY FREE FRED DARLING STKS (Gp 3) (3-Y.O F) (Class A)

3-10 (3-12) **7f 64y (round)** £20,400.00 (£7,635.00: £3,667.50: £1,597.50) Stalls: Low GOING minus 0.02 sec per fur (G)

	Runner	Dist	Pos	SP	RR	SF
	Dance Parade (USA) (106) (PFICole) **3-9-0** TQuinn(9) (lw: hld up: stdy hdwy over 3f out: rdn to ld ins fnl f: r.o wl)	—	1	16/1	111	52
	Seebe (USA) (110) (IABalding) **3-9-0** LDettori(1) (a.p: rdn over 2f out: swtchd rt over 1f out: r.o)	¾	2	5/1[2]	109	50
	Well Warned (95) (BWHills) **3-9-0** MHills(5) (led: rdn over 2f out: hdd ins fnl f)	½	3	50/1	108	49
	Sleepytime (IRE) (HRACecil) **3-9-0** KFallon(3) (h.d.w: hld up: nt clr run over 2f out: r.o ins fnl f)	1½	4	4/7[1]	105+	46
506*	**Supercal (95)** (DRCElsworth) **3-9-0** RCochrane(6) (s.s: rdn 3f out: nvr nr to chal)	2½	5	50/1	100	41
	Bianca Nera (DRLoder) **3-9-0** KDarley(8) (lw: chsd ldr: rdn over 2f out: hmpd over 1f out: wknd fnl f)	nk	6	13/2[3]	99	40
507*	**Calypso Grant (IRE) (100)** (PWHarris) **3-9-0** PatEddery(4) (lw: hld up & plld hrd: hdwy 3f out: btn whn sltly hmpd over 1f out)	2½	7	12/1	93	34
	Arethusa (108) (RHannon) **3-9-0** DaneO'Neill(2) (b: a bhd)	1¼	8	16/1	91	32
	Blues Queen (89) (MRChannon) **3-9-0** PPMurphy(10) (prom over 4f)	6	9	66/1	77	18
	Attitre (FR) (95) (CEBrittain) **3-9-0** MRoberts(7) (plld hrd in rr: rdn 3f out: no rspnse)	2½	10	66/1	72	13

(SP 120.0%) **10 Rn**

1m 31.99 (3.89) CSF £87.24 TOTE £15.40: £2.50 £1.90 £7.90 (£41.30) Trio £222.80 OWNER H R H Prince Fahd Salman (WHATCOMBE) BRED Newgate Stud Farm Inc

STEWARDS' ENQUIRY Dettori susp. 28-29/4/97 (careless riding)

Dance Parade (USA) completed her hat-trick when winning the Queen Mary. Not seen out again until below-par on soft ground in the Prix Marcel Boussac, she certainly showed she has trained on. (16/1)
Seebe (USA), whose rider picked up a two-day ban for careless riding, showed her appreciation for this extra furlong, and a mile should prove no problem. (5/1)
Well Warned turned around the Lowther form with Bianca Nera, having been beaten nearly ten lengths by that rival at York. (50/1)
Sleepytime (IRE), with nowhere to go when the pace quickened, stayed on in the last one hundred and fifty yards and should not be written off for the 1,000 Guineas where the longer trip will help. (4/7)
506* **Supercal**, stepping up considerably in class, found this longer distance coming to her aid in the closing stages. (50/1)
Bianca Nera, done no favours by the runner-up, should not be considered unlucky. (13/2)
507* **Calypso Grant (IRE)**, twice a winner over a mile last year, was always going to find this trip on the sharp side. (12/1)

725 PETER SMITH MEMORIAL MAIDEN STKS (3-Y.O) (Class D)

3-40 (3-49) **1m 3f 5y** £4,110.00 (£1,230.00: £590.00: £270.00) Stalls: Low GOING minus 0.02 sec per fur (G)

Runner	Dist	Pos	SP	RR	SF
Ghataas (JLDunlop) **3-9-0** RHills(7) (a.p: led on bit over 2f out: drvn out)	—	1	7/2[1]	97	43
Basman (IRE) (BSmart) **3-9-0** RHughes(2) (lw: hld up: nt clr run 3f out: swtchd rt & gd hdwy over 2f out: ev ch ins fnl f: r.o)	½	2	100/1	96	42
Redbridge (USA) (JHMGosden) **3-9-0** LDettori(9) (leggy: scope: hld up: hdwy over 3f out: ev ch over 2f out: one pce)	2½	3	4/1[2]	93	39
Pentad (USA) (RCharlton) **3-9-0** PatEddery(12) (str: scope: bit bkwd: a.p: led over 3f out tl over 2f out: eased whn btn ins fnl f)	6	4	9/1[3]	84	30
Catchable (HRACecil) **3-9-0** KFallon(3) (lw: prom tl rdn & wknd 2f out)	5	5	4/1[2]	77	23
Grapevine (IRE) (PWChapple-Hyam) **3-8-9** JReid(11) (b.nr hind: no hdwy fnl 2f)	hd	6	10/1	72	18
Right Wing (IRE) (MajorWRHern) **3-9-0** TSprake(10) (hld up: hdwy on bit over 3f out: ev ch over 2f out: sn rdn: wkng whn hung lft over 1f out)	5	7	9/1[3]	69	15
Mighty Flow (MrsPNDutfield) **3-8-9** MRoberts(15) (leggy: mid div whn hmpd & hung rt over 2f out)	4	8	33/1	59	5

				SP	RR	SF
	Walk On By (RHannon) **3-9-0** DaneO'Neill(1) (bit bkwd: no hdwy fnl 3f)	1¼	**9**	33/1	62	8
	Alhosaam (MajorWRHern) **3-9-0** PaulEddery(5) (w'like: scope: nvr nrr)	hd	**10**	33/1	62	8
	Hoh Explorer (IRE) (IABalding) **3-9-0** TQuinn(8) (w'like: bhd fnl 3f)	1½	**11**	16/1	59	5
	Milly of The Vally (HRACecil) **3-8-9** WRyan(18) (unf: sltly hmpd over 2f out: a bhd)	¾	**12**	20/1	53	—
539[5]	**Mazara (IRE)** (AGFoster) **3-8-9b[1]** RPerham(4) (b.nr hind: led over 6f)	½	**13**	66/1	53	—
	Royal Castle (IRE) (MajorWRHern) **3-9-0** MHills(19) (bit bkwd: hld up mid div: wkng whn bmpd over 2f out)	½	**14**	33/1	57	3
	Darien (RCharlton) **3-9-0** KDarley(13) (str: scope: lw: s.s: a bhd: t.o)	20	**15**	20/1	28	—
	Highly Prized (IABalding) **3-9-0** RCochrane(6) (bkwd: bhd fnl 3f: t.o)	¾	**16**	33/1	27	—
	Rear Window (LordHuntingdon) **3-9-0** DHarrison(16) (w'like: scope: bit bkwd: s.s: a bhd: t.o)	9	**17**	33/1	14	—
	Bint Rosie (MJFetherston-Godley) **3-8-9** DHolland(17) (prom 8f: t.o)	5	**18**	66/1	1	—
	Gee Bee Boy (APJarvis) **3-9-0** BDoyle(14) (Withdrawn not under Starter's orders: uns rdr & bolted bef s)		**W**	50/1	—	—
				(SP 130.3%)	**18 Rn**	

2m 24.59 (7.39) CSF £367.93 TOTE £3.50: £1.90 £38.40 £1.60 (£244.40) Trio £400.90 OWNER Mr Hamdan Al Maktoum (ARUNDEL) BRED Shadwell Estate Company Limited

Ghataas fulfilled the promise of his debut on soft ground at Haydock last October. He showed how well he stays by finding more to repel the challenge of the runner-up. A Dante and Derby entry, he can go on from here. (7/2: 5/2-4/1)

Basman (IRE), out of a half-sister to Sil Sila, stayed on well after meeting traffic problems and can soon go one better. (100/1)

Redbridge (USA), a well-bred colt, displayed plenty of promise for the future and will not have to improve much to win a race. (4/1)

Pentad (USA), a half-brother to two sprinters, gets his stamina from his sire. Not knocked about when his chance had gone, this kindness will be repaid. (9/1)

Catchable had two runs over a mile last back-end and should have been suited by this step-up in distance. (4/1: 3/1-9/2)

Grapevine (IRE) does not look like living up to her entry in the Oaks. (10/1: op 5/1)

Right Wing (IRE) (9/1: 5/1-10/1)

726 NEWBURY RACECOURSE SHOPPING ARCADE RATED STKS H'CAP (0-100) (4-Y.O+) (Class B)

4-10 (4-20) **5f 34y** £8,379.60 (£3,116.40: £1,508.20: £631.00: £265.50: £119.30) Stalls: Centre GOING minus 0.02 sec per fur (G)

				SP	RR	SF
	Repertory (88) (MSSaunders) **4-8-9** RPerham(16) (hdwy over 1f out: led last strides)	—	**1**	50/1	94	57
	To the Roof (IRE) (99) (PWHarris) **5-9-6** KFallon(9) (a.p: led ins fnl f: hdd last strides)	s.h	**2**	11/1	105	68
520*	**Eastern Prophets (85)** (GLewis) **4-8-6** PaulEddery(19) (w ldr: ev ch 1f out: nt qckn)	¾	**3**	8/1[2]	89	52
	That Man Again (86) (SCWilliams) **5-8-7** KDarley(10) (led tl ins fnl f)	s.h	**4**	14/1	89	52
520[2]	**Sea-Deer (85)** (CADwyer) **8-8-6** PatEddery(15) (a.p: r.o wl ins fnl f)	nk	**5**	3/1[1]	87	50
	Hoh Returns (IRE) (90) (MBell) **4-8-11** MFenton(13) (lw: a.p: one pce fnl f)	½	**6**	16/1	91	54
	Mr Bergerac (IRE) (83) (BPalling) **6-8-4** TSprake(20) (nvr nr to chal)	hd	**7**	16/1	84	47
520[10]	**Sir Joey (USA) (83)** (PGMurphy) **8-8-4** DHolland(12) (prom over 3f)	2½	**8**	25/1	76	39
	Midnight Escape (95) (CFWall) **4-9-2** NCarlisle(8) (prom over 3f)	1¼	**9**	11/1	84	47
	Bowden Rose (88) (MBlanshard) **5-8-9b** JQuinn(2) (w ldr far side: wknd over 1f out)	1¾	**10**	40/1	72	35
	Amazing Bay (98) (IABalding) **4-9-5** TQuinn(11) (lw: prom over 3f)	1	**11**	20/1	78	41
	Samwar (93) (MissGayKelleway) **5-9-0** OPeslier(17) (n.d)	½	**12**	9/1[3]	72	35
452[7]	**Warning Time (95)** (BJMeehan) **4-9-2** RHughes(14) (n.d)	1¼	**13**	20/1	70	33
	Dashing Blue (100) (IABalding) **4-9-7** LDettori(5) (lw: racd far side: outpcd)	s.h	**14**	9/1[3]	75	38
443[6]	**Bold Effort (FR) (88)** (KOCunningham-Brown) **5-8-9b** DaneO'Neill(1) (led far side: wknd over 1f out)	1½	**15**	16/1	58	21
	Kilvine (85) (WJHaggas) **4-8-6** RCochrane(18) (b.off fore: s.s: a bhd)	nk	**16**	16/1	54	17
	White Emir (84) (BJMeehan) **4-8-5** BDoyle(3) (swtg: bit bkwd: racd far side: outpcd)	3	**17**	33/1	44	7
	Depreciate (88) (CJames) **4-8-9** JReid(7) (lw: outpcd)	8	**18**	40/1	23	—
	Hello Mister (99) (TEPowell) **6-9-3(3)** PMcCabe(4) (bit bkwd: swtchd stands' side: a bhd)	4	**19**	40/1	22	—
	Major Quality (94) (JRFanshawe) **4-9-1** DHarrison(6) (racd far side: a bhd: eased whn no ch over 1f out)	13	**20**	14/1	—	—
				(SP 135.2%)	**20 Rn**	

62.29 secs (2.09) CSF £494.87 CT £4,514.37 TOTE £111.40: £14.00 £2.90 £2.20 £2.80 (£675.10) Trio £1,853.40; £522.09 to Newbury 19/4/97 OWNER Mr M. S. Saunders (WELLS) BRED W. H. Joyce

LONG HANDICAP Mr Bergerac (IRE) 8-3 Sir Joey (USA) 8-3

Repertory, plagued by muscle problems when trained by Mick Channon, never lived up to his seasonal debut last season when second to Westcourt Magic. Bought for only 8,500 guineas, he took advantage of an 8lb drop in the ratings. (50/1)

To the Roof (IRE), who shot up two stone in the ratings last season, seems to be continuing to improve with age. (11/1: 8/1-12/1)

520* Eastern Prophets did his best to defy a 6lb hike in the weights. (8/1)

That Man Again, who normally wears blinkers, had slipped to a mark 8lb lower than when he last won at Haydock in August 1995. (14/1)

520 Sea-Deer, raised 4lb for his half-length defeat by Eastern Prophets, found top gear too late to turn the tables over this shorter trip. (3/1: op 5/1)

Hoh Returns (IRE) may be better suited by six furlongs. (16/1)

Mr Bergerac (IRE) is another who appears to need six. (16/1)

727 BRIDGET MAIDEN STKS (UNRACED 3-Y.O F) (Class D)

4-40 (4-51) **7f (straight)** £3,980.00 (£1,190.00: £570.00: £260.00) Stalls: Centre GOING minus 0.02 sec per fur (G)

			SP	RR	SF
Kool Kat Katie (IRE) (DRLoder) **3-8-11** OPeslier(17) (leggy: scope: hld up: nt clr run over 2f out: qcknd to ld ins fnl f: r.o wl)	—	**1**	2/1[1]	98	55
Island Lore (IRE) (EALDunlop) **3-8-8(3)** DO'Donohoe(6) (leggy: lt-f: a.p: led over 2f out tl ins fnl f)	1	**2**	12/1	96	53
Selfish (HRACecil) **3-8-11** KFallon(9) (w'like: scope: lw: hld up: rdn & nt clr run over 1f out: swtchd rt: r.o ins fnl f)	3½	**3**	7/1[3]	88	45
Sceptre Lady (IRE) (BWHills) **3-8-11** DHolland(7) (b: leggy: trckd ldrs: rdn over 2f out: r.o ins fnl f)	½	**4**	25/1	87	44
Jafn (BHanbury) **3-8-11** RHills(16) (w'like: scope: lw: a.p: ev ch over 2f out: wknd over 1f out)	1¼	**5**	20/1	84	41
Fantastic Flame (IRE) (PJMakin) **3-8-11** MRoberts(2) (w'like: nvr nr to chal)	2½	**6**	50/1	78	35
Keyboogie (USA) (RCharlton) **3-8-11** PatEddery(5) (str: scope: bit bkwd: prom: rdn over 2f out: wknd over 1f out)	nk	**7**	5/2[2]	77	34
Marie Dora (FR) (IABalding) **3-8-11** TQuinn(11) (leggy: led over 4f)	2½	**8**	33/1	72	29
Anchored In Love (RCharlton) **3-8-11** TSprake(18) (w'like: bit bkwd: nvr nrr)	s.h	**9**	50/1	72	29
St Radegund (GWragg) **3-8-11** MHills(4) (leggy: prom 5f)	2½	**10**	10/1	66	23
Mystery Hill (USA) (JHMGosden) **3-8-11** LDettori(3) (w'like: scope: prom 5f)	1½	**11**	9/1	62	19
Fur Will Fly (IABalding) **3-8-8(3)** MartinDwyer(1) (unf: prom over 4f)	4	**12**	50/1	53	10

	Bellagrana (MJFetherston-Godley) **3-8-11** DHarrison(15) (leggy: scope: a bhd)	6	**13**	66/1	40	—
	Magic Hill (JHMGosden) **3-8-11** WRyan(19) (w'like: scope: a bhd)	1½	**14**	33/1	36	—
	Nanouche (JLDunlop) **3-8-11** KDarley(14) (w'like: scope: a bhd)	2	**15**	14/1	32	—
	Doyenne (GLewis) **3-8-8**(3) AWhelan(12) (w'like: s.v.s: a bhd)	2½	**16**	66/1	26	—
	Mamma Luigi (IRE) (GLewis) **3-8-11** PaulEddery(8) (w'like: a bhd)	5	**17**	33/1	14	—
	Prinia (GLewis) **3-8-11** NDay(13) (b.hind: leggy: a bhd)	4	**18**	66/1	5	—
	Miss Imp (IRE) (PMitchell) **3-8-11** AClark(10) (b.nr fore: b.off hind: lt-f: s.s: a bhd)	1¼	**19**	66/1	2	—
				(SP 137.1%)	**19 Rn**	

1m 27.3 (3.20) CSF £26.04 TOTE £3.30: £1.80 £3.10 £3.80 (£38.00) Trio £64.00 OWNER Lucayan Stud (NEWMARKET) BRED Lucayan Stud Ltd

Kool Kat Katie (IRE), an athletic filly who had been reported to have been working very well at home, looks one to keep on the right side of. (2/1)
Island Lore (IRE), a half-sister to Winter Romance, was another to have been reported going well on Newmarket gallops, and should be hard to beat next time. (12/1: 7/1-14/1)
Selfish, a half-sister to Aratos, would not have beaten the first two even with a trouble-free run, but there was a lot to like about the way she knuckled down in the closing stages. Normal improvement will see her find a suitable opening. (7/1: 5/1-8/1)
Sceptre Lady (IRE) gave the distinct impression that she found this trip inadequate. (25/1)
Jafn, a half-sister to a German Group Three winner, will be better for the experience. (20/1)
Fantastic Flame (IRE), a sister to Germano, should do better when tried over further. (50/1)
Keyboogie (USA), who will be sharper for the outing, is another bred to need further. (5/2)
St Radegund (10/1: op 5/1)
Nanouche (14/1: 10/1-16/1)

728 LEVY BOARD SEVENTH RACE H'CAP (0-100) (4-Y.O+) (Class C)

5-10 (5-18) **2m** £5,393.75 (£1,625.00: £787.50: £368.75) Stalls: Low GOING minus 0.02 sec per fur (G)

				SP	RR	SF
	Canon Can (USA) (92) (HRACecil) **4-9-10** KFallon(10) (lw: hld up: hdwy 4f out: led 3f out: drvn out)	—	**1**	11/8[1]	106	47
	Top Cees (86) (MrsJRRamsden) **7-9-8** JFortune(6) (lw: hld up & bhd: hdwy over 3f out: ev ch over 1f out: sn rdn: eased whn btn nr fin)	3	**2**	11/1	97	42
	Otto E Mezzo (71) (MJPolglase) **5-8-7** TGMcLaughlin(2) (hld up: rdn 4f out: hdwy over 1f out: styd on wl ins fnl f)	¾	**3**	33/1	81	26
	Captain Jack (85) (MCPipe) **7-9-7** MRoberts(12) (lw: led 13f: sn outpcd: styd on fnl f)	hd	**4**	12/1	95	40
650*	**Dancing Cavalier (71)** (RHollinshead) **4-8-0**(3)ow2 4x FLynch(1) (hld up & bhd: hdwy over 2f out: edgd lft ins fnl f: one pce)	1½	**5**	11/2[2]	80	19
430[22]	**Tonnerre (60)** (BAMcMahon) **5-7-10** NCarlisle(4) (hld up & plld hrd: lost pl on ins over 5f out: plld out 3f out: one pce fnl 2f)	3½	**6**	50/1	65	10
	Castle Courageous (90) (LadyHerries) **10-9-12** JReid(11) (b: hld up mid div: bhd fnl 3f)	12	**7**	25/1	83	28
	Bolivar (IRE) (73) (RAkehurst) **5-8-9b** TQuinn(7) (lw: prom tl wknd over 2f out)	3½	**8**	6/1[3]	63	8
	Zaforum (96) (LMontagueHall) **4-10-0b** RHughes(9) (b: plld hrd: sn chsng ldr: rdn over 4f out: wknd over 3f out)	9	**9**	12/1	77	18
	Nanton Point (USA) (79) (LadyHerries) **5-9-1** JQuinn(3) (bit bkwd: a bhd: eased whn no ch fnl 2f)	25	**10**	14/1	35	—
442[9]	**Magic Combination (IRE) (85)** (BJCurley) **4-9-3** LDettori(8) (prom tl rdn & wknd 4f out: eased whn btn fnl 2f)	8	**11**	8/1	33	—
521[15]	**Caudillo (IRE) (72)** (MrsPNDutfield) **4-8-4**ow1 DHolland(5) (lw: hld up & bhd: hdwy over 5f out: wkdn over 2f out: eased whn btn)	dist	**12**	50/1	—	—
				(SP 124.0%)	**12 Rn**	

3m 36.15 (11.95) CSF £17.21 CT £338.36 TOTE £2.50: £1.60 £3.10 £8.30 (£14.60) Trio £294.40 OWNER Canon (Anglia) O A Ltd (NEWMARKET) BRED Elkay Stables
WEIGHT FOR AGE 4yo-4lb

Canon Can (USA), 8lb higher than when narrowly beaten in the Cesarewitch, again showed just how well he stays. (11/8)
Top Cees, 4lb higher than when winning at Newmarket last July, had to concede he had met one too good. (11/1)
Otto E Mezzo, fit from hurdling, probably ran his best race on the Flat since his two-year-old days. (33/1)
Captain Jack, disappointing over hurdles, needs real marathon distances on this evidence. (12/1)
650* **Dancing Cavalier** did not help his rider by wanting to go left-handed. (11/2: 4/1-6/1)
Tonnerre refused to settle and gave Carlisle a horrible ride. (50/1)
Zaforum (12/1: op 8/1)
442 Magic Combination (IRE) (8/1: 5/1-9/1)

T/Jkpt: Not won; £35,341.73 to Newbury 19/4/97. T/Plpt: £887.50 (38.19 Tckts). T/Qdpt: £191.30 (8.59 Tckts) KH\

THIRSK (L-H) (Good to firm, Good patches)
Friday April 18th
WEATHER: Overcast WIND: mod half against

729 BRITON MEDIAN AUCTION MAIDEN STKS (3 & 4-Y.O) (Class D)

2-20 (2-20) **6f** £3,730.00 (£1,120.00: £540.00: £250.00) Stalls: High GOING minus 0.10 sec per fur (G)

				SP	RR	SF
	Divine Miss-P (APJarvis) **4-9-5** WJO'Connor(7) (trckd ldrs: effrt ½-wy: r.o u.p to ld towards fin)	—	**1**	8/1	70	21
524[6]	**Two On The Bridge (72)** (DenysSmith) **3-8-13** LCharnock(10) (led tl towards fin)	nk	**2**	9/2[3]	74	14
	Prince of Parkes (JBerry) **3-8-13** GCarter(9) (sn chsng ldrs: effrt ½-wy: styd on same pce appr fnl f)	2	**3**	14/1	69	9
649[11]	**Supercharmer (67)** (DNicholls) **3-8-13** AlexGreaves(8) (lw: w ldrs: nt qckn appr fnl f)	¾	**4**	12/1	67	7
	Truly Parched (USA) (PWChapple-Hyam) **3-8-10**(3) RHavlin(6) (lw: w ldrs: rdn ½-wy: hung lft: wknd over 1f out)	2½	**5**	9/4[1]	60	—
	Look Who's Calling (IRE) (77) (BAMcMahon) **4-9-10** SSanders(1) (w ldrs tl rdn & wknd over 1f out: eased)	9	**6**	4/1[2]	36	—
	Zalotto (IRE) (TJEtherington) **3-8-13** GHind(2) (unruly in stalls: reard s: rn green & sn outpcd: nvr nr ldrs)	1½	**7**	9/1	32	—
	Clean Swop (IRE) (TDEasterby) **3-8-13** JCarroll(5) (w'like: bit bkwd: s.i.s: a outpcd & bhd)	11	**8**	33/1	3	—

				SP	RR	SF
577[4]	**Gloria Imperator (IRE) (41)** (ABMulholland) **4-9-10b** MBirch(4) (w ldrs: hung bdly lft thrght: lost pl ½-wy: virtually p.u)	7	**9**	50/1	—	—
				(SP 109.3%)	**9 Rn**	

1m 14.9 (5.20) CSF £36.45 TOTE £16.80: £2.70 £1.10 £2.60 (£17.10) Trio £51.60 OWNER Mrs Ann Jarvis (ASTON UPTHORPE) BRED C. C. Bromley and Son and A. O. Nerses

WEIGHT FOR AGE 3yo-11lb

Divine Miss-P was only able to have two outings last year before she fractured her pelvis. Sticking on in determined fashion, she will be even better suited by seven. (8/1)

524 Two On The Bridge, who presumably failed to stay a mile on his reappearance, tended to hang away from the fence but was only worn down near the line. (9/2)

Prince of Parkes, speedily bred, showed little in two outings as a juvenile. Backward in his coat, he is almost certainly capable of better in due course. (14/1)

287 Supercharmer as usual raced keenly. (12/1)

Truly Parched (USA), who looked fit and well was taken to post quietly. Tending to hang left under pressure, he is only very moderate if this is the best he can do. (9/4: evens-5/2)

Look Who's Calling (IRE), who showed wayward tendencies at three, kept straight here but, with his chance gone, he was eased up. He is certainly does not lack ability if only connections can get him sorted out. (4/1)

74 73 69 74

730 CLIFTON NOVICE STKS (2-Y.O F) (Class D)

2-50 (2-52) **5f** £3,626.00 (£1,088.00: £524.00: £242.00) Stalls: High GOING minus 0.10 sec per fur (G)

				SP	RR	SF
594[4]	**Penniless (IRE)** (NTinkler) **2-8-8** JWeaver(3) (lw: led over 1f: rdn ½-wy: styd on to ld wl ins fnl f)	—	**1**	6/1[3]	68	14
594*	**Out Like Magic** (PDEvans) **2-9-0** JFEgan(7) (chsd ldrs: sn drvn along: swtchd & ev ch wl ins fnl f: r.o)	hd	**2**	5/2[2]	74	20
525[4]	**Antonia's Double** (JBerry) **2-8-8** GCarter(2) (lw: led over 3f out: rdn jst ins fnl f: wknd & hdd towards fin)	1	**3**	9/4[1]	65	11
	Bodfaridistinction (IRE) (ABailey) **2-8-8** SSanders(4) (lengthy: unf: scope: sn chsng ldrs: outpcd ½-wy: kpt on wl fnl f)	¾	**4**	5/2[2]	62	8
	Positive Air (BAMcMahon) **2-8-8** LNewton(5) (leggy: scope: bit bkwd: dwlt s: rn green & a bhd)	10	**5**	10/1	30	—
	Gifted Bairn (IRE) (DNicholls) **2-8-8** AlexGreaves(6) (w'like: bit bkwd: chsd ldrs tl outpcd ½-wy: sn lost pl)	1½	**6**	14/1	25	—
	Dancing Em (TDEasterby) **2-8-8** MBirch(1) (leggy: unf: bit bkwd: swvd lft s: rn green & hung lft: sn bhd)	2	**7**	10/1	19	—
				(SP 127.0%)	**7 Rn**	

61.7 secs (4.10) CSF £22.11 TOTE £8.40: £3.10 £2.10 (£7.40) OWNER Consultco Ltd (MALTON) BRED Clinton Investments

594 Penniless (IRE), who broke smartly, stuck on under a determined ride to get back up near the line. (6/1)

594* Out Like Magic, unimpressive in appearance, ran really well under her 6lb penalty. Forced to switch, in the end she was just denied. (5/2: 7/4-11/4)

525 Antonia's Double looked really well and showed a fluent action going down. Racing keenly, she looked to have the race in the bag at halfway but, treading water just inside the last, was worn down near the line. A very speedy type, she looks ideally suited to a sharp turning track like Chester. (9/4: 6/4-5/2)

Bodfaridistinction (IRE), who looked very green on the way down, was apparently well-fancied to make a winning debut. Tapped for foot at halfway, she kept on in promising fashion in the closing stages, and will improve considerably for the outing. (5/2)

Positive Air, lightly-backed at long odds, looked in need of the outing and, very green going to post, gave away several lengths at the start. (10/1)

Dancing Em (10/1: 8/1-12/1)

731 HAMBLETON LIMITED STKS (0-80) (3-Y.O+) (Class D)

3-20 (3-23) **5f** £3,470.00 (£1,040.00: £500.00: £230.00) Stalls: High GOING minus 0.10 sec per fur (G)

				SP	RR	SF
584[2]	**Lamarita (78)** (JMPEustace) **3-8-5** JTate(4) (hld up: hdwy ½-wy: r.o wl to ld fnl 75y)	—	**1**	5/1[3]	82	37
	Lunar Mist (80) (MartynMeade) **4-8-10**(5) DSweeney(8) (chsd ldr: led over 1f out: rdn & edgd lft: hdd ins fnl f)	2	**2**	12/1	76	41
473*	**Malibu Man (77)** (EAWheeler) **5-9-2**(5) ADaly(5) (lw: led: clr ½-wy: hdd over 1f out: kpt on)	s.h	**3**	11/4[1]	81	46
434[12]	**Weet Ees Girl (IRE) (76)** (PDEvans) **3-8-5** JFEgan(9) (sn outpcd & drvn along: hdwy over 1f out: kpt on)	3½	**4**	14/1	64	19
643[8]	**Friendly Brave (USA) (77)** (MissGayKelleway) **7-9-4** WJO'Connor(6) (lw: chsd ldrs: rdn & wandered over 1f out: no imp)	¾	**5**	6/1	65	30
596[5]	**The Happy Fox (IRE) (79)** (BAMcMahon) **5-9-3b**(7) SRighton(2) (sn outpcd & bhd)	5	**6**	6/1	55	20
555[6]	**Divide And Rule (76)** (RHollinshead) **3-8-5**(3) DGriffiths(3) (chsd ldrs over 3f: sn lost pl)	½	**7**	14/1	47	2
464[7]	**Sweet Magic (75)** (PHowling) **6-9-4** FNorton(7) (chsd ldrs tl lost pl over 1f out)	2½	**8**	6/1	39	4
443[7]	**Garnock Valley (80)** (JBerry) **7-9-4b** GCarter(1) (outpcd after 1f: sn bhd)	¾	**9**	7/2[2]	37	2
				(SP 129.4%)	**9 Rn**	

60.1 secs (2.50) CSF £64.37 TOTE £6.60: £1.70 £2.00 £1.80 (£54.90) Trio £40.70 OWNER Park Lane Racing / Mrs D A La Trobe (NEWMARKET) BRED Britton House Stud

WEIGHT FOR AGE 3yo-10lb

584 Lamarita, a keen type, finished with a flourish to lead and shoot clear inside the last one-hundred yards. (5/1)

Lunar Mist, a winner six times as two-year-old, showed precious little in three outings last season. Turned out in good trim she probably ran close to her best. (12/1)

473* Malibu Man, who looked outstanding in the paddock, is very speedy. Showing in a clear lead at halfway on this watered ground and racing into a head-wind, he was collared over a furlong out. (11/4: op 9/2)

Weet Ees Girl (IRE), who trod water after winning at Nottingham a year ago, was staying on when it was all over and may be better suited by six now. (14/1)

643 Friendly Brave (USA) tended to wander under pressure. (6/1)

443 Garnock Valley could never go the pace over this trip and on this fast ground. (7/2: 5/2-4/1)

732 SOWERBY MAIDEN STKS (3-Y.O) (Class D)

3-50 (3-50) **1m 4f** £3,574.00 (£1,072.00: £516.00: £238.00) Stalls: High GOING minus 0.30 sec per fur (GF)

				SP	RR	SF
	Regait (MAJarvis) **3-9-0** PBloomfield(1) (chsd ldrs: drvn along & outpcd over 3f out: hdwy u.p to ld over 1f out: sn clr: eased towards fin)	—	**1**	14/1[3]	81+	32
	Percy Isle (IRE) (84) (MRStoute) **3-9-0** MBirch(4) (chsd ldr: led over 2f out: rdn & edgd rt & hdd over 1f out: kpt on same pce)	2½	**2**	10/11[1]	78	29
559[2]	**Surtsey** (MJohnston) **3-9-0** JWeaver(2) (led: rn green & hung rt thrght: hdd over 2f out: wknd fnl f)	8	**3**	11/10[2]	67	18

				SP	RR	SF
	Markapen (IRE) (CNAllen) **3-8-4**(5) GFaulkner(3) (sn chsng ldrs: pushed along 5f out: sn wl outpcd: bhd fnl 3f)	8	**4**	20/1	51?	2
				(SP 111.4%)	**4 Rn**	

2m 37.1 (6.40) CSF £26.03 TOTE £12.20 (£7.60) OWNER Sheikh Ahmed Al Maktoum (NEWMARKET) BRED Sheikh Ahmed Bin Rashid Al Maktoum

Regait, who has plenty of size and scope, is essentially a stayer. After being tapped for foot turning in he was right on top at the finish. (14/1)
Percy Isle (IRE), a good-bodied colt, carried plenty of condition but he possibly needed this for, after taking it up travelling nicely, in the end he was well run out of it. (10/11: evens-11/10)
559 Surtsey, who looked very fit, tended to duck right on the bends and, passing the stables entering the back straight, for one minute looked like running out. Carrying his head high, he looked in some distress coming to the final furlong and when all chance had gone he was eased up. He presumably has some sort of problem. (11/10: op evens)
Markapen (IRE) looked on the backward side and was easily left trailing. (20/1)

733 OAKSTRIPE H'CAP (0-65) (3-Y.O+) (Class F)

4-20 (4-21) **1m** £3,281.00 (£916.00: £443.00) Stalls: Low GOING minus 0.30 sec per fur (GF)

				SP	RR	SF
468[17]	**Paint It Black (50)** (DNicholls) **4-8-13** AlexGreaves(8) (trckd ldrs gng wl: led on bit over 1f out: cheekily)	—	**1**	16/1	60+	30
599[6]	**Dispol Gem (60)** (PCalver) **4-9-9** JCarroll(4) (in tch: effrt over 2f out: styd on ins fnl f: no ch w wnr)	¾	**2**	6/1[2]	69	39
	Riccarton (48) (PCalver) **4-8-11** MBirch(3) (hld up: hdwy & nt clr run over 2f out: squeezed thro & r.o wl ins fnl f)	nk	**3**	16/1	56	26
571[13]	**Godmersham Park (63)** (PSFelgate) **5-9-12** GDuffield(7) (led tl over 1f out: no ex)	nk	**4**	16/1	70	40
461[10]	**Spanish Verdict (60)** (DenysSmith) **10-9-4**(5) DSweeney(5) (bhd: hdwy & nt clr run over 1f out: styd on wl towards fin)	¾	**5**	12/1	66	36
587*	**Eurobox Boy (56)** (APJarvis) **4-9-5** WJO'Connor(12) (lw: mid div: effrt on outside 2f out: kpt on: nvr nr to chal)	¾	**6**	5/2[1]	60	30
663[5]	**Rymer's Rascal (58)** (EJAlston) **5-9-7** SDrowne(6) (lw: a in tch: no hdwy fnl 2f)	s.h	**7**	25/1	62	32
571[12]	**Euro Sceptic (IRE) (53)** (TDEasterby) **5-8-13b**(3) RHavlin(9) (in tch: effrt over 2f out: nvr nr to chal)	½	**8**	10/1	56	26
571[16]	**Tinklers Folly (63)** (RMWhitaker) **5-9-12** DeanMcKeown(2) (s.i.s: bhd: hdwy on ins over 1f out: nvr nr ldrs)	½	**9**	16/1	65	35
448[11]	**Jack Flush (IRE) (65)** (BSRothwell) **3-9-0** LCharnock(13) (chsd ldrs: edgd lft & wknd ins fnl f: eased)	½	**10**	16/1	66	22
468[9]	**Cee-Jay-Ay (54)** (JBerry) **10-8-12**(5) PRoberts(10) (dwlt s: bhd tl sme hdwy fnl 2f)	nk	**11**	12/1	55	25
	My Millie (47) (DWBarker) **4-8-7**(3) DarrenMoffatt(16) (bit bkwd: a in rr)	s.h	**12**	25/1	48	18
294[7]	**Bernard Seven (IRE) (60)** (MDods) **5-9-9b** JWeaver(1) (chsd ldrs: wkng whn hmpd ins fnl f: eased)	1½	**13**	9/1[3]	58	28
	Polar Refrain (53) (JNorton) **4-9-2** GHind(11) (bit bkwd: racd wd: a bhd)	4	**14**	20/1	43	13
571[17]	**Superpride (58)** (MrsMReveley) **5-9-7** ACulhane(17) (sn drvn along: sn chsng ldrs: lost pl over 1f out: eased)	½	**15**	10/1	47	17
574[11]	**Stolen Music (IRE) (50)** (REBarr) **4-8-8**(5) PFessey(14) (s.s: racd wd: a bhd)	1½	**16**	25/1	36	6
	Mr Cube (IRE) (55) (JMBradley) **7-8-13b**(5) RFfrench(15) (mid div: hdwy on outside over 2f out: sn chsng ldrs: hung lft & wknd over 1f out)	¾	**17**	14/1	39	9
571[6]	**Lachesis (50)** (DShaw) **4-8-10b**(3) CTeague(18) (racd wd: bhd fnl 2f: t.o)	20	**18**	9/1[3]	—	—
				(SP 148.8%)	**18 Rn**	

1m 40.6 (4.10) CSF £114.28 CT £1,497.73 TOTE £20.70: £3.60 £2.00 £5.50 £6.80 (£50.30) Trio £304.20; £351.39 to Newbury 19/4/97
OWNER Mr M. A. Scaife (THIRSK) BRED Brian Winn
WEIGHT FOR AGE 3yo-14lb

OFFICIAL EXPLANATION **Paint It Black: had been gelded during the winter and had only recently come to himself. In addition, he was better suited by a furlong further and a more experienced rider on this occasion.**

233 Paint It Black, who has tumbled down the weights, is now a gelding. Travelling supremely well throughout, he never came off the bit. (16/1)
599 Dispol Gem, who looked very fit, never gave up trying, but her cause was always a forlorn one so easily was the winner travelling. (6/1)
Riccarton, still a maiden after ten outings, finished strongly after meeting plenty of trouble. (16/1)
Godmersham Park, an excitable type, ran easily his best race for his new trainer. (16/1)
Spanish Verdict, who has thirteen career wins, was putting in some good work at the finish after having a poor run. He loves firm ground and will certainly be adding to his record again this year. (12/1)
587* Eurobox Boy, who will race off a 6lb higher mark in the future, found this opposition much tougher than the weak handicap he claimed at Nottingham. (5/2)

734 BIRDFORTH H'CAP (0-70) (3-Y.O+) (Class E)

4-50 (4-52) **7f** £3,471.75 (£1,044.00: £504.50: £234.75) Stalls: Low GOING minus 0.30 sec per fur (GF)

				SP	RR	SF
702[4]	**Meranti (49)** (JMBradley) **4-8-2**(5) 6x RFfrench(3) (chsd ldrs: rdn to ld over 1f out: styd on)	—	**1**	2/1[1]	61	43
610*	**Foist (56)** (MWEasterby) **5-8-9**(5) 6x GParkin(15) (in tch: outpcd over 2f out: hdwy over 1f out: r.o wl towards fin)	¾	**2**	5/1[2]	66	48
468[7]	**Naughty Pistol (USA) (54)** (PDEvans) **5-8-12b[1]** JFEgan(10) (in tch: hdwy 2f out: styd on ins fnl f)	nk	**3**	14/1	64	46
571*	**Gulf Shaadi (64)** (EJAlston) **5-9-8** SDrowne(14) (hld up: hdwy on outside 2f out: styd on ins fnl f: nt rch ldrs)	hd	**4**	10/1	73	55
608*	**Rambo Waltzer (69)** (DNicholls) **5-9-6**(7) IonaWands(7) (lw: hld up: stdy hdwy 2f out: styd on ins fnl f: nt rch ldrs)	½	**5**	7/1[3]	77	59
201[8]	**Twin Creeks (52)** (VSoane) **6-8-10** CRutter(11) (lw: a chsng ldrs: kpt on same pce appr fnl f)	½	**6**	14/1	59	41
526[7]	**Kid Ory (46)** (DWChapman) **6-8-4** LCharnock(8) (chsd ldrs: one pce appr fnl f)	½	**7**	16/1	52	34
	Gymcrak Flyer (60) (GHolmes) **6-9-4** NConnorton(4) (b.nr hind: hdwy on ins 2f out: n.m.r 1f out: kpt on wl)	1¾	**8**	11/1	62	44
579[15]	**Komlucky (49)** (ABMulholland) **5-8-2v**(5) DSweeney(5) (w ldrs: led over 2f out tl over 1f out: sn wknd)	s.h	**9**	12/1	51	33
	Flying Pennant (IRE) (68) (JMBradley) **4-9-12** SSanders(1) (bit bkwd: unruly s: led tl over 2f out: wknd over 1f out)	5	**10**	16/1	58	40
275[9]	**Gormire (55)** (JHetherton) **4-8-13** ACulhane(6) (s.i.s: a bhd)	3	**11**	25/1	39	21
571[3]	**Genuine John (IRE) (67)** (JParkes) **4-9-6**(5) JBramhill(12) (in tch: rdn over 2f out: n.d)	nk	**12**	8/1	50	32
529[9]	**Somerton Boy (IRE) (66)** (PCalver) **7-9-10** MBirch(13) (sn drvn along & bhd)	1¼	**13**	14/1	46	28
560[8]	**Time of Night (USA) (67)** (RGuest) **4-9-8**(3) DGriffiths(9) (hld up & bhd: effrt over 2f out: n.d)	nk	**14**	16/1	46	28
	Midday Cowboy (USA) (68) (MDHammond) **4-9-12** GDuffield(2) (s.i.s: a in rr)	4	**15**	20/1	38	20
327[10]	**Ticka Ticka Timing (46)** (BWMurray) **4-8-4**ow1 VHalliday(16) (bhd fr ½-wy: t.o)	17	**16**	33/1	—	—
				(SP 147.9%)	**16 Rn**	

1m 26.9 (2.00) CSF £12.33 CT £129.97 TOTE £4.70: £1.20 £1.80 £2.50 £2.70 (£7.50) Trio £156.00 OWNER Mr John Wallis (CHEPSTOW)
BRED K. Birkinshaw

702 Meranti, having his second outing in two days, will have 6lb more on his back in the future. (2/1)

610* Foist, tapped for foot at one stage, was reeling in the winner at the line. He would not want the ground any firmer than this. (5/1: op 5/2)
254 Naughty Pistol (USA), in blinkers for the first time, is about a stone better mare on the All-Weather. (14/1)
571* Gulf Shaadi was racing from a 5lb higher mark. (10/1)
608* Rambo Waltzer, racing from a 4lb higher mark was certainly not knocked about. (7/1)
Gymcrak Flyer, racing from a mark 3lb lower than when successful at Yarmouth in July, shaped with plenty of promise and was by no means knocked about. (11/1)

T/Plpt: £2,947.60 (3.5 Tckts). T/Qdpt: £412.70 (2.22 Tckts) WG

0722-NEWBURY (L-H) (Good to firm)
Saturday April 19th
WEATHER: overcast WIND: mod half bhd

735 GRUNDON RECYCLE H'CAP (0-85) (3-Y.O+) (Class D)
2-00 (2-02) **1m 2f 6y** £6,352.50 (£1,920.00: £935.00: £442.50) Stalls: Low GOING minus 0.13 sec per fur (G)

	Horse	Dist	Pos	SP	RR	SF
450[22]	**Rockforce (83)** (MRChannon) **5-10-0** RHughes(11) (stdy hdwy 4f out: led on bit over 2f out: rdn over 1f out: r.o wl)	—	**1**	25/1	99	50
	Virtual Reality (72) (JARToller) **6-9-3** SSanders(2) (bkwd: a.p: chsd wnr over 1f out: unable qckn)	2½	**2**	25/1	84	35
	Ashby Hill (IRE) (69) (RRowe) **6-9-0** RCochrane(8) (bit bkwd: stdy hdwy over 2f out: rdn over 1f out: r.o one pce)	6	**3**	12/1	71	22
647[10]	**Punkah (USA) (76)** (GMMcCourt) **4-9-0**(7) RStudholme(10) (hdwy over 2f out: r.o one pce)	2½	**4**	33/1	74	25
*566**	**Anak-Ku (70)** (MissGayKelleway) **4-9-1** KFallon(6) (led 8f out tl over 2f out: wknd over 1f out)	nk	**5**	14/1	68	19
521[9]	**Royal Seaton (82)** (MrsPNDutfield) **8-9-13** DHolland(20) (bit bkwd: stdy hdwy fnl 2f: nvr nrr)	2	**6**	25/1	77	28
521[17]	**Docklands Limo (80)** (BJMcMath) **4-9-11** TQuinn(12) (hld up: rdn over 3f out: wknd over 2f out)	¾	**7**	16/1	74	25
	Shining Example (70) (PJMakin) **5-9-1** JFortune(21) (bkwd: hrd rdn over 2f out: nvr nrr)	1¼	**8**	20/1	62	13
	Bay of Islands (77) (DMorris) **5-9-8** NDay(19) (bkwd: a mid div)	2½	**9**	33/1	65	16
657[3]	**Pay Homage (68)** (IABalding) **9-8-6**(7) RFowley(7) (a mid div)	½	**10**	20/1	55	6
499[6]	**Myrtle Quest (76)** (RCharlton) **5-9-7** TSprake(22) (s.s: nvr nrr)	hd	**11**	11/1[3]	63	14
657[2]	**Vola Via (USA) (80)** (IABalding) **4-9-11** LDettori(15) (hdwy over 3f out: wknd wl over 1f out)	hd	**12**	11/2[2]	67	18
521[19]	**Serendipity (FR) (80)** (BRMillman) **4-9-11** WJO'Connor(4) (lw: hdwy over 3f out: wknd over 1f out)	2½	**13**	20/1	63	14
	Shaft of Light (80) (LordHuntingdon) **5-9-11** DHarrison(17) (bit bkwd: led 2f: wknd over 2f out)	1	**14**	25/1	61	12
	Edan Heights (77) (SDow) **5-9-3**(5) ADaly(1) (bit bkwd: hld up: rdn over 3f out: sn wknd)	1¾	**15**	20/1	55	6
521[5]	**Hardy Dancer (74)** (GLMoore) **5-9-5** SWhitworth(9) (bhd fnl 4f)	½	**16**	5/1[1]	51	2
	Grand Splendour (75) (LadyHerries) **4-9-6** AClark(14) (bkwd: prom over 4f)	12	**17**	12/1	33	—
	Fletcher (85) (HMorrison) **3-8-13** DaneO'Neill(5) (prom 6f)	5	**18**	40/1	35	—
	Green Bopper (USA) (68) (CPMorlock) **4-8-13** RPerham(16) (bhd fnl 5f)	11	**19**	66/1	1	—
	Pistol (IRE) (77) (CAHorgan) **7-9-8** PaulEddery(3) (b.nr hind: bit bkwd: dwlt: a bhd)	3	**20**	14/1	5	—
	Opalette (70) (LadyHerries) **4-9-1** DeclanO'Shea(13) (bkwd: bhd fnl 4f)	3	**21**	25/1	—	—
	Diminutive (USA) (80) (JWHills) **4-9-8**(3) MHenry(18) (bit bkwd: bhd fnl 3f)	1¾	**22**	25/1	—	—

(SP 126.9%) **22 Rn**

2m 10.34 (6.34) CSF £481.11 CT £6,973.43 TOTE £29.70: £5.00 £10.80 £3.30 £13.10 (£1,127.30) Trio £1,076.50; £1,364.64 to 21/4/97
OWNER Mr G. Z. Mizel (UPPER LAMBOURN) BRED Guest Leasing and Bloodstock Co
WEIGHT FOR AGE 3yo-17lb

Rockforce, reportedly claustrophobic, and with just one run under his belt since August 1995, bounced back to form in fine style. Cruising into the lead on the bridle over a quarter-of-a-mile from home, he was shaken up below the distance and, together with the second, pulled well clear of the remainder. (25/1)
Virtual Reality, who has changed stables since his last run back in October 1995, was carrying plenty of condition but still ran very well. Giving chase to the winner below the distance, he was unable to reel in that rival but still finished well clear of the remainder. He needs to be given time to recover from this, as horses who perform well after a lengthy lay-off often flop on their second start. (25/1)
Ashby Hill (IRE), looking in need of this seasonal bow, still gave a good account of herself, staying on nicely in the last three furlongs to take third prize. Despite rising considerably in the weights last year - her first win came off 41 and her last off 65 - she looks set for another successful campaign. (12/1)
291* Punkah (USA) began a forward move on the outside of the field over a quarter-of-a-mile from home, and struggled on for fourth prize. (33/1)
566* Anak-Ku did a lot of the donkey work, but he was collared over a quarter-of-a-mile from home and soon put in his place. (14/1)
Royal Seaton still looking in need of this, only his second run since October 1994, was not subjected to a hard time, but caught the eye as he steadily weaved his way through the pack in the final quarter-mile to be nearest at the line. He looks one to bear in mind as he comes to hand. (25/1)
499 Myrtle Quest (11/1: 8/1-12/1)
657 Vola Via (USA) (11/2: 7/1-9/2)

736 LANES END JOHN PORTER STKS (Gp 3) (4-Y.O+) (Class A)
2-30 (2-31) **1m 4f 5y** £20,940.00 (£7,842.00: £3,771.00: £1,647.00) Stalls: Low GOING minus 0.13 sec per fur (G)

	Horse	Dist	Pos	SP	RR	SF
	Whitewater Affair (107) (MRStoute) **4-8-8** OPeslier(13) (a.p: led wl over 1f out: drvn out)	—	**1**	20/1	119	44
	Ela-Aristokrati (IRE) (114) (MHTompkins) **5-8-12** RCochrane(2) (nt clr run over 3f out: hdwy over 2f out: n.m.r & swtchd rt ins fnl f: r.o wl)	½	**2**	10/1	121	47
	Kutta (111) (RWArmstrong) **5-8-12** RHills(10) (lw: hld up: rdn over 2f out: edgd lft & ev ch ins fnl f: r.o)	s.h	**3**	11/2[3]	121	47
	Salmon Ladder (USA) (113) (PFICole) **5-9-1** TQuinn(11) (led over 10f: wknd 1f out)	5	**4**	5/2[1]	118	44
	Election Day (IRE) (113) (MRStoute) **5-8-12** KFallon(9) (rdn over 4f out: nvr nr to chal)	6	**5**	12/1	107	33
522[3]	**Proper Blue (USA) (103)** (TGMills) **4-8-11** SSanders(1) (nt clr run & swtchd rt over 3f out: hdwy over 1f out: wknd fnl f)	1¾	**6**	14/1	104	29
	Sacrament (117) (MRStoute) **6-9-3** WRSwinburn(3) (bit bkwd: hdwy over 3f out: wknd 2f out)	3½	**7**	13/2	105	31
	Chief Contender (IRE) (110) (PWChapple-Hyam) **4-8-11** JReid(8) (lw: bhd fnl 6f)	5	**8**	16/1	93	18
	Lord Jim (IRE) (104) (LordHuntingdon) **5-8-12v** DaneO'Neill(12) (bit bkwd: prom over 9f)	2½	**9**	50/1	90	16
	Samraan (USA) (115) (JLDunlop) **4-8-11** LDettori(6) (lw: hdwy over 3f out: wknd over 2f out)	s.h	**10**	5/1[2]	90	15
	Mongol Warrior (USA) (LordHuntingdon) **4-9-2** DHarrison(7) (hld up: rdn over 3f out: wknd over 2f out)	nk	**11**	33/1	94	19

	Horse	Btn	Pos	SP	RR	SF
	Beauchamp Jade (100) (HCandy) **5-8-9** CRutter(4) (bhd fnl 3f)	3½	**12**	33/1	82	8
	Air Quest (RCharlton) **4-8-11** PatEddery(5) (bit bkwd: prom over 8f)	½	**13**	12/1	84	9

(SP 123.6%) **13 Rn**

2m 35.63 (5.63) CSF £189.94 TOTE £26.60: £5.40 £3.40 £2.40 (£80.10) Trio £197.90 OWNER Mr J. M. Greetham (NEWMARKET) BRED J. M. Greetham

WEIGHT FOR AGE 4yo-1lb

Whitewater Affair made a fine return to action, leading early in the final quarter-mile and responding to pressure to keep her two persistent rivals at bay. The Yorkshire Cup is next on the agenda. (20/1)

Ela-Aristokrati (IRE), formerly with Luca Cumani, made a very pleasing reappearance for his new stable. Managing to get a clear run to pick up ground over a quarter-of-a-mile from home, he was not done many favours by the third early inside the final furlong, but nevertheless ran on really strongly in the closing stages. Although he is yet to win a Listed or Group Three event, it would be a big disappointment if that was not remedied before long. (10/1)

Kutta made a very pleasing reappearance on ground livelier then he would have wanted. Throwing down a determined challenge in the final quarter-mile, he gave his all and only just lost out. (11/2)

Salmon Ladder (USA) developed into a really useful performer last season, showing tremendous battling qualities on countless occasions. Adopting his usual front-running role, he was collared early in the final quarter-mile and was soon put in his place. You are always guaranteed a good run for your money from this honest individual, and another successful campaign looks in store. (5/2)

Election Day (IRE) did not look happy from a long way out on this fast surface, and could never get in a blow. Cut in the ground looks the key to him. (12/1)

522 Proper Blue (USA), the only one with a recent run under his belt, failed to make that tell, finding this class and trip too much for him.(14/1)

Sacrament (13/2: 4/1-7/1)

Samraan (USA) (5/1: op 3/1)

737 TRIPLEPRINT GREENHAM STKS (Gp 3) (3-Y.O C & G) (Class A)

3-00 (3-01) **7f (straight)** £19,500.00 (£7,290.00: £3,495.00: £1,515.00) Stalls: Centre GOING minus 0.13 sec per fur (G)

	Horse	Btn	Pos	SP	RR	SF
	Yalaietanee (MRStoute) **3-9-0** LDettori(3) (a.p: rdn 2f out: led ins fnl f: r.o wl)	—	**1**	5/1 3	123	64
	Revoque (IRE) (PWChapple-Hyam) **3-9-0** JReid(4) (h.d.w: lw: chsd ldr: led over 1f out tl ins fnl f: r.o wl)	hd	**2**	11/8 1	123	64
	Muchea (118) (MRChannon) **3-9-0** RHughes(1) (lw: hld up: rdn over 2f out: unable qckn fnl f)	2	**3**	11/1	118	59
	In Command (IRE) (117) (BWHills) **3-9-0** MHills(6) (bit bkwd: led over 5f)	1½	**4**	5/1 3	115	56
	The West (USA) (113) (PFICole) **3-9-0** TQuinn(2) (h.d.w: lw: hld up: rdn 2f out: sn wknd)	6	**5**	100/30 2	101	42
449 4	**Hayes Way (IRE) (96)** (TGMills) **3-9-0** SSanders(5) (lw: hld up: rdn 3f out: wknd over 2f out)	17	**6**	66/1	62	3

(SP 108.3%) **6 Rn**

1m 26.07 (1.97) CSF £10.45 TOTE £5.10: £1.90 £1.60 (£4.10) OWNER Maktoum Al Maktoum (NEWMARKET) BRED Gainsborough Stud Management Ltd

Yalaietanee, the unknown quantity in the field, made a fine start to his three-year-old career. Woken up a quarter-of-a-mile from home, he just managed to poke a head in front inside the final furlong and held on well. At his best with some cut according to connections, he may well go for the French 2,000 Guineas where the ground is often easier. (5/1)

Revoque (IRE), unbeaten last season and rated the top juvenile, has done very well over the winter and, despite being a lazy individual at home, looked in good shape for this reappearance. However, the drop to seven furlongs and the moderate pace were both against him, although he managed to show with a narrow advantage below the distance. Collared inside the final furlong, he kept on really well but was unable to get back on top. This run will have sharpened him up and, over a mile and in a much faster-run race, he should be a different proposition in the 2,000 Guineas. (11/8: 11/10-evens)

Muchea, a useful sprinter last season, coped with this longer trip and was only about a length or so down on the front two below the distance before tapped for toe. (11/1: 8/1-12/1)

In Command (IRE), last year's Dewhurst winner, gave the impression the run would do him good - he is a laid-back individual according to connections - and so it proved for, after setting a moderate pace, he was collared below the distance and soon done with. (5/1: 7/2-11/2)

The West (USA) has done well over the winter, but was very disappointing and had shot his bolt early in the final quarter-mile. (100/30)

449 Hayes Way (IRE) was completely out of his depth. (66/1)

738 LADBROKE SPRING CUP H'CAP (0-105) (4-Y.O+) (Class B)

3-30 (3-31) **1m 7y (round)** £18,075.00 (£5,475.00: £2,675.00: £1,275.00) Stalls: Low GOING: minus 0.13 sec per fur (G)

	Horse	Btn	Pos	SP	RR	SF
450 9	**Hunters of Brora (IRE) (85)** (JDBethell) **7-8-11** DHolland(8) (in rr: hdwy, edgd rt & led over 1f out: hrd rdn & wandered ins fnl f: r.o wl: fin 1st: disq: plcd last)		**1d**	16/1	98	38
450 2	**Hawksley Hill (IRE) (94)** (MrsJRRamsden) **4-9-6** JFortune(17) (hdwy & edgd lft over 1f out: ev ch ins fnl f: unable qckn: fin 2nd, 2l: awrdd r)	—	**1**	5/1 1	103	43
433 6	**Lonely Leader (IRE) (100)** (RHannon) **4-9-12** DaneO'Neill(11) (lw: swtchd lft over 2f out: hdwy over 1f out: hrd rdn: r.o one pce: fin 3rd: plcd 2nd)	2	**2**	33/1	105	45
	Saifan (86) (DMorris) **8-8-12b** NDay(18) (n.m.r 3f out: hdwy over 2f out: hrd rdn & ev ch 1f out: one pce: fin 4th: plcd 3rd)	nk	**3**	25/1	90	30
	Almond Rock (96) (JRFanshawe) **5-9-8** DHarrison(9) (bit bkwd: stdy hdwy over 3f out: led wl over 1f out: sn hdd: wknd fnl f: fin 5th: plcd 4th)	nk	**4**	25/1	100	40
450 7	**Sky Dome (IRE) (87)** (MHTompkins) **4-8-13** RHills(7) (w ldr 6f: eased whn btn fnl f: fin 6th: plcd 5th)	5	**5**	15/2 2	81	21
	Medieval Lady (86) (IABalding) **4-8-12** RCochrane(19) (swtg: s.s: hdwy over 1f out: nvr nrr: fin 7th: plcd 6th)	nk	**6**	20/1	79	19
	Forza Figlio (86) (MissGayKelleway) **4-8-12** OPeslier(3) (bkwd: a.p: rdn over 3f out: eased whn btn fnl f: fin 8th: plcd 7th)	1	**7**	20/1	77	17
	Yalta (IRE) (86) (RCharlton) **4-8-12** PatEddery(16) (led over 6f: fin 9th: plcd 8th)	1¾	**8**	11/1	74	14
	Unitus (IRE) (95) (MRStoute) **4-9-7** JReid(2) (plld hrd: a mid div: fin 10th: plcd 9th)	3	**9**	9/1 3	77	17
	Cadeaux Tryst (102) (EALDunlop) **5-9-11**(3) DO'Donohoe(10) (b: bit bkwd: a.p: ev ch wl over 1f out: wkng whn hmpd over 1f out: fin 11th: plcd 10th)	nk	**10**	16/1	83	23
450*	**Kuala Lipis (USA) (92)** (PFICole) **4-9-4** TQuinn(15) (lw: nvr nrr: fin 12th: plcd 11th)	2½	**11**	9/1 3	68	8
	Lionize (USA) (94) (PWChapple-Hyam) **4-9-6** PaulEddery(14) (lw: hld up: rdn over 4f out: sn wknd: fin 13th: plcd 12th)	4	**12**	20/1	62	2
	Al Abraq (IRE) (92) (JWHills) **4-9-4** MHills(5) (lw: a bhd: fin 14th: plcd 13th)	½	**13**	14/1	59	—
521 2	**Secret Aly (CAN) (85)** (CEBrittain) **7-8-11** BDoyle(1) (mid div whn bdly hmpd on ins over 2f out: fin 15th: plcd 14th)	6	**14**	16/1	40	—

				SP	RR	SF
	Go Britannia (87) (DRLoder) **4-8-13** LDettori(4) (bit bkwd: hld up: rdn over 3f out: sn wknd: fin 16th: plcd 15th)	s.h	**15**	10/1	42	—
450[15]	**Grand Musica (92)** (IABalding) **4-9-1**(3) MartinDwyer(6) (lw: prom 6f: fin 17th: plcd 16th)	¾	**16**	20/1	46	—
450[5]	**Kala Sunrise (86)** (CSmith) **4-8-12** WJO'Connor(20) (bhd fnl 4f: fin 18th: plcd 17th)	½	**17**	14/1	39	—
433[3]	**Band on the Run (90)** (BAMcMahon) **10-9-2** SSanders(12) (prom over 5f: fin 19th: plcd 18th)	6	**18**	20/1	31	—

(SP 131.3%) **19 Rn**

1m 40.48 (4.48) CSF £176.18 CT £3,509.95 TOTE £4.30: £1.80 £6.80 £8.30 £5.20 (£185.70) Trio £3,692.10 OWNER Mr P. R. C. Morrison (THIRSK) BRED The Wickfield Stud Ltd

STEWARDS' ENQUIRY Holland susp 2-5/5/97 (careless riding). (Amended from irresponsible riding following appeal).

450 Hawksley Hill (IRE), who officially improved by over three stone last year, continues to run well. Picking up ground and drifting to his left below the distance, doing Cadeaux Tryst no favours, he threw down a very determined challenge inside the final furlong but found Hunters of Brora too good. However, he was awarded the race later on. (5/1: 7/1-9/2)

433 Lonely Leader (IRE) left his Doncaster reappearance well behind. Picking up ground below the distance, he stayed on well. (33/1)

Saifan made a pleasing reappearance. Launching his challenge below the distance, he had every chance entering the final furlong before tapped for toe. (25/1)

Almond Rock struck the front a furlong and a half from home, but he was soon collared and tired in the last two hundred yards. (25/1)

450 Sky Dome (IRE) disputed the lead until the quarter-mile marker, and was given an easy time of it when all chance had evaporated in the final furlong. (15/2)

Medieval Lady caught the eye on this reappearance, making steady progress from the back of the field in the final quarter-mile to be nearest at the line. She looks one to note. (20/1)

Cadeaux Tryst had every chance early in the final quarter-mile, but was beginning to feel the pinch when hampered by both Hawksley Hill and Hunters of Brora approaching the final furlong. (16/1)

450 Hunters of Brora (IRE) picked up ground nicely but, just before she struck the front below the distance, she was manoeuvred right, doing Cadeaux Tryst no favours. Engaged in a tremendous tussle with Hawksley Hill in the final furlong despite wandering about, she held on well. Unfortunately she was later disqualified and Holland handed a suspension. (16/1)

67 78+ 68 67

739 NETHERAVON MEDIAN AUCTION MAIDEN STKS (2-Y.O F) (Class D)

4-00 (4-03) **5f 34y** £3,817.50 (£1,140.00: £545.00: £247.50) Stalls: Centre GOING minus 0.13 sec per fur (G)

				SP	RR	SF
536[8]	**Supreme Angel** (MPMuggeridge) **2-8-8**(3) MHenry(9) (hld up: hdwy over 1f out: led ins fnl f: r.o)	—	**1**	33/1	69	10
557[2]	**Arian Da** (BPalling) **2-8-11** TSprake(5) (led tl ins fnl f)	nk	**2**	13/2 [3]	68	9
	Chrysalis (PFICole) **2-8-11** TQuinn(10) (w'like: b: bit bkwd: a.p: ev ch over 1f out: one pce)	2½	**3**	3/1 [1]	60	1
	Princess Londis (AGFoster) **2-8-11** RPerham(4) (b: neat: bkwd: a.p: rdn & ev ch 2f out: one pce)	s.h	**4**	33/1	60	1
	Ring The Rafters (IABalding) **2-8-11** LDettori(12) (w'like: bit bkwd: swvd rt s: sn rcvrd: wknd over 1f out)	3	**5**	3/1 [1]	51	—
	Face-Off (RHannon) **2-8-11** DaneO'Neill(1) (unf: s.s: nvr nrr)	hd	**6**	14/1	51	—
	Sun In The Morning (BJMeehan) **2-8-11** BDoyle(3) (w'like: mid div whn carried lft wl over 1f out: nt rcvr)	1½	**7**	12/1	46	—
	Dixie Crossroads (RHannon) **2-8-11** RHughes(6) (lengthy: scope: s.i.s: a bhd)	s.h	**8**	16/1	46	—
	Burning Love (JSMoore) **2-8-11** KFallon(11) (lengthy: unf: prom: rdn over 2f out: wknd wl over 1f out)	hd	**9**	8/1	45	—
583[5]	**Magical Dancer (IRE)** (MrsPNDutfield) **2-8-11** DHolland(7) (prom: wkng whn edgd lft wl over 1f out)	2	**10**	16/1	39	—
	Phone Alex (IRE) (RHannon) **2-8-11** PatEddery(2) (unf: bit bkwd: s.s: a bhd)	½	**11**	5/1 [2]	38	—
	Hamerra (IRE) (MartynMeade) **2-8-6**(5) DSweeney(8) (lt-f: bhd fnl 2f)	4	**12**	20/1	25	—

(SP 127.9%) **12 Rn**

64.77 secs (4.57) CSF £226.81 TOTE £75.20: £11.40 £1.90 £1.20 (£127.80) Trio £397.70; £280.09 to 21/4/97 OWNER Least Moved Partners (LAMBOURN) BRED K. J. and Mrs Sims

IN-FOCUS: **A poor race by Newbury standards.**

Supreme Angel, a sister to Patsy Grimes, was a springer in the market when slowly away in a similar event on her Warwick debut, and had obviously shown ability at home. (33/1)

557 Arian Da, a sister to Super High, put her previous experience to good use, but could not hold the winner. (13/2: 5/1-8/1)

Chrysalis, a half-sister to juvenile winners Vivienda and Thick As Thieves, gave the impression beforehand that her trainer had left something to work on. (3/1)

Princess Londis, a half-sister to two-year-old winner Satisfied Prince, ran well considering her paddock appearance, and is sure to come on for this. (33/1)

Ring The Rafters, a half-sister to Trumpet and Zenith, is fully entitled to require further on breeding. (3/1)

Face-Off, a 35,000 guineas half-sister to Sheer Face, could never recover from a poor start, but will have learnt from this. (14/1: 8/1-16/1)

Sun In The Morning, a half-sister to Able Sheriff, was hampered and this run is best forgotten. (12/1: op 8/1)

Phone Alex (IRE) (5/1: 5/2-6/1)

740 BOB RILEY 50TH BIRTHDAY MAIDEN STKS (I) (3-Y.O) (Class D)

4-30 (4-37) **1m (straight)** £3,427.50 (£1,020.00: £485.00: £217.50) Stalls: Centre GOING minus 0.13 sec per fur (G)

				SP	RR	SF
	Rashik (MajorWRHern) **3-9-0** RHills(10) (w'like: scope: a.p: led over 1f out: r.o wl)	—	**1**	12/1	103	57
	Alezal (WJarvis) **3-9-0** OPeslier(5) (bit bkwd: a.p: led over 2f out tl over 1f out: nt qckn)	1½	**2**	13/2	100	54
	Greek Palace (IRE) (MRStoute) **3-9-0** WRSwinburn(3) (unf: scope: hld up: hdwy over 2f out: sn rdn: one pce)	2½	**3**	100/30 [1]	95	49
	Memorise (USA) (HRACecil) **3-9-0** KFallon(15) (w ldr: rdn over 2f out: one pce)	s.h	**4**	6/1 [3]	95	49
	Praeditus (RHannon) **3-9-0** DaneO'Neill(2) (bit bkwd: led over 5f: wknd over 1f out)	8	**5**	20/1	79	33
518[3]	**Foreign Rule (IRE)** (PWChapple-Hyam) **3-9-0** JReid(9) (lw: no hdwy fnl 3f)	nk	**6**	11/2 [2]	78	32
	Smart Kid (IRE) (PFICole) **3-9-0** TQuinn(12) (unf: scope: prom over 6f)	2½	**7**	12/1	73	27
	Chief Monarch (BSmart) **3-9-0** RCochrane(8) (w'like: scope: bit bkwd: bhd fnl 3f)	1¼	**8**	33/1	71	25
	Mowelga (LadyHerries) **3-9-0** PaulEddery(7) (str: scope: bit bkwd: s.s: nvr nr ldrs)	½	**9**	20/1	70	24
	River Pilot (RCharlton) **3-9-0** TSprake(11) (w'like: scope: bhd fnl 3f)	1¾	**10**	20/1	66	20
	Walkabout (BWHills) **3-9-0** MHills(14) (str: scope: bkwd: s.s: bhd whn rdn over 3f out: t.o)	16	**11**	12/1	34	—
599[8]	**Premier Eclipse** (PWHarris) **3-9-0** PatEddery(16) (bit bkwd: a bhd: t.o)	7	**12**	25/1	20	—
	Legendary Lover (IRE) (RCharlton) **3-9-0** RHughes(1) (w'like: scope: bit bkwd: hrd rdn over 3f out: sn bhd: eased whn no ch fnl f)	1½	**13**	14/1	17	—
	Mistral Lord (IRE) (MMadgwick) **3-9-0** DHarrison(4) (unf: scope: a bhd: t.o)	1½	**14**	33/1	14	—
	Moonshift (MRStoute) **3-9-0** KBradshaw(13) (unf: scope: bhd whn hrd rdn over 4f out: t.o)	¾	**15**	33/1	13	—

Blewbury Hill (IRE) (RFJohnsonHoughton) **3-9-0** SSanders(6) (Withdrawn not under Starter's orders: ref to ent stalls)........ **W** — —

(SP 122.8%) **15 Rn**

1m 41.0 (3.00) CSF £73.66 TOTE £17.80: £3.80 £2.90 £2.10 (£87.20) Trio £247.10 OWNER Mr Hamdan Al Maktoum (LAMBOURN) BRED Shadwell Estate Company Limited

Rashik, a half-brother to Zuhair, took the eye in the paddock and travelled well through the race. He can go on to better things. (12/1: 6/1-16/1)

Alezal should come on for the outing, and there will be other days for him. (13/2: 3/1-7/1)

Greek Palace (IRE), a half-brother to Yorkshire Oaks winner Hellenic, gave the impression that a longer trip may help. (100/30)

Memorise (USA), a well-bred colt, should come into his own when stepped-up in distance. (6/1: 11/4-13/2)

Praeditus, who showed ability last season, unseated his jockey and got loose on the walkway leaving the paddock. He did nothing wrong in the race however, and is at least now qualified for handicaps. (20/1)

518 Foreign Rule (IRE) shaped as though he is going to need middle distances. (11/2)

Smart Kid (IRE), a half-brother to a couple of winners, ran well for a long way which was more than can be said for those finishing behind him. (12/1)

741 ARLINGTON INTERNATIONAL RACECOURSE CONDITIONS STKS (3-Y.O) (Class B)

5-00 (5-06) **1m 2f 6y** £7,962.00 (£2,958.00: £1,429.00: £595.00: £247.50: £108.50) Stalls: Centre GOING minus 0.13 sec per fur (G)

	Horse / details	Dist	Pos	SP	RR	SF
	Royal Amaretto (IRE) (109) (BJMeehan) **3-8-11** OPeslier(4) (mde all: clr 7f out: stdd 4f out: qckndclr wl over 1f out: r.o wl)	—	**1**	4/1 3	116+	40
	Falak (USA) (104) (MajorWRHern) **3-8-13** RHills(7) (lw: prom: chsd wnr 4f out: rdn 2f out: no imp)	9	**2**	10/1	104	28
	King Sound (JHMGosden) **3-9-1** LDettori(8) (hld up: hdwy over 4f out: one pce fnl 3f)	8	**3**	3/1 2	93	17
	Apache Star (84) (GWragg) **3-8-6** MHills(2) (bit bkwd: hld up & bhd: styd on fnl 2f: n.d)	¾	**4**	10/1	83	7
523*	**Single Empire (IRE)** (PWChapple-Hyam) **3-8-11** JReid(5) (lw: chsd wnr 6f: wknd 3f out)	1	**5**	8/1	86	10
524*	**Minersville (USA) (85)** (JHMGosden) **3-8-11** AClark(1) (lw: s.s: sme hdwy over 3f out: n.d)	13	**6**	10/1	65	—
507³	**Raindancing (IRE) (100)** (RHannon) **3-8-6** DaneO'Neill(3) (bhd fnl 6f)	5	**7**	16/1	52	—
365²	**Mersey Beat** (GLMoore) **3-8-11** KFallon(10) (lw: hld up: rdn 4f out: sn wknd)	3½	**8**	25/1	52	—
	Sophomore (BWHills) **3-8-11** PatEddery(6) (dwlt: bhd whn rdn 4f out: no rspnse)	8	**9**	11/4 1	39	—
	Out of Sight (IRE) (82) (BAMcMahon) **3-8-11** SSanders(9) (hld up & plld hrd: rdn 4f out: sn bhd)	1¼	**10**	50/1	37	—

(SP 121.7%) **10 Rn**

2m 9.63 (5.63) CSF £41.79 TOTE £6.10: £1.90 £2.30 £1.60 (£24.70) Trio £17.70 OWNER The Harlequin Partnership (UPPER LAMBOURN) BRED Patrick Doyle

Royal Amaretto (IRE) finished between this week's Craven Stakes and Free Handicap winners when runner-up in the Horris Hill. With stamina not a problem, he was an impressive winner under a canny ride from the front, by a French jockey who is certainly not going to put the punters off on his regular visits this season. (4/1: 9/4-4/1)

Falak (USA) tried to make a race of it coming to the quarter-mile marker, but proved no match for the cleverly-ridden winner. (10/1: op 5/1)

King Sound, third to Revoque in the Grand Criterium, let that form down badly and was another knock for the beaten Greenham favourite. (3/1)

Apache Star, not fully wound up, is going to have to rely on stamina rather than speed on this evidence. (10/1: op 6/1)

523* Single Empire (IRE), a half-brother to Court Of Honour and Italian Derby third Rubhahunish, only scraped home at Kempton and found this company a different kettle of fish. (8/1)

Sophomore (11/4: 4/1-5/2)

742 BOB RILEY 50TH BIRTHDAY MAIDEN STKS (II) (3-Y.O) (Class D)

5-30 (5-38) **1m (straight)** £3,427.50 (£1,020.00: £485.00: £217.50) Stalls: Centre GOING minus 0.13 sec per fur (G)

	Horse / details	Dist	Pos	SP	RR	SF
	Mamalik (USA) (JHMGosden) **3-9-0** RHills(10) (w'like: scope: hld up: swtchd lft & hdwy over 2f out: squeezed through: led over 1f out: easily)	—	**1**	8/11 1	84+	53
	Rainwatch (JLDunlop) **3-9-0** PatEddery(2) (lw: a.p: rdn over 3f out: ev ch whn bmpd over 2f out: one pce)	5	**2**	6/1 2	74	43
	Mystic Ridge (DRCElsworth) **3-9-0** RCochrane(13) (hld up: hdwy over 1f out: r.o)	1¼	**3**	12/1	72	41
	Hever Golf Glory (TJNaughton) **3-9-0** SSanders(4) (w'like: scope: hld up mid div: rdn whn bmpd over 2f out: hdwy over 1f out: r.o)	¾	**4**	33/1	70	39
	Royale Finale (IRE) (HRACecil) **3-9-0** KFallon(5) (lw: led: hrd rdn & hdd over 1f out: one pce)	½	**5**	7/1 3	69	38
	Island Sanctuary (IRE) (PJMakin) **3-9-0** JFortune(7) (leggy: scope: nvr nrr)	3	**6**	50/1	63	32
	Dalliance (IRE) (MRStoute) **3-9-0** AClark(11) (w'like: scope: swvd rt s: hld up: hmpd 3f out: nt clr run over 2f out: nt rcvr)	½	**7**	20/1	62	31
	Border Falcon (IABalding) **3-9-0** LDettori(14) (scope: rdn over 2f out: no hdwy)	½	**8**	12/1	61	30
495³	**Abajany** (MRChannon) **3-8-9**(5) PPMurphy(6) (hld up: a bhd)	2½	**9**	33/1	56	25
	Khafaaq (MajorWRHern) **3-9-0** PaulEddery(1) (bit bkwd: prom: rdn over 3f out: wknd over 1f out: eased whn btn ins fnl f)	3½	**10**	25/1	49	18
	Golden Saddle (USA) (PFICole) **3-9-0** TQuinn(8) (leggy: scope: prom over 5f)	4	**11**	33/1	41	10
	Good Reputation (BWHills) **3-8-9** DHolland(15) (b: leggy: unf: scope: s.s: bhd whn plld out over 3f out: sn rdn: no rspnse)	3½	**12**	16/1	29	—
	Bold Saint (IRE) (PWHarris) **3-9-0** WRSwinburn(9) (bit bkwd: a bhd)	1½	**13**	50/1	31	—
	Polished Steel (IRE) (LadyHerries) **3-9-0** DeclanO'Shea(12) (w'like: bit bkwd: s.s & swvd rt: a bhd: eased whn no ch fnl f)	2½	**14**	50/1	26	—
	Interregnum (AGFoster) **3-8-9** RPerham(3) (w ldr over 4f: wkng whn bmpd over 2f out)	5	**15**	50/1	11	—

(SP 131.2%) **15 Rn**

1m 41.33 (3.33) CSF £4.76 TOTE £1.80: £1.30 £1.60 £2.30 (£4.30) Trio £23.20 OWNER Mr Hamdan Al Maktoum (NEWMARKET) BRED Dorothy Alexander Matz

Mamalik (USA) lived up to his big home reputation and soon put the issue beyond doubt after wriggling through a narrow gap. He looks one to follow. (8/11)

Rainwatch chipped a bone in her knee after a promising debut here last September. Proving no match for the smart winner over this mile, he will be a different proposition when tackling longer distances. (6/1: op 4/1)

Mystic Ridge, backed down from long odds, can repay the faith shown in him when stepped-up in distance. (12/1)

Hever Golf Glory, a half-brother to a middle distance winner in France, is another who shaped as though he would get off the mark when trying a longer trip. (33/1)

Royale Finale (IRE) may not live up to his Derby and Dante entries, but should find a suitable opportunity over middle distances. (7/1: 4/1-8/1)

Island Sanctuary (IRE), a half-brother to among others the Triumph Hurdle third Shooting Light, made a promising debut in a race full of prospective middle distance animals. (50/1)
Dalliance (IRE), a half-brother to good French miler Marble Maiden, did not have the best of introductions, but seems sure to do better in due course. (20/1)
Border Falcon (12/1: op 5/1)
495 Abajany, dropping back to a mile, seems likely to get into handicaps on a useful mark. (33/1)

T/Jkpt: Not won; £47,332.98 to Nottingham 21/4/97. T/Plpt: £2,620.00 (14.69 Tckts). T/Qdpt: £10.40 (157.52 Tckts) AK/KH

0729-THIRSK (L-H) (Good to firm)
Saturday April 19th

WEATHER: fine WIND: fresh half against
50 49 60+

743 KNAYTON CLAIMING STKS (2-Y.O) (Class F)

2-20 (2-21) **5f** £2,652.50 (£740.00: £357.50) Stalls: High GOING minus 0.09 sec per fur (G)

				SP	RR	SF
594[12]	**Diamond Steve** (PDEvans) **2-8-7v[1]** JFEgan(12) (chsd ldrs: sn drvn along: styd on to ld towards fin)...........	—	**1**	4/1[1]	59	4
572[5]	**Ellenbrook (IRE)** (JBerry) **2-8-6** KDarley(10) (lw: led: rdn & edgd lft over 1f out: jst ct).................................	hd	**2**	9/2[2]	58	3
631[4]	**My Bet** (MWEasterby) **2-8-7**(5) GParkin(4) (a chsng ldrs: nt qckn appr fnl f).................................	3½	**3**	5/1[3]	53	—
631[3]	**Captain Bliss** (NTinkler) **2-8-12b[1]**(5) AimeeCook(2) (chsd ldrs on outside: rdn ½-wy: kpt on same pce appr fnl f).................................	½	**4**	6/1	56	1
572[8]	**Skippool Creek (IRE)** (TDEasterby) **2-8-8** MBirch(11) (s.i.s: sn outpcd & bhd: styd on fnl 2f)......................	2½	**5**	16/1	39	—
572[7]	**Daynabee** (NTinkler) **2-8-2** KimTinkler(7) (chsd ldrs: outpcd fnl 2f).................................	½	**6**	20/1	31	—
	Crafty Pet (IRE) (RAFahey) **2-8-12** ACulhane(1) (neat: w ldrs on outside: hung lft 2f out: wknd over 1f out: eased).................................	2	**7**	4/1[1]	35	—
	Toll's Times (MWEasterby) **2-9-3** DaleGibson(5) (unf: s.i.s: bhd tl styd on appr fnl f).................................	1	**8**	20/1	37	—
631[9]	**General Joey** (MDods) **2-8-5**(3)ow1 CTeague(8) (s.s: wl bhd: sme late hdwy).................................	1½	**9**	25/1	23	—
	Wait'n'see (MWEasterby) **2-9-3** TLucas(9) (lt-f: unf: s.v.s: wl bhd tl kpt on fnl 2f).................................	1¼	**10**	16/1	28	—
	Flea In Your Ear (MartynMeade) **2-7-10** LCharnock(6) (small: chsd ldrs tl lost pl ½-wy).................................	3	**11**	8/1	—	—
	Carnation King (WGMTurner) **2-8-6**(3) RHavlin(3) (small: lt-f: unf: chsd ldrs: rdn & hung lft 2f out: sn lost pl)..	3	**12**	8/1	1	—
				(SP 136.5%)		**12 Rn**

62.3 secs (4.70) CSF £22.77 TOTE £5.30: £1.90 £1.70 £2.40 (£11.40) Trio £40.20 OWNER Diamond Racing Ltd (WELSHPOOL) BRED R. Boland

Diamond Steve clmd NTinkler £5,000

Diamond Steve, fitted with a visor this time, looked very fit. He needed every yard of the five-furlong trip to get up near the line, and will be better suited by six or a stiffer track. (4/1: op 7/1)
572 Ellenbrook (IRE), who looked very fit, seemed to lose her action on the undulating ground and, edging away from the rail, was just caught. (9/2)
631 My Bet showed a fair bit of knee action going down. (5/1)
631 Captain Bliss, in blinkers this time, raced wide from a poor draw. (6/1: op 7/2)
Skippool Creek (IRE), very keen going to post, only got going when it was all over and, when she learns to settle better, a step up to six will be in her favour. (16/1)
Crafty Pet (IRE), the pick of the paddock, showed a good action going down. Drawn in stall one, she was always tending to hang towards the middle and, with her chance gone, was handled with consideration. She should improve and at least win a seller. (4/1)
Toll's Times, a narrow type, showed some ability, staying on nicely after a sluggish break. (20/1)
Wait'n'see, a narrow, unfurnished individual, walked out of the traps and gave away more ground than what he was eventually beaten by. (16/1)
Flea In Your Ear (8/1: op 5/1)

744 THOMAS LORD H'CAP (0-90) (3-Y.O+) (Class C)

2-50 (2-53) **5f** £7,668.00 (£2,304.00: £1,112.00: £516.00) Stalls: High GOING minus 0.09 sec per fur (G)

				SP	RR	SF
527*	**Surprise Mission (76)** (MrsJRRamsden) **5-9-3** SDrowne(21) (lw: hld up: smooth hdwy to ld ins fnl f: rdn out)	—	**1**	9/4[1]	86	46
529[18]	**Ziggy's Dancer (USA) (81)** (EJAlston) **6-9-8** GDuffield(1) (racd alone far side: w ldrs: r.o wl fnl f).................	s.h	**2**	16/1	91	51
	For the Present (83) (TDBarron) **7-9-10** KDarley(15) (bkwd: hdwy ½-wy: styd on wl u.p fnl f)........................	1¾	**3**	20/1	87	47
459[10]	**Squire Corrie (70)** (DWChapman) **5-8-11** ACulhane(11) (led stands' side tl ins fnl f).................................	hd	**4**	20/1	74	34
	Twice as Sharp (84) (PWHarris) **5-9-11** GHind(18) (a chsng ldrs: nt qckn fnl 2f).................................	1¼	**5**	12/1	84	44
	Stuffed (85) (MWEasterby) **5-9-7**(5) GParkin(16) (bit bkwd: hld up: hdwy 2f out: r.o fnl f).................................	1¼	**6**	10/1[3]	81	41
464[11]	**Insider Trader (71)** (MrsJRRamsden) **6-8-12** MDeering(19) (hld up & bhd: styd on strly fnl f: nt rch ldrs)	½	**7**	12/1	65	25
527[5]	**Captain Carat (60)** (DNicholls) **6-8-1** DaleGibson(10) (bhd tl styd on appr fnl f).................................	s.h	**8**	12/1	54	14
585[18]	**Cross The Border (63)** (DNicholls) **4-7-11**(7) IonaWands(2) (w ldrs over 3f).................................	s.h	**9**	25/1	57	17
473[2]	**Dande Flyer (70)** (DWPArbuthnot) **4-8-11** GCarter(9) (lw: w ldrs over 3f: grad wknd).................................	nk	**10**	16/1	63	23
585[13]	**Goretski (IRE) (56)** (NTinkler) **4-7-11** KimTinkler(8) (in tch over 3f).................................	nk	**11**	20/1	48	8
488[5]	**Tuscan Dawn (75)** (JBerry) **7-8-11**(5) PRoberts(17) (unruly in stalls: reard s: sn chsng ldrs: wknd fnl f)	3	**12**	10/1[3]	58	18
	Royal Dome (IRE) (71) (MartynWane) **5-8-12** JCarroll(20) (bkwd: chsd ldrs 3f: sn wknd).................................	s.h	**13**	8/1[2]	53	13
501[4]	**Swino (89)** (PDEvans) **3-9-6** JFEgan(12) (in tch over 3f: n.m.r & sn wknd).................................	1	**14**	10/1[3]	68	18
	Swynford Dream (86) (JFBottomley) **4-9-13** JLowe(13) (h.d.w: bit bkwd: trckd ldrs tl lost pl 2f out)	nk	**15**	20/1	64	24
494*	**Chemcast (74)** (JLEyre) **4-9-1b** RLappin(6) (w ldrs 3f: sn wknd).................................	s.h	**16**	14/1	52	12
	Here Comes a Star (60) (JMCarr) **9-8-1** LCharnock(14) (bhd: effrt & n.m.r on ins over 1f out: n.d)	hd	**17**	20/1	38	—
464[8]	**Blessingindisguise (62)** (MWEasterby) **4-8-3** TLucas(5) (nvr nr ldrs).................................	s.h	**18**	25/1	40	—
	Just Bob (73) (SEKettlewell) **8-8-7**(7) JennyBenson(7) (bit bkwd: s.v.s: a wl bhd).................................	2	**19**	14/1	44	4
	Bowlers Boy (72) (JJQuinn) **4-8-13** TWilliams(4) (bit bkwd: dwlt s: a wl bhd).................................	2	**20**	25/1	37	—
				(SP 152.7%)		**20 Rn**

60.3 secs (2.70) CSF £41.93 CT £628.95 TOTE £3.00: £1.60 £3.70 £5.10 £4.80 (£47.30) Trio £619.10 OWNER Mr D. R. Brotherton (THIRSK) BRED D. R. Brotherton

WEIGHT FOR AGE 3yo-10lb

OFFICIAL EXPLANATION **Bowlers Boy: the trainer reported that the gelding had received cuts to its head and mouth in the stalls and had lost ground as the stalls opened.**
Stuffed: the trainer reported that the gelding was found to be coughing after the race.

527* **Surprise Mission**, from a 5lb higher mark, was produced with fine timing to take charge on the stands' side but at the line connections must have had a shock to see Ziggy's Dancer, racing alone on the far side, almost upsides. Doing well physically, Surprise Mission should enjoy further success. (9/4: 3/1-2/1)
Ziggy's Dancer (USA) was taken to race alone on the far side and, in the end, was beaten by just a whisker. (16/1)
For the Present, who looked as if the outing would do him good, is better suited by six. (20/1)
364 **Squire Corrie**, who has speed to burn, has been busy on the All-Weather in the winter. (20/1)
Twice as Sharp prefers a stiffer track. (12/1)
Stuffed, 25lb higher in the weights compared with when he won this a year ago, was 6lb higher than when winning at Newcastle in October on his final outing last year. He shaped with promise, picking up ground nicely in the closing stages. (10/1)
Insider Trader, who has slipped down the weights, wore a visor when successful at Ripon last year. (12/1)
Swynford Dream, who has done really well from three to four, can prove himself better than ever in due course. (20/1)

745 MICHAEL FOSTER MEMORIAL CONDITIONS STKS (3-Y.O+) (Class C)

3-20 (3-21) **6f** £6,508.80 (£2,419.20: £1,169.60: £488.00: £204.00: £90.40) Stalls: High GOING minus 0.09 sec per fur (G)

			SP	RR	SF
	Soviet State (USA) (PWChapple-Hyam) **3-8-3**(3) RHavlin(5) (lw: trckd ldrs: led over 1f out: r.o wl u.p: readily)—	**1**	$5/1^{3}$	109+	27
573^{2}	**Cretan Gift (89)** (NPLittmoden) **6-9-0b** TGMcLaughlin(6) (sn outpcd & bhd: hdwy 2f out: styd on ins fnl f) 2½	**2**	16/1	99	28
452^{5}	**Venture Capitalist (110)** (DNicholls) **8-9-7** AlexGreaves(2) (hld up: hdwy over 2f out: sn chsng ldr: one pce appr fnl f) 1¾	**3**	$15/8^{1}$	102	31
519^{10}	**Watch Me (IRE) (105)** (RHannon) **4-8-12** JCarroll(3) (trckd ldrs: led over 2f out: edgd rt: hdd over 1f out: wknd towards fin) 1	**4**	13/2	90	19
	Young Bigwig (IRE) (97) (JBerry) **3-8-3** GCarter(7) (h.d.w: bit bkwd: a chsng ldrs: one pce fnl 2f) ....hd	**5**	10/1	92	10
573^{4}	**Westcourt Magic (100)** (MWEasterby) **4-9-7** LCharnock(4) (lw: led to ½-wy: rallied over 1f out: wknd towards fin) ....½	**6**	12/1	97	26
	Jhazi (103) (DRLoder) **3-8-6** KDarley(8) (w ldrs: led ½-wy: sn hdd: wkng whn hmpd over 1f out: eased) 9	**7**	$100/30^{2}$	69	—
519^{7}	**Sea Dane (100)** (PWHarris) **4-9-7** GHind(1) (b: in tch over 3f: sn lost pl & eased) 3	**8**	9/1	65	—

(SP 120.5%) **8 Rn**

1m 13.6 (3.90) CSF £75.05 TOTE £7.20: £2.80 £2.20 £1.20 (£46.20) OWNER Mr R. E. Sangster (MARLBOROUGH) BRED Echo Valley Horse Farm and Swettenham Stud
WEIGHT FOR AGE 3yo-11lb
Soviet State (USA), who was reported to have been unsuited by the soft ground in France on his final outing at two, took this in good style and is clearly a promising sprinter. Seven furlongs will be no problem. (5/1)
573 **Cretan Gift** ran another sound race. He would have been a stone better off with Venture Capitalist in a handicap, and is likely to take another hike in the weights. (16/1)
452 **Venture Capitalist**, who won this race two years ago, lacked a little of his normal dash. (15/8: 11/4-7/4)
Watch Me (IRE) has speed to burn. (13/2)
Young Bigwig (IRE) would have been 13lb better off with Venture Capitalist in a handicap. He looked as though the outing was needed.(10/1)
573 **Westcourt Magic**, who would have been 10lb better off with Venture Capitalist in a handicap, again failed to last out. (12/1)
Jhazi does not look a sprinter. (100/30)
Sea Dane ran another poor race. (9/1: 12/1-8/1)

746 RACING CHANNEL LIMITED STKS (0-70) (3-Y.O+) (Class E)

3-50 (3-50) **1m 4f** £2,880.25 (£862.00: £413.50: £189.25) Stalls: Low GOING minus 0.29 sec per fur (GF)

			SP	RR	SF
435^{3}	**Desert Fighter (68)** (MrsMReveley) **6-9-8** ACulhane(2) (mde all: shkn up over 3f out: styd on strly: eased nr fin) ....—	**1**	$4/1^{2}$	82	40
538^{8}	**Fairy Knight (68)** (RHannon) **5-9-10** KDarley(4) (chsd wnr: rdn over 2f out: styd on ins fnl f) 1	**2**	$6/1^{3}$	83	41
521^{7}	**Lookingforarainbow (IRE) (67)** (BobJones) **9-9-8** MWigham(5) (drvn along 7f out: styd on fnl 2f: nvr nr to chal) 2	**3**	$100/30^{1}$	78	36
	Pearl Venture (68) (SPCWoods) **5-9-5** DBiggs(3) (hld up: hdwy on outside over 2f out: hung lft: nvr nr to chal) 4	**4**	9/1	70	28
537^{5}	**Nile Valley (IRE) (68)** (PWChapple-Hyam) **3-7-7**(7)ow1 RCody-Boutcher(8) (chsd ldrs: effrt over 2f out: grad wknd) 4	**5**	$4/1^{2}$	65	2
	Kaitak (IRE) (68) (JMCarr) **6-9-8** LCharnock(7) (chsd ldrs: wknd over 2f out) 1¼	**6**	20/1	66	24
598^{8}	**Slasher Jack (IRE) (67)** (DNicholls) **6-9-8** AlexGreaves(1) (trckd ldrs tl lost pl over 4f out) 1¼	**7**	9/1	64	22
	Contrafire (IRE) (70) (MrsASwinbank) **5-9-8** JSupple(6) (hld up: effrt over 3f out: no imp) 1¼	**8**	$6/1^{3}$	62	20

(SP 116.4%) **8 Rn**

2m 37.1 (6.40) CSF £26.11 TOTE £3.70: £1.50 £2.00 £1.30 (£12.70) OWNER Mr A. Frame (SALTBURN) BRED P. D. and Mrs Player
WEIGHT FOR AGE 3yo-20lb
435 **Desert Fighter** was given an enterprising ride and always looked in control. (4/1)
380 **Fairy Knight** likes to come from behind. He never gave up trying and seems as good as ever. (6/1)
Lookingforarainbow (IRE), who has not won for two years, showed a very scratchy action going down and never looked happy in his work. (100/30)
Pearl Venture needs everything to go her own way and also needs further than this. (9/1)
537 **Nile Valley (IRE)** seems not to have progressed. (4/1)
Contrafire (IRE), a winner twice over hurdles for his new stable, looked in tremendous condition but ran no race at all. (6/1)

747 THIRSK CLASSIC TRIAL CONDITIONS STKS (3-Y.O) (Class B)

4-20 (4-20) **1m** £10,486.00 (£3,376.00: £1,638.00) Stalls: Low GOING minus 0.29 sec per fur (GF)

		SP	RR	SF
Starborough (107) (DRLoder) **3-9-0** KDarley(3) (h.d.w: mde all: shkn up & styd on strly fnl f) ....—	**1**	$4/5^{1}$	108	57
Intikhab (USA) (102) (DMorley) **3-9-5** GCarter(1) (trckd wnr: effrt over 2f out: ev ch over 1f out: unable qckn) .2	**2**	$7/4^{2}$	109	58
Caviar Royale (IRE) (99) (TDBarron) **3-9-0** JCarroll(2) (bit bkwd: hld up: effrt over 2f out: no imp) 4	**3**	$7/1^{3}$	96	45

(SP 104.4%) **3 Rn**

1m 38.1 (1.60) CSF £2.15 TOTE £1.80 (£1.20) OWNER Sheikh Mohammed (NEWMARKET) BRED Sheikh Mohammed Bin Rashid Al Maktoum
Starborough, a May foal, has grown and strengthened over the winter. He always looked in command, and a step-up to a mile-and-a-quarter will be no problem in due course. (4/5)
Intikhab (USA), forced to concede the winner 5lb, stayed the mile alright. (7/4)
Caviar Royale (IRE), sold for 62,000 guineas at the end of his two-year-old campaign, might struggle for opportunities. (7/1)

748 BYLAND RATING RELATED MAIDEN STKS (0-65) (3-Y.O+) (Class F)

4-50 (4-50) **7f** £2,722.50 (£760.00: £367.50) Stalls: Low GOING minus 0.29 sec per fur (GF)

			SP	RR	SF
	Star of Ring (IRE) (65) (MJHeaton-Ellis) **4-9-10** SDrowne(4) (trckd ldr: led over 2f out: pushed out: readily) .—	**1**	7/2[1]	67+	54
571[15]	**Serape (54)** (MrsLStubbs) **4-9-7** JFEgan(7) (b: trckd ldrs: styd on ins fnl f)....3½	**2**	25/1	56	43
634[7]	**In Good Nick (63)** (MWEasterby) **3-8-3b**(5) GParkin(9) (lw: led tl over 2f out: one pce)....s.h	**3**	9/2[2]	56	30
	Bewitching Lady (58) (DWPArbuthnot) **3-8-8** GCarter(10) (mid div: kpt on fnl 3f: nvr rchd ldrs)....3	**4**	5/1[3]	49	23
	Hong Kong Express (IRE) (65) (JBerry) **3-8-3**(5) PFessey(8) (a chsng ldrs: hung lft & one pce fnl 2f)....½	**5**	7/1	48	22
551[4]	**Swiss Coast (IRE) (65)** (NTinkler) **3-8-11** KDarley(6) (sn bhd & pushed along: kpt on fnl 2f: n.d)....1½	**6**	7/1	48	22
	Hadadabble (36) (PatMitchell) **4-9-7** MFenton(3) (swtg: s.i.s: hdwy ½-wy: one pce fnl 3f)....1	**7**	25/1	42	29
417[6]	**Hazel (55)** (MissGayKelleway) **5-9-0**(7) RSmith(2) (b: b.hind: dwlt s: bhd: sme hdwy 2f out: n.d)....nk	**8**	10/1	42	29
57[8]	**Santella Katie (60)** (MrsLStubbs) **4-9-7** MRimmer(11) (hld up: hrd rdn & styd on fnl 2f: nvr nr to chal)....1¾	**9**	20/1	38	25
	Dance Melody (48) (GROldroyd) **3-8-2**(7)ow1 RFarmer(5) (a in rr: drvn along ½-wy)....2½	**10**	33/1	33	6
	Carreamia (65) (JLEyre) **4-9-4**(3) OPears(1) (trckd ldrs tl lost pl fnl 2f: eased)....1¼	**11**	13/2	29	16
			(SP 119.9%)		**11 Rn**

1m 27.4 (2.50) CSF £92.14 TOTE £2.70: £1.50 £12.10 £1.80 (£55.10) Trio £230.60 OWNER Mrs Caroline Parker (WROUGHTON) BRED Mrs J. Costelloe

WEIGHT FOR AGE 3yo-13lb

Star of Ring (IRE), who had had only three previous outings spread over two seasons, took this in fine style and is potentially a good deal better than his current handicap mark. (7/2)

Serape, who changed hands cheaply, showed little on the All-Weather but ran much better here. (25/1)

In Good Nick tries hard but seems to possess nothing in the way of finishing speed. (9/2)

Bewitching Lady was always making hard work of this, and might be better suited by a mile. (5/1)

Hong Kong Express (IRE), who has had plenty of chances, hung under pressure. (7/1)

551 Swiss Coast (IRE) certainly does not lack ability but looks a bit of a softy. (7/1)

Carreamia was not knocked about at any stage, and connections will be hoping that this outing will help her slip down in the weights. (13/2: 9/2-7/1)

749 LEVY BOARD H'CAP (0-80) (3-Y.O+ F & M) (Class D)

5-20 (5-21) **1m** £3,730.00 (£1,120.00: £540.00: £250.00) Stalls: Low GOING minus 0.29 sec per fur (GF)

			SP	RR	SF
657*	**Angel Face (USA) (74)** (PDEvans) **4-9-10** JFEgan(13) (lw: unruly s: plld hrd: trckd ldrs: led 3f out: sn shkn up & qcknd clr: drvn out)....—	**1**	7/1	88	51
	Blessed Spirit (78) (CFWall) **4-10-0** ACulhane(12) (hld up & bhd: nt clr run over 2f out: swtchd & styd on strly appr fnl f: nt rch wnr)....3½	**2**	5/1[1]	85	48
608[6]	**Best of All (IRE) (62)** (JBerry) **5-8-12b** KDarley(5) (a in tch: styd on fnl 2f: no imp)....s.h	**3**	9/1	69	32
	Chorus Song (USA) (70) (PWChapple-Hyam) **3-8-3**(3) RHavlin(4) (b.hind: bit bkwd: mde most to 3f out: kpt on one pce: eased towards fin)....5	**4**	14/1	67	16
*317**	**Diamond Eyre (60)** (JLEyre) **3-7-5**(5) RMullen(9) (sn bhd: styd on wl fnl 2f)....½	**5**	14/1	56	5
	Lillibella (55) (MrsJRRamsden) **4-8-5** SDrowne(2) (bit bkwd: dwlt s: hld up: gd hdwy over 2f out: wknd over 1f out)....1	**6**	12/1	49	12
387[6]	**Perfect Poppy (73)** (JRFanshawe) **3-8-9** NVarley(6) (w ldrs: rdn over 2f out: wknd appr fnl f)....nk	**7**	14/1	66	15
423[10]	**Ballard Lady (IRE) (46)** (JSWainwright) **5-7-5**(5) JBramhill(10) (lw: plld hrd: trckd ldrs: outpcd fnl 2f)....1	**8**	20/1	37	—
571[11]	**Three Arch Bridge (65)** (MJohnston) **5-9-1b** DeanMcKeown(3) (s.i.s: bhd tl kpt on fnl 2f: n.d)....1¼	**9**	6/1[2]	54	17
587[11]	**Legend of Aragon (65)** (JAGlover) **3-8-1** GDuffield(8) (hld up & plld hrd: nvr rchd ldrs)....2	**10**	16/1	50	—
554*	**Sylvan Princess (69)** (DJSCosgrove) **4-9-5** MRimmer(14) (lw: trckd ldrs: effrt over 2f out: sn wknd)....¾	**11**	13/2[3]	52	15
444[10]	**Cashmere Lady (68)** (JLEyre) **5-9-4** RLappin(11) (mid div: hdwy on outside 3f out: shkn up 2f out: hung lft & sn wknd)....3	**12**	10/1	45	8
130[4]	**Marsh Marigold (60)** (JHetherton) **3-7-10** LCharnock(1) (trckd ldrs tl lost pl 3f out)....2	**13**	20/1	33	—
571[10]	**La Volta (65)** (JGFitzGerald) **4-9-1** JQuinn(15) (trckd ldrs tl lost pl over 2f out)....1	**14**	16/1	36	—
	Crissem (IRE) (72) (RHollinshead) **4-9-5**(3) FLynch(7) (s.i.s: a bhd)....1	**15**	25/1	41	4
			(SP 128.7%)		**15 Rn**

1m 39.6 (3.10) CSF £39.42 CT £309.80 TOTE £6.30: £3.10 £2.60 £2.90 (£25.90) Trio £51.60 OWNER Mrs E. J. Williams (WELSHPOOL) BRED Gainsborough Farm Inc.

LONG HANDICAP Diamond Eyre 7-4 Ballard Lady (IRE) 7-9

WEIGHT FOR AGE 3yo-14lb

657* Angel Face (USA), taken to post early, gave plenty of problems at the start but, once under way, she races with plenty of enthusiasm and had this won in a matter of strides after quickening clear off the bend. (7/1)

Blessed Spirit has plenty of ability but seems to make a habit of meeting trouble in running. When she did see daylight, she finished with a real flourish but the winner had flown. There is no doubt that, when things go her way, she is capable of adding to her record off this sort of mark. (5/1)

608 Best of All (IRE) ran a sound race. (9/1)

Chorus Song (USA), dropped 9lb since she last ran in a handicap, was eased right up towards the finish otherwise she would have finished only a couple of lengths behind the third. Connections will be hoping the Handicapper shows her more mercy. (14/1)

317* Diamond Eyre, staying on when it was all over, needs further. (14/1)

Lillibella, having her first outing since changing stables, possesses a fair bit of temperament but hopefully connections will be able to sort her out. (12/1)

T/Plpt: £65.10 (153.4 Tckts). T/Qdpt: £9.40 (43.41 Tckts) WG

0637-BRIGHTON (L-H) (Firm)

Monday April 21st

WEATHER: sunny WIND: almost nil

76 61 56 51

750 SIDNEY THOMPSON MEMORIAL NOVICE AUCTION STKS (2-Y.O) (Class F)

2-00 (2-00) **5f 59y** £2,277.00 (£627.00: £297.00) Stalls: Low GOING minus 0.33 sec per fur (GF)

				SP	RR	SF
637*	**Banningham Blade** (KTIvory) **2-8-10**(3) MartinDwyer(6) (a.p: led wl over 1f out: all out)	—	1	5/1	78	27
637^{3}	**Soft Touch (IRE)** (MissGayKelleway) **2-8-4** SSanders(1) (hld up: rdn over 1f out: r.o wl ins fnl f)	hd	2	12/1	69	18
	Fiveo'clock Shadow (IRE) (BJMeehan) **2-8-12** RHughes(8) (neat: bit bkwd: dwlt: hld up: swtchd rt 2f out: hrd rdn over 1f out: r.o wl ins fnl f)	nk	3	$4/1^{3}$	76	25
664*	**Heavenly Abstone** (PDEvans) **2-8-5v** JFEgan(5) (a.p: led over 3f out tl wl over 1f out: wandered: wknd fnl f)	3½	4	$3/1^{2}$	58	7
548*	**Mister Bankes** (WGMTurner) **2-8-13**(5) DSweeney(7) (lw: a.p: ev ch 2f out: wknd fnl f)	1¼	5	$9/4^{1}$	67	16
	Talaheart (CNAllen) **2-8-7** GHind(4) (neat: hld up: rdn over 2f out: sn wknd)	6	6	33/1	38	—
472^{7}	**Shannon (IRE)** (CADwyer) **2-8-1**(3) DO'Donohoe(3) (led over 1f: rdn 2f out: wkng whn n.m.r on ins 1f out)	2	7	20/1	29	—
	Katies Treat (IRE) (BAPearce) **2-8-4** DRMcCabe(2) (neat: bkwd: s.i.s: a wl bhd)	4	8	40/1	17	—

(SP 110.3%) **8 Rn**

62.5 secs (2.50) CSF £50.50 TOTE £6.20: £2.00 £2.40 £3.10 (£14.50) OWNER Crown Select (RADLETT) BRED K. T. Ivory

IN-FOCUS: **This was a decent early-season contest for this track.**

637* Banningham Blade put her experience and knowledge of this course to good use. In front early inside the final furlong, she had not an ounce to spare and found the line only just saving her. (5/1: 3/1-11/2)

637 Soft Touch (IRE), all the better for her recent run here, drifted in the market but she finished to great effect and would surely have prevailed in a few more strides. She should soon find a small race. (12/1: 6/1-14/1)

Fiveo'clock Shadow (IRE), who knocked himself in the box on the way to Kempton on his intended debut at the end of March, is a nippy sort. Despite looking just in need of this, he really got the hang of things from below the distance and, running on really strongly, only just failed. A race should be found for him in the near future. (4/1: 5/1-3/1)

664* Heavenly Abstone was soon at the head of affairs, but she was collared early in the final quarter-mile and, wandering about on this tricky course, tired inside the distance. (3/1)

548* Mister Bankes, quite a big individual, looked very well but he was racing on ground completely different than when successful at Hamilton, and was conceding weight all round. That told against him for, after racing up with the pace, he tired in the final furlong. (9/4: op 6/4)

751 ORLEANS LIMITED STKS (0-65) (3-Y.O) (Class F)

2-30 (2-30) **5f 213y** £2,277.00 (£627.00: £297.00) Stalls: Low GOING minus 0.33 sec per fur (GF)

				SP	RR	SF
155^{6}	**Hever Golf Mover (59)** (TJNaughton) **3-8-8** SSanders(1) (hld up: hrd rdn over 1f out: led wl ins fnl f: drvn out)	—	1	$10/1^{3}$	59	21
652^{2}	**Suite Factors (60)** (KRBurke) **3-8-11** RPerham(3) (lw: led: rdn over 1f out: hdd wl ins fnl f: r.o)	½	2	$2/1^{1}$	61	23
474^{9}	**Nampara Bay (39)** (GCBravery) **3-8-8** MRimmer(4) (w ldr: rdn over 2f out: ev ch over 1f out: unable qckn)	3½	3	16/1	48	10
642^{5}	**Nervous Rex (60)** (WRMuir) **3-8-11** JReid(2) (hld up: hrd rdn over 2f out: one pce)	nk	4	$2/1^{1}$	51	13
602^{4}	**Jukebox Jive (52)** (CADwyer) **3-8-1**(7) JoHunnam(5) (lw: outpcd: nvr nrr)	hd	5	$3/1^{2}$	47	9
602^{5}	**Whizz Kid (51)** (JJBridger) **3-8-3**(5) RMullen(6) (hld up: rdn over 2f out: sn wknd)	3½	6	$10/1^{3}$	38	—

(SP 115.7%) **6 Rn**

1m 10.1 (2.90) CSF £28.78 TOTE £9.00: £3.20 £1.10 (£10.70) OWNER Hever Racing Club (EPSOM) BRED Mrs L. Popely

Hever Golf Mover, who has shown only very moderate form, was given a very strong ride to lose her maiden tag. (10/1)

652 Suite Factors attempted to make all the running. It looked as if he may well hold on after he had shaken off the third entering the final furlong, but he was unable to prevent the winner going by in the closing stages. (2/1)

Nampara Bay ran her best race to date. Disputing the lead, she still had every chance below the distance before tapped for toe. (16/1)

642 Nervous Rex, who found a mile much too far last time, may have found this too sharp for, after coming under pressure over a quarter-of-a-mile from home, he could only go up and down in the same place. Seven furlongs is probably his trip. (2/1)

602 Jukebox Jive (3/1: 9/4-7/2)

602 Whizz Kid (10/1: 7/1-12/1)

752 OLD STEINE H'CAP (0-85) (3-Y.O+) (Class D)

3-00 (3-00) **6f 209y** £3,804.85 (£1,136.80: £543.90: £247.45) Stalls: Low GOING minus 0.33 sec per fur (GF)

				SP	RR	SF
567*	**Barbason (59)** (GLMoore) **5-8-5** CandyMorris(5) (hdwy & nt clr run over 2f out: hrd rdn over 1f out: led ins fnl f: r.o wl)	—	1	$9/4^{1}$	73	48
450^{19}	**Neuwest (USA) (82)** (NJHWalker) **5-10-0** RHughes(3) (b: lw: hld up: rdn over 2f out: led over 1f out tl ins fnl f: r.o)	½	2	$9/2^{3}$	95	70
567^{2}	**Ertlon (70)** (CEBrittain) **7-9-2** BDoyle(7) (lw: a.p: rdn over 2f out: unable qckn)	4	3	$3/1^{2}$	74	49
	Kings Harmony (IRE) (72) (PJMakin) **4-9-4** SSanders(2) (a.p: led 3f out tl over 1f out: wknd fnl f)	hd	4	11/1	75	50
532^{7}	**Penlop (67)** (BJMeehan) **3-7-11b**[1](3) MartinDwyer(4) (prom over 4f)	3½	5	13/2	62	24
294^{8}	**Regal Splendour (CAN) (65)** (RJO'Sullivan) **4-8-11** DHarrison(1) (lw: lost pl 5f out: rallied over 1f out: wknd fnl f)	5	6	9/1	49	24
	Jaazim (50) (MMadgwick) **7-7-5**(5) JBramhill(8) (bkwd: a bhd)	3½	7	33/1	26	1
601^{9}	**Astral Invader (IRE) (55)** (MSSaunders) **5-8-1v** JFEgan(6) (lw: led 4f)	5	8	25/1	19	—

(SP 112.4%) **8 Rn**

1m 21.0 (1.00) CSF £11.09 CT £26.97 TOTE £2.90: £1.20 £1.80 £1.40 (£11.70) OWNER Mr F. L. Hill (BRIGHTON) BRED Sheikh Mohammed bin Rashid al Maktoum

LONG HANDICAP Jaazim 7-7

WEIGHT FOR AGE 3yo-13lb

567* Barbason is in the form of his life and there seems to be no stopping him at present. Despite not getting the best of runs, he responded to pressure to get on top inside the final furlong. Full marks must go to his trainer who will surely try to get another quick victory into him before he is clobbered by the Handicapper. (9/4: op 6/4)

Neuwest (USA) comes from a stable that know how to turn their horses out looking really well. Eventually getting on top below the distance, he was collared by the winner inside the final furlong, but to his credit stuck on well to the line. All his wins have been on good to firm or firm ground. (9/2: op 3/1)
567 Ertlon has been labelled inconsistent but that has not been the case so far this year, although he was tapped for toe in the final quarter-mile on this occasion. (3/1)
Kings Harmony (IRE) moved to the front three furlongs from home, but he was collared below the distance and tired as lack of a recent run took its toll. (11/1: op 7/1)
532 Penlop, fitted with blinkers for the first time, played an active role until coming to the end of his tether over two furlongs from home. (13/2)

753 ROYAL PAVILION CLAIMING STKS (4-Y.O+) (Class F)
3-30 (3-32) **1m 3f 196y** £2,277.00 (£627.00: £297.00) Stalls: High GOING minus 0.33 sec per fur (GF)

				SP	RR	SF
595[3]	**Petoskin (54)** (JPearce) **5-8-12** MWigham(3) (led over 1f: rdn over 3f out: str run fnl f: led last stride)	—	1	5/1[2]	61	46
570[2]	**Bedouin Prince (USA) (39)** (MrsLStubbs) **10-8-8** SSanders(4) (b: chsd ldr 10f out: led 4f out to 2f out: rdn: led ins fnl f: hdd last stride)	s.h	2	11/2[3]	57	42
607[6]	**Roman Reel (USA) (63)** (GLMoore) **6-8-12** SWhitworth(2) (lw: stdy hdwy 5f out: led 2f out tl ins fnl f: one pce)	1¼	3	5/2[1]	59	44
680[14]	**English Invader (75)** (CADwyer) **6-8-11**(5) GFaulkner(6) (lw: hld up: rdn over 4f out: wknd over 2f out)	11	4	5/2[1]	48	33
487[3]	**Efficacious (IRE) (45)** (PEccles) **4-8-0** JFEgan(7) (lw: hld up: rdn over 4f out: wknd over 3f out)	8	5	16/1	23	7
511[3]	**Venice Beach** (CPEBrooks) **5-8-7**(3) JDSmith(5) (led over 10f out to 4f out: sn wknd)	7	6	11/2[3]	22	7
	Miss Pravda (49) (BJLlewellyn) **4-7-12**(5) JBramhill(8) (lw: a bhd)	4	7	25/1	11	—
607[11]	**Friar's Oak (30)** (PButler) **5-8-9**(5) DSweeney(1) (bhd fnl 10f: t.o fnl 4f)	dist	8	50/1	—	—
				(SP 116.3%)		**8 Rn**

2m 31.0 (3.40) CSF £30.11 TOTE £7.80: £1.80 £1.60 £1.60 (£9.30) OWNER Mrs Jean Routledge (NEWMARKET) BRED James Wigan
WEIGHT FOR AGE 4yo-1lb
595 Petoskin, whose last three victories have come over one mile seven furlongs, looked in some trouble as he was being bustled along over three furlongs from home. However, he came with a useful run in the final furlong to snatch the spoils right on the line. Claimers and sellers are his grade. (5/1: 3/1-11/2)
570 Bedouin Prince (USA), who ran much better on his return to Turf, only just failed to win his first race in over four years. Leading half-a-mile from home, he was collared by Roman Reel a quarter-of-a-mile out but, to his credit, managed to get back in front again inside the final furlong only to be caught by the winner right on the line. (11/2: 9/2-8/1)
401* Roman Reel (USA) has not run over this trip since 1994 and, after cruising into it at the top of the hill, his jockey did his very best to try and hold onto him until as late as possible. Showing with a narrow advantage a quarter-of-a-mile out, he was soon pushed along but he was collared inside the final furlong and had little left in the tank. This trip certainly stretches him to the very limit and a mile-and-a-quarter is his ideal distance. (5/2)
516 English Invader, winner of three All-Weather races this year, gained both his turf victories in France on heavy ground back in 1994. On this livelier surface, he was in trouble at the top of the hill. (5/2)
511 Venice Beach (11/2: 6/1-10/1)

754 CONFLANS MAIDEN STKS (3-Y.O+) (Class D)
4-00 (4-01) **7f 214y** £3,454.50 (£1,029.00: £490.00: £220.50) Stalls: Low GOING minus 0.33 sec per fur (GF)

			SP	RR	SF
Moon Blast (LadyHerries) **3-8-11** JReid(4) (hld up: led 2f out: clr over 1f out: comf)	—	1	13/8[2]	77+	24
Mystic Strand (WGMTurner) **4-9-1**(5) DSweeney(2) (hdwy over 1f out: chsd wnr fnl f: r.o one pce)	4	2	33/1	64?	25
Ghayyur (USA) (84) (JLDunlop) **3-8-6** RHills(1) (lw: chsd ldr: ev ch 2f out: wknd over 1f out)	6	3	8/11[1]	52	—
Polish Swinger (IRE) (MissGayKelleway) **4-9-11** WJO'Connor(3) (bit bkwd: led 6f)	3	4	12/1[3]	51?	12
			(SP 106.6%)		**4 Rn**

1m 35.2 (3.90) CSF £22.72 TOTE £3.10 (£15.70) OWNER Angmering Park Stud (LITTLEHAMPTON) BRED Lavinia Duchess of Norfolk
WEIGHT FOR AGE 3yo-14lb
Moon Blast, a half-brother to the high class Moon Madness and Sheriff's Star, had no problems on this return to action, leading a quarter-of-a-mile out and soon storming clear for a decisive victory. (13/8: op evens)
Mystic Strand, a workmanlike filly, looked big and well for this belated racecourse debut but, despite struggling into second place a furlong from home, had no hope of reeling in the winner. (33/1)
Ghayyur (USA) was the paddock pick and looked by far the fittest of the four runners, but she was unable to make that tell and tamely dropped away below the distance. (8/11: 4/5-10/1)
Polish Swinger (IRE), a good-bodied gelding who looked as though this belated racecourse debut would do him good, took the field along but, collared two furlongs from home, has soon shot his bolt. (12/1: 8/1-20/1)

755 TOWN PURSE H'CAP (0-70) (3-Y.O+) (Class E)
4-30 (4-30) **7f 214y** £3,044.25 (£909.00: £434.50: £197.25) Stalls: Low GOING minus 0.33 sec per fur (GF)

				SP	RR	SF
560[6]	**Safey Ana (USA) (59)** (BHanbury) **6-9-6** WRyan(10) (b: hdwy over 2f out: rdn over 1f out: led ins fnl f: drvn out)	—	1	5/1[2]	71	36
401[9]	**Czarna (IRE) (63)** (CEBrittain) **6-9-10** BDoyle(4) (a.p: led over 2f out: hrd rdn over 1f out: hdd ins fnl f: r.o)	nk	2	11/1	74	39
	Carlys Quest (60) (JNeville) **3-8-7** AClark(5) (rdn over 3f out: hdwy over 1f out: n.m.r ins fnl f: r.o wl)	nk	3	14/1	71	22
538[11]	**Whispered Melody (53)** (RAkehurst) **4-9-0** SSanders(3) (hld up: rdn over 2f out: unable qckn ins fnl f)	1	4	12/1	62	27
52[7]	**Doctor Bravious (IRE) (63)** (MBell) **4-9-5v**(5) GFaulkner(14) (hrd rdn & hdwy over 1f out: r.o one pce)	hd	5	16/1	72	37
	Alsahib (USA) (67) (WRMuir) **4-10-0** JReid(13) (rdn over 2f out: hdwy over 1f out: nvr nrr)	2	6	7/1[3]	72	37
269a[12]	**Confronter (64)** (SDow) **8-9-11** RHughes(2) (lw: hld up: rdn over 2f out: wknd fnl f)	1¼	7	7/1[3]	66	31
490[6]	**Rocky Waters (USA) (45)** (MDIUsher) **8-8-6** DRMcCabe(6) (b.hind: a.p: led over 3f out tl over 2f out: sn wknd)	1¼	8	8/1	45	10
390[4]	**Flagstaff (USA) (52)** (KRBurke) **4-8-6**(7) PWright(15) (nvr nrr)	2½	9	20/1	47	12
638[5]	**Pearl Dawn (IRE) (53)** (PCClarke) **7-8-7**(7) TField(8) (mid div whn bdly hmpd 3f out: nt rcvr)	2½	10	16/1	43	8
	Another Fiddle (IRE) (54) (JELong) **7-9-1** DHarrison(12) (b: b.hind: a bhd)	7	11	33/1	30	—
202[7]	**Ilandra (IRE) (40)** (GLMoore) **5-7-12**(3) MartinDwyer(1) (a.p: led over 4f out tl over 3f out: wknd over 2f out)	nk	12	33/1	15	—
490[2]	**Ki Chi Saga (USA) (60)** (MMadgwick) **5-9-7** DHolland(11) (prom over 5f)	5	13	4/1[1]	25	—
319[11]	**Shaynes Domain (42)** (RMFlower) **6-8-3b** GHind(7) (prom over 5f)	¾	14	33/1	5	—

				SP	RR	SF
538^{5}	**Sweet Ciseaux (IRE) (45)** (BJLlewellyn) **4-8-1b**(5) JBramhill(9) (led over 3f: wknd 3f out)	1½	**15**	14/1	5	—
				(SP 127.5%)		**15 Rn**

1m 34.9 (3.60) CSF £54.77 CT £685.03 TOTE £3.80: £1.60 £4.40 £6.80 (£28.60) Trio £366.00; £164.97 to Folkestone 22/4/97 OWNER The Optimists Racing Partnership (NEWMARKET) BRED Robert N. Clay
WEIGHT FOR AGE 3yo-14lb

560 Safey Ana (USA) began a forward move over a quarter-of-a-mile from home and, leading inside the final furlong, responded to pressure to gain his first victory over this trip. (5/1)
295 Czarna (IRE) bounced back to form. Showing in front over a quarter-of-a-mile from home, he was collared by the winner inside the final furlong but, to his credit, stuck on really well to the bitter end. (11/1)
Carlys Quest, off the track for six-and-a-half months, was being pushed along at the back of the field over three furlongs from home. Picking up ground in good style below the distance, he certainly did not have the clearest of passages but ran on really strongly and would surely have prevailed with a little further to go. (14/1)
Whispered Melody, who failed to stay one mile three furlongs last time out, was much happier over this trip, but failed to find the necessary turn of foot inside the final furlong. (12/1: op 7/1)
Doctor Bravious (IRE), off the track for over three months, picked up ground under pressure on the outside of the field below the distance and, staying on, only just failed to get into the prize money. (16/1)
Rocky Waters (USA) (8/1: 6/1-9/1)

756 LEVY BOARD H'CAP (0-70) (3-Y.O+) (Class E)
5-00 (5-00) **5f 59y** £2,862.25 (£853.00: £406.50: £183.25) Stalls: Low GOING minus 0.33 sec per fur (GF)

				SP	RR	SF
638^{4}	**Sharp Pearl (70)** (JWhite) **4-10-0b** RHughes(8) (lw: hdwy over 1f out: led ins fnl f: edgd lft: rdn out)	—	**1**	$6/1^{3}$	81	57
601^{7}	**Mister Raider (45)** (EAWheeler) **5-7-12b**(5)ow1 ADaly(6) (hld up: hrd rdn over 1f out: r.o ins fnl f)	1¾	**2**	$6/1^{3}$	51	26
638^{2}	**Justinianus (IRE) (42)** (JJBridger) **5-7-9**(5) RMullen(4) (hdwy over 2f out: n.m.r over 1f out & ins fnl f: r.o)	¾	**3**	$7/2^{1}$	45	21
319^{9}	**Bright Paragon (IRE) (40)** (KTIvory) **8-7-9**(3)ow2 MartinDwyer(3) (b: b.hind: led over 3f: hrd rdn over 1f out: unable qckn fnl f)	1	**4**	33/1	40	14
604^{2}	**Songsheet (62)** (MSSaunders) **4-9-6** RPerham(1) (a.p: led 2f out tl ins fnl f: btn whn n.m.r on ins wl ins fnl f)	1	**5**	$7/2^{1}$	59	35
488^{7}	**Princely Sound (66)** (MBell) **4-9-10** MFenton(7) (c stands' side st: bhd fnl 3f)	1½	**6**	$4/1^{2}$	59	35
569^{12}	**Tachycardia (46)** (RJO'Sullivan) **5-8-4** DHarrison(5) (spd 3f)	s.h	**7**	8/1	39	15
158^{5}	**Come Too Mamma's (55)** (GCBravery) **3-8-3** DRMcCabe(2) (bhd fnl 4f)	1¼	**8**	14/1	44	10
				(SP 113.7%)		**8 Rn**

61.5 secs (1.50) CSF £37.37 CT £132.43 TOTE £9.30: £1.90 £1.90 £1.30 (£51.10) OWNER Mr Dennis Yardy (ASTON ROWANT) BRED D. MacRae
LONG HANDICAP Bright Paragon (IRE) 7-8
WEIGHT FOR AGE 3yo-10lb

638 Sharp Pearl, whose only previous victory came over this course and distance, made smooth headway below the distance and, leading inside the final furlong, kept on well despite drifting left on the camber. (6/1)
541 Mister Raider chased the leaders. Responding to pressure, he stayed on well for second prize but was unable to trouble the winner. He has yet to win on turf. (6/1)
638 Justinianus (IRE) began to take closer order at halfway, and despite meeting traffic problems, he still managed to finish a commendable third. (7/2: 9/2-3/1)
Bright Paragon (IRE) took the field along to the quarter-mile marker and held on well until tapped for toe in the final furlong. He has not won since August 1994. (33/1)
323 Princely Sound (4/1: op 5/2)

T/Plpt: £230.30 (40.12 Tckts). T/Qdpt: £26.10 (24.44 Tckts) AK

0644-NOTTINGHAM (L-H) (Good to firm)
Monday April 21st
WEATHER: cloudy and overcast WIND: moderate half behind

757 OVAL (S) STKS (I) (3-Y.O) (Class G)
2-10 (2-12) **6f 15y** £1,634.50 (£447.00: £209.50) Stalls: High GOING minus 0.13 sec per fur (G)

				SP	RR	SF
649^{8}	**Cairn Dhu (53)** (MrsJRRamsden) **3-8-11** JFortune(2) (bit bkwd: led over 4f out: drvn clr appr fnl f: v.easily)	—	**1**	7/1	68+	22
556^{2}	**Terry's Rose (53)** (RHollinshead) **3-8-6** KDarley(1) (a.p: rdn over 2f out: kpt on wl towards fin)	1¼	**2**	$5/1^{3}$	60	14
588^{6}	**Rockaroundtheclock (58)** (PDEvans) **3-8-11b1** KFallon(11) (prom: outpcd 2f out: rdn & r.o wl ins fnl f)	½	**3**	15/2	63	17
569^{10}	**Blazing Castle (78)** (WGMTurner) **3-8-13**(3) RHavlin(7) (led over 1f: hrd rdn over 2f out: one pce fnl f)	s.h	**4**	12/1	68	22
659^{4}	**Bon Guest (IRE) (61)** (TJNaughton) **3-8-11** PaulEddery(6) (lw: hld up: hdwy & rdn 2f out: nt pce to chal)	2½	**5**	7/1	57	11
556^{7}	**Charlton Spring (IRE) (73)** (RJHodges) **3-8-11** SDrowne(9) (hld up: hmpd over 4f out: no imp fnl 2f)	2½	**6**	6/1	50	4
462^{2}	**Skyers Flyer (IRE) (66)** (RonaldThompson) **3-8-11** NConnorton(8) (hld up & plld hrd: rdn over 2f out: wknd over 1f out)	s.h	**7**	$7/2^{1}$	50	4
556^{10}	**Seamus** (CJHill) **3-8-11** JQuinn(10) (t: bit bkwd: a in rr)	nk	**8**	33/1	49	3
575^{9}	**Move The Clouds (54)** (DNicholls) **3-8-6** TSprake(3) (hld up mid div: rdn & wknd wl over 1f out)	¾	**9**	$4/1^{2}$	42	—
644^{10}	**Heavenly Dancer (56)** (MrsNMacauley) **3-8-6b1** CRutter(4) (s.s: a bhd & outpcd)	2½	**10**	33/1	36	—
	Frandickbob (JohnHarris) **3-8-11** DeanMcKeown(5) (a bhd: t.o)	5	**11**	50/1	27	—
				(SP 125.5%)		**11 Rn**

1m 16.0 (4.50) CSF £40.45 TOTE £9.80: £2.40 £1.90 £2.30 (£28.10) Trio £101.70 OWNER Mr Ronald Thorburn (THIRSK) BRED R. L. Cox
No bid

Cairn Dhu took advantage of this step down to selling company with a very comfortably-gained success and, if he remains in this class, he could run up a sequence. (7/1: 5/1-8/1)
556 Terry's Rose, a quick-actioned filly who raced keenly, was unable to match strides when the winner kicked for home below the distance and, though she kept persevering, was always fighting a lost cause. (5/1)
Rockaroundtheclock was tapped for toe at a crucial time, and a determined last-furlong effort was always going to be too late. (15/2: 5/1-8/1)
Blazing Castle, struggling to hold his place entering the last quarter-mile, did not fail for the want of trying but could not muster the speed to compete with the winner. (12/1: 8/1-14/1)
659 Bon Guest (IRE) is continuing to prove a big disappointment, and at present seems to be having trouble finding his right trip. (7/1: 5/1-8/1)

462 Skyers Flyer (IRE) could never quite get her head in front and, finding very little under pressure, was easily brushed aside. She has still to get her summer coat. (7/2)

758 OVAL (S) STKS (II) (3-Y.O) (Class G)

2-40 (2-43) **6f 15y** £1,634.50 (£447.00: £209.50) Stalls: High GOING minus 0.13 sec per fur (G)

Form	Horse	Dist	Pos	SP	RR	SF
	Municipal Girl (IRE) (45) (BPalling) **3-8-6** TSprake(9) (swtg: bit bkwd: a.p: rdn to ld wl ins fnl f)	—	**1**	33/1	52	15
	Juddy (JohnHarris) **3-8-11** JO'Reilly(8) (cmpt: bit bkwd: s.s: wnt lft: sn chsng ldrs: racd alone & led over 2f out: hdd wl ins fnl f)	1¼	**2**	33/1	54	17
506^{9}	**Gunners Glory (74)** (BJMeehan) **3-9-2b**[1] PatEddery(2) (lw: a.p: led over 3f out tl over 2f out: sn rdn: unable qckn)	1½	**3**	$5/4^{1}$	55	18
	Silver Lining (66) (APJones) **3-9-2** SDrowne(4) (a.p: rdn 2f out: r.o one pce)	hd	**4**	$5/1^{3}$	55	18
	Hi Mujtahid (IRE) (JMBradley) **3-8-6**(5) RFfrench(5) (w'like: bkwd: b: s.s: wl bhd tl hdwy fnl 2f: nvr nrr)	4	**5**	20/1	39	2
556^{8}	**Fit For The Job (IRE) (51)** (TWall) **3-8-13**(3) DGriffiths(10) (lw: led over 2f: rdn & wknd wl over 1f out)	1¼	**6**	25/1	41	4
546^{5}	**Heathyard's Flight (52)** (RHollinshead) **3-8-11** KDarley(7) (outpcd: a bhd)	5	**7**	33/1	23	—
546^{7}	**Antares (50)** (NTinkler) **3-8-11** KimTinkler(6) (sn outpcd)	nk	**8**	33/1	22	—
602^{3}	**Hever Golf Stormer (IRE) (58)** (TJNaughton) **3-8-11** PaulEddery(1) (sn drvn along: a bhd & outpcd)	2½	**9**	8/1	15	—
556^{3}	**Bellarula** (MDods) **3-8-7**ow1 SWebster(3) (chsd ldrs: rdn ½-wy: sn btn)	2	**10**	$3/1^{2}$	6	—
				(SP 117.6%)	**10 Rn**	

1m 16.2 (4.70) CSF £709.13 TOTE £36.20: £3.90 £5.20 £1.40 (£232.20) Trio £217.30; £165.32 to Folkestone 22/4/97 OWNER Merthyr Motor Auctions (COWBRIDGE) BRED K. and Mrs Cullen

No bid

Municipal Girl (IRE) opened her account at the first time of asking in her second season and, though she still looks to have a bit left to work on, there is no saying she will not win again. (33/1)

Juddy, a strongly-made half-brother to Burcroft, is sure to benefit from the run. He performed extremely well and, had he not drifted over to the far rail to race alone, he would definitely have made a winning debut. (33/1)

Gunners Glory, equipped with blinkers for the first time, looked a class apart from these rivals but, after striking the front, was unable to extend his advantage and his measure had been taken below the distance. (5/4)

Silver Lining, successful on his debut last year, is still clinging onto his winter coat, and he should be able to improve on this performance once the warmer weather arrives. (5/1: 3/1-11/2)

Hi Mujtahid (IRE), a very backward-looking half-brother to prolific winner Sooty Tern, walked out of the stalls and was well adrift until running on when it was all too late. He will definitely improve for the experience, and will also benefit from a stiffer test of stamina. (20/1)

602 Hever Golf Stormer (IRE) (8/1: op 5/1)

759 EDGBASTON H'CAP (0-70) (3-Y.O+) (Class E)

3-10 (3-12) **6f 15y** £3,330.25 (£997.00: £478.50: £219.25) Stalls: High GOING minus 0.13 sec per fur (G)

Form	Horse	Dist	Pos	SP	RR	SF
585^{3}	**Grey Kingdom (41)** (MBrittain) **6-7-9**(7) DMernagh(17) (mde all stands' side: clr fnl 2f)	—	**1**	$3/1^{1}$	58	47
593^{3}	**Stephensons Rocket (51)** (RAFahey) **6-8-12** ACulhane(16) (chsd wnr stands' side: no imp fnl 2f)	6	**2**	10/1	52	41
584^{6}	**Aquatic Queen (54)** (RJWeaver) **3-8-4** NConnorton(18) (b.hind: racd stands' side: hdwy over 1f out: r.o)	1½	**3**	40/1	51	29
569^{2}	**Robo Magic (USA) (46)** (LMontagueHall) **5-8-4**(3) FLynch(15) (b: lw: chsd ldrs stands' side: one pce fnl 2f)	2½	**4**	$9/2^{2}$	37	26
541*	**Napoleon Star (IRE) (49)** (SRBowring) **6-8-10b** NAdams(7) (prom far side: r.o wl fnl f)	hd	**5**	$9/1^{3}$	39+	28
	Souperficial (56) (NTinkler) **6-9-3v** KimTinkler(9) (bit bkwd: hdwy over 1f out: nrst fin)	1¾	**6**	25/1	42+	31
	Almasi (IRE) (67) (CFWall) **5-10-0** GDuffield(3) (lw: racd far side: dwlt: hdwy 2f out: nt rch ldrs)	¾	**7**	12/1	51+	40
596^{13}	**Halmanerror (59)** (MrsJRRamsden) **7-9-6** JFortune(8) (nvr nr ldrs)	½	**8**	10/1	42	31
109^{11}	**Tymeera (56)** (BPalling) **4-9-3** TSprake(14) (swtg: prom stands' side over 4f)	1¼	**9**	11/1	35	24
541^{4}	**Petraco (IRE) (57)** (NASmith) **9-9-4** JWeaver(5) (prom: led far side over 3f out tl wl over 1f out)	1	**10**	10/1	34	23
434^{6}	**Lunar Music (63)** (RonaldThompson) **3-8-13** TWilliams(4) (s.s: a bhd)	¾	**11**	20/1	38	16
	Paddy's Rice (56) (MBlanshard) **6-9-3** RCochrane(6) (bit bkwd: a in rr)	½	**12**	16/1	29	18
585^{11}	**Magazine Gap (47)** (PatMitchell) **4-8-3**(5) AmandaSanders(2) (lw: prom far side 4f)	½	**13**	25/1	19	8
	Welsh Mountain (58) (MJHeaton-Ellis) **4-9-5v** JCarroll(10) (led far side over 2f: wknd 2f out)	3	**14**	16/1	22	11
644^{9}	**Baptismal Rock (IRE) (56)** (BJCurley) **3-8-6** JQuinn(1) (outpcd)	¾	**15**	16/1	18	—
601^{5}	**Sir Tasker (46)** (JLHarris) **9-8-7** KDarley(11) (outpcd)	s.h	**16**	12/1	8	—
545^{14}	**Smart Guest (67)** (DShaw) **5-10-0b** JFanning(13) (b: t.o)	12	**17**	25/1	—	—
	Credite Risque (58) (JAGlover) **4-8-12**(7) TPengkerego(12) (t.o)	17	**18**	33/1	—	—
				(SP 143.5%)	**18 Rn**	

1m 13.5 (2.00) CSF £33.31 CT £771.76 TOTE £4.90: £1.50 £2.60 £3.10 £1.40 (£32.00) Trio £419.50 OWNER Mr Mel Brittain (WARTHILL) BRED Northgate Lodge Stud Ltd

WEIGHT FOR AGE 3yo-11lb

IN-FOCUS: **This race showed what a benefit a high draw was at this meeting. This was also Dean Mernagh's first winner.**

585 Grey Kingdom made short work of these rivals from the bottom of the handicap, to record his first success at sprinting and, as long as he can produce performances like this, there should be little to stop him from following up. (3/1)

593 Stephensons Rocket did his best to keep tabs on the winner, but that rival was always going a gear too fast and he was unable to make the slightest impression. (10/1)

Aquatic Queen has shown little sign of ability in the past, but she did well to make the frame here, and obviously has some when she decides to put it to good use. (40/1)

569 Robo Magic (USA) does most of his racing and all his winning at Lingfield, so this promising effort suggests that, when he returns there, another success is more than likely. (9/2: op 8/1)

541* Napoleon Star (IRE) did best of those racing on the far side, but they were always several lengths adrift. At least it shows he is still on song. (9/1)

Souperficial only wins in his turn, but he is probably more effective on Turf and is not past his sell-by date as yet. (25/1)

Almasi (IRE) recovered from a sluggish start and got to the front briefly in the latter stages over on the far rail, but they were always being led by the stands' side group, and she was never a serious factor. She can be improved in her coat and will be all the better for this run. (12/1)

760 LORDS CLAIMING STKS (3-Y.O+) (Class F)

3-40 (3-43) **5f 13y** £2,854.50 (£792.00: £379.50) Stalls: High GOING: Not Established

				SP	RR	SF
702^{9}	**Double Oscar (IRE) (52)** (DNicholls) **4-9-4b** AlexGreaves(3) (outpcd: hdwy 2f out: rdn to ld ins fnl f: all out)	—	**1**	11/2^{3}	59	29
*659**	**General Sir Peter (IRE) (69)** (NACallaghan) **5-9-3**(5) AmandaSanders(11) (lw: w ldr: led over 2f out tl over 1f out: rallied & ev ch fnl f: r.o)	s.h	**2**	6/4^{1}	63	33
386^{8}	**Chief's Lady (29)** (JMBradley) **5-8-2**(5) RFfrench(9) (a.p: led over 1f out tl ins fnl f)	1¾	**3**	33/1	42	12
429^{3}	**Sweet Mate (44)** (SRBowring) **5-8-7b**(7) FBoyle(1) (b.hind: chsd ldrs: rdn & outpcd over 1f out: kpt on towards fin)	nk	**4**	14/1	48	18
541^{12}	**Secret Miss (45)** (APJones) **5-8-9** TSprake(2) (chsd ldrs: rdn & ev ch over 1f out: no ex fnl f)	½	**5**	20/1	42	12
371^{6}	**Super Rocky (68)** (RBastiman) **8-9-1b**(5) HBastiman(7) (chsd ldrs: ev ch over 1f out: wknd ins fnl f)	1¾	**6**	6/1	47	17
593^{7}	**Southern Dominion (40)** (MissJFCraze) **5-9-2** SWebster(4) (b.hind: swtchd lft & effrt 2f out: nvr nrr)	½	**7**	33/1	42	12
593^{9}	**Featherstone Lane (40)** (MissLCSiddall) **6-8-13v**(7) TSiddall(8) (nvr trbld ldrs)	½	**8**	20/1	44	14
	Miss Fugit Penance (42) (PDEvans) **3-7-6**(7) AMcCarthy(5) (b.nr fore: outpcd)	¾	**9**	25/1	31	—
473^{12}	**Mister Sean (IRE) (28)** (JMBradley) **4-8-5**(7) JFowle(12) (b.hind: s.s: a outpcd)	¾	**10**	33/1	31	1
698^{7}	**Maydoro** (MDods) **4-9-3** RLappin(10) (s.i.s: a bhd)	½	**11**	33/1	35	5
656^{2}	**Captain Sinbad (69)** (KSBridgwater) **5-9-6b** SDrowne(13) (led over 2f: wknd wl over 1f out)	2½	**12**	4/1^{2}	30	—

(SP 121.5%) **12 Rn**

62.6 secs (3.70) CSF £12.07 TOTE £4.60: £1.20 £1.30 £8.70 (£4.10) Trio £138.00 OWNER Trilby Racing (THIRSK) BRED Tasia Limited

WEIGHT FOR AGE 3yo-10lb

STEWARDS' ENQUIRY Lappin susp. 30/4-9/5/97 & Dods fined £1,600 under Rule 151(ii) (schooling in public). Maydoro susp 30/4-29/5/97

303 Double Oscar (IRE) landed quite a touch with a hard-earned success, and a deal of the credit must go to the lass on top. (11/2)

659* General Sir Peter (IRE) does seem to need to get his toe in, but he did very little wrong on this occasion, and was probably a shade unfortunate to lose out on the nod. (6/4: op 4/6)

Chief's Lady, having her first try at the minimum trip, showed up with the pace and had every chance until finding herself out-gunned nearing the finish. This was one of her better efforts and she is capable of winning at this level. (33/1)

429 Sweet Mate had trouble handling this step-down to the minimum trip, and he was in trouble approaching the final furlong but, to his credit he was renewing his effort at the finish and has not stopped winning yet. (14/1)

Secret Miss has been struggling to recover her form for quite some time, and she moved very gingerly to post. Nevertheless she ran a race full of promise and, when the rain arrives, she will be worth keeping an eye on. (20/1)

371 Super Rocky, fighting for the lead approaching the final furlong, had to admit the principals too sharp for him this time, but this outing should help to put an edge on him. (6/1)

761 'MICHELOZZO' CONDITIONS STKS (4-Y.O+) (Class C)

4-10 (4-10) **1m 6f 15y** £4,401.49 (£1,638.50: £794.25: £333.75: £141.88: £65.13) Stalls: Low GOING: 0.15 sec per fur (G)

				SP	RR	SF
	Nabhaan (IRE) (94) (DMorley) **4-8-8** RCochrane(4) (hld up: hdwy over 3f out: rdn to ld wl ins fnl f)	—	**1**	7/2^{3}	109	54
630a^{4}	**Sheer Danzig (IRE) (104)** (RWArmstrong) **5-9-4** MHills(5) (lw: led: qcknd clr over 5f out: hrd rdn over 1f out: hdd wl ins fnl f)	½	**2**	5/2^{2}	116	63
	Key to My Heart (IRE) (113) (MissSEHall) **7-9-4** JWeaver(3) (b: lw: plld hrd: chsd ldr 5f out: ev ch over 1f out: one pce)	4	**3**	2/1^{1}	112	59
	Corradini (104) (HRACecil) **5-9-4** KFallon(6) (bit bkwd: hld up: rdn 5f out: styd on one pce fnl 2f)	1	**4**	2/1^{1}	111	58
	Blatant Outburst (68) (MissSJWilton) **7-8-10** DaneO'Neill(2) (hld up: wl bhd fnl 4f: t.o)	17	**5**	66/1	48 t	30
558^{4}	**Get A Life** (JohnHarris) **4-8-3** JO'Reilly(1) (bit bkwd: plld hrd: chsd ldr 9f: wknd over 3f out: t.o)	15	**6**	100/1	26 t	6

(SP 119.9%) **6 Rn**

3m 7.4 (8.90) CSF £12.54 TOTE £5.00: £3.60 £1.60 (£4.70) OWNER Mr Hamdan Al Maktoum (NEWMARKET) BRED Shadwell Estate Company Limited

WEIGHT FOR AGE 4yo-2lb

Nabhaan (IRE) seems to be progressing with age and looks to need this sort of trip now. (7/2)

630a Sheer Danzig (IRE) had plenty of use made of him this time, and the longer trip did not appear a problem. (5/2)

Key to My Heart (IRE) did not help his cause by proving a handful to settle and ,although he has won a Yorkshire Cup, his trainer thinks he barely gets this distance. (2/1)

Corradini did not look cherry-ripe, and it remains to be seen whether he will need two miles as a minimum now he is another year older. (2/1)

762 TRENT BRIDGE H'CAP (0-80) (4-Y.O+) (Class D)

4-40 (4-42) **1m 6f 15y** £3,900.40 (£1,166.20: £558.60: £254.80) Stalls: Low GOING: 0.15 sec per fur (G)

				SP	RR	SF
	The Butterwick Kid (45) (RAFahey) **4-7-7**(7) RWinston(13) (hld up: hdwy 6f out: styd on to ld nr fin)	—	**1**	20/1	55	27
	Samuel Scott (63) (MCPipe) **4-9-4** PatEddery(6) (chsd ldr: rdn to ld over 3f out: hdd nr fin)	nk	**2**	9/2^{2}	73	45
	Kintavi (39) (TWDonnelly) **7-7-10** JQuinn(8) (b: a.p: ev ch 1f out: r.o)	½	**3**	8/1	48	22
728^{5}	**Dancing Cavalier (70)** (RHollinshead) **4-9-8**(3) FLynch(10) (hld up: stdy hdwy 5f out: one pce fnl 2f)	4	**4**	5/1^{3}	75	47
552^{3}	**Moonraking (49)** (TJEtherington) **4-8-4** DaneO'Neill(7) (a.p: no hdwy fnl 2f)	1¾	**5**	14/1	52	24
481^{4}	**Reaganesque (USA) (53)** (PGMurphy) **5-8-10** SDrowne(2) (led over 10f: wknd over 1f out)	1¾	**6**	9/1	54	28
650^{2}	**Road Racer (IRE) (53)** (MrsJRRamsden) **4-8-8** JFortune(3) (hld up: nvr nr to chal)	1¾	**7**	6/1	52	24
	Gymcrak Tiger (IRE) (60) (GHolmes) **7-9-3** KFallon(11) (b.hind: lw: nvr trbld ldrs)	hd	**8**	14/1	59	33
481^{10}	**Jump The Lights (58)** (SPCWoods) **4-8-13** KDarley(14) (lw: dwlt: a bhd)	hd	**9**	14/1	56	28
607^{12}	**Arcady (62)** (JLHarris) **4-9-3** PaulEddery(5) (s.s: a bhd)	2½	**10**	25/1	58	30
499^{3}	**Midyan Blue (IRE) (70)** (JMPEustace) **7-9-13** RCochrane(4) (plld hrd: prom: racd alone centre in st: rdn & wknd 3f out)	1¼	**11**	4/1^{1}	64	38
	Temptress (64) (JLHarris) **4-9-5** DeanMcKeown(12) (bit bkwd: a bhd)	nk	**12**	16/1	58	30
613^{5}	**Heighth of Fame (50)** (JHetherton) **6-8-7** GDuffield(1) (bhd fnl 3f)	¾	**13**	16/1	43	17
	Beauchamp Knight (55) (HCandy) **4-8-10** CRutter(9) (bit bkwd: hld up mid div: bhd fnl 4f: t.o)	9	**14**	12/1	38	10

(SP 138.3%) **14 Rn**

3m 10.9 (12.40) CSF £112.44 CT £758.55 TOTE £27.80: £5.70 £2.30 £4.10 (£165.00) Trio £540.70; £388.41 to Folkestone 22/4/97 OWNER Mr Robert Chambers (MALTON) BRED Scorrier Stud

WEIGHT FOR AGE 4yo-2lb

IN-FOCUS: **Robert Winston was riding his first winner.**

The Butterwick Kid is considered by his trainer to have strengthened during the winter. (20/1)
Samuel Scott showed promise in one run over hurdles in March. Battling hard to keep Kintavi at bay, he could not hold the winner's late surge. (9/2: 3/1-5/1)
Kintavi, twice a winner over hurdles last winter, progressed from a mark of 82 to 99 so he was entitled to go close off only 39 here. (8/1)
728 Dancing Cavalier may have found this coming too soon after Newbury three days ago. (5/1)
552 Moonraking did have a longer trip this time, but this faster ground may not have been in his favour. (14/1)
481 Reaganesque (USA) seems more effective over a mile-and-a-half. (9/1)
Jump The Lights (14/1: 33/1-12/1)

763 NOTTINGHAM LADIES' H'CAP (0-75) (3-Y.O+) (Class F)

5-10 (5-14) **1m 1f 213y** £2,277.00 (£627.00: £297.00) Stalls: Low GOING: 0.15 sec per fur (G)

				SP	RR	SF
163^{5}	**Rasayel (USA) (65)** (PDEvans) **7-10-9**(7) MissKChilton(3) (hld up: hdwy over 4f out: led over 2f out: clr 1f out: r.o wl)	—	**1**	11/1	82	60
	Epic Stand (60) (MrsJRRamsden) **3-9-4**(4) MissERamsden(15) (lw: s.s: hdwy 6f out: wnt lft 2f out: styd on one pce fnl f)	6	**2**	$13/2^{2}$	67	28
435^{9}	**Squared Away (47)** (JWPayne) **5-9-8b**(4) MissCLake(4) (lw: bhd tl hdwy over 3f out: styd on fnl f)	nk	**3**	14/1	54	32
	Blaze of Oak (USA) (45) (JMBradley) **6-9-6**(4)ow2 MissVRoberts(18) (hld up: hdwy over 4f out: ev ch 2f out: one pce)	¾	**4**	33/1	51	27
607*	**Fresh Fruit Daily (70)** (PAKelleway) **5-11-3**(4) MissSKelleway(6) (a.p: ev ch over 2f out: one pce)	½	**5**	$9/2^{1}$	75	53
291^{5}	**Seattle Alley (USA) (68)** (PRWebber) **4-10-12**(7) MrsFWebber(13) (lw: hld up: hdwy 3f out: r.o ins fnl f)	s.h	**6**	8/1	73	51
	Breezed Well (44) (KGWingrove) **11-9-5**(4)ow1 MrsHNoonan(7) (nvr nr to chal)	2½	**7**	25/1	45	22
587^{12}	**Mezzoramio (48)** (KAMorgan) **5-9-9v**(4) MrsCWilliams(2) (no hdwy fnl 2f)	½	**8**	16/1	48	26
	Alfahaal (IRE) (60) (RFJohnsonHoughton) **4-10-11** MissEJohnsonHoughton(12) (bkwd: led over 6f: wknd fnl f)	hd	**9**	10/1	60	38
650^{9}	**Cohiba (43)** (BJCurley) **4-9-4**(4) MissABroderick(8) (n.d)	2½	**10**	9/1	39	17
544^{8}	**Fourdaned (IRE) (63)** (PWHarris) **4-11-0** MissAElsey(16) (prom: led over 3f out tl over 2f out: wknd over 1f out)	½	**11**	11/1	58	36
435^{7}	**Gold Blade (68)** (JPearce) **8-11-5** MrsLPearce(11) (hld up: hdwy over 2f out: eased whn btn ins fnl f)	½	**12**	$7/1^{3}$	62	40
	North Bear (53) (GMMcCourt) **5-9-11**(7) MissMO'Sullivan(14) (a bhd)	5	**13**	16/1	39	17
571^{9}	**Mybotye (66)** (RBastiman) **4-10-10**(7) MissRBastiman(17) (dwlt: a bhd)	1¾	**14**	20/1	49	27
	Master Millfield (IRE) (64) (CJHill) **5-11-1** MrsSBosley(1) (bkwd: prom tl wknd over 2f out)	nk	**15**	12/1	47	25
523^{6}	**Mac's Delight (67)** (NMBabbage) **3-10-1** MrsDKettlewell(5) (bkwd: prom over 7f)	1¾	**16**	20/1	47	8
	Tales Of Hearsay (GER) (67) (CFCJackson) **7-10-11**(7) MissSJackson(10) (bkwd: a bhd: t.o)	13	**17**	33/1	26	4
	Polly Peculiar (65) (BSmart) **6-10-12**(4) MissVMarshall(9) (bit bkwd: s.s: hld up mid div: bhd fnl 3f: t.o)	3½	**18**	10/1	19	—
				(SP 145.4%)	**18 Rn**	

2m 12.1 (9.60) CSF £81.69 CT £974.65 TOTE £18.60: £4.70 £2.50 £2.60 £7.20 (£136.90) Trio £380.70; £434.35 to Folkestone 22/4/97
OWNER Pentons Haulage and Cold Storage Ltd (WELSHPOOL) BRED Gainsborough Farm
WEIGHT FOR AGE 3yo-17lb
IN-FOCUS: **Karen Chilton was the third rider at the meeting to record their first winner.**
163 Rasayel (USA), rested after a busy midwinter campaign, spread-eagled this large field. (11/1: 8/1-12/1)
Epic Stand, the paddock pick, was 4lb higher than when winning a nursery at Redcar last back-end. (13/2: op 4/1)
Squared Away, appreciating this longer distance, was back to the same mark as when winning a Ladies' race at Redcar last June. (14/1)
Blaze of Oak (USA) has been given a chance by the Handicapper, having finishing third in a seller last September. (33/1)
607* Fresh Fruit Daily could not defy a 7lb hike in the weights. (9/2)
291 Seattle Alley (USA), twice a winner over this trip at Pontefract, may need further on a course as flat as this. (8/1)
544 Fourdaned (IRE) (11/1: op 7/1)

764 HEADINGLEY LIMITED STKS (0-70) (3-Y.O) (Class E)

5-40 (5-41) **1m 1f 213y** £3,044.25 (£909.00: £434.50: £197.25) Stalls: Low GOING: 0.15 sec per fur (G)

				SP	RR	SF
539*	**Dominant Duchess (65)** (JWHills) **3-8-10** KFallon(3) (lw: s.i.s: bhd tl hdwy 3f out: rdn to ld over 1f out: qcknd clr: easily)	—	**1**	$8/1^{3}$	79+	31
	Lady of The Lake (70) (JLDunlop) **3-8-8** PatEddery(4) (bit bkwd: hld up & bhd: rdn: swtchd lft & hdwy 3f out: chsd wnr over 1f out: no imp)	3½	**2**	$5/2^{2}$	71	23
	Imperial Or Metric (IRE) (70) (RAFahey) **3-8-11** ACulhane(2) (h.d.w: bit bkwd: a.p: led over 2f out tl over 1f out: one pce)	3	**3**	20/1	70	22
568^{3}	**Around Fore Alliss (70)** (TGMills) **3-8-11** KDarley(8) (plld hrd: prom: led over 4f out tl over 2f out: wknd over 1f out)	6	**4**	14/1	60	12
535^{11}	**Swan Island (68)** (BPalling) **3-8-8** TSprake(1) (b.hind: hld up & plld hrd: hdwy 3f out: wknd over 1f out)	¾	**5**	$8/1^{3}$	56	8
*513**	**Weet And See (67)** (RHollinshead) **3-8-10**(3) DGriffiths(10) (hld up: rdn & wknd over 2f out)	9	**6**	9/1	46	—
431^{9}	**Mogul (69)** (NAGraham) **3-8-11** AMcGlone(5) (prom tl rdn & wknd over 2f out)	hd	**7**	12/1	44	—
431^{3}	**The Deejay (IRE) (67)** (MrsMerritaJones) **3-8-11** JFortune(6) (led: rdn & hdd over 2f out: sn wknd)	¾	**8**	$8/1^{3}$	43	—
535*	**Freedom Chance (IRE) (70)** (JWHills) **3-8-10**(3) MHenry(9) (lw: a bhd)	3½	**9**	$7/4^{1}$	39	—
600^{9}	**Noirie (67)** (MBrittain) **3-8-11** JCarroll(7) (prom 7f: t.o)	12	**10**	12/1	18	—
				(SP 135.1%)	**10 Rn**	

2m 11.8 (9.30) CSF £30.11 TOTE £8.90: £3.50 £1.60 £2.40 (£8.40) Trio £126.30 OWNER Mr C. R. Nelson (LAMBOURN) BRED L. Godfrey
539* Dominant Duchess managed to overcome this shorter distance, but it was a case of the further she went the better she got. (8/1: op 5/1)
Lady of The Lake could not go with the winner from below the distance. (5/2)
Imperial Or Metric (IRE) soon found his measure taken once the winner took over. (20/1)
568 Around Fore Alliss did not settle as well as his rider would have liked. (14/1)
Swan Island had no chance of staying this longer trip given the way she pulled. (8/1: op 16/1)
513* Weet And See (9/1: 5/1-10/1)
431 The Deejay (IRE) (8/1: op 5/1)
463 Noirie (12/1: op 8/1)

T/Jkpt: Not won; £72,146.49 to Folkestone 22/4/97. T/Plpt: £229.80 (71.33 Tckts). T/Qdpt: £38.30 (25.89 Tckts) IM/KH

0601-FOLKESTONE (R-H) (Good to firm)
Tuesday April 22nd
WEATHER: fair WIND: almost nil

765 WALMER MAIDEN APPRENTICE STKS (3-Y.O) (Class F)
2-00 (2-00) **6f 189y** £2,277.00 (£627.00: £297.00) Stalls: Low GOING: 0.00 sec per fur (G)

				SP	RR	SF
	Barba Papa (IRE) (LMCumani) **3-8-6**(6) RFfrench(6) (w'like: a.p: led over 1f out: qcknd: easily)	—	**1**	7/4[1]	83+	40
	Pointe Fine (FR) (JWHills) **3-8-4**(3) MHenry(2) (a.p: rdn & ev ch over 2f out: unable qckn)	7	**2**	10/1	62	19
	Tisima (FR) (IABalding) **3-8-4**(3) MartinDwyer(9) (lw: led over 5f out tl over 1f out: one pce)	s.h	**3**	7/2[2]	62	19
685[3]	**Falls O'Moness (IRE) (70)** (KRBurke) **3-7-11**(10) PWright(4) (lw: hdwy over 3f out: one pce fnl 2f)	3½	**4**	9/2[3]	53	10
	Storyteller (IRE) (NJHWalker) **3-8-2**(10) BarrySmith(1) (w'like: no hdwy fnl 2f)	1¼	**5**	20/1	56	13
	Lucky Dip (70) (DRCElsworth) **3-8-7** DGriffiths(11) (led over 1f: wknd 3f out)	nk	**6**	13/2	50	7
	Dr Woodstock (MartynMeade) **3-8-9**(3) DSweeney(5) (nvr nrr)	hd	**7**	16/1	55	12
531[6]	**Geordie Lad (58)** (JABennett) **3-8-9**(3) SophieMitchell(8) (prom over 4f)	3½	**8**	33/1	46	3
	Blue Imperial (FR) (JWHills) **3-8-12** JDSmith(10) (bit bkwd: bhd fnl 3f)	¾	**9**	14/1	45	2
	Wheildon (SCWilliams) **3-8-2**(10) DarrenWilliams(3) (b.hind: w'like: lw: bhd fnl 3f)	s.h	**10**	33/1	45	2
	Dozen Roses (44) (TMJones) **3-8-7** ADaly(7) (a bhd)	¾	**11**	33/1	38	—
				(SP 125.3%)	**11 Rn**	

1m 26.0 (4.60) CSF £20.08 TOTE £2.40: £1.30 £3.90 £1.60 (£18.00) Trio £20.20 OWNER Dr M. Boffa (NEWMARKET) BRED Rathasker Stud

Barba Papa (IRE), who finished second in heavy ground in Italy on his only start as a two-year-old, has reportedly been working well at home and proved to be in a different class to these rivals, sweeping into the lead over a furlong out and quickening right away to win with a ton in hand. He can go on from here. (7/4)

Pointe Fine (FR), one of three almost in line entering the straight, just won the battle for second prize but had no hope with the winner. (10/1: 6/1-11/1)

Tisima (FR), a leggy filly, looked a picture in the paddock and was soon at the head of affairs. Collared below the distance, she was firmly put in her place by the winner and lost second place on the line. She should soon pick up a small race. (7/2)

685 Falls O'Moness (IRE) is a very lightly-made filly, and was made to look very pedestrian in the straight. She is very exposed and lack of substance is hardly helping her cause. (9/2: 5/2-5/1)

Storyteller (IRE), a medium-sized individual, moved up into midfield running down the hill but could make no further impression in the straight. (20/1)

Lucky Dip, who has changed stables since last season, broke best of all but, under tender handling, she lost her place running down the hill. (13/2)

Blue Imperial (FR) (14/1: 10/1-16/1)

766 FOLKESTONE TOWN LIMITED STKS (0-70) (3-Y.O+) (Class E)
2-30 (2-31) **6f 189y** £3,018.25 (£901.00: £430.50: £195.25) Stalls: Low GOING: 0.00 sec per fur (G)

				SP	RR	SF
560[5]	**Victory Team (IRE) (70)** (GBBalding) **5-9-6** RHughes(8) (a gng wl: stdy hdwy over 3f out: led on bit 1f out: easily)	—	**1**	3/1[1]	73	51
509[11]	**Manikato (USA) (70)** (DJSCosgrove) **3-8-7** MRimmer(2) (lw: lost pl over 3f out: rallied over 1f out: unable qckn ins fnl f)	1	**2**	6/1	71	36
643[2]	**Apollo Red (68)** (GLMoore) **8-10-0** CandyMorris(4) (led to 1f out: one pce)	1	**3**	9/2[2]	76	54
	Bon Luck (IRE) (70) (JABennett) **5-9-6** AClark(7) (rdn 3f out: hdwy over 1f out: r.o one pce)	nk	**4**	12/1	68	46
639[3]	**Gulliver (70)** (NJHWalker) **4-8-13**(7) BarrySmith(3) (b: b.hind: lw: rdn 3f out: hdwy over 1f out: nvr nrr)	1¾	**5**	13/2	64	42
477*	**Sharp 'n Smart (69)** (BSmart) **5-9-3**(5) ADaly(10) (lw: chsd ldr 6f out to 2f out: wknd fnl f)	s.h	**6**	5/1[3]	65	43
	Press On Nicky (70) (WRMuir) **4-9-3** JReid(9) (prom over 5f)	3½	**7**	9/2[2]	52	30
	No Extras (IRE) (70) (GLMoore) **7-9-6** SWhitworth(5) (bkwd: a bhd)	1½	**8**	14/1	52	30
585[7]	**Will Do (68)** (MartynMeade) **4-9-1**(5) DSweeney(1) (bhd fnl 4f)	nk	**9**	16/1	51	29
				(SP 125.9%)	**9 Rn**	

1m 25.7 (4.30) CSF £21.60 TOTE £4.30: £1.60 £2.00 £1.10 (£11.20) Trio £24.70 OWNER Mr R. J. Lavelle (ANDOVER) BRED Barronstown and Swettenham Studs and Ron Con Ltd

WEIGHT FOR AGE 3yo-13lb

560 Victory Team (IRE) won this in unbelievable fashion. To say Hughes had a double handful entering the straight would be something of an understatement, and the gelding cruised into the lead on the bridle a furlong from home to win with any amount in hand, and land his first Turf success. The winning distance is certainly no reflection of his superiority. Although both his All-Weather victories have come over a mile, this is his trip on grass. (3/1)

Manikato (USA) looked extremely well in the paddock, and was very well-supported in the market. Having been outpaced running down the hill, he managed to get back into it below the distance, but is greatly flattered to finish so close to the winner. (6/1: op 12/1)

643 Apollo Red, officially worse-in at the weights, nevertheless ran another fine race, setting the pace until collared a furlong from home. He has been a model of consistency so far this year despite a very hectic programme - this was his eleventh outing - and he is a real credit to his trainer. (9/2: 3/1-5/1)

Bon Luck (IRE), tailed off in two runs over hurdles this year, ran better here, staying on in the straight and only just failing to take third prize. Nevertheless he remains a maiden. (12/1: 8/1-14/1)

639 Gulliver looked extremely well beforehand, but the drop in distance was always against him and he was only staying on when it was all over. He needs a step-up in trip not a step-down. (13/2: 4/1-7/1)

477* Sharp 'n Smart raced in second place to the straight but had nothing more to give in the final furlong. He is not very consistent. (5/1: 4/1-6/1)

Press On Nicky (9/2: 6/1-4/1)

No Extras (IRE) (14/1: op 8/1) 60? 62+ 53+ 47

767 SANDLING (S) STKS (2-Y.O) (Class G)
3-00 (3-00) **5f** £1,984.50 (£547.00: £259.50) Stalls: Low GOING: 0.00 sec per fur (G)

				SP	RR	SF
	Lasham (NACallaghan) **2-8-11** SDrowne(2) (neat: hld up: led over 1f out: rdn & r.o wl)	—	**1**	8/1	72	21
536[7]	**Miss Scooter** (APJones) **2-8-6** TSprake(4) (hld up: rdn over 1f out: unable qckn)	3	**2**	4/1[2]	57	6
472[9]	**Swanmore Lady (IRE)** (SCWilliams) **2-8-6** DRMcCabe(9) (bit bkwd: lost pl over 3f out: rallied 2f out: one pce)	s.h	**3**	20/1	57	6

				SP	RR	SF
	Calliram (MBlanshard) **2-8-6** JQuinn(8) (small: bit bkwd: outpcd: hdwy over 1f out: nvr nrr)	3	**4**	33/1	48	—
	Primfaheights (TMJones) **2-8-6** RPerham(7) (neat: bit bkwd: lost pl over 3f out: r.o one pce fnl f)	3	**5**	25/1	38	—
592[4]	**Pink Ticket** (PDEvans) **2-8-6** JFEgan(1) (chsd ldrs 3f)	hd	**6**	10/1	38	—
648[3]	**Sea Imp (IRE)** (MartynMeade) **2-8-6** JReid(3) (led over 3f)	1¾	**7**	11/10[1]	32	—
	Ashjajon (JWhite) **2-8-7**[ow1] WJO'Connor(5) (w'like: bit bkwd: s.s: a bhd)	2½	**8**	8/1	25	—
682[9]	**Tinos Island (IRE)** (MHTompkins) **2-8-3**(3) MHenry(6) (prom over 2f)	2½	**9**	7/1[3]	16	—
				(SP 123.0%)		**9 Rn**

61.9 secs (4.30) CSF £38.05 TOTE £13.70: £4.10 £1.50 £8.10 (£22.10) Trio £152.10; £130.71 to Epsom 23/4/97 OWNER Mr N. A. Callaghan (NEWMARKET) BRED M. H. D. Madden and P. A. Tylor
Bt in 6,000 gns

OFFICIAL EXPLANATION **Swanmore Lady (IRE): the rider reported that he didn't ride out the filly for third place, as she had lost her action and he felt it prudent to hold her together.**

IN-FOCUS: **This was a very poor field with the majority of the runners lacking any scope whatsoever.**

Lasham is certainly on the small side, but the stable often do well in this type of event and he definitely looked fit enough, coming through to lead below the distance, and asserting his authority inside the final furlong. (8/1: 5/1-10/1)

Miss Scooter is very lightly-made. Unable to contain the winner in the final furlong, she had a battle for second prize. (4/1: 3/1-9/2)

Swanmore Lady (IRE), still not looking fully wound-up, broke well enough but soon got outpaced. She got back into it a quarter-of-a-mile from home and, in a battle for second place, only just lost out. (20/1)

Calliram is only tiny, but still looked as though the run would do her good. Unable to go the early pace, she was doing all her best work in the closing stages. (33/1)

Primfaheights is not very big and was carrying some condition. Outpaced over three furlongs from home, she plodded on again in the closing stages only to find the principals already home and dry. Another furlong would suit her. (25/1)

592 Pink Ticket has very little substance but raced in second place until the two-furlong marker. She certainly has early speed, but has now been beaten in four sellers. (10/1: 7/2-12/1)

Ashjajon (8/1: 20/1-7/1)

Tinos Island (IRE) (7/1: 7/2-8/1)

768 BARHAM MEDIAN AUCTION MAIDEN STKS (3-Y.O) (Class E)

3-30 (3-31) **6f** £3,148.25 (£941.00: £450.50: £205.25) Stalls: Low GOING: 0.00 sec per fur (G)

				SP	RR	SF
	Peppiatt (RAkehurst) **3-9-0** SSanders(2) (w'like: a.p: rdn over 1f out: led ins fnl f: r.o wl)	—	**1**	10/1	81	52
694[3]	**John Emms (IRE) (71)** (MBell) **3-9-0** JReid(10) (a.p: led over 2f out tl ins fnl f: unable qckn)	1¼	**2**	11/10[1]	78	49
474[5]	**Prince Zando** (CAHorgan) **3-9-0** PaulEddery(8) (hld up: rdn & ev ch over 1f out: wknd ins fnl f)	3½	**3**	11/2[3]	68	39
	Hever Golf Magic (IRE) (TJNaughton) **3-8-9** TSprake(9) (lw: rdn & hdwy 2f out: one pce)	nk	**4**	25/1	63	34
	Ocker (IRE) (79) (MHTompkins) **3-9-0** NDay(6) (lw: plld hrd: nt clr run & lost pl 2f out: one pce)	1¾	**5**	3/1[2]	63	34
	Third Party (74) (SDow) **3-8-4**(5) ADaly(4) (plld hrd: hld up: rdn wl over 1f out: sn wknd)	½	**6**	10/1	57	28
	Hippy Chick (JRJenkins) **3-8-9** JQuinn(3) (lw: a bhd)	3½	**7**	25/1	47	18
	Keen Alert (MBell) **3-8-9**(5) GFaulkner(1) (str: bit bkwd: s.s: a bhd)	nk	**8**	25/1	51	22
565[6]	**Little Annie** (GLMoore) **3-8-9** SWhitworth(5) (led over 3f)	1¾	**9**	25/1	42	13
	Mister Glum (IABalding) **3-8-11**(3) MartinDwyer(7) (leggy: unf: scope: spd 4f)	1¾	**10**	10/1	42	13
				(SP 130.7%)		**10 Rn**

1m 13.4 (3.20) CSF £21.23 TOTE £10.20: £2.40 £1.20 £1.50 (£12.80) Trio £19.80 OWNER Mr Kevin Reddington (EPSOM) BRED D. A. and Mrs Hicks

Peppiatt, like so many from the stable, knew what was required of him. Looking big and well beforehand, he was always close up and, rousted along, got on top inside the final furlong. (10/1: op 6/1)

694 John Emms (IRE) went on over a quarter-of-a-mile from home, but was unable to contain the winner inside the final furlong. He is running well at present, and there is a small race waiting for him. (11/10)

474 Prince Zando, who caught the eye in no uncertain fashion here last month, raced much closer to the pace on this occasion. He was certainly close enough if good enough below the distance, before tiring inside the final furlong. (11/2)

Hever Golf Magic (IRE), who has changed stables since last season, made her effort on the outside of the field a quarter-of-a-mile from home, but then failed to find another gear. (25/1)

Ocker (IRE) took a keen hold in the early stages, and was not helped when getting involved in scrimmaging a quarter-of-a-mile from home. He lost his pitch as a result and could only plod on at one pace. (3/1: op 7/4)

Third Party took a fierce hold and, not surprisingly, had run out of gas early in the final quarter-mile. (10/1: op 3/1)

Mister Glum (10/1: 5/1-11/1)

769 LEVY BOARD H'CAP (0-70) (4-Y.O+) (Class E)

4-00 (4-01) **1m 7f 92y** £2,992.25 (£893.00: £426.50: £193.25) Stalls: Low GOING: 0.00 sec per fur (G)

				SP	RR	SF
419[4]	**Paradise Navy (65)** (CREgerton) **8-9-10b** RHughes(5) (lw: stdy hdwy 6f out: swtchd lft over 1f out: shkn up: led nr fin)	—	**1**	2/1[1]	77	55
	Shirley Venture (68) (SPCWoods) **4-9-10** AClark(2) (hld up: chsd ldr over 6f out: led over 2f out: rdn: hdd nr fin)	nk	**2**	9/2[3]	80	55
660[2]	**Cuban Nights (USA) (52)** (BJLlewellyn) **5-8-6**(5) JBramhill(8) (lw: hdwy 5f out: rdn & ev ch over 1f out: one pce)	1¼	**3**	4/1[2]	62	40
324[5]	**Guest Alliance (IRE) (50)** (GLMoore) **5-8-9** CandyMorris(3) (lw: hdwy over 1f out: nvr nrr)	6	**4**	6/1	54	32
	Gentleman Sid (39) (PGMurphy) **7-7-12** NAdams(4) (lw: hdwy over 7f out: rdn over 5f out: wknd 3f out)	6	**5**	12/1	37	15
	Bresil (USA) (37) (JJBridger) **8-7-5**(5) RFfrench(9) (lw: prom 10f)	3	**6**	20/1	32	10
603[6]	**Kirov Protege (IRE) (37)** (MrsLCJewell) **5-7-3**(7) DarrenWilliams(6) (lw: w ldr: led 8f out tl over 2f out: sn wknd)	½	**7**	33/1	31	9
	Atienza (USA) (50) (SCWilliams) **4-8-3**(3) MHenry(1) (b.hind: prom over 7f: t.o)	dist	**8**	8/1	—	—
538[12]	**Talk Back (IRE) (65)** (GLewis) **5-9-7**(3) AWhelan(7) (led over 7f: wknd over 6f out: t.o)	24	**9**	14/1	—	—
				(SP 119.0%)		**9 Rn**

3m 28.3 (10.30) CSF £10.43 CT £30.64 TOTE £2.20: £1.30 £2.10 £1.70 (£6.30) Trio £6.60 OWNER Elite Racing Club (CHADDLEWORTH) BRED Stetchworth Park Stud Ltd

LONG HANDICAP Kirov Protege (IRE) 6-8 Bresil (USA) 7-0

WEIGHT FOR AGE 4yo-3lb

419 Paradise Navy is no easy ride and finds little off the bridle, but he was given an exquisite ride by Hughes. Far classier than these rivals, he was swinging off the bridle for much of the race with Hughes very keen to hold on to him until as late as possible. Switched to the outside approaching the final furlong, he had to be shaken up to get on top near the line. He is far better under big weights against inferior rivals and can score again in this company. (2/1)
Shirley Venture made her bid for glory over a quarter-of-a-mile from home but, despite desperately trying to hold on, was worried out of it near the line. (9/2: op 3/1)
660 Cuban Nights (USA), whose two wins to date have both come on the All-Weather, had every chance below the distance before tapped for toe. (4/1)
252 Guest Alliance (IRE), racing at the back of the field, stayed on in the closing stages without ever posing a threat. He seems better on the All-Weather. (6/1: op 4/1)
Talk Back (IRE) (14/1: 8/1-16/1)

770 DOVER H'CAP (0-70) (3-Y.O+) (Class E)

4-30 (4-30) **1m 4f** £3,070.25 (£917.00: £438.50: £199.25) Stalls: Low GOING: 0.00 sec per fur (G)

				SP	RR	SF
	Rising Spray (62) (CAHorgan) **6-9-8** PaulEddery(4) (lw: s.s: hdwy over 3f out: led ins fnl f: rdn out)	—	**1**	11/4[1]	72	36
559[5]	**Charnwood Jack (USA) (65)** (ICampbell) **4-9-10** RPrice(3) (a.p: chsd ldr over 5f out: led over 2f out tl ins fnl f: unable qckn)	¾	**2**	10/1	74	37
598[7]	**Almuhtaram (63)** (GLewis) **5-9-9b** RHughes(12) (hdwy over 3f out: hrd rdn over 1f out: r.o)	1¼	**3**	4/1[2]	70	34
640[3]	**Sapphire Son (IRE) (46)** (PCClarke) **5-8-6** NAdams(2) (lw: hdwy to ld over 9f out: hdd over 2f out: one pce)	1¾	**4**	12/1	51	15
607[3]	**Nails Tails (37)** (SDow) **4-7-10** JQuinn(8) (hdwy 5f out: rdn over 2f out: wknd over 1f out)	4	**5**	5/1	37	—
	Handson (40) (BRMillman) **5-8-0** TSprake(1) (lw: a.p: rdn over 3f out: wknd 2f out)	s.h	**6**	10/1	40	4
13[9]	**Ela Agapi Mou (USA) (52)** (GLMoore) **4-8-11** CandyMorris(7) (nvr nr to chal)	7	**7**	10/1	42	5
13[12]	**Mega Tid (36)** (JRPoulton) **5-7-10** GBardwell(10) (b.hind: plld hrd: prom 6f)	½	**8**	33/1	26	—
86[10]	**Executive Officer (38)** (RMFlower) **4-7-11**ow1 FNorton(9) (a bhd)	2½	**9**	33/1	24	—
	Anchor Venture (57) (SPCWoods) **4-9-2** AClark(5) (lw: bhd fnl 3f)	23	**10**	9/2[3]	13	—
338[9]	**Grey Legend (40)** (RMFlower) **4-7-13** DRMcCabe(11) (led over 2f: wknd over 5f out)	28	**11**	33/1	—	—

(SP 125.3%) **11 Rn**

2m 41.8 (10.60) CSF £30.88 CT £102.09 TOTE £4.50: £1.50 £2.50 £2.10 (£13.40) Trio £17.00 OWNER Mr J. T. Heritage (PULBOROUGH) BRED Pendley Farm
LONG HANDICAP Executive Officer 7-3 Nails Tails 7-9 Mega Tid 7-5
WEIGHT FOR AGE 4yo-1lb
Rising Spray loves this track and has yet to win anywhere else. Losing ground at the start, he was still at the tail-end of the field in the back straight, with apparently no hope. However, he began to make significant headway running down the hill and, getting into it in the straight, swept into the lead inside the final furlong to secure his third course victory. He relaxes and settles much better these days and will now be stepped up in trip. (11/4)
559 Charnwood Jack (USA), done no favours by the Handicapper, nevertheless ran a very promising race. Sent to the front over a quarter-of-a-mile from home, he gamely tried to hold on, but was unable to contain the winner inside the final furlong. (10/1)
Almuhtaram is not an easy individual but he ran much better here, staying on nicely in the last half-mile for third prize. (4/1: op 5/2)
640 Sapphire Son (IRE) was not going to hang around and swept into the lead setting out on the final circuit. Collared over a quarter-of-a-mile from home, he could then only go up and down in the same place. (12/1: op 8/1)
607 Nails Tails got into the action at the top of the hill, but had shot his bolt below the distance. (5/1)
Handson, in good form over hurdles this winter, was having his first run on the Flat since July 1995, but played an active role until calling it a day early in the straight. (10/1: 5/1-12/1)

771 TIM FREEMAN H'CAP (0-65) (3-Y.O) (Class F)

5-00 (5-01) **1m 1f 149y** £2,854.50 (£792.00: £379.50) Stalls: Low GOING: 0.00 sec per fur (G)

				SP	RR	SF
509[6]	**Pinchincha (FR) (65)** (DMorris) **3-9-7** NDay(12) (lw: hdwy 2f out: led over 1f out: hrd rdn & r.o wl)	—	**1**	5/1[3]	73	33
644[2]	**Aficionado (IRE) (65)** (RJHodges) **3-9-7** SSanders(9) (hdwy 2f out: hrd rdn over 1f out: unable qckn fnl f)	1½	**2**	10/1	71	31
	Philosophic (50) (SirMarkPrescott) **3-8-6** GDuffield(5) (rdn thrght: gd hdwy on ins over 1f out: one pce ins fnl f)	1½	**3**	9/4[1]	53	13
537[6]	**Right Man (58)** (GLewis) **3-9-0** PaulEddery(6) (hdwy 8f out: rdn over 5f out: ev ch over 1f out: one pce)	1	**4**	16/1	59	19
	Zorro (51) (RMFlower) **3-8-7** GHind(1) (hdwy over 1f out: r.o ins fnl f)	2	**5**	25/1	49	9
513[6]	**Scarrots (62)** (SCWilliams) **3-9-1**(3) MHenry(2) (lw: chsd ldr: led wl over 1f out: sn hdd & wknd)	¾	**6**	9/1	59	19
509[12]	**Sudest (IRE) (63)** (IABalding) **3-9-2**(3) MartinDwyer(4) (hld up: rdn over 5f out: one pce)	½	**7**	12/1	59	19
478[2]	**Herbshan Dancer (56)** (BRMillman) **3-8-12** TSprake(14) (lw: a.p: rdn over 3f out: ev ch wl over 1f out: sn wknd)	1¼	**8**	9/1	50	10
582*	**Riscatto (USA) (53)** (WRMuir) **3-8-9** JReid(7) (lw: hld up: rdn over 3f out: wknd wl over 1f out)	4	**9**	9/1	40	—
600[3]	**Chaluz (50)** (KRBurke) **3-8-6** RPerham(13) (lw: led 8f)	1¾	**10**	9/2[2]	34	—
537[8]	**Chief Predator (USA) (60)** (RHannon) **3-9-2** DaneO'Neill(15) (lw: bhd fnl 6f)	1¾	**11**	12/1	42	2
579[12]	**Our Kevin (50)** (BAPearce) **3-8-6b** GBardwell(8) (a bhd)	15	**12**	25/1	7	—
	Paddy Hurry (58) (NACallaghan) **3-9-0** SDrowne(11) (a bhd)	nk	**13**	16/1	14	—
535[13]	**Feel A Line (64)** (BJMeehan) **3-9-6** RHughes(3) (bhd fnl 2f)	11	**14**	25/1	2	—

(SP 143.4%) **14 Rn**

2m 6.2 (8.50) CSF £58.89 CT £138.64 TOTE £13.70: £3.50 £3.90 £1.70 (£28.30) Trio £132.70 OWNER Mr T. J. Wells (NEWMARKET) BRED Fluorocarbon Bloodstock
IN-FOCUS: **This race was run at a suicidal pace, and it was no surprise to see the complexion of the race change dramatically in the final quarter-mile.**
509 Pinchincha (FR), a handful for his trainer at home, came through to lead below the distance and, responding to pressure, kept on well. (5/1)
644 Aficionado (IRE) is only a selling plater, which does not say much for those below him, as he was allocated top weight. Getting into the action turning for home, he came under pressure below the distance, but failed to find another gear. (10/1: op 4/1)
Philosophic, a big boat of a horse, failed to cope with this suicidal pace and was being scrubbed along for the majority of the race. His cause looked hopeless, but Duffield must be given full marks for persevering with him, and the gelding began to make giant strides turning into the straight. He looked a serious threat entering the final furlong, but just failed to find another gear in the last one hundred yards. A long-striding individual, he will do better on a more galloping track, and is certainly up to winning a small race. (9/4)
537 Right Man was soon bustled up to the leaders, and had every chance below the distance before tapped for toe. (16/1)
Zorro, who showed nothing in three runs last year, raced at the back of the field but was noted making eye-catching headway under tender handling in the last furlong and a half. However, with so many horses stopping in front, this could well have flattered him. (25/1)

513 Scarrots chased the leader who went off at a break-neck pace. He managed to get to the front early in the final quarter-mile, but he was soon headed and not surprisingly tired. (9/1: 6/1-10/1)
Sudest (IRE) (12/1: 8/1-14/1)
478 Herbshan Dancer (9/1: 4/1-10/1)
600 Chaluz (9/2: 4/1-6/1)
491 Chief Predator (USA) (12/1: 6/1-14/1)

T/Jkpt: £23,547.20 (3.97 Tckts). T/Plpt: £39.90 (450.13 Tckts). T/Qdpt: £14.80 (43.07 Tckts) AK

0684-PONTEFRACT (L-H) (Good to firm, Firm ptchs between 15f & 12f markers)
Tuesday April 22nd
WEATHER: overcast WIND: almost nil

772 PONTEFRACT SERIES (ROUND ONE) APPRENTICE H'CAP (0-70) (3-Y.O+) (Class E)
2-15 (2-17) **5f** £2,721.75 (£834.00: £414.50: £204.75) Stalls: Low GOING minus 0.30 sec per fur (GF)

				SP	RR	SF
666^{4}	**Manolo (FR) (62)** (JBerry) **4-8-13b**(7) PBradley(1) (chsd ldr: led wl over 1f out: jst hld on)	—	**1**	$9/4^{1}$	70	52
666^{2}	**Able Sheriff (60)** (MWEasterby) **5-9-1b**(3) CLowther(5) (lw: a chsng ldrs: effrt over 1f out: styd on wl towards fin)	nk	**2**	$4/1^{2}$	67	49
	Henry the Hawk (48) (MDods) **6-8-6b** CWebb(8) (lw: bhd: hdwy 2f out: styd on: nrst fin)	2½	**3**	20/1	47	29
744^{4}	**Squire Corrie (70)** (DWChapman) **5-9-9**(5) TSiddall(3) (in tch: hdwy ½-wy: nvr rchd ldrs: sddle slipped)	s.h	**4**	$5/1^{3}$	69	51
702^{8}	**Dissentor (IRE) (40)** (JAGlover) **5-7-9b**(3) AMcCarthy(4) (lw: chsd ldrs: effrt 2f out: r.o one pce)	2½	**5**	12/1	31	13
333^{6}	**Spanish Stripper (USA) (40)** (MCChapman) **6-7-7**(5) JFowle(6) (dwlt: n.d)	1	**6**	50/1	28	10
222^{6}	**Playmaker (57)** (DNicholls) **4-8-10**(5) CarolynBales(7) (s.i.s: a wl bhd)	1¼	**7**	16/1	41	23
702^{3}	**Chadwell Hall (67)** (SRBowring) **6-9-4b**(7) FBoyle(9) (led tl hdd & wknd wl over 1f out)	¾	**8**	11/2	48	30
601*	**Summerville Wood (65)** (PMooney) **3-8-8b**(5) PFitzsimons(2) (s.s: a wl bhd)	2½	**9**	6/1	38	10

(SP 117.4%) **9 Rn**

63.4 secs (1.70) CSF £10.38 CT £130.60 TOTE £2.60: £1.20 £1.80 £5.10 (£5.10) Trio £120.70 OWNER Lucayan Stud (COCKERHAM) BRED Baron Guy De Rothschild
WEIGHT FOR AGE 3yo-10lb
OFFICIAL EXPLANATION **Squire Corrie: the rider reported that he had felt the saddle slip after hitting the stalls on loading.**
666 Manolo (FR), given a good ride by Paul Bradley, partnering his first winner, made no mistake this time, and getting first run just made the difference. (9/4)
666 Able Sheriff took time to get going and, despite finishing fast, the line was always going to come too soon. (4/1)
Henry the Hawk, normally at his best on softer ground, was nevertheless in tremendous form early on last year and that looks to be the case again. (20/1)
744 Squire Corrie, whose rider had problems with a slipping saddle from the start, ran a tremendous race in the circumstances. (5/1)
545 Dissentor (IRE), who took a strong hold going to post, ran quite well considering that. (12/1)
203 Spanish Stripper (USA) always found things happening too quickly, but he did stay on at the end and would prefer further. (50/1)
601* Summerville Wood had plenty on at this trip, and made the task hopeless with a very slow start. (6/1)

773 BEAST FAIR MEDIAN AUCTION MAIDEN STKS (3-Y.O) (Class E)
2-50 (2-51) **1m 2f 6y** £2,853.00 (£864.00: £422.00: £201.00) Stalls: Low GOING minus 0.30 sec per fur (GF)

				SP	RR	SF
	Will You Dance (JLDunlop) **3-8-9** PatEddery(2) (lw: chsd ldrs: effrt 3f out: slt ld ins fnl f: styd on u.p)	—	**1**	$15/8^{1}$	75	40
	Zinzari (FR) (DRLoder) **3-9-0** LDettori(7) (lw: led: rdn 3f out: hdd ins fnl f: kpt on wl)	¾	**2**	$8/1^{3}$	79	44
	In Question (BWHills) **3-9-0** DHolland(4) (stdd s: effrt 4f out: hung lft: styd on u.p fnl 2f: nrst fin)	1	**3**	9/1	77	42
	Miss Riviera Rose (GWragg) **3-8-9** MHills(6) (in tch: hdwy over 3f out: sn chsng ldrs: nt qckn fnl f)	1	**4**	16/1	71	36
	Winter Garden (LMCumani) **3-9-0** OUrbina(9) (h.d.w: bit bkwd: a chsng ldrs: effrt over 3f out: r.o one pce)	2	**5**	12/1	72	37
	Taunt (DMorley) **3-9-0** RCochrane(11) (hld up: hdwy over 3f out: hung rt & m wd st: sn btn & eased)	7	**6**	$2/1^{2}$	61	26
	Stakis Casinos Boy (IRE) (MJohnston) **3-9-0** JWeaver(3) (w'like: scope: bit bkwd: w ldr tl wknd fnl 3f)	2½	**7**	16/1	57	22
	Shilling (IRE) (ACStewart) **3-8-9** MRoberts(1) (w'like: bhd: sme hdwy 3f out: n.d)	2½	**8**	25/1	48	13
495^{5}	**Think Again (IRE)** (RCraggs) **3-9-0** DeanMcKeown(10) (a bhd)	9	**9**	100/1	39	4
	Marys Path (SGollings) **3-8-9** KFallon(5) (unf: outpcd over 4f out: sn wl bhd)	23	**10**	66/1	—	—
528^{5}	**Kissandy** (MrsVAAconley) **3-8-9** MDeering(8) (in tch tl outpcd 5f out: sn wl bhd)	½	**11**	100/1	—	—

(SP 116.0%) **11 Rn**

2m 13.5 (3.90) CSF £15.67 TOTE £2.90: £1.30 £2.40 £2.00 (£6.30) Trio £7.90 OWNER Mrs Mark Burrell (ARUNDEL) BRED Mrs M. Burrell
OFFICIAL EXPLANATION **Taunt: the rider reported that the colt hung badly right and felt wrong.**
Will You Dance looked particularly fit, but had to really battle to win this and will obviously get further. (15/8)
Zinzari (FR) made this a real test and proved very persistent when tackled, and over longer trips he will surely find races. (8/1)
In Question took time to find his stride, and did not help matters by continually hanging into the rails, but he was staying on particularly well at the end. (9/1: 5/1-10/1)
Miss Riviera Rose is only lightly-made, but she has an engine and should be all the better for this. (16/1)
Winter Garden has made up into a particularly nice sort, but he also needed this. Much better will be seen of him as he tries longer trips. (12/1: op 8/1)
Taunt hung badly right when he looked likely to get into it, throwing all chance away. The ability is certainly there. (2/1)
Stakis Casinos Boy (IRE) is a decent-looking newcomer who will certainly be better for the run. (16/1)

774 BENTLEY (S) STKS (3-Y.O+) (Class G)
3-20 (3-20) **6f** £2,679.00 (£744.00: £357.00) Stalls: Low GOING minus 0.30 sec per fur (GF)

				SP	RR	SF
17^{7}	**Standown (64)** (JBerry) **4-9-7** KDarley(3) (lw: trckd ldr: led over 1f out: rdn & styd on)	—	**1**	$9/4^{1}$	54	40
585^{12}	**Dashing Dancer (IRE) (48)** (DShaw) **6-9-7b**[1] JFanning(8) (lw: led tl hdd over 1f out: kpt on wl)	1	**2**	14/1	51	37
	Finisterre (IRE) (62) (JJO'Neill) **4-9-7** WRyan(4) (lw: mid div: styd on u.p fnl 2f: nrst fin)	1	**3**	$3/1^{2}$	49	35
263^{11}	**The Frisky Farmer (60)** (WGMTurner) **4-9-4**(3) RHavlin(9) (a chsng ldrs: nt qckn appr fnl f)	1¼	**4**	8/1	45	31
526^{13}	**Ohnonotagain (26)** (LRLloyd-James) **5-9-2** JFortune(6) (a chsng ldrs: one pce fnl 2f)	2	**5**	66/1	35	21
223^{8}	**Lucky Revenge (57)** (DNicholls) **4-9-2** AlexGreaves(5) (s.i.s: hdwy 2f out: nvr rchd ldrs)	2½	**6**	$4/1^{3}$	28	14
462^{8}	**Interaction** (RCraggs) **3-8-10** LCharnock(1) (nvr trbld ldrs)	1½	**7**	100/1	29	4

				SP	RR	SF
	Treasure Hill (IRE) (DWChapman) **3-8-10** ACulhane(11) (bit bkwd: bhd tl sme late hdwy)	s.h	**8**	6/1	29	4
303[7]	**Respectable Jones (38)** (RHollinshead) **11-9-0**(7) DHayden(7) (sn outpcd & bhd: n.d)	s.h	**9**	33/1	29	15
	Bold Engagement (MDods) **3-8-5** DaleGibson(10) (sn bhd)	1¼	**10**	100/1	21	—
	Skelton Countess (IRE) (55) (RHollinshead) **4-8-13**(3) FLynch(2) (lw: in tch tl rdn & wknd 2f out)	9	**11**	14/1	—	—
515[6]	**Deardaw (32)** (MissLCSiddall) **5-8-9**(7) TSiddall(12) (lw: prom to ½-wy)	2½	**12**	50/1	—	—
				(SP 122.9%)	**12 Rn**	

1m 18.1 (3.10) CSF £34.47 TOTE £3.50: £1.80 £4.20 £1.70 (£47.30) Trio £19.80 OWNER Mrs Chris Deuters (COCKERHAM) BRED Alan Gibson
WEIGHT FOR AGE 3yo-11lb
No bid
Standown always looked to be going best and, although he failed to streak away from his field, he was always doing just enough. (9/4)
Dashing Dancer (IRE) is six years old and has run thirty-five times without success, but he did little wrong here and does look particularly well at present. (14/1)
Finisterre (IRE) just found trouble at a vital stage entering the straight, and never got going until too late. He would also prefer a bit of cut.(3/1)
184 The Frisky Farmer ran quite well here after two months off. (8/1)
Ohnonotagain has changed stables this year and is showing signs of finding her form. (66/1)
166 Lucky Revenge was edgy and sweaty but, after proving disappointing on sand, she has ability on turf if she comes to hand. (4/1)

775 PONTEFRACT PARK LIMITED STKS (0-90) (3-Y.O+) (Class C)

3-50 (3-51) **1m 2f 6y** £5,498.00 (£1,664.00: £812.00: £386.00) Stalls: Low GOING minus 0.30 sec per fur (GF)

				SP	RR	SF
559*	**Stanton Harcourt (USA) (90)** (JLDunlop) **3-8-7** PatEddery(1) (lw: mde all: qcknd 3f out: r.o wl)	—	**1**	2/1[1]	101	37
	Billy Bushwacker (90) (MrsMReveley) **6-9-8** KDarley(3) (lw: hld up: effrt 2f out: r.o wl fnl f: nrst fin)	½	**2**	6/1[3]	98	51
	Rokeby Bowl (90) (IABalding) **5-9-8** LDettori(2) (lw: trckd ldrs: effrt 3f out: r.o: nt pce to chal)	nk	**3**	2/1[1]	98	51
	Cybertechnology (90) (BWHills) **3-8-5** DHolland(4) (h.d.w: bit bkwd: trckd ldrs: hdwy 4f out: rdn & btn 4f out)	4	**4**	7/2[2]	91	27
661[10]	**Van Gurp (90)** (BAMcMahon) **4-9-8** JFortune(5) (lw: hld up in last: effrt 3f out: wl outpcd fnl 2f)	16	**5**	20/1	66	19
				(SP 107.9%)	**5 Rn**	

2m 13.7 (4.10) CSF £12.31 TOTE £2.90: £1.60 £1.80 (£6.70) OWNER Mr Cyril Humphris (ARUNDEL) BRED Pamela H. Firman
WEIGHT FOR AGE 3yo-17lb
559* Stanton Harcourt (USA) was taken very steadily to post. In a race where most of his rivals needed holding up, he was given a cracking ride in front and pinched it. (2/1)
Billy Bushwacker is a frustrating individual who has so much ability but does not always put it to full use, but he showed he can shift in the final furlong here. (6/1)
Rokeby Bowl showed a particularly good action going to post and had his chances but, in the final sprint, the effort was always just beyond him. (2/1)
Cybertechnology has done particularly well physically, but ran as though this blow-out was needed. (7/2)
Van Gurp was most disappointing here, getting left way behind in the last quarter-mile. (20/1)

776 CORN MARKET H'CAP (0-85) (3-Y.O+) (Class D)

4-20 (4-20) **1m 4y** £3,785.00 (£1,130.00: £540.00: £245.00) Stalls: Low GOING minus 0.30 sec per fur (GF)

				SP	RR	SF
	Another Time (80) (SPCWoods) **5-9-12** DBiggs(1) (hld up: hdwy 2f out: led ins fnl f: r.o wl)	—	**1**	7/1[3]	90	67
646[5]	**Courtship (85)** (HRACecil) **3-9-3** KFallon(6) (lw: led tl hdd ins fnl f: kpt on wl)	1	**2**	6/4[1]	93	56
647[13]	**Forest Robin (71)** (MrsJRRamsden) **4-9-3** JFortune(2) (trckd ldrs: sltly outpcd over 1f out: no imp after)	5	**3**	8/1	69	46
	Sualtach (IRE) (77) (RHollinshead) **4-9-9** LDettori(8) (in tch: effrt over 2f out: kpt on one pce appr fnl f)	1	**4**	10/1	73	50
574[9]	**Sandblaster (51)** (JLEyre) **4-7-11**ow1 TWilliams(3) (hld up & bhd: hdwy ½-wy: sn in tch: nt qckn fnl 2f)	2	**5**	14/1	43	19
734[5]	**Rambo Waltzer (69)** (DNicholls) **5-8-10**(5) IonaWands(5) (lw: hld up: effrt over 3f out: sn outpcd & no imp after)	3	**6**	9/2[2]	55	32
734[12]	**Genuine John (IRE) (67)** (JParkes) **4-8-10**(3) RHavlin(7) (lw: chsd ldrs tl wknd fnl 2f)	11	**7**	9/1	31	8
653[3]	**King Athelstan (USA) (64)** (BAMcMahon) **9-8-10** KDarley(4) (cl up 5f: eased fnl 2f)	24	**8**	25/1	—	—
529[10]	**Keston Pond (IRE) (70)** (MrsVAAconley) **7-9-2** MDeering(9) (s.i.s: racd wd: wl bhd fnl 3f)	dist	**9**	14/1	—	—
				(SP 118.1%)	**9 Rn**	

1m 44.3 (1.90) CSF £16.67 CT £82.02 TOTE £8.30: £2.90 £1.40 £3.00 (£6.90) Trio £36.90 OWNER Mr D. Sullivan (NEWMARKET) BRED W. G. Barker
WEIGHT FOR AGE 3yo-14lb
OFFICIAL EXPLANATION **King Athelstan (USA): the rider reported that the gelding was hanging and as his stride shortened, he felt it prudent not to persevere.**
Another Time, from a yard in form, would have ideally preferred further but he won really well, and looks better than ever this year. (7/1)
646 Courtship, given an aggressive ride this time, ran much better. (6/4)
Forest Robin is beginning to show his first signs of form for his new stable, and looks one to keep an eye on. (8/1: op 5/1)
Sualtach (IRE) put in a reasonable first run of the season, but he had shot his bolt a furlong out. (10/1)
Sandblaster, taken to post early, again showed ability, but this wiry sort has yet to win a race. (14/1)
734 Rambo Waltzer, who looked as well as ever, never really fired this time. (9/2)

777 LEVY BOARD H'CAP (0-80) (4-Y.O+) (Class D)

4-50 (4-52) **2m 1f 22y** £3,687.50 (£1,100.00: £525.00: £237.50) Stalls: Low GOING minus 0.30 sec per fur (GF)

				SP	RR	SF
	Great Oration (IRE) (54) (FWatson) **8-8-4** NConnorton(5) (in tch: hdwy 4f out: chal over 1f out: styd on to ld cl home)	—	**1**	16/1	64	34
632[2]	**Shirley Sue (71)** (MJohnston) **4-9-3** JWeaver(9) (lw: led: rdn 3f out: styd on gamely: hdd & no ex towards fin)	nk	**2**	11/4[1]	81	47
442*	**Onefourseven (65)** (JLEyre) **4-8-11** TWilliams(3) (lw: hld up: hdwy 5f out: disp ld 2f out: nt qckn u.p fnl f)	nk	**3**	7/2[2]	74	40
470[8]	**Royal Expression (72)** (MrsMReveley) **5-9-8** ACulhane(1) (mid div: effrt 5f out: outpcd 3f out: styd on appr fnl f: no imp)	1½	**4**	4/1[3]	80	50
655[2]	**Embryonic (IRE) (78)** (MartinTodhunter) **5-10-0** JCarroll(8) (trckd ldrs: effrt & hmpd over 2f out: bmpd over 1f out: wknd fnl f)	5	**5**	5/1	81	51
73[12]	**Warning Reef (80)** (PEccles) **4-9-12** LDettori(4) (bhd: effrt 6f out: no imp)	2	**6**	20/1	82	48
570[8]	**Brodessa (60)** (MrsMReveley) **11-8-10** KDarley(7) (lw: cl up tl wknd fnl 3f)	2½	**7**	12/1	59	29

				SP	RR	SF
*55*4	**Sterling Fellow (58)** (DLWilliams) **4-8-4** DHarrison(6) (prom tl wknd over 4f out)	11	**8**	8/1	47	13
4425	**Invest Wisely (75)** (MDHammond) **5-9-11** JFortune(2) (chsd ldrs 6f: sn t.o: p.u over 1f out)		**P**	20/1	—	—
				(SP 119.8%)		**9 Rn**

3m 46.4 (6.90) CSF £56.65 CT £177.49 TOTE £10.80: £1.80 £1.50 £2.10 (£18.90) Trio £17.00 OWNER M D Hetherington (Packaging) Ltd (SEDGEFIELD) BRED P. F. I. Cole
WEIGHT FOR AGE 4yo-4lb
Great Oration (IRE) loves this track and, despite looking likely to be all the better for this, showed fine determination to get up. (16/1)
632 Shirley Sue battled as only she can, and will find her share of races again this year. (11/4)
442* Onefourseven looked likely to trot up here but was out-battled in the closing stages. He is nevertheless doing well and should continue to pay his way. (7/2)
470 Royal Expression does not as yet look quite right, but this was a better effort and he is obviously improving. (4/1)
655 Embryonic (IRE) again found trouble and is probably his own worst enemy. (5/1)
Warning Reef has been disappointing over hurdles and is yet to win a race of any kind, but there is ability there if the key can be found. (20/1)

778 SPRING MAIDEN STKS (3-Y.O F) (Class D)
5-20 (5-20) **6f** £3,598.75 (£1,090.00: £532.50: £253.75) Stalls: Low GOING minus 0.30 sec per fur (GF)

				SP	RR	SF
	Rosy Outlook (USA) (IABalding) **3-8-11** LDettori(4) (cl up: chal over 1f out: slt ld wl ins fnl f: edgd lft: r.o)	—	**1**	4/1 3	73	35
5843	**Silent Miracle (IRE) (77)** (MBell) **3-8-11** MFenton(3) (lw: led: qcknd 2f out: hdd wl ins fnl f: rallied)	hd	**2**	7/4 1	73	35
5844	**Tajrebah (USA) (75)** (PTWalwyn) **3-8-11** RHills(7) (a chsng ldrs: effrt 2f out: kpt on: nt pce to chal)	1¾	**3**	3/1 2	68	30
	Yabint El Sultan (BAMcMahon) **3-8-11** LNewton(1) (hld up: effrt over 2f out: kpt on wl: nrst fin)	½	**4**	50/1	67	29
	Sweet Patoopie (BHanbury) **3-8-11** JStack(2) (w'like: chsd ldrs tl grad wknd appr fnl f)	3	**5**	10/1	59	21
	Agift (RFJohnsonHoughton) **3-8-11** ACulhane(8) (w'like: leggy: hld up: effrt 2f out: rdn & nvr able to chal)	s.h	**6**	10/1	59	21
	Ella Lamees (WJMusson) **3-8-11** KFallon(5) (hld up & bhd: nvr plcd to chal)	hd	**7**	9/1	58	20
	Verasica (RHollinshead) **3-8-8**(3) FLynch(6) (w'like: bit bkwd: s.i.s: outpcd over 2f out: sn wknd)	22	**8**	33/1	—	—
				(SP 114.4%)		**8 Rn**

1m 17.7 (2.70) CSF £10.40 TOTE £3.40: £2.10 £1.10 £1.10 (£3.60) OWNER Mr J. C. Smith (KINGSCLERE) BRED Janus Bloodstock
STEWARDS' ENQUIRY Fenton susp. 1-4/5/97 (excessive use of whip).
Rosy Outlook (USA) was turned out looking particularly fit. and just had the edge in a rare battle. This should have taught her plenty. (4/1)
584 Silent Miracle (IRE) tried to steal this from the front, but it never quite came off despite a valiant attempt. (7/4)
584 Tajrebah (USA) is a rather edgy filly who gave the impression that she has more ability if she can be persuaded. (3/1)
Yabint El Sultan, who showed nothing in two runs previously, gave signs for hope here and will obviously appreciate a bit further. (50/1)
Sweet Patoopie needed this and showed some promise. She will do better in time, probably over longer trips. (10/1)
Agift has plenty to learn but was staying on under pressure. (10/1)
Ella Lamees, having her third run here, showed ability without getting into it and was not knocked about. In time we will see better. (9/1)

T/Plpt: £10.50 (1,506.16 Tckts). T/Qdpt: £6.10 (115.14 Tckts) AA

0466-CATTERICK (L-H) (Good, Good to firm patches)
Wednesday April 23rd
WEATHER: overcast WIND: fresh half against

779 5TH REGIMENT ROYAL ARTILLERY CHAMPAGNE POL ROGER APPRENTICE LIMITED STKS (0-55) (3-Y.O+) (Class G)
2-00 (2-02) **5f 212y** £2,258.50 (£631.00: £305.50) Stalls: High GOING minus 0.12 sec per fur (G)

				SP	RR	SF
702*	**Johayro (51)** (JSGoldie) **4-9-6**(5) JMcAuley(12) (lw: w ldr: styd on to ld wl ins fnl f: jst hld on)	—	**1**	9/2 2	60	48
	Millesime (IRE) (55) (MartynWane) **5-9-5** PFessey(2) (bkwd: a chsng ldrs: nt qckn towards fin)	hd	**2**	10/1	54	42
	Ivor's Deed (52) (CFWall) **4-9-0**(5) PClarke(10) (bit bkwd: stdd s: hld up & bhd: c wd ent st: gd hdwy & edgd lft over 1f out: fin fast)	nk	**3**	10/1	53	41
4668	**Keen To Please (55)** (DenysSmith) **3-8-5** DSweeney(8) (mde most tl fnl 75y)	½	**4**	10/1	49	26
46811	**Bollin Dorothy (52)** (TDEasterby) **4-9-2** RHavlin(4) (lw: dwlt: sn chsng ldrs: kpt on ins fnl f)	½	**5**	5/1 3	47	35
4693	**Merrily (54)** (MissSEHall) **4-9-2** GFaulkner(5) (b: b.hind: hld up: hdwy over 2f out: styd on fnl f)	nk	**6**	8/1	46	34
5278	**Grand Chapeau (IRE) (53)** (DNicholls) **5-9-2**(3) IonaWands(9) (lw: a chsng ldrs: rdn 2f out: kpt on one pce)	1¼	**7**	7/4 1	46	34
*659*6	**Thick as Thieves (40)** (RonaldThompson) **5-9-2**(3) GMilligan(3) (lw: chsd ldrs: rdn & outpcd over 2f out: kpt on fnl f)	nk	**8**	20/1	45	33
*513*10	**Skippy Was A Kiwi (IRE) (54)** (APJarvis) **3-8-0**(5) CCarver(13) (sn outpcd: kpt on fnl 2f: nvr nr ldrs)	s.h	**9**	16/1	42	19
*593*6	**Lochon (48)** (MrsNMacauley) **6-9-5b** CTeague(11) (b: hmpd after 100y: bhd: c v.wd ent st: sme hdwy fnl f: n.d)	3	**10**	16/1	37	25
*593*4	**Boffy (IRE) (47)** (BPJBaugh) **4-9-2v1**(3) JBramhill(1) (dwlt: sn chsng ldrs: lost pl over 1f out)	3	**11**	16/1	29	17
	Risky Flight (42) (ASmith) **3-8-3**(5) CLowther(7) (bit bkwd: sn outpcd & bhd)	1¾	**12**	50/1	24	1
	Aquado (55) (DShaw) **8-9-5b** FLynch(14) (sn bhd: hrd rdn & sme hdwy over 2f out: n.d: eased ins fnl f)	3½	**13**	16/1	15	3
	Chilled Wine (43) (GPKelly) **3-8-5** GParkin(6) (bkwd: bhd whn hmpd 3f out: t.o)	20	**14**	50/1	—	—
				(SP 141.8%)		**14 Rn**

1m 14.4 (3.50) CSF £53.13 TOTE £5.10: £3.30 £4.70 £4.00 (£48.30) Trio £211.60 OWNER Mr Frank Brady (GLASGOW) BRED R. M. Whitaker
WEIGHT FOR AGE 3yo-11lb
702* Johayro completed a hat-trick, but will have a lot more on his plate in future handicaps. He certainly stayed this easy six. (9/2)
Millesime (IRE), unplaced in four outings last year, showed a return to form for his new trainer. (10/1)
Ivor's Deed, dropped in at the start, would have won but for coming off a true line when making rapid strides over a furlong out. He is much better suited by seven. (10/1)
Keen To Please, who looked very fit, ran much better than on her reappearance but her stamina seemed to give out in the closing stages. (10/1: op 6/1)
Bollin Dorothy, awkward to load, was always up against it after missing the break. She is better over seven furlongs and on easier ground. (5/1)
Grand Chapeau (IRE), stepping up in trip, was sent off a ludicrous price but his supporters never looking like drawing. (7/4: 3/1-6/4)

48? 53+ 53+ 63+

780 FRAGGLES (S) STKS (2-Y.O) (Class G)

2-30 (2-31) **5f** £2,146.50 (£599.00: £289.50) Stalls: Low GOING: 0.01 sec per fur (G)

				SP	RR	SF
	Flash d'Or (IRE) (MWEasterby) **2-8-2**[(5)ow1] GParkin(6) (w'like: scope: bit bkwd: dwlt: sn outpcd & bhd: hdwy on outside 2f out: squeezed thro: r.o u.p to ld last strides)	—	**1**	12/1	47	—
631[2]	**Hopefully** (MRChannon) **2-8-6** RHills(1) (mde most: hdd nr fin)	s.h	**2**	5/4[1]	46	—
	Maedaley (PCHaslam) **2-8-6** JFortune(5) (neat: scope: hmpd s: sn trckng ldrs: chal & edgd rt ½-wy: nt qckn fnl f)	4	**3**	3/1[2]	33	—
	Chardania (IRE) (CaptJWilson) **2-8-6** JCarroll(7) (lt-f: unf: bit bkwd: swvd lft s: chsd ldrs: hung lft & nt qckn fnl 2f)	s.h	**4**	14/1	33	—
594[13]	**Vet's Deceit (IRE)** (RonaldThompson) **2-8-11** TWilliams(4) (w ldrs: edgd rt u.p ½-wy: wknd over 1f out)	2	**5**	10/1	32	—
536[10]	**Flirtina** (PDEvans) **2-8-6** JFEgan(8) (sn drvn along: nvr wnt pce)	1	**6**	5/1[3]	23	—
492[7]	**Sunshine Pet (IRE)** (JJO'Neill) **2-8-6** GDuffield(2) (chsd ldrs: outpcd ½-wy: sn lost pl)	¾	**7**	14/1	21	—
572[9]	**Companys Gamble** (BPJBaugh) **2-8-6** ACulhane(3) (trckd ldrs: hung lft & lost pl ½-wy: eased)	9	**8**	11/2	—	—

(SP 131.6%) **8 Rn**

63.9 secs (6.20) CSF £29.02 TOTE £13.50: £3.60 £1.10 £1.40 (£10.40) OWNER Mr Philip Jarvis (SHERIFF HUTTON) BRED Denis O'Brien
Bt in 6,800 gns

Flash d'Or (IRE), who has far more size and scope about her than the others in the field, had to overcome difficulties but showed the right sort of spirit to get up on the line. She will be much better suited by six furlongs. (12/1: op 8/1)
631 Hopefully ended up racing up the centre without the help of a rail on either side and was just pipped. (5/4: 8/11-11/8)
Maedaley, a sister to the four-year-old Galapino, raced keenly in the early stages after being hampered at the start. She should improve for the outing. (3/1)
Chardania (IRE) wanted to do nothing but go to her left. (14/1: op 8/1)
Vet's Deceit (IRE) looks as though he needs a little more time yet. (10/1: 7/1-12/1)
Flirtina was most unimpressive in the paddock. (5/1)

781 'WIN WITH THE TOTE' H'CAP (0-85) (4-Y.O+) (Class D)

3-00 (3-00) **1m 3f 214y** £3,496.00 (£1,048.00: £504.00: £232.00) Stalls: Low GOING minus 0.12 sec per fur (G)

				SP	RR	SF
	Ballpoint (72) (GMMoore) **4-9-11** ACulhane(7) (bit bkwd: sn pushed along: hdwy 5f out: sn outpcd: swtchd rt & hdwy over 1f out: hung lft: styd on to ld towards fin)	—	**1**	14/1	83	50
470[4]	**Hasta la Vista (46)** (MWEasterby) **7-8-0b**[ow2] JFEgan(4) (w ldr: led over 3f out: sn rdn: styd on: hdd towards fin)	¾	**2**	9/2[1]	56	22
	Tessajoe (72) (MJCamacho) **5-9-12** LCharnock(5) (b.hind: bit bkwd: hld up: wnt prom 7f out: chal over 2f out: sn rdn: nt qckn ins fnl f)	½	**3**	6/1[3]	81	49
598[2]	**Sherqy (IRE) (60)** (SEKettlewell) **5-9-0** JFortune(8) (lw: mde most tl over 3f out: wknd 2f out)	6	**4**	6/1[3]	61	29
598*	**Summerhill Special (IRE) (60)** (DWBarker) **6-9-0** DeanMcKeown(9) (lw: trckd ldrs: drvn along 6f out: lost pl over 3f out: styd on towards fin)	1	**5**	9/2[1]	60	28
633[2]	**Philistar (69)** (JMPEustace) **4-9-8b** RCochrane(1) (hld up & plld v.hrd: trckd ldrs tl wknd 2f out)	1¼	**6**	5/1[2]	67	34
552*	**Manful (74)** (MissLAPerratt) **5-10-0b** NKennedy(6) (chsd ldrs: drvn along 5f out: lost pl over 2f out)	1¾	**7**	15/2	70	38
	Highfield Fizz (44) (CWFairhurst) **5-7-5**[(7)ow1] PDoe(2) (sn bhd & pushed along: lost tch 6f out)	4	**8**	20/1	35	2
	Daira (63) (JDBethell) **4-9-2** SDrowne(3) (bit bkwd: trckd ldrs tl lost pl 3f out: eased whn btn)	1¼	**9**	7/1	52	19
	Cool Luke (IRE) (66) (FMurphy) **8-9-6** JFanning(10) (hld up & bhd: effrt 5f out: lost pl 3f out)	¾	**10**	20/1	54	22

(SP 122.1%) **10 Rn**

2m 38.8 (7.40) CSF £72.43 CT £390.00 TOTE £37.50: £8.80 £1.80 £1.30 (£100.70) Trio £156.00 OWNER Mr Geoffrey Hamilton (MIDDLEHAM) BRED R. D. Sears
WEIGHT FOR AGE 4yo-1lb

Ballpoint, who is now a gelding, looked as if he was in need of the outing. Sticking on after getting outpaced, he will be suited by further.(14/1)
470 Hasta la Vista won this event a year ago from a 5lb higher mark. (9/2)
Tessajoe, who looked just in need of the outing, has significantly won on his second appearance in each of the last two years. (6/1)
598 Sherqy (IRE) pulled out disappointingly little. (6/1)
598* Summerhill Special (IRE), from a 5lb higher mark, never seems to run two races alike. (9/2: op 3/1)
633 Philistar proved much too keen and gave himself no chance of getting the trip. (5/1)
552* Manful (15/2: 5/1-8/1)

782 HONDEGHEM CONDITIONS STKS (3-Y.O) (Class C)

3-30 (3-30) **1m 3f 214y** £6,876.25 (£2,207.50: £1,066.25) Stalls: Low GOING minus 0.12 sec per fur (G)

				SP	RR	SF
	Ivan Luis (FR) (106) (MBell) **3-9-3** MRoberts(2) (h.d.w: lw: hld up: smooth hdwy over 2f out: shkn up to ld jst ins fnl f: edgd lft: pushed out)	—	**1**	6/4[2]	96+	30
	Happy Minstral (USA) (82) (MJohnston) **3-9-3** MHills(1) (bit bkwd: led: pushed along 5f out: hdd jst ins fnl f: kpt on wl)	½	**2**	6/1[3]	95	29
445*	**Mithak (USA) (90)** (BWHills) **3-9-3** RHills(3) (trckd ldr: drvn along & chal over 3f out: ev ch tl wknd appr fnl f: eased)	5	**3**	5/6[1]	89	23

(SP 108.8%) **3 Rn**

2m 40.8 (9.40) CSF £6.97 TOTE £2.70 (£4.70) OWNER Mr Luciano Gaucci (NEWMARKET) BRED Rodrigo Investments

Ivan Luis (FR), a progressive juvenile, has grown and strengthened over the winter. Given a patient ride, in the end he did not have much to spare, and displayed an awkward head carriage. He now heads for the Italian Derby. (6/4)
Happy Minstral (USA), who looked as if the outing would do him good, is essentially a stayer. He would have been 24lb better off with the winner in a handicap and a stiff hike in the ratings is unfortunately now on the cards. (6/1: op 7/2)
445* Mithak (USA) had his limitations exposed. (5/6: 4/5-evens)

783 DRAGON TROOP H'CAP (0-80) (3-Y.O) (Class D)

4-00 (4-01) **5f** £3,509.00 (£1,052.00: £506.00: £233.00) Stalls: Low GOING: 0.01 sec per fur (G)

				SP	RR	SF
434*	**Brutal Fantasy (IRE) (78)** (JLEyre) **3-9-7** RLappin(6) (lw: w ldrs: shkn up to ld ins fnl f: eased towards fin)	—	**1**	9/4[1]	89	65
434[5]	**Ballymote (75)** (JBerry) **3-9-4** JFortune(10) (unruly in stalls: chsd ldrs: led & edgd rt over 1f out: hdd ins fnl f: styd on towards fin)	s.h	**2**	6/1[3]	86	62

				SP	RR	SF
	Tinker's Surprise (IRE) (54) (JBalding) **3-7-11**ow1 NCarlisle(8) (led: hdd & n.m.r over 1f out: grad wknd)	4	**3**	14/1	52	27
532[14]	**Soda (60)** (TDBarron) **3-8-3b** JCarroll(1) (racd far side: styd on ins fnl f: nvr nr to chal)	3	**4**	15/2	48	24
	Sylvan Dancer (IRE) (69) (CFWall) **3-8-12** GDuffield(4) (bit bkwd: s.s: bhd tl styd on appr fnl f)	½	**5**	12/1	56	32
221[4]	**Tear White (IRE) (70)** (TGMills) **3-8-13b** TWilliams(2) (led far side tl wknd ins fnl f)	1½	**6**	11/2[2]	52	28
434[10]	**Jedi Knight (71)** (MWEasterby) **3-8-9**(5) GParkin(7) (chsd ldrs: outpcd ½-wy: sn lost pl)	nk	**7**	12/1	52	28
731[4]	**Weet Ees Girl (IRE) (76)** (PDEvans) **3-9-5** JFEgan(5) (chsd ldrs: outpcd ½-wy: sn wknd)	¾	**8**	8/1	55	31
	Melbourne Princess (55) (RMWhitaker) **3-7-12** DWright(9) (bit bkwd: sn outpcd: sltly hmpd over 1f out: n.d)	1	**9**	9/1	31	7
494[9]	**Red Romance (57)** (DenysSmith) **3-8-0** LCharnock(3) (racd far side: chsd ldr tl wknd 2f out: eased)	6	**10**	12/1	13	—

(SP 123.1%) **10 Rn**

60.0 secs (2.30) CSF £15.17 CT £147.54 TOTE £2.50: £1.30 £2.50 £5.30 (£7.90) Trio £117.90 OWNER Diamond Racing Ltd (HAMBLETON) BRED Michael G. O'Brien

LONG HANDICAP Tinker's Surprise (IRE) 7-9

434* Brutal Fantasy (IRE) is doing well physically but had to be led round the paddock by a stable girl and his trainer. From a 6lb higher mark, he was always travelling smoothly but was almost caught unawares. Had the verdict gone the other way, his rider would have had egg on his face. (9/4)

434 Ballymote, drawn ten of ten, was able to race on the best ground towards the stands'-side rail. After giving trouble in the stalls, he stuck to his guns and almost caught the winner out. (6/1)

Tinker's Surprise (IRE), who has changed stables, has certainly started his three-year-old career on a handy mark. One thing is certain, he does not lack early toe. (14/1)

466 Soda came out best of the three who stuck to the far side. (15/2)

Sylvan Dancer (IRE) did as well as can be expected after losing several lengths at the start. (12/1)

221 Tear White (IRE) led the two others on the far side. (11/2: 4/1-6/1)

784 SANNA'S POST MAIDEN STKS (3-Y.O) (Class D)

4-30 (4-34) **7f** £3,665.00 (£1,100.00: £530.00: £245.00) Stalls: Low GOING minus 0.12 sec per fur (G)

				SP	RR	SF
475[3]	**Sharp Temper** (BWHills) **3-9-0** MHills(8) (chsd ldrs: effrt 2f out: r.o to ld ins fnl f: drvn out)	—	**1**	2/1[1]	75	39
586[8]	**Select Choice (IRE) (78)** (APJarvis) **3-9-0** SDrowne(10) (led tl ins fnl f: nt qckn)	1	**2**	10/1	73	37
446[5]	**Compatibility (IRE)** (JHMGosden) **3-9-0** GHind(2) (trckd ldrs gng wl: swtchd rt over 1f out: r.o steadily: nvr plcd to chal)	nk	**3**	6/1	72++	36
	Flourishing Way (81) (RCharlton) **3-8-9** TSprake(4) (lw: plld hrd: trckd ldrs: rdn over 1f out: sn wknd)	2	**4**	3/1[2]	63	27
485[3]	**Tabasco Jazz** (BJMeehan) **3-8-9** MRoberts(7) (b.nr hind: chsd ldrs: rdn along ½-wy: hung lft & swtchd rt over 1f out: sn wknd)	1	**5**	11/2[3]	60	24
576[3]	**Honourable** (JWWatts) **3-9-0** JCarroll(9) (lw: sn bhd: effrt over 2f out: kpt on: nvr nr ldrs)	3	**6**	6/1	58	22
	Keen Dancer (MBell) **3-9-0** MFenton(1) (dwlt: hld up & bhd: sme hdwy 2f out: nvr nr ldrs)	½	**7**	20/1	57?	21
676[16]	**Highly Respected (IRE)** (ABailey) **3-8-9** DWright(5) (sn pushed along: sn chsng ldrs: lost pl 2f out)	nk	**8**	12/1	52?	16
	Quarterstaff (CFWall) **3-9-0** GDuffield(3) (outpcd ½-wy: sn bhd)	nk	**9**	20/1	56?	20
551[6]	**Sweet Note (IRE)** (MissLAPerratt) **3-8-9** ACulhane(6) (bit bkwd: sn bhd & rdn along)	5	**10**	33/1	39?	3

(SP 131.5%) **10 Rn**

1m 27.7 (4.10) CSF £24.58 TOTE £3.10: £1.10 £4.20 £2.40 (£32.80) Trio £68.20 OWNER Mr K. Abdulla (LAMBOURN) BRED Juddmonte Farms

OFFICIAL EXPLANATION **Compatibility (IRE): the Stewards inquired into the apparent tender ride given to the colt in the home straight. The jockey reported that his instructions were to settle the colt in the early stages to enable him to get the trip, and also to keep a good hold of his head as he had suffered with knee problems in the past. He also felt that the colt became slightly unbalanced in the dip at approximately a furlong from home, and may have been unsuited by the firm ground.**

475 Sharp Temper, who has a scratchy action, only got up inside the last and will be better suited by a mile. (2/1)

Select Choice (IRE), a keen-going sort, ran another good race but his first success has been a long time coming. (10/1: 8/1-12/1)

446 Compatibility (IRE) travelled strongly on the heels of the leading group, but his rider showed no sense of urgency. With a token effort from the saddle he could surely have clinched second spot and could very likely have won. Even if he had been successful, he would only have earned a handicap mark of about 80. Various excuses were recorded by the Stewards and connections escaped without punishment. (6/1)

Flourishing Way proved too keen for her own good. (3/1: op 2/1)

485 Tabasco Jazz showed a very poor action and would prefer a more orthodox track and easier ground. (11/2)

576 Honourable, who was having his third outing, has now qualified for a handicap mark. (6/1)

Keen Dancer, who showed nothing at all in two runs as a juvenile, raced keenly after a slow break. Never knocked about at any stage, he now qualifies for a handicap mark. (20/1)

785 LILLIBULERO H'CAP (0-70) (3-Y.O) (Class E)

5-00 (5-04) **7f** £3,112.75 (£937.00: £453.50: £211.75) Stalls: Low GOING minus 0.12 sec per fur (G)

				SP	RR	SF
	Muscatana (58) (BWHills) **3-8-9** MHills(15) (stdd s: hld up: hdwy & c wd ent st: led over 1f out: readily)	—	**1**	12/1	65+	34
556*	**Brave Envoy (64)** (MJHeaton-Ellis) **3-9-1** SDrowne(9) (sn outpcd: drvn along and bhd: c wd ent st: styd on wl fnl 2f: no ch w wnr)	2½	**2**	8/1	65	34
378[2]	**Captain Carparts (63)** (JLEyre) **3-9-0** TWilliams(16) (lw: mde most: c wd ent st: hdd over 1f out: nt qckn)	¾	**3**	12/1	63	32
535[16]	**Abstone Queen (60)** (PDEvans) **3-8-11b** JFEgan(11) (prom: hmpd & lost pl after 2f: hdwy & hung rt over 1f out: styd on)	¾	**4**	13/2[3]	58	27
575[10]	**Rum Lad (60)** (JJQuinn) **3-8-6**(5) GParkin(1) (in tch: effrt over 2f out: styd on: nvr nr to chal)	1¼	**5**	14/1	55	24
634[5]	**Docklands Carriage (IRE) (60)** (NTinkler) **3-8-11v** RCochrane(6) (w ldr: ev ch tl wknd & eased fnl f)	½	**6**	6/1[2]	54	23
644[7]	**Joyful Joy (46)** (BPJBaugh) **3-7-8**(3)ow1 DarrenMoffatt(14) (trckd ldrs: c wd ent st: effrt 2f out: grad wknd)	s.h	**7**	33/1	40	8
610[15]	**Smokey From Caplaw (66)** (JJO'Neill) **3-9-3** GDuffield(7) (bhd whn hmpd after 2f: sme hdwy 2f out: nvr nr ldrs)	1½	**8**	16/1	56	25
575[12]	**Fullopep (63)** (MrsMReveley) **3-9-0** ACulhane(17) (unruly in stalls: s.i.s: bhd: drvn along & sme hdwy over 2f out: nvr nr to chal)	1½	**9**	16/1	50	19
535[18]	**Only Josh (IRE) (54)** (MrsJRRamsden) **3-8-5** JFortune(2) (sn outpcd & bhd: sme hdwy over 1f out: n.d)	1¼	**10**	9/1	38	7
685[5]	**La Dolce Vita (70)** (TDBarron) **3-9-0**(7) VictoriaAppleby(12) (trckd ldrs: c wd ent st: effrt over 2f out: sn wknd)	½	**11**	9/2[1]	53	22
549*	**I'm Still Here (65)** (JBerry) **3-8-11**(5) TEDurcan(8) (b: chsd ldrs: rdn 2f out: sn wknd)	¾	**12**	8/1	46	15
*287**	**Euroquest (48)** (DNicholls) **3-7-8**(5) IonaWands(4) (lw: lost pl after 2f: n.d after)	1¼	**13**	7/1	26	—
529[14]	**Bold Brief (64)** (DenysSmith) **3-9-1** LCharnock(5) (chsd ldrs: c wd ent st: lost pl 2f out)	½	**14**	16/1	41	10
600[11]	**Bali-Pet (48)** (JParkes) **3-7-8**(5) JBramhill(10) (a bhd: c wd ent st)	5	**15**	20/1	14	—

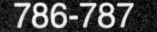

Form	Horse / details	Dist	Pos	SP	RR	SF
644[12]	**Tom Pladdey (52)** (RBastiman) **3-8-3** DaleGibson(3) (sn trckng ldrs: rdn over 2f out: sn wknd)	5	**16**	20/1	6	—
				(SP 142.7%)	**16 Rn**	

1m 27.7 (4.10) CSF £109.14 CT £1,128.73 TOTE £16.80: £2.10 £2.80 £3.40 £1.60 (£58.50) Trio £274.00; £154.40 to Beverley 24/4/97
OWNER K. Al-Said (LAMBOURN) BRED Charlton Down Stud
LONG HANDICAP Joyful Joy 7-5

Muscatana overcame a poor draw to score in good style. Beaten in selling company at two, she is clearly much improved and a good deal better than her current handicap mark. (12/1)
556* Brave Envoy, with the visor left off, took plenty of stoking up. Putting in some solid work towards the finish, he is probably still learning the ropes. (8/1)
378 Captain Carparts was amazingly racing off a 25lb higher mark than when second last time on the All-Weather. (12/1)
467* Abstone Queen, dropped back in distance, is certainly a tough sort. (13/2)
Rum Lad can do better on a more orthodox track. (14/1)
634 Docklands Carriage (IRE), with the visor back on, made the mistake of sticking to the far side. Easily the best ground was towards the stands'-side rail. (6/1)
685 La Dolce Vita, well supported in the market, broke on terms this time but was in trouble with over two furlongs left to run. (9/2: op 8/1)

T/Plpt: £176.20 (47.07 Tckts). T/Qdpt: £14.20 (31.33 Tckts) WG

EPSOM (L-H) (Good, Good to firm patches)
Wednesday April 23rd
WEATHER: fine WIND: almost nil

786 BANSTEAD H'CAP (0-95) (3-Y.O+) (Class C)
2-05 (2-05) **6f** £5,446.00 (£1,648.00: £804.00: £382.00) Stalls: High GOING minus 0.11 sec per fur (G)

Form	Horse / details	Dist	Pos	SP	RR	SF
	Lord Olivier (IRE) (75) (WJarvis) **7-8-11** LDettori(7) (a.p: chsd ldr over 2f out: rdn over 1f out: led last strides)	—	**1**	13/2[2]	87	68
	Selhurstpark Flyer (IRE) (91) (JBerry) **6-9-8**(5) PRoberts(9) (b: w ldr: led over 3f out: rdn over 1f out: hdd last strides)	hd	**2**	5/1[1]	103	84
596[6]	**Tiler (IRE) (81)** (MJohnston) **5-9-3** JWeaver(2) (lw: rdn over 2f out: hdwy over 1f out: r.o wl ins fnl f)	3½	**3**	8/1	83	64
540[4]	**My Best Valentine (92)** (JWhite) **7-10-0b** WJO'Connor(10) (lw: hdwy over 2f out: rdn over 1f out: one pce)	2½	**4**	7/1[3]	88	69
643[5]	**Willow Dale (IRE) (70)** (DRCElsworth) **4-8-6** TQuinn(1) (a.p: rdn 3f out: one pce)	¾	**5**	14/1	64	45
643*	**Spender (78)** (PWHarris) **8-9-0** JReid(8) (nvr nr to chal)	nk	**6**	5/1[1]	71	52
	Watch The Fire (70) (JEBanks) **4-8-1**(5) RMullen(5) (dwlt: a bhd)	½	**7**	12/1	62	43
520[11]	**So Intrepid (IRE) (74)** (JMBradley) **7-8-10** PatEddery(4) (a bhd)	½	**8**	5/1[1]	64	45
	Orange Place (IRE) (75) (TJNaughton) **6-8-11** DHolland(6) (swtg: bit bkwd: led over 2f: wknd wl over 1f out)	12	**9**	33/1	33	14
488[2]	**Mijas (70)** (LMontagueHall) **4-8-6** DaneO'Neill(3) (bhd fnl 2f)	1	**10**	11/1	26	7
				(SP 112.6%)	**10 Rn**	

1m 9.16 (1.16) CSF £34.18 CT £242.76 TOTE £8.50: £2.40 £1.90 £1.60 (£12.10) Trio £49.10 OWNER Miss V. R. Jarvis (NEWMARKET) BRED Michael Staunton in Ireland

Lord Olivier (IRE), who won first time out as a three-year-old and four-year-old, moved into second place over a quarter-of-a-mile from home and eventually managed to get on top in the last couple of strides, to gain his first-ever handicap victory. (13/2)
Selhurstpark Flyer (IRE) is a front-runner who is well suited by this downhill track - two of his three victories last year came here. Showing definitely in front in the straight, he grimly tried to hold off the winner but was caught in the last couple of strides. He is a winner without a penalty. (5/1)
596 Tiler (IRE) usually races up with the pace but, on this occasion, he was at the back of the field until running on strongly from below the distance to take third prize inside the final furlong. (8/1)
540 My Best Valentine, wearing blinkers for the first time since June 1995, was racing off a 7lb higher mark than he has ever won off before and, after creeping into the action in the straight, was tapped for toe in the final quarter-mile. All five of his victories to date have come at around seven furlongs. (7/1)
643 Willow Dale (IRE) was never far away but could only go up and down in the same place in the straight. She has not won since her two-year-old days. (14/1)
643* Spender (5/1: 3/1-11/2)
488 Mijas (11/1: 7/1-12/1)

787 CITY AND SUBURBAN H'CAP (0-105) (4-Y.O+) (Class B)
2-35 (2-40) **1m 2f 18y** £8,364.00 (£2,532.00: £1,236.00: £588.00) Stalls: Low GOING minus 0.11 sec per fur (G)

Form	Horse / details	Dist	Pos	SP	RR	SF
499[7]	**Major Change (86)** (MissGayKelleway) **5-8-9** KFallon(7) (hdwy over 3f out: led 2f out to 1f out: hrd rdn: led nr fin)	—	**1**	11/1	98	57
633[4]	**Champagne Prince (81)** (PWHarris) **4-8-4** AClark(6) (a.p: led 3f out to 2f out: led 1f out: hrd rdn: hdd nr fin)	hd	**2**	10/1	93	52
678[4]	**Behaviour (105)** (MrsJCecil) **5-10-0** JReid(2) (lw: hdwy over 3f out: hrd rdn over 1f out: one pce)	5	**3**	5/1[2]	109	68
	The Dilettanti (USA) (88) (JARToller) **4-8-11** SSanders(12) (bit bkwd: a.p: c stands' side st: hrd rdn over 2f out: hung lft over 1f out: one pce)	1¼	**4**	25/1	90	49
521[6]	**Silver Groom (IRE) (77)** (RAkehurst) **7-7-11**(3) MHenry(3) (hdwy over 1f out: nvr nrr)	1¼	**5**	7/1[3]	77	36
639*	**Sharp Shuffle (IRE) (74)** (RHannon) **4-7-8**(3) MartinDwyer(5) (b.off fore: hdwy 2f out: hrd rdn over 1f out: one pce)	½	**6**	10/1	73	32
482[6]	**Soviet Bride (IRE) (73)** (SDow) **5-7-10** JQuinn(9) (hrd rdn over 2f out: nvr nrr)	1½	**7**	14/1	70	29
	Burnt Offering (73) (CEBrittain) **4-7-10** JLowe(1) (nvr nrr)	1	**8**	33/1	68	27
521[14]	**Hoh Express (90)** (IABalding) **5-8-13** LDettori(10) (hdwy over 3f out: wknd over 2f out)	nk	**9**	9/2[1]	85	44
	Dance So Suite (90) (PFICole) **5-8-6**(7) DavidO'Neill(4) (s.i.s: c stands' side st: a bhd)	½	**10**	9/1	84	43
591[9]	**Trojan Risk (81)** (GLewis) **4-8-4** PaulEddery(14) (b: b.hind: led 9f out: c stands' side st: hdd 3f out: sn wknd)	nk	**11**	8/1	74	33
398[9]	**Royal Action (82)** (JEBanks) **4-8-0**(5) RMullen(13) (a.p: c stands' side st: wknd 3f out)	7	**12**	20/1	64	23
626a[5]	**Time for Action (IRE) (84)** (MHTompkins) **5-8-7** TQuinn(11) (lw: led 1f: wknd over 2f out)	17	**13**	20/1	39	—
				(SP 118.0%)	**13 Rn**	

2m 7.34 (3.34) CSF £99.10 CT £569.36 TOTE £10.70: £2.90 £3.70 £2.30 (£59.70) Trio £136.70 OWNER The Two In One Partnership (WHITCOMBE) BRED Shanbally House Stud
LONG HANDICAP Burnt Offering 7-8 Soviet Bride (IRE) 7-9

OFFICIAL EXPLANATION **Major Change: regarding the improved form, the trainer reported that the horse was suited by the shorter trip and softer ground here.**

451 Major Change has been running over a mile-and-a-half so far this year, but he has never won over that trip and seemed better suited by this shorter distance. Engaged in a tremendous battle with the runner-up, he managed to have his nose in front where it mattered most. (11/1)

633 Champagne Prince, winner of three races as a two-year-old, failed to score last year but almost got back in the winner's enclosure. Engaged in a ding-dong battle with the winner, he gave his all and only just lost out. (10/1)

678 Behaviour had to concede lumps of weight all round and that took its toll for, after creeping closer early in the straight, he could only keep on at one pace from below the distance. (5/1)

The Dilettanti (USA) was carrying some surplus flesh for this reappearance but still acquitted himself well. One of four who elected to come over to the stands' side in the straight, he came under pressure and, despite drifting into the centre of the course, kept on at one pace. (25/1)

521 Silver Groom (IRE) caught the eye, staying on from the back of the field under considerate handling in the closing stages to be nearest at the line. He is well and truly in the Handicapper's grip at present. (7/1)

639* Sharp Shuffle (IRE) began a forward move a quarter-of-a-mile from home but, over this longer trip, made no further impression. He may be better at a mile. (10/1)

591 Trojan Risk (8/1: 6/1-9/1)

788 BLUE RIBAND TRIAL CONDITIONS STKS (3-Y.O) (Class B)

3-10 (3-13) **1m 4f 10y** £8,301.60 (£2,685.60: £1,312.80) Stalls: Centre GOING minus 0.11 sec per fur (G)

				SP	RR	SF
505*	**Palio Sky (98)** (JLDunlop) **3-9-0** PatEddery(2) (chsd ldr: rdn over 3f out: led 2f out: edgd lft over 1f out: r.o wl)	—	**1**	8/13^{1}	102	54
508^{3}	**Papua (108)** (IABalding) **3-9-8** JReid(3) (lw: led 10f: unable qckn)	1¾	**2**	2/1^{2}	108	60
690^{12}	**Mister Pink (94)** (RFJohnsonHoughton) **3-8-10** SSanders(1) (hld up: rdn over 3f out: r.o ins fnl f)	hd	**3**	9/1^{3}	96	48
				(SP 105.2%)	**3 Rn**	

2m 39.94 (5.44) CSF £1.85 TOTE £1.60 (£1.20) OWNER Mr J. E. Nash (ARUNDEL) BRED Montealto Stud Establishment

505* Palio Sky appreciated this step-up in distance. Rousted along once in line for home, he got to the front a quarter-of-a-mile out and, despite drifting left on this notorious camber, proved too strong for his rivals. A promising but lazy individual, he will now go for the Italian Derby. (8/13)

508 Papua, who found a mile far too sharp at Kempton last month, was much happier over this longer trip but had no easy task conceding 8lb to the winner. Nevertheless he took the field along but, once collared a quarter-of-a-mile out, found the winner too good. (2/1)

502* Mister Pink, not in quite the same class as his two rivals, nevertheless acquitted himself well over this longer trip and, running on inside the final furlong, would probably have taken second place in a few more strides. (9/1: 5/1-10/1)

789 STANLEY RACING GREAT METROPOLITAN H'CAP (0-90) (3-Y.O+) (Class C)

3-40 (3-47) **1m 4f 10y** £5,810.00 (£1,760.00: £860.00: £410.00) Stalls: Centre GOING minus 0.11 sec per fur (G)

				SP	RR	SF
	Prince Kinsky (74) (JABOld) **4-9-2** DHarrison(6) (lw: stdy hdwy over 2f out: led over 1f out: hrd rdn: r.o wl)	—	**1**	33/1	86	62
538^{9}	**Urgent Swift (75)** (APJarvis) **4-9-3** WJO'Connor(9) (lw: stdy hdwy 2f out: hrd rdn over 1f out: r.o)	1½	**2**	16/1	85	61
	Artic Courier (83) (DJSCosgrove) **6-9-12** MRimmer(1) (a.p: ev ch over 1f out: unable qckn)	hd	**3**	14/1	93	70
	Pike Creek (USA) (75) (IABalding) **4-9-3** LDettori(3) (led 2f: led over 2f out tl over 1f out: one pce)	1	**4**	8/1^{3}	84	60
	Wild Rita (81) (WRMuir) **5-9-10** JReid(5) (lw: hld up: rdn over 2f out: one pce)	hd	**5**	11/1	89	66
207^{9}	**Cedez le Passage (FR) (69)** (KOCunningham-Brown) **6-8-12b** DaneO'Neill(15) (hdwy 2f out: hrd rdn over 1f out: r.o)	nk	**6**	50/1	77	54
647*	**White Plains (IRE) (79)** (MCPipe) **4-9-2**(5) RMullen(10) (lw: hdwy over 1f out: r.o)	¾	**7**	7/1^{2}	86	62
510^{6}	**Frozen Sea (USA) (63)** (GPEnright) **6-8-6** JWeaver(8) (lw: nvr nrr)	1	**8**	20/1	69	46
509*	**Northern Sun (86)** (TGMills) **3-8-9** KFallon(16) (nvr nrr)	½	**9**	12/1	91	48
510^{3}	**Shining Dancer (60)** (SDow) **5-8-3** JQuinn(19) (no hdwy fnl 3f)	hd	**10**	10/1	65	42
655^{6}	**Palamon (USA) (80)** (JWhite) **4-9-8** DBiggs(7) (rdn over 3f out: a mid div)	s.h	**11**	25/1	85	61
	Newport Knight (73) (RAkehurst) **6-9-2** TQuinn(2) (a.p: rdn 2f out: wknd over 1f out)	½	**12**	14/1	77	54
680^{3}	**Hazard a Guess (IRE) (83)** (DNicholls) **7-9-12** PatEddery(18) (nt clr run over 2f out & over 1f out: a mid div)	1	**13**	9/2^{1}	86	63
381^{2}	**Outstayed Welcome (53)** (MJHaynes) **5-7-10** GBardwell(17) (b.off hind: led 10f out tl over 2f out: sn wknd)	3	**14**	20/1	52	29
552^{10}	**Veridian (75)** (PWHarris) **4-9-3** AClark(13) (bhd fnl 4f)	1	**15**	20/1	73	49
	Chatham Island (72) (CEBrittain) **9-9-1** BDoyle(4) (b: bit bkwd: prom over 9f)	6	**16**	16/1	62	39
133^{4}	**General Haven (68)** (TJNaughton) **4-8-10** DHolland(14) (bit bkwd: a bhd)	3	**17**	12/1	54	30
	Wot No Fax (86) (BJMeehan) **4-10-0** RHughes(12) (prom over 9f)	3	**18**	33/1	68	44
205^{8}	**Glide Path (USA) (78)** (JRJenkins) **8-9-7** SWhitworth(11) (lw: a bhd)	10	**19**	33/1	46	23
				(SP 128.6%)	**19 Rn**	

2m 39.09 (4.59) CSF £430.16 CT £6,873.62 TOTE £60.30: £8.10 £7.10 £3.70 £2.20 (£552.80) Trio £1,568.30; £1,988.01 to Beverley 24/4/97
OWNER Mrs Anne Bickel (WROUGHTON) BRED J. L. and Mrs Hislop
LONG HANDICAP Outstayed Welcome 7-8
WEIGHT FOR AGE 3yo-20lb, 4yo-1lb

Prince Kinsky looked in good shape beforehand and made a winning debut for his new stable, leading below the distance and keeping on well under pressure. (33/1)

430 Urgent Swift bounced back from his poor run at Warwick last time out. Creeping closer a quarter-of-a-mile from home, he kept on well but was unable to reel in the winner. (16/1)

Artic Courier, 3lb higher than he has ever won off, made a pleasing reappearance and may well have shown in front for a brief time around the quarter-mile marker before tapped for toe from below the distance. (14/1)

Pike Creek (USA), a leading light from the outset, poked a whisker in front two out but, headed below the distance, failed to find another gear. She failed to stay two miles on her last two outings last year, and has subsequently fallen in the weights. (8/1)

Wild Rita chased the leaders but failed to find another gear in the final quarter-mile. (11/1)

160 Cedez le Passage (FR) is not up to this class but kept on in the final quarter-mile to be nearest at the line. This was his fortieth outing and he is yet to win on Turf. (50/1)

790 SPRING MEETING MAIDEN STKS (3-Y.O+) (Class D)

4-10 (4-16) **1m 114y** £3,532.00 (£1,066.00: £518.00: £244.00) Stalls: Low GOING minus 0.11 sec per fur (G)

				SP	RR	SF
	Supply And Demand (84) (GLMoore) **3-8-9** KFallon(3) (hmpd over 7f out: rdn & hdwy 2f out: led ins fnl f: r.o wl)	—	**1**	2/1^{1}	81	35
517^{3}	**Ijtinab** (RAkehurst) **3-8-9** TQuinn(1) (a.p: rdn & edgd rt over 2f out: led wl over 1f out tl ins fnl f: unable qckn)	2	**2**	2/1^{1}	77	31

				SP	RR	SF
523^{5}	**Seattle Swing** (JHMGosden) **3-8-5**^{ow1} LDettori(7) (a.p: hrd rdn over 2f out: one pce)	2	**3**	5/1 ^{2}	70	23
	Saxon Bay (KOCunningham-Brown) **5-9-10** JWeaver(5) (b: led tl wl over 1f out: sn wknd)	6	**4**	50/1	62	31
518^{2}	**The Negotiator** (MJHeaton-Ellis) **3-8-9** AClark(10) (lw: plld hrd: chsd ldr over 7f out tl over 2f out: wknd over 1f out)	4	**5**	5/1 ^{2}	55	9
	Midnight Romance (APJarvis) **3-8-5**^{ow1} DHolland(9) (hld up: rdn over 3f out: sn wknd)	5	**6**	25/1 ^{3}	41	—
	Honeyshan (DJSffrenchDavis) **5-9-5** JReid(8) (lw: hmpd over 7f out: bhd fnl 2f)	½	**7**	40/1	39	8
	Sipowitz (CACyzer) **3-8-9** AMorris(4) (lw: bmpd over 7f out: bhd fnl 6f)	2½	**8**	25/1 ^{3}	40	—
605^{9}	**Victor Blum (USA)** (CAHorgan) **4-9-10** PaulEddery(2) (lw: bdly hmpd over 7f out: a bhd)	7	**9**	50/1	27	—
	Gracious Imp (USA) (JRJenkins) **4-9-5** SWhitworth(6) (lw: reard s: a bhd)	16	**10**	33/1	—	—

(SP 117.0%) **10 Rn**

1m 47.08 (5.08) CSF £4.98 TOTE £3.20: £1.20 £1.40 £1.60 (£4.10) Trio £5.40 OWNER Action (BRIGHTON) BRED W. H. Joyce
WEIGHT FOR AGE 3yo-15lb

Supply And Demand appeared to be going far from well running down Tattenham Hill, but he began to pick up ground and, gradually reeling in the leader, managed to get on top inside the final furlong. (2/1)

517 Ijtinab, who drifted out into the centre of the track in the straight, went on early in the final quarter-mile and looked the likely winner. However, he was caught inside the final furlong. His turn is not far away. (2/1)

523 Seattle Swing, taking a step down in distance, was never far away but failed to quicken under pressure in the final quarter-mile. She is certainly one of the stable's lesser lights. (5/1)

Saxon Bay took the field along but, collared early in the final quarter-mile, soon had bellows to mend. (50/1)

518 The Negotiator took a fierce hold in the early stages, causing plenty of scrimmaging after only a furlong. Collared for second place early in the straight, he grimly tried to hold on but had shot his bolt below the distance. (5/1: 3/1-11/2)

791 WARREN LIMITED STKS (0-70) (3-Y.O+) (Class E)

4-40 (4-52) **1m 114y** £3,590.50 (£1,084.00: £527.00: £248.50) Stalls: Low GOING minus 0.11 sec per fur (G)

				SP	RR	SF
335^{3}	**La Modiste (70)** (MissGayKelleway) **4-9-5** KFallon(12) (hld up: hrd rdn over 2f out: led 1f out: edgd lft: r.o wl)	—	**1**	7/1 ^{3}	72	54
609^{*}	**Purchasing Power (IRE) (66)** (NACallaghan) **3-8-9** PatEddery(6) (led to 1f out: unable qckn ins fnl f)	1½	**2**	100/30 ^{1}	74	41
560^{4}	**Master M-E-N (IRE) (57)** (NMBabbage) **5-9-8v** VSlattery(9) (lw: hld up: hrd rdn over 2f out: one pce)	2½	**3**	12/1	68	50
186^{3}	**Sooty Tern (68)** (JMBradley) **10-9-3**$^{(5)}$ RFfrench(8) (a.p: ev ch 2f out: wknd fnl f)	nk	**4**	12/1	67	49
358^{4}	**Kingchip Boy (69)** (MJRyan) **8-9-7v**$^{(7)}$ AMcCarthy(2) (a.p: rdn over 3f out: wknd fnl f)	nk	**5**	10/1	72	54
	Laguna Bay (IRE) (70) (APJarvis) **3-8-5**^{ow1} DHolland(4) (rdn over 2f out: hdwy over 1f out: nvr nrr)	1¼	**6**	33/1	62	28
291^{8}	**Law Dancer (IRE) (65)** (TGMills) **4-9-8** TQuinn(3) (lw: hld up: rdn over 3f out: wknd over 1f out)	4	**7**	12/1	57	39
	Righty Ho (65) (PTWalwyn) **3-8-7** JReid(7) (prom 6f)	nk	**8**	25/1	56	23
	Rumbustious (66) (RHannon) **3-8-4** DaneO'Neill(13) (bhd fnl 3f)	nk	**9**	10/1	52	19
444^{18}	**Proud Monk (70)** (GLMoore) **4-9-8v** RHughes(10) (a bhd)	2	**10**	9/1	52	34
639^{5}	**Balance of Power (68)** (SDow) **5-9-8** SSanders(11) (lw: a bhd)	1½	**11**	9/1	49	31
642^{2}	**First Chance (IRE) (69)** (DRCElsworth) **3-8-6** BDoyle(14) (lw: a bhd)	2½	**12**	9/2 ^{2}	43	10
675^{6}	**Hoh Flyer (USA) (69)** (MBell) **3-7-13**$^{(5)}$ RMullen(1) (lw: bhd fnl 5f)	1¾	**13**	7/1 ^{3}	38	5
	Move With Edes (69) (WGMTurner) **5-9-8** LDettori(5) (Withdrawn not under Starter's orders: uns rdr & bolted bef s)		**W**	10/1	—	—

(SP 143.4%) **13 Rn**

1m 46.02 (4.02) CSF £31.39 TOTE £12.50: £4.10 £1.60 £4.00 (£22.40) Trio £200.20 OWNER Mr John Purcell (WHITCOMBE) BRED G. R. Smith (Thriplow) Ltd
WEIGHT FOR AGE 3yo-15lb

335 La Modiste, formerly with Simon Dow, made a winning debut for her new connections. Under pressure in the straight, she drifted left on this notorious camber, giving her jockey some steering problems, but she still managed to get to the front a furlong from home and keep the runner-up at bay. (7/1)

609* Purchasing Power (IRE) attempted to make all the running. Collared a furlong from home, he tried to get back at the hanging winner inside the final furlong, but just failed to find another gear. (100/30)

560 Master M-E-N (IRE) looked extremely well in the paddock, but was officially worst in at the weights and, despite all his rider's efforts, failed to quicken in the final quarter-mile. (12/1)

186 Sooty Tern had every chance, but he has been off the track for twelve weeks and that told in the final furlong. (12/1)

358 Kingchip Boy, whose last seven victories have all come on the Fibresand, had no easy task at the weights but played an active role until tiring in the final furlong. (10/1)

Laguna Bay (IRE) stayed on from the back of the field in the last furlong-and-a-half without ever threatening to get there in time. (33/1)

T/Jkpt: Not won; £3,919.95 to Beverley 24/4/97. T/Plpt: £341.40 (77.64 Tckts). T/Qdpt: £43.80 (23.95 Tckts) AK

0631-BEVERLEY (R-H) (Good to firm)

Thursday April 24th

WEATHER: fine & windy WIND: str half against

792 FULFORD MAIDEN STKS (3-Y.O+) (Class D)

2-10 (2-17) **5f** £3,743.00 (£1,124.00: £542.00: £251.00) Stalls: High GOING minus 0.31 sec per fur (GF)

				SP	RR	SF
531^{2}	**Cathedral (IRE)** (BJMeehan) **3-9-0** PatEddery(12) (mde all: qcknd 2f out: sn clr: easily)	—	**1**	2/5 ^{1}	97+	36
636^{5}	**Colway Ritz** (JWWatts) **3-9-0** GDuffield(10) (b: uns rdr gng to s: chsd ldrs: kpt on same pce fnl 2f: no ch w wnr)	6	**2**	20/1	78	17
636^{3}	**Archello (IRE) (71)** (GROldroyd) **3-8-4**$^{(5)}$ GParkin(5) (a chsng ldrs: one pce fnl 2f)	¾	**3**	20/1	70	9
	At Large (IRE) (JRFanshawe) **3-9-0** DHarrison(9) (w'like: lengthy: scope: mid div: styd on appr fnl f)	nk	**4**	14/1	74	13
693^{9}	**Hype Superior (IRE)** (ABailey) **3-9-0** DWright(13) (hld up & bhd: styd on fnl 2f: nvr nr to chal)	1½	**5**	50/1	70	9
636^{2}	**Marylebone (IRE) (73)** (JBerry) **3-9-0** JFortune(11) (chsd ldrs: rdn ½-wy: lost pl 2f out)	1	**6**	13/2 ^{2}	66	5
565^{4}	**Cambridge Blue (USA)** (GLewis) **3-9-0** PaulEddery(14) (chsd ldrs: rdn 2f out: no imp)	1¼	**7**	11/1 ^{3}	62	1
701^{8}	**Hever Golf Angel (IRE)** (PCHaslam) **3-8-9** JWeaver(7) (s.i.s: bhd: sme hdwy on ins 2f out: nvr nr ldrs)	nk	**8**	33/1	57	—
	Anetta (MissSEHall) **3-8-9** MRoberts(4) (s.i.s: bhd: sme hdwy on outside 2f out: n.d)	hd	**9**	50/1	56	—
	La Doyenne (IRE) (CBBBooth) **3-8-9** KHodgson(2) (mid div: rdn ½-wy: sn wl outpcd)	3½	**10**	50/1	45	—
636^{6}	**Star of The Road** (JMCarr) **3-9-0** ACulhane(6) (hld up: in tch to ½-wy: wkng whn n.m.r 1f out)	1¼	**11**	50/1	46	—

			Pos	SP	RR	SF
	Daintree (IRE) (68) (HJCollingridge) **3-8-9** MRimmer(1) (b.hind: sn cl up: lost pl 2f out)	1¾	**12**	50/1	35	—
759[13]	**Magazine Gap (47)** (PatMitchell) **4-9-5**(5) AmandaSanders(3) (sn bhd: sme hdwy on outside ½-wy: sn wknd)	2	**13**	50/1	34	—
656[3]	**Hoh Dancer (68)** (IABalding) **3-8-9** MHills(8) (hld up: a bhd)	¾	**14**	14/1	27	—

(SP 130.7%) **14 Rn**

64.1 secs (2.30) CSF £16.82 TOTE £1.50: £1.20 £6.30 £3.20 (£26.80) Trio £129.50 OWNER Kennet Valley Thoroughbreds (UPPER LAMBOURN) BRED P. D. and Mrs Player

WEIGHT FOR AGE 3yo-10lb

IN-FOCUS: **Kevin Hodgson was having his first ride for seven years.**

531 Cathedral (IRE), who had only one outing as a juvenile when there was a problem with his knees, was thought to have blown up first time at Nottingham when he met a decent horse. Showing a good action going down, once he injected some pace into the race at the two furlong from home marker he shot clear in a matter of strides and proved totally different class to this lot. Highly regarded, he should go on to much better things. (2/5)

636 Colway Ritz, on his toes beforehand, shied going to the start and unseated his rider and ran loose. Sticking on, he is now qualified for a handicap mark and a step up to six furlongs might be called for. (20/1)

636 Archello (IRE), who has a scrappy action, has now been placed on all her four outings. (20/1)

At Large (IRE), who moved very short going to post, stayed on in promising fashion and in due course will be suited by a step up in distance. (14/1: 6/1-16/1)

Hype Superior (IRE) has a bad case of stringhalt but he definitely possesses some ability despite showing a very poor action going down to the start. (50/1)

636 Marylebone (IRE), who has had plenty of chances, was unable to confirm her course running here two weeks ago with the third. (13/2)

565 Cambridge Blue (USA), a fair sort, moved very short going to the post. He might improve if given a little more time. (11/1: op 7/1)

793 PANNELL CLAIMING STKS (3-Y.O) (Class F)

2-40 (2-40) **1m 1f 207y** £2,574.00 (£714.00: £342.00) Stalls: High GOING minus 0.31 sec per fur (GF)

			Pos	SP	RR	SF
331[3]	**Going For Broke (68)** (PCHaslam) **3-8-13** JFortune(7) (trckd ldrs: led over 2f out: styd on wl fnl f: drvn out)	—	**1**	15/8[2]	70	35
654[9]	**Double Gold (73)** (BJMeehan) **3-8-12b** PatEddery(6) (trckd ldr: effrt over 2f out: rdn to chal over 1f out: kpt on one pce)	2½	**2**	7/4[1]	65	30
551[3]	**Manileno (42)** (JHetherton) **3-8-1** NKennedy(9) (led: hung badly lft ent s: hdd over 2f out: one pce fnl f)	1¾	**3**	16/1	51	16
471[7]	**Wildmoor (56)** (JDBethell) **3-8-13** JReid(1) (hld up: styd on u.p fnl 3f: nvr nr to chal)	¾	**4**	6/1	62	27
581[10]	**Maremma (48)** (DonEnricoIncisa) **3-8-0** KimTinkler(4) (hld up & bhd: hdwy on ins over 2f out: kpt on: nvr nr ldrs)	1¼	**5**	20/1	47	12
690[W]	**Red Embers (66)** (CADwyer) **3-8-2** DRMcCabe(3) (hld up & plld hrd: racd wd: lost pl over 3f out: n.d)	6	**6**	7/2[3]	39	4
	Forest Signal (MBrittain) **3-8-2**(7) DMernagh(2) (lengthy: dwlt: hld up & plld hrd: wnt prom 5f out: wknd over 2f out)	1	**7**	16/1	45	10
645[10]	**Misterton** (JAGlover) **3-8-6**(7) TPengkerego(5) (chsd ldrs tl lost pl over 2f out)	4	**8**	16/1	42	7
609[7]	**Willskip (USA) (45)** (JBerry) **3-8-11** JWeaver(8) (chsd ldrs tl lost pl over 2f out)	1¼	**9**	10/1	38	3

(SP 139.2%) **9 Rn**

2m 7.7 (4.60) CSF £6.48 TOTE £3.00: £1.30 £1.30 £2.80 (£3.30) Trio £14.70 OWNER Dunnington & Smart (MIDDLEHAM) BRED Mrs John Trotter

Manileno clmd SHolder £4,000

331 Going For Broke stuck on in most determined fashion and certainly stayed the trip okay. (15/8)

Double Gold was going up and down in the same place in the final furlong and possibly does not quite truly stay this far. (7/4: op 4/5)

551 Manileno, a fair sort, had real trouble handling the bend. He was claimed for only four thousand pounds and apparently now joins Martin Pipe. (16/1)

Wildmoor wore a tongue-strap. (6/1)

534 Maremma found this trip much too short. (20/1)

581 Red Embers, best in on official figures, raced wide and would not settle. (7/2)

794 GANTON RATED STKS H'CAP (0-90) (3-Y.O) (Class C)

3-10 (3-10) **7f 100y** £4,581.29 (£1,706.70: £828.35: £349.25: £149.63: £69.78) Stalls: High GOING minus 0.31 sec per fur (GF)

			Pos	SP	RR	SF
	Hawait (IRE) (83) (BWHills) **3-9-5** MHills(2) (hld up: hdwy over 3f out: qcknd to ld jst ins fnl f: r.o wl)	—	**1**	4/1[2]	93	59
*514**	**Nomore Mr Niceguy (85)** (EJAlston) **3-9-7** KFallon(3) (lw: trckd ldrs: plld hrd: effrt 2f out: kpt on wl ins fnl f)	¾	**2**	7/1[3]	93	59
	Can Can Lady (73) (MJohnston) **3-8-9** JWeaver(4) (led tl over 1f out: no ex)	½	**3**	14/1	80	46
642*	**Boater (72)** (DMorley) **3-8-8** MFenton(6) (trckd ldr: led over 1f out: hdd jst ins fnl f: wknd towards fin)	1	**4**	7/1[3]	77	43
	Tough Leader (80) (BHanbury) **3-9-2** JStack(5) (bit bkwd: trckd ldrs: effrt 2f out: kpt on one pce appr fnl f)	s.h	**5**	10/1	85	51
699*	**Hen Harrier (85)** (JLDunlop) **3-9-7** 3x PatEddery(7) (b: hld up: effrt on ins 2f out: sn rdn & hung rt: no imp)	1	**6**	11/10[1]	88	54
634[2]	**The Wyandotte Inn (72)** (RHollinshead) **3-8-5**(3) FLynch(1) (trckd ldrs: rdn & outpcd over 3f out: n.d after)	2	**7**	12/1	71	37

(SP 116.1%) **7 Rn**

1m 33.7 (1.70) CSF £29.46 TOTE £4.50: £2.50 £3.40 (£22.20) OWNER Maktoum Al Maktoum (LAMBOURN) BRED John R. Gaines

OFFICIAL EXPLANATION **Hen Harrier: no explanation offered.**

Hawait (IRE), 11lb lower than his first nursery mark, showed a nice turn of foot. A nicely-balanced sort, he looks made to measure for Chester. (4/1: 5/1-3/1)

514* Nomore Mr Niceguy, who is thriving physically, ran another fine race. (7/1)

Can Can Lady set what looked to be a strong pace and stuck on all the way to the line. (14/1: 10/1-16/1)

642* Boater was 3lb higher and in a tougher contest. (7/1)

Tough Leader looked and ran as if just needing the outing. This will put an edge on him. (10/1)

699* Hen Harrier looked even worse than she did in the paddock at Ripon and, always tending to hang to her right, was never giving her rider full co-operation. She has plenty of ability but time may show that she was flattered by her Ripon success. (11/10: 4/5-5/4)

795 MOORTOWN MAIDEN STKS (3-Y.O+) (Class D)

3-40 (3-41) **1m 100y** £3,860.00 (£1,160.00: £560.00: £260.00) Stalls: High GOING minus 0.31 sec per fur (GF)

			Pos	SP	RR	SF
	Teofilio (IRE) (DRLoder) **3-8-12** PatEddery(6) (lw: trckd ldrs: shkn up to ld over 1f out: drvn clr)	—	**1**	8/11[1]	80	52
599[2]	**Crystal Gold (77)** (MRStoute) **3-8-12** JReid(10) (lw: led: rn wd bnd 4f out: hdd over 1f out: no ch w wnr)	4	**2**	5/1[3]	72	44
586[11]	**Nobel Lad** (JLDunlop) **3-8-12** TSprake(11) (b: trckd ldrs: shkn up over 1f out: kpt on wl ins fnl f)	2½	**3**	16/1	68	40
	Begorrat (IRE) (BJMeehan) **3-8-12** PaulEddery(5) (plld hrd: trckd ldrs: drvn along 3f out: one pce)	1¼	**4**	16/1	65	37

				SP	RR	SF
	Gharib (USA) (ACStewart) **3-8-12** MRoberts(8) (b.hind: hld up & bhd: stdy hdwy 2f out: styd on towards fin)	¾	**5**	$7/2^{2}$	64	36
	Night Express (BHanbury) **3-8-12** MRimmer(3) (w'like: hld up: hdwy over 2f out: kpt on)	2	**6**	16/1	60	32
517^{6}	**Neronian (IRE)** (BWHills) **3-8-12** MHills(4) (sn bhd & pushed along: sme hdwy 2f out: n.d)	1¼	**7**	10/1	58	30
	Martindale (IRE) (RBastiman) **4-9-7**(5) HBastiman(1) (trckd ldrs tl lost pl 2f out)	8	**8**	50/1	43	29
	Glorious Dancer (JHetherton) **3-8-7** MBirch(2) (unf: bhd fnl 4f)	2	**9**	50/1	34	6
	Silver Moon (42) (BAMcMahon) **3-8-7** SSanders(7) (s.i.s: hdwy 4f out: wknd over 2f out)	5	**10**	50/1	24	—
	Blue Island (IRE) (ICampbell) **3-8-12** TGMcLaughlin(9) (unf: chsd ldrs: effrt over 3f out: wknd over 2f out)	2½	**11**	50/1	25	—

(SP 131.4%) **11 Rn**

1m 46.0 (2.00) CSF £5.25 TOTE £1.60: £1.10 £1.70 £3.50 (£3.30) Trio £59.60 OWNER Mr B. E. Nielsen (NEWMARKET) BRED Mrs J. Maxwell Moran

WEIGHT FOR AGE 3yo-14lb

Teofilio (IRE), beaten a length by Free Handicap winner Hidden Meadow at York last year, has plenty of size and scope. He took this in fine style and a step up to a mile and a quarter will be no problem. (8/11: op 4/9)

599 Crystal Gold, a keen-going sort, seems to lack anything in the way of finishing speed. Connections will be hoping the handicapper leaves him on 77. (5/1)

Nobel Lad, who showed a pronounced knee action going down, needs to learn to settle better. (16/1)

Begorrat (IRE) gave his rider problems, pulling very hard. (16/1)

Gharib (USA), who showed promise on his only outing at two, was given an educational outing. He needs one more run out to qualify for a handicap mark. (7/2: 3/1-9/2)

Night Express, who showed plenty of knee action going down, ran a satisfactory first race. (16/1)

517 Neronian (IRE) still has plenty to learn. (10/1)

Martindale (IRE), having his third ever outing, might be worth a try in a seven furlong handicap. (50/1)

796 ALWOODLY H'CAP (0-70) (4-Y.O+ F & M) (Class E)

4-10 (4-10) **1m 1f 207y** £2,922.50 (£875.00: £420.00: £192.50) Stalls: High GOING minus 0.31 sec per fur (GF)

				SP	RR	SF
689^{5}	**Tallulah Belle (57)** (NPLittmoden) **4-9-5** JWeaver(2) (hld up: hdwy & swtchd lft over 2f out: r.o wl u.p to ld jst ins fnl f)	—	**1**	$4/1^{1}$	62	57
608^{4}	**Portite Sophie (40)** (MBrittain) **6-7-9**(7) DMernagh(8) (trckd ldrs: led over 2f out tl jst ins fnl f: kpt on wl)	2	**2**	$9/2^{2}$	42	37
	Classic Beauty (IRE) (60) (SCWilliams) **4-9-8** KFallon(5) (a.p: drvn along over 3f out: one pce)	5	**3**	7/1	54	49
313^{8}	**Needwood Nutkin (36)** (BCMorgan) **4-7-12** LCharnock(6) (a chsng ldrs: one pce fnl 2f)	2	**4**	20/1	27	22
382^{7}	**Worldwide Elsie (USA) (62)** (ICampbell) **4-9-10** RPrice(10) (chsd ldrs: rdn over 2f out: no imp)	hd	**5**	16/1	52	47
	Mcgillycuddy Reeks (IRE) (40) (DonEnricoIncisa) **6-8-2** KimTinkler(1) (bhd: sme hdwy 2f out: nvr nr to chal)	½	**6**	16/1	30	25
733^{12}	**My Millie (47)** (DWBarker) **4-8-6**(3) DarrenMoffatt(4) (bit bkwd: plld hrd: sn led: hdd over 2f out: sn wknd)	4	**7**	16/1	30	25
	Tolepa (IRE) (34) (JJO'Neill) **4-7-10** JQuinn(3) (sn bhd & pushed along)	½	**8**	14/1	16	11
481^{8}	**On The Wildside (48)** (MRChannon) **4-8-3**(7) AEddery(9) (hld up: bdly hmpd & lost pl over 6f out: nt rcvr)	2½	**9**	8/1	26	21
578^{4}	**Noble Canonire (39)** (DShaw) **5-7-10b**(5) RFfrench(7) (mid div: drvn along over 3f out: sn wknd)	6	**10**	7/1	8	3
496^{11}	**Evening In Paris (35)** (MJohnston) **4-7-11** TWilliams(11) (led early: rdn & lost pl over 6f out: t.o whn p.u 4f out: lame)		**P**	$11/2^{3}$	—	—

(SP 118.8%) **11 Rn**

2m 5.6 (2.50) CSF £19.94 CT £112.91 TOTE £4.40: £2.00 £2.00 £1.70 (£7.90) Trio £51.20 OWNER Trojan Racing (WOLVERHAMPTON) BRED Bowler (Presswork) Services Ltd

LONG HANDICAP Tolepa (IRE) 7-8

689 Tallulah Belle, given a confident ride, took this low-grade handicap in decisive fashion. (4/1)

608 Portite Sophie, though very moderate, is running really well at present. (9/2)

Classic Beauty (IRE) ran a satisfactory first race. (7/1)

Needwood Nutkin ran easily her best outing so far this year. (20/1)

Worldwide Elsie (USA), who showed little on the All-Weather, ran better here. (16/1)

797 WOODHALL SPA H'CAP (0-85) (3-Y.O) (Class D)

4-40 (4-41) **1m 1f 207y** £3,522.00 (£1,056.00: £508.00: £234.00) Stalls: High GOING minus 0.31 sec per fur (GF)

				SP	RR	SF
517^{5}	**Regal Patrol (75)** (MRStoute) **3-8-12** JReid(2) (hld up: hdwy on outside over 2f out: edgd rt u.p: styd on to ld fnl 30y)	—	**1**	$4/1^{3}$	85	34
	Ajayib (USA) (76) (JLDunlop) **3-8-13** RHills(6) (trckd ldr: rdn to ld over 2f out: edgd rt: hdd & nt qckn wl ins fnl f)	nk	**2**	$6/4^{1}$	86	35
475^{11}	**Regal Reprimand (63)** (GLewis) **3-8-0** JQuinn(4) (b.hind: trckd ldrs: effrt over 3f out: chal over 1f out: edgd lft & nt qckn ins fnl f)	2	**3**	16/1	69	18
	Dream of Nurmi (84) (DRLoder) **3-9-7** PatEddery(5) (lw: trckd ldrs: rdn & hung rt over 1f out: one pce whn hmpd ins fnl f)	1¼	**4**	$7/2^{2}$	88	37
	Norman Conquest (USA) (77) (IABalding) **3-9-0** MHills(3) (bit bkwd: led tl over 2f out: styd on one pce)	1¼	**5**	12/1	79	28
535^{5}	**Shaded (IRE) (60)** (JWWatts) **3-7-11** LCharnock(7) (trckd ldrs: effrt over 2f out: no imp & eased)	8	**6**	7/1	49	—
	Jackson Falls (70) (TDEasterby) **3-8-7** MBirch(1) (bit bkwd: unruly in stalls: hld up: lost pl over 3f out: sn bhd: virtually p.u)	dist	**7**	20/1	—	—

(SP 113.1%) **7 Rn**

2m 7.7 (4.60) CSF £9.27 TOTE £4.80: £2.10 £1.30 (£3.50) OWNER Mr Saeed Suhail (NEWMARKET) BRED Cambremont Ltd Partnership

517 Regal Patrol, given a serious chance at the weights, was skillfully settled, but after making his effort on the outside, he almost threw it away by edging right and tightening up Dream of Nurmi. Though not a straightforward ride, there is no doubt that he is capable than better than this provided he goes the right way. (4/1)

Ajayib (USA), who looked very fit, dived to the rail once hitting the front. She stuck on strongly and will soon go one better. (6/4)

Regal Reprimand appreciated the step up in distance but, rolling off a straight line inside the last with the winner, contributed to the fourth's interference. (16/1)

Dream of Nurmi, who was fitted with a visor on his debut, is now a gelding. Hanging under pressure and coming off a true line himself, he was held when tightened up inside the last, and he would have only finished a length closer and only fourth at best. (7/2)

Norman Conquest (USA), who carries plenty of condition, was allowed to set his own pace. Though sticking on, he proved very one-paced and looks high in the handicap for what he has done. (12/1: 8/1-14/1)

535 Shaded (IRE) possibly found this trip too far. (7/1)

Jackson Falls, on his toes beforehand, misbehaved in the stalls and at present seems to have more temperament than ability. (20/1)

T/Jkpt: £2,994.20 (2.48 Tckts). T/Plpt: £27.30 (632.26 Tckts). T/Qdpt: £14.00 (61.15 Tckts) WG

0798a - 0805a : (Irish Racing) - See Computer Raceform

LEOPARDSTOWN (Dublin, Ireland) (L-H) (Good)
Saturday April 19th

806a LEOPARDSTOWN 1,000 GUINEAS TRIAL (Listed) (3-Y.O F)
3-20 (3-22) **7f** IR £12,900.00 (IR £3,700.00: IR £1,700.00: IR £500.00) GOING minus 0.21 sec per fur (GF)

Horse		SP	RR	SF
Classic Park (APO'Brien,Ireland) **3-8-10** SCraine (hld up: last st: hdwy to chal 1f out: rdn to ld last strides) .—	**1**	14/1	102	51
Chania (IRE) (JOxx,Ireland) **3-8-10** JPMurtagh (in tch: chal on ins early st: led over 1f out: hdd last trides) ..s.h	**2**	6/1	102	51
Almost Skint (IRE) (MissITOakes,Ireland) **3-8-10** NGMcCullagh (hld up: hdwy st: nt trble ldrs) 5½	**3**	16/1	89	38
Shell Ginger (IRE) (APO'Brien,Ireland) **3-9-1** CRoche (sn led: rdn bef st: hdd over 1f out: no ex) 1½	**4**	5/4 1	91	40
Token Gesture (IRE) (DKWeld,Ireland) **3-9-1** MJKinane (cl up: chsd ldrs st: kpt on same pce) 1½	**5**	7/2 2	88	37
Welsh Queen (IRE) (TStack,Ireland) **3-8-10** PJSmullen (in tch early: chsd ldrs early st: no imp) 2	**6**	14/1	78	27
Velvet Appeal (IRE) (MHalford,Ireland) **3-8-10** WJSupple (hld up: chsd ldrs 2f out: sn no imp) 2½	**7**	12/1	72	21
Azra (IRE) (JSBolger,Ireland) **3-8-13b** KJManning (sn chsng ldr: rdn & effrt st: wknd wl over 1f out) 2½	**8**	11/2 3	70	19
		(SP 123.2%)	**8 Rn**	

1m 27.2 (2.20) OWNER Mrs Seamus Burns (PILTOWN)

Classic Park, apparently totally unfancied, came from last to first in the straight, getting up in the last strides after a sustained run on the outside. On juvenile form, she was on a par with more fancied rivals and this just confirms that she is going the right way. The Irish 1,000 Guineas would appear the logical step. (14/1)

Chania (IRE) got to the front over a furlong out and was only thwarted in the last couple of strides. She only had one run last year and, on this sort of form, will not have to descend to maiden company to win. (6/1)

Almost Skint (IRE) is only a handicapper but she kept on well inside the last. (16/1)

Shell Ginger (IRE) was disappointing. She tried to make all the running but was being niggled along after half-way. Eased when headed over a furlong out, she will come on for this and a longer trip would be to her advantage. (5/4: op 4/5)

Token Gesture (IRE) found nothing when the button was pushed in the straight. (7/2)

Azra (IRE) ran second but, driven along before the straight, was not a contender once they straightened out and dropped away quickly enough. (11/2)

807a LEOPARDSTOWN 2,000 GUINEAS TRIAL (Listed) (3-Y.O C)
3-50 (3-50) **1m** IR £12,900.00 (IR £3,700.00: IR £1,700.00: IR £500.00) GOING: Not Established

Horse		SP	RR	SF
Lil's Boy (USA) (JSBolger,Ireland) **3-8-10** KJManning (rrn 3rd: chal st: led briefly ins last: rallied to ld nr fin) ....—	**1**	7/1 3	98	40
436* **Fly To The Stars** (MJohnston) **3-8-10** JWeaver (hld up: hdwy on outside st: led ins last: hdd nr fin: no ex)...s.h	**2**	4/6 1	98	40
Plaza De Toros (USA) (APO'Brien,Ireland) **3-8-10** CRoche (sn cl 2nd: led st: rdn & hdd ins last: one pce) ..1½	**3**	9/2 2	95	37
Beautiful Fire (IRE) (DKWeld,Ireland) **3-8-10b** MJKinane (hld up in tch: effrt 2f out: rdn & no ex over 1f out)..2	**4**	7/1 3	91	33
Sharemono (USA) (APO'Brien,Ireland) **3-8-10** WJSupple (s.i.s: hld up: trckd ldrs 3f out: rdn & nt rch ldrs over 1f out) 1½	**5**	20/1	88	30
Somerton Reef (JOxx,Ireland) **3-8-10** JPMurtagh (led: hdd st: rdn & no ex over 1f out) ....nk	**6**	7/1 3	87	29
Junikay (IRE) (JSBolger,Ireland) **3-8-10** SCraine (a rr: no imp fr 2f out) 6	**7**	16/1	75	17
		(SP 126.3%)	**7 Rn**	

1m 40.6 (3.60) OWNER Maktoum Al Maktoum (COOLCULLEN)

STEWARDS' ENQUIRY Manning & Weaver susp. 28-29/4/97 (excessive use of whip).

Lil's Boy (USA) got to the front early inside the last and fought back gamely when headed. He had a hard race and his jockey picked up a two-day suspension for whip abuse. He is tough and the Irish 2,000 Guineas will be his target. He went up 5lb for this for a new high of 101. (7/1)

436* Fly To The Stars would not give the outside to anyone and lost ground turning into the straight. He challenged on the outer over the last furlong and a half, got his head in front under pressure briefly inside the last, but couldn't come again to resist the winner's late effort. His jockey also received two days' suspension for use of the whip. (4/6: op 5/4)

Plaza De Toros (USA) was a real market drifter. He led over two furlongs out but looked very one-paced when the first pair went on. He will improve and this run saw him move up 5lb, to a new mark of 97. (9/2: op 7/4)

Beautiful Fire (IRE) held every chance two furlongs out, but again looked reluctant to go through with his effort. (7/1: op 4/1)

Sharemono (USA) ran promisingly enough, keeping on nicely in the straight without ever threatening. (20/1)

809a BALLYSAX STAKES (Listed) (3-Y.O)
4-50 (4-50) **1m 2f** IR £12,900.00 (IR £3,700.00: IR £1,700.00: IR £500.00) GOING minus 0.21 sec per fur (GF)

Horse		SP	RR	SF
Casey Tibbs (IRE) (DKWeld,Ireland) **3-9-0** MJKinane (hld up towards rr: hdwy on outside st: chal to ld over 1f out: rdn & r.o.) ....—	**1**	7/1 3	98	58
Zafarabad (IRE) (JOxx,Ireland) **3-9-0** JPMurtagh (led briefly early: in tch: chal st: led over 1½f out: hdd over 1f out: rdn & no ex ins fnl f) 1½	**2**	8/1	96	56
Caiseal Ros (IRE) (JSBolger,Ireland) **3-8-11** KJManning (led & disp ld: led st: hdd over 1½f out: kpt on same pce) 3½	**3**	4/1 2	87	47
Strawberry Roan (IRE) (APO'Brien,Ireland) **3-9-0** CRoche (hld up: 5th st: rdn 1½f out: no ex) ....hd	**4**	8/11 1	90	50
Rasin (IRE) (KPrendergast,Ireland) **3-9-0** SCraine (hld up: chsd ldrs 2f out: no imp) 5½	**5**	10/1	81	41
Saibhreas (IRE) (JSBolger,Ireland) **3-8-11** JMorgan (cl up: chsd ldrs st: no imp) 2½	**6**	20/1	74	34
Gunfire (IRE) (DGillespie,Ireland) **3-9-0** WJSupple (hld up towards rr: rdn st: no imp) 6	**7**	12/1	67	27
Moon Flower (IRE) (APO'Brien,Ireland) **3-8-11** PShanahan (led & disp ld: hdd st: rdn 2f out: sn wknd) ....¾	**8**	8/1	63	23
		(SP 134.2%)	**8 Rn**	

2m 6.9 (2.90) OWNER Michael Watt (CURRAGH)

Casey Tibbs (IRE) saw this trip out better than most and will appreciate even further. He came from just off the pace to lead a furlong out and was always in control. This run saw him move up 5lb to 102. (7/1)

Zafarabad (IRE) had only an ordinary maiden to his name last season and this was a fair step up. He led early in the straight until the winner took over. Some ease in the ground would help, but this run could be a good barometer to the stable's other three-year-old colts. He has gone up 14lb to 98. (8/1)
Caiseal Ros (IRE), always in the first two until one furlong out, had nothing more to give inside the last. (4/1)
Strawberry Roan (IRE) came through to hold every chance a furlong and a half out, but she was soon just going up and down on the spot. She didn't impress in the parade and this ground may have been a bit too fast, but it would be wrong to write her off on this display. (8/11)
Gunfire (IRE) (12/1: op 8/1)

0810a : (Irish Racing) - See Computer Raceform

0717a-MAISONS-LAFFITTE (France) (Good)
Wednesday April 16th

811a PRIX SERVANNE (Listed) (3-Y.O+)
3-20 (3-24) **5f 110y** £15,713.00 (£5,387.00: £4,040.00)

				SP	RR	SF
	Farhana (WJarvis) **4-9-1** OPeslier	—	1		112	—
	Waky Nao (France) **4-9-4** THellier	½	2		114	—
	Titus Livius (FR) (France) **4-9-4** CAsmussen	2	3		108	—
	Hever Golf Rose (TJNaughton) **6-9-1** SSanders (btn approx 4¼l)		6		—	—
452[6]	**Passion For Life** (GLewis) **4-9-4** FHead (btn approx 9¼l)		7		—	—
						10 Rn

Time Not Taken P-M 2.70F: 1.60F 4.10F 2.20F (28.20F) OWNER Mr A. Foustok (NEWMARKET) BRED Ahmed M. Foustok
Farhana looks an exciting sprinter in the making. She was given a lovely ride and was produced at exactly the right moment to win with something in hand. She looks sure to make her presence felt in Group company later in the season and she is sure to have benefited from this outing. She now heads for either the Duke of York or the Temple Stakes and, later in the season, the Prix Maurice de Gheest and the Prix de l'Abbaye de Longchamp.
Hever Golf Rose will come on considerably from the race. She led until inside the final furlong before gradually dropping back. She will strip fitter next time out and looks sure to visit the winner's enclosure again after missing out last season.
452 **Passion For Life** was well up early on, but was a beaten horse before the furlong marker and finished a rather distant seventh. It was a disappointing effort and one best forgotten.

SAN SIRO (Milan, Italy) (R-H) (Firm)
Wednesday April 16th

812a PREMIO PORTA ROMANA MAIDEN (3-Y.O)
4-20 (4-20) **1m 2f** £7,714.00

			SP	RR	SF
Rossi Osvaldo (ITY) (GColleo,Italy) **3-9-0** MLatorre	—	1		77?	—
Fools Honor (IRE) (GBotti,Italy) **3-8-12**ow1 MBotti	2½	2		71	—
Indulgent Toto (VValiani,Italy) **3-9-0** FJovine	1¼	3		71	—
North White Plains (CEBrittain) **3-8-11** VMezzatesta (btn 7 3/4l)		5		—	—
					15 Rn

2m 6.5 (12.50) TOTE 57L: 20L 53L 26L (1001L) OWNER Scuderia Andy Capp
North White Plains never threatened to take a hand in the finish, but ran very green and will be all the better for the experience.

0716a-SAINT-CLOUD (France) (L-H) (Good)
Thursday April 17th

813a PRIX PENELOPE (Gp 3) (3-Y.O F)
3-20 (3-22) **1m 2f 110y** £24,961.00 (£8,979.00: £4,489.00) GOING: Not Established

			SP	RR	SF
Brilliance (FR) (PBary,France) **3-9-0** SGuillot	—	1		104	—
Darashandeh (IRE) (AdeRoyerDupre,France) **3-9-0** GMosse	nk	2		104	—
La Nana (FR) (DSepulchre,France) **3-9-0** ODoleuze	nse	3		104	—
					8 Rn

2m 17.9 (7.90) P-M 9.20F: 2.00F 1.50F 2.00F (9.70F) OWNER Ecurie Skymarc Farm (CHANTILLY) BRED Skymarc Farm
Brilliance (FR) was given a decent ride here and, never far away from the leader, she took the advantage inside the final furlong and just held on in a desperate dash to the line. She has done well and has more scope for improvement. She is now likely to turn out for the Prix Saint-Alary as a prelude to the Prix de Diane.
Darashandeh (IRE) must be considered unlucky as she was not given the best of rides. She was held up on the rail and, last but one entering the straight, when produced to challenge she had to be snatched up as she had nowhere to go. Once a gap did appear, she motored and would have won this in another couple of strides. She will stay further and goes next to either the Prix Cleopatre or the Prix Saint-Alary.
La Nana (FR) put in a good effort here. In mid-division early on, she started her challenge two out and then ran on at one pace. She might be better suited to a slightly shorter distance and a listed race may come her way.

0812a-SAN SIRO (Milan, Italy) (R-H) (Good)
Saturday April 19th

814a PREMIO CAMPELLI MAIDEN (3-Y.O F)
2-50 (2-53) **1m 2f** £7,714.00

			SP	RR	SF
Swing And Brave (IRE) (LordHuntingdon) **3-8-13** MDemuro	—	1		—	—
Clara House (VValiani,Italy) **3-8-10** FJovine	1	2		—	—

Horse	Dist	Pos	SP	RR	SF
Evdokimova (GVerricelli,Italy) **3-8-13** SDettori	1	**3**		—	—

12 Rn

2m 9.1 (15.10) TOTE 26L: 14L 22L 21L (108L) OWNER Scuderia San Pancrazio (WEST ILSLEY)
Swing And Brave (IRE) had the benefit of a run in Rome last November. Always prominent, she led passing the two furlong pole and won with a bit in hand.

CAPANNELLE (Rome, Italy) (R-H) (Good)
Sunday April 20th

815a PREMIO REGINA ELENA (Gp 2) (3-Y.O F)
3-10 (3-40) **1m** £60,286.00 (£30,268.00: £17,607.00: £8,804.00)

Form	Horse	Dist	Pos	SP	RR	SF
	Nicole Pharly (AVerdesi,Italy) **3-8-11** LDettori (mid div: nt clr run 3f out: qcknd & led appr fnl f: r.o)	—	**1**		104	—
	Orange Jasmine (IRE) (APO'Brien,Ireland) **3-8-11v1** JAHeffernan (styd on fnl 2f: fin wl)	2¼	**2**		100	—
	Much Commended (GWragg) **3-8-11** MHills (a.p: led 2f out tl appr fnl f: one pce)	½	**3**		99	—
	Sopran Mariduff (RRossini,Italy) **3-8-11** EBotti (effrt 1½f out: sltly hmpd: styd on wl cl home)	¾	**4**		97	—
	Lady Bi (IRE) (RBrogi,Italy) **3-8-11** GBietolini (prom st: ev ch 2f out: nt qckn)	3	**5**		91	—
	She Bat (VCaruso,Italy) **3-8-11** FJovine (hdwy 2f out: nvr able to chal)	1	**6**		89	—
507^2	**Lycility (IRE)** (CEBrittain) **3-8-11** BDoyle (led early: 2nd st: wknd over 1f out)	¾	**7**		88	—
	Yxenery (IRE) (MmeCHead,France) **3-8-11** ODoleuze (in rr: effrt on outside: u.p when hmpd 2f out)	hd	**8**		87	—
	Regal Dynasty (IRE) (LCamici,Italy) **3-8-11** MCangiano (a bhd)	1	**9**		85	—
	Nilo of Time (ITY) (LBrogi,Italy) **3-8-11** CFiocchi (prom st: ev ch 2f out: wknd)	1¾	**10**		82	—
	Miss Carolina (IRE) (LCamici,Italy) **3-8-11** MPasquale (prom: chal over 2f out: wknd)	2¼	**11**		77	—
	Wooderine (USA) (Md'Auria,Italy) **3-8-11** MDemuro (led 2f to 2f out: sn wknd)	½	**12**		76	—
	Counterplot (IRE) (VSanMarzano,Italy) **3-8-11b1** JCaro (a bhd)	½	**13**		75	—
	Ilonka (ITY) (LCamici,Italy) **3-8-11** VMezzatesta (dwlt: sn prom: effrt over 3f out: sn btn)	¾	**14**		74	—
	Magic Surprise (ACalchetti,Italy) **3-8-11** OFancera (n.d)	5	**15**		64	—
	Perla Nera (IRE) (PGuarsegnati,Italy) **3-8-11** ACorniani (prom: cl up st: ev ch 2f out: wknd rapidly)	8	**16**		48	—

16 Rn

1m 39.1 TOTE 30L: 17L 32L 33L (276L) OWNER Scuderia Blu Horse BRED Stratford Place Stud
Nicole Pharly won with authority, despite having trouble getting a run approaching the quarter-mile pole. Dettori rates her highly and she will be very difficult to beat in the Italian Oaks. Already a winner over ten furlongs, she could be a potent force in some of Europe's better middle distance races later in the year.
Orange Jasmine (IRE), whose narrow Tipperary defeat was boosted when Lil's Boy won the Guineas Trial at Leopardstown twenty-four hours previously, stayed on strongly in the final furlong to snatch second.
Much Commended came on the outside to hit the front two furlongs from home, but had no answer when the winner swept past at the distance. She was the only one of the principals to be without a previous run this term, and improvement should be forthcoming. She will stay further.
507 Lycility (IRE) wore a visor for the first time and led for the first quarter-mile. Still in second place two furlongs from home, she could not raise her game thereafter.

DUSSELDORF (Germany) (R-H) (Good)
Sunday April 20th

816a DUSSELDORFER SPRINT CUP (Listed) (4-Y.O+)
3-55 (3-59) **5f** £9,091.00 (£3,636.00: £1,856.00)

Form	Horse	Dist	Pos	SP	RR	SF
$354a^2$	**Roseate Wood (FR)** (UweStoltefuss,Germany) **4-8-3** PHarley	—	**1**		99	—
	Munaaji (USA) (AWohler,Germany) **6-8-11b** EDubravka	s.h	**2**		107	—
354a*	**Le Rastaquouere (USA)** (ALowe,Germany) **6-8-9b1** KMarks	2	**3**		98	—
	My Cadeaux (RGuest) **5-8-3** GHind (btn just under 5½l)		**6**		—	—

9 Rn

59.5 secs TOTE 106DM: 24DM 21DM 22DM (996DM) OWNER R. Kopf
My Cadeaux was well in touch until dropping away in the last two furlongs.

HOPPEGARTEN (Berlin, Germany) (R-H) (Good)
Sunday April 20th

817a DR BUSCH MEMORIAL (Gp 3) (3-Y.O)
4-20 (4-32) **1m** £22,727.00 (£9,091.00: £4,545.00)

Horse	Dist	Pos	SP	RR	SF
Eden Rock (GER) (BSchutz,Germany) **3-9-0** AStarke	—	**1**		—	—
Happy Change (GER) (AWohler,Germany) **3-9-0** ABoschert	2½	**2**		—	—
Icemoon (GER) (HBlume,Germany) **3-9-0** THellier	¾	**3**		—	—

8 Rn

1m 38.2 TOTE 20DM: 11DM 16DM 14DM OWNER Mrs M. Herbert BRED Gestut Etzean

0629a-LONGCHAMP (Paris, France) (R-H) (Good)
Sunday April 20th

818a PRIX DE LA GROTTE (Gp 3) (3-Y.O F)
2-40 (2-39) **1m** £24,691.00 (£8,979.00: £4,489.00) GOING: 0.15 sec per fur (G)

Horse	Dist	Pos	SP	RR	SF
Always Loyal (USA) (MmeCHead,France) **3-9-0** FHead	—	**1**		104	45
Mousse Glacee (FR) (JLesbordes,France) **3-9-0** VVion	hd	**2**		104	45

			SP	RR	SF
Green Lady (IRE) (AFabre,France) 3-9-0 TJarnet	½	3		103	44
					5 Rn

1m 41.3 (6.30) P-M 2.50F: 1.50F 1.20F OWNER Maktoum Al Maktoum (CHANTILLY) BRED Gainsborough Farm

Always Loyal (USA) looked extremely well in the paddock and was given a fine ride by her jockey. She followed the leader and took the advantage halfway up the straight before battling on gamely to the finish. It was only her second race and this half-sister to Anabaa has considerable scope for improvement. She will now go for the Pouliches and will justifiably be one of the favourites for this Classic.

Mousse Glacee (FR) was given a very easy ride by her new jockey. Held up early on, she made progress in the straight and, flying at the finish, would have been the winner in a couple of extra strides. She is going to make endless progress after this run and is an exceptionally bright prospect for the future. This daughter of Mtoto will stay further and could still run in the Oaks, but first she will take on Always Loyal in the Pouliches. She looks certain to have an exceptional year.

Green Lady (IRE) ran a game race and stayed on right to the line. She was always well placed and never gave up the fight. She looks like a filly who will be much more effective over a longer distance.

819a PRIX GREFFULHE (Gp 2) (3-Y.O C & F)

3-10 (3-10) **1m 2f 110y** £35,718.00 (£14,169.00: £6,790.00: £2,806.00) GOING: 0.15 sec per fur (G)

			SP	RR	SF
Peintre Celebre (USA) (AFabre,France) **3-9-2** OPeslier (racd 3rd early: chal 1f out: led ins fnl f: r.o wl: impressive)	—	1		108	66
Astarabad (USA) (AdeRoyerDupre,France) **3-9-2** GMosse (dwlt: 2nd st: effrt 2f out: led briefly 1f out: outpcd cl home)	2	2		105	63
Kashwan (SPA) (ELellouche,France) **3-9-2** TThulliez (a cl up: led st tl 1f out: styd on one pce)	nk	3		105	63
New Frontier (IRE) (AFabre,France) **3-9-2** TJarnet (hld up: in rr st: late prog: r.o cl home)	2½	4		101	59
Rate Cut (USA) (PBary,France) **3-9-2** SGuillot (hld up: little prog)	1	5		99	57
Samapour (IRE) (AdeRoyerDupre,France) **3-9-2** CAsmussen (led tl st: hmpd & dropped back qckly)	6	6		90	48
					6 Rn

2m 14.0 (6.00) P-M 3.40F: 1.40F 1.20F OWNER Mr D. Wildenstein (CHANTILLY) BRED Allez France Stables

Peintre Celebre (USA) ran out an impressive winner of this event. Third early on, he came through in the straight to take the lead just inside the final furlong, showing a fine turn of foot in the process. He has done well between two and three and he looks as if a longer distance will not be a problem. He has a lot of stamina on his dam's side and the speed comes from his sire Nureyev. He is sure to improve for the race and could either go for the Prix Lupin or directly for the Prix du Jockey-Club. He is certainly a horse worth following this season.

Astarabad (USA) missed the break so did not make full use of his lead horse. He made up ground around the home turn and led halfway up the straight, but did not have the pace to go with the winner. His breeding suggests that he will stay further, so he should be judged when racing over a full mile and a half.

Kashwan (SPA) ran his usual game race. He was always close up and led for a short time in the straight and, although he is a battler, he is not of this class. He could well find a Group Three race within him this season.

New Frontier (IRE), held up early, was only put into the race in the closing stages and was running on well at the end.

820a PRIX DE FONTAINEBLEAU (Gp 3) (3-Y.O C)

4-10 (4-08) **1m** £24,691.00 (£8,418.00: £4,489.00) GOING: 0.15 sec per fur (G)

			SP	RR	SF
Daylami (IRE) (AdeRoyerDupre,France) **3-9-2** GMosse	—	1		115	62
Loup Sauvage (USA) (AFabre,France) **3-9-2** OPeslier	2	2		111	58
Fine Fellow (IRE) (MmeCHead,France) **3-9-2** GGuignard	s.h	3		111	58
					6 Rn

1m 39.8 (4.80) P-M 3.00F: 1.80F 2.20F OWNER H H Aga Khan (CHANTILLY) BRED Aga Khan's Studs

Daylami (IRE) ran a strange race and nearly fell five out when his jockey - suspended for four days - tried to move him on to the rail. He recovered to make a devastating late challenge, sweeping past the long-time leader inside the final furlong and winning going away. At this distance, he will be a force to reckon with in top events this season. He now heads for the Poulains and will start as one of the favourites.

Loup Sauvage (USA) fairly flew the last three hundred yards of this event. He was one of several hampered by the eventual winner on the descent to the straight while occupying last place. He picked up his bit halfway up the straight and stole second place on the line. This was a most promising effort and it would be no surprise if he reversed positions with the winner if they met in the Dubai Poule d'Essai des Poulains. It was just his second race and, looking set for a highly successful season, he deserves to go in the notebook in capital letters.

Fine Fellow (IRE) ran his heart out having tried to make all the running. He looked the likely winner just over a furlong out, but could not match the acceleration of the winner. He is a Group Three colt and he should pick another race in this category during the season.

0814a-SAN SIRO (Milan, Italy) (R-H) (Good to soft)
Sunday April 20th

821a PREMIO ASSIANO MAIDEN (3-Y.O)

2-20 (2-20) **1m** £7,714.00 (£3,394.00: £1,851.00)

			SP	RR	SF
Gracco (IRE) (GBotti,Italy) **3-8-13** MBotti	—	1		—	—
Ribot's Pearl (LordHuntingdon) **3-8-10** LSorrentino	9½	2		—	—
Reve Indien (EBorromeo,Italy) **3-8-13** MEsposito	1	3		—	—
					6 Rn

1m 42.9 (12.90) TOTE 37L: 15L 13L (27L) OWNER Scuderia Dioscuri (ITALY) BRED G. Gregori

Ribot's Pearl was sent off a short-priced favourite, but was put firmly in her place by the winner. Held up towards the rear, the winner had already gone beyond recall by the time she found her stride, and she only took second place close home.

CARLISLE (R-H) (Good, Good to firm patches)
Friday April 25th

WEATHER: unsettled WIND: fresh half against

71+ 74+ 73+ 73

822 TALBOTS MAIDEN STKS (2-Y.O) (Class D)

2-20 (2-21) **5f** £3,105.80 (£940.40: £459.20: £218.60) Stalls: High GOING: 0.28 sec per fur (G)

			SP	RR	SF
695[2] **Timekeeper (USA)** (MBell) **2-9-0** MFenton(9) (lw: mde virtually all: r.o strly fnl f: comf)	—	1	4/6[1]	82	30

		Pos	SP	RR	SF
	Prix Star (CWFairhurst) **2-9-0** LCharnock(8) (w'like: s.i.s: hdwy ½-wy: styd on ins fnl f: no ch w wnr) 2	**2**	20/1	76	24
	Oh Never Again (IRE) (MJohnston) **2-9-0** JFanning(7) (w'like: unf: w ldrs: rdn 2f out: kpt on same pce).......1¾	**3**	9/4[2]	70	18
	Thanks Keith (JJO'Neill) **2-9-0** GDuffield(2) (leggy: unf: sn outpcd: sme hdwy ½-wy: nvr rchd ldrs)..............2½	**4**	12/1[3]	62	10
	Tindaya (PDEvans) **2-9-0** JFEgan(6) (leggy: lt-f: sn outpcd: hdwy ½-wy: kpt on fnl f)..nk	**5**	12/1[3]	61	9
	Up The Clarets (IRE) (JJO'Neill) **2-9-0** JCarroll(5) (leggy: unf: in tch tl outpcd fr ½-wy) ....hd	**6**	16/1	61	9
	Ngaere Princess (WTKemp) **2-8-4**(5) JBramhill(1) (unf: w ldrs: rdn ½-wy: wandered: lost pl over 1f out) 4	**7**	33/1	43	—
	Black Jet (NPLittmoden) **2-9-0** TGMcLaughlin(4) (unf: bkwd: s.s: a outpcd & bhd)...7	**8**	16/1	26	—
			(SP 125.6%)	**8 Rn**	

65.7 secs (5.50) CSF £20.14 TOTE £1.20: £1.10 £3.90 £1.50 (£12.50) Trio £10.60 OWNER Mr C. M. Watt (NEWMARKET) BRED Adelphian Ltd

695 Timekeeper (USA), who looked unlucky first time, made no mistake and always had the situation well under control. (4/6)

Prix Star, a flashy chestnut, ran well, sticking on strongly inside the last. He is sure to come on for the outing. (20/1)

Oh Never Again (IRE) matched strides with the winner, but it was clear soon after halfway that he was not going to seriously trouble him. Green and noisy in the paddock, he should improve for the outing. (9/4)

Thanks Keith, a narrow sort, ran creditably on his debut. (12/1)

Tindaya, who lacks size and scope, probably needs six furlongs already. (12/1)

823 KESTREL CLAIMING STKS (4-Y.O+) (Class F)

2-55 (2-57) **6f 206y** £2,598.00 (£728.00: £354.00) Stalls: High GOING: 0.28 sec per fur (G)

		Pos	SP	RR	SF
550*	**High Premium (79)** (RAFahey) **9-9-0**(7) RWinston(1) (lw: sltly hmpd s: hdwy over 2f out: led over 1f out: hld on towards fin) ....—	**1**	7/2[2]	88	70
	Broctune Gold (65) (MrsMReveley) **6-9-3** ACulhane(3) (rn in snatches: chsd ldrs: rdn ½-wy: chal over 1f out: nt qckn nr fin).........nk	**2**	3/1[1]	83	65
	Kemo Sabo (CParker) **5-8-12**(3) FLynch(5) (bhd: hdwy over 2f out: styd on same pce fnl f)........................1½	**3**	10/1	78	60
	Desert Cat (IRE) (MartynWane) **4-8-13** JCarroll(9) (bhd: hdwy & swtchd lft over 2f out: nvr nr to chal) 8	**4**	8/1	57	39
599[9]	**Most Respectful** (DenysSmith) **4-8-9** LCharnock(13) (trckd ldrs: effrt over 2f out: grad wknd) 1½	**5**	25/1	50	32
698[3]	**Palacegate Touch (80)** (JBerry) **7-9-2b**(5) PRoberts(2) (swvd lft s: sn trckng ldrs: led over 2f out: hdd over 1f out: wknd)........nk	**6**	9/2[3]	61	43
	Fisiostar (34) (MDods) **4-8-10b**(3) CTeague(12) (s.i.s: t.o ½-wy: sme hdwy over 2f out: n.d)...........................8	**7**	25/1	35	17
668[9]	**Diet (44)** (MissLAPerratt) **11-8-3v** GDuffield(10) (chsd ldrs to ½-wy: sn btn)...2	**8**	16/1	20	2
571[7]	**Perilous Plight (56)** (MrsLStubbs) **6-8-13** JFEgan(7) (sn prom: rdn 3f out: sn lost pl)...7	**9**	12/1	14	—
698[8]	**The Wad (68)** (DNicholls) **4-8-9** AlexGreaves(6) (plld hrd: trckd ldrs tl wknd over 2f out) 1	**10**	9/1	8	—
	Beldray Park (IRE) (59) (MrsALMKing) **4-8-13** AClark(8) (plld hrd: in tch tl lost pl 3f out)................................nk	**11**	25/1	11	—
599[15]	**Samstotry** (MissLAPerratt) **7-8-7** JFanning(4) (sn bhd) 1½	**12**	33/1	2	—
411[10]	**Classic Victory (60)** (ICampbell) **4-8-3v**[1] RPrice(11) (led tl over 2f out: sn wknd)...½	**13**	20/1	—	—
			(SP 128.4%)	**13 Rn**	

1m 30.6 (4.90) CSF £13.24 TOTE £4.80: £2.20 £1.30 £3.90 (£5.80) Trio £24.00 OWNER Mr J. C. Parsons (MALTON) BRED M.E Wates

No bid

550* High Premium answered his young rider's every call to scrape home by the skin of his teeth. (7/2)

Broctune Gold, taken to post early, usually runs well on his first two or three outings. Tending to run in snatches, he was almost level through the final furlong, but could not quite poke his head in front. He would have been meeting the winner on 10lb better terms in a handicap.(3/1)

Kemo Sabo, who is hard to win with on the Flat, seemed to run right up to his very best. (10/1)

Desert Cat (IRE), who had only two outings at three, wore a tongue-strap and presumably has some sort of problem. (8/1: 6/1-10/1)

698 Palacegate Touch patently failed to stay the seven. (9/2)

824 OLD CAPTAIN'S HOUSE H'CAP (0-85) (3-Y.O+) (Class D)

3-25 (3-27) **7f 214y** £3,551.00 (£1,076.00: £526.00: £251.00) Stalls: High GOING: 0.28 sec per fur (G)

		Pos	SP	RR	SF
571[14]	**Thatched (IRE) (51)** (REBarr) **7-7-5**(5) PFessey(10) (lw: hld up: effrt on ins & nt clr run over 2f out: swtchd outside & hdwy over 1f out: led ins fnl f: r.o u.p) ....—	**1**	10/1	62	21
	Quilling (74) (MDods) **5-9-2**(3) FLynch(1) (sn trckng ldrs: led over 1f out: hdd & no ex ins fnl f) 1¼	**2**	16/1	83	42
635[3]	**Smarter Charter (73)** (MrsLStubbs) **4-9-4** JFEgan(11) (a chsng ldrs: rdn over 2f out: nt qckn appr fnl f)........1½	**3**	7/2[1]	79	38
733[11]	**Cee-Jay-Ay (54)** (JBerry) **10-7-6**(7) PBradley(6) (s.s: bhd: gd hdwy 2f out: kpt on one pce ins fnl f)................1½	**4**	10/1	57	16
	Bulsara (58) (CWFairhurst) **5-8-3** LCharnock(9) (hld up: hdwy ½-wy: kpt on same pce appr fnl f)....................¾	**5**	12/1	59	18
521[11]	**Royal Result (USA) (77)** (TDBarron) **4-9-8** DHarrison(2) (lw: led tl over 1f out: wknd ins fnl f) 3	**6**	11/2[3]	72	31
235[9]	**Gilling Dancer (IRE) (55)** (PCalver) **4-7-11**(3) DarrenMoffatt(5) (lw: sn bhd & drvn along: sme hdwy 2f out: n.d) 4	**7**	16/1	42	1
	Tertium (IRE) (83) (MartynWane) **5-10-0** JCarroll(12) (trckd ldrs tl wknd over 1f out: eased).............................2	**8**	11/2[3]	66	25
733[5]	**Spanish Verdict (60)** (DenysSmith) **10-8-5** ACulhane(3) (lw: bhd: rdn over 2f out: n.d)...1¾	**9**	5/1[2]	39	—
633[8]	**Celebration Cake (IRE) (74)** (MissLAPerratt) **5-9-5** GDuffield(7) (chsd ldrs: sn drvn along: lost pl over 2f out) ....hd	**10**	7/1	53	12
661[11]	**Classic Leader (79)** (ICampbell) **4-9-10** RPrice(4) (bhd: sme hdwy on outside over 2f out: sn wknd) 8	**11**	25/1	42	1
610[12]	**Naissant (69)** (RMMcKellar) **4-8-7**(7) KSked(8) (w ldrs tl wknd 3f out: sn bhd)...12	**12**	20/1	8	—
			(SP 128.4%)	**12 Rn**	

1m 45.1 (8.10) CSF £156.93 CT £633.32 TOTE £16.20: £4.50 £6.90 £1.90 (£73.30) Trio £240.70; £176.36 to Leicester 26/4/97 OWNER Mr C. W. Marwood (MIDDLESBROUGH) BRED D. P. O'Brien

OFFICIAL EXPLANATION **Thatched (IRE): regarding the improvement in form, he had too much daylight first time and had blown up.**

Thatched (IRE) is a funny old character who likes to come from behind, and often the more trouble he meets the better he runs, as was the case here. (10/1)

Quilling ran really well, but usually reserves his very best for the straight mile at Redcar. (16/1)

635 Smarter Charter was always making hard work of this, and seems better suited by the stiff uphill finish at Beverley. (7/2)

Cee-Jay-Ay as usual gave away plenty of ground at the start. (10/1)

Bulsara should be sharper for the outing. (12/1)

Royal Result (USA), gelded after being sold for 33,000 guineas, set a strong pace. Seven furlongs might suit him better. (11/2: op 7/2)

Tertium (IRE) raced without a tongue-strap. The outing should bring him on, and he was certainly not knocked about. (11/2)

825 SPARROW HAWK MAIDEN STKS (3-Y.O) (Class D)

4-00 (4-01) **1m 4f** £3,363.80 (£1,018.40: £497.20: £236.60) Stalls: High GOING: 0.28 sec per fur (G)

Form	Horse	Dist	Pos	SP	RR	SF
658^{2}	**Polyphony (USA)** (RCharlton) **3-9-0** DHarrison(6) (unruly s: chsd ldrs: sn pushed along: led over 2f out: drvn out)	—	**1**	7/2^{2}	76	23
605^{3}	**Rare Talent** (MRChannon) **3-9-0** ACulhane(4) (hld up: hdwy & nt clr run over 2f out: rdn to chal over 1f out: edgd lft & nt qckn)	1¼	**2**	5/1^{3}	74	21
463^{3}	**Indigo Dawn** (MJohnston) **3-8-9** JFanning(1) (led tl over 6f out: hung lft: led over 3f out tl over 2f out: edgd lft over 1f out: grad wknd)	6	**3**	15/8^{1}	61	8
670^{4}	**Not Forgotten (USA)** (PAKelleway) **3-9-0v** GDuffield(7) (w ldr: led over 6f out tl over 3f out: sn hrd rdn: wknd 2f out)	6	**4**	7/2^{2}	58	5
658^{6}	**Men Of Wickenby** (RMMcKellar) **3-8-7**$^{(7)}$ JMcAuley(5) (wnt prom 8f out: rdn & wknd over 2f out)	5	**5**	50/1	52	—
	Dawn Summit (BHanbury) **3-9-0** AClark(2) (bit bkwd: hld up & plld hrd: sme hdwy over 2f out: sn wknd & eased)	s.h	**6**	7/1	52	—
773^{9}	**Think Again (IRE)** (RCraggs) **3-9-0** LCharnock(3) (dwlt: bhd: hdwy to chse ldrs over 3f out: wknd over 2f out)	3	**7**	40/1	48	—

(SP 112.8%) **7 Rn**

2m 43.7 (14.70) CSF £18.73 TOTE £2.80: £2.30 £1.30 (£10.40) OWNER Mr K. Abdulla (BECKHAMPTON) BRED Juddmonte Farms
STEWARDS' ENQUIRY Clark susp. 5-6/5/97 (failure to ensure best possible placing).

658 Polyphony (USA) played up at the start and unseated his rider. Always making hard work of it, he looks only moderate if this is the best he can do. (7/2)

605 Rare Talent had trouble getting a run, but was only second-best anyway. (5/1)

463 Indigo Dawn, who continually swished her tail in the paddock, had difficulty handling the bends, hanging badly left. She is only moderate, and probably has her own ideas about the game. (15/8: 5/4-2/1)

670 Not Forgotten (USA) is clearly flattered by his Newmarket effort. (7/2)

Dawn Summit, a good-bodied colt, looked as if the outing would do him good. Making his third appearance, he walked past the line and down to the post and in the race simply would not settle. Only able to finish fifth at best, his rider eased him off in the closing stages and was pipped on the line. The Stewards decided Tony Clark had failed to ride his mount out for the best possible placing and suspended him for two days, in contrast with the leniency shown to Gary Hind at Catterick two days earlier. (7/1)

826 ST. NICHOLAS ARMS H'CAP (0-75) (3-Y.O) (Class D)

4-30 (4-31) **1m 4f** £3,566.60 (£1,080.80: £528.40: £252.20) Stalls: High GOING: 0.28 sec per fur (G)

Form	Horse	Dist	Pos	SP	RR	SF
471*	**Little Acorn (74)** (SCWilliams) **3-9-7** JCarroll(7) (trckd ldrs: led on bit over 2f out: sn rdn wl clr: eased towards fin)	—	**1**	11/4^{2}	82	43
558^{2}	**Night Mirage (USA) (74)** (MJohnston) **3-9-7** JFanning(6) (lw: set str pce: hdd over 2f out: kpt on: no ch w wnr)	5	**2**	9/4^{1}	75	36
528^{6}	**Arisaig (IRE) (59)** (PCalver) **3-8-3**$^{(3)}$ DarrenMoffatt(8) (chsd ldrs: rdn & lost pl ½-wy: styd on fnl 2f)	1¾	**3**	16/1	58	19
575^{6}	**Jack The Lad (IRE) (58)** (JHetherton) **3-8-5** NKennedy(1) (trckd ldrs: rdn ½-wy: one pce fnl 4f)	hd	**4**	8/1	57	18
537*	**Count Tony (70)** (SPCWoods) **3-9-3** DBiggs(3) (lw: bhd: hdwy ½-wy: hrd rdn over 3f out: nvr nr ldrs)	3	**5**	11/4^{2}	65	26
544^{7}	**Madam Lucy (50)** (WWHaigh) **3-7-6**$^{(5)ow1}$ JBramhill(4) (sn pushed along: lost tch 4f out)	18	**6**	25/1	21	—
471^{5}	**Pupil Master (IRE) (50)** (DenysSmith) **3-7-11** LCharnock(2) (chsd ldr: rdn 7f out: lost pl 4f out)	2	**7**	20/1	18	—
600^{6}	**Floating Devon (54)** (TDEasterby) **3-8-1** JFEgan(5) (hdwy ½-wy: sn rdn: lost pl over 3f out: virtually p.u over 1f out)	29	**8**	15/2^{3}	—	—

(SP 121.5%) **8 Rn**

2m 41.6 (12.60) CSF £9.20 CT £77.55 TOTE £3.60: £1.50 £1.10 £3.10 (£5.00) OWNER Mr Alasdair Simpson (NEWMARKET) BRED Alasdair J. Simpson
LONG HANDICAP Madam Lucy 7-8

471* Little Acorn, from a 9lb higher mark, proved much too good for this lot, despite again swishing his tail violently. Eased up considerably, he was value for ten lengths. (11/4)

558 Night Mirage (USA) set a strong gallop, and had all but the winner in trouble turning in. (9/4)

Arisaig (IRE) dropped himself right out at halfway. Staying on at the finish, he is presumably an out-and-out stayer. (16/1)

415 Jack The Lad (IRE) pulled hard in the early stages, but seemed to get the trip alright. (8/1)

537* Count Tony, raised 4lb, found this much tougher. Under the stick turning in, he never posed a threat. (11/4)

827 PEREGRINE FALCON H'CAP (0-65) (3-Y.O+) (Class F)

5-05 (5-07) **5f 207y** £2,794.00 (£784.00: £382.00) Stalls: High GOING: 0.28 sec per fur (G)

Form	Horse	Dist	Pos	SP	RR	SF
759*	**Grey Kingdom (48)** (MBrittain) **6-8-4**$^{(7)\ 7x}$ DMernagh(7) (mde virtually all: qcknd clr over 1f out: r.o strly)	—	**1**	11/4^{1}	65	47
527^{6}	**Amron (64)** (JBerry) **10-9-8**$^{(5)}$ TEDurcan(17) (lw: bhd: gd hdwy over 2f out: styd on fnl f: no ch w wnr)	4	**2**	9/1	70	52
	Winter Scout (USA) (55) (RAFahey) **9-8-11**$^{(7)}$ RWinston(16) (hld up: hdwy on ins 2f out: r.o fnl f)	nk	**3**	16/1	60	42
734^{7}	**Kid Ory (46)** (DWChapman) **6-8-9** ACulhane(11) (a chsng ldrs: styd on same pce fnl 2f)	½	**4**	20/1	50	32
529^{13}	**Birchwood Sun (50)** (MDods) **7-8-10b**$^{(3)}$ CTeague(9) (s.i.s: bhd tl hdwy on outside 2f out: nt rch ldrs)	½	**5**	33/1	53	35
	Bataleur (60) (MissJBower) **4-9-9** DHarrison(13) (a chsng ldrs: kpt on same pce fnl 2f)	¾	**6**	20/1	61	43
585^{14}	**Fairy Prince (IRE) (60)** (MrsALMKing) **4-9-6**$^{(3)}$ FLynch(3) (chsd ldrs: effrt over 2f out: grad wknd)	2	**7**	16/1	55	37
610^{6}	**Needle Match (55)** (JJO'Neill) **4-9-4** GDuffield(14) (mid div: effrt u.p over 2f out: nvr nr to chal)	¾	**8**	10/1	48	30
527^{4}	**Camionneur (IRE) (49)** (TDEasterby) **4-8-12** MBirch(15) (lw: trckd ldrs: effrt 2f out: grad wknd)	nk	**9**	6/1^{2}	42	24
587^{18}	**Shontaine (52)** (MJohnston) **4-8-8**$^{(7)}$ KSked(4) (sn bhd: sme hdwy 2f out: n.d)	nk	**10**	25/1	44	26
610^{10}	**Mister Westsound (55)** (MissLAPerratt) **5-9-4b** JCarroll(18) (s.s: bhd: hdwy whn nt clr run over 1f out: n.d)	1	**11**	12/1	44	26
585^{20}	**Zain Dancer (48)** (DNicholls) **5-8-11** AlexGreaves(8) (hld up: stdy hdwy 2f out: nvr nr to chal)	nk	**12**	20/1	36	18
610^{9}	**Sihafi (USA) (55)** (JMCarr) **4-9-4** AClark(5) (mid div: effrt ½-wy: no imp: b.b.v)	½	**13**	11/4^{1}	42	24
526^{17}	**Silent System (IRE) (33)** (DWChapman) **4-7-5**$^{(5)}$ PFessey(10) (a in rr: rdn ½-wy)	s.h	**14**	50/1	20	2
702^{7}	**Ramsey Hope (65)** (CWFairhurst) **4-10-0v** LCharnock(1) (lw: bhd: bmpd over 2f out: n.d)	¾	**15**	20/1	50	32
734^{3}	**Naughty Pistol (USA) (54)** (PDEvans) **5-9-3b** JFEgan(12) (chsd ldrs: wkng whn hmpd over 1f out)	1¼	**16**	8/1^{3}	35	17
663^{6}	**Another Nightmare (IRE) (47)** (RMMcKellar) **5-8-10** RLappin(2) (w ldrs tl lost pl over 2f out: eased)	11	**17**	16/1	—	—
203^{6}	**Lady Silk (41)** (MissJFCraze) **6-8-4** JFanning(6) (unruly gng to s: a bhd)	2½	**18**	20/1	—	—

608[14] **Take Notice (58)** (RMMcKellar) **4-9-0**(7) JMcAuley(19) (sn chsng ldrs: lost pl over 2f out: eased)....................¾ **19** 25/1 1 —
(SP 159.6%) **19 Rn**

1m 16.9 (5.10) CSF £30.59 CT £378.43 TOTE £3.80: £2.20 £2.20 £3.80 £5.20 (£24.80) Trio £357.10 OWNER Mr Mel Brittain (WARTHILL) BRED Northgate Lodge Stud Ltd

LONG HANDICAP Silent System (IRE) 7-0

OFFICIAL EXPLANATION Sihafi (USA): bled from the nose.

759* Grey Kingdom had the draw to overcome this time but, one of the few in the field with genuine early speed, he was soon showing his rivals a clean pair of heels. He is likely to be out very soon to try to complete a hat-trick, which looks a real possibility. (11/4)

527 Amron, who usually runs well in the first couple of months of the season, stuck on strongly up the hill. (9/1)

Winter Scout (USA), who ran over twelve furlongs on his final outing last term, has changed stables. Carrying condition, he was staying on in pleasing fashion at the line. (16/1)

526 Kid Ory is gradually finding his feet, and is better-suited by seven furlongs or even a mile. (20/1)

Birchwood Sun, having only his second outing since pulling up lame at Hamilton last summer, will have delighted connections with this effort. (33/1)

Zain Dancer was not knocked about at any stage. (20/1)

610 Sihafi (USA), who hinted at better to come at Hamilton last time, was well-supported in the market, but he was flat out and getting nowhere at halfway. (11/4: 7/1-5/2)

T/Plpt: £15.70 (603.28 Tckts). T/Qdpt: £15.90 (29.65 Tckts) WG

SANDOWN (R-H) (Good to firm St crse, Rnd crse Good to firm, Gd ptchs)

Friday April 25th

Race 3 & 5: hand-timed

WEATHER: raining WIND: almost nil

78+ 62+ 73 75

828 ALBERT MEDIAN AUCTION MAIDEN STKS (2-Y.O F) (Class D)

2-05 (2-07) **5f 6y** £3,566.25 (£1,080.00: £527.50: £251.25) Stalls: High GOING: 0.13 sec per fur (G)

			Pos	SP	RR	SF
	Daunting Lady (IRE) (RHannon) **2-8-11** PatEddery(15) (unf: lw: a.p: led over 3f out: rdn over 1f out: r.o wl)	—	**1**	100/30 1	78+	44
739[11]	**Phone Alex (IRE)** (RHannon) **2-8-11** DaneO'Neill(12) (hdwy on ins over 2f out: ev ch ins fnl f: unable qckn)	2	**2**	12/1	72	38
	Silent Pride (IRE) (MDIUsher) **2-8-11** MRoberts(9) (leggy: lt-f: s.i.s: gd hdwy on ins over 1f out: one pce fnl f)	2½	**3**	25/1	64	30
	Fast Tempo (IRE) (BPalling) **2-8-11** TSprake(6) (neat: bit bkwd: a.p: rdn over 1f out: one pce)	¾	**4**	25/1	61	27
739[7]	**Sun In The Morning** (BJMeehan) **2-8-11** BDoyle(8) (a.p: rdn over 1f out: one pce)	hd	**5**	8/1	61	27
	Patsy Culsyth (MJohnston) **2-8-11** JWeaver(2) (leggy: lt-f: hdwy over 1f out: nvr nr to chal)	2½	**6**	10/1	53	19
648[6]	**Fayrana (IRE)** (JWHills) **2-8-11** RHills(11) (prom 3f)	1¼	**7**	6/1 3	49	15
	Universal Lady (CJames) **2-8-11** MJKinane(4) (leggy: lt-f: spd over 3f)	1¾	**8**	25/1	44	10
651[5]	**Fleet Lady (IRE)** (MrsPNDutfield) **2-8-11** SDrowne(14) (hdwy over 3f out: wknd over 1f out)	¾	**9**	33/1	41	7
	Miss Hit (MRChannon) **2-8-11** RHughes(5) (scope: gd hdwy over 1f out: eased whn btn ins fnl f)	1	**10**	5/1 2	38	4
	Tundra (IRE) (KMcAuliffe) **2-8-11** JReid(10) (leggy: lt-f: bhd fnl 2f)	nk	**11**	20/1	37	3
	Blarney Park (CADwyer) **2-8-11** KFallon(1) (w'like: bit bkwd: a bhd)	2½	**12**	33/1	29	—
	Lisa's Pride (IRE) (MissGayKelleway) **2-8-11** SSanders(7) (w'like: bit bkwd: sme hdwy over 2f out: sn wknd)	s.h	**13**	9/1	29	—
648[11]	**After Dawn (IRE)** (MrsPNDutfield) **2-8-11** JQuinn(13) (prom over 2f)	¾	**14**	40/1	26	—
	Shalabella (IRE) (MRChannon) **2-8-11** TQuinn(3) (w'like: bit bkwd: bhd fnl 2f)	10	**15**	12/1	—	—

(SP 124.2%) **15 Rn**

63.53 secs (3.73) CSF £38.25 TOTE £2.90: £1.80 £2.90 £8.00 (£11.10) Trio £313.40 OWNER Mr T. J. Dale (MARLBOROUGH) BRED Mrs G. Doyle

Daunting Lady (IRE) needs time to develop, but she looked in good shape, and comes from a stable that has already produced five juvenile winners. She made full use of her good draw and, soon in front, was rousted along to put the runner-up in her place. (100/30: 9/4-7/2)

Phone Alex (IRE) left her debut effort behind. Moving into the action at halfway, she looked a serious threat to the winner inside the last, but could not find another gear. (12/1: 7/1-14/1)

Silent Pride (IRE), who cost just 2,000 guineas, lacks substance, but she made giant strides along the rail before running out of steam in the final furlong. (25/1)

Fast Tempo (IRE), a half-sister to several winners, looked as though the run would do her good, and failed to quicken from below the distance. (25/1)

739 Sun In The Morning, with the benefit of a previous run, played an active role until outpaced over a furlong out. (8/1: op 5/1)

Patsy Culsyth, a sparely-made individual, could never get into the race. (10/1: 6/1-12/1)

648 Fayrana (IRE) (6/1: op 7/2)

Miss Hit, with far more substance than most of her rivals, was not well-drawn. Nevertheless, she made eyecatching headway before being allowed to coast in when her chance had gone. She will be a different proposition next time. (5/1)

Lisa's Pride (IRE) (9/1: 5/1-10/1)

Shalabella (IRE) (12/1: 7/1-14/1)

829 TUDOR CONDITIONS STKS (3-Y.O C & G) (Class C)

2-35 (2-38) **1m 14y** £4,855.20 (£1,816.80: £888.40: £382.00: £171.00: £86.60) Stalls: High GOING: 0.13 sec per fur (G)

			Pos	SP	RR	SF
503*	**Romanov (IRE)** (PWChapple-Hyam) **3-9-0** JReid(1) (lw: hdwy over 1f out: hrd rdn: led nr fin)	—	**1**	7/2 3	104	66
	Harry Wolton (HRACecil) **3-9-0** WRyan(7) (lw: hld up: led over 1f out: hrd rdn: hdd nr fin)	nk	**2**	12/1	103	65
674[2]	**Komi** (MRStoute) **3-8-10** PatEddery(2) (lw: chsd ldr over 6f out: led 2f out tl over 1f out: wknd fnl f)	5	**3**	2/1 1	90	52
	Military (USA) (HRACecil) **3-8-7** KFallon(3) (wl grwn: dwlt: rdn over 3f out: hdwy over 1f out: wknd fnl f: rn green)	nk	**4**	7/2 3	86	48
586*	**Latalomne (USA)** (EALDunlop) **3-9-0** MJKinane(6) (led 6f: wknd fnl f)	1½	**5**	100/30 2	90	52
518*	**Greenaway Bay (USA)** (GWragg) **3-9-0** MHills(5) (plld hrd: a.p: rdn over 2f out: sn wknd)	1½	**6**	12/1	87	49

(SP 116.2%) **6 Rn**

1m 45.5 (4.30) CSF £38.56 TOTE £4.00: £2.60 £3.60 (£26.60) OWNER Mr R. E. Sangster (MARLBOROUGH) BRED Swettenham Stud

503* **Romanov (IRE)** is very well-regarded, but connections must have been anxious as he was being niggled along turning in. Galvanised into action, he picked up ground to get up near the line in what may prove to be a hot little race. The Heron Stakes at Kempton is his next objective. (7/2: 7/4-4/1)
Harry Wolton, without the advantage of a previous run, made his bid for glory below the distance and soon had his rivals in trouble, but he was worried out of it near the line. (12/1: 6/1-14/1)
674 **Komi** gained the advantage a quarter-of-a-mile out, but was soon headed and left for dead. (2/1)
Military (USA), a $250,000 yearling, is a massive individual who would not have been out of place in the Whitbread. Pitched in at the deep-end, he almost got into it below the distance, before tiring. A likeable colt, he should not take long to open his account. (7/2)
586* **Latalomne (USA)**, supplemented for the Derby after his winning debut, was rather disappointing. After leading, he increased the tempo in the straight, but folded rather tamely when headed. (100/30)
518* **Greenaway Bay (USA)** had far more on his plate this time. (12/1: 8/1-14/1)

830 SANDOWN MILE STKS (Gp 2) (4-Y.O+) (Class A)

3-10 (3-11) **1m 14y** £35,945.00 (£13,393.50: £6,384.25: £2,727.25) Stalls: High GOING: 0.13 sec per fur (G)

				SP	RR	SF
678[2]	**Wixim (USA)** (RCharlton) **4-9-0** PatEddery(6) (b.hind: hdwy over 2f out: led over 1f out: edgd rt ins fnl f: drvn out)	—	**1**	5/1[2]	121	82
	First Island (IRE) (120) (GWragg) **5-9-6** MHills(7) (hdwy 2f out: hrd rdn ins fnl f: r.o wl)	hd	**2**	5/6[1]	127	88
	Bin Rosie (116) (DRLoder) **5-9-0b** TQuinn(8) (a.p: rdn over 2f out: n.m.r & bmpd ins fnl f: r.o)	½	**3**	6/1[3]	120	81
627a[6]	**Gothenberg (IRE)** (MJohnston) **4-9-4** JWeaver(4) (lw: led over 6f: n.m.r on ins & bmpd ins fnl f: r.o)	s.h	**4**	33/1	124	85
678[5]	**Acharne (110)** (CEBrittain) **4-9-0** BDoyle(1) (hld up: n.m.r over 2f out: rdn: r.o wl ins fnl f)	½	**5**	40/1	119	80
	Beauchamp King (118) (JLDunlop) **4-9-0** JReid(5) (plld hrd: a bhd)	7	**6**	8/1	105	66
	Centre Stalls (IRE) (113) (RFJohnsonHoughton) **4-9-0** SSanders(2) (bit bkwd: s.s: plld hrd: bhd fnl 3f)	¾	**7**	14/1	103	64
	Royal Philosopher (105) (JWHills) **5-9-0** RHills(3) (bit bkwd: swtg: chsd ldr 6f)	7	**8**	33/1	90	51
				(SP 111.6%)	**8 Rn**	

1m 43.9 (2.70) CSF £8.25 TOTE £5.50: £1.30 £1.30 £1.40 (£3.80) OWNER Mr K. Abdulla (BECKHAMPTON) BRED Juddmonte Farms
678 **Wixim (USA)** missed the second half of 1996 with various problems, but confirmed the promise of his run at Headquarters last week. Striking the front over a furlong out, he just held off his challengers despite drifting to his right. (5/1)
First Island (IRE), who developed into a top-class miler in 1996, had won first-time-out in the two previous seasons, but probably needed a stronger pace. He made ground steadily in the last furlong, and was going on at the finish. Another rewarding season looks in store, with the Lockinge his next objective. (5/6)
Bin Rosie is not the easiest of rides, but did nothing wrong this time. He had every chance before getting involved in scrimmaging with Gothenberg in the last furlong. (6/1)
627a **Gothenberg (IRE)**, who failed to make much impression in Dubai this winter, only returned to England the day before this race. This did not prevent him putting up a bold show from the front. He wandered off the rails late on, but kept going all the way to the line. (33/1)
678 **Acharne**, with nowhere to go just as the race began in earnest, was putting in some really good work inside the last, and definitely needs further to be seen at his best. (40/1)
Beauchamp King, who went backwards after winning the 1996 Craven Stakes, showed no sign of a return to form. (8/1)

831 HEATHORNS BOOKMAKERS H'CAP (0-85) (4-Y.O+) (Class D)

3-40 (3-40) **2m 78y** £4,947.25 (£1,498.00: £731.50: £348.25) Stalls: High GOING: 0.13 sec per fur (G)

				SP	RR	SF
655[3]	**Etterby Park (USA) (74)** (MJohnston) **4-9-6** JWeaver(5) (lw: chsd ldr: led over 2f out: rdn out)	—	**1**	9/2[2]	89	53
	Jamaican Flight (USA) (63) (CSmith) **4-8-9** JFortune(6) (led tl over 2f out: unable qckn)	2½	**2**	9/1[3]	76	40
603[2]	**Soojama (IRE) (52)** (RMFlower) **7-8-2b** SDrowne(3) (lw: s.s: hdwy on ins 3f out: hrd rdn 2f out: one pce)	6	**3**	9/1[3]	59	27
	Northern Fleet (82) (MrsAJPerrett) **4-10-0** PatEddery(2) (lw: a.p: rdn over 3f out: one pce)	2½	**4**	9/2[2]	86	50
660[4]	**Coleridge (49)** (JJSheehan) **9-7-10b**(3)ow1 MHenry(8) (rdn over 2f out: nvr nr to chal)	2½	**5**	12/1	51	18
	Shadirwan (IRE) (76) (RAkehurst) **6-9-12** TQuinn(7) (lw: prom over 13f)	¾	**6**	9/2[2]	77	45
612[5]	**Sharaf (IRE) (61)** (WRMuir) **4-8-7**ow1 JReid(1) (lw: bhd fnl 3f)	nk	**7**	12/1	62	25
510[7]	**Unchanged (69)** (CEBrittain) **5-9-5** MRoberts(4) (lw: a bhd)	2	**8**	7/2[1]	68	36
				(SP 112.2%)	**8 Rn**	

3m 44.8 (12.80) CSF £38.37 CT £313.58 TOTE £4.30: £1.90 £2.20 £1.80 (£26.60) OWNER Mr & Mrs G Middlebrook (MIDDLEHAM) BRED Jayeff "B" Stables
WEIGHT FOR AGE 4yo-4lb
655 **Etterby Park (USA)**, five pounds higher than when last successful, struck the front some way out, and was vigorously ridden to shake off the long-time leader. (9/2)
Jamaican Flight (USA), fit from hurdling, has changed stables recently. Ahead from the start, he was put in his place by the winner, but finished well clear of the rest. (9/1)
603 **Soojama (IRE)** has been in good form on the All-Weather, but is 10lb higher than when last successful on Turf. He made a move early in the straight, but was making no impression in the closing stages. (9/1)
Northern Fleet, fit from hurdling, was made to look very pedestrian in the straight, and is becoming frustrating. (9/2)
660 **Coleridge** showed little on his return to grass. (12/1: 8/1-14/1)
Shadirwan (IRE) goes well fresh, but was in trouble early in the straight. (9/2)

832 ATHLONE RATED STKS H'CAP (0-95) (4-Y.O+) (Class C)

4-10 (4-14) **1m 14y** £6,359.00 (£2,381.00: £1,165.50: £502.50: £226.25: £115.75) Stalls: High GOING: 0.13 sec per fur (G)

				SP	RR	SF
653*	**Star Talent (USA) (82)** (IABalding) **6-8-12** RCochrane(9) (lw: stdy hdwy over 2f out: led over 1f out: rdn out)	—	**1**	10/1	95	77
	Give Me A Ring (IRE) (86) (CWThornton) **4-9-2** DeanMcKeown(4) (a.p: led over 2f out tl over 1f out: r.o one pce)	1¼	**2**	11/1	97	79
	Star Manager (USA) (85) (PFICole) **7-9-1** TQuinn(1) (lw: rdn over 2f out: hdwy over 1f out: r.o)	s.h	**3**	7/1[3]	95	77
	Alhawa (USA) (77) (RAkehurst) **4-8-7** SSanders(8) (lw: n.m.r & lost pl 3f out: rallied over 1f out: r.o one pce)	½	**4**	9/4[1]	86	68
450[13]	**Stone Ridge (IRE) (87)** (RHannon) **5-9-3** DaneO'Neill(13) (hdwy over 1f out: nvr nrr)	2½	**5**	14/1	92	74
567[3]	**Rakis (IRE) (78)** (MrsLStubbs) **7-8-8** KFallon(14) (hdwy over 1f out: nvr nrr)	¾	**6**	10/1	81	63
	Pomona (84) (PJMakin) **4-9-0** MRoberts(12) (hdwy over 2f out: ev ch over 1f out: eased whn btn fnl f)	1¾	**7**	11/1	84	66
450[24]	**Pater Noster (USA) (87)** (JohnHarris) **8-9-3** PaulEddery(7) (b: led 7f out tl over 2f out: sn wknd)	1½	**8**	33/1	84	66
398[10]	**Amber Fort (77)** (DRCElsworth) **4-8-4v**(3) DGriffiths(2) (lost pl 5f out: rallied over 1f out: wknd fnl f)	s.h	**9**	25/1	73	55
	Wakeel (USA) (81) (SDow) **5-8-11** JReid(10) (a.p: rdn over 3f out: ev ch over 1f out: sn wknd)	s.h	**10**	14/1	77	59
635*	**Night Dance (78)** (KAMorgan) **5-8-3**(5) RFfrench(3) (a.p: rdn over 3f out: ev ch over 1f out: sn wknd)	2	**11**	9/1	70	52

444[8] **Night Wink (USA) (80)** (GLMoore) **5-8-10** SWhitworth(11) (lw: led 1f: wknd over 2f out)....3½ **12** 16/1 65 47
444[12] **Therhea (IRE) (77)** (BRMillman) **4-8-7** TSprake(6) (lw: bhd fnl 2f)....nk **13** 25/1 62 44
Samara (IRE) (91) (JLDunlop) **4-9-7** PatEddery(5) (hdwy over 6f out: wknd over 4f out)....s.h **14** 11/2[2] 76 58
(SP 133.4%) **14 Rn**

1m 44.2 (3.00) CSF £114.51 CT £794.57 TOTE £12.40: £2.90 £3.20 £2.20 (£47.60) Trio £65.50 OWNER Mr R. P. B. Michaelson (KINGSCLERE) BRED Mrs Afaf A. Al Essa
LONG HANDICAP Amber Fort 8-5 Therhea (IRE) 8-5 Alhawa (USA) 8-6

653* Star Talent (USA), claimed out of Gay Kelleway's stable for £12,000 after winning at Warwick, travelled well throughout. Let loose below the distance, he was ridden along to stamp his authority on the race. (10/1)
Give Me A Ring (IRE), 9lb higher than when last successful, got his head in front briefly, but had no answer to the winner's challenge. (11/1)
Star Manager (USA), winner of this race in 1996, does best when fresh, and was putting in some good work from below the distance. In the last five years he has won just once each season. (7/1)
Alhawa (USA) who changed stables for 24,000 guineas in the autumn, was balloted out of the Newbury Spring Cup. Outpaced and with little room early in the straight, he stayed on but was just run out of third place close home. (9/4)
Stone Ridge (IRE), who has shown little since winning the 1996 Lincoln, made some late headway without posing a threat. (14/1)
567 Rakis (IRE) was putting in his best work in the closing stages. All ten of his victories have been over seven furlongs. (10/1)
Samara (IRE), reported to have cracked a hind sesamoid when finishing fourth at Ascot in June 1996, was given an extremely tender ride on her return. Soon pulling her way into the action, she ran wide on the home turn and gradually faded out of contention. Sure to come on for this, and possibly helped by dropping a few pounds in the handicap, she should leave this run well behind. (11/2)

833 APRIL MAIDEN STKS (3-Y.O F) (Class D)
4-45 (4-50) **1m 2f 7y** £3,993.50 (£1,208.00: £589.00: £279.50) Stalls: High GOING: 0.13 sec per fur (G)

SP RR SF

Ukraine Venture (SPCWoods) **3-8-7** WRyan(9) (w'like: scope: lw: hld up: rdn 3f out: led over 2f out: clr over 1f out: r.o wl)....— **1** 13/2 94++ 57
Alcalali (USA) (PAKelleway) **3-8-11** PatEddery(11) (w'like: scope: a.p: hmpd 5f out: rdn over 3f out: chsd wnr over 1f out: no imp)....10 **2** 100/30[1] 82 45
Go For Salt (USA) (MRStoute) **3-8-11** JReid(5) (a.p: led over 3f out tl over 2f out: one pce)....nk **3** 4/1[2] 82 45
Book At Bedtime (IRE) (CACyzer) **3-8-7** TQuinn(12) (str: bit bkwd: bhd whn hmpd 5f out: rdn over 4f out: hdwy over 1f out: nvr nrr)....3 **4** 25/1 73 36
Leading Note (USA) (LMCumani) **3-8-11** OUrbina(1) (led 9f out tl over 3f out: wknd over 2f out)....hd **5** 11/2[3] 77 40
La Curamalal (IRE) (GWragg) **3-8-11** MHills(8) (nvr nr to chal)....1½ **6** 12/1 74 37
Alifandango (IRE) (ACStewart) **3-8-11** MRoberts(6) (bhd fnl 5f)....nk **7** 16/1 74 37
Quest For Best (USA) (JHMGosden) **3-8-11** GHind(4) (sme hdwy over 2f out: eased whn btn over 1f out)....1 **8** 8/1 72 35
Divinity (CEBrittain) **3-8-7** BDoyle(10) (w'like: bit bkwd: bhd fnl 5f)....¾ **9** 14/1 67 30
Silankka (MRChannon) **3-8-7** RPerham(3) (unf: hdwy 7f out: wknd over 4f out)....6 **10** 25/1 57 20
Shouk (LMCumani) **3-8-6**(5) RFfrench(2) (led 1f: 3rd whn stumbled & uns rdr 5f out).... **U** 6/1 — —
Rocky Dance (FR) (APJarvis) **3-8-7** WJO'Connor(7) (Withdrawn not under Starter's orders: veterinary advice).... **W** 33/1 — —
(SP 128.1%) **11 Rn**

2m 12.29 (5.59) CSF £27.65 TOTE £7.80: £2.00 £1.60 £2.10 (£10.40) Trio £18.90 OWNER Dr Frank Chao (NEWMARKET) BRED Woodsway Stud and Chao Racing and Bloodstock Ltd

Ukraine Venture, an attractive individual, has been working well at home, but has proved hard to settle. Woken up in the straight, she stormed clear in impressive style. She is entered for the Oaks and can go on from here. (13/2: 10/1-6/1)
Alcalali (USA), a lengthy sort, was hampered by the fall of Shouk on the home turn. However, she was alongside the winner early in the straight, but was left standing when that filly made her effort. Her trainer believed she would have won but for the interference. Optimistic perhaps, but she should soon find a race. (100/30: 9/4-7/2)
Go For Salt (USA) moved to the front early in the straight, but could not find an extra gear. (4/1: op 9/4)
Book At Bedtime (IRE), a well-made filly, was carrying condition and, after being hampered on the bend, was last straightening-up. She made good ground in the closing stages to get into the frame. (25/1)
Leading Note (USA), was soon in front but, collared early in the straight, she was soon in trouble. (11/2: 4/1-6/1)
Quest For Best (USA), a plain filly, was given an interesting ride. Held up at the back, her jockey gave her a couple of reminders in the straight, but she was not given a hard time. She is one to note with interest. (8/1: 5/1-9/1)
Divinity (14/1: 12/1-20/1)

834 BOW STREET H'CAP (0-90) (3-Y.O+) (Class C)
5-20 (5-22) **5f 6y** £5,129.25 (£1,554.00: £759.50: £362.25) Stalls: High GOING: 0.13 sec per fur (G)

SP RR SF

698[2] **Gone Savage (75)** (WJMusson) **9-9-0** RCochrane(13) (b.nr fore: hdwy on ins 2f out: nt clr run over 1f out: led ins fnl f: r.o wl)....— **1** 6/1[3] 85 67
Literary Society (USA) (69) (JARToller) **4-8-8** SSanders(17) (a.p: led 1f out tl ins fnl f: unable qckn)....1¼ **2** 9/1 75 57
527[2] **Broadstairs Beauty (IRE) (72)** (DShaw) **7-8-11b** KFallon(15) (b: lw: led: rdn 2f out: hdd 1f out: one pce)....¾ **3** 5/1[2] 76 58
726[3] **Eastern Prophets (85)** (GLewis) **4-9-10** PaulEddery(10) (lw: a.p: rdn over 2f out: ev ch 1f out: one pce)....1½ **4** 7/1 84 66
585[4] **Pointer (57)** (MrsPNDutfield) **5-7-10** JQuinn(14) (a.p: rdn over 2f out: one pce)....¾ **5** 12/1 54 36
694[5] **Ellens Lad (IRE) (85)** (RHannon) **3-9-0** PatEddery(16) (lw: rdn & hdwy 2f out: 7th & btn whn hmpd ins fnl f).1¼ **6** 4/1[1] 78 50
520[17] **Longwick Lad (74)** (WRMuir) **4-8-13** JReid(11) (no hdwy fnl 2f)....¾ **7** 16/1 64 46
520[4] **Cim Bom Bom (IRE) (75)** (MBell) **5-8-9v**(5) GFaulkner(4) (a.p: rdn over 2f out: wknd fnl f)....nk **8** 11/1 64 46
High Domain (IRE) (68) (JLSpearing) **6-8-7** SDrowne(2) (prom 2f)....1¾ **9** 20/1 52 34
Half Tone (57) (RMFlower) **5-7-10b** JLowe(9) (nvr nrr)....hd **10** 14/1 40 22
731[8] **Sweet Magic (75)** (PHowling) **6-9-0** FNorton(7) (outpcd)....nk **11** 25/1 57 39
744[10] **Dande Flyer (70)** (DWPArbuthnot) **4-8-9** SWhitworth(3) (a bhd)....½ **12** 33/1 51 33
726[7] **Mr Bergerac (IRE) (82)** (BPalling) **6-9-7** TSprake(6) (a bhd)....3 **13** 14/1 53 35
364[5] **Rififi (66)** (RIngram) **4-8-5** AMcGlone(8) (b: a bhd)....hd **14** 16/1 37 19
Splicing (70) (WJHaggas) **4-8-9** MHills(12) (lw: a bhd)....½ **15** 12/1 39 21
443[16] **Lord High Admiral (CAN) (89)** (MJHeaton-Ellis) **9-10-0** MRoberts(5) (spd over 3f)....s.h **16** 16/1 58 40
541[9] **Mindrace (64)** (KTIvory) **4-8-0**(3) MartinDwyer(1) (prom over 2f)....3 **17** 33/1 24 6
(SP 142.6%) **17 Rn**

62.33 secs (2.53) CSF £60.90 CT £226.97 TOTE £5.80: £1.80 £4.50 £1.60 £2.00 (£65.80) Trio £43.90 OWNER The Square Table (NEWMARKET) BRED Mrs C. F. Van Straubenzee and R. Mead

WEIGHT FOR AGE 3yo-10lb

IN-FOCUS: At this first Flat meeting of the year, this event once again illustrated the importance of a high draw, when the stalls are on the far side on the straight course.

698 Gone Savage loves this track, but his come-from-behind style invariably gets him into trouble up the Sandown hill. Nevertheless, he managed a clear run on this occasion, and swept through to record his fifth course and distance victory. (6/1)

Literary Society (USA), always a leading player, was put in his place by the winner in the last furlong. (9/1)

527 Broadstairs Beauty (IRE) attempted to make all on the favoured far rail. Collared a furlong from home, he failed to find another gear. (5/1)

726 Eastern Prophets, always up with the pace, had every chance below the distance but could not quicken. (7/1)

585 Pointer found this trip too sharp and, although up with the pace, failed to quicken in the second half of the contest. He is yet to win at this distance. (12/1)

694 Ellens Lad (IRE) made a forward move after halfway, but had no chance with the principals when hampered inside the last. (4/1)

Half Tone (14/1: 16/1-25/1)

726 Mr Bergerac (IRE) (14/1: 10/1-16/1)

T/Jkpt: £6,454.50 (1.1 Tckts). T/Plpt: £48.70 (590.43 Tckts). T/Qdpt: £9.30 (163.07 Tckts) AK

0554-LEICESTER (R-H) (Good to soft, Good patches)

Saturday April 26th

WEATHER: rain WIND: almost nil

835 TOTE PLACEPOT H'CAP (0-85) (3-Y.O+) (Class D)

2-00 (2-02) **5f 218y** £3,900.40 (£1,166.20: £558.60: £254.80) Stalls: Low GOING minus 0.02 sec per fur (G)

				SP	RR	SF
	Oggi (72) (PJMakin) **6-9-1** MRoberts(14) (bit bkwd: chsd ldrs centre: led over 1f out: r.o wl)	—	**1**	8/1[3]	84	59
529[11]	**Knotty Hill (73)** (RCraggs) **5-9-2** DHolland(16) (led centre tl over 1f out: kpt on u.p)	1¾	**2**	12/1	80	55
	Mister Jolson (75) (RJHodges) **8-9-4** SDrowne(17) (b.nr fore: bkwd: chsd ldrs: effrt & ev ch 2f out: sn rdn: one pce)	3½	**3**	14/1	73	48
514[5]	**Weetman's Weigh (IRE) (74)** (RHollinshead) **4-9-0**(3) FLynch(4) (trckd ldrs: effrt & edgd rt appr fnl f: r.o)	½	**4**	12/1	71	46
610[7]	**Safio (66)** (ABailey) **4-8-9** DWright(13) (chsd ldrs: rdn & outpcd over 2f out: rallied fnl f)	nk	**5**	7/1[2]	62	37
541[10]	**Rockcracker (IRE) (55)** (GGMargarson) **5-7-12** GBardwell(15) (sn pushed along: hdwy 2f out: kpt on u.p ins fnl f)	2½	**6**	33/1	44	19
643[7]	**Bayin (USA) (72)** (MDIUsher) **8-9-1** RStreet(1) (s.i.s: r.o fnl 2f: nvr nrr)	5	**7**	9/1	48	23
529[8]	**Jo Mell (80)** (TDEasterby) **4-9-9** MBirch(9) (in tch: drvn along over 2f out: nt pce to chal)	nk	**8**	16/1	55	30
677[16]	**Pusey Street Girl (85)** (MRBosley) **4-9-9**(5) AimeeCook(2) (lw: chsd ldrs stands' side 4f)	1½	**9**	33/1	56	31
731[5]	**Friendly Brave (USA) (73)** (MissGayKelleway) **7-9-2** OPeslier(11) (nvr nr to chal)	hd	**10**	6/1[1]	44	19
	Pericles (78) (MJohnston) **3-8-10** RHills(8) (bkwd: spd over 3f)	nk	**11**	12/1	48	12
596[15]	**Benzoe (IRE) (71)** (MrsJRRamsden) **7-9-0** MDeering(12) (lw: dwlt: a in rr)	½	**12**	16/1	40	15
596[3]	**Maiteamia (72)** (SRBowring) **4-9-1b** JQuinn(7) (led stands' side 3f)	½	**13**	8/1[3]	39	14
569[7]	**Kildee Lad (78)** (APJones) **7-9-7** TSprake(3) (sn drvn along: outpcd fr ½-wy)	2½	**14**	20/1	39	14
450[14]	**La Petite Fusee (79)** (RJO'Sullivan) **6-9-3**(5) JBramhill(6) (b.hind: lw: w ldrs stands' side over 4f)	¾	**15**	12/1	38	13
	Enchanted Guest (IRE) (73) (VSoane) **4-9-2** CRutter(5) (bkwd: sn pushed along: a bhd: t.o)	17	**16**	20/1	—	—
357[R]	**Sailormaite (80)** (SRBowring) **6-9-9** SWebster(10) (ref to r: tk no part)		**R**	33/1	—	—
				(SP 126.6%)	**17 Rn**	

1m 12.7 (2.70) CSF £88.28 CT £779.50 TOTE £5.30: £2.00 £3.40 £5.90 £2.60 (£56.40) Trio £61.40 OWNER Skyline Racing Ltd (MARLBOROUGH) BRED H. D. and M. J. Gee

WEIGHT FOR AGE 3yo-11lb

OFFICIAL EXPLANATION Jo Mell: was found to have a dirty nose the following day.

Oggi did not look fit enough to win on this seasonal debut but, after striking the front over a furlong out, there was only going to be one winner. (8/1)

376 Knotty Hill, much better suited by this rain-softened ground, was in the firing line from the break and only the winner was able to match strides with him inside the distance. (12/1)

Mister Jolson ran extremely well considering he was carrying surplus condition and, if there is any improvement to come, should soon be paying his way. (14/1)

514 Weetman's Weigh (IRE) looked to be fighting a losing battle below the distance, but he was finding his feet again inside the final furlong, and another try at seven furlongs could be to his advantage. (12/1)

610 Safio, bustled along to hold his pitch soon after halfway, rallied gamely inside the distance and he his knocking at the door. (7/1: 4/1-15/2)

Rockcracker (IRE) was not helped by the continuous rain, for he had shown all his best form when he could hear his feet rattle. He did stay on though, and a small race is well within his reach. (33/1)

75+ 64 69+ 71

836 E.B.F. WILLOUGHBY MEDIAN AUCTION MAIDEN STKS (2-Y.O) (Class F)

2-30 (2-31) **5f 2y** £2,877.60 (£798.60: £382.80) Stalls: Low GOING minus 0.02 sec per fur (G)

				SP	RR	SF
	Ruzen (IRE) (BPalling) **2-9-0** TSprake(2) (w'like: leggy: a.p: nudged along ½-wy: led wl ins fnl f)	—	**1**	7/4[1]	84	32
594[3]	**Quiz Master** (EWeymes) **2-9-0** JQuinn(5) (led stands' side: ev ch ins fnl f: r.o)	¾	**2**	10/1	82	30
	Aurigny (SDow) **2-8-9** SSanders(8) (w'like: unf: dwlt: sn chsng ldrs: led over 1f out tl wl ins fnl f)	s.h	**3**	25/1	76	24
	Mari-Ela (IRE) (JRArnold) **2-8-9** DHarrison(13) (lengthy: led tl hdd over 1f out: r.o one pce)	3	**4**	33/1	67	15
	Blue Desert (MBell) **2-9-0** MFenton(4) (lt-f: unf: lw: racd stands' side: in tch: r.o wl ins fnl f)	½	**5**	11/1	70	18
722[2]	**Kennet** (PDCundell) **2-9-0** RPerham(10) (lw: prom: rdn 2f out: btn appr fnl f)	½	**6**	6/1[2]	69	17
	Cinder Hills (MWEasterby) **2-8-9** TLucas(14) (leggy: unf: bit bkwd: hld up mid div: hdwy appr fnl f: nvr nrr)	2½	**7**	25/1	56	4
557[6]	**Arm And A Leg (IRE)** (CADwyer) **2-9-0** JStack(16) (prom far side over 3f)	s.h	**8**	14/1	61	9
	Zig Zag (IRE) (MHTompkins) **2-8-9** DBiggs(11) (scope: prom over 3f)	nk	**9**	33/1	55	3
	Monopoly (IRE) (MJohnston) **2-9-0** MRoberts(9) (leggy: scope: spd 3f)	nk	**10**	8/1[3]	59	7
500[11]	**Latin Bay** (PWHarris) **2-9-0** AClark(6) (a in rr)	2½	**11**	25/1	51	—
	Bolero Kid (MWEasterby) **2-9-0** MWigham(12) (unf: scope: s.s: nvr plcd to chal)	½	**12**	25/1	49	—
	Lobuche (IRE) (RHannon) **2-9-0** WJO'Connor(7) (cmpt: s.s: a outpcd)	1¼	**13**	8/1[3]	45	—
730[5]	**Positive Air** (BAMcMahon) **2-8-9** RCochrane(1) (unruly stalls: a bhd)	½	**14**	8/1[3]	38	—
	Secret Tango (APJones) **2-8-9** SDrowne(3) (leggy: s.s: a bhd)	1¼	**15**	33/1	34	—

				SP	RR	SF
	Liberalis (GFHCharles-Jones) **2-8-9** CRutter(15) (unf: spd to ½-wy: sn outpcd: t.o)	11	**16**	33/1	—	—

(SP 135.2%) **16 Rn**

62.3 secs (3.80) CSF £18.86 TOTE £2.20: £1.10 £3.50 £7.40 (£16.40) Trio £257.20 OWNER Five To Follow (COWBRIDGE) BRED C. Farrell
Ruzen (IRE), a leggy May foal who was well supported on this debut, found all that was required to win a shade more easily than the margin suggests. (7/4)
594 Quiz Master had more use made of him than he did on his debut, and only lost out in an all-out battle to the line. (10/1: 7/1-11/1)
Aurigny, a full-sister to the speedy Tymeera, kicked for home below the distance but found the winner too strong for her in the final one hundred yards. (25/1)
Mari-Ela (IRE), a poor mover who may well need more time, held the overall lead until finding the quickening pace too much for her inside the last furlong. (33/1)
Blue Desert, an unfurnished half-brother to two winners and bred to need further, was finding his stride in the latter stages and will come good when the emphasis is more on stamina. (11/1: 6/1-12/1)
722 Kennet, off the bridle soon after halfway, is not cut-out for this much softer ground and his measure had been taken from some way out. (6/1)
Cinder Hills, who shows plenty of knee action, was getting down to some serious business in the closing stages and could be the one to keep in mind for the future. (25/1)
Monopoly (IRE) (8/1: 6/1-10/1)
Lobuche (IRE) (8/1: op 5/1)

837 TOTE BOOKMAKERS H'CAP (0-90) (3-Y.O) (Class C)

3-00 (3-01) **1m 3f 183y** £5,677.50 (£1,695.00: £810.00: £367.50) Stalls: Low GOING minus 0.02 sec per fur (G)

				SP	RR	SF
	Venetian Scene (64) (PFICole) **3-8-3** JQuinn(6) (hld up: swtchd lft & hdwy over 2f out: led over 1f out: rdn out)	—	**1**	16/1	75	27
676^{7}	**Recourse (USA) (82)** (HRACecil) **3-9-7** AMcGlone(9) (a.p: led wl over 2f out tl over 1f out: kpt on u.p)	1¼	**2**	8/1	91	43
505^{3}	**Drive Assured (80)** (CEBrittain) **3-9-5** MRoberts(7) (led after 3f tl wl over 2f out: rdn & wknd appr fnl f)	8	**3**	14/1	79	31
537^{7}	**Certain Magic (65)** (WRMuir) **3-8-1**(3) MHenry(4) (rdn & lost pl ent st: sme late hdwy: n.d)	7	**4**	20/1	54	6
	Henley (USA) (80) (DRLoder) **3-9-5** OPeslier(3) (h.d.w: lw: hld up in rr: effrt 3f out: no imp)	1¼	**5**	7/4 1	67	19
	Swallow Breeze (70) (DrJDScargill) **3-8-9** SDrowne(2) (bhd: rdn 3f out: no imp: t.o)	14	**6**	20/1	38	—
478*	**Tasik Chini (USA) (73)** (PFICole) **3-8-12** AClark(1) (chsd ldrs tl wknd wl over 2f out: t.o)	2½	**7**	13/2 3	38	—
700^{3}	**Mutabari (USA) (77)** (DMorley) **3-9-2** RHills(8) (lw: chsd ldrs: rdn & wknd 3f out: sn t.o)	2½	**8**	7/1	39	—
782^{2}	**Happy Minstral (USA) (82)** (MJohnston) **3-9-7** DHolland(5) (led 3f: drvn along ent st: wknd 3f out & eased: t.o)	2	**9**	3/1 2	41	—

(SP 120.4%) **9 Rn**

2m 37.3 (8.80) CSF £129.71 CT £1,676.53 TOTE £28.90: £3.10 £2.80 £3.70 (£88.40) Trio £115.50; £115.50 to Pontefract 28/4/97 OWNER Richard Green (Fine Paintings) (WHATCOMBE) BRED R. Green
OFFICIAL EXPLANATION **Happy Minstral (USA): rider reported that the colt seemed wrong and had given his all, so he felt it prudent to pull up.**
Venetian Scene, showed her appreciation for this longer trip and, despite still hanging on to her winter coat, won readily enough and should go on from here. (16/1)
Recourse (USA) struck the front early in the straight and tried hard to get away, but top weight took its toll and he was fighting a lost cause in the final two hundred yards. (8/1)
505 Drive Assured again attempted to do it from the front, but the leading pair proved much too good when a final effort was called for. (14/1)
Certain Magic had the softer ground that he requires, but he was in trouble turning in and was unable to make his presence felt. (20/1)
Henley (USA), sure to benefit from the run, failed to pick up when asked for his effort three furlongs out and proved a big disappointment. (7/4)
782 Happy Minstral (USA) found this race coming far too soon after such a promising effort four days ago, and he was under strong driving and galloping on the spot from the turn into the straight. (3/1: op 2/1)

838 TOTE TRIO H'CAP (0-70) (3-Y.O+) (Class E)

3-35 (3-45) **1m 1f 218y** £3,423.50 (£1,025.00: £492.00: £225.50) Stalls: Low GOING minus 0.02 sec per fur (G)

				SP	RR	SF
67^{4}	**Kinnescash (IRE) (53)** (PBowen) **4-8-13** RCochrane(6) (lw: hld up on outside: hdwy 5f out: led 3f out: hrd rdn: hld on)	—	**1**	13/2 2	68	51
589^{4}	**Premier Generation (IRE) (55)** (DWPArbuthnot) **4-9-1** SWhitworth(14) (plld hrd: chsd ldrs: ev ch over 1f out: r.o wl)	nk	**2**	20/1	70	53
587^{13}	**Arzani (USA) (46)** (DJSCosgrove) **6-8-6** RHills(17) (lw: a.p: led over 3f out: sn hdd: rdn & one pce appr fnl f)	5	**3**	16/1	53	36
400^{5}	**Aztec Flyer (USA) (49)** (CEBrittain) **4-8-9** MRoberts(4) (bhd: gd hdwy fnl 3f: nrst fin)	5	**4**	16/1	48	31
538^{3}	**Mono Lady (IRE) (55)** (DHaydnJones) **4-9-1b** CRutter(2) (hld up: hdwy 3f out: nvr able chal)	nk	**5**	8/1 3	53	36
689^{2}	**Father Dan (IRE) (56)** (MissGayKelleway) **8-9-2** GDuffield(5) (b: hld up: hdwy over 2f out: nt rch ldrs)	1¼	**6**	11/2 1	52	35
	Dormy Three (53) (RJHodges) **7-8-13** TSprake(8) (sme late hdwy: nvr nrr)	1	**7**	20/1	47	30
476^{3}	**South Eastern Fred (48)** (HJCollingridge) **6-8-8** JQuinn(16) (prom: ev ch 3f out: sn rdn: grad wknd)	3½	**8**	14/1	37	20
	Tonka (60) (PJMakin) **5-9-6** DHarrison(19) (lw: plld hrd: chsd ldrs: snatched up 6f out: btn 3f out)	hd	**9**	14/1	49	32
587^{7}	**Utmost Zeal (USA) (64)** (PWHarris) **4-9-3**(7) CLowther(10) (lw: prom: rdn 3f out: grad wknd)	1¼	**10**	20/1	51	34
	Dramatic Moment (66) (JRArnold) **4-9-12** SSanders(7) (mid div: rdn 3f out: no imp)	1¾	**11**	20/1	50	33
	Courageous Knight (47) (PHayward) **8-8-7**ow1 WJO'Connor(9) (bit bkwd: a in rr)	4	**12**	33/1	24	6
	Aurelian (62) (MBell) **3-8-5** MFenton(13) (s.i.s: a in rr)	½	**13**	16/1	39	5
	Mock Trial (IRE) (63) (MrsJRRamsden) **4-9-9** SDrowne(1) (a in rr: t.o)	5	**14**	11/2 1	32	15
521^{13}	**Zermatt (IRE) (68)** (MDIUsher) **7-10-0** MRimmer(15) (bit bkwd: led over 8f: sn rdn & wknd: t.o)	s.h	**15**	20/1	37	20
517^{10}	**Gain Line (USA) (62)** (BobJones) **4-9-8** AMcGlone(11) (s.s: a in rr: t.o)	12	**16**	33/1	11	—
689*	**Pendolino (IRE) (47)** (MBrittain) **6-8-7** GBardwell(3) (chsd ldrs 7f: sn wknd: t.o)	1¼	**17**	11/2 1	—	—
605^{7}	**Suleika Dancer (53)** (SGKnight) **4-8-13** RPerham(18) (lw: bolted bef s: prom over 4f: virtually p.u fnl 3f: t.o)	dist	**18**	33/1	—	—

(SP 134.2%) **18 Rn**

2m 9.2 (5.50) CSF £129.11 CT £1,855.55 TOTE £8.50: £2.70 £2.10 £3.10 £4.70 (£72.50) Trio £669.20 OWNER Mr D. R. James (HAVERFORDWEST) BRED Frank Barry
WEIGHT FOR AGE 3yo-17lb
67 Kinnescash (IRE), pulled wide to launch his challenge in the centre of the track, needed to be kept up to his work to hold on close home. (13/2)

589 **Premier Generation (IRE)**, restrained in behind the leaders, looked to be travelling best when putting in his bid approaching the final furlong, but the winner kept pulling out more and he was unable to get to terms. (20/1)
476 **Arzani (USA)**, sharing the lead from the turn for home, had to admit the principals too smart for him when the whips were cracking. (16/1)
Aztec Flyer (USA), taking a big step down in distance, made up a lot of ground in the latter stages but the leaders were not stopping. (16/1)
538 **Mono Lady (IRE)** made smooth headway three furlongs out, but did not maintain her progress when the leaders took one another on and she failed to land a blow. (8/1)
689 **Father Dan (IRE)** took a long time to find top gear and when he did the race was all but over. (11/2)
Mock Trial (IRE) attracted plenty of support in the ring but, on unsuitable ground, ran no race at all. (11/2)
689* **Pendolino (IRE)** was on a hat-trick, but the bubble had burst early in the straight and he was soon back-pedalling. (11/2)

839 TOTE LEICESTERSHIRE STKS (Listed) (4-Y.O+) (Class A)

4-05 (4-11) **7f 9y** £10,964.40 (£4,059.60: £1,949.80: £799.00: £319.50: £127.70) Stalls: Low GOING minus 0.02 sec per fur (G)

				SP	RR	SF
	Wizard King (116) (SirMarkPrescott) **6-9-6** GDuffield(6) (bit bkwd: a.p: led over 2f out: rdn & hld on gamely ins fnl f)	—	**1**	7/2 2	124	77
	Polar Prince (IRE) (110) (MAJarvis) **4-8-12** FLynch(2) (bit bkwd: trckd ldrs: ev ch 2f out: r.o nr fin)	½	**2**	9/2 3	115	68
	Ramooz (USA) (106) (BHanbury) **4-8-12** MRimmer(8) (lw: trckd ldrs: rdn 3f out: ev ch 1f out: unable qckn)	s.h	**3**	3/1 1	115	68
678 11	**Russian Music (106)** (MissGayKelleway) **4-8-12b** SSanders(10) (w ldr: rdn over 2f out: sn btn)	7	**4**	9/2 3	99	52
	El Opera (IRE) (96) (PFICole) **4-8-7** OPeslier(9) (hdwy over 1f out: nvr nrr)	1¾	**5**	12/1	90	43
	Miss Riviera (95) (GWragg) **4-8-7** AClark(5) (lw: plld hrd: in tch: rdn 2f out: sn btn)	1	**6**	10/1	88	41
	Sergeyev (IRE) (106) (RHannon) **5-8-12** WJO'Connor(3) (hld up: effrt over 2f out: fnd nil)	s.h	**7**	14/1	93	46
540 8	**Taoiste** (RWArmstrong) **4-8-12** RPrice(1) (lw: led over 4f)	1½	**8**	50/1	89?	42
726 19	**Hello Mister (99)** (TEPowell) **6-8-12** PMcCabe(7) (bit bkwd: a bhd)	1¾	**9**	50/1	85	38
	High Shot (GLewis) **7-8-12** AWhelan(4) (b: bkwd: a bhd: t.o)	21	**10**	20/1	37	—
				(SP 115.7%)	**10 Rn**	

1m 24.7 (2.10) CSF £17.47 TOTE £2.90: £1.20 £2.70 £1.20 (£10.10) Trio £22.00 OWNER Sheikh Ahmed bin Saeed Al Maktoum (NEWMARKET) BRED Sheikh Mohammed bin Rashid al Maktoum

Wizard King, taken to post very quietly after the others, looked just in need of the race but is proven on the ground and this was decisive and, although he was tying up in the last half-furlong, his admirable courage saw him home. (7/2: 5/2-4/1)
Polar Prince (IRE) looks to have done pretty well over the winter, and handled the ground better than might have been expected, although both his previous efforts on the surface came over a mile. A seven-furlong specialist, he can find an opening in Pattern races. (9/2)
Ramooz (USA) raced closer to the pace than he did for most of last season, but could not pick up on this rather dead ground. (3/1)
540* **Russian Music**, who dominated at Warwick in first-time blinkers, could not get to the front and was easily brushed aside. (9/2: op 11/4)
El Opera (IRE) appeared to move well on the ground, but did not get going soon enough and seems better over further. (12/1)
Miss Riviera looked rather too fresh, taking a fearsome hold despite a good early pace, and paying the penalty. (10/1)
Sergeyev (IRE) on softer ground than he had encountered before, settled well enough after the first furlong but his head went up when asked to pick up. (14/1)

840 TOTE CREDIT H'CAP (0-80) (3-Y.O) (Class D)

4-35 (4-37) **1m 8y** £4,123.35 (£1,234.80: £592.90: £271.95) Stalls: Low GOING minus 0.02 sec per fur (G)

				SP	RR	SF
	Kennemara Star (IRE) (70) (JLDunlop) **3-8-11** OPeslier(17) (dwlt: sn prom: led wl over 1f out: rdn out)	—	**1**	6/1 2	80	44
654 5	**Wild Sky (IRE) (75)** (MJHeaton-Ellis) **3-9-2** AClark(11) (lw: hdwy over 2f out: r.o wl fnl f: nt rch wnr)	2½	**2**	5/1 1	80+	44
483 11	**Doc Ryan's (75)** (MJRyan) **3-9-2** GBardwell(18) (bit bkwd: chsd ldrs: one pce appr fnl f)	½	**3**	9/1	79	43
535 7	**Carlton (IRE) (55)** (GLewis) **3-7-10** NAdams(10) (lw: led over 6f: no imp appr fnl f)	1¾	**4**	6/1 2	56	20
	Sun O'Tirol (IRE) (60) (JRArnold) **3-8-1** CRutter(5) (hdwy 2f out: one pce appr fnl f)	2½	**5**	25/1	56	20
	Inclination (72) (MBlanshard) **3-8-13** JQuinn(15) (bit bkwd: hdwy 2f out: nrst fin)	1¾	**6**	12/1	64	28
644 3	**Mardrew (62)** (TTClement) **3-7-12**(5)ow1 ADaly(7) (in tch: rdn 2f out: no imp)	½	**7**	12/1	53	16
654 8	**Puzzlement (67)** (CEBrittain) **3-8-8** MRoberts(1) (prom 5f)	1¾	**8**	7/1 3	55	19
	Euro Superstar (FR) (55) (SDow) **3-7-5**(5) RMullen(14) (lw: chsd ldrs over 5f)	5	**9**	33/1	33	—
	Keepsake (IRE) (62) (MDIUsher) **3-8-3** RStreet(16) (bit bkwd: s.s: nvr nr ldrs)	hd	**10**	20/1	39	3
675 16	**Smart Boy (IRE) (74)** (PFICole) **3-8-8**(7) JBosley(13) (prom 5f: sn rdn & wknd)	5	**11**	16/1	42	6
	Klondike Charger (USA) (70) (BWHills) **3-8-8**(3) JDSmith(19) (sn pushed along: nvr trbld ldrs)	1	**12**	10/1	36	—
	Beau Roberto (62) (MJohnston) **3-8-3** JFanning(3) (bit bkwd: chsd ldrs 4f)	1	**13**	16/1	26	—
	Dulas Bay (55) (MWEasterby) **3-7-10** DWright(8) (s.i.s: a bhd)	1½	**14**	25/1	16	—
341 2	**Jolly Jackson (68)** (RAkehurst) **3-8-9** SSanders(9) (w ldr over 4f: eased whn btn appr fnl f)	½	**15**	10/1	28	—
	Isca Maiden (56) (PHayward) **3-7-6**(5)ow1 AimeeCook(6) (bhd fnl 3f)	5	**16**	50/1	6	—
641 5	**The Green Grey (60)** (WRMuir) **3-7-12**(3) MHenry(2) (spd 4f)	hd	**17**	20/1	9	—
699 9	**Pension Fund (80)** (MWEasterby) **3-9-7** TLucas(4) (lw: w ldrs 5f)	s.h	**18**	14/1	29	—
	Canton Ron (66) (CADwyer) **3-8-7** DRMcCabe(12) (bhd fnl 3f)	6	**19**	16/1	3	—
				(SP 147.7%)	**19 Rn**	

1m 39.7 (4.70) CSF £36.41 CT £278.43 TOTE £6.40: £2.50 £2.10 £2.50 £1.70 (£18.60) Trio £89.90 OWNER Windflower Overseas Holdings Inc (ARUNDEL) BRED Windflower Overseas

LONG HANDICAP Isca Maiden 6-9 Euro Superstar (FR) 7-5

OFFICIAL EXPLANATION **Pension Fund: rider reported that his instructions were to lie handy and and make his way to the middle of the track, and to do his best. He was travelling until halfway, but the gelding was tired when asked for an effort on meeting the rising ground and clearly disliked the soft going. The trainer's representative added that he was disappointed with the run, using different tactics from last time, and that the gelding needed further. He was also later found to be coughing.**

Kennemara Star (IRE), gelded since qualifying for a handicap mark, was well drawn and took full advantage. A half-brother to Dawning Street and Special Dawn, he looks sure to stay ten furlongs. (6/1)
654 **Wild Sky (IRE)**, racing towards the stands' side, was set alight at the two-furlong pole and came well clear of those he was racing with. However, the winner was already clear up the centre and he could not close the gap in time. On this evidence, he looks well worth following. (5/1)
Doc Ryan's did well largely due to a good draw, but looks sure to do better over considerably further. (9/1)
535 **Carlton (IRE)** shaped quite well, but found trying to make all a very taxing task on the dead ground. (6/1: 8/1-12/1)
Sun O'Tirol (IRE) became very disappointing towards the end of last season, and this better effort was probably due to better ground and a good draw. (25/1)
Inclination, a front-runner at two, never got into the race with waiting tactics. She will come on for this and is worth keeping an eye on. (12/1: op 8/1)

644 Mardrew (12/1: 7/1-14/1)
Klondike Charger (USA) (10/1: 6/1-12/1)
341 Jolly Jackson raced prominently towards the stands' side, and was given an easy time of it once his chance had gone. He should not be written off on turf just yet. (10/1)
699 Pension Fund (14/1: 8/1-16/1)

841 REDMILE MAIDEN STKS (I) (3-Y.O+) (Class D)

5-05 (5-06) **1m 1f 218y** £3,572.80 (£1,065.40: £508.20: £229.60) Stalls: Low GOING minus 0.02 sec per fur (G)

				SP	RR	SF
	Tanaasa (IRE) (MRStoute) **3-8-7** OPeslier(12) (lw: a gng wl: led over 1f out: eased nr fin)	—	**1**	$1/3^{1}$	89+	25
	Spartan Royale (CEBrittain) **3-8-7** MRoberts(10) (w'like: scope: trckd ldrs: led over 3f out tl over 1f out: one pce)	1¾	**2**	25/1	86	22
	Machiavelli (HRACecil) **3-8-7** AMcGlone(13) (b: leggy: bit bkwd: chsd ldrs: ev ch over 1f out: r.o)	½	**3**	$6/1^{2}$	85	21
	Thornby Park (JLDunlop) **3-8-2** TSprake(2) (lw: hld up & bhd: rdn 3f out: r.o: nvr rchd ldrs)	2½	**4**	16/1	76	12
	Dancing Queen (IRE) (MBell) **3-8-2** MFenton(6) (s.i.s: hdwy 5f out: nvr rchd ldrs)	6	**5**	14/1	67	3
	Khayali (IRE) (DMorley) **3-8-7** RHills(7) (tall: in tch: lost pl 5f out: styd on fnl 2f)	1½	**6**	$12/1^{3}$	69	5
676^{10}	**Nichol Fifty** (MHTompkins) **3-8-7** DBiggs(15) (bhd: rdn & hdwy 3f out: nvr nr ldrs)	1¾	**7**	33/1	67	3
	Sadler's Blaze (IRE) (PWHarris) **3-8-7** AClark(11) (bit bkwd: in tch 6f)	3½	**8**	33/1	61	—
	Wontcostalotbut (MJWilkinson) **3-8-2** NAdams(14) (neat: bkwd: nvr nr to chal)	hd	**9**	33/1	56	—
	Tramline (MBlanshard) **4-9-10** JQuinn(3) (leggy: hld up: a bhd)	¾	**10**	50/1	60	13
	Media Star (USA) (JHMGosden) **4-9-10** GHind(8) (lengthy: bit bkwd: b.hind: s.i.s: hdwy 7f out: wknd over 3f out)	1½	**11**	16/1	57	10
686^{8}	**London's Heart (USA)** (PFICole) **3-8-2** CRutter(9) (led over 6f)	5	**12**	20/1	44	—
	Aquavita (RHannon) **3-8-4**^{ow2} RPerham(1) (bit bkwd: hdwy 6f out: wknd 4f out)	2½	**13**	25/1	42	—
	Mount Genius (USA) (DJSCosgrove) **4-9-10** MRimmer(4) (w'like: bhd: effrt 4f out: nvr rchd ldrs)	6	**14**	20/1	36	—
	Charcol (JEBanks) **4-9-5** MWigham(16) (a bhd)	13	**15**	50/1	10	—
606^{6}	**Purple Maize** (JAkehurst) **3-8-7** RCochrane(5) (lw: prom 7f)	4	**16**	50/1	8	—
				(SP 147.3%)	**16 Rn**	

2m 11.8 (8.10) CSF £22.49 TOTE £1.50: £1.10 £4.30 £2.60 (£16.00) Trio £39.10 OWNER Maktoum Al Maktoum (NEWMARKET) BRED Gainsborough Stud Management Ltd
WEIGHT FOR AGE 3yo-17lb
Tanaasa (IRE) was not in the least inconvenienced by the ground and was pulling over his rivals from the home turn, although he still showed signs of inexperience when briefly shaken up approaching the final furlong. He looks an interesting prospect. (1/3: op 1/2)
Spartan Royale, whose dam was a modest performer but a half-sister to Cormorant Wood, shaped really well and should win races if he does not fly too high. (25/1)
Machiavelli looked as if he would come on for this, and was in the thick of things all the way up the straight, although rather outclassed by the winner. (6/1: op 3/1)
Thornby Park, a full sister to the stayer Izza, was held up a long way off the pace. Put to work early in the straight, she stayed on all the way to the line. Now qualified for a handicap mark, she will be a very interesting prospect in that grade, particularly over a longer trip.(16/1)
Dancing Queen (IRE), not averse to the odd flash of the tail, missed the break but tried to get into the race early in the straight although the effort could not be sustained. Her trip has yet to be established. (14/1: 6/1-16/1)
Khayali (IRE), a tall, quite eye-catching newcomer, did not take the home turn very well but still shaped with promise. (12/1: 5/1-14/1)
Tramline, sold unraced out of the Cecil yard last year, is bred to stay longer than a double-glazing salesman, and did enough to give hope that he can find a race over a distance of ground. (50/1)
Media Star (USA), a rangy, long-backed half-brother to Park Hill winner Eva Luna, did not show a lot apart from making a brief move on the turn. (16/1)

842 REDMILE MAIDEN STKS (II) (3-Y.O+) (Class D)

5-35 (5-36) **1m 1f 218y** £3,540.95 (£1,055.60: £503.30: £227.15) Stalls: Low GOING minus 0.02 sec per fur (G)

				SP	RR	SF
678^{10}	**Rocky Oasis (USA) (100)** (MRStoute) **4-9-10** OPeslier(16) (lw: trckd ldrs: led over 1f out: rdn out)	—	**1**	$4/5^{1}$	98	48
586^{5}	**Mumaris (USA)** (ACStewart) **3-8-7** RHills(1) (prom: led over 2f out tl over 1f out: r.o wl nr fin)	nk	**2**	$6/1^{3}$	98	31
	King Kato (MrsAJPerrett) **4-9-10** AClark(14) (in tch: rdn & hdwy 4f out: ev ch 2f out: r.o ins fnl f)	1	**3**	$3/1^{2}$	96	46
693^{4}	**Bintang Timor (USA) (82)** (PFICole) **3-8-7** CRutter(2) (chsd ldrs: rdn 3f out: sn btn)	11	**4**	8/1	78	11
699^{4}	**Get The Point (75)** (RHollinshead) **3-8-4**$^{(3)}$ FLynch(15) (lw: prom: led 4f out tl over 2f out: sn btn)	nk	**5**	14/1	78	11
	Sarbaron (IRE) (PWHarris) **3-8-4**$^{(3)}$ DO'Donohoe(8) (tall: unf: bhd: r.o fnl 3f: nvr able to chal)	4	**6**	33/1	71	4
	Nick of Time (JLDunlop) **3-8-2** TSprake(6) (in tch: rdn 3f out: nvr trbld ldrs)	nk	**7**	14/1	66	—
605^{4}	**Urgent Reply (USA)** (CADwyer) **4-9-7**$^{(3)}$ JDSmith(9) (bhd: rdn 5f out: nvr rchd ldrs)	5	**8**	20/1	63	13
605^{6}	**Leatherneck (IRE)** (PMooney) **4-9-7**$^{(3)}$ PMcCabe(13) (s.s: nvr nr ldrs)	12	**9**	25/1	44	—
	Sassy Street (IRE) (RFJohnsonHoughton) **4-9-10** RPerham(4) (lw: led 6f)	2	**10**	50/1	41	—
	Welcome Heights (48) (MJFetherston-Godley) **3-8-7** DHolland(3) (chsd ldrs tl edgd rt & wknd fnl 3f)	10	**11**	25/1	25	—
686^{7}	**Needwood Legend** (BCMorgan) **4-9-10** DHarrison(10) (bit bkwd: in tch 6f)	7	**12**	50/1	13	—
586^{17}	**Gold Clipper** (MJRyan) **3-8-7** NDay(12) (chsd ldrs 5f)	18	**13**	33/1	—	—
	Glowing Moon (MissGayKelleway) **4-9-5** WJO'Connor(11) (tall: scope: bit bkwd: s.i.s: hdwy 6f out: wknd 4f out)	8	**14**	20/1	—	—
686^{6}	**Mr Montague (IRE)** (TWDonnelly) **5-9-10** JQuinn(7) (pushed along 6f out: sn bhd: t.o fnl 3f)	7	**15**	50/1	—	—
683^{19}	**Ratb** (SDow) **3-8-2**$^{(5)}$ ADaly(5) (s.i.s: bhd tl stumbled & p.u 1f out)		**P**	33/1	—	—
				(SP 151.2%)	**16 Rn**	

2m 10.9 (7.20) CSF £7.15 TOTE £1.80: £1.40 £1.80 £1.80 (£7.70) OWNER Maktoum Al Maktoum (NEWMARKET) BRED Gainsborough Farm Inc.
WEIGHT FOR AGE 3yo-17lb
Rocky Oasis (USA) might have been expected to outclass these, but was forced to struggle to lose his maiden tag. (4/5: 2/7-5/6)
586 Mumaris (USA) gave the favourite quite a fright and was coming back for more near the line. He is clearly useful but getting him a winning handicap mark will be all the harder after this. (6/1: tchd 10/1)
King Kato has grown into a tall, attractive gelding and certainly has ability. Now qualified for handicaps, he will find himself towards the top of the weights. (3/1: op 5/1)
693 Bintang Timor (USA) moved to post much more freely on this easier surface, but whether he gets this trip is open to doubt. (8/1)
699 Get The Point lacks the scope of those who beat him and seems very one-paced. (14/1)
Sarbaron (IRE) is not guaranteed to stay on pedigree, but was ridden to get the trip and came home quite well. (33/1)

Nick of Time is well worth bearing in mind when she steps up in trip, as she travelled pleasingly until short of pace when the tempo picked up. (14/1)
Leatherneck (IRE), a gelding by Sadler's Wells out of an unraced daughter of Lupe, lost a lot of ground at the start but was noted running on respectably in the last couple of furlongs without being knocked about. (25/1)

T/Plpt: £1,370.50 (10.88 Tckts). T/Qdpt: £117.00 (5.92 Tckts) IM/Dk

0697-RIPON (R-H) (Good)
Saturday April 26th
WEATHER: overcast WIND: almost nil

843 YORKSHIRE IMPERIAL BAND (S) STKS (3-Y.O+) (Class F)
2-05 (2-06) **1m 2f** £2,790.00 (£785.00: £384.00) Stalls: High GOING: 0.06 sec per fur (G)

				SP	RR	SF
635[5]	**Ten Past Six (57)** (MartynWane) **5-9-10** JCarroll(5) (mde most: kpt on wl fnl 3f)	—	**1**	5/1[2]	65	46
461[16]	**Action Jackson (50)** (BJMcMath) **5-9-10** JTate(13) (chsd ldr: rdn 3f out: kpt on same pce)	5	**2**	6/1[3]	57	38
687[6]	**Yuppy Girl (IRE) (43)** (CaptJWilson) **4-9-5v** JWeaver(6) (bhd: hdwy on outside 3f out: nrst fin)	3½	**3**	15/2	46	27
580[8]	**Durgams First (IRE) (58)** (MrsMReveley) **5-9-10** ACulhane(10) (lw: in tch: rdn 3f out: kpt on fnl f)	¾	**4**	6/1[3]	50	31
579[5]	**Northern Fan (IRE) (55)** (NTinkler) **5-10-0** DeanMcKeown(4) (a chsng ldrs: effrt over 3f out: r.o one pce)	3	**5**	9/1	49	30
570[9]	**Philgem (20)** (CWFairhurst) **4-9-5** NKennedy(9) (lw: bhd: effrt 4f out: nvr trbld ldrs)	4	**6**	100/1	34	15
526[14]	**Tajar (USA) (32)** (MDods) **5-9-10b** DaleGibson(12) (sme hdwy 4f out: n.d)	2½	**7**	33/1	35	16
	Safa Dancer (29) (BAMcMahon) **4-8-12**(7) SRighton(2) (chsd ldrs tl wknd fnl 3f)	1	**8**	100/1	28	9
	She's Simply Great (IRE) (51) (JJO'Neill) **4-9-5** WRyan(7) (b: in tch: effrt 4f out: wknd over 2f out)	2	**9**	5/1[2]	25	6
	Finsbury Flyer (IRE) (73) (RJHodges) **4-9-5**(5) PPMurphy(11) (prom: rdn over 3f out: sn wknd)	6	**10**	9/4[1]	21	2
729[8]	**Clean Swop (IRE)** (TDEasterby) **3-8-7** LCharnock(8) (bit bkwd: a bhd)	9	**11**	66/1	6	—
	Astrolabe (70) (JMBradley) **5-9-10b** JFEgan(1) (b: w wnr tl wknd fnl 3½f)	1¾	**12**	14/1	3	—
550[10]	**Incantrice** (WStorey) **4-9-5** JFanning(3) (rn wd st: a bhd)	1¾	**13**	100/1	—	—

(SP 128.5%) **13 Rn**

2m 11.7 (8.20) CSF £34.48 TOTE £7.40: £2.00 £2.20 £2.10 (£32.20) Trio £46.40 OWNER James S Kennerley and Miss Jenny Hall (RICHMOND) BRED T. D. Holland-Martin
WEIGHT FOR AGE 3yo-17lb
Bt in 6,400 gns
OFFICIAL EXPLANATION **Incantrice: had gurgled during the race.**
635 Ten Past Six is a funny customer, but showed here that when things go his way he is quite useful. (5/1)
Action Jackson, up with the pace as he likes to be, proved short of any change of speed in the last half-mile. (6/1)
687 Yuppy Girl (IRE) has failed to win a race after twenty-two starts, but she made useful ground in the straight to show she still retains some ability. (15/2: 8/1-12/1)
580 Durgams First (IRE) ran reasonably and, over further, he should find a similar race. (6/1)
579 Northern Fan (IRE) has done all his winning on the All-Weather and over shorter trips. (9/1)
Philgem was always finding this trip on the sharp side. (100/1)
Finsbury Flyer (IRE) looked fit enough but ran poorly, dropping tamely away in the last half-mile. (9/4)

81 77 78 82

844 YORKSHIRE TOURIST BOARD NOVICE AUCTION STKS (2-Y.O F) (Class E)
2-35 (2-40) **5f** £2,830.25 (£857.00: £418.50: £199.25) Stalls: Low GOING: Not Established

				SP	RR	SF
472*	**Lady Moll** (RBoss) **2-8-6** JCarroll(7) (mde all: jst hld on)	—	**1**	5/2[2]	77	40
611*	**Filey Brigg** (WTKemp) **2-7-11**(7)ow1 KSked(3) (chsd ldrs: nt clr run over 1f out: swtchd: styd on wl towards fin)	hd	**2**	8/1	75	37
682[3]	**Going Places** (KTIvory) **2-7-10**(3) MartinDwyer(4) (lw: hmpd after s: cl up: rdn 2f out: hung rt: nt qckn ins fnl f)	½	**3**	11/8[1]	68	31
	Petite Lady (PDEvans) **2-8-0**ow1 JFEgan(1) (lt-f: unf: chsd ldrs 3f: wknd)	8	**4**	12/1	44	6
	Golden Mirage (IRE) (MRChannon) **2-8-0**(5)ow3 PPMurphy(8) (leggy: scope: s.i.s: hdwy ½-wy: wknd over 1f out)	1¾	**5**	9/1	43	3
525[3]	**Flower O'Cannie (IRE)** (MWEasterby) **2-8-3**(5) GParkin(5) (sn outpcd)	s.h	**6**	13/2[3]	46	9
	Sylvan Cloud (CWFairhurst) **2-7-13** LCharnock(2) (neat: bit bkwd: s.i.s: n.d)	¾	**7**	50/1	34	—
	Sharp Pet (DMcCain) **2-7-13**(3) MBaird(6) (unf: s.i.s: a outpcd & wl bhd)	19	**8**	25/1	—	—

(SP 118.6%) **8 Rn**

61.0 secs (3.20) CSF £21.75 TOTE £2.80: £1.10 £2.40 £1.10 (£9.70) OWNER Ms Lynn Bell (NEWMARKET) BRED Longdon Stud Ltd
472* Lady Moll had the early pace to get the favoured stands' rails, and the line came just in time. (5/2)
611* Filey Brigg would have won this with any luck and seems to be improving. (8/1)
682 Going Places gave problems before the start and also during the race when hanging for most of the trip, and obviously has more ability then she cared to show here. (11/8)
Petite Lady has not much to recommend her on looks and, after showing early pace, she was left struggling soon after halfway. (12/1: 10/1-16/1)
Golden Mirage (IRE) never got into this, but looks the type to do better given time. (9/1: op 5/1)
525 Flower O'Cannie (IRE) failed to impress on looks and ran moderately. (13/2)

845 YORKSHIRE-TYNE TEES TELEVISION H'CAP (0-80) (3-Y.O) (Class D)
3-05 (3-10) **6f** £3,663.75 (£1,110.00: £542.50: £258.75) Stalls: Low GOING: 0.06 sec per fur (G)

				SP	RR	SF
	Denton Lad (64) (JWWatts) **3-8-10** NConnorton(2) (chsd ldrs: r.o to ld wl ins fnl f)	—	**1**	14/1	77	45
649[2]	**Always Alight (60)** (KRBurke) **3-8-6b** JFEgan(13) (dwlt: gd hdwy 2½f out: ev ch over 1f out: kpt on)	½	**2**	12/1	72	40
535[9]	**Swift (55)** (MJPolglase) **3-8-1** LCharnock(3) (led tl ct wl ins fnl f)	nk	**3**	14/1	66	34
610[2]	**Return of Amin (68)** (JDBethell) **3-8-11**(3) MartinDwyer(18) (lw: hdwy to ld far side over 2f out: veered lft: no imp)	5	**4**	7/2[1]	66	34
652[5]	**C-Harry (IRE) (65)** (RHollinshead) **3-8-11** ACulhane(12) (s.i.s: hdwy ½-wy: nvr rchd ldrs)	1¾	**5**	14/1	58	26
729[4]	**Supercharmer (65)** (DNicholls) **3-8-11** AlexGreaves(1) (chsd ldrs tl grad wknd appr fnl f)	5	**6**	9/1[3]	45	13
685[7]	**Express Girl (67)** (DMoffatt) **3-8-10**(3) DarrenMoffatt(6) (nvr trbld ldrs)	½	**7**	12/1	45	13
649[9]	**William's Well (51)** (MWEasterby) **3-7-11**ow1 DaleGibson(16) (spd far side over 3f)	1¼	**8**	25/1	26	—

				SP	RR	SF
259*	**Royal Cascade (IRE) (62)** (BAMcMahon) **3-8-8** LNewton(11) (swtchd far side after 1f: outpcd fr ½-wy)	2	**9**	14/1	32	—
602*	**Levelled (70)** (MRChannon) **3-8-11**(5) PPMurphy(9) (nvr nr to chal)	1¼	**10**	20/1	36	4
	Gipsy Princess (67) (MWEasterby) **3-8-8**(5) GParkin(7) (bit bkwd: chsd ldrs over 3f)	nk	**11**	20/1	32	—
503[6]	**Gablesea (64)** (BPJBaugh) **3-8-10** NCarlisle(10) (dwlt: a bhd)	3	**12**	16/1	21	—
634[3]	**Wagga Moon (IRE) (65)** (JJO'Neill) **3-8-11** WRyan(15) (racd far side: hdwy ½-wy: eased whn no ch fnl 1½f)	hd	**13**	16/1	22	—
588*	**Mon Bruce (72)** (WRMuir) **3-9-4** JWeaver(17) (lw: led far side 3½f: wknd)	hd	**14**	16/1	29	—
469[4]	**Splashed (62)** (TDBarron) **3-8-8** JCarroll(4) (chsd ldrs 4f: wknd)	2½	**15**	20/1	12	—
694[11]	**Rude Awakening (75)** (CWFairhurst) **3-9-7** DeanMcKeown(5) (prom over 3f)	2	**16**	16/1	20	—
685[8]	**Bold Gayle (59)** (MrsJRRamsden) **3-8-5** GCarter(14) (racd far side: a bhd)	4	**17**	11/1	—	—
413*	**Double-O (73)** (WJarvis) **3-9-5** OUrbina(8) (lw: a rr div)	½	**18**	9/2[2]	6	—
				(SP 142.4%)	**18 Rn**	

1m 14.3 (3.80) CSF £171.80 CT £2,303.09 TOTE £17.20: £2.90 £2.70 £4.30 £1.50 (£153.30) Trio £595.50; £419.40 to Pontefract 28/4/97
OWNER Mrs M. Irwin (RICHMOND) BRED Al Dahlawi Stud Co Ltd
OFFICIAL EXPLANATION **Supercharmer: hung badly right during the race.**
Denton Lad had a good draw and won without being knocked about, and would seem to be improving. (14/1)
649 Always Alight put in a really good effort here from a poor draw and a slow start, and if he gets it fully together there is certainly a race or two to be found. (12/1)
368* Swift had the speed to take the favoured stands' rails, but this moderate mover was outbattled late on. (14/1)
610 Return of Amin raced up the far side but, when leading that group, all he wanted to do was hang left and he finished up on the stands' side, making this a reasonable effort in the circumstances. (7/2)
652 C-Harry (IRE), after a poor start, only got going when the race was over. (14/1)
Express Girl likes plenty of give in the ground and is showing signs of coming back to form. (12/1)

846 C.B. HUTCHINSON MEMORIAL CHALLENGE CUP H'CAP (0-90) (4-Y.O+) (Class C)
3-40 (3-41) **2m** £6,287.50 (£1,900.00: £925.00: £437.50) Stalls: Low GOING: 0.06 sec per fur (G)

				SP	RR	SF
669[4]	**Here Comes Herbie (51)** (WStorey) **5-7-10**(5) PFessey(6) (trckd ldrs: qcknd to ld over 3f out: hld on wl)	—	**1**	9/1	64	37
612*	**Turnpole (IRE) (67)** (MrsMReveley) **6-9-3** ACulhane(3) (trckd ldrs: smooth hdwy to chal over 2f out: rdn over 1f out: nt qckn towards fin)	hd	**2**	7/2[2]	80	53
510[2]	**Siege Perilous (IRE) (68)** (SCWilliams) **4-8-11**(3) MartinDwyer(8) (lw: hld up: effrt 4f out: styd on: no imp)	10	**3**	100/30[1]	71	40
470[6]	**Dirab (73)** (TDBarron) **4-9-5** WRyan(9) (hld up & bhd: hdwy 3f out: nvr nr to chal)	6	**4**	6/1	70	39
	Jubran (USA) (52) (JLEyre) **11-8-2** TWilliams(1) (led tl hdd & wknd over 3f out)	12	**5**	40/1	37	10
	Berlin Blue (82) (JWWatts) **4-10-0** JCarroll(5) (trckd ldrs: effrt 3f out: wknd 2f out)	½	**6**	6/1	66	35
	Alwarqa (61) (MissJBower) **4-8-7** KHodgson(4) (bhd: drvn along over 4f out: sn no ch)	dist	**7**	20/1	—	—
	Highflying (76) (GMMoore) **11-9-12** JTate(7) (chsd ldrs tl wknd fnl 3½f)	3	**8**	20/1	—	—
465[2]	**La Brief (58)** (MJRyan) **5-8-8** GCarter(2) (lw: chsd ldrs: 4th & btn whn p.u lame ent fnl f)		**P**	9/2[3]	—	—
				(SP 114.0%)	**9 Rn**	

3m 36.0 (11.00) CSF £35.54 CT £116.09 TOTE £8.90: £1.30 £1.50 £1.40 (£19.90) Trio £17.30 OWNER Mr H. S. Hutchinson (CONSETT) BRED H. Hutchinson
WEIGHT FOR AGE 4yo-4lb
OFFICIAL EXPLANATION **Here Comes Herbie: regarding the improved form, the rider reported that the gelding is better suited to carrying smaller weights in better-class races.**
669 Here Comes Herbie again failed to impress on looks, but he is not all that big and seems better suited by receiving weight from better opposition such as this. (9/1)
612* Turnpole (IRE) improved going well early in the straight looking a question of when and how far but, in the end, he was outbattled. (7/2)
510 Siege Perilous (IRE) is looking and running well just now and, provided the ground remains on the easy side, he could well pick up a race before long. (100/30)
470 Dirab, given plenty to do, failed to land a blow and will find his mark in due course. (6/1: op 4/1)
Jubran (USA) has changed stables, and this step up in trip did not entirely seem to suit. (40/1)
Berlin Blue looked big and well, but ran as though this was needed. (6/1)

847 YORKSHIRE DALES MAIDEN STKS (3-Y.O) (Class D)
4-15 (4-16) **1m 2f** £3,550.00 (£1,075.00: £525.00: £250.00) Stalls: High GOING: 0.06 sec per fur (G)

				SP	RR	SF
528[3]	**Lawahik** (DMorley) **3-9-0** GCarter(6) (lw: trckd ldrs: led 2½f out: r.o wl appr fnl f)	—	**1**	5/1[3]	95+	42
	Double Alleged (USA) (MJohnston) **3-9-0** JWeaver(7) (b: led tl hdd 2½f out: kpt on same pce)	5	**2**	5/1[3]	87	34
503[3]	**Banbury (USA)** (JWWatts) **3-9-0** JCarroll(1) (lw: hld up: effrt 4f out: hdwy 3f out: styd on: nvr able to chal)	1½	**3**	100/30[2]	85	32
741[10]	**Out of Sight (IRE) (82)** (BAMcMahon) **3-9-0** LNewton(5) (prom: effrt 4f out: rdn & r.o one pce)	5	**4**	33/1	77	24
676[3]	**Monitor** (HRACecil) **3-9-0** WRyan(3) (lw: trckd ldrs: effrt 3f out: rdn & btn over 1f out)	1¾	**5**	6/5[1]	74	21
	Savu Sea (IRE) (CFWall) **3-8-9** ACulhane(2) (w'like: lengthy: scope: outpcd & bhd appr st: n.d)	12	**6**	40/1	50	—
	Tonight's Prize (IRE) (CFWall) **3-9-0** NCarlisle(4) (neat: bit bkwd: prom to st: sn outpcd & bhd)	5	**7**	40/1	47	—
	Bahr Alsalaam (USA) (JHMGosden) **3-8-9** AGarth(9) (leggy: scope: bit bkwd: prom tl outpcd 4f out: sn btn)	9	**8**	25/1	27	—
	Fatal Sahra (IRE) (JHMGosden) **3-9-0** DaleGibson(8) (bit bkwd: outpcd & lost tch appr st: n.d after)	6	**9**	25/1	23	—
				(SP 117.4%)	**9 Rn**	

2m 11.0 (7.50) CSF £25.94 TOTE £6.00: £1.60 £1.80 £1.70 (£19.70) Trio £31.20 OWNER Mr Hamdan Al Maktoum (NEWMARKET) BRED Olympic Bloodstock Ltd and Partners
528 Lawahik, dropping back in trip, got stronger as the race progressed, and fairly sprinted away in the closing stages to show he is improving. (5/1)
Double Alleged (USA) does not have the best of front legs, but he ran well here and looks likely to stay further. (5/1)
503 Banbury (USA) was stepping up in trip and wearing a tongue-strap, but proved a shade disappointing. (100/30: 7/4-7/2)
Out of Sight (IRE) had the experience but little else to recommend him, and ran quite well without getting in a blow. (33/1)
676 Monitor was most disappointing here, failing to pick up when the pace was on, and something would appear to be wrong with him. (6/5)

848 BBC RADIO YORK PRO-AM LADIES' H'CAP (0-70) (3-Y.O+) (Class E)
4-50 (4-53) **1m** £2,986.25 (£905.00: £442.50: £211.25) Stalls: High GOING: 0.06 sec per fur (G)

				SP	RR	SF
444[20]	**Knobbleeneeze (65)** (MRChannon) **7-11-0v** CandyMorris(19) (trckd ldrs: led 5f out: r.o wl fnl 2f)	—	**1**	14/1	84	66
	Marjaana (IRE) (62) (PTWalwyn) **4-10-6**(5) MissSSamworth(17) (led tl hdd 5f out: ev ch tl outpcd fnl 2f)	6	**2**	16/1	69•	51
668[2]	**Bedazzle (38)** (MBrittain) **6-9-1** JoHunnam(8) (lw: styd on wl fnl 3f: nrst fin)	1¼	**3**	11/1	43	25

				SP	RR	SF
	Abtaal (49) (RJHodges) **7-9-7**(5) MrsCWilliams(5) (a chsng ldrs: chal over 3f out: outpcd fnl 2f)	½	**4**	50/1	53	35
687[10]	**Sheraz (IRE) (42)** (NTinkler) **5-9-5b** KimTinkler(1) (in tch: effrt 3f out: styd on: no imp)	hd	**5**	33/1	45	27
401[5]	**Bellas Gate Boy (50)** (JPearce) **5-9-13** MrsLPearce(2) (bhd: hdwy 3f out: nrst fin)	½	**6**	20/1	52	34
763[3]	**Squared Away (47)** (JWPayne) **5-9-5b**(5) MissCLake(3) (lw: bhd tl r.o fnl 3f)	1¾	**7**	16/1	46	28
	Habeta (USA) (41) (JWWatts) **11-8-13**(5) MissERamsden(20) (hld up: effrt 4f out: styd on: n.d)	½	**8**	25/1	39	21
687[11]	**Asterix (40)** (JMBradley) **9-9-3b** KimberleyHart(15) (b: hdwy u.p 4f out: nvr rchd ldrs)	1¼	**9**	20/1	35	17
587[3]	**Return To Brighton (39)** (JMBradley) **5-9-2** AngelaGallimore(9) (nvr trbld ldrs)	½	**10**	10/1 [3]	33	15
733[8]	**Euro Sceptic (IRE) (50)** (TDEasterby) **5-9-13b** VictoriaAppleby(16) (trckd ldrs: effrt 4f out: wknd fnl 2½f)	¾	**11**	9/1 [2]	43	25
490[8]	**Eastleigh (35)** (RHollinshead) **8-8-7**(5) LisaWatson(11) (b.nr hind: bhd: c wd st: n.d)	½	**12**	16/1	27	9
733[2]	**Dispol Gem (61)** (PCalver) **4-10-10** MissDianaJones(6) (lw: in tch: rdn ½-wy: sn btn)	2	**13**	9/1 [2]	49	31
	Jungle Fresh (55) (JDBethell) **4-10-4** MissEJohnsonHoughton(14) (cl up tl wknd fnl 4f)	2½	**14**	100/1	38	20
99[9]	**Appearance Money (IRE) (35)** (FMurphy) **6-8-7**(5) JennyBenson(18) (hld up & bhd: n.d)	1¼	**15**	33/1	15	—
733*	**Paint It Black (58)** (DNicholls) **4-10-7** AlexGreaves(13) (cl up tl lost pl fnl 4f)	hd	**16**	Evens [1]	38	20
587[8]	**Shouldbegrey (44)** (WRMuir) **4-9-7** SophieMitchell(12) (prom over 4f: sn wknd)	1	**17**	25/1	22	4
721[8]	**High Low (USA) (50)** (MDHammond) **9-9-8**(5) MissAJSmith(7) (a bhd)	5	**18**	50/1	18	—
554[3]	**Charlton Imp (USA) (54)** (RJHodges) **4-10-3** AmandaSanders(10) (cl up: effrt ½-wy: sn lost pl)	2½	**19**	20/1	17	—
423[9]	**Katie Komaite (39)** (CaptJWilson) **4-8-11**(5) AngelaHartley(4) (Withdrawn not under Starter's orders: ref to ent stalls)		**W**	50/1	—	—

(SP 146.5%) **19 Rn**

1m 44.4 (6.20) CSF £212.15 CT £2,446.01 TOTE £15.30: £2.40 £6.40 £1.80 £26.40 (£131.30) Trio £436.90; £498.47 to Pontefract 28/4/97 OWNER Mr Anthony Andrews (UPPER LAMBOURN) BRED A. and Mrs Andrews

OFFICIAL EXPLANATION **Paint It Black: was unable to dominate the race on this slower surface.**

Knobbleeneeze, given a smashing ride, stuck to the rails like glue, saving lengths, and won most emphatically. (14/1)

Marjaana (IRE) contested the lead but gave ground away on the home turn, and then lacked pace in the last couple of furlongs. (16/1)

668 Bedazzle, from a yard going well, made up heaps of ground in the straight to show he is in good form. (11/1: 8/1-12/1)

Abtaal had his chances, but looked very one-paced in the last two furlongs. (50/1)

526 Sheraz (IRE) has the ability but does not often put it to full use. (33/1)

401 Bellas Gate Boy, given a lot to do, did pretty well to finish so close. (20/1)

763 Squared Away, as usual, did all his running late on but never soon enough to have any chance. (16/1)

849 YORKSHIRE CANCER RESEARCH CAMPAIGN CONDITIONS STKS (4-Y.O+) (Class C)

5-20 (5-20) **1m 4f 60y** £4,563.54 (£1,664.04: £813.52: £349.60: £156.30) Stalls: High GOING: 0.06 sec per fur (G)

				SP	RR	SF
	Harbour Dues (99) (LadyHerries) **4-9-1** WRyan(5) (chsd ldr: led over 3f out: styd on u.p)	—	**1**	5/4 [1]	106	36
	Star Selection (98) (JMackie) **6-8-12** JWeaver(3) (lw: hld up: hdwy ent st: brought wd & racd alone stands' side: ev ch over 2f out: styd on)	¾	**2**	6/1	101	32
	Greenstead (USA) (99) (JHMGosden) **4-9-1** JCarroll(4) (hld up: effrt ent st: rdn to chse ldrs 3f out: sn outpcd)	17	**3**	3/1 [2]	83	13
	Kailey Senor (USA) (RWArmstrong) **4-8-11** GCarter(2) (outpcd appr st: wl bhd after)	12	**4**	9/1	63?	—
625a[7]	**Legal Right (USA) (100)** (PWChapple-Hyam) **4-8-12b**[1](3) RHavlin(1) (lw: led & sn wl clr: rdn ent st: hdd over 3f out: sn btn: t.o)	dist	**5**	5/1 [3]	—	—

(SP 110.4%) **5 Rn**

2m 43.9 (10.40) CSF £8.36 TOTE £2.10: £1.20 £2.00 (£4.10) OWNER Hesmonds Stud (LITTLEHAMPTON) BRED Hesmonds Stud Ltd

WEIGHT FOR AGE 4yo-1lb

Harbour Dues is a useful performer, but he had to battle all the way here and will certainly know he has been in a race. (5/4)

Star Selection has improved tremendously over hurdles and has obviously carried that on and, if the ground remains on the soft side, there could be a decent race to be picked up. (6/1)

Greenstead (USA) is an edgy individual who found the effort required here all too much in the last three furlongs. (3/1)

Kailey Senor (USA), a French import, showed little here. (9/1: op 6/1)

625a Legal Right (USA) had the blinkers on for the first time and went off like a scalded cat but, ridden turning for home, he soon decided he wanted none of it. (5/1)

T/Plpt: £330.40 (41.71 Tckts). T/Qdpt: £45.40 (14.9 Tckts) AA

0828-SANDOWN (R-H) (Rnd crse Good to soft, 5f crse Good)

Saturday April 26th

Race 4 hand-timed. Other races under Rules of National Hunt Racing

WEATHER: overcast & damp WIND: almost nil

83 82 79+ 73

850 PIZZA HUT MAIDEN STKS (2-Y.O C & G) (Class D)

2-15 (2-17) **5f 6y** £3,571.00 (£1,078.00: £524.00: £247.00) Stalls: High GOING: 0.22 sec per fur (G)

				SP	RR	SF
557[5]	**Smooth Sailing** (KMcAuliffe) **2-8-11** JFortune(3) (a.p: rdn & carried lft over 1f out: hung rt & led ins fnl f: drvn out)	—	**1**	20/1	78	25
	Ron's Pet (RHannon) **2-8-11** RHughes(5) (leggy: scope: lw: hld up: led over 1f out: hung lft: hdd ins fnl f: carried rt: r.o)	nk	**2**	9/1	77	24
697[3]	**Prose (IRE)** (RHannon) **2-8-11** DaneO'Neill(1) (hdwy over 2f out: hrd rdn over 1f out: unable qckn)	1¾	**3**	4/1 [2]	72	19
695[5]	**Emperor Naheem (IRE)** (BJMeehan) **2-8-11** PatEddery(10) (led over 3f: hung lft: 3rd & btn whn hmpd ins fnl f)	1¾	**4**	100/30 [1]	66	13
	Alpen Wolf (IRE) (WRMuir) **2-8-11** JReid(6) (bit bkwd: a.p: rdn over 2f out: one pce)	1	**5**	14/1	63	10
	Swoosh (BJMeehan) **2-8-11** BDoyle(2) (w'like: bkwd: outpcd: nvr nrr)	1¾	**6**	25/1	57	4
	Hoh Justice (IABalding) **2-8-11** LDettori(4) (neat: bit bkwd: bhd fnl 2f)	1¾	**7**	4/1 [2]	52	—
	Batswing (MartynMeade) **2-8-11** KFallon(7) (neat: bhd fnl 3f)	nk	**8**	8/1 [3]	51	—
	Oisin (IRE) (MrsPNDutfield) **2-8-11** TQuinn(8) (neat: s.s: a bhd)	2½	**9**	50/1	43	—
	Basic Style (NACallaghan) **2-8-11** PaulEddery(9) (neat: bkwd: s.s: a bhd)	½	**10**	14/1	41	—

(SP 108.1%) **10 Rn**

65.16 secs (5.36) CSF £154.73 TOTE £17.40: £2.80 £2.20 £1.70 (£67.30) Trio £44.80 OWNER Mr A. R. Parrish (LAMBOURN) BRED C. R. Black

STEWARDS' ENQUIRY Obj. to Smooth Sailing by Hughes overruled.
557 Smooth Sailing, who suffered sore shins after his debut at Leicester, was carried left by the leader below the distance and then hung right himself as he came through to lead inside the final furlong. In a driving finish, he just held on to give his trainer his first winner of the season. (20/1)
Ron's Pet, quite a tall individual who cost 16,500 guineas as a yearling, has the scope to develop and looked in very good shape for this debut. Leading below the distance, he hung left but he was then carried right by the winner as he was headed inside the final furlong, and only just lost out. He should have no problems finding a race. (9/1: 6/1-10/1)
697 Prose (IRE), with experience on his side, took closer order at halfway but failed to quicken from below the distance. (4/1)
695 Emperor Naheem (IRE), with plenty of strength about him, had the best draw of all and took the field along against the favoured far rails. However, he drifted into the centre of the course and was headed below the distance and was held when tightened up for room inside the final furlong. (100/30: 2/1-7/2)
Alpen Wolf (IRE), a dipped-backed half-brother to numerous winners, looked big and well for this initial outing but, after racing up with the pace, failed to quicken in the second half of the race. (14/1: 10/1-16/1)
Swoosh was carrying plenty of condition for this debut and could never get into the argument. (25/1)
Hoh Justice (4/1: 3/1-9/2)
Basic Style (14/1: 8/1-16/1)

851 THRESHER CLASSIC TRIAL STKS (Gp 3) (3-Y.O) (Class A)

4-10 (4-16) **1m 2f 7y** £40,194.00 (£15,130.20: £7,340.10: £3,275.70) Stalls: High GOING: 0.22 sec per fur (G)

			SP	RR	SF
Voyagers Quest (USA) (PWChapple-Hyam) **3-8-12** JReid(4) (lw: chsd ldr: led over 2f out: rdn out)	—	1	11/2	125	67
Benny The Dip (USA) (113) (JHMGosden) **3-9-0** LDettori(5) (led over 7f: rdn: unable qckn ins fnl f)	1½	2	13/8[1]	125	67
Silver Patriarch (IRE) (104) (JLDunlop) **3-8-10** PatEddery(2) (bit bkwd: hld up: rdn over 3f out: edgd rt over 2f out: r.o wl ins fnl f)	hd	3	9/2[3]	120	62
Yavlensky (IRE) (JLDunlop) **3-8-10** TQuinn(1) (hdwy on ins over 4f out: wkng whn nt clr run over 2f out)	12	4	16/1	101	43
Further Outlook (USA) (102) (MrsAJPerrett) **3-8-10** MHills(3) (bit bkwd: hld up: rdn over 2f out: sn wknd)	4	5	20/1	95	37
Besiege (111) (HRACecil) **3-8-10** KFallon(6) (lw: hld up: rdn over 3f out: wknd over 2f out)	14	6	5/2[2]	73	15
			(SP 110.9%)		**6 Rn**

2m 12.54 (5.84) CSF £13.25 TOTE £7.10: £3.10 £1.40 (£6.30) OWNER Mr R. E. Sangster (MARLBOROUGH) BRED Gulf States Racing Stables II
Voyagers Quest (USA) has done really well over the winter and looked in tremendous shape in the paddock. Sent on over a quarter-of-a-mile from home, he was ridden along to put the runner-up in his place inside the final furlong. He looks a decent performer and will now head for the Prix Lupin at Longchamp before having a crack at the French Derby. (11/2: 4/1-6/1)
Benny The Dip (USA) did not impress in his coat and will come on for the run according to his trainer, but that did not stop him running a fine race. Bowling along in front, he was collared over a quarter-of-a-mile from home but, refusing to give way, was only put in his place in the last one hundred yards. He looks set for a very rewarding campaign with the Dante Stakes at York his next target. (13/8)
Silver Patriarch (IRE) found this trip far too sharp - he won twice over it last year - but, despite this and needing the run, he ran a tremendous race, running on really strongly up the hill and only just failing to take second prize. A mile-and-a-half should really bring out the best in him, and he will now head for the Lingfield Derby Trial. He looks a very useful prospect. (9/2: 7/1-4/1)
Yavlensky (IRE) has not grown much since last year. Picking up ground rounding the home turn, he was in trouble when tightened up over two furlongs from home. He will find life tough in this company in this country, and his trainer may well look for easier pickings abroad. (16/1)
Further Outlook (USA), trained by Michael Stoute last year, was sold for 160,000 guineas at the Newmarket Autumn Sales. Quite a tall individual, he has not filled out since last year and looked as though this run was just needed, eventually calling it a day a quarter-of-a-mile from home. He is probably not quite up to this class and may be difficult to place this season. (20/1)
Besiege looked very well in the paddock, but was a bitter disappointment and was the first beaten. He demonstrated last year that he does not do things quickly, and it may well be that he is not as good as was first thought. (5/2: op 6/4)

852 DAVID LLOYD LEISURE GORDON RICHARDS STKS (Gp 3) (4-Y.O+) (Class A)

4-45 (4-47) **1m 2f 7y** £19,110.00 (£7,233.00: £3,541.50: £1,615.50) Stalls: High GOING: 0.22 sec per fur (G)

				SP	RR	SF
	Sasuru (110) (GWragg) **4-9-1** MHills(2) (b: lw: a gng wl: stdy hdwy 2f out: led on bit over 1f out: qcknd ins fnl f: comf)	—	1	13/2[3]	125+	66
	Multicoloured (IRE) (102) (MRStoute) **4-8-10** JReid(6) (chsd ldr: led 7f out tl over 1f out: unable qckn)	2½	2	11/2[2]	116	57
678*	**Ali-Royal (IRE) (112)** (HRACecil) **4-8-13** KFallon(5) (swtg: hld up: rdn over 2f out: ev ch over 1f out: one pce)	hd	3	15/8[1]	119	60
	Tamure (IRE) (JHMGosden) **5-8-10** LDettori(1) (lost pl over 3f out: rallied over 1f out: r.o wl ins fnl f)	s.h	4	11/2[2]	116	57
	Bequeath (112) (HRACecil) **5-8-10** JLowe(7) (b: lw: hld up: rdn over 2f out: wknd wl over 1f out)	3½	5	12/1	110	51
627a[2]	**Needle Gun (IRE) (115)** (CEBrittain) **7-9-1** BDoyle(4) (led 3f: wknd 2f out)	¾	6	11/2[2]	114	55
678[8]	**Restructure (IRE) (114)** (MrsJCecil) **5-8-13** PaulEddery(3) (prom over 6f)	2	7	16/1	109	50
				(SP 107.8%)		**7 Rn**

2m 13.08 (6.38) CSF £33.41 TOTE £7.20: £2.80 £2.20 (£20.20) OWNER Mr A. E. Oppenheimer (NEWMARKET) BRED Hascombe and Valiant Studs
Sasuru was highly impressive on this return to action. Always travelling well, he cruised into the lead on the bridle approaching the final furlong and showed a tremendous turn of foot to quicken away from the opposition with the minimum of fuss. A real mile-and-a-quarter specialist it will be a major disappointment if he does not win further Group races this season. The Group One Premio Presidente Della Repubblica at Capannelle in Italy is his next target. (13/2)
Multicoloured (IRE) made a pleasing reappearance. Moving to the front after three furlongs, he remained at the head of affairs until firmly put in his place by the winner below the distance. He is certainly up to winning a listed event. (11/2)
678* Ali-Royal (IRE), who got very warm beforehand, was taking another small step up in distance. Asked for his effort over a quarter-of-a-mile from home, he was battling for the lead when the winner sailed by approaching the final furlong and left him standing. He did just stay this trip but is probably more effective at a mile. (15/8)
Tamure (IRE) looked big and well for his seasonal debut, only his second run since October 1995. Having lost his position turning into the straight, he was putting in some good work inside the final furlong and would have taken second prize in a few more strides. Over a mile-and-a-half, he should soon make up for lost time. (11/2: 4/1-6/1)
Bequeath, who jarred his suspensory ligaments last year, looked extremely well beforehand but was in trouble over a quarter-of-a-mile from home and soon beaten. He will do better when returning to a mile-and-a-half. (12/1: op 8/1)
627a Needle Gun (IRE), a real globe-trotting individual, may have won only three times in his career but he has amassed prize money in excess of half-a-million pounds. The early leader, he had given his all a quarter-of-a-mile from home. (11/2)

853 MARRIOTT HOTELS H'CAP (0-105) (3-Y.O) (Class B)

5-15 (5-19) **1m 14y** £9,495.00 (£3,555.00: £1,740.00: £750.00: £337.50: £172.50) Stalls: High GOING: 0.22 sec per fur (G)

				SP	RR	SF
	Amyas (IRE) (89) (BWHills) **3-8-13** MHills(4) (rdn over 2f out: hdwy over 1f out: led ins fnl f: r.o wl)	—	1	6/1[3]	99	67
599[3]	**Burning Truth (USA) (75)** (RCharlton) **3-7-8**(5) RFfrench(1) (lw: rdn 4f out: hdwy over 1f out: r.o wl ins fnl f)	nk	2	5/1[2]	84	52
635[2]	**No More Pressure (IRE) (82)** (NJHWalker) **3-8-6**ow1 PatEddery(6) (lw: led: rdn over 1f out: hdd ins fnl f: unable qckn)	2½	3	5/1[2]	86	53
	Kalinka (IRE) (85) (PFICole) **3-8-9** TQuinn(2) (lw: a.p: ev ch over 1f out: one pce)	1¼	4	6/1[3]	87	55
688[2]	**Rapier (86)** (RHannon) **3-8-10** DaneO'Neill(10) (a.p: rdn over 3f out: one pce)	1½	5	4/1[1]	85	53
654[7]	**Halowing (USA) (86)** (JGSmyth-Osbourne) **3-8-10** BDoyle(8) (lw: a.p: rdn over 2f out: wknd over 1f out)	4	6	33/1	77	45
555[3]	**Irish Accord (USA) (94)** (MrsJRRamsden) **3-9-4** JFortune(7) (prom over 4f)	2½	7	13/2	80	48
690[16]	**Sheer Face (88)** (WRMuir) **3-8-12** JReid(5) (hdwy 4f out: rdn over 3f out: wknd 2f out)	½	8	14/1	73	41
	Ortelius (78) (RHannon) **3-8-2**ow1 PaulEddery(9) (lw: bhd fnl 4f)	8	9	14/1	47	14
	Bride's Reprisal (88) (MRChannon) **3-8-12** RHughes(3) (sme hdwy over 2f out: eased whn btn over 1f out)	15	10	25/1	28	—
	Rich In Love (IRE) (97) (CACyzer) **3-9-7** KFallon(11) (bhd fnl 5f)	17	11	20/1	3	—

(SP 120.1%) **11 Rn**

1m 46.0 (4.80) CSF £32.81 CT £152.56 TOTE £8.50: £2.50 £2.30 £1.40 (£28.40) Trio £33.80 OWNER Mrs J. M. Corbett (LAMBOURN) BRED Mrs Helen Smith

Amyas (IRE), 11lb higher than when last successful, seemed well suited by the step up in trip, and came with a tremendous run to strike the front inside the final furlong and hold off the runner-up. (6/1)

599 Burning Truth (USA), bustled along and not going anywhere turning into the straight, really found his stride from below the distance and ran on in tremendous style. Well handicapped at present, he will do better over further, and should soon be winning. (5/1: op 3/1)

635 No More Pressure (IRE) ran another fine race, taking the field along until collared inside the final furlong. (5/1)

Kalinka (IRE) looked in good shape for this reappearance but looked far from enthusiastic, just as she had done on her final start last season. Throwing down her challenge in the straight, she carried her head very high and it was either a question of she could not or would not go past the leader. In the final furlong she was certainly tapped for toe. (6/1)

688 Rapier, a leading light from the off, failed to muster another gear in the straight despite all his rider's efforts. (4/1)

Halowing (USA) played an active role until coming to the end of her tether approaching the final furlong. (33/1)

555 Irish Accord (USA) (13/2: 9/2-7/1)

Bride's Reprisal, not guaranteed to get this trip, was given no ride whatsoever which leaves us none the wiser. With her jockey sitting as quiet as a church mouse, she certainly crept closer over a quarter-of-a-mile from home, but was then allowed to coast in from below the distance. She looks one to keep a very close eye on. (25/1)

854 BEEFEATER RESTAURANT RATED STKS H'CAP (0-100) (3-Y.O) (Class B)

5-50 (5-52) **5f 6y** £7,491.60 (£2,804.40: £1,372.20: £591.00: £265.50: £135.30) Stalls: High GOING: 0.22 sec per fur (G)

				SP	RR	SF
	Hattab (IRE) (91) (PTWalwyn) **3-8-13** RHughes(11) (lw: mde all: clr over 1f out: r.o wl)	—	1	16/1	99	67
	Sabina (82) (IABalding) **3-8-4** LDettori(10) (a.p: chsd wnr over 1f out: no imp)	1¼	2	9/2[2]	86	54
434[3]	**Bishops Court (83)** (MrsJRRamsden) **3-8-5**ow1 JFortune(4) (hdwy over 1f out: r.o wl ins fnl f)	1½	3	11/4[1]	82	49
453*	**Cadeaux Cher (89)** (BWHills) **3-8-11** MHills(1) (b: lw: hdwy on ins over 1f out: one pce)	3	4	9/1	79	47
694*	**Treasure Touch (IRE) (86)** (DNicholls) **3-8-3**(5) IonaWands(5) (a.p: rdn over 2f out: wknd 1f out)	½	5	7/1[3]	74	42
	Paddy Lad (IRE) (98) (RGuest) **3-9-6** PBloomfield(7) (lost pl 2f out: r.o one pce fnl f)	1¾	6	16/1	81	49
	Snap Crackle Pop (IRE) (92) (RFJohnsonHoughton) **3-9-0** JReid(6) (bit bkwd: hdwy over 2f out: wknd over 1f out)	1½	7	33/1	70	38
501[2]	**Myrmidon (96)** (MrsLStubbs) **3-9-4** KFallon(2) (prom over 3f)	nk	8	9/1	73	41
501[5]	**Vasari (IRE) (99)** (MRChannon) **3-9-7** TQuinn(3) (lw: bhd fnl 2f)	1½	9	25/1	71	39
506[5]	**Bilko (85)** (GLewis) **3-8-7** PatEddery(8) (bhd fnl 3f: b.b.v)	2	10	11/4[1]	51	19

(SP 122.6%) **10 Rn**

62.7 secs (2.90) CSF £82.89 CT £248.24 TOTE £22.40: £4.30 £1.40 £1.80 (£30.90) Trio £84.20 OWNER Mr Hamdan Al Maktoum (LAMBOURN) BRED Shadwell Estate Company Limited

OFFICIAL EXPLANATION **Bilko: finished distressed.**

Hattab (IRE) looked in good shape and could not have made a better start to the season, making every post a winning one and forging clear below the distance for a decisive victory. (16/1)

Sabina travelled well during the race and moved sweetly into second place below the distance. However, she failed to peg back the winner. There are races to be won with her this year. (9/2)

434 Bishops Court again caught the eye. Put to sleep at the back of the field, his jockey only got down to action below the distance and, from that point, the gelding sprinted up the hill. Unfortunately, the combination had left it too late. There is a race waiting for him just around the corner. (11/4)

453* Cadeaux Cher, 8lb higher than when beaten on his final start last season, made a forward move along the inside rail below the distance but could make no further impression. (9/1)

694* Treasure Touch (IRE) has been in tremendous form and has won all three of his turf races so far this season. Not surprisingly he has risen sharply in the weights from 63 to 86 and that was enough to stop him here. (7/1)

Paddy Lad (IRE) lost his pitch a quarter-of-a-mile from home, but struggled on in the closing stages to pass a few beaten horses. Successful over this course and distance last year, he subsequently ran over six furlongs and that is probably more his trip. (16/1)

506 Bilko ran no race at all and it was later explained by one of the Stewards' Secretaries, who reported the colt had broken a blood-vessel. He showed a great deal of promise at Kempton recently, and is well worth another chance. (11/4)

T/Jkpt: Not won; £10,160.32 to 28/4/97. T/Plpt: £515.20 (97.08 Tckts). T/Qdpt: £47.40 (65.09 Tckts) AK

0658-WOLVERHAMPTON (L-H) (Standard)

Saturday April 26th

WEATHER: raining WIND: almost nil

855 SARUMAN MAIDEN H'CAP (0-65) (3-Y.O+) (Class F)

7-00 (7-01) **6f (Fibresand)** £2,277.00 (£627.00: £297.00) Stalls: Low GOING: 0.09 sec per fur (STD)

			SP	RR	SF
Forcing Bid (65) (SirMarkPrescott) **3-9-12** GDuffield(7) (lw: mde virtually all: hrd rdn fnl f: hld on gamely)	—	1	9/2[2]	76	40

				SP	RR	SF
372^{3}	**Magic Fizz (56)** (TJEtherington) **3-9-3** LCharnock(12) (hdwy ½-wy: hrd rdn over 1f out: kpt on wl towards fin)	½	**2**	9/1	66	30
588^{2}	**Don't Worry Mike (60)** (FHLee) **3-9-7** ACulhane(9) (lw: a.p: drvn over 2f out: one pce fnl f)	5	**3**	$11/4^{1}$	56	20
	Prudent Princess (46) (AHide) **5-9-4** AMcGlone(1) (bit bkwd: a.p: ev ch wl over 1f out: wknd fnl f)	3	**4**	14/1	34	9
473^{5}	**Arnie (IRE) (35)** (JRPoulton) **5-8-4**(3) MartinDwyer(11) (hdwy 2f out: rdn & r.o ins fnl f)	½	**5**	$5/1^{3}$	22	—
577^{3}	**Sharp Holly (IRE) (41)** (JABennett) **5-8-13b** DWright(13) (effrt over 2f out: sn rdn: nt pce to chal)	½	**6**	10/1	27	2
469^{6}	**Blue Lugana (35)** (NBycroft) **5-8-2**(5) JBramhill(10) (sn pushed along: a outpcd)	1¼	**7**	8/1	17	—
554^{6}	**With The Tempo (IRE) (40)** (DrJDScargill) **4-8-12** SDrowne(6) (s.s: a bhd & outpcd)	2	**8**	12/1	17	—
	Express Routing (48) (VSoane) **5-9-6** FNorton(8) (b: bkwd: outpcd)	½	**9**	33/1	24	—
577^{5}	**Risky Lover (45)** (DShaw) **4-9-3b¹** JFanning(5) (lw: outpcd: t.o)	3½	**10**	14/1	11	—
	Primelta (48) (RAkehurst) **4-9-6** SSanders(3) (chsd ldrs to ½-wy: sn lost pl)	1½	**11**	14/1	10	—
	Toronto (59) (JBerry) **3-9-6** SWhitworth(4) (lw: spd over 4f: wknd qckly: t.o)	5	**12**	10/1	8	—
	Golborne Lad (45) (JBalding) **4-9-3** RLappin(2) (bkwd: w ldrs over 3f: wknd qckly: t.o)	9	**13**	33/1	—	—

(SP 134.4%) **13 Rn**

1m 16.7 (5.50) CSF £46.64 CT £126.98 TOTE £4.60: £2.10 £3.10 £1.40 (£13.30) Trio £11.90 OWNER Mr H. R. Moszkowicz (NEWMARKET) BRED Angley Stud Ltd

WEIGHT FOR AGE 3yo-11lb

Forcing Bid, from a yard just starting to fire, made his first appearance on the sand a winning one with a very brave all-the-way success. (9/2: op 3/1)

372 Magic Fizz would win no supporters with his very poor action in his slower paces, but he gets better as he warms up, and he certainly did not fail for the want of trying. (9/1: op 6/1)

588 Don't Worry Mike, always in the action, was under the strongest pressure turning in and had to admit the leading pair had too much pace for him. (11/4)

Prudent Princess stuck to the inside rail and was almost on terms on straightening up, but she was racing on the slower ground and was shaken off without much trouble. (14/1)

473 Arnie (IRE), still struggling to find a correct trip, was pegging back the leaders in the closing stages but had left his effort far too late. (5/1)

577 Sharp Holly (IRE), wound up for her challenge once in line for home, ran on but she lacked the speed to prove troublesome. (10/1)

Toronto (10/1: 6/1-12/1)

856 STRIDER CLAIMING STKS (3-Y.O+) (Class F)

7-30 (7-31) **5f (Fibresand)** £2,277.00 (£627.00: £297.00) Stalls: Low GOING: 0.09 sec per fur (STD)

				SP	RR	SF
698^{5}	**First Maite (80)** (SRBowring) **4-9-12b** SWebster(8) (chsd ldrs: rdn over 1f out: str run to ld wl ins fnl f)	—	**1**	9/1	73	52
760^{8}	**Featherstone Lane (51)** (MissLCSiddall) **6-9-4** MWigham(2) (outpcd & bhd tl r.o strly appr fnl f)	1¼	**2**	12/1	61	40
545^{6}	**Palacegate Jack (IRE) (66)** (JBerry) **6-9-1b**(7) CLowther(9) (w ldr: led 200y out: sn hdd: no ex)	½	**3**	$11/2^{3}$	63	42
659^{5}	**Chilling (60)** (NTinkler) **3-7-10b¹**(7)ow2 KSked(7) (hdwy u.p 2f out: kpt on wl ins fnl f)	½	**4**	9/1	53	20
702^{5}	**Kalar (74)** (DWChapman) **8-9-8b** ACulhane(6) (led tl hdd & no ex ins fnl f)	1¼	**5**	$9/4^{1}$	58	37
702^{10}	**Silk Cottage (55)** (RMWhitaker) **5-9-8** DeanMcKeown(10) (lw: chsd ldrs: hrd drvn over 2f out: hung lft & no imp fnl f)	1½	**6**	11/1	53	32
663^{10}	**Little Ibnr (65)** (PDEvans) **6-9-0v** JFEgan(5) (lw: chsd ldrs: rdn ent st: no imp)	nk	**7**	13/2	44	23
659^{2}	**Perfect Brave (63)** (JBalding) **6-9-4** RLappin(3) (lw: stumbled s: hdwy ½-wy: sn rdn: wknd fnl f)	6	**8**	$9/2^{2}$	29	8
	Susie's Sonny (JPLeigh) **3-8-8** LCharnock(4) (w'like: bit bkwd: outpcd: a bhd)	4	**9**	33/1	16	—
659^{7}	**Little Papoose** (BAMcMahon) **4-8-11** LNewton(1) (outpcd: a bhd)	1¼	**10**	33/1	5	—

(SP 119.6%) **10 Rn**

62.7 secs (3.80) CSF £103.80 TOTE £10.00: £2.90 £3.70 £2.00 (£49.40) Trio £110.60 OWNER Mr S. R. Bowring (EDWINSTOWE) BRED S. R. Bowring

WEIGHT FOR AGE 3yo-10lb

OFFICIAL EXPLANATION **Perfect Brave: the jockey reported that he had lost both irons as the gelding jumped in the air leaving the stalls.**

698 First Maite failed to match strides with the tearaway front-runners for the first three furlongs but, responding to a forceful ride, stormed through to pick them off inside the final hundred yards. (9/1)

515 Featherstone Lane ran much better under stronger handling but, not for the first time, had mistimed his run. (12/1)

178 Palacegate Jack (IRE) had a head-to-head with Kalar, and managed to win that battle two hundred yards out, but the pace had been furious and he had nothing left to repel the strong-finishing principals. (11/2)

427 Chilling showed a return to form in first-time blinkers. Another try at six furlongs could get her back to winning ways. (9/1)

702 Kalar, given no peace at the head of affairs, had run himself into the ground soon after reaching the final furlong. (9/4)

593 Silk Cottage would have been a leading contender had he not, once again, shown a tendency to hang left when pressure was applied inside the distance. (11/1)

857 WARLORD H'CAP (0-70) (3-Y.O+) (Class E)

8-00 (8-00) **1m 1f 79y (Fibresand)** £3,304.25 (£989.00: £474.50: £217.25) Stalls: Low GOING: 0.09 sec per fur (STD)

				SP	RR	SF
415^{7}	**Eurolink the Lad (48)** (DBurchell) **10-8-6** DeanMcKeown(9) (s.s: wl bhd tl hdwy 5f out: led appr fnl f: sn clr)	—	**1**	11/1	59	32
410^{16}	**Wildfire (SWI) (48)** (RAkehurst) **6-8-6** SSanders(2) (b: chsd ldr: led over 2f out tl appr fnl f: no ch w wnr)	3½	**2**	9/1	53	26
428^{9}	**Nicola's Princess (51)** (BAMcMahon) **4-8-9** LNewton(8) (bhd: hdwy 3f out: styd on appr fnl f)	4	**3**	25/1	49	22
578^{6}	**Bentico (63)** (MrsNMacauley) **8-9-7** SWebster(3) (lw: hdwy 3f out: styd on u.p appr fnl f)	nk	**4**	$6/1^{2}$	61	34
579^{6}	**Failed To Hit (49)** (NPLittmoden) **4-8-7v** TGMcLaughlin(7) (hdwy 5f out: hrd rdn 2f out: kpt on)	hd	**5**	16/1	47	20
476^{11}	**Captain's Day (58)** (HJCollingridge) **5-8-11**(5) RMullen(11) (b.hind: nvr plcd to chal)	2	**6**	$13/2^{3}$	52	25
	Mentalasanythin (70) (DHaydnJones) **8-10-0** CRutter(5) (bkwd: nvr gng pce of ldrs)	nk	**7**	9/1	64	37
566^{10}	**Tuigamala (58)** (RIngram) **6-9-2** AMcGlone(10) (sn outpcd: a bhd)	3½	**8**	14/1	46	19
537^{10}	**Big Bang (61)** (MBlanshard) **3-8-4** JQuinn(6) (outpcd: a bhd)	nk	**9**	8/1	48	6
589^{11}	**People Direct (55)** (KMcAuliffe) **4-8-13** JFEgan(13) (set str pce: sn clr: wknd & hdd over 2f out)	3½	**10**	11/1	36	9
566^{3}	**Shanghai Lil (55)** (MJFetherston-Godley) **5-8-13** FNorton(12) (a bhd & outpcd: t.o)	15	**11**	$11/2^{1}$	10	—
595^{20}	**Windyedge (USA) (50)** (MrsAMNaughton) **4-8-8** SDrowne(1) (chsd ldrs 6f: sn wknd: t.o)	¾	**12**	33/1	4	—
580^{5}	**Bailiwick (46)** (NAGraham) **4-8-4b** DHolland(4) (chsd ldrs tl wknd qckly over 2f out: t.o)	¾	**13**	12/1	—	—

(SP 117.8%) **13 Rn**

2m 3.6 (7.60) CSF £95.56 CT £2,202.02 TOTE £12.10: £3.40 £3.00 £7.20 (£75.40) Trio Not won; £224.56 to Pontefract 28/4/97 OWNER Mrs Elizabeth Stockton (EBBW VALE) BRED Mrs Jackie Ramos

WEIGHT FOR AGE 3yo-15lb

192 Eurolink the Lad, taken off his legs after losing ground at the start, was well suited by the strong early pace and, with the leaders tying up, was able to take over and forge clear inside the final furlong. (11/1)

206* Wildfire (SWI), taking a step down in distance, gained a decisive lead entering the straight, but the winner had the legs of him in the duel to the finish. (9/1)
Nicola's Princess, staying on from off the pace, ran one of her better races and these tactics could pay off in the not-too-distant future. (25/1)
578 Bentico began to close at the end of the back straight, but the progress was slow as his welter burden took its toll. (6/1)
Failed To Hit, taken wide to make progress down the back straight, kept staying on but lacked the turn of speed to prove troublesome. (16/1)
380* Captain's Day, restrained in the pack, was always finding the tempo too hot for him, and his final placing was as close as he could get. (13/2)
566 Shanghai Lil struggled with the pace from the break, and was always nearer last than first. She eventually finished tailed off and this poor performance must go down as a one-off. (11/2)
580 Bailiwick (12/1: op 7/1)

858 FOLEY STEELS H'CAP (0-95) (3-Y.O+) (Class C)

8-30 (8-33) **1m 6f 166y (Fibresand)** £5,732.15 (£1,713.20: £820.10: £373.55) Stalls: High GOING: 0.09 sec per fur (STD)

				SP	RR	SF
510^{10}	**Random Kindness (66)** (RIngram) **4-8-0** JFEgan(6) (lw: chsd ldrs: led over 4f out: sn drvn clr: unchal)	—	1	$7/1^{3}$	83	34
542^{7}	**All On (59)** (JHetherton) **6-7-5**(5) RMullen(10) (a.p: rdn 3f out: styd on same pce fnl 2f)	11	2	25/1	64	18
442^{2}	**Noufari (FR) (68)** (RHollinshead) **6-8-2**(3)ow3 FLynch(8) (hdwy 5f out: sn hrd drvn: wknd wl over 1f out)	9	3	$7/2^{2}$	63	14
	Dark Waters (IRE) (74) (NAGraham) **4-8-8** DHolland(9) (bkwd: hld up: hdwy 6f out: hrd drvn over 3f out: no imp)	8	4	12/1	61	12
299^{9}	**Super High (86)** (PHowling) **5-9-9b** FNorton(4) (lw: led tl over 4f out: sn rdn & lost tch)	3	5	20/1	69	23
516^{2}	**Premier Dance (66)** (DHaydnJones) **10-8-3** CRutter(1) (nvr plcd to chal)	4	6	$7/1^{3}$	45	—
660^{7}	**Royal Citizen (IRE) (60)** (JFBottomley) **8-7-11**ow1 LCharnock(11) (chsd ldrs 9f: sn lost tch: t.o)	7	7	25/1	32	—
591^{10}	**Opera Buff (IRE) (91)** (MissGayKelleway) **6-9-7**(7) AngelaGallimore(2) (s.s: hdwy 5f out: wknd over 2f out: t.o)	2	8	14/1	60	14
	Purple Splash (90) (PJMakin) **7-9-13v** SSanders(7) (hld up & bhd: effrt on ins 5f out: no imp: t.o)	6	9	12/1	53	7
591^{2}	**Sedbergh (USA) (70)** (MrsMReveley) **4-8-4** JQuinn(5) (lw: prom: rdn 5f out: sn wknd: t.o)	19	10	$6/4^{1}$	12	—
589^{10}	**Barbara's Jewel (59)** (ABailey) **5-7-10** DWright(3) (lw: uns rdr s)		U	25/1	—	—

(SP 125.6%) **11 Rn**

3m 18.2 (10.80) CSF £163.58 CT £653.99 TOTE £9.20: £2.20 £4.20 £1.40 (£50.30) Trio £137.80 OWNER 949 Racing (EPSOM) BRED Pendley Farm
LONG HANDICAP All On 7-3 Royal Citizen (IRE) 7-8 Barbara's Jewel 7-4
WEIGHT FOR AGE 4yo-3lb
STEWARDS' ENQUIRY Lynch fined £300 under Rule 161 (ii) (weighed in 3½lb heavy).
419* Random Kindness stays particularly well and, gaining the initiative down the back straight and driven into a clear lead, had caught his pursuers on the hop and the outcome was never in doubt. (7/1)
465 All On kept tabs on the leaders, but was caught flat-footed when the winner quickened things up and, from then on, the only prize that remained was the runner-up spot. (25/1)
442 Noufari (FR) had little chance of turning the tables on the winner on identical terms, and his run had come to an end before reaching the straight. (7/2)
Dark Waters (IRE), a very lightly-raced four-year-old needing the run after eight months out of action, did not fare badly but could never get near enough to cause concern. (12/1: op 8/1)
244* Super High will need to be ridden with restraint if he is going to get this trip, so his usual forceful tactics were doomed to failure from the word go. (20/1)
591 Sedbergh (USA) has won on the All-Weather but prefers a sounder surface and, with the continuous rain lying in places on the track, conditions here were far from suitable and he called enough halfway down the back straight. (6/4)

49 54 62+

859 STAR ENGINEERING (S) STKS (2-Y.O) (Class G)

9-00 (9-02) **5f (Fibresand)** £1,984.50 (£547.00: £259.50) Stalls: Low GOING: 0.09 sec per fur (STD)

				SP	RR	SF
592^{5}	**Wilfred Sherman (IRE)** (JBerry) **2-8-7**(5) PFessey(6) (lw: a.p: chal 1f out: r.o to ld nr fin)	—	1	$9/4^{2}$	52	6
592^{6}	**Jack-N-Jilly (IRE)** (JSMoore) **2-8-4**(3) MHenry(2) (led over 3f out: rdn fnl f: ct cl home)	hd	2	16/1	47	1
767^{6}	**Pink Ticket** (PDEvans) **2-8-7** JFEgan(5) (led over 1f out: rdn along ½-wy: kpt on same pce)	4	3	$7/2^{3}$	34	—
743*	**Diamond Steve** (NTinkler) **2-9-3v** KimTinkler(3) (outpcd: a bhd)	3½	4	$7/4^{1}$	33	—
	Lawless Bridget (MartynMeade) **2-8-2**(5) DSweeney(4) (small: bit bkwd: s.s: a bhd & outpcd)	8	5	5/1	—	—
743^{12}	***Carnation King*** (WGMTurner) **2-8-5**(7) DMcGaffin(1) (Withdrawn not under Starter's orders: broke out of stalls)		W	20/1	—	—

(SP 116.7%) **5 Rn**

64.8 secs (5.90) CSF £27.84 TOTE £3.30: £1.80 £2.50 (£21.70) OWNER Mr J. Berry (COCKERHAM) BRED Waterside Stud
No bid
OFFICIAL EXPLANATION **Diamond Steve: the jockey reported that gelding would appreciate further.**
592 Wilfred Sherman (IRE) gained his revenge over Pink Ticket, but won a poor race with nothing to spare. (9/4)
472 Jack-N-Jilly (IRE) made the winner fight to take her measure nearing the finish, and she does appear to be getting the hang of things. (16/1)
767 Pink Ticket, flat to the boards at halfway, could do little more than keep at the one pace. (7/2)
743* Diamond Steve failed to handle the Fibresand and was taken off his legs all the way. (7/4)
Lawless Bridget (5/1: op 2/1)

860 JOAN CHALK MEMORIAL H'CAP (0-60) (3-Y.O+) (Class F)

9-30 (9-30) **7f (Fibresand)** £2,277.00 (£627.00: £297.00) Stalls: High GOING: 0.09 sec per fur (STD)

				SP	RR	SF
589^{6}	**Theatre Magic (57)** (DShaw) **4-9-11** JFanning(12) (b: lw: chsd ldrs: hdwy over 2f out: led ins fnl f: sn clr)	—	1	11/1	72	54
477^{5}	**Sis Garden (58)** (JCullinan) **4-9-7b**(5) RFfrench(11) (lw: chsd ldrs: hdwy to ld 3f out: hdd & no ex ins fnl f)	3	2	7/1	66	48
578^{11}	**Johnnie the Joker (60)** (JPLeigh) **6-10-0b** DeanMcKeown(3) (chsd ldrs: outpcd 3f out: rallied u.p appr fnl f)	3½	3	$100/30^{1}$	60	42
589*	**Dragonjoy (60)** (NPLittmoden) **4-10-0b** RLappin(8) (s.i.s: sn drvn along: hdwy fnl 2f: nrst fin)	½	4	$5/1^{2}$	59	41
589^{8}	**Princess Efisio (57)** (BAMcMahon) **4-9-11** LNewton(10) (outpcd: sme hdwy fnl 2f: nvr nrr)	6	5	11/1	42	24
589^{2}	**Square Deal (FR) (60)** (SRBowring) **6-10-0** SWebster(1) (prom tl rdn & outpcd 2f out)	hd	6	10/1	45	27
	Samara Song (57) (IPWilliams) **4-9-11** JFEgan(7) (bkwd: prom tl wknd 2f out)	s.h	7	25/1	42	24
579^{4}	**Jigsaw Boy (55)** (PGMurphy) **8-9-9** SDrowne(4) (chsd ldrs: nvr able to chal)	hd	8	7/1	40	22
687^{8}	**Loch Style (50)** (RHollinshead) **4-9-1**(3) FLynch(9) (s.s: a bhd & outpcd)	nk	9	$6/1^{3}$	34	16
663^{4}	**Mercury (IRE) (60)** (JAGlover) **4-10-0** GDuffield(6) (led 4f: sn rdn & wknd)	¾	10	7/1	42	24

				SP	RR	SF
	Brandonville (52) (NTinkler) **4-9-6** KimTinkler(5) (bkwd: sn drvn along: a outpcd)	1¼	**11**	25/1	32	14
604[5]	**Polly Golightly (53)** (MBlanshard) **4-9-7** JQuinn(2) (in tch tl rdn & outpcd fnl 3f)	s.h	**12**	12/1	32	14
				(SP 132.7%)	**12 Rn**	

1m 29.9 (5.20) CSF £87.73 CT £299.60 TOTE £13.30: £3.30 £2.60 £2.00 (£46.30) Trio £164.00; £184.89 to Pontefract 28/4/97 OWNER Green Diamond Racing (NEWARK) BRED N. S. Yong

589 Theatre Magic has taken time to get on the winning track but he won readily here, and this could be the start of something good. (11/1: 8/1-12/1)

477 Sis Garden reserves her best for this track and, though she was forced to admit the winner too strong inside the last furlong, ran her race out to the finish and all is not lost yet. (7/1: 5/1-8/1)

Johnnie the Joker is not really happy on such a tight track as this and, though he has won here, he needs to be able to make full use of his long stride. (100/30: 8/1-3/1)

589* Dragonjoy overdid the waiting tactics on this return to a shorter trip, and it says much that he was able to finish as close as he did. (5/1)

Princess Efisio (11/1: 8/1-12/1)

589 Square Deal (FR) found the quickening pace too much for him off the turn into the home straight, and he appears to find this trip plenty short enough nowadays. (10/1: 8/1-12/1)

T/Plpt: £1,568.70 (9 Tckts). T/Qdpt: £479.10 (1.55 Tckts) IM

0772-PONTEFRACT (L-H) (Good)

Monday April 28th

WEATHER: showery WIND: fresh bhd

73 77+ 62+ 67

861 E.B.F. TOTE NOVICE STKS (2-Y.O) (Class D)

2-45 (2-46) **5f** £4,013.00 (£1,214.00: £592.00: £281.00) Stalls: Low GOING minus 0.15 sec per fur (GF)

				SP	RR	SF
572*	**Classy Cleo (IRE)** (RHannon) **2-8-9** PatEddery(7) (chsd ldrs: rdn to ld 1f out: r.o)	—	**1**	5/2 1	79	30
730[2]	**Out Like Magic** (PDEvans) **2-8-13** JFEgan(3) (w ldr: rdn 2f out: nt qckn ins fnl f)	1¾	**2**	4/1 3	77	28
684[3]	**Mamma's Boy** (JBerry) **2-8-7**(5) TEDurcan(2) (lw: mde most tl hdd 1f out: no ex)	¾	**3**	5/2 1	74	25
	Brookhouse Lady (IRE) (RHollinshead) **2-8-4**(3) FLynch(1) (lt-f: unf: outpcd early: hdwy ½-wy: styd on wl towards fin)	s.h	**4**	25/1	69	20
530*	**Lord Smith** (WGMTurner) **2-8-5**(7) DMcGaffin(9) (a chsng ldrs: rdn ½-wy: no imp)	1	**5**	16/1	71	22
695[3]	**Mamora Bay (IRE)** (MHTompkins) **2-8-12** RHills(5) (lw: sn outpcd & bhd: hdwy 2f out: nvr rchd ldrs)	1¾	**6**	3/1 2	65	16
	Cool Secret (ABMulholland) **2-8-12** MBirch(6) (lt-f: bit bkwd: s.i.s: outpcd tl styd on fnl 1½f)	hd	**7**	33/1	65	16
	Newhargen (IRE) (PDEvans) **2-8-12** ACulhane(4) (leggy: lt-f: outpcd & lost tch fr ½-wy)	5	**8**	25/1	49	—
	Linnetsong (GROldroyd) **2-8-7** MMcAndrew(10) (w'like: scope: bit bkwd: swtg: s.s: a wl bhd)	dist	**9**	66/1	—	—
				(SP 120.2%)	**9 Rn**	

64.9 secs (3.20) CSF £11.96 TOTE £3.20: £1.30 £1.40 £1.50 (£6.00) Trio £6.60 OWNER Mrs A. Kane (MARLBOROUGH) BRED Rathasker Stud

572* Classy Cleo (IRE) had to work hard to get on top but she did stay particularly well and should get further. (5/2: 7/4-11/4)

730 Out Like Magic ran her usual sound race and kept struggling on but was always second best. (4/1)

684 Mamma's Boy ran well but was tapped for toe in the final furlong and seems to need a stiffer test. (5/2)

Brookhouse Lady (IRE) would not win any prizes on looks at present but she showed plenty of ability, staying on nicely at the end. (25/1)

530* Lord Smith, stepping up in class, ran quite well but was never up to the task. (16/1)

695 Mamora Bay (IRE), judging from the way he finished, will come into his own once he goes over further. (3/1)

Cool Secret had not much idea early on but was learning as the race progressed. (33/1)

862 TOTE CREDIT (S) STKS (3-Y.O) (Class G)

3-15 (3-21) **1m 4f 8y** £2,427.00 (£672.00: £321.00) Stalls: Low GOING minus 0.15 sec per fur (GF)

				SP	RR	SF
662[2]	**Baby Jane (65)** (RGuest) **3-8-7** PBloomfield(7) (trckd ldrs: led 5f out: styd on strly: eased ins fnl f)	—	**1**	5/2 1	61+	16
	Lindrick Lady (IRE) (BSRothwell) **3-8-7** MFenton(5) (leggy: unf: bit bkwd: hdwy 5f out: chsd wnr fnl 3f: no imp)	1¾	**2**	12/1	59	14
	Fortune Hopper (JPearce) **3-8-12** GBardwell(6) (neat: bit bkwd: bhd tl styd on u.p fnl 3f: nrst fin)	9	**3**	12/1	52	7
581[8]	**Skelton Sovereign (IRE) (58)** (RHollinshead) **3-9-2**(3) FLynch(12) (lw: hld up: effrt over 3f out: rdn & no imp)	2	**4**	5/1 3	56	11
582[3]	**Rochea (58)** (MrsNMacauley) **3-8-7** SSanders(11) (lw: plld hrd: in tch: effrt over 4f out: no imp)	½	**5**	3/1 2	43	—
475[12]	**Arboreal (USA)** (MrsLStubbs) **3-8-8**ow1 KFallon(3) (hld up: sme hdwy 4f out: sn btn)	12	**6**	14/1	28	—
641[7]	**Rock It Rosie** (DrJDScargill) **3-8-7** MRoberts(13) (effrt over 4f out: sn rdn & no imp)	nk	**7**	16/1	27	—
	Ballydinero (IRE) (48) (CaptJWilson) **3-8-5**(7) AngelaHartley(9) (bit bkwd: chsd ldrs tl wknd fnl 4f)	4	**8**	25/1	27	—
582[7]	**Mechilie (30)** (JWPayne) **3-8-7** AMcGlone(10) (chsd ldrs tl wknd over 4f out)	4	**9**	33/1	16	—
773[10]	**Marys Path** (SGollings) **3-8-7** PaulEddery(1) (s.i.s: a outpcd & bhd)	2	**10**	33/1	14	—
	Guard A Dream (IRE) (MrsMReveley) **3-8-12** ACulhane(2) (leggy: scope: bkwd: s.i.s: a outpcd & bhd)	15	**11**	14/1	—	—
665[6]	**Missed May (30)** (BPJBaugh) **3-8-2**(5) RFfrench(14) (b: prom to ½-wy: wknd qckly)	12	**12**	66/1	—	—
582[8]	**Captain Flint (40)** (ASmith) **3-8-12** MBirch(4) (lw: led tl hdd 5f out: sn lost pl)	1½	**13**	20/1	—	—
	Smart Prospect (43) (BJMeehan) **3-8-12** PatEddery(8) (bit bkwd: w ldr tl wknd over 4f out)	2½	**14**	14/1	—	—
				(SP 127.5%)	**14 Rn**	

2m 44.3 (10.00) CSF £31.46 TOTE £3.20: £1.90 £4.80 £3.00 (£27.70) Trio £361.70; £157.94 to Nottingham 29/4/97 OWNER Mr Dick Low (NEWMARKET) BRED Lord Matthews

Bt in 7,000 gns

662 Baby Jane looked the part, had the form and turned this into a procession in the last three furlongs. She should stay further. (5/2)

Lindrick Lady (IRE) put up a useful first run here and similar events can be found. (12/1: 8/1-14/1)

Fortune Hopper took an age to get going but, despite staying on determinedly, he never had a hope. (12/1)

537 Skelton Sovereign (IRE) travelled quite well but then failed to pick up when asked a question. (5/1)

582 Rochea pulled both on the way to post and in the race, and did not find much when asked a question. (3/1)

Smart Prospect (14/1: op 8/1)

863 TOTE BOOKMAKERS H'CAP (0-80) (3-Y.O+) (Class D)

3-45 (3-49) **6f** £5,481.00 (£1,638.00: £784.00: £357.00) Stalls: Low GOING minus 0.15 sec per fur (GF)

				SP	RR	SF
	Night Flight (72) (JJO'Neill) **3-8-13** KFallon(4) (trckd ldrs: rdn to ld ins fnl f: r.o)	—	1	33/1	88	46
610^{4}	**Be Warned (56)** (MDods) **6-8-8b** JFEgan(17) (bhd: gd hdwy whn bdly hmpd 1½f out: r.o towards fin)	3½	2	16/1	63	32
827*	**Grey Kingdom (49)** (MBrittain) **6-7-8**(7) 7x DMernagh(7) (w ldrs: led over 1f tl ins fnl f: nt qckn)	1	3	5/4^{1}	53	22
744^{20}	**Bowlers Boy (70)** (JJQuinn) **4-9-8** JQuinn(14) (lw: trckd ldrs: effrt wl over 1f out: nt qckn ins fnl f)	¾	4	25/1	72	41
734^{6}	**Twin Creeks (52)** (VSoane) **6-8-4** CRutter(5) (in tch: effrt whn nt clr run 1½f out: swtchd & r.o)	s.h	5	16/1	54	23
	Gwespyr (64) (RHannon) **4-9-2** PatEddery(15) (s.i.s: hdwy 2f out: r.o)	nk	6	16/1	65	34
	Densben (52) (DenysSmith) **13-8-4** ACulhane(3) (bkwd: outpcd & bhd: hmpd over 2f out: hdwy whn n.m.r over 1f out: styd on)	1¼	7	33/1	50	19
835^{5}	**Safio (66)** (ABailey) **4-9-4** DWright(2) (cl up tl wknd over 1f out)	½	8	8/1^{3}	62	31
759^{6}	**Souperficial (56)** (NTinkler) **6-8-8v** KimTinkler(10) (pushed along ½-wy: nvr trbld ldrs)	2	9	20/1	47	16
	Sonderise (53) (NTinkler) **8-8-5**ow1 MRoberts(9) (bkwd: mid div & pushed along ½-wy: no imp)	5	10	16/1	31	—
702^{13}	**Ned's Bonanza (58)** (MDods) **8-8-7**(3) FLynch(16) (hdwy 2f out: n.m.r over 1f out: no imp)	1¾	11	25/1	31	—
702^{12}	**Barato (62)** (MrsJRRamsden) **6-9-0** JFortune(8) (b.hind: lw: chsd ldrs over 4f)	½	12	10/1	34	3
596^{4}	**Bollin Harry (73)** (TDEasterby) **5-9-11** MBirch(6) (lw: w ldrs tl wknd over 1f out)	nk	13	6/1^{2}	44	13
744^{18}	**Blessingindisguise (59)** (MWEasterby) **4-8-11** TLucas(12) (a rr div)	1¼	14	33/1	27	—
	Silver Purse (75) (APJones) **3-9-2** BDoyle(13) (bkwd: s.i.s: a rr div)	½	15	50/1	41	—
	Mousehole (73) (RGuest) **5-9-11** PaulEddery(1) (bkwd: led tl hdd & wknd over 1f out)	2½	16	20/1	33	2
444^{9}	**Barrel of Hope (71)** (JLEyre) **5-9-6b**(3) OPears(11) (a outpcd & bhd)	¾	17	16/1	29	—

(SP 136.3%) **17 Rn**

1m 17.9 (2.90) CSF £457.42 CT £1,117.00 TOTE £34.40: £4.60 £3.40 £1.10 £5.20 (£736.00) Trio £461.10 OWNER Mr C. H. Stevens (PENRITH) BRED Tarworth Bloodstock Investments Ltd

WEIGHT FOR AGE 3yo-11lb

STEWARDS' ENQUIRY Egan susp. 7-8/5/97 (careless riding)

OFFICIAL EXPLANATION Bollin Harry: had choked during the race.

Night Flight confirmed his promise of last year and won this in useful style. He should appreciate another furlong. (33/1)

610 Be Warned met with a fair deal of trouble when trying an ambitious run up the inner and did well to finish so close. (16/1)

827* Grey Kingdom was not made enough use of this time and was outsprinted in the final furlong. (5/4)

Bowlers Boy had plenty of running to do from his draw and put up a fair performance, but did not find quite as much as expected when ridden. (25/1)

146* Twin Creeks has never won over a trip as short as this, but was most unlucky here and should have been in the shake-up. He is obviously in top form just now. (16/1)

Gwespyr missed the break as he sometimes does and then made useful late progress to show he is going to pay his way again this year. (16/1)

Densben is now thirteen years old and this was his one hundred and seventy-fourth race, but he showed plenty of enthusiasm and, but for being hampered twice, would have been a deal closer. (33/1)

864 TOTE DUAL FORECAST LIMITED STKS (0-60) (3-Y.O+) (Class F)

4-15 (4-22) **1m 4y** £2,724.00 (£764.00: £372.00) Stalls: Low GOING minus 0.15 sec per fur (GF)

				SP	RR	SF
734^{8}	**Gymcrak Flyer (60)** (GHolmes) **6-9-5** KFallon(12) (b.hind: hld up: hdwy ½-wy: led ins fnl f: r.o)	—	1	4/1^{2}	68	34
763^{2}	**Epic Stand (60)** (MrsJRRamsden) **3-8-10** JFortune(18) (stdd s: hdwy ½-wy: swtchd wl over 1f out: r.o wl towards fin)	1	2	3/1^{1}	71	23
721^{9}	**Gadge (58)** (ABailey) **6-9-10** DWright(7) (b: cl up: led 3f out tl ins fnl f: no ex)	¾	3	8/1	70	36
	Moneghetti (28) (JLHarris) **6-9-8** ACulhane(3) (bit bkwd: in tch: effrt & nt clr run over 2f out: hdwy 1f out: nvr able to chal)	5	4	100/1	58	24
653^{5}	**Power Game (57)** (JBerry) **4-9-10** MRoberts(11) (hld up & bhd: hdwy 3f out: styd on wl)	3	5	12/1	54	20
	Bobbitt (60) (WJarvis) **3-8-5** PaulEddery(13) (mid div: effrt 3f out: no imp)	3	6	20/1	43	—
306^{3}	**Perang Polly (60)** (LordHuntingdon) **5-9-5v**^{1} DHarrison(17) (bhd tl styd on fnl 2f)	nk	7	20/1	42	8
	Parsa (USA) (60) (JLDunlop) **4-9-5** PatEddery(16) (stdd s: nvr plcd to chal)	3½	8	9/2^{3}	35	1
	Blockade (USA) (60) (MBell) **8-9-8** MFenton(2) (t: swtg: chsd ldrs: effrt 3f out: wknd over 1f out)	4	9	14/1	30	—
	Stone Cross (IRE) (50) (MartinTodhunter) **5-9-3**(5) PFessey(6) (b.off hind: s.i.s: nvr rchd ldrs)	s.h	10	66/1	30	—
	Delight of Dawn (59) (EAWheeler) **5-9-0**(5) ADaly(8) (bit bkwd: chsd ldrs tl wknd fnl 2f)	1¾	11	14/1	23	—
421^{9}	**Appeal Again (IRE) (46)** (DBurchell) **4-9-8** DeanMcKeown(10) (chsd ldrs tl wknd over 2f out)	2½	12	50/1	21	—
554^{4}	**Heathyards Lady (USA) (53)** (RHollinshead) **6-9-2**(3) FLynch(4) (b: prom: effrt 3f out: sn wknd)	½	13	25/1	17	—
368^{5}	**Mysterium (60)** (NPLittmoden) **3-8-10** BDoyle(1) (led tl hdd 3f out: wknd 1½f out)	¾	14	25/1	21	—
574^{15}	**Lila Pedigo (IRE) (58)** (MissJFCraze) **4-9-5** NConnorton(9) (chsd ldrs tl wknd fnl 2f)	1¼	15	25/1	13	—
579^{11}	**Oriole (38)** (DonEnricoIncisa) **4-9-8** KimTinkler(15) (bhd & pushed along ½-wy: n.d)	7	16	66/1	3	—
242^{6}	**Evan 'elp Us (60)** (JLEyre) **5-9-5b**(3) OPears(19) (bit bkwd: a outpcd & bhd)	3½	17	33/1	—	—
687^{5}	**Rafter-J (34)** (JohnHarris) **6-9-8** TGMcLaughlin(14) (effrt & hung lft ½-wy: sn bhd)	¾	18	50/1	—	—
83^{7}	**Holders Hill (IRE) (56)** (MGMeagher) **5-9-8** JQuinn(5) (bhd fr ½-wy)	4	19	20/1	—	—

(SP 132.0%) **19 Rn**

1m 48.3 (5.90) CSF £13.61 TOTE £5.30: £2.00 £1.60 £4.00 (£11.40) Trio £71.20 OWNER The Gymcrak Thoroughbred Racing Club (PICKERING) BRED D. G. Mason

WEIGHT FOR AGE 3yo-14lb

734 Gymcrak Flyer confirmed her promise of last time and, getting first run, stole enough advantage to see her home. (4/1)

763 Epic Stand finished strongly and will surely improve a good bit when tried over further. (3/1)

608 Gadge is in tremendous form just now. (8/1: 5/1-12/1)

Moneghetti has changed stables and has only ever won on the All-Weather, but he showed enough here to suggest that he is not a forlorn hope on turf. (100/1)

653 Power Game was without the blinkers that he won with four times last season and ran well, making steady late progress. (12/1)

Bobbitt never got into this but she did show something and should be all the better for it. (20/1)

Parsa (USA) seems a funny customer who needs things to go just right and, dropped out here, never saw daylight. This effort is best forgotten. (9/2: op 3/1)

Blockade (USA) (14/1: op 8/1)

Delight of Dawn (14/1: 10/1-16/1)

865 TOTE MARATHON H'CAP (0-70) (4-Y.O+) (Class E)

4-45 (4-51) **2m 5f 122y** £3,067.00 (£916.00: £438.00: £199.00) Stalls: Low GOING minus 0.15 sec per fur (GF)

				SP	RR	SF
858[2]	**All On (39)** (JHetherton) **6-7-6**(5) RFfrench(15) (hld up: stdy hdwy 8f out: led 4f out: sn clr: styd on wl)	—	**1**	10/1	57	18
	Aardwolf (52) (CPEBrooks) **6-8-10** KFallon(6) (a.p: chsd wnr fnl 3f: no imp)	7	**2**	5/1[2]	65	26
*381**	**High Five (IRE) (38)** (RIngram) **7-7-10** GBardwell(16) (b: bhd: hdwy 8f out: sltly hmpd 3f out: styd on: n.d)	14	**3**	11/2[3]	40	1
613[11]	**Thorntoun Estate (IRE) (38)** (MartinTodhunter) **4-7-5b**(5) PFessey(9) (bhd: hdwy 6f out: hung lft 3f out: no imp)	15	**4**	33/1	29	—
660[8]	**Castle Secret (57)** (DBurchell) **11-9-1** DeanMcKeown(1) (hdwy & in tch after 8f: outpcd over 3f out: n.d after)	¾	**5**	20/1	48	9
669*	**Tancred Mischief (39)** (DWBarker) **6-7-8**(3)ow1 DarrenMoffatt(10) (bhd: effrt 6f out: rdn & nvr rchd ldrs)	5	**6**	10/1	26	—
655[5]	**Upper Mount Clair (70)** (CEBrittain) **7-10-0** BDoyle(4) (lw: hld up: hdwy & prom 8f out: wknd fnl 3½f)	7	**7**	9/2[1]	52	13
632[10]	**Top Prize (38)** (MBrittain) **9-7-10v** JLowe(5) (bhd: drvn along 6f out: n.d)	11	**8**	25/1	12	—
632[6]	**Alcian Blue (40)** (MDHammond) **6-7-12** DaleGibson(14) (cl up: effrt 6f out: wknd 4f out)	nk	**9**	15/2	13	—
769[5]	**Gentleman Sid (39)** (PGMurphy) **7-7-11** FNorton(11) (b: mid div: rdn 8f out: wknd 6f out)	hd	**10**	33/1	12	—
	Black Ice Boy (IRE) (39) (RBastiman) **6-7-11**ow1 DWright(7) (prom tl wknd fnl 7f)	1¼	**11**	100/1	11	—
603[4]	**Stonecutter (44)** (MRChannon) **4-8-2v** PaulEddery(8) (cl up tl wknd fnl 6f)	1	**12**	20/1	16	—
	Precious Island (38) (PTDalton) **4-7-10** NKennedy(3) (lw: n.d)	1½	**13**	33/1	9	—
650[8]	**Chris's Lad (65)** (BJMeehan) **6-9-9b** PatEddery(2) (bit bkwd: led tl hdd 4f out: sn btn)	1	**14**	9/1	35	—
613[14]	**Mister Aspecto (IRE) (59)** (MJohnston) **4-9-3** MRoberts(12) (lw: prom tl wknd fnl 5f)	26	**15**	20/1	10	—
632[8]	**Sudden Spin (40)** (JNorton) **7-7-12** JQuinn(13) (lw: gd hdwy & prom 9f out: rdn & wknd 7f out)	1½	**16**	16/1	—	—
				(SP 124.0%)	**16 Rn**	

4m 57.4 (14.90) CSF £49.33 CT £286.25 TOTE £11.70: £2.50 £2.00 £1.70 £7.90 (£59.60) Trio £307.80 OWNER Mr N. Hetherton (MALTON) BRED N. Hetherton

LONG HANDICAP Mister Aspecto (IRE) 9-9 Stonecutter 8-8 Top Prize 7-2 High Five (IRE) 7-6 Precious Island 7-13 Thorntoun Estate (IRE) 8-0 Tancred Mischief 7-6 Black Ice Boy (IRE) 7-0

858 All On obviously stays forever and a day and, travelling well, won this a long way from home, but at this sort of distance there are not many opportunities. (10/1)

Aardwolf ran well at his first attempt on the Flat for three years but he was never anything like good enough to trouble the winner. (5/1)

381* High Five (IRE), 4lb out of the handicap, stays well but in his own time, which was never good enough. (11/2)

493 Thorntoun Estate (IRE) made useful progress with three-quarters of a mile to go but his stamina gave out in the last three furlongs. (33/1)

Castle Secret found this marathon trip beyond him. (20/1)

669* Tancred Mischief was 4lb wrong here and never gave any signs of hope. (10/1)

866 TOTE PLACEPOT H'CAP (0-75) (4-Y.O+) (Class D)

5-15 (5-21) **1m 2f 6y** £3,817.50 (£1,140.00: £545.00: £247.50) Stalls: Low GOING minus 0.15 sec per fur (GF)

				SP	RR	SF
762[7]	**Road Racer (IRE) (53)** (MrsJRRamsden) **4-8-7** JFortune(8) (lw: trckd ldrs: hdwy over 2f out: led ins fnl f: hrd drvn & hld on wl)	—	**1**	9/1	63	25
589[3]	**Shaffishayes (63)** (MrsMReveley) **5-9-3** DeanMcKeown(2) (lw: trckd ldrs: effrt 2f out: chal ins fnl f: hrd drvn & kpt on)	s.h	**2**	4/1[1]	73	35
574[4]	**Augustan (53)** (SGollings) **6-8-7** PatEddery(1) (lw: trckd ldrs: rdn to ld appr fnl f: sn hdd & one pce)	3	**3**	5/1[2]	58	20
426[8]	**Eagle Canyon (IRE) (74)** (BHanbury) **4-9-11**(3) DO'Donohoe(9) (hld up & bhd: hdwy 2f out: styd on wl towards fin)	1¾	**4**	14/1	76	38
476[8]	**Tomal (42)** (RIngram) **5-7-10** JQuinn(12) (b.hind: hld up: hdwy over 3f out: sn in tch: one pce appr fnl f)	nk	**5**	20/1	44	6
633[3]	**Night of Glass (58)** (JLEyre) **4-8-12** GHind(10) (led tl hdd appr fnl f: wknd)	3½	**6**	8/1	54	16
482[3]	**Danegold (IRE) (71)** (MRChannon) **5-9-11v** RHughes(13) (hld up: hdwy 6f out: outpcd 2f out: kpt on ins fnl f)	1¾	**7**	4/1[1]	65	27
657[8]	**Nosey Native (63)** (JPearce) **4-9-3** MWigham(4) (bhd: effrt 3f out: nvr rchd ldrs)	3	**8**	11/1	52	14
755[2]	**Czarna (IRE) (63)** (CEBrittain) **6-9-3** BDoyle(11) (prom tl wknd over 2f out)	5	**9**	13/2[3]	44	6
	Kernof (IRE) (53) (MDHammond) **4-8-4**(3) FLynch(3) (cl up tl wknd fnl 2½f)	½	**10**	20/1	33	—
734[15]	**Midday Cowboy (USA) (68)** (MDHammond) **4-9-8** KFallon(6) (lw: lost tch fnl 4f)	17	**11**	20/1	21	—
613[16]	**Sheemore (IRE) (43)** (MDHammond) **4-7-11**ow1 DaleGibson(7) (plld hrd: lost tch fnl 4f)	18	**12**	33/1	—	—
633[10]	**Terdad (USA) (74)** (TDBarron) **4-10-0** DHarrison(5) (chsd ldrs tl wknd fnl 3f)	2½	**13**	25/1	—	—
				(SP 127.2%)	**13 Rn**	

2m 16.8 (7.20) CSF £40.38 CT £192.04 TOTE £10.60: £3.60 £1.60 £2.50 (£30.70) Trio £51.40 OWNER Mr J. E. Swiers (THIRSK) BRED Michael M. Byrne

LONG HANDICAP Tomal 7-8

650 Road Racer (IRE), taking a dramatic drop in distance, saw his rider at his strongest to hold on. (9/1)

589 Shaffishayes is a hard-pulling individual who looked to have got it right here, but just failed to find enough when it mattered. (4/1)

574 Augustan had his chances but probably found this trip on the sharp side and could never quicken enough when it mattered. (5/1)

Eagle Canyon (IRE), who needs further, ran well, making steady late headway, and looks to be coming to form. (14/1)

Tomal, who has only won once and that was three years ago, showed signs of encouragement here. (20/1)

633 Night of Glass again left the impression that this trip is beyond his best. (8/1)

T/Jkpt: Not won; £15,882.37 to Nottingham 29/4/97. T/Plpt: £35.60 (678.66 Tckts). T/Qdpt: £18.30 (89.49 Tckts) AA

0576-SOUTHWELL (L-H) (Standard)

Monday April 28th

WEATHER: cloudy with heavy showers WIND: fresh half bhd

867 COLDSEAL 0800 221155 CLAIMING STKS (I) (4-Y.O+) (Class F)

2-00 (2-00) **1m 4f** **(Fibresand)** £1,927.00 (£527.00: £247.00) Stalls: Low GOING: 0.09 sec per fur (STD)

				SP	RR	SF
516[8]	**Carrolls Marc (IRE) (27)** (CMurray) **9-7-13**(5) IonaWands(9) (sn trckng ldrs: hdwy to ld over 1f out: jst hld on)	—	**1**	33/1	54	18
680[11]	**At Liberty (IRE) (80)** (RHannon) **5-9-8** DaneO'Neill(6) (trckd ldrs: rdn to ld 2f out: sn hdd: styd on: jst failed)	s.h	**2**	7/4[1]	72	36

Batabanoo (MrsMReveley) **8-9-8** MHills(5) (hld up: hdwy on outside over 4f out: shkn up over 2f out: styd on fnl f) ....4 **3** 2/1[2] 67 31
574[12] **Kilnamartyra Girl (43)** (JParkes) **7-8-0**(5) JBramhill(10) (hdwy 7f out: drvn along over 4f out: sn chsng ldrs: styd on ins fnl f) ....nk **4** 6/1[3] 49 13
Precedency (52) (KMcAuliffe) **5-9-4** WJO'Connor(3) (w ldrs: chal over 4f out: wknd over 1f out) 4 **5** 20/1 57 21
721[3] **Forzair (49)** (JJO'Neill) **5-8-10** WRyan(1) (led: edgd rt & hdd 2f out: grad wknd) ....1 **6** 6/1[3] 48 12
Apache Park (USA) (DBurchell) **4-8-4**(5) RMullen(8) (in tch: effrt over 3f out: sn rdn: wknd over 1f out) 1¼ **7** 12/1 46 9
579[7] **Jilly Beveled (36)** (RonaldThompson) **5-7-13** TWilliams(7) (bhd: gd hdwy 4f out: ev ch tl wknd 2f out) ....3½ **8** 20/1 30 —
721[16] **Anistop (45)** (JLEyre) **5-8-6** RLappin(2) (w ldrs: drvn along & outpcd over 4f out: hung lft & lost pl over 2f out) ....1 **9** 14/1 36 —
Red Light (61) (JRJenkins) **5-8-12b** GCarter(4) (trckd ldrs: pushed along 7f out: lost pl over 5f out: sn wl bhd: t.o) ....dist **10** 11/1 — —

(SP 133.4%) **10 Rn**

2m 45.0 (12.00) CSF £92.62 TOTE £18.80: £7.90 £1.30 £1.40 (£27.50) Trio £22.50 OWNER Mr C. J. Marvin (NEWMARKET) BRED John Connaughton

WEIGHT FOR AGE 4yo-1lb

Carrolls Marc (IRE), the outsider of the field, would have been meeting the favourite on 35lb worse terms in a handicap. Well handled, he did just enough to record his twelfth victory. (33/1)

486* At Liberty (IRE) looked to have been found an easy opening but, making hard work of getting to the front, he could not quite get back up. (7/4: op 11/10)

Batabanoo has had his fore-legs fired. Having his first outing for 583 days, he was by no means knocked about. (2/1)

410 Kilnamartyra Girl, who would have been 20lb better off with the favourite in a handicap, clearly likes the ground here. Though under pressure some way from home, was sticking on strongly at the finish. (6/1: op 10/1)

Precedency, a scratchy mover, ran as well as could be expected as he would have been meeting At Liberty on 24lb better terms in a handicap. (20/1)

721 Forzair, a scratchy mover at best, made the running but, edging right when headed, he dropped away. He too would have been considerably better off with the favourite in a handicap, and ran as well as could be expected. (6/1)

Red Light (11/1: 6/1-12/1)

868 COLDSEAL WINDOWS MEDIAN AUCTION MAIDEN STKS (I) (3-Y.O) (Class F)

2-30 (2-32) **1m (Fibresand)** £1,927.00 (£527.00: £247.00) Stalls: Low GOING: 0.09 sec per fur (STD)

SP RR SF

768[8] **Keen Alert** (MBell) **3-8-9**(5) GFaulkner(10) (dwlt: sn trckng ldrs: led over 2f out: edgd rt u.p: hld on towards fin) ....— **1** 12/1 65 13
Rheinbold (TJEtherington) **3-9-0** GCarter(6) (bit bkwd: hld up: stdy hdwy ½-wy: chal over 1f out: carried rt: kpt on wl) ....½ **2** 7/1[2] 64 12
576[2] **Mr Paradise (IRE) (69)** (TJNaughton) **3-9-0** MHills(8) (lw: w ldrs: chal over 2f out: wknd over 1f out) ....5 **3** 4/6[1] 54 2
341[7] **Isis Honda (IRE)** (CEBrittain) **3-8-2**(7) JGotobed(12) (b.hind: racd wd: gd hdwy ½-wy: one pce fnl 2f) ....2½ **4** 12/1 44 —
645[12] **Spanish Warrior** (JWHills) **3-9-0** NAdams(7) (w ldrs: chal over 2f out: wknd over 1f out) ....1¾ **5** 20/1 46 —
599[10] **Quezon City** (MJCamacho) **3-9-0** LCharnock(2) (s.i.s: drvn along & outpcd ½-wy: kpt on wl fnl 2f) ....¾ **6** 16/1 44 —
576[5] **Agent Mulder** (PDCundell) **3-9-0** JLowe(5) (chsd ldrs: sn pushed along: outpcd 2f out: eased) ....3½ **7** 40/1 37 —
609[5] **Father Eddie (43)** (JJO'Neill) **3-9-0** GDuffield(9) (bhd & drvn along ½-wy: n.d) ....1¾ **8** 33/1 34 —
Avanti Blue (KMcAuliffe) **3-9-0** WJO'Connor(3) (lw: led tl over 2f out: sn wknd) ....nk **9** 20/1 33 —
230[3] **Sliema Creek (67)** (TDBarron) **3-9-0** JCarroll(1) (outpcd & bhd fr ½-wy) ....½ **10** 10/1 32 —
Sweetchildofmine (HAkbary) **3-8-9** OUrbina(13) (leggy: unf: b: s.s: sn chsng ldrs: lost pl over 2f out) ....nk **11** 33/1 26 —
Sea Ya Maite (SRBowring) **3-9-0** SWebster(11) (b: racd wd: bhd fr ½-wy: t.o) ....17 **12** 25/1 — —
Regal Equity (63) (MCPipe) **3-9-0** DaneO'Neill(4) (chsd ldrs: sn drvn along: lost pl ½-wy) ....13 **13** 9/1[3] — —

(SP 134.5%) **13 Rn**

1m 48.3 (9.30) CSF £88.70 TOTE £19.00: £4.20 £2.20 £1.10 (£86.50) Trio £24.30 OWNER Ms Dawn Stagg (NEWMARKET) BRED Miss Dawn A. Stagg

Keen Alert soon stepped up on his initial effort. His rider persisted in using his whip in his correct hand, the right one, but he risked disqualification by not putting it down and attempting to keep his mount straight. (12/1)

Rheinbold is described by his trainer as of a nervous disposition, so being crowded could not have done him any good. (7/1: 6/1-4/1)

576 Mr Paradise (IRE) had no obvious excuse. (4/6: evens-6/4)

292 Isis Honda (IRE), an unfurnished filly, did as well as could be expected considering she raced very wide and made her effort on the turn. (12/1: 8/1-14/1)

Spanish Warrior stopped in two strides and might not stay this far. (20/1)

Quezon City, having his third run, was noted putting in some pleasing work in the final quarter-mile. Now qualified for a handicap mark, he probably needs a step up in distance. (16/1)

Agent Mulder, another having his third run, hinted at some ability. (40/1)

230 Sliema Creek (10/1: op 6/1)

Regal Equity (9/1: op 9/2)

869 COLDSEAL 0800 221155 CLAIMING STKS (II) (4-Y.O+) (Class F)

3-00 (3-00) **1m 4f (Fibresand)** £1,927.00 (£527.00: £247.00) Stalls: Low GOING: 0.09 sec per fur (STD)

SP RR SF

595[6] **Champagne Warrior (IRE) (44)** (MJCamacho) **4-8-0** LCharnock(9) (blind off eye: chsd ldrs: led over 5f out: sn rdn: styd on wl fnl f) ....— **1** 8/1 62 32
591[4] **Greenspan (IRE) (72)** (WRMuir) **5-9-8** AClark(7) (lw: chsd ldrs: chal over 1f out: nt qckn) ....2 **2** 13/8[1] 80 51
*580** **Grand Cru (64)** (RCraggs) **6-8-3**(7) DDenby(3) (lw: prom: drvn along 7f out: styd on same pce fnl 3f) ....6 **3** 6/1[3] 60 31
580[2] **Pharly Dancer (63)** (WWHaigh) **8-8-9**(3) PMcCabe(8) (sn wl bhd: hdwy on outside 6f out: kpt on fnl 2f: nt rch ldrs) ....1 **4** 4/1[2] 61 32
657[12] **Carol's Dream (USA) (70)** (MissJBower) **5-9-5**(3) MHenry(6) (chsd ldrs tl wknd 2f out) 7 **5** 10/1 62 33
209[8] **Duffertoes (48)** (MJRyan) **5-8-6** GCarter(5) (in tch: rdn & hung lft over 2f out: sn wknd) 3½ **6** 8/1 41 12
482[9] **Haroldon (IRE) (59)** (BPalling) **8-9-2** TSprake(10) (b: unruly: chsd ldrs tl lost pl over 3f out) ....½ **7** 14/1 50 21
653[8] **Lordan Velvet (IRE) (50)** (MrsWBAllen,Norway) **5-8-4** LNewton(1) (led tl over 5f out: lost pl over 3f out) ....10 **8** 50/1 25 —
231[6] **Ihtimaam (FR) (60)** (MrsASwinbank) **5-8-12** WRyan(2) (sn outpcd & bhd: sme hdwy on outside: sn wknd: eased) ....22 **9** 10/1 4 —

Master Showman (IRE) (DJWintle) **6-8-12** VSlattery(4) (bit bkwd: b: chsd ldrs: rdn & lost pl ½-wy: t.o 3f out) ....dist **10** 50/1 — —

(SP 123.4%) **10 Rn**

2m 42.2 (9.20) CSF £20.63 TOTE £13.00: £2.40 £1.60 £1.40 (£16.70) Trio £13.40 OWNER M K Slinger & A Stuart (MALTON) BRED Dr Peter C. Yorke

WEIGHT FOR AGE 4yo-1lb

Grand Cru clmd AScargo £6,000

595 Champagne Warrior (IRE) somehow seems a more genuine, sweeter filly since she lost her off-eye. Given a forceful ride, she showed the right sort of spirit to fight off the favourite coming to the final furlong. (8/1)

591 Greenspan (IRE) threw down a strong challenge but it was soon clear he was booked for second spot. (13/8)

580* Grand Cru found this trip on the short side. Flat out almost a mile from home, he kept on all the way to line and, claimed, looks sure to make his mark over hurdles. (6/1: op 7/2)

580 Pharly Dancer was given a strange ride. With the race run at a moderate pace, he was soon dropped right out. Making his ground on the outside at halfway, he kept on in his own time in the final two furlongs but had an impossible task. (4/1)

Carol's Dream (USA) (10/1: op 20/1)

209 Duffertoes (8/1: tchd 12/1)

66 Ihtimaam (FR), after an eighty-day absence, ran poorly, and his rider gave up a long way from home. (10/1: 8/1-12/1)

870 COLDSEAL ROTHERHAM PROMOTIONS AMATEUR H'CAP (0-70) (4-Y.O+) (Class G)

3-30 (3-32) **1m (Fibresand)** £2,070.00 (£570.00: £270.00) Stalls: Low GOING: 0.09 sec per fur (STD)

Form	Horse / details	Dist	Pos	SP	RR	SF
429^{7}	**Takhlid (USA) (63)** (DWChapman) **6-11-0** MissRClark(6) (trckd ldrs gng wl: led wl over 1f out: drvn out)	—	**1**	12/1	75	49
607^{9}	**Montone (IRE) (64)** (JRJenkins) **7-11-1v** DrMMannish(2) (chsd ldrs: sn drvn along: nt qckn fnl f)	2½	**2**	12/1	71	45
	Benjamins Law (68) (JAPickering) **6-10-12**(7) MissEGeorge(5) (dwlt: hdwy ½-wy: sn chsng ldrs: styd on same pce fnl 2f)	1	**3**	33/1	73	47
273^{8}	**Commin' Up (54)** (MissJBower) **4-9-12**(7)ow14 MrGWoodward(14) (a chsng ldrs: one pce fnl 2f)	4	**4**	33/1	51	11
123^{11}	**Pc's Cruiser (IRE) (40)** (NPLittmoden) **5-8-12**(7) MrJTyler-Morris(9) (s.i.s: bhd: hdwy on outside over 2f out: nvr rchd ldrs)	3½	**5**	12/1	30	4
753^{3}	**Roman Reel (USA) (59)** (GLMoore) **6-10-10** MrsJMoore(8) (mid div: sn drvn along: kpt on fnl 2f: nvr nr ldrs)	s.h	**6**	10/1	49	23
579^{3}	**Cats Bottom (55)** (AGNewcombe) **5-10-6** MrTMcCarthy(1) (trckd ldrs: led 5f out tl wl over 1f out: grad wknd)	¾	**7**	5/1 1	43	17
*579**	**The Barnsley Belle (IRE) (63)** (JLEyre) **4-11-0** MissDianaJones(12) (chsd ldrs tl lost pl ½-wy: n.d)	2	**8**	11/2 2	47	21
607^{4}	**Soldier Cove (USA) (60)** (MartynMeade) **7-10-11** MrCBonner(10) (swtg: bhd: hdwy on outside 2f out: nvr nr ldrs)	1¾	**9**	13/2	41	15
	Dancing Destiny (44) (RBastiman) **5-9-2**(7)ow1 MissRBastiman(4) (swtg: s.i.s: stdy hdwy on ins & hmpd over 3f out: nvr nr to chal)	2	**10**	33/1	21	—
407^{9}	**Private Fixture (IRE) (40)** (DMarks) **6-9-1b**(4) MrsAUsher(15) (racd wd: a rr div)	nk	**11**	20/1	16	—
552^{13}	**Domino Flyer (66)** (MrsASwinbank) **4-11-3** MrChrisWilson(16) (mid div: sn drvn along: n.d)	6	**12**	8/1	30	4
358^{9}	**Roar on Tour (54)** (MrsMReveley) **8-10-5** MrMHNaughton(7) (a in rr)	1¼	**13**	11/1	16	—
376^{6}	**Sea Spouse (65)** (MBlanshard) **6-11-2** MrRThornton(13) (chsd ldrs: rdn 3f out: sn lost pl)	6	**14**	6/1 3	15	—
579^{9}	**Sandmoor Denim (46)** (SRBowring) **10-9-7**(4) MrsMMorris(3) (chsd ldrs tl lost pl over 2f out)	nk	**15**	16/1	—	—
274^{10}	**Awesome Venture (70)** (MCChapman) **7-11-0**(7) MrNChapman(11) (b.off hind: led 3f: lost pl over 3f out)	7	**16**	25/1	5	—

(SP 134.6%) **16 Rn**

1m 47.2 (8.20) CSF £141.26 CT £2,425.02 TOTE £26.10: £3.10 £3.30 £8.00 £14.00 (£89.00) Trio Not won; £343.27 to Nottingham 29/4/97 OWNER Miss N. F. Thesiger (YORK) BRED Cheveley Park Stud Ltd

386* Takhlid (USA) could be named the winner some way from home. Judging by the market, his success was not unexpected. (12/1)

210* Montone (IRE) presumably needed it last time after a break. He can be relied on to run well in this type of event. (12/1)

Benjamins Law, having his first run for 282 days, will presumably come on for it. (33/1)

Commin' Up did really well to finish so close considering she was carrying a stone overweight. (33/1)

Pc's Cruiser (IRE), having his first outing for 98 days, shaped by no means badly. (12/1: op 33/1)

753 Roman Reel (USA), who found a mile and a half on turf too far last time, was soon being chopped for foot over this trip. (10/1)

579 Cats Bottom had a dream run through on the inner to take the lead turning out of the back stretch, but seemed to run out of stamina in the final furlong, her stride shortening markedly. (5/1)

579* The Barnsley Belle (IRE) (11/2: op 7/2)

871 COLDSEAL GOLDMINE H'CAP (0-75) (3-Y.O) (Class D)

4-00 (4-03) **6f (Fibresand)** £3,900.40 (£1,166.20: £558.60: £254.80) Stalls: Low GOING: 0.09 sec per fur (STD)

Form	Horse / details	Dist	Pos	SP	RR	SF
*855**	**Forcing Bid (72)** (SirMarkPrescott) **3-9-4** 7x GDuffield(4) (lw: trckd ldrs: led 2f out: edgd lft & sn clr: drvn out)	—	**1**	4/1 1	81	44
764^{5}	**Swan Island (68)** (BPalling) **3-9-0** TSprake(13) (b.hind: racd wd: in tch: styd on wl fnl f: no ch w wnr)	2½	**2**	10/1	70	33
845^{3}	**Swift (63)** (MJPolglase) **3-8-9** MRimmer(5) (trckd ldrs: kpt on one pce fnl 2f)	4	**3**	7/1 2	55	18
584^{7}	**Corinchili (56)** (GGMargarson) **3-7-13**(3) MHenry(3) (lw: led to 2f out: one pce)	nk	**4**	16/1	47	10
649^{7}	**Distinctive Dream (IRE) (50)** (KTIvory) **3-7-5b**(5) RMullen(10) (bhd: hdwy u.p over 2f out: nvr nr to chal)	¾	**5**	16/1	39	2
588^{5}	**Barwell Boy (50)** (JLHarris) **3-7-5**(5) JBramhill(2) (b.off hind: s.i.s: hdwy on ins to chse ldrs 3f out: sn rdn: no imp)	nk	**6**	12/1	38	1
459^{3}	**Roffey Spinney (IRE) (75)** (RHannon) **3-9-7** DaneO'Neill(1) (in tch: effrt u.p over 2f out: eased whn btn ins fnl f)	3	**7**	7/1 2	55	18
	Fine Times (64) (CWFairhurst) **3-8-10** LCharnock(8) (in tch: outpcd fnl 3f)	hd	**8**	16/1	44	7
581^{7}	**Gresatre (66)** (CADwyer) **3-8-5**(7) JoHunnam(14) (racd wd: hld up & bhd: sme hdwy 2f out: n.d)	1¾	**9**	12/1	41	4
694^{18}	**Enchanting Eve (70)** (CNAllen) **3-8-13**(3) MartinDwyer(9) (a in rr)	1¼	**10**	12/1	42	5
	Naivasha (65) (JBerry) **3-8-11** GCarter(12) (racd wd: hdwy on ins over 2f out: sn wknd)	¾	**11**	15/2 3	35	—
	Make Ready (67) (JNeville) **3-8-13** SDrowne(6) (chsd ldrs tl wknd 2f out)	1¼	**12**	14/1	34	—
649^{17}	**Parijazz (IRE) (68)** (MartynMeade) **3-9-0** NAdams(7) (hld up: a in rr)	2½	**13**	14/1	28	—
532^{9}	**Komasta (67)** (CaptJWilson) **3-8-13v** JCarroll(11) (racd wd: sn bhd)	6	**14**	16/1	11	—

(SP 125.8%) **14 Rn**

1m 18.3 (4.80) CSF £41.70 CT £264.38 TOTE £3.60: £2.00 £4.50 £2.20 (£38.90) Trio £79.10 OWNER Mr H. R. Moszkowicz (NEWMARKET) BRED Angley Stud Ltd

LONG HANDICAP Distinctive Dream (IRE) 7-3 Barwell Boy 7-8

855* Forcing Bid, a grand type, defied a 7lb penalty with something to spare. (4/1)

764 Swan Island, having her first outing on the All-Weather, stuck on strongly in the final furlong despite a tendency to carry her head high. Seven furlongs should suit her better. (10/1)
845 Swift,. like the winner, was having his second outing in three days. (7/1)
649 Distinctive Dream (IRE), who had the blinkers fitted again, was on his toes beforehand. Sticking on when it was all over, he is not a straightforward ride. (16/1)
588 Barwell Boy, nibbled at the market, was not disgraced after missing the break slightly. (12/1: op 25/1)
Naivasha (15/2: op 12/1) 49 67+ 56 47

872 COLDSEAL 'IN THE FRAME' (S) STKS (2-Y.O) (Class F)
4-30 (4-39) **5f (Fibresand)** £2,277.00 (£627.00: £297.00) Stalls: High GOING minus 0.42 sec per fur (FST)

				SP	RR	SF
743^{3}	**My Bet** (MWEasterby) **2-8-1**(5) GParkin(8) (w ldrs: rdn ½-wy: r.o to ld post)	—	**1**	9/2 2	55	5
	Branston Berry (IRE) (MJohnston) **2-8-6** JFanning(3) (w'like: leggy: led over 3f out: shkn up & hung lft over 1f out: r.o u.p: jst ct)	hd	**2**	11/10 1	55	5
743^{6}	**Daynabee** (NTinkler) **2-8-6** JCarroll(4) (chsd ldrs: rdn ½-wy: wknd over 1f out)	6	**3**	10/1	36	—
	Off And Running (JBerry) **2-8-11** GCarter(7) (leggy: unf: bit bkwd: s.i.s: sn wl outpcd & bhd: hung lft: sme hdwy fnl f: n.d)	7	**4**	6/1 3	18	—
697^{8}	**Statorhythm** (TDBarron) **2-8-11b1** LCharnock(6) (sn drvn along: outpcd after 2f)	1½	**5**	6/1 3	13	—
441^{7}	**Sipping Soda** (KTIvory) **2-8-3**(3) MartinDwyer(2) (sn outpcd)	3½	**6**	16/1	—	—
	Lady d'Abo (RCSpicer) **2-8-3**(3) RHavlin(1) (leggy: unf: s.s: a wl bhd: hung lft thrght)	10	**7**	14/1	—	—
651^{6}	***Frundin*** (MrsWBAllen,Norway) **2-8-6b1** LNewton(5) (Withdrawn not under Starter's orders: v.unruly going to s)		**W**	50/1	—	—
				(SP 118.0%)	**7 Rn**	

59.9 secs (2.90) CSF £9.26 TOTE £4.30: £2.90 £1.60 (£4.70) OWNER Mr W. T. Allgood (SHERIFF HUTTON) BRED M. W. Easterby
No Bid. Branston Berry (IRE) clmd KMeynell £6,000
743 My Bet, who became upset down at the stalls, used her experience to good effect, sticking on under a forceful ride to get up in the very last stride. She shows a fair bit of knee action and was clearly suited by this surface. (9/2: 7/2-6/1)
Branston Berry (IRE), a fair sort for a plater, had the legs of these at halfway but, showing signs of inexperience and coming off a straight line, she was pipped on the line. She looked as though she would be better for the outing and would certainly win a similar event next time if her new connections dare risk her. (11/10: 6/4-evens)
Daynabee, taken off her legs at halfway, seems very short on stamina. (10/1)
Off And Running, a May foal, looks very immature yet and ran like it. (6/1: op 11/4)
Statorhythm was tried in blinkers to no effect. (6/1)
Lady d'Abo (14/1: 10/1-16/1)

873 COLDSEAL NORTHERN REGION H'CAP (0-65) (3-Y.O F) (Class F)
5-00 (5-04) **7f (Fibresand)** £2,277.00 (£627.00: £297.00) Stalls: Low GOING: 0.09 sec per fur (STD)

				SP	RR	SF
662^{6}	**Sheraton Girl (38)** (NPLittmoden) **3-7-10**(3) MartinDwyer(9) (trckd ldr: led over 1f out: rdn out)	—	**1**	33/1	48	17
535^{8}	**Poker Princess (49)** (MBell) **3-8-5**(5) RMullen(8) (hdwy over 3f out: r.o wl fnl f: nt rch wnr)	1¾	**2**	10/1	55	24
590^{6}	**Dayrella (51)** (WRMuir) **3-8-12** DaneO'Neill(6) (lw: a chsng ldrs: styd on one pce fnl 2f)	5	**3**	20/1	46	15
378^{4}	**Lucy of Arabia (IRE) (53)** (JJSheehan) **3-9-0b1** SDrowne(13) (mid div: effrt on outside 2f out: kpt on: nvr nr to chal)	¾	**4**	20/1	46	15
*662**	**Mirror Four Sport (60)** (MJohnston) **3-9-0**(7) KSked(2) (bhd: sme hdwy 2f out: nvr nr to chal)	1½	**5**	10/1	49	18
	Showgirl (60) (CaptJWilson) **3-9-7** JCarroll(5) (bit bkwd: led tl over 1f out: sn wknd)	1	**6**	10/1	47	16
590^{5}	**Janglynyve (51)** (SPCWoods) **3-8-5**(7) CWebb(7) (in tch: effrt over 2f out: grad wknd)	5	**7**	8/1	27	—
751^{5}	**Jukebox Jive (52)** (CADwyer) **3-8-13** GDuffield(3) (chsd ldrs tl wknd over 1f out)	5	**8**	5/1 2	16	—
785*	**Muscatana (64)** (BWHills) **3-9-11** 6x MHills(4) (lw: stdd s: hld up & bhd: hdwy & nt clr run 2f out: nvr plcd to chal)	½	**9**	7/4 1	27	—
*577**	**Julia's Relative (52)** (RonaldThompson) **3-8-13** TWilliams(10) (chsd ldrs tl wknd over 2f out)	2	**10**	8/1	11	—
	Strelitza (IRE) (57) (MWEasterby) **3-8-13b**(5) GParkin(11) (racd wd: bhd & drvn along ½-wy: n.d)	9	**11**	13/2 3	—	—
652^{6}	**Royal Emblem (50)** (AGFoster) **3-8-11** RPerham(14) (racd wd: bhd fr ½-wy)	hd	**12**	20/1	—	—
	Trulyfan (IRE) (50) (RAFahey) **3-8-4**(7) RWinston(12) (racd wd: bhd fr ½-wy: t.o)	20	**13**	12/1	—	—
	Fontcaudette (IRE) (57) (JEBanks) **3-9-4** JStack(1) (sn wl bhd)	1¼	**14**	25/1	—	—
				(SP 144.6%)	**14 Rn**	

1m 33.0 (6.50) CSF £338.50 CT £6,142.34 TOTE £33.50: £4.50 £6.30 £9.70 (£580.30) Trio Not won; £230.55 to Nottingham 29/4/97 OWNER Happy Times Ahead Partnership (WOLVERHAMPTON) BRED Bearstone Stud
OFFICIAL EXPLANATION **Muscatana: resented the kick-back.**
Sheraton Girl, well beaten in a seller over further last time, took this poor handicap in decisive fashion. There was certainly no fluke. (33/1)
Poker Princess, who apparently failed to stay a mile last time, was racing from a 5lb lower mark. (10/1)
Dayrella showed her first worthwhile form. (20/1)
378 Lucy of Arabia (IRE), stepping up in distance and down in the weights, had blinkers on for the first time. (20/1)
662* Mirror Four Sport found this trip too sharp. (10/1)
590 Janglynyve (8/1: op 12/1)
602 Jukebox Jive (5/1: op 14/1)
785* Muscatana is not very big to be carrying such a big weight. Under a 6lb penalty and poorly drawn, she was again dropped in at the start. She apparently resented the kick-back, and her rider made just a token effort two furlongs from home before calling it a day. This can be safely overlooked when she returns to the turf. (7/4: op 11/10)
Trulyfan (IRE) (12/1: op 20/1)

874 COLDSEAL WINDOWS MEDIAN AUCTION MAIDEN STKS (II) (3-Y.O) (Class F)
5-30 (5-32) **1m (Fibresand)** £1,927.00 (£527.00: £247.00) Stalls: Low GOING: 0.09 sec per fur (STD)

				SP	RR	SF
742^{6}	**Island Sanctuary (IRE)** (PJMakin) **3-9-0** SSanders(9) (hld up: hdwy on outside ½-wy: led over 1f out: r.o u.p)	—	**1**	11/10 1	77	34
	Cartouche (66) (SirMarkPrescott) **3-9-0** GDuffield(2) (sn led: rdn 2f out: sn hdd: nt qckn towards fin)	nk	**2**	7/2 2	76	33
681^{11}	**Going Green** (JRFanshawe) **3-8-9** MHills(11) (b.hind: hdwy on outside over 3f out: sn chsng ldrs: eased fnl f)	19	**3**	10/1	33	—
361^{5}	**Crackerbox** (CADwyer) **3-8-2**(7) JoHunnam(6) (chsd ldrs to ½-wy: sn outpcd)	6	**4**	16/1	21	—

576^{4} **Bison Belting** (JAGlover) **3-9-0** GCarter(3) (trckd ldrs: shkn up & wknd over 1f out) ....¾ **5** $7/1^{3}$ 25 —
576^{6} **Impetuosity (IRE)** (CWThornton) **3-8-9** JFanning(8) (sn outpcd & bhd: sme hdwy 2f out: n.d) ....1 **6** 25/1 18 —
Bold Et Noir (WJarvis) **3-9-0** OUrbina(13) (rangy: s.i.s: sme hdwy ½-wy: nvr nr ldrs) ....1¼ **7** 9/1 20 —
588^{4} **Concer Arall** (SCWilliams) **3-8-11**(3) MHenry(5) (chsd ldrs: rdn & wknd over 2f out) ....7 **8** 8/1 6 —
652^{12} **Little Progress (35)** (TMJones) **3-9-0** RPerham(1) (s.s: a wl bhd) ....5 **9** 66/1 — —
485^{6} **Victoria House (IRE)** (MJHeaton-Ellis) **3-8-9** SDrowne(4) (chsd ldrs: drvn along over 4f out: lost pl over 2f out) ....3 **10** 25/1 — —
Hio Nod (MJCamacho) **3-9-0** LCharnock(7) (sn outpcd & drvn along) ....1 **11** 33/1 — —
Flying Esprit (GGMargarson) **3-9-0** LNewton(12) (rangy: unf: sn outpcd & drvn along) ....hd **12** 33/1 — —
576^{7} **Superapparos** (SRBowring) **3-9-0** SWebster(10) (racd wd: w ldrs tl wknd over 2f out: sn bhd) ....1 **13** 33/1 — —
(SP 136.4%) **13 Rn**

1m 46.1 (7.10) CSF £4.91 TOTE £1.80: £1.50 £1.80 £3.40 (£5.30) Trio £20.80 OWNER Dr Carlos Stelling (MARLBOROUGH) BRED The Earl of Harrington

742 Island Sanctuary (IRE) had a poor draw to overcome. After looking to have taken control, he had to dig deep when the runner-up fought back. (11/10: 4/5-5/4)
Cartouche, who has plenty of size and scope, had the run of the race on the inner. Sticking on strongly under pressure, in the end he was only just denied and the first two were a long way clear. (7/2: 4/1-6/1)
Going Green, who still does not look the finished article, was wisely asked to do just enough to secure third spot. She needs one more outing to qualify for a handicap mark. (10/1: op 6/1)
204 Crackerbox, having her third outing, kept on nicely after being outpaced at halfway. (16/1)
576 Bison Belting, who had finished behind Mr Paradise, a big disappointment in the first division, still has something to learn. (7/1: 7/2-8/1)
Impetuosity (IRE), still clueless, was staying on when it was all over. This was her third outing and a big step up in distance might suit. (25/1)

T/Plpt: £316.30 (41.78 Tckts). T/Qdpt: £138.80 (6.64 Tckts) WG

BATH (L-H) (Good to firm)
Tuesday April 29th
WEATHER: overcast WIND: fresh across

875 BLATHWAYT MAIDEN STKS (3-Y.O) (Class D)
2-00 (2-01) **1m 2f 46y** £3,783.75 (£1,140.00: £552.50: £258.75) Stalls: Low GOING minus 0.40 sec per fur (F)

SP RR SF

676^{6} **Maid of Camelot** (RCharlton) **3-8-9** PatEddery(5) (lw: chsd ldr: led over 2f out tl wl over 1f out: rdn to ld ins fnl f: r.o wl) ....— **1** $5/4^{1}$ 79 43
676^{5} **Natural Eight (IRE)** (BWHills) **3-9-0** MHills(6) (lw: a.p: led wl over 1f out tl ins fnl f) ....¾ **2** $3/1^{2}$ 83 47
645^{6} **Irsal** (ACStewart) **3-9-0** MRoberts(9) (hld up: carried wd over 4f out: hdwy 3f out: r.o one pce fnl 2f) ....9 **3** $8/1^{3}$ 69 33
Copper Shell (APJones) **3-9-0** SDrowne(2) (led: rdn & hdd over 2f out: wknd wl over 1f out) ....¾ **4** 50/1 68 32
Fantasy Girl (IRE) (JLDunlop) **3-8-9** PaulEddery(8) (lw: hld up: stdy hdwy over 2f out: nvr plcd to chal) 4 **5** 16/1 56 20
Arthur's Seat (LordHuntingdon) **3-9-0** RPerham(11) (lw: hld up: bdly hmpd on ins over 4f out: wknd 3f out) ...8 **6** 33/1 49 13
Cowtharee (MRStoute) **3-8-9** SSanders(10) (bit bkwd: hdwy 7f out: rdn over 3f out: wknd over 2f out) ....1 **7** $8/1^{3}$ 42 6
First Man (35) (BJLlewellyn) **3-9-0** JLowe(1) (lw: s.s: sme hdwy over 3f out: n.d) ....½ **8** 66/1 46 10
605^{5} **Laurel Seeker (USA)** (MrsAJPerrett) **3-8-7**(7) GayeHarwood(7) (prom: carried wd over 4f out: sn rdn: wknd over 3f out) 2½ **9** 16/1 43 7
Coincidence (MRChannon) **3-8-2**(7) AEddery(3) (leggy: s.s: a bhd: t.o) ....15 **10** 25/1 14 —
$812a^{5}$ **North White Plains** (CEBrittain) **3-9-0** BDoyle(4) (ref to r: tk no part) .... **R** 14/1 — —
(SP 120.3%) **11 Rn**

2m 8.8 (2.30) CSF £4.37 TOTE £2.60: £1.30 £1.30 £1.90 (£2.60) Trio £6.30 OWNER Mr A. E. Oppenheimer (BECKHAMPTON) BRED Hascombe and Valiant Studs

676 Maid of Camelot, who finished a short-head behind the runner-up on her debut, was described by Eddery as playing in front and responded when challenged. Her trainer thinks she will stay a mile and a half. (5/4)
676 Natural Eight (IRE), a half-brother to sprinter Watch Me, could not confirm his narrow Newmarket superiority over the winner, but beat the others easily enough. (3/1: op 2/1)
645 Irsal got messed about after leaving the back straight, and should do better when stepped up to an even longer distance. (8/1)
Copper Shell had shown nothing on his only run last season. (50/1)
Fantasy Girl (IRE), who only beat one home in two outings as a juvenile, caught the eye of the Stewards. Her rider described the filly as a poor mover who was never striding out until the rising ground, and the trainer added she was only moderate. These explanations were accepted. (16/1)
Arthur's Seat was badly hampered and this run is probably best forgotten. (33/1)
Cowtharee (8/1: op 5/1)
812a North White Plains (14/1: 12/1-8/1)

876 SPA (S) STKS (3-Y.O) (Class G)
2-30 (2-30) **5f 11y** £2,262.00 (£632.00: £306.00) Stalls: High GOING minus 0.10 sec per fur (G)

SP RR SF

Cauda Equina (75) (MRChannon) **3-8-7**(5) PPMurphy(9) (bhd tl hdwy 2f out: squeezed thro to ld 1f out: r.o wl) ....— **1** $3/1^{1}$ 69 38
339^{4} **Nopalea (72)** (TJNaughton) **3-8-7** SSanders(3) (led 4f: nt qckn) ....1½ **2** $9/2^{2}$ 59 28
758^{4} **Silver Lining (66)** (APJones) **3-9-3** BDoyle(5) (hdwy wl over 1f out: r.o one pce fnl f) ....nk **3** $9/2^{2}$ 68 37
751^{6} **Whizz Kid (51)** (JJBridger) **3-8-12** FNorton(10) (hdwy wl over 1f out: r.o ins fnl f) ....s.h **4** 20/1 63 32
783^{6} **Tear White (IRE) (70)** (TGMills) **3-9-0b**(3) AWhelan(8) (w ldr: ev ch 1f out: one pce) ....¾ **5** $9/2^{2}$ 66 35
765^{7} **Dr Woodstock** (MartynMeade) **3-8-9**(3) RHavlin(7) (s.i.s: nvr nr to chal) 2½ **6** 12/1 53 22
602^{7} **Littlestone Rocket (58)** (WRMuir) **3-8-12** PatEddery(1) (prom over 3f) ....1¾ **7** $6/1^{3}$ 47 16
758^{5} **Hi Mujtahid (IRE)** (JMBradley) **3-8-7**(5) RFfrench(6) (s.s: a bhd) ....hd **8** 16/1 47 16
757^{5} **Bon Guest (IRE) (61)** (TJNaughton) **3-8-12b**1 PaulEddery(2) (lw: prom 3f) 1¼ **9** 12/1 43 12
662^{8} **Our Drowsy Maggie** (WMBrisbourne) **3-8-4**(3) MartinDwyer(4) (chsd ldrs: rdn over 2f out: sn wknd) 1¾ **10** 50/1 33 2
(SP 121.8%) **10 Rn**

63.5 secs (3.00) CSF £15.70 TOTE £4.10: £1.70 £1.30 £1.50 (£10.10) Trio £23.20 OWNER Mr Michael Foy (UPPER LAMBOURN) BRED R. P. Williams
Bt in 4,000 gns

OFFICIAL EXPLANATION **Hi Mujtahid (IRE): missed the break but was stopped by weakening horses at the finish. He is big and weak and had been reluctent to leave the stalls last time.**
Cauda Equina who had lots of problems last year, was hobdayed during the winter and took advantage of a big drop in grade. (3/1: 2/1-100/30)
339 Nopalea, another dropped in class, was unable to cope with the winner but does seem better on grass than on sand. (9/2: op 3/1)
758 Silver Lining may be better suited by a return to six. (9/2: op 7/1)
602 Whizz Kid is another who could have found the minimum trip on the sharp side. (20/1)
783 Tear White (IRE) was reverting back to selling company. (9/2: 3/1-5/1)
758 Hi Mujtahid (IRE) was the subject of a Stewards' Enquiry and the explanations which included that, in the trainer's opinion, the gelding needs a longer trip, were accepted. (16/1)
757 Bon Guest (IRE) (12/1: op 8/1)

877 CORSTON CONDITIONS STKS (3-Y.O+) (Class C)
3-00 (3-00) **5f 11y** £4,713.89 (£1,760.10: £857.55: £365.25: £160.13: £78.08) Stalls: High GOING minus 0.10 sec per fur (G)

				SP	RR	SF
	Averti (IRE) (98) (WRMuir) **6-9-10** MRoberts(1) (lw: a.p: led ins fnl f: r.o)	—	1	16/1	112	73
726^{14}	**Dashing Blue (100)** (IABalding) **4-9-1**(3) MartinDwyer(7) (hld up: hdwy over 2f out: ev ch over 1f out: r.o)	nk	2	9/1	105	66
	Almaty (IRE) (JHMGosden) **4-9-4** MHills(9) (lw: a.p: led over 2f out tl ins fnl f)	1¾	3	11/4 1	100	61
726*	**Repertory (93)** (MSSaunders) **4-9-4** RPerham(2) (s.s: hdwy over 1f out: one pce fnl f)	2	4	10/1	93	54
	Crowded Avenue (101) (PJMakin) **5-9-4** SSanders(5) (hld up: ev ch over 1f out: wknd ins fnl f)	nk	5	4/1 3	92	53
501^{7}	**Jennelle (97)** (CADwyer) **3-8-2**(7) JoHunnam(3) (outpcd: nvr nrr)	nk	6	10/1	92	43
573^{6}	**Anotheranniversary (96)** (GLewis) **4-8-13** PaulEddery(4) (b.hind: led over 2f: eased whn btn ins fnl f)	2½	7	20/1	78	39
745^{4}	**Watch Me (IRE) (101)** (RHannon) **4-9-3** PatEddery(6) (chsd ldrs over 3f)	4	8	7/2 2	70	31
	Vax Star (100) (JLSpearing) **3-8-13** SDrowne(8) (w ldr 3f)	1½	9	12/1	71	22

(SP 115.4%) **9 Rn**

62.1 secs (1.60) CSF £137.15 TOTE £18.80: £4.30 £2.30 £1.90 (£155.40) Trio £87.00 OWNER Mr D. J. Deer (LAMBOURN) BRED D. J. and Mrs Deer
WEIGHT FOR AGE 3yo-10lb
Averti (IRE), disappointing since winning at Haydock last July, was turned out looking as though he could have just got off a plane from Dubai. His trainer said he will go for the King's Stand if he continues to improve. (16/1)
Dashing Blue, badly drawn on his reappearance, was much more like his old self here. (9/1: 5/1-10/1)
Almaty (IRE), third in last season's King's Stand when trained by Con Collins in Ireland, was without the visor he had worn when disappointing in the King George at Goodwood. (11/4: 2/1-7/2)
726* Repertory was not disgraced in this company especially when considering his poor start. (10/1)
Crowded Avenue should find this putting an edge on him. (4/1)
501 Jennelle would not have minded more give underfoot. (10/1: 8/1-12/1)
745 Watch Me (IRE) (7/2: 4/1-5/2)

878 RACING CHANNEL H'CAP (0-80) (3-Y.O) (Class D)
3-30 (3-39) **1m 2f 46y** £3,556.25 (£1,070.00: £517.50: £241.25) Stalls: Low GOING minus 0.40 sec per fur (F)

				SP	RR	SF
690^{8}	**Bold Oriental (IRE) (79)** (NACallaghan) **3-9-6** PatEddery(7) (lw: hld up & bhd: stdy hdwy over 3f out: led over 1f out: comf)	—	1	13/8 1	87+	52
667*	**Krosno (62)** (SCWilliams) **3-8-0**(3) MHenry(8) (a.p: rdn over 4f out: r.o one pce fnl f)	2½	2	10/1	66	31
700^{4}	**Time Can Tell (68)** (CMurray) **3-8-9** DeanMcKeown(11) (hrd rdn & hdwy 2f out: r.o ins fnl f)	¾	3	14/1	71	36
568^{2}	**Protocol (IRE) (73)** (JWHills) **3-9-0** MHills(10) (lw: a.p: rdn over 2f out: r.o one pce)	nk	4	8/1 3	75	40
	Indium (80) (JHMGosden) **3-9-7** GHind(9) (lw: hld up: stdy hdwy 6f out: led over 2f out tl over 1f out: wknd ins fnl f)	1¾	5	7/1 2	80	45
690^{15}	**Heart of Armor (79)** (PFICole) **3-8-13**(7) DavidO'Neill(6) (lw: nvr nrr)	3½	6	16/1	73	38
641*	**Here's To Howie (USA) (76)** (RHannon) **3-9-3** RPerham(3) (lw: a.p: led 3f out: sn hdd: wknd 2f out)	3	7	14/1	66	31
	Running Free (IRE) (56) (MJFetherston-Godley) **3-7-11** FNorton(4) (a bhd)	nk	8	33/1	45	10
	Eponine (70) (MRChannon) **3-8-11** BDoyle(12) (bhd fnl 4f)	hd	9	20/1	59	24
	Goodwood Lass (IRE) (73) (JLDunlop) **3-9-0** PaulEddery(2) (lw: prom 7f)	1¾	10	14/1	59	24
	Tartan Party (64) (PFICole) **3-8-0**(5) RFfrench(1) (bit bkwd: a bhd)	¾	11	12/1	49	14
700^{6}	**Miss Barcelona (IRE) (55)** (MJPolglase) **3-7-5**(5) RMullen(5) (led over 7f: sn wknd)	8	12	33/1	27	—

(SP 115.0%) **12 Rn**

2m 8.9 (2.40) CSF £15.54 CT £150.56 TOTE £2.60: £1.40 £2.60 £2.00 (£14.90) Trio £64.70 OWNER Mr M. Tabor (NEWMARKET) BRED Leo Collins
LONG HANDICAP Miss Barcelona (IRE) 7-7
Bold Oriental (IRE), 1lb lower than when not beaten far at Newmarket last, time had to be rousted along to assert, but was well on top at the end. (13/8)
667* Krosno, upped in trip, was not disgraced off a 7lb higher mark in a hotter race. (10/1)
700 Time Can Tell needs to revert to a mile and a half on this evidence. (14/1: 10/1-16/1)
568 Protocol (IRE) kept plugging away on this return to turf. (8/1)
Indium did not really prove he gets this trip, and it will be interesting to see if he is back to a shorter distance next time. (7/1: 4/1-15/2)
641* Here's To Howie (USA) (14/1: op 9/1)
Goodwood Lass (IRE) (14/1: op 8/1)

879 BRISTOL ROVERS H'CAP (0-70) (3-Y.O+) (Class E)
4-00 (4-08) **5f 11y** £3,015.25 (£907.00: £438.50: £204.25) Stalls: High GOING minus 0.10 sec per fur (G)

				SP	RR	SF
569^{3}	**Intiaash (IRE) (68)** (DHaydnJones) **5-9-13** PatEddery(12) (hld up: hdwy wl over 1f out: led ins fnl f: rdn & r.o wl)	—	1	8/1	80	62
477^{6}	**Flying Harold (42)** (MRChannon) **4-8-1** NAdams(10) (chsd ldrs: led wl over 1f out: edgd lft: hdd ins fnl f)	2	2	10/1	48	30
698^{6}	**John O'Dreams (50)** (MrsALMKing) **12-8-9** MRoberts(14) (b: bhd tl hdwy fnl 2f: r.o)	1½	3	8/1	51	33
	Tee-Emm (38) (RSimpson) **7-7-11b**ow1 FNorton(8) (b: a.p: bmpd 2f out: one pce)	¾	4	14/1	37	18
	Tinker Osmaston (63) (MSSaunders) **6-9-8** RPerham(13) (hdwy over 1f out: nvr nrr)	¾	5	12/1	59	41
756^{4}	**Bright Paragon (IRE) (40)** (KTIvory) **8-7-10**(3)ow3 MartinDwyer(3) (lw: b.hind: led 3f: one pce)	nk	6	20/1	35	14
643^{6}	**Crystal Heights (FR) (67)** (RJO'Sullivan) **9-9-12** SSanders(1) (b: no hdwy fnl 2f)	1	7	10/1	59	41
652^{4}	**Anokato (64)** (KTIvory) **3-8-10b**(3) MHenry(7) (prom: edgd rt 3f out: led 2f out: sn hdd: wknd fnl f)	1¾	8	6/1 3	51	23

702^{2} **River Tern (64)** (JMBradley) **4-9-4**(5) RFfrench(6) (s.s: sn rcvrd: ev ch whn hung rt 2f out: sn wknd)................½ **9** 9/2 ^{2} 49 31
541^{11} **Indian Wolf (37)** (BJLlewellyn) **4-7-10** NCarlisle(9) (bhd whn n.m.r wl over 1f out)..1½ **10** 50/1 17 —
604* **Beau Venture (USA) (69)** (BPalling) **9-10-0** BDoyle(4) (lw: w ldr 3f)..hd **11** 3/1 ^{1} 49 31
760^{10} **Mister Sean (IRE) (38)** (JMBradley) **4-7-4b**(7)ow1 JFowle(11) (b.hind: s.i.s: a bhd)..2 **12** 50/1 12 —
Sharp Stock (67) (RJHodges) **4-9-12** SDrowne(2) (plld hrd: w ldrs: hung rt bnd over 3f out: wkng whn bmpd 2f out)..4 **13** 33/1 28 10
(SP 123.9%) **13 Rn**

62.9 secs (2.40) CSF £78.38 CT £444.11 TOTE £8.10: £3.00 £3.00 £3.30 (£43.10) Trio £122.20 OWNER Mr Howard Thomas (PONTYPRIDD)
BRED Shadwell Estate Company Limited
LONG HANDICAP Indian Wolf 6-10 Mister Sean (IRE) 7-1 Bright Paragon (IRE) 7-9
WEIGHT FOR AGE 3yo-10lb
OFFICIAL EXPLANATION Beau Venture (USA): was unable to dominate and lost interest when passed.
569 Intiaash (IRE), whose two previous wins have come over six, did have the help of a stiff five. (8/1)
477 Flying Harold, dropped 3lb, has been making the running over seven furlongs and a mile, and the ploy of switching to the minimum distance nearly worked. (10/1: op 6/1)
John O'Dreams only got going late in the day but proved the ability is still there. (8/1)
Tee-Emm made a satisfactory reappearance for his new stable. (14/1)
Tinker Osmaston was 2lb lower than when scoring at Chepstow in October 1995. (12/1)
Crystal Heights (FR), dropped 3lb, was back to the mark off which he last won, but has never scored at less than six. A return to further looks on the cards. (10/1)

69 76+ 61 59

880 PENSFORD MAIDEN AUCTION STKS (2-Y.O) (Class D)

4-30 (4-36) **5f 11y** £3,187.50 (£960.00: £465.00: £217.50) Stalls: High GOING minus 0.10 sec per fur (G) — SP RR SF

Ballet Rambert (MJHeaton-Ellis) **2-7-7**(5) RFfrench(6) (lt-f: hld up: stdy hdwy over 2f out: led over 1f out: sn clr)..— **1** 20/1 64 13
682^{7} **Cloudberry** (BJMeehan) **2-8-1** BDoyle(3) (a.p: r.o one pce fnl 2f)...5 **2** 7/2 ^{2} 51 —
Whisky Mack (IRE) (RHannon) **2-8-6** PatEddery(1) (sn prom: led 3f out tl wl over 1f out: one pce)...............s.h **3** 6/5 ^{1} 56 5
Scene (IRE) (MartynMeade) **2-7-12** FNorton(2) (lt-f: unf: chsd ldrs: one pce fnl 2f)...3 **4** 14/1 39 —
Dande Times (DWPArbuthnot) **2-8-6** SSanders(8) (lt-f: prom: edgd rt bnd over 3f out: one pce fnl 2f)..........s.h **5** 14/1 46 —
648^{7} **Bliss (IRE)** (MrsPNDutfield) **2-7-7**(5) AimeeCook(10) (prom: carried rt bnd over 3f out: led wl over 1f out: sn hdd: wknd fnl f)..nk **6** 33/1 37 —
Eurofen (PDEvans) **2-8-5v**1ow2 SDrowne(5) (lt-f: a mid div)...1¾ **7** 9/1 39 —
Brandon Frank (IABalding) **2-8-0**(3) MartinDwyer(7) (w'like: scope: prom 3f)...hd **8** 7/1 ^{3} 37 —
Summer River (IRE) (CMurray) **2-8-6** DeanMcKeown(11) (neat: bhd whn hmpd over 1f out)............................¾ **9** 10/1 37 —
611^{5} **Solway Lass (IRE)** (PEccles) **2-7-12** JLowe(4) (led 2f)..2 **10** 20/1 23 —
Polly In Paris (IRE) (MartynMeade) **2-7-12** NAdams(9) (lt-f: unf: s.s: a bhd)..¾ **11** 16/1 20 —
(SP 130.9%) **11 Rn**

64.3 secs (3.80) CSF £88.22 TOTE £21.70: £3.90 £1.50 £1.20 (£85.70) Trio £33.50 OWNER Mrs Janet Wain (WROUGHTON) BRED Theakston Stud
Ballet Rambert, a half-sister to Kayus and Penny Forum, did not have to be on tiptoes to waltz away with this. (20/1)
682 Cloudberry, a first foal to a sister to Argentum, did much better than on her debut but had no chance with the winner. (7/2)
Whisky Mack (IRE) had more about him in the paddock than most of these, but got swept aside by the winner. (6/5)
Scene (IRE) is a half-sister to several winners including Te Amo. (14/1)
Dande Times is a half-brother to, amongst others, six-times five-furlong winner Lyndseylee. (14/1)
472 Bliss (IRE) is looking a bit of a short runner at the moment. (33/1)
Eurofen (9/1: 6/1-10/1)
Brandon Frank (7/1: op 4/1)

881 EMPIRE H'CAP (0-75) (4-Y.O+ F & M) (Class D)

5-00 (5-03) **1m 3f 144y** £3,488.00 (£1,049.00: £507.00: £236.00) Stalls: Low GOING minus 0.40 sec per fur (F) — SP RR SF

Last Laugh (IRE) (56) (NMBabbage) **5-8-9** BDoyle(6) (hld up: hdwy 3f out: led wl over 1f out: sn edgd lft: r.o wl)..— **1** 25/1 68 48
789^{4} **Pike Creek (USA) (75)** (IABalding) **4-9-13** PatEddery(9) (led: hrd rdn & hdd wl over 1f out: one pce).............2½ **2** 7/4 ^{1} 84 63
657^{11} **Hill Farm Dancer (55)** (WMBrisbourne) **6-8-3**(5) RMullen(1) (s.s: gd hdwy over 3f out: wknd over 1f out)..........7 **3** 10/1 54 34
796^{2} **Portite Sophie (45)** (MBrittain) **6-7-5**(7)ow2 DMernagh(8) (prom tl wknd over 1f out)..2½ **4** 7/1 41 19
Bronze Maquette (IRE) (43) (RSimpson) **7-7-5**(5) RFfrench(3) (nvr trbld ldrs)...nk **5** 14/1 38 18
Roufontaine (75) (WRMuir) **6-9-11**(3) RHavlin(7) (hld up: hdwy over 4f out: wknd over 2f out).........................1¾ **6** 4/1 ^{2} 68 48
796^{9} **On The Wildside (52)** (MRChannon) **4-7-13**(5)ow4 PPMurphy(5) (bhd fnl 4f)...2½ **7** 16/1 41 16
Mighty Phantom (USA) (73) (JWHills) **4-9-11** MHills(4) (prom 8f)..9 **8** 6/1 ^{3} 50 29
Afon Alwen (58) (SCWilliams) **4-8-7**(3) MHenry(2) (prom tl bdly hmpd on ins over 5f out: eased whn no ch fnl 2f)..dist **9** 12/1 — —
(SP 116.3%) **9 Rn**

2m 28.7 (2.00) CSF £63.48 CT £452.08 TOTE £12.40: £2.80 £1.10 £2.70 (£22.20) Trio £102.20 OWNER Charles Eden Ltd (CHELTENHAM)
BRED Brigitte Wolff in Ireland
LONG HANDICAP Bronze Maquette (IRE) 7-2 Portite Sophie 7-7
WEIGHT FOR AGE 4yo-1lb
Last Laugh (IRE) sprang a surprise for her new stable having failed to shine over hurdles for Martin Pipe. (25/1)
789 Pike Creek (USA) was well out-pointed by the winner. (7/4: 5/4-15/8)
482 Hill Farm Dancer regularly gives ground away at the start, but this was a slow exit even by her standards. (10/1: op 6/1)
796 Portite Sophie, 3lb out of the handicap, was reverting to a longer distance. (7/1)
Bronze Maquette (IRE) (14/1: 12/1-20/1)
Afon Alwen (12/1: op 8/1)

T/Plpt: £51.20 (267.79 Tckts). T/Qdpt: £41.70 (16.81 Tckts) KH

0757-NOTTINGHAM (L-H) (St Crse Good, Remainder Good, Good to firm patches)
Tuesday April 29th
WEATHER: cloudy & overcast WIND: fresh across

882 MEADOWS (S) STKS (3-Y.O) (Class G)
2-15 (2-18) **6f 15y** £1,984.50 (£547.00: £259.50) Stalls: High GOING: 0.23 sec per fur (G)

				SP	RR	SF
757[7]	**Skyers Flyer (IRE) (66)** (RonaldThompson) **3-8-13** NConnorton(16) (trckd ldrs: shkn up to ld over 1f out: qcknd clr)	—	**1**	8/1[3]	74	32
	Mystical (MrsLStubbs) **3-8-7v[1]** ACulhane(12) (leggy: unf: s.i.s: sn chsng ldrs: led over 2f tl over 1f out: outpcd fnl f)	4	**2**	7/2[1]	58	16
757[2]	**Terry's Rose (53)** (RHollinshead) **3-8-7** WRyan(17) (led tl over 2f out: rdn & one pce fnl f)	½	**3**	9/2[2]	56	14
	Miss Peregrine (RGuest) **3-8-7** PBloomfield(9) (cmpt: bkwd: s.i.s: hdwy 2f out: kpt on fnl f)	2	**4**	10/1	51	9
757[3]	**Rockaroundtheclock (58)** (PDEvans) **3-8-12b** JFEgan(10) (lw: mid div tl styd on fnl 2f)	1¾	**5**	8/1[3]	51	9
758[3]	**Gunners Glory (74)** (BJMeehan) **3-9-4b** JReid(6) (chsd ldrs over 4f)	¾	**6**	8/1[3]	55	13
757[4]	**Blazing Castle (78)** (WGMTurner) **3-8-11**(7) DMcGaffin(14) (prom: rdn over 2f out: edgd lft & wknd fnl f)	½	**7**	12/1	54	12
758*	**Municipal Girl (IRE) (45)** (BPalling) **3-8-13** TSprake(8) (w ldrs: rdn over 2f out: sn wknd)	2½	**8**	8/1[3]	42	—
	Patrita Park (53) (WWHaigh) **3-8-7** DaneO'Neill(15) (bit bkwd: a outpcd)	6	**9**	20/1	21	—
	Stravano (40) (BPJBaugh) **3-8-4**(3) DarrenMoffatt(13) (bit bkwd: outpcd fr ½-wy)	3	**10**	50/1	13	—
	Jib Jab (65) (MrsNMacauley) **3-8-9**(3) DO'Donohoe(18) (rdn ½-wy: a bhd)	s.h	**11**	8/1[3]	18	—
	Witney-La-Roche (JSMoore) **3-8-5**(7) KAxon(5) (chsd ldrs 3f: sn lost tch)	2½	**12**	25/1	11	—
*546**	**Advance Repro (60)** (JAkehurst) **3-8-13b** KFallon(11) (sn wl bhd: t.o)	19	**13**	8/1[3]	—	—

(SP 134.4%) **13 Rn**

1m 17.6 (6.10) CSF £36.51 TOTE £12.70: £3.00 £1.00 £2.90 (£36.40) Trio £44.30 OWNER Mrs J. Carney (DONCASTER) BRED Denis Brennan
Bt in 7,000 gns

OFFICIAL EXPLANATION **Skyers Flyer (IRE): regarding the improvement in form, the jockey reported that the filly had hung left after meeting interference last time.**

757 Skyers Flyer (IRE) recaptured her form under a very confident ride, and made up for a very disappointing reversal last week. (8/1: 6/1-9/1)

Mystical, fitted with a visor on her racecourse debut, failed to land the gamble but she showed plenty of promise after missing the break and, with a bit of summer sunshine on her back, should be able to recover losses. (7/2: 10/1-25/1)

757 Terry's Rose finished some way ahead of the winner over course and distance last week, and promised to do so again for most of the way, but the picture changed quickly approaching the final furlong and she was the one who was tapped for speed. (9/2: op 9/4)

Miss Peregrine, a not over-big, compact filly with plenty left to work on, was doing all her best work in the closing stages and will come into her own when tackling a longer trip. (10/1: 7/1-12/1)

757 Rockaroundtheclock takes time to find top gear, and as he seems to be fighting a losing battle to make his mark at this trip, maybe another furlong could be the answer. (8/1)

758 Gunners Glory sat in behind the leaders and looked to be waiting to pounce but, when push came to shove, he found absolutely nothing. (8/1: op 5/1)

758* Municipal Girl (IRE) (8/1: op 5/1)

546* Advance Repro (8/1: op 5/1)

883 BRADMORE H'CAP (0-70) (3-Y.O+ F & M) (Class E)
2-45 (2-49) **6f 15y** £3,226.25 (£965.00: £462.50: £211.25) Stalls: High GOING: 0.23 sec per fur (G)

				SP	RR	SF
585[8]	**Fame Again (54)** (MrsJRRamsden) **5-8-12** JFortune(9) (lw: hdwy ½-wy: r.o u.p to ld ins fnl f)	—	**1**	6/1[1]	66	44
545[12]	**Runs in the Family (46)** (GMMcCourt) **5-8-4b** DHarrison(5) (led: clr ½-wy: wknd & hdd ins fnl f)	3	**2**	25/1	50	28
	Corniche Quest (IRE) (54) (MRChannon) **4-8-12** RHughes(14) (hld up: hdwy over 2f out: kpt on one pce)	2½	**3**	9/1[3]	52	30
733[18]	**Lachesis (50)** (DShaw) **4-8-5**(3) CTeague(15) (a chsng ldrs: rdn & one pce appr fnl f)	¾	**4**	16/1	46	24
663[7]	**Delrob (42)** (DHaydnJones) **6-8-0b** CRutter(4) (hld up: hdwy fnl 2f: nvr nrr)	2½	**5**	14/1	31	9
749[8]	**Ballard Lady (IRE) (43)** (JSWainwright) **5-7-10**(5) JBramhill(11) (in tch: rdn ½-wy: kpt on: nt pce to chal)	nk	**6**	12/1	31	9
	Sharp 'n' Shady (56) (CFWall) **4-9-0** GDuffield(17) (bit bkwd: hld up & bhd: sme hdwy whn hmpd over 1f out)	2	**7**	7/1[2]	39	17
601[12]	**Time For Tea (IRE) (53)** (CACyzer) **4-8-11** DeclanO'Shea(18) (lw: nvr trbld ldrs)	hd	**8**	9/1[3]	36	14
	Robec Girl (IRE) (62) (KMcAuliffe) **3-8-9** JFEgan(1) (bit bkwd: in tch 4f)	½	**9**	14/1	43	10
545[8]	**Al Reet (IRE) (65)** (SRBowring) **6-9-2**(7) FBoyle(12) (chsd ldrs over 3f)	½	**10**	20/1	45	23
477[7]	**Aybeegirl (60)** (MrsJCecil) **3-8-7** JReid(16) (s.i.s: nvr nr to chal)	1¾	**11**	6/1[1]	35	2
749[10]	**Legend of Aragon (60)** (JAGlover) **3-8-7** MBirch(13) (chsd ldrs: effrt & hung lft 2f out: sn wknd)	6	**12**	6/1[1]	20	—
702[15]	**Sing With the Band (56)** (BAMcMahon) **6-9-0** LNewton(6) (chsd ldrs 4f: wknd qckly: t.o)	9	**13**	16/1	—	—
209[10]	**Cindy Kate (IRE) (50)** (WRMuir) **4-8-8** DaneO'Neill(3) (s.s: a in rr: t.o)	hd	**14**	25/1	—	—
	Emmas Breeze (55) (JSKing) **3-8-2** JQuinn(8) (a bhd: t.o)	¾	**15**	33/1	—	—
729*	**Divine Miss-P (69)** (APJarvis) **4-9-13** WJO'Connor(2) (trckd ldrs: rdn over 2f out: sn wknd: t.o)	1¾	**16**	10/1	—	—
436[8]	**April Jackson (49)** (PTDalton) **3-7-5**(5) PFessey(10) (a bhd: t.o)	½	**17**	33/1	—	—
	Rotherfield Park (IRE) (38) (CSmith) **5-7-7**(3) MBaird(7) (racd wd: bhd fr ½-wy: t.o)	5	**18**	20/1	—	—

(SP 140.3%) **18 Rn**

1m 16.6 (5.10) CSF £158.76 CT £1,308.42 TOTE £8.10: £1.70 £5.10 £2.80 £8.10 (£194.10) Trio £402.70 OWNER Mr James Ramsden (THIRSK) BRED R. Barbes

LONG HANDICAP April Jackson 7-9 Rotherfield Park (IRE) 7-7

WEIGHT FOR AGE 3yo-11lb

585 Fame Again, winning for the first time at this sprint distance, benefited from the hot pace set by the runner-up and, now that she has got back to winning ways, could be one to follow. (6/1)

Runs in the Family, attempting to gallop her rivals into the ground, looked to be in complete control below the distance but her stride shortened and she was legless when collared. (25/1)

Corniche Quest (IRE) comes to hand early but she was competing over longer trips for the majority of last season and, though she was into her stride in the latter stages, the principals were beyond recall. (9/1)

571 Lachesis, in the chasing group from the start, was never able to find the speed to mount a challenge, but this return to sprinting at least showed she has some ability when the right opportunity presents itself. (16/1)

429 Delrob, having her first outing on turf for over nine months, did well to finish as close as she did from one of the outside stalls, and she is capable of winning on this surface. (14/1)

203 Ballard Lady (IRE), always struggling with the pace, kept beavering away and, on more suitable soft ground, she is certainly no back number. (12/1)
Sharp 'n' Shady, far from fully wound up for this seasonal debut, was beginning to stay on when she was impeded below the distance, and what small chance she had quickly disappeared. She could be worth keeping in mind. (7/1)
Aybeegirl failed to recover from a sluggish start and was never a threat. (6/1: op 4/1)
Legend of Aragon, poised to challenge when hanging badly left inside the last quarter-mile, prevented her jockey from being able to really get serious with her when it was most needed. (6/1: op 12/1)

83 – 72+ 74

884 PORCHESTER NOVICE MEDIAN AUCTION STKS (2-Y.O) (Class F)

3-15 (3-18) **5f 13y** £2,277.00 (£627.00: £297.00) Stalls: High GOING: 0.23 sec per fur (G)

				SP	RR	SF
557[7]	**Rusty Babe (IRE)** (JJQuinn) **2-8-12** JQuinn(7) (chsd ldrs: led over 1f out: r.o wl)	—	**1**	10/1	81	23
684*	**Young Ibnr (IRE)** (PDEvans) **2-9-4** JFEgan(8) (w ldr: led ½-wy tl over 1f out: rdn & no ex fnl f)	2½	**2**	7/1	79	21
637[2]	**Prince Foley** (WGMTurner) **2-8-9**(7) DMcGaffin(2) (racd alone centre: a.p: rdn over 1f out: kpt on)	nk	**3**	7/2[1]	76	18
	Santa Faye (IRE) (BPalling) **2-8-7** TSprake(3) (w'like: bit bkwd: chsd ldrs: outpcd ½-wy: kpt on ins fnl f)	2½	**4**	4/1[2]	59	1
583*	**Blushing Victoria** (MartynMeade) **2-8-10**(5) DSweeney(4) (w ldrs tl outpcd 2f out: n.d after)	nk	**5**	4/1[2]	66	8
	Sweet Reward (JGSmyth-Osbourne) **2-8-12** DHarrison(12) (leggy: unf: bhd tl styd on appr fnl f)	¾	**6**	33/1	61	3
536[9]	**Swift Time** (MRBosley) **2-8-7** CRutter(10) (unruly: led to ½-wy: wknd wl over 1f out)	¾	**7**	25/1	54	—
536[11]	**Fey Rouge (IRE)** (RHollinshead) **2-8-4**(3) FLynch(1) (sn rdn along: a outpcd: t.o)	8	**8**	20/1	28	—
	Kantone (IRE) (JMPEustace) **2-8-12** RCochrane(9) (str: cmpt: bkwd: s.i.s: a bhd: t.o)	¾	**9**	10/1	31	—
557[10]	**O' Higgins (IRE)** (RBoss) **2-8-12** KFallon(6) (in tch tl ½-wy: sn wknd: t.o)	¾	**10**	5/1[3]	29	—
	Captain Jones (IRE) (BJMeehan) **2-8-12** RHughes(11) (w'like: cmpt: bit bkwd: a bhd & outpcd: t.o)	3	**11**	6/1	19	—
				(SP 135.4%)	**11 Rn**	

64.4 secs (5.50) CSF £80.53 TOTE £12.60: £3.60 £4.80 £1.60 (£81.60) Trio £55.80 OWNER Mrs K. Mapp (MALTON) BRED Rathasker Stud
557 Rusty Babe (IRE), supported at long odds on his debut, recovered some of his losses with a clear-cut success and he looks the type who can only get better. (10/1)
684* Young Ibnr (IRE) ran another brave race from the front, but the 6lb penalty for a hard-won race at Pontefract proved to be his undoing. (7/1)
637 Prince Foley ploughed a lone furrow up the centre of the track and was in the firing line all the way but, like the runner-up, had to admit he had met his match when the winner got down to business. (7/2)
Santa Faye (IRE) looked as if she would benefit from the run and, after losing her pitch at halfway, was beginning to realise what was required inside the distance. (4/1)
583* Blushing Victoria, one of three fighting for supremacy until past halfway, appeared to lose her action, and though she was renewing her efforts towards the finish, the principals had got away and her chance had gone. (4/1)
Sweet Reward, bred to need much further, was only finding his stride when the race was as good as over. (33/1)
Kantone (IRE) (10/1: 6/1-12/1)
447 O' Higgins (IRE) (5/1: 4/1-7/1)
Captain Jones (IRE) (6/1: 3/1-7/1)

885 RADFORD MAIDEN STKS (I) (3-Y.O F) (Class D)

3-45 (3-46) **1m 54y** £3,381.70 (£1,006.60: £478.80: £214.90) Stalls: Low GOING: 0.23 sec per fur (G)

				SP	RR	SF
681[3]	**Change For A Buck (USA)** (HRACecil) **3-8-11** KFallon(3) (lw: hld up: hdwy to ld over 2f out: sn clr: eased nr fin)	—	**1**	Evens[1]	81	34
586[4]	**Epworth** (JAGlover) **3-8-11** GCarter(2) (a.p: styd on ins fnl f: no ch w wnr)	½	**2**	12/1	80	33
60[3]	**Enlisted (IRE)** (SirMarkPrescott) **3-8-11** GDuffield(7) (sn trckng ldrs: effrt over 2f out: styd on same pce)	4	**3**	9/1	72	25
	Kilshanny (LMCumani) **3-8-11** OUrbina(10) (h.d.w: trckd ldrs: outpcd over 2f out: styd on fnl f)	4	**4**	6/1[3]	65	18
586[10]	**Top Jem** (MJRyan) **3-8-11** GBardwell(12) (bhd: rdn along ½-wy: styd on fnl 2f)	nk	**5**	33/1	64	17
	Arriving (JWHills) **3-8-11** JReid(8) (chsd ldrs: rdn over 2f out: no imp)	½	**6**	8/1	63	16
	Persian Blue (RHannon) **3-8-11** DaneO'Neill(4) (chsd ldrs: rdn & outpcd over 2f out)	nk	**7**	16/1	62	15
681[4]	**Sharkiyah (IRE)** (RWArmstrong) **3-8-11** RHills(1) (b.nr hind: led tl hdd & wknd over 2f out)	2	**8**	7/2[2]	59	12
	Cheek To Cheek (CACyzer) **3-8-11** AMorris(11) (bit bkwd: sn bhd & drvn along: n.d)	nk	**9**	25/1	58	11
727[16]	**Doyenne** (GLewis) **3-8-11** AClark(13) (bit bkwd: s.i.s: a bhd & outpcd: t.o)	9	**10**	25/1	40	—
	Oakbrook Rose (52) (MPMuggeridge) **3-8-11** TGMcLaughlin(6) (chsd ldrs 5f: sn wknd: t.o)	6	**11**	25/1	29	—
				(SP 135.7%)	**11 Rn**	

1m 49.4 (8.10) CSF £16.95 TOTE £1.60: £1.10 £3.50 £1.80 (£14.70) Trio £47.50 OWNER Buckram Oak Holdings (NEWMARKET) BRED Buckram Oak Farm
681 Change For A Buck (USA), very weak in the market, may not have had a lot to beat but she won without knowing she had been in a race and this can only do her confidence the world of good. (Evens)
586 Epworth showed she is going the right way with a much-improved performance and, though she is flattered to run the winner so close, will not always meet one so useful. (12/1)
60 Enlisted (IRE), whose previous runs have been on the All-Weather, may well need a stiffer test of stamina on turf when the ground rides lively, and she was never able to launch a bid. (9/1)
Kilshanny, an attractive filly who is a good walker, gave the impression she was finding this trip inadequate and she will be worth watching when her attentions are switched to middle-distances. (6/1: op 4/1)
Top Jem showed a considerable improvement on her previous run, staying on from off the pace to be nearest at the finish. (33/1)
Arriving, far from the finished article as yet, was being nudged along early in the straight, and all she could do was stay on at the one pace. (8/1)
681 Sharkiyah (IRE), less than two lengths behind the winner earlier in the month, had more use made of her but it backfired somewhat, for she stopped to nothing once her measure had been taken. This slightly longer trip may not have been in her favour. (7/2)

886 LEVY BOARD H'CAP (0-70) (3-Y.O) (Class E)

4-15 (4-17) **1m 54y** £3,616.25 (£1,085.00: £522.50: £241.25) Stalls: Low GOING: 0.23 sec per fur (G)

				SP	RR	SF
	Night Chorus (67) (BSRothwell) **3-9-4** MFenton(10) (lw: chsd ldrs: led over 1f out: hld on towards fin)	—	**1**	20/1	79	50
642[3]	**Interdream (59)** (RHannon) **3-8-10** WJO'Connor(5) (lw: a in tch: hdwy to chal over 1f out: nt qckn towards fin)	nk	**2**	12/1	70	41
840[7]	**Mardrew (61)** (TTClement) **3-8-7**(5) ADaly(18) (trckd ldrs: effrt over 2f out: styd on u.p ins fnl f)	¾	**3**	14/1	71	42
	Saffron Rose (65) (MBlanshard) **3-9-2** RCochrane(11) (hld up: hmpd 5f out: hdwy on ins 2f out: styd on wl towards fin)	hd	**4**	20/1	75	46
609[3]	**Barresbo (59)** (CWFairhurst) **3-8-10** JStack(12) (chsd ldrs: rdn & outpcd over 2f out: kpt on wl fnl f)	1	**5**	14/1	67	38

535^{2} **Pennywell (65)** (RFJohnsonHoughton) **3-9-2** JReid(6) (chsd ldrs: rdn & nt qckn fnl 2f)......1 **6** $7/1^{3}$ 71 42
Calamander (IRE) (62) (WRMuir) **3-8-13** DaneO'Neill(7) (a in tch: effrt over 2f out: wknd fnl f)......nk **7** 20/1 67 38
533^{6} **Baubigny (USA) (70)** (MRChannon) **3-9-7** RHughes(13) (lw: led: hrd rdn over 2f out: hdd & wknd over 1f out)5 **8** $11/2^{2}$ 66 37
Brynkir (67) (DJGMurraySmith) **3-9-4** GDuffield(2) (bit bkwd: s.i.s: bhd: sme hdwy 2f out: n.d)......1½ **9** 20/1 60 31
645^{9} **Viva Verdi (IRE) (68)** (JLDunlop) **3-9-5** TQuinn(16) (unruly s: trckd ldrs: rdn & ev ch over 1f out: sn wknd) ......1 **10** $7/2^{1}$ 59 30
581^{9} **Push A Venture (64)** (SPCWoods) **3-9-1** WRyan(1) (dwlt s: hld up & bhd: sme hdwy 2f out: n.d)......1¼ **11** 20/1 52 23
Santa Rosa (IRE) (65) (JLDunlop) **3-9-2** TSprake(3) (bhd: drvn along over 3f out: n.d) 5 **12** 10/1 44 15
Come Together (64) (DWPArbuthnot) **3-9-1** SWhitworth(17) (bkwd: racd wd: trckd ldrs: plld hrd: lost pl 3f out)......nk **13** 20/1 42 13
759^{11} **Lunar Music (63)** (RonaldThompson) **3-9-0** TWilliams(8) (bhd fnl 3f)......4 **14** 33/1 33 4
575^{8} **Mungo Park (63)** (MrsJRRamsden) **3-9-0** JFortune(4) (mid div: outpcd 3f out: sn lost pl)......4 **15** 8/1 26 —
600^{4} **Castles Burning (USA) (60)** (CACyzer) **3-8-11** DBiggs(9) (chsd ldrs tl lost pl 3f out)......1¼ **16** 12/1 20 —
279^{2} **Hever Golf Dancer (63)** (TJNaughton) **3-9-0** GCarter(14) (a bhd)......7 **17** 25/1 10 —
644* **Princess of Hearts (61)** (MCPipe) **3-8-12b** KFallon(15) (s.s: a bhd) ......½ **18** $7/1^{3}$ 7 —
(SP 146.9%) **18 Rn**

1m 48.4 (7.10) CSF £233.92 CT £3,294.42 TOTE £53.00: £7.50 £3.30 £4.20 £7.00 (£311.20) Trio Not won; £421.32 to Ascot 30/4/97 OWNER Mr R. M. J. MacNair (MALTON) BRED Roger Macnair
STEWARDS' ENQUIRY Hughes susp. 8-12/5/97 (excessive & improper use of whip).
OFFICIAL EXPLANATION Princess of Hearts: had reared in the stalls.

Night Chorus, who apparently hated the kick-back when beaten in a selling race at Southwell on his final outing last term, was turned out in good trim and showed the right sort of spirit to hang on in a tight finish. (20/1)
642 Interdream looked well and was just held at bay. (12/1)
644 Mardrew, having his second outing in three days, showed a fair bit of knee action going down and appreciated the well-watered track. (14/1)
Saffron Rose, who looked very fit, has taken a drop in the weights compared with last year. Meeting trouble on the turn, she stayed on strongly without being knocked about and should be knocking on the door again next time. (20/1)
609 Barresbo stuck on after being outpaced and will be suited by a step up to a mile and a quarter. (14/1)
535 Pennywell, who showed plenty of knee action going down, appreciated the amount of water put on the track. (7/1)
Calamander (IRE), having her first run for her new trainer, will have pleased connections. (20/1)
431 Baubigny (USA) (11/2: op 10/1)
645 Viva Verdi (IRE), having a first run in a handicap, proved troublesome at the start. She would not settle in the race and contributed to her own downfall. (7/2: 5/2-4/1)
Push A Venture hinted at better to come. (20/1)

887 COTMANHAY H'CAP (0-80) (3-Y.O+ F & M) (Class D)

4-45 (4-48) **1m 1f 213y** £4,027.80 (£1,205.40: £578.20: £264.60) Stalls: Low GOING: 0.23 sec per fur (G)

SP RR SF

Star Precision (65) (GBBalding) **3-7-10** NVarley(15) (unruly s: bhd: gd hdwy over 4f out: led 3f out: styd on wl fnl f)......— **1** 14/1 77 29
647^{3} **Peppers (IRE) (65)** (KRBurke) **4-8-13** KFallon(16) (lw: hld up: gd hdwy 2f out: chsd wnr fnl f: no imp)......2½ **2** $7/1^{2}$ 73 42
639^{4} **Scarlet Crescent (71)** (PTWalwyn) **3-8-2** TSprake(6) (bkwd: trckd ldrs: chal over 3f out: kpt on same pce fnl 2f)......4 **3** 10/1 73 25
533^{4} **Agony Aunt (79)** (MrsJCecil) **3-8-10** WRyan(11) (chsd ldrs: rdn & outpcd over 2f out: kpt on appr fnl f) ......1¾ **4** $11/2^{1}$ 78 30
Capilano Princess (80) (DHaydnJones) **4-10-0** CRutter(5) (bit bkwd: hld up: hdwy to chal over 3f out: sn rdn: kpt on one pce)......1¾ **5** 14/1 76 45
763* **Rasayel (USA) (70)** (PDEvans) **7-9-4** 5x JFEgan(1) (hld up: hdwy over 3f out: sn drvn along: nvr rchd ldrs)....nk **6** $11/2^{1}$ 66 35
647^{2} **Absolutelystunning (59)** (MrsBarbaraWaring) **4-8-7** TQuinn(9) (b: a in tch: effrt 3f out: no imp)......3½ **7** 12/1 49 18
796* **Tallulah Belle (60)** (NPLittmoden) **4-8-8** 5x TGMcLaughlin(2) (lw: hld up & plld hrd: hdwy over 3f out: sn chsng ldrs: wknd 2f out)......4 **8** $7/1^{2}$ 43 12
733^{14} **Polar Refrain (49)** (JNorton) **4-7-11** JQuinn(8) (bhd: sme hdwy over 2f out: n.d) ......1½ **9** 33/1 30 —
690^{7} **Princess Topaz (71)** (CACyzer) **3-8-2** DBiggs(3) (sn bhd: sme hdwy 3f out: n.d) ......½ **10** $11/2^{1}$ 51 3
Mazilla (54) (AStreeter) **5-7-11**(5) JBramhill(4) (hld up: sme hdwy over 3f out: sn wknd) ......¾ **11** $9/1^{3}$ 33 2
Polish Rhythm (IRE) (62) (GAHubbard) **4-8-10** GCarter(7) (bkwd: b: chsd ldrs: led over 4f out to 3f out: sn wknd)......1¾ **12** 16/1 38 7
601^{10} **Nellie North (53)** (GMMcCourt) **4-8-1v** GBardwell(10) (lw: trckd ldrs tl wknd 3f out: sn bhd)......16 **13** 25/1 4 —
485^{5} **Pretty Sharp (65)** (NMBabbage) **3-7-5**(5) PFessey(12) (lw: unruly s: s.s: rel to r: sme hdwy 4f out: sn wknd).1¾ **14** 20/1 13 —
759^{18} **Credite Risque (58)** (JAGlover) **4-8-6** NDay(13) (swtg: plld very hrd: led: racd wd: hdd over 4f out: sn lost pl: t.o)......25 **15** 33/1 — —
Daffodil Express (IRE) (48) (MJRyan) **4-7-7**(3) MBaird(14) (swtg: racd wd: in tch tl lost pl over 3f out: sn bhd: t.o)......hd **16** 40/1 — —
(SP 134.1%) **16 Rn**

2m 11.2 (8.70) CSF £103.49 CT £972.77 TOTE £37.00: £8.30 £2.00 £2.10 £2.20 (£114.50) Trio £329.60; £236.77 to Ascot 30/4/97 OWNER Miss B. Swire (ANDOVER) BRED Miss B. Swire
LONG HANDICAP Pretty Sharp 7-5 Star Precision 7-9 Daffodil Express (IRE) 6-13
WEIGHT FOR AGE 3yo-17lb
OFFICIAL EXPLANATION Princess Topaz: was probably unsuited by the going.

Star Precision from a late-developing family, showed little in three outings over shorter trips at two. Giving plenty of trouble at the start, she did nothing wrong in the race and, in the end, scored in most decisive fashion. (14/1: 8/1-16/1)
647 Peppers (IRE) ran another highly satisfactory race. (7/1)
639 Scarlet Crescent, who travelled strongly, still looked as if the race would do her good. (10/1)
533 Agony Aunt, who has plenty of scope, ran as if in need of a step up in distance. (11/2)
Capilano Princess ran a satisfactory first race. (14/1)
763* Rasayel (USA), taken very quietly to post, could never take a serious hand under her 5lb penalty. She needs a strongly-run race at this trip and is really better over a mile and a half. (11/2)
647 Absolutelystunning (12/1: op 8/1)
690 Princess Topaz never took hold of her bit at any stage. (11/2: 3/1-6/1)

888 ATTENBOROUGH H'CAP (0-70) (4-Y.O+) (Class E)

5-20 (5-21) **1m 6f 15y** £3,252.25 (£973.00: £466.50: £213.25) Stalls: Low GOING: 0.23 sec per fur (G)

Form	Horse / Details	Dist	Pos	SP	RR	SF
613*	**Sea Freedom (63)** (GBBalding) **6-9-7v** AClark(15) (reminders after s: bhd: hdwy 6f out: styd on u.p fnl 3f: led ins fnl f)	—	**1**	8/1^{3}	77	52
762*	**The Butterwick Kid (50)** (RAFahey) **4-7-13**(7) 5x RWinston(17) (trckd ldrs gng wl: led over 2f out tl ins fnl f: r.o)	½	**2**	8/1^{3}	63	36
650^{3}	**Chabrol (CAN) (60)** (TTClement) **4-8-11**(5) ADaly(9) (lw: led 2f: w ldrs: wandered & nt qckn fnl f)	s.h	**3**	14/1	73	46
770^{2}	**Charnwood Jack (USA) (62)** (ICampbell) **4-9-4** RPrice(16) (lw: hld up: hdwy 6f out: effrt & hung lft 3f out: one pce)	8	**4**	8/1^{3}	66	39
650^{5}	**Forgie (IRE) (60)** (PCalver) **4-9-2** MBirch(10) (chsd ldrs: led 4f out tl over 2f out: one pce)	1¼	**5**	12/1	63	36
762^{4}	**Dancing Cavalier (70)** (RHollinshead) **4-9-9**(3) FLynch(14) (hld up: hdwy 7f out: ev ch tl wknd over 1f out)	5	**6**	8/1^{3}	67	40
613^{3}	**He's Got Wings (IRE) (54)** (MrsJRRamsden) **4-8-10** JFortune(13) (lw: b.nr hind: bhd: effrt u.p over 3f out: nvr rchd ldrs)	1¼	**7**	7/1^{2}	50	23
762^{10}	**Arcady (62)** (JLHarris) **4-9-4** JCarroll(6) (hld up: sme hdwy 3f out: n.d)	4	**8**	20/1	53	26
728^{6}	**Tonnerre (55)** (BAMcMahon) **5-8-13** LNewton(5) (in tch: drvn along & outpcd over 3f out: n.d)	½	**9**	14/1	46	21
451^{4}	**Northern Drums (55)** (NMBabbage) **4-8-11** TSprake(1) (w ldrs tl lost pl over 3f out)	½	**10**	4/1^{1}	45	18
660^{3}	**Kalamata (50)** (JAGlover) **5-8-8** NDay(11) (in tch tl outpcd fnl 3f)	9	**11**	20/1	30	5
607^{5}	**Lalindi (IRE) (70)** (ACStewart) **6-10-0** SWhitworth(8) (bit bkwd: s.i.s: a bhd)	nk	**12**	20/1	50	25
	Sheriff (56) (JWHills) **6-9-0** RHills(7) (bkwd: chsd ldrs tl wknd over 3f out)	5	**13**	14/1	30	5
762^{13}	**Heighth of Fame (50)** (JHetherton) **6-8-8** GDuffield(4) (led after 2f out to 4f out: wknd 3f out)	¾	**14**	25/1	23	—
650^{6}	**Norsong (47)** (RAkehurst) **5-8-5** JQuinn(3) (bit bkwd: a in rr)	2½	**15**	12/1	17	—
	Sushi Bar (IRE) (48) (MrsMReveley) **6-8-6** DHarrison(2) (bkwd: bhd: hmpd bnd after 3f: styd far side: eased fnl 3f)	½	**16**	20/1	18	—
680^{4}	**Bowled Over (69)** (CACyzer) **4-9-11** KFallon(12) (in tch: effrt over 3f out: sn wknd: eased)	¾	**17**	8/1^{3}	38	11
	Belmarita (IRE) (70) (GAHubbard) **4-9-12** GCarter(18) (sn bhd: styd far side: t.o fnl 4f)	dist	**18**	20/1	—	—
				(SP 151.1%)	**18 Rn**	

3m 11.1 (12.60) CSF £71.60 CT £868.59 TOTE £12.80: £2.60 £3.00 £3.60 £1.70 (£127.20) Trio £230.20; £32.43 to Ascot 30/4/97 OWNER Miss B. Swire (ANDOVER) BRED Stetchworth Park Stud Ltd

WEIGHT FOR AGE 4yo-2lb

613* Sea Freedom took thirty-one attempts to get off the mark but here he made it two out of two thanks largely to the strength and determination of Clark. Giving his mount some sharp reminders after the start, he forced the gelding's head in front near the line. (8/1: 6/1-9/1)

762* The Butterwick Kid, under a 5lb penalty, proved his win here last time was no fluke. Travelling smoothly, he looked to have it in the bag when hitting the front, but near the line the winning combination proved just too strong. (8/1)

650 Chabrol (CAN), taken to post early, ran another sound race and would have finished even closer but for a tendency to come off a true line under pressure. (14/1)

770 Charnwood Jack (USA) showed his much-improved Folkestone effort was no fluke. (8/1)

650 Forgie (IRE), from a 3lb lower mark, ran another sound race but that first win is proving elusive. (12/1)

762 Dancing Cavalier stopped in two strides entering the final furlong. (8/1)

451 Northern Drums looked to have an outstanding chance at these weights after his effort in much better non-handicap company at Doncaster. Well supported in the morning, he dropped out tamely once in line for home. (4/1)

650 Norsong (12/1: op 8/1)

680 Bowled Over (8/1: 6/1-9/1)

889 RADFORD MAIDEN STKS (II) (3-Y.O F) (Class D)

5-50 (5-54) **1m 54y** £3,381.70 (£1,006.60: £478.80: £214.90) Stalls: Low GOING: 0.23 sec per fur (G)

Form	Horse / Details	Dist	Pos	SP	RR	SF
	Manazil (IRE) (RWArmstrong) **3-8-11** RHills(2) (leggy: lt-f: bit bkwd: hdwy over 3f out: styd on to ld ins fnl f: drvn out)	—	**1**	7/1	80	41
	Sellette (IRE) (76) (DHaydnJones) **3-8-11** RCochrane(6) (bit bkwd: hdwy to chse ldrs over 3f out: led over 1f out: wandered: hdd ins fnl f)	2	**2**	11/4^{2}	76	37
	Ciro's Pearl (IRE) (MHTompkins) **3-8-11** DBiggs(9) (bkwd: mde most to 3f out: one pce appr fnl f)	3	**3**	11/2^{3}	70	31
	Woodbeck (JAGlover) **3-8-11** NDay(8) (leggy: trckd ldrs: led 3f out tl over 1f out: grad wknd)	1	**4**	8/1	68	29
759^{3}	**Aquatic Queen (54)** (RJWeaver) **3-8-11** MWigham(10) (b.hind: swtg: sn outpcd: hrd rdn & styd on fnl 2f: nvr nr to chal)	4	**5**	25/1	61	22
	Oxbane (HCandy) **3-8-11** CRutter(12) (unf: bkwd: racd wd: trckd ldrs: plld hrd: effrt 3f out: edgd lft & grad wknd)	¾	**6**	25/1	59	20
	Chloe Nicole (USA) (PFICole) **3-8-11** TQuinn(13) (plld hrd: racd wd: w ldr tl wknd 3f out)	9	**7**	7/4^{1}	42	3
	Ar Hyd Y Knos (RCharlton) **3-8-11** TSprake(4) (lt-f: unf: bit bkwd: hld up & bhd: effrt over 3f out: sn btn)	1¼	**8**	16/1	39	—
	Cadbury Castle (MBlanshard) **3-8-11** JQuinn(5) (hld up: a bhd)	1¼	**9**	25/1	37	—
790^{6}	**Midnight Romance** (APJarvis) **3-8-11** WJO'Connor(1) (swtg: in tch: effrt over 3f out: sn wknd)	1	**10**	25/1	35	—
586^{14}	**Silver Jubilee** (BPalling) **3-8-11** DaneO'Neill(7) (hld up & plld hrd: a in rr)	1	**11**	33/1	33	—
	Phoenix Princess (BAMcMahon) **3-8-4**(7) SRighton(3) (unf: scope: reard s: a bhd)	2½	**12**	33/1	28	—
568^{5}	**Eileen's Lady** (GGMargarson) **3-8-11** GCarter(11) (a bhd)	¾	**13**	20/1	27	—
				(SP 133.9%)	**13 Rn**	

1m 48.7 (7.40) CSF £25.20 TOTE £6.60: £4.00 £1.10 £1.80 (£18.10) Trio £44.80 OWNER Mr Hamdan Al Maktoum (NEWMARKET) BRED Shadwell Estate Company Limited

Manazil (IRE), who looked in need of the outing, ran green but stuck on to get up inside the last one hundred yards. Though the time was faster, this was almost certainly the weaker of the two divisions. (7/1: op 4/1)

Sellette (IRE), loaded with the aid of a Monty Roberts blanket, wandered under pressure and had to give best inside the last. (11/4)

Ciro's Pearl (IRE) never gave up trying. (11/2)

Woodbeck, very keen going to post, was backed at long odds. After setting sail for home, her stride shortened in the final furlong and she should improve when she learns to settle better. (8/1: op 20/1)

759 Aquatic Queen, flattered by the draw here last time, only finished as close here because for some reason her rider seemed determined to give her a punishing race. (25/1)

Oxbane, very keen going to post, never settled in the race. (25/1)

Chloe Nicole (USA) took a fierce grip on the way to the start. Pulling hard and racing wide from her high draw, the needle was on empty three furlongs out. She will need to settle much better if she is to fulfil her potential. (7/4: op 4/5)

T/Jkpt: Not won; £20,143.06 to Ascot 30/4/97. T/Plpt: £766.00 (22.32 Tckts). T/Qdpt: £142.20 (7.57 Tckts) IM/WG

ASCOT (R-H) (Good to firm)
Wednesday April 30th
WEATHER: warm WIND: almost nil

890 INSULPAK CONDITIONS STKS (3-Y.O F) (Class B)
2-30 (2-30) **1m (round)** £8,134.10 (£2,966.60: £1,450.80: £624.00: £279.50) Stalls: High GOING minus 0.18 sec per fur (GF)

				SP	RR	SF
	Noisette (JHMGosden) **3-8-11** LDettori(2) (hld up in rr: hdwy over 2f out: led over 1f out: r.o wl)	—	**1**	11/1	89	62
*49**	**Flamboyance (USA)** (JRFanshawe) **3-9-0** DHarrison(4) (a.p: led over 2f out tl over 1f out: r.o)	2½	**2**	10/1	87	60
681[2]	**Delilah (IRE)** (MRStoute) **3-8-11** JReid(3) (lw: hld up in rr: hdwy over 2f out: r.o one pce)	½	**3**	6/5[1]	83	56
	Witching Hour (IRE) (MrsJCecil) **3-9-0** PatEddery(5) (chsd ldr tl wknd over 2f out)	5	**4**	9/2[3]	76	49
672[5]	**Imperial Scholar (IRE)** (JMPEustace) **3-8-11** RCochrane(1) (led tl wknd over 2f out)	2	**5**	100/30[2]	69	42

(SP 104.1%) **5 Rn**

1m 42.69 (1.89) CSF £78.33 TOTE £6.70: £2.20 £4.60 (£23.20) OWNER Sheikh Mohammed (NEWMARKET) BRED Sheikh Mohammed Bin Rashid Al Maktoum

OFFICIAL EXPLANATION **Imperial Scholar (IRE): was found to be in season.**

Noisette has been really thriving in the last week according to connections and, coming through to lead early in the final quarter-mile, soon put her stamp on the race. (11/1: 6/1-12/1)

49* Flamboyance (USA), winner of an All-Weather maiden at Wolverhampton in January on her only other racecourse appearance, gained control early in the straight but, collared well over a furlong from home, found the winner too good. (10/1: 5/1-12/1)

681 Delilah (IRE) began a forward move soon after the turn for home, but never looked like reeling in the front two. (6/5)

Witching Hour (IRE), without a run since last June, raced in second place until calling it a day early in the straight. Her only victory came with some cut. (9/2)

672 Imperial Scholar (IRE) took the field along but, collared over two furlongs from home, had soon shot her bolt. (100/30: 2/1-7/2)

891 INSULPAK SAGARO STKS (Gp 3) (4-Y.O+) (Class A)
3-05 (3-05) **2m 45y** £25,240.00 (£9,552.00: £4,676.00: £2,132.00) Stalls: High GOING minus 0.18 sec per fur (GF)

				SP	RR	SF
498[3]	**Orchestra Stall (104)** (JLDunlop) **5-8-12** TQuinn(1) (a.p: led over 2f out: pushed out)	—	**1**	9/1	117	70
451[2]	**Wilawander (107)** (BWHills) **4-8-9** MHills(4) (hdwy 3f out: chsd wnr fnl 2f: no imp)	3½	**2**	8/1	115	64
736[5]	**Election Day (IRE) (112)** (MRStoute) **5-8-12** JReid(6) (prom tl lost pl 3f out: rallied fnl f: r.o)	3½	**3**	6/1[3]	110	63
	Grey Shot (110) (IABalding) **5-9-3** LDettori(5) (lw: led tl over 2f out: r.o one pce)	1¾	**4**	3/1[2]	113	66
736[9]	**Lord Jim (IRE) (104)** (LordHuntingdon) **5-8-12v** DHarrison(8) (chsd ldr tl wknd 2f out)	2	**5**	40/1	106	59
	Garolo (FR) (CPEBrooks) **7-8-12** RHughes(3) (hld up in rr: gd hdwy 3f out: ev ch 2f out: wknd fnl f)	s.h	**6**	100/1	106	59
	Jiyush (100) (EALDunlop) **4-8-9** RHills(7) (a bhd)	3	**7**	12/1	104	53
	Double Trigger (IRE) (120) (MJohnston) **6-9-1** JWeaver(2) (drvn 6f out: sme hdwy 3f out: sn wknd)	1¼	**8**	6/4[1]	105	58

(SP 111.5%) **8 Rn**

3m 29.69 (2.49) CSF £67.20 TOTE £8.90: £1.80 £1.50 £1.70 (£18.90) OWNER Mr D. Sieff (ARUNDEL) BRED Alan Gibson

WEIGHT FOR AGE 4yo-4lb

OFFICIAL EXPLANATION **Double Trigger (IRE): no explanation offered.**

498 Orchestra Stall left his seasonal reappearance well behind and, leading soon after straightening for home, scooted clear for an impressive victory. (9/1)

451 Wilawander moved into second place a quarter of a mile from home but, although finishing clear of the remainder, had no hope of reeling in the winner. (8/1)

736 Election Day (IRE) gave a good account of himself on ground livelier than he would have liked. Bustled along from Swinley Bottom, he stayed on for third prize in the straight. Some cut in the ground would greatly be in his favour. (6/1)

Grey Shot, 12 kilos heavier than he was at this time last year, took the field along but, collared over a quarter-of-a-mile from home, was soon put in this place. He is better with some cut in the ground and, with so few suitable opportunities for him at home, connections are considering running him next in France. (3/1)

Lord Jim (IRE) raced in second place, but he was collared for that position early in the straight and soon done with. (40/1)

Garolo (FR), winner of a novice chase and a hurdle race this winter, has not raced on the Flat for over two years. However, he began to mount a useful-looking challenge early in the straight before tiring from below the distance. (100/1)

Double Trigger (IRE), such a firm favourite with the crowd, nearly missed this engagement after getting some poison in his left-fore foot last week, resulting in him having to swim rather than exercise. However, that can surely not be the reason for this abysmal display. Waited with in mid-division, Weaver was already bustling him along coming out of Swinley Bottom and the writing was on the wall early in the straight. The real reason for this appalling effort is surely that he has to be able to dominate from the front and, being restrained on this occasion, he simply lost interest. His trainer seems to be of this opinion and interestingly is considering putting blinkers on him. Allowed to stride out as he loves to do, he will hopefully bounce back to all his old glory in the near future. (6/4: evens-13/8)

892 INSULPAK VICTORIA CUP H'CAP (0-110) (4-Y.O+) (Class B)
3-40 (3-41) **7f** £22,567.50 (£6,840.00: £3,345.00: £1,597.50) Stalls: Low GOING minus 0.18 sec per fur (GF)

				SP	RR	SF
677[2]	**Tregaron (USA) (94)** (RAkehurst) **6-8-13** TQuinn(11) (lw: hdwy over 2f out: led 1f out: r.o wl)	—	**1**	9/1[2]	107	70
519[3]	**World Premier (93)** (CEBrittain) **4-8-12** BDoyle(16) (lw: a.p: led 3f out to 1f out: no ex)	2½	**2**	16/1	100	63
663[2]	**Waypoint (77)** (RCharlton) **4-7-5(5)** RFfrench(24) (lw: a.p: ev ch 2f out: r.o one pce)	2	**3**	25/1	80	43
560[2]	**Arterxerxes (83)** (MJHeaton-Ellis) **4-8-2**ow[1] SDrowne(15) (lw: a.p: ev ch over 1f out: r.o one pce)	2	**4**	33/1	81	43
514[2]	**Chewit (88)** (GLMoore) **5-8-7** CandyMorris(8) (gd hdwy 2f out: one pce fnl f)	1	**5**	20/1	84	47
677[3]	**Emerging Market (99)** (JLDunlop) **5-9-4** KDarley(1) (hld up: hdwy 2f out: nt qckn fnl f)	½	**6**	11/1	94	57
677*	**Chickawicka (IRE) (90)** (BPalling) **6-8-9** TSprake(22) (hdwy 2f out: nt rch ldrs)	s.h	**7**	16/1	85	48
	Resounder (USA) (94) (JHMGosden) **4-8-13** LDettori(14) (lw: gd hdwy over 2f out: rdn over 1f out: nt qckn)	hd	**8**	20/1	88	51
738[10]	**Cadeaux Tryst (102)** (EALDunlop) **5-9-4(3)** DO'Donohoe(13) (b: hdwy 3f out: rdn over 1f out: nvr nr to chal)	s.h	**9**	16/1	96	59
514[6]	**Tumbleweed Ridge (89)** (BJMeehan) **4-8-8b** PatEddery(9) (lw: hdwy over 2f out: hrd rdn over 1f out: wknd fnl f)	hd	**10**	13/2[1]	83	46
745[2]	**Cretan Gift (98)** (NPLittmoden) **6-9-3b** TGMcLaughlin(18) (nvr nr to chal)	2	**11**	33/1	88	51
529[15]	**Persian Fayre (85)** (JBerry) **5-8-4** GCarter(2) (prom tl wknd over 1f out)	s.h	**12**	33/1	74	37
726[12]	**Samwar (91)** (MissGayKelleway) **5-8-10** RHughes(3) (hdwy over 2f out: hrd rdn over 1f out: wknd ins fnl f)	2½	**13**	20/1	75	38

554[5]	**Tea Party (USA) (77)** (KOCunningham-Brown) **4-7-5b**(5) PFessey(21) (led 4f: sn wknd)	hd	**14**	100/1	60	23
	Kayvee (98) (MrsAJPerrett) **8-9-3** AClark(20) (prom tl wknd 2f out)	s.h	**15**	16/1	81	44
	Crumpton Hill (IRE) (90) (NAGraham) **5-8-9** MRoberts(7) (bit bkwd: nvr trbld ldrs)	3	**16**	11/1	66	29
	Zelda Zonk (77) (BJMeehan) **5-7-10** JQuinn(23) (in tch over 4f)	¾	**17**	66/1	52	15
	Master Charter (82) (MrsJRRamsden) **5-8-1** JFEgan(6) (nvr trbld ldrs)	½	**18**	12/1	56	19
752[2]	**Neuwest (USA) (82)** (NJHWalker) **5-8-1** CRutter(17) (bhd fnl 3f)	½	**19**	16/1	54	17
	Angel Chimes (77) (JEBanks) **4-7-5**(5) RMullen(5) (b.off hind: bit bkwd: nvr on terms)	¾	**20**	16/1	48	11
514[4]	**Dawalib (USA) (77)** (DHaydnJones) **7-7-10** JLowe(4) (a bhd)	2	**21**	150/1	43	6
443[15]	**Charlie Sillett (83)** (BWHills) **5-8-2** PaulEddery(10) (s.s: a bhd)	hd	**22**	25/1	49	12
786[3]	**Tiler (IRE) (81)** (MJohnston) **5-7-11**(3) MHenry(19) (bhd fnl 3f)	3	**23**	25/1	40	3
726[15]	**Bold Effort (FR) (87)** (KOCunningham-Brown) **5-8-6v** WRyan(12) (bhd fnl 4f)	1½	**24**	33/1	43	6
433[2]	**Yeast (109)** (WJHaggas) **5-10-0** RCochrane(25) (w ldr over 4f: sn wknd)	nk	**25**	10/1[3]	64	27
				(SP 132.8%)		**25 Rn**

1m 28.33 (1.13) CSF £117.85 CT £3,240.40 TOTE £9.00: £2.50 £3.40 £5.30 £4.60 (£58.00) Trio £1,498.20 OWNER Mr Hefin Jones (EPSOM) BRED Stonethorn Stud Farms

LONG HANDICAP Tea Party (USA) 7-0 Angel Chimes 7-9 Dawalib (USA) 6-4 Waypoint 7-6 Zelda Zonk 7-9

677 Tregaron (USA) was given a brilliant ride by Quinn, who decided to switch his mount from the stands' side to the far side, where the advantage undoubtedly was, soon after halfway. Striking the front a furlong out, he left his field for dead to give his trainer yet another big handicap success. (9/1)

519 World Premier, always close up, hit the front three furlongs from home but, collared by the winner entering the final furlong, had nothing in reserve. (16/1)

663 Waypoint, in a handy position throughout, was tapped for toe in the closing stages. (25/1)

560 Arterxerxes ran well and had every chance below the distance before failing to find another gear. (33/1)

514 Chewit had no easy task, but was one of four who elected to tack over to the far side over a quarter-of-a-mile from home. He stayed on from below the distance to be nearest at the line. (20/1)

677 Emerging Market picked up ground on the stands' side at the quarter-mile pole, but failed to quicken in the final furlong. He has done all his winning at six furlongs. (11/1: 8/1-12/1)

91+ 82+ 93+ 99

893 GARTER CONDITIONS STKS (2-Y.O) (Class B)

4-10 (4-11) **5f** £6,481.60 (£2,424.40: £1,184.70: £508.50: £226.75: £114.05) Stalls: Low GOING minus 0.18 sec per fur (GF)

				SP	RR	SF
432*	**Blueridge Dancer (IRE)** (BJMeehan) **2-9-1** PatEddery(9) (a.p: led over 1f out: r.o wl)	—	**1**	5/4[1]	96	45
648[5]	**Conectis (IRE)** (DJSCosgrove) **2-8-6** GCarter(2) (outpcd & bhd: gd hdwy over 1f out: fin wl)	2	**2**	50/1	81	30
750*	**Banningham Blade** (KTIvory) **2-8-10** MartinDwyer(7) (a.p: led over 2f out tl over 1f out: nt qckn)	nk	**3**	12/1	84	33
696[3]	**Miquelon** (RHollinshead) **2-9-1** KDarley(6) (lw: a.p: sltly hmpd over 2f out: one pce fnl f)	nk	**4**	12/1	88	37
	Hickory (IRE) (MJHaynes) **2-8-11** JReid(1) (w'like: s.s: wl in rr tl gd late hdwy)	2	**5**	33/1	77	26
697*	**Occhi Verdi (IRE)** (MJohnston) **2-8-10** JWeaver(4) (led: hung rt & hdd over 2f out: sn wknd)	4	**6**	2/1[2]	64	13
536*	**Vax Rapide** (JLSpearing) **2-8-6** SDrowne(3) (lw: w ldr over 2f: wknd qckly)	4	**7**	13/2[3]	47	—
				(SP 111.4%)		**7 Rn**

62.55 secs (2.35) CSF £52.49 TOTE £2.20: £1.40 £7.30 (£37.20) Trio £59.20 OWNER Mr Alan Cunliffe (UPPER LAMBOURN) BRED K. Molloy

432* Blueridge Dancer (IRE) put up a polished display, moving through to lead below the distance and quickly leaving the opposition for dead. A return visit for the Royal meeting is now on the cards. (5/4)

648 Conectis (IRE), unable to go with the early pace, put in some good work in the last furlong and a half, but found the winner was beyond recall. (50/1)

750* Banningham Blade has had an excellent spring winning three small races and, although she had a lot more on her plate here, acquitted herself well and showed in front at halfway. Collared below the distance, she failed to find another gear. (12/1)

696 Miquelon, done no favours by Occhi Verdi a quarter-of-a-mile from home, had every chance below the distance before tapped for toe. (12/1: 8/1-14/1)

Hickory (IRE) lost ground at the start and was completely taken off his feet until making some late headway. (33/1)

697* Occhi Verdi (IRE) set the pace to halfway, but she then hung right doing Miquelon no favours and was soon beaten. She has quite a high knee-action and may be helped by some give in the ground. (2/1)

536* Vax Rapide (13/2: 9/2-7/1)

894 CHOBHAM CONDITIONS STKS (4-Y.O+) (Class C)

4-40 (4-40) **1m (round)** £4,948.00 (£1,852.00: £906.00: £390.00: £175.00) Stalls: High GOING minus 0.18 sec per fur (GF)

				SP	RR	SF
	Nwaamis (USA) (110) (JLDunlop) **5-8-12** RHills(1) (lw: a.p: rdn over 1f out: r.o to ld last strides)	—	**1**	11/8[1]	111	67
	Charlotte Corday (85) (GWragg) **4-8-10** MHills(2) (swtg: hld up: qcknd to ld ins fnl f: hdd post)	s.h	**2**	10/1	109	65
	Cap Juluca (IRE) (RCharlton) **5-8-12** RHughes(6) (bit bkwd: led tl ins fnl f)	3	**3**	3/1[2]	105	61
	Winter Romance (102) (EALDunlop) **4-8-9**(3) DO'Donohoe(5) (lw: a bhd: rdn over 2f out: no rspnse)	7	**4**	9/2[3]	91	47
565*	**Intisab** (RWArmstrong) **4-8-10** GCarter(3) (prom tl wknd over 2f out)	1¾	**5**	8/1	85	41
				(SP 105.5%)		**5 Rn**

1m 42.31 (1.51) CSF £12.43 TOTE £2.30: £1.40 £2.60 (£9.00) OWNER Mr Hamdan Al Maktoum (ARUNDEL) BRED Shadwell Farm Inc & Shadwell Estate Co Ltd in USA

Nwaamis (USA) suffered from EPM last season which attacks the nervous system, and consequently has been off the course for a year. Nevertheless he returned looking in good shape and quickly made up for lost time. Never far away, he threw down a determined challenge in the straight and managed to get up in the last couple of strides. (11/8)

Charlotte Corday mounted her challenge in the straight and managed to get to the front inside the final furlong, but she just lost out on the nod. (10/1: 8/1-12/1)

Cap Juluca (IRE), winner of five races on the trot in 1995, ran just once last year through injury. He had to miss ten days' work recently and, not surprisingly, looked as though this run was needed. Nevertheless, he took the field along until tiring inside the final furlong. He should soon be winning. (3/1: 9/4-7/2)

Winter Romance, held up at the back of the field, was asked for his effort in the straight, but could never reel in the principals. His action suggests some cut is needed. (9/2: op 3/1)

565* Intisab was close up until tiring early in the straight. (8/1)

895 WHITE ROSE H'CAP (0-80) (3-Y.O+) (Class D)

5-15 (5-16) **1m (straight)** £7,782.50 (£2,360.00: £1,155.00: £552.50) Stalls: Low GOING minus 0.18 sec per fur (GF)

				SP	RR	SF
653[11]	**Broughtons Turmoil (70)** (BRMillman) **8-9-4** TSprake(28) (lw: a.p: led over 2f out: r.o wl)	—	**1**	33/1	83	65
	Family Man (70) (JRFanshawe) **4-9-4** DHarrison(12) (dwlt: gd hdwy 2f out: r.o ins fnl f)	1½	**2**	12/1[3]	80	62
	King of Tunes (FR) (76) (JJSheehan) **5-9-10** RCochrane(1) (lw: gd hdwy over 1f out: r.o ins fnl f)	nk	**3**	14/1	85	67
755[5]	**Doctor Bravious (IRE) (63)** (MBell) **4-8-6v**(5) GFaulkner(11) (hrd rdn 3f out: gd hdwy 2f out: r.o ins fnl f)	s.h	**4**	25/1	72	54
749[11]	**Sylvan Princess (69)** (DJSCosgrove) **4-9-3** MRimmer(6) (gd hdwy 2f out: nt qckn ins fnl f)	½	**5**	20/1	77	59
554[2]	**Mimosa (61)** (SDow) **4-8-4**(5) ADaly(7) (lw: styd on fnl 2f: nt rch ldrs)	2	**6**	20/1	65	47
755*	**Safey Ana (USA) (64)** (BHanbury) **6-8-12** 5x WRyan(24) (b: lw: hdwy over 2f out: one pce fnl f)	½	**7**	12/1[3]	67	49
749[9]	**Three Arch Bridge (65)** (MJohnston) **5-8-13b** JWeaver(27) (styd on fnl 2f: nt rch ldrs)	nk	**8**	14/1	68	50
791[5]	**Kingchip Boy (69)** (MJRyan) **8-9-3v** AClark(18) (brought lft after 1f: chsd ldrs: one pce fnl 2f)	½	**9**	20/1	71	53
	Dummer Golf Time (66) (LordHuntingdon) **4-8-9**(5) AimeeCook(22) (prom tl wknd over 2f out)	1¼	**10**	20/1	65	47
661[4]	**Duello (73)** (MBlanshard) **6-9-7** JQuinn(26) (nvr nr to chal)	2	**11**	14/1	68	50
763[9]	**Alfahaal (IRE) (60)** (RFJohnsonHoughton) **4-8-8** RHills(25) (led far side over 5f: sn wknd)	3	**12**	33/1	49	31
529[2]	**Impulsive Air (IRE) (65)** (EWeymes) **5-8-13** LDettori(4) (nvr on terms)	nk	**13**	6/1[2]	54	36
755[6]	**Alsahib (USA) (67)** (WRMuir) **4-9-1** JReid(20) (nvr trbld ldrs)	nk	**14**	20/1	55	37
578[14]	**Winston (63)** (JDBethell) **4-8-11** PaulEddery(21) (hrd rdn over 2f out: no rspnse)	1½	**15**	12/1[3]	48	30
	Missile Toe (IRE) (58) (DMorris) **4-8-6** NDay(10) (prom tl wknd qckly over 1f out)	1	**16**	20/1	41	23
654[11]	**My Beloved (IRE) (78)** (RHannon) **3-8-12** DaneO'Neill(2) (outpcd)	¾	**17**	33/1	60	28
	Q Factor (78) (DHaydnJones) **5-9-12** CRutter(29) (prom tl wknd over 2f out)	1¼	**18**	25/1	57	39
	Admirals Flame (IRE) (77) (CFWall) **6-9-11** GDuffield(14) (b: in tch tl wknd over 2f out)	1¾	**19**	16/1	53	35
748*	**Star of Ring (IRE) (70)** (MJHeaton-Ellis) **4-9-4** MRoberts(30) (prom tl wknd over 2f out)	1	**20**	5/1[1]	44	26
735[4]	**Punkah (USA) (74)** (GMMcCourt) **4-9-8** GCarter(9) (swtg: outpcd)	¾	**21**	20/1	46	28
	Sejaal (IRE) (60) (RAkehurst) **5-8-8** RPerham(8) (lw: chsd ldr tl wknd 3f out)	1½	**22**	20/1	29	11
657[9]	**Suez Tornado (IRE) (67)** (EJAlston) **4-9-1v**[1] JFortune(5) (lw: led tl wknd qckly over 2f out)	nk	**23**	33/1	35	17
	Phonetic (74) (GBBalding) **4-9-8** SDrowne(15) (lw: a bhd)	½	**24**	33/1	41	23
677[8]	**Zurs (IRE) (78)** (MissGayKelleway) **4-9-12b**[1] KFallon(13) (outpcd)	hd	**25**	14/1	45	27
	White Settler (70) (RJHodges) **4-9-4** SSanders(23) (bhd fnl 4f)	3½	**26**	20/1	30	12
	Courting Danger (70) (DRGandolfo) **4-9-4** MFenton(16) (swtg: wl bhd fnl 4f)	9	**27**	33/1	12	—
647[15]	**Kriscliffe (75)** (GLewis) **4-9-9** RHughes(19) (wl bhd fnl 4f)	nk	**28**	33/1	17	—

(SP 157.7%) **28 Rn**

1m 42.23 (2.23) CSF £339.93 CT £5,295.64 TOTE £34.30: £7.30 £4.10 £3.00 £14.10 (£506.60) Trio Not won; £2,777.52 to Redcar 1/5/97
OWNER Mr R. Marlow (CULLOMPTON) BRED Tally Ho Stud Co (U.K.) Ltd and Ninevah Ltd
WEIGHT FOR AGE 3yo-14lb
OFFICIAL EXPLANATION **Broughtons Turmoil: regarding the improvement in form, the trainer stated that he may have needed his previous run at Warwick.**

484 Broughtons Turmoil, never far away, struck the front over a quarter-of-a-mile from home and proved too strong for his rivals. (33/1)
Family Man, rather sluggish leaving the stalls, ran on strongly in the last furlong-and-a-half for second prize, but was unable to trouble the winner. (12/1)
King of Tunes (FR), without a run in nearly eleven months, was doing all his best work in the last furlong-and-a-half. (14/1)
755 Doctor Bravious (IRE), hard ridden soon after halfway. picked up ground and, running on strongly in the closing stages, may well have taken third place with a little further to go. (25/1)
554* Sylvan Princess made good strides a quarter-of-a-mile from home, but failed to find another gear inside the final furlong. (20/1)
554 Mimosa, pushed along and going nowhere at the back of the field fully five furlongs from home, struggled on in the final quarter-mile without posing a serious threat. (20/1)

T/Jkpt: Not won; £31,173.67 to Redcar 1/5/97. T/Plpt: £4,924.30 (7.31 Tckts). T/Qdpt: £150.20 (22.98 Tckts) AK

REDCAR (L-H) (Firm, Good to firm patches)

Thursday May 1st

WEATHER: fine & sunny WIND: slt half bhd

896 ELECTION DAY (S) STKS (3-Y.O+) (Class F)

2-30 (2-32) **7f** £2,985.00 (£835.00: £405.00) Stalls: Centre GOING minus 0.66 sec per fur (HD)

				SP	RR	SF
526[11]	**Dispol Diamond (52)** (GROldroyd) **4-9-0** KDarley(2) (chsd ldrs: led 3f out: sn clr)	—	**1**	14/1	50	44
760*	**Double Oscar (IRE) (50)** (DNicholls) **4-9-10b** AlexGreaves(21) (lw: w ldrs: r.o fnl f: no ch w wnr)	2	**2**	7/1[2]	55	49
734[9]	**Komlucky (49)** (ABMulholland) **5-9-0v** JQuinn(20) (trckd ldrs: effrt 2f out: kpt on same pce fnl f)	1¼	**3**	7/1[2]	43	37
	Move Smartly (IRE) (53) (MrsLStubbs) **7-9-0v**(5) RFfrench(23) (lw: w ldrs: one pce fnl 2f)	½	**4**	9/1[3]	46	40
823[7]	**Fisiostar (34)** (MDods) **4-9-2b**(3) CTeague(6) (swtchd rt after 1f: hdwy over 2f out: kpt on)	1¾	**5**	40/1	42	36
785[4]	**Abstone Queen (60)** (PDEvans) **3-8-7v** JFortune(7) (swtchd rt s: bhd tl styd on u.p fnl 2f)	1¾	**6**	11/4[1]	38	20
470[13]	**Born A Lady (42)** (MrsVAAconley) **4-9-0** MDeering(12) (lw: w ldrs: one pce fnl 2f)	½	**7**	25/1	32	26
587[17]	**Okay Baby (IRE) (27)** (JMBradley) **5-9-0** MRoberts(24) (hld up & bhd: styd on fnl 2f: nvr nr to chal)	½	**8**	50/1	31	25
496[6]	**Sounds Legal (41)** (PDEvans) **4-9-0b** JFEgan(18) (sn outpcd: sme hdwy 2f out: n.d)	¾	**9**	10/1	29	23
687[15]	**Mubariz (IRE) (50)** (CSmith) **5-9-5** WJO'Connor(13) (lw: w ldrs tl wknd over 2f out)	2	**10**	16/1	30	24
526[5]	**Miletrian City (51)** (JBerry) **4-8-12b**(7) PBradley(5) (lw: bhd: sme hdwy 2f out: n.d)	1	**11**	10/1	28	22
774[7]	**Interaction** (RCraggs) **3-8-7** LCharnock(19) (bhd: sme hdwy 2f out: n.d)	s.h	**12**	33/1	28	10
	Oriel Lad (49) (DonEnricoIncisa) **4-9-5** KimTinkler(17) (sn outpcd)	2½	**13**	33/1	22	16
772[6]	**Spanish Stripper (USA) (40)** (MCChapman) **6-9-0**(5) PFessey(16) (chsd ldrs 5f: sn lost pl)	hd	**14**	20/1	22	16
484[9]	**Auchinleck Judge** (JLHarris) **4-9-5** DWright(11) (sn outpcd)	½	**15**	100/1	20	14
685[12]	**Soviet Lady (IRE) (56)** (JLEyre) **3-8-2** TWilliams(14) (chsd ldrs: rdn ½-wy: eased whn no ch over 1f out)	3	**16**	7/1[2]	9	—
587[10]	**Cinnamon Stick (IRE) (33)** (PSFelgate) **4-9-5** GHind(4) (sn bhd)	½	**17**	40/1	12	6
774[10]	**Bold Engagement** (MDods) **3-8-2** DaleGibson(15) (outpcd fr ½-wy)	nk	**18**	33/1	7	—
779[14]	**Chilled Wine (43)** (GPKelly) **3-7-11**(5) JBramhill(9) (w ldrs 5f: sn wknd)	1¼	**19**	100/1	4	—
373[11]	**African Sun (IRE) (43)** (MCChapman) **4-9-2**(3) DO'Donohoe(22) (a in rr)	2	**20**	50/1	4	—
	Pecan Princess (IRE) (CASmith) **4-8-9**(5) IonaWands(1) (neat: bhd fr ½-wy)	nk	**21**	100/1	—	—

				SP	RR	SF
	Harvest Reaper (43) (JLHarris) **5-9-5** DeanMcKeown(3) (w ldrs 5f: sn lost pl)	3	**22**	33/1	—	—
	Wild Prospect (25) (ABailey) **9-9-5** MBirch(8) (w ldrs tl lost pl 3f out: eased)	2½	**23**	20/1	—	—
	My Achates (MBrittain) **4-8-9**(5) GParkin(10) (lt-f: s.s: a bhd: t.o)	22	**24**	50/1	—	—
				(SP 143.8%)	**24 Rn**	

1m 22.9 (-0.10) CSF £99.61 TOTE £16.80: £4.10 £3.00 £2.90 (£95.30) Trio £415.60 OWNER Mr W. B. Imison (YORK) BRED N. Stewart
WEIGHT FOR AGE 3yo-12lb
Bt in 4,200 gns
Dispol Diamond, who was originally rated 74 in handicaps, has slipped down the weights but proved much too good for this lot, racing in glorious isolation on the far side in the final two furlongs. (14/1)
760* Double Oscar (IRE) would have been meeting the winner on 6lb better terms in a handicap. He came out clear best on the stands' side but the winner was on the other wing. (7/1)
Komlucky, who was suited by fast ground, probably ran up to his best. (7/1)
Move Smartly (IRE) was having his first outing for his new trainer. (9/1: op 5/1)
Fisiostar would have been meeting the winner on 23lb better terms in a handicap and on paper looks to have run really well. (40/1)
785 Abstone Queen, switched right at the start, seems to reserve her best these days for Catterick. (11/4)

897 MONSTER RAVING LOONEY MAIDEN AUCTION STKS (2-Y.O F) (Class E)
3-00 (3-01) **5f** £2,898.25 (£871.00: £420.50: £195.25) Stalls: Centre GOING minus 0.66 sec per fur (HD)

				SP	RR	SF
682[4]	**Days of Grace** (MartynMeade) **2-8-4** FNorton(2) (led to ½-wy: led over 1f out: r.o)	—	**1**	6/1[3]	69	13
	Sharp Cracker (IRE) (MJohnston) **2-8-4** MRoberts(4) (w'like: scope: bit bkwd: s.i.s: bhd tl hdwy over 1f out: styd on wl towards fin)	2	**2**	6/1[3]	63	7
	Baby Grand (IRE) (TDBarron) **2-8-1** LCharnock(3) (neat: bit bkwd: w ldrs: rdn ½-wy: kpt on fnl f)	½	**3**	25/1	58	2
	Rhinefield Beauty (IRE) (JSGoldie) **2-8-1** JQuinn(1) (cmpt: lw: sn trckng ldrs: led ½-wy: hung rt: hdd over 1f out: sn wknd)	2	**4**	7/2[2]	52	—
536[3]	**Always Lucky** (JBerry) **2-7-13**(5) PFessey(6) (chsd ldrs: rdn & outpcd ½-wy: kpt on)	½	**5**	11/10[1]	53	—
500[6]	**Marske Machine** (NTinkler) **2-8-1** GHind(7) (sn drvn along & outpcd)	4	**6**	14/1	37	—
844[4]	**Petite Lady** (PDEvans) **2-8-1** JFEgan(5) (sn rdn & outpcd: bhd fr ½-wy)	9	**7**	12/1	8	—
				(SP 116.6%)	**7 Rn**	

58.6 secs (1.10) CSF £38.59 TOTE £5.80: £2.20 £2.50 (£17.10) OWNER Mr Stephen Bayless (MALMESBURY) BRED Peter McCalmont
682 Days of Grace, who has a fair bit about her, took this with something to spare. (6/1)
Sharp Cracker (IRE), who looked in need of the outing, ran green and had a lot to do at halfway. Picking up ground in good style inside the last, she will be a lot sharper for the outing. (6/1)
Baby Grand (IRE), outpaced at halfway, was sticking on at the finish and the outing will have done her a power of good. (25/1)
Rhinefield Beauty (IRE), a sharp sort, showed a quick action going down. Racing keenly, she tended to hang and faded in the final furlong. The outing should have taught her plenty. (7/2)
536 Always Lucky was very keen going to post but on the way back was never able to go the pace, though she was sticking on at the finish. (11/10)

898 PAT PHOENIX H'CAP (0-70) (3-Y.O+) (Class E)
3-30 (3-31) **1m 3f** £2,937.25 (£883.00: £426.50: £198.25) Stalls: Low GOING minus 0.66 sec per fur (HD)

				SP	RR	SF
574[18]	**Cottage Prince (IRE) (41)** (JJQuinn) **4-8-9** JFortune(5) (effrt u.p over 3f out: hdwy over 2f out: swtchd & styd on to ld nr fin)	—	**1**	7/1[3]	53	21
796[7]	**My Millie (44)** (DWBarker) **4-8-12** KDarley(1) (chsd ldrs: led & wnt lft over 1f out: hrd rdn: hdd nr fin)	nk	**2**	16/1	56	24
595[18]	**Cashmirie (30)** (JLEyre) **5-7-12** TWilliams(7) (trckd ldrs: led over 3f out tl wandered & hdd over 1f out: one pce)	3	**3**	20/1	37	5
796[6]	**Mcgillycuddy Reeks (IRE) (40)** (DonEnricoIncisa) **6-8-8** KimTinkler(6) (lw: w ldr: led over 4f out tl over 3f out: one pce appr fnl f)	3	**4**	16/1	43	11
	Keep Battling (50) (JSGoldie) **7-9-4** JQuinn(3) (hld up: stdy hdwy over 3f out: shkn up over 1f out: sn wknd)	6	**5**	9/2[2]	44	12
	Penny Peppermint (30) (REBarr) **5-7-7**(5) PFessey(9) (sn bhd & pushed along: sme hdwy 2f out: nvr nr to chal)	3	**6**	50/1	20	—
574*	**Brambles Way (54)** (MrsMReveley) **8-9-3b**(5) SCopp(10) (lw: led: hdd over 4f out: wknd over 2f out)	nk	**7**	13/8[1]	43	11
	Nornax Lad (USA) (57) (MartynMeade) **9-9-8**(3) RHavlin(8) (s.i.s: a in rr)	1½	**8**	9/1	44	12
595[17]	**Tagatay (35)** (MJCamacho) **4-8-3** LCharnock(4) (trckd ldrs tl wknd over 3f out)	2½	**9**	7/1[3]	19	—
608[13]	**Giftbox (USA) (42)** (NBycroft) **5-8-10** DeanMcKeown(2) (in tch: drvn along over 4f out: sn lost pl)	1¼	**10**	20/1	24	—
	Try Omnipotent (32) (MrsVAAconley) **5-8-0** MDeering(11) (hld up & bhd: plld hrd: a last)	12	**11**	33/1	—	—
				(SP 117.5%)	**11 Rn**	

2m 19.8 (2.80) CSF £96.10 CT £1,939.28 TOTE £10.10: £2.10 £4.80 £2.70 (£28.30) Trio £385.20; £173.65 to Newcastle 2/5/97 OWNER Mrs Kay Thomas (MALTON) BRED Owen Bourke
Cottage Prince (IRE), a winner over hurdles during the winter, owed this to his jockey who rode a most determined race, rousting him along to get up near the line. (7/1)
My Millie, still a maiden after fourteen starts, has tried a number of different trips. Diving left when she hit the front, she was worn down near the line. (16/1)
Cashmirie, who presumably needed it first time after a long absence, did not help her rider or her cause by ducking and diving under pressure. The outing might bring her on again. (20/1)
Mcgillycuddy Reeks (IRE) ran much better than on her reappearance, making the best of her way home. (16/1)
Keep Battling, having his first outing for ten months, as usual travelled strongly off the pace. After picking up ground on the bridle, just when he looked as though he might get into the argument he began to tire. The outing should bring him on a good deal. (9/2)
574* Brambles Way had the blinkers back on. Making his own running, he called it a day halfway up the straight. Over hurdles, he has shown his best form coming from off the pace. (13/8)
Nornax Lad (USA) (9/1: 7/1-12/1)
Tagatay (7/1: op 4/1)

899 RACING CHANNEL MAIDEN STKS (3-Y.O+) (Class D)
4-00 (4-04) **7f** £3,899.00 (£1,172.00: £566.00: £263.00) Stalls: Centre GOING minus 0.66 sec per fur (HD)

				SP	RR	SF
674[5]	**Broad River (USA)** (EALDunlop) **3-8-9**(3) DO'Donohoe(1) (lw: trckd ldr gng wl: shkn up to ld wl over 1f out: eased towards fin)	—	**1**	2/9[1]	79+	31

			SP	RR	SF
729^{6}	**Look Who's Calling (IRE) (73)** (BAMcMahon) **4-9-10** KDarley(6) (led tl wl over 1f out: kpt on towards fin) ...1½	**2**	$10/1^{2}$	76	40
	Raed (69) (MrsASwinbank) **4-9-10** JSupple(7) (swtg: chsd ldrs: outpcd ½-wy: styd on fnl f) ....½	**3**	$10/1^{2}$	74	38
645^{4}	**Madison Mist** (MrsJRRamsden) **3-8-7** JFortune(3) (trckd ldrs: outpcd ½-wy: kpt on wl appr fnl f) ....¾	**4**	$10/1^{2}$	68	20
	Digital Option (IRE) (MrsJRRamsden) **3-8-12** MDeering(5) (hld up: sn bhd) 12	**5**	50/1	45	—
	Heubach Boy (MrsASwinbank) **3-8-12** WJO'Connor(4) (unf: s.i.s: a outpcd) 5	**6**	50/1	34	—
599^{W}	**Makati** (MJCamacho) **3-8-12** LCharnock(2) (w'like: str: bkwd: s.s: a outpcd & sn pushed along) 2½	**7**	$25/1^{3}$	28	—
			(SP 116.9%)		**7 Rn**

1m 23.8 (0.80) CSF £3.41 TOTE £1.10: £1.10 £3.80 (£4.10) OWNER Maktoum Al Maktoum (NEWMARKET) BRED Barbara Hunter
WEIGHT FOR AGE 3yo-12lb

674 Broad River (USA) was found a soft option and took this easing down. It is doubtful if there has been a less competitive race for a long time. (2/9)

729 Look Who's Calling (IRE) led on sufferance but his rider seemed happy to accept that the winner was going to prove too good for him. (10/1: 8/1-12/1)

Raed, having his first outing since changing stables, sweated up at the start. Sticking on strongly under a quiet ride, he is probably better suited by a mile. (10/1)

645 Madison Mist, who was staying on over a mile last time, was dropped back a furlong. Taken off her legs at halfway, she was keeping on strongly at the finish without her rider ever getting serious. No doubt she will step back up in distance when she has had one more run and is qualified for a handicap mark. (10/1: op 5/1)

900 PARTY POLITICS MAIDEN APPRENTICE H'CAP (0-65) (3-Y.O+) (Class G)

4-30 (4-32) **1m 1f** £2,130.00 (£605.00: £300.00) Stalls: Low GOING minus 0.66 sec per fur (HD)

			SP	RR	SF
826^{4}	**Jack The Lad (IRE) (58)** (JHetherton) **3-8-9** TSiddall(4) (chsd ldrs: led 2f out: sn clr) ....—	**1**	16/1	75	29
733^{4}	**Godmersham Park (63)** (PSFelgate) **5-9-9**$^{(5)}$ DarrenWilliams(8) (lw: mde most to 2f out: no ch w wnr) 6	**2**	13/2	69	37
721^{10}	**Sing And Dance (43)** (EWeymes) **4-8-8** RWinston(16) (lw: mid div: hdwy over 3f out: styd on fnl f) 2½	**3**	14/1	45	13
	Grovefair Lad (IRE) (52) (MartynWane) **3-8-3** JMcAuley(13) (bit bkwd: bhd: hdwy 3f out: kpt on same pce fnl f) ....hd	**4**	14/1	54	8
755^{3}	**Carlys Quest (60)** (JNeville) **3-8-11** RCody-Boutcher(10) (lw: hdwy over 3f out: kpt on fnl 2f: nvr nr to chal) 2	**5**	$4/1^{1}$	58	12
	Advance East (54) (MDods) **5-9-5v¹** PFredericks(9) (trckd ldrs: plld hrd: chal over 4f out: wknd 2f out) ....hd	**6**	$6/1^{3}$	52	20
733^{16}	**Stolen Music (IRE) (44)** (REBarr) **4-8-9** DMernagh(5) (chsd ldrs: chal over 4f out: wknd over 2f out) 1½	**7**	33/1	39	7
580^{9}	**Whothehellisharry (45)** (PTDalton) **4-8-10v¹** RBrisland(12) (mid div: sme hdwy 3f out: n.d) ....nk	**8**	33/1	40	8
763^{4}	**Blaze of Oak (USA) (43)** (JMBradley) **6-8-8** JFowle(15) (bhd: sme hdwy 3f out: n.d) 5	**9**	12/1	29	—
	Gollaccia (47) (GMMoore) **3-7-12** PBradley(14) (hld up: hdwy on outside 6f out: lost pl over 3f) 4	**10**	33/1	26	—
687^{16}	**Ballet de Cour (38)** (TJEtherington) **4-8-3** CLowther(11) (a in rr) ....¾	**11**	50/1	15	—
538^{10}	**Severn Mill (34)** (JMBradley) **6-7-8**$^{(5)}$ JBosley(6) (in tch tl lost pl over 3f out) ....hd	**12**	16/1	11	—
668^{14}	**Nukud (USA) (33)** (GROldroyd) **5-7-12v** CCogan(2) (a in rr) 2½	**13**	12/1	6	—
642^{7}	**Mister Jay (50)** (PTWalwyn) **3-8-1** GHannon(1) (bhd: sme hdwy 4f out: sn wknd) 7	**14**	14/1	10	—
600^{2}	**Kingdom Emperor (52)** (MJCamacho) **3-7-12**$^{(5)}$ DHayden(7) (reluctant to r: sme hdwy on outside over 3f out: sn lost pl & eased) 6	**15**	$9/2^{2}$	2	—
570^{12}	**The Black Dubh (IRE) (31)** (JJQuinn) **4-7-10** NPollard(3) (prom tl lost pl over 3f out: sn bhd) 6	**16**	50/1	—	—
			(SP 125.7%)		**16 Rn**

1m 51.9 (1.20) CSF £105.81 CT £1,455.21 TOTE £13.90: £2.40 £2.50 £2.60 £5.30 (£56.40) Trio £233.40 OWNER Keith West Partnership (MALTON) BRED Thomas Healy
LONG HANDICAP The Black Dubh (IRE) 7-9
WEIGHT FOR AGE 3yo-14lb

826 Jack The Lad (IRE) was certainly happier over this shorter trip and his young rider left nothing to chance. (16/1)

733 Godmersham Park settled nicely in front but in the end proved no match. The trip was no problem. (13/2)

552 Sing And Dance was given a fair bit to do and in the circumstances did well to finish so close. She is probably happier over ten furlongs. (14/1)

Grovefair Lad (IRE) came from the back but his effort petered out in the final furlong. (14/1)

755 Carlys Quest was ridden to get the trip but his rider seemed to slightly overdo the tactics. (4/1)

Advance East, in a visor for the first time, pulled much too hard for his own good and got there far too early. He is better coming from off the pace. (6/1)

600 Kingdom Emperor was in a foul mood and virtually refused to race in the early stages. (9/2: op 3/1)

901 DON'T FORGET TO VOTE H'CAP (0-80) (3-Y.O+ F & M) (Class D)

5-00 (5-00) **5f** £3,535.00 (£1,060.00: £510.00: £235.00) Stalls: Centre GOING minus 0.66 sec per fur (HD)

			SP	RR	SF
596^{2}	**Kira (77)** (JLEyre) **7-9-9**$^{(3)}$ OPears(8) (b.hind: mde all: rdn over 1f out: r.o wl) ....—	**1**	$3/1^{1}$	86	61
702^{11}	**Lady Sheriff (66)** (MWEasterby) **6-8-10b**$^{(5)}$ GParkin(4) (lw: s.i.s: hdwy on ins ½-wy: styd on fnl f: no imp) 1½	**2**	$9/2^{2}$	70	45
596^{7}	**Time To Tango (68)** (GMMoore) **4-9-3** JFEgan(5) (w wnr: rdn ½-wy: kpt on same pce appr fnl f) 1¾	**3**	$5/1^{3}$	67	42
779^{5}	**Bollin Dorothy (52)** (TDEasterby) **4-8-1** LCharnock(10) (a chsng ldrs: rdn ½-wy: one pce) 1	**4**	9/1	47	22
	Amoeba (IRE) (50) (ABailey) **4-7-13** DWright(9) (lw: a chsng ldrs: rdn ½-wy: kpt on same pce) 1½	**5**	25/1	41	16
601^{14}	**Pharaoh's Joy (58)** (JWPayne) **4-8-7** MRoberts(3) (sn outpcd & bhd: kpt on appr fnl f: n.d) ....¾	**6**	6/1	46	21
	Oatey (65) (MrsJRRamsden) **4-9-0** JFortune(2) (effrt ½-wy: sme hdwy over 1f out: sn wknd) ....½	**7**	$5/1^{3}$	52	27
	Pathaze (49) (NBycroft) **4-7-7**$^{(5)}$ JBramhill(6) (s.i.s: hdwy on ins u.p ½-wy: no imp whn nt clr run over 1f out) 1½	**8**	50/1	31	6
	Antonia's Choice (80) (JBerry) **3-9-6** KDarley(7) (s.i.s: sn chsng ldrs: wknd & eased 2f out) 4	**9**	8/1	49	15
	Cinders Girl (55) (MrsMReveley) **7-8-4** TWilliams(1) (bolted 3f gng to s: sn wl bhd: virtually p.u over 1f out)..20	**10**	100/1	—	—
			(SP 118.7%)		**10 Rn**

57.0 secs (-0.50) CSF £15.15 CT £60.32 TOTE £3.30: £1.30 £1.20 £2.10 (£7.10) Trio £20.50 OWNER Mr J. E. Wilson (HAMBLETON) BRED J. S. Bell
WEIGHT FOR AGE 3yo-9lb

596 Kira has speed to burn and, much improved, has now won four times in the last year despite a rise in the weights of some 25lb. (3/1: op 2/1)

Lady Sheriff, who has tumbled down the weights and is now back with her old handler, stuck on strongly but the winner was never in any danger. (9/2)

596 Time To Tango is ideally suited by five furlongs and fast ground. (5/1)

779 Bollin Dorothy was being run off her legs from halfway but to her credit kept battling on. Six or seven furlongs and easier ground will help her cause. (9/1)

Amoeba (IRE) was far from disgraced though just lacking that vital bit of speed. (25/1)
Pharaoh's Joy seems to lack a little edge at present. (6/1)
Oatey will come on for the outing. (5/1)

T/Jkpt: Not won; £56,434.19 to Newmarket 2/5/97. T/Plpt: £1,272.00 (18.02 Tckts). T/Qdpt: £64.20 (23.83 Tckts) WG

0855-WOLVERHAMPTON (L-H) (Standard)
Thursday May 1st
WEATHER: fine & sunny WIND: nil

76 64 60

902 UTL MAIDEN AUCTION STKS (2-Y.O) (Class F)
2-15 (2-16) **5f** **(Fibresand)** £2,277.00 (£627.00: £297.00) Stalls: Low GOING: 0.03 sec per fur (STD)

				SP	RR	SF
	One Singer (MJohnston) **2-8-7** JWeaver(4) (leggy: lt-f: led to ½-wy: hrd rdn to ld cl home)	—	**1**	5/1[3]	78	27
	Blue Kite (NPLittmoden) **2-8-5** TGMcLaughlin(6) (cmpt: bit bkwd: chsd wnr: led ½-wy tl ct wl ins fnl f)	½	**2**	8/1	74	23
	Sweet Rosie (IRE) (RBoss) **2-7-7**(5) RMullen(13) (lt-f: unf: hdwy 2f out: rdn over 1f out: nt pce to chal)	7	**3**	2/1[1]	45	—
	Demolition Jo (PDEvans) **2-7-7**(7) AMcCarthy(10) (small: lt-f: unf: s.s: outpcd tl styd on appr fnl f)	1¾	**4**	16/1	41	—
	Flickan (RGuest) **2-7-11**(3) MartinDwyer(3) (lt-f: unf: bkwd: b: chsd ldrs: no hdwy fnl 2f)	hd	**5**	14/1	41	—
572[4]	**Summerseat** (CWFairhurst) **2-8-0** JLowe(2) (chsd ldrs over 3f: sn rdn & wknd)	¾	**6**	14/1	39	—
	Russian Romeo (IRE) (BAMcMahon) **2-8-7** GDuffield(8) (leggy: lt-f: outpcd: a bhd)	2	**7**	12/1	39	—
780[4]	**Chardania (IRE)** (CaptJWilson) **2-8-2** SSanders(12) (prom tl rdn & wknd qckly wl over 1f out)	3	**8**	14/1	25	—
	Super Rascal (NPLittmoden) **2-8-5** DaneO'Neill(9) (lt-f: bit bkwd: chsd ldrs over 3f: sn wknd)	½	**9**	16/1	26	—
592[2]	**Rosewood Lady (IRE)** (KRBurke) **2-7-12** CRutter(7) (outpcd)	½	**10**	8/1	18	—
	Hey Up Mate (IRE) (JBerry) **2-8-10** GCarter(11) (leggy: lt-f: s.s: a bhd & outcpd: t.o)	5	**11**	9/2[2]	14	—
	Lamoura (RBrotherton) **2-8-0** NAdams(5) (small: lt-f: bit bkwd: outpcd: t.o)	3	**12**	25/1	—	—
	Ruths Gem (IRE) (BAPearce) **2-7-12** GBardwell(1) (lt-f: bkwd: s.s: a bhd & outpcd: t.o)	10	**13**	25/1	—	—

(SP 137.6%) **13 Rn**

62.9 secs (0.70 under 2y best) (4.00) CSF £47.70 TOTE £4.20: £1.90 £4.50 £1.10 (£31.80) Trio £77.00 OWNER Clayton Bigley Partnership Ltd (MIDDLEHAM) BRED Zetland Stud

One Singer, a lightly-made colt who has only just reached his second birthday, is bred for speed and he proved the stronger to win this poor event a shade cosily. (5/1)
Blue Kite looked to have plenty left to work on but he dominated with the winner and, if he can improve on this, should have no trouble winning races. (8/1)
Sweet Rosie (IRE), a very fit-looking filly who may need time to fill to her frame, was never going the pace of the principals but she did run on and could benefit from being put away for twelve months. (2/1: op 4/1)
Demolition Jo, flat-footed as the stalls opened, was soon being bustled along in an attempt to close. Staying on inside the distance, she was never nearer than at the finish. A very small, unfurnished filly who looks very weak, it will be interesting to see how much a hardish race like this takes out of her. (16/1)
Flickan, in the chasing group all the way, just could not muster the pace to get serious. (14/1: op 8/1)
572 Summerseat, well beaten on her debut, would seem to be a short runner at present. (14/1: op 8/1)
Russian Romeo (IRE) (12/1: 7/1-14/1)
780 Chardania (IRE) (14/1: 8/1-16/1)
592 Rosewood Lady (IRE) (8/1: 6/1-9/1)
Hey Up Mate (IRE) (9/2: 9/4-5/1)

903 RPL AMATEUR CLAIMING STKS (I) (3-Y.O+) (Class G)
2-45 (2-45) **6f** **(Fibresand)** £1,634.50 (£447.00: £209.50) Stalls: Low GOING: 0.03 sec per fur (STD)

				SP	RR	SF
661[9]	**Zuhair (92)** (DMcCain) **4-11-5**(5) MrGLake(8) (swtg: bit bkwd: b: a.p: led 2f out: sn clr: hld on towards fin)	—	**1**	12/1	72	54
386[2]	**Dancing Sioux (59)** (RGuest) **5-10-11**(7) MissZBurkett(6) (b: outpcd: hdwy over 2f out: r.o wl ins fnl f)	1¾	**2**	7/2[2]	61	43
752[5]	**Penlop (67)** (BJMeehan) **3-10-6b** MissJAllison(4) (lw: s.i.s: sn wl outpcd: hdwy 2f out: r.o wl ins fnl f)	1	**3**	13/2[3]	57	29
681[12]	**Soura (USA) (55)** (PAKelleway) **3-10-4**(5) MrMSpillane(9) (swtg: prom tl rdn & outpcd over 2f out)	2½	**4**	13/2[3]	53	25
	Sea Dreams (IRE) (DMHyde) **6-11-4** MrMRimell(7) (chsd ldrs: drvn along ½-wy: hrd rdn over 2f out: sn outpcd)	5	**5**	16/1	39	21
856[5]	**Kalar (74)** (DWChapman) **8-11-8b** MissRClark(3) (led 4f: sn rdn & outpcd)	3	**6**	6/4[1]	35	17
774[5]	**Ohnonotagain (26)** (LRLloyd-James) **5-10-7** MrRThornton(5) (outpcd: a bhd)	1¾	**7**	10/1	15	—
	Verro (USA) (20) (KBishop) **10-10-5be**(5) MissAPurdy(2) (lw: outpcd: a wl bhd: t.o)	10	**8**	50/1	—	—
760[9]	**Miss Fugit Penance (42)** (PDEvans) **3-9-4**(5) MrVLukaniuk(1) (b.nr fore: s.i.s: a bhd: t.o)	25	**9**	20/1	—	—

(SP 118.3%) **9 Rn**

1m 17.1 (5.90) CSF £50.21 TOTE £11.10: £3.80 £1.30 £1.20 (£19.50) Trio £102.10 OWNER Clayton Bigley Partnership Ltd (CHOLMONDELEY) BRED Shadwell Estate Company Limited
WEIGHT FOR AGE 3yo-10lb

Zuhair, who won his maiden just less than two years ago, has done very little racing since then, but he must have shown something in his first season to be allowed to take his chance in the Group 3 July Stakes at Newmarket. (12/1: op 7/1)
386 Dancing Sioux has only ever won at seven furlongs, and he finds this trip on such a flat track nowhere near far enough. (7/2)
752 Penlop was unable to recover from a sluggish start, but he did plenty of running in the closing stages and a stiffer test looks a must. (13/2: 9/4-7/1)
Soura (USA), soon struggling with the pace on this step down to sprinting, did at least keep persevering and there could be a small race in her. (13/2)
856 Kalar should have made short work of these rivals but he was never allowed to get away, and he stopped to nothing on straightening up for home. (6/4)

904 DE TE WE H'CAP (0-85) (3-Y.O F) (Class D)
3-15 (3-16) **6f** **(Fibresand)** £3,486.35 (£1,038.80: £494.90: £222.95) Stalls: Low GOING: 0.03 sec per fur (STD)

				SP	RR	SF
778[2]	**Silent Miracle (IRE) (77)** (MBell) **3-8-8**(5) GFaulkner(7) (mde all: rdn & r.o wl fnl f)	—	**1**	5/2[1]	81+	25
*265**	**Shalstayholy (IRE) (67)** (GLMoore) **3-8-0**(3) MartinDwyer(9) (hdwy 3f out: chal & hung lft appr fnl f: unable qckn)	1¼	**2**	5/1[3]	68	12

				SP	RR	SF
555[4]	**Dancethenightaway (84)** (BJMeehan) **3-9-6** RHughes(1) (a.p: effrt & ev ch 2f out: kpt on u.p)	1¾	**3**	9/1	80	24
871[11]	**Naivasha (65)** (JBerry) **3-8-1** GCarter(6) (swtg: s.i.s: outpcd & bhd tl r.o appr fnl f)	2½	**4**	14/1	54	—
	Sally Green (IRE) (70) (CFWall) **3-8-6** GDuffield(3) (bkwd: prom: ev ch 2f out: sn drvn along & outpcd)	6	**5**	8/1	43	—
	Farewell My Love (IRE) (76) (PFICole) **3-8-12** TQuinn(4) (nt grwn: spd over 3f: grad wknd: t.o)	7	**6**	9/2[2]	31	—
	Chili Concerto (85) (PJMakin) **3-9-7** SSanders(2) (nt grwn: bit bkwd: trckd ldrs over 3f: sn lost tch: t.o)	hd	**7**	7/1	39	—
466[4]	**Bonyalua Mill (60)** (AStreeter) **3-7-5**(5) RMullen(5) (outpcd fr ½-wy: t.o)	4	**8**	14/1	4	—

(SP 110.4%) **8 Rn**

1m 16.6 (5.40) CSF £12.57 CT £80.54 TOTE £2.50: £1.40 £2.20 £2.10 (£11.70) Trio £22.30 OWNER Mr M. A. Khan (NEWMARKET) BRED Lady Richard Wellesley and Grange Nominees

LONG HANDICAP Bonyalua Mill 7-2

778 Silent Miracle (IRE) was able to open her account on this All-Weather debut with quite a comfortably-gained success, but she would have had a fight on her hands if the runner-up had gone through with her effort. (5/2)

265* Shalstayholy (IRE) has enjoyed a ten-week break since she last ran and this return to sprinting may have caught her out, but she was inclined to edge in behind the winner when asked for her effort, otherwise it is possible she would have won. (5/1)

555 Dancethenightaway, in the action all the way, did keep staying on but she lacked a turn of finishing speed to really pose a threat. (9/1)

Naivasha, flat to the boards after missing a beat at the start, did well to get so close at the finish and there are more prizes to be picked up. (14/1)

Sally Green (IRE) pushed the pace and had every chance until blowing up below the distance. (8/1)

Farewell My Love (IRE) was beginning to feel the strain soon after halfway, and this run may have been needed more than was apparent. (9/2)

905 VARIX H'CAP (0-100) (3-Y.O+) (Class C)

3-45 (3-45) **5f (Fibresand)** £5,352.55 (£1,596.40: £761.70: £344.35) Stalls: Low GOING: 0.03 sec per fur (STD)

				SP	RR	SF
759[4]	**Robo Magic (USA) (78)** (LMontagueHall) **5-8-6**(3) FLynch(10) (b: b.off hind: swtg: hld up: hdwy over 2f out: led ins fnl f: r.o wl)	—	**1**	8/1	91	45
744[2]	**Ziggy's Dancer (USA) (84)** (EJAlston) **6-9-1** KFallon(9) (trckd ldrs: effrt u.p appr fnl f: sn ev ch: no ex nr fin)	1½	**2**	7/4[1]	92	46
731[3]	**Malibu Man (70)** (EAWheeler) **5-8-1** TSprake(1) (swtg: led after 1f: clr ½-wy: hdd fnl 100y)	1¼	**3**	11/2[2]	74	28
698*	**Ansellman (85)** (JBerry) **7-9-2b** GCarter(4) (a.p: hrd rdn over 1f out: one pce)	2	**4**	8/1	83	37
856[8]	**Perfect Brave (65)** (JBalding) **6-7-10** NCarlisle(7) (led 1f: rdn 2f out: r.o one pce)	1¾	**5**	12/1	57	11
357[11]	**Stoppes Brow (93)** (GLMoore) **5-9-10v** GDuffield(5) (s.i.s: sn drvn along: nvr gng pce of ldrs)	½	**6**	14/1	84	38
879*	**Intiaash (IRE) (75)** (DHaydnJones) **5-8-6** 6x CRutter(2) (swtg: dwlt: nvr rcvrd)	nk	**7**	6/1[3]	65	19
760[2]	**General Sir Peter (IRE) (72)** (NACallaghan) **5-7-12**(5) AmandaSanders(6) (outpcd: a bhd)	s.h	**8**	7/1	62	16
883[13]	**Sing With the Band (75)** (BAMcMahon) **6-8-6** LNewton(8) (a bhd & outpcd)	2	**9**	14/1	58	12
*488**	**Lord Sky (72)** (ABailey) **6-8-3** SSanders(3) (lw: prom over 3f: eased whn btn fnl 2f: t.o)	26	**10**	6/1[3]	—	—

(SP 136.1%) **10 Rn**

61.9 secs (3.00) CSF £23.97 CT £88.78 TOTE £15.90: £2.90 £1.10 £1.90 (£27.00) Trio £29.90 OWNER Mr A D Green and Partners (EPSOM) BRED Curtis C. Green

LONG HANDICAP Perfect Brave 7-8

759 Robo Magic (USA) showed that he is capable of winning away from home with a very smoothly-gained clear cut win, and there is no doubting he is useful on his day. (8/1)

744 Ziggy's Dancer (USA), heavily supported in the ring, had just timed his run to take over when the winner appeared on his outside and did him for foot in the sprint to the post. (7/4)

731 Malibu Man did appear to have the prize safely in control turning in, but he began to tie up entering the final furlong and quite simply had no answer to the extra pace of his rivals. (11/2: 7/2-6/1)

698* Ansellman, pressing the leaders from the break, was always finding the tempo too hot and his measure had been taken approaching the final furlong. (8/1: 6/1-9/1)

659 Perfect Brave ran up to his best here and he is continuing to knock at the door. (12/1)

Stoppes Brow has been running over slightly longer trips and, on this return to five furlongs, he was always at full stretch in an attempt to keep tabs on the leaders. (14/1)

488* Lord Sky (6/1: 8/1-9/2)

906 ISDN (S) STKS (3-Y.O) (Class G)

4-15 (4-15) **1m 4f (Fibresand)** £1,984.50 (£547.00: £259.50) Stalls: Low GOING: 0.03 sec per fur (STD)

				SP	RR	SF
581[6]	**Kingsdown Trix (IRE) (62)** (GLMoore) **3-9-2** RPerham(3) (hld up: hdwy ½-wy: led over 3f out: clr 2f out: eased nr fin)	—	**1**	13/8[1]	63+	9
662[3]	**Spondulicks (IRE) (54)** (BPJBaugh) **3-8-11** ACulhane(5) (b: hld up: hdwy 6f out: rdn & outpcd over 2f out: kpt on fnl f)	3	**2**	9/4[3]	54	—
862[4]	**Skelton Sovereign (IRE) (50)** (RHollinshead) **3-8-13b**[1](3) FLynch(2) (s.s: hdwy to jn ldrs 4f out: hrd rdn over 2f out: sn btn)	4	**3**	2/1[2]	54	—
479[7]	**Sibor Star (44)** (DBurchell) **3-8-11** SDrowne(1) (swtg: led tl over 3f out: sn rdn & wknd)	3	**4**	14/1	45	—
	Silent Wells (45) (LRLloyd-James) **3-7-13**(7) KimberleyHart(4) (unf: bkwd: w ldr 5f: sn lost pl: t.o)	dist	**5**	14/1	—	—

(SP 115.5%) **5 Rn**

2m 47.1 (14.60) CSF £5.48 TOTE £2.20: £1.10 £1.50 (£3.90) OWNER Mr David Allen (BRIGHTON) BRED Owen Bourke

Bt in 5,000 gns

454* Kingsdown Trix (IRE) kicked for home entering the straight and, soon forging clear, was able to be eased to a walk crossing the line. (13/8)

662 Spondulicks (IRE), hard at work and outpaced on the home turn, stayed on again once into the straight but the winner had gone clear and was not for catching. He did seem to appreciate this longer trip. (9/4)

862 Skelton Sovereign (IRE) could have had the beating of the winner on these terms, especially as he was wearing blinkers for the first time, but a slow start did not help his cause and, when the final battle developed, he was left standing. (2/1)

Sibor Star, tackling the trip for the first time, tried to do it from the front but he was unable to respond when the winner came at him and his hopes soon disappeared. (14/1: op 7/1)

Silent Wells (14/1: op 7/1)

907 RPL AMATEUR CLAIMING STKS (II) (3-Y.O+) (Class G)

4-45 (4-47) **6f (Fibresand)** £1,634.50 (£447.00: £209.50) Stalls: Low GOING: 0.03 sec per fur (STD)

				SP	RR	SF
579[2]	**Desert Invader (IRE) (58)** (DWChapman) **6-11-2** MissRClark(6) (chsd ldrs: led 2f out: sn clr: canter)	—	**1**	13/8[1]	62+	21
856[7]	**Little Ibnr (65)** (PDEvans) **6-10-9v**(5) MrAEvans(4) (chsd ldrs: outpcd over 2f out: hrd rdn & kpt on fnl f)	5	**2**	9/2[3]	47	6
546[W]	**Coscoroba (IRE)** (JBerry) **3-10-5** MissDianaJones(5) (bhd & outpcd tl styd on appr fnl f)	3	**3**	13/2	40	—

653^{13}	**River Ensign** (WMBrisbourne) **4-10-0**(5) MissKChilton(9) (a.p: outpcd over 2f out: n.d after)	1¼	4	50/1	26	—
512^{4}	**Bold Aristocrat (IRE) (65)** (RHollinshead) **6-11-2** MrMRimell(1) (trckd ldrs: effrt 2f out: nt pce to chal)	2	5	4/1 2	32	—
487^{2}	**Hatta Sunshine (USA) (49)** (GLMoore) **7-11-4** MrsJMoore(8) (led after 2f to 2f out: sn pushed along: outpcd appr fnl f)	½	6	8/1	33	—
855^{6}	**Sharp Holly (IRE) (41)** (JABennett) **5-10-9** MrsSBosley(3) (outpcd)	1¼	7	20/1	20	—
	Espla (JSMoore) **6-10-11**(5) MrsSMoore(2) (b: bit bkwd: swtg: outpcd)	4	8	8/1	17	—
128^{10}	**Distant Dynasty (26)** (BAPearce) **7-10-9b**(7) MrsKHills(7) (b: b.hind: led 2f: wknd qckly ½-wy: t.o)	29	9	50/1	—	—
				(SP 120.5%)	**9 Rn**	

1m 19.0 (7.80) CSF £8.65 TOTE £2.20: £1.10 £2.50 £1.90 (£6.00) Trio £17.90 OWNER Mr David Chapman (YORK) BRED Gainsborough Stud Management Ltd
WEIGHT FOR AGE 3yo-10lb
Little Ibnr clmd PDCundell £4,000
579 Desert Invader (IRE), brought back to sprinting and ridden with any amount of confidence, gained command into the straight and justified the strong market support in the easiest possible fashion. (13/8)
515 Little Ibnr, claimed by Peter Cundell for £4,000, has gone off the boil a bit of late and the change of scenery might be just the tonic he needs. (9/2)
Coscoroba (IRE) looked well tuned up for this first run in over nine months, but the strong early pace proved too much and she was out with the washing until staying on when it was all over. (13/2)
River Ensign, led to post, ran by far her best race yet and, on this performance, there is a race in her. (50/1)
512 Bold Aristocrat (IRE) shows plenty of white in his eye and, more often than not, does not appear to be giving of his all. On this occasion, he just did as much as he wanted without being able to hold out much hope. (4/1: 5/2-9/2)
487 Hatta Sunshine (USA) has not got the speed to win at this trip, but he did his share of the pace-making before finding the quickening tempo too hot to handle. (8/1)

908 DECT H'CAP (0-70) (3-Y.O+) (Class E)
5-15 (5-16) **1m 4f (Fibresand)** £2,940.25 (£877.00: £418.50: £189.25) Stalls: Low GOING: 0.03 sec per fur (STD)

				SP	RR	SF
858^{6}	**Premier Dance (66)** (DHaydnJones) **10-9-7**(5) PPMurphy(7) (hld up & bhd: hdwy over 3f out: led ins fnl f: drvn clr)	—	1	8/1	74	34
580^{3}	**One Off the Rail (USA) (68)** (GLMoore) **7-10-0** KFallon(2) (b: chsd ldrs: hdwy 4f out: led over 1f out tl ins fnl f)	2½	2	12/1	73	33
762^{9}	**Jump The Lights (65)** (SPCWoods) **4-9-11** WRyan(9) (lw: hld up: hdwy 4f out: ev ch over 1f out: kpt on u.p)	¾	3	6/1 3	69	29
591^{7}	**Swan Hunter (63)** (DJSCosgrove) **4-9-9** MRimmer(8) (lw: a.p: led over 4f out tl over 1f out: sn rdn: one pce)	s.h	4	14/1	67	27
660^{6}	**State Approval (63)** (PEccles) **4-9-4**(5) GFaulkner(6) (chsd ldrs: rdn & ev ch 2f out: wknd appr fnl f)	6	5	7/2 2	59	19
544*	**Happy Brave (37)** (PDCundell) **5-7-11** JLowe(12) (b: hld up & bhd: effrt over 3f out: nt rch ldrs)	7	6	8/1	23	—
351^{5}	**Illegally Yours (45)** (LMontagueHall) **4-8-5** GCarter(1) (swtg: s.s: sn t.o: sme late hdwy: n.d)	4	7	16/1	26	—
284^{4}	**Shuttlecock (43)** (DWChapman) **6-8-3** SDrowne(11) (chsd ldrs tl wknd over 3f out)	5	8	7/1	17	—
591^{8}	**In the Money (IRE) (60)** (RHollinshead) **8-9-3**(3) DGriffiths(3) (trckd ldrs: effrt 3f out: wknd fnl 2f)	6	9	5/2 1	26	—
23^{9}	**Bayrak (USA) (48)** (PAKelleway) **7-8-8** DaneO'Neill(10) (b: swtg: bkwd: chsd ldrs to ½-wy: sn rdn & wknd: t.o)	11	10	16/1	—	—
	Bronhallow (43) (MrsBarbaraWaring) **4-8-3** RPrice(4) (bkwd: a bhd: t.o)	2	11	25/1	—	—
589^{9}	**Biya (IRE) (47)** (DMcCain) **5-8-7b** VSlattery(5) (led over 7f: wknd over 3f out: t.o)	11	12	14/1	—	—
				(SP 136.4%)	**12 Rn**	

2m 44.4 (11.90) CSF £105.33 CT £588.28 TOTE £13.50: £4.90 £3.70 £1.60 (£22.90) Trio £64.90 OWNER J S Fox and Sons (PONTYPRIDD) BRED Brick Kiln Stud Farm
OFFICIAL EXPLANATION **State Approval: was found to be lame on his off-fore the following morning.**
516 Premier Dance makes it look easy when he is on song and, in recording his eighth success on this track, has certainly paid his way over the years. (8/1)
580 One Off the Rail (USA) ran a fine race in defeat and a repeat will see him going one better in the near future. (12/1)
Jump The Lights showed a glimpse of his true ability on this return to the fibresand and he should now be cherry ripe for any near at hand engagements. (6/1: op 4/1)
Swan Hunter turned in an improved performance and, if he can continue to make progress, there is another prize waiting to be picked up. (14/1: op 8/1)
660 State Approval threatened danger on the home turn but he had been ridden to get there when the battle to the line really got underway. (7/2)
544* Happy Brave found this much tougher than the maiden he won on his previous outing and he was always struggling in the rear. (8/1: op 9/2)

T/Plpt: £29.70 (459.82 Tckts). T/Qdpt: £4.90 (230.84 Tckts) IM

0909a - 0915a : (Irish Racing) - See Computer Raceform

0818a-LONGCHAMP (Paris, France) (R-H) (Good)
Thursday April 24th

916a PRIX D'HEDOUVILLE (Gp 3) (4-Y.O+)
3-15 (3-15) **1m 4f** £24,691.00 (£8,979.00: £4,459.00: £2,245.00)

				SP	RR	SF
625a4	**Steward (FR)** (DSepulchre,France) **4-8-9** SGuillot	—	1		112	—
630a2	**Prussian Blue (USA)** (CLaffon-Parias,France) **5-8-9** ODoleuze	1½	2		109	—
	Si Seductor (USA) (AFabre,France) **4-8-9** OPeslier	hd	3		110	—
630a*	**Flyway (FR)** (ELellouche,France) **4-8-9** TThulliez	½	4		109	—
						5 Rn

2m 40.4 (14.40) P-M 4.80F: 2.10F 2.00F OWNER G. Coude BRED Jean-Charles Coude
625a Steward (FR) was given fine ride to win his first Group event. Held up in last place, he was produced with a late run which took him into the lead inside the final furlong. He is extremely consistent and genuine and will now be allowed to take his chance in the Grand Prix de Chantilly - the ex Grand Prix d'Evry - but may find this level beyond him. However, another good race should come his way this season.
Prussian Blue (USA) tried to make all the running but had no answer when tackled by the winner in the latter stages. He did battle on in an honest manner, but is not quite up to this level.
Si Seductor (USA) was given every chance, but failed to accelerate in the latter stages.

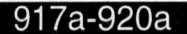

Flyway (FR) raced in second place and looked dangerous one and a half furlongs out, before staying on.

0815a-CAPANNELLE (Rome, Italy) (R-H) (Good)
Sunday April 27th

917a PREMIO PARIOLI (Gp 2) (3-Y.O)
3-35 (4-04) **1m** £62,369.00 (£31,830.00: £18,649.00: £9,324.00)

				SP	RR	SF
692⁴	**Air Express (IRE)** (CEBrittain) **3-9-2** BDoyle (s.i.s: sn rcvrd: hdwy over 3f out: chal 1f out: led nr fin)	—	1		114	—
	Risiat (IRE) (EBorromeo,Italy) **3-9-2b¹** CFiocchi (mid div st: hung rt over 1f out: led ins fnl f: ct cl home)	nse	2		114	—
	Gianky Gioffry (IRE) (RBrogi,Italy) **3-9-2** GBietolini (trckd ldr: led over 2f out: hdd over 1f out: styd on one pce)	2½	3		109	—
	Golden Biscayne (GFratini,Italy) **3-9-2** DJO'Donohoe (led tl over 2f out: styd on wl)	2½	4		104	—
679²	**Granny's Pet** (PFICole) **3-9-2** JFortune (mid div: hdwy over 2f out: no imp fnl f)	nk	5		103	—
	Hurricane State (USA) (PWChapple-Hyam) **3-9-2** JReid (s.i.s: last st: prog fnl 2f: nvr nrr)	¾	6		102	—
449⁵	**Poseidon** (MRChannon) **3-9-2** RHughes (prom tl wknd fnl 2f)	1¼	7		99	—
	Golden Aventura (IRE) (GFratini,Italy) **3-9-2** OFancera (mid div st: btn over 2f out)	s.h	8		99	—
	Woods of Cisterna (IRE) (LCamici,Italy) **3-9-2** MPasquale (n.d)	½	9		98	—
508⁶	**Royal Aty (IRE)** (PAKelleway) **3-9-2** KFallon (prom: effrt 2f out: wknd)	1¼	10		96	—
	Doctor Leckter (USA) (APeraino,Italy) **3-9-2** JCaro (a in rr)	8	11		80	—
	Miliardaire (IRE) (GColleo,Italy) **3-9-2** LSorrentino (a in rr)	1¼	12		77	—
*646**	***Sekari*** (DRLoder) **3-9-2v¹** KDarley (Withdrawn not under Starters' orders: lame gng to s)		W		—	—

12 Rn

1m 35.9 TOTE 19L: 14L 31L 20L (217L) OWNER Mr Mohamed Obaida (NEWMARKET) BRED Gainsborough Stud Management Ltd
692 Air Express (IRE) missed the break, but was soon back in touch though last of the twelve runners. Brought wide turning into the straight, he challenged the runner-up a furlong out and only got his nose in front in the last few strides.
679 Granny's Pet raced in mid-division until making his move on the rails approaching the two-furlong marker. His cause was not helped when he was squeezed up by Risiat a furlong out, and he made no further progress.
Hurricane State (USA) has wintered well and ran as if a longer trip would be in his favour. Soon amongst the back-markers, he was last turning for home but stayed on nicely in the closing stages.
449 Poseidon raced prominently and was in third place turning for home, but was back-pedalling in the final two furlongs.
508 Royal Aty (IRE) was close up until dropping away steadily from over two furlongs out.
646* Sekari was found to have injured a fetlock on the way down to the start. He will need surgery, but may be able to race again.

DIELSDORF (Zurich, Switzerland) (L-H) (Soft)
Sunday April 27th

918a GROSSER PREIS DER AMAG ZURICH (SWISS 2000 GUINEAS) (Listed) (3-Y.O)
1-30 (1-38) **1m** £6,316.00 (£2,526.00: £1,895.00)

				SP	RR	SF
	Le Chevalier (GER) (RStadelmann,Switzerland) **3-9-2** PCoppin	—	1		105	—
	Feliciano (SWI) (RStadelmann,Switzerland) **3-9-2** MissBRenk	s.h	2		105	—
690¹³	**Polar Flight** (MJohnston) **3-9-2** JWeaver	2	3		101	—

12 Rn

1m 45.9 TOTE 12.10SF: 2.00SF 1.50SF 1.20SF (68.50SF) OWNER M & J Buchi BRED Gestut Schloss Wald Erbach
Polar Flight made headway to hit the front turning into the short home straight, but could only keep on at the same pace when headed before the furlong pole.

919a ERICSSON GOLD CUP (Listed) (4-Y.O+)
2-45 (2-28) **1m** £8,421.00 (£3,368.00: £2,526.00: £1,684.00: £842.00)

				SP	RR	SF
	Transcript (USA) (USuter,Switzerland) **8-9-8** J-MBreux	—	1		113	—
	Street Rebel (CAN) (KKlein,Switzerland) **9-9-2b** MrAndiWyss	3¼	2		101	—
	Roger de Berksted (USA) (FGang,Germany) **9-9-0** MrMKeller	1	3		97	—
311a⁷	**Celestial Key (USA)** (MJohnston) **7-9-0** JWeaver (btn approx. 6l)		5		—	—

14 Rn

1m 46.0 TOTE 6.80SF: 2.80SF 4.70SF 4.60SF (747.30SF) OWNER A & D Furter
311a Celestial Key (USA), a Swiss-owned gelding, lost all chance when hampered and dropping to the rear at the start, but at least made up enough ground in the final quarter mile to sneak into the prize-money.

FRANKFURT (Germany) (L-H) (Good)
Sunday April 27th

920a QUOTENHAUS FRUHJAHRS DREIJAHRIGEN (Gp 3) (3-Y.O)
4-00 (4-12) **1m 2f** £26,515.00 (£10,606.00: £5,303.00)

				SP	RR	SF
	Ungaro (GER) (HBlume,Germany) **3-8-11** THellier	—	1		90?	—
	Baleno (GER) (BSchutz,Germany) **3-9-0** NGrant	½	2		92	—
	Ajano (GER) (HJGroschel,Germany) **3-8-9** ATylicki	1½	3		85	—

6 Rn

2m 12.7 TOTE 19DM: 19DM 28DM OWNER Gestut Rottgen BRED Gestut Rottgen
Ungaro (GER) produced a very fine turn of foot to come from last to first, striking the front fifty yards from the line. He looks sure to appreciate further, and may now step up to Group Two company for the Muller Brot-Preis at Munich.
Baleno (GER) could do little about the impressive speed of the winner.

0916a-LONGCHAMP (Paris, France) (R-H) (Soft)
Sunday April 27th

921a PRIX VANTEAUX (Gp 3) (3-Y.O F)
3-15 (3-15) **1m 1f 55y** £24,691.00 (£8,979.00: £4,489.00) GOING: 0.36 sec per fur (GS)

			Pos	SP	RR	SF
	Queen Maud (IRE) (JdeRoualle,France) **3-9-0** CAsmussen	—	1		102	47
	Tashiriya (IRE) (AdeRoyerDupre,France) **3-9-0** GMosse	¾	2		101	46
	Palacoona (GER) (AFabre,France) **3-9-0** TJarnet	½	3		100	45
						5 Rn

2m 1.0 (9.00) P-M 3.30F: 1.70F 2.10F OWNER Mr K. H. Eng BRED Barronstown Stud & Ron Con Ltd

Queen Maud (IRE) was given a fine ride. Her jockey took the initiative early in the straight and the others just could not catch her. Suited by the cut in the ground, she is a decent filly and will now be left alone until the Prix de Diane.

Tashiriya (IRE) followed the winner, but was one-paced throughout the final furlong. She may be suited by a longer trip, but is not thought to be one of the best in this powerful stable.

Palacoona (GER) made some late progress and was running on at the end. She has won a listed race but does not look up to Group company.

TF129

922a PRIX GANAY (Gp 1) (4-Y.O+)
3-55 (3-51) **1m 2f 110y** £56,117.00 (£22,447.00: £11,223.00: £5,612.00) GOING: 0.36 sec per fur (GS)

			Pos	SP	RR	SF
	Helissio (FR) (ELellouche,France) **4-9-2** OPeslier (trckd ldr: hdwy to ld 4f out: wnt clr st: impressive)	—	1	3/5 [1]	135+	99
439a[2]	**Le Destin (FR)** (PDemercastel,France) **4-9-2** TGillet (hld up in rr: prog 1½f out: fin wl)	9	2	279/10	121	85
	Pilsudski (IRE) (MRStoute) **5-9-2** MJKinane (a cl up: hrd rdn fr 2f out: styd on one pce)	1½	3	37/10 [2]	119	83
625a*	**River Bay (USA)** (JEHammond,France) **4-9-2** TJarnet (mid div: effrt over 2f out: styd on one pce)	2	4	4/1 [3]	116	80
	Strategic Choice (USA) (PFICole) **6-9-2** TQuinn (racd on outside: cl up st: hrd rdn & btn over 1f out)	3	5	164/10	111	75
	Bulington (FR) (H-APantall,France) **5-9-2** CAsmussen (mid div: dropped back st: no imp)	4	6	22/1	105	69
	Last Second (IRE) (SirMarkPrescott) **4-8-13** GDuffield (hld up: last st: sn btn)	15	7	103/10	79	43
716a[3]	**Trojan Sea (USA)** (DSmaga,France) **6-9-2** DBoeuf (led to 4f out: btn & dropped back sn after)	2	8	37/10 [2]	79	43
				(SP 147.5%)		**8 Rn**

2m 12.1 (4.10) P-M 1.60F: 1.10F 1.10F 1.10F (22.90F) OWNER Enrique Sarasola BRED Ecurie Skymarc Farm

Helissio (FR) could not have run a better race on his seasonal debut. There were rumours before this race that he was not working that well at Chantilly, but he put all doubters well and truly in their place with this performance. Cantering throughout, he struck the front four furlongs from home and, although idling a little in the straight, quickly drew right away from his rivals who were made to look very ordinary. He looked fairly fit and it is a great credit to his trainer who has brought him back from dirt to grass in just over three weeks. He looks better than ever and he will be racing in England next time out as his target is the Coronation Cup. He has an enormous amount of speed, and it has even been said that the one-mile Moulin de Longchamp might be used as a prep race for the Arc. It is difficult to envisage anything beating Helissio this season providing he maintains this form. (3/5)

Le Destin (FR) put in a decent effort and was running on at the end, though he had not the slightest chance of catching the winner. He has to be switched off early on if he is to show his best, and was held up here for a late run, taking second place inside the final furlong. His trainer would like him to race in England where he can be sure to find a decent pace, but he does not want to take on Helissio again. (279/10)

Pilsudski (IRE) had a small bandage on his near hind fetlock, but looked superb in the paddock, although carrying a fair amount of condition. He was given every chance in the race, but had no answer to the acceleration of the winner. He stayed on gamely nevertheless, but tired a little inside the final furlong. This outing would have done him a lot of good and he looks sure to have another successful season. (37/10)

625a* River Bay (USA) was another to look extremely well in the paddock. Racing in mid-division, he vainly tried to mount a challenge in the straight but could only stay on at the one pace in the closing stages. He probably did not quite stay this distance on ground which was rather testing. It would be no surprise to see him line up for the Prix d'Ispahan. (4/1)

Strategic Choice (USA) was well up on the outside for much of the race, but was beaten soon after entering the straight. He needs a good surface, but the Longchamp ground became soft during the forty-eight hours leading up to the Ganay. He will be a much better proposition on a firmer surface and he is sure to continue in his money spinning ways. (164/10)

Last Second (IRE) never looked likely to finish in the frame on this soft ground. Held up at the back of the field, she was being niggled along four out and this run is best forgotten. (103/10)

923a PRIX DE BARBEVILLE (Gp 3) (4-Y.O+)
4-30 (4-25) **1m 7f 110y** £24,691.00 (£8,979.00: £4,489.00: £2,245.00) GOING: 0.36 sec per fur (GS)

			Pos	SP	RR	SF
	Stretarez (FR) (DSepulchre,France) **4-8-9** FSanchez	—	1		120	77
310a[2]	**Philanthrop (FR)** (J-PGallorini,France) **5-8-9** ODoleuze	1½	2		116	76
	Heron Island (IRE) (PWChapple-Hyam) **4-8-9** MJKinane	3	3		115	72
	Tarator (USA) (ELellouche,France) **4-9-2** OPeslier	¾	4		122	79
						7 Rn

3m 24.8 (8.80) P-M 2.80F: 1.80F 3.20F OWNER Mr J-L Lagardere BRED SNC Lagardere Elevage

Stretarez (FR) arrived late on the scene and took control of this race with just over a furlong left to run. He is an improving sort of horse who is perfectly suited by long distances, and it would be no surprise if he made the grade next time out in the Prix Vicomtesse Vigier.

Philanthrop (FR) was always well up and is still going well even though he started his season at the beginning of the year at Cagnes. He battled on gamely, but did not have the acceleration of the winner.

Heron Island (IRE) made some late progress, but never looked like finishing in the first two. He was in mid division until making his effort from one and a half out, and will certainly improve for the outing.

Tarator (USA) was made quite a lot of use of early on and then just stayed on throughout the final furlong. He was reappearing and giving 7lb to the first three past the post. Considerable improvement should be expected, and he now heads for the Vicomtesse Vigier, and it is also hoped that he will make it to the Ascot Gold Cup.

0664-MUSSELBURGH (R-H) (Good to firm)
Friday May 2nd
WEATHER: fine

924 MCEWANS 80/- AMATEUR H'CAP (0-65) (3-Y.O+) (Class F)
2-15 (2-16) **5f** £2,670.00 (£745.00: £360.00) Stalls: Low GOING minus 0.15 sec per fur (GF)

				SP	RR	SF
760[7]	**Southern Dominion (40)** (MissJFCraze) **5-10-6** MissDianaJones(10) (lw: mde all: rdn & r.o wl fnl f)	—	1	12/1	46	21
666[6]	**Sunday Mail Too (IRE) (38)** (MissLAPerratt) **5-10-4** MissPRobson(5) (bhd: rdn ½-wy: hdwy & swtchd appr fnl f: r.o wl towards fin)	½	2	5/1	42	17
	Ready Teddy (IRE) (47) (MissLAPerratt) **4-10-13** MissERamsden(3) (a.p: ev ch wl over 1f out: styd on ins fnl f)	1½	3	20/1	47	22
702[6]	**Tropical Beach (62)** (JBerry) **4-12-0** MrsLPearce(7) (s.i.s: bhd: hdwy ½-wy: styd on wl ins fnl f)	¾	4	100/30[2]	59	34
652[3]	**Impish (IRE) (43)** (TJEtherington) **3-10-0** MissAElsey(9) (lw: bhd: rdn ½-wy: styd on fnl f: nvr nr to chal)	nk	5	8/1	39	5
666[3]	**Shadow Jury (59)** (DWChapman) **7-11-11b** MissRClark(8) (lw: cl up: ev ch tl rdn & one pce fnl f)	s.h	6	3/1[1]	55	30
429[6]	**Answers-To-Thomas (52)** (JMJefferson) **4-10-13(5)** MrWWenyon(6) (in tch over 3f: sn wknd)	3½	7	12/1	37	12
751[3]	**Nampara Bay (39)** (GCBravery) **3-9-5(5)** MissCHawe(2) (cl up tl wknd wl over 1f out)	1¾	8	4/1[3]	18	—
702[17]	**Gagajulu (45)** (PDEvans) **4-10-11** MrWMcLaughlin(4) (lw: rdn along ½-wy: a bhd)	1½	9	14/1	20	—
827[19]	**Take Notice (58)** (RMMcKellar) **4-11-10b[1]** MrsCWilliams(1) (wnt lft s: racd alone stands' side: nvr trbld ldrs)	4	10	50/1	20	—

(SP 124.6%) **10 Rn**

62.6 secs (4.90) CSF £69.14 CT £1,141.17 TOTE £16.10: £6.40 £2.60 £4.20 (£36.70) Trio £161.10 OWNER Miss J. F. Craze (YORK) BRED A. Wilkinson and J. W. Brown

WEIGHT FOR AGE 3yo-9lb

386 Southern Dominion, was given an excellent ride. Smartly away as usual, he found enough to hold on this time. (12/1: op 8/1)
666 Sunday Mail Too (IRE) was outpaced in the early stages, but stayed on well in the final furlong only to find the post arriving too soon. A stiffer track would probably suit her better. (5/1)
Ready Teddy (IRE), making her seasonal reappearance, stayed on in the closing stages and will come on for the race, though she is still a maiden. (20/1)
702 Tropical Beach stayed on well in the closing stages, and would be suited by another furlong. (100/30)
652 Impish (IRE) (8/1: op 5/1)
429 Answers-To-Thomas (12/1: op 8/1)
Gagajulu (14/1: 8/1-20/1)

925 MCEWANS LAGER LIMITED STKS (0-55) (3-Y.O+) (Class F)
2-45 (2-46) **1m 16y** £2,827.50 (£790.00: £382.50) Stalls: High GOING minus 0.41 sec per fur (F)

				SP	RR	SF
667[2]	**Murray Grey (52)** (EWeymes) **3-8-4** JQuinn(6) (lw: a.p: hdwy to ld 3 out: rdn over 1f out: kpt on wl)	—	1	9/1	61	28
687[3]	**Dictation (USA) (50)** (JJO'Neill) **5-9-6** JFortune(3) (hld up & bhd: gd hdwy 3f out: rdn over 1f out: kpt on ins fnl f)	½	2	9/1	63	43
636[7]	**Who's That Man (54)** (SCWilliams) **3-8-7** KDarley(11) (hld up mid div: stdy hdwy 3f out: rdn wl over 1f out: kpt on ins fnl f)	nk	3	5/2[1]	62	29
608[7]	**Running Green (55)** (DMoffatt) **6-9-6v[1](3)** DarrenMoffatt(14) (s.i.s: bhd tl styd on fnl 2f: nrst fin)	1	4	12/1	63	43
843[5]	**Northern Fan (IRE) (55)** (NTinkler) **5-9-9** DeanMcKeown(4) (lw: chsd ldrs: rdn 3f out: one pce)	2½	5	16/1	59	39
	Energy Man (55) (MDods) **4-9-6** DaleGibson(1) (bit bkwd: mid div: effrt & sme hdwy 2f out: kpt on: n.d)	1	6	50/1	54	34
653[4]	**Chinour (IRE) (55)** (EJAlston) **9-9-6** ACulhane(5) (bhd tl styd on fnl 2f)	1	7	12/1	52	32
748[2]	**Serape (54)** (MrsLStubbs) **4-9-3** JFEgan(8) (chsd ldrs: rdn 3f out: sn wknd)	2½	8	4/1[2]	44	24
477[14]	**Generous Present (54)** (JWPayne) **4-9-6** DWright(2) (hld up & bhd: sme hdwy 3f out: sn rdn & one pce)	¾	9	6/1[3]	45	25
	Mystic Times (39) (BMactaggart) **4-8-12(5)** PRoberts(12) (led to ½-wy: sn lost pl & bhd)	1½	10	33/1	39	19
827[18]	**Lady Silk (41)** (MissJFCraze) **6-9-6** SWebster(9) (a in rr)	¾	11	25/1	41	21
667[3]	**Music Express (IRE) (55)** (JLEyre) **3-7-13(5)** RFfrench(13) (chsd ldrs: rdn over 3f out: sn wknd)	¾	12	6/1[3]	36	3
701[7]	**The Tig (48)** (LRLloyd-James) **3-8-7** TWilliams(7) (a bhd)	14	13	25/1	11	—
687[14]	**Willie Miles (55)** (DWChapman) **4-9-6** NConnorton(10) (prom: led ½-wy tl rdn & hdd 3f out: sn wknd & bhd)	8	14	20/1	—	—

(SP 135.8%) **14 Rn**

1m 41.7 (2.70) CSF £85.47 TOTE £9.30: £2.50 £3.80 £1.10 (£41.10) Trio £265.10; £48.55 to Newmarket 3/5/97 OWNER Mrs A. Birkett (MIDDLEHAM) BRED Brook Stud Ltd

WEIGHT FOR AGE 3yo-13lb

667 Murray Grey led three furlongs out and stayed on well to the line. After the race she was found to have sustained a hair-line fracture of her off-fore canon-bone, but will hopefully make a full recovery. (9/1: 6/1-10/1)
687 Dictation (USA) was just outbattled by the winner in the closing stages. (9/1)
Who's That Man showed his first real sign of form here, and can improve a bit further. (5/2)
496 Running Green gave the impression that he would be suited by further. (12/1)

926 KRONENBOURG 1664 CLAIMING STKS (3-Y.O) (Class F)
3-20 (3-20) **1m 4f 31y** £2,425.00 (£675.00: £325.00) Stalls: High GOING minus 0.41 sec per fur (F)

				SP	RR	SF
862*	**Baby Jane (65)** (RGuest) **3-8-7** PBloomfield(3) (lw: mde all: drw clr appr st: unchal)	—	1	1/4[1]	46+	8
609[4]	**Tycoon Tina (50)** (WMBrisbourne) **3-8-3(5)** PFessey(2) (lw: dwlt: in tch after 4f: wnt 2nd ent st: sn rdn: no ch w wnr)	4	2	14/1[3]	42	4
533[10]	**Baaheth (USA) (68)** (SCWilliams) **3-9-3** KDarley(1) (chsd wnr tl rdn & wknd qckly ent st: sn eased: virtually p.u fnl 2f)	dist	3	7/2[2]	—	—

(SP 108.9%) **3 Rn**

2m 41.6 (8.10) CSF £3.95 TOTE £1.10 (£4.90) OWNER Mr Dick Low (NEWMARKET) BRED Lord Matthews

Baby Jane clmd BMacTaggart £6,500

862* Baby Jane, won this without turning a hair, though she had nothing to beat. (1/4)
609 Tycoon Tina chased the winner after turning into the straight, but never held out any real hope. (14/1: op 8/1)

927 MILLER PILSNER CLAIMING STKS (2-Y.O) (Class F)

3-55 (3-56) **5f** £2,565.00 (£715.00: £345.00) Stalls: Low GOING minus 0.15 sec per fur (GF)

				SP	RR	SF
648^{2}	**Theatre of Dreams** (PDEvans) **2-8-12** JFEgan(1) (lw: mde virtually all: rdn & hung rt 1½f out: sn drew clr)	—	1	Evens ^{1}	71	19
743^{2}	**Ellenbrook (IRE)** (JBerry) **2-8-8** KDarley(4) (lw: disp ld to ½-wy: rdn whn sltly hmpd 1½f out: one pce)	3½	2	6/4 ^{2}	56	4
594^{5}	**Inchalong** (MBrittain) **2-7-13**(7) DMernagh(3) (prom: rdn 2f out: rdr dropped whip ins fnl f: kpt on same pce)	1½	3	15/2 ^{3}	49	—
743^{4}	**Captain Bliss** (NTinkler) **2-8-11b** LCharnock(2) (spd over 3f out: eased whn btn ins fnl f)	2	4	10/1	48	—
				(SP 110.9%)	**4 Rn**	

61.5 secs (3.80) CSF £2.62 TOTE £1.70 (£1.30) OWNER Mr Mike Nolan (WELSHPOOL) BRED M. G. T. Stokes
Theatre of Dreams clmd BMacTaggart £10,000

648 Theatre of Dreams, in front from the start, had this poor race in safe keeping well over a furlong out. (Evens)
743 Ellenbrook (IRE) was already fighting a losing battle when slightly hampered by the winner over a furlong out. (6/4)
594 Inchalong was already beaten when her rider dropped his whip inside the final furlong. (15/2)
743 Captain Bliss (10/1: 4/1-11/1)

928 MCEWAN'S 70/- H'CAP (0-80) (3-Y.O+) (Class D)

4-25 (4-25) **1m 4f 31y** £3,509.00 (£1,052.00: £506.00: £233.00) Stalls: High GOING minus 0.41 sec per fur (F)

				SP	RR	SF
865*	**All On (44)** (JHetherton) **6-8-1**(5) 5x RFfrench(3) (lw: mde all: qckknd ent st: rdn along 2f out: hld on wl towards fin)	—	1	100/30 ^{2}	53	—
826*	**Little Acorn (79)** (SCWilliams) **3-9-8** 5x KDarley(2) (hld up & bhd: chsd wnr fr 7f out: rdn to disp ld ent fnl f: kpt on closing stages)	hd	2	2/7 ^{1}	88	15
	Recluse (34) (WTKemp) **6-7-10b** JQuinn(4) (lw: prom to ½-wy: wknd 3f out)	9	3	40/1	31	—
	Mowlaie (62) (DWChapman) **6-9-10** ACulhane(1) (bit bkwd: in tch to st: wl bhd fnl 3f: t.o)	26	4	20/1 ^{3}	25	—
				(SP 108.1%)	**4 Rn**	

2m 43.1 (9.60) CSF £4.37 TOTE £3.60 (£1.10) OWNER Mr N. Hetherton (MALTON) BRED N. Hetherton
LONG HANDICAP Recluse 7-8
WEIGHT FOR AGE 3yo-19lb

865* All On was running over a trip nine furlongs shorter than her previous win. Making all, she found enough to bravely hold off the favourite in the closing stages. (100/30: 9/4-7/2)
826* Little Acorn, held up in the early stages, looked likely to prevail when joining issue a furlong out. However, he found that the winner was not going to be denied but, although swishing his tail, kept on in the closing stages. (2/7)

929 BEAMISH RED IRISH ALE H'CAP (0-65) (3-Y.O+) (Class F)

5-00 (5-00) **7f 15y** £2,915.00 (£815.00: £395.00) Stalls: High GOING minus 0.41 sec per fur (F)

				SP	RR	SF
863^{3}	**Grey Kingdom (48)** (MBrittain) **6-8-11**(7) 6x DMernagh(3) (lw: mde all: styd on wl fnl 2f)	—	1	9/4 ^{1}	63	18
733^{7}	**Rymer's Rascal (54)** (EJAlston) **5-9-10** ACulhane(4) (chsd ldrs: rdn 2f out: kpt on same pce fnl f)	1½	2	9/1	66	21
779^{3}	**Ivor's Deed (52)** (CFWall) **4-9-8** NCarlisle(1) (lw: hld up & bhd: hdwy on outside over 2f out: no ex appr fnl f)	3½	3	3/1 ^{2}	56	11
827^{10}	**Shontaine (52)** (MJohnston) **4-9-8** DeanMcKeown(7) (chsd ldrs: outpcd 3f out: swtchd outside appr fnl f: styd on)	hd	4	14/1	56	11
785^{3}	**Captain Carparts (63)** (JLEyre) **3-9-7** TWilliams(11) (lw: cl up: rdn 3f out: one pce fnl 2f)	3½	5	15/2	59	2
749^{6}	**Lillibella (53)** (MrsJRRamsden) **4-9-9** JFortune(6) (lw: stdd s: hdwy ent st: n.m.r & rdn 2f out: one pce)	1½	6	7/1 ^{3}	45	—
668^{7}	**True Ballad (49)** (JSGoldie) **5-9-5** JQuinn(2) (in rr: effrt 3f out: n.d)	2½	7	16/1	36	—
526^{3}	**Seconds Away (26)** (JSGoldie) **6-7-3**(7) JMcAuley(8) (a in rr)	s.h	8	14/1	12	—
496^{7}	**Termon (45)** (MissLAPerratt) **4-9-1** KDarley(10) (cl up: rdn ent st: sn lost pl)	¾	9	14/1	30	—
796^{8}	**Tolepa (IRE) (32)** (JJO'Neill) **4-8-2** JFEgan(9) (bhd: rn v.wd ent st: hung bdly rt fnl f: n.d)	½	10	33/1	16	—
734^{11}	**Gormire (52)** (JHetherton) **4-9-8** KHodgson(12) (in tch: rdn 3f out: wl btn whn hmpd ins fnl f)	1¼	11	25/1	33	—
				(SP 122.7%)	**11 Rn**	

1m 30.4 (4.40) CSF £22.66 CT £59.17 TOTE £2.70: £2.40 £1.50 £1.10 (£17.10) Trio £33.00 OWNER Mr M. Brittain (WARTHILL) BRED Northgate Lodge Stud Ltd
WEIGHT FOR AGE 3yo-12lb

863 Grey Kingdom, attacking from the start as usual, kept on well to win his third race of the season. He is as game as they come, but is due to go up 14lb in the handicap now and is going to find life very tough. (9/4: 2/1-7/2)
663 Rymer's Rascal ran his best race for quite a while here, and was only denied by an in-form rival. He ought to be winning soon. (9/1)
779 Ivor's Deed, was not helped by his draw, but after making good progress two furlongs out, then looked a little one-paced. He may need either a mile or slower ground. (3/1)
484 Shontaine, who had shown little since returning to turf from the All-Weather, ran better here. (14/1)
785 Captain Carparts (15/2: 8/1-12/1)
749 Lillibella (7/1: op 4/1)

T/Plpt: £961.00 (8.08 Tckts). T/Qdpt: £22.40 (17.69 Tckts) GB

0690-NEWMARKET (R-H) (Good)

Friday May 2nd

WEATHER: sunny & very warm WIND: almost nil

930 LADBROKES ANIMAL HEALTH TRUST H'CAP (0-100) (3-Y.O) (Class C)

2-05 (2-06) **7f (Rowley)** £8,928.00 (£2,664.00: £1,272.00: £576.00) Stalls: Centre GOING minus 0.35 sec per fur (F)

				SP	RR	SF
	Green Jewel (84) (RHannon) **3-8-8** DaneO'Neill(10) (trckd ldrs: effrt over 1f out: led wl ins fnl f: r.o)	—	1	14/1	92	38
646^{6}	**Speedball (IRE) (94)** (IABalding) **3-9-4** LDettori(11) (lw: trckd ldrs: rdn to ld ins fnl f: sn hdd: kpt on)	nk	2	8/1	101	47
675^{2}	**Just Nick (80)** (WRMuir) **3-8-4** DHarrison(12) (s.i.s: sn chsng ldrs: ev ch over 1f out: kpt on)	¾	3	7/1	86	32
575^{2}	**Kaiser Kache (IRE) (81)** (KMcAuliffe) **3-8-5** MRoberts(5) (led: qcknd over 2f out: hdd over 1f out: kpt on)	s.h	4	9/1	87	33
	Triple Hay (89) (RHannon) **3-8-13** PatEddery(9) (hld up: hdwy to ld over 1f out: hdd ins fnl f: no ex)	s.h	5	9/2 ^{1}	94	40
675*	**Summer Queen (79)** (SPCWoods) **3-8-3** AClark(2) (lw: hld up: hdwy over 2f out: ch 1f out: nt qckn)	1¼	6	13/2 ^{3}	82	28

				SP	RR	SF
699[2]	**Baritone (76)** (JWWatts) **3-8-0** GDuffield(3) (hld up: effrt over 2f out: hung rt & no imp)	1¾	**7**	13/2[3]	75	21
685[9]	**Ivory Dawn (75)** (KTIvory) **3-7-10**(3)ow3 MartinDwyer(6) (chsd ldrs tl wknd over 1f out)	2	**8**	25/1	69	12
	Alphabet (84) (MRStoute) **3-8-8** JReid(4) (lw: prom tl grad wknd fnl 2½f)	½	**9**	5/1[2]	77	23
	Tal-Y-Llyn (IRE) (84) (BWHills) **3-8-8** MHills(7) (hld up: effrt over 2f out: sn wknd)	2½	**10**	11/1	71	17
449[12]	**Danetime (IRE) (97)** (NACallaghan) **3-9-7** SDrowne(8) (hld up: lost tch fnl 2½f)	3	**11**	16/1	77	23
723[15]	**Maladerie (IRE) (87)** (MRChannon) **3-8-11** TQuinn(1) (effrt 3f out: sn bhd)	10	**12**	33/1	44	—

(SP 122.8%) **12 Rn**

1m 26.64 (2.14) CSF £114.68 CT £570.50 TOTE £20.50: £4.40 £2.90 £2.10 (£102.40) Trio £229.60 OWNER Mr T. E. Bucknall (MARLBOROUGH) BRED Stetchworth Park Stud Ltd
LONG HANDICAP Ivory Dawn 7-5
Green Jewel was rather edgy beforehand, but showed a fine action going to post and, always travelling well, had the best turn of foot. (14/1)
Speedball (IRE) is doing well physically, and this was a much better effort, and he looks likely to progress further. (8/1)
675 Just Nick was up 4lb for a good run last time, and he again put up a bold show, and should be even better suited by easier ground (7/1: 5/1-8/1)
575 Kaiser Kache (IRE), who ideally needs further, tried to make full use of his stamina, but was tapped for speed late on. (9/1)
Triple Hay is a very tall individual, and he left the impression that he should be all the better for this run. He was reportedly sore afterwards. (9/2)
675* Summer Queen, up 7lb for her win last time, had her chances, but that final kick was blunted on this occasion. (13/2: 9/2-7/1)
699 Baritone has plenty more ability, but just wants to hang right, and is a difficult ride. (13/2)
Alphabet moved well, but gave the impression that she would be all the better for this. (5/1)
Tal-Y-Llyn (IRE) (11/1: 8/1-12/1)
449 Danetime (IRE) was extremely colty both in the pre-parade and the main parade ring, and an operation could well be needed to change his ways. (16/1)

931 KUWAIT GREEN RIDGE STABLES NEWMARKET STKS (Listed) (3-Y.O C) (Class A)

2-35 (2-36) **1m 2f (Rowley)** £12,676.00 (£4,684.00: £2,242.00: £910.00: £355.00: £133.00) Stalls: Low GOING minus 0.35 sec per fur (F)

				SP	RR	SF
646[3]	**Sandstone (IRE) (102)** (JLDunlop) **3-8-8** PatEddery(1) (hld up: stdy hdwy over 3f out: led over 1f out: r.o u.p)	—	**1**	8/1	107	60
	Haltarra (USA) (SbinSuroor) **3-8-8** LDettori(2) (h.d.w: cl up: led ½-wy: rdn 2f out: sn hdd: r.o wl u.p fnl f)	hd	**2**	11/10[1]	107	60
	Musical Dancer (USA) (105) (EALDunlop) **3-8-8** KFallon(3) (swtg: plld hrd: trckd ldr: ev ch over 1f out: rdn & nt qckn)	2½	**3**	5/1[2]	103	56
	Desert Horizon (JHMGosden) **3-8-8** TQuinn(6) (bit bkwd: trckd ldr: effrt 2f out: nt qckn)	3	**4**	13/2[3]	98	51
841[2]	**Spartan Royale** (CEBrittain) **3-8-8** MRoberts(5) (lw: chsd ldrs: rdn 4f out: wknd over 2f out)	16	**5**	20/1	72	25
	Royal Crusade (USA) (WJHaggas) **3-8-8** OPeslier(4) (h.d.w: bolted gng to post: led to ½-wy: wknd qckly 3f out: t.o)	dist	**6**	5/1[2]	—	—

(SP 110.2%) **6 Rn**

2m 5.23 (0.53) CSF £15.27 TOTE £8.90: £2.90 £1.40 (£6.10) OWNER Mr Peter Winfield (ARUNDEL) BRED Barouche Stud Ltd
OFFICIAL EXPLANATION Royal Crusade (USA): ran very freely on the way to the start and in the race.
646 Sandstone (IRE) came out of a warm race last time, and won this convincingly, showing a fine turn of foot. Once there, he battled on particularly well. (8/1: 6/1-9/1)
Haltarra (USA), who is improving looks-wise, put up a good show, and kept fighting back. Surely his winning turn will not be delayed much longer. (11/10)
Musical Dancer (USA) spoiled his chances by both sweating up and then running too freely. Once he gets into a race where there is a decent pace, he will come into his own. (5/1: 7/2-11/2)
Desert Horizon moves well, but probably just needed this, and that, combined with stamina doubts, found him out. (13/2: 7/2-7/1)
841 Spartan Royale, taken early to post, disappointed here, dropping out some way from home. (20/1)
Royal Crusade (USA) bolted going to post, and ran far too freely on the way back. This run is best completely ignored. (5/1: op 3/1)

932 GRANGEWOOD JOCKEY CLUB STKS (Gp 2) (4-Y.O+) (Class A)

3-10 (3-11) **1m 4f (Rowley)** £33,343.00 (£12,337.00: £5,918.50: £2,417.50: £958.75: £375.25) Stalls: High GOING minus 0.35 sec per fur (F)

				SP	RR	SF
	Time Allowed (109) (MRStoute) **4-8-6** JReid(3) (h.d.w: b: hld up: hdwy over 2f out: r.o wl to ld wl ins fnl f)	—	**1**	13/2	119	72
	Busy Flight (116) (BWHills) **4-8-9** MHills(8) (led: qcknd over 2f out: r.o u.p: hdd wl ins fnl f)	¾	**2**	5/1[2]	121	74
	Mons (117) (LMCumani) **4-8-9** JWeaver(5) (h.d.w: prom: hdwy u.p 3f out: kpt on wl fnl f: nrst fin)	¾	**3**	12/1	120	73
	Celeric (111) (DMorley) **5-8-9** PatEddery(10) (hld up & bhd: effrt 3f out: sn hrd drvn: styd on: no imp)	2½	**4**	10/1	117	70
628a[9]	**Luso (120)** (CEBrittain) **5-9-0** TQuinn(4) (chsd ldrs: rdn 3f out: wknd fnl 2f)	1¼	**5**	4/1[1]	120	73
736[10]	**Samraan (USA) (115)** (JLDunlop) **4-8-9** JCarroll(7) (lw: in tch: effrt over 3f out: nvr able to chal)	s.h	**6**	14/1	115	68
	Persian Punch (IRE) (107) (DRCElsworth) **4-8-9** RCochrane(6) (lw: dwlt: hld up & bhd: effrt over 3f out: n.d)	nk	**7**	33/1	115	68
736[3]	**Kutta (111)** (RWArmstrong) **5-8-9** RHills(2) (lw: in tch: effrt 3f out: grad wknd)	nk	**8**	11/2[3]	114	67
	Tulipa (USA) (SbinSuroor) **4-8-9** LDettori(9) (chsd ldrs: rdn 3f out: wknd wl over 1f out)	nk	**9**	6/1	114	67
736[7]	**Sacrament (117)** (MRStoute) **6-8-12** OPeslier(1) (cl up: rdn 4f out: wknd 3f out: t.o)	29	**10**	11/1	78	31

(SP 114.4%) **10 Rn**

2m 29.15 (-1.35) CSF £34.78 TOTE £7.70: £2.20 £2.20 £2.70 (£21.50) Trio £70.60 OWNER Mr R. Barnett (NEWMARKET) BRED W. and R. Barnett Ltd
Time Allowed looked really fit and, given a patient ride, showed a useful turn of foot coming down the hill, and settled it emphatically late on. (13/2)
Busy Flight is really going to make his mark this season, but will need stiffer tests to prove his worth. His particularly good attitude is a tremendous bonus. (5/1)
Mons is an edgy customer in the preliminaries, but he did nothing wrong in the race, and kept staying on, suggesting that further will suit. (12/1)
Celeric needed a run to put him straight last season, and it would seem that the same pattern is being followed. He should step up considerably on this, especially when put back over further. (10/1)
628a Luso looked magnificent after his trip to Dubai, but his performance failed to match his looks, and he was a shade disappointing. (4/1: op 6/1)
Samraan (USA) tried to get into it in the last half-mile, but lacked a real turn of foot and seems to need further. (14/1: 10/1-16/1)
Persian Punch (IRE) had a nice blow-out without looking likely to get into this, and once he is put back over longer distances, he is certainly one to keep an eye on. (33/1)
Tulipa (USA) (6/1: op 4/1)
Sacrament (11/1: 8/1-12/1)

933 MILCARS H'CAP (0-85) (3-Y.O+) (Class D)

3-45 (3-46) **1m 2f (Rowley)** £6,680.00 (£2,000.00: £960.00: £440.00) Stalls: Centre GOING minus 0.35 sec per fur (F)

				SP	RR	SF
787²	**Champagne Prince (81)** (PWHarris) **4-9-7**(7) CLowther(2) (a.p: effrt over 2f out: chal 1f out: r.o to ld wl ins fnl f)	—	1	7/1²	91	80
	Sharp Consul (IRE) (76) (HCandy) **5-9-9** CRutter(7) (hld up & bhd: gd hdwy over 2f out: led jst ins fnl f: sn hdd: kpt on wl)	nk	2	20/1	86	75
647⁵	**Fern's Governor (57)** (WJMusson) **5-8-4** GCarter(14) (hld up & bhd: gd hdwy to ld over 2f out: hung lft: hdd ins fnl f: no ex)	1¾	3	8/1³	64	53
688⁷	**Over To You (USA) (82)** (EALDunlop) **3-9-0** OPeslier(13) (lw: hld up: effrt over 2f out: kpt on: nt pce to chal)	1	4	12/1	87	61
735⁹	**Bay of Islands (75)** (DMorris) **5-9-8** NDay(1) (chsd ldrs: outpcd over 1f out: kpt on towards fin)	s.h	5	12/1	80	69
735³	**Ashby Hill (IRE) (69)** (RRowe) **6-9-2** RCochrane(4) (hld up & bhd: hdwy & n.m.r over 1f out: kpt on wl fnl f)	hd	6	8/1³	74	63
735²	**Virtual Reality (77)** (JARToller) **6-9-10** SSanders(3) (in tch: effrt over 2f out: sn chsng ldrs: nt qckn appr fnl f)	1	7	7/1²	80	69
735¹⁵	**Edan Heights (77)** (SDow) **5-9-5**(5) ADaly(12) (mid div: hdwy over 2f out: wknd over 1f out)	3	8	25/1	76	65
	Wafir (IRE) (81) (PCalver) **5-10-0** MBirch(15) (trckd ldrs: led 3f out: sn hdd & grad wknd)	2	9	33/1	76	65
	Raise A Prince (FR) (74) (JWHills) **4-9-7** MHills(5) (s.i.s: n.d)	1½	10	20/1	67	56
791²	**Purchasing Power (IRE) (66)** (NACallaghan) **3-7-7**(5) RMullen(9) (led 4f: wknd over 3f out)	2½	11	11/2¹	55	29
	Invermark (84) (JRFanshawe) **3-9-2** DHarrison(16) (lw: swtg: trckd ldrs: led over 3f out: sn hdd & wknd)	8	12	8/1³	60	34
689³	**Jean Pierre (56)** (JPearce) **4-8-3** AMcGlone(8) (swtg: dwlt: sn rcvrd & prom: wknd 3f out)	2	13	16/1	29	18
	Harvey White (IRE) (60) (JPearce) **5-8-4**(3) CTeague(11) (swtg: hld up & bhd: effrt 3f out: n.d)	d.h	13	25/1	36	25
	Blurred (IRE) (80) (MHTompkins) **4-9-13** RHills(10) (chsd ldrs tl wknd fnl 3f)	1¼	15	10/1	51	40
735¹³	**Serendipity (FR) (78)** (BRMillman) **4-9-11** WJO'Connor(6) (b.hind: plld hrd: led 6f out tl over 3f out: wknd qckly & t.o)	dist	16	16/1	—	—
				(SP 130.1%)	**16 Rn**	

2m 5.14 (0.44) CSF £138.93 CT £1,072.27 TOTE £8.60: £2.10 £4.80 £2.00 £3.10 (£127.00) Trio £391.70 OWNER Magnum Force (BERKHAMSTED) BRED Cheveley Park Stud Ltd

WEIGHT FOR AGE 3yo-15lb

787 Champagne Prince is a game and consistent sort who really deserved this. (7/1)

Sharp Consul (IRE) likes to come from behind and would ideally prefer softer ground, but was just outbattled here. (20/1)

647 Fern's Governor showed a useful turn of foot to take it up over two furlongs out, but it turned out she had done too much too soon, and ran out of fuel. (8/1)

688 Over To You (USA), stepping up in trip, got it well enough but was always short of the necessary speed. (12/1)

Bay of Islands ran well and, by the way he was staying on, he could appreciate a longer trip. (12/1: op 8/1)

735 Ashby Hill (IRE) tried to come from behind, but never had much luck in running. (8/1)

Wafir (IRE) gave the impression that this run was needed. (33/1)

934 DAHLIA STKS (Listed) (4-Y.O+ F & M) (Class A)

4-15 (4-15) **1m 1f (Rowley)** £10,007.40 (£3,696.60: £1,768.30: £716.50: £278.25: £102.95) Stalls: Low GOING minus 0.35 sec per fur (F)

				SP	RR	SF
	Balalaika (102) (LMCumani) **4-8-9** LDettori(5) (h.d.w: trckd ldr: led 2f out: rdn & r.o fnl f)	—	1	10/11¹	92	53
	Tsarnista (95) (JLDunlop) **4-8-9** PatEddery(2) (lw: trckd ldrs: hdwy u.p 2f out: kpt on)	1¼	2	8/1³	90	51
738⁶	**Medieval Lady (85)** (IABalding) **4-8-9** RCochrane(7) (hld up & bhd: effrt over 2f out: sn outpcd: styd on strly fnl f)	hd	3	11/1	90	51
738ᴰ	**Hunters of Brora (IRE) (92)** (JDBethell) **7-8-9** JReid(1) (prom tl outpcd over 2f out: hdwy u.p over 1f out: styd on wl)	s.h	4	9/2²	90	51
440a⁷	**Woodren (USA)** (RGuest) **4-8-9** OPeslier(3) (led tl hdd 2f out: rdn & r.o one pce)	1¼	5	50/1	87?	48
749²	**Blessed Spirit (78)** (CFWall) **4-8-9** GDuffield(6) (swtg: prom: effrt 2f out: rdn & nt qckn appr fnl f)	nk	6	9/1	87?	48
677¹⁷	**Defined Feature (IRE) (85)** (DrJDScargill) **4-8-9** MRoberts(4) (swtg: hld up: effrt on outside over 2f out: sn btn)	5	7	50/1	78?	39
				(SP 103.9%)	**7 Rn**	

1m 51.81 (1.31) CSF £6.30 TOTE £1.60: £1.10 £2.50 (£4.40) OWNER Helena Springfield Ltd (NEWMARKET) BRED Meon Valley Stud

Balalaika had the superior form in the race and always looked to be going best but, in the end, there was not a lot left and she may just have needed this. (10/11: 10/11-evens)

Tsarnista seems to continually get tapped for speed, but she responds to pressure and perhaps more use should be made of her. (8/1: 6/1-9/1)

738 Medieval Lady put in another eye-catching performance, responding really well in the last two furlongs, and looks to be coming to hand. (11/1: 6/1-12/1)

738 Hunters of Brora (IRE) is not the easiest of rides and, looking in trouble over two furlongs out, she ran on when it was all too late. (9/2: 5/2-5/1)

440a Woodren (USA) won over two miles last year in Ireland. Despite a fair performance here, she was done for speed in the closing stages. (50/1)

749 Blessed Spirit had plenty on in this company, and ran quite well in the circumstances. (9/1)

935 EQUITY FINANCIAL COLLECTIONS MAIDEN STKS (3-Y.O F) (Class D)

4-50 (4-50) **7f (Rowley)** £4,386.00 (£1,308.00: £624.00: £282.00) Stalls: Centre GOING minus 0.35 sec per fur (F)

				SP	RR	SF
727⁵	**Jafn** (BHanbury) **3-8-11** RHills(6) (b.off hind: trckd ldrs: ev ch & effrt over 1f out: hung lft: styd on to ld last strides)	—	1	5/4¹	77	28
681⁹	**Fonteyn** (ACStewart) **3-8-11** MRoberts(7) (lw: a cl up: led wl over 1f out: hrd rdn & r.o: jst ct)	hd	2	33/1	77	28
	Alikhlas (MajorWRHern) **3-8-11** TSprake(5) (hld up: hdwy 3f out: ev ch ins fnl f: kpt on wl)	s.h	3	8/1	77	28
681⁵	**Kaziranga (USA)** (LMCumani) **3-8-11** LDettori(3) (hld up: effrt 3f out: sn chsng ldrs: edgd rt appr fnl f: nt pce to chal)	3½	4	100/30²	69	20
	Khawafi (EALDunlop) **3-8-11** KFallon(2) (w'like: scope: bhd: outpcd over 2f out: styd on: no imp)	3	5	13/2³	62	13
	Zest (USA) (MBell) **3-8-11** MHills(1) (plld hrd: bhd: effrt over 2f out: no imp)	4	6	25/1	53	4
	Millpet (RGuest) **3-8-11** JReid(9) (cmpt: bkwd: wnt rt s: sn rcvrd & prom: outpcd fnl 3f)	2½	7	33/1	47	—
	Sugar Plum (RHannon) **3-8-11** PatEddery(4) (sn trckng ldrs: outpcd 3f out: wknd wl over 1f out)	nk	8	8/1	46	—

				SP	RR	SF
584[5]	**Sang d'Antibes (FR) (62)** (DJSCosgrove) **3-8-11** MRimmer(8) (lw: led tl hdd & wknd wl over 1f out)	2	**9**	25/1	42	—

(SP 116.7%) **9 Rn**

1m 27.73 (3.23) CSF £53.96 TOTE £2.50: £1.30 £4.80 £2.20 (£57.20) Trio £69.40 OWNER Mr Hamdan Al Maktoum (NEWMARKET) BRED P. and Mrs Venner

727 Jafn is not the easiest of rides but, well handled, she responded to pressure to just get up. (5/4)
Fonteyn put up a vastly-improved effort, and kept on despite swishing her tail. (33/1)
Alikhlas is a lengthy sort who is still developing, and she should have learnt plenty here. (8/1: 5/1-10/1)
681 Kaziranga (USA) is learning, but was inclined to hang when ridden and lacked a turn of foot. (100/30: 2/1-7/2)
Khawafi showed definite signs of inexperience just after halfway, but learnt as the race progressed and, over further, should improve. (13/2)
Zest (USA) took a strong hold both going down and on the way back, and must learn to settle. (25/1)
Sugar Plum (8/1: 12/1-7/1)

936 NEWMARKET CHALLENGE WHIP MAIDEN (3-Y.O) (Class G)

5-20 (5-20) **1m (Rowley)** Stalls: Centre GOING minus 0.35 sec per fur (F)

				SP	RR	SF
	Mythical (SirMarkPrescott) **3-8-9** GDuffield(2) (plld hrd: qcknd to ld over 1f out: easily)	—	**1**	Evens[2]	47+	—
	Zahir (USA) (SbinSuroor) **3-9-0** LDettori(1) (gd sort: led tl hdd over 1f out: sn btn)	8	**2**	10/11[1]	36	—

(SP 102.4%) **2 Rn**

1m 44.88 (7.58) TOTE £1.80 OWNER Lord Fairhaven (NEWMARKET) BRED Barton Stud

Mythical beat her sole opponent in very easy fashion and, although this form may not amount to anything, she is obviously improving. (Evens)
Zahir (USA) showed an action going to post that would have put off Stevie Wonder, and was a long way second-best. (10/11: op 1/3)

T/Jkpt: £59,223.30 (0.3 Tckts); £58,389.22 to Newmarket 3/4/97. T/Plpt: £279.50 (130.08 Tckts). T/Qdpt: £33.00 (62.15 Tckts) AA/IM

0930-NEWMARKET (R-H) (Good)

Saturday May 3rd

WEATHER: sunny & very warm WIND: almost nil

937 CULFORD STKS (3-Y.O) (Class C)

2-00 (2-01) **1m 4f (Rowley)** £4,666.49 (£1,723.50: £824.25: £333.75: £129.38: £47.63) Stalls: High GOING minus 0.29 sec per fur (GF)

				SP	RR	SF
741[5]	**Single Empire (IRE)** (PWChapple-Hyam) **3-9-0** JReid(2) (lw: hld up & plld hrd: hdwy 4f out: led 2f out: r.o wl)	—	**1**	10/1	95	57
	Bold Demand (SbinSuroor) **3-8-11** LDettori(5) (lw: a.p: led over 6f out to 5f out: rallied & ev ch 1f out: unable qckn)	3	**2**	9/2[2]	88	50
670*	**Street General** (HRACecil) **3-9-0** KFallon(1) (lw: hld up: hdwy to ld 5f out: sn drvn along: hdd 2f out: sn btn)	2	**3**	4/7[1]	88	50
	Sun Alert (USA) (MJPolglase) **3-8-3** MRoberts(3) (leggy: trckd ldrs: rdn & outpcd over 3f out: kpt on fnl f)	¾	**4**	66/1	76	38
	Windsor Castle (PFICole) **3-9-5** TQuinn(4) (bit bkwd: chsd ldrs: rdn & outpcd 4f out: styd on appr fnl f)	s.h	**5**	6/1[3]	92	54
	Bevier (CEBrittain) **3-8-8** BDoyle(6) (w'like: scope: b: unruly stalls: led over 5f: wknd over 3f out: t.o)	dist	**6**	25/1	—	—

(SP 110.5%) **6 Rn**

2m 33.15 (2.65) CSF £46.80 TOTE £11.10: £4.00 £1.70 (£25.00) OWNER Mr A. K. Collins (MARLBOROUGH) BRED Swettenham Stud

741 Single Empire (IRE), taking a fierce hold but restrained in the rear, got the better of the duel to lead entering the final quarter-mile, and stormed up the hill to win going away. With the choice of Derby engagements, a trip to Italy may be favoured as long as the ground rides fast. (10/1: 9/2-12/1)
Bold Demand, sure to benefit from the run, showed his battling qualities until lack of peak fitness took its toll. (9/2: 9/4-5/1)
670* Street General did his best to stretch the field over half-a-mile out, but on ground plenty fast enough, failed to get away and was well outpointed up the hill. (4/7: op evens)
Sun Alert (USA), a leggy half-sister to a couple of winners, looked done for when the tempo picked up over three furlongs out, but she was finding her stride again in the closing stages and will be all the wiser for the experience. (66/1)
Windsor Castle, winner of both his races in the autumn, was staying on strongly up the hill and will be all the sharper for the run. (6/1: 4/1-13/2)

8 84+ 86+ 77+ 80

938 MAYER PARRY MAIDEN STKS (2-Y.O) (Class D)

2-30 (2-30) **5f (Rowley)** £4,425.00 (£1,320.00: £630.00: £285.00) Stalls: Centre GOING minus 0.29 sec per fur (GF)

				SP	RR	SF
	Bodyguard (PFICole) **2-9-0** TQuinn(7) (nice colt: trckd ldrs: led over 1f out: qcknd clr)	—	**1**	4/7[1]	85+	41
	Legs Be Frendly (IRE) (KMcAuliffe) **2-9-0** RHughes(2) (w'like: scope: chsd ldrs: ev ch over 1f out: nt pce of wnr)	5	**2**	20/1	69	25
	Charlies Lad (IRE) (RGuest) **2-9-0** PBloomfield(9) (cmpt: bkwd: a.p: led 2f out tl over 1f out: sn rdn & outpcd)	2	**3**	20/1	63	19
	Festival Flyer (RBoss) **2-9-0** LDettori(1) (cmpt: bhd: rdn 2f out: styd on wl towards fin)	hd	**4**	5/1[2]	62	18
	Distinct Vintage (IRE) (RHannon) **2-9-0** DaneO'Neill(5) (neat: s.s: sn chsng ldrs: ev ch over 1f out: one pce)	½	**5**	6/1[3]	61	17
447[9]	**Livingstone** (CADwyer) **2-9-0** KFallon(4) (effrt ½-wy: no imp)	4	**6**	11/1	48	4
	Counsel (CEBrittain) **2-9-0** BDoyle(3) (neat: s.s: a bhd)	1¼	**7**	20/1	44	—
822[7]	**Ngaere Princess** (WTKemp) **2-8-9** PatEddery(6) (led 3f: sn wknd)	2½	**8**	20/1	31	—
850[8]	***Batswing*** (MartynMeade) **2-9-0** JReid(8) (Withdrawn not under Starter's orders: veterinary advice)		**W**		—	—

(SP 122.0%) **8 Rn**

60.62 secs (1.92) CSF £18.76 TOTE £1.80: £1.40 £2.00 £2.60 (£11.90) Trio £53.60 OWNER H R H Prince Fahd Salman (WHATCOMBE) BRED M. Rapp

Bodyguard, a very attractive son of Zafonic, provided that stallion with his first winner and, though there may be doubts about the strength of the opposition, he could have hardly made a more impressive start to his career. (4/7)
Legs Be Frendly (IRE) a newcomer with lots of scope, was fighting for the lead in the Dip but, once the winner showed his pace, like the rest he was left standing. He will not always meet one so useful. (20/1)
Charlies Lad (IRE), not so impressive cantering to post, ran well all the way and, though he was made to look pedestrian inside the last furlong, this was surely a signal of better things to come. (20/1)
Festival Flyer, a late-April foal bred for speed, was in trouble a quarter-of-a-mile out, but he was beginning to pick up again on meeting the rising ground and, given time, should be able to win races. (5/1: op 3/1)

Distinct Vintage (IRE) still has plenty of filling-out to do and, though he recovered from a tardy start to hold every chance in the Dip, he was only able to look on in amazement as the winner sprinted away. (6/1: 7/2-13/2)
447 Livingstone, a tall colt who had the advantage of a run, looks to need time and he will be better put away until he strengthens to his frame. (11/1: 6/1-12/1)

939 TORCH MOTOR POLICIES AT LLOYDS RATED STKS H'CAP (0-100) (4-Y.O+) (Class B)

3-00 (3-00) **1m 2f (Rowley)** £9,019.36 (£3,334.24: £1,597.12: £649.60: £254.80: £96.88) Stalls: Centre GOING minus 0.29 sec per fur (GF)

				SP	RR	SF
787[4]	**The Dilettanti (USA) (88)** (JARToller) **4-9-0** SSanders(5) (lw: mde all: sn clr: qcknd over 1f out: unchal)	—	**1**	7/1	101	83
738[7]	**Forza Figlio (86)** (MissGayKelleway) **4-8-12** PatEddery(1) (chsd ldrs: rdn 2f out: kpt on: no ch w wnr)	4	**2**	13/2	93	75
	Najm Mubeen (IRE) (92) (ACStewart) **4-9-4** MRoberts(2) (lw: plld hrd: chsd wnr ½-wy: rdn & one pce fnl 2f)	½	**3**	4/1[2]	98	80
521*	**Romios (IRE) (90)** (PFICole) **5-9-2** TQuinn(8) (hld up & bhd: styd on u.p fnl 2f: nvr nrr)	3	**4**	5/1[3]	91	73
776*	**Another Time (86)** (SPCWoods) **5-8-12** DBiggs(6) (plld hrd: hld up: hdwy over 2f out: sn rdn & no imp)	½	**5**	100/30[1]	86	68
	Clan Ben (IRE) (95) (HRACecil) **5-9-7b** KFallon(4) (bit bkwd: hld up: hdwy & rdn over 3f out: wknd fnl 2f)	1¼	**6**	7/1	93	75
	Manaloj (USA) (82) (RHannon) **4-8-8** DaneO'Neill(3) (lw: chsd ldrs 6f: sn rdn & btn: t.o)	19	**7**	33/1	50	32
787[9]	**Hoh Express (88)** (IABalding) **5-9-0** LDettori(9) (chsd ldrs: rdn over 3f out: sn btn & eased: t.o)	½	**8**	7/1	55	37
				(SP 113.5%)	**8 Rn**	

2m 3.7 (-1.00) CSF £46.11 CT £187.52 TOTE £9.90: £2.10 £1.70 £1.30 (£28.20) Trio £33.60 OWNER Duke of Devonshire (WHITSBURY) BRED Carmine Carcieri

787 The Dilettanti (USA), winner of his maiden twelve months ago, has done nothing since so this change to forcing tactics proved to be the right choice. Always going easily, he quickened well in the Dip and it will come as a surprise if he cannot follow up. (7/1)
Forza Figlio, a progressive, lightly-raced colt, turned in his best performance yet and, if he stays clear of the winner, will soon be paying his way. (13/2: 5/1-8/1)
Najm Mubeen (IRE) probably lost his race by taking such a strong pull and almost bolting to post. Poised to challenge all the way, he had nothing left when the final effort was called for but, if he can be taught to settle, he has the ability to go a long way. (4/1)
521* Romios (IRE), settled in the rear, always had too much to do with the winner keeping up a good gallop and then quickening, and he had a hardish race in finishing where he did. (5/1)
776* Another Time looked ill-at-ease cantering to post, but he ran up to his mark in this more competitive race. (100/30)
Clan Ben (IRE) has only ever won in the autumn and, with a bit left to work on on this seasonal debut, was unable to pose much of a threat. (7/1: 5/1-8/1)

940 PERTEMPS 2000 GUINEAS STKS (Gp 1) (3-Y.O C & F) (Class A)

3-40 (3-46) **1m (Rowley)** £131,832.00 (£48,888.00: £23,544.00: £9,720.00: £3,960.00: £1,656.00) Stalls: Low GOING minus 0.29 sec per fur (GF)

				SP	RR	SF
	Entrepreneur (103) (MRStoute) **3-9-0** MJKinane(4) (h.d.w: trckd ldrs: led over 2f out: rdn & r.o strly fnl f)	—	**1**	11/2[2]	127+	92
737[2]	**Revoque (IRE) (120)** (PWChapple-Hyam) **3-9-0** JReid(7) (lw: hld up & bhd: pushed along ½-wy: gd hdwy appr fnl f: fin wl)	¾	**2**	100/30[1]	126+	91
673*	**Poteen (USA) (115)** (LMCumani) **3-9-0** PatEddery(1) (drvn along & swtchd rt over 2f out: ev ch over 1f out: kpt on u.p)	1½	**3**	9/1	123	88
747*	**Starborough (111)** (DRLoder) **3-9-0** KDarley(15) (led tl hdd over 2f out: kpt on u.p fnl f)	s.h	**4**	33/1	122	87
	Zamindar (USA) (AFabre,France) **3-9-0** TJarnet(3) (wl grwn: hld up & bhd: hdwy 2f out: styd on wl towards fin)	¾	**5**	10/1	121+	86
692*	**Desert Story (IRE) (115)** (MRStoute) **3-9-0** RCochrane(12) (chsd ldrs: effrt 3f out: r.o one pce)	5	**6**	12/1	111	76
692[7]	**Shii-Take (104)** (RAkehurst) **3-9-0** AClark(11) (chsd ldr tl wknd fnl 2½f)	1½	**7**	100/1	108	73
692[3]	**Cape Cross (IRE) (110)** (JHMGosden) **3-9-0** OPeslier(9) (lw: b.hind: chsd ldrs: drvn along 3f out: sn outpcd)	¾	**8**	20/1	106	71
599*	**Green Card (USA)** (SPCWoods) **3-9-0** WRyan(2) (in rr: hmpd & swtchd 5f out: n.d)	1½	**9**	40/1	103	68
737[3]	**Muchea (118)** (MRChannon) **3-9-0** RHughes(16) (a in rr)	¾	**10**	50/1	102	67
	Tycoon Todd (USA) (SbinSuroor) **3-9-0** BDoyle(6) (trckd ldrs over 5f)	3½	**11**	50/1	95	60
673[2]	**Za-Im (106)** (BWHills) **3-9-0** RHills(14) (chsd ldrs over 5f: sn lost tch)	8	**12**	66/1	79	44
679*	**Hidden Meadow (118)** (IABalding) **3-9-0** MHills(13) (lw: trckd ldrs on outside: rdn over 3f out: sn btn)	1¼	**13**	7/1[3]	76	41
	Shamikh (SbinSuroor) **3-9-0** LDettori(5) (plld hrd: hmpd 5f out: sn btn & eased)	3½	**14**	7/1[3]	69	34
	Putra (USA) (PFICole) **3-9-0** TQuinn(10) (lw: bolted gng to post: chsd ldrs 5f: sn wknd)	nk	**15**	12/1	69	34
	Musical Pursuit (116) (MHTompkins) **3-9-0** KFallon(8) (h.d.w: plld hrd: in tch: sddle slipped: virtually p.u fnl 3f)	dist	**16**	22/1	—	—
				(SP 118.8%)	**16 Rn**	

1m 35.64 (-1.66) CSF £19.70 TOTE £6.80: £3.20 £1.40 £3.10 (£10.10) Trio £38.10 OWNER Mr M Tabor & Mrs John Magnier (NEWMARKET) BRED Cheveley Park Stud Ltd

Entrepreneur has been the talking horse in Newmarket with some impressive displays on the gallops this spring and, in confirming those opinions with this readily-gained success, will now go straight to the Derby. With his pedigree, the mile-and-a-half trip should be made-to-measure. (11/2)
737 Revoque (IRE), caught out by the fast early pace, was being bustled along at halfway. He did not find his stride until meeting the rising ground, where he fairly flew and failed by a couple of strides to reel in the winner. Present plans are to cross swords again in the Epsom Derby and, over that longer trip, he has obvious claims of gaining revenge. (100/30)
673* Poteen (USA) produced his best performance yet after finding trouble in running, and his jockey believes more cut in the ground is required for him. He also confirmed that this is his trip. (9/1: 12/1-8/1)
747* Starborough adopted the tactics that were successful in his previous race at Thirsk, and turned in a most pleasing performance, but in this company was just tapped for toe up the hill. (33/1)
Zamindar (USA) has a reputation as a bit of a tearaway, but he was dropped in here and, with the pace never slackening, was never able to deliver a challenge. He did little wrong in reaching his final placing, and dispelled thoughts that he may just be a sprinter. (10/1)
692* Desert Story (IRE) was unable to respond when the leaders took one another on in the Dip, and he was struggling to hold on up the hill. (12/1)
692 Shii-Take was reluctant to let himself down cantering to the start, but he ran his race out on the return journey, only to find this company too hot passing the Bushes. (100/1)

941 DUBAI RACING CLUB PALACE HOUSE STKS (Gp 3) (3-Y.O+) (Class A)

4-15 (4-18) **5f (Rowley)** £19,884.00 (£7,356.00: £3,528.00: £1,440.00: £570.00: £222.00) Stalls: Low GOING minus 0.29 sec per fur (GF)

				SP	RR	SF
501[6]	**Deep Finesse (113)** (MAJarvis) **3-8-6b[1]** MRoberts(2) (led after 2f: hrd rdn fnl f: r.o wl)	—	1	14/1	116	66
811a[6]	**Hever Golf Rose (113)** (TJNaughton) **6-8-9** SSanders(10) (b.hind: a w ldrs: rdn & ev ch ins fnl f: r.o)	½	2	5/1[1]	108	67
	Clever Caption (IRE) (SbinSuroor) **3-8-3** RHills(11) (lw: w ldrs: ev ch ins fnl f: r.o)	hd	3	6/1[2]	111	61
573*	**Bolshoi (IRE) (105)** (JBerry) **5-8-12b** EmmaO'Gorman(3) (hld up & bhd: rdn & hdwy 2f out: swtchd rt appr fnl f: fin fast)	s.h	4	5/1[1]	111	70
726[2]	**To the Roof (IRE) (102)** (PWHarris) **5-8-12** KFallon(13) (lw: sn chsng ldrs: rdn ½-wy: unable qckn ins fnl f)	nk	5	5/1[1]	110	69
671[6]	**Rambling Bear (111)** (MBlanshard) **4-9-1** RCochrane(5) (lw: chsd ldrs: hdwy over 1f out: hrd rdn: nt qckn)	1	6	7/1[3]	110	69
671[3]	**Sylva Paradise (IRE) (110)** (CEBrittain) **4-8-12** BDoyle(8) (chsd ldrs: rdn & stumbled wl over 1f out: sn btn)	¾	7	10/1	104	63
501*	**Superior Premium (102)** (RAFahey) **3-8-3** ACulhane(12) (lw: chsd ldrs: rdn ½-wy: outpcd appr fnl f)	¾	8	14/1	102	52
726[11]	**Amazing Bay (96)** (IABalding) **4-8-9** TQuinn(4) (in tch tl wknd fnl 2f)	2	9	33/1	93	52
726[9]	**Midnight Escape (95)** (CFWall) **4-8-12** NCarlisle(1) (led 2f: prom tl hmpd & eased over 1f out)	¾	10	33/1	93	52
573[3]	**Brave Edge (106)** (RHannon) **6-8-12** PatEddery(6) (outpcd fr ½-wy)	s.h	11	8/1	93	52
672[7]	**Connemara (IRE) (107)** (CADwyer) **3-8-0** JQuinn(9) (outpcd: a bhd)	1¾	12	14/1	84	34

(SP 122.9%) **12 Rn**

58.69 secs (-0.01) CSF £77.93 TOTE £21.40: £4.20 £2.10 £2.30 (£49.70) Trio £146.40 OWNER Mr John Sims (NEWMARKET) BRED D. A. and Mrs Hicks

WEIGHT FOR AGE 3yo-9lb

501 Deep Finesse, revitalised by the application of blinkers, needed to dig very deep in the closing stages to hold on in a breath-taking finish. He will stick to the minimum trip, and the King's Stand Stakes at Royal Ascot has been mentioned as a possible target. (14/1)

811a Hever Golf Rose has not won a race since the autumn of 1995, but she showed some of her old dash here and compensation awaits. (5/1)

Clever Caption (IRE), winner of his debut in France last year, showed he has what it takes with a very brave attempt in this competitive sprint, and was only half-a-stride down at the line. He will certainly make a name for himself as a sprinter. (6/1)

573* Bolshoi (IRE) needed to switch wide to find daylight approaching the final furlong and, fairly eating up the ground up the hill, found the line arriving a couple of strides too soon. (5/1)

726 To the Roof (IRE) lost a length at the start, probably by choice, but he soon recovered to press the leaders and, giving his all under a forceful ride, is getting back to something like his best. (5/1)

671 Rambling Bear, involved in a barging match in the Dip, responded willingly to pressure, but just lacked that bit extra nearing the line. (7/1)

671 Sylva Paradise (IRE) appeared to stumble on the downhill run into the Dip and, losing his momentum, was soon fighting a lost cause. (10/1)

Midnight Escape ran a deal better than his finishing position would suggest, but he looked held when hampered and eased entering the final furlong. (33/1)

942 LADBROKES H'CAP (0-95) (3-Y.O+) (Class C)

4-50 (4-51) **6f (Rowley)** £26,610.00 (£7,980.00: £3,840.00: £1,770.00) Stalls: Centre GOING minus 0.29 sec per fur (GF)

				SP	RR	SF
	Perryston View (78) (PCalver) **5-8-11** MJKinane(5) (a.p: led stands' side over 1f out: r.o wl u.p)	—	1	11/1[3]	86	67
726[8]	**Sir Joey (USA) (80)** (PGMurphy) **8-8-13** KFallon(3) (bhd: rapid hdwy over 1f out: fin fast)	½	2	14/1	87	68
675[3]	**Blue Goblin (USA) (90)** (LMCumani) **3-8-13b** LDettori(17) (racd far side: led wl over 1f out: r.o)	nk	3	7/1[2]	96+	67
675[5]	**Sharp Hat (84)** (RHannon) **3-8-7** DaneO'Neill(7) (led stands' side over 4f: kpt on u.p towards fin)	nk	4	20/1	89	60
726[5]	**Sea-Deer (85)** (CADwyer) **8-9-4** PatEddery(1) (a.p stands' side: rdn & r.o wl ins fnl f)	½	5	11/2[1]	89	70
*856**	**First Maite (73)** (SRBowring) **4-8-6b** GCarter(6) (chsd ldrs: kpt on u.p fnl 2f)	½	6	33/1	75	56
	Shining Cloud (68) (MBell) **4-7-10(5)** RMullen(9) (w ldrs stands' side tl rdn & wknd appr fnl f)	hd	7	20/1	70	51
786[8]	**So Intrepid (IRE) (71)** (JMBradley) **7-7-13(5)** RFfrench(21) (nvr nrr)	¾	8	16/1	71	52
786*	**Lord Olivier (IRE) (81)** (WJarvis) **7-9-0** TQuinn(27) (trckd ldrs far side: rdn 2f out: btn appr fnl f)	¾	9	16/1	79	60
835*	**Oggi (81)** (PJMakin) **6-9-0** MRoberts(10) (chsd ldrs stands' side: outpcd fnl 2f)	s.h	10	14/1	79	60
726[17]	**White Emir (82)** (BJMeehan) **4-9-1** OPeslier(20) (swtg: w ldrs far side over 4f)	½	11	25/1	79	60
	Galine (84) (WAO'Gorman) **4-9-3** EmmaO'Gorman(18) (hdwy far side 2f out: sn no imp)	¾	12	20/1	79	60
596*	**French Grit (IRE) (79)** (MDods) **5-8-12** AClark(4) (chsd ldrs stands' side: nvr able to chal)	hd	13	14/1	73	54
	Mallia (85) (TDBarron) **4-9-4** KDarley(2) (nvr nr ldrs)	s.h	14	25/1	79	60
	Top Banana (95) (HCandy) **6-9-7(7)** LJames(8) (in tch 3f)	1¼	15	14/1	86	67
834[13]	**Mr Bergerac (IRE) (82)** (BPalling) **6-9-1** TSprake(22) (m.n.s)	½	16	20/1	72	53
301[8]	**Antonias Melody (79)** (SRBowring) **4-8-12** SWebster(24) (w ldrs far side 4f)	nk	17	40/1	68	49
508[4]	**Zaretski (87)** (CEBrittain) **3-8-10** BDoyle(26) (lw: prom far side over 3f)	s.h	18	20/1	76	47
839[9]	**Hello Mister (95)** (TEPowell) **6-9-11(3)** PMcCabe(28) (outpcd)	nk	19	50/1	83	64
	Sandabar (84) (MRStoute) **4-9-3** JReid(13) (lw: outpcd fr ½-wy)	nk	20	14/1	71	52
726[13]	**Warning Time (91)** (BJMeehan) **4-9-10** RHughes(29) (lw: m.n.s)	s.h	21	40/1	78	59
731[2]	**Lunar Mist (77)** (MartynMeade) **4-8-7(3)** RHavlin(14) (chsd ldrs stands' side tl wknd over 2f out)	s.h	22	25/1	64	45
	Bajan Rose (85) (MBlanshard) **5-9-4** RCochrane(16) (outpcd)	s.h	23	33/1	72	53
	Thwaab (68) (FWatson) **5-8-1v** JQuinn(25) (bkwd: outpcd)	1½	24	33/1	51	32
610[5]	**Stylish Ways (IRE) (69)** (JPearce) **5-8-2** JLowe(30) (s.i.s: a bhd)	nk	25	20/1	51	32
	Indian Relative (76) (RGuest) **4-8-6(3)** DGriffiths(19) (prom far side 4f)	s.h	26	33/1	58	39
	Master Planner (90) (CACyzer) **8-9-9** DBiggs(23) (b: led far side over 4f)	hd	27	33/1	72	53
520[3]	**Denbrae (IRE) (72)** (DJGMurraySmith) **5-8-5** SSanders(15) (outpcd)	1¼	28	20/1	50	31
	Kind of Light (76) (RGuest) **4-8-9** PBloomfield(12) (outpcd)	1¼	29	33/1	51	32

(SP 150.7%) **29 Rn**

1m 12.09 (0.29) CSF £126.64 CT £1,112.52 TOTE £11.00: £2.70 £3.70 £1.80 £4.60 (£40.20) Trio £355.70 OWNER Mrs Janis MacPherson (RIPON) BRED Mrs V. E. Hughes

WEIGHT FOR AGE 3yo-10lb

Perryston View recovered his useful form of a couple of seasons ago with a very game display on this seasonal debut, helped in no small way by the man of the moment, Michael Kinane. (11/1)

Sir Joey (USA) showed here he still retains his enthusiasm for the game, with another strong-finishing performance that would have succeeded in another few strides. (14/1)

675 Blue Goblin (USA) was the unlucky one, for he finished clear of his rivals on the far side, only to find the nearside pair beating him to the punch. (7/1: op 12/1)
675 Sharp Hat led a tightly-packed group on the stands' side until the winner took over in the Dip, and then rallied bravely to go down fighting. He looks to be back to his best. (20/1)
726 Sea-Deer, always in the action, just failed to pick up entering the final furlong, but he was really into his stride again nearing the line. (11/2: 10/1-5/1)
856* First Maite ran a fine race in this much hotter company, and did not fail for the want of trying. (33/1)
Shining Cloud, in the firing-line all the way, only got left behind entering the last furlong. (20/1)
Top Banana (14/1: op 25/1)

943 NGK SPARK PLUGS CONDITIONS STKS (4-Y.O+) (Class C)

5-20 (5-20) **1m 2f (Rowley)** £5,014.49 (£1,855.50: £890.25: £363.75: £144.38: £56.63) Stalls: Centre GOING minus 0.29 sec per fur (GF)

				SP	RR	SF
522[2]	**Germano (103)** (GWragg) **4-8-10** MHills(3) (lw: a.p: led over 2f out: qcknd clr fnl f)	—	**1**	7/4[1]	112	64
	Forest Buck (USA) (108) (HRACecil) **4-9-3** KFallon(6) (hld up: hdwy over 2f out: edgd lft: nt pce of wnr fnl f)	3½	**2**	2/1[2]	113	65
	Wilcuma (104) (PJMakin) **6-9-5** PatEddery(5) (lw: hld up & bhd: hdwy 2f out: nt pce to chal)	1¾	**3**	4/1[3]	113	65
	Prince of Andros (USA) (110) (CFWall) **7-9-10** JReid(4) (bit bkwd: chsd ldrs 7f: rdn & hmpd over 1f out: sn btn)	2½	**4**	13/2	114	66
	Henry The Fifth (104) (CEBrittain) **4-8-10** BDoyle(1) (led tl over 2f out: sn rdn: btn appr fnl f)	nk	**5**	33/1	99	51
	Golden Ace (IRE) (RHannon) **4-8-10** DaneO'Neill(2) (prom tl wknd over 2f out)	3	**6**	20/1	94?	46
				(SP 110.7%)		**6 Rn**

2m 5.54 (0.84) CSF £4.88 TOTE £2.80: £1.70 £1.50 (£2.60) OWNER Baron G Von Ullmann (NEWMARKET) BRED Cambremont Ltd Partnership
522 Germano, always travelling supremely well, had the measure of his rivals approaching the final furlong and won with any amount in hand. He has not been easy to train, but looks useful. (7/4)
Forest Buck (USA) tried hard to take the winner on approaching the final furlong, but that rival proved much too strong and he was never able to land a blow. (2/1)
Wilcuma made a promising seasonal debut on ground far too lively for him, and he promises to be as good as ever. (4/1: 5/2-9/2)
Prince of Andros (USA) was unable to concede so much weight to the useful winner, and he was fighting a lost cause when impeded approaching the final furlong. (13/2: 4/1-7/1)
Henry The Fifth did a good job of pacemaking for almost a mile, before the quickening tempo proved beyond him. (33/1)

T/Jkpt: Not won; £81,506.87 to Newmarket 4/5/97. T/Plpt: £362.20 (145.7 Tckts). T/Qdpt: £36.80 (95.85 Tckts) AA/IM

0743-THIRSK (L-H) (St crse Good to firm, Rnd crse Firm)
Saturday May 3rd
WEATHER: fine

944 AYKBORNE MAIDEN STKS (3-Y.O+) (Class D)

2-20 (2-20) **1m 4f** £3,886.00 (£1,168.00: £564.00: £262.00) Stalls: High GOING minus 0.29 sec per fur (GF)

				SP	RR	SF
773[5]	**Winter Garden** (LMCumani) **3-8-5** OUrbina(11) (lw: trckd ldrs: shkn up to ld over 1f out: r.o wl)	—	**1**	11/8[1]	86+	49
	Nightlark (IRE) (DRLoder) **3-8-0** DRMcCabe(7) (led tl over 2f out: kpt on same pce: no ch w wnr)	2½	**2**	5/1[3]	78	41
	Valagalore (BWHills) **3-8-0** JFEgan(12) (b.hind: trckd ldrs: rdn to ld over 2f out: hdd & wknd over 1f out)	4	**3**	7/1	72	35
	Psicossis (HRACecil) **4-9-10** AMcGlone(5) (sn chsng ldrs: outpcd 3f out: n.d after)	4	**4**	3/1[2]	72	54
840[14]	**Dulas Bay (55)** (MWEasterby) **3-8-2**(5)ow2 GParkin(1) (bhd & drvn along 5f out: sme hdwy 2f out: nvr nr ldrs)	14	**5**	200/1	55	16
	Burn Out (JPearce) **5-9-7**(3) CTeague(9) (sn bhd & pushed along: t.o 7f out: sme late hdwy)	1¾	**6**	66/1	51	33
	Moon Colony (LadyHerries) **4-9-10** DeclanO'Shea(10) (rangy: unf: trckd ldrs: effrt over 3f out: wknd over 2f out: eased)	hd	**7**	20/1	51	33
511[2]	**Canadian Fantasy (82)** (MJohnston) **3-8-5** DeanMcKeown(6) (chsd ldrs: pushed along 5f out: sn wl outpcd)	½	**8**	12/1	50	13
	All Done (SMellor) **4-9-5** MWigham(3) (rangy: unf: sn outpcd & bhd)	2½	**9**	125/1	42	24
	Go Green Flag (MrsJCecil) **3-8-5** GBardwell(2) (w'like: s.i.s: bhd & drvn along: sme hdwy ½-wy: sn wknd)	3½	**10**	16/1	42	5
559[6]	**Taswib (USA)** (DMorley) **4-9-10** JStack(8) (bit bkwd: chsd ldrs: drvn along 5f out: sn lost pl: t.o)	24	**11**	20/1	10	—
				(SP 122.2%)		**11 Rn**

2m 33.3 (2.60) CSF £7.99 TOTE £2.60: £1.80 £2.20 £3.00 (£7.60) Trio £12.70 OWNER Sheikh Mohammed (NEWMARKET) BRED Darley Stud Management Co Ltd
WEIGHT FOR AGE 3yo-19lb
773 Winter Garden, who looked outstanding in the paddock, took this with a fair bit to spare. Obviously suited by the step-up in distance, it will be interesting to see what mark the Handicapper pitches him in at. (11/8)
Nightlark (IRE), who looked very lean, made the running, but was swept aside by the winner. (5/1)
Valagalore, a tall, narrow filly, looked a real danger when moving upsides, but she fell in a heap over a furlong out. She looks as though she needs more time. (7/1: op 9/2)
Psicossis, who had just one outing at three, was tapped for foot early in the straight, and was by no means knocked about. He looks a real stayer and will appreciate some give underfoot. (3/1)

945 RACING CHANNEL MAIDEN STKS (3-Y.O) (Class D)

2-50 (2-51) **7f** £4,094.00 (£1,232.00: £596.00: £278.00) Stalls: Low GOING minus 0.29 sec per fur (GF)

				SP	RR	SF
	Young Precedent (PWHarris) **3-9-0** AMcGlone(4) (trckd ldr: shkn up to ld over 1f out: r.o wl)	—	**1**	11/4[2]	77	47
784[5]	**Tabasco Jazz** (BJMeehan) **3-8-9** JCarroll(5) (b.nr hind: led: rdn over 2f out: hdd over 1f out: styd on one pce)	2½	**2**	11/2	66	36
693[3]	**Shadoof** (WRMuir) **3-9-0** JFortune(3) (lw: chsd ldrs: rdn over 2f out: styd on same pce appr fnl f)	hd	**3**	6/4[1]	71	41
	Van Chino (BAMcMahon) **3-9-0** LNewton(2) (hld up: hdwy & swtchd outside over 2f out: sn rdn: kpt on one pce)	5	**4**	12/1	60	30
	Tezaab (BHanbury) **3-9-0** JStack(1) (lengthy: trckd ldrs: effrt over 2f out: sn wknd)	5	**5**	5/1[3]	48	18
	Petite Risk (KWHogg) **3-8-9** LCharnock(9) (swvd rt s: sn trckng ldrs: plld hrd: rdn & wknd over 2f out)	¾	**6**	100/1	42	12
	Impetus (JHetherton) **3-9-0** NKennedy(7) (wl outpcd & bhd ½-wy: sme late hdwy)	4	**7**	25/1	37	7

Form	Horse / details	Pos	SP	RR	SF
	Nite Owler (JohnHarris) **3-9-0** JO'Reilly(6) (leggy: unf: hld up & plld hrd: hdwy on outside 3f out: sn wknd)....¾	8	25/1	36	6
			(SP 115.1%)		**8 Rn**

1m 27.2 (2.30) CSF £16.42 TOTE £3.90: £1.10 £1.50 £1.20 (£8.50) Trio £3.00 OWNER Pendley Knights (BERKHAMSTED) BRED P. V. and Mrs J. P. Jackson

Young Precedent stood out in the paddock. He has plenty of size and scope, and took this with something to spare. It was not a strong event, but he looks to have a decent future. (11/4)
784 Tabasco Jazz, happier on this more galloping track, proved very willing but, in the end, the winner was much too good. (11/2)
693 Shadoof was in trouble some way out. Staying on at the finish, he may be better suited by a mile. (6/4: 4/5-13/8)
Van Chino took a keen grip, but off the bit proved very one-paced. He may need a little more time yet. (12/1)
Tezaab was not knocked about on his debut, but he looks on the immature side at present. (5/1)

946 WALKER MORRIS H'CAP (0-90) (3-Y.O+) (Class C)
3-20 (3-20) **7f** £5,605.00 (£1,690.00: £820.00: £385.00) Stalls: Low GOING minus 0.29 sec per fur (GF)

Form	Horse / details	Pos	SP	RR	SF
835[4]	**Weetman's Weigh (IRE) (73)** (RHollinshead) **4-8-12**(3) FLynch(5) (lw: bhd: hdwy over 2f out: rdn to ld 1f out: r.o)...—	1	5/1[2]	82	57
832[6]	**Rakis (IRE) (78)** (MrsLStubbs) **7-9-6** JFEgan(6) (hdwy u.p 3f out: ev ch 1f out: styd on same pce)...½	2	13/2	86	61
433[5]	**Raheen (USA) (86)** (WGMTurner) **4-9-9b**(5) DSweeney(10) (swtg: racd wd: led: clr after 1f: hdd 1f out: kpt on wl)...s.h	3	6/1[3]	94	69
766*	**Victory Team (IRE) (75)** (GBBalding) **5-9-3** SDrowne(2) (trckd ldrs gng wl: effrt over 1f out: nt qckn)...½	4	9/4[1]	82	57
848[16]	**Paint It Black (58)** (DNicholls) **4-7-9**(5) IonaWands(1) (hdwy 3f out: sn chsng ldrs: rdn & nt qckn appr fnl f)...2½	5	5/1[2]	59	34
	Royal Mark (IRE) (85) (TDBarron) **4-9-13** DHarrison(4) (trckd ldrs: effrt 3f out: ev ch over 1f out: wknd towards fin)...hd	6	8/1	86	61
635[7]	**Royal South (IRE) (70)** (PSFelgate) **4-8-12** GHind(3) (hld up: hdwy over 2f out: n.m.r: nvr nr to chal)...¾	7	20/1	69	44
870[8]	**The Barnsley Belle (IRE) (55)** (JLEyre) **4-7-11** TWilliams(8) (chsd ldrs: wknd over 1f out)...2½	8	9/1	48	23
578[15]	**Pleasure Trick (USA) (54)** (DonEnricoIncisa) **6-7-10** KimTinkler(7) (sn pushed along: a in rr)...4	9	50/1	38	13
835[16]	**Enchanted Guest (IRE) (71)** (VSoane) **4-8-13** CRutter(9) (chsd ldrs tl wknd over 2f out)...7	10	33/1	39	14
			(SP 122.5%)		**10 Rn**

1m 26.4 (1.50) CSF £35.34 CT £191.11 TOTE £5.70: £2.00 £2.10 £2.80 (£17.70) Trio £54.20 OWNER Ed Weetman (Haulage & Storage) Ltd (UPPER LONGDON) BRED David Commins
LONG HANDICAP Pleasure Trick (USA) 7-1

835 Weetman's Weigh (IRE) came from last to first in the straight, and was particularly well handled. The step-up to seven furlongs suited him well. (5/1)
832 Rakis (IRE), a real seven-furlong specialist, ran right up to his best on turf. (13/2)
433 Raheen (USA), warm beforehand, raced keenly from his wide draw and, considering he did so much in the early stages, he kept on commendably. (6/1)
766* Victory Team (IRE) tracked the leaders going well but, when shaken up, did not pull out as much as expected. He is suited by exaggerated waiting tactics. (9/4)
733* Paint It Black was never doing enough on this occasion. (5/1)
Royal Mark (IRE), who has slipped down the weights, ran a pleasing race on his first outing for new connections. He looked as though the outing would bring him on (8/1)
Royal South (IRE) hinted at his first signs of ability since coming over from Ireland. He needs to drop another 2/3lb in the weights and he will be knocking on the door. (20/1)
579* The Barnsley Belle (IRE) (9/1: op 14/1)

947 THIRSK HUNT CUP H'CAP (0-90) (3-Y.O+) (Class C)
3-55 (3-56) **1m** £12,622.50 (£3,780.00: £1,815.00: £832.50) Stalls: Low GOING minus 0.29 sec per fur (GF)

Form	Horse / details	Pos	SP	RR	SF
864[3]	**Gadge (58)** (ABailey) **6-7-11** DWright(8) (b: trckd ldr: led over 3f out: jst hld on)...—	1	4/1[1]	69	39
734[4]	**Gulf Shaadi (65)** (EJAlston) **5-8-4** SDrowne(14) (hdwy over 2f out: styd on wl ins fnl f)...hd	2	10/1	76	46
823*	**High Premium (77)** (RAFahey) **9-8-9**(7) RWinston(10) (hld up: effrt over 2f out: swtchd rt over 1f out: hung lft: styd on wl towards fin)...s.h	3	4/1[1]	88	58
	Royal Ceilidh (IRE) (76) (DenysSmith) **4-8-12**(3) FLynch(18) (hdwy over 2f out: styd on fnl f: nt rch ldrs)...1½	4	25/1	84	54
398[12]	**Anonym (IRE) (64)** (JLEyre) **5-8-3b** TWilliams(3) (a chsng ldrs: ev ch over 2f out: r.o same pce fnl f)...hd	5	16/1	72	42
824[8]	**Tertium (IRE) (82)** (MartynWane) **5-9-7** JCarroll(12) (hld up: hdwy & nt clr run over 2f out: styd on fnl f)...hd	6	14/1	89	59
749*	**Angel Face (USA) (81)** (PDEvans) **4-9-6** JFEgan(2) (mid div: hdwy over 2f out: kpt on one pce fnl f)...1½	7	4/1[1]	85	55
824[6]	**Royal Result (USA) (75)** (TDBarron) **4-9-0** DHarrison(5) (chsd ldrs: wknd fnl f)...2	8	9/1[3]	75	45
738[18]	**Band on the Run (86)** (BAMcMahon) **10-9-11** LNewton(1) (hld up & bhd: hdwy on ins 2f out: nvr nr ldrs)...1¼	9	25/1	84	54
358[8]	**Karinska (58)** (MCChapman) **7-7-4**(7) PDoe(11) (s.i.s: hdwy over 2f out: no imp appr fnl f)...½	10	33/1	55	25
900[2]	**Godmersham Park (63)** (PSFelgate) **5-8-2** GDuffield(4) (led tl over 3f out: wknd over 1f out)...1¾	11	12/1	56	26
589[5]	**Queens Consul (IRE) (74)** (BSRothwell) **7-8-13** JFortune(13) (w ldrs: effrt on outside over 2f out: grad wknd)...1¼	12	11/1	65	35
444[4]	**Sandmoor Chambray (81)** (TDEasterby) **6-9-6** MBirch(6) (lw: a bhd & sn drvn along)...3	13	7/1[2]	66	36
661[6]	**Duke Valentino (58)** (RHollinshead) **5-7-11** DaleGibson(9) (swtg: hld up & bhd: n.d)...¾	14	50/1	41	11
832[12]	**Night Wink (USA) (78)** (GLMoore) **5-9-3** SWhitworth(17) (racd wd: prom tl lost pl ½-wy)...8	15	16/1	45	15
733[9]	**Tinklers Folly (60)** (RMWhitaker) **5-7-13** LCharnock(15) (swtg: in tch: rdn & outpcd over 3f out: sn wknd)...s.h	16	20/1	27	—
	Censor (88) (DNicholls) **4-9-13** AlexGreaves(16) (cl up tl lost pl over 3f out: eased)...5	17	16/1	45	15
			(SP 149.3%)		**17 Rn**

1m 38.3 (1.80) CSF £48.54 CT £174.32 TOTE £7.40: £2.00 £2.70 £2.50 £4.50 (£58.10) Trio £161.60 OWNER Mr J. B. Wilcox (TARPORLEY) BRED Snowdrop Stud Co Ltd

864 Gadge retains his form really well despite a busy schedule. Gambled on here, he kicked for home and did just enough. (4/1: op 10/1)
734 Gulf Shaadi is running really well this time, and was just denied. (10/1)
823* High Premium, fourth in this event last year, gave his young rider problems but, taking hold of the bit inside the last, was closing the gap on the first two at the line. (4/1: op 10/1)
Royal Ceilidh (IRE) ran well from a poor draw. (25/1)
136 Anonym (IRE) put two poor runs behind him. (16/1)
824 Tertium (IRE) again did not wear a tongue-strap. After meeting trouble, he was staying on in his own time at the end, and is definitely on the way back. (14/1)

749* Angel Face (USA) as usual was taken to post early and gave a problem or two. She ran well but could not overcome a 7lb rise in the weights. (4/1)
433 Band on the Run shaped as if on the way back. (25/1)

948 E.B.F. NORTON GROVE TIMELESS TIMES NOVICE MEDIAN AUCTION STKS (2-Y.O) (Class E)

4-25 (4-28) **5f** £3,140.25 (£942.00: £453.50: £209.25) Stalls: High GOING minus 0.14 sec per fur (G)

				SP	RR	SF
	Katy Thomas (JBerry) **2-8-2**(5) PFessey(6) (b.hind: leggy: unf: scope: mde all: hung lft thrght: hld on wl)	—	1	5/1[2]	55	18
	Turf Moor (IRE) (JJO'Neill) **2-8-7** JCarroll(5) (lt-f: unf: trckd ldrs: ev ch over 1f out: nt qckn ins fnl f)	¾	2	7/1[3]	53	16
	Adrenalin (MrsJRRamsden) **2-8-12** JFortune(9) (w'like: scope: s.i.s: hdwy ½-wy: hung lft & swtchd over 1f out: kpt on wl)	nk	3	5/1[2]	57	20
	Sandmoor Tartan (TDEasterby) **2-8-12** MBirch(8) (w'like: unf: swvd lft s: bhd: hdwy over 1f out: kpt on wl towards fin)	1	4	7/1[3]	53	16
861[8]	**Newhargen (IRE)** (PDEvans) **2-8-12** JFEgan(2) (lw: w ldr: hmpd 2f out: sn rdn: wknd appr fnl f)	1½	5	7/4[1]	49	12
	Cosmic Case (JSGoldie) **2-8-7** TWilliams(10) (unf: scope: bit bkwd: s.i.s: sn chsng ldrs: hung lft over 1f out: sn outpcd & eased)	2½	6	20/1	36	—
611[6]	**Mr Fund Switch** (DNicholls) **2-8-12** KHodgson(4) (lw: outpcd after 2f)	2½	7	50/1	33	—
	La Vaso Verdi (RMWhitaker) **2-8-7** DeanMcKeown(7) (neat: sn outpcd)	s.h	8	20/1	28	—
	Newgate Noblesse (BWMurray) **2-8-7** VHalliday(3) (leggy: unf: scope: s.i.s: a outpcd)	6	9	20/1	8	—
	Allmaites (DNicholls) **2-8-12** AlexGreaves(1) (Withdrawn not under Starter's orders: reard & uns rdr s: rider sltly injured)		W	10/1	—	—
				(SP 120.0%)	**9 Rn**	

61.2 secs (3.60) CSF £30.60 TOTE £3.80: £1.70 £2.00 £1.80 (£10.90) Trio £41.10 OWNER Mr N. Warburton (COCKERHAM) BRED N. and L. Warburton

Katy Thomas, who looked as if she might need the outing, hung to her left throughout, causing the favourite a few problems, but in the end she did just enough to take a purely run-of-the-mill event. (5/1)
Turf Moor (IRE), a sharp sort, is bred purely for speed. (7/1)
Adrenalin has far more size and scope than the remainder of these. From a stable not renowned for first-time-out two-year-old winners, he finished in pleasing style after hanging and taking time to find his stride. (5/1: 4/1-6/1)
Sandmoor Tartan, whose stable's two-year-olds seldom score first time, looked pretty fit. Forfeiting ground at the start and running green, he finished in pleasing fashion and should be a different proposition next time. (7/1)
Newhargen (IRE), a sharp sort, looked very fit. Gambled on to step-up on his initial effort five days earlier, he raced on the outside of the winner and took a bit of a buffeting soon after halfway. That was not the only reason for his defeat, and he dropped away in the final furlong. (7/4)
Cosmic Case was eased up when his chance had gone inside the last. (20/1)

949 BALDERSBY H'CAP (0-80) (3-Y.O+) (Class D)

5-00 (5-02) **5f** £4,640.00 (£1,400.00: £680.00: £320.00) Stalls: High GOING minus 0.14 sec per fur (G)

				SP	RR	SF
834[7]	**Longwick Lad (72)** (WRMuir) **4-9-7** DHarrison(15) (chsd ldrs: led over 1f out: drvn out)	—	1	9/2[1]	79	47
	Bee Health Boy (66) (MWEasterby) **4-8-10b**(5) GParkin(16) (a chsng ldrs: kpt on wl fnl f)	1	2	16/1	70	38
744[8]	**Captain Carat (59)** (DNicholls) **6-8-8b[1]** DaleGibson(17) (hld up & bhd: hdwy on ins & nt clr run over 1f out: swtchd & styd on wl towards fin)	s.h	3	6/1[2]	63	31
779*	**Johayro (64)** (JSGoldie) **4-8-6**(7) JMcAuley(2) (lw: chsd ldr far side: led over 1f out: r.o)	hd	4	15/2[3]	67+	35
659[8]	**Rennyholme (47)** (JHetherton) **6-7-10** NKennedy(1) (racd far side: hdwy ½-wy: styd on fnl f)	½	5	50/1	49+	17
827[9]	**Camionneur (IRE) (47)** (TDEasterby) **4-7-10b** GBardwell(14) (a chsng ldrs: rdn ½-wy: kpt on same pce)	½	6	10/1	47	15
772*	**Manolo (FR) (67)** (JBerry) **4-8-11b**(5) PRoberts(12) (led stands' side: edgd lft & hdd over 1f out: grad wknd)	1	7	9/2[1]	64	32
744[7]	**Insider Trader (70)** (MrsJRRamsden) **6-9-5** JFortune(7) (swtchd rt s: hld up & bhd: hdwy on ins over 1f out: nvr nr ldrs)	hd	8	8/1	67	35
527[9]	**Stolen Kiss (IRE) (68)** (MWEasterby) **5-9-3b** TLucas(6) (trckd ldrs far side tl wknd over 1f out)	½	9	20/1	63	31
593[5]	**Sotonian (HOL) (47)** (PSFelgate) **4-7-10** DWright(3) (led far side tl hdd over 1f out: grad wknd)	½	10	14/1	40	8
*593**	**Time To Fly (51)** (BWMurray) **4-8-0b**ow4 JFEgan(9) (b.hind: w ldrs 3f: sn wknd)	¾	11	12/1	42	6
744[17]	**Here Comes a Star (57)** (JMCarr) **9-8-6** LCharnock(5) (racd far side: sn outpcd)	nk	12	20/1	47	15
	Middle East (70) (TDBarron) **4-9-5** JCarroll(8) (swtg: chsd ldrs: rdn ½-wy: wknd & eased fnl f)	s.h	13	14/1	60	28
772[7]	**Playmaker (52)** (DNicholls) **4-7-10**(5) IonaWands(10) (s.s: sme hdwy ½-wy: n.d)	1	14	25/1	39	7
702[16]	**Rich Glow (54)** (NBycroft) **6-8-3** SDrowne(4) (racd far side: outpcd fr ½-wy)	½	15	25/1	39	7
744[19]	**Just Bob (73)** (SEKettlewell) **8-9-1**(7) JennyBenson(11) (s.s: nt rcvr)	1	16	14/1	55	23
	Elle Shaped (IRE) (79) (DNicholls) **7-10-0** KHodgson(13) (in tch to ½-wy: sn bhd)	4	17	33/1	48	16
				(SP 138.3%)	**17 Rn**	

60.2 secs (2.60) CSF £75.97 CT £330.31 TOTE £6.60: £1.60 £5.70 £1.70 £2.70 (£29.30) Trio £17.70 OWNER Mrs Marion Wickham (LAMBOURN) BRED Mrs Wickham

LONG HANDICAP Sotonian (HOL) 7-7 Camionneur (IRE) 7-9 Time To Fly 7-8 Rennyholme 7-5

OFFICIAL EXPLANATION Elle Shaped (IRE): Trainer reported that the gelding was found to be lame on its near fore the following morning.

IN-FOCUS: The result of this race again highlighted that the high draws have a definite advantage in sprint races here.

Longwick Lad made the best of his high draw. (9/2: op 8/1)
Bee Health Boy raced against the stand rail. He stuck on strongly and is probably better over six. (16/1)
527 Captain Carat, blinkered for the first time, met trouble in running and was reeling in the first two at the line. (6/1)
779* Johayro, 6lb higher than when winning at Ripon two outings ago, came out best of those on the far side. (15/2)
515 Rennyholme has won just one of his thirty-six starts but, from 5lb out of the handicap, gave a good account of himself here. (50/1)
772* Manolo (FR), from a 5lb higher mark, led on the stands' side, but was always tending to edge left. (9/2)
744 Insider Trader, with the visor again left off, was switched to race on the stands' side. By no means knocked about, he should strike form before much longer, especially when forcing tactics are adopted. (8/1)
593 Sotonian (HOL) (14/1: 10/1-16/1)

T/Plpt: £60.90 (201.6 Tckts). T/Qdpt: £135.70 (3.05 Tckts) WG

0608-HAMILTON (R-H) (Soft)

Sunday May 4th

WEATHER: unsettled with heavy showers WIND: fresh half bhd

950 LETHEBY AND CHRISTOPHER CATERING MADE SPECIAL CHALLENGE (FOR NATIONAL HUNT JOCKEYS) H'CAP (0-70) (4-Y.O+) (Class E)

2-20 (2-22) **1m 5f 9y** £3,025.25 (£917.00: £448.50: £214.25) Stalls: High GOING: 0.38 sec per fur (GS)

				SP	RR	SF
	Silver Pearl (39) (MrsAMNaughton) **6-10-0** JSupple(7) (b: s.i.s: hdwy over 5f out: c wd: r.o to ld jst ins fnl f)	—	**1**	33/1	49	28
777^{7}	**Brodessa (55)** (MrsMReveley) **11-11-2** PNiven(6) (hdwy 7f out: sn prom: ev ch over 2f out: nt qckn ins fnl f)	¾	**2**	8/1	64	43
613^{8}	**Rossel (USA) (55)** (PMonteith) **4-11-2** GCahill(4) (sn drvn along: wnt prom 9f out: ev ch over 2f out: kpt on same pce fnl f)	¾	**3**	11/1	63	42
721^{14}	**Philmist (45)** (MissLAPerratt) **5-10-6b** FPerratt(8) (lw: gd hdwy over 5f out: led on bit over 3f out: rdn over 1f out: wknd & hdd jst ins fnl f)	2	**4**	$7/1^{3}$	51	30
613^{6}	**Lord Hastie (USA) (55)** (CWThornton) **9-11-2** OPears(3) (hld up: hdwy 5f out: effrt over 2f out: nvr nr to chal)	8	**5**	$7/4^{1}$	51	30
669^{2}	**Anchorena (51)** (DWBarker) **5-10-12** RichardGuest(14) (swtg: hld up & bhd: hdwy over 3f out: nvr nr ldrs)	nk	**6**	$7/1^{3}$	47	26
721^{17}	**The Boozing Brief (USA) (57)** (CParker) **4-11-4b** DParker(15) (b: chsd ldrs: rdn over 3f out: wknd over 2f out)	5	**7**	14/1	46	25
272^{3}	**Mapengo (44)** (JCullinan) **6-10-5** DerekByrne(11) (bhd: hdwy u.p over 3f out: nvr nr ldrs)	nk	**8**	20/1	33	12
	Jarrow (39) (MrsAMNaughton) **6-10-0** RSupple(12) (lw: bhd: hdwy 8f out: lost pl 4f out)	hd	**9**	66/1	28	7
	American Hero (45) (RAllan) **9-10-6** BStorey(10) (lw: w ldr: led 9f out tl over 3f out: sn wknd)	6	**10**	$7/2^{2}$	27	6
493^{15}	**Nordisk Legend (42)** (MrsDThomson) **5-10-3**^{ow3} TReed(1) (chsd ldrs: rdn over 5f out: sn lost pl)	20	**11**	100/1	—	—
	Marsh's Law (39) (GPKelly) **10-10-0** LO'Hara(13) (sn bhd & rdn along)	3	**12**	100/1	—	—
	Marzocco (39) (TAKCuthbert) **9-10-0** CarolCuthbert(2) (lw: bhd: hdwy 10f out: sn prom: wknd 6f out)	13	**13**	100/1	—	—
612^{7}	**French Project (IRE) (60)** (MrsSCBradburne) **5-11-7** MFoster(5) (led to 9f out: lost pl 6f out: t.o)	25	**14**	33/1	—	—
				(SP 124.8%)	**14 Rn**	

3m 4.6 (18.90) CSF £257.19 CT £2,843.04 TOTE £25.80: £5.50 £2.50 £3.50 (£289.90) Trio Not won; £161.80 to Kempton 5/5/97 OWNER Mr Eric Scarth (RICHMOND) BRED M. H. Wrigley

LONG HANDICAP Jarrow 9-4 Silver Pearl 9-5 Marsh's Law 9-5 Marzocco 9-2 Nordisk Legend 9-2

IN-FOCUS: **Unusually the best ground, even though the going was soft, appeared to be up the centre and the far rail for once looked to be a disadvantage.**

Silver Pearl, who has been lightly raced for a long time now, mainly due to knee problems, showed a very poor action going down. Despite being 9lb out of the handicap, there looked to be no fluke about this. (33/1)

570 Brodessa appreciated the drop back in distance, and gave his jockey a good ride. (8/1: 5/1-9/1)

613 Rossel (USA), dropped 5lb, was under pressure some way from home but never gave up trying. (11/1)

553 Philmist took it up on the bridle but, under pressure, did not find as much as expected. (7/1)

613 Lord Hastie (USA), who looked very lean, tried to close once in line for home but, even with conditions in his favour, was never doing anything like enough. (7/4)

The Boozing Brief (USA) (14/1: 10/1-16/1)

951 SPECTRUM GOLD INTERNATIONAL BUSINESS & LEISURE CLUB (QUALIFIER) H'CAP (0-70) (4-Y.O+) (Class E)

2-50 (2-52) **1m 65y** £3,647.50 (£1,105.00: £540.00: £257.50) Stalls: High GOING: 0.38 sec per fur (GS)

				SP	RR	SF
	Stormless (53) (PMonteith) **6-8-7**$^{(5)}$ JBramhill(12) (bit bkwd: mid div: hdwy over 3f out: led over 1f out: drvn out)	—	**1**	9/1	65	49
578^{7}	**Broughton's Pride (IRE) (53)** (JLEyre) **6-8-12** MGallagher(9) (hdwy over 3f out: chsd wnr fnl f: no imp)	3½	**2**	10/1	58	42
689^{7}	**Nobby Barnes (37)** (DonEnricoIncisa) **8-7-10** KimTinkler(7) (bhd: hdwy over 3f out: one pce fnl 2f)	4	**3**	25/1	35	19
608^{11}	**Hutchies Lady (37)** (RMMcKellar) **5-7-3**$^{(7)}$ JennyBenson(2) (b.hind: sn wl bhd: gd hdwy 2f out: nt clr run jst ins fnl f: styd on)	2	**4**	16/1	31	15
521^{16}	**Chairmans Choice (61)** (APJarvis) **7-9-6** WJO'Connor(8) (lw: a.p: rdn & edgd lft over 1f out: kpt on one pce)	½	**5**	9/1	54	38
721^{13}	**Tibbi Blues (42)** (JSGoldie) **10-7-10**$^{(5)}$ PFessey(3) (bhd: hdwy on outside over 3f out: hung rt: nvr nr ldrs)	s.h	**6**	16/1	35	19
827^{11}	**Mister Westsound (55)** (MissLAPerratt) **5-9-0b** JCarroll(5) (bhd: hdwy over 3f out: edgd rt over 1f out: sn wknd)	5	**7**	12/1	38	22
721^{11}	**Western Venture (IRE) (37)** (RMMcKellar) **4-7-3**$^{(7)}$ JMcAuley(14) (b: hdwy u.p over 2f out: sn rdn & no imp)	hd	**8**	33/1	20	4
749^{3}	**Best of All (IRE) (62)** (JBerry) **5-9-7b** JFortune(10) (trckd ldrs: led over 2f out tl hdd & wknd over 1f out)	1¼	**9**	$7/2^{1}$	42	26
895^{8}	**Three Arch Bridge (65)** (MJohnston) **5-9-10b** DeanMcKeown(1) (lw: bhd: sme hdwy on outside 3f out: n.d)	4	**10**	$6/1^{3}$	38	22
585^{19}	**Magic Melody (47)** (JLSpearing) **4-8-6** SDrowne(16) (trckd ldrs tl lost pl over 1f out)	1¾	**11**	25/1	16	—
	Bowcliffe (44) (EJAlston) **6-8-3** LCharnock(6) (prom tl lost pl over 3f out)	4	**12**	10/1	6	—
	I'm a Nut Man (40) (CASmith) **6-7-8**$^{(5)}$ IonaWands(13) (bit bkwd: b: mid div: hdwy u.p over 3f out: sn wknd)	2½	**13**	10/1	—	—
668^{11}	**Ragtime Cowgirl (37)** (DANolan) **4-7-10** NVarley(11) (led tl over 2f out: wknd qckly)	1	**14**	25/1	—	—
*860**	**Theatre Magic (50)** (DShaw) **4-8-9** JFanning(4) (lw: b: prom: rdn & ev ch over 2f out: wknd qckly)	hd	**15**	$11/2^{2}$	5	—
495^{7}	**Nordic Gift (DEN) (37)** (MrsDThomson) **4-7-10** NKennedy(15) (swtg: chsd ldrs tl lost pl 4f out: t.o)	27	**16**	50/1	—	—
				(SP 135.1%)	**16 Rn**	

1m 52.2 (8.10) CSF £92.29 CT £2,043.22 TOTE £14.40: £3.80 £2.60 £2.40 £2.80 (£107.70) Trio £299.50 OWNER Mr D. St Clair (ROSEWELL) BRED D. V. St Clair

LONG HANDICAP Western Venture (IRE) 7-8 Hutchies Lady 7-5 Ragtime Cowgirl 7-7 Nobby Barnes 7-5 Nordic Gift (DEN) 7-8

Stormless, despite running over a trip short of his best and looking in need of the outing beforehand, scored in decisive fashion. (9/1)

428 Broughton's Pride (IRE) stayed this trip alright on this ground, but was never doing enough to trouble the winner. (10/1)

689 Nobby Barnes is on a losing run stretching back forty-nine races and almost three years. (25/1)

Hutchies Lady was just about last of all two furlongs from home. Coming between horses, she met trouble and, in the circumstances, did well to finish so close. Her only previous win was at 33-1 in this race last year. (16/1)

Chairmans Choice came off a true line under pressure and, along with Mister Westsound, managed to get in the way of Hutchies Lady. (9/1)

Tibbi Blues would have been even more closely involved but for giving her rider problems. (16/1)

Mister Westsound (12/1: op 8/1)

749 Best of All (IRE) took it up full of running but, when collared over a furlong out, found nothing at all. (7/2: op 6/1)

571 Three Arch Bridge (6/1: op 4/1)

952 LETHEBY AND CHRISTOPHER NEW FAMOUS FOODS CLAIMING STKS (3-Y.O) (Class F)

3-20 (3-21) **1m 1f 36y** £2,736.00 (£828.00: £404.00: £192.00) Stalls: High GOING: 0.38 sec per fur (GS)

				SP	RR	SF
793*	**Going For Broke (68)** (PCHaslam) **3-9-4** JFortune(5) (lw: dwlt: jnd ldr 9f out: led 3f out: hrd rdn & edgd lft fnl f: jst hld on)	—	1	4/5[1]	72	—
791[6]	**Laguna Bay (IRE) (68)** (APJarvis) **3-8-8** WJO'Connor(3) (led to 3f out: rallied & edgd rt ins fnl f: jst failed)	s.h	2	7/4[2]	62	—
784[10]	**Sweet Note (IRE)** (MissLAPerratt) **3-7-9**[(5)] PFessey(7) (lw: unruly s: hld up: effrt over 3f out: ev ch over 1f out: wandered & nt qckn ins fnl f)	2	3	20/1	50	—
556[6]	**Broadgate Flyer (IRE) (60)** (MrsLStubbs) **3-8-7** ACulhane(6) (hld up: effrt 4f out: ev ch tl outpcd fnl 2f)	5	4	13/2[3]	49	—
793[9]	**Willskip (USA) (40)** (JBerry) **3-7-13b**[1(7)ow3] CLowther(4) (lw: sn trckng ldr: chal over 3f out: wknd over 2f out)	7	5	25/1	36	—
				(SP 113.9%)	**5 Rn**	

2m 12.2 (17.90) CSF £2.35 TOTE £1.70: £1.30 £1.40 (£1.50) OWNER Dunnington & Smart (MIDDLEHAM) BRED Mrs John Trotter

793* Going For Broke, who had a bit to do on official figures, proved most willing. Edging left away from the far-side rail, he possibly ended up on just the better ground and, at the line, there was not an ounce to spare. (4/5: evens-11/10)

791 Laguna Bay (IRE) would have been meeting the winner on 10lb worse terms in a handicap. Despite coming off a true line, she rallied inside the last and only just failed to get there. (7/4: 11/10-2/1)

551 Sweet Note (IRE), who gave trouble at the start, ran easily her best race so far. (20/1)

556 Broadgate Flyer (IRE) ran better after three poor efforts. (13/2)

953 GUINNESS 'PERFECT PINT' H'CAP (0-90) (3-Y.O+) (Class C)

3-55 (3-55) **6f 5y** £7,197.50 (£2,180.00: £1,065.00: £507.50) Stalls: High GOING: 0.38 sec per fur (GS)

				SP	RR	SF
734[2]	**Foist (59)** (MWEasterby) **5-7-11** LCharnock(5) (hld up gng wl: shkn up over 2f out: led over 1f out: sn clr: easily)	—	1	7/4[1]	74+	29
824[12]	**Naissant (64)** (RMMcKellar) **4-7-9**[(7)] KSked(9) (led tl over 2f out: kpt on: no ch w wnr)	7	2	12/1	60	15
	Albert The Bear (78) (JBerry) **4-9-2** JFortune(8) (a chsng ldrs: drvn along ½-wy: styd on fnl f)	1¼	3	8/1	71	26
731[9]	**Garnock Valley (77)** (JBerry) **7-9-1b** SWebster(13) (lw: trckd ldrs: effrt over 2f out: kpt on wl towards fin)	s.h	4	9/2[2]	70	25
596[10]	**Lago Di Varano (87)** (RMWhitaker) **5-9-11** DeanMcKeown(10) (hdwy ½-wy: n.m.r over 1f out: kpt on wl)	s.h	5	10/1	80	35
610[13]	**Bold Street (IRE) (60)** (GMMoore) **7-7-12b** NCarlisle(3) (swtchd rt s: sme hdwy 2f out: n.d)	nk	6	20/1	52	7
883[16]	**Divine Miss-P (69)** (APJarvis) **4-8-7** WJO'Connor(2) (trckd ldr stands' side: kpt on fnl 2f: n.d)	½	7	14/1	60	15
	Biff-Em (IRE) (78) (MissLAPerratt) **3-8-6** ACulhane(14) (bhd: sme hdwy 2f out: nvr nr to chal)	½	8	16/1	67	12
529[5]	**Don't Care (IRE) (75)** (MissLAPerratt) **6-8-13** OUrbina(12) (outpcd after 2f: n.d)	½	9	7/1[3]	63	18
596[18]	**Mr Oscar (87)** (WMcKeown) **5-9-6**[(5)] PFessey(11) (cl up: led over 2f out tl over 1f out: sn wknd)	1	10	66/1	72	27
892[23]	**Tiler (IRE) (79)** (MJohnston) **5-9-3** JFanning(7) (lw: outpcd & rdn ½-wy: n.d)	2½	11	8/1	58	13
834[15]	**Splicing (68)** (WJHaggas) **4-8-6** JCarroll(1) (lw: led stands' side over 3f: wknd & eased)	10	12	11/1	20	—
924[10]	**Take Notice (58)** (RMMcKellar) **4-7-10** NVarley(4) (sn outpcd & bhd: edgd lft ½-wy)	3	13	66/1	2	—
				(SP 134.7%)	**13 Rn**	

1m 16.0 (6.00) CSF £26.99 CT £142.36 TOTE £2.60: £1.40 £3.20 £2.40 (£23.00) Trio £208.70 OWNER Mr D. F. Spence (SHERIFF HUTTON) BRED W. Cormack

LONG HANDICAP Take Notice 7-4

WEIGHT FOR AGE 3yo-10lb

734 Foist, happier on this easier ground, turned this race into a procession. The Handicapper will not forgive him for this performance. (7/4)

Naissant ran easily her best race this year after three poor efforts previously. (12/1)

Albert The Bear stuck on after being under pressure halfway. He is possibly better back over seven. (8/1)

731 Garnock Valley, who is well handicapped now, was sticking on in encouraging fashion at the line. (9/2)

Lago Di Varano, with the headgear again left off, did not enjoy the best of luck in running. It looks as though he is on the way back. (10/1)

786 Tiler (IRE) (8/1: op 9/2)

Splicing (11/1: 5/1-12/1)

71 - 69+

954 LINN MOTOR GROUP E.B.F. MAIDEN STKS (2-Y.O) (Class D)

4-30 (4-30) **5f 4y** £3,160.00 (£955.00: £465.00: £220.00) Stalls: High GOING: 0.38 sec per fur (GS)

				SP	RR	SF
844[5]	**Golden Mirage (IRE)** (MRChannon) **2-8-4**[(5)] PPMurphy(2) (led over 3f out: hrd rdn & edgd lft ins fnl f: kpt on)	—	1	12/1	76	25
594[6]	**Five of Spades (IRE)** (DNicholls) **2-9-0** AlexGreaves(5) (lw: trckd ldrs: effrt over 1f out: hung rt: kpt on wl)	2	2	13/2	75	24
	Llanasa (JBerry) **2-8-9** JFortune(6) (leggy: unf: sn chsng ldrs: shkn up over 1f out: kpt on wl)	1½	3	7/1	65	14
594[2]	**Happy Days** (DMoffatt) **2-8-11**[(3)] DarrenMoffatt(7) (sn outpcd: hdwy over 1f out: styd on wl towards fin)	1	4	7/4[1]	67	16
	Lochdene (IRE) (MJohnston) **2-9-0** DeanMcKeown(4) (w'like: scope: led over 1f: sn drvn along: outpcd appr fnl f)	s.h	5	7/2[2]	67	16
697[6]	**Winsome George** (CWFairhurst) **2-9-0** NKennedy(8) (sn outpcd & drvn along: hdwy over 1f out: nvr nr to chal)	2	6	5/1[3]	60	9
648[8]	**Dorton Grange** (JLSpearing) **2-8-2**[(7)] JBosley(1) (lw: chsd ldrs tl wknd over 1f out)	2½	7	20/1	47	—
	Solo Song (DANolan) **2-8-9** NVarley(3) (leggy: unf: s.s: sme hdwy u.p ½-wy: sn lost pl)	10	8	50/1	15	—
				(SP 115.5%)	**8 Rn**	

64.2 secs (5.90) CSF £79.81 TOTE £7.40: £2.10 £2.30 £2.80 (£9.50) OWNER Mr Stephen Crown (UPPER LAMBOURN) BRED Gainsborough Stud Management Ltd

844 Golden Mirage (IRE), who looked very fit, showed a poor action going down. After losing her chance at the start first time, she was again not the best away, but was in front after only a furlong or so. Hard-ridden, she stayed on grimly. (12/1: op 5/1)

594 Five of Spades (IRE), who is not the best of movers, appreciated the soft ground. Travelling strongly on the heels of the leaders when called on for an effort, he tended to hang in behind. (13/2)

Llanasa, who does not have the best of actions, ran a highly satisfactory first race. (7/1: op 3/1)

594 Happy Days, taken off his legs throughout, was putting in some solid work at the finish and, stoutly bred, needs at least six. (7/4)

Lochdene (IRE), a well-made sort, has a round action. He tired in the closing stages and should improve a fair bit for the outing. (7/2)

697 Winsome George had trouble coming down the hill. Staying on at the finish, he already needs at least six. (5/1: 7/1-4/1)

955 LETHEBY AND CHRISTOPHER EVENT CATERING SPECIALISTS H'CAP (0-80) (3-Y.O+) (Class D)

5-00 (5-01) **1m 3f 16y** £5,249.50 (£1,591.00: £778.00: £371.50) Stalls: High GOING: 0.38 sec per fur (GS)

				SP	RR	SF
781^{7}	**Manful (72)** (MissLAPerratt) **5-9-13b** NKennedy(15) (hld up & bhd: hdwy 7f out: styd on u.p fnl 3f: led towards fin: all out)	—	**1**	$6/1^{2}$	82	37
781^{5}	**Summerhill Special (IRE) (60)** (DWBarker) **6-9-1** TWilliams(4) (trckd ldrs: led over 3f out tl nr fin)	s.h	**2**	$8/1^{3}$	70	25
762^{5}	**Moonraking (52)** (TJEtherington) **4-8-2**(5)ow4 GParkin(14) (s.i.s: gd hdwy over 4f out: edgd lft & kpt on one pce fnl 2f)	7	**3**	14/1	52	3
647^{8}	**Nigel's Lad (IRE) (70)** (PCHaslam) **5-9-11** JFortune(8) (trckd ldrs: chal 4f out: wknd over 1f out)	½	**4**	$5/1^{1}$	69	24
858^{U}	**Barbara's Jewel (44)** (ABailey) **5-7-13** DWright(7) (led after 1f tl over 3f out: wknd fnl f)	½	**5**	10/1	42	—
669^{7}	**Lord Advocate (43)** (DANolan) **9-7-12b** NVarley(12) (prom: sn pushed along: edgd lft & lost pl over 2f out)	10	**6**	$8/1^{3}$	27	—
	Opulent (73) (MrsMReveley) **6-10-0** ACulhane(2) (hld up: hdwy over 3f out: wknd 2f out: eased)	10	**7**	10/1	43	—
689^{9}	**Shamokin (42)** (FWatson) **5-7-6**(5)ow1 PFessey(1) (hld up: effrt over 4f out: sn lost pl)	4	**8**	33/1	6	—
843*	**Ten Past Six (59)** (MartynWane) **5-9-0** JCarroll(5) (lw: led 1f: chsd ldrs: hung rt & wknd 2f out: eased)	3	**9**	$6/1^{2}$	18	—
595^{7}	**Slapy Dam (47)** (CASmith) **5-7-11**(5) IonaWands(9) (lw: hld up: gd hdwy over 4f out: sn chsng ldrs: wknd 3f out)	4	**10**	$5/1^{1}$	1	—
552^{5}	**Rapid Mover (43)** (DANolan) **10-7-9b**(3)ow2 DarrenMoffatt(3) (chsd ldrs tl wknd over 2f out)	3½	**11**	66/1	—	—
613^{15}	**Cois Na Farraige (IRE) (65)** (MissLAPerratt) **4-9-6** OUrbina(10) (bhd & drvn along 4f out: n.d)	1¼	**12**	25/1	12	—
669^{3}	**Breydon (46)** (PMonteith) **4-7-10**(5) JBramhill(13) (lw: hld up: sme hdwy 4f out: sn lost pl: virtually p.u)	11	**13**	10/1	—	—
	Fanadiyr (IRE) (49) (JSGoldie) **5-8-4** DeanMcKeown(11) (lost pl 7f out: sn wl bhd)	5	**14**	12/1	—	—

(SP 134.0%) **14 Rn**

2m 33.9 (14.50) CSF £54.00 CT £620.56 TOTE £10.20: £3.10 £5.70 £3.10 (£46.40) Trio £54.40 OWNER Mr C. D. Barber-Lomax (AYR) BRED John Rose

LONG HANDICAP Shamokin 6-13 Rapid Mover 6-11

552* Manful likes it here and is also at his best with some give underfoot. After a dour battle, he forced his head in front near the line. (6/1)

781 Summerhill Special (IRE) had one of her going days. Relishing the underfoot conditions, she gave her all but was just worn down. (8/1)

762 Moonraking made it hard work by missing the break slightly. He is willing but painfully one-paced, and is high enough in the handicap for what he has achieved. (14/1)

647 Nigel's Lad (IRE) called it a day with over a furlong left to run. (5/1)

589 Barbara's Jewel, who had cut little ice since winning at Wolverhampton's All-Weather track in March, ran much better here. (10/1: op 16/1)

595 Slapy Dam, who ought to have been suited by the mud, moved up looking a danger early in the straight, but dropped right out with three furlongs left to run. (5/1)

956 'TWO PART POUR' LIMITED STKS (0-55) (4-Y.O+) (Class F)

5-30 (5-32) **5f 4y** £2,850.00 (£800.00: £390.00) Stalls: High GOING: 0.38 sec per fur (GS)

				SP	RR	SF
666^{5}	**Leading Princess (IRE) (47)** (MissLAPerratt) **6-8-9b** OUrbina(1) (chsd ldrs: styd on to ld last 75y)	—	**1**	16/1	54	40
883^{3}	**Corniche Quest (IRE) (54)** (MRChannon) **4-8-4**(5) PPMurphy(11) (hld up: hdwy 2f out: hrd rdn & styd on fnl f)	1½	**2**	$4/1^{1}$	49	35
905^{10}	**Lord Sky (50)** (ABailey) **6-9-1**(3) OPears(2) (led: clr & hung rt ½-wy: hdd wl ins fnl f)	½	**3**	10/1	57	43
896^{2}	**Double Oscar (IRE) (56)** (DNicholls) **4-9-1b** AlexGreaves(6) (lw: hld up: hdwy stands' side 2f out: r.o same pce fnl f)	¾	**4**	$6/1^{3}$	51	37
779^{2}	**Millesime (IRE) (55)** (MartynWane) **5-8-12** JCarroll(4) (lw: hld up: effrt u.p 2f out: nvr rchd ldrs)	4	**5**	7/1	36	22
856^{6}	**Silk Cottage (52)** (RMWhitaker) **5-9-1** DeanMcKeown(3) (racd alone stands' side: sn pushed along: kpt on fnl 2f: nvr nr to chal)	1¼	**6**	16/1	35	21
464^{5}	**Present 'n Correct (49)** (CBBBooth) **4-8-12** KHodgson(16) (lw: unruly s: racd far side: chsd ldrs over 3f: grad wknd)	hd	**7**	10/1	31	17
827^{8}	**Needle Match (52)** (JJO'Neill) **4-9-4** JFortune(8) (sltly hmpd s: bhd tl hdwy over 2f out: edgd lft: nvr rchd ldrs)	½	**8**	13/2	36	22
924*	**Southern Dominion (38)** (MissJFCraze) **5-9-1** 3x SWebster(13) (lw: racd far side: outpcd fr ½-wy)	nk	**9**	10/1	32	18
	King of Show (IRE) (54) (RAllan) **6-8-12v** ACulhane(7) (sltly hmpd s: bhd & pushed along: n.d)	nk	**10**	9/1	28	14
243^{11}	**Mu-Arrik (30)** (GROldroyd) **9-8-5v**(7) RFarmer(12) (sn drvn along: in tch tl outpcd fr ½-wy)	½	**11**	50/1	26	12
779^{11}	**Boffy (IRE) (43)** (BPJBaugh) **4-8-7b**(5) PRoberts(9) (in tch to ½-wy: sn wknd)	4	**12**	33/1	13	—
929^{7}	**True Ballad (49)** (JSGoldie) **5-8-7**(5) PFessey(15) (chsd ldrs tl lost pl ½-wy: sn bhd)	8	**13**	14/1	—	—
	Forzara (50) (JLSpearing) **4-8-9** SDrowne(10) (chsd ldrs tl lost pl 2f out)	½	**14**	$11/2^{2}$	—	—
779^{13}	**Aquado (54)** (DShaw) **8-8-12b** JFanning(14) (virtually ref to r: a t.o last)	15	**15**	16/1	—	—

(SP 142.0%) **15 Rn**

63.3 secs (5.00) CSF £83.91 TOTE £25.70: £4.20 £1.80 £3.70 (£29.70) Trio £141.70 OWNER Mrs Ruth Wyllie (AYR) BRED Woodford Stud

666 Leading Princess (IRE) made it third time lucky, racing on what was almost certainly the better ground up the middle. (16/1)

883 Corniche Quest (IRE) lacked nothing in assistance from the saddle. Hard as she tried, she could not close the gap and is better over six. (4/1)

488* Lord Sky, who is over a stone better on the All-Weather, showed in a clear lead at halfway. Hanging right, he ended up on the worse ground on the far side, and was run out of it in the closing stages. (10/1)

896 Double Oscar (IRE), in no hurry to join issue, made ground towards the stands' side soon after halfway, but could find no more in the final furlong. (6/1)

856 Silk Cottage raced on the stands' side and was alone to past halfway. (16/1)

610 Needle Match (13/2: 10/1-6/1)

Aquado, not for the first time, virtually refused to race. (16/1)

T/Plpt: £556.40 (23.18 Tckts). T/Qdpt: £34.20 (20.33 Tckts) WG

0937-NEWMARKET (R-H) (Good)

Sunday May 4th

WEATHER: unsettled, sunny periods WIND: fresh across

957 BT RACEPAGER CONDITIONS STKS (3-Y.O) (Class C)

2-00 (2-00) **7f** **(Rowley)** £5,040.80 (£1,887.20: £923.60: £398.00: £179.00: £91.40) Stalls: Centre GOING minus 0.26 sec per fur (GF)

				SP	RR	SF
	Swiss Law (SbinSuroor) **3-8-12** LDettori(3) (lw: mde most: qcknd 2f out: hld on wl)	—	**1**	$7/2^{2}$	102	57

				SP	RR	SF
747[2]	**Intikhab (USA) (109)** (DMorley) **3-9-6** RHills(6) (w wnr: effrt over 2f out: nt qckn towards fin)	½	**2**	6/4[1]	109	64
	Showboat (BWHills) **3-9-1** MHills(1) (lw: dwlt: hld up: effrt over 2f out: styd on: nvr able chal)	3	**3**	15/2[3]	97	52
673[3]	**Sugarfoot** (NTinkler) **3-9-1** KDarley(4) (w ldrs: outpcd over 2f out: sn btn)	3	**4**	25/1	90	45
693[2]	**Midyan Call** (MBell) **3-8-12** MRoberts(5) (lw: hld up: effrt 3f out: sn btn)	½	**5**	7/2[2]	86	41
	Sambac (USA) (102) (HRACecil) **3-9-5** KFallon(2) (trckd ldrs tl outpcd fnl 2½f)	4	**6**	10/1	84	39

(SP 109.1%) **6 Rn**

1m 26.0 (1.50) CSF £7.87 TOTE £3.70: £1.80 £1.50 (£3.10) OWNER Godolphin (NEWMARKET) BRED J. M. Greetham
Swiss Law, looking particularly well, won this nicely quickening from the front, and showed a good attitude under pressure. (7/2: 5/2-4/1)
747 Intikhab (USA) has not the best of actions, but he does go on fast ground and had every chance throughout here. His penalties just made the difference. (6/4)
Showboat looked in good condition but left the impression that he would be all the better for this and, also, longer trips should suit. (15/2: 4/1-8/1)
673 Sugarfoot is looking and running quite well, but seems to be flying a bit high at the moment. (25/1)
693 Midyan Call looked a picture but proved disappointing, never really firing at the business end, and was not over-punished. (7/2)
Sambac (USA) got herself in a state beforehand and ran no sort of race. (10/1: op 4/1)

958 MAIL ON SUNDAY MILE (QUALIFIER) H'CAP (0-90) (3-Y.O) (Class C)

2-30 (2-31) **1m (Rowley)** £14,915.00 (£4,520.00: £2,210.00: £1,055.00) Stalls: Centre GOING minus 0.26 sec per fur (GF)

				SP	RR	SF
688[8]	**Brave Kris (IRE) (80)** (LMCumani) **3-8-11** LDettori(2) (hld up: smooth hdwy to ld over 1f out: rdn & r.o)	—	**1**	8/1[3]	98	55
790*	**Supply And Demand (84)** (GLMoore) **3-9-1** KFallon(7) (bhd: hdwy 3f out: chsng ldrs over 1f out: styd on wl)	1	**2**	8/1[3]	100	57
742[9]	**Abajany (65)** (MRChannon) **3-7-10** JQuinn(15) (lw: cl up: led 3f out tl over 1f out: wknd ins fnl f)	2½	**3**	16/1	76	33
690[6]	**Mantles Prince (79)** (GLewis) **3-8-10** PatEddery(6) (lw: stumbled s: sn chsng ldrs: effrt over 2f out: nt qckn appr fnl f)	3	**4**	7/1[2]	84	41
723[U]	**Maylane (90)** (ACStewart) **3-9-7** MRoberts(12) (rel to r: sn t.o: gd hdwy & prom ½-wy: eased whn btn appr fnl f)	3½	**5**	9/1	88	45
688*	**Future Perfect (85)** (PFICole) **3-9-2** TQuinn(13) (lw: hdwy over 3f out: sn rdn: btn 2f out)	nk	**6**	3/1[1]	82	39
764[3]	**Imperial Or Metric (IRE) (70)** (RAFahey) **3-8-1**ow1 JFEgan(10) (w ldrs: rdn over 2f out: wknd wl over 1f out)	2	**7**	16/1	63	19
654[12]	**Last Chance (70)** (DJSCosgrove) **3-8-1** GCarter(1) (led tl hdd & wknd 3f out)	s.h	**8**	33/1	63	20
	Nawasib (IRE) (84) (JLDunlop) **3-9-1** KDarley(4) (lt-f: unf: bhd: effrt over 3f out: n.d)	nk	**9**	11/1	77	34
	Caribbean Star (78) (MRStoute) **3-8-9** JReid(11) (lw: trckd ldrs: effrt 3f out: wknd fnl 2f)	hd	**10**	10/1	71	28
675[13]	**Share Delight (IRE) (81)** (BWHills) **3-8-12** MHills(14) (lw: hld up: effrt over 3f out: rdn & rspnse)	2	**11**	11/1	70	27
597[7]	**Millroy (USA) (82)** (PAKelleway) **3-8-13v** MJKinane(8) (outpcd & bhd fr ½-wy)	1¾	**12**	25/1	67	24
723[12]	**Golden Fact (USA) (80)** (RHannon) **3-8-11** GBardwell(9) (sn outpcd & a bhd)	½	**13**	33/1	64	21
675[18]	**Passiflora (76)** (JLDunlop) **3-8-7** RHills(5) (prom 5f: wknd)	½	**14**	25/1	59	16
	Solfegietto (80) (MBell) **3-8-11** OPeslier(3) (chsd ldrs 5f: sn wknd)	5	**15**	16/1	53	10

(SP 126.7%) **15 Rn**

1m 39.15 (1.85) CSF £64.84 CT £948.94 TOTE £7.20: £1.90 £3.20 £4.40 (£51.20) Trio £721.40 OWNER Mr Robert Smith (NEWMARKET) BRED Clare Dore Ltd
LONG HANDICAP Abajany 7-7
688 Brave Kris (IRE), an edgy filly, was a real handful in the paddock and took a strong hold in the race but, particularly well handled, she scored convincingly. (8/1)
790* Supply And Demand finished to some purpose here, suggesting that longer trips will see plenty of improvement. (8/1)
742 Abajany has shown he stays further than this, and was made plenty of use of here, only to be tapped for speed late on. From his draw this was not a bad effort. (16/1)
690 Mantles Prince, dropping back in trip, was done for speed in the last couple of furlongs. (7/1: 5/1-15/2)
Maylane needed two handlers in the paddock and was reluctant to jump off, but he then ran an incredible race and, if his head can be sorted out, he would be very useful. (9/1)
688* Future Perfect was disappointing this time, always struggling to get anywhere near and, although he won on fast ground at Pontefract previously, his action suggests that some give should suit. (3/1)
764 Imperial Or Metric (IRE) looked and ran quite well, but was tapped for speed in the last couple of furlongs. (16/1)
Nawasib (IRE) (11/1: 8/1-12/1)
Caribbean Star, a handful in the paddock, went freely to post and raced in similar fashion. (10/1)

959 R.L. DAVISON PRETTY POLLY STKS (Listed) (3-Y.O F) (Class A)

3-05 (3-05) **1m 2f (Rowley)** £12,428.00 (£4,652.00: £2,276.00: £980.00: £440.00: £224.00) Stalls: Low GOING minus 0.26 sec per fur (GF)

				SP	RR	SF
	Siyadah (USA) (SbinSuroor) **3-8-8** LDettori(1) (cl up: slt ld ins fnl f: styd on wl)	—	**1**	100/30[1]	101	68
724[10]	**Attitre (FR) (95)** (CEBrittain) **3-8-8** MRoberts(4) (led tl hdd jst ins fnl f: rallied)	¾	**2**	10/1	100	67
688[4]	**Vagabond Chanteuse (80)** (TJEtherington) **3-8-8** TQuinn(6) (lw: chsd ldrs: chal over 2f out: sn rdn: nt qckn towards fin)	s.h	**3**	33/1	100	67
	Crown of Light (MRStoute) **3-8-8** MJKinane(5) (plld hrd: bhd: effrt over 3f out: styd on: nvr able chal)	5	**4**	7/2[2]	92	59
	Mrs Miniver (USA) (100) (PAKelleway) **3-8-8** PatEddery(3) (in tch: rdn 4f out: sn chsng ldrs: wknd fnl 2½f)	7	**5**	15/2	81	48
724[5]	**Supercal (98)** (DRCElsworth) **3-8-8** RCochrane(7) (lw: hld up: effrt u.p over 3f out: sn btn)	3	**6**	4/1[3]	76	43
	Boojum (104) (BWHills) **3-8-13** MHills(9) (w'like: in tch: effrt over 3f out: sn btn)	6	**7**	6/1	71	38
853[11]	**Rich In Love (IRE) (97)** (CACyzer) **3-8-8** DBiggs(8) (w ldr tl wknd 3f out)	17	**8**	25/1	39	6
741[7]	**Raindancing (IRE) (92)** (RHannon) **3-8-9b**[1]ow1 OPeslier(2) (nvr gng wl: t.o fnl 3f)	dist	**9**	16/1	—	—

(SP 113.1%) **9 Rn**

2m 5.15 (0.45) CSF £32.88 TOTE £4.10: £1.60 £3.20 £5.00 (£25.10) Trio £176.30 OWNER Mr Hamdan Al Maktoum (NEWMARKET) BRED Shadwell Farm Inc
Siyadah (USA) appreciated this step-up in trip and showed fine determination under pressure, and looks to have improved a fair bit. (100/30)
Attitre (FR) settled better when in front this time and, certainly happier at this trip, kept fighting back when looking beaten. (10/1)
688 Vagabond Chanteuse, trying her longest trip to date, put up a tremendous performance and looks to be seriously getting her act together. (33/1)
Crown of Light spoiled her chances by going too freely to post and then pulling hard during the race, and did not give her true running. (7/2)
Mrs Miniver (USA) was off the bit a long way out, and had never looked good enough to make any impression. (15/2)
724 Supercal moved well but ran poorly, and probably did not stay. (4/1)
Boojum got a shade warm beforehand and ran no sort of race. (6/1: op 7/2)
507 Raindancing (IRE) was tried in blinkers and did not like them at all. (16/1)

960 PERTEMPS 1000 GUINEAS STKS (Gp 1) (3-Y.O F) (Class A)

3-45 (3-47) **1m (Rowley)** £104,730.00 (£38,670.00: £18,485.00: £7,475.00: £2,887.50: £1,052.50) Stalls: Low GOING minus 0.26 sec per fur (GF)

				SP	RR	SF
724^{4}	**Sleepytime (IRE) (111)** (HRACecil) **3-9-0** KFallon(3) (hld up & bhd: hdwy 3f out: qckdn to ld jst ins fnl f: r.o wl)	—	**1**	$5/1^{3}$	125	73
672^{2}	**Oh Nellie (USA)** (NACallaghan) **3-9-0** WRyan(11) (led tl hdd jst ins fnl f: kpt on same pce)	4	**2**	50/1	117	65
	Dazzle (110) (MRStoute) **3-9-0** JReid(2) (lw: hld up: hdwy over 3f out: chal over 1f out: no ex ins fnl f)	¾	**3**	16/1	116	64
718a*	**Pas De Reponse (USA)** (MmeCHead,France) **3-9-0** FHead(8) (plld hrd: trckd ldrs: chal 2f out: rdn & no ex appr fnl f)	hd	**4**	$5/2^{1}$	115	63
	Ocean Ridge (USA) (SbinSuroor) **3-9-0** TJarnet(9) (lw: effrt over 3f out: styd on wl: nrst fin)	¾	**5**	25/1	114	62
	Reams of Verse (USA) (114) (HRACecil) **3-9-0** PatEddery(14) (lw: in tch: effrt 3f out: r.o one pce)	1½	**6**	11/1	111	59
672^{3}	**Elegant Warning (IRE) (110)** (BWHills) **3-9-0** DHolland(13) (lw: b.nr hind: dwlt: bhd tl gd hdwy 3f out: rdn & no imp fnl 2f)	½	**7**	50/1	110	58
	Khassah (JHMGosden) **3-9-0** RHills(5) (h.d.w: hld up: hdwy 3f out: sn chsng ldrs: wknd wl over 1f out)	1¾	**8**	20/1	106	54
	Sarayir (USA) (MajorWRHern) **3-9-0** MRoberts(1) (h.d.w: chsd ldrs: outpcd over 3f out: wknd fnl 2f)	4	**9**	20/1	98	46
	Moonlight Paradise (USA) (SbinSuroor) **3-9-0** LDettori(4) (lw: prom: effrt over 2f out: wknd over 1f out)	½	**10**	$7/2^{2}$	97	45
724^{6}	**Bianca Nera (110)** (DRLoder) **3-9-0** KDarley(7) (chsd ldrs tl rdn & wknd fnl 3f)	1	**11**	50/1	95	43
724*	**Dance Parade (USA) (109)** (PFICole) **3-9-0** TQuinn(6) (drvn along ½-wy: nvr trbld ldrs)	3½	**12**	18/1	88	36
681*	**Rebecca Sharp** (GWragg) **3-9-0** MHills(10) (outpcd ½-wy: sn bhd)	nk	**13**	16/1	88	36
	Yashmak (USA) (HRACecil) **3-9-0** MJKinane(15) (outpcd & lost tch fr ½-wy)	3½	**14**	14/1	81	29
672*	**Reunion (IRE) (112)** (JWHills) **3-9-0** OPeslier(12) (s.i.s: rdn ½-wy: sn btn)	14	**15**	16/1	53	1

(SP 124.6%) **15 Rn**

1m 37.66 (0.36) CSF £236.74 TOTE £6.80: £2.70 £9.20 £4.20 (£550.00) Trio £579.30 OWNER Greenbay Stables Ltd (NEWMARKET) BRED C. H. Wacker III

724 Sleepytime (IRE), given a cracking ride, settled well and quickened impressively to win going right away. She is certainly a type who is suited by galloping tracks, and another couple of furlongs may well be her limit. (5/1)
672 Oh Nellie (USA) ran a storming race out in front and kept battling on, but was made to look ordinary by the very useful winner. Her turn will come. (50/1)
Dazzle, taken to post last, behaved herself well and put up a sound performance but her limitations were exposed late on. (16/1)
718a* Pas De Reponse (USA) went too freely for her own good, and failed to see out the trip because of this. (5/2)
Ocean Ridge (USA), who had stamina doubts, seemed to get the trip well and kept responding to pressure, but just lacked the speed to make it. Perhaps easier ground would help. (25/1)
Reams of Verse (USA) was always having to race on the unfavoured outside of the field, and was never going well enough to make a serious impression. She looks likely to be suited by further. (11/1)
672 Elegant Warning (IRE) has a good turn of foot and runs in the style of a sprinter. (50/1)
Khassah was one of the best-looking fillies in the race but her performance disappointed, as she dropped out in the last furlong-and-a-half. (20/1)
Sarayir (USA) looks on the lean side, and put up little fight when the race began in earnest. (20/1)
Moonlight Paradise (USA) always held a good-enough position, but proved disappointing when asked a question in the last three furlongs. (7/2)
724 Bianca Nera looked particularly fit but ran poorly. (50/1)
724* Dance Parade (USA) got mixed-up in some scrimmaging at halfway, but was not going well at the time. (18/1)
681* Rebecca Sharp got pretty warm beforehand and ran no sort of race. (16/1)
Yashmak (USA) never gave any signs of hope and probably needs much easier ground. (14/1: op 8/1)
672* Reunion (IRE) went very poorly to post and ran appallingly. (16/1)

961 INSTITUTE OF DIRECTORS/CHIFNEY RESTAURANT RATED STKS H'CAP (0-110) (4-Y.O+) (Class B)

4-20 (4-21) **6f (Rowley)** £7,241.04 (£2,709.36: £1,324.68: £569.40: £254.70: £128.82) Stalls: Centre GOING minus 0.26 sec per fur (GF)

				SP	RR	SF
677^{6}	**Cyrano's Lad (IRE) (98)** (CADwyer) **8-8-9** KFallon(3) (mde all: shkn up & r.o wl appr fnl f)	—	**1**	$5/2^{1}$	108	70
677^{4}	**How Long (98)** (LMCumani) **4-8-9** LDettori(1) (trckd ldrs: effrt 2f out: styd on one pce)	1¼	**2**	$11/4^{2}$	105	67
671^{4}	**Carranita (IRE) (106)** (BPalling) **7-9-3** PatEddery(6) (chsd ldrs: rdn 2f out: kpt on: nt pce to chal)	nk	**3**	$100/30^{3}$	112	74
677^{14}	**King of Peru (100)** (APJarvis) **4-8-11** DHolland(4) (chsd ldr: rdn ½-wy: r.o one pce)	1¾	**4**	14/1	101	63
942^{19}	**Hello Mister (96)** (TEPowell) **6-8-4**(3) PMcCabe(5) (bhd: effrt ½-wy: nvr rchd ldrs)	1¼	**5**	33/1	94	56
519^{4}	**Loch Patrick (100)** (MMadgwick) **7-8-11** JReid(7) (sn pushed along: hrd drvn ½-wy: n.d)	¾	**6**	11/2	96	58
	Daring Destiny (110) (KRBurke) **6-9-7b** TQuinn(2) (lw: in tch tl rdn & wknd 2f out: eased ins fnl f)	2½	**7**	8/1	99	61

(SP 114.4%) **7 Rn**

1m 11.92 (0.12) CSF £8.83 TOTE £4.00: £2.40 £1.90 (£4.50) OWNER Mr M. M. Foulger (NEWMARKET) BRED J. C. Condon
LONG HANDICAP Hello Mister 8-6

677 Cyrano's Lad (IRE) likes to dominate and really enjoyed himself here and, once he quickened two furlongs out, the race was his. (5/2)
677 How Long travelled well early on, but then failed to match the winner when the pressure was on, and is probably better over slightly further. (11/4)
671 Carranita (IRE) had her chances but could never quicken enough, and probably needs easier ground to help her. (100/30)
540 King of Peru took a strong hold going down and also in the first half of the race, but he was staying on at the end suggesting that a fast-run seven furlongs is ideal. (14/1: 10/1-16/1)
Hello Mister could never get into this, but is showing signs of coming to form. (33/1)
519 Loch Patrick was given plenty of help from the saddle, but was never fully co-operating. (11/2)
Daring Destiny has always needed her first run of the season. (8/1: 6/1-9/1)

962 EQUITY FINANCIAL COLLECTIONS H'CAP (0-105) (4-Y.O+) (Class B)

4-50 (4-53) **1m 4f (Rowley)** £7,456.80 (£2,791.20: £1,365.60: £588.00: £264.00: £134.40) Stalls: High GOING minus 0.26 sec per fur (GF)

				SP	RR	SF
	Valedictory (92) (HRACecil) **4-9-8** KFallon(3) (b: in tch: hdwy to ld 2f out: hung lft u.p: kpt on wl)	—	**1**	8/1	104	80
761*	**Nabhaan (IRE) (98)** (DMorley) **4-10-0** RHills(2) (lw: hld up: hdwy 4f out: chal 2f out: carried lft: nt qckn towards fin)	¾	**2**	$9/2^{2}$	109	85
775^{3}	**Rokeby Bowl (90)** (IABalding) **5-9-6** LDettori(6) (hld up: hdwy to chse ldrs over 2f out: sn rdn: kpt on one pce fnl f)	¾	**3**	$4/1^{1}$	100	76
762^{12}	**Temptress (67)** (JLHarris) **4-7-6**(5)ow1 RFfrench(4) (cl up: effrt over 3f out: one pce appr fnl f)	hd	**4**	33/1	77	52

General Assembly (IRE) (93) (HRACecil) **5-9-9** WRyan(9) (bkwd: trckd ldrs: led over 3f out to 2f out: grad wknd)....2 **5** 14/1 100 76
My Learned Friend (79) (AHide) **6-8-9** AMcGlone(12) (mid div: sme hdwy over 2f out: nvr nr to chal)....3 **6** 16/1 82 58
789[3] **Artic Courier (85)** (DJSCosgrove) **6-9-1** MRimmer(5) (in tch: effrt over 3f out: wknd wl over 1f out)....3½ **7** 11/2[3] 84 60
Domappel (70) (MrsJCecil) **5-8-0** GBardwell(11) (in tch: hrd rdn over 3f out: btn 2f out)....3½ **8** 7/1 64 40
Royal Scimitar (USA) (98) (MrsAJPerrett) **5-10-0** JReid(14) (in tch tl outpcd 4f out: n.d after)....1½ **9** 14/1 90 66
521[20] **Sofyaan (USA) (82)** (LadyHerries) **4-8-12** OPeslier(13) (chsd ldrs tl wknd fnl 3f)....4 **10** 20/1 69 45
680[9] **Classic Find (USA) (84)** (ICampbell) **4-9-0** RPrice(7) (b.off hind: mid div: drvn along over 4f out: wknd fnl 3f) .5 **11** 12/1 64 40
728[11] **Magic Combination (IRE) (80)** (BJCurley) **4-8-10** JQuinn(10) (led tl hdd & wknd over 3f out)....10 **12** 25/1 47 23
Ancient Quest (80) (NACallaghan) **4-8-10** PatEddery(1) (a bhd)....5 **13** 16/1 40 16
(SP 121.5%) **13 Rn**

2m 31.33 (0.83) CSF £39.66 CT £155.21 TOTE £9.10: £3.10 £2.20 £1.60 (£21.60) Trio £21.20 OWNER Lord Howard de Walden (NEWMARKET) BRED Lord Howard de Walden
LONG HANDICAP Temptress 7-6
Valedictory has a poor action, and hung badly into the whip in the closing stages and obviously has his problems, but he stays particularly well. (8/1)
761* Nabhaan (IRE) needs things to go his way and, with the winner hanging into him throughout the last two furlongs, he did not relish the struggle. (9/2)
775 Rokeby Bowl seems to flatter only to deceive and, when the pressure was on, he kept running but was never quite doing enough to make a real impression. (4/1)
Temptress put up a useful performance here from 4lb out of the handicap, and looks likely to pay her way for her new stable. (33/1)
General Assembly (IRE) has not run for twenty months and showed a terrible action going to post but, looking very much in need of this, ran with a deal of promise. (14/1)
My Learned Friend ran a nice race and was not over-punished, and he should repay the kindness in due course. (16/1)

963 HASTINGS MAIDEN STKS (3-Y.O) (Class D)
5-20 (5-22) **1m (Rowley)** £4,572.00 (£1,386.00: £678.00: £324.00) Stalls: Centre GOING minus 0.26 sec per fur (GF)

SP RR SF
Among Men (USA) (MRStoute) **3-9-0** MJKinane(8) (nice c: lw: plld hrd: trckd ldrs: smooth hdwy to ld ins fnl f: r.o wl)....— **1** 100/30[2] 93+ 64
683[4] **The Prince** (GWragg) **3-9-0** MHills(10) (hld up: smooth hdwy to ld over 1f out: hdd & no ex ins fnl f)....2½ **2** 6/4[1] 88 59
725[7] **Right Wing (IRE)** (MajorWRHern) **3-9-0** KDarley(6) (b: trckd ldrs: led wl over 1f out: sn hdd: kpt on same pce)....1¼ **3** 20/1 86 57
Super Monarch (EALDunlop) **3-9-0** TQuinn(4) (hld up: effrt over 3f out: styd on: nrst fin)....2½ **4** 16/1 81 52
Assailable (ACStewart) **3-9-0** MRoberts(3) (cmpt: bkwd: hld up: stdy hdwy over 2f out: shkn up & r.o wl fnl f)½ **5** 33/1 80 51
674[7] **Judicial Supremacy** (JRFanshawe) **3-9-0** PatEddery(2) (chsd ldrs: effrt 3f out: rdn & r.o one pce)....1½ **6** 10/1 77 48
Khalik (IRE) (EALDunlop) **3-9-0** OPeslier(1) (w'like: slt ld tl hdd wl over 1f out: wknd)....¾ **7** 25/1 75 46
Asef Alhind (BHanbury) **3-9-0** RHills(5) (w'like: b.off hind: trckd ldrs: effrt 3f out: rdn & btn over 1f out)....1½ **8** 7/1[3] 72 43
683[15] **Go Hence** (WJarvis) **3-9-0** RCochrane(14) (lw: mid div: outpcd over 3f out: n.d after)....1½ **9** 33/1 69 40
683[8] **Coble** (BWHills) **3-9-0** DHolland(11) (hld up & bhd: sme hdwy over 3f out: n.d)....¾ **10** 14/1 68 39
673[4] **Space Race** (CACyzer) **3-9-0** LDettori(7) (mid div: rdn over 3f out: wknd over 1f out)....hd **11** 14/1 67 38
742[5] **Royale Finale (IRE)** (HRACecil) **3-9-0** KFallon(9) (lw: w ldr tl wknd fnl 2½f)....7 **12** 11/1 53 24
670[9] **Flashtalkin' Flood** (CADwyer) **3-9-0** JStack(12) (cl up tl wknd over 2f out)....½ **13** 100/1 52 23
676[9] **Slipstream** (RGuest) **3-9-0** WRyan(15) (a bhd)....s.h **14** 25/1 52 23
Shahboor (USA) (MRStoute) **3-9-0** JReid(16) (plld hrd: a bhd)....hd **15** 25/1 52 23
Victory At Hart (48) (DMorris) **3-9-0** NDay(13) (w'like: leggy: struck into after 1½f: t.o fnl 3f)....dist **16** 100/1 — —
(SP 136.4%) **16 Rn**

1m 38.54 (1.24) CSF £8.24 TOTE £5.00: £1.80 £1.50 £6.00 (£3.60) Trio £49.10 OWNER Mr M Tabor & Mrs John Magnier (NEWMARKET) BRED Gail Beitz & Gainsborough Farm
Among Men (USA) took the eye in the paddock and, although going freely to post and racing in similar fashion, he did the business in good style and there looks to be plenty more to come. (100/30: 5/2-4/1)
683 The Prince travels well but lacks a finishing kick, nevertheless he is improving. (6/4)
Right Wing (IRE), dropping back in trip, ran well, only to be tapped for speed late on. (20/1)
Super Monarch is learning and, by the way he was keeping on, should make his mark before long. (16/1)
Assailable, given an educational, showed a deal of promise and was certainly finishing with a flourish. He looks one to follow. (33/1)
Judicial Supremacy showed up well, but looked one-paced when pressure was applied. (10/1)
Khalik (IRE) had a nice blow-out here, and should benefit from it in due course. (25/1)
Asef Alhind (7/1: 10/1-6/1)
683 Coble (14/1: 10/1-16/1)
742 Royale Finale (IRE) (11/1: 6/1-12/1)

T/Jkpt: £48,817.30 (1.78 Tckts). T/Plpt: £361.10 (125.79 Tckts). T/Qdpt: £37.00 (53.87 Tckts) AA

SALISBURY (R-H) (Good to firm, Firm patches)
Sunday May 4th
Race 6: flip start. Race 1 & 5: official times. Rest unofficial hand times.
WEATHER: overcast WIND: str half against

964 WOODFORD MAIDEN STKS (I) (3-Y.O+) (Class D)
2-10 (2-11) **6f** £3,143.75 (£950.00: £462.50: £218.75) Stalls: High GOING minus 0.26 sec per fur (GF)

SP RR SF
740[7] **Smart Kid (IRE)** (PFICole) **3-8-12** CRutter(3) (a.p: led over 1f out: hrd rdn & hung lft: r.o wl)....— **1** 10/11[1] 76 54
727[12] **Fur Will Fly** (IABalding) **3-8-4**(3) MartinDwyer(8) (hld up: hrd rdn & hung lft 2f out: r.o ins fnl f)....1¾ **2** 14/1 66 44
Bold Tina (IRE) (74) (RHannon) **3-8-7** DaneO'Neill(4) (hld up: hrd rdn over 1f out: 2nd & btn whn eased wl ins fnl f)....hd **3** 7/2[2] 66 44
Mutasawwar (EALDunlop) **3-8-9**(3) DO'Donohoe(7) (b: plld hrd: led over 4f: one pce)....2 **4** 6/1[3] 66 44
Verdi (IRE) (KMcAuliffe) **3-8-12** RHughes(9) (w'like: bit bkwd: a.p: rdn over 2f out: wknd over 1f out)....1¾ **5** 12/1 61 39
Sure To Dream (IRE) (RTPhillips) **4-9-3** RPerham(11) (bit bkwd: prom 4f)....7 **6** 50/1 37 25

	Croagh Patrick (51) (JCFox) **5-9-8** AClark(10) (a bhd)	½	**7**	66/1	41	29
792[7]	**Cambridge Blue (USA)** (GLewis) **3-8-12** PaulEddery(6) (nvr plcd to chal)	1	**8**	10/1	38	16
	Falcon Ridge (JCFox) **3-8-12** SWhitworth(1) (bit bkwd: dwlt: a bhd)	4	**9**	33/1	28	6
588[8]	**Hever Golf Charmer** (TJNaughton) **3-8-12** SSanders(5) (a bhd)	2½	**10**	33/1	21	—
638[12]	**Maraeinca** (PRHedger) **4-9-3** GDuffield(2) (dwlt: a bhd)	17	**11**	66/1	—	—

(SP 123.2%) **11 Rn**

1m 14.54 (1.54) CSF £15.96 TOTE £1.90: £1.40 £3.30 £1.50 (£15.40) Trio £16.50 OWNER H R H Sultan Ahmad Shah (WHATCOMBE) BRED Bernard Cooke

WEIGHT FOR AGE 3yo-10lb

OFFICIAL EXPLANATION **Cambridge Blue (USA): needed to be held up to get home, hung left and then ran on through beaten horses.**

740 Smart Kid (IRE), suited by this drop in distance, looks a very awkward ride if this is anything to go by. Striking the front below the distance, he carried his head high and looked far from enthusiastic, drifting to his left but, nevertheless, proved too strong for his rivals. He looks one to have reservations about. (10/11: evens-4/6)

Fur Will Fly improved on her recent debut at Newbury. Drifting left under pressure a quarter-of-a-mile from home, she nevertheless ran on inside the final furlong to snatch second prize in the last couple of strides. (14/1: op 7/1)

Bold Tina (IRE) chased the leaders. She managed to get into second place inside the final furlong, but her jockey took things easy in the closing stages and the combination was caught for second prize. O'Neill must consider himself very lucky not to have been suspended for not riding out. As for the filly, she does seem to lack a turn of foot at that vital stage. (7/2: 9/4-4/1)

Mutasawwar, who took a very keen hold, set the pace but, collared below the distance, failed to find another gear. (6/1: 4/1-8/1)

Verdi (IRE), a strongly-made individual, did not look fully wound up and so it proved for, after racing up with the pace, he had come to the end of his tether approaching the final furlong. (12/1: 8/1-16/1)

Sure To Dream (IRE), making a belated racecourse debut, looked big and well in the paddock and raced prominently until tiring a quarter-of-a-mile from home. (50/1)

792 Cambridge Blue (USA) was given an extremely quiet ride at the back of the field. He looks one to keep an eye on, especially as he is now qualified for handicaps. (10/1: 8/1-12/1)

81+ 67 95

965 SALISBURY CONDITIONS STKS (2-Y.O) (Class C)

2-40 (2-40) **5f** £4,268.60 (£1,597.40: £781.20: £336.00: £150.50: £76.30) Stalls: High GOING minus 0.26 sec per fur (GF)

				SP	RR	SF
722[3]	**Chips (IRE)** (DRCElsworth) **2-8-11** GDuffield(3) (lw: hld up: led over 1f out: edgd rt: rdn out: rn green)	—	**1**	6/4[1]	93	39
684[2]	**The Boy John (USA)** (RHannon) **2-8-11** RHughes(5) (lw: w ldrs: led over 2f out tl over 1f out: unable qckn)	1¾	**2**	6/4[1]	87	33
	Mighty Magic (MrsPNDutfield) **2-8-4**ow1 SSanders(4) (scope: bit bkwd: lost pl over 2f out: rallied fnl f: r.o)	1½	**3**	33/1	76	21
	Narrogin (USA) (MRChannon) **2-8-8** RPerham(6) (w'like: bit bkwd: outpcd: nvr nrr)	2½	**4**	14/1	72	18
739[4]	**Princess Londis** (AGFoster) **2-8-6** TSprake(1) (b: lw: a.p: ev ch 2f out: wknd over 1f out)	¾	**5**	7/1[3]	67	13
750[5]	**Mister Bankes** (WGMTurner) **2-8-6**(5) DSweeney(2) (lw: led over 2f: wknd over 1f out)	1½	**6**	13/2[2]	67	13

(SP 115.4%) **6 Rn**

62.1 secs (2.10) CSF £3.62 TOTE £2.40: £1.70 £1.50 (£1.90) OWNER Lucayan Stud (WHITCOMBE) BRED Mrs E. M. Gauvain

722 Chips (IRE) does not appear to have learnt a lot from his Newbury debut for he was still as green as grass. However, despite wandering about and carrying his head rather high, he gained a slender advantage below the distance and, in a tremendous battle with the runner-up, managed to assert his authority in the last one hundred yards. He is rated Royal Ascot material by his trainer. (6/4)

684 The Boy John (USA), who made such a promising debut at Pontefract, again ran well. Disputing the lead from the start, he was collared by the winner below the distance but, refusing to give way, was only put in his place in the last one hundred yards. His turn is not far away. (6/4)

Mighty Magic is rather on the leg at present, but nevertheless does have some substance about her. Looking as though the run would do her good, she got outpaced at halfway but stayed on again nicely in the closing stages. Another furlong would be in her favour. (33/1)

Narrogin (USA),a $30,000 yearling who is a half-brother to several winner in North America, comes from a stable that is not really firing with its juveniles at present. (14/1: 7/1-16/1)

739 Princess Londis played an active role until coming to the end of her tether below the distance. (7/1: 8/1-12/1)

750 Mister Bankes was again racing on very fast ground and, once again, ran poorly, dropping out of contention approaching the final furlong. His sire was the mud-loving Risk Me and cut in the ground would appear to be the key to him as well. (13/2: 4/1-7/1)

966 WEATHERBYS VAT SERVICES H'CAP (0-100) (3-Y.O) (Class C)

3-10 (3-10) **1m 1f 209y** £5,251.00 (£1,588.00: £774.00: £367.00) Stalls: High GOING minus 0.26 sec per fur (GF)

				SP	RR	SF
	Union Town (IRE) (95) (SirMarkPrescott) **3-9-7** GDuffield(3) (bit bkwd: led over 1f: led 5f out tl over 3f out: led wl over 1f out: rdn out)	—	**1**	3/1[1]	104	44
646[7]	**Ginzbourg (85)** (JLDunlop) **3-8-11** TSprake(2) (lw: hld up: rdn over 4f out: r.o ins fnl f)	1	**2**	6/1	92	32
586[13]	**Spy Knoll (75)** (MRStoute) **3-7-12**(3) MartinDwyer(6) (led over 8f out to 5f out: lost pl over 3f out: r.o one pce fnl f)	1	**3**	7/2[2]	81	21
789[9]	**Northern Sun (85)** (TGMills) **3-8-8**(3) AWhelan(1) (a.p: led over 3f out tl wl over 1f out: hrd rdn: one pce)	nk	**4**	11/2[3]	90	30
	Calypso Lady (IRE) (85) (RHannon) **3-8-11** DaneO'Neill(4) (hld up: rdn over 4f out: wknd over 2f out)	4	**5**	3/1[1]	84	24
	Beryllium (92) (RHannon) **3-9-4** RHughes(5) (bhd fnl 4f)	8	**6**	10/1	78	18

(SP 111.0%) **6 Rn**

2m 10.3 (5.00) CSF £18.59 TOTE £3.10: £1.70 £3.30 (£12.70) OWNER H R H Prince Fahd Salman (NEWMARKET) BRED Newgate Stud Co

Union Town (IRE), who drifted in the market, looked rather rough in the paddock and appeared in need of the run, but that did not stop him from making a winning reappearance. Battling his way back to the front early in the final quarter-mile, he was rousted along to keep his rivals at bay. He has done all his winning on a fast surface. (3/1: op 7/4)

Ginzbourg looked extremely well beforehand. Bustled along over half-a-mile from home, he eventually struggled on to take second place in the closing stages. (6/1)

Spy Knoll, taking a step-up in distance, showed in front in the first half of the race but he got outpaced over three furlongs from home, only to stay on again in the closing stages. He will surely appreciate a mile and a half. (7/2: 2/1-4/1)

509* Northern Sun made his bid for glory over three furlongs from home but, collared early in the final quarter-mile, could only go up and down in the same place. (11/2)

Calypso Lady (IRE) was certainly fit enough for this reappearance but never threatened to get in a serious challenge. (3/1)

Beryllium (10/1: op 6/1)

967 SMITH & WILLIAMSON MAIDEN STKS (3-Y.O) (Class D)

3-40 (3-40) **1m 4f** £3,680.00 (£1,115.00: £545.00: £260.00) Stalls: High GOING minus 0.26 sec per fur (GF)

				SP	RR	SF
732[2]	**Percy Isle (IRE) (83)** (MRStoute) **3-9-0** GDuffield(2) (lw: mde all: rdn over 2f out: r.o wl)	—	**1**	7/4[1]	84	44

		Dist	Pos	SP	RR	SF
725[16]	**Highly Prized** (IABalding) **3-8-11**(3) MartinDwyer(9) (chsd wnr over 6f: lost pl over 3f out: rallied 2f out: unable qckn)	2	**2**	20/1	81	41
	Tikopia (IABalding) **3-9-0** SWhitworth(7) (w'like: scope: lw: s.s: nt clr run & swtchd lft over 2f out: hdwy 2f out: chsd wnr over 1f out: one pce)	hd	**3**	10/1	81	41
	Tom Tailor (GER) (72) (DRCElsworth) **3-9-0** TSprake(6) (bit bkwd: a.p: chsd wnr over 5f out tl over 1f out: wknd)	6	**4**	100/30[2]	73	33
	Lahab Nashwan (MRChannon) **3-9-0** RHughes(8) (lw: hld up: hrd rdn over 2f out: wkng whn n.m.r on ins over 1f out)	10	**5**	100/30[2]	60	20
725[11]	**Hoh Explorer (IRE)** (IABalding) **3-9-0** DHarrison(3) (hdwy 7f out: rdn 6f out: wknd 4f out)	¾	**6**	16/1	59	19
725[8]	**Mighty Flow** (MrsPNDutfield) **3-8-9** AProcter(1) (lw: bhd fnl 3f)	2	**7**	8/1[3]	51	11
790[8]	**Sipowitz** (CACyzer) **3-9-0** AClark(4) (a bhd)	17	**8**	33/1	34	—
				(SP 116.3%)	**8 Rn**	

2m 36.0 (5.00) CSF £37.99 TOTE £2.40: £1.10 £2.70 £2.70 (£23.60) Trio £135.00 OWNER Sheikh Mohammed (NEWMARKET) BRED Sheikh Mohammed Bin Rashid Al Maktoum

732 Percy Isle (IRE) made every post a winning one and, rousted along over a quarter-of-a-mile from home, was not going to be caught. (7/4)

Highly Prized ran by far his best race to date and, after getting outpaced over three furlongs from home, got back into it. Although unable to challenge the winner, he just won the battle for second prize. (20/1)

Tikopia, a good-bodied gelding, looked in fine shape in the paddock and made a promising start to his racing career. Picking up ground to go second below the distance, he had a tremendous battle for the runner-up berth and only just lost out. He should soon find a race. (10/1: op 5/1)

Tom Tailor (GER), a half-brother to the stable's very useful hurdler Muse, looked as though the run was needed and so it proved for, after moving into second place just after halfway, he was collared for that position below the distance and had nothing more to offer. (100/30)

Lahab Nashwan looked in good shape for this seasonal debut and appeared to be travelling really well for a lot of the race. However, when his jockey got down to work on him, he failed to find what was expected and disappointingly dropped away. (100/30: 6/4-7/2)

968 WILTON RATED STKS H'CAP (0-100) (3-Y.O) (Class B)

4-10 (4-11) **6f** £7,409.24 (£2,773.16: £1,356.58: £583.90: £261.95: £133.17) Stalls: High GOING minus 0.26 sec per fur (GF)

		Dist	Pos	SP	RR	SF
555[2]	**Indian Spark (98)** (WGMTurner) **3-8-11**(5) DSweeney(10) (mde virtually all: hrd rdn over 1f out: r.o wl)	—	**1**	14/1	105	63
	Cryhavoc (93) (JRArnold) **3-8-11** SSanders(9) (hld up: rdn over 2f out: r.o one pce)	2½	**2**	10/1	93	51
694[6]	**Arruhan (IRE) (85)** (PTWalwyn) **3-8-3** GDuffield(1) (hld up: rdn over 2f out: r.o ins fnl f)	¾	**3**	9/1	83	41
	Meliksah (IRE) (94) (MBell) **3-8-7**(5) GFaulkner(3) (a.p: hrd rdn over 2f out: ev ch over 1f out: wknd ins fnl f)	½	**4**	10/1	91	49
854[6]	**Paddy Lad (IRE) (96)** (RGuest) **3-9-0** PBloomfield(12) (lost pl over 3f out: rallied fnl f: r.o)	½	**5**	20/1	92	50
531*	**Mile High (95)** (MRChannon) **3-8-13** PaulEddery(8) (a.p: rdn over 2f out: wknd fnl f)	nk	**6**	4/1[2]	90	48
778*	**Rosy Outlook (USA) (82)** (IABalding) **3-7-11**(3) MartinDwyer(11) (prom over 4f)	1½	**7**	8/1[3]	73	31
	Song of Skye (84) (TJNaughton) **3-8-2** TSprake(5) (nvr nrr)	1¼	**8**	20/1	72	30
	Salty Behaviour (IRE) (85) (RHannon) **3-8-3** DaneO'Neill(2) (lw: dwlt: a bhd)	¾	**9**	12/1	71	29
656*	**Darb Alola (USA) (99)** (MRStoute) **3-9-3** DHarrison(6) (lw: hdwy over 2f out: wknd wl over 1f out)	1½	**10**	2/1[1]	81	39
	Mayfair (85) (PFICole) **3-8-3** CRutter(4) (bit bkwd: bhd fnl 3f)	3	**11**	14/1	59	17
507[8]	**Lady Diesis (USA) (92)** (BWHills) **3-8-7**(3) JDSmith(7) (b.hind: dwlt: a bhd)	1¼	**12**	20/1	62	20
				(SP 127.9%)	**12 Rn**	

1m 14.16 (1.16) CSF £139.85 CT £1,240.22 TOTE £14.30: £3.00 £3.10 £2.40 (£58.10) Trio £350.70 OWNER Mr Frank Brady (SHERBORNE) BRED H. Young

LONG HANDICAP Rosy Outlook (USA) 7-11

555 Indian Spark made virtually all the running and, responding to pressure below the distance, was not going to be denied. He is better with some cut in the ground according to his trainer. (14/1)

Cryhavoc, 7lb higher than at the end of last season, chased the leaders and struggled on to take second place if having no hope with the winner. (10/1)

694 Arruhan (IRE) chased the leaders and, rousted along, eventually struggled on inside the final furlong to take third place. (9/1)

Meliksah (IRE) appeared to find this extra furlong just too far for him and, after having every chance below the distance, tired inside the last two hundred yards. A return to five furlongs is needed. (10/1)

854 Paddy Lad (IRE), better suited by the extra furlong, nevertheless got outpaced before halfway, although he stayed on again in the closing stages. (20/1)

531* Mile High played an active role until coming to the end of his tether inside the final furlong. He seems better at five furlongs. (4/1)

969 WESSEX H'CAP (0-90) (4-Y.O+) (Class C)

4-40 (4-40) **1m 6f** £5,407.00 (£1,636.00: £798.00: £379.00) Stalls: High GOING minus 0.26 sec per fur (GF)

		Dist	Pos	SP	RR	SF
770*	**Rising Spray (67)** (CAHorgan) **6-8-10** PaulEddery(5) (hld up: led 1f out: drvn out)	—	**1**	7/4[1]	77	1
	Desert Dunes (70) (NAGraham) **4-8-12** DaneO'Neill(8) (lw: w ldr: led over 2f out to 1f out: hrd rdn: r.o wl)	hd	**2**	5/1	80	3
	Viking Dream (IRE) (56) (JCFox) **5-7-8**(5) RMullen(6) (rdn over 3f out: hdwy 2f out: r.o one pce)	3½	**3**	20/1	62	—
728[7]	**Castle Courageous (85)** (LadyHerries) **10-9-7**(7) PDoe(4) (b: led over 11f: wknd over 1f out)	1	**4**	8/1	90	14
	Casual Water (IRE) (73) (AGNewcombe) **6-8-13**(3) DGriffiths(1) (nvr nr to chal)	4	**5**	4/1[3]	73	—
735[6]	**Royal Seaton (80)** (MrsPNDutfield) **8-9-9** AProcter(3) (lw: a bhd)	½	**6**	7/2[2]	80	4
216[12]	**Western Playboy (64)** (RJBaker) **5-8-7**ow2 VSlattery(7) (prom 11f: b.b.v)	20	**7**	33/1	41	—
				(SP 114.1%)	**7 Rn**	

3m 12.3 (13.60) CSF £9.95 CT £114.89 TOTE £2.20: £1.40 £2.90 (£5.40) OWNER Mr J. T. Heritage (PULBOROUGH) BRED Pendley Farm

WEIGHT FOR AGE 4yo-1lb

OFFICIAL EXPLANATION **Western Playboy: bled from the nose.**

IN-FOCUS: **This race was run at a farcical pace for the first three-quarters of a mile, and not too much should be read into the form.**

770* Rising Spray was taking a step-up in distance, but the ridiculous early pace gave him every chance of seeing it out. Held up in fourth pace, he was shaken up to lead a furlong out but, with the runner-up refusing to give way, he had to receive some stern reminders to remain in front. He gave the distinct impression that he was coming to the end of his tether. A return to a mile and a half would surely be the sensible thing to do. (7/4)

Desert Dunes looked fit for this reappearance and, after disputing the lead, showed with a definite advantage over a quarter-of-a-mile from home. Headed a furlong out, he refused to give way and proved a real thorn in the side of the winner. (5/1)

Viking Dream (IRE), fit from hurdling, picked up ground from the rear but, despite staying on, never looked like challenging the front two. (20/1)

Castle Courageous took the field along at a snail's pace for the first three-quarters of a mile. He had come to the end of his tether below the distance. (8/1: 6/1-9/1)

Casual Water (IRE), off the course since last August, never threatened to get into it. (4/1)

970 WOODFORD MAIDEN STKS (II) (3-Y.O+) (Class D)

5-10 (5-12) **6f** £3,143.75 (£950.00: £462.50: £218.75) Stalls: High GOING minus 0.26 sec per fur (GF)

	Horse	Dist	Pos	SP	RR	SF
	Mara River (IABalding) **3-8-4**(3) MartinDwyer(9) (a.p: rdn 2f out: chsd ldr over 1f out: led ins fnl f: r.o wl)	—	1	6/1	76	48
792[4]	**At Large (IRE)** (JRFanshawe) **3-8-12** DHarrison(2) (lw: chsd ldr: led 3f tl ins fnl f: unable qckn)	1¾	2	9/2	76	48
683[14]	**Butrinto** (MajorWRHern) **3-8-12** TSprake(7) (hld up: rdn over 2f out: one pce)	¾	3	3/1 [2]	74	46
765[6]	**Lucky Dip (70)** (DRCElsworth) **3-8-7** GDuffield(6) (led over 3f: wknd over 1f out)	6	4	8/1	53	25
	Bold Spring (IRE) (74) (RHannon) **3-8-12** RPerham(1) (hld up: rdn over 2f out: wknd over 1f out)	½	5	4/1 [3]	57	29
742[11]	**Golden Saddle (USA)** (PFICole) **3-8-5**(7) DavidO'Neill(4) (lw: dwlt: outpcd: nvr nrr)	½	6	20/1	56	28
	Taffs Well (RAkehurst) **4-9-8** SSanders(3) (dwlt: hld up: rdn 3f out: wknd 2f out)	½	7	5/2 [1]	54	36
	Fable (JARToller) **3-8-7** DaneO'Neill(8) (lw: bhd fnl 2f)	1¾	8	33/1	45	17
	Kilmeena Lady (JCFox) **3-8-7** AClark(5) (dwlt: a bhd)	nk	9	50/1	44	16

(SP 126.8%) **9 Rn**

1m 14.6 (1.60) CSF £32.78 TOTE £9.10: £2.50 £1.60 £1.60 (£15.70) Trio £17.80 OWNER Mr Nigel Harris (KINGSCLERE) BRED Mrs I. A. Balding

WEIGHT FOR AGE 3yo-10lb

Mara River, always close up, moved into second place below the distance and gradually reeled in the winner inside the final furlong. (6/1: op 7/2)

792 At Large (IRE), who showed promise on his debut at Beverley recently, struck the front at halfway but was unable to keep the winner at bay inside the final furlong. (9/2: 5/2-5/1)

Butrinto chased the leaders but, rousted along in the final quarter-mile, could only go up and down in the same place. (3/1)

765 Lucky Dip, in front to halfway, had shot her bolt below the distance. (8/1)

Bold Spring (IRE), without a run in nearly five months, chased the leaders until coming to the end of his tether below the distance. He remains a maiden after ten attempts. (4/1: 3/1-9/2)

Taffs Well (5/2: 5/2-4/1)

T/Plpt: £36.90 (298.19 Tckts). T/Qdpt: £21.40 (22.87 Tckts) AK

0447-DONCASTER (L-H) (Good becoming Good to soft)

Monday May 5th

WEATHER: raining WIND: slt bhd

71 75+ 72 63

971 WISETON NOVICE AUCTION STKS (2-Y.O) (Class D)

2-20 (2-28) **5f** £3,318.75 (£990.00: £472.50: £213.75) Stalls: High GOING: 0.31 sec per fur (G)

	Horse	Dist	Pos	SP	RR	SF
441*	**Jackerin (IRE)** (BSRothwell) **2-8-7** KFallon(6) (mde all: hld on wl)	—	1	9/2	79	35
648*	**Dim Ots** (BPalling) **2-8-2** JQuinn(4) (lw: a cl up: r.o u.p fnl f)	½	2	2/1 [1]	72	28
	Euro Venture (DNicholls) **2-8-9** AlexGreaves(5) (w'like: scope: bit bkwd: w ldrs: effrt 2f out: nt qckn towards fin)	½	3	7/1	78	34
	Mysticism (CEBrittain) **2-8-2**ow4 BDoyle(7) (small: neat: b: chsd ldrs: outpcd 2f out: no imp after)	2½	4	4/1 [3]	63	15
697[4]	**Erro Codigo** (MrsJRRamsden) **2-8-6** JFortune(1) (stdd s: nvr nr to chal)	½	5	7/2 [2]	65	21
	Moy (IRE) (MBrittain) **2-7-12** NCarlisle(8) (lt-f: s.i.s: plld hrd & sn prom: outpcd fnl 2f)	3	6	16/1	48	4
	Circuiteer (IRE) (JBerry) **2-8-6** GCarter(3) (leggy: outpcd ½-wy: sn lost tch)	1¼	7	13/2	52	8
	Ragford (IRE) (JMPEustace) **2-8-3** NKennedy(2) (Withdrawn not under Starter's orders: uns rdr & bolted bef s)		W	12/1	—	—

(SP 133.1%) **7 Rn**

63.27 secs (4.87) CSF £13.79 TOTE £4.40: £1.90 £1.90 (£3.80) OWNER Mr J. B. Young (MALTON) BRED Golden Vale Stud

441* Jackerin (IRE) has plenty of early pace, gets the trip well and is really tough. (9/2)

648* Dim Ots, a wiry sort, responded to pressure in gallant style but in the end had met one just too tough. (2/1)

Euro Venture put up a really good performance and left the impression that there is plenty more to come. (7/1)

Mysticism, a sharp little filly, should find a modest race in time. (4/1)

697 Erro Codigo was happy to give the rest a few lengths start, and could never get back on terms. Better will be seen in due course. (7/2)

Moy (IRE) races too freely for her own good at present. (16/1)

972 BAWTRY CLAIMING STKS (4-Y.O+) (Class E)

2-50 (2-55) **5f** £2,966.25 (£885.00: £422.50: £191.25) Stalls: High GOING: 0.31 sec per fur (G)

	Horse	Dist	Pos	SP	RR	SF
823[6]	**Palacegate Touch (78)** (JBerry) **7-9-2b** GCarter(6) (bhd: hdwy & sltly hmpd 3f out: qcknd to ld ins fnl f)	—	1	7/2 [2]	81	49
834[16]	**Lord High Admiral (CAN) (88)** (MJHeaton-Ellis) **9-9-4** MRoberts(2) (led: edgd rt fnl 2f: hdd & no ex ins fnl f)	2½	2	13/8 [1]	75	43
905[8]	**General Sir Peter (IRE) (64)** (NACallaghan) **5-8-7**(5) AmandaSanders(3) (squeezed out s: hdwy ½-wy: styd on)	2	3	6/1 [3]	63	31
856[3]	**Palacegate Jack (IRE) (75)** (JBerry) **6-8-3b**(7) CLowther(10) (disp ld to ½-wy: sltly hmpd over 1f out: wknd)	¾	4	7/2 [2]	58	26
870[16]	**Awesome Venture (50)** (MCChapman) **7-8-13** JFortune(1) (b.off hind: chsd ldrs tl outpcd fnl 2f)	¾	5	33/1	59	27
	Superfrills (44) (MissLCSiddall) **4-8-3** NCarlisle(8) (chsd ldrs: rdn over 2f out: grad wknd)	3½	6	33/1	38	6
760[6]	**Super Rocky (60)** (RBastiman) **8-8-6b** JQuinn(7) (a rr div)	½	7	10/1	39	7
429[11]	**Young Ben (IRE) (36)** (JSWainwright) **5-8-1v** BDoyle(5) (b: b.hind: spd to ½-wy: sn bhd)	½	8	33/1	32	—
759[17]	**Smart Guest (61)** (DShaw) **5-8-1** DWright(4) (lw: b.off fore: outpcd & lost tch fr ½-wy)	¾	9	20/1	30	—

(SP 119.5%) **9 Rn**

62.92 secs (4.52) CSF £8.75 TOTE £5.20: £1.60 £1.20 £1.90 (£3.60) Trio £9.70 OWNER Laurel (Leisure) Ltd (COCKERHAM) BRED The Woodhaven Stud

STEWARDS' ENQUIRY Obj. to Lord High Admiral (CAN) by Sanders overruled.

823 Palacegate Touch, back to his optimum trip here, won it well and is always to be considered in such events. (7/2)

Lord High Admiral (CAN) showed his first signs of form this season here, and this grand old handicapper will no doubt find his usual race or two. (13/8)

760 General Sir Peter (IRE) had plenty of running to do after getting carved up at the start and was making some late headway. (6/1)

856 Palacegate Jack (IRE) showed plenty of early pace but he didn't seem to like being taken on, and when the runner up squeezed him for room approaching the final furlong, he soon decided it was not for him. (7/2)

127 Awesome Venture was always finding things happening too quickly at this trip. (33/1)
760 Super Rocky found conditions against him here. (10/1)

973 CARR HILL CONDITIONS STKS (3-Y.O) (Class C)
3-20 (3-24) **1m (round)** £4,746.89 (£1,757.10: £843.55: £345.25: £137.63: £54.58) Stalls: High GOING: 0.31 sec per fur (G)

				SP	RR	SF
723[2]	**Peartree House (IRE) (95)** (WRMuir) **3-9-1** MRoberts(2) (b.hind: chsd ldrs: led over 2f out: r.o u.p)	—	**1**	8/1[3]	103	61
683*	**Dokos (USA)** (HRACecil) **3-9-1** KFallon(5) (lw: trckd ldrs: qcknd to chal 2f out: no ex u.p fnl f)	1	**2**	4/6[1]	101	59
	Cinema Paradiso (96) (PFICole) **3-9-1** JQuinn(4) (dwlt: hld up & bhd: effrt 3f out: hdwy over 1f out: nvr able to chal)	2	**3**	12/1	97	55
646[W]	**Premier Bay (103)** (PWHarris) **3-9-1** BDoyle(3) (outpcd & lost pl 3f out: hdwy over 1f out: styd on wl towards fin)	nk	**4**	9/2[2]	96	54
784*	**Sharp Temper** (BWHills) **3-9-1** GCarter(1) (led tl hdd & wknd over 2f out)	10	**5**	10/1	76	34
	Bachelors Pad (100) (WJarvis) **3-9-1** NDay(6) (chsd ldrs tl rdn & wknd 3f out)	nk	**6**	8/1[3]	76	34
				(SP 117.2%)		**6 Rn**

1m 44.63 (6.23) CSF £13.40 TOTE £8.80: £2.30 £1.40 (£4.50) OWNER Fayzad Thoroughbred Ltd (LAMBOURN) BRED Cocomo American Thoroughbred Exports Inc
723 Peartree House (IRE), whose enthusiasm was questioned last time when he seemed to throw his race away, did nothing wrong here and proved game under pressure. (8/1)
683* Dokos (USA), ridden with restraint this time, had his chances but failed to pick up late on and no doubt he will return to forcing tactics. (4/6: 4/5-evens)
Cinema Paradiso looks a bit of a handful but has ability if it can be channelled the right way. (12/1)
Premier Bay gave the impression finishing well here that, over further, much better will be seen. (9/2)
784* Sharp Temper set the race up and when passed, was certainly not knocked about. (10/1)
Bachelors Pad, whose yard is not really firing at present, ran disappointingly. (8/1: op 5/1)

974 CARBON LINK H'CAP (0-90) (3-Y.O+) (Class C)
3-55 (3-55) **1m 2f 60y** £5,328.25 (£1,591.00: £760.50: £345.25) Stalls: Low GOING: 0.41 sec per fur (GS)

				SP	RR	SF
633[11]	**Polar Champ (74)** (SPCWoods) **4-8-5**(7) CWebb(10) (mde most tl hdd ent fnl f: rallied to ld wl ins fnl f)	—	**1**	9/1	90	35
680[7]	**Remaadi Sun (78)** (MDIUsher) **5-9-2** JQuinn(4) (hld up: effrt 3f out: qcknd to ld ins fnl f: hung lft: no ex towards fin)	nk	**2**	5/1[3]	94	39
775[2]	**Billy Bushwacker (90)** (MrsMReveley) **6-10-0** KFallon(2) (lw: hld up: hdwy on outside over 3f out: nvr rchd ldrs)	6	**3**	7/2[1]	96	41
832[8]	**Pater Noster (USA) (84)** (JohnHarris) **8-9-1**(7) CLowther(7) (trckd ldrs: ev ch 3f out: one pce appr fnl f)	nk	**4**	9/1	90	35
789[13]	**Hazard a Guess (IRE) (84)** (DNicholls) **7-9-8** AlexGreaves(9) (trckd ldrs: effrt over 2f out: rdn & btn over 1f out)	hd	**5**	4/1[2]	90	35
787[8]	**Burnt Offering (70)** (CEBrittain) **4-8-8b[1]** BDoyle(8) (hld up: effrt 3f out: sn wknd)	11	**6**	10/1	58	3
450[4]	**Iamus (82)** (TDBarron) **4-9-6** WJO'Connor(1) (lw: hld up: effrt 3f out: n.d)	¾	**7**	11/2	69	14
	Tilaal (USA) (70) (MDHammond) **5-8-8** JFortune(3) (chsd ldrs tl wknd fnl 2½f)	8	**8**	8/1	45	—
776[9]	**Keston Pond (IRE) (66)** (MrsVAAconley) **7-8-4** MDeering(6) (stdd s: plld hrd & hdwy to jn ldr 6f out: wknd over 3f out)	28	**9**	20/1	—	—
				(SP 119.2%)		**9 Rn**

2m 19.8 (12.00) CSF £50.32 CT £174.64 TOTE £13.00: £3.20 £1.90 £1.30 (£29.70) Trio £19.30 OWNER Mr P. K. L. Chu (NEWMARKET) BRED High Point Bloodstock Ltd and Victor Sujanani
OFFICIAL EXPLANATION **Polar Champ: regarding the improved form, the trainer reported that the gelding had had to be chased up in the early stages last time, and had no more to give thereafter. He also appreciated having the visor left off here.**
Polar Champ was without the headgear he has been wearing for his last five races and he seemed to enjoy himself out in front in this falsely-run event. He showed fine determination in the closing stages. (9/1)
680 Remaadi Sun, over a shorter trip and in a slowly-run race, still came there looking likely to sluice in with a furlong to go, but then decided he had seen too much daylight too soon. When he gets it right he has plenty more ability and he is certainly in good form just now. (5/1)
775 Billy Bushwacker was always having to make his move on the outside of the field, and was never doing enough to get into it. (7/2)
396 Pater Noster (USA) loves cut in the ground and ran his best race on grass for a while to show he still retains some ability. (9/1)
680 Hazard a Guess (IRE) was not suited by this messy event and cried enough approaching the last furlong. (4/1)
Burnt Offering was tried in blinkers this time, but they had little effect. (10/1)
Keston Pond (IRE) would apparently have trouble in getting this trip in a horse box. (20/1)

975 JOE SIME MEMORIAL H'CAP (0-80) (3-Y.O) (Class D)
4-25 (4-26) **1m 6f 132y** £3,557.50 (£1,060.00: £505.00: £227.50) Stalls: Low GOING: 0.41 sec per fur (GS)

				SP	RR	SF
534*	**Ramike (IRE) (75)** (MJohnston) **3-9-7** MRoberts(5) (chsd ldr: pushed along 6f out: led over 2f out: styd on u.p)	—	**1**	7/4[1]	83	2
700[5]	**Sad Mad Bad (USA) (74)** (MJohnston) **3-9-6** WJO'Connor(4) (swtg: led tl hdd over 2f out: rallied ins fnl f)	1¼	**2**	15/2	81	—
	French Mist (71) (CEBrittain) **3-9-3** BDoyle(3) (lw: chsd ldrs: hdwy to chal over 2f out: wknd ins fnl f)	1¼	**3**	12/1	76	—
825[4]	**Not Forgotten (USA) (72)** (PAKelleway) **3-9-4** KFallon(2) (hld up: effrt over 4f out: no imp)	10	**4**	5/1[3]	66	—
533[3]	**Madison Welcome (IRE) (63)** (MrsJRRamsden) **3-8-9** JFortune(1) (hld up: effrt 4f out: rdn & no imp)	12	**5**	9/4[2]	44	—
	Ziggy's Viola (IRE) (62) (MrsMReveley) **3-8-8** DWright(6) (prom: rdn over 4f out: wknd over 2f out)	2½	**6**	11/1	40	—
				(SP 111.6%)		**6 Rn**

3m 28.96 (25.36) CSF £13.74 TOTE £2.40: £1.30 £2.80 (£6.90) OWNER Miss Belinda Lee (MIDDLEHAM) BRED Dene Investments N V
534* Ramike (IRE) looks an out and out stayer and got better the further they went. (7/4)
700 Sad Mad Bad (USA), trying his longest trip to date, left the impression that further yet should suit. (15/2)
French Mist, taking a big step up in distance, looked likely to win it halfway up the straight but then failed to last out. She is well worth keeping in mind if dropped back in trip. (12/1)
825 Not Forgotten (USA), after two runs in a visor, the second of which was disappointing, showed little spark without on this occasion. (5/1)
533 Madison Welcome (IRE) was stepped up in trip but disappointed this time, but this was not his true form as time will show. (9/4)
Ziggy's Viola (IRE), trying a much longer trip, ran out of fuel with over two furlongs left. (11/1)

976 MAY DAY HOLIDAY LIMITED STKS (0-70) (3-Y.O) (Class E)

4-55 (4-55) **1m 2f 60y** £2,966.25 (£885.00: £422.50: £191.25) Stalls: Low GOING: 0.41 sec per fur (GS)

Form	Horse	Dist	Pos	SP	RR	SF
771*	**Pinchincha (FR) (70)** (DMorris) **3-9-1** NDay(3) (hld up: hdwy over 4f out: led wl over 1f out: styd on strly)	—	**1**	4/1[2]	77	44
537[3]	**Mystic Quest (IRE) (63)** (KMcAuliffe) **3-8-4**(7) TField(6) (chsd ldrs: led over 4f out tl wl over 1f out: one pce)	3½	**2**	15/2	68	35
690[18]	**Top Shelf (65)** (CEBrittain) **3-8-10** BDoyle(5) (cl up: outpcd over 2f out: styd on fnl f)	6	**3**	13/2	57	24
826[5]	**Count Tony (69)** (SPCWoods) **3-8-6v**[1](7) CWebb(4) (lw: hld up: hdwy 5f out: sn chsng ldrs: rdn 3f out: wknd fnl 2f)	6	**4**	5/1[3]	51	18
878[3]	**Time Can Tell (68)** (CMurray) **3-8-11** JFortune(1) (led tl hdd over 4f out: wknd fnl 3f)	16	**5**	4/1[2]	24	—
641[3]	**Kalimat (70)** (WJarvis) **3-8-8** KFallon(2) (lw: prom tl outpcd over 4f out: sn lost tch)	18	**6**	9/4[1]	—	—

(SP 112.5%) **6 Rn**

2m 19.05 (11.25) CSF £29.46 TOTE £4.80: £2.10 £3.10 (£21.60) OWNER Mr T. J. Wells (NEWMARKET) BRED Fluorocarbon Bloodstock
OFFICIAL EXPLANATION **Kalimat: no explanation offered.**

771* Pinchincha (FR) revelled in the rain-softened ground and, the further they went, the stronger they got. (4/1)
537 Mystic Quest (IRE) is running consistently well just now and deserves to find a race. (15/2)
337* Top Shelf looks short of a change of gear but he does stay quite well. (13/2)
826 Count Tony is a very lean individual and was tried in a visor here for the first time, but it was all to no avail. (5/1)
878 Time Can Tell, who's already been busy on the All-Weather this winter, has now had five runs on turf this season and was disappointing on this ground. (4/1)
641 Kalimat ran as though something was amiss. (9/4)

977 COAL MINER H'CAP (0-85) (3-Y.O+) (Class D)

5-25 (5-27) **6f** £3,817.50 (£1,140.00: £545.00: £247.50) Stalls: High GOING: 0.41 sec per fur (GS)

Form	Horse	Dist	Pos	SP	RR	SF
759[8]	**Halmanerror (57)** (MrsJRRamsden) **7-8-5** JFortune(3) (hld up: smooth hdwy over 1f out: rdn to ld ins fnl f: r.o)	—	**1**	5/1[2]	66	32
	Mr Speaker (IRE) (63) (CFWall) **4-8-11** BDoyle(5) (trckd ldrs gng wl: rdn to ld over 1f out: nt qckn ins fnl f)	1¼	**2**	16/1	69	35
729[2]	**Two On The Bridge (72)** (DenysSmith) **3-8-10** KFallon(7) (led tl hdd over 1f out: kpt on same pce)	1	**3**	9/1	75	31
694[7]	**A Breeze (71)** (DMorris) **3-8-9** NDay(8) (bhd: hdwy u.p 2f out: nrst fin)	3½	**4**	10/1	65	21
	Palo Blanco (75) (TDBarron) **6-9-9** WJO'Connor(10) (hld up & bhd: hdwy 2f out: pushed along & nvr rchd ldrs)	3	**5**	12/1	61	27
827[2]	**Amron (64)** (JBerry) **10-8-12** NCarlisle(11) (trckd ldrs tl outpcd ½-wy: rdn & n.d after)	1½	**6**	5/2[1]	46	12
*545**	**Daawe (USA) (74)** (MrsVAAconley) **6-9-8** MDeering(9) (lw: chsd ldrs: ev ch 2f out: wknd ins fnl f)	1¼	**7**	7/1	52	18
835[12]	**Benzoe (IRE) (68)** (MrsJRRamsden) **7-9-2** LNewton(6) (trckd ldrs: rdn ½-wy: sn wknd)	7	**8**	12/1	28	—
469*	**Three For A Pound (72)** (JAGlover) **3-8-10** GCarter(13) (outpcd & lost tch fr ½-wy)	1¼	**9**	6/1[3]	28	—
	Spotted Eagle (76) (MartynWane) **4-9-10** DWright(2) (prom tl outpcd fnl 2f)	2	**10**	33/1	27	—
823[10]	**The Wad (66)** (DNicholls) **4-9-0** AlexGreaves(12) (racd alone stands' side: spd over 3f)	1¼	**11**	16/1	14	—
835[7]	**Bayin (USA) (70)** (MDIUsher) **8-9-4** JQuinn(4) (lw: dwlt: effrt ½-wy: n.d)	1¼	**12**	7/1	14	—

(SP 133.7%) **12 Rn**

1m 17.58 (6.58) CSF £85.35 CT £672.95 TOTE £7.00: £2.30 £9.00 £2.60 (£160.50) Trio £652.80; £505.71 to Chester 6/5/97 OWNER Mrs Joan Smith (Lincoln) (THIRSK) BRED Ulceby Vale Stud Ltd
WEIGHT FOR AGE 3yo-10lb

Halmanerror is good on his day and this was it as he travelled particularly well and won in most convincing style. (5/1)
Mr Speaker (IRE) travelled as well as the winner for much of the trip but, when it came down to a fight, he was plain and simply not as good, although he is obviously in fine form. (16/1)
729 Two On The Bridge put up a useful performance for a three-year-old and is obviously improving. (9/1)
448 A Breeze was staying on most determinedly in the closing stages to show he is coming to hand. (10/1)
Palo Blanco put up a useful effort here, and is coming down to a decent mark. (12/1)
827 Amron travelled too well early on and was too close to the pace, and needs dropping out. (5/2: op 4/1)
545* Daawe (USA) looked well enough but ran as though this was probably needed after five weeks off. (7/1)

T/Plpt: £27.30 (327.57 Tckts). T/Qdpt: £22.00 (16.89 Tckts) AA

0498-HAYDOCK (L-H) (Soft)

Monday May 5th

Race 6 - Flip start; hand-timed
WEATHER: raining WIND: mod half bhd

978 TAPSTER'S MOSS MAIDEN STKS (3-Y.O F) (Class D)

2-00 (2-00) **1m 2f 120y** £3,452.50 (£1,045.00: £510.00: £242.50) Stalls: High GOING: 0.89 sec per fur (S)

Form	Horse	Dist	Pos	SP	RR	SF
833[U]	**Shouk** (LMCumani) **3-8-11** OUrbina(6) (trckd ldrs: led 3f out: pushed clr appr fnl f: eased nr fin)	—	**1**	7/4[1]	83+	48
683[11]	**Georgia Venture** (SPCWoods) **3-8-11** JReid(4) (hld up in tch: hdwy to chse wnr 2f out: rdn & kpt on one pce)	1½	**2**	8/1	81	46
	Manuetti (IRE) (SbinSuroor) **3-8-11** PatEddery(3) (led 4f: led again 4f out: rdn & hdd 3f out: sn wknd)	19	**3**	9/4[2]	52	17
	Saintly Manner (USA) (DRLoder) **3-8-11** KDarley(2) (w'like: scope: bit bkwd: chsd ldr: led 6f out to 4f out: wknd over 2f out)	7	**4**	6/1	41	6
	Magaona (FR) (RHannon) **3-8-11** RHughes(1) (w'like: bit bkwd: in tch: pushed along over 3f out: sn wknd & eased: t.o)	24	**5**	12/1	5	—
	Arletty (HRACecil) **3-8-11** JLowe(7) (w'like: bkwd: s.i.s: racd wd: sn pushed along: dropped rr 6f out: t.o)	4	**6**	11/2[3]	—	—

(SP 115.6%) **6 Rn**

2m 27.09 (15.59) CSF £15.40 TOTE £3.00: £1.60 £2.60 (£6.50) OWNER Fittocks Stud (NEWMARKET) BRED Fittocks Stud

Shouk, always travelling well, had the race sewn up some way out and justified her strong market support in style. (7/4)
683 Georgia Venture put up a fine run although flattered by her proximity to the winner. She should be able to find a similar contest. (8/1: 6/1-9/1)
Manuetti (IRE) went out quite tamely once headed but should be given another chance as this race was run in deplorable conditions. (9/4: op evens)

Saintly Manner (USA) took a good hold going to post and raced quite freely but had shot her bolt over a quarter of a mile out. She should improve for the run. (6/1: 5/2-7/1)
Magaona (FR) looked just in need of the run and was weak in the market. Put under pressure early in the straight, she was soon outpointed and her jockey was very easy on her. (12/1: op 7/1)
Arletty, a workmanlike filly much in need of the run, was keen going to post but had to be chased along from the word go once the stalls opened. She was plum last after half a mile. (11/2)

67+ 73+ 87

979 E.B.F. GALLOWS HALL MAIDEN STKS (2-Y.O) (Class D)

2-30 (2-31) **5f** £3,403.75 (£1,030.00: £502.50: £238.75) Stalls: High GOING: 0.53 sec per fur (GS)

				SP	RR	SF
	Hoh Chi Min (MBell) **2-8-9** JReid(7) (scope: hmpd s: sn pushed along: hdwy to ld ins fnl f: rdn & edgd rt cl home)	—	1	6/1	72	26
850^{2}	**Ron's Pet** (RHannon) **2-9-0** RHughes(9) (lw: a.p: led over 1f out: hung lft & hdd ins fnl f: r.o)	s.h	2	$7/4^{1}$	77	31
	Peter's Imp (IRE) (JBerry) **2-9-0** KDarley(8) (scope: lw: led tl rdn & hdd over 1f out: hmpd jst ins fnl f)	3½	3	$11/2^{3}$	66	20
850^{6}	**Swoosh** (BJMeehan) **2-9-0** PatEddery(4) (chsd ldrs: ev ch appr fnl f: n.m.r ins fnl f: unable qckn)	s.h	4	$7/2^{2}$	66	20
	Kettlesing (IRE) (MWEasterby) **2-8-9b^{1}** TLucas(6) (neat: lw: towards rr: kpt on fnl 2f: n.d)	2	5	20/1	54	8
828^{6}	**Patsy Culsyth** (MJohnston) **2-8-9** DeanMcKeown(2) (chsd ldrs: rdn 2f out: wknd fnl f)	1¾	6	8/1	49	3
	Whacker-Do (IRE) (RHollinshead) **2-8-11**(3) FLynch(5) (small: in tch: rdn & ev ch appr fnl f: sn wknd)	6	7	14/1	34	—
	Cumbrian Caruso (TDEasterby) **2-9-0** MBirch(1) (w'like: bit bkwd: rdn & hdwy over 2f out: wknd appr fnl f)	2	8	12/1	28	—
	Sealed By Fate (IRE) (JSWainwright) **2-9-0** MRimmer(3) (str: bkwd: dwlt: a bhd)	10	9	20/1	—	—
				(SP 123.3%)	**9 Rn**	

66.2 secs (6.70) CSF £16.51 TOTE £6.80: £1.60 £1.10 £2.30 (£6.10) Trio £7.30 OWNER Mr D. F. Allport (NEWMARKET) BRED Christian Marner

Hoh Chi Min, a filly with a bit of scope about her, looked as if she would benefit from the run and battled on very gamely in a driving finish. (6/1: 4/1-7/1)
850 Ron's Pet, as on his debut, hung left in the final furlong despite his jockey doing all he could to keep him straight. He should soon go one better. (7/4)
Peter's Imp (IRE) looked really fit for his debut as you would expect from this yard, and ran well. Having just surrendered his lead, he looked held when checked inside the final furlong. He should not be long in winning. (11/2: 3/1-6/1)
850 Swoosh looked a real danger below the distance, but it appeared his measure had been taken when he was tightened up in the closing stages. (7/2)
Kettlesing (IRE), a small, fit filly who raced with her tongue tied, stayed on in the closing stages without getting in a blow. This experience will have done her good. (20/1)
828 Patsy Culsyth raced up with the pace here but was on the retreat in the final furlong. (8/1: op 5/1)
Cumbrian Caruso (12/1: 5/1-14/1)

980 LODGE LANE CONDITIONS STKS (3-Y.O+) (Class C)

3-00 (3-02) **6f** £4,768.20 (£1,783.80: £871.90: £374.50: £167.25: £84.35) Stalls: High GOING: 0.53 sec per fur (GS)

				SP	RR	SF
$717a^{4}$	**Tomba (105)** (BJMeehan) **3-9-3** KDarley(6) (swtg: sn pushed along: swtchd rt over 1f out: sn hrd rdn: r.o wl to ld nr fin)	—	1	8/1	104	67
671^{5}	**Cayman Kai (IRE) (116)** (RHannon) **4-9-3** RHughes(3) (lw: hld up: hdwy to ld 1f out: sn rdn & hdd: r.o wl)	nk	2	$6/4^{1}$	93	66
	Man Howa (IRE) (LMCumani) **3-8-10** OUrbina(8) (chsd ldrs: rdn to ld wl ins fnl f: hdd & no ex cl home)	s.h	3	$5/1^{3}$	96	59
663^{3}	**Nineacres (64)** (NMBabbage) **6-9-3v** DeanMcKeown(2) (w ldr: rdn ½-wy: wknd fnl f)	3	4	50/1	85	58
519^{8}	**Montendre (95)** (RJHodges) **10-9-3** MBirch(4) (in tch: rdn & r.o one pce fr over 1f out)	2	5	16/1	80	53
452^{8}	**Astrac (IRE) (106)** (MissGayKelleway) **6-9-13** JReid(7) (lw: led tl rdn & hdd 1f out: sn wknd)	hd	6	$4/1^{2}$	90	63
	The Puzzler (IRE) (104) (BWHills) **6-9-3** PatEddery(1) (b: prom: hdwy over 1f out: sn ev ch: wknd fnl f)	s.h	7	$5/1^{3}$	79	52
677^{15}	**Babsy Babe (90)** (JJQuinn) **4-8-12** JStack(5) (sn pushed along: wknd over 2f out: t.o)	27	8	20/1	2	—
				(SP 117.0%)	**8 Rn**	

1m 17.34 (5.64) CSF £19.11 TOTE £10.80: £1.80 £1.20 £1.90 (£12.10) OWNER Mr J. R. Good (UPPER LAMBOURN) BRED Mrs P. Good
WEIGHT FOR AGE 3yo-10lb

717a Tomba was under pressure and seemingly going nowhere below the distance when he was switched onto the stands rail. Once there, he sprouted wings and got up in the dying strides. (8/1)
671 Cayman Kai (IRE) travelled very well in behind the leaders and looked all over the winner when taking it up, only to be thwarted by the winner's late surge. (6/4)
Man Howa (IRE) was having his first run for over nine months and carrying quite a bit of condition, but he ran a blinder, only losing out in the final fifty yards. His shrewd handler will surely find something for him. (5/1: 5/2-11/2)
663 Nineacres has not won for well over two years but put in a creditable performance in this company. (50/1)
Montendre, on his toes in the preliminaries, never had the speed to threaten the principals. (16/1)
452 Astrac (IRE) ran well enough to suggest there are still races to be won with him. (4/1)

981 HAYDOCK PARK SPRING TROPHY RATED STKS H'CAP (0-110) (Listed) (3-Y.O+) (Class A)

3-30 (3-34) **7f 30y** £10,862.00 (£4,058.00: £1,979.00: £845.00: £372.50) Stalls: Low GOING: 0.53 sec per fur (GS)

				SP	RR	SF
449^{3}	**Craigievar (95)** (JRFanshawe) **3-7-13** NVarley(6) (lw: chsd ldr: led 2f out: rdn & edgd rt over 1f out: r.o)	—	1	$9/4^{1}$	99	72
839^{3}	**Ramooz (USA) (106)** (BHanbury) **4-9-8** MRimmer(2) (lw: hld up: hdwy over 2f out: chsd wnr fr over 1f out: rdn & unable qckn fnl f)	2½	2	$5/2^{2}$	104	80
	Musick House (IRE) (93) (PWChapple-Hyam) **4-8-9** JReid(1) (chsd ldrs: rdn 2f out: styd on cl home)	1¼	3	$7/2^{3}$	89	65
	Welville (93) (PJMakin) **4-8-9** PatEddery(5) (lw: led tl hdd 2f out: sn rdn & wknd)	12	4	9/2	62	38
	Everglades (IRE) (98) (RCharlton) **9-9-0** RHughes(3) (bit bkwd: hld up in tch: shkn up over 2f out: edgd lft: sn btn & eased)	21	5	10/1	20	—
				(SP 108.8%)	**5 Rn**	

1m 36.13 (8.13) CSF £7.24 TOTE £3.50: £1.80 £1.30 (£3.10) OWNER Mr D. I. Russell (NEWMARKET) BRED C. R. and V. M. Withers
WEIGHT FOR AGE 3yo-12lb
OFFICIAL EXPLANATION **Everglades (IRE): was not suited by the soft ground.**

449 Craigievar got loose by the saddling boxes and spread a plate, but was as cool as a cucumber in the paddock and never put a foot wrong in the race. He is still improving. (9/4)
839 Ramooz (USA), friendless in the market, put in a decent effort without ever looking like pegging back the winner. (5/2)

Musick House (IRE) couldn't go with the front two when the race started in earnest, and it was only in the final hundred yards that he was pegging them back. With this run under his belt he could be a different proposition. (7/2: 9/4-4/1)
Welville, although having his first run for over a year, appeared fit enough but went out like a light when headed. His form is all on fast ground and, when he encounters that again, he should leave this run behind. (9/2: 3/1-5/1)
Everglades (IRE) was held up on the heels of the leaders until weakening over a quarter of a mile out. His jockey quickly accepted the situation and connections cited the soft ground as the cause for his display. (10/1: 5/1-12/1)

982 DEAN MOOR H'CAP (0-85) (4-Y.O+) (Class D)
4-05 (4-06) **1m 6f** £3,501.25 (£1,060.00: £517.50: £246.25) Stalls: Centre GOING: 0.89 sec per fur (S)

	Horse	Dist	Pos	SP	RR	SF
613^{10}	**Turgenev (IRE) (63)** (RBastiman) **8-8-12b** MBirch(7) (lw: hld up: hdwy over 5f out: chsd wnr fr 2f out: styd on to ld wl ins fnl f)	—	**1**	5/1 ^{2}	75	53
470^{10}	**Welsh Mill (IRE) (76)** (MrsMReveley) **8-9-6**(5) SCopp(10) (a.p: led wl over 1f out: sn rdn: hdd & no ex wl ins fnl f)	1¼	**2**	10/1	87	65
660^{12}	**Bellara (58)** (NMBabbage) **5-8-7** JLowe(8) (lw: hld up: hdwy ½-wy: led 4f out tl wl over 1f out: sn wknd)	6	**3**	5/1 ^{2}	62	40
	Executive Design (72) (MrsMReveley) **5-9-7** KDarley(1) (hld up: hdwy over 4f out: kpt on one pce)	1¼	**4**	6/1 ^{3}	74	52
831^{7}	**Sharaf (IRE) (60)** (WRMuir) **4-8-8**ow2 JReid(3) (lw: in tch: rdn & wknd over 3f out: t.o)	15	**5**	12/1	45	20
	Rushen Raider (70) (KWHogg) **5-9-5** RHughes(4) (prom tl rdn & wknd over 2f out)	16	**6**	8/1	37	15
789^{15}	**Veridian (73)** (PWHarris) **4-9-7** PatEddery(9) (mid div: effrt over 5f out: sn wknd: t.o)	4	**7**	8/1	35	12
858^{3}	**Noufari (FR) (74)** (RHollinshead) **6-9-6**(3) FLynch(6) (a in rr: t.o)	2½	**8**	10/1	33	11
777^{2}	**Shirley Sue (75)** (MJohnston) **4-9-9** DeanMcKeown(11) (lw: led 8f: drvn along over 4f out: sn btn: t.o)	4	**9**	4/1 ^{1}	30	7
761^{5}	**Blatant Outburst (68)** (MissSJWilton) **7-9-3b^{1}** OUrbina(5) (chsd ldr tl led 6f out: hdd 4f out: wknd qckly: t.o)	11	**10**	16/1	10	—
	Batoutoftheblue (59) (WWHaigh) **4-8-7** MRimmer(2) (a bhd: t.o)	dist	**11**	14/1	—	—
				(SP 128.3%)	**11 Rn**	

3m 18.27 (20.07) CSF £54.37 CT £250.28 TOTE £5.30: £2.00 £4.80 £1.50 (£37.10) Trio £62.60 OWNER Mrs Bridget Tranmer (WETHERBY) BRED Paolo Tomei
WEIGHT FOR AGE 4yo-1lb
IN-FOCUS: Stalls 1 & 2 opened a fraction early.
Turgenev (IRE) came with a well-timed run to land his fourth course victory and give his handler a long-overdue win. (5/1)
Welsh Mill (IRE), always in the thick of things, looked set for a second course and distance victory when going down below the distance, but had no answer when the winner loomed up. (10/1: 7/1-12/1)
498 Bellara, back on a winning mark here, may need better ground if she is to exploit it. (5/1)
Executive Design, without a Flat win for over two years, never threatened to change that. (6/1: op 4/1)
612 Sharaf (IRE) has dropped nearly two stone in the ratings in nine months, but was still never a threat. (12/1)
Rushen Raider (8/1: 6/1-10/1)
777 Shirley Sue made the running for a mile but was soon under maximum pressure and dropped tamely away. (4/1: 3/1-9/2)
Batoutoftheblue (14/1: 10/1-16/1)

983 DERBYSHIRE HILL MAIDEN STKS (3-Y.O) (Class D)
4-35 (4-36) **7f 30y** £3,712.50 (£1,125.00: £550.00: £262.50) Stalls: Low GOING: 0.89 sec per fur (S)

	Horse	Dist	Pos	SP	RR	SF
	Rickenbacker (IRE) (PWChapple-Hyam) **3-9-0** JReid(7) (w'like: a.p: pushed along 3f out: hdwy to ld ins fnl f: edgd rt: r.o)	—	**1**	11/8 ^{1}	79	21
	Sky Commander (USA) (MRStoute) **3-9-0** MBirch(1) (h.d.w: lw: mid div: hmpd 5f out: rdn over 1f out: r.o wl fnl f)	½	**2**	9/2 ^{2}	78	20
599^{13}	**Welcome Home (42)** (PTDalton) **3-8-6**(3) FLynch(4) (led: rdn & hung lft over 2f out: hdd ins fnl f: r.o)	½	**3**	50/1	72	14
	Round Robin (IRE) (CWThornton) **3-9-0** NVarley(8) (w'like: scope: s.s: rdn & hdwy over 2f out: ev ch 1f out: no ex nr fin)	¾	**4**	50/1	75	17
503^{4}	**Compromise (IRE)** (BWHills) **3-9-0** PatEddery(12) (lw: in tch: rdn 2f out: hld whn n.m.r ins fnl f)	4	**5**	5/1 ^{3}	66	8
517^{2}	**Mr Majica** (BJMeehan) **3-9-0** RHughes(3) (hld up in tch: edgd lft over 1f out: n.d)	s.h	**6**	5/1 ^{3}	66	8
688^{11}	**Indian Blaze (79)** (PWHarris) **3-9-0** OUrbina(10) (chsd ldrs tl rdn & hung rt over 2f out: sn wknd)	3½	**7**	14/1	58	—
	Dargo (CWThornton) **3-9-0** JLowe(2) (mid div: hmpd 5f out: nvr nr ldrs)	½	**8**	14/1	57	—
	Jaza (NAGraham) **3-9-0** MRimmer(11) (str: scope: bit bkwd: mid div: rdn 3f out: btn over 1f out: eased)	s.h	**9**	12/1	57	—
	Tam O'Shanter (CWThornton) **3-9-0** DeanMcKeown(6) (neat: w ldr 3f: sn wknd)	6	**10**	25/1	44	—
	My Firebird (JJO'Neill) **3-8-9** KDarley(5) (tall: unf: bkwd: chsd ldrs: rdn & wknd over 2f out)	3	**11**	33/1	32	—
	Bernie's Star (IRE) (NBycroft) **3-9-0** JStack(9) (tall: bkwd: s.s: a bhd: t.o)	12	**12**	50/1	10	—
				(SP 127.3%)	**12 Rn**	

1m 41.22 (13.22) CSF £7.28 TOTE £2.50: £1.30 £2.00 £10.80 (£6.20) Trio Not won; £227.19 to Chester 6/5/97 OWNER Mr M. Tabor (MARLBOROUGH) BRED Kilcarn Stud
Rickenbacker (IRE), a 120,000gs yearling, moved well to post but had to be niggled along to hold his place over a quarter of a mile out. Taking it up inside the final furlong, he showed signs of greenness but was able to see off the challenges. He should go on from this. (11/8)
Sky Commander (USA) looked a picture and put in a fine display after being checked on the bend to the home straight. He gradually made his ground and finished best of all. (9/2: op 7/4)
Welcome Home put in far and away her best run to date, battling on with the utmost gameness when finally collared in the final furlong. (50/1)
Round Robin (IRE), from a yard yet to hit form, made a most encouraging run, coming to challenge at the furlong pole and only running out of steam in the last few yards. (50/1)
503 Compromise (IRE) was only a length or so off the leaders when getting squeezed out in the final furlong, although it is doubtful if he could have troubled the first two. Nevertheless, this was another good run. (5/1: 7/2-11/2)
517 Mr Majica travelled well but could never quite get amongst the leaders. His turn will come. (5/1)
Indian Blaze (14/1: op 8/1)

984 BOTANY BAY H'CAP (0-90) (3-Y.O+) (Class C)
5-05 (5-06) **1m 3f 200y** £5,218.50 (£1,578.00: £769.00: £364.50) Stalls: High GOING: 0.89 sec per fur (S)

	Horse	Dist	Pos	SP	RR	SF
746^{2}	**Fairy Knight (68)** (RHannon) **5-8-6** PatEddery(5) (hld up: hdwy 2f out: hrd rdn to ld nr fin)	—	**1**	5/2 ^{2}	76	48
680^{8}	**Al's Alibi (74)** (WRMuir) **4-8-12** RHughes(3) (trckd ldrs: led 3f out: rdn over 1f out: hdd & no ex cl home)	hd	**2**	2/1 ^{1}	82	54
	Ledgendry Line (68) (MrsMReveley) **4-8-6** KDarley(1) (bit bkwd: plld hrd: chsd ldrs: rdn 3 out: wknd over 1f out)	7	**3**	5/2 ^{2}	67	39

	Horse	Details	Dist	Pos	SP	RR	SF
605*	**Premier Night (76)**	(SDow) **4-9-0** DeanMcKeown(2) (led to 3f out: wknd 2f out: t.o)	20	**4**	5/1 3	48	20
					(SP 107.1%)		**4 Rn**

2m 46.28 (16.88) CSF £6.98 TOTE £2.10: (£2.50) OWNER P & S Lever Partners (MARLBOROUGH) BRED Peter McCalmont

746 Fairy Knight settled out the back going well and improved smoothly, but Eddery had to pull out all the stops in the end. This is by far the softest ground he has won on. (5/2: op 6/4)

499 Al's Alibi travelled well throughout the race until chased along to maintain his lead below the distance, and it was only in the last two strides that he was caught. (2/1)

Ledgendry Line took a good hold early on but his lack of peak fitness took its toll in the closing stages. (5/2)

605* Premier Night dropped right away once the leaders surrendered. This was very different ground than she encountered when winning last time out. (5/1: 5/2-11/2)

T/Plpt: £35.40 (287.53 Tckts). T/Qdpt: £8.90 (57.75 Tckts) J.

0517-KEMPTON (R-H) (Good)
Monday May 5th
WEATHER: fair WIND: almost nil

73+ 76+ 78+ 76

985 E.B.F. POLYANTHUS MAIDEN STKS (2-Y.O) (Class D)
2-10 (2-12) **5f** £3,338.75 (£1,010.00: £492.50: £233.75) Stalls: Low GOING minus 0.07 sec per fur (G)

	Horse	Details	Dist	Pos	SP	RR	SF
	Another Fantasy (IRE)	(RHannon) **2-8-9** DaneO'Neill(5) (neat: a.p: rdn over 2f out: led ins fnl f: r.o wl)	—	**1**	13/2	72	16
	Indian Silver	(MRChannon) **2-8-9** TQuinn(6) (unf: led tl ins fnl f: unable qckn)	2½	**2**	4/1 2	64	8
	Poetto	(BJMeehan) **2-9-0** OPeslier(3) (leggy: unf: hld up: rdn over 2f out: one pce)	3	**3**	9/2 3	59	3
	Memorial (IRE)	(RHannon) **2-9-0** LDettori(7) (w'like: a.p: rdn over 2f out: wknd over 1f out)	1½	**4**	5/2 1	55	—
	Angelique	(MJHaynes) **2-8-9** GBardwell(1) (w'like: s.s: outpcd: nvr nrr)	nk	**5**	8/1	49	—
	Sergeant Imp (IRE)	(PMitchell) **2-8-11**(3) MHenry(2) (str: bit bkwd: hld up: rdn over 3f out: wknd over 2f out)	s.h	**6**	25/1	54	—
	Really Done It Now (IRE)	(KRBurke) **2-8-9** PaulEddery(4) (leggy: unf: s.s: rdn & hdwy 2f out: wknd over 1f out)	1¾	**7**	25/1	43	—
828 13	**Lisa's Pride (IRE)**	(MissGayKelleway) **2-8-9** SSanders(8) (spd over 3f)	3	**8**	7/1	33	—
					(SP 111.4%)		**8 Rn**

62.4 secs (4.20) CSF £28.12 TOTE £8.30: £2.00 £1.70 £2.10 (£14.70) OWNER Mrs P. Jubert (MARLBOROUGH) BRED Jerry O'Brien

Another Fantasy (IRE), a half-sister to several winners, is not that big but, never far away, she was ridden along to get on top inside the final furlong for a decisive victory. (13/2)

Indian Silver, whose dam is a half-sister to the very useful Captain Horatius, has some filling out to do and comes from a stable that is not really firing with its juveniles at present. Nevertheless, she bowled along in front and, although eventually overhauled inside the final furlong, still finished well clear of the remainder. She should not be difficult to win with. (4/1)

Poetto, who needs time to develop, and is rather on the leg at present, drifted badly in the betting and, although lacking another gear in the second half of the race, did struggle on to win the battle for third prize. (9/2: 7/4-5/1)

Memorial (IRE), a sturdy individual, raced up with the pace but tired approaching the final furlong as lack of race fitness took its toll. (5/2: op 6/4)

Angelique, who cost a mere 3,600gs, comes from a stable that has a very bad record with its first time out two-year-olds. Very well supported in the market, she lost ground at the start and, taken off her feet, could never get into it despite making a little late headway. (8/1)

Sergeant Imp (IRE) comes from a stable for first time out juveniles. Not looking fully wound up, he had already shot his bolt by halfway. (25/1)

Lisa's Pride (IRE) (7/1: op 4/1)

986 SAXON HOUSE H'CAP (0-80) (3-Y.O+) (Class D)
2-40 (2-44) **1m 4f** £3,533.75 (£1,070.00: £522.50: £248.75) Stalls: High GOING minus 0.07 sec per fur (G)

	Horse	Details	Dist	Pos	SP	RR	SF
	Mr Wild (USA) (73)	(RAkehurst) **4-9-7** TQuinn(9) (chsd ldr 6f: rdn over 4f out: led wl over 1f out: sn hdd: led ins fnl f: r.o wl)	—	**1**	4/1 1	86	59
647 6	**Atlantic Mist (55)**	(BRMillman) **4-8-3** SSanders(7) (hdwy over 2f out: led over 1f out tl ins fnl f: unable qckn)	2½	**2**	9/2 2	65	38
680 6	**Tawafek (USA) (61)**	(SDow) **4-8-9** OPeslier(10) (rdn over 4f out: hdwy over 1f out: r.o one pce)	4	**3**	6/1 3	65	38
680 10	**Traceability (80)**	(SCWilliams) **4-10-0** LDettori(3) (led over 7f: led over 2f out tl wl over 1f out: wknd nl f)	nk	**4**	9/1	84	57
735 20	**Pistol (IRE) (77)**	(CAHorgan) **7-9-11** PaulEddery(2) (s.s: hdwy on ins over 2f out: wknd over 1f out)	2½	**5**	12/1	78	51
375 7	**Blue And Royal (IRE) (48)**	(VSoane) **5-7-10b** GBardwell(6) (lw: s.s: rdn over 4f out: hdwy over 1f out: nvr nrr)	s.h	**6**	66/1	49	22
690 19	**Supreme Sound (79)**	(PWHarris) **3-8-8** GHind(11) (bit bkwd: plld hrd: prom over 10f)	½	**7**	10/1	79	33
735 17	**Grand Splendour (75)**	(LadyHerries) **4-9-9** WRyan(8) (a.p: chsd ldr 6f out: led over 4f out tl over 2f out: wknd wl over 1f out)	2½	**8**	10/1	72	45
	Renzo (IRE) (78)	(MrsAJPerrett) **4-9-12** RHills(12) (prom 10f)	8	**9**	12/1	64	37
	Clouds Hill (FR) (67)	(RHannon) **4-9-1** DaneO'Neill(1) (b.off hind: hdwy 6f out: wknd over 4f out)	s.h	**10**	20/1	53	26
	Durham (65)	(GLMoore) **6-8-13** SWhitworth(4) (bhd fnl 5f)	1½	**11**	9/1	49	22
46 6	**Greenwich Fore (67)**	(TGMills) **3-7-5**(5) RFfrench(5) (bkwd: bhd fnl 4f)	½	**12**	25/1	50	4
					(SP 116.1%)		**12 Rn**

2m 35.96 (5.96) CSF £18.69 CT £97.30 TOTE £4.70: £2.10 £1.80 £2.50 (£9.60) Trio £15.80 OWNER Mr A. D. Spence (EPSOM) BRED Kinsman Farm

LONG HANDICAP Blue And Royal (IRE) 7-2

WEIGHT FOR AGE 3yo-19lb

Mr Wild (USA) made a very encouraging start to his hurdling career this winter, but then seemed to go the wrong way. Reverting back to the Flat, he certainly made Quinn work extremely hard and, after a tremendous tussle with the runner-up, eventually asserted inside the final furlong. He will be suited by further. (4/1)

647 Atlantic Mist, 4lb lower than when last successful, picked up ground and threw down a determined challenge in the final quarter-mile. He did get his head in front for a brief time, but he was unable to cope with the winner inside the final furlong. His turn is not far away. (9/2)

680 Tawafek (USA), bustled along turning for home, stayed on in the final quarter-mile but found the first two were already home and dry.(6/1)

Traceability, given his fair share of weight here, made the vast majority of the running until collared early in the final quarter-mile. (9/1)

Pistol (IRE) ran much better here and, after picking up ground along the inside rail early in the straight, tired below the distance. (12/1)

252 Blue And Royal (IRE), 8lb out of the handicap, stayed on from the back of the field in the closing stages, only to find it all over bar the shouting. (66/1)

Renzo (IRE) (12/1: op 8/1)

987 JUBILEE H'CAP (0-105) (4-Y.O+) (Class B)

3-10 (3-14) **1m (Jubilee)** £17,587.50 (£5,325.00: £2,600.00: £1,237.50) Stalls: High GOING minus 0.07 sec per fur (G)

	Horse		Pos	SP	RR	SF
	Autumn Cover (75) (PRHedger) **5-8-3** GHind(7) (lw: a.p: led over 3f out: rdn out)	—	**1**	33/1	85	61
738[2]	**Lonely Leader (IRE) (100)** (RHannon) **4-10-0** DaneO'Neill(6) (lw: hdwy over 2f out: hrd rdn over 1f out: r.o)	¾	**2**	12/1	109	85
	Gold Spats (USA) (84) (MRStoute) **4-8-12** RHills(5) (hld up: chsd wnr over 2f out: hrd rdn over 1f out: unable qckn ins fnl f)	s.h	**3**	12/1	92	68
	Welton Arsenal (88) (KBishop) **5-9-2** PaulEddery(13) (lw: nt clr run over 2f out: hdwy over 1f out: r.o wl ins fnl f: nt clr run nr fin)	1	**4**	33/1	94	70
832[9]	**Amber Fort (74)** (DRCElsworth) **4-7-13v**(3) MHenry(4) (rdn over 3f out: hdwy over 2f out: r.o)	nk	**5**	33/1	80	56
832*	**Star Talent (USA) (86)** (IABalding) **6-9-0** RCochrane(1) (lw: s.s: nt clr run over 2f out: hdwy over 1f out: one pce wl ins fnl f)	¾	**6**	13/2[3]	90	66
832[3]	**Star Manager (USA) (85)** (PFICole) **7-8-13** TQuinn(9) (lw: rdn over 2f out: hdwy over 1f out: nvr nrr)	nk	**7**	8/1	89	65
738[4]	**Almond Rock (96)** (JRFanshawe) **5-9-10** DHarrison(14) (nt clr run over 2f out: hdwy over 1f out: one pce)	2½	**8**	12/1	95	71
677[5]	**Concer Un (96)** (SCWilliams) **5-9-10** LDettori(12) (b: hld up: rdn over 2f out: sn wknd)	2	**9**	9/2[1]	91	67
444*	**Artful Dane (IRE) (79)** (MJHeaton-Ellis) **5-8-7v**ow2 OPeslier(2) (lw: prom over 6f)	¾	**10**	10/1	72	46
776[3]	**Forest Robin (69)** (MrsJRRamsden) **4-7-6**(5) RFfrench(15) (bhd fnl 2f)	¾	**11**	7/1	61	37
838[15]	**Zermatt (IRE) (68)** (MDIUsher) **7-7-10** JMarshall(11) (lw: a bhd)	1¼	**12**	50/1	57	33
735[16]	**Hardy Dancer (74)** (GLMoore) **5-8-2** DRMcCabe(8) (lw: prom 6f)	6	**13**	14/1	51	27
791*	**La Modiste (70)** (MissGayKelleway) **4-7-12** GBardwell(10) (prom over 5f)	1¼	**14**	10/1	45	21
832[4]	**Alhawa (USA) (77)** (RAkehurst) **4-8-5** SSanders(16) (lw: rdn 4f out: bhd fnl 2f)	8	**15**	6/1[2]	36	12
832[10]	**Wakeel (USA) (80)** (SDow) **5-8-8b[1]** WRyan(3) (led over 4f: wknd over 2f out)	1	**16**	25/1	37	13

(SP 132.0%) **16 Rn**

1m 39.7 (2.00) CSF £369.21 CT £4,566.37 TOTE £64.90: £9.20 £3.50 £2.80 £4.80 (£916.10) Trio £1,974.30 OWNER Mr G. A. Alexander (CHICHESTER) BRED P. and Mrs Venner

LONG HANDICAP Zermatt (IRE) 7-8

Autumn Cover, winner of five races last year - all over a mile on fast ground - gained his biggest career win to date on this reappearance, leading over three furlongs from home and being ridden along to keep his rivals at bay. (33/1)

738 Lonely Leader (IRE) ran another sound race. Picking up ground early in the straight, he kept on under pressure to finish on the heels of the winner. He looks ready to strike before long. (12/1)

Gold Spats (USA) made an encouraging reappearance. Moving into second place over a quarter of a mile from home, he grimly tried to get on terms with the winner but he failed to do so and just lost second place in the dying strides. A handicap should soon be found for him. (12/1)

Welton Arsenal, fit from hurdling, had no luck here, but it should be remembered he is a very awkward customer and is not easy to win with - his record now reads two victories from twenty-six starts. (33/1)

Amber Fort stayed on in the straight to be nearest at the line. (33/1)

832* Star Talent (USA), in fine form at present, did not have the best of runs early in the straight but, after picking up ground below the distance, just lacked another turn of foot in the closing stages. (13/2)

988 SKYLARK CONDITIONS STKS (3-Y.O F) (Class C)

3-40 (3-41) **6f** £4,672.49 (£1,747.50: £853.75: £366.25: £163.13: £81.88) Stalls: Low GOING minus 0.07 sec per fur (G)

	Horse		Pos	SP	RR	SF
	Tumbleweed Pearl (98) (BJMeehan) **3-8-13** OPeslier(6) (hld up: rdn over 1f out: led ins fnl f: r.o wl)	—	**1**	4/1[2]	96	39
	March Star (IRE) (93) (JARToller) **3-8-13** SSanders(5) (bit bkwd: a.p: led 2f out tl ins fnl f: unable qckn)	1	**2**	8/1	93	36
854[7]	**Snap Crackle Pop (IRE) (90)** (RFJohnsonHoughton) **3-8-9** PaulEddery(1) (led 4f: ev ch ins fnl f: one pce)	hd	**3**	7/1[3]	89	32
507[7]	**Carati (92)** (RBoss) **3-8-9** LDettori(2) (hld up: rdn over 2f out: one pce)	2½	**4**	8/1	82	25
672[10]	**Caerfilly Dancer (94)** (RAkehurst) **3-8-13** RCochrane(4) (lw: hld up: rdn over 2f out: one pce)	1	**5**	7/1[3]	84	27
724[9]	**Blues Queen (89)** (MRChannon) **3-8-9** DHarrison(8) (no hdwy fnl 2f)	1¼	**6**	9/1	76	19
	Simple Logic (78) (AGFoster) **3-8-9** SWhitworth(9) (b.nr hind: outpcd)	3½	**7**	20/1	67	10
602[6]	**Heavenly Miss (IRE) (64)** (JJBridger) **3-8-9** WRyan(10) (bhd fnl 4f)	6	**8**	50/1	51	—
889[7]	**Chloe Nicole (USA)** (PFICole) **3-8-9** TQuinn(7) (lw: prom 2f)	nk	**9**	14/1	50	—
	Sweet Bettsie (AGFoster) **3-8-6**(3) MHenry(11) (b: bhd fnl 4f)	11	**10**	25/1	21	—
	Ikdam (USA) (98) (MajorWRHern) **3-9-5** RHills(3) (spd over 3f)	3½	**11**	11/4[1]	22	—

(SP 121.1%) **11 Rn**

1m 14.95 (3.75) CSF £33.24 TOTE £4.50: £1.90 £3.00 £2.20 (£18.20) Trio £154.30 OWNER The Tumbleweed Partnership (UPPER LAMBOURN) BRED R. A. Dalton

OFFICIAL EXPLANATION **Ikdam(USA): was reported to be in season.**

Tumbleweed Pearl was due to have made her reappearance in the Fred Darling at Newbury but she was found to have a temperature the day before. Woken up in the final quarter-mile, she got on top inside the final furlong and kept on well. Connections are now contemplating running her in the German 1,000 Guineas on Sunday. (4/1)

March Star (IRE) looked as though this reappearance was needed but that did not stop her from running a fine race. Striking the front a quarter of a mile out, she grimly tried to hold on but was unable to fend off the winner inside the final furlong. (8/1)

Snap Crackle Pop (IRE) ran much better here and took the field along. Collared a quarter of a mile out, she refused to give way and still had every chance inside the final furlong before tapped for toe. (7/1)

Carati, who failed to stay a mile here on her reappearance, failed to quicken in the final quarter-mile. (8/1)

672 Caerfilly Dancer was made to look very pedestrian in the second half of the race. (7/1)

Blues Queen was making little impression on the principals in the final quarter-mile. (9/1)

Ikdam (USA) flopped badly on this return to action and connections reported afterwards that she was in season. (11/4)

989 STANLEY RACING MAIDEN STKS (I) (3-Y.O F) (Class D)

4-10 (4-12) **1m (Jubilee)** £3,062.50 (£925.00: £450.00: £212.50) Stalls: High GOING minus 0.07 sec per fur (G)

	Horse		Pos	SP	RR	SF
	Zalitzine (USA) (MRStoute) **3-8-11** OPeslier(13) (gd sort: a.p: chsd ldr 3f out: led ins fnl f: comf)	—	**1**	10/11[1]	79+	48
	Lonely Heart (70) (DRCElsworth) **3-8-11** RCochrane(12) (chsd ldr: led over 4f out tl ins fnl f: unable qckn)	1½	**2**	9/1[3]	76	45
	Henry's Mother (MRChannon) **3-8-11** TQuinn(4) (leggy: unf: gd hdwy over 1f out: r.o wl ins fnl f)	½	**3**	16/1	75	44
681[8]	**Dellua (IRE)** (RGuest) **3-8-11** GHind(10) (bit bkwd: shkn up over 2f out: hdwy over 1f out: r.o)	5	**4**	33/1	65	34
	Elegant Dance (JJSheehan) **3-8-11** DaneO'Neill(1) (a.p: rdn over 2f out: wknd over 1f out)	2	**5**	33/1	61	30
	Boss Lady (IRE) (RCharlton) **3-8-11** PaulEddery(9) (unf: scope: hdwy on ins over 3f out: wknd over 2f out)	1½	**6**	11/2[2]	58	27
	Limelight (JARToller) **3-8-11** SSanders(3) (w'like: bit bkwd: nvr nrr)	1¼	**7**	20/1	56	25

778^{6}	**Agift** (RFJohnsonHoughton) **3-8-11** DRMcCabe(2) (led over 3f: wknd over 2f out)	3	**8**	25/1	50	19
	Sandystones (NAGraham) **3-8-11** WRyan(5) (hld up: rdn over 3f out: sn wknd)	8	**9**	20/1	34	3
	Eternity (JRFanshawe) **3-8-11** DHarrison(8) (leggy: unf: scope: bhd fnl 3f)	1¼	**10**	$9/1^{3}$	31	—
	Gore Hill (MBlanshard) **3-8-6**(5) RFfrench(11) (bkwd: prom over 4f)	9	**11**	66/1	13	—
727^{17}	**Mamma Luigi (IRE)** (GLewis) **3-8-8**(3) AWhelan(6) (a bhd)	s.h	**12**	33/1	13	—
727^{19}	**Miss Imp (IRE)** (PMitchell) **3-8-8**(3) MHenry(7) (dwlt: a bhd)	3½	**13**	66/1	6	—
				(SP 118.8%)	**13 Rn**	

1m 41.72 (4.02) CSF £7.48 TOTE £1.80: £1.20 £1.50 £2.20 (£6.70) Trio £32.90 OWNER Maktoum Al Maktoum (NEWMARKET) BRED Gainsborough Farm Inc

Zalitzine (USA), an attractive, good-sized filly, stood out head and shoulders above her rivals in the paddock. Cruising into second place three furlongs from home, she had several lengths to make up on the leader but, nudged along, she gradually reeled him in and, striking the front inside the final furlong, won with plenty in hand. She looks a useful filly in the making and can certainly go on from here. A mile and a quarter will suit her according to her jockey. (10/11: evens-11/10)

Lonely Heart, who has changed stables since last year, made her bid for glory over half a mile from home, and had shaken off all bar the winner in the straight. With a useful advantage, she grimly tried to hold on, but was eventually overhauled inside the final furlong. Her turn is not far away. (9/1: op 4/1)

Henry's Mother, a tall, unfurnished filly, certainly grasped the hang of things in the straight and, making up a lot of ground in the last furlong and a half, flew through to take third prize. (16/1)

Dellua (IRE) still looked in need of the run but caught the eye under considerate handling, staying on well in the last furlong and a half, to finish fourth. She is going the right way. (33/1)

Elegant Dance played an active role until lack of a recent run took its toll in the final quarter-mile. (33/1)

Boss Lady (IRE), with the scope to develop, picked up ground along the inside rail turning for home, but had shot her bolt early in the straight. (11/2: 3/1-6/1)

Eternity (9/1: op 5/1)

990 ROTHMANS ROYALS NORTH SOUTH CHALLENGE SERIES H'CAP (0-90) (3-Y.O) (Class C)

4-40 (4-45) **1m 1f (round)** £7,262.50 (£2,200.00: £1,075.00: £512.50) Stalls: High GOING minus 0.07 sec per fur (G)

				SP	RR	SF
	Prince of Denial (76) (DWPArbuthnot) **3-8-10** SWhitworth(13) (s.s: j.path over 7f out: n.m.r over 2f out: hdwy over 1f out: hrd rdn ins fnl f: led last stride)	—	**1**	16/1	84	42
654*	**Strathmore Clear (85)** (GLewis) **3-9-5** PaulEddery(15) (a.p: led over 1f out: hrd rdn fnl f: hdd last stride)	s.h	**2**	$6/1^{2}$	93	51
878*	**Bold Oriental (IRE) (84)** (NACallaghan) **3-9-4** 5x LDettori(3) (hdwy over 1f out: ev ch whn carried lft ins fnl f: one pce)	1½	**3**	$4/1^{1}$	89	47
690^{17}	**Love Has No Pride (USA) (87)** (RHannon) **3-9-7** DaneO'Neill(7) (lw: hdwy over 1f out: ev ch whn edgd lft ins fnl f: one pce)	¾	**4**	16/1	91	49
754*	**Moon Blast (79)** (LadyHerries) **3-8-13** RCochrane(8) (s.s: nt clr run over 2f out: hdwy over 1f out: r.o)	2½	**5**	$13/2^{3}$	79	37
690^{10}	**Fantail (68)** (MHTompkins) **3-7-13**(3) MHenry(11) (rdn over 3f out: hdwy over 1f out: r.o one pce)	¾	**6**	12/1	66	24
676^{17}	**Padauk (75)** (MJHaynes) **3-8-9** GHind(5) (nvr nr to chal)	5	**7**	33/1	64	22
795^{4}	**Begorrat (IRE) (78)** (BJMeehan) **3-8-12** OPeslier(9) (s.s: rdn over 3f out: hdwy over 1f out: nvr nrr)	½	**8**	16/1	66	24
654^{10}	**Brandon Jack (83)** (IABalding) **3-9-3** DHarrison(10) (lw: hld up: rdn 3f out: wknd over 1f out)	nk	**9**	14/1	71	29
475^{6}	**Bathe In Light (USA) (63)** (LordHuntingdon) **3-7-6**(5) AimeeCook(4) (lw: prom 4f)	1¾	**10**	12/1	48	6
606*	**Bubbly (74)** (JLDunlop) **3-8-8** TQuinn(17) (lw: led over 7f)	nk	**11**	$4/1^{1}$	58	16
	Soden (IRE) (73) (TGMills) **3-8-4**(3) AWhelan(12) (prom 7f)	5	**12**	33/1	48	6
	Trooper (70) (RAkehurst) **3-8-4** SSanders(14) (prom over 7f)	¾	**13**	16/1	44	2
840^{3}	**Doc Ryan's (75)** (MJRyan) **3-8-9** GBardwell(6) (prom over 4f)	6	**14**	12/1	38	—
	Impulsif (USA) (80) (DJSffrenchDavis) **3-9-0** WRyan(1) (hdwy over 5f out: wknd over 2f out)	9	**15**	25/1	27	—
				(SP 130.6%)	**15 Rn**	

1m 55.76 (5.16) CSF £105.31 CT £442.23 TOTE £52.70: £9.00 £2.40 £2.20 (£136.10) Trio £138.30 OWNER Mr J. S. Gutkin (COMPTON) BRED R. E. Crutchley

Prince of Denial at last found his feet below the distance and, responding to pressure, burst through to hit the front right on the line. A little bit further would probably help. (16/1)

654* Strathmore Clear gained a narrow advantage below the distance and, in a tremendous battle royal, was only caught right on the line. He is a winner without a penalty. (6/1)

878* Bold Oriental (IRE) launched his challenge below the distance and, although carried left by the fourth inside the final furlong, it made little difference to the result. (4/1)

431 Love Has No Pride (USA), 11lb higher than when winning a handicap last year, picked up ground below the distance and had every chance when drifting left inside the final furlong. (16/1)

754* Moon Blast, who failed to get a clear run early in the straight, ran on in the last furlong and a half but never looked like getting there in time. (13/2)

Fantail struggled on from the back of the field in the last furlong and a half to be nearest at the line. (12/1)

991 WINDSOR PARK MAIDEN STKS (3-Y.O C & G) (Class D)

5-10 (5-14) **1m (Jubilee)** £3,712.50 (£1,125.00: £550.00: £262.50) Stalls: High GOING minus 0.07 sec per fur (G)

				SP	RR	SF
	Badlesmere (USA) (PFICole) **3-8-11** TQuinn(13) (lw: a.p: led over 2f out: hrd rdn fnl f: r.o wl)	—	**1**	5/1	93	55
586^{3}	**Shaheen (USA)** (HRACecil) **3-8-11** WRyan(11) (a.p: ev ch fnl 2f: r.o)	¾	**2**	$100/30^{2}$	92	54
740^{8}	**Chief Monarch** (BSmart) **3-8-11** RCochrane(8) (a.p: rdn over 2f out: r.o one pce)	2½	**3**	16/1	87	49
683^{5}	**Warningford** (JRFanshawe) **3-8-11** DHarrison(4) (hld up: rdn over 2f out: one pce)	s.h	**4**	$3/1^{1}$	86	48
742^{10}	**Khafaaq** (MajorWRHern) **3-8-11** RHills(15) (a.p: rdn over 2f out: wknd wl over 1f out)	5	**5**	20/1	76	38
683^{6}	**Patriot Games (IRE)** (MRStoute) **3-8-11** OPeslier(1) (nvr nr to chal)	2	**6**	$9/2^{3}$	72	34
693^{5}	**Masterpiece** (RHannon) **3-8-11** DaneO'Neill(16) (s.s: nvr nrr)	½	**7**	14/1	71	33
	Shaddad (USA) (JLDunlop) **3-8-11** GHind(9) (a mid div)	8	**8**	12/1	55	17
790^{2}	**Ijtinab (78)** (RAkehurst) **3-8-11** SSanders(10) (lw: led over 5f: wknd over 1f out)	½	**9**	10/1	54	16
645^{7}	**Travelmate** (JRFanshawe) **3-8-6**(5) RFfrench(12) (nvr nrr)	1¼	**10**	33/1	52	14
	Top of The Green (IRE) (PJMakin) **3-8-6**(5) DSweeney(3) (prom over 5f)	1¼	**11**	33/1	49	11
740^{12}	**Premier Eclipse** (PWHarris) **3-8-8**(3) MHenry(14) (bhd fnl 3f)	3½	**12**	33/1	42	4
436^{7}	**Khayal (USA)** (BWHills) **3-8-11** PaulEddery(7) (bit bkwd: s.s: a bhd)	¾	**13**	25/1	41	3
742^{14}	**Polished Steel (IRE)** (LadyHerries) **3-8-11** SWhitworth(17) (s.s: sme hdwy on ins 3f out: wknd over 2f out)	½	**14**	33/1	40	2
	Haydn James (USA) (PWHarris) **3-8-11** DRMcCabe(2) (prom 4f)	2	**15**	16/1	36	—

				SP	RR	SF
	Eben Albadou (USA) (ACStewart) **3-8-11** LDettori(5) (str: scope: bit bkwd: s.s: a bhd)	21	**16**	10/1	—	—
674[11]	**Chakra** (SDow) **3-8-8**(3) AWhelan(6) (bhd fnl 4f: t.o)	25	**17**	50/1	—	—
				(SP 149.6%)	**17 Rn**	

1m 41.06 (3.36) CSF £23.38 TOTE £7.60: £2.50 £1.80 £5.50 (£5.70) Trio £201.40 OWNER Exors of the late Lord Sondes (WHATCOMBE) BRED Peter J. Callahan

Badlesmere (USA) put up a very gutsy display. Leading over a quarter of a mile from home, he had a tremendous duel with the runner-up and just managed to prevail. His jockey reported he will get further and the Italian Derby is a possibility. (5/1: 7/2-11/2)

586 Shaheen (USA) launched a dangerous-looking challenge in the final quarter-mile but, despite giving his all, just failed to prevail. He should make no mistake next time out. (100/30: 2/1-7/2)

Chief Monarch, never far away, stayed on from below the distance if never looking likely to find that vital turn of foot. (16/1)

683 Warningford chased the leaders but, despite his rider's effort in the straight, failed to find the necessary turn of foot. (3/1)

Khafaaq played an active role until coming to the end of his tether early in the final quarter-mile. (20/1)

683 Patriot Games (IRE) never looked like posing a serious threat. (9/2)

693 Masterpiece (14/1: 8/1-16/1)

790 Ijtinab (10/1: 8/1-12/1)

Eben Albadou (USA) (10/1: 6/1-12/1)

992 STANLEY RACING MAIDEN STKS (II) (3-Y.O F) (Class D)

5-40 (5-41) **1m (Jubilee)** £3,062.50 (£925.00: £450.00: £212.50) Stalls: High GOING minus 0.07 sec per fur (G)

				SP	RR	SF
	Bint Baladee (SbinSuroor) **3-8-11** LDettori(5) (lw: chsd ldr: rdn over 1f out: led last strides)	—	**1**	5/2[2]	97	53
727[3]	**Selfish** (HRACecil) **3-8-11** WRyan(11) (led: clr over 2f out: wknd ins fnl f: hdd last strides)	hd	**2**	6/4[1]	97	53
	Nubile (BWHills) **3-8-11** GHind(2) (lw: s.s: stdy hdwy over 1f out: r.o: bttr for r)	14	**3**	16/1	69	25
	Academy Star (JRFanshawe) **3-8-11** DHarrison(3) (a.p: rdn 3f out: wknd over 2f out)	1	**4**	6/1[3]	67	23
727[9]	**Anchored In Love** (RCharlton) **3-8-11** PaulEddery(10) (hld up: rdn over 3f out: wknd over 2f out)	1½	**5**	14/1	64	20
727[6]	**Fantastic Flame (IRE)** (PJMakin) **3-8-11** SSanders(12) (prom over 5f)	2½	**6**	14/1	59	15
	Polska Princess (GER) (LordHuntingdon) **3-8-11** TQuinn(8) (scope: nvr nrr)	s.h	**7**	10/1	59	15
	Dulcinea (IABalding) **3-8-11** SWhitworth(9) (lw: plld hrd: prom 5f)	5	**8**	25/1	49	5
	Zibeth (LMCumani) **3-8-6**(5) RFfrench(7) (bhd fnl 4f)	1¼	**9**	25/1	46	2
841[13]	**Aquavita** (RHannon) **3-8-11** DaneO'Neill(6) (s.s: a bhd)	hd	**10**	33/1	46	2
656[4]	**La Chatelaine** (GLewis) **3-8-8**(3) AWhelan(1) (s.s: a bhd)	8	**11**	50/1	30	—
	Ghayah (IRE) (RWArmstrong) **3-8-11** RHills(4) (leggy: scope: lw: bhd fnl 2f)	7	**12**	10/1	16	—
				(SP 132.8%)	**12 Rn**	

1m 41.23 (3.53) CSF £6.68 TOTE £3.40: £1.60 £1.30 £6.90 (£1.90) Trio £21.70 OWNER Godolphin (NEWMARKET) BRED Gainsborough Stud Management Ltd

OFFICIAL EXPLANATION **Nubile: is a weak filly, was short of room two furlongs out and took time to get balanced again before running on.**

Bint Baladee has plenty of ability but looked an extremely awkward ride last year. Racing in second place, she looked booked for that position as the leader forged clear in the straight. However, she gradually managed to reel her in and got to the front in the last few strides. (5/2: 6/4-3/1)

727 Selfish attempted to make all the running and, forging clear early in the straight, appeared to have the race won. However, her stride shortened inside the final furlong and, going up and down on the spot, was collared in the last few strides. She looks nailed on next time out. (6/4)

Nubile was given considerate handling on this seasonal debut, but caught the eye staying on in the last furlong and a half to finish a moderate third. She should step up on this before long. (16/1)

Academy Star played an active role until coming to the end of her tether early in the straight. (6/1: op 10/1)

Anchored In Love chased the leaders but had shot her bolt over a quarter of a mile from home. (14/1)

727 Fantastic Flame (IRE) showed up until tiring over two furlongs from home. (14/1: 8/1-16/1)

Polska Princess (GER) (10/1: 9/2-12/1)

Ghayah (IRE) (10/1: op 6/1)

T/Jkpt: Not won; £4,237.74 to Chester 6/5/97. T/Plpt: £480.60 (68.04 Tckts). T/Qdpt: £113.50 (12.5 Tckts) AK

0524-NEWCASTLE (L-H) (Rnd crse Good to firm, St Good, Good to firm ptchs)
Monday May 5th

Races 2,4 & 6 hand-timed

WEATHER: raining WIND: fresh half against

61+ 63+ 67 60

993 AID ROMANIA MAIDEN AUCTION STKS (2-Y.O) (Class F)

2-25 (2-28) **5f** £2,599.50 (£732.00: £358.50) Stalls: Centre GOING minus 0.23 sec per fur (GF)

				SP	RR	SF
	Angel Hill (TDBarron) **2-7-12** LCharnock(14) (w'like: leggy: scope: chsd ldr: led jst ins fnl f: readily)	—	**1**	20/1	63+	5
822[3]	**Oh Never Again (IRE)** (MJohnston) **2-8-9** JWeaver(15) (lw: led stands' side tl jst ins fnl f: kpt on same pce)	1	**2**	2/1[1]	71	13
	Fairy Domino (MRChannon) **2-7-13**(5)ow2 PPMurphy(12) (neat: unf: chsd ldrs: edgd lft & kpt on same pce fnl f)	½	**3**	11/2[3]	64	4
	Sandside (JBerry) **2-8-2**(5) PFessey(4) (cmpt: led & sn clr far side: nt qckn ins fnl f)	hd	**4**	9/1	67	9
836[5]	**Blue Desert** (MBell) **2-8-2**(5) RMullen(6) (chsd ldrs: rdn 2f out: wandered & wknd fnl f)	4	**5**	11/4[2]	54	—
594[7]	**Durham Flyer** (TDEasterby) **2-8-6**(3) RHavlin(1) (chsd ldr far side: sn outpcd: styd on fnl f)	2	**6**	10/1	50	—
743[8]	**Toll's Times** (MWEasterby) **2-8-5** DaleGibson(2) (racd far side: a outpcd)	6	**7**	25/1	27	—
844[7]	**Sylvan Cloud** (CWFairhurst) **2-7-9**(3) DarrenMoffatt(10) (rdn & outpcd fr ½-wy)	2½	**8**	50/1	12	—
	Desire's Gold (MBrittain) **2-8-5** JCarroll(9) (leggy: unf: unruly s: chsd ldrs tl lost pl ½-wy)	1	**9**	25/1	15	—
880[7]	**Eurofen** (PDEvans) **2-8-6v**(5)ow6 PRoberts(11) (outpcd fr ½-wy)	¾	**10**	14/1	19	—
631[7]	**Just Nobby** (NTinkler) **2-8-3** KimTinkler(5) (outpcd fr ½-wy)	½	**11**	50/1	9	—
	Hayburner (MWEasterby) **2-8-1**(5)ow3 GParkin(3) (small: racd far side: swtchd stands' side after 2f: n.d)	3½	**12**	20/1	1	—
	Asprilla (IRE) (BEllison) **2-8-5** JTate(7) (neat: unf: sn wl outpcd)	½	**13**	25/1	—	—
	Wee Christy (IRE) (WMcKeown) **2-8-9** ACulhane(8) (leggy: unruly s: s.s: a wl bhd)	11	**14**	33/1	—	—
	Karenaragon (RonaldThompson) **2-7-12** TWilliams(13) (neat: s.v.s: a wl bhd)	5	**15**	50/1	—	—
				(SP 131.0%)	**15 Rn**	

61.87 secs (3.47) CSF £54.50 TOTE £35.50: £8.50 £1.40 £2.70 (£40.80) Trio £108.60 OWNER D K D Partnership (THIRSK) BRED T. D. and Mrs S. C. Barron

Angel Hill, a likeable filly, on the leg at present, took this in decisive fashion despite looking green beforehand. (20/1)

822 Oh Never Again (IRE) was again noisy in the paddock. With the benefit of the stands' side rail, he still found the winner much too good in the closing stages. (2/1)
Fairy Domino lacks size and substance but ran a sound first race. (11/2)
Sandside looked as if he knew his job. Clear of his two opponents on the far side, lack of company must have been a hindrance and he should soon find an opening. (9/1)
836 Blue Desert, very edgy in the paddock, dived left then badly right under pressure. (11/4: op 7/4)
Durham Flyer, who showed a round action going down, was staying on in the closing stages and can do better in time especially over further. (10/1)

994 FAT BINDER NATURAL WEIGHT MANAGEMENT H'CAP (0-80) (3-Y.O+) (Class D)
2-55 (2-55) **1m 4f 93y** £4,065.00 (£1,230.00: £600.00: £285.00) Stalls: Low GOING minus 0.23 sec per fur (GF)

				SP	RR	SF
746*	**Desert Fighter (68)** (MrsMReveley) **6-9-6** ACulhane(3) (trckd ldrs: effrt over 3f out: led over 1f out: jst hld on)	—	1	$5/2^{2}$	81	45
465^{8}	**Opaque (66)** (WStorey) **5-8-13**(5) PFessey(1) (hld up: pushed along over 3f out: hdwy over 1f out: styd on wl towards fin)	hd	2	9/1	79	43
781^{2}	**Hasta la Vista (48)** (MWEasterby) **7-8-0b** LCharnock(6) (plld hrd: led over 4f: led 2f out: sn hdd: r.o one pce)	2½	3	$9/2^{3}$	58	22
846^{8}	**Highflying (74)** (GMMoore) **11-9-12** JTate(5) (led over 8f out to 2f out: one pce)	1½	4	10/1	82	46
781*	**Ballpoint (76)** (GMMoore) **4-10-0** JFEgan(4) (in tch: effrt over 3f out: rdn over 2f out: nvr able to chal)	nk	5	$2/1^{1}$	83	47
838^{14}	**Mock Trial (IRE) (61)** (MrsJRRamsden) **4-8-13** JCarroll(2) (hld up: effrt over 3f out: sn in tch: rdn & wknd over 1f out: eased)	18	6	11/2	45	9

(SP 114.6%) **6 Rn**

2m 43.9 (6.40) CSF £22.45 TOTE £2.60: £2.20 £2.20 (£16.30) OWNER Mr A. Frame (SALTBURN) BRED P. D. and Mrs Player
746* Desert Fighter was inclined to hang fire once he hit the front and in the end the post came just in time. (5/2)
Opaque, who showed nothing over two miles first time, only found his stride inside the last and, without his rider resorting to the whip, almost got there. (9/1)
781 Hasta la Vista was too keen for his own good in the early stages. (9/2)
Highflying, now well into the veteran stage, still retains all his enthusiasm. (10/1)
781* Ballpoint, on this occasion, could never find the pace the get in a blow. (2/1)

995 CANTASSIUM H'CAP (0-70) (3-Y.O) (Class E)
3-25 (3-29) **6f** £3,615.00 (£1,095.00: £535.00: £255.00) Stalls: High GOING minus 0.23 sec per fur (GF)

				SP	RR	SF
785^{8}	**Smokey From Caplaw (62)** (JJO'Neill) **3-9-1** JFEgan(11) (unruly s: chsd ldrs: led 2f out: drvn out)	—	1	$8/1^{3}$	70	35
751*	**Hever Golf Mover (60)** (TJNaughton) **3-8-13** JWeaver(10) (w ldrs: ev ch over 1f out: nt qckn ins fnl f)	¾	2	10/1	66	31
845^{10}	**Levelled (67)** (MRChannon) **3-9-1**(5) PPMurphy(2) (trckd ldrs far side gng wl: led over 1f out: nt qckn ins fnl f)	¾	3	16/1	71	36
785^{11}	**La Dolce Vita (68)** (TDBarron) **3-9-7** JTate(9) (swtchd lft s: & racd far side: bhd tl hdwy 2f out: kpt on fnl f)	2	4	14/1	67	32
845^{8}	**William's Well (46)** (MWEasterby) **3-7-8b**(5) RMullen(8) (lw: unruly s: racd far side: hdwy 2f out: kpt on: nvr able chal)	¾	5	$5/1^{1}$	43	8
699^{5}	**High Spirits (IRE) (61)** (TDEasterby) **3-9-0** ACulhane(14) (hdwy u.p 2f out: styd on: nvr nr to chal)	2½	6	14/1	51	16
	Hurgill Lady (64) (JWWatts) **3-9-3** JCarroll(3) (chsd ldrs far side: rdn over 2f out: wknd fnl f)	1¼	7	10/1	51	16
882*	**Skyers Flyer (IRE) (66)** (RonaldThompson) **3-9-5** 7x TWilliams(1) (racd far side: hld up: hdwy & nt clr run over 1f out: eased)	½	8	$8/1^{3}$	51	16
845^{15}	**Splashed (57)** (TDBarron) **3-8-3**(7) KimberleyHart(17) (chsd ldrs: rdn ½-wy: wknd 2f out)	hd	9	33/1	42	7
	Mill End Boy (63) (MWEasterby) **3-8-11**(5) GParkin(5) (racd far side: effrt over 2f out: sn rdn & no imp)	1	10	20/1	45	10
785^{10}	**Only Josh (IRE) (51)** (MrsJRRamsden) **3-7-13**(5) PFessey(19) (s.i.s: swtchd lft & hdwy u.p over 2f out: n.d)	hd	11	16/1	33	—
757*	**Cairn Dhu (62)** (MrsJRRamsden) **3-8-12**(3) RHavlin(15) (lw: chsd ldrs tl rdn & wknd 2f out)	2	12	$7/1^{2}$	39	4
764^{10}	**Noirie (64)** (MBrittain) **3-8-12**(5) PRoberts(16) (s.i.s: a bhd: sn drvn along)	1¾	13	25/1	36	1
785^{14}	**Bold Brief (60)** (DenysSmith) **3-8-13** LCharnock(18) (led stands' side tl wknd 2f out)	1½	14	33/1	28	—
110^{6}	**Sharp Return (61)** (MJRyan) **3-8-11**(3) MBaird(7) (led far side tl over 1f out: wknd)	1¾	15	16/1	25	—
	Sparkling Harry (62) (MissLCSiddall) **3-8-8b**(7) TSiddall(4) (racd far side: sn bhd)	1¼	16	33/1	22	—
792^{9}	**Anetta (60)** (MissSEHall) **3-8-10**(3) DarrenMoffatt(6) (w ldrs far side tl wknd over 2f out)	hd	17	12/1	20	—
785^{6}	**Docklands Carriage (IRE) (60)** (NTinkler) **3-8-13v** KimTinkler(12) (sn bhd)	7	18	14/1	1	—
757^{9}	**Move The Clouds (50)** (DNicholls) **3-8-3b**[1] DaleGibson(13) (chsd ldrs tl lost pl ½-wy: sn bhd)	6	19	14/1	—	—

(SP 139.0%) **19 Rn**

1m 14.68 (3.18) CSF £82.77 CT £1,209.63 TOTE £10.90: £1.30 £1.90 £5.60 £5.70 (£246.00) Trio £366.80; £309.99 to Chester 6/5/97
OWNER Mr G. P. Bernacchi (PENRITH) BRED Gino P. Bernacchi
Smokey From Caplaw, who gave a problem or two at the start, did nothing at all wrong in the race. (8/1)
751* Hever Golf Mover gave her all and made the winner pull out all the stops. She seems to be improving on turf at least. (10/1)
602* Levelled travelled very strongly and came out best of the nine racing on the far side. This stiff uphill finish seemed to tax his stamina to the very limit. (16/1)
785 La Dolce Vita seemed to appreciate being dropped back to six. (14/1)
William's Well, with the blinkers back on, gave plenty of problems at the start. (5/1)
699 High Spirits (IRE) might be best suited by seven. (14/1)
882* Skyers Flyer (IRE), under a 7lb penalty, met some trouble and was by no means knocked about. She will be worth noting when connections slip her into a claimer once more. (8/1)

996 NATURES AID HEALTH PRODUCTS MAIDEN STKS (3-Y.O+) (Class D)
4-00 (4-00) **1m 2f 32y** £3,420.00 (£1,035.00: £505.00: £240.00) Stalls: High GOING minus 0.23 sec per fur (GF)

				SP	RR	SF
773^{7}	**Stakis Casinos Boy (IRE)** (MJohnston) **3-8-9** JWeaver(3) (lw: chsd ldr: led over 3f out: sn clr: drvn out)	—	1	$13/2^{2}$	77	28
740^{6}	**Foreign Rule (IRE)** (PWChapple-Hyam) **3-8-6**(3) RHavlin(4) (rdn along 7f out: wnt 2nd over 2f out: hung lft: no imp)	3	2	$1/2^{1}$	72	23
701^{4}	**Heart of Gold (IRE) (67)** (MissSEHall) **3-8-9** DaleGibson(2) (effrt over 4f out: sn rdn & outpcd: styd on ins fnl f)	1¾	3	$13/2^{2}$	70	21
	Well Armed (IRE) (JJO'Neill) **6-9-10** JFEgan(5) (bhd: hdwy u.p over 3f out: one pce)	¾	4	20/1	68	34
	Linea-G (MrsMReveley) **3-8-4** ACulhane(7) (rangy: unf: bit bkwd: sn bhd: sme hdwy over 2f out: sn wknd & eased)	10	5	$12/1^{3}$	48	—

	Horse		Dist	Pos	SP	RR	SF
	Society Times (USA)	(DANolan) **4-9-5**(5) PRoberts(1) (plld hrd: set str pce: hdd over 3f out: wknd qckly over 2f out)	20	**6**	16/1	21	—
	Trying Times (IRE)	(JBerry) **4-9-10** JCarroll(6) (sn outpcd: effrt 4f out: sn wknd)	2½	**7**	14/1	17	—

(SP 118.3%) **7 Rn**

2m 12.7 (6.00) CSF £9.75 TOTE £7.00: £2.30 £1.30 (£3.80) OWNER Stakis Casinos Racing Club (MIDDLEHAM) BRED Buckram Thoroughbred Enterprises Inc

WEIGHT FOR AGE 3yo-15lb

773 Stakis Casinos Boy (IRE) had clearly learnt plenty from his debut. The only one to keep tabs on the tearaway leader, he was kicked clear soon after hitting the front and, kept up to his work, was never going to be caught. He looks a real stayer in the making. (13/2)

740 Foreign Rule (IRE), most unimpressive in the paddock, wanted to do nothing but hang left after taking second spot and he was never going to reach the winner. (1/2)

701 Heart of Gold (IRE) has a high head carriage and gives his rider problems. Tapped for foot on the home turn, he decided to stay on inside the last. He probably needs a mile and a half but is not a straightforward ride. (13/2)

Well Armed (IRE), fit from hurdling, was made to look woefully one paced. (20/1)

Linea-G (12/1: op 8/1)

997 MILBURN HEALTH FOODS NEWGATE CENTRE CLAIMING STKS (3-Y.O+) (Class F)

4-30 (4-34) **7f** £2,473.50 (£696.00: £340.50) Stalls: High GOING minus 0.23 sec per fur (GF)

	Horse		Dist	Pos	SP	RR	SF
551*	**Rock Island Line (IRE)**	(JBerry) **3-8-8**(5) PRoberts(13) (hld up: stdy hdwy over 2f out: shkn up to ld ins fnl f: readily)	—	**1**	3/1[2]	68	36
823[3]	**Kemo Sabo (72)**	(CParker) **5-9-11** JCarroll(12) (trckd ldrs: led over 1f out: hdd & nt qckn ins fnl f)	2½	**2**	5/2[1]	62	42
601[13]	**Bon Secret (IRE) (53)**	(TJNaughton) **5-9-1** JWeaver(5) (hld up: hdwy ½-wy: sn chsng ldrs: kpt on same pce appr fnl f)	1¼	**3**	16/1	49	29
848[5]	**Sheraz (IRE) (40)**	(NTinkler) **5-9-7b** KimTinkler(11) (lw: led 1f: w ldrs: led over 2f out: edgd lft & hdd over 1f out: one pce)	1¼	**4**	16/1	53	33
550[5]	**Hanby**	(JSGoldie) **5-9-5** ACulhane(4) (b: chsd ldrs tl outpcd appr fnl f)	4	**5**	8/1	41	21
783[4]	**Soda (58)**	(TDBarron) **3-8-9** LCharnock(9) (sn outpcd & drvn along: hdwy over 2f out: nvr nr ldrs)	5	**6**	9/1	32	—
896[6]	**Abstone Queen (58)**	(PDEvans) **3-8-6v** JFEgan(7) (w ldrs: effrt over 2f out: eased whn btn ins fnl f)	1¼	**7**	11/2[3]	26	—
663[8]	**Hoh Majestic (IRE) (55)**	(RonaldThompson) **4-9-5** TWilliams(10) (hld up: hdwy ½-wy: sn rdn: wknd over 1f out)	2½	**8**	14/1	21	1
	Absolute Charlie	(CWFairhurst) **3-8-4**(3) DarrenMoffatt(8) (sn bhd & drvn along)	10	**9**	50/1	—	—
484[11]	**Dispol Prince**	(GROldroyd) **4-9-1** JTate(1) (sn bhd)	3	**10**	33/1	—	—
	Grey Prospect	(MBrittain) **3-8-2**(5) RMullen(6) (neat: unf: chsd ldrs tl lost pl over 2f out)	1¾	**11**	50/1	—	—
600[10]	**Not A Lot (50)**	(MWEasterby) **3-8-1b**(5)ow1 GParkin(3) (swtchd rt & led after 1f: hdd over 2f out: nt run on)	2½	**12**	16/1	—	—
774[6]	**Lucky Revenge (53)**	(DNicholls) **4-8-12** DaleGibson(2) (lw: sn bhd)	7	**13**	12/1	—	—

(SP 128.9%) **13 Rn**

1m 28.04 (3.54) CSF £10.76 TOTE £3.60: £2.30 £1.80 £3.40 (£5.90) Trio £62.60 OWNER Mr J. Berry (COCKERHAM) BRED Drumconrath Stud

WEIGHT FOR AGE 3yo-12lb

551* Rock Island Line (IRE) had his problems at two but he clearly possesses a fair bit of ability and, given a confident ride, took this with something to spare. (3/1)

823 Kemo Sabo ran up to his best but yet again showed that he is hard to win with. (5/2)

335 Bon Secret (IRE), a hard puller, was taken very quietly to post. (16/1)

848 Sheraz (IRE), who as usual wore a tongue-strap, did as well as could be expected considering he would have been two stone better off with Kemo Sabo in a handicap. (16/1)

550 Hanby, having his third run, was far from disgraced. He does possess some ability and is now qualified for a handicap mark. (8/1)

783 Soda, with the headgear left off, proved a very hard ride. (9/1)

896 Abstone Queen, mounted on the track, is possibly beginning to feel her racing. (11/2)

998 NEWCASTLE VOLUNTEER BUREAU H'CAP (0-80) (3-Y.O) (Class D)

5-00 (5-03) **1m 3y (straight)** £4,221.00 (£1,278.00: £624.00: £297.00) Stalls: High GOING minus 0.23 sec per fur (GF)

	Horse		Dist	Pos	SP	RR	SF
794[3]	**Can Can Lady (73)**	(MJohnston) **3-9-3** JWeaver(10) (lw: mde all: jst hld on)	—	**1**	11/4[1]	86	60
	Smart Spirit (IRE) (67)	(MrsMReveley) **3-8-11** ACulhane(8) (lw: hld up: stdy hdwy over 2f out: swtchd & chal ins fnl f: jst failed)	s.h	**2**	5/1[2]	80	54
647[11]	**Jalb (IRE) (74)**	(ACStewart) **3-9-4** JTate(6) (s.i.s: hld up: hdwy over 2f out: sn ev ch: nt qckn appr fnl f)	7	**3**	5/1[2]	73	47
699[3]	**Blooming Amazing (77)**	(JLEyre) **3-9-7** TWilliams(9) (trckd ldrs: rdn & ev ch over 2f out: wknd appr fnl f)	2½	**4**	11/2[3]	71	45
783[7]	**Jedi Knight (66)**	(MWEasterby) **3-8-5**(5) GParkin(2) (plld hrd: trckd ldrs: effrt 3f out: sn wl outpcd)	8	**5**	12/1	44	18
	Sparky (59)	(MWEasterby) **3-8-3** DaleGibson(3) (sn drvn along: sn chsng ldrs: wl outpcd fnl 3f)	8	**6**	14/1	21	—
785[5]	**Rum Lad (60)**	(JJQuinn) **3-8-4** LCharnock(4) (lost pl ½-wy: sn bhd)	2	**7**	10/1	18	—
845[13]	**Wagga Moon (IRE) (65)**	(JJO'Neill) **3-8-9** JFEgan(5) (w ldrs tl lost pl ½-wy: eased)	½	**8**	14/1	22	—
	Blue Hopper (62)	(MRChannon) **3-8-1**(5) PPMurphy(1) (trckd ldrs: effrt 3f out: sn wknd)	5	**9**	10/1	9	—
	Coral Strand (72)	(JWWatts) **3-9-2** JCarroll(7) (w ldrs tl lost pl over 2f out)	3½	**10**	14/1	12	—

(SP 121.3%) **10 Rn**

1m 40.8 (2.20) CSF £15.41 CT £61.57 TOTE £2.80: £1.70 £1.80 £2.20 (£11.50) Trio £33.30 OWNER Mr A. W. Robinson (MIDDLEHAM) BRED Godolphin Management Co Ltd

794 Can Can Lady, with the benefit of the stands' side rail, proved very willing but at the line there was not an ounce to spare. It took the judge twenty-seven minutes to give the verdict. (11/4)

Smart Spirit (IRE) has done well over the winter. Dropped in, she had to switch to throw down a determined challenge, but hard as she tried she could not quite force her head in front. (5/1: op 10/1)

647 Jalb (IRE) stumbled slightly leaving the stalls but, after having every chance, he found the first two running away from him. He looked to have more than his fair share of weight. (5/1)

699 Blooming Amazing, 5lb higher than when winning first time at Beverley, called it a day coming to the final furlong. (11/2)

Jedi Knight would not settle at any stage. (12/1)

Blue Hopper (10/1: 8/1-12/1)

T/Plpt: £26.50 (292.5 Tckts). T/Qdpt: £7.50 (52.15 Tckts) AA

0651-WARWICK (L-H) (Firm, Good to firm patches; Races 7 & 8: Good)
Monday May 5th
WEATHER: overcast, heavy showers WIND: mod bhd becoming mod against

999 E.B.F. PRIMROSE MAIDEN STKS (2-Y.O F) (Class D)
2-15 (2-16) **5f** £3,650.95 (£1,093.60: £525.30: £241.15) Stalls: Low GOING minus 0.41 sec per fur (F)

				SP	RR	SF
	Eastern Lyric (JBerry) **2-8-11** GDuffield(11) (small: lt-f: unf: hdwy 2f out: hrd drvn to ld wl ins fnl f)	—	1	6/1 3	65	34
828 4	**Fast Tempo (IRE)** (BPalling) **2-8-11** TSprake(6) (chsd ldr: led ½-wy: rdn & edgd lft over 1f out: ct nr fin)	½	2	11/4 2	63	32
682 6	**Composition** (MAJarvis) **2-8-11** PBloomfield(5) (led to ½-wy: rdn whn hmpd & swtchd over 1f out: nt qckn)	1¼	3	5/4 1	59	28
	First Dance (RHannon) **2-8-11** RPerham(8) (unf: scope: bkwd: in tch: effrt & rdn 2f out: nt pce to chal)	2	4	9/1	53	22
	Patricia Olive (IRE) (MHTompkins) **2-8-11** DBiggs(9) (neat: bkwd: a outpcd)	2½	5	20/1	45	14
	Tremonnow (JMBradley) **2-8-11** CRutter(10) (leggy: lt-f: dwlt: a bhd & outpcd)	2½	6	50/1	37	6
	Shalad'or (BRMillman) **2-8-8**(3) DO'Donohoe(1) (lt-f: s.s: sn rdn along: a outpcd)	3	7	50/1	27	—
	Persian Fortune (WGMTurner) **2-8-6**(5) DSweeney(7) (lt-f: outpcd)	1½	8	16/1	23	—
	Chiltern Emerald (JWhite) **2-8-11** KRutter(2) (lengthy: lt-f: s.s: a bhd & outpcd: t.o)	19	9	25/1	—	—

(SP 113.8%) **9 Rn**

59.5 secs (1.50) CSF £19.79 TOTE £6.40: £1.80 £1.60 £1.20 (£9.60) Trio £5.40 OWNER Mr R. Meredith (COCKERHAM) BRED A. Bromley

Eastern Lyric has plenty of growing to do but she knew what was required on this racecourse debut, finding all that was needed to land the spoils nearing the line. (6/1: op 7/2)

828 Fast Tempo (IRE), a late May foal who has not yet reached her second birthday, helped force the pace but she edged left when ridden approaching the final furlong, and failed to last home. (11/4: 2/1-3/1)

682 Composition, a beaten favourite on her debut, still looks to have a bit left to work on, and she had given best when the runner-up took her ground approaching the last furlong. (5/4)

First Dance does look to need time and, though she was steadily reducing the deficit at the finish, was never within striking range of the principals. (9/1: 4/1-10/1)

1000 STONELEIGH PARK POLO CLUB H'CAP (0-80) (3-Y.O) (Class D)
2-45 (2-47) **7f** £4,218.90 (£1,264.20: £607.60: £279.30) Stalls: Low GOING minus 0.18 sec per fur (GF)

				SP	RR	SF
636 4	**The Gay Fox (73)** (BAMcMahon) **3-9-0** GDuffield(7) (a.p: led over 1f out: sn rdn clr: jst hld on)	—	1	10/1	76	52
	Undercover Agent (IRE) (80) (JLDunlop) **3-9-7** TSprake(16) (still unf: hld up: effrt & nt clr run 2f out: swtchd rt: fin strly)	hd	2	13/2 2	83+	59
*590**	**Trading Aces (68)** (MBell) **3-8-9v1** MFenton(9) (hld up: hdwy 2f out: rdn & r.o wl fnl f)	nk	3	7/1 3	70	46
	Warring (58) (MSSaunders) **3-7-13** FNorton(13) (scope: bit bkwd: hdwy over 2f out: r.o wl ins fnl f)	1½	4	40/1	57	33
483 10	**Tycoon Girl (IRE) (80)** (BJMeehan) **3-9-0**(7) GHannon(1) (prom: rdn wl over 1f out: unable qckn fnl f)	nk	5	15/2	78	54
649 4	**Jupiter (IRE) (68)** (GCBravery) **3-8-9** MHills(2) (hld up mid div: nt clr run on ins over 1f out: squeezed thro fnl f: r.o)	hd	6	7/2 1	66	42
	Cherokee Flight (66) (SMellor) **3-8-7** AMcGlone(10) (bkwd: prom tl wknd over 1f out)	nk	7	25/1	63	39
	Rosenkavalier (IRE) (62) (LGCottrell) **3-7-12**(5)ow2 ADaly(5) (bkwd: plld hrd: chsd ldr: led 2f out: sn hdd: wknd fnl f)	1¾	8	33/1	55	29
	Lamorna (66) (MRChannon) **3-8-7** CandyMorris(11) (mid div: effrt over 3f out: wknd wl over 1f out)	1¾	9	12/1	55	31
	River of Fortune (IRE) (66) (MHTompkins) **3-8-7** DBiggs(8) (in tch over 4f: sn rdn & wknd)	½	10	9/1	54	30
685 11	**Oneknight With You (69)** (MJFetherston-Godley) **3-8-7**(3) DO'Donohoe(15) (s.s: a bhd)	nk	11	12/1	56	32
774 8	**Treasure Hill (IRE) (59)** (DWChapman) **3-8-0** JFanning(6) (bit bkwd: dwlt: a bhd)	½	12	20/1	45	21
723 11	**Mayflower (75)** (IABalding) **3-8-13**(3) MartinDwyer(4) (led 5f: sn rdn: wknd qckly)	3	13	14/1	54	30
794 7	**The Wyandotte Inn (70)** (RHollinshead) **3-8-8**(3) DGriffiths(3) (prom: hrd drvn & wknd over 2f out)	¾	14	16/1	48	24
97 4	**Come Dancing (60)** (MJohnston) **3-8-1** NAdams(12) (bit bkwd: s.i.s: a bhd)	4	15	25/1	28	4

(SP 124.7%) **15 Rn**

1m 27.2 (2.60) CSF £64.80 CT £464.79 TOTE £8.60: £1.90 £3.10 £2.10 (£32.30) Trio £51.90 OWNER Mr G. Whitaker (TAMWORTH) BRED Cheveley Park Stud Ltd

636 The Gay Fox, not winning out of turn, won the race by kicking clear passing the furlong marker, but lack of stamina began to tell and he was all out to hold on in the dying strides. (10/1)

Undercover Agent (IRE), with nowhere to go on straightening up, took time to find top gear again after being switched, but she was really into her stride late on, only for the post to arrive a brief second too soon. (13/2)

590* Trading Aces did not stride out freely to post but she put in a determined last-furlong challenge under pressure, and certainly went down fighting. (7/1)

Warring showed plenty of promise on this seasonal debut and a longer trip looks a must. (40/1)

Tycoon Girl (IRE), always poised to challenge, was making hard work of it below the distance, but she did keep plugging away and there is more improvement to come. (15/2)

649 Jupiter (IRE) had the trip he needs this time, but he endured a nightmare journey when about to mount his challenge, and the race was as good as over by the time he did wriggle free. (7/2: op 11/2)

Rosenkavalier (IRE) ran by far his best race yet and, with this badly-needed run under his belt, should be able to find an opening. (33/1)

Lamorna (12/1: op 7/1)

1001 WARWICK SPRING H'CAP (0-70) (4-Y.O+) (Class E)
3-15 (3-16) **1m 2f 169y** £3,564.25 (£1,069.00: £514.50: £237.25) Stalls: Low GOING minus 0.18 sec per fur (GF)

				SP	RR	SF
607 2	**Dauphin (IRE) (41)** (WJMusson) **4-7-13** FNorton(8) (prom: rdn & outpcd 3f out: str run fnl f: led cl home)	—	1	9/2 1	50	30
789 17	**General Haven (68)** (TJNaughton) **4-9-12** GDuffield(4) (a.p: hrd rdn & outpcd 2f out: r.o strly towards fin)	nk	2	10/1	77	57
647 13	**Golden Touch (USA) (54)** (DJSCosgrove) **5-8-12** DBiggs(14) (hld up: hdwy 5f out: led over 1f out tl ct fnl strides)	s.h	3	20/1	63	43
657 4	**Shalateeno (66)** (BRMillman) **4-9-10** TSprake(9) (w ldr: led 7f out to 6f out: led 5f out tl over 1f out: sn rdn: one pce)	2½	4	11/2 2	71	51
735 10	**Pay Homage (68)** (IABalding) **9-9-5**(7) RFowley(5) (lw: hld up: hdwy fnl 2f: r.o)	1	5	9/1 3	71	51
687 7	**Dannistar (52)** (PDEvans) **5-8-3**(7) AnthonyBond(6) (b.off hind: trckd ldrs: rdn 2f out: one pce)	2	6	11/1	52	32
442 8	**Evezio Rufo (53)** (NPLittmoden) **5-8-6b**(5) ADaly(13) (trckd ldrs: rdn & no hdwy fnl 3f)	2	7	33/1	50	30
54 7	**El Bardador (IRE) (51)** (RJHodges) **4-8-9** SDrowne(2) (s.s: nvr nrr)	1¼	8	20/1	47	27

Form	Horse / Trainer / Age-Weight / Jockey / Comment	Dist	Pos	SP	RR	SF
763[15]	**Master Millfield (IRE) (64)** (CJHill) **5-9-8** MFenton(18) (prom: mid div whn c stands' side st: nvr trbld ldrs)	¾	**9**	12/1	58	38
	Oscar Rose (43) (MJBolton) **4-8-1** JFanning(10) (nvr plcd to chal)	s.h	**10**	50/1	37	17
881[7]	**On The Wildside (46)** (MRChannon) **4-8-4** RPerham(1) (hld up: hdwy 3f out: nt rch ldrs)	1	**11**	25/1	39	19
869[6]	**Duffertoes (48)** (MJRyan) **5-7-13**(7) AMcCarthy(11) (hld up: nvr nr ldrs)	¾	**12**	33/1	40	20
735[21]	**Opalette (70)** (LadyHerries) **4-10-0** DeclanO'Shea(16) (lw: s.s: plld hrd: hdwy to ld 6f out: sn hdd: wknd over 2f out: t.o)	12	**13**	20/1	44	24
857[5]	**Failed To Hit (65)** (NPLittmoden) **4-9-9v** TGMcLaughlin(20) (a in rr: t.o)	¾	**14**	20/1	38	18
422[9]	**Rival Bid (USA) (69)** (MrsNMacauley) **9-9-13v** SWebster(15) (b: s.s: a bhd: t.o)	4	**15**	16/1	36	16
	Isitoff (69) (SCWilliams) **4-9-10**(3) PMcCabe(3) (bkwd: a bhd: t.o)	½	**16**	10/1	35	15
	Landlord (53) (PBowen) **5-8-6b**(5) GFaulkner(19) (prom: rdn over 3f out: sn wknd: t.o)	s.h	**17**	20/1	19	—
291[10]	**Baranov (IRE) (62)** (DJGMurraySmith) **4-9-6** MHills(12) (led over 3f: wknd over 4f out: t.o)	3½	**18**	14/1	23	3
796[5]	**Worldwide Elsie (USA) (58)** (ICampbell) **4-9-2** RPrice(17) (s.s: hdwy 6f out: rdn & wknd 3f out: t.o)	3	**19**	20/1	14	—
	Irish Kinsman (50) (GHYardley) **4-8-8b** NAdams(7) (lw: a in rr: t.o)	3	**20**	50/1	2	—
				(SP 132.5%)	**20 Rn**	

2m 19.3 (5.30) CSF £39.00 CT £783.99 TOTE £5.30: £1.60 £2.40 £4.20 £1.70 (£17.50) Trio £309.80 OWNER Mrs Rita Brown (NEWMARKET) BRED Patrick H. Dillon

607 Dauphin (IRE) was able to take advantage of his lenient handicap mark, but it was only within the shadow of the post that he surged through to poke his nose in front. His only previous success was at twelve furlongs and he does seem better the further he goes. (9/2)

133 General Haven, taking a step down in distance, pushed the pace, but he was caught out when the leaders quickened things up turning in. Answering his rider's every call, he was eating up ground at the finish but the winner matched him stride for stride and he was the one who had to miss out. (10/1)

56 Golden Touch (USA), at his best in the early part of the season, went for home below the distance and looked to be holding on until touched off right on the line. This was a good effort, and a repeat could see him back to winning ways. (20/1)

657 Shalateeno did not have quite so much use made of her, despite being in the firing line from the start, but her limitations were exposed once collared over a furlong out. She is handicapped to the hilt and would probably benefit from having 7lb taken off her back. (11/2)

657 Pay Homage has not yet won beyond nine furlongs and he was ridden to get the trip here but did not find top gear until far too late. (9/1: op 5/1)

687 Dannistar found this company too much for her in the latter stages, and she was beginning to throw out distress signals soon after turning for home. (11/1)

Isitoff (10/1: 6/1-11/1)

1002 MAY QUEEN H'CAP (0-80) (3-Y.O) (Class D)

3-45 (3-46) **1m 4f 115y** £3,709.30 (£1,107.40: £529.20: £240.10) Stalls: Low GOING minus 0.09 sec per fur (G)

Form	Horse / Trainer / Age-Weight / Jockey / Comment	Dist	Pos	SP	RR	SF
771[7]	**Sudest (IRE) (59)** (IABalding) **3-7-13**(3) MartinDwyer(1) (mde all: rdn over 1f out: hld on gamely)	—	**1**	7/2[3]	70	26
690[9]	**Maradi (IRE) (73)** (MBell) **3-9-2** MFenton(4) (hld up & bhd: hdwy ent st: jnd wnr ent fnl f: unable qckn)	¾	**2**	6/5[1]	83	39
690[11]	**City Gambler (74)** (GCBravery) **3-9-3** MHills(2) (plld hrd: a.p: wnt 2nd 4f out: hrd rdn & wknd fnl 2f)	17	**3**	5/2[2]	62	18
	Daylight Dreams (78) (CACyzer) **3-9-7** DBiggs(3) (dwlt: sn chsng wnr: rdn 3f out: sn lost tch: t.o)	21	**4**	6/1	40	—
				(SP 110.5%)	**4 Rn**	

2m 46.0 (8.50) CSF £7.61 TOTE £4.20: (£3.30) OWNER Robert & Elizabeth Hitchins (KINGSCLERE) BRED Airlie Stud

Sudest (IRE) waited in front at this first attempt at the trip, and made full use of the substantial weight allowance to worry the favourite out of it inside the last hundred yards. (7/2)

355* Maradi (IRE), settled in last place, looked likely to take over at will once he had joined the winner over a furlong out, but he realised he had a battle on his hands and the boot was on the other foot when the whips were cracking. (6/5)

City Gambler again raced keenly and tried to deliver her challenge early in the straight, but once the principals took one another on, she was left in their wake. (5/2)

Daylight Dreams (6/1: 4/1-7/1)

1003 ALBERT E. SHARP / T.B.O. LIMITED STKS (0-60) (4-Y.O+) (Class F)

4-15 (4-16) **6f** £2,715.90 (£752.40: £359.70) Stalls: Low GOING minus 0.09 sec per fur (G)

Form	Horse / Trainer / Age-Weight / Jockey / Comment	Dist	Pos	SP	RR	SF
924[6]	**Shadow Jury (59)** (DWChapman) **7-8-11b** GDuffield(3) (lw: mde all: rdn clr 2f out: drvn out)	—	**1**	4/1[2]	69	51
759[9]	**Tymeera (54)** (BPalling) **4-8-8** TSprake(2) (a.p: chsd wnr over 1f out: r.o)	½	**2**	9/1	65	47
864*	**Gymcrak Flyer (60)** (GHolmes) **6-8-11** NConnorton(8) (b.hind: hld up & bhd: gd hdwy fnl f: r.o)	½	**3**	11/4[1]	66	48
759[10]	**Petraco (IRE) (56)** (NASmith) **9-8-6**(5) JBramhill(9) (hdwy 2f out: one pce fnl f)	3½	**4**	11/2[3]	57	39
702[18]	**Barranak (IRE) (56)** (GMMcCourt) **5-8-8**(3) MartinDwyer(13) (lw: plld hrd: hdwy 4f out: wknd over 1f out)	1	**5**	10/1	54	36
883[8]	**Time For Tea (IRE) (53)** (CACyzer) **4-8-8** DBiggs(5) (nvr nr to chal)	½	**6**	12/1	50	32
	Northern Judge (43) (APJames) **4-8-11** MFenton(4) (bkwd: dwlt: nvr nrr)	nk	**7**	20/1	52	34
	Itsinthepost (55) (VSoane) **4-8-8** CRutter(1) (bit bkwd: nvr trbld ldrs)	¾	**8**	20/1	47	29
57[10]	**Red Time (50)** (MSSaunders) **4-8-11v**[1] RPerham(10) (prom: rdn over 3f out: wknd over 1f out)	1½	**9**	40/1	46	28
774[2]	**Dashing Dancer (IRE) (55)** (DShaw) **6-8-11b** JFanning(7) (lw: chsd wnr tl wknd over 1f out)	½	**10**	12/1	45	27
	Coastguards Hero (55) (MDIUsher) **4-8-11** FNorton(11) (bkwd: dwlt: a bhd)	½	**11**	14/1	44	26
	May Queen Megan (52) (MrsALMKing) **4-8-8** AMcGlone(6) (bkwd: chsd ldrs tl wknd 2f out)	1¾	**12**	16/1	36	18
653[14]	**Courting Newmarket (34)** (MissKMGeorge) **9-8-4b**(7) PDoe(12) (a bhd: t.o)	16	**13**	50/1	—	—
				(SP 123.0%)	**13 Rn**	

1m 14.6 (2.60) CSF £36.03 TOTE £5.00: £1.70 £2.50 £2.10 (£11.20) Trio £23.00 OWNER Mrs Jeanne Chapman (YORK) BRED J. S. Bell

666 Shadow Jury, enterprisingly ridden, recorded his sixteenth victory but only his second beyond the minimum trip. (4/1)

Tymeera ran well for a long way last time and seems to have come to hand. (9/1)

864* Gymcrak Flyer found this trip inadequate, especially on a course as sharp as this, but a return to further should see her resume winning ways. (11/4: 2/1-3/1)

541 Petraco (IRE) could not sustain his effort. (11/2)

473 Barranak (IRE), held up to get the trip, did not accept restraint and may be better off given his head over the minimum distance. (10/1: op 6/1)

Time For Tea (IRE) could never quite get to grips with the leaders but may be worth a try over seven. (12/1)

Northern Judge needs further than this but will be sharper for the outing. (20/1)

Coastguards Hero (14/1: 10/1-16/1)

1004 ALVESTON MAIDEN STKS (I) (3-Y.O+) (Class D)

4-45 (4-51) **1m** £3,349.85 (£996.80: £473.90: £212.45) Stalls: Low GOING minus 0.09 sec per fur (G)

				SP	RR	SF
723^{5}	**Tigrello (82)** (GLewis) **3-8-11** GDuffield(10) (chsd ldr: led 4f out: rdn clr over 2f out: r.o wl)	—	1	3/1 ^{2}	91	51
	Saddlers' Hope (JRFanshawe) **3-8-6** TSprake(9) (a.p: r.o one pce fnl f: no ch w wnr)	6	2	4/1 ^{3}	74	34
	Flint Knapper (GWragg) **3-8-11** MHills(4) (w'like: bit bkwd: plld hrd: a.p: one pce fnl 2f)	2½	3	15/8 ^{1}	74	34
795^{7}	**Neronian (IRE)** (BWHills) **3-8-8**(3) JDSmith(6) (no hdwy fnl 3f)	1¼	4	20/1	72	32
683^{9}	**Big Target (IRE)** (MRStoute) **3-8-11** KBradshaw(7) (bit bkwd: nvr nr ldrs)	1¼	5	5/1	69	29
645^{11}	**Hulal** (ACStewart) **3-8-11** WHollick(8) (led 4f: wknd qckly wl over 1f out)	3	6	33/1	63	23
	Run Or Bust (IRE) (RIngram) **4-9-5** AMcGlone(2) (b: hld up & plld hrd: a bhd)	2	7	50/1	54	27
	Jay-Em-Bee (JMBradley) **4-9-10** SDrowne(3) (bkwd: unruly s: a bhd: t.o fnl 3f)	dist	8	50/1	—	—
765^{3}	**Tisima (FR)** (IABalding) **3-8-3**(3) MartinDwyer(5) (reard & uns rdr stalls)		U	6/1	—	—
				(SP 122.4%)	**9 Rn**	

1m 39.9 (3.50) CSF £14.60 TOTE £3.60: £1.50 £1.50 £1.10 (£4.70) Trio £5.50 OWNER Mr A. M. Al-Midani (EPSOM) BRED L. C. and Mrs A. E. Sigsworth

WEIGHT FOR AGE 3yo-13lb

723 Tigrello took full advantage of a return to maiden company. (3/1: 9/4-7/2)

Saddlers' Hope could only win a separate race for the runner-up spot. (4/1: 11/4-9/2)

Flint Knapper, a half-brother to Don Micheletto, ran too freely and did not handle the home turn all that well. He will soon leave this form behind. (15/8)

795 Neronian (IRE) might be worth bearing in mind in handicaps over a longer trip. (20/1)

683 Big Target (IRE), a 60,000gs half-brother to a mile and three-quarters winner Primo Figlio, will be seen in a different light when tackling further. (5/1: 3/1-11/2)

Hulal, a half-brother to Mutabassim, showed his first sign of any ability. (33/1)

1005 LEVY BOARD APPRENTICE H'CAP (0-70) (3-Y.O+) (Class G)

5-15 (5-17) **1m** £2,175.50 (£618.00: £306.50) Stalls: Low GOING minus 0.09 sec per fur (G)

				SP	RR	SF
776^{8}	**King Athelstan (USA) (57)** (BAMcMahon) **9-9-2**(5) SRighton(7) (lw: w ldrs: led 5f out: pushed out)	—	1	12/1	66	47
848^{4}	**Abtaal (49)** (RJHodges) **7-8-8**(5) GHannon(20) (a.p: chsd wnr over 2f out: r.o ins fnl f)	¾	2	14/1	57	38
733^{17}	**Mr Cube (IRE) (50)** (JMBradley) **7-8-9b**(5) RWinston(17) (bit bkwd: hdwy 4f out: r.o one pce fnl 2f)	2	3	10/1	54	35
85^{5}	**Zahran (IRE) (36)** (JMBradley) **6-7-9**(5) JFowle(1) (hld up: hdwy on ins 2f out: rdn over 1f out: r.o one pce ins fnl f)	½	4	16/1	39	20
	Queen's Insignia (USA) (55) (PFICole) **4-8-12**(7) JBosley(12) (bit bkwd: a.p: no hdwy fnl 2f)	1¾	5	9/1 ^{3}	54	35
866^{5}	**Tomal (40)** (RIngram) **5-7-13**(5) PFitzsimons(10) (a.p: no hdwy fnl 2f)	½	6	16/1	38	19
848^{3}	**Bedazzle (38)** (MBrittain) **6-7-11**(5) DMernagh(9) (nvr nr to chal)	¾	7	6/1 ^{2}	35	16
860^{4}	**Dragonjoy (49)** (NPLittmoden) **4-8-13b** PDoe(15) (hdwy on outside 4f out: carried wd ent st: n.d after)	½	8	10/1	45	26
824^{4}	**Cee-Jay-Ay (53)** (JBerry) **10-8-12**(5) PBradley(11) (s.s: nrst fin)	hd	9	5/1 ^{1}	48	29
755^{7}	**Confronter (60)** (SDow) **8-9-3**(7) DSalt(14) (hdwy 4f out: wknd over 2f out)	¾	10	11/1	54	35
	With A Will (65) (HCandy) **3-8-9**(7) NicolaWright(16) (prom tl rn wd ent st: wknd 2f out)	1½	11	11/1	56	24
61^{13}	**Racing Hawk (USA) (49)** (MSSaunders) **5-8-8**(5) ClaireAngell(5) (swtg: bhd fnl 2f)	4	12	25/1	32	13
587^{5}	**Richard House Lad (43)** (RHollinshead) **4-8-0**(7) DHayden(4) (prom tl wknd over 2f out)	6	13	16/1	14	—
	Jona Holley (46) (IABalding) **4-8-3**(7)ow3 JaneLind(2) (leggy: lt-f: bhd fnl 3f)	2	14	25/1	13	—
61^{14}	**Daratown (35)** (CJHill) **4-7-8**(5) RBrisland(18) (plld hrd: led 3f: wknd over 2f out)	1½	15	20/1	—	—
	Fairly Sure (IRE) (45) (NEBerry) **4-8-4**(5) KerryBaker(8) (w'like: t.o)	8	16	20/1	—	—
774^{11}	**Skelton Countess (IRE) (51)** (RHollinshead) **4-8-10**(5) PFredericks(19) (hdwy 4f out: wknd over 2f out: t.o)	nk	17	33/1	—	—
				(SP 128.0%)	**17 Rn**	

1m 41.2 (4.80) CSF £149.94 CT £1,670.34 TOTE £19.30: £4.50 £3.30 £2.30 £3.20 (£292.00) Trio Not won; £355.92 to Chester 6/5/97 OWNER Mr Ian Guise (TAMWORTH) BRED Brushwood Stable

WEIGHT FOR AGE 3yo-13lb

653 King Athelstan (USA), dropped 7lb, put a disappointing run last time behind him. (12/1)

848 Abtaal, dropped back to a mile this season, ideally needs a stiffer course or a return to a longer trip. (14/1)

Mr Cube (IRE), dropped 5lb, was not helped by the heavy showers which had fallen during the afternoon. (10/1)

85 Zahran (IRE), 7lb lower than on the All-Weather, was another not aided by the ease in the ground. (16/1)

Queen's Insignia (USA), dropped 10lb since last running on grass, was 5lb lower than when she won a Goodwood nursery in September 1995. (9/1)

866 Tomal, in the handicap this time, again ran respectably on this drop back to a mile. (16/1)

With A Will (11/1: op 7/1)

1006 ALVESTON MAIDEN STKS (II) (3-Y.O+) (Class D)

5-45 (5-47) **1m** £3,318.00 (£987.00: £469.00: £210.00) Stalls: Low GOING minus 0.09 sec per fur (G)

				SP	RR	SF
701^{3}	**Zoom Up (IRE)** (MJHeaton-Ellis) **3-8-11** SDrowne(8) (s.s: sn rcvrd: outpcd 2f out: rdn & rallied fnl f: led nr fin)	—	1	7/1	88	31
742^{4}	**Hever Golf Glory** (TJNaughton) **3-8-11** TSprake(1) (lw: a.p: led over 1f out: hdd nr fin)	½	2	3/1 ^{2}	87	30
	Rhapsody In White (IRE) (80) (MAJarvis) **3-8-11** PBloomfield(5) (bit bkwd: led over 6f: one pce)	2½	3	14/1	82	25
446^{6}	**Zaahir (IRE)** (BWHills) **3-8-8**(3) JDSmith(4) (b.hind: a.p: ev ch 2f out: rdn over 1f out: one pce)	s.h	4	11/2	82	25
723^{16}	**Sturgeon (IRE) (87)** (PFICole) **3-8-11** CRutter(7) (a.p: ev ch 2f out: sn rdn: one pce)	nk	5	85/40 ^{1}	81	24
	Aerleon Pete (IRE) (MRStoute) **3-8-11** KBradshaw(11) (lw: hdwy over 1f out: nvr nr to chal)	1½	6	5/1 ^{3}	78	21
	Windrush Holly (55) (DRCElsworth) **4-9-2**(3) DGriffiths(10) (bkwd: prom over 5f)	4	7	20/1	65	21
841^{9}	**Wontcostalotbut** (MJWilkinson) **3-8-6** NAdams(6) (bhd fnl 3f)	5	8	50/1	55	—
683^{18}	**Sequoia Prince (CAN)** (MBell) **3-8-11** MFenton(9) (bit bkwd: s.s: sn rcvrd: racd wd: bhd fnl 3f)	1	9	16/1	58	1
	Stilett (IRE) (LMCumani) **3-8-4**(7) DYoung(2) (w'like: leggy: bhd fnl 3f)	2	10	16/1	54	—
855^{9}	**Express Routing (48)** (VSoane) **5-9-10** FNorton(3) (b: a bhd)	3½	11	50/1	47	3
				(SP 128.7%)	**11 Rn**	

1m 41.9 (5.50) CSF £27.99 TOTE £8.20: £1.70 £1.30 £5.20 (£10.20) Trio £119.60 OWNER Mr K. Maeda (WROUGHTON) BRED Michael Doyle

WEIGHT FOR AGE 3yo-13lb

701 Zoom Up (IRE) should stay further on this evidence. (7/1)

742 Hever Golf Glory, kept at a mile, seemed set to score until worn down at the death. (3/1)

Rhapsody In White (IRE) should find this putting an edge on him. (14/1)
446 Zaahir (IRE) was stepping up to a mile. (11/2)
Sturgeon (IRE), whose seasonal reappearance at Newbury can be ignored, has not lived up to his second to Benny The Dip at Newmarket last June. (85/40)
Aerleon Pete (IRE), now qualified for handicaps, is one to bear in mind when tried over a longer trip. (5/1: op 11/4)

T/Plpt: £46.10 (140.12 Tckts). T/Qdpt: £11.00 (24.38 Tckts) IM/

0750-BRIGHTON (L-H) (Good to Firm)
Tuesday May 6th
WEATHER: fair WIND: mod half against

78 65+ 71+

1007 E.B.F. ST ANN'S WELLS MAIDEN STKS (2-Y.O) (Class D) (71)
2-25 (2-25) **5f 59y** £3,091.95 (£921.60: £439.30: £198.15) Stalls: Low GOING minus 0.31 sec per fur (GF)

Form	Horse / details	Dist	Pos	SP	RR	SF
836[3]	**Aurigny** (SDow) **2-8-9** SSanders(5) (hld up: chsd ldr over 2f out: led over 1f out: comf)	—	1	9/2[3]	80+	46
750[3]	**Fiveo'clock Shadow (IRE)** (BJMeehan) **2-9-0** BDoyle(2) (led: rdn over 2f out: hdd over 1f out: unable qckn)	3½	2	8/11[1]	74	40
739[3]	**Chrysalis** (PFICole) **2-8-9** MRimmer(1) (lw: a.p: rdn over 2f out: r.o ins fnl f)	hd	3	4/1[2]	69	35
836[13]	**Lobuche (IRE)** (RHannon) **2-9-0** WJO'Connor(6) (lw: a.p: rdn over 2f out: sn wknd)	3	4	12/1	65	31
	Figawin (GLewis) **2-9-0** PaulEddery(4) (leggy: bit bkwd: bhd fnl 4f)	2	5	14/1	59	25
	Fred's In The Know (CMurray) **2-9-0** JStack(3) (leggy: scope: s.s: a wl bhd)	15	6	50/1	13	—

(SP 112.4%) **6 Rn**

61.2 secs (1.20) CSF £7.51 TOTE £9.90: £8.30 £1.10 (£3.60) OWNER J & S Kelly (EPSOM) BRED R. T. Lingwood
836 Aurigny, with plenty of substance about her, was always travelling supremely well, and strode clear to win with plenty in hand. (9/2: 3/1-5/1)
750 Fiveo'clock Shadow (IRE) knew much more about the game on this occasion and set the pace, but was firmly put in his place by the winner. (8/11)
739 Chrysalis, from a stable that has won with its only two previous juvenile runners this season, raced up with the pace but got slightly tapped for toe at halfway. However, she ran on again inside the final furlong and only just failed to take second prize. (4/1: op 2/1)
Lobuche (IRE) broke on level terms this time, and was close up until tiring a quarter of a mile from home. (12/1: 7/1-14/1)
Figawin, a tall, close-coupled individual, looked in need of this and was soon left behind. (14/1: op 6/1)

1008 HOLLINGBURY CLAIMING STKS (3-Y.O) (Class F)
2-55 (2-58) **6f 209y** £2,277.00 (£627.00: £297.00) Stalls: Low GOING minus 0.31 sec per fur (GF)

Form	Horse / details	Dist	Pos	SP	RR	SF
	Good News (IRE) (65) (MMadgwick) **3-8-8b[1]** RPerham(3) (b.hind: hld up: led over 1f out: r.o wl)	—	1	10/1	64	24
874[3]	**Going Green** (JRFanshawe) **3-8-12** DHarrison(9) (b.hind: hld up: ev ch over 1f out: unable qckn)	2	2	10/1	63	23
258[6]	**Siouxrouge (80)** (PCHaslam) **3-9-7** SDrowne(8) (a.p: led wl over 1f out: sn hdd: one pce)	1	3	9/4[1]	70	30
	Chopin (IRE) (53) (RFJohnsonHoughton) **3-8-7** SSanders(6) (hdwy over 1f out: r.o)	hd	4	20/1	56	16
876[9]	**Bon Guest (IRE) (57)** (TJNaughton) **3-8-2**(5) RFfrench(2) (hdwy over 1f out: nvr nrr)	hd	5	16/1	56	16
643[3]	**Without Friends (IRE) (72)** (JFfitch-Heyes) **3-9-3** SWhitworth(7) (nvr nr to chal)	4	6	5/2[2]	56	16
656[6]	**Sovereign** (MPMuggeridge) **3-7-10**(3)ow1 MartinDwyer(4) (lw: led over 5f)	1	7	33/1	36	—
329[3]	**Le Shuttle (47)** (MHTompkins) **3-8-0** DaleGibson(1) (prom over 4f)	6	8	14/1	23	—
535[15]	**Major Twist (IRE) (60)** (RHannon) **3-8-9** WJO'Connor(5) (prom 5f)	1	9	13/2[3]	30	—

(SP 111.1%) **9 Rn**

1m 23.4 (3.40) CSF £90.09 TOTE £15.40: £3.00 £2.10 £1.40 (£74.00) Trio £96.40 OWNER Mr T. G. N. Burrage (DENMEAD) BRED Rosemount House Stud
Good News (IRE), fitted with blinkers for the first time and taking a drop in class, found that helped her to make a winning return to action, striking the front approaching the final furlong and running on far too strongly for her rivals. She is a madam according to her trainer. (10/1)
874 Going Green was certainly close enough if good enough below the distance, but failed to find another gear. (10/1: op 6/1)
258 Siouxrouge, given a three-month break following a winter campaign on the All-Weather, had just poked his nose in front when passed by the winner. (9/4)
Chopin (IRE) is a poor plater that stayed on from the back of the field in the last furlong and a half. (20/1)
757 Bon Guest (IRE) has had plenty of opportunities and has been exposed as very moderate. (16/1)
643 Without Friends (IRE) could never get in a blow and was probably not helped by the extra furlong. He has done all his winning in claimers or sellers. (5/2)
535 Major Twist (IRE) (13/2: 3/1-7/1)

1009 LADBROKE H'CAP (0-70) (3-Y.O+) (Class E)
3-25 (3-27) **6f 209y** £3,148.25 (£941.00: £450.50: £205.25) Stalls: Low GOING minus 0.31 sec per fur (GF)

Form	Horse / details	Dist	Pos	SP	RR	SF
766[3]	**Apollo Red (68)** (GLMoore) **8-9-12** CandyMorris(17) (mde all: pushed out)	—	1	9/2[1]	82	65
756[3]	**Justinianus (IRE) (42)** (JJBridger) **5-8-0** GBardwell(16) (lw: chsd wnr: rdn 4f out: r.o one pce fnl 2f)	1¼	2	13/2	53	36
863[5]	**Twin Creeks (52)** (VSoane) **6-8-10** BDoyle(10) (lw: hld up: rdn over 2f out: r.o one pce)	½	3	11/2[2]	62	45
755[8]	**Rocky Waters (USA) (40)** (MDIUsher) **8-7-12v** JMarshall(6) (b.hind: rdn & hdwy over 1f out: r.o)	2½	4	9/1	44	27
791[8]	**Righty Ho (64)** (PTWalwyn) **3-8-10** SSanders(8) (hdwy over 1f out: nvr nrr)	1½	5	20/1	65	36
749[7]	**Perfect Poppy (70)** (JRFanshawe) **3-9-2** DHarrison(7) (hdwy over 2f out: wknd over 1f out)	1¾	6	14/1	67	38
601[4]	**Velvet Jones (49)** (GFHCharles-Jones) **4-8-0**(7) CharlotteCox(3) (s.s: hdwy over 1f out: nvr nrr)	nk	7	16/1	45	28
755[10]	**Pearl Dawn (IRE) (50)** (PCClarke) **7-8-8** NAdams(2) (hdwy & nt clr run on ins 2f out: n.m.r over 1f out: nvr nrr)	1	8	16/1	44	27
305[10]	**Mogin (52)** (TJNaughton) **4-8-7**(3) JDSmith(13) (lw: nvr nrr)	s.h	9	33/1	46	29
638*	**Sizzling (62)** (RHannon) **5-9-6** WJO'Connor(9) (prom over 4f)	2½	10	6/1[3]	50	33
864[11]	**Delight of Dawn (59)** (EAWheeler) **5-8-12**(5) ADaly(4) (a mid div)	2	11	11/1	42	25
756[7]	**Tachycardia (43)** (RJO'Sullivan) **5-8-1** DBiggs(5) (s.s: a bhd)	½	12	14/1	25	8
585[16]	**Into Debt (40)** (JRPoulton) **4-7-5**(7)ow2 AMcCarthy(11) (s.s: a bhd)	1¾	13	33/1	18	—
638[6]	**Halbert (41)** (MDIUsher) **8-7-13v** DRMcCabe(1) (prom over 5f)	4	14	16/1	10	—
642[8]	**Irish Fiction (IRE) (57)** (DJSCosgrove) **3-8-3** JStack(12) (a bhd)	2½	15	20/1	20	—
577[6]	**Shermood (41)** (KTIvory) **4-7-10**(3)ow3 MartinDwyer(14) (b: b.hind: bhd fnl 3f)	2½	16	33/1	—	—

				SP	RR	SF
638^{3}	**Jo Maximus (70)** (JGSmyth-Osbourne) **5-9-9**(5) RFfrench(15) (hld up: rdn over 2f out: sn wknd)	1¾	**17**	14/1	23	6

(SP 135.5%) **17 Rn**

1m 21.4 (1.40) CSF £30.99 CT £163.61 TOTE £6.10: £1.10 £2.50 £2.20 £2.10 (£16.10) Trio £25.40 OWNER Mr A. Moore (BRIGHTON) BRED Crest Stud Ltd
LONG HANDICAP Into Debt 7-7 Shermood 7-8
WEIGHT FOR AGE 3yo-12lb
766 Apollo Red is a real credit to his trainer and is yet to be out of the first four in twelve outings this season. Quickly tacking over to the rails, he made all the running for a very convincing victory. He gets on extremely well with Candy Morris, who has been the pilot on all bar one of his nine victories. (9/2)
756 Justinianus (IRE) ran another sound race. In pursuit of the winner throughout, he never threatened to get in a serious challenge. Unfortunately, he is very difficult to win with. (13/2)
863 Twin Creeks was happier for the return to seven furlongs and, chasing the leaders, struggled on in the final quarter-mile. (11/2)
Rocky Waters (USA) stayed on from the back of the field without ever threatening. (9/1)
Righty Ho found this easy seven furlongs too sharp and was only staying on when it was all over. (20/1)
Perfect Poppy had shot her bolt below the distance. (14/1: 10/1-16/1)

1010 LADBROKE BOOKMAKERS H'CAP (0-70) (4-Y.O+) (Class E)
3-55 (3-56) **1m 3f 196y** £3,018.25 (£901.00: £430.50: £195.25) Stalls: High GOING minus 0.31 sec per fur (GF)

				SP	RR	SF
410^{8}	**Mazurek (63)** (MCPipe) **4-9-8** PaulEddery(3) (lw: mde all: rdn out)	—	**1**	$9/2^{3}$	76	54
680^{5}	**Prince Danzig (IRE) (61)** (DJGMurraySmith) **6-9-1**(5) RFfrench(1) (lw: hdwy over 3f out: chsd wnr over 1f out: no imp)	5	**2**	$9/4^{1}$	67	45
640^{2}	**Duncombe Hall (39)** (CACyzer) **4-7-12** DeclanO'Shea(9) (hld up: rdn 3f out: one pce)	3	**3**	$4/1^{2}$	41	19
435^{10}	**Rising Dough (IRE) (66)** (GLMoore) **5-9-4**(7) MBatchelor(8) (hdwy over 4f out: rdn 3f out: one pce)	hd	**4**	$9/2^{3}$	68	46
283^{3}	**Nawaji (USA) (45)** (WRMuir) **4-8-4** DHarrison(5) (hdwy over 3f out: wknd wl over 1f out)	1	**5**	10/1	46	24
689^{10}	**May King Mayhem (39)** (MrsALMKing) **4-7-12**ow2 AGarth(7) (a bhd)	8	**6**	33/1	29	5
753^{2}	**Bedouin Prince (USA) (51)** (MrsLStubbs) **10-8-10** SSanders(4) (b: prom over 7f)	9	**7**	7/1	29	7
640^{5}	**Colour Counsellor (42)** (RMFlower) **4-8-1b** GHind(6) (prom 9f)	2	**8**	10/1	17	—
	Dazzling (65) (DCO'Brien) **4-9-10** GBardwell(2) (mid div whn hmpd on ins over 4f out: nt rcvr)	30	**9**	25/1	—	—

(SP 124.6%) **9 Rn**

2m 31.5 (3.90) CSF £14.92 CT £42.17 TOTE £5.10: £2.70 £1.10 £2.30 (£8.10) Trio £13.10 OWNER Kammac Plc (WELLINGTON) BRED Miss K. Rausing and Calogo Bloodstock AG
LONG HANDICAP May King Mayhem 7-4
Mazurek, who has flopped in three runs on the Fibresand so far this year, benefited from the golden touch of Martin Pipe and made a winning debut for his new stable, leading throughout. (9/2)
680 Prince Danzig (IRE) goes well round here, but could make little impression on the winner. (9/4)
640 Duncombe Hall chased the leaders but could only go up and down in the same place in the last three furlongs. He remains a maiden after twelve attempts. (4/1: op 5/2)
Rising Dough (IRE), fit from hurdling, was making little impression in the straight. (9/2: 4/1-6/1)
283 Nawaji (USA) began a forward move early in the straight, but had come to the end of her tether early in the final quarter-mile. She remains a maiden after thirteen attempts. (10/1: 7/1-12/1)
640 Colour Counsellor (10/1: 8/1-12/1)

1011 VARNDEAN (S) STKS (3-Y.O+) (Class G)
4-25 (4-27) **1m 1f 209y** £1,984.50 (£547.00: £259.50) Stalls: High GOING minus 0.31 sec per fur (GF)

				SP	RR	SF
639^{2}	**Stellar Line (USA) (72)** (DRCElsworth) **4-9-5**(3) DGriffiths(9) (lw: mde all: clr over 2f out: unchal)	—	**1**	$7/4^{1}$	68	47
791^{7}	**Law Dancer (IRE) (61)** (TGMills) **4-9-5**(3) AWhelan(5) (lw: hld up: chsd wnr over 2f out: no imp)	13	**2**	$9/2^{3}$	47	26
870^{6}	**Roman Reel (USA) (60)** (GLMoore) **6-9-12** SWhitworth(7) (lw: hdwy over 4f out: rdn over 2f out: one pce)	hd	**3**	$100/30^{2}$	51	30
662^{4}	**Leg Beforum (IRE) (50)** (LMontagueHall) **3-8-4b¹**(3) DO'Donohoe(2) (s.s: rdn over 2f out: hdwy over 1f out: nvr nrr)	¾	**4**	14/1	46	10
769^{7}	**Kirov Protege (IRE) (21)** (MrsLCJewell) **5-9-1**(7) DarrenWilliams(11) (lw: chsd wnr over 7f)	3½	**5**	33/1	40	19
88^{10}	**Burning Flame (37)** (RMFlower) **4-9-3b** GHind(4) (hdwy over 3f out: wknd over 1f out)	1¼	**6**	20/1	33	12
216^{11}	**Dia Georgy (31)** (CADwyer) **6-9-8** PaulEddery(8) (b: a.p: rdn over 3f out: wknd fnl f)	1	**7**	33/1	37	16
537^{9}	**Noble Hero (60)** (JJSheehan) **3-8-7** DeclanO'Shea(10) (a bhd)	hd	**8**	12/1	36	—
763^{16}	**Mac's Delight (60)** (NMBabbage) **3-8-7** VSlattery(1) (prom over 5f)	s.h	**9**	16/1	36	—
755^{11}	**Another Fiddle (IRE) (46)** (JELong) **7-9-8b¹** SSanders(3) (b.hind: bhd fnl 4f)	12	**10**	33/1	17	—
676^{18}	**Keenest Reluctance** (JRFanshawe) **3-8-2v¹** NVarley(6) (prom 5f)	¾	**11**	12/1	11	—

(SP 119.1%) **11 Rn**

2m 2.2 (3.90) CSF £8.45 TOTE £2.20: £1.40 £1.90 £1.90 (£5.00) Trio £6.50 OWNER Mr D. R. C. Elsworth (WHITCOMBE) BRED Juddmonte Farms
WEIGHT FOR AGE 3yo-15lb
Sold MPolglase 8,000 gns
639 Stellar Line (USA) appreciated the drop in class and had little more than an afternoon stroll, winning with any amount in hand. He can score again in a low grade. (7/4)
226 Law Dancer (IRE) but did not have a prayer with the winner. (9/2)
870 Roman Reel (USA) was in his right grade, but failed to find another gear in the straight despite all his rider's efforts. (100/30)
662 Leg Beforum (IRE), fitted with blinkers for the first time, stayed on from below the distance but by then it was far too late. (14/1: op 8/1)
Kirov Protege (IRE) is a very poor performer and one win from thirty-eight starts says it all. (33/1)
366 Noble Hero (12/1: op 8/1)
Keenest Reluctance (12/1: op 8/1)

1012 LADBROKE MAIDEN H'CAP (0-70) (3-Y.O+) (Class E)
4-55 (4-56) **5f 213y** £3,096.25 (£925.00: £442.50: £201.25) Stalls: Low GOING minus 0.31 sec per fur (GF)

				SP	RR	SF
585^{15}	**College Night (IRE) (39)** (SCWilliams) **5-8-2**(3) MHenry(9) (chsd ldrs: led over 2f out: r.o wl)	—	**1**	$7/1^{3}$	53	32
	Marengo (65) (JAkehurst) **3-9-7** SSanders(7) (a.p: hrd rdn over 1f out: r.o one pce)	1¼	**2**	$4/1^{1}$	76	45
601^{11}	**Ed's Folly (IRE) (52)** (SDow) **4-8-13**(5) ADaly(3) (led over 3f: one pce)	1½	**3**	10/1	59	38
879^{2}	**Flying Harold (42)** (MRChannon) **4-8-8** NAdams(15) (swtchd lft over 3f out: hdwy & swtchd rt 2f out: r.o)	3½	**4**	$5/1^{2}$	39	18

				SP	RR	SF
693^{7}	**Dandy Regent (70)** (CACyzer) **3-9-12** DBiggs(8) (lw: dwlt: rdn & hdwy over 2f out: one pce)	3½	**5**	14/1	58	27
649^{15}	**Fan of Vent-Axia (50)** (DJSCosgrove) **3-8-6** JStack(6) (nvr nr to chal)	1½	**6**	25/1	34	3
855^{5}	**Arnie (IRE) (35)** (JRPoulton) **5-7-12**(3) MartinDwyer(1) (chsd ldrs: rdn over 4f out: wknd over 1f out)	1	**7**	12/1	16	—
749^{4}	**Chorus Song (USA) (68)** (PWChapple-Hyam) **3-9-7**(3) RHavlin(12) (b.hind: lw: rdn over 3f out: nvr nrr)	½	**8**	4/1 1	48	17
518^{6}	**Out Line (62)** (MMadgwick) **5-9-9**(5) RFfrench(2) (lw: hdwy 2f out: nt clr run & hit rails over 1f out: sn wknd)	1½	**9**	5/1 2	38	17
855^{8}	**With The Tempo (IRE) (40)** (DrJDScargill) **4-8-6b**1 RPerham(4) (chsd ldrs: rdn over 2f out: wknd wl over 1f out)	1	**10**	16/1	13	—
693^{11}	**Joli's Prince (60)** (CMurray) **3-9-2** NicolaHowarth(11) (bhd fnl 2f)	2½	**11**	25/1	26	—
649^{14}	**Ludo (64)** (RHannon) **3-9-6** WJO'Connor(10) (bhd fnl 2f)	1½	**12**	11/1	26	—
694^{15}	**Saltimbanco (69)** (RAkehurst) **3-9-4**(7) DDenby(5) (lw: a bhd)	1	**13**	12/1	29	—
	Peter Perfect (57) (GLewis) **3-8-13** PaulEddery(13) (bit bkwd: a bhd)	1¾	**14**	11/1	12	—

(SP 147.2%) **14 Rn**

1m 9.2 (2.00) CSF £39.44 CT £288.21 TOTE £12.40: £2.60 £1.30 £5.50 (£15.30) Trio £232.80; £163.98 to Chester 7/5/97 OWNER Mrs Christine Dunnett (NEWMARKET) BRED Lady McAlpine

WEIGHT FOR AGE 3yo-10lb

473 College Night (IRE) made a winning debut for her new stable, breaking her duck at the twenty-fifth attempt. (7/1)

Marengo, who looked thoroughly ungenuine on two of his three starts last year, ran better here but still did not look to be enjoying himself. He carried his head extremely high and looked far from co-operative below the distance, but his jockey kept on beavering away and the colt eventually struggled on to take second prize. He looks one to avoid. (4/1: 7/1-7/2)

Ed's Folly (IRE) set a very brisk pace, but was then tapped for toe. (10/1)

879 Flying Harold, racing at the back of the field, encountered traffic problems as he tried to weave his way through the pack. (5/1)

Dandy Regent made a move on the outside of the field over a quarter of a mile from home, but then could make no further impression. (14/1)

Ludo (11/1: 8/1-12/1)

Saltimbanco (12/1: op 6/1)

Peter Perfect (11/1: 8/1-12/1)

T/Plpt: £60.00 (179.06 Tckts). T/Qdpt: £15.00 (57.61 Tckts) AK

CHESTER (L-H) (Soft)

Tuesday May 6th

WEATHER: sunny & v.cold WIND: fresh against

1013 JOSEPH HELER LILY AGNES CONDITIONS STKS (2-Y.O) (Class B)

2-10 (2-11) **5f 16y** £7,456.80 (£2,791.20: £1,365.60: £588.00: £264.00: £134.40) Stalls: Low GOING: 0.19 sec per fur (G)

				SP	RR	SF
828*	**Daunting Lady (IRE)** (RHannon) **2-8-8** PatEddery(1) (mde virtually all: drew clr appr fnl f: unchal)	—	**1**	10/11 1	97+	64
750^{4}	**Heavenly Abstone** (PDEvans) **2-8-5v** JFEgan(4) (chsd ldrs: rdn 2f out: kpt on: no ch w wnr)	5	**2**	12/1	78	45
682^{2}	**Kilcora (IRE)** (CADwyer) **2-8-6**ow1 KFallon(2) (trckd ldrs: outpcd 2f out: styd on ins fnl f)	2	**3**	4/1 2	73	39
651^{2}	**Salamanca** (JBerry) **2-8-5** KDarley(6) (lw: w wnr 3f: sn rdn & outpcd)	¾	**4**	6/1 3	70	37
884^{2}	**Young Ibnr (IRE)** (PDEvans) **2-8-10** JFortune(5) (sn drvn along: nvr gng pce of ldrs)	1¼	**5**	12/1	71	38
844^{2}	**Filey Brigg** (WTKemp) **2-8-5** JQuinn(7) (s.i.s: a outpcd)	1	**6**	12/1	63	30
730*	**Penniless (IRE)** (NTinkler) **2-8-8** JWeaver(8) (spd to ½-wy: sn wknd)	1¾	**7**	16/1	60	27
880^{4}	**Scene (IRE)** (MartynMeade) **2-8-5** FNorton(3) (bit bkwd: lost pl after 1f: sn bhd: t.o)	11	**8**	20/1	22	—

(SP 120.4%) **8 Rn**

62.85 secs (2.65) CSF £13.72 TOTE £1.80: £1.20 £3.30 £1.30 (£15.10) OWNER Mr T. J. Dale (MARLBOROUGH) BRED Mrs G. Doyle

828* Daunting Lady (IRE) followed up her comfortable win at Sandown with another clear-cut success, and there is no doubting she is sharp. The Queen Mary at Royal Ascot and the National Stakes are likely targets. (10/11: op evens)

750 Heavenly Abstone struggled to go the early pace, but she handled the ground better than many and battled on to secure a worthy runner-up prize. (12/1: op 8/1)

682 Kilcora (IRE), a filly who looks to have a future, had trouble handling the bends at racing pace, but she stuck to her task and was doing all her best work once in line for home. (4/1: 3/1-9/2)

651 Salamanca failed to get the better of the well-drawn winner and, on ground that could have been softer than she cares for, had nothing left once straightening up. (6/1: op 7/2)

884 Young Ibnr (IRE) had an impossible task conceding weight all round in this better-class event, and he was just not up to it. (12/1: op 8/1)

844 Filey Brigg, proven on softer going, missed the kick and was always at full stretch in an attempt to recover the lost ground. (12/1)

1014 T.H.I. LEISURE CRABWALL MANOR MAIDEN STKS (3-Y.O) (Class D)

2-40 (2-41) **1m 2f 75y** £8,458.00 (£2,554.00: £1,242.00: £586.00) Stalls: High GOING: 0.19 sec per fur (G)

				SP	RR	SF
	Conon Falls (IRE) (JHMGosden) **3-9-0** LDettori(4) (hld up: hdwy on ins over 3f out: led 2f out: sn clr)	—	**1**	9/2	93+	51
	Solo Mio (IRE) (98) (BWHills) **3-9-0** PatEddery(7) (bit bkwd: hld up: hdwy 4f out: rdn & styd on wl ins fnl f)	1¼	**2**	4/1 3	91+	49
	Montfort (USA) (PFICole) **3-9-0** TQuinn(3) (h.d.w: bit bkwd: w ldrs: led 7f out to 6f out: led 4f out to 3f out: kpt on one pce)	3½	**3**	20/1	86	44
740^{4}	**Memorise (USA)** (HRACecil) **3-9-0** KFallon(2) (hld up: hdwy 3f out: sn rdn: r.o one pce)	1½	**4**	100/30 2	83	41
676^{13}	**Fabled Light (IRE) (72)** (GWragg) **3-9-0** MHills(1) (bit bkwd: trckd ldrs: rdn 2f out: eased whn btn cl home)	¾	**5**	11/1	82	40
	Gulf Harbour (IRE) (PWChapple-Hyam) **3-9-0** JReid(10) (w'like: leggy: bit bkwd: hld up: gd hdwy 5f out: slt ld 3f out: hdd 2f out: sn btn)	2½	**6**	11/4 1	78	36
842^{5}	**Get The Point (75)** (RHollinshead) **3-8-11**(3) FLynch(8) (chsd ldrs over 7f: sn wknd: t.o)	22	**7**	25/1	44	2
740^{11}	**Walkabout** (BWHills) **3-9-0** DHolland(6) (bit bkwd: led over 3f: wknd 4f out: t.o)	10	**8**	20/1	29	—
683^{20}	**Behind The Scenes** (CACyzer) **3-9-0** JWeaver(5) (bkwd: dwlt: a bhd: t.o)	5	**9**	20/1	21	—
792^{5}	**Hype Superior (IRE)** (ABailey) **3-9-0** DWright(9) (w ldrs: led 6f out to 4f out: wknd qckly: t.o)	1½	**10**	40/1	19	—

(SP 116.8%) **10 Rn**

2m 16.72 (8.02) CSF £19.02 TOTE £3.80: £1.40 £1.40 £3.70 (£5.60) Trio £48.60 OWNER Sheikh Mohammed (NEWMARKET) BRED Darley Stud Management Co Ltd

Conon Falls (IRE) found this longer trip made-to-measure and, coming the shortest way round, had the prize sewn up as soon as he struck the front. He should go on from here. (9/2)

Solo Mio (IRE), by the same sire as the winner, was putting in some solid work in the closing stages and this impressive mover should have little trouble in opening his account. (4/1: op 5/2)

Montfort (USA), a good-looking colt who has done well physically since last year, looked as though he would benefit from the run. With the pace, he was a live contender turning into the straight before lack of peak condition took its toll. (20/1)
740 Memorise (USA) lacked the speed to mount a challenge, and even this step-up to ten furlongs did not seem sufficient on such an easy track. (100/30)
Fabled Light (IRE) is gradually getting the hang of the game, and was poised to challenge going as well as any until the winner appeared on the scene. (11/1)
Gulf Harbour (IRE), who comes from a useful winning family, went very freely to post. Settled once in action, he made up his ground quickly at halfway and briefly showed in front, but he had done too much too soon and was very leg-weary from the turn into the straight. The experience will not be wasted. (11/4)

1015 CHESTER VASE STKS (Gp 3) (3-Y.O) (Class A)

3-10 (3-10) **1m 4f 66y** £29,250.00 (£10,935.00: £5,242.50: £2,272.50) Stalls: Low GOING: 0.19 sec per fur (G)

				SP	RR	SF
691[2]	**Panama City (USA) (107)** (PWChapple-Hyam) **3-8-10** JReid(1) (lw: chsd ldrs: pushed along 4f out: hrd rdn 2f out: r.o strly to ld wl ins fnl f)	—	1	6/5[1]	104	42
782*	**Ivan Luis (FR) (106)** (MBell) **3-8-10** MRoberts(2) (lw: hld up & bhd: gd hdwy over 2f out: str chal fnl f: r.o)	hd	2	5/1[3]	104	42
	State Fair (99) (BWHills) **3-8-10** MHills(3) (h.d.w: set slow pce: rdn 2f out: ct cl home)	hd	3	8/1	104	42
725*	**Ghataas** (JLDunlop) **3-8-10** RHills(5) (chsd ldr: rdn & ev ch wl over 1f out: no ex fnl f)	1¾	4	11/4[2]	102	40
690[2]	**Generous Gift (90)** (EALDunlop) **3-8-10** LDettori(4) (hld up: hdwy 3f out: hrd drvn 2f out: eased whn btn fnl f)	4	5	9/1	96	34

(SP 109.9%) **5 Rn**

2m 46.64 (10.44) CSF £6.87 TOTE £1.90: £1.50 £1.80 (£4.40) OWNER Mr R. E. Sangster (MARLBOROUGH) BRED Swettenham Stud
691 Panama City (USA), in a race that hardly lived up to its billing as a Derby trial due to the mediocre early pace, was unable to respond when the tempo picked up half a mile out, and he looked held turning in. However, Reid really got to work on him once in line for home, and he found extra to land the spoils in the dying strides. (6/5: op evens)
782* Ivan Luis (FR), faced with by far his stiffest test to date, delivered a determined challenge inside the final furlong, but this only served to egg the winner on and he was a stride down at the line. He carries plenty of condition and did not really extend himself on the way to post, but he is up to this class and his future looks bright. (5/1)
State Fair, the only one without a previous outing this term, was prepared to do the donkey work and almost scored a major surprise until being forced to give best close home. On the evidence of this, he may well turn out the best of the lot in the long term. (8/1)
725* Ghataas had to dig deep to hold on over a slightly shorter trip on his seasonal debut against maidens, and lack of stamina seemed to be a problem here although, in this class, he may not be quite up to it as yet. (11/4)
690 Generous Gift tried to get himself into the action on the approach to the straight, but he was the first to crack and was not persevered with when all chance had gone. (9/1)

1016 WALKER SMITH & WAY H'CAP (0-95) (4-Y.O+) (Class C)

3-40 (3-41) **1m 2f 75y** £10,866.00 (£3,288.00: £1,604.00: £762.00) Stalls: High GOING: 0.19 sec per fur (G)

				SP	RR	SF
435*	**Break the Rules (79)** (MCPipe) **5-9-1** KDarley(17) (bhd: gd hdwy on outside 3f out: hrd rdn to ld ins fnl f: all out)	—	1	9/2[1]	89	56
738[11]	**Kuala Lipis (USA) (92)** (PFICole) **4-10-0** TQuinn(14) (a.p: led over 2f out tl over 1f out: rallied u.p cl home)	nk	2	11/1	102	69
925[5]	**Northern Fan (IRE) (60)** (NTinkler) **5-7-10** LCharnock(12) (a.p: led over 1f out tl ins fnl f)	1½	3	50/1	67	34
735*	**Rockforce (92)** (MRChannon) **5-10-0** RHughes(16) (lw: hld up: stdy hdwy 4f out: nt clr run ins fnl f: r.o)	s.h	4	8/1[3]	99	66
	Game Ploy (POL) (88) (DHaydnJones) **5-9-10** PatEddery(6) (bit bkwd: hld up: nt clr run over 2f out: swtchd rt & styd on ins fnl f)	3½	5	8/1[3]	90	57
	Brandon Magic (88) (IABalding) **4-9-10** LDettori(2) (bkwd: hld up: effrt over 3f out: nt rch ldrs)	3½	6	13/2[2]	84	51
789[6]	**Cedez le Passage (FR) (69)** (KOCunningham-Brown) **6-8-5b** MRoberts(8) (hld up: hdwy 4f out: wknd appr fnl f)	3	7	20/1	61	28
832[5]	**Stone Ridge (IRE) (85)** (RHannon) **5-9-7** DaneO'Neill(7) (rdn along ½-wy: nvr nrr)	1¼	8	13/2[2]	75	42
	Clifton Beat (USA) (71) (PJHobbs) **6-8-7** KFallon(1) (b: lw: bhd: styng on whn bmpd over 1f out: nvr nrr)	1	9	10/1	59	26
	Statajack (IRE) (80) (DRCElsworth) **9-9-2b** RCochrane(5) (b: bkwd: hld up & bhd: n.d)	nk	10	20/1	68	35
	Wentbridge Lad (IRE) (67) (PDEvans) **7-8-3v** JFEgan(13) (trckd ldrs: rdn 3f out: sn btn)	hd	11	12/1	55	22
405[4]	**Bardon Hill Boy (IRE) (90)** (BHanbury) **5-9-12** WRyan(4) (a in rr)	3	12	10/1	73	40
789[18]	**Wot No Fax (84)** (BJMeehan) **4-9-6** JWeaver(11) (bit bkwd: chsd ldr: led 3f out: sn hdd: rdn & wknd wl over 1f out)	2½	13	33/1	63	30
738[12]	**Lionize (USA) (90)** (PWChapple-Hyam) **4-9-12** JReid(10) (bit bkwd: prom over 6f)	nk	14	20/1	69	36
661[5]	**Polar Eclipse (78)** (MJohnston) **4-9-0b** MHills(9) (led to 3f out: sn hmpd & snatched up: t.o)	24	15	14/1	20	—
735[5]	**Anak-Ku (68)** (MissGayKelleway) **4-7-11**(7) AngelaGallimore(15) (lw: chsd ldrs 7f: sn lost pl: t.o)	3½	16	16/1	4	—

(SP 133.0%) **16 Rn**

2m 16.24 (7.54) CSF £50.80 CT £2,091.80 TOTE £5.10: £1.40 £2.80 £14.40 £2.40 (£43.70) Trio £1,108.20 OWNER Mr A. J. Lomas (WELLINGTON) BRED Cleaboy Farms Co
LONG HANDICAP Northern Fan (IRE) 7-2
435* Break the Rules, alternating between hurdles and the Flat, came from another county to win this and it was a very courageous performance to succeed with a host of rivals snapping at his heels. (9/2)
450* Kuala Lipis (USA) did not deserve to lose out after such a game weight-carrying effort, and another decent prize will be just reward. (11/1)
843 Northern Fan (IRE), beaten in a seller last month, ran the race of his life under this feather weight and, had his stamina not ebbed inside the final furlong, he may well have held on. (50/1)
735* Rockforce travelled well, but may have done the wrong thing in attempting to come through on the inside when delivering his challenge, for he was getting tightened up in the final hundred yards. He deserves the chance to make amends. (8/1)
Game Ploy (POL) enjoyed a rewarding time last year, and he looks on good terms with himself, turning in a very encouraging display even though he appeared to need this. (8/1)
Brandon Magic did not win a race last year but he does act on soft ground and, with this run to put an edge on him, can prove he is no back number yet. (13/2)

1017 S.I.S.10TH ANNIVERSARY EARL OF CHESTER H'CAP (0-100) (3-Y.O) (Class C)

4-10 (4-14) **7f 122y** £18,537.50 (£5,600.00: £2,725.00: £1,287.50) Stalls: Low GOING: 0.19 sec per fur (G)

				SP	RR	SF
675[11]	**Great Child (77)** (MRStoute) **3-8-6** KFallon(6) (lw: hld up: hdwy 3f out: led appr fnl f: hld on gamely)	—	1	9/2[1]	86	55

	Horse	Btn	Pos	SP	RR	SF
449[11]	**Jeffrey Anotherred (92)** (KMcAuliffe) **3-9-7** RHughes(3) (trckd ldrs: hdwy 2f out: str run u.p ins fnl f)	¾	**2**	16/1	99	68
654[2]	**Bollin Terry (72)** (TDEasterby) **3-8-1** LCharnock(2) (lw: a.p: hrd rdn wl over 1f out: kpt on towards fin)	nk	**3**	6/1[2]	79	48
699[6]	**I Can't Remember (76)** (PDEvans) **3-8-5** JFEgan(4) (led tl appr fnl f: hrd rdn: kpt on)	hd	**4**	14/1	83	52
794[2]	**Nomore Mr Niceguy (86)** (EJAlston) **3-9-1** JWeaver(8) (prom tl wknd over 1f out)	3	**5**	9/1	86	55
845[4]	**Return of Amin (67)** (JDBethell) **3-7-10** TWilliams(15) (lw: bhd: hdwy ½-wy: rdn over 1f out: sn btn)	1¾	**6**	6/1[2]	64	33
784[8]	**Highly Respected (IRE) (67)** (ABailey) **3-7-10b[1]** DWright(1) (hdwy over 2f out: nt rch ldrs)	½	**7**	16/1	62	31
597[6]	**Foot Battalion (IRE) (87)** (RHollinshead) **3-8-13**(3) FLynch(14) (effrt over 2f out: sn rdn & no imp)	¾	**8**	25/1	81	50
853[3]	**No More Pressure (IRE) (82)** (NJHWalker) **3-8-11** PatEddery(9) (hdwy ½-wy: rdn & wknd over 2f out)	1	**9**	15/2[3]	74	43
688[5]	**Rechullin (79)** (DRLoder) **3-8-8** LDettori(7) (nvr nr to chal)	2½	**10**	8/1	65	34
723[6]	**Test The Water (IRE) (91)** (RHannon) **3-9-6** DaneO'Neill(13) (lw: a bhd & outpcd)	1½	**11**	16/1	74	43
794*	**Hawait (IRE) (88)** (BWHills) **3-9-3** MHills(10) (a in rr)	nk	**12**	15/2[3]	71	40
729[5]	**Truly Parched (USA) (80)** (PWChapple-Hyam) **3-8-9** JReid(16) (trckd ldrs: rdn over 2f out: sn btn)	1¾	**13**	16/1	59	28
	What Happened Was (87) (MartynMeade) **3-8-11**(5) DSweeney(5) (bit bkwd: prom over 4f)	3	**14**	33/1	60	29
676[12]	**Party Romance (USA) (85)** (BHanbury) **3-9-0** WRyan(11) (plld hrd: in tch tl wknd over 2f out)	2	**15**	12/1	53	22
448[20]	**Effervescence (80)** (RHannon) **3-8-9** KDarley(12) (outpcd)	2½	**16**	20/1	43	12

(SP 140.8%) **16 Rn**

1m 36.68 (4.68) CSF £82.89 CT £334.29 TOTE £6.50: £1.90 £6.00 £1.90 £2.50 (£131.40) Trio £315.60 OWNER Mr Saeed Suhail (NEWMARKET) BRED Collin Stud and Coolmore Stud

LONG HANDICAP Highly Respected (IRE) 7-9

675 Great Child, much sharper for the run at Newmarket, landed the gamble readily and, now that he has got off the mark, should be able to follow up. (9/2: 3/1-5/1)

Jeffrey Anotherred has lost none of the ability that enabled him to win three races in the autumn, but top weight proved the deciding factor this time. (16/1)

654 Bollin Terry continues to knock at the door and he gave it all he had here, but that elusive first success is proving hard to come by. (6/1)

699 I Can't Remember enjoys himself round here and he proved a real tough nut to crack, but an extra effort was not forthcoming in an all-out battle to the post. (14/1)

794 Nomore Mr Niceguy ran another good race, being in the firing line until feeling the strain approaching the final furlong. (9/1)

845 Return of Amin had the going in his favour, but his bid for glory had come to an end below the distance. (6/1)

446 Highly Respected (IRE) showed much improved form in this first handicap courtesy of the headgear, and she should be able to pay her way. (16/1)

794* Hawait (IRE) either did not handle the ground or the track, for he was always towards the rear and never promised to improve. (15/2)

1018 PRINCE OF WALES H'CAP (0-100) (3-Y.O) (Class C)

4-40 (4-44) **5f 16y** £7,385.50 (£2,224.00: £1,077.00: £503.50) Stalls: Low GOING: 0.19 sec per fur (G)

	Horse	Btn	Pos	SP	RR	SF
904[3]	**Dancethenightaway (84)** (BJMeehan) **3-8-6** DaneO'Neill(2) (a.p: led over 2f out: qcknd clr fnl f)	—	**1**	10/1	96	68
652*	**Mangus (IRE) (77)** (KOCunningham-Brown) **3-7-8**(5) PFessey(1) (lw: chsd ldrs: effrt over 1f out: nt pce of wnr)	3	**2**	7/1[2]	80	52
731[7]	**Divide And Rule (74)** (RHollinshead) **3-7-10** JQuinn(3) (lw: a.p: rdn & one pce appr fnl f)	2½	**3**	25/1	69	41
854[2]	**Sabina (87)** (IABalding) **3-8-9** LDettori(4) (s.i.s: sn rcvrd: swtchd rt over 1f out: r.o)	1¼	**4**	2/1[1]	78	50
596[14]	**Double Action (90)** (TDEasterby) **3-8-12** MBirch(12) (lw: prom on outside: effrt over 1f out: nt pce to chal)	1¼	**5**	14/1	77	49
744[14]	**Swino (87)** (PDEvans) **3-8-9** JFEgan(14) (bhd & outpcd tl r.o wl fnl f)	1	**6**	14/1	71	43
854[9]	**Vasari (IRE) (96)** (MRChannon) **3-8-13**(5) PPMurphy(11) (nvr nr to chal)	½	**7**	16/1	78	50
	Bayford Thrust (88) (JBerry) **3-8-5**(5) TEDurcan(9) (b: b.hind: nvr nrr)	s.h	**8**	20/1	70	42
877[6]	**Jennelle (97)** (CADwyer) **3-9-5** KFallon(6) (hmpd sn after s: effrt ½-wy: eased whn btn appr fnl f)	s.h	**9**	7/1[2]	79	51
731*	**Lamarita (78)** (JMPEustace) **3-8-0** JTate(7) (n.m.r over 1f out: nvr nr ldrs)	2	**10**	8/1[3]	53	25
694[10]	**Cherry Blossom (IRE) (85)** (RHannon) **3-8-7** PatEddery(10) (prom: rdn & wknd over 1f out)	½	**11**	8/1[3]	59	31
501[3]	**Rudi's Pet (IRE) (96)** (RHannon) **3-9-4** JReid(5) (prom: pushed along ½-wy: btn whn bmpd over 1f out)	1¼	**12**	8/1[3]	66	38
	Fredrik The Fierce (IRE) (99) (JBerry) **3-9-7** KDarley(13) (sn pushed along: a outpcd)	2	**13**	16/1	63	35
694[19]	**Ice Age (80)** (RJRWilliams) **3-8-2** DWright(8) (led over 2f: sn drvn along & wknd: t.o)	11	**14**	33/1	9	—

(SP 137.4%) **14 Rn**

62.51 secs (2.31) CSF £80.11 CT £1,072.90 TOTE £10.30: £2.50 £2.20 £9.90 (£25.20) Trio £41.00 OWNER Mr G. A. Bosley (UPPER LAMBOURN) BRED G. A. Bosley and H. Clarkin

LONG HANDICAP Divide And Rule 7-8

904 Dancethenightaway appreciated this return to the minimum trip, and quickly showed her rivals a clean pair of heels inside the distance. (10/1)

652* Mangus (IRE) looked the part and nothing was going better turning in but, once the winner was let loose, he had to make do with the runner-up prize. (7/1)

555 Divide And Rule had the beating of the winner on the book and was a leading contender all the way but, when a turn of finishing pace was needed, he was unable to respond. (25/1)

854 Sabina looked a bit wintry in her coat on this very cold day, and probably lost what chance she had with a tardy start. The fact that she was able to finish on the heels of the leaders would suggest she can win once the warmer weather returns. (2/1: 3/1-6/4)

596 Double Action, thought to need a slightly longer trip, ran well throughout, but he was found wanting when the pace quickened below the distance. (14/1)

501 Swino, taken off his legs in the early stages from an outside draw, was running on best of all at the finish and he is worth keeping in mind. (14/1)

Cherry Blossom (IRE) (8/1: 6/1-9/1)

T/Jkpt: £7,763.80 (0.2 Tckts). T/Plpt: £192.50 (202.94 Tckts). T/Qdpt: £63.20 (24.24 Tckts) IM

0971-DONCASTER (L-H) (Good, Good to Soft patches)

Tuesday May 6th

WEATHER: sunny but cold WIND: mod half against

51 62? 61+

1019 CAPRICORN (S) STKS (2-Y.O) (Class F)

6-00 (6-03) **5f** £2,784.00 (£774.00: £372.00) Stalls: High GOING: 0.09 sec per fur (G)

	Horse	Btn	Pos	SP	RR	SF
	Mighty Sure (IRE) (PCalver) **2-8-3**(3) DarrenMoffatt(8) (lengthy: unf: outpcd: hdwy 2f out: r.o wl to ld nr fin)	—	**1**	25/1	58	15
884[7]	**Swift Time** (MRBosley) **2-8-6** CRutter(2) (b: led: hung lft & racd alone far side: ct cl home)	nk	**2**	4/1[2]	57	14

631^{8}	**Miss Beveled** (MBrittain) **2-8-6** GDuffield(6) (a chsng ldrs: kpt on fnl 2f)	3½	**3**	20/1	46	3
	Fleur-de-Lys (WJMusson) **2-8-6** AMcGlone(4) (neat: sn in tch: effrt ½-wy: styd on: nvr able chal)	1¼	**4**	20/1	42	—
948^{3}	**Adrenalin** (MrsJRRamsden) **2-8-11** JFortune(12) (in tch: hung lft most of wy: sme hdwy u.p 2f out: no imp)	hd	**5**	7/4^{1}	47	4
	Sixth Avenue (IRE) (RMWhitaker) **2-8-6** DeanMcKeown(7) (leggy: unf: s.s: outpcd tl hdwy over 1f out: r.o)	1¾	**6**	12/1	36+	—
859^{4}	**Diamond Steve** (NTinkler) **2-9-4v** KimTinkler(5) (sn pushed along: nvr trbld ldrs)	nk	**7**	7/1^{3}	47	4
780^{7}	**Sunshine Pet (IRE)** (JJO'Neill) **2-8-6** JCarroll(3) (nvr trbld ldrs)	nk	**8**	25/1	34	—
780^{8}	**Companys Gamble** (BPJBaugh) **2-8-6** ACulhane(1) (chsd ldrs: effrt ½-wy: wknd over 1f out)	½	**9**	20/1	32	—
767^{4}	**Calllram** (MBlanshard) **2-8-6** MFenton(11) (spd to ½-wy: sn outpcd)	2	**10**	9/1	26	—
441^{6}	**I'm Not Sure** (JBerry) **2-8-6** NCarlisle(13) (w ldrs 3f: wknd qckly)	4	**11**	9/1	13	—
	Slim Prior (KRBurke) **2-8-11** GCarter(9) (leggy: bkwd: dwlt: hung lft & a wl bhd)	hd	**12**	16/1	18	—
739^{12}	**Hamerra (IRE)** (MartynMeade) **2-8-6** FNorton(10) (spd 3f: wknd qckly)	5	**13**	10/1	—	—
				(SP 133.5%)	**13 Rn**	

63.32 secs (4.92) CSF £116.49 TOTE £83.60: £15.60 £1.30 £6.90 (£137.70) Trio Not won; £261.48 to Chester 8/5/97 OWNER Mrs Janis MacPherson (RIPON) BRED St Simon Foundation
Sold TStafford 5,000 gns

Mighty Sure (IRE) has not got the best of legs but she can motor, and there should be improvement in her. (25/1)
Swift Time did not help her chances by hanging badly and racing alone up the far rails, but she still put up a useful show and obviously has more ability. (4/1: op 8/1)
Miss Beveled improved a good deal on her debut, and this lightly-made individual may well find a little race. (20/1)
Fleur-de-Lys is a sharp, little, rather excitable filly who was deliberately taken last to post and ran reasonably. (20/1)
948 Adrenalin was always inclined to edge left and could never get in a blow. (7/4: evens-15/8)
Sixth Avenue (IRE) put paid to all chances by being very slowly away, but there is obviously plenty more there when she gets it together. (12/1)

1020 BEACHCOMBER H'CAP (0-75) (3-Y.O+) (Class D)

6-30 (6-34) **7f** £4,272.50 (£1,280.00: £615.00: £282.50) Stalls: High GOING: 0.09 sec per fur (G)

				SP	RR	SF
883*	**Fame Again (60)** (MrsJRRamsden) **5-9-1** ^{6x} JFortune(3) (lw: hld up: hdwy gng wl 2f out: rdn to ld ins fnl f: r.o)	—	**1**	3/1^{1}	69	52
734^{13}	**Somerton Boy (IRE) (63)** (PCalver) **7-9-4** NDay(12) (outpcd tl hdwy 2f out: ev ch ins fnl f: r.o)	nk	**2**	10/1	71	54
	Ochos Rios (IRE) (59) (BSRothwell) **6-9-0** OUrbina(18) (chsd ldrs: racd stands' side: kpt on wl fnl f)	½	**3**	14/1	66	49
	Nkapen Rocks (SPA) (53) (CaptJWilson) **4-8-8** ACulhane(5) (cl up: rdn to ld wl over 1f out: hdd ins fnl f: kpt on)	nk	**4**	33/1	60	43
*663**	**Barrack Yard (60)** (ACStewart) **4-9-1** MRoberts(21) (effrt 3f out: hung bdly lft: styd on: nrst fin)	2½	**5**	11/2^{2}	61	44
759^{5}	**Napoleon Star (IRE) (49)** (SRBowring) **6-8-4b** DeanMcKeown(8) (cl up: led 2f out: sn hdd & wknd)	hd	**6**	12/1	50	33
759^{7}	**Almasi (IRE) (66)** (CFWall) **5-9-7** WLord(22) (hld up: hdwy over 2f out: styd on: nvr rchd ldrs)	s.h	**7**	14/1	66	49
468^{5}	**Allinson's Mate (IRE) (62)** (TDBarron) **9-8-10b**$^{(7)}$ VictoriaAppleby(10) (styd on & edgd lft fnl 2f: nvr rchd ldrs)	1	**8**	16/1	60	43
	Legal Issue (IRE) (64) (WWHaigh) **5-9-2**$^{(3)}$ OPears(1) (lw: a chsng ldrs: nt qckn fnl 2f)	1	**9**	33/1	60	43
529^{5}	**Sagebrush Roller (56)** (JWWatts) **9-8-11** GDuffield(6) (effrt over 2f out: nvr trbld ldrs)	1½	**10**	9/1	48	31
596^{12}	**Carburton (73)** (JAGlover) **4-9-7**$^{(7)}$ TPengkerego(14) (hld up: effrt 3f out: n.d)	s.h	**11**	12/1	65	48
864^{16}	**Oriole (41)** (DonEnricoIncisa) **4-7-10** KimTinkler(7) (sn pushed along: nvr trbld ldrs)	5	**12**	50/1	22	5
766^{9}	**Will Do (62)** (MartynMeade) **4-9-3** FNorton(4) (led 5f: wknd)	1½	**13**	25/1	40	23
863^{2}	**Be Warned (56)** (MDods) **6-8-11b** GCarter(13) (hld up: effrt ½-wy: no imp)	s.h	**14**	6/1^{3}	33	16
	Persephone (41) (JLHarris) **4-7-3**$^{(7)}$ JFowle(2) (racd alone far side: chsd ldrs over 5f)	2½	**15**	50/1	13	—
756^{6}	**Princely Sound (66)** (MBell) **4-9-7** MFenton(19) (hld up: effrt 3f out: sn wknd)	5	**16**	16/1	26	9
687^{18}	**Saturiba (USA) (42)** (JohnHarris) **4-7-6**$^{(5)}$ RMullen(20) (cl up over 4f)	2½	**17**	50/1	—	—
	Dona Filipa (41) (MissLCSiddall) **4-7-10** NCarlisle(15) (chsd ldrs: rdn ½-wy: sn wknd)	nk	**18**	33/1	—	—
823^{4}	**Desert Cat (IRE) (70)** (MartynWane) **4-9-11** JCarroll(16) (chsd ldrs 4f: sn lost pl)	nk	**19**	20/1	23	6
	Girl of My Dreams (IRE) (48) (MJHeaton-Ellis) **4-8-3** JLowe(11) (lw: outpcd fr ½-wy)	2½	**20**	33/1	—	—
	Axeman (IRE) (58) (MissJBower) **5-8-13** RCochrane(17) (b: dwlt: a wl bhd)	6	**21**	33/1	—	—
				(SP 143.4%)	**21 Rn**	

1m 29.12 (4.62) CSF £31.93 CT £377.36 TOTE £4.10: £1.20 £3.60 £2.50 £8.00 (£36.00) Trio £224.90 OWNER Mr James Ramsden (THIRSK) BRED R. Barbes
LONG HANDICAP Oriole 7-7 Persephone 6-13 Dona Filipa 7-8

883* Fame Again is in top form at the moment and, after travelling on the bridle, she found enough when ridden to hold on. (3/1)
Somerton Boy (IRE) needs a fast-run race and things to go just right, and they almost did here. He is well worth keeping an eye on. (10/1)
Ochos Rios (IRE) is a difficult customer to win with these days, but this was a fair effort and he looks in good heart. (14/1)
Nkapen Rocks (SPA) goes well on this easier ground and, should this prevail, he may yet break his duck. (33/1)
663* Barrack Yard had a bad draw here considering all he wants to do is hang left, and he obviously needs to be against a left-hand rail. (11/2)
759 Napoleon Star (IRE), whose wins have been over shorter trips, seemed to have stamina problems here. (12/1)
759 Almasi (IRE) was noted finishing quite well and would seem to be coming to hand. (14/1)

1021 BRITISHRACING.COM LIMITED STKS (0-85) (3-Y.O+) (Class D)

7-00 (7-00) **6f** £3,427.50 (£1,020.00: £485.00: £217.50) Stalls: High GOING: 0.09 sec per fur (G)

				SP	RR	SF
	Bint Albaadiya (USA) (80) (MRStoute) **3-8-6**^{ow1} LDettori(5) (hld up: squeezed thro to ld wl over 1f out: qcknd clr & eased)	—	**1**	13/8^{1}	94+	20
596^{9}	**The Lambton Worm (84)** (DenysSmith) **3-8-8** KFallon(1) (chsd ldrs: rdn & styd on fnl 2f: no ch w wnr)	5	**2**	11/2	83	10
	Alpine Hideaway (IRE) (76) (BHanbury) **4-9-4** WRyan(7) (chsd ldr: bmpd 2f out: r.o one pce)	1	**3**	12/1	80	17
726^{18}	**Depreciate (85)** (CJames) **4-9-4** CRutter(4) (chsd ldrs: rdn over 2f out: nt qckn)	nk	**4**	14/1	79	16
584*	**Mouche (80)** (MrsJRRamsden) **3-8-8** JFortune(3) (hld up: hdwy over 2f out: nvr nr to chal)	3	**5**	4/1^{3}	71	—
942^{23}	**Bajan Rose (85)** (MBlanshard) **5-9-1** RCochrane(6) (led tl hdd & wknd wl over 1f out)	3	**6**	11/4^{2}	60	—
				(SP 114.5%)	**6 Rn**	

1m 16.58 (5.58) CSF £10.45 TOTE £2.10: £1.20 £3.00 (£10.30) OWNER Sheikh Ahmed Al Maktoum (NEWMARKET) BRED Swettenham Stud
WEIGHT FOR AGE 3yo-10lb

Bint Albaadiya (USA) sprinted clear once she saw the front to win in most emphatic style, and gave the impression that, when trying longer trips, there should be even better to come. (13/8: evens-7/4)
The Lambton Worm ran pretty well but was no match for the winner, but time could show this was still a decent effort. (11/2)
Alpine Hideaway (IRE) had plenty on here and, in the circumstances, ran well. (12/1)

Depreciate obviously has his problems, as this was only his seventh start in three seasons, but this was a big improvement on his previous effort this year. (14/1)
584* Mouche could never really get into this and was certainly not over-punished, and looks the sort who will do better in due course. (4/1: 3/1-9/2)
Bajan Rose, having her second run in four days, was a shade disappointing. (11/4)

1022 DONCASTER SPONSORSHIP CLUB H'CAP (0-75) (3-Y.O+) (Class D)

7-30 (7-30) **1m 4f** £3,720.00 (£1,110.00: £530.00: £240.00) Stalls: Low GOING: 0.09 sec per fur (G)

				SP	RR	SF
866[3]	**Augustan (53)** (SGollings) **6-8-11** KFallon(6) (lw: in tch: hdwy 3f out: swtchd over 1f out: r.o u.p to ld cl home)	—	1	7/1	65	31
	Tappeto (69) (HCandy) **5-9-13** CRutter(10) (in tch: hdwy 3f out: led over 1f out: r.o u.p: jst ct)	hd	2	12/1	81	47
866[2]	**Shaffishayes (63)** (MrsMReveley) **5-9-7** LDettori(7) (lw: hld up: stdy hdwy over 2f out: effrt over 1f out: no ex)	2½	3	9/4[1]	72	38
260[8]	**Sam Rockett (40)** (MissGayKelleway) **4-7-7**(5) RMullen(8) (lw: trckd ldrs: chal over 2f out tl outpcd fnl f)	1	4	14/1	47	13
598[9]	**Dashing Invader (USA) (40)** (PWHarris) **4-7-12** FNorton(9) (chsd ldrs: outpcd over 2f out: no imp after)	2	5	16/1	45	11
762[6]	**Reaganesque (USA) (51)** (PGMurphy) **5-8-9** SDrowne(5) (lw: led tl hdd over 1f out: wknd)	nk	6	7/1	55	21
866*	**Road Racer (IRE) (57)** (MrsJRRamsden) **4-9-1** 5x JFortune(11) (hld up: pushed along 3f out: nvr rchd ldrs)	1½	7	5/1[2]	59	25
612[2]	**Blenheim Terrace (62)** (CBBBooth) **4-9-6** KHodgson(3) (trckd ldrs: effrt 3f out: rdn & no imp)	1¾	8	6/1[3]	62	28
770[10]	**Anchor Venture (55)** (SPCWoods) **4-8-13** WRyan(4) (hld up: n.d)	19	9	16/1	30	—
	Faugeron (56) (NTinkler) **8-9-0** LCharnock(1) (bit bkwd: chsd ldrs tl outpcd fnl 2½f)	3	10	33/1	27	—
	Indiana Princess (56) (MrsMReveley) **4-9-0** ACulhane(2) (bit bkwd: plld hrd: bhd: hung bdly rt & virtually p.u)	30	11	14/1	—	—

(SP 122.5%) **11 Rn**

2m 40.71 (10.71) CSF £83.44 CT £230.43 TOTE £6.50: £2.20 £5.30 £1.40 (£63.90) Trio £78.60 OWNER Northern Bloodstock Racing (LOUTH) BRED Someries Stud
OFFICIAL EXPLANATION **Indiana Princess: was giving problems with her mouth.**
866 Augustan, happier at this trip, was brought with a perfectly-timed run to snatch it. (7/1)
Tappeto won his only race two seasons ago, but he showed here that he still has plenty of ability and is off a decent mark. (12/1)
866 Shaffishayes was given the kid glove treatment and looked to be going well but, when that final effort was required, he failed to pick up. (9/4: 3/1-2/1)
Sam Rockett, having his first run for his new stable, went well for a long way and may get off the mark at this game before long. (14/1)
Dashing Invader (USA) is a most attractive, strongly-made individual who seems to be coming to hand and may well stay further. (16/1)
762 Reaganesque (USA) was in cracking form last season and is slipping back down to a decent mark. He probably just needs faster ground than this. (7/1)

1023 GREAT LEGER RACING GAME GAMBLE MAIDEN STKS (3-Y.O+) (Class D)

8-00 (8-05) **1m (straight)** £4,435.00 (£1,330.00: £640.00: £295.00) Stalls: High GOING: 0.09 sec per fur (G)

				SP	RR	SF
683[3]	**Lord Eurolink (IRE)** (JLDunlop) **3-8-11** TQuinn(18) (chsd ldrs: led over 2f out: edgd rt: r.o wl)	—	1	3/1[2]	89	37
	Timissa (IRE) (LMCumani) **3-8-6** OUrbina(13) (leggy: scope: chsd ldrs: hdwy 2f out: kpt on one pce fnl f)	2½	2	12/1	79	27
829[4]	**Military (USA)** (HRACecil) **3-8-11** KFallon(15) (led tl hdd over 2f out: kpt on wl towards fin)	hd	3	11/10[1]	84	32
491[2]	**Western Sonata (IRE)** (LordHuntingdon) **4-9-5** DaneO'Neill(14) (cl up tl outpcd fnl 2f)	3	4	16/1	73	34
841[10]	**Tramline** (MBlanshard) **4-9-10** JQuinn(2) (racd far side: r.o fnl 2f: nrst fin)	1	5	50/1	76	37
	Tarradale (CBBBooth) **3-8-11** KHodgson(12) (in tch: hung bdly lft 3f out: n.d after)	6	6	50/1	64	12
	Strillo (NMBabbage) **3-8-11** WRyan(16) (w'like: bit bkwd: s.i.s: n.d)	½	7	50/1	63	11
	Atomic Shell (CAN) (CFWall) **4-9-10** GDuffield(9) (wnt lft s: nvr nr to chal)	1¼	8	33/1	60	21
	Waasef (MissGayKelleway) **4-9-10** RCochrane(3) (lengthy: unf: scope: led far side over 6f: eased whn btn)	hd	9	10/1[3]	60	21
	Aboo Hom (ACStewart) **3-8-11** MRoberts(7) (w'like: bit bkwd: s.i.s: drvn along thrght: n.d)	4	10	10/1[3]	52	—
683[17]	**Grand Hotel (IRE)** (PWHarris) **3-8-11** AMcGlone(17) (n.d)	½	11	33/1	51	—
795[9]	**Glorious Dancer** (JHetherton) **3-8-6** MBirch(5) (racd far side: wnt rt s: n.d)	4	12	50/1	38	—
	Fortune Hunter (IRE) (WJarvis) **3-8-11** JWeaver(1) (w'like: leggy: scope: racd far side: prom: hung lft 3f out: sn wknd & eased)	2	13	20/1	39	—
475[5]	**Eastern Eagle (IRE)** (JMPEustace) **3-8-11** JTate(4) (prom far side over 5f)	s.h	14	33/1	39	—
	Chief Connections (MPBielby) **4-9-10** DeanMcKeown(6) (wl grwn: nvr trbld ldrs)	6	15	50/1	27	—
	Top (JRFanshawe) **3-8-6** NDay(11) (Withdrawn not under Starter's orders: unruly in stalls)		W	16/1	—	—
	Prince Alex (IRE) (ACStewart) **3-8-11** KDarley(10) (Withdrawn not under Starter's orders: ref to ent stalls)		W	20/1	—	—

(SP 138.4%) **15 Rn**

1m 43.6 (6.40) CSF £34.39 TOTE £4.00: £1.30 £2.90 £1.30 (£31.00) Trio £8.10 OWNER Eurolink Group Plc (ARUNDEL) BRED A. G. Antoniades
WEIGHT FOR AGE 3yo-13lb
683 Lord Eurolink (IRE) continues his improvement and galloped on strongly to look as though there is more to come. (3/1)
Timissa (IRE) put up a decent show here and was not over-punished when obviously beaten, and should have learnt plenty. (12/1)
829 Military (USA) ran a fair race and left the impression that, over further, he will make his mark. (11/10: 4/7-5/4)
491 Western Sonata (IRE) had previously run twice on the All-Weather and twice in France on bad ground before that and this, her first effort on reasonable going, would seem a decent run. (16/1)
841 Tramline, likely to need further, put up an eye-catching performance, running on strongly up the unfavoured far side. (50/1)
Tarradale gave his rider problems throughout by continually hanging left. (50/1)
Waasef (10/1: 11/2-12/1)

1024 PORT LOUIS H'CAP (0-70) (3-Y.O+) (Class E)

8-30 (8-33) **1m 2f 60y** £3,640.50 (£1,089.00: £522.00: £238.50) Stalls: Low GOING: 0.09 sec per fur (G)

				SP	RR	SF
609[2]	**Step N Go (IRE) (61)** (MrsJRRamsden) **3-8-5** JFortune(13) (lw: hld up: effrt 3f out: rdn to ld wl ins fnl f)	—	1	100/30[1]	77	24
896[20]	**African Sun (IRE) (43)** (MCChapman) **4-8-2** FNorton(20) (bhd: hdwy over 2f out: r.o wl fnl f)	1	2	25/1	57	19
733[3]	**Riccarton (49)** (PCalver) **4-8-8** MBirch(15) (hld up: hdwy to ld over 2f out: hung bdly lft: no ex towards fin)	nk	3	6/1[3]	63	25
574[13]	**Cuban Reef (43)** (WJMusson) **5-8-2** JQuinn(12) (hld up: effrt 3f out: nt clr run: r.o u.p fnl f)	3	4	9/1	52	14
749[13]	**Marsh Marigold (57)** (JHetherton) **3-8-1** NCarlisle(10) (dwlt: bhd & nt clr run tl swtchd outside & hdwy 2f out: r.o)	1	5	25/1	65	12
733[10]	**Jack Flush (IRE) (60)** (BSRothwell) **3-8-4** MFenton(5) (b.nrr fore: in tch: effrt 3f out: one pce fnl 2f)	1¾	6	14/1	65	12

				SP	RR	SF
	Gold Desire (47) (MBrittain) **7-8-6** GCarter(6) (hld up: nt clr run over 2f out & over 1f out: nt rcvr)	¾	**7**	12/1	51	13
578^{16}	**Oneoftheoldones (42)** (JNorton) **5-8-1** JFanning(17) (chsd ldrs tl wknd fnl 2½f)	nk	**8**	33/1	45	7
	Essayeffsee (57) (MrsMReveley) **8-9-2** KDarley(11) (bit bkwd: hld up: nt clr run 3f out to 1f out: nt rcvr)	hd	**9**	11/1	60	22
900*	**Jack The Lad (IRE) (55)** (JHetherton) **3-7-13** NKennedy(3) (in tch: n.m.r over 2f out: no imp)	3	**10**	$7/2^{2}$	54	1
	Mr Rough (53) (DMorris) **6-8-12** NDay(8) (hld up: effrt over 2f out: no imp)	3	**11**	14/1	47	9
633^{9}	**Lapu-Lapu (54)** (MJCamacho) **4-8-13** LCharnock(4) (plld hrd: hdwy on ins 3f out: wknd fnl 2f)	½	**12**	14/1	47	9
733^{13}	**Bernard Seven (IRE) (60)** (MDods) **5-9-5** JWeaver(14) (led tl hdd over 2f out: btn whn n.m.r over 1f out)	1½	**13**	14/1	51	13
742^{13}	**Bold Saint (IRE) (58)** (PWHarris) **3-8-2** AMcGlone(19) (trckd ldrs: outpcd whn n.m.r over 2f out: n.d after)	s.h	**14**	12/1	49	—
870^{5}	**Pc's Cruiser (IRE) (40)** (NPLittmoden) **5-7-8**(5) RMullen(9) (nvr wnt pce)	2½	**15**	20/1	27	—
599^{14}	**Burlesque (55)** (JDBethell) **3-7-13** TWilliams(2) (cl up tl wknd fnl 2f)	17	**16**	16/1	15	—
				(SP 141.2%)	**16 Rn**	

2m 17.2 (9.40) CSF £96.05 CT £484.69 TOTE £4.60: £1.50 £11.30 £2.20 £2.90 (£360.80) Trio £536.80; £536.80 to Chester 8/5/97 OWNER Lord Petersham (THIRSK) BRED R. J. McAlpine and D. O. Pickering

WEIGHT FOR AGE 3yo-15lb

609 Step N Go (IRE) got the run required in this very messy race and, well-handled, did it nicely. (100/30)

African Sun (IRE) has failed to trouble the judge previously, but he finished fast to show he has ability. (25/1)

733 Riccarton has so much ability but just wanted to hang left when in front, and was picked off late on. (6/1)

Cuban Reef had no luck in running and, by the time he saw daylight, it was all too late. (9/1)

130 Marsh Marigold showed that when things go her way, she has plenty of ability. (25/1)

Jack Flush (IRE) had his chances but lacked a change of gear when the pace was really on. (14/1)

Gold Desire never saw daylight and looked as though he might well have been in the shake up. (12/1)

Essayeffsee needed this, but was denied a run all the way up the straight, and his rider just had to sit and suffer. (11/1: 8/1-12/1)

900* Jack The Lad (IRE) (7/2: op 9/4)

T/Plpt: £516.90 (34.31 Tckts). T/Qdpt: £4.00 (363.08 Tckts) AA

1013-**CHESTER (L-H) (Soft)**
Wednesday May 7th

WEATHER: showery WIND: mod against

1025 CHESHIRE REGIMENT H'CAP (0-95) (3-Y.O) (Class C)
2-10 (2-10) **1m 4f 66y** £8,552.00 (£2,576.00: £1,248.00: £584.00) Stalls: Low GOING: 0.39 sec per fur (GS)

				SP	RR	SF
528*	**Perfect Paradigm (IRE) (88)** (JHMGosden) **3-9-2** LDettori(1) (mde all: clr over 1f out: canter)	—	**1**	$11/8^{1}$	107+	54
524^{4}	**Flirting Around (USA) (84)** (MRStoute) **3-8-12** KFallon(2) (lw: a chsng ldrs: wnt 2nd over 2f out: styd on: no ch w wnr)	2½	**2**	$11/2^{2}$	100	47
690^{3}	**Ihtiyati (USA) (93)** (JLDunlop) **3-9-7** RHills(5) (hld up: effrt 3f out: nvr nr to chal)	16	**3**	$11/2^{2}$	88	35
600*	**Ibin St James (73)** (JDBethell) **3-8-1** TWilliams(3) (lw: chsd wnr tl rdn & wknd over 2f out)	½	**4**	14/1	67	14
788^{3}	**Mister Pink (93)** (RFJohnsonHoughton) **3-9-7** JReid(4) (dropped rr ½-wy: n.d after)	13	**5**	9/1	70	17
517^{8}	**Burundi (IRE) (75)** (PWChapple-Hyam) **3-8-3** BDoyle(7) (hld up & bhd: pushed along after 4f: no real imp: t.o)	6	**6**	$7/1^{3}$	45	—
*568**	**Davoski (80)** (BWHills) **3-8-8** MHills(6) (lw: trckd ldrs: rdn 5f out: sn lost tch: t.o)	16	**7**	8/1	29	—
				(SP 113.2%)	**7 Rn**	

2m 48.1 (11.90) CSF £8.23 TOTE £2.00: £1.50 £2.30 (£4.20) OWNER Sheikh Mohammed (NEWMARKET) BRED Airlie Stud

IN-FOCUS: **After the heavy squally showers of the past few days, the going was more reminiscent of the Festival at Cheltenham in March and most of the form will not hold up when the ground firms up.**

528* Perfect Paradigm (IRE) has improved out of all recognition and, making all on the bridle, did not need to be let down for an effortless success in this higher grade. (11/8)

524 Flirting Around (USA), tackling the trip for the first time, turned in a very pleasing performance. He stayed on strongly in the latter stages, but will need to steer clear of such as the winner if he is to make his mark. (11/2: 7/2-6/1)

690 Ihtiyati (USA) had his full quota of weight, but failed to handle the ground as well as the principals and was unable to get within striking range. (11/2: 4/1-6/1)

600* Ibin St James, a good-topped colt, did his best to make a race of it, but he was in trouble long before reaching the straight as this testing ground took its toll. (14/1)

Burundi (IRE) should have been in his element over this longer trip, but he is not built for mud-larking and was never going at any stage. (7/1: 9/2-8/1)

568* Davoski (8/1: 6/1-10/1)

82+ 80+ 87 68

1026 NWS BANK MAIDEN STKS (2-Y.O C & G) (Class D)
2-40 (2-41) **5f 16y** £6,930.50 (£2,084.00: £1,007.00: £468.50) Stalls: Low GOING: 0.39 sec per fur (GS)

				SP	RR	SF
	Only For Gold (JBerry) **2-8-11** KDarley(1) (w'like: leggy: mde all: shkn up over 1f out: r.o wl)	—	**1**	$4/1^{2}$	84	40
	Diligence (IRE) (PFICole) **2-8-11** TQuinn(4) (str: cmpt: bit bkwd: sn chsng wnr: rdn & effrt 2f out: nt pce to chal)	1½	**2**	$5/6^{1}$	79	35
722^{5}	**Chunito** (PWChapple-Hyam) **2-8-11** JReid(7) (prom: outpcd ½-wy: rallied u.p ent st: nvr able to chal)	3	**3**	$7/1^{3}$	70	26
	Estopped (IRE) (MRChannon) **2-8-6**(5) PPMurphy(5) (lt-f: unf: outpcd & bhd tl sme late hdwy)	6	**4**	8/1	51	7
948^{5}	**Newhargen (IRE)** (PDEvans) **2-8-11** JFortune(8) (lw: chsd ldrs: rdn 2f out: sn wknd)	¾	**5**	12/1	49	5
	Smart Venture (RHollinshead) **2-8-8**(3) FLynch(2) (lt-f: dwlt: a bhd & outpcd: t.o)	6	**6**	20/1	30	—
	Flame Tower (IRE) (RHannon) **2-8-11** DaneO'Neill(6) (w'like: bkwd: outpcd: a bhd: t.o)	2	**7**	10/1	23	—
				(SP 119.7%)	**7 Rn**	

65.53 secs (5.33) CSF £7.51 TOTE £3.50: £1.40 £1.50 (£2.60) OWNER Mr John Milner & Mr Stephen Milner (COCKERHAM) BRED C. J. Hill

Only For Gold looked far from fully wound-up for this racecourse debut but, with his stable striking form, adopted the ideal tactics round here and ran his rivals into the ground. (4/1: tchd 6/1)

Diligence (IRE), a strongly-made, compact colt with a daisy-cutting action, struggled in this bottomless ground, but he never stopped trying and will be more at home on a sounder surface. (5/6)

722 Chunito has probably not encountered conditions like this and, though he did stay on, was unable to get himself into the action. (7/1: 5/1-8/1)

Estopped (IRE), a lightly-made late-April foal, was all at sea in this ground but he should have learnt much from the experience. (8/1)

948 Newhargen (IRE) (12/1: op 8/1)

1027 TOTE CHESTER CUP H'CAP (4-Y.O+) (Class B)

3-10 (3-11) **2m 2f 147y** £35,678.75 (£10,805.00: £5,277.50: £2,513.75) Stalls: High GOING: 0.65 sec per fur (GS)

	Horse	Btn	Pos	SP	RR	SF
728²	**Top Cees (87)** (MrsJRRamsden) **7-8-11** JFortune(6) (dwlt: hld up in rr: stdy hdwy 6f out: led wl over 1f out: styd on strly)	—	**1**	11/2 ³	104	60
831*	**Etterby Park (USA) (77)** (MJohnston) **4-7-11** 3x NAdams(9) (a.p: led after 7f: qcknd clr 6f out: hdd wl over 1f out: sn btn)	10	**2**	8/1	85	37
655⁴	**Thaljanah (IRE) (80)** (BSmart) **5-8-4** SSanders(5) (lw: hld up in tch: effrt 6f out: hrd rdn & kpt on one pce fnl f)	hd	**3**	16/1	88	44
728*	**Canon Can (USA) (97)** (HRACecil) **4-9-3** KFallon(3) (a chsng ldrs: rdn 5f out: wknd over 2f out)	19	**4**	100/30 ¹	89	41
498²	**Old Rouvel (USA) (100)** (DJGMurraySmith) **6-9-10** KDarley(12) (lw: hld up & bhd: styd on fnl 3f: nvr nrr)	15	**5**	14/1	79	35
777⁶	**Warning Reef (80)** (PEccles) **4-8-0** CRutter(2) (prom: hrd drvn & lost pl 5f out)	6	**6**	50/1	54	6
	The Flying Phantom (78) (MHTompkins) **6-8-2** DaleGibson(7) (prom tl rdn & lost pl 7f out: t.o)	5	**7**	10/1	48	4
865⁷	**Upper Mount Clair (72)** (CEBrittain) **7-7-5**(5) RFfrench(11) (a bhd: t.o)	4	**8**	20/1	38	—
	Snow Princess (IRE) (99) (LordHuntingdon) **5-9-9** JReid(1) (bit bkwd: trckd ldrs tl lost pl 6f out: sn t.o)	10	**9**	6/1	57	13
	Danjing (IRE) (84) (MCPipe) **5-8-8b** TQuinn(4) (led 7f: rdn & wknd 6f out: t.o)	3½	**10**	11/1	39	—
	Mazamet (USA) (80) (OO'Neill) **4-8-0** DeclanO'Shea(8) (b.nr hind: bkwd: in tch 10f: grad wknd: t.o)	18	**11**	33/1	19	—
655*	**Bowcliffe Court (IRE) (77)** (RAkehurst) **5-8-1** JQuinn(10) (hld up & bhd: rdn 7f out: no imp: t.o)	22	**12**	7/2 ²	—	—

(SP 125.7%) **12 Rn**

4m 23.18 (20.68) CSF £46.83 CT £624.85 TOTE £6.50: £2.30 £2.40 £5.20 (£27.60) Trio £174.80 OWNER Mr R. E. Sangster (THIRSK) BRED Pendley Farm

LONG HANDICAP Upper Mount Clair 7-8

WEIGHT FOR AGE 4yo-4lb

OFFICIAL EXPLANATION Bowcliffe Court (IRE): spread a plate

728 Top Cees, successful in this event two years ago, has done all his winning on a sounder surface but he stays forever and, with the race run to suit, won going away in the easiest possible fashion. (11/2)

831* Etterby Park (USA) looked as though he had stolen the race when holding a healthy advantage three furlongs out, but the winner was only just finding top gear and, with his measure taken on the home turn, he had to work hard to retain the runner-up prize. (8/1)

655 Thaljanah (IRE) travelled extremely well for most of the way and always looked sure to be thereabouts, but he came off the bridle entering the final quarter-mile and could do little more than stay on. (16/1)

728* Canon Can (USA) finished three lengths ahead of the winner on 4lb better terms last month but, under these tiring conditions, he was feeling the strain from a long way out. (100/30)

498 Old Rouvel (USA) stayed on past beaten rivals in the last half-mile, but would have needed at least another circuit to get involved. (14/1)

Snow Princess (IRE) can act on the ground, but she had her full quota of weight for this first run of the season and she was back-pedalling soon after starting out on the final circuit. (6/1)

655* Bowcliffe Court (IRE), never going at any stage, was reported to have spread a plate and that would have had some bearing on such a below-par performance. (7/2)

1028 SHADWELL STUD CHESHIRE OAKS STKS (Listed) (3-Y.O F) (Class A)

3-45 (3-46) **1m 3f 79y** £24,205.00 (£7,240.00: £3,470.00: £1,585.00) Stalls: Low GOING: 0.65 sec per fur (GS)

	Horse	Btn	Pos	SP	RR	SF
686*	**Kyle Rhea (85)** (HRACecil) **3-8-9** KFallon(1) (a.p: led over 2f out: sn clr: comf)	—	**1**	9/4 ¹	99+	56
725⁶	**Grapevine (IRE)** (PWChapple-Hyam) **3-8-9** JReid(4) (b.off hind: led tl hdd over 2f out: sn rdn & btn)	11	**2**	8/1	84	41
741⁴	**Apache Star (84)** (GWragg) **3-8-9** MHills(2) (chsd ldrs tl rdn & wknd 3f out)	25	**3**	3/1 ³	48	5
	Desert Beauty (IRE) (MRStoute) **3-8-9** TQuinn(3) (bit bkwd: hld up & bhd: effrt & drvn along 5f out: no imp: t.o)	dist	**4**	5/2 ²	—	—
	Dundel (IRE) (BWHills) **3-8-9** LDettori(5) (bit bkwd: dropped rr ½-wy: sn t.o & eased)	dist	**5**	11/2	—	—

(SP 110.8%) **5 Rn**

2m 36.37 (12.77) CSF £17.47 TOTE £2.60: £1.60 £2.90 (£11.80) OWNER Sir David Wills (NEWMARKET) BRED Sir David Wills

686* Kyle Rhea is not a fluent mover so these conditions probably suited her better than most, but the way she brushed aside some highly thought-of rivals suggested she is very much on the upgrade. She will now be aimed at the Group Two Ribblesdale Stakes at Royal Ascot. (9/4)

725 Grapevine (IRE) adopted more forceful tactics on this step-up in class and she was the only one able to cause the winner any concern, but conditions took their toll and she was legless soon after entering the straight. (8/1)

741 Apache Star, driven along out in the country, could not pick up at all and she had to accept the situation. (3/1)

Desert Beauty (IRE), still to come to herself both in her coat and condition, could not get her feet out of the mud and she was always some way adrift of the principals. (5/2)

Dundel (IRE) has not come to herself as yet and, taking an instant dislike to the testing conditions, showed signs of temperament when Dettori got at her fully six furlongs out, and she was allowed to come home in her own time. (11/2)

1029 ROODEYE H'CAP (0-90) (3-Y.O) (Class C)

4-15 (4-16) **6f 18y** £11,178.00 (£3,384.00: £1,652.00: £786.00) Stalls: Low GOING: 0.65 sec per fur (GS)

	Horse	Btn	Pos	SP	RR	SF
854³	**Bishops Court (83)** (MrsJRRamsden) **3-9-3** JFortune(6) (lw: a.p: led on bit 1f out: canter)	—	**1**	5/2 ¹	94++	54
	Double-J (IRE) (86) (KMcAuliffe) **3-9-6** WJO'Connor(1) (trckd ldrs: effrt 2f out: nt clr run & swtchd rt over 1f out: r.o wl towards fin)	2	**2**	9/1	92	52
	Samsung Spirit (78) (EWeymes) **3-8-12** JQuinn(2) (gd sort: bkwd: hdwy 2f out: kpt on u.p ins fnl f)	hd	**3**	10/1	84	44
685²	**Song Mist (IRE) (75)** (PFICole) **3-8-9** TQuinn(3) (b.off fore: led tl hdd 1f out: rdn & no ex fnl f)	¾	**4**	11/2 ²	79	39
555⁵	**Nant Y Gamer (FR) (81)** (JBerry) **3-9-1** GCarter(10) (bhd: sn drvn along: nvr nrr)	5	**5**	20/1	71	31
768²	**John Emms (IRE) (74)** (MBell) **3-8-8** JReid(9) (lw: chsd ldrs: pushed along ½-wy: no imp)	1¼	**6**	13/2 ³	61	21
845¹⁸	**Double-O (70)** (WJarvis) **3-8-4** SSanders(5) (lw: prom tl rdn & wknd 2f out)	5	**7**	12/1	44	4
783⁸	**Weet Ees Girl (IRE) (71)** (PDEvans) **3-8-2**(3) FLynch(4) (prom over 4f: eased whn btn)	1	**8**	14/1	42	2
863*	**Night Flight (79)** (JJO'Neill) **3-8-13** 7x KFallon(14) (sn pushed along & bhd: eased whn btn)	3	**9**	7/1	42	2
506⁷	**Big Ben (87)** (RHannon) **3-9-7** DaneO'Neill(11) (outpcd)	1½	**10**	20/1	46	6
751²	**Suite Factors (62)** (KRBurke) **3-7-5**(5) RFfrench(8) (lw: prom 4f: sn wknd & eased)	3	**11**	16/1	14	—
652⁸	**Loch-Hurn Lady (66)** (KWHogg) **3-8-0** TSprake(13) (outpcd)	4	**12**	20/1	7	—

674[6]	**Moonshiner (USA) (86)** (GWragg) **3-9-6** MHills(7) (lost pl after 2f: sn t.o)	17	**13**	8/1	—	—
				(SP 134.5%)		**13 Rn**

1m 20.69 (7.39) CSF £26.27 CT £186.72 TOTE £3.50: £1.90 £3.90 £3.50 (£33.00) Trio £88.20 OWNER Mr D. R. Brotherton (THIRSK) BRED D. R. Brotherton

LONG HANDICAP Suite Factors 7-9

854 Bishops Court, close to the pace over this slightly longer trip, cruised to the front on the bridle passing the furlong marker and never needed to be asked any sort of question. He has been promising to do this since the start of the season and he is a useful youngster. (5/2: 7/4-11/4)

Double-J (IRE), forced to switch wide when beginning his run, did well to secure second prize close home and he is sure to strip fitter for the run. (9/1)

Samsung Spirit came to hand early last season and, though she did look very much in need of this, was really motoring inside the final furlong and could need a slightly longer trip now. (10/1)

685 Song Mist (IRE) behaved herself leaving the start this time, and set a good pace until fading after being overtaken going into the final furlong. Suited by a sounder surface, she is knocking at the door. (11/2)

555 Nant Y Gamer (FR) failed to go the pace and was only running on past beaten rivals at the finish. (20/1)

768 John Emms (IRE) could not handle the ground and he was in trouble before halfway. (13/2)

1030 EVELYN DELVES BROUGHTON MAIDEN STKS (3-Y.O F) (Class D)

4-45 (4-45) **7f 2y** £7,158.00 (£2,154.00: £1,042.00: £486.00) Stalls: Low GOING: 0.65 sec per fur (GS)

				SP	RR	SF
	Bea's Ruby (IRE) (81) (ABailey) **3-8-11** JWeaver(1) (a.p: hrd rdn over 1f out: r.o to ld last stride)	—	**1**	9/4[2]	73	56
	Radiancy (IRE) (JPLeigh) **3-8-11** DeanMcKeown(3) (lengthy: bit bkwd: led: clr 2f out: wknd nr fin: ct last stride)	nk	**2**	33/1	72	55
727[4]	**Sceptre Lady (IRE)** (BWHills) **3-8-11** DHolland(5) (a.p: rdn over 2f out: wknd fnl f)	11	**3**	7/4[1]	47	30
778[4]	**Yabint El Sultan (71)** (BAMcMahon) **3-8-11** TQuinn(10) (lost pl after 2f: rallied u.p over 2f out: nt rch ldrs)	nk	**4**	16/1	47	30
	Mystique Air (IRE) (EWeymes) **3-8-11** JQuinn(7) (bhd: hdwy fnl 2f: nvr nrr)	4	**5**	16/1	37	20
778[5]	**Sweet Patoopie** (BHanbury) **3-8-11** JStack(9) (chsd ldrs over 4f)	2	**6**	20/1	33	16
	Midyan Queen (67) (RHollinshead) **3-8-8**(3) FLynch(4) (still unf: dwlt: effrt 3f out: sn rdn: no imp)	9	**7**	25/1	12	—
1017[7]	**Highly Respected (IRE) (66)** (ABailey) **3-8-11b** DWright(11) (chsd ldrs 3f: sn rdn & wknd: t.o)	12	**8**	20/1	—	—
727[11]	**Mystery Hill (USA)** (JHMGosden) **3-8-11** LDettori(6) (bit bkwd: a bhd: t.o)	2½	**9**	5/1[3]	—	—
	Blushing Desert (RHannon) **3-8-11** DaneO'Neill(8) (bkwd: s.s: a wl bhd: t.o)	dist	**10**	13/2	—	—
				(SP 125.2%)		**10 Rn**

1m 33.05 (7.85) CSF £79.43 TOTE £3.00: £1.10 £7.20 £1.50 (£66.30) Trio £34.90 OWNER Mr M Tabor & Mrs John Magnier (TARPORLEY) BRED Green Ireland Properties Ltd

Bea's Ruby (IRE), still to get her summer coat, had to work very hard to get off the mark, but she thoroughly deserved to do so. She may now need time to recover. (9/4)

Radiancy (IRE), a lengthy filly from a good family, almost defied her burly looks on this racecourse debut and, if this is a sign of things to come, she could prove useful. (33/1)

727 Sceptre Lady (IRE), poised to challenge but appearing to be fighting a losing battle when ridden over two furlongs out, stopped very quickly once in line for home and this ground is certainly not for her. (7/4: 5/4-2/1)

778 Yabint El Sultan, inclined to run in snatches, was beginning to close again entering the straight, but was unable to maintain the progress. (16/1)

Mystique Air (IRE), still holding onto her winter coat, was only finding top gear when the race was all but over. (16/1)

Blushing Desert (13/2: 4/1-7/1)

T/Jkpt: £2,967.40 (4.98 Tckts). T/Plpt: £53.50 (770.32 Tckts). T/Qdpt: £24.00 (65.21 Tckts) IM

1025-CHESTER (L-H) (Heavy)

Thursday May 8th

Race 6 flip-start

WEATHER: heavy showers WIND: slt across

80? 73 78 63

1031 E.B.F. SEFTON MAIDEN STKS (2-Y.O F) (Class D) (73)

2-10 (2-13) **5f 16y** £6,970.00 (£2,110.00: £1,030.00: £490.00) Stalls: Low GOING: 1.44 sec per fur (HY)

				SP	RR	SF
730[4]	**Bodfaridistinction (IRE)** (ABailey) **2-8-11** KFallon(1) (hdwy ½-wy: led wl over 1f out: r.o wl)	—	**1**	2/1[1]	77	55
902[4]	**Demolition Jo** (PDEvans) **2-8-11** JFortune(5) (s.i.s: hdwy 2f out: hrd rdn & hung lft fnl f: no ch w wnr)	6	**2**	14/1	58	36
	Be My Wish (MissGayKelleway) **2-8-11** RCochrane(2) (gd sort: bit bkwd: led over 3f: wknd fnl f: fin tired)	3	**3**	7/1	49	27
	Sky Red (MBell) **2-8-11** TQuinn(3) (neat: bit bkwd: sn bhd & outpcd: sme late hdwy: n.d)	2½	**4**	6/1	41	19
682[5]	**Jewel (IRE)** (RHannon) **2-8-11** DaneO'Neill(4) (trckd ldrs: one pce fnl 2f)	1	**5**	3/1[2]	38	16
730[3]	**Antonia's Double** (JBerry) **2-8-11** KDarley(6) (lw: prom to ½-wy: sn wknd & eased: t.o)	25	**6**	5/1[3]	—	—
				(SP 108.5%)		**6 Rn**

69.94 secs (9.74) CSF £24.72 TOTE £2.50: £1.50 £4.20 (£21.80) OWNER Mr D. O. Pickering (TARPORLEY) BRED Frank Barry

IN-FOCUS: **Due to the persistent rain on top of what had already fallen, it is possible the meeting would not have gone ahead had it not been so important, for the ground was like a bog, and the form must be taken with a pinch of salt.**

730 Bodfaridistinction (IRE), foaled two years ago yesterday, had learned much from her debut and, proving the strongest in this bottomless ground, won very easily indeed. (2/1)

902 Demolition Jo is certainly not built for conditions like this, but she has obviously got plenty of courage and, if she is not over-faced, should be able to win races. (14/1)

Be My Wish, a grand-looking filly with plenty of strength and quality about her, showed good speed to lead the way for over three furlongs before lack of a previous race plus the prevailing conditions sapped her reserves, and she was very leg-weary inside the last furlong. She can soon leave this form behind. (7/1)

Sky Red, in need of the run and the experience, was beginning to grasp what was needed in the closing stages. (6/1)

682 Jewel (IRE) was always finding trouble handling the conditions, and she was unable to get close enough to mount a challenge. (3/1: op 2/1)

730 Antonia's Double (5/1: op 5/2)

1032 DEE STKS (Listed) (3-Y.O C & G) (Class A)

2-40 (2-40) **1m 2f 75y** £24,790.00 (£7,420.00: £3,560.00: £1,630.00) Stalls: High GOING: 1.44 sec per fur (HY)

				SP	RR	SF
646[2]	**Crystal Hearted (102)** (HCandy) **3-8-8** AMcGlone(4) (lw: mde all: clr over 2f out: unchal)	—	1	9/2[2]	110?	5
691[4]	**Barnum Sands (103)** (JLDunlop) **3-8-8** TQuinn(2) (lw: chsd wnr: rdn & dropped rr 3f out: n.d after)	13	2	5/4[1]	90	—
795*	**Teofilio (IRE) (94)** (DRLoder) **3-8-8** LDettori(1) (lw: hld up: hdwy 4f out: sn chsng wnr: rdn ent st: sn wknd & eased)	17	3	5/4[1]	64	—
				(SP 107.1%)		**3 Rn**

2m 35.14 (26.44) CSF £9.05 TOTE £4.70 (£3.40) OWNER Mrs C. M. Poland (WANTAGE) BRED Newgate Stud Co

646 Crystal Hearted made this look easy with an all-the-way success, and he only needed to keep galloping to draw right away inside the last quarter-mile. (9/2: op 3/1)

691 Barnum Sands, waiting on the winner travelling comfortably, faded rather quickly when they started to up the pace three furlongs out, but he stayed on again in the closing stages to gain a worthy runner-up prize. (5/4: evens-11/8)

795* Teofilio (IRE) has never been asked to tackle such conditions before and, though he did get within striking distance on the approach to the straight, he was soon flat-out and the task proved beyond him. (5/4)

1033 ORMONDE STKS (Gp 3) (4-Y.O+) (Class A)

3-10 (3-13) **1m 5f 89y** £29,520.00 (£11,038.50: £5,294.25: £2,297.25) Stalls: Low GOING: 1.44 sec per fur (HY)

				SP	RR	SF
	Royal Court (IRE) (114) (PWChapple-Hyam) **4-8-11** JReid(2) (b.nr fore: hld up: pushed along 6f out: hdwy over 3f out: styd on to ld wl ins fnl f)	—	1	9/4[1]	119	57
	Further Flight (109) (BWHills) **11-8-11** MHills(3) (b.hind: hld up & bhd: hdwy 5f out: c wd & led ent st: hrd rdn & hdd wl ins fnl f)	¾	2	20/1	118	56
	Moonax (IRE) (115) (BWHills) **6-8-11** DHolland(1) (bkwd: trckd ldrs: led over 3f out: hdd ent st: wknd appr fnl f)	7	3	13/2	110	48
498*	**Sweetness Herself (95)** (MJRyan) **4-8-8** GCarter(6) (swtg: chsd ldrs: rdn over 4f out: sn lost tch)	26	4	13/2	76	14
	Eva Luna (USA) (110) (HRACecil) **5-8-11** KFallon(7) (lw: sn pushed along: a in rr: lost tch over 4f out)	6	5	5/1[3]	72	10
891[3]	**Election Day (IRE) (112)** (MRStoute) **5-8-11** KDarley(5) (led tl over 3f out: sn hrd drvn & wknd)	2½	6	5/1[3]	69	7
736[4]	**Salmon Ladder (USA) (113)** (PFICole) **5-9-0** TQuinn(8) (bit bkwd: chsd ldr 8f: sn rdn & wknd: t.o fnl 4f)	dist	7	4/1[2]	—	—
				(SP 115.5%)		**7 Rn**

3m 15.85 (25.85) CSF £44.65 TOTE £3.40: £2.00 £3.80 (£52.80) Trio £57.20 OWNER Mr R. E. Sangster (MARLBOROUGH) BRED SWETTENHAM STUD AND RON CON LTD

Royal Court (IRE) takes a lot of driving but he does respond, and he needed all the courage he could summon up to forge ahead nearing the line. His trainer rates him highly and, after the Hardwicke Stakes at Royal Ascot, a tilt at the Prix de l'Arc de Triomphe has been pencilled in. (9/4)

Further Flight can handle all types of going and has won first time out for the past couple of years but, hard as he tried in the latter stages, he was forced to give best. What a grand campaigner to have in your yard. (20/1)

Moonax (IRE) gave problems in the preliminaries but he did nothing wrong once in action and, had he not blown up early in the straight, would have gone very close. (13/2)

498* Sweetness Herself is a real mud-lover and she had the edge on fitness, but she was unable to cope with this step-up in class and her future remains as a staying handicapper. (13/2: 10/1-6/1)

Eva Luna (USA) looked as though she had done plenty of work, but she was towards the rear and being nudged along with a circuit to race, and never looked likely to pick up. She has performed well on the soft in the past, but this ground was really something different. (5/1)

891 Election Day (IRE) enjoyed being able to dictate, but he found surprisingly little when taken on and his measure had soon been taken. (5/1: 3/1-11/2)

736 Salmon Ladder (USA) (4/1: 3/1-9/2)

1034 HILL DICKINSON WAYMAN-HALES RATED STKS H'CAP (0-100) (4-Y.O+) (Class B)

3-40 (3-43) **5f 16y** £9,145.20 (£3,406.80: £1,653.40: £697.00: £298.50: £139.10) Stalls: Low GOING: 1.44 sec per fur (HY)

				SP	RR	SF
744*	**Surprise Mission (83)** (MrsJRRamsden) **5-8-4** DaneO'Neill(8) (hld up & bhd: hdwy on ins to ld wl over 1f out: drvn clr)	—	1	11/2	98+	64
786[2]	**Selhurstpark Flyer (IRE) (95)** (JBerry) **6-8-11**(5) PRoberts(5) (b: chsd ldrs: kpt on u.p fnl f: no ch w wnr)	6	2	8/1	91	57
726[10]	**Bowden Rose (86)** (MBlanshard) **5-8-7b** JQuinn(2) (a.p: led over 2f out tl wl over 1f out: sn outpcd)	4	3	10/1	70	36
726[4]	**That Man Again (87)** (SCWilliams) **5-8-8** KDarley(1) (a.p: ev ch wl over 1f out: sn rdn & outpcd)	3	4	9/2[2]	61	27
	Speed On (100) (HCandy) **4-9-7** CRutter(7) (bit bkwd: prom: hrd drvn 2f out: sn btn)	1½	5	10/1	69	35
744[15]	**Swynford Dream (85)** (JFBottomley) **4-8-6**ow1 LDettori(4) (led over 3f out: sn hdd: wknd fnl 2f)	5	6	8/1	39	4
	Pride of Brixton (86) (CWThornton) **4-8-7** PaulEddery(6) (nvr gng pce of ldrs)	4	7	12/1	27	—
905[2]	**Ziggy's Dancer (USA) (86)** (EJAlston) **6-8-7**ow1 KFallon(9) (chsd ldrs on outside: sn drvn along: wknd 2f out)	1½	8	5/1[3]	22	—
	Tadeo (99) (MJohnston) **4-9-6** MRoberts(3) (bkwd: led over 1f: wknd 2f out)	6	9	7/2[1]	16	—
				(SP 120.6%)		**9 Rn**

69.01 secs (8.81) CSF £46.46 CT £399.42 TOTE £7.40: £2.30 £2.20 £4.00 (£40.00) Trio £151.40 OWNER Mr D. R. Brotherton (THIRSK) BRED D. R. Brotherton

LONG HANDICAP Surprise Mission 8-3

744* Surprise Mission did as his full-brother Bishops Court did yesterday, and simply annihilated his rivals to win a competitive sprint. His stable is in sparkling form. (11/2)

786 Selhurstpark Flyer (IRE), better at six furlongs nowadays, stayed on strongly to chase-up the winner in the closing stages without ever promising to get to terms. He is running well and deserves to gain reward. (8/1)

Bowden Rose got her head in front at halfway but the winner was waiting to pounce and, when he did, the race was as good as over. This outing should have blown away the cobwebs. (10/1: 6/1-12/1)

726 That Man Again, again running without blinkers, ran his race out but the testing ground was not for him and he was galloping on the spot from the turn into the straight. He can soon return to form. (9/2)

Speed On had a difficult task on his hands with top weight on his seasonal debut, and he was hard at work and held on straightening up. There was plenty of interest in him, and he will be much sharper next time. (10/1)

744 Swynford Dream, well behind the winner on his previous outing, helped set a strong pace before getting put in his place in the final quarter-mile. He looked to still have something left to work on. (8/1)

Tadeo had plenty left to work on on this first outing since the autumn, and he was a spent force two furlongs out. (7/2)

1035 WYNN H'CAP (0-90) (4-Y.O+) (Class C)

4-15 (4-19) **7f 122y** £9,280.00 (£2,800.00: £1,360.00: £640.00) Stalls: Low GOING: 1.44 sec per fur (HY)

				SP	RR	SF
953[3]	**Albert The Bear (78)** (JBerry) **4-9-2** KDarley(8) (a.p: led over 2f out: drvn out)	—	1	9/1[3]	93	31
848*	**Knobbleeneeze (75)** (MRChannon) **7-8-8v**(5) PPMurphy(5) (a.p: rdn 2f out: styd on ins fnl f)	3	2	9/2[1]	84	22
786[9]	**Orange Place (IRE) (75)** (TJNaughton) **6-8-13** TQuinn(6) (led tl over 2f out: kpt on u.p fnl f)	2	3	9/1[3]	79	17
947[2]	**Gulf Shaadi (65)** (EJAlston) **5-8-3** SDrowne(10) (a chsng ldrs: hdwy & ev ch over 1f out: one pce fnl f)	nk	4	11/1	69	7
520[6]	**Erupt (65)** (GBBalding) **4-8-3** AMcGlone(17) (effrt & rdn ½-wy: one pce fnl 2f)	3½	5	16/1	61	—
895[13]	**Impulsive Air (IRE) (65)** (EWeymes) **5-8-3** LCharnock(1) (lw: effrt 2f out: nt rch ldrs)	6	6	14/1	49	—
776[4]	**Sualtach (IRE) (77)** (RHollinshead) **4-9-1** LDettori(7) (bit bkwd: hdwy 3f out: rdn wl over 1f out: no imp)	nk	7	15/2[2]	60	—
*512**	**Walk the Beat (66)** (MartynMeade) **7-7-13**(5) DSweeney(2) (hdwy over 2f out: sn rdn & brought wd ent st: no imp)	2½	8	12/1	44	—
1016[11]	**Wentbridge Lad (IRE) (67)** (PDEvans) **7-8-5v** GHind(11) (nvr nr to chal)	nk	9	12/1	44	—
677[7]	**Highborn (IRE) (90)** (PSFelgate) **8-10-0** WRyan(18) (lw: nvr nr ldrs)	7	10	14/1	52	—
791[4]	**Sooty Tern (67)** (JMBradley) **10-8-0**(5) RFfrench(3) (trckd ldrs over 4f: sn wknd)	5	11	20/1	19	—
520[8]	**Delta Soleil (USA) (83)** (PWHarris) **5-9-7** JReid(12) (bit bkwd: prom 4f: wknd qckly)	7	12	10/1	20	—
734[10]	**Flying Pennant (IRE) (67)** (JMBradley) **4-8-5**[ow1] DHolland(4) (bit bkwd: a bhd: t.o)	30	13	25/1	—	—
895[11]	**Duello (73)** (MBlanshard) **6-8-11** JQuinn(13) (a in rr: t.o)	dist	14	14/1	—	—
316[4]	**Elite Hope (USA) (70)** (NTinkler) **5-8-8** GCarter(9) (swtg: virtually p.u ent st: t.o)	dist	15	16/1	—	—
	Sue's Return (78) (APJarvis) **5-9-2** WJO'Connor(16) (bkwd: s.s: a wl bhd: virtually p.u ent st: t.o)	12	16	25/1	—	—
786[4]	**My Best Valentine (89)** (JWhite) **7-9-13** MRoberts(14) (lw: a bhd: virtually p.u ent st: t.o)	2	17	12/1	—	—
	Oberon's Dart (IRE) (70) (PJMakin) **4-8-8** JFortune(15) (bkwd: a bhd: virtually p.u 2f out: t.o)	dist	18	16/1	—	—

(SP 140.5%) **18 Rn**

1m 49.23 (17.23) CSF £49.64 CT £367.52 TOTE £7.20: £2.10 £1.60 £2.70 £3.00 (£15.70) Trio £107.20 OWNER Mr Chris Deuters (COCKERHAM) BRED Rockhouse Farms Ltd

IN-FOCUS: **This race was run after a lengthy downpour and conditions must have been at their worst, and it is possible that there were plenty of excuses for many of the beaten animals.**

953 Albert The Bear, successful here last year, coped well with the testing conditions and ran out a most convincing winner. He could make a name for himself this season. (9/1)

848* Knobbleeneeze, at the top of his form at present, ran on gamely inside the distance after getting tapped for speed approaching the straight. A return to a mile would seem to be what he requires. (9/2)

Orange Place (IRE) forced the pace but could never get away though, to his credit, he stuck to his task right to the finish. There could be another race just around the corner. (9/1)

947 Gulf Shaadi, a reformed character nowadays, pressed the leaders all the way and had every chance until tying up approaching the final furlong. (11/1)

Erupt, tackling a slightly longer trip, could not muster the pace to deliver his challenge, but he was far from disgraced in this company and, once the visor is refitted, it could pay dividends. (16/1)

529 Impulsive Air (IRE) has only ever won on a sound surface so this effort was probably much better than it appears. (14/1)

776 Sualtach (IRE) could have still needed this and, though he was unable to get serious, he showed enough to suggest he is coming to himself. (15/2: 6/1-9/1)

Delta Soleil (USA) (10/1: 7/1-11/1)

1036 EATON H'CAP (0-80) (3-Y.O+) (Class D)

4-45 (4-51) **1m 4f 66y** £7,340.00 (£2,210.00: £1,070.00: £500.00) Stalls: Low GOING: 1.44 sec per fur (HY)

				SP	RR	SF
888[2]	**The Butterwick Kid (52)** (RAFahey) **4-7-11**(7) RWinston(8) (hld up: smooth hdwy 3f out: led wl ins fnl f)	—	1	11/2[3]	65	—
*591**	**Raffles Rooster (65)** (AGNewcombe) **5-8-10**(7) JoHunnam(1) (chsd ldrs: led over 6f out: sn hdd: led 4f out tl wl ins fnl f)	nk	2	3/1[1]	78	6
887[6]	**Rasayel (USA) (73)** (PDEvans) **7-9-11** JFortune(10) (a.p: brought stands' side st: ev ch fnl f: r.o)	hd	3	12/1	86	14
260[7]	**Slip Jig (IRE) (76)** (KRBurke) **4-10-0** KFallon(9) (lw: hld up: drvn along ½-wy: hdwy 3f out: chal over 1f out: sn rdn & wknd)	11	4	16/1	74	2
866[4]	**Eagle Canyon (IRE) (74)** (BHanbury) **4-9-12** WRyan(5) (lw: trckd ldrs: ev ch over 2f out: wknd appr fnl f)	9	5	16/1	61	—
781[3]	**Tessajoe (73)** (MJCamacho) **5-9-11** LCharnock(3) (b: bit bkwd: hld up: hdwy ½-wy: nt trble ldrs)	21	6	8/1	32	—
867[2]	**At Liberty (IRE) (72)** (RHannon) **5-9-10** DaneO'Neill(11) (a in rr: btn over 3f out: t.o)	dist	7	12/1	—	—
680[2]	**Galapino (61)** (MissGayKelleway) **4-8-13** GBardwell(13) (lw: prom: led over 5f out: sn hdd: rdn & wknd 3f out)	5	8	9/2[2]	—	—
781[9]	**Daira (61)** (JDBethell) **4-8-13** JReid(4) (bit bkwd: chsd ldrs over 7f: sn wknd: t.o)	11	9	16/1	—	—
858[5]	**Super High (54)** (PHowling) **5-8-6b** FNorton(12) (lw: led over 5f: wknd 5f out: t.o)	15	10	16/1	—	—
770[3]	**Almuhtaram (65)** (GLewis) **5-9-3b** PaulEddery(6) (racd wd: bhd fr ½-wy: t.o)	¾	11	12/1	—	—
888[6]	***Dancing Cavalier (70)*** (RHollinshead) **4-9-8** LDettori(7) (Withdrawn not under Starter's orders: veterinary advice)		W	8/1	—	—

(SP 127.4%) **11 Rn**

3m 9.58 (33.38) CSF £18.55 CT £134.41 TOTE £6.10: £2.00 £1.40 £3.50 (£6.10) Trio £36.10 OWNER Mr Robert Chambers (MALTON) BRED Scorrier Stud

888 The Butterwick Kid, ridden with any amount of confidence, looked the winner from some way out but, in the end, it was only his stamina that enabled him to scrape home. (11/2)

591* Raffles Rooster, dropped out at the start, soon pulled himself into contention and, taking over for a second time half-a-mile out, found the concession of almost a stone too much of a handicap in an all-out duel to the line. (3/1)

887 Rasayel (USA), pushing the pace from the start, was the only one to make a bee-line for the stand rail turning in and, though she rallied to such effect that she was only beaten in a photo, it is possible she gave away more ground than she was beaten by. (12/1)

260 Slip Jig (IRE) came from off the pace to put himself in with a chance below the distance, but lack of a recent race then began to tell and he was legless inside the final furlong. (16/1)

866 Eagle Canyon (IRE) had plenty of use made of him in these conditions and, after threatening danger on the approach to the straight, had had enough on straightening up. His turn will come. (16/1)

680 Galapino, several times a winner on the All-Weather, weakened quickly passing the three-furlong marker and left the impression that he did not see the trip out in these ever-worsening conditions. (9/2)

T/Jkpt: Not won; £6,497.34 to Lingfield 9/5/97. T/Plpt: £995.10 (38.79 Tckts). T/Qdpt: £32.00 (85.99 Tckts) IM

0950-HAMILTON (R-H) (Soft, Heavy patches)
Thursday May 8th
WEATHER: heavy showers with sunny periods WIND: almost nil

1037 CLYDE VALLEY H'CAP (0-70) (3-Y.O+) (Class E)
2-00 (2-01) **5f 4y** £2,908.25 (£881.00: £430.50: £205.25) Stalls: Low GOING: 0.32 sec per fur (G)

				SP	RR	SF
924^{5}	**Impish (IRE) (45)** (TJEtherington) **3-7-10** DaleGibson(11) (in tch: hdwy to ld wl over 1f out: r.o wl)	—	1	12/1	55	31
924^{4}	**Tropical Beach (62)** (JBerry) **4-9-1**(7) CLowther(9) (s.i.s: hdwy over 1f out: r.o: no ch w wnr)	6	2	$11/2^{3}$	53	38
951^{14}	**Ragtime Cowgirl (36)** (DANolan) **4-7-3**(7) PBradley(3) (styd on fnl 2f: nrst fin)	¾	3	100/1	25	10
772^{3}	**Henry the Hawk (48)** (MDods) **6-8-5b**(3) CTeague(1) (lw: b: disp ld tl led 2f out: sn hdd & no ex)	hd	4	$5/1^{2}$	36	21
951^{6}	**Tibbi Blues (42)** (JSGoldie) **10-8-2** TWilliams(4) (chsd ldrs: effrt ½-wy: sn outpcd)	3	5	25/1	21	6
924^{2}	**Sunday Mail Too (IRE) (38)** (MissLAPerratt) **5-7-12** NKennedy(5) (lw: sn pushed along: nvr trbld ldrs)	1¾	6	8/1	11	—
949^{9}	**Stolen Kiss (IRE) (68)** (MWEasterby) **5-10-0b** TLucas(6) (lw: cl up: rdn 2f out: sn wknd)	3½	7	7/1	30	15
924^{3}	**Ready Teddy (IRE) (47)** (MissLAPerratt) **4-8-7** OUrbina(10) (chsd ldrs: rdn ½-wy: wknd over 1f out)	nk	8	14/1	8	—
956^{3}	**Lord Sky (50)** (ABailey) **6-8-10** SSanders(8) (disp ld 3f: wknd)	2	9	$3/1^{1}$	5	—
698^{4}	**Antithesis (IRE) (65)** (JSHaldane) **4-9-11** JCarroll(2) (plld hrd early: outpcd fr ½-wy)	s.h	10	12/1	19	4
	Tribal Mischief (64) (DMoffatt) **3-8-12**(3) DarrenMoffatt(7) (s.i.s: racd stands' side: a outpcd & bhd)	2	11	14/1	12	—
				(SP 114.2%)	**11 Rn**	

62.8 secs (4.50) CSF £67.77 CT £5,718.12 TOTE £17.60: £2.60 £2.50 £5.60 (£26.80) Trio Not won; £498.50 to Lingfield 9/5/97 OWNER Mr Tim Etherington (MALTON) BRED Leinster Stud

LONG HANDICAP Ragtime Cowgirl 7-8 Impish (IRE) 7-8

WEIGHT FOR AGE 3yo-9lb

OFFICIAL EXPLANATION **Lord Sky: the race came too soon after his previous run four days earlier.**

652 Impish (IRE), on the ground he likes, won in tremendous style and, provided he behaves himself at the start, there are more races to be picked up. (12/1)

924 Tropical Beach looked on the lean side and ran his usual race, coming from off the pace, but he was never doing things fast enough to trouble the winner. (11/2)

Ragtime Cowgirl ran well over a trip that looks to be too short for her. (100/1)

772 Henry the Hawk likes the track, the trip and the going, but did not have the best of draws this time. (5/1)

951 Tibbi Blues ran quite well over a trip that would seem too short. (25/1)

Stolen Kiss (IRE) likes soft ground, but also likes things to go her way, and they never did here. (7/1: op 4/1)

924 Ready Teddy (IRE) (14/1: 10/1-16/1)

956 Lord Sky ran inexplicably badly and this is obviously not his true form. (3/1)

1038 TATTERSALLS (QUALIFIER) MAIDEN AUCTION STKS (2-Y.O) (Class E)
2-30 (2-31) **5f 4y** £2,752.25 (£833.00: £406.50: £193.25) Stalls: Low GOING: 0.32 sec per fur (G)

				SP	RR	SF
	Vice Presidential (TJEtherington) **2-8-8** JCarroll(5) (w'like: scope: lw: mde most: shkn up & qcknd clr appr fnl f)	—	1	$8/1^{3}$	93+	20
	Jacmar (IRE) (MissLAPerratt) **2-8-5** OUrbina(2) (cmpt: scope: bit bkwd: outpcd tl styd on fnl 2f: no ch w wnr)	6	2	20/1	71	—
897^{2}	**Sharp Cracker (IRE)** (MJohnston) **2-8-3** TWilliams(1) (a chsng ldrs: rdn ½-wy: r.o one pce)	1¼	3	$5/4^{1}$	65	—
861^{3}	**Mamma's Boy** (JBerry) **2-8-3**(5) TEDurcan(4) (lw: a chsng ldrs: rdn ½-wy: btn over 1f out)	hd	4	$5/4^{1}$	70	—
	Flying High (IRE) (FMurphy) **2-8-9** JFanning(3) (w'like: a outpcd & bhd)	7	5	$7/1^{2}$	48	—
948^{6}	**Cosmic Case** (JSGoldie) **2-8-3**ow3 SSanders(6) (cl up over 3f: wknd)	½	6	20/1	41	—
				(SP 122.0%)	**6 Rn**	

64.2 secs (5.90) CSF £122.14 TOTE £16.00: £4.40 £5.50 (£136.70) OWNER Mr P. D. Savill (MALTON) BRED Mrs M. E. Ward

Vice Presidential, a useful-looking sort, won this well and looks likely to be even better on faster ground. (8/1: 6/1-9/1)

Jacmar (IRE) took the eye in the paddock, but needed this and showed ability staying on and, over further, better will be seen. (20/1)

897 Sharp Cracker (IRE) jumped out on terms this time, but this ground found her out and she should be given another chance. (5/4)

861 Mamma's Boy, who had previously run well in similar conditions on this track, was a shade disappointing this time. (5/4: evens-11/8)

Flying High (IRE), an excitable newcomer, probably needed this to help settle him. (7/1)

948 Cosmic Case has plenty of speed but this testing ground found her out. (20/1)

1039 SCOTTISH EQUITABLE / JOCKEYS ASSOCIATION H'CAP (0-75) (4-Y.O+) (Class D)
3-00 (3-01) **1m 5f 9y** £5,083.75 (£1,540.00: £752.50: £358.75) Stalls: High GOING: 0.32 sec per fur (G)

				SP	RR	SF
493^{2}	**Golden Hadeer (37)** (MJRyan) **6-7-7**(3) MBaird(4) (lw: mde all: edgd lft 1f out: kpt on gamely)	—	1	$7/2^{2}$	50	17
762^{3}	**Kintavi (44)** (TWDonnelly) **7-8-3** JFanning(8) (b: hld up: hdwy on bit to chal over 2f out: rdn 1f out: no ex)	2	2	7/1	55	22
928*	**All On (44)** (JHetherton) **6-8-3** 5x SSanders(2) (chsd ldrs: ev ch over 2f out: rdn & r.o one pce)	5	3	$9/4^{1}$	48	15
721^{7}	**Karisma (IRE) (56)** (DenysSmith) **4-8-12**(3) DGriffiths(6) (lw: hld up: stdy hdwy 5f out: rdn 3f out: sn btn)	6	4	8/1	53	20
955^{6}	**Lord Advocate (46)** (DANolan) **9-7-12b**(7)ow3 CLowther(5) (hld up: effrt 4f out: no imp)	2½	5	12/1	40	4
950^{4}	**Philmist (45)** (MissLAPerratt) **5-8-4b** NKennedy(7) (in tch tl rdn & btn over 3f out)	17	6	7/1	18	—
950^{3}	**Rossel (USA) (55)** (PMonteith) **4-9-0** JCarroll(3) (lw: chsd wnr tl outpcd fnl 4f)	5	7	$13/2^{3}$	22	—
				(SP 110.1%)	**7 Rn**	

3m 0.6 (14.90) CSF £23.25 CT £55.31 TOTE £4.60: £1.90 £3.80 (£11.90) OWNER Four Jays Racing Partnership (NEWMARKET) BRED Stetchworth Park Stud Ltd

LONG HANDICAP Golden Hadeer 7-7

493 Golden Hadeer is well handicapped on turf and showed fine determination, and will certainly get further as he did on the All-Weather surface. (7/2)

762 Kintavi looked likely to trot up halfway up the straight but, in the end, was comprehensively outstayed, and the testing conditions probably made the difference. (7/1)

928* All On is having an amazingly busy time for a stayer and ran her usual game race, but was short of toe in the last three furlongs. (9/4: op 6/4)

721 Karisma (IRE) travelled well on the bridle, but did not do a lot once off it. (8/1)

552 Lord Advocate ridden with restraint this time, could never get into the argument. (12/1)

950 Philmist is an in-and-out performer and was disappointing, and it was probably too quick after her previous race. (7/1)

1040 BOLLINGER CHAMPAGNE CHALLENGE SERIES GENTLEMEN'S H'CAP (0-70) (3-Y.O+) (Class F)

3-30 (3-30) **1m 65y** £2,626.00 (£736.00: £358.00) Stalls: High GOING: 0.32 sec per fur (G)

Form	Horse / details	Dist	Pos	SP	RR	SF
721[5]	**Clued Up (46)** (PDEvans) **4-10-3v**(4) MrAEvans(4) (hdwy ½-wy: led wl over 1f out: hld on wl)	—	**1**	7/1	56	24
951[4]	**Hutchies Lady (32)** (RMMcKellar) **5-9-3**(4) MrVLukaniuk(3) (b.hind: sn outpcd & bhd: gd hdwy 2f out: ev ch ins fnl f: nt qckn towards fin)	¾	**2**	5/2[1]	41	9
870[13]	**Roar on Tour (32)** (MrsMReveley) **8-9-7v** MrMHNaughton(8) (cl up: disp ld 3f out tl wknd wl over 1f out)	7	**3**	12/1	27	—
895[9]	**Kingchip Boy (67)** (MJRyan) **8-11-10v**(4) MrSLavallin(9) (led tl hdd wl over 1f out: no ex)	1	**4**	11/2[3]	60	28
	Friendly Knight (34) (JSHaldane) **7-9-5**(4)ow2 MrOMcPhail(7) (a in tch: one pce fnl 4f)	1½	**5**	20/1	24	—
898[7]	**Brambles Way (54)** (MrsMReveley) **8-10-11b**(4) MrNEJones(2) (lw: effrt ½-wy: styd on: n.d)	¾	**6**	6/1	43	11
668[8]	**Rattle (42)** (DANolan) **4-9-13b**(4)ow10 MrTJBarry(1) (effrt & prom ent st: wknd fnl 4f)	11	**7**	20/1	10	—
951[8]	**Western Venture (IRE) (43)** (RMMcKellar) **4-10-0**(4)ow8 MrDDickenson(6) (b: chsd ldrs tl wknd fnl 3f)	4	**8**	14/1	3	—
36[2]	**In Good Faith (56)** (JJQuinn) **5-11-3** MrTMcCarthy(5) (bhd: outpcd ½-wy: nvr trbld ldrs)	nk	**9**	7/2[2]	15	—

(SP 116.8%) **9 Rn**

1m 56.7 (12.60) CSF £22.91 CT £187.46 TOTE £9.50: £2.00 £1.70 £3.30 (£14.10) Trio £53.60 OWNER Mrs E. J. Williams (WELSHPOOL) BRED C. R. and V. M. Withers

LONG HANDICAP Friendly Knight 9-3 Roar on Tour 9-5

721 Clued Up handled this soft ground well and certainly stays further, and her stamina won her the day. (7/1)

951 Hutchies Lady won this race in similar conditions last year, and did her utmost to follow up, but was just out-battled after racing through what was probably the slower ground. (5/2)

Roar on Tour last won on turf three seasons ago and has been disappointing of late, but showed signs of coming back to form. (12/1)

791 Kingchip Boy, a brave front-runner on the All-Weather, probably found these testing conditions too much. (11/2)

Friendly Knight has plenty of ability over fences when he decides to start, and ran reasonably here. (20/1)

898 Brambles Way is not the most reliable of customers, and is probably better on faster ground. (6/1: op 4/1)

668 Western Venture (IRE) (14/1: 10/1-16/1)

1041 BELLSHILL MEDIAN AUCTION MAIDEN STKS (3-Y.O) (Class E)

4-05 (4-05) **1m 65y** £2,944.00 (£892.00: £436.00: £208.00) Stalls: High GOING: 0.32 sec per fur (G)

Form	Horse / details	Dist	Pos	SP	RR	SF
740[2]	**Alezal** (WJarvis) **3-9-0** SSanders(2) (lw: a.gng wl: led 3f out: easily)	—	**1**	2/9[1]	88+	30
701[2]	**No Grousing (IRE)** (PCHaslam) **3-9-0** OUrbina(1) (disp ld tl hdd 3f out: sn btn)	18	**2**	4/1[2]	53	—
	Tipperary Sunset (IRE) (JJQuinn) **3-9-0** DaleGibson(4) (bit bkwd: last tl sme hdwy 3f out: n.d)	3	**3**	100/1	48?	—
	Paldost (55) (MDHammond) **3-9-0** JCarroll(3) (disp ld tl hdd & wknd 3f out)	12	**4**	20/1[3]	24?	—

(SP 107.6%) **4 Rn**

1m 53.9 (9.80) CSF £1.30 TOTE £1.20 (£1.40) OWNER Mr Howard Spooner (NEWMARKET) BRED Godolphin Management Co Ltd

740 Alezal, on soft ground for the first time, had no serious opposition and won pulling a bus, and this should have boosted his confidence no end. (2/9)

701 No Grousing (IRE) looked very slow here, and perhaps did not act in the ground. (4/1)

Tipperary Sunset (IRE), needing this, showed a little but plenty more is required. (100/1)

Paldost has yet to show anything positive. (20/1)

1042 EAGLESHAM LIMITED STKS (0-60) (4-Y.O+) (Class F)

4-35 (4-35) **1m 4f 17y** £2,556.00 (£716.00: £348.00) Stalls: High GOING: 0.32 sec per fur (G)

Form	Horse / details	Dist	Pos	SP	RR	SF
612[3]	**Sun Mark (IRE) (58)** (MrsASwinbank) **6-8-11** SSanders(3) (lw: chsd ldr: led wl over 1f out: hung lft ins fnl f: styd on wl)	—	**1**	3/1[2]	67	6
689[4]	**Kathryn's Pet (60)** (MrsMReveley) **4-8-6**(5) SCopp(2) (lw: trckd ldrs: chal gng wl 2f out: rdn & hung appr fnl f: nt qckn)	1¼	**2**	10/11[1]	65	4
	Six Clerks (IRE) (59) (JGFitzGerald) **4-8-11** JCarroll(4) (lw: a.p: effrt 3f out: styd on: nt pce to chal)	3½	**3**	7/1[3]	61	—
881[5]	**Bronze Maquette (IRE) (35)** (RSimpson) **7-8-8** MGallagher(1) (led: clr 7f out: hdd wl over 1f out: sn btn)	11	**4**	8/1	43	—
955[14]	**Fanadiyr (IRE) (49)** (JSGoldie) **5-8-8**(3) DGriffiths(5) (a last: rdn & no imp 4f out)	7	**5**	14/1	37	—

(SP 107.7%) **5 Rn**

2m 49.8 (17.80) CSF £5.35 TOTE £3.30: £1.10 £1.50 (£1.50) OWNER Scotnorth Racing Ltd (RICHMOND) BRED Matt Carr

612 Sun Mark (IRE), ridden with more restraint this time, got the trip well enough and battled on strongly. (3/1)

689 Kathryn's Pet looked to be going particularly well when challenging in the last quarter-mile, but she went to her left and, racing up the slower ground, was out-pointed late on. (10/11: 4/5-evens)

Six Clerks (IRE) was disappointing over hurdles last time but he showed here he has ability, staying on under pressure when it was all too late. (7/1: 4/1-8/1)

Bronze Maquette (IRE), wearing a tongue-strap, tried to gallop her rivals into the ground, but she found the testing conditions beyond her in the last quarter-mile. (8/1)

T/Plpt: £2,246.00 (4.25 Tckts). T/Qdpt: £18.90 (43.17 Tckts) AA

0867-SOUTHWELL (L-H) (Standard)

Thursday May 8th

WEATHER: heavy showers WIND: mod half bhd

1043 MAGNOLIA H'CAP (0-65) (3-Y.O) (Class F)

2-20 (2-21) **1m 4f (Fibresand)** £2,277.00 (£627.00: £297.00) Stalls: Low GOING minus 0.14 sec per fur (FST)

Form	Horse / details	Dist	Pos	SP	RR	SF
665[3]	**Sam Peeb (39)** (RAFahey) **3-7-10** DWright(12) (w ldrs: led 7f out: drvn clr over 1f out: styd on wl)	—	**1**	20/1	48	1
771[3]	**Philosophic (50)** (SirMarkPrescott) **3-8-7** GDuffield(1) (lw: sn pushed along: chsd ldrs: kpt on same pce appr fnl f: no imp)	3	**2**	6/4[1]	55	8
797[6]	**Shaded (IRE) (57)** (JWWatts) **3-9-0** NConnorton(10) (lw: trckd ldrs: kpt on same pce fnl 2f)	2½	**3**	12/1	59	12
581[3]	**Bonne Ville (62)** (BPalling) **3-9-5** TSprake(2) (chsd ldrs: one pce fnl 2f)	1¾	**4**	8/1[3]	61	14
862[8]	**Ballydinero (IRE) (43)** (CaptJWilson) **3-7-11**(3) MHenry(14) (mid div: hdwy u.p 3f out: hung lft: nvr rchd ldrs)	5	**5**	33/1	36	—
906[2]	**Spondulicks (IRE) (54)** (BPJBaugh) **3-8-11** RPerham(16) (racd wd: w ldrs tl wknd 2f out)	3½	**6**	20/1	42	—

355^{2}	**Good Day (57)** (CWThornton) **3-9-0** DeanMcKeown(13) (b: s.i.s: hdwy u.p 3f out: nvr nr ldrs) ....d.h	**7**	16/1	45	—
534^{5}	**Warrlin (53)** (CWFairhurst) **3-8-10** SWhitworth(15) (racd wd: mid div: drvn along ½-wy: nvr nr to chal)..........3½	**7**	20/1	36	—
582^{6}	**Kickonsun (IRE) (39)** (RAFahey) **3-7-5**(5) PFessey(6) (b.hind: in tch: drvn along over 3f out: sn wknd) 7	**9**	16/1	13	—
665*	**As-Is (64)** (MJohnston) **3-9-7** JWeaver(9) (bhd: sn drvn along: n.d)........6	**10**	11/2^{2}	30	—
539^{3}	**Ronquista d'Or (50)** (GAHam) **3-8-7** DHarrison(8) (sme hdwy u.p 4f out: sn wknd) 5	**11**	25/1	9	—
534^{2}	**Woodland Nymph (52)** (DJGMurraySmith) **3-8-9** DRMcCabe(4) (led to 7f out: lost pl over 4f out)........¾	**12**	16/1	10	—
*581**	**Broctune Line (59)** (MrsMReveley) **3-9-2** ACulhane(7) (racd wd: sn bhd) 5	**13**	11/2^{2}	11	—
	Wesley's Lad (IRE) (64) (JNeville) **3-9-7** BDoyle(3) (mid div: drvn along ½-wy: sn wknd) ....¾	**14**	20/1	15	—
825^{6}	**Dawn Summit (52)** (BHanbury) **3-8-9** JStack(5) (prom early: sn drvn along: t.o 3f out)........2	**15**	12/1	—	—
456^{7}	**Solar Dawn (48)** (MJohnston) **3-8-2**(3) DO'Donohoe(11) (sn wl bhd: t.o fnl 7f) 15	**16**	16/1	—	—
			(SP 146.6%)	**16 Rn**	

2m 43.9 (10.90) CSF £50.22 CT £416.57 TOTE £38.50: £4.70 £1.10 £4.10 £4.50 (£73.80) Trio £127.30 OWNER Mrs M. A. Brown (MALTON) BRED Biddestone Stud

LONG HANDICAP Kickonsun (IRE) 7-2 Sam Peeb 7-7

665 Sam Peeb turned in a much-improved effort, but there was no fluke about it and he will get further. (20/1)

771 Philosophic, on his All-Weather debut, found this slow surface very hard work, but he never gave up trying though unable to make any impression on the winner in the final furlong. There is no doubt he has started his second season on an attractive mark. (6/4)

797 Shaded (IRE), who seemed short of stamina over a mile-and-a-quarter on turf last time, travelled strongly and seemed to stay alright. (12/1: op 8/1)

581 Bonne Ville, from the same handicap mark, ran a similar sort of race. (8/1)

1044 CAMELLIA CLAIMING STKS (3-Y.O) (Class F)

2-50 (2-52) **1m (Fibresand)** £2,277.00 (£627.00: £297.00) Stalls: Low GOING minus 0.14 sec per fur (FST)

			SP	RR	SF
903^{3}	**Penlop (63)** (BJMeehan) **3-9-1b** BDoyle(8) (trckd ldrs: led over 5f out: drvn clr fnl f) ....—	**1**	11/4^{1}	60	22
904^{4}	**Naivasha (65)** (JBerry) **3-8-3**(5) PFessey(9) (chsd ldrs: kpt on fnl 2f: no ch w wnr) 6	**2**	5/1^{3}	41	3
826^{6}	**Madam Lucy (43)** (WWHaigh) **3-8-4** TSprake(14) (racd wd: hdwy over 2f out: styd on fnl f)........hd	**3**	33/1	37	—
889^{12}	**Phoenix Princess** (BAMcMahon) **3-8-5**(7) SRighton(13) (s.i.s: racd wd: bhd tl styd on fnl 3f) 1	**4**	25/1	43	5
841^{16}	**Purple Maize** (JAkehurst) **3-9-3** AClark(4) (hld up: hdwy 2f out: edgd lft: nvr nr to chal)........3½	**5**	16/1	41	3
497^{6}	**Italian Symphony (IRE) (70)** (MJohnston) **3-9-3b** JWeaver(7) (chsd ldrs: hrd rdn 2f out: hung lft & nt run on) 1½	**6**	4/1^{2}	38	—
	Grate Times (74) (EWeymes) **3-8-13** GDuffield(5) (bit bkwd: chsd ldrs: sn drvn along: lost pl over 4f out)......10	**7**	4/1^{2}	14	—
577^{8}	**Redspet** (SRBowring) **3-8-4** DeanMcKeown(10) (chsd ldrs tl lost pl over 4f) 3½	**8**	33/1	—	—
	Prince of Fortune (MBlanshard) **3-8-9** NAdams(3) (hld up: sme hdwy ½-wy: wknd over 2f out) 1	**9**	16/1	1	—
558^{6}	**Owdy** (MrsNMacauley) **3-8-11b^{1}** SWebster(2) (s.i.s: a bhd) 1½	**10**	33/1	—	—
871^{5}	**Distinctive Dream (IRE) (43)** (KTIvory) **3-8-11b** CScally(1) (b: b.hind: s.s: sme hdwy ½-wy: lost pl 2f out)......4	**11**	12/1	—	—
556^{11}	**Rock Fantasy (45)** (CMurray) **3-8-0** NicolaHowarth(6) (led: rdn & hdd over 5f out: sn lost pl)........2½	**12**	33/1	—	—
	My Betsy (MissSEHall) **3-8-6** NCarlisle(12) (bit bkwd: racd wd: lost pl 5f out: sn bhd) 1	**13**	11/1	—	—
874^{11}	**Hio Nod** (MJCamacho) **3-8-13** NConnorton(11) (prom early: sn bhd: t.o 3f out) 13	**14**	25/1	—	—
			(SP 130.6%)	**14 Rn**	

1m 45.6 (6.60) CSF £15.20 TOTE £4.10: £1.20 £1.80 £3.70 (£11.00) Trio £128.40; £79.58 to Lingfield 9/5/97 OWNER Lhendup Dorji (UPPER LAMBOURN) BRED N. S. Yong

OFFICIAL EXPLANATION **Purple Maize: resented the kickback, hung left in the back straight and ran on through beaten horses in the home straight.**

903 Penlop, an excitable sort, settled well in front and came right away in the final furlong. (11/4)

904 Naivasha, who would have met the winner on 7lb worse terms in a handicap, stuck on and stayed the trip okay. (5/1)

Madam Lucy, who would have been a stone better off with Naivasha in a handicap, ran easily her best race yet and could improve over further. The trouble is, she will take a hoist in the ratings after this. (33/1)

Phoenix Princess, dropped in class, showed much more than she had on her debut. (25/1)

Purple Maize, who had finished last on his two previous outings, looked very fit. Given a quiet ride and tending to edge left-handed, he is not without some ability. (16/1)

497 Italian Symphony (IRE), with the blinkers back on, wanted no part of it. (4/1: op 2/1)

Grate Times, making his All-Weather debut, looked backward in his coat and showed very little. (4/1: 3/1-9/2)

63 59 57

1045 TULIP MAIDEN AUCTION STKS (2-Y.O) (Class F)

3-20 (3-22) **5f (Fibresand)** £2,277.00 (£627.00: £297.00) Stalls: High GOING minus 0.14 sec per fur (FST)

			SP	RR	SF
	Piccolo Cativo (CaptJWilson) **2-7-5**(7) AngelaHartley(9) (neat: mde virtually all: styd on strly fnl f)........—	**1**	33/1	68	20
902^{2}	**Blue Kite** (NPLittmoden) **2-8-6** TGMcLaughlin(2) (trckd ldrs: kpt on wl appr fnl f: nt qckn towards fin)........¾	**2**	11/10^{1}	74	26
822^{4}	**Thanks Keith** (JJO'Neill) **2-8-7** JWeaver(10) (sn outpcd: hdwy ½-wy: styd on fnl f) 3	**3**	4/1^{2}	65	17
836^{12}	**Bolero Kid** (MWEasterby) **2-8-3**(5)ow1 GParkin(3) (sn outpcd: styd on u.p fr ½-wy: nt rch ldrs) ....¾	**4**	9/1	64	15
	Royal Dream (JBerry) **2-7-11**(5) PFessey(5) (unf: a chsng ldrs: one pce fnl 2f) 1¼	**5**	8/1^{3}	54	6
902^{7}	**Russian Romeo (IRE)** (BAMcMahon) **2-8-8** GDuffield(8) (w ldrs tl wknd 2f out) ....¾	**6**	12/1	57	9
664^{3}	**Rock From The Sun** (WGMTurner) **2-8-1** TSprake(11) (b.hind: chsd ldrs tl wknd 2f out) 4	**7**	10/1	37	—
872^{W}	**Frundin** (MrsWBAllen,Norway) **2-7-13**(5)ow5 ADaly(6) (unruly: reard s: nvr nr ldrs)........¾	**8**	33/1	38	—
730^{6}	**Gifted Bairn (IRE)** (DNicholls) **2-7-13**(5) IonaWands(4) (w ldrs tl wknd wl over 1f out) 1	**9**	25/1	35	—
	Glass River (PDEvans) **2-8-5** ACulhane(12) (leggy: lt-f: sn drvn along & outpcd) 3	**10**	12/1	26	—
	Robert's Daughter (JBalding) **2-8-1** NCarlisle(1) (neat: dwlt s: a bhd) 7	**11**	33/1	—	—
	Angry Albert (CSmith) **2-8-7** AClark(7) (leggy: s.s: wnt lft s: a wl bhd) 6	**12**	10/1	—	—
			(SP 135.0%)	**12 Rn**	

59.9 secs (2.90) CSF £70.55 TOTE £29.70: £8.00 £1.30 £1.50 (£84.80) Trio £46.10 OWNER Mr J. W. Gittins (PRESTON) BRED J. Gittins and J. H. Wilson

Piccolo Cativo lacks size but is well-made. Racing with plenty of enthusiasm and well handled, she was always going to hang on. (33/1)

902 Blue Kite never gave up trying, but the winner always just had the edge. (11/10: 4/7-5/4)

822 Thanks Keith failed hopelessly to go the pace. Putting in some good work at the finish, he is crying out for six furlongs. (4/1: 3/1-5/1)

Bolero Kid, run off his feet, stuck on under pressure and is the type to improve in nurseries over six or seven furlongs later on. (9/1)

Royal Dream, a narrow type, should be sharper next time. (8/1: op 5/1)

664 Rock From The Sun (10/1: 8/1-12/1)

Glass River (12/1: op 8/1)

Angry Albert (10/1: 14/1-25/1)

1046 FREESIA H'CAP (0-70) (3-Y.O+ F & M) (Class E)
3-50 (3-53) **5f (Fibresand)** £2,966.25 (£885.00: £422.50: £191.25) Stalls: High GOING minus 0.14 sec per fur (FST)

Form	Horse	Dist	Pos	SP	RR	SF
901[2]	**Lady Sheriff (63)** (MWEasterby) **6-9-4b**(5) GParkin(12) (lw: trckd ldrs: r.o to ld nr fin)	—	**1**	7/4[1]	70	52
663[9]	**Napier Star (61)** (MrsNMacauley) **4-9-7v** SWebster(10) (w ldr: hung lft ½-wy: led ins fnl f: r.o: hdd nr fin)	hd	**2**	11/1	68	50
871[4]	**Corinchili (56)** (GGMargarson) **3-8-4**(3) MHenry(11) (mde most tl ins fnl f: kpt on same pce)	½	**3**	9/1[3]	61	34
883[5]	**Delrob (46)** (DHaydnJones) **6-8-6b** AClark(1) (racd wd: a chsng ldrs: one pce fnl 2f)	4	**4**	9/1[3]	38	20
883[2]	**Runs in the Family (43)** (GMMcCourt) **5-8-3b**ow1 DHarrison(2) (racd wd: w ldrs tl wknd wl over 1f out)	½	**5**	4/1[2]	34	15
883[10]	**Al Reet (IRE) (65)** (SRBowring) **6-9-4**(7) FBoyle(13) (sn outpcd: sme hdwy ½-wy: nvr nr ldrs)	nk	**6**	20/1	55	37
871[12]	**Make Ready (67)** (JNeville) **3-9-4** JWeaver(5) (chsd ldrs tl wknd over 1f out)	1	**7**	11/1	54	27
760[5]	**Secret Miss (43)** (APJones) **5-8-3** TSprake(7) (sn outpcd: sme hdwy over 1f out: n.d)	hd	**8**	16/1	29	11
901[8]	**Pathaze (49)** (NBycroft) **4-8-4**(5) JBramhill(9) (chsd ldrs tl wknd over 1f out)	nk	**9**	20/1	34	16
901[5]	**Amoeba (IRE) (52)** (ABailey) **4-8-12** DWright(8) (lw: sn outpcd & drvn along: n.d)	3	**10**	11/1	28	10
427[9]	**Nefertiti (53)** (RFMarvin) **3-7-13**(5)ow8 ADaly(4) (w ldrs tl lost pl ½-wy)	5	**11**	66/1	13	—
	Fancy Clancy (36) (MissLCSiddall) **4-7-10bc** NCarlisle(3) (hld up: a in rr)	3½	**12**	33/1	—	—
	Positive Result (IRE) (36) (RJPrice) **5-7-5**(5) PFessey(6) (chsd ldrs 2f: sn lost pl)	4	**13**	50/1	—	—

(SP 123.2%) **13 Rn**

59.4 secs (2.40) CSF £20.23 CT £127.90 TOTE £2.40: £1.10 £3.60 £3.20 (£25.80) Trio £33.70 OWNER Mr E. J. Mangan (SHERIFF HUTTON) BRED Jeremy Green and Sons

LONG HANDICAP Nefertiti 6-4 Fancy Clancy 7-8 Positive Result (IRE) 7-4

WEIGHT FOR AGE 3yo-9lb

901 Lady Sheriff recorded her eighth win on her sixtieth outing. Racing from a 3lb higher mark, she was particularly well handled. Kept to the stands' side, she did not have the kickback to overcome, and stuck on to get up near the finish. (7/4)

137 Napier Star, with the visor back on, gave her rider problems, hanging left from halfway. (11/1: 7/1-12/1)

531 Corinchili is a speedy type and was well-suited by the drop back to five. (9/1: op 6/1)

883 Delrob, possibly racing on the slower ground on the far side, is better over six. (9/1)

883 Runs in the Family, from a 4lb higher mark, probably raced on the slower ground on the far side. (4/1: 5/2-9/2)

Al Reet (IRE) got going when it was all over and needs six. (20/1)

Make Ready (11/1: op 6/1)

901 Amoeba (IRE) (11/1: 8/1-12/1)

1047 BEGONIA (S) STKS (3-Y.O+) (Class G)
4-25 (4-26) **6f (Fibresand)** £2,070.00 (£570.00: £270.00) Stalls: Low GOING minus 0.14 sec per fur (FST)

Form	Horse	Dist	Pos	SP	RR	SF
856[4]	**Chilling (58)** (NTinkler) **3-8-2b**(7) KSked(4) (chsd ldrs: led over 1f out: drvn out)	—	**1**	20/1	68	18
*907**	**Desert Invader (IRE) (58)** (DWChapman) **6-9-10** ACulhane(5) (sn drvn along: hdwy over 2f out: chsd wnr fnl f: kpt on)	1¼	**2**	5/1[2]	70	30
907[5]	**Bold Aristocrat (IRE) (65)** (RHollinshead) **6-9-7**(3) FLynch(3) (dwlt: bhd: hdwy over 2f out: n.m.r over 1f out: styd on: no imp)	5	**3**	13/2[3]	56	16
404[4]	**Norling (IRE) (42)** (KOCunningham-Brown) **7-9-5** JWeaver(14) (racd wd: chsd ldrs: outpcd ½-wy: kpt on fnl 2f)	¾	**4**	12/1	49	9
882[13]	**Advance Repro (60)** (JAkehurst) **3-8-9b** GDuffield(8) (trckd ldrs gng wl: led over 3f out tl over 1f out: wknd fnl f)	1¼	**5**	8/1	46	—
288[2]	**Elton Ledger (IRE) (72)** (MrsNMacauley) **8-9-10v** EmmaO'Gorman(2) (b: in tch: effrt 2f out: sn btn)	1½	**6**	5/2[1]	47	7
24[8]	**Samsolom (40)** (MESowersby) **9-9-0**(5) PFessey(6) (bhd: swtchd outside & hdwy 2f out: nvr nr to chal)	½	**7**	33/1	41	1
484[5]	**Dahiyah (USA) (55)** (BSmart) **6-9-5v**(5) ADaly(1) (lw: hmpd & lost pl after 2f: n.d after)	1	**8**	10/1	43	3
759[16]	**Sir Tasker (46)** (JLHarris) **9-9-10** DeanMcKeown(10) (lw: racd wd: prom: sn drvn along: lost pl over 2f out)	nk	**9**	20/1	42	2
332[5]	**Klipspinger (52)** (BSRothwell) **4-9-0b** MFenton(13) (b.nr fore: racd wd: prom 2f: sn lost pl)	1¼	**10**	9/1	29	—
	Komaseph (RFMarvin) **5-9-5** TGMcLaughlin(9) (chsd ldrs tl wknd over 2f out)	1	**11**	50/1	31	—
585[17]	**Margaretrose Anna (35)** (BPJBaugh) **5-9-0** RPerham(11) (chsd ldrs tl lost pl over 2f out)	½	**12**	40/1	25	—
659[3]	**Hannah's Usher (62)** (CMurray) **5-9-5** NicolaHowarth(12) (racd wd: chsd ldrs tl lost pl over 2f out)	1	**13**	9/1	27	—
638[11]	**Cadford Jewel** (WGMTurner) **4-9-5** TSprake(7) (mde most tl over 3f out: virtually p.u 2f out)	22	**14**	33/1	—	—

(SP 126.3%) **14 Rn**

1m 18.3 (4.80) CSF £105.86 TOTE £16.90: £2.30 £4.40 £1.10 (£89.80) Trio £157.30; £177.33 to Lingfield 9/5/97 OWNER Speedlith Group (MALTON) BRED D. J. Simpson

WEIGHT FOR AGE 3yo-10lb

No bid

856 Chilling, whose biggest asset is certainly not consistency, ran right up to her best here under a highly capable ride. (20/1)

907* Desert Invader (IRE) ran another good race but, hard as he tried, he could not get in a serious blow at the winner. (5/1: 5/2-11/2)

907 Bold Aristocrat (IRE) finished much closer to Desert Invader this time, but he was never doing enough, even though he was short of room over a furlong out. (13/2)

404 Norling (IRE) ran as well as could be expected, as he would have been 16lb better off with the winner in a handicap. (12/1)

546* Advance Repro travelled strongly but, when tackled, found next to nothing. (8/1)

288 Elton Ledger (IRE) was having his first run for eighty days and was ring rusty. (5/2)

Samsolom, having his first run for his new trainer, extended his losing run to thirty-two, but he was far from disgraced considering he would have met the winner on 18lb better terms in a handicap. (33/1)

484 Dahiyah (USA) (10/1: 8/1-12/1)

1048 PETUNIA H'CAP (0-70) (3-Y.O+) (Class E)
4-55 (4-58) **7f (Fibresand)** £3,278.25 (£981.00: £470.50: £215.25) Stalls: Low GOING minus 0.14 sec per fur (FST)

Form	Horse	Dist	Pos	SP	RR	SF
*576**	**Water Garden (70)** (GWragg) **3-9-3** AClark(2) (lw: s.i.s: sn chsng ldrs: led over 1f out: rdn out)	—	**1**	9/4[1]	80	28
929[4]	**Shontaine (55)** (MJohnston) **4-9-0** JWeaver(6) (sn bhd: gd hdwy over 1f out: fin wl)	1¼	**2**	14/1	62	22
871[2]	**Swan Island (64)** (BPalling) **3-8-11** TSprake(5) (b.hind: chsd ldrs: outpcd over 3f out: styd on fnl 2f)	½	**3**	4/1[2]	70	18
*870**	**Takhlid (USA) (69)** (DWChapman) **6-10-0** 6x ACulhane(3) (trckd ldrs: led over 3f out tl over 1f out: no ex)	½	**4**	14/1	74	34
873[2]	**Poker Princess (49)** (MBell) **3-7-5**(5) RMullen(4) (chsd ldrs: outpcd over 2f out: kpt on fnl f)	1	**5**	8/1[3]	52	—
892[21]	**Dawalib (USA) (61)** (DHaydnJones) **7-9-6** JLowe(9) (a chsng ldrs: one pce fnl 2f)	1	**6**	10/1	61	21

				SP	RR	SF
860^{3}	**Johnnie the Joker (58)** (JPLeigh) **6-8-12b**$^{(5)}$ PFessey(12) (racd wd: bhd: effrt on outside over 2f out: hung lft: kpt on: nvr nr ldrs)	3	**7**	10/1	51	11
245^{5}	**Down The Yard (37)** (MCChapman) **4-7-5**$^{(5)}$ IonaWands(13) (sn bhd: gd hdwy u.p 2f out: nvr nr ldrs)	hd	**8**	33/1	30	—
663^{11}	**Leigh Crofter (62)** (PDCundell) **8-9-7b** RPerham(16) (chsd ldrs tl wknd appr fnl f)	nk	**9**	25/1	55	15
870^{14}	**Sea Spouse (65)** (MBlanshard) **6-9-10** NAdams(7) (chsd ldrs: sn drvn along: wknd fnl f)	1	**10**	16/1	55	15
925^{11}	**Lady Silk (51)** (MissJFCraze) **6-8-10** NConnorton(8) (unruly: a bhd)	¾	**11**	33/1	40	—
	Ladybower (IRE) (42) (LordHuntingdon) **5-7-8**$^{(7)}$ CCogan(14) (nvr bttr than mid div)	2	**12**	25/1	26	—
864^{4}	**Moneghetti (38)** (JLHarris) **6-7-11** NCarlisle(11) (sn bhd & drvn along)	¾	**13**	12/1	20	—
749^{14}	**La Volta (60)** (JGFitzGerald) **4-9-2**$^{(3)}$ FLynch(10) (hld up: effrt on outside over 2f out: n.d)	5	**14**	16/1	31	—
860^{6}	**Square Deal (FR) (59)** (SRBowring) **6-9-4** SWebster(15) (racd wd: chsd ldrs: hrd rdn & hung lft over 2f out: sn lost pl: eased)	8	**15**	16/1	12	—
790^{4}	**Saxon Bay (63)** (KOCunningham-Brown) **5-9-8** GDuffield(1) (led tl over 3f out: hung rt & sn lost pl)	9	**16**	20/1	—	—

(SP 137.1%) **16 Rn**

1m 31.9 (5.40) CSF £35.93 CT £119.94 TOTE £3.90: £1.70 £4.60 £1.40 £4.40 (£33.80) Trio £57.10 OWNER Mr A. E. Oppenheimer (NEWMARKET) BRED Hascombe and Valiant Studs
LONG HANDICAP Down The Yard 7-7
WEIGHT FOR AGE 3yo-12lb
576* Water Garden took this in decisive fashion. The form of his maiden race win here has been devalued since, but there is no doubt that he is capable of following-up. On turf he will almost certainly need some give underfoot. (9/4: op 7/2)
929 Shontaine is back to his very best. (14/1)
871 Swan Island appreciated the step up to seven, and a mile will be no problem. (4/1)
870* Takhlid (USA) probably ran up to his best under a 6lb penalty. (14/1: op 8/1)
873 Poker Princess was far from disgraced, but she is due to go up 5lb in the weights after her solid effort last time. (8/1: 5/1-12/1)
860 Johnnie the Joker (10/1: 8/1-12/1)
864 Moneghetti (12/1: op 8/1)

T/Plpt: £38.30 (307.67 Tckts). T/Qdpt: £4.50 (170.04 Tckts) WG

1049a - 1057a : (Irish Racing) - See Computer Raceform

0709a-CURRAGH (Newbridge, Ireland) (R-H) (Good)
Saturday May 3rd

1058a MOORESBRIDGE STKS(Listed) (4-Y.O+)
2-55 (2-56) **1m 2f** IR £12,900.00 (IR £3,700.00: IR £1,700.00: IR £500.00) GOING minus 0.45 sec per fur (F)

				SP	RR	SF
	Dance Design (IRE) (DKWeld,Ireland) **4-9-4** PShanahan (hld up: led under 3f out: hdd briefly 1f out: r.o u.p)	—	**1**	4/5^{1}	119	52
713a^{6}	**Raiyoun (IRE)** (JOxx,Ireland) **4-8-12** JPMurtagh (hld up: chal 2f out: narrow ld 1f out: edgd rt & hdd 150 yds fr fin: rallied)	s.h	**2**	9/2^{3}	113	46
	Tout A Coup (IRE) (GACusack,Ireland) **4-9-1** WJSupple (hld up: trckd ldrs st: one pce)	10	**3**	4/1^{2}	100	33
	Free To Speak (IRE) (DKWeld,Ireland) **5-8-12** PJSmullen (rdn to ld after 1½f: hdd under 3f out: wknd)	hd	**4**	16/1	97	30
	Wray (IRE) (LBrowne,Ireland) **5-8-12** SCraine (hld up towards rr: chsd ldrs over 2f out: no imp 1½f out)	hd	**5**	12/1	97	30
	Sharazan (IRE) (JOxx,Ireland) **4-8-12** DHogan (led 1½f: rn 2nd tl lost pl bef ½-wy)	8	**6**	20/1	84	17

(SP 112.1%) **6 Rn**

2m 5.7 (1.70) OWNER Moyglare Stud Farm (CURRAGH)
Dance Design (IRE) looked in good condition, but her trainer had left something to work on for what should be a profitable third season for the 1996 Irish Oaks winner. With no doubts about her stamina Shanahan, alert to the danger of being tapped for foot, sent her to the front on the last bend. She had to work to repel the second, but got her second wind before producing her final surge. She will come on a fair bit for this, but will take on stronger opposition in the Tattersalls Gold Cup later in the month. (4/5)
713a Raiyoun (IRE) derived benefit from his Gladness Stakes pipe-opener, and challenged persistently throughout the last quarter-mile. He edged left under pressure inside the last, but was coming back again at the finish. He seemed to get the trip alright. (9/2)
Tout A Coup (IRE), following a recent Listowel win on testing ground, was toiling throughout the last quarter-mile. (4/1: op 5/2)
Free To Speak (IRE) was forced to make the pace until dropping away in the straight. (16/1)

1060a OMNI RACING TETRARCH STKS(Gp 3) (3-Y.O C & F)
3-55 (3-58) **7f** IR £22,750.00 (IR £6,650.00: IR £3,150.00: IR £1,050.00) GOING minus 0.45 sec per fur (F)

				SP	RR	SF
713a^{2}	**Desert King (IRE)** (APO'Brien,Ireland) **3-9-2** CRoche (cl up: led 2f out: rdn clr fr over 1f out: r.o wl)	—	**1**	2/1^{1}	117	65
679^{3}	**Rich Ground** (JDBethell) **3-8-12** PaulEddery (hld up towards rr: hdwy ½-wy: u.p 1f out: no ch with wnr)	5½	**2**	6/1	100	48
807a*	**Lil's Boy (USA)** (JSBolger,Ireland) **3-8-10**ow1 KJManning (hld up: hdwy ½-wy: rdn 2f out: no ex 1f out)	nk	**3**	6/1	98	45
	Verglas (IRE) (KPrendergast,Ireland) **3-8-12** WJSupple (hld up: rdn 1½f out: kpt on same pce)	s.h	**4**	9/2^{3}	100	48
807a^{2}	**Fly To The Stars** (MJohnston) **3-8-6** JWeaver (prom: led after 2½f: hdd 2f out: rdn & no ex wl over 1f out)	½	**5**	5/2^{2}	93	41
807a^{5}	**Sharemono (USA)** (APO'Brien,Ireland) **3-8-6** JAHeffernan (led 2½f: lost pl bef ½-wy: t.o)	dist	**6**	20/1	—	—

(SP 113.4%) **6 Rn**

1m 22.8 (-0.20) OWNER Mr M. Tabor (PILTOWN)
713a Desert King (IRE) looked a lot fitter this time, and more positive tactics paid off. Always travelling well, he led with over just over two furlongs to run, and with no serious challenger, just drew clear. This was a smart performance giving weight away in what reads as a fast time. The race was run on a rarely-used inside track, and would be less testing than the usual seven furlongs. Raised to 119 for this effort, he looks the mainstay of the home defence for the Irish 2,000 Guineas. (2/1: op 5/4)
679 Rich Ground did not have the clearest of runs, but kept on willingly enough over the last furlong-and-a-half. (6/1: op 4/1)
807a* Lil's Boy (USA) was putting in his best work at the finish. (6/1)
Verglas (IRE), having his first run of the season, found trouble but will improve on this. (9/2)
807a Fly To The Stars tried to dominate, but found things much too hot when the pressure was turned on. (5/2)
807a Sharemono (USA) ran fast early, but was done with at halfway. (20/1)

1062a ATHASI STKS(Listed) (3 & 4-Y.O F)
4-55 (4-57) **7f** IR £12,900.00 (IR £3,700.00: IR £1,700.00: IR £500.00) GOING minus 0.45 sec per fur (F)

				SP	RR	SF
	Dangerous Diva (IRE) (APO'Brien,Ireland) **3-8-10**ow1 CRoche (mde all: drew clr½-wy: rdn ins last: kpt on)	—	**1**	2/1[2]	105	34
806a[8]	**Azra (IRE)** (JSBolger,Ireland) **3-8-13**ow1 KJManning (in tch: rdn & chsd wnr over 2f out: kpt on wl u.p)	½	**2**	6/1[3]	107	36
806a[2]	**Chania (IRE)** (JOxx,Ireland) **3-8-6** PJSmullen (in tch: rdn after ½-wy: btn over 2f out)	10	**3**	5/4[1]	77	7
	Orange Grouse (IRE) (LBrowne,Ireland) **4-9-7** JPSpencer (hld up: rdn & no imp over 2f out)	2	**4**	9/1	75	17
806a[7]	**Velvet Appeal (IRE)** (MHalford,Ireland) **3-8-6** WJSupple (sn chsng ldr: wknd after ½-wy)	5	**5**	10/1	61	—
	Daffodil Dale (IRE) (KPrendergast,Ireland) **3-8-9** SCraine (n.d: trailing over 2f out)	7	**6**	20/1	48	—
				(SP 115.9%)		**6 Rn**

1m 24.9 (1.90) OWNER Robert Lanigan (PILTOWN)

Dangerous Diva (IRE), coming back in distance after last month's course win, tried to run these into the ground. Clear over a furlong out, she was idling and had to be driven out. Raised to 105 for this, she is on the upgrade. (2/1)

806a Azra (IRE) showed improved form with a more patient ride. In pursuit throughout the last furlong, she made up plenty of ground in the closing stages. (6/1: op 4/1)

806a Chania (IRE) was never really travelling, being ridden along from halfway with no chance of getting on terms. (5/4)

Orange Grouse (IRE) was totally outpointed in the last two furlongs. (9/1: op 6/1)

Velvet Appeal (IRE) again demonstrated how much last year's Moyglare Stud Stakes result flattered her. (10/1)

1063a - 1066a : (Irish Racing) - See Computer Raceform

0813a-SAINT-CLOUD (France) (L-H) (Good to soft)
Thursday May 1st

1067a PRIX DU MUGUET (Gp 2) (4-Y.O+)
2-15 (2-13) **1m** £33,670.00 (£13,468.00: £6,734.00: £3,367.00)

				SP	RR	SF
	Spinning World (USA) (JEPease,France) **4-9-4** CAsmussen (qckly into stride: 6th st: forced wd: prog fr 1½f out: led fnl strides)	—	**1**		127	—
716a*	**Simon du Desert (FR)** (RCollet,France) **4-8-12** CHanotel (cl up early: mid div st: led 1f out: edgd lft: ct nr fin)	s.nk	**2**		121	—
	Accento (RSuerland,Germany) **4-9-1** AHelfenbein (led tl 1f out: styd on one pce)	2½	**3**		119	—
	Devil River Peek (USA) (BSchutz,Germany) **5-8-12** TJarnet (a cl up: chal 1½f out: one pce)	½	**4**		115	—
	Grey Risk (FR) (PDemercastel,France) **4-8-12** SGuillot (hld up rr: r.o fr 1f out: styng on at fin)	s.nk	**5**		114	—
625a[2]	**Nero Zilzal (USA)** (ELellouche,France) **4-8-12** TThulliez (mid div: effrt 1½f out: one pce)	1	**6**		112	—
	Nec Plus Ultra (FR) (AdeRoyerDupre,France) **6-8-12** GMosse (mid div: btn appr fnl f)	4	**7**		104	—
						7 Rn

1m 43.8 (5.30) P-M 1.50F: 1.20F 1.50F OWNER Niarchos Family (CHANTILLY)

Spinning World (USA), carrying a little condition in the paddock, has certainly done well between three and four. Quickly into his stride, he was then restrained and held up towards the back of the field. In sixth place entering the straight, he was pushed a little wide but, once he regained his balance, put up an impressive final run to pinch the race on the line. This effort is worthy of some credit as he was giving weight away to all of his rivals on this debut. He is sure to improve from this and he now heads for either the Lockinge Stakes or the Prix d'Ispahan, with the former preferred at the moment. A little cut in the ground is a definite advantage for him, and he now looks set for another highly successful season.

716a* Simon du Desert (FR) looked extremely well in the paddock. He was smartly into his stride but settled in mid-division until the straight, where he ran a little wide before making his challenge. Holding the advantage a furlong out, he veered left under pressure which probably cost him the race. He seems a much improved individual this season and he may even stay further.

Accento ran a decent race. He led from the start until a furlong out and stayed on. He looks capable of winning Group races again this season, but not in France.

Devil River Peek (USA) put in a decent performance, but is not up to this standard. Racing in mid-division, he looked quite dangerous soon after entering the straight, but his effort petered out.

0821a-SAN SIRO (Milan, Italy) (R-H) (Good to firm)
Thursday May 1st

1068a PREMIO TERRES (3-Y.O)
1-50 (1-55) **7f 110y** £9,642.00

			SP	RR	SF
Special Lad (ITY) (MCiciarelli,Italy) **3-8-9** MEsposito	—	**1**		84	—
Forbes (ITY) (GBotti,Italy) **3-8-11** EBotti	s.nk	**2**		86	—
Minarello (USA) (GVerricelli,Italy) **3-8-7** SDettori	2¼	**3**		77	—
Scoss (LMCumani) **3-8-6** MDemuro (btn approx 7l)		**6**		—	—
					6 Rn

1m 34.0 (9.50) TOTE 56L: 28L 25L (115L) OWNER Scuderia Briantea BRED Az Agr delle Groane

Scoss ran very green. Slowly away, he gradually closed up at halfway, but was soon beaten. He should be better for the experience.

1069a PREMIO EMANUELE FILIBERTO (Listed) (3-Y.O)
3-50 (4-03) **1m 2f** £38,570.00

				SP	RR	SF
686[2]	**Jaunty Jack** (LMCumani) **3-9-2** FJovine	—	**1**		89+	—
	Sunny Sample (IRE) (BGrizzetti,Italy) **3-9-2** MTellini	4¼	**2**		82	—
	Setmatt (GBotti,Italy) **3-9-2** EBotti	1	**3**		81	—
						7 Rn

2m 4.0 (10.00) TOTE 22L: 16L 47L (239L) OWNER Allevamento Gialloblu (NEWMARKET) BRED Fonthill Stud

686 Jaunty Jack, who is held in high regard by connections, duly repaid that confidence with a very solid performance. The son of Midyan made all, went clear two furlongs out, and never looked in any danger. He is definitely one to follow.

CHANTILLY (France) (R-H) (Good)
Saturday May 3rd

1070a PRIX HOCQUART (Gp 2) (3-Y.O C & F)
3-20 (3-19) **1m 3f** £43,883.00 (£17,396.00: £8,305.00: £8,305.00)

				SP	RR	SF
629a[3]	**Shaka** (J-CRouget,France) **3-9-2** J-RDubosc (hld up: gd prog 2f out: led ins fnl f: r.o wl)	—	**1**		112	—
	Oscar (IRE) (PBary,France) **3-9-2** SGuillot (3rd ent st: disp ld 1½f out: outpcd fnl f)	1	**2**		111	—
	Alekos (USA) (CLaffon-Parias,France) **3-9-2** DBoeuf (mid div: effrt 2f out: r.o one pce)	¾	**3**		110	—
	Ithaki (IRE) (JEPease,France) **3-9-2** CAsmussen (a.p: disp ld 1½f out: r.o one pce fnl f)	d.h	**3**		110	—
629a[2]	**Sendoro (IRE)** (AdeRoyerDupre,France) **3-9-2** GMosse (mid div st: no ex fr 2f out)	2	**5**		107	—
	Fier Danseur (FR) (JLesbordes,France) **3-9-2** VVion (hld up rr: squeezed through 2f out: one pce)	½	**6**		106	—
819a[4]	**New Frontier (IRE)** (AFabre,France) **3-9-2** TGillet (led to 2f out: grad fdd)	s.nk	**7**		106	—

7 Rn

2m 22.8 (9.10) P-M 3.90F: 2.00F 2.50F OWNER Mr R. Bousquet (PAU) BRED Petra Bloodstack Agency Ltd

629a Shaka stripped a lot fitter and was given an enterprising ride. He was dropped out in last place where he stayed until entering the straight. He then came with a well-timed run and stayed on well. This event was not really a test of stamina after a moderate early pace, but he looks certain to improve again after this. He now heads for the Prix du Jockey-Club.

Oscar (IRE) put up a really decent effort considering this was only his third race and his first attempt at this level. He was forced to race on the outside throughout, and shared the lead for a short time in the straight. He was not suited by the lack of early pace and he is sure to improve further before the Jockey-Club.

Alekos (USA) raced on the rail and made good late progress to share third place. He is on the upgrade and should win a Group race before the end of the season.

Ithaki (IRE) raced in second place, but was outpaced early in the straight before running on again in the closing stages. The way the race was run did not suit this promising colt. He will appreciate a little further and the Epsom Derby remains a possibility.

CHURCHILL DOWNS (Louisville, USA) (L-H) (Fast)
Saturday May 3rd

1071a KENTUCKY DERBY (Gp 1) (3-Y.O)
10-32 (10-34) **1m 2f** £416,667.00 (£101,190.00: £50,595.00)

			SP	RR	SF
Silver Charm (USA) (BBaffert,USA) **3-9-0** GaryStevens	—	**1**		124	—
Captain Bodgit (USA) (GCapuano,USA) **3-9-0** ASolis	hd	**2**		124	—
Free House (USA) (JGonzalez,USA) **3-9-0** DFlores	3½	**3**		118	—

13 Rn

2m 2.44 P-M $10.00: (1-2) $4.80 $4.80 (1-2-3) $3.00 $2.80 $2.80 OWNER R & B Lewis BRED Mary Lou Wootton

Silver Charm (USA), a lightly-raced sort, was tackling ten furlongs for the first time. Tracking the leaders for most of the way, Stevens finally let him go at the top of the home straight. Challenged inside the final furlong, he dug deep and was holding on at the line.

Captain Bodgit (USA) came off the rail around horses to challenge in the straight, and seemed to be getting the better of the winner half-a-furlong from home, but he found that rival just too resolute.

0440a-COLOGNE (Germany) (R-H) (Good)
Sunday May 4th

1072a BEHR MEMORIAL (3-Y.O)
2-30 (2-31) **1m** £5,568.00

				SP	RR	SF
918a[3]	**Polar Flight** (MJohnston) **3-9-0** JWeaver	—	**1**		101	—
	Le Battant (GER) (HJentzsch,Germany) **3-9-0** PSchiergen	¾	**2**		100	—
	Burberry (GER) (BSchutz,Germany) **3-9-4** AStarke	nk	**3**		103	—

7 Rn

1m 38.43 (8.43) TOTE 61DM: 17DM 13DM 12DM (228DM) OWNER The Middleham Partnership (MIDDLEHAM) BRED P. and Mrs Venner

918a Polar Flight put up what can only be described as a strange performance. He quickly took up the running but, with two-and-a-half furlongs to run, was outpaced and headed. However, he renewed his challenge and ran on again to lead thirty yards from the line.

1073a GERLING PREIS (Gp 2) (4-Y.O+)
3-40 (3-55) **1m 4f** £27,462.00 (£10,985.00: £5,492.00)

				SP	RR	SF
	Wurftaube (GER) (HRemmert,Germany) **4-9-0** KWoodburn	—	**1**		117	—
	Surako (GER) (HJentzsch,Germany) **4-9-2** PSchiergen	1¼	**2**		117	—
736[11]	**Mongol Warrior (USA)** (LordHuntingdon) **4-9-4** JWeaver	nk	**3**		119	—
719a[2]	**Try Again (GER)** (AWohler,Germany) **6-9-0** ABoschert	nse	**4**		115	—
	Protektor (GER) (ALowe,Germany) **8-9-4** GBocskai	2½	**5**		116	—
	Bon Jovi (GER) (HJentzsch,Germany) **4-9-0** LHammer-Hansen	¾	**6**		111	—
440a*	**Leconte (GER)** (MWeber,Germany) **6-9-0** TMundry	½	**7**		110	—
	Narrabeth (IRE) (HJentzsch,Germany) **4-9-0** ASuborics	nk	**8**		110	—
	Pacajas (GER) (Germany) **5-9-0** WNewnes	6	**9**		102	—
440a[2]	**Ocean Sea (USA)** (BSchutz,Germany) **4-9-0** AStarke	8	**10**		91	—
	Humbel (USA) (Germany) **5-9-0** ATylicki	4½	**11**		85	—

11 Rn

2m 28.64 (1.64) TOTE 19DM: 13DM 18DM 26DM (99DM) OWNER Gestut Ravensberg BRED Gestut Ravensberg

Wurftaube (GER) continued her winning ways in impressive style here, and it will take something special to end her unbeaten run of seven victories.

Mongol Warrior (USA) put up a solid performance on ground that was probably a bit on the firm side for him. Always close up, he was in fourth place entering the straight, but was unable to quicken when asked and kept on at the same pace from two furlongs out.

1074a WEIDENPESCHER MEILE (Listed) (4-Y.O+)
4-45 (5-07) **1m** £7,576.00

				SP	RR	SF
	Landsuitor (GER) (AWohler,Germany) **5-8-11** ABoschert	—	1		113	—
	Catoki (USA) (PRau,Germany) **4-8-9** TMundry	nk	2		110	—
	La Blue (GER) (BSchutz,Germany) **4-9-2** AStarke	s.h	3		117	—
919a5	**Celestial Key (USA)** (MJohnston) **7-8-9** JWeaver (btn approx 4l)		5		—	—
						12 Rn

1m 35.86 (5.86) TOTE 179DM: 36DM 39DM 16DM (3,063DM) OWNER R. Klostermann BRED Dr A. Viebrock
919a Celestial Key (USA), held up in the rear, came with a run from two furlongs out. He looked to have every chance approaching the final furlong, but was unable to find any extra.

1068a-SAN SIRO (Milan, Italy) (R-H) (Good)
Sunday May 4th

1075a PREMIO BAGGIO (Listed) (3-Y.O F)
5-00 (5-28) **1m 2f** £23,142.00 (£10,183.00: £5,554.00)

				SP	RR	SF
	Bedside Story (GBotti,Italy) **3-8-8** EBotti	—	1		101	—
815a4	**Sopran Mariduff** (RRossini,Italy) **3-8-8** AMarcialis	2½	2		97	—
	Viscoumtess Brave (IRE) (LordHuntingdon) **3-8-8** CColombi	2¼	3		93	—
						8 Rn

2m 4.6 (10.60) TOTE 14L: 11L 12L 13L (28L) OWNER Grundy Bloodstock Ltd (ITALY) BRED Grundy Bloodstock
Viscoumtess Brave (IRE) was beaten by what could turn out to be a very useful filly. Racing in mid-division, she went third over a furlong out but, despite staying on well, was never able to get on terms with the winner. She would have preferred the ground a lot softer.

0822-CARLISLE (R-H) (Good to Soft, Soft patches)
Friday May 9th
WEATHER: unsetted, heavy rain last 2 races WIND: almost nil

70 68+ 77+ 69

1076 E.B.F. CALDEW MAIDEN STKS (2-Y.O) (Class D)
2-10 (2-10) **5f** £3,403.75 (£1,030.00: £502.50: £238.75) Stalls: High GOING: 0.15 sec per fur (G)

				SP	RR	SF
6972	**Hirst Bridge (IRE)** (MWEasterby) **2-9-0** TLucas(2) (led tl hd wl ins fnl f: rallied to ld post)	—	1	7/4 1	76	30
8222	**Prix Star** (CWFairhurst) **2-9-0** LCharnock(6) (lw: cl up: rdn to ld wl ins fnl f: nt qckn towards fin: hdd post)	s.h	2	11/4 2	76	30
	Alconleigh (MJohnston) **2-9-0** JWeaver(4) (w'like: scope: s.i.s: chsng ldrs after 2f: nt qckn appr fnl f)	1¾	3	7/4 1	70+	24
5579	**Seventh Heaven** (JBerry) **2-8-9**(5) TEDurcan(3) (chsd ldrs: rdn 2f out: one pce)	¾	4	10/1	68	22
	Lakeland Pride (IRE) (PDEvans) **2-9-0** JFEgan(5) (w'like: scope: s.i.s: rdn ½-wy: nvr trbld ldrs)	4	5	7/1 3	55	9
	Petara (IRE) (JSWainwright) **2-8-9**(5) JBramhill(1) (w'like: bit bkwd: s.i.s: hdwy & prom ½-wy: wknd over 1f out)	2	6	20/1	49	3
				(SP 125.7%)		**6 Rn**

65.1 secs (4.90) CSF £7.41 TOTE £2.10: £2.10 £1.10 (£3.40) OWNER Mr I. Bray (SHERIFF HUTTON) BRED Mrs P. H. Burns
697 Hirst Bridge (IRE) again did not help his rider by continually hanging right but, well handled, he met the line on the right stride to get the verdict. (7/4)
822 Prix Star looked to have done everything right only just to get touched off. (11/4)
Alconleigh, like the vast majority of newcomers from this yard, he was green early on but still had his chances and will no doubt improve for the experience. (7/4)
Seventh Heaven both walks and moves really well, and this was a much better effort. (10/1)
Lakeland Pride (IRE), unlike the majority of juveniles from this yard, he had plenty of size and scope about him and may take a bit longer to come to hand. (7/1)
Petara (IRE) needed this, but did show something and time should see improvement. (20/1)

1077 DERWENT CLAIMING STKS (3-Y.O+) (Class F)
2-40 (2-40) **6f 206y** £2,472.00 (£692.00: £336.00) Stalls: High GOING: 0.15 sec per fur (G)

				SP	RR	SF
10208	**Allinson's Mate (IRE) (62)** (TDBarron) **9-8-12b**(7) VictoriaAppleby(3) (lw: bhd: swtchd outside over 2f out: r.o to ld ins fnl f)	—	1	7/2 2	65	46
9073	**Coscoroba (IRE)** (JBerry) **3-7-13**(5) PFessey(4) (in tch: hdwy to chal 1f out: nt qckn)	1½	2	8/1 3	59	28
5798	**First Gold (47)** (JWharton) **8-9-6** GDuffield(1) (lw: bhd: hdwy u.p 2f out: n.m.r 1f out: styd on towards fin)	1½	3	8/1 3	59	40
9972	**Kemo Sabo (72)** (CParker) **5-9-11** JCarroll(8) (lw: cl up: rdn to ld over 1f out: hdd & no ex ins fnl f)	nk	4	7/2 2	63	44
8232	**Broctune Gold (65)** (MrsMReveley) **6-9-13** ACulhane(7) (led tl hdd over 1f out: sn btn)	nk	5	6/4 1	65	46
	My Handsome Prince (27) (PJBevan) **5-9-2v** NCarlisle(6) (lw: sn bhd: sme hdwy 2f out: n.d)	2	6	12/1	49	30
6445	**Champagne On Ice (45)** (PDEvans) **3-8-1**ow1 JFEgan(2) (prom tl wknd fnl 2f)	6	7	8/1 3	32	—
	Indian Serenade (37) (RSimpson) **6-9-3** MGallagher(5) (cl up tl wknd fnl 2f)	2½	8	25/1	31	12
				(SP 129.3%)		**8 Rn**

1m 31.6 (5.90) CSF £32.81 TOTE £8.40: £2.00 £2.50 £2.00 (£44.70) OWNER Mr D. Courtier (THIRSK) BRED Gay O'Callaghan
WEIGHT FOR AGE 3yo-12lb
468 Allinson's Mate (IRE) looked a picture and, coming from off the pace, quickened splendidly to settle it late on. He is is obviously in top form. (7/2)
907 Coscoroba (IRE), after two modest efforts on the All-Weather recently, put in a much better performance, and she seems to be coming right. (8/1)
480* First Gold won this last year and ran well again but was never quite doing enough, and being slightly hampered made little difference. (8/1)
997 Kemo Sabo ran another sound race but just lacked that finishing kick. (7/2)

823 Broctune Gold needs things to go all his own way, and could never shake off his challengers here. (6/4)
My Handsome Prince looked fit for his seasonal debut, but he has yet to win a race and was always finding this trip too sharp. (12/1)
644 Champagne On Ice (8/1: op 5/1)

1078 CARLISLE, GREAT RAILWAY CITY, 1997 H'CAP (0-70) (3-Y.O) (Class E)

3-10 (3-11) **7f 214y** £3,215.95 (£973.60: £475.30: £226.15) Stalls: High GOING: 0.15 sec per fur (G)

				SP	RR	SF
1024^{10}	**Jack The Lad (IRE) (55)** (JHetherton) **3-8-10** LCharnock(6) (trckd ldrs: led over 2f out: r.o)	—	1	6/1^{3}	67	26
958^{3}	**Abajany (62)** (MRChannon) **3-8-12**(5) PPMurphy(7) (trckd ldrs: ev ch 2f out: nt qckn ins fnl f)	¾	2	4/1^{2}	73	32
945^{6}	**Petite Risk (41)** (KWHogg) **3-7-5**(5) JBramhill(9) (a chsng ldrs: kpt on one pce fnl 2½f)	4	3	33/1	44	3
701^{5}	**Fauna (IRE) (65)** (NAGraham) **3-9-6** DeanMcKeown(2) (a chsng ldrs: effrt over 2f out: nt pce to chal)	hd	4	12/1	67	26
124^{5}	**Samspet (44)** (RAFahey) **3-7-6**(7)ow2 RWinston(8) (plld hrd: trckd ldrs: effrt 3f out: sn btn)	3	5	7/1	40	—
926^{2}	**Tycoon Tina (50)** (WMBrisbourne) **3-8-0**(5) PFessey(10) (s.s: hdwy ½-wy: nvr trbld ldrs)	1	6	12/1	44	3
840^{13}	**Beau Roberto (58)** (MJohnston) **3-8-13** JWeaver(5) (lw: mid div: effrt over 2f out: no hdwy)	5	7	12/1	42	1
535^{12}	**King Uno (51)** (MrsJRRamsden) **3-8-6** JFortune(3) (lw: bhd: shkn up over 3f out: n.d)	3	8	10/1	29	—
873^{11}	**Strelitza (IRE) (57)** (MWEasterby) **3-8-12b** TLucas(11) (s.s: a bhd)	8	9	12/1	19	—
	Emily-Jayne (52) (MrsMReveley) **3-8-7** ACulhane(1) (outpcd & bhd most of wy)	1	10	16/1	12	—
874^{2}	**Cartouche (66)** (SirMarkPrescott) **3-9-7** GDuffield(4) (led tl hdd & wknd over 2f out)	3½	11	Evens^{1}	19	—
				(SP 145.5%)	**11 Rn**	

1m 44.9 (7.90) CSF £34.63 CT £743.09 TOTE £7.70: £1.60 £1.80 £12.30 (£9.20) Trio £166.70; £98.66 to Beverley 10/5/97 OWNER Keith West Partnership (MALTON) BRED Thomas Healy
LONG HANDICAP Petite Risk 7-0
OFFICIAL EXPLANATION Cartouche: no explanation offered.
900* Jack The Lad (IRE), unlucky at Doncaster last time, made no mistake this time and scored convincingly. (6/1: op 7/2)
958 Abajany looked to be going well when challenging early in the straight but, inclined to edge left when ridden, he failed to come up with the goods. The ability is there when he gets it together. (4/1)
Petite Risk handled this easier ground well and seems to be improving. (33/1)
701 Fauna (IRE) was always close enough if good enough, but proved one-paced when ridden in the home straight. (12/1)
124 Samspet, well supported in the market, did not help his cause by pulling very hard and should be given another chance. (7/1)
926 Tycoon Tina needs to learn to jump out on terms and she may well then have a chance. (12/1: op 8/1)

1079 BORDER ESK H'CAP (0-70) (3-Y.O+) (Class E)

3-40 (3-40) **5f 207y** £2,960.25 (£897.00: £438.50: £209.25) Stalls: High GOING: 0.15 sec per fur (G)

				SP	RR	SF
827^{5}	**Birchwood Sun (50)** (MDods) **7-8-8b**ow1 JWeaver(9) (lw: outpcd & bhd: swtchd outside 2f out: r.o wl to ld ins fnl f)	—	1	9/2^{1}	65	34
977^{6}	**Amron (64)** (JBerry) **10-9-3**(5) TEDurcan(8) (bhd: hdwy over 2f out: led wl over 1f out tl wl ins fnl f: no ex)	1¼	2	5/1^{2}	76	46
929^{2}	**Rymer's Rascal (54)** (EJAlston) **5-8-12** JFortune(5) (hdwy ½-wy: chsng ldrs appr fnl f: kpt on same pce)	3½	3	9/2^{1}	56	26
1012^{4}	**Flying Harold (42)** (MRChannon) **4-8-0** JFanning(4) (chsd ldrs: chal 2f out: nt qckn fnl f)	1½	4	11/1	40	10
759^{2}	**Stephensons Rocket (51)** (RAFahey) **6-8-9** ACulhane(2) (disp ld tl hdd appr fnl f: sn btn)	¾	5	5/1^{2}	47	17
827^{4}	**Kid Ory (45)** (DWChapman) **6-7-12**(5) PFessey(6) (disp ld tl hdd & wknd appr fnl f)	nk	6	8/1	40	10
823^{5}	**Most Respectful (54)** (DenysSmith) **4-8-12** LCharnock(10) (lw: in tch: effrt 2f out: one pce)	5	7	12/1	36	6
956^{8}	**Needle Match (52)** (JJO'Neill) **4-8-10b^{1}** JCarroll(3) (bhd: hdwy ½-wy: wknd over 1f out)	3	8	9/1	26	—
953^{2}	**Naissant (64)** (RMMcKellar) **4-9-1**(7) KSked(1) (spd 4f)	2½	9	13/2	31	1
901^{4}	**Bollin Dorothy (50)** (TDEasterby) **4-8-8** MBirch(11) (lw: dwlt: hdwy ½-wy: sn wknd)	1	10	11/2^{3}	14	—
				(SP 135.6%)	**10 Rn**	

1m 16.9 (5.10) CSF £29.11 CT £106.19 TOTE £6.80: £1.80 £2.60 £1.20 (£11.40) Trio £45.30 OWNER Mr A. G. Watson (DARLINGTON) BRED The Hall Stud Ltd
827 Birchwood Sun goes well on this track, and produced a devastating burst to come from last to first and win going away. (9/2)
977 Amron, dropped out this time, quickened well when asked, but probably hit the front too soon and was worried out of it late on. (5/1)
929 Rymer's Rascal ran well over further last time and put up another good performance here, but was just short of speed when he saw daylight. (9/2)
1012 Flying Harold, happy to track the leaders, failed to pick up when an effort was required. (11/1)
759 Stephensons Rocket is well handicapped, having not won for three years, but all his victories were over the minimum trip. (5/1)
827 Kid Ory gives the impression that another furlong may well see improvement. (8/1)

1080 IRTHING LIMITED STKS (0-60) (3-Y.O+) (Class F)

4-10 (4-11) **5f** £2,542.00 (£712.00: £346.00) Stalls: High GOING: 0.15 sec per fur (G)

				SP	RR	SF
956^{2}	**Corniche Quest (IRE) (54)** (MRChannon) **4-8-9**(5) PPMurphy(2) (lw: outpcd & bhd: hdwy 2f out: r.o to ld wl ins fnl f)	—	1	7/4^{1}	69	51
593^{8}	**Afaan (IRE) (59)** (RFMarvin) **4-9-3** DeanMcKeown(3) (chsd ldrs: led over 1f out tl wl ins fnl f: nt qckn)	1¼	2	7/1	68	50
995^{8}	**Skyers Flyer (IRE) (59)** (RonaldThompson) **3-8-8** TWilliams(4) (mid div: drvn along: hdwy 2f out: nt qckn ins fnl f)	1¼	3	3/1^{2}	64	37
1003*	**Shadow Jury (59)** (DWChapman) **7-9-6b** 3x LCharnock(8) (led tl hdd appr fnl f: sn btn)	5	4	9/2^{3}	51	33
1003^{4}	**Petraco (IRE) (56)** (NASmith) **9-8-12**(5) JBramhill(5) (a chsng ldrs: rdn ½-wy: one pce)	nk	5	7/1	47	29
855^{12}	**Toronto (59)** (JBerry) **3-8-8b^{1}** JWeaver(1) (bhd tl sme late hdwy)	2	6	9/1	41	14
905^{9}	**Sing With the Band (56)** (BAMcMahon) **6-9-0** GDuffield(6) (lw: chsd ldrs: outpcd ½-wy: grad wknd)	7	7	7/1	15	—
924^{7}	**Answers-To-Thomas (52)** (JMJefferson) **4-9-3** JFortune(9) (chsd ldrs over 3f: wknd)	4	8	14/1	5	—
886^{14}	**Lunar Music (60)** (RonaldThompson) **3-8-5** NConnorton(10) (nvr trbld ldrs)	1	9	12/1	—	—
783^{10}	**Red Romance (51)** (DenysSmith) **3-8-8** ACulhane(7) (nvr wnt pce)	8	10	14/1	—	—
				(SP 148.1%)	**10 Rn**	

63.8 secs (3.60) CSF £18.80 TOTE £2.60: £1.60 £3.00 £1.80 (£15.00) Trio £28.60 OWNER Mr M. Bishop (UPPER LAMBOURN) BRED K. Molloy
WEIGHT FOR AGE 3yo-9lb
956 Corniche Quest (IRE) acts on a soft surface and certainly stays further than this. Her stamina came into play in the closing stages and she won going away. (7/4)
545 Afaan (IRE), after some creditable efforts on the All-Weather, was having his first run on turf. He acquitted himself well, and ought to find a modest event. (7/1)

995 Skyers Flyer (IRE), unlucky last time, had no such excuses here and was done for speed in the closing stages. (3/1)
1003* Shadow Jury likes things to go his way and it was never on this time. (9/2: op 3/1)
1003 Petraco (IRE) was always close enough, but he seems to have lost his finishing kick these days. (7/1)
Toronto, tried in blinkers this time, never gave any signs of hope. (9/1)

1081 EDEN H'CAP (0-70) (3-Y.O+) (Class E)

4-40 (4-40) **1m 6f 32y** £2,791.25 (£845.00: £412.50: £196.25) Stalls: Low GOING: 0.15 sec per fur (G)

				SP	RR	SF
1039[3]	**All On (44)** (JHetherton) **6-8-6** [5x] GDuffield(6) (mde all: pushed clr 4f out: unchal)	—	1	11/4[1]	61	—
781[8]	**Highfield Fizz (42)** (CWFairhurst) **5-8-4** LCharnock(3) (bhd: effrt & c wd st: styd on: no ch w wnr)	9	2	12/1	49	—
	Well Appointed (IRE) (59) (BMactaggart) **8-9-7** JCarroll(2) (lw: wnt prom after 4f: rdn 4f out: one pce)	6	3	11/2	59	—
888[9]	**Tonnerre (55)** (BAMcMahon) **5-9-3** JFortune(1) (lw: sn chsng wnr: rdn 4f out: grad wknd fnl 3f)	¾	4	4/1[2]	54	—
570[5]	**Charity Crusader (38)** (MrsMReveley) **6-7-9b**(5) PFessey(9) (lw: dwlt: outpcd & bhd tl sme hdwy u.p fnl 3f)	3½	5	6/1	33	—
950[5]	**Lord Hastie (USA) (55)** (CWThornton) **9-9-3** DeanMcKeown(7) (prom: effrt over 4f out: sn btn)	2	6	9/2[3]	48	—
613[9]	**Trilby (63)** (GRichards) **4-9-10** ACulhane(4) (outpcd fnl 5f: a rr div)	10	7	11/2	45	—
	Lady Swift (44) (KWHogg) **6-8-1**(5) JBramhill(8) (chsd ldrs tl outpcd 3f out: sn wknd: t.o)	30	8	16/1	—	—
928[3]	**Recluse (34)** (WTKemp) **6-7-10b** NCarlisle(5) (prom tl wknd 6f out: wn wl bhd: t.o)	2	9	12/1	—	—

(SP 131.2%) **9 Rn**

3m 20.5 (19.50) CSF £40.08 CT £169.43 TOTE £3.20: £2.40 £5.60 £2.70 (£32.10) Trio £151.00; £72.33 to Beverley 10/5/97 OWNER Mr N. Hetherton (MALTON) BRED N. Hetherton
LONG HANDICAP Recluse 7-8
WEIGHT FOR AGE 4yo-1lb

1039 All On, who has been extremely busy of late, showed just how tough she is and, once she stepped on the pace half a mile out, the race was hers. (11/4: 2/1-3/1)
Highfield Fizz came wide in the straight trying to find better ground, but the winner was in a different league. (12/1)
Well Appointed (IRE) has been flying over hurdles this winter but was made to look very one-paced here. (11/2)
728 Tonnerre was always close enough but, when the struggle began with half a mile to go, he soon decided it was not for him. (4/1)
570 Charity Crusader never looked happy, and brought up the rear until deciding to stay on when it was all over. (6/1)
950 Lord Hastie (USA) ran miserably, running out of fuel once ridden approaching the last half-mile. (9/2)

T/Plpt: £77.70 (148.95 Tckts). T/Qdpt: £9.10 (83.64 Tckts) AA

0564-LINGFIELD (L-H) (Turf Good, Good to soft patches, AWT Standard)

Friday May 9th

WEATHER: unsettled WIND: mod half against

1082 KAHYASI H'CAP (0-80) (4-Y.O+) (Class D)

1-50 (1-53) **1m (Equitrack)** £3,645.60 (£1,087.80: £519.40: £235.20) Stalls: High GOING minus 0.48 sec per fur (FST)

				SP	RR	SF
677[9]	**Pengamon (74)** (HJCollingridge) **5-9-10** JQuinn(3) (b.hind: hld up: hrd rdn over 1f out: led nr fin)	—	1	3/1[1]	84	66
567[7]	**Banzhaf (USA) (78)** (GLMoore) **4-10-0** CandyMorris(11) (a.p: led over 1f out: hrd rdn fnl f: hdd nr fin)	hd	2	20/1	88	70
566[5]	**Sweet Supposin (IRE) (64)** (CADwyer) **6-9-0v** LDettori(2) (lw: hld up: rdn over 4f out: r.o wl ins fnl f)	¾	3	15/2[3]	72	54
	Resist the Force (USA) (55) (CACyzer) **7-8-5** DBiggs(6) (led over 5f out tl over 1f out: one pce)	2½	4	7/1[2]	58	40
	Prime Light (75) (GWragg) **4-9-11** MHills(1) (hdwy over 1f out: nvr nrr)	6	5	15/2[3]	66	48
755[13]	**Ki Chi Saga (USA) (65)** (MMadgwick) **5-9-1** DHolland(10) (lw: led over 1f: lost pl 5f out: rallied over 3f out: wknd over 2f out)	4	6	12/1	48	30
403[5]	**Soaking (75)** (MDIUsher) **7-9-11** DRMcCabe(4) (nvr nr to chal)	¾	7	16/1	57	39
578[2]	**Young Annabel (USA) (71)** (CADwyer) **4-9-7** GCarter(9) (b: led over 6f out tl over 5f out: wknd over 2f out)	1½	8	15/2[3]	50	32
477[13]	**Oberons Boy (IRE) (62)** (SDow) **4-8-12** TQuinn(12) (lw: a bhd)	1¾	9	12/1	37	19
490[9]	**Hawaii Storm (FR) (55)** (DJSffrenchDavis) **9-7-12**(7) KerryBaker(5) (a bhd)	2½	10	25/1	25	7
	Farmost (72) (SirMarkPrescott) **4-9-8** SSanders(7) (lw: prom over 4f)	hd	11	3/1[1]	42	24
	Sand Star (70) (DHaydnJones) **5-9-6** AClark(8) (hld up: rdn over 3f out: sn wknd)	7	12	25/1	26	8

(SP 131.5%) **12 Rn**

1m 37.59 (0.19) CSF £75.69 CT £404.89 TOTE £4.80: £2.30 £5.00 £1.50 (£84.20) Trio £188.60 OWNER Miss Arabella Smallman (EXNING) BRED John Smallman

Pengamon chased the leaders. Throwing down his challenge in the straight, he responded to pressure to get up in the closing stages. (3/1)
Banzhaf (USA) bounced back to form. Sent to the front below the distance, he had a tremendous tussle with the winner and only just lost out. All three wins to date have come on this surface. (20/1)
566 Sweet Supposin (IRE), who has gained all thirteen of his victories on the All-Weather, gets on incredibly well with Dettori who has won on five of the six previous occasions he has ridden him. However, this trip proved far too sharp for him and he was being bustled along before halfway. However, the combination ran on really strongly in the closing stages. A return to a mile and a quarter is required. (15/2)
Resist the Force (USA), who won a novice hurdle for Josh Gifford in November, has returned to Charles Cyzer who trained him when he was last seen on the Flat back in September 1993. Well supported in the market, he was in front before halfway but, collared below the distance, failed to find another gear. (7/1: op 12/1)
Prime Light has been gelded since last year, and was certainly fit enough for this first run in eleven months but, although staying on from the back of the field from below the distance, never threatened to get into it. (15/2: 5/1-8/1)
490 Ki Chi Saga (USA) was outpaced five furlongs from home but, after trying to get back into it running down the hill, was a spent force over two furlongs from home. (12/1: 8/1-14/1)
Farmost was a model of consistency last year, winning six of his ten starts and finishing second on another three occasions. He looked in tremendous shape for this reappearance but was a bitter disappointment, and was going in reverse over three furlongs from home. This run was surely far too bad to be true. (3/1)

1083 GOLDEN HORSESHOE H'CAP (0-70) (3-Y.O+) (Class E)

2-20 (2-22) **5f** £3,018.25 (£901.00: £430.50: £195.25) Stalls: High GOING minus 0.35 sec per fur (F)

				SP	RR	SF
1046[5]	**Runs in the Family (46)** (GMMcCourt) **5-8-4b** DHarrison(13) (mde all: rdn out)	—	1	6/1[2]	59	42
786[5]	**Willow Dale (IRE) (67)** (DRCElsworth) **4-9-11** TQuinn(14) (a.p: rdn over 2f out: chsd wnr over 1f out: r.o one pce)	4	2	7/2[1]	67	50

				SP	RR	SF
860[12]	**Polly Golightly (53)** (MBlanshard) **4-8-11b** KDarley(6) (a.p: rdn over 2f out: one pce)	1¾	**3**	14/1	48	31
879[3]	**John O'Dreams (50)** (MrsALMKing) **12-8-8** TSprake(12) (b: rdn over 3f out: hdwy over 1f out: r.o)	hd	**4**	6/1[2]	44	27
834[14]	**Rififi (64)** (RIngram) **4-9-8** SWhitworth(10) (b: lw: rdn over 2f out: hdwy over 1f out: one pce)	2	**5**	10/1[3]	52	35
786[10]	**Mijas (66)** (LMontagueHall) **4-9-7**(3) FLynch(11) (a.p: rdn over 2f out: wknd fnl f)	s.h	**6**	10/1[3]	54	37
	Shavinsky (64) (PHowling) **4-9-8** MRoberts(7) (lw: outpcd: nvr nrr)	½	**7**	14/1	50	33
834[17]	**Mindrace (62)** (KTIvory) **4-9-3**(3) MartinDwyer(9) (b.hind: hld up: rdn over 2f out: sn wknd)	2½	**8**	16/1	40	23
834[10]	**Half Tone (56)** (RMFlower) **5-9-0b** DaneO'Neill(2) (lw: outpcd: nvr nrr)	s.h	**9**	6/1[2]	34	17
792[12]	**Daintree (IRE) (65)** (HJCollingridge) **3-9-0** MRimmer(5) (b.hind: bhd fnl 2f)	3	**10**	20/1	33	7
473[7]	**Superlao (BEL) (39)** (JJBridger) **5-7-11**ow1 FNorton(3) (rdn thrght: chsd ldrs tl wknd 2f out)	1¼	**11**	20/1	3	—
759[15]	**Baptismal Rock (IRE) (51)** (BJCurley) **3-8-0** JQuinn(8) (lw: a bhd)	1	**12**	25/1	12	—
768[6]	**Third Party (70)** (SDow) **3-9-5** WRyan(1) (a bhd)	3	**13**	14/1	22	—
				(SP 122.5%)	**13 Rn**	

57.91 secs (0.91) CSF £24.68 CT £273.69 TOTE £5.90: £2.30 £1.40 £4.70 (£9.60) Trio £125.40 OWNER Mr Geoffrey Greenwood (WANTAGE)
BRED Mr and Mrs J. K. S. Cresswell
LONG HANDICAP Superlao (BEL) 7-6
WEIGHT FOR AGE 3yo-9lb

1046 Runs in the Family, unplaced on the sand at Southwell the previous day, was a different proposition on this rain-softened ground. Happier for the return to grass, she made every post a winning one and was ridden along to keep her rivals at bay. Her only previous victory also came with some cut. (6/1)

786 Willow Dale (IRE), who has been falling down the handicap, was rousted along to take second place below the distance but, try as she might, failed to reel in the winner. (7/2)

Polly Golightly, whose only handicap win came in November 1995 off a mark of 77, has tumbled in the weights following a string of poor efforts and was racing off just 53 here. Consequently she ran a lot better, playing a leading role from the outset before tapped for toe in the final quarter-mile. (14/1)

879 John O'Dreams may be an old-age pensioner, but he struggled on from the back of the field, only just failing to take third prize. (6/1: 4/1-13/2)

364 Rififi tried to get closer below the distance, but could then make no further impression. (10/1)

488 Mijas is not very consistent and, having played an active role, tired in the final furlong. (10/1)

1084 RACING CHANNEL STEVE WOOD MEMORIAL NOVICE STKS (2-Y.O) (Class D)

2-50 (2-57) **5f** £3,064.00 (£913.00: £435.00: £196.00) Stalls: High GOING minus 0.35 sec per fur (F)

				SP	RR	SF
884[3]	**Prince Foley** (WGMTurner) **2-8-7**(7) DMcGaffin(8) (lw: mde virtually all: pushed out)	—	**1**	2/1[2]	80	29
850*	**Smooth Sailing** (KMcAuliffe) **2-9-4** JReid(3) (a.p: ev ch over 1f out: unable qckn)	1¾	**2**	7/4[1]	78	27
880[3]	**Whisky Mack (IRE)** (RHannon) **2-8-12** DaneO'Neill(5) (lw: bolted bef s: rdn & lost pl over 3f out: rallied over 1f out: r.o)	nk	**3**	3/1[3]	71	20
	English Lady (IRE) (MJHaynes) **2-8-7** TQuinn(2) (unf: lw: rdn thrght: chsd ldrs: hrd rdn over 1f out: one pce)	½	**4**	20/1	65	14
	High Money (GLewis) **2-8-12** PaulEddery(6) (w'like: bit bkwd: dwlt: outpcd: hdwy fnl f: nvr nrr)	2½	**5**	7/1	62	11
850[10]	**Basic Style** (NACallaghan) **2-8-12** SDrowne(1) (a bhd)	7	**6**	16/1	39	—
880[10]	**Solway Lass (IRE)** (PEccles) **2-8-7** CRutter(9) (spd over 3f)	½	**7**	50/1	33	—
	Highbury Legend (BobJones) **2-8-12** NDay(4) (neat: lw: a bhd)	s.h	**8**	14/1	38	—
985[6]	**Sergeant Imp (IRE)** (PMitchell) **2-8-9**(3) MHenry(7) (lw: spd over 3f)	1	**9**	20/1	35	—
				(SP 131.2%)	**9 Rn**	

59.23 secs (2.23) CSF £6.21 TOTE £3.20: £1.40 £1.40 £1.30 (£3.40) Trio £3.30 OWNER Foley Steelstock (SHERBORNE) BRED Ian Slocock

884 Prince Foley has been running really well this season and, travelling strongly, made all the running, needing only to be shaken up to have the situation nicely in hand. (2/1)

850* Smooth Sailing probably appreciated the rain-softened conditions - he suffered from sore shins on the firm ground on his Leicester debut - and had every chance below the distance before put in his place by the winner. (7/4)

880 Whisky Mack (IRE) looked really well beforehand but unfortunately, having got down to the start safely, then took off with his jockey for another two-and-a-half furlongs. His rider wisely dismounted and ambled back with him, but the incident must have taken quite a bit out of the colt. Losing his pitch over three furlongs from home, O'Neill got down to some serious work, and the combination ran on nicely from below the distance. He should soon be winning. (3/1: op 7/4)

English Lady (IRE) needs time to develop, but looked in good shape in the paddock. Bustled along virtually throughout, she chased the leaders but failed to quicken from below the distance. (20/1)

High Money has got some strength about him but looked in need of this and, after failing to go the early pace, made a little late headway. (7/1: 5/1-8/1)

1085 HAVANA HORSE (UK) LIMITED STKS (0-90) (3-Y.O+) (Class C)

3-20 (3-22) **7f 140y** £5,162.75 (£1,538.00: £732.50: £329.75) Stalls: High GOING minus 0.35 sec per fur (F)

				SP	RR	SF
	Lilli Claire (86) (AGFoster) **4-9-4** TSprake(5) (hld up: led 2f out: shkn up over 1f out: comf)	—	**1**	8/1	98+	41
	Crown Court (USA) (89) (LMCumani) **4-9-7** JReid(2) (b: lw: hld up: led over 2f out: sn hdd: unable qckn)	4	**2**	13/8[1]	93	36
892[5]	**Chewit (88)** (GLMoore) **5-9-7** CandyMorris(1) (hld up: hrd rdn over 2f out: one pce)	7	**3**	15/8[2]	78	21
	Lynton Lad (70) (CPEBrooks) **5-9-7** TQuinn(7) (a.p: rdn over 2f out: sn wknd)	4	**4**	25/1	70	13
450[16]	**Whittle Rock (86)** (MrsMReveley) **4-9-4** KDarley(3) (a bhd)	2	**5**	5/1[3]	62	5
791[W]	**Move With Edes (69)** (WGMTurner) **5-9-2**(5) DSweeney(6) (w ldr: led over 3f out tl over 2f out: sn wknd)	8	**6**	25/1	49	—
738[13]	**Al Abraq (IRE) (89)** (JWHills) **4-9-7** DHolland(4) (lw: led 4f: wkng whn virtually p.u over 1f out)	15	**7**	7/1	17	—
				(SP 120.8%)	**7 Rn**	

1m 31.76 (2.76) CSF £21.04 TOTE £16.80: £5.80 £1.60 (£23.30) OWNER Mr C. Leafe (LAMBOURN) BRED Roger C. Denton

Lilli Claire made a very pleasing return to action. Cruising into the lead on the bridle, she was shaken up to comfortably dispose of her rivals. (8/1: 11/2-9/1)

Crown Court (USA), who was only going to run if there was overnight rain, got the ground he wanted. Looking big and well beforehand, he gained a slender advantage over a quarter-of-a-mile from home, but he was soon passed by the winner and put in his place. (13/8)

892 Chewit, who ran well in last week's Victoria Cup, came under pressure over two furlongs from home but, racing with his tongue hanging out, could only go up and down in the same place. He has gained all five of his wins here - two on grass and three on the All-Weather. (15/8)

Lynton Lad, who ran badly after his seasonal debut last year, was having his first run in eleven months and played an active role until lack of a recent run took its toll. (25/1)

Whittle Rock made the long journey down from the north, but was always at the back of the field. (5/1)

Move With Edes had a very stiff task at the weights - he was up to 20lb worse off with many of his rivals on adjusted ratings - and, after showing in front in the middle part of the race, was a spent force two furlongs from home. (25/1)
Al Abraq (IRE) (7/1: 5/1-8/1)

1086 LADY O H'CAP (0-70) (3-Y.O+ F & M) (Class E)

3-50 (3-50) **1m 2f (Equitrack)** £3,018.25 (£901.00: £430.50: £195.25) Stalls: Low GOING minus 0.48 sec per fur (FST)

				SP	RR	SF
838[5]	**Mono Lady (IRE) (63)** (DHaydnJones) **4-9-7b** AClark(11) (dwlt: gd hdwy over 3f out: led over 1f out: pushed out)	—	**1**	10/1	77	57
566[7]	**Calendula (57)** (DMorley) **4-9-1** GCarter(1) (led over 8f: unable qckn)	6	**2**	10/1	61	41
1001[19]	**Worldwide Elsie (USA) (55)** (ICampbell) **4-8-13b**[1] RPrice(3) (lw: a.p: ev ch over 1f out: one pce)	1¾	**3**	25/1	57	37
895[6]	**Mimosa (56)** (SDow) **4-9-0** TQuinn(12) (lw: rdn over 4f out: hdwy over 1f out: nvr nrr)	5	**4**	9/2[2]	50	30
753[5]	**Efficacious (IRE) (38)** (PEccles) **4-7-10b** JLowe(2) (lw: chsd ldrs over 7f)	nk	**5**	25/1	31	11
	Bubble Wings (FR) (70) (SPCWoods) **5-10-0** WRyan(6) (nvr nr to chal)	10	**6**	15/8[1]	47	27
	Sandicliffe (USA) (50) (BWHills) **4-8-8** MHills(8) (sme hdwy 5f out: wknd over 3f out)	nk	**7**	14/1	27	7
857[11]	**Shanghai Lil (55)** (MJFetherston-Godley) **5-8-13** FNorton(5) (hld up: rdn over 4f out: wknd over 3f out)	1¾	**8**	7/1[3]	29	9
796[3]	**Classic Beauty (IRE) (58)** (SCWilliams) **4-9-2** KDarley(7) (prom over 6f)	4	**9**	7/1[3]	25	5
532[12]	**Biba (IRE) (53)** (RBoss) **3-7-10** JQuinn(4) (prom 5f)	9	**10**	25/1	6	—
	Alisura (49) (DTThom) **4-8-7** NVarley(9) (bhd fnl 6f)	5	**11**	25/1	—	—
1009[8]	**Pearl Dawn (IRE) (40)** (PCClarke) **7-7-12** NAdams(10) (bhd fnl 5f)	¾	**12**	14/1	—	—

(SP 124.9%) **12 Rn**

2m 5.38 (1.08) CSF £96.85 CT £2,186.49 TOTE £15.00: £2.40 £4.30 £7.20 (£41.20) Trio £488.70; £68.84 to Beverley 10/5/97 OWNER Monolithic Refractories Ltd (PONTYPRIDD) BRED Dr. Michael Smurfit
LONG HANDICAP Biba (IRE) 7-7 Efficacious (IRE) 7-4
WEIGHT FOR AGE 3yo-15lb
OFFICIAL EXPLANATION **Bubble Wings (FR): did not act on the ground and resented the kickback.**
838 Mono Lady (IRE) put up a polished display to win off her highest-ever mark. Making giant strides through the field over three furlongs from home, she cruised into the lead below the distance and needed only to be shaken up to sprint away. (10/1: 7/1-11/1)
400 Calendula attempted to make all the running but, collared by the winner below the distance, was firmly put in her place. Both her wins to date have come over a mile and a half, and a step back up in trip would surely help. (10/1)
796 Worldwide Elsie (USA), fitted with blinkers for the first time, ran much better as a result, and had every chance below the distance before tapped for toe. (25/1)
895 Mimosa is not easy to win with, and one victory from twenty-nine starts says it all. (9/2)
487 Efficacious (IRE) is a poor performer and remains a maiden after thirty-one attempts. (25/1)
Bubble Wings (FR) never threatened to get in a serious challenge, and her trainer reported that she failed to handle the surface or the kickback. (15/8: 3/1-7/4)
857 Shanghai Lil (7/1: 4/1-8/1)
796 Classic Beauty (IRE) (7/1: op 4/1)

1087 TEENOSO MAIDEN STKS (I) (3-Y.O+) (Class D)

4-20 (4-23) **7f** £3,190.60 (£947.80: £449.40: £200.20) Stalls: High GOING minus 0.35 sec per fur (F)

				SP	RR	SF
	Rock Falcon (IRE) (LadyHerries) **4-9-10** AClark(12) (hld up: led 1f out: rdn out)	—	**1**	33/1	86	36
	Giko (MissGayKelleway) **3-8-5**(7) AngelaGallimore(8) (w'like: a.p: led over 2f out to 1f out: unable qckn)	1¾	**2**	25/1	82	20
795[6]	**Night Express** (BHanbury) **3-8-12** MRimmer(11) (a.p: rdn over 2f out: wknd over 1f out)	8	**3**	12/1[3]	64	2
795[5]	**Gharib (USA)** (ACStewart) **3-8-12** MRoberts(10) (lw: led over 2f: lost pl over 3f out: one pce)	1½	**4**	9/4[2]	60	—
	Mowjood (USA) (MRStoute) **3-8-12** KDarley(5) (lost pl over 4f out: no hdwy fnl 3f)	1	**5**	12/1[3]	58	—
768[3]	**Prince Zando** (CAHorgan) **3-8-12** MFenton(6) (lost pl over 4f out: no hdwy fnl 3f)	1¼	**6**	20/1	55	—
	Flying Colours (IRE) (CJBenstead) **3-8-7** AMcGlone(1) (bkwd: nvr nrr)	4	**7**	66/1	41	—
503[2]	**Musharak** (JLDunlop) **3-8-12** RHills(2) (b.hind: a.p: led over 4f out tl over 2f out: sn wknd)	s.h	**8**	4/5[1]	46	—
	Sharp Deed (IRE) (PJMakin) **3-8-12** DHolland(4) (a bhd)	5	**9**	33/1	35	—
768[9]	**Little Annie** (GLMoore) **3-8-7** CandyMorris(7) (bhd fnl 3f)	7	**10**	66/1	14	—
	My Girl Lucy (PMitchell) **3-8-4**(3) MHenry(9) (a bhd)	14	**11**	66/1	—	—
	Barbury Ballad (IRE) (MJHeaton-Ellis) **3-8-12** SSanders(3) (w'like: bhd fnl 4f)	22	**12**	33/1	—	—

(SP 123.6%) **12 Rn**

1m 24.62 (3.42) CSF £592.67 TOTE £35.30: £4.70 £3.00 £2.10 (£366.80) Trio £383.50 OWNER Mr E. Reitel (LITTLEHAMPTON) BRED Juddmonte Farms
WEIGHT FOR AGE 3yo-12lb
OFFICIAL EXPLANATION **Musharak: lost his action over a furlong out.**
Rock Falcon (IRE), a half-brother to Lancashire Oaks winner Rainbow Lake, was sold by Khalid Abdullah for 8,500 gns at the 1995 December Sales. Making a belated debut, this chestnut gelding travelled well throughout the contest and, shaken up to lead a furlong from home, pulled well clear with the runner-up. (33/1)
Giko, a very plain individual who was sold by Sheikh Mohammed for just 4,500 gns at the Autumn Sales last year, has since been gelded. Nevertheless, he made a very pleasing debut, moving to the front over a quarter of a mile from home. Headed a furlong out, he failed to quicken with the winner but still finished well clear of the remainder. (25/1)
795 Night Express was never far away, but was left for dead by the front two from below the distance. (12/1: 8/1-14/1)
795 Gharib (USA) was running over a patently inadequate trip, and it was no surprise to see him lose his pitch at halfway. He struggled on again in the closing stages but never threatened to get near the front three. He is now qualified for handicaps and, when stepped up considerably in distance, looks one to note with interest. (9/4)
Mowjood (USA), making his seasonal bow, got outpaced over half a mile from home and was making little impression in the last three furlongs. He is now qualified for handicaps and will do better over further. (12/1: 5/1-14/1)

1088 TEENOSO MAIDEN STKS (II) (3-Y.O+) (Class D)

4-50 (4-52) **7f** £3,190.60 (£947.80: £449.40: £200.20) Stalls: High GOING minus 0.35 sec per fur (F)

				SP	RR	SF
740[5]	**Praeditus (77)** (RHannon) **3-8-12** DaneO'Neill(10) (mde virtually all: drvn out)	—	**1**	7/4[1]	82	18
73[10]	**Perfect Pal (IRE)** (MissGayKelleway) **6-9-10** NDay(9) (hdwy over 2f out: ev ch ins fnl f: r.o)	nk	**2**	11/2[3]	81	29
674[9]	**Regal Thunder (USA)** (MRStoute) **3-8-12** KDarley(12) (a.p: rdn over 2f out: unable qckn)	1¾	**3**	9/4[2]	77	13
586[9]	**March Crusader** (BHanbury) **3-8-12** WRyan(5) (lw: a.p: rdn over 2f out: one pce)	1½	**4**	6/1	74	10

				SP	RR	SF
	Ardent (CJBenstead) **3-8-12** AMcGlone(3) (bit bkwd: a.p: ev ch over 2f out: wknd over 1f out)	6	**5**	33/1	60	—
	Balfour Lady (JARToller) **3-8-7** SSanders(6) (w'like: bkwd: a.p: rdn over 2f out: sn wknd)	hd	**6**	20/1	55	—
	Such Boldness (RAkehurst) **3-8-12** AClark(8) (lw: nvr nr to chal)	3	**7**	16/1	53	—
484^{10}	**Fancy Design (IRE) (31)** (PMitchell) **4-9-5v** MRoberts(2) (racd alone far side: prom over 5f)	2½	**8**	100/1	42	—
	Durable George (JJBridger) **3-8-12** FNorton(11) (neat: s.s: a bhd)	5	**9**	66/1	36	—
	Keen Companion (TJNaughton) **4-9-2**(3) JDSmith(7) (bit bkwd: s.s: a bhd)	3	**10**	33/1	24	—
	Secret Strength (LadyHerries) **3-8-12** DeclanO'Shea(1) (unf: scope: bhd fnl 3f)	½	**11**	16/1	28	—
989^{13}	**Miss Imp (IRE)** (PMitchell) **3-8-4**(3) MHenry(4) (b.nr fore: bhd fnl 4f: t.o)	dist	**12**	100/1	—	—
				(SP 122.7%)	**12 Rn**	

1m 25.2 (4.00) CSF £10.90 TOTE £3.20: £1.40 £2.00 £1.70 (£12.60) Trio £5.80 OWNER Mr B. A. Kilpatrick (MARLBOROUGH) BRED Deerfield Farm

WEIGHT FOR AGE 3yo-12lb

740 Praeditus made virtually all the running and, responding to pressure, just managed to hold off the persistent runner-up. (7/4)

73 Perfect Pal (IRE), winner of two National Hunt Flat races in the spring of 1995, has shown nothing in three runs over hurdles or an All-Weather maiden since his return from a twenty-month absence. This distance looked far too sharp for him but he ran surprisingly well and, launching his challenge from below the distance, had a tremendous tussle with the winner, only just losing out. Over a more suitable trip, he should soon find a race. (11/2)

674 Regal Thunder (USA) was a leading light from the off, but failed to quicken in the final quarter-mile. (9/4: 6/4-5/2)

586 March Crusader looked extremely well beforehand and stepped up on considerably on his debut, if failing to find another gear in the last two furlongs. (6/1)

Ardent did not look fully fit for this return, but still had every chance over a quarter-of-a-mile from home before lack of a recent run took its toll. (33/1)

Balfour Lady, a medium-sized filly, was carrying a lot of surplus flesh and, after playing an active role, tired two furlongs from home as lack of peak fitness took its toll. (20/1)

T/Jkpt: Not won; £10,783.03 to Beverley 10/5/97. T/Plpt: £3,537.00 (4.91 Tckts). T/Qdpt: £846.50 (0.5 Tckts); £571.99 to Beverley 10/5/97 AK

0882-NOTTINGHAM (L-H) (Good, Good to soft patches)
Friday May 9th
WEATHER: fine WIND: slt against

1089 COLWICK PARK APPRENTICE H'CAP (0-70) (3-Y.O+) (Class G)
6-00 (6-01) **6f 15y** £1,984.50 (£547.00: £259.50) Stalls: Low GOING: 0.53 sec per fur (GS)

				SP	RR	SF
760^{4}	**Sweet Mate (45)** (SRBowring) **5-7-10b**(7)ow1 FBoyle(10) (b.hind: chsd ldrs: led ins fnl f: drvn clr)	—	**1**	10/1	47	37
887^{13}	**Nellie North (53)** (GMMcCourt) **4-8-8b**(3) AEddery(8) (s.i.s: hdwy ½-wy: ev ch over 1f out: unable qckn)	3½	**2**	20/1	46	37
585^{10}	**Gay Breeze (42)** (PSFelgate) **4-7-7**(7) DarrenWilliams(7) (a.p: led over 1f out tl ins fnl f)	nk	**3**	12/1	34	25
	Great Hall (40) (PDCundell) **8-7-7**(5) CCogan(9) (b.hind: mid div: rdn 2f out: styd on wl fnl f)	nk	**4**	33/1	31	22
889^{5}	**Aquatic Queen (56)** (RJWeaver) **3-7-13**(5)ow3 TField(2) (b.hind: lw: led & sn clr: drifted rt fr ½-wy: hdd over 1f out: wknd)	2	**5**	16/1	42	20
779^{10}	**Lochon (48)** (MrsNMacauley) **6-8-3**(3) JoHunnam(1) (b: prom far side: rdn & wknd appr fnl f)	2½	**6**	25/1	27	18
980^{4}	**Nineacres (64)** (NMBabbage) **6-9-8v** SophieMitchell(16) (dwlt: sn rcvrd: led stands' side after 2f: no ch appr fnl f)	nk	**7**	7/1^{2}	43	34
	Croeso Cynnes (70) (BPalling) **4-9-9**(5) CLowther(3) (bhd far side: r.o fnl 2f: nvr nrr)	s.h	**8**	14/1	48	39
1048^{9}	**Leigh Crofter (50)** (PDCundell) **8-8-5b**(3) AimeeCook(13) (prom stands' side: rdn 2f out: sn btn)	1¾	**9**	20/1	24	15
956^{5}	**Millesime (IRE) (55)** (MartynWane) **5-8-13** GParkin(6) (swvd lft s: spd far side 4f)	3	**10**	12/1	21	12
873^{12}	**Royal Emblem (55)** (AGFoster) **3-8-0**(3) GMilligan(18) (spd 2f: sn bhd)	s.h	**11**	25/1	21	2
*361**	**Polgwynne (54)** (BSmart) **3-8-2** ADaly(4) (lw: hmpd s: sn bhd & outpcd)	½	**12**	10/1	18	—
	Lorins Gold (38) (AndrewTurnell) **7-7-5**(5) PDoe(15) (b.nr hind: led stands' side 2f: wknd 2f out)	¾	**13**	20/1	—	—
734*	**Meranti (55)** (JMBradley) **4-8-10**(3) RFfrench(12) (lw: prom: ev ch over 1f out: wknd qckly)	1	**14**	5/2^{1}	15	6
827^{6}	**Bataleur (59)** (MissJBower) **4-9-3** RMullen(5) (lw: hmpd s: a bhd)	3½	**15**	8/1^{3}	10	1
638^{7}	**Mellors (IRE) (60)** (MJHeaton-Ellis) **4-8-13v**1(5) JFowle(14) (a in rr)	1¾	**16**	14/1	6	—
896^{4}	**Move Smartly (IRE) (53)** (MrsLStubbs) **7-8-11v** GFaulkner(17) (lw: wl bhd fr ½-wy: t.o)	4	**17**	16/1	—	—
	Expectation (IRE) (64) (PRWebber) **3-8-7**(5) DavidO'Neill(11) (bit bkwd: a bhd: t.o)	nk	**18**	20/1	—	—
				(SP 140.5%)	**18 Rn**	

1m 18.3 (6.80) CSF £194.93 CT £2,269.80 TOTE £16.60: £4.10 £6.00 £2.90 £3.20 (£164.60) Trio £397.90; £336.27 to Beverley 11/5/97

OWNER Mr S. R. Bowring (EDWINSTOWE) BRED T. Barratt

LONG HANDICAP Lorins Gold 7-8

WEIGHT FOR AGE 3yo-10lb

STEWARDS' ENQUIRY Parkin susp. 18-22/5/97 (careless riding).

IN-FOCUS: **This was Finbarr Boyle's first winner.**

760 Sweet Mate, gaining his first success on turf, burst through to lead two hundred yards out and won going away. (10/1)

Nellie North, brought back to sprinting, showed a return to form and, if she remains in her own class, is still capable of winning races. (20/1)

Gay Breeze, showing a good action to post, ran his best race yet and he would now seem to be getting it together. (12/1: 7/1-14/1)

Great Hall only does as much as he wants, but his young pilot was getting him working in the latter stages, and he was staying on stoutly nearing the finish. (33/1)

889 Aquatic Queen, allowed to bowl along at the head of affairs, veered over to the centre of the track from halfway, and she had run her race approaching the final furlong. (16/1)

593 Lochon showed up with the pace on the far rail, but could never summon up the speed to deliver her challenge. (25/1)

980 Nineacres, drawn on the less favoured stands' side, soon led that group but they were always some way adrift of the principals. (7/1)

734* Meranti pressed the leaders all the way, and still had a chance approaching the final furlong, but he stopped to nothing as if something was amiss. (5/2)

512 Mellors (IRE) (14/1: 10/1-16/1)

1090 BRITISH BUS MEDIAN AUCTION MAIDEN STKS (3-Y.O) (Class E)
6-25 (6-25) **6f 15y** £3,226.25 (£965.00: £462.50: £211.25) Stalls: Low GOING: 0.53 sec per fur (GS)

				SP	RR	SF
693^{8}	**Soviet Leader** (RGuest) **3-9-0** KFallon(11) (trckd ldrs: rdn to ld over 1f out: r.o strly)	—	**1**	5/1^{3}	81	48

	Frederick James (MJHeaton-Ellis) **3-9-0** SWhitworth(9) (hdwy ½-wy: rdn to ld wl over 1f out: sn hdd: one pce) 4	**2**	5/1 3	71	38
	Farley Green (HCandy) **3-8-9** GHind(12) (lengthy: unf: bit bkwd: hdwy 2f out: r.o wl fnl f)....nk	**3**	6/1	65	32
	Tellion (MajorWRHern) **3-9-0** TSprake(7) (leggy: lt-f: hld up & plld hrd: hdwy 2f out: r.o wl fnl f)....1¼	**4**	8/1	66	33
	Inflation (RFJohnsonHoughton) **3-8-9** JReid(4) (prom tl wknd appr fnl f)....1	**5**	100/30 1	59	26
768 5	**Ocker (IRE) (76)** (MHTompkins) **3-9-0** RCochrane(13) (chsd ldrs: rdn 2f out: no imp) 5	**6**	4/1 2	51	18
	Alpine Music (IRE) (JMBradley) **3-8-9**(5) RFfrench(3) (bit bkwd: a outpcd) 1	**7**	50/1	48	15
845 2	**Always Alight (65)** (KRBurke) **3-9-0b** WJO'Connor(1) (lw: led: sn clr: wknd & hdd wl over 1f out) 2	**8**	5/1 3	43	10
	Prospering (JGSmyth-Osbourne) **3-8-9** DHarrison(6) (neat: unf: bit bkwd: s.i.s: a outpcd)....1¾	**9**	12/1	33	—
868 12	**Sea Ya Maite** (SRBowring) **3-9-0** SWebster(10) (b: lw: prom 4f)....2½	**10**	25/1	31	—
768 7	**Hippy Chick** (JRJenkins) **3-8-9** BDoyle(5) (lw: a bhd & outpcd)....½	**11**	20/1	25	—
874 5	**Bison Belting** (JAGlover) **3-8-7**(7) TPengkerego(2) (early spd: bhd fr ½-wy: t.o)....16	**12**	10/1	—	—
	Blue Cheese (MrsNMacauley) **3-8-6**(3) DO'Donohoe(8) (leggy: bkwd: s.s: a bhd: t.o fnl 2f) ....dist	**13**	16/1	—	—
			(SP 151.7%)		**13 Rn**

1m 18.3 (6.80) CSF £35.21 TOTE £6.20: £2.40 £2.40 £5.30 (£40.50) Trio £116.00; £102.94 to Beverley 11/5/97 OWNER Matthews Breeding and Racing (NEWMARKET) BRED Lord Matthews

OFFICIAL EXPLANATION **Blue Cheese: was found to be distressed.**

Soviet Leader, taking a step down in class, won very easily indeed and could be the sort to go on improving. (5/1)

Frederick James turned in a very promising performance on this seasonal debut and, if he remains in this grade, should have little trouble in going one better. (5/1)

Farley Green needed the run to put an edge on her, but she performed with credit and there are races to be won. (6/1)

Tellion, a lightly-made gelding who is bred to need much further, took some settling in the early stages, but he was picking up well inside the final furlong and, if brought along steadily, should make the grade. (8/1)

Inflation, who showed promise on both his outings last year, was in the firing line holding every chance until fading approaching the final furlong. She is bred for speed and may do better at the minimum trip. (100/30)

768 Ocker (IRE) held his pitch in the chasing group until demands proved too much for him from below the distance. (4/1)

845 Always Alight broke smartly to set a scorching pace on the far rail, but he obviously did too much too soon for he was down to a walk on reaching the final furlong. (5/1)

1091 E.B.F. MEDIAN AUCTION NOVICE STKS (2-Y.O F) (Class F)

6-50 (6-54) **5f 13y** £2,600.40 (£719.40: £343.20) Stalls: Low GOING: 0.39 sec per fur (GS)

			SP	RR	SF
	Star (MAJarvis) **2-8-8** DHarrison(8) (w'like: scope: mde virtually all: qcknd clr appr fnl f)....—	**1**	2/1 1	81+	43
836 14	**Positive Air** (BAMcMahon) **2-8-8** KFallon(6) (swtg: chsd ldrs: drvn along over 2f out: kpt on: no ch w wnr).....6	**2**	9/2 2	62	24
	High Gain (PHowling) **2-8-8** PaulEddery(7) (w'like: unf: dwlt: sn trckng ldrs: rdn & r.o appr fnl f).....nk	**3**	10/1	61	23
682 8	**Summer Day Blues (IRE)** (CMurray) **2-8-8** JReid(9) (w ldrs: shkn up over 2f out: sn outpcd) 3½	**4**	8/1	50	12
*872**	**My Bet** (MWEasterby) **2-8-7**(5) GParkin(4) (lw: prom: rdn 2f out: sn btn)....nk	**5**	13/2	53	15
	Scolding (KAMorgan) **2-8-8** RCochrane(5) (lengthy: unf: s.s: a bhd: t.o)....11	**6**	6/1 3	14	—
739 10	**Magical Dancer (IRE)** (MrsPNDutfield) **2-8-8** SDrowne(1) (racd alone far side: spd to ½-wy: t.o) 1	**7**	7/1	11	—
	Jaybee Silver (MHTompkins) **2-8-8** DBiggs(3) (lt-f: bit bkwd: s.i.s: rdn ½-wy: a bhd: t.o) 3	**8**	8/1	2	—
	Lady Anna (JRJenkins) **2-8-8** BDoyle(2) (lengthy: unf: s.i.s: a outpcd: t.o)....1¼	**9**	14/1	—	—
			(SP 129.6%)		**9 Rn**

64.5 secs (5.60) CSF £11.59 TOTE £2.70: £2.00 £2.40 £3.90 (£6.80) Trio £103.80 OWNER Mr T. G. Warner (NEWMARKET) BRED Red House Stud

Star, home-bred from a very useful family, is not quite the finished article as yet and she is still clinging on to her winter coat, but she simply outclassed this opposition to start her career in the best possible fashion. (2/1: evens-9/4)

730 Positive Air is beginning to get the hang of things, and she will not always meet one as useful as the winner. (9/2)

High Gain, an unfurnished filly related to three winners, should have learnt much from this debut and immediate improvement can follow. (10/1)

Summer Day Blues (IRE) appeared much sharper than she did on her debut, but there is still more improvement to come and she is gaining experience all the time. (8/1)

872* My Bet, always struggling to remain in the action, was unable to respond when the winner set sail for home, and she may have been out of her class here. (13/2)

Scolding (6/1: op 10/1)

583 Magical Dancer (IRE) (7/1: 6/1-10/1)

1092 WEATHERBYS PRODUCTION SERVICES LIMITED STKS (0-80) (3-Y.O+) (Class D)

7-20 (7-20) **1m 1f 213y** £3,390.80 (£1,009.40: £480.20: £215.60) Stalls: Low GOING: 0.39 sec per fur (GS)

			SP	RR	SF
887 5	**Capilano Princess (80)** (DHaydnJones) **4-9-5** SDrowne(4) (chsd ldrs: led over 1f out: rdn clr) ....—	**1**	9/2 2	86	51
*395**	**Cyrian (IRE) (75)** (PFICole) **3-8-9** TQuinn(1) (lw: chsd ldr: rdn over 3f out: ev ch over 1f out: nt pce of wnr).....3	**2**	2/1 1	86	36
634 8	**Dawam Allail (IRE) (77)** (MAJarvis) **3-8-7** RCochrane(5) (led tl hdd over 1f out: sn rdn: no ex)....1¼	**3**	6/1 3	82	32
	Alaflak (IRE) (79) (MajorWRHern) **6-9-8** TSprake(6) (b: b.hind: bkwd: trckd ldrs: effrt over 3f out: outpcd 2f out: styd on fnl f)....1½	**4**	7/1	80	45
787 11	**Trojan Risk (80)** (GLewis) **4-9-8** PaulEddery(3) (b: b.hind: stdd s: hld up: hdwy 5f out: no imp fnl 3f) 7	**5**	2/1 1	69	34
789 11	**Palamon (USA) (78)** (JWhite) **4-9-8b1** WJO'Connor(2) (hld up: lost 4f out: sn t.o) 19	**6**	7/1	38	3
			(SP 124.1%)		**6 Rn**

2m 12.7 (10.20) CSF £14.31 TOTE £6.20: £1.90 £1.70 (£13.90) OWNER Mr H. G. Collis (PONTYPRIDD) BRED Mrs O. M. Collis

WEIGHT FOR AGE 3yo-15lb

887 Capilano Princess appreciated the easing of the ground and, gaining command on the run to the final furlong, had no trouble pulling clear. (9/2)

395* Cyrian (IRE), very impressive on his All-Weather success two months ago, was making hard work of it from some way out, and the more-experienced winner left him for dead inside the distance. (2/1: op 5/4)

Dawam Allail (IRE), trying his luck at this longer trip, forced the pace until the winner took his measure and he then had nothing more to give. (6/1)

Alaflak (IRE) carries a lot of condition and he looked far from fully wound-up for this seasonal reappearance, but he was coming back for more after getting outpaced two furlongs out, and he can only improve on this. (7/1)

1093 'STUDENTS IN HALF PRICE' H'CAP (0-60) (3-Y.O+) (Class F)

7-50 (7-52) **1m 1f 213y** £2,277.00 (£627.00: £297.00) Stalls: Low GOING: 0.39 sec per fur (GS)

				SP	RR	SF
838^{9}	**Tonka (58)** (PJMakin) **5-9-12** DHarrison(15) (lw: hld up: hdwy 4f out: rdn to ld wl ins fnl f)	—	**1**	6/1^{1}	69	51
418^{7}	**Elly Fleetfoot (IRE) (51)** (GLMoore) **5-9-5v^{1}** SWhitworth(18) (lw: hdwy 7f out: led wl over 1f out: hdd & no ex fnl 100y)	1¼	**2**	12/1	60	42
933^{13}	**Jean Pierre (56)** (JPearce) **4-9-10** JWeaver(7) (hld up: hdwy 3f out: rdn & r.o wl ins fnl f)	1¾	**3**	7/1^{2}	62	44
857^{3}	**Nicola's Princess (50)** (BAMcMahon) **4-9-4** KFallon(12) (hld up: hdwy over 2f out: nrst fin)	3	**4**	10/1	51	33
330^{5}	**What A Fuss (60)** (BHanbury) **4-10-0** JStack(4) (lw: led tl wl over 1f out: sn hrd rdn: r.o one pce)	¾	**5**	14/1	60	42
*76**	**Arcatura (51)** (CJames) **5-9-5** CRutter(17) (lw: chsd ldrs tl wknd wl over 1f out)	1¼	**6**	10/1	49	31
	Double Rush (IRE) (50) (TGMills) **5-9-4** TQuinn(16) (hld up: hdwy over 3f out: hrd rdn over 1f out: no imp)	3	**7**	6/1^{1}	43	25
476^{10}	**Kristal Breeze (56)** (WRMuir) **5-9-10** JReid(14) (hdwy 7f out: rdn over 3f out: nt trble ldrs)	3½	**8**	9/1	44	26
1001^{20}	**Irish Kinsman (50)** (GHYardley) **4-8-11**(7) CLowther(9) (bit bkwd: prom: no hdwy fnl 3f)	2	**9**	33/1	35	17
857^{4}	**Bentico (53)** (MrsNMacauley) **8-9-7** SWebster(5) (hld up & bhd: nvr nr to chal)	4	**10**	16/1	31	13
687*	**Gold Lance (USA) (50)** (RJO'Sullivan) **4-9-4** RCochrane(6) (trckd ldrs: rdn 3f out: sn btn)	1	**11**	8/1^{3}	27	9
763^{13}	**North Bear (53)** (GMMcCourt) **5-9-0**(7) RStudholme(8) (chsd ldrs 7f: sn lost tch)	5	**12**	20/1	22	4
516^{9}	**Cashaplenty (52)** (NPLittmoden) **4-9-6** TGMcLaughlin(3) (swtg: racd keenly: prom over 6f)	½	**13**	12/1	20	2
	Errant (54) (DJSCosgrove) **5-9-5**(3) DO'Donohoe(11) (b: bit bkwd: reard s: plld hrd: a bhd)	½	**14**	16/1	21	3
864^{15}	**Lila Pedigo (IRE) (58)** (MissJFCraze) **4-9-7**(5) RFfrench(2) (w ldr tl wknd 4f out)	1	**15**	20/1	23	5
516^{6}	**Golden Fawn (50)** (NMBabbage) **4-9-4** VSlattery(1) (chsd ldrs 6f: sn wknd)	nk	**16**	16/1	15	—
567^{6}	**Saltando (IRE) (58)** (PatMitchell) **6-9-9**(3) MartinDwyer(13) (in tch to ½-wy: sn rdn & wknd)	nk	**17**	16/1	22	4
	Comedy River (50) (NEBerry) **10-9-4** GHind(10) (bkwd: hld up: hdwy whn hmpd ent st & over 3f out: wknd 2f out: fin lame)	7	**18**	16/1	3	—
				(SP 144.3%)	**18 Rn**	

2m 13.5 (11.00) CSF £80.59 CT £504.43 TOTE £8.60: £2.30 £3.60 £2.10 £2.00 (£76.30) Trio £321.50; £321.59 to Beverley 11/5/97 OWNER Mrs J. M. West (MARLBOROUGH) BRED Mrs J. Murray-Smith and N. Bowyer

Tonka is not very big but he can carry weight and, ridden with restraint, put his stamp on proceedings inside the final furlong. (6/1)

Elly Fleetfoot (IRE) showed something of a return to form here, but she has proved very in-and-out in the past and is not one to stake your life on. (12/1)

689 Jean Pierre is still struggling to make his mark, but he is running well and fortune will favour him before long. (7/1)

857 Nicola's Princess was certainly not disgraced on this return to the turf, and she is capable of more success. (10/1)

330 What A Fuss, fit from the All-Weather and taking a step down in trip, did a brave job of trying to make all, but he was in trouble soon after passing the quarter-mile post. (14/1)

76* Arcatura, winner of his previous two races on the All-Weather, has had a four-month break since he last ran, and lack of peak fitness began to take its toll below the distance. He should be capable of winning a race on turf. (10/1)

Double Rush (IRE), out of action since the turn of the year, came with a promising-looking run up the centre of the track over two furlongs out, but was unable to pick up when pressure was applied and could well have needed the spin. (6/1)

1094 'NEXT GENERATION OF RACEGOERS' H'CAP (0-70) (3-Y.O) (Class E)

8-20 (8-21) **1m 6f 15y** £3,252.25 (£973.00: £466.50: £213.25) Stalls: Low GOING: 0.39 sec per fur (GS)

				SP	RR	SF
537^{2}	**Tango King (69)** (JLDunlop) **3-9-7** PaulEddery(3) (a chsng ldrs: chal 2f out: hrd rdn to ld wl ins fnl f)	—	**1**	2/1^{1}	76	23
665^{5}	**Jucinda (56)** (JPearce) **3-8-8** BDoyle(15) (a.p: led over 3f out: rdn & edgd rt over 1f out: hdd nr fin)	½	**2**	12/1	62	9
658^{4}	**Mountaineer (IRE) (64)** (MBell) **3-9-2** MFenton(8) (hld up: hdwy over 3f out: styd on u.p fnl f)	½	**3**	8/1^{3}	70	17
670^{7}	**Bisquet-de-Bouche (50)** (RDickin) **3-8-2** CRutter(5) (hld up: hdwy 4f out: rdn & edgd lft: nvr able to chal)	3½	**4**	12/1	52	—
1043^{6}	**Spondulicks (IRE) (54)** (BPJBaugh) **3-8-6** GHind(16) (a.p: ev ch over 3f out: btn 2f out)	½	**5**	14/1	55	2
	Mellwood (IRE) (46) (MHTompkins) **3-7-12** DaleGibson(14) (bkwd: bhd tl sme late hdwy)	6	**6**	16/1	41	—
581^{2}	**Touch'n'go (67)** (MJohnston) **3-9-5** JWeaver(17) (lw: prom: led 8f out tl over 3f out: sn rdn & wknd)	2½	**7**	11/2^{2}	59	6
725^{13}	**Mazara (IRE) (55)** (AGFoster) **3-8-7** TSprake(11) (lw: chsd ldrs tl wknd over 2f out)	2	**8**	16/1	44	—
793^{5}	**Maremma (47)** (DonEnricoIncisa) **3-7-13** KimTinkler(4) (s.i.s: nvr nrr)	¾	**9**	16/1	36	—
793^{4}	**Wildmoor (56)** (JDBethell) **3-8-8** JReid(7) (plld hrd: in tch tl wknd over 2f out)	8	**10**	12/1	35	—
	Le Grand Gousier (USA) (63) (RJRWilliams) **3-9-1** RCochrane(6) (bit bkwd: prom: rdn 6f out: wknd over 3f out)	10	**11**	14/1	31	—
640^{8}	**Warrior King (IRE) (50)** (MrsPNDutfield) **3-8-2** SDrowne(9) (lw: a in rr)	5	**12**	25/1	12	—
837^{6}	**Swallow Breeze (68)** (DrJDScargill) **3-9-3**(3) DO'Donohoe(1) (a in rr)	2	**13**	11/1	28	—
	Clear The Air (59) (PFICole) **3-8-11** TQuinn(13) (chsd ldrs 10f)	4	**14**	8/1^{3}	15	—
658^{5}	**Moorbird (IRE) (62)** (JLHarris) **3-9-0v^{1}** KFallon(10) (nvr trbld ldrs)	1¾	**15**	16/1	16	—
875^{8}	**First Man (44)** (BJLlewellyn) **3-7-10** JLowe(12) (lw: stdd s: hdwy 5f out: wknd 3f out)	1¼	**16**	25/1	—	—
539^{4}	**Alimerjam (45)** (JWhite) **3-7-8**(3) MBaird(2) (led 6f: wknd 4f out: t.o)	16	**17**	14/1	—	—
				(SP 153.6%)	**17 Rn**	

3m 18.7 (20.20) CSF £33.36 CT £180.09 TOTE £2.30: £1.70 £4.30 £1.90 £4.00 (£23.10) Trio £111.90 OWNER Lord Swaythling (ARUNDEL) BRED B. J. Warren

LONG HANDICAP First Man 7-1

STEWARDS' ENQUIRY Rutter susp. 18-19/5/97 (careless riding).

537 Tango King delayed his challenge as late as possible and, though he moved upsides entering the final quarter-mile, was only asked for his effort two hundred yards out. Even then he had to pull out all the stops to get the better of a very persistent rival. (2/1)

665 Jucinda kicked on early in the straight, and battled on despite a tendency to edge right under pressure inside the distance. She was only forced to give best nearing the line. This was by far her best effort yet and compensation awaits. (12/1: op 8/1)

658 Mountaineer (IRE), restrained in the rear over this longer trip, made relentless progress once in line for home and, despite staying on strongly, could not quite reach the leading pair. Out of a mare who won at two miles, this looks to be his kind of trip. (8/1)

Bisquet-de-Bouche, showing her first signs of ability, was unable to mount a serious challenge but she stayed on and is going the right way.(12/1)

906 Spondulicks (IRE) has been promising to win a race, but this extended trip appeared to catch him out and he was labouring for the last quarter-mile. (14/1)

Mellwood (IRE) never got into it, but he stayed on and, with plenty of improvement to come, must not be written off yet. (16/1)

581 Touch'n'go, a very poor mover even on this rain-softened ground, helped share the lead until fading out of contention in the last couple of furlongs. Twice a winner on the All-Weather at shorter trips, that looks to be more his game. (11/2: 4/1-6/1)

T/Plpt: £731.70 (21.15 Tckts). T/Qdpt: £12.90 (95.61 Tckts) IM

0792-**BEVERLEY (R-H) (Good becoming Soft)**

Saturday May 10th

WEATHER: overcast with heavy rain at times WIND: fresh across

1095 KIPLINGCOTE (S) STKS (3-Y.O) (Class F)

2-15 (2-16) **1m 1f 207y** £2,721.00 (£756.00: £363.00) Stalls: High GOING: 0.07 sec per fur (G)

	Horse	Dist	Pos	SP	RR	SF
868[8]	**Father Eddie (50)** (JJO'Neill) **3-8-12** GDuffield(2) (b.nr fore: lw: trckd ldrs: led over 1f out: rdn & r.o)	—	1	6/1[3]	58	25
906[3]	**Skelton Sovereign (IRE) (58)** (RHollinshead) **3-8-9**(3) FLynch(6) (hld up: hdwy 3f out: n.m.r 2f out: ch ins fnl f: nt qckn)	1½	2	15/8[1]	56	23
862[7]	**Rock It Rosie** (DrJDScargill) **3-8-7** MFenton(1) (in tch: hdwy & ev ch over 3f out: rdn & no ex)	3	3	14/1	46	13
862[6]	**Arboreal (USA) (49)** (MrsLStubbs) **3-8-7** SSanders(8) (cl up: led wl over 2f out tl over 1f out: one pce)	hd	4	11/1	46	13
862[5]	**Rochea (58)** (MrsNMacauley) **3-8-7** SWebster(11) (lw: plld hrd: led tl hdd wl over 2f out: rdn & grad wknd)	2½	5	11/4[2]	42	9
582[11]	**Foolish Flutter (IRE) (37)** (RBastiman) **3-8-7** DaleGibson(4) (in tch: no hdwy fnl 3f)	3	6	14/1	37	4
862[11]	**Guard A Dream (IRE)** (MrsMReveley) **3-8-12** ACulhane(9) (lw: outpcd & bhd fr ½-wy)	8	7	12/1	29	—
785[15]	**Bali-Pet (45)** (JParkes) **3-8-12** DHarrison(7) (dwlt: sn prom: wknd fnl 3f)	10	8	15/2	13	—
862[12]	**Missed May (30)** (BPJBaugh) **3-8-0**(7) RWinston(5) (plld hrd: chsd ldrs to st: sn lost pl)	6	9	33/1	—	—
862[10]	**Marys Path** (SGollings) **3-8-7** PaulEddery(3) (lost tch fnl 4f)	2½	10	25/1	—	—
				(SP 123.6%)	**10 Rn**	

2m 12.7 (9.60) CSF £17.08 TOTE £6.40: £1.90 £1.40 £2.90 (£8.70) Trio £43.70 OWNER Mr C. H. Stevens (PENRITH) BRED The Earl of Suffolk
Bt in 6,800 gns

609 Father Eddie took a drop in class here and did the job well, staying on strongly. (6/1)
906 Skelton Sovereign (IRE) has seen plenty of action, but is a difficult customer to win with and he was comprehensively out-battled here. (15/8)
Rock It Rosie, wearing a tongue-strap for the first time, showed her first signs of form and there could be a race in her. (14/1)
Arboreal (USA) had her chances until the stiff finish found her out. (11/1)
862 Rochea pulls hard and is her own worst enemy. (11/4: 4/1-2/1)

1096 HYPAC H'CAP (0-70) (3-Y.O) (Class E)

2-45 (2-47) **7f 100y** £3,874.75 (£1,168.00: £566.50: £265.75) Stalls: High GOING: 0.07 sec per fur (G)

	Horse	Dist	Pos	SP	RR	SF
840[4]	**Carlton (IRE) (53)** (GLewis) **3-8-4** PaulEddery(16) (lw: chsd ldrs: led wl over 1f out: styd on strly)	—	1	2/1[1]	66	36
748[3]	**In Good Nick (63)** (MWEasterby) **3-8-9b**(5) GParkin(8) (chsd ldrs: chal 3f out: led 2f out: sn hdd & kpt on same pce)	3½	2	12/1	69	39
886[3]	**Mardrew (61)** (TTClement) **3-8-7**(5) ADaly(6) (mid div: hdwy 3f out: styd on: nvr able chal)	1½	3	7/1[2]	63	33
845[16]	**Rude Awakening (70)** (CWFairhurst) **3-9-7** DeanMcKeown(9) (lw: hmpd st: mid div: styd on u.p fnl 2f: nrst fin)	1¼	4	25/1	70	40
883[12]	**Legend of Aragon (56)** (JAGlover) **3-8-7** GDuffield(14) (cl up: led wl over 2f out: hdd 2f out: wknd)	½	5	12/1	55	25
	Bollero (IRE) (67) (JBerry) **3-8-13**(5) PFessey(7) (s.i.s: hdwy 3f out: nrst fin)	2½	6	16/1	60	30
855[3]	**Don't Worry Mike (57)** (FHLee) **3-8-8** ACulhane(5) (chsd ldrs tl wknd fnl 2½f)	4	7	14/1	42	12
	Dee Pee Tee Cee (IRE) (54) (MWEasterby) **3-8-5** TLucas(12) (bit bkwd: nvr nr to chal)	2½	8	20/1	33	3
	Hiltons Executive (IRE) (46) (EJAlston) **3-7-11** DWright(15) (led tl hdd & wknd wl over 2f out)	4	9	25/1	17	—
845[5]	**C-Harry (IRE) (63)** (RHollinshead) **3-8-11**(3) FLynch(1) (in tch: effrt ent st: outpcd fnl 2f)	s.h	10	12/1	34	4
	Ginger Rogers (58) (DWPArbuthnot) **3-8-9** CRutter(10) (in tch over 4f)	½	11	25/1	27	—
	Court Express (67) (TJEtherington) **3-9-4** LCharnock(2) (bit bkwd: dwlt: a rr div)	½	12	20/1	35	5
886[15]	**Mungo Park (59)** (MrsJRRamsden) **3-8-10** JFortune(13) (lw: hld up & a bhd)	2½	13	8/1[3]	22	—
547[7]	**Al Ava Consonant (60)** (JDBethell) **3-8-11** OUrbina(17) (sn pushed along: hmpd after 2f: sn bhd)	½	14	20/1	22	—
*873**	**Sheraton Girl (47)** (NPLittmoden) **3-7-7**(5) RMullen(4) (lw: chsd ldrs tl wknd fnl 3f)	½	15	10/1	8	—
995[13]	**Noirie (64)** (MBrittain) **3-9-1b[1]** JCarroll(11) (a bhd)	2½	16	25/1	20	—
475[7]	**Hajat (62)** (NAGraham) **3-8-13** DHarrison(3) (swtg: in tch: effrt over 3f out: sn btn)	2	17	14/1	13	—
				(SP 138.0%)	**17 Rn**	

1m 37.4 (5.40) CSF £25.35 CT £144.94 TOTE £2.80: £1.30 £2.40 £2.10 £4.20 (£19.80) Trio £59.90 OWNER Mr George Moore (EPSOM) BRED Theo Waddington (UK) Ltd

OFFICIAL EXPLANATION **Hiltons Executive (IRE): hung badly right.**

840 Carlton (IRE) looked the part and did the business well, and there seems to be more to come. (2/1)
748 In Good Nick again did her utmost, but the winner proved far too good late on. (12/1)
886 Mardrew finished really well, suggesting that a bit further should make a lot of difference. (7/1)
Rude Awakening, trying his longest trip to date, was given plenty of assistance from the saddle and finished well, suggesting that he should get further yet. (25/1)
883 Legend of Aragon raced up with the pace until the trip on this stiff track eventually found her out. (12/1)
Bollero (IRE), stepping up in distance, finished quite well after a poor start and looks to be in good heart. (16/1)
Dee Pee Tee Cee (IRE) never really got into this, but did show a little and should be all the better for it. (20/1)

1097 ROTHMANS ROYALS NORTH SOUTH CHALLENGE SERIES H'CAP (0-85) (3-Y.O+) (Class D)

3-15 (3-17) **1m 100y** £4,536.00 (£1,368.00: £664.00: £312.00) Stalls: High GOING: 0.07 sec per fur (G)

	Horse	Dist	Pos	SP	RR	SF
947[3]	**High Premium (79)** (RAFahey) **9-9-1**(7) RWinston(15) (lw: trckd ldrs: hdwy to ld over 1f out: rdn out)	—	1	7/2[1]	90	46
633[7]	**Golden Thunderbolt (FR) (66)** (NTinkler) **4-8-9** JWeaver(4) (lw: bhd: gd hdwy on ins 2f out: swtchd & r.o wl towards fin)	nk	2	33/1	76	32
738[17]	**Kala Sunrise (85)** (CSmith) **4-10-0** JFortune(9) (lw: rr div: drvn along & hdwy 3f out: r.o wl towards fin)	1½	3	16/1	93	49
895[23]	**Suez Tornado (IRE) (63)** (EJAlston) **4-8-6v** GDuffield(16) (cl up: ev ch 3f out tl rdn & btn appr fnl f)	1½	4	33/1	68	24
895[2]	**Family Man (72)** (JRFanshawe) **4-9-1** DHarrison(2) (lw: hld up: hdwy to chse ldrs over 2f out: kpt on fnl f)	½	5	11/2[2]	76	32
947[8]	**Royal Result (USA) (72)** (TDBarron) **4-9-1** KDarley(19) (led tl hdd appr fnl f: no ex)	2½	6	16/1	71	27
895[15]	**Winston (61)** (JDBethell) **4-8-4b[1]** PaulEddery(6) (bhd: effrt over 2f out: nrst fin)	1¼	7	16/1	58	14
947[6]	**Tertium (IRE) (82)** (MartynWane) **5-9-11** JCarroll(18) (lw: hld up: gd hdwy 3f out: sn prom: nt qckn appr fnl f)	½	8	13/2[3]	78	34
824[2]	**Quilling (76)** (MDods) **5-9-2**(3) FLynch(12) (prom: effrt over 2f out: nt qckn)	½	9	12/1	71	27
824[3]	**Smarter Charter (73)** (MrsLStubbs) **4-9-2** SSanders(8) (bhd: brought wd st: nvr rchd ldrs)	¾	10	12/1	66	22
444[2]	**Shinerolla (80)** (CParker) **5-9-9** DRMcCabe(3) (s.i.s: bhd tl sme late hdwy)	1¼	11	12/1	71	27
315[6]	**Up in Flames (IRE) (67)** (SRBowring) **6-8-10** SWebster(1) (effrt 3f out: nvr trbld ldrs)	½	12	33/1	57	13

				SP	RR	SF
947[12]	**Queens Consul (IRE) (71)** (BSRothwell) **7-9-0** MFenton(10) (b.nr hind: in tch tl outpcd fnl 3f)	hd	**13**	25/1	61	17
776[7]	**Genuine John (IRE) (65)** (JParkes) **4-8-8** OUrbina(5) (n.d)	1¼	**14**	25/1	52	8
947[5]	**Anonym (IRE) (64)** (JLEyre) **5-8-7b** MGallagher(13) (chsd ldrs tl wknd 3f out)	¾	**15**	12/1	49	5
610[14]	**No Cliches (71)** (DNicholls) **4-9-0** AlexGreaves(11) (s.i.s: n.d)	2½	**16**	20/1	51	7
866[13]	**Terdad (USA) (70)** (TDBarron) **4-8-13** RLappin(7) (in tch: effrt ent st: sn wknd)	9	**17**	33/1	33	—
	Gladys Althorpe (IRE) (70) (JLEyre) **4-8-13** TWilliams(14) (in tch tl wknd fnl 3f)	6	**18**	12/1	22	—
766[4]	**Bon Luck (IRE) (67)** (JABennett) **5-8-10** JQuinn(17) (lw: prom tl wknd 3f out & eased)	dist	**19**	12/1	—	—
				(SP 139.0%)	**19 Rn**	

1m 50.8 (6.80) CSF £135.65 CT £1,600.92 TOTE £5.20: £1.80 £8.50 £4.90 £8.40 (£259.40) Trio £1,157.30; £1,320.38 to Beverley 11/5/97
OWNER Mr J. C. Parsons (MALTON) BRED M.E Wates
947 High Premium is in tremendous form and showed fine courage to hold on. (7/2)
463 Golden Thunderbolt (FR) showed his first signs of form for his new stable, and a repeat of this will surely find him a race. (33/1)
450 Kala Sunrise is a game performer who finished well, suggesting that he is in really good heart. (16/1)
Suez Tornado (IRE) raced freely but still put up a fair performance, and is slipping down the weights. (33/1)
895 Family Man keeps finishing well, suggesting that a bit further might well help his cause. (11/2)
824 Royal Result (USA) has won over a mile previously, but is failing to get home at the moment. (16/1)
Winston, in blinkers for the first time, only got going when it was all over. (16/1)
947 Tertium (IRE) is coming to hand and looks one to keep an eye on. (13/2)
766 Bon Luck (IRE) (12/1: op 20/1)

1098 WILLIAM HILL H'CAP (0-80) (3-Y.O+) (Class D)

3-45 (3-51) **5f** £4,614.00 (£1,392.00: £676.00: £318.00) Stalls: High GOING: 0.07 sec per fur (G)

				SP	RR	SF
942[6]	**First Maite (72)** (SRBowring) **4-9-11b** SWebster(16) (lw: chsd ldrs: rdn to ld ins fnl f: r.o)	—	**1**	9/4[1]	81	53
863[14]	**Blessingindisguise (54)** (MWEasterby) **4-8-7b** TLucas(12) (lw: in tch: hdwy 2f out: styd on wl fnl f)	1¾	**2**	11/1	57	29
51[7]	**Sue Me (IRE) (59)** (DNicholls) **5-8-12** AlexGreaves(1) (bhd: hdwy ½-wy: r.o wl: nrst fin)	hd	**3**	20/1	62	34
772[4]	**Squire Corrie (69)** (DWChapman) **5-9-8** ACulhane(13) (w ldrs: led 2f out tl ins fnl f: sn btn)	1¼	**4**	7/1[2]	68	40
585[6]	**Sound the Trumpet (IRE) (51)** (RCSpicer) **5-8-4** DeanMcKeown(19) (unruly s: led 3f: grad wknd fnl f)	nk	**5**	16/1	49	21
949[6]	**Camionneur (IRE) (46)** (TDEasterby) **4-7-13b** LCharnock(11) (lw: effrt ½-wy: styd on: nvr rchd ldrs)	½	**6**	10/1	43	15
863[9]	**Souperficial (53)** (NTinkler) **6-8-6v** KimTinkler(6) (outpcd & bhd: racd wd: styd on fnl 2f)	1	**7**	25/1	46	18
779[8]	**Thick as Thieves (43)** (RonaldThompson) **5-7-5**(5) JBramhill(10) (a chsng ldrs: sn dvn along: one pce fnl 2f)	hd	**8**	20/1	36	8
949[8]	**Insider Trader (68)** (MrsJRRamsden) **6-9-7** JFortune(3) (lw: racd wd: spd over 3f: grad wknd)	¾	**9**	8/1[3]	59	31
863[11]	**Ned's Bonanza (55)** (MDods) **8-8-8** JFEgan(2) (racd wd: n.d)	1¾	**10**	25/1	40	12
834[12]	**Dande Flyer (68)** (DWPArbuthnot) **4-9-7** SWhitworth(4) (dwlt & swvd rt: n.d)	½	**11**	14/1	51	23
792[11]	**Star of The Road (53)** (JMCarr) **3-7-11** NKennedy(18) (mid div: sn pushed along: no imp fnl 2f)	¾	**12**	33/1	34	—
949[14]	**Playmaker (49)** (DNicholls) **4-8-2b** DaleGibson(17) (chsd ldrs 3f: sn lost pl)	¾	**13**	14/1	28	—
949[15]	**Rich Glow (50)** (NBycroft) **6-8-3** FNorton(9) (nvr trbld ldrs)	2½	**14**	33/1	21	—
1029[12]	**Loch-Hurn Lady (66)** (KWHogg) **3-8-10** JQuinn(5) (racd wd: outpcd fr ½-wy)	¾	**15**	25/1	34	—
863[10]	**Sonderise (53)** (NTinkler) **8-8-6**ow2 JWeaver(15) (n.d)	3	**16**	10/1	12	—
	Saunders Wren (63) (MrsLStubbs) **3-8-7** SSanders(14) (in tch: sn drvn along: wknd 2f out)	2	**17**	20/1	15	—
	L A Touch (55) (JJQuinn) **4-8-8** JStack(7) (bit bkwd: bhd fr ½-wy)	1¼	**18**	33/1	3	—
				(SP 134.8%)	**18 Rn**	

65.6 secs (3.80) CSF £23.47 CT £404.38 TOTE £4.00: £1.70 £2.60 £9.40 £1.90 (£21.00) Trio £797.00 OWNER Mr S. R. Bowring (EDWINSTOWE) BRED S. R. Bowring
LONG HANDICAP Thick as Thieves 7-7
WEIGHT FOR AGE 3yo-9lb
942 First Maite last won on turf two seasons ago but, he is in top form just now and, with the necessary high draw here, did it nicely. (9/4: 9/2-2/1)
Blessingindisguise put up a useful effort and kept on really well at the finish, and looks on good terms with himself. (11/1)
Sue Me (IRE), having his first run for his new stable, put up an amazing show from the worst draw and looks one to keep on the right side of. (20/1)
772 Squire Corrie, well-drawn, showed plenty of speed but failed to get home on this occasion. (7/1)
585 Sound the Trumpet (IRE) is an awkward customer at the start, but has ability when he decides to use it. (16/1)
527 Camionneur (IRE) is a frustrating character who will probably win a race or two this season, though he needs things to go just right.(10/1)
759 Souperficial ran pretty well from a poor draw and was making fair late progress. (25/1)

1099 BLACK MILL CONDITIONS STKS (3-Y.O) (Class C)

4-15 (4-17) **1m 1f 207y** £5,712.00 (£1,842.00: £896.00) Stalls: High GOING: 0.07 sec per fur (G)

				SP	RR	SF
	Indiscreet (CAN) (DRLoder) **3-9-1** KDarley(2) (trckd ldr: chal on bit 2f out: sn hrd drvn: led nr fin)	—	**1**	6/5[1]	97	14
851[4]	**Yavlensky (IRE)** (JLDunlop) **3-9-5** JWeaver(3) (led: qcknd 2f out: r.o u.p: jst ct)	hd	**2**	4/1[3]	101	18
765*	**Barba Papa (IRE)** (LMCumani) **3-8-12** OUrbina(1) (lw: chsd ldrs: effrt over 2f out: sn outpcd: styd on towards fin)	1½	**3**	5/4[2]	91?	8
				(SP 109.9%)	**3 Rn**	

2m 14.4 (11.30) CSF £4.98 TOTE £1.70: (£2.90) OWNER Mrs Virginia Kraft Payson (NEWMARKET) BRED Virginia Kraft Payson
Indiscreet (CAN) was touted early season as likely to carry all before him, but has since lost his way on home gallops and had to really struggle to get on top here. (6/5: 4/6-11/8)
851 Yavlensky (IRE) likes plenty of cut in the ground and put up a fair show, but did have things his own way, quickening from the front, and was still just touched off. (4/1)
765* Barba Papa (IRE) got outpaced when the tempo increased early in the straight, but he was keeping on well at the end, and plenty of opportunities will be found for him. (5/4)

1100 BURTON BUSHES H'CAP (0-70) (4-Y.O+) (Class E)

4-45 (4-50) **2m 35y** £3,783.75 (£1,140.00: £552.50: £258.75) Stalls: High GOING: 0.07 sec per fur (G)

				SP	RR	SF
846[4]	**Dirab (70)** (TDBarron) **4-9-11** KDarley(18) (hld up: hdwy 3f out: led appr fnl f: r.o)	—	**1**	10/1	83	3
481[11]	**Contrarie (41)** (MJRyan) **4-7-5**(5) RMullen(10) (bhd: gd hdwy over 3f out: chsng wnr ins fnl f: kpt on wl)	¾	**2**	20/1	53	—
1039*	**Golden Hadeer (38)** (MJRyan) **6-7-7**(3) 4x MBaird(13) (lw: hld up: gd hdwy on outside ½-wy: led over 4f out tl appr fnl f: no ex)	6	**3**	2/1[1]	44	—

				SP	RR	SF
632^{3}	**Romalito (38)** (MBlanshard) **7-7-10** JQuinn(5) (lw: hdwy 6f out: styd on u.p fnl 3f: nvr rchd ldrs)	5	**4**	12/1	39	—
831^{2}	**Jamaican Flight (USA) (65)** (CSmith) **4-9-6** JWeaver(1) (lw: led tl hdd over 4f out: wknd fnl f)	4	**5**	$7/2^{2}$	62	—
865^{14}	**Chris's Lad (62)** (BJMeehan) **6-9-6b** GDuffield(4) (chsd ldrs tl wknd fnl 3f)	4	**6**	12/1	55	—
888^{7}	**He's Got Wings (IRE) (52)** (MrsJRRamsden) **4-8-7v** JFortune(8) (b.nr hind: lw: chsd ldrs: rdn 4f out: wknd fnl 3f)	2½	**7**	$7/1^{3}$	43	—
632*	**Kinoko (48)** (KWHogg) **9-8-6** LCharnock(17) (chsd ldrs tl wknd fnl 3f)	6	**8**	$7/1^{3}$	33	—
	Gymcrak Cyrano (IRE) (39) (NChamberlain) **8-7-11**^{ow1} NKennedy(11) (nvr trbld ldrs)	1¼	**9**	50/1	23	—
	Mudlark (41) (JNorton) **5-7-13v** DaleGibson(19) (prom tl wknd fnl 3f)	s.h	**10**	50/1	25	—
950^{6}	**Anchorena (49)** (DWBarker) **5-8-7** TWilliams(7) (lw: chsd ldrs: shkn up ½-wy: hrd drvn ent st: sn wknd)	3	**11**	16/1	30	—
632^{11}	**French Ivy (USA) (65)** (FMurphy) **10-9-9** JFanning(20) (b: bhd: hdwy 7f out: nvr rchd ldrs)	5	**12**	12/1	41	—
865^{8}	**Top Prize (38)** (MBrittain) **9-7-10v** GBardwell(6) (bhd fnl 4f)	8	**13**	25/1	6	—
982^{6}	**Rushen Raider (70)** (KWHogg) **5-9-9**$^{(5)}$ ADaly(15) (a bhd)	1¾	**14**	14/1	36	—
	Hullbank (63) (WWHaigh) **7-9-7** JTate(2) (bkwd: bhd fnl 6f)	3	**15**	16/1	26	—
580^{6}	**El Nido (49)** (DWChapman) **9-8-7** ACulhane(16) (outpcd fr ½-wy)	¾	**16**	20/1	12	—
888^{8}	**Arcady (58)** (JLHarris) **4-8-13** PaulEddery(9) (prom to ½-wy: sn bhd)	2	**17**	14/1	19	—
762^{8}	**Gymcrak Tiger (IRE) (55)** (GHolmes) **7-8-13** AlexGreaves(12) (chsd ldrs tl wknd 5f out)	½	**18**	25/1	15	—
650^{4}	**Lawful Love (IRE) (40)** (TWDonnelly) **7-7-5b**$^{1(7)ow2}$ RWinston(3) (mid div: rdn & wknd 6f out)	¾	**19**	20/1	—	—
	Sharp to Oblige (38) (RMWhitaker) **10-7-10** DWright(14) (sn drvn along: t.o fr ½-wy)	dist	**20**	50/1	—	—

(SP 165.7%) **20 Rn**

3m 54.4 (23.90) CSF £217.59 CT £542.36 TOTE £12.70: £2.90 £7.10 £1.20 £2.90 (£604.60) Trio £781.80; £220.24 to Beverley 11/5/97
OWNER Mr Alex Gorrie (THIRSK) BRED Nawara Stud Co Ltd
LONG HANDICAP Gymcrak Cyrano (IRE) 7-4 Romalito 7-9 Contrarie 7-3 Top Prize 7-2 Lawful Love (IRE) 7-2
WEIGHT FOR AGE 4yo-3lb

846 Dirab, patiently ridden, did it well in these very wet conditions and seems to be improving. (10/1: op 6/1)
Contrarie likes cut in the ground and came from way off the pace to give the winner a fright. She looks to be getting it together. (20/1)
1039* Golden Hadeer, held up, suddenly quickened past the field from halfway to lead approaching the straight. Not surprisingly, he had done too much too soon and was worried out of it in the last furlong. (2/1: tchd 7/2)
632 Romalito just gallops and stays, but was never doing things fast enough to offer a threat. (12/1)
831 Jamaican Flight (USA) tried to gallop his rivals into the ground but, in these testing conditions, he was found out in the home straight. (7/2: op 8/1)
613 He's Got Wings (IRE) ran reasonably but is probably better on faster ground. (7/1)

T/Jkpt: Not won; £16,735.27 to Beverley 11/5/97. T/Plpt: £23.00 (1,074.96 Tckts). T/Qdpt: £15.20 (111.1 Tckts) AA

1082-LINGFIELD (L-H) (Good, Good-soft patches st becoming Soft after Race 1)
Saturday May 10th

WEATHER: rain with sunny periods WIND: mod half against

1101 MILCARS CHARTWELL STKS (Listed) (3-Y.O+ F & M) (Class A)
2-00 (2-00) **7f** £10,580.00 (£3,920.00: £1,885.00: £775.00: £312.50: £127.50) Stalls: High GOING: 0.30 sec per fur (G)

				SP	RR	SF
959^{6}	**Supercal (98)** (DRCElsworth) **3-8-5** PatEddery(4) (lw: hdwy 2f out: chsd ldr over 1f out: led ins fnl f: r.o wl)	—	**1**	6/1	104	48
672^{6}	**Baked Alaska** (ACStewart) **3-8-5** MRoberts(7) (chsd ldr 3f: rdn over 3f out: chsd ldrs over 2f out tl over 1f out: r.o one pce)	2	**2**	$7/2^{2}$	99	43
	Lochangel (IABalding) **3-8-5** RCochrane(6) (lw: led: hrd rdn over 1f out: wknd & hdd ins fnl f)	1	**3**	$5/2^{1}$	97	41
	West Humble (94) (LadyHerries) **4-9-3** DeclanO'Shea(1) (lw: hld up: rdn over 2f out: one pce)	¾	**4**	14/1	95	51
677^{18}	**Prends Ca (IRE) (90)** (WRMuir) **4-9-3** DaneO'Neill(5) (rdn & hdwy wl over 1f out: one pce)	hd	**5**	12/1	95	51
957^{6}	**Sambac (USA) (102)** (HRACecil) **3-8-7**^{ow2} KFallon(2) (a.p: chsd ldrs 4f out tl over 2f out: sn wknd)	6	**6**	$5/1^{3}$	84	26
839^{5}	**El Opera (IRE) (95)** (PFICole) **4-9-3** TQuinn(3) (b.hind: prom 5f)	20	**7**	7/1	36	—

(SP 108.6%) **7 Rn**

1m 26.68 (5.48) CSF £22.22 TOTE £7.10: £2.50 £1.90 (£8.80) OWNER The Caledonian Racing Society (WHITCOMBE) BRED Stetchworth Park Stud Ltd
WEIGHT FOR AGE 3yo-12lb

959 Supercal, who failed to stay a mile-and-a-quarter last time out, was back over her optimum trip, and came with a good run to strike the front inside the final furlong and land her first listed event. (6/1)
672 Baked Alaska was a leading light from the off and stayed on to regain second prize in the last fifty yards. (7/2)
Lochangel looked in good heart for her seasonal debut, but she found this trip on this ground just too far for her. She may just stay seven furlongs on faster ground, but six would surely suit her better. (5/2: 7/4-11/4)
West Humble looked in good shape for this first run since last June, but failed to quicken in the last two furlongs. (14/1)
Prends Ca (IRE), sold out of Richard Hannon's stable for 34,000guineas at the Newmarket Autumn Sales, came home last on her debut for her new connections recently, but ran better here if never getting in a serious challenge. (12/1)
957 Sambac (USA) again flopped and was going in reverse a quarter-of-a-mile from home. (5/1)

1102 LINGFIELD OAKS TRIAL STKS (Listed) (3-Y.O F) (Class A)
2-30 (2-30) **1m 3f 106y** £12,464.00 (£4,514.00: £2,182.00: £910.00: £380.00) Stalls: High GOING: 0.60 sec per fur (GS)

				SP	RR	SF
959^{4}	**Crown of Light** (MRStoute) **3-8-8** OPeslier(4) (hld up: hmpd on ins over 2f out: led over 1f out: rdn out)	—	**1**	$11/2^{2}$	100	64
833^{4}	**Book At Bedtime (IRE)** (CACyzer) **3-8-8** KFallon(3) (rdn over 7f out: hdwy 2f out: ev ch over 1f out: r.o)	1	**2**	14/1	99	63
833*	**Ukraine Venture** (SPCWoods) **3-8-8** WRyan(5) (lw: hld up: hrd rdn over 2f out: ev ch over 1f out: unable qckn)	7	**3**	$8/15^{1}$	89	53
833^{3}	**Go For Salt (USA)** (MRStoute) **3-8-8** JReid(1) (chsd ldr: led over 9f out tl over 1f out: sn wknd)	5	**4**	9/1	82	46
$815a^{7}$	**Lycility (IRE) (94)** (CEBrittain) **3-8-8** BDoyle(2) (led 2f: rdn over 2f out: wknd wl over 1f out)	6	**5**	$7/1^{3}$	74	38

(SP 109.8%) **5 Rn**

2m 35.72 (11.02) CSF £55.35 TOTE £4.70: £1.80 £2.30 (£20.50) OWNER Sheikh Mohammed (NEWMARKET) BRED Sheikh Mohammed Bin Rashid Al Maktoum

959 Crown of Light, a plain filly, caused an upset here. Hampered along the inside rail over a quarter-of-a-mile from home, she recovered well to lead below the distance and, ridden along, kept the persistent runner-up at bay. She is bound for the Oaks and, whilst there can be no doubting that this year's event is extremely open with no obvious hot-shots, she is surely not going to be good enough. (11/2)

833 Book At Bedtime (IRE), who finished thirteen lengths behind the hot favourite at Sandown recently, dramatically turned the tables. However, the signs did not look good as she was being niggled along in the back straight. Nevertheless, she picked up well once in line for home and, throwing down a determined challenge in the final quarter-mile, made sure the winner did not have things all her own way. Connections are now looking forward to the Oaks, but she must be an outsider. (14/1)
833* Ukraine Venture was a major flop after such an impressive debut at Sandown and, though strong riding got her to have every chance below the distance, she was left for dead. She now has it all to prove and the jury is out over whether her Sandown run was a fluke, or this awful performance was down to the soft ground. (8/15)
833 Go For Salt (USA) was soon at the head of affairs but, collared below the distance, she soon capitulated. (9/1)
815a Lycility (IRE), quite a tall, unfurnished filly, had shot her bolt early in the final quarter-mile. (7/1)

1103 TRIPLEPRINT DERBY TRIAL STKS (Gp 3) (3-Y.O) (Class A)

3-00 (3-00) **1m 3f 106y** £31,927.50 (£11,490.00: £5,495.00: £2,225.00: £862.50) Stalls: High GOING: 0.60 sec per fur (GS)

				SP	RR	SF
851^{3}	**Silver Patriarch (IRE) (108)** (JLDunlop) **3-8-7** PatEddery(4) (lw: hdwy over 3f out: led over 2f out: clr over 1f out: r.o wl)	—	**1**	5/4^{1}	108+	72
841*	**Tanaasa (IRE)** (MRStoute) **3-8-7** OPeslier(2) (b.off hind: hld up: led over 3f out tl over 2f out: unable qckn)	7	**2**	13/8^{2}	98	62
725^{2}	**Basman (IRE)** (BSmart) **3-8-7** RCochrane(3) (lw: chsd ldr over 2f: chsd ldr 5f out tl over 2f out: sn wknd)	2	**3**	7/1^{3}	96	60
788^{2}	**Papua (106)** (IABalding) **3-8-7v^{1}** JReid(5) (lw: plld hrd: hdwy to chse ldr 9f out: led over 5f out tl over 3f out: sn wknd)	26	**4**	7/1^{3}	59	23
700^{8}	**Michael Venture (82)** (SPCWoods) **3-8-7b^{1}** WRyan(1) (led 6f: t.o fnl 3f)	dist	**5**	50/1	—	—
				(SP 109.5%)		**5 Rn**

2m 34.44 (9.74) CSF £3.19 TOTE £1.90: £1.20 £1.40 (£1.60) OWNER Mr Peter Winfield (ARUNDEL) BRED Peter Winfield
851 Silver Patriarch (IRE) was in his element over this longer trip and, with some cut in the ground, his stamina really came into play. He forged clear approaching the final furlong and won with plenty of hand. He is a resolute galloper and one just wonders that if the ground is fast at Epsom, he may well get caught out. However, if the ground was to come up on the soft side, putting more of an emphasis on stamina, he could run an extremely big race. Not surprisingly, his odds have tumbled from 20/1 to 8/1. (5/4)
841* Tanaasa (IRE), who had a nice stroll round on his reappearance, had far more on his plate here. Nudged into a slender lead early in the straight, it soon became plain the winner was too good for him. (13/8: 11/10-7/4)
725 Basman (IRE), taking a big step-up in class, acquitted himself well and may have even poked his head in front for a few strides early in the straight before tiring. His trainer has a high opinion of him and he should soon lose his maiden tag. (7/1)
788 Papua, tried in a visor for the first time, stopped as if shot once collared early in the straight. (7/1)
700 Michael Venture was totally out of his league. (50/1)

1104 HSBC JAMES CAPEL H'CAP (0-100) (3-Y.O) (Class C)

3-30 (3-31) **1m 1f** £5,823.75 (£1,740.00: £832.50: £378.75) Stalls: Low GOING: 0.60 sec per fur (GS)

				SP	RR	SF
958^{2}	**Supply And Demand (90)** (GLMoore) **3-9-5** KFallon(3) (a.p: led over 2f out: rdn: r.o wl)	—	**1**	7/4^{1}	99	68
853^{8}	**Sheer Face (85)** (WRMuir) **3-9-0** DaneO'Neill(1) (hdwy on ins over 2f out: chsd wnr over 1f out: r.o one pce)	1¾	**2**	10/1	91	60
797*	**Regal Patrol (79)** (MRStoute) **3-8-8** JReid(4) (hld up: rdn over 2f out: hung rt over 1f out: one pce)	2	**3**	5/2^{2}	81	50
	Our People (92) (MJohnston) **3-9-7** DHolland(5) (lw: chsd ldr 6f: wknd over 1f out)	6	**4**	5/1^{3}	84	53
700^{7}	**Noble Investment (75)** (JMPEustace) **3-8-1**(3) MartinDwyer(2) (led over 6f)	11	**5**	16/1	47	16
	Orontes (USA) (82) (RHannon) **3-8-11** PatEddery(7) (bhd fnl 7f)	¾	**6**	6/1	53	22
				(SP 110.9%)		**6 Rn**

1m 59.78 (9.28) CSF £17.34 TOTE £2.30: £1.30 £5.10 (£13.00) OWNER Action (BRIGHTON) BRED W. H. Joyce
958 Supply And Demand enjoyed the soft ground and the extra furlong and brushed aside a 6lb rise in the weights. A little further should suit him even better. (7/4)
Sheer Face, who has failed to shine in two runs so far this season, ran much better but, despite moving into second place below the distance, was unable to reel-in the winner. (10/1: 7/1-12/1)
797* Regal Patrol has shown himself to be a very temperamental character despite being gelded, and that was again evident here. He has plenty of ability, but he is not at all keen to use it and is one to avoid. (5/2: 7/4-11/4)
Our People looked in good shape for this reappearance, but was on a stiff mark for this handicap debut and had shot his bolt below the distance. (5/1)
Noble Investment, who has been gelded over the winter, finished tailed-off on his reappearance and, after taking the field along here, had nothing more to offer when collared. (16/1)

1105 TESTERS OF EDENBRIDGE MAIDEN STKS (I) (3-Y.O+) (Class D)

4-00 (4-04) **1m 2f** £3,460.00 (£1,030.00: £490.00: £220.00) Stalls: Low GOING: 0.60 sec per fur (GS)

				SP	RR	SF
670^{2}	**Salamah** (RCharlton) **3-8-11** PatEddery(10) (lw: chsd ldr: led over 2f out: drvn out)	—	**1**	Evens^{1}	93	56
	Eshtiaal (USA) (JLDunlop) **3-8-11** RHills(2) (hdwy over 2f out: hrd rdn over 1f out: ev ch ins fnl f: r.o)	¾	**2**	4/1^{2}	92	55
	Danish Rhapsody (IRE) (LadyHerries) **4-9-12** DeclanO'Shea(12) (a.p: ev ch over 2f out: unable qckn)	5	**3**	6/1^{3}	84	62
	Eagle Dancer (LadyHerries) **5-9-12** AClark(5) (hld up: rdn over 2f out: one pce)	1½	**4**	33/1	81	59
	Yak Alfaraj (MRStoute) **3-8-11** DHolland(7) (unf: scope: nvr nr to chal)	14	**5**	8/1	59	22
	Utah (IRE) (BGubby) **3-8-11** DaneO'Neill(3) (prom 6f)	½	**6**	33/1	58	21
	Joli's Son (MJHaynes) **4-9-12** KFallon(1) (bkwd: s.s: nvr nrr)	nk	**7**	33/1	58	36
	Slipstream Star (IABalding) **3-8-3**(3) MartinDwyer(9) (led over 7f)	1¼	**8**	25/1	51	14
771^{5}	**Zorro (51)** (RMFlower) **3-8-11** GHind(11) (a mid div)	2½	**9**	50/1	52	15
	Moonlight Invader (IRE) (EALDunlop) **3-8-8**(3) DO'Donohoe(4) (a bhd)	nk	**10**	12/1	51	14
790^{9}	**Victor Blum (USA)** (CAHorgan) **4-9-12** WRyan(13) (lw: a bhd)	2½	**11**	50/1	47	25
	Canadian Jive (DWPArbuthnot) **4-9-7** RPrice(6) (mid div 8f)	7	**12**	50/1	31	9
645^{13}	**Craven Hill (IRE)** (NAGraham) **3-8-11** AMcGlone(8) (bhd fnl 6f)	3½	**13**	33/1	30	—
				(SP 124.6%)		**13 Rn**

2m 15.58 (10.88) CSF £4.32 TOTE £1.90: £1.20 £1.80 £2.00 (£3.60) Trio £6.00 OWNER Mr K. Abdulla (BECKHAMPTON) BRED Juddmonte Farms
WEIGHT FOR AGE 3yo-15lb
IN-FOCUS: **The time of this race was considerably faster than the other division.**
670 Salamah confirmed the promise shown on his debut at Newmarket last month. Showing a nice turn of foot to get rid of the third, he was soon being tackled by the runner-up, but responding to pressure, he quickened again inside the final furlong to settle the issue. (Evens)

Eshtiaal (USA), who has spent the winter in Dubai, coped with this longer trip in these testing conditions. Throwing down his challenge from below the distance, it looked as if he was going to prevail, but he had met a real tartar in the winner. He should soon go one better. (4/1)
Danish Rhapsody (IRE) had every chance before being left standing by the front two. This was a pleasing reappearance. (6/1)
Eagle Dancer, who finished in mid-division in a bumper at Sandown in March, before unseating his rider on his only other start, chased the leaders but could only go up and down in the same place in the final quarter-mile. (33/1)

1106 TESTERS OF EDENBRIDGE MAIDEN STKS (II) (3-Y.O+) (Class D)
4-30 (4-35) **1m 2f** £3,460.00 (£1,030.00: £490.00: £220.00) Stalls: Low GOING: 0.60 sec per fur (GS)

	Horse	Dist	Pos	SP	RR	SF
	Gentilesse (HRACecil) **3-8-8**^{ow2} KFallon(5) (w'like: hdwy over 3f out: led over 2f out: hrd rdn over 1f out: r.o wl)	—	**1**	$11/4^{1}$	78	40
	Hachiyah (IRE) (DMorley) **3-8-6** RHills(3) (chsd ldr over 8f out: ev ch 1f out: 2nd & btn whn n.m.r on ins ins fnl f)	3	**2**	$13/2^{3}$	71	35
	Height of Heights (IRE) (LadyHerries) **4-9-12** JReid(1) (rdn over 2f out: hdwy over 1f out: r.o)	3	**3**	$5/1^{2}$	71	50
	Bear Hug (LadyHerries) **4-9-12** DeclanO'Shea(8) (hld up: rdn over 2f out: one pce)	3	**4**	$5/1^{2}$	67	46
842^{8}	**Urgent Reply (USA)** (CADwyer) **4-9-9**$^{(3)}$ JDSmith(13) (hld up: rdn over 3f out: one pce)	2	**5**	33/1	63	42
	Whirlawhile (USA) (EALDunlop) **3-8-8**$^{(3)}$ DO'Donohoe(2) (b.hind: s.s: nvr nr to chal)	nk	**6**	7/1	63	27
842^{6}	**Sarbaron (IRE)** (PWHarris) **3-8-11** AClark(11) (no hdwy fnl 3f)	2½	**7**	7/1	59	23
842^{9}	**Leatherneck (IRE)** (PMooney) **4-9-9**$^{(3)}$ PMcCabe(10) (b.nr hind: a bhd)	9	**8**	50/1	45	24
875^{R}	**North White Plains** (CEBrittain) **3-8-11** BDoyle(4) (virtually ref to r: a t.o)	11	**9**	33/1	27	—
	Oh So Misty (SDow) **4-9-7** MRoberts(6) (bhd fnl 7f: t.o)	7	**10**	20/1	11	—
	Tulsa (IRE) (55) (BGubby) **3-8-11v** DaneO'Neill(9) (led: sn clr: hdd over 2f out: sn wknd: t.o)	8	**11**	50/1	3	—
740^{15}	**Moonshift** (MRStoute) **3-8-11** DHolland(12) (chsd ldr over 1f: wknd over 6f out: t.o)	23	**12**	25/1	—	—
				(SP 116.7%)	**12 Rn**	

2m 17.23 (12.53) CSF £17.14 TOTE £2.60: £1.50 £2.60 £1.90 (£9.30) Trio £12.30 OWNER H R H Prince Fahd Salman (NEWMARKET) BRED Newgate Stud Co
WEIGHT FOR AGE 3yo-15lb
Gentilesse, whose dam was a smart French miler, is a half-sister to numerous winners including May Hill winner Intimate Guest. Picking up ground nicely entering the straight, she responded to pressure to assert in the final furlong. (11/4: op 6/4)
Hachiyah (IRE) made a very pleasing debut for her new stable, and threw down a determined challenge in the final quarter-mile. Still in with every chance entering the final furlong, she was getting the worst of the argument when slightly tightened up by the winner in the last one hundred yards. She should soon find a race. (13/2: 3/1-7/1)
Height of Heights (IRE), a half-brother to Serious, was making a belated racecourse debut but stayed on in the last furlong-and-a-half to take third prize. (5/1)
Bear Hug chased the leaders but never looked like quickening up in the straight. (5/1: 7/2-11/2)
605 Urgent Reply (USA) was made to look very pedestrian in the last three furlongs. (33/1)
842 Sarbaron (IRE) (7/1: 8/1-12/1)

1107 SLIP ANCHOR H'CAP (0-85) (3-Y.O+) (Class D)
5-00 (5-04) **6f** £3,486.35 (£1,038.80: £494.90: £222.95) Stalls: High GOING: 0.30 sec per fur (G)

	Horse	Dist	Pos	SP	RR	SF
	Youdontsay (80) (TJNaughton) **5-10-0** DaneO'Neill(8) (lw: hdwy over 2f out: led over 1f out: all out)	—	**1**	10/1	87	70
835^{15}	**La Petite Fusee (77)** (RJO'Sullivan) **6-9-8**$^{(3)}$ DO'Donohoe(4) (b.nr hind: a.p: rdn over 2f out: ev ch fnl f: r.o wl)	s.h	**2**	$9/2^{3}$	84	67
357^{7}	**Mr Frosty (64)** (WJarvis) **5-8-12** JReid(5) (rdn over 2f out: hdwy over 1f out: r.o)	1	**3**	7/1	68	51
180^{4}	**Just Loui (80)** (WGMTurner) **3-8-13**$^{(5)}$ DSweeney(9) (bit bkwd: led over 4f: one pce)	1	**4**	8/1	82	55
835^{3}	**Mister Jolson (75)** (RJHodges) **8-9-9** SDrowne(1) (lw: racd far side: rdn over 2f out: hdwy over 1f out: nvr nrr)	½	**5**	$11/4^{1}$	75	58
995^{15}	**Sharp Return (62)** (MJRyan) **3-8-0**^{ow1} TSprake(7) (hld up: rdn over 2f out: one pce)	1	**6**	8/1	60	32
186^{4}	**Sea Danzig (65)** (JJBridger) **4-8-13** RCochrane(3) (lw: racd far side: outpcd)	2½	**7**	8/1	56	39
942^{28}	**Denbrae (IRE) (72)** (DJGMurraySmith) **5-9-6** TQuinn(6) (bhd fnl 4f)	12	**8**	6/1	31	14
	Rise 'n Shine (72) (CACyzer) **3-8-10** MRoberts(11) (lw: w ldr over 3f)	1	**9**	5/1	28	1
*752**	***Barbason (65)*** (GLMoore) **5-8-13** CandyMorris(10) (Withdrawn not under Starter's orders: veterinary advice)		**W**	$7/2^{2}$	—	—
				(SP 152.9%)	**9 Rn**	

1m 13.63 (4.63) CSF £56.38 CT £324.98 TOTE £15.40: £6.40 £2.00 £2.20 (£31.40) Trio £51.30 OWNER Mr Tom Nicholls (EPSOM) BRED Mrs and Exors of the late Col F. R. Hue-Williams
WEIGHT FOR AGE 3yo-10lb
Youdontsay had done all her winning previously on a fast surface, but she coped well with these underfoot conditions. Leading below the distance, she responded to strong pressure to hold on in a desperate finish. (10/1)
La Petite Fusee bounced back to form. Going at it hammer and tongs with the winner from below the distance, she gave her all and failed by only a whisker. She should gain compensation shortly. (9/2)
89 Mr Frosty stayed on in the last furlong-and-a-half but was unable to get to the front two in time. All four of his wins to date have come on the All-Weather. (7/1)
62* Just Loui had a tremendous campaign on the All-Weather this winter winning four times, but his trainer stated that he was useless on turf. Looking in need of this first run in three-and-a-half months, he certainly dispelled his handler's fears as he held a slender advantage until below the distance. Although he is yet to win on grass, he may well soon put that to rights. (8/1)
835 Mister Jolson, one of two who elected to race on the far side, stayed on without being able to get to the principals racing on the opposite side of the track. Nine of his ten victories have come over five furlongs. (11/4)
Sharp Return chased the leaders but failed to quicken in the last two furlongs. (8/1)

T/Plpt: £64.40 (425.16 Tckts). T/Qdpt: £2.50 (497.53 Tckts) AK

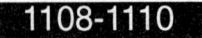

0875-BATH (L-H) (Good becoming Good to Soft becoming Heavy)
Sunday May 11th
WEATHER: thundery showers WIND: fresh against

1108 SUNDAY CONDITIONS STKS (4-Y.O+) (Class C)
2-00 (2-01) **1m 3f 144y** £4,523.65 (£1,647.40: £803.70: £343.50: £151.75) Stalls: Low GOING: 0.21 sec per fur (G)

	Horse	Dist	Pos	SP	RR	SF
	King Alex (RCharlton) **4-8-10** PatEddery(1) (sn chsng ldr: led on bit over 1f out: easily)	—	1	4/9 1	102+	67
	Taufan's Melody (106) (LadyHerries) **6-9-2** MRoberts(4) (led: hdd over 1f out: no ch w wnr)	2	2	9/4 2	105	70
	Male-Ana-Mou (IRE) (92) (DRCElsworth) **4-9-0** DaneO'Neill(3) (lw: plld hrd: prom: rdn wl over 1f out: sn wknd)	3½	3	8/1 3	98?	63
849[4]	**Kailey Senor (USA)** (RWArmstrong) **4-8-10** RPrice(5) (lw: hld up: rdn over 3f out: sn wknd)	11	4	33/1	62 t	44
	Light Reflections (PGMurphy) **4-8-10** SDrowne(2) (hld up: rdn 3f out: sn bhd)	3½	5	66/1	58 t	40
				(SP 115.5%)		**5 Rn**

2m 33.1 (6.40) CSF £1.74 TOTE £1.50: £1.10 £1.40 (£1.50) OWNER Mr Wafic Said (BECKHAMPTON) BRED Jon Hanson

King Alex, who went lame last June when looking a promising three-year-old, seems set to make up for lost time. Appreciating the cut in the ground, he is well entered up abroad and may even go for the Hardwicke at Royal Ascot. (4/9)

Taufan's Melody proved no match for the winner at these weights. (9/4: op 5/4)

Male-Ana-Mou (IRE) would have been 12lb better off with the runner-up in a handicap. (8/1)

74 63 68† 55 (65)

1109 TATTERSALLS NOVICE AUCTION STKS (2-Y.O) (Class E)
2-30 (2-33) **5f 11y** £2,869.25 (£869.00: £424.50: £202.25) Stalls: High GOING: 0.21 sec per fur (G)

	Horse	Dist	Pos	SP	RR	SF
536[14]	**Gypsy Hill** (DHaydnJones) **2-8-2** SDrowne(8) (wnt rt s: gd hdwy 2f out: rdn to ld nr fin)	—	1	33/1	78	27
	Contrary Mary (GLewis) **2-8-1**(3) AWhelan(1) (lt-f: unruly stalls: a.p: led ins fnl f: hdd nr fin)	nk	2	9/1	79	28
	Country Garden (RHannon) **2-8-2** DaneO'Neill(6) (lt-f: s.s: gd hdwy over 1f out: r.o)	2½	3	5/1 3	69	18
	Lord Kintyre (BRMillman) **2-8-8** TSprake(10) (w'like: hld up: hdwy over 2f out: nt clr run & swtchd rt over 1f out: r.o ins fnl f)	1¼	4	10/1	71	20
651[3]	**Mai Tai (IRE)** (MrsPNDutfield) **2-7-10**(5) RFfrench(9) (a.p: one pce fnl 2f)	s.h	5	9/1	64	13
1007*	**Aurigny** (SDow) **2-8-5**(5) 8x ADaly(2) (led tl hdd & wknd ins fnl f)	2½	6	9/4 1	65	14
	Imperial Prince (KMcAuliffe) **2-8-12** WJO'Connor(7) (lt-f: chsd ldrs: ev ch 2f out: wknd over 1f out)	½	7	12/1	66	15
828[3]	**Silent Pride (IRE)** (MDIUsher) **2-8-1**ow2 MRoberts(4) (spd 3f)	4	8	100/30 2	42	—
	Regalo (DMHyde) **2-8-5**(3)ow4 RHavlin(3) (w'like: prom: rdn over 2f out: wknd wl over 1f out)	8	9	50/1	24	—
	Miss Equal (MCPipe) **2-8-1**ow1 GCarter(5) (lt-f: outpcd: t.o)	9	10	10/1	—	—
				(SP 121.3%)		**10 Rn**

65.2 secs (4.70) CSF £286.80 TOTE £43.90: £5.80 £1.50 £2.00 (£109.40) Trio £203.60 OWNER Mr Kevan Kynaston (PONTYPRIDD) BRED Mrs A. V. Ferguson

Gypsy Hill, a half-sister to among others Lee Artiste, again lost ground at the start but not so much as on her debut. (33/1)

Contrary Mary, a half-sister to La Belle Dominique, had to be taken out of the stalls and eventually went in last. (9/1: 5/1-10/1)

Country Garden, a half-sister to Cherokee Flight, has apparently been showing ability at home, and will have learned a lot from this promising debut. (5/1)

Lord Kintyre, a half-brother to Crofters Ceilidh and Highland Fawn, was a springer in the market. The unlucky horse of the race, he deserves a chance to recoup losses. (10/1: 20/1-9/1)

651 Mai Tai (IRE) was a little disappointing and may need further. (9/1)

1007* Aurigny failed to get home over this stiffer course in rain-softened ground. (9/4)

1110 WILLIE CARSON MAIDEN STKS (3-Y.O F) (Class D)
3-00 (3-03) **1m 5y** £3,550.00 (£1,075.00: £525.00: £250.00) Stalls: Low GOING: 0.21 sec per fur (G)

	Horse	Dist	Pos	SP	RR	SF
	Irish Light (USA) (MRStoute) **3-8-11** DHolland(15) (scope: b: b.hind: hld up: hdwy 3f out: led ins fnl f: rdn out)	—	1	4/1 2	84	36
889[2]	**Sellette (IRE) (76)** (DHaydnJones) **3-8-11** SDrowne(8) (a.p: led over 2f out tl ins fnl f: r.o)	½	2	4/1 2	83	35
	Persevere (LordHuntingdon) **3-8-6**(5) AimeeCook(3) (lengthy: scope: a.p: ev ch 2f out: one pce)	4	3	16/1	75	27
754[3]	**Ghayyur (USA) (73)** (JLDunlop) **3-8-11** RHills(12) (hld up & bhd: hdwy over 2f out: nt rch ldrs)	2½	4	5/1 3	70	22
	Blue Lamp (USA) (MAJarvis) **3-8-11** MRoberts(10) (a.p: no hdwy fnl 2f)	2	5	9/1	66	18
	Listed Account (USA) (LMCumani) **3-8-11** PatEddery(11) (no hdwy fnl 2f)	s.h	6	9/4 1	66	18
	Kanawa (APJones) **3-8-11** TSprake(13) (no hdwy fnl 4f)	8	7	66/1	50	2
	Silvery (JARToller) **3-8-11** WRyan(2) (leggy: lt-f: dwlt: nvr nr ldrs)	1½	8	14/1	47	—
	My Jess (SGKnight) **3-8-11** RPerham(6) (w'like: scope: led over 5f: wknd wl over 1f out)	¾	9	66/1	46	—
935[8]	**Sugar Plum** (RHannon) **3-8-11** DaneO'Neill(1) (prom 3f)	1¾	10	16/1	42	—
	Tetris (IRE) (CFWall) **3-8-11** NCarlisle(7) (a bhd)	hd	11	25/1	42	—
885[10]	**Doyenne** (GLewis) **3-8-8**(3) AWhelan(14) (a bhd)	1½	12	66/1	39	—
840[16]	**Isca Maiden (40)** (PHayward) **3-8-11** NAdams(9) (a bhd)	2½	13	66/1	34	—
	Kara Queen (CJHill) **3-8-6**(5) RFfrench(4) (unf: s.s: a bhd)	3	14	50/1	28	—
				(SP 127.6%)		**14 Rn**

1m 45.7 (7.50) CSF £19.34 TOTE £5.70: £2.10 £2.10 £5.00 (£14.60) Trio £176.10 OWNER Cheveley Park Stud (NEWMARKET) BRED Newgate Stud Farm Inc.

Irish Light (USA) is the first foal of a dual six-furlong winner from the family of Soviet Line and Pure Grain. Enhancing her paddock value, she won a race run in a rainstorm. (4/1)

889 Sellette (IRE) keeps knocking at the door and deserves a change of luck. (4/1)

Persevere made a satisfactory enough start to her career. (16/1)

754 Ghayyur (USA), who broke a blood-vessel on her final outing last season, was left with quite a bit to do when going in pursuit of the leading half dozen early in the home straight. (5/1: 4/1-7/1)

Blue Lamp (USA) was apparently injured after making quite a promising debut at the Newmarket July meeting. (9/1: op 6/1)

Listed Account (USA) should be given a chance to atone on some better ground. (9/4)

1111 MAIL ON SUNDAY MILE (QUALIFIER) H'CAP (0-95) (3-Y.O+) (Class C)

3-30 (3-34) **1m 5y** £7,067.50 (£2,140.00: £1,045.00: £497.50) Stalls: Low GOING: 0.21 sec per fur (G)

				SP	RR	SF
947*	**Gadge (61)** (ABailey) **6-7-10** DWright(5) (b: led over 4f: led on bit over 2f out: rdn out)	—	1	7/2[2]	72	34
895[5]	**Sylvan Princess (69)** (DJSCosgrove) **4-8-1**(3) MartinDwyer(10) (hld up: hdwy over 2f out: r.o ins fnl f)	1½	2	10/1	77	39
895*	**Broughtons Turmoil (76)** (BRMillman) **8-8-11** DaneO'Neill(6) (a.p: one pce fnl f)	½	3	15/2	83	45
766[7]	**Press On Nicky (70)** (WRMuir) **4-8-5** MRoberts(4) (hdwy fnl 2f: r.o)	½	4	14/1	76	38
791[3]	**Master M-E-N (IRE) (61)** (NMBabbage) **5-7-5v**(5) RMullen(2) (plld hrd: sn prom: one pce fnl 2f)	1¼	5	7/1	65	27
	Law Commission (93) (DRCElsworth) **7-9-11**(3) DGriffiths(3) (nvr nr to chal)	3½	6	16/1	90	52
832[13]	**Therhea (IRE) (70)** (BRMillman) **4-8-5b** TSprake(1) (w wnr: led over 3f out tl over 2f out: sn wknd)	3	7	6/1[3]	61	23
1035[2]	**Knobbleeneeze (75)** (MRChannon) **7-8-5v**(5) PPMurphy(11) (prom over 5f)	3	8	3/1[1]	60	22
	Sandy Floss (IRE) (75) (RHBuckler) **4-8-10** SDrowne(7) (a bhd)	3½	9	14/1	53	15
1001[9]	**Master Millfield (IRE) (64)** (CJHill) **5-7-13** FNorton(9) (hld up mid div: bhd fnl 4f)	7	10	11/1	28	—
				(SP 122.4%)		**10 Rn**

1m 44.5 (6.30) CSF £37.10 CT £232.98 TOTE £4.00: £1.80 £2.70 £2.60 (£15.00) Trio £32.40 OWNER Mr J. B. Wilcox (TARPORLEY) BRED Snowdrop Stud Co Ltd

LONG HANDICAP Master M-E-N (IRE) 7-8

947* Gadge, up 3lb, had scored twice on soft ground in his younger days and continues on the crest of a wave. (7/2)

895 Sylvan Princess, 2lb higher than when making a successful seasonal debut, ran another good race on ground softer than she prefers. (10/1)

895* Broughtons Turmoil was 6lb worse off than when beating the runner-up two-and-a-half lengths at Ascot. (15/2: 5/1-8/1)

Press On Nicky, stepping-up to a mile, caught the eye running on nicely without being knocked about, and seems to be coming to hand. (14/1)

791 Master M-E-N (IRE), despite being raised 5lb, was still just out of the handicap and ran too freely on a surface softer than ideal for him. (7/1)

Law Commission has yet to score beyond seven or on ground worse than good-to-firm. (16/1)

1112 SOMERSET STKS (Listed) (3-Y.O+ F & M) (Class A)

4-00 (4-00) **5f 161y** £10,903.09 (£4,082.90: £1,998.95: £862.25: £388.63: £199.18) Stalls: High GOING: 0.21 sec per fur (G)

				SP	RR	SF
	Royale Figurine (IRE) (103) (MJFetherston-Godley) **6-9-0** DHolland(1) (hdwy over 2f out: sn hrd rdn: led over 1f out: r.o wl)	—	1	7/2[2]	108	77
724[8]	**Arethusa (108)** (RHannon) **3-8-8** DaneO'Neill(6) (hdwy over 2f out: hrd rdn over 1f out: r.o ins fnl f)	3½	2	9/2[3]	102	61
	Blue Iris (102) (MAJarvis) **4-9-0** MRoberts(7) (lw: plld hrd early: led over 3f out tl over 1f out: edgd lft ins fnl f: one pce)	hd	3	100/30[1]	98	67
941[12]	**Connemara (IRE) (107)** (CADwyer) **3-8-4** TSprake(4) (prom tl wknd over 1f out)	5	4	11/1	84	43
685*	**Dayville (USA) (86)** (JBerry) **3-8-4** GCarter(5) (spd over 2f)	7	5	5/1	65	24
	Conspiracy (102) (JLDunlop) **3-8-8** PatEddery(3) (led over 2f: wknd over 1f out)	2	6	7/2[2]	63	22
853[10]	**Bride's Reprisal (88)** (MRChannon) **3-8-4** PPMurphy(2) (s.i.s: hdwy over 2f out: eased whn btn over 1f out)	18	7	25/1	9	—
				(SP 114.5%)		**7 Rn**

1m 12.2 (2.70) CSF £17.85 TOTE £5.10: £2.20 £2.40 (£20.20) OWNER Mr Craig Pearman (EAST ILSLEY) BRED Craig Pearman

WEIGHT FOR AGE 3yo-10lb

STEWARDS' ENQUIRY Roberts susp. 20-24/5/97 (failure to ensure best possible placing).

Royale Figurine (IRE), who is in-foal to Most Welcome, can only run up to July 3rd and may now go for the Temple Stakes at Sandown. (7/2)

Arethusa, brought back to sprinting, kept on to snatch second place on the line and is probably better-suited by six. (9/2)

Blue Iris, on whom Roberts was seemingly under instructions not to use his whip, came under very little pressure, and getting pipped for second place meant a five-day ban for Roberts for failing to ride out. (100/30)

672 Connemara (IRE) found the extended five in rain-softened ground too demanding. (11/1: 8/1-12/1)

685* Dayville (USA) found this company a different kettle of fish. (5/1)

Conspiracy is going to need fast ground to stay beyond the bare minimum. (7/2)

1113 HOLSTEN PILS H'CAP (0-90) (3-Y.O+) (Class C)

4-30 (4-31) **5f 11y** £5,173.00 (£1,564.00: £762.00: £361.00) Stalls: High GOING: 0.21 sec per fur (G)

				SP	RR	SF
905[7]	**Intiaash (IRE) (75)** (DHaydnJones) **5-9-7** PatEddery(7) (lw: hld up: hdwy 2f out: squeezed thro over 1f out: led ins fnl f: r.o wl)	—	1	4/1[2]	85	51
835[14]	**Kildee Lad (75)** (APJones) **7-9-7** TSprake(8) (hdwy over 2f out: bmpd over 1f out: r.o ins fnl f)	¾	2	10/1	83	49
942[22]	**Lunar Mist (74)** (MartynMeade) **4-9-3**(3) RHavlin(3) (a.p: led over 2f out tl ins fnl f)	hd	3	9/1	81	47
879[5]	**Tinker Osmaston (61)** (MSSaunders) **6-8-7** RPerham(9) (lw: a.p: ev ch over 1f out: nt qckn)	1¼	4	5/1[3]	64	30
834[2]	**Literary Society (USA) (71)** (JARToller) **4-9-3** SDrowne(4) (a.p: ev ch whn bmpd over 1f out: one pce)	1¾	5	11/4[1]	69	35
879[8]	**Anokato (62)** (KTIvory) **3-7-10b**(3) MartinDwyer(1) (led over 2f: wknd over 1f out)	nk	6	16/1	59	16
756*	**Sharp Pearl (77)** (JWhite) **4-9-9b** MRoberts(6) (lw: s.s: a bhd)	nk	7	13/2	73	39
786[6]	**Spender (78)** (PWHarris) **8-9-7**(3) DO'Donohoe(2) (lw: chsd ldrs: rdn over 2f out: sn wknd)	2½	8	6/1	66	32
				(SP 115.9%)		**8 Rn**

64.8 secs (4.30) CSF £39.61 CT £312.75 TOTE £3.50: £1.70 £2.00 £2.10 (£20.00) Trio £44.20 OWNER Mr Howard Thomas (PONTYPRIDD) BRED Shadwell Estate Company Limited

WEIGHT FOR AGE 3yo-9lb

STEWARDS' ENQUIRY Eddery susp. 20-24/5/97 (careless riding).

879* Intiaash (IRE), 7lb higher than when scoring over course and distance last month, forced her way through a narrow gap. With Eddery picking up a five-day ban for careless riding, she was fortunate to keep the race, although there is no doubt she was the best horse on merit. (4/1)

Kildee Lad bounced back to form, and it should be noted that all three of his victories here have come over the extended five. (10/1)

731 Lunar Mist was 3lb lower than when not beaten that far in a big field at Newmarket on 2,000 Guineas day. (9/1: 6/1-10/1)

879 Tinker Osmaston could not take advantage of being 9lb better off with the winner than when beaten five lengths here last month. (5/1)

834 Literary Society (USA), up 2lb, was done no favours by the winner but did not appear particularly unlucky. (11/4)

652 Anokato ran better than when behind the winner here last month on 11lb better terms, but did not get home on this softer surface. (16/1)

756* Sharp Pearl, raised 7lb, lost his chance at the start in this tougher race. (13/2)

643* Spender (6/1: 4/1-13/2)

1114 KATH AND DOUG WOOTTEN BIRTHDAY H'CAP (0-70) (4-Y.O+) (Class E)

5-00 (5-03) **2m 1f 34y** £2,869.25 (£869.00: £424.50: £202.25) Stalls: High GOING: 0.21 sec per fur (G)

Form	Horse	Dist	Pos	SP	RR	SF
865[3]	**High Five (IRE) (40)** (RIngram) **7-7-9**(3)ow2 MartinDwyer(3) (hld up & bhd 7f out: led over 2f out: clr whn edgd lft over 1f out: pushed out)	—	1	7/2[1]	53	35
	Fortunes Course (IRE) (50) (JSKing) **8-8-3**(5) RFfrench(6) (lw: a.p: r.o one pce fnl 2f)	8	2	7/1	56	40
660[9]	**Bridie's Pride (40)** (GAHam) **6-7-12** NCarlisle(4) (prom: led over 8f out tl over 2f out: one pce)	2	3	33/1	44	28
603*	**Coh Sho No (58)** (SDow) **4-8-13** WRyan(1) (hld up mid div: hdwy over 6f out: one pce fnl 2f)	5	4	4/1[2]	57	38
	Fieldridge (70) (MPMuggeridge) **8-10-0** PatEddery(8) (hld up: hdwy & c wd 3f out: nvr trbld ldrs)	2½	5	15/2	67	51
769*	**Paradise Navy (70)** (CREgerton) **8-10-0b** DaneO'Neill(12) (lw: hld up: stdy hdwy over 6f out: wknd over 2f out)	2	6	9/2[3]	65	49
481[6]	**Kashan (IRE) (38)** (PHayward) **9-7-5**(5) RMullen(9) (rdn 8f out: a bhd)	16	7	25/1	18	2
838[7]	**Dormy Three (51)** (RJHodges) **7-8-9** SDrowne(5) (hld up mid div: hdwy 6f out: wknd over 2f out)	2½	8	16/1	29	13
603[3]	**Ginka (39)** (JWMullins) **6-7-11**ow1 FNorton(10) (prom over 7f)	2	9	7/1	15	—
43[5]	**Rose of Glenn (41)** (BPalling) **6-7-13**ow1 TSprake(2) (prom over 12f: t.o)	14	10	10/1	4	—
865[10]	**Gentleman Sid (38)** (PGMurphy) **7-7-10** NAdams(11) (led over 8f: rdn 6f out: wknd over 3f out: t.o)	18	11	25/1	—	—
487[6]	**Wicklow Boy (IRE) (38)** (RIngram) **6-7-7**(3) MBaird(7) (ref to r: t.n.p)		R	33/1	—	—

(SP 125.7%) **12 Rn**

3m 55.7 (14.30) CSF £26.53 CT £652.25 TOTE £4.40: £1.40 £2.30 £8.60 (£30.90) Trio £128.40 OWNER Mr D. A. Wilson (EPSOM) BRED Rosemount House Stud

LONG HANDICAP High Five (IRE) 7-6 Ginka 7-7 Kashan (IRE) 7-2 Gentleman Sid 7-7

WEIGHT FOR AGE 4yo-3lb

865 High Five (IRE), effectively carrying 3lb more than his long handicap mark, found no difficulty turning this race into a procession. (7/2)

Fortunes Course (IRE), 6lb higher than when winning at Chepstow last July, stayed on to win the separate race for second. (7/1: 5/1-8/1)

Bridie's Pride reached the prize-money for the first time in nine attempts. (33/1)

603* Coh Sho No, penalised 4lb, probably requires faster ground. (4/1)

Fieldridge presumably came wide in search of better ground. (15/2: 5/1-8/1)

769* Paradise Navy was always going to find it difficult to do it all on the bridle in this ground, and also had a 5lb higher mark to contend with. (9/2: op 3/1)

603 Ginka (7/1: 5/1-8/1)

T/Plpt: £472.60 (27.96 Tckts). T/Qdpt: £100.80 (5.92 Tckts) KH

1095-BEVERLEY (R-H) (Soft becoming Heavy)

Sunday May 11th

WEATHER: heavy showers WIND: fresh half against

1115 BEVERLEY LIONS CLAIMING STKS (3-Y.O) (Class F)

2-20 (2-21) **7f 100y** £2,822.00 (£792.00: £386.00) Stalls: High GOING: 0.44 sec per fur (GS)

Form	Horse	Dist	Pos	SP	RR	SF
862[2]	**Lindrick Lady (IRE)** (BSRothwell) **3-8-8** MFenton(2) (lw: mde all: kpt on wl fnl 2f)	—	1	11/2[3]	68	38
1078[3]	**Petite Risk (50)** (KWHogg) **3-8-4** JQuinn(12) (in tch: hdwy 2f out: styd on: nrst fin)	3½	2	7/1	57	27
448[18]	**Ultra Boy (78)** (PCHaslam) **3-9-1** JFortune(9) (lw: a chsng ldrs: nt qckn fnl 2f)	1¼	3	7/2[2]	65	35
896[16]	**Soviet Lady (IRE) (50)** (JLEyre) **3-7-13v1** TWilliams(11) (a chsng ldrs: effrt over 2f out: no imp)	4	4	13/2	40	10
952[4]	**Broadgate Flyer (IRE) (60)** (MrsLStubbs) **3-8-7** ACulhane(10) (outpcd tl styd on fnl 2f)	½	5	12/1	47	17
748[6]	**Swiss Coast (IRE) (60)** (NTinkler) **3-8-7** LCharnock(5) (a.p: effrt & ch 3f out: wknd fnl 2f)	6	6	8/1	34	4
	Ocean Breeze (JSWainwright) **3-8-4**(5) JBramhill(3) (drvn along & bhd 3f out: n.d)	hd	7	33/1	36	6
882[9]	**Patrita Park (51)** (WWHaigh) **3-8-2** JTate(6) (nvr rchd ldrs)	3	8	20/1	23	—
792[8]	**Hever Golf Angel (IRE)** (PCHaslam) **3-8-7** JWeaver(1) (swvd lft s: a bhd)	2½	9	12/1	22	—
871[9]	**Gresatre (64)** (CADwyer) **3-8-11** KFallon(7) (cl up tl wknd over 2f out)	¾	10	3/1[1]	25	—
547[6]	**Apiculate (IRE) (35)** (SRBowring) **3-8-4** JCarroll(8) (trckd ldrs tl wknd over 2f out)	8	11	20/1	1	—
793[8]	**Misterton** (JAGlover) **3-8-2**(7) TPengkerego(13) (outpcd & bhd fr ½-wy)	3½	12	20/1	—	—
882[10]	**Stravano (40)** (BPJBaugh) **3-7-12**(3) DarrenMoffatt(4) (in tch tl rdn & wknd over 3f out)	5	13	33/1	—	—

(SP 135.1%) **13 Rn**

1m 40.3 (8.30) CSF £42.45 TOTE £4.10: £1.60 £2.20 £1.90 (£24.60) Trio £15.90 OWNER Mr S. P. Hudson (MALTON) BRED F. D. McAuley

862 Lindrick Lady (IRE), despite taking a big drop in distance, still had the speed to lead and, revelling in the soft conditions, was not going to stop. (11/2)

1078 Petite Risk has certainly nothing to recommend her on looks, but she is tough and was keeping on determinedly at the end. (7/1)

155 Ultra Boy won on firm ground last season and was always struggling in these soft conditions. (7/2: 9/4-4/1)

467 Soviet Lady (IRE), tried in a visor here, was never giving full co-operation. (13/2: op 4/1)

952 Broadgate Flyer (IRE) seems to be having trouble in finding his correct trip. (12/1)

748 Swiss Coast (IRE) had his chances but, when ridden early in the straight, he soon cried enough. (8/1)

1116 MR LAZENBY'S H'CAP (0-70) (3-Y.O+ F & M) (Class E)

2-50 (2-51) **1m 100y** £4,377.00 (£1,326.00: £648.00: £309.00) Stalls: High GOING: 0.44 sec per fur (GS)

Form	Horse	Dist	Pos	SP	RR	SF
951[10]	**Three Arch Bridge (65)** (MJohnston) **5-9-10b** JWeaver(6) (lw: mde all: rdn over 1f out: kpt on wl)	—	1	11/2[2]	79	31
574[16]	**Snowy Mantle (42)** (JDBethell) **4-8-1** LCharnock(11) (a chsng ldrs: kpt on one pce fnl 3f)	5	2	14/1	47	—
776[5]	**Sandblaster (47)** (JLEyre) **4-8-6** TWilliams(1) (s.i.s: hdwy 3f out: no ex fnl f)	1½	3	10/1	49	1
843[6]	**Philgem (37)** (CWFairhurst) **4-7-10** NKennedy(4) (a.p: rdn 3f out: one pce)	5	4	25/1	29	—
898[4]	**Mcgillycuddy Reeks (IRE) (37)** (DonEnricoIncisa) **6-7-10** KimTinkler(13) (outpcd & bhd tl sme hdwy fnl 2f)	1	5	12/1	27	—
881[4]	**Portite Sophie (40)** (MBrittain) **6-7-6**(7) DMernagh(3) (a chsng ldrs: grad wknd fnl 2f)	½	6	6/1[3]	29	—
929[10]	**Tolepa (IRE) (37)** (JJO'Neill) **4-7-10** GBardwell(12) (prom early: sn outpcd & lost pl: sme hdwy 2f out: n.d)	9	7	25/1	9	—
887[9]	**Polar Refrain (45)** (JNorton) **4-8-4** JQuinn(7) (hdwy u.p ½-wy: sn wknd)	6	8	12/1	6	—
296[10]	**Sweet Seventeen (40)** (HJCollingridge) **4-7-8**(5) IonaWands(2) (in tch tl st)	2½	9	20/1	—	—
864[8]	**Parsa (USA) (58)** (JLDunlop) **4-9-3** KFallon(9) (lw: hdwy & prom ½-wy: rdn 3f out: sn wknd)	hd	10	7/4[1]	14	—
748[4]	**Bewitching Lady (54)** (DWPArbuthnot) **3-8-0** CRutter(8) (sn outpcd & bhd)	3½	11	11/2[2]	4	—

848^{13} **Dispol Gem (60)** (PCalver) **4-9-5** JCarroll(5) (lw: chsd wnr tl wknd fnl 3f)....4 **12** 8/1 2 —
1020^{15} **Persephone (38)** (JLHarris) **4-7-11**^{ow1} DaleGibson(10) (sn outpcd & wl bhd) ....13 **13** 20/1 — —
(SP 140.9%) **13 Rn**

1m 55.7 (11.70) CSF £82.54 CT £744.69 TOTE £6.80: £2.30 £5.00 £2.00 (£65.30) Trio £247.10 OWNER Mr R. N. Pennell (MIDDLEHAM) BRED R. Taylor
LONG HANDICAP Tolepa (IRE) 6-12 Philgem 6-11 Mcgillycuddy Reeks (IRE) 7-9 Persephone 7-3
WEIGHT FOR AGE 3yo-13lb
571 Three Arch Bridge has been missing the break of late but, back to her normal front-running tactics here, she was always in command. This was her first-ever win on soft ground. (11/2: 4/1-6/1)
Snowy Mantle had her chances, but looked one-paced when ridden early in the straight. (14/1)
776 Sandblaster is a law unto herself and she showed ability at times here, but was never doing enough when it mattered. (10/1)
843 Philgem has yet to win a race and, from 13lb out of the handicap, she was always fighting a lost cause here. (25/1)
898 Mcgillycuddy Reeks (IRE) ran as though this trip was too short. (12/1)
Polar Refrain (12/1: op 20/1)

1117 MAGIC 1161 H'CAP (0-80) (3-Y.O+) (Class D)
3-20 (3-23) **1m 1f 207y** £7,035.00 (£2,130.00: £1,040.00: £495.00) Stalls: High GOING: 0.44 sec per fur (GS)

SP RR SF

608^{3} **Mels Baby (IRE) (71)** (JLEyre) **4-9-4**$^{(3)}$ OPears(9) (hld up: smooth hdwy to ld appr fnl f: rdn & r.o wl)....— **1** 9/4 ^{1} 82 14
838^{2} **Premier Generation (IRE) (60)** (DWPArbuthnot) **4-8-10** SWhitworth(7) (hld up & bhd: hdwy 3f out: ev ch over 1f out: rdn & r.o wl)....½ **2** 7/2 ^{2} 70 2
1024^{7} **Gold Desire (47)** (MBrittain) **7-7-11** GBardwell(10) (lw: trckd ldrs: led 2f out tl appr fnl f: sn outpcd)....7 **3** 6/1 46 —
633* **Gymcrak Premiere (78)** (GHolmes) **9-10-0** KFallon(3) (b.hind: trckd ldrs: ev ch 3f out: wknd wl over 1f out)....9 **4** 11/2 ^{3} 62 —
860^{10} **Mercury (IRE) (50)** (JAGlover) **4-8-0** DaleGibson(5) (hld up: effrt over 2f out: sn outpcd)....1¾ **5** 12/1 32 —
565^{5} **William Wallace (74)** (DHaydnJones) **3-8-9** LCharnock(1) (set slow pce: qcknd ent st: hdd 2f out: wknd)....hd **6** 25/1 56 —
Mr Teigh (67) (MrsJRRamsden) **5-9-3** JFortune(6) (hld up & bhd: effrt over 2f out: n.d)....hd **7** 8/1 48 —
840^{18} **Pension Fund (78)** (MWEasterby) **3-8-13** TLucas(4) (cl up tl lost pl over 2f out: n.d after)....7 **8** 12/1 48 —
*140** **Onefortheditch (USA) (65)** (JRFanshawe) **4-9-1** NVarley(8) (prom: hdwy to chal ent st: sn wknd: fin lame) ..13 **9** 11/2 ^{3} 14 —
(SP 128.4%) **9 Rn**

2m 18.9 (15.80) CSF £10.53 CT £41.59 TOTE £2.80: £1.50 £1.50 £1.90 (£6.40) Trio £15.10 OWNER Mr John Roberts (Wakefield) (HAMBLETON) BRED A. F. O'Callaghan
WEIGHT FOR AGE 3yo-15lb
OFFICIAL EXPLANATION Onefortheditch (USA): was lame behind.
608 Mels Baby (IRE) goes well with give in the ground, travels particularly well and, given a good ride, always had the edge in a driving finish. (9/4: op 7/2)
838 Premier Generation (IRE) has yet to win a race, but he did nothing wrong and there was a lot to like about the way he responded to pressure. His turn should come before long. (7/2)
1024 Gold Desire ran well on ground that did not really suit, and the pace was also too slow for his liking. (6/1)
633* Gymcrak Premiere ran reasonably on ground far too soft. (11/2: op 7/2)
663 Mercury (IRE) could never make any impression, but this was a messy race in very testing ground. (12/1: op 20/1)
William Wallace found the trip in these testing conditions beyond him. (25/1)

1118 TRYTON FOODS H'CAP (0-70) (3-Y.O+) (Class E)
3-50 (3-51) **1m 3f 216y** £3,631.25 (£1,100.00: £537.50: £256.25) Stalls: High GOING: 0.44 sec per fur (GS)

SP RR SF

857^{7} **Mentalasanythin (63)** (DHaydnJones) **8-9-2**$^{(5)}$ GFaulkner(10) (lw: cl up: led 1½f out: styd on)....— **1** 11/2 76 13
Campaspe (52) (JGFitzGerald) **5-8-10** KFallon(5) (lw: bhd: hdwy on outside & prom ent st: chal over 1f out: no ex towards fin)....1 **2** 7/2 ^{2} 64 1
888^{5} **Forgie (IRE) (60)** (PCalver) **4-9-4** MBirch(6) (lw: trckd ldrs: ev ch over 2f out: btn appr fnl f)....7 **3** 5/1 ^{3} 62 —
In A Tizzy (38) (ABMulholland) **4-7-5**$^{(5)}$ IonaWands(11) (led tl hdd & wknd 1½f out)....1½ **4** 25/1 38 —
746^{3} **Lookingforarainbow (IRE) (64)** (BobJones) **9-9-8** NConnorton(9) (trckd ldrs: effrt over 3f out: sn wknd) ....3½ **5** 3/1 ^{1} 60 —
746^{8} **Contrafire (IRE) (70)** (MrsASwinbank) **5-10-0** JSupple(8) (lw: prom tl outpcd & lost pl 6f out: n.d after)....14 **6** 10/1 47 —
687^{4} **Monis (IRE) (38)** (RonaldThompson) **6-7-5**$^{(5)}$ JBramhill(1) (sn outpcd & bhd)....7 **7** 10/1 6 —
848^{14} **Jungle Fresh (47)** (JDBethell) **4-8-5** OUrbina(2) (chsd ldrs tl outpcd 4f out: sn wknd)....1¾ **8** 16/1 12 —
898* **Cottage Prince (IRE) (46)** (JJQuinn) **4-8-4** JQuinn(4) (outpcd over 3f out: sn lost tch)....1½ **9** 6/1 9 —
Dramatic Pass (IRE) (39) (MCChapman) **8-7-8**$^{(3)ow1}$ DarrenMoffatt(7) (bit bkwd: drvn along & bhd after 4f) ..15 **10** 33/1 — —
(SP 124.4%) **10 Rn**

2m 52.6 (19.60) CSF £24.52 CT £97.61 TOTE £6.30: £1.90 £1.70 £1.90 (£11.80) Trio £33.40 OWNER Mr Hugh O'Donnell (PONTYPRIDD) BRED R. B. Warren
LONG HANDICAP Monis (IRE) 7-7 In A Tizzy 7-3 Dramatic Pass (IRE) 6-6
Mentalasanythin goes in the soft which many of his rivals did not, and this probably won him the day. (11/2)
Campaspe, racing on soft ground for the first time, put up a good performance but was always just being held. (7/2)
888 Forgie (IRE), from a yard going well at the moment, had his chances but he is happier on faster ground and over further. (5/1)
In A Tizzy managed to win over hurdles and has changed stables since, and her correct trip on the level has yet to be settled. (25/1)
746 Lookingforarainbow (IRE) ran reasonably for a horse who is better on faster ground. (3/1)
746 Contrafire (IRE) has done all his winning on turf on a much faster surface. (10/1)

1119 SAVOURY KITCHEN MAIDEN STKS (3-Y.O) (Class D)
4-20 (4-25) **5f** £3,631.25 (£1,100.00: £537.50: £256.25) Stalls: High GOING: 0.44 sec per fur (GS)

SP RR SF

Nifty Norman (66) (JBerry) **3-9-0** KFallon(1) (mde all: qcknd clr fnl 2f)....— **1** 9/1 ^{3} 88? 62
792^{3} **Archello (IRE) (71)** (GROldroyd) **3-8-4**$^{(5)}$ GParkin(6) (in tch: hdwy ½-wy: styd on: no ch w wnr)....6 **2** 10/1 64 38
970^{2} **At Large (IRE)** (JRFanshawe) **3-9-0** DHarrison(16) (lw: chsd ldrs: outpcd ½-wy: kpt on fnl f)....4 **3** 6/4 ^{1} 56 30
845^{6} **Supercharmer (63)** (DNicholls) **3-9-0b** JCarroll(12) (lw: chsd ldrs: kpt on fnl f: no imp)....2½ **4** 16/1 48 22
729^{7} **Zalotto (IRE)** (TJEtherington) **3-9-0** GHind(3) (s.i.s: hdwy after 2f: nvr nr to chal)....1½ **5** 25/1 43 17
448^{13} **Rainbow Rain (USA) (80)** (MJohnston) **3-9-0** JWeaver(18) (lw: chsd ldrs: outpcd ½-wy: no imp after)....2½ **6** 5/2 ^{2} 35 9
1014^{10} **Hype Superior (IRE)** (ABailey) **3-9-0** NConnorton(7) (hdwy 2f out: nvr nr to chal)....hd **7** 20/1 35 9
Locksill (ASmith) **3-9-0** MBirch(2) (str: bkwd: s.s: bhd tl sme late hdwy)....nk **8** 33/1 34 8
871^{8} **Fine Times (62)** (CWFairhurst) **3-9-0** SWhitworth(19) (nvr trbld ldrs)....1¾ **9** 14/1 28 2

				SP	RR	SF
882[2]	**Mystical** (MrsLStubbs) **3-8-9v** ACulhane(10) (chsd ldrs to ½-wy: grad wknd)	½	**10**	10/1	22	—
792[10]	**La Doyenne (IRE)** (CBBBooth) **3-8-9** KHodgson(20) (racd alone far side: n.d)	nk	**11**	33/1	21	—
	Just Typical (NTinkler) **3-8-9** KimTinkler(4) (spd to ½-wy)	1¼	**12**	33/1	17	—
995[16]	**Sparkling Harry (62)** (MissLCSiddall) **3-8-11**(3) PMcCabe(14) (sn bhd)	nk	**13**	25/1	21	—
	Gadroon (PCHaslam) **3-9-0** JFortune(11) (bkwd: a bhd)	1½	**14**	25/1	16	—
855[2]	**Magic Fizz (62)** (TJEtherington) **3-9-0** CRutter(13) (hdwy ½-wy: sn wknd)	2	**15**	11/1	10	—
377[8]	**Love Over Gold** (MCChapman) **3-8-9** GBardwell(5) (s.s: a bhd)	3½	**16**	33/1	—	—
	Ioulios (JEBanks) **3-9-0** JQuinn(8) (bit bkwd: spd to ½-wy: sn bhd)	5	**17**	16/1	—	—
899[7]	**Makati** (MJCamacho) **3-9-0** LCharnock(9) (bit bkwd: dwlt: a bhd)	½	**18**	33/1	—	—
531[7]	**Astral Crown (IRE)** (JBerry) **3-8-9** TWilliams(15) (b.hind: a bhd)	15	**19**	25/1	—	—

(SP 158.4%) **19 Rn**

66.2 secs (4.40) CSF £101.77 TOTE £11.90: £2.90 £2.40 £1.40 (£110.90) Trio £24.40 OWNER Mrs Norma Peebles (COCKERHAM) BRED Mrs Norma Peebles

Nifty Norman, who had the necessary low draw for soft ground, turned this into a procession and seems to have improved immensely. (9/1: op 6/1)

792 Archello (IRE) kept plugging away under pressure, but is basically short of any change of speed. (10/1: 5/1-12/1)

970 At Large (IRE), because of the rain-softened ground, had a bad draw and, in the circumstances, this was not a bad effort. (6/4)

729 Supercharmer has more ability if he ever decides to use it. (16/1)

Zalotto (IRE) is showing signs of improvement and looks one to keep an eye on. (25/1)

448 Rainbow Rain (USA) had what turned out to be a poor draw in the conditions, and was always fighting a lost cause. (5/2)

792 Hype Superior (IRE), who ran over ten furlongs last time, put up a much better effort here and looks one to bear in mind. (20/1)

Locksill needed this and, after a poor start, showed definite signs of ability. (33/1)

882 Mystical (10/1: op 6/1)

1120 E.B.F. WILLIAM JACKSON BAKERY MEDIAN AUCTION MAIDEN STKS (2-Y.O) (Class E)

4-50 (4-53) **5f** £3,647.50 (£1,105.00: £540.00: £257.50) Stalls: High GOING: 0.44 sec per fur (GS)

				SP	RR	SF
872[2]	**Branston Berry (IRE)** (JLEyre) **2-8-9** MGallagher(12) (mde all: clr 1f out: styd on)	—	**1**	6/1[2]	79	31
836[2]	**Quiz Master** (EWeymes) **2-9-0** KFallon(7) (lw: chsd ldrs: effrt 2f out: styd on wl towards fin)	¾	**2**	Evens[1]	82	34
884[6]	**Sweet Reward** (JGSmyth-Osbourne) **2-9-0** OUrbina(4) (in tch: kpt on fnl f: no imp)	3	**3**	7/1	72	24
	Reap Rewards (JGFitzGerald) **2-9-0** JFortune(10) (w'like: lengthy: scope: in tch: hdwy ½-wy: styd on: nrst fin)	6	**4**	14/1	53+	5
	The Cannie Rover (MWEasterby) **2-8-9**(5) GParkin(3) (unf: s.i.s: hdwy 2f out: nvr nr to chal)	1¾	**5**	16/1	47	—
	Gymcrak Mystery (GHolmes) **2-8-9** AlexGreaves(6) (unf: bkwd: chsd ldrs tl outpcd appr fnl f)	4	**6**	20/1	29	—
	Shawdon (SirMarkPrescott) **2-9-0** JCarroll(14) (neat: cl up tl wknd appr fnl f)	1	**7**	13/2[3]	31	—
	Top Floor (IRE) (NTinkler) **2-9-0** KimTinkler(1) (w'like: s.i.s: outpcd & bhd: styng on whn hmpd ent fnl f)	¾	**8**	20/1	29	—
	Townville Cee Cee (JSWainwright) **2-8-4**(5) JBramhill(2) (leggy: scope: spd 3f: wknd)	¾	**9**	25/1	21	—
	Tom Dougal (CSmith) **2-9-0** JWeaver(8) (leggy: unf: wnt lft s: hdwy ½-wy: hung rt: sn wknd)	3	**10**	14/1	17	—
	I'm Tef (TDEasterby) **2-9-0** MBirch(11) (neat: spd 3f: wknd)	1¾	**11**	14/1	11	—
	Are Yer There (MWEasterby) **2-9-0** TLucas(13) (tall: unf: s.i.s: a bhd)	2½	**12**	20/1	3	—
	Averham Star (DShaw) **2-9-0** JQuinn(9) (str: cmpt: dwlt: a bhd)	11	**13**	20/1	—	—

(SP 138.9%) **13 Rn**

67.9 secs (6.10) CSF £12.16 TOTE £6.10: £1.90 £1.50 £2.00 (£6.00) Trio £12.50 OWNER Diamond Racing Ltd (HAMBLETON) BRED J. D. and Mrs Abell

872 Branston Berry (IRE), a handful beforehand, did nothing wrong in the race and, given a fine ride by Gallagher - on his first British winner for more than eight years - was always going to hang on. (6/1)

836 Quiz Master battled away well in these testing conditions, and should certainly stay further and his turn will come. (Evens)

884 Sweet Reward gave the impression that he will come into his own over longer trips. (7/1)

Reap Rewards, a big sort, took time to realise what was required but he showed enough to suggest that there is better to come. (14/1: op 8/1)

The Cannie Rover showed definite signs of ability and is one likely to improve. (16/1)

Shawdon is not all that big, and the ground coupled with a poor draw found him out. (13/2: 4/1-7/1)

Top Floor (IRE), completely outpaced early on, was picking up well at the end suggesting that there is ability there. (20/1)

T/Jkpt: Not won; £21,270.92 to Windsor 12/5/97. T/Plpt: £72.30 (221.99 Tckts). T/Qdpt: £5.80 (122.43 Tckts) AA

0902-WOLVERHAMPTON (L-H) (Standard)

Sunday May 11th

WEATHER: sunny intervals WIND: slt half bhd

Other races under Rules of national hunt Racing

1121 FAMILY DAY OUT MEDIAN AUCTION MAIDEN STKS (3 & 4-Y.O) (Class E)

2-10 (2-14) **1m 100y (Fibresand)** £2,596.25 (£785.00: £382.50: £181.25) Stalls: Low GOING minus 0.24 sec per fur (FST)

				SP	RR	SF
	Absolute Liberty (USA) (66) (SPCWoods) **3-8-11** DBiggs(2) (bit bkwd: a.p: led over 3f out: rdn & r.o wl ins fnl f)	—	**1**	14/1	80	32
936*	**Mythical** (SirMarkPrescott) **3-8-6** CNutter(8) (a.p: chsd wnr over 2f out: no imp fnl f)	3½	**2**	6/4[1]	68	20
765[2]	**Pointe Fine (FR) (64)** (JWHills) **3-8-3**(3) MHenry(6) (hld up: hdwy 3f out: nvr nr to chal)	3	**3**	3/1[2]	63	15
681[7]	**Misty Rain** (BWHills) **3-8-3**(3) JDSmith(9) (hdwy over 4f out: hrd drvn ent st: styd on)	1¾	**4**	7/2[3]	59	11
425[5]	**Robbo** (CWThornton) **3-8-11** DeanMcKeown(7) (prom: drvn along 4f out: effrt & rdn over 2f out: sn wknd)	3	**5**	16/1	59	11
	Mr Music (KMcAuliffe) **3-8-11** JFEgan(4) (chsd ldrs: rdn 4f out: wknd over 2f out)	3½	**6**	20/1	52	4
	Gilding The Lily (IRE) (63) (MJohnston) **3-8-6** JFanning(5) (nt grwn: bit bkwd: led 2f: lost pl 5f out: sn rdn & btn)	2½	**7**	12/1	42	—
	Petuntse (JGSmyth-Osbourne) **3-8-11** KDarley(1) (lengthy: unf: bolted bef s: s.s: led after 2f tl over 3f out: wknd qckly: t.o)	24	**8**	14/1	2	—

(SP 118.9%) **8 Rn**

1m 49.6 (4.60) CSF £33.71 TOTE £17.00: £2.90 £1.30 £1.10 (£13.30) Trio £27.10 OWNER Mr S. P. C. Woods (NEWMARKET) BRED C.Weston

Absolute Liberty (USA), getting off the mark on his first outing as a three-year-old, threw down the gauntlet three furlongs out and only needed to keep going to win comfortably. (14/1: 8/1-16/1)

936* Mythical had only one to beat to score at Newmarket and, though she did give it her best shot here, she was never better than second best. (6/4)
765 Pointe Fine (FR) was a bit of a disappointment on his debut on the Fibresand, and was never going well enough to stake a claim. (3/1: op 7/4)
681 Misty Rain has been brought along steadily and, doing all her best work in the latter stages, is gaining experience all the time. (7/2)
Robbo was never far away, but he was being bustled along on the home turn and lacked the pace to mount a challenge. (16/1)
Gilding The Lily (IRE) (12/1: op 8/1)

1122 DAY OF REST H'CAP (0-85) (4-Y.O+) (Class D)
2-40 (2-42) **2m 46y (Fibresand)** £3,220.00 (£970.00: £470.00: £220.00) Stalls: High GOING minus 0.24 sec per fur (FST)

				SP	RR	SF
865^{5}	**Castle Secret (47)** (DBurchell) **11-8-1** JLowe(3) (disp ld to 4f out: sn hrd rdn: styd on gamely to ld post)	—	1	6/1	58	—
982^{8}	**Noufari (FR) (65)** (RHollinshead) **6-9-2**(3) FLynch(2) (disp ld: led wl over 1f out tl ct fnl stride)	s.h	2	$5/2^{2}$	76	7
869^{2}	**Greenspan (IRE) (73)** (WRMuir) **5-9-13** AClark(4) (lw: hld up: hdwy 5f out: hrd drvn 3f out: styd on)	3½	3	$4/1^{3}$	81	12
*858**	**Random Kindness (77)** (RIngram) **4-10-0** JFEgan(1) (lw: hld up: hdwy to ld over 3f out: hrd rdn & hdd wl over 1f out: sn btn)	2	4	$11/10^{1}$	83	11
				(SP 110.5%)		**4 Rn**

3m 43.8 (16.80) CSF £18.68 TOTE £8.40: (£7.80) OWNER Mrs Ruth Burchell (EBBW VALE) BRED Lavinia Duchess of Norfolk
WEIGHT FOR AGE 4yo-3lb
865 Castle Secret, who stays further, looked out of it turning out of the back straight, but he put in a renewed effort once in line for home, and forced his way to the front right on the line. (6/1: op 10/1)
858 Noufari (FR) made the majority of the running and always looked to be going best but, with his stamina failing inside the distance, he was worried out of it close home. (5/2)
869 Greenspan (IRE) settled in the rear, did not pick up as well as was expected and he was unable to get himself into the action. (4/1: 3/1-9/2)
858* Random Kindness had plenty on his plate conceding weight all round and he had shot his bolt below the distance. (11/10)

1123 SUNDAY MEETING H'CAP (0-100) (3-Y.O+) (Class C)
4-10 (4-11) **1m 1f 79y (Fibresand)** £7,725.00 (£2,325.00: £1,125.00: £525.00) Stalls: Low GOING minus 0.24 sec per fur (FST)

				SP	RR	SF
795^{2}	**Crystal Gold (81)** (MRStoute) **3-7-11**(3) MHenry(8) (lw: led 3f: led 2f out: edgd lft: drvn clr)	—	1	$100/30^{2}$	96	38
661^{3}	**Effectual (81)** (MissGayKelleway) **4-8-11**(3) FLynch(6) (b: chsd ldrs: led over 3f out to 2f out: kpt on u.p)	2½	2	$7/2^{3}$	92	48
947^{7}	**Angel Face (USA) (80)** (PDEvans) **4-8-13** JFEgan(4) (hld up: hdwy over 4f out: hrd rdn 2f out: nt pce to chal)	1	3	9/2	89	45
749^{12}	**Cashmere Lady (78)** (JLEyre) **5-8-11** RLappin(2) (trckd ldrs: drvn along 6f out: styd on one pce fnl 2f)	3½	4	20/1	81	37
	Ground Game (87) (DRLoder) **4-9-6** KDarley(3) (b: bit bkwd: led over 6f out tl over 3f out: hrd drvn & one pce fnl 2f)	1	5	$5/2^{1}$	88	44
*61**	**Tribal Peace (IRE) (68)** (BGubby) **5-8-1** DBiggs(1) (bit bkwd: prom: ev ch 3f out: sn hrd drvn: wknd wl over 1f out)	5	6	12/1	61	17
	Pekay (65) (MJohnston) **4-7-12** JFanning(5) (prom tl ½-wy: sn rdn & lost tch)	8	7	12/1	44	—
838^{8}	**South Eastern Fred (91)** (HJCollingridge) **6-9-10** MRimmer(7) (a bhd: rdn over 5f out: no imp)	6	8	8/1	60	16
	Moving Arrow (95) (MissSEHall) **6-10-0** DeanMcKeown(10) (bkwd: s.i.s: effrt 5f out: rdn 3f out)	nk	9	12/1	63	19
				(SP 131.0%)		**9 Rn**

1m 59.2 (3.20) CSF £16.36 CT £52.59 TOTE £4.70: £1.70 £1.40 £1.50 (£9.70) Trio £9.90 OWNER Maktoum Al Maktoum (NEWMARKET)
BRED Gainsborough Stud Management Ltd
WEIGHT FOR AGE 3yo-14lb
795 Crystal Gold, taking on handicappers for the first time and making his debut on the sand, did not really need to get serious to break his duck, and he looks a progressive sort. (100/30)
661 Effectual turned in another pleasing performance and, though the winner proved too good, he ran his race out to the finish and will find easier tasks than this. (7/2)
947 Angel Face (USA) had more than her fair share of weight in this company, but she is a trier and she never gave up. (9/2)
Cashmere Lady has only ever won here, but she was always finding the pace stretching her and, though she kept battling away, lacked the speed to prove troublesome. (20/1)
Ground Game won first time out last season but she looked to have a bit left to work on this time, and she did not have a lot left once headed and the position had to be accepted. (5/2)
61* Tribal Peace (IRE) is an All-Weather specialist but he was stepping-up in grade on this first outing since January, and was feeling the strain soon after entering the straight. (12/1)

1124 SUNDAY ROAST AT DUNSTALL PARK (S) STKS (2-Y.O) (Class G)
4-40 (4-41) **5f (Fibresand)** £1,992.50 (£555.00: £267.50) Stalls: Low GOING minus 0.24 sec per fur (FST)

				SP	RR	SF
902^{6}	**Summerseat** (CWFairhurst) **2-8-7** DeanMcKeown(2) (chsd ldrs: hdwy on ins to ld appr fnl f: r.o wl)	—	1	6/1	56	—
	Impulse (IRE) (APJarvis) **2-8-12** KDarley(4) (neat: bit bkwd: sn pushed along & outpcd: hdwy u.p appr fnl f: fin wl)	1½	2	11/2	56	—
859^{2}	**Jack-N-Jilly (IRE)** (JSMoore) **2-8-4**(3) MHenry(7) (a.p: led over 2f out tl appr fnl f: one pce)	1¼	3	$7/2^{3}$	47	—
	Medina Miss (WGMTurner) **2-8-2**(5) DSweeney(3) (lt-f: unf: led tl over 2f out: wknd appr fnl f)	2½	4	$9/4^{1}$	39	—
*859**	**Wilfred Sherman (IRE)** (JBerry) **2-8-12**(5) PFessey(6) (a.p: rdn wl over 1f out: one pce)	1½	5	$100/30^{2}$	44	—
	Raazi (RMStronge) **2-8-0**(7) AEddery(1) (leggy: lt-f: s.s: a in rr)	6	6	20/1	15	—
1019^{12}	**Slim Prior** (KRBurke) **2-8-12v¹** DRMcCabe(8) (trckd ldrs on outside: outpcd fnl 2f)	2½	7	20/1	12	—
844^{8}	**Sharp Pet** (DMcCain) **2-8-7** VSlattery(5) (b.off hind: gd spd over 3f)	1½	8	25/1	2	—
				(SP 119.1%)		**8 Rn**

63.9 secs (5.00) CSF £35.48 TOTE £8.00: £1.60 £2.20 £2.00 (£30.30) OWNER Mr M. R. Handy (MIDDLEHAM) BRED Roy Matthews
No bid
902 Summerseat won well on this step-down to selling company and connections were lucky to retain her without a bid. (6/1)
Impulse (IRE) could not handle the early pace, but he got better the further he went and was eating up ground at the finish. (11/2)
859 Jack-N-Jilly (IRE) made the winner work to wear her down below the distance, and she then found an extra effort beyond her. Her turn will come before long. (7/2: op 2/1)
Medina Miss, well-supported to open her account at this first time of asking, did nothing wrong, but she is out of a mare with plenty of stamina in her breeding and will obviously need further in time. (9/4: op 7/2)
859* Wilfred Sherman (IRE) pressed the leaders, but he was always at full stretch and his measure had been taken below the distance. (100/30)

1125 STEWARDS AS JOCKEYS H'CAP (0-60) (4-Y.O+) (Class G)

5-10 (5-11) **1m 4f (Fibresand)** £1,997.50 (£560.00: £272.50) Stalls: Low GOING minus 0.24 sec per fur (FST)

				SP	RR	SF
763⁵	**Fresh Fruit Daily (49)** (PAKelleway) **5-11-11** MrsDWilliams(8) (trckd ldrs: hdwy 4f out: led appr fnl f: r.o wl)	—	1	5/2 1	58	42
955⁵	**Barbara's Jewel (53)** (ABailey) **5-12-1** MrRSandys-Clarke(6) (sn wl bhd: hdwy over 3f out: styd on ins fnl f)	¾	2	9/1	61	45
1081*	**All On (64)** (JHetherton) **6-12-12** 5x MrCBealby(5) (led tl appr fnl f: r.o one pce)	1½	3	5/2 1	70	54
*867*⁶	**Forzair (47)** (JJO'Neill) **5-11-9** MrAOrkney(4) (hld up: hdwy 5f out: hrd rdn 2f out: nt rch ldrs)	7	4	3/1 2	44	28
982⁵	**Sharaf (IRE) (58)** (WRMuir) **4-12-6** MrTWhales(2) (lw: chsd ldrs: drvn along 4f out: sn lost tch)	7	5	7/1 3	45	29
848¹²	**Eastleigh (48)** (RHollinshead) **8-11-10** MrsSLeader(3) (b.hind: prom: jnd ldr 4f out: ev ch tl wknd wl over 1f out)	1¼	6	11/1	34	18
	More Bills (IRE) (31) (JNeville) **5-10-7v** MajorCWSLane(7) (prom tl ½-wy: wknd qckly: t.o)	17	7	33/1	—	—
	Mrs Drummond (IRE) (39) (APJarvis) **4-11-1** MrMEChamberlayne(1) (bkwd: a t.o)	28	8	20/1	—	—

(SP 120.7%) **8 Rn**

2m 43.9 (11.40) CSF £25.30 CT £57.88 TOTE £4.20: £1.70 £2.40 £1.10 (£19.30) OWNER Mr Kevin Hudson (NEWMARKET) BRED Worksop Manor Stud Farm

LONG HANDICAP More Bills (IRE) 10-4

763 Fresh Fruit Daily, a fourteenth success for her lady jockey, was always travelling like a winner and, once in front, she only had to keep galloping to score readily. (5/2)

955 Barbara's Jewel came from a long way off the pace and stayed on strongly towards the finish, but the winner had kicked first and was not for catching. (9/1: op 6/1)

1081* All On, having her sixth outing in fifteen days, was further penalised for winning at Carlisle three days ago and 12st 12lb proved just too much for her in the dash to the line. She thoroughly deserves a decent break from racing. (5/2)

867 Forzair, ill at ease cantering to post, made an effort from off the pace down the back straight, but it did not amount to much and he was never a factor. (3/1)

982 Sharaf (IRE) is possibly better on a sounder surface, but he remained in the action for over a mile before beating a retreat. (7/1)

407 Eastleigh took the leader on and looked to have his measure three furlongs out, but he was the one to call enough and downed tools once into the straight. (11/1)

T/Plpt: £128.80 (68.23 Tckts). T/Qdpt: £6.80 (58.35 Tckts) IM

0896-REDCAR (L-H) (Good, Good to firm patches)

Monday May 12th

WEATHER: sunny periods WIND: str half bhd

83 69+ 61 65

1126 'CROW'S NEST RESTAURANT' NOVICE MEDIAN AUCTION STKS (2-Y.O) (Class F) (69)

2-15 (2-16) **5f** £2,617.50 (£730.00: £352.50) Stalls: Centre GOING minus 0.36 sec per fur (F)

				SP	RR	SF
*902**	**One Singer** (MJohnston) **2-9-2** JWeaver(8) (mde all: r.o wl fnl 2f)	—	1	7/2 2	92	51
884*	**Rusty Babe (IRE)** (JJQuinn) **2-9-2** JFortune(6) (lw: chsd ldrs: hdwy 2f out: r.o: nt pce of wnr)	2½	2	6/4 1	84	43
	Miss Puci (JBerry) **2-8-7** KDarley(3) (leggy: a chsng ldrs: rdn & nt qckn fnl 2f)	4	3	11/2 3	62	21
	King of Dance (BSRothwell) **2-8-12** LCharnock(1) (str: s.i.s: hdwy & hung rt ½-wy: nrst fin)	2½	4	8/1	59	18
	Imperial Honey (IRE) (MrsASwinbank) **2-8-7** JStack(2) (neat: unf: s.i.s: hdwy 2f out: nvr nr to chal)	1½	5	20/1	49	8
	Leather And Scrim (IRE) (DNicholls) **2-8-0**(7) CarolynBales(7) (w'like: bit bkwd: nvr wnt pce)	2½	6	25/1	41	—
993¹³	**Asprilla (IRE)** (BEllison) **2-8-7**(5) SCopp(4) (nvr wnt pce)	1¾	7	33/1	41	—
948⁴	**Sandmoor Tartan** (TDEasterby) **2-8-12** MBirch(9) (wnt rt s: gd spd to ½-wy: wknd)	½	8	6/1	39	—
938⁸	**Ngaere Princess** (WTKemp) **2-8-7** KFallon(5) (prom tl outpcd fr ½-wy)	¾	9	14/1	32	—

(SP 121.2%) **9 Rn**

58.5 secs (1.00) CSF £8.60 TOTE £5.00: £1.90 £1.10 £1.70 (£3.90) Trio £4.80 OWNER Clayton Bigley Partnership Ltd (MIDDLEHAM) BRED Zetland Stud

902* One Singer looks even better on Turf than on the All-Weather and obviously has bags of speed. (7/2)

884* Rusty Babe (IRE) ran his heart out but always found the winner too quick and, over further, he should really come into his own. (6/4)

Miss Puci looked fairly straight and showed plenty of speed, and should benefit from the experience. (11/2)

King of Dance, a sturdy type, needed this and, after running green, gave definite signs of ability and looks likely to improve. (8/1)

Imperial Honey (IRE) is nothing special on looks, but she showed enough without getting into it to suggest that better is likely. (20/1)

Leather And Scrim (IRE), one of the better lookers in the race, needed it and never showed. (25/1)

1127 'VOLTIGEUR RESTAURANT' CLAIMING STKS (3-Y.O+) (Class F)

2-45 (2-48) **6f** £2,810.00 (£785.00: £380.00) Stalls: Centre GOING minus 0.36 sec per fur (F)

				SP	RR	SF
879⁹	**River Tern (64)** (JMBradley) **4-8-12** JWeaver(5) (a.p: led over 2f out: hung rt u.p ins fnl f: kpt on)	—	1	6/1 2	71	48
977⁵	**Palo Blanco (75)** (TDBarron) **6-9-3** JFortune(11) (lw: hld up: effrt over 2f out: rdn & ev ch ins fnl f: nt qckn towards fin)	¾	2	10/11 1	74	51
977¹⁰	**Spotted Eagle (76)** (MartynWane) **4-9-12** JCarroll(8) (a chsng ldrs: kpt on fnl 2f: nvr able to chal)	2½	3	20/1	76	53
896⁷	**Born A Lady (38)** (MrsVAAconley) **4-8-7** MDeering(12) (hdwy ½-wy: kpt on: nvr able to chal)	2	4	33/1	52	29
774*	**Standown (64)** (JBerry) **4-9-8** KDarley(13) (lw: hdwy ½-wy: styd on: no imp)	¾	5	8/1	65	42
997¹²	**Not A Lot (50)** (MWEasterby) **3-8-2b** DaleGibson(9) (s.i.s: styd on fnl 2f)	4	6	25/1	44	11
	Assignment (29) (MrsLStubbs) **11-8-12** ACulhane(3) (led centre over 3f: wknd)	s.h	7	50/1	44	21
	Forecast (40) (KAMorgan) **4-8-12** DeanMcKeown(15) (b: dwlt: nvr nrr)	1¼	8	50/1	41	18
*332*¹⁰	**Ragazzo (IRE) (29)** (JSWainwright) **7-9-0b** LCharnock(10) (b.hind: in tch over 3f)	1¼	9	50/1	40	17
876⁸	**Hi Mujtahid (IRE)** (JMBradley) **3-8-1**(5) AmandaSanders(7) (b: a rr div)	½	10	20/1	40	7
668¹⁰	**Napoleon's Return (37)** (JLEyre) **4-9-0v** MGallagher(2) (drvn along & chsd ldrs 3f: sn wknd)	s.h	11	20/1	38	15
	Monkey Face (33) (WWHaigh) **6-8-2**(5) AimeeCook(4) (chsd ldrs over 3f)	s.h	12	50/1	31	8
896¹³	**Oriel Lad (45)** (DonEnricoIncisa) **4-8-12** KimTinkler(6) (a outpcd & bhd)	d.h	12	50/1	36	13
956⁴	**Double Oscar (IRE) (53)** (DNicholls) **4-9-4b** AlexGreaves(1) (racd alone far side: disp ld tl hdd & wknd over 2f out)	4	14	7/1 3	31	8

779^{4}	**Keen To Please (51)** (DenysSmith) **3-7-12**(3) MBaird(14) (sn disp ld: hdd over 2f out: wknd qckly)	6	**15**	7/1^{3}	8	—
				(SP 133.7%)		**15 Rn**

1m 11.4 (1.20) CSF £10.82 TOTE £9.50: £2.10 £1.20 £4.00 (£6.30) Trio £51.90 OWNER Mr M. B. Carver (CHEPSTOW) BRED Bearstone Stud
WEIGHT FOR AGE 3yo-10lb
Palo Blanco clmd DBlower £8,000. Hi Mujtahid (IRE) clmd SKettlewell £5,000.

OFFICIAL EXPLANATION **Hi Mujtahid (IRE): rider reported that the gelding had an awkward head carriage and was unbalanced leaving the stalls. It took her to the three-furlong pole to get him balanced and he continued to run green. The trainer expressed himself satisfied with the ride given.**

702 River Tern looks a real character, but he is certainly in good form and, jumping off on terms this time, he found enough when ridden, despite wandering about. (6/1)
977 Palo Blanco had the form to win this but, when the chips were down, there were no excuses. (10/11)
Spotted Eagle, having only his second run for his new stable, put up a much better effort. (20/1)
Born A Lady had plenty on at these weights and over this trip, and ran quite well in the circumstances. (33/1)
774* Standown found this company just too good, and his stands' side draw was probably a handicap. (8/1)
Not A Lot found this trip a bit sharp, but was staying on well after a poor start. (25/1)
779 Keen To Please (7/1: op 4/1)

1128 KISS AND CUDDLE PROFESSIONAL LADY JOCKEYS' H'CAP (0-70) (3-Y.O+) (Class E)
3-15 (3-20) **1m** £3,054.25 (£919.00: £444.50: £207.25) Stalls: Centre GOING minus 0.36 sec per fur (F)

				SP	RR	SF
1020^{12}	**Oriole (33)** (DonEnricoIncisa) **4-7-13v**^{1} KimTinkler(5) (hdwy ½-wy: led 3f out: hld on wl)	—	**1**	50/1	45	22
763^{8}	**Mezzoramio (46)** (KAMorgan) **5-8-5v**(7) JoHunnam(8) (b: a cl up: kpt on one pce fnl 2f)	1¼	**2**	9/1	56	33
1024^{6}	**Jack Flush (IRE) (60)** (BSRothwell) **3-8-6**(7) ClaireWest(12) (in tch: hdwy 3f out: kpt on fnl f)	1	**3**	12/1	68	32
	Murphy's Gold (IRE) (49) (RAFahey) **6-9-1** AlexGreaves(4) (hld up: hdwy & ch 1f out: rdn & no ex)	nk	**4**	6/1^{2}	56	33
	Maurangi (33) (BWMurray) **6-7-8b**(5) AimeeCook(14) (hdwy stands' side 3f out: kpt on wl fnl f)	½	**5**	12/1	39	16
824^{9}	**Spanish Verdict (58)** (DenysSmith) **10-9-3**(7) JennyBenson(6) (cl up tl wknd over 2f out)	hd	**6**	9/1	64	41
848^{10}	**Return To Brighton (39)** (JMBradley) **5-8-0**(5) AmandaSanders(3) (lw: in tch: no hdwy fnl 3f)	1½	**7**	12/1	42	19
689^{12}	**Rinus Magic (30)** (EJAlston) **4-7-3**(7) NicolaWright(13) (nvr trbld ldrs)	½	**8**	50/1	32	9
896^{5}	**Fisiostar (34)** (MDods) **4-7-7b**(7) KimberleyHart(2) (led tl hdd & wknd 3f out)	½	**9**	8/1	35	12
313^{11}	**Bad News (34)** (JMBradley) **5-7-7**(7) LisaMoncrieff(1) (t: in tch: effrt 3f out: sn wknd)	1¾	**10**	50/1	31	8
578^{3}	**Bagshot (50)** (GLMoore) **6-9-2** CandyMorris(9) (lw: chsd ldrs: rdn 3f out: grad wknd)	2½	**11**	9/2^{1}	42	19
1005^{9}	**Cee-Jay-Ay (53)** (JBerry) **10-9-5** EmmaO'Gorman(11) (s.s: hdwy over 2f out: hrd rdn & n.d)	1¼	**12**	13/2^{3}	43	20
900^{6}	**Advance East (54)** (MDods) **5-8-13v**(7) AngelaGallimore(10) (hld up: effrt over 3f out: n.d)	2½	**13**	10/1	39	16
	Champagne N Dreams (44) (DNicholls) **5-8-3**(7) CarolynBales(16) (prom stands' side tl wknd fnl 3f)	1½	**14**	25/1	26	3
848^{9}	**Asterix (38)** (JMBradley) **9-7-11b**(7) KerryBaker(17) (b: prom stands' side 5f)	6	**15**	16/1	8	—
953^{13}	**Take Notice (49)** (RMMcKellar) **4-8-8**(7) FionaBrown(7) (cl up 5f: wknd)	6	**16**	50/1	7	—
91^{10}	**Our Tom (42)** (JWharton) **5-8-1**(7) VictoriaAppleby(15) (t.o fr ½-wy)	8	**17**	33/1	—	—
				(SP 129.6%)		**17 Rn**

1m 38.0 (3.00) CSF £425.59 CT £5,382.20 TOTE £49.70: £6.60 £2.20 £3.00 £1.90 (£218.00) Trio £445.00; £256.98 to York 13/5/97 OWNER Don Enrico Incisa (MIDDLEHAM) BRED Red House Stud
LONG HANDICAP Rinus Magic 7-8
WEIGHT FOR AGE 3yo-13lb
Oriole, wearing a visor for the first time, was completely transformed and showed fine determination to hold on. (50/1)
Mezzoramio had his chances two out but just lacked a change of gear in the closing stages. (9/1)
1024 Jack Flush (IRE) does not look the easiest of rides as he was always tending to hang left, but he was keeping on well, suggesting that there is a race in him. (12/1)
Murphy's Gold (IRE) travelled well and had his chances but, when an effort was required, he was found wanting. (6/1: op 4/1)
Maurangi ran well, but was probably not helped by his high draw. (12/1: 25/1-10/1)
733 Spanish Verdict, who ran miserably last time, put up a much better performance. (9/1)

1129 'CLASSIC SUITE' H'CAP (0-70) (3-Y.O) (Class E)
3-45 (3-46) **1m 2f** £3,112.75 (£937.00: £453.50: £211.75) Stalls: Low GOING minus 0.36 sec per fur (F)

				SP	RR	SF
1078*	**Jack The Lad (IRE) (71)** (JHetherton) **3-9-12** 5x JWeaver(4) (a cl up: led wl over 2f out: r.o wl)	—	**1**	9/1	83	22
797^{3}	**Regal Reprimand (63)** (GLewis) **3-9-4** PaulEddery(2) (b.hind: in tch: effrt 3f out: n.m.r 2f out: r.o fnl f)	1¼	**2**	5/1^{2}	73	12
864^{2}	**Epic Stand (60)** (MrsJRRamsden) **3-9-1** JFortune(10) (hld up: effrt 4f out: ch 1f out: nt qckn)	1	**3**	5/4^{1}	68	7
771^{6}	**Scarrots (61)** (SCWilliams) **3-9-2** KFallon(11) (lw: chsd ldrs: rdn over 2f out: r.o one pce)	4	**4**	10/1	63	2
749^{5}	**Diamond Eyre (54)** (JLEyre) **3-8-4**(5) RMullen(9) (bhd tl styd on fnl 3f)	1¼	**5**	10/1	54	—
524^{8}	**Monarch's Pursuit (59)** (TDEasterby) **3-9-0** MBirch(1) (led tl hdd wl over 2f out: grad wknd)	nk	**6**	20/1	59	—
497*	**Polarize (55)** (TDBarron) **3-8-10** KDarley(12) (chsd ldrs tl wknd fnl 2½f)	hd	**7**	10/1	54	—
868^{6}	**Quezon City (56)** (MJCamacho) **3-8-11** LCharnock(7) (effrt over 3f out: nvr trbld ldrs)	½	**8**	10/1	55	—
886^{5}	**Barresbo (57)** (CWFairhurst) **3-8-12** PatEddery(6) (bhd tl sme late hdwy)	2	**9**	7/1^{3}	52	—
1024^{5}	**Marsh Marigold (57)** (JHetherton) **3-8-12** NCarlisle(3) (dwlt: hld up & a bhd)	7	**10**	16/1	41	—
900^{4}	**Grovefair Lad (IRE) (52)** (MartynWane) **3-8-7** JCarroll(5) (cl up tl wknd 3f out)	2	**11**	16/1	33	—
825^{5}	**Men Of Wickenby (51)** (RMMcKellar) **3-8-6** JLowe(8) (prom tl wknd over 3f out)	2½	**12**	33/1	28	—
609^{8}	**My Saltarello (IRE) (55)** (ABMulholland) **3-8-10b**^{1} DeanMcKeown(13) (in tch to st: sn wknd)	10	**13**	33/1	16	—
				(SP 142.4%)		**13 Rn**

2m 11.0 (7.40) CSF £57.50 CT £92.20 TOTE £10.10: £4.10 £2.20 £1.10 (£24.50) Trio £16.60 OWNER Keith West Partnership (MALTON) BRED Thomas Healy
1078* Jack The Lad (IRE) is in tremendous form just now, and once in front, he was not going to give it up. (9/1)
797 Regal Reprimand looked a shade unlucky, and is one to keep on the right side of from now on. (5/1)
864 Epic Stand, who looks likely to appreciate this trip, was very much on his toes in the paddock. His performance was a shade disappointing, and this was not his true running. (5/4)
771 Scarrots, who probably went too fast last time, found the pace just the opposite here and was done for speed late on. (10/1)
749 Diamond Eyre did well considering the slow early pace, making up a lot of ground in the straight. (10/1)
Monarch's Pursuit is gradually getting the hang of this game, and there is more to come in due course. (20/1)
868 Quezon City (10/1: op 11/2)

1130 'CLASSIC BOXES' MAIDEN STKS (3-Y.O) (Class D)
4-15 (4-18) **1m 2f** £3,847.00 (£1,156.00: £558.00: £259.00) Stalls: Low GOING minus 0.36 sec per fur (F)

				SP	RR	SF
847^{3}	**Banbury (USA)** (JWWatts) **3-9-0** JCarroll(8) (lw: hld up: hdwy 4f out: led 1f out: r.o wl)	—	**1**	6/1	100	33
842^{2}	**Mumaris (USA)** (ACStewart) **3-9-0** RHills(10) (lw: a.p: led 2f out to 1f out: r.o)	3	**2**	7/2 [2]	95	28
773^{6}	**Taunt** (DMorley) **3-9-0** PatEddery(9) (chsd ldrs: chal 3f out: rdn & one pce fnl 2f)	3	**3**	7/2 [2]	90	23
	Mengaab (USA) (JHMGosden) **3-9-0** JWeaver(3) (b.hind: mid div: hdwy over 2f out: chsng ldrs appr fnl f: nt qckn u.p)	2½	**4**	9/4 [1]	86	19
742^{7}	**Dalliance (IRE)** (MRStoute) **3-9-0** KDarley(5) (chsd ldrs: ev ch 2f out: wknd appr fnl f)	5	**5**	9/2 [3]	78	11
	Speedboat (USA) (JLEyre) **3-9-0**(3)ow3 OPears(11) (plld hrd: led & sn clr: racd wd: rn v.wd st: hdd & wknd 2f out)	10	**6**	12/1	65	—
	Kayfiyah (IRE) (DMorley) **3-8-9** JStack(4) (lengthy: unf: hld up & bhd: hdwy 4f out: nvr nr to chal)	½	**7**	20/1	57	—
	Briggs Turn (WJarvis) **3-9-0** OUrbina(1) (prom tl wknd fnl 3f)	4	**8**	33/1	55	—
	Avro Avian (MJCamacho) **3-8-9** LCharnock(6) (w'like: bkwd: dwlt: hld up & bhd tl sme late hdwy)	2½	**9**	50/1	46	—
	San Glamore Melody (FR) (JHMGosden) **3-9-0** JLowe(12) (cmpt: hld up & a bhd)	6	**10**	20/1	42	—
	Northern Maestro (MrsMReveley) **3-9-0** ACulhane(2) (w'like: bit bkwd: hld up & a bhd)	¾	**11**	33/1	40	—
997^{9}	**Absolute Charlie** (CWFairhurst) **3-9-0** DeanMcKeown(7) (a bhd)	11	**12**	100/1	23	—
				(SP 133.7%)	**12 Rn**	

2m 8.1 (4.50) CSF £26.73 TOTE £7.30: £2.20 £1.30 £1.50 (£14.30) Trio £21.50 OWNER Sheikh Mohammed (RICHMOND) BRED Darley Stud Management Inc

847 Banbury (USA), again wearing the tongue-strap, got it right this time and did it particularly well, staying on really strongly. (6/1)
842 Mumaris (USA) is running consistently well and should stay further, and will surely not be a maiden for much longer. (7/2)
773 Taunt had no excuses this time and just proved short of pace in the last two furlongs. (7/2)
Mengaab (USA) needed the Monty Roberts rug to enter the stalls, wears bandages behind and is not the best of movers and, after looking dangerous approaching the final furlong, ran out of fuel. (9/4)
742 Dalliance (IRE) looks the type to improve and showed something here until running out of steam in the last couple of furlongs. (9/2: 6/1-4/1)
Speedboat (USA), wearing a cross-noseband, took charge from the start but obviously has ability if he can be taught to settle. (12/1)
Kayfiyah (IRE) showed a little here without getting into it and has plenty of scope for improvement. (20/1)
Avro Avian is a full-sister to Avro Anson and, although very much in need of this, she showed ability without looking likely to trouble the principals. Time should see plenty of improvement. (50/1)

1131 'SEE THE DIFFERENCE' H'CAP (0-80) (3-Y.O+ F & M) (Class D)
4-45 (4-46) **7f** £3,535.00 (£1,060.00: £510.00: £235.00) Stalls: Centre GOING minus 0.36 sec per fur (F)

				SP	RR	SF
1003^{3}	**Gymcrak Flyer (60)** (GHolmes) **6-8-11** KFallon(2) (lw: b.hind: trckd ldrs: hdwy 2f out: led ins fnl f: r.o)	—	**1**	15/8 [1]	69	51
995^{4}	**La Dolce Vita (68)** (TDBarron) **3-8-7** JFortune(10) (in tch: effrt over 2f out: r.o towards fin)	¾	**2**	9/1	75	45
892^{17}	**Zelda Zonk (76)** (BJMeehan) **5-9-13** PatEddery(5) (lw: disp ld tl led 2f out: hdd & no ex ins fnl f)	nk	**3**	11/2 [3]	83	65
1000^{3}	**Trading Aces (68)** (MBell) **3-8-2v**(5) RMullen(9) (hld up: effrt 3f out: r.o towards fin)	nk	**4**	6/1	74	44
1012*	**College Night (IRE) (46)** (SCWilliams) **5-7-4**(7) 7x DarrenWilliams(8) (prom: effrt over 2f out: nt qckn)	3½	**5**	7/1	44	26
593^{13}	**Magic Lake (45)** (EJAlston) **4-7-7**(3) MBaird(1) (lw: disp ld 5f: sn rdn & btn)	6	**6**	20/1	29	11
723^{14}	**Our Way (72)** (CEBrittain) **3-8-11** JWeaver(7) (prom 4f: sn wknd)	1¼	**7**	5/1 [2]	53	23
953^{9}	**Don't Care (IRE) (72)** (MissLAPerratt) **6-9-9** OUrbina(6) (prom 4f: eased whn btn)	nk	**8**	11/1	53	35
	Pride of Pendle (70) (MartynWane) **8-9-7** JCarroll(4) (hld up: effrt over 2f out: n.d)	s.h	**9**	12/1	51	33
652^{9}	**Sarabi (59)** (JPearce) **3-7-12** DaleGibson(3) (hld up: effrt 3f out: sn rdn & btn)	11	**10**	20/1	14	—
				(SP 129.2%)	**10 Rn**	

1m 24.1 (1.10) CSF £21.05 CT £79.83 TOTE £3.10: £1.10 £2.40 £2.30 (£12.90) Trio £21.90 OWNER The Gymcrak Thoroughbred Racing Club (PICKERING) BRED D. G. Mason
LONG HANDICAP Magic Lake 7-8
WEIGHT FOR AGE 3yo-12lb

1003 Gymcrak Flyer, happy at this trip, picked up well from halfway and won with a little in hand. (15/8)
995 La Dolce Vita, an edgy filly, has ability and responded well to pressure late on. (9/1)
Zelda Zonk won this last year and looks magnificent at the moment, and ran a cracking race off what appears a stiffish mark. (11/2)
1000 Trading Aces was a shade unlucky but finished particularly well and gave the impression that, over further, better looks likely. (6/1)
1012* College Night (IRE) was always close enough if good enough, but her penalty proved to be the stumbling block. (7/1)
464 Magic Lake looks well at present, but stopped as though shot here when the pressure was on. She is a moody customer who certainly has more ability when things go her way. (20/1)
Our Way (5/1: op 10/1)
529 Don't Care (IRE) (11/1: 8/1-12/1)

T/Plpt: £34.30 (505.32 Tckts). T/Qdpt: £18.30 (52.68 Tckts) AA

1043-SOUTHWELL (L-H) (Standard)
Monday May 12th
WEATHER: sunny WIND: mod half bhd

1132 SPAIN CLAIMING STKS (I) (3-Y.O+) (Class F)
2-00 (2-01) **7f** **(Fibresand)** £1,927.00 (£527.00: £247.00) Stalls: Low GOING: 0.17 sec per fur (SLW)

				SP	RR	SF
1047^{2}	**Desert Invader (IRE) (65)** (DWChapman) **6-9-0**(5) PFessey(5) (lw: trckd ldrs: led over 2f out: edgd lft & hdd ins fnl f: rallied to ld cl home)	—	**1**	2/1 [2]	69	43
1047^{3}	**Bold Aristocrat (IRE) (63)** (RHollinshead) **6-9-0**(3) FLynch(1) (hld up: effrt on ins over 2f out: swtchd rt: led ins fnl f: hdd cl home)	hd	**2**	5/1 [3]	67	41
1082^{8}	**Young Annabel (USA) (71)** (CADwyer) **4-9-3**(5) GFaulkner(3) (sn chsng ldrs: led over 4f out tl over 2f out: swtchd rt over 1f out: sn wknd)	5	**3**	5/4 [1]	60	34
870^{4}	**Commin' Up (42)** (MissJBower) **4-9-2** DHarrison(4) (chsd ldrs: rdn over 3f out: one pce fnl 2f)	¾	**4**	14/1	53	27
1047^{7}	**Samsolom (40)** (MESowersby) **9-8-6**(7) KSked(7) (outpcd ½-wy: kpt on fnl 2f: nvr nr to chal)	3½	**5**	33/1	42	16
	Gunner B Special (33) (SRBowring) **4-9-1b** SWebster(9) (b: sn drvn along: outpcd & lost tch ½-wy)	10	**6**	25/1	21	—

864[12] **Appeal Again (IRE) (38)** (DBurchell) **4-8-13b1** JQuinn(2) (sn bhd & drvn along)	5	**7**	16/1	7	—
Sylvania Lights (AGNewcombe) **3-7-10** JMarshall(6) (unruly: led: plld hrd: hdd over 4f out: sn lost pl: eased)	dist	**8**	33/1	—	—
956[15] **Aquado (48)** (DShaw) **8-8-10**(3) CTeague(8) (ref to r: t.n.p)		**R**	20/1	—	—
			(SP 121.5%)	**9 Rn**	

1m 32.9 (6.40) CSF £11.57 TOTE £4.20: £1.00 £1.80 £1.80 (£4.90) Trio £1.60 OWNER Mr David Chapman (YORK) BRED Gainsborough Stud Management Ltd
WEIGHT FOR AGE 3yo-12lb
1047 Desert Invader (IRE) never looked happy, but still showed more resolution than the runner-up. (2/1: tchd 3/1)
1047 Bold Aristocrat (IRE), who had the same chance as the winner on official figures, was brought with a well-timed run to go a head up inside the last but, once there, he put the brakes on and threw it away. (5/1)
578 Young Annabel (USA) was having her second run in just three days. (5/4: evens-4/5)
870 Commin' Up did as well as could be expected considering she would have been meeting the first and second on 20lb better terms in a handicap. (14/1)

1133 ITALY H'CAP (0-65) (4-Y.O+) (Class F)
2-30 (2-32) **1m 6f (Fibresand)** £2,277.00 (£627.00: £297.00) Stalls: Low GOING: 0.17 sec per fur (SLW)

			SP	RR	SF
888[11] **Kalamata (54)** (JAGlover) **5-9-5** NDay(8) (trckd ldrs: led over 7f out: clr 4f out: eased towards fin)	—	**1**	9/1	72+	36
1114* **High Five (IRE) (38)** (RIngram) **7-8-3** 4x GBardwell(10) (b: sn bhd & pushed along: hdwy 6f out: styd on one pce fnl 3f)	12	**2**	7/2[1]	38	2
384[6] **Stalled (IRE) (48)** (PTWalwyn) **7-8-13** DHolland(9) (b: hld up & bhd: hdwy on outside 5f out: styd on wl fnl 2f)	hd	**3**	12/1	52	16
994[3] **Hasta la Vista (41)** (MWEasterby) **7-8-1b**(5)ow2 GParkin(1) (lw: led tl over 7f out: one pce fnl 4f)	6	**4**	7/2[1]	38	—
580[10] **Another Quarter (IRE) (40)** (MCChapman) **4-7-13**(5) PFessey(6) (chsd ldrs tl wknd over 2f out)	5	**5**	25/1	32	—
*867** **Carrolls Marc (IRE) (40)** (CMurray) **9-8-0**(5) IonaWands(12) (sn bhd & pushed along: hdwy 6f out: nvr nr ldrs)	12	**6**	8/1	18	—
763[10] **Cohiba (43)** (BJCurley) **4-8-7** WRyan(14) (hld up & bhd: drvn along 4f out: n.d)	8	**7**	13/2[3]	12	—
218P **Swandale Flyer (31)** (NBycroft) **5-7-5**(5) JBramhill(11) (chsd ldrs: sn drvn along: wknd 4f out)	½	**8**	16/1	—	—
1100[16] **El Nido (53)** (DWChapman) **9-8-11**(7) RWinston(16) (chsd ldrs tl lost pl over 5f out)	2	**9**	20/1	19	—
908[3] **Jump The Lights (64)** (SPCWoods) **4-9-7**(7) CWebb(15) (hld up: a bhd)	¾	**10**	10/1	29	—
867[5] **Precedency (52)** (KMcAuliffe) **5-9-3** JFEgan(7) (trckd ldrs: rdn & lost pl over 3f out)	3½	**11**	14/1	13	—
869[4] **Pharly Dancer (61)** (WWHaigh) **8-9-12** LNewton(2) (chsd ldrs: drvn along 8f out: lost pl 6f out)	5	**12**	8/1	16	—
888[16] **Sushi Bar (IRE) (48)** (MrsMReveley) **6-8-13** DHarrison(4) (chsd ldrs: drvn along 8f out: lost pl over 4f out)	9	**13**	20/1	—	—
660[4] **Tiaphena (42)** (JMackie) **6-8-7** JQuinn(5) (b: trckd ldrs: wknd over 5f out)	7	**14**	11/2[2]	—	—
Tip it In (35) (ASmith) **8-8-0** NAdams(3) (b: sn bhd: t.o 5f out)	12	**15**	20/1	—	—
Glowing Mantle (IRE) (31) (BPreece) **9-7-10** DWright(13) (sn bhd: t.o 7f out)	½	**16**	50/1	—	—
			(SP 154.8%)	**16 Rn**	

3m 12.4 (14.40) CSF £44.31 CT £393.34 TOTE £17.90: £3.30 £2.20 £2.30 £1.10 (£62.50) Trio £62.50 OWNER Mr B. H. Farr (WORKSOP) BRED Worksop Manor Stud Farm
LONG HANDICAP Swandale Flyer 7-8 Glowing Mantle (IRE) 7-4
WEIGHT FOR AGE 4yo-1lb
660 Kalamata, obviously well-suited by the testing conditions, recorded his third victory here this year. Out on his own in the final half-mile, he won pulling up. (9/1)
1114* High Five (IRE), attempting to make it two wins in two days on very different surfaces, was soon being pushed along. Sticking on under pressure, he never got within hailing distance of the winner. (7/2: 5/2-9/2)
205 Stalled (IRE), who is slipping down the weights, is now on a long losing run, but the way he finished here with a professional in the saddle suggests that another victory is just round the corner. (12/1)
994 Hasta la Vista, 9lb lower on this surface, was making hard work of it a long way from home. (7/2: 6/1-3/1)
Cohiba (13/2: 5/1-8/1)

1134 SPAIN CLAIMING STKS (II) (3-Y.O+) (Class F)
3-00 (3-01) **7f (Fibresand)** £1,927.00 (£527.00: £247.00) Stalls: Low GOING: 0.17 sec per fur (SLW)

			SP	RR	SF
860[8] **Jigsaw Boy (53)** (PGMurphy) **8-9-3** DHarrison(6) (lw: chsd ldrs: drvn along 5f out: led on bit over 1f out: sn clr: easily)	—	**1**	Evens[1]	55+	36
1047[11] **Komaseph** (RFMarvin) **5-9-5** TGMcLaughlin(8) (s.i.s: bhd tl hdwy 2f out: styd on wl ins fnl f: no ch w wnr)	6	**2**	25/1	43	24
Kustom Kit Klassic (SRBowring) **3-8-11** SWebster(3) (b: sn wl bhd: styd on wl fnl 2f: nt rch ldrs)	½	**3**	20/1	46	15
105[9] **Medland (IRE) (36)** (BJMcMath) **7-8-13** DBiggs(7) (b: a chsng ldrs: sn pushed along: one pce fnl 2f)	3	**4**	10/1	29	10
772[5] **Dissentor (IRE) (38)** (JAGlover) **5-8-13b** GCarter(4) (set str pce: hdd over 1f out: wknd qckly ins fnl f)	1	**5**	100/30[2]	27	8
1003[10] **Dashing Dancer (IRE) (34)** (DShaw) **6-8-13** JFanning(1) (lw: chsd ldr: rdn over 2f out: wknd over 1f out)	¾	**6**	5/1[3]	25	6
896[14] **Spanish Stripper (USA) (30)** (MCChapman) **6-9-0**(3) DO'Donohoe(2) (s.i.s: sn wl bhd: sme late hdwy)	nk	**7**	14/1	29	10
856[10] **Little Papoose** (BAMcMahon) **4-8-12** LNewton(9) (trckd ldrs: rdn & wknd over 2f out)	2	**8**	25/1	19	—
903[8] **Verro (USA) (20)** (KBishop) **10-8-13e** GBardwell(5) (sn wl bhd & drvn along)	1½	**9**	40/1	17	—
			(SP 120.4%)	**9 Rn**	

1m 33.3 (6.80) CSF £35.46 TOTE £1.90: £1.10 £6.70 £2.20 (£57.30) Trio £161.80; £100.27 to York 13/5/97 OWNER Mrs Louise Murphy (BRISTOL) BRED Mrs J. A. Rawding
WEIGHT FOR AGE 3yo-12lb
579 Jigsaw Boy, clear best-in on official figures, looked to have been found an easy opening. After being troubled to go the strong pace, he took it up on the bridle and, in the end, won with any amount in hand. (Evens)
Komaseph had shown very little on his two previous outings, one in a National Hunt Flat race and the other in a seller. Taking time to find his stride, he came from some way off the pace to secure second spot. (25/1)
Kustom Kit Klassic, who showed very little in two outings at two, was another to come from off the pace in what was a strongly-run race. (20/1)
Medland (IRE) had the blinkers left off. (10/1)
772 Dissentor (IRE) set a very strong pace and, after being collared, he fell away to nothing inside the last. (100/30)
774 Dashing Dancer (IRE) (5/1: op 3/1)

1135 FRANCE H'CAP (0-70) (3-Y.O+ F & M) (Class E)

3-30 (3-31) **1m (Fibresand)** £3,174.25 (£949.00: £454.50: £207.25) Stalls: Low GOING minus 0.19 sec per fur (FST)

Form	Horse / Trainer / Weight / Jockey / Comment	Dist	Pos	SP	RR	SF
587^{4}	**Queens Stroller (IRE) (38)** (REPeacock) **6-7-5**(5) JBramhill(1) (sn chsng ldrs: drvn along ½-wy: led over 1f out: hld on towards fin)	—	1	14/1	44	10
868^{4}	**Isis Honda (IRE) (57)** (CEBrittain) **3-8-2** GBardwell(4) (b.hind: chsd ldrs: drvn along over 4f out: hrd rdn & outpcd over 2f out: kpt on fnl f)	nk	2	12/1	62	15
687^{17}	**David James' Girl (43)** (ABailey) **5-7-8**(7) RWinston(15) (b: lost pl after 2f: gd hdwy 2f out: n.m.r: styd on wl ins fnl f)	½	3	4/1 1	47	13
526^{16}	**Efipetite (39)** (NBycroft) **4-7-11**ow1 NKennedy(9) (sn trckng ldrs: effrt on outside over 2f out: r.o fnl f)	nk	4	25/1	43	8
864^{13}	**Heathyards Lady (USA) (66)** (RHollinshead) **6-9-7**(3) FLynch(14) (b: lw: hld up: rdn & hung lft 2f out: styd on ins fnl f)	1	5	16/1	68	34
860^{2}	**Sis Garden (60)** (JCullinan) **4-9-1b**(3) DO'Donohoe(5) (a chsng ldrs: rdn to chal over 2f out: one pce fnl f)	1	6	8/1	60	26
870^{7}	**Cats Bottom (54)** (AGNewcombe) **5-8-12** JQuinn(7) (hld up: hdwy over 2f out: sn chsng ldrs: hung lft & one pce fnl f: eased nr fin)	2	7	9/2 2	50	16
857^{10}	**People Direct (52)** (KMcAuliffe) **4-8-10** JFEgan(6) (led tl over 1f out: wknd ins fnl f)	1	8	10/1	46	12
951^{9}	**Best of All (IRE) (65)** (JBerry) **5-9-9e** GCarter(8) (lw: hdwy over 4f out: sn chsng ldrs: rdn & wknd 2f out)	3½	9	8/1	52	18
748^{7}	**Hadadabble (38)** (PatMitchell) **4-7-10** NVarley(11) (lw: chsd ldrs: sn drvn along: outpcd ½-wy: n.d after)	8	10	20/1	9	—
791^{13}	**Hoh Flyer (USA) (67)** (MBell) **3-8-12** MFenton(10) (chsd ldrs: sn drvn along: outpcd over 2f out: sn wknd)	1¼	11	7/1 3	35	—
1048^{8}	**Down The Yard (38)** (MCChapman) **4-7-5**(5) IonaWands(2) (sn bhd)	s.h	12	20/1	6	—
883^{4}	**Lachesis (38)** (DShaw) **4-7-10** DWright(13) (racd wd: w ldrs tl lost pl over 3f out)	8	13	7/1 3	—	—
867^{8}	**Jilly Beveled (40)** (RonaldThompson) **5-7-12**ow2 TWilliams(12) (hdwy on outside over 3f out: sn lost pl)	¾	14	20/1	—	—
795^{10}	**Silver Moon (56)** (BAMcMahon) **3-7-8**(7)ow5 SRighton(3) (sn bhd: virtually p.u 2f out)	dist	15	40/1	—	—

(SP 135.3%) **15 Rn**

1m 47.5 (8.50) CSF £162.96 CT £766.47 TOTE £10.20: £5.60 £2.20 £1.70 (£96.90) Trio £150.00 OWNER Mr R. E. Peacock (MALMESBURY) BRED Ardenode Stud Ltd

LONG HANDICAP Queens Stroller (IRE) 7-2 Hadadabble 7-5 Efipetite 7-3 Down The Yard 7-6 Lachesis 7-6 Jilly Beveled 7-8 Silver Moon 7-1

WEIGHT FOR AGE 3yo-13lb

587 Queens Stroller (IRE) won twice in March last year, and was 18lb lower than her winning grass mark and 28lb lower than her previous All-Weather success. She proved very game, but the post came just in time. (14/1)

868 Isis Honda (IRE) stuck on after being outpaced turning in. A slightly longer trip will not come amiss. (12/1)

428 David James' Girl, 9lb lower than when she last won, was well-supported to regain the winning streak. Short of room over a furlong out, she stayed on strongly inside the last, but needed another fifty yards. (4/1)

428 Efipetite has only won once from forty-seven starts, but there is no doubt that she is now back on a mark from which she can add to her record. (25/1)

554 Heathyards Lady (USA) ran easily her best race so far this year. (16/1)

860 Sis Garden was 2lb higher than when runner-up last time. The Handicapper looks to have her form assessed to a tee. (8/1)

951 Best of All (IRE) (8/1: 6/1-9/1)

58+ 66 65+ 50

1136 SWEDEN MAIDEN AUCTION STKS (2-Y.O) (Class F) (59)

4-00 (4-02) **5f (Fibresand)** £2,277.00 (£627.00: £297.00) Stalls: High GOING minus 0.19 sec per fur (FST)

Form	Horse / Trainer / Weight / Jockey / Comment	Dist	Pos	SP	RR	SF
	Malozza (PDEvans) **2-8-2** JFEgan(8) (cmpt: a chsng ldrs: r.o u.p to ld wl ins fnl f)	—	1	12/1	59	12
938^{3}	**Charlies Lad (IRE)** (RGuest) **2-8-7** PBloomfield(11) (led: hung bdly lft thrght: hdd wl ins fnl f)	nk	2	7/4 1	63	16
	Minetta (MBell) **2-8-4** MFenton(6) (w'like: leggy: scope: swvd lft s: sn chsng ldr: sltly hmpd ½-wy: nt qckn appr fnl f)	1¾	3	11/2 3	54	7
	Elleysanta (AGNewcombe) **2-7-13** JMarshall(13) (leggy: unf: prom tl outpcd ½-wy: kpt on fnl f)	6	4	33/1	30	—
	Benrock (IRE) (CaptJWilson) **2-7-13**(7) AngelaHartley(4) (wl grwn: w ldrs tl wknd over 1f out)	hd	5	8/1	37	—
664^{2}	**Moss Side Monkey** (JBerry) **2-8-7** GCarter(12) (s.i.s: sn outpcd: nvr nr ldrs)	3½	6	11/2 3	27	—
447^{14}	**Margaret's Dancer** (CSmith) **2-8-1**(3) DO'Donohoe(9) (dwlt: bhd: sme hdwy over 1f out: n.d)	¾	7	33/1	21	—
	Life Sentence (JGSmyth-Osbourne) **2-8-9** DHarrison(3) (small: str: s.i.s: sn in tch: rdn & outpcd ½-wy)	s.h	8	20/1	26	—
	Heavenly Falls (IRE) (CADwyer) **2-8-5** NVarley(10) (leggy: s.i.s: a bhd)	s.h	9	12/1	22	—
	Kagsi (DCO'Brien) **2-7-12** GBardwell(1) (unf: chsd ldrs tl lost pl 2f out)	3½	10	33/1	4	—
	Gralmano (IRE) (NPLittmoden) **2-8-8** TGMcLaughlin(5) (w'like: sltly hmpd s: a outpcd & bhd)	1¾	11	5/1 2	8	—
993^{7}	**Toll's Times** (MWEasterby) **2-8-2**(5) GParkin(7) (s.i.s: sn drvn along & outpcd)	3	12	16/1	—	—
	Dispol Lass (PCalver) **2-7-10**(3) DarrenMoffatt(2) (w'like: s.i.s: a outpcd & bhd)	s.h	13	12/1	—	—

(SP 137.5%) **13 Rn**

60.4 secs (3.40) CSF £33.88 TOTE £21.30: £6.10 £1.20 £3.60 (£18.40) Trio £28.90 OWNER Mr D. Maloney (WELSHPOOL) BRED W. R. Jones

Malozza, by the 'Tartan St Leger' winner Michelozzo out of a point-to-point mare, is hardly bred to be a sharp two-year-old. Probably racing on the better ground, she ran on willingly to get up near the line. (12/1: op 8/1)

938 Charlies Lad (IRE) made the running but hung badly left throughout, despite his rider's efforts, ending up on the slower ground towards the far side. Swishing his tail violently, he is obviously one to have severe reservations about. (7/4)

Minetta was intimidated and slightly hampered by the hanging Charlies Lad at the halfway mark. Keeping on, she should be sharper next time. (11/2: 3/1-6/1)

Elleysanta, a narrow May foal, stuck on again when it was all over and will be suited by six. (33/1)

Benrock (IRE), a typical son of Ballad Rock, showed ability and will do better in time. (8/1: op 12/1)

Heavenly Falls (IRE) (12/1: op 8/1)

Gralmano (IRE), who has plenty of size and scope, lost his chance when hampered at the start. He ought to be capable of a good deal better. (5/1: 3/1-11/2)

53 53 60

1137 DENMARK (S) STKS (2-Y.O F) (Class F)

4-30 (4-32) **5f (Fibresand)** £2,277.00 (£627.00: £297.00) Stalls: High GOING minus 0.19 sec per fur (FST)

Form	Horse / Trainer / Weight / Jockey / Comment	Dist	Pos	SP	RR	SF
999^{8}	**Persian Fortune** (WGMTurner) **2-8-4**(5) DSweeney(6) (mde all: hld on wl towards fin)	—	1	14/1	57	6
927^{2}	**Ellenbrook (IRE)** (JBerry) **2-8-4**(5) PFessey(5) (lw: unruly s: w ldr: nt qckn wl ins fnl f)	nk	2	5/1 3	56	5
	Beechwood Quest (IRE) (BSRothwell) **2-8-9** MFenton(4) (w'like: dwlt: sn w ldrs: hung lft ½-wy: nt qckn appr fnl f)	3	3	5/1 3	46	—

				SP	RR	SF
1091^{5}	**My Bet** (MWEasterby) **2-8-9**$^{(5)}$ GParkin(7) (sn drvn along: chsd ldrs: rdn & outpcd ½-wy: edgd lft & kpt on same pce appr fnl f)	½	**4**	3/1^{2}	50	—
979^{6}	**Patsy Culsyth** (MJohnston) **2-8-9** JFanning(1) (lw: w ldrs: rdn ½-wy: lost pl over 1f out)	9	**5**	5/2^{1}	16	—
902^{8}	**Chardania (IRE)** (CaptJWilson) **2-8-2**$^{(7)}$ AngelaHartley(3) (w ldrs: rdn 2f out: sn lost pl)	2	**6**	14/1	10	—
780^{3}	**Maedaley** (PCHaslam) **2-8-9** TWilliams(2) (chsd ldrs: rdn ½-wy: sn lost pl & eased)	28	**7**	6/1	—	—
				(SP 114.5%)	**7 Rn**	

61.2 secs (4.20) CSF £74.00 TOTE £13.40: £2.60 £2.20 (£28.80) OWNER Mr G. L. Barker (SHERBORNE) BRED J. G. Charlton
Bt in 4,400 gns

Persian Fortune, who had shown very little on her debut seven days earlier, showed the right sort of spirit to fight off the second's determined challenge. She is not very big but six furlongs will be no problem. (14/1)
927 Ellenbrook (IRE) gave problems at the start but did nothing wrong in the race, throwing down a determined challenge. (5/1: op 3/1)
Beechwood Quest (IRE), who had more size and scope than the others in the field, missed the break slightly but was soon upsides. Tending to hang left, the experience will not be lost on her. (5/1)
1091 My Bet, having her second outing in three days, was on edge beforehand and was flat-out from start to finish. (3/1)
979 Patsy Culsyth, dropped in class, was possibly racing on the slower ground. Certainly the three who raced away from the stands' side rail dropped right out in the final furlong-and-a-half. (5/2: op 11/10)

1138 GERMANY APPRENTICE H'CAP (0-65) (3-Y.O+) (Class G)
5-00 (5-00) **1m 3f (Fibresand)** £1,984.50 (£547.00: £259.50) Stalls: Low GOING: 0.17 sec per fur (SLW)

				SP	RR	SF
1001^{7}	**Evezio Rufo (45)** (NPLittmoden) **5-8-8v** PRoberts(5) (sn bhd & pushed along: gd hdwy 5f out: styd on to ld wl ins fnl f)	—	**1**	14/1	56	9
867^{4}	**Kilnamartyra Girl (43)** (JParkes) **7-8-6** DSweeney(9) (lw: sn outpcd & pushed along: bhd tl hdwy 3f out: ev ch ins fnl f: nt qckn nr fin)	nk	**2**	9/2^{1}	54	7
888^{14}	**Heighth of Fame (64)** (JHetherton) **6-9-10**$^{(3)}$ IonaWands(8) (chsd ldrs: led over 7f out: clr 3f out: hdd wl ins fnl f)	1¼	**3**	8/1	73	26
	Diego (64) (CEBrittain) **4-9-8**$^{(5)}$ KParkin(3) (lw: chsd ldrs tl lost pl over 5f out: sn bhd: swtchd outside 2f out: r.o wl)	2½	**4**	13/2^{2}	69	22
	Burning Cost (37) (REPeacock) **7-7-11**$^{(3)ow4}$ KSked(1) (lost pl 7f out: sme hdwy 4f out: nvr nr to chal)	13	**5**	50/1	23	—
598^{12}	**Carol Again (45)** (NBycroft) **5-8-5**$^{(3)}$ JBramhill(2) (lw: gd hdwy over 7f out: sn chsng ldrs: rdn over 4f out: wknd over 2f out)	1¾	**6**	7/1^{3}	29	—
908^{6}	**Happy Brave (37)** (PDCundell) **5-7-9**$^{(5)}$ CCogan(13) (dwlt: hdwy u.p over 6f out: wknd over 1f out)	1½	**7**	7/1^{3}	19	—
928^{4}	**Mowlaie (50)** (DWChapman) **6-8-13** PFessey(14) (bit bkwd: gd hdwy 7f out: rdn & lost pl over 2f out)	½	**8**	16/1	31	—
544^{3}	**Evaporate (33)** (MJHeaton-Ellis) **5-7-5**$^{(5)}$ JFowle(11) (b: chsd ldrs tl lost pl ½-wy: bhd whn hung bdly rt over 2f out)	4	**9**	10/1	8	—
324^{8}	**Illuminate (65)** (DCO'Brien) **4-9-7**$^{(7)}$ DanielBurchell(7) (swtg: led tl over 7f out: wknd over 3f out)	½	**10**	16/1	39	—
944^{5}	**Dulas Bay (51)** (MWEasterby) **3-7-6**$^{(5)}$ RWinston(6) (chsd ldrs tl lost pl: 7f out: sn bhd)	2½	**11**	12/1	22	—
	Perfect Angel (IRE) (50) (MHTompkins) **3-7-5**$^{(5)}$ RBrisland(12) (prom tl lost pl ½-wy: sn bhd)	8	**12**	20/1	9	—
495^{6}	**Stretching (IRE) (55)** (ABailey) **4-8-13b**$^{1(5)}$ TSiddall(4) (b: sn pushed along: gd hdwy 7f out: lost pl 4f out)	1¾	**13**	7/1^{3}	11	—
843^{8}	**Safa Dancer (39)** (BAMcMahon) **4-7-11**$^{(5)}$ SRighton(10) (w ldrs tl wknd over 3f out)	nk	**14**	12/1	—	—
				(SP 129.8%)	**14 Rn**	

2m 33.8 (13.80) CSF £74.41 CT £516.83 TOTE £12.30: £2.40 £2.60 £2.10 (£32.30) Trio £122.40 OWNER Mr T. Clarke (WOLVERHAMPTON)
BRED Lode Moors Farm
LONG HANDICAP Evaporate 7-6 Burning Cost 6-11
WEIGHT FOR AGE 3yo-17lb

Evezio Rufo was unable to go the frantic gallop and came from last to first. Dropped 8lb in the ratings, he did just enough. (14/1)
867 Kilnamartyra Girl, as usual, was soon in trouble. Sticking to her guns, in the end she was only just denied. This trip is on the sharp side for her. (9/2)
613 Heighth of Fame, back on his favourite surface, helped set a strong pace. Kicking clear off the bend, he did really well to last-out in front until the final seventy-five yards. Considering the pace at which the race was run, this was a most creditable effort. (8/1)
Diego, who has dropped down the weights, looked in good trim. Coming from well off the pace on possibly the best ground towards the stands' side, he finished with quite a flourish. There is no doubt that he is now on a mark from which he can win again. (13/2)
Safa Dancer (12/1: op 25/1)

T/Plpt: £42.20 (249.98 Tckts). T/Qdpt: £33.80 (17.13 Tckts) WG

WINDSOR (Fig. 8) (Good to soft becoming Soft)
Monday May 12th
WEATHER: fair WIND: almost nil

1139 FIFIELD CLAIMING STKS (3 & 4-Y.O) (Class F)
6-00 (6-00) **1m 67y** £2,738.00 (£768.00: £374.00) Stalls: High GOING: 0.13 sec per fur (G)

				SP	RR	SF
668*	**Scathebury (62)** (KRBurke) **4-9-7** DHolland(12) (hld up: chsd ldr over 2f out: led over 1f out: pushed out)	—	**1**	9/2^{1}	70	29
1012^{12}	**Ludo (64)** (RHannon) **3-8-5** DaneO'Neill(18) (rdn over 3f out: gd hdwy over 1f out: r.o wl ins fnl f)	1½	**2**	9/1	64	10
197^{8}	**Mad Alex** (MJHaynes) **4-9-0** MRoberts(4) (lw: rdn over 3f out: hdwy over 1f out: r.o)	1½	**3**	33/1	57	16
771^{11}	**Chief Predator (USA) (56)** (RHannon) **3-8-8** RPerham(9) (rdn 5f out: nt clr run on ins over 2f out: hdwy over 2f out: r.o)	2	**4**	14/1	60	6
264^{4}	**Pastiche (69)** (TGMills) **3-7-11**$^{(5)}$ RFfrench(13) (a.p: led over 3f out tl over 1f out: wknd fnl f)	¾	**5**	11/2^{2}	53	—
843^{10}	**Finsbury Flyer (IRE) (68)** (RJHodges) **4-9-3** SDrowne(10) (lw: chsd ldrs: rdn over 5f out: one pce)	3	**6**	8/1	49	8
297^{7}	**Bold Faith** (WJMusson) **4-9-4** GHind(2) (b: hdwy over 1f out: nvr nrr)	nk	**7**	14/1	50	9
	Valise (39) (GGMargarson) **4-8-8**$^{(3)}$ MHenry(3) (rdn over 3f out: nvr nrr)	3	**8**	20/1	37	—
964^{6}	**Sure To Dream (IRE)** (RTPhillips) **4-8-10** TSprake(7) (rdn & hdwy over 2f out: wknd fnl f)	½	**9**	25/1	35	—
131^{8}	**Mutadarra (IRE) (79)** (WJMusson) **4-9-8** JReid(5) (a mid div)	½	**10**	8/1	46	5
	Schisandra (48) (MJFetherston-Godley) **3-7-13** FNorton(8) (rdn 5f out: a mid div)	5	**11**	33/1	26	—
895^{27}	**Courting Danger (63)** (DRGandolfo) **4-9-0b** AMcGlone(14) (led over 6f out tl over 3f out: sn wknd)	s.h	**12**	16/1	28	—
824^{11}	**Classic Leader (74)** (ICampbell) **4-9-5v**^{1} RCochrane(15) (prom over 5f)	2½	**13**	16/1	28	—
476^{14}	**Challenger (IRE) (40)** (JJSheehan) **4-9-4** CRutter(16) (prom 5f)	5	**14**	50/1	18	—

				SP	RR	SF
790^{10}	**Gracious Imp (USA)** (JRJenkins) **4-8-9**(5) ADaly(1) (a bhd)	4	**15**	50/1	6	—
	All Stand (55) (MajorDNChappell) **4-8-12** AClark(17) (a bhd)	2	**16**	16/1	—	—
	Orange Order (IRE) (71) (JWhite) **4-9-7** TQuinn(11) (prom over 5f)	¾	**17**	$6/1^{3}$	8	—
422^{10}	**Hever Golf Eagle (40)** (TJNaughton) **4-9-4** SSanders(6) (led over 1f: wknd over 3f out)	16	**18**	16/1	—	—

(SP 135.3%) **18 Rn**

1m 51.1 (8.90) CSF £41.85 TOTE £4.40: £1.80 £6.50 £5.60 (£73.50) Trio £178.60; £226.47 to York 14/5/97 OWNER Mr Nigel Shields (WANTAGE) BRED The Duke Of Marlborough

WEIGHT FOR AGE 3yo-13lb

668* Scathebury had no easy task at the weights but he coped well with the soft ground and, woken-up to lead below the distance, needed only to be nudged along for a decisive victory. This is his grade. (9/2: op 11/4)

Ludo appreciated this longer trip and drop in class, and made up a tremendous amount of ground in the last furlong-and-a-half, if finding the line always going to beat him. (9/1: 6/1-10/1)

128 Mad Alex was making his debut on grass and, with a drop in class, ran his best race to date, staying on well in the last furlong-and-a-half to be nearest at the finish. (33/1)

491 Chief Predator (USA) had no easy task at the weights, and did not have a trouble-free run. However, he stayed on nicely from below the distance to take fourth prize. This is his grade. (14/1)

264 Pastiche was making her debut on grass and taking a drop in class. Sent on over three furlongs from home, she was collared below the distance and soon tired. (11/2)

843 Finsbury Flyer (IRE) was off the bridle a long way out, and could only go up and down in the same place in the straight. (8/1)

213 Bold Faith (14/1: 10/1-16/1)

Mutadarra (IRE) (8/1: 6/1-9/1)

1140 STORACALL H'CAP (0-70) (3-Y.O) (Class E)

6-30 (6-31) **1m 3f 135y** £3,160.00 (£955.00: £465.00: £220.00) Stalls: High GOING: 0.13 sec per fur (G)

				SP	RR	SF
771^{4}	**Right Man (57)** (GLewis) **3-8-8** AClark(13) (a.p: led over 1f out: rdn out)	—	**1**	$9/1^{3}$	74	30
878^{2}	**Krosno (63)** (SCWilliams) **3-8-11**(3) MHenry(4) (led 10f: unable qckn)	3½	**2**	$7/1^{1}$	75	31
	Dizzy Tilly (56) (TJNaughton) **3-8-7** DHolland(18) (hdwy 4f out: hrd rdn over 2f out: one pce)	¾	**3**	33/1	67	23
1002*	**Sudest (IRE) (64)** (IABalding) **3-8-12**(3) 5x MartinDwyer(1) (hdwy 3f out: hrd rdn 2f out: wknd fnl f)	8	**4**	$7/1^{1}$	64	20
	Classic Line (59) (JLDunlop) **3-8-10** GDuffield(7) (hdwy over 1f out: nvr nrr)	2½	**5**	12/1	56	12
	Moonspell (65) (RCharlton) **3-9-2** TSprake(5) (prom 9f)	nk	**6**	12/1	61	17
998^{9}	**Blue Hopper (62)** (MRChannon) **3-8-13** RPainter(12) (lw: hdwy 3f out: hrd rdn over 1f out: one pce)	1	**7**	25/1	57	13
658^{3}	**Masrrah (IRE) (62)** (RWArmstrong) **3-8-13** RPrice(10) (b.hind: nvr nr to chal)	1¾	**8**	20/1	55	11
771^{2}	**Aficionado (IRE) (67)** (RJHodges) **3-9-4** SSanders(11) (a mid div)	4	**9**	$7/1^{1}$	54	10
	Tommy Tortoise (70) (MissGayKelleway) **3-9-7** RCochrane(15) (shkn up over 2f out: nt clr run over 1f out: nvr nrr)	¾	**10**	$8/1^{2}$	56	12
	Beauchamp Lion (62) (JLDunlop) **3-8-13** BDoyle(20) (lw: nvr nrr)	1½	**11**	12/1	46	2
837^{4}	**Certain Magic (63)** (WRMuir) **3-9-0v¹** JReid(8) (prom 9f)	1½	**12**	12/1	45	1
878^{11}	**Tartan Party (62)** (PFICole) **3-8-13** TQuinn(6) (a mid div)	1	**13**	12/1	42	—
838^{13}	**Aurelian (58)** (MBell) **3-8-9** MHills(17) (a bhd)	1	**14**	25/1	37	—
889^{9}	**Cadbury Castle (57)** (MBlanshard) **3-8-8** RPerham(3) (prom 8f)	4	**15**	33/1	31	—
878^{9}	**Eponine (68)** (MRChannon) **3-9-0**(5) PPMurphy(19) (prom 8f)	s.h	**16**	25/1	42	—
700^{P}	**Classic Mystery (IRE) (62)** (BJMeehan) **3-8-6**(7) GHannon(16) (a bhd)	nk	**17**	33/1	35	—
857^{9}	**Big Bang (61)** (MBlanshard) **3-8-12** MRoberts(2) (bhd fnl 6f)	28	**18**	25/1	—	—
	Sand Cay (USA) (65) (RHannon) **3-9-2** DaneO'Neill(14) (prom tl hmpd on ins 6f out: nt rcvr)	21	**19**	20/1	—	—
	Select Star (IRE) (66) (APJarvis) **3-9-3** WJO'Connor(9) (prom 7f)	hd	**20**	25/1	—	—

(SP 134.7%) **20 Rn**

2m 36.7 (10.70) CSF £60.42 CT £1,864.13 TOTE £8.80: £2.00 £2.10 £10.10 £2.40 (£31.20) Trio Not won; £413.65 to York 14/5/97 OWNER Mr G. V. Wright (EPSOM) BRED A. C. Birkle

771 Right Man was in his element over this longer trip on soft ground, where stamina rather than acceleration was the order of the day. (9/1)

878 Krosno handles this ground and coped well with the step-up in trip. (7/1)

Dizzy Tilly, making her seasonal debut, coped with the big step-up in distance. (33/1)

1002* Sudest (IRE), who won over this trip on fast ground last Monday, was not as happy on this soft ground and tired in the final furlong. (7/1)

Classic Line stayed on from the back of the field without ever posing a threat. (12/1: op 8/1)

Moonspell, who ran poorly on rain-softened ground last year, was taking a step-up in distance and had given her all over two furlongs from home. A sound surface would help. (12/1: 8/1-14/1)

Tommy Tortoise, who has changed stables since last year, was not given a hard time on this return to action. A drop in the handicap would be a great help. (8/1)

Beauchamp Lion (12/1: op 8/1)

1141 BEALE DOBIE & CO H'CAP (0-80) (3-Y.O) (Class D)

7-00 (7-01) **5f 217y** £3,935.00 (£1,190.00: £580.00: £275.00) Stalls: High GOING: 0.01 sec per fur (G)

				SP	RR	SF
532^{17}	**Strat's Quest (64)** (DWPArbuthnot) **3-8-9** SWhitworth(3) (a.p: hrd rdn over 1f out: led nr fin)	—	**1**	20/1	64	43
988^{8}	**Heavenly Miss (IRE) (64)** (JJBridger) **3-8-9** RCochrane(1) (led: hrd rdn over 1f out: hdd nr fin)	hd	**2**	33/1	64	43
904^{5}	**Sally Green (IRE) (65)** (CFWall) **3-8-10** GDuffield(8) (a.p: ev ch 1f out: one pce)	1½	**3**	20/1	61	40
*399**	**Will To Win (55)** (PGMurphy) **3-8-0** CRutter(7) (hdwy over 1f out: nvr nrr)	¾	**4**	16/1	49	28
930^{8}	**Ivory Dawn (65)** (KTIvory) **3-8-7**(3) MartinDwyer(18) (racd stands' side: hld up: rdn over 1f out: one pce)	1¾	**5**	20/1	54	33
694^{9}	**Marsad (IRE) (75)** (RAkehurst) **3-9-6** AClark(20) (racd stands' side: a.p: one pce fnl 2f)	¾	**6**	$6/1^{1}$	62	41
652^{10}	**Wild Nettle (51)** (JCFox) **3-7-10** DeclanO'Shea(2) (s.s: hdwy over 4f out: hrd rdn 2f out: one pce)	¾	**7**	33/1	36	15
904^{6}	**Farewell My Love (IRE) (76)** (PFICole) **3-9-7** TQuinn(6) (w ldr over 4f)	nk	**8**	12/1	60	39
	Savona (IRE) (75) (PJMakin) **3-9-6** DHolland(11) (hdwy 2f out: eased whn btn ins fnl f)	1½	**9**	20/1	55	34
413^{3}	**V I P Charlie (74)** (JRJenkins) **3-9-5** SSanders(4) (lw: nt clr run 2f out: nvr nrr)	2	**10**	10/1	49	28
602^{8}	**Village Pub (FR) (60)** (KOCunningham-Brown) **3-8-0**(5) RFfrench(9) (prom over 3f)	s.h	**11**	33/1	35	14
	Stock Hill Dancer (63) (BJMeehan) **3-8-8** BDoyle(22) (racd stands' side: spd 4f)	s.h	**12**	20/1	38	17
	Tailwind (65) (WRMuir) **3-8-10** DHarrison(13) (a mid div)	1¼	**13**	20/1	36	15
1008^{6}	**Without Friends (IRE) (72)** (JFfitch-Heyes) **3-9-0b¹**(3) MHenry(24) (racd stands' side: prom 4f)	nk	**14**	25/1	43	22
652^{11}	**Hype Energy (70)** (GLewis) **3-9-1** PaulEddery(5) (outpcd)	hd	**15**	$7/1^{2}$	40	19
876^{3}	**Silver Lining (64)** (APJones) **3-8-9** TSprake(25) (racd stands' side: prom 4f)	nk	**16**	16/1	33	12

				SP	RR	SF
685[10]	**Midnight Shift (IRE) (73)** (RGuest) **3-9-4** MRoberts(12) (prom over 3f)	½	**17**	16/1	41	20
964[3]	**Bold Tina (IRE) (74)** (RHannon) **3-9-5** DaneO'Neill(21) (racd stands' side: a bhd)	3	**18**	8/1[3]	34	13
863[15]	**Silver Purse (74)** (APJones) **3-9-5** SDrowne(17) (racd stands' side: prom 3f)	hd	**19**	50/1	34	13
1107[6]	**Sharp Return (61)** (MJRyan) **3-8-6** GCarter(23) (racd stands' side: prom over 3f)	2	**20**	20/1	15	—
694[8]	**Papita (IRE) (72)** (SDow) **3-8-12**(5) ADaly(10) (bhd fnl 4f)	½	**21**	16/1	25	4
694[17]	**Batsman (60)** (WJMusson) **3-8-5** GHind(19) (racd stands' side: a bhd)	3	**22**	33/1	5	—
	Shifting Time (73) (IABalding) **3-9-4** MHills(15) (lw: racd stands' side: a bhd)	2½	**23**	12/1	11	—
845[14]	**Mon Bruce (68)** (WRMuir) **3-8-13** JReid(14) (lw: bhd fnl 2f)	4	**24**	20/1	—	—
	Class Distinction (IRE) (73) (RHannon) **3-8-11**(7) GGallagher(16) (lw: racd stands' side: a bhd)	8	**25**	20/1	—	—
				(SP 146.3%)	**25 Rn**	

1m 14.1 (3.60) CSF £522.12 CT £11,546.80 TOTE £24.60: £5.90 £10.00 £8.90 £2.60 (£584.40) Trio £1,266.90; £1,249.10 to York 14/5/97
OWNER Mr Jack Blumenow (COMPTON) BRED Miss P. E. Decker
LONG HANDICAP Wild Nettle 7-8

Strat's Quest, whose only previous victory came on this surface, clearly handles it well and, always close up on the far side, managed to get on top near the line. (20/1)

602 Heavenly Miss (IRE) showed blistering pace from the stalls and took the field along until eventually overhauled near the line. Although she has never won on this surface, she handles it well. (33/1)

904 Sally Green (IRE) was always close-up on the far side, and had every chance entering the final furlong before tapped for toe. (20/1)

399* Will To Win stayed on well in the last furlong-and-a-half without ever looking likely to get there in time. Her two wins to date have come in sellers on the sand. (16/1)

506 Ivory Dawn did best of the stands' side group, winning that battle inside the final furlong, but found the return to six furlongs too sharp for her. (20/1)

694 Marsad (IRE) led the stands' side group over a quarter-of-a-mile from home, but he did not have overall control and was passed by Ivory Dawn inside the final furlong. (6/1)

413 V I P Charlie, who has shown all his form on the sand - winning twice on that surface this year - failed to get a clear run but stayed on to be nearest at the line. (10/1)

1142 ROBERT WALTERS LIMITED STKS (0-75) (4-Y.O+) (Class D)
7-30 (7-31) **1m 2f 7y** £3,642.50 (£1,100.00: £535.00: £252.50) Stalls: High GOING: 0.13 sec per fur (G)

				SP	RR	SF
881[6]	**Roufontaine (75)** (WRMuir) **6-8-11** JReid(13) (lw: hld up: led 2f out: rdn out)	—	**1**	4/1[2]	81	40
647[14]	**Zidac (71)** (PJMakin) **5-9-0** SSanders(9) (lw: hld up: led over 2f out: sn hdd: unable qckn fnl f)	3	**2**	14/1	79	38
1016[7]	**Cedez le Passage (FR) (69)** (KOCunningham-Brown) **6-9-2b** BDoyle(10) (a.p: ev ch over 1f out: one pce)	2	**3**	20/1	78	37
657[6]	**Ocean Park (72)** (LadyHerries) **6-9-0** DeclanO'Shea(5) (b: lw: hdwy over 1f out: r.o one pce)	1¼	**4**	4/1[2]	74	33
	Farringdon Hill (72) (JHMGosden) **6-9-0** LDettori(7) (lw: hdwy over 1f out: one pce)	1¾	**5**	9/2[3]	71	30
781[6]	**Philistar (69)** (JMPEustace) **4-9-0b** RCochrane(3) (led 4f: led over 4f out tl over 2f out: sn wknd)	½	**6**	12/1	70	29
	Classic Parisian (IRE) (73) (ICampbell) **4-8-11** RPrice(12) (bit bkwd: prom over 7f)	5	**7**	12/1	60	19
369[7]	**Myfontaine (65)** (KTIvory) **10-8-7**(7) CCassidy(2) (b: b.hind: bhd fnl 7f)	2½	**8**	20/1	59	18
63[9]	**Whippers Delight (IRE) (25)** (GFHCharles-Jones) **9-8-7**(7) CharlotteCox(8) (a bhd)	5	**9**	33/1	51	10
333[9]	**Just Flamenco (38)** (MJRyan) **6-9-0** GCarter(11) (a bhd)	3	**10**	33/1	46	5
558*	**Kota (75)** (JWharton) **4-9-2** PatEddery(6) (lw: hdwy 8f out: led 6f out tl over 4f out: wknd 3f out)	5	**11**	100/30[1]	40	—
	Hawanafa (40) (MissKMGeorge) **4-8-11** GDuffield(4) (lw: bhd fnl 7f)	17	**12**	40/1	8	—
				(SP 121.2%)	**12 Rn**	

2m 13.1 (8.20) CSF £50.40 TOTE £4.80: £1.60 £4.40 £3.70 (£45.50) Trio £159.40 OWNER Piercefield Stables (LAMBOURN) BRED D. J. and Mrs Deer

Roufontaine was rated 75 in a race restricted to horses rated no more than that. She likes this ground according to her trainer. (4/1)

482 Zidac ran much better here but, having got to the front, was soon passed by the winner and put in his place. (14/1: 10/1-16/1)

789 Cedez le Passage (FR) is very exposed and, although he every chance over a furlong from home, was then tapped for toe. Two wins from forty-two starts says it all. (20/1)

657 Ocean Park stayed on in the last furlong-and-a-half without posing a serious threat. (4/1)

Farringdon Hill, who has changed stables since last year, found this trip too sharp and never had the pace to get into it. Both his wins to date have come on fast ground. (9/2)

781 Philistar cut out a lot of the running, but weakened quickly when collared. (12/1: op 7/1)

Classic Parisian (IRE) (12/1: op 8/1)

88+ 72 77+ 78 (79)

1143 BONUSPRINT CONDITIONS STKS (2-Y.O) (Class C)
8-00 (8-01) **5f 10y** £4,333.20 (£1,618.80: £789.40: £337.00: £148.50: £73.10) Stalls: High GOING: 0.01 sec per fur (G)

				SP	RR	SF
893[3]	**Banningham Blade** (KTIvory) **2-8-7**(3) MartinDwyer(6) (a.p: rdn over 1f out: led ins fnl f: r.o wl)	—	**1**	9/1	87	48
965*	**Chips (IRE)** (DRCElsworth) **2-9-3** LDettori(1) (lw: a.p: rdn over 1f out: ev ch ins fnl f: r.o)	nk	**2**	5/6[1]	93	54
954*	**Golden Mirage (IRE)** (MRChannon) **2-8-5**(5) PPMurphy(2) (a.p: led 2f out tl ins fnl f: r.o)	hd	**3**	7/1[3]	86	47
965[2]	**The Boy John (USA)** (RHannon) **2-8-11** PatEddery(3) (lw: led 3f: wknd over 1f out)	4	**4**	4/1[2]	74	35
	Jay Gee (IRE) (GGMargarson) **2-8-3** GCarter(7) (unf: bit bkwd: s.s: outpcd: nvr nrr)	hd	**5**	40/1	66	27
850[5]	**Alpen Wolf (IRE)** (WRMuir) **2-8-11** JReid(5) (spd over 2f)	1	**6**	16/1	71	32
	Truth Teller (RHannon) **2-8-8** DaneO'Neill(4) (scope: s.s: a bhd)	1½	**7**	12/1	63	24
				(SP 113.1%)	**7 Rn**	

62.5 secs (2.80) CSF £15.17 TOTE £8.30: £3.40 £1.90 (£5.40) OWNER Crown Select (RADLETT) BRED K. T. Ivory

IN-FOCUS: **This was a very decent little event.**

893 Banningham Blade has turned out to be an extremely shrewd investment by her owners, who bought her for a mere 600 guineas, yet she has already earned over £13,000 in prize money so far this season. Having only raced on a fast surface up to this point, she coped very well with the underfoot conditions, and gained control inside the final furlong to register her fourth victory from six starts. She may come back here next week, but she is definitely bound for the Queen Mary Stakes at Royal Ascot, although she will surely find a few too good for her there. (9/1: 9/2-10/1)

965* Chips (IRE) is rated highly by his trainer but, although handling the ground, he found the concession of 10lb to the winner too much and just lost out in a three-way battle in the final furlong. (5/6: evens-11/10)

954* Golden Mirage (IRE) won on this ground eight days ago. Narrowly headed inside the final furlong, she refused to give way and only just lost out in a tight finish. (7/1)

965 The Boy John (USA), 6lb better off with Chips for a one-and-three-quarter length beating at Salisbury eight days ago, finished even further behind on this rain-softened ground. On a sounder surface, he should find a race. (4/1: op 9/4)

Jay Gee (IRE) looked as though the run would do her good and, after getting completely outpaced, made some late headway. (40/1)

850 Alpen Wolf (IRE) was rather colty in the paddock, and had been seen off at halfway in this strong contest. (16/1)
Truth Teller (12/1: 5/1-14/1)

1144 BULLBROOK MEDIAN AUCTION MAIDEN STKS (3-Y.O) (Class E)
8-30 (8-31) **1m 2f 7y** £3,030.00 (£915.00: £445.00: £210.00) Stalls: High GOING: 0.13 sec per fur (G)

				SP	RR	SF
967^{4}	**Tom Tailor (GER) (72)** (DRCElsworth) **3-9-0** LDettori(16) (a.p: led over 1f out: rdn out)	—	**1**	$9/2^{2}$	80	19
$1068a^{6}$	**Scoss** (LMCumani) **3-8-9**(5) RFfrench(5) (hdwy & edgd lft over 1f out: r.o)	1	**2**	14/1	78	17
773^{3}	**In Question (84)** (BWHills) **3-9-0** DHolland(8) (hdwy over 3f out: hrd rdn over 1f out: unable qckn)	1	**3**	$2/1^{1}$	77	16
641^{6}	**Northern Touch** (SCWilliams) **3-8-9** DHarrison(7) (led: styd stands' side st: hdd over 1f out: one pce)	2½	**4**	100/1	68	7
	Farhan (USA) (PTWalwyn) **3-9-0** RHills(1) (a.p: ev ch over 1f out: wknd fnl f)	¾	**5**	$9/2^{2}$	72	11
868^{11}	**Sweetchildofmine** (HAkbary) **3-8-9** GHind(10) (b: rdn over 2f out: nvr nr to chal)	1	**6**	100/1	65	4
875^{4}	**Copper Shell** (APJones) **3-9-0** SDrowne(15) (prom over 8f)	1	**7**	50/1	68	7
725^{10}	**Alhosaam** (MajorWRHern) **3-9-0** SWhitworth(9) (nvr nrr)	2	**8**	25/1	65	4
773^{4}	**Miss Riviera Rose (77)** (GWragg) **3-8-9** MHills(14) (s.s: hdwy over 4f out: wknd over 1f out)	1	**9**	$11/2^{3}$	59	—
	Pardan (BPalling) **3-9-0** TSprake(13) (w'like: nvr nrr)	nk	**10**	50/1	63	2
	Expialiodoocius (JRFanshawe) **3-9-0** MRoberts(11) (scope: hdwy over 4f out: wknd over 2f out)	1¾	**11**	9/1	60	—
990^{8}	**Begorrat (IRE) (78)** (BJMeehan) **3-9-0** PatEddery(12) (stdd s: hdwy 8f out: rdn over 3f out: wknd over 1f out)	¾	**12**	12/1	59	—
	Marx Mistress (ICampbell) **3-8-9** RPrice(6) (w'like: a bhd)	9	**13**	50/1	40	—
	Despina (HCandy) **3-8-9** CRutter(4) (prom 6f)	7	**14**	50/1	29	—
874^{7}	**Bold Et Noir** (WJarvis) **3-9-0** SSanders(2) (a bhd: t.o)	dist	**15**	100/1	—	—
874^{12}	**Flying Esprit** (GGMargarson) **3-8-11**(3) MHenry(3) (bhd fnl 4f: t.o)	s.h	**16**	100/1	—	—

(SP 125.1%) **16 Rn**

2m 16.2 (11.30) CSF £59.35 TOTE £5.00: £2.00 £4.70 £1.40 (£58.40) Trio £92.70 OWNER The A A Partnership (WHITCOMBE) BRED V. Kaufling

967 Tom Tailor (GER), all the fitter for his recent run, appreciated the shorter trip and underfoot conditions. (9/2)
1068a Scoss, who finished last in Italy on his debut recently, ran much better here over this longer trip on soft ground and, despite drifting left, ran on nicely. (14/1: 7/1-16/1)
773 In Question took closer order in the straight but, under pressure below the distance, failed to find the necessary turn of foot. (2/1)
Northern Touch was given an enterprising ride and, setting the pace, was the only horse who elected to stay on the stands' side in the straight. (100/1)
Farhan (USA) actually led the far side group in the straight, but did not have overall control. He tired as lack of a recent run took its toll. (9/2)
Sweetchildofmine struggled on in the final quarter-mile without posing a threat. (100/1)
773 Miss Riviera Rose (11/2: 3/1-6/1)
Expialiodoocius (9/1: 5/1-10/1)
795 Begorrat (IRE) (12/1: 8/1-14/1)

T/Jkpt: Not won; £26,043.44 to York 13/5/97. T/Plpt: £508.50 (39.58 Tckts). T/Qdpt: £186.10 (6.47 Tckts) AK

YORK (L-H) (Good, Good to soft patches)
Tuesday May 13th
WEATHER: sunny periods WIND: fresh half bhd

1145 YORKSHIRE LIFE MAGAZINE H'CAP (0-95) (4-Y.O+) (Class C)
2-05 (2-12) **1m 3f 195y** £7,375.00 (£2,200.00: £1,050.00: £475.00) Stalls: Low GOING: 0.01 sec per fur (G)

				SP	RR	SF
680^{*}	**Angus-G (88)** (MrsMReveley) **5-9-11** KDarley(9) (hld up: hdwy 4f out: slt ld appr fnl f: rdn & r.o)	—	**1**	$2/1^{1}$	99	56
974^{2}	**Remaadi Sun (78)** (MDIUsher) **5-9-1v1** JQuinn(8) (hld up & bhd: stdy hdwy 3f out: edgd lft: ch ins fnl f: kpt on)	¾	**2**	$5/1^{2}$	88	45
962^{4}	**Temptress (67)** (JLHarris) **4-8-4** DHolland(12) (lw: chsd ldr: rdn to ld over 2f out: hdd appr fnl f: kpt on)	¾	**3**	$9/1^{3}$	76	33
846^{6}	**Berlin Blue (80)** (JWWatts) **4-9-3** LDettori(3) (lw: outpcd & bhd 3f out: styd on wl u.p fnl 2f)	3	**4**	10/1	85	42
	Zaralaska (90) (LMCumani) **6-9-8**(5) RFfrench(7) (hld up & bhd: hdwy on outside 3f out: nvr plcd to chal)	s.h	**5**	16/1	95+	52
908^{4}	**Swan Hunter (69)** (DJSCosgrove) **4-8-3**(3) DO'Donohoe(6) (lw: hld up & bhd: swtchd outside 2f out: styd on u.p: nrst fin)	2½	**6**	25/1	71	28
974^{5}	**Hazard a Guess (IRE) (84)** (DNicholls) **7-9-7** AlexGreaves(11) (prom: outpcd 3f out: no imp after)	½	**7**	$9/1^{3}$	85	42
1022^{*}	**Augustan (59)** (SGollings) **6-7-10** 5x LCharnock(2) (lw: prom tl n.m.r & swtchd over 2f out: n.d after)	2½	**8**	12/1	57	14
499^{9}	**Prospector's Cove (85)** (JPearce) **4-9-8** GBardwell(10) (chsd ldrs tl outpcd fnl 3f)	2½	**9**	33/1	79	36
686^{5}	**Duraid (IRE) (69)** (DenysSmith) **5-8-6** ACulhane(5) (lw: in tch tl wknd fnl 3f)	5	**10**	11/1	56	13
1024^{2}	**African Sun (IRE) (59)** (MCChapman) **4-7-5**(5) PFessey(1) (led tl hdd & wknd over 2f out)	1¼	**11**	66/1	45	2
	Jazz King (78) (MissGayKelleway) **4-9-1** KFallon(4) (outpcd appr st: wl bhd fnl 3f)	10½	**12**	16/1	50	7

(SP 115.2%) **12 Rn**

2m 35.67 (7.87) CSF £9.47 CT £65.84 TOTE £2.60: £1.30 £1.80 £2.80 (£3.90) Trio £18.90 OWNER Mr W. Ginzel (SALTBURN) BRED W. Ginzel

LONG HANDICAP Augustan 7-4 African Sun (IRE) 6-4
STEWARDS' ENQUIRY Ffrench susp. 22-24 & 26/05/97 & Cumani fined £700 under Rule 151 (ii) schooling in public. Zaralaska banned 16/5-16/6/97.
680* Angus-G always had the situation in hand, but he appeared a bit lazy when in front and there would seem to be plenty more to come. (2/1)
974 Remaadi Sun, trying to win this for the second year running, had a visor on for the first time, but he basically met one too good. (5/1: op 3/1)
962 Temptress is as honest as they come, and that should find her success. (9/1)
846 Berlin Blue ran as though at least another couple of furlongs are needed. (10/1)
Zaralaska had what can only be described as a pipe-opener here and was in no way knocked about, and the Stewards took the appropriate action. (16/1)
908 Swan Hunter, given a lot to do, finished well after switching for a clear run, and looks likely to do better. (25/1)
974 Hazard a Guess (IRE) saw too much daylight too soon. (9/1)
1022* Augustan was already feeling the pace when getting cramped for room halfway up the straight. (12/1: op 8/1)

1146 SHEPHERD TROPHY RATED STKS H'CAP (0-100) (3-Y.O) (Class B)

2-35 (2-40) **1m 2f 85y** £13,534.40 (£5,009.60: £2,404.80: £984.00: £392.00: £155.20) Stalls: Low GOING: 0.01 sec per fur (G)

				SP	RR	SF
	The Fly (93) (BWHills) **3-9-2** MHills(12) (lw: hld up & bhd: stdy hdwy 3f out: qcknd to ld 1f out: r.o)	—	1	4/1^{1}	108+	75
701*	**Silverani (IRE) (89)** (LMCumani) **3-8-12** LDettori(11) (lw: hld up & bhd: smooth hdwy 4f out: disp ld wl over 1f out: sn rdn: hdd 1f out: kpt on)	2	2	4/1^{1}	101	68
690^{5}	**Blue River (IRE) (90)** (TGMills) **3-8-13** MJKinane(1) (chsd ldrs: rdn to disp ld wl over 1f out: hdd 1f out: kpt on)	nk	3	8/1	102	69
890^{3}	**Delilah (IRE) (87)** (MRStoute) **3-8-10** JReid(9) (prom tl outpcd 4f out: kpt on u.p fnl 2f)	5	4	8/1	91	58
646^{4}	**Bali Paradise (USA) (97)** (PFICole) **3-9-6** TQuinn(4) (led tl hdd wl over 2f out: grad wknd)	¾	5	15/2^{3}	100	67
1072a*	**Polar Flight (90)** (MJohnston) **3-8-13** JWeaver(5) (cl up: rdn to ld wl over 2f out: hdd wl over 1f out: sn outpcd)	nk	6	10/1	92	59
502^{2}	**Mr Bombastique (IRE) (87)** (BWHills) **3-8-10** DHolland(6) (bhd: effrt over 3f out: nvr rchd ldrs)	3½	7	12/1	84	51
675^{9}	**Stone Flower (USA) (85)** (PWChapple-Hyam) **3-8-5**(3) RHavlin(7) (chsd ldrs tl rdn & wknd fnl 2f)	nk	8	14/1	81	48
723^{4}	**Noble Dane (IRE) (82)** (PWHarris) **3-8-5**ow1 PatEddery(8) (bhd: gd hdwy 3f out: rdn 2f out: sn btn)	1¼	9	13/2^{2}	76	42
747^{3}	**Caviar Royale (IRE) (98)** (TDBarron) **3-9-7** JCarroll(3) (outpcd over 3f out: n.d)	hd	10	25/1	92	59
957^{4}	**Sugarfoot (92)** (NTinkler) **3-9-1** KDarley(13) (prom: outpcd: n.m.r 2f out: no imp after)	½	11	25/1	85	52
990^{4}	**Love Has No Pride (USA) (87)** (RHannon) **3-8-10** DaneO'Neill(2) (chsd ldrs tl rdn & wknd fnl 2½f)	2½	12	14/1	77	44
	Marathon Maid (89) (RAFahey) **3-8-12** ACulhane(10) (in tch tl outpcd ent st: sn btn)	4	13	25/1	72	39

(SP 129.0%) **13 Rn**

2m 12.31 (3.31) CSF £17.80 CT £114.54 TOTE £4.90: £2.00 £1.60 £2.00 (£5.50) Trio £14.50 OWNER Mrs J. M. Corbett (LAMBOURN) BRED S. Wingfield Digby

LONG HANDICAP Noble Dane (IRE) 8-3

IN-FOCUS: **This was the 1,000th British Flat winner of Michael Hills' career.**

The Fly adopted his usual come-from-way-behind tactics, and did this in impressive fashion. He looks very useful indeed when in this mood. He is entered in the Derby, and connections are tempted to let him take his chance. (4/1)

701* Silverani (IRE), trying a longer trip, went really well for much of the race, but was outclassed late on and had to struggle to hold on for second. (4/1)

690 Blue River (IRE) is an honest sort who gives the impression that he will improve as he tries longer distances. (8/1)

890 Delilah (IRE) was trying her longest trip to date, and left the impression that she needs further yet. (8/1)

646 Bali Paradise (USA) likes to be out in front, but this extended trip seemed beyond him. (15/2)

1072a* Polar Flight is honest and stays, but he was short of the pace required. (10/1)

502 Mr Bombastique (IRE), ridden from behind this time, found this company too hot and could never summon the pace to get on terms. (12/1)

1147 TATTERSALLS MUSIDORA STKS (Gp 3) (3-Y.O F) (Class A)

3-10 (3-12) **1m 2f 85y** £26,048.00 (£9,632.00: £4,616.00: £1,880.00: £740.00: £284.00) Stalls: Low GOING: 0.01 sec per fur (G)

				SP	RR	SF
960^{6}	**Reams of Verse (USA) (114)** (HRACecil) **3-8-11** KFallon(9) (lw: hld up: stdy hdwy to ld 2f out: rdn & r.o strly)	—	1	11/10^{1}	120	74
959^{3}	**Vagabond Chanteuse (97)** (TJEtherington) **3-8-8** TQuinn(2) (lw: chsd ldr: chal over 2f out: r.o one pce)	11	2	14/1	100	54
	Etoile (FR) (100) (PWChapple-Hyam) **3-8-8** JReid(8) (led tl hdd 2f out: kpt on same pce)	hd	3	11/1	100	54
	Entice (FR) (SbinSuroor) **3-8-8** LDettori(5) (lw: plld hrd early: effrt 4f out: sn in tch: edgd lft: no imp fnl 2f)	4	4	5/1^{2}	94	48
	Society Rose (MRStoute) **3-8-8** MJKinane(4) (hld up & bhd: gd hdwy 3f out: rdn: hung lft: wknd fnl 2f)	3½	5	7/1^{3}	88	42
833^{2}	**Alcalali (USA)** (PAKelleway) **3-8-8** KDarley(1) (chsd ldrs: outpcd over 3f out: no imp after)	3½	6	33/1	83	37
975^{3}	**French Mist (71)** (CEBrittain) **3-8-8** BDoyle(3) (swtg: in tch tl rdn & wknd over 3f out)	8	7	100/1	71	25
890*	**Noisette** (JHMGosden) **3-8-8** RCochrane(7) (hld up: effrt over 3f out: sn btn)	1	8	7/1^{3}	69	23
724^{7}	**Calypso Grant (IRE) (100)** (PWHarris) **3-8-8** PatEddery(6) (chsd ldrs tl rdn & wknd fnl 3f)	3	9	9/1	65	19
672^{8}	**Dame Laura (IRE) (106)** (HMorrison) **3-8-8** CRutter(10) (prom: rdn over 3f out: wknd over 2f out)	9	10	33/1	51	5

(SP 121.2%) **10 Rn**

2m 11.81 (2.81) CSF £18.60 TOTE £2.10: £1.10 £3.10 £3.20 (£12.30) Trio £49.50 OWNER Mr K. Abdulla (NEWMARKET) BRED Juddmonte Farms

960 Reams of Verse (USA) appreciated this trip and won most impressively. Although not bred to, there seems no reason why she should not get the mile-and-a-half, and she will take all the beating in the Oaks. (11/10: evens-6/5)

959 Vagabond Chanteuse is running consistently well and is a real battler, but was completely outclassed by a useful opponent. (14/1)

Etoile (FR) seemed to stay well enough, but was well and truly outpointed in the last two furlongs. (11/1)

Entice (FR) gave problems by pulling hard early on as she did last year, and ran no sort of race. She must learn to settle. (5/1)

Society Rose showed a useful turn of foot early in the straight, but did not appear to stay. (7/1)

833 Alcalali (USA) has been highly-tried in all her races to date, and deserves a drop in class to boost her confidence. (33/1)

975 French Mist was comprehensively outclassed, and always outpaced at the business end. (100/1)

890* Noisette would seem to have her problems as she ran no sort of race here. (7/1)

1148 STANLEY RACING SPRINT TROPHY RATED STKS H'CAP (0-105) (3-Y.O+) (Class B)

3-40 (3-41) **6f** £11,862.89 (£4,391.10: £2,108.05: £862.75: £343.88: £136.33) Stalls: High GOING: 0.01 sec per fur (G)

				SP	RR	SF
	Bollin Joanne (95) (TDEasterby) **4-8-8**(5) GParkin(2) (b: cl up: led appr fnl f: r.o u.p)	—	1	10/1	105	85
892^{10}	**Tumbleweed Ridge (89)** (BJMeehan) **4-8-7b** PatEddery(7) (s.s: hdwy u.str.p 2f out: ev ch ins fnl f: nt qckn)	nk	2	15/2^{3}	98	78
892^{2}	**World Premier (97)** (CEBrittain) **4-9-1** BDoyle(13) (in tch: outpcd over 2f out: kpt on wl fnl f)	1¼	3	8/1	103	83
961*	**Cyrano's Lad (IRE) (103)** (CADwyer) **8-9-7** KFallon(1) (lw: led tl hdd appr fnl f: no ex)	1¼	4	9/1	106	86
	Double Splendour (IRE) (97) (PSFelgate) **7-9-1** KDarley(10) (lw: in tch: hdwy & prom 2f out: sn rdn & nt qckn)	¾	5	7/2^{1}	98	78
892^{11}	**Cretan Gift (98)** (NPLittmoden) **6-8-11b**(5) ADaly(4) (lw: prom tl outpcd 2f out: kpt on wl towards fin)	¾	6	16/1	97	77
*903**	**Zuhair (90)** (DMcCain) **4-8-8** JCarroll(8) (b: swtg: cl up 4f: grad wknd)	3	7	33/1	81	61
877^{2}	**Dashing Blue (102)** (IABalding) **4-9-6** LDettori(14) (in tch: outpcd over 2f out: no imp after)	2	8	8/1	87	67
961^{4}	**King of Peru (99)** (APJarvis) **4-9-3** WJO'Connor(6) (chsd ldrs: rdn over 3f out: sn wknd)	1½	9	14/1	80	60
892^{22}	**Charlie Sillett (89)** (BWHills) **5-8-2**(5) RMullen(11) (s.s: nvr rchd ldrs)	hd	10	16/1	70	50
726^{6}	**Hoh Returns (IRE) (90)** (MBell) **4-8-8** MFenton(12) (chsd ldrs 4f)	1½	11	12/1	67	47
694^{12}	**Yorkie George (89)** (LMCumani) **3-7-6**(5) RFfrench(3) (chsd ldrs: rdn ½-wy: wknd fnl 2f)	2	12	7/1^{2}	61	31
892^{13}	**Samwar (90)** (MissGayKelleway) **5-8-8** RCochrane(15) (nvr trbld ldrs)	¾	13	10/1	60	40
	Unconditional Love (IRE) (98) (MJohnston) **4-9-2** JWeaver(16) (outpcd & bhd fr ½-wy)	hd	14	25/1	67	47

				SP	RR	SF
745[8]	**Sea Dane (100)** (PWHarris) **4-9-4** MJKinane(9) (sn outpcd & bhd)	1½	**15**	25/1	65	45
745[6]	**Westcourt Magic (98)** (MWEasterby) **4-9-2** TQuinn(5) (sn outpcd & t.o: virtually p.u)	dist	**16**	20/1	—	—

(SP 138.4%) **16 Rn**

1m 11.49 (0.99) CSF £82.57 CT £628.06 TOTE £9.80: £2.20 £2.00 £2.40 £2.60 (£55.70) Trio £179.00 OWNER Lady Westbrook (MALTON) BRED Sir Neil and Lady Westbrook
LONG HANDICAP Charlie Sillett 8-0
WEIGHT FOR AGE 3yo-10lb
OFFICIAL EXPLANATION **Westcourt Magic: ran free to post and had no more to give in the race.**
Bollin Joanne had the speed to lay-up with the strong pace and the stamina to see the trip out well, and seems to be on the upgrade. (10/1)
514 Tumbleweed Ridge was given plenty of assistance from the saddle and made up a tremendous amount of ground, but is proving very difficult to win with. (15/2)
892 World Premier ran well, and with a better draw would have been in the shake up. (8/1)
961* Cyrano's Lad (IRE) has speed to burn, but is at his best on faster ground and failed to last out. (9/1)
Double Splendour (IRE) had won first time out for the two previous seasons but, on this occasion, the effort was always just beyond him. He will do better in due course. (7/2)
745 Cretan Gift looks to have been harshly treated by the Handicapper, but did run quite well here, sticking on doggedly at the end. (16/1)
877 Dashing Blue likes faster ground and was not well drawn. (8/1)

75+ 88+ 76 76 (79)

1149 E.B.F. AER LINGUS LEEDS-BRADFORD AIRPORT NOVICE STKS (2-Y.O F) (Class D)
4-10 (4-11) **5f** £5,848.00 (£1,744.00: £832.00: £376.00) Stalls: High GOING: 0.01 sec per fur (G)

				SP	RR	SF
	Balance The Books (RHannon) **2-8-8** PatEddery(3) (leggy: scope: chsd ldrs: rdn to ld ins fnl f: carried lft: r.o)	—	**1**	3/1 [2]	83	28
985[2]	**Indian Silver** (MRChannon) **2-8-8** TQuinn(1) (led tl hdd & hung badly lft ins fnl f)	1¼	**2**	11/4 [1]	79	24
	Child Prodigy (IRE) (JWWatts) **2-8-8** JReid(5) (w'like: chsd ldrs: outpcd 2f out: styd on u.p fnl f)	¾	**3**	11/4 [1]	77+	22
1013[6]	**Filey Brigg** (WTKemp) **2-8-10** KFallon(2) (sn outpcd & bhd: styd on wl fnl 2f: no imp)	1¼	**4**	12/1 [3]	75	20
999*	**Eastern Lyric** (JBerry) **2-9-0** KDarley(4) (cl up tl wknd appr fnl f)	2½	**5**	3/1 [2]	71	16

(SP 111.0%) **5 Rn**

61.47 secs (3.77) CSF £10.60 TOTE £3.30: £1.70 £1.80 (£4.60) OWNER Mr Mohamed Suhail (MARLBOROUGH) BRED John Wynne Morris
Balance The Books looks the type to improve as he strengthens, will certainly stay further and won this well under a determined drive. (3/1)
985 Indian Silver has bags of speed, but she threw it away by hanging badly into the whip. (11/4)
Child Prodigy (IRE) left the impression that she should be all the sharper for this, and there should be a nice prize or two to be picked up. (11/4)
1013 Filey Brigg showed yet again that over further she will be all the better, but this was also her seventh race of the campaign. (12/1)
999* Eastern Lyric had plenty on trying to give weight all round, and ran out of fuel with a furlong to go. (3/1)

1150 NEWTON INVESTMENT MANAGEMENT CONDITIONS STKS (3-Y.O) (Class B)
4-40 (4-40) **1m 5f 194y** £7,758.75 (£2,790.00: £1,332.50: £537.50: £206.25) Stalls: Low GOING: 0.01 sec per fur (G)

				SP	RR	SF
1025[2]	**Flirting Around (USA) (84)** (MRStoute) **3-8-12** KFallon(4) (lw: trckd ldrs: hdwy to ld wl over 2f out: edgd lft: r.o)	—	**1**	13/8 [1]	100	32
937[5]	**Windsor Castle (95)** (PFICole) **3-9-6** TQuinn(2) (cl up: disp ld 8f out tl wl over 2f out: sn outpcd: hdwy appr fnl f: swtchd & r.o towards fin)	hd	**2**	3/1 [2]	108	40
773[2]	**Zinzari (FR)** (DRLoder) **3-8-12** LDettori(1) (lw: chsd ldrs: rdn to disp ld appr fnl f: wknd wl ins fnl f)	2	**3**	3/1 [2]	98	30
931[5]	**Spartan Royale** (CEBrittain) **3-8-12** MRoberts(5) (mde most tl hdd & wknd wl over 2f out)	12	**4**	8/1 [3]	55 t	16
670[6]	**Autumn Time (IRE)** (PWChapple-Hyam) **3-8-7** JReid(3) (in tch tl outpcd fnl 4f)	1¼	**5**	9/1	48 t	9

(SP 109.2%) **5 Rn**

3m 5.01 (11.41) CSF £6.02 TOTE £2.00: £1.10 £1.70 (£2.90) OWNER Maktoum Al Maktoum (NEWMARKET) BRED Once Over Farm
1025 Flirting Around (USA) stays well but is not the easiest of rides as he tends to hang, but he did battle on well. (13/8)
937 Windsor Castle, trying his longest trip to date, left the distinct impression that he needs further yet. (3/1)
773 Zinzari (FR), stepping-up in distance, looked likely to win this until the final furlong proved just too far. (3/1)
931 Spartan Royale had his limitations exposed when tackled halfway up the straight. (8/1: 6/1-9/1)
670 Autumn Time (IRE) has yet to show anything positive. (9/1: 6/1-10/1)

T/Jkpt: £3,697.50 (8.33 Tckts). T/Plpt: £17.50 (2,675.99 Tckts). T/Qdpt: £8.20 (169.46 Tckts) AA

1101-LINGFIELD (L-H) (Standard)
Wednesday May 14th
WEATHER: warm WIND: almost nil

1151 SANTANDER H'CAP (0-65) (3-Y.O) (Class F)
2-15 (2-17) **6f (Equitrack)** £2,277.00 (£627.00: £297.00) Stalls: Low GOING minus 0.51 sec per fur (FST)

				SP	RR	SF
873[3]	**Dayrella (49)** (WRMuir) **3-8-6** MRoberts(1) (lw: a.p: rdn 3f out: led last strides)	—	**1**	14/1	54	26
924[8]	**Nampara Bay (48)** (GCBravery) **3-8-5** DHarrison(6) (led: clr over 1f out: hrd rdn fnl f: hdd last strides)	hd	**2**	20/1	53	25
694[16]	**Signs And Wonders (63)** (CACyzer) **3-9-6** DeclanO'Shea(5) (lw: lost pl over 4f out: rallied over 1f out: r.o wl ins fnl f)	nk	**3**	20/1	67	39
531[5]	**Castle Ashby Jack (62)** (PHowling) **3-9-5b** PaulEddery(2) (chsd ldr tl ins fnl f: one pce)	1½	**4**	12/1	62	34
868[9]	**Avanti Blue (52)** (KMcAuliffe) **3-8-9** WJO'Connor(8) (a.p: hrd rdn over 1f out: one pce)	2	**5**	6/1 [3]	47	19
873[4]	**Lucy of Arabia (IRE) (51)** (JJSheehan) **3-8-8b** SDrowne(7) (nvr nr to chal)	2½	**6**	20/1	39	11
606[5]	**Muara Bay (41)** (GLewis) **3-7-12** JQuinn(11) (rdn & no hdwy fnl 3f)	¾	**7**	16/1	27	—
876[5]	**Tear White (IRE) (64)** (TGMills) **3-9-4(3)** AWhelan(13) (nvr nrr)	½	**8**	20/1	49	21
649[6]	**Chasetown Flyer (USA) (58)** (NEBerry) **3-9-1** CRutter(9) (nvr nrr)	nk	**9**	9/1	42	14
995[2]	**Hever Golf Mover (59)** (TJNaughton) **3-9-2** SSanders(12) (b: b.hind: bhd fnl 3f)	2½	**10**	7/2 [1]	36	8
	Bapsford (58) (GLMoore) **3-9-1** GDuffield(14) (bit bkwd: a bhd)	½	**11**	14/1	34	6
883[11]	**Aybeegirl (56)** (MrsJCecil) **3-8-10v(3)** MartinDwyer(4) (bhd fnl 3f)	nk	**12**	4/1 [2]	31	3
606[3]	**Wing of A Prayer (52)** (WJarvis) **3-8-9** OUrbina(3) (hld up: rdn over 2f out: sn wknd)	4	**13**	9/1	16	—

	Jingoist (IRE) (53) (JLHarris) **3-8-10b** BDoyle(10) (a bhd)	2½	**14**	16/1	11	—
				(SP 128.3%)		**14 Rn**

1m 12.65 (1.55) CSF £256.88 CT £4,990.88 TOTE £14.10: £2.80 £9.30 £18.20 (£174.90) Trio £290.60 OWNER Dulverton Equine (LAMBOURN) BRED R. B. Warren

873 Dayrella confirmed the promise shown at Southwell recently, and at last managed to get up in the dying strides to lose her maiden tag. (14/1)

751 Nampara Bay attempted to make all the running and had poached a useful advantage in the straight. She looked as if she was just going to hold on, but was worried out of it in the last few strides. She can soon gain compensation. (20/1)

Signs And Wonders seemed to cope with the sand on this All-Weather debut and, after losing her good early pitch, ran on strongly from below the distance. (20/1)

531 Castle Ashby Jack runs well here, but he is yet to get his head in front after thirteen attempts. A return to five furlongs would probably help. (12/1: 6/1-14/1)

Avanti Blue appreciated the drop in distance and ran his best race to date, playing an active role until tapped for toe in the straight. (6/1: op 16/1)

873 Lucy of Arabia (IRE) has dropped 13lb in the handicap since the beginning of the year, but she is no nearer getting to the winner's enclosure. (20/1)

Bapsford (14/1: 10/1-16/1)

606 Wing of A Prayer (9/1: 4/1-10/1)

1152 VIGO CLAIMING STKS (4-Y.O+) (Class F)

2-45 (2-46) **2m (Equitrack)** £2,277.00 (£627.00: £297.00) Stalls: Low GOING minus 0.51 sec per fur (FST)

				SP	RR	SF
753*	**Petoskin (72)** (JPearce) **5-9-1** MWigham(1) (mde all: pushed out)	—	**1**	15/8 ^{1}	74	28
908 ^{2}	**One Off the Rail (USA) (68)** (GLMoore) **7-9-1** SWhitworth(6) (b: hld up: rdn over 3f out: chsd wnr ins fnl f: r.o one pce)	3½	**2**	5/2 ^{2}	71	25
869 ^{5}	**Carol's Dream (USA) (66)** (JWHills) **5-9-4**(3) MHenry(5) (lw: a.p: chsd wnr over 6f out tl ins fnl f: one pce)	1	**3**	10/1 ^{3}	76	30
867 ^{3}	**Batabanoo (70)** (MrsMReveley) **8-9-7** WJO'Connor(3) (s.s: hld up: rdn 4f out: sn wknd)	7	**4**	15/8 ^{1}	69	23
	Red Whirlwind (55) (RSimpson) **7-8-13** MFenton(4) (b: bit bkwd: chsd wnr over 9f: wknd over 4f out)	26	**5**	25/1	35	—
	Arch Angel (IRE) (40) (GFHCharles-Jones) **4-8-2**(7) CharlotteCox(2) (lw: plld hrd: bhd fnl 8f)	nk	**6**	50/1	33	—
				(SP 113.0%)		**6 Rn**

3m 27.16 (6.16) CSF £6.40 TOTE £2.40: £1.20 £1.40 (£2.90) OWNER Mrs Jean Routledge (NEWMARKET) BRED James Wigan
WEIGHT FOR AGE 4yo-3lb

753* Petoskin goes well on the All-Weather and, making all the running, needed only to be nudged along for a cosy success. He has now gained six of his seven victories in claimers or sellers. (15/8)

908 One Off the Rail (USA) loves it around here, and has gained nine of his ten victories on this surface. Coping well with this longer trip, he stayed on to take second place inside the final furlong if never threatening the winner. He should soon add to his tally. (5/2)

Carol's Dream (USA) ran his best race for some time over this much longer trip. (10/1)

867 Batabanoo has won eleven times in his career but only one of those was on the All-Weather and, after a lengthy lay-off, has now disappointed in two lowly claimers. (15/8)

1153 BILBAO LIMITED STKS (0-70) (3-Y.O+) (Class E)

3-20 (3-20) **1m 2f (Equitrack)** £2,888.25 (£861.00: £410.50: £185.25) Stalls: Low GOING minus 0.51 sec per fur (FST)

				SP	RR	SF
840 ^{11}	**Smart Boy (IRE) (70)** (PFICole) **3-8-4** CRutter(4) (chsd ldr over 8f out: led over 3f out: clr wl over 1f out: r.o wl)	—	**1**	10/1	75	40
871 ^{10}	**Enchanting Eve (70)** (CNAllen) **3-8-2**(3) MartinDwyer(2) (lw: rdn & hdwy over 3f out: chsd wnr wl over 1f out: no imp)	5	**2**	7/1	68	33
1022 ^{9}	**Anchor Venture (56)** (SPCWoods) **4-9-5** WRyan(6) (lw: led over 6f: wknd wl over 1f out)	3	**3**	14/1	62	42
887 ^{3}	**Scarlet Crescent (70)** (PTWalwyn) **3-8-2**ow1 PaulEddery(1) (lw: hld up: rdn over 4f out: wknd wl over 1f out)	2½	**4**	15/8 ^{1}	56	20
976 ^{3}	**Top Shelf (65)** (CEBrittain) **3-8-3** BDoyle(5) (s.s: bhd fnl 4f)	12	**5**	4/1 ^{3}	38	3
1010 ^{4}	**Rising Dough (IRE) (66)** (GLMoore) **5-9-5** SSanders(7) (prom 5f)	7	**6**	5/2 ^{2}	28	8
				(SP 111.6%)		**6 Rn**

2m 5.25 (0.95) CSF £66.06 TOTE £11.20: £2.60 £2.90 (£23.10) OWNER H R H Sultan Ahmad Shah (WHATCOMBE) BRED Peter Savill
WEIGHT FOR AGE 3yo-15lb

Smart Boy (IRE) has been very disappointing since winning here on grass on his two-year-old debut, but he had no problems with this surface and scooted up in this lower-grade event. (10/1: op 6/1)

489 Enchanting Eve, taking a step-up in trip, goes well on the sand but, after moving into second place early in the short straight, never looked like reeling in the winner. (7/1)

Anchor Venture had no easy task at the weights, but nevertheless took the field along until collared over three furlongs from home. He remains a maiden. (14/1: op 7/1)

887 Scarlet Crescent had a very good chance at the weights, but she was making her debut on the All-Weather, and is certainly not as effective on it if this run is anything to go by. (15/8)

1010 Rising Dough (IRE) had a good chance at the weights, and was well-supported in the market, but he failed to handle this surface, and punters knew their fate at halfway. (5/2: 7/2-9/4)

1154 LIMA H'CAP (0-90) (3-Y.O+) (Class C)

3-50 (3-50) **1m (Equitrack)** £5,226.45 (£1,557.60: £742.30: £334.65) Stalls: High GOING minus 0.51 sec per fur (FST)

				SP	RR	SF
1082 ^{4}	**Resist the Force (USA) (58)** (CACyzer) **7-7-5**(5) RFfrench(5) (w ldr: shkn up over 1f out: led ins fnl f: pushed out)	—	**1**	9/2 ^{3}	66	43
752 ^{3}	**Ertlon (75)** (CEBrittain) **7-8-13** BDoyle(4) (lw: led: hrd rdn over 1f out: hdd ins fnl f: r.o)	nk	**2**	7/2 ^{1}	82	59
*1082**	**Pengamon (79)** (HJCollingridge) **5-9-3** 5x JQuinn(2) (b.hind: hld up: rdn over 2f out: unable qckn)	3	**3**	4/1 ^{2}	80	57
886 ^{16}	**Castles Burning (USA) (77)** (CACyzer) **3-8-2** DBiggs(3) (hld up: rdn over 3f out: one pce)	1¾	**4**	8/1	75	39
1017 ^{16}	**Effervescence (88)** (RHannon) **3-8-13** RHughes(6) (a.p: hrd rdn over 2f out: wknd wl over 1f out)	2	**5**	8/1	82	46
905 ^{6}	**Stoppes Brow (90)** (GLMoore) **5-9-7v**(7) MBatchelor(7) (s.s: hdwy over 2f out: sn wknd)	1¼	**6**	5/1	81	58
947 ^{14}	**Duke Valentino (80)** (RHollinshead) **5-9-1**(3) DGriffiths(1) (b.off fore: hld up: rdn over 2f out: sn wknd)	¾	**7**	14/1	70	47
857 ^{8}	**Tuigamala (58)** (RIngram) **6-7-10** NAdams(8) (lw: bhd fnl 4f)	13	**8**	16/1	22	—
				(SP 111.8%)		**8 Rn**

1m 37.0 (-0.40) CSF £17.91 CT £59.97 TOTE £7.40: £1.40 £1.10 £2.10 (£11.40) OWNER Mrs Barbara Hogan (HORSHAM) BRED Ron Con & Barronstown
LONG HANDICAP Resist the Force (USA) 7-7 Tuigamala 7-8

WEIGHT FOR AGE 3yo-13lb
1082 Resist the Force (USA) confirmed the promise shown here last Friday. Disputing the lead, he needed only to be shaken up to gain control inside the final furlong, and cheekily keep the runner-up at bay. (9/2)
752 Ertlon ran another sound race. Merrily bowling along in front, he was collared inside the final furlong and, although failing by only a neck, is rather flattered to have finished so close. He would not want to go up any higher in the weights. (7/2)
1082* Pengamon, successful here on Friday, found the 5lb penalty too much. (4/1: op 9/4)
600 Castles Burning (USA) had no easy task at the weights, being 8lb higher than when winning his only race to date. (8/1)
12* Effervescence, who disappointed on his two previous starts, was close up until tiring entering the straight. All three of his victories to date have come over seven furlongs, and a return to that trip is required. (8/1: 5/1-9/1)
297* Duke Valentino (14/1: 10/1-16/1)

1155 SAN SEBASTIAN MAIDEN STKS (3-Y.O) (Class D)

4-20 (4-25) **7f (Equitrack)** £3,947.50 (£1,180.00: £565.00: £257.50) Stalls: Low GOING minus 0.51 sec per fur (FST)

				SP	RR	SF
983[2]	**Sky Commander (USA)** (MRStoute) **3-9-0** DHarrison(11) (a.p: chsd ldr over 2f out: led ins fnl f: pushed out)	—	**1**	2/5[1]	93	55
	Goodbye Gatemen (IRE) (BAPearce) **3-8-11**(3) MartinDwyer(5) (chsd ldr: led over 2f out tl ins fnl f: unable qckn)	2	**2**	100/1	88	50
	Juggler (LordHuntingdon) **3-9-0** MRoberts(6) (w'like: bit bkwd: chsd ldrs: rdn over 4f out: one pce)	6	**3**	10/1[2]	75	37
1104[5]	**Noble Investment (75)** (JMPEustace) **3-9-0b[1]** JTate(12) (led over 4f)	6	**4**	16/1	61	23
945[5]	**Tezaab** (BHanbury) **3-9-0** JStack(4) (5th whn nt clr run on ins 5f out: no hdwy fnl 3f)	1¼	**5**	14/1[3]	58	20
645[8]	**Kristopher** (JWHills) **3-9-0** NAdams(8) (lw: plld hrd: nvr nr to chal)	¾	**6**	33/1	56	18
	Sifwa (DCO'Brien) **3-8-9** GBardwell(2) (leggy: lt-f: nvr nrr)	2½	**7**	100/1	46	8
784[9]	**Quarterstaff** (CFWall) **3-9-0** GDuffield(3) (nvr nrr)	1¾	**8**	20/1	47	9
	Yanavanavano (IRE) (GLewis) **3-8-7**(7) JDennis(13) (bit bkwd: s.i.s: a wl bhd)	2½	**9**	50/1	41	3
	Showcase (JWHills) **3-8-6**(3) MHenry(1) (bhd fnl 3f)	3	**10**	16/1	29	—
935[6]	**Zest (USA)** (MBell) **3-8-9** MFenton(9) (rel to r: a wl bhd)	5	**11**	14/1[3]	18	—
	Soda Pop (IRE) (CEBrittain) **3-9-0** BDoyle(10) (bhd fnl 3f)	½	**12**	14/1[3]	22	—
	Nite Bites (CACyzer) **3-9-0** DBiggs(7) (str: a bhd: t.o fnl 4f: lame)	dist	**13**	20/1	—	—
				(SP 128.7%)	**13 Rn**	

1m 24.46 (0.06) CSF £118.63 TOTE £1.50: £1.10 £17.10 £1.70 (£70.70) Trio £88.00 OWNER Maktoum Al Maktoum (NEWMARKET) BRED Heronwood Farm Inc
OFFICIAL EXPLANATION **Nite Bites: was lame.**
983 Sky Commander (USA) had little to beat here and, shaken up in the straight, gained control inside the final furlong. (2/5)
Goodbye Gatemen (IRE) left his previous run well behind. He grimly tried to keep the hot favourite at bay, but was eventually forced to concede inside the final furlong. He can find find a small race. (100/1)
Juggler, a medium-sized gelding, looked as though the run was just needed and was made to look extremely one-paced in the last half-mile. (10/1: op 5/1)
1104 Noble Investment, making a quick reappearance, was fitted with blinkers for the first time, but they failed to have the desired effect. He started to flash his tail when pressure was applied. (16/1)
945 Tezaab was made to look woefully one-paced in the last three furlongs. He looks very moderate. (14/1: op 7/1)

1156 SANTIAGO H'CAP (0-75) (3-Y.O+) (Class D)

4-50 (4-51) **1m 4f (Equitrack)** £3,720.00 (£1,110.00: £530.00: £240.00) Stalls: Low GOING minus 0.51 sec per fur (FST)

				SP	RR	SF
	Canton Venture (74) (SPCWoods) **5-9-13** WRyan(13) (chsd ldr: led over 3f out: clr over 2f out: comf)	—	**1**	7/1[3]	85+	66
865[15]	**Mister Aspecto (IRE) (68)** (MJohnston) **4-9-7b** BDoyle(12) (lw: led over 8f: rdn: unable qckn)	5	**2**	16/1	72	53
908[9]	**In the Money (IRE) (59)** (RHollinshead) **8-8-9**(3) FLynch(2) (hrd rdn over 3f out: hdwy over 2f out: r.o one pce)	3	**3**	10/1	59	40
1001[2]	**General Haven (75)** (TJNaughton) **4-10-0** GDuffield(1) (lw: a.p: rdn 5f out: one pce)	hd	**4**	4/1[1]	75	56
1010[5]	**Nawaji (USA) (43)** (WRMuir) **4-7-5**(5) RFfrench(10) (nvr nr to chal)	5	**5**	20/1	37	18
1086[2]	**Calendula (57)** (DMorley) **4-8-10** GCarter(5) (hld up: rdn over 4f out: wknd over 2f out)	hd	**6**	13/2[2]	50	31
986[6]	**Blue And Royal (IRE) (43)** (VSoane) **5-7-10b** GBardwell(8) (s.s: rdn over 4f out: nvr nrr)	2½	**7**	33/1	33	14
838[3]	**Arzani (USA) (51)** (DJSCosgrove) **6-7-13**(5) RMullen(4) (lw: nvr nrr)	2	**8**	10/1	38	19
	Willie Rushton (58) (GLMoore) **4-8-11** SWhitworth(9) (hld up: rdn 4f out: wknd over 2f out)	5	**9**	16/1	39	20
888[17]	**Bowled Over (69)** (CACyzer) **4-9-8** MRoberts(7) (prom over 9f)	½	**10**	9/1	49	30
566[9]	**Awesome Power (50)** (JWHills) **11-8-3** AClark(3) (hld up: rdn over 4f out: wknd over 2f out)	1¾	**11**	16/1	28	9
1002[2]	**Maradi (IRE) (73)** (MBell) **3-8-7** MFenton(11) (lw: bhd fnl 4f)	2½	**12**	4/1[1]	47	9
789[12]	**Newport Knight (73)** (RAkehurst) **6-9-12e** SSanders(6) (b.hind: bhd fnl 4f)	11	**13**	8/1	33	14
				(SP 130.5%)	**13 Rn**	

2m 30.58 (0.58) CSF £113.54 CT £1,051.22 TOTE £11.00: £4.50 £6.60 £3.00 (£100.70) Trio £224.50; £158.17 to York 15/5/97 OWNER Dr Frank Chao (NEWMARKET) BRED High Point B/stock Ltd & Chao Racing & B/stock Ltd
LONG HANDICAP Nawaji (USA) 7-7 Blue And Royal (IRE) 6-6
WEIGHT FOR AGE 3yo-19lb
Canton Venture, winner of seven races last year and one over hurdles this winter, got off to the perfect start on his seasonal debut, forging clear for a very comfortable victory. (7/1)
402 Mister Aspecto (IRE), who has flopped three times on grass this season, bounced back to form on this return to sand, although he had no hope with the winner. (16/1)
591 In the Money (IRE) has already won five times this year but, after two recent disappointments, ran better here, if never threatening to trouble the front two. All his twelve wins have come over this trip. (10/1)
1001 General Haven was returning to a more suitable trip, but failed to find the necessary turn of foot under his big weight. (4/1)
1010 Nawaji (USA) was not given a particularly hard time, but she never threatened to get into it and remains a maiden. (20/1)
1086 Calendula was back over a more suitable trip, but was held up on this occasion, which may account for this poor show. (13/2)
Newport Knight (8/1: 5/1-9/1)

T/Plpt: £3,770.00 (2.52 Tckts). T/Qdpt: £102.90 (6.67 Tckts) AK

1145-YORK (L-H) (Good)
Wednesday May 14th

WEATHER: cloudy WIND: almost nil becoming slt across

1157 GROSVENOR CASINOS MIDDLETON STKS (Listed) (4-Y.O+ F & M) (Class A)

2-05 (2-05) **1m 2f 85y** £11,386.80 (£4,096.80: £1,958.40: £792.00: £306.00) Stalls: Low GOING: 0.11 sec per fur (G)

				SP	RR	SF
	Papering (IRE) (112) (LMCumani) **4-8-12** LDettori(1) (mde all: shkn up appr fnl f: hld on wl)	—	**1**	8/11^{1}	113	84
894^{2}	**Charlotte Corday (104)** (GWragg) **4-8-9** MHills(3) (chsd wnr: effrt over 2f out: kpt on u.p towards fin)	½	**2**	11/4^{2}	109	80
	Ball Gown (95) (DTThom) **7-8-9** DHolland(2) (stdd s: hdwy over 2f out: nvr nr to chal)	9	**3**	6/1^{3}	95	66
1145^{3}	**Temptress (67)** (JLHarris) **4-8-9** OPeslier(5) (chsd ldrs: pushed along over 3f out: sn btn)	3½	**4**	33/1	79 t	61
	Spirito Libro (USA) (87) (DJSCosgrove) **4-8-9** MRimmer(4) (trckd ldrs: outpcd over 2f out)	hd	**5**	10/1	79 t	61
				(SP 110.9%)	**5 Rn**	

2m 11.77 (2.77) CSF £2.74 TOTE £1.60: £1.20 £1.40 (£1.50) OWNER Sheikh Mohammed (NEWMARKET) BRED Sheikh Mohammed bin Rashid al Maktoum

Papering (IRE), slightly warm in the preliminaries but looking well tuned-up, made sure this was a true test of stamina, and always had the measure of her rivals. (8/11)

894 Charlotte Corday had the edge on fitness and battled on willingly in the closing stages, but the winner was always finding enough when the chips were down. (11/4)

Ball Gown was slightly out of her depth, especially on her seasonal debut, but she battled on to the end without ever threatening to prove troublesome. (6/1)

1145 Temptress was not beaten far in a competitive handicap twenty-four hours previously, but these rivals proved far too good and she was never in a position to land a blow. (33/1)

Spirito Libro (USA) improved no end last year but is only a handicapper, and she was out of her depth here. (10/1)

1158 GROSVENOR CASINO LEEDS SPRINT H'CAP (0-105) (3-Y.O+) (Class B)

2-35 (2-36) **5f** £15,270.00 (£4,560.00: £2,180.00: £990.00) Stalls: High GOING: 0.11 sec per fur (G)

				SP	RR	SF
744^{5}	**Twice as Sharp (83)** (PWHarris) **5-8-12** GHind(6) (swtg: mde virtually all centre: rdn over 1f out: r.o wl)	—	**1**	10/1	92	65
953^{5}	**Lago Di Varano (86)** (RMWhitaker) **5-9-1v** DeanMcKeown(8) (lw: sn drvn along: a chsng ldrs: r.o wl ins fnl f)	¾	**2**	20/1	93	66
1029*	**Bishops Court (89)** (MrsJRRamsden) **3-8-9** ^{6x} JFortune(4) (trckd ldrs: effrt & ev ch ins fnl f: unable qckn)	¾	**3**	13/8^{1}	93	57
1034*	**Surprise Mission (88)** (MrsJRRamsden) **5-9-3** ^{6x} ACulhane(7) (hld up: hdwy over 1f out: nrst fin)	½	**4**	11/2^{2}	91	64
901*	**Kira (84)** (JLEyre) **7-8-13** KFallon(9) (b: b.hind: chsd ldrs: rdn & one pce ins fnl f)	¾	**5**	9/1	84	57
1034^{6}	**Swynford Dream (84)** (JFBottomley) **4-8-13** JLowe(3) (sltly hmpd s: sn w wnr: rdn & one pce fnl f)	nk	**6**	33/1	83	56
834*	**Gone Savage (82)** (WJMusson) **9-8-11** RCochrane(5) (lw: hld up: effrt over 1f out: nvr nrr)	½	**7**	10/1	80	53
942^{11}	**White Emir (80)** (BJMeehan) **4-8-9** OPeslier(13) (chsd ldrs stands' side 3f)	nk	**8**	16/1	77	50
834^{6}	**Ellens Lad (IRE) (85)** (RHannon) **3-8-5** DaneO'Neill(11) (sn outpcd)	s.h	**9**	14/1	82	46
972*	**Palacegate Touch (84)** (JBerry) **7-8-8b**$^{(5)\ 6x}$ PFessey(2) (swvd rt s: nvr rchd ldrs)	¾	**10**	25/1	78	51
744^{6}	**Stuffed (84)** (MWEasterby) **5-8-13** TQuinn(12) (prom stands' side: rdn along ½-wy: sn btn)	1	**11**	8/1^{3}	75	48
877^{4}	**Repertory (93)** (MSSaunders) **4-9-8** RPerham(10) (sn chsng ldrs: rdn & wknd 2f out)	2	**12**	16/1	78	51
744^{16}	**Chemcast (75)** (JLEyre) **4-8-4b**^{ow1} RLappin(1) (w ldrs over 3f)	1	**13**	33/1	56	28
941^{9}	**Amazing Bay (95)** (IABalding) **4-9-10** LDettori(14) (chsd ldrs stands' side over 3f)	½	**14**	25/1	75	48
				(SP 129.5%)	**14 Rn**	

60.07 secs (2.37) CSF £190.43 CT £455.28 TOTE £10.80: £2.60 £4.00 £1.90 (£57.20) Trio £197.20 OWNER Formula Twelve (BERKHAMSTED) BRED R. and A. Craddock

WEIGHT FOR AGE 3yo-9lb

744 Twice as Sharp, always holding the call down the centre of the track, had to work really hard in the latter stages to hold on. He had conditions in his favour, but this was by far his best display yet. (10/1)

953 Lago Di Varano, stepping back to the minimum trip, put in a determined last-furlong effort but the winner kept pulling out more. This was his best effort for quite some time, and an early success will come as no surprise. (20/1)

1029* Bishops Court ran well all the way and did not fail for the want of trying but, over the minimum trip on such a flat track, he lacked the extra pace to launch a challenge. (13/8)

1034* Surprise Mission had probably not fully recovered from his easy success in the testing ground at Chester six days ago, and he was only getting into top gear when the race was over. (11/2)

901* Kira is a credit to her stable but, on ground softer than she really cares for, was fighting a losing battle inside the distance. (9/1)

1034 Swynford Dream has shown his best form on a sounder surface, but he ran a fine race in defeat and is ready to score again. (33/1)

834* Gone Savage, very free to post, was pegging back the leaders in the closing stages, but the line was always going to arrive too soon. (10/1)

1159 GROSVENOR CASINOS DANTE STKS (Gp 2) (3-Y.O) (Class A)

3-10 (3-12) **1m 2f 85y** £79,190.00 (£29,739.50: £14,369.75: £6,350.75) Stalls: Low GOING: 0.11 sec per fur (G)

				SP	RR	SF
851^{2}	**Benny The Dip (USA) (113)** (JHMGosden) **3-8-11** OPeslier(4) (swtg: mde all: qcknd over 2f out: r.o wl)	—	**1**	100/30^{1}	116	82
940^{6}	**Desert Story (IRE) (115)** (MRStoute) **3-8-11** MJKinane(7) (hld up: hdwy to chse wnr over 2f out: unable qckn fnl f)	2½	**2**	4/1^{2}	112	78
449*	**Musalsal (IRE) (104)** (BWHills) **3-8-11** MHills(9) (dwlt: hld up: hdwy over 3f out: styd on wl fnl f)	¾	**3**	8/1	111	77
676*	**Kingfisher Mill (USA)** (MrsJCecil) **3-8-11** PatEddery(2) (lw: hld up: rdn over 2f out: styd on wl fnl f)	nk	**4**	15/2	111	77
692^{8}	**Monza (USA) (108)** (PWChapple-Hyam) **3-8-11** JReid(3) (lw: prom: hrd drvn over 2f out: kpt on same pce)	2½	**5**	16/1	107	73
	Apprehension (DRLoder) **3-8-11** KDarley(5) (h.d.w: trckd ldrs: outpcd over 4f out: n.d afterwards)	½	**6**	13/2	106	72
	Yorkshire (IRE) (PFICole) **3-8-11** TQuinn(6) (h.d.w: plld hrd: sn chsng wnr: wknd wl over 1f out)	5	**7**	6/1^{3}	98	64
	Medaaly (SbinSuroor) **3-8-11** LDettori(8) (bit bkwd: chsd ldrs: drvn along over 3f out: sn wknd)	8	**8**	6/1^{3}	86	52
691^{3}	**Crimson Tide (IRE) (105)** (JWHills) **3-8-11** RHills(1) (stdd s: a bhd)	4	**9**	12/1	80	46
				(SP 121.4%)	**9 Rn**	

2m 11.97 (2.97) CSF £16.08 TOTE £4.50: £1.70 £1.60 £2.20 (£6.10) Trio £22.90 OWNER Mr Landon Knight (NEWMARKET) BRED Landon Knight

851 Benny The Dip (USA) was able to dictate from the front and, stepping up the tempo to draw a couple of lengths clear entering the final quarter-mile, soon had the rest in trouble, and only had to keep going to win comfortably. His price now varies between 7/1 and 12/1 for the Derby and, in a race where previous Dante winners have figured prominently, he could well be the value. (100/30)
940 Desert Story (IRE), playing second fiddle to the winner for the third time in three meetings, did nothing wrong and ran his race out to the finish, but he had to make do with the runner-up prize once again. (4/1)
449* Musalsal (IRE), restrained in the rear, was doing all his best work in the closing stages and, if he can be taught to settle, he is one who has a sporting chance of turning the tables at Epsom. (8/1)
676* Kingfisher Mill (USA) is a very progressive colt who is short on experience, and the way he was staying on in the latter stages suggests he is set to go a long way. (15/2)
692 Monza (USA) ran much better than he did on his seasonal debut, but he was being made to work early in the straight and his measure was soon taken. (16/1)
Apprehension, who has done well physically since last year, was content to wait on the leaders, but he got tapped for toe early in the straight and, from then on, was always fighting a lost cause. (13/2: 4/1-7/1)
Yorkshire (IRE) has grown into a very handsome colt and he looked as though he had done plenty of work, but he almost took charge going to post, refused to settle once in action and had run himself out below the distance. It is possible he will be more settled with this run under his belt and, if things go his way, he could prove very useful. (6/1)
Medaaly looked as though the run was needed and, showing plenty of knee action, was in trouble early in the straight. (6/1)
691 Crimson Tide (IRE), dropped out at the start, was unable to pick up when popped the question early in the straight, and he ran no race at all. (12/1)

1160 GROSVENOR CASINOS HAMBLETON RATED STKS H'CAP (0-110) (Listed) (4-Y.O+) (Class A)
3-40 (3-42) **7f 202y** £13,604.00 (£5,036.00: £2,418.00: £990.00: £395.00: £157.00) Stalls: Low GOING: 0.11 sec per fur (G)

				SP	RR	SF
830^{7}	**Centre Stalls (IRE) (110)** (RFJohnsonHoughton) **4-9-7** TQuinn(8) (hld up: hdwy over 2f out: led ent fnl f: drvn out)	—	**1**	10/1	123	94
678^{9}	**Prince Babar (100)** (JEBanks) **6-8-11** PatEddery(2) (a.p: ev ch over 1f out: nt pce of wnr fnl f)	2½	**2**	6/1^{2}	108	79
	Insatiable (IRE) (96) (MRStoute) **4-8-7** MJKinane(7) (hld up: hdwy over 2f out: rdn & no ex fnl f)	1¼	**3**	6/1^{2}	101	72
894^{4}	**Winter Romance (100)** (EALDunlop) **4-8-11** OPeslier(11) (lw: hld up: hdwy over 2f out: kpt on fnl f: nvr nrr)	¾	**4**	6/1^{2}	104	75
839^{4}	**Russian Music (105)** (MissGayKelleway) **4-9-2b** KFallon(12) (led: hrd rdn over 1f out: hdd ent fnl f: sn btn)	1¾	**5**	14/1	105	76
981^{3}	**Musick House (IRE) (96)** (PWChapple-Hyam) **4-8-7b^{1}** JReid(6) (chsd ldrs: rdn over 3f out: kpt on same pce)	1	**6**	11/1	94	65
677^{10}	**New Century (USA) (96)** (DNicholls) **5-8-7** JCarroll(3) (a chsng ldrs: hrd rdn over 1f out: sn btn)	2½	**7**	16/1	89	60
987^{9}	**Concer Un (96)** (SCWilliams) **5-8-7** MHills(14) (b: lw: chsd ldrs: rdn 3f out: sn btn)	½	**8**	9/1^{3}	88	59
	Hi Nod (100) (MJCamacho) **7-8-11** LCharnock(9) (bkwd: chsd ldrs tl wknd over 2f out)	7	**9**	12/1	78	49
519^{6}	**Patsy Grimes (96)** (JSMoore) **7-8-7** DaneO'Neill(10) (hld up in rr: effrt & rdn 3f out: no imp)	hd	**10**	25/1	74	45
	Master Boots (102) (DRLoder) **4-8-13** KDarley(4) (lw: chsd ldrs: effrt over 3f out: wknd over 2f out)	3½	**11**	10/1	73	44
1074a^{5}	**Celestial Key (USA) (102)** (MJohnston) **7-8-13b** JWeaver(1) (lw: a bhd)	3	**12**	12/1	67	38
409a^{2}	**Hammerstein (105)** (SbinSuroor) **4-9-2** LDettori(5) (lw: trckd ldrs: rdn 3f out: eased whn btn fnl 2f: t.o)	11	**13**	5/1^{1}	48	19
892^{8}	**Resounder (USA) (96)** (JHMGosden) **4-8-7** RHills(13) (hld up: a bhd: t.o)	15	**14**	12/1	8	—

(SP 135.5%) **14 Rn**

1m 39.01 (2.01) CSF £70.76 CT £386.62 TOTE £13.70: £3.80 £2.10 £2.00 (£49.40) Trio £80.70 OWNER Mr Anthony Pye-Jeary (DIDCOT) BRED Limestone Stud
LONG HANDICAP New Century (USA) 8-2 Patsy Grimes 8-5 Insatiable (IRE) 8-3 Musick House (IRE) 8-4 Resounder (USA) 8-5
Centre Stalls (IRE), back in his own class here, began to pick up ground over two furlongs out and, going through with his effort, won going away. A long-striding colt who needs a galloping track, he will stay further and is on the way up. (10/1)
Prince Babar, upsides the winner at the distance, was unable to contain him in the duel to the finish, but he lost no caste in defeat. His turn cannot be far away. (6/1)
Insatiable (IRE) has not been out since running North Song to a head in the Britannia Handicap at Royal Ascot eleven months ago, but he looked wound-up, and this impressive, staying-on performance could be a sure sign that he is out to make up for lost time. There is no reason why he should not get further. (6/1)
894 Winter Romance was never able to land a blow despite staying on. He may well benefit from a slightly longer trip in this grade, and he is certainly ready to strike. (6/1)
839 Russian Music set a very strong pace and, in the end, only succeeded in beating himself. He has not yet won beyond seven furlongs, and these tactics at that trip could well pay off. (14/1)
981 Musick House (IRE), a half-brother to Rodrigo de Triano and blinkered for the first time, was off the bridle three furlongs out but he kept staying on, and he is capable of better than he has produced so far. (11/1)
409a Hammerstein, who has wintered in Dubai, was very much on his toes in the preliminaries. Held up just off the pace, he failed to pick up when given the office and was eased when all chance had gone. He has done all his winning on a sounder surface and may well need to hear his feet rattle. (5/1)

93 93 94 82

1161 GROSVENOR CASINO SHEFFIELD CONDITIONS STKS (2-Y.O) (Class B) (90)
4-10 (4-11) **6f** £7,309.00 (£2,529.00: £1,214.50: £497.50) Stalls: High GOING: 0.11 sec per fur (G)

				SP	RR	SF
938*	**Bodyguard** (PFICole) **2-8-13** TQuinn(3) (lw: hld up: hdwy on ins over 2f out: led wl over 1f out: r.o)	—	**1**	2/7^{1}	87	28
861^{2}	**Out Like Magic** (PDEvans) **2-8-8** JFEgan(2) (b.hind: chsd ldr: reminders ½-wy: kpt on wl ins fnl f)	1¾	**2**	12/1	77	18
971*	**Jackerin (IRE)** (BSRothwell) **2-8-13** KFallon(4) (b.off hind: led tl hdd wl over 1f out: outpcd fnl f)	6	**3**	15/2^{3}	66	7
836*	**Ruzen (IRE)** (BPalling) **2-8-11** TSprake(1) (lw: hld up & plld hrd: effrt over 2f out: sn rdn: no imp)	2½	**4**	5/1^{2}	58	—

(SP 113.9%) **4 Rn**

1m 16.1 (5.60) CSF £4.86 TOTE £1.30 (£3.10) OWNER H R H Prince Fahd Salman (WHATCOMBE) BRED M. Rapp
938* Bodyguard was made to work over this extra furlong, but he always looked in control and he will now chance his arm in the Group Three Coventry Stakes at Royal Ascot. (2/7)
861 Out Like Magic was the first to be ridden, but she stuck to her task willingly, and will not always meet one as useful as the winner. (12/1)
971* Jackerin (IRE), again attempted to make all, but in this class he was found wanting and was left for dead approaching the final furlong. (15/2: 6/1-9/1)
836* Ruzen (IRE), waited with to make sure he got the trip, could not respond when asked to quicken. (5/1)

1162 GROSVENOR CASINO MANCHESTER H'CAP (0-90) (4-Y.O+) (Class C)

4-40 (4-43) **1m 5f 194y** £7,830.00 (£2,340.00: £1,120.00: £510.00) Stalls: Low GOING: 0.11 sec per fur (G)

				SP	RR	SF
846^{2}	**Turnpole (IRE) (70)** (MrsMReveley) **6-8-8** ACulhane(5) (lw: hld up in tch: led 2f out tl ins fnl f: rallied u.p to ld cl home)	—	**1**	$6/1^{2}$	84	48
994^{2}	**Opaque (66)** (WStorey) **5-7-13**(5) PFessey(4) (b.off hind: s.s: hdwy on outside ent st: jnd ldrs 2f out: led ins fnl f: hrd rdn & hdd nr fin)	s.h	**2**	$6/1^{2}$	80	44
762^{11}	**Midyan Blue (IRE) (68)** (JMPEustace) **7-8-6** RCochrane(11) (led to 3f out: rallied gamely towards fin)	¾	**3**	$11/2^{1}$	81	45
846^{3}	**Siege Perilous (IRE) (68)** (SCWilliams) **4-8-5** TQuinn(16) (hld up: hdwy 3f out: rdn & swtchd rt over 1f out: kpt on)	¾	**4**	10/1	80	43
1036^{2}	**Raffles Rooster (65)** (AGNewcombe) **5-7-10**(7) JoHunnam(10) (a chsng ldrs: styd on same pce fnl 2f)	2½	**5**	$6/1^{2}$	74	38
680^{16}	**Totem Dancer (78)** (JLEyre) **4-9-1** KFallon(6) (hld up: hdwy 4f out: edgd lft 2f out: styd on)	2	**6**	14/1	85	48
858^{9}	**Purple Splash (90)** (PJMakin) **7-10-0v** PatEddery(9) (lw: hld up: hdwy over 2f out: staying on whn nt clr run appr fnl f: eased)	1¼	**7**	14/1	96	60
982^{*}	**Turgenev (IRE) (67)** (RBastiman) **8-8-5b** 4x MBirch(13) (hld up: hdwy over 3f out: rdn 2f out: wknd)	hd	**8**	10/1	73	37
955^{2}	**Summerhill Special (IRE) (62)** (DWBarker) **6-8-0** TWilliams(1) (b.near hind: w ldrs: slt ld 3f out: hdd & wknd 2f out)	nk	**9**	16/1	67	31
982^{3}	**Bellara (58)** (NMBabbage) **5-7-10** NVarley(3) (nvr trbld ldrs)	2	**10**	16/1	61	25
	Arctic Fancy (USA) (80) (PWHarris) **4-9-3** MJKinane(14) (hld up & bhd: effrt & rdn ent st: no imp)	10	**11**	14/1	71	34
	Campaign (74) (MDHammond) **6-8-12** JFortune(12) (chsd ldrs: rdn 3f out: sn wknd)	1¼	**12**	33/1	64	28
982^{11}	**Batoutoftheblue (59)** (WWHaigh) **4-7-10** LCharnock(7) (bit bkwd: trckd ldrs 10f: sn rdn & wknd)	3½	**13**	33/1	45	8
	Samim (USA) (60) (SGollings) **4-7-11b** JLowe(2) (trckd ldrs: rdn over 3f out: sn lost pl)	1½	**14**	33/1	44	7
881^{2}	**Pike Creek (USA) (75)** (IABalding) **4-8-12** LDettori(15) (swtg: prom tl rdn & wknd over 3f out: eased whn btn)	nk	**15**	$7/1^{3}$	59	22
982^{4}	***Executive Design (72)*** (MrsMReveley) **5-8-10** KDarley(8) (Withdrawn not under Starter's orders: ref to ent stalls)		**W**		—	—
				(SP 129.5%)	**15 Rn**	

3m 2.82 (9.22) CSF £40.31 CT £196.93 TOTE £7.70: £2.60 £2.30 £2.10 (£17.40) Trio £24.50 OWNER Mr W. J. Williams (SALTBURN) BRED Old Meadow Stud

WEIGHT FOR AGE 4yo-1lb

846 Turnpole (IRE) stays well and is much happier when he can get his toe in, and that, plus the fact that he had the rail to race against in the closing stages, enabled him to fight back and land the spoils nearing the line. (6/1)

994 Opaque made relentless progress up the centre of the track and joined issue two furlongs out. He appeared to have the edge when gaining a slight lead inside the final furlong, but he was inclined to lean on the winner and that rival proved the stronger in an all-out battle to the line. (6/1)

499 Midyan Blue (IRE), a close-up fourth in this race twelve months ago after winning it the previous year, had far more use made of him this time and, staying on particularly well in the latter stages, ran up to his mark. (11/2)

846 Siege Perilous (IRE) finished much closer to the winner despite meeting him on 3lb worse terms than on his most recent outing, but that was over two miles and, though he did not stride out with any freedom, he is surely knocking at the door. (10/1)

1036 Raffles Rooster had probably not recovered from his duel in the mud at Chester six days ago, and he was always at full stretch and unable to make any impression on the leaders. (6/1)

Totem Dancer, back over a more suitable trip, began to peg back the leaders inside the last half-mile, but she was inclined to edge left and failed to make much progress. (14/1)

Purple Splash needs to come from behind, and he was staying on, but with it all to do, when Raffles Rooster took his ground on the approach to the final furlong, and the position was accepted. If given a chance by the Handicapper, he is one to keep in mind. (14/1)

T/Jkpt: £7,889.80 (0.29 Tckts); £7,889.88 to York 15/5/97. T/Plpt: £15.90 (2747.13 Tckts). T/Qdpt: £8.80 (189.35 Tckts) IM

0964-SALISBURY (R-H) (Good to Firm, Firm patches)

Thursday May 15th

All races hand-timed

WEATHER: fine but cloudy WIND: almost nil

89+ 79+ 74+ 69

1163 WARMINSTER MAIDEN STKS (2-Y.O) (Class D) (77)

2-15 (2-15) **5f** £3,281.50 (£982.00: £471.00: £215.50) Stalls: High GOING minus 0.60 sec per fur (F)

				SP	RR	SF
	Pool Music (RHannon) **2-9-0** RHughes(4) (scope: lw: hld up: led over 1f out: pushed out)	—	**1**	$3/1^{2}$	85+	48
	Compradore (MBlanshard) **2-8-9** JQuinn(5) (unf: a.p: ev ch over 1f out: nt qckn)	1¼	**2**	25/1	76	39
500^{5}	**Percy-P** (WRMuir) **2-9-0** JReid(6) (lw: plld hrd: chsd ldr: led 2f out: sn hdd: one pce)	1½	**3**	$7/2^{3}$	76	39
	Rodinia (USA) (GLewis) **2-9-0** PaulEddery(7) (scope: lw: led 3f: wknd fnl f)	1¾	**4**	5/1	71	34
	Lincolnshire (USA) (PFICole) **2-9-0** RCochrane(2) (leggy: s.s: rdn over 2f out: nvr nr to chal)	nk	**5**	$9/4^{1}$	70	33
	Striding King (MRChannon) **2-9-0** RPerham(3) (unf: scope: bit bkwd: prom over 2f)	½	**6**	12/1	68	31
850^{9}	**Oisin (IRE)** (MrsPNDutfield) **2-8-9**(5) RFfrench(1) (wnt lft s: a bhd)	2	**7**	33/1	62	25
	Petaling (IRE) (BJMeehan) **2-8-9** BDoyle(9) (leggy: bit bkwd: s.s: outpcd)	3½	**8**	14/1	45	8
				(SP 115.8%)	**8 Rn**	

60.0 secs (0.00) CSF £64.72 TOTE £3.30: £1.10 £3.50 £1.20 (£20.00) Trio £84.40; £96.38 to Thirsk 16/5/97 OWNER Mrs Caroline Parker (MARLBOROUGH) BRED Mrs N. F. M. Sampson

Pool Music, a 60,000gns brother to Russian Music, seemed rather green when noisy in the paddock. However, he had certainly been taught his job and, well regarded by his trainer, may go for the Norfolk at Royal Ascot. (3/1)

Compradore, out of a mare who won over a mile and twelve furlongs, came up against a sharp sort in the winner. (25/1)

500 Percy-P had a sounder surface this time but did not help his cause by not accepting restraint. (7/2)

Rodinia (USA), a brother to Group Three winner Gneiss, made a satisfactory start to his career. (5/1)

Lincolnshire (USA) lost his chance at the start. (9/4)

Striding King, out of a mare who won from five furlongs up to a mile and a quarter, will be sharper for the outing. (12/1: op 8/1)

Petaling (IRE) (14/1: op 8/1)

1164 DRUIDS H'CAP (0-70) (3-Y.O) (Class E)

2-45 (2-47) **1m** £3,330.25 (£997.00: £478.50: £219.25) Stalls: High GOING minus 0.60 sec per fur (F)

Form	Horse	Dist	Pos	SP	RR	SF
765^{9}	**Blue Imperial (FR) (54)** (JWHills) **3-8-4**(3) MHenry(7) (bit bkwd: mde all: rdn 3f out: r.o wl)	—	1	20/1	65+	34
868^{7}	**Agent Mulder (52)** (PDCundell) **3-8-5** RPerham(18) (w wnr: rdn over 2f out: ev ch ins fnl f: nt qckn)	½	2	33/1	62	31
900^{5}	**Carlys Quest (62)** (JNeville) **3-9-1** AMcGlone(11) (lw: hld up: hdwy 3f out: r.o ins fnl f)	½	3	12/1	71	40
886^{2}	**Interdream (61)** (RHannon) **3-9-0** RHughes(10) (hld up & bhd: hdwy & swtchd lft over 2f out: r.o)	¾	4	8/1 3	69	38
1078^{2}	**Abajany (66)** (MRChannon) **3-9-0**(5) PPMurphy(17) (a.p: one pce fnl 2f)	hd	5	3/1 1	73	42
535^{14}	**Hadawah (USA) (65)** (JLDunlop) **3-9-4** BDoyle(15) (prom: rdn over 2f out: eased whn btn wl ins fnl f)	2½	6	16/1	67	36
	Racing Heart (52) (PJMakin) **3-8-5**ow1 DHolland(9) (nvr nr to chal)	4	7	33/1	46	14
886^{4}	**Saffron Rose (65)** (MBlanshard) **3-9-4** RCochrane(6) (nvr nr to chal)	1¼	8	7/1 2	57	26
840^{10}	**Keepsake (IRE) (58)** (MDIUsher) **3-8-11** MRoberts(1) (nvr nrr)	½	9	33/1	49	18
791^{12}	**First Chance (IRE) (68)** (DRCElsworth) **3-9-7** PaulEddery(14) (prom over 6f)	nk	10	14/1	58	27
785^{2}	**Brave Envoy (64)** (MJHeaton-Ellis) **3-9-3** SDrowne(8) (hld up mid div: rdn over 2f out: wknd wl over 1f out)	1½	11	10/1	51	20
	Palaemon (66) (GBBalding) **3-9-5** AClark(4) (a bhd)	2½	12	14/1	48	17
889^{8}	**Ar Hyd Y Knos (60)** (RCharlton) **3-8-13** TSprake(2) (prom over 5f)	s.h	13	20/1	42	11
876^{6}	**Dr Woodstock (55)** (MartynMeade) **3-8-8** FNorton(13) (bhd fnl 2f)	hd	14	20/1	37	6
886^{9}	**Brynkir (61)** (DJGMurraySmith) **3-9-0** DHarrison(3) (a bhd)	3	15	25/1	37	6
	Myosotis (58) (PJMakin) **3-8-11** SSanders(16) (rdn after 2f: bhd fnl 3f)	¾	16	25/1	32	1
840^{5}	**Sun O'Tirol (IRE) (60)** (JRArnold) **3-8-13** CRutter(5) (bhd fnl 2f)	hd	17	16/1	34	3
764^{4}	**Around Fore Alliss (67)** (TGMills) **3-9-3**(3) AWhelan(12) (s.s: rdn over 3f out: a bhd: t.o)	20	18	16/1	1	—

(SP 127.2%) **18 Rn**

1m 41.0 (1.00) CSF £494.13 CT £7,471.07 TOTE £66.30: £8.70 £8.50 £3.30 £2.30 (£340.60) Trio £326.00; £293.89 to Thirsk 16/5/97 OWNER Mr George Tong (LAMBOURN) BRED Haras de Clairfeuille

Blue Imperial (FR) was described by his trainer as hard to motivate but had been working well. He held on gamely over a course where it is none too easy to front-run over a mile. (20/1)

868 Agent Mulder, giving the first indication that the truth is out there, looked set to score in the last two hundred yards but his supporters had been foxed by the winner. (33/1)

900 Carlys Quest had been raised 2lb for this return to a mile. (12/1: op 8/1)

886 Interdream, raised 2lb, had difficulty obtaining a clear run and seems suited to a stiff mile like this. (8/1)

1078 Abajany was 4lb higher than when runner-up at Carlisle last week. (3/1)

Hadawah (USA) may have found this stiff mile beyond her best. (16/1)

Racing Heart, a stone lower than when running in a nursery on her final outing last season, gave the impression she might be capable of better things. (33/1)

886 Saffron Rose was on the same mark as when unlucky at Nottingham. (7/1)

1165 DURNFORD CONDITIONS STKS (3-Y.O) (Class C)

3-20 (3-20) **1m 4f** £4,910.00 (£1,710.00: £830.00: £350.00) Stalls: High GOING minus 0.60 sec per fur (F)

Form	Horse	Dist	Pos	SP	RR	SF
991*	**Badlesmere (USA)** (PFICole) **3-9-1** CRutter(2) (lw: plld hrd: led 2f: led over 2f out: all out)	—	1	10/11 1	93	16
847^{2}	**Double Alleged (USA)** (MJohnston) **3-8-12** MRoberts(3) (b: plld hrd: led after 2f tl over 2f out: hrd rdn & ev ch fnl f: r.o wl)	s.h	2	13/8 2	90	13
735^{18}	**Fletcher (83)** (HMorrison) **3-8-12** RHughes(4) (hld up: hdwy 3f out: hrd rdn over 1f out: r.o)	½	3	16/1	89	12
	Royal Crown (IRE) (PWChapple-Hyam) **3-8-12** JReid(1) (hld up: wknd 3f out)	5	4	6/1 3	83?	6

(SP 110.6%) **4 Rn**

2m 36.6 (5.60) CSF £2.50 TOTE £1.70: (£1.80) OWNER Exors of the late Lord Sondes (WHATCOMBE) BRED Peter J. Callahan

991* Badlesmere (USA) just scrambled home over this extra half-mile, and the Italian Derby looks a long way off on this evidence. (10/11: evens-4/5)

847 Double Alleged (USA) appreciated this extra quarter-mile and fought the winner tooth and nail. (13/8)

Fletcher, not one to trust when with Paul Cole last year, gave every indication he might be going straight in his new surroundings. (16/1)

Royal Crown (IRE), a brother to Royal Court and a half-brother to Dr Devious, took a walk in the market and ran accordingly. (6/1: op 5/2)

1166 TRYON H'CAP (0-80) (3-Y.O+) (Class D)

3-50 (3-51) **6f 212y** £4,120.00 (£1,240.00: £600.00: £280.00) Stalls: High GOING minus 0.60 sec per fur (F)

Form	Horse	Dist	Pos	SP	RR	SF
131^{5}	**Ben Gunn (60)** (PTWalwyn) **5-8-8** RCochrane(13) (hdwy 2f out: led ins fnl f: r.o wl)	—	1	12/1	72	44
987^{5}	**Amber Fort (74)** (DRCElsworth) **4-9-5v**(3) DGriffiths(11) (hdwy over 1f out: r.o: fin 3rd, 2l & hd: plcd 2nd)	2¼	2	7/2 1	81	53
	Mihriz (IRE) (61) (RAkehurst) **5-8-9** AClark(3) (gd hdwy over 1f out: fin wl: fin 4th, 1l: plcd 3rd)	1	3	12/1	66	38
895^{26}	**White Settler (70)** (RJHodges) **4-8-13**(5) RFfrench(6) (hdwy 2f out: one pce fnl f: fin 5th, 1 3/4l: plcd 4th)	1¾	4	20/1	71	43
987^{10}	**Artful Dane (IRE) (77)** (MJHeaton-Ellis) **5-9-11v** MRoberts(8) (lw: hdwy over 1f out: edgd rt: one pce fnl f: fin 6th, hd: plcd 5th)	hd	5	7/1 2	78	50
520^{13}	**Newlands Corner (58)** (JAkehurst) **4-8-6b** DBiggs(5) (hld up: hdwy, nt clr run & swtchd lft 2f out: one pce fnl f: fin 7th, nk: plcd 6th)	nk	6	12/1	58	30
892^{14}	**Tea Party (USA) (65)** (KOCunningham-Brown) **4-8-13b** TSprake(4) (lw: tk keen hold: hdwy over 3f out: ev ch 2f out: wknd over 1f out: fin 8th, ½l: plcd 7th)	½	7	20/1	64	36
483^{7}	**Kewarra (75)** (BRMillman) **3-8-11** BDoyle(9) (lw: hld up & bhd: hdwy whn nt clr run over 1f out: nt rch ldrs: fin 9th, 3/4l: plcd 8th)	¾	8	20/1	72	32
1012^{9}	**Out Line (62)** (MMadgwick) **5-8-10** NVarley(19) (prom 5f: fin 10th, hd: plcd 9th)	hd	9	16/1	59	31
895^{25}	**Zurs (IRE) (78)** (MissGayKelleway) **4-9-12** DHolland(2) (nvr nrr: fin 11th, ½l: plcd 10th)	½	10	20/1	74	46
1083^{5}	**Rififi (64)** (RIngram) **4-8-12** SWhitworth(17) (b: lw: dwlt: hdwy 2f out: nt clr run over 1f out: eased: fin 12th, sh hd; plcd 11th)	s.h	11	14/1	60	32
	Sharp Rebuff (79) (PJMakin) **6-9-13** SSanders(20) (prom: ev ch 2f out: wknd over 1f out: fin 13th, 1½l: plcd 12th)	1½	12	10/1 3	71	43
	Havago (71) (RHannon) **3-8-7** RPerham(15) (lw: led over 5f: fin 14th, 2l: plcd 13th)	2	13	10/1 3	59	19
	Flotilla (77) (SMellor) **3-8-13** MWigham(10) (a bhd: fin 15th, nk: plcd 14th)	nk	14	33/1	64	24
791^{11}	**Balance of Power (65)** (SDow) **5-8-8**(5) ADaly(1) (swtchd rt s: a bhd: fin 16th, sh hd: plcd 15th)	s.h	15	20/1	52	24
	Sovereigns Court (65) (LGCottrell) **4-8-13** JReid(18) (lw: prom: wkng whn hmpd over 2f out: fin 17th, 2½l: plcd 16th)	2½	16	11/1	46	18

				SP	RR	SF
1020[13]	**Will Do (62)** (MartynMeade) **4-8-10** FNorton(14) (prom over 4f: fin 18th, 2½l: plcd 17th)	2½	**17**	33/1	37	9
450[21]	**Barossa Valley (IRE) (80)** (PButler) **6-9-9**(5) PPMurphy(16) (prom over 4f: fin 19th, 8l: plcd 18th)	8	**18**	33/1	37	9
	Elfland (IRE) (80) (LadyHerries) **6-9-7**(7) PDoe(12) (hld up & plld hrd: hdwy & squeezed thro over 2f out: led wl over 1f out: hdd ins fnl f: fin 2nd, 2l: disq: plcd last)		**D**	11/1	87	59
				(SP 137.8%)	**19 Rn**	

1m 26.0 (0.00) CSF £47.95 CT £514.20 TOTE £10.90: £2.00 £1.40 £4.00 £3.80 (£34.70) Trio £233.20 OWNER Mr Michael White (LAMBOURN) BRED Michael White and Peter Walwyn
WEIGHT FOR AGE 3yo-12lb
STEWARDS' ENQUIRY Doe susp. 24 & 26-29/5/97 (irresponsible riding).
131 Ben Gunn, dropping back in trip, was well handicapped on his best form and had shown signs of a return to form on the sand at Lingfield during the winter. (12/1)
987 Amber Fort was suited by this testing seven furlongs. (7/2)
Mihriz (IRE) has dropped to a useful mark and looks to be coming to hand. (12/1)
White Settler, still 6lb higher than when winning at Chepstow last July, appreciated this return to seven. (20/1)
444* Artful Dane (IRE), 5lb higher than when winning at Doncaster's Lincoln meeting, has never scored at less than a mile. (7/1)
Newlands Corner is one to consider when reverting to six. (12/1)
554 Tea Party (USA) needs to be covered up. (20/1)
Havago (10/1: 7/1-11/1)
Elfland (IRE), although his rider landed in hot water, made a highly satisfactory comeback, especially when considering he refused to settle. (11/1)

1167 REDENHAM CLAIMING STKS (3-Y.O) (Class F)

4-20 (4-21) **6f 212y** £2,763.00 (£768.00: £369.00) Stalls: High GOING minus 0.60 sec per fur (F)

				SP	RR	SF
	Forget To Remindme (JSMoore) **3-8-0**(5)ow3 PPMurphy(11) (lw: bhd: rdn 3f out: gd hdwy over 1f out: str run to ld wl ins fnl f)	—	**1**	33/1	56	15
895[17]	**My Beloved (IRE) (74)** (RHannon) **3-9-2** RHughes(4) (lw: hld up: rdn & hdwy over 2f out: ev ch wl ins fnl f: r.o)	nk	**2**	5/2[1]	66	28
958[8]	**Last Chance (68)** (DJSCosgrove) **3-9-1** MRimmer(7) (led tl wl ins fnl f)	1¼	**3**	8/1[3]	62	24
1044[9]	**Prince of Fortune** (MBlanshard) **3-8-7** NAdams(5) (hld up mid div: hdwy 2f out: r.o ins fnl f)	s.h	**4**	25/1	54	16
	Circle of Magic (52) (PJMakin) **3-8-8** SSanders(17) (hdwy over 1f out: r.o)	s.h	**5**	16/1	55	17
	Impala (52) (WGMTurner) **3-8-13** TSprake(2) (plld hrd: a.p: one pce fnl 2f)	2	**6**	12/1	56	18
871[13]	**Parijazz (IRE) (68)** (MartynMeade) **3-8-4** FNorton(10) (prom: ev ch 2f out: wknd fnl f)	1½	**7**	8/1[3]	43	5
882[4]	**Miss Peregrine** (RGuest) **3-8-12** PBloomfield(12) (nvr nr to chal)	s.h	**8**	9/1	51	13
	Over The Moon (MJFetherston-Godley) **3-9-2** CRutter(16) (lw: nvr nrr)	s.h	**9**	20/1	55	17
740[14]	**Mistral Lord (IRE)** (MMadgwick) **3-8-13** NVarley(8) (prom: rdn over 3f out: wknd fnl f)	1¼	**10**	33/1	49	11
1023[13]	**Fortune Hunter (IRE)** (WJarvis) **3-9-7** OUrbina(13) (a mid div)	s.h	**11**	12/1	57	19
	Ginny Wossername (53) (MartynMeade) **3-7-13**(3) MHenry(1) (prom: rdn over 3f out: wknd over 1f out)	3½	**12**	14/1	30	—
379[8]	**Not Out Lad** (PButler) **3-8-9** SDrowne(9) (s.s: a bhd)	hd	**13**	33/1	37	—
535[17]	**Folly Foot Fred (55)** (BRMillman) **3-8-7** BDoyle(3) (prom over 4f)	nk	**14**	16/1	34	—
458[4]	**Cheval Roc (62)** (RHannon) **3-8-9** RPerham(15) (lw: bhd fnl 2f)	hd	**15**	7/1[2]	36	—
779[9]	**Skippy Was A Kiwi (IRE) (50)** (APJarvis) **3-7-7**(5) RFfrench(6) (prom over 4f)	3	**16**	12/1	18	—
				(SP 132.2%)	**16 Rn**	

1m 28.3 (2.30) CSF £107.71 TOTE £46.00: £6.00 £1.60 £2.50 (£72.10) Trio £154.30 OWNER Mrs P. M. Ratcliffe (HUNGERFORD) BRED New Hall Farms Estate
Forget To Remindme showed signs of ability on her debut last back-end and mounted a whirlwind finish. (33/1)
My Beloved (IRE) appreciated this drop in grade. (5/2)
483 Last Chance was reverting back to seven for this descent into a claimer. (8/1)
Prince of Fortune, showing his first signs of ability, shaped as though he might appreciate further. (25/1)
Circle of Magic seems to have improved a bit with another year on his back, but found this trip inadequate. (16/1)
Impala did not look an easy ride last season and may be better off given his head over sprint distances. (12/1)
Parijazz (IRE) did not see out this longer trip. (8/1)
Fortune Hunter (IRE) (12/1: op 8/1)

1168 NETHERHAMPTON MAIDEN STKS (3-Y.O+ F & M) (Class D)

4-50 (4-53) **1m 1f 209y** £3,847.00 (£1,156.00: £558.00: £259.00) Stalls: High GOING minus 0.60 sec per fur (F)

				SP	RR	SF
	Western Hour (USA) (PWChapple-Hyam) **3-8-6** JReid(10) (led 1f: led 2f out tl over 1f out: led ins fnl f: rdn out)	—	**1**	3/1[2]	81	27
989[2]	**Lonely Heart (70)** (DRCElsworth) **3-8-6** RCochrane(8) (lw: hld up: hdwy 3f out: hung rt & led over 1f out: hdd ins fnl f: nt qckn)	1¼	**2**	7/1[3]	79	25
	Silver Whirl (USA) (RCharlton) **3-8-6** TSprake(12) (w'like: scope: lw: hld up: hdwy over 4f out: wknd over 1f out)	5	**3**	9/1	71	17
	Kilma (USA) (LMCumani) **3-8-6** OUrbina(3) (w'like: reard s: hdwy 4f out: ev ch over 2f out: wknd over 1f out)	1	**4**	15/8[1]	69	15
	Tangshan (CAN) (MRStoute) **3-8-6** DHolland(5) (lw: a.p: ev ch over 2f out: wknd over 1f out)	2½	**5**	10/1	65	11
	Inimitable (JLDunlop) **3-8-6** BDoyle(4) (bit bkwd: hdwy 7f out: rdn 2f out: sn wknd)	nk	**6**	20/1	65	11
885[7]	**Persian Blue** (RHannon) **3-8-6** RPerham(14) (nvr nrr)	2	**7**	25/1	62	8
	Jude (PFICole) **3-8-6** CRutter(13) (leggy: lt-f: s.v.s: sme hdwy over 2f out: n.d)	nk	**8**	14/1	61	7
	Itatinga (USA) (MRStoute) **3-8-6** AClark(9) (prom over 7f)	1¾	**9**	14/1	58	4
	Flagship (MajorWRHern) **3-8-6** PaulEddery(11) (led after 1f: hdd 2f out: sn wknd)	½	**10**	8/1	58	4
989[10]	**Eternity** (JRFanshawe) **3-8-6** DHarrison(18) (prom tl wknd over 2f out)	3	**11**	25/1	53	—
1006[7]	**Windrush Holly (55)** (DRCElsworth) **4-9-4**(3) DGriffiths(7) (a bhd)	3½	**12**	33/1	47	8
	War Shanty (LadyHerries) **4-9-0**(7) PDoe(1) (bit bkwd: hdwy over 5f out: wknd over 2f out)	1	**13**	40/1	46	7
725[18]	**Bint Rosie** (MJFetherston-Godley) **3-8-3**(3) DO'Donohoe(2) (a bhd)	1¾	**14**	66/1	43	—
	Puteri Wentworth (MissGayKelleway) **3-8-6** SSanders(17) (b: b.hind: leggy: scope: dwlt: a bhd)	8	**15**	14/1	30	—
	Miss Mezzanine (EAWheeler) **3-8-1**(5) ADaly(16) (bit bkwd: a bhd)	nk	**16**	50/1	29	—
				(SP 143.8%)	**16 Rn**	

2m 7.4 (2.10) CSF £25.54 TOTE £4.60: £1.60 £1.90 £2.70 (£12.00) Trio £30.60 OWNER Mrs B. V. Sangster (MARLBOROUGH) BRED Roncon Ltd and Barronstown Stud
WEIGHT FOR AGE 3yo-15lb

Western Hour (USA) came into her own over this longer trip but was helped by the runner-up's antics. (3/1)
989 Lonely Heart, stepping up from a mile, would undoubtedly have made it harder for the winner had she kept straight. (7/1)
Silver Whirl (USA), a $125,000 half-sister to a Listed winner in Spain, is out of a mare who won a nine-furlong Grade Three event in the States as a five-year-old. (9/1)
Kilma (USA), a $210,000 yearling, is out of a Grade Two nine-furlong winner as a four-year-old in the States who went on to be placed in Grade One events the following season. Taking some persuading to load up, she then fly-jumped leaving the stalls and gave the general impression that she will be better for the experience. (15/8)
Tangshan (CAN) was not knocked about once her chance had gone and it could be that a mile is far enough for her for the time being. (10/1: op 6/1)
Inimitable seemed to find lack of peak fitness finding her out. (20/1)
Jude (14/1: 10/1-16/1)
Flagship (8/1: op 3/1)

1169 LEVY BOARD H'CAP (0-80) (3-Y.O+) (Class D)

5-20 (5-20) **1m 4f** £3,743.00 (£1,124.00: £542.00: £251.00) Stalls: High GOING minus 0.60 sec per fur (F)

				SP	RR	SF
1010*	**Mazurek (68)** (MCPipe) **4-9-4** 5x PaulEddery(1) (lw: chsd ldr: led 3f out: clr over 1f out: r.o wl)	—	**1**	$6/4^{1}$	81	39
	Serious Trust (58) (MrsLCJewell) **4-8-3**(5) SophieMitchell(5) (bit bkwd: a.p: chsd wnr over 2f out: no imp)	3½	**2**	33/1	66	24
986^{2}	**Atlantic Mist (55)** (BRMillman) **4-8-5** BDoyle(13) (hdwy 2f out: hung rt over 1f out: one pce)	5	**3**	$9/2^{2}$	57	15
	Russian Rose (IRE) (70) (JARToller) **4-9-6** AClark(10) (hld up: nt clr run over 2f out: hdwy over 1f out: r.o ins fnl f)	s.h	**4**	25/1	72	30
898^{8}	**Nornax Lad (USA) (53)** (MartynMeade) **9-8-3b** FNorton(12) (chsd ldrs: btn whn n.m.r on ins over 1f out)	nk	**5**	33/1	54	12
	Sovereign Crest (IRE) (50) (CAHorgan) **4-8-0** JQuinn(7) (s.i.s: hdwy 3f out: wandered over 2f out: sn btn)	3	**6**	20/1	47	5
	Gumair (USA) (70) (RHannon) **4-9-6** RPerham(4) (lw: nvr trbld ldrs)	4	**7**	20/1	62	20
1022^{2}	**Tappeto (69)** (HCandy) **5-9-5** CRutter(14) (a mid div)	nk	**8**	$6/1^{3}$	61	19
426^{6}	**Nikita's Star (IRE) (63)** (DJGMurraySmith) **4-8-13** DHarrison(3) (b.hind: bhd fnl 3f)	1	**9**	20/1	53	11
	Prospero (74) (MrsAJPerrett) **4-9-10** JReid(2) (bit bkwd: chsd ldrs: wknd over 2f out)	1½	**10**	16/1	62	20
	Mr Browning (USA) (63) (RAkehurst) **6-8-13b** SSanders(6) (led 9f)	1¼	**11**	7/1	50	8
	High Desire (IRE) (54) (JRArnold) **4-8-1**(3) MHenry(8) (a bhd)	2½	**12**	16/1	37	—
858^{8}	**Opera Buff (IRE) (70)** (MissGayKelleway) **6-8-13**(7) AngelaGallimore(9) (dwlt: a bhd: t.o)	6	**13**	20/1	45	3
	Astral Weeks (IRE) (55) (MJBolton) **6-8-5** MRoberts(11) (bit bkwd: a bhd: t.o)	10	**14**	33/1	17	—
				(SP 128.4%)	**14 Rn**	

2m 33.3 (2.30) CSF £71.34 CT £186.06 TOTE £3.40: £3.10 £5.90 £1.60 (£33.10) Trio £34.70 OWNER Kammac Plc (WELLINGTON) BRED Miss K. Rausing and Calogo Bloodstock AG

1010* Mazurek would have had another 7lb to carry had the Handicapper been able to have his way. (6/4)
Serious Trust, who changed hands for 12,500gns at Newmarket Autumn Sales, came up against a handicap good thing and will find this putting an edge on him. (33/1)
986 Atlantic Mist, due to go up 4lb, hung over to the rails and his rider could do little more than keep him off Nornax Lad. (9/2)
Russian Rose (IRE), off course since finishing with a muscle problem at Ripon at the end of August, gave the impression she may be ready to tackle a mile and a half. (25/1)
Nornax Lad (USA), down 4lb, had the blinkers refitted this time. (33/1)

T/Plpt: £141.10 (70.85 Tckts). T/Qdpt: £13.20 (45.43 Tckts) KH

1157-YORK (L-H) (Good)

Thursday May 15th

WEATHER: mostly fine with heavy shower 1st race WIND: slt half bhd

1170 WILLIAM HILL H'CAP (0-105) (3-Y.O) (Class B)

2-05 (2-09) **6f 214y** £20,387.50 (£6,100.00: £2,925.00: £1,337.50) Stalls: High GOING: 0.01 sec per fur (G)

				SP	RR	SF
	Tayseer (USA) (89) (EALDunlop) **3-8-11** WRyan(5) (hld up & bhd: hdwy on ins ½-wy: nt clr run: qcknd to ld ins fnl f: r.o wl)	—	**1**	$9/1^{2}$	101	50
930^{3}	**Just Nick (80)** (WRMuir) **3-7-13**(3) MartinDwyer(3) (chsd ldrs: styd on to ld over 1f out: hdd ins fnl f: nt qckn)	2	**2**	$9/1^{2}$	87	36
1017^{5}	**Nomore Mr Niceguy (86)** (EJAlston) **3-8-8** JFortune(2) (trckd ldrs: ev ch over 1f out: styd on same pce)	1½	**3**	14/1	90	39
930^{2}	**Speedball (IRE) (96)** (IABalding) **3-9-4** LDettori(13) (lw: outpcd & drvn along ½-wy: hung lft: hdwy on outside 2f out: styd on wl ins fnl f)	3	**4**	$9/1^{2}$	93	42
973^{3}	**Cinema Paradiso (96)** (PFICole) **3-9-4** TQuinn(9) (dwlt s: hdwy ½-wy: styd on one pce fnl 2f)	hd	**5**	16/1	93	42
*904**	**Silent Miracle (IRE) (77)** (MBell) **3-7-8**(5) RMullen(4) (led tl over 1f out: wknd towards fin)	hd	**6**	14/1	74	23
930^{5}	**Triple Hay (89)** (RHannon) **3-8-11** PatEddery(18) (hld up & bhd: gd hdwy on outside 2f out: hung lft: wknd towards fin)	½	**7**	$7/1^{1}$	85	34
1029^{2}	**Double-J (IRE) (86)** (KMcAuliffe) **3-8-8** MJKinane(10) (hld up & plld hrd: kpt on fnl 2f: nvr nr to chal)	2½	**8**	12/1	76	25
	Fun Galore (USA) (99) (BWHills) **3-9-7** MHills(1) (bit bkwd: hld up: hdwy 2f out: eased towards fin)	nk	**9**	14/1	88	37
	For Your Eyes Only (92) (TDEasterby) **3-9-0** KFallon(14) (lt-f: unf: bhd: sme hdwy whn nt clr run over 1f out: n.d)	5	**10**	20/1	70	19
1000*	**The Gay Fox (79)** (BAMcMahon) **3-8-1** 6x GDuffield(12) (mid div: effrt & nt clr run ½-wy: n.d)	½	**11**	20/1	55	4
930^{7}	**Baritone (75)** (JWWatts) **3-7-11** NCarlisle(15) (racd wd: trckd ldrs: effrt over 2f out: grad wknd)	2½	**12**	20/1	46	—
853^{6}	**Halowing (USA) (84)** (JGSmyth-Osbourne) **3-8-3**(3) FLynch(7) (chsd ldr tl wknd 2f out)	nk	**13**	33/1	54	3
1029^{9}	**Night Flight (81)** (JJO'Neill) **3-8-3** JCarroll(11) (chsd ldrs: rdn over 2f out: sn wknd)	½	**14**	20/1	50	—
968^{3}	**Arruhan (IRE) (84)** (PTWalwyn) **3-8-6** RHills(19) (lw: unruly in stalls: s.s: a bhd)	1½	**15**	20/1	49	—
1017^{2}	**Jeffrey Anotherred (92)** (KMcAuliffe) **3-9-0** JFEgan(17) (racd wd: chsd ldrs tl lost pl over 2f out)	s.h	**16**	$10/1^{3}$	57	6
792^{2}	**Colway Ritz (77)** (JWWatts) **3-7-13** LCharnock(16) (mid div: n.m.r ½-wy: sn outpcd & eased)	5	**17**	20/1	31	—
835^{11}	**Pericles (76)** (MJohnston) **3-7-12** TWilliams(8) (bit bkwd: chsd ldrs: rdn ½-wy: wknd over 2f out)	3½	**18**	33/1	22	—
699^{7}	**Jay-Owe-Two (IRE) (77)** (RMWhitaker) **3-7-13** DWright(6) (unruly in stalls: chsd ldrs: drvn along ½-wy: lost pl over 2f out)	1½	**19**	25/1	19	—

654[3]	*Cosmic Prince (IRE) (88)* (MAJarvis) **3-8-10** KDarley(20) (bolted 3½f gng to s: Withdrawn not under Starter's orders: veterinary advice)		**W**	12/1	—	—
				(SP 131.2%)	**19 Rn**	

1m 26.8 (3.80) CSF £62.54 CT £596.50 TOTE £9.60: £2.80 £2.20 £2.80 £2.00 (£35.40) Trio £95.90 OWNER Mr Hilal Salem (NEWMARKET) BRED Gainsborough Farm Inc

OFFICIAL EXPLANATION **Jay-Owe-Two (IRE): was unruly in the stalls and lost a plate leaving the stalls.**

Tayseer (USA) is not very big but he has started his three-year old career potentially well handicapped. Overcoming difficulties in running, in the end he took this in good style, and looks sure to improve again. A step up to a mile should not be a problem. (9/1)

930 Just Nick ran another good race but the trouble is he keep going up in the ratings without getting his head in front. (9/1)

1017 Nomore Mr Niceguy, a grand type, ran another fine race. (14/1)

930 Speedball (IRE), tapped for foot at halfway, gave his rider problems but was staying on in fine style at the death. (9/1)

973 Cinema Paradiso, who showed plenty of knee action going down, was not suited by the drop back to seven furlongs. He needs at least a mile. (16/1)

904* Silent Miracle (IRE), who showed a poor action going down, seemed to run out of stamina in the closing stages. (14/1)

930 Triple Hay, who wore a crossed noseband, ran as if just in need of the outing. Six furlongs could prove his optimum distance and he is well worth keeping on the right side. (7/1)

Fun Galore (USA), who was not seen out again after losing his unbeaten record at Glorious Goodwood last July, showed a round action going down. Not knocked about and eased off when his chance had gone, he is capable of better. (14/1)

1171 DUKE OF YORK INTERNATIONAL FACTORS STKS (Gp 3) (3-Y.O+) (Class A)

2-35 (2-38) **6f** £28,400.00 (£10,640.00: £5,120.00: £2,240.00) Stalls: High GOING: 0.01 sec per fur (G)

				SP	RR	SF
452*	**Royal Applause (111)** (BWHills) **4-9-0** MHills(1) (lw: mde all: r.o wl u.p fnl 2f)	—	1	3/1[1]	122	76
811a*	**Farhana (108)** (WJarvis) **4-8-11** TQuinn(4) (b.off hind: trckd wnr: kpt on same pce ins fnl f)	1¼	2	9/2[3]	116	70
	Blue Duster (USA) (SbinSuroor) **4-8-11** LDettori(9) (trckd ldrs: effrt 2f out: styd on same pce fnl f)	3	3	100/30[2]	108	62
877*	**Averti (IRE) (109)** (WRMuir) **6-9-0** KFallon(7) (lw: stumbled s: bhd tl styd on appr fnl f)	nk	4	20/1	110	64
	Diffident (FR) (SbinSuroor) **5-9-6** KDarley(5) (lw: trckd ldrs: n.m.r after 2f: kpt on same pce fnl 2f)	s.h	5	10/1	116	70
941[5]	**To the Roof (IRE) (105)** (PWHarris) **5-9-0** GHind(6) (chsd ldrs: hung lft ½-wy: sn rdn: wknd appr fnl f)	s.h	6	10/1	110	64
	Danehill Dancer (IRE) (118) (NACallaghan) **4-9-4** PatEddery(2) (bit bkwd: swtg: chsd ldrs: rdn ½-wy: sn outpcd: kpt on wl fnl f)	s.h	7	6/1	114	68
671[8]	**Wildwood Flower (98)** (RHannon) **4-8-11** DaneO'Neill(3) (lw: sn outpcd: hdwy u.p ½-wy: wknd over 1f out)	2½	8	33/1	100	54
961[3]	**Carranita (IRE) (106)** (BPalling) **7-8-11** JCarroll(8) (s.i.s: a outpcd & bhd)	6	9	12/1	84	38
968*	**Indian Spark (107)** (WGMTurner) **3-8-5** MJKinane(10) (drvn along & wl outpcd fr ½-wy)	3½	10	20/1	79	23
				(SP 118.9%)	**10 Rn**	

1m 12.13 (1.63) CSF £15.10 TOTE £3.40: £1.40 £1.60 £1.60 (£6.40) Trio £6.30 OWNER Maktoum Al Maktoum (LAMBOURN) BRED Gainsborough Stud Management Ltd

WEIGHT FOR AGE 3yo-10lb

452* Royal Applause took this in decisive fashion and is obviously back to the smart sort of form he showed as a juvenile. (3/1)

811a* Farhana, the only one to seriously trouble the winner, is probably better suited by five furlongs and some give underfoot. (9/2)

Blue Duster (USA) probably ran very well considering the way some of the other Godolphin horses are running at present. (100/30)

877* Averti (IRE) did well to finish so close considering he completely lost his back legs exiting the stalls. (20/1)

Diffident (FR), winner of seven of his previous fourteen starts, shouldered a 6lb penalty. Considering the cloud over the stable, he ran with credit. (10/1: 7/1-11/1)

941 To the Roof (IRE), who improved hand over fist at four, gave his rider problems here, leaning on Diffident at the halfway mark. (10/1: 14/1-9/1)

Danehill Dancer (IRE), who looked in need of the outing, was soon being taken off his legs. Keeping on at the finish, seven furlongs should prove his optimum distance this time. (6/1)

1172 YORKSHIRE CUP STKS (Gp 2) (4-Y.O+) (Class A)

3-10 (3-11) **1m 5f 194y** £55,338.60 (£20,447.40: £9,786.20: £3,971.00: £1,548.00: £578.80) Stalls: Low GOING: 0.01 sec per fur (G)

				SP	RR	SF
932[4]	**Celeric (111)** (DMorley) **5-8-9** PatEddery(2) (hld up: hdwy over 3f out: squeezed thro & led ins fnl f: hrd rdn: jst hld on)	—	1	7/2[2]	121	61
932[3]	**Mons (117)** (LMCumani) **4-8-9** JWeaver(1) (lw: trckd ldrs: effrt over 4f out: hrd rdn: wandered & led jst ins fnl f: sn hdd: rallied cl home)	s.h	2	13/2	122	61
736*	**Whitewater Affair (110)** (MRStoute) **4-8-6** MJKinane(8) (b: trckd ldrs: styd on wl & ev ch ins fnl f: nt qckn towards fin)	¾	3	6/1[3]	118	57
932[6]	**Samraan (USA) (115)** (JLDunlop) **4-8-9** TQuinn(6) (plld hrd: sn trckng ldrs: chal over 2f out: n.m.r & kpt on same pce ins fnl f)	1½	4	14/1	119	58
932[8]	**Kutta (112)** (RWArmstrong) **5-8-9** RHills(4) (lw: hld up: effrt on ins & nt clr run over 2f out: sn outpcd: styd on wl fnl f)	½	5	14/1	118	58
761[3]	**Key to My Heart (IRE) (113)** (MissSEHall) **7-8-9** KFallon(5) (lw: b: trckd ldrs: led over 2f out tl jst ins fnl f: wknd nr fin)	hd	6	16/1	118	58
891[2]	**Wilawander (107)** (BWHills) **4-8-9** MHills(9) (hld up: effrt over 3f out: wknd 2f out)	7	7	25/1	111	50
932[10]	**Sacrament (117)** (MRStoute) **6-8-12** KDarley(7) (trckd ldrs: led over 3f out: hdd over 2f out: sn wknd)	nk	8	33/1	112	52
	Classic Cliche (IRE) (SbinSuroor) **5-9-0** LDettori(3) (led tl over 3f out: sn lost pl & eased)	18	9	Evens[1]	94	34
				(SP 125.8%)	**9 Rn**	

2m 59.39 (5.79) CSF £26.73 TOTE £3.80: £1.40 £1.90 £1.90 (£9.90) Trio £21.90 OWNER Mr Christopher Spence (NEWMARKET) BRED Chieveley Manor Enterprises

WEIGHT FOR AGE 4yo-1lb

STEWARDS' ENQUIRY Eddery susp. 26-27/5/97 (improper use of whip).

OFFICIAL EXPLANATION **Classic Cliche (IRE): no explanation offered.**

932 Celeric, held up as usual, had to squeeze through between horses. Answering his rider's every call, he did just enough. Whether he will stay the two and a half miles at Ascot remains to be seen. (7/2: 5/2-4/1)

932 Mons, who has a pronounced knee action, lacks a finishing kick, but to his credit he fought back all the way to the line and in the end was only just denied. (13/2)

736* Whitewater Affair never gave up trying and certainly stayed the trip. (6/1)

932 Samraan (USA), who finished ahead of Mons when third in the St Leger, was held when short of room inside the last. (14/1)

736 Kutta did not have the run of the race. It would be interesting to see exaggerated waiting tactics adopted, especially when there is some give underfoot. (14/1)
761 Key to My Heart (IRE), who stole this in 1994, ran his heart out but seemed to run out of stamina in the closing stages. (16/1)
Classic Cliche (IRE), the class act in the race - winner of the 1995 St Leger and last year's Ascot Gold Cup - was backed as if defeat was out of the question, but he went flat like a pricked balloon and trailed in almost pulled up. Something is obviously drastically wrong with the Godolphin horses at present. (Evens)

1173 MICHAEL SEELY MEMORIAL GLASGOW CONDITIONS STKS (3-Y.O C & G) (Class B)
3-40 (3-41) **1m 2f 85y** £9,681.00 (£3,579.00: £1,714.50: £697.50: £273.75: £104.25) Stalls: Low GOING: 0.01 sec per fur (G)

				SP	RR	SF
	Symonds Inn (105) (JGFitzGerald) **3-8-9** KFallon(4) (h.d.w: trckd ldrs: rdn over 2f out: led & edgd lft over 1f out: styd on wl)	—	1	4/1[3]	98	40
	Shaya (MajorWRHern) **3-8-9** RHills(5) (bit bkwd: trckd ldr: chal over 2f out: nt qckn fnl f)	3½	2	3/1[1]	93	35
740[3]	**Greek Palace (IRE)** (MRStoute) **3-8-9** MJKinane(2) (hld up: effrt & outpcd 3f out: styd on fnl f)	2½	3	7/2[2]	89	31
741[9]	**Sophomore** (BWHills) **3-8-12** MHills(6) (bit bkwd: led tl over 1f out: sn wknd)	4	4	5/1	86	28
742[2]	**Rainwatch** (JLDunlop) **3-8-9** PatEddery(3) (lw: hld up: hdwy 6f out: rdn over 3f out: sn btn)	2½	5	6/1	79	21
	Asas (SbinSuroor) **3-8-12** LDettori(1) (hld up: effrt over 3f out: wknd qckly 2f out)	2	6	11/2	79	21

(SP 113.6%) **6 Rn**

2m 16.02 (7.02) CSF £15.15 TOTE £4.00: £1.80 £1.90 (£4.60) OWNER Marquesa de Moratalla (MALTON) BRED B. Freiha
Symonds Inn, who showed plenty of ability in three outings at two, took this in decisive fashion in the end despite a tendency to edge left and also to thrash his tail. He obviously has a lot to find if he is to figure in the Derby picture. (4/1)
Shaya, runner-up on his only outing as a juvenile, wintered in Dubai but has apparently had his problems since. Outstayed by the winner in the end, he is sure to improve. (3/1: 2/1-100/30)
740 Greek Palace (IRE), who showed plenty of knee action going down, stuck on in pleasing fashion in the final furlong after being outpaced. He will be suited by a step up to a mile and a half and is sure to win races. (7/2)
Sophomore, well supported in the market, ran another disappointing race and presumably shows in better light at home. (5/1)
742 Rainwatch was left toiling when the race began in earnest. (6/1)
Asas, a particularly good mover, was yet another Godolphin-trained horse to run deplorably. (11/2: 7/2-6/1)

79 81 95+ 82

1174 E.B.F. TRAVELLING THE TURF RACECOURSE OF THE YEAR 1997 MAIDEN STKS (2-Y.O) (Class D) (84)
4-10 (4-10) **6f** £5,692.00 (£1,696.00: £808.00: £364.00) Stalls: High GOING: 0.01 sec per fur (G)

				SP	RR	SF
	Belladera (IRE) (NTinkler) **2-8-9** KDarley(3) (lt-f: unf: dwlt: sn drvn along: hdwy ½-wy: hung lft & led jst ins fnl f: drvn out)	—	1	33/1	76	38
954[4]	**Happy Days** (DMoffatt) **2-8-11**(3) DarrenMoffatt(2) (led over 2f: ev ch over 1f out: kpt on wl)	1½	2	20/1	77	39
	Wales (PFICole) **2-9-0** TQuinn(4) (lt-f: chsd ldrs: rdn & outpcd over 2f out: kpt on wl ins fnl f)	¾	3	2/1[1]	75	37
	Monsajem (USA) (SbinSuroor) **2-9-0** LDettori(8) (w'like: scope: chsd ldrs: outpcd ½-wy: styd on wl fnl f)	½	4	9/2[3]	74	36
1076[5]	**Lakeland Pride (IRE)** (PDEvans) **2-9-0** JFEgan(6) (bit bkwd: chsd ldrs: outpcd ½-wy: kpt on fnl f)	1¼	5	25/1	70	32
	After The Rain (BWHills) **2-9-0** MHills(1) (w'like: scope: bkwd: hld up: outpcd over 2f out: styd on fnl f)	hd	6	7/1	70	32
	Atlantic Viking (IRE) (MJohnston) **2-9-0** JWeaver(9) (leggy: scope: bit bkwd: w ldr: led over 3f out: rdn & hung lft over 1f out: hdd jst ins fnl f: wknd towards fin)	nk	7	11/4[2]	69+	31
	Harnage (IRE) (MRChannon) **2-9-0** PatEddery(5) (lt-f: trckd ldrs tl lost pl ½-wy: sn bhd)	14	8	7/1	32	—
	Julies Jewel (IRE) (MCChapman) **2-9-0** GDuffield(7) (leggy: bkwd: s.s: a wl bhd)	3	9	50/1	24	—

(SP 116.7%) **9 Rn**

1m 14.5 (4.00) CSF £481.75 TOTE £49.80: £5.30 £1.70 £1.50 (£196.70) Trio £102.40 OWNER Mrs D. Wright (MALTON) BRED Massimo Marchetti
Belladera (IRE), who lacks substance and looks as though she needs more time yet, showed a good action going down. She made things hard for herself after giving away ground at the start and running green. Hanging left, she ended up on the far side but took this very ordinary two-year-old maiden by York standards in decisive fashion in the end. (33/1)
954 Happy Days, the most experienced runner in the field, emphasised the low quality of this event. (20/1)
Wales, who lacks substance, proved very keen going to post. Sticking on at the finish, the way he ran and his breeding suggests he already needs seven furlongs or possibly a mile later on. (2/1: 11/8-9/4)
Monsajem (USA), who has a choppy, powerful action, gave a good account of himself especially considering he was rather isolated towards the stands side. Considering the way some of the other Godolphin horses are running at present, this was probably a most creditable effort. (9/2: 3/1-5/1)
1076 Lakeland Pride (IRE), who still looked in need of the outing, ran better than on his debut. (25/1)
After The Rain, a decent sort, showed a fair bit of knee action going down. Not bred for speed, he will improve over seven furlongs or even a mile. (7/1: 9/2-8/1)
Atlantic Viking (IRE), very coltish beforehand, showed a round action. Hanging left, he faded badly near the line. The stable's two-year-olds generally improve a good deal for their first outing and the way he was supported in the market suggests he has been showing plenty at home. (11/4: op 9/2)
Harnage (IRE) (7/1: 5/1-8/1)

1175 BERRY MAGICOAL CENTENARY H'CAP (0-95) (3-Y.O) (Class C)
4-40 (4-42) **7f 202y** £8,285.00 (£2,480.00: £1,190.00: £545.00) Stalls: Low GOING: 0.01 sec per fur (G)

				SP	RR	SF
847[4]	**Out of Sight (IRE) (75)** (BAMcMahon) **3-8-4** LNewton(17) (swtg: in tch: styd on to ld over 1f out: drvn out)	—	1	33/1	85	54
1017*	**Great Child (82)** (MRStoute) **3-8-11** 5x MJKinane(1) (lw: trckd ldrs: led over 2f out: hdd over 1f out: unable qckn)	1	2	11/2[2]	90	59
933[4]	**Over To You (USA) (82)** (EALDunlop) **3-8-11** KFallon(7) (dwlt: bhd tl styd on wl fnl 2f)	½	3	10/1	89	58
853[4]	**Kalinka (IRE) (85)** (PFICole) **3-9-0** TQuinn(18) (swtg: bhd: gd hdwy 3f out: styd on same pce appr fnl f)	hd	4	14/1	92	61
688[3]	**Captain Scott (IRE) (81)** (JAGlover) **3-8-10** GCarter(10) (hdwy over 2f out: kpt on same pce appr fnl f)	½	5	14/1	87	56
958[11]	**Share Delight (IRE) (80)** (BWHills) **3-8-9** MHills(12) (hld up & plld hrd: hdwy 3f out: styd on fnl f)	nk	6	25/1	85	54
1017[8]	**Foot Battalion (IRE) (87)** (RHollinshead) **3-8-13**(3) FLynch(19) (bhd: hdwy on outside over 2f out: nvr nr to chal)	4	7	33/1	84	53
1029[5]	**Nant Y Gamer (FR) (81)** (JBerry) **3-8-10** KDarley(3) (lw: sn in tch: pushed along: outpcd fnl 3f)	5	8	25/1	68	37
1017[4]	**I Can't Remember (76)** (PDEvans) **3-8-5** JFEgan(14) (chsd ldrs: drvn along over 3f out: outpcd fnl 2f)	1¼	9	16/1	60	29
1017[3]	**Bollin Terry (72)** (TDEasterby) **3-8-1** LCharnock(15) (lw: trckd ldrs: ev ch over 2f out: edgd lft: sn wknd: eased)	3	10	10/1	50	19

				SP	RR	SF
966^{5}	**Calypso Lady (IRE) (83)** (RHannon) **3-8-12** DaneO'Neill(9) (mid div: rdn 3f out: n.d)	nk	**11**	16/1	61	30
	Caution (80) (MrsJRRamsden) **3-8-9** JFortune(2) (still unf: s.s: wnt prom over 5f out: outpcd fnl 2f)	½	**12**	14/1	57	26
990^{9}	**Brandon Jack (83)** (IABalding) **3-8-9**$^{(3)}$ MartinDwyer(13) (bhd: hdwy on ins over 2f out: nt clr run over 1f out: n.d)	¾	**13**	20/1	58	27
1004*	**Tigrello (87)** (GLewis) **3-9-2** ^{5x} GDuffield(11) (lw: chsd ldrs: sn drvn along: ev ch tl wknd over 1f out)	¾	**14**	11/1	61	30
840*	**Kennemara Star (IRE) (77)** (JLDunlop) **3-8-6** PatEddery(4) (hld up & bhd: smooth hdwy over 3f out: nt clr run: nt rcvr: eased over 1f out)	nk	**15**	5/2 [1]	50	19
998^{2}	**Smart Spirit (IRE) (67)** (MrsMReveley) **3-7-10** JLowe(5) (lw: w ldrs tl wknd over 2f out)	3	**16**	8/1 [3]	34	3
990^{3}	**Bold Oriental (IRE) (85)** (NACallaghan) **3-9-0** LDettori(16) (lw: chsd ldrs: ev ch tl wknd over 1f out)	nk	**17**	12/1	52	21
930^{4}	**Kaiser Kache (IRE) (81)** (KMcAuliffe) **3-8-10** WJO'Connor(8) (lw: in tch: drvn along over 3f out: sn wknd)	1¾	**18**	16/1	44	13
853^{7}	**Irish Accord (USA) (92)** (MrsJRRamsden) **3-9-7** JCarroll(6) (mde most tl over 2f out: sn lost pl)	3	**19**	25/1	49	18
				(SP 149.1%)	**19 Rn**	

1m 40.45 (3.45) CSF £209.30 CT £1,908.38 TOTE £49.50: £5.90 £1.80 £2.80 £3.50 (£662.20) Trio £790.40 OWNER Mr D. J. Allen (TAMWORTH) BRED Floors Farming

847 Out of Sight (IRE), who has been set some stiff tasks previously, was very keen going to post but on the way back he showed a good attitude and there was certainly no fluke about this. (33/1)

1017* Great Child, under a 5lb penalty, was full of running when taking it up but, in the end, was beaten to the punch. He might have done better had he made his way home earlier. (11/2)

933 Over To You (USA), back against his own age group, gave away ground at the start. Sticking on really strongly, he would have troubled the winner with a little further to go. (10/1)

853 Kalinka (IRE), a very keen sort, did nothing wrong here. (14/1)

688 Captain Scott (IRE), who was apparently involved in some scrimmaging soon after the start, gave a good account of himself despite his marked lacked of experience. Unfortunately he suffered a leg injury and he will be on the sidelines for quite awhile. (14/1)

675 Share Delight (IRE), who again wore a tongue-strap, did as well as could be expected and put her poor run behind her last time, taking into account she was 10lb higher in the weights than when winning at Doncaster first time. (25/1)

840* Kennemara Star (IRE), from a 7lb higher mark, had a nightmare run. Trying to make ground on the inner and on the bridle at halfway, he saw no daylight at all and his jockey gave up with over a furlong left to run. He showed a smooth action going down and there should be a valuable handicap to be won with him. (5/2)

1176 LEVY BOARD SEVENTH RACE RATED STKS H'CAP (0-105) (4-Y.O+) (Class B)

5-10 (5-17) **1m 2f 85y** £9,024.49 (£3,345.50: £1,610.25: £663.75: £269.38: £111.63) Stalls: Low GOING: 0.01 sec per fur (G)

				SP	RR	SF
832^{2}	**Give Me A Ring (IRE) (86)** (CWThornton) **4-8-9** DeanMcKeown(6) (trckd ldr: led over 3f out: sn qcknd clr: kpt on strly: unchal)	—	**1**	9/1	100	55
787*	**Major Change (92)** (MissGayKelleway) **5-9-1** GDuffield(13) (lw: trckd ldrs: rdn over 3f out: kpt on: no imp)	4	**2**	10/1	100	55
1016^{5}	**Game Ploy (POL) (88)** (DHaydnJones) **5-8-11** PatEddery(12) (a in tch: effrt 4f out: hrd rdn & kpt on fnl 2f)	½	**3**	7/2 [1]	95	50
939^{6}	**Clan Ben (IRE) (93)** (HRACecil) **5-9-2b** KFallon(3) (lw: a in tch: effrt over 3f out: sn rdn: kpt on one pce)	nk	**4**	8/1 [3]	100	55
	Wahiba Sands (94) (JLDunlop) **4-9-3** KDarley(5) (bit bkwd: hld up & bhd: stdy hdwy & nt clr run over 2f out: r.o fnl f: nvr plcd to chal)	¾	**5**	16/1	100	55
987^{7}	**Star Manager (USA) (85)** (PFICole) **7-8-8** TQuinn(7) (lw: hld up: stdy hdwy 3f out: nt clr run 2f out: kpt on: nvr nr to chal)	1½	**6**	10/1	88	43
1016^{6}	**Brandon Magic (88)** (IABalding) **4-8-11** MHills(14) (lw: hld up & bhd: hdwy over 2f out: kpt on: nvr nr to chal)	nk	**7**	16/1	91	46
	Maiden Castle (91) (JHMGosden) **4-9-0** LDettori(11) (bit bkwd: b: hld up: stdy hdwy over 2f out: sn wknd & eased)	4	**8**	14/1	88	43
	Story Line (94) (DWPArbuthnot) **4-9-3** JFortune(1) (bit bkwd: b.hind: led tl over 3f out: wknd over 1f out)	1¾	**9**	25/1	88	43
775^{5}	**Van Gurp (87)** (BAMcMahon) **4-8-10** LNewton(8) (lw: hld up: sme hdwy 3f out: hung lft & nt run on)	¾	**10**	25/1	80	35
842*	**Rocky Oasis (USA) (98)** (MRStoute) **4-9-7** MJKinane(2) (lw: trckd ldrs: effrt over 3f out: lost pl over 2f ut)	2½	**11**	6/1 [2]	87	42
	Red Robbo (CAN) (90) (RAkehurst) **4-8-13** RHills(10) (bkwd: trckd ldrs: effrt over 3f out: lost pl 2f out)	9	**12**	10/1	65	20
*933**	***Champagne Prince (86)*** (PWHarris) **4-8-2**$^{(7)}$ CLowther(9) (Withdrawn not under Starter's orders: reard in stalls & uns rdr)		**W**	6/1 [2]	—	—
				(SP 125.3%)	**12 Rn**	

2m 14.02 (5.02) CSF £74.02 CT £255.61 TOTE £7.40: £2.20 £2.60 £1.50 (£36.90) Trio £34.50 OWNER Mr G. Reed (MIDDLEHAM) BRED W. Maxwell Ervine

OFFICIAL EXPLANATION **Wahiba Sands: rider reported that his instructions were to drop the gelding in and switch him off, due to the horses's physical and mental disposition at home. He asked a question three furlongs out but had nowhere to go and did not persevere.**

832 Give Me A Ring (IRE), from the same mark, was given an intelligent ride. Quickening clear off what had been just a moderate pace, he certainly stayed the trip alright and will now head for the Zetland Gold Cup on Whit Monday. (9/1)

787* Major Change, from a 6lb higher mark, kept on gallantly in vain pursuit. (10/1)

1016 Game Ploy (POL) took time to get going but stayed on in determined fashion. He is happier on faster ground. (7/2)

939 Clan Ben (IRE) is finding it tough going in handicaps, the assessor seems to have him weighed up to the pound. (8/1)

Wahiba Sands, who had just two outings at three, looked in need of the outing. Done no favours by the Handicapper, he certainly took the eye here. Short of room two furlongs out, instead of making his effort on the outside he was kept towards the inner. Running on as sweet as a nut, the impression was that, with any encouragement at all, he could have taken second spot at least. (16/1)

832 Star Manager (USA), a keen-going sort, kept on after meeting trouble. He seemed to stay the trip okay. (10/1)

Maiden Castle, who has presumably had his problems, looked backward and wore bandages. He shaped as if at least some of his old ability is still there. (14/1)

842* Rocky Oasis (USA) found this much too tough from an official handicap mark of 98. (6/1)

T/Jkpt: Not won; £16,672.39 to Thirsk 16/5/97. T/Plpt: £54.80 (815.54 Tckts). T/Qdpt: £19.70 (83.65 Tckts) WG

1177a - 1185a : (Irish Racing) - See Computer Raceform

0800a-TIPPERARY (Ireland) (L-H) (Good to yielding)
Thursday May 8th

1186a TOPAZ SPRINT STAKES (Listed) (3-Y.O+)
6-30 (6-31) **5f** IR £9,675.00 (IR £2,775.00: IR £1,275.00: IR £375.00)

	Horse	Dist	Pl	SP	RR	SF
	Carhue Lass (IRE) (PO'Leary,Ireland) **3-8-8**ow1 NGMcCullagh (led tl hdd over 1f out: rallied ins fnl f: led again cl home)	—	1	14/1	91	—
	Check The Band (USA) (APO'Brien,Ireland) **3-9-3** CRoche (prom: led over 1f out: rdn ins fnl f: hdd nr fin)	hd	2	8/11[1]	100	—
	Ailleacht (USA) (JSBolger,Ireland) **5-9-9** KJManning (chsd ledrs: sn rdn: 3rd & no imp fr over 2f out)	5½	3	13/8[2]	81	—
	Trickery (IRE) (ALeahy,Ireland) **3-8-7** PJSmullen (bhd: kpt on fr over 1f out: never nrr)	½	4	20/1	71	—
	Lady Shannon (USA) (DKWeld,Ireland) **3-8-7** MJKinane (chsd ledrs: no imp last 2f)	2½	5	6/1[3]	63	—
				(SP 121.7%)	**5 Rn**	

59.9 secs OWNER P. O'Leary (FRIARSTOWN)

IN-FOCUS: The ground had become yielding to soft by the time of this race.

Carhue Lass (IRE), a maiden after five starts, including one in handicap company, had no apparent chance at these weights, but she was fit and that edge enabled her to fight back and gain the verdict close home. She has gone up 10lb for this but is still rated some 15lb behind the runner-up. (14/1)

Check The Band (USA), like so many of the better performers from his stable, seemed to need the run first time out. Faster ground would have helped, but he will make amends without any difficulty. (8/11)

Ailleacht (USA) was another who found the ground against her and she showed no sparkle whatsoever, being totally outpaced over the last one and a half furlongs. (13/8)

1187a - 1191a : (Irish Racing) - See Computer Raceform

0804a-LEOPARDSTOWN (Dublin, Ireland) (L-H) (Yielding to soft)
Sunday May 11th

89

1192a STEPASIDE E.B.F. STAKES (2-Y.O)
2-30 (2-32) **5f** IR £6,165.00 (IR £1,395.00: IR £585.00: IR £315.00)

	Horse	Dist	Pl	SP	RR	SF
	Sideman (IRE) (APO'Brien,Ireland) **2-8-10** CRoche (mde all: clr fr 2f out easily)	—	1	2/5[1]	93	37
	Holly Hedge (IRE) (CCollins,Ireland) **2-8-10** PShanahan (rn 2nd: no imp fr 2f out)	6	2	7/1[3]	74	18
	Proof Positive (DKWeld,Ireland) **2-8-10** MJKinane (a same pl: n.d last 2f)	2½	3	11/4[2]	66	10
				(SP 110.6%)	**3 Rn**	

63.9 secs (6.40) OWNER Mr M. Tabor (PILTOWN)

Sideman (IRE) dominated everywhere, the paddock, the ring and in the race. Always travelling well, he made all the running and effortlessly drew clear. The opposition may not have amounted to much, but the Coventry Stakes is on the agenda. (2/5)

Holly Hedge (IRE) could make no impression over the last one-and-a-half furlongs. (7/1: op 4/1)

Proof Positive went through the motions without having anything but an educational run. (11/4)

1193a DERRINSTOWN STUD 1,000 GUINEAS TRIAL STAKES (Listed) (3-Y.O)
3-00 (3-01) **1m** IR £13,900.00 (IR £3,700.00: IR £1,700.00: IR £500.00)

	Horse	Dist	Pl	SP	RR	SF
809a[4]	**Strawberry Roan (IRE)** (APO'Brien,Ireland) **3-8-12** CRoche (rn 3rd: w.w: hdwy to ld ent st: rdn clr 1½f out: r.o.)	—	1	2/5[1]	88+	50
806a[6]	**Welsh Queen (IRE)** (TStack,Ireland) **3-8-9** PJSmullen (bhd: pushed along 3f out: hdwy 1½f out: styd on fnl f)	3½	2	16/1	78	40
	Magical Cliche (USA) (DKWeld,Ireland) **3-8-9b** MJKinane (rn 2nd: rdn over 2f out: no imp on wnr last 1½f)	¾	3	10/1[3]	77	39
	Ciste (IRE) (JSBolger,Ireland) **3-8-9** KJManning (s.s: w.w: 3rd st: rdn 2f out: sn btn)	3½	4	3/1[2]	70	32
	Prairie Flame (IRE) (JOxx,Ireland) **3-8-9** JPMurtagh (led tl hdd ent st: wknd qckly 2f out)	6	5	10/1[3]	58	20
				(SP 120.5%)	**5 Rn**	

1m 46.4 (9.40) OWNER Mrs John Magnier (PILTOWN)

809a Strawberry Roan (IRE) went on early in the straight and won virtually unchallenged. She will be one of five in her trainer's Irish 1,000 Guineas team, but already seems to need further. (2/5)

Welsh Queen (IRE), out the back door for most of the way, ran on well inside the last one-and-a-half furlongs, and apparently achieved the objective. (16/1)

Magical Cliche (USA) looked rather one-paced once the winner went on. (10/1)

Ciste (IRE) had her limitations exposed here, as she is really no more than a handicapper. (3/1: op 2/1)

Prairie Flame (IRE), needing the run, weakened quickly in the straight to finish a lot further behind the winner than she had done as a juvenile. (10/1: op 4/1)

1195a DERRINSTOWN STUD DERBY TRIAL STAKES (Gp 3) (3-Y.O F)
4-00 (4-02) **1m 2f** IR £27,000.00 (IR £7,600.00: IR £3,600.00: IR £1,200.00)

	Horse	Dist	Pl	SP	RR	SF
	Ashley Park (IRE) (CO'Brien,Ireland) **3-8-11** CRoche (hld up in rr: hdwy 2f out: nt clr run, swtchd rt & strong run fnl f: led last stride)	—	1	8/1	98	54
809a*	**Casey Tibbs (IRE)** (DKWeld,Ireland) **3-8-11** MJKinane (hld up in rr: gd hdwy to ld over 1½f out: edgd lft: rdn & kpt on ins fnl f: ct post)	s.h	2	9/4[2]	98	54
	Ebadiyla (IRE) (JOxx,Ireland) **3-8-8** JPMurtagh (hld up in tch: effrt 2f out: rdn & styd on wl)	s.h	3	2/1[1]	95	51
807a[3]	**Plaza De Toros (USA)** (APO'Brien,Ireland) **3-8-11** JAHeffernan (sn cl 3rd: u.p ent st: wknd over 1f out)	4½	4	13/2[3]	91	47

	Buddy Marvel (IRE) (JJMcLoughlin,Ireland) **3-8-11** NGMcCullagh (rn 2nd: led briefly over 1½f out: rdn & no ex ins fnl f)	¾	**5**	7/1	89	45
	Candereli (IRE) (JOxx,Ireland) **3-8-11** PJSmullen (led tl hdd 2f out: kpt on same pce)	2	**6**	33/1	86	42
713a[3]	**Mosconi (IRE)** (JSBolger,Ireland) **3-8-11** KJManning (hld up in tch: 4th st: sn rdn: wknd under 2f out: eased whn btn fnl f)	10	**7**	8/1	70	26
				(SP 115.1%)		**7 Rn**

2m 15.3 (11.30) OWNER Mrs M. V. O'Brien
Ashley Park (IRE), successful in a maiden here last month, was supposed to have improved dramatically since. With Roche opting to ride him instead of Plaza De Toros, many took the hint. Settled at the rear of the field, he was being ridden along approaching the straight, but then found his way blocked on more than one occasion before finally switching to the outside. He ran on really well inside the last to get his head in front virtually on the line. Future plans are fluid, but this was a good performance. (8/1: op 4/1)
809a* Casey Tibbs (IRE), a course and distance winner, looked all set for a repeat when going to the front over a furlong and a half out. He was inclined to idle a bit and edged left at one stage, but he still seemed to be in complete control with Kinane content to put his stick down near the finish, and he was caught napping. He may have seen too much daylight, and a pair of blinkers might suit. (9/4: op 6/4)
Ebadiyla (IRE) faltered slightly when the winner delivered his challenge on her outside, but she battled back again and her trainer is still considering the Vodafone Oaks. She will be suited by the extra two furlongs. (2/1)
807a Plaza De Toros (USA) is getting there slowly, and was not abused once he came under pressure early in the straight. He is making up into a fair horse, and could well turn the tables on these by midsummer. (13/2)
Buddy Marvel (IRE) found things too hot for him in the straight. (7/1)
713a Mosconi (IRE) has no pretensions of staying this trip. (8/1: op 4/1)

1196a - 1197a : (Irish Racing) - See Computer Raceform

1198a AMETHYST STAKES (Listed) (3-Y.O+)
5-30 (5-36) **1m** IR £12,900.00 (IR £3,700.00: IR £1,700.00: IR £500.00)

				SP	RR	SF
	Burden Of Proof (IRE) (CO'Brien,Ireland) **5-9-11** JPMurtagh (hld up in tch: wnt 2nd st: led over 1f out: r.o wl)	—	**1**	5/1[3]	114	50
839*	**Wizard King** (Trained) **6-10-2** MJKinane (led: came off rail ent st: sn rdn: hdd over 1f out: no ex ins fnl f)	2½	**2**	Evens[1]	114	50
	Theano (IRE) (APO'Brien,Ireland) **4-9-8** CRoche (hld up in rr: 3rd & rdn 1½f out: kpt on)	1½	**3**	4/1[2]	103	39
	Mr Lightfoot (IRE) (CCollins,Ireland) **3-8-11** PShanahan (rn 3rd: cl up appr st: rdn 1½f out: no ex)	2½	**4**	5/1[3]	100	23
	Fairy Lake (IRE) (JGMurphy,Ireland) **4-9-8** PJSmullen (in tch tl lost pl & last st)	5½	**5**	40/1	87	23
	Wandering Thoughts (IRE) (PJFlynn,Ireland) **8-10-0** NGMcCullagh (rn 2nd tl lost pl st)	3½	**6**	12/1	86	22
				(SP 113.5%)		**6 Rn**

1m 47.6 (10.60) OWNER M. V. O'Brien BRED Lyonstown Stud in Ireland
Burden Of Proof (IRE) showed a lot more enthusiasm on his first outing of the season, and was always travelling like a winner after coming wide into the straight. He could drop back in distance successfully. (5/1)
839* Wizard King found the concession of 5lb too much over the last furlong after holding every chance. (Evens)
Theano (IRE), the choice of Roche who could have ridden the winner, will improve from this, her first outing of the season. (4/1)
Wandering Thoughts (IRE) (12/1: op 7/1)

LYON PARILLY (Lyon, France) (Holding)
Thursday May 8th

1199a TIERCE MAGAZINE PRIX CORRIDA (Gp 3) (4-Y.O+)
3-45 (3-45) **1m 3f** £24,691.00 (£8,979.00: £4,489.00)

			SP	RR	SF
Camporese (IRE) (PWChapple-Hyam) **4-8-11** OPeslier	—	**1**		112	—
Maroussie (FR) (NClement,France) **4-9-2** J-MBreux	5	**2**		110	—
Reine Wells (IRE) (PBary,France) **4-8-9** SGuillot	1	**3**		101	—
					7 Rn

2m 22.4 P-M 2.30F: 1.80F 2.30F OWNER Mr M. Tabor (MARLBOROUGH) BRED M. Tabor
Camporese (IRE) ran out an easy winner of this Group Three event. She was given the perfect ride and after being restrained early, she was moved up closer to the leader and then took the advantage early in the straight. She drew clear a furlong and a half out and totally outclassed her opposition. Cut in the ground is essential for her and that will determine her next outing. A long term target is the Prix de Pomone at Deauville.
Maroussie (FR) was always close up and had every chance, but was rather one-paced in the straight. She was giving 5lb to the winner and looks capable of winning another Group race this season.
Reine Wells (IRE) was waited with before making some late progress in the straight. She only looks listed material.

0917a-CAPANNELLE (Rome, Italy) (R-H) (Good)
Sunday May 11th

1200a PREMIO PRESIDENTE DELLA REPUBBLICA (Gp 1) (4-Y.O+ C & F)
3-30 (3-38) **1m 2f** £69,042.00 (£33,962.00: £19,555.00: £9,778.00)

				SP	RR	SF
	Artan (IRE) (MRolke,Germany) **5-9-2** RCochrane	—	**1**		123	—
852[6]	**Needle Gun (IRE)** (CEBrittain) **7-9-2** BDoyle	2½	**2**		119	—
	Taxi de Nuit (USA) (AVerdesi,Italy) **5-9-2** MHills	nse	**3**		119	—
	Supreme Commander (FR) (VCaruso,Italy) **4-9-2** FJovine	nse	**4**		119	—
	Grey Way (USA) (GBotti,Italy) **4-8-13** EBotti	2½	**5**		112	—
	Dancer Mitral (LBrogi,Italy) **4-9-2** CFiocchi	nk	**6**		114	—
	Broken Detraeh (IRE) (ATortorella,Italy) **6-9-2** ACorniani	7	**7**		103	—
	Germignana (ITY) (LCamici,Italy) **4-8-13** MCangiano		**U**		—	—
						8 Rn

2m 2.7 TOTE 37L: 14L 13L 13L (60L) OWNER Stall Brandenburg BRED J. Brennen
852 Needle Gun (IRE) finished second in this race for the third time in four years. He made most of the running until collared by the winner approaching the two-furlong marker, and only just held on for the runner-ups prize.

1201a PREMIO MELTON-TUDINI (Gp 3) (3-Y.O+)
4-30 (4-39) **6f** £33,433.00 (£15,509.00: £8,694.00: £4,347.00)

				SP	RR	SF
	Armando Carpio (ARenzoni,Italy) **4-9-5** JacquelineFreda	—	1		104	—
	Plumbird (ACalchetti,Italy) **3-8-9** OFancera	s.h	2		104	—
	Nil (IRE) (SBenedetti,Italy) **4-9-5** PPerlanti	s.h	3		104	—
941[7]	**Sylva Paradise (IRE)** (CEBrittain) **4-9-5** BDoyle (btn approx 5¼l)		6		—	—
						11 Rn

1m 8.1 TOTE 116L: 27L 17L 23L (240L) OWNER Scuderia Jerome BRED Super King Srl
941 Sylva Paradise (IRE) dead-heated for sixth. He overcame a slow start to race in touch, but was flat to the boards and going nowhere passing the furlong pole.

0816a-DUSSELDORF (Germany) (R-H) (Heavy)
Sunday May 11th

1202a HENKEL RENNEN (Gp 2) (3-Y.O F)
4-20 (4-27) **1m** £45,454.00 (£18,182.00: £9,091.00: £4,545.00)

				SP	RR	SF
	Que Belle (USA) (HRemmert,Germany) **3-9-2** KWoodburn	—	1		109	—
	El Zulia (GER) (AWohler,Germany) **3-9-2** ABoschert	4½	2		100	—
815a[3]	**Much Commended** (GWragg) **3-9-2** WNewnes	½	3		99	—
	Anna Thea (IRE) (Germany) **3-9-2** THellier	3	4		93	—
	Mandellicht (IRE) (Germany) **3-9-2** ASuborics	¾	5		92	—
	Ramblin Rose (GER) (Germany) **3-9-2** AHelfenbein	2½	6		87	—
	Adorea (GER) (Germany) **3-9-2** ABrockhausen	3	7		81	—
	Miss Kypros (GER) (Germany) **3-9-2** PHeugl	4	8		73	—
	Genevra (IRE) (Germany) **3-9-2** WHickst	s.h	9		72	—
	Praia Grande (GER) (Germany) **3-9-2** ATylicki	¾	10		71	—
	Ariosta (GER) (Germany) **3-9-2** PPiatkowski	9	11		53	—
	Alte Kunst (IRE) (Germany) **3-9-2** ABest		12		—	—
	Nirvana (USA) (Germany) **3-9-2** TMundry		13		—	—
	Enigma (GER) (Germany) **3-9-2** AStarke		14		—	—
	Glenturret (GER) (Germany) **3-9-2** PVanDeKeere		15		—	—
						15 Rn

1m 46.82 TOTE 29DM: 17DM 40DM 25DM OWNER M & U Stoof BRED Hedgestone Management
815a Much Commended broke well and, from her inside draw, was left to make the running. She remained in front until the winner swept past approaching the furlong pole, and lost second place close home. This looked to be a decent renewal of the German Guineas, as did the Italian version in which she finished third three weeks before. Given her ideal conditions, which are probably faster ground, waiting tactics and a slightly longer trip, she should be winning a decent prize before too long.

0921a-LONGCHAMP (Paris, France) (R-H) (Very Soft)
Sunday May 11th

1203a DUBAI POULE D'ESSAI DES POULICHES (Gp 1) (3-Y.O F)
2-10 (2-09) **1m** £112,233.00 (£44,893.00: £22,447.00: £11,223.00) GOING: 0.47 sec per fur (GS)

				SP	RR	SF
818a*	**Always Loyal (USA)** (MmeCHead,France) **3-9-0** FHead (a cl up: rdn 2f out: led ins fnl f: hrd rdn & r.o wl)	—	1	14/10[2]	115	84
724[2]	**Seebe (USA)** (IABalding) **3-9-0** CAsmussen (cl up: rdn 1f out: qcknd to chal cl home)	hd	2	39/10[3]	115	84
	Red Camellia (SirMarkPrescott) **3-9-0** GDuffield (led tl hdd ins fnl f: r.o one pce)	¾	3	74/10	113	82
	Dances With Dreams (PWChapple-Hyam) **3-9-0** JReid (s.s: rr st: prog fr 2f out: r.o wl ins fnl f)	nk	4	28/1	113	82
	Nightbird (IRE) (SbinSuroor) **3-9-0** LDettori (hld up: hrd rdn st: no ex fnl f)	4	5	14/10[2]	105	74
818a[2]	**Mousse Glacee (FR)** (JLesbordes,France) **3-9-0** VVion (plld early: mid div st: sn btn)	1	6	Evens[1]	103	72
	Star Profile (IRE) (SbinSuroor) **3-9-0** OPeslier (hld up: sn btn st)	2	7	14/10[2]	99	68
					(SP 210.8%)	**7 Rn**

1m 40.2 (5.20) P-M 2.40F: 2.50F 2.90F OWNER Maktoum Al Maktoum (CHANTILLY) BRED Gainsborough Farm
IN-FOCUS: **For betting purposes, Always Loyal (USA), Nightbird (IRE) & Star Profile (IRE) were cpld**
818a* Always Loyal (USA) is a thoroughly game and top-class filly who always finds a little extra at the end of her races. She was always well up and battled her way into the lead half a furlong out before bravely holding off the runner-up. A half-sister to Anabaa, she is improving with every race and her trainer still thinks there is a little more scope. She was reported to be extremely well after this and judging by the way she races, she will stay further. She is now being aimed at the ten and a half furlong Prix de Diane at Chantilly, where she will be a difficult nut to crack. (14/10)
724 Seebe (USA) was given every chance and was coming back at the winner in the final stages. She acted pretty well on the soft ground which connections thought she might not appreciate. She may now take her chance in the Irish 1,000 Guineas. (39/10)
Red Camellia made a brave effort to make every yard of the running. She looked the likely winner halfway up the straight, but ran out of puff shortly before the post. She loved the soft ground, but it over-tested her stamina. She will now be dropped in distance and her next major race will be the July Cup. (74/10)
Dances With Dreams was held up in last place but made excellent late progress to take fourth place. She will be suited by a longer trip and it would be no surprise if she was back in France for the Prix de Diane. (28/1)
Nightbird (IRE) did not look up to this class. She was held up near the tail of the field and made a little progress in the straight. (14/10)
Star Profile (IRE) never looked like taking a hand in the finish and was another out of her depth in this company. (14/10)

1204a DUBAI POULE D'ESSAI DES POULAINS (Gp 1) (3-Y.O C)
3-15 (3-16) **1m** £112,233.00 (£44,893.00: £22,447.00: £11,223.00) GOING: 0.47 sec per fur (GS)

				SP	RR	SF
820a*	**Daylami (IRE)** (AdeRoyerDupre,France) **3-9-2** GMosse (hld up: last pl st: effrt 2f out: rapid hdwy to ld ins fnl f: r.o wl)	—	1	16/10[2]	124	60

820a² **Loup Sauvage (USA)** (AFabre,France) **3-9-2** OPeslier (mid div st: rdn to ld over 1f out: hdd ins fnl f: r.o one pce) 2 **2** 32/10³ 120 56
Visionary (FR) (AFabre,France) **3-9-2** TJarnet (mid div: outpcd st: styd on wl fnl f) 2½ **3** 71/10 115 51
737* **Yalaietanee** (MRStoute) **3-9-2** TQuinn (a cl up: led over 3f out tl over 1f out: no ex fnl f) ....¾ **4** 11/10¹ 114 50
717a* **Fantastic Fellow (USA)** (CEBrittain) **3-9-2** JReid (mid div: squeezed whn chal 2f out: hmpd & sn btn) 3 **5** 225/10 108 44
Bahamian Bounty (SbinSuroor) **3-9-2** LDettori (cl up: 2nd st: wknd & sn btn) 10 **6** 11/10¹ 88 24
(SP 174.1%) **6 Rn**

1m 42.6 (7.60) P-M 2.60F: 1.40F 1.50F OWNER Aga Khan (CHANTILLY) BRED Aga Khan's Studs
IN-FOCUS: For betting purposes, Yalaietanee & Bahamian Bounty were cpld
820a* Daylami (IRE) put up another excellent performance here. Held up for most of the way, he was brought with a sweeping run in the straight. Taking up the running inside the last, he proved his dominance by showing his superior acceleration. Connections had doubts about the soft ground after his below-par run in the Criterium de Saint-Cloud, but it was the distance that caught him out on that occasion. His targets include the Prix Jean Prat and the St. James's Palace Stakes. It will take a good horse to lower his colours this season. (16/10)
820a Loup Sauvage (USA) put up a decent effort but was one-paced inside the final furlong. Always close up on the outside, he took the lead halfway up the straight but then failed to match the acceleration of the winner. He is still slightly inexperienced and would seem to be crying out for a longer distance. He can now be expected to run in the Prix Jean Prat or the Grand Prix de Paris and later on in the International at York. (32/10)
Visionary (FR) ran well up to expectations. He was ridden for a place and ran on well to take third off Yalaietanee inside the final furlong. A Group Three race should come the way of this colt later on in the season. (71/10)
737* Yalaietanee was made favourite for this race, but he started to fade as the field entered the final furlong. He was one-paced in the latter stages and was probably unsuited by the ground, although most Sadler's Wells' appreciate cut. Always close up, he gave way to Loup Sauvage halfway up the straight and a lack of pace might have been another factor not in his favour. He should be given another chance and may be suited by a longer distance. (11/10)
717a* Fantastic Fellow (USA) made his challenge from two furlongs out but was hampered coming into the final furlong. This was an unlucky run and the soft ground may have also been against him. He should be given another chance. (225/10)
Bahamian Bounty made the running until early in the straight and then dropped back quickly. He evidently did not stay the trip and should be given another chance over a shorter distance. (11/10)

1205a PRIX LUPIN (Gp 1) (3-Y.O C & F)
3-45 (3-47) **1m 2f 110y** £44,893.00 (£17,957.00: £8,979.00: £4,489.00) GOING: 0.47 sec per fur (GS)

SP RR SF
Cloudings (IRE) (AFabre,France) **3-9-2** OPeslier (cl up: hrd rdn 1½f out: r.o wl to ld fnl 50y) ....— **1** 9/10¹ 111 59
Zenith Rose (FR) (PLenogue,France) **3-9-2** SGuillot (mde all tl hdd fnl 50y) ....nk **2** 18/1 111 59
Kalimisik (FR) (AFabre,France) **3-9-2** TJarnet (hld up: styd on wl fnl f) 3 **3** 69/10 106 54
819a² **Astarabad (USA)** (AdeRoyerDupre,France) **3-9-2** GMosse (mid div tl st: u.p 2f out: r.o one pce) ....¾ **4** 21/10² 105 53
Eleos (NClement,France) **3-9-2** CAsmussen (a in rr: m.n.s) 4 **5** 34/10³ 99 47
(SP 125.5%) **5 Rn**

2m 18.2 (10.20) P-M 1.90F: 1.50F 3.30F OWNER Sheikh Mohammed (CHANTILLY) BRED Calogo Bloodstock Ag and M3 Elevage
Cloudings (IRE) gave his supporters a nasty fright here. Halfway up the straight, the rank outsider Zenith Rose was still bowling along, and it was only well inside the final furlong that he got down to business, albeit under pressure. He always appears to pull out a little extra at the end of his races and he is improving with experience. He could go to Epsom for the Derby, but on this form, would have to improve a lot to have a leading chance. A decision will be made after the trials and his jockey deserves recognition for his strong and well-timed run on this occasion. (9/10)
Zenith Rose (FR) ran a cracker of a race considering he was moving up from handicaps. He was given a great ride trying to make all the running, and halfway up the straight a major shock looked on the cards. However, he faded inside the final fifty yards and just failed to last out to the line. He will not be returning to handicap company as he is to be aimed at the Grand Prix de Paris. (18/1)
Kalimisik (FR) was ridden for a place in this Group One event and that is what he got. He is not up to this standard, but is sure to be successful in lesser company. (69/10)
819a Astarabad (USA) was a neck behind Cloudings first time out, and this may show how much the winner has improved. Racing in third place, his measure had been taken halfway up the straight and he had soon run out of steam. (21/10)

1206a PRIX DE SAINT-GEORGES (Gp 3) (3-Y.O+)
4-15 (4-19) **5f** £24,691.00 (£8,979.00: £4,489.00) GOING: 0.47 sec per fur (GS)

SP RR SF
941² **Hever Golf Rose** (TJNaughton) **6-8-12** SSanders ....— **1** 108 43
811a³ **Titus Livius (FR)** (JEPease,France) **4-9-2** CAsmussen ....s.nk **2** 111 46
Wardara (FBellenger,France) **5-8-10b** MdeSmyter ....¾ **3** 103 38
7 Rn

59.8 secs (5.30) P-M 2.80F: 1.80F 1.80F OWNER Hever Racing Club (EPSOM) BRED Ronald Popely
941 Hever Golf Rose stayed on bravely to hold off the fast-finishing runner-up. This was her first victory since winning the Prix de L'Abbaye de Longchamp over course and distance in October 1995. She appears as game as ever and never runs a bad race, and she may now either go for the Temple Stakes or the Prix du Gros Chene before another crack at the L'Abbaye at the end of the season.
Titus Livius (FR) was a little outpaced early on but really slipped into overdrive inside the final furlong. He was closing rapidly on the winner at the post and would have won in a few more strides. He is sure to pick up a decent sprint this season and he will probably take on this winner again if she goes for the Gros Chene.
Wardara tried to make every yard of the running and she managed to hold on until a furlong out.

0735-NEWBURY (L-H) (Good to soft)
Friday May 16th
WEATHER: Overcast

1207 CROOKHAM MAIDEN STKS (3-Y.O) (Class D)
2-10 (2-13) **1m (straight)** £4,016.00 (£1,208.00: £584.00: £272.00) Stalls: High GOING minus 0.01 sec per fur (G)

SP RR SF
Faithful Son (USA) (MRStoute) **3-9-0** JReid(8) (w'like: scope: hdwy over 2f out: shkn up over 1f out: qcknd & led wl ins fnl f: pushed out) ....— **1** 12/1 97 75
991² **Shaheen (USA)** (HRACecil) **3-9-0** KFallon(16) (led: rdn over 2f out: hdd wl ins fnl f: unable qckn) 1¼ **2** 11/4² 95 73
Generous Libra (DRLoder) **3-9-0** LDettori(5) (lw: plld hrd: a.p: chsd ldr over 2f out tl wl ins fnl f: one pce) ...1½ **3** 2/1¹ 92 70
479² **Titta Ruffo (80)** (BJMeehan) **3-9-0** CAsmussen(6) (rdn over 2f out: hdwy over 1f out: r.o one pce) 5 **4** 10/1³ 82 60
963⁸ **Asef Alhind** (BHanbury) **3-9-0** MHills(3) (lw: hld up: rdn over 2f out: sn wknd) 9 **5** 12/1 64 42

				SP	RR	SF
	Snow Partridge (USA) (PFICole) **3-9-0** TQuinn(4) (rdn over 3f out: nvr nr to chal)	½	**6**	10/1[3]	63	41
	Kafil (USA) (MajorWRHern) **3-9-0** SWhitworth(17) (rdn over 2f out: nvr nrr)	hd	**7**	33/1	62	40
	Sharbadarid (IRE) (LMCumani) **3-9-0** JWeaver(7) (w'like: scope: s.s: rdn over 3f out: nvr nrr)	1	**8**	14/1	60	38
	Easy Song (USA) (RCharlton) **3-9-0** PaulEddery(14) (leggy: scope: lw: rdn thrght: prom over 5f)	¾	**9**	16/1	59	37
	After Hours (DJSffrenchDavis) **3-8-9** RPerham(15) (a bhd)	4	**10**	66/1	46	24
740[W]	**Blewbury Hill (IRE)** (RFJohnsonHoughton) **3-9-0** PatEddery(10) (leggy: scope: bkwd: hdwy 3f out: wknd over 1f out)	¾	**11**	10/1[3]	49	27
790[5]	**The Negotiator** (MJHeaton-Ellis) **3-9-0** RCochrane(13) (lw: s.s: plld hrd: a bhd)	3½	**12**	25/1	42	20
	Misellina (FR) (JSMoore) **3-8-9** NAdams(9) (bit bkwd: a bhd)	1¼	**13**	66/1	35	13
683[16]	**Prince of Bhutan (IRE)** (RHannon) **3-9-0** DaneO'Neill(12) (prom over 4f)	s.h	**14**	33/1	40	18
1105[6]	**Utah (IRE)** (BGubby) **3-9-0** AClark(11) (hld up: rdn over 2f out: sn wknd)	s.h	**15**	66/1	40	18
	Change (CEBrittain) **3-9-0** BDoyle(2) (w'like: prom over 4f)	10	**16**	40/1	20	—

(SP 131.9%) **16 Rn**

1m 40.22 (2.22) CSF £42.70 TOTE £14.80: £3.60 £1.50 £1.10 (£29.90) Trio £31.80 OWNER Maktoum Al Maktoum (NEWMARKET) BRED Gainsborough Farm Inc

Faithful Son (USA), a medium-sized individual who has already been gelded, looked to be carrying a little bit of condition, but that was not going to stop him from making an extremely pleasing debut, showing a very useful turn of foot to quicken into the lead in the closing stages. (12/1: 8/1-14/1)

991 Shaheen (USA) again ran a first-class race in defeat, and towed the field along from the start. Really trying to stretch his field in the final quarter-mile, he was given no peace by the third, but looked as if he was going to hold on, until the late swoop of the winner beat him in the closing stages. He looks nailed-on next time out. (11/4)

Generous Libra, a half-brother to Bin Rosie - a talented individual, but not the easiest of rides - has yet to fill out fully. Taking a keen hold, he gave chase to the leader over a quarter of a mile from home, but did tend to carry his head rather high. Unable to master that rival, he was passed by the winner in the closing stages. (2/1)

479 Titta Ruffo stayed on in the last furlong and a half, but never threatened the principals. (10/1: 7/1-11/1)

Asef Alhind raced on the outside in midfield, but could do nothing to prevent the leaders pulling right away in the final quarter-mile. (12/1: 7/1-14/1)

Snow Partridge (USA), who ran over this trip as a two-year-old, not surprisingly found it on the sharp side on this seasonal debut, and could never get in a blow. (10/1: op 5/1)

Sharbadarid (IRE) (14/1: op 7/1)

Easy Song (USA), a tall, attractive colt with plenty of scope, was being pushed along virtually throughout, but nevertheless showed up well until tiring over two furlongs from home. Improvement can be expected from this likeable individual when stepped up in distance. (16/1)

Blewbury Hill (IRE), a tall colt with plenty of substance, looked far from fit for this debut, and so it proved. Nevertheless he still showed promise as he moved into contention three furlongs from home, before tiring below the distance as lack of a recent run took its toll. He should come on in leaps and bounds for this, and improvement can certainly be expected. (10/1: 8/1-12/1)

1208 LONDON AND MANCHESTER ASSURANCE H'CAP (0-90) (3-Y.O+) (Class C)

2-40 (2-43) **1m 4f 5y** £5,800.00 (£1,750.00: £850.00: £400.00) Stalls: High GOING minus 0.01 sec per fur (G)

				SP	RR	SF
310a[7]	**Whitechapel (USA) (80)** (LordHuntingdon) **9-9-10** LDettori(6) (a.p: led 3f out tl ins fnl f: hrd rdn: led wl ins fnl f: r.o wl)	—	**1**	5/2[1]	95	48
933[2]	**Sharp Consul (IRE) (80)** (HCandy) **5-9-10** CRutter(1) (stdy hdwy over 3f out: chsd ldr 2f out: led ins fnl f: sn hdd: r.o)	nk	**2**	4/1[2]	95	48
	Voila Premiere (IRE) (68) (MHTompkins) **5-8-12** TQuinn(2) (lw: a.p: rdn over 2f out: unable qckn)	6	**3**	5/1	75	28
969[6]	**Royal Seaton (77)** (MrsPNDutfield) **8-9-7** KFallon(5) (lw: rdn over 4f out: hdwy over 3f out: wknd 2f out)	7	**4**	13/2	74	27
1016[9]	**Clifton Beat (USA) (71)** (PJHobbs) **6-9-1** JWeaver(7) (chsd ldr: led over 10f out to 3f out: wknd over 2f out)	2	**5**	10/1	66	19
789[7]	**White Plains (IRE) (79)** (MCPipe) **4-9-9** CAsmussen(4) (lw: bhd fnl 2f)	2	**6**	9/2[3]	71	24
505[4]	**Happy Go Lucky (85)** (RJO'Sullivan) **3-8-12** RCochrane(3) (led over 1f: wknd 3f out)	nk	**7**	14/1	77	13

(SP 112.5%) **7 Rn**

2m 38.76 (8.76) CSF £11.07 TOTE £2.70: £1.40 £1.90 (£5.60) OWNER The Queen (WEST ILSLEY) BRED The Queen

WEIGHT FOR AGE 3yo-17lb

310a Whitechapel (USA), who had a couple of unsuccessful runs at Cagnes-Sur-Mer in February, had conditions in his favour. He was given a masterly ride by Dettori, who refused to accept defeat when the gelding was headed inside the final furlong, and conjured up a little bit extra out of him to get back in front in the closing stages. (5/2)

933 Sharp Consul (IRE) was tackling this longer trip for the first time. He had the ground in his favour, and with his jockey having a double handful, appeared to be hacking over the winner. Let down and into a slender advantage inside the final furlong, he had not bargained on such a tenacious rival, and was worried out of it in the closing stages. (4/1)

Voila Premiere (IRE), who finished distressed on his only try over hurdles at Plumpton in January, grimly tried to get on terms with the front two, but was tapped for toe from below the distance. (5/1)

735 Royal Seaton unseated his rider and had a nice jog before the race. Whether that had any effect on his performance is open to debate, as he was beaten off two furlongs from home. He is yet to win beyond a mile and a quarter. (13/2: 4/1-7/1)

Clifton Beat (USA), a useful handicap hurdler, was soon at the head affairs, but he was collared three furlongs from home, and was soon a spent force. (10/1)

1209 VODAFONE GROUP FILLIES' TRIAL STKS (Listed) (3-Y.O F) (Class A)

3-10 (3-11) **1m 2f 6y** £12,315.00 (£3,720.00: £1,810.00: £855.00) Stalls: High GOING minus 0.01 sec per fur (G)

				SP	RR	SF
960[14]	**Yashmak (USA) (112)** (HRACecil) **3-8-9** KFallon(1) (hld up: led over 3f out: rdn: clr 2f out: r.o wl)	—	**1**	1/2[1]	116	37
	Tempting Prospect (LordHuntingdon) **3-8-9** LDettori(2) (chsd ldr 6f: chsd wnr fnl 3f: no imp)	9	**2**	4/1[2]	102	23
959[7]	**Boojum (102)** (BWHills) **3-8-12v[1]** MHills(3) (led over 6f)	7	**3**	14/1	94	15
	Gretel (105) (MRStoute) **3-8-9** JReid(4) (lw: plld hrd: a in rr)	½	**4**	5/1[3]	90	11

(SP 110.0%) **4 Rn**

2m 10.84 (6.84) CSF £2.68 TOTE £1.50 (£1.90) OWNER Mr K. Abdulla (NEWMARKET) BRED Juddmonte Farms

960 Yashmak (USA) has been working well since her bad run in the 1,000 Guineas and, well suited by the step-up in distance, gave a real drubbing to her rivals, being ridden along to lead over three furlongs from home, and forging clear for a decisive victory. Whilst it has to be said she did not beat a great deal, she could hardly have been more authoritative, and connections are now in the enviable position of whether to let her join her stable-companion in the Oaks, or go for the Prix de Diane, although with the ground often softer in France, the latter is probably the more attractive option. (1/2)

Tempting Prospect is only lightly-made, and therefore probably does not take much getting fit. Giving chase to the winner in the last three furlongs, she had no hope with that rival. (4/1: op 5/2)

959 Boojum again failed to see out this trip, and after setting the pace had nothing more to offer when collared over three furlongs from home. (14/1: 5/1-16/1)
Gretel looked in good shape for her reappearance, but unfortunately she has learnt nothing, for just like last year she refused to settle, and took a fierce hold. Not surprisingly, she had used up all her energy by the time it was most needed. There is no doubting she has ability, but she looks one to avoid until she learns to settle. (5/1: 3/1-11/2)

1210 JUDDMONTE LOCKINGE STKS (Gp 1) (4-Y.O+) (Class A)
3-40 (3-44) **1m (straight)** £73,320.99 (£27,335.55: £13,042.78: £5,585.68) Stalls: High GOING minus 0.01 sec per fur (G)

				SP	RR	SF
830²	**First Island (IRE) (123)** (GWragg) **5-9-0** MHills(1) (stdy hdwy over 3f out: led over 1f out: edgd lft ins fnl f: rdn out)	—	**1**	11/4²	131	77
852³	**Ali-Royal (IRE) (112)** (HRACecil) **4-9-0** KFallon(2) (hld up: led over 3f out: rdn over 2f out: hdd over 1f out: unable qckn)	1½	**2**	9/1³	128	74
628a⁷	**Even Top (IRE)** (MHTompkins) **4-9-0** TQuinn(4) (a.p: rdn over 3f out: one pce)	5	**3**	9/1³	118	64
1067a*	**Spinning World (USA)** (JEPease,France) **4-9-0** CAsmussen(7) (lw: hdwy over 2f out: hrd rdn over 1f out: one pce)	hd	**4**	6/4¹	118	64
830⁴	**Gothenberg (IRE) (115)** (MJohnston) **4-9-0** JWeaver(9) (swtg: prom over 4f)	2	**5**	33/1	114	60
	Decorated Hero (117) (JHMGosden) **5-9-0** LDettori(8) (bit bkwd: nvr nr to chal)	1	**6**	10/1	112	58
830⁵	**Acharne (110)** (CEBrittain) **4-9-0** BDoyle(5) (hdwy over 6f out: wknd 3f out)	¾	**7**	50/1	110	56
830³	**Bin Rosie (116)** (DRLoder) **5-9-0b** KDarley(3) (lw: rdn over 3f out: sme hdwy over 2f out: sn wknd)	¾	**8**	12/1	109	55
830⁶	**Beauchamp King (118)** (JLDunlop) **4-9-0** JReid(6) (led over 4f: wknd over 2f out)	8	**9**	40/1	93	39
980²	**Cayman Kai (IRE) (116)** (RHannon) **4-9-0** DaneO'Neill(11) (lw: a bhd)	s.h	**10**	25/1	93	39

(SP 114.6%) **10 Rn**

1m 40.04 (2.04) CSF £23.75 TOTE £4.00: £1.30 £2.10 £2.70 (£17.40) Trio £36.80 OWNER Mollers Racing (NEWMARKET) BRED Citadel Stud
830 First Island (IRE) is at his best when he can really hear his feet rattle, which makes his performance even more impressive. Covering Ali-Royal's move over three furlongs from home, he gained control approaching the final furlong, and although drifting left in the soft ground, was rousted along for a decisive victory. There is no doubting he is going to be a leading contender for top mile honours, and the Group Two Queen Anne Stakes at Royal Ascot is his next likely target, for which he must take all the beating. (11/4)
852 Ali-Royal (IRE) got a bit warm and keen beforehand, so instead of going directly up the straight course to the mile start, his jockey went the scenic route via the round course to try and settle him. It worked, for he ran the race of his life. Shooting into the lead over three furlongs from home, he soon had all bar the winner at it, but was unable to hold off that rival approaching the final furlong. Nevertheless, he still finished well clear of the remainder, and another Group victory is surely not far away. (9/1)
628a Even Top (IRE), returning to a mile for the first time since last year's 2,000 Guineas, is probably better suited by further these days, and after getting rather outpaced as the race began in earnest over three furlongs from home, stayed on again in the closing stages for third prize. (9/1)
1067a* Spinning World (USA), who stamped himself as a top-class miler last year, had the ground in his favour, but was well and truly put in his place in the final quarter-mile. He will have a break now until the Prix du Haras de Fresnay le Buffard Jacques le Marois at Deauville in August. (6/4)
830 Gothenberg (IRE), who sweated up beforehand, had shot his bolt over three furlongs from home, and is not really up to this class. (33/1)
Decorated Hero won four decent prizes last year, including two Listed races, but he was certainly up against it on this seasonal debut, and could never get in a blow. Sure to strip fitter for this, he needs to lower his sights, but is up to winning a Group Three event. (10/1)
830 Bin Rosie (12/1: 8/1-14/1) 88+ 90+ 92+ 82

1211 HIGHCLERE STUD CONDITIONS STKS (2-Y.O F) (Class C) (88)
4-15 (4-17) **5f 34y** £4,880.00 (£1,820.00: £885.00: £375.00: £162.50) Stalls: High GOING minus 0.01 sec per fur (G)

				SP	RR	SF
	Nadwah (USA) (PTWalwyn) **2-8-5** KDarley(1) (str: scope: s.s: hld up: w ldr over 2f out: led ins fnl f: pushed out)	—	**1**	12/1	76+	24
682*	**Pacifica** (RBoss) **2-8-11** LDettori(4) (a.p: led over 2f out tl ins fnl f: unable qckn)	1¼	**2**	4/1³	78	26
979*	**Hoh Chi Min** (MBell) **2-8-11** JReid(6) (dwlt: hld up: rdn over 1f out: one pce)	2	**3**	7/1	72	20
985*	**Another Fantasy (IRE)** (RHannon) **2-8-11** DaneO'Neill(3) (spd over 2f)	2	**4**	5/1	66	14
1031*	**Bodfaridistinction (IRE)** (ABailey) **2-8-11** KFallon(2) (led over 2f: wknd over 1f out)	7	**5**	2/1¹	44	—
	Summer Deal (USA) (PFICole) **2-8-5** TQuinn(5) (Withdrawn not under Starter's orders: veterinary advice)		**W**	100/30²	—	—

(SP 113.3%) **5 Rn**

64.11 secs (3.91) CSF £33.55 TOTE £11.60: £2.60 £1.80 (£26.90) OWNER Mr Hamdan Al Maktoum (LAMBOURN) BRED Shadwell Farm Inc
Nadwah (USA), an attractive, well-made filly, was certainly the paddock pick, but she has not been the easiest of horses to handle at home, and consequently was fitted with a neck-strap for this debut. Racing with the leader from halfway, she only needed to be shaken up to get on top inside the final furlong. (12/1)
682* Pacifica went to the front at halfway, but immediately had the winner breathing down her neck. Collared inside the final furlong, she was then put in her place. (4/1: 3/1-9/2)
979* Hoh Chi Min had more on her plate on this occasion, and failed to quicken from below the distance. (7/1)
985* Another Fantasy (IRE) was taking a step up in class, and had been seen off at halfway. (5/1: 3/1-11/2)
1031* Bodfaridistinction (IRE) may have won easily on heavy ground at Chester eight days ago, but this outing may well have come too soon, for he was a bitter disappointment, dropping tamely away having set the pace to halfway. (2/1)
Summer Deal (USA) (100/30: op 6/4)

1212 FURLONG CLUB CONDITIONS STKS (3-Y.O) (Class B)
4-45 (4-45) **6f 8y** £7,668.80 (£2,859.20: £1,389.60: £588.00: £254.00: £120.40) Stalls: High GOING minus 0.01 sec per fur (G)

				SP	RR	SF
980*	**Tomba (105)** (BJMeehan) **3-9-9** KDarley(4) (rdn over 3f out: hdwy over 1f out: led ins fnl f: r.o wl)	—	**1**	9/2³	118	65
679⁶	**Referendum (IRE) (112)** (GLewis) **3-9-0** PaulEddery(3) (lw: led: rdn over 2f out: hdd ins fnl f: r.o)	½	**2**	2/1¹	108	55
854*	**Hattab (IRE) (100)** (PTWalwyn) **3-9-0** PatEddery(2) (lw: a.p: rdn over 2f out: ev ch over 1f out: unable qckn)	1¾	**3**	100/30²	103	50
	Johnny Staccato (96) (JMPEustace) **3-8-11** MHills(1) (hld up: rdn over 2f out: ev ch over 1f out: one pce)	s.h	**4**	14/1	100	47
679¹¹	**Omaha City (IRE) (105)** (BGubby) **3-9-0** AClark(7) (hld up: rdn over 3f out: wknd wl over 1f out)	5	**5**	12/1	90	37
1018*	**Dancethenightaway (84)** (BJMeehan) **3-8-9** DaneO'Neill(5) (prom over 3f)	3½	**6**	11/2	75	22
679⁹	**Mukaddar (USA) (107)** (CJBenstead) **3-9-0** RCochrane(6) (lw: a bhd)	2½	**7**	11/1	74	21

(SP 112.7%) **7 Rn**

1m 14.74 (2.94) CSF £12.30 TOTE £4.80: £2.80 £1.90 (£6.20) OWNER Mr J. R. Good (UPPER LAMBOURN) BRED Mrs P. Good
980* Tomba had a 12lb penalty to contend with, but he had the cut in the ground he needs, and although being nudged along for much of the contest, came with a nice run from below the distance to grab the initiative inside the final furlong. (9/2: 3/1-5/1)

679 Referendum (IRE) ran much better here, and ran a gutsy race from the front, only being passed inside the final furlong. (2/1)
854* Hattab (IRE), a leading light from the off, was one of four with every chance below the distance before tapped for toe. Five furlongs may suit him better. (100/30)
Johnny Staccato, whose only win last year came in the mud, was the only runner without a recent outing under his belt, but still gave a good performance, holding every chance below the distance before failing to find another gear. (14/1: 10/1-16/1)
Omaha City (IRE), who ran well in Group and Listed events last year, was well beaten on his reappearance, and had been seen off here early in the final quarter mile. (12/1: 8/1-14/1)
1018* Dancethenightaway was close up until tiring over two furlongs from home. (11/2)

T/Plpt: £53.10 (423.49 Tckts). T/Qdpt: £28.30 (27.11 Tckts) AK

0957-NEWMARKET (R-H) (Good)
Friday May 16th
WEATHER: Sunny & warm WIND: slt across

81+ 83+ 81+

1213 E.B.F. DITCH MAIDEN STKS (2-Y.O F) (Class D)
2-00 (2-01) **6f (Rowley)** £3,525.00 (£1,050.00: £500.00: £225.00) Stalls: Centre GOING: 0.03 sec per fur (G)

				SP	RR	SF
	Silent Tribute (IRE) (MBell) **2-8-11** MFenton(1) (leggy: scope: a.p: rdn to ld ins fnl f)	—	1	9/2^{3}	83	36
	Diamond White (GCBravery) **2-8-11** MRimmer(3) (neat: lw: prom: led 2f out: hdd & unable qckn ins fnl f)	¾	2	11/2	81	34
	Saffron Lane (IRE) (RHannon) **2-8-11** RHughes(2) (cmpt: scope: dwlt: hld up: rdn over 2f out: r.o fnl f)	3½	3	11/4^{1}	72	25
	Petarga (JARToller) **2-8-11** SSanders(6) (neat: chsd ldrs over 4f)	2½	4	11/2	65	18
971^{4}	**Mysticism** (CEBrittain) **2-8-11** MRoberts(7) (racd alone centre: led 4f)	¾	5	3/1^{2}	63	16
750^{6}	**Talaheart** (CNAllen) **2-8-8**(3) MartinDwyer(4) (lw: dwlt: sn rcvrd: wknd 2f out)	15	6	25/1	23	—
	Funny Howithappens (CMurray) **2-8-11** NicolaHowarth(8) (w'like: racd alone far side: spd 3f)	10	7	33/1	—	—

(SP 107.4%) **7 Rn**

1m 16.21 (4.41) CSF £23.16 TOTE £3.60: £1.50 £2.10 (£18.50) OWNER Mrs E. A. Harris (NEWMARKET) BRED Rathbarry Stud
Silent Tribute (IRE), the paddock pick by common consent, responded gamely to wear down the leader, but had a hard race in the process. (9/2: op 3/1)
Diamond White looked fit but is bred to stay further, so it was a creditable debut performance. (11/2: 3/1-7/1)
Saffron Lane (IRE) looked a sharp sort but gave trouble before the start and lost ground as the stalls opened. Running on nicely towards the finish, she should learn plenty from this. (11/4: 7/4-3/1)
Petarga, rather keen to post and possibly just in need of the run fitness-wise, didn't do too badly as she only folded on meeting the rising ground. (11/2)
971 Mysticism showed a lot of pace, but racing alone in the centre of the track probably did her no favours. (3/1)
Talaheart, quite keen going down, missed the break but then did too much too soon to get back into contention, and stopped quickly in the final quarter-mile. Bred to stay middle-distances, she is going to have to settle better to achieve anything. (25/1)

1214 NGK SPARK PLUGS RATED STKS H'CAP (0-100) (4-Y.O+) (Class B)
2-30 (2-31) **7f (Rowley)** £7,349.01 (£2,716.18: £1,300.59: £528.45: £206.73: £78.04) Stalls: Centre GOING: 0.03 sec per fur (G)

				SP	RR	SF
987^{4}	**Welton Arsenal (88)** (KBishop) **5-7-11**(5) RFfrench(7) (trckd ldrs: qcknd to ld over 1f out: rdn out)	—	1	5/1^{3}	99	62
450^{10}	**Sabot (88)** (CWThornton) **4-8-2** SDrowne(5) (hld up: gd hdwy over 1f out: r.o wl)	¾	2	14/1	97	60
892^{9}	**Cadeaux Tryst (100)** (EALDunlop) **5-8-11**(3) DO'Donohoe(8) (b: trckd ldrs: outpcd & plld out & wl over 1f out: kpt on fnl f)	¾	3	100/30^{1}	108	71
738^{3}	**Saifan (88)** (DMorris) **8-8-2b**ow2 NDay(2) (lw: in tch: rdn after 2f: r.o strly fnl f: nrst fin)	hd	4	9/2^{2}	95	56
892^{7}	**Chickawicka (IRE) (90)** (BPalling) **6-8-4** TSprake(9) (lw: led over 4f: kpt on)	s.h	5	13/2	97	60
	Mullitover (86) (MJHeaton-Ellis) **7-8-0** JQuinn(4) (w ldr: led over 2f out: hdd over 1f out: wknd fnl f)	1¼	6	12/1	90	53
1035^{10}	**Highborn (IRE) (90)** (PSFelgate) **8-8-4** GHind(1) (prom: lost pl 2f out: styng on whn n.m.r wl ins fnl f)	½	7	13/2	93	56
	General Academy (IRE) (100) (PAKelleway) **4-9-0** RHughes(3) (b.hind: hld up: rdn over 1f out: nvr trbld ldrs)	1	8	33/1	101	64
	Almuhimm (USA) (88) (TDBarron) **5-8-2**ow1 MRoberts(6) (hld up & plld hrd: hdwy over 4f out: wknd fnl f)	5	9	7/1	78	40

(SP 114.4%) **9 Rn**

1m 26.8 (2.30) CSF £64.42 CT £241.13 TOTE £5.00: £1.80 £4.80 £1.80 (£28.90) Trio £127.70 OWNER Business Forms Express (BRIDGWATER) BRED Ian H. Wills
LONG HANDICAP Mullitover 7-13
987 Welton Arsenal has been called all sorts of names in the past, but seems to have been sweetened up by a change of yards and confirmed the view that he would have won at Kempton with a clear run, which was very difficult to believe at the time. The handicapper has relented a little as he started this season on a 10lb lower mark than he did last, but it is worth noting that his best runs in the previous two seasons have been second time out. (5/1)
450 Sabot is beginning to look a bit of a bridesmaid, but to catch the winner on such a going day was just rank bad luck. (14/1)
738 Cadeaux Tryst encountered similar conditions to when he won the '95 Bunbury Cup, as an early-morning downpour left a nice cut in the ground. Moving well to post, it looked a matter of how far, until he was suddenly outpaced in the Dip. He battled on strongly to the line, but the damage was done and it appears that a mile is now his optimum trip. (100/30)
738 Saifan ran a splendid race over a trip short of his best, picking up in tremendous style once hitting the rising ground. (9/2)
677* Chickawicka (IRE) ran a similar race to when winning here last month, but the 5lb he has gone up since that success proved too much for him. (13/2)
Mullitover, taken on by Chickawicka from the off, probably found that the rain had sent the ground against him and was the first to crack. (12/1: op 8/1)
677 Highborn (IRE), off a pound higher mark than he has ever won off, caught the eye when his good late run was halted inside the final furlong, and is close to coming to hand. (13/2)

1215 EQUITY FINANCIAL COLLECTIONS H'CAP (0-80) (3-Y.O+) (Class D)
3-00 (3-01) **1m 6f (Rowley)** £4,163.50 (£1,243.00: £594.00: £269.50) Stalls: High GOING: 0.03 sec per fur (G)

				SP	RR	SF
831^{3}	**Soojama (IRE) (52)** (RMFlower) **7-8-3b** GHind(7) (hld up: stdy hdwy to ld over 2f out: shkn up & sn qcknd clr)	—	1	13/2	66	48
888*	**Sea Freedom (68)** (GBBalding) **6-9-5v** SDrowne(1) (a.p: ev ch over 2f out: one pce appr fnl f)	7	2	11/4^{1}	74	56

				SP	RR	SF
552^{6}	**Express Gift (55)** (MrsMReveley) **8-8-6** DHarrison(2) (hld up: hdwy 4f out: ev ch over 2f out: kpt on same pce)	1½	**3**	13/2	59	41
962^{13}	**Ancient Quest (77)** (NACallaghan) **4-10-0** RHughes(6) (lw: s.i.s: hld up: stdy hdwy 4f out: shkn up & wknd over 1f out)	14	**4**	16/1	65	47
	Noble Lord (60) (RHBuckler) **4-8-11** AMcGlone(5) (led 4f: led 5f out tl over 3f out: sn btn)	3½	**5**	$6/1^{3}$	44	26
982^{2}	**Welsh Mill (IRE) (76)** (MrsMReveley) **8-9-8**(5) SCopp(4) (plld hrd: trckd ldrs: chal on bit 5f out: led over 3f out: hdd & wknd over 2f out)	7	**6**	$3/1^{2}$	52	34
	Full Throttle (70) (MHTompkins) **4-9-7** MRoberts(8) (lw: chsd ldrs 11f)	2½	**7**	7/1	43	25
962^{12}	**Magic Combination (IRE) (77)** (BJCurley) **4-10-0** JQuinn(3) (w ldr: led 10f out to 5f out: sn wknd)	dist	**8**	20/1	—	—
				(SP 115.8%)	**8 Rn**	

3m 3.43 (7.43) CSF £22.84 CT £111.12 TOTE £8.30: £2.00 £1.70 £2.00 (£13.80) OWNER Mr M. G. Rogers (JEVINGTON) BRED E. and Mrs Hanley

831 Soojama (IRE), taken down quietly after the others, was travelling ominously well fully six furlongs out, and quickened decisively when let down. (13/2)

888* Sea Freedom took so long to get off the mark due to his lack of gears, and that was exposed by the winner to floor his hat-trick bid. (11/4: 2/1-3/1)

552 Express Gift, better known as a hurdler, is on a fair mark on the level, but has not won on the flat for three and a half years, and never beyond an extended ten furlongs. (13/2)

Ancient Quest seemed to be travelling as well as any, and began to creep forward still going well. Once asked to go about his business, he faltered and faded. This may have been needed more than it appeared. (16/1)

Noble Lord, much improved over hurdles during the winter, was on a lower mark than when he last ran on the Flat, but didn't appear to see out the trip. (6/1)

982 Welsh Mill (IRE) wouldn't settle on Newmarket's wide open spaces either on the way down or on the way back, and paid the price. (3/1)

1216 KING CHARLES II STKS (Listed) (3-Y.O) (Class A)

3-35 (3-35) **7f (Rowley)** £10,842.60 (£4,013.40: £1,926.70: £788.50: £314.25: £124.55) Stalls: Centre GOING: 0.03 sec per fur (G)

				SP	RR	SF
679^{4}	**Andreyev (IRE) (109)** (RHannon) **3-8-12** RHughes(5) (lw: hld up: hdwy over 1f out: led ins fnl f: rdn out)	—	**1**	$3/1^{2}$	106	52
$917a^{10}$	**Royal Aty (IRE)** (PAKelleway) **3-8-12** GHind(7) (led: rdn & edgd lft over 1f out: hdd ins fnl f: r.o)	¾	**2**	33/1	104	50
$917a^{5}$	**Granny's Pet (102)** (PFICole) **3-8-12** JQuinn(2) (hld up & plld hrd: hdwy over 1f out: no imp fnl f)	2	**3**	8/1	100	46
988*	**Tumbleweed Pearl (98)** (BJMeehan) **3-8-7** MRoberts(3) (lw: trckd ldr: ev ch over 2f out: sn rdn & one pce)	1½	**4**	$5/1^{3}$	91	37
674*	**Shawaf (USA)** (JLDunlop) **3-8-12** RHills(4) (lw: plld hrd: trckd ldrs: ev ch over 2f out: sn rdn & btn)	4	**5**	$6/4^{1}$	87	33
	Serenity (102) (JRFanshawe) **3-8-7** DHarrison(6) (plld hrd: trckd ldrs 5f)	1¾	**6**	$5/1^{3}$	78	24
				(SP 112.4%)	**6 Rn**	

1m 28.44 (3.94) CSF £65.24 TOTE £4.70: £1.90 £6.60 (£108.90) OWNER Mr J. Palmer-Brown (MARLBOROUGH) BRED T. F. Moorhead

OFFICIAL EXPLANATION **Shawaf (USA): no explanation offered.**

679 Andreyev (IRE) is a tough and experienced campaigner, and settled down well despite the slow pace, before proving gutsy in a struggle. This wasn't the greatest Listed race ever staged. (3/1)

917a Royal Aty (IRE), targeted at this race for some time, dictated matter from the front and seemed to have stolen it when going a couple of lengths to the good in the Dip. However, the winner just managed to peg him back. (33/1)

917a Granny's Pet, last to post and unwilling to settle, still did plenty of strong, late running. (8/1: 5/1-10/1)

988* Tumbleweed Pearl, keen to post, settled upsides the runner-up, but couldn't match strides with that rival once the tempo quickened. (5/1: 4/1-6/1)

674* Shawaf (USA), a quality colt, looks still to have growing up to do and showed his inexperience by failing to accept the slow early pace, paying the penalty once the chips were down. He is anything but a lost cause. (6/4)

Serenity got warm and ran far too freely to do herself justice. (5/1)

1217 EQUITY FINANCIAL COLLECTIONS CLAIMING STKS (3-Y.O) (Class D)

4-05 (4-06) **1m (Rowley)** £3,785.00 (£1,130.00: £540.00: £245.00) Stalls: Centre GOING: 0.03 sec per fur (G)

				SP	RR	SF
873^{7}	**Janglynyve (51)** (SPCWoods) **3-7-9**(5) RFfrench(5) (lw: trckd ldrs: led 3f out: rdn clr fnl f)	—	**1**	8/1	65	24
903^{4}	**Soura (USA) (55)** (PAKelleway) **3-8-2** GHind(3) (swtg: hld up: hdwy over 3f out: ev ch 2f out: no imp fnl f)	5	**2**	8/1	57	16
1029^{10}	**Big Ben (87)** (RHannon) **3-9-3** RHughes(4) (hld up: hdwy on bit over 2f out: shkn up over 1f out: edgd lft & fnd nil)	3½	**3**	$9/4^{2}$	65	24
*1044**	**Penlop (63)** (BJMeehan) **3-8-0b**(7) GHannon(6) (lw: trckd ldrs: rdn 2f out: no rspnse)	s.h	**4**	$6/4^{1}$	55	14
862^{3}	**Fortune Hopper** (JPearce) **3-8-1v**[1] GBardwell(1) (led 5f)	9	**5**	$15/2^{3}$	31	—
	Bella Daniella (TTClement) **3-7-7**(5) RMullen(2) (w ldr 5f)	¾	**6**	25/1	26	—
				(SP 108.6%)	**6 Rn**	

1m 43.48 (6.18) CSF £55.85 TOTE £11.70: £2.90 £3.10 (£22.10) OWNER The Storm Again Syndicate (NEWMARKET) BRED S. J. Mear
Penlop clmd C Ransom £9,000

590 Janglynyve is genuine and stays the trip, little more being required on this occasion. (8/1)

903 Soura (USA) did her best to chase the winner from the Bushes, but was getting nowhere in the last half-furlong, and may not quite see out a full mile. (8/1)

Big Ben looked to be cruising when moving up to the leaders but, once let down, fell in a heap in a couple of strides. This was his first try beyond six furlongs and he did not appear to stay. (9/4: op 6/4)

1044* Penlop raced with his head high and did little to help his pilot once put to work. He may need things all his own way. (6/4)

862 Fortune Hopper, dropped half a mile in trip from his debut and given a totally different ride, failed to last home. Bred to stay middle-distances, there might be a race in him once he learns the ropes. (15/2: 4/1-8/1)

1218 ASHLEY MAIDEN STKS (3-Y.O) (Class D)

4-35 (4-36) **1m 4f (Rowley)** £3,557.50 (£1,060.00: £505.00: £227.50) Stalls: High GOING: 0.03 sec per fur (G)

				SP	RR	SF
670^{3}	**Assured Gamble** (CEBrittain) **3-9-0** DHolland(6) (lw: mde all: rdn clr appr fnl f)	—	**1**	$11/8^{1}$	88	39
	Silver Wonder (USA) (LMCumani) **3-9-0** TSprake(7) (wl grwn: chsd ldrs: rdn & outpcd 4f out: r.o appr fnl f)	3	**2**	$13/2^{3}$	84	35
937^{4}	**Sun Alert (USA)** (MJPolglase) **3-8-9** MRoberts(2) (chsd ldr tl rdn & btn over 1f out)	3½	**3**	$13/2^{3}$	74	25
975^{4}	**Not Forgotten (USA) (72)** (PAKelleway) **3-9-0v** RHughes(5) (hld up: rdn 3f out: kpt on fnl f)	2½	**4**	33/1	76	27
	Awesome Wells (IRE) (HRACecil) **3-9-0** AMcGlone(3) (wl grwn: bkwd: dwlt: hdwy 5f out: rdn over 2f out: sn btn)	3	**5**	$7/4^{2}$	72	23

				SP	RR	SF
944^{10}	**Go Green Flag** (MrsJCecil) **3-9-0** GBardwell(4) (in tch 9f: sn rdn & bhd)	dist	**6**	25/1	—	—
				(SP 111.9%)	**6 Rn**	

2m 39.84 (9.34) CSF £9.93 TOTE £3.00: £1.50 £2.20 (£5.20) OWNER Mr Peter Head (NEWMARKET) BRED Mrs John Van Geest
670 Assured Gamble has the sort of action that suggests he might not take to faster ground, but did this in fine style, confirming course and distance form with the fourth horse in a manner that suggests he is on the upgrade. (11/8)
Silver Wonder (USA) looked straight enough and moved down well, but appeared to become very tired with half a mile left. Getting a second wind, he finished in good style to show a deal of promise. (13/2: 7/2-7/1)
937 Sun Alert (USA) ran another sound race and shouldn't be hard to place if she can be kept sweet. (13/2: 5/1-8/1)
975 Not Forgotten (USA), with the visor back on, ran a decent race, staying on after appearing well held. Both his good efforts have been at Newmarket. (33/1)
Awesome Wells (IRE) is clearly named after his rotund near-namesake, and will surely improve as the season goes on. (7/4: 5/4-15/8)

1219 TUDDENHAM LIMITED STKS (0-70) (3-Y.O+) (Class E)
5-10 (5-11) **7f (Rowley)** £3,720.00 (£1,110.00: £530.00: £240.00) Stalls: Centre GOING: 0.03 sec per fur (G)

				SP	RR	SF
933^{11}	**Purchasing Power (IRE) (66)** (NACallaghan) **3-8-10** MRoberts(2) (lw: racd alone stands' side: mde all: rdn & r.o wl fnl f)	—	**1**	$4/1^{2}$	78	52
	Mountgate (70) (MPBielby) **5-9-4** DeanMcKeown(4) (trckd ldrs: rdn over 2f out: r.o wl ins fnl f)	2	**2**	$11/2^{3}$	70	55
1009^{6}	**Perfect Poppy (70)** (JRFanshawe) **3-8-4** DHarrison(10) (lw: hdwy 3f out: ev ch 1f out: no ex ins fnl f)	nk	**3**	12/1	67	41
1085^{4}	**Lynton Lad (70)** (CPEBrooks) **5-9-4** RHughes(9) (hld up: hdwy over 2f out: one pce fnl f)	2½	**4**	16/1	64	49
1093^{17}	**Saltando (IRE) (58)** (PatMitchell) **6-9-4v^{1}** TSprake(5) (lw: sn in ld centre: one pce appr fnl f)	¾	**5**	25/1	62	47
	Broughtons Error (69) (WJMusson) **3-8-7** GHind(12) (hld up: styd hdwy over 1f out: r.o)	nk	**6**	12/1	62	36
942^{25}	**Stylish Ways (IRE) (67)** (JPearce) **5-9-4** GBardwell(8) (in tch: effrt 2f out: nt trble ldrs)	1½	**7**	12/1	58	43
1111^{2}	**Sylvan Princess (69)** (DJSCosgrove) **4-9-1**(3) MartinDwyer(1) (lw: s.i.s: sn swtchd centre: wl bhd tl r.o fnl f)	1½	**8**	$3/1^{1}$	55	40
895^{20}	**Star of Ring (IRE) (66)** (MJHeaton-Ellis) **4-9-7** SDrowne(7) (w ldrs 5f)	7	**9**	6/1	42	27
864^{9}	**Blockade (USA) (60)** (MBell) **8-9-4** MFenton(6) (swtg: w ldrs over 4f)	1	**10**	12/1	37	22
786^{7}	**Watch The Fire (70)** (JEBanks) **4-9-1** JStack(3) (stdd s: sn chsng ldrs: wknd over 2f)	1¾	**11**	13/2	30	15
895^{7}	**Safey Ana (USA) (62)** (BHanbury) **6-9-4**(3) DO'Donohoe(11) (b: s.s: a bhd)	nk	**12**	10/1	35	20
				(SP 137.6%)	**12 Rn**	

1m 28.26 (3.76) CSF £28.47 TOTE £5.40: £2.00 £2.60 £4.80 (£28.50) Trio £196.70 OWNER Mr M. Tabor (NEWMARKET) BRED Barronstown Stud and Roncon Ltd
WEIGHT FOR AGE 3yo-11lb
OFFICIAL EXPLANATION **Sylvan Princess: was found to be in season.**
791 Purchasing Power (IRE), back over a suitable trip, was left alone with a rail to race up, and always looked on top. (4/1)
Mountgate, back on a winning mark, has to come late, but with the winner alone under the stands rail, couldn't be given an ideal ride. He is in good heart and a race should come his way during the summer off this sort of mark, probably here. (11/2)
1009 Perfect Poppy, not inconvenienced by this easier ground, looked dangerous in the Dip before being found wanting for another change of gear. (12/1)
1085 Lynton Lad, ridden with far more restraint his time, lacked the pace in the final furlong after making a promising run. (16/1)
Saltando (IRE) ran freely at the head of affairs in the main centre bunch in a first-time visor, but did stick on quite well once headed. (25/1)
Broughtons Error, held up in rear, made eyecatching late progress, seemingly without being popped a serious question, and is worth keeping a close eye on. (12/1: 8/1-14/1)
1111 Sylvan Princess, having missed the break, opted to tack over to the centre group, and this run is best forgotten. It later transpired she was in season. (3/1)
748* Star of Ring (IRE) (6/1: 7/2-7/1)

T/Plpt: £1,463.70 (8.01 Tckts). T/Qdpt: £120.00 (6.51 Tckts) Dk

0944-THIRSK (L-H) (Good)
Friday May 16th
WEATHER: Cloudy

1220 MOWBRAY (S) STKS (3-Y.O+) (Class G)
2-15 (2-17) **7f** £2,617.50 (£730.00: £352.50) Stalls: Low GOING minus 0.14 sec per fur (G)

				SP	RR	SF
896^{3}	**Komlucky (45)** (ABMulholland) **5-8-11v**(5) GFaulkner(4) (a.p: rdn to ld ins fnl f: styd on wl)	—	**1**	10/1	61	55
925^{2}	**Dictation (USA) (55)** (JJO'Neill) **5-9-7** JFortune(8) (lw: in tch: effrt over 2f out: chal ins fnl f: no ex towards fin)	hd	**2**	$6/1^{2}$	66	60
	Super Benz (80) (JLEyre) **11-9-4**(3) OPears(5) (b: led: clr appr st: hdd & wknd ins fnl f)	5	**3**	$13/8^{1}$	54	48
774^{4}	**The Frisky Farmer (56)** (WGMTurner) **4-9-0**(7) DMcGaffin(14) (lw: sn chsng ldr: rdn 3f out: grad wknd)	2	**4**	10/1	50	44
	Sir Arthur Hobbs (55) (JLEyre) **10-9-7** RLappin(10) (in tch: effrt ½-wy: styd on: no imp)	4	**5**	9/1	41	35
1077^{3}	**First Gold (47)** (JWharton) **8-9-12** GDuffield(7) (outpcd & bhd: styd on fnl 3f: nrst fin)	¾	**6**	$7/1^{3}$	44	38
925^{8}	**Serape (54)** (MrsLStubbs) **4-9-2** ACulhane(13) (b: hld up & bhd: nvr nr to chal)	nk	**7**	9/1	33	27
	Prime Partner (39) (TDEasterby) **4-9-7** MBirch(9) (nvr bttr than mid div)	¾	**8**	20/1	37	31
956^{11}	**Mu-Arrik (30)** (GROldroyd) **9-9-0v**(7) RFarmer(12) (lw: a in rr)	1	**9**	33/1	34	28
	Frugal (BWMurray) **4-9-7** VHalliday(3) (a rr div)	hd	**10**	33/1	34	28
	Sacred Spirit (APJarvis) **5-9-7** WJO'Connor(6) (chsd ldrs tl wknd fnl 3f)	1	**11**	$6/1^{2}$	32	26
843^{12}	**Astrolabe (55)** (JMBradley) **5-9-7b** GCarter(2) (s.s: a outpcd & bhd)	2½	**12**	50/1	26	20
896^{19}	**Chilled Wine (34)** (GPKelly) **3-8-5** DaleGibson(1) (chsd ldrs to st: sn wknd)	4	**13**	50/1	12	—
175^{6}	**Cross of Valour (76)** (PHowling) **4-9-7** FNorton(11) (sn bhd)	5	**14**	12/1	5	—
				(SP 139.6%)	**14 Rn**	

1m 27.7 (2.80) CSF £70.47 TOTE £11.20: £2.70 £1.40 £1.70 (£26.70) Trio £40.20 OWNER Hambleton Lodge Equine Premix Ltd (HAMBLETON) BRED T. Barratt
WEIGHT FOR AGE 3yo-11lb
No bid
896 Komlucky, normally better on faster ground, showed she is an honest sort here. (10/1)
925 Dictation (USA) has yet to win a race, but he is running consistently well just now, and deserves a change of luck. (6/1)

Super Benz, having his first run for almost a year, has been off with leg problems and showed he still possesses all his speed, but needed this and blew up. (13/8)
774 The Frisky Farmer had his chances, but just seemed to find this trip stretching his stamina. (10/1)
Sir Arthur Hobbs ran well here over a trip too sharp, and despite his years he should again find his share of races. (9/1)
1077 First Gold runs when he decides to, and his effort was always too late on this occasion. (7/1)
748 Serape, given a lot to do, failed to make any impression, but she has the ability to do better when things go her way. (9/1)

1221 GORDON FOSTER MAIDEN STKS (3-Y.O+) (Class D)
2-45 (2-47) **1m** £4,016.00 (£1,208.00: £584.00: £272.00) Stalls: Low GOING minus 0.14 sec per fur (G)

				SP	RR	SF
829[3]	**Komi** (MRStoute) **3-8-9**(3) FLynch(5) (lw: trckd ldrs: rdn over 2f out: edgd rt & r.o to ld wl ins fnl f)	—	**1**	11/8[1]	91	40
674[3]	**Darnaway** (HRACecil) **3-8-12** WRyan(12) (led: qcknd clr 3f out: rdn & no ex wl ins fnl f)	1¼	**2**	11/8[1]	89	38
	Blot (MrsJCecil) **3-8-12** JCarroll(8) (neat: hld up: effrt 3f out: r.o: nrst fin)	4	**3**	14/1[3]	81	30
1006[4]	**Zaahir (IRE) (76)** (BWHills) **3-8-12** GCarter(1) (lw: chsd ldrs: rdn 3f out: r.o one pce)	3½	**4**	11/1[2]	74	23
1006[10]	**Stilett (IRE)** (LMCumani) **3-8-12** OUrbina(3) (chsd ldrs: outpcd ent st: no imp after)	½	**5**	16/1	73	22
	Jack Doyle (IRE) (JJO'Neill) **6-9-10** JFEgan(10) (lw: hld up & bhd: hdwy 2f out: styd on towards fin)	1¼	**6**	33/1	70	31
1023[6]	**Tarradale** (CBBBooth) **3-8-12** KHodgson(11) (hld up: effrt 3f out: n.d)	8	**7**	66/1	54	3
842[15]	**Mr Montague (IRE)** (TWDonnelly) **5-9-10** JFanning(4) (bhd: brought wd & rdn over 3f out: n.d)	¾	**8**	100/1	53	14
899[4]	**Madison Mist** (MrsJRRamsden) **3-8-7** JFortune(2) (hld up: shkn up over 2f out: n.d)	1½	**9**	20/1	45	—
	Miami Moon (CWThornton) **3-8-7** LCharnock(7) (bit bkwd: prom to st: sn outpcd)	1¾	**10**	100/1	41	—
524[9]	**Cochiti** (CWThornton) **3-8-7** DaleGibson(9) (bhd: rdn ent st: n.d)	1¼	**11**	50/1	39	—
1023[15]	**Chief Connections** (MPBielby) **4-9-10** ACulhane(6) (chsd ldrs tl wknd fnl 3f)	1	**12**	100/1	42	3
				(SP 119.2%)	**12 Rn**	

1m 40.8 (4.30) CSF £2.70 TOTE £2.90: £1.10 £1.10 £3.30 (£1.30) Trio £9.00 OWNER Sheikh Mohammed (NEWMARKET) BRED Sheikh Mohammed Bin Rashid Al Maktoum
WEIGHT FOR AGE 3yo-12lb
829 Komi showed fine courage to win this despite hanging slightly, and will obviously improve when trying longer distances. (11/8)
674 Darnaway did his best to pinch this, quickening clear early in the straight, but in the end he had to admit he had met one just too good. (11/8)
Blot put in a useful first effort here, and is one likely to improve a fair bit from the experience. (14/1: 8/1-16/1)
1006 Zaahir (IRE) seems to lack a change of gear, and should stay a bit further. (11/1)
Stilett (IRE) improved on his debut, and seems to be learning with experience. (16/1)
Jack Doyle (IRE), who has had his problems chasing, gave definite signs of hope here, staying on well over an inadequate trip. (33/1)

1222 STATION ROAD CLAIMING STKS (4-Y.O+) (Class F)
3-20 (3-21) **1m 4f** £2,757.50 (£770.00: £372.50) Stalls: High GOING minus 0.14 sec per fur (G)

				SP	RR	SF
	Heathyards Rock (RHollinshead) **5-8-9**(3) FLynch(1) (lw: hld up: hdwy on outside over 2f out: hung bdly lft: led appr fnl f: hung lft again: r.o)	—	**1**	5/1[3]	49	20
	Junior Ben (IRE) (36) (MESowersby) **5-8-3**(5) PFessey(5) (led tl hdd appr fnl f: kpt on)	1¾	**2**	12/1	43	14
689[8]	**Bold Top (36)** (BSRothwell) **5-8-8** JFortune(7) (lw: a chsng ldrs: rdn 2f out: one pce)	½	**3**	20/1	42	13
900[8]	**Whothehellisharry (42)** (PTDalton) **4-8-11**(3) PMcCabe(8) (lw: chsd ldrs: chal ent st: nt qckn appr fnl f)	nk	**4**	16/1	48	19
1010[7]	**Bedouin Prince (USA) (51)** (MrsLStubbs) **10-8-8** JFEgan(12) (lw: b: chsd ldrs tl lost pl appr st: kpt on fnl 2f)	½	**5**	5/1[3]	41	12
843[4]	**Durgams First (IRE) (50)** (MrsMReveley) **5-8-12** ACulhane(9) (hld up: effrt 3f out: styd on: nt pce to chal)	¾	**6**	9/2[2]	44	15
*869**	**Champagne Warrior (IRE) (52)** (MJCamacho) **4-8-3** LCharnock(2) (trckd ldrs: effrt 3f out: n.m.r over 1f out: eased whn btn)	1¼	**7**	7/4[1]	33	4
1010[6]	**May King Mayhem (31)** (MrsALMKing) **4-8-6** AGarth(3) (in tch: outpcd whn hmpd over 2f out: n.d after)	3	**8**	25/1	32	3
	Club Elite (23) (MissAStokell) **5-8-0**(5)ow1 PPMurphy(4) (swtg: prom tl lost pl appr st)	7	**9**	25/1	22	—
493[12]	**Finestatetobein (31)** (FWatson) **4-8-5** NConnorton(11) (hdwy & prom ½-wy: wknd fnl 3f)	1½	**10**	33/1	20	—
864[10]	**Stone Cross (IRE) (50)** (MartinTodhunter) **5-8-8** JCarroll(10) (b.off hind: plld hrd: hdwy on outside 5f out: wknd fnl 3f)	¾	**11**	16/1	22	—
114[11]	**Double Vintage (IRE) (25)** (MCChapman) **4-8-10b** GDuffield(6) (drvn along thrght: nt keen & t.o)	dist	**12**	33/1	—	—
				(SP 125.7%)	**12 Rn**	

2m 40.6 (9.90) CSF £56.93 TOTE £4.60: £2.10 £5.40 £3.20 (£64.70) Trio £345.50; £77.86 to Newbury 17/5/97 OWNER Mr L. A. Morgan (UPPER LONGDON) BRED N. E. and Mrs Poole
Heathyards Rock clmd Robert McKellar £6,000
Heathyards Rock, who has been off the track for well over a year, and only ever won on the All-Weather, showed a useful turn of foot to win this, despite steering a most erratic course. (5/1: op 5/2)
Junior Ben (IRE), given a good ride out in front, put up a decent performance for his new stable, but he had no answer to the winner's turn of foot. (12/1)
Bold Top has ability, but has yet to win a race. (20/1)
273 Whothehellisharry had his chances, but had plenty on at these weights, and was outbattled late on. (16/1)
753 Bedouin Prince (USA) was not helped by the steady pace here, and got messed about approaching the turn, which put paid to his chances. (5/1: op 8/1)
843 Durgams First (IRE) needs this trip, but also needs a much stronger gallop. (9/2)
869* Champagne Warrior (IRE), unsuited by the pace, was short of room at vital stages, and this is best forgotten. (7/4)

1223 KILBURN H'CAP (0-80) (3-Y.O+) (Class D)
3-50 (3-51) **5f** £4,406.00 (£1,328.00: £644.00: £302.00) Stalls: High GOING minus 0.14 sec per fur (G)

				SP	RR	SF
1098[4]	**Squire Corrie (69)** (DWChapman) **5-9-3** ACulhane(5) (chsd ldrs: led ½-wy: all out)	—	**1**	12/1	76	44
834[3]	**Broadstairs Beauty (IRE) (73)** (DShaw) **7-9-4b**(3) CTeague(12) (lw: b: a chsng ldrs: ev ch over 1f out: kpt on)	¾	**2**	9/2[1]	78	46
1037*	**Impish (IRE) (56)** (TJEtherington) **3-7-5**(5) 7x JBramhill(1) (lw: racd alone far side: cl up: nt qckn fnl f)	2½	**3**	12/1	53	13
949[3]	**Captain Carat (60)** (DNicholls) **6-8-8b** DaleGibson(3) (sn drvn along: hdwy 2f out: styd on: nrst fin)	nk	**4**	9/1	56	24
702[19]	**Dominelle (55)** (TDEasterby) **5-8-3** GDuffield(4) (racd centre: w ldrs tl btn appr fnl f)	1½	**5**	20/1	46	14
905[3]	**Malibu Man (77)** (EAWheeler) **5-9-11** JCarroll(8) (lw: cl up tl wknd over 1f out)	1¾	**6**	7/1	62	30
949[4]	**Johayro (64)** (JSGoldie) **4-8-5**(7) JMcAuley(10) (disp ld to ½-wy: wknd)	5	**7**	11/2[2]	33	1
	U-No-Harry (IRE) (70) (RHollinshead) **4-9-1**(3) FLynch(2) (sn outpcd & bhd)	hd	**8**	20/1	39	7

357^{8}	**Master of Passion (70)** (JMPEustace) **8-9-4** JTate(7) (dwlt: outpcd & bhd: bdly hmpd 2f out: eased)	dist	**9**	20/1	—	—
772^{2}	**Able Sheriff (63)** (MWEasterby) **5-8-6b**(5) GParkin(6) (chsd ldrs tl b.d 2f out: dead)		**B**	15/2	—	—
901^{7}	**Oatey (64)** (MrsJRRamsden) **4-8-12** JFortune(9) (hld up: effrt whn b.d 2f out)		**B**	$6/1^{3}$	—	—
772^{8}	**Chadwell Hall (67)** (SRBowring) **6-8-8b**(7) FBoyle(11) (disp ld to ½-wy: cl up whn fell 2f out: dead)		**F**	9/1	—	—
956^{7}	**Present 'n Correct (48)** (CBBBooth) **4-7-10** LCharnock(13) (chsd ldrs tl bdly hmpd & uns rdr 2f out)		**U**	9/1	—	—

(SP 131.8%) **13 Rn**

60.2 secs (2.60) CSF £63.85 CT £640.79 TOTE £14.50: £4.10 £1.90 £3.90 (£28.40) Trio £611.40; £51.67 to Newbury 17/5/97 OWNER Miss N. F. Thesiger (YORK) BRED Whitsbury Manor Stud
LONG HANDICAP Impish (IRE) 6-10
WEIGHT FOR AGE 3yo-8lb

1098 Squire Corrie, although not well drawn, has the speed and saw it out well under a most determined ride. (12/1)
834 Broadstairs Beauty (IRE) is running his socks off, but just lacks that bit of dash these days. (9/2)
1037* Impish (IRE) didn't quite have the ground he really likes, but still ran a fine race, although the handicapper is about to take swift revenge for his convincing win last time. (12/1)
949 Captain Carat is running reasonably just now, but he always gives the impression that there is more to come if he can be persuaded.(9/1)
Dominelle likes fast ground, but seems to be high enough in the weights in the moment. (20/1)
905 Malibu Man couldn't get away from his field this time, and it would seem the handicapper has him taped just now. (7/1)

1224 HELMSLEY H'CAP (0-90) (4-Y.O+) (Class C)

4-25 (4-28) **2m** £5,442.50 (£1,640.00: £795.00: £372.50) Stalls: Low GOING minus 0.14 sec per fur (G)

				SP	RR	SF
777^{3}	**Onefourseven (68)** (JLEyre) **4-9-0** TWilliams(3) (hld up: effrt & nt clr run over 1f out: swtchd & r.o wl fnl f to ld post)	—	**1**	$7/1^{3}$	78	10
777^{4}	**Royal Expression (74)** (MrsMReveley) **5-9-8** ACulhane(2) (a.p: led over 1f out: r.o u.p: jst ct)	hd	**2**	8/1	84	18
846*	**Here Comes Herbie (55)** (WStorey) **5-7-12**(5) PFessey(4) (hld up: hdwy & prom appr st: ev ch 1f out: kpt on)	½	**3**	$7/4^{1}$	64	—
1100*	**Dirab (74)** (TDBarron) **4-9-3**(3) 4x FLynch(5) (lw: hld up & bhd: effrt 3f out: nrst fin)	2	**4**	$4/1^{2}$	81	13
777*	**Great Oration (IRE) (60)** (FWatson) **8-8-8** NConnorton(10) (lw: hld up: effrt on outside 3f out: edgd lft: nt pce to chal)	½	**5**	8/1	67	1
858^{10}	**Sedbergh (USA) (70)** (MrsMReveley) **4-9-2** WJO'Connor(8) (led: qcknd ent st: hdd over 1f out: edgd lft & grad wknd)	d.h	**5**	10/1	77	9
777^{5}	**Embryonic (IRE) (78)** (MartinTodhunter) **5-9-12** JCarroll(1) (hld up: effrt & nt clr run fnl 2f: nt rcvr)	1¼	**7**	9/1	84	18
1100^{14}	**Rushen Raider (70)** (KWHogg) **5-8-13**(5) ADaly(7) (chsd ldrs tl outpcd fnl 3f)	5	**8**	20/1	71	5
315^{11}	**Charter (72)** (WStorey) **6-9-6** GCarter(6) (hld up & bhd: n.d)	nk	**9**	20/1	72	6
1022^{10}	**Faugeron (56)** (NTinkler) **8-8-4** KimTinkler(9) (cl up tl wknd fnl 3f)	6	**10**	20/1	50	—

(SP 124.5%) **10 Rn**

3m 39.0 (16.00) CSF £58.21 CT £127.55 TOTE £8.50: £2.20 £1.50 £1.70 (£29.70) Trio £17.30 OWNER Mr J. Roundtree (HAMBLETON) BRED Peter Storey
WEIGHT FOR AGE 4yo-2lb

777 Onefourseven won this messy contest after finding trouble, and would seem to be improving. (7/1)
777 Royal Expression is running well, and will no doubt find a suitable race. (8/1)
846* Here Comes Herbie ran a useful race, but would have been better suited by a stronger gallop. (7/4)
1100* Dirab had plenty on here, trying to come from behind in this moderately-run event, and in the end did well to get so close. (4/1)
777* Great Oration (IRE) likes to come from off a strong pace, and this was certainly not run to suit him. (8/1)
858 Sedbergh (USA) gave the impression that more will be seen of him when he gets faster ground. (10/1)
777 Embryonic (IRE) has plenty of ability, but does not always put it to full use, but he was denied any sort of run on this occasion and appeared very unlucky. (9/1)

1225 DICK PEACOCK SPRINT H'CAP (0-75) (3-Y.O+) (Class D)

4-55 (4-59) **6f** £4,523.00 (£1,364.00: £662.00: £311.00) Stalls: High GOING minus 0.14 sec per fur (G)

				SP	RR	SF
995*	**Smokey From Caplaw (69)** (JJO'Neill) **3-8-13** 7x WRyan(2) (racd far side: in tch: hdwy over 1f out: r.o wl to ld nr fin)	—	**1**	12/1	76	35
1098^{2}	**Blessingindisguise (54)** (MWEasterby) **4-8-7b** TLucas(7) (racd far side: led tl ct cl home)	hd	**2**	10/1	61	29
977^{8}	**Benzoe (IRE) (68)** (MrsJRRamsden) **7-9-4**(3) FLynch(13) (lw: bhd: hdwy 2f out: r.o fnl f: nrst fin)	3	**3**	$4/1^{1}$	67	35
998^{7}	**Rum Lad (60)** (JJQuinn) **3-8-4** JLowe(20) (led stands' side 5f: no ex)	1½	**4**	33/1	55	14
827^{13}	**Sihafi (USA) (55)** (JMCarr) **4-8-8** PBloomfield(24) (hdwy over 2f out: styd on: nvr able to chal)	¾	**5**	$8/1^{3}$	48	16
1089^{14}	**Meranti (55)** (JMBradley) **4-8-3**(5) PPMurphy(10) (lw: a cl up: nt qckn appr fnl f)	nk	**6**	12/1	47	15
951^{15}	**Theatre Magic (50)** (DShaw) **4-8-3** JFanning(4) (lw: b: chsd ldrs tl wknd fnl 2f)	¾	**7**	25/1	40	8
901^{3}	**Time To Tango (66)** (GMMoore) **4-9-5** JFEgan(9) (cl up far side tl wknd wl over 1f out)	½	**8**	14/1	55	23
863^{7}	**Densben (52)** (DenysSmith) **13-8-5** TWilliams(23) (outpcd & bhd tl styd on fnl 2f)	s.h	**9**	25/1	41	9
827^{3}	**Winter Scout (USA) (55)** (RAFahey) **9-8-1**(7) RWinston(21) (lw: outpcd & bhd tl styd on fnl 2f)	hd	**10**	9/1	43	11
1098^{7}	**Souperficial (53)** (NTinkler) **6-8-6v** KimTinkler(16) (some hdwy u.p over 2f out: n.d)	½	**11**	20/1	40	8
863^{16}	**Mousehole (73)** (RGuest) **5-9-9**(3) DGriffiths(17) (cl up over 4f: wknd)	nk	**12**	12/1	59	27
	Melodic Drive (60) (JAGlover) **7-8-13b** GCarter(6) (racd far side: dwlt: n.d)	1	**13**	25/1	43	11
953^{7}	**Divine Miss-P (67)** (APJarvis) **4-9-6** WJO'Connor(19) (cl up over 4f: wknd)	¾	**14**	20/1	48	16
942^{7}	**Shining Cloud (67)** (MBell) **4-9-1**(5) GFaulkner(1) (lw: w ldrs far side tl wknd fnl 2f)	¾	**15**	$6/1^{2}$	46	14
946^{7}	**Royal South (IRE) (70)** (PSFelgate) **4-9-6**(3) PMcCabe(22) (lw: prom tl wknd fnl 2f)	1¾	**16**	16/1	45	13
694^{13}	**Style Dancer (IRE) (75)** (RMWhitaker) **3-9-5** OUrbina(5) (racd far side: n.d)	¾	**17**	20/1	48	7
949^{13}	**Middle East (70)** (TDBarron) **4-9-9** JCarroll(3) (racd far side: a bhd)	4	**18**	20/1	32	—
*1132**	**Desert Invader (IRE) (60)** (DWChapman) **6-8-13** 7x ACulhane(14) (outpcd most of way)	1¼	**19**	20/1	19	—
863^{17}	**Barrel of Hope (68)** (JLEyre) **5-9-4v**(3) OPears(15) (a outpcd & bhd)	1	**20**	20/1	24	—
977^{2}	**Mr Speaker (IRE) (63)** (CFWall) **4-9-2** GDuffield(8) (racd far side: outpcd fr ½-wy)	¾	**21**	12/1	17	—
998^{5}	**Jedi Knight (66)** (MWEasterby) **3-8-10** DaleGibson(12) (in tch to ½-wy: wknd)	¾	**22**	20/1	18	—
845*	**Denton Lad (71)** (JWWatts) **3-9-1** NConnorton(18) (sn outpcd & bhd)	5	**23**	12/1	10	—
	Double Matt (IRE) (75) (MrsPSly) **5-10-0** NCarlisle(11) (outpcd fr ½-wy)	9	**24**	33/1	—	—

(SP 166.3%) **24 Rn**

1m 13.2 (3.50) CSF £126.86 CT £559.64 TOTE £22.90: £4.00 £3.80 £1.90 £19.10 (£346.40) Trio £406.90 OWNER Mr G. P. Bernacchi (PENRITH) BRED Gino P. Bernacchi
WEIGHT FOR AGE 3yo-9lb

995* Smokey From Caplaw is in superb form at present, and showed a really good attitude here. (12/1)
1098 Blessingindisguise is running particularly well just now, and ought to be able to find a suitable race. (10/1: 8/1-12/1)
Benzoe (IRE) was trying to win this for the third year running, but was denied the services of his usual brilliant rider, and that probably made all the difference as he is a real character. (4/1: op 6/1)
785 Rum Lad had a good draw, and ran a fair race. (33/1)
827 Sihafi (USA) has the ability to do better when caught in the mood. (8/1)
1089 Meranti is still running well, despite a rise of 12lb this season, and this was a fair effort from his draw. (12/1)
827 Winter Scout (USA) had the right draw, but he lacks the speed over this trip to take advantage of it. (9/1: op 9/2)

1226 EASINGWOLD RATING RELATED MAIDEN LIMITED STKS (0-70) (3-Y.O) (Class E)
5-25 (5-26) **1m** £2,888.50 (£868.00: £419.00: £194.50) Stalls: Low GOING minus 0.14 sec per fur (G)

				SP	RR	SF
	Janie's Boy (68) (MrsJCecil) **3-9-0** GDuffield(2) (cl up: led over 3f out: hld on wl)	—	**1**	8/1	77	25
885^{4}	**Kilshanny (70)** (LMCumani) **3-8-11** OUrbina(4) (lw: a.p: effrt over 2f out: ch 1f out: kpt on u.p)	nk	**2**	$2/1^{1}$	73	21
840^{12}	**Klondike Charger (USA) (68)** (BWHills) **3-9-0** GCarter(7) (rr div: outpcd 3f out: hdwy u.p 2f out: kpt on wl)	1¼	**3**	17/2	74	22
766^{2}	**Manikato (USA) (68)** (DJSCosgrove) **3-9-0** MRimmer(6) (hld up: effrt 3f out: styd on: nrst fin)	1¼	**4**	$9/2^{3}$	71	19
	Kweilo (66) (JWPayne) **3-9-0** WRyan(3) (lw: hld up: hdwy gng wl over 2f out: effrt over 1f out)	½	**5**	$11/4^{2}$	70	18
1096^{2}	**In Good Nick (63)** (MWEasterby) **3-8-11b** TLucas(1) (b.nr fore: led tl hdd over 3f out: wknd fnl 2f)	2½	**6**	6/1	62	10
110^{7}	**Heathyards Pearl (USA) (60)** (RHollinshead) **3-8-8**(3) DGriffiths(8) (s.s: effrt 3f out: n.m.r: wknd fnl 2f)	5	**7**	33/1	52	—
	Colonel's Pride (63) (RMWhitaker) **3-9-0** DWright(5) (chsd ldrs tl wknd fnl 2f)	2½	**8**	14/1	50	—
				(SP 123.7%)	**8 Rn**	

1m 42.5 (6.00) CSF £24.20 TOTE £8.90: £2.00 £1.10 £2.30 (£14.60) OWNER Mr R. Auchincloss (NEWMARKET) BRED Brook Stud Ltd
Janie's Boy had previously been tried on sand and in blinkers without success, but this step up in trip proved to be the answer. (8/1)
885 Kilshanny doesn't do anything quickly, but she does stay on well, and over further will come into her own. (2/1)
Klondike Charger (USA) looks short of speed, and will appreciate longer distances. (17/2)
766 Manikato (USA) was staying on really well when ridden in the straight, and there are opportunities to be found for him. (9/2)
Kweilo is the type who travels particularly well during the race, but is as yet disappointing once off the bit. (11/4)
1096 In Good Nick just found this company too hot when the pace was really on in the home straight. (6/1)

T/Jkpt: Not won; £23,518.48 to Newbury 17/5/97. T/Plpt: £118.50 (127.39 Tckts). T/Qdpt: £302.40 (2.69 Tckts) AA

1037-HAMILTON (R-H) (Soft, Good to Soft patches)
Saturday May 17th
WEATHER: Overcast WIND: almost nil

1227 PIONEER AT STEPEK SERIES (ROUND 2) APPRENTICE H'CAP (0-70) (3-Y.O+) (Class F)
6-15 (6-15) **5f 4y** £2,511.50 (£714.00: £354.50) Stalls: Low GOING: 0.13 sec per fur (G)

				SP	RR	SF
744^{11}	**Goretski (IRE) (54)** (NTinkler) **4-8-9**(3) PFredericks(7) (mde all: hld on wl)	—	**1**	$7/1^{3}$	65	31
949^{16}	**Just Bob (70)** (SEKettlewell) **8-9-8**(6) JennyBenson(6) (lw: s.i.s: swtchd far side & racd alone: ev ch ins fnl f: kpt on)	½	**2**	14/1	79	45
1098^{3}	**Sue Me (IRE) (61)** (DNicholls) **5-8-13**(6) CarolynBales(4) (lw: stdd s & sn bhd: rdn & r.o fnl 2f: nrst fin)	2½	**3**	$7/2^{1}$	62	28
1037^{4}	**Henry the Hawk (44)** (MDods) **6-8-2b** AMcCarthy(8) (lw: b: cl up tl rdn & btn appr fnl f)	1¾	**4**	$5/1^{2}$	40	6
827^{17}	**Another Nightmare (IRE) (44)** (RMMcKellar) **5-7-10**(6) JMcAuley(2) (cl up: hung rt & grad wknd fr ½-wy)	2½	**5**	16/1	32	—
949^{2}	**Bee Health Boy (68)** (MWEasterby) **4-9-12b** RWinston(9) (lw: sn drvn along: in tch tl outpcd fr ½-wy)	s.h	**6**	$7/2^{1}$	56	22
956*	**Leading Princess (IRE) (52)** (MissLAPerratt) **6-8-4b**(6) MSemple(10) (prom: rdn ½-wy: no imp after)	hd	**7**	$5/1^{2}$	39	5
1079^{9}	**Naissant (60)** (RMMcKellar) **4-9-1**(3) SBuckley(5) (s.i.s: sn drvn along: n.d)	hd	**8**	14/1	47	13
685^{13}	**Morning Star (68)** (WMcKeown) **3-9-4** TSiddall(1) (racd alone stands' side: spd to ½-wy: wknd qckly: t.o)	26	**9**	25/1	—	—
				(SP 113.3%)	**9 Rn**	

62.8 secs (4.50) CSF £87.94 CT £362.75 TOTE £9.60: £3.20 £2.80 £1.80 (£21.70) Trio £43.50 OWNER Mr P. D. Savill (MALTON) BRED Pierre Brichart
WEIGHT FOR AGE 3yo-8lb
494 Goretski (IRE) has gone well on this track previously in similar conditions, but this was his first victory here. (7/1)
Just Bob, a course winner in the soft, tried his best here, switching to the far rails, and he is obviously coming to hand fast. (14/1)
1098 Sue Me (IRE) gave a lot of ground away at the start, and did remarkably well to finish so close. He looks worth keeping in mind. (7/2: op 7/4)
1037 Henry the Hawk looked superb, and had his chances, but at present he seems to have lost the dash that he showed early last season. (5/1)
663 Another Nightmare (IRE) likes the soft ground, but is probably better over another furlong, and trying to keep up caused her to hang. (16/1)
949 Bee Health Boy loves the soft, but needs six furlongs, and was always being taken off his legs. (7/2)

1228 ZANUSSI AT STEPEK MAIDEN AUCTION STKS (2-Y.O) (Class E)
6-45 (6-45) **5f 4y** £2,830.25 (£857.00: £418.50: £199.25) Stalls: Low GOING: 0.13 sec per fur (G)

				SP	RR	SF
	Colours To Gold (IRE) (RAFahey) **2-8-4**ow2 ACulhane(2) (leggy: scope: stdd s: hdwy 2f out: r.o wl to ld wl ins fnl f: fin 1st: disq: plcd last)	—	**1d**	10/1	67+	9
993^{3}	**Fairy Domino** (MRChannon) **2-7-13**(5)ow6 PPMurphy(6) (w ldr: led ½-wy tl wl ins fnl f: no ex: fin 2nd, 1¼l: awrdd r)	—	**1**	$7/2^{2}$	63	1
	Crazee Mental (DHaydnJones) **2-8-2** NKennedy(4) (w'like: bit bkwd: s.s: stdy hdwy 2f out: r.o: nvr plcd to chal: fin 3rd, 1¼l & 2l: plcd 2nd)	3¼	**2**	7/1	55+	—
897^{6}	**Marske Machine** (NTinkler) **2-7-12** DaleGibson(5) (chsd ldrs: effrt ½-wy: rdn & r.o one pce: fin 4th, 1l: plcd 3rd)	1	**3**	20/1	47	—
	Junior Muffin (IRE) (JBerry) **2-8-6**(5) PRoberts(3) (unf: scope: s.i.s: sn chsng ldrs: nt qckn appr fnl f: fin 5th, 3l: plcd 4th)	3	**4**	$11/4^{1}$	51	—
	Makahu Don (WTKemp) **2-8-3** TWilliams(7) (cmpt: led to ½-wy: wknd: fin 6th, 4l: plcd 5th)	4	**5**	25/1	30	—
	Falkenberg (FR) (MJohnston) **2-8-7** JWeaver(8) (cmpt: bit bkwd: cl up over 3f: wandered u.p & grad wknd: fin 7th, 2l: plcd 6th)	2	**6**	$4/1^{3}$	28	—

				SP	RR	SF
	Ellenber (WMcKeown) **2-7-12**(5) PFessey(9) (w'like: unf: outpcd most of wy: lost tch fnl 2f: fin 8th, ¾l: pl 7th)	¾	**7**	20/1	27	—
	Queen Sigi (IRE) (SirMarkPrescott) **2-8-6** JCarroll(1) (cmpt: scope: s.s: a bhd: fin 9th, 3l: plcd 8th)	3	**8**	9/2	15	—
				(SP 122.0%)	**9 Rn**	

63.7 secs (5.40) CSF £42.21 TOTE £13.30: £3.00 £1.10 £2.00 (£24.00) Trio £95.80 OWNER Mr I. Bray (MALTON) BRED Knocktoran Stud

SUBSEQUENT STEWARDS' ENQUIRY: Colours To Gold (IRE) disq. (prohibited substance (procaine) in urine). Fahey fined £400.

993 Fairy Domino, a free-runner, has plenty of speed, and a sharp track would surely help. (7/2)

Crazee Mental, the pick of the bunch on looks, needed this and, given an educational run, showed plenty of promise. (7/1: 4/1-8/1)

500 Marske Machine looks a bit of a handful, but has ability if she can be persuaded. (20/1)

Junior Muffin (IRE) showed ability, running right up the unfavoured stands' rails, and should improve for the experience. (11/4)

Makahu Don, likely to need further, showed speed here until blowing up just after halfway. (25/1)

Falkenberg (FR), who was coltish beforehand, needed this and blew up approaching the last furlong. (4/1: 11/4-9/2)

Colours To Gold (IRE) did not look anything special in the paddock, but was fit and, after giving much of the field a start, she picked up in splendid style. She ought to appreciate further. (10/1: op 5/1)

1229 TOSHIBA AT STEPEK (S) H'CAP (0-60) (3-Y.O+) (Class G)

7-15 (7-16) **1m 3f 16y** £2,458.00 (£688.00: £334.00) Stalls: High GOING: 0.13 sec per fur (G)

				SP	RR	SF
1116[4]	**Philgem (27)** (CWFairhurst) **4-8-11** NKennedy(16) (hdwy 5f out: led 1f out: styd on wl)	—	**1**	5/1[1]	34	24
873[5]	**Mirror Four Sport (45)** (MJohnston) **3-9-0** JWeaver(1) (wl away: lost pl after 2f: effrt 4f out: hrd rdn & styd on: nvr able to chal)	1½	**2**	6/1[3]	50	25
900[11]	**Ballet de Cour (32)** (TJEtherington) **4-8-11b**[1](5) JBramhill(2) (in tch: hdwy over 3f out: hrd rdn & edgd lft appr fnl f: no ex)	1¼	**3**	16/1	35	25
1116[6]	**Portite Sophie (40)** (MBrittain) **6-9-3**(7) DMernagh(3) (led after 3f to 1f out: sn btn)	2½	**4**	10/1	39	29
796[4]	**Needwood Nutkin (32)** (BCMorgan) **4-8-13**(3) DarrenMoffatt(5) (a chsng ldrs: effrt 3f out: btn over 1f out)	1	**5**	12/1	30	20
493[5]	**Bruz (27)** (LLungo) **6-8-11** DaleGibson(15) (hdwy u.p 3f out: styd on: nvr rchd ldrs)	nk	**6**	12/1	25	15
874[6]	**Impetuosity (IRE) (40)** (CWThornton) **3-8-6**(3) CTeague(12) (sn outpcd & wl bhd: styd on u.p fnl 3f)	hd	**7**	10/1	37	12
	Craigary (30) (MrsASwinbank) **6-9-0v**[1] ACulhane(8) (bhd: effrt & brought wd 3f out: btn appr fnl f)	1¾	**8**	11/2[2]	25	15
1001[11]	**On The Wildside (40)** (MRChannon) **4-9-5**(5) PPMurphy(13) (chsd ldrs tl wknd fnl 3f)	10	**9**	11/1	20	10
950[9]	**Jarrow (24)** (MrsAMNaughton) **6-8-8** TWilliams(6) (s.s: effrt 4f out: sn rdn & no imp)	1½	**10**	25/1	2	—
869[9]	**Ihtimaam (FR) (32)** (MrsASwinbank) **5-8-11b**(5) PFessey(4) (led 3f: cl up tl wknd fnl 3f)	6	**11**	14/1	2	—
1078[9]	**Strelitza (IRE) (52)** (MWEasterby) **3-9-2**(5) GFaulkner(10) (lw: hdwy appr st: sn in tch: c wd & wknd fnl 4f)	9	**12**	9/1	9	—
1040[8]	**Western Venture (IRE) (30)** (RMMcKellar) **4-9-0b**[1] JCarroll(14) (plld hrd: cl up tl st: sn wknd)	3	**13**	16/1	—	—
1043[5]	**Ballydinero (IRE) (46)** (CaptJWilson) **3-8-8**(7) AngelaHartley(9) (nvr trbld ldrs)	3½	**14**	16/1	—	—
887[16]	**Daffodil Express (IRE) (37)** (MJRyan) **4-9-7** KRutter(7) (n.d)	1	**15**	14/1	—	—
925[10]	**Mystic Times (35)** (BMactaggart) **4-9-0**(5) PRoberts(11) (plld hrd: cl up tl wknd fnl 5f)	3	**16**	12/1	—	—
				(SP 140.8%)	**16 Rn**	

2m 30.9 (11.50) CSF £36.04 CT £445.71 TOTE £5.80: £2.00 £1.60 £5.10 £2.40 (£15.10) Trio £138.70; £138.76 to 19/5/97 OWNER Mr C. D. Barber-Lomax (MIDDLEHAM) BRED Mrs M. Morley

WEIGHT FOR AGE 3yo-15lb

No bid

1116 Philgem got off the mark at last, responding to pressure in good style, and should get further. (5/1)

873 Mirror Four Sport an All-Weather winner, looks a hard ride but responds to pressure, and will no doubt find a race on turf. (6/1)

312 Ballet de Cour, from a stable bang in form, had blinkers on for the first time, and put in his best effort on turf to date. (16/1)

881 Portite Sophie keeps running reasonably, but gives the impression faster ground may suit her better. (10/1)

796 Needwood Nutkin, stepping up slightly in trip and on more testing ground, was found out approaching the final furlong. (12/1: 9/1-14/1)

493 Bruz looks a hard ride, but was staying on when it was all over. (12/1)

874 Impetuosity (IRE) is slow but she stays well and, over further, is likely to find a modest race. (10/1)

1230 LEBUS UPHOLSTERY AT STEPEK MAIDEN STKS (3-Y.O+) (Class D)

7-45 (7-53) **1m 4f 17y** £3,663.75 (£1,110.00: £542.50: £258.75) Stalls: High GOING: 0.13 sec per fur (G)

				SP	RR	SF
445[4]	**One For Baileys** (MJohnston) **3-8-7** JWeaver(11) (mde most: hld on wl)	—	**1**	3/1[1]	81	33
	Colour Code (MrsASwinbank) **5-9-10** JSupple(13) (a cl up: chal 4f out: hrd rdn over 2f out: kpt on wl)	nk	**2**	7/2[2]	81	50
875[3]	**Irsal (78)** (ACStewart) **3-8-7** TWilliams(14) (trckd ldrs: chal over 3f out: rdn 2f out: nt qckn)	2	**3**	9/2[3]	78	30
825[2]	**Rare Talent (73)** (MRChannon) **3-8-2**(5) PPMurphy(2) (trckd ldrs: effrt 3f out: wknd over 1f out)	7	**4**	6/1	69	21
	Ardarroch Prince (MrsMReveley) **6-9-10** ACulhane(1) (bhd tl styd on wl fnl 3f: nrst fin)	3	**5**	16/1	65	34
841[11]	**Media Star (USA)** (JHMGosden) **4-9-10** JCarroll(3) (b.hind: chsd ldrs tl outpcd appr st: kpt on fnl 4f: n.d)	7	**6**	8/1	55	24
761[6]	**Get A Life** (JohnHarris) **4-9-2**(3) DarrenMoffatt(7) (hdwy ½-wy: nvr trbld ldrs)	1½	**7**	50/1	48	17
996[6]	**Society Times (USA)** (DANolan) **4-9-10** KRutter(4) (in tch: effrt 4f out: no imp)	3	**8**	50/1	50	19
983[10]	**Tam O'Shanter** (CWThornton) **3-8-7** DaleGibson(12) (hdwy ent st: n.d)	3½	**9**	33/1	45	—
996[4]	**Well Armed (IRE)** (JJO'Neill) **6-9-10** RLappin(6) (n.d)	2	**10**	14/1	42	11
944[8]	**Canadian Fantasy (78)** (MJohnston) **3-8-0**(7) KSked(9) (lw: outpcd & lost tch 7f out: n.d after)	2½	**11**	12/1	39	—
558[5]	**Wellcome Inn** (JohnHarris) **3-8-7** JO'Reilly(15) (s.s: a bhd)	¾	**12**	50/1	38	—
	Banneret (USA) (JohnHarris) **4-9-10** VHalliday(10) (hld up & bhd: n.d)	2½	**13**	33/1	35	4
551[7]	**Eurolink Windsong (IRE)** (RMMcKellar) **3-7-9**(7) JMcAuley(8) (b.hind: plld hrd early: bhd most of way)	2	**14**	50/1	27	—
	Comic's Future (USA) (JJO'Neill) **4-9-5**(5) JBramhill(16) (bhd & swvd lft over 3f out: t.o)	dist	**15**	33/1	—	—
996[7]	**Trying Times (IRE)** (JBerry) **4-9-5**(5) PRoberts(5) (in tch to st: sn wknd: t.o)	15	**16**	25/1	—	—
				(SP 131.6%)	**16 Rn**	

2m 42.5 (10.50) CSF £12.33 TOTE £3.40: £1.90 £2.10 £1.40 (£9.50) Trio £47.00 OWNER G R Bailey Ltd (Baileys Horse Feeds) (MIDDLEHAM) BRED P. and Mrs Venner

WEIGHT FOR AGE 3yo-17lb

445 One For Baileys looked lean and exceptionally fit and, given a most positive ride, showed the right spirit to hold on. (3/1)

Colour Code, a very useful bumper winner on faster ground, put up a good show here under a most vigorous ride. He kept battling on all the way to the line, and will surely not be long in breaking his duck at this game. (7/2)

875 Irsal, who was awkward before the start, travelled well in the race, but the combination of the trip and soft ground probably sapped all reserves late on. (9/2)

825 Rare Talent, racing on soft ground for the first time, found it all too much in the last couple of furlongs. (6/1)

Ardarroch Prince, a bumper winner, found this trip on the sharp side, but was making useful late headway. (16/1)

841 Media Star (USA), coltish beforehand, was either not co-operating or is very slow. (8/1: op 9/2)

1231 SHARP AT STEPEK H'CAP (0-70) (3-Y.O+) (Class E)

8-15 (8-19) **1m 65y** £3,468.75 (£1,050.00: £512.50: £243.75) Stalls: High GOING: 0.13 sec per fur (G)

				SP	RR	SF
152[12]	**Principal Boy (IRE) (35)** (TJEtherington) **4-7-13** DaleGibson(8) (trckd ldrs tl outpcd & lost pl 3f out: hdwy over 1f out: led ins fnl f: r.o strly)	—	**1**	20/1	51	29
951[3]	**Nobby Barnes (32)** (DonEnricoIncisa) **8-7-10** KimTinkler(3) (wnt prom ½-wy: swtchd 2f out: ev ch 1f out: r.o one pce)	5	**2**	12/1	38	16
951*	**Stormless (58)** (PMonteith) **6-9-3**(5) JBramhill(4) (rr div: c wd st: led wl over 1f out tl ins fnl f: one pce)	1¼	**3**	6/4[1]	62	40
	One Life To Live (IRE) (48) (SEKettlewell) **4-8-12** ACulhane(2) (bhd: gd hdwy 2f out: sn chsng ldrs: nt qckn fnl f)	1¼	**4**	33/1	50	28
1117[3]	**Gold Desire (45)** (MBrittain) **7-8-9** JCarroll(7) (drvn along ½-wy: styd on: nt pce to chal)	hd	**5**	8/1	46	24
1040[2]	**Hutchies Lady (35)** (RMMcKellar) **5-7-8**(5) PFessey(5) (b.hind: prom tl outpcd 3f out: kpt on appr fnl f: n.d)	1½	**6**	9/2[2]	33	11
1005[7]	**Bedazzle (34)** (MBrittain) **6-7-5**(7) DMernagh(9) (dwlt: hdwy & prom appr st: ch 3f out: outpcd fnl 2f)	hd	**7**	16/1	32	10
955[11]	**Rapid Mover (32)** (DANolan) **10-7-3b**(7) PBradley(6) (led tl hdd & wknd over 1f out)	4	**8**	33/1	23	1
1016[3]	**Northern Fan (IRE) (60)** (NTinkler) **5-9-10** DeanMcKeown(1) (lw: w ldr tl wknd over 2f out)	¾	**9**	13/2[3]	49	27
997[5]	**Hanby (45)** (JSGoldie) **5-8-9** TWilliams(10) (b: plld hrd early: in tch: effrt over 3f out: wknd fnl 2f: eased)	18	**10**	7/1	—	—

(SP 119.3%) **10 Rn**

1m 51.0 (6.90) CSF £218.35 CT £542.08 TOTE £44.00: £5.70 £3.40 £1.10 (£62.40) Trio £88.20 OWNER Mr Chris Moreno (MALTON) BRED Mrs M. Mansergh

LONG HANDICAP Rapid Mover 7-6 Nobby Barnes 7-9

Principal Boy (IRE) won his first race on turf and, after looking in trouble halfway up the straight, did it in some style. It looks as though longer trips will be appreciated. (20/1)

951 Nobby Barnes ran another decent race and seems to be knocking on the door. (12/1)

951* Stormless was always racing wide on what appeared the slightly slower ground, but he still had his chances until getting outbattled in the last furlong. (6/4)

One Life To Live (IRE) showed some ability here and should improve for the run. (33/1)

1117 Gold Desire is running well and, once he gets faster ground, he should come into his own. (8/1)

1040 Hutchies Lady seems to run when in the mood, and was not on this occasion. (9/2)

1232 SILHOUETTE UPHOLSTERY AT STEPEK H'CAP (0-70) (4-Y.O+) (Class E)

8-45 (8-45) **1m 5f 9y** £2,892.00 (£876.00: £428.00: £204.00) Stalls: High GOING: 0.13 sec per fur (G)

				SP	RR	SF
1039[2]	**Kintavi (46)** (TWDonnelly) **7-8-2**(5) PFessey(8) (b: hld up: hdwy 4f out: effrt 2f out: r.o u.p to ld post)	—	**1**	7/2[3]	59	32
1039[5]	**Lord Advocate (42)** (DANolan) **9-7-10b**(7) KSked(2) (led: qcknd over 3f out: r.o: jst ct)	s.h	**2**	16/1	55	28
1118*	**Mentalasanythin (67)** (DHaydnJones) **8-9-9**(5) GFaulkner(5) (a cl up: effrt 3f out: nt qckn fnl f)	3½	**3**	3/1[2]	76	49
613[4]	**Northern Motto (48)** (JSGoldie) **4-8-9** DeanMcKeown(4) (trckd ldrs: effrt & swtchd 3f out: rdn & styd on: nt pce to chal)	hd	**4**	11/4[1]	57	30
	Clash of Swords (54) (PCalver) **4-8-12**(3) DarrenMoffatt(9) (hld up: effrt over 3f out: sn rdn & no imp)	8	**5**	20/1	53	26
	Needwood Poppy (35) (BCMorgan) **9-7-5**(5) JBramhill(6) (drvn along & bhd appr st: sme hdwy over 2f out: n.d)	2½	**6**	33/1	31	4
1100[2]	**Contrarie (46)** (MJRyan) **4-8-0**(7) AMcCarthy(1) (prom tl outpcd fnl 3f)	1½	**7**	9/2	40	13
1081[2]	**Highfield Fizz (42)** (CWFairhurst) **5-8-3** DaleGibson(7) (b.off hind: outpcd & lost tch 4f out: n.d after)	3	**8**	14/1	32	5
	Vintage Taittinger (IRE) (37) (JSGoldie) **5-7-12**ow2 TWilliams(10) (s.i.s: hld up: effrt 5f out: sn btn)	7	**9**	50/1	19	—
1133[13]	**Sushi Bar (IRE) (48)** (MrsMReveley) **6-8-9** JCarroll(3) (sn chsng ldrs: rdn & wknd fnl 3f)	4	**10**	25/1	25	—

(SP 118.1%) **10 Rn**

2m 57.4 (11.70) CSF £49.69 CT £172.18 TOTE £3.90: £1.30 £3.00 £1.60 (£22.30) Trio £10.70 OWNER Mr S. Taberner (SWADLINCOTE) BRED S. Taberner

LONG HANDICAP Needwood Poppy 7-0 Vintage Taittinger (IRE) 7-7

STEWARDS' ENQUIRY McKeown susp. 26-28/5/97 (excessive use of whip).

1039 Kintavi, settled off the pace, was brought with a perfectly-timed run to snatch it late on. (7/2: 5/2-4/1)

1039 Lord Advocate at his best when out in front, did his utmost to make all but, despite a gallant effort, was just caught. (16/1)

1118* Mentalasanythin loves this track and ran another fine race, but was never quite good enough off his present mark. (3/1)

613 Northern Motto again left the impression that he will be happier over further. (11/4: 6/1-5/2)

Clash of Swords managed to win a race over hurdles, but is still a maiden on the Flat and was never fully co-operating here. (20/1)

Needwood Poppy ran as though longer trips are needed. (33/1)

1100 Contrarie, who ran well last time over further, is a very lightly-made and lean individual, and was always struggling at this trip. (9/2)

T/Plpt: £54.70 (259.09 Tckts). T/Qdpt: £6.30 (178.72 Tckts) AA

1151-LINGFIELD (L-H) (Good, Good to firm patches)

Saturday May 17th

WEATHER: Fine WIND: alm nil

1233 BOLLINGER CHAMPAGNE CHALLENGE SERIES GENTLEMEN'S H'CAP (0-70) (3-Y.O+) (Class F)

6-00 (6-03) **1m 2f** £2,877.60 (£798.60: £382.80) Stalls: High GOING minus 0.47 sec per fur (F)

				SP	RR	SF
1024[4]	**Cuban Reef (43)** (WJMusson) **5-10-1** MrTMcCarthy(4) (hld up mid div: hdwy on ins over 2f out: led 1f out: r.o wl)	—	**1**	5/1[1]	—	20
870[3]	**Benjamins Law (45)** (JAPickering) **6-9-13**(4) MrVLukaniuk(16) (a.p: led over 4f out: hdd 1f out: one pce)	2	**2**	20/1	—	19
1040*	**Clued Up (50)** (PDEvans) **4-10-4v**(4) MrAEvans(2) (mid div: hdwy over 2f out: ev ch over 1f out: one pce)	s.h	**3**	9/1[3]	4	24
763[6]	**Seattle Alley (USA) (67)** (PRWebber) **4-11-11** MrPScott(15) (hdwy 3f out: rdn 2f out: kpt on one pce ins fnl f)	2	**4**	10/1	18	38
984*	**Fairy Knight (69)** (RHannon) **5-11-13** MrCVigors(9) (lw: hld up: hdwy 2f out: rdn over 1f out: kpt on one pce ins last)	½	**5**	5/1[1]	19	39
838[6]	**Father Dan (IRE) (56)** (MissGayKelleway) **8-11-0** MrMArmytage(8) (hdwy over 3f out: rdn 2f out: one pce)	1¾	**6**	8/1[2]	3	23
	Printers Quill (48) (MajorDNChappell) **5-10-2**(4) MrPO'Keeffe(7) (bit bkwd: chsd ldrs tl wknd over 1f out)	nk	**7**	33/1	50	14
888[12]	**Lalindi (IRE) (70)** (ACStewart) **6-11-10**(4)ow2 MrCRanson(3) (nvr nrr)	½	**8**	25/1	72	34
	Westminster (IRE) (63) (MHTompkins) **5-11-3**(4) MrMJenkins(6) (prom tl wknd over 2f out)	5	**9**	20/1	57	21

141[4]	**Suitor (47)** (SDow) **4-10-1**(4) MrJGoldstein(10) (bhd fnl 3f)	1½	**10**	14/1	38	2
857[6]	**Captain's Day (47)** (HJCollingridge) **5-10-5** MrRWakley(1) (nvr bttr than mid div)	½	**11**	12/1	37	1
350[5]	**Lily Jaques (69)** (RGuest) **3-10-9**(4)ow14 MrVCoogan(14) (a bhd)	s.h	**12**	66/1	59	—
188[3]	**Zamalek (USA) (44)** (RMFlower) **5-10-2** MrKGoble(13) (swtg: hdwy 4f out: wknd over 2f out)	1¼	**13**	10/1	32	—
	Sheilas Dream (50) (GLMoore) **4-10-4**(4) MrIMongan(12) (bit bkwd: a bhd)	2	**14**	25/1	35	—
147[12]	**In Cahoots (46)** (CJHill) **4-10-0**(4) MrSDurack(5) (led: hdd over 4f out: wknd 3f out)	1½	**15**	25/1	29	—
1125*	**Fresh Fruit Daily (70)** (PAKelleway) **5-11-10**(4) MrMSpillane(11) (mid div whn clipped heels & uns rdr over 3f out)		**U**	9/1[3]	—	—

(SP 122.5%) **16 Rn**

2m 11.77 (7.07) CSF £101.22 CT £813.94 TOTE £6.60: £1.60 £3.50 £2.80 £3.30 (£77.20) Trio Not won; £341.09 to 19/5/97 OWNER Mr K. L. West (NEWMARKET) BRED Angley Stud Ltd

WEIGHT FOR AGE 3yo-14lb

1024 Cuban Reef was given a peach of a ride by her competent amateur, saving ground on the inside the whole way. (5/1)

870 Benjamins Law tried to steal the race when kicking clear early in the straight, but had no response to the winner's late thrust. (20/1)

1040* Clued Up moved up to have every chance below the distance, but could not find a turn of foot. (9/1: 6/1-11/1)

763 Seattle Alley (USA), who had been running well over hurdles, ran a sound race here, but looked a little one-paced in the final two furlongs. He is worth a try over further. (10/1: 8/1-12/1)

984* Fairy Knight made some headway in the final two furlongs, but never looked like reaching the principals. (5/1)

838 Father Dan (IRE) made an effort early in the straight, but this amounted to little. (8/1)

61 Suitor (14/1: 10/1-16/1)

1234 SGB/YOUNGMAN MEDIAN AUCTION MAIDEN STKS (3-Y.O) (Class E)

6-30 (6-32) **1m 1f** £3,070.25 (£917.00: £438.50: £199.25) Stalls: High GOING minus 0.47 sec per fur (F)

				SP	RR	SF
991[6]	**Patriot Games (IRE)** (MRStoute) **3-9-0** JReid(1) (a.p: led over 2f out: hrd rdn ins fnl f: r.o)	—	**1**	6/1[3]	85	13
853[2]	**Burning Truth (USA) (80)** (RCharlton) **3-9-0** RHughes(3) (lw: hld up: rn wd home turn: gd hdwy over 2f out: ev ch ins fnl f: unable qckn)	¾	**2**	6/4[1]	84	12
	Ridaiyma (IRE) (LMCumani) **3-8-4**(5) RFfrench(5) (unf: scope: bit bkwd: dwlt: bhd: gd hdwy over 2f out: nt clr run over 1f out: swtchd rt: styd on wl ins last)	4	**3**	16/1	72	—
675[15]	**Topatori (IRE) (77)** (MHTompkins) **3-8-9** DBiggs(2) (lw: hld up: hdwy over 2f out: rdn over 1f out: one pce)	s.h	**4**	40/1	72	—
725[W]	**Gee Bee Boy** (APJarvis) **3-9-0** WJO'Connor(6) (rr: sme hdwy over 2f out: sn rdn: one pce)	2	**5**	50/1	73	1
833[8]	**Quest For Best (USA)** (JHMGosden) **3-8-9** GHind(4) (sn led: hdd 6f out: wknd over 2f out)	5	**6**	10/1	59	—
	Indian Brave (MJohnston) **3-9-0** LDettori(7) (bit bkwd: prom: rdn 3f out: grad wknd)	½	**7**	100/30[2]	63	—
586[6]	**Final Warning** (JEBanks) **3-9-0** MWigham(8) (led 6f out: hdd over 2f out: sn wknd)	nk	**8**	6/1[3]	63	—
475[13]	**Hippios (45)** (SDow) **3-8-11**(3) AWhelan(9) (a bhd)	4	**9**	100/1	56	—

(SP 112.0%) **9 Rn**

1m 55.92 (5.42) CSF £13.43 TOTE £6.40: £1.80 £1.10 £2.40 (£5.80) Trio £25.10 OWNER Mr Basil Sellers (NEWMARKET) BRED Adstock Manor Stud

991 Patriot Games (IRE), who had run well in the Wood Ditton, confirmed that promise here with a game display. He looks likes he would be suited by further. (6/1)

853 Burning Truth (USA) moved up to have every chance, but found the winner too strong. (6/4)

Ridaiyma (IRE) ran a race full of promise. Green and behind in the early stages, she was making very good headway when stopped in her tracks below the distance. Switched right, she stayed on strongly in the final furlong, but the leaders were beyond recall. She looks sure to find a race. (16/1)

Topatori (IRE) ran a sound enough race, but was put in her place in the final furlong. (40/1)

586 Final Warning (6/1: 3/1-7/1)

72 66+ 73+ 64

1235 E.B.F. CIDER MAIDEN STKS (2-Y.O) (Class D) (69)

7-00 (7-01) **5f** £3,348.00 (£999.00: £477.00: £216.00) Stalls: High GOING minus 0.47 sec per fur (F)

				SP	RR	SF
999[2]	**Fast Tempo (IRE)** (BPalling) **2-8-9** TSprake(1) (broke wl: mde all: clr over 1f out: easily)	—	**1**	9/2[2]	81	26
1084[4]	**English Lady (IRE)** (MJHaynes) **2-8-9** JReid(3) (chsd wnr: edgd rt over 3f out: rdn 2f out: one pce)	5	**2**	9/2[2]	65	10
979[2]	**Ron's Pet** (RHannon) **2-9-0** RHughes(4) (lw: dwlt: sn bhd & rdn along: sme hdwy over 2f out: rdn over 1f out: one pce)	1¼	**3**	5/6[1]	66	11
844[3]	**Going Places** (KTIvory) **2-8-6**(3) MartinDwyer(5) (chsd ldrs: n.m.r over 3f out: rdn & hung lft over 2f out: sn btn)	1¾	**4**	5/1[3]	55	—
	Corsecan (SDow) **2-9-0** SSanders(2) (leggy: bit bkwd: in tch 2f)	14	**5**	25/1	16	—

(SP 111.4%) **5 Rn**

58.54 secs (1.54) CSF £21.82 TOTE £5.10: £1.60 £2.20 (£8.80) OWNER Mrs M. M. Palling (COWBRIDGE) BRED W. H. Elliott

999 Fast Tempo (IRE) broke extremely fast and never saw another runner. (9/2)

1084 English Lady (IRE) ran a sound race, but was tapped for foot in the final two furlongs. (9/2)

979 Ron's Pet looked far from keen in the early stages. (5/6: evens-11/10)

844 Going Places was ridden to challenge over two furlongs out, but hung away her chance. (5/1)

1236 SARAH J WATSON BIRTHDAY (S) H'CAP (0-60) (3-Y.O+) (Class G)

7-30 (7-34) **5f** £1,984.50 (£547.00: £259.50) Stalls: High GOING minus 0.47 sec per fur (F)

				SP	RR	SF
879[6]	**Bright Paragon (IRE) (36)** (KTIvory) **8-8-7**(3) MartinDwyer(6) (b: b.hind: a.p: led ins fnl f: r.o)	—	**1**	20/1	43	25
1086[12]	**Pearl Dawn (IRE) (50)** (PCClarke) **7-9-5**(5) RFfrench(20) (mid div: hdwy over 1f out: str run fnl f: fin wl)	hd	**2**	20/1	57	39
1083[11]	**Superlao (BEL) (34)** (JJBridger) **5-8-8** JQuinn(18) (a.p: ev ch ins fnl f: one pce)	nk	**3**	14/1	40	22
879[4]	**Tee-Emm (37)** (RSimpson) **7-8-11b** MGallagher(19) (b: led: hdd ins fnl f: unable qckn)	nk	**4**	11/2[1]	42	24
1098[8]	**Thick as Thieves (40)** (RonaldThompson) **5-8-7**(7) DDenby(9) (lw: a.p: rdn over 1f out: one pce)	1½	**5**	9/1[3]	40	22
876[7]	**Littlestone Rocket (55)** (WRMuir) **3-9-7v**[1] JReid(2) (led far side: no ch with stands' side group fnl f)	1¼	**6**	16/1	51	25
882[8]	**Municipal Girl (IRE) (54)** (BPalling) **3-9-6** TSprake(12) (mid div: rdn 2f out: one pce)	s.h	**7**	10/1	50	24
756[2]	**Mister Raider (46)** (EAWheeler) **5-9-1b**(5) ADaly(10) (swtg: chsd ldrs: rdn 2f out: one pce)	hd	**8**	11/2[1]	42	24
907[4]	**River Ensign (40)** (WMBrisbourne) **4-8-11**(3) AWhelan(13) (a mid div)	1½	**9**	33/1	31	13
956[9]	**Southern Dominion (45)** (MissJFCraze) **5-9-5** SWebster(4) (racd far side: spd 3f)	s.h	**10**	12/1	36	18
876[4]	**Whizz Kid (57)** (JJBridger) **3-9-2**(7) MBatchelor(7) (racd far side: prom over 3f)	¾	**11**	14/1	45	19
1046[8]	**Secret Miss (37)** (APJones) **5-8-11** BDoyle(15) (dwlt: sn in mid div: wknd over 2f out)	¾	**12**	8/1[2]	23	5

1009^{14}	**Halbert (36)** (MDIUsher) **8-8-10v** CandyMorris(5) (lw: bhd fnl 3f)	½	**13**	14/1	20	2
1088^{8}	**Fancy Design (IRE) (38)** (PMitchell) **4-8-12v** DaneO'Neill(8) (a bhd)	1½	**14**	33/1	17	—
758^{9}	**Hever Golf Stormer (IRE) (54)** (TJNaughton) **3-9-6** SSanders(3) (lw: racd far side: a bhd)	1½	**15**	20/1	29	3
1012^{7}	**Arnie (IRE) (33)** (JRPoulton) **5-8-7** LDettori(16) (dwlt: a bhd)	½	**16**	10/1	6	—
907^{9}	**Distant Dynasty (30)** (BAPearce) **7-8-4** GBardwell(11) (bhd fnl 3f)	1¼	**17**	40/1	—	—
883^{15}	**Emmas Breeze (50)** (JSKing) **3-8-11**(5) SophieMitchell(1) (racd far side: a bhd)	½	**18**	33/1	17	—
	Poppy My Love (46) (ICampbell) **4-8-13**(7) SRussell(17) (swtg: bhd fnl 3f)	4	**19**	33/1	1	—
	Daughter In Law (IRE) (35) (PRWebber) **4-8-9** RPerham(14) (sddle slipped, swvd lft & uns rdr after 1f)		**U**	33/1	—	—
				(SP 135.1%)	**20 Rn**	

58.67 secs (1.67) CSF £337.04 CT £5,309.66 TOTE £20.30: £2.80 £4.40 £2.90 £1.80 (£176.50) Trio Not won; £500.88 to 19/5/97 OWNER Mr D. C. G. Cooper (RADLETT) BRED B. Kennedy
WEIGHT FOR AGE 3yo-8lb
No bid
756 Bright Paragon (IRE) was always prominent and just lasted home in a driving finish. (20/1)
638 Pearl Dawn (IRE) produced a storming run in the final furlong, and would have won in a few more strides. (20/1)
304 Superlao (BEL) was never far away, but could not quicken up in the final furlong. (14/1)
879 Tee-Emm tried to make all up the favoured stand rail, but just lost out in the final furlong. (11/2)
391 Thick as Thieves ran a sound enough race, but only had the one pace to give late on. (9/1)
756 Mister Raider hunted up the leaders, but was under pressure shortly after halfway, and had little more to give. (11/2)
924* Southern Dominion (12/1: op 8/1)
876 Whizz Kid (14/1: op 8/1)
855 Arnie (IRE) (10/1: op 6/1)

1237 C.T.T. PRE-PRESS MAIDEN STKS (3-Y.O+) (Class D)
8-00 (8-08) **6f** £4,218.90 (£1,264.20: £607.60: £279.30) Stalls: High GOING minus 0.47 sec per fur (F)

				SP	RR	SF
942^{3}	**Blue Goblin (USA) (93)** (LMCumani) **3-8-12** LDettori(14) (lw: a.p: led over 1f out: easily)	—	**1**	8/13 ^{1}	90+	36
784^{4}	**Flourishing Way (78)** (RCharlton) **3-8-7** SSanders(15) (led: hdd over 1f out: one pce)	2½	**2**	8/1 ^{3}	78	24
	Musafi (USA) (MajorWRHern) **3-8-12** RHills(17) (scope: bit bkwd: mid div: rdn 2f out: styd on ins fnl f)	1¾	**3**	15/2 ^{2}	79	25
1088^{2}	**Perfect Pal (IRE)** (MissGayKelleway) **6-9-7** RHughes(16) (chsd ldrs: rdn 2f out: kpt on one pce fnl f)	hd	**4**	14/1	78	33
970^{5}	**Bold Spring (IRE) (70)** (RHannon) **3-8-12** DaneO'Neill(19) (prom tl wknd over 1f out)	1	**5**	10/1	76	22
970^{3}	**Butrinto** (MajorWRHern) **3-8-12** TSprake(5) (led far side: ev ch over 1f out: one pce)	1½	**6**	8/1 ^{3}	72	18
31^{7}	**The Fugative** (PMitchell) **4-8-13**(3) AWhelan(7) (w ldr far side: wknd over 1f out)	7	**7**	50/1	48	3
	Nicker (WJarvis) **3-8-12** OUrbina(3) (w'like: swtchd stands' side after 1f: nvr nrr)	2	**8**	25/1	48	—
935^{7}	**Millpet** (RGuest) **3-8-7** JReid(1) (swtchd stands' side after 1f: nvr nrr)	2	**9**	50/1	37	—
	Lobkov (RSimpson) **5-9-2** MGallagher(12) (prom to ½-wy)	5	**10**	100/1	24	—
681^{10}	**Perlethorpe** (MBell) **3-8-0**(7) DMulhall(8) (racd far side: a bhd)	1¾	**11**	25/1	19	—
970^{9}	**Kilmeena Lady** (JCFox) **3-8-7** DeclanO'Shea(13) (dwlt a bhd)	hd	**12**	50/1	19	—
1006^{9}	**Sequoia Prince (CAN)** (MBell) **3-8-12** MFenton(2) (racd far side: a bhd)	hd	**13**	50/1	24	—
991^{17}	**Chakra (62)** (SDow) **3-8-12** JQuinn(4) (racd far side: bhd fr ½-wy)	nk	**14**	100/1	23	—
970^{6}	**Golden Saddle (USA)** (PFICole) **3-8-5**(7) DavidO'Neill(11) (bhd fnl 4f)	hd	**15**	20/1	23	—
1088^{9}	**Durable George** (JJBridger) **3-8-12** GBardwell(10) (swtchd far side after 1f: bhd ½-wy)	3	**16**	100/1	15	—
1139^{15}	**Gracious Imp (USA)** (JRJenkins) **4-8-11v**^{1}(5) ADaly(6) (dwlt: brought stands' side after 1f: a bhd)	2	**17**	100/1	5	—
	Kildee Boy (APJones) **3-8-12** BDoyle(9) (Withdrawn not under Starter's orders: unruly)		**W**	50/1	—	—
				(SP 137.9%)	**17 Rn**	

1m 10.38 (1.38) CSF £6.19 TOTE £1.70: £1.20 £2.00 £2.00 (£5.60) Trio £9.60 OWNER Sheikh Mohammed (NEWMARKET) BRED Darley Stud Management Inc
WEIGHT FOR AGE 3yo-9lb
942 Blue Goblin (USA) had by far the best form before the race, and won this in very easy fashion. He was not blinkered as he had been on the last two occasions, but it appeared to make no difference. (8/13)
784 Flourishing Way made a brave attempt to lead throughout, but the winner was much too strong. (8/1: op 5/1)
Musafi (USA) is quite a nice sort, but looked just in need of the race. He made steady headway in the final two furlongs, and an opportunity should be found. (15/2)
1088 Perfect Pal (IRE) kept on in the final furlong, and is better over further. (14/1: 10/1-16/1)
970 Bold Spring (IRE) showed some pace, but weakened below the distance. (10/1: 7/1-11/1)
970 Butrinto ran a good race considering he was racing down the slower far side, and is an interesting runner now he is qualified for handicaps. (8/1)

1238 OASTWELL WINES H'CAP (0-80) (3-Y.O) (Class D)
8-30 (8-38) **7f** £3,964.10 (£1,185.80: £568.40: £259.70) Stalls: High GOING minus 0.47 sec per fur (F)

				SP	RR	SF
	Gee Bee Dream (72) (APJarvis) **3-9-0** WJO'Connor(3) (a.p: led 2f out: readily)	—	**1**	16/1	71+	26
958^{13}	**Golden Fact (USA) (75)** (RHannon) **3-9-3** RPerham(7) (chsd ldrs: rdn 2f out: ev ch appr fnl f: one pce)	1½	**2**	12/1	71	26
1088*	**Praeditus (77)** (RHannon) **3-9-5** DaneO'Neill(2) (a.p: led over 2f out: sn hdd: ev ch appr fnl f: one pce)	nk	**3**	4/1 ^{1}	72	27
1012^{5}	**Dandy Regent (67)** (CACyzer) **3-8-9** OUrbina(4) (chsd ldrs: rdn 2f out: one pce)	3	**4**	25/1	55	10
675^{10}	**Al Masroor (USA) (75)** (JWPayne) **3-9-3** AMcGlone(14) (hld up: hdwy ½-wy: rdn over 2f out: one pce)	2½	**5**	6/1 ^{3}	57	12
649^{10}	**Eager To Please (65)** (MissGayKelleway) **3-8-7b** DHolland(1) (led: hdd over 2f out: wknd over 1f out)	1½	**6**	16/1	44	—
988^{7}	**Simple Logic (75)** (AGFoster) **3-9-3** TSprake(8) (chsd ldrs tl wknd 2f out)	3	**7**	10/1	47	2
575^{7}	**Globetrotter (IRE) (71)** (MJohnston) **3-8-13** LDettori(13) (nvr nrr)	¾	**8**	11/2 ^{2}	41	—
1012^{11}	**Joli's Prince (56)** (CMurray) **3-7-12** NicolaHowarth(5) (racd wd: mid div: rdn ½-wy: sn btn)	1½	**9**	33/1	23	—
693^{6}	**Blood Orange (67)** (GGMargarson) **3-8-9** NDay(6) (mid div tl wknd 2f out)	1½	**10**	14/1	31	—
840^{19}	**Canton Ron (62)** (CADwyer) **3-8-4** DRMcCabe(9) (bhd fnl 3f)	½	**11**	33/1	24	—
*868**	**Keen Alert (75)** (MBell) **3-9-3** MFenton(12) (bhd fnl 3f)	nk	**12**	9/1	37	—
930^{6}	**Summer Queen (79)** (SPCWoods) **3-9-0**(7) CWebb(15) (hld up in rr: hmpd over 3f out: sn rdn & btn)	1½	**13**	11/2 ^{2}	37	—
	Mirror Four Life (IRE) (73) (MHTompkins) **3-9-1** DBiggs(10) (a bhd: t.o)	28	**14**	33/1	—	—
420^{7}	**Cold Steel (75)** (WJarvis) **3-9-3** SSanders(11) (a bhd: t.o)	4	**15**	12/1	—	—
				(SP 130.6%)	**15 Rn**	

1m 23.87 (2.67) CSF £185.95 CT £850.24 TOTE £37.80: £6.40 £5.60 £2.00 (£211.80) Trio £309.00 OWNER Grant & Bowman Ltd (ASTON UPTHORPE) BRED J. R. C. and Mrs Wren

Gee Bee Dream was never far away, and won this more comfortably than the margin suggests. She can defy a penalty. (16/1)
Golden Fact (USA) ran his best race for some time and, after having every chance entering the final furlong, could not match the winner's turn of foot. (12/1: op 7/1)
1088* Praeditus ran another good race. Never far away, he could not find a burst of speed in the final furlong. (4/1)
1012 Dandy Regent was not knocked about in the closing stages, and could be one to keep an eye on. (25/1)
Al Masroor (USA) caught the eye, staying on late on, and will be an interesting proposition over another furlong. (6/1: op 12/1)
489* Eager To Please showed the way, but was done with below the distance. (16/1)
Simple Logic (10/1: 8/1-12/1)
868* Keen Alert (9/1: 6/1-10/1)
930 Summer Queen, although hampered shortly after halfway, never looked like taking a hand anyway. (11/2: 4/1-13/2)
50* Cold Steel (12/1: op 8/1)

T/Plpt: £173.10 (77.95 Tckts). T/Qdpt: £71.60 (11.98 Tckts) SM

1207-NEWBURY (L-H) (Soft)
Saturday May 17th
WEATHER: Humid WIND: alm nil

1239 BARBARA E. MAIDEN STKS (3-Y.O) (Class D)
2-00 (2-01) **1m 2f 6y** £3,860.00 (£1,160.00: £560.00: £260.00) Stalls: High GOING: 0.36 sec per fur (GS)

	Horse		Pos	SP	RR	SF
676[4]	**Garuda (IRE)** (JLDunlop) **3-9-0** JReid(2) (lw: a.p: led over 3f out tl over 2f out: hrd rdn & led ins fnl f: r.o wl)	—	1	2/1 [1]	90	47
	Scattergun (JHMGosden) **3-9-0** LDettori(9) (str: scope: stdy hdwy over 3f out: led over 2f out tl ins fnl f: r.o)	¾	2	7/2 [2]	89	46
	Life of Riley (GLewis) **3-9-0** PaulEddery(3) (str: scope: s.s: rdn & hdwy 3f out: r.o one pce)	12	3	33/1	70	27
676[14]	**Final Stage (IRE)** (PWChapple-Hyam) **3-9-0** SWhitworth(1) (s.s: hrd rdn over 3f out: hdwy over 2f out: r.o one pce)	3	4	33/1	65	22
725[17]	**Rear Window** (LordHuntingdon) **3-9-0** KFallon(7) (rdn over 4f out: hdwy 3f out: wknd 2f out)	11	5	50/1	47	4
	Dina Line (USA) (MBell) **3-8-9** MFenton(4) (w'like: scope: bit bkwd: hdwy on ins over 3f out: wknd over 2f out)	10	6	40/1	26	—
963[10]	**Coble** (BWHills) **3-9-0** DHolland(5) (hdwy 8f out: wknd over 2f out)	¾	7	12/1	30	—
	Wathbat Nashwan (LMCumani) **3-9-0** OUrbina(8) (bit bkwd: prom over 7f)	2½	8	33/1	26	—
742[3]	**Mystic Ridge** (DRCElsworth) **3-9-0** RCochrane(12) (prom over 4f)	2	9	6/1 [3]	23	—
967[5]	**Lahab Nashwan** (MRChannon) **3-9-0** RHughes(13) (lw: a bhd)	1	10	33/1	21	—
	Badge of Fame (IRE) (LMCumani) **3-9-0** PatEddery(6) (w'like: scope: bit bkwd: s.s: a bhd)	s.h	11	8/1	21	—
	Supremism (CEBrittain) **3-9-0** BDoyle(15) (prom over 5f)	3½	12	16/1	16	—
967[7]	**Mighty Flow** (MrsPNDutfield) **3-8-9** AProcter(10) (swtg: led over 6f)	13	13	50/1	—	—
599[4]	**Fooled You (USA)** (EALDunlop) **3-8-11**(3) DO'Donohoe(11) (lw: bhd fnl 4f)	3	14	10/1	—	—
	Pleasure Boat (NAGraham) **3-9-0** DHarrison(16) (w'like: prom over 6f)	8	15	40/1	—	—

(SP 124.2%) **15 Rn**

2m 13.96 (9.96) CSF £7.32 TOTE £3.50: £1.70 £1.80 £3.60 (£6.60) Trio £73.50 OWNER Mr Bob Demuyser (ARUNDEL) BRED Grangemore Stud
676 Garuda (IRE) settled much better on this occasion and, together with the runner-up, pulled well clear of the rest of the field in the last three furlongs. After a tremendous scrap, he just managed to win the battle inside the final furlong. (2/1)
Scattergun, a deep-girthed individual with plenty of strength about him, showed much promise on this racecourse debut. He gave his all, and although just losing out, finished well clear of the remainder. He should have little problem opening his account. (7/2)
Life of Riley, a tall, well-made colt, struggled on in the last three furlongs. (33/1)
Final Stage (IRE), a half-brother to Chester Vase winner High Baroque, was under pressure at the back of the field over three furlongs from home, but struggled on to finish a moderate fourth. (33/1)
683 Coble (12/1: 16/1-25/1)
742 Mystic Ridge (6/1: op 7/2)
Badge of Fame (IRE) (8/1: 3/1-10/1)
599 Fooled You (USA) (10/1: op 6/1)

86+ 79 81 77 (81)

1240 KINGWOOD STUD MAIDEN STKS (2-Y.O F) (Class D)
2-30 (2-31) **6f 8y** £3,808.00 (£1,144.00: £552.00: £256.00) Stalls: High GOING: 0.36 sec per fur (GS)

	Horse		Pos	SP	RR	SF
	Dance Trick (USA) (PWChapple-Hyam) **2-8-11** JReid(12) (leggy: unf: lw: a.p: led over 2f out tl over 1f out: rallied nr fin: led last stride)	—	1	5/4 [1]	93	40
	Ajig Dancer (MRChannon) **2-8-11** RPerham(13) (leggy: unf: hld up: led over 1f out: hrd rdn ins fnl f: hdd last stride)	s.h	2	16/1	93	40
	Tadwiga (RHannon) **2-8-11** DaneO'Neill(14) (neat: rdn over 3f out: hdwy over 1f out: r.o wl ins fnl f)	1	3	11/1	90	37
	Lady In Waiting (PFICole) **2-8-11** TQuinn(6) (w'like: w ldr: led 3f out tl over 2f out: unable qckn)	1½	4	11/2 [2]	86	33
739[6]	**Face-Off** (RHannon) **2-8-11** PatEddery(4) (led 3f: wknd wl over 1f out)	9	5	9/1 [3]	62	9
965[5]	**Princess Londis** (AGFoster) **2-8-11** DHolland(2) (hld up: rdn over 2f out: sn wknd)	hd	6	14/1	62	9
722[7]	**Distinctly Lillie (IRE)** (JSMoore) **2-8-11** WJO'Connor(3) (s.s: nvr nrr)	1½	7	50/1	58	5
	Gipsy Moth (BJMeehan) **2-8-11** OPeslier(10) (w'like: bit bkwd: s.s: hld up: rdn over 2f out: wknd wl over 1f out)	1¾	8	11/1	54	1
	Respond (GLMoore) **2-8-11** CandyMorris(11) (leggy: prom over 2f)	1	9	50/1	51	—
	Primavera (MJHaynes) **2-8-11** RCochrane(7) (unf: bit bkwd: bhd fnl 3f)	8	10	40/1	30	—
	Miss Muffett (IRE) (PMooney) **2-8-11** DeclanO'Shea(5) (unf: s.s: a wl bhd)	nk	11	50/1	29	—
	No Shame (JGSmyth-Osbourne) **2-8-11** DHarrison(8) (str: bkwd: bhd fnl 3f)	10	12	50/1	2	—
739[9]	**Burning Love** (JSMoore) **2-8-11** LDettori(1) (bhd fnl 2f)	½	13	16/1	1	—
	Miss Chief Maker (WRMuir) **2-8-11** KFallon(9) (cmpt: bkwd: bhd fnl 3f)	12	14	25/1	—	—

(SP 119.1%) **14 Rn**

1m 17.93 (6.13) CSF £20.66 TOTE £2.00: £1.30 £5.00 £3.30 (£20.50) Trio £58.10 OWNER Mr R. E. Sangster (MARLBOROUGH) BRED Swettenham Stud
Dance Trick (USA), a speedy sort who is well regarded at home, comes from a stable with a thirty-eight per cent strike rate with its juveniles here over the last five years. The signs did not look good as she was headed below the distance, but Reid conjured up another run out of her in the

closing stages, and the combination lunged to the front right on the line. (5/4)
Ajig Dancer, a tall filly, needs time to strengthen, but made a fine start to her racing career. Cruising into the lead over a furlong out, she appeared to have the race in the bag, but was caught right on the line. She should soon gain compensation. (16/1)
Tadwiga is not that big, but she was well drawn and showed plenty of promise, running on really nicely for third prize. She should soon find a race. (11/1: 6/1-12/1)
Lady In Waiting, a medium-sized filly, came down the centre of the track where the ground was undoubtedly slower. (11/2: 3/1-6/1)
739 Face-Off was racing down the unfavoured centre of the course, but still took the field along to halfway. (9/1: 6/1-10/1)
965 Princess Londis, the most experienced runner in the field, was beaten some way out. A return to five furlongs may help. (14/1: 10/1-16/1)
Gipsy Moth (11/1: 6/1-12/1)

1241 QUANTEL ASTON PARK STKS (Listed) (4-Y.O+) (Class A)
3-00 (3-00) **1m 5f 61y** £11,990.00 (£3,620.00: £1,760.00: £830.00) Stalls: High GOING: 0.36 sec per fur (GS)

				SP	RR	SF
932[7]	**Persian Punch (IRE) (107)** (DRCElsworth) **4-9-1** RCochrane(6) (mde all: hrd rdn over 2f out: r.o wl)	—	**1**	4/1[2]	122	58
1033[2]	**Further Flight (109)** (BWHills) **11-8-12** MHills(5) (b.hind: rdn over 3f out: hdwy over 1f out: r.o ins fnl f)	3½	**2**	5/1[3]	115	51
1033[4]	**Sweetness Herself (95)** (MJRyan) **4-8-9**ow2 OPeslier(7) (chsd wnr over 4f: chsd wnr over 3f out tl ins fnl f: unable qckn)	1	**3**	8/1	111	45
849*	**Harbour Dues (103)** (LadyHerries) **4-8-12** PatEddery(4) (lw: chsd wnr 9f out tl over 3f out: rdn over 2f out: one pce)	2	**4**	4/1[2]	111	47
852[5]	**Bequeath (112)** (HRACecil) **5-9-1** KFallon(1) (b: lw: rdn over 3f out: nvr nr to chal)	2½	**5**	9/4[1]	111	47
962[2]	**Nabhaan (IRE) (100)** (DMorley) **4-8-12v**[1] RHills(3) (lw: hld up: rdn over 3f out: wknd over 1f out)	6	**6**	5/1[3]	101	37
				(SP 115.2%)	**6 Rn**	

2m 58.07 (11.57) CSF £22.32 TOTE £5.20: £2.30 £2.10 (£10.50) OWNER Mr J. C. Smith (WHITCOMBE) BRED Adstock Manor Stud
932 Persian Punch (IRE) was much happier over this longer trip, and was given a masterly ride by Cochrane, who dictated matters from the front, and he was never going to be caught. (4/1)
1033 Further Flight, despite his advancing years and a very hard race at Chester, still gave a good account of himself. He really needs further, and has not won over a trip as short as this since 1991. (5/1: 3/1-11/2)
1033 Sweetness Herself again had the ground in her favour and, although running better than at Chester, again showed she is not quite up to this class. (8/1)
849* Harbour Dues was taking a step up in class, but travelled well for a long way. (4/1)
852 Bequeath was very disappointing, especially considering the step-up in trip was in his favour. He flashed his tail when asked for an effort, and could never get near the leaders. (9/4)
962 Nabhaan (IRE) is not the easiest of rides, and was tried in a visor for the first time. Unfortunately it did not have the desired effect, as he flashed his tail and wandered before weakening. He has done all his winning on a fast surface. (5/1)

1242 LONDON GOLD CUP RATED STKS H'CAP (0-95) (3-Y.O) (Class C)
3-35 (3-35) **1m 4f 5y** £9,365.60 (£3,490.40: £1,695.20: £716.00: £308.00: £144.80) Stalls: High GOING: 0.36 sec per fur (GS)

				SP	RR	SF
1092[2]	**Cyrian (IRE) (79)** (PFICole) **3-8-7** TQuinn(2) (a.p: led over 3f out: all out)	—	**1**	14/1	91	47
944*	**Winter Garden (93)** (LMCumani) **3-9-7** LDettori(1) (stdy hdwy over 3f out: chsd wnr 2f out: ev ch fnl f: r.o wl)	s.h	**2**	5/2[1]	105	61
967*	**Percy Isle (IRE) (84)** (MRStoute) **3-8-12** JReid(4) (a.p: rdn over 2f out: unable qckn)	12	**3**	9/2[3]	80	36
976*	**Pinchincha (FR) (79)** (DMorris) **3-8-7** NDay(10) (stdy hdwy over 5f out: rdn over 3f out: one pce)	1	**4**	9/1	74	30
725[5]	**Catchable (85)** (HRACecil) **3-8-13** KFallon(8) (lw: a.p: rdn over 4f out: ev ch over 2f out: wknd over 1f out)	10	**5**	9/1	66	22
597[3]	**Iechyd-Da (IRE) (90)** (MBell) **3-9-4** MFenton(3) (lw: nvr nr to chal)	6	**6**	16/1	63	19
1104[4]	**Our People (90)** (MJohnston) **3-9-4** RHills(5) (lw: led 11f out tl over 3f out: wknd over 2f out)	4	**7**	25/1	58	14
967[2]	**Highly Prized (79)** (IABalding) **3-8-7** MHills(6) (led 1f: wknd 4f out)	6	**8**	11/1	39	—
	Bandore (IRE) (87) (DRLoder) **3-9-1** DRMcCabe(9) (lw: s.s: a bhd)	13	**9**	20/1	30	—
773*	**Will You Dance (83)** (JLDunlop) **3-8-11** PatEddery(7) (lw: a bhd)	¾	**10**	4/1[2]	25	—
				(SP 116.2%)	**10 Rn**	

2m 41.04 (11.04) CSF £44.57 CT £172.50 TOTE £17.40: £5.10 £1.50 £1.50 (£30.40) Trio £31.00 OWNER Lord Donoughmore (WHATCOMBE) BRED Cahalane O'Hanlon
LONG HANDICAP Pinchincha (FR) 8-3
1092 Cyrian (IRE) will not forget this race in a hurry. Coming under severe pressure, Quinn used his whip eleven times, and he held on by the skin of his teeth. This was a tremendous ride from Quinn, but he surely transgressed the Rules, although he went unpunished. As for Cyrian, he needs to be given a good break to get over his exertions. (14/1: 10/1-16/1)
944* Winter Garden was given an over-confident ride. Absolutely hacking over the hard-ridden Cyrian below the distance, he may have got his head in front for a few strides inside the final furlong, but the winner was too tenacious. (5/2)
967* Percy Isle (IRE) was never far away, but was left to scrap for minor honours in the final quarter-mile. (9/2)
976* Pinchincha (FR) had far more on his plate this time after two small wins, and could only struggle on in the straight. (9/1)
725 Catchable certainly made Fallon work hard, but this trip may be too far for him. (9/1)
597 Iechyd-Da (IRE) gained both of his wins to date with some cut in the ground, but never threatened to get into it. (16/1)

1243 WINCHESTER H'CAP (0-90) (3-Y.O) (Class C)
4-05 (4-06) **6f 8y** £5,637.50 (£1,700.00: £825.00: £387.50) Stalls: High GOING: 0.36 sec per fur (GS)

				SP	RR	SF
942[4]	**Sharp Hat (85)** (RHannon) **3-9-4** DaneO'Neill(13) (lw: hld up: led over 1f out: drvn out)	—	**1**	4/1[1]	96	45
	Alumisiyah (USA) (85) (RWArmstrong) **3-9-4** RHills(12) (lw: led over 4f: unable qckn)	3	**2**	10/1[3]	88	37
970*	**Mara River (82)** (IABalding) **3-9-1** LDettori(10) (rdn over 2f out: hdwy over 1f out: r.o)	1½	**3**	4/1[1]	81	30
1090[8]	**Always Alight (65)** (KRBurke) **3-7-12** DeclanO'Shea(8) (lw: rdn over 3f out: hdwy over 1f out: one pce)	4	**4**	12/1	54	3
1029[4]	**Song Mist (IRE) (74)** (PFICole) **3-8-7** TQuinn(2) (hld up: rdn over 2f out: wknd fnl f)	4	**5**	10/1[3]	52	1
1029[3]	**Samsung Spirit (78)** (EWeymes) **3-8-11** JQuinn(5) (swtg: hld up: rdn over 3f out: wknd wl over 1f out)	½	**6**	11/2[2]	55	4
871[3]	**Swift (63)** (MJPolglase) **3-7-10** NVarley(7) (lw: s.s: rdn & hdwy over 3f out: wknd wl over 1f out)	1	**7**	33/1	37	—
723[13]	**Braveheart (IRE) (85)** (MRChannon) **3-8-11**(7) AEddery(11) (swtg: bhd fnl 2f)	2½	**8**	20/1	52	1
	Restless Spirit (USA) (88) (MJohnston) **3-9-7** MHills(3) (lw: spd over 4f)	4	**9**	12/1	45	—
	Nor-Do-I (86) (JMPEustace) **3-9-2b**(3) MartinDwyer(9) (spd over 3f)	2½	**10**	16/1	36	—
	Unshaken (88) (JRFanshawe) **3-9-7** PatEddery(1) (s.s: a bhd)	2½	**11**	14/1	31	—
953[8]	**Biff-Em (IRE) (76)** (MissLAPerratt) **3-8-9** OUrbina(4) (spd over 3f)	1¼	**12**	16/1	16	—

				SP	RR	SF
988[10]	**Sweet Bettsie (63)** (AGFoster) **3-7-5**(5) RFfrench(6) (swtg: bhd fnl 4f)	14	**13**	16/1	—	—

(SP 121.0%) **13 Rn**

1m 18.04 (6.24) CSF £41.02 CT £141.94 TOTE £4.10: £2.20 £3.30 £1.50 (£18.50) Trio £27.90 OWNER Mr J. C. Smith (MARLBOROUGH) BRED Littleton Stud

LONG HANDICAP Swift 7-6 Sweet Bettsie 7-8

942 Sharp Hat confirmed the promise shown at Newmarket two weeks ago, and coped well with the soft ground. (4/1: 3/1-9/2)
Alumisiyah (USA), who wintered in Dubai, took the field along but, collared by the winner over a furlong out, failed to find another gear. (10/1)
970* Mara River found her feet below the distance, and ran on nicely for third prize. An extra furlong may well be in her favour. (4/1)
1090 Always Alight, rousted along before halfway, picked up ground below the distance, but could make no further impression. (12/1)
1029 Song Mist (IRE) did not have the ground in her favour and, after chasing the leaders, tired inside the distance. (10/1: 7/1-11/1)
1029 Samsung Spirit goes well in the ground, but had been hung out to dry early in the final quarter-mile. (11/2)
Restless Spirit (USA) (12/1: 7/1-14/1)
Unshaken (14/1: op 8/1)

1244 MAY H'CAP (0-80) (3-Y.O+) (Class D)

4-35 (4-39) **1m 2f 6y** £4,146.00 (£1,248.00: £604.00: £282.00) Stalls: High GOING: 0.36 sec per fur (GS)

				SP	RR	SF
1117[2]	**Premier Generation (IRE) (63)** (DWPArbuthnot) **4-8-13** SWhitworth(21) (s.s: stdy hdwy on ins 3f out: led over 1f out: hrd rdn: r.o wl)	—	**1**	7/1[2]	76	35
380[7]	**Bakers Daughter (53)** (JRArnold) **5-8-0**(3) MartinDwyer(4) (swtg: led over 8f: unable qckn)	3	**2**	25/1	61	20
	Princess Danielle (59) (WRMuir) **5-8-9** JReid(20) (hdwy over 2f out: r.o one pce)	2½	**3**	14/1	63	22
887[2]	**Peppers (IRE) (67)** (KRBurke) **4-9-3** KFallon(11) (rdn & hdwy 3f out: one pce fnl 2f)	1¾	**4**	8/1[3]	68	27
933[5]	**Bay of Islands (75)** (DMorris) **5-9-11** NDay(22) (lw: a.p: rdn over 2f out: wknd over 1f out)	2½	**5**	8/1[3]	72	31
	Ballyranter (57) (HJCollingridge) **8-8-7** JQuinn(1) (b: stdy hdwy 3f out: wknd over 1f out)	¾	**6**	33/1	53	12
1111[7]	**Therhea (IRE) (66)** (BRMillman) **4-9-2** BDoyle(16) (lw: prom over 8f)	7	**7**	20/1	51	10
735[8]	**Shining Example (68)** (PJMakin) **5-9-4** DHolland(9) (lw: hdwy over 2f out: wknd over 1f out)	hd	**8**	10/1	53	12
	Koraloona (IRE) (47) (GBBalding) **4-7-11** NVarley(10) (nvr nrr)	hd	**9**	50/1	32	—
1016[10]	**Statajack (IRE) (78)** (DRCElsworth) **9-10-0b** TQuinn(15) (b: hdwy on ins over 2f out: wknd over 1f out)	1¼	**10**	16/1	61	20
933[3]	**Fern's Governor (58)** (WJMusson) **5-8-8** LDettori(12) (a mid div)	hd	**11**	3/1[1]	41	—
544[W]	**Formidable Flame (55)** (WJMusson) **4-8-5** OUrbina(5) (lw: nvr nrr)	¾	**12**	25/1	36	—
	Spring Campaign (IRE) (55) (MCPipe) **4-8-5** DaneO'Neill(6) (lw: prom 8f)	hd	**13**	20/1	36	—
1082[9]	**Oberons Boy (IRE) (59)** (SDow) **4-8-9** RPerham(18) (nvr nrr)	½	**14**	33/1	39	—
	Infatuation (75) (LadyHerries) **4-9-11** PaulEddery(3) (swtg: prom over 5f)	15	**15**	16/1	32	—
763[11]	**Fourdaned (IRE) (60)** (PWHarris) **4-8-10b**[1] DRMcCabe(13) (prom over 3f)	4	**16**	33/1	10	—
895[28]	**Kriscliffe (70)** (GLewis) **4-9-3**(3) AWhelan(2) (prom over 4f)	8	**17**	50/1	7	—
1001[5]	**Pay Homage (66)** (IABalding) **9-8-9**(7) JaneLind(17) (hdwy over 5f out: wknd over 3f out)	½	**18**	33/1	3	—
	Deevee (51) (CJBenstead) **8-8-1** JLowe(8) (a bhd)	11	**19**	25/1	—	—
986[8]	**Grand Splendour (72)** (LadyHerries) **4-9-8** DeclanO'Shea(7) (prom over 6f)	2½	**20**	16/1	—	—
14[8]	**Ruby Angel (52)** (MissBSanders) **4-7-13**(3)ow2 DO'Donohoe(14) (a bhd: t.o)	dist	**21**	50/1	—	—
866[7]	**Danegold (IRE) (70)** (MRChannon) **5-9-6v** RHughes(19) (swtg: a bhd: t.o)	15	**22**	16/1	—	—

(SP 137.7%) **22 Rn**

2m 15.35 (11.35) CSF £170.42 CT £2,228.83 TOTE £6.20: £1.70 £7.20 £3.40 £1.80 (£237.70) Trio £706.50 OWNER Mrs W. A. Oram (COMPTON) BRED The Mount Coote Partnership

1117 Premier Generation (IRE) goes well in these conditions, and was given a confident ride by Whitworth, who was quite content to bide his time at the back of the field. Steadily creeping closer in the straight, the combination struck the front below the distance, and ran on strongly. (7/1)
340 Bakers Daughter attempted to make all the running but, collared below the distance, failed to match the winner. (25/1)
Princess Danielle, making her seasonal debut, stayed on, without finding that vital turn of foot. (14/1)
887 Peppers (IRE), who has shown promise on both her previous outings this season, but could not quicken in the straight. She remains a maiden. (8/1)
933 Bay of Islands played an active role until coming to the end of his tether over a furlong out. (8/1)
Ballyranter, fit from an unsuccessful spell over hurdles with Micky Hammond, had not raced on the Flat for over two years. He looked dangerous until fading below the distance. (33/1)
Shining Example (10/1: 8/1-12/1)

1245 HEADLEY H'CAP (0-80) (3-Y.O F) (Class D)

5-05 (5-08) **7f 64y (round)** £3,886.00 (£1,168.00: £564.00: £262.00) Stalls: High GOING: 0.36 sec per fur (GS)

				SP	RR	SF
675[4]	**Sleepless (78)** (NAGraham) **3-9-7** DHolland(6) (hld up: chsd ldr over 2f out: led over 1f out: hrd rdn: r.o wl)	—	**1**	6/1[2]	96	48
1131[4]	**Trading Aces (71)** (MBell) **3-9-0v** MFenton(7) (hdwy over 2f out: chsd wnr over 1f out: r.o)	1¼	**2**	13/2[3]	86	38
886[7]	**Calamander (IRE) (62)** (WRMuir) **3-8-5** DHarrison(10) (lw: stdy hdwy over 3f out: rdn over 2f out: unable qckn)	8	**3**	14/1	60	12
904[2]	**Shalstayholy (IRE) (64)** (GLMoore) **3-8-7** SWhitworth(8) (hdwy over 2f out: one pce)	2	**4**	11/2[1]	57	9
765[4]	**Falls O'Moness (IRE) (68)** (KRBurke) **3-8-11** DRMcCabe(2) (led 6f out tl over 1f out: sn wknd)	hd	**5**	16/1	61	13
841[12]	**London's Heart (USA) (60)** (PFICole) **3-7-10**(7) JBosley(4) (rdn thrght: nvr nr to chal)	3	**6**	14/1	47	—
723[7]	**Sound Appeal (67)** (AGFoster) **3-8-10b** RPerham(11) (lost pl over 5f out: r.o one pce fnl 2f)	3	**7**	12/1	47	—
945[2]	**Tabasco Jazz (70)** (BJMeehan) **3-8-13** OPeslier(15) (b.nr hind: a.p: c centre st: wknd 3f out)	2½	**8**	11/2[1]	44	—
791[9]	**Rumbustious (64)** (RHannon) **3-8-7** KFallon(12) (sme hdwy whn nt clr run over 2f out: nt rcvr)	3	**9**	14/1	32	—
649[16]	**Keen Waters (54)** (JRArnold) **3-7-11** JLowe(5) (prom over 5f)	1	**10**	33/1	20	—
1000[9]	**Lamorna (60)** (MRChannon) **3-8-3** CandyMorris(14) (stdy hdwy 3f out: wknd over 2f out)	1	**11**	14/1	24	—
778[3]	**Tajrebah (USA) (73)** (PTWalwyn) **3-9-2** RHills(1) (lw: prom 5f)	1¾	**12**	8/1	33	—
840[6]	**Inclination (72)** (MBlanshard) **3-9-1** JQuinn(9) (swtg: bhd fnl 3f)	22	**13**	10/1	—	—
	Impy Fox (IRE) (55) (PMooney) **3-7-12** DeclanO'Shea(3) (led over 1f: wknd over 2f out)	2½	**14**	25/1	—	—

(SP 125.6%) **14 Rn**

1m 35.72 (7.62) CSF £42.68 CT £494.26 TOTE £6.00: £2.80 £2.50 £6.10 (£21.90) Trio £178.20 OWNER Mrs Audrey Scotney (NEWMARKET) BRED Biddestone Stud

675 Sleepless gained control over a furlong out, and ran on strongly to give her trainer his first winner for over nine months. (6/1)
1131 Trading Aces came through to take second place below the distance, but despite pulling well clear of the remainder, failed to peg back the winner. (13/2)
886 Calamander (IRE) steadily crept closer in the straight, but was left for dead in the final quarter-mile. (14/1)

904 Shalstayholy (IRE) was made to look woefully one-paced. (11/2)
765 Falls O'Moness (IRE) is extremely exposed and, after cutting out the running, had nothing more to offer when collared below the distance. (16/1)
559 London's Heart (USA) failed to cope with the drop in distance, and was being bustled along virtually throughout. (14/1)

T/Jkpt: £22,.588.10 (0.28 Tckts); £22,906.31 to Newbury 18/5/97. T/Plpt: £49.90 (591.03 Tckts). T/Qdpt: £15.40 (77.4 Tckts) AK

1089-NOTTINGHAM (L-H) (Good, Good to soft patches)
Saturday May 17th
WEATHER: cloudy WIND: nil

1246 'CUP FINAL' (S) STKS (I) (3-Y.O+) (Class G)
2-25 (2-27) **1m 1f 213y** £1,634.50 (£447.00: £209.50) Stalls: Low GOING minus 0.04 sec per fur (G)

				SP	RR	SF
	Esperto (44) (JPearce) **4-9-7** GBardwell(7) (hld up & plld hrd: gd hdwy over 3f out: hrd rdn over 2f out: edgd lft: led over 1f out: r.o)	—	**1**	$9/2^{3}$	59	29
843^{2}	**Action Jackson (50)** (BJMcMath) **5-9-7** GDuffield(3) (led: qcknd clr over 3f out: rdn 2f out: hdd over 1f out: nt qckn ins fnl f)	1¼	**2**	$7/4^{1}$	57	27
1095^{5}	**Rochea (55)** (MrsNMacauley) **3-8-2** SSanders(5) (lw: hld up: hdwy over 3f out: edgd lft 2f out: r.o one pce)	3½	**3**	11/2	46	2
511^{6}	**Persian Sunset (IRE) (47)** (MissJBower) **5-9-2** LNewton(9) (lw: prom: rdn over 3f out: r.o one pce fnl 2f)	nk	**4**	40/1	46	16
1121^{7}	**Gilding The Lily (IRE) (63)** (MJohnston) **3-8-2** MRoberts(2) (no hdwy fnl 3f)	7	**5**	$7/2^{2}$	35	—
235^{13}	**Alpheton Prince (35)** (JohnHarris) **4-9-2**(5) RMullen(10) (lw: prom over 6f)	3½	**6**	50/1	34	4
	Tocco Jewel (20) (MJRyan) **7-8-13**(3) MBaird(4) (bkwd: a bhd)	1¼	**7**	33/1	27	—
896^{17}	**Cinnamon Stick (IRE) (27)** (PSFelgate) **4-9-7** DWright(8) (chsd ldr: rdn over 4f out: wknd over 2f out)	¾	**8**	25/1	31	1
	Timely Example (USA) (42) (BRCambidge) **6-9-7** NAdams(6) (s.i.s: a bhd: t.o fnl 4f)	11	**9**	50/1	13	—
	Apartments Abroad (38) (KMcAuliffe) **4-8-9b**(7) TField(1) (prom 7f: t.o)	5	**10**	12/1	—	—
				(SP 113.0%)	**10 Rn**	

2m 11.5 (9.00) CSF £10.80 TOTE £7.90: £1.90 £1.10 £1.20 (£6.90) OWNER Mrs Anne Holman-Chappell (NEWMARKET) BRED Roldvale Ltd
WEIGHT FOR AGE 3yo-14lb
No bid
Esperto, appreciating the cut in the ground, had been off with leg trouble since winning a selling handicap over course and distance over a year ago. (9/2)
843 Action Jackson tried to slip his field inside the half-mile marker, but the winner soon had him in his sights. (7/4)
1095 Rochea settled better this time, but did not help her rider by drifting into the fourth in the final quarter-mile. (11/2)
Gilding The Lily (IRE) was down in class and up in distance, and it is difficult to see where this daughter of a runner-up in the Irish 1,000 Guineas goes from here. (7/2: 7/4-4/1)

1247 'CUP FINAL' (S) STKS (II) (3-Y.O+) (Class G)
2-55 (2-56) **1m 1f 213y** £1,634.50 (£447.00: £209.50) Stalls: Low GOING minus 0.04 sec per fur (G)

				SP	RR	SF
1093^{2}	**Elly Fleetfoot (IRE) (53)** (GLMoore) **5-9-2v** GDuffield(6) (hld up & plld hrd: stdy hdwy on bit over 3f out: led over 1f out: r.o wl)	—	**1**	$10/11^{1}$	57+	11
	Shabanaz (55) (WRMuir) **12-9-7** CRutter(1) (lw: hld up & bhd: stdy hdwy over 3f out: r.o one pce fnl 2f)	2½	**2**	$4/1^{2}$	58	12
457^{10}	**River Run (IRE) (42)** (RHollinshead) **5-9-4**(3) FLynch(2) (hld up: hdwy on ins to ld wl over 1f out: sn hdd: one pce)	2½	**3**	11/1	54	8
1011^{8}	**Noble Hero (53)** (JJSheehan) **3-8-4**(3) MHenry(8) (lw: a.p: one pce fnl 2f)	3½	**4**	$7/1^{3}$	48	—
1106^{10}	**Oh So Misty** (SDow) **4-8-11**(5) ADaly(10) (lw: hld up & bhd: nvr trbld ldrs)	9	**5**	16/1	29	—
1132^{6}	**Gunner B Special (33)** (SRBowring) **4-9-7** SWebster(9) (b: prom over 7f)	4	**6**	12/1	28	—
896^{15}	**Auchinleck Judge (20)** (JLHarris) **4-9-7** MRoberts(5) (swtg: led over 8f: wknd qckly)	3	**7**	33/1	23	—
1044^{10}	**Owdy** (MrsNMacauley) **3-8-7v¹** SSanders(3) (chsd ldrs: rdn & ev ch over 2f out: sn wknd)	s.h	**8**	20/1	23	—
997^{10}	**Dispol Prince** (GROldroyd) **4-9-7** JTate(4) (b.hind: prom tl lost pl on ins & hmpd bnd over 5f out: t.o fnl 4f)	dist	**9**	40/1	—	—
	T'Niel (GFierro) **6-9-2** MWigham(7) (ref to r: t.n.p.)		**R**	50/1	—	—
				(SP 118.9%)	**10 Rn**	

2m 13.2 (10.70) CSF £4.07 TOTE £1.80: £1.10 £1.50 £2.20 (£2.40) Trio £13.30 OWNER Mr A. S. Reid (BRIGHTON) BRED B. Barnes, Dr S. Barnes, Brick Kiln Stud & V. D'Ha
WEIGHT FOR AGE 3yo-14lb
Bt in 6,600 gns
1093 Elly Fleetfoot (IRE) was considered to have hit the front too soon last time, and Duffield took a pull going to the two furlong pole. (10/11: op 13/8)
Shabanaz would have been a little better off with the winner had this been a handicap, and confirmed he is no back number in this grade. (4/1: op 2/1)
River Run (IRE) the winner of two handicaps at Clonmel a year ago, had previously disappointed in five runs on the sand since coming across the Irish Sea. (11/1: 7/1-14/1)
366 Noble Hero at least fared better than last time. (7/1: 5/1-8/1)
Gunner B Special (12/1: op 6/1)

1248 'WATCH FOOTBALL HERE' LIMITED STKS (0-65) (3-Y.O+) (Class F)
3-25 (3-28) **1m 54y** £2,277.00 (£627.00: £297.00) Stalls: Low GOING minus 0.04 sec per fur (G)

				SP	RR	SF
886^{10}	**Viva Verdi (IRE) (65)** (JLDunlop) **3-8-5** TSprake(12) (hld up: hdwy over 3f out: rdn to ld over 1f out: r.o wl)	—	**1**	$11/2^{2}$	69	39
	Baba Au Rhum (IRE) (60) (IPWilliams) **5-9-6** SSanders(8) (hdwy 3f out: rdn & ev ch over 1f out: one pce)	1¾	**2**	12/1	69	51
1123^{7}	**Pekay (65)** (MJohnston) **4-9-6** MRoberts(11) (swtg: plld hrd: a.p: c centre st: r.o wl ins fnl f)	¾	**3**	14/1	67	49
1096^{3}	**Mardrew (61)** (TTClement) **3-8-6**(5) ADaly(10) (hdwy over 2f out: r.o one pce fnl f)	½	**4**	$8/1^{3}$	69	39
947^{11}	**Godmersham Park (63)** (PSFelgate) **5-9-6** GDuffield(17) (lw: led over 6f out tl over 1f out: wknd fnl f)	hd	**5**	12/1	66	48
1020^{9}	**Legal Issue (IRE) (59)** (WWHaigh) **5-9-3**(3) OPears(13) (lw: hdwy fnl 2f: nt rch ldrs)	2½	**6**	12/1	61	43
895^{4}	**Doctor Bravious (IRE) (64)** (MBell) **4-9-1v**(5) RMullen(4) (s.i.s: hdwy 3f out: one pce fnl 2f)	1¼	**7**	$11/2^{2}$	59	41
866^{9}	**Czarna (IRE) (65)** (CEBrittain) **6-9-6** GBardwell(9) (tk keen hold: hdwy over 3f out: wknd over 2f out)	1¾	**8**	10/1	55	37
	Classic Ballet (FR) (61) (ICampbell) **4-9-3** RPrice(7) (bkwd: nvr trbld ldrs)	5	**9**	16/1	43	25

				SP	RR	SF
1020^{3}	**Ochos Rios (IRE) (59)** (BSRothwell) **6-9-3**$^{(3)}$ FLynch(5) (prom tl rdn & wknd 2f out)	3	**10**	9/2^{1}	40	22
866^{11}	**Midday Cowboy (USA) (64)** (MDHammond) **4-9-6** FNorton(16) (a bhd)	1	**11**	33/1	38	20
778^{7}	**Ella Lamees (65)** (WJMusson) **3-8-5** JStack(18) (a bhd)	s.h	**12**	12/1	35	5
544^{5}	**Acerbus Dulcis (25)** (MCChapman) **6-9-1**$^{(5)}$ AmandaSanders(15) (swtg: prom over 7f)	s.h	**13**	50/1	38	20
734^{14}	**Time of Night (USA) (65)** (RGuest) **4-9-0**$^{(3)}$ DGriffiths(6) (swtg: led over 1f: wknd over 2f out)	s.h	**14**	12/1	35	17
181^{10}	**Sherzetto (65)** (RTPhillips) **3-8-5** AMcGlone(2) (swtg: hld up: a bhd)	2½	**15**	16/1	30	—
532^{16}	**Kustom Kit Xpres (57)** (SRBowring) **3-8-5** NAdams(3) (a bhd)	4	**16**	33/1	22	—
	Homestead (62) (RHannon) **3-8-8** JTate(1) (sn prom: wknd over 2f out: t.o)	12	**17**	14/1	2	—
				(SP 140.6%)	**17 Rn**	

1m 46.1 (4.80) CSF £73.05 TOTE £6.60: £2.60 £11.30 £5.20 (£95.30) Trio £209.10; £126.69 to Newbury 18/5/97 OWNER Mrs Sonia Rogers (ARUNDEL) BRED Airlie Stud
WEIGHT FOR AGE 3yo-12lb
886 Viva Verdi (IRE) came on song, having settled better than over course and distance last month. (11/2: 4/1-6/1)
Baba Au Rhum (IRE) was not persevered with over hurdles this winter, having seemingly been considered not to have got the trip. (12/1)
Pekay finished in a style which suggests he needs further, especially considering the way he pulled. (14/1)
1096 Mardrew was 13lb worse off than when finishing ten lengths in front of the winner here last month. (8/1)
900 Godmersham Park appears best on a faster surface. (12/1: 7/1-14/1)
Legal Issue (IRE) has never won beyond seven, but this return to a mile did not look a problem. (12/1)
1020 Ochos Rios (IRE) (9/2: op 7/1)
778 Ella Lamees (12/1: op 8/1)
Time of Night (USA) (12/1: op 8/1)

1249 PRINT 4 H'CAP (0-80) (3-Y.O) (Class D)

3-55 (3-57) **1m 54y** £3,868.55 (£1,156.40: £553.70: £252.35) Stalls: Low GOING minus 0.24 sec per fur (GF)

				SP	RR	SF
*874**	**Island Sanctuary (IRE) (74)** (PJMakin) **3-9-1** SSanders(9) (lw: hld up: hdwy over 3f out: rdn to ld ins fnl f: r.o wl)	—	**1**	3/1^{1}	84	42
958^{4}	**Mantles Prince (78)** (GLewis) **3-9-5b^{1}** GDuffield(7) (lw: led: rdn over 3f out: hdd over 2f out: hrd rdn & ev ch whn n.m.r on ins wl ins fnl f: r.o)	hd	**2**	3/1^{1}	88	46
886*	**Night Chorus (70)** (BSRothwell) **3-8-8**$^{(3)}$ FLynch(8) (a.p: led over 2f out: edgd lft & hdd ins fnl f: r.o)	hd	**3**	5/1^{2}	80	38
764^{6}	**Weet And See (64)** (RHollinshead) **3-8-5** AMcGlone(1) (hdwy 2f out: nvr nr to chal)	3	**4**	9/1	68	26
1115^{2}	**Petite Risk (56)** (KWHogg) **3-7-6**$^{(5)ow1}$ RMullen(6) (hld up: hdwy over 3f out: ev ch over 2f out: wknd over 1f out)	1½	**5**	12/1	57	14
1000^{5}	**Tycoon Girl (IRE) (80)** (BJMeehan) **3-9-0**$^{(7)}$ GHannon(4) (s.s: nvr nrr)	1½	**6**	11/1	78	36
	Java Bay (58) (MBlanshard) **3-7-13** NAdams(5) (lw: bhd fnl 2f)	4	**7**	25/1	48	6
	Heart Full of Soul (77) (PFICole) **3-9-4** CRutter(3) (chsd ldr: ev ch over 2f out: sn wknd)	1½	**8**	7/1^{3}	64	22
991^{7}	**Masterpiece (76)** (RHannon) **3-9-3** JTate(2) (lw: prom over 5f: eased whn btn over 1f out)	dist	**9**	9/1	—	—
				(SP 119.0%)	**9 Rn**	

1m 46.8 (5.50) CSF £10.89 CT £40.02 TOTE £5.10: £1.20 £1.30 £1.90 (£7.30) Trio £13.20 OWNER Dr C. E. Stelling (MARLBOROUGH) BRED The Earl of Harrington
STEWARDS' ENQUIRY Duffield susp. 26-27/5/97 (excessive use of whip).
874* Island Sanctuary (IRE) found Night Chorus leaning on him in the closing stages, and in turn tightened Mantles Prince against the rails. (3/1)
958 Mantles Prince, well backed, was sharpened up by the blinkers. Running out of room towards the finish, it was not the winner's fault and Duffield picked up a two-day ban for using his whip in a way which reflected that the money was down. (3/1)
886* Night Chorus, up 3lb, caused the problems in the final one hundred yards, but still ran a fine race in this hotter contest. (5/1)
513* Weet And See, who appeared not to stay last time, was reverting to a mile and appreciated the cut in the ground. (9/1)
1115 Petite Risk had been put up a stone for her last two efforts. (12/1: op 8/1)
1000 Tycoon Girl (IRE), stepping up to a mile, ambled out of the stalls. (11/1: 8/1-12/1)
Heart Full of Soul (7/1: 5/1-15/2)

1250 HOLSTEN PILS H'CAP (0-70) (3-Y.O+) (Class E)

4-25 (4-27) **5f 13y** £3,252.25 (£973.00: £466.50: £213.25) Stalls: High GOING minus 0.24 sec per fur (GF)

				SP	RR	SF
	Pleasure Time (58) (CSmith) **4-9-3b** GDuffield(7) (bit bkwd: mde all far side: jst hld on)	—	**1**	14/1	69	51
1083^{3}	**Polly Golightly (51)** (MBlanshard) **4-8-10b** MRoberts(9) (racd centre: a.p: r.o wl ins fnl f)	s.h	**2**	7/1^{2}	62	44
949^{10}	**Sotonian (HOL) (44)** (PSFelgate) **4-8-3** DWright(13) (chsd ldrs: outpcd 3f out: rallied over 1f out: r.o wl)	1¼	**3**	16/1	51	33
883^{6}	**Ballard Lady (IRE) (40)** (JSWainwright) **5-7-13b^{1}** CRutter(3) (hrd rdn & hdwy over 1f out: nvr nrr)	¾	**4**	14/1	45	27
541^{6}	**Night Harmony (IRE) (52)** (MissSJWilton) **4-8-8**$^{(3)}$ RHavlin(18) (b: swtg: hdwy fnl f: fin wl)	1	**5**	14/1	53	35
1083*	**Runs in the Family (57)** (GMMcCourt) **5-8-9b**$^{(7)}$ RStudholme(17) (prom over 3f)	½	**6**	2/1^{1}	57	39
1012^{3}	**Ed's Folly (IRE) (52)** (SDow) **4-8-6**$^{(5)}$ ADaly(12) (no hdwy fnl 2f)	1¼	**7**	16/1	48	30
1020^{6}	**Napoleon Star (IRE) (49)** (SRBowring) **6-8-8b** NAdams(10) (s.s: nvr nrr)	nk	**8**	11/1	44	26
879^{11}	**Beau Venture (USA) (69)** (BPalling) **9-10-0** TSprake(1) (prom 3f)	¾	**9**	12/1	62	44
1037^{7}	**Stolen Kiss (IRE) (63)** (MWEasterby) **5-9-5**$^{(3)}$ MHenry(6) (n.d)	hd	**10**	14/1	55	37
1003^{5}	**Barranak (IRE) (54)** (GMMcCourt) **5-8-10**$^{(3)}$ JDSmith(2) (lw: hdwy over 1f out: wknd fnl f)	1¾	**11**	14/1	41	23
1047^{10}	**Klipspinger (48)** (BSRothwell) **4-8-7be** JStack(4) (a bhd)	¾	**12**	20/1	32	14
972^{3}	**General Sir Peter (IRE) (61)** (NACallaghan) **5-9-1**$^{(5)}$ AmandaSanders(11) (swtg: outpcd)	nk	**13**	12/1	44	26
949^{12}	**Here Comes a Star (54)** (JMCarr) **9-8-13** PBloomfield(14) (s.s: a bhd)	3	**14**	10/1^{3}	28	10
972^{6}	**Superfrills (44)** (MissLCSiddall) **4-8-3** AMcGlone(15) (a bhd)	1	**15**	20/1	15	—
758^{6}	**Fit For The Job (IRE) (46)** (TWall) **3-7-11** FNorton(16) (lw: a bhd)	nk	**16**	25/1	16	—
1098^{15}	**Loch-Hurn Lady (63)** (KWHogg) **3-8-11**$^{(3)}$ FLynch(8) (a bhd)	1¼	**17**	16/1	29	3
	Fleeting Footsteps (40) (DShaw) **5-7-8**$^{(5)}$ RMullen(5) (b: bkwd: spd 3f)	¾	**18**	33/1	3	—
				(SP 145.9%)	**18 Rn**	

60.6 secs (1.70) CSF £111.93 CT £1,523.35 TOTE £38.40: £5.40 £1.70 £3.50 £4.00 (£157.60) Trio £501.10; £564.66 to Newbury 18/5/97 OWNER Mr A. E. Needham (WELLINGORE) BRED John David Abell
WEIGHT FOR AGE 3yo-8lb
Pleasure Time, dropped 5lb, has always been a speedy individual, and has obviously benefited from being gelded. (14/1)
1083 Polly Golightly, down a further 2lb, was 13lb better off than when beaten nearly six lengths by Runs In The Family at Lingfield last time. (7/1)
593 Sotonian (HOL) was 4lb higher than when pipped at Warwick in March. (16/1)

883 Ballard Lady (IRE), down 3lb, ran better in the first-time blinkers, but this minimum trip was always likely to be inadequate. (14/1)
541 Night Harmony (IRE) only found top gear when the race was virtually over. (14/1)
1083* Runs in the Family, backed as if defeat was out of the question, could not overcome an 11lb hike in the weights. (2/1: op 7/2)
1003 Barranak (IRE) (14/1: op 8/1)

1251 'ENJOY RACING & FOOTBALL' MEDIAN AUCTION MAIDEN STKS (2-Y.O) (Class E)
4-55 (4-56) **6f 15y** £3,590.25 (£1,077.00: £518.50: £239.25) Stalls: High GOING minus 0.24 sec per fur (GF)

				SP	RR	SF
11207	**Shawdon** (SirMarkPrescott) **2-9-0** GDuffield(11) (w ldr: rdn to ld wl ins fnl f: r.o)	—	1	5/1 3	80	23
	Tamerin Bay (RBoss) **2-9-0** RPrice(14) (w'like: scope: led: rn green over 1f out: hdd wl ins fnl f)	¾	2	14/1	78	21
6954	**Opposition Leader** (BWHills) **2-8-11**(3) JDSmith(7) (lw: a.p: rdn over 2f out: r.o one pce)	3½	3	2/1 1	69	12
11242	**Impulse (IRE)** (APJarvis) **2-9-0** AMcGlone(8) (prom tl wknd over 1f out)	2	4	8/1	64	7
	Catch The Rainbow (JGSmyth-Osbourne) **2-8-6**(3) FLynch(3) (lengthy: unf: outpcd: gd hdwy fnl f: nvr nrr)	½	5	25/1	57	—
9799	**Sealed By Fate (IRE)** (JSWainwright) **2-9-0** MRimmer(13) (no hdwy fnl 2f)	¾	6	33/1	60	3
	Hiding Place (MBell) **2-8-4**(5) RMullen(9) (scope: s.s: nrst fin)	hd	7	7/1	55	—
	Balanita (IRE) (BPalling) **2-9-0** FNorton(5) (neat: plld hrd: prom over 4f: eased whn btn ins fnl f)	s.h	8	14/1	60	3
9854	**Memorial (IRE)** (RHannon) **2-8-11**(3) DGriffiths(2) (prom over 4f: eased whn btn ins fnl f)	3½	9	9/2 2	51	—
	Won't Forget Me (IRE) (MHTompkins) **2-9-0** MRoberts(4) (lengthy: prom 4f: eased whn btn fnl f)	½	10	10/1	49	—
	Filgrave (IRE) (CADwyer) **2-9-0** JStack(6) (leggy: prom 4f)	3	11	14/1	41	—
	Espresso (JWHills) **2-8-11**(3) MHenry(1) (w'like: leggy: wnt lft s: a bhd)	hd	12	12/1	41	—
104512	**Angry Albert** (CSmith) **2-9-0** CRutter(10) (s.s: a bhd)	3½	13	33/1	32	—
				(SP 138.3%)	**13 Rn**	

1m 15.5 (4.00) CSF £76.85 TOTE £6.80: £1.40 £5.40 £1.30 (£69.20) Trio £91.80; £68.57 to Newbury 18/5/97 OWNER Mr Cyril Humphris (NEWMARKET) BRED C. Humphris

1120 Shawdon, out of a half-sister to an Italian Oaks winner, was much better drawn this time. Well-supported in the ring, he took advantage of the runner-up's inexperience. (5/1)
Tamerin Bay, a half-brother to Chilibang Bang and Heathyards Gem, looks a real bargain at 2,800 guineas, because it was only inexperience that prevented him making a winning debut. (14/1)
695 Opposition Leader found the first two pulling the curtain down coming to the distance. (2/1)
1124 Impulse (IRE) found this hotter than his Wolverhampton debut. (8/1: tchd 12/1)
Catch The Rainbow only began to get the message late on, and finished in a style which showed promise for the future. (25/1)
Sealed By Fate (IRE) fared much better than on his debut. (33/1)
Hiding Place, a half-sister to selling winner Amnesty Bay, could never overcome a poor start. (7/1)
Balanita (IRE), a 40,000 guineas half-brother to an Irish twelve-furlong winner, ran much better than his finishing position suggests, and will soon step up on this. (14/1: op 8/1)
985 Memorial (IRE) is another who could have finished a lot closer. (9/2: 3/1-5/1)

1252 'CUP FINAL DAY' H'CAP (0-75) (4-Y.O+) (Class D)
5-25 (5-25) **2m 9y** £3,741.15 (£1,117.20: £534.10: £242.55) Stalls: Low GOING minus 0.04 sec per fur (G)

				SP	RR	SF
11003	**Golden Hadeer (43)** (MJRyan) **6-7-8**(3) MBaird(2) (mde all: clr over 3f out: eased nr fin)	—	1	11/8 1	55+	19
110017	**Arcady (53)** (JLHarris) **4-8-5** GDuffield(3) (chsd wnr: no imp fnl 3f)	3½	2	16/1	62	24
8652	**Aardwolf (54)** (CPEBrooks) **6-8-8** CRutter(6) (a.p: r.o one pce fnl 2f)	¾	3	11/4 2	62	26
8315	**Coleridge (45)** (JJSheehan) **9-7-10b**(3) MHenry(7) (hld up: lost pl 5f out: styd on fnl 2f)	1¼	4	11/1	52	16
11222	**Noufari (FR) (74)** (RHollinshead) **6-9-11**(3) FLynch(1) (hld up: rdn 5f out: no hdwy fnl 3f)	¾	5	15/2	80	44
11008	**Kinoko (48)** (KWHogg) **9-7-11**(5) RMullen(4) (hld up: bhd fnl 5f)	8	6	7/1 3	46	10
2028	**Children's Choice (IRE) (53)** (WJMusson) **6-8-7** JStack(5) (lw: hld up: hdwy 6f out: wknd over 3f out: t.o)	20	7	12/1	31	—
				(SP 114.9%)	**7 Rn**	

3m 35.3 (12.30) CSF £23.56 TOTE £2.40: £1.40 £6.60 (£33.00) OWNER Four Jays Racing Partnership (NEWMARKET) BRED Stetchworth Park Stud Ltd
WEIGHT FOR AGE 4yo-2lb

1100 Golden Hadeer, reverting to front-running tactics, was 27lb lower than for his last run on the sand, despite being raised 5lb. (11/8)
Arcady must have been all at sea on the soft ground, when miles behind the winner at Beverley last time. (16/1)
865 Aardwolf, raised 2lb, did not find this a stiff a test as the Pontefract marathon. (11/4)
831 Coleridge was 4lb lower than at Sandown. (11/1)
1122 Noufari (FR) was trying to concede lumps of weight to the well-handicapped winner. (15/2)

T/Plpt: £106.90 (111.66 Tckts). T/Qdpt: £67.80 (6.68 Tckts) KH

1220-THIRSK (L-H) (Good becoming Soft)
Saturday May 17th
WEATHER: overcast, thunderstorm after 1st race WIND: almost nil

1253 SKIPTON CLAIMING STKS (2-Y.O) (Class F)
2-15 (2-16) **5f** £2,757.50 (£770.00: £372.50) Stalls: High GOING: 0.35 sec per fur (G)

				SP	RR	SF
5948	**Laurel Pleasure** (JBerry) **2-8-4**(5) TEDurcan(11) (mde all: r.o wl fnl f)	—	1	10/1	69	27
9273	**Inchalong** (MBrittain) **2-8-1** GCarter(5) (lw: racd centre: in tch: hdwy ½-wy: styd on wl fnl f)	2½	2	9/1	53	11
10137	**Penniless (IRE)** (NTinkler) **2-8-9** JWeaver(1) (trckd ldrs: effrt over 1f out: kpt on same pce)	1¼	3	2/1 1	57	15
10265	**Newhargen (IRE)** (PDEvans) **2-8-7b1** JFEgan(9) (chsd ldrs: rdn 2f out: one pce)	2½	4	9/2 2	47	5
11266	**Leather And Scrim (IRE)** (DNicholls) **2-7-8**(5) IonaWands(10) (chsd ldrs: rdn and hung lft ½-wy: lost pl over 1f out)	1¾	5	10/1	33	—
780*	**Flash d'Or (IRE)** (MWEasterby) **2-8-4** KDarley(7) (lw: unrully in stalls: chsd ldrs: outpcd fnl 2f)	hd	6	5/1 3	38	—
10196	**Sixth Avenue (IRE)** (RMWhitaker) **2-8-3**ow1 DeanMcKeown(12) (lw: chsd ldrs: rdn 2f out: sn wknd)	1	7	6/1	34	—
	Docklands Dispatch (IRE) (NTinkler) **2-8-11** KimTinkler(6) (s.i.s: bhd tl sme hdwy fnl 2f)	2½	8	25/1	34	—
	Kara-Lovo (JBalding) **2-8-4** NCarlisle(2) (w'like: scope: bkwd: s.s: sn wl bhd: sme late hdwy)	1	9	25/1	24	—
	Gala Miss (PDEvans) **2-8-3v1**ow1 SDrowne(4) (unf: s.i.s: a bhd)	hd	10	20/1	22	—
	Miss Main Street (IRE) (JJQuinn) **2-8-5** DaleGibson(3) (w'like: bit bkwd: sn outpcd & bhd)	nk	11	20/1	23	—

				SP	RR	SF
	Mabli (MWEasterby) **2-8-4** TLucas(8) (leggy: unf: bit bkwd: s.s: a wl bhd: lame)	1½	**12**	25/1	18	—

(SP 131.7%) **12 Rn**

63.2 secs (5.60) CSF £90.39 TOTE £14.10: £3.10 £2.30 £1.40 (£86.50) Trio £96.70 OWNER Laurel (Leisure) Ltd (COCKERHAM) BRED Laurel (Leisure) Ltd

Laurel Pleasure clmd MPBurke £15,000

594 Laurel Pleasure, favourably drawn, stepped up appreciably on her first effort, and had this won coming to the final furlong, to give her apprentice, who has forty winners in his native Ireland to his credit, his first taste of success here. (10/1)

927 Inchalong was meeting Penniless on 8lb better terms for a length-and-a-half beating at Ripon. Racing wide on probably the slower ground, she stuck on strongly in the final furlong, and will be suited by a step-up to six. (9/1)

730* Penniless (IRE), who had an impossible task at Chester last time, still ran below her best here. (2/1)

948 Newhargen (IRE) was fitted with blinkers for the first time, but they had no appreciable effect. (9/2)

1126 Leather And Scrim (IRE), very keen going to post, wanted to do nothing but hang, and this outing probably came too soon after her debut only five days earlier. (10/1)

780* Flash d'Or (IRE), who gave problems in the stalls, needs six at least. (5/1)

1019 Sixth Avenue (IRE) went to post very keenly. (6/1)

Docklands Dispatch (IRE), who showed plenty of knee action, showed a little promise after a sluggish break. (25/1)

1254 BUSINESS FURNITURE CENTRE (HOLDINGS) H'CAP (0-100) (3-Y.O) (Class C)

2-45 (2-48) **5f** £7,200.00 (£2,160.00: £1,040.00: £480.00) Stalls: High GOING: 0.42 sec per fur (GS)

				SP	RR	SF
854[5]	**Treasure Touch (IRE) (85)** (DNicholls) **3-8-4**(5) IonaWands(7) (lw: chsd ldrs: styd on wl to ld last 75y)	—	**1**	15/2	91+	40
1018[6]	**Swino (85)** (PDEvans) **3-8-9** JFEgan(5) (in tch: rdn ½-wy: edgd rt: styd on strly towards fin)	hd	**2**	12/1	91	40
968[4]	**Meliksah (IRE) (93)** (MBell) **3-8-12**(5) GFaulkner(11) (mde most tl hdd & wknd wl ins fnl f)	1	**3**	3/1 [1]	96	45
783[2]	**Ballymote (78)** (JBerry) **3-7-11**(5) PFessey(8) (w ldrs: nt qckn fnl f)	hd	**4**	7/1 [3]	80	29
854[8]	**Myrmidon (95)** (MrsLStubbs) **3-9-5** ACulhane(3) (bmpd s: swtchd rt: bhd tl styd on fnl 2f)	¾	**5**	16/1	95	44
	Polish Warrior (IRE) (86) (TDBarron) **3-8-10** KDarley(10) (sn chsng ldrs: nt qckn appr fnl f)	¾	**6**	5/1 [2]	83	32
1018[5]	**Double Action (88)** (TDEasterby) **3-8-12** MBirch(1) (in tch: racd centre: outpcd fnl 2f)	2	**7**	10/1	79	28
783*	**Brutal Fantasy (IRE) (87)** (JLEyre) **3-8-4**(7) SBuckley(9) (lw: chsd ldrs: hrd rdn & lost pl 2f out)	5	**8**	7/1 [3]	62	11
977[3]	**Two On The Bridge (73)** (DenysSmith) **3-7-11**ow1 TWilliams(2) (racd centre: outpcd fr ½-wy)	1¾	**9**	15/2	42	—
636*	**Prince Dome (IRE) (77)** (MartynWane) **3-8-1** GCarter(6) (sn outpcd & drvn along)	1	**10**	12/1	43	—
1018[13]	**Fredrik The Fierce (IRE) (97)** (JBerry) **3-9-0**(7) CLowther(4) (bmpd s: a wl bhd: hung lft fr ½-wy)	2	**11**	20/1	57	6

(SP 125.3%) **11 Rn**

62.8 secs (5.20) CSF £91.25 CT £311.86 TOTE £7.60: £2.40 £3.70 £1.70 (£80.50) Trio £100.60 OWNER Mr N. Honeyman (THIRSK) BRED St Simon Foundation

854 Treasure Touch (IRE), 22lb higher than when recording his first handicap success, found the drop back to five and the change in the going no problem. Skilfully handled, he did just enough, and deserves a crack at a better prize. (15/2)

1018 Swino, badly drawn at Chester last time, stayed on strongly in the closing stages despite edging right, and almost caught out the winner. (12/1)

968 Meliksah (IRE), who apparently had a wind operation during the winter, had the best of the draw. After showing his usual poor action going down, his stamina seemed to give out in the last one hundred yards. (3/1)

783 Ballymote, 6lb better of with Brutal Fantasy compared with Catterick, ran another sound race. (7/1)

501 Myrmidon, taken to post very early, was hampered at the start. Drawn low, he was switched to race on the favoured stands' side rails, and in the circumstances did as well as could be expected. (16/1)

Polish Warrior (IRE), who has been gelded, was supported to make a winning debut for his new yard, but he ran as if just in need of the outing. (5/1)

783* Brutal Fantasy (IRE), hoisted 9lb in the ratings for his narrow success at Catterick, hardly surprisingly seemed to resent the brutal treatment handed out to him by his apprentice. (7/1)

1255 E.B.F. CARLTON MINIOTT NOVICE STKS (2-Y.O) (Class D)

3-15 (3-16) **5f** £3,600.00 (£1,080.00: £520.00: £240.00) Stalls: High GOING: 0.49 sec per fur (GS)

				SP	RR	SF
	Forest Treasure (IRE) (JBerry) **2-8-7** GCarter(6) (leggy: scope: hmpd s: sn bhd: gd hdwy & swtchd centre ½-wy: r.o wl to ld ins fnl f: sn clr)	—	**1**	13/2	75+	38
684[6]	**Carambo** (JLEyre) **2-8-7** RLappin(3) (chsd ldrs: led over 1f out tl ins fnl f: no ch w wnr)	2½	**2**	12/1	67	30
1076*	**Hirst Bridge (IRE)** (MWEasterby) **2-9-4** TLucas(5) (lw: hmpd s: sn w ldrs: rdn to chal over 1f out: nt qckn)	¾	**3**	7/2 [1]	76	39
985[3]	**Poetto** (BJMeehan) **2-8-12** KDarley(7) (chsd ldrs: sn drvn along: outpcd fnl 2f)	4	**4**	7/2 [1]	57	20
971[3]	**Euro Venture** (DNicholls) **2-8-12** AlexGreaves(2) (lw: sn in tch: effrt 2f out: wknd fnl f)	5	**5**	9/2 [2]	41	4
1013[5]	**Young Ibnr (IRE)** (PDEvans) **2-9-2v**[1] JFEgan(4) (swtchd rt s: led tl hung bdly lft & hdd over 1f out: sn wknd)	1	**6**	8/1	42	5
	Night People (WJarvis) **2-8-12** EmmaO'Gorman(9) (w'like: scope: s.i.s: nvr wnt pce)	¾	**7**	6/1 [3]	35	—
	Cumbrian Cadet (TDEasterby) **2-8-12** MBirch(8) (lengthy: scope: bit bkwd: chsd ldrs: rdn & outpcd 2f out: sn wknd)	1¼	**8**	14/1	31	—
	Scotch Time (RAFahey) **2-8-12** ACulhane(10) (str: cmpt: bit bkwd: sn outpcd & bhd)	3½	**9**	12/1	20	—
948[7]	**Mr Fund Switch** (DNicholls) **2-8-12** KHodgson(1) (s.i.s: a wl bhd)	8	**10**	33/1	—	—

(SP 126.3%) **10 Rn**

63.1 secs (5.50) CSF £80.50 TOTE £11.50: £3.20 £3.00 £1.80 (£53.80) Trio £275.70; £174.79 to Newbury 18/5/97 OWNER Mrs John Magnier (COCKERHAM) BRED M. J. Foley

STEWARDS' ENQUIRY Egan susp. 26-31/5/97 (irresponsible riding).

Forest Treasure (IRE), who cost 64.000 guineas as a yearling, is on the leg at present. She did really well to win this for, after being hampered at the start, she was left to make her effort on probably the slower ground towards the centre. Really taking hold of her bit at halfway, she shot clear inside the last. She will appreciate six furlongs, but connections will be tempted to go for the Queen Mary over the stiff five at Royal Ascot. (13/2)

684 Carambo, a poor mover, appreciated the rain-softened ground. (12/1)

1076* Hirst Bridge (IRE), very keen to post, was hampered by Young Ibnr at the start. After getting almost upsides on the stands' side rail over a furlong out, he was then left for dead by the winner. (7/2: op 8/1)

985 Poetto showed a very choppy action going down, and was left behind in the final quarter-mile. (7/2: 5/2-4/1)

971 Euro Venture, taken very quietly to post, got tired in the ground, and he will be seen to better advantage in nurseries in the second half of the season. (9/2)

1013 Young Ibnr (IRE), in a visor for the first time, was switched right leaving the stalls to secure the favoured stands' side rail, but he did no favours to Hirst Bridge and the winner. Hanging badly left under pressure, his jockey apparently claimed his bit had slipped, but his deliberate manoeuvre at the start was quite rightly punished by the Stewards. (8/1)

1256 ROTHMANS ROYALS NORTH SOUTH CHALLENGE SERIES H'CAP (0-80) (3-Y.O) (Class D)

3-45 (3-46) **1m** £7,512.00 (£2,256.00: £1,088.00: £504.00) Stalls: Low GOING: 0.56 sec per fur (GS)

	Horse / details	Dist	Pos	SP	RR	SF
1128[3]	**Jack Flush (IRE) (59)** (BSRothwell) **3-8-4**[ow1] JFEgan(5) (b.nr fore: chsd ldrs: led over 1f out: hld on towards fin)	—	**1**	9/1[3]	70	40
794[4]	**Boater (71)** (DMorley) **3-9-2** WRyan(4) (lw: mde most tl over 1f out: kpt on wl u.p)	nk	**2**	13/2[2]	82	52
446[7]	**Just Grand (IRE) (76)** (MJohnston) **3-9-7** JWeaver(10) (hld up & bhd: hdwy over 2f out: styd on fnl f)	6	**3**	14/1	75	45
1117[6]	**William Wallace (70)** (DHaydnJones) **3-9-1** SDrowne(7) (lw: s.i.s: hld up & bhd: hdwy over 2f out: nvr nr to chal)	7	**4**	14/1	55	25
840[2]	**Wild Sky (IRE) (76)** (MJHeaton-Ellis) **3-9-7** AClark(15) (lw: in tch: hdwy over 3f out: sn rdn & hung lft: no imp)	2½	**5**	5/2[1]	56	26
1000[12]	**Treasure Hill (IRE) (54)** (DWChapman) **3-7-8**(5) PFessey(2) (bit bkwd: a in tch: styd on: one pce fnl 2f)	s.h	**6**	25/1	34	4
372[6]	**Pet Express (60)** (PCHaslam) **3-8-5** MBirch(13) (mid div: sme hdwy whn n.m.r over 1f out: nvr nr ldrs)	4	**7**	20/1	32	2
1117[8]	**Pension Fund (74)** (MWEasterby) **3-9-5** TLucas(14) (mid div: sn drvn along: kpt on fnl 2f)	2	**8**	16/1	42	12
1096[4]	**Rude Awakening (70)** (CWFairhurst) **3-9-1** DeanMcKeown(12) (lw: in tch: effrt over 2f out: grad wknd)	3	**9**	10/1	32	2
995[6]	**High Spirits (IRE) (58)** (TDEasterby) **3-8-3b**[1] JFanning(9) (chsd ldrs tl wknd over 2f out)	1¾	**10**	12/1	17	—
599[11]	**American Whisper (68)** (PWHarris) **3-8-13** ACulhane(3) (s.i.s: bhd & drvn along)	2½	**11**	14/1	22	—
	Thahabyah (USA) (75) (DMorley) **3-9-6** GCarter(6) (in tch: drvn along over 2f out: no imp: virtually p.u fnl f)	20	**12**	14/1	—	—
998[6]	**Sparky (59)** (MWEasterby) **3-8-4** DaleGibson(1) (a bhd: virtually p.u over 1f out)	14	**13**	12/1	—	—
771[10]	**Chaluz (51)** (KRBurke) **3-7-5**(5) IonaWands(16) (plld hrd: w ldr tl wknd over 2f out)	4	**14**	16/1	—	—
	Ninth Symphony (65) (PCHaslam) **3-8-10** KDarley(8) (bit bkwd: sn bhd & drvn along: virtually p.u 2f out)	dist	**15**	16/1	—	—
958[7]	**Imperial Or Metric (IRE) (67)** (RAFahey) **3-8-12** JCarroll(11) (lw: in tch tl p.u over 3f out: dismntd)		**P**	12/1	—	—
				(SP 137.0%)	**16 Rn**	

1m 45.6 (9.10) CSF £67.95 CT £783.75 TOTE £8.40: £1.90 £1.60 £3.70 £4.20 (£21.10) Trio £234.60 OWNER Mr Derek Smith (MALTON) BRED D. Maher

LONG HANDICAP Chaluz 7-9

OFFICIAL EXPLANATION **Imperial Or Metric (IRE): went lame during the race.**

IN-FOCUS: **Though the official going at this stage was Good to soft, it looked more like Heavy ground, and the last four to finish were virtually pulled up.**

1128 Jack Flush (IRE), from a 2lb higher mark, did just enough in a race in which only two were seriously involved in the straight. (9/1: 7/1-12/1)

794 Boater, despite carrying his head high, stuck to his guns, but could not quite find sufficient. (13/2)

446 Just Grand (IRE), who ran poorly first time, was settled off the pace. Sticking on at the finish, he looks capable of better. (14/1)

1117 William Wallace, dropped in distance, was steadied at the start. He gave the impression there was better to come (14/1)

840 Wild Sky (IRE), who wore a tongue-strap, was badly drawn. When asked to join issue all he did was hang, and he never looked like justifying the gamble. (5/2: op 9/2)

Treasure Hill (IRE), ex-Irish, still looks some way short of peak fitness, and did not shape too badly. (25/1)

1257 DISHFORTH CONDITIONS STKS (3-Y.O) (Class B)

4-15 (4-16) **1m** £8,208.00 (£2,848.00: £1,374.00: £570.00) Stalls: Low GOING: 0.63 sec per fur (GS)

	Horse / details	Dist	Pos	SP	RR	SF
	Catienus (USA) (96) (MRStoute) **3-9-6** KDarley(2) (lw: mde all: shkn up over 2f out: styd on strly fnl f: drvn out)	—	**1**	3/1[2]	113	76
957[2]	**Intikhab (USA) (109)** (DMorley) **3-9-6** GCarter(3) (trckd ldrs: chal over 2f out: nt qckn ins fnl f)	1¾	**2**	7/2[3]	110	73
973[4]	**Premier Bay (103)** (PWHarris) **3-9-1** AClark(1) (trckd ldrs: drvn along ½-wy: wknd 2f out)	6	**3**	11/2	93	56
829[2]	**Harry Wolton (103)** (HRACecil) **3-9-1** WRyan(4) (hld up: effrt over 3f out: sn rdn: no imp)	2½	**4**	11/8[1]	88	51
				(SP 104.7%)	**4 Rn**	

1m 44.2 (7.70) CSF £10.99 TOTE £3.90 (£6.50) OWNER Sheikh Mohammed (NEWMARKET) BRED Darley Stud Management Inc

OFFICIAL EXPLANATION **Harry Wolton: was unsuited by the soft going.**

Catienus (USA), who showed improved form and won his final two outings as a juvenile, clearly relishes getting his toe in. Making his own running, he quickened it up once in line for home, and outstayed the runner-up in the final furlong. (3/1)

957 Intikhab (USA) as usual travelled well, but found the winner too strong in the final furlong. Seven furlongs may prove his optimum trip, and he may even be worth a try over six. (7/2: 9/4-4/1)

973 Premier Bay, who seemed to have problems handling the bend, found the first two running away from him in the final quarter-mile. (11/2)

829 Harry Wolton, dropped in at the start, found nothing under pressure. His rider reported that he was unsuited by the soft ground. (11/8)

1258 YORKSHIRE-TYNE TEES TELEVISION MAIDEN STKS (3-Y.O F) (Class D)

4-45 (4-46) **1m 4f** £3,626.00 (£1,088.00: £524.00: £242.00) Stalls: High GOING: 0.70 sec per fur (GS)

	Horse / details	Dist	Pos	SP	RR	SF
725[12]	**Milly of The Vally** (HRACecil) **3-8-11** WRyan(2) (in tch: pushed along 8f out: outpcd 5f out: hdwy u.p to chal 2f out: led over 1f out: styd on wl)	—	**1**	5/1[3]	88	47
	Vicki Romara (MJohnston) **3-8-11** GCarter(1) (led tl over 2f out: styd on fnl f)	2½	**2**	7/1	85	44
944[2]	**Nightlark (IRE)** (DRLoder) **3-8-11** KDarley(4) (lw: trckd ldr: led over 2f out: hdd over 1f out: wknd ins fnl f)	3	**3**	5/4[1]	81	40
978[2]	**Georgia Venture** (SPCWoods) **3-8-11** AClark(8) (sn trckng ldrs: pushed along 5f out: ev ch & rdn 3f out: edgd lft & wknd over 1f out: eased towards fin)	7	**4**	7/2[2]	71	30
825[3]	**Indigo Dawn** (MJohnston) **3-8-11** DeanMcKeown(6) (chsd ldrs: sn pushed along: rdn & lost pl 4f out)	6	**5**	8/1	63	22
	Gymcrak Gorjos (GHolmes) **3-8-11** AlexGreaves(3) (bit bkwd: b.hind: hld up & plld hrd: lost tch 5f out)	5	**6**	50/1	57	16
	Stoned Imaculate (IRE) (FMurphy) **3-8-11** JFanning(5) (leggy: unf: scope: sn outpcd & bhd)	2½	**7**	50/1	53	12
847[6]	**Savu Sea (IRE)** (CFWall) **3-8-11** NCarlisle(7) (rn green & sn bhd: sme hdwy 7f out: sn wknd)	1½	**8**	25/1	51	10
				(SP 114.7%)	**8 Rn**	

2m 46.4 (15.70) CSF £35.18 TOTE £6.00: £1.40 £2.70 £1.10 (£30.30) OWNER Cliveden Stud (NEWMARKET) BRED Cliveden Stud

Milly of The Vally, who showed plenty of knee action going down, proved well-suited by the mud. Having to work hard to get into the race, in the end she won going away. She looks an out-and-out stayer. (5/1)

Vicki Romara showed plenty of ability when fourth on both her outings as a juvenile. Making her own running, she battled back when headed. Clearly stamina is her strong suit, and she should have no difficulty finding an opening or two. (7/1: op 4/1)

944 Nightlark (IRE), a particularly good mover, took it up travelling best but, soon challenged, fell in a heap. She is now qualified for a handicap mark, and should make amends on better ground. (5/4)

978 Georgia Venture, a poor mover, is suited by the mud. Struggling to keep up under strong pressure, she edged to her left and, booked for fourth, was eased off considerably near the line, which should help her handicap mark. (7/2)

825 Indigo Dawn again looked anything but a straightforward ride. (8/1)

1259 NORTHALLERTON H'CAP (0-95) (4-Y.O+) (Class C)

5-15 (5-17) **6f** £7,564.00 (£2,272.00: £1,096.00: £508.00) Stalls: High GOING: 0.77 sec per fur (S)

Form	Horse	Dist	Pos	SP	RR	SF
942[8]	**So Intrepid (IRE) (70)** (JMBradley) **7-9-0** WRyan(12) (hld up: nt clr run 2f out: swtchd appr fnl f: r.o strly to ld towards fin)	—	1	11/2[3]	82	62
953[4]	**Garnock Valley (76)** (JBerry) **7-9-6b** GCarter(10) (chsd ldrs: led jst ins fnl f: hdd nr fin)	1	2	9/1	85	65
1225[3]	**Benzoe (IRE) (65)** (MrsJRRamsden) **7-8-9** MBirch(8) (dwlt s: sn trckng ldrs: nt clr run 2f out: swtchd 1f out: kpt on one pce)	5	3	4/1[2]	61	41
953*	**Foist (73)** (MWEasterby) **5-9-3** TLucas(13) (lw: w ldrs: led over 2f out: hdd jst ins fnl f: sn wknd)	1	4	11/4[1]	66	46
953[11]	**Tiler (IRE) (77)** (MJohnston) **5-9-7** DeanMcKeown(7) (mde most: sn rdn along: hdd over 2f out: wknd over 1f out)	4	5	14/1	60	40
942[24]	**Thwaab (66)** (FWatson) **5-8-10v** NConnorton(11) (sn outpcd: hdwy u.p ½-wy: n.m.r: nvr nr to chal)	¾	6	16/1	47	27
942[9]	**Lord Olivier (IRE) (80)** (WJarvis) **7-9-3**(7) CLowther(6) (lw: w ldrs tl wknd over 1f out)	2	7	9/1	55	35
942[13]	**French Grit (IRE) (77)** (MDods) **5-9-7** AClark(4) (lw: trckd ldrs: rdn 2f out: sn wknd)	1¼	8	9/1	49	29
1079[2]	**Amron (65)** (JBerry) **10-8-4**(5) TEDurcan(3) (lw: sn outpcd: hdwy u.p on outside over 2f out: sn wknd)	1½	9	15/2	33	13
942[14]	**Mallia (83)** (TDBarron) **4-9-13** KDarley(1) (chsd ldrs: rdn ½-wy: lost pl over 1f out)	1	10	16/1	48	28
	Antarctic Storm (60) (RAFahey) **4-8-4** JFanning(9) (bit bkwd: plld hrd: chsd ldrs tl rdn & lost pl ½-wy)	7	11	33/1	7	—

(SP 125.2%) **11 Rn**

1m 16.8 (7.10) CSF £52.94 CT £206.62 TOTE £6.80: £1.90 £2.70 £1.70 (£19.20) Trio £28.10 OWNER Mr E. A. Hayward (CHEPSTOW) BRED Crest Stud Ltd

443 So Intrepid (IRE), who won four times last year, was racing from a mark 7lb below that from which he last won. In tip-top shape beforehand, he showed a good action going down and, after having to bide his time for an opening, he showed a good turn of foot get up near the line. He should follow up this success. (11/2)

953 Garnock Valley ran right up to his best, but was picked off by the winner in the shadow of the post. (9/1)

1225 Benzoe (IRE), having his second outing in two days, as usual gave away ground at the start. Soon on the heels of the leaders and travelling strongly, he had to search for an opening but, when it came, in truth he found very little. (4/1)

953* Foist was 14lb higher in the weights than when winning at Hamilton. (11/4)

786 Tiler (IRE) is now on a winning mark, but he needs to dominate and have everything go his own way. (14/1)

Thwaab did not have the run of the race, but looks to be close to his best again. (16/1)

T/Plpt: £334.80 (39.96 Tckts). T/Qdpt: £92.10 (5.34 Tckts) WG

1239-NEWBURY (L-H) (Soft)

Sunday May 18th

WEATHER: overcast WIND: almost nil

1260 YOU H'CAP (0-90) (4-Y.O+) (Class C)

2-00 (2-00) **2m** £5,524.00 (£1,672.00: £816.00: £388.00) Stalls: High GOING: 0.34 sec per fur (G)

Form	Horse	Dist	Pos	SP	RR	SF
869[3]	**Grand Cru (62)** (JCullinan) **6-8-7**(3) DO'Donohoe(6) (lw: hdwy over 7f out: rdn over 4f out: led over 1f out: edgd lft ins fnl f: all out)	—	1	20/1	73	35
1027[3]	**Thaljanah (IRE) (80)** (BSmart) **5-10-0** RCochrane(8) (rdn & hdwy over 3f out: ev ch ins fnl f: r.o wl)	s.h	2	11/2[2]	91	53
762[2]	**Samuel Scott (69)** (MCPipe) **4-9-1** PatEddery(3) (lw: a.p: led over 9f out: rdn over 3f out: hdd over 1f out: 3rd & btn whn nt clr run ins fnl f)	2½	3	7/4[1]	77	37
888[3]	**Chabrol (CAN) (64)** (TTClement) **4-8-5**(5) ADaly(5) (a.p: rdn over 4f out: wknd 3f out)	7	4	15/2[3]	65	25
858[4]	**Dark Waters (IRE) (74)** (NAGraham) **4-9-6** DHolland(9) (lw: hld up: rdn over 4f out: sn wknd)	18	5	16/1	57	17
984[2]	**Al's Alibi (74)** (WRMuir) **4-9-6** DHarrison(7) (lw: hdwy 8f out: rdn over 4f out: wknd over 2f out)	¾	6	11/2[2]	57	17
	Spring Marathon (USA) (67) (MrsPNDutfield) **7-9-1** AProcter(2) (a bhd)	5	7	25/1	45	7
831[6]	**Shadirwan (IRE) (73)** (RAkehurst) **6-9-7** TQuinn(1) (led 4f: wknd over 8f out)	15	8	8/1	36	—
	Kadastrof (FR) (75) (RDickin) **7-9-9** DaneO'Neill(4) (led 12f out tl over 9f out: wknd over 4f out)	9	9	11/2[2]	29	—

(SP 119.9%) **9 Rn**

3m 41.69 (17.49) CSF £118.83 CT £272.64 TOTE £27.80: £4.40 £2.10 £1.10 (£80.90) Trio £83.90 OWNER Alan Spargo Ltd Toolmakers (AYLESBURY) BRED A. Dimmock

WEIGHT FOR AGE 4yo-2lb

STEWARDS' ENQUIRY O'Donohoe susp. 27-29/5/97 (careless riding).

869 Grand Cru, who changed hands for £6,000 after finishing third in a Southwell claimer last month, was making his debut on grass, having already won twice on the sand. Well-suited by the step up in trip and soft ground, he came through to gain a narrow lead but then drifted left doing the third no favours. His jockey was later suspended for three days for careless riding. (20/1)

1027 Thaljanah (IRE) threw down a determined challenge in the final quarter-mile. Battling hard, he lost out by only a whisker in an attempt to land his first race since 1995. (11/2)

762 Samuel Scott, 6lb higher for his narrow defeat at Nottingham, moved to the front halfway down the back straight. Collared below the distance, he was feeling the pinch when done no favours by the winner inside the final furlong. (7/4)

888 Chabrol (CAN), tackling a longer trip, had been hung out to dry three furlongs from home. (15/2)

858 Dark Waters (IRE) was a spent force early in the straight. (16/1)

984 Al's Alibi, who looked well despite getting rather warm, goes well with some cut, but this longer trip was beyond him. A return to a mile-and-a-half is needed. (11/2: 7/2-6/1)

1261 NIGHT AND DAY RATED STKS H'CAP (0-105) (3-Y.O+) (Class B)

2-30 (2-35) **1m 1f** £7,408.08 (£2,772.72: £1,356.36: £583.80: £261.90: £133.14) Stalls: High GOING: 0.34 sec per fur (G)

Form	Horse	Dist	Pos	SP	RR	SF
522[5]	**Prince of My Heart (100)** (BWHills) **4-9-4** MHills(8) (lw: led over 7f out: styd far side st: clr 2f out: eased wl ins fnl f)	—	1	8/1	114?	50
	Wijara (IRE) (100) (RHannon) **5-9-4** DaneO'Neill(6) (lw: rdn over 3f out: hdwy over 2f out: r.o one pce)	7	2	10/1	102	38
987[8]	**Almond Rock (95)** (JRFanshawe) **5-8-13** DHarrison(13) (hdwy over 5f out: rdn over 3f out: one pce)	hd	3	13/2[2]	96	32
943[6]	**Golden Ace (IRE) (91)** (RHannon) **4-8-9** RPerham(10) (a.p: rdn over 3f out: wknd fnl f)	3½	4	33/1	86	22
939[2]	**Forza Figlio (92)** (MissGayKelleway) **4-8-10**ow1 RHughes(4) (hld up: rdn over 3f out: wknd over 2f out)	8	5	15/2	73	8

				SP	RR	SF
	Arabian Story (100) (LordHuntingdon) **4-9-4** DHolland(1) (b: hld up: rdn over 3f out: sn wknd)	2½	**6**	10/1	77	13
934[3]	**Medieval Lady (91)** (IABalding) **4-8-6**(3) MartinDwyer(12) (lw: hld up: rdn 4f out: wknd over 3f out)	5	**7**	10/1	59	—
943[3]	**Wilcuma (105)** (PJMakin) **6-9-9** PatEddery(11) (hld up: rdn over 3f out: sn wknd)	2½	**8**	9/4[1]	68	4
830[8]	**Royal Philosopher (105)** (JWHills) **5-9-9** RHills(7) (led over 1f: wknd 2f out)	4	**9**	7/1[3]	61	—
591[5]	**Cotteir Chief (IRE) (97)** (JNeville) **6-9-1** SDrowne(2) (swtg: hdwy over 4f out: wknd over 3f out)	3½	**10**	33/1	47	—
738[9]	**Unitus (IRE) (95)** (MRStoute) **4-8-13** TQuinn(3) (hdwy over 3f out: wknd over 2f out)	14	**11**	8/1	20	—
	Night City (100) (LadyHerries) **6-9-4** DeclanO'Shea(9) (Withdrawn not under Starter's orders: bolted bef s)		**W**	9/1	—	—
				(SP 133.7%)		**11 Rn**

1m 59.06 (8.76) CSF £81.91 CT £517.83 TOTE £12.50: £3.40 £3.40 £1.90 (£90.50) Trio £179.80 OWNER Mr G. J. Hicks (LAMBOURN) BRED George Joseph Hicks

LONG HANDICAP Medieval Lady 8-4 Golden Ace (IRE) 8-8 Forza Figlio 8-6

OFFICIAL EXPLANATION **Wilcuma: was hampered on the home bend and then lost interest.**

IN-FOCUS: **From both the previous days it had become evident that the slowest ground was down the centre of the track, so it seemed quite amazing that all the jockeys, with the exception of Hills on the winner, decided to come down the middle. In the circumstances, the result was hardly surprising and the form is therefore rather suspect.**

522 Prince of My Heart was given a superb ride by Hills, who stuck to the far rails and, as a result, was well clear of his rivals halfway up the straight. With the race in the bag, he was eased down in the closing stages. (8/1)

Wijara (IRE) is suited by some cut and, struggling on in the straight, won the battle for second prize if having no hope with the winner. He has done all his winning in September. (10/1)

738 Almond Rock likes some cut in the ground but, after moving into the action turning for home, was only scrapping for minor honours in the straight. (13/2)

Golden Ace (IRE), never far away, was at the end of his tether inside the final furlong. (33/1)

939 Forza Figlio was beaten over two furlongs from home. (15/2)

Arabian Story had things all against him here - he was making his seasonal debut over a trip well short of his best and was 12lb higher than he has ever won off before - so it was no surprise that he could never make his presence felt. (10/1)

943 Wilcuma ran no race at all on ground that was right up his street. (9/4)

1262 MAIL ON SUNDAY MILE (QUALIFIER) H'CAP (0-85) (3-Y.O+) (Class D)

3-00 (3-03) **1m (straight)** £7,782.50 (£2,360.00: £1,155.00: £552.50) Stalls: High GOING: 0.34 sec per fur (G)

				SP	RR	SF
895[24]	**Phonetic (71)** (GBBalding) **4-9-0** RPrice(9) (lw: hdwy 2f out: led ins fnl f: drvn out)	—	**1**	25/1	83	66
647[4]	**Master Beveled (71)** (PDEvans) **7-9-0b** JFEgan(11) (b.nr fore: lw: lost pl 3f out: nt clr run over 2f out: swtchd lft: rallied over 1f out: ev ch ins fnl f: r.o)	nk	**2**	7/1[1]	82	65
987[16]	**Wakeel (USA) (75)** (SDow) **5-9-4** RPerham(19) (nt clr run over 2f out: hdwy over 1f out: r.o wl ins fnl f)	1	**3**	25/1	84	67
1035[14]	**Duello (71)** (MBlanshard) **6-9-0** JQuinn(17) (lw: a.p: rdn over 2f out: ev ch ins fnl f: unable qckn)	1¾	**4**	15/2[2]	77	60
933[6]	**Ashby Hill (IRE) (69)** (RRowe) **6-8-12** RCochrane(7) (hld up: rdn over 2f out: r.o one pce)	¾	**5**	7/1[1]	73	56
895[14]	**Alsahib (USA) (65)** (WRMuir) **4-8-8** DaneO'Neill(10) (hld up: rdn over 3f out: one pce)	s.h	**6**	10/1	69	52
895[18]	**Q Factor (78)** (DHaydnJones) **5-9-7** SDrowne(16) (led over 6f)	1¼	**7**	10/1	80	63
*325**	**Sweet Wilhelmina (60)** (LordHuntingdon) **4-8-3** DHarrison(4) (stdy hdwy over 3f out: led over 1f out tl ins fnl f: sn wknd)	¾	**8**	8/1[3]	60	43
738[8]	**Yalta (IRE) (85)** (RCharlton) **4-10-0** PatEddery(20) (swtchd lft 3f out: hdwy over 1f out: wknd ins fnl f)	2	**9**	7/1[1]	81	64
	Koathary (USA) (80) (LGCottrell) **6-9-9** DHolland(18) (lw: nt clr run on ins over 2f out & over 1f out: nvr nrr)	¾	**10**	14/1	75	58
	Fionn de Cool (IRE) (67) (RAkehurst) **6-8-10** SSanders(14) (chsd ldrs 5f: wknd over 2f out)	nk	**11**	11/1	61	44
352[7]	**Whatever's Right (IRE) (65)** (MDIUsher) **8-8-8** JMarshall(12) (sme hdwy 2f out: wknd over 1f out)	¾	**12**	33/1	58	41
	Fahs (USA) (71) (RAkehurst) **5-8-7**(7) DDenby(5) (hld up: rdn over 3f out: wknd wl over 1f out)	s.h	**13**	16/1	64	47
	Kentucky Fall (FR) (68) (LadyHerries) **4-8-11** AClark(13) (hdwy 2f out: wknd over 1f out)	4	**14**	25/1	53	36
968[11]	**Mayfair (83)** (PFICole) **3-9-0** TQuinn(6) (lw: prom 6f)	9	**15**	20/1	50	21
	Lucky Begonia (IRE) (60) (WJMusson) **4-8-3**ow1 BDoyle(3) (swtg: a bhd)	6	**16**	25/1	15	—
363[7]	**Dances With Hooves (77)** (DJSffrenchDavis) **5-9-6** SWhitworth(8) (a bhd)	1¼	**17**	25/1	29	12
				(SP 126.4%)		**17 Rn**

1m 43.89 (5.89) CSF £167.23 CT £4,180.30 TOTE £52.30: £9.50 £1.40 £3.40 £3.40 (£125.10) Trio £733.80 OWNER Miss B. Swire (ANDOVER) BRED Miss B. Swire

WEIGHT FOR AGE 3yo-12lb

Phonetic needs this ground according to his trainer and, sweeping into the lead inside the final furlong, held on under pressure. (25/1)

647 Master Beveled had the ground in his favour and, fitted with blinkers for the first time since his three-year-old days, ran a tremendous race. He looked in trouble as he lost his place three furlongs from home, and then got no sort of run at all. However, his jockey managed to get him back into contention below the distance and, one of several with every chance inside the final furlong, he only just failed. (7/1)

Wakeel (USA) is not easy to win with and is yet to win a handicap. Nevertheless, he ran his best race for some time and, after meeting traffic problems, was running on really strongly in the last furlong-and-a-half. (25/1)

661 Duello, a leading player from the outset, threw down his challenge in the final quarter-mile, but was tapped for toe in the last one hundred yards. Although successful twice last season, he is not that easy to win with, and his record now stands at three victories from fifty starts. (15/2)

933 Ashby Hill (IRE) chased the leaders but failed to find that vital turn of foot in the final quarter-mile. She has won with some cut in the ground, but is at her best when she can really hear her feet rattle. (7/1)

Alsahib (USA) chased the leaders but could only go up and down in the same place in the last three furlongs. He remains a maiden. (10/1: 8/1-12/1)

325* Sweet Wilhelmina, rated 10lb lower on grass than on the All-Weather, gave a good account of herself and gained a narrow advantage below the distance before collared inside the final furlong. All four of her victories to date have come on the sand. (8/1)

Koathary (USA), 25lb higher than when first successful last season, looked in good shape for this reappearance, but was trapped against the rails and got no sort of run whatsoever. (14/1)

Fionn de Cool (IRE) (11/1: 8/1-12/1)

81+ 88 95

1263 FINANCIAL MAIL ON SUNDAY MAIDEN STKS (2-Y.O C & G) (Class D)

3-35 (3-35) **6f 8y** £3,566.25 (£1,080.00: £527.50: £251.25) Stalls: High GOING: 0.34 sec per fur (G)

				SP	RR	SF
	Bold Edge (RHannon) **2-8-11** PatEddery(2) (leggy: scope: lw: led 4f out: rdn over 1f out: r.o wl)	—	**1**	2/1[1]	94+	40
696[5]	**Anvil (USA)** (GLewis) **2-8-11** PaulEddery(5) (lw: led 2f: rdn over 2f out: ev ch over 1f out: unable qckn)	1¾	**2**	7/1	89	35
938[2]	**Legs Be Frendly (IRE)** (KMcAuliffe) **2-8-11** JFEgan(11) (a.p: rdn over 2f out: one pce)	1¾	**3**	13/2[3]	85	31

	Exbourne's Wish (USA) (BWHills) **2-8-11** MHills(13) (str: scope: plld hrd: hdwy over 2f out: rdn over 1f out: one pce)	s.h	**4**	100/30 2	85	31
	Red Maple (USA) (PFICole) **2-8-11** TQuinn(14) (leggy: nt clr run on ins over 2f out: hdwy over 1f out: nvr nrr)	3	**5**	9/1	77	23
965[4]	**Narrogin (USA)** (MRChannon) **2-8-11** RPerham(1) (rdn over 2f out: nvr nr to chal)	3½	**6**	12/1	67	13
	Ben Rinnes (RFJohnsonHoughton) **2-8-11** AClark(10) (unf: lw: chsd ldrs: rdn 4f out: wknd over 1f out)	¾	**7**	33/1	65	11
	Kim's Brave (BJMeehan) **2-8-4**(7) GHannon(6) (w'like: bkwd: hdwy 2f out: wknd over 1f out)	1½	**8**	33/1	61	7
	Swift Alliance (RAkehurst) **2-8-11** SSanders(12) (str: bit bkwd: lost pl over 2f out: swtchd lft & rallied over 1f out: sn wknd)	1	**9**	14/1	59	5
	Night Vigil (IRE) (BWHills) **2-8-11** DHolland(3) (str: bkwd: hld up: rdn over 2f out: sn wknd)	12	**10**	20/1	27	—
	Royal Axminster (MrsPNDutfield) **2-8-11** SDrowne(4) (w'like: bit bkwd: bhd fnl 3f)	1½	**11**	33/1	23	—
	Blue Shadow (RHannon) **2-8-11** DaneO'Neill(9) (w'like: bit bkwd: prom over 3f)	4	**12**	14/1	12	—
				(SP 126.9%)	**12 Rn**	

1m 17.84 (6.04) CSF £15.75 TOTE £3.20: £1.90 £4.00 £2.20 (£23.90) Trio £21.20 OWNER Lady Whent (MARLBOROUGH) BRED Lady Whent

Bold Edge, quite a tall colt with room for development, looked in good shape beforehand and made a fine start to his racing career. Well regarded at home, he was soon at the head of affairs and, set alight below the distance, proved far too good for his rivals. A trip to Royal Ascot looks on the cards. (2/1)

696 Anvil (USA) looked extremely well in the paddock and ran a race full of promise, still having every chance below the distance before the winner asserted. He should soon go one better. (7/1: op 4/1)

938 Legs Be Frendly (IRE), who made a promising debut at Newmarket, was never far away. (13/2: 4/1-7/1)

Exbourne's Wish (USA) is a mature two-year-old with plenty of substance and scope. Unfortunately, he took a very keen hold at the back of the field and refused to settle in the early stages. He found his early exertions taking their toll from below the distance but, once he learns to settle, he should have no problems opening his account. (100/30)

Red Maple (USA), quite a tall, close-coupled individual, made late headway without ever threatening to get into it. (9/1: 5/1-10/1)

965 Narrogin (USA) (12/1: 8/1-14/1)

Swift Alliance (14/1: 20/1-12/1)

Blue Shadow (14/1: 10/1-16/1)

1264 PROGRAMME LIMITED STKS (0-85) (3-Y.O+) (Class D)

4-05 (4-05) **7f 64y (round)** £3,533.75 (£1,070.00: £522.50: £248.75) Stalls: High GOING: 0.34 sec per fur (G)

				SP	RR	SF
930[10]	**Tal-Y-Llyn (IRE) (84)** (BWHills) **3-8-7** MHills(6) (mde all: drvn out)	—	**1**	6/1	85	44
946[2]	**Rakis (IRE) (79)** (MrsLStubbs) **7-9-7** JFEgan(4) (lw: chsd wnr: hrd rdn & ev ch fnl 2f: r.o wl)	s.h	**2**	11/2 3	88	58
832[7]	**Pomona (84)** (PJMakin) **4-9-1** PatEddery(5) (hld up: rdn over 3f out: unable qckn)	4	**3**	11/10 1	73	43
939[7]	**Manaloj (USA) (79)** (RHannon) **4-9-4** DaneO'Neill(2) (stdy hdwy over 3f out: wknd over 2f out)	18	**4**	20/1	37	7
	My Valentina (82) (BWHills) **3-8-4** DHolland(7) (swtg: a.p: rdn 3f out: wknd over 2f out)	2½	**5**	3/1 2	28	—
				(SP 107.1%)	**5 Rn**	

1m 34.71 (6.61) CSF £30.83 TOTE £7.70: £2.20 £2.10 (£17.50) OWNER Tilstone Lodge Stud (LAMBOURN) BRED Ardenode Stud Ltd

WEIGHT FOR AGE 3yo-11lb

Tal-Y-Llyn (IRE) left his reappearance run at Newmarket well behind, and just won a tremendous scrap with the runner-up. (6/1: 4/1-13/2)

946 Rakis (IRE) ran a tremendous race in defeat, especially considering he was officially worst in at the weights. All ten of his victories have come over this trip, and he should soon be adding to that tally. (11/2)

Pomona was very disappointing. She appeared to have things in her favour - she was 13lb better off for being beaten one-and-three-quarter lengths by Rakis at Sandown last month - yet ended up finishing further behind. (11/10: 5/4-4/5)

Manaloj (USA) was getting left behind over a quarter-of-a-mile from home. (20/1)

My Valentina, the only runner without a recent outing under her belt, was well-beaten. (3/1: 2/1-100/30)

1265 CHARLES WINTOUR MAIDEN STKS (3-Y.O) (Class D)

4-40 (4-41) **7f 64y (round)** £3,550.00 (£1,075.00: £525.00: £250.00) Stalls: High GOING: 0.34 sec per fur (G)

				SP	RR	SF
	Hornbeam (JRJenkins) **3-9-0** RCochrane(5) (a.p: led over 1f out: rdn out)	—	**1**	100/30 1	92	56
	Icy Guest (USA) (PJMakin) **3-8-9** SSanders(1) (bit bkwd: led over 6f out tl over 1f out: unable qckn)	7	**2**	16/1	72	36
945[3]	**Shadoof** (WRMuir) **3-9-0** DaneO'Neill(6) (hld up: rdn over 2f out: r.o one pce)	2	**3**	5/1	72	36
	Topton (IRE) (IABalding) **3-9-0** SWhitworth(9) (unf: scope: s.s: hdwy over 2f out: swtchd rt: one pce)	nk	**4**	10/1	72	36
889[6]	**Oxbane** (HCandy) **3-8-9** NAdams(4) (hdwy over 2f out: wknd over 1f out)	3½	**5**	20/1	59	23
964[2]	**Fur Will Fly** (IABalding) **3-8-9** TQuinn(10) (led 1f: rdn over 2f out: wknd over 1f out)	12	**6**	4/1 2	33	—
	Smart Dominion (LordHuntingdon) **3-9-0** MHills(7) (bit bkwd: a bhd)	½	**7**	5/1	37	1
673[5]	**Churchill's Shadow (IRE)** (BAPearce) **3-8-11**(3) MartinDwyer(2) (lw: prom over 4f)	9	**8**	10/1	17	—
	Davids Revenge (MajorDNChappell) **3-9-0** PatEddery(3) (bit bkwd: s.s: bhd fnl 3f)	4	**9**	9/2 3	8	—
				(SP 123.4%)	**9 Rn**	

1m 34.26 (6.16) CSF £56.79 TOTE £4.70: £1.60 £4.50 £2.90 (£59.40) Trio £59.70 OWNER Mr K. C. Payne (ROYSTON) BRED K. Payne

Hornbeam made a winning return to action, leading over a furlong out and being kept right up to his work to the bitter end. (100/30)

Icy Guest (USA), who has changed stables since last year, looked in need of this reappearance, but soon moved to the head of affairs. Collared below the distance, she was then left standing by the winner. (16/1)

945 Shadoof chased the leaders but was made to look very pedestrian in the last three furlongs. He looks to need further. (5/1: op 2/1)

Topton (IRE), quite a tall gelding, is rather weak behind at present. (10/1: 5/1-12/1)

889 Oxbane edged closer in the straight, but was left for dead below the distance. (20/1)

964 Fur Will Fly found this trip in this ground far too much for her. A return to six furlongs is needed. (4/1)

Davids Revenge (9/2: op 3/1)

T/Jkpt: Not won; £31,117.18 to Bath 19/5/97. T/Plpt: £317.70 (87.07 Tckts). T/Qdpt: £24.10 (43.12 Tckts) AK

0843-RIPON (R-H) (Good to soft)
Sunday May 18th
WEATHER: overcast WIND: almost nil

1266 SUNDAY IS FUNDAY AT THE RACES (S) STKS (3-Y.O+) (Class F)
2-15 (2-16) **1m** £2,866.00 (£868.00: £424.00: £202.00) Stalls: High GOING: 0.25 sec per fur (G)

				SP	RR	SF
461^{8}	**Flag Fen (USA) (56)** (JParkes) **6-9-4** KFallon(2) (mid div: hdwy to ld 2f out: hung bdly rt: r.o wl)	—	**1**	9/1	71	53
870^{15}	**Sandmoor Denim (48)** (SRBowring) **10-9-4** SWebster(11) (hdwy ½-wy: ch 2f out: kpt on one pce)	4	**2**	12/1	63	45
864^{5}	**Power Game (54)** (JBerry) **4-9-4b** KDarley(10) (in tch: hdwy & ev ch over 2f out: rdn & one pce)	3½	**3**	$2/1^{1}$	56	38
1077^{6}	**My Handsome Prince (27)** (PJBevan) **5-9-4** NCarlisle(1) (bhd: styd on fnl 3f: nrst fin)	4	**4**	20/1	48	30
755^{9}	**Flagstaff (USA) (47)** (KRBurke) **4-9-4v** OUrbina(5) (lw: trckd ldrs: led 3f out to 2f out: wknd)	2	**5**	11/1	44	26
997^{4}	**Sheraz (IRE) (40)** (NTinkler) **5-8-11b**(7) KSked(7) (lw: cl up: led appr st tl hdd 3f out: sn outpcd)	nk	**6**	14/1	43	25
	Mbulwa (62) (RAFahey) **11-9-4** ACulhane(4) (prom: effrt & ch 3f out: wknd fnl 2f)	2	**7**	13/2	39	21
686^{9}	**Dario's Girl** (DMoffatt) **4-8-10**(3) DarrenMoffatt(6) (a bhd)	10	**8**	33/1	14	—
955^{9}	**Ten Past Six (59)** (MartynWane) **5-9-9** JCarroll(12) (effrt ½-wy: hrd rdn 3f out: sn btn & eased)	nk	**9**	$9/2^{2}$	24	6
	Bold Patriot (IRE) (BobJones) **4-9-4** NDay(3) (b: chsd ldrs tl wknd fnl 2f: eased fnl f: broke down)	1	**10**	$6/1^{3}$	17	—
	Mystic Maid (IRE) (JLHarris) **4-8-13** JWeaver(8) (led to st: ev ch tl wknd fnl 3f)	nk	**11**	10/1	11	—
	Rambo's Rumtime (30) (FWatson) **5-8-8**(5) PFessey(9) (bit bkwd: prom tl outpcd fnl 3½f)	5	**12**	50/1	1	—
901^{10}	**Cinders Girl (55)** (MrsMReveley) **7-8-13** DWright(13) (plld hrd early: a bhd: t.o)	dist	**13**	25/1	—	—
				(SP 134.4%)	**13 Rn**	

1m 45.0 (6.80) CSF £111.07 TOTE £11.40: £3.10 £3.40 £1.70 (£145.10) Trio £198.40 OWNER Mr Vince Dolan (MALTON) BRED Mrs Paul Little
No bid
411 Flag Fen (USA) goes well with cut in the ground but is not an easy ride as he hangs quite badly. (9/1: 6/1-10/1)
526 Sandmoor Denim does not win very often these days and this was one of his better efforts. (12/1)
864 Power Game had the blinkers back on but, despite holding every chance, he was never really firing under pressure. (2/1)
1077 My Handsome Prince came from behind as usual and looks likely to need further yet. (20/1)
313 Flagstaff (USA) had his chances but, once a struggle developed in the last two furlongs, he soon dropped away. (11/1: 8/1-12/1)
Mbulwa, taking a drop in class here, probably needed this. (13/2: op 4/1)

82+ 76 71+

1267 FUN FOR ALL THE FAMILY MAIDEN STKS (2-Y.O) (Class D)
2-45 (2-47) **6f** £3,391.10 (£1,026.80: £501.40: £238.70) Stalls: Low GOING: 0.25 sec per fur (G)

				SP	RR	SF
1076^{3}	**Alconleigh** (MJohnston) **2-9-0** JWeaver(11) (lw: mde all: hung rt fr ½-wy: kpt on wl)	—	**1**	$5/2^{1}$	77	58
850^{3}	**Prose (IRE)** (RHannon) **2-9-0** KFallon(4) (a chsng ldrs: swtchd over 1f out: styd on wl towards fin)	½	**2**	$3/1^{2}$	76	57
954^{6}	**Winsome George** (CWFairhurst) **2-9-0** NKennedy(2) (sn pushed along: hdwy ½-wy: r.o fnl f)	2	**3**	12/1	70	51
1076^{6}	**Petara (IRE)** (JSWainwright) **2-9-0** GCarter(8) (bhd: swtchd outside 2f out: styd on wl)	7	**4**	33/1	52	33
	Wathbat Lion (MAJarvis) **2-9-0** PBloomfield(1) (small: lengthy: a chsng ldrs: kpt on same pce fnl 2f)	1	**5**	$9/2^{3}$	49	30
1076^{4}	**Seventh Heaven** (JBerry) **2-8-9**(5) TEDurcan(13) (chsd wnr tl wknd over 1f out)	1	**6**	8/1	46	27
	Dangerman (IRE) (MWEasterby) **2-9-0** TLucas(5) (rangy: unf: bit bkwd: bhd: hdwy over 1f out: nvr nr to chal)	1¾	**7**	25/1	42	23
1084^{8}	**Highbury Legend** (BobJones) **2-9-0** NDay(9) (sn drvn along: nvr trbld ldrs)	1¼	**8**	25/1	38	19
730^{7}	**Dancing Em** (TDEasterby) **2-8-9** MBirch(6) (outpcd ½-wy: n.d after)	½	**9**	25/1	32	13
	Grand Estate (TDEasterby) **2-9-0** KDarley(7) (cmpt: unf: hld up: nvr plcd to chal)	¾	**10**	14/1	35	16
880^{9}	**Summer River (IRE)** (CMurray) **2-9-0** DeanMcKeown(3) (chsd ldrs over 4f: wknd qckly)	4	**11**	12/1	24	5
971^{W}	**Ragford (IRE)** (JMPEustace) **2-9-0** JTate(10) (cmpt: sn bhd)	9	**12**	9/1	—	—
993^{14}	**Wee Christy (IRE)** (WMcKeown) **2-9-0** ACulhane(14) (nvr wnt pce)	1½	**13**	33/1	—	—
	Marton Moss (SWE) (TDEasterby) **2-9-0** JCarroll(12) (leggy: spd 4f: wknd qckly)	½	**14**	20/1	—	—
				(SP 137.1%)	**14 Rn**	

1m 14.8 (4.30) CSF £9.58 TOTE £3.90: £1.80 £1.10 £3.90 (£2.70) Trio £33.70 OWNER Mr David Abell (MIDDLEHAM) BRED Maristow Farms Partnership
1076 Alconleigh had the speed to take the stands rails from a poor draw and, despite hanging in the closing stages, was always in command. He is going the right way. (5/2)
850 Prose (IRE), stepping up in distance here, finished well to show that even stiffer tests will suit. (3/1)
954 Winsome George appreciated this extra furlong and finished to some purpose, showing he is improving. (12/1)
1076 Petara (IRE) again showed ability, and there seems to be some improvement yet to come. (33/1)
Wathbat Lion showed ability and will no doubt improve for the experience. He should appreciate further yet. (9/2)
1076 Seventh Heaven is such a good mover that faster ground should bring improvement. (8/1)
Dangerman (IRE), needing this, showed enough to suggest that there is improvement likely in due course. (25/1)
Grand Estate never got a run at any stage and should benefit a good deal from the experience. (14/1)
Ragford (IRE) (9/1: op 16/1)

1268 MIDDLEHAM TRAINERS ASSOCIATION H'CAP (0-85) (3-Y.O+) (Class D)
3-15 (3-17) **1m 2f** £4,377.00 (£1,326.00: £648.00: £309.00) Stalls: High GOING: 0.25 sec per fur (G)

				SP	RR	SF
1123^{2}	**Effectual (77)** (MissGayKelleway) **4-9-11** GDuffield(10) (chsd ldrs: led over 3f out: r.o wl)	—	**1**	$13/2^{3}$	92	52
	Leviticus (IRE) (73) (TPTate) **3-8-7** MBirch(6) (lw: in tch: effrt & ev ch 2f out: kpt on wl)	½	**2**	16/1	87	33
735^{7}	**Docklands Limo (78)** (BJMcMath) **4-9-12** GBardwell(8) (lw: trckd ldrs: chal 3f out: hrd rdn & kpt on fnl 2f)	s.h	**3**	14/1	92	52
735^{12}	**Vola Via (USA) (80)** (IABalding) **4-10-0** WRyan(2) (bhd: effrt 4f out: styd on wl towards fin)	3½	**4**	16/1	89	49
1117^{*}	**Mels Baby (IRE) (76)** (JLEyre) **4-9-7**(3) OPears(4) (lw: in tch: effrt & ch 2f out: no ex)	hd	**5**	$5/2^{1}$	84	44
1129^{10}	**Marsh Marigold (62)** (JHetherton) **3-7-5**(5) IonaWands(1) (hld up & bhd: gd hdwy on outside over 3f out: prom 2f out: nt qckn appr fnl f)	1½	**6**	33/1	68	14
	Flying North (IRE) (73) (MrsMReveley) **4-9-7** ACulhane(15) (bhd: hdwy whn n.m.r over 1f out: nrst fin)	½	**7**	20/1	78	38
1040^{9}	**In Good Faith (53)** (JJQuinn) **5-8-1** DaleGibson(5) (swtg: bhd: rdn 4f out: styd on fnl 2f)	nk	**8**	25/1	58	18
	Stackattack (IRE) (61) (MrsJRRamsden) **4-8-6**(3) FLynch(16) (lw: hld up: nvr nr to chal)	2½	**9**	16/1	62	22
1024^{9}	**Essayeffsee (57)** (MrsMReveley) **8-8-5** KDarley(3) (bhd: sme hdwy 2f out: n.d)	3	**10**	12/1	53	13
680^{17}	**Mukhlles (USA) (72)** (BobJones) **4-9-6** NDay(11) (prom tl wknd fnl 2½f)	nk	**11**	9/1	67	27
1117^{4}	**Gymcrak Premiere (78)** (GHolmes) **9-9-12** JCarroll(9) (b.hind: hld up & bhd: nt clr run 3f out: nt rcvr)	4	**12**	14/1	67	27

				SP	RR	SF
898^{5}	**Keep Battling (50)** (JSGoldie) **7-7-12** TWilliams(12) (lw: hld up: effrt on ins 3f out: rdn & wknd wl over 1f out)	1½	**13**	25/1	37	—
	Vanishing Trick (USA) (80) (HRACecil) **3-9-0** KFallon(13) (h.d.w: chsd ldrs: rdn 4f out: grad wknd)	3½	**14**	$11/2^{2}$	61	7
1117^{7}	**Mr Teigh (65)** (MrsJRRamsden) **5-8-13** GCarter(7) (hld up: hdwy 5f out: ev ch over 2f out: wknd wl over 1f out)	2	**15**	14/1	43	3
723^{17}	**Shoumatara (USA) (83)** (MRStoute) **3-9-3** JWeaver(14) (lw: led tl hdd over 3f out: sn wknd)	¾	**16**	11/1	60	6

(SP 136.4%) **16 Rn**

2m 12.9 (9.40) CSF £104.20 CT £1,337.97 TOTE £5.50: £1.50 £7.90 £2.80 £3.60 (£162.20) Trio £565.40; £637.07 to Bath 19/5/97 OWNER Blandford Thoroughbreds (WHITCOMBE) BRED Miss Sarah Hollinshead
LONG HANDICAP Marsh Marigold 7-5
WEIGHT FOR AGE 3yo-14lb

1123 Effectual, back on turf for the first time for his new stable, continues his improvement. (13/2)
Leviticus (IRE) got this trip well and looks likely to appreciate further. He really deserves a change of luck. (16/1)
Docklands Limo put up a really good show and kept responding to pressure when looking beaten. He should get further. (14/1: op 25/1)
657 Vola Via (USA), poorly drawn, had a lot of running to do from the home turn and did well to finish so close.He might well appreciate a bit further. (16/1)
1117* Mels Baby (IRE), because of his draw, was having to race wide to get a run, and he can be forgiven this. (5/2)
1024 Marsh Marigold showed here that she has plenty of ability when things go her way. (33/1)
Flying North (IRE) has proved difficult to win with but he certainly has ability and this was a fair first effort of the season. (20/1)
1024 Essayeffsee (12/1: op 8/1)
1117 Gymcrak Premiere never got a run and was certainly not knocked about. This is best ignored. (14/1)
Vanishing Trick (USA) (11/2: 4/1-6/1)

1269 RIPON SUNDAY SPRINT CHALLENGE H'CAP (0-90) (3-Y.O+) (Class C)
3-45 (3-46) **5f** £7,100.00 (£2,150.00: £1,050.00: £500.00) Stalls: Low GOING: 0.25 sec per fur (G)

				SP	RR	SF
	Canovas Heart (78) (BobJones) **8-9-8** NDay(7) (mde all: r.o wl appr fnl f)	—	**1**	$6/1^{3}$	90	72
*1046**	**Lady Sheriff (68)** (MWEasterby) **6-8-12b** TLucas(9) (lw: chsd wnr tl rdn & btn 1f out)	3	**2**	$5/1^{2}$	70	52
845^{7}	**Express Girl (65)** (DMoffatt) **3-7-12**(3) DarrenMoffatt(1) (a chsng ldrs: kpt on wl ins fnl f)	1¼	**3**	12/1	63	37
903^{6}	**Kalar (55)** (DWChapman) **8-7-8b**(5) PFessey(3) (cl up tl rdn & btn appr fnl f)	2½	**4**	11/1	45	27
1227^{3}	**Sue Me (IRE) (62)** (DNicholls) **5-8-6**ow1 AlexGreaves(11) (bhd: hdwy ½-wy: prom over 1f out: no ex)	1½	**5**	7/1	48	29
942^{17}	**Antonias Melody (77)** (SRBowring) **4-9-7** SWebster(2) (outpcd tl styd on fnl 2f: nrst fin)	s.h	**6**	12/1	62	44
863^{4}	**Bowlers Boy (69)** (JJQuinn) **4-8-13** DaleGibson(4) (sn pushed along: nvr trbld ldrs)	¾	**7**	10/1	52	34
905^{4}	**Ansellman (83)** (JBerry) **7-9-13b** GCarter(6) (b: in tch: sn drvn along: no imp fnl 2f)	nk	**8**	8/1	65	47
1098^{9}	**Insider Trader (66)** (MrsJRRamsden) **6-8-5**(5) GFaulkner(8) (lw: in tch: effrt ½-wy: sn outpcd)	hd	**9**	$7/2^{1}$	48	30
827^{15}	**Ramsey Hope (63)** (CWFairhurst) **4-8-7v** NKennedy(12) (lw: sn outpcd & bhd)	4	**10**	25/1	32	14
1034^{8}	**Ziggy's Dancer (USA) (84)** (EJAlston) **6-10-0** GDuffield(10) (lw: spd over 3f)	2½	**11**	17/2	45	27

(SP 124.0%) **11 Rn**

61.0 secs (3.20) CSF £34.79 CT £335.72 TOTE £7.60: £2.20 £2.40 £3.10 (£37.60) Trio £154.70 OWNER Mr M J Osborne and Mrs J Woods (NEWMARKET) BRED M. J. Hall
WEIGHT FOR AGE 3yo-8lb

Canovas Heart has bags of speed and was winning off his highest mark to date here, and this was the third consecutive season he has scored first time out. (6/1)
1046* Lady Sheriff is a tough sort but, despite a gallant effort, she was well second best. (5/1)
845 Express Girl had the best draw, likes soft ground and kept on well, suggesting that another furlong is probably what she needs. (12/1)
903 Kalar is better on sand but this was not a bad effort of his present mark. (11/1)
1227 Sue Me (IRE), who ran the previous evening, had a poor draw here which probably made all the difference. (7/1: op 4/1)
301 Antonias Melody was always finding this trip too sharp. (12/1)
863 Bowlers Boy gave the impression that he is better over six furlongs. (10/1: 8/1-12/1)

1270 GARDEN RACECOURSE H'CAP (0-85) (3-Y.O) (Class D)
4-20 (4-20) **1m 4f 60y** £4,201.50 (£1,272.00: £621.00: £295.50) Stalls: Low GOING: 0.25 sec per fur (G)

				SP	RR	SF
1014^{5}	**Fabled Light (IRE) (80)** (GWragg) **3-9-2**(5) GMilligan(2) (lw: a gng wl: led appr fnl f: qcknd: comf)	—	**1**	$2/1^{1}$	89+	13
841^{4}	**Thornby Park (77)** (JLDunlop) **3-9-4** TSprake(3) (b: swtg: trckd ldrs: effrt over 2f out: r.o: no ch w wnr)	1¾	**2**	$4/1^{3}$	84	8
966^{3}	**Spy Knoll (75)** (MRStoute) **3-9-2** KFallon(5) (lw: trckd ldr: led wl over 1f out tl hdd appr fnl f: nt qckn)	½	**3**	$5/2^{2}$	81	5
	Double Flight (71) (MJohnston) **3-8-12** JWeaver(6) (hld up: effrt over 2f out: swtchd over 1f out: styd on)	2½	**4**	6/1	74	—
887^{4}	**Agony Aunt (77)** (MrsJCecil) **3-9-4** KDarley(1) (led tl hdd wl over 1f out: wknd)	3	**5**	11/2	76	—

(SP 111.6%) **5 Rn**

2m 50.9 (17.40) CSF £9.45 TOTE £3.40: £1.70 £2.10 (£7.20) OWNER Mollers Racing (NEWMARKET) BRED Churchtown House Stud

1014 Fabled Light (IRE) is certainly going the right way and is very useful indeed judging from this. Plenty more will be seen of him. (2/1)
841 Thornby Park, first time in a handicap, put up a gallant effort but always found the winner too good. Her turn will come. (4/1: 5/2-9/2)
966 Spy Knoll, in a race where there was no real pace on, always held a good position but failed to pick up when asked. (5/2)
Double Flight, stepping up in trip, got it well and would have preferred a stronger gallop. (6/1)
887 Agony Aunt, trying a longer trip, was most disappointing, dropping tamely away in the last two furlongs after setting only a moderate pace. (11/2)

1271 GO SUNDAY RACING IN YORKSHIRE MAIDEN STKS (3-Y.O) (Class D)
4-50 (4-54) **1m 1f** £3,947.40 (£1,195.20: £583.60: £277.80) Stalls: High GOING: 0.25 sec per fur (G)

				SP	RR	SF
683^{7}	**Darcy** (MRStoute) **3-9-0** KDarley(1) (s.i.s & drvn along: sn prom: rdn over 3f out: styd on wl to ld ins fnl f)	—	**1**	$6/1^{3}$	97	49
885^{2}	**Epworth (78)** (JAGlover) **3-8-9** GCarter(5) (trckd ldrs: effrt 3f out: styd on to ld ins fnl f: sn hdd: kpt on)	1¼	**2**	8/1	90	42
645^{2}	**Barrier Ridge** (HRACecil) **3-9-0** KFallon(6) (lw: led: rdn 3f out: hdd & no ex fnl f)	2½	**3**	$6/5^{1}$	90	42
963^{7}	**Khalik (IRE)** (EALDunlop) **3-9-0** WRyan(2) (b: hld up & bhd: gd hdwy 3f out: wknd over 1f out)	13	**4**	8/1	67	19
795^{3}	**Nobel Lad** (JLDunlop) **3-9-0** TSprake(9) (b: a.p: outpcd fnl 3f)	1½	**5**	$5/1^{2}$	65	17
	Pharly Star (DShaw) **3-9-0** JFanning(10) (rangy: unf: bkwd: nvr nr to chal)	5	**6**	50/1	56	8
899^{6}	**Heubach Boy** (MrsASwinbank) **3-9-0** GDuffield(4) (sn outpcd & bhd)	s.h	**7**	66/1	56	8
	Robban Hendi (USA) (MAJarvis) **3-9-0** PBloomfield(8) (w'like: bit bkwd: outpcd appr st: a bhd)	¾	**8**	12/1	54	6
1023^{12}	**Glorious Dancer** (JHetherton) **3-8-9** MBirch(7) (cl up tl wknd over 3f out)	7	**9**	50/1	37	—

				SP	RR	SF
945[7]	**Impetus** (JHetherton) **3-9-0** NKennedy(3) (plld hrd: chsd ldrs tl wknd over 3f out)	hd	**10**	50/1	42	—
				(SP 113.7%)	**10 Rn**	

1m 58.7 (7.70) CSF £46.08 TOTE £6.70: £1.70 £1.70 £1.10 (£26.40) Trio £8.50 OWNER Cheveley Park Stud (NEWMARKET) BRED Cheveley Park Stud Ltd
683 Darcy is a hard ride but certainly stays well and should improve as he tries longer distances. (6/1)
885 Epworth keeps running well and deserves to find a race or two. (8/1)
645 Barrier Ridge has not much of an action and his limitations were exposed some way from home. (6/5: evens-10/11)
963 Khalik (IRE), ridden from behind this time, certainly has a useful turn of foot, but he stopped dramatically in the closing stages. (8/1)
795 Nobel Lad found this well beyond him when the pace was really on in the last three furlongs. (5/1)
Pharly Star needs time and never looked likely to get into this. (50/1)
Robban Hendi (USA) (12/1: op 8/1)

T/Plpt: £77.50 (178.95 Tckts). T/Qdpt: £25.90 (25.86 Tckts) AA

1108-**BATH (L-H) (Good becoming Good to soft)**
Monday May 19th
WEATHER: heavy rain with sunny periods WIND: mod half against

1272 50 YEARS OF TIMEFORM MEDIAN AUCTION MAIDEN STKS (3-Y.O) (Class F)
2-15 (2-21) **1m 5y** £2,556.00 (£716.00: £348.00) Stalls: Low GOING: 0.30 sec per fur (G)

				SP	RR	SF
963[11]	**Space Race** (CACyzer) **3-9-0** LDettori(8) (led over 3f: led over 2f out: drvn out)	—	**1**	13/2[3]	76	46
161[3]	**Twin Time** (MJHeaton-Ellis) **3-8-9** SDrowne(17) (bit bkwd: trckd ldrs: hdwy over 2f out: sn ev ch: rdn & kpt on ins fnl f)	1¼	**2**	16/1	69	39
868[3]	**Mr Paradise (IRE) (69)** (TJNaughton) **3-9-0** DHolland(16) (lw: mid div: rdn along over 4f out: swtchd rt & hdwy over 2f out: r.o ins fnl f)	1¾	**3**	13/2[3]	70	40
784[7]	**Keen Dancer (69)** (MBell) **3-9-0** MRoberts(10) (bkwd: hld up: hdwy over 1f out: fin wl)	s.h	**4**	10/1	70	40
1164[5]	**Abajany (66)** (MRChannon) **3-8-9**(5) PPMurphy(9) (lw: prom: led over 4f out tl over 2f out: wknd ins fnl f)	nk	**5**	3/1[1]	69	39
885[6]	**Arriving** (JWHills) **3-8-9** MHills(3) (trckd ldrs: rdn over 2f out: sn btn)	¾	**6**	6/1[2]	63	33
1000[4]	**Warring (58)** (MSSaunders) **3-9-0** FNorton(2) (mid div: effrt ½-wy: no hdwy fnl 2f)	3½	**7**	14/1	61	31
964[10]	**Hever Golf Charmer** (TJNaughton) **3-9-0** SSanders(12) (chsd ldrs: rdn 2f out: sn wknd)	2	**8**	50/1	57	27
	Khamsin (IRE) (MJHeaton-Ellis) **3-8-9** AClark(14) (w'like: str: bkwd: nvr plcd to chal)	3½	**9**	10/1	45	15
989[5]	**Elegant Dance** (JJSheehan) **3-8-9** DaneO'Neill(1) (bit bkwd: plld hrd: prom over 5f)	1¾	**10**	11/1	41	11
785[7]	**Joyful Joy (40)** (BPJBaugh) **3-8-9** GHind(5) (a in rr)	2½	**11**	66/1	36	6
	Certain Surprise (MMadgwick) **3-8-9** RPerham(4) (w'like: scope: bit bkwd: s.s: a in rr)	½	**12**	66/1	35	5
1140[13]	**Tartan Party (62)** (PFICole) **3-9-0b**[1] TQuinn(15) (dwlt: sn prom: rdn & wknd over 2f out: eased)	1¼	**13**	14/1	38	8
757[8]	**Seamus (47)** (CJHill) **3-9-0** AMcGlone(13) (t: s.s: a bhd)	1¼	**14**	20/1	35	5
795[11]	**Blue Island (IRE)** (ICampbell) **3-8-11**(3) AWhelan(11) (a rr div: t.o)	7	**15**	66/1	22	—
	Blue Calvine (CJHill) **3-9-0** NAdams(7) (leggy: lt-f: s.s: a bhd: t.o)	6	**16**	66/1	10	—
	Another Victim (MBlanshard) **3-9-0** JQuinn(6) (lt-f: unf: s.s: a bhd: t.o)	20	**17**	33/1	—	—
				(SP 127.3%)	**17 Rn**	

1m 45.7 (7.50) CSF £96.65 TOTE £7.90: £2.20 £4.20 £2.60 (£76.00) Trio £81.20 OWNER Mr R. M. Cyzer (HORSHAM) BRED Mrs S. M. Sands and M. Yiapatos
673 Space Race found his true mark on this step down in class, and the rain-softened ground also seemed to suit him. (13/2: op 4/1)
161 Twin Time, whose only previous outing was on the All-Weather almost four months ago, looked far from fully wound-up for this return to action, but she was really into her stride inside the distance and the ability is there. (16/1)
868 Mr Paradise (IRE), in no hurry to take on the leaders, picked up well when switched for daylight entering the final quarter-mile, but the winner had got away and his effort was always going to be too late. (13/2)
784 Keen Dancer still has plenty left to work on, but he finished best of all and only just failed to make the frame. If he can continue to progress, he should not be too hard to place. (10/1)
1164 Abajany has been running well in handicaps of late, and he had a chance second to none on this return to maiden company but, after being in the firing line from the break, was tapped for toe in the closing stages. It would seem he needs a much stiffer test of stamina to get to the bottom of him. (3/1)
885 Arriving, made to work soon after straightening up for home, did not find a lot and she is not yet getting it together. (6/1: op 4/1)
1000 Warring (14/1: op 8/1)
Khamsin (IRE), a good-quartered filly very much in need of the run and the experience, was starting to realise what it was all about in the latter stages, and she is worth keeping in mind. (10/1: 8/1-12/1)
989 Elegant Dance (11/1: 8/1-12/1)

1273 TIMEFORM BLACK BOOK & RATINGS H'CAP (0-70) (3-Y.O+) (Class E)
2-45 (2-52) **1m 5y** £3,366.25 (£1,015.00: £492.50: £231.25) Stalls: Low GOING: 0.30 sec per fur (G)

				SP	RR	SF
	Vanborough Lad (37) (MJBolton) **8-7-6**(5) RFfrench(1) (hld up: hdwy over 2f out: led ins fnl f: comf)	—	**1**	14/1	45	31
	Noeprob (USA) (55) (RJHodges) **7-8-10**(5) AmandaSanders(15) (lw: a.p: led over 2f out tl ins fnl f: r.o)	nk	**2**	14/1	62	48
	Castel Rosselo (59) (ICampbell) **7-9-5** RPrice(4) (a.p: ev ch 2f out: hrd rdn & wandered: no ex nr fin)	1	**3**	14/1	64	50
1093[11]	**Gold Lance (USA) (48)** (RJO'Sullivan) **4-8-8** SSanders(11) (hld up: hdwy over 2f out: rdn & one pce ins fnl f)	3	**4**	8/1[3]	47	33
848[17]	**Shouldbegrey (42)** (WRMuir) **4-8-2v**[1] DaneO'Neill(18) (hdwy over 4f out: ev ch over 2f out: one pce appr fnl f)	nk	**5**	7/1[2]	41	27
721[6]	**Proud Brigadier (IRE) (41)** (MRBosley) **9-8-1** TSprake(7) (s.s: hdwy 2f out: nrst fin)	2	**6**	16/1	36	22
838[10]	**Utmost Zeal (USA) (61)** (PWHarris) **4-9-0b**[1](7) CLowther(13) (hdwy 4f out: sn rdn: wknd fnl 2f)	nk	**7**	14/1	55	41
1009[11]	**Delight of Dawn (49)** (EAWheeler) **5-8-4b**[1](5) ADaly(8) (prom: led wl over 2f out: sn hdd & wknd)	3½	**8**	16/1	36	22
608[10]	**Ca'd'oro (55)** (GBBalding) **4-9-1** SDrowne(3) (prom 4f: sn drvn along & lost pl: n.d after)	2½	**9**	4/1[1]	37	23
653[7]	**Ethbaat (USA) (55)** (MJHeaton-Ellis) **6-9-1** AClark(14) (hld up: hdwy on outside over 3f out: rdn & wknd fnl 2f)	7	**10**	12/1	23	9
759[12]	**Paddy's Rice (53)** (MBlanshard) **6-8-13** JQuinn(9) (a in rr)	½	**11**	16/1	20	6
	Absolute Utopia (USA) (64) (NEBerry) **4-9-10** RPerham(5) (bkwd: led 2f: wknd over 2f out: t.o)	13	**12**	25/1	5	—
598[14]	**Great Chief (50)** (BobJones) **4-8-10** AMcGlone(17) (b.hind: led after 2f tl wl over 2f out: wknd qckly: t.o)	2½	**13**	25/1	—	—
1111[10]	**Master Millfield (IRE) (60)** (CJHill) **5-9-6** MRoberts(2) (plld hrd: hld up in tch: wknd 3f out: t.o)	2½	**14**	14/1	—	—

848[19]	**Charlton Imp (USA) (54)** (RJHodges) **4-9-0** LDettori(16) (chsd ldrs 5f: sn wknd: t.o)	1	**15**	8/1 3	—	—
476[7]	**Country Thatch (52)** (CAHorgan) **4-8-12** PaulEddery(6) (prom: rdn ½-wy: sn wknd: t.o)	½	**16**	16/1	—	—
	Eric's Bett (63) (PGMurphy) **4-9-9** DHarrison(10) (bkwd: a bhd: t.o)	5	**17**	14/1	—	—
				(SP 133.6%)	**17 Rn**	

1m 45.6 (7.40) CSF £194.76 CT £2,650.27 TOTE £10.30: £1.70 £5.20 £3.10 £3.50 (£176.10) Trio £1,121.10 OWNER Mr A. R. M. Galbraith (SHREWTON) BRED Small Breeders' Group

Vanborough Lad reserves his best for this track and, fit from hurdling, stormed through to gain command inside the final furlong and win far more easily than the margin suggests. (14/1)

Noeprob (USA), twice a winner at this venue, was produced in tip-top condition for this belated seasonal reappearance. Doing nothing wrong, she had to admit the concession of 18lb just too much in the duel to the line. She deserves the chance to make amends. (14/1)

Castel Rosselo has not won a race for three years, but this change of tactics may well have paid off, had he not wandered about when the pressure was applied entering the final furlong. (14/1)

687* Gold Lance (USA) came from off the pace to reach his final placing, and was never in a position to cause concern. (8/1)

Shouldbegrey performs best when produced as late as possible, but he got there too soon in a first-time visor, and had shot his bolt when a final effort was called for. (7/1)

721 Proud Brigadier (IRE) is running well enough to win another race, but he has lost the habit of winning, and he may have to take a step down in grade if he is to succeed again. (16/1)

608 Ca'd'oro should have been thereabouts if producing the form he is capable of, but he lost his pitch starting the long home turn and was unable to recover the lost ground. (4/1)

79 85 85+ 73

1274 TIMEFORM RACE CARD NOVICE STKS (2-Y.O) (Class D) (80)

3-15 (3-20) **5f 11y** £3,246.00 (£978.00: £474.00: £222.00) Stalls: Low GOING minus 0.04 sec per fur (G)

				SP	RR	SF
971[2]	**Dim Ots** (BPalling) **2-8-9** TSprake(1) (mde all: edgd rt fr ½-wy: clr fnl f)	—	**1**	2/1 1	72	39
	Caversfield (RHannon) **2-8-12** DaneO'Neill(4) (leggy: chsd wnr: rdn ½-wy: no imp appr fnl f)	5	**2**	4/1 3	59	26
	The Rich Man (IRE) (BWHills) **2-8-12** MHills(5) (w'like: scope: bit bkwd: s.s: outpcd: hdwy 2f out: kpt on fnl f)	hd	**3**	5/2 2	59+	26
583[7]	**Means Business (IRE)** (BJMeehan) **2-8-12** RHughes(2) (chsd ldrs: eased whn btn appr fnl f)	5	**4**	8/1	43	10
	Carver John (PDCundell) **2-8-12** RPerham(6) (lt-f: outpcd)	3	**5**	12/1	34	1
	Hugger-Mugger (JRArnold) **2-8-12b1** PBloomfield(3) (neat: lt-f: swvd rt s: outpcd fr ½-wy: t.o)	22	**6**	20/1	—	—
				(SP 105.5%)	**6 Rn**	

63.6 secs (3.10) CSF £8.13 TOTE £2.80: £1.40 £2.50 (£6.30) OWNER Mrs D. J. Hughes (COWBRIDGE) BRED R. Bowers

971 Dim Ots put her previous experience to good use and, even though she was racing on ground far softer than she had encountered before, she was never in the slightest danger. (2/1)

Caversfield, a leggy colt from a winning family, was the only one able to make a race of it, but he was feeling the strain before reaching the final furlong. (4/1)

The Rich Man (IRE) lost what chance he had at the start, but he was getting down to some serious work in the latter stages, and the experience will not be lost. (5/2)

Means Business (IRE) ran much better than he did on his racecourse debut, but the softer ground took its toll, and he was eased when held inside the last furlong. (8/1: op 4/1)

Carver John (12/1: 6/1-14/1)

1275 TIMEFORM PHONE SERVICE LIMITED STKS (0-75) (3-Y.O) (Class D)

3-45 (3-45) **5f 11y** £3,351.50 (£1,007.00: £486.00: £225.50) Stalls: Low GOING minus 0.04 sec per fur (G)

				SP	RR	SF
876*	**Cauda Equina (75)** (MRChannon) **3-8-9**(5) PPMurphy(2) (hld up: swtchd rt & hdwy 2f out: rdn to ld ent fnl f: r.o wl)	—	**1**	11/4 3	77	12
964[4]	**Mutasawwar (74)** (EALDunlop) **3-8-11** RHills(4) (b: a.p: led over 2f out to 1f out: one pce)	2½	**2**	6/4 1	66	1
1141[19]	**Silver Purse (74)** (APJones) **3-8-8** SDrowne(3) (swtg: a.p: ev ch ins fnl f: unable qckn)	hd	**3**	9/1	63	—
1018[3]	**Divide And Rule (72)** (RHollinshead) **3-8-8**(3) DGriffiths(1) (lw: led to ½-wy: ev ch ins fnl f: wknd towards fin)	1½	**4**	9/4 2	61	—
				(SP 107.4%)	**4 Rn**	

65.6 secs (5.10) CSF £6.55 TOTE £3.00 (£3.00) OWNER Mr Michael Foy (UPPER LAMBOURN) BRED R. P. Williams

876* Cauda Equina carries a lot of condition, but he has the makings of quite a useful individual. Settled in the rear, he picked up readily to take charge into the final furlong and won very much as he pleased. (11/4: 2/1-3/1)

964 Mutasawwar did not race as freely as he did over a slightly longer trip at Salisbury, but he still held the call from halfway until the winner proved much too good for him. (6/4)

Silver Purse, showing her first signs of form this term, disputed the lead two hundred yards out, but found an extra effort beyond her when the winner got down to business. (9/1: 6/1-10/1)

1018 Divide And Rule attempted to make every post a winning one and did not fail for the want of trying, but he was the first to crack when it developed into a last-furlong dash. (9/4)

1276 TIMEFORM SILVER TANKARD MAIDEN STKS (I) (3-Y.O+) (Class D)

4-15 (4-20) **1m 2f 46y** £3,101.25 (£930.00: £447.50: £206.25) Stalls: Low GOING: 0.30 sec per fur (G)

				SP	RR	SF
1014[2]	**Solo Mio (IRE) (98)** (BWHills) **3-8-12** PatEddery(9) (lw: mde all: rdn over 2f out: r.o wl)	—	**1**	1/8 1	91	56
992[6]	**Fantastic Flame (IRE)** (PJMakin) **3-8-7** MRoberts(7) (hld up & bhd: gd hdwy 3f out: wnt 2nd over 1f out: nt trble wnr)	5	**2**	20/1 3	78	43
740[13]	**Legendary Lover (IRE)** (RCharlton) **3-8-12** TSprake(4) (prom tl wknd over 1f out)	5	**3**	33/1	75	40
1004[5]	**Big Target (IRE)** (MRStoute) **3-8-12** RHills(8) (hdwy 7f out: sn chsng wnr: wknd over 1f out)	1½	**4**	14/1 2	73	38
1023[5]	**Tramline** (MBlanshard) **4-9-12** JQuinn(5) (bit bkwd: nvr nr to chal)	2	**5**	33/1	70	49
	Bright Fountain (IRE) (HCandy) **3-8-7** AMcGlone(1) (unf: scope: bit bkwd: prom tl wknd over 2f out)	5	**6**	33/1	57	22
	Woody's Boy (IRE) (MJHeaton-Ellis) **3-8-12** SDrowne(12) (wl grwn: bkwd: hdwy over 4f out: wknd 3f out)	12	**7**	50/1	43	8
	Nigels Choice (CJHill) **5-9-12** DeclanO'Shea(10) (swtg: bhd fnl 3f)	1¾	**8**	100/1	41	20
1108[5]	**Light Reflections** (PGMurphy) **4-9-12** NAdams(2) (bit bkwd: plld hrd: prom over 7f)	5	**9**	100/1	33	12
754[2]	**Mystic Strand** (WGMTurner) **4-9-0**(7) DMcGaffin(11) (lw: s.s: a bhd)	2½	**10**	33/1	24	3
1105[12]	**Canadian Jive** (DWPArbuthnot) **4-9-7** RPrice(6) (a bhd)	1¼	**11**	100/1	22	1

				SP	RR	SF
842[10]	**Sassy Street (IRE)** (RFJohnsonHoughton) **4-9-12** SSanders(3) (rdn 4f out: bhd fnl 3f)	6	**12**	100/1	17	—
				(SP 118.0%)		**12 Rn**

2m 14.6 (8.10) CSF £5.74 TOTE £1.10: £1.10 £1.80 £3.10 (£5.10) Trio £13.70 OWNER Mr Wafic Said (LAMBOURN) BRED London Thoroughbred Services Ltd and Roncon Ltd
WEIGHT FOR AGE 3yo-14lb
1014 Solo Mio (IRE) ran here instead of in tomorrow's Predominate Stakes, and was workmanlike rather than impressive. His trainer is thinking in terms of the King Edward VII at Royal Ascot rather than the Derby, but he could go for the St Leger later on. (1/8)
992 Fantastic Flame (IRE), appreciating this step-up in distance, put in some eyecatching work in the home straight and looks a ready-made future winner. (20/1)
Legendary Lover (IRE), out of a half-sister to Guns of Navarone, had obviously learnt something from his Newbury debut. (33/1)
1004 Big Target (IRE) had softer ground to contend with this time, but is at least now qualified for handicaps. (14/1: op 8/1)
Bright Fountain (IRE) is a sister to the seven-furlong and mile winner Brighstone. (33/1)

1277 TIMEFORM SILVER TANKARD MAIDEN STKS (II) (3-Y.O+) (Class D)
4-45 (4-47) **1m 2f 46y** £3,101.25 (£930.00: £447.50: £206.25) Stalls: Low GOING: 0.30 sec per fur (G)

				SP	RR	SF
740[10]	**River Pilot** (RCharlton) **3-8-12** TSprake(3) (swtg: hld up: hdwy over 3f out: rdn to ld ins fnl f: r.o)	—	**1**	12/1	88	50
991[3]	**Chief Monarch** (BSmart) **3-8-12** PatEddery(7) (lw: a.p: led over 1f out tl ins fnl f)	¾	**2**	7/4[2]	87	49
875[2]	**Natural Eight (IRE) (88)** (BWHills) **3-8-12** MHills(9) (lw: w ldr: led over 2f out tl over 1f out: wknd fnl f)	7	**3**	11/10[1]	76	38
1106[6]	**Whirlawhile (USA)** (EALDunlop) **3-8-9**(3) DO'Donohoe(1) (b.hind: bit bkwd: hld up mid div: rdn over 2f out: one pce)	2	**4**	10/1[3]	73	35
725[14]	**Royal Castle (IRE)** (MajorWRHern) **3-8-12** PaulEddery(10) (nvr nr to chal)	1	**5**	16/1	71	33
944[7]	**Moon Colony** (LadyHerries) **4-9-12** DeclanO'Shea(6) (led 7f out tl over 2f out: wknd over 1f out)	2	**6**	16/1	68	44
	Stahr (HCandy) **3-8-12** NAdams(4) (mid div: rdn over 4f out: sn bhd)	5	**7**	33/1	60	22
373[4]	**Happy Medium (IRE)** (GPEnright) **4-9-7**(5) ADaly(11) (led over 3f: wknd over 2f out)	5	**8**	50/1	52	28
841[8]	**Sadler's Blaze (IRE)** (PWHarris) **3-8-12** AClark(8) (bkwd: a bhd: t.o)	10	**9**	33/1	37	—
989[11]	**Gore Hill (38)** (MBlanshard) **3-8-7** JQuinn(2) (lw: a bhd: t.o)	16	**10**	50/1	7	—
				(SP 122.3%)		**10 Rn**

2m 15.4 (8.90) CSF £31.52 TOTE £7.80: £1.80 £1.20 £1.20 (£10.60) Trio £6.50 OWNER Lady Rothschild (BECKHAMPTON) BRED Lord Rothschild
WEIGHT FOR AGE 3yo-14lb
River Pilot, a half-brother to Far Ahead, relished this extra quarter-mile in the rain-softened ground and should stay further. (12/1: 8/1-14/1)
991 Chief Monarch, appreciating this longer trip, simply met one too good on the day, but he is knocking at the door. (7/4)
875 Natural Eight (IRE) ought to be capable of staying further, but did not get home on this yielding surface. (11/10)
Whirlawhile (USA) failed to pick up in the home straight in the rain-softened ground, but will now be eligible for handicaps. (10/1)
Royal Castle (IRE), a well-bred colt, was another having his third run and should do better over a mile-and-a-half. (16/1)
Moon Colony, who moved from Andre Fabre to Maurice Zilber in France, was bought for 14,000 guineas at Newmarket Autumn Sales, having been placed in minor events. (16/1)

1278 TIMEFORM PERSPECTIVE & RATINGS H'CAP (0-80) (3-Y.O+ F & M) (Class D)
5-15 (5-18) **1m 5f 22y** £3,488.00 (£1,049.00: £507.00: £236.00) Stalls: High GOING: 0.30 sec per fur (G)

				SP	RR	SF
887*	**Star Precision (72)** (GBBalding) **3-8-5** SDrowne(3) (lw: hld up: hdwy over 4f out: led on bit over 2f out: r.o wl)	—	**1**	15/8[1]	88+	46
1036[3]	**Rasayel (USA) (73)** (PDEvans) **7-9-11** KFallon(6) (hld up: hdwy over 4f out: rdn & ev ch over 2f out: one pce)	6	**2**	3/1[3]	82	59
826[2]	**Night Mirage (USA) (74)** (MJohnston) **3-8-7** LDettori(8) (hld up: hdwy 3f out: one pce fnl 2f)	2	**3**	5/2[2]	80	38
151[6]	**Daily Sport Girl (44)** (BJLlewellyn) **8-7-10** JQuinn(7) (lw: chsd ldrs: led over 3f out tl over 2f out: wknd over 1f out)	5	**4**	14/1	44	21
1142[7]	**Classic Parisian (IRE) (73)** (ICampbell) **4-9-11** RPrice(1) (bit bkwd: swtg: hld up: hdwy 7f out: rdn & wknd over 3f out)	11	**5**	20/1	60	37
881[8]	**Mighty Phantom (USA) (72)** (JWHills) **4-9-7**(3) MHenry(2) (led: rdn & hdd over 3f out: sn wknd)	1¾	**6**	10/1	57	34
753[7]	**Miss Pravda (44)** (BJLlewellyn) **4-7-10** DeclanO'Shea(4) (bit bkwd: w ldr tl wknd 5f out: t.o fnl 3f)	dist	**7**	50/1	—	—
				(SP 110.8%)		**7 Rn**

2m 56.9 (11.20) CSF £6.60 CT £11.22 TOTE £3.40: £1.40 £2.20 (£4.90) OWNER Miss B. Swire (ANDOVER) BRED Miss B. Swire
LONG HANDICAP Daily Sport Girl 7-9 Miss Pravda 7-7
WEIGHT FOR AGE 3yo-19lb
887* Star Precision, raised 7lb, relished this longer trip, coming from a family with a reputation for staying well in this sort of ground. (15/8)
1036 Rasayel (USA), raised 8lb for winning at Nottingham last month, was two stone higher than when winning this race two years ago, and 17lb higher than when finishing third in it last season. (3/1)
826 Night Mirage (USA) did not find the combination of an extra furlong and softer ground offsetting her lack of acceleration. (5/2)
Daily Sport Girl was fit from hurdling. (14/1: 10/1-16/1)

1279 TIMEFORM DAY AT BATH H'CAP (0-70) (3-Y.O+) (Class E)
5-45 (5-48) **5f 161y** £3,268.75 (£985.00: £477.50: £223.75) Stalls: High GOING minus 0.04 sec per fur (G)

				SP	RR	SF
1250[5]	**Night Harmony (IRE) (52)** (MissSJWilton) **4-9-0** KFallon(9) (b: hdwy 2f out: r.o to ld nr fin)	—	**1**	10/1	60	42
1250[6]	**Runs in the Family (57)** (GMMcCourt) **5-9-5b** DHarrison(12) (led: rdn over 2f out: hdd nr fin)	¾	**2**	4/1[1]	63	45
1079[4]	**Flying Harold (43)** (MRChannon) **4-8-0**(5)ow2 PPMurphy(2) (hdwy over 2f out: rdn & hung lft over 1f out: r.o)	½	**3**	8/1	48	28
1141[4]	**Will To Win (55)** (PGMurphy) **3-8-8** SDrowne(17) (gd hdwy over 1f out: fin wl)	s.h	**4**	8/1	59	32
	Deerly (44) (RDickin) **4-8-6** GHind(1) (bkwd: a.p: ev ch over 1f out: one pce)	hd	**5**	16/1	48	30
835[6]	**Rockcracker (IRE) (51)** (GGMargarson) **5-8-10b**(3) MHenry(16) (hdwy over 1f out: r.o)	1	**6**	10/1	52	34
604[7]	**Ivory's Grab Hire (55)** (KTIvory) **4-9-3b** DBiggs(14) (swtg: prom: rdn over 1f out: eased whn btn wl ins fnl f)	1¼	**7**	20/1	53	35
390[8]	**Amnesty Bay (36)** (MDIUsher) **5-7-5**(7)ow2 RBrisland(7) (nvr nrr)	2½	**8**	66/1	27	7
1003[2]	**Tymeera (58)** (BPalling) **4-8-13**(7) CLowther(13) (nvr trbld ldrs)	nk	**9**	11/1	48	30
1003[8]	**Itsinthepost (51)** (VSoane) **4-8-13** NAdams(15) (b.nr hind: bit bkwd: chsd ldrs: rdn over 2f out: sn wknd)	s.h	**10**	25/1	41	23
588[7]	**Dancing Mystery (52)** (EAWheeler) **3-8-0**(5) ADaly(8) (s.s: a bhd)	s.h	**11**	33/1	42	15
1083[4]	**John O'Dreams (48)** (MrsALMKing) **12-8-10** MRoberts(5) (b: lw: n.d)	½	**12**	7/1[3]	36	18
1236[16]	**Arnie (IRE) (34)** (JRPoulton) **5-7-3**(7) JFowle(10) (a bhd)	nk	**13**	40/1	22	4
1113[4]	**Tinker Osmaston (60)** (MSSaunders) **6-9-8** RHughes(18) (lw: hld up: rdn over 2f out: sn bhd)	1¼	**14**	6/1[2]	44	26

				SP	RR	SF
	The Noble Oak (IRE) (34) (MJBolton) **9-7-3**(7) CCogan(19) (bkwd: a bhd)	1¾	**15**	66/1	13	—
	Don Pepe (62) (RBoss) **6-9-10** LDettori(4) (lw: prom 3f)	8	**16**	10/1	19	1
	Perchance To Dream (IRE) (58) (BRMillman) **3-8-11** WJO'Connor(11) (bkwd: prom 3f)	nk	**17**	25/1	14	—
*1046*13	**Positive Result (IRE) (34)** (RJPrice) **5-7-10** DeclanO'Shea(6) (bit bkwd: a bhd: t.o)	12	**18**	66/1	—	—

(SP 132.8%) **18 Rn**

1m 13.2 (3.70) CSF £45.49 CT £333.11 TOTE £10.90: £2.50 £1.20 £1.80 £2.60 (£28.50) Trio £67.20 OWNER Gilberts Animal Feed Products (STOKE-ON-TRENT) BRED Tally-Ho Stud

LONG HANDICAP The Noble Oak (IRE) 7-3 Arnie (IRE) 7-9 Amnesty Bay 7-9 Positive Result (IRE) 7-6

WEIGHT FOR AGE 3yo-9lb

1250 Night Harmony (IRE) had also finished well to pip Runs in the Family at Nottingham on Saturday, but this time it was for first place rather than fifth. (10/1)

1250 Runs in the Family again proved an expensive failure in the ring, but went much closer than two days ago. (4/1)

1079 Flying Harold, who very-nearly collided with the rails when drifting over to race alone on the inside, at least saved ground at the elbow. (8/1)

1141 Will To Win found this extended five too sharp despite the give underfoot. (8/1)

Deerly, who dropped 16lb down the ratings last season, ran her best race for a long time. (16/1)

835 Rockcracker (IRE), down 4lb, had the headgear on for the first time this season, but again had to contend with ground softer than he likes. (10/1: 8/1-12/1)

T/Jkpt: £25,381.30 (1.59 Tckts). T/Plpt: £32.80 (512.63 Tckts). T/Qdpt: £5.10 (135.13 Tckts) IM/KH

0924-MUSSELBURGH (R-H) (Good to soft)

Monday May 19th

WEATHER: overcast WIND: moderate half behind

63 70 64+ 61

1280 MAY MAIDEN AUCTION STKS (2-Y.O) (Class F) (64)

6-30 (6-31) **5f** £2,687.50 (£750.00: £362.50) Stalls: High GOING minus 0.03 sec per fur (G)

				SP	RR	SF
993[4]	**Sandside** (JBerry) **2-8-7** GCarter(2) (lw: cl up: led 2f out: hung lft: r.o u.p)	—	**1**	10/11[1]	70	12
548[4]	**Oriel Girl** (PDEvans) **2-8-2**ow1 JFEgan(3) (b.nr fore: a cl up: chal 2f out: nt qckn ins fnl f)	½	**2**	6/1[3]	63	4
743[7]	**Crafty Pet (IRE)** (RAFahey) **2-7-7**(7) RWinston(4) (w ldrs: effrt 2f out: r.o one pce)	3	**3**	8/1	52	—
897[3]	**Baby Grand (IRE)** (TDBarron) **2-7-13** JFanning(5) (led 3f: rdn & btn appr fnl f)	2	**4**	7/1	44	—
948[2]	**Turf Moor (IRE)** (JJO'Neill) **2-8-6** JCarroll(1) (dwlt: hdwy & ch ½-wy: sn rdn & btn)	2½	**5**	5/1[2]	43	—

(SP 106.9%) **5 Rn**

62.2 secs (4.50) CSF £5.69 TOTE £1.90: £1.10 £3.00 (£4.30) OWNER Mr J. K. Brown (COCKERHAM) BRED P. Young

993 Sandside was the pick of these on looks, but it was never easy and he will probably be better on faster ground. (10/11: evens-11/10)

548 Oriel Girl keeps running well and ought to find a race in due course. (6/1)

743 Crafty Pet (IRE) goes well on the bridle and looks the type to pick up a race, especially if dropped in class. (8/1)

897 Baby Grand (IRE) was a shade flattered first time, and this is probably as good as she is. (7/1: 4/1-8/1)

948 Turf Moor (IRE) came out of a moderate race at Thirsk last time and, very edgy beforehand here, she ran poorly. (5/1: 4/1-6/1)

1281 EAST LOTHIAN H'CAP (0-65) (3-Y.O+) (Class F)

7-00 (7-00) **1m 4f 31y** £2,827.50 (£790.00: £382.50) Stalls: High GOING minus 0.03 sec per fur (G)

				SP	RR	SF
1036*	**The Butterwick Kid (54)** (RAFahey) **4-8-10**(7) RWinston(7) (lw: hld up: effrt 2f out: led ins fnl f: r.o)	—	**1**	2/1[1]	63+	39
1042[2]	**Kathryn's Pet (60)** (MrsMReveley) **4-9-9** ACulhane(3) (lw: hld up: smooth hdwy ent st: led 2f out tl ins fnl f: kpt on)	2	**2**	6/1[3]	66	42
574[8]	**Ambidextrous (IRE) (48)** (EJAlston) **5-8-11** DWright(5) (lw: hld up & bhd: hdwy 4f out: chsng ldrs 2f out: kpt on)	1¾	**3**	9/1	52	28
608[9]	**Teejay'n'aitch (IRE) (33)** (JSGoldie) **5-7-5**(5) JBramhill(6) (mde most tl hdd 2f out: one pce)	1¾	**4**	9/2[2]	35	11
846[5]	**Jubran (USA) (50)** (JLEyre) **11-8-13** MGallagher(2) (b.nr hind: hdwy to jn ldrs 6f out: outpcd fnl 2½f)	6	**5**	20/1	44	20
1095*	**Father Eddie (60)** (JJO'Neill) **3-8-6** JCarroll(1) (b.nr fore: in tch: effrt over 3f out: no imp)	5	**6**	14/1	47	6
650[10]	**General Glow (54)** (PDEvans) **4-9-3** JFEgan(8) (chsd ldrs tl wknd fnl 2½f)	6	**7**	20/1	33	9
1232[2]	**Lord Advocate (42)** (DANolan) **9-8-5b** VHalliday(11) (disp ld 4f: wknd appr st)	1	**8**	8/1	20	—
955[12]	**Cois Na Farraige (IRE) (62)** (MissLAPerratt) **4-9-11** OUrbina(9) (chsd ldrs tl wknd 3f out)	hd	**9**	50/1	40	16
1042*	**Sun Mark (IRE) (62)** (MrsASwinbank) **6-9-11** JSupple(4) (lw: in tch tl wknd fnl 3f)	1¾	**10**	10/1	38	14
	Dunrowan (51) (MrsMReveley) **4-8-9**(5) SCopp(10) (bit bkwd: a bhd)	6	**11**	25/1	19	—

(SP 118.0%) **11 Rn**

2m 42.6 (9.10) CSF £11.99 CT £81.76 TOTE £3.20: £1.30 £2.10 £2.70 (£5.20) Trio £26.80 OWNER Mr Robert Chambers (MALTON) BRED Scorrier Stud

LONG HANDICAP Teejay'n'aitch (IRE) 7-9

WEIGHT FOR AGE 3yo-17lb

1036* The Butterwick Kid both looked and travelled well and, given a confident ride, won nicely. (2/1: 11/4-7/4)

1042 Kathryn's Pet likes cut in the ground and has a useful turn of foot, but the winner was always too good for her. (6/1)

574 Ambidextrous (IRE) likes this track but ideally prefers faster ground, so this was not a bad effort. (9/1)

Teejay'n'aitch (IRE) has been a revelation over hurdles recently. This was a fair effort and he may well find a suitable race. (9/2)

846 Jubran (USA), dropped back in trip, ran a good deal better. (20/1)

1095* Father Eddie found this company a different proposition. (14/1: 10/1-16/1)

1282 LEVENHALL MEDIAN AUCTION MAIDEN STKS (3-Y.O) (Class F)

7-30 (7-31) **1m 4f 31y** £2,617.50 (£730.00: £352.50) Stalls: High GOING minus 0.03 sec per fur (G)

				SP	RR	SF
868[2]	**Rheinbold** (TJEtherington) **3-9-0** GCarter(3) (lw: trckd ldr gng wl: shkn up to ld 1f out: comf)	—	**1**	6/4[2]	70+	12
641[2]	**High On Life (71)** (ACStewart) **3-9-0** SWhitworth(2) (led tl hdd 1f out: kpt on same pce)	1¾	**2**	11/10[1]	68	10
	In The Genes (JLEyre) **3-9-0** MGallagher(1) (str: trckd ldrs: effrt over 2f out: kpt on wl: nt pce to chal)	2½	**3**	5/1[3]	64	6
1095[4]	**Arboreal (USA) (48)** (MrsLStubbs) **3-8-2v**1(7) RWinston(5) (chsd ldr tl outpcd fnl 3f)	7	**4**	33/1	50	—

Form	Horse	Dist	Pos	SP	RR	SF
996^{5}	**Linea-G** (MrsMReveley) **3-8-9** ACulhane(4) (hld up & bhd: nvr nr to chal)	2½	**5**	20/1	47	—
				(SP 112.0%)		**5 Rn**

2m 46.6 (13.10) CSF £3.26 TOTE £2.50: £1.30 £1.10 (£1.40) OWNER Mr E. Oliver (MALTON) BRED Witney Stud Farm
868 Rheinbold, unlucky not to get the race in the Stewards' room last time, made no mistake here and won in useful style. (6/4)
641 High On Life, trying another step-up in trip, did his utmost but was always second best when the pressure was on. (11/10: evens-10/11)
In The Genes, a sturdy newcomer, ran well and should have learnt plenty from the experience. (5/1)
1095 Arboreal (USA) wore a visor for the first time, which did not seem to have the desired effect. (33/1)
Linea-G never got into this, but she is learning and there looks to be something there. (20/1)

1283 FISHERROW (S) STKS (3-Y.O+) (Class G)

8-00 (8-00) **1m 16y** £2,234.00 (£624.00: £302.00) Stalls: High GOING minus 0.03 sec per fur (G)

Form	Horse	Dist	Pos	SP	RR	SF
1266^{3}	**Power Game (54)** (JBerry) **4-9-7b** GCarter(1) (trckd ldr: led wl over 2f out: r.o: clr fnl f)	—	**1**	$5/6^{1}$	60	—
	Diamond Crown (IRE) (47) (MartynWane) **6-9-7** JCarroll(5) (hld up: effrt & ev ch over 2f out: nt qckn)	5	**2**	$3/1^{3}$	50	—
	She's A Winner (IRE) (40) (PMonteith) **4-8-11**(5) JBramhill(6) (led tl hdd wl over 2f out: sn outpcd)	1¾	**3**	$9/4^{2}$	42	—
				(SP 110.3%)		**3 Rn**

1m 50.5 (11.50) CSF £3.29 TOTE £1.70: (£1.50) OWNER Countrywide Racing (COCKERHAM) BRED Bearstone Stud
Bt in 5,600gns
1266 Power Game always had the measure of his two rivals and won with something to spare. (5/6: evens-4/5)
Diamond Crown (IRE) had plenty on with the winner on official figures, and was well out-pointed. (3/1: 11/4-9/2)
She's A Winner (IRE) likes the easy ground and looked fit, but proved very disappointing when ridden. (9/4: 6/4-5/2)

1284 MUSSELBURGH HONEST TOUN H'CAP (0-65) (3-Y.O) (Class F)

8-30 (8-31) **1m 16y** £2,687.50 (£750.00: £362.50) Stalls: High GOING minus 0.03 sec per fur (G)

Form	Horse	Dist	Pos	SP	RR	SF
1078^{6}	**Tycoon Tina (46)** (WMBrisbourne) **3-8-6**(5) JBramhill(6) (in tch: hdwy 3f out: rdn to ld ins fnl f: styd on wl)	—	**1**	10/1	57	31
1078^{5}	**Samspet (40)** (RAFahey) **3-7-12**(7) RWinston(8) (led tl hdd ins fnl f: no ex)	2½	**2**	$4/1^{3}$	46	20
1129^{7}	**Polarize (55)** (TDBarron) **3-9-6b¹** ACulhane(9) (lw: plld hrd: trckd ldrs: hrd rdn over 2f out: no ex)	4	**3**	$7/2^{2}$	53	27
842^{13}	**Gold Clipper (35)** (MJRyan) **3-8-0** GCarter(4) (a chsng ldrs: rdn & one pce fnl 3f)	nk	**4**	14/1	33	7
1043^{3}	**Shaded (IRE) (56)** (JWWatts) **3-9-7** JCarroll(1) (lw: in tch: effrt 3f out: no imp)	2	**5**	$3/1^{1}$	50	24
997^{7}	**Abstone Queen (55)** (PDEvans) **3-9-6v** JFEgan(2) (bhd: sme hdwy u.p fnl 2f: n.d)	2	**6**	9/1	45	19
550^{7}	**See You Soon (40)** (CWThornton) **3-8-5** DeanMcKeown(5) (b.nr hind: lw: in tch tl outpcd ½-wy: n.d after)	8	**7**	16/1	14	—
497^{4}	**Manhattan Diamond (50)** (ABailey) **3-9-1** KHodgson(7) (prom tl wknd fnl 3½f)	1	**8**	16/1	22	—
1024^{16}	**Burlesque (48)** (JDBethell) **3-8-13b¹** SWhitworth(3) (outpcd & bhd fr ½-wy)	hd	**9**	20/1	20	—
952^{3}	**Sweet Note (IRE) (50)** (MissLAPerratt) **3-9-1** OUrbina(10) (drvn along ½-wy: n.d)	nk	**10**	12/1	21	—
				(SP 117.2%)		**10 Rn**

1m 45.2 (6.20) CSF £45.59 CT £156.10 TOTE £11.70: £1.50 £1.70 £1.90 (£29.20) Trio £10.60 OWNER Mr Brooke Rankin (NESSCLIFFE) BRED A. H. Brisbourne
1078 Tycoon Tina jumped off on terms for once, then proved determined under pressure and thoroughly deserved this. (10/1)
1078 Samspet, a free-runner, made it and kept trying hard, but was well out-pointed late on. (4/1)
497* Polarize had blinkers on for the first time, and this caused him to pull quite hard early on. However, they failed to have their desired effect when the pressure was applied in the home straight. (7/2)
Gold Clipper, first-time in a handicap, ran a good deal better. (14/1)
1043 Shaded (IRE) keeps trying all sorts of trips on various surfaces, but so far without any luck. (3/1)
997 Abstone Queen showed a little here, trying to come from behind, but was still never doing enough. (9/1: 5/1-10/1)

1285 MUSSELBURGH LINKS H'CAP (0-70) (3-Y.O+) (Class E)

9-00 (9-02) **7f 15y** £3,168.00 (£954.00: £462.00: £216.00) Stalls: High GOING minus 0.03 sec per fur (G)

Form	Horse	Dist	Pos	SP	RR	SF
	Miss Pigalle (35) (MissLAPerratt) **6-7-11** NKennedy(12) (in tch: hdwy 3f out: led ins fnl f: styd on wl)	—	**1**	25/1	50	5
1077^{5}	**Broctune Gold (65)** (MrsMReveley) **6-9-13** ACulhane(13) (cl up: led 2f out: hdd ins fnl f: kpt on u.p)	½	**2**	$4/1^{2}$	79	34
1079^{3}	**Rymer's Rascal (57)** (EJAlston) **5-9-5** DeanMcKeown(11) (a chsng ldrs: kpt on one pce fnl 2f)	2½	**3**	$6/1^{3}$	65	20
903^{2}	**Dancing Sioux (53)** (RGuest) **5-9-1** JFanning(10) (b: led tl hdd 2f out: grad wknd)	2½	**4**	8/1	56	11
929^{8}	**Seconds Away (37)** (JSGoldie) **6-7-6**(7)ow3 JMcAuley(5) (lost pl appr st: r.o fnl 2f: nrst fin)	nk	**5**	20/1	36	—
848^{11}	**Euro Sceptic (IRE) (46)** (TDEasterby) **5-8-5b**(3) RHavlin(4) (lw: rr div: effrt 3f out: nvr trbld ldrs)	nk	**6**	10/1	47	2
1020^{4}	**Nkapen Rocks (SPA) (53)** (CaptJWilson) **4-9-1** GCarter(2) (prom: effrt 3f out: sn rdn & btn)	s.h	**7**	7/1	54	9
1040^{7}	**Rattle (35)** (DANolan) **4-7-6**(5)ow1 JBramhill(8) (bhd: effrt ½-wy: n.d)	2	**8**	33/1	32	—
827^{16}	**Naughty Pistol (USA) (55)** (PDEvans) **5-9-3b** JFEgan(6) (chsd ldrs tl wknd fnl 3f)	1½	**9**	8/1	48	3
1131^{2}	**La Dolce Vita (65)** (TDBarron) **3-9-2** JCarroll(9) (lw: prom: effrt 3f out: rdn & wknd 2f out)	6	**10**	$11/4^{1}$	45	—
1079^{7}	**Most Respectful (51)** (DenysSmith) **4-8-6**(7) RWinston(3) (w ldrs tl wknd fnl 3f)	6	**11**	25/1	17	—
	King Chestnut (53) (MDods) **6-9-1** SWhitworth(7) (a bhd)	12	**12**	33/1	—	—
				(SP 123.1%)		**12 Rn**

1m 32.5 (6.50) CSF £110.27 CT £508.97 TOTE £40.90: £8.30 £1.70 £2.70 (£22.20) Trio £137.70 OWNER Miss Heather Galbraith (AYR) BRED Miss Heather Galbraith
LONG HANDICAP Rattle 7-8 Seconds Away 7-1
WEIGHT FOR AGE 3yo-11lb
Miss Pigalle has gained both of her wins on this track, and there was plenty to like about the way she did this. (25/1)
1077 Broctune Gold loves this track, but found one too determined in a driving finish. (4/1)
1079 Rymer's Rascal had his chances but lacked a turn of foot. (6/1)
903 Dancing Sioux has plenty of ability, but does not always give it his best when the pressure is on. (8/1)
526 Seconds Away is a funny customer who certainly has ability, but ran pretty well here from 9lb out of the handicap. (20/1)
Euro Sceptic (IRE) looks on good terms with himself just now and ran reasonably. Should he return to Beverley (his favourite track) he could be well worth bearing in mind. (10/1)
1020 Nkapen Rocks (SPA) ran disappointingly as he often does. (7/1: op 7/2)

T/Plpt: £17.60 (714.25 Tckts). T/Qdpt: £9.00 (78.86 Tckts) AA

1132-SOUTHWELL (L-H) (Standard)

Monday May 19th

WEATHER: fine WIND: almost nil

66+ 53

1286 E.B.F. CARDIFF MEDIAN AUCTION MAIDEN STKS (2-Y.O) (Class F)

2-30 (2-31) **5f (Fibresand)** £2,646.60 (£732.60: £349.80) Stalls: High GOING: 0.16 sec per fur (SLW)

				SP	RR	SF
897[5]	**Always Lucky** (JBerry) **2-8-4**(5) PFessey(5) (mde virtually all: edgd rt & styd on wl fnl f)	—	1	100/30[2]	76	25
902[5]	**Flickan** (RGuest) **2-8-6**(3) MartinDwyer(9) (w wnr: nt qckn ins fnl f)	1¾	2	6/1	70	19
611[4]	**Captain Brady (IRE)** (WGMTurner) **2-8-11**(3) RHavlin(10) (swtg: unruly s: swvd rt s: w ldrs tl wknd over 1f out)	5	3	13/2	59	8
1045[9]	**Gifted Bairn (IRE)** (DNicholls) **2-8-9** AlexGreaves(2) (a chsng ldrs: one pce fnl 2f)	s.h	4	20/1	54	3
836[10]	**Monopoly (IRE)** (MJohnston) **2-9-0** JWeaver(11) (chsd ldrs: outpcd fnl 2f)	¾	5	2/1[1]	57	6
	Angie Minor (JWharton) **2-8-9** MBirch(6) (cmpt: bit bkwd: s.i.s: hdwy ½-wy: nvr nr to chal)	2½	6	33/1	44	—
	Lawful Contract (IRE) (RHollinshead) **2-8-11**(3) FLynch(7) (tall: sn outpcd)	1¼	7	16/1	45	—
1120[13]	**Averham Star** (DShaw) **2-8-11**(3) CTeague(4) (prom: outpcd after 2f: rdn & hung lft 2f out: sn wknd)	¾	8	33/1	42	—
	Jen's In The Know (CMurray) **2-8-9** DeanMcKeown(8) (leggy: chsd ldrs: edgd rt & wknd over 1f out)	8	9	16/1	12	—
	Liberte Bell (IRE) (SirMarkPrescott) **2-8-9** GDuffield(3) (leggy: scope: s.i.s: racd wd: a outpcd)	5	10	11/2[3]	—	—
	Risknowt Getnowt (TWall) **2-9-0** RLappin(1) (leggy: s.i.s: racd wd: a bhd)	2½	11	33/1	—	—

(SP 124.8%) **11 Rn**

61.7 secs (4.70) CSF £22.23 TOTE £3.50: £1.20 £1.50 £2.30 (£16.60) Trio £33.30 OWNER Miss Lilo Blum (COCKERHAM) BRED Ridgebarn Farm Stud, Mrs L. Jenkins and Mrs T. She

IN-FOCUS: **This was trainer Jack Berry's 1,400th winner, including Flat, Jumps and races abroad.**

897 Always Lucky was much happier getting her toe in. Despite edging right under pressure, she was always doing more than enough. (100/30)

902 Flickan showed the benefit of her initial outing, and pushed the winner hard all the way to the line. (6/1: op 7/2)

611 Captain Brady (IRE), warm beforehand, was reluctant to go behind the stalls and had to be dismounted. Swerving right leaving them, he raced upsides but his stamina seemed to give out in the final furlong. On turf he will be suited by a sharp downhill track, and a seller may be more his mark. (13/2)

Gifted Bairn (IRE) does not lack speed but, at this stage of her career, seems to have trouble lasting out the five. (20/1)

Monopoly (IRE), tucked away on the stands' side rail, had the worst of the kick-back and was left behind in the final two furlongs. (2/1)

Angie Minor did not shape too badly, but probably needs six furlongs already. (33/1)

Liberte Bell (IRE) (11/2: 7/2-6/1)

1287 EDINBURGH CLAIMING LIMITED STKS (0-55) (3-Y.O+) (Class F)

3-00 (3-00) **1m 3f (Fibresand)** £2,277.00 (£627.00: £297.00) Stalls: Low GOING: 0.16 sec per fur (SLW)

				SP	RR	SF
236[8]	**Royal Legend (50)** (JPearce) **5-9-5v[1]** MWigham(2) (trckd ldrs: plld hrd: rdn to ld over 1f out: styd on)	—	1	5/1[2]	57	30
721[15]	**Zatopek (48)** (JCullinan) **5-9-9** VSlattery(1) (led tl over 1f out: kpt on same pce)	3½	2	8/1	56	29
*1138**	**Evezio Rufo (40)** (NPLittmoden) **5-9-6v**(5) PRoberts(5) (sn bhd & drvn along: hdwy on outside ½-wy: styd on one pce fnl 2f)	2½	3	5/1[2]	54	27
1024[15]	**Pc's Cruiser (IRE) (38)** (NPLittmoden) **5-9-7** JWeaver(6) (sn bhd: reminders & hdwy on outside ½-wy: hrd rdn & hung lft over 2f out: nvr nr to chal)	2	4	7/1[3]	47	20
908[8]	**Shuttlecock (40)** (DWChapman) **6-9-3** GDuffield(4) (w ldr tl outpcd fnl 3f)	2	5	9/2[1]	41	14
1133[6]	**Carrolls Marc (IRE) (40)** (CMurray) **9-8-12**(5) IonaWands(10) (b.hind: in tch: wnt prom 7f out: drvn along over 4f out: sn wl outpcd)	7	6	5/1[2]	30	3
595[12]	**Dino's Mistral (32)** (FHLee) **4-9-5** DeanMcKeown(8) (w ldrs: rdn & wknd 2f out)	3½	7	20/1	27	—
1114[8]	**Dormy Three (48)** (RJHodges) **7-9-5** JLowe(9) (trckd ldrs: effrt 3f out: sn wknd)	5	8	7/1[3]	20	—
1001[8]	**El Bardador (IRE) (42)** (RJHodges) **4-9-5** NVarley(7) (sn bhd & pushed along: rdn 5f out: t.o 3f out)	7	9	12/1	10	—
1247[6]	**Gunner B Special (33)** (SRBowring) **4-9-7b** SWebster(3) (b: sn bhd & pushed along: t.o 3f out)	6	10	20/1	3	—

(SP 121.5%) **10 Rn**

2m 32.1 (12.10) CSF £42.58 TOTE £7.10: £2.30 £3.50 £1.50 (£51.80) Trio £60.30 OWNER Mrs K. J. Crangle (NEWMARKET) BRED Newgate Stud Co

Royal Legend, in a visor for the first time, took a keen grip but, when sent about his business, did enough to take a modest event. (5/1)

328 Zatopek, who lacks any finishing speed, set out to make the running. He would have met the winner on 6lb better terms in a handicap. (8/1)

1138* Evezio Rufo, who would have been 16lb better off with the winner in a handicap, as usual took some stoking up. (5/1: op 3/1)

870 Pc's Cruiser (IRE), who would have been a stone better off with the winner in a handicap, as usual got behind and looked reluctant to exert himself under pressure. (7/1: op 12/1)

284 Shuttlecock started favourite despite the fact that he would have met the winner on 8lb better terms in a handicap. He was in trouble on the turn. (9/2: op 3/1)

1288 BIRMINGHAM H'CAP (0-70) (4-Y.O+) (Class E)

3-30 (3-30) **1m 6f (Fibresand)** £2,784.25 (£829.00: £394.50: £177.25) Stalls: Low GOING: 0.16 sec per fur (SLW)

				SP	RR	SF
*1133**	**Kalamata (59)** (JAGlover) **5-9-4** 5x NDay(4) (trckd ldrs: shkn up to ld over 5f out: clr over 3f out: eased fin)	—	1	7/4[2]	85+	35
1027[2]	**Etterby Park (USA) (69)** (MJohnston) **4-10-0** JWeaver(1) (lw: trckd ldrs: pushed along 7f out: wl outpcd over 5f out: styd on fnl 2f: no ch w wnr)	19	2	11/8[1]	73	23
769[3]	**Cuban Nights (USA) (67)** (BJLlewellyn) **5-9-12** TWilliams(3) (trckd ldrs: rdn over 4f out: kpt on one pce)	3	3	11/2[3]	68	18
950[8]	**Mapengo (37)** (JCullinan) **6-7-3**(7) PDoe(5) (led: drvn along & hdd over 5f out: wknd fnl f)	½	4	50/1	37	—
	High Summer (63) (TThomsonJones) **7-9-8** DeanMcKeown(6) (b: trckd ldrs: rdn & lost pl 5f out)	9	5	14/1	53	3
1125[4]	**Forzair (47)** (JJO'Neill) **5-8-3**(3)ow3 FLynch(2) (lw: hld up: drvn along & wl outpcd over 5f out: sn bhd)	10	6	12/1	26	—

(SP 110.2%) **6 Rn**

3m 12.2 (14.20) CSF £3.93 TOTE £3.30: £1.10 £1.60 (£1.90) OWNER Mr B. H. Farr (WORKSOP) BRED Worksop Manor Stud Farm

LONG HANDICAP Mapengo 6-12

1133* Kalamata enjoyed his second course and distance success in the space of a week. Slipping through on the inner and injecting some pace, he was out on his own in the final three furlongs. He is sure to take a stiff rise in the weights now. (7/4)

1027 Etterby Park (USA), racing from a handicap mark 8lb lower than in the Chester Cup on turf, could not dominate and was finding this hard work a long way from home. To his credit, he stuck on to finish second best, but the winner was in a different parish. He seems best when forcing the pace. (11/8)

769 Cuban Nights (USA) was flat-out fully half-a-mile from home. (11/2)
272 Mapengo, who set just a sensible gallop, ran as well as could be expected until tiring in the final furlong, considering he was 12lb wrong at the weights. (50/1)

1289 LIVERPOOL H'CAP (0-60) (3-Y.O+) (Class F)

4-00 (4-04) **6f (Fibresand)** £2,277.00 (£627.00: £297.00) Stalls: Low GOING: 0.16 sec per fur (SLW)

				SP	RR	SF
1089*	**Sweet Mate (45)** (SRBowring) **5-9-1b** SWebster(5) (b.hind: mid div: sn pushed along: gd hdwy on outside 2f out: fin wl to ld nr fin)	—	1	5/2^{1}	55	35
956^{6}	**Silk Cottage (55)** (RMWhitaker) **5-9-8**$^{(3)}$ OPears(1) (lw: led tl wl ins fnl f: no ex)	2	2	12/1	60	40
1079^{6}	**Kid Ory (37)** (DWChapman) **6-8-7** GDuffield(2) (w ldrs: rdn to chal 2f out: nt qckn ins fnl f)	hd	3	10/1	41	21
1127^{4}	**Born A Lady (38)** (MrsVAAconley) **4-8-8** MDeering(11) (unruly s: hdwy on outside 2f out: styd on fnl f)	s.h	4	14/1	42	22
997^{8}	**Hoh Majestic (IRE) (58)** (RonaldThompson) **4-9-9v**$^{(5)}$ GMilligan(3) (lw: trckd ldrs: ev ch over 1f out: nt qckn)	¾	5	11/1	60	40
1046^{4}	**Delrob (43)** (DHaydnJones) **6-8-8b**$^{(5)}$ GFaulkner(13) (s.i.s: bhd tl hdwy on outside 2f out: nvr nr to chal)	1¼	6	5/1^{2}	42	22
827^{12}	**Zain Dancer (45)** (DNicholls) **5-9-1** AlexGreaves(6) (lw: sn trckng ldrs: shkn up 2f out: kpt on steadily)	nk	7	14/1	43	23
1089^{6}	**Lochon (45)** (MrsNMacauley) **6-8-12b**$^{(3)}$ CTeague(4) (b: s.i.s: sn chsng ldrs: rdn & outpcd over 2f out)	¾	8	14/1	41	21
1047^{12}	**Margaretrose Anna (35)** (BPJBaugh) **5-8-5** RLappin(12) (hld up & bhd: sme hdwy on outside 2f out: n.d)	3	9	33/1	23	3
1079^{5}	**Stephensons Rocket (44)** (RAFahey) **6-9-0** MBirch(15) (sme hdwy on outside ½-wy: nvr nr ldrs)	1¾	10	7/1^{3}	28	8
855^{4}	**Prudent Princess (44)** (AHide) **5-8-7v**$^{(7)}$ CWebb(10) (racd wd: sn chsng ldrs: wknd 2f out)	nk	11	16/1	27	7
	Bent Raiwand (USA) (38) (DonEnricoIncisa) **4-8-8** KimTinkler(7) (chsd ldrs tl wknd over 2f out)	¾	12	33/1	19	—
332^{7}	**Guy's Gamble (40)** (JWharton) **4-8-5**$^{(5)}$ SophieMitchell(14) (bhd fr ½-wy)	¾	13	14/1	19	—
751^{4}	**Nervous Rex (55)** (WRMuir) **3-9-2b** JWeaver(8) (hld up: a bhd)	½	14	12/1	32	3
1048^{11}	**Lady Silk (46)** (MissJFCraze) **6-9-2** NConnorton(9) (sn bhd)	8	15	16/1	2	—
1250^{18}	**Fleeting Footsteps (40)** (DShaw) **5-8-7**$^{(3)}$ FLynch(16) (b: swtg: s.i.s: a bhd)	14	16	33/1	—	—
				(SP 137.8%)	**16 Rn**	

1m 19.2 (5.70) CSF £35.39 CT £219.81 TOTE £5.50: £2.40 £3.50 £1.90 £2.90 (£41.00) Trio £116.00 OWNER Mr S. R. Bowring (EDWINSTOWE) BRED T. Barratt
WEIGHT FOR AGE 3yo-9lb
1089* Sweet Mate, racing off the same mark as Nottingham but 10lb lower than when winning on this surface in February, came with a late surge to get up in the last twenty yards and win going away. In this sort of mood, he is obviously capable of a follow-up. (5/2: 9/4-7/2)
956 Silk Cottage has only won twice in forty-one starts, but he showed plenty of resolution here. (12/1)
1079 Kid Ory never gave up trying but his effort lacked a final dash. He is probably better over seven furlongs. (10/1)
1127 Born A Lady, who gave trouble at the start, ran another creditable race. (14/1)
429* Hoh Majestic (IRE), taken to post quietly, gave a good account of himself under top weight. (11/1)
1046 Delrob, undeniably well-handicapped, put in some good late work after a sluggish break. (5/1)
827 Zain Dancer again hinted at better to come. Ideally suited by seven furlongs and a sound surface on turf, the market will no doubt tell the story. (14/1)
71 Guy's Gamble (14/1: op 8/1)

1290 HULL (S) STKS (2-Y.O) (Class G)

4-30 (4-32) **5f (Fibresand)** £1,984.50 (£547.00: £259.50) Stalls: High GOING: 0.16 sec per fur (SLW)

				SP	RR	SF
1137^{2}	**Ellenbrook (IRE)** (JBerry) **2-8-2b**$^{1(5)}$ PFessey(1) (unruly s: mde virtually all: clr ½-wy: drvn out)	—	1	4/5^{1}	56	4
1124^{4}	**Medina Miss** (WGMTurner) **2-8-0**$^{(7)}$ PDoe(3) (w wnr over 1f: kpt on fr ½-wy: no imp)	7	2	9/4^{2}	34	—
993^{15}	**Karenaragon** (RonaldThompson) **2-8-7** NConnorton(6) (outpcd & hung lft after 2f: kpt on fnl f)	6	3	33/1	14	—
648^{14}	**Ivory's Joy** (KTIvory) **2-8-7** CScally(4) (b: s.i.s: outpcd & hung lft ½-wy: sn chsng ldrs: wknd fnl f)	7	4	12/1	—	—
743^{9}	**General Joey** (MDods) **2-8-9b**$^{1(3)}$ CTeague(5) (v.unruly & uns rdr bef s: reard s: sn bhd: nt keen)	10	5	10/1	—	—
	Wideyedbushytailed (PatMitchell) **2-8-2**$^{(5)}$ RMullen(2) (leggy: lt-f: sn drvn along & outpcd: wl bhd fr ½-wy)	4	6	4/1^{3}	—	—
				(SP 126.0%)	**6 Rn**	

62.9 secs (5.90) CSF £3.20 TOTE £1.40: £1.00 £2.10 (£1.80) OWNER Mr J. K. Brown (COCKERHAM) BRED M. Bourke
Bt in 4,600gns
1137 Ellenbrook (IRE) again gave problems at the start. In blinkers this time, she was out on her own after two furlongs but had to be kept right up to her work. (4/5)
1124 Medina Miss, well-backed first time, kept on in pursuit of the winner but was never going to get in a blow. (9/4)
Karenaragon, last of fifteen in a maiden first time, was soon being taken off her legs. Sticking on under pressure in the final furlong, she needs six but will have to improve a good deal to win even a poor seller. (33/1)
Ivory's Joy, last of fourteen in a maiden first time, wanted to do nothing but hang left. (12/1)
General Joey, excitable on the way to the start wearing blinkers for the first time, gave all sorts of problems and unseated his rider before he was eventually loaded. Weary leaving the stalls, he wanted nothing to do with it. (10/1)

1291 LONDON H'CAP (0-65) (3-Y.O+) (Class F)

5-00 (5-01) **1m (Fibresand)** £2,277.00 (£627.00: £297.00) Stalls: Low GOING: 0.16 sec per fur (SLW)

				SP	RR	SF
1048^{7}	**Johnnie the Joker (57)** (JPLeigh) **6-9-3b**$^{(3)}$ CTeague(2) (mde most tl over 2f out: led ins fnl f: all out)	—	1	5/1^{2}	67	49
598^{5}	**Monte Cavo (35)** (MBrittain) **6-7-5**$^{(7)ow1}$ DMernagh(10) (chsd ldrs: led over 2f out tl over 1f out: nt qckn ins fnl f)	½	2	9/1^{3}	44	25
1093^{10}	**Bentico (61)** (MrsNMacauley) **8-9-5v**$^{(5)}$ GFaulkner(6) (lw: w ldrs: led over 2f out tl over 1f out: nt qckn towards fin)	s.h	3	14/1	70	52
668^{3}	**Kass Alhawa (35)** (DWChapman) **4-7-7**$^{(5)}$ PFessey(9) (s.i.s: hdwy 2f out: nvr nr ldrs)	7	4	10/1	30	12
1117^{5}	**Mercury (IRE) (52)** (JAGlover) **4-9-1** NDay(13) (racd wd: chsd ldrs: outpcd over 2f out: kpt on)	nk	5	9/1^{3}	46	28
1005^{8}	**Dragonjoy (60)** (NPLittmoden) **4-9-9b** RLappin(7) (chsd ldrs: rdn over 2f out: grad wknd)	2½	6	12/1	49	31
1135^{3}	**David James' Girl (43)** (ABailey) **5-8-1**$^{(5)}$ IonaWands(14) (lw: b: bhd & pushed along: sme hdwy 2f out: kpt on: nvr nr ldrs)	2	7	4/1^{1}	28	10
972^{5}	**Awesome Venture (65)** (MCChapman) **7-9-9**$^{(5)}$ TEDurcan(16) (lw: racd wd: hld up & bhd: effrt ½-wy: n.d)	6	8	14/1	38	20
1135^{14}	**Jilly Beveled (36)** (RonaldThompson) **5-7-13** TWilliams(4) (in tch: rdn over 2f out: sn wknd: virtually p.u nr fin)	1¼	9	33/1	7	—
578^{10}	**Chadleigh Lane (USA) (64)** (ABMulholland) **5-9-13** MBirch(5) (b: sn bhd & drvn along: sme hdwy ½-wy: n.d)	nk	10	10/1	34	16
547^{3}	**Hever Golf Charger (IRE) (59)** (TJNaughton) **3-8-10** DaleGibson(11) (unruly gng to s: chsd ldrs: lost pl over 2f out)	5	11	14/1	19	—

				SP	RR	SF
689[13]	**Scenicris (IRE) (42)** (RHollinshead) **4-8-2**(3)ow2 FLynch(15) (hld up: sme hdwy over 3f out: sn wknd)	¾	**12**	16/1	1	—
424[5]	**Quinzii Martin (42)** (DHaydnJones) **9-7-12b**(7) JoeleneRichards(3) (hld up & bhd: sme hdwy over 3f out: sn wknd)	3	**13**	14/1	—	—
1127[12]	**Oriel Lad (45)** (DonEnricoIncisa) **4-8-8** KimTinkler(8) (a bhd)	2	**14**	33/1	—	—
675[17]	**Saratoga Red (USA) (63)** (WAO'Gorman) **3-9-0** EmmaO'Gorman(12) (s.s: a bhd)	2	**15**	12/1	8	—
1024[13]	**Bernard Seven (IRE) (63)** (MDods) **5-9-12b** JWeaver(1) (lw: w ldrs: rdn 3f out: sn lost pl)	9	**16**	14/1	—	—
				(SP 135.3%)	**16 Rn**	

1m 45.7 (6.70) CSF £50.62 CT £589.96 TOTE £9.10: £2.90 £1.80 £3.20 £3.70 (£27.40) Trio £276.20; £202.36 to Goodwood 20/5/97 OWNER Miss M. Carrington-Smith (GAINSBOROUGH) BRED Miss M. Carrington-Smith
WEIGHT FOR AGE 3yo-12lb
IN-FOCUS: **Chadleigh Lane was Mark Birch's last ride before his retirement. He rode a total of 1,339 winners.**
860 Johnnie the Joker has recorded five of his seven victories on the All-Weather, and is clearly best when fitted with blinkers. (5/1)
598 Monte Cavo, walked down to the start, proved well-suited by the drop back in distance and gave his all. (9/1: 12/1-8/1)
857 Bentico ran easily his best race for some time. (14/1)
668 Kass Alhawa was racing from a mark 16lb lower than when third in a seller on Turf last time. (10/1)
1117 Mercury (IRE), who has slipped down the weights, ran an encouraging race. (9/1)
1135 David James' Girl was always making hard work of this, and never looked like entering the argument at any stage. (4/1: op 5/2)
461 Chadleigh Lane (USA) (10/1: 8/1-12/1)

T/Plpt: £39.20 (280.36 Tckts). T/Qdpt: £11.00 (62.21 Tckts) WG

1139-WINDSOR (Fig. 8) (Good to soft becoming Soft)
Monday May 19th

WEATHER: sunny WIND: almost nil

1292 EDWARD SYMMONS & PARTNERS CLAIMING STKS (3-Y.O+) (Class F)
6-15 (6-16) **1m 67y** £2,780.00 (£780.00: £380.00) Stalls: High GOING: 0.31 sec per fur (G)

				SP	RR	SF
1139[6]	**Finsbury Flyer (IRE) (68)** (RJHodges) **4-8-9**(5) RFfrench(14) (hdwy 3f out: led 2f out: drvn out)	—	**1**	7/1	71	43
728[12]	**Caudillo (IRE) (65)** (MrsPNDutfield) **4-8-5**(5) AimeeCook(10) (lw: a.p: ev ch fnl 2f: r.o)	¾	**2**	12/1	66	38
1142[6]	**Philistar (69)** (JMPEustace) **4-9-4** JTate(18) (a.p: ev ch 2f out: r.o one pce)	1¾	**3**	4/1[2]	70	42
	Queen of Shannon (IRE) (43) (AWCarroll) **9-8-7**(7)ow4 RStudholme(15) (bhd tl gd hdwy fnl 2f)	1¾	**4**	10/1	63	31
1005[14]	**Jona Holley (40)** (IABalding) **4-8-6**(7) LeanneMasterson(13) (bhd tl styd on fnl 2f)	6	**5**	33/1	50	22
1048[16]	**Saxon Bay (58)** (KOCunningham-Brown) **5-8-11**(7) TField(8) (lw: a.p: led over 2f out: sn hdd: one pce)	2½	**6**	33/1	50	22
*578**	**Jibereen (70)** (PHowling) **5-9-10** PaulEddery(3) (b: lw: hdwy over 3f out: sn rdn: one pce fnl 2f)	¾	**7**	5/1[3]	55	27
	Cape Pigeon (USA) (65) (LGCottrell) **12-8-13v** DHolland(9) (lw: w ldrs: led over 3f out tl over 2f out: sn wknd)	hd	**8**	7/2[1]	44	16
735[19]	**Green Bopper (USA) (65)** (CPMorlock) **4-9-3** RPerham(2) (lw: nvr nr to chal)	¾	**9**	33/1	46	18
	Switch To Senate (DJSCosgrove) **3-8-10** MRimmer(11) (bhd tl sme late hdwy)	nk	**10**	16/1	51	11
1009[16]	**Shermood (30)** (KTIvory) **4-8-5**(3) MartinDwyer(16) (b.hind: lw: a bhd)	8	**11**	33/1	21	—
1001[14]	**Failed To Hit (58)** (NPLittmoden) **4-9-0v**(3) DGriffiths(1) (outpcd)	5	**12**	25/1	21	—
874[9]	**Little Progress (35)** (TMJones) **3-7-12**(3) AWhelan(4) (a bhd)	1¾	**13**	33/1	13	—
1008[7]	**Sovereign** (MPMuggeridge) **3-7-12** NVarley(17) (prom 4f)	1	**14**	20/1	8	—
	Camp Follower (DCO'Brien) **4-9-8** GBardwell(5) (a bhd)	6	**15**	12/1	9	—
903[5]	**Sea Dreams (IRE)** (DMHyde) **6-8-13**(3) JDSmith(6) (a bhd)	5	**16**	14/1	—	—
765[11]	**Dozen Roses (44)** (TMJones) **3-7-10b** NCarlisle(7) (led tl over 3f out: wknd qckly)	nk	**17**	33/1	—	—
				(SP 134.7%)	**17 Rn**	

1m 50.4 (8.20) CSF £80.89 TOTE £9.70: £2.40 £3.20 £2.40 (£32.90) Trio £46.10 OWNER Mr P. Slade (SOMERTON) BRED Gordon Patterson
WEIGHT FOR AGE 3yo-12lb
Philistar clmd KRBurke £8,000
1139 Finsbury Flyer (IRE), all the better for his race here last week, improved gradually to take the lead at the two-furlong marker. Staying on strongly, he won decisively. (7/1)
Caudillo (IRE), well-suited by racing over a much shorter trip, was always close up and had every chance. Although well-ridden, she could not quicken near the finish. (12/1: op 20/1)
1142 Philistar elected to come up the stands' rails. Prominent all the way, he had every chance but could not quicken in the final furlong. (4/1: 5/2-9/2)
Queen of Shannon (IRE) was among the back-markers in a well strung-out field until staying on strongly in the closing stages. (10/1)
Jona Holley, well behind for a long way, was going on at the finish and may be capable of a little better. (33/1)
790 Saxon Bay led momentarily over two furlongs out, but was soon under maximum pressure and could find no more. (33/1)
578* Jibereen (5/1: op 3/1)
Sea Dreams (IRE) (14/1: op 8/1)

89+ 65

1293 E.B.F. DIBB LUPTON ALSOP MAIDEN STKS (2-Y.O) (Class D)
6-45 (6-45) **5f 10y** £3,143.75 (£950.00: £462.50: £218.75) Stalls: High GOING: 0.07 sec per fur (G)

				SP	RR	SF
	Carrowkeel (IRE) (BWHills) **2-9-0** MHills(7) (leggy: unf: hld up gng wl: qcknd to ld 1f out: comf)	—	**1**	9/4[1]	81+	52
	Jilted (IRE) (RHannon) **2-8-9** PatEddery(2) (neat: w ldr: led over 2f out to 1f out)	2½	**2**	5/2[2]	68	39
	Al's Fella (IRE) (PFICole) **2-9-0** TQuinn(3) (neat: led over 2f: hmpd over 1f out: r.o ins fnl f)	4	**3**	11/2[3]	60	31
880[6]	**Bliss (IRE)** (MrsPNDutfield) **2-8-4**(5) AimeeCook(5) (a.p: r.o one pce fnl 2f)	1	**4**	33/1	52	23
	Allasella (IRE) (BPalling) **2-8-9** TSprake(1) (neat: spd 3f)	1	**5**	9/1	49	20
739[8]	**Dixie Crossroads** (RHannon) **2-8-9** DaneO'Neill(4) (b.hind: prom 3f)	3	**6**	9/1	40	11
	Ready Fontaine (JNeville) **2-9-0** AMcGlone(8) (str: outpcd: nvr on terms)	2	**7**	33/1	38	9
	Bandbox (IRE) (SMellor) **2-9-0** MWigham(6) (w'like: plld hrd: prom over 2f)	1½	**8**	20/1	33	4
	The Honorable Lady (MRChannon) **2-8-2**(7) AEddery(10) (neat: bit bkwd: s.s: a wl bhd)	s.h	**9**	14/1	28	—
767[3]	**Swanmore Lady (IRE)** (SCWilliams) **2-8-9** DRMcCabe(9) (a bhd)	½	**10**	14/1	27	—
	Twentytwo Black (MJHaynes) **2-8-9** JReid(11) (leggy: s.s: a wl bhd)	9	**11**	16/1	—	—
				(SP 124.6%)	**11 Rn**	

62.8 secs (3.10) CSF £7.59 TOTE £4.20: £1.70 £1.70 £1.60 (£4.40) Trio £7.90 OWNER Mr John Grant (LAMBOURN) BRED D. Houlihan

Carrowkeel (IRE), very confidently ridden, quickened readily when asked approaching the final furlong and soon settled the issue. He has scope for improvement. (9/4)
Jilted (IRE), a sharp sort, disputed the lead from the start but could not quicken under pressure when challenged by the winner. (5/2: op evens)
Al's Fella (IRE) disputed the lead and, after receiving a bump below the distance, did well to run on again inside the final furlong. (11/2: op 3/1)
880 Bliss (IRE), easily the most experienced in the field, was always up there but could not quicken under pressure in the closing stages. (33/1)
Allasella (IRE), from a stable with some useful early two-year-olds, ran fast for more than three furlongs and should be capable of winning a race. (9/1: op 5/1)
Dixie Crossroads, always chasing the leaders, could make no headway in the final quarter-mile. (9/1)
The Honorable Lady (14/1: op 8/1)

1294 NAISMITHS H'CAP (0-85) (3-Y.O) (Class D)
7-15 (7-16) **5f 10y** £3,467.00 (£1,046.00: £508.00: £239.00) Stalls: High GOING: 0.07 sec per fur (G)

				SP	RR	SF
652^{7}	**Bramble Bear (62)** (MBlanshard) **3-7-12** JQuinn(7) (dwlt: hdwy over 2f out: led over 1f out: r.o wl)	—	**1**	16/1	70	35
904^{7}	**Chili Concerto (85)** (PJMakin) **3-9-7** SSanders(1) (swtg: led tl over 1f out: hrd rdn: r.o)	1¼	**2**	$8/1^{3}$	89	54
1018^{10}	**Lamarita (78)** (JMPEustace) **3-9-0** JTate(5) (a.p: ev ch over 1f out: nt qckn)	s.h	**3**	9/1	82	47
1158^{9}	**Ellens Lad (IRE) (85)** (RHannon) **3-9-7** JReid(9) (lw: hdwy 2f out: hrd rdn & r.o fnl f)	hd	**4**	$9/2^{2}$	89	54
1151^{3}	**Signs And Wonders (63)** (CACyzer) **3-7-8**(5) RFfrench(10) (b.off hind: lw: racd alone stands' side: ev ch over 1f out: edgd lft: nt qckn)	1¼	**5**	10/1	63	28
1141^{10}	**V I P Charlie (74)** (JRJenkins) **3-8-7**(3) AWhelan(11) (lw: hld up & bhd: gd hdwy over 1f out: nt rch ldrs)	1½	**6**	12/1	69	34
1113^{6}	**Anokato (63)** (KTIvory) **3-7-10b**(3)ow3 MartinDwyer(3) (w ldrs: hrd rdn over 2f out: no rspnse)	½	**7**	20/1	56	18
783^{5}	**Sylvan Dancer (IRE) (67)** (CFWall) **3-8-3** GDuffield(4) (swtg: in tch tl wknd 2f out)	2	**8**	10/1	54	19
1018^{14}	**Ice Age (72)** (RJRWilliams) **3-8-8** MHills(2) (spd over 3f)	1¾	**9**	33/1	53	18
1141^{2}	**Heavenly Miss (IRE) (61)** (JJBridger) **3-7-11** GBardwell(6) (w ldrs tl wknd over 2f out)	4	**10**	$9/2^{2}$	30	—
1018^{2}	**Mangus (IRE) (77)** (KOCunningham-Brown) **3-8-13** TQuinn(8) (lw: w ldrs over 2f: wknd qckly)	8	**11**	$4/1^{1}$	20	—
				(SP 116.9%)	**11 Rn**	

62.9 secs (3.20) CSF £125.20 CT £1,143.93 TOTE £28.10: £5.20 £2.00 £4.00 (£170.30) Trio £358.30 OWNER Mrs Michael Hill & Mrs Heather Chakko (UPPER LAMBOURN) BRED E. A. Badger
LONG HANDICAP Anokato 7-9
OFFICIAL EXPLANATION Mangus (IRE): no explanation offered.
Bramble Bear, last away, moved up steadily approaching the two-furlong marker. She struck the front at the distance and won readily. (16/1)
Chili Concerto made a bold bid to lead throughout under joint top weight, but could not hold the winner from the distance. (8/1)
731* Lamarita, always with the leaders, looked dangerous approaching the final furlong but could not quicken under pressure. (9/1)
834 Ellens Lad (IRE) came with a good run from two furlongs out but, though staying on, lacked a final turn of foot. (9/2)
1151 Signs And Wonders raced all alone on the stands' rails until hanging out into the centre of the course in the last furlong. She was certainly close enough at the distance, but lacked the final pace. (10/1)
1141 V I P Charlie was dropped out at the start and was last for a long way. He came with a promising-looking run below the distance, but could not quite sustain the effort in the final furlong. (12/1)
783 Sylvan Dancer (IRE) (10/1: 8/1-12/1)

72+ 75 74

1295 RICHARD & JACK WISEMAN TRUST CONDITIONS STKS (2-Y.O F) (Class C)
7-45 (7-47) **5f 10y** £4,470.10 (£1,627.60: £793.80: £339.00: £149.50) Stalls: High GOING: 0.07 sec per fur (G)

				SP	RR	SF
1235^{4}	**Going Places** (KTIvory) **2-8-5**(3) MartinDwyer(4) (led 1f: qcknd & led over 2f out: drvn out)	—	**1**	$6/1^{3}$	70	27
1091^{3}	**High Gain** (PHowling) **2-8-8** PaulEddery(3) (chsd ldrs: hrd rdn 2f out: r.o ins fnl f)	1	**2**	9/1	67	24
1211^{W}	**Summer Deal (USA)** (PFICole) **2-8-5** TQuinn(2) (unf: lw: led after 1f tl over 2f out: r.o ins fnl f)	nk	**3**	$1/2^{1}$	63	20
1109^{8}	**Silent Pride (IRE)** (MDIUsher) **2-8-8** SSanders(1) (bhd fnl 2f)	3½	**4**	14/1	55	12
985^{5}	**Angelique** (MJHaynes) **2-8-8** JReid(5) (lw: s.s: bhd most of wy)	1¼	**5**	$11/2^{2}$	51	8
				(SP 113.0%)	**5 Rn**	

64.0 secs (4.30) CSF £46.48 TOTE £6.00: £1.70 £2.60 (£16.30) OWNER Mr K. T. Ivory (RADLETT) BRED K. T. Ivory
1235 Going Places disputed the lead from the start. She quickened clear at halfway and, though coming to the end of her tether in the final furlong, never appeared likely to be caught. (6/1: 7/2-13/2)
1091 High Gain, always chasing the leaders, stayed on inside the last furlong but never appeared likely to catch the winner. (9/1: op 5/1)
Summer Deal (USA), an unfurnished filly, failed to live up to her home reputation. She disputed the lead from the start, but was left floundering when the winner quickened clear at the halfway stage. However, she stayed on again at the finish. (1/2: tchd 18/13)
828 Silent Pride (IRE), in touch to halfway, was soon fighting a losing battle. (14/1: 7/1-16/1)
985 Angelique missed the break and was at the back of the field for most of the race. (11/2: op 7/2)

1296 MOORE STEPHENS BOOTH WHITE H'CAP (0-80) (3-Y.O) (Class D)
8-15 (8-15) **1m 3f 135y** £3,584.00 (£1,082.00: £526.00: £248.00) Stalls: High GOING: 0.31 sec per fur (G)

				SP	RR	SF
878^{6}	**Heart of Armor (77)** (PFICole) **3-9-4** DaneO'Neill(2) (lw: hdwy 5f out: led over 1f out: r.o wl)	—	**1**	14/1	87	52
1129^{2}	**Regal Reprimand (63)** (GLewis) **3-8-4** PaulEddery(10) (b.hind: hdwy 3f out: ev ch & hrd rdn over 1f out: nt qckn)	1¾	**2**	$3/1^{1}$	71	36
771^{8}	**Herbshan Dancer (55)** (BRMillman) **3-7-10** JQuinn(12) (gd hdwy fnl 2f: nrst fin)	s.h	**3**	$12/1^{3}$	63	28
523^{4}	**Pennys From Heaven (80)** (HCandy) **3-9-7** TQuinn(3) (led tl over 1f out: wknd ins fnl f)	1½	**4**	$3/1^{1}$	86	51
878^{8}	**Running Free (IRE) (55)** (MJFetherston-Godley) **3-7-10** FNorton(1) (prom tl wknd 2f out)	8	**5**	33/1	49	14
925^{3}	**Who's That Man (58)** (SCWilliams) **3-7-10**(3)ow3 MHenry(4) (no hdwy fnl 3f)	2	**6**	$10/1^{2}$	50	12
1140^{10}	**Tommy Tortoise (70)** (MissGayKelleway) **3-8-11** RCochrane(9) (lw: nvr bttr than mid div)	s.h	**7**	$3/1^{1}$	62	27
1043^{14}	**Wesley's Lad (IRE) (64)** (JNeville) **3-8-5** SDrowne(6) (nvr trbld ldrs)	1½	**8**	50/1	54	19
990^{7}	**Padauk (72)** (MJHaynes) **3-8-13** JReid(5) (nvr nr to chal)	½	**9**	25/1	61	26
634^{4}	**Cee-N-K (IRE) (73)** (MJohnston) **3-9-0** DHolland(8) (lw: prom tl wknd 3f out)	3	**10**	$10/1^{2}$	58	23
1094^{11}	**Le Grand Gousier (USA) (60)** (RJRWilliams) **3-8-1** GDuffield(11) (chsd ldr tl wknd over 3f out)	2½	**11**	33/1	41	6
840^{9}	**Euro Superstar (FR) (55)** (SDow) **3-7-5**(5) RMullen(7) (a bhd: t.o)	15	**12**	50/1	16	—
				(SP 121.2%)	**12 Rn**	

2m 36.9 (10.90) CSF £50.23 CT £491.07 TOTE £16.50: £2.90 £1.80 £2.90 (£26.70) Trio £53.30 OWNER Mr J. S. Gutkin (WHATCOMBE) BRED The Wickfield Stud Ltd
LONG HANDICAP Who's That Man 7-9 Herbshan Dancer 7-9 Running Free (IRE) 7-9 Euro Superstar (FR) 7-5
502 Heart of Armor made smooth headway on the home turn. He struck the front approaching the final furlong and stayed on strongly. (14/1)

1129 Regal Reprimand came with a promising run from three furlongs out but, having reached second place at the distance, could make no impression on the winner. (3/1: op 2/1)
478 Herbshan Dancer was at the back of the field for much of the way. He stayed on well in the final quarter-mile to almost snatch second place, but was never on terms with the winner. (12/1: op 8/1)
523 Pennys From Heaven tried to make all the running and had the field well strung-out early in the straight. Headed approaching the final furlong, he then weakened, but is capable of improvement. (3/1)
Running Free (IRE) was close up until gradually weakening in the last two-and-a-half furlongs. (33/1)
925 Who's That Man (10/1: 6/1-12/1)
634 Cee-N-K (IRE) (10/1: 7/1-12/1)

1297 QUEEN CHARLOTTES HOSPITAL MAIDEN STKS (3-Y.O+) (Class D)

8-45 (8-47) **1m 67y** £3,779.00 (£1,142.00: £556.00: £263.00) Stalls: High GOING: 0.31 sec per fur (G)

				SP	RR	SF
645[5]	**Green Power** (JRFanshawe) **3-8-12** DHarrison(17) (lw: hdwy 4f out: led over 2f out: r.o wl)	—	**1**	9/4[1]	75	21
989[6]	**Boss Lady (IRE)** (RCharlton) **3-8-7** TSprake(1) (stdy hdwy 3f out: ev ch fnl f: r.o)	¾	**2**	6/1[3]	69	15
1088[10]	**Keen Companion** (TJNaughton) **4-9-2**(3) JDSmith(15) (gd hdwy fnl 2f: fin wl)	4	**3**	50/1	61	19
991[13]	**Khayal (USA)** (BWHills) **3-8-12** RHills(12) (a.p: r.o one pce fnl 2f)	1¼	**4**	12/1	63	9
727[13]	**Bellagrana** (MJFetherston-Godley) **3-8-7** DHolland(18) (sn prom: r.o one pce fnl 2f)	2½	**5**	50/1	54	—
1110[11]	**Tetris (IRE)** (CFWall) **3-8-7** NCarlisle(14) (led tl over 3f out)	s.h	**6**	25/1	54	—
	Krabloonik (FR) (SirMarkPrescott) **3-8-12** GDuffield(4) (leggy: scope: lw: dwlt: nrst fin)	1½	**7**	15/2	56	2
	Northern Angel (IRE) (MrsJCecil) **3-8-12** RCochrane(10) (lw: led over 3f out tl over 2f out: wknd fnl f)	hd	**8**	20/1	55	1
	Classic Ribbon (IRE) (ICampbell) **4-9-5** RPrice(11) (bit bkwd: prom tl wknd 3f out)	¾	**9**	50/1	49	7
1023[9]	**Waasef** (MissGayKelleway) **4-9-10** TQuinn(8) (lw: prom tl wknd over 2f out)	4	**10**	7/2[2]	46	4
1144[15]	**Bold Et Noir** (WJarvis) **3-8-12** SSanders(5) (nvr bttr than mid div)	1	**11**	50/1	44	—
	Be Valiant (JRFanshawe) **3-8-12** NVarley(16) (b: w'like: bit bkwd: s.s: a bhd)	1¾	**12**	16/1	41	—
1023[11]	**Grand Hotel (IRE)** (PWHarris) **3-8-9**(3) MHenry(6) (lw: a bhd)	nk	**13**	25/1	40	—
991[15]	**Haydn James (USA) (76)** (PWHarris) **3-8-12** FNorton(7) (wl bhd fnl 4f)	3	**14**	7/1	35	—
	Crescent's Whisper (IRE) (BHanbury) **3-8-12** JStack(3) (w'like: bit bkwd: a bhd)	5	**15**	16/1	25	—
1087[12]	**Barbury Ballad (IRE)** (MJHeaton-Ellis) **3-8-12** AClark(9) (bhd fnl 4f)	10	**16**	50/1	6	—

(SP 133.3%) **16 Rn**

1m 52.6 (10.40) CSF £14.88 TOTE £3.30: £1.50 £1.70 £9.90 (£13.90) Trio £165.80 OWNER Dexa'tex Ltd (NEWMARKET) BRED Gainsborough Stud Management Ltd
WEIGHT FOR AGE 3yo-12lb
645 Green Power, confidently ridden, moved smoothly into the lead over two furlongs from home. He had to be shaken up to hold the strong challenge of the second, the pair of them drawing clear. (9/4: 6/4-5/2)
989 Boss Lady (IRE), patiently ridden, tracked the winner through and challenged strongly from the distance. She had every chance but was held near the finish. This was an improvement on her debut and she will soon be winning. (6/1)
Keen Companion had plenty to do from the junction, but finished in tremendous style and would have troubled the leading pair with a little further to go. (50/1)
Khayal (USA), one of the leaders throughout, ran on at one pace under pressure in the final quarter-mile. (12/1: op 8/1)
Tetris (IRE) made much of the running, but proved one-paced when headed over three furlongs out. (25/1)
Krabloonik (FR) has plenty of scope for improvement. One of the last away, he was at the rear of the field until staying on in the last two furlongs. (15/2)

T/Plpt: £498.00 (32.71 Tckts). T/Qdpt: £94.60 (8.71 Tckts) AK/Hn

1115-BEVERLEY (R-H) (Good to soft)
Tuesday May 20th

WEATHER: fine & sunny WIND: slt half bhd

65 56+ 53 58

1298 TIGER INN (S) STKS (2-Y.O) (Class F) (58)

2-25 (2-27) **5f** £2,530.00 (£705.00: £340.00) Stalls: High GOING: 0.04 sec per fur (G)

				SP	RR	SF
1045[5]	**Royal Dream** (JBerry) **2-8-1**(5) PFessey(4) (mde all: clr over 1f out)	—	**1**	2/1[1]	71	28
780[2]	**Hopefully** (MRChannon) **2-8-6** PaulEddery(2) (swtg: a chsng ldrs: styd on fnl 2f: no ch w wnr)	6	**2**	5/2[2]	52	9
1019[3]	**Miss Beveled** (MBrittain) **2-8-6** GDuffield(9) (w ldrs to ½-wy: kpt on one pce)	1¾	**3**	5/1	46	3
	Step In To The Sun (RAFahey) **2-8-6** JCarroll(3) (unf: bkwd: s.i.s: outpcd & bhd tl kpt on appr fnl f)	6	**4**	10/1	27	—
1019[13]	**Hamerra (IRE)** (MartynMeade) **2-8-6** FNorton(1) (bolted gng to s: chsd ldrs tl lost pl ½-wy)	1½	**5**	25/1	22	—
684[10]	**Collacar** (DShaw) **2-8-8**(3) CTeague(7) (hung rt thrght: effrt ½-wy: wknd over 1f out)	2½	**6**	33/1	19	—
1019[5]	**Adrenalin** (MrsJRRamsden) **2-8-11v**[1] WRyan(5) (hld up: effrt ½-wy: hung lft: nt r.o)	2	**7**	9/2[3]	13	—
1136[12]	**Toll's Times** (MWEasterby) **2-8-11b**[1] TLucas(8) (unruly & uns rdr bef s: w ldrs tl wknd 2f out)	hd	**8**	20/1	13	—
441[8]	**Valslastchance** (NTinkler) **2-8-11b**[1] KimTinkler(6) (s.i.s: sme hdwy & edgd lft ½-wy: sn wknd)	6	**9**	20/1	—	—

(SP 122.2%) **9 Rn**

65.9 secs (4.10) CSF £6.62 TOTE £3.90: £1.70 £1.10 £1.90 (£4.80) Trio £5.70 OWNER Mrs B. A. Matthews (COCKERHAM) BRED P. J. and Mrs Sands
Bt in 8,400 gns
1045 Royal Dream proved much too good for this lot. Though she scored in good style, the opposition was very moderate indeed. (2/1: 3/1-15/8)
780 Hopefully stuck on under pressure, but the winner was far too good. (5/2)
1019 Miss Beveled, who is only small, was flat-out at halfway. (5/1)
Step In To The Sun, a plain, backward filly, showed a degree of promise. (10/1)
Hamerra (IRE) bolted going to the start. (25/1)
Collacar wants to do nothing but hang right. (33/1)
1019 Adrenalin, on his toes beforehand, wore a visor for the first time but it had no effect. All he wanted to do was hang left and, when called on for an effort at halfway, he said no thank-you. (9/2: op 3/1)

1299 ROSE & CROWN H'CAP (0-70) (3-Y.O) (Class E)
2-55 (2-55) **1m 3f 216y** £3,039.50 (£911.00: £438.00: £201.50) Stalls: High GOING: 0.04 sec per fur (G)

				SP	RR	SF
1115*	**Lindrick Lady (IRE) (65)** (BSRothwell) **3-9-2** MFenton(10) (mde all: c stands' side st: r.o wl fnl f)	—	**1**	6/1[3]	72	32
1043[10]	**As-Is (64)** (MJohnston) **3-9-1** JWeaver(6) (trckd ldrs: ev ch fnl 2f: nt qckn wl ins fnl f)	1	**2**	10/1	70	30
606[4]	**Alagna (48)** (SCWilliams) **3-7-10**(3)ow3 MHenry(3) (hld up: hdwy u.p 2f out: hung bdly lft: styd on wl towards fin)	4	**3**	12/1	48	5
1094[10]	**Wildmoor (55)** (JDBethell) **3-8-6** TWilliams(9) (hld up & bhd: styd on wl fnl 2f)	hd	**4**	14/1	55	15
1043*	**Sam Peeb (45)** (RAFahey) **3-7-10** DWright(2) (trckd ldrs: kpt on one pce fnl 2f)	1	**5**	5/1[2]	44	4
1043[15]	**Dawn Summit (49)** (BHanbury) **3-8-0** DaleGibson(14) (trckd ldrs: effrt over 2f out: one pce)	1¼	**6**	25/1	46	6
952[2]	**Laguna Bay (IRE) (58)** (APJarvis) **3-8-9** WJO'Connor(11) (lw: rr div: sn trckng ldrs: rdn over 3f out: grad wknd)	5	**7**	6/1[3]	49	9
1095[2]	**Skelton Sovereign (IRE) (58)** (RHollinshead) **3-8-6**(3) FLynch(4) (hld up: hdwy over 3f out: nvr nr ldrs)	hd	**8**	12/1	48	8
581[11]	**Propellant (60)** (CWThornton) **3-8-11** DeanMcKeown(13) (hdwy 6f out: sn in tch: rdn over 2f out: no imp)	1¾	**9**	20/1	48	8
670[8]	**Pertemps Mission (67)** (JPearce) **3-9-4** MWigham(5) (in tch: effrt over 3f out: sn lost pl)	1¼	**10**	14/1	53	13
1094[9]	**Maremma (46)** (DonEnricoIncisa) **3-7-11** KimTinkler(12) (hld up: a in rr)	s.h	**11**	20/1	32	—
764[2]	**Lady of The Lake (70)** (JLDunlop) **3-9-7** PaulEddery(8) (prom: drvn along 5f out: lost pl over 3f out)	2½	**12**	3/1[1]	53	13
1138[11]	**Dulas Bay (51)** (MWEasterby) **3-8-2** TLucas(7) (sme hdwy u.p 7f out: lost pl over 4f out: sn bhd)	8	**13**	20/1	23	—
	Lady Salome (52) (JGFitzGerald) **3-8-3** JCarroll(1) (swtg: sn in tch: drvn along over 4f out: wknd 3f out)	13	**14**	20/1	7	—
				(SP 130.9%)	**14 Rn**	

2m 43.9 (10.90) CSF £58.98 CT £664.22 TOTE £5.80: £2.40 £2.80 £4.40 (£27.10) Trio £166.30 OWNER Mr S. P. Hudson (MALTON) BRED F. D. McAuley
LONG HANDICAP Sam Peeb 7-1 Alagna 7-8
1115* Lindrick Lady (IRE), back over a much more suitable trip, made all the running. Hanging left, she ended up alone under the stands' side but, to her credit, kept on strongly. Her action suggests she appreciated the give underfoot. (6/1)
665* As-Is, who ran poorly on the All-Weather last time, was almost upsides the winner but on the opposite side two furlongs out. He ran on under pressure but could not bridge the gap. (10/1: op 6/1)
606 Alagna has more ability than she wants to show. Hanging badly left and meeting trouble when starting her effort, she took it into her head to stay on strongly towards the line. (12/1: 14/1-7/1)
793 Wildmoor, who wore a tongue-strap, made up an appreciable amount of late ground. (14/1)
1043* Sam Peeb, 9lb out of the handicap, was in effect racing from a 6lb higher mark than when he won on the All-Weather at Southwell. He was far from disgraced and looks a potential stayer. (5/1)
825 Dawn Summit took a keen grip but, off the bridle, looked slow. (25/1)
764 Lady of The Lake was in trouble almost three-quarters-of-a-mile from home, and dropped right out turning in. Possibly the ground was against her. (3/1)

1300 DAVID SWANNELL MEMORIAL RATED STKS H'CAP (0-90) (3-Y.O+) (Class C)
3-25 (3-25) **1m 100y** £4,566.80 (£1,701.20: £825.60: £348.00: £149.00: £69.40) Stalls: High GOING: 0.04 sec per fur (G)

				SP	RR	SF
1129*	**Jack The Lad (IRE) (73)** (JHetherton) **3-7-5**(5) 4x RFfrench(5) (sn prom: drvn along over 3f out: led over 1f out: edgd lft & styd on wl)	—	**1**	11/4[1]	83	33
1097[3]	**Kala Sunrise (86)** (CSmith) **4-9-7** GDuffield(2) (hld up: effrt over 3f out: hdwy 2f out: styd on same pce ins fnl f)	¾	**2**	9/2[3]	95	57
1097*	**High Premium (84)** (RAFahey) **9-8-12**(7) RWinston(9) (lw: in tch: sn pushed along: hdwy on ins 2f out: nt qckn fnl f)	1	**3**	7/2[2]	91	53
1097[2]	**Golden Thunderbolt (FR) (73)** (NTinkler) **4-8-8** JWeaver(7) (hld up: hdwy over 2f out: kpt on wl fnl f: nvr nr to chal)	1¾	**4**	13/2	76	38
1016[12]	**Bardon Hill Boy (IRE) (87)** (BHanbury) **5-9-8** JStack(3) (w ldrs tl wknd 2f out)	2½	**5**	16/1	86	48
947[4]	**Royal Ceilidh (IRE) (76)** (DenysSmith) **4-8-11** JCarroll(6) (led tl over 1f out: wknd fnl f)	nk	**6**	5/1	74	36
1097[10]	**Smarter Charter (73)** (MrsLStubbs) **4-8-8** ACulhane(4) (sn drvn along: hdwy on outside over 3f out: nvr nr to chal)	1½	**7**	11/1	68	30
934[7]	**Defined Feature (IRE) (80)** (DrJDScargill) **4-9-1** MFenton(8) (drvn along 5f out: sme hdwy on outside 3f out: n.d)	2	**8**	20/1	72	34
974[4]	**Pater Noster (USA) (84)** (JohnHarris) **8-9-5** PaulEddery(1) (b: chsd ldrs tl lost pl 3f out)	5	**9**	8/1	66	28
				(SP 127.2%)	**9 Rn**	

1m 49.3 (5.30) CSF £15.73 CT £43.46 TOTE £3.60: £1.70 £3.60 £1.80 (£15.60) Trio £17.40 OWNER Keith West Partnership (MALTON) BRED Thomas Healy
LONG HANDICAP Golden Thunderbolt (FR) 8-5 Smarter Charter 8-6 Jack The Lad (IRE) 7-3
WEIGHT FOR AGE 3yo-12lb
1129* Jack The Lad (IRE), 18lb higher in the weights than when winning at Carlisle two runs ago, raced with plenty of enthusiasm to complete the hat-trick and make it four wins from his last five starts. He will not be resting on his laurels either, and will be out again at Lingfield on Saturday night. (11/4)
1097 Kala Sunrise ran really well, especially considering he is better on fast ground. (9/2)
1097* High Premium, from a 5lb higher mark, was tucked away on the inside but was being pushed along some way from home. The pace was not that fast and, on this occasion, he did not pick up in the closing stages. (7/2)
1097 Golden Thunderbolt (FR), 3lb out of the handicap, was in effect 2lb worse off with High Premium. Given plenty to do, he was putting in his best work at the finish. (13/2)
405 Bardon Hill Boy (IRE) was outpaced in the final quarter-mile. This trip is really too short for him. (16/1)
947 Royal Ceilidh (IRE) took a keen grip, but her stamina gave out on this stiff track inside the last. (5/1)
974 Pater Noster (USA) (8/1: op 14/1)

1301 H & P FREIGHTWAYS H'CAP (0-80) (3-Y.O F) (Class D)
3-55 (3-55) **1m 1f 207y** £3,548.00 (£1,064.00: £512.00: £236.00) Stalls: High GOING: 0.04 sec per fur (G)

				SP	RR	SF
1024*	**Step N Go (IRE) (65)** (MrsJRRamsden) **3-8-6** WRyan(2) (lw: hld up: hdwy over 2f out: shkn up to ld over 1f out: r.o wl: readily)	—	**1**	6/4[1]	73	29
998*	**Can Can Lady (79)** (MJohnston) **3-9-6** JWeaver(4) (lw: led tl over 1f out: kpt on wl: no ch w wnr)	3½	**2**	9/2[2]	81	37
1140[16]	**Eponine (68)** (MRChannon) **3-8-9** JFEgan(3) (trckd ldr: drvn along over 3f out: styd on same pce fnl f)	s.h	**3**	20/1	70	26

				SP	RR	SF
1004[2]	**Saddlers' Hope (74)** (JRFanshawe) **3-9-1** TSprake(1) (lw: trckd ldrs: effrt & c wd over 2f out: styd on same pce)	1½	**4**	6/1	74	30
534[7]	**Native Princess (IRE) (56)** (BWHills) **3-7-6**(5) RMullen(6) (effrt over 3f out: sn wl outpcd: styd on fnl f)	4	**5**	20/1	49	5
875[5]	**Fantasy Girl (IRE) (66)** (JLDunlop) **3-8-7** PaulEddery(7) (hld up: effrt u.p 2f out: sn wknd)	3	**6**	5/1[3]	55	11
1078[4]	**Fauna (IRE) (63)** (NAGraham) **3-8-4** DeanMcKeown(5) (chsd ldrs: rdn over 2f out: sn wknd)	¾	**7**	8/1	50	6
1017[14]	**What Happened Was (80)** (MartynMeade) **3-9-7** FNorton(8) (trckd ldrs: hung lft ½-wy: drvn along over 3f out: sn lost pl & eased)	14	**8**	16/1	45	1
				(SP 115.7%)		**8 Rn**

2m 11.1 (8.00) CSF £7.71 CT £81.15 TOTE £2.40: £1.30 £1.10 £4.90 (£3.80) OWNER Lord Petersham (THIRSK) BRED R. J. McAlpine and D. O. Pickering

1024* Step N Go (IRE), who looked in particularly good trim, showed a nice turn of foot. Hanging fire in front, she will improve when stepped up to a mile-and-a-half, and looks several steps ahead of the Handicapper. (6/4)

998* Can Can Lady, from a 6lb higher mark, ran her usual gallant race but, in the winner, met an improving, well-handicapped filly. (9/2)

Eponine proved very willing, and ran easily her best race so far this term. (20/1)

1004 Saddlers' Hope, done no favours by the Handicapper, raced alone on the stands' side and, to her credit, kept on all the way to the line. (6/1)

Native Princess (IRE), who looked backward in her coat, was left behind in a moderately-run race. Sticking on at the finish she looks, despite her breeding, as though she needs a stiffer test. (20/1)

875 Fantasy Girl (IRE), who caught plenty of eyes last time, is nothing much to look at and, done no favours by the Handicapper, never looked like taking a hand. (5/1)

1302 WINDMILL INN MAIDEN STKS (3-Y.O) (Class D)

4-25 (4-25) **7f 100y** £3,561.00 (£1,068.00: £514.00: £237.00) Stalls: High GOING: 0.04 sec per fur (G)

				SP	RR	SF
	Raaha (RWArmstrong) **3-8-9** GCarter(2) (trckd ldrs: drvn along over 3f out: led over 1f out: edgd lft & styd on wl)	—	**1**	9/1[2]	80	52
889[4]	**Woodbeck** (JAGlover) **3-8-9** NDay(8) (hld up: effrt over 3f out: swtchd rt & styd on same pce ins fnl f)	1¼	**2**	9/1[2]	77	49
983[4]	**Round Robin (IRE)** (CWThornton) **3-9-0** DeanMcKeown(6) (hld up: effrt over 3f out: styd on same pce appr fnl f)	4	**3**	9/1[2]	74	46
586[2]	**Shawm** (DRLoder) **3-9-0** DRMcCabe(4) (lw: w ldr: led over 3f out: rdn & hdd over 1f out: sn wknd)	3	**4**	1/3[1]	67	39
	Broadway Melody (APJarvis) **3-8-9** WJO'Connor(5) (unf: scope: hld up: effrt over 2f out: sn wl outpcd)	14	**5**	25/1	32	4
1014[7]	**Get The Point (75)** (RHollinshead) **3-8-11**(3) FLynch(7) (led tl over 3f out: wknd over 1f out)	4	**6**	14/1[3]	29	1
				(SP 115.5%)		**6 Rn**

1m 36.1 (4.10) CSF £75.08 TOTE £6.00: £1.80 £4.00 (£43.60) OWNER Mr Hamdan Al Maktoum (NEWMARKET) BRED Shadwell Estate Company Limited

OFFICIAL EXPLANATION **Shawm: choked from two and a half furlongs out. This was reportedly caused by an ill-fitting tongue bit.**

Raaha, a lazy walker, took time to get into full stride but, in the end, scored in decisive fashion. She will be suited by a step-up in distance. (9/1: op 6/1)

889 Woodbeck, a keen-going sort, had to be switched in behind the winner, but was beaten entirely on merit. (9/1: op 5/1)

983 Round Robin (IRE), who has plenty of strength and scope, again showed ability. He needs one more run for a handicap mark. (9/1: op 6/1)

586 Shawm looked outstanding in the paddock. Tending to race keenly, under pressure he pulled out next to nothing, and was very leg-weary near the line. The stable is not in the best of form and there is a possibility he did not appreciate the overnight rain. The jockey told the Stewards that he felt his mount had choked two-and-a-half furlongs from home, and the trainer's representative added that the bit had spun round causing the tongue to lift in the horse's mouth. (1/3)

1303 ANGEL CONDITIONS STKS (3-Y.O+) (Class C)

5-00 (5-00) **5f** £4,665.37 (£1,693.50: £821.75: £346.25: £148.13) Stalls: High GOING: 0.04 sec per fur (G)

				SP	RR	SF
573[5]	**Ya Malak (95)** (DNicholls) **6-9-0** AlexGreaves(4) (lw: hld up: stdy hdwy ½-wy: swtchd lft & rdn to ld jst ins fnl f: styd on wl)	—	**1**	3/1[3]	92	74
1034[9]	**Tadeo (97)** (MJohnston) **4-9-6** JWeaver(2) (w ldr: led ½-wy tl jst ins fnl f)	2	**2**	13/8[1]	92	74
977[7]	**Daawe (USA) (71)** (MrsVAAconley) **6-9-0** MDeering(1) (sn outpcd: hdwy u.p ½-wy: styd on wl ins fnl f)	1¼	**3**	8/1	82	64
839[8]	**Taoiste** (RWArmstrong) **4-9-8** RPrice(5) (led to ½-wy: w ldr tl wknd qckly fnl f)	7	**4**	11/4[2]	67	49
1148[16]	**Westcourt Magic (98)** (MWEasterby) **4-9-0** JCarroll(3) (bolted 5f gng to s: lost pl after 1f: t.o ½-wy: virtually p.u)	30	**5**	7/1	—	—
				(SP 113.4%)		**5 Rn**

63.5 secs (1.70) CSF £7.85 TOTE £3.00: £2.20 £1.20 (£2.90) OWNER Contrac Promotions Ltd (THIRSK) BRED Mrs R. B. Kennard

573 Ya Malak, who looked in good trim beforehand, sensibly wanted nothing to do with the break-neck gallop. Produced to lead just inside the last, he was clear in a matter of strides. (3/1)

1034 Tadeo battled for the lead with Taoiste, and it was hardly surprising that he had nothing left when the winner swept by. (13/8)

977 Daawe (USA), taken off his legs at halfway, stuck on strongly inside the last. He would have been receiving 20lb from Tadeo in a handicap. (8/1)

Taoiste, a heavy-topped ex-French sprinter, took on Tadeo for the lead but the needle was on empty entering the last. (11/4)

745 Westcourt Magic bolted five furlongs going to the start, and his rider had to take him onto the round course to pull him up. He was legless after a furlong and tailed off from halfway, and he should surely not have been allowed to run. (7/1: op 11/4)

T/Plpt: £163.00 (104.26 Tckts). T/Qdpt: £45.80 (23.49 Tckts) WG

GOODWOOD (R-H) (St Crse Good to Soft, Rnd Good)

Tuesday May 20th

WEATHER: overcast WIND: almost nil

1304 TREHEARNE & NORMAN MAIDEN STKS (3-Y.O) (Class D)

2-10 (2-11) **1m** £4,889.50 (£1,456.00: £693.00: £311.50) Stalls: High GOING: 0.22 sec per fur (G)

				SP	RR	SF
674[8]	**Wasp Ranger (USA) (92)** (PFICole) **3-9-0** TQuinn(1) (lw: chsd ldr: rdn over 1f out: led wl ins fnl f: r.o wl)	—	**1**	13/2[3]	87	29
992[2]	**Selfish** (HRACecil) **3-8-9** KFallon(2) (hld up: led over 3f out: hrd rdn over 1f out: hdd wl ins fnl f: r.o)	nk	**2**	11/10[1]	81	23
	Star Invader (MRStoute) **3-9-0** JReid(4) (w'like: scope: bit bkwd: s.s: hld up: rdn over 2f out: unable qckn: lame off fore)	5	**3**	11/8[2]	76	18

	Love Venture (SPCWoods) **3-8-9** KDarley(3) (b: unf: scope: led over 6f)	10	**4**	25/1	51	—
				(SP 106.9%)		**4 Rn**

1m 45.76 (8.56) CSF £12.80 TOTE £5.20: (£2.90) OWNER Mr Christopher Wright (WHATCOMBE) BRED Jane C. Hinkle & Vinery
OFFICIAL EXPLANATION Star Invader: finished lame.
674 Wasp Ranger (USA), who was found to be suffering from a sore throat after his Newmarket run, has always shown a lot at home according to his trainer. Enjoying this rain-softened ground, he put up a good battling display and, after a good tussle with the runner-up in the straight, eventually got on top in the closing stages. (13/2: 3/1-7/1)
992 Selfish, who was very tired when caught in the last few strides at Kempton last time out having set the pace, had less use made of her here. It looked as if she was going to prevail inside the final furlong, but she was just worried out of it close home. Her turn is surely not far away, but a mile seems to be stretching her to the limit, and a return to seven furlongs would help. (11/10: 4/5-5/4)
Star Invader, an attractive, good-bodied colt, looked as though the run would do him good and, after travelling sweetly in the race, failed to quicken once asked. He was subsequently found to be lame on his off fore and is well worth another chance. (11/8)
Love Venture, a half-sister to Pearl Venture, still has some developing to do but took the field along until collared over three furlongs from home. (25/1)

1305 CHICHESTER FESTIVAL THEATRE H'CAP (0-100) (3-Y.O) (Class C)
2-40 (2-41) **7f** £7,375.00 (£2,200.00: £1,050.00: £475.00) Stalls: High GOING: 0.22 sec per fur (G)

				SP	RR	SF
693*	**Captain Collins (IRE) (95)** (PWChapple-Hyam) **3-9-7** JReid(1) (a.p: led over 1f out: rdn & edgd rt ins fnl f: r.o wl)	—	**1**	9/2[3]	109	77
654[4]	**Zaima (IRE) (84)** (JLDunlop) **3-8-10** KDarley(5) (a.p: led wl over 1f out: sn hdd: ev ch & n.m.r on ins wl ins fnl f: r.o wl)	s.h	**2**	6/1	98	66
1170[2]	**Just Nick (80)** (WRMuir) **3-8-3**(3) MartinDwyer(4) (lw: rdn & hdwy wl over 1f out: unable qckn)	4	**3**	11/4[1]	85	53
930*	**Green Jewel (87)** (RHannon) **3-8-13** DaneO'Neill(3) (w ldr 5f)	3	**4**	7/2[2]	85	53
990[15]	**Impulsif (USA) (78)** (DJSffrenchDavis) **3-8-4** JQuinn(6) (led over 5f)	1½	**5**	25/1	73	41
899*	**Broad River (USA) (87)** (EALDunlop) **3-8-13** LDettori(7) (a bhd)	1¾	**6**	9/2[3]	78	46
1018[12]	**Rudi's Pet (IRE) (93)** (RHannon) **3-9-5** RHughes(9) (bhd fnl 2f)	hd	**7**	14/1	83	51
				(SP 110.1%)		**7 Rn**

1m 28.72 (3.92) CSF £26.12 CT £73.34 TOTE £5.20: £2.70 £2.90 (£20.60) Trio £16.20 OWNER Mr R. E. Sangster (MARLBOROUGH) BRED Swettenham Stud
693* Captain Collins (IRE), reverting back to seven furlongs, gained a narrow lead below the distance and, despite drifting right in the closing stages, doing the runner-up no favours, held on by the skin of his teeth. He is a bit of a monkey according to connections and would prefer good or faster ground. He will now go for either the Jersey Stakes at Royal Ascot, or a Listed or Group race abroad. (9/2: 3/1-5/1)
654 Zaima (IRE), reverting back to seven furlongs, had a tremendous battle with the winner and, although done no favours by that rival in the closing stages, only just lost out. Compensation awaits. (6/1)
1170 Just Nick had the ground in his favour - his only win to date came in the mud - which makes this performance rather disappointing. The slow early pace was against him and he needs further according to connections. The Britannia Handicap at Royal Ascot is his mid-season target. (11/4)
930* Green Jewel disputed the lead to the two-furlong pole before giving best. (7/2)

90 97 75+ 80 (85)

1306 SOUTHERNPRINT MAIDEN STKS (2-Y.O) (Class D)
3-10 (3-10) **5f** £4,889.50 (£1,456.00: £693.00: £311.50) Stalls: Low GOING: 0.22 sec per fur (G)

				SP	RR	SF
1026[2]	**Diligence (IRE)** (PFICole) **2-9-0** TQuinn(2) (led over 3f: hrd rdn: led wl ins fnl f: r.o wl)	—	**1**	Evens[1]	82	66
	Shegardi (DRLoder) **2-9-0** LDettori(3) (w'like: chsd wnr: led over 1f out: rdn: hdd wl ins fnl f: unable qckn)	¾	**2**	5/2[2]	80+	64
	Taalluf (USA) (MajorWRHern) **2-8-9** RHills(1) (str: scope: bit bkwd: bmpd s: lost pl over 3f out: r.o one pce fnl f)	7	**3**	5/1[3]	52	36
1031[3]	**Be My Wish** (MissGayKelleway) **2-8-9** RCochrane(4) (b.hind: a.p: rdn 2f out: wknd over 1f out)	1½	**4**	7/1	47	31
	Pure Coincidence (GLewis) **2-9-0** AClark(6) (str: scope: bit bkwd: chsd ldrs: rdn over 2f out: wknd over 1f out)	3	**5**	20/1	43	27
594[11]	**Last Knight (IRE)** (MRChannon) **2-8-9**(5) PPMurphy(7) (a bhd)	4	**6**	33/1	30	14
				(SP 115.4%)		**6 Rn**

59.61 secs (2.91) CSF £3.56 TOTE £1.90: £1.20 £1.60 (£2.20) OWNER Axom (WHATCOMBE) BRED N. Hartery
1026 Diligence (IRE) is a very mature, strongly-made colt who is reminiscent of his sire Dilum. An extremely laid-back individual according to his trainer, he set the pace but looked in trouble once passed by the runner-up below the distance. However, showing the right attitude, he responded well to pressure and rallied to get back up in the closing stages and give Dilum his first winner as a stallion. Royal Ascot surely beckons. (Evens)
Shegardi was the first two-year-old runner of the season for David Loder. Not as big as his rivals in the paddock, he nevertheless made a very promising debut and looked set for victory as he moved into the lead below the distance. However, despite doing little wrong, he was worried out of it in the closing stages. He will now go straight for the Norfolk Stakes at Royal Ascot. (5/2: 5/4-11/4)
Taalluf (USA), an attractive, round-bodied filly, did not look fully wound-up. She had no hope with the front two, but should come on for this. (5/1: op 3/1)
1031 Be My Wish played an active role until coming to the end of her tether over a furlong from home. (7/1)
Pure Coincidence, a well-made newcomer, looked in need of this and so it proved, as he was forced to give best over a furlong out. (20/1)

1307 WESTMINSTER TAXI INSURANCE PREDOMINATE STKS (Listed) (3-Y.O C & G) (Class A)
3-40 (3-41) **1m 2f** £22,320.00 (£6,660.00: £3,180.00: £1,440.00) Stalls: High GOING: 0.22 sec per fur (G)

				SP	RR	SF
692[2]	**Grapeshot (USA) (110)** (LMCumani) **3-8-11** JReid(6) (swtg: chsd ldr: led over 2f out: pushed out)	—	**1**	2/1[1]	114+	64
692[5]	**Running Stag (USA) (106)** (PMitchell) **3-8-8** KFallon(4) (swtg: hdwy over 3f out: rdn over 2f out: chsd wnr over 1f out: no imp)	2½	**2**	12/1	107	57
940[7]	**Shii-Take (105)** (RAkehurst) **3-8-8** AClark(3) (led over 7f: rdn: one pce)	1	**3**	9/2	105	55
1014*	**Conon Falls (IRE) (100)** (JHMGosden) **3-8-8** LDettori(2) (lw: hld up: rdn over 2f out: one pce)	1¼	**4**	11/4[2]	103	53
1099*	**Indiscreet (CAN)** (DRLoder) **3-8-8** KDarley(1) (lw: prom over 7f)	6	**5**	4/1[3]	94	44
851[5]	**Further Outlook (USA) (100)** (MrsAJPerrett) **3-8-8** MHills(5) (lw: a bhd)	2	**6**	25/1	91	41
				(SP 109.7%)		**6 Rn**

2m 12.7 (6.10) CSF £22.29 TOTE £3.00: £1.80 £4.70 (£16.60) OWNER Mrs T Von Halle & Mr M Kerr-Dineen (NEWMARKET) BRED Jody Huckabay and Dr Stuart Brown
692 Grapeshot (USA) was ideally suited by the step-up in distance, and put up a very polished display. His odds have been cut for the Derby, but his participation is still in the balance as his trainer believes nothing can beat Entrepreneur. There is certainly a Group race to be won with him before long. (2/1: 11/8-9/4)

692 Running Stag (USA) was certainly happier with this return to a longer trip and enjoyed the rain-softened ground. Still a baby who needs to grow up according to his trainer, he is still a possible for the Belmont Stakes in America. (12/1)
940 Shii-Take took the field along but had no chance with the winner. His trainer believes he is capable of winning a Group race but admits he may have to go to Germany to do it. (9/2)
1014* Conon Falls (IRE) showed here that he is not good enough for the Derby. (11/4)
1099* Indiscreet (CAN) was very disappointing and, after racing up with the pace, was a spent force over two furlongs out. (4/1)
851 Further Outlook (USA) once again demonstrated he is not in this league. It is going to be difficult to place him this season. (25/1)

1308 ANNE FRANCES STEVENS MEMORIAL H'CAP (0-100) (4-Y.O+) (Class C)
4-10 (4-11) **1m** £7,375.00 (£2,200.00: £1,050.00: £475.00) Stalls: High GOING: 0.22 sec per fur (G)

				SP	RR	SF
987³	**Gold Spats (USA) (86)** (MRStoute) **4-9-7** JReid(7) (lw: chsd ldrs over 6f out: led 2f out: pushed out)	—	**1**	100/30 ¹	99	81
787⁶	**Sharp Shuffle (IRE) (73)** (RHannon) **4-8-8** DaneO'Neill(10) (b: swtg: hld up: rdn over 2f out: chsd wnr fnl f: unable qckn)	2	**2**	10/1	82	64
	Orsay (76) (WRMuir) **5-8-11** KFallon(3) (bit bkwd: rdn over 3f out: hdwy over 2f out: r.o one pce)	1½	**3**	8/1	82	64
987⁶	**Star Talent (USA) (86)** (IABalding) **6-9-7** RCochrane(5) (lw: nt clr run over 2f out & over 1f out: hdwy fnl f: r.o wl)	nk	**4**	4/1 ²	91	73
892⁴	**Arterxerxes (82)** (MJHeaton-Ellis) **4-9-3** AClark(11) (lw: led 6f: wknd fnl f)	1	**5**	10/1	85	67
895³	**King of Tunes (FR) (77)** (JJSheehan) **5-8-12** DHolland(9) (swtg: chsd ldr over 1f out: wknd over 2f out)	nk	**6**	5/1 ³	80	62
1111⁶	**Law Commission (93)** (DRCElsworth) **7-10-0** TQuinn(6) (stdy hdwy over 2f out: hmpd over 1f out: eased whn btn fnl f)	1	**7**	16/1	94	76
1021³	**Alpine Hideaway (IRE) (76)** (BHanbury) **4-8-11** LDettori(2) (a.p: rdn over 2f out: wknd 1f out)	nk	**8**	12/1	76	58
	Conspicuous (IRE) (84) (LGCottrell) **7-9-5** KDarley(1) (bit bkwd: hdwy 3f out: rdn over 2f out: wknd over 1f out)	2½	**9**	20/1	79	61
1092*	**Capilano Princess (80)** (DHaydnJones) **4-9-1** SDrowne(8) (bhd fnl 2f)	2	**10**	9/1	71	53
	Volley (IRE) (85) (MajorDNChappell) **4-9-6** DHarrison(4) (a bhd)	6	**11**	40/1	64	46

(SP 119.8%) **11 Rn**

1m 41.26 (4.06) CSF £34.93 CT £235.11 TOTE £4.90: £2.40 £2.90 £2.20 (£32.70) Trio £96.10 OWNER Cheveley Park Stud (NEWMARKET) BRED Christiana Stables
987 Gold Spats (USA) confirmed the promise shown at Kempton on his reappearance, needing only to be nudged along for a cosy success. (100/30: 9/4-7/2)
787 Sharp Shuffle (IRE) was better-suited by the return to a mile but, after moving up along the inside rail to take second place, was unable to reel in the winner. (10/1)
Orsay looked as though this first run in eight months was needed. (8/1)
987 Star Talent (USA) had a nightmare run as he continually found his passage blocked in the straight. In the circumstances, he did well to finish so close. In fine form at present, he should soon return to the winner's enclosure. (4/1)
892 Arterxerxes found this trip in this ground just beyond him. Seven furlongs is his distance. (10/1: 6/1-11/1)
1111 Law Commission certainly caught the eye. Steadily weaving his way through the pack, he had to be snatched up below the distance and, from that point, his jockey was incredibly easy on him. All five of his wins to date have come over six or seven furlongs on a fast surface and, given those conditions, he looks one to give very close consideration to. (16/1)
1021 Alpine Hideaway (IRE) (12/1: 8/1-14/1)
1092* Capilano Princess (9/1: 6/1-10/1)

1309 EQUITY FINANCIAL COLLECTIONS CONDITIONS STKS (3-Y.O+) (Class C)
4-45 (4-45) **6f** £4,878.37 (£1,756.50: £840.75: £341.25: £133.13) Stalls: Low GOING: 0.22 sec per fur (G)

				SP	RR	SF
671*	**Monaassib (111)** (EALDunlop) **6-9-11**(3) DO'Donohoe(3) (chsd ldr: rdn over 1f out: led last strides)	—	**1**	6/5 ¹	116	96
	Jayannpee (107) (IABalding) **6-10-0** LDettori(5) (lw: led: rdn over 1f out: hdd last strides)	hd	**2**	5/1 ³	116	96
877⁵	**Crowded Avenue (101)** (PJMakin) **5-9-2** SSanders(1) (swtg: hld up: rdn over 1f out: one pce)	5	**3**	7/2 ²	90	70
942¹⁵	**Top Banana (93)** (HCandy) **6-8-9**(7) NicolaWright(4) (bhd fnl 2f)	4	**4**	7/1	80	60
981⁵	**Everglades (IRE) (98)** (RCharlton) **9-9-2** JReid(2) (swtg: hld up: rdn over 1f out: sn wknd)	s.h	**5**	10/1	80	60

(SP 105.9%) **5 Rn**

1m 12.27 (2.47) CSF £6.20 TOTE £1.80: £1.20 £1.50 (£3.30) OWNER Maktoum Al Maktoum (NEWMARKET) BRED Side Hill Stud in Ireland
671* Monaassib, whose connections were concerned about the soft ground, was given a super-cool ride by his talented apprentice. Racing in second place, he was shaken up below the distance and, with his jockey not being in the slightest bit flustered, eased his way into the lead with only yards to go. He is at his best on a fast surface. (6/5)
Jayannpee looked in good shape for this reappearance and ran a fine race, setting the pace, and grimly holding on until passed in the last few strides. All nine of his victories have come on good ground or faster. (5/1)
877 Crowded Avenue did not have the ground in his favour and is yet to win beyond five furlongs. If the ground is fast, the Vodac Dash at the Derby meeting is a possibility. (7/2)
Top Banana was officially worst in at the weights, and it was no surprise to see him getting left behind in the final quarter-mile. (7/1)
981 Everglades (IRE) is yet to win on ground worse than good and, on this rain-softened ground, he stopped to nothing from below the distance. (10/1: 5/1-11/1)

T/Jkpt: £528.20 (13.44 Tckts). T/Plpt: £188.70 (145.94 Tckts). T/Qdpt: £5.40 (324.79 Tckts) AK

0721-AYR (L-H) (Soft)
Wednesday May 21st
Race 1: hand timed.
WEATHER: sunny periods WIND: mod bhd

79 75 68

1310 E.B.F. AYR MAY NOVICE STKS (2-Y.O) (Class D)
2-30 (2-35) **5f** £3,220.00 (£970.00: £470.00: £220.00) Stalls: High GOING: 0.75 sec per fur (S)

				SP	RR	SF
1013²	**Heavenly Abstone** (PDEvans) **2-8-9v** JFEgan(3) (lw: chsd ldrs: rdn to ld wl ins fnl f)	—	**1**	11/2 ²	78	31
1126*	**One Singer** (MJohnston) **2-9-2** JWeaver(6) (chsd ldrs: outpcd 2f out: styd on strly towards fin)	1	**2**	7/4 ¹	82	35
1038*	**Vice Presidential** (TJEtherington) **2-9-2** JCarroll(4) (lw: led: rdn 2f out: hdd & no ex wl ins fnl f)	2	**3**	7/4 ¹	75	28

			Pos	SP	RR	SF
	Selkirk Rose (IRE) (MissLAPerratt) **2-8-7** OUrbina(5) (w'like: scope: bit bkwd: in tch: hdwy over 2f out: nt qckn appr fnl f)	¾	**4**	25/1	64	17
954^{8}	**Solo Song** (DANolan) **2-8-2**(5) JBramhill(1) (cl up: rdn & hung lft 2f out: sn btn)	4	**5**	66/1	51	4
696^{6}	**Risky Whisky** (JBerry) **2-9-2** GCarter(7) (sn pushed along: nvr trbld ldrs)	2½	**6**	8/1^{3}	52	5
861^{9}	**Linnetsong** (GROldroyd) **2-8-2**(7)ow2 RFarmer(2) (sn outpcd & wl bhd)	9	**7**	100/1	16	—

(SP 105.6%) **7 Rn**

64.3 secs (7.30) CSF £11.99 TOTE £9.10: £2.90 £1.10 (£7.00) OWNER Mr J. E. Abbey (WELSHPOOL) BRED Ridgebarn Farm

1013 Heavenly Abstone showed at Chester last time that she handles these conditions and, seeing the trip out well, scored in determined fashion. (11/2)

1126* One Singer found this testing ground blunting his speed, but he picked up well at the end, suggesting that he should get further. (7/4: 5/4-2/1)

1038* Vice Presidential looked a bit of a handful both in the paddock and before the start, and his temperament may well be a problem. He is worth a chance on better ground. (7/4: 5/4-2/1)

Selkirk Rose (IRE) is not the best of movers, but needed this and showed enough to suggest that there is a race or two in the pipeline. (25/1)

Solo Song showed ability until running green and tiring in the last quarter-mile. (66/1)

696 Risky Whisky showed a moderate action and was never happy with the pace. (8/1: op 9/2)

1311 BALLANTRAE H'CAP (0-70) (3-Y.O+) (Class E)

3-00 (3-03) **5f** £3,065.50 (£928.00: £453.00: £215.50) Stalls: High GOING: 0.75 sec per fur (S)

			Pos	SP	RR	SF
1098^{14}	**Rich Glow (46)** (NBycroft) **6-8-4** SDrowne(5) (lw: hdwy ½-wy: styd on wl to ld wl ins fnl f)	—	**1**	11/2^{2}	55	35
1227*	**Goretski (IRE) (54)** (NTinkler) **4-8-5**(7) PFredericks(1) (lw: cl up: led ½-wy tl wl ins fnl f)	½	**2**	3/1^{1}	61	41
1227^{2}	**Just Bob (70)** (SEKettlewell) **8-10-0** JStack(3) (lw: s.i.s: hdwy 2f out: nvr rchd ldrs)	3½	**3**	3/1^{1}	66	46
1037^{8}	**Ready Teddy (IRE) (45)** (MissLAPerratt) **4-8-3** JCarroll(4) (chsd ldrs: rdn 2f out: no ex)	1½	**4**	20/1	36	16
956^{10}	**King of Show (IRE) (52)** (RAllan) **6-8-10** GDuffield(9) (lw: sn drvn along & bhd: sme late hdwy)	6	**5**	12/1	24	4
744^{9}	**Cross The Border (61)** (DNicholls) **4-9-5** AlexGreaves(8) (lw: sn drvn along & bhd: n.d)	2	**6**	8/1	27	7
972^{4}	**Palacegate Jack (IRE) (70)** (JBerry) **6-9-9b**(5) PRoberts(6) (led to ½-wy: wknd)	nk	**7**	8/1	35	15
1227^{7}	**Leading Princess (IRE) (52)** (MissLAPerratt) **6-8-10b** OUrbina(7) (lw: spd to ½-wy: sn lost pl)	3	**8**	7/1^{3}	7	—
	Lord Cornelious (39) (DANolan) **4-7-6**(5)ow1 JBramhill(2) (spd to ½-wy: sn wknd)	2	**9**	100/1	—	—

(SP 113.6%) **9 Rn**

63.82 secs (6.82) CSF £19.98 CT £52.98 TOTE £5.10: £1.20 £1.70 £1.30 (£11.20) Trio £9.00 OWNER Mr M. J. Bateson (BRANDSBY) BRED P. Young

LONG HANDICAP Lord Cornelious 7-1

OFFICIAL EXPLANATION **Ready Teddy (IRE): rider reported that the filly's tongue-strap had been removed at the start and that she had gurgled in the last furlong.**

Rich Glow loves this track and won his fifth race here. This was the most testing ground he has successfully encountered. (11/2: 4/1-6/1)

1227* Goretski (IRE) is obviously in tremendous form, but these conditions just sapped his stamina. (3/1)

1227 Just Bob is both looking and running well just now, and no doubt his turn will come. (3/1)

924 Ready Teddy (IRE) has yet to win, but there is ability there if the key can be found. (20/1)

King of Show (IRE) came good over this course and distance last year, but on much faster ground. (12/1)

Cross The Border is looking well, but seems to hate these soft conditions. (8/1: 5/1-10/1)

1312 FENWICK MAIDEN CLAIMING STKS (3-Y.O+) (Class F)

3-30 (3-31) **1m 2f** £2,612.00 (£732.00: £356.00) Stalls: High GOING: 0.75 sec per fur (S)

			Pos	SP	RR	SF
1043^{7}	**Good Day (57)** (CWThornton) **3-8-12b**^{1} DeanMcKeown(1) (b: lw: mde all: rdn 2f out: styd on)	—	**1**	15/8^{2}	71	—
1095^{7}	**Guard A Dream (IRE)** (MrsMReveley) **3-8-10** ACulhane(2) (hdwy 6f out: chsd wnr fnl 4f: rdn & no imp fnl 2f)	25	**2**	11/2^{3}	29	—
900^{13}	**Nukud (USA) (28)** (GROldroyd) **5-9-2b** GDuffield(3) (outpcd & lost tch appr st: sn t.o)	dist	**3**	7/1	—	—
1044^{6}	**Italian Symphony (IRE) (64)** (MJohnston) **3-8-6** JWeaver(4) (chsd wnr to st: sn rdn & wknd qckly)	12	**4**	6/4^{1}	—	—

(SP 102.7%) **4 Rn**

2m 32.39 (26.59) CSF £9.12 TOTE £2.90 (£6.60) OWNER Mr G. Reed (MIDDLEHAM) BRED Sir Stephen Hastings

WEIGHT FOR AGE 3yo-14lb

OFFICIAL EXPLANATION **Italian Symphony (IRE): no explanation offered.**

355 Good Day had blinkers on for the first time and, against very moderate opposition, he had galloped them into the ground with two furlongs left. (15/8)

Guard A Dream (IRE) was the only one able to keep within sight of the winner in the straight but, once pressure was applied two furlongs out, his limitations were well exposed. (11/2)

312 Nukud (USA) looked very moderate in these conditions. (7/1: 5/1-8/1)

1044 Italian Symphony (IRE), who has had his attitude questioned several times in the past, ran as though there is something seriously wrong with him. (6/4: 10/11-13/8)

1313 TORRANYARD H'CAP (0-85) (4-Y.O+) (Class D)

4-00 (4-00) **1m 2f 192y** £3,387.50 (£1,025.00: £500.00: £237.50) Stalls: High GOING: 0.75 sec per fur (S)

			Pos	SP	RR	SF
1231^{5}	**Gold Desire (45)** (MBrittain) **7-7-11** GBardwell(5) (lw: trckd ldrs: led over 5f out: pushed clr: eased ins fnl f)	—	**1**	11/4^{2}	59+	—
955*	**Manful (75)** (MissLAPerratt) **5-9-13b** NKennedy(6) (lw: led tl hdd over 5f out: sn wl outpcd)	9	**2**	2/1^{1}	76	11
	Ordained (56) (EJAlston) **4-8-8** SDrowne(4) (in tch: effrt 4f out: one pce)	3	**3**	14/1	52	—
1268^{13}	**Keep Battling (50)** (JSGoldie) **7-8-2** TWilliams(2) (stdd s: hld up: effrt over 3f out: n.d)	8	**4**	6/1	35	—
955^{7}	**Opulent (73)** (MrsMReveley) **6-9-11** ACulhane(3) (hld up: effrt appr st: sn btn)	5	**5**	7/2^{3}	50	—
900^{3}	**Sing And Dance (44)** (EWeymes) **4-7-5**(5) PFessey(1) (lw: cl up tl wknd rapidly appr st: sn wl t.o: virtually p.u)	dist	**6**	9/1	—	—

(SP 113.2%) **6 Rn**

2m 36.31 (20.41) CSF £8.04 TOTE £3.90: £2.50 £1.10 (£4.50) OWNER Northgate Lodge Racing Club (WARTHILL) BRED Northgate Lodge Stud Ltd

LONG HANDICAP Sing And Dance 7-9

OFFICIAL EXPLANATION **Sing And Dance: was found to have a heart irregularity. The rider had not pulled up as the filly had retained her action and he felt it would be all right to let her finish in her own time.**

1231 Gold Desire, back over a longer trip, turned this into a procession early in the straight to gain his first win on really testing ground. (11/4)
955* Manful, who likes the soft and has been in tremendous form this season, was trying to win this for the second year running, but was made to look very pedestrian by the easy winner. (2/1: 5/4-9/4)
Ordained has always seemed better on faster ground, and this was not a bad effort in the circumstances. (14/1)
898 Keep Battling has won his three races on much faster going and was never firing. (6/1)
Opulent has something about him on looks, but his two runs this season on soft ground have left plenty to be desired. (7/2)
900 Sing And Dance ran a stinker and looked distressed. (9/1: 8/1-12/1)

1314 CROSSHILL LIMITED STKS (0-85) (3-Y.O) (Class D)
4-30 (4-31) **1m** £3,355.00 (£1,015.00: £495.00: £235.00) Stalls: High GOING: 0.75 sec per fur (S)

				SP	RR	SF
1030*	**Bea's Ruby (IRE) (83)** (ABailey) **3-8-11** JWeaver(4) (mde all: qcknd over 3f out: sn clr: styd on wl)	—	**1**	10/11 ^{1}	91	8
	Brave Montgomerie (83) (MissLAPerratt) **3-8-11** JCarroll(5) (hld up: hdwy 3f out: chsd wnr fnl 2f: rdn & no imp)	6	**2**	10/1	79	—
699^{11}	**Right Tune (82)** (BHanbury) **3-8-8** MRimmer(2) (chsd wnr: rdn 3f out: sn outpcd)	8	**3**	8/1	60	—
1006*	**Zoom Up (IRE) (82)** (MJHeaton-Ellis) **3-9-0** SDrowne(3) (lw: chsd ldrs tl rdn & btn over 2f out)	9	**4**	4/1 ^{2}	48	—
	Mudflap (84) (SirMarkPrescott) **3-8-8** GDuffield(1) (prom tl rdn & wknd qckly over 4f out: sn t.o & virtually p.u)	dist	**5**	5/1 ^{3}	—	—
				(SP 109.2%)		**5 Rn**

1m 52.13 (14.73) CSF £9.50 TOTE £1.60: £1.90 £2.20 (£4.10) OWNER Mr M Tabor & Mrs John Magnier (TARPORLEY) BRED Green Ireland Properties Ltd
1030* Bea's Ruby (IRE), stepping up a furlong, made full use of her stamina and had it sewn up approaching the final furlong. (10/11: op 6/4)
Brave Montgomerie looked likely to be all the better for this and ran a fine race, suggesting that there is plenty of improvement to come. (10/1: op 5/1)
699 Right Tune is certainly a nice type, and gave the impression that on faster ground plenty more will be seen of her. (8/1: op 5/1)
1006* Zoom Up (IRE) was extremely fit, but he proved disappointing once asked a question early in the straight. This ground did not appear to suit. (4/1)
Mudflap ran terribly, being beaten before the home turn, and there was obviously something wrong with her. (5/1: op 3/1)

1315 KILMACOLM H'CAP (0-60) (3-Y.O+) (Class F)
5-05 (5-07) **7f** £3,165.00 (£960.00: £470.00: £225.00) Stalls: Low GOING: 0.75 sec per fur (S)

				SP	RR	SF
860^{11}	**Brandonville (52)** (NTinkler) **4-9-6** DeanMcKeown(9) (lw: in tch: led over 1f out: hung lft ins fnl f: rdn & swvd bdly rt: styd on)	—	**1**	25/1	62	47
733^{15}	**Superpride (56)** (MrsMReveley) **5-9-10** ACulhane(14) (cl up: led ½-wy tl over 1f out: kpt on one pce)	2½	**2**	14/1	60	45
1037^{5}	**Tibbi Blues (37)** (JSGoldie) **10-8-0**(5) JBramhill(3) (mid div tl hdwy 3f out: styd on wl: nrst fin)	½	**3**	14/1	40	25
929^{9}	**Termon (38)** (MissLAPerratt) **4-8-6** OUrbina(11) (swtg: styd on fnl 3f: nrst fin)	s.h	**4**	25/1	41	26
925^{4}	**Running Green (55)** (DMoffatt) **6-9-6**(3) DarrenMoffatt(8) (in tch: drvn along appr st: styd on fnl 2f: no imp)	4	**5**	12/1	49	34
1077*	**Allinson's Mate (IRE) (58)** (TDBarron) **9-9-5b**(7) VictoriaAppleby(10) (lw: bhd: effrt & bmpd ent st: styd on wl fnl 2f)	1½	**6**	7/1 ^{3}	49	34
1020^{10}	**Sagebrush Roller (54)** (JWWatts) **9-9-8** GDuffield(2) (bhd: hdwy 3f out: nvr rchd ldrs)	3½	**7**	6/1 ^{1}	37	22
1220^{9}	**Mu-Arrik (30)** (GROldroyd) **9-7-7v**(5) PFessey(18) (prom tl wknd fnl 2½f)	6	**8**	33/1	—	—
423^{4}	**Ring the Chief (37)** (MDIUsher) **5-8-5** JMarshall(7) (drvn along ½-wy: nvr rchd ldrs)	1½	**9**	25/1	2	—
774^{3}	**Finisterre (IRE) (59)** (JJO'Neill) **4-9-13** JWeaver(1) (lw: bhd tl styd on fnl 2f)	1	**10**	10/1	22	7
795^{8}	**Martindale (IRE) (54)** (RBastiman) **4-9-3**(5) HBastiman(6) (lw: led to ½-wy: sn wknd)	¾	**11**	13/2 ^{2}	15	—
1098^{13}	**Playmaker (45)** (DNicholls) **4-8-13** AlexGreaves(12) (unruly in stalls: n.d)	2	**12**	33/1	2	—
1131^{6}	**Magic Lake (43)** (EJAlston) **4-8-11** SDrowne(16) (unruly in stalls: sn chsng ldrs: effrt 3f out: wknd fnl 2f)	s.h	**13**	16/1	—	—
527^{11}	**Craigie Boy (43)** (NBycroft) **7-8-11** TWilliams(13) (chsd ldrs 4f: wknd)	¾	**14**	20/1	—	—
1291^{2}	**Monte Cavo (29)** (MBrittain) **6-7-11** GBardwell(17) (lw: prom 4f)	1¼	**15**	13/2 ^{2}	—	—
1020^{14}	**Be Warned (57)** (MDods) **6-9-11b** GCarter(4) (rr div & bmpd ent st: n.d)	1¼	**16**	9/1	6	—
951^{7}	**Mister Westsound (50)** (MissLAPerratt) **5-9-4b** JCarroll(15) (s.i.s: a bhd)	3½	**17**	25/1	—	—
1119^{5}	**Zalotto (IRE) (52)** (TJEtherington) **3-8-9** GHind(5) (lw: wl off: sn drvn along & lost pl: virtually p.u)	dist	**18**	6/1 ^{1}	—	—
				(SP 139.8%)		**18 Rn**

1m 34.43 (10.03) CSF £326.59 CT £4,738.42 TOTE £71.00: £17.20 £3.30 £6.10 £6.90 (£324.60) Trio £497.40 OWNER Mr Philip Grundy (MALTON) BRED Cheveley Park Stud Ltd
WEIGHT FOR AGE 3yo-11lb
Brandonville is without doubt a real character, but there is plenty of ability there if it can be channelled in the right direction. (25/1)
Superpride has gained his only two wins on this track and, taken last and very slowly to post, tried hard again, but was well outpointed in the last furlong. (14/1: 12/1-20/1)
1037 Tibbi Blues made up a lot of ground in the straight, but the task was always too much. Despite her years, she is obviously in really good form. (14/1)
Termon made useful progress all the way up the straight, and may well need further. (25/1)
925 Running Green was off the bridle for much of the trip and would seem to need further. (12/1)
1077* Allinson's Mate (IRE) had a lot of running to do from the home turn, and in the end did quite well. (7/1)
529 Sagebrush Roller runs when he is ready, and it was never going to be soon enough here. (6/1)
1119 Zalotto (IRE), edgy beforehand, was off the bit immediately after the start and ran as though something was seriously amiss. (6/1)

T/Plpt: £809.80 (12.62 Tckts). T/Qdpt: £322.00 (1.23 Tckts) AA

1304-GOODWOOD (R-H) (St crse Good to soft, Rnd Good)
Wednesday May 21st
WEATHER: overcast WIND: almost nil

1316 METSA-SERLA PAPERBOARD LTD MAIDEN STKS (3-Y.O F) (Class D)
2-10 (2-13) **7f** £5,526.50 (£1,652.00: £791.00: £360.50) Stalls: Low GOING minus 0.04 sec per fur (G)

				SP	RR	SF
727^{10}	**St Radegund** (GWragg) **3-8-11** MHills(3) (lw: hld up in tch: led gng wl over 1f out: pushed clr ins fnl f)	—	**1**	3/1 ^{1}	72	52
	Blueygreen (PWChapple-Hyam) **3-8-11** JReid(7) (led: hdd over 1f out: one pce)	2½	**2**	20/1	66	46

				SP	RR	SF
	Doyella (IRE) (DRLoder) **3-8-11** LDettori(17) (mid div: rdn 2f out: styd on ins fnl f)	¾	**3**	8/1	65	45
	Chinaberry (CEBrittain) **3-8-11** BDoyle(6) (neat: b: rr: hdwy over 2f out: styd on ins fnl f: nvr nrr)	¾	**4**	20/1	63	43
935^{3}	**Alikhlas (87)** (MajorWRHern) **3-8-11** RHills(11) (chsd ldr 5f: rdn & one pce fnl 2f)	1	**5**	$6/1^{2}$	61	41
935^{5}	**Khawafi** (EALDunlop) **3-8-11** KFallon(15) (nvr nrr)	2½	**6**	8/1	55	35
992^{5}	**Anchored In Love** (RCharlton) **3-8-11** TSprake(8) (a mid div)	nk	**7**	20/1	54	34
1147^{6}	**Alcalali (USA)** (PAKelleway) **3-8-11** KDarley(4) (a mid div)	½	**8**	7/1	53	33
1087^{7}	**Flying Colours (IRE)** (CJBenstead) **3-8-11** AMcGlone(1) (a mid div)	nk	**9**	66/1	52	32
	Senorita Matilda (USA) (RHannon) **3-8-11** DaneO'Neill(9) (bit bkwd: chsd ldrs tl wknd wl over 1f out)	1½	**10**	14/1	49	29
1110^{5}	**Blue Lamp (USA)** (MAJarvis) **3-8-11** RCochrane(16) (prom tl wknd over 1f out)	5	**11**	12/1	38	18
1030^{3}	**Sceptre Lady (IRE)** (BWHills) **3-8-11** DHolland(10) (chsd ldrs tl wknd 2f out)	1¾	**12**	$13/2^{3}$	34	14
885^{9}	**Cheek To Cheek** (CACyzer) **3-8-11** AClark(12) (mid div: rdn over 5f out: wknd over 2f out)	1¾	**13**	50/1	30	10
	Wintered Out (GLMoore) **3-8-11** MWigham(5) (a bhd)	15	**14**	66/1	—	—
989^{12}	**Mamma Luigi (IRE)** (GLewis) **3-8-4**(7) JDennis(14) (a bhd)	¾	**15**	100/1	—	—
	Marisa's Pet (GLewis) **3-8-8**(3) AWhelan(2) (w'like: bit bkwd: a bhd)	4	**16**	100/1	—	—

(SP 122.9%) **16 Rn**

1m 28.16 (3.36) CSF £65.62 TOTE £4.80: £2.00 £4.70 £2.30 (£65.40) Trio £114.60 OWNER Mr A. E. Oppenheimer (NEWMARKET) BRED Hascombe and Valiant Studs

St Radegund looked well in the paddock and, well supported in the ring, stepped up on her debut to score readily. (3/1)
Blueygreen set out to try and make all and plugged on gamely when headed. A race can be found. (20/1)
Doyella (IRE) is out of a ten-furlong winner in Ireland, and the way she kept on here suggests improvement will come as she steps up in trip. (8/1: 6/1-10/1)
Chinaberry was another to stay on promisingly and will improve over further. (20/1)
935 Alikhlas ran her race, but simply was not good enough. (6/1: 9/2-7/1)
935 Khawafi kept on from way back to show plenty of promise. (8/1: op 9/2)
1147 Alcalali (USA) (7/1: 4/1-8/1)
1110 Blue Lamp (USA) (12/1: 8/1-14/1)

1317 MARRIOTT GOODWOOD PARK HOTEL H'CAP (0-95) (3-Y.O+) (Class C)

2-40 (2-43) **6f** £7,960.00 (£2,380.00: £1,140.00: £520.00) Stalls: Low GOING minus 0.04 sec per fur (G)

				SP	RR	SF
942^{10}	**Oggi (79)** (PJMakin) **6-9-0** RCochrane(6) (racd stands' side: a.p: led wl over 1f out: rdn ins fnl f: r.o wl)	—	**1**	11/1	87	57
942^{2}	**Sir Joey (USA) (83)** (PGMurphy) **8-9-4** KFallon(12) (dwlt: brought stands' side: in tch: rdn over 1f out: styd on ins fnl f)	1¾	**2**	$6/1^{2}$	86	56
942^{5}	**Sea-Deer (85)** (CADwyer) **8-9-6** LDettori(18) (lw: racd far side: hdwy 2f out: ev ch 1f out: unable qckn)	s.h	**3**	$5/1^{1}$	88	58
942^{21}	**Warning Time (89)** (BJMeehan) **4-9-10** RHughes(1) (led stands' side tl over 1f out: one pce)	hd	**4**	33/1	92	62
540^{5}	**Marl (84)** (RAkehurst) **4-9-5** TQuinn(2) (racd stands' side: chsd ldrs: rdn over 1f out: one pce)	s.h	**5**	$10/1^{3}$	87	57
	Double Bounce (89) (PJMakin) **7-9-10** DHolland(5) (racd stands' side: rdn & hdwy over 1f out: styd on ins fnl f)	1	**6**	12/1	89	59
930^{11}	**Danetime (IRE) (92)** (NACallaghan) **3-9-4** PaulEddery(14) (stdd s: swtchd stands' side after 2f: hld up: hdwy fnl f: nvr nrr)	½	**7**	16/1	91	52
1148^{10}	**Charlie Sillett (82)** (BWHills) **5-9-3** MHills(4) (dwlt: racd stands' side: towards rr tl styd on ins fnl f: nvr nrr)	½	**8**	11/1	80	50
569^{6}	**Purple Fling (70)** (LGCottrell) **6-8-5** SSanders(13) (racd centre: a.p: rdn over 1f out: wknd ins fnl f)	hd	**9**	$10/1^{3}$	67	37
	Akalim (66) (LGCottrell) **4-7-12**(3) AWhelan(20) (racd far side: a.p: ev ch 1f out: wknd ins fnl f)	hd	**10**	33/1	63	33
1034^{3}	**Bowden Rose (84)** (MBlanshard) **5-9-5b** JQuinn(16) (racd centre: spd over 4f)	1¾	**11**	11/1	76	46
892^{24}	**Bold Effort (FR) (85)** (KOCunningham-Brown) **5-9-6b** BDoyle(11) (racd centre: led 4f out tl wl over 1f out: wknd ins fnl f)	nk	**12**	25/1	77	47
942^{26}	**Indian Relative (74)** (RGuest) **4-8-6**(3) DGriffiths(3) (spd over 4f)	1¾	**13**	20/1	61	31
1009^{*}	**Apollo Red (73)** (GLMoore) **8-8-8** CandyMorris(19) (racd far side: led 2f: wknd 2f out)	1½	**14**	12/1	56	26
1113^{2}	**Kildee Lad (77)** (APJones) **7-8-12** TSprake(8) (bhd fnl 2f)	1¼	**15**	14/1	57	27
942^{27}	**Master Planner (87)** (CACyzer) **8-9-3**(5) RFfrench(15) (b: racd centre: spd 4f)	1	**16**	33/1	64	34
980^{5}	**Montendre (93)** (RJHodges) **10-10-0** JReid(9) (a bhd)	1	**17**	20/1	67	37
	Hard to Figure (91) (RJHodges) **11-9-7**(5) AmandaSanders(10) (a bhd)	4	**18**	40/1	55	25
540^{7}	**Varnishing Day (IRE) (90)** (PWChapple-Hyam) **5-9-11** SWhitworth(17) (a bhd)	3	**19**	33/1	46	16

(SP 129.6%) **19 Rn**

1m 12.41 (2.61) CSF £64.81 CT £361.48 TOTE £10.50: £2.20 £1.80 £1.50 £9.10 (£31.60) Trio £26.50 OWNER Skyline Racing Ltd (MARLBOROUGH) BRED H. D. and M. J. Gee

WEIGHT FOR AGE 3yo-9lb

835* Oggi won this readily off a mark 7lb higher than his Leicester success, and is obviously improving. (11/1)
942 Sir Joey (USA) ran another sound race and should find a similar event soon. (6/1)
942 Sea-Deer was once again unlucky with the draw, comfortably winning the race on his side. (5/1)
Warning Time ran his best race for some time. (33/1)
540 Marl has not won since her two-year-old days, but the way she ran here suggests her turn is near. (10/1)
Double Bounce ran a sound race on his seasonal debut, staying on nicely in the closing stages. (12/1)
Charlie Sillett (11/1: 8/1-12/1)

1318 TRIPLEPRINT LUPE STKS (Listed) (3-Y.O F) (Class A)

3-10 (3-14) **1m 2f** £17,610.00 (£5,280.00: £2,540.00: £1,170.00) Stalls: Low GOING minus 0.04 sec per fur (G)

				SP	RR	SF
875^{*}	**Maid of Camelot** (RCharlton) **3-8-8** TSprake(6) (set slow pce: hdd over 3f out: regained ld over 1f out: r.o wl)	—	**1**	10/1	93	37
	Priena (IRE) (DRLoder) **3-8-8** KDarley(1) (lw: chsd wnr: led over 3f out: hdd over 1f out: hrd rdn ins fnl f: unable qckn)	1¼	**2**	7/1	91	35
727^{7}	**Keyboogie (USA)** (RCharlton) **3-8-8** JReid(7) (lw: dwlt: hld up: hdwy 3f out: hrd rdn over 1f out: styd on ins fnl f)	hd	**3**	$3/1^{2}$	91	35
	Meshhed (USA) (BHanbury) **3-8-8** RHills(4) (hld up: hdwy over 3f out: ev ch over 1f out: no ex ins fnl f)	1¼	**4**	$9/4^{1}$	89	33
485^{*}	**Dust Dancer (81)** (JLDunlop) **3-8-8** TQuinn(3) (a bhd)	6	**5**	$4/1^{3}$	79	23
1102^{5}	**Lycility (IRE) (94)** (CEBrittain) **3-8-8b**[1] BDoyle(8) (lw: chsd ldrs tl wknd 3f out)	2	**6**	10/1	76	20

1028[5]	**Dundel (IRE) (80)** (BWHills) **3-8-8** MHills(2) (in tch: rdn over 2f out: sn btn)	nk	**7**	20/1	76	20

(SP 111.2%) **7 Rn**

2m 13.26 (6.66) CSF £65.31 TOTE £10.80: £3.30 £3.30 (£32.80) OWNER Mr A. E. Oppenheimer (BECKHAMPTON) BRED Hascombe and Valiant Studs

875* Maid of Camelot was given a good ride in a tactical race. (10/1)
Priena (IRE) was always up with the pace in a slowly-run race. (7/1: 5/1-15/2)
727 Keyboogie (USA) is bred to be a staying filly, and was not suited by the slow gallop. (3/1)
Meshhed (USA) ran well but could find no more in the closing stages. (9/4)
485* Dust Dancer was disappointing, never looking likely to get into it. (4/1)
1102 Lycility (IRE) dropped away tamely up the straight. (10/1: 7/1-11/1)

1319 ABN AMRO RATED STKS H'CAP (0-105) (4-Y.O+) (Class B)

3-40 (3-42) **1m 6f** £9,454.80 (£3,493.20: £1,671.60: £678.00: £264.00: £98.40) Stalls: Low GOING: 0.04 sec per fur (G)

				SP	RR	SF
891[7]	**Jiyush (100)** (EALDunlop) **4-9-7** RHills(7) (lw: mde all: clr 2f out: easily)	—	**1**	11/1	112+	65
	Bahamian Sunshine (USA) (95) (RAkehurst) **6-9-2** TQuinn(3) (chsd wnr: hrd rdn over 2f out: one pce)	3	**2**	8/1	104	57
736[13]	**Air Quest (99)** (RCharlton) **4-9-6** KDarley(5) (hld up: hdwy 3f out: rdn over 2f out: one pce)	¾	**3**	8/1	107	60
1027[9]	**Snow Princess (IRE) (97)** (LordHuntingdon) **5-9-4** JReid(8) (chsd ldrs: hrd rdn over 2f out: one pce)	s.h	**4**	7/1[3]	105	58
	Benatom (USA) (95) (HRACecil) **4-9-2** WRyan(1) (hld up: hdwy over 3f out: rdn over 2f out: one pce)	¾	**5**	8/1	102	55
962[3]	**Rokeby Bowl (90)** (IABalding) **5-8-11** LDettori(9) (hld up: effrt & n.m.r over 2f out: sn rdn & btn)	2½	**6**	4/1[2]	94	47
1108[3]	**Male-Ana-Mou (IRE) (92)** (DRCElsworth) **4-8-13** DaneO'Neill(4) (keen hold: hld up: rdn over 3f out: sn btn)	6	**7**	7/1[3]	89	42
962[9]	**Royal Scimitar (USA) (98)** (MrsAJPerrett) **5-9-5** AClark(6) (lw: towards rr: rdn 6f out: sn btn)	3	**8**	16/1	92	45
962[5]	**General Assembly (IRE) (93)** (HRACecil) **5-9-0** MHills(2) (chsd ldrs tl rdn & wknd over 3f out)	9	**9**	3/1[1]	76	29

(SP 117.5%) **9 Rn**

3m 5.52 (6.52) CSF £88.25 CT £683.63 TOTE £15.50: £3.40 £2.50 £3.20 (£79.50) Trio £258.60 OWNER Mr Hamdan Al Maktoum (NEWMARKET) BRED Shadwell Estate Company Limited

OFFICIAL EXPLANATION **General Assembly (IRE): rider reported that the horse appeared not to act on the track, so he didn't persevere in the last two furlongs.**

Jiyush bounced back to form under top-weight to win in emphatic fashion. (11/1)
Bahamian Sunshine (USA) chased vainly throughout but, ridden halfway up the straight, was unable to get to the winner. (8/1)
Air Quest appears to have plenty of weight for what he has done and, although keeping on in the final three furlongs, never looked like winning. (8/1: 6/1-9/1)
1027 Snow Princess (IRE) ran better than at Chester and could be running into form. (7/1)
Benatom (USA) made an effort early in the straight, but was just going up and down in the closing stages. (8/1: 6/1-9/1)
962 Rokeby Bowl, although finding trouble over two furlongs out, made little impression once he was in the clear. (4/1)
962 General Assembly (IRE) dropped away very tamely in the closing stages, and something could well have been amiss. (3/1)

1320 NPI RECOGNITION OF ACHIEVEMENT H'CAP (0-80) (3-Y.O+) (Class D)

4-10 (4-15) **1m** £5,726.25 (£1,710.00: £817.50: £371.25) Stalls: Low GOING minus 0.04 sec per fur (G)

				SP	RR	SF
363[3]	**Hurtleberry (IRE) (70)** (LordHuntingdon) **4-9-6** LDettori(9) (hld up mid div: hdwy 3f out: led wl ins fnl f: comf)	—	**1**	7/1[2]	75+	66
1035[3]	**Orange Place (IRE) (75)** (TJNaughton) **6-9-11** TQuinn(6) (lw: led: hdd over 1f out: rallied to ld again ins fnl f: hdd nr fin)	¾	**2**	6/1[1]	79	70
991[5]	**Khafaaq (76)** (MajorWRHern) **3-9-0** RHills(16) (lw: a.p: led over 1f out: hdd ins fnl f: unable qckn)	½	**3**	6/1[1]	79	58
963[6]	**Judicial Supremacy (80)** (JRFanshawe) **3-9-4** MHills(3) (lw: dwlt: rr: rdn 3f out: kpt on one pce fnl 2f)	3	**4**	7/1[2]	77	56
1035[16]	**Sue's Return (78)** (APJarvis) **5-10-0** WJO'Connor(8) (chsd ldrs: rdn 2f out: one pce)	s.h	**5**	11/1	74	65
383[5]	**Superior Force (58)** (MissBSanders) **4-8-8** SSanders(14) (chsd ldr over 5f: wknd over 1f out)	2	**6**	25/1	50	41
1005[10]	**Confronter (57)** (SDow) **8-8-7** RPerham(17) (chsd ldrs tl wknd 2f out)	3	**7**	10/1[3]	43	34
	Tremplin (USA) (75) (NACallaghan) **5-9-11** RHughes(18) (dwlt: rr: n.m.r over 2f out tl ins fnl f: styd on: nvr nrr)	hd	**8**	12/1	61	52
752[6]	**Regal Splendour (CAN) (59)** (RJO'Sullivan) **4-8-9** KDarley(2) (a mid div)	s.h	**9**	20/1	45	36
1082[2]	**Banzhaf (USA) (70)** (GLMoore) **4-9-6** MWigham(10) (chsd ldrs: rdn over 2f out: grad wknd)	s.h	**10**	10/1[3]	56	47
1024[11]	**Mr Rough (53)** (DMorris) **6-8-3**ow2 NDay(5) (nvr bttr than mid div)	¾	**11**	16/1	38	27
752[7]	**Jaazim (46)** (MMadgwick) **7-7-10** NVarley(7) (nvr bttr than mid div)	hd	**12**	33/1	30	21
1035[18]	**Oberon's Dart (IRE) (70)** (PJMakin) **4-9-6** DHolland(13) (hld up in rr: hmpd over 2f out: nt rcvr)	3	**13**	14/1	48	39
853[9]	**Ortelius (77)** (RHannon) **3-9-1** DaneO'Neill(11) (nvr bttr than mid div)	¾	**14**	20/1	54	33
1003[11]	**Coastguards Hero (55)** (MDIUsher) **4-8-5** JQuinn(1) (dwlt: a bhd)	½	**15**	16/1	31	22
	Moi Canard (52) (BAPearce) **4-7-13**(3) MartinDwyer(12) (a bhd)	nk	**16**	33/1	27	18
	Warren Knight (55) (CAHorgan) **4-8-5** MFenton(4) (chsd ldrs tl wknd over 2f out)	11	**17**	16/1	8	—

(SP 131.3%) **17 Rn**

1m 40.53 (3.33) CSF £44.24 CT £262.34 TOTE £5.80: £1.50 £1.60 £3.00 £2.20 (£10.50) Trio £28.30 OWNER Mrs Ian Pilkington (WEST ILSLEY) BRED D. Maher

LONG HANDICAP Jaazim 7-6
WEIGHT FOR AGE 3yo-12lb

363 Hurtleberry (IRE) won this much more cosily than the margin suggests and can score again. (7/1)
1035 Orange Place (IRE) put up a very brave front-running performance, but is flattered by his proximity to the winner. (6/1: op 4/1)
991 Khafaaq ran a sound first race in a handicap, and should have no trouble finding a similar event. (6/1: 10/1-11/2)
963 Judicial Supremacy stayed on in the final two furlongs and is worth a try over further. (7/1)
Sue's Return ran better than of late, but could do with the Handicapper relenting. (11/1)
Tremplin (USA) (12/1: 8/1-14/1)

88+ 73+79

1321 E.B.F. EQUITY FINANCIAL COLLECTIONS MAIDEN STKS (2-Y.O) (Class D)

4-45 (4-47) **6f** £4,542.00 (£1,356.00: £648.00: £294.00) Stalls: Low GOING minus 0.04 sec per fur (G)

				SP	RR	SF
	Shadow of Doubt (IRE) (PWChapple-Hyam) **2-9-0** JReid(2) (scope: lw: a.p: led over 2f out: edgd rt ins fnl f: r.o wl)	—	**1**	5/6[1]	80	30
696[2]	**Arpeggio** (RHannon) **2-9-0** LDettori(7) (lw: trckd ldrs: n.m.r & swtchd rt over 1f out: chal strly & ev ch ins fnl f: r.o)	nk	**2**	2/1[2]	79	29
	Indian Missile (JLDunlop) **2-9-0** RHills(6) (w'like: bit bkwd: rdn ½-wy: hdwy over 2f out: no ex ins fnl f)	5	**3**	13/2[3]	66+	16

				SP	RR	SF
	Supacalifragilistk (CEBrittain) **2-8-9** BDoyle(8) (neat: swtg: dwlt: hdwy 2f out: wknd ins fnl f)	6	**4**	20/1	45	—
	Carouse (MRChannon) **2-9-0** TQuinn(4) (w'like: bit bkwd: spd 4f)	1¼	**5**	16/1	47	—
	Sassy (IRE) (APJarvis) **2-8-9** WJO'Connor(3) (w'like: dwlt: rdn ½-wy: nvr nrr)	nk	**6**	50/1	41	—
1084[6]	**Basic Style** (NACallaghan) **2-9-0** RHughes(9) (led over 3f: wknd over 1f out)	nk	**7**	50/1	45	—
	Argumentative (SDow) **2-9-0** RPerham(1) (w'like: bit bkwd: spd over 3f)	1	**8**	50/1	42	—
	Solo Spirit (JRJenkins) **2-8-4**(5) RFfrench(5) (Withdrawn not under Starter's orders)		**W**	50/1	—	—
				(SP 119.7%)	**8 Rn**	

1m 14.38 (4.58) CSF £2.46 TOTE £2.40: £1.40 £1.20 £1.60 (£2.10) Trio £2.50 OWNER Mr R. E. Sangster (MARLBOROUGH) BRED Mull Enterprizes

Shadow of Doubt (IRE), a most attractive, lengthy colt, won this race despite looking green in the closing stages. More will be heard of him, and he looks possible Ascot material. (5/6)

696 Arpeggio looked very well beforehand and ran accordingly, but he met a smart opponent here. Compensation awaits. (2/1: 6/4-5/2)

Indian Missile ran a very promising race. Not fully fit and green in the early stages, he moved up menacingly at the two pole but, once it was obvious he could not win, his rider was sympathetic. This kindness will be repaid. (13/2: 3/1-7/1)

Supacalifragilistk showed her greenness by missing the break. (20/1)

Carouse ran quite well until lack of fitness told in the closing stages. (16/1)

T/Jkpt: Not won; £4,851.99 to Goodwood 22/5/97. T/Plpt: £695.20 (48.82 Tckts). T/Qdpt: £70.80 (22.77 Tckts) SM

1316-GOODWOOD (R-H) (Good Rnd crse, Good to soft St crse)
Thursday May 22nd

WEATHER: overcast WIND: almost nil

1322 A & J BULL MAIDEN STKS (3-Y.O) (Class D)
2-10 (2-11) **1m 1f** £3,752.50 (£1,120.00: £535.00: £242.50) Stalls: High GOING: 0.07 sec per fur (G)

				SP	RR	SF
1014[9]	**Behind The Scenes** (CACyzer) **3-9-0** LDettori(1) (led over 6f out: rdn over 2f out: hdd nr fin: fin 2nd, ½l: awrdd r)	—	**1**	13/2	71	39
833[W]	**Rocky Dance (FR)** (APJarvis) **3-8-9** WJO'Connor(5) (unf: scope: a.p: rdn over 2f out: ev ch over 1f out: btn whn bmpd ins fnl f: fin 3rd, ½l & 2l: plcd 2nd)	½	**2**	5/1[3]	63	31
742[12]	**Good Reputation** (BWHills) **3-8-9** MHills(6) (led over 2f: rdn over 2f out: barged thro ins fnl f: led nr fin: fin 1st: disq: plcd 3rd)	2	**3**	4/1[1]	67	35
989[9]	**Sandystones** (NAGraham) **3-8-9** JReid(8) (a.p: rdn over 2f out: one pce)	½	**4**	9/1	62	30
	Chandler's Hall (MJHeaton-Ellis) **3-9-0** AClark(4) (gd sort: rdn over 3f out: nvr nr to chal)	3	**5**	6/1	61	29
	Liquid Gold (IRE) (WAO'Gorman) **3-9-0** EmmaO'Gorman(3) (str: scope: bkwd: hld up: rdn over 3f out: wknd wl over 1f out)	1	**6**	9/2[2]	60	28
	Mashkorah (USA) (RHannon) **3-8-9** DaneO'Neill(7) (bhd fnl 5f)	1¾	**7**	9/2[2]	51	19
	Dazla's Double (RRowe) **3-8-9** AProcter(2) (neat: bhd fnl 3f)	2	**8**	33/1	48	16
	Halavadream (MJBolton) **3-9-0** SSanders(9) (leggy: s.s: a wl bhd: t.o fnl 6f)	dist	**9**	33/1	—	—
				(SP 116.5%)	**9 Rn**	

2m 0.24 (7.24) CSF £35.80 TOTE £5.70: £1.80 £2.40 £1.60 (£36.60) Trio £30.70 OWNER Mr R. M. Cyzer (HORSHAM) BRED Fittocks Stud

STEWARDS' ENQUIRY Hills susp. 31/5 & 2-4/6/97 (irresponsible riding)

Behind The Scenes left previous form well behind. Soon pulling his way to the head of affairs, he was rousted along in the straight but was just worried out of it in the closing stages. He was later awarded the race on the disqualification of Good Reputation but his trainer admitted afterwards that his horse was second best on the day. (13/2)

Rocky Dance (FR) needs time to fully develop but still showed promise on this initial run. Still in with every chance below the distance, he was getting the worst of the argument when given a bump by Good Reputation inside the final furlong. (5/1)

Good Reputation left her initial run well behind. With nowhere to go entering the final furlong, her jockey decided to make an opening and barged through a non-existent gap inside the final furlong, giving Rocky Dance a hefty bump. It came as no surprise to see her disqualified and, although Hills disagreed, the Stewards quite rightly handed him a four-day ban for irresponsible riding. (4/1: 3/1-9/2)

Sandystones ran her best race by far and was a leading light from the outset if failing to quicken in the final quarter mile. This was her first encounter with soft ground and it obviously suited her well. (9/1: 5/1-10/1)

Chandler's Hall, a really attractive, deep-girthed individual with bags of scope, struggled on but never had the pace to get in a serious blow. (6/1)

Liquid Gold (IRE), a well-built colt with any amount of strength, was colty in the paddock and was carrying a lot of surplus flesh, so it came as no surprise to see him drop away in the final quarter-mile. (9/2: 9/4-5/1)

1323 ROYAL SUSSEX REGIMENT FESTIVAL STKS (Listed) (4-Y.O+) (Class A)
2-40 (2-41) **1m 2f** £14,620.00 (£4,360.00: £2,080.00: £940.00) Stalls: High GOING: 0.07 sec per fur (G)

				SP	RR	SF
943*	**Germano (105)** (GWragg) **4-8-12** MHills(8) (chsd ldr: led over 3f out: drvn out)	—	**1**	4/1[2]	118	74
1108*	**King Alex (107)** (RCharlton) **4-8-12** LDettori(3) (hdwy over 4f out: hung rt & chsd wnr over 1f out: r.o wl)	hd	**2**	5/4[1]	118	74
	Medaille Militaire (109) (JLDunlop) **5-9-1** KDarley(9) (hdwy over 4f out: rdn over 2f out: unable qckn)	3½	**3**	8/1	115	71
943[4]	**Prince of Andros (USA) (110)** (CFWall) **7-9-1** JReid(4) (lost pl over 4f out: nt clr run over 2f out: rallied over 1f out: r.o wl)	s.h	**4**	10/1	115	71
678[3]	**Amrak Ajeeb (IRE) (107)** (BHanbury) **5-8-12** MRimmer(10) (lw: s.s: rdn over 2f out: hdwy over 1f out: nvr nrr)	2	**5**	7/1[3]	109	65
736[6]	**Proper Blue (USA) (103)** (TGMills) **4-9-1** TQuinn(1) (hdwy over 4f out: hrd rdn over 2f out: wknd over 1f out)	hd	**6**	12/1	112	68
987[2]	**Lonely Leader (IRE) (102)** (RHannon) **4-8-12** DaneO'Neill(7) (lw: a.p: rdn over 2f out: wknd over 1f out)	1½	**7**	16/1	106	62
522[4]	**Captain Horatius (IRE) (107)** (JLDunlop) **8-9-1** TSprake(2) (a bhd)	¾	**8**	12/1	108	64
1157[3]	**Ball Gown (95)** (DTThom) **7-8-7** DHolland(6) (hdwy over 3f out: wknd over 2f out)	3½	**9**	40/1	95	51
	Brighstone (DRCElsworth) **4-8-12** AMcGlone(5) (led over 6f: wknd over 2f out)	18	**10**	66/1	71	27
				(SP 122.3%)	**10 Rn**	

2m 10.14 (3.54) CSF £8.96 TOTE £4.90: £1.60 £1.60 £2.00 (£3.60) Trio £9.80 OWNER Baron G Von Ullmann (NEWMARKET) BRED Cambremont Ltd Partnership

IN-FOCUS: **This looked a very hot Listed event.**

943* Germano suffered from back trouble last year but a spell of treatment in Germany over the winter has certainly worked wonders and he gained his first Listed victory, leading over three furlongs from home and finding the line just saving him from the fast-finishing runner-up. His first Group success will surely not be far away but it may well come abroad. (4/1: op 5/2)

1108* King Alex was suited by the ground but not by the drop in distance. Hanging right as he was asked for his effort and, moving into second place below the distance, he was cutting back the winner's advantage in the closing stages and may well have prevailed with a few more strides. He will now return to a mile and a half and a first Group success should not be long in coming. (5/4)
Medaille Militaire made a pleasing return to action and, although failing to quicken in the final quarter-mile, just held on for third prize. (8/1)
943 Prince of Andros (USA) lost his pitch running down the hill and then failed to get a clear run over a quarter of a mile from home. Nevertheless, he rallied nicely from below the distance and failed by only a whisker to take third prize. (10/1: 7/1-12/1)
678 Amrak Ajeeb (IRE), bustled along at the back of the field in the straight, never threatened to get near the principals in time. (7/1)
736 Proper Blue (USA) was probably not suited by the soft conditions and, after smoothly running into contention down the hill, had shot his bolt below the distance. A return to a sound surface will be in his favour. (12/1)
522 Captain Horatius (IRE) (12/1: 8/1-14/1)

1324 KIDSONS IMPEY TROPHY H'CAP (0-90) (4-Y.O+) (Class C)

3-10 (3-14) **7f** £9,552.00 (£2,856.00: £1,368.00: £624.00) Stalls: High GOING: 0.07 sec per fur (G)

				SP	RR	SF
1111*	**Gadge (66)** (ABailey) **6-8-5** DWright(12) (b: made all: rdn out)	—	**1**	4/1[1]	78	60
	Dancing Image (85) (IABalding) **4-9-10** LDettori(3) (swtg: stdy hdwy wl over 1f out: chsd wnr fnl f: r.o one pce)	¾	**2**	10/1[3]	95	77
1111[8]	**Knobbleeneeze (75)** (MRChannon) **7-9-0v** RHughes(10) (lw: hdwy 2f out: rdn over 1f out: r.o one pce)	¾	**3**	11/1	84	66
766[8]	**No Extras (IRE) (64)** (GLMoore) **7-8-3** CandyMorris(15) (swtg: rdn ovr 2f out: hdwy & bmpd over 1f out: r.o one pce)	¾	**4**	33/1	71	53
1035[17]	**My Best Valentine (89)** (JWhite) **7-10-0** WJO'Connor(16) (lw: a.p: rdn 2f out: one pce)	nk	**5**	20/1	95	77
1154[6]	**Stoppes Brow (75)** (GLMoore) **5-9-0v** AClark(6) (hld up: rdn over 2f out: n.m.r 1f out: one pce)	1¾	**6**	11/1	77	59
*1154**	**Resist the Force (USA) (62)** (CACyzer) **7-7-12**(3) 7x DO'Donohoe(4) (lw: hdwy over 2f out: hrd rdn over 1f out: sn wknd)	¾	**7**	12/1	63	45
567[4]	**Statoyork (65)** (BWHills) **4-8-4** DHolland(9) (lw: stdy hdwy 3f out: nt clr run 2f out: hmpd wl over 1f out: nt rcvr)	hd	**8**	12/1	65	47
	Wild Palm (72) (WAO'Gorman) **5-8-11b** EmmaO'Gorman(13) (lw: s.s: hdwy over 1f out: nvr nrr)	1¼	**9**	14/1	69	51
942[20]	**Sandabar (84)** (MRStoute) **4-9-9** JReid(7) (lw: nt clr run over 2f out: nvr nrr)	2	**10**	6/1[2]	77	59
766[6]	**Sharp 'n Smart (69)** (BSmart) **5-8-3**(5) ADaly(5) (lw: a.p: rdn 3f out: wkng whn squeezed out over 2f out)	1½	**11**	33/1	58	40
1035*	**Albert The Bear (84)** (JBerry) **4-9-9** KDarley(2) (hld up: rdn over 3f out: wkng whn hmpd over 2f out)	1	**12**	10/1[3]	71	53
929*	**Grey Kingdom (62)** (MBrittain) **6-8-1** GBardwell(1) (w wnr 5f)	½	**13**	20/1	48	30
834[8]	**Cim Bom Bom (IRE) (75)** (MBell) **5-8-9v**(5) GFaulkner(8) (mid div & wkng whn n.m.r over 2f out)	s.h	**14**	14/1	61	43
1107[3]	**Mr Frosty (64)** (WJarvis) **5-8-3** SSanders(11) (prom over 4f)	2½	**15**	16/1	44	26
				(SP 119.1%)	**15 Rn**	

1m 27.79 (2.99) CSF £36.49 CT £380.31 TOTE £4.30: £2.50 £2.20 £4.00 (£13.30) Trio £59.10 OWNER Mr J. B. Wilcox (TARPORLEY) BRED Snowdrop Stud Co Ltd

IN-FOCUS: **As can often be the case in big-field handicaps at Goodwood, there was plenty of rough and tumble with numerous horses failing to get a clear run or getting interfered with.**
1111* Gadge is in terrific form at present and coped well with the drop in distance, making all the running and needing only a couple of slaps to keep his rivals at bay. (4/1)
Dancing Image ran well after an absence of nine and a half months and steadily crept closer in the final quarter-mile. Bustled along, he took second place entering the final furlong but, despite staying on, failed to get to the winner in time. Both his wins have come over a mile and a return to that trip may well help. (10/1)
1035 Knobbleeneeze is high in the handicap at present but he picked up ground a quarter of a mile from home and stayed on for third prize. (11/1: 8/1-12/1)
No Extras (IRE) has slumped down the handicap after a string of bad efforts last year but bounced back here, staying on well in the last furlong and a half, despite getting a bump, to take fourth place. (33/1)
786 My Best Valentine was never far away but failed to quicken in the final quarter-mile. He has done all his winning at around seven furlongs on ground no worse than good. (20/1)
905 Stoppes Brow chased the leaders but failed to quicken in the final quarter-mile. (11/1: 8/1-12/1)
1154* Resist the Force (USA) (12/1: 8/1-14/1)
520 Cim Bom Bom (IRE) (14/1: 10/1-16/1)

1325 BOOKER FOODSERVICE H'CAP (0-100) (4-Y.O+) (Class C)

3-40 (3-42) **1m 4f** £7,310.00 (£2,180.00: £1,040.00: £470.00) Stalls: Low GOING: 0.07 sec per fur (G)

				SP	RR	SF
939[8]	**Hoh Express (85)** (IABalding) **5-9-3** KDarley(7) (lw: rdn over 2f out: hdwy & nt clr run on ins over 1f out: swtchd lft ins fnl f: led nr fin)	—	**1**	20/1	94	55
962*	**Valedictory (96)** (HRACecil) **4-10-0** RHughes(9) (b: lw: a.p: rdn over 3f out: led ins fnl f: hdd nr fin)	½	**2**	11/4[1]	104	65
	Humourless (93) (LMCumani) **4-9-11** LDettori(5) (b.hind: led: rdn over 2f out: hdd ins fnl f: one pce)	¾	**3**	7/2[2]	100	61
	Transom (USA) (82) (MrsAJPerrett) **6-9-0** JReid(4) (stdy hdwy over 1f out: nvr plcd to chal)	3	**4**	40/1	85	46
986*	**Mr Wild (USA) (81)** (RAkehurst) **4-8-13** TQuinn(2) (lw: chsd ldr 10f: wknd over 1f out)	¾	**5**	7/2[2]	83	44
	Captain's Guest (IRE) (83) (MrsAJPerrett) **7-9-1** AClark(8) (swtg: hld up: rdn over 3f out: wknd over 1f out)	1½	**6**	40/1	83	44
1036[4]	**Slip Jig (IRE) (76)** (KRBurke) **4-8-8** DHolland(1) (lw: a bhd)	1¼	**7**	12/1	75	36
962[6]	**My Learned Friend (78)** (AHide) **6-8-10** AMcGlone(3) (lw: hld up: rdn over 3f out: wknd over 2f out)	s.h	**8**	6/1[3]	77	38
789*	**Prince Kinsky (79)** (JABOld) **4-8-11** DHarrison(6) (lw: bhd fnl 2f)	7	**9**	13/2	68	29
				(SP 116.1%)	**9 Rn**	

2m 41.03 (7.83) CSF £67.46 CT £223.34 TOTE £21.30: £3.60 £1.70 £1.30 (£29.20) Trio £22.80 OWNER Mr D. F. Allport (KINGSCLERE) BRED Mrs M. Upsdell

OFFICIAL EXPLANATION **Hoh Express: regarding the improved form, the trainer reported that the gelding had appreciated the longer trip here.**
Hoh Express bounced back to form after three disappointing runs this season. Coping well with the step up to a mile and a half, he was just making smooth headway when failing to get a clear run at a critical point approaching the final furlong. Switched left, he found a useful turn of foot to get up in the shadow of the post. (20/1)
962* Valedictory is a real stayer and that was certainly evident here as he was being bustled along as the Bugler called. He eventually got on top inside the final furlong, only to be worried out of it near the line. (11/4)
Humourless put up a good display following a twelve-month absence and attempted to make all the running, only being passed inside the final furlong. (7/2)

Transom (USA) was given a very tender ride on this first outing in just over two years, but showed plenty of promise as he stayed on under sympathetic handling in the last furlong and a half to finish an eye-catching fourth. Given time to recover from this, improvement can be expected.(40/1)
986* Mr Wild (USA), 8lb higher for his Kempton win, raced in second place to the two-furlong pole before tiring. (7/2)
Captain's Guest (IRE), winner of the 1994 Cesarewitch, has not won since and had called it a day over a furlong from home. (40/1)
1036 Slip Jig (IRE) (12/1: op 8/1)

1326 RUINART CHAMPAGNE CONQUEROR STKS (Listed) (3-Y.O+ F & M) (Class A)

4-10 (4-11) **1m** £11,954.25 (£3,564.00: £1,699.50: £767.25) Stalls: High GOING: 0.07 sec per fur (G)

				SP	RR	SF
	Out West (USA) (HRACecil) **3-8-2** AMcGlone(6) (lw: a.p: led over 1f out: edgd rt ins fnl f: rdn out)	—	1	$6/1^{3}$	105	54
1085*	**Lilli Claire (94)** (AGFoster) **4-9-0** TSprake(2) (lw: stdy hdwy over 2f out: edgd rt over 1f out: hrd rdn: unable qckn ins fnl f)	¾	2	7/1	104	65
839^{6}	**Miss Riviera (95)** (GWragg) **4-9-0** MHills(4) (lw: stdy hdwy over 2f out: n.m.r over 1f out: r.o ins fnl f)	1	3	10/1	102	63
934*	**Balalaika (102)** (LMCumani) **4-9-3** LDettori(9) (lw: hld up: nt clr run over 2f out, over 1f out & ins fnl f: nt rcvr)	s.h	4	$7/4^{1}$	104+	65
935*	**Jafn** (BHanbury) **3-8-2** BDoyle(3) (b.off hind: lw: nt clr run over 2f out & 2f out: swtchd lft over 1f out: gd hwy fnl f: fin wl)	nk	5	14/1	101	50
934^{2}	**Tsarnista (95)** (JLDunlop) **4-9-0** JReid(8) (a.p: rdn over 2f out: sn wknd)	2½	6	7/1	96	57
1209^{4}	**Gretel (105)** (MRStoute) **3-8-2** AClark(1) (lw: led over 6f: 3rd & btn whn hmpd on ins ins fnl f)	½	7	10/1	95	44
1101*	**Supercal (99)** (DRCElsworth) **3-8-5** TQuinn(5) (lw: dwlt: sme hdwy 2f out: wknd over 1f out)	10	8	$11/2^{2}$	78	27
507^{6}	**Blane Water (USA) (99)** (JRFanshawe) **3-8-2** DHarrison(7) (lw: prom over 5f)	1¾	9	20/1	71	20

(SP 120.6%) **9 Rn**

1m 40.92 (3.72) CSF £45.23 TOTE £8.60: £2.30 £1.80 £2.80 (£33.20) Trio £254.30 OWNER Buckram Oak Holdings (NEWMARKET) BRED Buckram Oak Farm
WEIGHT FOR AGE 3yo-12lb
Out West (USA) fourth to Benny The Dip at Doncaster last September, struck the front below the distance and, despite edging right, held on well. (6/1)
1085* Lilli Claire had much more on her plate on this occasion but still ran really well, if just failing to find that necessary turn of foot inside the final furlong. (7/1)
839 Miss Riviera is certainly not easy to win with. Cruising into the action over a quarter of a mile from home, she was done no favours below the distance but, nevertheless, ran on to snatch third prize right on the line. She is going to be covered for a fourth time by Salse on Friday and this will be her last chance to get in foal. (10/1)
934* Balalaika had a nightmare run and was not helped by the drop in distance. With nowhere to go along the inside rail over a quarter of a mile from home, and again below the distance, she was just picking up inside the final furlong when again done no favours. This run is best ignored and she can certainly win another Pattern race this season. (7/4)
935* Jafn was taking a big step up in class but, despite having an horrendous run, still showed a great deal of promise for the future. Failing to get a clear run over a quarter of a mile from home, her jockey would have been wise to take her to the outside but, instead, he persisted in trying to go for a run where there was a conglomeration of horses. The penny eventually dropped and Doyle switched him to the outside below the distance but by this time she was in last place. Nevertheless, she sprouted wings in the final furlong and came tearing through, only just failing to take fourth prize. She is certainly up to winning a similar event. (14/1)
934 Tsarnista was close up until calling it a day a quarter of a mile from home. She has just one victory to her name. (7/1: op 9/2)

1327 RACING CHANNEL APPRENTICE H'CAP (0-70) (3-Y.O+) (Class E)

4-45 (4-46) **5f** £3,485.00 (£1,055.00: £515.00: £245.00) Stalls: Low GOING: 0.07 sec per fur (G)

				SP	RR	SF
1083^{9}	**Half Tone (52)** (RMFlower) **5-8-12b** GMilligan(5) (lw: outpcd: gd hdwy fnl f: led last stride)	—	1	$100/30^{2}$	59	36
1083^{2}	**Willow Dale (IRE) (67)** (DRCElsworth) **4-9-13** PPMurphy(7) (hld up: rdn over 2f out: led ins fnl f: slipped last strides: hdd last stride)	s.h	2	$3/1^{1}$	74	51
1250^{10}	**Stolen Kiss (IRE) (63)** (MWEasterby) **5-9-9b** GFaulkner(3) (a.p: rdn over 2f out: r.o ins fnl f)	½	3	$5/1^{3}$	68	45
879^{13}	**Sharp Stock (63)** (RJHodges) **4-9-9** SophieMitchell(4) (led over 1f: rdn over 2f out: ev ch ins fnl f: unable qckn)	s.h	4	25/1	68	45
1236^{3}	**Superlao (BEL) (36)** (JJBridger) **5-7-10** RMullen(8) (a.p: rdn over 2f out: ev ch ins fnl f: one pce)	s.h	5	10/1	41	18
604^{4}	**Village Native (FR) (60)** (KOCunningham-Brown) **4-9-1**(5) TField(6) (lw: rdn over 2f out: hdwy over 1f out: nt clr run ins fnl f: r.o)	hd	6	9/1	65	42
	Another Batchworth (67) (EAWheeler) **5-9-13b** ADaly(1) (a.p: led over 3f out tl ins fnl f: wknd)	1¾	7	13/2	66	43
	La Spagna (36) (MDIUsher) **6-7-5**(5) RBrisland(9) (nvr nr to chal)	1½	8	33/1	30	7
1029^{11}	**Suite Factors (60)** (KRBurke) **3-8-7**(5) RWinston(2) (prom over 2f)	¾	9	10/1	52	21

(SP 113.0%) **9 Rn**

60.46 secs (3.76) CSF £12.22 CT £43.54 TOTE £4.10: £1.30 £1.60 £1.60 (£5.80) Trio £7.40 OWNER Mrs G. M. Temmerman (JEVINGTON) BRED T. M. Jennings
LONG HANDICAP Superlao (BEL) 7-8 La Spagna 7-9
WEIGHT FOR AGE 3yo-8lb
Half Tone bounced back to form. Unable to go the early pace, he really found his stride in the final furlong and came flying through to snatch the spoils right on the line. (100/30)
1083 Willow Dale (IRE) is not the easiest of rides but was very unlucky not to have won this. Despite carrying her head awkwardly to one side, her jockey coaxed her to the front inside the final furlong, only for her to lose her hind legs momentarily strides from the line, but that was enough for her to get caught right on the post. Her trainer admitted afterwards that she can often stop to nothing when in front. (3/1)
1037 Stolen Kiss (IRE), an extremely rare runner for Mick Easterby at the Sussex venue, ran her best race for a long time, being a leading light from the outset and staying on nicely in the closing stages. (5/1)
Sharp Stock ran his best race for a long time and was one of several scrapping for the lead inside the final furlong before tapped for toe.(25/1)
1236 Superlao (BEL), never far away, was in there with every chance inside the final furlong before failing to find another gear. She is yet to win in this country. (10/1: 8/1-12/1)
604 Village Native (FR) picked up ground below the distance and, although stopped in his tracks inside the final furlong, kept on again in the closing stages. (9/1: 5/1-10/1)
751 Suite Factors (10/1: 6/1-12/1)

T/Jkpt: Not won; £10,515.95 to Brighton 23/5/97. T/Plpt: £71.40 (564.41 Tckts). T/Qdpt: £33.80 (75.1 Tckts) AK

0993-NEWCASTLE (L-H) (Good)

Thursday May 22nd

Races 2, 4 & 6: hand-timed
WEATHER: overcast WIND: slt bhd

1328 EDUCATION BUSINESS PARTNERSHIP NOVICE STKS (2-Y.O) (Class D)

2-30 (2-31) **5f** £3,067.50 (£930.00: £455.00: £217.50) Stalls: High GOING minus 0.29 sec per fur (GF)

				SP	RR	SF
1084*	**Prince Foley** (WGMTurner) **2-8-13**(7) DMcGaffin(4) (lw: chsd ldrs: led appr fnl f: pushed out)	—	**1**	5/1^{3}	89	39
893^{6}	**Occhi Verdi (IRE)** (MJohnston) **2-8-13** JWeaver(9) (disp ld tl hdd appr fnl f: r.o towards fin)	hd	**2**	13/8^{1}	82	32
1120*	**Branston Berry (IRE)** (JLEyre) **2-8-11** GCarter(5) (disp ld tl hdd appr fnl f: kpt on)	½	**3**	5/1^{3}	78	28
1076^{2}	**Prix Star** (CWFairhurst) **2-8-12** DeanMcKeown(10) (lw: chsd ldrs: sn drvn along: kpt on wl towards fin)	1	**4**	4/1^{2}	76	26
500^{9}	**Premium Pursuit** (RAFahey) **2-8-12** ACulhane(2) (chsd ldrs tl outpcd fnl 2f)	5	**5**	25/1	60	10
	Frisky Lady (TDEasterby) **2-8-7** GDuffield(7) (neat: bit bkwd: s.i.s: styd on fnl 2f: nvr nr to chal)	1¾	**6**	16/1	49	—
	Inshallah (MartinTodhunter) **2-8-7** JCarroll(8) (neat: s.i.s: bhd tl sme late hdwy)	3	**7**	25/1	40	—
1255^{4}	**Poetto** (BJMeehan) **2-8-12b**^{1} PaulEddery(6) (sn drvn along: lost tch fr ½-wy)	2½	**8**	9/1	37	—
1126^{9}	**Ngaere Princess** (WTKemp) **2-8-7** JQuinn(3) (spd to ½-wy: sn bhd)	3½	**9**	50/1	21	—

(SP 117.0%) **9 Rn**

60.72 secs (2.32) CSF £12.28 TOTE £6.30: £1.80 £1.10 £1.40 (£5.10) Trio £8.20 OWNER Foley Steelstock (SHERBORNE) BRED Ian Slocock

1084* Prince Foley is taking his racing well and still seems to be improving, but the line only just came in time here. (5/1)
893 Occhi Verdi (IRE) is an excitable filly who obviously boiled over at Ascot last time. She was taken early to post on this occasion and in another furlong she would have won. Provided her temperament does not get the better of her, there is plenty more to come. (13/8)
1120* Branston Berry (IRE) has bags of speed and looks a tough sort who should continue to pay her way. (5/1)
1076 Prix Star found things happening too quickly early on and may well need another furlong. (4/1: 5/2-9/2)
Premium Pursuit improved on his first run and seems to be going the right way. (25/1)
Frisky Lady needed this both fitness and experience-wise and there should be better to come. (16/1)
1255 Poetto (9/1: 5/1-10/1)

1329 RAMSIDE EVENT CATERING H'CAP (0-80) (3-Y.O+) (Class D)

3-00 (3-00) **1m 4f 93y** £3,420.00 (£1,035.00: £505.00: £240.00) Stalls: Low GOING minus 0.29 sec per fur (GF)

				SP	RR	SF
1022^{3}	**Shaffishayes (65)** (MrsMReveley) **5-9-4** DeanMcKeown(4) (plld hrd: hdwy 3f out: led 1½f out: styd on u.p)	—	**1**	11/4^{3}	75	38
1036^{5}	**Eagle Canyon (IRE) (72)** (BHanbury) **4-9-11** WRyan(1) (lw: trckd ldrs: outpcd 3f out: hdwy whn n.m.r & swtchd 1f out: styd on)	¾	**2**	5/2^{2}	81	44
1081^{6}	**Lord Hastie (USA) (43)** (CWThornton) **9-7-10** JQuinn(3) (trckd ldr: led wl over 2f out to 1½f out: r.o one pce)	½	**3**	11/4^{3}	51	14
926*	**Baby Jane (67)** (BMactaggart) **3-8-3** PBloomfield(2) (lw: led tl hdd wl over 2f out: sn outpcd)	8	**4**	9/4^{1}	65	11

(SP 112.7%) **4 Rn**

2m 44.0 (6.50) CSF £9.17 TOTE £3.30: (£4.60) OWNER Mr P. Davidson-Brown (SALTBURN) BRED W. G. Barker
WEIGHT FOR AGE 3yo-17lb

1022 Shaffishayes took a fierce grip but this was not the most competitive of events and, once in front approaching the final furlong, even he was doing enough. (11/4: 6/4-3/1)
1036 Eagle Canyon (IRE), not suited by the steady pace, should have been made more use of. (5/2)
1081 Lord Hastie (USA) is coming to hand looks-wise and he certainly has the Handicapper on his side. (11/4)
926* Baby Jane won two egg and spoon races previously and, against racehorses this time, had her limitations exposed. (9/4)

1330 'IT CERTAINLY BEATS WORKING' CLAIMING STKS (2-Y.O) (Class F)

3-30 (3-31) **6f** £2,514.00 (£704.00: £342.00) Stalls: High GOING minus 0.29 sec per fur (GF)

				SP	RR	SF
861^{5}	**Lord Smith** (WGMTurner) **2-8-3**(7) DMcGaffin(9) (a cl up: led ins fnl f: r.o)	—	**1**	3/1^{2}	71	19
979^{4}	**Swoosh** (BJMeehan) **2-8-12** JWeaver(11) (lw: led tl hdd ins fnl f: kpt on wl)	nk	**2**	2/1^{1}	72	20
	Bali Dance (CBBBooth) **2-8-6** KHodgson(3) (neat: unf: lw: s.i.s: hdwy ½-wy: rdn to chal ins fnl f: no ex towards fin)	s.h	**3**	10/1	66+	14
1007^{5}	**Figawin** (GLewis) **2-8-6** PaulEddery(8) (lw: chsd ldrs: effrt 2f out: r.o one pce)	3½	**4**	10/1	57	5
836^{8}	**Arm And A Leg (IRE)** (CADwyer) **2-9-0** JStack(10) (chsd ldrs tl rdn & btn appr fnl f)	1¼	**5**	7/1^{3}	61	9
1137^{4}	**My Bet** (MWEasterby) **2-8-3** DaleGibson(5) (in tch: sn drvn along: no imp fnl 2f)	5	**6**	11/1	37	—
1253^{6}	**Flash d'Or (IRE)** (MWEasterby) **2-8-9** TLucas(4) (outpcd ½-wy: n.d after)	7	**7**	20/1	24	—
743^{5}	**Skippool Creek (IRE)** (TDEasterby) **2-8-1b**^{1} JQuinn(6) (lw: hld up: effrt over 2f out: sn rdn & btn)	hd	**8**	16/1	16	—
	Blue Anchor (MrsMReveley) **2-9-0** ACulhane(1) (cmpt: bkwd: s.s: a bhd)	1½	**9**	25/1	25	—
1136^{6}	**Moss Side Monkey** (JBerry) **2-8-10** GCarter(7) (s.s: hdwy ½-wy: sn wknd)	2½	**10**	12/1	15	—

(SP 119.5%) **10 Rn**

1m 15.21 (3.71) CSF £8.80 TOTE £3.70: £1.60 £1.40 £1.80 (£4.50) Trio £34.20 OWNER Mrs M. S. Teversham (SHERBORNE) BRED Mrs M. S. Teversham

861 Lord Smith, trying an extra furlong here, got it well and won nicely. (3/1)
979 Swoosh, stepped up a furlong and dropped in class, tried hard but was just out-battled. (2/1: op 5/4)
Bali Dance, a fit-looking newcomer, was beaten by both greenness and her low draw. (10/1)
1007 Figawin ran better on this stiff track and over this extra distance and looks to be improving. (10/1)
557 Arm And A Leg (IRE) had his chances but just found this too competitive in the closing stages. (7/1: 6/1-10/1)
1137 My Bet was always finding things happening too quickly for her liking. (11/1: 6/1-12/1)
664 Moss Side Monkey (12/1: op 7/1)

1331 JAMES FLETCHER MARQUEES MAIDEN STKS (3-Y.O) (Class D)

4-00 (4-01) **1m 2f 32y** £3,485.00 (£1,055.00: £515.00: £245.00) Stalls: High GOING minus 0.29 sec per fur (GF)

				SP	RR	SF
1014^{4}	**Memorise (USA) (85)** (HRACecil) **3-9-0** WRyan(5) (lw: cl up: led 1f out: r.o u.p)	—	**1**	2/1^{2}	88	33
797^{4}	**Dream of Nurmi (84)** (DRLoder) **3-9-0** DRMcCabe(1) (lw: led: edgd rt fnl 2f: hdd 1f out: no ex towards fin)	nk	**2**	13/2^{3}	88	33
1105^{2}	**Eshtiaal (USA) (86)** (JLDunlop) **3-9-0** RHills(2) (lw: hld up: effrt 3f out: hung lft u.p: nt run on)	3½	**3**	10/11^{1}	82	27
841^{6}	**Khayali (IRE)** (DMorley) **3-9-0** GCarter(3) (trckd ldrs: n.m.r 2f out: sn outpcd)	4	**4**	10/1	76	21

	Down Hearted (IRE) (WTKemp) **3-9-0** JQuinn(4) (leggy: lt-f: dwlt: a last)	15	**5**	100/1	52	—
				(SP 109.1%)	**5 Rn**	

2m 12.0 (5.30) CSF £12.92 TOTE £3.00: £1.10 £4.10 (£10.20) OWNER Mr K. Abdulla (NEWMARKET) BRED Juddmonte Farms

1014 Memorise (USA) stays well and, more importantly in this company, he showed the right attitude which some of his rivals certainly did not. (2/1: 6/4-9/4)

797 Dream of Nurmi does not look the most resolute of characters but he did keep on despite hanging right. (13/2: 9/2-7/1)

1105 Eshtiaal (USA) has the looks and plenty of ability but it is his attitude that is the problem, and it seems a very big one. (10/11: evens-4/5)

841 Khayali (IRE) is a big sort who was coltish in the paddock and seems to need time to get his mind on the job in hand. (10/1)

Down Hearted (IRE), a very tall, leggy and lean newcomer, was well out-classed here. (100/1)

1332 SEATON BURN DISTAFF H'CAP (0-75) (3-Y.O+ F & M) (Class D)

4-30 (4-33) **5f** £3,501.25 (£1,060.00: £517.50: £246.25) Stalls: High GOING minus 0.29 sec per fur (GF)

				SP	RR	SF
1269[2]	**Lady Sheriff (68)** (MWEasterby) **6-10-0b** TLucas(8) (lw: mde all: shkn up 1f out: r.o)	—	**1**	11/10[1]	75	45
1250[4]	**Ballard Lady (IRE) (40)** (JSWainwright) **5-7-9b**(5) JBramhill(2) (lw: a chsng ldrs: rdn 2f out: r.o: nt pce of wnr)	1¼	**2**	7/2[2]	43	13
*1047**	**Chilling (52)** (NTinkler) **3-7-11b**(7) KSked(6) (hdwy 2f out: styd on: nrst fin)	1½	**3**	9/1	50	12
1250[15]	**Superfrills (44)** (MissLCSiddall) **4-8-4** DeanMcKeown(4) (a chsng ldrs: rdn 2f out: kpt on same pce)	nk	**4**	25/1	41	11
702[13]	**Sunset Harbour (IRE) (43)** (SEKettlewell) **4-8-3** JStack(7) (bhd: hdwy 2f out: nvr rchd ldrs)	2	**5**	16/1	34	4
1037[10]	**Antithesis (IRE) (61)** (JSHaldane) **4-9-7** JCarroll(9) (chsd ldrs: rdn ½-wy: no imp after)	2½	**6**	8/1[3]	44	14
	Madam Zando (37) (JBalding) **4-7-8**(3) DarrenMoffatt(5) (bhd tl sme hdwy fnl 2f)	1	**7**	25/1	17	—
903[7]	**Ohnonotagain (36)** (LRLloyd-James) **5-7-10** JQuinn(10) (spd to ½-wy: sn btn)	1¼	**8**	16/1	12	—
1046[9]	**Pathaze (46)** (NBycroft) **4-8-6** ACulhane(3) (effrt ½-wy: btn whn hmpd ins fnl f)	½	**9**	16/1	20	—
1046[12]	**Fancy Clancy (36)** (MissLCSiddall) **4-7-10b** NCarlisle(1) (s.i.s: hdwy ½-wy: sn rdn & wknd)	3	**10**	50/1	—	—
				(SP 118.3%)	**10 Rn**	

60.82 secs (2.42) CSF £4.33 CT £21.44 TOTE £1.70: £1.10 £1.60 £1.50 (£2.50) Trio £4.90 OWNER Mr E. J. Mangan (SHERIFF HUTTON) BRED Jeremy Green and Sons

LONG HANDICAP Ohnonotagain 7-4 Fancy Clancy 7-8

WEIGHT FOR AGE 3yo-8lb

1269 Lady Sheriff had the draw and the speed and the race was always hers. (11/10: 4/5-11/8)

1250 Ballard Lady (IRE), happier over a bit further, looked tremendously well and ran a useful race here but always found the winner too good. (7/2: 9/2-3/1)

1047* Chilling has been running consistently well on the All-Weather and, by the looks of things, she will find a race on turf. (9/1)

Superfrills has not shown previously and this was certainly one of her better efforts. (25/1)

Sunset Harbour (IRE) is slipping back down the handicap and this was a reasonable effort. (16/1)

698 Antithesis (IRE) (8/1: 5/1-9/1)

Madam Zando looked in good condition but always found this trip too sharp. (25/1)

1333 BRANDLING HOUSE H'CAP (0-70) (3-Y.O) (Class E)

5-05 (5-05) **1m 3y (straight)** £2,882.25 (£873.00: £426.50: £203.25) Stalls: Low GOING minus 0.29 sec per fur (GF)

				SP	RR	SF
1129[3]	**Epic Stand (60)** (MrsJRRamsden) **3-8-11**(3) FLynch(6) (hld up: hdwy & gng wl whn nt clr run over 2f out: qcknd to ld appr fnl f: r.o wl)	—	**1**	13/8[1]	76+	61
997*	**Rock Island Line (IRE) (67)** (JBerry) **3-9-2**(5) PRoberts(11) (in tch: hdwy over 2f out: disp ld appr fnl f: r.o: nt pce of wnr)	3	**2**	7/2[3]	77	62
1096*	**Carlton (IRE) (63)** (GLewis) **3-9-3** PaulEddery(7) (lw: in tch: hdwy over 1f out: styd on: nt pce to chal)	5	**3**	3/1[2]	63	48
1078[8]	**King Uno (47)** (MrsJRRamsden) **3-8-1v**[1] JQuinn(8) (cl up: ev ch 2f out: no ex)	2	**4**	12/1	43	28
925[12]	**Music Express (IRE) (49)** (JLEyre) **3-8-3v**[1] TWilliams(9) (cl up: btn whn sltly hmpd appr fnl f)	5	**5**	25/1	35	20
771[14]	**Feel A Line (60)** (BJMeehan) **3-9-0b** GDuffield(10) (led tl hdd over 1f out: sn btn)	1	**6**	25/1	44	29
667[4]	**Why O Six (52)** (RAFahey) **3-8-6v**[1] DeanMcKeown(2) (w ldrs tl rdn & btn appr fnl f)	nk	**7**	16/1	36	21
	Kippilaw (66) (MJohnston) **3-9-6** JWeaver(4) (chsd ldrs tl wknd appr fnl f)	4	**8**	20/1	42	27
1096[14]	**Al Ava Consonant (55)** (JDBethell) **3-8-9** WRyan(3) (a outpcd & bhd)	1	**9**	33/1	29	14
1078[10]	**Emily-Jayne (48)** (MrsMReveley) **3-8-2** GCarter(5) (a outpcd & bhd)	s.h	**10**	25/1	21	6
1256[6]	**Treasure Hill (IRE) (54)** (DWChapman) **3-8-8** ACulhane(1) (a outpcd & bhd)	1¼	**11**	16/1	25	10
797[7]	**Jackson Falls (67)** (TDEasterby) **3-9-7** JCarroll(12) (a bhd)	6	**12**	33/1	26	11
				(SP 127.0%)	**12 Rn**	

1m 39.9 (1.30) CSF £12.94 CT £108.19 TOTE £3.80: £1.10 £1.60 £4.30 (£5.10) Trio £35.20 OWNER Mr Colin Webster (THIRSK) BRED Cleaboy Farms Co

STEWARDS' ENQUIRY Lynch susp. 2-5/6/97 (irresponsible riding), changed to susp. 31/5 & 2-4/6/97 (careless riding) on appeal.

IN-FOCUS: **The Disciplinary Committee rightly reinstated Epic Stand a week after his original disqualification. All win bets were settled on Rock Island Line.**

1129 Epic Stand, always going much the best, took a narrow gap to lead approaching the final furlong and won going right away. However, despite the interference appearing to be minimal, the Stewards threw him out, and imposed a ban on his apprentice jockey for irresponsible riding. The decision was later reversed on appeal, although Lynch received four days for careless riding. Punters who backed him down from 9/4 however, lost their money. (13/8)

997* Rock Island Line (IRE) was a long way second best. (7/2)

1096* Carlton (IRE) has been assaulted by the Handicapper for winning a moderate race and was never able to get in a blow. (3/1)

King Uno ran a deal better with the visor on for the first time, but was still nothing like good enough. (12/1: op 7/1)

667 Music Express (IRE), in a visor for the first time, had her chances but was well outpaced in the final furlong. (25/1)

Feel A Line was the one who caused much of the trouble by tending to edge left, and he does not look one to rely on. (25/1)

667 Why O Six had a visor on for the first time but, once a struggle developed, he soon stopped. (16/1)

T/Plpt: £31.80 (353.61 Tckts). T/Qdpt: £5.20 (144.95 Tckts) AA

1334a - 1357a : (Irish Racing) - See Computer Raceform

1070a-CHANTILLY (France) (R-H) (Soft)
Monday May 12th

1358a PRIX DE PONTARME (Listed) (3-Y.O C & G)
2-20 (2-20) **1m** £15,713.00 (£5,387.00: £4,040.00) GOING minus 0.06 sec per fur (G)

				SP	RR	SF
	Kaldou Star (ELellouche,France) **3-9-2** TThulliez	—	1		101	71
	Bartex (FR) (France) **3-9-2** VVion	1	2		99	69
1006[2]	**Hever Golf Glory** (TJNaughton) **3-9-2** CAsmussen	1½	3		96	66
						7 Rn

1m 38.9 (2.40) P-M 2.20F: 1.60F 2.50F OWNER Mr J. C. Seroul
1006 Hever Golf Glory was held up for a late run and was putting in his best work at the finish. He now goes for the Swedish 2,000 Guineas and should not be far away if he repeats this form.

1359a PRIX DE LA PORTE DE MADRID (Listed) (4-Y.O+)
3-20 (3-18) **1m 4f** £15,713.00 (£5,387.00: £4,040.00) GOING minus 0.06 sec per fur (G)

				SP	RR	SF
	Surgeon (JdeRoualle,France) **4-8-11** CAsmussen	—	1		113	51
	Yokohama (USA) (Mme CHead,France) **6-8-11** FHead	1½	2		111	49
852[4]	**Tamure (IRE)** (JHMGosden) **5-8-11** LDettori	½	3		110	48
						9 Rn

2m 32.6 (5.80) P-M 4.70F: 1.30F 2.10F 1.10F (63.50F) OWNER Mr K. H. Eng BRED George Strawbridge
852 Tamure (IRE) was one of the joint leaders in this race. He battled on well up the straight, but was only one-paced in the final furlong. Apparently, the ground was not soft enough for him.

1067a-SAINT-CLOUD (France) (L-H) (Soft)
Tuesday May 13th

1360a PRIX CLEOPATRE (Gp 3) (3-Y.O F)
2-20 (2-17) **1m 2f 110y** £24,691.00 (£8,979.00: £4,489.00)

			SP	RR	SF
Allurement (IRE) (AFabre,France) **3-8-9** TJarnet	—	1		106	—
Silver Fun (FR) (MmeCHead,France) **3-8-9** ODoleuze	nse	2		106	—
Deflagration (FR) (ELellouche,France) **3-8-9** TThulliez	½	3		105	—
					7 Rn

2m 20.4 (10.40) P-M 16.70F: 6.20F 7.30F OWNER Sheikh Mohammed (CHANTILLY) BRED Sheikh Mohammed
Allurement (IRE) raced just behind the leaders before having a ding-dong battle with the runner-up, getting up by only a whisker. She could be supplemented into the Epsom Oaks but this will depend on the European trials
Silver Fun (FR) was asked to make all and ran her heart out before going under by a nose. She had reportedly been coughing earlier in the year and was making her seasonal debut. She may well be allowed to take her chance in the Prix de Diane.
Deflagration (FR) was always well up before fading a little inside the final furlong.

1203a-LONGCHAMP (Paris, France) (R-H) (Very Soft)
Thursday May 15th

1361a PRIX DE GUICHE (Gp 3) (3-Y.O C)
2-20 (2-18) **1m 1f** £24,691.00 (£8,979.00: £4,489.00) GOING: 1.02 sec per fur (S)

			SP	RR	SF
Kirkwall (AFabre,France) **3-9-2** TJarnet	—	1		108	69
Aneysar (IRE) (AdeRoyerDupre,France) **3-9-2** GMosse	1	2		106	67
Varxi (FR) (DSmaga,France) **3-9-2** DBoeuf	1	3		104	65
					5 Rn

2m 0.6 (12.60) P-M 1.90F: 1.30F 2.00F OWNER Mr K. Abdulla (CHANTILLY) BRED Juddmonte Farms
Kirkwall is one of the most improved colts in France. At the beginning of the year he was no more than a maiden, but since then he has reeled off four consecutive victories. Dropped back into last place in the straight, he balanced himself well before coming with a sweeping late run, striding clear at the finish. Connections feared that he might not handle the very soft ground, but he put that doubt to rest here and, if this level of improvement continues, he may well make his presence felt in the Prix Jean Prat.
Aneysar (IRE) attempted to make all the running and he stuck to his task right up to the post. He was making his seasonal debut so this effort deserves some credit, but this may be as good as he is.
Varxi (FR) had his ground and was given every possible chance. Connections will be slightly disappointed with this performance, as last October he beat Aneysar by five lengths in the Prix Thomas Bryon. He may be more effective over a shorter distance.

1362a PRIX LA FORCE (Gp 3) (3-Y.O)
3-20 (3-18) **1m 4f** £24,691.00 (£8,979.00: £4,489.00) GOING: 1.02 sec per fur (S)

			SP	RR	SF
Magellano (USA) (AFabre,France) **3-9-2** OPeslier	—	1		110	60
Six Zero (FR) (AFabre,France) **3-9-2** TJarnet	1½	2		108	58
With Fire (USA) (JEPease,France) **3-9-2** CAsmussen	½	3		107	57
					6 Rn

2m 44.1 (18.10) P-M 1.90F: 1.20F 1.50F OWNER Sultan Al Kabeer (CHANTILLY) BRED Prince Sultan bin Mohammed bin Saud Al Kabeer
Magellano (USA) is definitely going the right way. He moved smoothly into the lead halfway up the straight, and won his first Group race with plenty in hand. He will probably have a rest until July, when he will be aimed at the Prix Eugene Adam. He is an interesting son of Miswaki, who could go on to better things.
Six Zero (FR) was always close up and held second place fairly comfortably. A son of Linamix, a shorter trip may suit.
With Fire (USA) was always well-placed, but appears to lack acceleration, and may do better on good or faster ground.

1360a-SAINT-CLOUD (France) (L-H) (Holding)
Friday May 16th

1363a PRIX JEAN DE CHAUDENAY (Gp 2) (4-Y.O+)
2-50 (2-49) **1m 4f** £33,670.00 (£13,468.00: £6,734.00: £3,367.00)

				SP	RR	SF
916a4	**Flyway (FR)** (ELellouche,France) **4-8-12** TThulliez (a cl up: outpcd st: r.o to ld over 1f out: gng clr at fin)	—	1		123	—
	De Quest (AFabre,France) **5-8-12** TJarnet (hld up: 4th st: effrt 2f out: led briefly 1f out: r.o one pce: p.u lame)	2	2		120	—
9322	**Busy Flight** (BWHills) **4-8-12** OPeslier (led tl over 1f out: r.o one pce)	2½	3		117	—
	Darazari (IRE) (AdeRoyerDupre,France) **4-9-2** GMosse (hld up: prog to 2nd st: slt chal 1½f out: styd on one pce)	hd	4		121	—
	Key Change (IRE) (JOxx,Ireland) **4-9-1** JPMurtagh (prom 6f tl hrd rdn: dropped away qckly: eased)	dist	5		—	—
						5 Rn

2m 41.0 (11.70) P-M 19.20F: 5.60F 3.40F OWNER Mr B. Clin BRED Petra Bloodstock Agency Ltd

916a Flyway (FR), who was bought out of a seller last June, put some useful horses in their place. He was always close up and, after being outpaced in the straight, ran on really well in the closing stages. He is a very honest colt and deserved this victory, although some of his main rivals were slightly off-colour. A number of engagements are envisaged for him now, with either the Grand Prix de Chantilly, the Grand Prix de Saint-Cloud or even the Prix Maurice de Nieuil in July, all possibilities.

De Quest looked to have this race in the bag as he challenged at the furlong marker, but he did not go through with his effort. It appeared that on passing the post he seemed lame, and this was later confirmed. In the circumstances this was a useful reappearance.

932 Busy Flight attempted to make all the running, but just ran on at the one pace throughout the last furlong-and-a-half. He was not favoured by the extremely sticky ground and this race is best forgotten.

Darazari (IRE) was given every chance, but tired in the straight. He was carrying a Group Two penalty and was another not suited by the underfoot conditions. He has been known to get a little nervous before a race, and his mental attitude may have to be questioned if he does not live up to expectations next time out. In his defence, there is a possibility that he may not be suited by a left-handed track. He is entered in the Hardwicke Stakes at Ascot and another possible target is the Grand Prix de Saint-Cloud.

Key Change (IRE) was never at the races and was tailed off entering the straight. Ridden seven furlongs out, something must have been amiss, as her performance was a total mystery to her trainer.

PIMLICO (Baltimore, USA) (L-H) (Fast)
Saturday May 17th

1364a PREAKNESS STKS (GRADE 1) (3-Y.O)
10-31 (10-31) **1m 1f 110y (Dirt)** £290,565.00 (£89,286.00: £44,702.00)

				SP	RR	SF
1071a*	**Silver Charm (USA)** (BBaffert,USA) **3-9-0** GaryStevens	—	1		125	—
1071a3	**Free House (USA)** (JGonzalez,USA) **3-9-0** KDesormeaux	hd	2		125	—
1071a2	**Captain Bodgit (USA)** (GCapuano,USA) **3-9-0** ASolis	hd	3		125	—
						10 Rn

1m 54.8 P-M 8.20: (1-2) 4.00 3.60 (1-2-3) 2.60 2.60 2.40 OWNER R & B Lewis BRED Mary Lou Wootton

1071a* Silver Charm (USA) kept Triple Crown hopes alive with this thrilling success. The first three finishers were the same as those in the Kentucky Derby, except for the runner-up positions being reversed. His trainer believes that the final leg at Belmont will be a lot easier.

Free House (USA) put up a brave display but just could not find that little extra when headed close home. He will reportedly not take on the winner at Belmont Park.

1071a Captain Bodgit (USA) has been retired due to an old tendon problem. Over a twelve-race career, he never finished out of the first three, amassing $1,014,819 in prize money.

1361a-LONGCHAMP (Paris, France) (R-H) (Very Soft)
Sunday May 18th

1365a PRIX VICOMTESSE VIGIER (Gp 2) (4-Y.O+)
2-35 (2-35) **1m 7f 110y** £33,670.00 (£13,468.00: £6,734.00: £3,367.00) GOING: 0.59 sec per fur (GS)

				SP	RR	SF
923a*	**Stretarez (FR)** (DSepulchre,France) **4-8-12** FSanchez (bhd early: n.m.r & nt clr run 1½f out: opening 1f out: r.o to ld cl home)	—	1		117	78
8914	**Grey Shot** (IABalding) **5-9-1** OPeslier (led tl ct cl home)	s.h	2		119	81
923a2	**Philanthrop (FR)** (J-PGallorini,France) **5-8-12** TGillet (hld up in rr: gd hdwy 1f out: r.o wl)	1	3		115	77
916a2	**Prussian Blue (USA)** (CLaffon-Parias,France) **5-8-12** ODoleuze (a.p: effrt 1½f out: styd on one pce)	1½	4		113	75
	Fairhonor (FR) (AFabre,France) **4-8-12** TJarnet (hld up: sme prog fr 1½f out)	½	5		114	75
	Nononito (FR) (JLesbordes,France) **6-9-4** GMosse (cl up early: mid div st: effrt 2f out: one pce cl home)	2½	6		116	78
1073a3	**Mongol Warrior (USA)** (LordHuntingdon) **4-9-1** FHead (cl up tl st: rdn & btn fnl f)	1	7		113	74
						7 Rn

3m 28.8 (12.80) P-M 1.80F: 1.40F 2.60F OWNER Mr J-L Lagardere BRED SNC Lagardere Elevage

923a* Stretarez (FR) has turned into a really decent stayer. This was his second Group victory in a row and he would have won by further but for being boxed-in soon after entering the straight. Waited with as usual, he could not get out at precisely the right moment, but finally got a run a furlong out and struck the front in the last few strides. He loves cut in the ground, and his trainer hopes to rest him before bringing him back for an autumn campaign. However, he still remains a possibility for the Prix Kergorlay at Deauville.

891 Grey Shot took the lead rounding the first turn. After setting a fair pace, he was given a breather before the straight and, when sent on, looked to have the race in the bag, but could not hold off the late surge of the winner. He was giving 3lb to Stretarez and his trainer hoped that the gelding would have set a faster pace, but it should not be forgotten that, with a clear run, the winner would have won by even further. He is an out-and-out stayer and goes for the Gold Cup at Royal Ascot.

923a Philanthrop (FR), running for the ninth time this season, put up another decent performance. He is a thoroughly genuine individual, but was no match for his old rival here.

916a Prussian Blue (USA) was always close up and ran wide for part of the back straight, before joining the pack running down into the straight. He could only run on at the one pace to the line, but is a very game and consistent performer who should pick up a Group race this season.

1073a Mongol Warrior (USA) found the step-up in distance on the very heavy ground too much in the closing stages. A well-travelled individual, a drop in trip and grade could see him back to winning ways.

1366a PRIX SAINT-ALARY (Gp 1) (3-Y.O F)

3-35 (3-36) **1m 2f** £56,128.00 (£22,278.00: £10,707.00: £4,489.00) GOING: 0.59 sec per fur (GS)

				SP	RR	SF
813a*	**Brilliance (FR)** (PBary,France) **3-9-0** OPeslier (in rr: pushed along fr 5f out: chal 2f out: led over 1f out: r.o wl)	—	1	35/10[2]	111+	72
	Fleeting Glimpse (AFabre,France) **3-9-0** TJarnet (a.p: led 1½f out: sn hdd: r.o fnl f)	4	2	44/10[3]	105	66
	Gazelle Royale (FR) (JEHammond,France) **3-9-0** TThulliez (mid div: chal over 1f out: no ex cl home)	s.h	3	25/1	105	66
813a[2]	**Darashandeh (IRE)** (AdeRoyerDupre,France) **3-9-0** GMosse (a.p: 3rd pl st: sn rdn & r.o one pce)	1½	4	9/10[1]	102	63
	Gracie Lady (IRE) (RCollet,France) **3-9-0** DBoeuf (hld up: effrt u.p 2f out: one pce)	4	5	22/1	96	57
815a[8]	**Yxenery (IRE)** (MmeCHead,France) **3-9-0** ODoleuze (hld up: prog st: hmpd & lost pl 1½f out: one pce)	s.nk	6	65/10	95	56
	Family Tradition (IRE) (APO'Brien,Ireland) **3-9-0** CAsmussen (led tl 1½f out: wknd rapidly)	4½	7	79/10	88	49

(SP 126.1%) **7 Rn**

2m 9.1 (9.10) P-M 4.50F: 2.40F 2.90F OWNER Ecurie Skymarc Farm (CHANTILLY) BRED Skymarc Farm

813a* Brilliance (FR) won this in great style. With no apparent chance and being niggled along entering the straight, once sent for home she was a totally different filly. Brought up the middle of the track, she surged into the lead at the furlong marker before outclassing the field. A great credit to her trainer, she relished the soft ground and, showing such improvement, will start one of the favourites for the Prix de Diane. (35/10)

Fleeting Glimpse showed no sign of inexperience, although this was only her second racecourse appearance. She was always close up and led briefly in the straight before being passed by the winner. Running on again close home, she narrowly took second place and, given plenty of time, looks a top-class filly in the making. It would be no surprise to see her line up for the Prix Vermeille in September. (44/10)

Gazelle Royale (FR) ran with great credit as she was making her seasonal debut. Racing on the rail, she probably lost second place as she was not as fit as the runner-up. She will be allowed to take her chance in the Prix de Diane, and she certainly looks like a filly who acts on a testing surface. (25/1)

813a Darashandeh (IRE) looked in trouble soon after entering the straight and stayed on one-paced to the line. She finished an unlucky second to Brilliance in the Prix Penelope and, on this occasion, was beaten nearly six lengths, only to be found to have hurt her off-fore ankle. (9/10)

Family Tradition (IRE) finished last having attempted to make all the running. (79/10)

1075a-SAN SIRO (Milan, Italy) (R-H) (Good)
Sunday May 18th

1367a PREMIO GAMBASCA MAIDEN (3-Y.O F)

3-20 (3-33) **1m 2f** £5,786.00

				SP	RR	SF
	Schwarz Fairy (MGuarnieri,Italy) **3-9-0** CColombi	—	1		—	—
	Armungia (VCaruso,Italy) **3-9-0** LPanici	1¼	2		—	—
	Kaberlaba (ITY) (Ld'Auria,Italy) **3-9-0** MDemuro	5½	3		—	—
821a[2]	**Ribot's Pearl** (LordHuntingdon) **3-9-0** LDettori (btn approx 15¼l)		7		—	—

12 Rn

2m 5.3 (11.30) TOTE 52L: 18L 15L 19L (80L) OWNER Scuderia San Pancrazio BRED Dietrich von Boetticher

821a Ribot's Pearl put up what can only be described as a slightly disappointing display. In fourth place for most of the way, the pace quickened with two furlongs to go and she was unable to go with them. She gave the indication that this trip may have been a bit too far for her.

1368a OAKS D'ITALIA (Gp 1) (3-Y.O F)

4-20 (4-43) **1m 3f** £130,832.00 (£68,232.00: £40,345.00: £20,172.00)

				SP	RR	SF
815a*	**Nicole Pharly** (AVerdesi,Italy) **3-8-11** LDettori (mid div st: pushed along 2f out: hrd rdn wl over 1f out: r.o to ld wl ins fnl f)	—	1		103	—
959[2]	**Attitre (FR)** (CEBrittain) **3-8-11** MRoberts (a.p: led over 3f out tl ct ins fnl f)	1	2		102	—
1075a[2]	**Sopran Mariduff** (RRossini,Italy) **3-8-11** JReid (hld up: gng wl whn n.m.r 1f out: r.o)	1	3		100	—
1075a*	**Bedside Story** (GBotti,Italy) **3-8-11** EBotti (mid div: ev ch over 1f out: one pce)	2½	4		97	—
815a[2]	**Orange Jasmine (IRE)** (APO'Brien,Ireland) **3-8-11** JAHeffernan (trckd ldr ½-wy: btn 2f out)	1¼	5		95	—
815a[5]	**Lady Bi (IRE)** (RBrogi,Italy) **3-8-11** GBietolini (nvr nr to chal)	8½	6		82	—
814a[2]	**Clara House** (VValiani,Italy) **3-8-11** FJovine (a in rr)	2¼	7		79	—
	Alfa Daisy (IRE) (LCamici,Italy) **3-8-11** MDemuro (mid div: wknd over 3f out)	12	8		62	—
	Slipping (GBotti,Italy) **3-8-11** SDettori (led tl over 3f out: wknd rapidly: t.o)	dist	9		—	—

9 Rn

2m 15.5 (7.50) TOTE 21L: 12L 13L 18L (30L) OWNER Scuderia Blu Horse BRED Stratford Place Stud

815a* Nicole Pharly, bought for only 4,500 guineas, has proved an unbelievable acquisition. Completing an impressive double, she proved very tough here. She will now take a rest and return for an autumn campaign.

959 Attitre (FR) put up a gallant display to finish second to a very useful filly. Up with the pace throughout, she moved into second place approaching the straight and hit the front well over three furlongs out, only to be caught well inside the final furlong. The next stop may be Epsom.

815a Orange Jasmine (IRE) was clearly beaten by better horses on the day. Prominent for the first six furlongs and third turning for home, she soon came under pressure and was beaten two furlongs from home. She is better over shorter distances.

1369a PREMIO ORIANO (3-Y.O+ F & M)

5-20 (5-53) **1m 2f** £13,500.00

				SP	RR	SF
	Croa (IRE) (GMaggi,Italy) **4-9-10** EBotti	—	1		—	—
	Sispre (ITY) (Ld'Auria,Italy) **4-9-5** MDemuro	2½	2		—	—
	Bazelle (FR) (BGrizzetti,Italy) **4-9-5** MTellini	¾	3		—	—
814a*	**Swing And Brave (IRE)** (LordHuntingdon) **3-8-6** LDettori (btn approx 10½l)		6		—	—

7 Rn

2m 5.8 (11.80) TOTE 31L: 16L 17L (50L) OWNER Scuderia Gabriella

814a* Swing And Brave (IRE) looked somewhat outclassed in this field and never really got into contention. Racing in fourth when the pace quickened at the two-furlong marker, she was outpaced and gradually weakened.

1007-BRIGHTON (L-H) (Firm)
Friday May 23rd
WEATHER: fair WIND: mod half behind
55 50

1370 VICTORIA GARDENS (S) STKS (2-Y.O) (Class G)
2-10 (2-14) **5f 213y** £1,984.50 (£547.00: £259.50) Stalls: Low GOING minus 0.49 sec per fur (F)

Last	Horse	Dist	Pos	SP	RR	SF
631^{6}	**Who Nose (IRE)** (BJMeehan) **2-8-11b** RHughes(6) (lw: hld up: rdn over 1f out: nt clr run on ins 1f out: swtchd rt: nt rcvr: fin 2nd, 1l: awrdd r)	—	1	$7/1^{2}$	59	9
1007^{4}	**Lobuche (IRE)** (RHannon) **2-8-11** DaneO'Neill(1) (lw: led 5f out: edgd lft 1f out: rdn out: fin 1st: disq & plcd 2nd)	1	2	$2/1^{1}$	62+	12
1019^{10}	**Calliram** (MBlanshard) **2-8-6** NAdams(2) (a.p: ev ch 2f out: unable qckn)	2½	3	20/1	48	—
592^{7}	**The Hobby Lobby (IRE)** (MRChannon) **2-8-6**(5) PPMurphy(4) (lost pl over 4f out: hung lft & hdwy over 1f out: one pce)	1	4	20/1	50	—
880^{5}	**Dande Times** (DWPArbuthnot) **2-8-11** SWhitworth(8) (bmpd s: hdwy over 3f out: wknd over 1f out)	s.h	5	$2/1^{1}$	50	—
	Chika Shan (IRE) (BSmart) **2-8-11** RCochrane(7) (unf: bmpd s: hld up: rdn over 2f out: sn wknd)	3½	6	$12/1^{3}$	40	—
767^{5}	**Primfaheights** (TMJones) **2-8-1**(5) ADaly(3) (led 1f: wknd over 2f out)	2	7	20/1	30	—
	Greenbrook (WGMTurner) **2-8-8**(3) RHavlin(5) (leggy: wnt rt s: a bhd: t.o)	dist	8	$7/1^{2}$	—	—

(SP 113.6%) **8 Rn**

1m 10.0 (2.80) CSF £18.81 TOTE £5.10: £1.10 £1.10 £12.90 (£5.20) OWNER Abbott Racing Ltd (UPPER LAMBOURN) BRED Martin Flattery
Bt in 5,000gns
STEWARDS' ENQUIRY O'Neill susp. 2-3/6/97 (careless riding).
OFFICIAL EXPLANATION **Who Nose (IRE): regarding the apparent improvement in form, trainer explained that the gelding dwelt last time and never got into it, but that he was given a positive ride up with the pace here.**

631 Who Nose (IRE), together with Lobuche, stood out in the paddock in this low-grade race. Travelling well just in behind the front rank, his jockey went for a very small gap along the inside rail below the distance - not the best of ideas on this notorious course - and not surprisingly got interefered with by Lobuche as that rival edged marginally over towards the rails. Hughes switched his mount but the damage had already been done. He was later awarded the race in the Stewards' room. (7/1)
1007 Lobuche (IRE), taking a drop in class, was soon at the head of affairs and he edged slightly to his left a furlong out doing Who Nose no favours. It was very touch and go, but in the end the Stewards decided O'Neill was guilty of careless riding - he had not brought his whip through - and suspended him for two days and demoted Lobuche to second place. (2/1)
767 Calliram had every chance a quarter of a mile from home but then failed to find the necessary turn of foot. (20/1)
530 The Hobby Lobby (IRE) completely failed to handle this notoriously difficult course and, with his action all over the place and throwing his head around at the top of the hill, completely lost his position. He began to pick up ground below the distance but then started rolling in on the camber and could only plod on at one pace. He looks one to avoid if returning to this course. (20/1)
880 Dande Times is very much on the small side and a forward move just before halfway had petered out below the distance. (2/1)
Chika Shan (IRE) looked extremely weak in the paddock and it was no surprise that he could never really make his presence felt. (12/1: 6/1-20/1)
Greenbrook (7/1: 4/1-8/1)

1371 GRAND PARADE LIMITED STKS (0-70) (3-Y.O+) (Class E)
2-40 (2-42) **1m 3f 196y** £2,940.25 (£877.00: £418.50: £189.25) Stalls: High GOING minus 0.49 sec per fur (F)

Last	Horse	Dist	Pos	SP	RR	SF
1169^{13}	**Opera Buff (IRE) (70)** (MissGayKelleway) **6-9-7**(3) AWhelan(11) (hdwy 5f out: chsd ldr over 4f out: rdn over 3f out: led ins fnl f: r.o wl)	—	1	14/1	76	57
680^{15}	**Florentino (IRE) (70)** (BWHills) **4-9-8** DHolland(1) (b: bdly hmpd & lost pl 5f out: swtchd rt over 3f out: rallied over 2f out: hrd rdn & hung lft: r.o wl ins fnl f)	nk	2	$9/4^{1}$	74	55
521^{10}	**Renown (67)** (LordHuntingdon) **5-9-8** TQuinn(5) (lost pl over 5f out: rallied over 2f out: r.o wl ins fnl f)	hd	3	$9/4^{1}$	74	55
1036^{7}	**At Liberty (IRE) (70)** (RHannon) **5-9-10** RPerham(8) (lw: hld up: rdn over 3f out: carried lft wl over 1f out: one pce: fin 5th, 2½l: plcd 4th)	4½	4	11/1	69	50
419^{6}	**Montecristo (70)** (RGuest) **4-9-8** PBloomfield(9) (hmpd 5f out: nvr nr to chal: fin 6th: plcd 5th)	10	5	16/1	54	35
888^{4}	**Charnwood Jack (USA) (68)** (ICampbell) **4-9-8** RPrice(4) (lw: led 10f out to 9f out: hmpd on ins 5f out: sn wknd: fin 7th, plcd 6th)	hd	6	$6/1^{2}$	54	35
1042^{4}	**Bronze Maquette (IRE) (35)** (RSimpson) **7-9-5** MGallagher(3) (prom over 9f: fin 8th, plcd 7th)	6	7	40/1	43	24
1156^{10}	**Bowled Over (69)** (CACyzer) **4-9-8** RCochrane(7) (prom over 6f: fin 9th, plcd 8th)	3	8	$8/1^{3}$	42	23
	Apollono (67) (RLee) **5-9-8** GCarter(2) (led 2f: wknd over 8f out: fin 10th, plcd 9th)	4	9	14/1	36	17
976^{4}	**Count Tony (69)** (SPCWoods) **3-8-7v** AClark(10) (lw: prom over 8f: fin 11th, plcd 10th)	28	10	10/1	1	—
1001^{16}	**Isitoff (67)** (SCWilliams) **4-9-5**(3) PMcCabe(6) (led 9f out: rdn over 3f out: hdd ins fnl f: unable qckn: fin 4th, 2l: disq)		D	16/1	—	—

(SP 131.9%) **11 Rn**

2m 29.2 (1.60) CSF £46.66 TOTE £16.80: £8.40 £2.40 £1.60 (£51.80) Trio £49.40 OWNER Mr D. W. Watson (WHITCOMBE) BRED Juddmonte Farms
WEIGHT FOR AGE 3yo-17lb
STEWARDS' ENQUIRY McCabe susp. 2-7 & 9-12/6/97 (reckless riding).

591 Opera Buff (IRE) bounced back to form following a number of bad performances and, having moved into second place at the top of the hill, eventually got on top inside the final furlong. (14/1: 10/1-16/1)
Florentino (IRE) can be counted incredibly unlucky. Travelling well at the top of the hill, he was badly hampered and completely lost his pitch, ending up at the back of the field. His jockey then had to bring him round the whole field and he had plenty of ground to make up. He did so in the straight despite drifting left, but despite running on really strongly, found the line always just beating him. Losses are only leant. (9/4)
405 Renown, who lost his pitch soon after halfway, ran on really strongly in the closing stages and only just failed. (9/4)
867 At Liberty (IRE) has gained his last two wins in claimers and that may well be his level. (11/1: 8/1-12/1)
419 Montecristo, hampered at the back of the field five furlongs from home, could never get in a blow. (16/1)
888 Charnwood Jack (USA) (6/1: op 4/1)
680 Bowled Over (8/1: op 5/1)
976 Count Tony (10/1: 6/1-11/1)
Isitoff moved to the front after three furlongs but his jockey manoeuvered him over to the rails at the top of the hill, resulting in several horses, most notably Florentino, getting hampered. Grimly trying to hold on, he was eventually collared inside the final furlong. His jockey was later suspended for ten days for reckless riding. (16/1)

1372 FESTIVAL MAIDEN STKS (3-Y.O+) (Class D)

3-10 (3-11) **1m 3f 196y** £3,518.20 (£1,048.60: £499.80: £225.40) Stalls: High GOING minus 0.49 sec per fur (F)

				SP	RR	SF
1014[3]	**Montfort (USA)** (PFICole) **3-8-10** TQuinn(4) (a.p: chsd ldr 6f out: led 2f out: shkn up: comf)	—	1	1/3[1]	86	43
996[2]	**Foreign Rule (IRE) (72)** (PWChapple-Hyam) **3-8-7**(3) RHavlin(1) (lw: hld up: rdn 5f out: r.o one pce fnl f)	6	2	6/1[2]	78	35
	Hope Chest (DRLoder) **3-8-5** DRMcCabe(3) (bit bkwd: led 10f: wknd fnl f)	1½	3	6/1[2]	71	28
875[9]	**Laurel Seeker (USA)** (MrsAJPerrett) **3-8-3**(7) GayeHarwood(5) (lw: chsd ldrs 6f)	3½	4	50/1[3]	71?	28
944[6]	**Burn Out** (JPearce) **5-9-13** MWigham(6) (a bhd)	½	5	66/1	71?	45
842[14]	**Glowing Moon** (MissGayKelleway) **4-9-8** RHughes(2) (b: b.hind: a bhd)	15	6	50/1[3]	45?	19

(SP 109.0%) **6 Rn**

2m 29.4 (1.80) CSF £2.34 TOTE £1.20: £1.10 £1.70 (£2.40) OWNER Sir George Meyrick (WHATCOMBE) BRED Timothy J. Rooney
WEIGHT FOR AGE 3yo-17lb

1014 Montfort (USA) could hardly have been found an easier opportunity to lose his maiden tag, cruising into the lead a quarter of a mile from home and needing only to be shaken up to have the situation well in hand. (1/3)

996 Foreign Rule (IRE) is certainly one of the stable's lesser lights and was being bustled along at the top of the hill. He did struggle on to take second place inside the final furlong, but had absolutely no hope with the winner. He looks a hard ride. (6/1: op 3/1)

Hope Chest looked big and well for this reappearance and took the field along until collared a quarter of a mile from home. (6/1: op 3/1)

605 Laurel Seeker (USA), in second place to halfway, had soon shot his bolt. (50/1)

1373 JIM TAYLOR MEMORIAL H'CAP (0-70) (3-Y.O+ F & M) (Class E)

3-40 (3-44) **7f 214y** £3,174.25 (£949.00: £454.50: £207.25) Stalls: Low GOING minus 0.49 sec per fur (F)

				SP	RR	SF
1135[6]	**Sis Garden (47)** (JCullinan) **4-8-2**(3) DO'Donohoe(8) (a.p: led over 4f out: rdn out)	—	1	16/1	56	26
590[3]	**Tayovullin (IRE) (63)** (HMorrison) **3-8-9** RCochrane(6) (b.hind: a.p: rdn over 2f out: chsd wnr fnl f: unable qckn)	1¼	2	14/1	70	28
305[8]	**Passage Creeping (IRE) (64)** (SDow) **4-9-3**(5) ADaly(13) (lw: led over 1f: rdn over 2f out: one pce)	1½	3	16/1	68	38
755[4]	**Whispered Melody (53)** (RAkehurst) **4-8-11** TQuinn(2) (hdwy over 5f out: swtchd rt over 1f out: r.o ins fnl f)	¾	4	4/1[1]	55	25
1003[6]	**Time For Tea (IRE) (50)** (CACyzer) **4-8-8** DeclanO'Shea(15) (lw: rdn & no hdwy fnl 2f)	1¼	5	20/1	50	20
226[6]	**Always Happy (70)** (MissGayKelleway) **4-10-0** RHughes(4) (lost pl 4f out: rallied over 1f out: r.o)	hd	6	12/1	69	39
1245[9]	**Rumbustious (64)** (RHannon) **3-8-10** DaneO'Neill(10) (hdwy over 3f out: wknd over 1f out)	1¼	7	4/1[1]	61	19
1009[9]	**Mogin (47)** (TJNaughton) **4-8-2**(3)ow1 JDSmith(14) (a mid div)	4	8	8/1[3]	36	5
1151[6]	**Lucy of Arabia (IRE) (53)** (JJSheehan) **3-7-10b**(3)ow3 MartinDwyer(5) (lw: nvr nrr)	hd	9	50/1	42	—
1236[2]	**Pearl Dawn (IRE) (50)** (PCClarke) **7-8-8** CandyMorris(11) (lw: hdwy over 3f out: wknd over 2f out)	2	10	7/1[2]	35	5
1012[8]	**Chorus Song (USA) (63)** (PWChapple-Hyam) **3-8-6**(3) RHavlin(9) (b.nr hind: bhd fnl 5f)	7	11	9/1	34	—
1086[3]	**Worldwide Elsie (USA) (53)** (ICampbell) **4-8-11b** RPrice(1) (b: lw: led over 6f out tl stumbled, hit rails & hdd over 4f out: wknd over 2f out)	2	12	14/1	20	—
566[4]	**Harlequin Walk (IRE) (40)** (RJO'Sullivan) **6-7-12b** JLowe(12) (mid div & wkng whn bmpd over 4f out)	nk	13	10/1	6	—
	Risking (55) (MRChannon) **4-8-8**(5) PPMurphy(3) (lw: bhd fnl 4f)	6	14	33/1	9	—
*1008**	***Good News (IRE) (65)*** (MMadgwick) **3-8-11b** RPerham(7) (Withdrawn not under starter's orders: ref to ent stalls)		W	7/1[2]	—	—

(SP 137.7%) **14 Rn**

1m 33.2 (1.90) CSF £187.32 CT £2,534.36 TOTE £17.10: £3.80 £3.30 £3.90 (£99.20) Trio Not won; £823.27 to Kempton 24/5/97 OWNER Alan Spargo Ltd Toolmakers (AYLESBURY) BRED Mrs J. Mackie and Major W. R. Paton Smith
WEIGHT FOR AGE 3yo-12lb

1135 Sis Garden, whose three previous wins had all come over seven furlongs, struck the front over half a mile from home and, ridden along, was not going to be caught. (16/1)

590 Tayovullin (IRE), who has been running well on the Fibresand this spring, put up a good show on this return to grass, moving into second place entering the final furlong if failing to peg back the winner. (14/1)

173 Passage Creeping (IRE), given a three-month break, has had plenty of chances, but she still remains a maiden and lack of acceleration was once again her downfall here. (16/1)

755 Whispered Melody took closer order at the top of the hill, and after being switched towards the outside below the distance, kept on well inside the final furlong. (4/1: op 5/2)

1003 Time For Tea (IRE) was made to look woefully onepaced in the last three furlongs. She remains a maiden after twenty-five attempts. (20/1)

226 Always Happy, winner of three hurdles races during this National Hunt season, found this trip too sharp and was doing all her best work in the closing stages. A step up to a mile and a half is needed. (12/1: op 6/1)

1236 Pearl Dawn (IRE) (7/1: 5/1-8/1)

749 Chorus Song (USA) (9/1: 6/1-10/1)

566 Harlequin Walk (IRE) (10/1: 8/1-12/1)

1374 DOME H'CAP (0-70) (3-Y.O+) (Class E)

4-10 (4-13) **5f 213y** £3,148.25 (£941.00: £450.50: £205.25) Stalls: Low GOING minus 0.49 sec per fur (F)

				SP	RR	SF
1279[7]	**Ivory's Grab Hire (55)** (KTIvory) **4-9-1b**(3) MartinDwyer(5) (b: a.p: hrd rdn & edgd lft over 1f out: led wl ins fnl f: r.o wl)	—	1	16/1	65	48
643[4]	**Sharp Imp (55)** (RMFlower) **7-9-4b** DHolland(9) (stdy hdwy 2f out: squeezed thro to ld 1f out: hrd rdn: hdd wl ins fnl f: unable qckn)	1¼	2	5/1[2]	62	45
1009[2]	**Justinianus (IRE) (43)** (JJBridger) **5-8-6**ow1 RCochrane(13) (lw: rdn over 2f out: hdwy over 1f out: r.o wl)	1	3	9/2[1]	47	29
1131[5]	**College Night (IRE) (46)** (SCWilliams) **5-8-6**(3) PMcCabe(8) (a.p: hrd rdn over 2f out: one pce)	2½	4	13/2[3]	43	26
325[2]	**Lancashire Legend (55)** (SDow) **4-8-13**(5) ADaly(4) (a.p: led over 1f out: sn hdd & wknd)	s.h	5	14/1	52	35
1292[11]	**Shermood (33)** (KTIvory) **4-7-10** JLowe(12) (lw: outpcd: gd hdwy fnl f: r.o)	2	6	33/1	25	8
863[6]	**Gwespyr (64)** (RHannon) **4-9-13** DaneO'Neill(7) (lw: nvr nr to chal)	nk	7	8/1	55	38
	Super Park (45) (JPearce) **5-8-8** AClark(6) (nvr nrr)	¾	8	33/1	34	17
1089[13]	**Lorins Gold (35)** (AndrewTurnell) **7-7-12** NAdams(3) (led 1f: led over 2f out tl hdd & hmpd over 1f out: sn wknd)	1½	9	25/1	20	3
	Invigilate (41) (MRChannon) **8-7-13**(5)ow1 PPMurphy(11) (lw: sme hdwy over 2f out: wknd over 1f out)	nk	10	16/1	25	7
1098[11]	**Dande Flyer (65)** (DWPArbuthnot) **4-10-0v**[1] SWhitworth(10) (hld up: rdn over 1f out: 5th whn hmpd on ins 1f out: nt rcvr)	1¼	11	12/1	46	29

879[7]	**Crystal Heights (FR) (65)** (RJO'Sullivan) **9-9-11**(3) DO'Donohoe(2) (b: s.s: a wl bhd)	6	**12**	5/1[2]	30	13
1012[2]	**Marengo (68)** (JAkehurst) **3-9-8** TQuinn(1) (lw: led 5f out tl over 2f out: sn wknd)	3	**13**	5/1[2]	25	—
				(SP 128.5%)	**13 Rn**	

1m 7.9 (0.70) CSF £90.78 CT £410.03 TOTE £20.90: £5.00 £2.20 £2.00 (£54.70) Trio £82.60 OWNER Mr Dean Ivory (RADLETT) BRED Japan Bloodstock Ltd

LONG HANDICAP Shermood 7-7

WEIGHT FOR AGE 3yo-9lb

OFFICIAL EXPLANATION **Marengo: bolted to post, which contributed to his poor showing.**

488 Ivory's Grab Hire, making a quick reappearance, threw down his challenge from below the distance and eventually managed to get on top in the last one hundred yards, gaining his first win away from Lingfield. (16/1)

643 Sharp Imp goes well here - he has won three times - and squeezed through to lead a furlong from home. Responding to pressure, he was only worried out of it in the last one hundred yards. (5/1)

1009 Justinianus (IRE) once again got into the prize money, running on nicely in the last furlong and a half for third place, and is running well on grass at present. However, he is now easy to win with. (9/2)

1131 College Night (IRE), a leading light from the off, could only go up and down in the same place in the last two furlongs. She is not easy to win with as one victory from twenty-seven starts shows. (13/2)

325 Lancashire Legend lacks acceleration and his record now stands at one win from twenty-one starts which say it all. (14/1)

Shermood, making a quick reappearance, failed to go the pace but she eventually found her stride in the final furlong and ran on really strongly. She remains a maiden after twenty-three attempts. (33/1)

863 Gwespyr (8/1: op 5/1)

1375 BRIGHTON CENTRE H'CAP (0-70) (3-Y.O) (Class E)

4-40 (4-43) **5f 59y** £2,914.25 (£869.00: £414.50: £187.25) Stalls: Low GOING minus 0.49 sec per fur (F)

				SP	RR	SF
1294[7]	**Anokato (59)** (KTIvory) **3-8-11b**(3) MartinDwyer(1) (b: a.p: nt clr run on ins 4f out: led wl over 1f out: rdn out)	—	**1**	9/2[2]	66	40
466[3]	**Gold Edge (54)** (MRChannon) **3-8-4**(5) PPMurphy(8) (lw: stdy hdwy over 2f out: hrd rdn over 1f out: r.o wl ins fnl f)	2	**2**	7/1	55	29
876[2]	**Nopalea (66)** (TJNaughton) **3-9-4**(3) JDSmith(6) (lw: a.p: rdn over 2f out: chsd wnr over 1f out: unable qckn)	s.h	**3**	5/1[3]	67	41
	Bestelina (53) (DJSCosgrove) **3-8-5**(3) DO'Donohoe(4) (stdd s: outpcd: hdwy fnl f: r.o)	2½	**4**	33/1	46	20
988[9]	**Chloe Nicole (USA) (61)** (PFICole) **3-9-2** TQuinn(7) (b.off hind: outpcd: hdwy fnl f: r.o)	hd	**5**	6/1	54	28
132[4]	**Formidable Spirit (41)** (MJHeaton-Ellis) **3-7-10v** JLowe(2) (lw: hld up: rdn 2f out: n.m.r & swtchd lft over 1f out: one pce)	½	**6**	20/1	32	6
1141[12]	**Stock Hill Dancer (63)** (BJMeehan) **3-8-11b**[1](7) GHannon(5) (a.p: ev ch wl over 1f out: wknd fnl f)	1¼	**7**	14/1	51	25
1238[6]	**Eager To Please (65)** (MissGayKelleway) **3-9-6b** DHolland(9) (lw: bhd fnl 2f)	nk	**8**	7/2[1]	52	26
1151[2]	**Nampara Bay (48)** (GCBravery) **3-8-3** DeclanO'Shea(3) (led over 3f: wknd fnl f)	3	**9**	7/2[1]	26	—
	Eaton Park (IRE) (54) (RAkehurst) **3-8-9** AClark(10) (bhd fnl 2f)	6	**10**	12/1	13	—
				(SP 128.1%)	**10 Rn**	

60.9 secs (0.90) CSF £36.50 CT £159.60 TOTE £7.00: £1.70 £2.90 £1.50 (£28.10) Trio £43.40 OWNER Mr K. T. Ivory (RADLETT) BRED Mrs P. A. Brown

LONG HANDICAP Formidable Spirit 7-5

1113 Anokato, making a quick reappearance, was happier with the return to a sounder surface and, leading early in the final quarter-mile, was rousted along to assert his authority. (9/2: op 7/1)

466 Gold Edge crept closer at halfway and, responding to pressure, ran on strongly in the closing stages to snatch second place right on the line. (7/1: op 4/1)

876 Nopalea, never far away, moved into second place below the distance but she failed to reel in the winner and was caught for the runner-up berth right on the line. She is still looking for her first victory. (5/1)

Bestelina, making her seasonal debut, was taken off her legs for much of the race and was still out with the washing below the distance. However, she eventually found her feet in the final furlong and ran on to snatch fourth prize. (33/1)

889 Chloe Nicole (USA) was taking a drop in class but found this trip too sharp and was only running on when it was all over. (6/1)

132 Formidable Spirit, 5lb out of the handicap and without a run in five months, chased the leaders. He did not have a great deal of room early in the final quarter-mile and was switched as a result, but could then only struggle on at one pace. (20/1)

1151 Nampara Bay (7/2: 5/2-4/1)

Eaton Park (IRE) (12/1: 6/1-14/1)

T/Jkpt: Not won; £15,992.61 to Kempton 24/5/97. T/Plpt: £70.00 (249.01 Tckts). T/Qdpt: £31.80 (31.31 Tckts) AK

0978-HAYDOCK (L-H) - Friday May 23rd

1376 Abandoned-Waterlogged

1246-NOTTINGHAM (L-H) (Good)

Friday May 23rd

WEATHER: cloudy WIND: mod half behind

1383 ARNOLD (S) H'CAP (0-60) (3-Y.O+) (Class G)

2-25 (2-25) **1m 1f 213y** £1,984.50 (£547.00: £259.50) Stalls: Low GOING minus 0.11 sec per fur (G)

				SP	RR	SF
	Hill Farm Blues (49) (WMBrisbourne) **4-9-3** AGarth(10) (hld up: stdy hdwy over 3f out: led over 1f out: r.o wl)	—	**1**	25/1	63	29
1246*	**Esperto (49)** (JPearce) **4-9-3** 5x GBardwell(15) (trckd ldrs: led 2f out: sn hdd: unable qckn fnl f)	2	**2**	3/1[1]	60	26
	Acquittal (IRE) (39) (AStreeter) **5-8-7v** TSprake(12) (bit bkwd: in tch: styd on u.p over 2f out)	2	**3**	14/1	47	13
951[13]	**I'm a Nut Man (37)** (CASmith) **6-8-5** DeanMcKeown(11) (plld hrd: hld up & bhd: hdwy over 3f out: kpt on fnl f)	¾	**4**	8/1[3]	43	9
721[2]	**Captain Marmalade (43)** (DTThom) **8-8-11** GDuffield(9) (b: lw: bhd tl styd on u.p fnl 2f)	2	**5**	8/1[3]	46	12
647[9]	**Rehaab (58)** (DMorris) **4-9-7**(5) GFaulkner(8) (trckd ldrs: rdn & wknd over 3f out)	½	**6**	6/1[2]	60	26
1283[2]	**Diamond Crown (IRE) (47)** (MartynWane) **6-9-1** JCarroll(18) (hld up & bhd: styd on fnl 2f: nrst fin)	2	**7**	8/1[3]	46	12
900[9]	**Blaze of Oak (USA) (43)** (JMBradley) **6-8-11** SDrowne(16) (lw: chsd ldrs: led over 2f out: sn hdd & wknd)	hd	**8**	14/1	42	8
1128[7]	**Return To Brighton (39)** (JMBradley) **5-8-7** JWeaver(13) (lw: w ldr tl wknd over 2f out)	1½	**9**	14/1	36	2

			SP	RR	SF
	Guesstimation (USA) (60) (JPearce) **8-9-11**(3) CTeague(14) (hld up & bhd tl styd on fnl 2f)......1¼	**10**	16/1	55	21
1093[9]	**Irish Kinsman (44)** (GHYardley) **4-8-5**(7) CLowther(3) (lw: hld up: hdwy u.p over 2f out: sn wknd)......nk	**11**	33/1	38	4
1273[6]	**Proud Brigadier (IRE) (41)** (MRBosley) **9-8-9** CRutter(6) (b: lw: s.i.s: a bhd)......¾	**12**	16/1	34	—
748[9]	**Santella Katie (54)** (MrsLStubbs) **4-9-8** ACulhane(4) (a in rr)......1½	**13**	25/1	45	11
1247[3]	**River Run (IRE) (42)** (RHollinshead) **5-8-7**(3) FLynch(7) (plld hrd: hld up: wknd 3f out)......2½	**14**	8/1[3]	29	—
1118[8]	**Jungle Fresh (43)** (JDBethell) **4-8-11** OUrbina(2) (lw: bhd fr ½-wy)......1¼	**15**	25/1	28	—
1008[4]	**Chopin (IRE) (53)** (RFJohnsonHoughton) **3-8-7** SSanders(1) (b.off hind: plld hrd: prom over 6f: sn lost tch) .1¼	**16**	10/1	36	—
1005[12]	**Racing Hawk (USA) (46)** (MSSaunders) **5-9-0v** AMcGlone(5) (led: rdn & hdd over 2f out: wknd qckly)......¾	**17**	20/1	27	—
1246[3]	**Rochea (55)** (MrsNMacauley) **3-8-9** SWebster(17) (chsd ldrs over 6f: sn wknd)......3½	**18**	12/1	31	—

(SP 151.5%) **18 Rn**

2m 10.3 (7.80) CSF £103.73 CT £1,112.22 TOTE £29.00: £5.70 £1.60 £2.90 £5.40 (£36.40) Trio £347.10; £366.76 to Kempton 24/5/97
OWNER Mr Dennis Newton (NESSCLIFFE) BRED D. Newton
WEIGHT FOR AGE 3yo-14lb
Bt in 4200 gns

Hill Farm Blues, from a yard running into form, defied a long absence from the racecourse to record her first success with a fairly easy-gained win, stepping down to selling company. (25/1)

1246* Esperto, attempting a quick follow-up, did nothing wrong and gave it his best shot, but he did find this run coming too soon and he was fighting a lost cause throughout the final furlong. (3/1)

Acquittal (IRE), out of action since the autumn, ran really well since he was carrying so much surplus condition, and he will not have much trouble finding an opening in this company. (14/1)

I'm a Nut Man, still struggling to get off the mark, took a lot of settling and stayed on particularly well in the closing stages. He has the ability to win a race if he only gives himself a chance. (8/1: op 12/1)

721 Captain Marmalade stayed on under a forceful ride in the latter stages, but had given himself too much to do and was never going to get there. (8/1: 6/1-9/1)

487 Rehaab looked sure to take a hand in proceedings when joining issue three furlongs out, but she did not find much when pressure was applied and she gradually dropped away. (6/1: op 14/1)

1283 Diamond Crown (IRE) (8/1: 6/1-10/1)

1247 River Run (IRE) (8/1: op 5/1)

1008 Chopin (IRE) ran far too freely over this longer trip and he was in trouble early in the straight. (10/1)

1246 Rochea (12/1: op 8/1)

1384 NORTHWEST HOLST CONSTRUCTION H'CAP (0-70) (3-Y.O+) (Class E)

2-55 (2-56) **1m 1f 213y** £3,486.25 (£1,045.00: £502.50: £231.25) Stalls: Low GOING minus 0.11 sec per fur (G)

			SP	RR	SF
991[10]	**Travelmate (66)** (JRFanshawe) **3-8-11** DHarrison(12) (lw: hld up: hdwy 4f out: led over 2f out: rdn & r.o wl) .—	**1**	5/2[1]	80+	29
1244[9]	**Koraloona (IRE) (47)** (GBBalding) **4-8-6** SDrowne(16) (lw: hld up in tch: hdwy over 3f out: styd on ins fnl f) 3	**2**	14/1	56	19
1001[3]	**Golden Touch (USA) (58)** (DJSCosgrove) **5-9-3** DBiggs(8) (lw: hld up: hdwy 3f out: styd on u.p appr fnl f)...1½	**3**	6/1[3]	65	28
1024[3]	**Riccarton (50)** (PCalver) **4-8-9** JCarroll(2) (s.s: hld up & plld hrd: hdwy 4f out: hung lft & kpt on fnl f)......1½	**4**	4/1[2]	54	17
	Runic Symbol (38) (MBlanshard) **6-7-11** JQuinn(13) (hld up: hdwy over 2f out: rdn appr fnl f: nvr nrr)......2	**5**	14/1	39	2
1097[12]	**Up in Flames (IRE) (65)** (SRBowring) **6-9-10** SWebster(1) (lw: dwlt: hld up: effrt on outside over 2f out: nt pce to chal)......2	**6**	20/1	63	26
	Renata's Prince (IRE) (52) (KRBurke) **4-8-11** ACulhane(18) (lw: trckd ldrs: effrt 3f out: nt pce to chal)......nk	**7**	33/1	50	13
1097[7]	**Winston (59)** (JDBethell) **4-9-4** PaulEddery(10) (sn drvn along: hdwy & hung lft 3f out: nt rch ldrs)......5	**8**	7/1	48	11
755[15]	**Sweet Ciseaux (IRE) (40)** (MJHeaton-Ellis) **4-7-6**(7) JFowle(14) (led: clr ½-wy: wknd & hdd over 2f out) 6	**9**	14/1	20	—
887[11]	**Mazilla (52)** (AStreeter) **5-8-11** TSprake(5) (chsd ldrs: rdn along 3f out: grad lost tch) ......s.h	**10**	15/2	32	—
759[14]	**Welsh Mountain (55)** (MJHeaton-Ellis) **4-9-0** JWeaver(17) (trckd ldrs over 7f)......3½	**11**	16/1	29	—
1291[15]	**Saratoga Red (USA) (63)** (WAO'Gorman) **3-8-8** EmmaO'Gorman(4) (dwlt: a in rr)......½	**12**	20/1	36	—
1036[10]	**Super High (54)** (PHowling) **5-8-13v[1]** FNorton(9) (chsd ldrs: rdn over 2f out: sn wknd)......hd	**13**	16/1	27	—
	Conic Hill (IRE) (44) (JPearce) **6-8-3** GBardwell(3) (bit bkwd: a bhd: t.o)......6	**14**	16/1	8	—
	The Roundsills (54) (RFJohnsonHoughton) **3-7-8**(5) RMullen(7) (dwlt: hdwy & plld hrd: a bhd: t.o: sddle slipped)......10	**15**	20/1	2	—
	Tomashenko (47) (TWDonnelly) **8-8-6** NConnorton(11) (b: chsd clr ldr over 6f: sn wknd: t.o)......4	**16**	33/1	—	—

(SP 144.9%) **16 Rn**

2m 9.6 (7.10) CSF £42.55 CT £200.64 TOTE £5.30: £1.20 £3.30 £1.80 £1.20 (£50.80) Trio £234.90 OWNER Barford Bloodstock II (NEWMARKET) BRED London Thoroughbred Services Ltd
WEIGHT FOR AGE 3yo-14lb

OFFICIAL EXPLANATION **The Roundsills: the trainer reported that the saddle had slipped, preventing the jockey from riding out.**

Travelmate, well supported in his first handicap, won with a bit to spare, and though the company was moderate, he brushed them aside with ease. (5/2)

Koraloona (IRE) took time to find top gear, but stayed on pleasingly inside the distance and there is a small race in him. (14/1)

1001 Golden Touch (USA), making progress from off the pace, lacked the speed to deliver a challenge, but he appeared to give his all which was just not good enough on the day. (6/1: op 4/1)

1024 Riccarton lost far more ground at the start than he was eventually beaten. He looks dull in his coat and listless and he definitely needs some sunshine on his back. (4/1)

Runic Symbol, taken out of the seller to run in this race, would probably have won if he had been allowed to take his chance in that event, but he had to work hard here to finish where did. (14/1: 10/1-16/1)

315 Up in Flames (IRE), still to succeed beyond a mile, did not fair badly conceding weight all round and all is not lost yet. (20/1)

538 Sweet Ciseaux (IRE) (14/1: 10/1-16/1)

1385 RADCLIFFE LIMITED STKS (0-65) (3-Y.O+) (Class F)

3-25 (3-27) **6f 15y** £2,277.00 (£627.00: £297.00) Stalls: High GOING minus 0.47 sec per fur (F)

			SP	RR	SF
1080*	**Corniche Quest (IRE) (56)** (MRChannon) **4-8-11**(7) AEddery(18) (a.p stands' side: led over 1f out: drvn out)—	**1**	8/1[3]	74	56
1020[7]	**Almasi (IRE) (63)** (CFWall) **5-9-1** JReid(3) (lw: racd far side: hdwy 2f out: r.o wl fnl f)......½	**2**	7/2[1]	70	52
1080[2]	**Afaan (IRE) (56)** (RFMarvin) **4-9-4** TGMcLaughlin(13) (lw: chsd ldr stands' side: kpt on u.p fnl f)......2	**3**	14/1	67	49
1127*	**River Tern (64)** (JMBradley) **4-9-7** JWeaver(17) (lw: s.s: hdwy 2f out: r.o wl fnl f)......2	**4**	9/1	65	47
895[12]	**Alfahaal (IRE) (57)** (RFJohnsonHoughton) **4-9-4** SSanders(2) (b.hind: led far side tl ins fnl f)......1¼	**5**	14/1	59	41
1285[10]	**La Dolce Vita (65)** (TDBarron) **3-8-9** KDarley(15) (racd stands' side: r.o fnl 2f: nvr nrr)......¾	**6**	7/1[2]	57	30
1046[6]	**Al Reet (IRE) (61)** (SRBowring) **6-9-1** SWebster(14) (led stands' side over 4f)......½	**7**	20/1	53	35

				SP	RR	SF
756^{5}	**Songsheet (62)** (MSSaunders) **4-9-1** SDrowne(9) (trckd ldrs over 4f)	1¼	**8**	12/1	49	31
1083^{7}	**Shavinsky (62)** (PHowling) **4-9-4** PaulEddery(12) (nvr nrr)	½	**9**	20/1	51	33
	Rambold (62) (NEBerry) **6-9-1** BDoyle(4) (bkwd: in tch far side 4f: sn wknd)	1½	**10**	16/1	44	26
1223^{4}	**Captain Carat (60)** (DNicholls) **6-9-4** LDettori(7) (racd far side: hld up: effrt over 2f out: no imp)	hd	**11**	$7/2^{1}$	47	29
675^{19}	**Royal Blackbird (65)** (JEBanks) **3-8-1**(5) RMullen(16) (racd stands' side: effrt & hung lft ½-wy: sn wknd)	1¾	**12**	12/1	39	12
929^{5}	**Captain Carparts (61)** (JLEyre) **3-8-9v¹** TWilliams(11) (plld hrd: w ldrs stands' side over 3f)	¾	**13**	14/1	40	13
1121^{2}	**Mythical (64)** (SirMarkPrescott) **3-8-6** GDuffield(10) (racd stands' side: wandered bdly ½-wy: sn outpcd & eased)	7	**14**	$7/1^{2}$	19	—
1089^{15}	**Bataleur (59)** (MissJBower) **4-9-4** DHarrison(6) (racd far side: sn outpcd)	1¼	**15**	20/1	18	—
550^{9}	**Amany (IRE) (40)** (DBurchell) **5-9-1** DeanMcKeown(8) (racd centre: bhd fr ½-wy)	2	**16**	25/1	10	—
638^{10}	**Lady Westbury (IRE) (33)** (PCRitchens) **6-9-1** JQuinn(1) (chsd ldrs far side to ½-wy: sn outpcd)	1¼	**17**	33/1	7	—

(SP 152.9%) **17 Rn**

1m 11.9 (0.40) CSF £38.56 TOTE £11.10: £3.60 £1.30 £5.00 (£24.70) Trio £88.90 OWNER Mr M. Bishop (UPPER LAMBOURN) BRED K. Molloy

WEIGHT FOR AGE 3yo-9lb

1080* Corniche Quest (IRE), a versatile filly who can win at anything from five furlongs to a mile, won this courtesy of a high draw, but she confirmed her form with Afaan so there is no fluke about the result. (8/1)

1020 Almasi (IRE) finished way ahead of her rivals on the far side, but the draw had played its part again and she had to accept the inevitable. (7/2: 9/2-5/2)

1080 Afaan (IRE), a consistent but luckless colt, had more than his fair share of weight for a maiden, but he ran his usual game race and connections must be crying out for a change of fortune. (14/1)

1127* River Tern, flat-footed as the stalls opened, was getting down to some serious business nearing the finish, and he may have been more than a shade unlucky. (9/1)

Alfahaal (IRE) again dictated at this step down to sprinting, but he had the misfortune to be drawn on the slower far side and that helped to beat him on the end. (14/1)

1131 La Dolce Vita, having her second outing of the week, did not begin to pick up until far too late and she does look to need seven furlongs nowadays. (7/1)

1046 Al Reet (IRE), twice a winner in Ireland, has not fired over here as yet but she showed plenty of pace and she could be coming to herself. (20/1)

Royal Blackbird (12/1: op 8/1)

71+ 72+ 76+ 92

1386 E.B.F. NOVICE STKS (2-Y.O F) (Class D) (78)

3-55 (3-57) **6f 15y** £3,542.00 (£1,058.00: £506.00: £230.00) Stalls: High GOING minus 0.47 sec per fur (F)

				SP	RR	SF
1213^{3}	**Saffron Lane (IRE)** (RHannon) **2-8-8** LDettori(5) (chsd ldr: led over 2f out: r.o strly fnl f)	—	**1**	$6/4^{1}$	77	15
	Muftuffenuf (PRWebber) **2-8-8** DHarrison(1) (w'like: unf: scope: led tl over 2f out: rdn & edgd lft over 1f out: sn outpcd)	1¾	**2**	14/1	72	10
1109*	**Gypsy Hill** (DHaydnJones) **2-8-12** SDrowne(4) (lw: chsd ldrs on outside: rdn over 2f out: r.o one pce)	1¾	**3**	$9/4^{2}$	72	10
739*	**Supreme Angel** (MPMuggeridge) **2-8-11**(3) MHenry(2) (chsd ldrs: effrt & rdn ½-wy: no imp appr fnl f)	2	**4**	$4/1^{3}$	69	7
	Meadgate's Dreamer (IRE) (BPalling) **2-8-8** TSprake(3) (unf: scope: s.s: a outpcd)	7	**5**	7/1	44	—

(SP 109.9%) **5 Rn**

1m 14.3 (2.80) CSF £18.82 TOTE £2.00: £1.40 £3.50 (£16.90) OWNER S L Partnership (MARLBOROUGH) BRED Saffron Breeders Club

1213 Saffron Lane (IRE) knew much more on this occasion and, after leading into the final quarter-mile, lengthened up to draw right away in the last two hundred yards. (6/4: op evens)

Muftuffenuf, a nice, easy mover, bred for speed, would probably do better over the minimum trip and she looks a sure future winner. (14/1: 10/1-16/1)

1109* Gypsy Hill had more to do in this company and, when the whips were cracking, she was just not up to it. (9/4)

739* Supreme Angel, a poor mover in her slower paces, was close enough if good enough entering the last quarter-mile, but once she came off the bridle, there was not a lot left to come. (4/1)

Meadgate's Dreamer (IRE) (7/1: op 4/1)

1387 NORWEST HOLST CONSTRUCTION H'CAP (0-80) (3-Y.O) (Class D)

4-25 (4-25) **1m 6f 15y** £3,645.60 (£1,087.80: £519.40: £235.20) Stalls: Low GOING minus 0.11 sec per fur (G)

				SP	RR	SF
1140*	**Right Man (61)** (GLewis) **3-8-6** 4x PaulEddery(7) (hld up: hdwy over 3f out: led jst ins fnl f: r.o wl)	—	**1**	$7/4^{1}$	68	29
1094^{2}	**Jucinda (60)** (JPearce) **3-8-5** BDoyle(5) (chsd ldrs: led 2f out tl hdd & no ex jst ins fnl f)	2	**2**	$5/1^{3}$	65	26
1094^{4}	**Bisquet-de-Bouche (51)** (RDickin) **3-7-5**(5) RMullen(9) (hld up: hdwy 6f out: led over 2f out: sn hdd: r.o one pce)	1½	**3**	12/1	54	15
825*	**Polyphony (USA) (75)** (RCharlton) **3-9-6** DHarrison(2) (rn in snatches: hdwy to chse ldrs 3f out: styd on one pce)	nk	**4**	$7/2^{2}$	78	39
1140^{15}	**Cadbury Castle (57)** (MBlanshard) **3-8-2** JQuinn(8) (plld hrd: hld up: effrt 4f out: sn rdn & no imp)	7	**5**	50/1	52	13
837^{7}	**Tasik Chini (USA) (71)** (PFICole) **3-9-2** CRutter(10) (chsd ldr: led over 3f out tl over 2f out: sn rdn & btn)	4	**6**	12/1	61	22
1140^{8}	**Masrrah (IRE) (62)** (RWArmstrong) **3-8-7b¹** JWeaver(3) (b.hind: chsd ldrs tl rdn & wknd over 2f out)	2½	**7**	20/1	49	10
878^{10}	**Goodwood Lass (IRE) (71)** (JLDunlop) **3-9-2** LDettori(1) (lw: hld up: effrt & swtchd outside 3f out: no imp)	3	**8**	8/1	55	16
764^{7}	**Mogul (62)** (NAGraham) **3-8-7b¹** AMcGlone(4) (lw: hld up: hdwy over 4f out: rdn & wknd 3f out)	1¼	**9**	14/1	45	6
975^{2}	**Sad Mad Bad (USA) (76)** (MJohnston) **3-9-7** WJO'Connor(6) (led: reminders 6f out: hdd over 3f out: sn wknd: t.o)	21	**10**	9/1	35	—

(SP 125.1%) **10 Rn**

3m 7.9 (9.40) CSF £10.67 CT £79.77 TOTE £2.70: £1.10 £3.00 £3.90 (£4.30) Trio £45.10 OWNER Mr G. V. Wright (EPSOM) BRED A. C. Birkle

LONG HANDICAP Bisquet-de-Bouche 7-8

1140* Right Man, continuing his step up in distance, won this poorish contest with the minimum of fuss. Looking very dull in his coat and winning no awards with his action to post, he has benefited from the easing of the ground and it would seem he is only just coming to himself. (7/4)

1094 Jucinda ran up to her mark and confirmed the promise she showed here earlier in the month, but once again she was found wanting in the last two hundred yards. (5/1)

1094 Bisquet-de-Bouche, improving with every run, was only tapped for toe inside the distance and that initial success can not be far away. (12/1)

825* Polyphony (USA) has not had the three runs to qualify him for a proper handicap mark and, though he did stay on in the closing stages, showed his lack of experience. There will be better to come when he does get his act together. (7/2)

478* Tasik Chini (USA) did not appear to see the trip out for he was only forced to give best on the approach to the two-furlong pole, and then stopped as if shot. (12/1: op 8/1)

1388 COLWICK MAIDEN APPRENTICE H'CAP (0-70) (3-Y.O+) (Class G)

4-55 (4-56) **1m 54y** £2,002.50 (£565.00: £277.50) Stalls: Low GOING minus 0.11 sec per fur (G)

Form	Horse / details	Dist	Pos	SP	RR	SF
1008[5]	**Bon Guest (IRE) (52)** (TJNaughton) **3-7-5**(10) RachaelMoody(17) (hld up: hdwy 4f out: led & hung lft appr fnl f: drvn out)	—	**1**	16/1	62	22
653[6]	**Chalky Dancer (35)** (HJCollingridge) **5-7-5**(5) PBradley(6) (b.hind: led: clr over 2f out: edgd lft appr fnl f: sn hdd: hmpd & swtchd rt: nr fin)	2	**2**	14/1	41	13
1248[14]	**Time of Night (USA) (65)** (RGuest) **4-9-9**(3) SRighton(3) (hld up: hdwy over 2f out: styd on ins fnl f)	hd	**3**	14/1	71	43
1097[17]	**Terdad (USA) (65)** (TDBarron) **4-9-9**(3) VictoriaAppleby(7) (lw: a chsng ldrs: one pce appr fnl f)	nk	**4**	20/1	70	42
1266[5]	**Flagstaff (USA) (48)** (KRBurke) **4-7-13v**(10)ow1 PWright(12) (s.i.s: bhd: hdwy over 2f out: nrst fin)	3	**5**	12/1	48	19
1220[8]	**Prime Partner (39)** (TDEasterby) **4-7-11**(3) RWinston(14) (in tch: kpt on u.p fnl 2f)	nk	**6**	14/1	38	10
886[11]	**Push A Venture (59)** (SPCWoods) **3-8-5**(3) CWebb(13) (hld up & bhd: styd on fnl 2f)	¾	**7**	8/1	57	17
864[7]	**Perang Polly (52)** (LordHuntingdon) **5-8-5v**(8) CCogan(4) (chsd ldrs: sn drvn along: grad wknd fnl 2f)	1¼	**8**	9/2[2]	47	19
	Spiral Flyer (IRE) (38) (MDIUsher) **4-7-5**(8) RBrisland(9) (mid div: hmpd over 5f out: n.d afterwards)	3½	**9**	25/1	26	—
882[11]	**Jib Jab (62)** (MrsNMacauley) **3-8-6**(5) CCarver(2) (rdn & swtchd rt & racd alone fnl 3f: no imp)	2	**10**	20/1	46	6
687[2]	**Square Mile Miss (IRE) (42)** (PHowling) **4-8-3** JDennis(8) (nvr nr to chal)	1¼	**11**	4/1[1]	24	—
1128[10]	**Bad News (44)** (JMBradley) **5-7-12**(7)ow9 DHayden(1) (t: a in rr)	3½	**12**	25/1	19	—
896[10]	**Mubariz (IRE) (44)** (CSmith) **5-8-5** CLowther(10) (t: lw: sn drvn along: a bhd)	2½	**13**	16/1	14	—
1090[7]	**Alpine Music (IRE) (60)** (JMBradley) **3-8-4**(5) JFowle(16) (prom tl lost pl 3f out: sn bhd)	nk	**14**	16/1	30	—
874[4]	**Crackerbox (47)** (CADwyer) **3-7-3**(7) DarrenWilliams(18) (chsd ldrs: rdn ½-wy: sn lost pl)	2½	**15**	16/1	12	—
868[13]	**Regal Equity (57)** (MCPipe) **3-8-6** JWilkinson(11) (chsd ldrs tl ½-wy: sn wknd: t.o)	¾	**16**	14/1	20	—
868[5]	**Spanish Warrior (58)** (JWHills) **3-8-4**(3) AMcCarthy(5) (prom tl lost pl over 5f out: t.o)	15	**17**	7/1[3]	—	—
476[13]	**Scottish Hero (51)** (LadyHerries) **4-8-9b**[1](3) PDoe(15) (hmpd & uns rdr over 5f out)		**U**	12/1	—	—

(SP 144.6%) **18 Rn**

1m 46.9 (5.60) CSF £226.89 CT £3,051.41 TOTE £15.70: £3.00 £3.40 £7.70 £5.00 (£230.80) Trio Not won; £390.53 to Kempton 24/5/97
OWNER Mr T. J. Naughton (EPSOM) BRED Mrs Heather Glendinning
LONG HANDICAP Chalky Dancer 7-7 Bad News 7-9 Crackerbox 7-8
WEIGHT FOR AGE 3yo-12lb
IN-FOCUS: **This was the rider's first winner.**

1008 Bon Guest (IRE) managed to open his account at the first time of asking over this longer trip, but he did contravene the rules inside the final furlong and may have been a shade fortunate to escape scot-free. (16/1)
Chalky Dancer, falling out of the bottom of the handicap, run up to his best here and, though he was impeded late on, the Stewards may have thought, quite rightly, that he was beaten at the time. (14/1)
Time of Night (USA) shows her best form when ridden from behind and, though she may have left it just too late on this occasion, she did finish best of all and there is a race in her. (14/1)
463 Terdad (USA) has shown signs of ability in the past, but he has taken time to get together and, once he does, he could go on and win a couple of races. (20/1)
1266 Flagstaff (USA) was unable to recover after losing ground at the start, but he did keep staying on and he could get it right one of these days. (12/1: op 8/1)
Prime Partner ran much better than he did earlier in the month in a seller, but he does seem to lack a turn of speed and that will always count against him. (14/1)
886 Push A Venture, restrained in the rear, stayed on steadily to reach her final placing and, as she is bred to need further, will come into her own when tackling twelve furlongs plus. (8/1)
306 Perang Polly (9/2: 7/1-4/1)

T/Plpt: £176.20 (115.1 Tckts). T/Qdpt: £59.40 (21.37 Tckts) IM

0861-PONTEFRACT (L-H) (Good, Good to soft patches)
Friday May 23rd

WEATHER: overcast WIND: slight against

1389 FRIENDS OF THE NORTHERN RACING COLLEGE CLAIMING STKS (4-Y.O+) (Class F)

6-40 (6-41) **1m 4y** £2,742.00 (£762.00: £366.00) Stalls: Low GOING minus 0.17 sec per fur (GF)

Form	Horse / details	Dist	Pos	SP	RR	SF
1300[4]	**Golden Thunderbolt (FR) (70)** (NTinkler) **4-9-2** JWeaver(10) (hld up: hdwy 3f out: chal ins fnl f: rdn to ld wl ins fnl f)	—	**1**	11/4[1]	73	47
1085[5]	**Whittle Rock (83)** (MrsMReveley) **4-9-2** ACulhane(5) (lw: hld up: gd hdwy 3f out: rdn to disp ld ins fnl f: faltered: styd on towards fin)	hd	**2**	4/1[2]	73	47
951[12]	**Bowcliffe (39)** (EJAlston) **6-8-11** MFenton(7) (prom: hdwy to ld wl over 1f out: hdd & no ex wl ins fnl f)	½	**3**	50/1	67	41
	Scaraben (76) (SEKettlewell) **9-8-13** JStack(3) (hld up: nt clr run & swtchd wl over 1f out: kpt on wl: nt pce to chal)	1¼	**4**	13/2	66	40
776[6]	**Rambo Waltzer (69)** (DNicholls) **5-8-8**(5) IonaWands(4) (lw: cl up: outpcd 3f out: no imp after)	5	**5**	4/1[2]	56	30
1220[6]	**First Gold (47)** (JWharton) **8-8-6** GDuffield(6) (bhd: effrt ½-wy: styd on fnl 2f: n.d)	4	**6**	25/1	41	15
896[11]	**Miletrian City (45)** (JBerry) **4-8-6v**[1] KDarley(2) (led tl hdd & wknd wl over 1f out)	3	**7**	25/1	35	9
	Rush Me Not (IRE) (MPBielby) **4-8-6** DeanMcKeown(11) (effrt on outside over 3f out: n.d)	4	**8**	100/1	27	1
1048[13]	**Moneghetti (42)** (JLHarris) **6-8-8** SSanders(8) (chsd ldrs tl wknd wl over 1f out)	6	**9**	33/1	17	—
	Equerry (79) (MDods) **6-8-10**(3) FLynch(1) (chsd ldrs tl wknd fnl 2f)	3	**10**	9/2[3]	16	—
946[9]	**Pleasure Trick (USA) (40)** (DonEnricoIncisa) **6-9-2** KimTinkler(9) (a bhd)	7	**11**	33/1	6	—

(SP 114.7%) **11 Rn**

1m 46.47 (4.07) CSF £11.37 TOTE £3.30: £1.30 £1.80 £7.60 (£12.20) Trio £259.50; £274.13 to 26/5/97 OWNER Contrac Promotions Ltd (MALTON) BRED L. T. Al Swaidi

1300 Golden Thunderbolt (FR) has been running well of late and, given some strong assistance, he showed a good attitude. (11/4)
1085 Whittle Rock should have won this but threw it away by hesitating when challenging, and she obviously has plenty more ability when she puts it in. (4/1: 3/1-9/2)
Bowcliffe ran a blinder here and the change of surroundings seems to have made the world of difference. (50/1)
Scaraben ran really well and by the looks of things he is going to be one to be reckoned with before long. (13/2)
776 Rambo Waltzer has had a month off and that might have just have made the difference. (4/1)

1220 First Gold runs when he thinks and it was never soon enough on this occasion. (25/1)
Equerry (9/2: op 3/1)

1390 TOTE H'CAP (0-70) (3-Y.O+ F & M) (Class E)

7-05 (7-10) **1m 2f 6y** £3,405.00 (£1,020.00: £490.00: £225.00) Stalls: Low GOING minus 0.17 sec per fur (GF)

Prev	Horse	Dist	Pos	SP	RR	SF
1001^{13}	**Opalette (63)** (LadyHerries) **4-9-8** JWeaver(1) (trckd ldrs: led 3f out & qcknd: hld on wl)	—	1	16/1	72	56
1138^{2}	**Kilnamartyra Girl (37)** (JParkes) **7-7-10** GBardwell(12) (outpcd tl hdwy u.p 2f out: styd on wl towards fin)	½	2	16/1	45	29
1024^{12}	**Lapu-Lapu (54)** (MJCamacho) **4-8-8**(5) GParkin(8) (in tch: effrt & ch ins fnl f: kpt on u.p)	½	3	16/1	61	45
1123^{4}	**Cashmere Lady (65)** (JLEyre) **5-9-7**(3) OPears(14) (bhd: stdy hdwy 4f out: ev ch ins fnl f: kpt on u.p)	s.h	4	$10/1^{3}$	72	56
1301^{*}	**Step N Go (IRE) (70)** (MrsJRRamsden) **3-9-1** 5x KFallon(10) (lw: in tch: drvn along over 3f out: hdwy 2f out: btn whn hmpd ins fnl f)	1¾	5	$Evens^{1}$	75	45
1116^{5}	**Mcgillycuddy Reeks (IRE) (37)** (DonEnricoIncisa) **6-7-10** KimTinkler(7) (s.i.s: hdwy 3f out: kpt on: nt pce to chal)	4	6	33/1	35	19
	Forest Fantasy (55) (JWharton) **4-9-0** GDuffield(4) (s.i.s: hld up: hmpd over 2f out: stdy hdwy 2f out: nvr nr to chal)	2	7	25/1	50	34
1096^{6}	**Bollero (IRE) (63)** (JBerry) **3-8-3**(5) PFessey(11) (s.i.s: styd on fnl 3f: nrst fin)	1½	8	20/1	56	26
1093^{8}	**Kristal Breeze (54)** (WRMuir) **5-8-13** JReid(17) (effrt 4f out: nvr bttr than mid div)	nk	9	14/1	46	30
	Cruz Santa (47) (TDBarron) **4-8-6** KDarley(18) (in tch: wnt 2nd 2f out: wknd wl over 1f out)	1½	10	25/1	37	21
553^{13}	**Winnebago (50)** (CWThornton) **4-8-9** DeanMcKeown(5) (chsd ldrs tl nt clr run & wknd over 2f out)	14	11	33/1	17	1
574^{3}	**Petit Flora (38)** (GHolmes) **5-7-11** JQuinn(2) (b.hind: chsd ldrs tl wknd 2f out)	nk	12	14/1	5	—
1138^{12}	**Perfect Angel (IRE) (52)** (MHTompkins) **3-7-11**ow1 DaleGibson(16) (a outpcd & bhd)	7	13	25/1	8	—
1020^{18}	**Dona Filipa (38)** (MissLCSiddall) **4-7-11**ow1 NCarlisle(6) (lw: bhd fnl 5f)	½	14	50/1	—	—
1299^{*}	**Lindrick Lady (IRE) (70)** (BSRothwell) **3-9-1** 5x MFenton(3) (set str pce tl hdd & wknd 3f out)	1	15	$6/1^{2}$	23	—
1229^{4}	**Portite Sophie (40)** (MBrittain) **6-7-6**(7) DMernagh(9) (w ldr tl wknd qckly 3f out)	hd	16	16/1	—	—
	Welcome Lu (43) (JLHarris) **4-8-2** SSanders(15) (a bhd)	23	17	25/1	—	—

(SP 138.2%) **17 Rn**

2m 14.3 (4.70) CSF £233.35 CT £3,817.21 TOTE £26.20: £3.60 £2.60 £3.50 £2.00 (£313.20) Trio Not won; £701.43 to 26/5/97 OWNER Angmering Park Stud (LITTLEHAMPTON) BRED Lavinia Duchess Of Norfolk
LONG HANDICAP Perfect Angel (IRE) 7-9 Mcgillycuddy Reeks (IRE) 7-3 Dona Filipa 7-6
WEIGHT FOR AGE 3yo-14lb
Opalette twice ran miserably this season, but she got it right here in a big way and there was certainly no fluke about it. (16/1)
1138 Kilnamartyra Girl was never on the bridle at any stage but she did finish well and would seem to need further. (16/1)
Lapu-Lapu travelled well and seems to be coming to hand. (16/1)
1123 Cashmere Lady, trying her longest trip to date, got it well and put up a tremendous show. A win on turf can not be far away. (10/1)
1301* Step N Go (IRE) never looked happy from halfway but did keep responding to pressure albeit in vain. She should be forgiven this lapse. (Evens)
1116 Mcgillycuddy Reeks (IRE) ran well from 7lb wrong in the handicap and is obviously in good heart. (33/1)
Forest Fantasy ran well after getting murdered approaching the home turn and looks one to keep in mind. (25/1)
1299* Lindrick Lady (IRE) being taken on in the lead, went far too fast and ran herself into the ground with three furlongs left. (6/1)

1391 NORTHERN RACING COLLEGE CONDITIONS STKS (2-Y.O) (Class C)

7-30 (7-32) **6f** £4,296.60 (£1,566.60: £765.80: £329.00: £147.00) Stalls: Low GOING minus 0.17 sec per fur (GF)

Prev	Horse	Dist	Pos	SP	RR	SF
1126^{2}	**Rusty Babe (IRE)** (JJQuinn) **2-8-11** JQuinn(3) (lw: hld up: hdwy ½-wy: led 1½f out: edgd lft: r.o u.p)	—	1	$4/1^{3}$	83	22
1161^{2}	**Out Like Magic** (PDEvans) **2-8-10** JFEgan(5) (b.hind: chsd ldrs: effrt whn nt clr run wl over 1f out: styd on wl fnl f)	¾	2	$9/4^{2}$	80	19
861^{*}	**Classy Cleo (IRE)** (RHannon) **2-8-10** KDarley(2) (mde most tl hdd 1½f out: kpt on)	nk	3	$2/1^{1}$	79	18
965^{6}	**Mister Bankes** (WGMTurner) **2-8-13** TSprake(4) (lw: w ldr tl wknd 1½f out)	3½	4	6/1	73	12
1084^{5}	**High Money** (GLewis) **2-8-11** PaulEddery(1) (outpcd ½-wy: sn lost tch)	24	5	5/1	7	—

(SP 115.1%) **5 Rn**

1m 19.5 (4.50) CSF £12.75 TOTE £5.30: £2.20 £1.40 (£6.70) OWNER Mrs K. Mapp (MALTON) BRED Rathasker Stud
1126 Rusty Babe (IRE) appreciated this trip and put in some really good work from the two-furlong to the one-furlong marker which won him the race. Ridden with even more patience, better looks likely. (4/1)
1161 Out Like Magic might well have made a race of this but for running into trouble over a furlong out, but in the end she did battle on well. (9/4)
861* Classy Cleo (IRE) tried hard to make it all but, taken on in the lead, probably went too fast too soon, but to give her credit she did battle on. (2/1)
965 Mister Bankes took the leader on and this proved his undoing as he was out on his feet approaching the final furlong. (6/1)
1084 High Money was very edgy here and, once the tempo increased from halfway, dropped tamely away. (5/1)

1392 WILLIAM HILL H'CAP (0-80) (3-Y.O) (Class D)

8-00 (8-00) **1m 4y** £3,817.50 (£1,140.00: £545.00: £247.50) Stalls: Low GOING minus 0.17 sec per fur (GF)

Prev	Horse	Dist	Pos	SP	RR	SF
	Southerly Wind (78) (MrsJRRamsden) **3-9-7** KFallon(7) (hld up: effrt 3f out: rdn to ld ins fnl f: edgd lft & r.o wl)	—	1	$3/1^{1}$	88	49
784^{6}	**Honourable (70)** (JWWatts) **3-8-13** JCarroll(2) (trckd ldrs: rdn to ld wl over 1f out: hdd ins fnl f: r.o)	1¼	2	$4/1^{2}$	78	39
1164^{4}	**Interdream (61)** (RHannon) **3-8-4** KDarley(8) (prom: outpcd 3f out: styd on strly fnl f)	¾	3	$7/1^{3}$	67	28
1009^{5}	**Righty Ho (59)** (PTWalwyn) **3-8-2** SSanders(4) (in tch: styd on u.p fnl 2f: nt pce to chal)	½	4	10/1	64	25
998^{4}	**Blooming Amazing (76)** (JLEyre) **3-9-5** TWilliams(1) (led & sn clr: hdd wl over 1f out: rdn & grad wknd)	2	5	8/1	77	38
	Bally Souza (IRE) (76) (MJohnston) **3-9-5** JWeaver(5) (bhd: effrt 3f out: styd on: no imp)	¾	6	14/1	76	37
1249^{3}	**Night Chorus (70)** (BSRothwell) **3-8-13** MFenton(9) (chsd ldrs: ev ch 2f out: rdn & wknd 1f out)	¾	7	$4/1^{2}$	68	29
977^{4}	**A Breeze (70)** (DMorris) **3-8-13** JReid(6) (lw: hld up & bhd: n.d)	18	8	10/1	32	—
1041^{4}	**Paldost (55)** (MDHammond) **3-7-12** DaleGibson(3) (a bhd: lost tch fnl 3f)	4	9	50/1	9	—

(SP 115.4%) **9 Rn**

1m 46.7 (4.30) CSF £13.57 CT £69.85 TOTE £3.10: £1.50 £2.00 £2.00 (£9.20) Trio £35.00 OWNER Mr M. J. Simmonds (THIRSK) BRED M. J. Simmonds
Southerly Wind looked good here and has obviously progressed from two to three and plenty more will be seen of him. (3/1)
784 Honourable, first time in a handicap, ran well and, by the way he stayed on, further will be appreciated. (4/1: 3/1-9/2)

1164 Interdream always seems to be in the shake up but never quite does enough and leaves the impression that if the key can be found, there is more to come. (7/1)
1009 Righty Ho is a rather weak-looking individual but he did stay on here after looking well beaten. (10/1)
998 Blooming Amazing, back to his front-running tactics here, tried hard, but was well outpointed in the last furlong and a half. (8/1)
Bally Souza (IRE), patiently ridden, got this trip well and should appreciate further. (14/1)

1393 MICK MCCOY MEMORIAL H'CAP (0-70) (3-Y.O+) (Class E)

8-30 (8-34) **1m 4f 8y** £3,223.00 (£964.00: £462.00: £211.00) Stalls: Low GOING minus 0.17 sec per fur (GF)

				SP	RR	SF
1022[7]	**Road Racer (IRE) (56)** (MrsJRRamsden) **4-9-5** KFallon(9) (lw: prom: squeezed thro to ld 1f out: r.o)	—	**1**	11/4[1]	67	34
1162[9]	**Summerhill Special (IRE) (62)** (DWBarker) **6-9-11** TWilliams(7) (b.nr hind: trckd ldrs: hdwy to chal 1f out: kpt on)	1¼	**2**	7/2[2]	71	38
1022[4]	**Sam Rockett (39)** (MissGayKelleway) **4-7-11**(5) RMullen(3) (chsd ldrs: chal 4f out: disp ld wl over 1f out: nt qckn ins fnl f)	3	**3**	5/1[3]	44	11
866[10]	**Kernof (IRE) (51)** (MDHammond) **4-8-11**(3) FLynch(4) (bhd tl styd on wl appr fnl f)	hd	**4**	20/1	56	23
1222[2]	**Junior Ben (IRE) (36)** (MESowersby) **5-7-8**(5) PFessey(5) (led tl hdd 1f out: no ex)	s.h	**5**	13/2	41	8
553[6]	**Passing Strangers (USA) (55)** (PWHarris) **4-9-4** JReid(8) (cl up tl rdn & wknd over 1f out)	4	**6**	9/1	55	22
1036[11]	**Almuhtaram (64)** (GLewis) **5-9-13b** PaulEddery(6) (swtg: bhd: effrt over 3f out: n.d)	1¼	**7**	13/2	62	29
	Dalwhinnie (63) (JWharton) **4-9-12** GDuffield(1) (chsd ldrs tl rdn & wknd over 2f out: btn whn hmpd over 1f out)	4	**8**	16/1	56	23

(SP 112.9%) **8 Rn**

2m 42.9 (8.60) CSF £10.97 CT £39.88 TOTE £3.00: £1.40 £1.80 £1.90 (£4.50) Trio £11.20 OWNER Mr J. E. Swiers (THIRSK) BRED Michael M. Byrne
866* Road Racer (IRE) is honest and stays well and that was all that was needed against this opposition. (11/4)
955 Summerhill Special (IRE) is running well at present but was always second best. (7/2)
1022 Sam Rockett is running well but is just failing to see the trip out at the moment. (5/1)
Kernof (IRE), again without the visor he won with last season, put in an eyecatching run, finishing strongly. (20/1)
1222 Junior Ben (IRE) tried his front-running tactics again, but his lack of a change of gear was exposed in the closing stages. (13/2)
553 Passing Strangers (USA) had his chances but proved disappointing when pressure was applied in the home straight. (9/1: op 6/1)
770 Almuhtaram is a law unto himself and he was not in a cooperative mood on this occasion. (13/2)

1394 RACING AND THOROUGHBRED BREEDING TRAINING BOARD MAIDEN STKS (3-Y.O) (Class D)

9-00 (9-01) **6f** £3,615.00 (£1,095.00: £535.00: £255.00) Stalls: Low GOING minus 0.17 sec per fur (GF)

				SP	RR	SF
	Wellspring (IRE) (DRLoder) **3-8-9** KDarley(6) (w'like: trckd ldrs: led & qcknd over 1f out: all out)	—	**1**	4/1[2]	81	38
	Present Chance (BAMcMahon) **3-9-0** LNewton(5) (hld up: effrt appr fnl f: r.o wl: jst failed)	hd	**2**	25/1	86	43
	Polish Romance (USA) (MRStoute) **3-8-9** JReid(1) (stdd s: swtchd & effrt 2f out: ch 1f out: no ex)	6	**3**	4/7[1]	65	22
1087[3]	**Night Express** (BHanbury) **3-9-0** MRimmer(2) (b: b.nr hind: chsd ldrs: outpcd 2f out: kpt on fnl f)	1	**4**	10/1[3]	67	24
	Balladara (IRE) (RHannon) **3-9-0** SSanders(4) (w'like: s.i.s: drvn along ½-wy: styd on: no imp)	2½	**5**	10/1[3]	60	17
1119[13]	**Sparkling Harry (53)** (MissLCSiddall) **3-8-7b**(7) TSiddall(7) (hld up: effrt on outside 2f out: rdn & n.d)	hd	**6**	100/1	60	17
758[2]	**Juddy** (JohnHarris) **3-9-0** JO'Reilly(3) (led: hung lft, hdd & wknd over 1f out)	2½	**7**	11/1	54	11
1119[8]	**Locksill** (ASmith) **3-9-0** DeanMcKeown(8) (cl up 4f: wknd)	3	**8**	100/1	46?	3

(SP 116.0%) **8 Rn**

1m 18.1 (3.10) CSF £76.45 TOTE £4.00: £1.30 £4.90 £1.10 (£152.80) OWNER Mr E. J. Loder (NEWMARKET) BRED E. J. Loder
Wellspring (IRE) is nothing special to look at, but she has an engine and getting first run made all the difference. (4/1: op 5/2)
Present Chance, having his first outing of the season, was given plenty of time to find his stride and then finished in tremendous style. He looks one to keep in mind. (25/1)
Polish Romance (USA) obviously has problems as she wears a net-muzzle and still took a very strong hold. Once asked the question, the response this time was very disappointing. There is plenty more ability if she can ever learn to settle. (4/7)
1087 Night Express, wearing bandages all round and a tongue-strap, just looked very one-paced. (10/1)
Balladara (IRE) not the best of movers, was very green early on but, given plenty of assistance from the saddle, did pick up a little. (10/1)
Sparkling Harry just wanted to hang left yet again and, continually hitting the rails, was easily picked off. (100/1)

T/Plpt: £137.30 (143.87 Tckts). T/Qdpt: £4.70 (242.85 Tckts) AA

1019-DONCASTER (L-H) (Good, Good to firm patches)

Saturday May 24th

WEATHER: sunny periods WIND: mod across

1395 RACING SCHOOLS FURNITURE FACTORS APPRENTICE H'CAP (0-70) (4-Y.O+) (Class F)

2-20 (2-25) **7f** £2,683.50 (£756.00: £370.50) Stalls: High GOING minus 0.47 sec per fur (F)

				SP	RR	SF
1315[6]	**Allinson's Mate (IRE) (58)** (TDBarron) **9-9-4b** KimberleyHart(2) (lw: in tch: stdy hdwy to ld 1½f out: r.o)	—	**1**	10/1	70	52
579[13]	**Octavia Hill (50)** (PWHarris) **4-8-10b[1]** GMilligan(5) (cl up: led over 2f out tl wl over 1f out: sn outpcd: kpt on wl towards fin)	1	**2**	14/1	60	42
1097[14]	**Genuine John (IRE) (62)** (JParkes) **4-9-8** RHavlin(1) (lw: chsd ldrs: led wl over 1f out: sn hdd & nt qckn)	¾	**3**	12/1	70	52
	Morocco (IRE) (58) (MRChannon) **8-9-4** AEddery(8) (in tch: hdwy 2f out: kpt on: nvr able chal)	¾	**4**	16/1	64	46
1035[8]	**Walk the Beat (64)** (MartynMeade) **7-9-6**(4) JWilkinson(6) (chsd ldrs: rdn over 2f out: kpt on towards fin)	nk	**5**	9/1	70	52
1024[8]	**Oneoftheoldones (39)** (JNorton) **5-7-13** KSked(4) (chsd ldrs: effrt over 2f out: kpt on same pce)	hd	**6**	33/1	44	26
1079*	**Birchwood Sun (55)** (MDods) **7-9-1b** CTeague(7) (bhd tl styd on fnl 2f)	¾	**7**	11/2[2]	59	41
834[5]	**Pointer (58)** (MrsPNDutfield) **5-9-0**(4) JFowle(3) (lw: led over 4f: sn outpcd)	2	**8**	6/1[3]	57	39
1315[8]	**Mu-Arrik (36)** (GROldroyd) **9-7-6v**(4) PBradley(9) (spd to ½-wy)	nk	**9**	50/1	34	16
1269[5]	**Sue Me (IRE) (59)** (DNicholls) **5-9-5** IonaWands(12) (lw: hld up: smooth hdwy over 2f out: wknd wl over 1f out)	1	**10**	7/1	55	37
1289[4]	**Born A Lady (47)** (MrsVAAconley) **4-8-7** SCopp(14) (effrt ½-wy: sn rdn & btn)	1¼	**11**	14/1	40	22
352[4]	**Piquant (64)** (LordHuntingdon) **10-9-2**(8) RLake(10) (cl up 5f: wknd)	1¼	**12**	12/1	54	36
1089[4]	**Great Hall (40)** (PDCundell) **8-7-10**(4) CCogan(15) (lw: b.hind: sn outpcd & bhd)	½	**13**	14/1	29	11
929[6]	**Lillibella (50)** (MrsJRRamsden) **4-8-10** DGriffiths(13) (outpcd fr ½-wy)	1½	**14**	11/1	36	18

977*	**Halmanerror (63)** (MrsJRRamsden) **7-9-9** RMullen(11) (hld up: effrt over 2f out: sn rdn & btn)..........2	**15**	5/1 1	44	26
			(SP 132.4%)		**15 Rn**

1m 25.4 (0.90) CSF £142.02 CT £1,006.59 TOTE £10.50: £3.10 £10.00 £4.30 (£402.20) Trio £500.70; £359.72 to 26/5/97 OWNER Mr D. Courtier (THIRSK) BRED Gay O'Callaghan

LONG HANDICAP Mu-Arrik 7-4

OFFICIAL EXPLANATION Halmanerror: no explanation offered.

1315 Allinson's Mate (IRE) is in tremendous form at present, and this type of race suits him particularly well. (10/1)

Octavia Hill had blinkers on for the first time and they certainly made a difference and, by the look of things, she should stay further. (14/1)

571 Genuine John (IRE) looks really well at the moment and this was a decent effort. (12/1)

Morocco (IRE) put in a fair first effort of the season, and looks in good form. (16/1)

512* Walk the Beat has been in tremendous form on the All-Weather, and he certainly appreciates this faster ground compared with Chester's testing conditions last time. (9/1)

206 Oneoftheoldones ran reasonably, but this trip was probably just too sharp for him. (33/1)

1079* Birchwood Sun is a hard ride and only ran on when it was too late. (11/2)

834 Pointer (6/1: 10/1-5/1)

977* Halmanerror was a disappointing favourite, and connections could offer no explanation for the performance. (5/1)

91+ 78 82 74 81 (81)

1396 E.B.F. ZETLAND MAIDEN STKS (2-Y.O) (Class D)

2-50 (2-51) **6f** £3,640.50 (£1,089.00: £522.00: £238.50) Stalls: High GOING minus 0.47 sec per fur (F)

			SP	RR	SF
	Desert Prince (IRE) (DRLoder) **2-9-0** KDarley(2) (w'like: leggy: scope: hld up: effrt 2f out: qcknd to ld ins fnl f)..........—	**1**	2/5 1	80+	29
	Hayil (USA) (DMorley) **2-9-0** RHills(12) (cmpt: scope: cl up: led after 2f: qcknd 2f out: hdd ins fnl f: r.o)..........½	**2**	9/1 2	79+	28
	Premium Rate (USA) (EALDunlop) **2-9-0** KFallon(6) (w'like: scope: s.i.s: hdwy ½-wy: chsng ldrs & rdn 2f out: eased whn btn ins fnl f)..........2½	**3**	9/1 2	72	21
	Herminius (IRE) (JLDunlop) **2-9-0** PaulEddery(5) (w'like: stdd after s: in tch: hdwy 2f out: kpt on wl)..........2	**4**	11/1	67	16
	Saddlers' Roe (IRE) (BWHills) **2-9-0** MHills(4) (w'like: hld up: pushed along 2f out: r.o towards fin)..........2½	**5**	12/1	60	9
1120 8	**Top Floor (IRE)** (NTinkler) **2-9-0** KimTinkler(9) (led 2f: cl up tl outpcd appr fnl f)..........1	**6**	66/1	57	6
	The Thruster (MajorWRHern) **2-9-0** TSprake(10) (cmpt: scope: hld up & bhd: stdy hdwy 2f out: nvr nr tochal)1	**7**	14/1	55	4
	Dutch Lad (MHTompkins) **2-9-0** DaleGibson(8) (w'like: bit bkwd: bhd: pushed along ½-wy: sme late hdwy) .hd	**8**	66/1	54	3
743 10	**Wait'n'see** (MWEasterby) **2-9-0** TLucas(7) (nvr nr to chal)..........½	**9**	50/1	53	2
	Hogaif (IRE) (JHMGosden) **2-9-0** TQuinn(13) (cmpt: w ldrs 4f: wknd)..........s.h	**10**	10/1 3	53	2
	Gift of Gold (ICampbell) **2-9-0** RPrice(11) (cmpt: bit bkwd: hld up & bhd: effrt ½-wy: n.d)..........2	**11**	66/1	48	—
	On The Mat (JJO'Neill) **2-9-0** RLappin(1) (cmpt: bit bkwd: chsd ldrs: sn pushed along: wknd fnl 3f)..........¾	**12**	66/1	46	—
1120 11	**I'm Tef** (TDEasterby) **2-9-0** CRutter(3) (cl up 4f: sn lost pl)..........2½	**13**	50/1	39	—
			(SP 133.1%)		**13 Rn**

1m 13.14 (2.14) CSF £5.69 TOTE £1.70: £1.50 £2.30 £1.60 (£9.20) Trio £10.90 OWNER Lucayan Stud (NEWMARKET) BRED Tarworth Bloodstock Investments Ltd

STEWARDS ENQUIRY: Easterby fined £2,500 & Lucas susp. 9-18/9/ 97 under Rule 151(ii) (schooling in public). Wait'n'See susp. 30 days

Desert Prince (IRE) came with a big reputation and, despite showing signs of greenness in a messy race, he did it nicely. There would seem to be plenty of improvement to come. (2/5: 1/2-1/3)

Hayil (USA), given a good ride, tried to pinch this but had to admit he had met one just too good. To his credit, he kept trying and has a good attitude. (9/1: 6/1-11/1)

Premium Rate (USA), one of the better lookers in the race, was clueless early on, but then showed plenty and should not be long in finding compensation. (9/1: op 6/1)

Herminius (IRE) gave the impression that this was needed, but still ran well and should now improve. (11/1: 6/1-12/1)

Saddlers' Roe (IRE), given plenty of time to find his stride, finished well and will obviously do better when the longer trips come in. (12/1)

1120 Top Floor (IRE) is improving with experience, and is worth keeping in mind for a modest race or two. (66/1)

The Thruster had a nice educational and will no doubt improve with time and a trip. (14/1)

Dutch Lad took a long time to get going and is going to need further. (66/1)

743 Wait'n'see keeps showing ability without getting into the race and is one to keep an eye on. (50/1)

Hogaif (IRE) (10/1: op 6/1)

1397 MERLIN LAND ROVER H'CAP (0-100) (3-Y.O+) (Class C)

3-20 (3-22) **7f** £6,160.00 (£1,840.00: £880.00: £400.00) Stalls: High GOING minus 0.47 sec per fur (F)

			SP	RR	SF
892 3	**Waypoint (77)** (RCharlton) **4-8-5** TSprake(3) (a cl up: led ins fnl f: rdn out)..........—	**1**	4/1 2	85	49
892 12	**Persian Fayre (82)** (JBerry) **5-8-10** KDarley(1) (lw: led: qcknd after 3f: hdd ins fnl f: rallied)..........hd	**2**	13/2	90	54
	Mawingo (IRE) (82) (GWragg) **4-8-5**(5) GMilligan(7) (outpcd & lost tch after 3f: r.o wl u.p fnl f)..........2	**3**	5/2 1	85	49
1214 7	**Highborn (IRE) (90)** (PSFelgate) **8-9-4** KFallon(2) (lw: a chsng ldrs: effrt 3f out: nt qckn appr fnl f)..........s.h	**4**	13/2	93	57
1214 9	**Almuhimm (USA) (85)** (TDBarron) **5-8-13** RHills(5) (s.i.s: stdy hdwy to chse ldrs 2f out: rdn & sn btn)..........2½	**5**	10/1	82	46
	Pleading (92) (HCandy) **4-9-6** CRutter(4) (in tch: rdn & wl outpcd over 2f out: no imp after)..........1	**6**	8/1	87	51
1160 9	**Hi Nod (100)** (MJCamacho) **7-10-0** TLucas(8) (lw: bhd: outpcd ½-wy: n.d)..........1	**7**	6/1 3	93	57
987 11	**Forest Robin (68)** (MrsJRRamsden) **4-7-5**(5) RMullen(6) (hld up: effrt 3f out: edgd lft & n.d)..........2	**8**	7/1	56	20
			(SP 122.2%)		**8 Rn**

1m 24.62 (0.12) CSF £29.44 CT £72.91 TOTE £4.60: £1.60 £1.40 £1.20 (£12.10) OWNER Mr Ray Richards (BECKHAMPTON) BRED Berkshire Equestrian Services Ltd

LONG HANDICAP Forest Robin 7-9

STEWARDS' ENQUIRY Fallon susp. 2-5/6/97 (failure to ensure best possible placing).

892 Waypoint is in really good form this season but, after looking in command, the line came just in time. (4/1)

Persian Fayre was able to dictate things, and then showed fine determination after being headed. This is by far his best effort of the season. (13/2)

Mawingo (IRE) found this trip too sharp, especially the way in which the race was run, but he finished with a tremendous flourish to show he is particularly well at present. (5/2)

1214 Highborn (IRE) had his chances and kept trying hard, but was always short of toe. (13/2)

Almuhimm (USA) is a hard-pulling sort who needs things to go just right, and this messy event was not for him. (10/1)

Pleading did not show any real spark, and may well have needed this. (8/1)

Hi Nod looked big and well and was trying to win this for the second year running, but he needs a much stronger gallop than was set here. (6/1: op 4/1)

1398 NAPOLEONS RACING H'CAP (0-85) (3-Y.O+) (Class D)

3-50 (3-50) **1m 4f** £4,386.00 (£1,308.00: £624.00: £282.00) Stalls: Low GOING minus 0.30 sec per fur (GF)

Form	Horse	Dist	Pos	SP	RR	SF
982[7]	**Veridian (68)** (PWHarris) **4-9-0** KFallon(1) (hld up: hdwy 4f out: led 1½f out: r.o wl u.p)	—	**1**	8/1	84	66
984[3]	**Ledgendry Line (68)** (MrsMReveley) **4-9-0** ACulhane(6) (lw: hld up: shkn up 4f out: r.o fnl 2f: nrst fin)	2	**2**	7/2[3]	81	63
1208[3]	**Voila Premiere (IRE) (68)** (MHTompkins) **5-9-0** TQuinn(2) (lw: cl up: led over 4f out: rdn & qcknd over 2f out: hdd 1½f out: sn btn)	7	**3**	15/8[1]	72	54
1145[8]	**Augustan (56)** (SGollings) **6-8-2**ow1 PaulEddery(3) (hld up: effrt 4f out: sn outpcd: kpt on fnl 2f: nvr able to chal)	1¼	**4**	11/2	58	39
1157[4]	**Temptress (72)** (JLHarris) **4-9-4** KDarley(7) (lw: cl up: chal 4f out: rdn & btn wl over 1f out)	nk	**5**	100/30[2]	74	56
962[11]	**Classic Find (USA) (82)** (ICampbell) **4-10-0** RPrice(4) (b: drvn along & hdwy 7f out: sn prom: outpcd fnl 3f)	15	**6**	14/1	64	46
151[9]	**Spa Lane (60)** (MPBielby) **4-8-3**(3)ow2 RHavlin(5) (led tl hdd over 4f out: wknd fnl 3f)	½	**7**	14/1	41	21
				(SP 119.9%)		**7 Rn**

2m 31.17 (1.17) CSF £34.83 TOTE £8.40: £3.30 £2.90 (£20.30) OWNER Mrs P. W. Harris (BERKHAMSTED) BRED A. L. Penfold and H. Lascelles

OFFICIAL EXPLANATION **Veridian: regarding the improvement in form, the trainer stated that the gelding was suited by today's shorter trip and faster ground.**

Veridian has run poorly previously this season, mostly on ground too soft and, in this event which finished up a sprint, he always had the edge for pace. (8/1: 6/1-9/1)

984 Ledgendry Line, held up, had next to no chance the way the race was run and did remarkably well to finish so close. (7/2)

1208 Voila Premiere (IRE) was always well enough placed if good enough but, when the tempo increased dramatically in the home straight, he was tapped for toe in the last furlong and a half. Surely a stronger pace is needed for him. (15/8)

1145 Augustan needed a stronger pace than was set here, and was completely tapped for speed when the tempo increased in the home straight. (11/2)

1157 Temptress would have been better-suited by more forceful tactics, and was well outpaced in the closing stages. (100/30)

680 Classic Find (USA) looks to have problems at present. (14/1)

1399 ROSEHILL CONDITIONS STKS (3-Y.O) (Class B)

4-20 (4-21) **1m 2f 60y** £8,109.40 (£3,004.60: £1,444.80: £594.00: £239.50: £97.70) Stalls: Low GOING minus 0.30 sec per fur (GF)

Form	Horse	Dist	Pos	SP	RR	SF
741[2]	**Falak (USA) (104)** (MajorWRHern) **3-9-2** KFallon(3) (lw: a.p: led wl over 1f out: styd on strly towards fin)	—	**1**	11/2	114	82
	Stowaway (SbinSuroor) **3-9-0** ACulhane(4) (dwlt: hdwy 4f out: chal ins fnl f: no ex towards fin)	½	**2**	8/1	111	79
1159[6]	**Apprehension** (DRLoder) **3-9-0** KDarley(1) (lw: led tl hdd wl over 1f out: kpt on same pce)	3½	**3**	11/4[1]	106	74
847*	**Lawahik** (DMorley) **3-9-0** RHills(2) (trckd ldrs: hdwy to chal 2f out: rdn & btn appr fnl f)	1½	**4**	3/1[2]	103	71
	Passi d'Orlando (IRE) (JLDunlop) **3-9-4** JWeaver(9) (bhd tl styd on fnl 3f: nvr rchd ldrs)	2½	**5**	25/1	104	72
	Isle of Man (USA) (PFICole) **3-8-11** TQuinn(10) (cl up tl rdn & wknd 2f out)	1	**6**	5/1[3]	95	63
1105*	**Salamah** (RCharlton) **3-9-0** TSprake(6) (outpcd & bhd 5f out: n.d)	5	**7**	9/1	90	58
1023*	**Lord Eurolink (IRE)** (JLDunlop) **3-9-0** PaulEddery(5) (chsd ldrs: hrd rdn over 2f out: wknd over 1f out)	½	**8**	10/1	89	57
	Attitude (HCandy) **3-9-0** CRutter(7) (outpcd & bhd fnl 5f)	½	**9**	25/1	89	57
829[6]	**Greenaway Bay (USA)** (GWragg) **3-9-0** MHills(8) (lw: hld up: effrt 4f out: sn rdn & btn)	½	**10**	14/1	88	56
				(SP 128.3%)		**10 Rn**

2m 7.02 (-0.78) CSF £49.44 TOTE £5.20: £1.90 £3.00 £1.60 (£27.30) Trio £31.30 OWNER Mr Hamdan Al Maktoum (LAMBOURN) BRED Shadwell Farm Inc

741 Falak (USA) is not very big but he does stay well, and has a heart for the game which will always stand him in good stead. This could well turn out to be a useful event. (11/2)

Stowaway, having only his second run of his career, had to work hard to get into contention, only to find the struggle beyond him late on. However, he should come on for the experience. (8/1: 6/1-9/1)

1159 Apprehension took the eye in the paddock and tried to gallop his rivals into the ground, but was made to look one-paced in the closing stages. (11/4: 9/4-7/2)

847* Lawahik, who won what looked like a decent race last time, was a shade disappointing, but the ground was certainly faster. (3/1)

Passi d'Orlando (IRE) has done most of his racing on testing ground in Italy and, despite staying on well, things were always happening too quickly. (25/1)

Isle of Man (USA) was disappointing, dropping away when the race began in earnest in the last two-and-a-half furlongs but, to give him the benefit of the doubt, it was his first outing of the season. (5/1)

1105* Salamah was never going the pace, and turned in a disappointing effort. (9/1)

1400 HAREWOOD RATED STKS H'CAP (0-95) (4-Y.O+) (Class C)

4-50 (4-50) **2m 110y** £4,588.20 (£1,693.80: £809.40: £327.00: £126.00: £45.60) Stalls: High GOING minus 0.30 sec per fur (GF)

Form	Horse	Dist	Pos	SP	RR	SF
1224[7]	**Embryonic (IRE) (76)** (MartinTodhunter) **5-8-12** KFallon(3) (lw: hld up: hdwy to ld over 2f out: r.o u.p)	—	**1**	11/4[2]	87	38
1162*	**Turnpole (IRE) (74)** (MrsMReveley) **6-8-10** ACulhane(4) (trckd ldrs: chal over 2f out: sn rdn & outpcd: kpt on towards fin)	1¼	**2**	6/4[1]	84	35
738[15]	**Go Britannia (87)** (DRLoder) **4-9-7** KDarley(6) (hld up: effrt over 3f out: kpt on u.p: nrst fin)	nk	**3**	9/1	97	46
969[4]	**Castle Courageous (84)** (LadyHerries) **10-9-6** MHills(1) (b: trckd ldrs: led over 4f out tl over 2f out: sn outpcd)	7	**4**	11/1	87	38
1288[2]	**Etterby Park (USA) (80)** (MJohnston) **4-9-0** RHills(2) (chsd ldr: chal 5f out: wknd fnl 2f)	nk	**5**	9/2[3]	82	31
982[9]	**Shirley Sue (77)** (MJohnston) **4-8-11** JWeaver(5) (lw: led tl hdd over 4f out: sn lost pl)	1½	**6**	13/2	78	27
				(SP 116.5%)		**6 Rn**

3m 37.26 (7.26) CSF £7.01 TOTE £3.90: £1.60 £1.50 (£3.70) OWNER Mrs D. Miller (ULVERSTON) BRED Tsarina Stud

WEIGHT FOR AGE 4yo-2lb

1224 Embryonic (IRE) had his mind made up for him on this occasion and did it well, responding to pressure. (11/4)

1162* Turnpole (IRE) had his chances and kept trying hard, but always found the winner too strong. (6/4)

Go Britannia, held up presumably to get this big step-up in trip, stayed on despite carrying his head at an angle. (9/1)

969 Castle Courageous knows plenty about the game and, although running reasonably, he is not anything like the force he was. (11/1: 8/1-12/1)

1288 Etterby Park (USA) has had some very hard races already this season and, on this occasion, he was not up to scratch. (9/2)

982 Shirley Sue, normally a most game and consistent sort, just did not look in the mood here. (13/2)

1401 RIFLE BUTTS MEDIAN AUCTION MAIDEN STKS (3-Y.O) (Class E)
5-20 (5-22) **5f** £2,810.25 (£837.00: £398.50: £179.25) Stalls: High GOING minus 0.47 sec per fur (F)

				SP	RR	SF
	Alamode (JGSmyth-Osbourne) **3-8-9** TSprake(2) (str: scope: lw: trckd ldrs gng wl: shkn up to ld ins fnl f: r.o)	—	**1**	$8/1^{3}$	54+	30
1237^{9}	**Millpet** (RGuest) **3-8-9** KFallon(7) (bhd: hdwy to chal appr fnl f: kpt on: nt pce of wnr)	1¾	**2**	$3/1^{1}$	48	24
1119^{15}	**Magic Fizz (53)** (TJEtherington) **3-9-0** KDarley(5) (lw: mde most tl hdd ins fnl f: no ex)	nk	**3**	$3/1^{1}$	52	28
1151^{5}	**Avanti Blue** (KMcAuliffe) **3-9-0b¹** JWeaver(3) (lw: chsd ldrs tl wknd appr fnl f)	4	**4**	$9/2^{2}$	40	16
1167^{8}	**Miss Peregrine** (RGuest) **3-8-9** PBloomfield(6) (outpcd & bhd tl sme late hdwy)	2½	**5**	$8/1^{3}$	27	3
1119^{17}	**Ioulios** (JEBanks) **3-9-0** PaulEddery(1) (w ldrs tl wknd over 1f out)	1½	**6**	$8/1^{3}$	27	3
1119^{12}	**Just Typical** (NTinkler) **3-8-9** KimTinkler(4) (prom: rdn 2f out: no imp after)	s.h	**7**	9/1	22	—
1119^{19}	**Astral Crown (IRE)** (JBerry) **3-8-2**(7) CLowther(8) (b.hind: disp ld to ½-wy: wknd over 1f out)	2	**8**	14/1	15	—
				(SP 118.2%)	**8 Rn**	

59.74 secs (1.34) CSF £30.43 TOTE £11.90: £2.70 £1.50 £1.10 (£19.60) OWNER Mrs M V Dawes & Partners (TOWCESTER) BRED T. H. Rossiter

IN-FOCUS: **This was Julian Smyth-Osbourne's first winner.**

Alamode, a well-made newcomer, looked the pick of the bunch and won this modest race particularly well. Better looks likely. (8/1: 9/2-9/1)
Millpet had to work hard to get into it, and was then outpointed late on. (3/1)
855 Magic Fizz went much better on this faster ground, but his limitations were exposed late on. (3/1)
1151 Avanti Blue had the blinkers on for the first time, but they were not much help. (9/2)
882 Miss Peregrine found this trip far too sharp and only got going when it was all over. (8/1: 5/1-9/1)
Ioulios finished within sight of the leaders for the first time, but there is still plenty more needed. (8/1: op 5/1)
Just Typical (9/1: op 5/1)

T/Plpt: £395.90 (58.63 Tckts). T/Qdpt: £18.90 (73.09 Tckts) AA

1376-HAYDOCK (L-H) (Good to soft, Soft patches)
Saturday May 24th
WEATHER: sunny & bright WIND: slight half behind

1402 BE FRIENDLY H'CAP (0-90) (3-Y.O+) (Class C)
2-00 (2-00) **5f** £5,322.50 (£1,610.00: £785.00: £372.50) Stalls: Low GOING minus 0.03 sec per fur (G)

				SP	RR	SF
	Tedburrow (88) (EJAlston) **5-10-0** ACulhane(1) (bit bkwd: a.p: led over 1f out: drvn out)	—	**1**	16/1	100	77
1269^{8}	**Ansellman (80)** (JBerry) **7-9-6b** GCarter(6) (b: a.p: kpt on u.p ins fnl f: no ch w wnr)	2	**2**	10/1	86	63
1227^{6}	**Bee Health Boy (66)** (MWEasterby) **4-8-1b**(5) GParkin(4) (lw: a chsng ldrs: swtchd rt & r.o wl ins fnl f)	nk	**3**	10/1	71	48
1098*	**First Maite (79)** (SRBowring) **4-9-5b** SWebster(3) (lw: s.i.s: rdn ½-wy: hdwy wl over 1f out: nrst fin)	1¾	**4**	$4/1^{2}$	78	55
1223^{2}	**Broadstairs Beauty (IRE) (73)** (DShaw) **7-8-13b** DHolland(7) (b: lw: led after 1f tl hdd over 1f out: sn rdn: one pce)	s.h	**5**	$5/1^{3}$	72	49
972^{2}	**Lord High Admiral (CAN) (83)** (MJHeaton-Ellis) **9-9-9** JCarroll(9) (lw: racd alone: a.w ldrs: rdn over 1f out: sn btn)	nk	**6**	$11/4^{1}$	81	58
1223^{8}	**U-No-Harry (IRE) (68)** (RHollinshead) **4-8-5**(3) FLynch(2) (bit bkwd: dwlt: a outpcd)	1¾	**7**	20/1	60	37
1021^{6}	**Bajan Rose (81)** (MBlanshard) **5-9-7** JQuinn(10) (lw: s.i.s: a outpcd: t.o)	7	**8**	14/1	51	28
1080^{7}	**Sing With the Band (62)** (BAMcMahon) **6-7-9b**¹(7)ow6 SRighton(5) (lw: gd spd 3f: sn wknd: t.o)	hd	**9**	25/1	32	3
1037^{9}	**Lord Sky (56)** (ABailey) **6-7-10** DWright(8) (b: led 1f: rdn & wknd ½-wy: sn bhd: t.o)	7	**10**	12/1	3	—
				(SP 110.4%)	**10 Rn**	

61.38 secs (1.88) CSF £141.70 CT £1,486.02 TOTE £17.10: £3.90 £2.90 £2.40 (£57.00) Trio £688.30; £339.31 to 26/5/97 OWNER Mr Philip Davies (PRESTON) BRED Lady Matthews

LONG HANDICAP Sing With the Band 7-4 Lord Sky 7-8

Tedburrow did not look fully wound up for this first run since changing stables, but he delivered his challenge up the inside rail to nose ahead below the distance, and proved much the stronger on the run to the line. (16/1)
905 Ansellman was only a neck behind the winner when they last clashed in the Autumn, and he had a 10lb pull in the weights this time, but he was unable to summon the speed to mount a serious challenge. (10/1)
1227 Bee Health Boy finds this minimum trip just that bit too sharp for him and, though he needed to be switched to obtain a clear run inside the final furlong, he was beaten on merit. (10/1)
1098* First Maite missed the beat at the start and was at full stretch all the way, so it says much that he was able to finish as close as he did. (4/1)
972 Lord High Admiral (CAN), winner of this race twice in the past, ploughed a lone furrow up the centre of the track but he was never able to gain control on ground that was more lively than he needs, and his measure had been taken approaching the final furlong. (11/4)

1403 LEAHURST SANDY LANE RATED STKS H'CAP (0-110) (Listed) (3-Y.O+) (Class A)
2-30 (2-30) **6f** £12,323.60 (£4,612.40: £2,256.20: £971.00: £435.50: £221.30) Stalls: Low GOING minus 0.03 sec per fur (G)

				SP	RR	SF
1212*	**Tomba (109)** (BJMeehan) **3-9-7** DeanMcKeown(2) (lw: a.p: rdn to ld ins fnl f: r.o wl)	—	**1**	$4/1^{2}$	115	66
980^{3}	**Man Howa (IRE) (99)** (LMCumani) **3-8-11** OUrbina(4) (lw: chsd ldr: led 2f out tl hdd & no ex ins fnl f)	1¼	**2**	$13/8^{1}$	102	53
1112^{4}	**Connemara (IRE) (100)** (CADwyer) **3-8-12** DHarrison(1) (hld up & plld hrd: effrt & rdn over 1f out: r.o wl)	nk	**3**	14/1	102	53
1216^{3}	**Granny's Pet (102)** (PFICole) **3-9-0** JQuinn(5) (lw: trckd ldrs: rdn & nt clr run over 1f out: r.o wl towards fin)	½	**4**	$5/1^{3}$	103	54
745^{5}	**Young Bigwig (IRE) (95)** (JBerry) **3-8-7** PRoberts(6) (lw: led 4f: rdn over 1f out: unable qckn)	½	**5**	12/1	94	45
1254^{5}	**Myrmidon (95)** (MrsLStubbs) **3-8-7** ACulhane(3) (hld up: hdwy on outside over 2f out: rdn & outpcd appr fnl f)	2½	**6**	9/1	88	39
1212^{4}	**Johnny Staccato (95)** (JMPEustace) **3-8-7** JCarroll(7) (lw: prom 4f: sn drvn along & outpcd)	2½	**7**	7/1	81	32
				(SP 111.6%)	**7 Rn**	

1m 14.3 (2.60) CSF £9.45 TOTE £4.00: £2.40 £1.70 (£2.50) OWNER Mr J. R. Good (UPPER LAMBOURN) BRED Mrs P. Good

LONG HANDICAP Myrmidon 8-6

1212* Tomba has improved out of all recognition this term, and showed here that he does not need it hock deep to produce his best. He earned himself a day out at Royal Ascot with a choice of engagements, namely the Cork & Orrery Stakes or a step-up to seven furlongs for the Jersey Stakes. (4/1)

980 Man Howa (IRE) enjoyed a 3lb pull in the weights with the winner for a narrow defeat over course and distance earlier in the month but, once again, that rival proved his master as the duel to the finish developed. (13/8: 9/4-6/4)
1112 Connemara (IRE) is not giving herself a chance to truly get this trip because she refuses to settle, but she still produced a promising performance, and showed she retains all her ability. (14/1)
1216 Granny's Pet, not the most impressive of movers in his slower paces, was making a return to sprinting. Although staying just off the pace, he was denied a clear run more than once inside the distance, otherwise he may have given the winner something to think about. He really deserves a change of fortune. (5/1)
745 Young Bigwig (IRE) has earned the right to take his chance in such a hot handicap, but he adopted more forceful tactics and only succeeded in beating himself. He must not be written off just yet. (12/1: op 8/1)
1254 Myrmidon, whose previous outings this season have all been at the minimum trip, did his best to mount a challenge entering the final quarter-mile, but he was soon hard at work and had to admit the task beyond him. (9/1)

1404 TOTE CREDIT SILVER BOWL H'CAP (0-110) (3-Y.O) (Class B)

3-00 (3-02) **1m 30y** £21,202.50 (£6,420.00: £3,135.00: £1,492.50) Stalls: Low GOING minus 0.03 sec per fur (G)

				SP	RR	SF
1041*	**Alezal (90)** (WJarvis) **3-9-1** SSanders(6) (lw: mde all: qcknd clr over 1f out: comf)	—	**1**	5/2[1]	100+	44
958[6]	**Future Perfect (85)** (PFICole) **3-8-10** JQuinn(5) (lw: stdd s: plld hrd: hld up: hdwy & swtchd lft over 1f out: nt clr run: r.o wl nr fin)	2½	**2**	5/1	90	34
1146[10]	**Caviar Royale (IRE) (96)** (TDBarron) **3-9-7** JCarroll(4) (hld up: hdwy 2f out: rdn & drifted lft appr fnl f: unable qckn)	nk	**3**	20/1	101	45
1175*	**Out of Sight (IRE) (79)** (BAMcMahon) **3-8-4** LNewton(2) (chsd wnr: ev ch over 1f out: sn rdn: one pce)	2	**4**	11/2	80	24
*1155**	**Sky Commander (USA) (88)** (MRStoute) **3-8-13** DHarrison(1) (lw: hld up: hdwy 3f out: btn whn hmpd over 1f out)	½	**5**	9/2[3]	88	32
853*	**Amyas (IRE) (95)** (BWHills) **3-9-6** DHolland(3) (lw: prom: pushed along over 3f out: outpcd fnl 2f)	2	**6**	3/1[2]	91	35
				(SP 108.6%)		**6 Rn**

1m 45.86 (5.26) CSF £12.86 TOTE £3.10: £1.90 £2.70 (£10.00) OWNER Mr Howard Spooner (NEWMARKET) BRED Godolphin Management Co Ltd
1041* Alezal had plenty on his plate in this first handicap but he decided to attack from the front and, pinching a valuable couple of lengths when stepping-up the pace below the distance, won very much as he pleased. The Britannia Handicap on the opening day could be his Royal Ascot target. (5/2)
958 Future Perfect, settled in the rear, had a nightmare run when trying to deliver his challenge inside the distance, but he may have caused most of the trouble himself and, in the circumstances, was never in a position to hold out much hope for his followers. He deserves a chance to show his true worth. (5/1)
1175* Out of Sight (IRE) caused quite an upset when successful at York, but he looked to perform best when produced from off the pace. He had a bit too much use made of him here, and was found wanting when the battle to the line got under way. (11/2)
1155* Sky Commander (USA) found this opposition much stronger than he had met in maiden events, and the ever-drying ground was probably not as testing as he requires. He was beginning to back-pedal when the runner-up took his ground approaching the final furlong. (9/2)
853* Amyas (IRE) has done all his winning when ridden with restraint, but he pushed the pace this time, and was in trouble passing the quarter-mile marker. (3/1)

1405 MOBBERLEY MAIDEN STKS (3-Y.O) (Class D)

3-30 (3-32) **1m 2f 120y** £3,615.00 (£1,095.00: £535.00: £255.00) Stalls: High GOING minus 0.03 sec per fur (G)

				SP	RR	SF
445[3]	**Heritage** (JHMGosden) **3-9-0** JCarroll(3) (mde all: pushed clr wl over 1f out: unchal)	—	**1**	1/2[1]	77++	46
	Vrennan (JRFanshawe) **3-8-9** DHarrison(1) (lengthy: unf: hld up: hdwy to chse wnr over 2f out: no imp)	6	**2**	6/1[3]	63	32
992[9]	**Zibeth** (LMCumani) **3-8-9** OUrbina(4) (prom: ev ch & rdn 3f out: grad wknd & eased)	13	**3**	4/1[2]	43	12
1130[10]	**San Glamore Melody (FR)** (JHMGosden) **3-9-0** JLowe(2) (bit bkwd: chsd wnr over 4f: sn lost tch)	4	**4**	16/1	42	11
1130[11]	**Northern Maestro** (MrsMReveley) **3-9-0** DeanMcKeown(5) (bit bkwd: s.i.s: hld up: a bhd: t.o fnl 3f)	14	**5**	11/1	21	—
				(SP 115.2%)		**5 Rn**

2m 17.99 (6.49) CSF £4.12 TOTE £1.50: £1.10 £2.40 (£2.70) OWNER Highclere Thoroughbred Racing Ltd (NEWMARKET) BRED Mrs C. R. Philipson
445 Heritage, faced with a simple task to open his account, was allowed to bowl along from the start, and did not need to get serious to coast home at his leisure. (1/2)
Vrennan, a lengthy, unfurnished filly with a bit about her, failed to get in a blow against a more experienced winner, but she will have learnt a lot and can be expected to improve on this in the near future. (6/1)
Zibeth should have been suited by this longer trip, and she promised to make a race of it when joining issue three furlongs out, but she has probably not quite come to herself as yet, and was given as easy time as possible when all chance had gone. (4/1)

1406 BELLCHARM VAUXHALL MAIDEN STKS (3-Y.O+) (Class D)

4-00 (4-00) **7f 30y** £3,468.75 (£1,050.00: £512.50: £243.75) Stalls: Low GOING minus 0.03 sec per fur (G)

				SP	RR	SF
	Sweet Contralto (DRLoder) **3-8-8** DRMcCabe(2) (lt-f: scope: trckd ldrs: hdwy 2f out: squeezed thro to ld wl ins fnl f)	—	**1**	8/1	85	59
	Geimhriuil (IRE) (83) (LMCumani) **3-8-13** OUrbina(3) (w'like: scope: hld up: hdwy 3f out: led 2f out tl hrd rdn & hdd wl ins fnl f: sn btn)	1¼	**2**	13/8[2]	87	61
899[2]	**Look Who's Calling (IRE) (73)** (BAMcMahon) **4-9-10** LNewton(4) (led 2f: ev ch & rdn 2f out: outpcd appr fnl f)	8	**3**	14/1	69	54
	Furnish (BWHills) **3-8-8** DHolland(1) (bit bkwd: led after 2f to 2f out: sn rdn & wknd)	3½	**4**	11/8[1]	56	30
	Swift Sovereign (JHMGosden) **3-8-13** JCarroll(5) (lt-f: unf: a bhd & outpcd: rdn 3f out: no imp)	½	**5**	7/1[3]	60?	34
				(SP 110.5%)		**5 Rn**

1m 30.75 (2.75) CSF £19.69 TOTE £10.20: £3.30 £1.40 (£20.80) OWNER Mr S. Frisby (NEWMARKET) BRED Patrick Eddery Ltd
WEIGHT FOR AGE 3yo-11lb
OFFICIAL EXPLANATION Furnish: no explanation offered.
Sweet Contralto, a May foal who is a sister to Group Three winner Alriffa, had to show her true grit when coming between the runner-up and the rails, for she was tightened-up two hundred yards out, but she stuck her head out and forced her way through to win going away. Still far from the finished article, she looks to have a future. (8/1)
Geimhriuil (IRE), who raced in Ireland in his first season, looked well in control when forging ahead two furlongs out, but he wandered about when pressured inside the final furlong, and may have been more in need of the run than the winner. He is a strongly-made colt and should certainly win races. (13/8)

899 Look Who's Calling (IRE), in the firing-line from the start, was beginning to feel the pinch entering the final quarter-mile, and found his younger rivals too smart for him. (14/1)
Furnish pitted against top-class opposition in both her outings as a juvenile, gave the impression that she had not come to herself as yet this year and, though she was allowed to bowl along, she did not put up much resistance when taken on two furlongs out. She was wisely not knocked about when her measure had been taken. (11/8)
Swift Sovereign, a lightly-made gelded son of Petong, is closely related to several useful winners. Taken off his legs in the early exchanges, he was given a couple of reminders three out but, failing to pick up at all, was always the back marker. (7/1)

68+ 54 65 78

1407 E.B.F. ST HELENS MAIDEN STKS (2-Y.O F) (Class D) (66)
4-30 (4-31) **5f** £3,473.50 (£1,048.00: £509.00: £239.50) Stalls: Low GOING minus 0.03 sec per fur (G)

				SP	RR	SF
	Sea Magic (IRE) (BWHills) **2-8-11** DHolland(2) (lengthy: scope: bit bkwd: dwlt: hdwy 2f out: led wl ins fnl f: rn green)	—	**1**	2/1[2]	76	16
	Miss Dangerous (MRChannon) **2-8-11** JCarroll(1) (unf: bit bkwd: led: rdn wl over 1f out: hdd fnl 100y)	½	**2**	9/4[3]	74	14
954[3]	**Llanasa** (JBerry) **2-8-11** GCarter(4) (chsd ldr: ev ch fr 2f out: rdn & btn whn n.m.r ins fnl f)	3	**3**	11/8[1]	65	5

(SP 106.2%) **3 Rn**

64.17 secs (4.67) CSF £5.53 TOTE £2.50: (£3.90) OWNER Mr Ray Richards (LAMBOURN) BRED Jim O'Hara and Christian Healy
Sea Magic (IRE), the only one who looks as though she can improve, did not catch the eye striding to post. Sluggish as the stalls opened, she proved the stronger in the battle to the line, despite showing signs of greenness. (2/1)
Miss Dangerous, a late foal who looks to need time, did her best to make all but she had been collared a hundred yards out, and had little more to give. (9/4)
954 Llanasa is not much to look at but she did have previous experience, though she failed to put that to good use and, at this stage of her career, she looks very moderate. (11/8: op evens)

1408 SHEVINGTON H'CAP (0-80) (4-Y.O+) (Class D)
5-05 (5-05) **1m 6f** £3,582.50 (£1,085.00: £530.00: £252.50) Stalls: Low GOING minus 0.03 sec per fur (G)

				SP	RR	SF
1215[3]	**Express Gift (52)** (MrsMReveley) **8-8-6** DHarrison(8) (hld up: hdwy on outside 3f out: styd on strly to ld wl ins fnl f)	—	**1**	100/30[1]	62	43
1145[6]	**Swan Hunter (67)** (DJSCosgrove) **4-9-7** GCarter(7) (hld up: hdwy over 2f out: ev ch ins fnl f: r.o)	nk	**2**	11/1	77	58
	General Mouktar (56) (MCPipe) **7-8-10** DHolland(9) (hld up in rr: gd hdwy 3f out: styd on u.p fnl f)	hd	**3**	8/1	66	47
419[3]	**Secret Service (IRE) (70)** (CWThornton) **5-9-10** DeanMcKeown(3) (lw: chsd ldrs: hdwy to ld over 2f out: hrd rdn & hdd wl ins fnl f)	hd	**4**	6/1[3]	79	60
1162[8]	**Turgenev (IRE) (66)** (RBastiman) **8-9-1b(5)** HBastiman(2) (chsd ldrs: rdn over 2f out: styd on same pce)	3½	**5**	9/2[2]	71	52
613[7]	**Compass Pointer (58)** (JMPEustace) **4-8-12** DRMcCabe(4) (plld hrd: hld up: hdwy 3f out: rdn & wknd wl over 1f out)	5	**6**	20/1	58	39
	Salska (56) (AStreeter) **6-8-5(5)** GParkin(10) (bit bkwd: plld hrd: hld up: hdwy 8f out: rdn & btn 3f out: t.o)	12	**7**	6/1[3]	42	23
1106[5]	**Urgent Reply (USA) (67)** (CADwyer) **4-9-7** JCarroll(1) (b.off hind: led 10f: rdn & wknd over 2f out: t.o)	1¾	**8**	14/1	51	32
	So Keen (52) (ABailey) **4-8-6** SSanders(5) (bkwd: chsd ldr: led 4f out tl over 2f out: sn rdn & wknd: t.o)	9	**9**	25/1	26	7
1036[W]	**Dancing Cavalier (67)** (RHollinshead) **4-9-4(3)** FLynch(6) (lost pl after 4f: n.d afterwards: t.o)	4	**10**	7/1	36	17

(SP 117.0%) **10 Rn**

3m 6.15 (7.95) CSF £37.76 CT £249.91 TOTE £4.20: £1.80 £2.70 £2.30 (£40.40) Trio £197.50 OWNER M W Horner, H Young, and D S Arnold (SALTBURN) BRED H. Young
1215 Express Gift, winning for the first time at such an extended trip, timed his run to perfection and showed the right battling qualities when they were needed in the hectic all-out duel to the line. (100/30)
1145 Swan Hunter, a peculiar mover who does not seem to extend himself to the full, produced a determined challenge inside the last furlong, but the concession of 15lb swayed the balance against him in the dying strides. (11/1)
General Mouktar has won at extended trips over hurdles, but he has not succeeded at beyond twelve furlongs on the Flat. Delaying his challenge, he was little more than a stride down at the finish, and is certainly capable of winning again when the mood takes him. (8/1)
419 Secret Service (IRE) kicked on over two furlongs out and tried to slip his field, but the challenges came in thick and fast and, with top weight taking its toll, he was forced to give best nearing the finish. Another success is long overdue. (6/1)
982* Turgenev (IRE) is not an ideal ride for an apprentice because he knows too much about the game, and lack of strength from the saddle played a big part in proceedings in the latter stages. (9/2: op 3/1)
613 Compass Pointer took a very strong hold when restrained in the rear and, though he did close up to put himself in with a shout two furlongs out, he was a spent force when a final effort was called for. (20/1)
Salska (6/1: op 10/1)

T/Plpt: £468.10 (38.23 Tckts). T/Qdpt: £36.00 (20.58 Tckts) IM

0985-KEMPTON (R-H) (Good)
Saturday May 24th
WEATHER: sunny WIND: slight half against

1409 CALIFORNIAN MAIDEN STKS (I) (3-Y.O) (Class D)
2-05 (2-09) **1m (Jubilee)** £2,997.50 (£905.00: £440.00: £207.50) Stalls: High GOING minus 0.21 sec per fur (GF)

				SP	RR	SF
727[8]	**Marie Dora (FR)** (IABalding) **3-8-9** SWhitworth(4) (a.p: led over 2f out: rdn out)	—	**1**	11/2[2]	82	49
	Mount Holly (USA) (JHMGosden) **3-9-0** GHind(7) (hdwy over 4f out: ev ch over 2f out: chsd wnr over 1f out: unable qckn)	5	**2**	11/2[2]	77	44
	Reward (PFICole) **3-9-0** DaneO'Neill(1) (wl grwn: led over 5f: hrd rdn over 1f out: one pce)	1¼	**3**	10/1	75	42
	Massyar Seventeen (HJCollingridge) **3-9-0** MRimmer(8) (w'like: bit bkwd: rdn & hdwy over 2f out: one pce)	4	**4**	33/1	67	34
	Grand Ovation (IRE) (BHanbury) **3-9-0** WRyan(3) (b: unf: scope: lw: dwlt: rdn over 2f out: hdwy over 1f out: nvr nrr)	1½	**5**	7/1[3]	64	31
	Loganlea (IRE) (WJMusson) **3-8-9** JStack(2) (nvr nr to chal: bttr for r)	hd	**6**	33/1	58	25
1297[15]	**Crescent's Whisper (IRE)** (BHanbury) **3-9-0** JTate(5) (bit bkwd: prom 3f)	1¾	**7**	33/1	60	27
	Aurora Bay (IRE) (MBell) **3-8-9** MFenton(9) (b.off hind: lengthy: bit bkwd: rdn over 3f out: sme hdwy over 1f out: sn wknd)	4	**8**	16/1	47	14
1006[8]	**Wontcostalotbut** (MJWilkinson) **3-8-9** NAdams(12) (a bhd)	1	**9**	50/1	45	12

				SP	RR	SF
	Colour Key (USA) (DRCElsworth) **3-9-0** GDuffield(11) (a bhd)	nk	**10**	33/1	49	16
	Enthrone (USA) (JHMGosden) **3-8-9** AMcGlone(13) (unf: bit bkwd: prom over 4f)	7	**11**	7/1[3]	30	—
991[14]	**Polished Steel (IRE)** (LadyHerries) **3-9-0b[1]** WJO'Connor(6) (chsd ldr 5f)	7	**12**	33/1	21	—
	Fatal Baraari (MRStoute) **3-9-0** RCochrane(10) (Withdrawn not under Starter's orders: ref to ent stalls)		**W**	11/4[1]	—	—
				(SP 114.1%)		**12 Rn**

1m 40.32 (2.62) CSF £15.75 TOTE £4.90: £1.30 £1.40 £1.90 (£8.80) Trio £19.80 OWNER Lord Roborough (KINGSCLERE) BRED Ecurie Bader
Marie Dora (FR) left her initial run well behind, and was ridden along to put daylight between herself and her rivals. (11/2)
Mount Holly (USA) may not be that big, but what there is of him is strongly-made. Racing with his tongue tied down, he was one of three almost in line before the winner asserted. (11/2: 7/2-6/1)
Reward, a big individual, took the field along but, once collared, could only keep on at the same pace. (10/1: op 7/2)
Massyar Seventeen, a plain, medium-sized gelding, did not look fully wound-up and, after taking closer order, was only treading water in the closing stages. (33/1)
Grand Ovation (IRE) looked in good shape for his racecourse debut, but needs time to develop. Nevertheless, he struggled on in the last furlong-and-a-half to be nearest at the line. (7/1)
Loganlea (IRE) was given one or two cosmetic reminders, but basically received considerate handling in midfield. (33/1)
Enthrone (USA) (7/1: 3/1-8/1)
Fatal Baraari (11/4: evens-3/1)

1410 SINGAPORE H'CAP (0-90) (3-Y.O+) (Class C)

2-35 (2-38) **6f** £5,317.75 (£1,612.00: £788.50: £376.75) Stalls: High GOING minus 0.21 sec per fur (GF)

				SP	RR	SF
1107[5]	**Mister Jolson (74)** (RJHodges) **8-8-12** RCochrane(12) (stdy hdwy on ins 2f out: led ins fnl f: pushed out)	—	**1**	5/1[1]	82	65
1327[2]	**Willow Dale (IRE) (67)** (DRCElsworth) **4-8-0**(5) PPMurphy(6) (a.p: ev ch ins fnl f: unable qckn)	½	**2**	15/2[3]	74	57
1148[7]	**Zuhair (86)** (DMcCain) **4-9-10** RHughes(10) (b: a.p: ev ch 1f out: one pce)	1½	**3**	20/1	89	72
567[5]	**Natural Key (71)** (DHaydnJones) **4-8-9** SDrowne(5) (lw: a.p: rdn over 2f out: one pce)	1¼	**4**	8/1	70	53
1158[8]	**White Emir (78)** (BJMeehan) **4-9-2** WJO'Connor(4) (lw: hld up: rdn over 2f out: one pce)	nk	**5**	11/1	77	60
1035[12]	**Delta Soleil (USA) (82)** (PWHarris) **5-9-6** GDuffield(13) (led tl ins fnl f: sn wknd)	¾	**6**	7/1[2]	79	62
1259*	**So Intrepid (IRE) (77)** (JMBradley) **7-9-1** WRyan(2) (lw: hdwy over 1f out: nvr nrr)	1½	**7**	8/1	70	53
1141[5]	**Ivory Dawn (70)** (KTIvory) **3-7-10**(3)ow3 MartinDwyer(14) (lw: nvr nr to chal)	1¼	**8**	8/1	59	30
1021[4]	**Depreciate (81)** (CJames) **4-9-5** RPerham(8) (lw: plld hrd: hdwy over 4f out: wknd 2f out)	¾	**9**	16/1	68	51
488[6]	**Sally Slade (73)** (CACyzer) **5-8-11** MRimmer(1) (a bhd)	3	**10**	20/1	52	35
323[9]	**Krystal Max (IRE) (75)** (JCullinan) **4-8-10**(3) DO'Donohoe(11) (prom over 2f)	2½	**11**	33/1	48	31
	Osomental (90) (DHaydnJones) **3-9-0**(5) GFaulkner(3) (lw: s.i.s: a bhd)	1¼	**12**	33/1	59	33
949*	**Longwick Lad (78)** (WRMuir) **4-9-2** DaneO'Neill(7) (a bhd)	s.h	**13**	11/1	47	30
1243[11]	**Unshaken (85)** (JRFanshawe) **3-9-0** NVarley(9) (lw: bhd fnl 4f)	12	**14**	14/1	22	—
				(SP 118.9%)		**14 Rn**

1m 12.17 (0.97) CSF £34.89 CT £644.00 TOTE £5.10: £2.10 £2.50 £6.50 (£11.10) Trio £99.20 OWNER Mr Bob Froome (SOMERTON) BRED Mrs D. D. Scott
LONG HANDICAP Ivory Dawn 7-8
WEIGHT FOR AGE 3yo-9lb
1107 Mister Jolson is a grand old servant and, coming through to lead inside the final furlong, needed only to be nudged along to record his eleventh victory. (5/1)
1327 Willow Dale (IRE), making a quick reappearance after her unlucky defeat at Goodwood on Thursday, was never far away, and may have even got her head in front for a few strides before the winner asserted. For the third consecutive time she had to settle for being the bridesmaid. She is becoming rather frustrating. (15/2)
903* Zuhair, rather warm beforehand, was an extremely rare runner here for his trainer. He had plenty of weight for what he has achieved this year, but still ran very well and had every chance entering the final furlong. (20/1)
567 Natural Key was 6lb higher than she has ever won off before, and failed to quicken in the final quarter-mile. (8/1)
White Emir is gradually coming down the handicap but, after chasing the leaders, could find no extra in the last two furlongs. (11/1)
Delta Soleil (USA) is gradually coming down the weights after a number of poor efforts, and did not run badly. (7/1)
1259* So Intrepid (IRE) (8/1: 6/1-9/1)
949* Longwick Lad (11/1: 7/1-12/1)
Unshaken (14/1: op 8/1) 91+ 89+ 89+ 97

1411 NEW ENGLAND CONDITIONS STKS (2-Y.O) (Class C) (91)

3-05 (3-06) **6f** £4,248.29 (£1,589.70: £777.35: £334.25: £149.63: £75.78) Stalls: High GOING minus 0.21 sec per fur (GF)

				SP	RR	SF
1143[2]	**Chips (IRE)** (DRCElsworth) **2-9-3** RHughes(7) (lw: mde all: shkn up over 1f out: r.o wl)	—	**1**	6/4[1]	83+	52
1084[2]	**Smooth Sailing** (KMcAuliffe) **2-9-0** JFEgan(4) (a.p: chsd wnr over 3f out: hrd rdn over 1f out: unable qckn)	¾	**2**	10/1	78	47
1211[4]	**Another Fantasy (IRE)** (RHannon) **2-8-9** DaneO'Neill(5) (lw: chsd ldrs: rdn over 2f out: r.o one pce)	hd	**3**	8/1	73	42
	Central Park (IRE) (PFICole) **2-8-7** MRimmer(1) (unf: scope: bit bkwd: s.s: outpcd: hdwy over 1f out: r.o: bttr for r)	1¾	**4**	7/1[3]	66+	35
1007[2]	**Fiveo'clock Shadow (IRE)** (BJMeehan) **2-8-10** WJO'Connor(3) (hld up: rdn over 2f out: wknd over 1f out)	1¾	**5**	12/1	64	33
	Bemsha Swing (IRE) (RHannon) **2-8-7** RPerham(2) (w'like: bkwd: a bhd)	2½	**6**	10/1	55	24
822*	**Timekeeper (USA)** (MBell) **2-9-0** MFenton(6) (chsd wnr over 2f: wknd over 1f out)	1¼	**7**	7/2[2]	58	27
				(SP 111.7%)		**7 Rn**

1m 13.38 (2.18) CSF £15.29 TOTE £2.00: £1.20 £3.60 (£11.20) OWNER Lucayan Stud (WHITCOMBE) BRED Mrs E. M. Gauvain
1143 Chips (IRE) is certainly being kept on the go for one who is so highly-rated by his trainer. The paddock pick, he put up a polished display as he made all the running, and needed only to be woken up to keep his rivals at bay. Royal Ascot is surely on the agenda. (6/4)
1084 Smooth Sailing, a leggy individual with not much substance, again gave a good account of himself but, although in second place from halfway, found the winner was always holding him. (10/1: 7/1-11/1)
1211 Another Fantasy (IRE) is not that big and was being niggled along for the majority of the race. Nevertheless, she stayed on in the final furlong and only just failed to take the runner-up birth. (8/1: 6/1-9/1)
Central Park (IRE), a lengthy individual who still has some strengthening to do, did not look fully wound-up but, despite being thrown in at the deep end, showed promise for the future. Given a nudge and losing ground at the start, he was then taken off his feet and done no favours by Bemsha Swing in the early stages. Only grasping the hang of things from below the distance, he ran on in encouraging style to finish fourth. With this experience under his belt, he should soon be winning. (7/1: 3/1-8/1)
1007 Fiveo'clock Shadow (IRE) had far more on his plate this time, and had come to the end of his tether below the distance. (12/1: 8/1-14/1)
Bemsha Swing (IRE) looked far from fit, so it was no surprise to see him always struggling at the back of the field. (10/1: 3/1-12/1)

1412 CRAWLEY WARREN HERON STKS (Listed) (3-Y.O) (Class A)

3-35 (3-37) **1m (Jubilee)** £13,810.00 (£4,180.00: £2,040.00: £970.00) Stalls: High GOING minus 0.21 sec per fur (GF)

Form	Horse	Dist	Pos	SP	RR	SF
963*	**Among Men (USA)** (MRStoute) **3-8-12** RCochrane(5) (lw: hld up: nt clr run over 2f out: rdn over 1f out: led ins fnl f: r.o wl)	—	**1**	10/11[1]	106	77
723*	**Amid Albadu (USA) (105)** (JLDunlop) **3-8-12** RHughes(2) (lw: a.p: rdn over 2f out: led 1f out tl ins fnl f: r.o wl)	s.h	**2**	9/2[2]	106	77
940[9]	**Green Card (USA) (100)** (SPCWoods) **3-8-12** WRyan(6) (a.p: rdn over 2f out: unable qckn fnl f)	1½	**3**	5/1[3]	103	74
957*	**Swiss Law (105)** (SbinSuroor) **3-8-12** GHind(4) (led to 1f out: one pce)	½	**4**	7/1	102	73
679[7]	**Nigrasine (105)** (JLEyre) **3-8-12** MGallagher(7) (prom 6f)	3½	**5**	20/1	95	66
	Natalia Bay (IRE) (99) (PFICole) **3-8-7** MRimmer(3) (plld hrd: bhd fnl 4f)	hd	**6**	40/1	90	61
957[3]	**Showboat (98)** (BWHills) **3-8-12** GDuffield(1) (a bhd)	10	**7**	20/1	75	46

(SP 111.7%) **7 Rn**

1m 37.95 (0.25) CSF £4.46 TOTE £1.90: £1.40 £2.30 (£2.80) OWNER Mr M Tabor & Mrs John Magnier (NEWMARKET) BRED Gail Beitz & Gainsborough Farm

963* Among Men (USA) looked absolutely tremendous in the paddock, but looked in trouble as he failed to get a clear run early in the straight. Picking up nicely when a gap appeared, he had a tremendous battle with the runner-up and succeeded by only the skin of his teeth. (10/11: evens-4/5)

723* Amid Albadu (USA) ran a tremendous race on his first venture into Listed company. Launching his challenge from below the distance, he had a tremendous battle with the winner, and failed by only a whisker. A similar event should soon come his way. (9/2)

599* Green Card (USA) was never far away, but lacked that vital turn of foot in the final furlongs. He is worth a try at further. (5/1)

957* Swiss Law, from a stable that has had to shut up shop for a week following several inexplicably bad performances, must have allowed connections a big sigh of relief after running a sound race, taking the field along to the furlong pole. (7/1: 9/2-8/1)

679 Nigrasine, tackling a mile for the first time, was close up until tiring a quarter-of-a-mile out. (20/1)

1413 CRAWLEY WARREN H'CAP (0-90) (4-Y.O+) (Class C)

4-05 (4-05) **2m** £7,524.00 (£2,277.00: £1,111.00: £528.00) Stalls: High GOING minus 0.21 sec per fur (GF)

Form	Horse	Dist	Pos	SP	RR	SF
789[10]	**Shining Dancer (60)** (SDow) **5-8-4** JFEgan(1) (hdwy over 4f out: led over 2f out: clr over 1f out: rdn out)	—	**1**	6/1[3]	70	32
510*	**Inchcailloch (IRE) (83)** (JSKing) **8-9-10**(3) MartinDwyer(4) (lw: hdwy over 3f out: chsd wnr over 1f out: r.o)	1¼	**2**	4/1[1]	92	54
1260*	**Grand Cru (68)** (JCullinan) **6-8-9**(3) DO'Donohoe(7) (lw: hdwy 7f out: rdn 3f out: unable qckn)	1¼	**3**	11/2[2]	76	38
1215[2]	**Sea Freedom (66)** (GBBalding) **6-8-10v** SDrowne(3) (a.p: led 4f out tl over 2f out: one pce)	s.h	**4**	4/1[1]	73	35
1114[3]	**Bridie's Pride (52)** (GAHam) **6-7-10** NCarlisle(10) (prom over 13f)	9	**5**	66/1	50	12
1114[5]	**Fieldridge (68)** (MPMuggeridge) **8-8-12** DaneO'Neill(9) (nvr nr to chal)	1½	**6**	20/1	65	27
831[4]	**Northern Fleet (80)** (MrsAJPerrett) **4-9-8** AClark(5) (prom over 12f)	10	**7**	7/1	67	27
728[8]	**Bolivar (IRE) (70)** (RAkehurst) **5-9-0b** RCochrane(6) (lw: bhd fnl 3f)	1½	**8**	6/1[3]	55	17
	Greenback (BEL) (52) (PJHobbs) **6-7-10** NAdams(2) (led 15f out to 7f out: sn wknd)	22	**9**	16/1	15	—
1152[5]	**Red Whirlwind (52)** (RSimpson) **7-7-10** FNorton(8) (led 1f: led 7f out to 4f out: sn wknd)	18	**10**	66/1	—	—

(SP 110.1%) **10 Rn**

3m 32.91 (8.31) CSF £25.36 CT £117.75 TOTE £7.40: £1.40 £1.40 £1.80 (£14.70) Trio £23.20 OWNER The Lalemaha Partnership (EPSOM) BRED Gainsborough Stud Management Ltd

LONG HANDICAP Bridie's Pride 6-10 Greenback (BEL) 7-7 Red Whirlwind 7-4

WEIGHT FOR AGE 4yo-2lb

510 Shining Dancer was given a lovely ride. Moving to the front soon after the turn for home, she stole a march on her rivals and was not going to be caught. (6/1)

510* Inchcailloch (IRE) allowed the winner to get first run and, although moving into second place below the distance and cutting back the advantage, was never going to get there in time. (4/1)

1260* Grand Cru needs a thorough test of stamina, which he got last Sunday in the mud at Newbury. This sharp, flat track on good ground was a different kettle of fish, and he failed to find the necessary turn of foot in the straight. (11/2: 7/2-6/1)

1215 Sea Freedom moved to the front on the home turn, but once again found lack of acceleration his undoing. (4/1: 3/1-9/2)

1114 Bridie's Pride, a stone out of the handicap, was close up until tiring early in the straight. (66/1)

1414 NEW SOUTH WALES H'CAP (0-90) (3-Y.O+) (Class C)

4-35 (4-38) **1m 2f** £5,249.50 (£1,591.00: £778.00: £371.50) Stalls: High GOING minus 0.21 sec per fur (GF)

Form	Horse	Dist	Pos	SP	RR	SF
1268*	**Effectual (82)** (MissGayKelleway) **4-9-6** RHughes(7) (hdwy over 2f out: led over 1f out: rdn out)	—	**1**	11/2[1]	93	67
457[4]	**Quiet Arch (IRE) (65)** (WRMuir) **4-8-3** DaneO'Neill(6) (lw: hdwy over 2f out: hrd rdn over 1f out: r.o one pce)	¾	**2**	25/1	75	49
	Bit on the Side (IRE) (82) (NEBerry) **8-9-6** SDrowne(3) (hld up: rdn over 1f out: r.o one pce)	nk	**3**	16/1	91	65
	Monument (62) (JSKing) **5-7-11**(3) MartinDwyer(4) (led over 1f: led over 2f out tl over 1f out: one pce)	1	**4**	20/1	70	44
962[10]	**Sofyaan (USA) (79)** (LadyHerries) **4-9-3** RCochrane(12) (rdn & hdwy over 2f out: one pce)	1¾	**5**	25/1	84	58
986[5]	**Pistol (IRE) (75)** (CAHorgan) **7-8-13** MFenton(13) (hdwy over 1f out: nvr nrr)	7	**6**	8/1[3]	69	43
	Tykeyvor (IRE) (88) (LadyHerries) **7-9-12** GDuffield(11) (bit bkwd: hdwy over 2f out: wknd over 1f out)	1	**7**	16/1	80	54
	Sovereign Page (USA) (79) (BHanbury) **8-9-3** JStack(1) (b: nvr nr to chal)	2	**8**	25/1	68	42
	Arctiid (USA) (90) (JHMGosden) **4-10-0** GHind(10) (prom over 8f)	¾	**9**	13/2[2]	78	52
974*	**Polar Champ (80)** (SPCWoods) **4-9-4** WRyan(9) (prom over 7f)	2½	**10**	13/2[2]	64	38
933[8]	**Edan Heights (76)** (SDow) **5-8-9**(5) ADaly(15) (lw: a bhd)	3½	**11**	11/1	54	28
1261[4]	**Golden Ace (IRE) (89)** (RHannon) **4-9-13** RPerham(8) (lw: prom over 7f)	1¾	**12**	16/1	64	38
986[7]	**Supreme Sound (77)** (PWHarris) **3-8-1**ow1 AMcGlone(16) (prom over 7f)	2½	**13**	14/1	48	7
	Tissue of Lies (USA) (65) (MJohnston) **4-8-0**(3) DO'Donohoe(14) (lw: in rr fnl 8f)	1¼	**14**	11/1	34	8
1011*	**Stellar Line (USA) (72)** (MJPolglase) **4-8-10** MRimmer(2) (lw: led over 8f out: clr 5f out: hdd over 2f out: sn wknd)	1¼	**15**	14/1	39	13
	Antiguan Jane (67) (RWArmstrong) **4-8-5** AClark(5) (bkwd: a bhd)	6	**16**	25/1	25	—

(SP 121.0%) **16 Rn**

2m 4.9 (2.40) CSF £137.39 CT £1,851.55 TOTE £4.90: £1.80 £3.20 £2.40 £2.80 (£59.00) Trio £496.90 OWNER Blandford Thoroughbreds (WHITCOMBE) BRED Miss Sarah Hollinshead

WEIGHT FOR AGE 3yo-14lb

1268* Effectual continues in fine form, coming through to lead below the distance and being ridden along to keep his rivals at bay. (11/2)

457 Quiet Arch (IRE), who has been in good form on the All-Weather so far this year, has yet to win on grass but ran a fine race, staying on well in the straight. (25/1)
Bit on the Side (IRE), making her seasonal bow, found this trip too sharp. Racing in touch, she was ridden along from below the distance and, staying on, only just failed to take second prize. Given some cut in the ground and a step-up to a mile-and-a-half, she can find a race. (16/1)
Monument, off the course since last September, showed in front early in the straight but was collared below the distance. (20/1)
Sofyaan (USA) ran his best race since coming over from Ireland, taking closer order early in the straight before making no further impression. (25/1)
986 Pistol (IRE) has never won anything better than a Class D race and, although staying on, never threatened to get near the principals.(8/1)

1415 CALIFORNIAN MAIDEN STKS (II) (3-Y.O) (Class D)

5-05 (5-06) **1m (Jubilee)** £2,997.50 (£905.00: £440.00: £207.50) Stalls: High GOING minus 0.21 sec per fur (GF)

				SP	RR	SF
	Byzantium (LordHuntingdon) **3-9-0** RPerham(10) (w'like: bit bkwd: a.p: led over 2f out: clr over 1f out: rdn out)	—	**1**	7/1	84	56
	Illusion (MRStoute) **3-9-0** GHind(12) (str: scope: lw: shkn up 5f out: nt clr run over 2f out: hdwy over 1f out: fin wl: bttr for r)	½	**2**	2/1 1	83	55
1002 3	**City Gambler (72)** (GCBravery) **3-8-9** MRimmer(4) (hld up: rdn over 2f out: unable qckn)	3½	**3**	15/2	71	43
	Misty Point (IABalding) **3-8-9** SWhitworth(11) (unf: scope: lw: hld up: n.m.r over 2f out: rdn: one pce)	½	**4**	6/1 3	70	42
	Cordate (IRE) (JHMGosden) **3-8-9** AGarth(1) (unf: nt clr run & swtchd lft over 2f out: nvr nr to chal)	½	**5**	10/1	69	41
	Swing West (USA) (PFICole) **3-9-0** GDuffield(8) (bit bkwd: a.p: rdn over 2f out: sn wknd)	3	**6**	6/1 3	68	40
	Gold Millenium (IRE) (CAHorgan) **3-9-0** AMcGlone(3) (leggy: bit bkwd: dwlt: a bhd)	2	**7**	20/1	64	36
1088 11	**Secret Strength** (LadyHerries) **3-9-0** WJO'Connor(5) (lw: led over 5f)	8	**8**	16/1	48	20
983 9	**Jaza** (NAGraham) **3-9-0** RHughes(6) (chsd ldr over 5f: wknd over 1f out)	2½	**9**	4/1 2	43	15
727 18	**Prinia** (GLewis) **3-8-9** NAdams(7) (s.s: a bhd)	2½	**10**	20/1	33	5
				(SP 130.7%)	**10 Rn**	

1m 40.11 (2.41) CSF £21.96 TOTE £17.00: £3.20 £1.40 £1.90 (£11.10) Trio £90.40 OWNER Mr R. Van Gelder (WEST ILSLEY) BRED Mrs B. Long
Byzantium, a medium-sized colt, belied his burly paddock appearance under a fine ride. Sent on early in the straight, he forged clear below the distance, which proved vital as the runner-up was closing hand over fist inside the final furlong. (7/1: 5/1-8/1)
Illusion, an attractive, round-bodied colt who is a half-brother to Time Allowed and Zinaad, did not seem entirely sure what was required of him. Nudged along fully five furlongs from home, he failed to get a clear run at a vital stage but, after being given a couple of smacks of the whip, he picked up in tremendous style and was absolutely flying inside the final furlong. There is no doubt he would have won with a little further to go and he looks a ready-made winner. (2/1: evens-5/2)
1002 City Gambler is only lightly-made and, once again when the race began in earnest, she was found wanting. She is very exposed. (15/2)
Misty Point, a scopey individual who needs time, nevertheless looked in good order, but failed to find the necessary turn of foot. (6/1: 4/1-13/2)
Cordate (IRE) is not the kind of horse one usually associates with the Gosden stable, being not that big and rather lacking strength. Switched to the outside to get a clear passage early in the straight, she was then only treading water. (10/1: op 6/1)
Swing West (USA) was close up until lack of race fitness took its toll. (6/1: 3/1-13/2)
Jaza (4/1: op 9/4)

T/Jkpt: £17,071.30 (0.1 Tckts); £21,639.79 to 26/5/97. T/Plpt: £15.90 (1797.38 Tckts). T/Qdpt: £6.70 (165.84 Tckts) AK

1233-LINGFIELD (L-H) (Turf Good to firm, AWT Standard)

Saturday May 24th

Race 3: hand timed
WEATHER: fine WIND: fresh against

1416 GABLE APPRENTICE H'CAP (0-80) (3-Y.O) (Class E)

6-10 (6-13) **1m 2f** £2,682.75 (£822.00: £408.50: £201.75) Stalls: High GOING minus 0.38 sec per fur (F)

				SP	RR	SF
889 3	**Ciro's Pearl (IRE) (74)** (MHTompkins) **3-9-2**(3) PClarke(5) (lw: mde all: edgd rt over 2f out: rdn ins fnl f: r.o wl)	—	**1**	3/1 2	84	32
1300*	**Jack The Lad (IRE) (81)** (JHetherton) **3-9-12** 5x TSiddall(4) (lw: chsd wnr after 2f: rdn & ev ch ins fnl f: unable qckn)	1½	**2**	10/11 1	89	37
990 12	**Soden (IRE) (70)** (TGMills) **3-8-7**(8) JCornally(2) (hdwy on ins 3f out: ev ch 2f out: rdn over 1f out: one pce)	2½	**3**	10/1	74	22
1106 11	**Tulsa (IRE) (55)** (BGubby) **3-8-0** GGallagher(3) (chsd ldrs: c wd fnl bnd: sn wknd)	9	**4**	33/1	44	—
*906**	**Kingsdown Trix (IRE) (60)** (GLMoore) **3-8-5** GHannon(1) (hld up: rdn over 2f out: sn btn)	1	**5**	6/1 3	48	—
1044 5	**Purple Maize (53)** (JAkehurst) **3-7-12** PFitzsimons(6) (prom over 6f)	5	**6**	20/1	33	—
				(SP 108.5%)	**6 Rn**	

2m 9.85 (5.15) CSF £5.15 TOTE £4.10: £1.20 £1.40 (£1.90) OWNER Mr J. H. Shannon (NEWMARKET) BRED Johnny Kelly
889 Ciro's Pearl (IRE) looked well in the paddock beforehand, and would have run out a more emphatic winner had she not edged to her right around the two pole. She stayed on strongly at the finish and was obviously well-suited by the step-up in trip. (3/1)
1300* Jack The Lad (IRE) had won four of his previous five races, and ran well under a 5lb penalty. (10/11)
Soden (IRE) ran much better than on her seasonal debut, and should be cherry-ripe next time. (10/1: 8/1-16/1)
906* Kingsdown Trix (IRE) (6/1: 3/1-13/2)

1417 PATIO (S) H'CAP (0-60) (3-Y.O+) (Class G)

6-40 (6-40) **2m (Equitrack)** £1,984.50 (£547.00: £259.50) Stalls: High GOING minus 0.38 sec per fur (FST)

				SP	RR	SF
1287 6	**Carrolls Marc (IRE) (40)** (CMurray) **9-9-10** RCochrane(2) (hld up in tch: chsd ldr over 2f out: led over 1f out: r.o wl)	—	**1**	4/1 2	58	24
	Side Bar (28) (PMooney) **7-8-5v**(7) JBosley(6) (set slow pce: qcknd ½-wy: hdd over 1f out: one pce)	7	**2**	12/1	39	5
640 7	**Lucy Tufty (30)** (JPearce) **6-9-0** GHind(4) (dwlt: hld up: hdwy over 3f out: rdn over 2f out: kpt on one pce)	1¼	**3**	5/1	40	6
908 7	**Illegally Yours (42)** (LMontagueHall) **4-9-7**(3) DO'Donohoe(9) (dwlt: hld up: hdwy 4f out: rdn over 2f out: one pce)	1¾	**4**	5/2 1	50	14
1125 8	**Mrs Drummond (IRE) (34)** (APJarvis) **4-9-2** WJO'Connor(8) (chsd ldr tl over 2f out: sn rdn: wknd over 1f out)	2½	**5**	12/1	40	4

*356*7	**Dutch Dyane (28)** (GPEnright) **4-8-10** NAdams(1) (in tch tl wknd 5f out)	3	**6**	20/1	31	—
1222[9]	**Club Elite (28)** (MissAStokell) **5-8-5**(7) JoHunnam(5) (chsd ldrs tl wknd 5f out)	5	**7**	20/1	26	—
*487*7	**Circus Colours (40)** (JRJenkins) **7-9-10** NDay(3) (b: keen hold: prom tl wknd over 6f out)	½	**8**	9/2[3]	37	3
1114R	**Wicklow Boy (IRE) (30)** (RIngram) **6-9-0v** AMcGlone(7) (b: ref to r: t.n.p)		**R**	33/1	—	—
				(SP 111.3%)	**9 Rn**	

3m 31.86 (10.86) CSF £42.35 CT £214.24 TOTE £3.50: £1.20 £3.60 £2.50 (£29.20) Trio £158.80 OWNER Mr A. Piller (NEWMARKET) BRED John Connaughton
WEIGHT FOR AGE 4yo-2lb
No bid
867* Carrolls Marc (IRE), already proven on this surface, appeared suited by the step-up in trip. (4/1)
Side Bar set a pace to suit himself, but was firmly put in his place in the final furlong. (12/1: 10/1-16/1)
Lucy Tufty made some headway coming down the hill but, already under pressure, could not quicken. (5/1: 3/1-6/1)
262 Illegally Yours was struggling to make headway throughout the final four furlongs. (5/2)
Mrs Drummond (IRE) (12/1: op 8/1)

77+ 76 83+ 71 (77)

1418 E.B.F. LINGFIELD MAIDEN STKS (2-Y.O) (Class D)
7-10 (7-14) **6f** £3,669.75 (£1,098.00: £526.50: £240.75) Stalls: High GOING minus 0.38 sec per fur (F)

				SP	RR	SF
	Deki (USA) (DMorley) **2-9-0** JStack(10) (leggy: lw: a.p: led 2f out: r.o wl)	—	**1**	7/2[2]	75+	24
	Blundell Lane (IRE) (APJarvis) **2-9-0** WJO'Connor(7) (w'like: bit bkwd: mid div: rdn over 3f out: hdwy over 1f out: styd on to go 2nd ent fnl f: r.o)	1	**2**	8/1	72	21
	Mohawk (IRE) (JLDunlop) **2-8-11**(3) DO'Donohoe(1) (w'like: bit bkwd: mid div: rdn over 2f out: styd on ins fnl f)	2½	**3**	6/1[3]	66	15
	Fire Goddess (JSMoore) **2-8-9** SWhitworth(4) (unf: bit bkwd: led: hdd 2f out: wknd ins fnl f)	½	**4**	25/1	59	8
*1136*9	**Heavenly Falls (IRE)** (CADwyer) **2-8-7**(7) JoHunnam(5) (mid div: hrd rdn over 2f out: kpt on one pce ins fnl f)	hd	**5**	33/1	64	13
	Celtic Pageant (RAkehurst) **2-9-0** TQuinn(11) (w'like: bit bkwd: prom: ev ch 2f out: wknd over 1f out)	½	**6**	2/1[1]	63	12
	Campione (IRE) (MHTompkins) **2-9-0** DBiggs(3) (leggy: prom: wknd 2f out: eased)	16	**7**	16/1	20	—
	Pianist (IRE) (GLewis) **2-8-11**(3) AWhelan(8) (cmpt: bit bkwd: dwlt: sltly hmpd over 3f out: a bhd)	2½	**8**	16/1	13	—
	Rebalza (IRE) (JMPEustace) **2-9-0** RCochrane(6) (w'like: towards rr whn bdly hmpd over 3f out: nt rcvr)	hd	**9**	12/1	13	—
	Sky Mountain (IRE) (GLewis) **2-9-0** NDay(9) (w'like: dwlt: sn rdn: hmpd over 3f out: a bhd)	1	**10**	12/1	11	—
	Bettron (RHannon) **2-9-0** NAdams(2) (unf: bit bkwd: dwlt: rr whn swvd rt & uns rdr over 3f out)		**U**	11/1	—	—
				(SP 123.2%)	**11 Rn**	

1m 11.9 (2.90) CSF £30.63 TOTE £5.10: £1.70 £2.50 £2.10 (£26.60) Trio £101.20 OWNER Mr Hadi Al-Tajir (NEWMARKET) BRED Hadi Al Tajir
Deki (USA) looked the fittest of the newcomers, was always going best, and ran out a ready winner. (7/2)
Blundell Lane (IRE) looked a little burly beforehand and ran a bit green early in the race but, once the penny had dropped, he stayed on promisingly. A race can be found. (8/1: 6/1-10/1)
Mohawk (IRE) ran a promising race. Decidedly burly beforehand, the way he stayed on in the closing stages suggests the connections should have no trouble finding a similar event. (6/1: 4/1-7/1)
Fire Goddess showed plenty of speed and can be made fitter. (25/1)
Heavenly Falls (IRE) kept on in the final two furlongs without threatening to take a hand. (33/1)
Celtic Pageant was made favourite despite looking backward in the preliminaries. He showed some speed but was done with below the distance. He will know more about it next time. (2/1)
Rebalza (IRE) (12/1: 8/1-14/1)
Bettron (11/1: 5/1-12/1)

1419 ROB & BETTY THOMAS 40-YEARS-AND-STILL-RUNNING H'CAP (0-70) (3-Y.O+) (Class E)
7-40 (7-42) **5f** £2,862.25 (£853.00: £406.50: £183.25) Stalls: High GOING minus 0.38 sec per fur (F)

				SP	RR	SF
1250[2]	**Polly Golightly (54)** (MBlanshard) **4-9-3b** NAdams(3) (mde all: edgd lft over 1f out: drvn out)	—	**1**	11/2[3]	63	46
	Kilcullen Lad (IRE) (65) (PMooney) **3-9-6** WJO'Connor(1) (chsd ldrs: rdn over 1f out: r.o)	½	**2**	12/1	72	47
901[6]	**Pharaoh's Joy (56)** (JWPayne) **4-9-5** GHind(8) (hld up: swtchd lft & hdwy over 2f out: rdn over 1f out: r.o ins fnl f)	½	**3**	5/1[2]	62	45
1327*	**Half Tone (52)** (RMFlower) **5-9-1b** TQuinn(5) (sn rdn along: hdwy 3f out: hrd rdn over 1f out: styd on ins fnl f)	½	**4**	11/4[1]	56	39
1236*	**Bright Paragon (IRE) (40)** (KTIvory) **8-8-0**(3) MartinDwyer(2) (a.p: rdn over 1f out: r.o one pce)	s.h	**5**	11/1	44	27
1327[5]	**Superlao (BEL) (35)** (JJBridger) **5-7-12** JLowe(10) (prom: rdn over 2f out: one pce)	1¼	**6**	8/1	35	18
1374[11]	**Dande Flyer (65)** (DWPArbuthnot) **4-10-0v** SWhitworth(7) (hdwy 3f out: n.m.r over 1f out: swtchd rt: kpt on one pce fnl f)	½	**7**	6/1	63	46
1327[6]	**Village Native (FR) (60)** (KOCunningham-Brown) **4-9-6**(3) AWhelan(6) (towards rr: rdn 3f out: no hdwy fnl 2f)	2½	**8**	10/1	50	33
	Il Doria (IRE) (54) (AHide) **4-9-3** AMcGlone(9) (a bhd)	6	**9**	33/1	25	8
1083[6]	**Mijas (62)** (LMontagueHall) **4-9-11** RCochrane(4) (prom tl wknd over 1f out)	nk	**10**	16/1	32	15
				(SP 118.1%)	**10 Rn**	

58.25 secs (1.25) CSF £63.98 CT £330.82 TOTE £6.80: £2.20 £1.60 £1.60 (£38.40) Trio £86.80 OWNER Mr David Sykes (UPPER LAMBOURN) BRED Aston Park Stud and T. R. Lock
WEIGHT FOR AGE 3yo-8lb
1250 Polly Golightly made most of the running and, despite hanging away from the stands' rail, was always just doing enough. (11/2)
Kilcullen Lad (IRE) had been absent for four months, but ran a great race. He should be spot-on next time. (12/1: op 7/1)
901 Pharaoh's Joy was switched to the outside and made promising headway over two furlongs out but, though staying on, never looked like reaching the first two. (5/1)
1327* Half Tone ran another sound race. Ridden along as normal to go the pace, he stayed on nicely in the final two furlongs, but could not reach the principals in time. (11/4)
1236* Bright Paragon (IRE) (11/1: 7/1-12/1)
1327 Village Native (FR) (10/1: 5/1-12/1)

1420 HALL MAIDEN STKS (3-Y.O F) (Class D)
8-10 (8-13) **1m 2f** £3,581.90 (£1,068.20: £509.60: £230.30) Stalls: High GOING minus 0.38 sec per fur (F)

				SP	RR	SF
1023[2]	**Timissa (IRE)** (LMCumani) **3-8-11** GHind(4) (hld up: hdwy to ld 3f out: rdn ins fnl f: r.o)	—	**1**	4/5[1]	77	19

				SP	RR	SF
	Melodica (MRStoute) **3-8-11** RCochrane(1) (chsd ldrs: led briefly over 3f out: rdn 2f out: styd on ins fnl f)	1¼	**2**	7/2[2]	75	17
	Off The Rails (HCandy) **3-8-11** AMcGlone(3) (led: rn wd & hdd over 3f out: rdn 2f out: one pce)	4	**3**	12/1	69	11
1168[8]	**Jude** (PFICole) **3-8-11** TQuinn(6) (stdd s: hld up: rdn over 2f out: kpt one pce fnl f)	2	**4**	6/1[3]	65	7
	Across The Water (CACyzer) **3-8-11** WJO'Connor(5) (leggy: chsd ldrs: hrd rdn over 2f out: wknd ins fnl f)	½	**5**	33/1	65	7
1023[W]	**Top** (JRFanshawe) **3-8-11** DHarrison(8) (w'like: bit bkwd: hld up: hdwy over 3f out: rdn over 2f out: wknd over 1f out)	6	**6**	10/1	55	—
1207[13]	**Misellina (FR)** (JSMoore) **3-8-11** NAdams(2) (dwlt: a bhd)	3	**7**	50/1	50	—
978[5]	**Magaona (FR)** (RHannon) **3-8-11** DBiggs(7) (chsd ldrs: carried wd over 3f out: sn rdn: wknd over 2f out)	¾	**8**	25/1	49	—

(SP 117.6%) **8 Rn**

2m 10.54 (5.84) CSF £3.53 TOTE £1.80: £1.10 £2.00 £2.90 (£3.00) OWNER H H Aga Khan (NEWMARKET) BRED His Highness the Aga Khans Studs S. C.

1023 Timissa (IRE) made a promising debut at Doncaster, and confirmed that promise with an emphatic success. (4/5: evens-11/10)
Melodica looked a bit of a madam going down, but did nothing wrong in the race. (7/2: op 2/)
Off The Rails failed to handle the home turn, but kept on quite nicely once straightened-up, and should improve. (12/1: op 7/1)
Jude stayed on in the final two furlongs, and will be seen in a better light over further. (6/1)
Top (10/1: 8/1-12/1)

1421 KING POST LIMITED STKS (0-70) (3-Y.O+) (Class E)

8-40 (8-40) **1m 2f (Equitrack)** £2,862.25 (£853.00: £406.50: £183.25) Stalls: High GOING minus 0.38 sec per fur (FST)

				SP	RR	SF
*1153**	**Smart Boy (IRE) (75)** (PFICole) **3-8-9** TQuinn(7) (mde all: rdn ins fnl f: r.o wl)	—	**1**	2/1[1]	75	35
1023[4]	**Western Sonata (IRE) (67)** (LordHuntingdon) **4-9-4** DHarrison(3) (hld up in tch: chsd wnr over 1f out: rdn ins fnl f: unable qckn)	2	**2**	3/1[2]	67	41
1153[2]	**Enchanting Eve (68)** (CNAllen) **3-8-5**(3) MartinDwyer(8) (chsd wnr tl over 1f out: sn rdn: one pce)	¾	**3**	12/1	70	30
1093[7]	**Double Rush (IRE) (65)** (TGMills) **5-9-4**(3) AWhelan(1) (hld up: hdwy on outside 2f out: rdn over 1f out: r.o one pce fnl f)	1¼	**4**	11/2[3]	67	41
510[9]	**Amadour (IRE) (70)** (PMitchell) **4-9-4**(3) DO'Donohoe(2) (hld up in rr: rdn over 2f out: kpt on one pce ins fnl f)	1¾	**5**	10/1	64	38
1082[3]	**Sweet Supposin (IRE) (64)** (CADwyer) **6-9-11v** RCochrane(5) (hld up: sme hdwy 2f out: sn rdn: wknd ins fnl f)	nk	**6**	10/1	67	41
1123[6]	**Tribal Peace (IRE) (68)** (BGubby) **5-9-9** JStack(6) (mid div: rdn over 2f out: wknd ins fnl f)	s.h	**7**	10/1	65	39
764[9]	**Freedom Chance (IRE) (64)** (JWHills) **3-8-9** NAdams(4) (chsd ldrs tl wknd over 2f out)	2	**8**	10/1	62	22

(SP 117.8%) **8 Rn**

2m 7.76 (3.46) CSF £7.58 TOTE £2.30: £1.40 £1.20 £2.40 (£4.60) OWNER H R H Sultan Ahmad Shah (WHATCOMBE) BRED Peter Savill
WEIGHT FOR AGE 3yo-14lb

1153* Smart Boy (IRE) was given a sound tactical ride by Quinn, and was not troubled to score. (2/1)
1023 Western Sonata (IRE) moved up threateningly on the inside turning for home but, soon ridden along, never really looked like pegging back the winner. (3/1)
1153 Enchanting Eve was up with the pace throughout but had no more to give in the final furlong. (12/1: op 8/1)
1093 Double Rush (IRE) made his move turning for home but had to go wide to do so. Once straightened up, he only kept on at the one pace. (11/2)
334* Amadour (IRE) was ridden along coming down the hill, but took a long time to get going. He was staying on when the race was all over. (10/1)
1082 Sweet Supposin (IRE) (10/1: op 6/1)
535* Freedom Chance (IRE) (10/1: 7/1-12/1)

T/Plpt: £20.60 (486.44 Tckts). T/Qdpt: £9.80 (52.56 Tckts) SM

0999-WARWICK (L-H) (Good to firm)

Saturday May 24th

WEATHER: fine but cloudy WIND: slight against

1422 LEAM AMATEUR H'CAP (0-70) (3-Y.O+) (Class G)

6-20 (6-22) **1m** £2,592.10 (£720.60: £346.30) Stalls: Low GOING minus 0.22 sec per fur (GF)

				SP	RR	SF
848[2]	**Marjaana (IRE) (62)** (PTWalwyn) **4-10-8**(5) MissSSamworth(10) (a.p: led over 1f out: sn clr: r.o wl)	—	**1**	14/1	76	64
1005[3]	**Mr Cube (IRE) (48)** (JMBradley) **7-9-8b**(5) MissVRoberts(19) (hld up mid div: hdwy over 2f out: r.o ins fnl f)	4	**2**	16/1	54	42
1128[4]	**Murphy's Gold (IRE) (49)** (RAFahey) **6-9-9**(5) MrCRussell(11) (dwlt: gd hdwy over 1f out: fin wl)	s.h	**3**	14/1	55	43
848[7]	**Squared Away (47)** (JWPayne) **5-9-7b**(5) MissCLake(13) (lw: hdwy over 1f out: nvr nrr)	2½	**4**	20/1	48	36
1268[15]	**Mr Teigh (63)** (MrsJRRamsden) **5-10-9**(5) MissERamsden(3) (a.p: ev ch over 1f out: wknd fnl f)	1¼	**5**	12/1	61	49
1233[3]	**Clued Up (51)** (PDEvans) **4-9-11v**(5)ow1 MrAEvans(15) (no hdwy fnl 2f)	1¾	**6**	12/1	46	33
1035[9]	**Wentbridge Lad (IRE) (65)** (PDEvans) **7-10-11b**(5) MrWMcLaughlin(2) (hld up mid div: swtchd rt wl over 1f out: no hdwy)	¾	**7**	11/1	58	46
1005[2]	**Abtaal (49)** (RJHodges) **7-9-9**(5) MrsCWilliams(20) (prom 6f)	1¾	**8**	12/1	39	27
1248[2]	**Baba Au Rhum (IRE) (60)** (IPWilliams) **5-10-11** MrTMcCarthy(17) (lw: prom tl wknd wl over 1f out)	hd	**9**	9/2[1]	50	38
1011[3]	**Roman Reel (USA) (56)** (GLMoore) **6-10-7** MrsJMoore(18) (nvr bttr than mid div)	2	**10**	20/1	42	30
866[6]	**Night of Glass (57)** (JLEyre) **4-10-8v** MissDianaJones(16) (lw: led over 6f: sn wknd)	½	**11**	13/2[3]	42	30
870[2]	**Montone (IRE) (64)** (JRJenkins) **7-11-1v** DrMMannish(5) (n.d)	nk	**12**	5/1[2]	48	36
*1134**	**Jigsaw Boy (55)** (PGMurphy) **8-10-1**(5) MissLGreen(8) (nvr nr ldrs)	nk	**13**	16/1	39	27
763[18]	**Polly Peculiar (65)** (BSmart) **6-10-11**(5) MissVMarshall(1) (bit bkwd: s.s: a bhd)	nk	**14**	14/1	48	36
	Merciless Cop (67) (BJMeehan) **3-10-6b** MissJAllison(7) (bkwd: s.s: a bhd)	nk	**15**	20/1	49	25
1138[8]	**Mowlaie (55)** (DWChapman) **6-10-6** MissRClark(6) (chsd ldrs 5f)	nk	**16**	50/1	37	25
1040[4]	**Kingchip Boy (65)** (MJRyan) **8-10-11v**(5) MrSLavallin(12) (prom 5f)	½	**17**	12/1	46	34
	Lime Street Blues (IRE) (70) (TKeddy) **6-11-2**(5) MrJGoldstein(9) (a bhd)	hd	**18**	50/1	51	39
	Everset (FR) (55) (ABailey) **9-10-1**(5)ow5 MissALHutchinson(4) (b: prom over 5f)	4	**19**	50/1	28	11

566^{8}	**Digpast (IRE) (58)** (JJBridger) **7-10-4b**$^{(5)ow3}$ MrDBridger(14) (t.o)	dist	**20**	25/1	—	—
				(SP 143.1%)	**20 Rn**	

1m 40.4 (4.00) CSF £215.12 CT £3,004.29 TOTE £15.30: £4.20 £4.80 £1.60 £7.30 (£149.50) Trio £282.50; £362.14 to 26/5/97 OWNER Mrs D. C. Samworth (LAMBOURN) BRED Shadwell Estate Company Limited
WEIGHT FOR AGE 3yo-12lb
848 Marjaana (IRE) gave her rider her first winner with a most convincing victory. (14/1)
1005 Mr Cube (IRE), dropped 2lb, had faster ground this time but found the winner was already home and dry. (16/1)
1128 Murphy's Gold (IRE) finished full of running and, although the form of these races can be misleading, he looks ready to strike. (14/1)
848 Squared Away, poorly drawn when finishing less than five lengths behind the winner last time, needs a longer trip or a stiffer mile. (20/1)
Mr Teigh, dropping back to a mile, has already come down 4lb this season, but seems a better animal on the sand. (12/1)
1233 Clued Up, 4lb higher than when winning at Hamilton, needs further on ground as lively as this. (12/1)
Wentbridge Lad (IRE) (11/1: 8/1-12/1)
1248 Baba Au Rhum (IRE) (9/2: op 8/1)
866 Night of Glass (13/2: 4/1-7/1)

1423 SANDRETTO MAIDEN STKS (3-Y.O+) (Class D)
6-50 (6-54) **7f** £3,900.40 (£1,166.20: £558.60: £254.80) Stalls: Low GOING minus 0.22 sec per fur (GF)

				SP	RR	SF
983^{5}	**Compromise (IRE)** (BWHills) **3-8-10**$^{(3)}$ JDSmith(2) (a.p: rdn to ld ins fnl f: r.o)	—	**1**	3/1^{2}	82	42
963^{4}	**Super Monarch** (EALDunlop) **3-8-13** RHughes(7) (chsd ldr: led over 2f out: hrd rdn & hdd ins fnl f)	¾	**2**	5/4^{1}	80	40
1030^{4}	**Yabint El Sultan (71)** (BAMcMahon) **3-8-8** LNewton(11) (a.p: ev ch over 1f out: nt qckn ins fnl f)	nk	**3**	14/1	75	35
1088^{4}	**March Crusader** (BHanbury) **3-8-13** TLucas(3) (lw: plld hrd: a.p: one pce fnl 2f)	2½	**4**	13/2	74	34
	Mary Culi (HCandy) **3-8-8** CRutter(5) (bkwd: hld up: stdy hdwy fnl 2f: r.o)	3½	**5**	33/1	61	21
	Summerosa (USA) (85) (PWChapple-Hyam) **3-8-5**$^{(3)}$ RHavlin(10) (b.nr fore: lw: led over 4f: wknd over 1f out)	s.h	**6**	11/2^{3}	61	21
	Las Vistas (HJCollingridge) **3-8-8** DaleGibson(14) (lengthy: nvr trbld ldrs)	2	**7**	40/1	56	16
	Matoaka (RJRWilliams) **3-8-8** JQuinn(1) (bkwd: nvr nr to chal)	1½	**8**	14/1	53	13
989^{8}	**Agift** (RFJohnsonHoughton) **3-8-8** AClark(15) (no hdwy fnl 3f)	hd	**9**	25/1	53	13
	Imperial Glen (IRE) (MDIUsher) **3-8-8** JMarshall(9) (w'like: bkwd: a bhd)	s.h	**10**	40/1	52	12
1139^{9}	**Sure To Dream (IRE)** (RTPhillips) **4-9-5** RPerham(6) (a bhd)	2	**11**	50/1	48	19
	Nite Wonder (GLMoore) **3-8-13** CandyMorris(13) (w'like: s.s: hdwy 5f out: wknd qckly 2f out)	4	**12**	40/1	44	4
840^{15}	**Jolly Jackson (64)** (RAkehurst) **3-8-13** FNorton(12) (a bhd)	2	**13**	20/1	39	—
874^{10}	**Victoria House (IRE)** (MJHeaton-Ellis) **3-8-8** SDrowne(8) (a bhd)	1¾	**14**	50/1	30	—
	Damanka (IRE) (MBell) **3-8-8** MFenton(4) (s.s: a bhd)	½	**15**	25/1	29	—
				(SP 138.1%)	**15 Rn**	

1m 27.7 (3.10) CSF £6.85 TOTE £4.40: £1.70 £1.10 £3.10 (£2.90) Trio £25.20 OWNER Sheikh Mohammed (LAMBOURN) BRED Sheikh Mohammed Bin Rashid Al Maktoum
WEIGHT FOR AGE 3yo-11lb
OFFICIAL EXPLANATION **Matoaka: the filly stumbled leaving the stalls and the jockey felt it prudent to give her a chance to find her feet. She was outpaced and unbalanced on the home bend and ran on through beaten horses. She also needs a longer trip.**
983 Compromise (IRE), well-backed, did the business on this faster surface. (3/1)
963 Super Monarch, a half-brother to Fancy Heights and Tajannab, obviously came up against a well-fancied rival in the winner. However, it was a bit surprising to see him come back in distance when, if anything, he may require further. (5/4)
1030 Yabint El Sultan showed her appreciation for a longer trip here, having been bogged down in the Chester mud last time. (14/1)
1088 March Crusader is learning all the time, and would have been entitled to have folded-up, having run too freely early on. (13/2: 4/1-7/1)
Mary Culi had a much needed pipe-opener, and is one to keep an eye on in handicaps over a longer trip. (33/1)
Summerosa (USA) is one of her stable's lesser-lights. (11/2: 4/1-6/1)
Matoaka, who split a pastern on her only outing as a juvenile, caught the eye of the Stewards. The various explanations, which included that she needed a longer trip, were accepted. (14/1)

1424 ANGLO HOLT H'CAP (0-70) (3-Y.O+) (Class E)
7-20 (7-21) **1m 6f 194y** £3,252.25 (£973.00: £466.50: £213.25) Stalls: Low GOING minus 0.22 sec per fur (GF)

				SP	RR	SF
1252*	**Golden Hadeer (47)** (MJRyan) **6-8-5** AClark(4) (lw: chsd ldr: hrd rdn over 1f out: led ins fnl f: all out)	—	**1**	7/4^{1}	59	35
1100^{4}	**Romalito (38)** (MBlanshard) **7-7-10** JQuinn(2) (hld up: hdwy 5f out: hrd rdn 3f out: ev ch fnl f: r.o wl)	s.h	**2**	9/1	50	26
1114^{6}	**Paradise Navy (68)** (CREgerton) **8-9-12b** RHughes(9) (hld up & bhd: hdwy 2f out: edgd lft ins fnl f: r.o)	2½	**3**	7/1^{3}	77	53
1001^{17}	**Landlord (48)** (PBowen) **5-8-6b** MFenton(7) (led: rdn over 2f out: hdd ins fnl f)	s.h	**4**	33/1	57	33
	Badawi (FR) (38) (NMBabbage) **7-7-10** FNorton(12) (hld up: hdwy 4f out: sn hrd rdn: one pce fnl 2f)	1	**5**	16/1	46	22
1252^{4}	**Coleridge (41)** (JJSheehan) **9-7-13b** CRutter(6) (a.p: no hdwy fnl 3f)	¾	**6**	12/1	48	24
1133^{3}	**Stalled (IRE) (50)** (PTWalwyn) **7-8-8** KFallon(3) (hld up mid div: hdwy whn nt clr run over 1f out: btn whn nt clr run ins fnl f)	½	**7**	8/1	57	33
1215*	**Soojama (IRE) (57)** (RMFlower) **7-9-1b** SDrowne(1) (s.s: stdy hdwy 7f out: rdn over 3f out: wknd wl over 1f out)	2½	**8**	4/1^{2}	61	37
888^{15}	**Norsong (45)** (RAkehurst) **5-8-3** SSanders(10) (prom: rdn 3f out: wknd wl over 1f out)	1¼	**9**	20/1	48	24
1222^{4}	**Whothehellisharry (46)** (PTDalton) **4-8-3** JFEgan(8) (prom over 11f)	3½	**10**	16/1	45	20
	Arian Spirit (IRE) (52) (JLEyre) **6-8-10** MGallagher(5) (a bhd: t.o fnl 6f)	15	**11**	14/1	35	11
	Couchant (IRE) (57) (JWhite) **6-9-1** RPrice(11) (bkwd: a bhd: t.o fnl 8f)	dist	**12**	50/1	—	—
				(SP 125.8%)	**12 Rn**	

3m 17.2 (7.20) CSF £17.93 CT £89.82 TOTE £2.70: £1.60 £3.50 £1.10 (£18.60) Trio £103.90 OWNER Four Jays Racing Partnership (NEWMARKET) BRED Stetchworth Park Stud Ltd
LONG HANDICAP Romalito 7-9 Badawi (FR) 7-9
WEIGHT FOR AGE 4yo-1lb
1252* Golden Hadeer, up a further 4lb, registered his seventh victory of 1997, but it was only by the skin of his teeth. (7/4)
1100 Romalito was only beaten by the shortest of short heads, and being just out of the handicap must have made the difference. (9/1)
1114 Paradise Navy, down 2lb, was never going to reach the principals in time. (7/1)
Landlord, bought for only 800 guineas at Ascot October Sales, showed nothing in two runs over hurdles but looked capable of springing a surprise early in the short home straight. (33/1)
Badawi (FR) should be sharper for the run, and it will be interesting to see if he returns to the All-Weather. (16/1)
1252 Coleridge was down a further 4lb here. (12/1: op 8/1)
1133 Stalled (IRE), 1lb lower than when last seen on grass, would have finished closer but for twice running into trouble. (8/1)

1215* Soojama (IRE), raised 5lb, was rather reluctant to leave the stalls and did not have things his own way this time. (4/1)
Arian Spirit (IRE) (14/1: 10/1-16/1)

1425 EDGEHILL NOVICE MEDIAN AUCTION STKS (2-Y.O) (Class E)
7-50 (7-51) **5f** £3,226.25 (£965.00: £462.50: £211.25) Stalls: Low GOING minus 0.22 sec per fur (GF)

				SP	RR	SF
564[3]	**Flaming Ember (IRE)** (BJMeehan) **2-8-12** RHughes(2) (lw: s.s: sn rcvrd: led wl over 1f out: r.o wl)	—	**1**	2/1[1]	72	13
684[7]	**Yorkies Boy** (BAMcMahon) **2-8-12** LNewton(12) (wnt lft s: hrd rdn & hdwy over 1f out: r.o ins fnl f)	½	**2**	33/1	70	11
	Great Lyth Lass (IRE) (PDEvans) **2-8-7** JFEgan(6) (leggy: lt-f: unf: hdwy over 2f out: hrd rdn over 1f out: r.o on ins fnl f)	hd	**3**	16/1	65	6
	Magic Rainbow (MBell) **2-8-12** MFenton(9) (leggy: s.s: hdwy 3f out: ev ch over 1f out: one pce)	2	**4**	5/1	64	5
828[8]	**Universal Lady** (CJames) **2-8-7** TLucas(5) (s.i.s: nvr nrr)	2½	**5**	12/1	51	—
1026[3]	**Chunito** (PWChapple-Hyam) **2-8-9**(3) RHavlin(4) (led over 2f: wknd over 1f out)	nk	**6**	9/2[3]	55	—
1109[9]	**Regalo** (DMHyde) **2-8-9**(3) JDSmith(1) (w ldrs: led over 2f out tl wl over 1f out: sn wknd)	3½	**7**	33/1	44	—
1274[2]	**Caversfield** (RHannon) **2-8-12** DaneO'Neill(10) (lw: prom: c wd bnd over 2f out: sn wknd)	¾	**8**	13/2	41	—
	Desert Native (RHannon) **2-8-7** RPerham(14) (cmpt: bkwd: outpcd)	1¼	**9**	16/1	32	—
828[9]	**Fleet Lady (IRE)** (MrsPNDutfield) **2-8-7** SDrowne(13) (a bhd)	¾	**10**	20/1	30	—
739[2]	**Arian Da** (BPalling) **2-8-7** TSprake(8) (spd 3f)	4	**11**	4/1[2]	17	—
	Heiress of Meath (IRE) (MDIUsher) **2-8-7** JQuinn(7) (lt-f: s.i.s: a bhd)	3½	**12**	33/1	6	—
999[9]	**Chiltern Emerald** (JWhite) **2-8-7** RPrice(3) (prom 3f)	1	**13**	40/1	3	—
836[16]	**Liberalis** (GFHCharles-Jones) **2-8-7** CRutter(11) (hmpd s: a bhd: t.o)	19	**14**	33/1	—	—

(SP 139.9%) **14 Rn**

61.8 secs (3.80) CSF £92.99 TOTE £3.00: £2.30 £5.00 £6.20 (£48.90) Trio £138.20; £155.82 to 26/5/97 OWNER Mr B. Schmidt-Bodner (UPPER LAMBOURN) BRED Fort Union Stud Ltd

564 Flaming Ember (IRE) was friendless in the market when narrowly beaten on his debut, but it was a different story this time. Recovering remarkably quickly from a slow start, he was by no means hard pressed to hold on in the closing stages. (2/1)
500 Yorkies Boy got the trip better, having been forced to come from behind after a tardy start. (33/1)
Great Lyth Lass (IRE) is a half-sister to a mile winner in Ireland who went on to win three hurdles. She may be no oil painting, but her attitude could not be faulted. An extra furlong should help. (16/1)
Magic Rainbow, a half-brother to five-furlong winner Blue Sioux, will not have to improve much to take a similar event. (5/1: op 3/1)
Universal Lady, a half-sister to five-furlong winner Had A Girl, only cost 3,000 guineas but seems to be going the right way. (12/1)
1026 Chunito does not appear to be progressing. (9/2)

1426 RADWAY CLAIMING STKS (3-Y.O) (Class F)
8-20 (8-21) **1m 2f 169y** £2,669.70 (£739.20: £353.10) Stalls: Low GOING minus 0.22 sec per fur (GF)

				SP	RR	SF
793[2]	**Double Gold (64)** (BJMeehan) **3-8-6** KFallon(2) (plld hrd: mde all: clr over 2f out: easily)	—	**1**	4/6[1]	65+	7
1043[11]	**Ronquista d'Or (45)** (GAHam) **3-8-8** NCarlisle(6) (hld up: hdwy over 2f out: wnt 2nd over 1f out: no ch w wnr)	8	**2**	25/1	55	—
1139[4]	**Chief Predator (USA) (56)** (RHannon) **3-8-11** DaneO'Neill(4) (hld up: hdwy 5f out: one pce fnl 3f)	1¼	**3**	100/30[2]	56	—
1094[12]	**Warrior King (IRE) (46)** (MrsPNDutfield) **3-8-5** SDrowne(7) (hld up: hdwy over 3f out: one pce fnl 2f)	s.h	**4**	20/1	50	—
	Greenacres Goddess (TWall) **3-8-3** SSanders(5) (leggy: lt-f: prom: chsd wnr 4f out: outpcd over 2f out: wknd over 1f out)	6	**5**	33/1	39	—
1094[14]	**Clear The Air (55)** (PFICole) **3-8-8** CRutter(3) (prom: rdn 5f out: wknd 3f out)	9	**6**	7/1[3]	31	—
	Pow Wow (55) (PEccles) **3-8-7** JQuinn(1) (stdd s: a bhd: t.o fnl f)	dist	**7**	14/1	—	—

(SP 113.8%) **7 Rn**

2m 23.0 (9.00) CSF £22.28 TOTE £1.80: £1.10 £4.30 (£10.90) OWNER Mr Michael Edwards (UPPER LAMBOURN) BRED Catridge Farm Stud Ltd

793 Double Gold, well in at the weights, was a facile winner over this longer trip despite pulling like a train down the hill on the far side. (4/6)
539 Ronquista d'Or could well be facing eight flights of hurdles come August. (25/1)
1139 Chief Predator (USA) was reverting to a longer trip. (100/30: 2/1-7/2)
478 Warrior King (IRE) is another probably set to try his luck over timber. (20/1)

1427 RATLEY H'CAP (0-80) (3-Y.O+) (Class D)
8-50 (8-51) **1m 2f 169y** £4,027.80 (£1,205.40: £578.20: £264.60) Stalls: Low GOING minus 0.22 sec per fur (GF)

				SP	RR	SF
	North Reef (IRE) (69) (JPearce) **6-9-4** MWigham(7) (lw: a.p: rdn 4f out: led 2f out: r.o wl)	—	**1**	14/1	80	41
1244[14]	**Oberons Boy (IRE) (56)** (SDow) **4-8-5** RPerham(6) (hld up: hdwy 3f out: chsd wnr over 1f out: r.o one pce)	1	**2**	25/1	66	27
866[8]	**Nosey Native (60)** (JPearce) **4-8-6**(3) CTeague(8) (hld up in rr: swtchd rt wl over 1f out: gd hdwy fnl f: fin wl)	nk	**3**	14/1	69	30
990[5]	**Moon Blast (79)** (LadyHerries) **3-8-13** RHughes(3) (plld hrd early: lost pl 6f out: rdn 3f out: swtchd rt & hdwy over 1f out: hung lft ins fnl f: r.o)	½	**4**	3/1[1]	87	33
538*	**Mad Militant (IRE) (56)** (AStreeter) **8-8-5** TSprake(10) (hld up: hdwy 3f out: eased whn btn wl ins fnl f)	4	**5**	11/2[3]	58	19
986[4]	**Traceability (78)** (SCWilliams) **4-9-13** KFallon(11) (hld up: rdn over 3f out: eased whn btn ins fnl f)	5	**6**	9/2[2]	73	34
1226*	**Janie's Boy (71)** (MrsJCecil) **3-8-5** JQuinn(12) (lw: prom tl wknd over 1f out)	1¼	**7**	6/1	64	10
	Well Drawn (68) (HCandy) **4-9-3** CRutter(9) (lw: hld up & plld hrd: a bhd)	1¼	**8**	16/1	59	20
533[11]	**Kalinini (USA) (78)** (LMCumani) **3-8-12** OUrbina(5) (led tl hdd 2f out: eased whn btn fnl f)	5	**9**	8/1	62	8
1156[13]	**Newport Knight (73)** (RAkehurst) **6-9-8** SSanders(4) (rdn 5f out: a bhd)	¾	**10**	16/1	56	17
657[7]	**Askern (62)** (DHaydnJones) **6-8-11** MFenton(1) (prom: rdn over 3f out: ev ch 2f out: wknd over 1f out: eased whn btn)	1¼	**11**	6/1	43	4
1256[4]	**William Wallace (68)** (DHaydnJones) **3-8-2** SDrowne(2) (lw: hld up & plld hrd: a bhd)	9	**12**	12/1	36	—

(SP 134.9%) **12 Rn**

2m 19.8 (5.80) CSF £326.07 CT £4,529.31 TOTE £25.60: £4.50 £4.80 £7.40 (£98.50) Trio £214.80; £272.35 to 26/5/97 OWNER Storeforce Ltd (NEWMARKET) BRED Limestone Stud
WEIGHT FOR AGE 3yo-15lb

North Reef (IRE) took advantage of being 6lb lower than when second on the sand at Lingfield in December. (14/1)
120 Oberons Boy (IRE), dropped 6lb on grass this season, ran his best race for a while on turf. (25/1)
Nosey Native, now only 3lb higher than when winning at Haydock last October, finds this trip the bare minimum on ground as fast this. (14/1)
990 Moon Blast, one way and another did not give Hughes the best of rides, and seems the type who keeps the bookmakers smoking big cigars. (3/1)

538* Mad Militant (IRE) looked dangerous turning into the short home straight, but could not overcome a 4lb hike in the ratings for his course and distance win. (11/2)
533 Kalinini (USA) (8/1: tchd 12/1)
1256 William Wallace (12/1: 10/1-16/1)

T/Plpt: £2,479.70 (5.43 Tckts). T/Qdpt: £395.70 (1.7 Tckts) KH

1121-**WOLVERHAMPTON (L-H) (Standard)**
Saturday May 24th
WEATHER: sunny

1428 EDGBASTON H'CAP (0-65) (3-Y.O+ F & M) (Class F)
7-00 (7-00) **5f (Fibresand)** £2,277.00 (£627.00: £297.00) Stalls: Low

				SP	RR	SF
1046^{2}	**Napier Star (63)** (MrsNMacauley) **4-10-0v** SWebster(4) (b.off hind: chsd ldr: led over 1f out: r.o u.p)	—	**1**	4/1^{3}	69	50
1289^{6}	**Delrob (43)** (DHaydnJones) **6-8-8b** DHolland(8) (lw: a.p: rdn 2f out: r.o wl fnl f)	hd	**2**	7/2^{2}	49	30
1236^{9}	**River Ensign (39)** (WMBrisbourne) **4-7-13**(5) RMullen(7) (mid div: rdn over 2f out: kpt on)	6	**3**	14/1	26	7
1046^{10}	**Amoeba (IRE) (48)** (ABailey) **4-8-13b^{1}** DWright(6) (lw: towards rr: sn rdn along: kpt on fr over 1f out: n.d)	hd	**4**	9/4^{1}	34	15
1046^{3}	**Corinchili (57)** (GGMargarson) **3-8-11**(3) MHenry(3) (lw: led tl rdn & hdd over 1f out: sn wknd)	nk	**5**	9/2	42	15
1236^{U}	**Daughter In Law (IRE) (35)** (PRWebber) **4-7-9**(5) JBramhill(2) (lw: in tch tl rdn & wknd over 1f out)	1¾	**6**	33/1	15	—
	Lawsimina (37) (DShaw) **4-8-2** JFanning(11) (bkwd: racd wd: nvr nr ldrs)	s.h	**7**	16/1	16	—
	Hi Hoh (IRE) (40) (NPLittmoden) **4-8-5** TGMcLaughlin(5) (bkwd: chsd ldrs tl rdn & wknd wl over 1f out)	2	**8**	33/1	13	—
882^{3}	**Terry's Rose (44)** (RHollinshead) **3-7-10**(5) PFessey(10) (a bhd)	s.h	**9**	7/1	17	—
1134^{8}	**Little Papoose (37)** (BAMcMahon) **4-7-9**(7)ow4 SRighton(1) (prom 3f)	hd	**10**	33/1	10	—
756^{8}	**Come Too Mamma's (55)** (GCBravery) **3-8-12** ACulhane(9) (outpcd)	7	**11**	12/1	5	—
				(SP 132.7%)	**11 Rn**	

62.0 secs (3.10) CSF £19.02 CT £172.47 TOTE £5.00: £3.10 £1.90 £2.10 (£9.50) Trio £45.20 OWNER Mr P. M. Heaton (MELTON MOWBRAY) BRED P. M. Heaton
WEIGHT FOR AGE 3yo-8lb
1046 Napier Star landed her third course and distance win, having just enough in reserve to hold off the late challenge of the runner-up. (4/1)
1289 Delrob put in a determined late challenge to no avail. A step-up to six furlongs should have its reward off her present mark. (7/2)
907 River Ensign, very worked-up in the paddock, could not go the early pace but stuck gamely to her task. (14/1: 10/1-16/1)
901 Amoeba (IRE), well-supported for her first run in blinkers, struggled from the word go. (9/4: 4/1-2/1)
1046 Corinchili again showed plenty of speed but, at the moment, she does not even seem to get the minimum trip. (9/2)
158 Come Too Mamma's (12/1: op 8/1)

1429 TRENT BRIDGE APPRENTICE CLAIMING STKS (3-Y.O) (Class G)
7-30 (7-30) **1m 100y (Fibresand)** £1,984.50 (£547.00: £259.50) Stalls: Low

				SP	RR	SF
952*	**Going For Broke (66)** (PCHaslam) **3-9-1**(3) GFaulkner(5) (lw: trckd ldr: led over 6f out: rdn & r.o fnl f)	—	**1**	4/7^{1}	74	33
1044^{3}	**Madam Lucy (47)** (WWHaigh) **3-8-0**(3) JBramhill(3) (a.p: rdn 2f out: unable qckn fnl f)	2	**2**	9/1	55	14
*6**	**Royal Roulette (57)** (SPCWoods) **3-8-2v**(5) CWebb(2) (plld hrd: a.p: rdn & r.o one pce fnl f)	¾	**3**	7/2^{2}	58	17
1044^{4}	**Phoenix Princess** (BAMcMahon) **3-8-2**(7) SRighton(1) (lw: plld hrd: in tch: dropped rr 4f out: n.d after)	3	**4**	12/1	54	13
1096^{15}	**Sheraton Girl (47)** (NPLittmoden) **3-8-2**(3) RMullen(4) (lw: led 2f: chsd wnr tl rdn & wknd over 1f out)	7	**5**	5/1^{3}	37	—
				(SP 120.2%)	**5 Rn**	

1m 51.4 (6.40) CSF £7.22 TOTE £1.70: £1.10 £2.10 (£5.10) OWNER Dunnington & Smart (MIDDLEHAM) BRED Mrs John Trotter
952* Going For Broke completed a hat-trick in his usual gutsy style, and never looked like being denied. (4/7)
1044 Madam Lucy moved well to post and threw down a challenge early in the straight, but found the winner too strong. She can find a race on this showing. (9/1)
6* Royal Roulette was found wanting in the closing stages, but this was her first run for over five months. (7/2)
1044 Phoenix Princess looked a bit of handful, refusing to settle and dropping right away half-a-mile out, though she ran on again turning for home. (12/1: op 8/1)
873* Sheraton Girl shaped as though this was just too far for her, stopping to nothing in the final furlong. (5/1)

1430 OVAL MAIDEN STKS (3-Y.O+) (Class D)
8-00 (8-03) **1m 1f 79y (Fibresand)** £3,773.00 (£1,127.00: £539.00: £245.00) Stalls: Low

				SP	RR	SF
1130^{5}	**Dalliance (IRE)** (MRStoute) **3-8-10** KDarley(11) (hdwy 4f out: led 2f out: clr ent fnl f: r.o wl)	—	**1**	Evens^{1}	87	56
1092^{3}	**Dawam Allail (IRE) (75)** (MAJarvis) **3-8-10** WRyan(3) (led tl rdn & hdd 2f out: r.o one pce)	8	**2**	11/4^{2}	73	42
933^{10}	**Raise A Prince (FR) (72)** (JWHills) **4-9-6**(3) MHenry(2) (b.hind: a.p: rdn & one pce fnl 2f)	1	**3**	8/1	72	54
1090^{4}	**Tellion** (MajorWRHern) **3-8-10** DHolland(8) (bhd: hdwy over 3f out: rdn 2f out: sn wknd)	½	**4**	8/1	71	40
1105^{4}	**Eagle Dancer** (LadyHerries) **5-9-9** DeclanO'Shea(10) (hld up & bhd: stdy hdwy 5f out: no imp fnl 2f)	2	**5**	10/1	67	49
1121^{5}	**Robbo** (CWThornton) **3-8-10** DeanMcKeown(6) (bhd tl mod late hdwy: n.d)	7	**6**	33/1	55	24
1138^{14}	**Safa Dancer (34)** (BAMcMahon) **4-8-11**(7) SRighton(7) (prom tl rdn & wknd 3f out)	1¼	**7**	50/1	48	30
1297^{7}	**Krabloonik (FR)** (SirMarkPrescott) **3-8-10** GDuffield(4) (hld up: plld hrd: btn over 3f out)	½	**8**	5/1^{3}	52	21
1155^{5}	**Tezaab** (BHanbury) **3-8-10** MRimmer(5) (chsd ldr 6f: sn rdn & wknd)	4	**9**	33/1	46	15
	Shark (IRE) (KAMorgan) **4-9-9** ACulhane(9) (bkwd: plld hrd: prom: dropped rr ½-wy: t.o)	24	**10**	40/1	5	—
				(SP 134.9%)	**10 Rn**	

1m 59.5 (3.50) CSF £4.28 TOTE £2.50: £1.30 £1.40 £3.70 (£4.00) Trio £12.20 OWNER Sheikh Mohammed (NEWMARKET) BRED Sheikh Mohammed Bin Rashid Al Maktoum
WEIGHT FOR AGE 3yo-13lb
1130 Dalliance (IRE) marked his All-Weather debut with a most emphatic win, outclassing this opposition and forging clear in the closing stages. (Evens)
1092 Dawam Allail (IRE) cut out the running but was made to look very one-paced when the winner went on. It could be that he was unlucky to meet such an opponent on the All-Weather. (11/4)
Raise A Prince (FR) was up in the firing line but, like the rest, he was only running for second place turning for home. (8/1: op 5/1)
1090 Tellion was stepped-up in trip and moved well to post, but was well outpointed on reaching the home straight. His turn may come when his yard hits form. (8/1)

1105 Eagle Dancer, taken early to the start, was steadied back when the stalls opened. He made headway on the wide outside up the back straight and, although making no ground in the final three furlongs, he was not knocked about. He will be handicapped after his next run, and is worth keeping a close eye on. (10/1)
1121 Robbo was right out the back and just kept on through beaten horses. (33/1)

1431 FRANKIE GOES TO EPSOM H'CAP (0-95) (3-Y.O+) (Class C)

8-30 (8-31) **1m 4f (Fibresand)** £5,067.85 (£1,508.80: £717.90: £322.45) Stalls: Low

				SP	RR	SF
283^{2}	**Glow Forum (73)** (LMontagueHall) **6-8-9**(3) FLynch(5) (a.p: rdn 2f out: str run to ld last stride)	—	1	$7/2^{3}$	81	40
1123^{5}	**Ground Game (84)** (DRLoder) **4-9-9** KDarley(4) (chsd ldr: led over 2f out: sn rdn: hdd post)	s.h	2	$5/2^{2}$	92	51
881^{3}	**Hill Farm Dancer (78)** (WMBrisbourne) **6-8-12**(5) RMullen(2) (hld up: hdwy 4f out: rdn & ev ch fr 2f out: no ex ins fnl f)	1½	3	13/2	84	43
*908**	**Premier Dance (70)** (DHaydnJones) **10-8-4**(5) PPMurphy(1) (hld up: dropped rr & pushed along 4f out: kpt on fnl 2f: n.d)	2½	4	4/1	73	32
*1156**	**Canton Venture (85)** (SPCWoods) **5-9-10** WRyan(3) (led tl rdn & hdd over 2f out: sn wknd: eased ins fnl f)	3½	5	$7/4^{1}$	83	42
				(SP 120.5%)	**5 Rn**	

2m 39.9 (7.40) CSF £12.63 TOTE £4.90: £1.70 £1.80 (£6.00) OWNER Miss J D Anstee & Partners (EPSOM) BRED Forum Bloodstock Ltd
283 Glow Forum once again showed she can produce her best after a lay-off, coming with a storming late run to land the spoils. (7/2)
1123 Ground Game appeared to have fought off her main rival, only to be collared in the last stride by another. With her yard not yet firing on all cylinders, her turn may come when their fortunes pick up. (5/2)
881 Hill Farm Dancer is a course and distance specialist, but is weighted to the hilt at the moment. (13/2)
908* Premier Dance was never able to get in this race after losing touch half-a-mile out. (4/1)
1156* Canton Venture found an 11lb rise in his mark too much to handle. His pilot soon accepted the position once his chance had gone. (7/4)

1432 LORDS (S) STKS (2-Y.O F) (Class G)

9-00 (9-02) **6f (Fibresand)** £1,984.50 (£547.00: £259.50) Stalls: Low

				SP	RR	SF
*1290**	**Ellenbrook (IRE)** (JBerry) **2-8-9b**(5) PFessey(1) (lw: mde virtually all: clr over 2f out: easily)	—	1	Evens[1]	65+	15
1124^{3}	**Jack-N-Jilly (IRE)** (JSMoore) **2-8-6**(3) MHenry(4) (lw: w wnr 2f: outpcd over 2f out: rdn & no imp)	5	2	7/1	47	—
993^{8}	**Sylvan Cloud** (CWFairhurst) **2-8-9** DeanMcKeown(6) (chsd ldrs: rdn & outpcd fr ½-wy)	4	3	20/1	36	—
1045^{7}	**Rock From The Sun** (WGMTurner) **2-8-2**(7) DMcGaffin(5) (chsd ldrs: rdn & wknd 3f out)	2	4	$13/2^{3}$	31	—
	Keen Lady (NPLittmoden) **2-8-9** TGMcLaughlin(2) (cmpt: leggy: unruly stalls: s.s: a bhd)	4	5	10/1	20	—
1298^{3}	**Miss Beveled** (MBrittain) **2-8-9** GDuffield(3) (dwlt & sn pushed along: outpcd)	1¼	6	$2/1^{2}$	17	—
				(SP 123.0%)	**6 Rn**	

1m 16.6 (5.40) CSF £9.46 TOTE £1.70: £1.20 £3.10 (£3.40) OWNER Mr J. K. Brown (COCKERHAM) BRED M. Bourke
Bt in 5,000gns
1290* Ellenbrook (IRE), whose blinkers appeared to have had the desired effect, was always travelling well and she won this in effortless fashion. (Evens)
1124 Jack-N-Jilly (IRE) kept tabs on the winner early on, but was left flat-footed early in the straight. (7/1)
Sylvan Cloud was under pressure to hold her place a long way out. (20/1)
664 Rock From The Sun took a keen hold to post but lacked the pace to lay up with them. (13/2)
Keen Lady (10/1: op 6/1)
1298 Miss Beveled (2/1: op 5/1)

1433 OLD TRAFFORD H'CAP (0-65) (3-Y.O+) (Class F)

9-30 (9-30) **7f (Fibresand)** £2,277.00 (£627.00: £297.00) Stalls: High

				SP	RR	SF
1225^{7}	**Theatre Magic (64)** (DShaw) **4-9-13** JFanning(3) (b: lw: in tch: rdn & hdwy over 2f out: qcknd to ld ins fnl f)	—	1	8/1	74	47
1048^{6}	**Dawalib (USA) (59)** (DHaydnJones) **7-9-8** DHolland(12) (chsd ldrs fr ½-wy: rdn to ld over 1f out: hdd & no ex ins fnl f)	1¼	2	$11/4^{1}$	66	39
466^{6}	**Molly Music (55)** (GGMargarson) **3-8-4**(3) MHenry(11) (a.p: led over 2f out: hdd over 1f out: no ex ins fnl f)	nk	3	20/1	62	24
1035^{11}	**Sooty Tern (53)** (JMBradley) **10-9-2** JFEgan(7) (lw: led after 1f: hdd over 4f out: rdn & one pce fnl f)	½	4	$9/2^{3}$	58	31
1248^{6}	**Legal Issue (IRE) (53)** (WWHaigh) **5-9-2** RLappin(9) (s.s: bhd tl styd on fr over 1f out: nvr nrr)	½	5	$4/1^{2}$	57	30
972^{9}	**Smart Guest (57)** (DShaw) **5-9-3**(3) OPears(6) (b: b.hind: sn bhd & rdn along: kpt on fnl 2f)	1¼	6	25/1	58	31
1135^{4}	**Efipetite (39)** (NBycroft) **4-8-2** NKennedy(1) (chsd ldrs: ev ch whn nt clr run wl over 1f out: n.d after)	hd	7	16/1	40	13
1096^{5}	**Legend of Aragon (52)** (JAGlover) **3-8-4** GDuffield(10) (lw: chsd ldrs: led over 4f out: rdn & hdd over 3f out: wknd appr fnl f)	1½	8	5/1	50	12
1291^{6}	**Dragonjoy (60)** (NPLittmoden) **4-9-4v**(5) PRoberts(8) (lw: outpcd)	1	9	15/2	55	28
	Best Kept Secret (46) (LJBarratt) **6-8-2**(7) CLowther(5) (a bhd)	nk	10	33/1	41	14
	Opening Range (36) (NEBerry) **6-7-6**(7)ow1 RWinston(2) (bkwd: led 1f: led over 3f out: hdd over 2f out: wknd qckly)	1	11	40/1	28	—
	Four of Spades (60) (RJHodges) **6-9-4b**(5) AmandaSanders(4) (b: b.hind: bkwd: prom to ½-wy)	10	12	12/1	30	3
				(SP 132.0%)	**12 Rn**	

1m 29.4 (4.70) CSF £29.77 CT £425.33 TOTE £10.60: £2.90 £2.80 £6.30 (£15.60) Trio £159.80; £202.61 to 26/5/97 OWNER Green Diamond Racing (NEWARK) BRED N. S. Yong
WEIGHT FOR AGE 3yo-11lb
860* Theatre Magic, 7lb higher than when winning here last month, looked in some trouble turning in but found a nice turn of foot in the final furlong. (8/1: op 9/2)
514 Dawalib (USA) looked all set to land another prize for his in-form yard, only to be foiled in the last hundred yards. (11/4: op 5/1)
Molly Music put in by far her best run to date and, as long as the Handicapper is not too harsh, she may find a similar race. (20/1)
791 Sooty Tern produced another consistent effort, and it was only in the final furlong that his challenge petered out. (9/2)
1248 Legal Issue (IRE) lost any chance with a tardy start and did well to get as close as he did under the circumstances. (4/1)
1096 Legend of Aragon was right in the thick of things until dropping out in the final furlong. Maybe a drop back to six furlongs will help exploit what looks a favourable handicap mark. (5/1)
860 Dragonjoy (15/2: 5/1-8/1)

T/Plpt: £21.20 (398.15 Tckts). T/Qdpt: £9.30 (48.72 Tckts) J

CHEPSTOW (L-H) (Good)

Monday May 26th

WEATHER: fine WIND: slt against

1434 ST ARVANS MAIDEN STKS (3-Y.O+) (Class D)

2-30 (2-32) **1m 4f 23y** £3,715.50 (£1,119.00: £542.00: £253.50) Stalls: Low GOING minus 0.07 sec per fur (G)

				SP	RR	SF
670^{5}	**Prairie Falcon (IRE) (88)** (BWHills) **3-8-6**(3) JDSmith(5) (hld up: hdwy over 4f out led over 2f out: r.o wl)	—	**1**	7/2 ^{2}	86	51
967^{3}	**Tikopia** (IABalding) **3-8-9** SWhitworth(12) (hdwy over 3f out: chsd wnr fnl 2f: r.o one pce)	2½	**2**	11/4 ^{1}	83	48
	Badenoch (IRE) (JHMGosden) **3-8-9** GHind(8) (unf: a.p: one pce fnl 2f)	5	**3**	12/1	76	41
944^{4}	**Psicossis** (HRACecil) **4-9-12** AMcGlone(6) (swtg: prom: chsd ldr 9f out: led 3f out tl over 2f out: wknd wl over 1f out)	1½	**4**	4/1 ^{3}	74	56
605^{2}	**Mardi Gras (IRE) (80)** (JLDunlop) **3-8-10**ow1 RHughes(9) (lw: led 9f: wknd wl over 1f out)	1	**5**	6/1	74	38
1105^{5}	**Yak Alfaraj** (MRStoute) **3-8-9** DHarrison(1) (s.i.s: sn chsng ldrs: rdn & wknd 3f out)	1¼	**6**	10/1	71	36
1144^{8}	**Alhosaam** (MajorWRHern) **3-8-9** DeclanO'Shea(4) (s.i.s: stdy hdwy fnl 3f: nvr plcd to chal)	½	**7**	33/1	71	36
1168^{15}	**Puteri Wentworth** (MissGayKelleway) **3-8-1**(3) AWhelan(10) (bhd fnl 4f)	5	**8**	33/1	59	24
	Sheep Stealer (REPeacock) **9-9-12** RPrice(11) (bhd tl rdn & hdwy over 4f out: wknd over 3f out)	1	**9**	100/1	63	45
949^{9}	**All Done** (SMellor) **4-9-7** MWigham(3) (chsd ldr 3f: wknd over 4f out: t.o)	12	**10**	100/1	42	24
1144^{7}	**Copper Shell (74)** (APJones) **3-8-6**(3) DO'Donohoe(2) (plld hrd in rr: t.o fnl 4f)	2½	**11**	33/1	43	8
	Eastbury Rose (APJones) **3-8-4** NAdams(7) (w'like: s.s: a bhd: t.o fnl 4f)	6	**12**	50/1	30	—
1276^{8}	**Nigels Choice** (CJHill) **5-9-9**(3) RHavlin(13) (bit bkwd: a bhd: t.o)	8	**13**	100/1	25	7
				(SP 113.7%)	**13 Rn**	

2m 38.0 (5.60) CSF £11.19 TOTE £3.50: £2.00 £1.50 £3.20 (£4.30) Trio £28.60 OWNER Lady Harrison (LAMBOURN) BRED Holborn Trust Co

WEIGHT FOR AGE 3yo-17lb

670 Prairie Falcon (IRE), described by the trainer's son as having run flat last time, lived up to his narrow defeat by the subsequent Italian Derby winner on his seasonal reappearance. (7/2: 9/4-4/1)

967 Tikopia beat the others easily enough, and came up against an above-average sort in the winner. (11/4: 2/1-3/1)

Badenoch (IRE), a half-brother to Irresistible Lady and Ceilidh Star, did not appear to possess a lot of scope on paddock inspection. (12/1: op 4/1)

944 Psicossis is not living up to his Gold Cup and Hardwicke Stakes entries at Royal Ascot. (4/1: op 5/2)

605 Mardi Gras (IRE) is possibly more effective at shorter distances. (6/1)

Yak Alfaraj is a half-brother to several winners including Zilclare and an Irish staying juvenile winner. (10/1: 7/1-11/1)

Alhosaam, a half-brother to Namoodaj and Pfalz, is now qualified for handicaps, and it will come as no surprise if he does not turn out to be a good deal better than he has shown so far. (33/1)

1435 ST ATHAN H'CAP (0-80) (3-Y.O+ F & M) (Class D)

3-00 (3-01) **1m 4f 23y** £3,442.50 (£1,035.00: £500.00: £232.50) Stalls: Low GOING minus 0.07 sec per fur (G)

				SP	RR	SF
1278*	**Star Precision (78)** (GBBalding) **3-9-0** 6x RPrice(1) (lw: hld up: hdwy over 4f out: led on bit over 3f out: shkn up: sn clr)	—	**1**	2/1 ^{1}	98++	67
1142*	**Roufontaine (75)** (WRMuir) **6-9-11**(3) RHavlin(2) (lw: hld up & bhd: stdy hdwy on ins over 4f out: chsd wnr over 2f out: no imp)	7	**2**	11/2 ^{3}	86	72
1001^{4}	**Shalateeno (65)** (BRMillman) **4-9-4** MWigham(5) (plld hrd: led over 1f: rdn over 4f out: styd on one pce fnl 2f)	1¼	**3**	12/1	74	60
1247*	**Elly Fleetfoot (IRE) (53)** (GLMoore) **5-8-6v** SWhitworth(7) (hld up: stdy hdwy 5f out: wknd wl over 1f out)	4	**4**	10/1	57	43
797^{2}	**Ajayib (USA) (79)** (JLDunlop) **3-9-1** RHughes(4) (lw: hld up: rdn 5f out: hdwy over 3f out: eased whn btn ins fnl f)	½	**5**	11/4 ^{2}	82	51
1278^{4}	**Daily Sport Girl (43)** (BJLlewellyn) **8-7-10** DeclanO'Shea(6) (led over 10f out: hdd over 3f out: sn wknd)	7	**6**	20/1	37	23
1140^{6}	**Moonspell (66)** (RCharlton) **3-8-2**ow1 AMcGlone(8) (prom: wnt 2nd 6f out: wknd over 3f out)	6	**7**	8/1	52	20
	Contract Bridge (IRE) (51) (PGMurphy) **4-8-4v**1ow1 DHarrison(3) (dwlt: a bhd)	5	**8**	12/1	30	15
				(SP 115.7%)	**8 Rn**	

2m 36.3 (3.90) CSF £12.47 CT £95.08 TOTE £2.20: £1.10 £1.60 £3.70 (£3.60) OWNER Miss B. Swire (ANDOVER) BRED Miss B. Swire

WEIGHT FOR AGE 3yo-17lb

OFFICIAL EXPLANATION **Ajayib (USA): rider reported that the filly had been fractious in the stalls, hung right and became unco-ordinated. He felt it prudent not to persevere.**

1278* Star Precision was effectively 13lb higher for her two previous wins, but still looked some way ahead of the Handicapper. (2/1)

1142* Roufontaine, something of a course specialist, came up against a horse in top form. (11/2)

1001 Shalateeno plugged on for the minor berth after looking held early in the long home straight. (12/1: 8/1-14/1)

1247* Elly Fleetfoot (IRE), reverting to a mile and a half, only won a seller at Nottingham and was 2lb higher than the time before. (10/1)

797 Ajayib (USA), up 3lb over this longer trip, can be considered fourth on merit, and lengthy explanations as to why she was not ridden out in the closing stages were accepted. (11/4)

1436 ST MELLONS LIMITED STKS (0-75) (3-Y.O+) (Class D)

3-30 (3-32) **1m 14y** £3,510.75 (£1,056.00: £510.50: £237.75) Stalls: High GOING minus 0.07 sec per fur (G)

				SP	RR	SF
	Mo-Addab (IRE) (74) (ACStewart) **7-9-6** SWhitworth(3) (swtg: a.p: led wl over 1f out: rdn out)	—	**1**	4/1 ^{2}	75	41
1166^{8}	**Kewarra (70)** (BRMillman) **3-8-5**(3) AWhelan(1) (hld up: hdwy to ld 2f out: sn hdd: r.o ins fnl f)	½	**2**	12/1 ^{3}	74	28
1308^{2}	**Sharp Shuffle (IRE) (73)** (RHannon) **4-9-8** RHughes(4) (b: hld up: rdn & hdwy over 1f out: one pce fnl f)	3½	**3**	5/6 ^{1}	69	35
1110^{4}	**Ghayyur (USA) (73)** (JLDunlop) **3-8-2**(3) DO'Donohoe(5) (plld hrd: sn chsng ldr: wknd over 1f out)	1¼	**4**	4/1 ^{2}	62	16
1017^{13}	**Truly Parched (USA) (75)** (PWChapple-Hyam) **3-8-5**(3) RHavlin(2) (plld hrd: led 6f: wknd over 1f out)	s.h	**5**	12/1 ^{3}	65	19
560^{7}	**Attarikh (IRE) (67)** (MrsALMKing) **4-9-6** AMcGlone(6) (lw: hld up: swtchd lft over 4f out: rdn over 2f out: sn bhd)	7	**6**	33/1	51	17
				(SP 112.9%)	**6 Rn**	

1m 36.4 (5.20) CSF £42.28 TOTE £4.90: £1.50 £2.60 (£13.50) OWNER Mr S. J. Hammond (NEWMARKET) BRED Mrs M. Upsdell

WEIGHT FOR AGE 3yo-12lb

Mo-Addab (IRE) took a walk in the market, probably because he was awash with sweat in the paddock. He may now go for the Royal Hunt Cup. (4/1: op 5/2)

Kewarra relished this step up to a mile, and a stiffer course could well be in his favour. (12/1: 8/1-14/1)

1308 Sharp Shuffle (IRE) was disappointing here and displayed a rather awkward head carriage when making his move. (5/6: evens-5/4)
1110 Ghayyur (USA) saw too much daylight in this small field on a straight course. (4/1)
729 Truly Parched (USA) is another who ran too freely. (12/1: op 8/1)

1437 ST BRIAVELS MAIDEN STKS (3-Y.O+) (Class D)
4-00 (4-02) **1m 14y** £3,761.00 (£1,133.00: £549.00: £257.00) Stalls: High GOING minus 0.07 sec per fur (G)

				SP	RR	SF
1221^{5}	**Stilett (IRE)** (LMCumani) **3-8-12** OUrbina(2) (hld up: hdwy to ld over 2f out: comf)	—	**1**	6/1	84+	28
	Cugina (70) (GBBalding) **3-8-7** RPrice(1) (unruly paddock: a.p: ev ch 2f out: r.o one pce)	1½	**2**	12/1	76	20
	Fayik (MRStoute) **3-8-12** DHarrison(7) (lw: a.p: led over 3f out tl over 2f out: one pce)	3	**3**	$7/4^{1}$	75	19
1023^{8}	**Atomic Shell (CAN)** (CFWall) **4-9-10** NDay(6) (lw: hld up: rdn over 2f out: styd on fnl f)	1	**4**	$5/1^{3}$	73	29
	Danzas (RCharlton) **3-8-12** AMcGlone(5) (w'like: scope: s.s: no hdwy fnl 2f)	9	**5**	15/2	55	—
1110^{14}	**Kara Queen** (CJHill) **3-8-7** NAdams(3) (chsd ldr over 4f: sn wknd: t.o)	14	**6**	100/1	22	—
565^{3}	**Deep Water (USA) (82)** (PFICole) **3-8-5**(7) DavidO'Neill(8) (lw: led: rdn & hdd over 3f out: sn wknd: t.o)	1	**7**	$9/2^{2}$	26	—
1272^{16}	**Blue Calvine** (CJHill) **3-8-12** MWigham(4) (s.s: a bhd: t.o)	5	**8**	100/1	16	—

(SP 106.9%) **8 Rn**

1m 36.9 (5.70) CSF £58.29 TOTE £8.00: £1.30 £2.20 £1.30 (£62.00) OWNER Scuderia Rencati Srl (NEWMARKET) BRED James M. Egan
WEIGHT FOR AGE 3yo-12lb
1221 Stilett (IRE) really got his act together and scored with a fair bit in hand. (6/1: 4/1-13/2)
Cugina, who eventually had to be mounted just before coming on to the racecourse, was as good as gold thereafter but met one too sharp in the winner. (12/1: 7/1-14/1)
Fayik is bred to require further than this. (7/4: 11/10-2/1)
Atomic Shell (CAN), a springer in the market, shaped as though he may require further. (5/1)
Danzas, a well-bred gelding, could never recover from a poor start. (15/2: 5/2-8/1)
565 Deep Water (USA) is unfortunately showing why his trainer took the unusual step of sending him to Southwell for his seasonal debut.(9/2)

54 43 60+

1438 ST WEONARDS (S) STKS (2-Y.O) (Class G)
4-30 (4-32) **6f 16y** £2,262.00 (£632.00: £306.00) Stalls: High GOING minus 0.07 sec per fur (G)

				SP	RR	SF
536^{6}	**Island Girl (IRE)** (DWPArbuthnot) **2-8-6** SWhitworth(1) (a.p: led over 1f out: r.o)	—	**1**	$3/1^{2}$	66	9
	Huxleen (WGMTurner) **2-8-3**(3) RHavlin(4) (lt-f: unf: hdwy over 1f out: r.o wl ins fnl f)	hd	**2**	12/1	66	9
1330^{2}	**Swoosh** (BJMeehan) **2-8-11** RHughes(6) (led 1f: rdn & ev ch over 1f out: edgd lft ins fnl f: nt qckn)	1	**3**	$11/10^{1}$	68	11
999^{6}	**Tremonnow** (JMBradley) **2-8-6** GHind(5) (led after 1f tl over 2f out: one pce)	1¾	**4**	7/1	59	2
1293^{6}	**Dixie Crossroads** (RHannon) **2-8-6** DHarrison(2) (lw: w ldrs: led over 2f out tl over 1f out: sn wknd)	1¼	**5**	$6/1^{3}$	55	—
	Goldenacres (JNeville) **2-8-11** AMcGlone(7) (neat: outpcd)	2½	**6**	16/1	54	—
	Flibbertigibbet (CJHill) **2-8-6** NAdams(3) (lt-f: bkwd: s.s: a t.o)	dist	**7**	33/1	—	—

(SP 115.9%) **7 Rn**

1m 14.5 (5.30) CSF £34.72 TOTE £3.70: £1.90 £6.00 (£52.30) OWNER Mr Philip Banfield (COMPTON) BRED Leo Collins
No bid
536 Island Girl (IRE), dropped into a seller, saw the extra furlong out well enough. (3/1)
Huxleen really grasped what was required in the last two hundred yards, and would have overhauled the winner in another few strides. (12/1: op 5/1)
1330 Swoosh was taking another drop in grade here. (11/10: evens-5/4)
Tremonnow is a sister to mile-and-a-half winner Bark 'n' Bite, and half-sister to ten furlong winner Flockton's Own. (7/1)
1293 Dixie Crossroads could not take advantage of a drop in grade. (6/1)

1439 ST BRIDES H'CAP (0-80) (3-Y.O+ F & M) (Class D)
5-00 (5-01) **6f 16y** £3,783.75 (£1,140.00: £552.50: £258.75) Stalls: High GOING minus 0.07 sec per fur (G)

				SP	RR	SF
1279^{5}	**Deerly (47)** (RDickin) **4-7-5**(5) APolli(11) (mde all: r.o wl)	—	**1**	10/1	54	32
1166^{6}	**Newlands Corner (58)** (JAkehurst) **4-8-4b**(3) JDSmith(1) (s.s: gd hdwy over 1f out: fin wl)	2	**2**	9/1	60	38
1046^{7}	**Make Ready (63)** (JNeville) **3-8-3** JTate(13) (hld up: gd hdwy wl over 1f out: r.o one pce fnl f)	s.h	**3**	20/1	65	34
883^{7}	**Sharp 'n' Shady (56)** (CFWall) **4-8-5** NDay(10) (swtg: a.p: one pce fnl 2f)	½	**4**	$13/2^{2}$	56	34
1245^{12}	**Tajrebah (USA) (70)** (PTWalwyn) **3-8-10** GHind(7) (chsd ldrs: rdn over 2f out: one pce)	4	**5**	11/1	60	29
1275^{3}	**Silver Purse (71)** (APJones) **3-8-11** MWigham(14) (swtg: a.p: no hdwy fnl 2f)	1	**6**	16/1	58	27
1127^{2}	**Palo Blanco (73)** (GLMoore) **6-9-8** SWhitworth(6) (prom over 4f)	nk	**7**	$15/2^{3}$	59	37
1166^{7}	**Tea Party (USA) (62)** (KOCunningham-Brown) **4-8-11b** AMcGlone(5) (hdwy over 2f out: wknd over 1f out)	nk	**8**	20/1	48	26
1141*	**Strat's Quest (69)** (DWPArbuthnot) **3-8-9** DHarrison(12) (mid div: rdn over 2f out: sn bhd)	5	**9**	$6/1^{1}$	41	10
	Calandrella (47) (GBBalding) **4-7-10** NAdams(2) (bhd fnl 2f)	2½	**10**	25/1	13	—
1141^{18}	**Bold Tina (IRE) (72)** (RHannon) **3-8-12** RHughes(15) (a bhd)	nk	**11**	8/1	37	6
1107^{2}	**La Petite Fusee (79)** (RJO'Sullivan) **6-9-11**(3) DO'Donohoe(8) (prom: rdn over 2f out: wknd over 1f out)	nk	**12**	$6/1^{1}$	43	21
1110^{10}	**Sugar Plum (60)** (RHannon) **3-7-11**(3) AWhelan(9) (a bhd)	2	**13**	20/1	19	—
1279^{14}	**Tinker Osmaston (60)** (MSSaunders) **6-8-9v**[1] RPrice(4) (lw: spd over 3f)	1¼	**14**	10/1	16	—
1141^{7}	**Wild Nettle (56)** (JCFox) **3-7-10** DeclanO'Shea(3) (swtg: a bhd: t.o)	16	**15**	25/1	—	—

(SP 129.2%) **15 Rn**

1m 12.2 (3.00) CSF £86.82 CT £1,672.61 TOTE £12.10: £3.30 £2.20 £7.30 (£120.00) Trio £322.60; £408.94 to Redcar 27/5/97 OWNER Derek & Cheryl Holder (STRATFORD) BRED Stetchworth Park Stud Ltd
LONG HANDICAP Calandrella 7-3 Deerly 7-7 Wild Nettle 7-1
WEIGHT FOR AGE 3yo-9lb
1279 Deerly, 3lb out of the handicap, was sharpened up by her run at Bath last week. Getting her Italian rider off the mark on his first ride in this country, her trainer told him the quieter you sit the faster she runs. (10/1)
1166 Newlands Corner, back to her optimum trip, lost more ground at the start than the margin of defeat. (9/1)
Make Ready, having her first run on grass, was 4lb lower than her last outing on the sand. (20/1)
883 Sharp 'n' Shady needs to return to seven. (13/2)
778 Tajrebah (USA), who did not stay the extended seven in soft ground last time, was not unduly knocked about once her chance had gone. (11/1)
1275 Silver Purse, dropped 4lb this season, has yet to convince that she really stays six. (16/1)
1107 La Petite Fusee has been raised 2lb for her narrow defeat last time and was 6lb higher than the highest mark off which she has won. (6/1: 4/1-13/2)

T/Plpt: £839.60 (11.35 Tckts). T/Qdpt: £290.20 (1.19 Tckts) KH

0835-LEICESTER (R-H) (Good)

Monday May 26th

WEATHER: fine & sunny WIND: mod across

71+ 72 72+

1440 LIONESS MAIDEN STKS (2-Y.O F) (Class D)

2-20 (2-23) **5f 218y** £3,444.00 (£1,032.00: £496.00: £228.00) Stalls: High GOING minus 0.15 sec per fur (GF)

				SP	RR	SF
	Sapphire Ring (RCharlton) **2-8-11** TSprake(2) (lt-f: unf: trckd ldrs: led 1f out: rn green: r.o wl)	—	**1**	9/2[2]	77+	26
1031[2]	**Demolition Jo** (PDEvans) **2-8-11** DRMcCabe(7) (a.p: ev ch 1f out: rallied u.p towards fin)	¾	**2**	13/2	75	24
	Latin Nexus (USA) (PFICole) **2-8-11** CRutter(4) (leggy: lt-f: hld up: hdwy 2f out: rdn & r.o wl fnl f)	nk	**3**	8/1	74+	23
999[4]	**First Dance** (RHannon) **2-8-11** RPerham(3) (a.p: rdn & outpcd fnl f)	1¾	**4**	7/2[1]	70	19
1007[3]	**Chrysalis** (PFICole) **2-8-4**(7) JBosley(10) (led to 1f out: sn rdn: wknd)	nk	**5**	6/1[3]	69	18
	Mrs Middle (NACallaghan) **2-8-11** SDrowne(8) (lt-f: unf: nvr trbld ldrs)	4	**6**	10/1	58	7
	Flow By (JLDunlop) **2-8-11** MRimmer(1) (w'like: scope: s.s: effrt ½-wy: wknd wl over 1f out)	2	**7**	9/2[2]	53	2
	Bobbydazzle (DrJDScargill) **2-8-11** GBardwell(9) (lt-f: drvn along ½-wy: a bhd)	2	**8**	20/1	47	—
	Katie's Cracker (MRChannon) **2-8-11** RPainter(5) (lt-f: unf: outpcd)	hd	**9**	14/1	47	—
	Ghorapani (IRE) (MrsNMacauley) **2-8-11** SWebster(6) (w'like: leggy: dwlt: a bhd & outpcd)	2½	**10**	33/1	40	—
1240[11]	**Miss Muffett (IRE)** (PMooney) **2-8-4**(7) PFitzsimons(11) (swvd rt s: chsd ldrs 4f: wknd qckly)	4	**11**	20/1	30	—

(SP 125.5%) **11 Rn**

1m 14.0 (4.00) CSF £32.35 TOTE £3.50: £1.90 £2.00 £3.00 (£21.50) Trio £73.80 OWNER The Thoroughbred Corporation (BECKHAMPTON) BRED Mrs Mary Taylor

Sapphire Ring has plenty of speed in her breeding and, having been taught the job, won readily enough despite showing signs of greenness, and her future should be secure. (9/2: 3/1-5/1)

1031 Demolition Jo, having her first run on such lively ground, stuck to her guns in the latter stages and her turn is surely close at hand. (13/2)

Latin Nexus (USA), whose dam was a prolific winner in the States, did not really get into her stride until it was all too late, but she gave the right vibes and she will win her share of races. (8/1)

999 First Dance, in the action all the way, was unable to respond when the pace lifted inside the distance and was soon fighting a lost cause. (7/2)

1007 Chrysalis, a not over-big filly who is a good walker, attempted to make it all but she was swallowed up entering the final furlong and had shot her bolt. (6/1)

Mrs Middle is bred to be sharp, but she shows a fair bit of knee action and may well benefit from more yielding ground. (10/1: 7/1-11/1)

Flow By has more scope than most of her rivals, but she was flat-footed as the stalls opened and, over a trip that could turn out far from ideal, she was unable to make her presence felt. (9/2)

1441 ANSTEY (S) H'CAP (0-60) (3-Y.O+) (Class G)

2-55 (2-56) **1m 1f 218y** £3,036.00 (£846.00: £408.00) Stalls: High GOING minus 0.29 sec per fur (GF)

				SP	RR	SF
1156[8]	**Arzani (USA) (46)** (DJSCosgrove) **6-9-6** MRimmer(5) (b: lw: hld up: hdwy 3f out: swtchd rt: rdn to ld ins fnl f)	—	**1**	7/1[3]	60	39
1383[3]	**Acquittal (IRE) (39)** (AStreeter) **5-8-13v** TSprake(10) (chsd ldrs: led over 2f out tl hdd & no ex ins fnl f)	2½	**2**	13/2[2]	49	28
1246[2]	**Action Jackson (50)** (BJMcMath) **5-9-10** GBardwell(12) (led 3f: led over 3f out tl over 2f out: kpt on u.p)	1½	**3**	6/1[1]	58	37
236[6]	**Blue Jumbo (IRE) (36)** (WJMusson) **4-8-10** MHills(8) (hld up: hdwy over 3f out: one pce appr fnl f)	¾	**4**	10/1	42	21
1383[14]	**River Run (IRE) (48)** (RHollinshead) **5-9-5**(3) FLynch(7) (hld up: hdwy over 2f out: kpt on u.p ins fnl f)	1½	**5**	20/1	52	31
	Northern Grey (46) (DrJDScargill) **5-9-3**(3) DGriffiths(1) (hdwy on outside 3f out: nt pce to chal)	1½	**6**	25/1	48	27
	Rock The Barney (IRE) (40) (MDIUsher) **8-9-0** DRMcCabe(11) (hld up: effrt & nt clr run 2f out: nt rcvr)	hd	**7**	16/1	41	20
1001[6]	**Dannistar (49)** (PDEvans) **5-9-2**(7) AnthonyBond(2) (in tch: jnd ldrs over 3f out: rdn 2f out: grad wknd)	1	**8**	20/1	49	28
1011[6]	**Burning Flame (37)** (RMFlower) **4-8-8b**(3) MartinDwyer(19) (swtg: nvr trbld ldrs)	2	**9**	12/1	34	13
147[14]	**Tauten (IRE) (36)** (MDIUsher) **7-8-10** JMarshall(13) (bit bkwd: a in rr)	½	**10**	25/1	32	11
1233[11]	**Captain's Day (44)** (HJCollingridge) **5-8-13**(5) RMullen(16) (b.hind: nvr nr to chal)	1¾	**11**	9/1	37	16
	Araboybill (49) (JNeville) **6-9-9b** SDrowne(15) (bit bkwd: chsd ldrs: rdn over 3f out: wknd over 2f out)	3½	**12**	14/1	36	15
1266[4]	**My Handsome Prince (37)** (PJBevan) **5-8-11** NCarlisle(9) (a in rr)	½	**13**	14/1	24	3
318[13]	**Speedy Snaps Pride (41)** (PDCundell) **5-8-10**(5) GFaulkner(14) (bit bkwd: hld up: effrt ½-wy: sn rdn & noimp)	4	**14**	20/1	21	—
	Persian Dawn (41) (RTPhillips) **4-9-1** RPerham(18) (a in rr)	1¾	**15**	14/1	18	—
1116[8]	**Polar Refrain (40)** (JNorton) **4-8-7b1**(7) KSked(4) (hld up: hdwy on outside 4f out: sn ev ch: rdn & wknd over 2f out)	3	**16**	16/1	13	—
1282[4]	**Arboreal (USA) (48)** (MrsLStubbs) **3-8-3**(5) PRoberts(17) (led after 3f tl over 3f out: wknd qckly)	2	**17**	25/1	17	—
1128[17]	**Our Tom (35)** (JWharton) **5-8-9b** FNorton(6) (w ldrs 7f: sn rdn & wknd qckly: t.o)	12	**18**	25/1	—	—
582[2]	**Sidney The Kidney (56)** (MJRyan) **3-8-11**(5) TEDurcan(3) (chsd ldrs 6f: sn wknd: t.o)	3	**19**	7/1[3]	1	—

(SP 140.8%) **19 Rn**

2m 8.8 (5.10) CSF £48.67 CT £275.90 TOTE £9.10: £2.20 £1.70 £1.80 £2.70 (£16.90) Trio £22.80 OWNER Mr D. J. S. Cosgrove (NEWMARKET) BRED Eaton and Thorne and Robert N. Clay

WEIGHT FOR AGE 3yo-14lb

Bt in 4,200gns

838 Arzani (USA), appreciating the step down in class, won this with quite a bit to spare and, if he remains in this company, more success should follow. (7/1)

1383 Acquittal (IRE) found this coming far too quickly after such a promising effort four days ago, but he gave his followers a run for their money and he is going in the right direction. (13/2)

1246 Action Jackson battled back willingly after losing control approaching the final quarter-mile, but the winner had come fresh on the scene and easily had the legs of him in the run to the line. (6/1)

Blue Jumbo (IRE) has little form to her name and was returning after almost four months out of action, but she showed a bit of what she is made of and there could be a race for her. (10/1: 7/1-12/1)

1247 River Run (IRE) stayed on doggedly in the latter stages, but he had been hard at work from some way out and lacked the speed to get involved. (20/1)

Northern Grey, having his first try at a longer trip, made progress up the centre of the track and kept staying on without ever threatening to reach the leaders. (25/1)

Rock The Barney (IRE), a dual course winner who has not won for almost two years, may well have troubled the judge on this first run for his present stable had he enjoyed any sort of run throughout the final quarter-mile. Compensation awaits. (16/1)

1442 ROTHMANS ROYALS NORTH SOUTH CHALLENGE SERIES H'CAP (0-85) (3-Y.O+) (Class D)
3-25 (3-25) **1m 8y** £5,481.00 (£1,638.00: £784.00: £357.00) Stalls: High GOING minus 0.15 sec per fur (GF)

	Horse	Dist	Pos	SP	RR	SF
1262^{8}	**Sweet Wilhelmina (60)** (LordHuntingdon) **4-7-12**(5) AimeeCook(5) (lw: a.p: led over 2f out: clr fnl f)	—	1	$6/1^{2}$	74	56
1020^{11}	**Carburton (65)** (JAGlover) **4-8-8** CRutter(4) (hld up: hdwy wl over 1f out: kpt on u.p fnl f)	3½	2	16/1	72	54
974^{7}	**Iamus (82)** (TDBarron) **4-9-11** MHills(1) (prom tl lost pl 2f out: rallied u.p appr fnl f: r.o)	1	3	8/1	87	69
951^{2}	**Broughton's Pride (IRE) (53)** (JLEyre) **6-7-10** DWright(2) (a.p: led over 3f out tl over 2f out: sn rdn: one pce)	nk	4	8/1	57	39
376^{4}	**Iblis (IRE) (85)** (GWragg) **5-9-9**(5) GMilligan(9) (bit bkwd: swtchd lft sn after s: chsd ldrs: ev ch over 2f out: sn rdn: one pce appr fnl f)	hd	5	$9/2^{1}$	89	71
1244^{7}	**Therhea (IRE) (64)** (BRMillman) **4-8-7** MRimmer(8) (led over 4f: rdn & one pce fnl 2f)	1	6	20/1	66	48
1262^{3}	**Wakeel (USA) (77)** (SDow) **5-9-6** RPerham(7) (lw: hld up: effrt 2f out: sn rdn: nvr able to chal)	3	7	$9/2^{1}$	73	55
1262^{7}	**Q Factor (77)** (DHaydnJones) **5-9-1**(5) GFaulkner(3) (prom tl rdn & wknd 2f out)	¾	8	10/1	72	54
1146^{9}	**Noble Dane (IRE) (79)** (PWHarris) **3-8-10** GBardwell(10) (lw: prom tl wknd qckly wl over 2f out: t.o)	5	9	$13/2^{3}$	64	34
1166^{5}	**Artful Dane (IRE) (76)** (MJHeaton-Ellis) **5-9-5v** SDrowne(6) (trckd ldrs: drvn along 3f out: sn lost tch: t.o)	6	10	8/1	49	31
1111^{5}	**Master M-E-N (IRE) (59)** (NMBabbage) **5-8-2v** TSprake(11) (lw: prom 5f: sn wknd: t.o)	4	11	8/1	24	6

(SP 128.2%) **11 Rn**

1m 36.8 (1.80) CSF £97.00 CT £726.88 TOTE £8.10: £2.00 £3.50 £3.60 (£53.20) Trio £188.40; £193.71 to Redcar 27/5/97 OWNER Mr Chris van Hoorn (WEST ILSLEY) BRED D. Walker
WEIGHT FOR AGE 3yo-12lb

1262 Sweet Wilhelmina has only ever won on the All-Weather, but she turned the tables on the favourite in no uncertain terms with a run-away success and, in this form, she is some way ahead of the Handicapper. (6/1)
Carburton, without being able to cope with the winner, ran his best race this term and he would seem to be on the way back. (16/1)
450 Iamus, caught out when the winner quickened the pace two furlongs out, responded willingly to strong pressure and he was pegging them back again at the finish. (8/1)
951 Broughton's Pride (IRE) rarely runs a bad race and she did not fail for the want of trying, but she did get tapped for speed once the battle to the finish developed. (8/1)
376 Iblis (IRE), still with something left to work on, somehow managed to work his way into the centre of the track and he was challenging for the lead two furlongs out but, as yet, he does not appear to truly get this trip and his measure had been taken inside the distance. (9/2)
Therhea (IRE) is running well enough to pick up another prize, but he may fare better if not quite so much use is made of him. (20/1)
1262 Wakeel (USA), not quite so effective on this more livelier ground, tries hard but was never able to mount a serious challenge. (9/2)

1443 MARKET BOSWORTH MEDIAN AUCTION MAIDEN STKS (3-Y.O) (Class F)
3-55 (3-57) **1m 8y** £2,637.00 (£732.00: £351.00) Stalls: High GOING minus 0.15 sec per fur (GF)

	Horse	Dist	Pos	SP	RR	SF
989^{3}	**Henry's Mother** (MRChannon) **3-8-9** RPerham(4) (hld up: hdwy 3f out: led over 1f out: comf)	—	1	$7/4^{1}$	71+	42
1272^{3}	**Mr Paradise (IRE) (69)** (TJNaughton) **3-9-0** DRMcCabe(1) (mde most tl hdd over 1f out: r.o one pce)	1½	2	8/1	73	44
568^{4}	**Farley Mount** (LordHuntingdon) **3-8-9**(5) AimeeCook(3) (hld up in tch: effrt over 1f out: nt pce to chal)	1¼	3	12/1	71	42
586^{12}	**Occam (IRE)** (GWragg) **3-9-0** MHills(5) (sn chsng ldrs: rdn over 2f out: sn outpcd)	5	4	$4/1^{3}$	61	32
1272^{2}	**Twin Time** (MJHeaton-Ellis) **3-8-9** SDrowne(10) (chsd ldrs: ev ch 2f out: sn rdn & wknd)	1¾	5	6/1	52	23
885^{5}	**Top Jem** (MJRyan) **3-8-9** GBardwell(2) (a in rr)	4	6	14/1	44	15
1023^{7}	**Strillo** (NMBabbage) **3-9-0** TSprake(7) (bit bkwd: bhd most of wy)	3	7	20/1	43	14
	Lakota Brave (CNAllen) **3-8-11**(3) MartinDwyer(6) (lengthy: unf: prom: rdn & rn green over 2f out: sn btn)	¾	8	$7/2^{2}$	42	13
	Pot of Tea (AStreeter) **3-8-4**(5) JBramhill(9) (lt-f: bit bkwd: trckd ldrs over 5f: sn wknd: t.o)	9	9	33/1	19	—
1144^{16}	**Flying Esprit** (GGMargarson) **3-8-9**(5) TEDurcan(8) (w ldrs to ½-wy: sn rdn & wknd: t.o)	9	10	100/1	6	—

(SP 127.0%) **10 Rn**

1m 38.7 (3.70) CSF £17.22 TOTE £2.70: £1.30 £1.60 £2.80 (£8.00) Trio £16.10 OWNER Mr G. Z. Mizel (UPPER LAMBOURN) BRED Guest Leasing and Bloodstock Co

OFFICIAL EXPLANATION **Top Jem: regarding his apparently tender ride, the jockey reported that his instructions were to settle the filly and make his effort in the closing stages. The trainer's representative added that the filly did not come down the hill well and did not run on until meeting the rising ground two furlongs out. He added that she needed softer ground and had finished with sore shins.**

989 Henry's Mother knew what was required this time and, gaining control on the approach to the final furlong, won a shade more easily than the margin would suggest. (7/4)
1272 Mr Paradise (IRE) reverted to his previous front-running tactics and proved tough enough to crack but, once the winner delivered her challenge, the writing was on the wall. (8/1)
568 Farley Mount, having his first outing on turf, sat in behind the leaders going well but, once the pace lifted, he was being made to work and over this trip was always finding the task beyond him. (12/1: op 7/1)
Occam (IRE), a full-brother to Henry Island, was one of the first off the bridle over a quarter-mile out, and the quickening pace proved too much for him. He is short on experience, but should be getting the hang of things now. (4/1)
1272 Twin Time, pushing the pace and holding every chance two furlongs out, found very little when the pressure was applied and she quickly beat a retreat. (6/1)

bl 60 60+

1444 LOUGHBOROUGH CLAIMING STKS (2-Y.O) (Class F)
4-25 (4-26) **5f 2y** £2,553.00 (£708.00: £339.00) Stalls: High GOING minus 0.15 sec per fur (GF)

	Horse	Dist	Pos	SP	RR	SF
828^{5}	**Sun In The Morning** (BJMeehan) **2-8-12** MHills(5) (a.p: led ent fnl f: jst hld on)	—	1	$5/2^{1}$	66	12
	Deri Fach (BPalling) **2-8-2** TSprake(3) (lt-f: unf: dwlt: hdwy 2f out: str chal ins fnl f: r.o)	hd	2	6/1	56	2
530^{4}	**Sandy Shore** (JWharton) **2-8-8** FNorton(4) (a.p: outpcd 2f out: rallied fnl f)	1½	3	16/1	57	3
767*	**Lasham** (NACallaghan) **2-8-13** SDrowne(7) (chsd ldrs: effrt & ev ch over 1f out: unable qckn)	1½	4	$3/1^{3}$	57	3
1019^{2}	**Swift Time** (MRBosley) **2-7-12** CRutter(9) (prom: led 2f out to 1f out: wknd fnl f)	3	5	$11/4^{2}$	33	—
1253^{8}	**Docklands Dispatch (IRE)** (NTinkler) **2-8-9** GBardwell(6) (bit bkwd: chsd ldrs 3f: sn rdn & outpcd)	1¼	6	33/1	40	—
1019^{4}	**Fleur-de-Lys** (WJMusson) **2-7-9**(5) RMullen(8) (s.i.s: a in rr)	5	7	8/1	15	—
1298^{5}	**Hamerra (IRE)** (MartynMeade) **2-7-7**(5) JBramhill(2) (led & sn clr: wknd & hdd 2f out)	nk	8	40/1	12	—
1109^{10}	**Miss Equal** (MCPipe) **2-8-1**(3) MartinDwyer(1) (ref to r: t.n.p)		R	25/1	—	—

(SP 120.7%) **9 Rn**

62.8 secs (4.30) CSF £17.13 TOTE £3.80: £1.70 £1.90 £2.20 (£10.30) Trio £61.30 OWNER Mr David Powell (UPPER LAMBOURN) BRED Theakston Stud
Deri Fach clmd CBjorling £7,000

828 Sun In The Morning set sail for home entering the final furlong and looked well in control, but she did not find as much as was expected when taken on, and the line arrived not a stride too soon. (5/2)
Deri Fach, a sparely-made unfurnished filly, did extremely well to finish so close after forfeiting ground at the start and, if remaining in this class, should have little trouble in going one better. (6/1: 4/1-13/2)
530 Sandy Shore again left the impression that a longer trip is needed and it should not be long before she gets off the mark. (16/1)
767* Lasham, close enough to pose a threat at the distance, was unable to pick up when the winner kicked for home and, from then on, he was fighting for the places. (3/1)
1019 Swift Time, very much on her toes in the preliminaries, was in the firing line with a chance as good as any until tying up rather quickly inside the last furlong. (11/4)
1298 Hamerra (IRE) has got speed to burn, but she is a very short runner and, until she learns to settle, will continue to run herself into the ground. (40/1)

1445 TIGERS APPRENTICE H'CAP (0-65) (4-Y.O+) (Class F)
4-55 (5-03) **1m 3f 183y** £2,641.50 (£744.00: £364.50) Stalls: High GOING minus 0.29 sec per fur (GF)

				SP	RR	SF
1138[9]	**Evaporate (27)** (MJHeaton-Ellis) **5-7-6**(5) JFowle(6) (mde most: drvn clr over 1f out: styd on wl)	—	**1**	20/1	40	22
1232*	**Kintavi (51)** (TWDonnelly) **7-9-7** KSked(12) (b: hld up: hdwy on outside ent st: str chal fnl f: nt rch wnr)	2	**2**	11/4[1]	61	43
1222[8]	**May King Mayhem (27)** (MrsALMKing) **4-7-6**(5)ow1 RWinston(15) (hld up in tch: hdwy 3f out: styd on fnl f)	1	**3**	16/1	36	17
	Schnozzle (IRE) (48) (KSBridgwater) **6-8-13**(5) TSiddall(9) (hld up & bhd: hdwy over 2f out: nrst fin)	4	**4**	12/1	52	34
1388[9]	**Spiral Flyer (IRE) (38)** (MDIUsher) **4-8-3**(5) RBrisland(4) (swtg: trckd ldrs: hrd drvn & outpcd 2f out: styd on same pce)	5	**5**	25/1	35	17
1156[5]	**Nawaji (USA) (40)** (WRMuir) **4-8-7**(3) JWilkinson(10) (hld up in tch: effrt 3f out: nvr able to chal)	2½	**6**	12/1	33	15
1244[13]	**Spring Campaign (IRE) (53)** (MCPipe) **4-9-9** AEddery(13) (prom: drvn along over 3f out: grad wknd)	1¼	**7**	14/1	45	27
1246[7]	**Tocco Jewel (26)** (MJRyan) **7-7-5**(5) DMernagh(14) (nvr nr to chal)	1	**8**	33/1	16	—
1169[5]	**Nornax Lad (USA) (52)** (MartynMeade) **9-9-8b** GMilligan(2) (lw: disp ld: rdn 3f out: wknd fnl 2f)	1	**9**	7/1[3]	41	23
	Haydown (IRE) (34) (MRBosley) **5-7-11**(7) JBosley(16) (prom tl wknd 3f out)	2	**10**	20/1	20	2
1106[8]	**Leatherneck (IRE) (54)** (PMooney) **4-9-5**(5) PFitzsimons(5) (s.s: hdwy 5f out: veered bdly lft over 3f out: rdn & wnt rt over 2f out: no imp)	1½	**11**	16/1	38	20
770[9]	**Executive Officer (33)** (RMFlower) **4-7-12**(5)ow3 TField(7) (hdwy 5f out: wknd 3f out)	½	**12**	33/1	17	—
1001*	**Dauphin (IRE) (46)** (WJMusson) **4-8-11**(5) PBradley(8) (lw: hld up: effrt & c wd st: hmpd 3f out: nt rcvr)	3	**13**	7/2[2]	26	8
1246[4]	**Persian Sunset (IRE) (41)** (MissJBower) **5-8-6**(5) GHannon(3) (chsd ldrs over 8f)	s.h	**14**	25/1	21	3
1133[10]	**Jump The Lights (55)** (SPCWoods) **4-9-8**(3) CWebb(11) (swtg: hld up: a bhd: t.o)	14	**15**	9/1	16	—
653[10]	***Prove The Point (IRE) (38)*** (MrsPNDutfield) **4-8-8** AimeeCook(1) (Withdrawn not under Starter's orders: uns rdr & bolted bef s)		**W**	33/1	—	—
				(SP 131.2%)	**15 Rn**	

2m 34.1 (5.60) CSF £66.77 CT £874.45 TOTE £62.50: £6.70 £1.80 £3.50 (£114.20) Trio £189.40; £240.21 to Redcar 27/5/97 OWNER Mr R. W. Floyd (WROUGHTON) BRED Manor Grange Stud Co Ltd
LONG HANDICAP Tocco Jewel 7-4
544 Evaporate, fit from the All-Weather, was allowed to put her stamina to good use and, slipping her field inside the quarter-mile marker, had gone beyond recall. (20/1)
1232* Kintavi did the wrong thing making ground on the wide outside turning in and, though he stayed on willingly in the closing stages, the winner had got away and was not for catching. (11/4)
481 May King Mayhem ran up to his best and will not need to improve to pick up a run-of-the-mill claimer. (16/1)
Schnozzle (IRE), fit from hurdling and ridden with restraint over this longer trip, stayed on pleasingly in the latter stages, and that elusive first success could be near at hand. (12/1: op 25/1)
Spiral Flyer (IRE) was flat to the boards a long way out but she kept persevering, and at least her heart is in the right place. (25/1)
1156 Nawaji (USA), a springer in the market, was unable to increase her tempo from the three-furlong pole and was never a serious factor. (12/1)

1446 GROBY H'CAP (0-85) (3-Y.O+) (Class D)
5-25 (5-26) **5f 218y** £3,665.00 (£1,100.00: £530.00: £245.00) Stalls: High GOING minus 0.15 sec per fur (GF)

				SP	RR	SF
942[16]	**Mr Bergerac (IRE) (80)** (BPalling) **6-9-10** TSprake(5) (hld up: hdwy 2f out: led wl ins fnl f)	—	**1**	2/1[1]	88	57
1250[7]	**Ed's Folly (IRE) (58)** (SDow) **4-7-11**(5)ow6 ADaly(1) (led & sn clr: hdd wl ins fnl f)	½	**2**	12/1	65	28
1113[3]	**Lunar Mist (76)** (MartynMeade) **4-9-6** FNorton(7) (trckd ldrs: hrd drvn 2f out: r.o wl ins fnl f)	hd	**3**	4/1[2]	82	51
	Faith Alone (62) (CFWall) **4-8-6** NCarlisle(4) (in tch: hdwy 2f out: ev ch appr fnl f: unable qckn)	1½	**4**	10/1	64	33
1269[7]	**Bowlers Boy (66)** (JJQuinn) **4-8-10** MRimmer(10) (hld up: hdwy 2f out: sn drvn along: kpt on)	2	**5**	5/1[3]	63	32
1166[4]	**White Settler (68)** (RJHodges) **4-8-12** SDrowne(2) (bhd: effrt & rdn over 1f out: nvr nrr)	1	**6**	4/1[2]	62	31
	Macgillycuddy (IRE) (64) (MrsPNDutfield) **8-8-3**(5) AimeeCook(6) (a bhd & outpcd)	½	**7**	20/1	57	26
823[11]	**Beldray Park (IRE) (54)** (MrsALMKing) **4-7-12** AGarth(3) (a in rr)	½	**8**	16/1	46	15
1080[5]	**Petraco (IRE) (54)** (NASmith) **9-7-7**(5) JBramhill(9) (prom: rdn wl over 1f out: sn wknd)	½	**9**	10/1	44	13
	Celandine (70) (AndrewTurnell) **4-9-0** MHills(8) (bit bkwd: a bhd & outpcd: t.o)	8	**10**	20/1	39	8
				(SP 131.3%)	**10 Rn**	

1m 12.6 (2.60) CSF £30.78 CT £90.28 TOTE £2.80: £2.10 £2.30 £1.90 (£37.60) Trio £41.00 OWNER Mr P. R. John (COWBRIDGE) BRED Red House Stud
LONG HANDICAP Ed's Folly (IRE) 7-9
726 Mr Bergerac (IRE) had to put his best foot forward to reel in the long-time leader, but he always looked likely to do so and he was well on top at the finish. (2/1)
1012 Ed's Folly (IRE) will be something to bet on if he adopts forceful tactics in a maiden over the minimum trip for, at that trip today, he would not have been caught. (12/1)
1113 Lunar Mist responded to strong pressure to make the frame and she was still galloping on at the finish, but the Handicapper seems to have her measure at present. (4/1: 3/1-9/2)
Faith Alone looked set to take over entering the final furlong but the leader just would not give best and, with lack of a recent outing beginning to take its toll, she was the one who had to admit defeat. (10/1)
1269 Bowlers Boy was never able to get in a blow, despite staying on, and he seems to need a stiffer test of stamina. (5/1)
1166 White Settler found things happening far too quickly on this step down to sprinting, and was only just getting into his stride when the race was over. (4/1)

T/Plpt: £213.30 (44.88 Tckts). T/Qdpt: £38.50 (10.77 Tckts) IM

1126-REDCAR (L-H) (Good to firm, Good patches)

Monday May 26th

WEATHER: sunny periods WIND: slt against

74 78+ 70 71

1447 YARM NOVICE AUCTION STKS (2-Y.O) (Class E)

2-15 (2-16) **5f** £3,015.25 (£907.00: £438.50: £204.25) Stalls: High GOING minus 0.24 sec per fur (GF)

				SP	RR	SF
1280*	**Sandside** (JBerry) **2-8-3**(5) PFessey(12) (lw: cl up: hung lft ½-wy: kpt on wl fnl f to ld post)	—	1	7/2^{2}	70	23
993*	**Angel Hill** (TDBarron) **2-8-3** LCharnock(6) (lw: cl up: led over 1f out: r.o: jst ct)	s.h	2	3/1^{1}	65	18
1255^{8}	**Cumbrian Cadet** (TDEasterby) **2-8-8** JCarroll(8) (chsd ldrs: chal 1f out: nt qckn towards fin)	1	3	20/1	67	20
999^{5}	**Patricia Olive (IRE)** (MHTompkins) **2-7-10**(3) MHenry(2) (in tch: sn drvn along: kpt on fnl 2f: nvr able to chal)	1	4	8/1	54	7
583^{8}	**Tippitt Boy** (KMcAuliffe) **2-8-12** JFortune(9) (led tl hdd & wknd over 1f out)	3	5	7/2^{2}	58	11
1045^{4}	**Bolero Kid** (MWEasterby) **2-8-4** TLucas(10) (styd on fnl 2f: no imp)	s.h	6	14/1	50	3
1126^{4}	**King of Dance** (BSRothwell) **2-8-12** MFenton(5) (in tch: outpcd ½-wy: n.d after)	2½	7	6/1^{3}	50	3
	Jacobina (TDBarron) **2-8-3** RLappin(1) (unf: outpcd after 2f)	1	8	50/1	38	—
664^{5}	**Snappy Times** (MDods) **2-8-5b^{1}**(3) CTeague(4) (plld hrd: lost tch fr ½-wy)	1¼	9	33/1	39	—
948^{W}	**Allmaites** (DNicholls) **2-8-3**(5) IonaWands(11) (cmpt: scope: bit bkwd: sn outpcd)	1	10	20/1	35	—
971^{6}	**Moy (IRE)** (MBrittain) **2-7-13** JQuinn(3) (s.i.s: a bhd)	5	11	20/1	10	—
	Behind The Veil (MrsMReveley) **2-7-13** TWilliams(7) (neat: s.i.s: a outpcd & wl bhd)	14	12	50/1	—	—

(SP 122.7%) **12 Rn**

60.3 secs (2.80) CSF £12.44 TOTE £2.90: £1.20 £1.80 £5.30 (£2.90) Trio £78.60 OWNER Mr J. K. Brown (COCKERHAM) BRED P. Young

1280* Sandside, despite hanging left to join the other runners at halfway, proved game under pressure and ought to stay further. (7/2: 5/2-4/1)

993* Angel Hill put up a brave attempt on 4lb worse terms with the winner, and looks the sort to find other success as she strengthens. (3/1: 5/2-4/1)

Cumbrian Cadet is improving and will surely find a modest race in due course. (20/1)

Patricia Olive (IRE) kept responding to pressure, but lacked the pace to make it and may well need further. (8/1)

504 Tippitt Boy was taken early to post this time as he misbehaved at Nottingham. He did little wrong before the start, but in the race he failed to see it out. (7/2)

1045 Bolero Kid is going to come into his own over longer trips in due course. (14/1)

1126 King of Dance is still learning and gives the impression that longer trips will be needed. (6/1: op 4/1)

1448 BANK HOLIDAY (S) STKS (3-Y.O+) (Class G)

2-45 (2-46) **7f** £2,407.50 (£670.00: £322.50) Stalls: High GOING minus 0.24 sec per fur (GF)

				SP	RR	SF
1220^{3}	**Super Benz (80)** (JLEyre) **11-9-4**(3) OPears(9) (b: trckd ldrs: rdn to ld over 1f out: styd on wl)	—	1	6/5^{1}	62	17
896*	**Dispol Diamond (52)** (GROldroyd) **4-9-5** JCarroll(2) (hld up: hdwy to chal ins fnl f: kpt on)	nk	2	11/4^{2}	59	14
1167^{6}	**Impala (52)** (WGMTurner) **3-8-3**(7) DMcGaffin(7) (led tl hdd over 1f out: hrd rdn & kpt on same pce)	½	3	13/2	60	4
1225^{9}	**Densben (49)** (DenysSmith) **13-9-7** MRoberts(10) (effrt ½-wy: styd on: nvr able to chal)	5	4	11/2^{3}	49	4
	Sun Fairy (JAGlover) **3-8-5** LCharnock(6) (lt-f: drvn along ½-wy: styd on: no imp)	2½	5	25/1	38	—
	That Old Feeling (IRE) (DWChapman) **5-9-7** ACulhane(8) (outpcd & bhd tl styd on fnl 2f)	hd	6	16/1	43	—
1220^{10}	**Frugal** (BWMurray) **4-9-7** VHalliday(4) (sn drvn along & bhd: n.d)	1¼	7	100/1	40	—
	Hotcake (MissSEHall) **4-9-4**(3) MHenry(5) (plld hrd early: outpcd fnl 3f)	¾	8	16/1	38	—
1291^{14}	**Oriel Lad (38)** (DonEnricoIncisa) **4-9-7b** KimTinkler(1) (chsd ldrs: rdn 3f out: sn lost pl)	¾	9	25/1	37	—
1220^{7}	**Serape (54)** (MrsLStubbs) **4-9-2** WRyan(3) (b: outpcd fnl 3f)	1	10	10/1	29	—

(SP 130.4%) **10 Rn**

1m 28.7 (5.70) CSF £4.75 TOTE £1.90: £1.10 £1.40 £1.80 (£3.40) OWNER Whitestonecliffe Racing Partnership (HAMBLETON) BRED Scarteen Stud

WEIGHT FOR AGE 3yo-11lb

No bid

STEWARDS' ENQUIRY McGaffin susp. 4-5/6/97 & another day to be arranged (incorrect use of whip).

1220 Super Benz, ridden with restraint this time, got on top in the final furlong under a cool ride. (6/5: evens-5/4)

896* Dispol Diamond is an excitable sort, but she has a useful turn of foot and further races can be found. (11/4: op 5/1)

1167 Impala, a free-runner, had his own way out in front but was tapped for toe late on. He deserves to pick up a race such as this. (13/2)

863 Densben needs a flat-out gallop and never got it here. (11/2)

Sun Fairy is nothing to look at, but she showed a little ability under some vigorous driving. (25/1)

That Old Feeling (IRE), having his first run for his new stable, showed he still has some ability if he can be coaxed back to form, and he is certainly in the right yard to do that. (16/1)

1449 VAUX SAMSON H'CAP (0-75) (3-Y.O) (Class D)

3-15 (3-19) **1m 3f** £5,706.00 (£1,728.00: £844.00: £402.00) Stalls: Low GOING minus 0.24 sec per fur (GF)

				SP	RR	SF
990^{6}	**Fantail (67)** (MHTompkins) **3-9-4**(3) MHenry(9) (a.p: slt ld over 2f out: edgd lft: styd on u.p)	—	1	3/1^{1}	83	46
1129^{8}	**Quezon City (54)** (MJCamacho) **3-8-8** LCharnock(1) (cl up: disp ld wl over 2f out: sn rdn & kpt on same pce)	1½	2	7/1	68	31
975^{5}	**Madison Welcome (IRE) (63)** (MrsJRRamsden) **3-9-3** JFortune(8) (lw: trckd ldrs: outpcd 3f out: styd on wl appr fnl f)	1	3	13/2^{3}	75	38
1140^{2}	**Krosno (65)** (SCWilliams) **3-9-5** JCarroll(6) (cl up: led over 3f out tl over 2f out: one pce)	2	4	3/1^{1}	75	38
1135^{11}	**Hoh Flyer (USA) (63)** (MBell) **3-9-3** MFenton(7) (mid div: effrt over 3f out: nt pce to chal)	1	5	15/2	71	34
1164^{9}	**Keepsake (IRE) (51)** (MDIUsher) **3-8-5** JQuinn(3) (in tch tl outpcd over 3f out: n.d after)	7	6	10/1	49	12
	Cimmerian (54) (MJohnston) **3-8-8** MRoberts(4) (lw: led tl hdd over 3f out: sn btn)	6	7	25/1	43	6
899^{5}	**Digital Option (IRE) (52)** (MrsJRRamsden) **3-8-6** MDeering(5) (s.i.s: n.d)	2	8	25/1	38	1
1226^{5}	**Kweilo (66)** (JWPayne) **3-9-6** WRyan(2) (hld up: effrt over 3f out: sn rdn & n.d)	2	9	5/1^{2}	49	12
609^{6}	**Fearless Sioux (50)** (CWThornton) **3-8-4** DaleGibson(11) (a rr div)	nk	10	16/1	33	—
1078^{7}	***Beau Roberto (54)*** (MJohnston) **3-8-8b^{1}** JFanning(10) (Withdrawn not under Starter's orders: veterinary advice)		W	25/1	—	—

(SP 130.8%) **10 Rn**

2m 22.4 (5.40) CSF £24.98 CT £120.96 TOTE £3.80: £1.60 £3.00 £2.40 (£20.20) Trio £96.10 OWNER Pamela, Lady Nelson of Stafford (NEWMARKET) BRED Skyline Racing Limited

990 Fantail, trying his longest trip to date, got his head in front and saw it out really well. (3/1)

868 Quezon City showed his first signs of form, appreciated the trip and, although always second best, he kept staying on. (7/1)
975 Madison Welcome (IRE) keeps showing signs of form and, by the way he responded to pressure late on, better will be seen in due course. (13/2)
1140 Krosno keeps getting punished by the Handicapper for some useful efforts, but is basically short of a real turn of foot. (3/1: op 2/1)
675 Hoh Flyer (USA) was stepping-up in trip, and ran reasonably without getting into it, but looks a tricky customer to place. (15/2)
Keepsake (IRE) took the eye with a good action going down, but she looked slow once off the bit in the race. (10/1: op 16/1)
1226 Kweilo, trying a longer trip, got a shade warm beforehand and seems to be his own worst enemy. (5/1)

1450 TOTE ZETLAND GOLD CUP H'CAP (0-105) (3-Y.O+) (Class B)
3-45 (3-50) **1m 2f** £14,785.00 (£4,480.00: £2,190.00: £1,045.00) Stalls: Low GOING minus 0.24 sec per fur (GF)

				SP	RR	SF
1176[W]	**Champagne Prince (87)** (PWHarris) **4-8-9**(7) CLowther(7) (mde all: hld on wl fnl 3f)	—	**1**	6/1[2]	100	62
933[9]	**Wafir (IRE) (80)** (PCalver) **5-8-6**(3) DarrenMoffatt(1) (lw: in tch: effrt over 3f out: styd on wl & ev ch ins fnl f: kpt on)	nk	**2**	12/1	93	55
1123[3]	**Angel Face (USA) (81)** (PDEvans) **4-8-10** LCharnock(4) (trckd ldrs: nt clr run 2f out: hdwy 2f out: r.o towards fin)	½	**3**	14/1	93	55
939[4]	**Romios (IRE) (90)** (PFICole) **5-9-5** JFortune(6) (hld up: effrt 3f out: n.m.r: styd on wl towards fin)	1	**4**	8/1	100	62
974[3]	**Billy Bushwacker (90)** (MrsMReveley) **6-9-5** ACulhane(3) (hdwy & prom ent st: outpcd 2f out: kpt on fnl f)	1¼	**5**	13/2[3]	98	60
1097[8]	**Tertium (IRE) (80)** (MartynWane) **5-8-9** JCarroll(10) (hld up: hdwy 3f out: ev ch over 1f out: sn rdn & wknd)	¾	**6**	6/1[2]	87	49
939[3]	**Najm Mubeen (IRE) (93)** (ACStewart) **4-9-8** MRoberts(12) (chsd ldr: chal 4f out: wknd fnl 2f)	2½	**7**	9/2[1]	96	58
1268[12]	**Gymcrak Premiere (76)** (GHolmes) **9-8-5** MFenton(9) (lw: b.hind: hld up & bhd: swtchd & hdwy over 2f out: btn 2f out)	nk	**8**	14/1	78	40
1176[4]	**Clan Ben (IRE) (93)** (HRACecil) **5-9-8** WRyan(8) (lw: chsd ldrs: effrt 3f out: wknd fnl 2f)	2	**9**	15/2	92	54
1145[2]	**Remaadi Sun (83)** (MDIUsher) **5-8-12v** JQuinn(5) (hld up: effrt 3f out: rdn & wknd fnl 2f)	6	**10**	6/1[2]	73	35
1097[18]	**Gladys Althorpe (IRE) (70)** (JLEyre) **4-7-13** TWilliams(2) (mid div tl outpcd fnl 3½f)	1½	**11**	20/1	57	19
1123[9]	**Moving Arrow (95)** (MissSEHall) **6-9-10** TLucas(11) (a bhd)	s.h	**12**	25/1	82	44
				(SP 126.9%)		**12 Rn**

2m 5.9 (2.30) CSF £74.43 CT £906.90 TOTE £7.00: £2.20 £4.70 £3.40 (£75.20) Trio £560.70; £7.90 to Redcar 27/5/97 OWNER Magnum Force (BERKHAMSTED) BRED Cheveley Park Stud Ltd
933* Champagne Prince is a game sort who stays well, and fought off several challengers for a much-deserved victory. (6/1)
933 Wafir (IRE), third in the race last year, kept responding to pressure, but the winner was always holding him. He does not win very often, but there seems nothing wrong with his attitude and he should stay a bit further. (12/1)
1123 Angel Face (USA) was a real handful beforehand and looked unlucky, getting shut-in entering the last two furlongs, and may well have given the winner a shock otherwise. (14/1)
939 Romios (IRE) certainly stays further and was short of room at a vital stage which put paid to his chances, but he looks in tremendous form just now. (8/1)
974 Billy Bushwacker had his chances, but needs things to go his way and was never doing enough at the right time. (13/2)
1097 Tertium (IRE), unlucky in this event last year, had no such excuses this time and, if anything, did not really stay. (6/1: 4/1-13/2)
939 Najm Mubeen (IRE) looked as though he had been sweating before entering the paddock, and this free-runner was a shade disappointing. (9/2)
1268 Gymcrak Premiere, wearing a pricker on his off-side, needed a stronger pace and, trying to come from behind, always had an impossible task. (14/1)

1451 STOKESLEY MEDIAN AUCTION MAIDEN STKS (3-Y.O) (Class D)
4-15 (4-17) **6f** £3,561.00 (£1,068.00: £514.00: £237.00) Stalls: High GOING minus 0.24 sec per fur (GF)

				SP	RR	SF
1141[13]	**Tailwind (61)** (WRMuir) **3-9-0** MRoberts(8) (a.p: rdn to ld 1f out: hdd wl ins fnl f: rallied to ld post)	—	**1**	2/1[2]	71	8
	Bongo (CWThornton) **3-9-0** ACulhane(3) (leggy: dwlt: outpcd & wl bhd after 2f: gd hdwy 2f out: led wl ins fnl f: edgd rt & no ex towards fin)	s.h	**2**	10/1	71	8
729[3]	**Prince of Parkes (67)** (JBerry) **3-9-0** JFortune(6) (mde most tl hdd 1f out: btn whn sltly hmpd wl ins fnl f)	2	**3**	13/8[1]	66	3
	Alisadara (45) (NBycroft) **3-8-9** JQuinn(2) (chsd ldrs: ev ch 2f out: btn 1f out)	5	**4**	33/1	47	—
1119[4]	**Supercharmer (63)** (DNicholls) **3-9-0b** JCarroll(1) (lw: w ldrs 4f: sn rdn & btn)	1¾	**5**	9/2[3]	48	—
	Onemoretime (45) (BWMurray) **3-8-9** VHalliday(7) (v.unruly in paddock: cl up tl rdn & wknd wl over 1f out)	4	**6**	33/1	32	—
1220[13]	**Chilled Wine (30)** (GPKelly) **3-8-9** DaleGibson(9) (w ldrs over 4f: wknd)	2½	**7**	66/1	25	—
1119[18]	**Makati** (MJCamacho) **3-9-0** LCharnock(5) (dwlt: a bhd)	1¼	**8**	25/1	27	—
	Running Bear (MissSEHall) **3-9-0** WRyan(4) (w'like: spd over 3f: sn btn)	2	**9**	6/1	22	—
				(SP 124.2%)		**9 Rn**

1m 15.2 (5.00) CSF £21.32 TOTE £3.30: £1.10 £4.20 £1.10 (£13.40) Trio £13.40 OWNER Mr R. Haim (LAMBOURN) BRED Miss C. Tagart
Tailwind broke his duck, but it was a desperate affair in a modest race. (2/1)
Bongo, after a poor start, was soon virtually tailed off, but he then showed amazing ability to get into it only for greenness to beat him. (10/1)
729 Prince of Parkes had no excuses and was beaten fair and square. (13/8)
Alisadara showed some ability, but there is plenty more required. (33/1)
1119 Supercharmer raced upsides until a real effort was required in the last two furlongs. (9/2: op 3/1)
Onemoretime reared over twice in the paddock and is obviously one to be wary of. (33/1)

1452 ROSE GARDEN H'CAP (0-70) (3-Y.O+) (Class E)
4-50 (4-52) **1m 6f 19y** £2,976.25 (£895.00: £432.50: £201.25) Stalls: Centre GOING minus 0.24 sec per fur (GF)

				SP	RR	SF
1118[2]	**Campaspe (54)** (JGFitzGerald) **5-8-12** JFortune(6) (lw: hld up: hdwy ent st: led 2f out: rdn & r.o wl)	—	**1**	11/4[1]	64	45
962[8]	**Domappel (68)** (MrsJCecil) **5-9-12** MRoberts(4) (a chsng ldrs: wnt 2nd appr fnl f: kpt on u.p: nt pce of wnr)	1½	**2**	9/2[2]	76	57
1232[8]	**Highfield Fizz (40)** (CWFairhurst) **5-7-9**(3) DarrenMoffatt(3) (bhd: effrt 4f out: styd on: nrst fin)	2½	**3**	10/1	46	27
1224[5]	**Sedbergh (USA) (70)** (MrsMReveley) **4-10-0** ACulhane(2) (in tch: effrt ent st: rdn & one pce fnl 3f)	2	**4**	6/1[3]	73	54
1329[3]	**Lord Hastie (USA) (43)** (CWThornton) **9-8-1** TWilliams(1) (chsd ldrs: led 3f out to 2f out: sn btn)	3½	**5**	9/2[2]	42	23
950[2]	**Brodessa (58)** (MrsMReveley) **11-8-11**(5) SCopp(7) (lw: prom: led 9f out to 3f out: sn outpcd)	1¾	**6**	7/1	55	36
1022[5]	**Dashing Invader (USA) (38)** (PWHarris) **4-7-10** JQuinn(5) (lw: led tl hdd 9f out: sn drvn along: wknd over 3f out)	5	**7**	8/1	30	11
1224[10]	**Faugeron (50)** (NTinkler) **8-8-3**(5) IonaWands(10) (prom to st: sn bhd)	3½	**8**	14/1	38	19
955[3]	**Moonraking (48)** (TJEtherington) **4-8-6** JCarroll(9) (in tch tl outpcd fnl 4f)	2	**9**	15/2	33	14

				SP	RR	SF
595^{13}	**Ship's Dancer (38)** (DonEnricoIncisa) **4-7-10v** KimTinkler(8) (lw: a bhd)	11	**10**	25/1	11	—

(SP 132.3%) **10 Rn**

3m 5.0 (5.70) CSF £15.92 CT £108.91 TOTE £3.90: £1.60 £2.60 £3.60 (£8.10) Trio £114.40 OWNER Mr J. G. FitzGerald (MALTON) BRED J. G. Fitzgerald
LONG HANDICAP Dashing Invader (USA) 7-9 Ship's Dancer 7-2
1118 Campaspe, the best on looks, did it nicely and showed a good attitude under pressure. (11/4: op 9/2)
Domappel, given every chance to get this trip, was seriously put into it approaching the final furlong, but was never doing enough under pressure. (9/2: op 3/1)
1081 Highfield Fizz has only ever won on this track, and this was another reasonable effort. (10/1)
1224 Sedbergh (USA), wearing a tongue-strap, looked short of pace and seems to have lost his edge for the moment. (6/1)
1329 Lord Hastie (USA) has never won over quite this far, and ran out of fuel in the last couple of furlongs. (9/2)
950 Brodessa is better with a drop in class when he can dominate. (7/1)
1022 Dashing Invader (USA), trying a longer trip, looked none too keen when taken on. (8/1)

T/Plpt: £90.30 (137.94 Tckts). T/Qdpt: £90.90 (4.84 Tckts) AA

0850-SANDOWN (R-H) (Rnd crse Gd-frm, Gd ptchs, 5f crse Gd, Gd-frm ptchs) Monday May 26th

WEATHER: warm WIND: slt half against

1453 BONUSPHOTO H'CAP (0-100) (3-Y.O+ F & M) (Class C)

2-05 (2-06) **7f 16y** £6,872.50 (£2,080.00: £1,015.00: £482.50) Stalls: High GOING minus 0.29 sec per fur (GF)

				SP	RR	SF
1166^{9}	**Out Line (58)** (MMadgwick) **5-7-10** NVarley(4) (rdn over 3f out: hdwy over 1f out: squeezed thro ins fnl f: led last stride)	—	**1**	16/1	67	44
1170^{15}	**Arruhan (IRE) (82)** (PTWalwyn) **3-8-9** RCochrane(7) (swtg: s.s: hdwy 2f out: led 1f out: hrd rdn: hdd last stride)	s.h	**2**	8/1	91	57
	Dancing Drop (97) (RHannon) **3-9-10** DaneO'Neill(1) (hld up: rdn over 2f out: r.o ins fnl f)	¾	**3**	8/1	104	70
	Alpine Time (IRE) (86) (DRLoder) **3-8-13** LDettori(2) (a.p: hrd rdn over 1f out: one pce)	½	**4**	5/1 3	92	58
968^{8}	**Song of Skye (80)** (TJNaughton) **3-8-7** DHolland(3) (rdn over 2f out: hdwy over 1f out: r.o)	s.h	**5**	20/1	86	52
894^{5}	**Intisab (88)** (RWArmstrong) **4-9-12** RHills(5) (chsd ldr: led over 2f out to 1f out: one pce)	nk	**6**	9/1	93	70
1131^{3}	**Zelda Zonk (77)** (BJMeehan) **5-9-1** OPeslier(8) (lw: jinked s: a.p: rdn over 2f out: ev ch over 1f out: one pce)	¾	**7**	4/1 2	81	58
694^{4}	**Plaisir d'Amour (IRE) (82)** (NACallaghan) **3-8-9** MJKinane(9) (plld hrd: a.p: rdn over 2f out: n.m.r wl over 1f out: one pce)	1	**8**	3/1 1	83	49
1035^{15}	**Elite Hope (USA) (70)** (NTinkler) **5-8-8** GCarter(6) (swtg: led over 4f)	8	**9**	20/1	53	30

(SP 109.3%) **9 Rn**

1m 29.82 (1.22) CSF £114.43 CT £930.56 TOTE £16.50: £3.40 £2.40 £2.20 (£89.50) Trio £261.50 OWNER Miss D. M. Green (DENMEAD) BRED Miss D. M. Green
LONG HANDICAP Out Line 7-9
WEIGHT FOR AGE 3yo-11lb
518 Out Line has fallen in the handicap and took full advantage. Only finding her feet below the distance, she squeezed through a gap inside the final furlong and, in a blanket finish, got up right on the line to lose her maiden tag. (16/1)
968 Arruhan (IRE) had no problems with the trip and looked set to score as she moved to the front. Given no peace by a whole host of rivals, she was caught right on the line. Compensation awaits. (8/1)
Dancing Drop, making her seasonal bow, chased the leaders and, in a tremendous finish, ran on to snatch third prize. Although both her wins have come over six furlongs, this trip suits her well. (8/1: 6/1-9/1)
Alpine Time (IRE), off the track since disappointing at Ripon last June, was always close up but, despite pressure from the saddle, failed to find that vital turn of foot. (5/1)
Song of Skye, racing at the back of the field, ran on from below the distance, only just failing to get into the prize money. (20/1)
894 Intisab was given a very stiff mark for this handicap debut, considering what she has achieved so far, but still ran a very pleasing race. (9/1: op 6/1)
1131 Zelda Zonk, never far away, threatened to take the lead in the straight but was tapped for toe from below the distance. The Handicapper appears to have her measure at present. (4/1)
694 Plaisir d'Amour (IRE) was never far away but, although not having a great deal of room as she tried to mount a challenge in the straight, was tapped for toe in the final furlong. (3/1)

1454 BONUSPRINT HENRY II STKS (Gp 3) (4-Y.O+) (Class A)

2-35 (2-35) **2m 78y** £25,240.00 (£9,552.00: £4,676.00: £2,132.00) Stalls: High GOING minus 0.29 sec per fur (GF)

				SP	RR	SF
1241*	**Persian Punch (IRE) (110)** (DRCElsworth) **4-8-10** RCochrane(1) (chsd ldr: led over 2f out: rdn out)	—	**1**	3/1 2	121	62
1172*	**Celeric (117)** (DMorley) **5-9-3** LDettori(2) (rdn over 2f out: hdwy over 1f out: ev ch ins fnl f: unable qckn nr fin)	¾	**2**	7/4 1	125	68
1033^{5}	**Eva Luna (USA) (110)** (HRACecil) **5-8-12** MJKinane(5) (rdn over 2f out: swtchd lft over 1f out: hdwy fnl f: r.o wl)	1	**3**	11/1	119	62
761^{4}	**Corradini (100)** (HRACecil) **5-8-12** KFallon(3) (lw: rdn over 6f out: hdwy over 4f out: lost pl over 2f out: rallied fnl f: r.o)	¾	**4**	11/1	119	62
$923a^{3}$	**Heron Island (IRE) (111)** (PWChapple-Hyam) **4-8-10** JReid(4) (hld up: rdn over 3f out: one pce)	hd	**5**	12/1	119	60
1172^{5}	**Kutta (112)** (RWArmstrong) **5-8-12** RHills(7) (lw: led tl over 2f out: hrd rdn: wknd fnl f)	2½	**6**	10/1	116	59
891*	**Orchestra Stall (110)** (JLDunlop) **5-9-1** TQuinn(6) (b: a.p: hrd rdn over 2f out: eased whn btn ins fnl f)	4	**7**	4/1 3	115	58

(SP 114.8%) **7 Rn**

3m 34.15 (2.15) CSF £7.97 TOTE £4.20: £2.60 £1.40 (£3.60) OWNER Mr J. C. Smith (WHITCOMBE) BRED Adstock Manor Stud
WEIGHT FOR AGE 4yo-2lb
STEWARDS' ENQUIRY Elsworth fined £230 (failure to inform rdr of horse's hypersensitive skin).
1241* Persian Punch (IRE) continues to improve and kept the persistent runner-up at bay to land his first Group victory. He returned marked as a result of Cochrane's use of the stick, but the jockey was found not to be in breach of whip regulations, although the trainer was fined. All systems are now go for the Ascot Gold Cup. (3/1)
1172* Celeric had no easy task conceding weight all-round. Produced on the outside, he probably saw too much daylight but looked like overhauling the winner until that rival produced a little extra in the closing stages. A return clash in the Ascot Gold Cup is on the cards. (7/4)

1033 Eva Luna (USA), back on a more suitable surface, only found her stride in the final furlong and, despite running on strongly, found the line coming far too soon. (11/1: 8/1-12/1)
761 Corradini was suited by the step-up to two miles, but he looks a far from easy ride. Having taken closer order on the home turn, he then lost his pitch again, and violently flashed his tail when shown the persuader. He looks one to have reservations about. (11/1: 8/1-12/1)
923a Heron Island (IRE) chased the leaders, but failed to quicken in the straight. (12/1)
1172 Kutta, taking a step-up in trip, took the field along and grimly tried to hold on until tiring in the last two hundred yards. This distance may have been just beyond him. (10/1: 8/1-12/1)
891* Orchestra Stall found life a lot tougher, and had been hung out to dry below the distance. (4/1)

1455 TRIPLEPRINT TEMPLE STKS (Gp 2) (3-Y.O+) (Class A)
3-05 (3-08) **5f 6y** £39,114.99 (£14,685.75: £7,092.88: £3,131.38) Stalls: High GOING minus 0.14 sec per fur (G)

				SP	RR	SF
	Croft Pool (107) (JAGlover) **6-9-3** GCarter(9) (lw: hld up: rdn wl over 1f out: led ins fnl f: r.o wl)	—	**1**	20/1	114	60
941[11]	**Brave Edge (105)** (RHannon) **6-9-3** DaneO'Neill(10) (w ldr: led over 1f out tl ins fnl f: unable qckn)	¾	**2**	25/1	112	58
941[4]	**Bolshoi (IRE) (106)** (JBerry) **5-9-3b** EmmaO'Gorman(1) (rdn & hdwy over 1f out: hung rt ins fnl f: r.o wl)	hd	**3**	15/2	111	57
1112*	**Royale Figurine (IRE) (103)** (MJFetherston-Godley) **6-9-0** DHolland(7) (hdwy & nt clr run over 1f out: r.o wl ins fnl f)	s.h	**4**	7/1	108	54
1303*	**Ya Malak (95)** (DNicholls) **6-9-3** AlexGreaves(3) (lw: nt clr run & dropped rr over 2f out: hdwy fnl f: r.o wl)	nk	**5**	25/1	110	56
1201a[6]	**Sylva Paradise (IRE) (110)** (CEBrittain) **4-9-3** BDoyle(8) (lw: led over 3f: one pce)	½	**6**	25/1	109	55
1171[2]	**Farhana (108)** (WJarvis) **4-9-0** TQuinn(4) (lw: rdn over 2f out: hdwy over 1f out: wknd ins fnl f)	2	**7**	9/4[1]	99	45
	Easycall (118) (BJMeehan) **3-8-13** OPeslier(6) (a.p: rdn over 1f out: wkng whn n.m.r ins fnl f)	nk	**8**	4/1[2]	105	43
1206a*	**Hever Golf Rose (111)** (TJNaughton) **6-9-0** JWeaver(2) (a.p: hrd rdn over 1f out: wkng whn n.m.r ins fnl f)	1¾	**9**	6/1[3]	93	39
	Abou Zouz (USA) (113) (DRLoder) **3-8-13** KDarley(5) (lw: spd 3f)	10	**10**	9/1	68	6
				(SP 115.6%)	**10 Rn**	

61.55 secs (1.75) CSF £375.46 TOTE £28.90: £4.50 £4.00 £1.90 (£53.00) Trio £73.70 OWNER Countrywide Classics Ltd (WORKSOP) BRED J. S. Bell
WEIGHT FOR AGE 3yo-8lb
Croft Pool, who got an infection in his hind leg and had to miss his intended reappearance in the Palace House Stakes at Newmarket, made a tremendous return to action, coming with a nice run to snatch the spoils inside the final furlong to land the biggest prize of his career and give his trainer his first Group success. (20/1)
573 Brave Edge, who had finished well behind Bolshoi on both his starts this season, reversed his form here. With the best draw of all, he made his bid for glory below the distance, but was unable to cope with the winner inside the final furlong. (25/1)
941 Bolshoi (IRE), who goes particularly well for Emma O'Gorman, had the worst possible draw but still ran well. Really finding his stride from below the distance, he hung badly to his right inside the final furlong, doing no favours to a couple of rivals but, nevertheless, kept on really well. His first Pattern victory does not look far away. (15/2)
1112* Royale Figurine (IRE), in-foal to Most Welcome, was picking up ground when failing to get a clear run below the distance. With little room to manoeuvre from that point, she nevertheless ran on strongly, and only just failed to take third prize. She is due to end her career in the King's Stand at Royal Ascot. (7/1)
1303* Ya Malak had no luck in running and, after finding his way blocked, dropped back to last at halfway. However, he really motored in the final furlong and finished in fine style. All seven of his victories to date have come over the minimum trip. (25/1)
1201a Sylva Paradise (IRE) took the field along but, collared below the distance, had nothing in reserve. (25/1)
1171 Farhana was very disappointing and was one of the first off the bridle. She made an effort below the distance but was a spent force early inside the final furlong. She would prefer cut in the ground. (9/4)

1456 DOUBLEPRINT WHITSUN CUP RATED STKS H'CAP (0-105) (3-Y.O+) (Class B)
3-40 (3-42) **1m 14y** £15,709.00 (£5,881.00: £2,878.00: £1,240.00: £557.50: £284.50) Stalls: High GOING minus 0.29 sec per fur (GF)

				SP	RR	SF
1160[3]	**Insatiable (IRE) (96)** (MRStoute) **4-9-4** MJKinane(7) (hrd rdn & hdwy over 1f out: led wl ins fnl f: r.o wl)	—	**1**	5/2[1]	111	89
691[5]	**Bold Words (CAN) (104)** (EALDunlop) **3-9-0** KFallon(17) (a.p: hrd rdn 3f out: led ins fnl f: edgd rt: sn hdd: unable qckn)	1¼	**2**	8/1[2]	117	83
832[14]	**Samara (IRE) (91)** (JLDunlop) **4-8-13** OPeslier(18) (a.p: led over 1f out tl ins fnl f: one pce)	1¼	**3**	9/1[3]	101	79
892[16]	**Crumpton Hill (IRE) (90)** (NAGraham) **5-8-12** LDettori(5) (nt clr run 2f out: hdwy over 1f out: r.o wl)	nk	**4**	10/1	99	77
939[5]	**Another Time (86)** (SPCWoods) **5-8-8** DBiggs(12) (hdwy over 1f out: r.o)	2½	**5**	12/1	91	69
1176[2]	**Major Change (94)** (MissGayKelleway) **5-9-2** JWeaver(8) (chsd ldr: led over 2f out tl over 1f out: wknd fnl f)	2	**6**	14/1	95	73
1016[2]	**Kuala Lipis (USA) (95)** (PFICole) **4-9-3** TQuinn(3) (lost pl over 2f out: r.o one pce fnl f)	nk	**7**	12/1	95	73
1214[8]	**General Academy (IRE) (98)** (PAKelleway) **4-9-6** SSanders(16) (hdwy over 1f out: nvr nrr)	nk	**8**	50/1	97	75
1160[8]	**Concer Un (95)** (SCWilliams) **5-9-3** GCarter(6) (b: a.p: rdn over 2f out: wknd over 1f out)	¾	**9**	14/1	93	71
	Aunty Jane (95) (JLDunlop) **4-9-3** JReid(9) (lw: led over 5f: wknd over 1f out)	nk	**10**	33/1	92	70
934[4]	**Hunters of Brora (IRE) (92)** (JDBethell) **7-9-0** DHolland(1) (lw: nvr nrr)	1¼	**11**	12/1	87	65
*661**	**Hal's Pal (96)** (DRLoder) **4-9-4v[1]** KDarley(10) (swtg: hld up: rdn over 3f out: wknd over 1f out)	1½	**12**	8/1[2]	88	66
1166[2]	**Amber Fort (86)** (DRCElsworth) **4-8-3v(5)** PPMurphy(4) (a bhd)	2½	**13**	33/1	73	51
892[15]	**Kayvee (98)** (MrsAJPerrett) **8-9-6** AClark(14) (hdwy on ins over 1f out: wknd fnl f)	8	**14**	33/1	69	47
1214*	**Welton Arsenal (92)** (KBishop) **5-9-0** RHills(15) (lw: hld up: rdn over 2f out: wknd over 1f out)	hd	**15**	10/1	63	41
	Lomberto (87) (VSoane) **4-8-9** RCochrane(13) (lw: bhd fnl 2f)	3	**16**	50/1	52	30
1261[W]	**Night City (100)** (LadyHerries) **6-9-8** PaulEddery(11) (a bhd)	3	**17**	33/1	59	37
				(SP 131.1%)	**17 Rn**	

1m 40.21 (-0.99) CSF £20.11 CT £159.06 TOTE £3.70: £1.40 £2.00 £2.70 £1.80 (£12.70) Trio £133.70 OWNER Sir Evelyn De Rothschild (NEWMARKET) BRED W. Maxwell Ervine
LONG HANDICAP Amber Fort 7-10
WEIGHT FOR AGE 3yo-12lb
1160 Insatiable (IRE) is only lightly-raced and is a progressive individual. He ran on really strongly to snatch the spoils in this extremely competitive event. (5/2)
691 Bold Words (CAN) is another progressive individual, and did extremely well considering he was the only three-year-old in the field. (8/1)
832 Samara (IRE) left her eye-catching reappearance well behind. Striking the front below the distance, she was unable to get away from her rivals and was collared inside the final furlong. She should not take long to get off the mark. (9/1)
Crumpton Hill (IRE) did not have the clearest of runs but, nevertheless, weaved his way through the pack to finish a very creditable fourth. (10/1)
939 Another Time, 6lb higher than at the beginning of the season, was doing all his best work in the closing stages. (12/1)

1176 Major Change, 8lb higher than he has ever won off before, was collared below the distance and had soon run out of gas. (14/1)

79 83 89 80

1457 E.B.F. MAIDEN STKS (2-Y.O F) (Class D)

4-10 (4-16) **5f 6y** £3,550.00 (£1,075.00: £525.00: £250.00) Stalls: High GOING minus 0.14 sec per fur (G)

				SP	RR	SF
1013[3]	**Kilcora (IRE)** (CADwyer) **2-8-11** KFallon(9) (led 3f out: edgd lft over 2f out: hdd over 1f out: led nr fin)	—	1	6/1[3]	80	37
	Folklore (DRLoder) **2-8-11** LDettori(8) (scope: lw: a.p: led over 1f out: hrd rdn ins fnl f: hdd nr fin)	hd	2	4/5[1]	80+	37
	Sada (MajorWRHern) **2-8-11** JReid(1) (unf: bit bkwd: rdn over 2f out: hdwy over 1f out: r.o)	1¾	3	20/1	74	31
985[7]	**Really Done It Now (IRE)** (KRBurke) **2-8-11** PaulEddery(4) (a.p: nt clr run over 2f out: one pce)	3	4	50/1	65	22
	Ratiyya (IRE) (BHanbury) **2-8-11** RHills(6) (scope: bit bkwd: hdwy over 2f out: wknd over 1f out)	1	5	12/1	61	18
1143[5]	**Jay Gee (IRE)** (GGMargarson) **2-8-11** GCarter(3) (nvr nr to chal)	s.h	6	33/1	61	18
1091[4]	**Summer Day Blues (IRE)** (CMurray) **2-8-11** JWeaver(2) (led 2f: j.path over 2f out: wknd over 1f out)	1	7	50/1	58	15
1293[2]	**Jilted (IRE)** (RHannon) **2-8-11** DaneO'Neill(5) (bhd fnl 2f)	nk	8	9/2[2]	57	14
	Ffestiniog (IRE) (PFICole) **2-8-11** TQuinn(10) (leggy: lt-f: dwlt: hdwy on ins 4f out: wknd wl over 1f out)	1½	9	9/1	52	9
	Isabella (TKeddy) **2-8-11** DHolland(7) (unf: scope: a bhd)	¾	10	50/1	50	7

(SP 119.3%) **10 Rn**

62.58 secs (2.78) CSF £10.11 TOTE £7.60: £1.70 £1.30 £4.40 (£5.50) Trio £74.80 OWNER Dr A. Haloute (NEWMARKET) BRED Rathasker Stud

1013 Kilcora (IRE), with experience on her side, did not give her jockey an easy time of it, drifting to her left from halfway. She looked booked for second place but, to her credit, rallied to get back up near the line. (6/1: 4/1-7/1)
Folklore, an attractive, nippy sort, was the subject of very encouraging reports and they appeared to be well-founded, as she travelled well throughout the race and cruised to the front below the distance. The race appeared to be in the bag, but she stumbled slightly inside the final furlong and then, coming under pressure, was caught near the line. She looks a ready-made winner. (4/5)
Sada needs time to develop, but ran on in pleasing style to finish third. She should come on a lot for this. (20/1)
Really Done It Now (IRE) left her initial run behind. (50/1)
Ratiyya (IRE), a scopey individual, looked as though the run was needed and so it proved. (12/1: 5/1-14/1)
1143 Jay Gee (IRE) did not have the pace to get in a blow, and already needs further. (33/1)
1293 Jilted (IRE) (9/2: 5/2-5/1)
Ffestiniog (IRE) (9/1: 3/1-10/1)

1458 FAMILY DAY OUT H'CAP (0-80) (3-Y.O) (Class D)

4-45 (4-49) **7f 16y** £3,517.50 (£1,065.00: £520.00: £247.50) Stalls: High GOING minus 0.29 sec per fur (GF)

				SP	RR	SF
675[12]	**Plan For Profit (IRE) (75)** (MJohnston) **3-9-3** JWeaver(4) (gd hdwy & nt clr run over 1f out: nt clr run & swtchd lft ins fnl f: led last strides)	—	1	16/1	82	56
1294[5]	**Signs And Wonders (64)** (CACyzer) **3-8-6**ow1 TQuinn(14) (lw: hld up: rdn over 2f out: led wl ins fnl f: hdd last strides)	hd	2	12/1	71	44
699[10]	**Rotor Man (IRE) (64)** (JDBethell) **3-8-6** DHolland(9) (led: rdn over 2f out: hdd wl ins fnl f: one pce)	¾	3	25/1	69	43
1000[7]	**Cherokee Flight (66)** (SMellor) **3-8-8** PaulEddery(11) (lw: hdwy over 1f out: r.o wl)	hd	4	33/1	71	45
1219*	**Purchasing Power (IRE) (70)** (NACallaghan) **3-8-12** LDettori(10) (swtg: a.p: rdn over 2f out: one pce fnl f)	nk	5	7/4[1]	74	48
1265[3]	**Shadoof (75)** (WRMuir) **3-9-3** KFallon(6) (rdn over 2f out: hdwy over 1f out: r.o)	nk	6	15/2[2]	79	53
1166[13]	**Havago (69)** (RHannon) **3-8-11** WJO'Connor(5) (swtg: a.p: rdn 2f out: ev ch ins fnl f: sn wknd)	1½	7	14/1	69	43
958[10]	**Caribbean Star (77)** (MRStoute) **3-9-5** JReid(3) (swtg: hdwy 4f out: wknd over 1f out: no ch whn hmpd ins fnl f)	1¼	8	10/1	74	48
675[14]	**Linden's Lad (IRE) (60)** (JRJenkins) **3-8-2**ow2 GCarter(8) (nvr nrr)	1¼	9	33/1	54	26
1104[6]	**Orontes (USA) (79)** (RHannon) **3-9-7** DaneO'Neill(2) (swtg: a.p: rdn over 2f out: wkng whn nt clr run ins fnl f)	nk	10	25/1	73	47
958[14]	**Passiflora (70)** (JLDunlop) **3-8-12** KDarley(13) (swtg: rdn over 3f out: sme hdwy on ins over 1f out: sn wknd)	nk	11	25/1	63	37
1245[8]	**Tabasco Jazz (70)** (BJMeehan) **3-8-12b1** MJKinane(7) (b.nr hind: hld up: rdn over 2f out: wknd over 1f out)	2½	12	8/1[3]	57	31
1167*	**Forget To Remindme (54)** (JSMoore) **3-7-10** NVarley(15) (bhd fnl 2f)	1¼	13	10/1	39	13
227[3]	**Supreme Maimoon (75)** (MJPolglase) **3-9-3** TGMcLaughlin(1) (hdwy 4f out: wknd over 1f out)	3½	14	25/1	52	26
1012[13]	**Saltimbanco (63)** (RAkehurst) **3-8-5** SSanders(12) (lw: a bhd)	5	15	25/1	28	2

(SP 122.8%) **15 Rn**

1m 30.51 (1.91) CSF £165.38 CT £4,409.39 TOTE £19.80: £4.10 £3.20 £10.60 (£99.10) Trio £1,163.50; £16.39 to Redcar 27/5/97 OWNER Professional Racing Partnership (MIDDLEHAM) BRED P. D. Savill
STEWARDS' ENQUIRY Weaver susp. 3-4/6/97 (careless riding).

413 Plan For Profit (IRE) had anything but a clear passage, but he picked up ground in good style and, with his jockey having to switch him left inside the final furlong, managed to get up in the last couple of strides. His jockey was later suspended for two days for careless riding. (16/1)
1294 Signs And Wonders appreciated the return to this longer trip and eventually managed to force his head in front in the closing stages, only to be caught in the last couple of strides. She is a winner without a penalty. (12/1)
518 Rotor Man (IRE) ran by far his best race to date. Taking the field along, he only conceded defeat in the closing stages. (25/1)
Cherokee Flight found his stride from below the distance and ran on in really good style. (33/1)
1219* Purchasing Power (IRE), in good form this spring, was never far away. (7/4: 5/2-13/8)
1265 Shadoof ran well on this handicap debut and was doing all his best work late on. He needs further. (15/2)
958 Caribbean Star (10/1: 8/1-12/1)
945 Tabasco Jazz (8/1: 6/1-9/1)

1459 LADBROKE H'CAP (0-80) (4-Y.O+) (Class D)

5-20 (5-26) **1m 2f 7y** £3,663.75 (£1,110.00: £542.50: £258.75) Stalls: High GOING minus 0.29 sec per fur (GF)

				SP	RR	SF
1262[13]	**Fahs (USA) (70)** (RAkehurst) **5-9-4** TQuinn(2) (lw: hld up: led over 2f out: clr over 1f out: r.o wl)	—	1	13/2[2]	86	66
	Nordansk (53) (MMadgwick) **8-8-1** NVarley(5) (lw: hdwy over 1f out: chsd wnr fnl f: no imp)	5	2	16/1	61	41
	Typhoon Eight (IRE) (70) (RWArmstrong) **5-9-4** GCarter(4) (nt clr run over 2f out: hdwy & nt clr run over 1f out: r.o)	1¼	3	20/1	76	56
1313*	**Gold Desire (49)** (MBrittain) **7-7-11** 6x JLowe(1) (lw: hld up: rdn over 3f out: one pce fnl 2f)	½	4	6/1[1]	54	34
1248[3]	**Pekay (60)** (MJohnston) **4-8-8** JWeaver(7) (led over 1f: led over 3f out tl over 2f out: one pce)	1	5	6/1[1]	64	44
	Mattimeo (IRE) (71) (APJarvis) **4-9-5** WJO'Connor(9) (n.m.r over 2f out: hdwy over 1f out: r.o one pce)	s.h	6	9/1	75	55
1384[3]	**Golden Touch (USA) (58)** (DJSCosgrove) **5-8-6** DBiggs(11) (lw: nvr nr to chal)	1½	7	10/1	59	39
1244[15]	**Infatuation (73)** (LadyHerries) **4-9-7** PaulEddery(3) (swtg: nvr nrr)	hd	8	11/1	74	54

				SP	RR	SF
987[12]	**Zermatt (IRE) (64)** (MDIUsher) **7-8-12** JReid(8) (lw: prom over 8f)	1¼	**9**	33/1	63	43
	Mawared (IRE) (72) (JLDunlop) **4-9-6** RHills(13) (b: nvr nrr)	1¼	**10**	12/1	69	49
1142[2]	**Zidac (71)** (PJMakin) **5-9-5** SSanders(6) (prom over 8f)	4	**11**	7/1[3]	62	42
	Desert Time (68) (CAHorgan) **7-9-2** DHolland(16) (a bhd)	1½	**12**	33/1	56	36
986[10]	**Clouds Hill (FR) (64)** (RHannon) **4-8-12** DaneO'Neill(14) (b.off hind: swtg: a bhd)	s.h	**13**	25/1	52	32
1166[15]	**Balance of Power (62)** (SDow) **5-8-10** OPeslier(17) (prom over 8f)	2½	**14**	16/1	46	26
892[20]	**Angel Chimes (76)** (JEBanks) **4-9-10** JStack(12) (swtg: a bhd)	4	**15**	11/1	54	34
1016[13]	**Wot No Fax (80)** (BJMeehan) **4-10-0b[1]** MJKinane(15) (swtg: led over 8f out tl over 3f out: wknd over 2f out)	3	**16**	16/1	53	33

(SP 130.0%) **16 Rn**

2m 8.28 (1.58) CSF £99.24 CT £1,831.79 TOTE £8.20: £2.40 £4.10 £4.40 £1.80 (£101.00) Trio £483.00 OWNER City Industrial Supplies Ltd (EPSOM) BRED Shadwell Farm Inc

Fahs (USA) turned this race into a non-event for, once he had got to the front, he left his rivals for dead. (13/2)

Nordansk, off the course since falling in a novice chase at Kempton back in November, looked really well for this return. Racing over an inadequate trip, he came through to take second place, but had no hope of reeling in the winner. He should soon find a race. (16/1)

Typhoon Eight (IRE), without a run in over five months, continually met traffic problems and, in the circumstances, did well to take third prize. A return to a mile-and-a-half could see him winning before long. (20/1)

1313* Gold Desire has never won off a mark as high as this. (6/1)

Mattimeo (IRE), making his seasonal reappearance, struggled on without ever posing a threat. (9/1)

1384 Golden Touch (USA) (10/1: 7/1-12/1)

T/Jkpt: £23,288.10 (0.1 Tckts); £29,520.16 to Redcar 27/5/97. T/Plpt: £3,407.00 (11.79 Tckts). T/Qdpt: £267.70 (6.79 Tckts) AK

1440-LEICESTER (R-H) (Good to firm)
Tuesday May 27th

WEATHER: overcast WIND: slight half behind

1460 SHARNFORD CONDITIONS STKS (3-Y.O) (Class C)

2-30 (2-30) **5f 218y** £5,231.00 (£1,811.00: £870.50: £357.50) Stalls: High GOING minus 0.16 sec per fur (GF)

				SP	RR	SF
	Wolf Mountain (99) (RHannon) **3-9-1** DaneO'Neill(1) (a.p: led over 2f out: shkn up appr fnl f: hld on wl)	—	**1**	2/1[2]	101	52
	Imroz (USA) (101) (HRACecil) **3-9-2** KFallon(2) (outpcd early: hdwy over 2f out: jnd wnr appr fnl f: rdn & unable qckn nr fin)	nk	**2**	11/8[1]	101	52
1090*	**Soviet Leader** (RGuest) **3-8-13** JReid(3) (stdd s: drvn along & outpcd over 1f out: sn btn)	5	**3**	9/2[3]	85	36
745[7]	**Jhazi (103)** (DRLoder) **3-9-1b[1]** LDettori(4) (bit bkwd: led over 3f: wknd & eased wl over 1f out)	23	**4**	13/2	25	—

(SP 107.0%) **4 Rn**

1m 12.3 (2.30) CSF £4.60 TOTE £3.50: (£2.10) OWNER Lord Carnarvon (MARLBOROUGH) BRED Highclere Stud Ltd

Wolf Mountain, a winner at this trip in the autumn, looked well tuned-up for his seasonal debut and, although he had to work hard in the closing stages, kept pulling out sufficient to hold off the hard-driven favourite. (2/1)

Imroz (USA), much leaner and more streamlined then she was as a two-year-old, looked to have the measure of the winner when joining forces at the distance but, over a trip that could be on the short side for her now, she was unable to find the pace to wear him down. (11/8)

1090* Soviet Leader, with an outing under his belt already this term, was content to wait on the leaders but, when the pace lifted below the distance, he quite simply had no answer and was easily brushed aside. (9/2)

745 Jhazi still looks to have a bit left to work on and, running very freely in his first-time blinkers, was beginning to back-pedal entering the last quarter-mile and the position was accepted. (13/2: 4/1-7/1)

64+ 62 61+ 62

1461 HATHERN (S) STKS (2-Y.O) (Class G)

3-00 (3-01) **5f 218y** £2,343.00 (£648.00: £309.00) Stalls: High GOING minus 0.16 sec per fur (GF)

				SP	RR	SF
1370*	**Who Nose (IRE)** (BJMeehan) **2-8-9b**(7) 5x GHannon(2) (lw: swvd lft s: hld up: hdwy 2f out: led over 1f out: pushed out)	—	**1**	9/4[3]	59	7
1293[9]	**The Honorable Lady** (MRChannon) **2-8-6** TQuinn(1) (sltly hmpd s: a.p: led ½-wy tl over 1f out: rallied u.p towards fin)	1¼	**2**	7/4[1]	46	—
836[9]	**Zig Zag (IRE)** (MHTompkins) **2-8-6** DBiggs(6) (bit bkwd: plld hrd: prom: ev ch & rdn 2f out: outpcd appr fnl f)	5	**3**	2/1[2]	32	—
1136[7]	**Margaret's Dancer** (CSmith) **2-8-11b[1]** LDettori(4) (lw: plld hrd: chsd ldrs: hrd drvn & edgd lft 2f out: sn btn)	1¼	**4**	11/1	34	—
1286[8]	**Averham Star** (DShaw) **2-8-11** GCarter(3) (led to ½-wy: sn rdn along: wknd over 1f out)	¾	**5**	33/1	32	—

(SP 111.7%) **5 Rn**

1m 15.7 (5.70) CSF £6.13 TOTE £2.20: £1.30 £1.10 (£3.80) OWNER Abbott Racing Ltd (UPPER LAMBOURN) BRED Martin Flattery

No bid

1370* Who Nose (IRE), awarded the race in the Stewards' room at Brighton five days ago, had no such trouble here and, always travelling like a winner, won very much as he pleased. (9/4)

The Honorable Lady, lowered in class, ran much better than she did on her debut, and the way she was fighting back suggests she may be better-suited by an even longer trip. (7/4)

Zig Zag (IRE) covers a lot of ground and, taking a keen hold, pushed the pace but, once the winner quickened things up, she was unable to respond. (2/1)

Margaret's Dancer, wearing blinkers this time, at least held his pitch in the chasing group, but he drifted left into the centre of the track when pressure was applied, and was one of the first beaten. (11/1)

Averham Star, smartly into his stride to set the pace, did not remain in pole position for long and he is not yet getting it together. (33/1)

1462 ABBEY PARK CONDITIONS STKS (3-Y.O) (Class C)

3-30 (3-31) **7f 9y** £5,010.80 (£1,857.20: £893.60: £368.00: £149.00: £61.40) Stalls: High GOING minus 0.16 sec per fur (GF)

				SP	RR	SF
1207*	**Faithful Son (USA)** (MRStoute) **3-9-0** JReid(3) (hld up: hdwy to ld 200y out: qcknd impressively)	—	**1**	8/13[1]	112+	48
940[12]	**Za-Im (102)** (BWHills) **3-9-0** RHills(6) (a.p: shkn up to ld wl over 1f out: hdd & outpcd ins fnl f)	3	**2**	4/1[2]	105	41
1216[2]	**Royal Aty (IRE) (106)** (PAKelleway) **3-9-0** GHind(4) (lw: led far side tl wl over 1f out: sn rdn: one pce)	3	**3**	8/1[3]	98	34
973[6]	**Bachelors Pad (98)** (WJarvis) **3-9-0b[1]** LDettori(1) (swtg: racd alone: led 4f: hrd drvn fnl f: sn btn)	1¼	**4**	16/1	96	32
889*	**Manazil (IRE)** (RWArmstrong) **3-8-9** GCarter(5) (a outpcd & bhd)	6	**5**	14/1	77	13

				SP	RR	SF
1212^{7}	**Mukaddar (USA) (101)** (CJBenstead) **3-9-0** TQuinn(2) (chsd ldrs 5f: sn hrd drvn & wknd)	5	**6**	20/1	71	7

(SP 110.3%) **6 Rn**

1m 25.6 (3.00) CSF £2.90 TOTE £1.60: £1.10 £1.50 (£2.10) OWNER Maktoum Al Maktoum (NEWMARKET) BRED Gainsborough Farm Inc

1207* Faithful Son (USA) had more to beat than he did on his racecourse debut, but he accomplished it in impressive style, and he is still very much on the upgrade. (8/13)

673 Za-Im, back in his own company this time, did nothing wrong and beat the rest easily enough, but the winner proved to be in a class of his own. (4/1)

1216 Royal Aty (IRE) held the call on the far rail for over five furlongs, but he was found wanting when the winner appeared on the scene, and his measure was soon taken. (8/1)

973 Bachelors Pad, brought into the centre of the track to race alone, forced the pace for the first half-mile, but he was soon being bustled along and had to admit the leading pair too smart for him. (16/1)

1463 FOREST H'CAP (0-70) (3-Y.O+) (Class E)

4-00 (4-01) **1m 1f 218y** £3,509.00 (£1,052.00: £506.00: £233.00) Stalls: High GOING minus 0.42 sec per fur (F)

				SP	RR	SF
1244^{3}	**Princess Danielle (59)** (WRMuir) **5-9-3** JReid(12) (hld up: hdwy 4f out: hrd rdn to ld wl ins fnl f)	—	**1**	5/1 [1]	70	39
1266^{2}	**Sandmoor Denim (49)** (SRBowring) **10-8-7**ow1 SWebster(15) (hld up & bhd: gd hdwy 2f out: rdn & r.o wl fnl f)	nk	**2**	9/1	60	28
1156^{6}	**Calendula (60)** (DMorley) **4-9-4** GCarter(6) (trckd ldrs: ev ch 2f out: hrd rdn & kpt on towards fin)	s.h	**3**	16/1	70	39
1116^{2}	**Snowy Mantle (40)** (JDBethell) **4-7-7**(5)ow1 RMullen(8) (a.p: led over 3f out tl wl ins fnl f)	1	**4**	14/1	49	17
1244^{8}	**Shining Example (66)** (PJMakin) **5-9-10** DHolland(5) (hld up: hdwy & nt clr run over 2f out: rdn & hung rt over 1f out: unable qckn)	hd	**5**	7/1 [3]	75	44
1291^{5}	**Mercury (IRE) (43)** (JAGlover) **4-8-1** TSprake(1) (hld up & bhd: hdwy centre over 2f out: nrst fin)	¾	**6**	14/1	51	20
1459^{4}	**Gold Desire (48)** (MBrittain) **7-8-6** 5x GBardwell(18) (in tch: effrt over 2f out: nt pce to chal)	3	**7**	11/2 [2]	51	20
1248^{9}	**Classic Ballet (FR) (58)** (ICampbell) **4-9-2** RPrice(10) (swtg: prom: rdn 2f out: kpt on same pce)	¾	**8**	14/1	60	29
	Absolutely Fayre (60) (VSoane) **6-9-4** GHind(16) (bkwd: in tch: effrt & rdn 3f out: nt rch ldrs)	1¼	**9**	50/1	60	29
1142^{11}	**Kota (70)** (JWharton) **4-10-0** LDettori(9) (hld up: hdwy 4f out: rdn over 2f out: nvr able chal)	1¼	**10**	5/1 [1]	68	37
1262^{16}	**Lucky Begonia (IRE) (56)** (WJMusson) **4-9-0** MRimmer(14) (swtg: nvr plcd to chal)	1	**11**	16/1	52	21
360^{3}	**African-Pard (IRE) (60)** (DHaydnJones) **5-9-4** TQuinn(11) (bit bkwd: w ldr: rdn over 2f out: grad wknd)	¾	**12**	16/1	55	24
1233^{2}	**Benjamins Law (45)** (JAPickering) **6-8-3** RLappin(4) (hld up: hdwy 4f out: ev ch 2f out: wknd)	nk	**13**	12/1	39	8
1162^{14}	**Samim (USA) (57)** (SGollings) **4-9-1b** PaulEddery(7) (chsd ldrs: drvn along ent st: wknd 3f out)	s.h	**14**	33/1	51	20
1118^{4}	**In A Tizzy (38)** (ABMulholland) **4-7-5**(5) IonaWands(13) (led over 6f: wknd over 2f out)	1½	**15**	25/1	30	—
544^{10}	**Gulf of Siam (55)** (JMackie) **4-8-13** JQuinn(3) (a rr div: t.o)	8	**16**	25/1	34	3
	Woodlands Lad Too (38) (PAPritchard) **5-7-10** NAdams(2) (a bhd: t.o)	11	**17**	100/1	—	—
1273^{17}	**Eric's Bett (63)** (PGMurphy) **4-9-7** SDrowne(17) (a in rr: t.o)	3½	**18**	25/1	19	—

(SP 134.0%) **18 Rn**

2m 7.2 (3.50) CSF £46.22 CT £648.63 TOTE £6.60: £1.10 £3.10 £3.10 £4.60 (£24.80) Trio £346.50; £258.69 to Yarmouth 28/5/97 OWNER Mrs Marion Wickham (LAMBOURN) BRED Mrs Wickham

LONG HANDICAP Woodlands Lad Too 6-12 In A Tizzy 7-3

1244 Princess Danielle knew she had been in a race and had to fight hard to force her head in front, but she answered her rider's every call and deservedly won the day. (5/1)

1266 Sandmoor Denim may have found the ground plenty fast enough for him, but he delivered a determined last-furlong challenge which only just failed. (9/1)

1156 Calendula has done all her winning over a longer tip, and her determined late bid was always being comfortably held. (16/1)

1116 Snowy Mantle has still to get off the mark but she ran a very genuine race, and it was only late on that she was forced to give best. Her turn is long overdue. (14/1)

Shining Example was held by the winner on their most recent running but, if he had not been impeded and had not hung right towards the inside rail, he may well have gained his revenge. (7/1)

1291 Mercury (IRE) stayed on relentlessly in the last quarter-mile, but the post was always going to arrive too soon. With the stable striking form, he is one to keep in mind. (14/1)

1459 Gold Desire could not muster the pace to mount a challenge, and he may have found the ground had dried out too quickly. (11/2)

1464 WOODHOUSE EAVES CLAIMING STKS (3-Y.O) (Class F)

4-30 (4-31) **1m 8y** £2,595.00 (£720.00: £345.00) Stalls: High GOING minus 0.16 sec per fur (GF)

				SP	RR	SF
1217*	**Janglynyve (60)** (SPCWoods) **3-8-7** LDettori(6) (hld up: hdwy to ld over 2f out: hrd drvn fnl f: hld on gamely)	—	**1**	13/8 [1]	66	18
886^{18}	**Princess of Hearts (60)** (MCPipe) **3-8-7b** JReid(7) (hld up & bhd: hdwy 2f out: str chal fnl f: jst failed)	hd	**2**	7/2 [2]	66	18
1217^{2}	**Soura (USA) (55)** (PAKelleway) **3-8-7** GHind(3) (hld up: hdwy ½-wy: rdn over 1f out: nt qckn)	4	**3**	7/1 [3]	58	10
765^{10}	**Wheildon** (SCWilliams) **3-8-10** SDrowne(2) (chsd ldrs: rdn 2f out: r.o one pce)	4	**4**	25/1	53	5
264^{3}	**Hint of Victory** (MBell) **3-9-2** TQuinn(4) (bit bkwd: prom: led 4f out tl over 2f out: sn rdn: no ex appr fnl f)	1½	**5**	9/1	56	8
963^{16}	**Victory At Hart (48)** (DMorris) **3-8-6** PBloomfield(8) (chsd ldrs tl rdn & wknd over 2f out)	3	**6**	20/1	40	—
1207^{16}	**Change** (CEBrittain) **3-8-12** DHolland(5) (led to ½-wy: rdn over 2f out: sn wknd)	hd	**7**	10/1	46	—
1139^{5}	**Pastiche (61)** (TGMills) **3-8-9** JQuinn(1) (prom: drvn along over 2f out: sn outpcd)	1¾	**8**	10/1	39	—

(SP 109.6%) **8 Rn**

1m 40.8 (5.80) CSF £5.89 TOTE £1.70: £1.10 £2.10 £2.20 (£2.60) OWNER The Storm Again Syndicate (NEWMARKET) BRED S. J. Mear

1217* Janglynyve poked her nose in front over two furlongs out and then stepped up a gear, but she had to dig even deeper when the runner-up launched a serious last-furlong challenge, and she was all out at the line. (13/8)

644* Princess of Hearts delayed her challenge until the last possible moment and looked sure to take over in the final hundred yards but, with the winner finding extra, she was still half-a-stride down at the line. (7/2: 9/4-4/1)

1217 Soura (USA), poised to challenge entering the final furlong, lacked the extra speed of the principals and she was well outpaced in the battle to the finish. (7/1)

Wheildon turned in a promising display for one so short on experience, and he is heading in the right direction. (25/1)

264 Hint of Victory, making his turf debut, looked just in need of the run after over three months out of action, but he remained in the heat of the battle until feeling the strain approaching the final furlong. He could be one to be on next time. (9/1)

Change (10/1: op 5/1)

1139 Pastiche (10/1: op 5/1)

1465 CORONATION H'CAP (0-70) (3-Y.O) (Class E)

5-00 (5-01) **1m 3f 183y** £3,275.00 (£980.00: £470.00: £215.00) Stalls: High GOING minus 0.42 sec per fur (F)

			Pos	SP	RR	SF
1129^{4}	**Scarrots (59)** (SCWilliams) **3-9-2** SDrowne(5) (mde virtually all: rdn over 1f out: edgd lft ins fnl f: all out)	—	**1**	11/1	69	31
976^{2}	**Mystic Quest (IRE) (63)** (KMcAuliffe) **3-9-6** JReid(6) (b: trckd ldrs: ev ch fnl 2f: hrd rdn: r.o)	nk	**2**	$3/1^{1}$	73	35
1168^{7}	**Persian Blue (61)** (RHannon) **3-9-4** DaneO'Neill(8) (lw: hld up: hdwy over 2f out: r.o strly nr fin)	s.h	**3**	7/1	71	33
1140^{11}	**Beauchamp Lion (60)** (JLDunlop) **3-9-3** GCarter(3) (bit bkwd: hld up: reminder 4f out: swtchd ins & styd on strly ins fnl f)	½	**4**	9/1	69	31
1284*	**Tycoon Tina (50)** (WMBrisbourne) **3-8-2**(5) 4x RMullen(1) (s.s: hdwy 2f out: nvr nrr)	1½	**5**	9/1	57	19
1299^{2}	**As-Is (64)** (MJohnston) **3-9-7** DHolland(12) (lw: prom: rdn & wandered appr fnl f: squeezed out ins fnl f: nt rcvr)	nk	**6**	$4/1^{2}$	70+	32
842^{7}	**Nick of Time (64)** (JLDunlop) **3-9-7** PaulEddery(9) (dwlt: sn chsng ldrs: wknd 3f out: t.o)	9	**7**	$9/2^{3}$	58	20
1234^{9}	**Hippios (45)** (SDow) **3-8-2** JQuinn(7) (hld up: effrt 4f out: sn rdn: no imp: t.o)	½	**8**	50/1	39	1
1134^{3}	**Kustom Kit Klassic (51)** (SRBowring) **3-8-8** SWebster(2) (b: a in rr: t.o)	8	**9**	25/1	34	—
1043^{4}	**Bonne Ville (62)** (BPalling) **3-9-5** TSprake(10) (hld up: effrt & rdn over 2f out: no imp: t.o)	1½	**10**	10/1	43	5
534^{6}	**Yangtze (IRE) (49)** (BRMillman) **3-8-6b¹** WJO'Connor(4) (w wnr 8f: wknd 3f out: eased whn btn: t.o)	½	**11**	25/1	29	—

(SP 122.8%) **11 Rn**

2m 33.9 (5.40) CSF £41.27 CT £237.04 TOTE £10.40: £2.10 £1.60 £2.40 (£27.40) Trio £88.10 OWNER Mr Bruce Wyatt (NEWMARKET) BRED R. G. Percival

STEWARDS' ENQUIRY Drowne susp. 5 & 9/6/97 (careless riding).

1129 Scarrots, having his first try at such an extended trip, attacked from the front and, though he drifted left under strong pressure nearing the finish, he showed the right attitude to hang on in an all-out duel to the line. (11/1)

976 Mystic Quest (IRE) joined issue two furlongs out and may have briefly shown ahead, but the winner kept the pressure on and he was always getting the worst of the argument. (3/1: 5/1-11/4)

Persian Blue runs as if she needs a slightly stiffer test of stamina, for she was only finding top gear when the race was as good as over. (7/1)

Beauchamp Lion, given a back-hander soon after entering the straight, took a long time to really find his stride, but he was staying on strongly towards the finish and would seem to be coming to himself. (9/1)

1284* Tycoon Tina, sluggish leaving the start, was doing all her best work late on and seems to get the trip. (9/1)

1299 As-Is, battling for supremacy but looking to be fighting a lost cause, became the meat in the sandwich two hundred yards out and, forced to check, had no hope at all of recovering. (4/1)

842 Nick of Time (9/2: 3/1-5/1)

T/Plpt: £37.00 (273.37 Tckts). T/Qdpt: £5.40 (166.42 Tckts) IM

1447-REDCAR (L-H) (Good to firm, Firm patches)
Tuesday May 27th

WEATHER: sunny periods WIND: slight against

65+ 63 71+ 66

1466 E.B.F. MEDIAN AUCTION MAIDEN STKS (2-Y.O F) (Class E)

2-15 (2-16) **6f** £3,015.25 (£907.00: £438.50: £204.25) Stalls: High GOING minus 0.41 sec per fur (F)

			Pos	SP	RR	SF
	Behold (JRFanshawe) **2-8-11** DHarrison(3) (lt-f: unf: lw: in tch: qcknd to ld appr fnl: r.o)	—	**1**	$5/1^{3}$	74+	19
828^{7}	**Fayrana (IRE)** (JWHills) **2-8-8**(3) FLynch(7) (in tch: hdwy 2f out: kpt on wl towards fin)	1	**2**	6/1	71	16
1038^{3}	**Sharp Cracker (IRE)** (MJohnston) **2-8-11** JWeaver(10) (lw: w ldrs: disp ld 2f out: hdd appr fnl f: kpt on)	hd	**3**	$2/1^{1}$	68	16
	Ella Falls (IRE) (TDBarron) **2-8-11** KDarley(5) (neat: bit bkwd: in tch: effrt 3f out: kpt on fnl f: nt pce to chal)	1½	**4**	$4/1^{2}$	64	12
844^{6}	**Flower O'Cannie (IRE)** (MWEasterby) **2-8-6**(5) GParkin(4) (led 4f: kpt on again towards fin)	hd	**5**	10/1	64	12
1253^{2}	**Inchalong** (MBrittain) **2-8-11** WRyan(2) (chsd ldrs: chal 2f out: nt qckn fnl f)	1	**6**	12/1	61	9
1126^{5}	**Imperial Honey (IRE)** (MrsASwinbank) **2-8-11** WSupple(1) (w ldrs: led 2f out: sn hdd & wknd)	½	**7**	20/1	60	8
	Bollinger Rose (IRE) (JJO'Neill) **2-8-11** JCarroll(8) (w'like: scope: bkwd: sn pushed along: lost tch fnl 3f)	7	**8**	12/1	41	—
	Shalyah (IRE) (MrsJRRamsden) **2-8-11** JFortune(6) (w'like: bkwd: in tch tl outpcd fnl 2½f)	¾	**9**	12/1	39	—
1253^{9}	**Kara-Lovo** (JBalding) **2-8-11** NCarlisle(9) (bit bkwd: outpcd & wl bhd fr ½-wy)	7	**10**	50/1	21	—
	Patricius (TDEasterby) **2-8-11** ACulhane(11) (unf: bkwd: s.s: sn t.o: sme late hdwy)	3	**11**	12/1	13	—

(SP 130.9%) **11 Rn**

1m 13.2 (3.00) CSF £36.01 TOTE £6.20: £2.20 £2.20 £1.20 (£15.90) Trio £8.80 OWNER Cheveley Park Stud (NEWMARKET) BRED Cheveley Park Stud Ltd

Behold had nothing to recommend her on looks but she was fit. She did it nicely and obviously has an engine. (5/1: op 5/2)

648 Fayrana (IRE) appreciated this extra distance and finished well, suggesting that either stiffer tracks or further yet will also help. (6/1)

1038 Sharp Cracker (IRE) had no excuses this time and just failed to pick up when the pressure was on. She is such a big filly, she will probably get better as she strengthens. (2/1: op 3/1)

Ella Falls (IRE) looks the type that can go, but lack of experience was the difference here. (4/1)

844 Flower O'Cannie (IRE), after a month off, ran much better and certainly appreciated the extra furlong. (10/1: op 5/1)

1253 Inchalong ran her usual race, but was tapped for speed when it mattered. (12/1)

1126 Imperial Honey (IRE) was a shade disappointing this time, and perhaps too much use was made of her. (20/1)

Shalyah (IRE) (12/1: op 7/1)

1467 REDCAR MAIDEN AMATEUR H'CAP (0-60) (3-Y.O+) (Class G)

2-45 (2-50) **6f** £2,440.50 (£683.00: £331.50) Stalls: High GOING minus 0.41 sec per fur (F)

			Pos	SP	RR	SF
1385^{3}	**Afaan (IRE) (56)** (RFMarvin) **4-11-7**(5) MrsMMorris(15) (a chsng ldrs: led wl over 1f out: r.o)	—	**1**	$7/2^{1}$	70	55
1089^{3}	**Gay Breeze (38)** (PSFelgate) **4-10-3**(5) MrJGoldstein(17) (lw: a cl up: led ½-wy tl wl over 1f out: kpt on one pce)	2½	**2**	$6/1^{2}$	45	30
1256^{10}	**High Spirits (IRE) (56)** (TDEasterby) **3-10-12b**(5) MissADeniel(22) (chsd ldrs: kpt on u.p fnl 3f: nvr able chal)	1	**3**	12/1	61	37
	Priory Gardens (IRE) (42) (JMBradley) **3-9-12**(5) MissVRoberts(21) (in tch stands' side: kpt on fnl 2f)	½	**4**	25/1	45	21
1284^{8}	**Manhattan Diamond (51)** (ABailey) **3-10-5b**(7)ow1 MissALHutchinson(13) (a in tch: kpt on one pce fnl 2f)	nk	**5**	25/1	54	29
	Belbay Star (37) (JLEyre) **4-10-7** MissDianaJones(12) (swtg: bit bkwd: hdwy to chse ldrs ½-wy: sn rdn: btn appr fnl f)	nk	**6**	16/1	39	24

1127^{10}	**Hi Mujtahid (IRE) (43)** (SEKettlewell) **3-10-4** MrsDKettlewell(25) (lw: styd on fnl 3f: nrst fin)	1	**7**	$8/1^{3}$	42	18
900^{12}	**Severn Mill (30)** (JMBradley) **6-9-9**(5) MrOMcPhail(24) (swtg: hung lft ½-wy: styd on u.p fnl 2f: n.d)	1¼	**8**	25/1	26	11
1115^{6}	**Swiss Coast (IRE) (52)** (NTinkler) **3-10-13** MissJAllison(23) (lw: sn wl bhd: styd on wl fnl 2f)	½	**9**	16/1	46	22
1128^{9}	**Fisiostar (34)** (MDods) **4-10-4b** MrMHNaughton(9) (lw: prom tl outpcd fnl 2f)	3½	**10**	14/1	19	4
827^{14}	**Silent System (IRE) (23)** (DWChapman) **4-9-2**(5) MrVLukaniuk(14) (nvr nr ldrs)	s.h	**11**	25/1	8	—
995^{9}	**Splashed (53)** (TDBarron) **3-10-9**(5) MissMKeuthen(11) (nvr trbld ldrs)	s.h	**12**	20/1	38	14
1096^{9}	**Hiltons Executive (IRE) (40)** (EJAlston) **3-10-1** MissPRobson(4) (cl up far side tl wknd fnl 2f)	1½	**13**	16/1	21	—
896^{12}	**Interaction (35)** (RCraggs) **3-9-3**(7) MissNicolaCraggs(16) (n.d)	½	**14**	50/1	15	—
760^{3}	**Chief's Lady (38)** (JMBradley) **5-10-3**(5) MrAEvans(1) (led far side tl hdd ½-wy: wknd qckly)	nk	**15**	12/1	17	2
588^{9}	**Thewrightone (IRE) (40)** (GROldroyd) **3-9-8b**(7) MrWWenyon(20) (n.d)	¾	**16**	50/1	17	—
900^{7}	**Stolen Music (IRE) (41)** (REBarr) **4-10-11** MrRHale(6) (n.d)	1	**17**	20/1	15	—
1132^{4}	**Commin' Up (55)** (MissJBower) **4-11-4**(7) MrGWoodward(5) (n.d)	nk	**18**	25/1	28	13
758^{10}	**Bellarula (52)** (MDods) **3-10-13** MrSSwiers(18) (s.s: a bhd)	1½	**19**	20/1	21	—
1266^{11}	**Mystic Maid (IRE) (58)** (JLHarris) **4-11-9**(5) MrsCWilliams(26) (bhd fr ½-wy)	nk	**20**	20/1	26	11
995^{11}	**Only Josh (IRE) (48)** (MrsJRRamsden) **3-10-4**(5) MissERamsden(7) (lw: nvr trbld ldrs)	½	**21**	14/1	15	—
1020^{17}	**Saturiba (USA) (39)** (JohnHarris) **4-10-4**(5)ow7 MrMMackley(8) (n.d)	3	**22**	50/1	—	—
925^{14}	**Willie Miles (45)** (DWChapman) **4-11-1** MissRClark(2) (cl up over 3f: sn wknd)	4	**23**	16/1	—	—
	Rustic Song (IRE) (27) (JWharton) **4-9-6**(5) MissBridgetGatehouse(3) (cl up tl ½-wy: wknd qckly)	2	**24**	50/1	—	—
1238^{11}	**Canton Ron (52)** (CADwyer) **3-10-13b**^{1} MrTMcCarthy(10) (lw: cl up 4f: wknd qckly)	1½	**25**	16/1	—	—
				(SP 151.9%)	**25 Rn**	

1m 13.4 (3.20) CSF £20.26 CT £236.60 TOTE £5.80: £1.70 £2.30 £2.40 £30.30 (£10.80) Trio £26.50 OWNER Mr E. Gray (NEWARK) BRED Shadwell Estate Company Limited
WEIGHT FOR AGE 3yo-9lb
1385 Afaan (IRE) does not know how to run a bad race, and scored authoritatively to break his duck. (7/2: op 7/1)
1089 Gay Breeze is running consistently well at present and will surely find a modest opportunity. (6/1)
995 High Spirits (IRE) put in his best effort this season, but was short of a real turn of foot in the last furlong-and-a-half. (12/1)
Priory Gardens (IRE), who showed little last season, gave signs of hope here. (25/1)
497 Manhattan Diamond was dropping back in trip, and this was her best effort for a while. (25/1)
Belbay Star needed this but did not run badly, and there is obviously some ability there. (16/1)
876 Hi Mujtahid (IRE), having his first run for his new stable, gave the impression that further may well see improvement. (8/1: 5/1-9/1)
387 Only Josh (IRE) (14/1: 16/1-25/1)

1468 DORMANSTOWN SPRINT H'CAP (0-90) (3-Y.O+) (Class C)
3-15 (3-21) **5f** £5,328.75 (£1,605.00: £777.50: £363.75) Stalls: High GOING minus 0.41 sec per fur (F)

				SP	RR	SF
1225^{2}	**Blessingindisguise (58)** (MWEasterby) **4-7-13b** LCharnock(9) (lw: chsd ldrs: rdn to ld 1½f out: r.o)	—	**1**	$11/2^{2}$	67	39
	Moon Strike (FR) (79) (HAkbary) **7-9-6** OUrbina(12) (b: hld up & bhd: nt clr run fr ½-wy tl swtchd rt 1f out: fin wl)	½	**2**	9/1	86	58
1259^{11}	**Antarctic Storm (60)** (RAFahey) **4-8-1** FNorton(1) (bolted 3f bef s: hld up: effrt ½-wy: styd on: nrst fin)	1¼	**3**	100/1	63	35
1269^{9}	**Insider Trader (63)** (MrsJRRamsden) **6-8-4** MDeering(11) (in tch: styd on wl fnl f: nrst fin)	1	**4**	$6/1^{3}$	63	35
1113^{8}	**Spender (77)** (PWHarris) **8-8-11**(7) CLowther(5) (lw: hdwy ½-wy: ch over 1f out: nt qckn)	s.h	**5**	10/1	77	49
1223*	**Squire Corrie (72)** (DWChapman) **5-8-13** ACulhane(6) (lw: a chsng ldrs: pushed along thrght: no imp fnl 2f)	2	**6**	8/1	66	38
	Brecongill Lad (67) (MissSEHall) **5-8-8v**^{1} WRyan(13) (sn pushed along: nvr able chal)	½	**7**	20/1	59	31
744^{3}	**For the Present (83)** (TDBarron) **7-9-10** KDarley(8) (lw: s.i.s: drvn along ½-wy: no imp)	nk	**8**	$5/2^{1}$	74	46
	Top of The Form (IRE) (85) (MJohnston) **3-9-4** JWeaver(10) (drvn along ½-wy: nvr trbld ldrs)	1¼	**9**	25/1	72	36
1018^{8}	**Bayford Thrust (86)** (JBerry) **3-9-0**(5) TEDurcan(4) (b.hind: outpcd & bhd fr ½-wy)	s.h	**10**	25/1	73	37
744^{13}	**Royal Dome (IRE) (69)** (MartynWane) **5-8-10** JCarroll(7) (sn pushed along: nvr trbld ldrs)	1½	**11**	12/1	51	23
	Tart and a Half (72) (JLEyre) **5-8-13b** MGallagher(2) (led & sn clr: hdd & wknd qckly over 1f out)	hd	**12**	16/1	54	26
1158^{6}	**Swynford Dream (82)** (JFBottomley) **4-9-9** JLowe(3) (lw: spd to ½-wy: sn wknd)	1¼	**13**	$6/1^{3}$	60	32
				(SP 129.7%)	**13 Rn**	

58.2 secs (0.70) CSF £52.15 CT £4,279.03 TOTE £5.20: £2.20 £2.10 £12.50 (£33.00) Trio £476.40; £536.84 to Yarmouth 28/5/97 OWNER Mr A. G. Black (SHERIFF HUTTON) BRED Mrs A. Meller
WEIGHT FOR AGE 3yo-8lb
OFFICIAL EXPLANATION **For the Present: missed the break and was never able thereafter to get into a challenging position in a fast-run race.**
1225 Blessingindisguise gained just reward for his consistency, but was a shade lucky as the runner-up met with all sorts of trouble. (11/2)
Moon Strike (FR), without doubt, would have won this with any sort of run. (9/1)
Antarctic Storm is a real handful, but there is plenty of ability there and he ran really well. (100/1)
949 Insider Trader is on a useful mark at present and is running quite well. (6/1)
643* Spender ran more encouragingly after two moderate efforts. (10/1)
1223* Squire Corrie was never really firing on this occasion. (8/1)
Tart and a Half has changed stables and was having her first run of the season, but showed blistering early pace which will surely bring success in due course. (16/1)

1469 SKELTON MAIDEN H'CAP (0-60) (3-Y.O) (Class F)
3-45 (3-46) **1m 6f 19y** £2,722.50 (£760.00: £367.50) Stalls: Centre GOING minus 0.41 sec per fur (F)

				SP	RR	SF
1140^{14}	**Aurelian (52)** (MBell) **3-9-1** MFenton(9) (mid div: hdwy on outside 3f out: hung lft 2f out: led 1f out: r.o)	—	**1**	10/1	58	16
1299^{3}	**Alagna (43)** (SCWilliams) **3-8-6** KDarley(4) (lw: hld up: hdwy 3f out: led over 1f out: sn hdd: kpt on u.p)	nk	**2**	$2/1^{1}$	49	7
1129^{6}	**Monarch's Pursuit (56)** (TDEasterby) **3-9-5** JFortune(7) (lw: led 3f: chsd ldrs: chal 2f out: hrd rdn & one pce)	5	**3**	$6/1^{3}$	56	14
1043^{9}	**Kickonsun (IRE) (35)** (RAFahey) **3-7-5b**^{1}(7)ow2 RWinston(15) (in tch: hdwy 3f out: sltly hmpd wl over 1f out: r.o one pce)	s.h	**4**	20/1	35	—
975^{6}	**Ziggy's Viola (IRE) (58)** (MrsMReveley) **3-9-7** ACulhane(6) (hdwy 3f out: styd on u.p: nt pce to chal)	nk	**5**	16/1	58	16
826^{3}	**Arisaig (IRE) (56)** (PCalver) **3-9-2**(3) DarrenMoffatt(8) (lw: in tch: kpt on fnl 3f: no imp)	1	**6**	$5/1^{2}$	54	12
1094^{5}	**Spondulicks (IRE) (53)** (BPJBaugh) **3-9-2** JWeaver(12) (lw: led after 3f tl over 1f out: wknd)	nk	**7**	7/1	51	9
1115^{7}	**Ocean Breeze (44)** (JSWainwright) **3-8-2**(5) JBramhill(11) (hdwy u.p 4f out: n.d)	1¾	**8**	33/1	40	—
878^{12}	**Miss Barcelona (IRE) (50)** (MJPolglase) **3-8-13** TGMcLaughlin(3) (hdwy 4f out: rdn & btn 2f out)	1	**9**	25/1	45	3
1094^{6}	**Mellwood (IRE) (46)** (MHTompkins) **3-8-9** DaleGibson(14) (bhd: rdn 4f out: n.d)	2	**10**	15/2	39	—
900^{10}	**Gollaccia (44)** (GMMoore) **3-8-7** JTate(5) (in tch tl wknd 3½f)	1	**11**	33/1	36	—

1299[11] **Maremma (46)** (DonEnricoIncisa) **3-8-9** KimTinkler(2) (a bhd)	½	**12**	20/1	37	—
1129[11] **Grovefair Lad (IRE) (50)** (MartynWane) **3-8-13** JCarroll(13) (cl up: chal 4f out: wknd fnl 2f)	½	**13**	20/1	40	—
608[12] **Bout (40)** (RMMcKellar) **3-8-3** JLowe(10) (chsd ldrs tl wknd fnl 3f)	3	**14**	16/1	27	—
773[11] **Kissandy (35)** (MrsVAAconley) **3-7-12** MDeering(1) (bhd fr ½-wy)	22	**15**	50/1	—	—
			(SP 135.4%)		**15 Rn**

3m 8.6 (9.30) CSF £28.46 CT £134.57 TOTE £23.20: £5.20 £1.30 £1.90 (£25.00) Trio £106.70 OWNER Mr Desmond Fitzgerald (NEWMARKET) BRED D. Fitzgerald

LONG HANDICAP Kickonsun (IRE) 7-8

Aurelian, stepped up in trip and given a chance by the Handicapper after two moderate efforts so far this season, showed just what he can do, and won well despite hanging left. (10/1)

1299 Alagna took well to the extra distance but looks a really hard ride and was never helping her jockey. There is obviously plenty more ability there if she can be persuaded. (2/1)

1129 Monarch's Pursuit is running well just now and was taking a big step-up in trip, but proved too slow at the business end. (6/1)

582 Kickonsun (IRE) had blinkers on for the first time and they made a difference, but he was still never good enough. (20/1)

975 Ziggy's Viola (IRE), ridden from behind on this occasion, stayed on well at the end to put up a much better effort. (16/1)

826 Arisaig (IRE) does not do anything quickly, but certainly stays and is going to need further yet. (5/1)

1470 KIRKLEATHAM RATING RELATED MAIDEN STKS (0-70) (3-Y.O+) (Class E)

4-15 (4-17) **1m 2f** £2,859.25 (£859.00: £414.50: £192.25) Stalls: Low GOING minus 0.41 sec per fur (F)

			SP	RR	SF
996[3] **Heart of Gold (IRE) (69)** (MissSEHall) **3-8-10** WRyan(8) (cl up: led over 3f out: r.o wl)	—	**1**	5/1[3]	81	39
1226[3] **Klondike Charger (USA) (68)** (BWHills) **3-8-10** JWeaver(1) (a.p: effrt over 2f out: sn chsng wnr: r.o: nt pce to chal)	2½	**2**	7/4[1]	77	35
841[5] **Dancing Queen (IRE) (70)** (MBell) **3-8-7** MFenton(3) (hdwy & in tch 4f out: wl outpcd fnl f)	7	**3**	9/2[2]	63	21
1234[6] **Quest For Best (USA) (70)** (JHMGosden) **3-8-4v**[1](3) FLynch(4) (chsd ldrs: ev ch over 2f out: wknd over 1f out)	3	**4**	6/1	58	16
535[6] **Allied Academy (67)** (SCWilliams) **3-8-10** KDarley(5) (hdwy 4f out: sn pushed along & in tch: one pce fnl 2f)	3	**5**	6/1	56	14
1221[9] **Madison Mist (68)** (MrsJRRamsden) **3-8-7** JFortune(10) (lw: bhd: sme hdwy over 2f out: nvr trbld ldrs)	2½	**6**	6/1	49	7
425[6] **Lightning Rebel (70)** (CWThornton) **3-8-10** LCharnock(2) (lw: bhd: hdwy 4f out: sn drvn along & no imp)	½	**7**	12/1	51	9
245[8] **Degree (70)** (SCWilliams) **4-9-0**(7) DarrenWilliams(9) (led tl hdd over 3f out: sn outpcd)	3½	**8**	50/1	43	15
1096[12] **Court Express (63)** (TJEtherington) **3-8-10** TLucas(6) (lw: hmpd & lost tch appr st: n.d after)	2	**9**	20/1	43	1
1020[19] **Desert Cat (IRE) (64)** (MartynWane) **4-9-10** JCarroll(7) (a rr div)	11	**10**	33/1	25	—
			(SP 131.4%)		**10 Rn**

2m 6.4 (2.80) CSF £14.50 TOTE £5.70: £1.30 £1.60 £1.80 (£7.10) Trio £13.60 OWNER Mr C. Platts (MIDDLEHAM) BRED Miss Fiona Meehan

WEIGHT FOR AGE 3yo-14lb

996 Heart of Gold (IRE) showed just what he can do, and there was a lot to like about the performance. Now he has got his head in front, he should continue to improve and ought to stay further. (5/1)

1226 Klondike Charger (USA), appreciated the extra distance and kept running on when ridden, but always found the winner too strong. (7/4: op 3/1)

841 Dancing Queen (IRE) was close enough if good enough in the last half-mile but, when serious pressure was on, she failed to pull out any extra. (9/2: op 5/2)

833 Quest For Best (USA), tried in a visor for the first time, had her chances but gave up once a real effort was needed. (6/1)

535 Allied Academy was trying a longer trip, but still looked very one-paced. (6/1)

899 Madison Mist, given a patient ride over her longest trip to date, was gradually getting the hang of things at the finish. (6/1: op 4/1)

1471 BILLINGHAM LIMITED STKS (0-75) (3-Y.O+) (Class D)

4-45 (4-48) **7f** £3,431.00 (£1,028.00: £494.00: £227.00) Stalls: High GOING minus 0.41 sec per fur (F)

			SP	RR	SF
946* **Weetman's Weigh (IRE) (75)** (RHollinshead) **4-9-4**(3) FLynch(2) (lw: hld up: effrt over 2f out: led ins fnl f: r.o)	—	**1**	3/1[2]	87	40
1097[9] **Quilling (75)** (MDods) **5-9-4** JFortune(3) (lw: unruly bef & in stalls: trckd ldrs: led over 1f out tl ins fnl f: no ex)	1	**2**	11/4[1]	82	35
Toujours Riviera (73) (JPearce) **7-9-1**(3) CTeague(1) (bit bkwd: led tl hdd over 1f out: kpt on)	2	**3**	11/2	77	30
1219[2] **Mountgate (68)** (MPBielby) **5-9-4** JWeaver(6) (lw: s.s: hdwy over 2f out: rdn & no imp)	1	**4**	100/30[3]	75	28
1127[3] **Spotted Eagle (71)** (MartynWane) **4-9-4** JCarroll(5) (in tch 4f)	12	**5**	10/1	47	—
701[6] **Prominent (59)** (MrsVAAconley) **3-8-7** MDeering(4) (prom 4f: sn btn)	½	**6**	40/1	46	—
1085[6] **Move With Edes (69)** (WGMTurner) **5-8-11**(7) DMcGaffin(7) (cl up over 5f: wknd qckly)	5	**7**	7/1	35	—
			(SP 114.2%)		**7 Rn**

1m 25.5 (2.50) CSF £10.62 TOTE £3.30: £2.00 £1.80 (£5.00) OWNER Ed Weetman (Haulage & Storage) Ltd (UPPER LONGDON) BRED David Commins

WEIGHT FOR AGE 3yo-11lb

946* Weetman's Weigh (IRE) travelled well and won nicely, suggesting that he is in really good form. (3/1)

824 Quilling gave problems both in the paddock and at the start, but still ran well. His temperament has always been his undoing. (11/4)

Toujours Riviera, looking likely to benefit from this, put up a fair performance and probably needs further. (11/2)

1219 Mountgate has plenty more ability when he decides to use it, but this was not one of those days. (100/30)

1127 Spotted Eagle ran poorly, but his rider did not seem happy with him and he was not knocked about when beaten. (10/1)

1472 LEVY BOARD H'CAP (0-70) (3-Y.O+) (Class E)

5-15 (5-17) **1m 1f** £3,132.25 (£943.00: £456.50: £213.25) Stalls: Low GOING minus 0.41 sec per fur (F)

			SP	RR	SF
1116[12] **Dispol Gem (58)** (PCalver) **4-9-3** KDarley(14) (lw: hld up: nt clr run over 3f out: hdwy 2f out: r.o to ld wl ins fnl f: cleverly)	—	**1**	10/1	62	37
1231[2] **Nobby Barnes (37)** (DonEnricoIncisa) **8-7-10** KimTinkler(5) (lw: bhd: hdwy on ins 4f out: led 1f out: hdd & no ex towards fin)	½	**2**	12/1	40	15
848[8] **Habeta (USA) (37)** (JWWatts) **11-7-10** JLowe(4) (hld up: hdwy & ev ch appr fnl f: nt qckn)	1¾	**3**	8/1[2]	37	12
1128[6] **Spanish Verdict (56)** (DenysSmith) **10-8-12**(3) FLynch(2) (cl up: led over 4f out tl hdd 1f out: kpt on)	s.h	**4**	10/1	56	31
689[6] **Leif the Lucky (USA) (57)** (MissSEHall) **8-8-13**(3) OPears(13) (in tch: effrt over 2f out: styd on one pce appr fnl f)	hd	**5**	8/1[2]	57	32
Majal (IRE) (49) (JSWainwright) **8-8-3**(5) JBramhill(15) (bit bkwd: chsd ldrs: ev ch over 2f out: btn appr fnl f)	¾	**6**	50/1	47	22
925[6] **Energy Man (50)** (MDods) **4-8-9** JWeaver(9) (rr div: effrt 3f out: styd on towards fin)	s.h	**7**	10/1	48	23

1131[9]	**Pride of Pendle (68)** (MartynWane) **8-9-13** JCarroll(12) (hld up & bhd: hdwy & swtchd over 2f out: sn chsng ldrs: kpt on fnl f)	½	**8**	9/1[3]	65	40
687[13]	**Major Mouse (47)** (WWHaigh) **9-8-6** DHarrison(6) (hld up & bhd: effrt 3f out: nvr rchd ldrs)	s.h	**9**	33/1	44	19
1231[7]	**Bedazzle (38)** (MBrittain) **6-7-4**(7)ow1 DMernagh(10) (rr div: effrt on outside 3f out: styd on: n.d)	nk	**10**	10/1	35	9
1256[P]	**Imperial Or Metric (IRE) (67)** (RAFahey) **3-8-13** ACulhane(7) (chsd ldrs: rdn over 3f out: wknd fnl 2f)	3	**11**	20/1	59	21
824[5]	**Bulsara (58)** (CWFairhurst) **5-9-3** LCharnock(16) (hld up & bhd: hdwy whn nt clr run & swtchd 2f out: no imp)	3	**12**	8/1[2]	44	19
899[3]	**Raed (69)** (MrsASwinbank) **4-10-0** WSupple(1) (trckd ldrs: ev ch 4f out: wknd fnl 3f)	3	**13**	9/2[1]	50	25
1256[8]	**Pension Fund (70)** (MWEasterby) **3-9-2** TLucas(3) (led tl hdd over 4f out: wkng whn hmpd over 1f out)	nk	**14**	8/1[2]	50	12
933[13]	**Harvey White (IRE) (58)** (JPearce) **5-9-0**(3) CTeague(11) (outpcd & bhd fnl 4f)	1¾	**15**	8/1[2]	35	10
	Talented Ting (IRE) (49) (PCHaslam) **8-8-1**(7) PGoode(8) (bit bkwd: chsd ldrs tl wknd fnl 2f)	2½	**16**	25/1	22	—

(SP 141.3%) **16 Rn**

1m 54.1 (3.40) CSF £127.45 CT £991.39 TOTE £11.30: £2.10 £2.00 £2.70 £2.90 (£78.00) Trio £620.20 OWNER Mr W. B. Imison (RIPON) BRED R. S. A. Urquhart

LONG HANDICAP Bedazzle 7-5 Nobby Barnes 7-4

WEIGHT FOR AGE 3yo-13lb

733 Dispol Gem, given a more patient ride this time, won nicely but this was a messy event. (10/1)
1231 Nobby Barnes got a tremendous run up the inner to come from last to take it up, but then just found one too good late on. (12/1)
Habeta (USA) has a dreadful action these days but still has the ability, and will probably pick up a race yet again. (8/1)
1128 Spanish Verdict ran well and is on a useful mark, and will no doubt find a race or two when the ground is fast. (10/1)
689 Leif the Lucky (USA) has plenty more ability if he can be persuaded to put it to full use. (8/1)
Majal (IRE), after over a year off, put up a fair performance. (50/1)
Energy Man was sticking on well at the end, suggesting that he should stay further. (10/1)
Pride of Pendle got messed about a fair bit, but put in a decent run suggesting that she is coming to form. (9/1)

T/Jkpt: Not won; £34,557.17 to Folkestone 28/5/97. T/Plpt: £18.20 (975.25 Tckts). T/Qdpt: £12.70 (108.7 Tckts) AA

1453-SANDOWN (R-H) (Good to firm, Firm patches Rnd Course)
Tuesday May 27th

WEATHER: sunny WIND: almost nil

1473 ADDLESTONE CLAIMING STKS (3-Y.O+) (Class E)

6-20 (6-25) **1m 14y** £2,921.25 (£885.00: £432.50: £206.25) Stalls: High GOING minus 0.48 sec per fur (F)

				SP	RR	SF
987[14]	**La Modiste (68)** (MissGayKelleway) **4-9-3** KFallon(11) (b: nt clr run over 3f out: hdwy over 2f out: led ins fnl f: rdn out)	—	**1**	3/1[1]	72	60
1292[3]	**Philistar (67)** (KRBurke) **4-9-8** BDoyle(7) (plld hrd: rdn over 3f out: hdwy over 2f out: r.o ins fnl f)	3½	**2**	14/1	70	58
1085[7]	**Al Abraq (IRE) (85)** (JWHills) **4-9-1**(3) MHenry(4) (lw: a.p: led over 2f out tl ins fnl f: unable qckn)	hd	**3**	7/1[3]	66	54
1292[5]	**Jona Holley (40)** (IABalding) **4-8-6**(7) RFowley(3) (a.p: ev ch 2f out: one pce)	2½	**4**	33/1	56	44
1292*	**Finsbury Flyer (IRE) (63)** (RJHodges) **4-8-10**(5) RFfrench(8) (rdn over 3f out: hdwy over 1f out: nvr nrr)	¾	**5**	5/1[2]	56	44
1300[9]	**Pater Noster (USA) (84)** (JohnHarris) **8-9-6** SSanders(9) (b: hrd rdn over 2f out: nvr nr to chal)	1¾	**6**	7/1[3]	58	46
1244[10]	**Statajack (IRE) (76)** (DRCElsworth) **9-9-6b** RCochrane(2) (b: rdn over 2f out: nvr nrr)	1	**7**	10/1	56	44
1093[6]	**Arcatura (51)** (CJames) **5-9-0** CRutter(13) (prom over 5f)	5	**8**	12/1	40	28
1219[4]	**Lynton Lad (67)** (CPEBrooks) **5-9-6** RPerham(12) (prom over 5f)	6	**9**	9/1	34	22
1082[6]	**Ki Chi Saga (USA) (57)** (MMadgwick) **5-9-4** RHughes(1) (swtg: led over 5f)	4	**10**	16/1	24	12
	Spirit of Sport (AGNewcombe) **4-8-10b[1]** SWhitworth(5) (bit bkwd: prom over 3f)	1¼	**11**	66/1	14	2
	Barbrallen (36) (MrsLCJewell) **5-8-6**(5) SophieMitchell(10) (b: s.i.s: a bhd)	2½	**12**	66/1	10	—

(SP 111.9%) **12 Rn**

1m 41.44 (0.24) CSF £40.34 TOTE £3.30: £1.60 £3.60 £2.70 (£19.00) Trio £83.70 OWNER Mr John Purcell (WHITCOMBE) BRED G. R. Smith (Thriplow) Ltd

Jona Holley clmd CJBates £3,000

791* La Modiste was far more at home back in this class and, coming through to lead inside the final furlong, was ridden along to pull clear. (3/1)
1292 Philistar took a keen hold in midfield in the early stages. He began to pick up ground over a quarter-of-a-mile from home but, despite running on to snatch second prize, was unable to get in a blow at the winner. (14/1: 7/1-16/1)
Al Abraq (IRE), who ran as though something was amiss last time out, appreciated the drop in class. Headed inside the final furlong, he then failed to find another gear. (7/1)
1292 Jona Holley appears to be being used as the schoolmaster for the stable's apprentices this year. He ran probably his best race to date, but he remains a maiden and is a very moderate performer. (33/1)
1292* Finsbury Flyer (IRE) stayed on when it was all over bar the shouting. (5/1)
974 Pater Noster (USA) found the drop in class still not enough to get him into the action. He is at his best with cut in the ground, but has not scored since picking up an Italian Group Two event back in November 1994, and is very much on the downgrade. (7/1)
Statajack (IRE) (10/1: 8/1-12/1)
1093 Arcatura (12/1: 8/1-14/1)

1474 EVENING STANDARD H'CAP (0-80) (3-Y.O) (Class D)

6-50 (6-53) **1m 3f 91y** £3,533.75 (£1,070.00: £522.50: £248.75) Stalls: High GOING minus 0.48 sec per fur (F)

				SP	RR	SF
878[4]	**Protocol (IRE) (73)** (JWHills) **3-9-3** RHills(1) (hdwy & swtchd rt 2f out: hung lft & led ins fnl f: rdn out)	—	**1**	13/2	80	46
	Madame Chinnery (77) (JMPEustace) **3-9-7** RCochrane(8) (hld up: rdn over 3f out: led 1f out tl edgd rt & hdd ins fnl f: r.o)	nk	**2**	5/1[3]	84	50
1153[5]	**Top Shelf (62)** (CEBrittain) **3-8-6** BDoyle(6) (a.p: led over 2f out to 1f out: 3rd & btn whn nt clr run & snatched up ins fnl f)	4	**3**	12/1	63	29
944[3]	**Valagalore (76)** (BWHills) **3-9-6** MHills(3) (swtg: hdwy 10f out: rdn over 3f out: ev ch over 2f out: wknd over 1f out)	2½	**4**	11/4[1]	74	40
976[5]	**Time Can Tell (68)** (CMurray) **3-8-7**(5) RFfrench(10) (lw: rdn & no hdwy fnl 3f)	1¼	**5**	15/2	64	30
1164[12]	**Palaemon (62)** (GBBalding) **3-8-6** AClark(2) (lw: nvr nr to chal)	hd	**6**	9/2[2]	58	24
	Motcombs Club (56) (NACallaghan) **3-8-0** CRutter(4) (lw: a bhd)	1¼	**7**	16/1	50	16
840[17]	**The Green Grey (56)** (WRMuir) **3-7-11**(3) MartinDwyer(7) (led 9f: wknd over 1f out:)	hd	**8**	25/1	50	16

878[7]	**Here's To Howie (USA) (72)** (RHannon) **3-9-2** DaneO'Neill(5) (bhd fnl 3f)	¾	**9**	10/1	65	31

(SP 113.1%) **9 Rn**

2m 25.74 (2.34) CSF £34.67 CT £344.58 TOTE £5.90: £1.80 £1.90 £2.80 (£14.80) Trio £61.80 OWNER Highclere Thoroughbred Racing Ltd (LAMBOURN) BRED Derek Veitch

878 Protocol (IRE), switched to the rails as he picked up ground, hung left briefly inside the final furlong doing the third no favours. Nevertheless, he was soon in front and proved more resolute than the runner-up. (13/2)

Madame Chinnery has a very high head carriage, but she managed to show in front a furlong from home. Edging slightly to the right, she was soon collared and, although sticking on, did not look as game as the winner. This longer trip appeared to suit her well. (5/1)

976 Top Shelf ran by far her best race on grass. Headed a furlong out, she was getting the worst of the argument when becoming the meat in the sandwich soon afterwards. (12/1)

944 Valagalore was soon in a handy position but, after having every chance early in the straight, was at the end of her tether below the distance. (11/4)

976 Time Can Tell, whose only victory in nineteen previous attempts was in a seller, was made to look extremely slow in the straight. (15/2)

641* Here's To Howie (USA) (10/1: 8/1-12/1)

96+ 104 88 81

1475 NATIONAL STKS (Listed) (2-Y.O) (Class A) (92)

7-20 (7-21) **5f 6y** £9,386.00 (£2,843.00: £1,389.00: £662.00) Stalls: High GOING minus 0.33 sec per fur (GF)

				SP	RR	SF
1163*	**Pool Music** (RHannon) **2-9-1** RHughes(5) (lw: a.p: chsd ldr over 2f out: led ins f: rdn out) —	**1**		6/1	94+	56
1143*	**Banningham Blade** (KTIvory) **2-8-12** MartinDwyer(6) (led: hrd rdn over 1f out: hdd ins fnl f: unable qckn) 1¼	**2**		12/1	87	49
1211*	**Nadwah (USA)** (PTWalwyn) **2-8-12** RHills(4) (lw: nt clr run over 1f out: hdwy 1f out: r.o wl ins fnl f) s.h	**3**		7/2[3]	87+	49
	Danyross (IRE) (APO'Brien,Ireland) **2-8-7** LDettori(1) (scope: plld hrd: hld up: rdn over 2f out: one pce) 2½	**4**		5/2[2]	74	36
893*	**Blueridge Dancer (IRE)** (BJMeehan) **2-9-5** OPeslier(2) (lw: lost pl 3f out: one pce fnl 2f) 1¾	**5**		2/1[1]	80	42
525*	**Stately Princess** (MRChannon) **2-8-10** TQuinn(3) (chsd ldr over 2f: wknd over 1f out) 8	**6**		16/1	46	8

(SP 112.0%) **6 Rn**

60.72 secs (0.92) CSF £60.81 TOTE £6.70: £3.00 £2.70 (£14.60) OWNER Mrs Caroline Parker (MARLBOROUGH) BRED Mrs N. F. M. Sampson

IN-FOCUS: This was a very hot two-year-old event, but Richard Hannon has made this race his own and was winning it for the fifth time in the last six years.

1163* Pool Music, an attractive, speedy colt, had far more on his plate this time but still came through with flying colours, getting the better of the runner-up inside the final furlong. Not surprisingly, Royal Ascot now beckons. (6/1)

1143* Banningham Blade continues to go from strength to strength and ran a first-class race in this very tough event. (12/1: op 6/1)

1211* Nadwah (USA), an attractive individual, did not have the best of runs below the distance, but she was putting in some really good work inside the final furlong and would have taken second prize in a few more strides. She looks Royal Ascot-bound and is certain to run well but, however she fares there, there are more races to be won with her this season. (7/2)

Danyross (IRE), winner of a Navan maiden earlier in the month, had far more to do here and, after being nicely placed at halfway, was then tapped for toe. (5/2)

893* Blueridge Dancer (IRE) may have been conceding weight all-round, but this was an extremely disappointing display - he was only 2lb worse off with Banningham Blade for beating her two lengths at Ascot. This was surely not his true running. (2/1)

525* Stately Princess was out of her class, and had shot her bolt below the distance. (16/1)

1476 BRIGADIER GERARD STKS (Gp 3) (4-Y.O+) (Class A)

7-50 (7-50) **1m 2f 7y** £18,840.00 (£7,129.50: £3,489.75: £1,590.75) Stalls: High GOING minus 0.48 sec per fur (F)

			SP	RR	SF
	Bosra Sham (USA) (131) (HRACecil) **4-9-0** KFallon(1) (bit bkwd: hld up: led over 1f out: rdn out) —	**1**	1/5[1]	126	55
	Predappio (SbinSuroor) **4-9-1** LDettori(3) (bit bkwd: chsd ldr: led 3f out tl over 1f out: hrd rdn: r.o) ½	**2**	12/1[3]	126	55
1160*	**Centre Stalls (IRE) (116)** (RFJohnsonHoughton) **4-8-10** JReid(2) (lw: hld up: ev ch 2f out: wknd over 1f out) 5	**3**	8/1[2]	113	42
1176[11]	**Rocky Oasis (USA) (96)** (MRStoute) **4-8-10** OPeslier(6) (lw: hld up: rdn over 2f out: one pce) ½	**4**	50/1	112	41
	Posidonas (118) (PFICole) **5-9-1** TQuinn(5) (lw: plld hrd: a.p: rdn over 2f out: sn wknd) nk	**5**	12/1[3]	117	46
943[5]	**Henry The Fifth (98)** (CEBrittain) **4-8-10** BDoyle(4) (led 7f: wknd over 2f out) 14	**6**	100/1	90	19

(SP 112.8%) **6 Rn**

2m 7.37 (0.67) CSF £3.67 TOTE £1.20: £1.10 £2.30 (£2.70) OWNER Mr Wafic Said (NEWMARKET) BRED Gerald W. Leigh

Bosra Sham (USA) was gleaming in the paddock and has really thickened up since last year, but needed the run. Settling really well, she cruised up on the outside in the straight and quickened into the lead below the distance. Probably idling in front, she had to be ridden along to keep the very persistent runner-up at bay. She will come on considerably for the run, and it will take something special to beat her in the Prince of Wales's Stakes at Royal Ascot. (1/5)

Predappio, trained last season by John Oxx in Ireland, looked as though this run would do him good but ran a tremendous race, sticking to his guns to make sure the filly did not have things all her own way. Connections were delighted after the recent poor form of the stable and, over a mile and a half with possibly a bit of cut, he looks certain to win some decent prizes. (12/1: 8/1-14/1)

1160* Centre Stalls (IRE), taking a step-up in distance, had every chance before being left for dead by the front two. He has two listed victories to his credit, and that is more his level. (8/1)

1176 Rocky Oasis (USA) is not up to this class and, when the race began in earnest, he was tapped for toe. (50/1)

Posidonas looked in good shape for this reappearance. Tackling this trip for the first time since his two-year-old days, he played an active role until a quarter-of-a-mile from home. (12/1: 8/1-14/1)

943 Henry The Fifth was outclassed in both the paddock and the race. (100/1)

1477 LILLIAN & MARTIN WHITE MAIDEN STKS (3-Y.O+) (Class D)

8-20 (8-26) **1m 2f 7y** £3,696.25 (£1,120.00: £547.50: £261.25) Stalls: High GOING minus 0.48 sec per fur (F)

			SP	RR	SF
937[2]	**Bold Demand** (SbinSuroor) **3-8-11** LDettori(1) (lw: a.p: led over 2f out: r.o wl) —	**1**	2/1[2]	89	40
1173[2]	**Shaya** (MajorWRHern) **3-8-11** RHills(3) (lw: led over 7f: ev ch over 1f out: unable qckn) 1¼	**2**	5/4[1]	87	38
1106[2]	**Hachiyah (IRE)** (DMorley) **3-8-6** GCarter(15) (a.p: rdn & swtchd lft over 2f out: r.o one pce) 1¾	**3**	20/1	79	30
841[3]	**Machiavelli** (HRACecil) **3-8-11** KFallon(2) (lw: hdwy 7f out: rdn over 3f out: r.o one pce) 1¾	**4**	13/2[3]	81	32
	Dancing Feather (BWHills) **3-8-6** MHills(18) (w'like: scope: bit bkwd: stdy hdwy over 1f out: r.o wl: bttr for r) 6	**5**	14/1	67	18
	Graceful Lass (DRLoder) **3-8-6** KDarley(5) (b.nr hind: a.p: rdn over 3f out: wknd over 2f out) nk	**6**	20/1	66	17
937[6]	**Bevier** (CEBrittain) **3-8-11** BDoyle(17) (b: nvr nr to chal) 2	**7**	33/1	68	19
1144[10]	**Pardan** (BPalling) **3-8-11** TSprake(10) (a mid div) 1¼	**8**	100/1	66	17
1144[11]	**Expialiodoocius** (JRFanshawe) **3-8-11** NDay(4) (hdwy over 5f out: wknd over 3f out) 1½	**9**	50/1	64	15
	Tarxien (KRBurke) **3-8-11** WJO'Connor(11) (str: scope: bkwd: nvr nrr) nk	**10**	100/1	63	14

				SP	RR	SF
1106[4]	**Bear Hug** (LadyHerries) **4-9-11** AClark(6) (nvr nrr)	¾	**11**	50/1	62	27
	Bonanza Peak (USA) (MrsJCecil) **4-9-11** RCochrane(14) (lw: nvr nrr)	2	**12**	33/1	59	24
	Capsoff (IRE) (GAHubbard) **4-9-6** NAdams(7) (bhd fnl 8f)	nk	**13**	100/1	54	19
1106[3]	**Height of Heights (IRE)** (LadyHerries) **4-9-11** JReid(13) (prom over 4f)	nk	**14**	20/1	58	23
1105[7]	**Joli's Son** (MJHaynes) **4-9-11** TQuinn(12) (hdwy 6f out: wknd over 3f out)	2½	**15**	100/1	54	19
1372[5]	**Burn Out** (JPearce) **5-9-11** MWigham(8) (a bhd)	hd	**16**	66/1	54	19
	Olivo (IRE) (86) (CAHorgan) **3-8-11** PaulEddery(16) (bhd fnl 6f)	2½	**17**	33/1	50	1
1277[6]	**Moon Colony** (LadyHerries) **4-9-11** DeclanO'Shea(9) (prom over 4f)	3½	**18**	100/1	44	9
				(SP 131.3%)	**18 Rn**	

2m 8.89 (2.19) CSF £4.15 TOTE £3.10: £1.50 £1.20 £3.90 (£2.60) Trio £20.60 OWNER Godolphin (NEWMARKET) BRED Gainsborough Stud Management Ltd
WEIGHT FOR AGE 3yo-14lb

937 Bold Demand kept on far too strongly for the runner-up to give Godolphin their first winner in twenty-two days. He could turn out to be useful. (2/1: op 3/1)
1173 Shaya looked in good shape beforehand and attempted to make all the running. He refused to lie down, and time may show this was a good performance. He should have no problem losing his maiden tag. (5/4)
1106 Hachiyah (IRE) is only lightly-made but was never far away. She flashed her tail when given a reminder approaching the final furlong, but kept on well to the line. (20/1)
841 Machiavelli stayed on without ever looking likely to find that vital turn of foot. He can find a race, but it may well be over further. (13/2: 4/1-7/1)
Dancing Feather, a good-bodied filly, looked as though the run was needed but caught the eye under considerate handling, finishing a very promising fifth. She will come on in leaps and bounds for this and should soon find a race. (14/1: 12/1-7/1)
Graceful Lass played an active role until coming to the end of her tether after a mile. (20/1)

1478 EFFINGHAM H'CAP (0-80) (3-Y.O+) (Class D)
8-50 (8-56) **1m 6f** £3,501.25 (£1,060.00: £517.50: £246.25) Stalls: High GOING minus 0.48 sec per fur (F)

				SP	RR	SF
1252[2]	**Arcady (50)** (JLHarris) **4-7-10**(5) RFfrench(12) (lw: a.p: led over 2f out: drvn out)	—	**1**	5/1[2]	63	26
974[6]	**Burnt Offering (67)** (CEBrittain) **4-9-4** BDoyle(5) (lw: rdn over 3f out: hdwy over 1f out: str run fnl f: fin wl)	hd	**2**	14/1	80	43
1162[11]	**Arctic Fancy (USA) (77)** (PWHarris) **4-10-0** JReid(8) (rdn & hdwy on ins over 2f out: r.o wl ins fnl f)	nk	**3**	14/1	90	53
969[5]	**Casual Water (IRE) (71)** (AGNewcombe) **6-9-8** SDrowne(2) (lw: hld up: rdn over 2f out: unable qckn)	1¼	**4**	8/1	82	45
986[9]	**Renzo (IRE) (76)** (MrsAJPerrett) **4-9-13** AClark(9) (hdwy & nt clr run on ins over 1f out: r.o)	s.h	**5**	16/1	87	50
	Veronica Franco (45) (RIngram) **4-7-10** DeclanO'Shea(6) (hdwy over 2f out: hrd rdn over 1f out: one pce)	hd	**6**	50/1	56	19
1162[3]	**Midyan Blue (IRE) (70)** (JMPEustace) **7-9-7** RCochrane(4) (lost pl 3f out: r.o one pce fnl 2f)	1½	**7**	3/1[1]	79	42
510[4]	**Hattaafeh (IRE) (60)** (MissBSanders) **6-8-11** SSanders(7) (lw: a.p: hrd rdn over 2f out: wknd fnl f)	¾	**8**	7/1[3]	68	31
1100[6]	**Chris's Lad (60)** (BJMeehan) **6-8-11b** KDarley(10) (lw: rdn over 3f out: nt clr run 2f out: nvr nrr)	¾	**9**	12/1	68	31
869[7]	**Haroldon (IRE) (72)** (BPalling) **8-9-9** TSprake(1) (hdwy 4f out: wknd over 2f out)	2½	**10**	50/1	77	40
1169[2]	**Serious Trust (62)** (MrsLCJewell) **4-8-8**(5) SophieMitchell(13) (led over 11f)	7	**11**	12/1	59	22
888[18]	**Belmarita (IRE) (65)** (GAHubbard) **4-9-2** NAdams(3) (a bhd)	8	**12**	33/1	53	16
	Academy House (IRE) (73) (RAkehurst) **4-9-10** TQuinn(11) (lw: prom over 8f)	4	**13**	5/1[2]	56	19
				(SP 123.4%)	**13 Rn**	

3m 2.86 (3.96) CSF £68.38 CT £852.60 TOTE £6.70: £2.30 £3.50 £3.30 (£59.40) Trio £857.70 OWNER Mr J. H. Henderson (MELTON MOWBRAY) BRED A. D. G. Oldrey
LONG HANDICAP Veronica Franco 7-8

1252 Arcady, 12lb lower than at the beginning of the year, took full advantage, but would surely have been caught in a couple more strides. (5/1)
974 Burnt Offering had no problems with this longer trip. Going nowhere at the back of the field entering the straight, he went into overdrive and, absolutely flying, would have prevailed in a few more strides. (14/1)
Arctic Fancy (USA) ran much better, keeping on well inside the final furlong. (14/1)
969 Casual Water (IRE) chased the leaders but, despite his rider's efforts, failed to find that vital turn of foot. (8/1)
Renzo (IRE) looks a far from easy ride and carries his head extremely high. Not getting a great deal of room along the inside rail, he ran on but did not look as if he was putting it all in. He looks one to avoid. (16/1)
Veronica Franco, fit from hurdling, has changed stables since her last run. (50/1)
1169 Serious Trust (12/1: op 8/1)
Academy House (IRE) (5/1: 7/2-11/2)

T/Plpt: £454.90 (56.47 Tckts). T/Qdpt: £34.70 (38.57 Tckts) AK

0765-FOLKESTONE (R-H) (Good to firm, Good patches)
Wednesday May 28th
WEATHER: sunny WIND: fresh across

1479 BREDE H'CAP (0-70) (3-Y.O+ F & M) (Class E)
2-20 (2-27) **5f** £3,494.25 (£1,044.00: £499.50: £227.25) Stalls: Low GOING minus 0.07 sec per fur (G)

				SP	RR	SF
1385[8]	**Songsheet (62)** (MSSaunders) **4-9-3**(5) PPMurphy(4) (chsd ldrs: led 1f out: drvn out)	—	**1**	11/2[3]	72	47
1237[7]	**The Fugative (48)** (PMitchell) **4-8-5**(3) AWhelan(5) (rr: rdn over 3f out: hdwy over 2f out: styd on to take 2nd wl ins fnl f)	1¾	**2**	14/1	52	27
1279[2]	**Runs in the Family (57)** (GMMcCourt) **5-9-3b** DHarrison(9) (broke wl: led: swtchd to stands' side: hdd 1f out: one pce)	½	**3**	7/4[1]	60	35
1141[23]	**Shifting Time (70)** (IABalding) **3-9-8** KDarley(6) (lw: prom tl wknd over 1f out)	4	**4**	9/2[2]	60	27
1373[10]	**Pearl Dawn (IRE) (52)** (PCClarke) **7-8-12** NAdams(2) (outpcd in rr tl mod late hdwy)	nk	**5**	10/1	41	16
1374[4]	**College Night (IRE) (46)** (SCWilliams) **5-8-3**(3) MHenry(7) (chsd ldrs: rdn 3f out: wknd over 2f out)	1½	**6**	6/1	30	5
	Midnight Times (50) (DCO'Brien) **3-8-2** GDuffield(1) (chsd ldrs tl wknd wl over 1f out)	2½	**7**	33/1	26	—
1327[7]	**Another Batchworth (67)** (EAWheeler) **5-9-8b**(5) ADaly(3) (rel to go to post: s.s: rcvrd to r in tch tl wknd 2f out)	11	**8**	8/1	8	—

				SP	RR	SF
1236^{19}	**Poppy My Love (43)** (ICampbell) **4-8-3** RPrice(8) (prom tl wknd qckly ½-wy)	1	**9**	33/1	—	—

(SP 117.0%) **9 Rn**

60.6 secs (3.00) CSF £72.18 CT £171.16 TOTE £7.90: £2.40 £3.90 £1.10 (£43.10) Trio £28.10 OWNER Mr M. S. Saunders (WELLS) BRED Lord Matthews

WEIGHT FOR AGE 3yo-8lb

604 Songsheet was always travelling quite well, and was not hard-pressed to score. (11/2)
The Fugative struggled with the early pace but kept on well late on. Seven could prove her optimum trip. (14/1)
1279 Runs in the Family showed tremendous early speed to cross over to the stands' rails but, collared a furlong out, had no more to give. She is probably in the Handicapper's grip now. (7/4)
Shifting Time showed some pace, but weakened tamely late on. (9/2: 11/4-5/1)
1236 Pearl Dawn (IRE) could not go the early pace. (10/1)
Another Batchworth was very mulish beforehand and during the race. (8/1)

76 73 70+ 73

1480 WESTENHANGER MAIDEN STKS (2-Y.O) (Class D)

2-50 (2-52) **6f** £3,640.50 (£1,089.00: £522.00: £238.50) Stalls: Low GOING minus 0.07 sec per fur (G)

				SP	RR	SF
1263^{9}	**Swift Alliance** (RAkehurst) **2-9-0** DHarrison(2) (hld up: n.m.r over 3f out: swtchd rt over 2f out: led 1f out: r.o wl)	—	**1**	12/1	78+	26
	Bermuda Triangle (IRE) (MJHaynes) **2-8-6**(3) AWhelan(11) (leggy: s.i.s: hdwy 2f out: rdn over 1f out: styd on ins fnl f)	2½	**2**	40/1	66	14
1163^{6}	**Striding King** (MRChannon) **2-9-0** RHughes(12) (a.p: ev ch 1f out: edgd lft ins fnl f: one pce)	1¼	**3**	12/1	68	16
	Master Mac (USA) (RAkehurst) **2-9-0** SSanders(7) (w'like: bit bkwd: dwlt: sn pushed along in rr: hdwy over 1f out: kpt on whn n.m.r cl home)	¾	**4**	12/1	66	14
	Saint Malo (USA) (DRLoder) **2-9-0** KDarley(10) (unf: scope: bit bkwd: led 4f out: hdd 1f out: one pce)	hd	**5**	5/4 1	66	14
1251^{4}	**Impulse (IRE)** (APJarvis) **2-9-0** WJO'Connor(5) (lw: hld up bhd ldrs: hdwy over 1f out: ev ch ent fnl f: edgd lft: no ex)	½	**6**	11/1 3	64	12
1263^{5}	**Red Maple (USA)** (PFICole) **2-9-0** TQuinn(3) (lw: chsd ldrs: rdn ½-wy: kpt on whn n.m.r ins fnl f: eased)	3	**7**	4/1 2	56	4
750^{2}	**Soft Touch (IRE)** (MissGayKelleway) **2-8-9** GDuffield(13) (lw: chsd ldrs: rdn 2f out: wknd over 1f out)	¾	**8**	4/1 2	49	—
648^{13}	**Far-So-La** (TMJones) **2-8-9**(5) ADaly(6) (led 2f: prom tl wknd over 2f out)	10	**9**	50/1	28	—
1263^{7}	**Ben Rinnes** (RFJohnsonHoughton) **2-9-0** AClark(8) (mid div tl wknd over 1f out)	½	**10**	14/1	26	—
	Temujin (DCO'Brien) **2-9-0** RCochrane(9) (unf: a bhd)	6	**11**	50/1	10	—
836^{6}	**Kennet** (PDCundell) **2-9-0** RPerham(4) (b.hind: prom: wknd over 1f out: btn whn hmpd & uns rdr ins fnl f)		**U**	11/1 3	—	—

(SP 137.2%) **12 Rn**

1m 14.9 (4.70) CSF £415.63 TOTE £23.00: £5.00 £11.30 £3.10 (£386.50) Trio Not won; £199.21 to Carlisle 29/5/97 OWNER Fernray Ltd (EPSOM) BRED Devonia Stud

Swift Alliance improved tremendously on his debut run, and his trainer says that he will now think about the Coventry. (12/1)
Bermuda Triangle (IRE) ran promisingly, staying on well after a tardy start. (40/1)
1163 Striding King showed good speed, and a small race can be found. (12/1)
Master Mac (USA) was very green early on, but stayed on well once the penny had dropped. He can be made fitter and will improve. (12/1: 5/1-14/1)
Saint Malo (USA), unusually for one from this stable, looked as though the run would do him good and, after showing plenty of pace, he weakened late on. (5/4)
1251 Impulse (IRE) looked dangerous entering the final furlong, but could not find a change of gear. (11/1: 8/1-12/1)
1263 Red Maple (USA) (4/1: 5/2-9/2)
750 Soft Touch (IRE) (4/1: 5/2-9/2)
836 Kennet (11/1: 6/1-12/1)

1481 LYMPNE LIMITED STKS (0-70) (3-Y.O+) (Class E)

3-20 (3-20) **1m 4f** £3,231.00 (£963.00: £459.00: £207.00) Stalls: Low GOING minus 0.07 sec per fur (G)

				SP	RR	SF
1371^{D}	**Isitoff (67)** (SCWilliams) **4-9-9** KDarley(8) (a.p: led over 1f out: r.o wl)	—	**1**	14/1	80	39
1169^{4}	**Russian Rose (IRE) (70)** (JARToller) **4-9-6** AClark(9) (lw: hld up: hdwy 4f out: rdn over 1f out: styd on to take 2nd ins fnl f)	2½	**2**	11/2 3	74	33
1169^{7}	**Gumair (USA) (68)** (RHannon) **4-9-9** RPerham(1) (lw: a.p: led 6f out: hdd over 1f out: one pce)	1	**3**	14/1	75	34
1142^{4}	**Ocean Park (69)** (LadyHerries) **6-9-9** DeclanO'Shea(10) (mid div: lost pl 8f out: hdwy over 2f out: kpt on one pce ins fnl f)	1	**4**	3/1 2	74	33
1371^{2}	**Florentino (IRE) (70)** (BWHills) **4-9-9** MHills(6) (hld up: hdwy 4f out: rdn 2f out: one pce)	hd	**5**	11/10 1	74	33
1371*	**Opera Buff (IRE) (68)** (MissGayKelleway) **6-9-10**(3) AWhelan(7) (hld up in rr: hdwy 3f out: rdn 2f out: wknd ins fnl f)	3	**6**	9/1	74	33
1371^{8}	**Bowled Over (69)** (CACyzer) **4-9-9** WJO'Connor(2) (hdwy 7f out: rdn 3f out: wknd wl over 1f out)	3½	**7**	14/1	65	24
1152^{3}	**Carol's Dream (USA) (70)** (JWHills) **5-9-6**(3) MHenry(5) (chsd ldrs: lost pl 5f out: wknd over 2f out)	4	**8**	12/1	60	19
1138^{10}	**Illuminate (65)** (DCO'Brien) **4-9-11** RCochrane(4) (chsd ldrs tl wknd 2f out)	6	**9**	40/1	54	13
	Esta Maria (IRE) (34) (PaulSmith,Belgium) **4-9-6b**1 GDuffield(3) (led to ½-wy)	15	**10**	50/1	29	—

(SP 130.1%) **10 Rn**

2m 40.6 (9.40) CSF £90.46 TOTE £15.50: £2.60 £2.90 £2.30 (£106.50) Trio £110.80 OWNER Mr James Brown (NEWMARKET) BRED Mrs Celia Miller

1371 Isitoff travelled well throughout and, after taking it up below the distance, ran out a ready winner. (14/1)
1169 Russian Rose (IRE) made her effort early in the straight but took time to find top speed. (11/2: 7/2-6/1)
Gumair (USA) cut out much of the running. (14/1: 10/1-16/1)
1142 Ocean Park shaped quite promisingly and, not being given a hard race, he should be spot-on next time. (3/1)
1371 Florentino (IRE) was well-fancied after his unlucky run at Brighton, but proved disappointing. (11/10)
1371* Opera Buff (IRE) (9/1: 6/1-10/1)

1482 GLANMOOR GROUP CHALLENGE CUP H'CAP (0-90) (3-Y.O+) (Class C)

3-55 (3-56) **1m 1f 149y** £5,580.00 (£1,665.00: £795.00: £360.00) Stalls: Low GOING minus 0.07 sec per fur (G)

				SP	RR	SF
1105^{3}	**Danish Rhapsody (IRE) (80)** (LadyHerries) **4-9-12** DeclanO'Shea(1) (led after 2f: hdd over 1f out: rallied to ld ins fnl f: r.o)	—	**1**	12/1	91	60

				SP	RR	SF
933^{7}	**Virtual Reality (76)** (JARToller) **6-9-8** SSanders(7) (lw: led 2f: chsd wnr after tl led over 1f out: hdd ins fnl f: unable qckn)	nk	**2**	$13/2^{3}$	87	56
1414^{*}	**Effectual (88)** (MissGayKelleway) **4-10-6** ^{6x} RHughes(5) (lw: hld up in tch: rdn 2f out: one pce)	6	**3**	$2/1^{1}$	89	58
1146^{12}	**Love Has No Pride (USA) (86)** (RHannon) **3-9-4** DaneO'Neill(3) (hld up: hdwy over 2f out: rdn over 1f out: one pce)	1	**4**	12/1	85	40
1262^{5}	**Ashby Hill (IRE) (68)** (RRowe) **6-9-0** AClark(10) (hld up in tch: rdn 2f out: wknd over 1f out)	1½	**5**	$11/4^{2}$	65	34
1164^{3}	**Carlys Quest (67)** (JNeville) **3-7-10**$^{(3)ow3}$ MartinDwyer(2) (nvr nrr)	s.h	**6**	8/1	63	15
1145^{9}	**Prospector's Cove (81)** (JPearce) **4-9-13** MWigham(8) (hld up in rr: sme hdwy over 2f out: sn rdn & btn)	1½	**7**	50/1	75	44
1139^{*}	**Scathebury (62)** (KRBurke) **4-8-8** DHolland(9) (hld up in rr: sme hdwy on ins over 2f out: sn rdn & btn)	9	**8**	11/1	41	10
1244^{17}	**Kriscliffe (66)** (GLewis) **4-8-9**$^{(3)}$ AWhelan(6) (prom tl wknd over 3f out)	4	**9**	25/1	38	7
1242^{9}	**Bandore (IRE) (85)** (DRLoder) **3-9-3** KDarley(4) (chsd ldrs tl wknd 3f out)	nk	**10**	12/1	57	12

(SP 121.7%) **10 Rn**

2m 2.8 (5.10) CSF £83.42 CT £206.10 TOTE £11.10: £2.20 £2.20 £1.80 (£33.70) Trio £55.80 OWNER Mr Chris Hardy (LITTLEHAMPTON) BRED Grangemore Stud
WEIGHT FOR AGE 3yo-14lb

1105 Danish Rhapsody (IRE), in a handicap for the first time, ran out a game winner, rallying bravely after being headed below the distance. Well on top at the finish, he probably has further improvement in him. (12/1: op 8/1)
735 Virtual Reality looked sure to win below the distance, but the winner was just too strong. (13/2)
1414* Effectual found his big weight slowing him down in the final two furlongs. (2/1: 6/4-9/4)
990 Love Has No Pride (USA) could do with being dropped a few pounds. (12/1)
1262 Ashby Hill (IRE) weakened tamely approaching the final furlong. (11/4)
1139* Scathebury (11/1: 8/1-12/1)
Bandore (IRE) (12/1: op 7/1)

1483 SELLINDGE CLAIMING LIMITED STKS (0-55) (I) (3-Y.O+) (Class F)

4-25 (4-30) **6f 189y** £1,927.00 (£527.00: £247.00) Stalls: Low GOING minus 0.07 sec per fur (G)

				SP	RR	SF
1086^{7}	**Sandicliffe (USA) (50)** (BWHills) **4-9-5** MHills(1) (hld up: hdwy 2f out: led 1f out: r.o)	—	**1**	$13/2^{3}$	58	39
1164^{13}	**Ar Hyd Y Knos (50)** (RCharlton) **3-8-6** TSprake(2) (chsd ldrs: rdn 2f out: ev ch 1f out: unable qckn)	1¾	**2**	$11/2^{2}$	52	22
	Clytha Hill Lad (29) (JMBradley) **6-9-0** GHind(4) (hld up in tch: shkn up ent fnl f: r.o)	1	**3**	33/1	47	28
1128^{15}	**Asterix (36)** (JMBradley) **9-8-9b**$^{(5)}$ SophieMitchell(11) (hld up: hdwy over 1f out: styd on ins fnl f: nvr plcd to chal)	1¾	**4**	20/1	43	24
644^{8}	**Don't Forget Shoka (IRE) (40)** (JSMoore) **3-7-11**$^{(5)}$ AimeeCook(3) (hld up: hdwy 2f out: rdn 1f out: kpt on one pce)	nk	**5**	33/1	41	11
199^{7}	**Dark Menace (47)** (EAWheeler) **5-8-13b**$^{(5)}$ ADaly(13) (sn led: clr 2f out: hdd 1f out: no ex)	s.h	**6**	12/1	46	27
	Old Hook (IRE) (55) (PaulSmith,Belgium) **6-9-3**$^{(3)}$ AWhelan(7) (chsd ldrs: rdn over 1f out: wknd ins fnl f)	¾	**7**	$11/2^{2}$	46	27
1389^{6}	**First Gold (47)** (JWharton) **8-9-4b** GDuffield(5) (rr: hdwy over 1f out: styng on whn nt clr run ent fnl f: nt rcvr)	1¼	**8**	10/1	41	22
1422^{8}	**Abtaal (49)** (RJHodges) **7-9-6** RCochrane(6) (a.p: chsd ldr briefly over 1f out: wknd ins fnl f)	nk	**9**	$7/2^{1}$	42	23
1116^{9}	**Sweet Seventeen (35)** (HJCollingridge) **4-8-11** NAdams(12) (chsd ldr tl wknd over 1f out)	2½	**10**	25/1	28	9
1008^{8}	**Le Shuttle (41)** (MHTompkins) **3-7-13v**$^{1(3)}$ MHenry(14) (hld up: hdwy u.p 3f out: n.m.r over 1f out: wknd ins fnl f)	s.h	**11**	14/1	29	—
1374^{6}	**Shermood (30)** (KTIvory) **4-8-9** CScally(9) (dwlt: a bhd)	6	**12**	7/1	11	—
1279^{13}	**Arnie (IRE) (30)** (JRPoulton) **5-8-9**$^{(3)}$ MartinDwyer(10) (a bhd)	4	**13**	25/1	5	—
1151^{14}	**Jingoist (IRE) (54)** (JLHarris) **3-8-4b** SSanders(8) (prom tl wknd over 2f out)	7	**14**	$11/2^{2}$	—	—

(SP 136.0%) **14 Rn**

1m 26.3 (4.90) CSF £41.21 TOTE £9.40: £2.90 £2.20 £4.80 (£66.50) Trio Not won; £411.17 to Carlisle 29/5/97 OWNER Mrs J. R. Woodhouse (LAMBOURN) BRED Brereton C. Jones
WEIGHT FOR AGE 3yo-11lb
Ar Hyd Y Knos clmd CSparrowhawk £6,000. Sandicliffe (USA) clmd GHeald £7,000.

Sandicliffe (USA) was brought with a well-timed challenge to lead at the furlong pole, and won this readily. (13/2: 4/1-7/1)
Ar Hyd Y Knos was never that far away, but could not match the winner's turn of foot late on. (11/2: 4/1-6/1)
Clytha Hill Lad stayed on nicely in the last two furlongs, and was given anything but a hard ride. (33/1)
Asterix was never nearer than at the finish, and can certainly do better under more forceful handling. (20/1)
1005 Abtaal threatened briefly below the distance but dropped away tamely late on. (7/2)
1374 Shermood (7/1: 4/1-8/1)

1484 SELLINDGE CLAIMING LIMITED STKS (0-55) (II) (3-Y.O+) (Class F)

4-55 (4-56) **6f 189y** £1,927.00 (£527.00: £247.00) Stalls: Low GOING minus 0.07 sec per fur (G)

				SP	RR	SF
929^{3}	**Ivor's Deed (54)** (CFWall) **4-9-6** GDuffield(12) (hld up in tch: chsd ldr over 1f out: led ins fnl f: r.o)	—	**1**	$5/4^{1}$	57	39
1048^{12}	**Ladybower (IRE) (32)** (LordHuntingdon) **5-8-4**$^{(5)}$ AimeeCook(11) (chsd ldrs: led over 1f out: hdd ins fnl f: unable qckn)	1½	**2**	14/1	43	25
1005^{4}	**Zahran (IRE) (33)** (JMBradley) **6-8-13**$^{(5)}$ ADaly(2) (rr: rdn over 2f out: styd on ins fnl f)	1½	**3**	20/1	48	30
1245^{10}	**Keen Waters (54)** (JRArnold) **3-8-6** DHarrison(1) (rr: rdn 2f out: styd on ins fnl f)	½	**4**	14/1	46	17
873^{8}	**Jukebox Jive (52)** (CADwyer) **3-8-2** GHind(8) (rr: hdwy over 1f out: sn rdn: one pce)	2½	**5**	$13/2^{2}$	36	7
487^{8}	**Komodo (USA) (32)** (JELong) **5-8-12** LeesaLong(14) (prom: rdn over 1f out: wknd ins last)	1	**6**	33/1	33	15
1473^{12}	**Barbrallen (36)** (MrsLCJewell) **5-8-12**$^{(5)}$ SophieMitchell(5) (dwlt: nvr nrr)	1¼	**7**	33/1	35	17
896^{8}	**Okay Baby (IRE) (25)** (JMBradley) **5-8-8**$^{(3)}$ MHenry(6) (chsd ldrs: rdn over 2f out: wknd ins fnl f)	1	**8**	25/1	26	8
1320^{12}	**Jaazim (42)** (MMadgwick) **7-9-3b**$^{(7)}$ AEddery(7) (mid div: rdn 2f out: wknd 1f out)	s.h	**9**	9/1	39	21
458^{7}	**Rawi (55)** (MissGayKelleway) **4-9-3**$^{(7)}$ AngelaGallimore(9) (rr: n.m.r on ins over 2f out: swtchd lft: no hdwy)	1¼	**10**	$7/1^{3}$	36	18
1151^{13}	**Wing of A Prayer (52)** (WJarvis) **3-8-13** SSanders(13) (prom tl wknd over 1f out)	1½	**11**	10/1	33	4
	No Class (55) (ICampbell) **3-8-4** RPrice(10) (led: hdd over 1f out: sn wknd)	1	**12**	25/1	22	—
1236^{14}	**Fancy Design (IRE) (35)** (PMitchell) **4-8-13v** MHills(3) (rr: effrt over 2f out: sn btn)	1½	**13**	33/1	16	—
1167^{16}	**Skippy Was A Kiwi (IRE) (45)** (APJarvis) **3-7-11v**$^{1(3)}$ AWhelan(4) (mid div tl wknd over 2f out)	3	**14**	14/1	7	—

(SP 130.6%) **14 Rn**

1m 26.4 (5.00) CSF £19.72 TOTE £2.30: £1.50 £4.30 £2.50 (£12.50) Trio £102.10 OWNER Mr Mervyn Ayers (NEWMARKET) BRED David Sinden, Mervyn Ayers and Richard Brunger
WEIGHT FOR AGE 3yo-11lb

Ivor's Deed clmd CSparrowhawk £6,000
929 Ivor's Deed was never far away and travelled quite nicely throughout. Brought with a well-timed challenge to lead inside the final furlong, he won with a shade in hand. (5/4)
Ladybower (IRE) tracked the leaders throughout. She led below the distance but had no answer to the winner's late surge. (14/1)
1005 Zahran (IRE) was in trouble some way from home and did not stay on until the race was over. (20/1)
Keen Waters was another to make late headway, having never really been in the race. (14/1)
Jaazim (9/1: 16/1-8/1)
383 Rawi (7/1: op 4/1)

1485 SMEETHE MEDIAN AUCTION MAIDEN STKS (3-Y.O) (Class F)
5-25 (5-30) **6f 189y** £3,200.50 (£888.00: £425.50) Stalls: Low GOING minus 0.07 sec per fur (G)

				SP	RR	SF
1090[3]	**Farley Green** (HCandy) **3-8-9** CRutter(7) (a.p: chsd ldr 2f out: hrd rdn ins fnl f: led cl home)	—	1	11/8[1]	73	35
1155[2]	**Goodbye Gatemen (IRE)** (BAPearce) **3-8-11**(3) MartinDwyer(8) (led: rdn & edgd lft ins fnl f: hdd cl home)	nk	2	11/2[3]	77	39
	Juvenilia (IRE) (JARToller) **3-8-9** SSanders(2) (w'like: bit bkwd: mid div: rdn 3f out: kpt on one pce fnl 2f)	5	3	6/1	61	23
474[3]	**Moon Song** (APJarvis) **3-8-9** WJO'Connor(4) (chsd ldrs: hrd rdn over 2f out: one pce)	½	4	9/2[2]	60	22
1155[7]	**Sifwa** (DCO'Brien) **3-8-9** GDuffield(6) (nvr nrr)	1½	5	33/1	56	18
1110[7]	**Kanawa** (APJones) **3-8-9** GHind(3) (dwlt: nvr nrr)	½	6	40/1	55	17
1012[14]	**Peter Perfect (54)** (GLewis) **3-8-11b**(3) AWhelan(9) (chsd ldr to 2f out: wknd over 1f out)	¾	7	25/1	58	20
	Beveled Crystal (CJames) **3-8-6**(3) MHenry(11) (bit bkwd: chsd ldrs tl wknd over 2f out)	1	8	40/1	51	13
1008[2]	**Going Green (60)** (JRFanshawe) **3-8-9** DHarrison(5) (b: b.hind: dwlt: hdwy ½-wy: wknd 2f out)	½	9	11/2[3]	50	12
446[8]	**Dorado Beach (48)** (LGCottrell) **3-8-9** NAdams(1) (stdd s: hld up: effrt ½-wy: sn btn)	4	10	33/1	40	2
1237[W]	**Kildee Boy** (APJones) **3-9-0** RPrice(10) (str: lw: dwlt: a bhd)	13	11	33/1	15	—
				(SP 122.9%)		**11 Rn**

1m 25.9 (4.50) CSF £8.38 TOTE £2.70: £1.40 £2.20 £1.10 (£6.70) Trio £19.80 OWNER Major M. G. Wyatt (WANTAGE) BRED Dunchurch Lodge Stud
1090 Farley Green raced just behind the leaders. She was hard ridden approaching the final furlong and, keeping a straighter line than the runner-up, gained the upper hand close home. (11/8)
1155 Goodbye Gatemen (IRE) was unco-operative going in the stalls and was not very keen under pressure inside the final furlong, hanging away to his left. This threw away a winning chance and for good measure he unseated his rider after the line. (11/2: 5/2-6/1)
Juvenilia (IRE) was being ridden along before the home turn but, to her credit, stayed on in the final two furlongs. She can be made fitter and can improve. (6/1)
474 Moon Song was never far away. Hard at work early in the straight, she only had the one pace to give. (9/2)
Sifwa was out the back until staying on promisingly in the closing stages. (33/1)

T/Jkpt: Not won; £52,828.89 to Carlisle 29/5/97. T/Plpt: £9,217.20 (1.88 Tckts). T/Qdpt: £174.00 (5.02 Tckts) SM

1260-NEWBURY (L-H) (Good to firm, Good bk st)
Wednesday May 28th
WEATHER: sunny WIND: alm nil

82 83 88+ 81 (83)

1486 E.B.F. BOXFORD MAIDEN STKS (2-Y.O) (Class D)
5-55 (5-56) **5f 34y** £3,610.00 (£1,090.00: £530.00: £250.00) Stalls: High GOING minus 0.51 sec per fur (F)

				SP	RR	SF
1163[2]	**Compradore** (MBlanshard) **2-8-9** JQuinn(6) (w ldr: led 4f out: rdn out)	—	1	5/1[3]	76	44
	Hadid (USA) (BWHills) **2-9-0** RHills(5) (leggy: hld up: rdn over 1f out: r.o ins fnl f)	¾	2	3/1[2]	79	47
	Shalford's Honour (IRE) (WJarvis) **2-9-0** JReid(2) (scope: bit bkwd: hld up: hung lft over 2f out: ev ch ins fnl f: unable qckn)	½	3	14/1	77	45
	Cortachy Castle (IRE) (BJMeehan) **2-9-0** PatEddery(7) (leggy: led 1f: ev ch wl over 1f out: wknd fnl f)	3½	4	7/1	66	34
	Katah (JHMGosden) **2-8-9** LDettori(9) (b.hind: leggy: s.s: outpcd: nvr nrr)	4	5	5/1[3]	49	17
1263[12]	**Blue Shadow** (RHannon) **2-9-0** DaneO'Neill(1) (outpcd)	nk	6	25/1	53	21
	John Ferneley (PFICole) **2-9-0** TQuinn(3) (leggy: unf: scope: a.p: hung lft over 2f out: wkng whn hung bdly lft over 1f out)	nk	7	9/4[1]	52	20
	Russian About (IRE) (MRChannon) **2-8-9** RPerham(4) (leggy: a bhd)	nk	8	33/1	46	14
	Santone (IRE) (RHannon) **2-9-0** RHughes(10) (neat: hld up: rdn over 2f out: sn wknd)	1¼	9	25/1	47	15
	Water Force (GBBalding) **2-9-0** SDrowne(8) (neat: a bhd)	4	10	50/1	35	3
				(SP 120.9%)		**10 Rn**

60.55 secs (0.05 under 2y best) (0.35) CSF £18.68 TOTE £6.00: £1.90 £1.60 £3.20 (£10.40) Trio £43.40 OWNER Mrs James Watkins (UPPER LAMBOURN) BRED B. Freiha
IN-FOCUS: **This did not look a particularly strong Newbury maiden.**
1163 Compradore, second to Tuesday's National Stakes winner Pool Music on her debut, put her experience to good use. Soon at the head of affairs, she was ridden along to repel her persistent rivals. The Queen Mary at Royal Ascot could be next on the agenda. (5/1)
Hadid (USA), out of a million dollar-earning mare whose wins included a Grade One nine furlong event, was tucked in behind the leaders. Bustled along from below the distance, he really found his feet inside the final furlong and ran on nicely to finish on the heels of the winner. Given another furlong, he should soon get off the mark. (3/1: op 2/1)
Shalford's Honour (IRE), with more substance than many in the field, looked as though the run would do him good. Drifting right out into the centre of the course at halfway, he nevertheless still had every chance inside the final furlong before tapped for toe. He should soon find a race. (14/1)
Cortachy Castle (IRE), quite a leggy newcomer, had every chance early in the final quarter-mile before tiring in the last two hundred yards. (7/1: op 7/2)
Katah, rather on the leg at present, lost ground at the start and failed to go the pace. (5/1: 5/2-11/2)
Blue Shadow was quickly taken off his feet. (25/1)
John Ferneley (9/4: 2/1-3/1)

1487 BASINGSTOKE CLAIMING STKS (3-Y.O) (Class E)
6-20 (6-22) **1m 2f 6y** £3,109.50 (£936.00: £453.00: £211.50) Stalls: Low GOING minus 0.51 sec per fur (F)

				SP	RR	SF
1426*	**Double Gold (64)** (BJMeehan) **3-8-7** KFallon(3) (mde all: hrd rdn over 1f out: r.o wl)	—	1	3/1[2]	73	33

1139^{2}	**Ludo (56)** (RHannon) **3-9-4** DaneO'Neill(2) (hld up: rdn over 3f out: chsd wnr fnl f: no imp)	5	**2**	14/1	76	36
1146^{7}	**Mr Bombastique (IRE) (86)** (BWHills) **3-9-7** PatEddery(5) (rdn & hdwy over 3f out: chsd wnr over 2f out to 1f out: one pce)	1¾	**3**	8/11 ^{1}	76	36
1301^{3}	**Eponine (64)** (MRChannon) **3-8-7** TQuinn(7) (lw: chsd wnr over 7f: wkng whn hmpd on ins wl over 1f out)	7	**4**	8/1 ^{3}	51	11
1096^{11}	**Ginger Rogers (52)** (DWPArbuthnot) **3-8-6** SWhitworth(4) (lw: hld up: rdn over 4f out: wknd 3f out)	6	**5**	50/1	41	1
875^{6}	**Arthur's Seat** (LordHuntingdon) **3-9-7** LDettori(1) (shkn up & sme hdwy over 3f out: swtchd rt: sn wknd)	13	**6**	10/1	35	—
771^{13}	**Paddy Hurry (51)** (NACallaghan) **3-8-9** SDrowne(6) (bhd fnl 4f)	9	**7**	33/1	8	—
	Hot Shot (GLMoore) **3-8-8** CandyMorris(8) (bit bkwd: s.s: bhd whn p.u 3f out: dismntd)		**P**	66/1	—	—

(SP 116.2%) **8 Rn**

2m 6.21 (2.21) CSF £38.67 TOTE £3.50: £1.30 £1.50 £1.20 (£15.60) Trio £4.90 OWNER Mr Michael Edwards (UPPER LAMBOURN) BRED Catridge Farm Stud Ltd

Mr Bombastique (IRE) clmd DMorgan £18,000

1426* Double Gold followed up her Saturday victory in this grade at Warwick with another pillar to post victory. Given a few slaps below the distance, she lengthened her stride in great style to dispose of a very moderate field. There were seven claims for her but, luckily for her connections, their name was first out of the hat. (3/1: 2/1-100/30)

1139 Ludo has certainly found his right grade. Not inconvenienced by the step-up in trip, he struggled into second place entering the final furlong but had no hope with the winner. (14/1: 8/1-16/1)

1146 Mr Bombastique (IRE) was taking a big drop in class but, even so, failed to summon up the necessary turn of foot when the real race developed. (8/11)

1301 Eponine, in second place until over two furlongs from home, was feeling the pinch when hampered along the inside rail early in the final quarter-mile. (8/1: op 4/1)

Ginger Rogers is a very bad performer and had been seen off three furlongs from home. (50/1)

875 Arthur's Seat looks a very moderate individual but he was given considerate handling on this occasion, and may at least be kindly treated by the Handicapper. (10/1)

1488 KINGSTON SMITH H'CAP (0-80) (3-Y.O+) (Class D)

6-50 (6-51) **6f 8y** £3,704.00 (£1,112.00: £536.00: £248.00) Stalls: High GOING minus 0.51 sec per fur (F)

				SP	RR	SF
1243^{4}	**Always Alight (62)** (KRBurke) **3-8-3** JQuinn(5) (lw: hdwy over 1f out: led ins fnl f: rdn out)	—	**1**	9/1	75	49
1410^{5}	**White Emir (78)** (BJMeehan) **4-10-0b** PatEddery(4) (lw: w ldr: led over 1f out tl ins fnl f: unable qckn)	1	**2**	100/30 ^{1}	84	71
1166^{11}	**Rififi (60)** (RIngram) **4-8-10** SWhitworth(9) (b: lw: a.p: ev ch 1f out: one pce)	2	**3**	8/1	61	48
1107^{7}	**Sea Danzig (63)** (JJBridger) **4-8-13** LDettori(1) (lw: led over 4f: one pce)	hd	**4**	8/1	64	51
1395^{5}	**Walk the Beat (64)** (MartynMeade) **7-9-0** JReid(3) (hld up: rdn over 1f out: one pce)	¾	**5**	11/2	63	50
977^{12}	**Bayin (USA) (67)** (MDIUsher) **8-9-3** RStreet(7) (s.s: rdn & hdwy over 1f out: one pce)	hd	**6**	9/2 ^{3}	66	53
1279*	**Night Harmony (IRE) (57)** (MissSJWilton) **4-8-7**ow1 6x KFallon(2) (a.p: ev ch wl over 1f out: sn wknd)	2½	**7**	4/1 ^{2}	49	35

(SP 108.9%) **7 Rn**

1m 11.79 (-0.01) CSF £32.07 CT £205.91 TOTE £12.20: £3.70 £2.10 (£11.80) Trio £178.00 OWNER Mr M. Nelmes-Crocker (WANTAGE) BRED Bylon Farmers Ltd

WEIGHT FOR AGE 3yo-9lb

1243 Always Alight, still in last place below the distance, came with a real rattle to sweep into the lead inside the final furlong and lose his maiden tag. (9/1)

1410 White Emir had the blinkers on for the first time this season and consequently ran a lot better, showing in front below the distance before passed by the winner inside the final furlong. The headgear seems to be the key to him. (100/30)

1083 Rififi, whose two wins to date have both come on the All-Weather, ran much better here and still had every chance entering the final furlong before tapped for toe. (8/1)

121 Sea Danzig, whose two victories to date have both come over seven furlongs, took the field along but, collared below the distance, failed to find another gear. (8/1)

1395 Walk the Beat, making a quick reappearance, chased the leaders but failed to summon up another turn of foot in the last furlong and a half. (11/2)

Bayin (USA) has been dropped 8lb in the handicap since the beginning of the season and ran better as a result, taking closer order below the distance, before failing to find another gear. (9/2: 3/1-5/1)

1489 MARSH BENHAM H'CAP (0-85) (4-Y.O+) (Class D)

7-20 (7-23) **7f 64y (round)** £5,345.00 (£1,610.00: £780.00: £365.00) Stalls: Low GOING minus 0.51 sec per fur (F)

				SP	RR	SF
	Winsome Wooster (60) (PGMurphy) **6-8-4**ow5 DHarrison(3) (a.p: led over 3f out: hrd rdn over 1f out: r.o wl)	—	**1**	33/1	67	47
1324^{6}	**Stoppes Brow (75)** (GLMoore) **5-9-5v** AClark(1) (hdwy over 3f out: n.m.r on ins over 2f out: chsd wnr over 1f out: ev ch fnl f: r.o)	½	**2**	12/1	81	66
1166^{12}	**Sharp Rebuff (79)** (PJMakin) **6-9-9** SSanders(13) (nt clr run 3f out: hdwy over 1f out: r.o wl ins fnl)	1¼	**3**	16/1	82	67
1097^{4}	**Suez Tornado (IRE) (63)** (EJAlston) **4-8-7v** SDrowne(7) (lw: a.p: hrd rdn over 1f out: unable qckn)	½	**4**	16/1	65	50
1262^{4}	**Duello (71)** (MBlanshard) **6-9-1** JQuinn(8) (lw: nt clr run over 3f out & over 2f out: gd hdwy fnl f: fin wl)	2	**5**	12/1	69	54
1166*	**Ben Gunn (65)** (PTWalwyn) **5-8-9** RHills(16) (lw: rdn over 3f out: hdwy over 1f out: nvr nrr)	1½	**6**	13/2 ^{2}	59	44
946^{4}	**Victory Team (IRE) (75)** (GBBalding) **5-9-5** TQuinn(14) (led 4f: wknd over 1f out)	nk	**7**	12/1	69	54
733^{6}	**Eurobox Boy (63)** (APJarvis) **4-8-0**(7)ow1 CCarver(11) (lw: nvr nr to chal)	½	**8**	16/1	56	40
1166^{10}	**Zurs (IRE) (75)** (MissGayKelleway) **4-9-5** KFallon(12) (rdn & hdwy over 3f out: swtchd rt over 2f out: wknd fnl f)	½	**9**	33/1	67	52
1324^{3}	**Knobbleeneeze (75)** (MRChannon) **7-9-5v** LDettori(10) (lw: rdn over 3f out: hdwy over 1f out: wknd ins fnl f)	¾	**10**	4/1 ^{1}	65	50
1264^{2}	**Rakis (IRE) (80)** (MrsLStubbs) **7-9-10** PatEddery(15) (b: lw: bhd fnl 2f)	4	**11**	13/2 ^{2}	61	46
263^{13}	**Xenophon of Cunaxa (IRE) (70)** (MJFetherston-Godley) **4-9-0** DaneO'Neill(2) (prom 5f)	1	**12**	33/1	49	34
1166^{16}	**Sovereigns Court (65)** (LGCottrell) **4-8-9** JReid(9) (lw: prom over 5f)	½	**13**	14/1	43	28
1237^{4}	**Perfect Pal (IRE) (76)** (MissGayKelleway) **6-9-6** RHughes(5) (bhd fnl 3f)	15	**14**	11/1	21	6
1020^{5}	**Barrack Yard (58)** (ACStewart) **4-8-2** DeclanO'Shea(6) (bhd fnl 2f)	16	**15**	10/1 ^{3}	—	—

(SP 120.3%) **15 Rn**

1m 28.0 (-0.10) CSF £349.39 CT £5,980.68 TOTE £44.00: £8.60 £4.50 £4.60 (£228.20) Trio £876.90; £864.59 to 30/5/97 OWNER Miss Amanda Rawding (BRISTOL) BRED Mrs J. A. Rawding and G. C. Greenwood

Winsome Wooster, currently in foal to Cyrano de Bergerac, was running for the first time since she had been covered. Gaining a narrow lead over three furlongs from home, she responded to pressure and, in a tremendous battle royal with the runner-up, just prevailed. (33/1)

1324 Stoppes Brow ran a first-class race. Throwing down a very determined challenge in the final furlong, he went at it hammer and tongs with the winner but found he had met a real tartar in that rival and could not get by. (12/1)

Sharp Rebuff, 5lb higher than he has ever won off before, put in some really good work in the last furlong and a half but found the line always just coming too soon. (16/1)
1097 Suez Tornado (IRE), a leading light from the off, failed to quicken when it mattered in the last furlong and a half. (16/1)
1262 Duello continually met traffic problems and was in last place a quarter of a mile from home. However, he sprouted wings in the final furlong and, absolutely flying, came through to take fifth place. He is not that easy to win with. (12/1: op 8/1)
1166* Ben Gunn stayed on in the last furlong and a half without ever threatening to get into it. (13/2)
1237 Perfect Pal (IRE) (11/1: 8/1-12/1)

1490 TARMAC CONDITIONS STKS (4-Y.O+) (Class C)
7-50 (7-51) **1m 2f 6y** £4,858.75 (£1,765.00: £857.50: £362.50: £156.25) Stalls: Low GOING minus 0.51 sec per fur (F)

				SP	RR	SF
894[3]	**Cap Juluca (IRE) (107)** (RCharlton) **5-8-10** RHughes(3) (mde all: rdn out)	—	1	5/4[1]	110	52
	Helicon (IRE) (SbinSuroor) **4-8-10** LDettori(2) (lw: hld up: chsd wnr fnl 2f: rdn: r.o)	¾	2	11/4[2]	109	51
1241[5]	**Bequeath (110)** (HRACecil) **5-9-5** KFallon(5) (b: lw: chsd wnr 8f: wknd over 1f out)	5	3	4/1[3]	110	52
	River North (IRE) (102) (LadyHerries) **7-8-10** JReid(7) (b: bit bkwd: a bhd)	8	4	12/1	88	30
	My Lewicia (IRE) (98) (PWHarris) **4-8-6**[ow1] MRoberts(4) (bit bkwd: a bhd)	1½	5	9/1	82	23

(SP 108.8%) **5 Rn**

2m 4.05 (0.05) CSF £4.34 TOTE £2.00: £1.40 £1.50 (£2.30) OWNER Mr Martin Myers (BECKHAMPTON) BRED Mrs N. Myers
894 Cap Juluca (IRE), who had some muck in his lungs a couple of weeks ago, made every post a winning one. With his jockey oozing confidence in the straight, he was ridden along from below the distance to keep the runner-up at bay. He does not like going right-handed according to his trainer. (5/4: evens-11/8)
Helicon (IRE), winner of a Newmarket maiden in September 1995 for Henry Cecil, subsequently joined Godolphin but he suffered from a stress fracture of his near fore last spring and, as a result, failed to make it to the racecourse last year. Looking in tremendous shape for this reappearance, he moved into second place a quarter of a mile out and, although unable to overhaul the winner, kept on well to the bitter end. he should soon make up for lost time. (11/4)
1241 Bequeath, in second place to the two furlong marker, was then left for dead by the front two. (4/1)
River North (IRE), who nearly died last year from a major sinus operation, was running over a trip short of his best and on ground faster than ideal. Carrying condition for this reappearance, he was wisely nursed around and never threatened at any stage. (12/1: 7/1-14/1)
My Lewicia (IRE), tackling a longer trip, was always at the back of the field. (9/1)

1491 KENNETH ROBERTSON H'CAP (0-80) (3-Y.O+) (Class D)
8-20 (8-21) **1m 5f 61y** £3,600.00 (£1,080.00: £520.00: £240.00) Stalls: Low GOING minus 0.51 sec per fur (F)

				SP	RR	SF
984[4]	**Premier Night (76)** (SDow) **4-10-0** JReid(8) (stdy hdwy over 3f out: swtchd rt 2f out: led ins fnl f: r.o wl)	—	1	14/1	84	45
1424*	**Golden Hadeer (52)** (MJRyan) **6-8-1**[(3) 5x] MBaird(10) (lw: led over 12f out: rdn over 3f out: hdd ins fnl f: unable qckn)	1	2	7/2[1]	59	20
1022[6]	**Reaganesque (USA) (50)** (PGMurphy) **5-8-2** SDrowne(5) (led 1f: ev ch wl over 1f out: one pce)	1	3	9/1	56	17
*658**	**Brand New Dance (75)** (DWPArbuthnot) **3-8-8** TQuinn(6) (a.p: chsd wnr 8f out: ev ch over 1f out: one pce)	1¼	4	9/2[2]	79	21
1215[4]	**Ancient Quest (72)** (NACallaghan) **4-9-10** PatEddery(1) (hdwy over 4f out: rdn 3f out: one pce)	1¼	5	5/1[3]	75	36
1093*	**Tonka (63)** (PJMakin) **5-9-1** DHarrison(3) (lw: plld hrd: hdwy 4f out: wknd over 2f out)	8	6	7/1	56	17
969*	**Rising Spray (72)** (CAHorgan) **6-9-10** PaulEddery(9) (s.s: sme hdwy 3f out: wknd over 2f out)	13	7	7/2[1]	49	10
986[11]	**Durham (64)** (GLMoore) **6-9-2** SWhitworth(4) (a bhd)	2½	8	16/1	38	—
1027[6]	**Warning Reef (75)** (PEccles) **4-9-13** JQuinn(7) (lw: bhd fnl 3f)	1¼	9	25/1	48	9

(SP 118.2%) **9 Rn**

2m 50.83 (4.33) CSF £58.38 CT £437.09 TOTE £16.20: £3.20 £1.60 £2.10 (£31.50) Trio £153.70 OWNER Mr D. G. Churston (EPSOM) BRED Sheikh Mohammed Bin Rashid Al Maktoum
WEIGHT FOR AGE 3yo-19lb
984 Premier Night, who hated the mud at Haydock last time out, revelled on this lively ground. Throwing down her challenge from below the distance, she managed to assert her authority inside the final furlong. (14/1: 10/1-16/1)
1424* Golden Hadeer ran a first-class race. Soon at the head of affairs, he looked certain to be swallowed up in the straight but he showed tremendous battling qualities and simply refused to give way, only conceding defeat in the last one hundred yards. (7/2: 5/2-4/1)
1022 Reaganesque (USA), a leading light from the outset, had every chance early in the final quarter-mile before tapped for toe. (9/1)
658* Brand New Dance, one of several with every chance entering the final quarter-mile, then failed to find the necessary turn of foot. (9/2)
1215 Ancient Quest took closer order early in the straight but could only go up and down in the same place in the last three furlongs. (5/1)
1093* Tonka took a very keen hold in the early stages. He took closer order early in the straight but the longer trip proved too much for him and he was a spent force over two furlongs from home. (7/1: 9/2-15/2)

T/Plpt: £228.40 (78.86 Tckts). T/Qdpt: £190.10 (6.02 Tckts) AK

1266-RIPON (R-H) (Good to firm)
Wednesday May 28th
WEATHER: sunny WIND: almost nil

73+ 92+ 76 69

1492 LISHMAN, SIDWELL, CAMPBELL AND PRICE MAIDEN STKS (2-Y.O) (Class D) (77)
6-40 (6-41) **5f** £3,220.20 (£975.60: £476.80: £227.40) Stalls: Low GOING minus 0.38 sec per fur (F)

				SP	RR	SF
	Princely Heir (IRE) (MJohnston) **2-9-0** JWeaver(12) (lengthy: scope: s.i.s: sn in tch: led ins fnl f: r.o)	—	1	11/4[1]	76+	34
938[W]	**Batswing** (MartynMeade) **2-9-0** FNorton(1) (swtg: chsd ldrs: ev ch over 1f out: kpt on)	2	2	10/1	70	28
	Leofric (MJPolglase) **2-9-0** TGMcLaughlin(19) (unf: scope: bit bkwd: racd centre: led 3f: kpt on u.p)	½	3	20/1	68	26
	Happy Days Again (IRE) (JWharton) **2-8-9** JFanning(16) (unf: scope: w ldrs: led 2f out tl ins fnl f: no ex)	¾	4	33/1	61	19
1120[10]	**Tom Dougal** (CSmith) **2-9-0** JTate(14) (in tch: hdwy 2f out: styd on towards fin)	2	5	25/1	59	17
	Prince Ashleigh (PCHaslam) **2-9-0** DaleGibson(10) (str: cmpt: scope: bit bkwd: w ldrs tl rdn & btn appr fnl f)	nk	6	25/1	58	16
	Sharp Shooter (IRE) (MrsJRRamsden) **2-9-0** JFortune(7) (w'like: scope: bkwd: chsd ldrs tl btn appr fnl f)	nk	7	14/1	57	15
1267[14]	**Marton Moss (SWE)** (TDEasterby) **2-9-0** ACulhane(11) (hdwy 2f out: nvr nr to chal)	1	8	11/1	54	12
	Three Tenners (JBerry) **2-8-4**[(5)] TEDurcan(8) (cmpt: scope: nvr rchd ldrs)	2	9	4/1[2]	43	1
	Ra Ra Rasputin (BAMcMahon) **2-9-0** LNewton(6) (unf: scope: bkwd: dwlt: nvr trbld ldrs)	1¾	10	10/1	42	—
	Dibola (JSWainwright) **2-9-0** LCharnock(9) (neat: bit bkwd: w ldrs tl wknd appr fnl f)	¾	11	25/1	40	—
	Welcome Sunset (JWharton) **2-8-11**[(3)] PFessey(4) (leggy: bkwd: s.s: a bhd)	hd	12	33/1	39	—

				SP	RR	SF
1120[12]	**Are Yer There** (MWEasterby) **2-8-9**(5) GParkin(15) (n.d)	hd	**13**	50/1	39	—
	Reach For A Star (CWThornton) **2-9-0** NCarlisle(17) (w'like: bit bkwd: s.i.s: n.d)	nk	**14**	33/1	38	—
836[7]	**Cinder Hills** (MWEasterby) **2-8-9** TLucas(5) (a in rr)	s.h	**15**	6/1[3]	33	—
	Velvet Story (NTinkler) **2-9-0** KimTinkler(3) (neat: nvr wnt pce)	2	**16**	20/1	32	—
	Cue Man (IRE) (JLEyre) **2-9-0** TWilliams(18) (small: neat: w ldrs 4f: wknd)	4	**17**	11/1	19	—
	College Clipper (MPBielby) **2-9-0** OUrbina(13) (str: scope: bkwd: sn t.o)	17	**18**	66/1	—	—
				(SP 135.8%)	**18 Rn**	

59.6 secs (1.80) CSF £27.92 TOTE £3.70: £2.10 £2.30 £6.10 (£19.90) Trio Not won; £249.06 to 30/5/97 OWNER Maktoum Al Maktoum (MIDDLEHAM) BRED Gainsborough Stud Management Ltd

OFFICIAL EXPLANATION **Cinder Hills: was coughing after the race.**

Princely Heir (IRE) was very coltish in the paddock but won well, despite giving ground away at the start, and there is obviously plenty more there if it can be channelled in the right direction. (11/4: 7/4-3/1)

Batswing came into the paddock late and was sweating profusely but he ran really well and, if he can be settled, there is obviously more to come. (10/1)

Leofric looked likely to be all the better for his and had an impossible draw but ran a fine race and will obviously find compensation. (20/1)

Happy Days Again (IRE) ran well from a poor draw and this tall filly looks likely to be all the better for the experience. (33/1)

Tom Dougal put in a much-improved effort and is obviously going the right way. (25/1)

Prince Ashleigh ran a fair race until blowing up in the final furlong, and looks the sort to do better as the season progresses. (25/1)

Sharp Shooter (IRE), a useful type, needed this but showed plenty and, in time, much more will be seen of him. (14/1)

Marton Moss (SWE) caught the eye running on steadily in the closing stages. (11/1)

Three Tenners (4/1: op 9/4)

836 Cinder Hills (6/1: tchd 4/1)

Cue Man (IRE), who is only small, has bags of speed but tends to hang left. (11/1: 6/1-12/1)

1493 'RIPON FESTIVAL' CLAIMING STKS (3-Y.O) (Class F)

7-10 (7-13) **1m** £2,598.00 (£728.00: £354.00) Stalls: High GOING minus 0.38 sec per fur (F)

				SP	RR	SF
1115[3]	**Ultra Boy (71)** (PCHaslam) **3-9-0**(5) RFfrench(5) (lw: mde all: qcknd ½-wy: kpt on wl)	—	**1**	9/4[2]	89	54
1080[3]	**Skyers Flyer (IRE) (67)** (RonaldThompson) **3-8-10** TWilliams(2) (plld hrd: bhd: effrt ½-wy: styd on towards fin)	1½	**2**	4/1[3]	77	42
329[2]	**Bonnie Lassie (72)** (CWThornton) **3-8-10** KDarley(4) (lw: chsd ldrs: wnt 2nd over 4f out: rdn 3f out: sn btn)	5	**3**	15/8[1]	67	32
1256[15]	**Ninth Symphony (65)** (PCHaslam) **3-9-3** JFortune(3) (in tch: rdn ½-wy: no imp)	2	**4**	14/1	70	35
1167[11]	**Fortune Hunter (IRE)** (WJarvis) **3-8-11** OUrbina(6) (drvn along over 4f out: n.d)	1¾	**5**	7/1	61	26
1229[12]	**Strelitza (IRE) (52)** (MWEasterby) **3-7-12b** DaleGibson(1) (chsd wnr: rdn & wandered over 4f out: sn btn)	5	**6**	12/1	38	3
				(SP 112.4%)	**6 Rn**	

1m 39.9 (1.70) CSF £10.62 TOTE £3.00: £2.10 £1.90 (£8.70) OWNER Pet Express (W&R) Ltd (MIDDLEHAM) BRED Cheveley Park Stud Ltd

1115 Ultra Boy enjoyed this faster ground and, given a most promising ride, had it won some way out. (9/4)

1080 Skyers Flyer (IRE), held up to get the trip, then took time to find his stride and when he finally did, it was all too late. (4/1)

329 Bonnie Lassie, an All-Weather winner, was always being tapped for toe on this faster surface. (15/8)

Ninth Symphony, a stable companion of the winner, was off the bit at halfway and never anything like good enough. (14/1: op 7/1)

Fortune Hunter (IRE) has not much of an action and, as yet, has not shown any real ability. (7/1)

Strelitza (IRE) wanted to go every which way when ridden and does not look a co-operative type. (12/1)

1494 RIPON FARM SERVICES H'CAP (0-75) (4-Y.O+) (Class D)

7-40 (7-40) **2m** £3,452.50 (£1,045.00: £510.00: £242.50) Stalls: Low GOING minus 0.38 sec per fur (F)

				SP	RR	SF
955[4]	**Nigel's Lad (IRE) (70)** (PCHaslam) **5-9-6**(5) RFfrench(2) (lw: trckd ldrs: qcknd to ld 3½f out: sn clr: pushed out)	—	**1**	5/2[1]	91	73
1133[4]	**Hasta la Vista (48)** (MWEasterby) **7-8-3b** LCharnock(1) (lw: trckd ldrs: ev ch 4f out: one pce)	14	**2**	6/1	55	37
1100[11]	**Anchorena (47)** (DWBarker) **5-8-2** TWilliams(3) (chsd ldrs: effrt & ev ch 4f out: sn rdn & one pce)	nk	**3**	8/1	54	36
1100[12]	**French Ivy (USA) (65)** (FMurphy) **10-9-6** JFanning(8) (b: bhd: effrt over 3f out: hdwy 2f out: no imp)	s.h	**4**	8/1	72	54
	Amiarge (50) (MBrittain) **7-8-5** JCarroll(9) (chsd ldrs tl outpcd fnl 3f)	1¾	**5**	14/1	55	37
1224[9]	**Charter (67)** (WStorey) **6-9-8** JSupple(5) (bit bkwd: outpcd 6f out: nvr plcd to chal after)	1½	**6**	12/1	70	52
	Zamhareer (USA) (50) (WStorey) **6-8-5** NKennedy(4) (bit bkwd: bhd: effrt 4f out: n.d)	6	**7**	11/2[3]	47	29
994[4]	**Highflying (72)** (GMMoore) **11-9-13** JTate(7) (cl up: chal 4f out: wknd fnl 2½f)	3	**8**	7/2[2]	66	48
1133[9]	**El Nido (45)** (DWChapman) **9-7-11**(3) PFessey(6) (led tl hdd & wknd 3½f out)	3	**9**	25/1	36	18
				(SP 120.9%)	**9 Rn**	

3m 26.2 (0.40 under best) (1.20) CSF £17.28 CT £98.87 TOTE £3.20: £1.60 £1.50 £2.00 (£5.40) Trio £26.40 OWNER Mr N. C. Dunnington (MIDDLEHAM) BRED Nikita Investments

955 Nigel's Lad (IRE) got this extra distance particularly well, and his rider left nothing to chance. Presumably the Handicapper will now do the same. (5/2)

1133 Hasta la Vista, happy to track the leaders this time, was made to look very pedestrian in the last half-mile. (6/1)

669 Anchorena travelled well but just cannot quicken when asked a question. (8/1)

French Ivy (USA) ran his best race of the season and seems to be coming to hand steadily. (8/1: op 5/1)

Amiarge put in a reasonable first effort of the season but he was treading water a long way out. (14/1)

Charter never got into this but was certainly not knocked about and looks the type to improve for this useful stable. (12/1)

994 Highflying dropped disappointingly away in the last three furlongs and did not look happy on pulling up. (7/2)

1495 AMEC CIVIL ENGINEERING H'CAP (0-85) (3-Y.O+) (Class D)

8-10 (8-12) **1m** £4,240.50 (£1,284.00: £627.00: £298.50) Stalls: High GOING minus 0.38 sec per fur (F)

				SP	RR	SF
1116*	**Three Arch Bridge (70)** (MJohnston) **5-9-0b** JWeaver(8) (bhd: hdwy 3f out: led ins fnl f: r.o wl)	—	**1**	11/2[3]	83	58
945*	**Young Precedent (81)** (PWHarris) **3-8-13** AMcGlone(11) (lw: w ldrs: led over 1f out tl ins fnl f: no ex)	3	**2**	11/4[1]	88	51
	Lay The Blame (73) (MDHammond) **4-9-3** JCarroll(13) (bit bkwd: led tl hdd over 1f out: kpt on wl)	½	**3**	40/1	79	54
	Bollin Frank (69) (TDEasterby) **5-8-13** LCharnock(7) (bit bkwd: bhd: hdwy on ins 3f out: kpt on wl)	nk	**4**	14/1	74	49
824[7]	**Gilling Dancer (IRE) (53)** (PCalver) **4-7-8**(3)ow1 DarrenMoffatt(10) (chsd ldrs: n.m.r 3f out: kpt on one pce)	s.h	**5**	16/1	58	32
1414[15]	**Stellar Line (USA) (72)** (MJPolglase) **4-9-2** MRimmer(12) (chsd ldrs: effrt & swtchd 2f out: btn appr fnl f)	½	**6**	16/1	76	51
947[9]	**Band on the Run (84)** (BAMcMahon) **10-10-0** LNewton(3) (bhd tl styd on fnl 2f)	s.h	**7**	11/1	88	63
1048[4]	**Takhlid (USA) (70)** (DWChapman) **6-9-0** ACulhane(5) (lw: bhd tl styd on fnl 2f)	1¼	**8**	12/1	72	47

				SP	RR	SF
824*	**Thatched (IRE) (55)** (REBarr) **7-7-10**(3) PFessey(4) (bhd effrt 4f out: wknd fnl 2f)	nk	**9**	8/1	56	31
1266*	**Flag Fen (USA) (56)** (JParkes) **6-7-9**(5) RFfrench(1) (lw: hdwy on outside to jn ldrs ent st: effrt & hung rt 4f out: wknd fnl 2½f)	6	**10**	11/2[3]	45	20
1384[6]	**Up in Flames (IRE) (65)** (SRBowring) **6-8-9** SWebster(2) (chsd ldrs: effrt over 3f out: wkng whn hmpd wl over 1f out)	2	**11**	16/1	50	25
1248[11]	**Midday Cowboy (USA) (55)** (MDHammond) **4-7-13** DaleGibson(9) (lw: in tch tl grad lost pl fnl 3f)	nk	**12**	40/1	40	15
1021[5]	**Mouche (80)** (MrsJRRamsden) **3-8-12** JFortune(6) (unruly in stalls: in tch to st: wknd qckly: p.u appr fnl f)		**P**	5/1[2]	—	—

(SP 130.4%) **13 Rn**

1m 39.1 (0.90) CSF £20.91 CT £535.92 TOTE £4.70: £1.70 £1.80 £9.40 (£7.30) Trio £148.80 OWNER Mr R. N. Pennell (MIDDLEHAM) BRED R. Taylor

WEIGHT FOR AGE 3yo-12lb

1116* Three Arch Bridge at one time could only win from the front but nowadays it does not seem to matter and she came from way off the pace to win this. (11/2)

945* Young Precedent is a free-runner and put in a useful performance against older rivals here, but was well outpointed late on. (11/4)

Lay The Blame ran well for his new stable and looks likely to be all the better for it. (40/1)

Bollin Frank is obviously in good heart but he is high enough in the handicap and is probably at his best on easier ground. (14/1: 10/1-16/1)

235 Gilling Dancer (IRE) ran quite well, despite being short of room at times. (16/1)

1011* Stellar Line (USA) seems happier over a bit further and was never doing enough when the pressure was on. (16/1)

947 Band on the Run is running reasonably and is well worth keeping in mind for the return to form. (11/1)

1048 Takhlid (USA) spends most of his time on the All-Weather but he showed enough here to suggest that a race can be found on turf. (12/1: op 8/1)

1496 ST MARYGATE H'CAP (0-70) (3-Y.O) (Class E)

8-40 (8-41) **6f** £2,934.25 (£889.00: £434.50: £207.25) Stalls: Low GOING minus 0.38 sec per fur (F)

				SP	RR	SF
1243[7]	**Swift (57)** (MJPolglase) **3-8-8** MRimmer(8) (lw: s.i.s: hdwy after 2f: styd on to ld ins fnl f)	—	**1**	7/1[3]	69	29
1119[9]	**Fine Times (58)** (CWFairhurst) **3-8-9v1** JWeaver(12) (b.hind: chsd ldrs: rdn to ld 1f out: sn hdd: hung rt & kpt on)	¾	**2**	16/1	68	28
1141[17]	**Midnight Shift (IRE) (68)** (RGuest) **3-9-5** PBloomfield(3) (lw: drvn along to chse ldrs after 2f: kpt on u.p towards fin)	¾	**3**	7/1[3]	76	36
1225[4]	**Rum Lad (56)** (JJQuinn) **3-8-7** JLowe(14) (lw: chsd ldrs: outpcd whn hmpd 1½f out: kpt on wl)	½	**4**	6/1[2]	63	23
995[14]	**Bold Brief (55)** (DenysSmith) **3-8-6b1** LCharnock(16) (led tl hdd 1f out: hmpd & swtchd ins fnl f: kpt on)	s.h	**5**	33/1	62	22
1098[12]	**Star of The Road (50)** (JMCarr) **3-8-1** NKennedy(9) (w ldrs tl rdn & btn ins fnl f)	hd	**6**	25/1	56	16
1394[6]	**Sparkling Harry (54)** (MissLCSiddall) **3-8-5b**ow1 KDarley(15) (bhd tl hdwy u.p 2f out: nvr able to chal)	hd	**7**	25/1	60	19
1332[3]	**Chilling (52)** (NTinkler) **3-7-10b**(7) KSked(6) (lw: mid div: effrt & nt clr run 2f out: swtchd & styd on: n.d)	½	**8**	3/1[1]	57	17
1096[8]	**Dee Pee Tee Cee (IRE) (49)** (MWEasterby) **3-8-0** DaleGibson(11) (lw: outpcd & bhd tl styd on fnl 2f)	1	**9**	16/1	51	11
1221[7]	**Tarradale (58)** (CBBBooth) **3-8-9** KHodgson(1) (dwlt: a outpcd & bhd)	3	**10**	12/1	52	12
995[17]	**Anetta (57)** (MissSEHall) **3-8-8** ACulhane(2) (cl up: hung rt most of wy: wknd appr fnl f)	s.h	**11**	12/1	51	11
977[9]	**Three For A Pound (70)** (JAGlover) **3-9-7** GCarter(13) (lw: chsd ldrs 4f: eased whn btn)	s.h	**12**	6/1[2]	64	24
785[13]	**Euroquest (45)** (DNicholls) **3-7-5b1**(5) RFfrench(10) (sn outpcd & wl bhd: wandered u.p: sme late hdwy)	¾	**13**	9/1	37	—
845[11]	**Gipsy Princess (67)** (MWEasterby) **3-8-13b**(5) GParkin(5) (in tch 4f: wknd)	1	**14**	12/1	56	16
1226[8]	**Colonel's Pride (61)** (RMWhitaker) **3-8-12** JCarroll(7) (spd to ½-wy: sn bhd)	1½	**15**	20/1	46	6
1044[8]	**Redspet (45)** (SRBowring) **3-7-5**(5) JBramhill(4) (a outpcd & bhd)	5	**16**	50/1	17	—

(SP 140.8%) **16 Rn**

1m 12.7 (2.20) CSF £114.09 CT £807.27 TOTE £8.80: £1.90 £2.90 £2.80 £1.80 (£193.00) Trio £162.30 OWNER Gen Sir Geoffrey Howlett (NEWMARKET) BRED Mrs Amschel Rothschild

LONG HANDICAP Euroquest 7-8 Redspet 6-9

871 Swift has speed and stays the trip well and, after a poor start, did it nicely. (7/1)

Fine Times, in a visor for the first time, ran better but then threw his chances away by hanging under pressure late on. (16/1)

Midnight Shift (IRE) was always struggling with the pace but she did keep responding to pressure and may well need a bit further. (7/1)

1225 Rum Lad is running well at the moment and deserves a change of luck. (6/1)

Bold Brief, in blinkers for the first time, showed bags of speed from a poor draw and was then hampered when beaten. (33/1)

Star of The Road ran pretty well but just lacks a change of gear. (25/1)

1332 Chilling was always short of room and was certainly short of the necessary pace to get out of trouble. (3/1)

1096 Dee Pee Tee Cee (IRE) ran well, staying on over a trip too short. (16/1)

1023 Tarradale (12/1: op 8/1)

469* Three For A Pound (6/1: 9/2-7/1)

1497 ST AGNESGATE MAIDEN STKS (3-Y.O+) (Class D)

9-10 (9-11) **1m 2f** £3,566.25 (£1,080.00: £527.50: £251.25) Stalls: High GOING minus 0.38 sec per fur (F)

				SP	RR	SF
1173[3]	**Greek Palace (IRE)** (MRStoute) **3-8-10** KDarley(10) (lw: trckd ldrs gng wl: chal on bit over 2f out: led 1f out: qcknd: cleverly)	—	**1**	1/3[1]	91+	31
1130[3]	**Taunt (85)** (DMorley) **3-8-10** GCarter(1) (lw: cl up: led wl over 3f out to 1f out: r.o wl)	nk	**2**	3/1[2]	91	31
1130[7]	**Kayfiyah (IRE)** (DMorley) **3-8-5** MFenton(11) (chsd ldrs: chal 3f out: outpcd fnl 2f)	7	**3**	25/1	74	14
	Derby Darbak (USA) (JHMGosden) **4-9-10** JCarroll(3) (gd sort: str: bkwd: a.p: effrt over 3f out: outpcd fnl 2f)	3½	**4**	16/1[3]	74	28
1230[10]	**Well Armed (IRE)** (JJO'Neill) **6-9-10** JFortune(7) (led tl hdd wl over 3f out: wknd over 2f out)	8	**5**	100/1	61	15
	Northern Flash (FMurphy) **3-8-10** JWeaver(6) (lengthy: bkwd: s.i.s: hld up & bhd: sme late hdwy)	7	**6**	100/1	50	—
	Euphoric Illusion (MrsSJSmith) **6-9-7**(3) OPears(2) (chsd ldrs tl wknd fnl 3f)	2	**7**	100/1	47	1
	Spick And Span (CWThornton) **3-8-10** NCarlisle(8) (leggy: unf: bit bkwd: a rr div)	1¼	**8**	66/1	45	—
1221[11]	**Cochiti** (CWThornton) **3-8-5** DaleGibson(12) (hld up & a bhd)	½	**9**	66/1	39	—
1130[9]	**Avro Avian** (MJCamacho) **3-8-5** LCharnock(9) (bit bkwd: hld up & a bhd)	2½	**10**	66/1	35	—
	Notary (JWWatts) **3-8-10** NConnorton(4) (cmpt: scope: bit bkwd: hld up & bhd: sme hdwy ent st: sn lost pl)	1¼	**11**	16/1[3]	38	—
983[11]	**My Firebird** (JJO'Neill) **3-8-6**ow1 ACulhane(13) (plld hrd early: a bhd)	1¾	**12**	100/1	31	—

(SP 124.0%) **12 Rn**

2m 7.6 (4.10) CSF £1.56 TOTE £1.50: £1.10 £1.60 £2.70 (£2.00) Trio £4.80 OWNER Lord Weinstock (NEWMARKET) BRED Ballymacoll Stud Farm Ltd

WEIGHT FOR AGE 3yo-14lb

1173 Greek Palace (IRE) always had this in hand but he did need to quicken to put it beyond doubt late on, and will surely stay further. (1/3)
1130 Taunt, always second best, kept running on under pressure and deserves to find a race. (3/1)
1130 Kayfiyah (IRE) is improving and this should have taught her plenty. (25/1)
Derby Darbak (USA), a useful sort, was very much in need of this and showed enough to suggest that, in time, much better is likely. (16/1)
996 Well Armed (IRE), one of the few no-hopers allowed to take serious part in this, was left behind in the last two and a half furlongs. (100/1)
Northern Flash, needing this, made some late headway without getting into it and the future would seem to be long-term. (100/1)
Notary had what can only be described as an educational. (16/1)

T/Plpt: £24.10 (475.92 Tckts). T/Qdpt: £7.90 (79.18 Tckts) AA

YARMOUTH (L-H) (Firm, Good to Firm patches)
Wednesday May 28th
WEATHER: Overcast with sunny periods WIND: fresh across

51+

1498 REPPS (S) STKS (2-Y.O) (Class G)
2-10 (2-10) **5f 43y** £2,239.30 (£619.80: £295.90) Stalls: Low GOING minus 0.65 sec per fur (HD)

				SP	RR	SF
1330^{5}	**Arm And A Leg (IRE)** (CADwyer) **2-8-11** JStack(5) (chsd ldrs: rdn ½-wy: styd on to ld nr fin)	—	1	$8/1^{3}$	61	13
993^{10}	**Eurofen** (PDEvans) **2-8-11b**[1] WRyan(1) (led & sn clr: hdd over 1f out: rallied u.p ins fnl f)	hd	2	33/1	61	13
	Sans Rivale (BJMeehan) **2-8-6** BDoyle(3) (neat: bit bkwd: chsd ldr: led over 1f out tl hdd cl home)	s.h	3	$3/1^{2}$	56	8
1228^{2}	**Fairy Domino** (MRChannon) **2-8-6** LDettori(4) (hld up: effrt 2f out: sn hrd rdn: nt pce to chal)	2	4	$4/6^{1}$	49	1
1461^{3}	**Zig Zag (IRE)** (MHTompkins) **2-8-0**(7)ow1 PClarke(6) (trckd ldrs: pushed along 3f out: no imp)	1¼	5	9/1	47	—
767^{8}	**Ashjajon** (JWhite) **2-8-6** DBiggs(2) (sn pushed along: a in rr)	2½	6	33/1	38	—

(SP 112.0%) **6 Rn**

62.7 secs (1.70) CSF £154.07 TOTE £6.90: £1.90 £5.00 (£78.70) OWNER A K K Financial Futures Ltd (NEWMARKET) BRED Martyn J. McEnery
Bt in 4,000 gns
1330 Arm And A Leg (IRE), returning to the minimum trip, was struggling with the pace at halfway but, responding to a forceful ride, ran on to nose ahead in the dying strides. (8/1: op 5/1)
Eurofen ran very free in the first-time blinkers and, battling hard, may well have regained control in another stride. (33/1)
Sans Rivale gave the impression she would benefit from the race, but she made the principals fight hard to take her measure in the shadow of the post. (3/1)
1228 Fairy Domino has had a couple of hard races this month and she ran a bit flat on this occasion and could have been feeling the effects. (4/6)
1461 Zig Zag (IRE), having her second outing in twenty-four hours, was always at full stretch and never a factor. (9/1: 6/1-10/1)

1499 SOUTH NORFOLK CATERERS MAIDEN STKS (3-Y.O) (Class D)
2-40 (2-42) **1m 3y** £3,836.70 (£1,146.60: £548.80: £249.90) Stalls: Low GOING minus 0.65 sec per fur (HD)

				SP	RR	SF
485^{2}	**Heavenly Ray (USA)** (JRFanshawe) **3-8-9** KFallon(4) (a.p: led over 2f out: r.o wl)	—	1	$2/1^{1}$	78+	28
	Muhtafel (JLDunlop) **3-9-0** GCarter(5) (w'like: leggy: bit bkwd: hld up & bhd: rdn ½-wy: hdwy 2f out: r.o strly towards fin)	1	2	$11/4^{2}$	81	31
	Blowing Away (IRE) (MHTompkins) **3-8-9** DBiggs(1) (still unf: chsd ldrs: effrt over 1f out: kpt on u.p)	2	3	16/1	72	22
	Bint Shihama (USA) (CEBrittain) **3-8-9** BDoyle(7) (lengthy: unf: a.p: led wl over 3f out: sn hdd: ev ch 1f out: one pce fnl f)	½	4	12/1	71	21
	Dukhan (USA) (RWArmstrong) **3-9-0** RHills(9) (leggy: bit bkwd: chsd ldrs: led 3f out: tl over 2f out: one pce fnl f)	½	5	8/1	75	25
	Real Estate (CFWall) **3-9-0** WLord(6) (bkwd: nvr rchd ldrs)	4	6	16/1	67	17
	Swan Lane (USA) (JHMGosden) **3-8-9** LDettori(2) (lt-f: unf: hld up in tch: effrt over 2f out: sn drvn along & wknd)	s.h	7	$9/2^{3}$	62	12
1234^{8}	**Final Warning** (JEBanks) **3-9-0** JStack(3) (a in rr)	2	8	25/1	63	13
	River Tweed (JHMGosden) **3-8-9** WRyan(8) (leggy: scope: s.s: sn chsng ldrs: wknd 3f out: t.o)	12	9	12/1	34	—
	Caribbee Beach (IRE) (GGMargarson) **3-8-9** GBardwell(10) (small: unf: bkwd: led over 4f: wknd wl over 2f out: t.o)	11	10	50/1	12	—

(SP 122.2%) **10 Rn**

1m 37.8 (1.80) CSF £7.20 TOTE £2.70: £1.50 £1.20 £2.50 (£4.30) Trio £57.40 OWNER Cheveley Park Stud (NEWMARKET) BRED Runnymede Farm Inc and Peter J. Callahan
485 Heavenly Ray (USA), given time to recover from a narrow defeat on her seasonal debut two months ago, did not appear to relish this lively ground but she still won well, despite being inclined to edge right inside the distance. (2/1)
Muhtafel, a leggy colt out of a full sister to Last Tycoon, took time to realise what was required but he was really motoring inside the final furlong and will be much wiser when he next appears. (11/4: 4/1-5/2)
Blowing Away (IRE) did not show much on her debut in the Autumn but she ran a fine race in defeat here and she is certainly one for the note-book. (16/1)
Bint Shihama (USA), an unfurnished newcomer in the firing line from the break, only got shaken off inside the final furlong and, when she strengthens up, could prove useful. (12/1)
Dukhan (USA), a leggy half-brother to two winners, ran a race full of promise and he should come on no end for the experience. (8/1)
Real Estate, very much in need of the run, was given the kid-glove treatment and was never nearer than at the finish. (16/1)
Swan Lane (USA) has not yet come to herself or in her coat and does look to need more time. (9/2: 5/2-5/1)
River Tweed (12/1: op 8/1)

1500 APPLEGATE H'CAP (0-70) (3-Y.O F) (Class E)
3-10 (3-11) **1m 3y** £3,018.25 (£901.00: £430.50: £195.25) Stalls: Low GOING minus 0.65 sec per fur (HD)

				SP	RR	SF
1131^{7}	**Our Way (68)** (CEBrittain) **3-9-7** BDoyle(6) (a.p: led 3f out to 2f out: rallied under str pressure to ld last stride)	—	1	$8/1^{3}$	78	36
1245^{3}	**Calamander (IRE) (59)** (WRMuir) **3-8-12** KFallon(3) (hld up: hdwy ½-wy: led 2f out tl ct post)	hd	2	$3/1^{1}$	69	27
1048^{5}	**Poker Princess (52)** (MBell) **3-8-5** MFenton(10) (chsd ldrs: effrt 2f out: one pce fnl f)	2	3	$8/1^{3}$	58	16
1164^{7}	**Racing Heart (45)** (PJMakin) **3-7-12** JQuinn(2) (swtg: prom: jnd ldr 3f out: rdn & wknd appr fnl f)	5	4	$3/1^{1}$	41	—
1388^{15}	**Crackerbox (45)** (CADwyer) **3-7-7**(5) RMullen(8) (s.i.s: hdwy over 2f out: wknd appr fnl f)	nk	5	20/1	40	—
1090^{11}	**Hippy Chick (49)** (JRJenkins) **3-8-2**ow1 GCarter(11) (dwlt: effrt & rdn 3f out: no imp)	3	6	16/1	38	—

				SP	RR	SF
	Singforyoursupper (53) (GGMargarson) **3-8-6** GBardwell(9) (bkwd: a bhd: rdn ½-wy: no rspnse)	7	**7**	16/1	28	—
1000[10]	**River of Fortune (IRE) (63)** (MHTompkins) **3-9-2** DBiggs(7) (lw: prom: ev ch 3f out: sn rdn & wknd)	¾	**8**	4/1[2]	37	—
873[14]	**Fontcaudette (IRE) (57)** (JEBanks) **3-8-10** JStack(5) (lw: plld hrd: prom over 5f: t.o)	6	**9**	33/1	19	—
	Pirongia (43) (PHowling) **3-7-5**(5) APolli(1) (b: led 5f: sn rdn & wknd: t.o)	13	**10**	66/1	—	—
642[6]	**Junie (IRE) (62)** (TGMills) **3-9-1** WRyan(4) (prom 3f: sn lost pl: t.o)	22	**11**	14/1	—	—

(SP 119.8%) **11 Rn**

1m 37.4 (1.40) CSF £29.45 CT £189.98 TOTE £8.00: £2.10 £1.90 £2.70 (£18.30) Trio £19.60 OWNER Mr Ward Hill (NEWMARKET) BRED S. Tindall and Stowell Hill Ltd

LONG HANDICAP Pirongia 7-7

Our Way produced a very gutsy performance to open her account and, unless she is super-tough, could need time to get over it. (8/1)

1245 Calamander (IRE) is slowly but surely finding her way and, with any luck at all, should be able to atone for this last-stride defeat. (3/1)

1048 Poker Princess must have found this surface much firmer than she had been used to on the All-Weather recently, but she did not fail for the want of trying and her turn will come. (8/1)

1164 Racing Heart joined issue three furlongs out but failed to get the better of the winner and she had had enough entering the final furlong. She did nothing wrong and would seem to be one to keep in mind. (3/1)

874 Crackerbox made up a lot of ground after missing a beat at the start, but her run had come to an end before reaching the final furlong. (20/1)

Hippy Chick was never able to maker her presence felt over this longer trip but must not be written off yet. (16/1)

Junie (IRE) (14/1: 10/1-16/1)

1501 DAVID STOTT H'CAP (0-70) (3-Y.O+) (Class E)

3-45 (3-47) **7f 3y** £3,122.25 (£933.00: £446.50: £203.25) Stalls: Low GOING minus 0.65 sec per fur (HD)

				SP	RR	SF
1219[12]	**Safey Ana (USA) (61)** (BHanbury) **6-9-5** WRyan(13) (b: racd stands' side: led ins fnl f: r.o wl)	—	**1**	9/1	73	58
1128[2]	**Mezzoramio (46)** (KAMorgan) **5-7-11v**(7) JoHunnam(2) (b: overall ldr far side: hrd rdn & ct cl home)	¾	**2**	6/1[3]	56	41
1154[2]	**Ertlon (70)** (CEBrittain) **7-10-0** BDoyle(14) (a.p stands' side: led after 3f tl hdd & no ex ins fnl f)	½	**3**	9/2[2]	79	64
838[16]	**Gain Line (USA) (58)** (BobJones) **4-9-2** NDay(5) (racd far side: hdwy over 2f out: nrst fin)	3	**4**	9/1	60	45
1248[5]	**Godmersham Park (62)** (PSFelgate) **5-9-6** LDettori(7) (w ldr far side: rdn 2f out: sn btn)	1¾	**5**	6/1[3]	60	45
1292[7]	**Jibereen (70)** (PHowling) **5-10-0** PaulEddery(3) (chsd ldrs far side: hrd drvn 2f out: one pce)	4	**6**	12/1	59	44
1131*	**Gymcrak Flyer (64)** (GHolmes) **6-9-8** KFallon(1) (b.hind: lw: hld up far side: hdwy over 2f out: sn rdn: nvr able to chal)	3	**7**	5/2[1]	46	31
1135[10]	**Hadadabble (38)** (PatMitchell) **4-7-5**(5) APolli(4) (racd far side: bhd tl sme late hdwy)	nk	**8**	50/1	20	5
1116[13]	**Persephone (38)** (JLHarris) **4-7-10b** JLowe(10) (nvr plcd to chal)	1¾	**9**	66/1	16	1
1011[7]	**Dia Georgy (38)** (CADwyer) **6-7-10** JQuinn(9) (b: a in rr)	2	**10**	50/1	11	—
1225[13]	**Melodic Drive (57)** (JAGlover) **7-9-1b** GCarter(12) (bit bkwd: s.s: racd stands' side: a bhd)	1	**11**	14/1	28	13
686[10]	**On The Green (47)** (AHide) **4-8-5** DBiggs(6) (s.i.s: a bhd)	1	**12**	33/1	16	1
	Bear To Dance (40) (PHowling) **4-7-7**(5) RMullen(8) (bit bkwd: bhd fr ½-wy)	2	**13**	50/1	4	—
1134[7]	**Spanish Stripper (USA) (38)** (MCChapman) **6-7-10** GBardwell(15) (led stands' side 3f: sn lost tch)	¾	**14**	50/1	—	—
1219[11]	**Watch The Fire (67)** (JEBanks) **4-9-11** JStack(11) (lw: hld up: hdwy u.p over 3f out: wknd fnl 2f)	s.h	**15**	14/1	29	14

(SP 128.6%) **15 Rn**

1m 23.4 (-0.80) CSF £58.63 CT £266.06 TOTE £11.20: £2.60 £2.10 £1.90 (£33.10) Trio £59.90 OWNER The Optimists Racing Partnership (NEWMARKET) BRED Robert N. Clay

LONG HANDICAP Persephone 6-12 Dia Georgy 7-3 Spanish Stripper (USA) 7-2 Hadadabble 7-5

OFFICIAL EXPLANATION **Gymcrak Flyer: was found to be coughing.**

755* Safey Ana (USA) only seems to win in his turn but this was his second success this season, so he is at least paying his way. (9/1)

1128 Mezzoramio made a brave attempt to make it all and he did finish clear on the far side but the winner, under the stands rail, beat him to the punch in the final fifty yards. Losses are only lent. (6/1)

1154 Ertlon looked to have control on the stands side until the winner beat him for toe in the battle to the finish. (9/2)

Gain Line (USA) has shown little of note in the past but he was gradually working his way into it in the closing stages, and there could be more improvement to come. (9/1)

1248 Godmersham Park did his best to match strides with the far-side leader, but he was in trouble entering the final quarter-mile and could do nothing more than stay on at the one pace. (6/1: op 4/1)

578* Jibereen, ill at ease on this lively ground, still ran well and, when he does get cut in the ground, should never be left out of calculations. (12/1)

1131* Gymcrak Flyer, according to her jockey, was never going at any stage and she was reported to be coughing after the race. (5/2)

Melodic Drive (14/1: 16/1-33/1)

1502 SOMERTON CLAIMING STKS (3-Y.O) (Class F)

4-15 (4-18) **2m** £2,461.80 (£679.80: £323.40) Stalls: High GOING minus 0.65 sec per fur (HD)

				SP	RR	SF
1299[6]	**Dawn Summit (49)** (BHanbury) **3-8-13** JStack(4) (led 2f: led 10f out: hrd rdn fnl f: hld on gamely)	—	**1**	11/4[2]	57	21
377[W]	**Zafarelli** (SCWilliams) **3-8-11** WLord(1) (hld up: hmpd & lost tch ent st: hdwy on ins over 2f out: nt clr run appr fnl f: fin wl)	nk	**2**	8/1	55	19
1217[5]	**Fortune Hopper** (JPearce) **3-8-9** GBardwell(3) (sn drvn along in rr: hdwy 3f out: ev ch appr fnl f: unable qckn)	2	**3**	13/8[1]	51	15
1094[15]	**Moorbird (IRE) (56)** (JLHarris) **3-8-7b**[1] BDoyle(5) (prom: chsd wnr 6f out: rdn over 3f out: one pce appr fnl f)	2	**4**	9/2[3]	47	11
1094[17]	**Alimerjam (43)** (JWhite) **3-9-2b** DBiggs(6) (lw: led after 2f to 10f out: hrd drvn ent st: sn wknd: t.o)	dist	**5**	25/1	—	—
	Shoreleave (BobJones) **3-8-9** NDay(2) (leggy: lt-f: s.s: t.o fr ½-wy)	dist	**6**	9/1	—	—

(SP 107.9%) **6 Rn**

3m 28.9 (2.90 under best) (5.40) CSF £19.93 TOTE £3.10: £1.10 £3.40 (£14.80) OWNER Mr A. Merza (NEWMARKET) BRED Mrs Carol Merza

Zafarelli clmd JJenkins £7,000

1299 Dawn Summit found his true mark over this extended trip with more use made of him, and this success was thoroughly deserved. (11/4)

Zafarelli did look an extremely lucky loser and most of it could be put down to his lack of racing experience. He was claimed by John Jenkins for £7,000. (8/1)

1217 Fortune Hopper wore a visor on his previous outing and he took a lot of driving to get him going without the help of that aid this time but, in the end, it was to no avail and he was well held in the closing stages. (13/8)

Moorbird (IRE), in pursuit of the winner from the end of the back straight, did keep persevering but he had met his match on the approach to the final furlong. (9/2)

Shoreleave (9/1: 6/1-10/1)

1503 SEA PALLING APPRENTICE H'CAP (0-60) (3-Y.O+) (Class E)
4-45 (4-45) **1m 2f 21y** £2,715.25 (£832.00: £413.50: £204.25) Stalls: Low GOING minus 0.65 sec per fur (HD)

Form	Horse	Dist	Pos	SP	RR	SF
1219^{10}	**Blockade (USA) (55)** (MBell) **8-9-1**$^{(8)}$ NicolaCole(3) (t: hld up: smooth hdwy to ld on bit over 2f out: comf)	—	**1**	8/1	63	35
1135^{2}	**Isis Honda (IRE) (59)** (CEBrittain) **3-8-10**$^{(3)}$ JGotobed(6) (a.p: rdn 2f out: kpt on: no ch w wnr)	3	**2**	7/2 ^{2}	62	20
1383^{2}	**Esperto (52)** (JPearce) **4-8-12**$^{(8)}$ LisaMoncrieff(4) (s.i.s: bhd: hdwy wl over 1f out: fin wl)	¾	**3**	5/2 ^{1}	54	26
1248^{13}	**Acerbus Dulcis (28)** (MCChapman) **6-7-10** AMcCarthy(7) (hld up in tch: effrt u.p over 2f out: kpt on same pce)	½	**4**	25/1	29	1
1011^{2}	**Law Dancer (IRE) (53)** (TGMills) **4-9-7v**^{1} TSiddall(8) (chsd ldrs: drvn along & ev ch 2f out: r.o one pce)	½	**5**	8/1	54	26
1388^{3}	**Time of Night (USA) (60)** (RGuest) **4-10-0** SRighton(10) (prom: led over 3f out tl over 2f out: hrd drvn & btn appr fnl f)	2½	**6**	9/2 ^{3}	57	29
864^{6}	**Bobbitt (53)** (WJarvis) **3-7-13**$^{(8)}$ TThomas(9) (chsd ldrs over 7f: grad wknd)	2	**7**	10/1	46	4
124^{14}	**Lycius Touch (45)** (AGNewcombe) **3-7-13** PBradley(5) (a in rr)	2	**8**	12/1	35	—
566^{2}	**Paronomasia (28)** (JLHarris) **5-7-10** JFowle(1) (bit bkwd: dwtl: effrt 3f out: sn rdn & wknd)	s.h	**9**	12/1	18	—
1139^{8}	**Valise (39)** (GGMargarson) **4-8-2**$^{(5)}$ DarrenWilliams(11) (led 2f: wknd over 3f out: t.o)	9	**10**	20/1	15	—
1390^{13}	**Perfect Angel (IRE) (48)** (MHTompkins) **3-7-13v**$^{1(3)ow3}$ PClarke(12) (led after 2f tl over 3f out: sn lost tch: t.o)	½	**11**	33/1	23	—
595^{15}	**Antartictern (USA) (30)** (GROldroyd) **7-7-12b** DMernagh(2) (bit bkwd: rel to r: a t.o)	dist	**12**	33/1	—	—
				(SP 130.2%)	**12 Rn**	

2m 6.2 (2.40) CSF £34.94 CT £86.85 TOTE £7.50: £1.90 £1.80 £1.90 (£12.40) Trio £27.00 OWNER Mr A. M. Warrender (NEWMARKET) BRED Patricia C. Warrender
LONG HANDICAP Acerbus Dulcis 7-7 Paronomasia 7-9
WEIGHT FOR AGE 3yo-14lb

Blockade (USA), a most consistent individual throughout the years, was given a dream of a ride from his inexperienced jockey - on her first winner - and came from off the pace to win this in a canter. It was a pleasure to watch. (8/1)
1135 Isis Honda (IRE), fit from the All-Weather, did her best to make a race of it but, on this occasion, the winner was in a class of his own. She still has to get off the mark but her turn is merely delayed. (7/2)
1383 Esperto had more to do here and he did not find top gear until the outcome had virtually been decided. (5/2)
122 Acerbus Dulcis, driven along to improve over two furlongs out, had let the winner take first run and from then on the race was only for the places. (25/1)
1011 Law Dancer (IRE) wore a visor for the first time and was never far away but, on this lively ground, he was never giving it his full co-operation. (8/1)
1388 Time of Night (USA) found the concession of so much weight more than she could cope with in the last couple of furlongs. (9/2)

T/Plpt: £499.20 (20.63 Tckts). T/Qdpt: £22.40 (35.26 Tckts) IM

1370-BRIGHTON (L-H) (Firm)
Thursday May 29th
WEATHER: sunny WIND: mod half bhd

68 75 68 77

1504 E.B.F. FRESHFIELD NOVICE MEDIAN AUCTION STKS (2-Y.O) (Class E) (72)
2-10 (2-11) **5f 213y** £2,888.25 (£861.00: £410.50: £185.25) Stalls: Low GOING minus 0.57 sec per fur (F)

Form	Horse	Dist	Pos	SP	RR	SF
1143^{7}	**Truth Teller** (RHannon) **2-8-12** DaneO'Neill(2) (lw: mde all: hrd rdn over 1f out: r.o wl)	—	**1**	11/4 ^{2}	66	5
1425*	**Flaming Ember (IRE)** (BJMeehan) **2-9-4** RHughes(4) (chsd wnr: ev ch fnl 2f: r.o wl)	s.h	**2**	8/13 ^{1}	72	11
1293^{11}	**Twentytwo Black** (MJHaynes) **2-8-7** MRoberts(3) (plld hrd: hld up: rdn over 2f out: sn wknd)	14	**3**	33/1	23	—
*1137**	**Persian Fortune** (WGMTurner) **2-8-4**$^{(7)}$ DMcGaffin(1) (reard s: a wl bhd)	8	**4**	11/2 ^{3}	6	—
				(SP 106.9%)	**4 Rn**	

1m 10.1 (2.90) CSF £4.41 TOTE £3.90 (£1.60) OWNER Mr J. C. Smith (MARLBOROUGH) BRED Elsdon Farms

Truth Teller looked in very good shape beforehand. Making all the running, he had a tremendous duel with the runner-up in the final quarter-mile and held on by the skin of his teeth. (11/4)
1425* Flaming Ember (IRE) raced in second place. Engaged in a tremendous ding-dong battle with the winner in the final quarter-mile, he only just failed. (8/13)
Twentytwo Black, a tall filly, took a very keen hold and was left behind in the final quarter-mile. (33/1)
1137* Persian Fortune is not very big and showed nothing on this return to turf. (11/2)

1505 SHOREHAM LIMITED STKS (0-65) (3-Y.O+) (Class F)
2-40 (2-41) **6f 209y** £2,277.00 (£627.00: £297.00) Stalls: Low GOING minus 0.57 sec per fur (F)

Form	Horse	Dist	Pos	SP	RR	SF
376^{3}	**Stand Tall (60)** (LadyHerries) **5-9-6** MRoberts(4) (a.p: rdn over 2f out: led wl ins fnl f: r.o wl)	—	**1**	11/2 ^{2}	67	44
1324^{8}	**Statoyork (65)** (BWHills) **4-9-6** MHills(5) (lw: stdy hdwy over 1f out: rdn: r.o)	½	**2**	4/5 ^{1}	66	43
1374^{7}	**Gwespyr (64)** (RHannon) **4-9-6** DaneO'Neill(1) (lw: hld up: n.m.r 2f out: led ins fnl f: sn hdd: unable qckn)	½	**3**	14/1	65	42
1226^{4}	**Manikato (USA) (65)** (DJSCosgrove) **3-8-9** MRimmer(3) (lw: rdn over 2f out: hdwy over 1f out: r.o)	2	**4**	11/2 ^{2}	60	26
	Dancing Lawyer (57) (BJMeehan) **6-9-6** RHughes(7) (bit bkwd: chsd ldr: led 2f out tl ins fnl f: sn wknd)	nk	**5**	20/1	59	36
1291^{11}	**Hever Golf Charger (IRE) (63)** (TJNaughton) **3-8-11b**^{1} SSanders(2) (led 5f: wkng whn bmpd on ins over 1f out)	4	**6**	25/1	52	18
1373^{2}	**Tayovullin (IRE) (63)** (HMorrison) **3-8-8** CRutter(6) (b.hind: hld up: rdn over 2f out: sn wknd)	1¼	**7**	6/1 ^{3}	46	12
				(SP 115.9%)	**7 Rn**	

1m 20.8 (0.80) CSF £9.67 TOTE £6.50: £2.50 £1.20 (£3.20) OWNER Mr Chris Hardy (LITTLEHAMPTON) BRED Mrs E. Longton
WEIGHT FOR AGE 3yo-11lb

376 Stand Tall, given a three-month break, was never far away and managed to get up in the closing stages. (11/2)
567 Statoyork, held up travelling well, began to creep closer below the distance still going sweetly. However, when his jockey asked him for his effort it was another matter and although running on, he did not look overenthusiastic about the job in hand and did not find as much as was expected. He could have won this and looks one to leave alone. (4/5)
863 Gwespyr coped well with this slightly longer trip and managed to get in front inside the final furlong only to be passed by the winner soon afterwards. (14/1: op 7/1)

1226 Manikato (USA) did not appreciate the drop in distance and was doing all his best work in the last furlong and a half. A return to a mile would help. (11/2: op 7/2)
Dancing Lawyer ran well on this seasonal debut. Sent on a quarter of a mile from home, he was collared inside the final furlong and tired as lack of peak fitness took its toll. (20/1)
547 Hever Golf Charger (IRE), fitted with blinkers for the first time, took the field along but he was collared a quarter of a mile out and was already feeling the pinch when given a hefty bump along the inside rail soon afterwards. He has yet to win on grass. (25/1)
1373 Tayovullin (IRE) (6/1: op 3/1)

1506 FLANAGAN AND ALLEN H'CAP (0-60) (3-Y.O+) (Class F)

3-10 (3-11) **7f 214y** £3,108.60 (£864.60: £415.80) Stalls: Low GOING minus 0.57 sec per fur (F)

				SP	RR	SF
1273^{11}	**Paddy's Rice (53)** (MBlanshard) **6-9-7** FNorton(14) (a.p: chsd ldr 2f out: led wl ins fnl f: rdn out)	—	**1**	16/1	58	42
1005^{5}	**Queen's Insignia (USA) (50)** (PFICole) **4-9-4** MRimmer(15) (chsd ldr: led over 2f out tl wl ins fnl f: r.o)	nk	**2**	$7/1^{3}$	54	38
1273^{4}	**Gold Lance (USA) (48)** (RJO'Sullivan) **4-9-2** TGMcLaughlin(12) (rdn 3f out: hdwy 2f out: r.o ins fnl f)	2½	**3**	11/1	47	31
1422^{2}	**Mr Cube (IRE) (48)** (JMBradley) **7-9-2b** NDay(7) (mid div whn n.m.r on ins over 4f out: n.m.r 2f out: swtchd rt & hrd rdn over 1f out: hdwy fnl f: r.o wl)	4	**4**	$5/1^{1}$	39	23
211^{4}	**Fort Knox (IRE) (55)** (RMFlower) **6-9-9b** DBiggs(1) (rdn 3f out: hdwy over 2f out: unable qckn)	1¾	**5**	12/1	43	27
	Hannalou (FR) (60) (TGMills) **4-10-0** GBardwell(4) (swtg: a.p: rdn over 2f out: wknd fnl f)	hd	**6**	20/1	48	32
1248^{17}	**Homestead (59)** (RHannon) **3-9-1** WJO'Connor(13) (dwlt: nvr nr to chal)	nk	**7**	25/1	46	18
1273^{5}	**Shouldbegrey (42)** (WRMuir) **4-8-10v** JLowe(5) (led over 5f)	1¼	**8**	20/1	27	11
210^{8}	**Multi Franchise (52)** (RMFlower) **4-9-6** RPrice(3) (hld up: shkn up over 3f out: sn wknd)	1	**9**	25/1	35	19
1296^{12}	**Euro Superstar (FR) (50)** (SDow) **3-8-6** RPerham(10) (dwlt: nvr nrr)	¾	**10**	50/1	31	3
1388^{*}	**Bon Guest (IRE) (52)** (TJNaughton) **3-8-8** DaleGibson(8) (swtg: lost pl over 4f out: sme hdwy over 1f out: sn wknd)	hd	**11**	$11/2^{2}$	33	5
1503^{6}	**Time of Night (USA) (60)** (RGuest) **4-10-0** PBloomfield(11) (dwlt: a bhd)	½	**12**	9/1	40	24
1169^{6}	**Sovereign Crest (IRE) (48)** (CAHorgan) **4-9-2** NAdams(2) (s.s: hdwy 5f out: wknd 2f out)	1½	**13**	9/1	25	9
907^{6}	**Hatta Sunshine (USA) (42)** (GLMoore) **7-8-10** JTate(9) (b: lw: sme hdwy on ins over 1f out: sn wknd)	3	**14**	16/1	13	—
895^{22}	**Sejaal (IRE) (57)** (RAkehurst) **5-9-11** DeclanO'Shea(6) (lw: a bhd)	3	**15**	$7/1^{3}$	22	6
				(SP 124.0%)	**15 Rn**	

1m 32.5 (1.20) CSF £107.93 CT £798.77 TOTE £22.90: £4.10 £1.90 £4.70 (£63.60) Trio £394.10; £388.57 to Ayr 30/5/97 OWNER Mrs R. G. Wellman (UPPER LAMBOURN) BRED Mrs H. Lawson
WEIGHT FOR AGE 3yo-12lb
OFFICIAL EXPLANATION **Paddy's Rice: considering the improvement in form, the trainer reported that the gelding was better suited by the firm ground. Bon Guest (IRE): sweated up at the start, and the run may have come too soon.**
Paddy's Rice enjoyed this firm surface and left his two previous runs this season well behind, being rousted along to get up in the closing stages. This is his surface. (16/1)
1005 Queen's Insignia (USA), 9lb lower than when last successful, tried to make that tell and moved to the front over a quarter of a mile from home. Grimly trying to fend off the winner, she was eventually overhauled in the closing stages. (7/1)
1273 Gold Lance (USA), rousted along to take closer order a quarter of a mile from home, stayed on for third prize without threatening to get on terms with the front two. (11/1: op 7/1)
1422 Mr Cube (IRE) did not have the best of runs and, when he did begin to pick up his feet in the final furlong, it was all far too late. (5/1)
211 Fort Knox (IRE), given a three-month break, began a forward over a quarter of a mile from home but could then make no further impression. (12/1)
Hannalou (FR), rather warm beforehand, has changed stables since last year. Never far away, she had come to the end of her tether entering the final furlong. She remains a maiden. (20/1)
1503 Time of Night (USA) (9/1: 5/1-10/1)

1507 SEAFORD (S) H'CAP (0-60) (3-Y.O+) (Class G)

3-40 (3-41) **1m 3f 196y** £1,984.50 (£547.00: £259.50) Stalls: High GOING minus 0.57 sec per fur (F)

				SP	RR	SF
793^{3}	**Manileno (45)** (MCPipe) **3-8-5** MRoberts(5) (lw: chsd ldr: led 7f out: rdn out)	—	**1**	$Evens^{1}$	54	40
	Hillswick (24) (JSKing) **6-7-12**(3) MartinDwyer(13) (a.p: chsd wnr over 4f out: rdn 2f out: r.o one pce)	½	**2**	20/1	32	35
870^{11}	**Private Fixture (IRE) (38)** (DMarks) **6-8-12**(3) AWhelan(6) (lw: rdn over 4f out: hdwy over 1f out: r.o wl)	3	**3**	20/1	42	45
992^{10}	**Aquavita (50)** (RHannon) **3-8-10** DaneO'Neill(4) (hld up: rdn over 2f out: one pce)	¾	**4**	$15/2^{3}$	53	39
1247^{4}	**Noble Hero (48)** (JJSheehan) **3-8-8** SDrowne(12) (hld up: rdn over 2f out: wknd over 1f out)	5	**5**	12/1	45	31
1011^{5}	**Kirov Protege (IRE) (28)** (MrsLCJewell) **5-7-12**(7) DarrenWilliams(7) (a.p: rdn over 3f out: wknd 2f out)	¾	**6**	16/1	24	27
595^{4}	**Open Affair (51)** (HAkbary) **4-10-0** OUrbina(8) (hld up: rdn over 2f out: wknd over 1f out)	1½	**7**	$4/1^{2}$	45	48
	Digwana (IRE) (29) (TMJones) **4-8-1**(5) ADaly(1) (led 5f: wknd over 4f out)	19	**8**	33/1	—	—
1220^{12}	**Astrolabe (45)** (JMBradley) **5-9-1**(7) JFowle(11) (s.s: a bhd)	1½	**9**	25/1	11	14
769^{6}	**Bresil (USA) (27)** (JJBridger) **8-8-4** GBardwell(10) (b: lw: a bhd)	3½	**10**	16/1	—	—
1383^{8}	**Blaze of Oak (USA) (43)** (JMBradley) **6-9-1**(5) RFfrench(3) (b: a bhd)	¾	**11**	12/1	3	6
1086^{5}	**Efficacious (IRE) (45)** (PEccles) **4-9-1b**(7) AEddery(2) (lw: reluctant to r: a bhd)	hd	**12**	25/1	5	8
				(SP 129.1%)	**12 Rn**	

2m 28.2 (0.60) CSF £30.64 CT £282.78 TOTE £1.90: £1.30 £7.20 £4.10 (£41.60) Trio £213.50; £129.32 to Ayr 30/5/97 OWNER Mr Stuart Mercer (WELLINGTON) BRED Mrs C. Ashworth and C. Barber-Lomax
WEIGHT FOR AGE 3yo-17lb
No bid
793 Manileno, who has changed stables since his last run, is only moderate but, sent to the front seven furlongs from home, his jockey vigorously rousted him along in the straight to win this bad race and give Martin Pipe a winner on his fifty-second birthday. (Evens)
Hillswick, without a run in eleven months, moved into second place over half a mile from home but was unable to overhaul the winner. He is a very poor performer. (20/1)
327 Private Fixture (IRE) coped with this much longer trip and ran on nicely in the last furlong and a half to take third prize. He has not won since December 1993. (20/1)
Aquavita, who has shown nothing to date, was taking a drop in class and was made to look extremely pedestrian in the final quarter-mile. (15/2)
1247 Noble Hero found this longer trip too much and had run out of gas below the distance. (12/1: 8/1-14/1)
1011 Kirov Protege (IRE) was close up until tiring a quarter of a mile from home. One win from thirty-nine starts says it all. (16/1)
595 Open Affair (4/1: 3/1-5/1)
763 Blaze of Oak (USA) (12/1: op 8/1)

1508 REGENCY MEDIAN AUCTION MAIDEN STKS (3-Y.O) (Class F)
4-10 (4-10) **7f 214y** £2,277.00 (£627.00: £297.00) Stalls: Low GOING minus 0.57 sec per fur (F)

Form	Horse	Dist	Pos	SP	RR	SF
1006[3]	**Rhapsody In White (IRE) (79)** (MAJarvis) **3-9-0** PBloomfield(1) (mde all: rdn 2f out: r.o wl)	—	1	1/3[1]	55+	11
970[8]	**Fable (56)** (JARToller) **3-8-9** SSanders(2) (plld hrd: a.p: rdn & bmpd 2f out: unable qckn)	1¾	2	16/1[3]	47	3
1297[16]	**Barbury Ballad (IRE)** (MJHeaton-Ellis) **3-9-0** SDrowne(3) (a.p: rdn & bmpd 2f out: wknd over 1f out)	5	3	40/1	42?	—
	Aegean (RHannon) **3-9-0** DaneO'Neill(4) (wl grwn: s.s: hdwy 4f out: wknd over 3f out)	9	4	100/30[2]	23?	—

(SP 106.4%) **4 Rn**

1m 34.9 (3.60) CSF £5.81 TOTE £1.40 (£3.50) OWNER Mrs Christine Stevenson (NEWMARKET) BRED Mrs A. C. Peters

1006 Rhapsody In White (IRE) had nothing to beat and, making all the running, was woken up a quarter of a mile from home to assert his authority. (1/3)

Fable, who took a keen hold in the early stages, won the battle for second prize early in the final quarter-mile but was unable to cope with the winner. (16/1)

Barbury Ballad (IRE), who has finished last on his only two other outings, actually beat one home on this occasion. (40/1)

Aegean already looks like a steeplechaser and so it was a bit of a surprise to see him running here as large-framed horses often have problems negotiating this track. That was the case with him and, although he closed up on his three rivals at the top of the hill, the tricky downhill bend proved a problem for him and he was soon in trouble. (100/30)

1509 CLAYTON H'CAP (0-70) (3-Y.O+) (Class E)
4-40 (4-41) **5f 213y** £3,200.25 (£957.00: £458.50: £209.25) Stalls: Low GOING minus 0.57 sec per fur (F)

Form	Horse	Dist	Pos	SP	RR	SF
1374*	**Ivory's Grab Hire (62)** (KTIvory) **4-9-11b**(3) 7x MartinDwyer(4) (b: swtg: a.p: rdn 2f out: led 1f out: r.o wl)	—	1	9/2[2]	73	49
1374[2]	**Sharp Imp (55)** (RMFlower) **7-9-7b** OUrbina(7) (bmpd s: squeezed out 5f out: hdwy over 1f out: r.o wl ins fnl f)	1	2	11/4[1]	63	39
1151[8]	**Tear White (IRE) (62)** (TGMills) **3-9-2**(3) AWhelan(12) (lw: a.p: rdn 2f out: led & edgd lft over 1f out: sn hdd: unable qckn)	2	3	25/1	65	32
1220[4]	**The Frisky Farmer (51)** (WGMTurner) **4-8-10**(7) DMcGaffin(3) (led over 1f: ev ch wl over 1f out: hmpd over 1f out: one pce)	¾	4	8/1[3]	52	28
1009[10]	**Sizzling (62)** (RHannon) **5-10-0** DaneO'Neill(2) (lw: lost pl 5f out: rallied over 1f out: r.o one pce)	s.h	5	8/1[3]	63	39
1374[3]	**Justinianus (IRE) (42)** (JJBridger) **5-8-3**(5) ADaly(11) (lw: chsd ldrs: rdn 5f out: r.o one pce fnl f)	s.h	6	9/2[2]	43	19
1009[12]	**Tachycardia (38)** (RJO'Sullivan) **5-8-4** SSanders(10) (w ldr: led over 4f out tl hdd & hmpd over 1f out: sn wknd)	1¼	7	11/1	35	11
	Smiling Bess (43) (JSKing) **4-8-4**(5) RFfrench(6) (bmpd s: bhd fnl 2f)	4	8	33/1	30	6
1236[13]	**Halbert (33)** (MDIUsher) **8-7-13v** DRMcCabe(8) (lw: a bhd)	1	9	25/1	17	—
	Pride of Hayling (IRE) (61) (PRHedger) **6-9-13** SDrowne(5) (bhd fnl 2f)	2	10	10/1	40	16
1248[15]	**Sherzetto (55)** (RTPhillips) **3-8-12** AMcGlone(1) (bhd fnl 4f)	1¼	11	33/1	30	—
1141[14]	**Without Friends (IRE) (68)** (JFfitch-Heyes) **3-9-11b** DBiggs(9) (swtg: a bhd)	4	12	12/1	33	—

(SP 123.9%) **12 Rn**

1m 8.0 (0.80) CSF £15.85 CT £264.14 TOTE £10.40: £3.10 £1.40 £8.40 (£12.10) Trio £103.00 OWNER Mr Dean Ivory (RADLETT) BRED Japan Bloodstock Ltd

WEIGHT FOR AGE 3yo-9lb

STEWARDS' ENQUIRY Sanders susp. 9-10/6/97 (careless riding).

1374* Ivory's Grab Hire followed up last week's course and distance victory, leading a furlong from home and keeping on too well for the runner-up. (9/2)

1374 Sharp Imp, 7lb better off with the winner for being beaten a length and a quarter here last week, was unable to reverse the form but did not have much luck in the first furlong of the race. Picking up ground below the distance, he ran on strongly but was never going to overhaul the winner in time. (11/4)

876 Tear White (IRE) was something of a surprise runner considering his trainer had told officials last year that the gelding failed to act on this track. Leading below the distance, he drifted left and, soon headed, failed to find another gear. (25/1)

1220 The Frisky Farmer had every chance early in the final quarter-mile but was just beginning to feel the pinch when hampered soon afterwards. Both his wins to date have come in sellers and a drop in class is required. (8/1)

638* Sizzling soon lost his pitch but did stay on again from below the distance. (8/1: 6/1-9/1)

1374 Justinianus (IRE) chased the leaders but was soon off the bridle and, although struggling on in the final furlong, never looked like finding that vital turn of foot. (9/2)

1008 Without Friends (IRE) (12/1: 8/1-14/1)

T/Plpt: £193.40 (51.03 Tckts). T/Qdpt: £21.60 (33.99 Tckts) AK

1076-CARLISLE (R-H) (Firm)
Thursday May 29th
WEATHER: sunny & warm WIND: slt across

66+ 57

1510 SANDS MAIDEN AUCTION STKS (2-Y.O) (Class E)
2-20 (2-20) **5f 207y** £2,986.25 (£905.00: £442.50: £211.25) Stalls: High GOING minus 0.78 sec per fur (HD)

Form	Horse	Dist	Pos	SP	RR	SF
1136[3]	**Minetta** (MBell) **2-8-2** MFenton(1) (lw: trckd ldrs: led ins fnl f: jst hld on)	—	1	7/2[1]	66	—
1267[3]	**Winsome George** (CWFairhurst) **2-8-10** NKennedy(5) (lw: bhd: hdwy u.p 2f out: r.o wl towards fin)	s.h	2	9/1	74	6
1174[5]	**Lakeland Pride (IRE)** (PDEvans) **2-8-10** KFallon(10) (lw: chsd ldrs: kpt on fnl f: nrst fin)	1½	3	7/2[1]	70	2
954[5]	**Lochdene (IRE)** (MJohnston) **2-8-10** JWeaver(2) (cl up: led over 2f out tl ins fnl f: no ex)	nk	4	12/1	69	1
	Half A Knicker (RAFahey) **2-8-4** ACulhane(4) (unf: scope: dwlt: wl bhd tl hdwy on outside 2f out: r.o)	½	5	7/1[2]	62+	—
1120[2]	**Quiz Master** (EWeymes) **2-8-7** JQuinn(9) (lw: a chsng ldrs: effrt over 2f out: nt qckn fnl f)	1	6	7/2[1]	62	—
979[7]	**Whacker-Do (IRE)** (RHollinshead) **2-8-4** JCarroll(12) (in tch: effrt over 2f out: no imp)	3	7	20/1	51	—
1251[5]	**Catch The Rainbow** (JGSmyth-Osbourne) **2-8-2** TSprake(6) (in tch: hung lft ½-wy: hung rt over 1f out: styd on one pce)	1	8	8/1[3]	46	—
	Lord of Love (TDEasterby) **2-8-4** DeanMcKeown(14) (leggy: unf: s.s: hdwy ½-wy: n.d)	hd	9	33/1	48	—
1120[5]	**The Cannie Rover** (MWEasterby) **2-8-2**(5)ow3 GParkin(7) (s.i.s: n.d)	¾	10	33/1	49	—
1045[6]	**Russian Romeo (IRE)** (BAMcMahon) **2-8-4** LNewton(3) (outpcd ½-wy: n.d after)	3	11	33/1	38	—

822⁵	**Tindaya** (PDEvans) **2-8-4** RLappin(11) (a bhd) ....½	**12**	33/1	37	—
1126⁷	**Asprilla (IRE)** (BEllison) **2-8-1**(3) PFessey(8) (spd over 3f: wknd qckly) 16	**13**	100/1	—	—
*902*¹¹	**Hey Up Mate (IRE)** (JBerry) **2-8-7** KDarley(13) (led tl hdd & wknd over 2f out) 1½	**14**	20/1	—	—

(SP 130.2%) **14 Rn**

1m 13.8 (2.00) CSF £34.62 TOTE £4.60: £2.00 £1.80 £2.20 (£57.50) Trio £30.80 OWNER Mrs G. Rowland-Clark (NEWMARKET)
1136 Minetta, making her debut on turf and stepping up a furlong in trip, spent much of the race on the bridle but in the end only just lasted home. (7/2)
1267 Winsome George just stays and would have won in another stride, and is obviously going to like it when the longer trips come in. (9/1)
1174 Lakeland Pride (IRE) looked fit this time and ran well, and is improving. (7/2)
954 Lochdene (IRE) again ran well but was inclined to wander about on this fast ground when put under pressure. (12/1: 6/1-14/1)
Half A Knicker did not realise what was required early on and was soon a long way behind. He showed plenty in the latter half of the race and improvement now looks likely. (7/1: op 12/1)
1120 Quiz Master was trying six furlongs for the first time and it should have suited but for some reason he put in a mediocre run. This grand sort is well worth another chance. (7/2)
1251 Catch The Rainbow (8/1: 6/1-9/1)
Lord of Love looked pretty straight but after a very slow start had no chance, and in the circumstances ran quite well. (33/1)

1511 BATTLE HOLM H'CAP (0-70) (3-Y.O+) (Class E)
2-50 (2-51) **6f 206y** £3,038.25 (£921.00: £450.50: £215.25) Stalls: High GOING minus 0.57 sec per fur (F)

			SP	RR	SF
*1048*²	**Shontaine (50)** (MJohnston) **4-8-12** JWeaver(10) (mde all: hld on wl) ....—	**1**	8/1³	62	44
1268⁹	**Stackattack (IRE) (60)** (MrsJRRamsden) **4-9-8** JFortune(15) (trckd ldrs: effrt & swtchd ins over 1f out: styd on towards fin) ....½	**2**	10/1	71	53
1285³	**Rymer's Rascal (57)** (EJAlston) **5-9-5** ACulhane(6) (in tch: hdwy over 1f out: kpt on towards fin) ....¾	**3**	9/1	66	48
1395*	**Allinson's Mate (IRE) (58)** (TDBarron) **9-8-13b**(7) KimberleyHart(14) (lw: mid div: effrt over 2f out: nt clr run & swtchd ins fnl f: r.o towards fin) ....s.h	**4**	7/2¹	67	49
687⁹	**Java Red (IRE) (44)** (JGFitzGerald) **5-8-6** LCharnock(11) (b: lw: a chsng ldrs: effrt over 2f out: nt qckn ins fnl f) 2	**5**	12/1	48	30
1448⁴	**Densben (49)** (DenysSmith) **13-8-11** KFallon(7) (mid div: effrt over 2f out: kpt on same pce) ....s.h	**6**	14/1	53	35
1128¹²	**Cee-Jay-Ay (50)** (JBerry) **10-8-12** KDarley(3) (s.i.s: hdwy u.p 3f out: no imp whn sltly hmpd ins fnl f) 1	**7**	10/1	52	34
1389¹¹	**Pleasure Trick (USA) (40)** (DonEnricoIncisa) **6-8-2** KimTinkler(9) (bhd: hdwy 2f out: styd on towards fin) ....s.h	**8**	40/1	42	24
*371*³	**Myttons Mistake (62)** (ABailey) **4-9-5**(5) GFaulkner(8) (b: chsd ldrs: rdn over 2f out: ev ch over 1f out: sn wknd) ....½	**9**	20/1	63	45
1285⁶	**Euro Sceptic (IRE) (46)** (TDEasterby) **5-8-1b**(7) RWinston(13) (lw: cl up tl rdn & wknd fnl 2f) 3	**10**	6/1²	40	22
*1289*³	**Kid Ory (44)** (DWChapman) **6-8-3**(3) PFessey(1) (cl up tl wknd over 2f out) ....nk	**11**	12/1	37	19
1395⁷	**Birchwood Sun (55)** (MDods) **7-9-3b** TSprake(12) (lw: bhd: hdwy on ins over 2f out: wknd over 1f out: lame).3	**12**	6/1²	41	23
1390¹⁴	**Dona Filipa (34)** (MissLCSiddall) **4-7-10** NCarlisle(2) (lw: a rr div) 1¼	**13**	50/1	17	—
1285⁸	**Rattle (34)** (DANolan) **4-7-10** JQuinn(5) (sn outpcd & bhd) 4	**14**	66/1	8	—
1003⁷	**Northern Judge (49)** (APJames) **4-8-11** MFenton(4) (bhd: drvn along 3f out: n.d) 2	**15**	14/1	18	—

(SP 129.5%) **15 Rn**

1m 26.2 (0.50) CSF £81.54 CT £705.14 TOTE £8.90: £2.80 £4.70 £2.40 (£42.90) Trio £113.90 OWNER Mr Paul Dean (MIDDLEHAM) BRED Mark Johnston Racing Ltd
LONG HANDICAP Dona Filipa 7-9 Rattle 7-8
OFFICIAL EXPLANATION **Birchwood Sun: was found to be lame.**
1048 Shontaine has slipped down the handicap after some in and out performances on turf but he was back to something like his best here and proved most determined when challenged. (8/1)
Stackattack (IRE) ran well here and was keeping on stoutly at the end and seems to be coming to hand. (10/1: 6/1-12/1)
1285 Rymer's Rascal keeps running well but is never quite doing enough but the ability is certainly there if he can be persuaded. (9/1)
1395* Allinson's Mate (IRE) is in tremendous form and with any luck at all would have gone very close. (7/2)
Java Red (IRE) last won a race two seasons ago and showed here he still has ability. (12/1)
1448 Densben has yet to win over further than six furlongs and in the last two seasons has not found a race until the back end. He is running reasonably just now. (14/1)
358 Pleasure Trick (USA) ran well, producing his usual late burst. (40/1)
1285 Euro Sceptic (IRE) looked particularly well again but ran disappointingly. (6/1: op 4/1)
1395 Birchwood Sun was very disappointing and was later found to be lame (6/1)

1512 SORCERIES MAIDEN STKS (3-Y.O+) (Class D)
3-20 (3-24) **7f 214y** £3,566.60 (£1,080.80: £528.40: £252.20) Stalls: High GOING minus 0.57 sec per fur (F)

			SP	RR	SF
	St Blaine (CAN) (DRLoder) **3-8-7** KDarley(2) (lw: trckd ldrs: led over 2f out: r.o wl) ....—	**1**	6/5²	78	31
	Raivue (EWeymes) **3-8-12** JQuinn(3) (in tch: hdwy to chse wnr 2f out: no imp) 3½	**2**	50/1³	76	29
1207⁸	**Sharbadarid (IRE)** (LMCumani) **3-8-12** JWeaver(7) (lw: chsd ldrs: rdn 3f out: wl outpcd fnl 2f) 8	**3**	Evens¹	60	13
	Kwikpoint (MartinTodhunter) **3-8-12** JCarroll(6) (w'like: hdwy ½-wy: styd on: nvr able to chal) 2	**4**	50/1³	56	9
	Sabu (JIACharlton) **5-9-7**(3) PFessey(8) (leggy: dwlt: hdwy 3f out: nrst fin) 1	**5**	100/1	54	19
1230⁸	**Society Times (USA)** (DANolan) **4-9-10** KRutter(10) (unruly gng to s: led & sn clr: hdd & wknd over 2f out) 3½	**6**	50/1³	47	12
	Imperial Line (IRE) (ABMulholland) **3-8-7**(5) GFaulkner(9) (b: chsd ldrs to st: sn lost pl) 8	**7**	50/1³	31	—
	Spare My Blushes (BAMcMahon) **3-8-7** LNewton(1) (neat: bit bkwd: s.i.s: n.d) 1¾	**8**	50/1³	22	—
	General Monty (TDBarron) **5-9-3**(7) VictoriaAppleby(5) (chsd ldrs 5f: sn wknd) 1¾	**9**	100/1	24	—
	Lake Aria (MrsAMNaughton) **4-9-5** NConnorton(4) (leggy: sn outpcd & bhd: t.o) 30	**10**	66/1	—	—

(SP 108.7%) **10 Rn**

1m 38.3 (1.30) CSF £50.18 TOTE £1.90: £1.10 £2.80 £1.10 (£32.00) Trio £5.20 OWNER Mrs Virginia Kraft Payson (NEWMARKET) BRED Virginia Kraft Payson
WEIGHT FOR AGE 3yo-12lb
St Blaine (CAN), a lengthy sort, was very fit and won really well. This should have done her no end of good. (6/5: evens-5/4)
Raivue took a strong hold but showed plenty here only to find the winner too good. The experience should stand him in good stead. (50/1)
Sharbadarid (IRE) looked well enough but ran disappointingly, and was beaten a long way out. Perhaps this ground was too fast. (Evens)
Kwikpoint ran well and should improve, and looks the type for hurdling in due course. (50/1)
Sabu has failed to make the frame in bumpers and looks a bit of a handful but he did show ability here, staying on well at the end. (100/1)
Society Times (USA) went off far too fast and had run himself into the ground approaching the last quarter-mile. (50/1)

1513 SWIFTS H'CAP (0-70) (3-Y.O) (Class E)

3-50 (3-50) **7f 214y** £2,908.25 (£881.00: £430.50: £205.25) Stalls: High GOING minus 0.57 sec per fur (F)

Form	Horse	Dist	Pos	SP	RR	SF
	Coral Island (55) (JGFitzGerald) **3-8-8** KFallon(3) (lw: chsd ldrs: chal over 2f out: outpcd 1f out: styd on to ld post)	—	**1**	7/1	61	6
1256*	**Jack Flush (IRE) (63)** (BSRothwell) **3-9-2** MFenton(5) (b.nr fore: b.off hind: led: qcknd 2f out: jst ct)	s.h	**2**	7/4^{1}	69	14
1256^{13}	**Sparky (57)** (MWEasterby) **3-8-5b**$^{(5)}$ GParkin(6) (outpcd & bhd ½-wy: hdwy over 1f out: styd on u.p towards fin)	nk	**3**	8/1	62	7
1256^{9}	**Rude Awakening (68)** (CWFairhurst) **3-9-7** DeanMcKeown(7) (hld up: effrt 2f out: rdn & no rspnse)	1	**4**	13/2^{3}	71	16
1496^{13}	**Euroquest (43)** (DNicholls) **3-7-10** JQuinn(2) (lw: prom tl wknd fnl 2f)	6	**5**	16/1	34	—
1249^{4}	**Weet And See (62)** (RHollinshead) **3-8-12**$^{(3)}$ DGriffiths(4) (prom tl wknd over 2f out)	s.h	**6**	9/2^{2}	53	—
1229^{2}	**Mirror Four Sport (45)** (MJohnston) **3-7-5**$^{(7)}$ MeeiCheah(1) (stdd s: racd wd & sn cl up: wknd over 2f out)	2	**7**	9/2^{2}	32	—

(SP 115.6%) **7 Rn**

1m 41.0 (4.00) CSF £18.36 TOTE £6.40: £3.70 £1.60 (£17.80) OWNER Mr Stephen Curtis (MALTON) BRED W. H. F. Carson

Coral Island had to really battle to win this and gave the impression that he should stay further yet. (7/1: op 9/2)
1256* Jack Flush (IRE), racing on much faster ground this time, put up a brave show but this stiff finish just found him out. (7/4)
Sparky had the blinkers back on and was really galvanised into action in the last two furlongs, in the end finishing best of all. He does not look one to fully rely on. (8/1)
1096 Rude Awakening goes well on the bridle but his response off it is most disappointing and he would seem to have a problem. (13/2)
287* Euroquest looked none too keen in the blinkers the previous evening and was disappointing without them here. (16/1)
1249 Weet And See looked warm and edgy beforehand and ran no sort of race. (9/2)

1514 DENTON HOLM LIMITED STKS (0-55) (3-Y.O+) (Class F)

4-20 (4-21) **5f** £2,710.00 (£760.00: £370.00) Stalls: High GOING minus 0.78 sec per fur (HD)

Form	Horse	Dist	Pos	SP	RR	SF
1096^{13}	**Mungo Park (55)** (MrsJRRamsden) **3-8-9** JFortune(13) (hld up: hdwy 2f out: led ins fnl f: r.o)	—	**1**	9/1	57	32
1250^{11}	**Barranak (IRE) (50)** (GMMcCourt) **5-9-3** JWeaver(8) (led tl hdd ins fnl f: kpt on)	1¼	**2**	5/1^{2}	53	36
1098^{10}	**Ned's Bonanza (52)** (MDods) **8-9-3** SWhitworth(4) (lw: hld up: effrt over 1f out: styd on towards fin)	s.h	**3**	6/1^{3}	53	36
856^{2}	**Featherstone Lane (40)** (MissLCSiddall) **6-9-3** DeanMcKeown(7) (hdwy 2f out: styd on u.p: nrst fin)	hd	**4**	6/1^{3}	53	36
1223^{5}	**Dominelle (53)** (TDEasterby) **5-9-0** JCarroll(6) (w ldr tl rdn & btn appr fnl f)	nk	**5**	3/1^{1}	49	32
949^{5}	**Rennyholme (46)** (ABMulholland) **6-8-12**$^{(5)}$ GFaulkner(2) (chsd ldrs tl rdn & btn 1f out)	½	**6**	12/1	50	33
1402^{9}	**Sing With the Band (50)** (BAMcMahon) **6-9-0** LNewton(3) (chsd ldrs: outpcd 2f out: kpt on fnl f)	nk	**7**	12/1	46	29
1080^{9}	**Lunar Music (52)** (RonaldThompson) **3-8-6** NConnorton(10) (chsd ldrs tl wknd over 1f out)	2	**8**	20/1	40	15
1250^{14}	**Here Comes a Star (50)** (JMCarr) **9-9-3** ACulhane(12) (lw: bhd & hmpd after 1f: hdwy 2f out: n.d)	1¼	**9**	6/1^{3}	39	22
1048^{14}	**La Volta (55)** (JGFitzGerald) **4-9-0** KFallon(5) (a rr div)	1	**10**	14/1	32	15
1127^{7}	**Assignment (29)** (MrsLStubbs) **11-9-3** TSprake(1) (outpcd & lost tch fr ½-wy)	2	**11**	66/1	29	12
423^{6}	**Soaked (55)** (DWChapman) **4-9-0**$^{(3)}$ PFessey(9) (s.s: a bhd)	½	**12**	25/1	27	10
1332^{8}	**Ohnonotagain (30)** (LRLloyd-James) **5-9-0v^{1}** LCharnock(11) (spd 3f: wknd)	1½	**13**	50/1	20	3

(SP 128.6%) **13 Rn**

60.0 secs (-0.20) CSF £51.17 TOTE £7.20: £2.50 £3.00 £2.50 (£71.20) Trio £129.70 OWNER Mrs H. M. Carr (THIRSK) BRED Hyde Park Racing

WEIGHT FOR AGE 3yo-8lb

448 Mungo Park, back to sprinting, did the business well and this should have boosted his confidence. (9/1)
1003 Barranak (IRE) put up his best effort of the season here. (5/1)
Ned's Bonanza finished well and looks to be coming to hand. (6/1: op 7/2)
856 Featherstone Lane is a frustrating character who has more ability than he really cares to show. (6/1)
1223 Dominelle was very edgy beforehand but still ran well until finding it all too much in the last furlong. (3/1)
949 Rennyholme had plenty on here and this was not a bad effort in the circumstances. (12/1)
Here Comes a Star (6/1: op 4/1)

1515 WILLY HOLM H'CAP (0-70) (4-Y.O+) (Class E)

4-50 (4-50) **1m 6f 32y** £2,843.25 (£861.00: £420.50: £200.25) Stalls: Centre GOING minus 0.57 sec per fur (F)

Form	Horse	Dist	Pos	SP	RR	SF
1222^{6}	**Durgams First (IRE) (42)** (MrsMReveley) **5-8-12** ACulhane(4) (hld up: hdwy on bit 3f out: led & qcknd ins fnl f: r.o wl)	—	**1**	5/1^{2}	53	—
1281*	**The Butterwick Kid (57)** (RAFahey) **4-9-6**$^{(7)}$ 5x RWinston(2) (lw: hld up: hdwy on bit 3f out: shkn up ent fnl f: r.o: nt pce of wnr)	2	**2**	8/11^{1}	66	4
1156^{3}	**In the Money (IRE) (54)** (RHollinshead) **8-9-7**$^{(3)}$ DGriffiths(1) (trckd ldr: led over 3f out tl jst ins fnl f: sn outpcd)	6	**3**	5/1^{2}	56	—
1494^{3}	**Anchorena (47)** (DWBarker) **5-9-3** KDarley(3) (lw: led tl hdd over 3f out: sn wknd)	2½	**4**	11/2^{3}	46	—

(SP 106.6%) **4 Rn**

3m 12.8 (11.80) CSF £8.31 TOTE £6.20 (£2.10) OWNER The Mary Reveley Racing Club (SALTBURN) BRED William McGladdery in Ireland

1222 Durgams First (IRE) appreciated this trip and, in a tactical event, he produced the best turn of foot. (5/1)
1281* The Butterwick Kid spent much of the race swinging off the bridle, but once the winner got first run on him he had no answer. He is best suited by a stronger pace. (8/11)
1156 In the Money (IRE) failed to impress with a moderate action going to post and, once off the bridle early in the straight, soon gave up. (5/1: op 3/1)
1494 Anchorena, who ran the previous evening, looked very slow here. (11/2)

T/Jkpt: £30,862.50 (2.47 Tckts). T/Plpt: £375.90 (46 Tckts). T/Qdpt: £72.10 (8.25 Tckts) AA

1516a - 1530a : (Irish Racing) - See Computer Raceform

1057a-CURRAGH (Newbridge, Ireland) (R-H) (Good to yielding)
Saturday May 24th

1531a ORAL B. MARBLE HILL STKS (Listed) (2-Y.O)
2-50 (2-54) **5f** IR £12,900.00 (IR £3,700.00: IR £1,700.00: IR £500.00) GOING: 0.14 sec per fur (G)

				SP	RR	SF
1143[3]	**Golden Mirage (IRE)** (MRChannon) **2-8-11** MJKinane (trckd ldrs: chal over 1½f out: rdn to ld over 100y fr fin: kpt on wl)	—	**1**	10/1	96	36
	Hopping Higgins (IRE) (APO'Brien,Ireland) **2-8-11** PVGilson (led & disp ld: hdd over 100y fr fin: kpt on)	½	**2**	7/1	94	34
	Dixie Dynamo (USA) (CCollins,Ireland) **2-9-0** PShanahan (prom: 3rd ½-wy: ev ch 1½f out: rdn & no ex ins last: kpt on)	1	**3**	8/1	94	34
	Marigot Bay (IRE) (APO'Brien,Ireland) **2-8-6** WJSupple (chsd ldrs: 5th ½-wy: nt trble ldrs over 1f out: kpt on ins last)	1½	**4**	14/1	81	21
	Magical Baba (IRE) (PatrickPrendergast,Ireland) **2-9-0** TEDurcan (towards rr: rdn & hdwy ½-wy: kpt on last 2f: nt rch ldrs)	1	**5**	11/1	86	26
	Flame Violet (IRE) (APO'Brien,Ireland) **2-8-11** JAHeffernan (cl up: 4th ½-wy: rdn & ev ch over 1f out: no ex ins last)	hd	**6**	6/1[3]	83	23
	Harbour Master (FR) (APO'Brien,Ireland) **2-9-0** CRoche (outpcd early: 7th & rdn ½-wy: nt trble ldrs)	1	**7**	9/4[1]	83	23
	Law Library (IRE) (JMRyan,Ireland) **2-8-9** SCraine (prom: 2nd ½-wy: rdn & wknd fr 1½f out)	3½	**8**	4/1[2]	67	7
	Fiddler's Rock (IRE) (GMLyons,Ireland) **2-9-0** PJSmullen (dwlt: in tch on outside: rdn & no imp 1½f out)	4	**9**	10/1	59	—
	Apache Red (IRE) (JSBolger,Ireland) **2-8-9b[1]** KJManning (chsd ldrs: 6th ½-wy: rdn & no imp over 1½f out)	¾	**10**	12/1	51	—
				(SP 129.5%)	**10 Rn**	

62.2 secs (4.20) OWNER Stephen Crown (UPPER LAMBOURN) BRED Gainsborough Stud Management Ltd

1143 Golden Mirage (IRE), with little apparent fancy for her, really put one over the six previous winners here. Once she got the split when switched to challenge over one furlong out, she was always in command. Maybe it was her experience that told, but she was well in command throughout the last half furlong. (10/1)

Hopping Higgins (IRE) made the running until headed by the winner, and it was an uneven tussle inside the last. (7/1)

Dixie Dynamo (USA) had his chance but just could not quicken inside the last. (8/1)

Marigot Bay (IRE), still a maiden after three attempts, but this was her best effort so far. (14/1)

Magical Baba (IRE) stayed on from behind without ever threatening. (11/1: op 7/1)

Flame Violet (IRE), possibly best backed of the O'Brien quartet, ran fast for three furlongs but could make no impression once the pressure was turned on. (6/1: op 10/1)

Harbour Master (FR), an uneasy favourite, never went the pace, although he was keeping on at the end. (9/4: op 6/4)

Apache Red (IRE) (12/1: op 8/1)

1532a WEATHERBYS IRELAND GREENLANDS STKS (Gp 3) (3-Y.O+)
3-20 (3-24) **6f** IR £19,500.00 (IR £5,700.00: IR £2,700.00: IR £900.00) GOING: 0.14 sec per fur (G)

				SP	RR	SF
1198a*	**Burden Of Proof (IRE)** (CO'Brien,Ireland) **5-9-4** JPMurtagh (trckd ldrs: closing 3rd ½-wy: disp ld over 1½f out: led 1f out: r.o.)	—	**1**	5/2[1]	118	48
	Catch The Blues (IRE) (APO'Brien,Ireland) **5-9-1b** CRoche (prom: rn 2nd: disp ld ½-wy: sn led: hdd 1f out: rdn & no ex: r.o.)	½	**2**	5/1[2]	114	44
	Lucayan Prince (USA) (DRLoder) **4-9-8b** OPeslier (hld up: 3rd & trckd ldrs over 1½f out: swtchd & effrt: nt rch ldrs early ins last: rdn & r.o.)	1	**3**	5/2[1]	118	48
	Symboli Kildare (IRE) (JOxx,Ireland) **4-9-4** PJSmullen (towards rr: 5th & no imp 1½f out: kpt on)	6	**4**	12/1	98	28
	Ger's Royale (IRE) (PJFlynn,Ireland) **6-9-4** JReid (led: jnd ½-wy: hdd over 1f out: 4th & btn 1½f out)	1	**5**	5/1[2]	95	25
	Air Of Distinction (IRE) (APO'Brien,Ireland) **3-8-10** JAHeffernan (chsd ldrs: rn 4th early: rdn & btn over 2f out)	4½	**6**	10/1[3]	84	5
1171[8]	***Wildwood Flower*** (RHannon) **4-9-1** MJKinane (w/drawn)		**W**	12/1	—	—
				(SP 115.0%)	**6 Rn**	

1m 15.2 (4.70) OWNER M. V. O'Brien BRED Lyonstown Stud in Ireland

1198a* Burden Of Proof (IRE) certainly seems a reformed character and was always calling the shots over the runner-up, despite not gaining the advantage until the last furlong. He has plenty of options open to him, the Cork And Orrery possibly the most attractive. (5/2)

Catch The Blues (IRE), in front from two furlongs out, possible just needed this run. She looks set for a good season. (5/1)

Lucayan Prince (USA), held up, was given every chance over one furlong out, but found precious little under pressure inside the last. (5/2: op 6/4)

Symboli Kildare (IRE) led until outpaced from two furlongs out, and has yet to prove he is anything more than a handicapper (12/1: op 8/1)

1533a AIRLIE/COOLMORE IRISH 1,000 GUINEAS (Gp 1) (3-Y.O F)
3-55 (3-56) **1m** IR £84,250.00 (IR £28,750.00: IR £13,750.00: IR £4,750.00) GOING: 0.14 sec per fur (G)

				SP	RR	SF
806a*	**Classic Park** (APO'Brien,Ireland) **3-9-0** SCraine (hld up towards rr: cld on ins over 2f out: trckd ldr: chal 1½f out: led 1f out: rdn clr: r.o.)	—	**1**	20/1	114	35
1193a*	**Strawberry Roan (IRE)** (APO'Brien,Ireland) **3-9-0** CRoche (hld up: trckd ldrs whn nt clr run fr over 2f out: 6th & swtchd to outside over 1f out: r.o wl fnl f)	1	**2**	4/1[2]	112	33
809a[3]	**Caiseal Ros (IRE)** (JSBolger,Ireland) **3-9-0** KJManning (cl up: 3rd ½-wy: rdn & ev ch over 2f out: nt qckn over 1f out: kpt on wl ins last)	2½	**3**	20/1	107	28
	Ryafan (USA) (JHMGosden) **3-9-0** LDettori (hld up in tch: rdn & chsd ldrs ½-wy: 4th u.p 2f out: edgd rt over 1f out: kpt on)	s.h	**4**	3/1[1]	107	28
960[2]	**Oh Nellie (USA)** (NACallaghan) **3-9-0** MJKinane (sn led to 1f out: no ex: wknd last 100y)	¾	**5**	9/2[3]	105	26
1203a[2]	**Seebe (USA)** (IABalding) **3-9-0** CAsmussen (cl up: rn 2nd: ev ch over 2f out: rdn & no ex u.p over 1f out: wknd ins last)	¾	**6**	9/2[3]	104	25
806a[3]	**Almost Skint (IRE)** (MissITOakes,Ireland) **3-9-0** NGMcCullagh (towards rr: rdn 3f out: kpt on: never nrr)	2½	**7**	100/1	99	20
	Via Verbano (IRE) (JSBolger,Ireland) **3-9-0** CEverard (towards rr: rdn & kpt on last 2f: never nrr)	s.h	**8**	40/1	99	20
960[3]	**Dazzle** (MRStoute) **3-9-0** JReid (plld hrd: hld up: 6th & chsd ldrs 3f out: sn btn)	4½	**9**	5/1	90	11
	Royale (IRE) (APO'Brien,Ireland) **3-9-0** JAHeffernan (in tch early: rdn & lost pl ½-wy: dropped bhd fr 3f out: t.o)	dist	**10**	50/1	—	—
				(SP 112.9%)	**10 Rn**	

1m 42.2 (7.20) OWNER Mrs Seamus Burns (PILTOWN)

806a* Classic Park showed a serious turn of foot to quicken clear inside the last. She seemed to relish this trip and now goes for the Coronation Stakes. She went up 11lb for this to 114. (20/1)
1193a* Strawberry Roan (IRE) was desperately unlucky. She met all the trouble going, was hit across the face, inadvertently by Dettori, but still rallied with tremendous effect. She should have won this by a couple of lengths and with no stamina doubts, has to rate a serious Epsom Oaks prospect. She goes up 11lb to 112. (4/1)
809a Caiseal Ros (IRE) just failed to quicken but stayed on well inside the final furlong. She looks an Irish Oaks candidate. (20/1)
Ryafan (USA) was under strong pressure two and a half furlongs out but kept rallying despite edging right a furlong and a half out. (3/1: op 2/1)
960 Oh Nellie (USA) held the lead until headed one furlong out. (9/2: op 3/1)
1203a Seebe (USA) looked a real possibility two furlongs out but seemed not to get the trip. (9/2: op 3/1)
806a Almost Skint (IRE) ran above her ordinary form. (100/1)
Via Verbano (IRE) was another showing similar improvement. (40/1)
960 Dazzle took a strong hold and was done with fully three furlongs from home. (5/1: op 3/1)

1534a - 1537a & 1539a : (Irish Racing) - See Computer Raceform

1530a-CURRAGH (Newbridge, Ireland) (R-H) (Good to yielding)
Sunday May 25th

1538a GLENGARRIF E.B.F. MAIDEN (2-Y.O)
2-35 (2-37) **6f** IR £4,795.00 (IR £1,085.00: IR £455.00: IR £245.00) GOING minus 0.14 sec per fur (G)

Horse	Dist	Pos	SP	RR	SF
King Of Kings (IRE) (APO'Brien,Ireland) **2-9-0** CRoche (led briefly early: plld hrd: w.w: close 3rd ½-wy: led 2f out: qcknd clr ins last: v.easily)	—	**1**	2/7[1]	102++	32
Jimmy The Greek (IRE) (PatrickPrendergast,Ireland) **2-8-10**(4) TEDurcan (5th & chsd ldrs ½-wy: cld over 2f out: 2nd over 1f out: kpt on: no ch with wnr)	8	**2**	12/1	81	11
Hillside Rose (IRE) (CO'Brien,Ireland) **2-8-11** JPMurtagh (wnt mod 6th over 2f out: 5th & nt trble ldrs over 1f out: kpt on)	2	**3**	10/1[3]	72	2
Bismarck (IRE) (DKWeld,Ireland) **2-9-0** MJKinane (towards rr: rdn over 2f out: kpt on last 1½f: never nrr)	2½	**4**	20/1	69	—
Crown Point (DGillespie,Ireland) **2-8-11** RKRagbirsingh (towards rr: kpt on last 2f: never nrr)	s.h	**5**	20/1	66	—
Yulara (IRE) (GMLyons,Ireland) **2-8-11** PJSmullen (sn disp ld tl appr ½-wy: 4th u.p 2f out: sn btn)	4	**6**	20/1	55	—
Prince Minata (IRE) (JSBolger,Ireland) **2-9-0** KJManning (prom: 2nd ½-wy: led briefly over 2f out: 2nd & rdn 1½f out: no ex: wknd ins last)	s.h	**7**	8/1[2]	58	—
Antrim Coast (CCollins,Ireland) **2-9-0** PShanahan (dwlt: sn prom: led briefly ½-wy: 3rd & rdn 2f out: wknd over 1f out)	6	**8**	10/1[3]	42	—
Prilora (IRE) (MissITOakes,Ireland) **2-8-11** NGMcCullagh (in tch early: towards rr & n.d ½-wy)	2½	**9**	33/1	32	—

(SP 132.0%) **9 Rn**

1m 14.4 (3.90) OWNER Mrs John Magnier (PILTOWN)
King Of Kings (IRE), a half-brother to General Monash, has been the subject of hype for some weeks. He justified every word and, rocketing out of the stalls going right and then left, raced with the leaders until Roche let him go. He quickened clear inside the last and is good value for more than the winning distance. He looks a superb prospect and will really come into his own in the autumn. One gets the impression that Royal Ascot is not high on the list of priorities. (2/7)
Jimmy The Greek (IRE), despite finding himself totally outclassed, showed ability. (12/1)
Prince Minata (IRE) (8/1: op 5/1)
Antrim Coast (10/1: op 5/1)

1540a CONRAD INTERNATIONAL DUBLIN SILVER STKS (Listed) (3-Y.O)
3-35 (3-37) **1m 2f** IR £12,900.00 (IR £3,700.00: IR £1,700.00: IR £500.00) GOING minus 0.14 sec per fur (G)

	Horse	Dist	Pos	SP	RR	SF
	Dr Johnson (USA) (CO'Brien,Ireland) **3-8-11** JPMurtagh (rn 2nd: cld 2nd fr½-wy: led 3f out: rdn & kpt on wl)	—	**1**	4/1[2]	100	69
	Sublime Beauty (USA) (JSBolger,Ireland) **3-8-9**ow1 KJManning (hld up towards rr: cld 4f out: chal on outside early st: 2nd & edgd rt 2f out: chal u.p: nt rch wnr: kpt on)	2	**2**	10/1	95	63
806a[5]	**Token Gesture (IRE)** (DKWeld,Ireland) **3-8-13** MJKinane (hel dup: 3rd fr½-wy: rdn & chsd ledrs over 2f out: edgd lft: nt rch ledrs u.p 1f out: kpt on)	1½	**3**	9/2[3]	96	65
806a[4]	**Shell Ginger (IRE)** (APO'Brien,Ireland) **3-8-13** CRoche (rn 3rd: 4th & pushed along 4f out: rdn st: btn 2f out: wknd: eased: lame)	14	**4**	5/4[1]	74d	43
	Chauncy Lane (IRE) (MJPO'Brien,Ireland) **3-8-8** PatEddery (led: jnd bef st: hdd 3f out: no ex: 4th & btn 2f out)	½	**5**	5/1	68	37

(SP 108.4%) **5 Rn**

2m 5.9 (1.90) OWNER M. V. O'Brien
Dr Johnson (USA) continued his rate of improvement, backing up his Leopardstown maiden win with an impressive success here. He had to be set alight over two furlongs out, but quickly learned what it was all about and was in total command over the last furlong and a half. He would have some sort of chance in the Irish Derby and could prove very useful as he develops. He goes up 15lb to 105. (4/1)
Sublime Beauty (USA) chased the winner from over two furlongs out, but was never getting on terms. (10/1: op 6/1)
806a Token Gesture (IRE) found herself outpaced but stayed on inside the last. (9/2: op 3/1)
806a Shell Ginger (IRE), unable to dominate as usual, was never travelling and dropped right away in the straight. She was subsequently discovered to be lame on her off-fore. (5/4)

1541a LEXUS IRISH 2,000 GUINEAS (Gp 1) (3-Y.O C & F)
4-10 (4-12) **1m** IR £112,700.00 (IR £38,700.00: IR £18,700.00: IR £6,700.00) GOING minus 0.14 sec per fur (G)

	Horse	Dist	Pos	SP	RR	SF
1060a*	**Desert King (IRE)** (APO'Brien,Ireland) **3-9-0** CRoche (hld up: trckd ldrs ½-wy: cld 3f out: led under 2f out: rdn clr: edgd rt: r.o wl)	—	**1**	3/1[2]	124	52
1060a[4]	**Verglas (IRE)** (KPrendergast,Ireland) **3-9-0** WJSupple (hld up towards rr: hdwy 3f out: 2nd & chsd wnr 1f out: r.o: nt trble wnr)	3	**2**	33/1	118	46
829*	**Romanov (IRE)** (PWChapple-Hyam) **3-9-0** RHughes (hld up in tch: hdwy ½-wy: disp ld & ev ch 2f out: sn hdd: rdn & no ex wl over 1f out: kpt on)	2	**3**	11/1	114	42

1204a4	**Yalaietanee** (MRStoute) **3-9-0** MJKinane (hld up towards rr: hdwy 3f out: 6th 2f out: 4th u.p 1f out: kpt on: nt trble ldrs)	2	**4**	8/1	110	38
1204a5	**Fantastic Fellow (USA)** (CEBrittain) **3-9-0** BDoyle (towards rr: hdwy to 7th & chsd ldrs 2f out: kpt on: nrst fin)	2½	**5**	33/1	105	33
940²	**Revoque (IRE)** (PWChapple-Hyam) **3-9-0** JReid (hld up in tch: closing 3rd 3f out: sn disp ld: ev ch 2f out: btn 1½f out)	¾	**6**	11/10 1	104	32
1195a7	**Mosconi (IRE)** (JSBolger,Ireland) **3-9-0** KJManning (towards rr: sme hdwy on ins over 3f out: 7th & nt trble ledrs 1½f out: kpt on)	¾	**7**	50/1	102	30
	Bob The Broker (IRE) (PJFlynn,Ireland) **3-9-0** PVGilson (towards rr ½-wy: sme hdwy 3f out: 8th 1½f out: kpt on: no imp)	3	**8**	200/1	96	24
973*	**Peartree House (IRE)** (WRMuir) **3-9-0** DO'Neill (chsd ldrs: 4th & rdn over 3f out: wknd: n.d over 2f out)	3	**9**	50/1	90	18
940[16]	**Musical Pursuit** (MHTompkins) **3-9-0** PatEddery (sn 2nd: rdn & chsd ldr ½-wy: 4th u.p 2f out: sn wknd)	1	**10**	20/1	88	16
741*	**Royal Amaretto (IRE)** (BJMeehan) **3-9-0** OPeslier (in tch: 5th & chsd ldrs 3f out: sn wknd & n.d)	2	**11**	7/1 3	84	12
1060a6	**Sharemono (USA)** (APO'Brien,Ireland) **3-9-0** JAHeffernan (rdn clr after 1f: hdd under 3f out: wknd qckly: dropped bhd)	12	**12**	100/1	60	—

(SP 120.6%) **12 Rn**

1m 38.3 (3.30) OWNER Mr M. Tabor (PILTOWN)

1060a* Desert King (IRE), without a tongue strap, was always travelling well within himself. Roche made his move towards the outer over two furlongs out, led well over a furlong and a half out and, under the riders usual vigorous bustling, went clear. This was impressive and on the evidence we have seen, a mile and a half would not be out of the question. He has been upped 4lb to 123. (3/1)

1060a Verglas (IRE) ran his best race of the season and is certainly going the right way. He chased the winner over a furlong and a half out, without ever getting on challenging terms. (33/1)

829* Romanov (IRE) held a nice position on the inside throughout, and flattered briefly two and a half furlongs down, but the effort was not sustained. He kept on well enough, but found the task beyond him. The vet reported a case of nasal discharge after the race. (11/1: op 7/1)

1204a Yalaietanee, once finding room on the inside, plugged on in fourth place over the last furlong and a half without ever threatening. (8/1)

1204a Fantastic Fellow (USA) travelled well enough but was only staying on at the one pace over the last two furlongs. (33/1)

940 Revoque (IRE) had his chances on the outside with two furlongs to race, but was soon showing distress signals. (11/10)

1195a Mosconi (IRE), under pressure well over a furlong out, just ran on at the one pace. (50/1)

Bob The Broker (IRE), behind after a slow break, stayed on late in the day. (200/1)

973* Peartree House (IRE) was prominent until after halfway before fading. (50/1)

Musical Pursuit, in second place over two furlongs out, dropped away pretty tamely. (20/1)

741* Royal Amaretto (IRE) was a slow starter and had some early traffic problems. He was beaten well over two and a half furlongs out. (7/1)

1060a Sharemono (USA) set off like a scolded cat. He was soon clear until headed, and dropped away quickly two and a half furlongs out. (100/1)

1542a TATTERSALLS GOLD CUP (Gp 2) (4-Y.O+)

4-45 (4-45) **1m 2f** IR £48,750.00 (IR £14,250.00: IR £6,750.00: IR £2,250.00) GOING minus 0.14 sec per fur (G)

				SP	RR	SF
1058a*	**Dance Design (IRE)** (DKWeld,Ireland) **4-9-1** MJKinane (mde all: shaken up 2f out: r.o.)	—	**1**	5/2 2	122	75
	Oscar Schindler (IRE) (KPrendergast,Ireland) **5-9-4** SCraine (hld up: 5th ½-wy: cld bef st: chal 2f out: sn chsng ldr: rdn & nt rch wnr over 1f out: kpt on)	3	**2**	8/1 3	120	73
	Taipan (IRE) (JLDunlop) **5-8-12** JReid (hld up: wnt 3rd ½-wy: 2nd & effrt over 2f out: 3rd & no ex 1½f out: kpt on same pce)	3	**3**	9/1	109	62
1210⁷	**Acharne** (CEBrittain) **4-8-12** BDoyle (sn chsng ldr: rdn & chsd wnr 3f out: 4th & btn 2f out)	1	**4**	20/1	108	61
	Damancher (PMullins,Ireland) **5-8-12** CRoche (hld up towards rr: 5th & chsd ldrs early st: no imp 1½f out: kpt on)	2½	**5**	33/1	104	57
1058a4	**Free To Speak (IRE)** (DKWeld,Ireland) **5-8-12** PShanahan (rn 2nd early: 4th ½-wy: 5th & rdn st: sn no imp)	8	**6**	40/1	91	44
522*	**Dr Massini (IRE)** (MRStoute) **4-8-12** PEddery (ref to race)		**R**	4/7 1	—	—

(SP 123.5%) **7 Rn**

2m 5.6 (1.60) OWNER Moyglare Stud Farm (CURRAGH)

1058a* Dance Design (IRE) soon in front, made all the running and repelled her challengers with some ease. She is going to have good season with either Coronation Cup at Epsom or the Prince Of Wales's Stakes at Royal Ascot as her next target. (5/2)

Oscar Schindler (IRE) looked to be travelling well on the outside, in fourth place turning into the straight, but this trip is too short. He went second over one furlong out but just could not quicken. He seems as good as ever. (8/1: op 5/1)

Taipan (IRE), a flattering third into the straight, was just one paced from a furlong and a half out. (9/1: op 6/1)

830 Acharne ran in second and was still travelling nicely on the last bend, but once asked for his effort, he quickly cried enough. (20/1)

522* Dr Massini (IRE), a rather surprising odds-on favourite, just refused to have anything to do with racing once the stalls opened. He literally walked out and refused to budge, until the rest of the field had gone over a furlong. (4/7)

1543a (Irish Racing) - See Computer Raceform

1072a-COLOGNE (Germany) (R-H) (Soft)
Monday May 19th

1544a MEHL-MULHENS-RENNEN (Gp 2) (3-Y.O)

3-40 (3-45) **1m** £71,970.00 (£29,167.00: £14,394.00: £7,576.00)

				SP	RR	SF
917a*	**Air Express (IRE)** (CEBrittain) **3-9-2** BDoyle (a.p: disp ld 2½f out: led 2f out: r.o wl)	—	**1**		114	—
	Is Tirol (IRE) (MHofer,Germany) **3-9-2** ASuborics (mid div: gd hdwy 1½f out: nt rch wnr)	1¼	**2**		112	—
820a3	**Fine Fellow (IRE)** (MmeCHead,France) **3-9-2** FHead (in rr: styd on wl fnl 2f: nvr nrr)	1¾	**3**		108	—
817a3	**Icemoon (GER)** (HBlume,Germany) **3-9-2** THellier (mid div: kpt on wl cl home)	1¾	**4**		105	—
817a*	**Eden Rock (GER)** (BSchutz,Germany) **3-9-2** AStarke (a.p: ev ch 2f out: no imp)	nk	**5**		104	—
817a2	**Happy Change (GER)** (AWohler,Germany) **3-9-2** RCochrane (mid div: styd on fnl 2f)	¾	**6**		102	—
	Fan (GER) (AWohler,Germany) **3-9-2** WRyan (a mid div)	½	**7**		101	—
	Orsuno (GER) (HJentzsch,Germany) **3-9-2** SEccles (set pce: hdd 2½f out: sn wknd)	2½	**8**		96	—
	Abou Lahab (MHofer,Germany) **3-9-2** KWoodburn (a in rr)	hd	**9**		96	—
	Mr Finch (USA) (BSchutz,Germany) **3-9-2** GBocskai (a bhd)	s.h	**10**		96	—
679⁵	**Groom's Gordon (FR)** (JLDunlop) **3-9-2** KDarley (prom: disp ld 2½f out: wknd qckly)	¾	**11**		95	—
	Vision Of Spirit (USA) (HJentzsch,Germany) **3-9-2** LHammer-Hansen (mid div: sn btn)	2	**12**		91	—

				SP	RR	SF
	Tarictic (GER) (TTheilkuhl,Germany) **3-9-2** WNewnes (cl up: wknd rapidly 2f out)	1	**13**		89	—
						13 Rn

1m 36.75 (6.75) TOTE 65DM: 24DM 30DM 23DM OWNER Mr Mohamed Obaida (NEWMARKET) BRED Gainsborough Stud Management Ltd
917a* Air Express (IRE) completed a Guineas double following his win in the Premio Parioli. Always prominent, he hit the front two furlongs out and ran on well to win comfortably. He will almost certainly head for Royal Ascot with the St James's Palace Stakes his target.
679 Groom's Gordon (FR) looked to be going well when disputing the lead with the eventual winner, two and a half furlongs from home. However, when the button was pushed there was little response and he weakened quickly from nearly two furlongs out.

MUNICH (Germany) (L-H) (Good)
Monday May 19th

1545a GROSSER MULLER BROT-PREIS (Gp 2) (3-Y.O)
3-25 (3-28) **1m 3f** £53,030.00 (£11,364.00: £5,682.00: £3,788.00)

				SP	RR	SF
920a[3]	**Ajano (GER)** (HJGroschel,Germany) **3-9-2** ATylicki (a.p: chal 2f out: hmpd ins fnl f: fin 2nd, 1l: plcd 1st)	—	**1**		101	—
	Caitano (BSchutz,Germany) **3-9-2** NGrant (prom: led 2½f out: hung rt ins fnl f: rdn out: fin 1st: disq & plcd 2nd)	1	**2**		102	—
	Damus (GER) (AWohler,Germany) **3-9-2** ABoschert (hld up: styd on wl fnl 2f)	3½	**3**		97	—
	Asolo (GER) (BSchutz,Germany) **3-9-2** DBoeuf (prom: rdn 4f out: kpt on u.p fnl 3f)	½	**4**		96	—
	Augustus Rex (IRE) (HBlume,Germany) **3-9-2** TMundry (mid div: sn rdn & one pce)	3	**5**		92	—
	Irish Fighter (IRE) (HJentzsch,Germany) **3-9-2** PSchiergen (hld up in rr: slt hdwy)	¾	**6**		91	—
	Lakota Dance (GER) (RSuerland,Germany) **3-9-2** AHelfenbein (nvr nrr)	8	**7**		79	—
	Etmal (BSchutz,Germany) **3-9-2b[1]** OPeslier (set gd pce: wknd qckly 2½f out)	3½	**8**		74	—
						8 Rn

2m 23.4 TOTE 103DM: 19DM 14DM 14DM OWNER Dr R. Rudolph BRED Gestut Schlenderhan
Ajano (GER) always held a prominent position and, after a decent challenge two furlongs from home, he was hampered inside the last and was not given a hard time of it once his chance had gone. He won the race in the Stewards' room.

1363a-SAINT-CLOUD (France) (L-H) (Holding)
Wednesday May 21st

1546a PRIX BASILEUS (3-Y.O C & G)
3-25 (3-23) **1m 2f 110y** £7,856.00

				SP	RR	SF
	Gonzaga (IRE) (JLDunlop) **3-8-12** MBoutin	—	**1**		79?	—
	Legat de France (FR) (France) **3-8-12** ODoleuze	1	**2**		78	—
	Hung Jury (France) **3-8-12** GMosse	1	**3**		76	—
						12 Rn

2m 28.2 (18.20) P-M 26.50F: 6.80F 3.10F 2.70F (93.40F) OWNER Sultan Al Kabeer (ARUNDEL) BRED Prince Sultan Al Kabeer
Gonzaga (IRE), a lightly-raced two-year-old last term, made a winning seasonal debut. He got this extra distance well and improvement seems likely.

1547a PRIX DE SAINT-CHERON APPRENTICE (4-Y.O+)
3-55 (3-55) **1m 2f 110y** £6,173.00

				SP	RR	SF
	Eudoxe (IRE) (BSecly,France) **4-8-4**(7) MSautjeau	—	**1**		96	—
	Kapatchi (FR) (France) **6-8-8**(6) NPerret	nk	**2**		99	—
	Lapon (USA) (France) **6-8-4**(7) SJesus	5	**3**		88	—
1142[3]	**Cedez le Passage (FR)** (KOCunningham-Brown) **6-8-8**(6) JWindrif (btn approx 16¼l)		**8**		—	—
						19 Rn

2m 23.1 (13.10) P-M 5.90F: 1.80F 1.40F 2.50F (9.70F) OWNER Mr L. Gautier BRED Ecurie Takeflash
1142 Cedez le Passage (FR) is a highly-tried individual both in Britain and in France, but has only two wins to his name.

BADEN-BADEN (Germany) (L-H) (Good to soft)
Saturday May 24th

1548a BETTY BARCLAY-RENNEN-OLEANDER-RENNEN (Gp 3) (4-Y.O+)
3-43 (3-46) **2m** £28,409.00 (£11,364.00: £5,682.00)

				SP	RR	SF
	Camp David (GER) (AWohler,Germany) **7-9-0** ABoschert	—	**1**		117	—
1241[3]	**Sweetness Herself** (MJRyan) **4-8-3** MBaird	1½	**2**		107	—
891[5]	**Lord Jim (IRE)** (LordHuntingdon) **5-8-7b** KWoodburn	nk	**3**		108	—
						8 Rn

3m 23.0 TOTE 20DM: 12DM 20DM 16DM (171DM) OWNER Mr D. Gabel BRED Frau & I. Brunotte
Camp David (GER) made progress form the rear at halfway, and tracked his two British rivals turning into the straight. He hit the front inside the final furlong, and quickened up well before hanging right in the closing stages when clear. He now goes for the Ascot Gold Cup, but will face much stiffer opposition.
1241 Sweetness Herself continues to go from strength to strength and posted a career best effort. In second pace with three furlongs to race, she was collared by the winner soon after hitting the front at the furlong pole. She was tying up in the last few yards and was almost caught for second.
891 Lord Jim (IRE) took it up with more than half-a-mile to race, but was tapped for toe approaching the furlong marker. Stamina is his strong suit, and he was staying on again at the finish.

1200a-CAPANNELLE (Rome, Italy) (R-H) (Good to firm)
Saturday May 24th

1549a PREMIO ELLINGTON (Gp 2) (4-Y.O+)
3-00 (3-08) **1m 4f** £51,275.00 (£23,510.00: £13,102.00)

				SP	RR	SF
932[5]	**Luso** (CEBrittain) **5-9-1** BDoyle (mde all: rdn clr appr fnl f: r.o wl)	—	1		127	—
	Toto le Moko (IRE) (AVerdesi,Italy) **4-8-10** EBotti (a.p: chal over 2f out: ev ch 1f out: no ex)	¾	2		121	—
	Febrar (ITY) (Ld'Auria,Italy) **4-8-10** MDemuro (hld up: slt prog fnl 2f: nvr nrr)	5½	3		114	—
	Pay Me Back (IRE) (GVerricelli,Italy) **7-8-10** SDettori (broke wl: mid div st: one pce fnl 3f)	2	4		111	—
1200a[U]	**Germignana (ITY)** (LCamici,Italy) **4-8-7** MPasquale (a in rr)	6	5		100	—
1200a[6]	**Dancer Mitral** (LBrogi,Italy) **4-8-10** CFiocchi (mid div: bhd fnl 3f)	3	6		99	—
	Sugarland Express (IRE) (AVerdesi,Italy) **6-8-12** GPucciatti (prom: wknd qckly 2f out)	3	7		97	—
						7 Rn

2m 25.3 TOTE 15L: 11L 13L (18L) OWNER Mr Saeed Manana (NEWMARKET) BRED Saeed Manana
932 Luso made all the running for the second successive year in this event. Challenged by the runner-up approaching the furlong pole, he had a little more in hand than the winning margin suggests. Very successful on his travels, the Gran Premio di Milano and the Arlington Million are his next targets.

1548a-BADEN-BADEN (Germany) (L-H) (Good)
Sunday May 25th

1550a LAURENT-PERRIER MEILE (Gp 3) (3-Y.O+)
3-25 (3-34) **1m** £28,409.00 (£11,364.00: £5,682.00: £5,682.00)

				SP	RR	SF
1074a[3]	**La Blue (GER)** (BSchutz,Germany) **4-9-3** WNewnes	—	1		120	—
1067a[4]	**Devil River Peek (USA)** (BSchutz,Germany) **5-9-5** AStarke	hd	2		122	—
	Jashin (IRE) (ALowe,Germany) **4-8-12** PVanDeKeere	2½	3		110	—
	Tajawall (USA) (DRichardson,Germany) **5-8-12** KWoodburn	d.h	3		110	—
						15 Rn

1m 38.07 TOTE 52DM: 21DM 21DM J 54DM T 12DM OWNER Gestut Wittekindshof BRED Gestut Wittekindshof
La Blue (GER) was brought with a strong run to lead a furlong out, and got the better of a hard-fought duel with her stable companion. She has plenty of big-race entries to choose from.

1551a SCHERPING-RENNEN (Listed) (3-Y.O)
4-35 (4-48) **6f** £15,152.00 (£6,061.00: £3,409.00: £1,894.00)

				SP	RR	SF
	Bandira (GER) (HBlume,Germany) **3-8-7b[1]** ABrockhausen	—	1		100	—
	Platin Queen (IRE) (ALowe,Germany) **3-8-7** ASuborics	1½	2		96	—
	Arpista (GER) (RSuerland,Germany) **3-8-5** NGrant	nk	3		93	—
968[2]	**Cryhavoc** (JRArnold) **3-9-0** SSanders	1¾	4		98	—
						10 Rn

1m 9.37 TOTE 88DM: 26DM 32DM 36DM (787DM) OWNER Mr H. von Finck BRED H. von Fink
968 Cryhavoc was sent off the even-money favourite. Racing prominently, he held every chance at the two-furlong pole, but was unable to raise his game.

1549a-CAPANNELLE (Rome, Italy) (R-H) (Good to firm)
Sunday May 25th

1552a PREMIO W.W.F. (Listed) (4-Y.O+)
3-00 (3-05) **7f** £23,142.00 (£10,183.00: £5,554.00)

				SP	RR	SF
839[2]	**Polar Prince (IRE)** (MAJarvis) **4-8-12** RCochrane	—	1		107	—
961[2]	**How Long** (LMCumani) **4-8-12** LDettori	¾	2		105	—
	Robins (IRE) (ACalchetti,Italy) **5-8-12** OFancera	½	3		104	—
						9 Rn

1m 22.3 TOTE 17L: 12L 15L 31L (24L) OWNER Mrs Christine Stevenson (NEWMARKET) BRED Michael Morrin
839 Polar Prince (IRE) had the form to win this, but was not particularly impressive in doing so. In mid division on the inside, he was switched off the rails to find room at the two-furlong pole. He quickened to lead with a furlong to run and kept on well.
961 How Long tried to follow the winner through, but did not get a clear run and may have been a little unlucky. Running on strongly in the closing stages, this was a good effort.

1553a DERBY ITALIANO (Gp 1) (3-Y.O)
4-10 (4-15) **1m 4f** £242,190.00 (£127,836.00: £74,967.00: £37,984.00)

				SP	RR	SF
937*	**Single Empire (IRE)** (PWChapple-Hyam) **3-9-2** DHarrison (mid div: gd hdwy fnl 2f: r.o wl to ld fin)	—	1	148/10	107	—
920a*	**Ungaro (GER)** (HBlume,Germany) **3-9-2** THellier (led over 5f out tl ct cl home)	nse	2	49/10[3]	107	—
1015*	**Panama City (USA)** (PWChapple-Hyam) **3-9-2** LDettori (hdwy ½-wy: hrd rdn over 2f out: rallied 1f out: kpt on one pce)	1	3	13/10[1]	106	—
1165*	**Badlesmere (USA)** (PFICole) **3-9-2** RCochrane (prom st: ev ch over 1f out: one pce)	hd	4	17/1	106	—
931[3]	**Musical Dancer (USA)** (EALDunlop) **3-9-2** KFallon (trckd ldrs st: hdwy over 2f out: hung lft over 1f out: fin 5th, ¼l, disq & plcd last)		**5d**	39/1	105	—
917a[2]	**Risiat (IRE)** (EBorromeo,Italy) **3-9-2** MDemuro (mid div ent st: hdwy over 2f out: ev ch whn carried lft 1f out: dead-heated 6th, 1l & ¼l: plcd equal 5th)	1¼	5	29/1	104	—
1015[2]	**Ivan Luis (FR)** (MBell) **3-9-2** MRoberts (prom: ev ch over 1f out: styd on wl: dead-heated 6th, 1l & ¼l: plcd equal 5th)	d.h	5	34/10[2]	104	—

				SP	RR	SF
	Honey Colour (IRE) (AColella,Italy) **3-9-2** OFancera (nvr nr to chal: fin 8th, plcd 7th)	3½	**7**	61/1	99	—
	Rio Napo (IRE) (LCamici,Italy) **3-9-2** MPasquale (hdwy 5f out: ev ch 2f out: sn wknd: fin 9th, plcd 8th)	2	**8**	18/1	97	—
775*	**Stanton Harcourt (USA)** (JLDunlop) **3-9-2** FJovine (prom tl ½-wy: wknd over 2f out: fin 10th, plcd 9th)	1¼	**9**	28/1	95	—
	Special Star (PGuarsegnati,Italy) **3-9-2** ACorniani (prom tl wknd ½-wy: fin 11th, plcd 10th)	2	**10**	106/1	92	—
1015[3]	**State Fair** (JLDunlop) **3-9-2** DHolland (trckd ldrs st: btn over 2f out: fin 12th, plcd 11th)	nse	**11**	57/10	92	—
1099[2]	**Yavlensky (IRE)** (JLDunlop) **3-9-2** JWeaver (a bhd: fin 13th, plcd 12th)	hd	**12**	85/1	92	—
	Hahnio (IRE) (LBrogi,Italy) **3-9-2** CFiocchi (a bhd: fin 14th, plcd 13th)	1½	**13**	138/1	90	—
	Pariofige (USA) (OPessi,Italy) **3-9-2** VMezzatesta (a bhd: fin 15th, plcd 14th)	2	**14**	73/1	88	—
	Solitario Wells (OPessi,Italy) **3-9-2** LPolito (led tl over 5f out: wknd rapidly: t.o: fin 16th, plcd 15th)	dist	**15**	34/10[2]	—	—

(SP 153.0%) **16 Rn**

2m 26.2 TOTE 158L: 35L 21L 15L (734L) OWNER Mr A. K. Collins (MARLBOROUGH) BRED Swettenham Stud
STEWARDS' ENQUIRY Fallon susp. 6-15/6/97. Changed on appeal to 22/6-2/7/97

937* Single Empire (IRE), in mid-division entering the straight, made good headway on the outside in the final two furlongs, running on strongly and being forced up on the line by Harrison. He is in the Epsom Derby, but looks more likely to go for the King Edward VII Stakes at Royal Ascot. (148/10)

1015* Panama City (USA), in second place coming into the straight, was hard ridden over two furlongs out. He rallied approaching the final furlong but did not reach the leaders, only staying on at the one pace. (13/10)

1165* Badlesmere (USA) looked to have every chance approaching the final furlong, but kept on at the one pace. (17/1)

931 Musical Dancer (USA) was in seventh place as the field turned into the straight, but his unfortunate jockey dropped his whip, and subsequently had no control as his mount veered violently left over a furlong out. This resulted in interference with Risiat for which Fallon, regardless of losing his whip, was given a ten-day suspension. (39/1)

1015 Ivan Luis (FR), with every chance over a furlong out, stayed on and dead-heated with Risiat. (34/10)

775* Stanton Harcourt (USA) was prominent until halfway and then began to weaken from over two furlongs out. (28/1)

1015 State Fair, in sixth place entering the straight, was soon beaten. (57/10)

1099 Yavlensky (IRE) was always towards the rear of the field. (85/1)

1365a-LONGCHAMP (Paris, France) (R-H) (Very Soft)
Sunday May 25th

1554a PRIX D'ISPAHAN (Gp 1) (4-Y.O+ C & F)
3-10 (3-14) **1m 1f 55y** £56,117.00 (£22,447.00: £11,223.00: £5,612.00)

				SP	RR	SF
852*	**Sasuru** (GWragg) **4-9-2** MHills (3rd pl tl 2f out: effrt & pushed lft ins fnl f: hrd rdn to ld cl home)	—	**1**	6/5[1]	124	—
830*	**Wixim (USA)** (RCharlton) **4-9-2** TJarnet (trckd ldr tl led over 1f out: hung lft ins fnl f: btn cl home)	s.nk	**2**	3/1[2]	124	—
1067a[2]	**Simon du Desert (FR)** (RCollet,France) **4-9-2** CHanotel (hld up: prod 2f out: veered rt over 1f out: one pce cl home)	3	**3**	36/10[3]	119	—
625a[3]	**Baroud d'Honneur (FR)** (JBernard,France) **4-9-2** FBlondel (hld up in last pl: prog 2f out: r.o one pce)	s.h	**4**	76/10	118	—
1067a[6]	**Nero Zilzal (USA)** (ELellouche,France) **4-9-2** TThulliez (hld up: one pce)	3	**5**	14/1	113	—
*627a**	**Tamayaz (CAN)** (SbinSuroor) **5-9-2** SGuillot (led tl 1½f out: wknd qckly)	3	**6**	5/1	108	—

(SP 127.2%) **6 Rn**

1m 55.6 (3.60) P-M 2.20F: 1.40F 1.60F OWNER Mr A. E. Oppenheimer (NEWMARKET) BRED Hascombe and Valiant Studs

852* Sasuru ducked out on two occasions going down to the start, but these antics are normal when he is in strange surroundings. Doing nothing wrong in the race, he bowled along in third place and began his serious challenge with a furlong and a half left to run. Leant on by the persistent runner-up during the final furlong, he still managed to get in front at the post. The interference was so blatant that if he had been beaten, the Stewards would have been forced to award him the race. The target now is either the Prince of Wales's or the Hardwicke Stakes at Royal Ascot. A longer-term plan is a tilt at the King George and then possibly the Arc de Triomphe. He looks a horse to follow this season. (6/5)

830* Wixim (USA) ran his heart out. In second place for much of the way, he took the advantage over a furlong out but then hung persistently left. He was at the end of his tether at the finish, so will now be brought back to a mile. He, like the winner, is an improved colt, and now heads for the Queen Anne Stakes at Royal Ascot. Connections are also talking about the Prix Jacques le Marois at Deauville in August. (3/1)

1067a Simon du Desert (FR) arrived late on the scene and battled on well for third place. He veered right over a furlong out but still managed to hold his position. This distance seemed a little beyond him and he will now come back to a mile. He does not appear to be the easiest of rides and his trainer may be using a more experienced jockey in the future. (36/10)

625a Baroud d'Honneur (FR) was held up in last place but made some progress in the final two furlongs. He was rather one-paced and it was evident that this distance was short of his best. He will now return to longer trips, and the Grand Prix de Vichy at the end of July will be one of his targets. (76/10)

627a* Tamayaz (CAN) looked well and led from the start until halfway up the straight. He then weakened very rapidly and certainly did not show his best. He should not be judged on this performance, as his stable has been under a bit of a cloud. (5/1)

1367a-SAN SIRO (Milan, Italy) (R-H) (Good to firm)
Sunday May 25th

1555a PREMIO ROVIGO (3-Y.O)
2-50 (-) **1m 1f** £11,571.00 (£5,091.00: £2,777.00)

				SP	RR	SF
1099[3]	**Barba Papa (IRE)** (LMCumani) **3-8-12** CColombi	—	**1**		86	—
	Alonso De Castillo (IRE) (GBotti,Italy) **3-8-12** MBotti	2½	**2**		82	—
821a*	**Gracco (IRE)** (GBotti,Italy) **3-9-2** MLatorre	2½	**3**		81	—

5 Rn

1m 54.7 (12.50) TOTE 16L: 12L 15L (28L) OWNER Dr M. Boffa (NEWMARKET) BRED Rathasker Stud

1099 Barba Papa (IRE) tracked the leader until taking over and going on from two furlongs out. He was soon in command and won easily.

1556a PREMIO PISTOIA MAIDEN (3-Y.O)
4-50 (-) **1m 110y** £5,786.00 (£2,314.00: £1,388.00)

				SP	RR	SF
	Icy Love (CVittorio,Italy) **3-9-0** LPanici	—	**1**		—	—
	Sopran Newar (VValiani,Italy) **3-9-0** GForte	7	**2**		—	—
	Sopran Tycoon (ITY) (GVerricelli,Italy) **3-9-0** MBotti	½	**3**		—	—

	Gomanta (LMCumani) **3-8-10** CColombi (btn approx 15 3/4l)		6		—	—
	Rufalda (IRE) (LMCumani) **3-8-10** LSorrentino (btn approx 20l)		7		—	—
						10 Rn

1m 47.7 TOTE 16L: 23L 52L 16L (555L) OWNER Laghi SNC BRED L. Murphy & J. Stack & J. Francome
Gomanta was never in a position to challenge for the lead.
Rufalda (IRE) was always towards the rear.

1310-AYR (L-H) (Good to firm, Good last 6f rnd crse)
Friday May 30th

WEATHER: sunny WIND: slt against

80 63 66+ 64

1557 GREIG MIDDLETON PEP MEDIAN AUCTION MAIDEN STKS (2-Y.O) (Class E) (68)

2-00 (2-02) **6f** £2,934.00 (£882.00: £426.00: £198.00) Stalls: Low GOING: 0.07 sec per fur (G)

				SP	RR	SF
1120[4]	**Reap Rewards** (JGFitzGerald) **2-9-0** KFallon(4) (lw: a.p: hdwy to ld 1f out: r.o)	—	1	3/1[3]	72	16
	Lend A Hand (MJohnston) **2-9-0** JWeaver(1) (cmpt: scope: bit bkwd: hld up: nt clr run 2f out: hdwy over 1f out: styd on wl towards fin)	½	2	2/1[2]	71+	15
979[3]	**Peter's Imp (IRE)** (JBerry) **2-9-0** GCarter(6) (cl up: led wl over 1f out: hdd 1f out: no ex)	1¾	3	13/8[1]	66	10
	Aberkeen (MDods) **2-9-0** DaleGibson(2) (w'like: hld up: hdwy 2f out: kpt on: nvr able chal)	3½	4	33/1	57	1
	Pleasant Dreams (DenysSmith) **2-8-9** ACulhane(5) (leggy: s.i.s: hld up: effrt over 2f out: no imp)	3	5	16/1	44	—
822[6]	**Up The Clarets (IRE)** (JJO'Neill) **2-9-0** JFortune(7) (mde most tl hdd & wknd wl over 1f out)	3	6	25/1	41	—
611[3]	**Anka Lady** (DMoffatt) **2-8-6**(3) DarrenMoffatt(3) (lw: disp ld 2f: wknd ½-wy)	12	7	25/1	4	—
				(SP 112.9%)		**7 Rn**

1m 16.05 (6.25) CSF £8.33 TOTE £4.80: £1.80 £1.80 (£6.20) OWNER Marquesa de Moratalla (MALTON) BRED North Cheshire Trading and Storage Ltd
1120 Reap Rewards is improving and certainly appreciated this longer trip. He showed a really good attitude. (3/1)
Lend A Hand needed this both fitness- and experience-wise and there should be plenty of improvement next time. (2/1: 6/4-9/4)
979 Peter's Imp (IRE) ran pretty well but the combination of the fast ground and extra distance just seemed to find him out. (13/8)
Aberkeen put up a reasonable first effort and ought to improve for the run. (33/1)
Pleasant Dreams looks the type to need further and a bit more time. (16/1)

1558 GILT-EDGED MAIDEN STKS (3-Y.O+) (Class D)

2-30 (2-34) **1m 2f** £3,626.00 (£1,088.00: £524.00: £242.00) Stalls: Low GOING: 0.07 sec per fur (G)

				SP	RR	SF
1017[15]	**Party Romance (USA) (80)** (BHanbury) **3-8-10** WRyan(5) (lw: mde most: hld on wl u.p fnl f)	—	1	4/1[2]	91	59
1230[2]	**Colour Code** (MrsASwinbank) **5-9-10** GDuffield(2) (w wnr: rdn & edgd lft appr fnl f: kpt on towards fin)	s.h	2	10/1	91	73
1165[2]	**Double Alleged (USA) (88)** (MJohnston) **3-8-10** JWeaver(4) (b: lw: trckd ldrs: effrt 3f out: sn rdn & no imp)	1¾	3	4/7[1]	88	56
1230[5]	**Ardarroch Prince** (MrsMReveley) **6-9-10** ACulhane(3) (dwlt: sn t.o: sme late hdwy)	18	4	50/1	59	41
1221[6]	**Jack Doyle (IRE)** (JJO'Neill) **6-9-10** JFortune(6) (dwlt: sn in tch: effrt 3f out: sn btn)	3½	5	25/1	54	36
	Kalisz (IRE) (DRLoder) **3-8-5** DRMcCabe(1) (w'like: lengthy: trckd ldrs tl outpcd 3f out: sn btn & eased: lame)	18	6	6/1[3]	20?	—
				(SP 112.8%)		**6 Rn**

2m 10.9 (5.10) CSF £36.85 TOTE £6.20: £1.90 £2.70 (£17.20) OWNER Mr Abdullah Ali (NEWMARKET) BRED Mollie E. Boyd & Vinery
WEIGHT FOR AGE 3yo-14lb
OFFICIAL EXPLANATION Kalisz (IRE): lame.
Party Romance (USA) looked superb and really got his act together, showing fine battling qualities. (4/1)
1230 Colour Code was dropping back in trip and this probably just the made the difference as he was keeping on really well at the end. He will surely not be long in breaking his duck at this game. (10/1)
1165 Double Alleged (USA), who seems better over further, was always being taken off his legs here early in the straight, but to his credit he did keep on well. (4/7)
1230 Ardarroch Prince, over a trip too short, was in no hurry early on and better will be seen when he qualifies for handicaps. (50/1)
1221 Jack Doyle (IRE), despite the extra distance, always found this company too hot. (25/1)
Kalisz (IRE) is a fine-looking type but her action here left a lot to be desired and, when asked to stretch early in the straight, she was soon in trouble. She was later said to be lame. (6/1: op 7/2)

1559 GREIG MIDDLETON STOCKBROKERS CUP H'CAP (0-90) (3-Y.O+) (Class C)

3-00 (3-01) **1m 2f** £5,150.00 (£1,550.00: £750.00: £350.00) Stalls: Low GOING: 0.07 sec per fur (G)

				SP	RR	SF
1450[2]	**Wafir (IRE) (80)** (PCalver) **5-9-7**(3) DarrenMoffatt(2) (lw: led after 2f: qcknd over 2f out: eased ins fnl f)	—	1	11/4[1]	89+	59
1390[3]	**Lapu-Lapu (52)** (MJCamacho) **4-7-10** LCharnock(3) (led 2f: stdd & plld hrd: effrt over 2f out: no ch w wnr)	2	2	11/4[1]	58	28
1244*	**Premier Generation (IRE) (70)** (DWPArbuthnot) **4-9-0** SWhitworth(5) (sn trckng ldrs: effrt over 2f out: r.o one pce)	1¼	3	3/1[2]	74	44
1313[4]	**Keep Battling (52)** (JSGoldie) **7-7-5**(5) JBramhill(4) (hld up & bhd: hdwy 3f out: rdn & btn 2f out)	s.h	4	14/1	56	26
1262[2]	**Master Beveled (75)** (PDEvans) **7-9-5b** KFallon(1) (b.nr fore: lw: hld up: rdn 3f out: no imp)	¾	5	7/2[3]	78	48
				(SP 107.2%)		**5 Rn**

2m 12.52 (6.72) CSF £9.07 TOTE £3.60: £2.10 £1.30 (£6.20) OWNER Mr Kenneth MacPherson (RIPON) BRED Ronnie Boland
LONG HANDICAP Keep Battling 7-6
1450 Wafir (IRE), in a race where there were no confirmed front-runners, went on after two furlongs, and once he quickened early in the straight it was a case of how far. (11/4)
1390 Lapu-Lapu took a strong hold and needed a much stronger pace than was set here, being well outpointed in the final sprint. (11/4)
1244* Premier Generation (IRE) found this ground faster than he really prefers and once the sprint was on in the last three furlongs he was soon left struggling. (3/1: tchd 100/3)
1313 Keep Battling was 4lb out of the handicap and needs a much stronger pace than was set here. (14/1)
1262 Master Beveled likes the ground much softer and was never happy here. (7/2)

1560 GREIG MIDDLETON PRIVATE CLIENT H'CAP (0-70) (3-Y.O+) (Class E)
3-30 (3-39) **1m** £3,148.50 (£948.00: £459.00: £214.50) Stalls: Low GOING: 0.07 sec per fur (G)

	Horse	Dist	Pos	SP	RR	SF
1020[2]	**Somerton Boy (IRE) (64)** (PCalver) **7-9-13** GDuffield(12) (lw: hld up & bhd: effrt 3f out: str run to ld wl ins fnl f)	—	1	5/1[2]	79	50
1315[5]	**Running Green (55)** (DMoffatt) **6-9-1v**(3) DarrenMoffatt(3) (cl up: led wl over 1f out: r.o u.p: hdd & nt qckn wl ins fnl f)	2	2	12/1	66	37
1389[3]	**Bowcliffe (39)** (EJAlston) **6-8-2** DWright(4) (trckd ldrs: hdwy to chal 1½f out: nt qckn ins fnl f)	1½	3	9/2[1]	47	18
1231[3]	**Stormless (58)** (PMonteith) **6-9-7** WRyan(13) (a chsng ldrs: effrt 3f out: r.o one pce)	1½	4	7/1	63	34
1315[3]	**Tibbi Blues (37)** (JSGoldie) **10-7-9**(5) JBramhill(1) (led tl hdd wl over 1f out: grad wknd)	s.h	5	14/1	42	13
1315*	**Brandonville (58)** (NTinkler) **4-9-7** 6x DeanMcKeown(10) (lw: mid div: outpcd 3f out: sme hdwy 2f out: n.d)	1¾	6	7/1	59	30
1128[13]	**Advance East (51)** (MDods) **5-9-0** JWeaver(6) (lw: s.i.s: hld up & bhd: effrt over 2f out: n.d)	nk	7	25/1	52	23
1035[6]	**Impulsive Air (IRE) (65)** (EWeymes) **5-10-0** KFallon(7) (in tch: effrt over 2f out: no imp)	½	8	6/1[3]	65	36
1128[5]	**Maurangi (34)** (BWMurray) **6-7-11b**ow1 MDeering(11) (lw: in tch: effrt 3f out: one pce)	1¼	9	10/1	31	1
	Highspeed (IRE) (59) (SEKettlewell) **5-9-8** JFortune(2) (prom tl wknd fnl 2½f)	1½	10	20/1	53	24
1128*	**Oriole (36)** (DonEnricoIncisa) **4-7-13v** KimTinkler(9) (bhd: effrt on outside ent st: n.d)	1¾	11	12/1	27	—
1315[17]	**Mister Westsound (50)** (MissLAPerratt) **5-8-13b** OUrbina(8) (hld up: effrt 3f out: rdn & no imp)	½	12	25/1	40	11
1285[12]	**King Chestnut (53)** (MDods) **6-9-2** SWhitworth(5) (lw: s.i.s: a bhd: virtually p.u fnl 2f)	dist	13	50/1	—	—

(SP 119.7%) **13 Rn**

1m 43.83 (6.43) CSF £55.41 CT £275.38 TOTE £4.60: £1.60 £2.90 £2.50 (£25.90) Trio £197.00 OWNER Mrs Janis MacPherson (RIPON) BRED Mrs A. Whitehead
LONG HANDICAP Maurangi 7-9

1020 Somerton Boy (IRE) likes the track, is well handicapped at present and loves fast ground, and produced his customary late burst to settle it in most emphatic style. (5/1)
1315 Running Green seemed happier on this faster ground and proved game under pressure but the winner's turn of foot left him floundering. (12/1)
1389 Bowcliffe, due to take a 13lb rise in the weights, ran well, but his limitations were exposed in the closing stages. No doubt the Handicapper will be just as quick to drop him to a realistic mark. (9/2)
1231 Stormless had his chances but the struggle always proved beyond him when the pressure was on over this trip and on this faster ground. (7/1)
1315 Tibbi Blues, ridden the opposite way to last time, had run himself into the ground approaching the last furlong. (14/1)
1315* Brandonville looked the part but is a tricky ride and never got in a blow. (7/1)
900 Advance East needs everything to go just right and may well need a bit further. (25/1)
1035 Impulsive Air (IRE) spread a plate on the way to post which delayed the start for some time, and was then never happy during the race.(6/1)

1561 ST. VINCENT HIGH INCOME H'CAP (0-85) (3-Y.O+) (Class D)
4-00 (4-04) **6f** £3,730.00 (£1,120.00: £540.00: £250.00) Stalls: Low GOING: 0.07 sec per fur (G)

	Horse	Dist	Pos	SP	RR	SF
1324*	**Gadge (72)** (ABailey) **6-9-2** 6x DWright(7) (b: mde all: qcknd ½-wy: eased ins fnl f)	—	1	4/1[2]	86+	57
1259[9]	**Amron (63)** (JBerry) **10-8-2**(5) TEDurcan(9) (trckd ldrs: hdwy to chse wnr 2f out: no imp)	2½	2	16/1	70	41
1311[3]	**Just Bob (73)** (SEKettlewell) **8-9-3** JFortune(4) (lw: s.i.s: effrt 2f out: sn chsng ldrs: no ex fnl f)	1½	3	9/1	76	47
1259[2]	**Garnock Valley (80)** (JBerry) **7-9-10b** GCarter(2) (bhd: rdn 2f out: r.o fnl f)	nk	4	7/1	83	54
1021[2]	**The Lambton Worm (82)** (DenysSmith) **3-9-3** KFallon(8) (prom: hdwy u.p 2f out: btn 1f out)	nk	5	8/1	84	46
1225*	**Smokey From Caplaw (74)** (JJO'Neill) **3-8-9** GDuffield(10) (chsd ldrs: rdn 2f out: sn btn)	5	6	5/2[1]	62	24
1131[8]	**Don't Care (IRE) (70)** (MissLAPerratt) **6-9-0b** OUrbina(3) (lw: in tch tl outpcd fnl 2f)	1¼	7	12/1	55	26
1225[8]	**Time To Tango (64)** (GMMoore) **4-8-8** ACulhane(6) (cl up 4f: wknd qckly)	5	8	12/1	36	7
1259[8]	**French Grit (IRE) (74)** (MDods) **5-9-4** JWeaver(1) (plld hrd: cl up 4f)	2½	9	11/2[3]	39	10
953[10]	**Mr Oscar (84)** (WMcKeown) **5-9-7**(7) JMcAuley(5) (reluctant to r: sn wl t.o)	dist	10	33/1	—	—

(SP 121.8%) **10 Rn**

1m 13.21 (3.41) CSF £62.85 CT £516.22 TOTE £5.50: £1.90 £6.10 £1.40 (£40.40) Trio £84.30 OWNER Mr J. B. Wilcox (TARPORLEY) BRED Snowdrop Stud Co Ltd
WEIGHT FOR AGE 3yo-9lb

1324* Gadge last won over this trip four years ago but he was presented with this as no-one wanted to make it. He was allowed things all his own way and in the end won pulling up. (4/1)
1079 Amron likes to come from off a strong pace and in the circumstances this was not a bad effort. (16/1)
1311 Just Bob is best over five furlongs with a strong gallop, which he never had here, and did well to finish so close. (9/1)
1259 Garnock Valley was set an impossible task in this slowly-run event and finished like the proverbial train, but far too late. (7/1)
1021 The Lambton Worm was disappointing here but his stable is yet to strike any form. (8/1)

1562 GREIG MIDDLETON PORTFOLIO CHARITY STAKES FOR THE HANSEL VILLAGE LIMITED STKS (0-60) (3-Y.O+) (Class F)
4-30 (4-30) **1m 5f 13y** £2,637.00 (£732.00: £351.00) Stalls: Low GOING: 0.07 sec per fur (G)

	Horse	Dist	Pos	SP	RR	SF
1393[2]	**Summerhill Special (IRE) (60)** (DWBarker) **6-9-8** WRyan(3) (trckd ldrs: led 1½f out: r.o wl)	—	1	4/1[2]	66	30
1222*	**Heathyards Rock (50)** (RMMcKellar) **5-9-11** GDuffield(7) (in tch: stdy hdwy 3f out: effrt over 1f out: nt pce of wnr)	1½	2	14/1	67	31
1281[2]	**Kathryn's Pet (60)** (MrsMReveley) **4-9-8** ACulhane(1) (lw: hld up: nt clr run 2f out: swtchd appr fnl f: r.o: nrst fin)	nk	3	9/2[3]	64	28
781[4]	**Sherqy (IRE) (60)** (SEKettlewell) **5-9-9** JFortune(6) (hld up: effrt 2f out: nt pce to chal)	3½	4	7/1	61	25
1125[2]	**Barbara's Jewel (44)** (ABailey) **5-9-11** KFallon(5) (b: hld up & bhd: effrt 3f out: nvr trbld ldrs)	hd	5	14/1	62	26
	John Lee Hooker (60) (DWPArbuthnot) **5-9-9** SWhitworth(4) (b: trckd ldrs: chal 3f out: sn rdn: wknd 1½f out)	4	6	9/2[3]	56	20
1156[2]	**Mister Aspecto (IRE) (60)** (MJohnston) **4-9-9b** JWeaver(2) (led: rdn 3f out: hdd & wknd 1½f out)	2½	7	5/2[1]	52	16

(SP 110.8%) **7 Rn**

2m 58.25 (13.45) CSF £46.76 TOTE £5.20: £2.60 £3.30 (£7.90) OWNER Alba Racing Syndicate (RICHMOND) BRED Miss Audrey F. Thompson

1393 Summerhill Special (IRE) travelled well and certainly has a useful turn of foot, which made all the difference here. (4/1)
1222* Heathyards Rock, having his first run for his new stable, was a bit edgy beforehand but still put up a fair performance, although he was well outsprinted in the closing stages. (14/1: op 8/1)

1281 Kathryn's Pet looked to be the unlucky one here and had she seen daylight sooner she might well have given the winner a fright. (9/2: 3/1-5/1)
781 Sherqy (IRE), after over five weeks off, ran a useful race and should be all the better for it. (7/1)
1125 Barbara's Jewel looked to have a stiff task here and could never get into it despite staying on. (14/1)
John Lee Hooker, after an absence of twenty-one months, was supported to win this, but his lack of a recent run told once pressure was applied early in the straight. (9/2)
1156 Mister Aspecto (IRE) likes this ground and this trip but was most disappointing, dropping tamely away once collared inside the last couple of furlongs. (5/2)

T/Plpt: £567.60 (22.44 Tckts). T/Qdpt: £24.80 (34.79 Tckts) AA

1272-BATH (L-H) (Good to firm, Firm patches)
Friday May 30th
WEATHER: fine WIND: almost nil

1563 GRITTLETON MEDIAN AUCTION MAIDEN STKS (3 & 4-Y.O) (Class F)
6-20 (6-20) **1m 2f 46y** £2,584.00 (£724.00: £352.00) Stalls: Low GOING minus 0.52 sec per fur (F)

				SP	RR	SF
1144[2]	**Scoss** (LMCumani) **3-8-10** PatEddery(4) (w'like: lw: hld up: hdwy to ld over 2f out: rdn wl over 1f out: r.o wl)	—	1	8/13[1]	74	39
1144[9]	**Miss Riviera Rose (76)** (GWragg) **3-8-5** MHills(6) (hld up: hdwy 6f out: rdn & ev ch over 2f out: one pce)	2½	2	4/1[2]	65	30
	Little Miss Rocker (IABalding) **3-8-5** TQuinn(3) (chsd ldr over 6f: rdn 3f out: one pce)	1	3	9/1[3]	64	29
989[7]	**Limelight** (JARToller) **3-8-5** TSprake(1) (hld up: rdn over 3f out: hdwy over 2f out: one pce)	2	4	11/1	60	25
1272[9]	**Khamsin (IRE)** (MJHeaton-Ellis) **3-8-5** SDrowne(2) (a bhd: t.o fnl 2f)	13	5	50/1	40	5
1110[9]	**My Jess** (SGKnight) **3-8-5** RPerham(5) (tk keen hold: led 8f: sn wknd)	s.h	6	40/1	40	5
				(SP 104.6%)	**6 Rn**	

2m 8.2 (1.70) CSF £2.44 TOTE £1.70: £1.10 £1.60 (£1.90) OWNER Scuderia Rencati Srl (NEWMARKET) BRED The Overbury Stud
1144 Scoss was well on top in the closing stages and, although out of a sprinter, gave the impression he might stay further. (8/13)
773 Miss Riviera Rose, a half-sister to Riviera Magic, had finished over nine lengths behind the winner at Windsor and seemed to appreciate this sounder surface. A longer trip should help. (4/1)
Little Miss Rocker benefited from this longer distance and may need an even stiffer test. (9/1)
Limelight is yet another who probably wants further. (11/1: 6/1-12/1)

79+ 64 79

1564 E.B.F. SWAINSWICK MAIDEN STKS (2-Y.O F) (Class D) (74)
6-50 (6-51) **5f 161y** £3,421.50 (£1,032.00: £501.00: £235.50) Stalls: High GOING minus 0.52 sec per fur (F)

				SP	RR	SF
	Ascot Cyclone (USA) (BWHills) **2-8-11** MHills(8) (w'like: scope: hld up: hdwy & nt clr run wl over 1f out: swtchd rt: led ins fnl f: comf)	—	1	1/2[1]	72+	42
1213[4]	**Petarga** (JARToller) **2-8-11** SSanders(13) (a.p: led 2f out tl ins fnl f)	2½	2	16/1	65	35
	Tajmil (IRE) (MajorWRHern) **2-8-11** RHills(6) (neat: a.p: one pce fnl 2f)	1¾	3	12/1[3]	60	30
965[3]	**Mighty Magic** (MrsPNDutfield) **2-8-8**(3) AWhelan(10) (chsd ldrs: wknd over 1f out)	6	4	8/1[2]	43	13
	Cherished (IRE) (PFICole) **2-8-11** TQuinn(3) (small: lt-f: s.i.s: sn rcvrd: nt clr run on ins wl over 2f out: swtchd rt: hdwy fnl f: r.o)	1¾	5	12/1[3]	39+	9
	Aspen (IRE) (RHannon) **2-8-11** PatEddery(12) (leggy: unf: nvr nr to chal)	¾	6	12/1[3]	36	6
	Make Believe (RCharlton) **2-8-11** TSprake(9) (unf: bkwd: chsd ldrs: wkng whn edgd rt wl over 1f out)	nk	7	12/1[3]	36	6
	Phantom Waters (RFJohnsonHoughton) **2-8-11** JReid(11) (w'like: s.i.s: nvr nr ldrs)	1	8	33/1	33	3
	Jackies Webb (BSmart) **2-8-11** RPerham(7) (neat: a.p: led over 3f out to 2f out: sn wknd)	nk	9	50/1	32	2
	Francesca's Folly (JWHills) **2-8-11** RHughes(2) (small: outpcd)	11	10	33/1	1	—
	Apple Sauce (JRArnold) **2-8-11** DHarrison(5) (str: scope: bkwd: prom 3f)	3½	11	50/1	—	—
	Tempus Fugit (BRMillman) **2-8-11** SDrowne(4) (unf: scope: led 4f out: sn hdd & wknd)	2½	12	66/1	—	—
902[12]	**Lamoura** (RBrotherton) **2-8-11** NAdams(14) (s.s: a bhd: t.o)	6	13	100/1	—	—
	Silvazine (DJSffrenchDavis) **2-8-11** RPrice(1) (leggy: scope: bkwd: led over 1f: wknd over 3f out: t.o)	3½	14	100/1	—	—
				(SP 127.7%)	**14 Rn**	

1m 10.2 (0.70) CSF £10.91 TOTE £1.80: £1.40 £3.10 £2.10 (£18.80) Trio £77.50 OWNER Mr Salem Bel Obaida (LAMBOURN) BRED Gainsborough Farm Inc
Ascot Cyclone (USA), a half-sister to, amongst others, Magellan and Bin Nashwan, was well touted beforehand. Weaving her way through in the final quarter-mile, there was plenty to like about this performance and she may go for the Queen Mary at Royal Ascot. (1/2: evens-4/9)
1213 Petarga, a half-sister to Silver Standard and Opulent, came up against a well-regarded filly and will not always meet one so smart. (16/1)
Tajmil (IRE), a half-sister to Juwwi and Sariah, ought to be capable of taking a similar event on this evidence. (12/1: op 6/1)
965 Mighty Magic, a half-sister to seven-furlong juvenile winner Mighty Forum, rather surprisingly did not seem to benefit from this extended trip. (8/1: 4/1-10/1)
Cherished (IRE), a half-sister to a dual five-furlong juvenile winner, did not get the best of runs but finished with a bit of a flourish and seems sure to improve. (12/1: op 9/2)
Aspen (IRE) (12/1: op 9/2)
Make Believe (12/1: op 5/1)

1565 FRIDAY EVENING H'CAP (0-75) (3-Y.O) (Class D)
7-20 (7-21) **2m 1f 34y** £3,397.00 (£1,021.00: £493.00: £229.00) Stalls: High GOING minus 0.52 sec per fur (F)

				SP	RR	SF
1140[4]	**Sudest (IRE) (64)** (IABalding) **3-9-4** PatEddery(5) (hld up: rdn & hdwy 3f out: led 2f out: rdn out)	—	1	9/4[2]	75	34
746[5]	**Nile Valley (IRE) (65)** (PWChapple-Hyam) **3-9-5** JReid(7) (tk keen hold: chsd ldr: led 3f out to 2f out: rallied 1f out: one pce)	1¾	2	7/2[3]	74	33
	Old Colony (60) (PFICole) **3-9-0** TQuinn(6) (a.p: rdn over 3f out: one pce fnl 2f)	6	3	7/1	64	23
1094[8]	**Mazara (IRE) (51)** (AGFoster) **3-8-5** TSprake(4) (hld up: pushed along 6f out: no hdwy fnl 2f)	3½	4	25/1	52	11
1094[3]	**Mountaineer (IRE) (67)** (MBell) **3-9-7** MFenton(2) (hld up & bhd: hrd rdn & hung lft wl over 2f out: no rspnse)	¾	5	7/4[1]	67	26
534[4]	**Foxford Lad (42)** (TMJones) **3-7-10** NAdams(3) (led: rdn over 4f out: hdd 3f out: wknd qckly: t.o)	16	6	33/1	27	—

				SP	RR	SF
1094^{16}	**First Man (42)** (BJLlewellyn) **3-7-10** DeclanO'Shea(1) (stdd s: plld hrd in rr: t.o fnl 3f)	9	**7**	50/1	19	—

(SP 110.6%) **7 Rn**

3m 47.5 (6.10) CSF £8.85 TOTE £2.60: £1.40 £2.50 (£5.60) OWNER Robert & Elizabeth Hitchins (KINGSCLERE) BRED Airlie Stud
LONG HANDICAP Foxford Lad 7-8 First Man 7-3

1140 Sudest (IRE), again 5lb higher than when successful at Warwick, appreciated this return to faster ground and had no problem with the stamina test. (9/4: 3/1-2/1)
746 Nile Valley (IRE), down 5lb, benefited from this step up in distance but wanted to go a stride quicker than Reid wanted for much of the trip. (7/2)
Old Colony, whose three runs as a two-year-old were all over a mile, seemed blessed with stamina rather than speed. (7/1)
Mazara (IRE), dropped 4lb, was yet another trying a longer trip. (25/1)
1094 Mountaineer (IRE), raised 3lb and set to go up a further 1lb, looked none too co-operative early in the home straight and soon had a mountain to climb. (7/4)

1566 HAYMAKING CLAIMING STKS (3-Y.O) (Class F)

7-50 (7-53) **5f 11y** £2,626.00 (£736.00: £358.00) Stalls: High GOING minus 0.52 sec per fur (F)

				SP	RR	SF
970^{4}	**Lucky Dip (64)** (DRCElsworth) **3-9-2** TQuinn(2) (mde virtually all: rdn 2f out: r.o wl)	—	**1**	$8/1^{3}$	73	42
1375^{3}	**Nopalea (66)** (TJNaughton) **3-9-0** SSanders(5) (lw: a.p: r.o ins fnl f)	1¼	**2**	$9/2^{1}$	67	36
1236^{11}	**Whizz Kid (52)** (JJBridger) **3-7-13**(5) RMullen(14) (hrd rdn & hdwy over 2f out: r.o one pce fnl f)	1	**3**	11/1	54	23
602^{9}	**College Princess (46)** (SCWilliams) **3-8-0** DeclanO'Shea(8) (a.p: ev ch 2f out: one pce)	nk	**4**	40/1	49	18
1119^{10}	**Mystical** (MrsLStubbs) **3-8-10** MFenton(7) (lw: nvr nrr)	¾	**5**	10/1	57	26
882^{7}	**Blazing Castle (63)** (WGMTurner) **3-8-11** TSprake(4) (lw: a.p: one pce fnl f)	½	**6**	14/1	56	25
379^{3}	**Sparkling Edge (57)** (CADwyer) **3-8-6** JStack(11) (swtg: hrd rdn & hdwy over 2f out: wknd ins fnl f)	¾	**7**	10/1	49	18
964^{8}	**Cambridge Blue (USA) (66)** (GLewis) **3-8-13b¹** PatEddery(9) (hdwy over 2f out: wknd over 1f out)	nk	**8**	$9/2^{1}$	55	24
1141^{16}	**Silver Lining (61)** (APJones) **3-8-6**(5) PPMurphy(10) (prom over 2f)	1	**9**	10/1	50	19
1236^{6}	**Littlestone Rocket (53)** (WRMuir) **3-8-11v** JReid(12) (lw: a bhd)	hd	**10**	11/1	49	18
1167^{14}	**Folly Foot Fred (45)** (BRMillman) **3-8-11** SDrowne(3) (lw: a bhd)	¾	**11**	25/1	47	16
1294^{10}	**Heavenly Miss (IRE) (67)** (JJBridger) **3-8-12** PaulEddery(1) (lw: w wnr tl wknd over 1f out)	1¾	**12**	$13/2^{2}$	42	11
1292^{14}	**Sovereign** (MPMuggeridge) **3-7-11**(3) MartinDwyer(13) (a bhd)	4	**13**	50/1	18	—
1250^{16}	**Fit For The Job (IRE) (42)** (TWall) **3-8-7** LNewton(6) (lw: a bhd: t.o)	8	**14**	50/1	—	—

(SP 121.6%) **14 Rn**

61.4 secs (0.90) CSF £39.36 TOTE £9.10: £2.70 £1.80 £3.90 (£15.80) Trio £80.70 OWNER Mr C. J. Harper (WHITCOMBE) BRED Whitsbury Manor Stud

970 Lucky Dip has gradually dropped back to the minimum trip and managed to draw first prize here. (8/1: tchd 12/1)
1375 Nopalea continues to run well on turf and may be worth a try at six. (9/2)
876 Whizz Kid was trying to overcome the worst of the draw for the second time in succession. (11/1: 5/1-12/1)
345 College Princess ran her best race on grass for a while. (40/1)
882 Mystical was again without the visor she wore on her debut and might appreciate a return to six. (10/1: op 6/1)
757 Blazing Castle was reverting to the minimum distance. (14/1)
876 Silver Lining (10/1: 6/1-12/1)
Littlestone Rocket (11/1: 6/1-12/1)

1567 HAMSWELL MAIDEN STKS (3-Y.O+ F & M) (Class D)

8-20 (8-21) **1m 5y** £3,692.75 (£1,112.00: £538.50: £251.75) Stalls: Low GOING minus 0.52 sec per fur (F)

				SP	RR	SF
1297^{2}	**Boss Lady (IRE)** (RCharlton) **3-8-9** PatEddery(4) (lw: a.p: led over 2f out: rdn out)	—	**1**	$5/4^{1}$	77	38
1168^{5}	**Tangshan (CAN)** (MRStoute) **3-8-9** JReid(7) (hld up & plld hrd: hdwy over 2f out: r.o ins fnl f: nt trble wnr)	1¾	**2**	$5/2^{2}$	74	35
	Bold Becky (APJones) **3-8-9** TSprake(8) (w'like: a.p: chsd wnr over 2f out: rdn & rn green over 1f out: one pce)	¾	**3**	40/1	72	33
992^{3}	**Nubile** (BWHills) **3-8-9** MHills(10) (lw: outpcd over 4f out: styd on fnl 2f)	8	**4**	$3/1^{3}$	56	17
	Flyaway Hill (FR) (PWHarris) **3-8-9** RHills(9) (bkwd: bhd: rdn over 3f out: nvr nr ldrs)	2½	**5**	10/1	51	12
1207^{10}	**After Hours** (DJSffrenchDavis) **3-8-9** RPerham(5) (s.i.s: nvr nr ldrs)	2½	**6**	66/1	46	7
1322^{7}	**Mashkorah (USA)** (RHannon) **3-8-9** TQuinn(2) (led 2f: wknd over 2f out)	1¼	**7**	16/1	44	5
	Naburn Loch (DMHyde) **7-9-4**(3) RHavlin(1) (led 6f out tl over 2f out: wknd qckly)	1¼	**8**	150/1	41	14
	Inchella (APJones) **4-9-7** RPrice(3) (a bhd)	5	**9**	100/1	31	4
	Bairn Atholl (RJHodges) **4-9-7** SDrowne(6) (a bhd)	3	**10**	66/1	25	—

(SP 120.1%) **10 Rn**

1m 39.5 (1.30) CSF £4.32 TOTE £1.90: £1.10 £1.40 £3.20 (£2.90) Trio £57.30 OWNER Lord Weinstock (BECKHAMPTON) BRED Ballymacoll Stud Farm Ltd
WEIGHT FOR AGE 3yo-12lb

1297 Boss Lady (IRE), out of a mile and three-quarters winner, did not mind this faster ground and will stay further in time. (5/4: 11/10-evens)
1168 Tangshan (CAN), back to a mile, did not help her cause by proving difficult to settle. (5/2)
Bold Becky, a half-sister to dual five-furlong winner Silca-Cisa, belied her long odds quoted in the ring. (40/1)
992 Nubile is going to need further if this effort is anything to go by. (3/1)

1568 END OF THE DAY H'CAP (0-70) (3-Y.O) (Class E)

8-50 (9-04) **1m 5y** £3,210.25 (£967.00: £468.50: £219.25) Stalls: Low GOING minus 0.52 sec per fur (F)

				SP	RR	SF
1164^{*}	**Blue Imperial (FR) (58)** (JWHills) **3-8-9** RHills(2) (lw: mde all: rdn over 1f out: jst hld on)	—	**1**	$5/2^{1}$	65	26
1272^{7}	**Warring (58)** (MSSaunders) **3-8-4**(5) PPMurphy(4) (a.p: hrd rdn over 1f out: r.o wl ins fnl f)	nk	**2**	$8/1^{3}$	64	25
963^{13}	**Flashtalkin' Flood (55)** (CADwyer) **3-8-6** JStack(11) (a.p: r.o ins fnl f)	¾	**3**	12/1	60	21
1164^{17}	**Sun O'Tirol (IRE) (58)** (JRArnold) **3-8-9** CRutter(6) (chsd wnr: ev ch over 1f out: one pce)	hd	**4**	33/1	63	24
1164^{11}	**Brave Envoy (64)** (MJHeaton-Ellis) **3-9-1** SDrowne(3) (lw: dwlt: hdwy over 2f out: nvr nr to chal)	3	**5**	12/1	63	24
1140^{19}	**Sand Cay (USA) (65)** (RHannon) **3-9-2** RHughes(5) (hld up: hdwy 3f out: one pce fnl 2f)	nk	**6**	25/1	63	24
1048^{3}	**Swan Island (64)** (BPalling) **3-9-1** TSprake(10) (prom: rdn over 2f out: wknd over 1f out)	¾	**7**	$6/1^{2}$	61	22
1167^{4}	**Prince of Fortune (52)** (MBlanshard) **3-8-3** NAdams(8) (hld up & plld hrd: nvr trbld ldrs)	½	**8**	10/1	48	9
1121^{4}	**Misty Rain (70)** (BWHills) **3-9-7** MHills(9) (bhd fnl 2f)	hd	**9**	$6/1^{2}$	65	26
1140^{12}	**Certain Magic (60)** (WRMuir) **3-8-11** JReid(7) (a bhd)	1¾	**10**	12/1	52	13
1140^{9}	**Aficionado (IRE) (67)** (RJHodges) **3-9-4** TQuinn(12) (a bhd)	s.h	**11**	$6/1^{2}$	59	20

				SP	RR	SF
1024[14]	**Bold Saint (IRE) (55)** (PWHarris) **3-8-6** AMcGlone(13) (a bhd)	½	**12**	16/1	46	7
1110[12]	***Doyenne (49)*** (GLewis) **3-7-11**(3) AWhelan(1) (withdrawn not under Starter's orders: uns rdr & bolted bef s)		**W**	25/1	—	—
				(SP 131.2%)	**12 Rn**	

1m 40.7 (2.50) CSF £22.65 CT £201.06 TOTE £3.90: £1.90 £3.00 £3.40 (£33.80) Trio £444.70; £100.24 to 2/6/97 OWNER Mr George Tong (LAMBOURN) BRED Haras de Clairfeuille

1164* Blue Imperial (FR), up 4lb, was given a canny ride from the front, which was just as well for in the end the post came plenty soon enough. (5/2)
1000 Warring, already due to go up 2lb, was much more at home back on this faster ground but took a long time to really find his stride and the line arrived just too soon. (8/1)
Flashtalkin' Flood seems to have found the right trip. (12/1)
840 Sun O'Tirol (IRE) was 6lb better off with the winner than when beaten nearly twenty lengths last time. (33/1)
785 Brave Envoy was meeting the winner on 4lb better terms than when beaten twelve lengths at Salisbury. (12/1)
Sand Cay (USA) was reverting to a mile. (25/1)
1167 Prince of Fortune (10/1: 8/1-12/1)

T/Plpt: £48.80 (274.31 Tckts). T/Qdpt: £23.80 (36.4 Tckts) KH

0779-CATTERICK (L-H) (Good to firm, Good patches)
Friday May 30th
WEATHER: sunny WIND: almost nil

64+ 64 65 60

1569 STAPLETON MAIDEN AUCTION STKS (2-Y.O F) (Class F) (63)
2-20 (2-21) **5f** £2,792.50 (£780.00: £377.50) Stalls: Low GOING minus 0.31 sec per fur (GF)

				SP	RR	SF
1280[4]	**Baby Grand (IRE)** (TDBarron) **2-7-8**(7) KimberleyHart(7) (chsd ldrs: styd on to ld jst ins fnl f)	—	**1**	14/1	60	35
1137[5]	**Patsy Culsyth** (MJohnston) **2-8-7** BDoyle(9) (chsd ldrs: rdn & outpcd ½-wy: styd on fnl f)	1¼	**2**	20/1	62	37
1109[3]	**Country Garden** (RHannon) **2-8-7** DaneO'Neill(2) (a chsng ldrs: rdn ½-wy: kpt on same pce)	nk	**3**	11/10[1]	61	36
	Its All Relative (JBerry) **2-8-7** KDarley(4) (rangy: unf: scope: led tl jst ins fnl f)	s.h	**4**	8/1	61+	36
	Bow Peep (IRE) (MWEasterby) **2-8-2**(5)ow3 GParkin(6) (chsd ldrs tl wknd appr fnl f)	2½	**5**	33/1	53	25
1328[6]	**Frisky Lady** (TDEasterby) **2-8-7** WJO'Connor(10) (chsd ldrs tl wknd over 1f out)	½	**6**	14/1	51	26
	Sing For Me (IRE) (RHollinshead) **2-8-1** JQuinn(1) (chsd ldrs tl wknd over 1f out)	2	**7**	25/1	39	14
1280[2]	**Oriel Girl** (PDEvans) **2-8-4** JFanning(12) (chsd ldrs: rdn ½-wy: lost pl over 1f out)	5	**8**	7/2[2]	26	1
750[7]	**Shannon (IRE)** (CADwyer) **2-8-4** NVarley(14) (swvd rt s: a bhd)	1¾	**9**	16/1	20	—
902[3]	**Sweet Rosie (IRE)** (RBoss) **2-7-12**(3) MHenry(15) (bmpd s: a outpcd)	nk	**10**	7/1[3]	16	—
572[6]	**Blitz** (MWEasterby) **2-8-3**ow2 TLucas(3) (sn outpcd & bhd)	1¾	**11**	16/1	13	—
	Chikapenny (MrsLStubbs) **2-8-1** GHind(11) (dwlt: a wl bhd)	hd	**12**	10/1	10	—
	Musical Pet (IRE) (JLEyre) **2-8-4** MGallagher(8) (s.i.s: a outpcd)	2½	**13**	20/1	5	—
1091[6]	**Scolding** (KAMorgan) **2-7-13**(5) RFfrench(5) (swvd bdly lft s: sn uns rdr)		**U**	12/1	—	—
				(SP 151.6%)	**14 Rn**	

59.1 secs (1.40) CSF £290.15 TOTE £21.30: £4.50 £3.70 £1.50 (£208.90) Trio £56.40 OWNER Mrs D. E. Sharp (THIRSK) BRED Rathbarry Stud

1280 Baby Grand (IRE) took a race that looked no better than a seller. (14/1)
1137 Patsy Culsyth, very keen going to post, stuck on after being outpaced and either needs a stiffer track or six furlongs. (20/1)
1109 Country Garden was flat out at halfway and this sharp downhill track was not in her favour. (11/10)
Its All Relative, who has plenty of size and scope, showed bags of toe to lead these until tiring. The outing should bring her on. (8/1: op 5/1)
Bow Peep (IRE) ran surprisingly well considering she looked backward and showed a poor action going down. (33/1)
1328 Frisky Lady, who missed the break first time, showed plenty of speed from her outside draw. (14/1)
Scolding (12/1: 16/1-10/1)

1570 CROFT (S) STKS (4-Y.O+) (Class G)
2-50 (2-52) **1m 5f 175y** £2,174.50 (£607.00: £293.50) Stalls: Low GOING minus 0.31 sec per fur (GF)

				SP	RR	SF
1114[10]	**Rose of Glenn (38)** (BPalling) **6-8-7** JQuinn(3) (trckd ldrs: led 4f out: styd on wl fnl 2f)	—	**1**	16/1	55	37
570[4]	**Risky Rose (40)** (RHollinshead) **5-8-6**(3)ow2 DGriffiths(5) (hld up: hdwy over 3f out: chsd wnr fnl 2f: no imp)	3	**2**	9/1	54	34
1152[4]	**Batabanoo (68)** (MrsMReveley) **8-8-12** KDarley(9) (hld up: hdwy over 5f out: sn chsng ldrs: rdn over 2f out: one pce)	1¾	**3**	Evens[1]	55	37
1133[12]	**Pharly Dancer (58)** (WWHaigh) **8-8-7**(5) GParkin(2) (led tl over 6f out: hung lft & lost pl over 2f out)	13	**4**	5/1[3]	39	21
1229[10]	**Jarrow (24)** (MrsAMNaughton) **6-8-12** NConnorton(10) (hld up: hdwy 5f out: lost pl 3f out)	5	**5**	50/1	34	16
*1152**	**Petoskin (55)** (JPearce) **5-9-4** MWigham(6) (chsd ldrs: led over 6f out: hdd 4f out: wknd over 2f out)	1½	**6**	11/4[2]	38	20
	Bobby's Dream (35) (MHTompkins) **5-8-4**(3) MHenry(1) (outpcd 8f out: hdwy on outside over 4f out: sn lost pl)	19	**7**	14/1	5	—
1229[8]	**Craigary (30)** (MrsASwinbank) **6-8-12b** WJO'Connor(8) (chsd ldrs: rdn 6f out: lost pl 4f out)	6	**8**	20/1	3	—
	Paperwork Pete (IRE) (WStorey) **5-8-12** JFanning(7) (prom: rdn 6f out: sn lost pl)	12	**9**	14/1	—	—
	Bristol Gold (PSFelgate) **4-8-12** GHind(4) (bhd & pushed along 8f out: t.o 5f out)	dist	**10**	33/1	—	—
				(SP 132.2%)	**10 Rn**	

3m 1.4 (5.40) CSF £152.60 TOTE £16.40: £3.10 £1.80 £1.10 (£15.70) Trio £14.90 OWNER Mr S. Sullivan (COWBRIDGE) BRED Mrs M. J. Dandy
No bid

Rose of Glenn made it four wins from four starts here. She certainly proved very willing. (16/1)
570 Risky Rose, who is by no means a consistent individual, took second place two furlongs out but was never making any real impression. (9/1)
1152 Batabanoo does not seem as good as he once was after having a year off and being fired. (Evens)
869 Pharly Dancer is off the boil at present. (5/1)
Jarrow, who wore a tongue-strap, found little under pressure. (50/1)
1152* Petoskin, who had beaten Batabanoo on the All-Weather, folded tamely. (11/4)

1571 WENSLEY SPRINT H'CAP (0-80) (3-Y.O) (Class D)
3-20 (3-21) **5f** £3,379.00 (£1,012.00: £486.00: £223.00) Stalls: Low GOING minus 0.31 sec per fur (GF)

Form	Horse / details	Dist	Pos	SP	RR	SF
1294*	**Bramble Bear (69)** (MBlanshard) **3-8-12** 7x JQuinn(4) (trckd ldrs: effrt over 1f out: styd on to ld last 75y)	—	**1**	2/1^{2}	73	32
549^{5}	**Northern Sal (58)** (MissLAPerratt) **3-7-12**(3) PFessey(2) (unruly in stalls: dwlt: hdwy to chse ldrs over 3f out: led over 1f out tl wl ins fnl f)	½	**2**	10/1	60	19
783^{3}	**Tinker's Surprise (IRE) (53)** (JBalding) **3-7-10** NCarlisle(1) (trckd ldr: plld hrd: led 2f out: sn hdd: wknd ins fnl f)	2½	**3**	5/1^{3}	47	6
1254^{4}	**Ballymote (78)** (JBerry) **3-9-7** KDarley(3) (led to 2f out: wknd jst ins fnl f)	1¼	**4**	10/11^{1}	68	27

(SP 111.5%) **4 Rn**

59.9 secs (2.20) CSF £15.68 TOTE £2.50: (£13.10) OWNER Mrs Michael Hill & Mrs Heather Chakko (UPPER LAMBOURN) BRED E. A. Badger
LONG HANDICAP Tinker's Surprise (IRE) 7-9

1294* Bramble Bear found this different ground no problem and was produced with a well-timed run. (2/1)
549 Northern Sal, a nervous type, played up badly in the stalls and missed the break. Even so, she was only run out of it inside the last one hundred yards. (10/1: 6/1-11/1)
783 Tinker's Surprise (IRE), meeting Ballymote on 4lb better terms for a four-length beating, contributed to his own downfall by refusing to settle. (5/1)
1254 Ballymote gave problems going to the start and produced little under pressure. (10/11)

1572 PEN HILL CLAIMING STKS (3-Y.O+) (Class F)
3-50 (3-51) **5f** £1,617.50 (£1,617.50: £340.00) Stalls: Low GOING minus 0.31 sec per fur (GF)

Form	Horse / details	Dist	Pos	SP	RR	SF
1158^{10}	**Palacegate Touch (78)** (JBerry) **7-9-10**(3) PFessey(3) (trckd ldrs: led 2f out: jst hld on)	—	**1**	13/8^{1}	70	57
1385^{11}	**Captain Carat (59)** (DNicholls) **6-9-1b** AlexGreaves(10) (hld up: hdwy ½-wy: sn rdn: styd on ins fnl f)	—	**1**	5/1^{3}	63	45
	Donna's Dancer (IRE) (66) (NTinkler) **3-7-10b**(5) RFfrench(7) (s.i.s: sn bhd: hdwy over 1f out: styd on towards fin)	1½	**3**	4/1^{2}	46	26
1236^{10}	**Southern Dominion (43)** (MissJFCraze) **5-8-11b** SWebster(9) (b.hind: chsd ldrs: edgd rt ½-wy: styd on u.p fnl f)	s.h	**4**	14/1	47	36
1332^{6}	**Antithesis (IRE) (61)** (JSHaldane) **4-8-8** KDarley(5) (a chsng ldrs: kpt on same pace fnl f)	½	**5**	8/1	43	31
58^{5}	**Windrush Boy (50)** (MRBosley) **7-8-6**(5) AimeeCook(4) (hdwy ½-wy: ev ch over 1f out: one pce)	1¼	**6**	8/1	42	30
760^{12}	**Captain Sinbad (56)** (KSBridgwater) **5-8-13b** VSlattery(6) (led to 2f out: wknd fnl f)	¾	**7**	14/1	41	30
	Bashful Brave (60) (BPJBaugh) **6-9-1** GHind(8) (trckd ldrs: ev ch over 1f out: wknd fnl f)	2½	**8**	12/1	35	24
1451^{7}	**Chilled Wine (30)** (GPKelly) **3-7-10** JQuinn(2) (prom to ½-wy: sn bhd)	5	**9**	50/1	8	—
1046^{11}	**Nefertiti (30)** (RFMarvin) **3-7-5**(7) RWinston(1) (w ldrs to ½-wy: sn lost pl)	5	**10**	50/1	—	—

(SP 121.9%) **10 Rn**

59.2 secs (1.50) CSF PT & CC £4.75 CC & PT £6.44 TOTE PT £1.50 CC £2.60: PT £1.10 CC £2.40 £1.40 (£8.00) Trio £5.30 OWNER Laurel (Leisure) Ltd (COCKERHAM)/Mr V. Greaves (THIRSK) BRED The Woodhaven Stud/Lt-Col J. H. Scott
WEIGHT FOR AGE 3yo-8lb

972* Palacegate Touch, with the headgear left off, carried his head at an awkward angle and had to share the spoils right on the line. (13/8)
1223 Captain Carat, who would have been meeting the winner on 7lb better terms in a handicap, came from off the pace to get up on the line. (5/1)
Donna's Dancer (IRE), who had 6lb in hand on official figures, not for the first time threw away a winning chance at the start. (4/1)
924* Southern Dominion, who would have been meeting Palacegate Touch on 19lb better terms in a handicap, edged right and ended up under the stands' side rail. (14/1)
698 Antithesis (IRE), back in a claimer, ran better than she had in two handicaps. (8/1)
58 Windrush Boy would have been meeting Palacegate Touch on 12lb better terms in a handicap. (8/1)

1573 GRINTON H'CAP (0-70) (3-Y.O) (Class E)
4-20 (4-21) **5f 212y** £3,054.25 (£919.00: £444.50: £207.25) Stalls: Low GOING minus 0.31 sec per fur (GF)

Form	Horse / details	Dist	Pos	SP	RR	SF
995^{18}	**Docklands Carriage (IRE) (55)** (NTinkler) **3-8-3b**(3) PMcCabe(2) (chsd ldrs: sn drvn along: led over 1f out: styd on)	—	**1**	7/1	67	38
1236^{7}	**Municipal Girl (IRE) (52)** (BPalling) **3-8-0**(3) MHenry(3) (swtg: led after 2f tl over 1f out: kpt on same pce)	2	**2**	12/1	59	30
1096^{10}	**C-Harry (IRE) (60)** (RHollinshead) **3-8-11** MWigham(5) (sn bhd & drvn along: hdwy over 2f out: kpt on one pce appr fnl f)	2	**3**	6/1^{3}	61	32
995^{12}	**Cairn Dhu (61)** (DWBarker) **3-8-12** AlexGreaves(6) (chsd ldrs: rdn & hung lft 2f out: no imp)	1¾	**4**	9/1	58	29
1141^{24}	**Mon Bruce (64)** (WRMuir) **3-8-12**(3) JDSmith(4) (lw: trckd ldrs: ev ch over 1f out: sn wknd)	nk	**5**	12/1	60	31
1237^{5}	**Bold Spring (IRE) (70)** (RHannon) **3-9-7** DaneO'Neill(7) (lw: sn bhd & drvn along: kpt on fnl 2f: nvr nr ldrs)	1¾	**6**	2/1^{1}	61	32
1284^{6}	**Abstone Queen (55)** (PDEvans) **3-8-6v** WJO'Connor(1) (hld up & bhd: swtchd ins: hdwy over 1f out: nvr nrr ldrs)	2½	**7**	5/1^{2}	39	10
1245^{5}	**Falls O'Moness (IRE) (68)** (KRBurke) **3-9-0**(5) RFfrench(8) (bhd fr ½-wy)	1¼	**8**	13/2	49	20
656^{5}	**Changed To Baileys (IRE) (63)** (JBerry) **3-9-0** KDarley(10) (drvn along & bhd ½-wy)	7	**9**	10/1	25	—
1131^{10}	**Sarabi (55)** (JPearce) **3-8-6v^{1}** JQuinn(9) (plld hrd: led 2f: chsd ldrs tl wknd over 2f out)	1¾	**10**	14/1	13	—

(SP 131.3%) **10 Rn**

1m 12.8 (1.90) CSF £89.75 CT £505.82 TOTE £15.20: £3.70 £4.20 £2.70 (£44.50) Trio £65.70 OWNER Mrs Lisa Olley (MALTON) BRED Topazio Est Vaduz
OFFICIAL EXPLANATION **Docklands Carriage (IRE): had been unsuited by the straight track last time.**

785 Docklands Carriage (IRE), who was apparently unsuited by the straight track last time, took what was a seller in all but name. (7/1)
758* Municipal Girl (IRE), who was awash with sweat even taking into account the hot day, proved suited by the step back up to six. (12/1)
845 C-Harry (IRE) stayed on from off the pace and is better over seven. (6/1)
757* Cairn Dhu, who changed hands for 4,800 gns, wanted to do nothing but hang left. (9/1)
588* Mon Bruce raced keenly and had nothing left with over a furlong left to run. (12/1)
1237 Bold Spring (IRE) is proving a disappointing sort. (2/1: 4/1-7/4)
1284 Abstone Queen, dropped in at the start, really needs seven furlongs now. (5/1: op 3/1)

1574 MUKER RATING RELATED MAIDEN STKS (0-60) (3-Y.O+) (Class F)

4-50 (4-52) **1m 3f 214y** £2,617.50 (£730.00: £352.50) Stalls: Low GOING minus 0.31 sec per fur (GF)

	Horse	Dist	Pos	SP	RR	SF
785[9]	**Fullopep (60)** (MrsMReveley) **3-8-6** KDarley(2) (hld up: hdwy over 6f out: shkn up to ld over 1f out: sn clr: eased towards fin)	—	1	11/2[3]	63+	22
1042[3]	**Six Clerks (IRE) (58)** (JGFitzGerald) **4-9-9** DaneO'Neill(1) (sn trckng ldrs: rdn & outpcd over 2f out: hdwy & swtchd over 1f out: kpt on wl)	3½	2	8/1	58	34
1258[5]	**Indigo Dawn (59)** (MJohnston) **3-8-3** BDoyle(9) (bhd & drvn along 5f out: hdwy over 2f out: styd on one pce fnl f)	nk	3	11/2[3]	55	14
1296[11]	**Le Grand Gousier (USA) (60)** (RJRWilliams) **3-8-6** GHind(3) (led tl over 1f out: one pce)	½	4	14/1	57	16
1153[3]	**Anchor Venture (52)** (SPCWoods) **4-9-2**(7) CWebb(5) (hdwy to trck ldrs 7f out: chal over 2f out: sn rdn: wknd over 1f out)	5	5	10/1	51	27
1093[3]	**Jean Pierre (55)** (JPearce) **4-9-9** MWigham(6) (dwlt: hld up: hdwy 7f out: rdn over 2f out: edgd rt & no imp)	2	6	9/4[1]	48	24
1222[10]	**Finestatetobein (31)** (FWatson) **4-9-3**(3) PFessey(8) (w ldrs tl wknd 2f out:)	2	7	33/1	42	18
	Cascatelle Bleue (IRE) (60) (MHTompkins) **4-9-6** WJO'Connor(4) (trckd ldrs: effrt u.p over 2f out: grad wknd)	½	8	10/1	42	18
1155[10]	**Showcase (60)** (JWHills) **3-8-0**(3) MHenry(10) (sn trckng ldrs: effrt & ev ch over 2f out: sn wknd)	3½	9	9/2[2]	37	—
	Opera Fan (IRE) (41) (KAMorgan) **5-9-4**(5) RFfrench(7) (trckd ldrs: drvn along 7f out: lost pl over 4f out: sn bhd)	7	10	14/1	31	7

(SP 125.3%) **10 Rn**

2m 38.2 (6.80) CSF £48.21 TOTE £7.90: £2.40 £1.60 £1.60 (£18.40) Trio £20.30 OWNER Mr P. D. Savill (SALTBURN) BRED M. H. Easterby
WEIGHT FOR AGE 3yo-17lb

Fullopep, a keen-going sort, proved well suited by the step up in distance and, coming from off the pace, in the end did it in good style. He looks a potential hurdler but there is another race or two to be won with him on the level. (11/2)

1042 Six Clerks (IRE), who ran poorly in a handicap hurdle two weeks earlier, was badly chopped for foot on the home turn but recovered to be staying on at the finish. (8/1)

1258 Indigo Dawn has ability but is clearly something of a madam. Dropping herself out halfway down the back straight, she consented to stay on once in line for home. (11/2)

Le Grand Gousier (USA) proved well suited by this much faster ground and ran a genuine race from the front. (14/1)

1153 Anchor Venture, a keen-going sort, not for the first time flattered only to deceive. (10/1)

1093 Jean Pierre, presumably a headstrong sort, was walked all the way down to the start. After missing the break, he made things hard for himself and, under pressure once in line for home, was never doing anything like enough. (9/4)

T/Jkpt: Not won; £2,707.10 to Newmarket 31/5/97. T/Plpt: £117.50 (96.82 Tckts). T/Qdpt: £48.30 (13.52 Tckts) WG

1428-**WOLVERHAMPTON (L-H) (Standard)**

Friday May 30th

WEATHER: fine & sunny WIND: slt half bhd

1575 CLOWN AMATEUR H'CAP (0-85) (3-Y.O+) (Class G)

2-10 (2-14) **1m 100y (Fibresand)** £1,984.50 (£547.00: £259.50) Stalls: Low GOING minus 0.14 sec per fur (FST)

	Horse	Dist	Pos	SP	RR	SF
1097[15]	**Anonym (IRE) (68)** (JLEyre) **5-10-9b** MissDianaJones(6) (a.p: shkn up to chal fnl f: r.o to ld last stride)	—	1	11/2[3]	80	54
176[7]	**Waikiki Beach (USA) (69)** (GLMoore) **6-10-6**(4) MrsJMoore(9) (b: bit bkwd: swtg: led after 1f tl ct post)	s.h	2	12/1	81	55
1285[4]	**Dancing Sioux (62)** (RGuest) **5-9-10**(7) MissZBurkett(8) (b: hld up & bhd: hdwy over 3f out: rdn over 1f out: nt pce to chal)	2	3	7/1	70	44
1422[19]	**Everset (FR) (70)** (ABailey) **9-10-4**(7) MissALHutchinson(3) (b: bit bkwd: hld up: hdwy 4f out: one pce fnl 2f)	2½	4	33/1	73	47
1225[19]	**Desert Invader (IRE) (65)** (DWChapman) **6-10-6** MissRClark(2) (w ldrs: rdn over 1f out: one pce)	4	5	6/1	61	35
1422[7]	**Wentbridge Lad (IRE) (65)** (PDEvans) **7-10-2v**(4) MrWMcLaughlin(4) (chsd ldrs: effrt & rdn wl over 1f out: no rspnse)	2½	6	5/1[2]	56	30
490[4]	**Dream Carrier (IRE) (57)** (REPeacock) **9-9-5**(7)ow12 MrsCPeacock(1) (a in rr)	5	7	14/1	39	1
763[7]	**Breezed Well (51)** (KGWingrove) **11-9-2**(4)ow6 MrsHNoonan(10) (led 1f: wknd 3f out: t.o)	17	8	50/1	1	—
210[4]	**Sarum (53)** (JELong) **11-9-1**(7)ow8 MrTWaters(11) (b: bkwd: prom: stmbld & lost pl over 6f out: t.o)	28	9	50/1	—	—
1450[3]	***Angel Face (USA) (80)*** (PDEvans) **4-11-3**(4) MrAEvans(5) (Withdrawn not under Starter's orders: ref to ent stalls)		W	6/4[1]	—	—

(SP 120.1%) **9 Rn**

1m 50.7 (5.70) CSF £26.09 CT £94.79 TOTE £3.10: £1.50 £2.50 £1.80 (£10.40) Trio £26.10 OWNER Wetherby Racing Bureau 28 (HAMBLETON) BRED T. G. Mooney
LONG HANDICAP Breezed Well 7-13 Sarum 7-10 Dream Carrier (IRE) 8-8

947 Anonym (IRE) regained his form on this step down in class but he only just managed it and a lot of the credit must go to the ride he received. (11/2)

105 Waikiki Beach (USA), reappearing after a four-month break, always looked to be in control, but lack of a recent race must have told in the closing stages and he was touched off right on the line. (12/1: op 7/1)

1285 Dancing Sioux, ridden to get the trip, made significant progress at the end of the back straight, but was feeling the strain once in line for home and found an extra effort beyond him. (7/1)

Everset (FR), making a quick reappearance, was given more of a chance to get the trip, but he only plugged on at the one pace from the turn for home and probably found the run coming too soon. (33/1)

1132* Desert Invader (IRE) pressed the leaders and still had a live chance on straightening up but he does appear to find this trip beyond his best and was galloping on the spot inside the distance. (6/1: op 4/1)

Wentbridge Lad (IRE) was entitled to be thereabouts on this return to the sand but he was flat to the boards turning in and all hopes soon disappeared. (5/1: 3/1-6/1)

1576 GROUPER CLAIMING STKS (3-Y.O+) (Class F)

2-40 (2-45) **1m 1f 79y (Fibresand)** £2,277.00 (£627.00: £297.00) Stalls: Low GOING minus 0.14 sec per fur (FST)

	Horse	Dist	Pos	SP	RR	SF
1238[8]	**Globetrotter (IRE) (85)** (MJohnston) **3-9-0** DHolland(2) (lw: stumbled s: hdwy over 3f out: led wl over 1f out: drvn clr)	—	1	5/4[1]	70	22

1125[6]	**Eastleigh (48)** (RHollinshead) **8-9-0**(3) FLynch(11) (b.nr hind: swtg: a.p: rdn ent st: styd on wl fnl f)	1¾	**2**	20/1	57	22
1389[5]	**Rambo Waltzer (82)** (DNicholls) **5-9-5**(5) IonaWands(12) (hld up in rr: hdwy over 2f out: kpt on u.p fnl f)	nk	**3**	5/4[1]	64	29
1448[6]	**That Old Feeling (IRE)** (DWChapman) **5-9-4** JCarroll(7) (lw: a.p: ev ch over 2f out: sn rdn & wknd)	7	**4**	16/1	46	11
1287[4]	**Pc's Cruiser (IRE) (38)** (NPLittmoden) **5-9-3b** TGMcLaughlin(10) (hdwy 6f out: led over 4f out tl hdd & wknd wl over 1f out)	1¾	**5**	10/1[2]	42	7
1291[10]	**Chadleigh Lane (USA) (64)** (ABMulholland) **5-9-1v**(5) GFaulkner(1) (b: trckd ldrs: rdn over 2f out: sn btn)	3	**6**	14/1	39	4
	Scottish Park (46) (MCPipe) **8-8-10** MRoberts(8) (nvr plcd to chal)	2	**7**	10/1[2]	26	—
1134[4]	**Medland (IRE) (36)** (BJMcMath) **7-9-1** GBardwell(9) (bit bkwd: prom: ev ch 2f out: sn rdn & wknd)	4	**8**	50/1	24	—
	Frans Lad (BPJBaugh) **5-9-3v** RPerham(6) (led tl hdd over 4f out: sn rdn & wknd)	2	**9**	66/1	23	—
1441[13]	**My Handsome Prince (38)** (PJBevan) **5-8-12**(5) GMilligan(3) (a bhd)	¾	**10**	50/1	21	—
1289[13]	**Guy's Gamble (40)** (JWharton) **4-9-1**(3) OPears(5) (a bhd: t.o fr ½-wy:)	7	**11**	50/1	11	—
1273[10]	***Ethbaat (USA) (65)*** (MJHeaton-Ellis) **6-9-10v**[1] SDrowne(4) (Withdrawn not under Starter's orders: ref to ent stalls)		**W**	12/1[3]	—	—

(SP 139.4%) **11 Rn**

2m 3.6 (7.60) CSF £34.63 TOTE £2.50: £1.40 £4.50 £1.10 (£30.60) Trio £12.20 OWNER Brian Yeardley Continental Ltd (MIDDLEHAM) BRED Norelands Bloodstock

WEIGHT FOR AGE 3yo-13lb

388* Globetrotter (IRE) lost his footing as he bounded out of the stalls and was lucky to remain upright. Beginning to pick up at the end of the back straight, he took over once in line for home and from then on the race was as good as over. (5/4: tchd evens)

1125 Eastleigh has never won at this track despite being trained nearby, but he ran well here and in this kind of form is capable of finding another race. (20/1)

1389 Rambo Waltzer sat way off the pace on this occasion and, though he did stay on particularly well in the closing stages, always seemed to have to much to do. (5/4)

1448 That Old Feeling (IRE) found this race coming far too soon after making his seasonal debut five days ago and what chance he had had come to an end on reaching the straight. He has not won a race for close on three years but he is with the right man to put the record straight. (16/1)

1287 Pc's Cruiser (IRE), taking a step down in trip, moved easily to the front entering the last half-mile, but the winner took his measure without much difficulty and he was soon fighting a lost cause. (10/1: op 16/1)

461 Chadleigh Lane (USA) has not improved his ways since changing stables and he had shot his bolt on the home turn. (14/1: 10/1-16/1)

68 80 64+

1577 STAR MAIDEN STKS (2-Y.O) (Class D)

3-10 (3-11) **6f (Fibresand)** £3,318.75 (£990.00: £472.50: £213.75) Stalls: Low GOING minus 0.14 sec per fur (FST)

				SP	RR	SF
993[2]	**Oh Never Again (IRE)** (MJohnston) **2-9-0** DHolland(8) (chsd ldrs: hrd drvn over 2f out: styd on to ld wl ins fnl f)	—	**1**	2/1[1]	70	21
	Tangerine Flyer (JBerry) **2-8-9**(5) PRoberts(5) (small: unf: bit bkwd: a.p: led 3f out: sn wl clr: wknd & ct cl home)	¾	**2**	9/2[3]	68	19
1136[11]	**Gralmano (IRE)** (NPLittmoden) **2-9-0** TGMcLaughlin(6) (mid div: drvn along ½-wy: styd on ins fnl f)	2½	**3**	10/1	61	12
	Ringleader (PFICole) **2-9-0** CRutter(9) (leggy: lt-f: sn drvn along & outpcd: effrt over 1f out: nvr nrr)	3	**4**	11/4[2]	53	4
	Press Ahead (BAMcMahon) **2-9-0** RCochrane(1) (w'like: bkwd: led to ½-wy: wknd 2f out)	10	**5**	16/1	27	—
1286[6]	**Angie Minor** (JWharton) **2-8-9** SSanders(4) (w ldrs over 3f: sn pushed along & lost pl)	½	**6**	16/1	20	—
	Stravsea (BPJBaugh) **2-8-9** RPerham(3) (w'like: scope: s.s: a in rr)	2	**7**	25/1	15	—
1045[3]	**Thanks Keith** (JJO'Neill) **2-9-0** JCarroll(7) (outpcd fr ½-wy)	1	**8**	11/4[2]	17	—
1370[8]	**Greenbrook** (WGMTurner) **2-8-7b**[1](7) DMcGaffin(10) (a outpcd)	1	**9**	20/1	15	—
648[12]	**Red Risk** (PWHarris) **2-9-0** MRoberts(2) (outpcd: a bhd)	3½	**10**	14/1	5	—

(SP 141.0%) **10 Rn**

1m 15.9 (4.70) CSF £13.39 TOTE £3.00: £1.30 £1.90 £1.70 (£10.30) Trio £23.50 OWNER Mr F. McNamee (MIDDLEHAM) BRED Airlie Stud

993 Oh Never Again (IRE) found the extra furlong and the more testing ground of the All-Weather made to measure and, gaining command in the final fifty yards, won going away. (2/1)

Tangerine Flyer, a son of a very speedy racemare, looked set to make a winning debut when driven clear two furlongs out, but had given the impression in the paddock that he would be all the better for the run and the race-fit winner had the legs of him in the sprint to the line. He can soon make amends. (9/2: op 5/2)

1136 Gralmano (IRE), bred to come into his own when tackling a more suitable trip, was doing all his best work late on, and if brought along quietly could be the sort to make amends when the nurseries arrive. (10/1: op 5/1)

Ringleader is out of a winning sprinter but he was always being made to work from an outside stall and was unable to find top gear until it was far too late. (11/4)

1578 MINNOW H'CAP (0-100) (3-Y.O+) (Class C)

3-40 (3-40) **6f (Fibresand)** £5,352.55 (£1,596.40: £761.70: £344.35) Stalls: Low GOING minus 0.14 sec per fur (FST)

				SP	RR	SF
1317[12]	**Bold Effort (FR) (90)** (KOCunningham-Brown) **5-9-6b** MRoberts(7) (lw: hld up: hdwy 2f out: led 200y out: r.o strly)	—	**1**	14/1	100	48
1324[14]	**Cim Bom Bom (IRE) (95)** (MBell) **5-9-6v**(5) GFaulkner(5) (chsd ldrs: led over 2f out: rdn & hdd jst ins fnl f: nt pce of wnr)	2	**2**	6/1	100	48
*905**	**Robo Magic (USA) (84)** (LMontagueHall) **5-8-11**(3) FLynch(9) (b: hdwy u.p 2f out: r.o wl ins fnl f)	2	**3**	9/2[2]	83	31
731[6]	**The Happy Fox (IRE) (82)** (BAMcMahon) **5-8-12b** RCochrane(4) (hdwy over 2f out: kpt on u.p fnl f)	hd	**4**	8/1	81	29
1158[5]	**Kira (74)** (JLEyre) **7-8-4** RLappin(8) (b: b.hind: led after 1f: sn hdd: rdn 2f out: one pce)	1¾	**5**	7/2[1]	68	16
1410[3]	**Zuhair (80)** (DMcCain) **4-8-10** JCarroll(3) (swtg: chsd ldrs: rdn & no hdwy fnl 2f)	1½	**6**	8/1	70	18
1160[11]	**Master Boots (98)** (DRLoder) **4-10-0** DHolland(6) (lw: nvr gng pce of ldrs)	nk	**7**	6/1	88	36
1029[7]	**Double-O (82)** (WJarvis) **3-8-3** SSanders(2) (lw: swtg: led 1f: led 4f out tl over 2f out: sn wknd)	6	**8**	25/1	56	—
1107[4]	**Just Loui (90)** (WGMTurner) **3-8-4**(7) DMcGaffin(11) (in tch: hrd drvn over 2f out: no imp)	nk	**9**	16/1	63	2
1269[10]	**Ramsey Hope (79)** (CWFairhurst) **4-8-9v** NKennedy(1) (a outpcd)	5	**10**	33/1	39	—
1317[4]	**Warning Time (89)** (BJMeehan) **4-9-5b**[1] RHughes(10) (lw: prom tl rdn & outpcd wl over 1f out)	1	**11**	11/2[3]	46	—

(SP 125.9%) **11 Rn**

1m 14.3 (3.10) CSF £93.30 CT £414.07 TOTE £7.50: £2.00 £3.40 £2.20 (£28.60) Trio £128.50 OWNER Mr A. J. Richards (STOCKBRIDGE) BRED Ewar Stud Farm

WEIGHT FOR AGE 3yo-9lb

443 Bold Effort (FR) appreciated these more patient tactics and,set alight to lead inside the final furlong, had no trouble in storming clear. This is certainly the way to ride him. (14/1)

520 Cim Bom Bom (IRE) did look the one to beat when moving smoothly into the lead on the home turn and, with the winner, was able to draw right away from the pursuing group. When it developed into a sprint, he was found wanting. (6/1)
905* Robo Magic (USA), like the majority of his rivals, was caught out when the tempo lifted entering the last quarter-mile and, though he did extremely well to finish so close, was never able to make his presence felt. (9/2)
596 The Happy Fox (IRE) does the majority of his racing at the minimum trip and he was intent on delaying his challenge as late as possible, but the principals had got away and his final placing was as close as he could manage. (8/1)
1410 Zuhair (8/1: 6/1-9/1)

1579 LION (S) STKS (3, 4 & 5-Y.O) (Class G)

4-10 (4-11) **1m 4f (Fibresand)** £1,984.50 (£547.00: £259.50) Stalls: Low GOING minus 0.14 sec per fur (FST)

				SP	RR	SF
1299^{8}	**Skelton Sovereign (IRE) (50)** (RHollinshead) **3-8-4**$^{(3)}$ FLynch(4) (lw: s.s: wl bhd ½-wy: hdwy 3f out: led appr fnl f: sn clr)	—	**1**	9/2^{3}	63	9
1288^{3}	**Cuban Nights (USA) (67)** (BJLlewellyn) **5-9-10** TWilliams(3) (b.off fore: a.p: rdn 4f out: led over 2f out tl appr fnl f)	5	**2**	8/15^{1}	56	19
1288^{6}	**Forzair (44)** (JJO'Neill) **5-10-0** JCarroll(2) (led 4f: led 7f out tl over 2f out: sn rdn & btn)	5	**3**	15/2	54	17
	Glen Garnock (IRE) (50) (RTJuckes) **5-9-10** MFenton(5) (hld up: effrt & hrd drvn 3f out: no imp)	nk	**4**	25/1	49	12
	Slightly Special (IRE) (DTThom) **5-9-10** DHolland(6) (b: bit bkwd: prom: led after 4f to 7f out: wknd wl over 3f out)	4	**5**	33/1	44	7
*1287**	**Royal Legend (50)** (JPearce) **5-10-0b^{1}** GBardwell(1) (trckd ldrs: rdn & outpcd 6f out: sn bhd)	6	**6**	7/2^{2}	40	3
				(SP 124.2%)		**6 Rn**

2m 43.6 (11.10) CSF £7.54 TOTE £5.90: £2.00 £1.10 (£5.30) OWNER Mr G. Bailey (UPPER LONGDON) BRED Patrick Brady
WEIGHT FOR AGE 3yo-17lb
No bid
1095 Skelton Sovereign (IRE), coming from a long way off the pace, won in a common canter in the end, but the company was moderate to say the least and not too much should be written into the ease of this victory. (9/2)
1288 Cuban Nights (USA) has only ever won at this trip but he performs best when the emphasis is on stamina and he was left standing once the winner appeared on the scene. (8/15: evens-1/2)
1125 Forzair, a well-made individual on short legs, is being asked the impossible to carry so much weight, and his chance had come to an end early in the straight. (15/2)
Glen Garnock (IRE), still struggling to win a race, was trying his luck over a much longer trip here, but the result was very much the same and he was never a factor. (25/1)
1287* Royal Legend (7/2: op 2/1)

1580 ANGEL H'CAP (0-65) (3-Y.O+ F & M) (Class F)

4-40 (4-41) **7f (Fibresand)** £2,277.00 (£627.00: £297.00) Stalls: High GOING minus 0.14 sec per fur (FST)

				SP	RR	SF
1439^{8}	**Tea Party (USA) (62)** (KOCunningham-Brown) **4-9-11b** RCochrane(12) (lw: hld up: rdn & hdwy over 2f out: led ins fnl f: r.o)	—	**1**	3/1^{1}	70	23
1433^{3}	**Molly Music (55)** (GGMargarson) **3-8-7** DBiggs(11) (swtg: bhd: hdwy & swtchd outside 2f out: r.o wl towards fin)	¾	**2**	13/2	61	3
*1151**	**Dayrella (52)** (WRMuir) **3-8-4** MRoberts(9) (s.i.s: wl bhd tl r.o strly ins fnl f)	1	**3**	4/1^{3}	56	—
1077^{7}	**Champagne On Ice (44)** (PDEvans) **3-7-3**$^{(7)}$ AMcCarthy(8) (bhd: hdwy over 2f out: r.o wl fnl f: nrst fin)	nk	**4**	16/1	47	—
590^{4}	**Patina (52)** (RHollinshead) **3-8-1**$^{(3)ow1}$ FLynch(2) (swtg: led 4f out: rdn clr over 2f out: hdd & no ex appr fnl f)	1	**5**	8/1	53	—
1433^{8}	**Legend of Aragon (52)** (JAGlover) **3-8-4b^{1}** NDay(3) (led 1f: led appr fnl f: sn rdn & wandered: hdd & no ex ins fnl f)	nk	**6**	12/1	52	—
1433^{7}	**Efipetite (39)** (NBycroft) **4-8-2** NKennedy(1) (hdwy over 3f out: sn hrd drvn: nt pce to chal)	¾	**7**	14/1	38	—
1044^{2}	**Naivasha (59)** (JBerry) **3-8-4**$^{(7)}$ CLowther(5) (bhd & outpcd tl sme late hdwy)	1¼	**8**	13/2	55	—
1030^{8}	**Highly Respected (IRE) (63)** (ABailey) **3-8-10b**$^{(5)}$ PRoberts(6) (lw: led after 1f to 4f out: rdn over 2f out: sn btn)	nk	**9**	100/30^{2}	58	—
1116^{3}	**Sandblaster (43)** (JLEyre) **4-8-6** TWilliams(4) (dwlt: sn pushed along: a bhd: t.o)	6	**10**	8/1	24	—
1327^{8}	**La Spagna (35)** (MDIUsher) **6-7-5**$^{(7)}$ RBrisland(10) (a bhd & outpcd: t.o)	15	**11**	25/1	—	—
				(SP 141.1%)		**11 Rn**

1m 31.1 (6.40) CSF £26.08 CT £80.50 TOTE £4.00: £2.00 £2.90 £3.40 (£14.80) Trio £55.30 OWNER Mr A. J. Richards (STOCKBRIDGE) BRED W. S. Farish and Bayard Sharp
LONG HANDICAP Champagne On Ice 7-6
WEIGHT FOR AGE 3yo-11lb
1166 Tea Party (USA), completing the double for her owner and trainer, returned to form over this more suitable trip and, in conceding so much weight all round, this was not a bad performance. (3/1)
1433 Molly Music adopted more patient tactics than when narrowly defeated over course and distance seven days ago and there is no doubting she is coming to herself fast just now. (13/2)
1151* Dayrella came from a different county to reach her finishing position and, ridden this way, a mile would be well within her reach. (4/1: tchd 6/1)
644 Champagne On Ice, racing with her tongue tied down, did a lot of running to finish so close and on evidence of this will get further. (16/1)
590 Patina looked to be well in control when kicked clear two furlongs out, but she appeared to be knocked out of her stride by the antics of the challenging Legend of Aragon inside the distance and an extra effort proved beyond her. (8/1: 6/1-9/1)
1433 Legend of Aragon probably has more ability than she cares to show and even the application of blinkers failed to bring out the best in her. (12/1)
1135 Efipetite (14/1: 10/1-16/1)
1116 Sandblaster (8/1: 6/1-10/1)

T/Plpt: £72.20 (138.61 Tckts). T/Qdpt: £13.40 (45.95 Tckts) IM

1569-CATTERICK (L-H) (Good to firm)
Saturday May 31st
WEATHER: fine but heat haze WIND: mod half against

1581 SKIPTON-ON-SWALE (S) STKS (2-Y.O) (Class G)
2-00 (2-02) **5f 212y** £2,244.50 (£627.00: £303.50) Stalls: Low GOING minus 0.26 sec per fur (GF)

	Horse	Dist	Pos	SP	RR	SF
	Pigeon (DWBarker) **2-8-6** TWilliams(3) (leggy: unf: bit bkwd: dwlt: sn chsng ldrs: hdwy to ld appr fnl f: r.o wl)	—	1	6/1[3]	63	15
	Final Claim (JGFitzGerald) **2-8-11** JFortune(8) (w'like: bit bkwd: b: dwlt: bhd tl hdwy 2f out: rdn & edgd lft fnl f: r.o)	¾	2	7/1	66	18
1298[2]	**Hopefully** (MRChannon) **2-7-13**(7) AEddery(1) (led tl hdd appr fnl f: sn rdn: one pce)	1¼	3	11/10[1]	58	10
1330[10]	**Moss Side Monkey** (JBerry) **2-8-6b[1]**(5) TEDurcan(4) (lw: s.s: hdwy ½-wy: rdn 2f out: wknd appr fnl f)	2	4	8/1	57	9
1330[8]	**Skippool Creek (IRE)** (TDEasterby) **2-8-6** JCarroll(6) (chsd ldrs: rdn 2f out: wknd appr fnl f)	4	5	11/2[2]	42	—
780[6]	**Flirtina** (PDEvans) **2-8-6b[1]** LCharnock(9) (sn drvn along: nvr gng pce of ldrs)	½	6	11/1	40	—
1298[6]	**Collacar** (DShaw) **2-8-8**(3) CTeague(2) (chsd ldr: ev ch 2f out: rdn & wknd appr fnl f)	2½	7	33/1	39	—
1330[7]	**Flash d'Or (IRE)** (MWEasterby) **2-8-7**(5) GParkin(5) (b.hind: lw: a bhd & outpcd)	hd	8	6/1[3]	39	—
1253[10]	**Gala Miss** (PDEvans) **2-8-6v** ACulhane(7) (a bhd & outpcd: t.o)	22	9	11/1	—	—

(SP 134.8%) **9 Rn**

1m 14.8 (3.90) CSF £50.83 TOTE £11.40: £2.40 £3.20 £1.10 (£66.00) Trio £27.50 OWNER Mr D. W. Barker (RICHMOND) BRED Exors of the late T. F. M. Corrie
Bt in 5,400 gns

Pigeon, a sparely-made debutante, missed the break but soon recovered to chase the leaders. Running about before poking her head in front at the distance, she always had too much pace for the runner-up. (6/1: op 4/1)
Final Claim, like the winner a racecourse debutant, began to peg back the leaders inside the final quarter-mile but, running green and inclined to drift in behind, could not summon the speed to get to terms. There could be a deal of improvement to come and he should be able to win races. (7/1)
1298 Hopefully, who could not be made fitter, forced the pace but failed to last home over this extra furlong. (11/10: 7/4-evens)
664 Moss Side Monkey once again forfeited ground at the start despite the fitting of blinkers, and it certainly cost him the race. If he can get his act together, there is a similar event waiting to be picked up. (8/1)
743 Skippool Creek (IRE) had the blinkers left off, and pressed the leaders until feeling the strain and getting shaken off approaching the final furlong. (11/2: 6/1-9/1)
780 Flirtina (11/1: 8/1-12/1)
Gala Miss (11/1: 8/1-12/1)

1582 SINDERBY MEDIAN AUCTION MAIDEN STKS (3-Y.O) (Class E)
2-35 (2-37) **7f** £2,820.25 (£847.00: £408.50: £189.25) Stalls: Low GOING minus 0.26 sec per fur (GF)

	Horse	Dist	Pos	SP	RR	SF
1302[2]	**Woodbeck** (JAGlover) **3-8-9** NDay(5) (lw: led 1f: led wl over 1f out: r.o wl)	—	1	11/8[1]	77	39
1423[3]	**Yabint El Sultan (71)** (BAMcMahon) **3-8-9** LNewton(9) (lw: chsd ldrs: rdn 2f out: r.o wl ins fnl f)	1¼	2	2/1[2]	74	36
1030[5]	**Mystique Air (IRE) (70)** (EWeymes) **3-8-9** LCharnock(4) (swtg: a.p: rdn & ev ch over 1f out: unable qckn)	1¼	3	5/1[3]	71	33
1226[6]	**In Good Nick (65)** (MWEasterby) **3-8-4b**(5) GParkin(1) (led after 1f tl wl over 1f out: one pce)	3½	4	11/2	63	25
	Ohio Royale (30) (GROldroyd) **3-9-0** MMcAndrew(6) (bkwd: s.i.s: sn chsng ldrs: outpcd fnl 2f)	9	5	50/1	48	10
	Kalousion (TJEtherington) **3-9-0** JCarroll(7) (still unf: in tch: rdn over 2f out: no imp)	½	6	20/1	47	9
	Dissington Times (WMcKeown) **3-9-0** JWeaver(8) (bit bkwd: a bhd & outpcd)	1½	7	33/1	43	5
997[11]	**Grey Prospect** (MBrittain) **3-9-0** TWilliams(3) (b: b.hind: in tch: hrd drvn ½-wy: sn btn)	3½	8	50/1	35	—
1394[8]	**Locksill** (ASmith) **3-9-0** NConnorton(2) (bit bkwd: outpcd: a bhd: t.o)	8	9	50/1	17	—

(SP 121.1%) **9 Rn**

1m 26.3 (2.70) CSF £4.02 TOTE £2.40: £1.10 £1.30 £1.30 (£2.40) Trio £2.40 OWNER Mr B. H. Farr (WORKSOP) BRED Worksop Manor Stud Farm

1302 Woodbeck had this won from some way out but, with the runner-up staying on strongly, she was never able to take things easy and was punched out to the finish. (11/8)
1423 Yabint El Sultan responded to pressure early in the straight and finished with quite a flourish, but the winner had first run and had gone beyond recall. (2/1)
1030 Mystique Air (IRE) finished closer to the runner-up than she did on identical terms at Chester, and she would seem very much on the upgrade. (5/1)
1226 In Good Nick, taking a step down in trip, hardly gives herself a chance by running so freely but, once she learns to settle, she could have the ability to make her mark. (11/2)

1583 ROTHMANS ROYALS NORTH SOUTH CHALLENGE SERIES H'CAP (0-85) (3-Y.O+) (Class D)
3-05 (3-07) **7f** £4,402.50 (£1,320.00: £635.00: £292.50) Stalls: Low GOING minus 0.26 sec per fur (GF)

	Horse	Dist	Pos	SP	RR	SF
1017[10]	**Rechullin (76)** (DRLoder) **3-8-10** JFortune(10) (hld up in tch: hdwy over 1f out: rdn to ld wl ins fnl f)	—	1	5/1[3]	80	45
1175[8]	**Nant Y Gamer (FR) (78)** (JBerry) **3-8-7**(5) TEDurcan(2) (lw: led after 2f tl wl ins fnl f)	¾	2	10/1	80	45
635[6]	**Magic Mill (IRE) (79)** (JLEyre) **4-9-10** TWilliams(3) (led 2f: rdn wl over 1f out: kpt on fnl f)	1½	3	10/1	78	54
925[7]	**Chinour (IRE) (51)** (EJAlston) **9-7-3**(7) JFowle(1) (s.s: bhd tl r.o wl appr fnl f)	nk	4	16/1	49	25
1300[6]	**Royal Ceilidh (IRE) (75)** (DenysSmith) **4-9-6** JCarroll(5) (lw: prom: rdn wl over 1f out: unable qckn)	½	5	4/1[2]	72	48
1035[4]	**Gulf Shaadi (67)** (EJAlston) **5-8-12** SDrowne(8) (a chsng ldrs: effrt wl over 1f out: nt pce to chal)	s.h	6	5/2[1]	64	40
1397[8]	**Forest Robin (66)** (MrsJRRamsden) **4-8-4**(7)ow1 ClaireWest(4) (s.s: rdn & bhd 2f out: kpt on fnl f)	hd	7	14/1	63	38
835[8]	**Jo Mell (77)** (TDEasterby) **4-9-8** LCharnock(9) (hld up: hdwy 2f out: nt rch ldrs)	¾	8	9/1	72	48
*306**	**Agent (56)** (JLEyre) **4-8-1** DWright(6) (bit bkwd: swtg: a outpcd)	3	9	9/1	44	20
	Formidable Liz (61) (MDHammond) **7-8-6** DaleGibson(7) (bkwd: outpcd: a bhd)	3½	10	16/1	41	17

(SP 121.9%) **10 Rn**

1m 25.9 (2.30) CSF £51.67 CT £459.10 TOTE £6.30: £2.40 £2.90 £4.00 (£57.70) Trio £210.70; £92.02 to 2/6/97 OWNER Mrs P. D. Player (NEWMARKET) BRED P. D. Player and Mrs J. Shipway-Pratt
LONG HANDICAP Chinour (IRE) 7-8
WEIGHT FOR AGE 3yo-11lb

688 Rechullin, stepping-up on what she has achieved so far, won this competitive handicap readily and could now be finding her way. (5/1: op 3/1)

1029 Nant Y Gamer (FR), who has been highly tried, adopted more forceful tactics and they almost paid off. (10/1)
635 Magic Mill (IRE) certainly has his full quota of weight, having only won a maiden in his first season, but he ran a fine race here and it should have put an edge on him. (10/1)
653 Chinour (IRE) has not won for a couple of years and he looks to carry plenty of condition, but he performed with credit after losing the odd length at the start, and could be on the way back. (16/1)
1300 Royal Ceilidh (IRE), returning to seven furlongs, was restrained just behind the leaders. Asked for an effort below the distance, she kept plugging away without having the speed to deliver her challenge. She looks one to keep in mind. (4/1)
1035 Gulf Shaadi seems to need a mile nowadays especially on such a sharp track as this, for he was close enough if good enough below the distance. (5/2)
776 Forest Robin, still to open his account, ran extremely well after a slow start and there could be a race for him. (14/1)
Jo Mell is gradually coming to himself and another success is long overdue. (9/1)

1584 YORKSHIRE-TYNE TEES TELEVISION LIMITED STKS (0-60) (3-Y.O+) (Class F)

3-35 (3-36) **7f** £2,705.00 (£755.00: £365.00) Stalls: Low GOING minus 0.26 sec per fur (GF)

			SP	RR	SF
1511[2]	**Stackattack (IRE) (60)** (MrsJRRamsden) **4-9-6** JFortune(9) (lw: hld up: hdwy 2f out: led ent fnl f: rdn out) ....—	**1**	11/4[2]	61	54
1225[22]	**Jedi Knight (60)** (MWEasterby) **3-8-4**(5) GParkin(10) (bhd: rdn along 3f out: gd hdwy fnl f: fin wl)..................1¼	**2**	14/1	58	40
1220*	**Komlucky (51)** (ABMulholland) **5-9-0v**(5) TEDurcan(7) (prom: led wl over 1f out: hdd ent fnl f: unable qckn) 1	**3**	12/1	55	48
579[10]	**Surf City (50)** (WWHaigh) **4-9-6** LCharnock(2) (hld up: hdwy on ins over 2f out: no ex fnl f) ....nk	**4**	25/1	55	48
1273[3]	**Castel Rosselo (62)** (ICampbell) **7-9-6** JWeaver(4) (dwlt: gd hdwy whn hmpd over 1f out: r.o ins fnl f)...........hd	**5**	4/1[3]	55	48
1095[8]	**Bali-Pet (38)** (JParkes) **3-8-9** JFanning(8) (bhd: hrd drvn over 2f out: nvr nrr) 2½	**6**	40/1	49	31
1005*	**King Athelstan (USA) (59)** (BAMcMahon) **9-9-6** LNewton(3) (swtg: chsd ldrs: rdn 2f out: swtchd rt: sn outpcd) ....½	**7**	9/1	48	41
1009[3]	**Twin Creeks (51)** (VSoane) **6-9-8** JCarroll(1) (lw: prom tl outpcd wl over 1f out) ....nk	**8**	11/1	49	42
1385*	**Corniche Quest (IRE) (65)** (MRChannon) **4-9-0**(7) AEddery(6) (swtg: prom: ev ch whn bdly hmpd wl over 1f out: nt rcvr) 3	**9**	5/2[1]	42	35
	Just Dissident (IRE) (60) (RMWhitaker) **5-9-6** ACulhane(5) (bkwd: led tl hdd & wknd wl over 1f out) 3	**10**	14/1	34	27
1132[5]	**Samsolom (54)** (MESowersby) **9-9-3**(3) PFessey(11) (lw: chsd ldrs on outside: effrt ent st: wknd 2f out) ....¾	**11**	25/1	32	25
			(SP 124.7%)	**11 Rn**	

1m 25.9 (2.30) CSF £39.42 TOTE £3.90: £1.70 £3.80 £2.80 (£24.10) Trio £99.90 OWNER Miss E. L. Ramsden (THIRSK) BRED John Bernard O'Connor
WEIGHT FOR AGE 3yo-11lb
1511 Stackattack (IRE), narrowly beaten at Carlisle three days ago, got off the mark with a readily-attained win, and this could be just the start. (11/4)
998 Jedi Knight, one of the back-markers and hard at work over two furlongs out, really found his stride inside the distance and, finishing fast, gave notice of better things to come. (14/1)
1220* Komlucky did not impress to post, but she can act on this ground and did her best to get away below the distance. However, the winner powered past at the furlong pole and she was easily tapped for toe. (12/1)
164 Surf City, running by far his best race for some time, persevered up the inside rail and, on the strength of this performance, there is a prize waiting to be won. (25/1)
1273 Castel Rosselo, stopped in his tracks when poised to challenge below the distance, ran on strongly once free, but the damage had been done. He is effectively a winner without a penalty. (4/1)
41 Bali-Pet had to work hard to reach his final placing, and it would seem he finds this trip inadequate. (40/1)
1385* Corniche Quest (IRE), about to deliver her challenge when short of room just inside the quarter-mile marker, was forced to take avoiding action and this effort can safely be ignored. (5/2)

1585 PICKHILL H'CAP (0-70) (4-Y.O+) (Class E)

4-10 (4-10) **1m 7f 177y** £2,820.25 (£847.00: £408.50: £189.25) Stalls: Low GOING minus 0.26 sec per fur (GF)

			SP	RR	SF
1494*	**Nigel's Lad (IRE) (74)** (PCHaslam) **5-10-4** 4x JFortune(3) (hld up: pushed along 4f out: hrd rdn 2f out: styd on to ld fnl 50y)..........—	**1**	1/3[1]	85	61
	Cloud Inspector (IRE) (66) (MJohnston) **6-9-10** JWeaver(6) (bit bkwd: dropped rr ½-wy: rallied over 3f out: hrd rdn & kpt on towards fin) ....½	**2**	8/1[2]	77	53
	Marsayas (IRE) (54) (MJCamacho) **4-8-10** LCharnock(1) (swtg: lw: led: rdn over 2f out: wknd & hdd wl ins fnl f) ....nk	**3**	12/1	64	38
1081[7]	**Trilby (58)** (GRichards) **4-9-0** ACulhane(5) (hld up: hdwy 7f out: wnt 2nd 5f out: rdn & one pce fnl f) 3	**4**	12/1	65	39
1424[11]	**Arian Spirit (IRE) (49)** (JLEyre) **6-8-7** MGallagher(2) (bit bkwd: chsd ldr over 10f: wknd fnl 2f) 7	**5**	10/1[3]	49	25
898[6]	**Penny Peppermint (38)** (REBarr) **5-7-7**(3) PFessey(4) (hld up: a in rr) ....s.h	**6**	50/1	32 t	14
			(SP 112.5%)	**6 Rn**	

3m 28.7 (6.70) CSF £3.48 TOTE £1.30: £1.20 £2.50 (£4.10) OWNER Mr N. C. Dunnington (MIDDLEHAM) BRED Nikita Investments
LONG HANDICAP Penny Peppermint 6-12
WEIGHT FOR AGE 4yo-2lb
1494* Nigel's Lad (IRE), having his second outing of the week, looked to have taken the opportunity of easy pickings but, from the turn out of the back straight, he was the only one not going to win, until the leader weakened and his superior fitness and stamina enabled him to pinch the race close home. (1/3)
Cloud Inspector (IRE), winner of the Swiss St Leger as a three-year-old, looked far from fully wound-up for his first outing in this country. Running in snatches, he gave it his best shot in the latter stages and should not be hard to place. (8/1)
Marsayas (IRE) would definitely have won this with a previous run under his belt, for he was only worn down in the final fifty yards. (12/1)
Trilby, far from happy striding to the start, was in the firing line with every chance in the home straight, but she could never get the better of Marsayas and she called enough inside the final furlong. (12/1)

1586 ALDBROUGH RATING RELATED MAIDEN STKS (0-60) (3-Y.O+) (Class F)

4-40 (4-40) **5f 212y** £2,477.50 (£690.00: £332.50) Stalls: Low GOING minus 0.26 sec per fur (GF)

			SP	RR	SF
1496[4]	**Rum Lad (56)** (JJQuinn) **3-8-10** JLowe(5) (led after 1f: rdn over 1f out: hld on wl)...—	**1**	10/11[1]	59	32
1514[13]	**Ohnonotagain (30)** (LRLloyd-James) **5-9-2** KimTinkler(2) (bhd & outpcd tl gd hdwy appr fnl f: fin wl)...............1	**2**	33/1	53	35
882[5]	**Rockaroundtheclock (57)** (PDEvans) **3-8-10** JFortune(7) (hld up: hdwy u.p 2f out: nvr nrr) 1	**3**	11/2	54	27
748[11]	**Carreamia (60)** (JLEyre) **4-8-13**(3) OPears(6) (hld up: effrt 2f out: sn rdn: nvr able to chal) ....nk	**4**	9/2[3]	50	32

748[5] **Hong Kong Express (IRE) (60)** (JBerry) **3-8-4b¹**(3) PFessey(1) (lw: s.i.s: sn chsng ldrs: disp ld 3f out to 2f out: sn rdn & wknd) 3½ **5** 4/1 2 40 13
Good To Talk (43) (TDEasterby) **4-9-5** LCharnock(3) (bkwd: led 1f: hrd drvn over 2f out: sn btn) 2 **6** 9/1 38 20
(SP 118.9%) **6 Rn**

1m 13.8 (2.90) CSF £32.33 TOTE £1.90: £1.40 £7.20 (£60.40) OWNER Mr B. Shaw (MALTON) BRED Mrs M. Shaw
WEIGHT FOR AGE 3yo-9lb

1496 Rum Lad, having his fourth outing of the month, looked something to bet on in this poor event, but he gave cause for concern cantering to post and, in the end, he only did just enough to score. (10/11: evens-11/10)
774 Ohnonotagain, much sharper for the run at Carlisle three days ago, took time to find top gear and, when she looked likely to take the measure of the favourite inside the last furlong, strength from the saddle proved the deciding factor. (33/1)
882 Rockaroundtheclock is very moderate and, without the help of blinkers, only did as much as he needed to. (11/2)
748 Carreamia, a choppy mover not suited to fast ground, could not muster the pace to get involved. (9/2)
748 Hong Kong Express (IRE) joined the winner three furlongs out and may have poked her nose in front, but she was struggling on the approach to the final furlong and faded tamely. (4/1)
Good To Talk will strip much fitter for this first outing since the autumn, and he has the ability to pick up a small race. (9/1)

T/Plpt: £44.70 (210.54 Tckts). T/Qdpt: £32.20 (9.06 Tckts) IM

1409-KEMPTON (R-H) (Good to firm)
Saturday May 31st
WEATHER: Sunny WIND: slt half against

1587 WATERLOO MAIDEN STKS (3-Y.O) (Class D)
6-25 (6-29) **7f (Jubilee)** £3,582.50 (£1,085.00: £530.00: £252.50) Stalls: High GOING minus 0.46 sec per fur (F)

				SP	RR	SF
1207[2]	**Shaheen (USA) (90)** (HRACecil) **3-9-0** KFallon(17) (lw: mde virtually all: rdn out)	—	**1**	1/3 1	91	70
674[12]	**Satin Stone (USA)** (JHMGosden) **3-9-0** LDettori(2) (chsd wnr: rdn 2f out: unable qckn)	2½	**2**	12/1 3	85	64
	Mr Sponge (USA) (IABalding) **3-8-11**(3) MartinDwyer(12) (str: scope: stdy hdwy over 3f out: nt clr run over 2f out: r.o one pce)	1½	**3**	33/1	82	61
1207[11]	**Blewbury Hill (IRE)** (RFJohnsonHoughton) **3-9-0** JReid(11) (bit bkwd: hdwy over 2f out: r.o one pce)	s.h	**4**	14/1	82	61
784[3]	**Compatibility (IRE) (83)** (JHMGosden) **3-9-0** GHind(10) (lw: a.p: shkn up 2f out: wknd over 1f out)	6	**5**	16/1	68	47
992[5]	**Dulcinea** (IABalding) **3-8-9** SWhitworth(1) (hdwy over 1f out: nvr nrr)	nk	**6**	50/1	62	41
	Always On My Mind (PJMakin) **3-8-9** SSanders(4) (b: plld hrd: a.p: rdn over 2f out: wknd over 1f out)	½	**7**	33/1	61	40
	Atnab (USA) (PTWalwyn) **3-8-9** RHills(5) (bkwd: prom over 3f)	¾	**8**	33/1	60	39
1088[5]	**Ardent** (CJBenstead) **3-9-0** CRutter(16) (hld up: rdn over 2f out: sn wknd)	1	**9**	66/1	62	41
	Pointelle (AHide) **3-8-9** DBiggs(3) (bkwd: a mid div)	hd	**10**	66/1	57	36
1087[2]	**Giko** (JRPoulton) **3-9-0** RCochrane(6) (prom over 4f)	hd	**11**	25/1	62	41
	Dick Turpin (USA) (LordHuntingdon) **3-9-0** DaneO'Neill(9) (bkwd: bhd fnl 3f)	2	**12**	25/1	57	36
	Blazer's Baby (JRFanshawe) **3-8-9** DHarrison(7) (unf: mid div over 5f)	¾	**13**	40/1	51	30
	Sahara River (USA) (RCharlton) **3-8-9** PatEddery(15) (bit bkwd: a bhd)	2½	**14**	13/2 2	45	24
	Sandweld (72) (CADwyer) **3-8-7**(7) JoHunnam(13) (bit bkwd: a bhd)	nk	**15**	66/1	49	28
1409[6]	**Loganlea (IRE)** (WJMusson) **3-8-9** JStack(14) (a bhd)	1½	**16**	100/1	41	20
	Beckenham Insight (DCO'Brien) **3-8-9** GBardwell(8) (neat: bit bkwd: bhd fnl 4f)	26	**17**	100/1	—	—
				(SP 135.9%)	**17 Rn**	

1m 23.63 (0.16 under best) (-0.87) CSF £5.68 TOTE £1.50: £1.00 £3.80 £6.40 (£11.80) Trio £37.10 OWNER The Thoroughbred Corporation (NEWMARKET) BRED Howard B. Keck
OFFICIAL EXPLANATION **Dick Turpin (USA): the trainer reported the colt had coughed after the race.**
IN-FOCUS: **Generally speaking they did not look a particularly good lot in the paddock and this was certainly not one of the hot maiden three-year-old-races we have come to expect from Kempton.**
1207 Shaheen (USA) at last came good after three very promising efforts, needing only to be rousted along to assert his authority in the final quarter-mile. (1/3: 4/7-2/7)
Satin Stone (USA) stepped-up on his initial run. Racing in second place, he was unable to contain the winner in the final quarter-mile. (12/1: 7/1-14/1)
Mr Sponge (USA), quite an attractive individual with far more scope than the majority in this field, stayed on nicely in the second-half of the race to take third prize right on the line. This was a pleasing debut and he should soon find a race. (33/1)
1207 Blewbury Hill (IRE), a good-bodied colt with far more substance than the majority of his rivals, still did not look fully-fit despite having a very promising debut at Newbury under his belt. Nevertheless, he again showed plenty for the future, staying on nicely in the straight and only just losing third prize. Sure to strip a lot fitter for this, he should now be ready to win a race. (14/1: 10/1-20/1)
784 Compatibility (IRE), who caught the eye of the Catterick Stewards last time out, was again given the kid-glove treatment. Always close up, his rider did a bit of knitting in the straight and the combination gradually dropped away from below the distance. He looks one to note with interest. (16/1)
Dulcinea, racing at the back of the field, passed some rivals in the final quarter-mile. (50/1)
Sahara River (USA) (13/2: 4/1-7/1)

1588 FLORENCE NAGLE GIRL APPRENTICE H'CAP (0-80) (3-Y.O+) (Class E)
6-55 (7-00) **1m 1f (round)** £2,830.25 (£857.00: £418.50: £199.25) Stalls: High GOING minus 0.46 sec per fur (F)

				SP	RR	SF
1268[4]	**Vola Via (USA) (79)** (IABalding) **4-9-9**(5) LeanneMasterson(6) (hdwy over 2f out: rdn over 1f out: led nr fin)	—	**1**	4/1 3	89	50
1016[16]	**Anak-Ku (65)** (MissGayKelleway) **4-9-0** AngelaGallimore(2) (b: led: hrd rdn over 2f out: hdd nr fin)	hd	**2**	100/30 2	75	36
1395[12]	**Piquant (60)** (LordHuntingdon) **10-8-9** AimeeCook(1) (a.p: ev ch ins fnl f: r.o)	nk	**3**	8/1	69	30
1273[12]	**Absolute Utopia (USA) (56)** (NEBerry) **4-8-5** GayeHarwood(3) (lw: a.p: ev ch over 1f out: one pce)	1½	**4**	12/1	63	24
1139[10]	**Mutadarra (IRE) (65)** (WJMusson) **4-9-0** JoHunnam(7) (lw: prom over 5f)	5	**5**	14/1	63	24
1244[18]	**Pay Homage (64)** (IABalding) **9-8-8**(5) JaneLind(10) (mid div whn stumbled on ins over 4f out: nvr nr to chal)	nk	**6**	13/2	61	22
1111[4]	**Press On Nicky (70)** (WRMuir) **4-9-5** SophieMitchell(8) (lw: s.s: hld up: shkn up 2f out: wknd over 1f out)	s.h	**7**	3/1 1	67	28
1384[5]	**Runic Symbol (47)** (MBlanshard) **6-7-10** KerryBaker(9) (bhd fnl 5f)	1¼	**8**	14/1	42	3
1166[14]	**Flotilla (73)** (SMellor) **3-8-9** EmilyJoyce(5) (lw: hld up: shkn up 2f out: wknd over 1f out)	1	**9**	20/1	66	14
1262[17]	**Dances With Hooves (73)** (DJSffrenchDavis) **5-9-3**(5) SarahSpong(11) (s.s: a bhd)	7	**10**	12/1	54	15

*1427**	***North Reef (IRE) (73)*** (JPearce) **6-9-3**(5) LisaMoncrieff(4) (Withdrawn not under Starter's orders: bolted bef s)..		**W**	9/2	—	—
				(SP 144.2%)		**10 Rn**

1m 53.19 (2.59) CSF £17.68 CT £98.21 TOTE £5.80: £1.70 £2.90 £2.00 (£8.30) Trio £42.70 OWNER Mr G. M. Smart (KINGSCLERE) BRED Hurstland Farm Inc.
LONG HANDICAP Runic Symbol 7-1
WEIGHT FOR AGE 3yo-13lb
OFFICIAL EXPLANATION Mutadarra (IRE): rider reported that the gelding ran very free early on and was forced wide on the home turn before running on without being able to close on the placed horses. The trainer added that the gelding is hard to settle and needs to be switched off in order to relax.
1268 Vola Via (USA), whose only previous victory came as a two-year-old, came with a nice run to snatch the spoils near the line and give his rider her very first winner. (4/1)
735 Anak-Ku attempted to make every post a winning one and, after grimly trying to hold off her persistent rivals, was caught near the line. (100/30: 3/1-7/2)
352 Piquant may be at the OAP stage, but he ran a fine race over a more suitable trip. Throwing down his challenge in the straight, he did little wrong and only just failed. (8/1)
Absolute Utopia (USA), never far away, was one of three battling for the lead below the distance, but just failed to find that vital turn of foot. He remains a maiden. (12/1)
Mutadarra (IRE), who had previously shown little for his new connections, was given a quiet ride by one of the more experienced jockeys in the race, and he was close-up until allowed to coast in in the straight. He is very hard to settle at home according to his trainer. (14/1)
1001 Pay Homage stumbled badly on the inside rail turning out of the back straight, and could never get into the action. He is very hard to win with these days and has not scored since May 1995. (13/2)
1111 Press On Nicky chased the leaders but had come to the end of her tether below the distance. The extra furlong seemed beyond her. (3/1)
108* Dances With Hooves (12/1: 10/1-16/1)

1589 GEORGE LADLEY MEMORIAL H'CAP (0-85) (3-Y.O) (Class D)

7-25 (7-31) **7f (round)** £4,455.00 (£1,350.00: £660.00: £315.00) Stalls: High GOING minus 0.46 sec per fur (F)

				SP	RR	SF
1175[18]	**Kaiser Kache (IRE) (81)** (KMcAuliffe) **3-9-5** JReid(11) (mde all: drvn out)	—	**1**	12/1	89	46
1000[2]	**Undercover Agent (IRE) (82)** (JLDunlop) **3-9-6** PatEddery(9) (chsd wnr: ev ch fnl 2f: r.o)	½	**2**	15/8[1]	89	46
1245[4]	**Shalstayholy (IRE) (60)** (GLMoore) **3-7-12v[1]** JQuinn(8) (lw: a.p: ev ch over 1f out: unable qckn fnl f)	nk	**3**	7/1[2]	66	23
	Irtifa (72) (PTWalwyn) **3-8-10** RHills(10) (a.p: rdn over 1f out: r.o wl ins fnl f)	s.h	**4**	10/1	78	35
	Secret Combe (IRE) (80) (PJMakin) **3-9-4** SSanders(5) (stdy hdwy over 2f out: hrd rdn over 1f out: r.o)	1	**5**	25/1	84	41
1458[4]	**Cherokee Flight (66)** (SMellor) **3-8-4** PaulEddery(3) (lw: rdn over 2f out: hdwy over 1f out: r.o)	¾	**6**	8/1[3]	68	25
842[4]	**Bintang Timor (USA) (79)** (PFICole) **3-9-3** TQuinn(14) (lw: a.p: rdn over 1f out: wknd fnl f)	1¾	**7**	8/1[3]	77	34
	Another Night (IRE) (82) (RHannon) **3-9-6** DaneO'Neill(1) (lw: hdwy over 1f out: nvr nrr)	1½	**8**	12/1	77	34
983[7]	**Indian Blaze (70)** (PWHarris) **3-8-8** AClark(7) (nt clr run over 2f out: nvr nrr)	3	**9**	10/1	58	15
930[12]	**Maladerie (IRE) (83)** (MRChannon) **3-9-7** RPerham(4) (prom over 4f)	1	**10**	33/1	69	26
1151[11]	**Bapsford (60)** (GLMoore) **3-7-12**ow2 CRutter(6) (prom over 4f)	nk	**11**	33/1	45	—
794[5]	**Tough Leader (80)** (BHanbury) **3-9-4** JStack(12) (lw: dwlt: a bhd)	¾	**12**	10/1	63	20
1000[13]	**Mayflower (70)** (IABalding) **3-8-8b[1]** RCochrane(13) (lw: hld up: rdn over 2f out: sn wknd)	2½	**13**	16/1	47	4
	Chain Reaction (IRE) (70) (MAJarvis) **3-8-3**(5) RFfrench(2) (b: bit bkwd: a bhd)	5	**14**	20/1	36	—
				(SP 132.5%)		**14 Rn**

1m 25.59 (1.59) CSF £33.51 CT £171.93 TOTE £12.10: £2.20 £1.50 £2.50 (£17.80) Trio £57.00 OWNER Mr Peter Barclay (LAMBOURN) BRED St Simon Foundation
930 Kaiser Kache (IRE) put up a good battling display from the front, and grimly held off the very persistent challenges of the second and third. (12/1: 8/1-14/1)
1000 Undercover Agent (IRE) is still rather weak, but nevertheless produced a very determined challenge in the straight. However, she had met a real tartar in the winner and was unable to get by. (15/8)
1245 Shalstayholy (IRE), fitted with a visor for the first time, threw down her challenge once in line for home, but was just tapped for that vital turn of foot in the final furlong. (7/1)
Irtifa, without a run since September, made a very pleasing reappearance. Never far away, she failed by only a whisker to take third prize. (10/1: 8/1-14/1)
Secret Combe (IRE), making her seasonal reappearance, stayed on in the straight to be nearest at the line. (25/1)
1458 Cherokee Flight, as at Sandown on Monday, was doing all his best work in the closing stages. (8/1: 5/1-9/1)
842 Bintang Timor (USA) (8/1: 6/1-9/1)
Another Night (IRE) (12/1: 7/1-14/1)
Indian Blaze (10/1: 8/1-12/1)
794 Tough Leader (10/1: op 6/1)

1590 HOLSTEN PILS ACHILLES STKS (Listed) (3-Y.O+) (Class A)

7-55 (7-59) **5f** £10,319.40 (£3,864.60: £1,892.30: £816.50: £368.25: £188.95) Stalls: Low GOING minus 0.46 sec per fur (F)

				SP	RR	SF
877[3]	**Almaty (IRE)** (JHMGosden) **4-9-3** LDettori(3) (mde all: comf)	—	**1**	7/2[1]	114+	75
	Compton Place (112) (JARToller) **3-8-9** SSanders(1) (lw: a.p: chsd wnr over 2f out: rdn over 1f out: unable qckn)	2½	**2**	7/2[1]	106	59
941[6]	**Rambling Bear (109)** (MBlanshard) **4-9-10** RCochrane(6) (outpcd: hdwy over 1f out: r.o)	¾	**3**	5/1[2]	111	72
1171[6]	**To the Roof (IRE) (105)** (PWHarris) **5-9-7** KFallon(8) (lw: a.p: rdn over 2f out: one pce)	s.h	**4**	6/1[3]	107	68
1148[8]	**Dashing Blue (99)** (IABalding) **4-9-3** KDarley(5) (a.p: hrd rdn over 1f out: one pce)	½	**5**	14/1	102	63
1455[2]	**Brave Edge (105)** (RHannon) **6-9-7** DaneO'Neill(7) (a.p: rdn over 2f out: one pce)	¾	**6**	5/1[2]	103	64
1034[5]	**Speed On (98)** (HCandy) **4-9-3** CRutter(9) (lw: a.p: rdn over 2f out: wknd fnl f)	s.h	**7**	20/1	99	60
1212[3]	**Hattab (IRE) (99)** (PTWalwyn) **3-8-9** RHills(2) (lw: prom over 2f)	nk	**8**	15/2	98	51
1018[9]	**Jennelle (95)** (CADwyer) **3-8-4** JoHunnam(4) (a bhd)	1½	**9**	25/1	89	42
				(SP 119.1%)		**9 Rn**

57.42 secs (0.65 under best) (-0.78) CSF £14.59 TOTE £3.50: £1.70 £2.00 £1.70 (£5.00) Trio £11.40 OWNER Mr P. D. Savill (NEWMARKET) BRED P. E. Banahan
WEIGHT FOR AGE 3yo-8lb
877 Almaty (IRE) put up a very polished display, making every post a winning one and needing only to be shaken-up from below the distance for a very cosy success. He smashed the course record set eleven years ago by over half-a-second. (7/2: 5/2-4/1)

Compton Place was 10lb clear on official adjusted ratings, but was the only runner without a recent outing under his belt. Moving into second place at halfway, he was unable to cope with the winner. (7/2)
941 Rambling Bear, with a 7lb Group Three penalty to shoulder, failed to go the early pace, but stayed on from below the distance to snatch third prize right on the line. Six furlongs is probably more his trip. (5/1)
1171 To the Roof (IRE) ran another sound race, if failing to find the necessary turn of foot in the last two furlongs. (6/1)
1148 Dashing Blue was never far away but, shown the persuader below the distance, could only go up and down in the same place. (14/1: op 7/1)
1455 Brave Edge, winner of this race last year, could only keep on in his own time in the final quarter-mile. (5/1)

1591 KEMPTON EXHIBITION CENTRE MAIDEN STKS (3-Y.O F) (Class D)
8-25 (8-26) **1m 1f (round)** £3,566.25 (£1,080.00: £527.50: £251.25) Stalls: High GOING minus 0.46 sec per fur (F)

				SP	RR	SF
	Maroulla (IRE) (MRStoute) **3-8-11** JReid(10) (lw: hdwy over 1f out: str run to ld nr fin)	—	1	9/1	84	32
1316[3]	**Doyella (IRE)** (DRLoder) **3-8-11** KDarley(2) (lw: chsd ldr: led over 2f out: hrd rdn over 1f out: hdd nr fin)	¾	2	6/4 1	83	31
	Kawa-Ib (IRE) (PTWalwyn) **3-8-11** RHills(3) (bit bkwd: hld up: rdn over 1f out: ev ch ins fnl f: one pce)	nk	3	7/1 3	82	30
	Elbaaha (83) (MAJarvis) **3-8-11** RCochrane(9) (bit bkwd: hld up: rdn over 2f out: one pce)	1¼	4	7/1 3	80	28
1168[2]	**Lonely Heart (77)** (DRCElsworth) **3-8-11** TQuinn(4) (lw: led over 6f: wknd fnl f)	2½	5	9/4 2	76	24
	Kristal Bridge (PWHarris) **3-8-11** AClark(8) (leggy: s.s: sme hdwy on ins over 1f out: sn wknd)	½	6	20/1	75	23
992[7]	**Polska Princess (GER)** (LordHuntingdon) **3-8-11** DHarrison(1) (lw: prom over 7f)	s.h	7	16/1	75	23
1168[16]	**Miss Mezzanine** (EAWheeler) **3-8-6**(5) ADaly(6) (bit bkwd: dwlt: a bhd)	23	8	66/1	34	—

(SP 117.9%) **8 Rn**

1m 53.45 (2.85) CSF £21.62 TOTE £12.70: £2.50 £1.30 £1.60 (£13.60) Trio £7.60 OWNER Mr Athos Christodoulou (NEWMARKET) BRED A. Christodoulou

Maroulla (IRE), without a recent run under her belt, really took off in the final furlong and swept through to snatch the spoils near the line. (9/1)
1316 Doyella (IRE) appreciated the step-up in trip but, from the second she struck the front over two furlongs out, she had a fight on her hands. Grimly fending off the challenge of the third, she had just won that battle when the winner swept by. She should soon go one better. (6/4: evens-7/4)
Kawa-Ib (IRE), an attractive filly, did not look fully tuned-up but still ran a very promising race. Throwing down her challenge below the distance, she looked to have the measure of the runner-up but failed to get past, and was unable to cope with the winner. She should soon be winning. (7/1: 5/1-8/1)
Elbaaha did not look fully wound-up, but she was nicely placed entering the straight if tapped for toe in the last two furlongs. Lack of acceleration at that vital stage was her undoing last year and it could well be the same this season. (7/1)
1168 Lonely Heart took the field along. Collared early in the straight, she had nothing more to offer in the final furlong. (9/4: 7/2-2/1)

1592 BLACKBIRD H'CAP (0-80) (3-Y.O+) (Class D)
8-55 (8-57) **1m 4f** £3,468.75 (£1,050.00: £512.50: £243.75) Stalls: High GOING minus 0.46 sec per fur (F)

				SP	RR	SF
	Roisin Clover (61) (RRowe) **6-8-10** RCochrane(12) (stdy hdwy & n.m.r 2f out: swtchd rt: led over 1f out: pushed out)	—	1	4/1 2	74	39
1296*	**Heart of Armor (82)** (PFICole) **3-9-0** TQuinn(5) (lw: hld up: ev ch over 1f out: unable qckn)	5	2	11/2	88	36
1325[9]	**Prince Kinsky (79)** (JABOld) **4-10-0** DHarrison(4) (lw: hld up: rdn over 4f out: ev ch over 1f out: one pce)	s.h	3	12/1	85	50
	Silently (77) (JSKing) **5-9-7**(5) RFfrench(3) (a.p: ev ch over 1f out: one pce)	½	4	20/1	83	48
	Taufan Boy (74) (PWHarris) **4-9-9** AClark(2) (bit bkwd: rdn over 2f out: hdwy over 1f out: r.o)	¾	5	14/1	79	44
725[9]	**Walk On By (70)** (RHannon) **3-8-2** DaneO'Neill(6) (swtchd rt over 2f out: hdwy wl over 1f out: nvr nrr)	1¼	6	20/1	73	21
	Credit Squeeze (64) (RFJohnsonHoughton) **7-8-13** JReid(7) (b: bkwd: w ldr: led 9f out tl over 2f out: wknd over 1f out)	2	7	25/1	64	29
1208[6]	**White Plains (IRE) (79)** (MCPipe) **4-10-0** KDarley(1) (lw: hdwy over 3f out: wknd 2f out)	1	8	7/1	78	43
1036[8]	**Galapino (61)** (MissGayKelleway) **4-8-10** KFallon(11) (a.p: chsd ldr 6f out: led over 2f out tl over 1f out: sn wknd)	1½	9	2/1 1	58	23
1169[12]	**High Desire (IRE) (52)** (JRArnold) **4-7-12**(3) MHenry(13) (a bhd)	1¼	10	16/1	47	12
990[13]	**Trooper (68)** (RAkehurst) **3-8-0** JQuinn(9) (bhd fnl 3f)	7	11	5/1 3	54	2
1292[15]	**Camp Follower (70)** (DCO'Brien) **4-9-5** GBardwell(8) (led 3f: wknd 4f out)	25	12	50/1	23	—

(SP 133.5%) **12 Rn**

2m 32.8 (2.80) CSF £26.28 CT £239.91 TOTE £5.00: £2.20 £2.00 £3.50 (£18.50) Trio £105.20 OWNER The Clockhouse Press Ltd (PULBOROUGH) BRED D. A. and Mrs Hicks
WEIGHT FOR AGE 3yo-17lb

Roisin Clover goes particularly well round here and, sweeping into the lead approaching the final furlong, needed only to be nudged along to put daylight between herself and her rivals, and register her fourth course and distance victory. (4/1)
1296* Heart of Armor had every chance over a furlong out before firmly put in his place by the winner. (11/2)
789* Prince Kinsky was much happier with this return to a sounder surface and, although being bustled along turning for home, was one of several with every chance below the distance. (12/1: 7/1-14/1)
Silently, sold out of Ian Balding's stable for 10,000 guineas, may have got his head in front for a couple of strides over a furlong out before failing to find another gear. All three of his victories to date came in 1995. (20/1)
Taufan Boy did not look fully tuned-up, but stayed on in the last furlong-and-a-half to be nearest at the line. He has yet to win on grass. (14/1)
Walk On By struggled on in the last two furlongs without ever posing a threat. (20/1)
Trooper (5/1: op 8/1)

T/Plpt: £33.70 (532.03 Tckts). T/Qdpt: £7.90 (84.87 Tckts) AK

1416-LINGFIELD (L-H) (St crse Good to firm, Rnd Good to firm, Firm bk st)
Saturday May 31st
WEATHER: fine WIND: fresh across

1593 SMUGGLERS NOVICE AUCTION STKS (2-Y.O) (Class E)
1-45 (1-48) **5f** £3,148.25 (£941.00: £450.50: £205.25) Stalls: High GOING minus 0.26 sec per fur (GF)

				SP	RR	SF
1109[2]	**Contrary Mary** (GLewis) **2-8-1**(3) AWhelan(8) (lw: mde all: clr over 1f out: pushed out)	—	1	2/1 1	82+	47
1274*	**Dim Ots** (BPalling) **2-8-13** TSprake(4) (chsd wnr: hrd rdn over 1f out: one pce)	6	2	100/30 2	72	37

				SP	RR	SF
880^{8}	**Brandon Frank** (IABalding) **2-8-6** SWhitworth(6) (mid div: rdn over 2f out: r.o one pce fnl 2f)	1	**3**	9/1	62	27
1418^{4}	**Fire Goddess** (JSMoore) **2-7-12**(3) MHenry(1) (mid div: sn rdn along: kpt on one pce fnl 2f)	hd	**4**	9/1	56	21
	Persian Sabre (VSoane) **2-8-1** CRutter(11) (unf: bit bkwd: chsd ldrs: rdn over 2f out: one pce)	1	**5**	20/1	53	18
836^{4}	**Mari-Ela (IRE)** (JRArnold) **2-7-10**(5) RFfrench(2) (sn rdn along: nvr nrr)	1¼	**6**	$6/1^{3}$	49	14
	Emperor's Gold (ICampbell) **2-8-12** RPrice(3) (tall: dwlt: sn in tch: rdn over 2f out: no hdwy)	hd	**7**	33/1	60	25
1091^{7}	**Magical Dancer (IRE)** (MrsPNDutfield) **2-7-13**(5) AimeeCook(9) (bhd fr ½-wy)	nk	**8**	33/1	51	16
	The Druidess (IRE) (GCBravery) **2-8-1** GDuffield(5) (w'like: bit bkwd: chsd ldrs tl wknd over 1f out)	nk	**9**	16/1	47	12
	Clear View (BJMeehan) **2-8-2**(7) GHannon(7) (leggy: lt-f: sn outpcd)	2½	**10**	14/1	47	12
1136^{10}	**Kagsi** (DCO'Brien) **2-8-1** DRMcCabe(10) (dwlt: a bhd: eased over 1f out: t.o)	22	**11**	33/1	—	—
				(SP 116.8%)	**11 Rn**	

58.07 secs (1.07) CSF £7.14 TOTE £2.00: £1.10 £1.40 £2.90 (£2.20) Trio £19.00 OWNER Mr W. J. P. Jackson (EPSOM) BRED C. R. and V. M. Withers

1109 Contrary Mary looked a different class both in the paddock and in the race. (2/1)
1274* Dim Ots was in vain pursuit throughout. (100/30: 9/4-7/2)
Brandon Frank kept on in the final two furlongs and is bred to need further. (9/1: 6/1-10/1)
1418 Fire Goddess was always flat to the boards. (9/1: 6/1-10/1)
Persian Sabre showed some promise, racing to the fore until lack of condition told late on. (20/1)
836 Mari-Ela (IRE) was never going the pace. (6/1)
Clear View (14/1: 7/1-16/1)

1594 TOTE BOOKMAKERS H'CAP (0-85) (3-Y.O+) (Class D)

2-15 (2-16) **6f** £5,952.00 (£1,776.00: £848.00: £384.00) Stalls: High GOING minus 0.26 sec per fur (GF)

				SP	RR	SF
1419^{2}	**Kilcullen Lad (IRE) (69)** (PMooney) **3-8-6v**ow2 WJO'Connor(7) (lw: a.p: led over 1f out: all out)	—	**1**	$4/1^{1}$	80	47
1259^{6}	**Thwaab (62)** (FWatson) **5-8-8v** KFallon(5) (hld up: hdwy 2f out: str run fnl f: jst failed)	s.h	**2**	$11/2^{3}$	73	51
1410^{7}	**So Intrepid (IRE) (76)** (JMBradley) **7-9-3**(5) RFfrench(6) (lw: chsd ldrs: rdn & outpcd 2f out: kpt on one pce ins last)	2½	**3**	10/1	80	58
1317^{13}	**Indian Relative (71)** (RGuest) **4-9-0**(3) DGriffiths(1) (lw: chsd ldrs: ev ch over 1f out: sn rdn: one pce)	nk	**4**	$11/2^{3}$	74	52
1317^{15}	**Kildee Lad (76)** (APJones) **7-9-8** TSprake(10) (lw: sltly hmpd after s: hld up: swtchd lft 3f out: hrd rdn over 1f out: one pce)	2½	**5**	16/1	73	51
1410*	**Mister Jolson (79)** (RJHodges) **8-9-11** RCochrane(4) (lw: prom tl wknd over 1f out)	nk	**6**	$9/2^{2}$	75	53
1419^{4}	**Half Tone (56)** (RMFlower) **5-8-2v**1 GDuffield(2) (towards rr: rdn ½-wy: sme hdwy over 2f out: sn btn)	½	**7**	12/1	51	29
1311*	**Rich Glow (53)** (NBycroft) **6-7-13** NVarley(3) (mid div: rdn 3f out: wknd over 1f out)	¾	**8**	12/1	46	24
	Faraway Lass (78) (LordHuntingdon) **4-9-5**(5) AimeeCook(9) (bit bkwd: bhd fnl 3f)	1¼	**9**	12/1	67	45
1018^{11}	**Cherry Blossom (IRE) (82)** (RHannon) **3-9-5** PatEddery(8) (led: hdd over 1f out: sn wknd: broke down ins fnl f: broke leg: dead)	10	**10**	12/1	45	14
				(SP 114.7%)	**10 Rn**	

1m 10.43 (1.43) CSF £23.11 CT £185.60 TOTE £4.60: £1.50 £1.80 £3.30 (£14.60) Trio £75.20 OWNER Mr George Tobitt (ASTON UPTHORPE) BRED S. W. D. McIlveen
WEIGHT FOR AGE 3yo-9lb
STEWARDS' ENQUIRY O'Connor susp. 9-11/6/97 (careless riding).

1419 Kilcullen Lad (IRE) had run promisingly last week, and confirmed that with a game display. He has plenty of speed and will be just as effective over a stiff five furlongs. (4/1: op 6/1)
1259 Thwaab bounced back to his best, and his strong run in the final furlong only just failed. (11/2)
1259* So Intrepid (IRE) was outpaced just after halfway and, though staying on again, never threatened to get back to the leaders. (10/1)
Indian Relative was always to the fore and she is finding her form. (11/2)
1113 Kildee Lad was slightly short of room early and, as a consequence, his good draw was of no use. He had to switch round the whole field and never looked likely to make up the leeway. (16/1)
1410* Mister Jolson raced more prominently than usual, and had burnt himself out by the distance. (9/2)

1595 BET WITH THE TOTE H'CAP (0-100) (3-Y.O) (Class C)

2-45 (2-47) **1m 2f** £9,318.00 (£2,784.00: £1,332.00: £606.00) Stalls: High GOING minus 0.26 sec per fur (GF)

				SP	RR	SF
837^{5}	**Henley (USA) (80)** (DRLoder) **3-8-2** DRMcCabe(7) (mde all: hrd rdn ins fnl f: r.o wl)	—	**1**	15/2	91	51
1104^{3}	**Regal Patrol (79)** (MRStoute) **3-7-12**(3) MHenry(1) (chsd wnr: hrd rdn & ev ch ins fnl f: unable qckn)	1¾	**2**	11/1	87	47
1156^{12}	**Maradi (IRE) (77)** (MBell) **3-7-8**(5) RMullen(9) (hld up in mid div: rdn 2f out: styd on ins fnl f)	1¾	**3**	14/1	82	42
794^{6}	**Hen Harrier (90)** (JLDunlop) **3-8-12** RCochrane(8) (hld up in rr: pushed wd 4f out: rdn 3f out: styd on fnl 2f)	2½	**4**	12/1	91	51
1146^{5}	**Bali Paradise (USA) (97)** (PFICole) **3-9-5** CRutter(2) (chsd ldrs: rdn 2f out: wknd over 1f out)	2	**5**	$11/2^{3}$	95	55
959^{8}	**Rich In Love (IRE) (93)** (CACyzer) **3-8-10**(5) RFfrench(6) (nvr nrr)	4	**6**	50/1	85	45
1175^{13}	**Brandon Jack (80)** (IABalding) **3-8-2** TSprake(3) (hld up in rr: rdn 3f out: nvr nrr)	nk	**7**	20/1	71	31
990*	**Prince of Denial (81)** (DWPArbuthnot) **3-8-3** SWhitworth(5) (lw: hld up in rr: hit rail & stumbled 4f out: nt rcvr)	nk	**8**	$4/1^{1}$	72	32
1104^{2}	**Sheer Face (86)** (WRMuir) **3-8-8** KFallon(4) (lw: hld up in tch: rdn over 2f out: grad wknd)	1¾	**9**	8/1	74	34
1173^{6}	**Asas (99)** (SbinSuroor) **3-9-7** RHills(11) (lw: chsd ldrs tl wknd 2f out)	¾	**10**	$5/1^{2}$	86	46
853^{5}	**Rapier (84)** (RHannon) **3-8-6** PatEddery(10) (racd wd thrght: a bhd: virtually p.u 6f out)	dist	**11**	6/1	—	—
				(SP 118.6%)	**11 Rn**	

2m 6.47 (1.77) CSF £80.01 CT £1,036.28 TOTE £7.50: £2.50 £2.70 £3.50 (£54.90) Trio £275.70 OWNER Mrs Virginia Kraft Payson (NEWMARKET) BRED Jesse M. Henley Jr

OFFICIAL EXPLANATION **Hen Harrier: rider reported he had been told to ride a normal race, but to keep the filly on the fence as she tends to hang both ways. She was fractious leaving the paddock and could not go the gallop in the race or come down the hill. When her cause was lost, he pushed her out with hands and heels. Prince of Denial: injured his right-fore fetlock.**

837 Henley (USA) put up a good performance, staying on strongly when challenged by the runner-up. (15/2: 9/2-8/1)
1104 Regal Patrol ran well and clearly appreciated the faster ground. He carried his head slightly high in the final furlong but, to be fair, the winner was finding plenty in front. (11/1: 7/1-12/1)
1002 Maradi (IRE) kept on well in the final two furlongs and can win a handicap soon. (14/1)
794 Hen Harrier was the unlucky horse of the race. He was forced wide four furlongs out and lost some valuable momentum. She kept on nicely in the final two furlongs and should have been considerably closer. (12/1: 8/1-14/1)
1146 Bali Paradise (USA) had every chance, but was done with shortly after the two pole. (11/2)
Rich In Love (IRE) kept on for a distant sixth. (50/1)

990* Prince of Denial appeared to strike the rail coming down the hill and was not a factor after. (4/1: 3/1-9/2)

1596 TOTE CREDIT LEISURE STKS (Listed) (3-Y.O+) (Class A)
3-15 (3-22) **6f** £13,078.80 (£4,849.20: £2,334.60: £963.00: £391.50: £162.90) Stalls: High GOING minus 0.26 sec per fur (GF)

				SP	RR	SF
1148[4]	**Cyrano's Lad (IRE) (103)** (CADwyer) **8-9-0** KFallon(1) (broke wl: swtchd stands' side: led: hdd ins fnl f: hrd rdn: regained ld cl home)	—	1	11/2[3]	114	72
1324[5]	**My Best Valentine (87)** (JWhite) **7-9-0** RFfrench(6) (lw: chsd ldrs: pushed along to improve over 2f out: led ins fnl f: hrd rdn: hdd cl home)	hd	2	33/1	114	72
	Russian Revival (USA) (SbinSuroor) **4-9-4** RHills(4) (lw: prom: rdn over 2f out: wknd over 1f out)	5	3	7/2[2]	104	62
1309[2]	**Jayannpee (107)** (IABalding) **6-9-4** RCochrane(7) (dwlt: hld up: rdn over 2f out: sme hdwy over 1f out: sn btn)	1	4	2/1[1]	102	60
961[5]	**Hello Mister (92)** (TEPowell) **6-9-0** PMcCabe(3) (hld up: rdn 2f out: no hdwy)	1¼	5	40/1	94	52
1171[10]	**Indian Spark (105)** (WGMTurner) **3-8-6** DSweeney(2) (in tch: hrd rdn over 2f out: sn wknd)	s.h	6	12/1	95	44
1212[2]	**Referendum (IRE) (108)** (GLewis) **3-8-6** PatEddery(8) (chsd ldr: rdn over 3f out: wknd 2f out)	3½	7	2/1[1]	86	35

(SP 117.3%) **7 Rn**

1m 9.25 (0.25) CSF £130.67 TOTE £5.80: £2.50 £6.00 (£85.10) OWNER Mr M. M. Foulger (NEWMARKET) BRED J. C. Condon
WEIGHT FOR AGE 3yo-9lb
OFFICIAL EXPLANATION **Referendum (IRE): hung left throughout and was later found to be sore.**
1148 Cyrano's Lad (IRE) is in the form of his life. He quickly crossed over to the favoured stands' rail and looked cooked when headed inside the final furlong but, under a brilliant ride from Fallon, he got back up in the shadow of the post. (11/2: op 7/2)
1324 My Best Valentine had no chance at the weights and ran an incredible race. He is obviously back to his best. (33/1)
Russian Revival (USA), like a few of his stablemates, ran a lucklustre race. (7/2: 5/2-4/1)
1309 Jayannpee lost whatever chance he had with a tardy start. (2/1)
961 Hello Mister travelled quite well to halfway and is gradually finding some form. (40/1)
968* Indian Spark ran well for four furlongs. (12/1: 6/1-14/1)
1212 Referendum (IRE) was never going well. (2/1)

1597 CROWHURST CONDITIONS STKS (4-Y.O+) (Class C)
3-50 (3-50) **1m 3f 106y** £4,807.50 (£1,657.50: £791.25: £318.75) Stalls: High GOING minus 0.26 sec per fur (GF)

				SP	RR	SF
1108[2]	**Taufan's Melody (105)** (LadyHerries) **6-9-1** RCochrane(5) (lw: chsd ldr: led 3f out: hrd rdn ins fnl f: eased sltly cl home)	—	1	2/5[1]	109+	75
1241[6]	**Nabhaan (IRE) (100)** (DMorley) **4-9-1** RHills(1) (lw: hld up in tch: chsd wnr over 2f out: hrd rdn ins fnl f: r.o)	nk	2	9/4[2]	109	75
1482[7]	**Prospector's Cove (81)** (JPearce) **4-8-10** MWigham(3) (led: hdd 3f out: wknd 2f out)	15	3	20/1[3]	83	49
1108[4]	**Kailey Senor (USA)** (RWArmstrong) **4-8-10** RPrice(4) (in tch tl wknd 3f out)	1	4	20/1[3]	65 t	47

(SP 111.7%) **4 Rn**

2m 25.15 (0.45) CSF £1.53 TOTE £1.60 (£1.20) OWNER All At Sea (LITTLEHAMPTON) BRED Midhurst Farm Inc
1108 Taufan's Melody won a shade more easily than the winning margin suggests. (2/5)
1241 Nabhaan (IRE) gave chase to the winner over the final two furlongs or so, but is flattered to finish as close as he did. (9/4)

1598 FERRENDONS CONDITIONS STKS (4-Y.O+) (Class C)
4-25 (4-25) **7f 140y** £4,676.29 (£1,683.04: £805.02: £326.10: £126.55) Stalls: High GOING minus 0.26 sec per fur (GF)

				SP	RR	SF
894*	**Nwaamis (USA) (110)** (JLDunlop) **5-9-2** RHills(4) (chsd ldr: led over 1f out: edgd rt: r.o wl)	—	1	10/11[1]	112	71
1148[2]	**Tumbleweed Ridge (94)** (BJMeehan) **4-8-10** PatEddery(2) (hld up: hdwy over 2f out: rdn ins fnl f: one pce)	3	2	11/4[2]	100	59
1160[5]	**Russian Music (105)** (MissGayKelleway) **4-9-2b** KFallon(5) (led: hdd over 1f out: one pce)	2½	3	7/2[3]	101	60
946[3]	**Raheen (USA) (87)** (WGMTurner) **4-8-9v[1](5)** DSweeney(1) (chsd ldrs: rdn 3f out: wknd over 1f out)	1¾	4	25/1	95	54
1087*	**Rock Falcon (IRE)** (LadyHerries) **4-9-0** DeclanO'Shea(3) (in tch 5f)	16	5	10/1	61	20

(SP 114.2%) **5 Rn**

1m 29.56 (0.56) CSF £3.57 TOTE £1.60: £1.10 £2.10 (£2.90) OWNER Mr Hamdan Al Maktoum (ARUNDEL) BRED Shadwell Farm Inc & Shadwell Estate Co Ltd in USA
894* Nwaamis (USA) travelled best throughout and won this a shade cosily. (10/11)
1148 Tumbleweed Ridge gave chase in the final furlong but gave the impression that seven-and-a-half furlongs is as far as he wants to go. He will be suited by dropping back a little in distance. (11/4: 3/1-9/2)
1160 Russian Music tried to make all but was put in his place from the distance. (7/2: 5/2-4/1)
946 Raheen (USA) tracked the leaders, but he came under pressure shortly after halfway and had little more to give in the final two furlongs. (25/1)

1599 O.C.S. LADIES' H'CAP (0-75) (3-Y.O+) (Class E)
4-55 (4-57) **7f** £3,122.25 (£933.00: £446.50: £203.25) Stalls: High GOING minus 0.26 sec per fur (GF)

				SP	RR	SF
848[6]	**Bellas Gate Boy (46)** (JPearce) **5-9-10** MrsLPearce(12) (rr: sn pushed along: hdwy 2f out: str run to ld wl ins fnl f)	—	1	7/1	57	43
1422*	**Marjaana (IRE) (68)** (PTWalwyn) **4-11-4** MissSSamworth(7) (a.p: ev ch wl ins fnl f: unable qckn)	½	2	2/1[1]	78	64
1317[14]	**Apollo Red (71)** (GLMoore) **8-11-7** MrsJMoore(8) (led: edgd lft over 1f out: hdd wl ins fnl f: unable qckn)	nk	3	7/2[2]	80	66
1035[13]	**Flying Pennant (IRE) (62)** (JMBradley) **4-10-12** MissVRoberts(9) (hld up: hdwy 2f out: rdn over 1f out: one pce)	3	4	20/1	64	50
1505[5]	**Dancing Lawyer (57)** (BJMeehan) **6-10-7** MissJAllison(10) (nvr nrr)	3	5	4/1[3]	53	39
401[3]	**Love Legend (38)** (DWPArbuthnot) **12-9-2** MrsDArbuthnot(5) (mid div: rdn 3f out: grad wknd)	4	6	12/1	24	10
1385[4]	**River Tern (65)** (JMBradley) **4-11-1** MissRClark(6) (chsd ldrs tl wknd over 1f out)	hd	7	7/1	51	37
601[6]	**Spectacle Jim (42)** (BAPearce) **8-9-2v(4)** MrsKHills(11) (prom tl wknd over 2f out)	3	8	20/1	21	7
1324[11]	**Sharp 'n Smart (67)** (BSmart) **5-11-3** MissVMarshall(1) (prom tl wknd over 2f out)	1½	9	10/1	43	29
	Roy Boy (65) (CAHorgan) **5-10-11(4)** MissLCourier(3) (wnt lft s: in tch tl wknd over 2f out)	2½	10	20/1	35	21
	Flashfeet (46) (KBishop) **7-9-10** MissAPurdy(2) (hmpd s: a bhd)	¾	11	33/1	14	—

(SP 134.6%) **11 Rn**

1m 24.59 (3.39) CSF £21.45 CT £60.05 TOTE £9.50: £1.90 £1.40 £1.50 (£25.20) Trio £19.80 OWNER Mr Jeff Pearce (NEWMARKET) BRED Mrs J. H. Weller-Poley
848 Bellas Gate Boy appeared to be struggling early on but, picking up two furlongs out, produced a strong run in the final furlong to get up close home. (7/1)

1422* Marjaana (IRE) was never far away but, after having every chance inside the final furlong, just lost out. (2/1: tchd 3/1)
1009* Apollo Red made a brave attempt to make all, but did not help his cause by edging left. (7/2)
Flying Pennant (IRE) made a promising move two furlongs out, but could only plug on at the one speed in the final furlong. (20/1)
1505 Dancing Lawyer never really got into it. (4/1: op 6/1)
766 Sharp 'n Smart (10/1: 8/1-12/1)

T/Plpt: £183.70 (95.79 Tckts). T/Qdpt: £110.20 (4.96 Tckts) SM

1280-**MUSSELBURGH (R-H) (Good to firm)**

Saturday May 31st

WEATHER: sunny but cool WIND: mod bhd

51 47+

1600 DON'T BLINK (S) STKS (2-Y.O) (Class F)

6-45 (6-45) **5f** £2,770.00 (£835.00: £405.00: £190.00) Stalls: High GOING minus 0.29 sec per fur (GF)

				SP	RR	SF
1228[6]	**Makahu Don** (WTKemp) **2-8-8**(3) PFessey(5) (cl up: led wl over 1f out: edgd lft: r.o)	—	1	12/1	53	10
1253[4]	**Newhargen (IRE)** (PDEvans) **2-8-11** JFortune(4) (led over 3f: r.o one pce)	1¼	2	2/1[2]	49	6
1498[4]	**Fairy Domino** (MRChannon) **2-8-3**(3) PPMurphy(6) (a chsng ldrs: rdn ½-wy: nt qckn)	2½	3	5/4[1]	36	—
1019[8]	**Sunshine Pet (IRE)** (JJO'Neill) **2-8-6** JCarroll(3) (lw: outpcd: hdwy ½-wy: no imp)	s.h	4	10/1	36	—
1019[11]	**I'm Not Sure** (JBerry) **2-7-13**(7) CLowther(2) (spd 3f: sn wknd)	5	5	16/1	20	—
1432[6]	**Miss Beveled** (MBrittain) **2-8-6** DaleGibson(1) (s.i.s: hdwy u.p ½-wy: sn wknd)	1½	6	7/1[3]	15	—
				(SP 112.9%)		**6 Rn**

61.3 secs (3.60) CSF £33.57 TOTE £12.80: £5.80 £1.70 (£15.30) OWNER Mr W. T. Kemp (DUNS) BRED Mrs M. A. Hall
No bid
1228 Makahu Don has come on a ton from his first run. The only one in the race with any real substance about him, he did it well. (12/1: 8/1-14/1)
1253 Newhargen (IRE) had everything in his favour and was given a fine ride, but still was not good enough. (2/1)
1498 Fairy Domino has rather lost her way since the ground firmed up. (5/4)
Sunshine Pet (IRE) looked particularly well and ran her best race to date, but was always being taken off her legs. (10/1: 8/1-12/1)
441 I'm Not Sure looked a short runner. (16/1)
1298 Miss Beveled was always struggling after a poor start. (7/1)

1601 SHERATON GRAND CLAIMING STKS (4-Y.O+) (Class F)

7-15 (7-16) **1m 4f 31y** £2,635.00 (£735.00: £355.00) Stalls: High GOING minus 0.29 sec per fur (GF)

				SP	RR	SF
	Latvian (57) (RAllan) **10-8-13** JFortune(6) (trckd ldrs: rdn to ld over 2f out: styd on u.p fnl f)	—	1	5/2[1]	58	35
	Indonesian (IRE) (59) (PCalver) **5-8-6**(3) DarrenMoffatt(1) (plld hrd: trckd ldrs: effrt 4f out: styd on fnl f: edgd rt)	1¾	2	6/1[3]	52	29
	Sun of Spring (DWChapman) **7-8-10**(3) PFessey(11) (in tch: hdwy on ins 3f out: nt clr run wl over 1f out: kpt on fnl f)	½	3	10/1	55	32
1229*	**Philgem (27)** (CWFairhurst) **4-8-2** NKennedy(5) (bhd: hdwy 5f out: styd on: nt pce to chal)	2	4	9/1	41	18
1481[8]	**Carol's Dream (USA) (70)** (JWHills) **5-9-7** JCarroll(4) (lw: led tl hdd over 2f out: wknd over 1f out)	3	5	7/2[2]	56	33
1281[9]	**Cois Na Farraige (IRE) (57)** (MissLAPerratt) **4-9-3** RLappin(7) (lw: a.p: effrt 4f out: sn outpcd)	2½	6	16/1	49	26
68[15]	**Fenian Court (IRE)** (PDEvans) **6-8-3**(5) GParkin(8) (hdwy to trck ldrs after 4f: wknd over 3f out)	2	7	16/1	38	15
1229[6]	**Bruz (27)** (LLungo) **6-8-9** DaleGibson(2) (lw: prom tl lost pl 6f out: n.d after)	6	8	16/1	31	8
	Snow Domino (IRE) (JMJefferson) **4-8-9** LCharnock(9) (lost tch fnl 5f)	12	9	33/1	15	—
1283[3]	**She's A Winner (IRE) (40)** (PMonteith) **4-7-13**(5) JBramhill(3) (a outpcd & bhd)	½	10	9/1	9	—
				(SP 114.8%)		**10 Rn**

2m 39.5 (6.00) CSF £15.77 TOTE £3.10: £2.00 £3.30 £3.60 (£13.20) Trio £20.30 OWNER Mr I. Bell (CORNHILL-ON-TWEED) BRED Fittocks Stud Ltd
Latvian won first time out last year, and this unreliable character did it again under a forceful ride. (5/2)
Indonesian (IRE), from a yard in good form, seems to stay well and this was his best effort for some time. (6/1: op 4/1)
Sun of Spring is a sturdy sort who ran well and would have been closer had he had a clear run. (10/1: 8/1-12/1)
1229* Philgem found this ground too fast, but was keeping on determinedly at the end. (9/1: 6/1-10/1)
1152 Carol's Dream (USA), wearing a tongue-strap, was happy bowling along in front but, once tackled, he found little when ridden. (7/2)

1602 SHERATON GRAND CUP H'CAP (0-80) (3-Y.O+) (Class D)

7-45 (7-49) **5f** £4,276.00 (£1,288.00: £624.00: £292.00) Stalls: High GOING minus 0.29 sec per fur (GF)

				SP	RR	SF
1080[4]	**Shadow Jury (60)** (DWChapman) **7-9-0b** LCharnock(1) (disp ld tl hdd ins fnl f: rallied to ld cl home)	—	1	7/1	66	42
1332*	**Lady Sheriff (74)** (MWEasterby) **6-10-0b** TLucas(5) (lw: mde most tl ct cl home)	s.h	2	5/4[1]	80	56
1332[5]	**Sunset Harbour (IRE) (42)** (SEKettlewell) **4-7-3**(7) JennyBenson(2) (in tch: swtchd rt wl over 1f out: r.o towards fin)	1½	3	14/1	43	19
	Pallium (IRE) (45) (DANolan) **9-7-8**(5) JBramhill(4) (in tch: hdwy 2f out: nvr able to chal)	hd	4	33/1	46	22
1223[7]	**Johayro (63)** (JSGoldie) **4-9-3** ACulhane(6) (in tch: rdn ½-wy: nt pce to chal)	1¾	5	4/1[2]	58	34
1311[7]	**Palacegate Jack (IRE) (66)** (JBerry) **6-8-13**(7) CLowther(3) (in tch: effrt ½-wy: no imp)	½	6	12/1	60	36
1311[4]	**Ready Teddy (IRE) (43)** (MissLAPerratt) **4-7-8**(3) PFessey(7) (lw: sltly hmpd s: outpcd: hdwy 2f out: sn btn)	hd	7	11/2[3]	36	12
1468[11]	**Royal Dome (IRE) (69)** (MartynWane) **5-9-9** JCarroll(8) (chsd ldrs tl wknd appr fnl f)	1¼	8	10/1	58	34
				(SP 118.7%)		**8 Rn**

59.5 secs (1.80) CSF £15.36 CT £115.54 TOTE £7.60: £2.10 £1.10 £3.60 (£5.40) OWNER Mrs Jeanne Chapman (YORK) BRED J. S. Bell
LONG HANDICAP Sunset Harbour (IRE) 7-6
1080 Shadow Jury had everything going his way and, given a fine ride up the stands' rails, he showed great spirit to make it. (7/1)
1332* Lady Sheriff has never won off a mark as high as this, but she put up a brave effort. (5/4)
1332 Sunset Harbour (IRE) made a dramatic switch right round the field approaching the final furlong, and showed she is in good heart to finish so close. (14/1: 8/1-16/1)
Pallium (IRE) has changed yards, and this was not a bad effort from this rather unreliable character. (33/1)
949 Johayro ran a shade better this time. (4/1)
972 Palacegate Jack (IRE) could never dominate, and was always fighting a lost cause. (12/1: 8/1-14/1)
1311 Ready Teddy (IRE) (11/2: 6/1-10/1)

1603 SMARTS ADVERTISING H'CAP (0-60) (3-Y.O+) (Class F)

8-15 (8-17) **1m 16y** £3,002.50 (£840.00: £407.50) Stalls: High GOING minus 0.29 sec per fur (GF)

				SP	RR	SF
1283*	**Power Game (51)** (JBerry) **4-9-1b**(5) TEDurcan(7) (hld up: hdwy to ld ins fnl f: r.o)	—	**1**	4/1^{1}	65	47
1129^{9}	**Barresbo (57)** (CWFairhurst) **3-8-7**(7) TSiddall(14) (chsd ldrs: chal over 2f out: led over 1f out: hdd ins fnl f: kpt on)	½	**2**	8/1	70	40
1220^{2}	**Dictation (USA) (55)** (JJO'Neill) **5-9-10** JFortune(13) (in tch: hdwy to disp ld over 2f out: hdd over 1f out: no ex)	2½	**3**	4/1^{1}	63	45
1291^{4}	**Kass Alhawa (54)** (DWChapman) **4-9-9** ACulhane(12) (hld up: gd hdwy to disp ld 2f out: hdd & no ex appr fnl f)	½	**4**	11/2^{2}	61	43
1383^{7}	**Diamond Crown (IRE) (46)** (MartynWane) **6-9-1** JCarroll(10) (mid div: effrt 4f out: nt pce to chal)	3½	**5**	14/1	46	28
496^{10}	**Roseate Lodge (38)** (SEKettlewell) **11-8-0**(7) JennyBenson(11) (cl up: led 4f out tl over 2f out: grad wknd)	2½	**6**	25/1	33	15
	Charisse Dancer (50) (CWThornton) **4-9-5** DaleGibson(4) (bhd: sme hdwy fnl 3f: n.d)	¾	**7**	20/1	44	26
1128^{16}	**Take Notice (46)** (RMMcKellar) **4-8-12**(3)ow1 OPears(3) (bhd: styd on fnl 3f: n.d)	hd	**8**	50/1	40	21
1285*	**Miss Pigalle (37)** (MissLAPerratt) **6-8-6** NKennedy(8) (lw: prom tl outpcd fnl 3f)	3	**9**	7/1^{3}	25	7
1266^{6}	**Sheraz (IRE) (40)** (NTinkler) **5-8-9b** LCharnock(6) (lw: chsd ldrs tl wknd wl over 2f out)	1	**10**	7/1^{3}	26	8
823^{9}	**Perilous Plight (53)** (MrsLStubbs) **6-9-1**(7) CLowther(1) (s.i.s: c wd ent st: wknd 2f out)	2	**11**	20/1	35	17
	Special-K (54) (EWeymes) **5-9-4**(5) GParkin(2) (lw: chsd ldrs 5f: wknd)	2	**12**	14/1	32	14
1284^{2}	**Samspet (42)** (RAFahey) **3-7-6**(7) RWinston(9) (led tl hdd 4f out: sn wknd)	4	**13**	7/1^{3}	12	—
1080^{8}	**Answers-To-Thomas (44)** (JMJefferson) **4-8-10**(3) PFessey(5) (lw: chsd ldrs 5f: wknd)	1¼	**14**	50/1	11	—
				(SP 134.6%)	**14 Rn**	

1m 42.3 (3.30) CSF £35.62 CT £136.66 TOTE £3.90: £2.00 £3.90 £1.50 (£51.00) Trio £82.40 OWNER Countrywide Racing (COCKERHAM) BRED Bearstone Stud

WEIGHT FOR AGE 3yo-12lb

STEWARDS' ENQUIRY Durcan susp: 9-10/06/97 (excessive use of whip)

1283* Power Game was given the far rails all to himself as the field spread out in the straight and, sticking to his task well, he won in good style. (4/1)

886 Barresbo is running well and there would seem to be a race in him. (8/1)

1220 Dictation (USA) is running consistently well but just lacks that finishing kick. (4/1)

1291 Kass Alhawa has plenty more ability but needs a more patient ride. (11/2)

1283 Diamond Crown (IRE) comes from a yard that has yet to strike real form this season, but he showed something on this occasion. (14/1)

Roseate Lodge showed his first signs of form of the season, but this old campaigner cried enough once the pressure was on early in the straight. (25/1)

1604 BAILEYS ORIGINAL IRISH CREAM RATING RELATED MAIDEN STKS (0-60) (3-Y.O+) (Class F)

8-45 (8-47) **5f** £2,652.50 (£740.00: £357.50) Stalls: High GOING minus 0.29 sec per fur (GF)

				SP	RR	SF
1080^{6}	**Toronto (54)** (JBerry) **3-8-8b**(3) PFessey(1) (lw: w ldrs: disp ld ½-wy tl ins fnl f: r.o to ld cl home)	—	**1**	7/1^{3}	62	32
1375^{2}	**Gold Edge (54)** (MRChannon) **3-8-5**(3) PPMurphy(4) (disp ld: led ins fnl f: hdd & nt qckn towards fin)	nk	**2**	4/6^{1}	58	28
1332^{4}	**Superfrills (40)** (MissLCSiddall) **4-8-13**(3) OPears(5) (cl up: drvn along ½-wy: r.o one pce)	4	**3**	8/1	45	23
1129^{13}	**My Saltarello (IRE) (48)** (ABMulholland) **3-8-4b**(7) CLowther(3) (a chsng ldrs: rdn ½-wy: no imp after)	½	**4**	20/1	47	17
1119^{11}	**La Doyenne (IRE) (51)** (CBBBooth) **3-8-8** KHodgson(8) (disp ld 3f: sn rdn & btn)	3½	**5**	7/1^{3}	32	2
1332^{10}	**Fancy Clancy (29)** (MissLCSiddall) **4-8-9b**(7) TSiddall(7) (lw: chsd ldrs tl outpcd fnl 2f)	5	**6**	50/1	16	—
	Midas Man (25) (DANolan) **6-9-5** VHalliday(2) (nvr wnt pce)	2½	**7**	100/1	11	—
1311^{9}	**Lord Cornelious (29)** (DANolan) **4-9-0b**^{1}(5) JBramhill(9) (outpcd & bhd fr ½-wy)	3½	**8**	100/1	—	—
995^{10}	**Mill End Boy (60)** (MWEasterby) **3-8-11** TLucas(6) (bolted gng to s: sn bhd)	8	**9**	11/2^{2}	—	—
				(SP 120.2%)	**9 Rn**	

59.9 secs (2.20) CSF £11.40 TOTE £7.20: £2.00 £1.00 £2.20 (£4.20) Trio £5.10 OWNER Mr John Hulme (COCKERHAM) BRED M. G. T. Stokes

WEIGHT FOR AGE 3yo-8lb

1080 Toronto, well handled, won this poor race by conjuring up a good burst of speed late on. (7/1)

1375 Gold Edge is proving very difficult to win with, and will have to go a long way to find another race as bad as this. (4/6)

1332 Superfrills keeps showing bits of form but does not come up with the goods. (8/1)

My Saltarello (IRE), dropping back in trip, ran reasonably but was never on the bridle at any stage. (20/1)

La Doyenne (IRE) apparently gave problems in the saddling boxes and cut a leg and, after showing speed, dropped tamely away and was later found to be lame. (7/1: 5/1-8/1)

Mill End Boy ran his race on the way to post. (11/2: 7/2-6/1)

1605 SHERATON GRAND H'CAP (0-60) (3-Y.O+) (Class F)

9-15 (9-18) **2m** £2,687.50 (£750.00: £362.50) Stalls: High GOING: 0.00 sec per fur (G)

				SP	RR	SF
1494^{2}	**Hasta la Vista (48)** (MWEasterby) **7-9-5b**(5) GParkin(9) (lw: a cl up: led over 2f out to 1f out: rallied to ld post)	—	**1**	9/4^{1}	59	—
1081^{5}	**Charity Crusader (35)** (MrsMReveley) **6-8-11b** ACulhane(4) (lw: unruly in stalls: s.s: hdwy 4f out: disp ld 1f out: edgd rt: no ex towards fin)	s.h	**2**	6/1^{3}	46	—
1232^{4}	**Northern Motto (48)** (JSGoldie) **4-9-5**(3) RHavlin(2) (hld up: hdwy 4f out: disp ld 1f out: r.o: jst ct)	hd	**3**	5/2^{2}	59	—
1081^{9}	**Recluse (26)** (WTKemp) **6-7-11b**(5) JBramhill(8) (lw: a.p: hdwy & ch over 1f out: sn btn)	5	**4**	66/1	32	—
865^{6}	**Tancred Mischief (34)** (DWBarker) **6-8-7**(3) DarrenMoffatt(3) (b.nr fore: hld up & bhd: effrt 4f out: nvr able to chal)	½	**5**	6/1^{3}	39	—
	Suselja (IRE) (32) (JMJefferson) **6-8-5**(3) PFessey(5) (chsd ldr tl lost pl st: n.d after)	6	**6**	14/1	31	—
1232^{5}	**Clash of Swords (52)** (PCalver) **4-9-12** JFortune(6) (led 3f: cl up tl outpcd fnl 3f)	2½	**7**	12/1	49	—
1452^{8}	**Faugeron (50)** (NTinkler) **8-9-12b** LCharnock(1) (led after 3f tl over 2f out: sn wknd)	16	**8**	9/1	31	—
1229^{3}	**Ballet de Cour (32)** (TJEtherington) **4-8-6b** JCarroll(7) (prom tl rn wd & lost pl ent st: n.d after)	14	**9**	14/1	—	—
				(SP 120.4%)	**9 Rn**	

3m 33.7 CSF £15.73 CT £33.76 TOTE £3.80: £1.10 £1.60 £1.50 (£8.10) Trio £10.00 OWNER Mr K. Hodgson (SHERIFF HUTTON) BRED Clanville Lodge Stud

WEIGHT FOR AGE 4yo-2lb

1494 Hasta la Vista gained his reward for some gallant efforts, and showed fine spirit to make it. (9/4)

1081 Charity Crusader looked particularly well but gave all sorts of problems in the stalls. He showed he has the ability, only to throw it away late on. (6/1: op 4/1)
1232 Northern Motto, happier at this trip, had his chances but tended to hang under pressure and was just worried out of it. (5/2)
Recluse took the eye in the paddock and ran his best race for some time. (66/1)
865 Tancred Mischief has only ever won once, and that was over this track earlier in the season, and this was a reasonable effort from 6lb higher. (6/1)
Suselja (IRE) (14/1: 10/1-16/1)
1232 Clash of Swords (12/1: 8/1-14/1)
Faugeron (9/1: 12/1-8/1)
1229 Ballet de Cour (14/1: 10/1-16/1)

T/Plpt: £31.30 (344.38 Tckts). T/Qdpt: £2.80 (240.17 Tckts) AA

1213-NEWMARKET (R-H) (Good to firm)
Saturday May 31st
Races 1 & 2 hand-timed
WEATHER: warm & sunny WIND: mod half against

1606 ALDANITI MEMORIAL H'CAP (0-80) (4-Y.O+) (Class D)
2-10 (2-12) **1m (Rowley)** £3,893.85 (£1,162.80: £555.90: £252.45) Stalls: High GOING minus 0.20 sec per fur (GF)

				SP	RR	SF
1097[5]	**Family Man (72)** (JRFanshawe) **4-9-9** DHarrison(9) (trckd ldrs: led over 1f out: shkn up & qcknd clr: easily)	—	1	11/4[1]	84+	66
1308[3]	**Orsay (76)** (WRMuir) **5-9-13** JReid(7) (trckd ldrs: rdn 2f out: r.o fnl f)	3	2	5/1[3]	82	64
1308[8]	**Alpine Hideaway (IRE) (76)** (BHanbury) **4-9-13** JStack(8) (lw: hld up: hdwy over 1f out: r.o wl ins fnl f)	nk	3	16/1	81	63
1324[7]	**Resist the Force (USA) (55)** (CACyzer) **7-8-6** TQuinn(11) (lw: prom: led over 2f out tl over 1f out: wknd wl ins fnl f)	½	4	7/1	59	41
1093[14]	**Errant (52)** (DJSCosgrove) **5-8-3** JQuinn(6) (b: dwlt: bhd tl sme hdwy fnl 2f)	7	5	33/1	42	24
1324[9]	**Wild Palm (70)** (WAO'Gorman) **5-9-7** EmmaO'Gorman(1) (hld up: effrt over 3f out: no imp)	nk	6	8/1	60	42
1495*	**Three Arch Bridge (75)** (MJohnston) **5-9-12b** 5x DeanMcKeown(4) (lw: sn prom: ev ch over 2f out: sn wknd)	nk	7	9/2[2]	64	46
1219[5]	**Saltando (IRE) (56)** (PatMitchell) **6-8-4v**(3) MartinDwyer(5) (led: rdn 3f out: hdd & btn over 2f out)	2½	8	16/1	40	22
346[4]	**Tart (FR) (70)** (JPearce) **4-9-7** GBardwell(3) (swtchd rt s: a bhd)	1	9	33/1	52	34
1248[7]	**Doctor Bravious (IRE) (64)** (MBell) **4-9-1v** MFenton(10) (prom over 5f)	7	10	14/1	32	14
1082[7]	**Soaking (52)** (MDIUsher) **7-8-3** MRoberts(2) (lw: prom 5f)	3	11	20/1	14	—
				(SP 114.2%)	**11 Rn**	

1m 39.6 (2.30) CSF £13.73 CT £162.50 TOTE £3.40: £1.40 £2.10 £4.10 (£12.50) Trio £154.00 OWNER Family Man Partnership (NEWMARKET) BRED Mrs Celia Miller
1097 Family Man, heavily-supported throughout the day, was always travelling well and never gave his supporters a moment's concern, quickening clear in fine style when let down. Already soundly beaten twice off this mark, he could be improving fast and looks one to keep on the right side of. (11/4)
1308 Orsay ran another sound race, but consistency does not see his handicap mark drop. He carries weight well and would have a good chance in a 0-75 handicap should he ever get the opportunity. (5/1)
1021 Alpine Hideaway (IRE), ridden with the restraint that was used when scoring at Leicester last October, finished with a real flourish once he saw daylight. (16/1)
1154* Resist the Force (USA) cruised to the front looking the part, but was no match for the winner once he pounced. Tying up in the final furlong, he surrendered second place late on and may be better over seven on turf. (7/1)
Errant, rather keen on the way to post, only ran on past beaten horses. (33/1)
Wild Palm may have seen too much daylight racing towards the centre of the track, as his effort came to little, but he is still off a mark 6lb higher than that off which he won last season. (8/1)
1495* Three Arch Bridge (9/2: 3/1-5/1)

95+ 77

1607 E.B.F. SUNLEY BUILDS MAIDEN STKS (2-Y.O) (Class D)
2-40 (2-43) **6f (Rowley)** £4,012.50 (£1,200.00: £575.00: £262.50) Stalls: High GOING minus 0.20 sec per fur (GF)

				SP	RR	SF
	Cape Verdi (IRE) (PWChapple-Hyam) **2-8-9** JReid(12) (gd sort: dwlt: sn prom: led 2f out: rdn out)	—	1	8/13[1]	86++	39
	Trans Island (IABalding) **2-9-0** KDarley(7) (w'like: scope: prom: led 3f out to 2f out: kpt on wl)	2	2	12/1	86	39
	Way Out Yonder (BWHills) **2-9-0** DHolland(9) (cmpt: scope: in tch: rdn 3f out: r.o wl appr fnl f)	1	3	25/1	83+	36
1321[2]	**Arpeggio** (RHannon) **2-9-0** DaneO'Neill(11) (chsd ldrs: rdn & one pce appr fnl f)	1½	4	11/2[3]	79	32
	Mumtaaz (SbinSuroor) **2-9-0** LDettori(4) (gd sort: lw: hld up: plld out over 1f out: r.o wl fnl f)	1¼	5	5/1[2]	76+	29
	Muhtathir (JHMGosden) **2-9-0** GHind(2) (leggy: scope: chsd ldrs: one pce fnl 2f)	1½	6	20/1	72	25
	Outsourcing (USA) (PFICole) **2-9-0** TQuinn(10) (neat: chsd ldrs 4f: sn btn)	nk	7	16/1	71	24
	Dashing Chief (IRE) (MAJarvis) **2-9-0** MRoberts(3) (cmpt: in tch 4f)	1½	8	33/1	67	20
1213[2]	**Diamond White** (GCBravery) **2-8-9** MRimmer(13) (plld hrd: led 3f)	4	9	14/1	51	4
	Yajtahed (IRE) (JHMGosden) **2-9-0** AGarth(1) (w'like: dwlt: sn pushed along: nvr nr ldrs)	s.h	10	50/1	56	9
	Dancing Al (JSMoore) **2-9-0** NAdams(8) (neat: s.s: a bhd)	¾	11	66/1	54	7
	Sabre Butt (MHTompkins) **2-9-0** DBiggs(5) (w'like: bit bkwd: a bhd)	1¾	12	66/1	49	2
				(SP 130.7%)	**12 Rn**	

1m 14.5 (2.70) CSF £10.09 TOTE £1.90: £1.10 £3.50 £4.90 (£8.40) Trio £71.90 OWNER Mr R. E. Sangster (MARLBOROUGH) BRED Swettenham Stud
Cape Verdi (IRE) was not so much the course whisper as a nationwide loud hailer. She managed to confirm the promise she had been showing at home in determined style. By Caerleon out of a sister of the Breeders' Cup Classic winner Arcangues, whose only previous progeny was considered good enough to take his chance in last year's Prix du Jockey-Club, her pedigree strongly suggests she will be better-suited to further, making this performance, in may what turn out to have been a very decent race, all the more creditable. (8/13)
Trans Island, a tall, scopey colt, gave trouble in the stalls. However, he did little wrong in the race and looks sure to win races over this sort of trip. (12/1: 8/1-14/1)
Way Out Yonder, hardly a typical Shirley Heights, being not over-big but strongly-made, he really caught the eye coming with a late rattle after struggling to go the pace at halfway. His dam won over six but some of her progeny have stayed. (25/1)
1321 Arpeggio seemed to run his race, suggesting this is a very useful contest (11/2: 7/2-6/1)
Mumtaaz, a tall, attractive colt, finished in fine style and must have a future. (5/1: 4/1-6/1)

Muhtathir, a good-looking son of May Hill Stakes winner Majmu, was rather keen going down and was outpaced once the temperature rose. Seven may already be needed. (20/1)
Outsourcing (USA), a flashy-looking chestnut, is a good walker and mover, and showed some promise in the race. (16/1)
1213 Diamond White, with little early pace on, pulled far too hard and ruined his chance. (14/1: 12/1-20/1)

1608 HAMELLS H'CAP (0-100) (3-Y.O+) (Class C)

3-10 (3-14) **5f (Rowley)** £5,628.75 (£1,680.00: £802.50: £363.75) Stalls: High GOING minus 0.20 sec per fur (GF)

				SP	RR	SF
1113^{5}	**Literary Society (USA) (71)** (JARToller) **4-8-9** SSanders(10) (lw: chsd ldrs: led ins fnl f: rdn out)	—	**1**	13/2	80	52
1158*	**Twice as Sharp (90)** (PWHarris) **5-10-0** GHind(6) (lw: led over 4f: unable qckn)	1	**2**	$6/1^{3}$	96	68
1158^{7}	**Gone Savage (81)** (WJMusson) **9-9-5** LDettori(11) (hld up: hdwy 2f out: r.o fnl f)	½	**3**	$5/1^{2}$	85	57
	Crofters Ceilidh (84) (BAMcMahon) **5-9-8** KDarley(7) (chsd ldrs: kpt on same pce appr fnl f)	1¼	**4**	25/1	84	56
1254^{3}	**Meliksah (IRE) (94)** (MBell) **3-9-5**(5) GFaulkner(4) (chsd ldrs: one pce appr fnl f)	nk	**5**	7/1	93	57
1212^{6}	**Dancethenightaway (92)** (BJMeehan) **3-9-8** RHughes(5) (hld up: hdwy 2f out: n.m.r 1f out: swtchd & no imp)	¾	**6**	20/1	89	53
1158^{2}	**Lago Di Varano (90)** (RMWhitaker) **5-10-0v** DeanMcKeown(9) (dwlt: sn chsng ldrs: wknd over 1f out)	2	**7**	7/1	80	52
1243^{10}	**Nor-Do-I (83)** (JMPEustace) **3-8-10**(3) MartinDwyer(8) (bhd: rdn & hung lft 2f out: nvr trbld ldrs)	½	**8**	33/1	72	36
1317^{11}	**Bowden Rose (81)** (MBlanshard) **5-9-5b** JQuinn(3) (w ldr: rdn over 2f out: sn wknd)	1½	**9**	$9/2^{1}$	65	37
1303^{4}	**Taoiste (89)** (RWArmstrong) **4-9-13** MRoberts(1) (rdn 2f out: a bhd)	nk	**10**	20/1	72	44
1402^{2}	**Ansellman (81)** (JBerry) **7-9-5b** GCarter(2) (in tch tl rdn & btn 2f out)	2½	**11**	15/2	56	28
				(SP 115.5%)		**11 Rn**

60.09 secs (1.39) CSF £38.13 CT £195.82 TOTE £7.70: £2.20 £2.40 £1.60 (£31.90) Trio £40.30 OWNER Lady Celina Carter (WHITSBURY) BRED William R. and Mrs Buster
WEIGHT FOR AGE 3yo-8lb
1113 Literary Society (USA) moved to post exceptionally well, and was able to hold his pitch against the far rail, having been drawn just one off it. Put to work in the Dip, he soon got on top. (13/2)
1158* Twice as Sharp again tried to make all and, given that he was raised 7lb for his York win, this must be as well as he has ever run. (6/1)
1158 Gone Savage might have been expected to find trouble, being a finisher drawn against a rail, but he had a pretty clear run when making a bid and ran his race. (5/1)
Crofters Ceilidh has yet to be forgiven by the Handicapper for finishing fourth in a conditions race at Newbury last September, in first-time blinkers. She is clearly in good heart and will win in her turn. (25/1)
1254 Meliksah (IRE) could not dominate against some experienced campaigners. (7/1)
1212 Dancethenightaway did not get a clear run when making her effort, and might have gone a deal closer given racing room. She races with her head rather high and does not look an easy ride. (20/1)
1034 Bowden Rose, second in this race last year off a 2lb higher mark, took the runner-up on from the gun and paid the penalty. (9/2)

1609 CORAL SPRINT H'CAP (0-105) (3-Y.O) (Class B)

3-40 (3-42) **6f (Rowley)** £22,515.00 (£6,720.00: £3,210.00: £1,455.00) Stalls: High GOING minus 0.20 sec per fur (GF)

				SP	RR	SF
1237*	**Blue Goblin (USA) (94)** (LMCumani) **3-8-13** LDettori(10) (hld up: hdwy to ld over 1f out: qcknd clr: easily)	—	**1**	$11/10^{1}$	109++	66
1403^{3}	**Connemara (IRE) (100)** (CADwyer) **3-9-5** DHarrison(4) (lw: stdd s: hdwy 2f out: r.o wl fnl f: no ch w wnr)	2½	**2**	14/1	108	65
1243*	**Sharp Hat (92)** (RHannon) **3-8-11** DaneO'Neill(11) (in tch: hdwy 3f out: rdn & ev ch over 1f out: one pce)	1¾	**3**	$7/1^{2}$	96	53
1453^{8}	**Plaisir d'Amour (IRE) (82)** (NACallaghan) **3-7-10**(5) APolli(6) (w ldr: led over 3f out tl over 1f out: sn btn)	nk	**4**	16/1	85	42
1254^{6}	**Polish Warrior (IRE) (85)** (TDBarron) **3-8-4** KDarley(8) (lw: plld hrd: chsd ldrs: nt clr run over 2f out: swtchd rt: no imp fnl f)	nk	**5**	10/1	87	44
854^{4}	**Cadeaux Cher (88)** (BWHills) **3-8-7** DHolland(3) (b: hld up: hdwy 2f out: nvr rchd ldrs)	6	**6**	$7/1^{2}$	74	31
1403^{5}	**Young Bigwig (IRE) (94)** (JBerry) **3-8-8**(5) PRoberts(9) (lw: led over 2f: sn wknd)	2	**7**	16/1	75	32
988^{3}	**Snap Crackle Pop (IRE) (90)** (RFJohnsonHoughton) **3-8-9b1** JReid(12) (w ldrs over 3f)	1	**8**	16/1	68	25
1170^{11}	**The Gay Fox (77)** (BAMcMahon) **3-7-10** JQuinn(2) (chsd ldr 4f)	1¼	**9**	20/1	52	9
968^{5}	**Paddy Lad (IRE) (93)** (RGuest) **3-8-12** PBloomfield(5) (chsd ldrs: rdn 3f out: sn bhd)	1¼	**10**	25/1	64	21
1243^{2}	**Alumisiyah (USA) (85)** (RWArmstrong) **3-8-4** GCarter(7) (chsd ldrs: rdn 3f out: sn btn)	3	**11**	$8/1^{3}$	48	5
1403^{4}	**Granny's Pet (102)** (PFICole) **3-9-7** TQuinn(1) (hld up: rdn & btn over 2f out)	¾	**12**	12/1	63	20
				(SP 133.4%)		**12 Rn**

1m 12.84 (1.04) CSF £21.02 CT £88.34 TOTE £2.20: £1.30 £3.70 £2.70 (£20.80) Trio £51.90 OWNER Sheikh Mohammed (NEWMARKET) BRED Darley Stud Management Inc
LONG HANDICAP The Gay Fox 7-8
1237* Blue Goblin (USA) was very impressive, destroying his rivals in what ought to have been a competitive handicap. The drop back to six furlongs has proved the key and, while he remains none too easy a ride, he may well follow last year's winner of this race, Atraf, into the Cork and Orrery winner's enclosure. (11/10: op 7/4)
1403 Connemara (IRE), put to sleep in rear more easily this time due to the fast early pace, produced a run that would normally have won this sort of race, only to catch a Group horse in waiting. She is not going to be easy to place off her current mark, but retains her ability and deserves an opening. (14/1)
1243* Sharp Hat went down keenly and challenged against the rails moments before the winner shot past. He finished behind the winner over course and distance two outings ago, despite racing in the favoured stands' side group that day, and did not have a prayer or reversing form on 4lb worse terms. (7/1: 5/1-8/1)
1453 Plaisir d'Amour (IRE), whose wins have come over seven, races like a sprinter and is capable of winning again if her sights are lowered a little. (16/1)
1254 Polish Warrior (IRE) gave his pilot few options by failing to settle, and may be better forcing the issue over the minimum trip judged on this. (10/1)
854 Cadeaux Cher did not find a great deal when let down, and may now need seven. (7/1)

1610 BAIRSTOW EVES CHARLOTTE STKS (Listed) (3-Y.O+ F & M) (Class A)

4-15 (4-17) **6f (Rowley)** £10,935.40 (£4,048.60: £1,944.30: £796.50: £318.25: £126.95) Stalls: High GOING minus 0.20 sec per fur (GF)

				SP	RR	SF
$1203a^{5}$	**Nightbird (IRE) (104)** (SbinSuroor) **3-8-11** LDettori(5) (mde all: qcknd clr 2f out: unchal)	—	**1**	$2/1^{1}$	122	66
960^{7}	**Elegant Warning (IRE) (107)** (BWHills) **3-8-11** DHolland(4) (hld up: hdwy 2f out: r.o wl fnl f: nt trble wnr)	3½	**2**	$2/1^{1}$	113	57
$1532a^{W}$	**Wildwood Flower (97)** (RHannon) **4-9-2** RHughes(6) (lw: trckd ldrs: rdn & one pce fnl 2f)	3½	**3**	8/1	99	52
1101^{7}	**El Opera (IRE) (91)** (PFICole) **4-9-2** TQuinn(9) (sn pushed along: chsd ldrs: outpcd 2f out: kpt on nr fin)	2	**4**	16/1	94	47
1112^{2}	**Arethusa (105)** (RHannon) **3-8-11** DaneO'Neill(8) (in tch: effrt over 2f out: sn btn)	1¾	**5**	$13/2^{2}$	93	37

1112[6]	**Conspiracy (102)** (JLDunlop) **3-8-11** KDarley(3) (hld up: rdn 2f out: no imp)	½	**6**	12/1	92	36
	Crystal Crossing (IRE) (PWChapple-Hyam) **3-8-11** JReid(2) (hld up: hdwy over 2f out: sn rdn: wknd over 1f out)	s.h	**7**	15/2[3]	92	36
1112[5]	**Dayville (USA) (86)** (JBerry) **3-8-7** SSanders(7) (prom 3f)	nk	**8**	33/1	87	31
988[4]	**Carati (89)** (RBoss) **3-8-7** MRoberts(1) (racd alone centre: spd over 3f)	8	**9**	33/1	66	10
				(SP 122.3%)		**9 Rn**

1m 12.68 (0.88) CSF £5.48 TOTE £2.80: £1.20 £1.40 £2.20 (£2.80) Trio £15.70 OWNER Godolphin (NEWMARKET) BRED S. Tindall and Stowell Hill Ltd

WEIGHT FOR AGE 3yo-9lb

1203a Nightbird (IRE), led round the paddock by two handlers, looked magnificent and moved well to post. Dictating matters from the front, she stole an unassailable advantage with two furlongs left. Such tactics clearly suit her and she looks Royal Ascot bound. (2/1: op 3/1)

960 Elegant Warning (IRE), settled in rear despite the drop in trip, finished strongly but the winner had got first run. (2/1)

Wildwood Flower moved down moderately and got worked up after being installed last, but ran a sound race although comprehensively out-paced in the closing stages. (8/1: 6/1-10/1)

839 El Opera (IRE), whose trip remains a mystery, stayed on under a firm ride to hang on to fourth place. (16/1)

1112 Arethusa ran below her best, fading in the last couple of furlongs. (13/2)

1112 Conspiracy looked another hindered by making her move towards the centre of the track. (12/1: 8/1-14/1)

Crystal Crossing (IRE) looked in tip-top condition for his seasonal bow, and was moving up promisingly until losing her action going into the Dip. She does not look a straightforward ride, but is better than this. (15/2: 4/1-8/1)

1611 UNICOIN HOMES MAIDEN STKS (3-Y.O) (Class D)

4-45 (4-46) **1m (Rowley)** £4,163.50 (£1,243.00: £594.00: £269.50) Stalls: High GOING minus 0.20 sec per fur (GF)

				SP	RR	SF
963[2]	**The Prince** (GWragg) **3-9-0** AClark(3) (lw: trckd ldrs: led over 2f out: eased nr fin)	—	**1**	4/7[1]	88	51
	Bombazine (IRE) (LMCumani) **3-8-9** OUrbina(7) (w'like: leggy: hld up: hdwy 2f out: r.o fnl f: nt rch wnr)	1¼	**2**	7/1[3]	81	44
1207[9]	**Easy Song (USA)** (RCharlton) **3-9-0** SSanders(9) (lw: chsd ldrs: rdn over 2f out: one pce)	3	**3**	33/1	80	43
	Vain Tempest (PWChapple-Hyam) **3-9-0** JReid(8) (wl grwn: hld up & plld hrd: hdwy over 2f out: n.m.r over 1f out: one pce)	2	**4**	15/2	76	39
1239[12]	**Supremism (75)** (CEBrittain) **3-9-0** BDoyle(1) (w ldr over 5f: wknd fnl f)	hd	**5**	33/1	75	38
	Sheltering Sky (IRE) (JLDunlop) **3-9-0** KDarley(6) (leggy: scope: hdwy over 2f out: no imp appr fnl f)	nk	**6**	25/1	75	38
989[4]	**Dellua (IRE)** (RGuest) **3-8-9** PBloomfield(5) (rdn over 3f out: sn bhd)	18	**7**	33/1	34	—
1221[3]	**Blot** (MrsJCecil) **3-9-0** LDettori(4) (led over 5f: sn wknd)	hd	**8**	4/1[2]	39	2
				(SP 120.6%)		**8 Rn**

1m 40.25 (2.95) CSF £5.14 TOTE £1.60: £1.10 £1.50 £4.00 (£4.30) Trio £40.90 OWNER Mr I. R. MacNicol (NEWMARKET) BRED Bottisham Heath Stud

OFFICIAL EXPLANATION **Dellua (IRE): bled slightly from the nose.**

963 The Prince took this in good style and will be interesting in handicaps, as he seems to be going the right way. (4/7)

Bombazine (IRE), a Generous half-sister to Barathea, is a good mover and came home well. She looks likely to stay further and should win races. (7/1)

1207 Easy Song (USA) again made his jockey work hard, but this run suggests he has improved. (33/1)

Vain Tempest took a strong hold and is going to need to settle better than this to fulfil his potential. (15/2)

Supremism was again something of a disappointment, but ran as though not quite getting this trip. (33/1)

Sheltering Sky (IRE), a tall newcomer, cut little ice but should come on for the run. (25/1)

1221 Blot allowed to bowl along this time, was always doing a little too much and faded dramatically once headed. His initial effort suggests he is capable of much better. (4/1: 5/2-9/2)

1612 MILTON PARK STUD MAIDEN STKS (3-Y.O) (Class D)

5-20 (5-21) **1m 6f (Rowley)** £3,841.75 (£1,144.00: £544.50: £244.75) Stalls: High GOING minus 0.20 sec per fur (GF)

				SP	RR	SF
558[3]	**Three Cheers (IRE)** (JHMGosden) **3-9-0v1** AGarth(2) (lw: chsd ldrs: rdn 4f out: led over 2f out: drew clr fnl f)	—	**1**	16/1	84	53
1218[5]	**Awesome Wells (IRE)** (HRACecil) **3-9-0** AMcGlone(7) (prom: led 4f out tl over 2f out: wknd fnl f)	7	**2**	9/2[3]	76	45
1218[3]	**Sun Alert (USA)** (MJPolglase) **3-8-9** MRoberts(4) (hdwy 3f out: r.o fnl f)	nk	**3**	9/1	71	40
1014[8]	**Walkabout** (BWHills) **3-9-0** DHolland(6) (hld up: hdwy 6f out: nvr rchd ldrs)	8	**4**	14/1	67	36
1258[2]	**Vicki Romara (80)** (MJohnston) **3-8-9** GCarter(1) (lw: led 10f)	7	**5**	100/30[2]	54	23
1218[2]	**Silver Wonder (USA)** (LMCumani) **3-9-0** TSprake(5) (lw: prom: rdn 4f out: sn wknd)	7	**6**	Evens[1]	51	20
1106[9]	**North White Plains** (CEBrittain) **3-9-0** BDoyle(3) (reluctant to r: a t.o)	30	**7**	66/1	16	—
				(SP 115.3%)		**7 Rn**

3m 1.1 (5.10) CSF £78.91 TOTE £10.30: £3.20 £2.10 (£21.20) OWNER Sheikh Mohammed (NEWMARKET) BRED Sheikh Mohammed Bin Rashid Al Maktoum

558 Three Cheers (IRE), noisy in the paddock and tried in a visor for the first time, showed that stamina is his strong suit. He is anything but an easy ride, as he showed when hanging once in charge. (16/1)

1218 Awesome Wells (IRE), fitter this time, was colty in the paddock, but gave the winner a sustained duel until tying up in the last furlong. (9/2)

1218 Sun Alert (USA) has stamina aplenty but does not do anything quickly. (9/1: 6/1-10/1)

Walkabout tried to close on the two clear leaders with three furlongs left, but was never able to do so. (14/1)

1258 Vicki Romara found making all over this trip over Newmarket's wide open spaces too daunting a task, and ran poorly. (100/30)

1218 Silver Wonder (USA) failed to confirm form with Awesome Wells and Sun Alert, being first of the main group beaten. He was gone too far from home to blame the distance alone. (Evens)

T/Jkpt: £703.60 (10.09 Tckts). T/Plpt: £25.90 (1,460.17 Tckts). T/Qdpt: £3.20 (533.93 Tckts) Dk

1227-HAMILTON (R-H) (Good to Firm)
Monday June 2nd
WEATHER: sunny & warm WIND: almost nil

1613 EAST KILBRIDE SERIES (ROUND 3) APPRENTICE H'CAP (0-65) (3-Y.O+) (Class F)
2-30 (2-30) **6f 5y** £2,808.00 (£788.00: £384.00) Stalls: Low GOING minus 0.38 sec per fur (F)

				SP	RR	SF
1227[4]	**Henry the Hawk (42)** (MDods) **6-8-5** SCopp(15) (b: lw: chsd ldrs: led 1½f out: r.o)	—	**1**	16/1	52	29
1315[14]	**Craigie Boy (40)** (NBycroft) **7-8-3b** PRoberts(14) (w ldr: nt qckn fnl f)	¾	**2**	16/1	48	25
1602[4]	**Pallium (IRE) (45)** (DANolan) **9-8-5**(3) KSked(13) (w ldrs: nt qckn ins fnl f)	hd	**3**	20/1	53	30
1285[5]	**Seconds Away (33)** (JSGoldie) **6-7-5v**(5) JennyBenson(10) (chsd ldrs: kpt on u.p fnl 2f)	½	**4**	33/1	39	16
1225[10]	**Winter Scout (USA) (53)** (RAFahey) **9-8-11**(5) RWinston(8) (lw: in tch centre: kpt on fnl 2f: nrst fin)	¾	**5**	6/1[2]	57	34
823[8]	**Diet (36)** (MissLAPerratt) **11-7-8v**(5) NPollard(16) (led tl hdd 1½f out: no ex)	¾	**6**	12/1	38	15
1315[4]	**Termon (38)** (MissLAPerratt) **4-7-10**(5) MSemple(5) (racd centre: in tch: no hdwy fnl 2f)	nk	**7**	12/1	40	17
1037[2]	**Tropical Beach (60)** (JBerry) **4-9-4**(5) CLowther(3) (hdwy centre ½-wy: nvr able chal)	hd	**8**	11/2[1]	61	38
1037[6]	**Sunday Mail Too (IRE) (41)** (MissLAPerratt) **5-8-4** DSweeney(12) (lw: in tch tl outpcd fnl 2f)	½	**9**	14/1	41	18
1584[9]	**Corniche Quest (IRE) (65)** (MRChannon) **4-10-0** PPMurphy(2) (lw: spd stands' side: no ch fr ½-wy)	1	**10**	8/1[3]	62	39
	Suedoro (40) (JSGoldie) **7-8-3** TEDurcan(4) (cl up stands' side 4f: wknd)	1	**11**	20/1	35	12
1227[5]	**Another Nightmare (IRE) (39)** (RMMcKellar) **5-7-11**(5) JMcAuley(1) (spd stands' side 4f)	1½	**12**	25/1	30	7
1395[10]	**Sue Me (IRE) (58)** (DNicholls) **5-9-2**(5) CarolynBales(9) (lw: hld up: effrt 2f out: sn btn)	½	**13**	6/1[2]	47	24
1223[3]	**Impish (IRE) (55)** (TJEtherington) **3-8-10** JBramhill(7) (dwlt: hdwy centre ½-wy: wknd over 1f out)	5	**14**	8/1[3]	31	—
	Marino Street (54) (PDEvans) **4-8-12v**(5) AnthonyBond(11) (outpcd & bhd fr ½-wy)	½	**15**	33/1	29	6
1037[3]	**Ragtime Cowgirl (33)** (DANolan) **4-7-5**(5) PBradley(6) (outpcd & lost tch ½-wy: sn t.o)	dist	**16**	16/1	—	—
				(SP 125.1%)	**16 Rn**	

1m 12.0 (2.00) CSF £218.61 CT £2,573.17 TOTE £13.30: £2.50 £3.60 £4.00 £4.00 (£51.60) Trio £145.40 OWNER Mr S. Barras (DARLINGTON) BRED Mrs Celia Miller
LONG HANDICAP Seconds Away 7-2 Ragtime Cowgirl 7-9
WEIGHT FOR AGE 3yo-8lb

1227 Henry the Hawk normally likes cut in the ground and the minimum trip, but he had the necessary good draw, and did the business for the first time season. (16/1)
233 Craigie Boy is well-handicapped after some modest efforts and he really prefers easy ground but, with a big draw advantage here, he put up his best performance for a while. (16/1)
1602 Pallium (IRE) showed promise on his first run a couple of days earlier, and confirmed that with another decent effort here. (20/1)
1285 Seconds Away has yet to win a race, seems better over further and was 8lb out of the handicap, but this unpredictable sort ran really well. (33/1)
1225 Winter Scout (USA) put up a fair performance and there would seem to be a race in him again this year. (6/1)
Diet had the best draw and put up his best performance of the season. (12/1: 10/1-16/1)
1315 Termon put up a fair effort from a poor draw. (12/1)
1037 Tropical Beach ran well despite being badly drawn. (11/2)
924 Sunday Mail Too (IRE) (14/1: 10/1-16/1)

1614 BURNBANK CLAIMING STKS (2-Y.O) (Class F)
3-00 (3-00) **5f 4y** £2,430.00 (£680.00: £330.00) Stalls: Low GOING minus 0.38 sec per fur (F)

				SP	RR	SF
	Pierpoint (IRE) (RAFahey) **2-8-6**(7) RWinston(1) (cmpt: scope: lw: s.i.s: hdwy 2f out: qcknd to ld wl ins fnl f)	—	**1**	9/1	69+	24
1600*	**Makahu Don** (WTKemp) **2-8-4**(3) PFessey(2) (cl up: kpt on fnl f: nt pce of wnr)	1	**2**	11/2[3]	60	15
1444*	**Sun In The Morning** (BJMeehan) **2-9-0** KDarley(7) (lw: trckd ldr: led 2f out: edgd lft & hdd wl ins fnl f)	nk	**3**	4/5[1]	66	21
1045[10]	**Glass River** (PDEvans) **2-8-11** JFEgan(5) (lw: cl up: outpcd over 1f out & edgd rt: no ex)	2½	**4**	12/1	55	10
1444[6]	**Docklands Dispatch (IRE)** (NTinkler) **2-8-13** KimTinkler(3) (chsd ldrs: rdn ½-wy: nt qckn)	2	**5**	25/1	51	6
1267[6]	**Seventh Heaven** (JBerry) **2-8-12**(5) TEDurcan(8) (lw: led 3f: sn outpcd)	hd	**6**	100/30[2]	54	9
	Michelee (PDEvans) **2-8-4** DaleGibson(6) (leggy: unf: s.i.s: rdn ½-wy: n.d)	1	**7**	20/1	38	—
				(SP 120.3%)	**7 Rn**	

60.7 secs (2.40) CSF £55.02 TOTE £15.10: £3.50 £2.30 (£32.10) OWNER Mr R. A. Fahey (MALTON) BRED Mrs C. L. Weld
Pierpoint (IRE) took the eye in the paddock and won well, despite having a few problems in getting a run, and there would seem to be more to come. (9/1: 6/1-10/1)
1600* Makahu Don showed he is on the upgrade and stayed on really well and should have no difficulty in getting further. (11/2)
1444* Sun In The Morning travelled particularly well but, yet again, disappointed when in front and, inclined to hang, was worried out of it late on. (4/5: tchd evens)
Glass River is learning and this should help bring him on. (12/1)
1253 Docklands Dispatch (IRE) ran reasonably and looks the type to keep an eye on if dropped in class. (25/1)
1267 Seventh Heaven is proving a shade disappointing at the moment. (100/30)

1615 SUNDAY MAIL H'CAP (0-70) (3-Y.O+) (Class E)
3-30 (3-30) **1m 1f 36y** £3,420.00 (£1,035.00: £505.00: £240.00) Stalls: High GOING minus 0.38 sec per fur (F)

				SP	RR	SF
1459[5]	**Pekay (60)** (MJohnston) **4-9-10** JWeaver(8) (lw: chsd ldrs: led appr fnl f: r.o wl)	—	**1**	9/4[1]	70	52
1231*	**Principal Boy (IRE) (44)** (TJEtherington) **4-8-8** DaleGibson(3) (hld up: hdwy 3f out: ev ch 1f out: r.o)	2	**2**	11/4[2]	51	33
1229[13]	**Western Venture (IRE) (32)** (RMMcKellar) **4-7-5**(5) JBramhill(4) (led & sn clr: hdd appr fnl f: no ex)	4	**3**	16/1	32	14
1472[2]	**Nobby Barnes (32)** (DonEnricoIncisa) **8-7-10** KimTinkler(2) (hdwy & prom ent st: ev ch 3½f out: one pce)	3	**4**	3/1[3]	26	8
1231[8]	**Rapid Mover (33)** (DANolan) **10-7-4b**(7)ow1 PBradley(7) (effrt ½-wy: nvr trbld ldrs)	9	**5**	33/1	12	—
1284[10]	**Sweet Note (IRE) (46)** (MissLAPerratt) **3-7-12** NKennedy(1) (in tch tl outpcd fnl 3f)	2½	**6**	25/1	20	—
1230[15]	**Comic's Future (USA) (40)** (JJO'Neill) **4-8-4** JFEgan(6) (chsd ldrs tl lost pl 3f out)	1½	**7**	16/1	12	—
1472[7]	**Energy Man (50)** (MDods) **4-9-0** TWilliams(5) (in tch: effrt on ins 3f out: sn btn)	½	**8**	8/1	21	3
				(SP 112.1%)	**8 Rn**	

1m 57.2 (2.90) CSF £7.48 CT £66.69 TOTE £2.50: £1.40 £1.50 £3.70 (£4.70) OWNER Mr T G & Mrs M E Holdcroft (MIDDLEHAM) BRED Bearstone Stud
LONG HANDICAP Rapid Mover 7-4 Nobby Barnes 7-9 Western Venture (IRE) 7-8
WEIGHT FOR AGE 3yo-12lb

1248 Pekay, given a forceful ride, showed good attitude and won really well. Longer trips should prove no problem. (9/4: op 6/4)
1231* Principal Boy (IRE), on ground much faster than he won on last time, ran a useful race but he had to admit that he had met one too good in the end. (11/4)
668 Western Venture (IRE) had the run of the race when being allowed to go clear, but was comfortably picked off late on. (16/1)
1472 Nobby Barnes came down the outside of the field in the straight on the slower ground, and was fighting a lost cause in the last two-and-a-half furlongs. (3/1)
552 Rapid Mover, normally up with pace, was held up and then got hampered halfway up the straight, but it made little difference. (33/1)

53-54

1616 MANDORA MAIDEN AUCTION STKS (2-Y.O) (Class F)
4-00 (4-00) **6f 5y** £2,528.00 (£708.00: £344.00) Stalls: Low GOING minus 0.38 sec per fur (F)

				SP	RR	SF
1038^{2}	**Jacmar (IRE)** (MissLAPerratt) **2-8-6** NKennedy(3) (lw: swtchd centre after 2f: hdwy ½-wy: r.o wl fnl f to ld cl home)	—	**1**	14/1	79	32
1440^{2}	**Demolition Jo** (PDEvans) **2-8-2** JFEgan(10) (bmpd s: cl up far side: led 2f out: hung lft: nt qckn towards fin)	hd	**2**	$11/4^{1}$	75	28
	Just Another Time (JBerry) **2-8-2**(5) TEDurcan(1) (leggy: scope: cl up stands' side: nt qckn fnl f)	5	**3**	14/1	67	20
1255^{9}	**Scotch Time** (RAFahey) **2-7-10**(7) RWinston(6) (w ldrs stands' side: edgd rt: one pce fnl f)	¾	**4**	33/1	61	14
1228^{4}	**Marske Machine** (NTinkler) **2-8-2** DaleGibson(8) (chsd ldrs far side: nt qckn fnl 2f)	1¼	**5**	20/1	56	9
1013^{8}	**Scene (IRE)** (MartynMeade) **2-7-9**(5) JBramhill(4) (racd stands' side: prom: one pce fnl 2f)	nk	**6**	16/1	53	6
1438^{3}	**Swoosh** (BJMeehan) **2-8-11b**[1] DeanMcKeown(9) (wnt rt s: racd far side: spd over 4f)	hd	**7**	10/1	64	17
1407^{2}	**Miss Dangerous** (MRChannon) **2-8-0**(3) PPMurphy(11) (racd far side: led 4f: sn wknd)	s.h	**8**	9/2	56	9
954^{2}	**Five of Spades (IRE)** (DNicholls) **2-8-9** AlexGreaves(7) (lw: chsd ldrs stands' side: effrt 2f out: wknd over 1f out)	1¼	**9**	$7/2^{2}$	59	12
1447^{9}	**Snappy Times** (MDods) **2-8-11** TWilliams(5) (lw: dwlt: racd stands' side: a bhd)	2	**10**	33/1	55	8
	John Bowdler Music (MJohnston) **2-8-8** JWeaver(2) (w'like: bit bkwd: led stands' side over 4f: wknd)	5	**11**	$4/1^{3}$	39	—
				(SP 126.0%)	**11 Rn**	

1m 11.8 (1.80) CSF £50.39 TOTE £17.70: £4.70 £1.10 £8.40 (£22.40) Trio £220.50 OWNER Mr J. G. Marett (AYR) BRED Lodge Park Stud
1038 Jacmar (IRE) appreciated the trip but was not well drawn, but this good-looking colt worked his way into the centre of the track and showed a fine attitude to get up late on. (14/1)
1440 Demolition Jo, although she has nothing to recommend her on looks, certainly has an engine. She had a good draw, but then threw it away by hanging left. (11/4)
Just Another Time ran a fine race from a poor draw and looks the type to improve a fair bit. (14/1)
Scotch Time looked in really good trim and ran a useful race but proved a shade green under pressure. (33/1)
1228 Marske Machine was again a handful in the paddock and his performance from a good draw was slightly disappointing. (20/1)
880 Scene (IRE), a rather edgy individual, went better on this faster ground but was always struggling from her draw, and was fighting a lost cause in the last couple of furlongs. (16/1)
1407 Miss Dangerous had the right draw but disappointed on this much faster ground. (9/2)
John Bowdler Music, a big, plain sort, needed the run and showed signs of temperament in the paddock, but did show a fair amount of speed in the race. (4/1: op 5/2)

1617 RAMILLES LIMITED STKS (0-55) (3-Y.O+) (Class F)
4-30 (4-30) **1m 4f 17y** £2,416.00 (£676.00: £328.00) Stalls: High GOING minus 0.38 sec per fur (F)

				SP	RR	SF
1449^{2}	**Quezon City (54)** (MJCamacho) **3-8-7** JWeaver(3) (lw: mde all: r.o wl fnl 2f)	—	**1**	$13/8^{2}$	67	19
1574^{6}	**Jean Pierre (55)** (JPearce) **4-9-8** MWigham(2) (lw: trckd ldrs: effrt 3f out: kpt on: nt pce of wnr)	4	**2**	$5/1^{3}$	62	29
1452*	**Campaspe (54)** (JGFitzGerald) **5-9-0**(7) RWinston(1) (lw: trckd wnr: effrt 3f out: wandered u.p: wknd 2f out)	2	**3**	$10/11^{1}$	58	25
				(SP 107.1%)	**3 Rn**	

2m 38.7 (6.70) CSF £6.76 TOTE £2.50: (£3.80) OWNER Middleham Park Racing XI (MALTON) BRED Mrs S. Camacho
WEIGHT FOR AGE 3yo-15lb
1449 Quezon City looked a picture and really got it right for a most emphatic win. (13/8)
1574 Jean Pierre had his chances but, when the pressure was seriously on, he proved slightly disappointing. (5/1: op 3/1)
1452* Campaspe won on similar ground last week and gave the impression that he was feeling it, as he continually changed his legs when put under pressure and certainly did not give his running. (10/11: 8/11-evens)

1618 BLENHEIM H'CAP (0-70) (4-Y.O+) (Class E)
5-00 (5-00) **1m 5f 9y** £3,051.50 (£923.00: £450.00: £213.50) Stalls: High GOING minus 0.38 sec per fur (F)

				SP	RR	SF
1281^{8}	**Lord Advocate (46)** (DANolan) **9-8-6b**(7) KSked(3) (mde all: kpt on wl fnl 2f: fin 1st: disq)	—	**1d**	$7/4^{2}$	49	15
1445^{9}	**Nornax Lad (USA) (52)** (MartynMeade) **9-9-5** JWeaver(1) (lw: chsd ldrs: outpcd over 2f out: hdwy u.p appr fnl f: styd on wl towards fin: fin 2nd, nk: awrdd r)	—	**1**	$11/8^{1}$	55	21
1601^{6}	**Cois Na Farraige (IRE) (57)** (MissLAPerratt) **4-9-5**(5) TEDurcan(2) (hld up: hdwy & ch 2f out: hrd rdn & no ex fnl f: fin 3rd, nk & 3/4l: plcd 2nd)	1	**2**	9/1	59	25
1138^{6}	**Carol Again (32)** (NBycroft) **5-7-8**(5) JBramhill(4) (lw: sn chsng wnr: effrt 3f out: outpcd fnl 2f: fin 4th: plcd 3rd)	5	**3**	$4/1^{3}$	28	—
				(SP 108.5%)	**4 Rn**	

2m 54.6 (8.90) CSF £4.14 TOTE £2.30: (£1.70) OWNER Mrs J. McFadyen-Murray (WISHAW) BRED London Thoroughbred Services Ltd
SUBSEQUENT STEWARDS' ENQUIRY: Lord Advocate disq. (prohibited substance (isoxsuprine) in urine). Nolan fined £400.
1232 Lord Advocate was winning off his highest mark to date, and this was his fifth course victory. (7/4)
1169 Nornax Lad (USA) was in trouble halfway up the straight but he suddenly found his stride approaching the final furlong and, now off a decent mark, looks to be coming to hand. (11/8)
Cois Na Farraige (IRE) ran his best race for a long time, and is worth keeping in mind for a modest event. (9/1)
553 Carol Again looked particularly well and ran a fair race until the pressure was seriously on in the last two furlongs but, to date, she has only ever won on sand. (4/1)

T/Plpt: £1,287.90 (9.85 Tckts). T/Qdpt: £27.90 (31.47 Tckts) AA

1460-LEICESTER (R-H) (Good to Firm)
Monday June 2nd
WEATHER: fine and sunny WIND: strong half against 83

1619 E.B.F. WOLVEY MAIDEN STKS (2-Y.O F) (Class D)
2-15 (2-16) **5f 2y** £3,366.00 (£1,008.00: £484.00: £222.00) Stalls: High GOING minus 0.09 sec per fur (G)

				SP	RR	SF
1240^{4}	**Lady In Waiting** (PFICole) **2-8-11** TQuinn(2) (lw: sn pushed along: hdwy ½-wy: rdn to ld wl ins fnl f)	—	**1**	6/5^{1}	86	40
	Asfurah (USA) (SbinSuroor) **2-8-11** LDettori(7) (w'like: scope: chsd ldrs: led wl over 1f out: edgd lft & hdd wl ins fnl f)	½	**2**	9/4^{2}	84	38
1425^{11}	**Arian Da** (BPalling) **2-8-11** TSprake(5) (lw: led over 3f: rdn whn bmpd over 1f out: sn outpcd)	4	**3**	16/1	72	26
	Saint Ann (USA) (MJohnston) **2-8-11** RHills(6) (str: scope: bkwd: dwlt: bhd & rdn ½-wy: r.o wl ins fnl f)	1	**4**	12/1	68+	22
1149^{2}	**Indian Silver** (MRChannon) **2-8-12**^{ow1} RHughes(9) (prom: rdn 2f out: r.o one pce)	1¼	**5**	6/1^{3}	65	18
	Lady Yavanna (KMcAuliffe) **2-8-11** JReid(3) (w'like: bit bkwd: sn drvn along: nvr gng pce of ldrs)	nk	**6**	25/1	64	18
	Wild Lilly (MJRyan) **2-8-11** GCarter(4) (lt-f: unf: s.i.s: a bhd & outpcd)	4	**7**	33/1	51	5
	Sentinella Key (IRE) (MJHeaton-Ellis) **2-8-11** SDrowne(8) (neat: a bhd & outpcd)	3½	**8**	20/1	40	—
1321^{4}	**Supacalifragilistk** (CEBrittain) **2-8-11** BDoyle(10) (prom: rdn over 2f out: sn wknd: t.o)	5	**9**	14/1	24	—
	Helenes Hill (CSmith) **2-8-11** JFortune(1) (lt-f: unf: s.s: a outpcd: t.o)	6	**10**	50/1	4	—

(SP 124.3%) **10 Rn**

61.3 secs (2.80) CSF £3.73 TOTE £2.10: £1.10 £1.80 £1.90 (£3.60) Trio £31.10 OWNER Pegasus Racing Ltd (WHATCOMBE) BRED Mrs J. Haigh

1240 Lady In Waiting, tackling the minimum trip this time on ground totally different than she had on her debut, needed all the encouragement she could get to prove the master nearing the finish. (6/5: 5/4-evens)

Asfurah (USA) has plenty of speed in her breeding and she looked to have the edge when leading into the final furlong but, feeling the full effect of this strong, almost head-on wind, plus showing signs of greenness, she drifted left and was eventually worn down in the sight of the post. (9/4)

739 Arian Da held the call for over three furlongs, but she was beginning to throw out distress signals when the winner was blown into her path approaching the final furlong, although it had no bearing on the outcome. (16/1)

Saint Ann (USA), a strongly-made filly who seemed ill at ease on this ever-drying ground, was taken off her legs in the early stages but she did pick up well inside the distance and can only improve on this. (12/1: op 8/1)

1149 Indian Silver, restrained on the heels of the leaders, did not find a lot when a serious question was asked and her measure had been taken approaching the final furlong. (6/1: op 7/2)

Lady Yavanna, whose dam was three times a winner at this minimum trip, could never quicken enough to get herself into contention. She will benefit from the experience and may well fare better with a stiffer test of stamina. (25/1)

1620 PETRACO '100 NOT OUT' (S) H'CAP (0-60) (3-Y.O+) (Class G)
2-45 (2-48) **5f 218y** £2,847.00 (£792.00: £381.00) Stalls: High GOING minus 0.09 sec per fur (G)

				SP	RR	SF
1236^{8}	**Mister Raider (44)** (EAWheeler) **5-8-8b**$^{(5)}$ ADaly(7) (lw: hdwy ½-wy: chal over 1f out: led wl ins fnl f)	—	**1**	12/1	52	30
1467^{15}	**Chief's Lady (38)** (JMBradley) **5-8-2**$^{(5)}$ RFfrench(11) (a.p: led over 1f out tl wl ins fnl f: r.o)	hd	**2**	16/1	46	24
1250^{8}	**Napoleon Star (IRE) (48)** (SRBowring) **6-9-3b** SWebster(4) (hdwy 2f out: rdn & r.o strly nr fin)	s.h	**3**	6/1^{2}	56	34
1098^{5}	**Sound the Trumpet (IRE) (50)** (RCSpicer) **5-9-2**$^{(3)}$ RHavlin(8) (hdwy over 2f out: disp ld ent fnl f: unable qckn)	hd	**4**	7/1^{3}	57	35
1395^{9}	**Mu-Arrik (30)** (GROldroyd) **9-7-8v**$^{(5)}$ RMullen(12) (hdwy over 2f out: nt clr run appr fnl f: fin wl)	¾	**5**	33/1	35	13
1446^{9}	**Petraco (IRE) (54)** (NASmith) **9-9-9** LDettori(10) (trckd ldrs: effrt & nt clr run over 1f out: nt rcvr)	1¼	**6**	9/2^{1}	56	34
1047^{9}	**Sir Tasker (43)** (JLHarris) **9-8-12** DHolland(13) (w ldrs stands' side: rdn & one pce appr fnl f)	1¼	**7**	14/1	42	20
1467^{9}	**Swiss Coast (IRE) (52)** (NTinkler) **3-8-13b** GCarter(2) (wl bhd & outpcd tl r.o wl fnl f)	1½	**8**	14/1	47	17
752^{8}	**Astral Invader (IRE) (48)** (MSSaunders) **5-9-3** RPerham(22) (chsd ldrs far side over 4f)	nk	**9**	12/1	42	20
1279^{9}	**Tymeera (56)** (BPalling) **4-9-11** TSprake(16) (lw: hdwy ½-wy: rdn over 1f out: one pce)	hd	**10**	10/1	50	28
1003^{9}	**Red Time (50)** (MSSaunders) **4-9-5v** RPrice(20) (nvr trbld ldrs)	2½	**11**	14/1	37	15
734^{16}	**Ticka Ticka Timing (35)** (BWMurray) **4-8-4** SSanders(3) (chsd ldrs stands' side over 4f)	½	**12**	33/1	21	—
1509^{4}	**The Frisky Farmer (51)** (WGMTurner) **4-8-13**$^{(7)}$ DMcGaffin(19) (lw: spd far side over 4f)	1½	**13**	10/1	33	11
1289^{8}	**Lochon (43)** (MrsNMacauley) **6-8-9b**$^{(3)}$ CTeague(21) (b: led over 4f: wknd qckly)	2	**14**	20/1	19	—
1439^{15}	**Wild Nettle (47)** (JCFox) **3-8-8** MFenton(6) (prom stands' side 4f)	3½	**15**	25/1	14	—
1279^{8}	**Amnesty Bay (33)** (MDIUsher) **5-7-9**$^{(7)}$ RBrisland(1) (nvr nr to chal)	2	**16**	33/1	—	—
1135^{15}	**Silver Moon (42)** (BAMcMahon) **3-8-3** LNewton(14) (s.s: a bhd & outpcd)	nk	**17**	33/1	3	—
1374^{10}	**Invigilate (37)** (MRChannon) **8-8-6** TQuinn(15) (outpcd)	1½	**18**	8/1	—	—
	Mazzarello (IRE) (37) (RIngram) **7-8-3v**$^{(3)}$ MBaird(17) (bkwd: gd spd far side over 3f)	2	**19**	33/1	—	—
1141^{20}	**Sharp Return (57)** (MJRyan) **3-9-4b^{1}** AClark(9) (s.s: a bhd & outpcd: t.o)	17	**20**	12/1	—	—
1428^{7}	**Lawsimina (40)** (DShaw) **4-8-9** JFanning(5) (Withdrawn not under Starter's orders: ref to ent stalls)		**W**	25/1	—	—

(SP 150.4%) **20 Rn**

1m 14.2 (4.20) CSF £191.26 CT £1,185.40 TOTE £19.60: £3.70 £4.00 £1.80 £2.40 (£192.40) Trio £561.30; £474.34 to Brighton 3/6/97
OWNER Raiders Partnership (PANGBOURNE) BRED Alan Hogan
WEIGHT FOR AGE 3yo-8lb
No bid

1236 Mister Raider has previously only won on the All-Weather, but he handled this lively ground surprisingly well and showed the right commitment in an all-out sprint to the line. (12/1)

760 Chief's Lady looked set to open her account when holding a narrow advantage halfway through the final furlong, but the last gasp effort of the winner proved just too much. She did everything right and fortune must favour her before long. (16/1)

1020 Napoleon Star (IRE) was unable to find his stride until far too late, but he finished best of all and would have made it in another couple of yards. (6/1)

1098 Sound the Trumpet (IRE) got to the front of the stands' side group entering the final furlong, but the principals in the centre of the track matched him stride for stride and he was the one who had to miss out. He is running well this term and another success would not come out of turn. (7/1)

Mu-Arrik, stepping back down to the only trip he has won at, was the meat in a tightly-packed sandwich entering the final furlong and, though he never stopped trying, was unable to land a blow. If he could be relied on, a race of this description could be his for the taking. (33/1)

1080 Petraco (IRE), in the race named after him, may have been an unlucky loser, but there seemed to be excuses for several of his beaten rivals. (9/2)

1115 Swiss Coast (IRE), off the bridle and one of the tail-enders at halfway, was really into his stride in the closing stages and he seems to need a seventh furlong. (14/1)

1621 SILVER PHEASANT CONDITIONS STKS (3-Y.O F) (Class C)
3-15 (3-16) **7f 9y** £4,850.65 (£1,749.40: £839.70: £343.50: £136.75) Stalls: High GOING minus 0.09 sec per fur (G)

				SP	RR	SF
1318^{4}	**Meshhed (USA) (92)** (BHanbury) **3-9-0** RHills(2) (mde all: hrd drvn over 1f out: drew clr towards fin)	—	**1**	11/4^{3}	111	49
1412^{6}	**Natalia Bay (IRE) (99)** (PFICole) **3-8-10** TQuinn(5) (hld up: hdwy over 2f out: kpt on ins fnl f: no ch w wnr)	3½	**2**	9/1	99	37
1203a^{7}	**Star Profile (IRE)** (SbinSuroor) **3-9-2** LDettori(1) (lw: trckd ldrs: hdwy to disp ld 2f out: sn rdn: one pce)	hd	**3**	5/2^{2}	105	43
724^{3}	**Well Warned (106)** (BWHills) **3-9-0** PatEddery(3) (lw: prom: rdn & ev ch 2f out: kpt on same pce)	2	**4**	5/4^{1}	98	36
1316^{4}	**Chinaberry** (CEBrittain) **3-8-10** BDoyle(4) (prom: pushed along 3f out: outpcd fnl 2f)	8	**5**	20/1	42 t	14
				(SP 114.4%)		**5 Rn**

1m 26.0 (3.40) CSF £23.04 TOTE £5.40: £2.20 £3.40 (£12.20) OWNER Mr Hamdan Al Maktoum (NEWMARKET) BRED Shadwell Farm Inc

1318 Meshhed (USA) adopted more forceful tactics on this return to a shorter trip, and she showed what a useful filly she really is with a very comfortable all-the-way success. (11/4)

Natalia Bay (IRE) stayed on strongly to gain the runner-up prize in the final stride, but by then the winner was going away, and it was more than possible that she needs a stiffer test of stamina. (9/1: 6/1-10/1)

1203a Star Profile (IRE), beaten in the French One Thousand Guineas on her previous outing this term, has been highly-tried throughout her short career, and failure in this company must raise doubts as to whether she has trained on. (5/2: 7/4-11/4)

724 Well Warned, content to be given the lead, was almost on terms two furlongs out but she had been nudged along to get there and, with the winner showing no signs of stopping, she was the one who threw in the towel. (5/4)

1316 Chinaberry may have been outclassed, but she looked ill at ease cantering to post and should not be written off until she does get the opportunity to prove herself. (20/1)

1622 SWANNINGTON CLAIMING STKS (3-Y.O+) (Class F)
3-45 (3-47) **1m 8y** £2,784.00 (£774.00: £372.00) Stalls: High GOING minus 0.09 sec per fur (G)

				SP	RR	SF
	Trojan Hero (SAF) (BWHills) **6-10-0** PatEddery(3) (mde all: qcknd clr wl over 1f out: comf)	—	**1**	13/2^{3}	76+	58
1383^{18}	**Rochea (50)** (MrsNMacauley) **3-8-2**^{ow2} BDoyle(9) (trckd ldrs: swtchd ins 2f out: r.o wl cl home)	1	**2**	5/1^{2}	59	28
1389^{4}	**Scaraben (75)** (SEKettlewell) **9-10-0** JFortune(7) (hld up: hdwy 3f out: hrd rdn appr fnl f: kpt on)	2	**3**	2/1^{1}	70	52
	The Executor (RJO'Sullivan) **7-9-2** SSanders(8) (bit bkwd: hld up: hdwy 3f out: effrt & rdn over 1f out: wknd ins fnl f)	3	**4**	16/1	52	34
1389^{9}	**Moneghetti (28)** (JLHarris) **6-8-11**$^{(5)}$ RFfrench(4) (hld up: hdwy 4f out: effrt 2f out: wknd appr fnl f)	3½	**5**	33/1	45	27
1247^{5}	**Oh So Misty** (SDow) **4-8-4**$^{(5)}$ ADaly(10) (effrt over 2f out: no imp appr fnl f)	2	**6**	33/1	34	16
1389*	**Golden Thunderbolt (FR) (70)** (NTinkler) **4-10-0** LDettori(5) (hld up: hdwy ½-wy: wknd fnl 2f)	½	**7**	2/1^{1}	52	34
1388^{U}	**Scottish Hero (51)** (LadyHerries) **4-8-13b**$^{(7)}$ PDoe(2) (lw: chsd wnr over 5f: sn rdn & wknd: t.o)	7	**8**	16/1	30	12
896^{22}	**Harvest Reaper (39)** (JLHarris) **5-8-12** SDrowne(6) (a in rr: t.o)	4	**9**	33/1	14	—
	Bluebell Miss (62) (MJRyan) **3-7-12** GBardwell(1) (bit bkwd: in tch tl outpcd 3f out: t.o)	½	**10**	12/1	10	—
				(SP 124.9%)		**10 Rn**

1m 39.3 (4.30) CSF £37.68 TOTE £6.00: £2.20 £1.50 £1.70 (£32.60) Trio £40.50 OWNER Mr Laurence Jaffee (LAMBOURN) BRED Mr & Mrs L. Jaffee

WEIGHT FOR AGE 3yo-11lb

Trojan Hero (SAF) clmd CBuckley £12,000

Trojan Hero (SAF), six times a winner in South Africa and placed in a Group Two race over there, is reported to have had leg trouble and did not impress to post. Jumping off in front, he got his rivals at it when stepping up the pace to draw clear inside the last quarter-mile and was able to take things easily nearing the line. Claimed for £12,000, it is doubtful if he will be seen in a race of this description for some time to come. (13/2: 9/2-7/1)

1246 Rochea was rather surprisingly the subject of strong market support, seeing that she has still to win a race, but she did show improved form and, with the winner out of the way, her followers would have collected. (5/1: op 10/1)

1389 Scaraben gained his revenge over the favourite on slightly worse terms, but he had to admit the winner too much of a handful when the battle to the line really developed. (2/1)

The Executor had a summer bloom on his coat for this first outing in almost eleven months, and his first on the Flat since July 1993, but he also had quite a bit left to work on so, if he remains sound after this promising effort, the ability is there. (16/1)

864 Moneghetti, twice successful on the All-Weather, promised to make his presence felt a quarter-of-a-mile out but, on this ground, a turn of finishing speed was missing when it was most needed. (33/1)

Oh So Misty, very short on experience, was unable to get herself into the action but she was far from disgraced and all is not lost yet. (33/1)

1623 JOHN FERNELEY H'CAP (0-70) (3-Y.O+ F & M) (Class E)
4-15 (4-16) **1m 3f 183y** £3,041.00 (£908.00: £434.00: £197.00) Stalls: High GOING minus 0.39 sec per fur (F)

				SP	RR	SF
1226^{2}	**Kilshanny (68)** (LMCumani) **3-9-3** LDettori(3) (b.nr hind: led after 2f: shkn up appr fnl f: hld on wl)	—	**1**	11/10^{1}	78	36
1313^{3}	**Ordained (56)** (EJAlston) **4-9-6** SDrowne(4) (trckd ldrs: drvn along ent st: gd hdwy to chse wnr appr fnl f: r.o wl)	¾	**2**	9/1	65	38
881^{9}	**Afon Alwen (57)** (SCWilliams) **4-9-7** RHughes(7) (hld up & bhd: hdwy & rdn over 2f out: r.o wl fnl f)	½	**3**	20/1	65	38
1463^{3}	**Calendula (60)** (DMorley) **4-9-10** GCarter(5) (a.p: jnd wnr & pushed along 3f out: styd on same pce appr fnl f)	1¼	**4**	3/1^{2}	67	40
1383^{6}	**Rehaab (56)** (DMorris) **4-9-6** PatEddery(8) (hld up: hdwy over 2f out: hrd drvn & one pce appr fnl f)	4	**5**	14/1	57	30
1093^{4}	**Nicola's Princess (48)** (BAMcMahon) **4-8-12** TQuinn(1) (lw: chsd ldrs: rdn wl over 2f out: sn btn)	8	**6**	6/1^{3}	38	11
1387^{5}	**Cadbury Castle (50)** (MBlanshard) **3-7-13** CRutter(6) (led 2f: wknd wl over 2f out)	1	**7**	25/1	39	—
1420^{7}	**Misellina (FR) (55)** (JSMoore) **3-8-4** NAdams(2) (s.s: effrt ent st: wknd 3f out: t.o)	dist	**8**	20/1	—	—
				(SP 116.9%)		**8 Rn**

2m 33.6 (5.10) CSF £11.15 CT £120.64 TOTE £1.70: £1.10 £1.60 £2.50 (£5.30) OWNER Sheikh Mohammed (NEWMARKET) BRED Sheikh Mohammed Bin Rashid Al Maktoum

WEIGHT FOR AGE 3yo-15lb

1226 Kilshanny, taking on handicappers this time, was given a classical ride from the front by Dettori, who nursed her along and then found just enough to withstand a couple of determined challenges close home. (11/10: evens-10/11)

1313 Ordained had the ground she thrives on but took a lot of driving to find top gear, and her sustained last-furlong challenge was never quite going to get her there. (9/1)

Afon Alwen won her maiden on fast ground in the autumn but she moved gingerly to post and, taking time to find her stride, did in the end run possibly her best race yet. Once the sting is taken out of the ground, she could show what she is made of. (20/1)
1463 Calendula had the longer trip that she needs but she had it all to do conceding weight all round and, though she kept staying on, could not muster the speed to compete inside the distance. (3/1)
1383 Rehaab stepped up on her previous run and briefly threatened danger entering the last quarter-mile, but she was unable to maintain the run and, as yet, appears to find this trip beyond her. (14/1: 10/1-16/1)

1624 OLD DALBY H'CAP (0-70) (3-Y.O) (Class E)

4-45 (4-46) **1m 1f 218y** £3,509.00 (£1,052.00: £506.00: £233.00) Stalls: High GOING minus 0.39 sec per fur (F)

				SP	RR	SF
1487^{2}	**Ludo (56)** (RHannon) **3-8-7** RPerham(11) (trckd ldrs: sltly hmpd & lost pl 6f out: hdwy to ld over 1f out: rdn out)	—	**1**	5/1 ^{3}	65	34
1155^{12}	**Soda Pop (IRE) (60)** (CEBrittain) **3-8-11** BDoyle(10) (chsd ldrs: rallied appr fnl f: nt pce of wnr)	3	**2**	25/1	64	33
990^{10}	**Bathe In Light (USA) (60)** (LordHuntingdon) **3-8-11** DHarrison(9) (hld up: hdwy 5f out: rdn & one pce appr fnl f)	3	**3**	12/1	59	28
1284^{4}	**Gold Clipper (45)** (MJRyan) **3-7-7**(3) MBaird(7) (hld up: hdwy over 2f out: kpt on u.p fnl f)	3	**4**	33/1	40	9
1087^{9}	**Sharp Deed (IRE) (57)** (PJMakin) **3-8-8** DHolland(6) (lw: hld up: hdwy ent st: ev ch 2f out: sn rdn & wknd)	1¾	**5**	8/1	49	18
533^{9}	**Swiftway (65)** (KWHogg) **3-9-2** TSprake(14) (nvr plcd to chal)	6	**6**	25/1	47	16
1487*	**Double Gold (69)** (BJMeehan) **3-9-6** 5x PatEddery(13) (led tl hdd & wknd over 1f out)	¾	**7**	9/2 ^{2}	50	19
1116^{11}	**Bewitching Lady (49)** (DWPArbuthnot) **3-7-9**(5) RMullen(2) (nvr nrr)	½	**8**	20/1	29	—
1272^{4}	**Keen Dancer (69)** (MBell) **3-9-6** MFenton(12) (hld up in rr: effrt & rdn 4f out: no imp)	¾	**9**	7/2 ^{1}	48	17
1297^{13}	**Grand Hotel (IRE) (52)** (PWHarris) **3-8-3** AClark(5) (sn rdn along: a in rr)	½	**10**	16/1	30	—
1270^{4}	**Double Flight (70)** (MJohnston) **3-9-7** LDettori(8) (chsd ldrs over 7f: eased whn btn fnl 2f)	8	**11**	11/2	35	4
1121^{3}	**Pointe Fine (FR) (64)** (JWHills) **3-9-1** TQuinn(4) (b.off fore: chsd ldr: rdn over 2f out: sn lost tch)	½	**12**	10/1	29	—
	Good Judge (IRE) (59) (MDHammond) **3-8-10** JReid(3) (nt grwn: a in rr: t.o)	3½	**13**	20/1	18	—
1388^{10}	**Jib Jab (55)** (MrsNMacauley) **3-8-3**(3) AWhelan(1) (a in rr: t.o)	12	**14**	33/1	—	—

(SP 129.3%) **14 Rn**

2m 6.9 (3.20) CSF £126.21 CT £1,332.45 TOTE £6.80: £1.60 £14.70 £2.60 (£131.90) Trio £379.00; £74.75 to Brighton 3/6/97 OWNER Mr Michael Pescod (MARLBOROUGH) BRED Pigeon House Stud
LONG HANDICAP Gold Clipper 6-9
1487 Ludo, forced to take a pull when a rival took his ground at the end of the back straight, picked up really well on meeting the rising ground and, leading below the distance, strode clear without much difficulty. (5/1)
Soda Pop (IRE), in a handicap for the first time and relishing this step-up in distance, could not match the finishing speed of the winner, but this was a big improvement on what he has achieved before and he is beginning to find his way. (25/1)
475 Bathe In Light (USA) could not quite reach a challenging position but she did show how much she is improving and, if she can continue the progress, there is a race in store. (12/1)
1284 Gold Clipper, more patiently ridden on this return to ten furlongs, was still galloping on at the finish without ever being in a position to cause concern. (33/1)
Sharp Deed (IRE) showed his first signs of form over this more suitable trip and, though he was outpaced late on, should have little trouble in finding a suitable opening. (8/1)
1272 Keen Dancer had much more to do against these handicappers and, failing to fire, was always out with the washing. (7/2)

1625 LEVY BOARD MAIDEN STKS (3-Y.O) (Class D)

5-15 (5-17) **1m 3f 183y** £3,639.00 (£1,092.00: £526.00: £243.00) Stalls: High GOING minus 0.39 sec per fur (F)

				SP	RR	SF
1168^{4}	**Kilma (USA)** (LMCumani) **3-8-9** LDettori(4) (lw: hld up: swtchd lft & hdwy 2f out: rdn to chal & swished tail ins fnl f: led nr fin)	—	**1**	7/2 ^{2}	84	49
676^{2}	**Purist** (MRStoute) **3-9-0** JReid(6) (chsd ldr: hrd drvn to ld 200y out: hdd & no ex cl home)	hd	**2**	4/7 ^{1}	89	54
1331^{4}	**Khayali (IRE)** (DMorley) **3-9-0** RHills(1) (led: qcknd clr ½-wy: hdd & one pce ins fnl f)	3	**3**	8/1	85	50
978^{6}	**Arletty** (HRACecil) **3-8-9** AMcGlone(3) (hld up in tch: effrt & pushed along over 3f out: outpcd fnl 2f)	12	**4**	14/1	64	29
1168^{3}	**Silver Whirl (USA)** (RCharlton) **3-8-9** TSprake(2) (chsd ldrs: effrt 3f out: outpcd fnl 2f)	6	**5**	6/1 ^{3}	56	21
1106^{7}	**Sarbaron (IRE)** (PWHarris) **3-9-0** AClark(5) (dwlt: a bhd: t.o fr ½-wy)	dist	**6**	50/1	—	—

(SP 119.9%) **6 Rn**

2m 30.4 (1.90) CSF £5.83 TOTE £3.50: £1.60 £1.10 (£2.20) OWNER Sheikh Ahmed Al Maktoum (NEWMARKET) BRED Heronwood Farm Inc
1168 Kilma (USA), much the wiser for the experience gained on her debut at Salisbury, again swished her tail when pressure was applied but she went through with her effort this time, and there is no reason why she should not go on improving. (7/2)
676 Purist gave the impression that he will benefit from an easing of the ground, but he did work hard to nose ahead two hundred yards out, before the winner took his measure nearing the finish. (4/7)
1331 Khayali (IRE), once again colty in the paddock, settled to gallop his rivals into the ground and he was only forced to give best in the duel to the line. This could prove the ideal way to ride him and that initial success is near at hand. (8/1: tchd 12/1)
978 Arletty, waiting on the leaders, had no answer when the tempo quickened early in the straight and, though she did not drop away until inside the quarter-mile marker, she was very soon trailing. (14/1)
1168 Silver Whirl (USA) impressed to post and threatened danger three furlongs out but, when the race began in earnest, she was left standing. (6/1: op 3/1)

T/Jkpt: £5,461.50 (1.3 Tckts). T/Plpt: £118.30 (129.21 Tckts). T/Qdpt: £23.70 (32.93 Tckts) IM

1253-THIRSK (L-H) (St Good to firm, Rnd Firm)
Monday June 2nd

WEATHER: fine & sunny WIND: fresh half against

1626 PICKERING (S) STKS (2-Y.O F) (Class G)

6-15 (6-16) **6f** £2,792.50 (£780.00: £377.50) Stalls: High GOING minus 0.38 sec per fur (F)

				SP	RR	SF
	Edna's Gift (IRE) (JBerry) **2-8-9** KDarley(7) (cmpt: s.i.s: hdwy ½-wy: led over 1f out: drvn out)	—	**1**	6/1 ^{3}	67	7
1498^{3}	**Sans Rivale** (BJMeehan) **2-8-9** JFortune(4) (trckd ldrs: effrt 2f out: nt qckn ins fnl f)	1¼	**2**	11/4 ^{2}	64	4
1438^{2}	**Huxleen** (WGMTurner) **2-8-4**(5) DSweeney(9) (led: hung lft & hdd over 1f out: sn wknd: eased towards fin)	8	**3**	11/8 ^{1}	42	—

1136^{13}	**Dispol Lass** (PCalver) **2-8-6**(3) DarrenMoffatt(5) (b.nr hind: s.i.s: sn chsng ldrs: rdn & edgd lft 2f out: one pce)	s.h	**4**	20/1	42	—
	Dutch Patriarch (MWEasterby) **2-8-4**(5) GParkin(6) (cmpt: s.s: wl bhd tl sme late hdwy)	5	**5**	10/1	29	—
1330^{6}	**My Bet** (MWEasterby) **2-9-0** TLucas(2) (w ldrs: rdn & hung lft ½-wy: lost pl over 1f out)	¾	**6**	14/1	32	—
	Gay da Cheen (IRE) (JMCarr) **2-8-9** PBloomfield(1) (neat: unf: bit bkwd: sn wl outpcd)	hd	**7**	20/1	27	—
1298^{4}	**Step In To The Sun** (RAFahey) **2-8-9** JCarroll(8) (bit bkwd: w ldrs: rdn over 2f out: wknd over 1f out)	1¼	**8**	10/1	23	—
	Baroness Noble (TDEasterby) **2-8-9** LCharnock(3) (unf: b.hind: trckd ldrs tl wknd 2f out)	1¼	**9**	20/1	20	—
				(SP 122.2%)		**9 Rn**

1m 13.6 (3.90) CSF £21.49 TOTE £5.10: £2.20 £1.50 £1.10 (£8.70) Trio £6.90 OWNER Mr Sam Berry (COCKERHAM) BRED Mrs E. Thompson
No bid. Sans Rivale claimed £6,000
OFFICIAL EXPLANATION **Huxleen: did not appreciate the ground, lost her action and was hanging badly left handed.**
Edna's Gift (IRE), who showed a poor action going down, recovered from a tardy start to take this in decisive fashion. (6/1: op 4/1)
1498 Sans Rivale, like the winner, travelled strongly, but had to give best inside the last. Significantly she finished clear second best. (11/4: 9/2-5/2)
1438 Huxleen, whose action going down left plenty to be desired, hung badly and looked to be feeling the firm ground. (11/8)
Dispol Lass, who is not the best of movers, ran much better than on her first outing when she finished last of thirteen. (20/1)
Dutch Patriarch (10/1: op 3/1)

1627 LEEMING BAR H'CAP (0-75) (3-Y.O+) (Class D)
6-45 (6-45) **5f** £3,860.00 (£1,160.00: £560.00: £260.00) Stalls: High GOING minus 0.38 sec per fur (F)

				SP	RR	SF
1259^{3}	**Benzoe (IRE) (64)** (MrsJRRamsden) **7-9-4** JFortune(7) (lw: s.i.s: hdwy on stands' side 2f out: led jst ins fnl f: sn clr)	—	**1**	7/2^{1}	71	46
1098^{6}	**Camionneur (IRE) (45)** (TDEasterby) **4-7-13b** LCharnock(12) (hld up: hdwy stands' side to ld over 1f out: hdd & nt qckn ins fnl f)	1½	**2**	9/1	47	22
1468^{4}	**Insider Trader (63)** (MrsJRRamsden) **6-9-3** WRyan(3) (chsd ldr centre: rdn & nt qckn appr fnl f)	6	**3**	6/1^{2}	46	21
1250^{3}	**Sotonian (HOL) (44)** (PSFelgate) **4-7-12** DWright(5) (hdwy 2f out: nt clr run ins fnl f: styd on towards fin)	s.h	**4**	12/1	27	2
494^{W}	**Swan At Whalley (65)** (RAFahey) **5-9-5** DBiggs(8) (led tl over 1f out: kpt on same pce)	1¼	**5**	25/1	44	19
1514^{5}	**Dominelle (53)** (TDEasterby) **5-8-4**(3) DarrenMoffatt(2) (sn outpcd centre: styd on fnl 2f: nvr nr to chal)	¾	**6**	10/1	29	4
406^{7}	**Bowcliffe Grange (IRE) (53)** (DWChapman) **5-8-4**(3) PFessey(10) (lw: prom: outpcd 2f out: kpt on fnl f)	s.h	**7**	16/1	29	4
949^{7}	**Manolo (FR) (66)** (JBerry) **4-9-6b** KDarley(11) (lw: chsd ldr stands' side: rdn over 1f out: eased towards fin)	¾	**8**	7/1^{3}	40+	15
1098^{18}	**L A Touch (52)** (JJQuinn) **4-8-6** NConnorton(13) (sn outpcd: sme hdwy over 1f out: n.d)	nk	**9**	25/1	25	—
1158^{13}	**Chemcast (71)** (JLEyre) **4-9-4**(7) SBuckley(1) (w ldr centre over 3f: sn wknd)	¾	**10**	20/1	42	17
1083^{8}	**Mindrace (58)** (KTIvory) **4-8-12** JCarroll(9) (a bhd)	hd	**11**	25/1	28	3
	Oh Whataknight (60) (RMWhitaker) **4-9-0** DeanMcKeown(6) (bit bkwd: b: sn outpcd & bhd)	s.h	**12**	40/1	30	5
	Allwight Then (IRE) (54) (TDBarron) **6-8-1**(7) KimberleyHart(15) (trckd ldr stands' side: edgd lft ½-wy: ev ch over 1f out: wknd)	hd	**13**	16/1	24	—
1327^{3}	**Stolen Kiss (IRE) (63)** (MWEasterby) **5-9-3b** TLucas(4) (lw: chsd ldrs centre 3f: sn wknd)	1¼	**14**	10/1	29	4
1269^{4}	**Kalar (53)** (DWChapman) **8-8-7b** ACulhane(14) (w ldr stands' side: carried lft ½-wy: lost pl 2f out)	¾	**15**	7/1^{3}	16	—
				(SP 127.9%)		**15 Rn**

58.9 secs (1.30) CSF £31.38 CT £180.42 TOTE £4.90: £2.70 £2.80 £2.30 (£42.20) Trio £84.80 OWNER Mr Tony Fawcett (THIRSK) BRED Mrs P. Grubb
1259 Benzoe (IRE), as usual, missed the break slightly, but it enabled him to switch over to race on the favoured stands' side. He took this in most decisive fashion and clearly likes it here. Five or six furlongs all come alike to him and, these days, he seems to like the ground fast. (7/2)
1098 Camionneur (IRE) has only won once from thirty-five starts but he travelled strongly and will surely go one better. It will have to be soon, for having finished six lengths clear of the third, he is sure to take a hike in the weights. (9/1)
1468 Insider Trader ran another good race and almost certainly had little chance from his low draw. (6/1)
1250 Sotonian (HOL), another not favoured by the draw, stuck on strongly after running out of room inside the last. (12/1)
Swan At Whalley behaved himself in the stalls this time and showed all his old speed. (25/1)
1514 Dominelle ran as well as could be expected from a poor draw. (10/1)
949 Manolo (FR) was eased off inside the last, Darley repeatedly looking down at the gelding's legs as if something was amiss. (7/1)

1628 MARTON H'CAP (0-80) (3-Y.O+) (Class D)
7-15 (7-15) **1m 4f** £3,444.00 (£1,032.00: £496.00: £228.00) Stalls: High GOING minus 0.38 sec per fur (F)

				SP	RR	SF
1036^{6}	**Tessajoe (73)** (MJCamacho) **5-9-11** LCharnock(2) (b.hind: led 3f: led over 2f out: jst hld on)	—	**1**	2/1^{1}	83	50
1398^{4}	**Augustan (55)** (SGollings) **6-8-7** JFortune(3) (lw: trckd ldrs: pushed along 4f out: styd on wl ins fnl f)	s.h	**2**	6/1	65	32
1036^{9}	**Daira (59)** (JDBethell) **4-8-8**(3) PFessey(1) (lw: hld up: outpcd over 3f out: hdwy 2f out: hung lft & kpt on fnl f: nvr able chal)	1¼	**3**	12/1	67	34
994*	**Desert Fighter (73)** (MrsMReveley) **6-9-11** ACulhane(5) (led after 3f: hdd over 2f out: ev ch tl wknd over 1f out)	6	**4**	9/4^{2}	73	40
1390^{4}	**Cashmere Lady (65)** (JLEyre) **5-9-0**(3) OPears(4) (lw: hld up: effrt & outpcd over 3f out: rdn & wknd 2f out)	1¼	**5**	11/4^{3}	64	31
				(SP 112.7%)		**5 Rn**

2m 34.9 (4.20) CSF £12.97 TOTE £3.80: £1.50 £2.30 (£8.40) OWNER Riley Partnership (MALTON) BRED A. and Mrs Rhodes
781 Tessajoe, unsuited by the mud at Chester, was given a fine ride but, in the end, the post came just in time. (2/1: 6/4-9/4)
1398 Augustan, 2lb higher compared with when he won at Doncaster three runs ago, stuck to his guns and, staying on in determined fashion inside the last, needed two more strides. A more truly-run race would have suited him much better. (6/1)
Daira, who has slipped down the weights, gave her rider no help, persisting in hanging in behind the first two. (12/1)
994* Desert Fighter, 5lb higher, went on after three furlongs but only set a moderate gallop. Swept aside coming to the final furlong, the Handicapper probably has his measure for the time being. (9/4)
1390 Cashmere Lady, stepping up in distance, ran a flat race and pulled out little under pressure. She is about a stone better on the All-Weather. (11/4)

1629 BEDALE LIMITED STKS (0-75) (3-Y.O+) (Class D)
7-45 (7-45) **7f** £3,470.00 (£1,040.00: £500.00: £230.00) Stalls: Low GOING minus 0.38 sec per fur (F)

				SP	RR	SF
1471*	**Weetman's Weigh (IRE) (75)** (RHollinshead) **4-9-8**(3) DGriffiths(1) (lw: hld up: effrt over 2f out: rdn to ld over 1f out: hld on wl towards fin)	—	**1**	10/11^{1}	87	69

Spanish Knot (USA) (75) (LordHuntingdon) **3-8-6** KDarley(5) (trckd ldr: led over 2f out tl over 1f out: kpt on wl ins fnl f) ....½ **2** 9/4[2] 77 49
1225[17] **Style Dancer (IRE) (72)** (RMWhitaker) **3-8-9** DeanMcKeown(2) (hld up: effrt over 2f out: ev ch 1f out: kpt on same pce) 1¼ **3** 9/1 77 49
1044[7] **Grate Times (74)** (EWeymes) **3-8-9b[1]** JCarroll(4) (led tl over 2f out: hung rt & one pce appr fnl f) 1¼ **4** 20/1 74 46
*1121** **Absolute Liberty (USA) (75)** (SPCWoods) **3-8-12** DBiggs(3) (chsd ldrs: drvn along ½-wy: hung lft & lost pl over 2f out: eased towards fin) ....12 **5** 6/1[3] 50 22
(SP 112.2%) **5 Rn**

1m 25.6 (0.70) CSF £2.99 TOTE £2.20: £1.10 £1.70 (£2.00) OWNER Ed Weetman (Haulage & Storage) Ltd (UPPER LONGDON) BRED David Commins
WEIGHT FOR AGE 3yo-10lb

1471* Weetman's Weigh (IRE), a grand type, looked to be feeling the firm ground but always had it under control. (10/11: evens-5/4)
Spanish Knot (USA), who looked very fit, never gave up trying but the winner always had the upper hand. (9/4)
506 Style Dancer (IRE), stepping up in trip, proved very keen. He seemed to stay the seven alright. (9/1)
1044 Grate Times, who wore blinkers for the first time, ducked and dived under pressure and is not one to rely on. (20/1)
1121* Absolute Liberty (USA) hobbled to post. Hanging and never looking happy, his rider soon called it a day. Presumably he needs either the All-Weather or some give underfoot. (6/1)

1630 SPROXTON MAIDEN STKS (3-Y.O+) (Class D)
8-15 (8-16) **1m** £3,678.00 (£1,104.00: £532.00: £246.00) Stalls: Low GOING minus 0.38 sec per fur (F)

SP RR SF
1271[3] **Barrier Ridge** (HRACecil) **3-8-12** WRyan(5) (mde all: drvn out) ....— **1** 3/10[1] 65++ 54
Dantesque (IRE) (GWragg) **4-9-9** KDarley(4) (lw: trckd ldrs: effrt over 2f out: nt qckn ins fnl f) ....1 **2** 4/1[2] 63++ 63
Billy Nomaite (MrsSJSmith) **3-8-12**(3)ow3 OPears(7) (leggy: unf: sn chsng ldrs: styd on same pce fnl 2f) 8 **3** 50/1 50 36
1512[9] **General Monty** (TDBarron) **5-9-2**(7) VictoriaAppleby(1) (s.i.s: hdwy over 3f out: sn chsng ldrs: rdn & wknd over 1f out) 2½ **4** 66/1 42 42
841[14] **Mount Genius (USA)** (BobJones) **4-9-9** NConnorton(3) (trckd ldrs: pushed along over 3f out: outpcd over 2f out) 3 **5** 33/1 36 36
765[5] **Storyteller (IRE)** (MrsJRRamsden) **3-8-12** JFortune(2) (trckd ldrs: pushed along over 3f out: sn lost pl) ....8 **6** 16/1[3] 20 9
1282[5] **Linea-G** (MrsMReveley) **3-8-7** ACulhane(6) (unruly gng to s: s.i.s: sn bhd: virtually p.u 3f out) ....30 **7** 20/1 — —
(SP 114.0%) **7 Rn**

1m 37.5 (1.00) CSF £1.59 TOTE £1.30: £1.20 £1.20 (£1.80) OWNER Buckram Oak Holdings (NEWMARKET) BRED Buckram Oak Holdings
WEIGHT FOR AGE 3yo-11lb

1271 Barrier Ridge, whose action left plenty to be desired, was always doing just enough to hold his sole challenger at bay, but he had to be kept right up to his work all the way to the line. (3/10: 1/2-2/7)
Dantesque (IRE), an attractive colt and a good mover, had just two outings at three. Somewhat headstrong, he never gave up trying but the winner always had the edge. Unfortunately for him, the Handicapper will do him no favours. (4/1: op 2/1)
Billy Nomaite, a plain sort, was bought cheaply as a yearling. Making a belated debut, he was by no means disgraced but will need two more outings before he qualifies for a handicap mark. (50/1)
General Monty is a five-year-old who was having only his third ever outing. (66/1)
Mount Genius (USA) has a poor action. (33/1)
1282 Linea-G continually fly-jumped on the way to the start. Almost refusing to race, her rider gave up soon after the halfway mark. There was clearly something badly amiss here. (20/1)

1631 SALTERSGATE H'CAP (0-70) (3-Y.O+) (Class E)
8-45 (8-47) **1m** £3,130.50 (£939.00: £452.00: £208.50) Stalls: Low GOING minus 0.38 sec per fur (F)

SP RR SF
766[5] **Gulliver (70)** (MrsJRRamsden) **4-10-0** JFortune(6) (lw: hld up: hdwy ½-wy: sn prom: styd on strly to ld towards fin) ....— **1** 10/1 79 59
1220[5] **Sir Arthur Hobbs (55)** (JLEyre) **10-8-13** RLappin(5) (lw: trckd ldrs: led over 1f out: edgd lft u.p: hdd wl ins fnl f) ....¾ **2** 10/1 63 43
1511[8] **Pleasure Trick (USA) (38)** (DonEnricoIncisa) **6-7-10** KimTinkler(2) (bhd: hdwy 2f out: swtchd ins & bdly hmpd jst ins fnl f: swtchd rt: fin wl) ....nk **3** 20/1 45 25
1268[11] **Mukhlles (USA) (69)** (BobJones) **4-9-13** NConnorton(14) (hdwy over 2f out: ev ch over 1f out: edgd rt & nt qckn) 1½ **4** 12/1 73 53
1388[4] **Terdad (USA) (62)** (TDBarron) **4-9-6** KDarley(12) (lw: led 1f: led over 2f out: hdd over 1f out: hrd rdn & edgd lft: one pce) ....nk **5** 9/1 65 45
946[5] **Paint It Black (56)** (DNicholls) **4-9-0** AlexGreaves(11) (lw: sn chsng ldrs: effrt 2f out: kpt on one pce whn n.m.r ins fnl f) ....¾ **6** 7/2[1] 58 38
1603[6] **Roseate Lodge (38)** (SEKettlewell) **11-7-3**(7) JennyBenson(7) (bhd: hdwy 2f out: styng on same pce whn hmpd jst ins fnl f) ....nk **7** 20/1 39 19
1472[4] **Spanish Verdict (56)** (DenysSmith) **10-8-11**(3) PFessey(10) (lw: a chsng ldrs: rdn over 2f out: one pce) ....¾ **8** 5/1[3] 56 36
1285[2] **Broctune Gold (65)** (MrsMReveley) **6-9-9** ACulhane(9) (hld up & bhd: kpt on fnl 2f: n.d) ....3 **9** 4/1[2] 59 39
1467[11] **Silent System (IRE) (38)** (DWChapman) **4-7-7**(3) MBaird(3) (hld up & bhd: shkn up & hdwy over 2f out: nvr nr to chal) 1 **10** 50/1 30 10
1289[10] **Stephensons Rocket (49)** (RAFahey) **6-8-7** TLucas(13) (w ldrs tl wknd over 2f out) 1¼ **11** 14/1 38 18
1390[17] **Welcome Lu (43)** (JLHarris) **4-8-1** LCharnock(1) (lw: sn bhd) ....¾ **12** 25/1 31 11
947[16] **Tinklers Folly (57)** (RMWhitaker) **5-9-1** DeanMcKeown(15) (racd wd: bhd fr ½-wy) ....¾ **13** 16/1 43 23
Mustard (39) (ABMulholland) **4-7-11**ow1 DWright(8) (in tch tl lost pl over 3f out) ....½ **14** 50/1 24 3
1291[16] **Bernard Seven (IRE) (54)** (MDods) **5-8-12b** WRyan(16) (racd wd: in tch: rdn & lost pl 2f out) ....½ **15** 20/1 38 18
1333[12] **Jackson Falls (60)** (TDEasterby) **3-8-7b[1]** JCarroll(4) (plld hrd: led after 1f tl over 2f out: sn lost pl: virtually p.u) ....dist **16** 20/1 — —
(SP 134.1%) **16 Rn**

1m 38.5 (2.00) CSF £97.65 CT £1,142.40 TOTE £10.20: £2.30 £2.10 £3.40 £4.70 (£41.40) Trio £426.40; £450.49 to 4/6/97 OWNER Mr P. Green (THIRSK) BRED Juddmonte Farms
LONG HANDICAP Mustard 7-2 Silent System (IRE) 6-9
WEIGHT FOR AGE 3yo-11lb

766 Gulliver, having his first outing for Lynda Ramsden, showed a nice turn of foot to seal it late in the day. Another two furlongs will be no problem. (10/1)

1220 Sir Arthur Hobbs, five of whose thirteen victories have been recorded at Hamilton, edged left under strong pressure contributing to Terdad interfering with Pleasure Trick. (10/1)
1511 Pleasure Trick (USA), whose last three victories have been recorded on the All-Weather, again did not wear blinkers. Forced to search for an opening when he was switched inside just inside the last, he was badly hampered by Terdad. Switched again, he finished strongly and can be accounted an unlucky loser. (20/1)
559 Mukhiles (USA), who changed hands cheaply last back-end, wore a tongue-strap. Nibbled at in the market, he had every chance. (12/1)
1388 Terdad (USA), cool and calm on this occasion, edged left and was left short of room by Sir Arthur Hobbs and as a result, he completely blocked the passage of Pleasure Trick on his inner. (9/1)
946 Paint It Black, 6lb higher than when winning on the bridle here three outings ago, gave the impression that another success is just around the corner. (7/2)
1603 Roseate Lodge, a sprightly veteran, was sticking on at the same pace when hampered just inside the last. (20/1)
Silent System (IRE), who was racing from 15lb out of the handicap, hinted at better to come. (50/1)
797 Jackson Falls, in blinkers for the first time, took a fierce grip on the way to the start. After running himself to a standstill, he was virtually pulled up. (20/1)

T/Plpt: £38.50 (381.49 Tckts). T/Qdpt: £17.00 (38.29 Tckts) WG

1292-WINDSOR (Fig. 8) (Good to firm, Firm bk crse)
Monday June 2nd
WEATHER: overcast WIND: mod half against

1632 STORACALL TELECOMMUNICATIONS H'CAP (0-70) (3-Y.O+) (Class E)
6-30 (6-32) **1m 2f 7y** £3,051.25 (£925.00: £452.50: £216.25) Stalls: High GOING minus 0.37 sec per fur (F)

				SP	RR	SF
1442^{2}	**Carburton (65)** (JAGlover) **4-9-10** NDay(3) (s.s: stdy hdwy 5f out: led ins fnl f: drvn out)	—	**1**	8/1	76	54
1248^{4}	**Mardrew (61)** (TTClement) **3-8-2**$^{(5)}$ ADaly(14) (lw: a.p: ev ch fnl 2f: r.o)	2	**2**	14/1	69	34
1390^{9}	**Kristal Breeze (52)** (WRMuir) **5-8-11** WJO'Connor(10) (lw: gd hdwy 2f out: ev ch whn edgd lft ins fnl f: r.o)	hd	**3**	20/1	60	38
1244^{2}	**Bakers Daughter (56)** (JRArnold) **5-8-12**$^{(3)}$ MartinDwyer(19) (swtg: led 7f out tl ins fnl f)	hd	**4**	9/1	64	42
1384^{7}	**Renata's Prince (IRE) (50)** (KRBurke) **4-8-4**$^{(5)}$ RFfrench(18) (lost pl over 3f out: rallied over 1f out: r.o)	1	**5**	12/1	56	34
1315^{9}	**Ring the Chief (37)** (MDIUsher) **5-7-3**$^{(7)}$ RBrisland(15) (a.p: ev ch over 1f out: wknd ins fnl f)	2	**6**	33/1	40	18
1233^{5}	**Fairy Knight (69)** (RHannon) **5-10-0** PatEddery(1) (hdwy fnl 2f: nrst fin)	½	**7**	$7/1^{3}$	71	49
1168^{12}	**Windrush Holly (55)** (DRCElsworth) **4-9-0** MRimmer(24) (dwlt: nrst fin)	1½	**8**	25/1	55	33
1292^{2}	**Caudillo (IRE) (60)** (MrsPNDutfield) **4-9-0**$^{(5)}$ AimeeCook(5) (lw: prom tl wknd over 1f out)	nk	**9**	20/1	59	37
838^{12}	**Courageous Knight (42)** (PHayward) **8-7-12**$^{(3)}$ MHenry(23) (nvr bttr than mid div)	nk	**10**	33/1	41	19
587^{6}	**One In The Eye (38)** (JRPoulton) **4-7-11** NVarley(20) (b.hind: nvr nr to chal)	½	**11**	33/1	36	14
1233^{6}	**Father Dan (IRE) (55)** (MissGayKelleway) **8-9-0** GDuffield(21) (b: b.hind: a mid div)	1	**12**	14/1	51	29
1273^{16}	**Country Thatch (44)** (CAHorgan) **4-8-3** PaulEddery(22) (bhd tl sme late hdwy)	hd	**13**	33/1	40	18
1421^{4}	**Double Rush (IRE) (50)** (TGMills) **5-8-9** SSanders(2) (lw: hdwy 4f out: wknd over 1f out)	1¼	**14**	12/1	44	22
1383^{10}	**Guesstimation (USA) (60)** (JPearce) **8-9-2**$^{(3)}$ CTeague(17) (b.nr fore: nvr nr ldrs)	1¼	**15**	20/1	52	30
116^{10}	**Chieftain's Crown (USA) (37)** (THind) **6-7-3b**$^{(7)}$ PDoe(25) (prom tl wknd qckly over 1f out)	nk	**16**	14/1	29	7
1145^{11}	**African Sun (IRE) (44)** (MCChapman) **4-8-3** DRMcCabe(11) (nvr on terms)	s.h	**17**	20/1	36	14
1273^{2}	**Noeprob (USA) (50)** (RJHodges) **7-8-4**$^{(5)}$ AmandaSanders(7) (prom tl wknd 2f out)	1	**18**	$13/2^{2}$	40	18
1445^{13}	**Dauphin (IRE) (46)** (WJMusson) **4-8-5** GHind(8) (nvr trbld ldrs)	1¼	**19**	12/1	34	12
1441^{10}	**Tauten (IRE) (37)** (MDIUsher) **7-7-10v** JMarshall(16) (s.s: a bhd)	hd	**20**	33/1	25	3
1384^{9}	**Sweet Ciseaux (IRE) (38)** (MJHeaton-Ellis) **4-7-11** JLowe(12) (led 3f: wknd over 2f out)	nk	**21**	20/1	25	3
	Impetuous Lady (USA) (45) (WJMusson) **4-8-4** JStack(13) (prom tl wknd over 3f out)	6	**22**	33/1	23	1
1244^{6}	**Ballyranter (57)** (HJCollingridge) **8-9-2v** JQuinn(4) (b: wl bhd fnl 3f)	11	**23**	$6/1^{1}$	17	—
				(SP 149.6%)	**23 Rn**	

2m 7.9 (3.00) CSF £104.82 CT £2,029.64 TOTE £8.90: £2.60 £4.20 £5.40 £3.30 (£47.30) Trio £557.20; £470.89 to 4/6/97 OWNER Mr B. H. Farr (WORKSOP) BRED Worksop Manor Stud Farm
LONG HANDICAP Ring the Chief 7-9 Tauten (IRE) 7-9
WEIGHT FOR AGE 3yo-13lb
1442 Carburton, trying a longer trip and very slowly away, had the class to move very smoothly through his field. He struck the front inside the final furlong and won decisively. He looks sure to follow up. (8/1: 6/1-9/1)
1248 Mardrew, like the winner trying a longer trip, was always well placed. He had every chance but could not quicken inside the last furlong. (14/1)
Kristal Breeze found a clear run near the inside from two furlongs out and looked very dangerous as she moved up to challenge, only to spoil her chance by edging to the left. (20/1)
1244 Bakers Daughter, always in the first two, battled on strongly until outpaced inside the final furlong. (9/1: 8/1-12/1)
Renata's Prince (IRE) failed to hold his place when the pace quickened approaching the junction, but he rallied strongly in the closing stages. (12/1)
423 Ring the Chief was one of the three disputing the lead at the two-furlong marker but his effort petered out inside the final furlong. (33/1)
1273 Noeprob (USA) raced rather too prominently and weakened at the two-furlong marker and is better at coming from behind. (13/2)
1244 Ballyranter, surprisingly made favourite, was well behind in the latter stages of the race. (6/1)

1633 EVENING STANDARD H'CAP (0-70) (3-Y.O) (Class E)
7-00 (7-01) **1m 67y** £3,078.75 (£930.00: £452.50: £213.75) Stalls: High GOING minus 0.37 sec per fur (F)

				SP	RR	SF
1164^{2}	**Agent Mulder (55)** (PDCundell) **3-8-7** RPerham(5) (lw: 2nd tl led 2f out: r.o wl)	—	**1**	$7/1^{3}$	67	16
532^{8}	**Chingachgook (59)** (PWHarris) **3-8-11** NDay(8) (led to 2f out: r.o one pce)	1½	**2**	20/1	68	17
1464^{2}	**Princess of Hearts (60)** (MCPipe) **3-8-12b** GDuffield(11) (hmpd over 4f out: gd hdwy on ins 3f out: ev ch 1f out: nt qckn)	½	**3**	15/2	68	17
1392^{3}	**Interdream (61)** (RHannon) **3-8-13** PatEddery(3) (gd hdwy over 1f out: fin wl)	¾	**4**	$9/2^{1}$	68	17
1164^{18}	**Around Fore Alliss (62)** (TGMills) **3-9-0** GBardwell(16) (lw: hdwy fnl 2f: nvr nrr)	nk	**5**	33/1	68	17
1392^{4}	**Righty Ho (58)** (PTWalwyn) **3-8-10** RPrice(12) (a.p: r.o one pce fnl 2f)	s.h	**6**	12/1	64	13
1083^{10}	**Daintree (IRE) (60)** (HJCollingridge) **3-8-12** MRimmer(1) (b.hind: styd on fnl 2f: nt rch ldrs)	2	**7**	20/1	62	11
1423^{13}	**Jolly Jackson (55)** (RAkehurst) **3-8-7** SSanders(15) (dwlt: nrst fin)	1¼	**8**	12/1	55	4
1458^{9}	**Linden's Lad (IRE) (58)** (JRJenkins) **3-8-10** GCarter(10) (lw: prom tl wknd over 2f out)	s.h	**9**	$6/1^{2}$	58	7

				SP	RR	SF
1155[6]	**Kristopher (64)** (JWHills) **3-9-2** RHughes(14) (lw: prom tl wknd over 2f out)	nk	**10**	11/1	63	12
1333[6]	**Feel A Line (50)** (BJMeehan) **3-8-2b** PaulEddery(18) (hdwy 5f out: wknd over 2f out)	hd	**11**	25/1	49	—
1164[16]	**Myosotis (50)** (PJMakin) **3-8-2b** DRMcCabe(9) (nvr on terms)	1¾	**12**	25/1	46	—
1219[6]	**Broughtons Error (69)** (WJMusson) **3-9-7** GHind(6) (a bhd)	1½	**13**	9/1	62	11
1297[11]	**Bold Et Noir (52)** (WJarvis) **3-7-13**(5) RFfrench(2) (a bhd)	¾	**14**	25/1	43	—
1249[7]	**Java Bay (55)** (MBlanshard) **3-8-7** JQuinn(13) (bhd fnl 3f)	4	**15**	25/1	39	—
1141[11]	**Village Pub (FR) (55)** (KOCunningham-Brown) **3-8-7b** MRoberts(4) (lw: plld hrd: prom tl wknd 3f out)	hd	**16**	33/1	38	—
842[11]	**Welcome Heights (48)** (MJFetherston-Godley) **3-8-0** CRutter(17) (prom tl wknd over 2f out)	1	**17**	25/1	29	—
1167[2]	**My Beloved (IRE) (65)** (RHannon) **3-9-3** WJO'Connor(7) (bhd fnl 4f)	nk	**18**	11/1	46	—

(SP 133.4%) **18 Rn**

1m 47.0 (4.80) CSF £137.61 CT £1,013.78 TOTE £7.30: £2.00 £4.70 £1.60 £1.80 (£173.90) Trio £239.80 OWNER Mr P. D. Cundell (NEWBURY) BRED Roden House Stud

1164 Agent Mulder raced in second place until leading two furlongs out. He ran on to win readily and, lightly-raced, can continue to improve. (7/1)
Chingachgook went off in front although trying a longer trip and appeared to stay well enough. He found the winner too good in the last furlong-and-a-half. (20/1)
1464 Princess of Hearts had to be snatched up when hampered over four furlongs from home, but found a clear run on the inside to challenge and had every chance in the last furlong. She could not quicken in the final one hundred yards. (15/2)
1392 Interdream, pulled to the outside with well under two furlongs to race, finished to great purpose but too late to trouble the leaders. (9/2)
764 Around Fore Alliss made good headway in the closing stages but could not reach the leaders. (33/1)
1167 My Beloved (IRE) (11/1: 8/1-12/1)

1634 FRENCH HORN AT SONNING LIMITED STKS (0-90) (3-Y.O+) (Class C)

7-30 (7-30) **5f 217y** £5,033.25 (£1,521.00: £740.50: £350.25) Stalls: High GOING minus 0.11 sec per fur (G)

				SP	RR	SF
1170[7]	**Triple Hay (89)** (RHannon) **3-8-10** PatEddery(2) (lw: rdn along: hdwy over 2f out: led over 1f out: r.o wl)	—	**1**	13/8 [1]	99	47
1148[12]	**Yorkie George (87)** (LMCumani) **3-8-10** LDettori(5) (b.hind: hdwy on ins 2f out: ev ch 1f out: r.o wl nr fin)	nk	**2**	9/4 [2]	98	46
1578[11]	**Warning Time (90)** (BJMeehan) **4-8-11**(7) GHannon(7) (a.p: ev ch 2f out: nt qckn)	3½	**3**	7/1	89	45
	Paris Babe (88) (DMorris) **5-9-1** NDay(3) (w ldr: led over 3f out tl over 1f out: one pce)	1	**4**	20/1	83	39
988[6]	**Blues Queen (86)** (MRChannon) **3-8-7** TQuinn(9) (chsd ldrs: rdn 2f out: one pce)	½	**5**	10/1	82	30
1113[7]	**Sharp Pearl (76)** (JWhite) **4-9-7b** RHughes(6) (lw: hrd rdn over 2f out: no hdwy)	4	**6**	25/1	77	33
677[13]	**Wild Rice (89)** (GWragg) **5-9-4b[1]** PaulEddery(8) (b: lw: led over 2f: wknd qckly)	11	**7**	6/1 [3]	45	1
	Rivers Magic (76) (JJBridger) **4-9-4** DHarrison(1) (a bhd)	8	**8**	33/1	23	—

(SP 116.3%) **8 Rn**

1m 13.2 (2.70) CSF £4.90 TOTE £2.40: £1.40 £1.40 £1.70 (£2.80) Trio £16.10 OWNER The Broadgate Partnership (MARLBOROUGH) BRED S. C. Palmer

WEIGHT FOR AGE 3yo-8lb

1170 Triple Hay, dropped in trip, found difficulty going the early pace. He moved up strongly approaching the two-furlong marker and, after taking the lead a furlong and a half out, in the end he won a shade more easily than the neck verdict would suggest. (13/8)
Yorkie George found a clear run near the inside in the final two furlongs and looked dangerous entering the last two hundred yards. Though he ran on well, he is a little flattered by running the winner quite so close. (9/4)
1317 Warning Time, without the blinkers this time, went with the leaders. He kept on well enough in the last two furlongs without being able to quicken. (7/1: 5/1-8/1)
Paris Babe went to the front over three furlongs from home but was gradually outpaced in the last furlong-and-a-half. Compensation should follow. (20/1)
988 Blues Queen was always tracking the leaders but could make no headway under pressure in the final quarter-mile. (10/1: 6/1-12/1)
Wild Rice, blinkered for the first time, shot off in front but weakened rapidly before the halfway stage. (6/1)

1635 E.B.F. CHISWICK NOVICE STKS (2-Y.O) (Class D)

8-00 (8-02) **5f 10y** £3,176.25 (£960.00: £467.50: £221.25) Stalls: High GOING minus 0.11 sec per fur (G)

				SP	RR	SF
	Alfiglia (PJMakin) **2-8-7** SSanders(6) (unf: hdwy 2f out: hung lft over 1f out: led wl ins fnl f: drvn out)	—	**1**	16/1	76+	40
	Islamabad (GLewis) **2-8-12** PaulEddery(4) (b.hind: leggy: hdwy over 2f out: led over 1f out tl wl ins fnl f)	½	**2**	7/2 [3]	79+	43
1235*	**Fast Tempo (IRE)** (BPalling) **2-8-13** TSprake(13) (w ldr: led over 2f out tl over 1f out: nt qckn)	3	**3**	13/8 [1]	71	35
1149[5]	**Eastern Lyric** (JBerry) **2-8-13** GCarter(1) (a.p: r.o one pce fnl 2f)	hd	**4**	100/30 [2]	71	35
1293[8]	**Bandbox (IRE)** (SMellor) **2-8-12** JQuinn(14) (hdwy 2f out: nt qckn fnl f)	¾	**5**	50/1	67	31
1290[4]	**Ivory's Joy** (KTIvory) **2-8-7b[1]** CScally(7) (b: led over 2f: wknd over 1f out)	5	**6**	50/1	46	10
1084[9]	**Sergeant Imp (IRE)** (PMitchell) **2-8-9**(3) MHenry(11) (lw: sn rdn along: nvr on terms)	hd	**7**	25/1	51	15
1274[6]	**Hugger-Mugger** (JRArnold) **2-8-12b** CRutter(3) (prom 3f)	2½	**8**	50/1	43	7
	Mislead (IRE) (JSMoore) **2-8-7** MFenton(12) (str: bit bkwd: spd over 2f)	¾	**9**	20/1	36	—
1124[6]	**Raazi** (RMStronge) **2-8-0**(7) AEddery(8) (a bhd)	½	**10**	50/1	34	—
	Courtney Gym (IRE) (MRChannon) **2-8-12** RHughes(5) (cmpt: bit bkwd: s.s: a bhd)	2	**11**	10/1	33	—
	Street Singer (MissCJohnsey) **2-8-12** NAdams(9) (str: bit bkwd: s.s: a bhd)	nk	**12**	25/1	32	—

(SP 118.7%) **12 Rn**

62.2 secs (2.50) CSF £61.56 TOTE £20.70: £3.00 £2.10 £1.10 (£35.60) Trio £39.00 OWNER Bakewell Bloodstock Ltd (MARLBOROUGH) BRED Highfield Stud Ltd and the Glen Andred Stud

Alfiglia, well enough placed early, was slightly tapped for toe at the two-furlong marker but soon began to run on again. Despite edging to the left, she put in a good run to snatch the lead well inside the final furlong. (16/1)
Islamabad, patiently ridden, came with what appeared to be a winning run to take the lead approaching the final furlong, but was run out of it in the last seventy-five yards. Compensation should follow. (7/2: 6/4-4/1)
1235* Fast Tempo (IRE) disputed the lead from the start and went to the front at halfway. Headed approaching the final furlong, she could not quicken but time may tell if she was taking on two useful performers. (13/8)
1149 Eastern Lyric was always well placed and had every chance but failed to quicken in the closing stages. (100/30: 9/2-3/1)
Bandbox (IRE) came with a promising-looking run two furlongs out but could not quite sustain it in the closing stages. (50/1)
1290 Ivory's Joy, blinkered for the first time, shot off in front but weakened approaching the final furlong. (50/1)
Courtney Gym (IRE) (10/1: 4/1-11/1)

1636 SLOANE STREET H'CAP (0-60) (3-Y.O+) (Class F)

8-30 (8-33) **1m 3f 135y** £2,836.00 (£796.00: £388.00) Stalls: High GOING minus 0.37 sec per fur (F)

				SP	RR	SF
1140[3]	**Dizzy Tilly (57)** (TJNaughton) **3-8-10** DHolland(16) (led 5f: led over 2f out: sn clr: easily)	—	**1**	13/2[2]	70+	38
115[6]	**Nothing Doing (IRE) (42)** (WJMusson) **8-8-10** JQuinn(8) (a.p: styd on fnl 2f: no ch w wnr)	5	**2**	12/1	48	31
908[5]	**State Approval (58)** (PEccles) **4-9-12** PatEddery(5) (led after 5f tl over 2f out: r.o one pce)	nk	**3**	13/2[2]	64	47
770[4]	**Sapphire Son (IRE) (46)** (PCClarke) **5-8-9**(5) RFfrench(4) (lw: hdwy 3f out: hrd rdn & one pce fnl 2f)	2	**4**	14/1	49	32
1421[5]	**Amadour (IRE) (60)** (PMitchell) **4-10-0** OUrbina(13) (lw: a.p: one pce fnl 3f)	4	**5**	16/1	57	40
1441[7]	**Rock The Barney (IRE) (40)** (MDIUsher) **8-8-8** DRMcCabe(3) (gd hdwy over 2f out: styd on: nt rch ldrs)	nk	**6**	6/1[1]	37	20
1408[6]	**Compass Pointer (52)** (JMPEustace) **4-9-3**(3) MartinDwyer(12) (hdwy 3f out: hrd rdn 2f out: nt rch ldrs)	1¾	**7**	16/1	47	30
1287[2]	**Zatopek (45)** (JCullinan) **5-8-13** VSlattery(1) (nvr bttr than mid div)	2½	**8**	20/1	36	19
	Admirals Secret (USA) (57) (CFWall) **8-9-11** GDuffield(14) (hdwy 4f out: grad wknd fnl 2f)	s.h	**9**	10/1[3]	48	31
1156[7]	**Blue And Royal (IRE) (42)** (VSoane) **5-8-10** GBardwell(2) (nvr bttr than mid div)	½	**10**	25/1	32	15
1445[11]	**Leatherneck (IRE) (50)** (PMooney) **4-9-4v[1]** WJO'Connor(20) (prom tl wknd over 2f out)	s.h	**11**	12/1	40	23
1001[10]	**Oscar Rose (41)** (MJBolton) **4-8-6**(3) MHenry(9) (bhd fnl 3f)	1¼	**12**	33/1	30	13
1277[9]	**Sadler's Blaze (IRE) (60)** (PWHarris) **3-8-13** AClark(15) (nvr trbld ldrs)	1¾	**13**	25/1	46	14
1233[10]	**Suitor (45)** (SDow) **4-8-13** JFEgan(7) (lw: a bhd)	2½	**14**	25/1	28	11
	Crest Wing (USA) (52) (TPMcGovern) **4-9-6** TSprake(19) (wl bhd fnl 5f)	7	**15**	20/1	25	8
1105[11]	**Victor Blum (USA) (48)** (CAHorgan) **4-9-2** PaulEddery(10) (lw: bhd most of wy)	1¼	**16**	33/1	19	2
284[13]	**Seventh Edition (55)** (PGMurphy) **4-9-9** SDrowne(6) (wl bhd fnl 5f)	1¼	**17**	25/1	25	8
1272[13]	**Tartan Party (60)** (PFICole) **3-8-13** TQuinn(11) (prom tl wknd 3f out)	hd	**18**	20/1	30	—
1435[4]	**Elly Fleetfoot (IRE) (53)** (GLMoore) **5-9-7v** SWhitworth(18) (lw: wl bhd fr 4f out: t.o whn p.u & dsmntd ins fnl f)		**P**	6/1[1]	—	—
				(SP 133.7%)	**19 Rn**	

2m 29.9 (3.90) CSF £69.31 CT £500.16 TOTE £5.20: £1.80 £4.80 £2.50 £3.40 (£39.10) Trio £113.70 OWNER Mrs S. Leech (EPSOM) BRED Dandy's Farm

WEIGHT FOR AGE 3yo-15lb

1140 Dizzy Tilly ran in the style of a fast-improving filly. Always in the first two, she readily shot clear when given the office at the two-furlong marker. (13/2: 4/1-7/1)

43 Nothing Doing (IRE), well placed all the way, had every chance but could not quicken with the easy winner. (12/1: 8/1-14/1)

908 State Approval took up the running after five furlongs, but was quickly outpaced when the winner was unleashed approaching the two furlong marker. (13/2)

770 Sapphire Son (IRE) was driven on to the heels of the leaders at the two-furlong marker but could make no further progress. (14/1: 8/1-16/1)

1421 Amadour (IRE), in much the same place throughout, could make no headway in the final quarter-mile. (16/1)

1441 Rock The Barney (IRE), towards the back of the field in the slowly-run race, did extremely well to reach his final position and may be about to strike form. (6/1: 8/1-5/1)

Admirals Secret (USA) ran a satisfactory first race of the season. He improved from mid-division on to the heels of the leaders approaching the two-furlong marker, but gradually weakened and was not given a hard time. (10/1: op 6/1)

842 Leatherneck (IRE) (12/1: op 33/1)

1637 PALL MALL MEDIAN AUCTION MAIDEN STKS (3-Y.O) (Class E)

9-00 (9-02) **1m 2f 7y** £2,965.00 (£895.00: £435.00: £205.00) Stalls: High GOING minus 0.37 sec per fur (F)

				SP	RR	SF
	Arctic Owl (JRFanshawe) **3-9-0** DHarrison(12) (unf: scope: gd hdwy 2f out: r.o wl to ld cl home)	—	**1**	25/1	84	34
1239[9]	**Mystic Ridge (76)** (DRCElsworth) **3-9-0** RHughes(6) (lw: a.p: hrd rdn over 2f out: led 1f out tl nr fin)	¾	**2**	7/2[2]	83	33
1207[4]	**Titta Ruffo (80)** (BJMeehan) **3-9-0** PatEddery(8) (a.p: led over 2f out to 1f out: nt qckn)	½	**3**	9/4[1]	82	32
1155[3]	**Juggler** (LordHuntingdon) **3-9-0** LDettori(11) (hdwy on ins 2f out: ev ch 1f out: wknd nr fin)	1¾	**4**	5/1[3]	79	29
723[9]	**Contentment (IRE) (72)** (JWHills) **3-8-11**(3) MHenry(13) (hdwy fnl 2f: nvr nrr)	5	**5**	33/1	71	21
	Foleys Quest (IRE) (JSMoore) **3-8-9** JFEgan(5) (b.off hind: leggy: scope: nrst fin)	4	**6**	50/1	60	10
1409[3]	**Reward** (PFICole) **3-9-0** TQuinn(4) (led: unbalanced all turns: hdd & wknd over 2f out)	½	**7**	5/1[3]	64	14
1144[6]	**Sweetchildofmine** (HAkbary) **3-8-9** GHind(7) (b: nvr on terms)	½	**8**	50/1	58	8
1272[12]	**Certain Surprise** (MMadgwick) **3-8-9** RPerham(9) (nvr bttr than mid div)	3	**9**	50/1	54	4
1110[8]	**Silvery** (JARToller) **3-8-9** SSanders(1) (bhd fnl f)	3½	**10**	33/1	48	—
239[3]	**Sixties Melody** (RBoss) **3-9-0** MRoberts(10) (nvr nr ldrs)	5	**11**	50/1	45	—
	Shirazan (IRE) (LMCumani) **3-9-0** OUrbina(2) (str: scope: dwlt: hdwy 4f out: wknd 2f out)	2½	**12**	7/1	41	—
	Forestry (JGSmyth-Osbourne) **3-9-0** TSprake(3) (leggy: scope: prom tl wknd over 3 out)	6	**13**	33/1	31	—
				(SP 119.3%)	**13 Rn**	

2m 9.2 (4.30) CSF £97.10 TOTE £27.70: £4.50 £2.00 £1.30 (£204.70) Trio £145.80 OWNER The Owl Society (NEWMARKET) BRED J. M. Greetham

Arctic Owl made a most impressive debut. Steadily moving up from halfway, he really found his stride from the two-furlong marker and ran on to snatch the race close home. He looks an exciting prospect. (25/1)

742 Mystic Ridge was in third place for much of the way and, hard ridden over two furlongs from home, appeared unlikely to pass the two in front. He did eventually do so, only to be run out of it near the finish. (7/2: 3/1-5/1)

1207 Titta Ruffo, always close up, took up the running over two furlongs from home but was soon under maximum pressure. He kept on when headed but could not quicken. (9/4)

1155 Juggler, whose only previous outing was a modest third on the All-Weather, gave promise of better things to come. He came with a good run on the inside in the straight and, after looking really dangerous, was struggling in the last hundred yards. He should pay to follow. (5/1)

Contentment (IRE) stayed on in the last two furlongs to reach a remote fifth place, but never promised to catch the leaders. (33/1)

1409 Reward tried to make all the running but turned very badly and soon weakened when headed over two furlongs from home. (5/1: 4/1-6/1)

Shirazan (IRE) (7/1: 2/1-8/1)

T/Plpt: £41.90 (575.25 Tckts). T/Qdpt: £8.20 (129.92 Tckts) AK

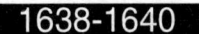

1504-BRIGHTON (L-H) (Firm)

Tuesday June 3rd

WEATHER: sunny WIND: mod half bhd

1638 MOULSECOMBE MEDIAN AUCTION MAIDEN STKS (3-Y.O) (Class E)

2-30 (2-30) **5f 213y** £2,862.25 (£853.00: £406.50: £183.25) Stalls: High GOING minus 0.57 sec per fur (F)

Form	Horse / details	Dist	Pos	SP	RR	SF
1083^{13}	**Third Party (64)** (SDow) **3-8-9** TQuinn(5) (chsd ldr: rdn over 1f out: led wl ins fnl f: r.o wl)	—	1	7/2^{2}	72	41
1485^{2}	**Goodbye Gatemen (IRE)** (BAPearce) **3-9-0** SSanders(1) (hung rt s: led: hrd rdn over 1f out: hdd wl ins fnl f: unable qckn)	½	2	4/7^{1}	76	45
1423^{7}	**Las Vistas** (HJCollingridge) **3-8-9** MRimmer(2) (rdn & no hdwy fnl 2f)	6	3	10/1^{3}	55	24
1289^{14}	**Nervous Rex (55)** (WRMuir) **3-9-0v^{1}** JReid(4) (hld up: rdn over 2f out: sn wknd)	3	4	14/1	52	21
1044^{11}	**Distinctive Dream (IRE) (43)** (KTIvory) **3-8-11**(3) MartinDwyer(6) (b: s.s: a bhd)	½	5	20/1	50	19
	Hot News (JRJenkins) **3-9-0** GBardwell(3) (b.hind: w'like: s.s: a bhd)	1¼	6	20/1	47?	16

(SP 111.1%) **6 Rn**

1m 7.3 (0.20 under best) (0.10) CSF £5.23 TOTE £4.00: £1.30 £1.20 (£2.20) OWNER Mrs G. R. Smith (EPSOM) BRED G.R. Smith(Thriplow) Ltd

768 Third Party raced in second place and eventually managed to overhaul the favourite in the closing stages to win this very poor race. (7/2: 5/2-4/1)

1485 Goodbye Gatemen (IRE), who misbehaved before his race at Folkestone last week, did so again here. Tearing off in front, he looked to have the measure of his rivals, only to be worried out of it in the closing stages. A pair of blinkers look needed. (4/7)

Las Vistas looked ill at ease on this very tricky switch back track and was making little impression in the final quarter mile. She looks very moderate. (10/1: op 6/1)

751 Nervous Rex had been hung out to dry a quarter-of-a-mile from home and is a very poor individual. (14/1: 7/1-16/1)

1639 PEACEHAVEN APPRENTICE H'CAP (0-60) (3-Y.O+) (Class F)

3-00 (3-01) **6f 209y** £2,305.00 (£655.00: £325.00) Stalls: High GOING minus 0.57 sec per fur (F)

Form	Horse / details	Dist	Pos	SP	RR	SF
1483^{6}	**Dark Menace (47)** (EAWheeler) **5-9-3b**(3) SCarson(10) (led over 5f out: clr over 4f out: r.o wl)	—	1	14/1	58	36
1484^{8}	**Okay Baby (IRE) (25)** (JMBradley) **5-7-12** JFowle(2) (a.p: chsd wnr 5f out: rdn over 2f out: r.o one pce)	2	2	16/1	31	9
1373^{5}	**Time For Tea (IRE) (49)** (CACyzer) **4-9-0**(8)ow2 RSawyer(3) (lw: a.p: rdn over 2f out: r.o one pce)	nk	3	14/1	55	31
992^{11}	**La Chatelaine (42)** (GLewis) **3-8-5** PFredericks(8) (lost pl over 4f out: rallied over 1f out: r.o)	nk	4	10/1^{3}	47	15
1009^{7}	**Velvet Jones (44)** (GFHCharles-Jones) **4-8-9**(8) CharlotteCox(13) (bmpd s: hdwy over 1f out: 4th & no ch whn n.m.r ins fnl f)	¾	5	7/1^{2}	47	25
1506^{11}	**Bon Guest (IRE) (54)** (TJNaughton) **3-9-0**(3) RachaelMoody(14) (lw: edgd rt over 3f out: wl bhd over 5f: gd hdwy fnl f: fin wl)	1	6	10/1^{3}	55	23
1506^{5}	**Fort Knox (IRE) (55)** (RMFlower) **6-10-0b** TField(9) (lw: hld up: rdn 3f out: one pce)	hd	7	7/1^{2}	56	34
1506^{4}	**Mr Cube (IRE) (48)** (JMBradley) **7-9-7b** RWinston(11) (hld up: rdn 3f out: one pce)	½	8	3/1^{1}	48	26
1506^{14}	**Hatta Sunshine (USA) (42)** (GLMoore) **7-8-7v^{1}**(8) CherylBone(7) (lw: s.s: hdwy fnl f: nvr nrr)	s.h	9	33/1	42	20
907^{7}	**Sharp Holly (IRE) (38)** (JABennett) **5-8-11v** RStudholme(1) (prom over 4f)	1½	10	25/1	34	12
1484^{10}	**Rawi (55)** (MissGayKelleway) **4-10-0** PFitzsimons(12) (lw: a bhd)	1¾	11	14/1	47	25
1388^{2}	**Chalky Dancer (32)** (HJCollingridge) **5-8-5** PBradley(5) (b.hind: led over 1f: wknd over 2f out)	3	12	7/1^{2}	17	—
1082^{10}	**Hawaii Storm (FR) (33)** (DJSffrenchDavis) **9-7-12b**(8) SarahSpong(4) (s.s: a wl bhd)	2	13	20/1	14	—
879^{12}	**Mister Sean (IRE) (28)** (JMBradley) **4-8-1b** GHannon(6) (b.hind: hld up: rdn over 2f out: wknd over 1f out)	4	14	33/1	—	—

(SP 121.1%) **14 Rn**

1m 21.5 (1.50) CSF £193.12 CT £2,957.74 TOTE £14.50: £4.30 £8.00 £3.10 (£205.80) Trio £657.80 OWNER Austin Stroud & Co Ltd (PANGBOURNE) BRED Roger C. Denton

WEIGHT FOR AGE 3yo-10lb

IN-FOCUS: **This was an Apprentice race restricted to riders who had not ridden more than five winners and, whilst races like this should be encouraged for the jockeys of tomorrow, it seemed quite bizarre that a race of this nature should find its way onto this notoriously tricky course, where even the most experienced jockeys can often have difficulties.**

Dark Menace was given a nice ride by his young jockey, partnering his first winner in Britain. Soon at the head of affairs, he quickly put daylight between himself and his rivals and was never going to get caught to win this poor race. (14/1)

Okay Baby (IRE) moved into second place five furlongs from home but never looked like reeling in the winner. She is a very moderate performer whose record now reads one win from twenty-three starts. (16/1)

1373 Time For Tea (IRE) was a leading player from the outset but never looked like finding that vital turn of foot. She is a moderate individual who remains a maiden after twenty-six attempts. (14/1: op 8/1)

La Chatelaine ran her best race to date and, after getting outpaced at the top of the hill, stayed on from below the distance. (10/1: op 6/1)

601 Velvet Jones had little help from the saddle. The gelding did pick up ground but was held when not having much room in the closing stages. He is very moderate and remains a maiden after twenty-four attempts. (7/1)

1388* Bon Guest (IRE) took the scenic route. Having negotiated the tricky top turn, he ended up coming down the centre of the track, and was still miles adrift of the winner at the quarter-mile pole. However, the colt began to pick up ground in the final furlong and, sprouting wings, came flying through to finish sixth. He would surely have been involved in the finish with a stronger apprentice in the saddle. (10/1: op 6/1)

383 Rawi (14/1: op 8/1)

1640 BRIGHTON MILE CHALLENGE TROPHY H'CAP (0-80) (3-Y.O+) (Class D)

3-30 (3-30) **7f 214y** £3,677.45 (£1,097.60: £524.30: £237.65) Stalls: High GOING minus 0.57 sec per fur (F)

Form	Horse / details	Dist	Pos	SP	RR	SF
1433^{4}	**Sooty Tern (64)** (JMBradley) **10-9-3**(5) RFfrench(7) (chsd ldrs: rdn over 2f out: led ins fnl f: r.o wl)	—	1	8/1	74	45
1262^{14}	**Kentucky Fall (FR) (66)** (LadyHerries) **4-9-10** AClark(2) (a.p: rdn over 2f out: ev ch ins fnl f: unable qckn)	2	2	16/1	72	43
1373*	**Sis Garden (55)** (JCullinan) **4-8-10b**(3) DO'Donohoe(4) (led: hrd rdn over 2f out: hdd ins fnl f: one pce)	s.h	3	8/1	61	32
1320^{7}	**Confronter (55)** (SDow) **8-8-13** JReid(5) (lw: rdn over 2f out: hdwy over 1f out: r.o one pce)	1¼	4	7/1	58	29
1107^{W}	**Barbason (65)** (GLMoore) **5-9-9** CandyMorris(1) (hld up: rdn over 2f out: one pce)	1¾	5	9/4^{1}	65	36
1262^{11}	**Fionn de Cool (IRE) (66)** (RAkehurst) **6-9-10** TQuinn(6) (lw: hld up: shkn up over 2f out: one pce)	1½	6	13/2^{3}	63	34
1506*	**Paddy's Rice (54)** (MBlanshard) **6-8-12** 5x FNorton(8) (hld up: rdn over 3f out: wknd over 2f out)	1¾	7	11/4^{2}	47	18
1135^{7}	**Cats Bottom (53)** (AGNewcombe) **5-8-11** SDrowne(3) (a bhd)	15	8	14/1	16	—

(SP 118.0%) **8 Rn**

1m 32.3 (1.00) CSF £114.32 CT £972.38 TOTE £7.40: £2.10 £3.00 £2.00 (£66.20) Trio £346.90; £58.64 to Warwick 4/6/97 OWNER Mr J. M. Bradley (CHEPSTOW) BRED Sheikh Mohammed bin Rashid al Maktoum

1433 Sooty Tern may be an O.A.P. but he was still able to show his younger rivals a clean pair of heels, getting on top in the last one hundred yards. He has won every year since 1990. (8/1: 6/1-10/1)
Kentucky Fall (FR) was much happier with the return to a firm surface and was still battling for the lead inside the final furlong before the winner went by. (16/1)
1373* Sis Garden, 8lb higher than when successful here recently, attempted to make all the running but was unable to withstand the late surge of the winner inside the final furlong. (8/1: 6/1-9/1)
269a Confronter is not the force of old and, although staying on in the last furlong-and-a-half, has not won since September 1995. (7/1)
752* Barbason found his terrific winning run coming to an end and the Handicapper may well have got the measure of him for the time being. (9/4)
Fionn de Cool (IRE) was certainly looked after. Chasing the leaders, his jockey did a bit of knitting and looked down a couple of times as though something may have been wrong. In the final quarter-mile, the gelding could only struggle on at one pace. One win from forty-three starts does not exactly inspire confidence but, if he is dropped a few pounds in the handicap, he looks one to keep an eye on, especially if there is a market move. (13/2)
870 Cats Bottom (14/1: 10/1-16/1)

1641 LEVY BOARD H'CAP (0-70) (3-Y.O+) (Class E)

4-00 (4-00) **1m 3f 196y** £2,836.25 (£845.00: £402.50: £181.25) Stalls: Low GOING minus 0.57 sec per fur (F)

Form	Horse	Dist	Pos	SP	RR	SF
1169^{11}	**Mr Browning (USA) (61)** (RAkehurst) **6-9-12b** TQuinn(6) (mde all: unchal)	—	1	9/2^{2}	71	56
1010^{8}	**Colour Counsellor (37)** (RMFlower) **4-7-13b**$^{(3)}$ MartinDwyer(4) (chsd wnr: hrd rdn over 3f out: no imp)	4	2	25/1	42	27
1393^{7}	**Almuhtaram (60)** (GLewis) **5-9-8b**$^{(3)}$ AWhelan(8) (hdwy over 5f out: rdn 4f out: one pce)	5	3	9/1	58	43
640*	**Yet Again (45)** (MissGayKelleway) **5-8-10** SSanders(7) (b: lw: s.s: hdwy 10f out: hrd rdn over 2f out: one pce)	2	4	5/2^{1}	40	25
1010^{2}	**Prince Danzig (IRE) (63)** (DJGMurraySmith) **6-9-9**$^{(5)}$ RFfrench(3) (lw: nvr nr to chal)	1¾	5	5/2^{1}	56	41
1427^{2}	**Oberons Boy (IRE) (58)** (SDow) **4-9-9** RPerham(5) (lw: a bhd)	2	6	7/1^{3}	48	33
1408^{8}	**Urgent Reply (USA) (60)** (CADwyer) **4-9-11** DHarrison(1) (b: bhd fnl 5f)	3½	7	20/1	45	30
887^{10}	**Princess Topaz (70)** (CACyzer) **3-9-6** AClark(2) (lw: hld up: rdn over 4f out: wknd over 1f out)	6	8	8/1	47	17

(SP 117.5%) **8 Rn**

2m 28.7 (1.10) CSF £95.00 CT £890.13 TOTE £5.70: £1.60 £4.30 £1.80 (£37.60) OWNER Mrs M. E. O'Shea (EPSOM) BRED Lord Carnarvon
WEIGHT FOR AGE 3yo-15lb
Mr Browning (USA) was given a masterly ride by Quinn who took the gelding off in front. With only the runner-up keeping tabs on him, the combination had a healthy advantage at the top of the hill and, really injecting pace in the straight, were never going to get caught. This is his trip. (9/2)
640 Colour Counsellor was the only runner to go after the winner. Coming under strong pressure over three furlongs from home, his jockey used his whip above shoulder height on at least two occasions, but the combination could make little impression on the winner. (25/1)
1393 Almuhtaram, racing with his tongue hanging out, took closer order at the top of the hill but failed to find the necessary turn of foot to get on terms with the front two. (9/1)
640* Yet Again failed to find the necessary turn of foot in the straight. (5/2: op 5/4)
1010 Prince Danzig (IRE) goes well round here but, on this occasion, could never get in a blow. (5/2)
887 Princess Topaz (8/1: 6/1-9/1)

1642 HOVE CLAIMING LIMITED STKS (0-60) (3-Y.O+) (Class F)

4-30 (4-30) **1m 1f 209y** £2,277.00 (£627.00: £297.00) Stalls: Low GOING minus 0.57 sec per fur (F)

Form	Horse	Dist	Pos	SP	RR	SF
1422^{10}	**Roman Reel (USA) (53)** (GLMoore) **6-9-3** SWhitworth(1) (lw: hdwy 5f out: bmpd over 2f out: rdn & r.o one pce: fin 2nd, 1½l: awrdd r)	—	1	3/1^{2}	61	38
	Marchman (48) (JSKing) **12-8-8**$^{(5)}$ RFfrench(6) (bkwd: hld up: squeezed thro over 2f out: led over 1f out: comf: fin 1st: disq: plcd 2nd)	1½	2	10/1	59	36
1441^{12}	**Araboybill (49)** (JNeville) **6-8-13** SDrowne(3) (lost pl 4f out: rallied fnl f: r.o)	2	3	16/1	53	30
1301^{5}	**Native Princess (IRE) (52)** (BWHills) **3-8-7** TQuinn(2) (lw: chsd ldr: ev ch over 1f out: one pce)	1	4	9/2^{3}	59	23
1469^{9}	**Miss Barcelona (IRE) (50)** (MJPolglase) **3-8-3** SSanders(4) (lw: led: rdn over 3f out: hdd over 1f out: wknd fnl f)	2½	5	20/1	51	15
578^{13}	**Silver Harrow (55)** (AGNewcombe) **4-8-12**$^{(3)}$ DGriffiths(7) (nvr nr to chal)	3½	6	9/1	44	21
748^{8}	**Hazel (49)** (MissGayKelleway) **5-8-11b**$^{(5)}$ RMullen(9) (b: rdn & no hdwy fnl 3f)	2	7	20/1	42	19
1247^{2}	**Shabanaz (55)** (WRMuir) **12-9-3** JReid(5) (bhd fnl 5f)	nk	8	9/4^{1}	42	19
1472^{15}	**Harvey White (IRE) (58)** (JPearce) **5-9-4**$^{(3)}$ CTeague(8) (s.s: a bhd)	11	9	8/1	29	6
1011^{4}	**Leg Beforum (IRE) (50)** (LMontagueHall) **3-8-6v^{1}** AClark(10) (a bhd)	5	10	25/1	19	—

(SP 123.4%) **10 Rn**

1m 59.9 (1.60) CSF £31.21 TOTE £3.50: £1.70 £4.30 £3.50 (£34.50) Trio £123.40 OWNER Mr K. Higson (BRIGHTON) BRED Dorothy Price, Jackie W. Ramos & Ken Hickson
WEIGHT FOR AGE 3yo-13lb
STEWARDS' ENQUIRY Ffrench susp. 12-14 & 16-18/6/97 (irresponsible riding)
1011 Roman Reel (USA) goes well round here, especially over this trip in this grade. His jockey was keeping the winner in when he was given a nudge as that rival created a gap, but it had little effect on Roman Reel's chances and he was certainly second best on the day. (3/1)
Marchman belied his burly paddock appearance on this first run in nine months. Kept in by Roman Reel over a quarter of a mile from home, Ffrench made a gap for himself, giving Roman Reel a gentle nudge. Leading below the distance, he soon put daylight between himself and his rivals for a very decisive victory. There is absolutely no doubt that he was the best horse on the day, but the Stewards quite rightly decided that it could not have been careless riding as Ffrench had made a gap for himself. Even though the interference was minimal, the Stewards therefore had no option but to call it irresponsible riding, handing Ffrench a six-day ban and demoting Marchman to second. (10/1)
Araboybill got outpaced at the top of the hill but stayed on again in the final furlong to take third prize. He is very moderate. (16/1)
1301 Native Princess (IRE) raced in second place and still had every chance below the distance before tapped for toe. (9/2)
700 Miss Barcelona (IRE) took the field along but, headed below the distance, soon capitulated. She is extremely exposed and remains a maiden after twenty-two attempts. (20/1)

1643 BEVENDEAN MAIDEN STKS (3-Y.O+) (Class D)

5-00 (5-00) **6f 209y** £3,422.65 (£1,019.20: £485.10: £218.05) Stalls: High GOING minus 0.57 sec per fur (F)

Form	Horse	Dist	Pos	SP	RR	SF
1268^{16}	**Shoumatara (USA) (80)** (MRStoute) **3-8-11v^{1}** JReid(1) (lw: led over 5f: hrd drvn: led wl ins fnl f: all out)	—	1	4/1^{3}	73	41
	Tithcar (BHanbury) **3-8-6** SSanders(3) (lw: hld up: chsd wnr over 3f out: led over 1f out tl wl ins fnl f: hrd rdn: r.o wl)	s.h	2	15/8^{2}	68	36

				SP	RR	SF
	Literary (85) (JHMGosden) **3-8-6** GHind(4) (hld up: rdn 2f out: unable qckn)	2½	**3**	10/11^{1}	62	30
	Cabcharge Glory (GGMargarson) **3-8-1**$^{(7)ow2}$ JGotobed(2) (leggy: unf: lw: a wl bhd)	22	**4**	40/1	14	—
1423^{12}	**Nite Wonder** (GLMoore) **3-8-11** CandyMorris(5) (chsd wnr over 3f)	1½	**5**	25/1	13	—
				(SP 113.4%)	**5 Rn**	

1m 20.4 (0.40) CSF £11.23 TOTE £4.70: £1.50 £1.40 (£6.60) OWNER Maktoum Al Maktoum (NEWMARKET) BRED Northwest Farms
STEWARDS' ENQUIRY Reid susp. 12-13/6/97 (excessive use of whip).
Shoumatara (USA) looked in great shape in the paddock and left his two disappointments this season well behind. Setting the pace, he was collared over a furlong from home but, with Reid getting down to serious work - he hit the colt twelve times in the last furlong-and-a-half - managed to get the colt back up in the closing stages. There is no doubt he would not have won had Reid not been so forceful, but he did transgress the Rules and was handed a two-day ban for excessive use of the whip. Shoumatara will not forget this race in a hurry. (4/1)
Tithcar looked in fine fettle for this return to action and moved into a narrow lead below the distance. However, she was unable to shake off the attentions of the winner and was worried out of it in the closing stages. (15/8)
Literary was taking a drop in class for this seasonal debut but failed to find the necessary turn of foot. (10/11: 2/5-evens)

1644 KEMP TOWN H'CAP (0-70) (3-Y.O) (Class E)
5-30 (5-30) **5f 59y** £2,836.25 (£845.00: £402.50: £181.25) Stalls: High GOING minus 0.57 sec per fur (F)

				SP	RR	SF
1509^{3}	**Tear White (IRE) (62)** (TGMills) **3-9-1** TQuinn(6) (lw: hld up: swtchd rt over 1f out: led ins fnl f: rdn out)	—	**1**	11/4^{1}	68	44
1327^{9}	**Suite Factors (57)** (KRBurke) **3-8-10** RPerham(1) (led: rdn over 2f out: hdd ins fnl f: r.o)	nk	**2**	4/1^{3}	62	38
1375*	**Anokato (66)** (KTIvory) **3-9-2b**$^{(3)}$ MartinDwyer(2) (b: a.p: rdn over 2f out: ev ch whn edgd lft over 1f out: unable qckn)	¾	**3**	3/1^{2}	69	45
	Caspian Morn (62) (WGMTurner) **3-8-10**$^{(5)}$ DSweeney(9) (nvr nr to chal)	5	**4**	12/1	50	26
1107^{9}	**Rise 'n Shine (68)** (CACyzer) **3-9-2**$^{(5)}$ RFfrench(4) (lw: spd 3f)	9	**5**	10/1	28	4
1375^{7}	**Stock Hill Dancer (58)** (BJMeehan) **3-8-4b**$^{(7)}$ GHannon(8) (a bhd)	2½	**6**	20/1	11	—
1375^{4}	**Bestelina (51)** (DJSCosgrove) **3-8-1**$^{(3)}$ DO'Donohoe(5) (s.s: a wl bhd)	16	**7**	4/1^{3}	—	—
				(SP 113.2%)	**7 Rn**	

60.3 secs (0.30) CSF £12.55 CT £30.67 TOTE £3.30: £1.50 £2.20 (£7.80) Trio £6.60 OWNER A W Lawson & Co Ltd (EPSOM) BRED A. F. O'Callaghan
1509 Tear White (IRE) seemed to cope with the track perfectly well, in contrast to his trainer's remarks to the Stewards last year when he reported the gelding failed to handle the course. Switched to get a decent run below the distance, he found a nice turn of foot to get on top inside the final furlong. He is a different horse since he has been gelded in the winter, and the blinkers and pricker have been left off, according to his trainer. (11/4)
751 Suite Factors attempted to make all the running but was unable to cope with the winner inside the final furlong. He has now won just once from twenty-three starts and has finished runner-up in four of his last six races. (4/1: 3/1-9/2)
1375* Anokato, 7lb higher than when winning over this course and distance eleven days ago, had every chance when drifting left under pressure below the distance, and then failed to find another gear. (3/1)
Caspian Morn, making her seasonal reappearance, could never make her presence felt. (12/1: 7/1-14/1)
Rise 'n Shine is coming down in the handicap but, after playing an active role, had little more to offer entering the last two furlongs. (10/1: op 5/1)

T/Jkpt: Not won; £4,581.74 to Warwick 4/6/97. T/Plpt: £1,611.70 (11.12 Tckts). T/Qdpt: £79.00 (14.19 Tckts) AK

1389-PONTEFRACT (L-H) (Good to firm)
Tuesday June 3rd
WEATHER: sunny & warm WIND: slt across

1645 E.B.F. THORNE MAIDEN STKS (2-Y.O F) (Class D)
2-45 (2-49) **6f** £4,013.00 (£1,214.00: £592.00: £281.00) Stalls: Low GOING minus 0.45 sec per fur (F)

				SP	RR	SF
	Land of Dreams (MJohnston) **2-8-11** DHolland(11) (w'like: str: hld up: smooth hdwy to ld 1½f out: r.o wl: comf)	—	**1**	4/1^{2}	88+	44
	Filfilah (PTWalwyn) **2-8-11** RHills(5) (w'like: scope: bit bkwd: trckd ldrs: chal 1½f out: r.o: no ch w wnr)	1¾	**2**	9/2^{3}	83	39
	First Village (IRE) (JBerry) **2-8-11** KDarley(1) (w'like: scope: led tl hdd 1½f out: no ex)	5	**3**	9/4^{1}	70	26
1120^{9}	**Townville Cee Cee** (JSWainwright) **2-8-6**$^{(5)}$ JBramhill(9) (chsd ldrs: rn wd st: rdn & no imp after)	4	**4**	100/1	59	15
651^{4}	**Dawn Patrol** (KWHogg) **2-8-11** DeanMcKeown(6) (disp ld 4f: grad wknd)	1¼	**5**	33/1	56	12
	Bint Nadia (JDBethell) **2-8-11** TWilliams(2) (w'like: lengthy: outpcd ½-wy: kpt on fnl f)	hd	**6**	50/1	56	12
	Elsinore (IRE) (MrsJRRamsden) **2-8-11** JFortune(10) (w'like: bit bkwd: s.i.s: plld hrd: hdwy ½-wy: shkn up 2f out: grad wknd)	1½	**7**	20/1	52	8
	Spice Girl (PDEvans) **2-8-11** JFEgan(3) (lt-f: sn drvn along & bhd: sme late hdwy)	s.h	**8**	25/1	52	8
1386^{5}	**Meadgate's Dreamer (IRE)** (BPalling) **2-8-11** TSprake(4) (sn outpcd & bhd: n.d)	1	**9**	33/1	49	5
861^{4}	**Brookhouse Lady (IRE)** (RHollinshead) **2-8-11** WRyan(7) (spd 4f)	2½	**10**	13/2	42	—
	Thundering Papoose (APJames) **2-8-11** MFenton(8) (s.i.s: a outpcd & bhd)	2½	**11**	33/1	36	—
	Dooze (IRE) (JHMGosden) **2-8-11** LDettori(12) (w'like: unf: prom to ½-wy: wknd)	½	**12**	5/1	34	—
				(SP 119.3%)	**12 Rn**	

1m 16.1 (1.10) CSF £19.11 TOTE £5.90: £1.70 £1.90 £1.40 (£21.20) Trio £28.30 OWNER Maktoum Al Maktoum (MIDDLEHAM) BRED Gainsborough Stud Management Ltd
Land of Dreams is a particularly nice sort and is obviously extremely useful. There looks to be plenty more to come and she should be followed in any company. (4/1)
Filfilah, a useful type of filly, certainly needed this and showed plenty and, by the looks of things, there is much better to come. (9/2)
First Village (IRE) was certainly not out of place in this very useful race and, after doing the donkey work, she had run herself out approaching the final furlong. She should improve for the experience. (9/4)
Townville Cee Cee has improved a good bit from her debut and, although she was beaten over ten lengths, this was a high-class event. (100/1)
651 Dawn Patrol keeps showing enough to suggest a run-of-the-mill event can be found. (33/1)
Bint Nadia has the scope for improvement and, after getting taken off her legs at halfway, she was picking up nicely at the end. (50/1)
Elsinore (IRE) needed this and raced too freely early on and, in time, she will do better. (20/1)
Dooze (IRE) (5/1: op 5/2)

1646 NEIL WYATT GROUNDSTAFF AWARDS MAIDEN STKS (3-Y.O) (Class D)

3-15 (3-18) **1m 2f 6y** £3,582.50 (£1,085.00: £530.00: £252.50) Stalls: Low GOING minus 0.45 sec per fur (F)

	Horse	Dist	Pos	SP	RR	SF
1239^3	**Life of Riley** (GLewis) **3-9-0** PaulEddery(7) (a cl up: effrt 2f out: styd on to ld post)	—	1	3/1^2	80	45
1271^8	**Robban Hendi (USA)** (MAJarvis) **3-9-0** MRoberts(1) (led: qcknd 4f out: r.o: jst ct)	s.h	2	20/1	80	45
	Vicious Circle (LMCumani) **3-9-0** OUrbina(10) (w'like: lengthy: pushed along after s: sn in tch: rdn 3f out: kpt on wl towards fin)	2	3	12/1	77	42
1316^8	**Alcalali (USA) (80)** (PAKelleway) **3-8-9** JFortune(8) (a.p: effrt 3f out: ch over 1f out: nt qckn)	hd	4	11/4^1	72	37
	Ikhtisar (USA) (PTWalwyn) **3-8-9** RHills(5) (prom: outpcd 2f out: n.d after)	7	5	10/1	60	25
1430^4	**Tellion** (MajorWRHern) **3-9-0** TSprake(6) (hld up & bhd: effrt 2f out: nvr trbld ldrs)	3	6	10/1	61	26
599^5	**Yours In Sport** (JWWatts) **3-9-0** JCarroll(9) (nvr nr to chal)	2	7	13/2	57	22
1304^4	**Love Venture** (SPCWoods) **3-8-9** KDarley(2) (b: chsd ldrs tl rdn & wknd over 2f out)	¾	8	16/1	51	16
	Straffan Gold (USA) (GWragg) **3-9-0** WRyan(11) (hld up: outpcd over 4f out: n.d after)	11	9	20/1	39	4
	Classical Dance (IRE) (MrsMReveley) **3-9-0** ACulhane(4) (w'like: dwlt: a bhd)	1¾	10	50/1	36	1
1372^3	***Hope Chest*** (DRLoder) **3-8-9** LDettori(3) (Withdrawn not under Starter's orders: spread plate at s)		W	4/1^3	—	—

(SP 128.2%) **10 Rn**

2m 12.0 (2.40) CSF £43.27 TOTE £3.10: £1.40 £4.10 £2.10 (£60.00) Trio £64.30 OWNER Mr John Manley (EPSOM) BRED Chippenham Lodge Stud

1239 Life of Riley always held a good position in this messy race and, in the final sprint, he did just enough to get his nose in front on the stick. This should have taught him plenty. (3/1: op 2/1)

Robban Hendi (USA) set a steady gallop and then went for home four furlongs out and almost pinched it. He is obviously improving fast. (20/1)

Vicious Circle, a decent-looking newcomer, was very green and needed constant attention from the saddle, but he finished well and should improve no end for the experience. (12/1: op 7/1)

1147 Alcalali (USA), a shade warm beforehand, had her chances but lacked the speed in the final sprint. (11/4: 4/1-5/2)

Ikhtisar (USA), a tall filly, has filled out a good bit since last year and should improve for this run. (10/1: op 20/1)

1430 Tellion, held up in a race that turned out to be sprint, had no chance of getting into it and will no doubt do better when handicapped. (10/1)

1647 KALAMAZOO SECURITY PRINT H'CAP (0-90) (3-Y.O) (Class C)

3-45 (3-46) **1m 2f 6y** £6,056.00 (£1,808.00: £864.00: £392.00) Stalls: Low GOING minus 0.45 sec per fur (F)

	Horse	Dist	Pos	SP	RR	SF
1242^4	**Pinchincha (FR) (75)** (DMorris) **3-8-9** NDay(5) (a cl up: led over 2f out: r.o wl)	—	1	7/1	84	51
1392*	**Southerly Wind (83)** (MrsJRRamsden) **3-9-3** JFortune(2) (lw: hld up: hdwy 3f out: rdn & r.o wl appr fnl f: nrst fin)	1	2	7/4^1	90	57
690^4	**Sausalito Bay (87)** (IABalding) **3-9-7** KDarley(3) (trckd ldrs: effrt 3f out: r.o one pce)	6	3	3/1^3	85	52
1110^6	**Listed Account (USA) (77)** (LMCumani) **3-8-11** LDettori(4) (trckd ldrs: qcknd to chal over 2f out: wknd over 1f out)	1¼	4	5/2^2	73	40
1150^3	**Zinzari (FR) (86)** (DRLoder) **3-9-6** DRMcCabe(6) (hld up & bhd: r.o fnl 2f: nvr plcd to chal)	s.h	5	12/1	82	49
1242^7	**Our People (87)** (MJohnston) **3-9-7b^1** DHolland(7) (led tl hdd over 2f out: sn wknd)	¾	6	33/1	82	49
1144^5	**Farhan (USA) (84)** (PTWalwyn) **3-9-4** RHills(1) (lw: prom tl outpcd fnl 3f)	9	7	16/1	64	31

(SP 119.0%) **7 Rn**

2m 10.5 (0.90) CSF £19.00 TOTE £7.50: £1.90 £1.30 (£4.60) OWNER Mr T. J. Wells (NEWMARKET) BRED Fluorocarbon Bloodstock

1242 Pinchincha (FR) seems to act on any going and is as honest as they come and, getting first run in the final sprint, he was not going to stop. (7/1)

1392* Southerly Wind looked magnificent but the pace was not a strong one and, despite trying his hardest, he could never peg the winner back. Plenty more opportunities will be found, especially when there is some serious pace on. (7/4)

690 Sausalito Bay is a really good-looking sort who just seems to stay and this messy event was not to his liking. (3/1)

1110 Listed Account (USA), well supported at early morning prices, gave punters hope when quickening to challenge on the home turn but then seemed to blow up. She looks the sort to do better in time. (5/2)

1150 Zinzari (FR), dropped back four furlongs in trip, was given next to no chance by sitting way off the pace. He did remarkably well to finish so close and was certainly not knocked about. (12/1)

1104 Our People had blinkers on for the first time and, after racing freely, he soon stopped when tackled approaching the straight. (33/1)

1648 TONY BETHELL MEMORIAL H'CAP (0-80) (3-Y.O+) (Class D)

4-15 (4-15) **2m 1f 22y** £4,560.00 (£1,260.00: £600.00) Stalls: Centre GOING minus 0.45 sec per fur (F)

	Horse	Dist	Pos	SP	RR	SF
1585*	**Nigel's Lad (IRE) (73)** (PCHaslam) **5-9-8** 3x JFortune(3) (lw: mde all: easily)	—	1	4/5^1	83+	26
1138^4	**Diego (67)** (CEBrittain) **4-9-1** BDoyle(1) (hld up: effrt 3f out: sn chsng wnr: no imp)	1½	2	5/1^3	76	18
1224^2	**Royal Expression (79)** (MrsMReveley) **5-10-0** ACulhane(2) (lw: chsd wnr tl rdn & wknd wl over 2f out)	25	3	15/8^2	64	7

(SP 107.0%) **3 Rn**

3m 49.5 (10.00) CSF £4.10 TOTE £1.50: (£3.00) OWNER Mr N. C. Dunnington (MIDDLEHAM) BRED Nikita Investments

WEIGHT FOR AGE 4yo-1lb

1585* Nigel's Lad (IRE) went off in front this time as he likes to, and the situation was always well in hand. (4/5)

1138 Diego seemed to stay well enough but he found the winner far too good. (5/1)

1224 Royal Expression looked well but was a disappointment here, stopping quickly once the pressure was on in the last three furlongs. (15/8)

1649 YORKSHIRE-TYNE TEES TELEVISION H'CAP (0-80) (3-Y.O) (Class D)

4-45 (4-46) **1m 4f 8y** £3,720.00 (£1,110.00: £530.00: £240.00) Stalls: Low GOING minus 0.45 sec per fur (F)

	Horse	Dist	Pos	SP	RR	SF
1277^5	**Royal Castle (IRE) (70)** (MajorWRHern) **3-9-0** TSprake(3) (lw: chsd ldrs: drvn along over 3f out: styd on to ld appr fnl f: kpt on wl)	—	1	4/1^2	79	45
996*	**Stakis Casinos Boy (IRE) (77)** (MJohnston) **3-9-7** DHolland(4) (lw: hld up: hdwy over 2f out: ev ch 1f out: kpt on)	1¼	2	4/1^2	84	50
686^4	**Nordic Crest (IRE) (75)** (PWHarris) **3-9-5** GDuffield(6) (lw: cl up: effrt 3f out: sn outpcd: kpt on fnl f)	2½	3	8/1	79	45
1094*	**Tango King (75)** (JLDunlop) **3-9-5** LDettori(1) (hld up & bhd: effrt over 2f out: sn rdn & nt pce to chal)	2	4	2/1^1	76	42
1025^4	**Ibin St James (73)** (JDBethell) **3-9-3b^1** TWilliams(7) (chsd ldrs: rdn 3f out: outpcd fnl 2f)	hd	5	10/1	74	40

				SP	RR	SF
1147^{7}	**French Mist (71)** (CEBrittain) **3-9-1** BDoyle(5) (lw: led tl hdd & wknd appr fnl f)	3	**6**	12/1	68	34
1282*	**Rheinbold (75)** (TJEtherington) **3-9-5** GCarter(2) (outpcd 3f out: sn btn)	25	**7**	6/1^{3}	39	5

(SP 115.5%) **7 Rn**

2m 37.0 (2.70) CSF £18.87 TOTE £5.70: £3.00 £2.30 (£22.90) OWNER Lord Weinstock (LAMBOURN) BRED Ballymacoll Stud Farm Ltd
OFFICIAL EXPLANATION **Rheinbold: was subsequently found to have a low blood count.**
1277 Royal Castle (IRE) just gallops and stays and, although off the bit at various stages, he did all that was needed in the end. (4/1)
996* Stakis Casinos Boy (IRE) takes a good grip but he does seem to stay well, and was always second best in the closing stages. (4/1)
686 Nordic Crest (IRE) looked short of pace at various stages but he was keeping on well at the end, suggesting that even further should suit. (8/1)
1094* Tango King, dropping back in trip this time, this free-runner was held up and then lacked the pace to get on terms. He did, however, look very lean on this occasion. (2/1)
1025 Ibin St James had blinkers on for the first time and they did not appear to help. (10/1)
1147 French Mist set a good pace until running out of fuel approaching the final furlong. (12/1)

1650 FERRYBRIDGE FLYERS' MAIDEN STKS (3-Y.O+) (Class D)

5-15 (5-15) **6f** £3,566.25 (£1,080.00: £527.50: £251.25) Stalls: Low GOING minus 0.45 sec per fur (F)

				SP	RR	SF
	Elnadim (USA) (JLDunlop) **3-9-0** RHills(2) (hld up: hdwy to ld over 1f out: shkn up & r.o wl)	—	**1**	1/2^{1}	92	51
1394^{2}	**Present Chance (80)** (BAMcMahon) **3-9-0** LNewton(4) (lw: trckd ldrs: effrt 2f out: r.o: no ch w wnr)	4	**2**	7/2^{2}	81	40
	Husun (USA) (PTWalwyn) **3-8-9** JCarroll(3) (lw: mde most tl hdd appr fnl f: no ex)	hd	**3**	16/1	76	35
1030^{7}	**Midyan Queen (67)** (RHollinshead) **3-8-9** WRyan(10) (bhd tl styd on appr fnl f)	5	**4**	25/1	63	22
1451^{3}	**Prince of Parkes (67)** (JBerry) **3-9-0** KDarley(5) (chsd ldrs tl outpcd fnl 2f)	1¾	**5**	16/1	63	22
1134^{2}	**Komaseph** (RFMarvin) **5-9-8** TGMcLaughlin(8) (bhd: effrt over 2f out: sme late hdwy)	2	**6**	66/1	58	25
1119^{7}	**Hype Superior (IRE) (64)** (ABailey) **3-9-0** PaulEddery(6) (bhd: hdwy u.p 2f out: n.d)	hd	**7**	10/1^{3}	58	17
760^{11}	**Maydoro** (MDods) **4-9-3** RLappin(7) (disp ld 4f: sn wknd)	nk	**8**	100/1	52	19
	Babe (IRE) (54) (MHTompkins) **3-8-9e** DBiggs(9) (spd to ½-wy: wknd qckly)	dist	**9**	50/1	—	—

(SP 118.0%) **9 Rn**

1m 15.8 (0.80) CSF £2.29 TOTE £1.60: £1.20 £1.10 £2.00 (£2.10) Trio £5.60 OWNER Mr Hamdan Al Maktoum (ARUNDEL) BRED Shadwell Farm Inc
WEIGHT FOR AGE 3yo-8lb
Elnadim (USA) looked likely to benefit from this and did not show the best of actions, but he did the job required well and should now improve. (1/2: op 1/3)
1394 Present Chance is doing well physically and is running consistently well, which will surely pay dividends before long. (7/2)
Husun (USA) set the race up but was easily picked off approaching the final furlong. (16/1)
Midyan Queen sat off the pace for much of the trip and then showed ability, staying on when it was all over. (25/1)
1451 Prince of Parkes is struggling to find an opportunity. (16/1)
1134 Komaseph was outpaced and behind until picking up ground when it was all over, suggesting that longer trips might well help, and he is now qualified for handicaps. (66/1)

T/Plpt: £40.90 (459.58 Tckts). T/Qdpt: £13.50 (66.73 Tckts) AA

1298-BEVERLEY (R-H) (Good to firm)
Wednesday June 4th

WEATHER: fine & sunny WIND: almost nil

1651 TEAM RATING RELATED MAIDEN STKS (0-70) (3-Y.O) (Class E)

6-30 (6-30) **1m 100y** £2,854.25 (£854.00: £409.50: £187.25) Stalls: High GOING minus 0.24 sec per fur (GF)

				SP	RR	SF
1443^{2}	**Mr Paradise (IRE) (67)** (TJNaughton) **3-8-11**(3) JDSmith(2) (w ldr: rdn to ld 2f out: all out)	—	**1**	3/1^{2}	79	40
1004^{4}	**Neronian (IRE) (70)** (BWHills) **3-9-0** RHills(1) (trckd ldrs: effrt over 2f out: rdn & ev ch over 1f out: styd on towards fin)	½	**2**	4/1^{3}	78	39
1458^{2}	**Signs And Wonders (61)** (CACyzer) **3-8-11** LDettori(3) (led to 2f out: wknd over 1f out)	7	**3**	8/13^{1}	62	23
998^{10}	**Coral Strand (67)** (JWWatts) **3-8-11** NConnorton(4) (trckd ldrs: plld hrd: rdn over 2f out: lost pl over 1f out)	6	**4**	12/1	51	12

(SP 114.6%) **4 Rn**

1m 48.0 (4.00) CSF £13.32 TOTE £3.30: (£9.00) OWNER Mr G. E. Archer (EPSOM) BRED Airlie Stud
1443 Mr Paradise (IRE), who looked very fit, had finished runner-up on five of his previous nine starts. He did just enough to take a very modest event with not an ounce to spare. (3/1)
1004 Neronian (IRE) looked to walk stiff behind in the paddock and his action left something to be desired. Almost upsides over a furlong out, he rolled about under pressure but was closing the gap at the line. (4/1)
1458 Signs And Wonders, who looked very fit, started at a ludicrous price considering that on official figures she was worst in. Allowed to set her own pace, she produced very little when challenged and her stamina soon gave out completely. (8/13)
Coral Strand would not settle at any stage. (12/1)

1652 KENNEDY WATTS PARTNERSHIP CONSULTING ENGINEERS H'CAP (0-80) (4-Y.O+) (Class D)

7-00 (7-00) **1m 100y** £3,444.00 (£1,032.00: £496.00: £228.00) Stalls: High GOING minus 0.24 sec per fur (GF)

				SP	RR	SF
1422^{3}	**Murphy's Gold (IRE) (50)** (RAFahey) **6-7-5**(7)ow1 RWinston(1) (lw: plld hrd: racd wd: sn w ldr: led over 1f out: edgd rt: rdn out)	—	**1**	2/1^{2}	61	33
1450^{6}	**Tertium (IRE) (80)** (MartynWane) **5-10-0** JCarroll(3) (lw: trckd ldrs gng wl: hdwy on ins over 2f out: chal over 1f out: sn rdn & nt qckn)	1	**2**	7/4^{1}	89	62
1615*	**Pekay (66)** (MJohnston) **4-9-0** 6x LDettori(2) (trckd ldrs: effrt over 3f out: sn rdn & outpcd: kpt on appr fnl f)	1¾	**3**	7/2^{3}	72	45
1606^{7}	**Three Arch Bridge (76)** (MJohnston) **5-9-10b** 6x DeanMcKeown(4) (led: rdn over 2f out: sn hdd: wknd 1f out)	3	**4**	7/2^{3}	76	49

(SP 114.1%) **4 Rn**

1m 47.2 (3.20) CSF £5.68 TOTE £2.90: (£2.60) OWNER Mr D. A. Read (MALTON) BRED Anthony Byrne
1422 Murphy's Gold (IRE) has now recorded three of his five victories here. In such a small field and drawn on the outside, he took a keen grip and, after hitting the front, tended to edge right on to the far rail. He was always doing more than enough for his promising young rider. (2/1)
1450 Tertium (IRE) looked a real danger when moving up on the inner to challenge but, under pressure though keeping on, he did not find the anticipated burst of finishing speed. He is proving hard to win with. (7/4)

1615* Pekay, having his second outing in three days and under a 6lb penalty, stuck on after being outpaced. (7/2)
1495* Three Arch Bridge, under a 6lb penalty and having her second outing in five days, did not move well to post. Making the running, she rolled off the fence, leaving a gap for Tertium to come up her inside, and she was leg-weary a furlong out. (7/2)

1653 HILARY NEEDLER TROPHY CONDITIONS STKS (2-Y.O F) (Class B)

7-30 (7-30) **5f** £9,277.49 (£3,472.50: £1,698.75: £731.25: £328.13: £166.88) Stalls: High GOING minus 0.24 sec per fur (GF)

				SP	RR	SF
1149[4]	**Filey Brigg** (WTKemp) **2-8-8** JQuinn(3) (chsd ldrs: led 1f out: hld on wl)	—	**1**	16/1	84	34
1255*	**Forest Treasure (IRE)** (JBerry) **2-8-12** GCarter(2) (b.hind: swvd lft s: sn chsng ldrs: rdn ½-wy: styd on wl towards fin)	¾	**2**	4/1[2]	86	36
1447[2]	**Angel Hill** (TDBarron) **2-8-8** KDarley(6) (chsd ldrs: rdn ½-wy: sn outpcd: styd on ins fnl f)	1¼	**3**	16/1	78	28
844*	**Lady Moll** (RBoss) **2-8-8** JCarroll(7) (led to 1f out: wknd towards fin)	hd	**4**	12/1	77	27
1457*	**Kilcora (IRE)** (CADwyer) **2-8-12** JReid(8) (lw: chsd ldrs: nt qckn appr fnl f)	nk	**5**	7/1[3]	80	30
1310*	**Heavenly Abstone** (PDEvans) **2-8-12v** ACulhane(10) (sn outpcd & drvn along: styng on whn sltly hmpd jst ins fnl f)	¾	**6**	10/1	78	28
1457[2]	**Folklore** (DRLoder) **2-8-8** LDettori(5) (lw: hld up: effrt over 1f out: sn rdn & no imp)	nk	**7**	4/7[1]	73	23
1457[3]	**Sada** (MajorWRHern) **2-8-8** RHills(1) (sltly hmpd s: effrt ½-wy: nvr nr ldrs)	1¼	**8**	8/1	69	19
1295*	**Going Places** (KTIvory) **2-9-0** MartinDwyer(4) (b.hind: swvd lft s: a outpcd & sn bhd)	19	**9**	25/1	14	—
	The Prussian Queen (CSmith) **2-8-5** GDuffield(9) (leggy: unf: scope: bit bkwd: sn outpcd & wl bhd: t.o ½-wy)	19	**10**	33/1	—	—
				(SP 142.6%)	**10 Rn**	

64.2 secs (2.40) CSF £87.91 TOTE £34.00: £4.00 £1.70 £3.00 (£62.50) Trio £371.30; £266.74 to 6/6/97 OWNER Drakemyre Racing (DUNS) BRED L. T. and M. Foster

IN-FOCUS: **In the past this race has proved a useful guide to the Queen Mary at Royal Ascot and twelve months ago Dance Parade followed up her victory here. This year's renewal looked decidedly sub-standard.**

1149 Filey Brigg, having her eighth outing already, landed something of a touch. There is no denying she is very willing but it is hard to know what to make of the form. (16/1)
1255* Forest Treasure (IRE), who was kept on the grass in the paddock, swerved left leaving the stalls making it even harder work from her stall two. Under pressure at halfway, she stuck on strongly towards the finish and, still inexperienced, will be seen to better advantage over six. (4/1)
1447 Angel Hill, on her toes beforehand, was tapped for foot at halfway. The way she was sticking on at the finish, she will be suited by a step up to six. (16/1)
844* Lady Moll, who is not very big, is a keen-going sort. After making the running, her stamina seemed to give out towards the finish. She will be better suited by a less stiff track and faster ground, it was well watered here. (12/1)
1457* Kilcora (IRE) confirmed her Sandown superiority over the favourite Folklore and Sada. (7/1)
1310* Heavenly Abstone, on her toes beforehand, could not go the pace. Left short of room inside the last, she is a much better filly on soft ground. (10/1)
1457 Folklore, who continually swished her tail in the paddock, showed a choppy action going down. Held up off the pace, she made a brief effort one and a half furlongs out but in truth found very little. It might be interesting to see her allowed to stride on and get on with the job. (4/7: op 10/11)
1457 Sada, who showed a good action going down, was pushed sideways at the start and finished behind Kilcora and Folklore as she had done on her debut at Sandown. (8/1)

1654 DON & RAYMOND GIBBON MEMORIAL H'CAP (0-70) (3-Y.O+) (Class E)

8-00 (8-00) **2m 35y** £3,117.50 (£935.00: £450.00: £207.50) Stalls: High GOING minus 0.24 sec per fur (GF)

				SP	RR	SF
1100[15]	**Hullbank (63)** (WWHaigh) **7-9-9** ACulhane(5) (hld up: hdwy over 5f out: chal over 1f out: hrd rdn to ld last 50y)	—	**1**	7/2[3]	74	43
1424[2]	**Romalito (42)** (MBlanshard) **7-8-2** JQuinn(2) (lw: sn trckng ldrs: effrt over 3f out: edgd rt & led 2f out: hdd towards fin)	nk	**2**	5/2[2]	53	22
1424[3]	**Paradise Navy (68)** (CREgerton) **8-10-0b** LDettori(6) (hld up: hdwy 4f out: kpt on one pce fnl 2f)	3½	**3**	2/1[1]	75	44
1232[10]	**Sushi Bar (IRE) (40)** (MrsMReveley) **6-8-0** JFanning(1) (hld up: stdy hdwy on outside over 3f out: ev ch 2f out: wknd jst ins fnl f)	½	**4**	16/1	47	16
1494[5]	**Amiarge (50)** (MBrittain) **7-8-10** JCarroll(8) (chsd ldrs: outpcd & n.m.r over 2f out: kpt on one pce)	2	**5**	8/1	55	24
1393[5]	**Junior Ben (IRE) (36)** (MESowersby) **5-7-7**(3) PFessey(3) (led to 2f out: sn wknd)	5	**6**	10/1	36	5
632[5]	**Regal Eagle (68)** (MDHammond) **4-9-13** GDuffield(9) (trckd ldrs: drvn along over 4f out: rdn over 2f out: sn wknd)	5	**7**	8/1	63	31
1452[10]	**Ship's Dancer (37)** (DonEnricoIncisa) **4-7-10b** KimTinkler(7) (hld up: effrt over 2f out: sn wknd)	7	**8**	33/1	25	—
1408[9]	**So Keen (47)** (ABailey) **4-8-6** GCarter(4) (trckd ldr: chal over 5f out: rdn & wknd over 2f out)	8	**9**	20/1	27	—
				(SP 129.0%)	**9 Rn**	

3m 40.0 (9.50) CSF £13.16 CT £21.58 TOTE £5.50: £1.40 £1.90 £1.30 (£8.80) Trio £8.40 OWNER Mrs P. Gibbon (MALTON) BRED D. Gibbon
LONG HANDICAP Ship's Dancer 7-3
WEIGHT FOR AGE 4yo-1lb
OFFICIAL EXPLANATION **Hullbank: regarding the improvement in form, the gelding had been unsuited by the ground and had needed the run last time.**

Hullbank likes it round here and likes to hear his hooves rattle. Given a patient ride, he did just enough to run out a narrow but highly appropriate winner of this event. (7/2)
1424 Romalito, who has only won once from forty-six outings, dived right when he hit the front and in the end found the winner too tough. (5/2)
1424 Paradise Navy was never doing enough. A reluctant hero, he seems to reserve his best for when Richard Hughes is in the saddle. (2/1)
Sushi Bar (IRE), who has had his fore-legs fired, has slipped down the weights. He came there looking a real danger but, under pressure, pulled out very little. (16/1)
1494 Amiarge, short of room early in the straight, was sticking on at the finish and prefers extreme distances. (8/1)

1655 RACING PAGES H'CAP (0-70) (3-Y.O+) (Class E)

8-30 (8-30) **7f 100y** £3,163.00 (£949.00: £457.00: £211.00) Stalls: High GOING minus 0.24 sec per fur (GF)

				SP	RR	SF
1511[5]	**Java Red (IRE) (44)** (JGFitzGerald) **5-8-2b1** JQuinn(7) (b: lw: sn bhd: effrt u.p 2f out: styd on wl to ld last 50y)	—	**1**	5/1	49	39
1433[5]	**Legal Issue (IRE) (55)** (WWHaigh) **5-8-13** RLappin(2) (lw: trckd ldrs: effrt over 2f out: led jst ins fnl f: hdd nr fin)	1	**2**	7/2[2]	58	48
1448[9]	**Oriel Lad (38)** (DonEnricoIncisa) **4-7-10b** KimTinkler(5) (sn wl bhd: hdwy 2f out: styd on wl towards fin)	s.h	**3**	20/1	41	31

1448[2] **Dispol Diamond (52)** (GROldroyd) **4-8-10** KDarley(6) (sn trckng ldrs: rdn over 2f out: led & edgd rt over 1f out: hdd jst ins fnl f: one pce) 1¼ **4** 9/2 52 42
1511[10] **Euro Sceptic (IRE) (42)** (TDEasterby) **5-7-7b**(7) RWinston(8) (lw: trckd ldrs: hdwy on ins 2f out: styng whn hmpd jst ins fnl f) ....¾ **5** 4/1[3] 41 31
1471[4] **Mountgate (68)** (MPBielby) **5-9-12** DeanMcKeown(3) (led tl over 1f out: sn wknd) ....2 **6** 3/1[1] 62 52
1225[5] **Sihafi (USA) (53)** (JMCarr) **4-8-11** PBloomfield(4) (hld up & plld hrd: drvn along over 3f out: no imp) 1¼ **7** 10/1 45 35
1315[11] **Martindale (IRE) (50)** (RBastiman) **4-8-8** RHills(1) (w ldr tl wknd qckly over 1f out) 7 **8** 12/1 27 17
(SP 123.6%) **8 Rn**

1m 34.6 (2.60) CSF £22.69 CT £306.23 TOTE £5.10: £1.60 £1.60 £5.80 (£10.30) OWNER Mr M. Ng (MALTON) BRED Rathasker Stud
LONG HANDICAP Oriel Lad 7-8
1511 Java Red (IRE), in blinkers for the first time, came from off the pace in a strongly-run race. (5/1)
1433 Legal Issue (IRE) travelled strongly but, after hitting the front just inside the last, was worn down near the line. (7/2)
Oriel Lad came from out of the wilderness. Soon well behind in a strongly-run race, he was staying on best of all at the finish. (20/1)
1448 Dispol Diamond edged right as she hit the front, closing the door on Euro Sceptic on her inside. (9/2)
1511 Euro Sceptic (IRE), who has slipped down the weights, chose to make his effort on the inside. He was staying on when squeezed out just inside the final furlong, but would probably only have finished fourth at best. (4/1)
1471 Mountgate, as usual, gave a problem or two going to the start and he is clearly something of a character. (3/1)
1225 Sihafi (USA) (10/1: 8/1-12/1)
795 Martindale (IRE) (12/1: op 8/1)

1656 EDWIN STARR NIGHT MAIDEN STKS (3-Y.O+) (Class D)
9-00 (9-01) **7f 100y** £3,535.00 (£1,060.00: £510.00: £235.00) Stalls: High GOING minus 0.24 sec per fur (GF)

SP RR SF
1207[3] **Generous Libra** (DRLoder) **3-8-11** LDettori(4) (trckd ldr: shkn up: hung rt & led wl over 1f out: pushed clr fnl f: eased towards fin) ....— **1** 1/5[1] 94+ 55
1316[5] **Alikhlas (83)** (MajorWRHern) **3-8-6** RHills(2) (trckd ldrs: effrt & ev ch over 1f out: kpt on same pce) ....8 **2** 13/2[2] 72 33
793[7] **Forest Signal** (MBrittain) **3-8-11** JCarroll(3) (sn outpcd: sme hdwy over 3f out: kpt on fnl 2f: nvr nr ldrs) 8 **3** 14/1 60 21
1130[6] **Speedboat (USA)** (JLEyre) **3-8-11** DeanMcKeown(5) (plld v.hrd: led & sn clr: wknd & hdd wl over 1f out) ....5 **4** 7/1[3] 49 10
1221[12] **Chief Connections** (MPBielby) **4-9-7** ACulhane(1) (unruly in stalls: dwlt: sn wl bhd) 5 **5** 66/1 38 9
(SP 117.3%) **5 Rn**

1m 33.9 (1.90) CSF £2.44 TOTE £1.10: £1.20 £1.20 (£1.60) OWNER Mr Wafic Said (NEWMARKET) BRED Addison Racing Ltd Inc
WEIGHT FOR AGE 3yo-10lb
1207 Generous Libra has plenty of ability but also a fair degree of temperament. After giving a problem or two at the start, he carried his head high and at an awkward angle but in the end proved far too much for this very moderate lot. (1/5)
1316 Alikhlas, who is not very big, got on to the winner's quarters over a furlong out but was then left for dead. (13/2: 4/1-7/1)
Forest Signal, who was well beaten in a claimer on his debut, still has plenty to learn. (14/1: 33/1-50/1)
1130 Speedboat (USA), taken to post early, ran away in front and gave his rider steering problems. It was no surprise to see him fall in a heap with two furlongs left to run. Connections must now be tempted to try him in a sprint on a straight track and to just let him get on with it. (7/1)

T/Plpt: £347.10 (29.08 Tckts). T/Qdpt: £23.10 (34.64 Tckts) WG

1031-CHESTER (L-H) (Good to firm)
Wednesday June 4th
WEATHER: fine and sunny WIND: slight behind

1657 BRYMAU ESTATES MAIDEN STKS (2-Y.O) (Class D)
6-40 (6-43) **5f 16y** £3,649.00 (£1,102.00: £536.00: £253.00) Stalls: Low GOING minus 0.27 sec per fur (GF)

SP RR SF
1425[2] **Yorkies Boy** (BAMcMahon) **2-9-0** LNewton(5) (mde all: drvn clr appr fnl f: comf) ....— **1** 5/1[3] 76+ 41
Iris May (JBerry) **2-8-4**(5) TEDurcan(9) (lt-f: sn chsng wnr: rdn over 1f out: r.o one pce) ....2½ **2** 5/1[3] 63 28
Jimmy Too (BAMcMahon) **2-9-0** MWigham(6) (unf: scope: bkwd: a.p: rdn over 1f out: one pce) 1 **3** 14/1 65 30
1425[3] **Great Lyth Lass (IRE)** (PDEvans) **2-8-9** JFEgan(4) (chsd ldrs: n.m.r ent st: sn rdn: no imp) ....¾ **4** 3/1[1] 58 23
1447[10] **Allmaites** (DNicholls) **2-8-9**(5) IonaWands(3) (bit bkwd: prom tl rdn & outpcd appr fnl f) 2½ **5** 25/1 55 20
Chasetown Cailin (RHollinshead) **2-8-9** PatEddery(8) (small: lt-f: trckd ldrs: effrt 2f out: nt pce to chal) 3 **6** 11/2 40 5
Gorgeous (NPLittmoden) **2-8-9** TGMcLaughlin(1) (lt-f: unf: s.s: sn wl outpcd: a bhd) 1½ **7** 8/1 36 1
Dernier Croise (FR) (BJMeehan) **2-9-0** PaulEddery(7) (lt-f: chsd ldrs 2f: sn pushed along & outpcd) ....¾ **8** 9/2[2] 38 3
Mister Damask (EJAlston) **2-9-0** MRimmer(2) (wl grwn: bkwd: s.s: a outpcd: t.o) ....5 **9** 20/1 22 —
(SP 118.3%) **9 Rn**

62.27 secs (2.07) CSF £28.23 TOTE £4.90: £1.60 £2.00 £4.10 (£15.80) Trio £32.80 OWNER Mrs M. Beddis (TAMWORTH) BRED J. and Mrs M. Beddis
1425 Yorkies Boy put his previous experience to good use and adopted the choice tactics on this track with a clear-cut success. (5/1)
Iris May, an early May foal, did well from an outside stall and, although out-battled in the closing stages, she can only improve with this experience under her belt. (5/1: op 3/1)
Jimmy Too, an unfurnished half-brother to Princess Efisio and too backward to do himself justice, was also very green so this promising effort behind his stablemate should be a sign of better things to come. (14/1)
1425 Great Lyth Lass (IRE), a very lightly-made filly who could need time to strengthen, finished further behind the winner than she did on her debut, and that was probably due to the fact that she was tightened up and short of space on the entrance to the straight. (3/1)
Allmaites showed more pace than he did on his debut but he had kept nothing in hand and was treading ground on the run to the final furlong. (25/1)
Chasetown Cailin is hardly bred for sprinting and, after clinging on to the tail-end of the leaders, she was made to look slow when the battle to the finish really got underway. (11/2: 4/1-6/1)
Gorgeous (8/1: op 5/1)

1658 NWS BANK H'CAP (0-95) (3-Y.O+) (Class C)
7-10 (7-12) **7f 2y** £8,481.00 (£2,568.00: £1,254.00: £597.00) Stalls: Low GOING minus 0.27 sec per fur (GF)

SP RR SF
1324[12] **Albert The Bear (84)** (JBerry) **4-8-13**(5) TEDurcan(12) (hdwy over 4f out: led 2f out: swtchd lft & hld on gamely) ....— **1** 14/1 93 69

				SP	RR	SF
1170[3]	**Nomore Mr Niceguy (86)** (EJAlston) **3-8-10** JFortune(4) (lw: a.p: hrd rdn to chal ins fnl f: no ex cl home)	nk	**2**	7/1[3]	94	60
1176[10]	**Van Gurp (83)** (BAMcMahon) **4-9-3** MRoberts(3) (swtg: bhd & outpcd: hdwy wl over 1f out: fin wl)	2	**3**	33/1	87	63
1489[2]	**Stoppes Brow (72)** (GLMoore) **5-8-6v** CandyMorris(11) (lw: hdwy 3f out: kpt on fnl f: nt pce to chal)	½	**4**	9/1	75	51
1561*	**Gadge (78)** (ABailey) **6-8-12** 6x DWright(8) (b: chsd ldr: led 4f out to 2f out: rdn & n.m.r over 1f out: one pce)	s.h	**5**	9/4[1]	81	57
1214[5]	**Chickawicka (IRE) (90)** (BPalling) **6-9-10** TSprake(7) (lw: led 3f: rdn & outpcd over 2f out: n.d after)	3	**6**	11/1	86	62
1511[9]	**Myttons Mistake (62)** (ABailey) **4-7-5**(5) IonaWands(2) (hdwy ½-wy: rdn over 1f out: r.o one pce)	nk	**7**	25/1	57	33
1035[7]	**Sualtach (IRE) (75)** (RHollinshead) **4-8-9** PatEddery(5) (nvr gng pce of ldrs)	2½	**8**	12/1	64	40
1489[10]	**Knobbleeneeze (75)** (MRChannon) **7-8-6v**(3) PPMurphy(6) (chsd ldrs 5f: sn drvn along & wknd)	hd	**9**	8/1	64	40
1442[5]	**Iblis (IRE) (85)** (GWragg) **5-9-5** PaulEddery(13) (lw: s.s: swtchd lft sn after s: a in rr)	s.h	**10**	12/1	74	50
1032[3]	**Teofilio (IRE) (94)** (DRLoder) **3-9-4** DRMcCabe(1) (lw: sn pushed along: a bhd)	5	**11**	5/1[2]	72	38
1175[9]	**I Can't Remember (76)** (PDEvans) **3-8-0** JFEgan(9) (trckd ldrs: pushed along 3f out: sn lost tch)	s.h	**12**	16/1	53	19
1300[8]	**Defined Feature (IRE) (77)** (DrJDScargill) **4-8-11b[1]** MRimmer(10) (lw: chsd ldrs to ½-wy: sn lost pl: t.o)	12	**13**	33/1	27	3

(SP 127.0%) **13 Rn**

1m 26.12 (0.92) CSF £103.67 CT £3,027.86 TOTE £14.20: £3.20 £1.70 £8.90 (£46.80) Trio £447.60 OWNER Mr Chris Deuters (COCKERHAM) BRED Rockhouse Farms Ltd

WEIGHT FOR AGE 3yo-10lb

OFFICIAL EXPLANATION **Teofilio (IRE): choked**

1035* Albert The Bear finds all conditions alike and, continuing his love affair with this track, readily dug deep to withstand the determined late rally of the runner-up. (14/1)

1170 Nomore Mr Niceguy is running extremely well this term but he is not enjoying the best of fortune and, though he ran his heart out against these older rivals, could do no more in the dying strides. (7/1)

775 Van Gurp, taken off his legs in the early exchanges on this step down to seven furlongs, did a lot of running in the latter stages to reach his final placing and, to come from behind on this track in a field of this size, it is doubtful if he did enjoy a clear passage. (33/1)

1489 Stoppes Brow acts well on such a tight track and he did not fail for the want of trying, but an extra burst of speed was missing in a frenzied battle to the post. (9/1: 5/1-10/1)

1561* Gadge has taken all before him in the past month or so but he has been steadily rising in the weights and, though he was being squeezed for room below the distance, looked at the time to have met his match. (9/4)

1214 Chickawicka (IRE) lost out in his attempt to force the pace after three furlongs and, though he did keep plugging away, was fighting a lost cause from the turn for home. (11/1)

1442 Iblis (IRE) (12/1: op 8/1)

1659 BODFARI STUD CONDITIONS STKS (4-Y.O+) (Class C)

7-40 (7-40) **1m 4f 66y** £6,356.00 (£1,764.00) Stalls: Low GOING minus 0.27 sec per fur (GF)

				SP	RR	SF
	Maralinga (IRE) (97) (LadyHerries) **5-9-3** PaulEddery(2) (mde all: drew clr fnl 3f: unchal)	—	**1**	4/7[1]	91?	44
	Night Watch (USA) (IABalding) **4-8-11** PatEddery(1) (bit bkwd: stdd s: pushed along 5f out: wknd 3f out: eased appr fnl f)	18	**2**	11/8[2]	62	15

(SP 105.7%) **2 Rn**

2m 41.74 (5.54) TOTE £1.40: OWNER Mr D K R & Mrs J B C Oliver (LITTLEHAMPTON) BRED W. H. Elliott

Maralinga (IRE) did look the more forward of the pair although they were both making their seasonal debut and, making sure it was a true-run race, had the measure of his rival inside the last half-mile. (4/7)

Night Watch (USA), a useful two-year-old who looked set to go places, did not run at all last year and, though he had obviously done plenty of work, there is nothing like a race to put an edge on and that was the one thing missing here. (11/8)

1660 PAT WHELAN H'CAP (0-80) (3-Y.O+) (Class D)

8-10 (8-10) **1m 2f 75y** £3,473.50 (£1,048.00: £509.00: £239.50) Stalls: High GOING minus 0.27 sec per fur (GF)

				SP	RR	SF
1244[5]	**Bay of Islands (75)** (DMorris) **5-9-11** NDay(1) (a.p: led on bit over 3f out: clr ent fnl f: r.o wl)	—	**1**	4/1[2]	87	59
1414[2]	**Quiet Arch (IRE) (67)** (WRMuir) **4-9-3** MRoberts(5) (lw: bhd: hdwy over 2f out: rdn & r.o wl ins fnl f)	3	**2**	5/1	74	46
1393*	**Road Racer (IRE) (61)** (MrsJRRamsden) **4-8-11** JFortune(3) (lw: hld up: gd hdwy over 2f out: rdn appr fnl f: nvr able to chal)	nk	**3**	3/1[1]	68	40
*1135**	**Queens Stroller (IRE) (46)** (REPeacock) **6-7-5**(5) JBramhill(8) (prom tl outpcd over 2f out: rallied u.p ins fnl f)	¾	**4**	20/1	52	24
1281[3]	**Ambidextrous (IRE) (46)** (EJAlston) **5-7-10** DWright(6) (lw: bhd: hdwy 5f out: hrd drvn over 2f out: one pce)	½	**5**	7/1	51	23
1291[12]	**Scenicris (IRE) (62)** (RHollinshead) **4-8-12** PatEddery(7) (lw: hld up: hdwy 3f out: rdn wl over 1f out: sn btn)	5	**6**	16/1	59	31
1278[2]	**Rasayel (USA) (74)** (PDEvans) **7-9-10** JFEgan(2) (lw: prom tl hrd rdn & outpcd over 2f out)	4	**7**	9/2[3]	65	37
1231[9]	**Northern Fan (IRE) (60)** (NTinkler) **5-8-10** LCharnock(4) (led over 6f: sn hrd drvn: wknd fnl 2f: t.o)	5	**8**	16/1	43	15
1287[3]	**Evezio Rufo (48)** (NPLittmoden) **5-7-7v**(5) RFfrench(9) (outpcd: a bhd: t.o)	1	**9**	14/1	30	2

(SP 115.5%) **9 Rn**

2m 12.28 (3.58) CSF £22.18 CT £61.63 TOTE £6.60: £1.60 £2.40 £1.90 (£21.40) Trio £33.00 OWNER Bloomsbury Stud (NEWMARKET) BRED Bloomsbury Stud

LONG HANDICAP Queens Stroller (IRE) 7-2

1244 Bay of Islands, well supported despite top weight, won this with quite a bit in hand and, with his stable now striking form, a follow-up is very much on the cards. (4/1)

1414 Quiet Arch (IRE), possibly much better when he can get his toe in, did not find top gear until far too late and, by then, the winner was home and dried. (5/1)

1393* Road Racer (IRE) had more to do here on this step back to ten furlongs, but he was in hot pursuit of the winner entering the final furlong before having to admit his measure taken. (3/1)

1135* Queens Stroller (IRE) lost her pitch when the tempo lifted on the approach to the straight but she renewed her challenge once in line for home, and is on good terms with herself. (20/1)

1281 Ambidextrous (IRE) finds this trip on such a sharp track inadequate and he could never get in a blow against the principals. (7/1)

125 Scenicris (IRE), poised to challenge on straightening up, seemed to find this trip just too far and, as she has shown a preference for more cut in the ground, she could be worth watching in a mile event on the All-Weather. (16/1)

1661 DENTON CLARKE & CO. CLAIMING STKS (3-Y.O) (Class D)

8-40 (8-41) **6f 18y** £3,551.50 (£1,072.00: £521.00: £245.50) Stalls: Low GOING minus 0.27 sec per fur (GF)

				SP	RR	SF
1175[12]	**Caution (80)** (MrsJRRamsden) **3-8-11** JFortune(1) (lw: s.i.s: hdwy ½-wy: led wl over 1f out: hrd rdn: all out)	—	**1**	5/2[1]	76	51

1573[3] **C-Harry (IRE) (60)** (RHollinshead) **3-8-12** MWigham(2) (hld up: hdwy over 2f out: jnd wnr ent fnl f: hrd rdn: r.o wl) ....s.h **2** 12/1 77 52
1468[10] **Bayford Thrust (86)** (JBerry) **3-8-7**(5) TEDurcan(9) (b: b.hind: dwlt: hdwy on ins over 2f out: hrd drvn ent fnl f: one pce) 2½ **3** 8/1 70 45
1573[2] **Municipal Girl (IRE) (52)** (BPalling) **3-8-2** TSprake(3) (a.p: hrd drvn & c wd st: kpt on one pce) 4 **4** 9/1 50 25
1141[8] **Farewell My Love (IRE) (72)** (PFICole) **3-8-13** MRimmer(5) (lw: prom: hrd drvn wl over 1f out: one pce)....1¾ **5** 5/1[3] 56 31
Davis Rock (66) (WRMuir) **3-8-12**(7) JWilkinson(6) (h.d.w: bhd & outpcd: hdwy & hmpd wl over 1f out: r.o wl towards fin)....1½ **6** 25/1 58 33
1272[11] **Joyful Joy (39)** (BPJBaugh) **3-7-6**(5) IonaWands(4) (swtg: outpcd) 3 **7** 50/1 28 3
1029[8] **Weet Ees Girl (IRE) (67)** (PDEvans) **3-8-1** JFEgan(10) (sn outpcd: btn whn carried lft ins fnl f)....nk **8** 8/1 32 7
1008[3] **Siouxrouge (74)** (PCHaslam) **3-8-5b**[1](5) RFfrench(7) (swtg: led: clr ½-wy: rdn, hdd & rn wd ent st: sn btn)...3½ **9** 9/2[2] 31 6
1496[8] **Chilling (49)** (NTinkler) **3-7-13b** LCharnock(8) (s.i.s: sn chsng ldrs: rdn & wknd wl over 1f out: t.o)....8 **10** 12/1 — —

(SP 116.8%) **10 Rn**

1m 14.89 (1.59) CSF £31.83 TOTE £2.90: £1.50 £2.90 £2.60 (£17.30) Trio £54.60 OWNER L C and A E Sigsworth (THIRSK) BRED L. C. and Mrs A. E. Sigsworth

Caution needed to show all her true grit on this return to sprinting for she had a head-to-head with the runner-up throughout the final furlong and neither was prepared to give an inch. (5/2)
1573 C-Harry (IRE) would have preferred slightly easier ground but he gave it all he had got and, had he had the rail to race against like the winner, the verdict would have gone his way. He is a winner without a penalty. (12/1)
Bayford Thrust, showing a return to form, did well to put himself in with every chance after missing a beat at the start but he was stuck in behind the leading pair with nowhere to go approaching the final furlong and had to accept the position. (8/1: op 4/1)
1573 Municipal Girl (IRE), inclined to forfeit ground when she failed to handle the bend into the straight, did her best to rally under pressure but the task was always beyond her. (9/1: op 6/1)
904 Farewell My Love (IRE) is gradually coming to herself and she should be able to find an opening in the near future. (5/1)
Davis Rock, making a belated seasonal reappearance, is not an impressive mover on turf, but she was into her stride in the closing stages after getting hopelessly outpaced and she has certainly not lost any of her ability. (25/1)
731 Weet Ees Girl (IRE) (8/1: op 5/1)
1008 Siouxrouge (9/2: op 3/1)
1496 Chilling (12/1: op 8/1)

1662 SWETTENHAM STUD H'CAP (0-85) (3-Y.O+) (Class D)

9-10 (9-11) **5f 16y** £4,123.50 (£1,248.00: £609.00: £289.50) Stalls: Low GOING minus 0.27 sec per fur (GF)

SP RR SF

1269[11] **Ziggy's Dancer (USA) (81)** (EJAlston) **6-9-12** JFEgan(6) (hld up: led 1f out: rdn & r.o strly)....— **1** 5/1[3] 88 63
1439[7] **Palo Blanco (73)** (GLMoore) **6-9-4** CandyMorris(3) (lw: chsd ldrs: rdn over 1f out: r.o wl towards fin)....nk **2** 12/1 79 54
977[11] **The Wad (61)** (DNicholls) **4-8-1**(5) IonaWands(1) (lw: mde most 4f: kpt on u.p fnl f) ....¾ **3** 16/1 65 40
1250[9] **Beau Venture (USA) (67)** (BPalling) **9-8-12** TSprake(5) (a.p: disp ld ent st tl no ex wl ins fnl f) ....¾ **4** 15/2 68 43
1402[7] **U-No-Harry (IRE) (66)** (RHollinshead) **4-8-11** MWigham(2) (s.i.s: bhd: hdwy whn hmpd over 1f out: nt rcvr) ..hd **5** 8/1 67 42
1627[3] **Insider Trader (63)** (MrsJRRamsden) **6-8-8** JFortune(7) (lw: s.i.s: bhd: effrt wl over 1f out: no imp)....nk **6** 11/4[1] 63 38
1578[4] **The Happy Fox (IRE) (74)** (BAMcMahon) **5-9-5b** MRoberts(8) (sn pushed along: trckd ldrs over 3f) 4 **7** 6/1 61 36
854[10] **Bilko (85)** (GLewis) **3-9-9** PaulEddery(4) (disp ld over 3f: sn wknd & eased)....2 **8** 7/2[2] 66 34

(SP 116.3%) **8 Rn**

61.59 secs (1.39) CSF £57.13 CT £820.65 TOTE £5.00: £1.60 £3.80 £3.30 (£59.00) OWNER Mr John Patrick Barry (PRESTON) BRED Warren W. Rosenthal

WEIGHT FOR AGE 3yo-7lb

905 Ziggy's Dancer (USA) has failed to trouble the judge since December 1995, but he was back on song here and, surging through to nose ahead entering the final furlong, had to pull out all the stops to hold on in the dying strides. (5/1)
1127 Palo Blanco, who has moved south recently to join her present stable, delivered a determined late challenge up the inside rail and only just failed to peg back the winner. Possibly better suited by six furlongs now, she looks a ready-made winner. (12/1)
The Wad has yet to succeed at this minimum trip but he ran a fine race in defeat and an early return to form is ear-marked. (16/1)
604* Beau Venture (USA), fighting for supremacy all the way, had to admit younger rivals had the legs of him in the sprint to the line. (15/2)
U-No-Harry (IRE) was undoubtedly the unlucky one, for he was into his stride and closing down on the leaders when Palo Blanco edged in front of him below the distance and, though he did rally inside the final furlong, the damage had been done. This is his time of year and losses can soon be recovered. (8/1)
1627 Insider Trader has had a busy time of it of late but he has not won a race since this time last year, and to find excuses can sometimes prove costly. (11/4)

T/Plpt: £510.40 (33.49 Tckts). T/Qdpt: £34.80 (28.35 Tckts) IM

1479-FOLKESTONE (R-H) (Good to firm)
Wednesday June 4th

WEATHER: fair WIND: mod across

1663 PEDLINGE AMATEUR LIMITED STKS (0-70) (3-Y.O+) (Class F)

6-20 (6-20) **6f 189y** £2,484.90 (£686.40: £326.70) Stalls: Low GOING minus 0.16 sec per fur (GF)

SP RR SF

1599[2] **Marjaana (IRE) (68)** (PTWalwyn) **4-10-8**(5) MissSSamworth(4) (lw: chsd ldr: led 3f out: r.o wl) ....— **1** 7/4[1] 80 62
1495[8] **Takhlid (USA) (70)** (DWChapman) **6-11-4** MissRClark(2) (hld up: chsd wnr over 2f out: no imp) ....2 **2** 3/1[3] 80 62
1436[2] **Kewarra (70)** (BRMillman) **3-10-4** MrLJefford(1) (lw: hdwy over 2f out: wandered over 1f out: one pce)....1¼ **3** 9/4[2] 73 45
873[9] **Muscatana (66)** (BWHills) **3-10-0**(5)ow2 MrCBHills(6) (bhd fnl 2f) 6 **4** 7/1 60 30
1599[8] **Spectacle Jim (42)** (BAPearce) **8-10-9**(5) MrsKHills(3) (prom 4f)....9 **5** 40/1 38 20
1575[9] **Sarum (35)** (JELong) **11-10-9**(5) MrTWaters(5) (b: led over 3f) 1 **6** 50/1 36 18

(SP 109.0%) **6 Rn**

1m 25.5 (4.10) CSF £6.27 TOTE £1.90: £1.10 £2.20 (£5.10) OWNER Mrs D. C. Samworth (LAMBOURN) BRED Shadwell Estate Company Limited

WEIGHT FOR AGE 3yo-10lb

1599 Marjaana (IRE) seems to go particularly well for her rider, even though she received little assistance. Sent to the front three furlongs from home, the combination kept on too well for their rivals. (7/4)

1495 Takhlid (USA) gave a good account of himself but, despite moving into second place over a quarter of a mile from home, was unable to reel in the winner. (3/1)
1436 Kewarra, who seemed suited by the step up to a mile at Chepstow last week, was reverting back to seven furlongs and failed to quicken in the short home-straight. A return to a mile is needed. (9/4)

1664 E.B.F. HYTHE MAIDEN STKS (2-Y.O F) (Class D)
6-50 (6-52) **6f** £3,287.60 (£981.80: £469.40: £213.20) Stalls: Low GOING minus 0.16 sec per fur (GF)

				SP	RR	SF
1457^{9}	**Ffestiniog (IRE)** (PFICole) **2-8-11** TQuinn(1) (mde all: qcknd over 2f out: r.o wl)	—	**1**	9/2^{2}	77	23
1440^{4}	**First Dance** (RHannon) **2-8-11** DaneO'Neill(5) (a.p: rdn over 2f out: chsd wnr over 1f out: no imp)	2½	**2**	9/2^{2}	70	16
1386^{2}	**Muftuffenuf** (PRWebber) **2-8-11** RPerham(2) (lw: chsd wnr over 4f: one pce)	1½	**3**	Evens^{1}	66	12
1440^{6}	**Mrs Middle** (NACallaghan) **2-8-11** SDrowne(7) (hld up: rdn over 2f out: one pce)	hd	**4**	8/1^{3}	66	12
1286^{2}	**Flickan** (RGuest) **2-8-8**(3) DGriffiths(6) (a.p: rdn over 2f out: one pce)	hd	**5**	8/1^{3}	66	12
828^{14}	**After Dawn (IRE)** (MrsPNDutfield) **2-8-6**(5) AimeeCook(4) (nvr nr to chal)	1¾	**6**	50/1	61	7
	Make It So (JSMoore) **2-8-11** WJO'Connor(3) (unf: bit bkwd: prom over 2f)	20	**7**	33/1	8	—
				(SP 113.5%)	**7 Rn**	

1m 14.4 (4.20) CSF £22.26 TOTE £4.30: £2.00 £1.80 (£9.10) OWNER Elite Racing Club (WHATCOMBE) BRED Theo Waddington
Ffestiniog (IRE) knew more about the game this time and, making every post a winning one, quickened away from her rivals soon after halfway for a cosy victory. (9/2: 7/4-5/1)
1440 First Dance struggled into second place over a furlong out but had little hope of getting near the winner. She is certainly one of the stable's lesser likes. (9/2: 3/1-5/1)
1386 Muftuffenuf looked in good shape beforehand and was all the rage in the market. However, once the winner quickened away over a quarter of a mile from home, the writing was soon on the wall. (Evens)
1440 Mrs Middle is only lightly-made and could only go up and down in the same place in the last two furlongs. (8/1: 6/1-12/1)
1286 Flickan, making her turf debut, was never far away but could only struggle on in her own time in the final quarter-mile. (8/1: 6/1-9/1)

1665 BROADSTAIRS H'CAP (0-65) (3-Y.O+) (Class F)
7-20 (7-24) **2m 93y** £2,692.80 (£745.80: £356.40) Stalls: Low GOING minus 0.16 sec per fur (GF)

				SP	RR	SF
1424^{4}	**Landlord (48)** (PBowen) **5-8-11b** MFenton(6) (lw: mde all: rdn out)	—	**1**	11/2^{2}	59	31
381^{6}	**Matthias Mystique (55)** (MissBSanders) **4-9-3** DaneO'Neill(9) (hdwy 7f out: rdn over 2f out: chsd wnr over 1f out: r.o)	½	**2**	12/1	66	37
1010^{3}	**Duncombe Hall (39)** (CACyzer) **4-7-12**(3) AWhelan(7) (hld up: rdn over 2f out: r.o)	nk	**3**	7/1	49	20
1441^{3}	**Action Jackson (50)** (BJMcMath) **5-8-13** TQuinn(4) (chsd wnr tl over 1f out: unable qckn)	3	**4**	8/1	57	29
1424^{6}	**Coleridge (40)** (JJSheehan) **9-8-3b** SDrowne(8) (a.p: rdn over 2f out: one pce)	s.h	**5**	6/1^{3}	47	19
	Pleasureland (IRE) (60) (RCurtis) **4-9-8** GBardwell(10) (lw: rdn over 8f out: hdwy over 2f out: one pce)	5	**6**	6/1^{3}	62	33
1260^{7}	**Spring Marathon (USA) (65)** (MrsPNDutfield) **7-9-9**(5) AimeeCook(1) (nvr nrr)	8	**7**	33/1	60	32
1114^{9}	**Ginka (33)** (JWMullins) **6-7-10** NVarley(5) (lw: bhd fnl 9f)	½	**8**	11/1	27	—
324^{6}	**Chez Catalan (45)** (RAkehurst) **6-8-8b** RPerham(11) (lw: prom over 9f)	hd	**9**	12/1	39	11
1507^{6}	**Kirov Protege (IRE) (33)** (MrsLCJewell) **5-7-3**(7) DarrenWilliams(3) (hdwy 7f out: wknd over 3f out)	5	**10**	40/1	22	—
1478^{6}	**Veronica Franco (43)** (RIngram) **4-8-5** DeclanO'Shea(2) (hld up: rdn over 2f out: sn wknd)	nk	**11**	9/2^{1}	32	3
				(SP 114.8%)	**11 Rn**	

3m 41.0 (11.00) CSF £61.90 CT £424.92 TOTE £4.20: £2.70 £3.80 £2.30 (£21.50) Trio £81.60 OWNER Mrs J. E. Hawkins (HAVERFORD-WEST) BRED Fonthill Stud and Philip Wroughton
LONG HANDICAP Kirov Protege (IRE) 7-5
WEIGHT FOR AGE 4yo-1lb
1424 Landlord confirmed the promise shown at Warwick recently. Serving it up to his rivals, he made it all and was nudged along to maintain his superiority in the straight. (11/2: 4/1-6/1)
381 Matthias Mystique, given a three-month break, moved into second place over a furlong out but, despite staying on, never looked like overhauling the winner in time. She has yet to win on grass. (12/1: 8/1-14/1)
1010 Duncombe Hall kept on in the final furlong and only just lost out in the battle for second prize. He remains a maiden. (7/1)
1441 Action Jackson, whose two wins to date have both come in mile and a quarter sellers, coped with this longer trip and raced in second place until over a furlong from home. A drop in class would help. (8/1)
1424 Coleridge continues to fall in the handicap but is still unable to take advantage of it. (6/1: op 10/1)
Pleasureland (IRE), who showed himself to be a useful staying novice hurdler this winter, was being shoved along for the majority of the final circuit and could never make his presence felt. (6/1: op 4/1)
603 Ginka (11/1: 7/1-12/1)
93 Chez Catalan (12/1: op 20/1)

1666 ROMNEY MARSH H'CAP (0-70) (3-Y.O+) (Class E)
7-50 (7-56) **6f** £3,148.25 (£941.00: £450.50: £205.25) Stalls: Low GOING minus 0.16 sec per fur (GF)

				SP	RR	SF
1279^{6}	**Rockcracker (IRE) (48)** (GGMargarson) **5-8-6b** GBardwell(6) (hdwy over 2f out: led wl over 1f out: hrd rdn: r.o wl)	—	**1**	13/2	57	40
1485^{7}	**Peter Perfect (54)** (GLewis) **3-8-1b**(3) AWhelan(3) (a.p: rdn over 3f out: r.o one pce)	3	**2**	16/1	55	30
	Texas Cowgirl (IRE) (57) (HVanderdussen,Belgium) **7-8-8b**(7) SMaertens(9) (s.s: swtchd far side: hld up: rdn over 1f out: ev ch ins fnl f: one pce)	s.h	**3**	10/1	58	41
1225^{12}	**Mousehole (70)** (RGuest) **5-9-11**(3) DGriffiths(11) (hld up: rdn over 2f out: ev ch over 1f out: one pce)	½	**4**	11/2^{3}	70	53
883^{9}	**Robec Girl (IRE) (59)** (KMcAuliffe) **3-8-9v^{1}** WJO'Connor(4) (led over 4f)	3	**5**	12/1	51	26
	Always Grace (60) (MissGayKelleway) **5-9-4** DaneO'Neill(1) (s.s: hdwy & nt clr run 2f out: nvr nrr)	hd	**6**	9/1	51	34
1410^{2}	**Willow Dale (IRE) (70)** (DRCElsworth) **4-10-0** RHughes(14) (racd far side: a.p: rdn over 2f out: ev ch over 1f out: wknd fnl f)	3	**7**	4/1^{1}	53	36
	Waders Dream (IRE) (47) (PatMitchell) **8-8-5v** MFenton(13) (lw: s.s: outpcd: nvr nrr)	nk	**8**	16/1	30	13
1077^{8}	**Indian Serenade (38)** (RSimpson) **6-7-3**(7) JFowle(8) (prom over 2f)	1¾	**9**	33/1	16	—
1446^{2}	**Ed's Folly (IRE) (51)** (SDow) **4-8-4**(5) ADaly(12) (lw: racd centre: hld up: rdn over 2f out: wknd over 1f out)	½	**10**	5/1^{2}	28	11
1428^{2}	**Delrob (39)** (DHaydnJones) **6-7-11b** FNorton(10) (prom over 4f)	1¼	**11**	8/1	12	—
1003^{12}	**May Queen Megan (52)** (MrsALMKing) **4-8-10** AGarth(2) (lw: a bhd)	1¾	**12**	20/1	21	4
1385^{9}	**Shavinsky (60)** (PHowling) **4-9-4** SDrowne(7) (lw: prom 4f)	6	**13**	20/1	13	—
1439*	**Deerly (51)** (RDickin) **4-8-4**(5) 7x APolli(15) (lw: racd far side: bhd fnl 2f)	hd	**14**	5/1^{2}	3	—

			SP	RR	SF
1107^{8}	*Denbrae (IRE) (68)* (DJGMurraySmith) **5-9-12** TQuinn(5) (Withdrawn not under Starter's orders: veterinary advice)	**W**	11/2^{3}	—	—
			(SP 159.6%)	**14 Rn**	

1m 12.8 (2.60) CSF £113.99 CT £997.50 TOTE £8.40: £2.80 £5.70 £1.50 (£122.70) Trio £269.50; £132.85 to 6/6/97 OWNER Mr P. E. Axon (NEWMARKET) BRED Mrs Amanda Skiffington
LONG HANDICAP Indian Serenade 7-4
WEIGHT FOR AGE 3yo-8lb
OFFICIAL EXPLANATION **Deerly: The trainer reported that the filly was never travelling on the fast ground.**
1279 Rockcracker (IRE), who has been dropped 9lb since the beginning of the season, took full advantage of it here and, leading early in the final quarter-mile, was rousted along to prevail. This is his ground. (13/2)
Peter Perfect ran much better here. Never far away, he stayed on to take second prize but was unable to trouble the winner. (16/1)
Texas Cowgirl (IRE), a Belgian raider who won twice in her native country last year and was runner-up on her reappearance there, was one of three who elected to race on the far rails. She appeared to still have every chance inside the final furlong before tapped for toe. (10/1: 20/1-12/1)
Mousehole ran his best race so far this season and had every chance below the distance before failing to quicken. His best form last year came in blinkers. (11/2)
Robec Girl (IRE) took the field along but, collared below the distance, had little more to offer. A drop in class would help. (12/1)
Always Grace, making her seasonal debut, did not have the best of runs but could never get into it. All three of her wins to date have come over six furlongs. (9/1)
1428 Delrob (8/1: 20/1-9/1)
1439* Deerly (5/1: 4/1-6/1)

1667 HASTINGS (S) STKS (3-Y.O+) (Class G)

8-20 (8-21) **5f** £2,278.50 (£631.00: £301.50) Stalls: Low GOING minus 0.16 sec per fur (GF)

				SP	RR	SF
1566^{10}	**Littlestone Rocket (53)** (WRMuir) **3-8-10b**[1] DaneO'Neill(1) (hld up: rdn over 1f out: led ins fnl f: r.o wl)	—	**1**	8/1	61	27
1572^{8}	**Bashful Brave (60)** (BPJBaugh) **6-9-3** GHind(3) (lw: a.p: led wl over 1f out tl ins fnl f: unable qckn)	3	**2**	9/2^{3}	51	24
1566^{5}	**Mystical** (MrsLStubbs) **3-8-5v** SSanders(5) (rdn over 1f out: hdwy fnl f: r.o)	s.h	**3**	7/2^{1}	46	12
1566^{6}	**Blazing Castle (63)** (WGMTurner) **3-8-5**(5) DSweeney(4) (lw: a.p: rdn over 2f out: ev ch wl over 1f out: one pce)	¾	**4**	4/1^{2}	49	15
1236^{4}	**Tee-Emm (37)** (RSimpson) **7-9-3b** SDrowne(2) (b: led over 3f)	2	**5**	5/1	42	15
1620^{4}	**Sound the Trumpet (IRE) (50)** (RCSpicer) **5-9-0**(3) RHavlin(7) (spd over 3f)	3½	**6**	5/1	31	4
	Hinton Rock (IRE) (AlexVanderhaeghen,Belgium) **5-9-3b** MServranckx(6) (b: spd 3f)	¾	**7**	7/2^{1}	29	2
				(SP 127.1%)	**7 Rn**	

60.7 secs (3.10) CSF £44.51 TOTE £12.70: £4.70 £2.50 (£41.00) OWNER Mr J. R. Bailey (LAMBOURN) BRED Mrs S. M. Sands and Mrs D. M. Paul
WEIGHT FOR AGE 3yo-7lb
No bid
Littlestone Rocket found the application of blinkers for the first time just what the doctor ordered, and showed a nice turn of foot to lead inside the final furlong. (8/1)
Bashful Brave loves to hear his feet rattle and has gained all bar one of his wins over five furlongs. Taking a drop in class, he eased his way to the front early in the final quarter-mile, but he was unable to cope with the winner's surge early inside the final furlong. He goes particularly well here where he has gained three of his five victories and can pick up a similar event before long. (9/2: 3/1-5/1)
1566 Mystical only began to find her feet in the final furlong, by which time, it was all far too late. (7/2)
1566 Blazing Castle had every chance early in the final quarter-mile before tapped for toe. (4/1: 3/1-9/2)
1236 Tee-Emm took the field along but, collared below the distance, had little more to offer. (5/1)
1620 Sound the Trumpet (IRE), making a quick reappearance, showed up well until tiring in the last furlong and a half. One win from thirty-three starts says it all. (5/1: 4/1-6/1)

1668 DEAL H'CAP (0-70) (3-Y.O+ F & M) (Class E)

8-50 (8-50) **1m 1f 149y** £3,070.25 (£917.00: £438.50: £199.25) Stalls: Low GOING minus 0.16 sec per fur (GF)

				SP	RR	SF
1390*	**Opalette (65)** (LadyHerries) **4-9-9** WRyan(4) (hld up: chsd ldr over 1f out: hrd rdn fnl f: led last strides)	—	**1**	6/4^{1}	70	31
1373^{3}	**Passage Creeping (IRE) (64)** (SDow) **4-9-3**(5) ADaly(5) (lw: chsd ldr over 2f out: led 2f out: rdn: hdd last strides)	hd	**2**	8/1	69	30
*1086**	**Mono Lady (IRE) (55)** (DHaydnJones) **4-8-13b** AClark(7) (rdn & hdwy over 2f out: one pce)	3	**3**	4/1^{3}	55	16
1506^{2}	**Queen's Insignia (USA) (50)** (PFICole) **4-8-8** TQuinn(1) (led over 7f: wknd fnl f)	½	**4**	3/1^{2}	49	10
1503^{2}	**Isis Honda (IRE) (59)** (CEBrittain) **3-8-4** GBardwell(2) (b.hind: chsd ldr 8f out: ev ch 2f out: wknd over 1f out)	2½	**5**	6/1	54	2
1458^{13}	**Forget To Remindme (54)** (JSMoore) **3-7-8**(5) AimeeCook(6) (lw: bhd fnl 2f)	6	**6**	20/1	39	—
				(SP 115.2%)	**6 Rn**	

2m 5.1 (7.40) CSF £13.59 CT £37.16 TOTE £2.20: £1.60 £2.70 (£9.20) OWNER Angmering Park Stud (LITTLEHAMPTON) BRED Lavinia Duchess Of Norfolk
WEIGHT FOR AGE 3yo-13lb
1390* Opalette certainly made heavy weather of this and it needed Ryan to be at his very strongest to get the filly up in the last couple of strides. Ryan reported afterwards that a more galloping track would suit her. (6/4)
1373 Passage Creeping (IRE) at long last looked as if she was going to lose her maiden tag as she moved to the front a quarter of a mile from home and appeared to have the others at full stretch below the distance. However, despite doing nothing wrong, she was caught in the last couple of strides. (8/1: 5/1-10/1)
1086* Mono Lady (IRE) began a forward move turning into the straight but could then only go up and down in the same place. Three of her four wins have come on the All-Weather. (4/1)
1506 Queen's Insignia (USA) took the field along but she was collared a quarter of a mile out and had run out of gas in the final furlong. A return to a mile may well suit her better. (3/1: op 2/1)
1503 Isis Honda (IRE) had every chance entering the straight but had come to the end of her tether below the distance. (6/1)

T/Plpt: £1,552.90 (6.37 Tckts). T/Qdpt: £604.70 (0.45 Tckts); £449.47 to Beverley 5/6/97. AK

1328-NEWCASTLE (L-H) (Firm, Good to firm patches)
Wednesday June 4th

Race 2 & 6: hand-timed.
WEATHER: sunny & warm WIND: mod bhd

1669 'BET COMPELLING TIMEFORM COMMENTARIES' MAIDEN STKS (2-Y.O) (Class D)
2-30 (2-31) **5f** £3,067.50 (£930.00: £455.00: £217.50) Stalls: High GOING minus 0.48 sec per fur (F)

				SP	RR	SF
1174^{7}	**Atlantic Viking (IRE)** (MJohnston) **2-9-0** DHolland(8) (lw: mde all: edgd lft: shkn up 2f out: r.o v.wl)	—	1	$11/4^{2}$	97+	49
1306^{2}	**Shegardi** (DRLoder) **2-9-0** LDettori(2) (lw: trckd ldrs: effrt 2f out: r.o: no ch w wnr)	4	2	$3/10^{1}$	84	36
1447^{8}	**Jacobina** (TDBarron) **2-8-9** RLappin(7) (in tch: kpt on fnl 2f: no imp)	5	3	50/1	63	15
	Rich Choice (JDBethell) **2-8-9** TWilliams(5) (leggy: scope: sn pushed along: styd on fnl 2f: n.d)	2	4	$20/1^{3}$	57	9
1466^{7}	**Imperial Honey (IRE)** (MrsASwinbank) **2-8-9** GDuffield(4) (in tch tl outpcd fnl 2f)	½	5	50/1	55	7
1328^{7}	**Inshallah** (MartinTodhunter) **2-8-9** JCarroll(6) (hld up: effrt ½-wy: n.d)	2½	6	66/1	47	—
	Stephangeorge (MBrittain) **2-9-0** KDarley(1) (leggy: lt-f: gd spd 3f: sn wknd)	3	7	66/1	43	—
	Deeceebee (WStorey) **2-9-0** SWhitworth(3) (w'like: dwlt: hld up: outpcd fr ½-wy)	6	8	25/1	23	—
				(SP 119.1%)	**8 Rn**	

58.83 secs (0.37 under 2y best) (0.43) CSF £3.72 TOTE £3.40: £1.10 £1.10 £9.40 (£1.20) OWNER Atlantic Racing Ltd (MIDDLEHAM) BRED Kilcarn Stud

1174 Atlantic Viking (IRE) got it right this time in brilliant style and, although he did tend to go to his left, he kept straight in the closing stages. He also broke the two-year-old track record which has stood since 1962. (11/4)
1306 Shegardi a much more finely-made colt than the winner, travelled well but, try as he might, he was well outclassed. This may well turn out to be a decent event. (3/10)
Jacobina put in a much improved effort and looks to be going the right way. (50/1)
Rich Choice, a half-sister to the useful two-year-old of last year Rich Ground, found this trip too sharp but was staying on, suggesting that better is now likely. (20/1)
1466 Imperial Honey (IRE) ran reasonably in a hot race here. (50/1)
Inshallah needs time and is gradually learning. (66/1)
Stephangeorge, a very tall and lightly-made colt, has bags of speed and probably blew up here. (66/1)

1670 BUCKNALL AUSTIN H'CAP (0-95) (3-Y.O) (Class C)
3-00 (3-01) **1m (round)** £5,889.50 (£1,781.00: £868.00: £411.50) Stalls: Low GOING minus 0.48 sec per fur (F)

				SP	RR	SF
1175^{10}	**Bollin Terry (72)** (TDEasterby) **3-8-6** LCharnock(2) (lw: trckd ldrs: hdwy over 2f out: led 1f out: r.o wl)	—	1	5/1	85	51
597^{5}	**Atlantic Desire (IRE) (87)** (MJohnston) **3-9-7** LDettori(8) (lw: chsd ldr: ev ch over 1f out: kpt on)	3	2	8/1	94	60
1256^{2}	**Boater (74)** (DMorley) **3-8-3**(5) RFfrench(5) (led: pushed along over 2f out: hdd 1f out: no ex)	½	3	$100/30^{2}$	80	46
1314^{2}	**Brave Montgomerie (83)** (MissLAPerratt) **3-9-3** JCarroll(3) (s.i.s: rdn & styd on fnl 3f: n.d)	6	4	11/1	77	43
1423^{2}	**Super Monarch (83)** (EALDunlop) **3-9-3** KDarley(4) (b.hind: lw: unruly in stalls: hld up: effrt 3f out: rdn & no imp)	s.h	5	$5/2^{1}$	77	43
	Kadeena (82) (MJohnston) **3-9-2** DHolland(7) (chsd ldrs: pushed along ½-wy: wknd fnl 3f)	nk	6	14/1	75	41
	Silver Secret (71) (MJHeaton-Ellis) **3-8-5** GDuffield(6) (chsd ldrs tl wknd fnl 3f)	3	7	12/1	58	24
1017^{9}	**No More Pressure (IRE) (82)** (MrsJRRamsden) **3-9-2** JFortune(1) (in tch tl lost pl fnl 3f)	5	8	$4/1^{3}$	59	25
				(SP 122.1%)	**8 Rn**	

1m 39.1 (0.10) CSF £43.04 CT £143.48 TOTE £6.40: £1.60 £1.80 £1.40 (£14.30) OWNER Sir Neil Westbrook (MALTON) BRED Sir Neil and Lady Westbrook

OFFICIAL EXPLANATION **Bollin Terry: regarding the improvement in form, the trainer reported that the colt had boiled over, run too freely and hung left last time.**
1017 Bollin Terry looked magnificent and won this really well and, now he has broken his duck, he should improve further. (5/1)
597 Atlantic Desire (IRE) is fast coming to hand and this was a sound effort and she should not be long in finding winning form. (8/1)
1256 Boater looks a bit of a character as he carries his head high and also had problems with the turn. He did seem to do his best, but was well and truly out-pointed late on. (100/30)
1314 Brave Montgomerie won on fast ground last year but, judging from his action, he has problems with it and, never happy here, only ran on when it was too late. (11/1)
1423 Super Monarch went berserk in the stalls and, not surprisingly, ran no sort of race. (5/2: op 4/1)
Kadeena, a tall, lean filly, looked fairly straight but was obviously in need of it judging from the way she ran, as she was struggling some way out. (14/1)

1671 RAMSIDE HALL HOTEL (S) STKS (3-Y.O+) (Class G)
3-30 (3-30) **5f** £2,155.00 (£605.00: £295.00) Stalls: High GOING minus 0.48 sec per fur (F)

				SP	RR	SF
1602^{6}	**Palacegate Jack (IRE) (66)** (JBerry) **6-9-5v** KDarley(1) (lw: led: sn wl clr: wknd fnl f: jst lasted)	—	1	$13/8^{1}$	55	49
1514^{4}	**Featherstone Lane (40)** (MissLCSiddall) **6-9-5** DeanMcKeown(3) (lw: chsd wnr: kpt on fnl f: nrst fin)	½	2	$4/1^{3}$	53	47
1514^{9}	**Here Comes a Star (50)** (JMCarr) **9-9-5** ACulhane(2) (lw: hld up: effrt ½-wy: nvr able to chal)	2	3	7/1	47	41
1127^{14}	**Double Oscar (IRE) (49)** (DNicholls) **4-9-3**(7) JoanneDavies(7) (in tch: no imp fr ½-wy)	2½	4	11/1	44	38
1572*	**Captain Carat (59)** (DNicholls) **6-9-10b** AlexGreaves(6) (hld up: effrt ½-wy: no imp)	nk	5	$15/8^{2}$	43	37
1514^{6}	**Rennyholme (46)** (ABMulholland) **6-9-5** JQuinn(8) (lw: effrt ½-wy: sn rdn & n.d)	4	6	11/1	25	19
	Petaz (MWEasterby) **3-8-7** TLucas(5) (leggy: s.i.s: a bhd)	13	7	25/1	—	—
				(SP 125.9%)	**7 Rn**	

59.12 secs (0.72) CSF £9.14 TOTE £2.40: £1.30 £2.40 (£5.40) OWNER Mr William Burns (COCKERHAM) BRED Brendan and Sheila Powell
WEIGHT FOR AGE 3yo-7lb
No bid

1602 Palacegate Jack (IRE) likes his own way and, showing blistering early pace, certainly got it here, but the line only just came in time. (13/8)
1514 Featherstone Lane has won twice in eighty-four starts and had a big chance here but was never doing quite enough. (4/1)
Here Comes a Star gave signs of coming back to form here but was never finding enough late on. (7/1)
956 Double Oscar (IRE) looked to have plenty on here, but ran well and was certainly not knocked about. (11/1: 8/1-12/1)
1572* Captain Carat is a moody customer and was not on one of his going days here. (15/8)

1672 '50 YEARS OF TIMEFORM' H'CAP (0-85) (3-Y.O+) (Class D)
4-00 (4-00) **2m 19y** £4,026.00 (£1,218.00: £594.00: £282.00) Stalls: High GOING minus 0.48 sec per fur (F)

				SP	RR	SF
1400*	**Embryonic (IRE) (78)** (MartinTodhunter) **5-10-0** GCarter(6) (hld up: a.gng wl: led appr fnl f: shkn up & r.o wl)	—	1	3/1 2	89	39
1252 5	**Noufari (FR) (70)** (RHollinshead) **6-9-6** LDettori(4) (led to ½-wy: chsd ldr: drvn along 4f out: kpt on: no ch w wnr)	2	2	9/2 3	79	29
1224 5	**Great Oration (IRE) (61)** (FWatson) **8-8-11** JQuinn(5) (hld up: effrt 3f out: styd on fnl f: nvr able to chal)	nk	3	9/2 3	70	20
994 5	**Ballpoint (76)** (GMMoore) **4-9-6**(5) RFfrench(3) (cl up: led ½-wy tl appr fnl f: sn btn)	2	4	13/2	83	32
1162 2	**Opaque (69)** (WStorey) **5-9-5** SWhitworth(2) (lw: hdwy ½-wy: chal 4f out: wknd 2f out)	10	5	6/4 1	66	16
				(SP 114.7%)	**5 Rn**	

3m 32.77 (7.27) CSF £15.38 TOTE £4.70: £1.80 £2.60 (£5.90) OWNER Mrs D. Miller (ULVERSTON) BRED Tsarina Stud
WEIGHT FOR AGE 4yo-1lb
OFFICIAL EXPLANATION **Opaque: was unsuited by the fast ground.**
1400* Embryonic (IRE) has really got his act together at the moment and won this with plenty to spare. (3/1)
1252 Noufari (FR) has yet to win in Turf and, although he kept on after looking in trouble, he was never in danger of losing his record. (9/2)
1224 Great Oration (IRE) is running well and just needs a race with a strong pace and he will come into his own. (9/2)
994 Ballpoint, stepping up in trip, helped force the pace but he was easily picked off in the closing stages. (13/2)
1162 Opaque was disappointing here, dropping out tamely in the last two furlongs, and perhaps this ground was just too firm. (6/4)

1673 'WIN WITH TIMEFORM' H'CAP (0-85) (3-Y.O) (Class D)
4-30 (4-30) **6f** £3,533.75 (£1,070.00: £522.50: £248.75) Stalls: High GOING minus 0.48 sec per fur (F)

				SP	RR	SF
1254 10	**Prince Dome (IRE) (74)** (MartynWane) **3-8-11** JCarroll(5) (w ldr: led 2f out: all out)	—	1	14/1	87	51
1488*	**Always Alight (68)** (KRBurke) **3-8-5** 6x JQuinn(2) (in tch: hdwy 2f out: hung rt: chal ins fnl f: kpt on)	s.h	2	9/4 1	81	45
1170 14	**Night Flight (80)** (JJO'Neill) **3-9-3** GDuffield(3) (lw: trckd ldrs: ev ch over 1f out: btn whn sltly hmpd ins fnl f)	3	3	14/1	85	49
1170 8	**Double-J (IRE) (84)** (KMcAuliffe) **3-9-7** BDoyle(8) (in tch: effrt 2f out: kpt on: nvr able to chal)	½	4	9/2 2	88	52
1586*	**Rum Lad (62)** (JJQuinn) **3-7-13** 6x JLowe(6) (chsd ldrs: effrt & n.m.r 2f out: nt qckn)	1½	5	8/1 3	62	26
1254 9	**Two On The Bridge (71)** (DenysSmith) **3-8-8** ACulhane(1) (chsd ldrs: rdn 2f out: sn btn)	3½	6	14/1	61	25
1119*	**Nifty Norman (79)** (JBerry) **3-9-2** KDarley(7) (led 4f: sn wknd)	3	7	9/2 2	61	25
1269 3	**Express Girl (64)** (DMoffatt) **3-7-12**(3) DarrenMoffatt(4) (spd over 3f: sn wknd)	5	8	9/1	33	—
				(SP 108.2%)	**8 Rn**	

1m 11.75 (0.25) CSF £37.34 CT £368.28 TOTE £32.90: £4.10 £1.30 £3.00 (£49.60) OWNER Mr G. W. Jones (RICHMOND) BRED Airlie Stud
636* Prince Dome (IRE) goes well on the fast ground, has plenty of toe and showed fine courage under pressure. (14/1)
1488* Always Alight is certainly a bit of a character and, if he had run straight here, he would have won. (9/4)
863* Night Flight travelled well but when let down seemed to be feeling this firm ground and failed to quicken. (14/1)
1029 Double-J (IRE) chased the leaders but was short of both pace and room at a vital stage and was fighting a lost cause thereafter. (9/2)
1586* Rum Lad never had room in which to manoeuvre and was not given a hard time. (8/1: 6/1-9/1)
977 Two On The Bridge was always struggling and seems to have just lost his way at the moment. (14/1: op 8/1)
1119* Nifty Norman, hiked up the weights for winning a poor race on bad ground, was all at sea here. (9/2)
1269 Express Girl (9/1: op 6/1)

1674 'TIP-TOP TIMEFORM RATINGS' LIMITED STKS (0-65) (3-Y.O+) (Class F)
5-00 (5-02) **1m 1f 9y** £2,379.00 (£669.00: £327.00) Stalls: Low GOING minus 0.48 sec per fur (F)

				SP	RR	SF
1473 2	**Philistar (65)** (KRBurke) **4-9-6** BDoyle(3) (hld up: effrt 2f out: r.o wl ins fnl f to ld nr fin)	—	1	7/4 2	67	30
1472*	**Dispol Gem (58)** (PCalver) **4-9-5** KDarley(6) (lw: trckd ldrs: led ins fnl f: r.o u.p: jst ct)	hd	2	6/4 1	66	29
1470 10	**Desert Cat (IRE) (64)** (MartynWane) **4-9-6** JCarroll(2) (trckd ldrs: led 2f out tl ins fnl f: rallied: no ex towards fin)	1½	3	25/1	64	27
1281 10	**Sun Mark (IRE) (62)** (MrsASwinbank) **6-9-8** GDuffield(5) (led tl hdd 2f out: btn appr fnl f)	2	4	13/2	63	26
1395 3	**Genuine John (IRE) (64)** (JParkes) **4-9-8** SWhitworth(4) (hld up: effrt 2f out: rdn & nt qckn fnl f)	s.h	5	9/2 3	63	26
	Dark Midnight (IRE) (28) (DALamb) **8-8-13b**(7) KSked(1) (a last: wl outpcd & bhd fnl 3f)	18	6	100/1	29	—
				(SP 112.7%)	**6 Rn**	

1m 56.3 (4.00) CSF £4.37 TOTE £2.50: £2.20 £1.20 (£2.10) OWNER Mr Nigel Shields (WANTAGE) BRED John A. Jones Morgan
1473 Philistar looks a real character but was given a superb ride and, produced at the exact moment, he hit the front on the line. (7/4)
1472* Dispol Gem took the eye in the paddock and always looked to be going best in the race but she was tapped for toe in the sprint for the line. She is obviously in top form at the moment. (6/4)
823 Desert Cat (IRE) is coming to hand and this was a fair effort. (25/1)
1042* Sun Mark (IRE) showed a liking for soft ground early in the season but, after trying hard here, was well outpaced in the closing stages. (13/2)
1395 Genuine John (IRE) looked to be going well enough until an effort was required in the last two furlongs when he found nothing. (9/2)

T/Plpt: £26.60 (544.45 Tckts). T/Qdpt: £12.70 (49.58 Tckts) AA

1422-WARWICK (L-H) (Firm, Good to firm st)
Wednesday June 4th
WEATHER: fine WIND: nil

1675 KENILWORTH NOVICE AUCTION STKS (2-Y.O) (Class D)
2-15 (2-22) **6f** £3,287.60 (£981.80: £469.40: £213.20) Stalls: Low GOING minus 0.48 sec per fur (F)

				SP	RR	SF
1447 5	**Tippitt Boy** (KMcAuliffe) **2-8-9** JReid(3) (lw: a.p: led ins fnl f: pushed out)	—	1	16/1	67	25
1447*	**Sandside** (JBerry) **2-8-12**(3) PFessey(1) (led tl hrd rdn & hdd ins fnl f)	1¼	2	9/2 2	70	28
	Lido (IRE) (BWHills) **2-8-7** RHills(2) (leggy: s.s: hdwy over 2f out: rdn over 1f out: one pce)	4	3	4/6 1	51+	9
	Signatory (RHannon) **2-8-7** WJO'Connor(9) (lengthy: unf: nvr trbld ldrs)	5	4	14/1	38	—
	Donegal Sean (KMcAuliffe) **2-8-9** TSprake(7) (lt-f: unf: nvr nr ldrs)	hd	5	33/1	39	—

880*	**Ballet Rambert** (MJHeaton-Ellis) **2-8-8** SDrowne(4) (hld up: rdn 3f out: sn bhd)	2½	**6**	13/2[3]	32	—
*1136**	**Malozza** (PDEvans) **2-8-4** JFEgan(6) (prom tl bit slipped & rn wd bnd 3f out: eased whn btn over 1f out)	11	**7**	8/1	—	—
1295[4]	**Silent Pride (IRE)** (MDIUsher) **2-8-0** JMarshall(10) (chsd ldr tl wknd over 2f out: t.o)	8	**8**	16/1	—	—
1240[7]	**Distinctly Lillie (IRE)** (JSMoore) **2-7-11**(3) MHenry(8) (ref to r: t.n.p)		**R**	33/1	—	—
				(SP 126.9%)	**9 Rn**	

1m 14.1 (2.10) CSF £86.44 TOTE £31.30: £4.20 £1.80 £1.00 (£44.90) Trio £36.60 OWNER Highgrove Developments Ltd (LAMBOURN) BRED Cheveley Park Stud Ltd

OFFICIAL EXPLANATION **Malozza: the trainer reported that the filly's bit had slipped through her mouth.**

1447 Tippitt Boy has always been well thought of by his trainer, and came into his own over this longer trip on fast ground. (16/1)

1447* Sandside, stepping up to six, had the rails to prevent him hanging left from his inside draw. (9/2: 3/1-5/1)

Lido (IRE), out of a juvenile winner in Germany, was reported to have been working well at home. He could easily have found this ground too lively and should be given another chance. (4/6: 4/5-evens)

Signatory, a half-brother to three winners, failed to cut much ice on this debut. (14/1: 2/1-16/1)

Donegal Sean, who lacks scope, was another who was never in the hunt. (33/1)

880* Ballet Rambert probably found this ground a bit quicker than at Bath. (13/2: 7/2-7/1)

1136* Malozza ran wide when the bit slipped three furlongs out, and this run can be safely ignored. (8/1: op 4/1)

1676 QUEEN BESS CLAIMING STKS (3-Y.O+) (Class F)

2-45 (2-55) **6f** £2,762.10 (£765.60: £366.30) Stalls: Low GOING minus 0.48 sec per fur (F)

				SP	RR	SF
1127[5]	**Standown (61)** (JBerry) **4-8-12**(3) PFessey(5) (mde all: qcknd clr over 2f out: rdn over 1f out: comf)	—	**1**	4/1[2]	57	28
1317[17]	**Montendre (90)** (RJHodges) **10-9-11** JReid(9) (hdwy 3f out: chsd wnr over 1f out: no imp)	2½	**2**	2/1[1]	60	31
1419[6]	**Superlao (BEL) (35)** (JJBridger) **5-8-3**(5) ADaly(4) (a.p: rdn over 2f out: r.o one pce)	½	**3**	12/1	42	13
610[16]	**Ultra Beet (66)** (PCHaslam) **5-9-4**(7) PGoode(8) (swtg: a.p: hrd rdn over 1f out: one pce)	1	**4**	7/1	56	27
1317[18]	**Hard to Figure (87)** (RJHodges) **11-9-2**(5) AmandaSanders(1) (lw: bhd tl hdwy fnl f: nvr nrr)	½	**5**	11/2[3]	51	22
1047[4]	**Norling (IRE) (39)** (KOCunningham-Brown) **7-8-11** RCochrane(11) (chsd wnr over 4f: wknd ins fnl f)	1¼	**6**	10/1	38	9
	Culsyth Flyer (PJBevan) **6-9-1** NCarlisle(3) (s.i.s: hld up & plld hrd: rdn over 2f out: n.d)	s.h	**7**	33/1	42	13
1639[14]	**Mister Sean (IRE) (28)** (JMBradley) **4-8-11** JFEgan(10) (b.hind: sme hdwy over 2f out: sn wknd)	3½	**8**	33/1	28	—
1410[11]	**Krystal Max (IRE) (72)** (JCullinan) **4-8-12**(3) DO'Donohoe(2) (a bhd: t.o)	9	**9**	13/2	8	—
1620[2]	***Chief's Lady (38)*** (JMBradley) **5-7-13**(7) JFowle(6) (Withdrawn not under Starter's orders: bolted bef s)		**W**	8/1	—	—
				(SP 128.3%)	**9 Rn**	

1m 14.3 (2.30) CSF £11.48 TOTE £6.60: £2.70 £1.00 £2.40 (£12.10) Trio £21.20 OWNER Mrs Chris Deuters (COCKERHAM) BRED Alan Gibson

1127 Standown ran out a convincing winner, despite seeming to have a bit to do based on official ratings. (4/1)

980 Montendre is not getting any younger but did his best on this drop into a claimer. (2/1)

1327 Superlao (BEL) has not lived up to her five wins in Belgium. (12/1)

224 Ultra Beet would have been much better off in a handicap. (7/1)

Hard to Figure, well treated at the weights on this drop in class, only got going late in the day. (11/2)

1047 Norling (IRE) had not run on grass since last August. (10/1)

1677 BOLLINGER CHAMPAGNE CHALLENGE SERIES GENTLEMEN'S H'CAP (0-70) (3-Y.O+) (Class E)

3-15 (3-18) **1m** £3,044.25 (£909.00: £434.50: £197.25) Stalls: Low GOING minus 0.48 sec per fur (F)

				SP	RR	SF
1374[9]	**Lorins Gold (32)** (AndrewTurnell) **7-9-12** MrJRees(1) (lw: hld up mid div: stdy hdwy over 4f out: rdn to ld wl ins fnl f)	—	**1**	14/1	46	31
860[7]	**Samara Song (50)** (IPWilliams) **4-11-2** MrTMcCarthy(5) (a.p: wnt 2nd 3f out: led over 1f out: hdd wl ins fnl f)	½	**2**	11/1	63	48
1511[7]	**Cee-Jay-Ay (50)** (JBerry) **10-11-2** MrRHale(2) (s.s: hdwy on ins over 2f out: plld out over 1f out: r.o one pce fnl f)	3	**3**	15/2[2]	57	42
1484[3]	**Zahran (IRE) (33)** (JMBradley) **6-9-9**(4) MrJGoldstein(7) (lw: hdwy fnl f: nvr nr to chal)	2½	**4**	11/2[1]	35	20
1422[17]	**Kingchip Boy (61)** (MJRyan) **8-11-9v**(4) MrSLavallin(8) (led over 6f: wknd ins fnl f)	¾	**5**	8/1[3]	62	47
1633[12]	**Myosotis (50)** (PJMakin) **3-10-1b**(4) MrLBaker(4) (hld up: stdy hdwy over 4f out: rdn over 2f out: one pce)	1¼	**6**	20/1	48	22
1575[6]	**Wentbridge Lad (IRE) (60)** (PDEvans) **7-11-8v**(4) MrAEvans(13) (nvr nrr)	1	**7**	15/2[2]	56	41
1483[4]	**Asterix (36)** (JMBradley) **9-10-2b** MrRThornton(11) (b: chsd ldrs tl wknd over 1f out)	2	**8**	11/2[1]	28	13
1445[10]	**Haydown (IRE) (39)** (MRBosley) **5-10-1**(4)ow5 MrPPhillips(9) (s.i.s: a bhd)	1¾	**9**	40/1	28	8
	Euro Singer (53) (TKeddy) **5-11-5** MrPScott(10) (a bhd)	nk	**10**	8/1[3]	41	26
1422[12]	**Montone (IRE) (62)** (JRJenkins) **7-12-0v** DrMMannish(12) (chsd ldr tl rdn 3f out: wknd over 1f out)	3	**11**	8/1[3]	44	29
1384[16]	**Tomashenko (47)** (TWDonnelly) **8-10-13** MrMHNaughton(6) (a bhd)	1¾	**12**	33/1	25	10
1422[20]	**Digpast (IRE) (53)** (JJBridger) **7-11-1**(4) MrDBridger(3) (s.s: sn rcvrd: bhd fnl 3f)	3½	**13**	25/1	24	9
				(SP 116.6%)	**13 Rn**	

1m 40.2 (3.80) CSF £135.75 CT £774.53 TOTE £16.80: £4.20 £1.90 £2.30 (£104.70) Trio £316.90 OWNER Mrs M. R. Taylor (WANTAGE) BRED E. and G. Bosley

WEIGHT FOR AGE 3yo-11lb

Lorins Gold was only 2lb higher than when registering his only ever success at Brighton on the firm, just over a year ago. He keeps earning a reprieve by running well on the Flat when his trainer is tempted to run him over hurdles. (14/1)

Samara Song, who has changed stables this season, was 5lb lower than when second in a Bath seller last September. (11/1: 8/1-12/1)

824 Cee-Jay-Ay ran into traffic problems in the short home straight after his customary poor start. (15/2)

1484 Zahran (IRE) was 3lb lower than when fourth over course and distance a month ago. (11/2)

1040 Kingchip Boy, whose last seven victories have been on the sand at Southwell, has already dropped 8lb on grass this season. (8/1)

Myosotis was making a quick reappearance after having the blinkers refitted at Windsor on Monday night. (20/1)

1678 MIDSUMMER H'CAP (0-80) (3-Y.O+) (Class D)

3-45 (3-45) **1m 2f 169y** £3,518.20 (£1,048.60: £499.80: £225.40) Stalls: Low GOING minus 0.48 sec per fur (F)

				SP	RR	SF
1427[5]	**Mad Militant (IRE) (55)** (AStreeter) **8-8-5** TSprake(6) (lw: hld up in rr: hdwy over 2f out: led over 1f out: sn clr & edgd lft: easily)	—	**1**	11/2	66	29
1430[2]	**Dawam Allail (IRE) (75)** (MAJarvis) **3-8-11** RCochrane(3) (plld hrd early: led over 8f out: hrd rdn over 2f out: hdd over 1f out: no ch w wnr)	3½	**2**	7/1	81	30
1393[3]	**Sam Rockett (46)** (MissGayKelleway) **4-7-5**(5) RMullen(4) (hld up: rdn over 3f out: hdwy over 1f out: styd on one pce fnl f)	nk	**3**	16/1	51	14

				SP	RR	SF
1111^{9}	**Sandy Floss (IRE) (72)** (RHBuckler) **4-9-3**(5) SophieMitchell(5) (a.p: one pce fnl 2f)	1	**4**	25/1	76	39
1414^{8}	**Sovereign Page (USA) (78)** (BHanbury) **8-10-0** JStack(1) (hld up: nt clr run on ins & swtchd rt wl over 1f out: sn rdn: one pce fnl f)	nk	**5**	$3/1^{1}$	81	44
1481*	**Isitoff (72)** (SCWilliams) **4-9-8** 5x JReid(8) (hld up: pushed along after 2f: hdwy over 4f out: wknd over 1f out)	3	**6**	$9/2^{3}$	71	34
1156^{4}	**General Haven (72)** (TJNaughton) **4-9-8** SSanders(7) (prom: rdn over 4f out: wknd over 1f out)	3½	**7**	7/1	66	29
1503*	**Blockade (USA) (55)** (MBell) **8-8-5** MFenton(2) (t: led 2f: rdn over 2f out: wknd over 1f out)	1½	**8**	$7/2^{2}$	47	10

(SP 115.5%) **8 Rn**

2m 17.0 (3.00) CSF £39.83 CT £527.73 TOTE £7.30: £2.60 £2.40 £2.60 (£17.10) Trio £34.30 OWNER Mr K. Nicholls (UTTOXETER) BRED Cloghran Stud Farm Co in Ireland
LONG HANDICAP Sam Rockett 7-2
WEIGHT FOR AGE 3yo-14lb

1427 Mad Militant (IRE), down 1lb, made mincemeat of this opposition. (11/2)
1430 Dawam Allail (IRE) would not have beaten the winner even if he had settled better. (7/1)
1393 Sam Rockett, the winner of a selling hurdle at Taunton in January, was out of the handicap here. (16/1)
Sandy Floss (IRE) was bought out of Henry Cecil's yard for 16,000 guineas at Newmarket Autumn Sales, presumably with jumping in mind. (25/1)
Sovereign Page (USA), 5lb higher than when winning this race last season, was confronted by a wall of horses in the short home-straight but should not be considered unlucky. (3/1)
1481* Isitoff never really looked like defying his penalty. (9/2)

1679 KING HAMLET LIMITED STKS (0-85) (3-Y.O) (Class D)

4-15 (4-15) **1m 2f 169y** £3,454.50 (£1,029.00: £490.00: £220.50) Stalls: Low GOING minus 0.48 sec per fur (F)

				SP	RR	SF
1208^{7}	**Happy Go Lucky (80)** (RJO'Sullivan) **3-8-8** SSanders(1) (mde all: clr over 1f out: drvn out)	—	**1**	$6/1^{3}$	84	27
1144*	**Tom Tailor (GER) (84)** (DRCElsworth) **3-8-13** RCochrane(4) (hld up: rdn over 2f out: chsd wnr & edgd lft over 1f out: no imp)	5	**2**	$8/11^{1}$	82	25
1249^{6}	**Tycoon Girl (IRE) (78)** (BJMeehan) **3-8-8** JReid(2) (a.p: chsd wnr over 2f out tl over 1f out: one pce)	3	**3**	$7/2^{2}$	72	15
1103^{5}	**Michael Venture (82)** (SPCWoods) **3-8-11** AClark(3) (plld hrd: chsd wnr: rdn over 3f out: wknd wl over 1f out)	12	**4**	13/2	57	—

(SP 107.7%) **4 Rn**

2m 17.6 (3.60) CSF £10.08 TOTE £4.80: (£2.80) OWNER Whitcombe Manor Racing Stables Ltd (WHITCOMBE) BRED Casterbridge Stud
505 Happy Go Lucky did not mind this fast ground. (6/1)
1144* Tom Tailor (GER) found this ground in total contrast to his soft-going win at Windsor. (8/11)
1249 Tycoon Girl (IRE) did not appear to benefit from this longer trip. (7/2)
1103 Michael Venture had been tried in blinkers in the Lingfield Derby Trial. (13/2)

1680 KINGSBURY LIMITED STKS (0-60) (3-Y.O+) (Class F)

4-45 (4-46) **7f** £2,831.40 (£785.40: £376.20) Stalls: Low GOING minus 0.48 sec per fur (F)

				SP	RR	SF
1584^{8}	**Twin Creeks (51)** (VSoane) **6-9-6** CRutter(2) (lw: s.i.s: sn prom: led 1f out: r.o wl)	—	**1**	16/1	62	46
1489*	**Winsome Wooster (55)** (PGMurphy) **6-9-3** JReid(3) (a.p: rdn over 2f out: r.o one pce)	2½	**2**	$7/2^{2}$	53	37
1273^{8}	**Delight of Dawn (43)** (EAWheeler) **5-9-0** SSanders(4) (hdwy 3f out: one pce fnl 2f)	¾	**3**	16/1	49	33
*364**	**Speedy Classic (USA) (60)** (MJHeaton-Ellis) **8-9-9** AClark(1) (led 6f: one pce)	1¼	**4**	$5/1^{3}$	55	39
1439^{2}	**Newlands Corner (58)** (JAkehurst) **4-9-0b** DBiggs(5) (bhd tl hdwy 2f out: nt rch ldrs)	3	**5**	11/2	39	23
1089^{5}	**Aquatic Queen (53)** (RJWeaver) **3-8-4** NAdams(6) (b.hind: stdd s: sn wl bhd: nvr nrr)	nk	**6**	25/1	38	12
1442^{11}	**Master M-E-N (IRE) (59)** (NMBabbage) **5-9-3v** VSlattery(9) (lw: nvr trbld ldrs)	hd	**7**	12/1	41	25
1219^{3}	**Perfect Poppy (59)** (JRFanshawe) **3-8-4** DHarrison(7) (prom over 4f)	¾	**8**	$7/4^{1}$	36	10
1000^{8}	**Rosenkavalier (IRE) (60)** (LGCottrell) **3-8-7** MRoberts(8) (swtg: bhd fnl 3f)	9	**9**	12/1	19	—
1374^{5}	**Lancashire Legend (53)** (SDow) **4-8-12**(5) ADaly(10) (w ldr tl rdn & wknd over 2f out: t.o)	7	**10**	25/1	3	—

(SP 125.5%) **10 Rn**

1m 26.1 (1.50) CSF £70.03 TOTE £26.80: £4.30 £1.30 £3.70 (£47.90) Trio £134.00 OWNER The Armchair Jockeys-Four Seasons Racing (ASTON ROWANT) BRED Crest Stud Ltd
WEIGHT FOR AGE 3yo-10lb
1009 Twin Creeks acts on a sound surface and put a disappointing recent run at Catterick behind him. (16/1)
1489* Winsome Wooster had a sharper track and quicker ground than at Newbury a week ago. (7/2: 5/2-4/1)
Delight of Dawn, tried in blinkers last time, was arguably back to her best trip. (16/1)
364* Speedy Classic (USA), supported in the ring, was returning after a three-month break. (5/1)
1439 Newlands Corner got loose when her rider attempted to mount her on the course, and was briefly loose amongst the crowd near the paddock. (11/2: op 3/1)
1089 Aquatic Queen rather overdid the waiting tactics in an attempt to get the trip. (25/1)
1111 Master M-E-N (IRE) (12/1: op 6/1)

1681 PRINCE RUPERT MAIDEN H'CAP (0-75) (3-Y.O+ F & M) (Class D)

5-15 (5-17) **5f** £3,613.75 (£1,078.00: £514.50: £232.75) Stalls: Low GOING minus 0.48 sec per fur (F)

				SP	RR	SF
1566^{2}	**Nopalea (66)** (TJNaughton) **3-9-10** SSanders(2) (trckd ldrs: rdn to ld ins fnl f: r.o)	—	**1**	$9/4^{2}$	72	36
1316^{11}	**Blue Lamp (USA) (63)** (MAJarvis) **3-9-7** RCochrane(7) (lw: led tl ins fnl f)	1¼	**2**	$7/4^{1}$	65	30
	Brin-Lodge (IRE) (32) (KSBridgwater) **4-7-6**(5)ow1 JBramhill(5) (b.nr hind: bkwd: swtg: prom: hrd rdn over 2f out: wknd over 1f out)	6	**3**	50/1	15	—
1401^{8}	**Astral Crown (IRE) (38)** (JBerry) **3-7-10b1** NAdams(3) (b.hind: a.p: ev ch over 1f out: wknd ins fnl f)	1¾	**4**	$12/1^{3}$	15	—
1401^{2}	**Millpet (56)** (RGuest) **3-9-0** JReid(6) (prom: rdn over 2f out: sn wknd)	1½	**5**	$9/4^{2}$	28	—
	Breffni (IRE) (51) (RDickin) **3-8-2**(7) PMundy(1) (reard stalls: a bhd)	1	**6**	14/1	20	—
1500^{10}	**Pirongia (40)** (PHowling) **3-7-12** NCarlisle(4) (b.hind: prom over 3f)	4	**7**	25/1	—	—

(SP 118.1%) **7 Rn**

59.8 secs (1.80) CSF £6.35 TOTE £3.00: £1.60 £1.40 (£6.20) OWNER Mr T. J. Naughton (EPSOM) BRED Sheikh Marwan Al Maktoum
LONG HANDICAP Brin-Lodge (IRE) 7-8 Astral Crown (IRE) 7-8
WEIGHT FOR AGE 3yo-7lb
1566 Nopalea made it thirteenth time lucky and was hardly winning out of turn. (9/4)

1110 Blue Lamp (USA) was having her first run over the minimum distance. (7/4)
Brin-Lodge (IRE) did not look fit enough to do herself justice, which does not say a lot for those who finished behind. (50/1)
Astral Crown (IRE) hails from a stable in cracking form, but not even the first-time blinkers could do the trick. (12/1: op 7/1)
1401 Millpet is going to struggle to find a race on this evidence, unless she found the ground too firm. (9/4)
Breffni (IRE) (14/1: 10/1-16/1)

T/Jkpt: Not won; £8,041.63 to Beverley 5/6/97. T/Plpt: £1,214.90 (11.84 Tckts). T/Qdpt: £536.10 (0.38 Tckts); £449.24 to Beverley 5/6/97 KH

1651-BEVERLEY (R-H) (Good to firm)
Thursday June 5th
WEATHER: fine & sunny WIND: fresh half bhd

1682 ETTON MAIDEN STKS (3-Y.O+) (Class D)
2-20 (2-23) **1m 100y** £3,457.00 (£1,036.00: £498.00: £229.00) Stalls: High GOING minus 0.36 sec per fur (F)

				SP	RR	SF
1207^{5}	**Asef Alhind** (BHanbury) **3-8-10** JStack(6) (lw: mde all: rdn & styd on fnl f: hld on wl towards fin)	—	**1**	2/1^{2}	83	51
	Coretta (IRE) (LMCumani) **3-8-5** JFortune(3) (trckd ldrs: pushed along over 3f out: rdn & ev ch over 1f out: styd on towards fin)	nk	**2**	10/11^{1}	77	45
	Polenka (IRE) (JWWatts) **3-8-5** JCarroll(1) (leggy: unf: hld up & bhd: effrt over 2f out: styd on appr fnl f)	6	**3**	12/1^{3}	66	34
	Tassili (IRE) (LadyHerries) **4-9-7** KDarley(5) (bit bkwd: unruly s: trckd wnr: wknd fnl f)	hd	**4**	20/1	71	50
	Portuguese Lil (70) (JLEyre) **4-9-2b^{1}** MGallagher(7) (hld up: hdwy 4f out: effrt over 2f out: one pce)	1	**5**	16/1	64	43
524^{7}	**Zibak (USA)** (DMorley) **3-8-10** GCarter(2) (hld up & plld hrd: rdn & wandered over 2f out: sn lost pl)	19	**6**	12/1^{3}	33	1
	Snow Carnival (LadyHerries) **4-9-7** GDuffield(4) (w'like: bit bkwd: s.i.s: sn in tch: pushed along 5f out: lost pl over 2f out)	7	**7**	20/1	20	—
				(SP 116.5%)		**7 Rn**

1m 45.4 (1.40) CSF £3.91 TOTE £3.10: £1.30 £1.40 (£1.90) OWNER Mr Hamdan Al Maktoum (NEWMARKET) BRED Mascalls Stud
WEIGHT FOR AGE 3yo-11lb
1207 Asef Alhind, who took the eye in the paddock, made all the running and, despite flashing his tail under pressure, was always doing enough. (2/1: op 3/1)
Coretta (IRE), a narrow type, seemed to find trouble handling the track but, sticking to her guns despite showing an ungainly action under pressure, she was closing the gap all the way to the line. Still immature, she is sure to do better especially over further. (10/11: 4/6-evens)
Polenka (IRE), a narrow type showing a fair amount of knee action going down, showed some ability, staying on from off the pace coming to the final furlong. (12/1: op 8/1)
Tassili (IRE), who carried plenty of condition, was having his third ever run. After giving trouble at the start, he showed ability, tracking the winner until tiring coming to the final furlong. Providing his temperament does not get the better of him, he looks capable of showing improvement now he is qualified for a handicap mark. (20/1)
Portuguese Lil, who last year ran in both the One Thousand Guineas and Derby, possesses some ability but is high enough in the ratings. On her toes beforehand, she probably found this trip too sharp. (16/1)
524 Zibak (USA) (12/1: 7/1-14/1)

1683 TOUCH ABOVE H'CAP (0-70) (3-Y.O+) (Class E)
2-50 (2-50) **1m 1f 207y** £3,345.00 (£1,005.00: £485.00: £225.00) Stalls: High GOING minus 0.36 sec per fur (F)

				SP	RR	SF
1422^{5}	**Mr Teigh (60)** (MrsJRRamsden) **5-9-4** JFortune(9) (lw: mde all: qcknd clr over 3f out: unchal)	—	**1**	9/2^{2}	70	52
1390^{6}	**Mcgillycuddy Reeks (IRE) (38)** (DonEnricoIncisa) **6-7-10** KimTinkler(7) (bhd: hdwy over 3f out: styd on fnl 2f: no ch w wnr)	2	**2**	25/1	45	27
1268^{10}	**Essayeffsee (55)** (MrsMReveley) **8-8-13** KDarley(10) (lw: hld up & bhd: hdwy on outside over 2f out: nvr rchd ldrs)	½	**3**	4/1^{1}	61	43
1244^{20}	**Grand Splendour (70)** (LadyHerries) **4-10-0** DHolland(8) (hld up & bhd: hdwy over 2f out: styd on wl ins fnl f)	nk	**4**	14/1	76	58
	Hawkish (USA) (50) (DMorley) **8-8-8** GCarter(3) (hld up & bhd: styd on fnl 2f)	2	**5**	7/1^{3}	52	34
1390^{2}	**Kilnamartyra Girl (38)** (JParkes) **7-7-10** GBardwell(12) (mid div: sn drvn along: kpt on fnl 2f: nvr nrr to chal)	1½	**6**	9/2^{2}	38	20
1138^{3}	**Heighth of Fame (45)** (JHetherton) **6-7-12**(5) IonaWands(4) (sn chsng ldrs: sltly hmpd over 5f out: rdn 3f out: sn outpcd)	1¼	**7**	16/1	43	25
1388^{6}	**Prime Partner (38)** (TDEasterby) **4-7-3**(7) RWinston(14) (chsd ldrs: effrt over 3f out: grad wknd)	2½	**8**	20/1	32	14
1128^{14}	**Champagne N Dreams (44)** (DNicholls) **5-8-2** DaleGibson(5) (hld up: hdwy on outside over 3f out: grad wknd)	1¼	**9**	8/1	36	18
1472^{12}	**Bulsara (58)** (CWFairhurst) **5-9-2** DeanMcKeown(1) (hdwy over 3f out: rdn & wnt rt 2f out: n.d)	nk	**10**	10/1	49	31
1588^{8}	**Runic Symbol (38)** (MBlanshard) **6-7-10** JQuinn(11) (sn rr div: sme hdwy u.p 3f out: sn wknd)	2½	**11**	10/1	25	7
	Farfields Prince (38) (DNicholls) **5-7-10** LCharnock(13) (hld up: hdwy u.p 5f out: lost pl 3f out)	nk	**12**	25/1	25	7
1281^{6}	**Father Eddie (57)** (JJO'Neill) **3-8-2** GDuffield(6) (chsd ldrs: sltly hmpd over 5f out: drvn along over 3f out: sn lost pl)	nk	**13**	14/1	43	12
1445^{14}	**Persian Sunset (IRE) (41)** (MissJBower) **5-7-13** LNewton(2) (racd wd: sn chsng ldrs: lost pl 4f out: t.o 2f out)	13	**14**	33/1	6	—
				(SP 132.8%)		**14 Rn**

2m 5.7 (2.60) CSF £116.58 CT £467.29 TOTE £5.90: £2.80 £4.80 £2.40 (£64.90) Trio £55.40 OWNER Platinum Racing Ltd (THIRSK) BRED K. G. Bridges
LONG HANDICAP Mcgillycuddy Reeks (IRE) 7-2 Prime Partner 7-5
WEIGHT FOR AGE 3yo-13lb
1422 Mr Teigh had this won the minute he quickened clear on turning for home. But for being eased, he would have had five lengths to spare at the line. (9/2)
1390 Mcgillycuddy Reeks (IRE) as usual wore a tongue-strap. Racing from 8lb out of the handicap, she stayed on from off the pace to snatch second spot near the line. (25/1)
1024 Essayeffsee took this event a year ago from a 1lb higher mark. Making ground on the outside early in the straight, he gave the impression that he can do better next time. (4/1)
Grand Splendour, a maiden carrying top weight in a handicap, showed ability, staying on in good style late in the day. Connections will be hoping the handicapper shows her some mercy. (14/1)
Hawkish (USA), on his reappearance, stayed on towards the finish and should be sharper as a result of the outing. (7/1)

1684 BRIAN YEARDLEY CONTINENTAL TWO YEAR OLD TROPHY CONDITIONS STKS (2-Y.O C & G) (Class B)

3-20 (3-21) **5f** £8,729.80 (£3,308.20: £1,651.60: £748.00: £371.50: £220.90) Stalls: High GOING minus 0.44 sec per fur (F)

				SP	RR	SF
1026*	**Only For Gold** (JBerry) **2-8-13** KDarley(4) (mde all: styd on wl fnl f: drvn out)	—	**1**	4/5^{1}	84	44
1391*	**Rusty Babe (IRE)** (JJQuinn) **2-9-1** JQuinn(6) (lw: chsd ldrs: outpcd 2f out: styd on wl u.p fnl f: nt rch wnr)	¾	**2**	11/2^{2}	84	44
1557*	**Reap Rewards** (JGFitzGerald) **2-8-11** JFortune(5) (lw: sn chsng ldrs: nt qckn appr fnl f)	1	**3**	9/1	76	36
1328*	**Prince Foley** (WGMTurner) **2-9-3** DSweeney(1) (lw: a chsng ldrs: kpt on same pce appr fnl f)	¾	**4**	6/1^{3}	80	40
1255^{3}	**Hirst Bridge (IRE)** (MWEasterby) **2-8-13** TLucas(7) (lw: chsd ldrs: drvn along ½-wy: hung rt: lost pl over 1f out)	2½	**5**	15/2	68	28
1251^{6}	**Sealed By Fate (IRE)** (JSWainwright) **2-8-9** MRimmer(3) (sn wl outpcd: sn drvn along & hung lft: styd on appr fnl f)	nk	**6**	50/1	63	23
1228^{7}	**Falkenberg (FR)** (MJohnston) **2-8-9** DHolland(8) (chsd ldrs: rdn & outpcd ½-wy: n.d)	hd	**7**	14/1	63	23
1492^{11}	**Dibola** (JSWainwright) **2-8-9** LCharnock(2) (bit bkwd: s.i.s: a bhd)	9	**8**	33/1	34	—

(SP 118.6%) **8 Rn**

62.9 secs (1.10) CSF £5.48 TOTE £1.60: £1.30 £1.20 £1.60 (£3.50) OWNER Mr John Milner & Mr Stephen Milner (COCKERHAM) BRED C. J. Hill

1026* Only For Gold has plenty of speed. Soon showing his rivals a clean pair of heels on the far rail, he stuck on strongly under pressure and never looked in danger of being overhauled. He will probably attempt to emulate his stable-mate Mind Games who took this event in 1994 before going on to take the Norfolk Stakes at Royal Ascot. (4/5: op 5/4)

1391* Rusty Babe (IRE), dropping back to six, struggled to go the pace soon after halfway. Making his ground on the wide outside, he stuck on grimly in the final furlong but could not reel in the winner. Progressing with every outing, he is better suited by six. (11/2: op 7/2)

1557* Reap Rewards, a grand type, ran really well. He should improve as the season progressess and will be happier back over six. (9/1)

1328* Prince Foley, giving weight away all round, was worst drawn, and in the circumstances was far from disgraced. He was ridden by an apprentice unable to claim his allowance. (6/1: 4/1-13/2)

1255 Hirst Bridge (IRE), who looked really well, again showed a tendency to hang under pressure. (15/2: 6/1-9/1)

1251 Sealed By Fate (IRE), who gave his rider problems, is clearly not without some ability. (50/1)

1228 Falkenberg (FR) (14/1: op 8/1)

1685 112TH YEAR OF THE WATT MEMORIAL H'CAP (0-90) (3-Y.O+) (Class C)

3-50 (3-50) **1m 3f 216y** £5,150.00 (£1,550.00: £750.00: £350.00) Stalls: High GOING minus 0.44 sec per fur (F)

				SP	RR	SF
182^{6}	**Far Ahead (82)** (JLEyre) **5-9-6** RLappin(4) (trckd ldrs: rdn over 2f out: led on ins 2f out: hung lft: hdd jst ins fnl f: sn led again: jst hld on)	—	**1**	4/1^{3}	92	43
1414^{7}	**Tykeyvor (IRE) (87)** (LadyHerries) **7-9-11** GDuffield(2) (hld up: stdy hdwy on ins to ld jst ins fnl f: hung rt & sn hdd: nt qckn nr fin)	s.h	**2**	Evens^{1}	97	48
1329^{2}	**Eagle Canyon (IRE) (71)** (BHanbury) **4-8-9** MRimmer(3) (lw: trckd ldrs: chal over 2f out: ev ch whn n.m.r ins fnl f: kpt on wl)	hd	**3**	13/8^{2}	81	32
1398^{7}	**Spa Lane (58)** (MPBielby) **4-7-5(5)** RMullen(1) (led to 2f out: wkng whn n.m.r appr fnl f)	4	**4**	25/1	63	14

(SP 111.9%) **4 Rn**

2m 38.0 (5.00) CSF £8.06 TOTE £6.50: (£3.90) OWNER Sunpak Potatoes (HAMBLETON) BRED Sir John Astor

LONG HANDICAP Spa Lane 7-7

Far Ahead, who has been in action over hurdles, poked through on the inner to take it up two furlongs out. With his rider persisting in using his whip in his right hand, he edged off the rail contributing to the interference to the third. (4/1: 3/1-9/2)

Tykeyvor (IRE) won this last year from a 10lb lower mark before going on to land the Bessborough. He moved up on the outside travelling best to show ahead just inside the final furlong, but once there he hung right, tightening up the third. In the end just denied, he should be spot on next time. (Evens)

1329 Eagle Canyon (IRE), a frustrating sort, stuck on despite the winner and the second hanging into him from either side inside the final furlong. (13/8)

Spa Lane ran slightly better than he had on his first two outings this time. (25/1)

1686 HURN CLAIMING STKS (4-Y.O+) (Class F)

4-20 (4-20) **1m 3f 216y** £2,448.00 (£678.00: £324.00) Stalls: High GOING minus 0.36 sec per fur (F)

				SP	RR	SF
1601^{3}	**Sun of Spring** (DWChapman) **7-8-5(3)** PFessey(8) (lw: chsd ldrs: led over 1f out: sn clr: pushed out)	—	**1**	5/1^{3}	59	31
1622^{7}	**Golden Thunderbolt (FR) (70)** (NTinkler) **4-9-12** KDarley(5) (s.i.s: drvn along over 3f out: hdwy & hung rt over 1f out: styd on wl towards fin: nt rch wnr)	1¼	**2**	7/2^{2}	75	47
1229^{5}	**Needwood Nutkin (32)** (BCMorgan) **4-8-1** LCharnock(3) (w ldrs: led over 3f out tl over 1f out: kpt on same pce)	½	**3**	16/1	50	22
1371^{4}	**At Liberty (IRE) (67)** (RHannon) **5-9-6** RPerham(1) (lw: chsd ldrs: rdn over 3f out: edgd rt 2f out: no imp)	5	**4**	11/10^{1}	62	34
1222^{3}	**Bold Top (40)** (BSRothwell) **5-8-6** MFenton(7) (pushed along over 5f out: swtchd lft over 1f out: one pce)	3	**5**	10/1	44	16
	Skiddaw Samba (MrsMReveley) **8-8-3** DWright(4) (hld up: hdwy on outside over 2f out: sn wknd)	3	**6**	11/1	37	9
	Eden Dancer (47) (MrsMReveley) **5-8-10** ACulhane(2) (lw: led tl over 3f out: wknd over 1f out)	3	**7**	15/2	40	12
1389^{8}	**Rush Me Not (IRE)** (MPBielby) **4-8-6** DeanMcKeown(6) (hld up: effrt over 3f out: sn lost pl)	11	**8**	40/1	21	—

(SP 124.0%) **8 Rn**

2m 38.1 (5.10) CSF £22.77 TOTE £5.70: £1.50 £1.50 £3.40 (£7.50) OWNER Mr S. B. Clark (YORK) BRED R. H. Cowell

1601 Sun of Spring, making a quick reappearance, was given a positive ride and, after dashing to the front, had only to be pushed out. Dropped no less than 20lb in the ratings after his run at Musselburgh five days ago, he could be very interesting if turning out in a handicap soon under a penalty. (5/1)

1389* Golden Thunderbolt (FR) as usual wore a tongue-strap. Lethargic in the early stages, he was still last turning in. Hanging fire, he consented to stay on strongly inside the last and would have troubled the winner with a bit further to go. (7/2: 5/2-4/1)

1229 Needwood Nutkin ran surprisingly well considering she would have been meeting the first two on much better terms in a handicap. (16/1)

1371 At Liberty (IRE) had more use made of him than usual but, under pressure, all he wanted to do was hang right. (11/10)

1687 FIGHAM MAIDEN APPRENTICE H'CAP (0-75) (3-Y.O+) (Class G)

4-50 (4-50) **5f** £2,232.50 (£620.00: £297.50) Stalls: High GOING minus 0.44 sec per fur (F)

				SP	RR	SF
	Reinhardt (IRE) (40) (DNicholls) **4-8-7** CarolynBales(5) (sn wl bhd: gd hdwy on outside over 1f out: styd on strly to ld nr fin)	—	**1**	16/1	50	32

1119^{2}	**Archello (IRE) (67)** (GROldroyd) **3-9-8**$^{(5)}$ RFarmer(1) (racd wd: chsd ldrs: rdn over 1f out: styd on ins fnl f)	1¾	**2**	9/4^{1}	71	46
972^{8}	**Young Ben (IRE) (36)** (JSWainwright) **5-8-3b** DMernagh(2) (b: b.hind: w ldr: hung lft ½-wy: led ins fnl f: hdd nr fin)	s.h	**3**	9/2^{2}	40	22
1496^{3}	**Midnight Shift (IRE) (68)** (RGuest) **3-10-0** SRighton(4) (sn drvn along: chsd ldrs: nt qckn fnl f)	1½	**4**	9/4^{1}	67	42
1604^{9}	**Mill End Boy (60)** (MWEasterby) **3-9-6** TSiddall(6) (outpcd ½-wy: hdwy over 1f out: styng on whn nt clr run ins fnl f)	s.h	**5**	7/1^{3}	59	34
1586^{6}	**Good To Talk (43)** (TDEasterby) **4-8-10** PBradley(3) (led tl hdd & wknd ins fnl f)	s.h	**6**	7/1^{3}	42	24
				(SP 110.6%)	**6 Rn**	

63.3 secs (1.50) CSF £46.05 TOTE £11.20: £2.70 £1.70 (£18.80) OWNER Mrs Sheila Walker (THIRSK) BRED Swettenham Stud
WEIGHT FOR AGE 3yo-7lb

Reinhardt (IRE), who has changed stables and whose last run was over eleven furlongs, has tumbled down the weights since showing promise as a two-year-old. Having nothing to do with the fast and furious pace, he was at least ten lengths behind at halfway. Making ground on the wide outside, he shot through to lead near the finish. He has clearly kicked off on a favourable mark for his able new handler. (16/1)
1119 Archello (IRE), who raced wide, is finding that first win elusive. (9/4)
Young Ben (IRE), still a maiden after twenty-two starts, gave his rider problems by hanging left. (9/2)
1496 Midnight Shift (IRE) was soon being driven along and five furlongs is really too short for her. (9/4: op 5/4)
1604 Mill End Boy, who bolted last time, was taken to post early. He was sticking on at the one pace when running out of room inside the last. He would only have finished fourth at best. (7/1: 5/1-8/1)
1586 Good To Talk, with the headgear again left off, was two lengths clear on the far rail two furlongs out but his stride shortened inside the final furlong. He seems barely to stay the minimum trip. (7/1)

T/Jkpt: £12,722.70 (0.1 Tckts); £16,127.49 to Epsom Downs 6/6/97. T/Plpt: £164.30 (91.3 Tckts). T/Qdpt: £46.20 (29.15 Tckts) WG

1498-**YARMOUTH (L-H) (Firm)**
Thursday June 5th
WEATHER: sunny WIND: fresh across

1688 AMEC PROCESS AND ENERGY MAIDEN STKS (3-Y.O) (Class D)
2-00 (2-01) **1m 3y** £3,613.75 (£1,078.00: £514.50: £232.75) Stalls: Low GOING minus 0.48 sec per fur (F)

				SP	RR	SF
1477^{7}	**Bevier** (CEBrittain) **3-9-0** MRoberts(1) (b: lw: mde all: rdn & hld on wl ins fnl f)	—	**1**	6/4^{1}	75	31
1423^{8}	**Matoaka** (RJRWilliams) **3-8-9** RCochrane(2) (hld up: hdwy & n.m.r 2f out: unable qckn ins fnl f)	nk	**2**	5/2^{2}	69	25
1237^{8}	**Nicker** (WJarvis) **3-9-0** SSanders(3) (lw: w wnr: one pce appr fnl f)	2½	**3**	9/2^{3}	69	25
1409^{7}	**Crescent's Whisper (IRE)** (BHanbury) **3-9-0** WRyan(4) (b: hld up: hdwy over 3f out: sn rdn & btn)	5	**4**	5/1	59	15
				(SP 103.4%)	**4 Rn**	

1m 38.6 (2.60) CSF £4.48 TOTE £1.80: (£1.90) OWNER Mr Saeed Manana (NEWMARKET) BRED Sheikh Mohammed Bin Rashid Al Maktoum
Bevier, taking another drop in trip, always looked just in control in a moderate race. (6/4: op evens)
1423 Matoaka looked much fitter this time and retains some ability after her injury. (5/2)
Nicker is a moderate mover and was easily outpaced in the last furlong and a half. (9/2)
Crescent's Whisper (IRE) moved poorly to post and only briefly looked dangerous in the race. (5/1: op 3/1)

1689 FLEGGS (S) H'CAP (0-60) (3-Y.O+) (Class G)
2-30 (2-35) **1m 3y** £2,670.50 (£743.00: £357.50) Stalls: Low GOING minus 0.48 sec per fur (F)

				SP	RR	SF
1320^{11}	**Mr Rough (50)** (DMorris) **6-9-4** NDay(13) (prom: chsd ldr 4f out: led 2f out: drvn out)	—	**1**	7/2^{1}	63	39
1483^{3}	**Clytha Hill Lad (29)** (JMBradley) **6-7-6**$^{(5)}$ RFfrench(5) (b: lw: trckd ldr far side: stumbled 4f out: led far side over 2f out: jst failed)	nk	**2**	9/2^{2}	41	17
	Nabjelsedr (40) (AGNewcombe) **7-8-8**^{ow1} RCochrane(19) (b: bit bkwd: rdn 2f out: r.o wl appr fnl f: nrst fin)	3	**3**	7/1^{3}	46	21
1501^{8}	**Hadadabble (36)** (PatMitchell) **4-8-4**^{ow3} DHarrison(20) (led: rdn clr 4f out: hdd 2f out: kpt on)	s.h	**4**	14/1	42	15
662^{5}	**Battle Ground (IRE) (50)** (NACallaghan) **3-8-7** MRoberts(8) (a.p: ev ch 2f out: one pce)	s.h	**5**	9/1	56	21
1632^{15}	**Guesstimation (USA) (60)** (JPearce) **8-9-11v**$^{1(3)}$ CTeague(3) (b.nr fore: hld up far side: hdwy fnl 2f: r.o)	¾	**6**	10/1	65	41
1115^{12}	**Misterton (42)** (JAGlover) **3-7-13b**^{1} JFEgan(12) (in tch: rdn 2f out: r.o ins fnl f)	½	**7**	20/1	46	11
1388^{11}	**Square Mile Miss (IRE) (42)** (PHowling) **4-8-10** PaulEddery(15) (lw: hdwy over 1f out: r.o)	½	**8**	14/1	45	21
1449^{7}	**Cimmerian (54)** (MJohnston) **3-8-11** LDettori(7) (prom over 5f)	hd	**9**	14/1	57	22
1388^{13}	**Mubariz (IRE) (40)** (CSmith) **5-8-8** TQuinn(17) (t: lw: nvr trbld ldrs)	½	**10**	20/1	42	18
1501^{14}	**Spanish Stripper (USA) (32)** (MCChapman) **6-7-7**$^{(7)ow2}$ KimberleyHart(11) (in tch: rdn 2f out: sn btn)	1¼	**11**	33/1	31	5
1383^{9}	**Return To Brighton (36)** (JMBradley) **5-7-11**$^{(7)}$ JFowle(6) (chsd ldrs far side 5f)	4	**12**	20/1	27	3
1487^{7}	**Paddy Hurry (51)** (NACallaghan) **3-8-8b**^{1} WRyan(18) (in tch over 5f)	1¼	**13**	16/1	40	5
1005^{13}	**Richard House Lad (41)** (RHollinshead) **4-8-9** FLynch(4) (led far side over 5f)	2	**14**	14/1	26	2
1430^{7}	**Safa Dancer (29)** (BAMcMahon) **4-7-11** NCarlisle(2) (swtg: racd far side: a bhd)	3	**15**	16/1	8	—
1247^{7}	**Auchinleck Judge (28)** (JLHarris) **4-7-10** FNorton(1) (racd far side: a bhd)	2	**16**	25/1	3	—
	Madison's Touch (30) (RMFlower) **4-7-12** JLowe(10) (bit bkwd: a bhd)	½	**17**	25/1	4	—
1135^{12}	**Down The Yard (30)** (MCChapman) **4-7-12** DeclanO'Shea(16) (lw: n.d)	1½	**18**	20/1	1	—
1503^{10}	**Valise (39)** (GGMargarson) **4-8-7** GHind(9) (s.i.s: a bhd)	2	**19**	33/1	6	—
1441^{9}	**Burning Flame (37)** (RMFlower) **4-8-5b** SSanders(14) (a bhd)	8	**20**	33/1	—	—
				(SP 146.0%)	**20 Rn**	

1m 38.2 (2.20) CSF £16.88 CT £109.72 TOTE £4.50: £1.10 £2.00 £2.30 £5.20 (£13.60) Trio £50.20 OWNER Mr Robin Akehurst (NEWMARKET) BRED Ahmed M. Foustok
LONG HANDICAP Auchinleck Judge 7-2
WEIGHT FOR AGE 3yo-11lb
No bid
Mr Rough, who made the frame on both his visits here last season, was running in a seller for the first time since winning as a two-year-old. (7/2)
1483 Clytha Hill Lad looked a handicap certainty on his latest effort, and was very unfortunate to run out a clear winner on the slower side of the track. (9/2)
Nabjelsedr, who was disqualified after scoring on his final attempt last season, looked to just need the run but finished strongly and ought to find a race. (7/1)

Hadadabble made the most of the best ground against the stands' rail but was easily outpaced in the last quarter-mile. She has had plenty of chances. (14/1: 7/1-16/1)
556 Battle Ground (IRE) with trip and ground to suit but it probably did not help his chance that her was drawn so far from the stands' rail. (9/1)
Guesstimation (USA) ran a decent race from a poor draw and is no back number. (10/1)
Cimmerian (14/1: op 8/1)

1690 ROYAL ANGLIAN REGIMENT MEDIAN AUCTION MAIDEN STKS (3-Y.O F) (Class E)
3-00 (3-02) **7f 3y** £2,784.25 (£829.00: £394.50: £177.25) Stalls: Low GOING minus 0.48 sec per fur (F)

				SP	RR	SF
	Eurolink Profile (LMCumani) **3-8-11** LDettori(7) (hld up: plld out over 2f out: hdwy to ld 1f out: comf)	—	1	15/8 [1]	70+	39
	Free As A Bird (MRChannon) **3-8-11** RHills(1) (led 6f: one pce)	1	2	7/2 [3]	68	37
1485[3]	**Juvenilia (IRE)** (JARToller) **3-8-11** SSanders(2) (prom: outpcd over 2f out: styd on wl fnl f)	3	3	3/1 [2]	61	30
1485[4]	**Moon Song** (APJarvis) **3-8-11** TQuinn(5) (chsd ldr: one pce appr fnl f)	hd	4	11/2	61	30
	Go For Green (62) (DrJDScargill) **3-8-11** RCochrane(4) (lw: hld up: hdwy over 3f out: rdn 2f out: sn btn)	1	5	10/1	58	27
1500[5]	**Crackerbox (39)** (CADwyer) **3-8-11** DHarrison(6) (lw: chsd ldrs: rdn over 2f out: sn wknd)	10	6	33/1	36	5
	Pisum Sativum (JLHarris) **3-8-6**(5) RFfrench(3) (str: bkwd: sn t.o)	25	7	25/1	—	—
				(SP 113.3%)		**7 Rn**

1m 25.6 (1.40) CSF £7.77 TOTE £2.50: £2.00 £2.10 (£6.70) OWNER Eurolink Group Plc (NEWMARKET) BRED Mrs Carolyn Antoniades
Eurolink Profile was given plenty to do in a poor race but did the job in good style and should leave this ordinary from behind in time. (15/8)
Free As A Bird, on her toes beforehand, did little wrong but was not in the same league as the winner. (7/2)
1485 Juvenilia (IRE), despite her pedigree, shaped like one that would appreciate further. (3/1)
1485 Moon Song reproduced Folkestone form with Juvenilia to the pound. (11/2)
Go For Green, whose promising-looking run quickly petered out as the race warmed up, may do better over six. (10/1: 7/1-12/1)
1500 Crackerbox begins to look thoroughly exposed. (33/1)

1691 AMEC PROCESS AND ENERGY H'CAP (0-80) (3-Y.O) (Class D)
3-30 (3-30) **6f 3y** £3,613.75 (£1,078.00: £514.50: £232.75) Stalls: Low GOING minus 0.48 sec per fur (F)

				SP	RR	SF
	Zugudi (70) (KMahdi) **3-9-2** RPrice(5) (lw: chsd ldrs: rdn 2f out: led ins fnl f: r.o)	—	1	20/1	79	53
1423[4]	**March Crusader (72)** (BHanbury) **3-9-4** WRyan(6) (stdd s: hld up: hdwy 2f out: unable qckn ins fnl f)	¾	2	7/2 [2]	79	53
1243[5]	**Song Mist (IRE) (72)** (PFICole) **3-9-4** TQuinn(1) (lw: w ldr: led over 2f out: hdd & one pce ins fnl f)	1½	3	2/1 [1]	75	49
1392[8]	**A Breeze (68)** (DMorris) **3-9-0** NDay(4) (bhd: rdn 3f out: styd on appr fnl f)	3	4	7/2 [2]	63	37
1151[4]	**Castle Ashby Jack (64)** (PHowling) **3-8-10v** PaulEddery(2) (b.hind: led over 3f)	4	5	16/1	48	22
845[9]	**Royal Cascade (IRE) (58)** (BAMcMahon) **3-8-4** SSanders(7) (lw: in tch: rdn 2f out: no imp)	1¾	6	8/1	38	12
1451*	**Tailwind (67)** (WRMuir) **3-8-13** 6x MRoberts(3) (chsd ldrs: tl wknd over 2f out)	½	7	6/1 [3]	45	19
1458[14]	**Supreme Maimoon (75)** (MJPolglase) **3-9-7** TGMcLaughlin(8) (lw: dwlt: hdwy 3f out: wknd over 1f out)	2	8	14/1	48	22
				(SP 120.5%)		**8 Rn**

1m 11.3 (0.40) CSF £85.16 CT £193.27 TOTE £18.10: £2.30 £1.30 £1.40 (£50.70) OWNER Sheik Ahmad Yousuf Al Sabah (NEWMARKET) BRED Cliveden Stud Ltd
Zugudi gave his trainer his first winner with his first runner in this country, battling on in fine style to cause another upset at the track. (20/1)
1423 March Crusader took a good hold but looked in control when beginning his move, not finding quite as much as might have been expected. There are races to be won with him once he gets his act together. (7/2)
1243 Song Mist (IRE) acted well on the fast ground and made good use of the rail she was drawn against. There seemed no excuses. (2/1:op7/2)
977 A Breeze found this trip too sharp on such quick ground. (7/2)
1151 Castle Ashby Jack did not seem to see out the trip but is proving very hard to place. (16/1)
259* Royal Cascade (IRE) was suited by racing close to the pace on the All-Weather but has yet to match those efforts on Turf. (8/1: 11/2-9/1)

1692 E.B.F. BRECKLAND MAIDEN STKS (2-Y.O) (Class D)
4-00 (4-00) **6f 3y** £3,260.25 (£972.00: £463.50: £209.25) Stalls: Low GOING minus 0.48 sec per fur (F)

				SP	RR	SF
	Baltic State (USA) (HRACecil) **2-9-0** WRyan(3) (leggy: scope: bit bkwd: plld hrd: trckd ldr far side: led 1f out: rdn & r.o wl)	—	1	5/6 [1]	77+	52
583[6]	**Mishraak (IRE)** (RWArmstrong) **2-9-0** RHills(1) (led far side: led 3f out: hdd 1f out: unable qckn)	4	2	4/1 [3]	66	41
	Moothyeb (USA) (SbinSuroor) **2-9-0** LDettori(2) (w'like: scope: s.i.s: sn trckng ldrs far side: rdn & one pce appr fnl f)	2½	3	3/1 [2]	60	35
1418[9]	**Rebalza (IRE)** (JMPEustace) **2-9-0** RCochrane(4) (racd centre: led 3f: sn btn)	6	4	33/1	44	19
1418[2]	**Blundell Lane (IRE)** (APJarvis) **2-9-0** TQuinn(5) (trckd ldr centre effrt over 2f out: sn rdn & btn)	2	5	8/1	38	13
				(SP 113.6%)		**5 Rn**

1m 11.3 (0.40) CSF £4.41 TOTE £2.40: £1.40 £2.00 (£3.70) OWNER Mr K. Abdulla (NEWMARKET) BRED Juddmonte Farms
Baltic State (USA), a tall, weak-looking sort, has the frame to grow into a very attractive colt. A half-brother to last year's hat-trick scorer Sambac, he has a fine action and did this in great style. (5/6: 4/7-10/11)
583 Mishraak (IRE), quietly fancied in the ring, ran a much improved race and is capable of finding an opening. (4/1)
Moothyeb (USA) never looked like fully recovering after a slightly tardy start, looking short of speed in the closing stages. This brother to the useful filly Ikdam should do better in time. (3/1)
Rebalza (IRE) took the rather odd step of coming down the centre but at least had a clear run this time although he cut little ice. (33/1)
1418 Blundell Lane (IRE) probably saw too much daylight in the centre of the track and did run his race. (8/1)

1693 RIVER YARE LIMITED STKS (0-65) (4-Y.O+) (Class F)
4-30 (4-31) **1m 6f 17y** £2,392.50 (£660.00: £313.50) Stalls: High GOING minus 0.48 sec per fur (F)

				SP	RR	SF
1371[6]	**Charnwood Jack (USA) (65)** (ICampbell) **4-8-10** RPrice(1) (b: dropped rr 10f out: hdwy over 3f out: led 2f out: rdn out)	—	1	3/1 [3]	72	37
1260[4]	**Chabrol (CAN) (62)** (TTClement) **4-8-5**(5) ADaly(5) (led 12f: rdn & r.o fnl f)	1¼	2	7/4 [1]	71	36
1414[14]	**Tissue of Lies (USA) (62)** (MJohnston) **4-8-10** LDettori(4) (lw: plld hrd: sn chsng ldr: ev ch 4f out: one pce appr fnl f)	2	3	2/1 [2]	68	33
1081[4]	**Tonnerre (52)** (BAMcMahon) **5-8-10** SSanders(2) (chsd ldrs: rdn over 3f out: no imp)	3	4	9/1	65	30

632[9]	**Lucky Hoof (60)** (KAMorgan) **4-8-0v**(7) GHannon(3) (stdd s: hld up & plld hrd: pushed along 5f out: sn wl bhd)	dist	**5**	20/1	—	—
				(SP 109.5%)	**5 Rn**	

3m 1.4 (3.40) CSF £7.81 TOTE £3.50: £1.30 £1.20 (£3.60) OWNER Mr T. J. Dawson (NEWMARKET) BRED Virginia Kraft Payson
888 Charnwood Jack (USA) may have been suited by the sedate early pace, reversing Nottingham form with Chabrol. (3/1)
1260 Chabrol (CAN), racing with his tongue tied down as usual to minimise his wind trouble, looked to be struggling once the pace picked up but responded gamely in the final furlong. (7/4)
Tissue of Lies (USA) seemed to pull too hard to get this trip and it would be 'case not proven' in a more truly-run race. (2/1: 6/4-9/4)
1081 Tonnerre would have been 10lb and more better off than these in a handicap, and ran as well as could be expected. (9/1)
Lucky Hoof, once she stopped pulling, quickly gave up the ghost. (20/1)

1694 HEYDON HALL APPRENTICE H'CAP (0-70) (3-Y.O+) (Class G)

5-00 (5-00) **1m 2f 21y** £2,168.50 (£616.00: £305.50) Stalls: Low GOING minus 0.48 sec per fur (F)

				SP	RR	SF
1105[9]	**Zorro (54)** (RMFlower) **3-8-0**ow3 JWilkinson(5) (hdwy over 3f out: led over 2f out: rdn & r.o wl fnl f)	—	**1**	4/1[2]	63	30
1677[4]	**Zahran (IRE) (37)** (JMBradley) **6-7-5**(5) JFowle(4) (lw: chsd ldrs: outpcd 3f out: rdn & edgd lft appr fnl f: r.o wl)	3	**2**	9/1	41	24
1503[4]	**Acerbus Dulcis (37)** (MCChapman) **6-7-5**(5) SCarson(2) (chsd ldrs: led 6f out: tl over 2f out: btn whn n.m.r ins fnl f & nr fin: fin 4th, s.h: plcd 3rd)	s.h	**3**	25/1	36	19
1632[2]	**Mardrew (61)** (TTClement) **3-8-2**(5) PClarke(3) (lw: a.p: one pce & n.m.r ins fnl f: wnt lft & eased nr fin: fin 3rd, 3l: disq: plcd 4th)	3	**4**	5/2[1]	61	31
1459[7]	**Golden Touch (USA) (58)** (DJSCosgrove) **5-8-9**(8) SGaillard(10) (lw: in tch: rdn over 2f out: r.o fnl f)	2	**5**	7/1[3]	54	37
1500[3]	**Poker Princess (52)** (MBell) **3-7-4**(8) NicolaCole(7) (prom tl wknd over 2f out)	s.h	**6**	4/1[2]	48	18
1273[7]	**Utmost Zeal (USA) (60)** (PWHarris) **4-9-5b** CLowther(11) (sn pushed along bhd fnl 5f)	1	**7**	10/1	55	38
1371[5]	**Montecristo (65)** (RGuest) **4-9-0**(10) LucyBrown(9) (s.v.s: nvr nrr)	3½	**8**	14/1	54	37
1388[12]	**Bad News (37)** (JMBradley) **5-7-10** PDoe(1) (t: hld up: hdwy 4f out: rdn 3f out: sn btn)	¾	**9**	33/1	25	8
1140[20]	**Select Star (IRE) (66)** (APJarvis) **3-8-4**(8) CCarver(8) (w ldrs: rdn & wknd over 3f out)	3½	**10**	16/1	48	18
1632[17]	**African Sun (IRE) (44)** (MCChapman) **4-8-3** VictoriaAppleby(6) (lw: led over 4f: wknd 4f out: eased whn btn)	20	**11**	11/1	—	—
				(SP 127.8%)	**11 Rn**	

2m 5.7 (1.90) CSF £40.09 CT £760.72 TOTE £5.50: £1.20 £2.90 £2.30 (£28.00) Trio £106.60 OWNER Mr G. George (JEVINGTON) BRED T. M. Jennings
LONG HANDICAP Bad News 6-12 Zahran (IRE) 7-6 Acerbus Dulcis 6-12
WEIGHT FOR AGE 3yo-13lb
771 Zorro apparently hated the soft ground last time and showed his Folkestone effort was no fluke by landing quite a touch. (4/1)
1677 Zahran (IRE) stayed on strongly towards the finish but looked to be edging towards the far rail, doing those on his inside no favours. (9/1)
1503 Acerbus Dulcis, made plenty of use of, was short of room in the closing stages, but it made little difference as he was already well held. (25/1)
1632 Mardrew ran his second good race of the week off this mark, and would have finished considerably closer had his pilot been able to ride him right out, rather than contend with hanging. (5/2)
1384 Golden Touch (USA) never looked like doing enough to take a hand. (7/1)
1500 Poker Princess, stepping up in trip, didn't seem to last the trip after the quick early pace. (4/1)
Utmost Zeal (USA) (10/1: 8/1-12/1)
1371 Montecristo took some persuading to start, but showed enough from an impossible position to suggest he is capable of stepping up before too long. (14/1: 10/1-16/1)
1024 African Sun (IRE) (11/1: 7/1-12/1)

T/Plpt: £16.80 (568.31 Tckts). T/Qdpt: £10.20 (54.55 Tckts) Dk

1695a - 1697a (Irish Racing) - See Computer Raceform

1192a-LEOPARDSTOWN (Dublin, Ireland) (L-H) (Good)
Wednesday May 28th

1698a JONES LANG WOOTTON SAVAL BEG STKS (Listed) (3-Y.O+)

7-30 (7-33) **1m 6f** IR £12,900.00 (IR £3,700.00: IR £1,700.00: IR £500.00) GOING minus 0.07 sec per fur (G)

				SP	RR	SF
	French Ballerina (IRE) (PJFlynn,Ireland) **4-9-7** JAHeffernan (rn 2nd: trckd ldr: chal st: led 2f out: sn qcknd clr: styd on wl: easily)	—	**1**	11/8[1]	105+	56
1542a[5]	**Damancher** (PMullins,Ireland) **5-9-10** CRoche (rn 3rd: rdn & chsd ldrs 4f out: 4th st: mod 2nd u.p over 1f out: s.o: no ch w wnr)	8	**2**	11/2[3]	99	50
	Sadlers Home (IRE) (JSBolger,Ireland) **3-7-11** JoannaMorgan (hld up: rn 6th: chsd ldrs 2f out: styd on last 1½f: nt trble wnr)	nk	**3**	8/1	92	23
	Kris Green (IRE) (DKWeld,Ireland) **3-8-0** WJSupple (hld up: 5th ½-wy: chsd ldrs st: kpt on last 2f: no imp)	¾	**4**	10/1	94	25
	Miltonfield (JEMulhern,Ireland) **8-9-6** PJSmullen (hld up towards rr: rdn st: styd on last 1½f: nvr nr to chal)	nk	**5**	20/1	93	44
1195a[5]	**Buddy Marvel (IRE)** (JJMcLoughlin,Ireland) **3-8-0** NGMcCullagh (rn 4th: 3rd, rdn & chsd ldrs st: edgd lft u.p 2f out: 2nd & nt trble wnr 1½f out: one pce)	4½	**6**	3/1[2]	88	19
	Lady Arpel (IRE) (PO'Leary,Ireland) **5-9-3** KJManning (hld up towards rr: 7th & rdn st: no imp 1½f out)	4½	**7**	14/1	80	31
	Mount Row (CCollins,Ireland) **4-9-3** PShanahan (led: hdd & nt qckn 2f out: sn wknd)	8	**8**	7/1	71	22
				(SP 126.6%)	**8 Rn**	

3m 4.7 (7.70) OWNER Mrs John Magnier (CARRICK-ON-SUIR)
French Ballerina (IRE), trying this trip for the first time, continued the rate of progress she displayed towards the end of last season. She ran right away from the opposition in the straight, and there are plenty of options for her. Distance seems to be absolutely no object. (11/8)
Damancher was flying a bit high here and was not disgraced. (11/2: op 3/1)
Sadlers Home (IRE) ran well for a three-year-old, staying on well but never holding out any hope of getting on terms with the winner. (8/1)
Kris Green (IRE) was another for whom this distance now seems essential. (10/1)
Miltonfield, the Irish Cesarewitch winner, underlined his limitations that he is just a handicapper. (20/1)

1699a - 1718a (Irish Racing) - See Computer Raceform

1554a-LONGCHAMP (Paris, France) (R-H) (Good)
Thursday May 29th

1719a PRIX DU PALAIS-ROYAL (Gp 3) (3-Y.O+)
3-05 (3-04) **7f** £24,691.00 (£8,979.00: £4,489.00: £2,694.00)

				SP	RR	SF
717a^{2}	**Nombre Premier** (AdeRoyerDupre,France) **3-8-12** GMosse	—	**1**		120	—
	Earl Of March (AFabre,France) **3-8-7** TJarnet	1½	**2**		112	—
1198a^{2}	**Wizard King** (SirMarkPrescott) **6-9-9** GDuffield	s.h	**3**		117	—
981*	**Craigievar** (JRFanshawe) **3-8-7** DHarrison	2½	**4**		106	—

6 Rn

1m 19.3 (0.30) P-M 2.00F: 1.30F 1.70F OWNER Marquesa de Moratella (CHANTILLY) BRED Marquesa de Moratalla

717a Nombre Premier is a top-class performer when the ground is on the fast side. He moved sweetly to take the lead at the furlong marker and was not extended, winning with a lot in hand. The time was just 0.40 seconds outside the course record. He had apparently worked on very soft ground leading up to this event with disastrous results. He now goes for the Jersey Stakes at Royal Ascot and will take all the beating on this form.

Earl Of March is a rapidly-improving colt and he will definitely make it in Group company by the end of the season. He made a forward move halfway up the straight and was running on really well at the finish, taking second place close home. It would be no surprise to see him run in the Prix de la Porte Maillot over the same course and distance

1198a Wizard King made a courageous effort to make all, but began to weaken as the weight burden started to tell inside the final furlong. He is one of the most consistent horses in training, and will now go for the Ballychorus Stakes in Ireland and then the Beeswing at Newcastle.

981* Craigievar put up a gallant effort, but he could not show his best due to the fast ground. His connections will now wait for an easier surface and then confirm his future programme. This was, however, a solid performance in unfavourable conditions.

1550a-BADEN-BADEN (Germany) (L-H) (Good to firm)
Friday May 30th

1720a BENAZET RENNEN (Gp 3) (3-Y.O+)
3-25 (3-31) **6f** £28,409.00 (£11,364.00: £5,681.00)

				SP	RR	SF
1309*	**Monaassib** (EALDunlop) **6-9-6** DO'Donohoe	—	**1**		113	—
816a*	**Roseate Wood (FR)** (UweStoltefuss,Germany) **4-9-2** PHarley	nk	**2**		108	—
671^{2}	**Easy Dollar** (BGubby) **5-9-6** AClark	1¾	**3**		108	—
1171^{5}	**Diffident (FR)** (SbinSuroor) **5-9-6** LDettori (btn over 2¼l)		**5**		—	—

13 Rn

1m 7.91 TOTE 67DM: 24DM 41DM 41DM OWNER Maktoum Al Maktoum (NEWMARKET) BRED Side Hill Stud in Ireland

1309* Monaassib was always disputing the lead. He kept on well to take the advantage close home, breaking the course record in the process.

671 Easy Dollar, always prominent, took the lead two furlongs out and hung left over a furlong out, slightly hampering Diffident in the process. Still with the advantage inside the final furlong, he was headed and unable to quicken close home.

1171 Diffident (FR), in mid-division, made headway over two furlongs out but did not get a clear run over a furlong out. He was one-paced inside the final furlong.

1358a-CHANTILLY (France) (R-H) (Good)
Saturday May 31st

1721a PRIX DU GROS-CHENE (Gp 2) (3-Y.O+)
3-00 (2-57) **5f** £33,670.00 (£13,468.00: £6,734.00: £3,367.00)

				SP	RR	SF
1206a^{2}	**Titus Livius (FR)** (JEPease,France) **4-9-3** CAsmussen (hld up: n.m.r 2f out: rapid prog 1f out: tk ld cl home)	—	**1**		115	—
1206a^{3}	**Wardara** (FBellenger,France) **5-9-0b** MdeSmyter (hld up: effrt fr 1½f out: gd late prog: wnt 2nd cl home)	¾	**2**		110	—
1455^{9}	**Hever Golf Rose** (TJNaughton) **6-9-0** OPeslier (a.p: led ins fnl f: outpcd cl home)	s.h	**3**		109	—
	Don't Worry Me (IRE) (GHenrot,France) **5-9-0** AJunk (prom early: led over 1f out: outpcd fnl 100y)	¾	**4**		107	—
	Winning Smile (FR) (TClout,France) **7-9-0b** TGillet (s.s: prog 1½f out: fin wl)	2½	**5**		99	—
1309^{3}	**Crowded Avenue** (PJMakin) **5-9-0** GMosse (mid div: one pce fnl f)	hd	**6**		99	—
	Hambye (VCaruso,Italy) **3-8-3** TThulliez (prom 1½f out: sn fdd)	s.nk	**7**		95	—
811a^{7}	**Passion For Life** (GLewis) **4-9-0b^{1}** PaulEddery (led tl 1½f out: fdd qckly)	2	**8**		92	—

8 Rn

59.5 secs (3.00) P-M 1.80F: 1.10F 1.40F 1.10F (14.00F) OWNER Niarchos Family (CHANTILLY) BRED S.Niarchos

1206a Titus Livius (FR) was given a fine waiting race ride by Asmussen. He had plenty to do entering the final furlong but showed a fine turn of foot to mow down his rivals in the final stages. After having a busy two-year-old campaign, he was unsuccessful at three, running in decent company on several occasions, but looks back to his best. He is now being aimed at the King's Stand Stakes at Royal Ascot and, in his present form, it will take a good horse to beat him.

1206a Wardara was putting in her best work at the finish and stole second place close home. She has improved considerably since being trained at Deauville and a Group race could come her way before the season is out. She will now be heading for the Prix de Ris-Orangis at her local track in July.

1206a* Hever Golf Rose ran her usual game and genuine race. Never far off the lead, she showed ahead inside the final furlong but just ran out of steam in the final twenty yards. She is now back on top form and still retains enormous ability.

Don't Worry Me (IRE) is still coming back to her best. Well up throughout, she led a furlong out before being passed in the final one hundred yards. She loves a firm surface and is entered in the King's Stand Stakes and the Cork And Orrery Stakes at Royal Ascot. Six furlongs may be her best distance now.

1309 Crowded Avenue was thereabouts until a furlong and a half out but then proved rather one paced. His cause was hindered by the fact that he was not covered up in the race, and he may well go for the Vodac Dash at Epsom.

811a Passion For Life showed up well for most of the way, but dropped out rather quickly with a furlong and a half to travel. He is yet to find his form of last year, but will be more of a force with cut in the ground.

1722a PRIX DE ROYAUMONT (Gp 3) (3-Y.O F)
3-30 (3-27) **1m 4f** £24,691.00 (£8,979.00: £4,489.00)

				SP	RR	SF
	Legend Maker (IRE) (AFabre,France) **3-9-0** TJarnet	—	1		102	—
	Kassana (IRE) (AdeRoyerDupre,France) **3-9-0** GMosse	1½	2		100	—
1147²	**Vagabond Chanteuse** (TJEtherington) **3-9-0** OPeslier	½	3		99	—
1028*	**Kyle Rhea** (HRACecil) **3-9-0** WRyan (btn over 3l)		6		—	—
						8 Rn

2m 33.6 (6.80) P-M 22.10F: 4.10F 2.20F 3.40F (45.90F) OWNER Mr M. Tabor (CHANTILLY) BRED Sir Thomas Pilkington and Mrs E. Burke
Legend Maker (IRE) ran out a rather impressive winner. She was well placed throughout and took control halfway up the straight. She then stretched out impressively to the line and won virtually unchallenged. Although by Sadler's Wells, she acted well on the surface, and will now take in the Prix de Malleret at Longchamp at the end of the month.
Kassana (IRE) was unlucky on her seasonal debut and again here. She was hampered at a crucial moment one and a half furlongs out and the race was virtually over by the time she was balanced to make her challenge. Making up a lot of ground inside the final furlong, she could never get close enough to threaten the winner. She is still a maiden but one of the most useful ones in training. Like the winner, she may be allowed to take her chance in the Prix de Malleret.
1147 Vagabond Chanteuse needed a decent pace but as there were no takers, she had to do the donkey work herself. She set a sound gallop but could not accelerate with the others halfway up the straight, although she did stay on gamely under pressure. Now due a rest, her main autumn targets will be the Park Hill Stakes and a tilt at the Prix de Pomone at Deauville. She cannot be ruled out if the ground becomes soft.
1028* Kyle Rhea was close up down the back straight and still there with every chance when the field entered the straight. She was beaten because she could not stride out on the firm ground, and was not given a hard time in the latter stages. She will no doubt be racing on a soft surface next time.

1720a-BADEN-BADEN (Germany) (L-H) (Good)
Sunday June 1st

1723a BADENER JUGEND PREIS (UNRACED) (2-Y.O)
2-45 (2-55) **5f** £11,364.00 (£4,545.00: £2,655.00)

				SP	RR	SF
	El Maimoun (MHofer,Germany) **2-9-0** ASuborics	—	1		—	—
	Norbello (GER) (PRemmert,Germany) **2-9-0** THellier	1½	2		—	—
	Supermodel (GER) (MRChannon) **2-8-9** BDoyle	7	3		—	—
						8 Rn

57.75 secs TOTE 28DM: 18DM 28DM 18DM (572DM) OWNER Stall Mabrouk BRED Belgravia Bloodstock Ltd
Supermodel (GER), making her debut for Mick Channon, raced in mid-division and stayed on from two furlongs out, but was unable to catch the winner.

1724a GROSSER PREIS DER WIRTSCHAFT (Gp 2) (4-Y.O+)
3-25 (3-27) **1m 3f** £60,606.00 (£24,621.00: £11,364.00: £6,439.00)

				SP	RR	SF
719a*	**Oxalagu (GER)** (BSchutz,Germany) **5-9-2** AStarke (hld up in tch: hdwy to ld 1f out: all out)	—	1		119	—
1073a*	**Wurftaube (GER)** (HRemmert,Germany) **4-9-0** KWoodburn (hld up: hdwy over 3f out & over 1f out: ev ch wl ins fnl f: unable qckn cl home)	½	2		116	—
1200a²	**Needle Gun (IRE)** (CEBrittain) **7-9-4** BDoyle (led to 1f out: kpt on)	1¼	3		119	—
1073a⁸	**Narrabeth (IRE)** (HJentzsch,Germany) **4-9-0** MLarsen (mid div: one pce cl home)	s.h	4		114	—
1200a*	**Artan (IRE)** (MRolke,Germany) **5-9-6** RCochrane (a.p: ev ch wl over 1f out: one pce)	1½	5		118	—
	Night Petticoat (GER) (BSchutz,Germany) **4-9-0** NGrant (a.p: one pce fnl 2f)	4	6		106	—
1073a²	**Surako (GER)** (HJentzsch,Germany) **4-9-2** PSchiergen (prom: rdn st: wknd wl over 1f out)	3½	7		103	—
						7 Rn

2m 12.92 TOTE 83DM: 15DM 12DM 19DM (141DM) OWNER Gestut Rietberg
1200a Needle Gun (IRE) set an even pace and stayed at the head of affairs until a furlong from home, where he kept on to take third prize. He will now have a well-earned rest.

1721a-CHANTILLY (France) (R-H) (Good)
Sunday June 1st

1725a D'ABU DHABI AIRPORT DUTY FREE PRIX JEAN PRAT (Gp 1) (3-Y.O C & F)
2-00 (1-58) **1m 1f** £44,893.00 (£17,957.00: £8,979.00: £4,489.00) GOING minus 0.07 sec per fur (G)

				SP	RR	SF
940⁴	**Starborough** (DRLoder) **3-9-2** LDettori (broke wl: mde all: styd on wl fnl f)	—	1	2/1²	111	79
742*	**Mamalik (USA)** (JHMGosden) **3-9-2** RHills (m free early: trckd ldr: hrd rdn 1½f out: styd on one pce)	1½	2	67/10	108	76
1361a*	**Kirkwall** (AFabre,France) **3-9-2** TJarnet (mid div: sn outpcd: r.o fr 1½f out: fin wl)	s.h	3	6/5¹	108	76
1204a³	**Visionary (FR)** (AFabre,France) **3-9-2** OPeslier (hld up bhd: rapid prog fr 1f out: fin wl)	nse	4	33/10³	108	76
	Cirino (USA) (MmeCHead,France) **3-9-2** FHead (prom early: bdly hmpd over 5f out: 4th st: effrt & one pce cl home)	2½	5	63/10	104	72
				(SP 128.7%)		**5 Rn**

1m 51.7 (1.70) P-M 3.00F: 2.10F 3.60F OWNER Sheikh Mohammed (NEWMARKET) BRED Sheikh Mohammed Bin Rashid Al Maktoum
STEWARDS' ENQUIRY Hills susp. 10-13/6/97 (dangerous riding)
940 Starborough won this Group One race in excellent style. Making virtually every yard of the running, he was given a breather rounding the final turn, which took some of his rivals by surprise. He built up a good lead of a length by the furlong marker and kept it easily to the line without being given a hard time in the final furlong. On the upgrade, he should stay further. His trainer is now looking seriously at the St James's Palace Stakes over Ascot's stiff mile. (2/1)

742* Mamalik (USA) put up a most promising performance considering it was just his second appearance on a racecourse. He badly interfered with Cirino some six furlongs out and the Stewards suspended his jockey for four days. He ran a little green in the straight but battled on well to hold second place by the smallest of margins. He will improve for the outing and may be allowed to take his chance in the St James's Palace Stakes. (67/10)
1361a* Kirkwall was held up and then outpaced when the leader accelerated early in the straight. He ran on strongly from one and a half furlongs out and only failed by inches to steal second place. He will be suited by a slightly longer distance, but may now be given a rest, having had five races already this season, (6/5)
1204a Visionary (FR) was in last place for much of the race. He did come with a late run and was still making progress at the line. (33/10)

1726a LES EMIRATES PRIX DU JOCKEY-CLUB (Gp 1) (3-Y.O C & F)
3-20 (3-21) **1m 4f** £280,548.00 (£112,233.00: £56,117.00: £28,058.00: £14,029.00) GOING minus 0.07 sec per fur (G)

				SP	RR	SF
819a*	**Peintre Celebre (USA)** (AFabre,France) **3-9-2** OPeslier (trckd ldrs: gd prog fr 1½f out: hdd 1f out: wnt clr u.p ½f out: r.o wl)	—	**1**	31/10[1]	122	76
1070a[2]	**Oscar (IRE)** (PBary,France) **3-9-2** SGuillot (mid div: prog 2f out: led briefly 1f out: hdd & r.o one pce)	2	**2**	9/1[3]	119	73
1205a[4]	**Astarabad (USA)** (AdeRoyerDupre,France) **3-9-2** GMosse (hld up: prog ent st: qcknd to ld 2f out: no ex fnl f)	½	**3**	138/10	119	73
629a*	**Fragrant Mix (FR)** (AFabre,France) **3-9-2b[1]** TJarnet (a cl up: chal 2f out: one pce cl home)	4	**4**	38/10[2]	113	67
1070a[3]	**Ithaki (IRE)** (JEPease,France) **3-9-2** CAsmussen (hld up: effrt 2f out: one pce fnl f)	5	**5**	217/10	107	61
1070a*	**Shaka** (J-CRouget,France) **3-9-2b[1]** J-RDubosc (hld up: hdwy 2f out: nvr nrr)	¾	**6**	31/10[1]	106	60
851*	**Voyagers Quest (USA)** (PWChapple-Hyam) **3-9-2** JReid (disp ld fr s: led st: hdd 2f out: wknd rapidly fr 1½f out)	hd	**7**	97/10	106	60
819a[3]	**Kashwan (SPA)** (ELellouche,France) **3-9-2** TThulliez (nvr cl to chal: one pce fr 2f out)	s.h	**8**	504/10	106	60
	Bonapartiste (FR) (PDemercastel,France) **3-9-2** FHead (last st: styd on one pce)	4	**9**	242/10	100	54
	Fier Danseur (FR) (JLesbordes,France) **3-9-2** VVion (n.d)	¾	**10**	638/10	99	53
1195a[2]	**Casey Tibbs (IRE)** (DKWeld,Ireland) **3-9-2v[1]** MJKinane (hld up: effrt 2f out: sn btn)	2	**11**	172/10	97	51
	Arabian King (AFabre,France) **3-9-2** DBoeuf (cl up early: u.p 2f out: wknd fnl f)	2	**12**	139/10	94	48
1025*	**Perfect Paradigm (IRE)** (JHMGosden) **3-9-2b[1]** LDettori (disp ld st: sn btn: dropped out)	5	**13**	172/10	87	41
	Speedfriend (GER) (RCollet,France) **3-9-2** CHanotel (mid div st: wknd qckly)	4	**14**	618/10	82	36

(SP 126.9%) **14 Rn**

2m 29.6 (2.80) P-M 4.10F: 2.10F 3.10F 4.20F (25.70F) OWNER Mr D. Wildenstein (CHANTILLY) BRED Allez France Stables
819a* Peintre Celebre (USA) has improved considerably. Prominent on the rail nearly the whole way, he briefly looked a little hemmed in early in the straight. Once he got a run over a furlong out he produced a devastating burst under pressure one hundred yards from the line, showing true class. This was his fourth appearance in public and he has only been beaten once, when things went against him in the autumn. He seems a really classy individual and could go for the Irish Derby, although connections appear to be leaning towards the King George VI and Queen Elizabeth Diamond Stakes. He will take all the beating from now on and should improve as he is still learning the game. (31/10)
1070a Oscar (IRE) lost nothing in defeat and was running on at the finish. Held up early on, he came to challenge on the outside halfway up the straight and might just have had his head in front at the furlong pole, but had no answer to the late surge of the winner. He is still a little inexperienced and has scope for further improvement. He will now be rested and trained for the Arc de Triomphe, via the Prix Neil. He will almost certainly benefit from a softer surface. (9/1)
1205a Astarabad (USA) put up his best performance to date. He took control of the race one and a half furlongs out and at that point looked the likely winner, but could not keep up late on. He loves a firm surface so will be campaigned over the summer, and the Prix Maurice de Nieuil at the end of July looks a likely target. (138/10)
629a* Fragrant Mix (FR) was always well placed but could only stay on at the one pace inside the final furlong. He was given every chance but may have been found out by the distance. He may now be aimed at the Grand Prix de Paris. (38/10)
851* Voyagers Quest (USA) was given every chance and was prominent until shortening his stride over a furlong out. Once beaten, he was not given a hard time and his trainer thought that this below-par performance may well be linked with a bug in his stable. On the other hand, he may have preferred more cut in the ground and should be given another chance. (97/10)
1025* Perfect Paradigm (IRE) led from the start and then dropped out of contention rather quickly. This ground was much faster than that at Chester and his jockey reported that the colt chopped and changed his legs on many occasions during the race. (172/10)

1727a PRIX DE SANDRINGHAM (Gp 3) (3-Y.O F)
4-40 (4-32) **1m** £24,691.00 (£8,979.00: £4,489.00) GOING minus 0.07 sec per fur (G)

			SP	RR	SF
Orford Ness (FR) (PBary,France) **3-8-11** SGuillot	—	**1**		104	60
Basse Besogne (IRE) (CLaffon-Parias,France) **3-8-11** CAsmussen	s.nk	**2**		104	60
Veiled Threat (IRE) (RCollet,France) **3-8-11** TJarnet	s.nk	**3**		103	59

7 Rn

1m 39.4 (2.90) P-M 5.70F: 2.50F 2.90F OWNER Mr K. Abdulla (CHANTILLY) BRED Juddmonte Farms
Orford Ness (FR) held a good position behind the leaders and took a little time before delivering her challenge, which was perfectly timed. She only really goes on a firm surface and now heads for the Prix d'Astarte at Deauville.
Basse Besogne (IRE) always held a handy position and kept on gamely to the line. She was just run out of it in the final stages and may be better suited to a shorter distance.
Veiled Threat (IRE) was putting in her best work at the finish in this slowly-run race.

1555a-SAN SIRO (Milan, Italy) (R-H) (Heavy)
Sunday June 1st

1728a PREMIO EMILIO TURATI (Gp 2) (3-Y.O+)
5-05 (5-20) **1m** £50,692.00 (£23,275.00: £12,945.00: £6,473.00)

				SP	RR	SF
1210[5]	**Gothenberg (IRE)** (MJohnston) **4-9-4** JWeaver (mde all: r.o wl)	—	**1**		124	—
719a[3]	**Zero Problemo (IRE)** (BSchutz,Germany) **4-9-4** WNewnes (mid div st: r.o fnl 2f: tk 2nd cl home)	3¾	**2**		117	—
	Morigi (ITellini,Italy) **6-9-4** MTellini (mid div: chsd wnr appr fnl f: wknd cl home)	1	**3**		115	—
	Kierkegaard (DDucci,Italy) **4-9-4** FJovine (prom: chal wl over 2f out: wknd appr fnl f)	1	**4**		113	—
917a[3]	**Gianky Gioffry (IRE)** (RBrogi,Italy) **3-8-7** GBietolini (hld up in rr: effrt 2f out: sn one pce)	3¼	**5**		106	—
	Ravier (ITY) (EBorromeo,Italy) **6-9-4** MEsposito (in rr: no hdwy fnl 3f)	½	**6**		105	—
1550a[2]	**Devil River Peek (USA)** (BSchutz,Germany) **5-9-4** RHughes (in rr: a bhd)	1½	**7**		102	—

	Sensation (SbinSuroor) **4-9-1** PatEddery (3rd st: btn over 2f out)	2½	**8**		94	—
						8 Rn

1m 41.8 (11.80) TOTE 33L: 16L 23L 25L (177L) OWNER Brian Yeardley Continental Ltd (MIDDLEHAM) BRED Brownstown Stud Farm
1210 Gothenberg (IRE) made all and ran on well to record his first win from his last thirteen starts. He could now go to Royal Ascot, but his main target will be the Premio Vittorio di Capua at San Siro in October.

1581-CATTERICK (L-H) (Good, Good to firm patches)
Friday June 6th

Racing delayed - only one doctor present.
WEATHER: overcast WIND: mod half bhd

1729 E.B.F. NOVICE STKS (2-Y.O) (Class D)
2-35 (3-45) **5f** £3,093.00 (£924.00: £442.00: £201.00) Stalls: Low GOING minus 0.28 sec per fur (GF)

				SP	RR	SF
1569*	**Baby Grand (IRE)** (TDBarron) **2-8-2**(7) KimberleyHart(1) (swtg: mde all: hrd rdn 2f out: kpt on wl fnl f)	—	**1**	100/30^{3}	80	25
*1286**	**Always Lucky** (JBerry) **2-8-6**(3) PFessey(2) (a chsng wnr: ev ch & hung lft jst ins fnl f: nt qckn)	1¾	**2**	11/4^{2}	74	19
1328^{3}	**Branston Berry (IRE)** (JLEyre) **2-8-11** RLappin(3) (swtg: trckd ldrs: rdn & outpcd 3f out: wknd over 1f out)	3½	**3**	6/4^{1}	65	10
1255^{6}	**Young Ibnr (IRE)** (PDEvans) **2-9-2** JFEgan(4) (outpcd & rdn over 3f out: n.d after)	1½	**4**	7/2	65	10
				(SP 112.0%)		**4 Rn**

60.3 secs (2.60) CSF £11.49 TOTE £4.30: (£6.20) OWNER Mrs D. E. Sharp (THIRSK) BRED Rathbarry Stud
1569* Baby Grand (IRE) was awash with sweat when first brought into the paddock. None the worse for the long delay, she proved willing under a hard ride. (100/30: 5/1-3/1)
1286* Always Lucky spoilt her chance by persistently hanging in behind the winner. (11/4: 9/4-7/2)
1328 Branston Berry (IRE) was on her toes and in a muck sweat when first brought into the paddock. After the long delay she took a keen grip going to the start, and was almost certainly not seen at her best. (6/4: op 4/5)
1255 Young Ibnr (IRE) with the visor left off and trying to give weight away all round, was soon being taken off his legs. (7/2)

1730 JERVAULX H'CAP (0-65) (3-Y.O) (Class F)
3-05 (4-08) **5f** £2,635.00 (£735.00: £355.00) Stalls: Low GOING minus 0.28 sec per fur (GF)

				SP	RR	SF
995^{5}	**William's Well (43)** (MWEasterby) **3-7-13b** DaleGibson(7) (w ldrs: hrd rdn to ld jst ins fnl f: sn clr)	—	**1**	6/1^{2}	50	25
1571^{3}	**Tinker's Surprise (IRE) (52)** (JBalding) **3-8-8** TWilliams(10) (led tl jst ins fnl f)	2½	**2**	8/1	51	26
1604^{2}	**Gold Edge (54)** (MRChannon) **3-8-10** JFEgan(6) (a chsng ldrs: rdn ½-wy: kpt on same pce appr fnl f)	hd	**3**	100/30^{1}	53	28
1514^{8}	**Lunar Music (52)** (RonaldThompson) **3-8-3b**^{1}(5) RFfrench(8) (s.s: bhd tl styd on wl appr fnl f)	1¾	**4**	12/1	45	20
1571^{2}	**Northern Sal (58)** (MissLAPerratt) **3-8-11**(3) PFessey(9) (swtg: hdwy over 1f out: kpt on towards fin)	½	**5**	6/1^{2}	50	25
1496^{6}	**Star of The Road (50)** (JMCarr) **3-8-6** NKennedy(12) (sn outpcd: hdwy 2f out: kpt on fnl f)	3	**6**	8/1	32	7
1428^{5}	**Corinchili (56)** (GGMargarson) **3-8-12** GBardwell(4) (w ldrs tl wknd jst ins fnl f)	hd	**7**	9/1	38	13
1083^{12}	**Baptismal Rock (IRE) (45)** (BJCurley) **3-8-1** JFanning(13) (sn outpcd: hdwy over 1f out: nvr nr to chal)	hd	**8**	16/1	26	1
1496^{5}	**Bold Brief (55)** (DenysSmith) **3-8-11b** LCharnock(11) (in tch: rdn ½-wy: sn wknd)	4	**9**	13/2^{3}	23	—
1294^{9}	**Ice Age (65)** (RJRWilliams) **3-9-4**(3) DGriffiths(3) (chsd ldrs over 3f: sn wknd)	hd	**10**	8/1	33	8
1451^{4}	**Alisadara (45)** (NBycroft) **3-7-10**(5) JBramhill(2) (s.s: a bhd)	1¼	**11**	14/1	9	—
	Five-O-Fifty (53) (JLEyre) **3-8-9** MGallagher(1) (sn outpcd: drvn along fr ½-wy)	2½	**12**	14/1	9	—
1375^{6}	**Formidable Spirit (40)** (MJHeaton-Ellis) **3-7-10v** JLowe(5) (sn outpcd: wl bhd fr ½-wy)	2½	**13**	10/1	—	—
				(SP 144.3%)		**13 Rn**

59.7 secs (2.00) CSF £59.61 CT £184.27 TOTE £5.80: £2.60 £2.10 £3.80 (£30.90) Trio £17.60 OWNER Mr K. Hodgson (SHERIFF HUTTON) BRED M. W. Easterby and K. Hodgson
LONG HANDICAP Formidable Spirit 7-6
995 William's Well took the advantage of a 3lb drop in the weights to take this in decisive fashion. (6/1)
1571 Tinker's Surprise (IRE), a keen sort, was allowed to get on with it this time. (8/1)
1604 Gold Edge ran her usual game race but is finding it hard to get her head in front. (100/30)
427 Lunar Music, who has tumbled down the weights, was tried in blinkers. She gave away more ground at the start than that which she was eventually beaten by. (12/1)
1571 Northern Sal behaved herself better at the stalls this time. (6/1)
Ice Age (8/1: 8/1-12/1)

1731 SCORTON CLAIMING STKS (3-Y.O) (Class F)
3-40 (4-28) **1m 5f 175y** £2,425.00 (£675.00: £325.00) Stalls: Low GOING minus 0.05 sec per fur (G)

				SP	RR	SF
1487^{4}	**Eponine (66)** (MRChannon) **3-8-8** JFEgan(6) (mde all: rdn wl clr fnl 2f)	—	**1**	1/2^{1}	71	14
	Aunt Daphne (BAMcMahon) **3-7-9**(5) KSked(1) (trckd ldrs: outpcd over 3f out: styd on appr fnl f)	9	**2**	4/1^{2}	53	—
600^{8}	**Silver Button (42)** (SEKettlewell) **3-8-2**(5) RFfrench(5) (trckd ldrs: drvn along & lost pl 5f out: n.d after)	8	**3**	10/1	50	—
94^{5}	**Zanabay (55)** (WStorey) **3-7-12** NKennedy(2) (trckd wnr: plld hrd: rdn over 2f out: wknd over 1f out: eased towards fin)	½	**4**	11/2^{3}	41	—
1331^{5}	**Down Hearted (IRE)** (WTKemp) **3-8-2**(3) PFessey(3) (s.i.s: hdwy u.p 6f out: sn wl outpcd)	nk	**5**	16/1	47	—
				(SP 117.0%)		**5 Rn**

3m 9.4 (13.40) CSF £3.00 TOTE £1.50: £1.10 £2.20 (£2.40) OWNER Mr Robin Olley (UPPER LAMBOURN) BRED Mrs A. L. Wood
1487 Eponine was out on her own in this very moderate event in the final quarter-mile, her rider having no doubts about her stamina. (1/2: op 2/7)
Aunt Daphne proved suited by the step-up in distance but, when she got into top gear, the winner had flown. (4/1)
497 Silver Button has shown precious little in three outings this time. (10/1)
Zanabay was very keen, and was exhausted when eased up near the line, costing her third place. (11/2)
1331 Down Hearted (IRE) is still inexperienced. (16/1)

1732 LESLIE PETCH H'CAP (0-70) (3-Y.O+) (Class E)
4-10 (4-50) **1m 3f 214y** £2,742.25 (£823.00: £396.50: £183.25) Stalls: Low GOING minus 0.05 sec per fur (G)

				SP	RR	SF
1118^{9}	**Cottage Prince (IRE) (46)** (JJQuinn) **4-9-2** JFEgan(6) (lw: chsd ldr: rdn over 2f out: led over 1f out: styd on wl)	—	**1**	4/1^{2}	55	36

1472[6] **Majal (IRE) (49)** (JSWainwright) **8-9-0**(5) JBramhill(2) (dwlt: hld up & plld hrd: effrt over 3f out: rdn & ev ch over 1f out: nt qckn)........1½ **2** 11/2 56 37
Course Fishing (41) (BAMcMahon) **6-8-11** LNewton(1) (hld up: effrt over 3f out: ev ch over 1f out: one pce)2½ **3** 5/1[3] 45 26
1494[7] **Zamhareer (USA) (50)** (WStorey) **6-9-1v**[1](5) RFfrench(4) (drvn along & lost pl 6f out: sn bhd: kpt on fnl f)........6 **4** 6/1 46 27
1559[2] **Lapu-Lapu (54)** (MJCamacho) **4-9-10** LCharnock(5) (lw: led: clr over 2f out: sn rdn: hdd & wknd over 1f out)2½ **5** 4/5[1] 46 27
Arif (IRE) (37) (BJCurley) **5-8-7** JFanning(3) (trckd ldrs: pushed along over 4f out: rdn & lost pl over 2f out: eased)........17 **6** 9/1 7 —
(SP 131.9%) **6 Rn**

2m 40.5 (9.10) CSF £27.63 TOTE £7.90: £1.70 £2.70 (£23.50) OWNER Mrs Kay Thomas (MALTON) BRED Owen Bourke
898* Cottage Prince (IRE), who won over hurdles only a week earlier, is a lazy sort but, responding to his rider's urgings, was always going to do enough. (4/1)
1472 Majal (IRE) has only won twice from forty-four starts on the Flat but, suited by the step up in distance, gave his all. (11/2)
Course Fishing proved very keen, but after having every chance coming to the final furlong, off the bit he proved woefully one-paced. (5/1)
Zamhareer (USA) is out of sorts at present. Tried in a visor, he soon dropped himself out before staying on when it was all over. (6/1)
1559 Lapu-Lapu, a keen-going sort, set sail for home off the bend but the stamina gave out with over a furlong left to run. (4/5: op 5/4)
Arif (IRE) walked round in the paddock with two huge blankets on despite it being a warm day. The parade ring is supposed to be the place where punters can inspect the horses, and racegoers, who paid good money, were deprived once again. (9/1)

1733 ELLERY HILL RATING RELATED MAIDEN APPRENTICE STKS (0-60) (3-Y.O+) (Class G)

4-45 (5-12) **7f** £2,067.00 (£587.00: £291.00) Stalls: Low GOING minus 0.05 sec per fur (G)

SP RR SF

1467[3] **High Spirits (IRE) (56)** (TDEasterby) **3-8-8b** DMcGaffin(2) (sn pushed along: hdwy on ins to trck ldrs over 4f out: led over 3f out: clr 2f out: rdn out)........— **1** 7/4[1] 61 37
1448[10] **Serape (54)** (MrsLStubbs) **4-9-1** JGotobed(6) (w ldrs: outpcd after 2f: c wd ent st: styd on fnl f)........6 **2** 10/1 44 30
1385[13] **Captain Carparts (60)** (JLEyre) **3-8-8** JFowle(8) (lw: chsd ldrs: outpcd over 3f out: hdwy 2f out: kpt on same pce)........hd **3** 3/1[3] 47 23
1333[8] **Kippilaw (60)** (MJohnston) **3-8-5** NPollard(1) (led to 4f out: hung rt: wknd over 1f out)........5 **4** 5/2[2] 33 9
1586[5] **Hong Kong Express (IRE) (60)** (JBerry) **3-8-5v**[1] PBradley(4) (s.i.s: bhd: c wd ent st: some hdwy fnl 2f)........nk **5** 9/1 32 8
1115[9] **Hever Golf Angel (IRE) (57)** (PCHaslam) **3-8-0**(5) PGoode(5) (sn bhd: some late hdwy)........3 **6** 10/1 25 1
1467[6] **Belbay Star (37)** (JLEyre) **4-9-1** TSiddall(7) (chsd ldrs: outpcd ½-wy: rdn over 2f out. n.d after)........1½ **7** 14/1 22 8
Blazing Imp (USA) (42) (MrsJJordan) **4-8-13**(5) JennyMurphy(3) (swtg: w ldrs: led 4f out: sn hdd: c wd: wknd qckly 2f out)........16 **8** 33/1 — —
(SP 127.7%) **8 Rn**

1m 27.9 (4.30) CSF £21.99 TOTE £2.80: £1.10 £2.90 £1.80 (£31.40) OWNER Mrs J. B. Mountifield (MALTON) BRED Sean Twomey
WEIGHT FOR AGE 3yo-10lb
1467 High Spirits (IRE) found this trip ideal. Well handled, he saved lengths sticking to the inside throughout. (7/4)
1220 Serape finished last in a seller last time, sufficient to tell the class of this event. (10/1)
785 Captain Carparts settled better with the visor left off. (3/1)
Kippilaw, a weak-looking sort, was dropped in class and distance but she gave her rider little help. (5/2: op 6/4)
1586 Hong Kong Express (IRE), in a visor for the first time, stayed on when it was all over and might be better suited by a mile. (9/1)
Hever Golf Angel (IRE) (10/1: 9/1-14/1)

1734 SCOTCH CORNER H'CAP (0-70) (3-Y.O+) (Class E)

5-20 (5-35) **5f 212y** £2,937.25 (£883.00: £426.50: £198.25) Stalls: Low GOING minus 0.05 sec per fur (G)

SP RR SF

1620[3] **Napoleon Star (IRE) (48)** (SRBowring) **6-8-6b** DaleGibson(2) (s.i.s: bhd & drvn along: hdwy over 1f out: squeezed thro to ld cl home)........— **1** 5/1[2] 58 38
1493[2] **Skyers Flyer (IRE) (67)** (RonaldThompson) **3-9-3** TWilliams(11) (hld up: effrt on outside over 2f out: led wl ins fnl f: hdd cl home)........½ **2** 9/1 76 48
1468[7] **Brecongill Lad (67)** (MissSEHall) **5-9-6v**(5) JBramhill(4) (trckd ldr: rdn to ld jst ins fnl f: edgd rt: hdd & no ex fnl 75y)........1 **3** 8/1 73 53
Superbit (61) (BAMcMahon) **5-9-5** LNewton(10) (a chsng ldrs: kpt on appr fnl f: n.m.r towards fin)........1¼ **4** 16/1 64 44
1584[10] **Just Dissident (IRE) (60)** (RMWhitaker) **5-9-4** RPerham(1) (led tl jst ins fnl f: wknd cl home)........hd **5** 5/1[2] 62 42
1098[16] **Sonderise (47)** (NTinkler) **8-8-5** NCarlisle(8) (sn outpcd: hdwy over 1f out: nvr rchd ldrs)........hd **6** 16/1 49 29
1332[9] **Pathaze (39)** (NBycroft) **4-7-11** NKennedy(3) (s.i.s: bhd: hdwy & edgd lft over 1f out: n.m.r: nvr nr to chal)....1½ **7** 14/1 37 17
1089[10] **Millesime (IRE) (52)** (MartynWane) **5-8-7**(3) PFessey(6) (in tch: no imp whn hmpd over 1f out)........nk **8** 10/1 49 29
1259[4] **Foist (70)** (MWEasterby) **5-10-0** JFanning(12) (lw: racd wd: nvr nr ldrs)........2½ **9** 11/2[3] 61 41
1627[2] **Camionneur (IRE) (45)** (TDEasterby) **4-8-3b** LCharnock(7) (chsd ldrs: wkng whn hmpd over 1f out)........4 **10** 3/1[1] 25 5
1332[7] **Madam Zando (38)** (JBalding) **4-7-10** JLowe(5) (bit bkwd: in tch: effrt over 2f out: no imp whn hmpd over 1f out)........1¼ **11** 14/1 15 —
(SP 129.0%) **11 Rn**

1m 14.3 (3.40) CSF £49.97 CT £344.54 TOTE £7.60: £2.70 £2.60 £4.00 (£24.20) Trio £70.70 OWNER Mr Roland Wheatley (EDWINSTOWE) BRED Eamon O'Mahony
LONG HANDICAP Madam Zando 7-6
WEIGHT FOR AGE 3yo-8lb
1620 Napoleon Star (IRE), who likes to run round a bend, was still last of all one-and-a-half furlongs out. Weaving his way through, his rider deserves full marks. (5/1)
1493 Skyers Flyer (IRE) came from off the pace, but no sooner had she put her head in front than the winner touched her off. (9/1)
Brecongill Lad as usual raced keenly. Carrying his head high, even when he took the lead he did not look as if he really had the will to win. Anyone who puts him up as a horse to follow needs a stay in a funny farm. (8/1)
Superbit was held when running out of room near the finish. (16/1)
Just Dissident (IRE), well supported in the market, showed his rivals a clean pair of heels until inside the last. He might be worth trying over five. (5/1: op 12/1)
Sonderise ran his best race so far this year. (16/1)
1627 Camionneur (IRE), making a quick reappearance, was already on the on the retreat when tightened up over a furlong out. (3/1)

T/Plpt: £179.80 (43.04 Tckts). T/Qdpt: £12.60 (30.37 Tckts) WG

0786-**EPSOM (L-H) (Good, Good to firm bk st)**
Friday June 6th
WEATHER: unsettled WIND: strong half bhd

1735 VODATA WOODCOTE STKS (Listed) (2-Y.O) (Class A)
2-10 (2-11) **6f** £16,937.50 (£5,125.00: £2,500.00: £1,187.50) Stalls: High GOING minus 0.16 sec per fur (GF)

				SP	RR	SF
1240*	**Dance Trick (USA)** (PWChapple-Hyam) **2-8-9** JReid(1) (lw: a.p: led 4f out: rdn out)	—	**1**	11/8^{1}	78+	54
1411^{3}	**Another Fantasy (IRE)** (RHannon) **2-8-9** LDettori(3) (lw: led 2f: rdn over 2f out: unable qckn)	1¾	**2**	10/1	73	49
1504^{2}	**Flaming Ember (IRE)** (BJMeehan) **2-8-11** PatEddery(6) (a.p: c centre st: rdn over 2f out: one pce)	¾	**3**	15/2^{3}	73	49
1475^{2}	**Banningham Blade** (KTIvory) **2-8-11** MartinDwyer(4) (plld hrd: hdwy on ins over 2f out: one pce)	4	**4**	11/2^{2}	63	39
1411^{2}	**Smooth Sailing** (KMcAuliffe) **2-9-0v^{1}** JFortune(8) (a.p: carried centre st: rdn over 2f out: wkng whn edgd lft ins fnl f)	s.h	**5**	14/1	66	42
893^{2}	**Conectis (IRE)** (DJSCosgrove) **2-8-6** MJKinane(5) (bhd fnl 4f)	2½	**6**	12/1	51	27
1263^{6}	**Narrogin (USA)** (MRChannon) **2-8-11** TQuinn(7) (lw: a bhd)	2	**7**	16/1	51	27
1504*	**Truth Teller** (RHannon) **2-8-11** DaneO'Neill(2) (lw: bhd fnl 2f)	1¼	**8**	14/1	47	23
				(SP 105.3%)	**8 Rn**	

1m 9.68 (1.68) CSF £11.87 TOTE £2.20: £1.20 £1.50 £1.80 (£8.00) OWNER Mr R. E. Sangster (MARLBOROUGH) BRED Swettenham Stud
1240* Dance Trick (USA), whose trainer was worried beforehand that this trip on this course might be too sharp for her, put up a fine display. Leading before halfway and winning convincingly. Connections did think of her aiming her at the Queen Mary Stakes at Royal Ascot over five furlongs, but have wisely decided to go instead for the Cherry Hinton Stakes at Newmarket in July over a more suitable six furlongs. She will have no problem getting seven furlongs. (11/8: evens-6/4)
1411 Another Fantasy (IRE) the early leader, gave chase to the winner but, despite her rider's efforts, was unable to reel in that rival. Connections will now look for conditions races over six furlongs for her. (10/1)
1504 Flaming Ember (IRE) elected to come down the centre of the course in the straight. (15/2)
1475 Banningham Blade owes connections absolutely nothing after a string of first-class efforts, but on this occasion she had problems coming down Tattenham Hill, and found the opposition too hot. (11/2: 4/1-6/1)
1411 Smooth Sailing, carried into the centre of the track by Flaming Ember turning into the straight, failed to find another gear and was feeling the pinch when drifting left on the camber inside the final furlong. (14/1: op 8/1)
893 Conectis (IRE) (12/1: 8/1-14/1)
1504* Truth Teller (14/1: op 8/1)

1736 VODAFONE CORONATION CUP STKS (Gp 1) (4-Y.O+) (Class A)
2-45 (2-48) **1m 4f 10y** £113,895.00 (£42,503.50: £20,314.25: £8,737.25) Stalls: Centre GOING minus 0.16 sec per fur (GF)

				SP	RR	SF
*628a**	**Singspiel (IRE) (128)** (MRStoute) **5-9-0** LDettori(3) (led over 4f: led over 3f out: clr over 2f out: easily)	—	**1**	5/4^{1}	132+	65
	Dushyantor (USA) (120) (HRACecil) **4-9-0** KFallon(2) (hld up: rdn 4f out: chsd wnr wl over 1f out: no imp)	5	**2**	9/2^{3}	125	58
922a^{2}	**Le Destin (FR)** (PDemercastel,France) **4-9-0** TGillet(5) (rdn over 3f out: hdwy over 1f out: r.o one pce)	½	**3**	14/1	125	58
736^{2}	**Ela-Aristokrati (IRE) (114)** (MHTompkins) **5-9-0** TQuinn(1) (lw: hdwy to ld over 7f out: hdd over 3f out: wknd wl over 1f out)	4	**4**	14/1	119	52
1542a^{2}	**Oscar Schindler (IRE)** (KPrendergast,Ireland) **5-9-0** SCraine(4) (lw: chsd wnr over 4f: hrd rdn over 2f out: wknd wl over 1f out)	1¼	**5**	9/4^{2}	118	51
				(SP 106.7%)	**5 Rn**	

2m 37.72 (3.22) CSF £6.12 TOTE £1.80: £1.10 £2.70 (£2.50) OWNER Sheikh Mohammed (NEWMARKET) BRED Sheikh Mohammed bin Rashid al Maktoum
628a* Singspiel (IRE) has turned into an International superstar with victories in the Japan Cup and the Dubai World Cup, and seems to be getting better with age. He recorded his first Group One race win in Britain in breathtaking style. After setting a slow pace, he breezed back into the lead entering the straight and forged clear to win with a ton in hand. It is going to take something pretty special to beat him this season, and he will be a major contender for the King George VI and Queen Elizabeth Diamond Stakes, his next engagement. (5/4: 4/5-11/8)
Dushyantor (USA), runner-up in last year's Derby and St Leger, looked fit enough to do himself justice on this seasonal debut, but he had met a real star in Singspiel and, even though he lost his off-fore shoe during the race, it made not the slightest difference. The Hardwicke Stakes at Royal Ascot is a possibility. (9/2)
922a Le Destin (FR), third in last year's French Derby and sixth in the Arc, has nevertheless just one victory to his name. He needs a really strong pace to be seen at his best, and did not get that here. (14/1)
736 Ela-Aristokrati (IRE) looked in good shape beforehand, but this was a very tough assignment. Unhappy with the slow early pace, he moved to the front over seven furlongs from home but he was collared early in the straight and soon folded. (14/1)
1542a Oscar Schindler (IRE) looked absolutely magnificent in the paddock, but put up a dismal display, although the slow early pace was all against him. His trainer remarked afterwards that whilst the King George VI and Queen Elizabeth Diamond Stakes is being kept in mind, it would be nice to avoid Singspiel. (9/4)

1737 PEOPLES PHONE H'CAP (0-100) (3-Y.O) (Class C)
3-20 (3-20) **7f** £25,077.50 (£7,595.00: £3,710.00: £1,767.50) Stalls: Low GOING minus 0.16 sec per fur (GF)

				SP	RR	SF
1170^{W}	**Cosmic Prince (IRE) (88)** (MAJarvis) **3-8-11** RCochrane(10) (lw: a.p: led over 1f out: rdn out)	—	**1**	7/1^{2}	95	55
1238*	**Gee Bee Dream (80)** (APJarvis) **3-8-3** SDrowne(5) (a.p: rdn over 2f out: r.o one pce)	2½	**2**	14/1	81	41
973^{5}	**Sharp Temper (83)** (BWHills) **3-8-6** MHills(9) (lw: hld up: rdn over 3f out: r.o one pce)	s.h	**3**	12/1	84	44
1243^{9}	**Restless Spirit (USA) (86)** (MJohnston) **3-8-9** JWeaver(8) (lw: chsd ldr: led over 2f out tl over 1f out: one pce)	nk	**4**	20/1	87	47
1017^{6}	**Return of Amin (73)** (JDBethell) **3-7-5(5)** RMullen(13) (rdn over 3f out: hdwy over 1f out: r.o)	¾	**5**	20/1	72	32
1302^{4}	**Shawm (90)** (DRLoder) **3-8-13** LDettori(12) (lw: rdn over 2f out: hdwy over 1f out: r.o)	s.h	**6**	10/1^{3}	89	49
1170^{16}	**Jeffrey Anotherred (93)** (KMcAuliffe) **3-9-2** JReid(6) (lw: prom over 5f)	½	**7**	16/1	91	51
1305^{5}	**Impulsif (USA) (74)** (DJSffrenchDavis) **3-7-11** JQuinn(2) (lw: rdn over 2f out: hdwy over 1f out: nvr nrr)	1	**8**	25/1	69	29
1175^{2}	**Great Child (84)** (MRStoute) **3-8-7** MJKinane(4) (lw: hld up: rdn over 2f out: one pce)	hd	**9**	3/1^{1}	79	39
1458*	**Plan For Profit (IRE) (79)** (MJohnston) **3-7-13**(3) 4x MHenry(11) (lw: nvr nrr)	1¾	**10**	12/1	70	30
1245*	**Sleepless (84)** (NAGraham) **3-8-7** DHolland(3) (a mid div)	3½	**11**	7/1^{2}	67	27
1453^{5}	**Song of Skye (80)** (TJNaughton) **3-8-3** TSprake(17) (bhd fnl 3f)	nk	**12**	25/1	62	22
958^{12}	**Millroy (USA) (79)** (PAKelleway) **3-8-2v** SSanders(7) (led over 4f)	¾	**13**	33/1	60	20

455*	**Assume (USA) (85)** (JWHills) **3-8-8** RHills(1) (lw: a bhd) 2½	**14**	11/1	60	20
1462⁴	**Bachelors Pad (98)** (WJarvis) **3-9-7b** OPeslier(15) (mid div whn hmpd 5f out: bhd fnl 3f) 1¾	**15**	33/1	69	29
1305⁷	**Rudi's Pet (IRE) (89)** (RHannon) **3-8-12** DaneO'Neill(14) (prom 3f) 2½	**16**	33/1	54	14
1305²	**Zaima (IRE) (89)** (JLDunlop) **3-8-12** KDarley(16) (lw: mid div whn hmpd 5f out: bhd whn hmpd over 2f out) 4	**17**	10/1 ³	45	5

(SP 130.5%) **17 Rn**

1m 22.42 (2.12) CSF £89.72 CT £1,074.50 TOTE £8.00: £1.90 £3.80 £3.40 £3.90 (£109.30) Trio £1,043.50 OWNER Cosmic Greyhound Racing Partnership (NEWMARKET) BRED R. V. Young

LONG HANDICAP Return of Amin 7-3

654 Cosmic Prince (IRE), a hyper-nervous horse according to his trainer, bolted before the start and had to be withdrawn last time out, but was much more settled on this occasion. Gaining control below the distance, he was rousted along to assert his superiority. He loves fast ground and fast tracks. (7/1)

1238* Gee Bee Dream, 8lb higher than when winning an ordinary Lingfield handicap last time out, had problems with the course, but kept on well to finish second. (14/1)

973 Sharp Temper gave a good account of himself and only just failed to take second prize. A return to a mile would be in his favour. (12/1)

Restless Spirit (USA) looked absolutely tremendous beforehand and ran a first-class race, but failed to find another gear in the closing stages. (20/1)

1017 Return of Amin found it all happening too quickly on this lively ground and was doing all his best work in the last furlong-and-a-half. He is at his best with some cut. (20/1)

1302 Shawm, racing at the back of the field, stayed on to be nearest at the line. A return to a mile would surely help. (10/1)

455* Assume (USA) (11/1: 8/1-12/1)

1305 Zaima (IRE) (10/1: 8/1-12/1)

1738 VODAFONE OAKS STKS (Gp 1) (3-Y.O F) (Class A)

4-00 (4-02) **1m 4f 10y** £182,250.00 (£68,012.50: £32,506.25: £13,981.25) Stalls: Centre GOING minus 0.16 sec per fur (GF)

			SP	RR	SF
1147*	**Reams of Verse (USA) (119)** (HRACecil) **3-9-0** KFallon(6) (lw: stdy hdwy over 3f out: bmpd & nt clr run over 2f out: hrd rdn over 1f out: led ins fnl f: r.o wl) ....—	**1**	5/6 ¹	117+	79
1366a³	**Gazelle Royale (FR)** (JEHammond,France) **3-9-0** JFortune(9) (leggy: unf: hdwy over 3f out: led over 2f out: edgd lft over 1f out: hdd ins fnl f: unable qckn) 1½	**2**	33/1	115	77
1102*	**Crown of Light (98)** (MRStoute) **3-9-0** OPeslier(8) (rdn over 2f out: hdwy over 1f out: r.o wl) ....¾	**3**	11/1	114	76
1209*	**Yashmak (USA) (114)** (HRACecil) **3-9-0** MJKinane(7) (hld up: rdn over 3f out: ev ch whn edgd lft over 2f out: one pce) ....½	**4**	6/1 ²	113	75
1147³	**Etoile (FR) (100)** (PWChapple-Hyam) **3-9-0** JReid(4) (stdy hdwy 6f out: rdn over 3f out: bmpd over 2f out: r.o one pce) ....hd	**5**	66/1	113	75
1195a³	**Ebadiyla (IRE)** (JOxx,Ireland) **3-9-0** JPMurtagh(2) (cmpt: lw: a.p: rdn over 4f out: led over 3f out tl over 2f out: hmpd on ins over 1f out: one pce) 1¼	**6**	15/2 ³	112	74
992*	**Bint Baladee (94)** (SbinSuroor) **3-9-0** KDarley(3) (lw: hld up: rdn over 3f out: sn wknd) 8	**7**	50/1	101	63
1102²	**Book At Bedtime (IRE)** (CACyzer) **3-9-0** PatEddery(11) (lw: bhd ½-wy: late hdwy) 5	**8**	33/1	94	56
890⁵	**Imperial Scholar (IRE) (100)** (JMPEustace) **3-9-0** RCochrane(5) (a bhd) ....nk	**9**	150/1	94	56
1368a²	**Attitre (FR) (102)** (CEBrittain) **3-9-0** MRoberts(12) (a.p: led over 4f out tl over 3f out: sn wknd) 14	**10**	33/1	75	37
959*	**Siyadah (USA) (102)** (SbinSuroor) **3-9-0v¹** LDettori(10) (lw: led over 7f) 15	**11**	11/1	55	17
1102³	**Ukraine Venture** (SPCWoods) **3-9-0** WRyan(1) (lw: prom 8f) 4	**12**	25/1	50	12

(SP 114.0%) **12 Rn**

2m 35.59 (1.09) CSF £39.26 TOTE £1.90: £1.10 £3.90 £2.00 (£37.80) Trio £83.00 OWNER Mr K. Abdulla (NEWMARKET) BRED Juddmonte Farms

STEWARDS' ENQUIRY Fortune susp. 16 & 20/6/97 (careless riding).

1147* Reams of Verse (USA), who has improved since her Musidora victory according to her trainer, looked a picture in the paddock and had no problems with this longer trip, indeed she needed it after getting no run early in the straight. She gave Henry Cecil his fifth Oaks winner and fulfilled owner Khalid Abdulla's dreams to land this Classic for the very first time. She is an extremely high-class filly and is now all set to take on the colts. (5/6)

1366a Gazelle Royale (FR), a tall filly who still looks very weak, ran a tremendous race. She drifted left on the camber under extreme pressure from the saddle as she made her move, doing a couple of her rivals no favours. Headed inside the final furlong, she than had to admit defeat. Fortune was later suspended for two days for careless riding (33/1)

1102* Crown of Light ran a first-class race and was putting in some really good work in the last furlong-and-a-half. She is a lazy filly according to her jockey. (11/1)

1209* Yashmak (USA) was running because her owner Khalid Abdulla was keen to win this race. Despite not having the ground in her favour she ran a tremendous race, and had every chance before tapped for toe. Given the cut in the ground she loves, she should not take long to win her first Group race. (6/1)

1147 Etoile (FR), well beaten by the winner in the Musidora Stakes, got much closer on this occasion despite not having the best of runs. (66/1)

1195a Ebadiyla (IRE) did not have experience on her side but looked in great heart in the paddock - many from her stable have had a touch of a virus. Gaining control early in the straight, she was soon collared, and was tightened up on the inside rail below the distance. It did not affect her chance as she was already struggling. (15/2)

992* Bint Baladee, beaten a neck by Reams of Verse in a Newmarket maiden on her debut last year, looked in tremendous shape beforehand but had been hung out to dry early in the straight. She has shown more at home than on the racecourse according to connections. (50/1)

1102 Book At Bedtime (IRE) was out of her league but, despite being left behind as she failed to come down Tattenham Hill, she passed beaten horses in the straight. (33/1)

890 Imperial Scholar (IRE) was outclassed from start to finish. (150/1)

1368a Attitre (FR) had far more on her plate in the definitive Oaks, and after showing briefly in front rounding Tattenham Corner had soon been hung out to dry. (33/1)

959* Siyadah (USA) took the field along, but she totally failed to handle Tattenham Corner and quickly dropped away. (11/1)

1102 Ukraine Venture was close up until tamely dropping out of the action rounding Tattenham Corner. (25/1)

1739 VODAFONE H'CAP (0-95) (3-Y.O+) (Class C)

4-35 (4-38) **1m 114y** £17,993.75 (£5,450.00: £2,662.50: £1,268.75) Stalls: Low GOING minus 0.16 sec per fur (GF)

			SP	RR	SF
1674*	**Philistar (69)** (KRBurke) **4-8-2** 4x BDoyle(1) (lw: hdwy over 2f out: hrd rdn over 1f out: led ins fnl f: r.o wl) ....—	**1**	20/1	83	66
1442*	**Sweet Wilhelmina (64)** (LordHuntingdon) **4-7-6**(5) 4x AimeeCook(12) (stdy hdwy over 2f out: led over 1f out tl ins fnl f: unable qckn) 1½	**2**	6/1 ²	75	58

				SP	RR	SF
1308[4]	**Star Talent (USA) (86)** (IABalding) **6-9-5** RCochrane(13) (lw: hdwy over 2f out: hrd rdn over 1f out: r.o)	1¼	**3**	8/1[3]	95	78
1482[2]	**Virtual Reality (76)** (JARToller) **6-8-9** SSanders(9) (lw: a.p: ev ch over 1f out: one pce)	½	**4**	10/1	84	67
1249[2]	**Mantles Prince (80)** (GLewis) **3-8-1bow1** PaulEddery(8) (b.nr fore: led tl over 1f out: one pce)	½	**5**	14/1	87	57
1495[2]	**Young Precedent (81)** (PWHarris) **3-7-9(7)** CLowther(6) (a.p: hrd rdn over 2f out: wknd over 1f out)	4	**6**	12/1	80	51
1148[14]	**Unconditional Love (IRE) (95)** (MJohnston) **4-10-0** JWeaver(10) (lw: no hdwy fnl 3f)	½	**7**	33/1	94	77
1219[8]	**Sylvan Princess (70)** (DJSCosgrove) **4-8-0(3)** MartinDwyer(4) (dwlt: rdn over 3f out: nvr nrr)	½	**8**	12/1	68	51
1320[8]	**Tremplin (USA) (74)** (NACallaghan) **5-8-7** MRoberts(14) (rdn over 3f out: nvr nrr)	½	**9**	5/1[1]	71	54
1472[8]	**Pride of Pendle (70)** (MartynWane) **8-8-3ow2** DaneO'Neill(15) (nvr nrr)	hd	**10**	25/1	66	47
1471[3]	**Toujours Riviera (73)** (JPearce) **7-8-6** LDettori(2) (lw: a.p: rdn over 2f out: wknd over 1f out)	¾	**11**	11/1	68	51
1473*	**La Modiste (72)** (MissGayKelleway) **4-8-5** 4x KDarley(16) (b: nvr nrr)	½	**12**	16/1	66	49
1170[5]	**Cinema Paradiso (95)** (PFICole) **3-9-2** TQuinn(7) (lw: a bhd)	1¾	**13**	16/1	86	57
947[15]	**Night Wink (USA) (76)** (GLMoore) **5-8-9** SWhitworth(18) (hld up: rdn over 3f out: sn wknd)	nk	**14**	33/1	66	49
1501[3]	**Ertlon (70)** (CEBrittain) **7-8-3** JQuinn(19) (lw: bhd fnl 2f)	3	**15**	20/1	55	38
1324[10]	**Sandabar (80)** (MRStoute) **4-8-13** JReid(5) (hld up: rdn over 3f out: wknd over 2f out)	5	**16**	10/1	55	38
1456[13]	**Amber Fort (74)** (DRCElsworth) **4-8-7v** KFallon(3) (a bhd)	¾	**17**	16/1	48	31
1320[2]	**Orange Place (IRE) (78)** (TJNaughton) **6-8-11** MHills(11) (chsd ldr 6f)	9	**18**	14/1	35	18
				(SP 134.2%)	**18 Rn**	

1m 42.8 (0.80) CSF £126.71 CT £1,012.13 TOTE £34.50: £6.40 £1.80 £2.50 £2.40 (£50.20) Trio £123.10 OWNER Mr Nigel Shields (WANTAGE) BRED John A. Jones Morgan
WEIGHT FOR AGE 3yo-12lb

1674* Philistar followed up his win at Newcastle on Wednesday and, weaving his way through the field, responded to pressure to get on top inside the final furlong. (20/1)

1442* Sweet Wilhelmina is in tremendous heart at present - she had won three of her four previous races this year, and was receiving weight all round. She looked set for another victory as she struck the front below the distance, but had not bargained on the late flourish of the winner inside the final furlong. (6/1)

1308 Star Talent (USA), whose come-from-behind style has got him into trouble on his last two outings, had no problems here as he picked up ground on the outside of the field over a quarter of a mile from home. Responding to pressure, he stayed on well to take third prize. He remains in good form. (8/1)

1482 Virtual Reality, who has not run over a mile since his two-year-old days, had every chance below the distance before tapped for toe. A return to a mile and a quarter would suit. (10/1: 8/1-12/1)

1249 Mantles Prince took the field along but, collared below the distance, could then only go up and down in the same place. He remains a maiden. (14/1)

1495 Young Precedent was close up until calling it a day approaching the final furlong. A return to seven furlongs might help. (12/1)

1740 VODACALL VICTRESS STKS (Listed) (3-Y.O+ F & M) (Class A)

5-10 (5-10) **1m 114y** £24,281.25 (£7,350.00: £3,587.50: £1,706.25) Stalls: Low GOING minus 0.16 sec per fur (GF)

				SP	RR	SF
1456[3]	**Samara (IRE) (91)** (JLDunlop) **4-9-6** PatEddery(3) (chsd ldr over 6f out: led over 2f out: hrd rdn over 1f out: r.o wl)	—	**1**	6/1	111	69
1157[2]	**Charlotte Corday (107)** (GWragg) **4-9-6** MHills(1) (hmpd over 7f out: stdy hdwy over 2f out: r.o one pce)	1½	**2**	11/4[1]	108	66
1326*	**Out West (USA) (100)** (HRACecil) **3-8-11** KFallon(4) (bdly hmpd over 7f out: rdn over 4f out: hdwy over 1f out: r.o one pce: fin 4th; 13/4l: plcd 3rd)	nk	**3**	3/1[2]	107	53
627a[10]	**Fatefully (USA)** (SbinSuroor) **4-9-9** LDettori(6) (a.p: rdn over 2f out: chsd wnr over 1f out: edgd lft ins fnl f: one pce: fin 3rd; nk: disq: plcd 4th)	1¾	**4**	9/2[3]	111	69
1101[2]	**Baked Alaska (95)** (ACStewart) **3-8-8** MRoberts(5) (hmpd over 7f out: bhd fnl 3f)	5	**5**	12/1	95	41
1326[7]	**Gretel (97)** (MRStoute) **3-8-8** AClark(7) (lw: led 6f: wknd over 1f out)	½	**6**	20/1	94	40
1409*	**Marie Dora (FR) (83)** (IABalding) **3-8-8** TQuinn(2) (lw: prom 6f)	10	**7**	10/1	75	21
				(SP 105.7%)	**7 Rn**	

1m 44.21 (2.21) CSF £17.63 TOTE £5.30: £2.10 £1.90 (£12.80) OWNER Aylesfield Farms Stud Ltd (ARUNDEL) BRED Mount Coote Stud
WEIGHT FOR AGE 3yo-12lb
STEWARDS' ENQUIRY Dettori susp. 16 & 20/6/97 (careless riding).

1456 Samara (IRE) confirmed the promise shown at Sandown recently, leading over a quarter of a mile from home and responding well to pressure to keep her rivals at bay. (6/1)

1157 Charlotte Corday steadily crept closer in the straight and, staying on, snatched second prize in the last few yards. (11/4)

1326* Out West (USA) was seriously hampered after only a furlong and than appeared to be all at sea coming down Tattenham Hill. However, despite these problems she stayed on in the last furlong-and-a-half, and was later promoted to third place. Winner of a listed race already this season, she should find another before long. (3/1)

Fatefully (USA), winner of four races last year including two Listed events, was conceding weight all round. Never far away, she moved into second place below the distance but was just worried out of that position in the last few yards. Dettori was later suspended for two days for careless riding over an incident soon after the start, and as a result will miss the last day of Royal Ascot. (9/2: op 3/1)

1101 Baked Alaska was getting left behind in the straight. (12/1)

1209 Gretel continues to disappoint, and after taking the field along was collared over a quarter of a mile from home and was soon in trouble. (20/1)

1409* Marie Dora (FR) (10/1: 12/1-8/1)

1741 VODACOM TOKYO TROPHY H'CAP (0-100) (3-Y.O) (Class C)

5-40 (5-46) **1m 2f 18y** £18,400.00 (£5,575.00: £2,725.00: £1,300.00) Stalls: Low GOING minus 0.16 sec per fur (GF)

				SP	RR	SF
1069a*	**Jaunty Jack (98)** (LMCumani) **3-9-5** LDettori(2) (lw: hdwy over 2f out: led over 1f out: rdn out)	—	**1**	4/1[1]	109	64
1104*	**Supply And Demand (96)** (GLMoore) **3-9-3** KFallon(5) (hdwy over 2f out: hrd rdn over 1f out: hung lft ins fnl f: unable qckn)	2½	**2**	8/1[3]	103	58
1331[2]	**Dream of Nurmi (84)** (DRLoder) **3-8-5** KDarley(3) (lw: a.p: rdn over 3f out: n.m.r over 1f out: swtchd rt: r.o ins fnl f)	nk	**3**	10/1	91	46
1060a[5]	**Fly To The Stars (100)** (MJohnston) **3-9-7** OPeslier(6) (chsd ldr: ev ch over 1f out: one pce)	hd	**4**	15/2[2]	106	61
1277[2]	**Chief Monarch (88)** (BSmart) **3-8-9** RCochrane(4) (lw: led over 8f)	5	**5**	12/1	87	42
990[2]	**Strathmore Clear (89)** (GLewis) **3-8-10** PaulEddery(10) (a.p: rdn over 3f out: wknd wl over 1f out)	6	**6**	8/1[3]	78	33
1399[6]	**Isle of Man (USA) (90)** (PFICole) **3-8-11** TQuinn(7) (lw: prom over 6f)	3	**7**	10/1	74	29
1006[6]	**Aerleon Pete (IRE) (80)** (MRStoute) **3-7-12(3)** MHenry(9) (a bhd)	1	**8**	4/1[1]	63	18
1651*	**Mr Paradise (IRE) (75)** (TJNaughton) **3-7-5(5)** 4x RMullen(8) (lw: hdwy over 4f out: wknd over 2f out)	½	**9**	25/1	57	12

690*	**River's Source (USA) (85)** (BWHills) **3-8-6** MHills(1) (a bhd)	¾	**10**	9/1	66	21

(SP 113.7%) **10 Rn**

2m 7.16 (3.16) CSF £32.02 CT £269.36 TOTE £3.30: £1.50 £2.50 £3.40 (£12.30) Trio £81.60 OWNER Mr M. Marchetti (NEWMARKET) BRED Fonthill Stud
LONG HANDICAP Mr Paradise (IRE) 7-2
1069a* Jaunty Jack, winner of a Listed race in Italy last month, came through to lead below the distance and was rousted along for a decisive victory. He will now head back to Italy for another valuable Listed event at the end of the month. (4/1: 3/1-9/2)
1104* Supply And Demand, who has jumped up the handicap following a good start to the season, began a forward move in the straight, but he hung left on the camber inside the final furlong, and failed to find another gear. (8/1: 6/1-9/1)
1331 Dream of Nurmi, always close up, did not have a great deal of room in which to manoeuvre below the distance and had to be switched as a result. He kept on well inside the final furlong and only just failed to take second prize. (10/1: 6/1-11/1)
1060a Fly To The Stars coped well with this longer trip, and had every chance below the distance before tapped for toe. (15/2: 5/1-8/1)
1277 Chief Monarch set the pace but, collared below the distance, had little more to offer. (12/1: 16/1-25/1)
990 Strathmore Clear is in fine form this season, and was close up until coming to the end of his tether below the distance. (8/1)
1006 Aerleon Pete (IRE) (4/1: 3/1-9/2)

T/Jkpt: £11,538.80 (1.99 Tckts). T/Plpt: £61.80 (771.99 Tckts). T/Qdpt: £46.30 (44.1 Tckts) AK

1322-GOODWOOD (R-H) (Good to firm, Rnd crse Firm patches)
Friday June 6th
Race 5: no time taken or official distances
WEATHER: overcast then heavy rain WIND: mod bhd

1742 WEALD & DOWNLAND MUSEUM MAIDEN STKS (3-Y.O) (Class D)
6-30 (6-30) **1m 4f** £3,850.00 (£1,150.00: £550.00: £250.00) Stalls: Low GOING minus 0.26 sec per fur (GF)

				SP	RR	SF
1015^{5}	**Generous Gift (97)** (EALDunlop) **3-8-11**(3) DO'Donohoe(2) (dwlt: hld up: hdwy 4f out: led gng wl over 2f out: pushed out ins fnl f)	—	**1**	$2/9^{1}$	80	15
1150^{5}	**Autumn Time (IRE)** (PWChapple-Hyam) **3-8-6**(3) RHavlin(3) (prom: rdn & outpcd 4f out: rallied to chse wnr over 1f out: kpt on one pce ins fnl f)	2½	**2**	$9/1^{2}$	72	7
1296^{9}	**Padauk (66)** (MJHaynes) **3-9-0** SSanders(5) (chsd ldrs: rdn over 2f out: one pce)	2	**3**	14/1	74	9
599^{16}	**Action Stations** (CACyzer) **3-9-0** AMorris(1) (led: hdd over 2f out: one pce)	1	**4**	50/1	73	8
1234^{5}	**Gee Bee Boy** (APJarvis) **3-9-0** WJO'Connor(4) (hld up: shkn up over 2f out: kpt on one pce ins fnl f)	1½	**5**	$10/1^{3}$	71	6
1420^{5}	**Across The Water** (CACyzer) **3-8-9** SDrowne(6) (prom: rdn over 2f out: wknd over 1f out)	6	**6**	11/1	58	—

(SP 117.9%) **6 Rn**

2m 43.07 (9.87) CSF £3.43 TOTE £1.20: £1.10 £2.70 (£3.20) OWNER Maktoum Al Maktoum (NEWMARKET) BRED Gainsborough Stud Management Ltd
1015 Generous Gift, as the odds suggest, won this in easy fashion. (2/9: op 2/5)
1150 Autumn Time (IRE) lost her pitch when the tempo increased early in the straight. She kept on again in the final two furlongs but the winner had flown. (9/1: op 7/2)
Padauk was tapped for foot in the final two furlongs. (14/1: op 7/1)
Gee Bee Boy was never really put in the race and could improve now he is qualified for handicaps. (10/1: op 5/1)
Across The Water (11/1: 6/1-12/1)

1743 BILL WIGHTMAN H'CAP (0-75) (3-Y.O+) (Class D)
7-00 (7-02) **5f** £3,752.50 (£1,120.00: £535.00: £242.50) Stalls: Low GOING minus 0.26 sec per fur (GF)

				SP	RR	SF
1419*	**Polly Golightly (59)** (MBlanshard) **4-8-12b** NAdams(5) (led: sn clr: rdn ins fnl f: jst hld on)	—	**1**	$100/30^{1}$	70	53
1279^{3}	**Flying Harold (43)** (MRChannon) **4-7-10** JQuinn(6) (hld up: hdwy to chse wnr over 1f out: str run fnl f: jst failed)	s.h	**2**	$13/2^{2}$	54	37
1666^{7}	**Willow Dale (IRE) (70)** (DRCElsworth) **4-9-6**(3) PPMurphy(3) (rr: rdn ½-wy: hdwy appr fnl f: r.o)	3	**3**	$13/2^{2}$	71	54
1488^{5}	**Walk the Beat (64)** (MartynMeade) **7-9-3** FNorton(4) (rr: hdwy appr fnl f: styd on one pce ins fnl f)	2½	**4**	14/1	57	40
1410^{10}	**Sally Slade (71)** (CACyzer) **5-9-10** JReid(7) (mid div: rdn 2f out: one pce)	1¾	**5**	$7/1^{3}$	59	42
1488^{4}	**Sea Danzig (63)** (JJBridger) **4-9-2** GHind(10) (racd centre: in tch: rdn 2f out: one pce)	nk	**6**	12/1	50	33
1223^{6}	**Malibu Man (75)** (EAWheeler) **5-10-0** TSprake(8) (dwlt: sn rcvrd to chse wnr: wknd ent fnl f)	hd	**7**	8/1	61	44
1225^{14}	**Divine Miss-P (64)** (APJarvis) **4-9-3** WJO'Connor(9) (chsd ldrs tl wknd over 1f out)	nk	**8**	33/1	49	32
834^{11}	**Sweet Magic (70)** (PHowling) **6-9-9** AMcGlone(12) (racd centre: prom tl wknd appr fnl f)	1½	**9**	20/1	51	34
1279^{12}	**John O'Dreams (45)** (MrsALMKing) **12-7-12** AGarth(2) (b: dwlt: a bhd)	s.h	**10**	12/1	25	8
323^{5}	**Scissor Ridge (70)** (JJBridger) **5-9-9** SSanders(11) (racd centre: in tch to ½-wy)	nk	**11**	12/1	50	33
1327^{4}	**Sharp Stock (63)** (RJHodges) **4-8-11**(5) SophieMitchell(1) (keen hold: bhd fr ½-wy)	5	**12**	8/1	27	10

(SP 121.9%) **12 Rn**

57.84 secs (1.14) CSF £22.61 CT £126.06 TOTE £3.80: £1.60 £2.00 £1.90 (£12.20) Trio £28.50 OWNER Mr David Sykes (UPPER LAMBOURN) BRED Aston Park Stud and T. R. Lock
LONG HANDICAP Flying Harold 7-9
1419* Polly Golightly broke well and showed very good speed to go clear. Her stride shortened a little inside the final furlong and she only just held on. (100/30)
1279 Flying Harold produced a strong, late challenge which only just failed to get up. He is in good form at present and can surely find a race soon. (13/2)
1410 Willow Dale (IRE) is an infuriating filly, as sometimes she races prominently and weakens, and other times like today she is unable to go the pace and then stays on when the race is all over. (13/2)
1488 Walk the Beat kept on towards the finish having been unable to go the early pace. (14/1)
488 Sally Slade was tapped for speed in the final two furlongs. (7/1)
1223 Malibu Man lost his chance with a tardy start. (8/1)
1327 Sharp Stock (8/1: 6/1-9/1)

1744 E.B.F. SOUTHERN DAILY ECHO MAIDEN STKS (2-Y.O) (Class D)

7-30 (7-33) **6f** £4,581.00 (£1,368.00: £654.00: £297.00) Stalls: Low GOING minus 0.26 sec per fur (GF)

			SP	RR	SF
	Bold Fact (USA) (HRACecil) **2-9-0** KFallon(7) (unf: lw: a.p: led 3f out: rdn ins fnl f: r.o) ——	**1**	4/9[1]	73+	47
1411[6]	**Bemsha Swing (IRE)** (RHannon) **2-9-0** DaneO'Neill(2) (lw: led: hdd 3f out: ev ch 1f out: unable qckn) 1¼	**2**	16/1	70	44
	Night Flyer (JWHills) **2-9-0** AClark(1) (unf: chsd ldrs: rdn over 2f out: styd on ins fnl f) 1¾	**3**	16/1	65	39
	Carry The Flag (PFICole) **2-9-0** TQuinn(10) (neat: a.p: ev ch 2f out: one pce) s.h	**4**	7/1[2]	65	39
	Middle Temple (EALDunlop) **2-8-11**(3) DO'Donohoe(4) (w'like: bit bkwd: rr: sn pushed along: nvr nrr) 5	**5**	16/1	52	26
	Cut Diamond (PFICole) **2-9-0** JReid(6) (w'like: mid div: pushed along 2f out: one pce) s.h	**6**	16/1	51	25
1321[5]	**Carouse** (MRChannon) **2-9-0** RHughes(9) (stdd s: hld up: hdwy 2f out: wknd 1f out) 1¾	**7**	16/1	47	21
1492[2]	**Batswing** (MartynMeade) **2-9-0** FNorton(5) (prom tl wknd over 2f out) 5	**8**	16/1	33	7
	Eastwell Hall (RCurtis) **2-9-0** SDrowne(8) (leggy: mid div tl wknd over 2f out) 4	**9**	33/1	23	—
	Naayel (IRE) (CJBenstead) **2-9-0** AMcGlone(11) (cmpt: bit bkwd: dwlt: sn rcvrd to r prom: wknd qckly 2f out) 3	**10**	16/1	15	—
	Goodwood Cavalier (JLDunlop) **2-9-0** PatEddery(3) (unf: bit bkwd: dwlt: a bhd: t.o) 8	**11**	9/1[3]	—	—
			(SP 135.8%)	**11 Rn**	

1m 11.79 (1.99) CSF £12.74 TOTE £1.70: £1.30 £4.60 £3.30 (£11.10) Trio £63.00 OWNER Mr K. Abdulla (NEWMARKET) BRED Juddmonte Farms

Bold Fact (USA), quite an attractive colt who is a brother to the useful So Factual, knew his job well like most of his stable's youngster's, and won this with a little in hand. (4/9)
1411 Bemsha Swing (IRE) improved on his debut and can find a small race. (16/1)
Night Flyer ran promisingly here, keeping on nicely towards the finish. (16/1)
Carry The Flag, like his sire, isn't very big, but is quite attractive and showed enough here to suggest a race should soon be found. (7/1: op 4/1)
Middle Temple looked backward beforehand and was very green in the early stages of the race. He did stay on a bit at the finish and will improve. (16/1)
Cut Diamond wasn't given a hard time and can improve. (16/1)
Goodwood Cavalier (9/1: op 6/1)

1745 CHELSEA CONSTRUCTION TEAM H'CAP (0-90) (3-Y.O+) (Class C)

8-00 (8-02) **1m** £5,628.75 (£1,680.00: £802.50: £363.75) Stalls: Low GOING minus 0.26 sec per fur (GF)

			SP	RR	SF
1436[3]	**Sharp Shuffle (IRE) (75)** (RHannon) **4-9-1** RHughes(2) (hld up: gd hdwy on ins to ld 1f out: comf) ——	**1**	7/2[2]	84+	57
1320[5]	**Sue's Return (78)** (APJarvis) **5-9-4** WJO'Connor(8) (lw: hld up: n.m.r over 3f out: swtchd lft over 1f out: styd on to chse wnr ins fnl f) 1	**2**	6/1[3]	85	58
1261[5]	**Forza Figlio (88)** (MissGayKelleway) **4-10-0** JReid(7) (hld up: hdwy 4f out: rdn over 1f out: one pce) 1	**3**	6/1[3]	93	66
	Thatchmaster (IRE) (59) (CAHorgan) **6-7-10**(3) AWhelan(5) (a.p: led 4f out: hdd 2f out: one pce) s.h	**4**	6/1[3]	64	37
1320[10]	**Banzhaf (USA) (68)** (GLMoore) **4-8-8** KFallon(3) (keen hold: chsd ldrs: led 2f out: hdd 1f out: one pce) 1¼	**5**	10/1	70	43
1489[5]	**Duello (71)** (MBlanshard) **6-8-11** JQuinn(4) (hld up: hdwy over 2f out: rdn over 1f out: wknd ins fnl f) 3	**6**	6/1[3]	67	40
895[10]	**Dummer Golf Time (65)** (LordHuntingdon) **4-8-5v** TQuinn(6) (keen hold: hld up: rdn 3f out: sn btn: eased) 15	**7**	11/4[1]	31	4
	Civil Liberty (87) (GLewis) **4-9-13** PatEddery(9) (led 5f out: hdd 4f out: sn wknd: eased) 4	**8**	7/1	45	18
1166[18]	**Barossa Valley (IRE) (70)** (PButler) **6-8-5**(5) DSweeney(1) (racd wd: led 3f: wknd over 3f out) 2½	**9**	33/1	23	—
			(SP 130.6%)	**9 Rn**	

1m 39.22 (2.02) CSF £26.11 CT £120.61 TOTE £3.50: £1.40 £2.40 £2.20 (£14.70) Trio £24.40 OWNER Mrs H. F. Prendergast (MARLBOROUGH) BRED W. Tierney

1436 Sharp Shuffle (IRE) was held up under a confident ride. He quickened smartly to lead entering the final furlong, and won much more easily than the winning margin suggests. (7/2)
1320 Sue's Return ran another good race here but is flattered to finish as close to the winner as she did. (6/1)
1261 Forza Figlio was held up and made an effort just after the two-pole, but found his weight anchoring him in the closing stages. (6/1)
Thatchmaster (IRE) ran a good race on his seasonal debut, leading early in the straight and keeping on well once headed two furlongs out. (6/1)
1082 Banzhaf (USA) didn't help himself by pulling hard early on, and as a consequence had little more to give in the final furlong. (10/1)
1489 Duello made an effort over two furlongs out, but dropped away rather disappointingly shortly after. (6/1)

1746 CELER ET AUDAX CLAIMING STKS (3-Y.O) (Class D)

8-30 (8-30) **7f** £3,730.00 (£1,030.00: £490.00) Stalls: Low GOING minus 0.26 sec per fur (GF)

			SP	RR	SF
1217[3]	**Big Ben (73)** (RHannon) **3-8-11** PatEddery(1) (hld up: a.gng wl: smooth hdwy to ld over 1f out: easily) ——	**1**	5/6[1]	77+	—
1505[6]	**Hever Golf Charger (IRE) (63)** (TJNaughton) **3-8-4b** SSanders(2) (chsd ldr: led 3f out: hdd over 1f out: one pce) 2	**2**	9/4[2]	65	—
1151[12]	**Aybeegirl (56)** (MrsJCecil) **3-7-12v**(3) MartinDwyer(3) (led 4f: sn wknd) dist	**3**	5/2[3]	—	—
			(SP 113.9%)	**3 Rn**	

0m CSF £2.93 TOTE £1.40: (£1.40) OWNER Lady Davis (MARLBOROUGH) BRED Mrs M. Lingwood

1217 Big Ben won this very poor race in effortless fashion. (5/6)
1505 Hever Golf Charger (IRE) is very flattered to finish as close as he did to the winner. (9/4)

1747 GEORGE STUBBS H'CAP (0-80) (3-Y.O) (Class D)

9-00 (9-01) **1m 2f** £4,698.00 (£1,404.00: £672.00: £306.00) Stalls: Low GOING minus 0.26 sec per fur (GF)

			SP	RR	SF
1256[11]	**American Whisper (64)** (PWHarris) **3-7-12**(7) CLowther(8) (a.p: led 5f out: hrd rdn ins fnl f: r.o) ——	**1**	25/1	73	35
1558*	**Party Romance (USA) (85)** (BHanbury) **3-9-12** 5x RHughes(6) (led: hdd 5f out: outpcd 3f out: rallied appr fnl f: r.o) 1½	**2**	8/1	92	54
1296[2]	**Regal Reprimand (65)** (GLewis) **3-8-6** PaulEddery(2) (b.hind: a.p: chsd wnr 3f out: ev ch ins fnl f: unable qckn) hd	**3**	4/1[2]	71	33
1482[6]	**Carlys Quest (64)** (JNeville) **3-8-5** SDrowne(10) (hld up: hdwy 4f out: rdn over 2f out: one pce) 3	**4**	14/1	66	28
878[5]	**Indium (79)** (JHMGosden) **3-9-6** GHind(1) (lw: hld up: rdn 3f out: one pce) 5	**5**	5/2[1]	73	35
1164[8]	**Saffron Rose (65)** (MBlanshard) **3-8-6** JQuinn(9) (mid div: rdn 3f out: grad wknd) 4	**6**	14/1	52	14
1624*	**Ludo (61)** (RHannon) **3-8-2** 5x DaneO'Neill(5) (lw: a bhd) ½	**7**	5/2[1]	47	9
1322*	**Behind The Scenes (77)** (CACyzer) **3-9-4** KFallon(3) (dwlt: a bhd) 5	**8**	14/1	55	17

1271^{5}	**Nobel Lad (76)** (JLDunlop) **3-9-3** PatEddery(7) (lw: chsd ldrs: rdn 3f out: sn wknd)	2½	**9**	7/1	50	12
1276^{2}	**Fantastic Flame (IRE) (79)** (PJMakin) **3-9-6** MRoberts(4) (plld hrd: hld up in rr: effrt 4f out: sn btn: t.o)	27	**10**	5/1 ^{3}	10	—
				(SP 141.3%)		**10 Rn**

2m 10.88 (4.28) CSF £230.50 CT £921.07 TOTE £34.90: £5.60 £3.00 £2.10 (£96.30) Trio £506.10; £71.29 to 9/6/97 OWNER The Confederates (BERKHAMSTED) BRED Cambremont Ltd Partnership

American Whisper, who had showed promise on his first racecourse outing as a two-year-old, came back to form here with a game display. He led just before the home turn, and saw it out in the bravest fashion when challenged inside the final furlong. (25/1)

1558* Party Romance (USA) put up a very good performance under his welter-weight. He looked to be dropping away early in the straight, but to his credit rallied strongly approaching the final furlong and none was finishing better. (8/1)

1296 Regal Reprimand ran another sound race and can surely pick up a race soon. (4/1)

1164 Carlys Quest made a little headway early in the straight but was only plugging on at the one speed at the finish. (14/1)

878 Indium was a little disappointing, finding very little in the final three furlongs. (5/2)

1271 Nobel Lad (7/1: op 7/2)

T/Plpt: £16.90 (688.18 Tckts). T/Qdpt: £13.10 (34.86 Tckts) SM

1402-HAYDOCK (L-H) (Good to firm, Firm patches)

Friday June 6th

Meeting abandoned after Race 2 - slippery state of ground

WEATHER: raining WIND: fresh half bhd

1748 RED ROSE AMATEUR H'CAP (0-70) (3-Y.O+) (Class G)

6-40 (6-43) **1m 2f 120y** £2,472.00 (£692.00: £336.00) Stalls: High GOING minus 0.53 sec per fur (F)

				SP	RR	SF
1422^{16}	**Mowlaie (49)** (DWChapman) **6-10-7** MissRClark(11) (mde virtually all: hrd drvn fnl f: hld on wl)	—	**1**	33/1	61	42
1233^{*}	**Cuban Reef (47)** (WJMusson) **5-10-5** MrTMcCarthy(2) (lw: hld up in tch: hdwy to chal 2f out: sn hrd rdn: kpt on)	hd	**2**	11/4 ^{1}	59	40
1142^{5}	**Farringdon Hill (70)** (JHMGosden) **6-11-10**(4) MrCRanson(1) (b.hind: a chsng ldrs: ev ch 2f out: wknd appr fnl f)	6	**3**	6/1 ^{2}	73	54
1562^{5}	**Barbara's Jewel (44)** (ABailey) **5-9-9**(7) MrDBShaw(3) (hld up: hdwy 2f out: r.o wl towards fin)	¾	**4**	12/1	46	27
1233^{9}	**Westminster (IRE) (63)** (MHTompkins) **5-11-3v**(4) MrMJenkins(6) (lw: hld up & bhd: hdwy 3f out: nvr plcd to chal)	1¾	**5**	12/1	62	43
1422^{15}	**Merciless Cop (65)** (BJMeehan) **3-10-9** MissJAllison(12) (bit bkwd: hmpd & c wd ent st: nvr nrr)	¾	**6**	16/1	63	30
1422^{4}	**Squared Away (47)** (JWPayne) **5-10-1b**(4) MissCLake(14) (in tch tl wknd over 2f out)	1¼	**7**	15/2 ^{3}	43	24
	Rex Mundi (61) (PDEvans) **5-11-1**(4) MrWMcLaughlin(5) (bkwd: hld up: hmpd over 4f out: nt rcvr)	½	**8**	10/1	56	37
151^{8}	**Phanan (39)** (REPeacock) **11-9-4**(7)ow4 MrsCPeacock(17) (b: bkwd: plld hrd: racd wd: w ldrs 6f: sn wknd: t.o)	10	**9**	50/1	19	—
1579^{3}	**Forzair (53)** (JJO'Neill) **5-10-7**(4) MrGLake(9) (lw: prom tl wknd over 3f out: t.o)	2	**10**	16/1	30	11
1383^{12}	**Proud Brigadier (IRE) (51)** (MRBosley) **9-10-2**(7)ow13 MrSJEdwards(13) (b: lw: w ldrs over 7f: wknd qckly: t.o)	12	**11**	25/1	10	—
1433^{10}	**Best Kept Secret (49)** (LJBarratt) **6-10-0**(7)ow1 MissALHutchinson(7) (bit bkwd: a bhd: t.o)	6	**12**	25/1	—	—
1231^{6}	**Hutchies Lady (35)** (RMMcKellar) **5-9-3**(4) MrsCWilliams(16) (b.hind: in rr tl b.d over 4f out)		**B**	14/1	—	—
763^{12}	**Gold Blade (67)** (JPearce) **8-11-11** MrsLPearce(15) (bhd whn p.u over 4f out)		**P**	8/1	—	—
1422^{6}	**Clued Up (50)** (PDEvans) **4-10-4v**(4) MrAEvans(8) (trckd ldrs tl slipped & fell bnd over 4f out)		**S**	10/1	—	—
				(SP 128.4%)		**15 Rn**

2m 15.92 (4.42) CSF £114.91 CT £608.89 TOTE £79.40: £14.40 £1.70 £2.70 (£249.70) Trio £295.80; £104.19 to 9/6/97 OWNER Mr J. M. Chapman (YORK) BRED Gainsborough Stud Management Ltd

LONG HANDICAP Phanan 9-5

WEIGHT FOR AGE 3yo-14lb

Mowlaie, lightly-raced in recent years, came back to form with a hard-fought, all-the-way success, and his rider did a good job in keeping him going when strongly pressed through the final quarter-mile. (33/1)

1233* Cuban Reef looked set to take over at will after ranging upsides but the winner stuck to the task in hand and worried him out of it towards the finish. (11/4)

1142 Farringdon Hill ran up to his mark with top weight but he does lack a turn of finishing speed, especially over such an inadequate trip. (6/1)

1562 Barbara's Jewel has been running over longer trips of late and he did not find top gear until the race was all but decided. (12/1)

Westminster (IRE), probably best when ridden from behind, was given far too much to do, and his final placing was as close as he could manage. (12/1)

Merciless Cop, continuing his step up in distance, was being restrained off the pace when he was impeded by the fallers on the home turn and, forced to run wide, had little chance of getting himself into the action. (16/1)

1422 Squared Away (15/2: 5/1-8/1)

1749 E.B.F. WEAVER MAIDEN STKS (2-Y.O) (Class D)

7-10 (7-14) **6f** £3,647.50 (£1,105.00: £540.00: £257.50) Stalls: Low GOING minus 0.53 sec per fur (F)

				SP	RR	SF
1411^{4}	**Central Park (IRE)** (PFICole) **2-9-0** CRutter(7) (lw: a.p: led ½-wy: drew clr fnl 2f)	—	**1**	11/10 ^{1}	92+	41
	Lady From Limerick (IRE) (JBerry) **2-8-4**(5) TEDurcan(1) (w'like: leggy: hld up: hdwy 3f out: chsd wnr & veered rt fnl 2f: no imp)	10	**2**	6/1 ^{3}	60	9
884^{11}	**Captain Jones (IRE)** (BJMeehan) **2-9-0** WRyan(2) (bit bkwd: led 1f: hrd drvn over 2f out: sn outpcd)	1½	**3**	16/1	61	10
	The Groveller (PDEvans) **2-9-0** JFEgan(8) (unf: scope: bkwd: chsd ldrs: hrd rdn 2f out: sn lost tch)	2½	**4**	11/1	55	4
	Durar (JLDunlop) **2-9-0** RHills(3) (neat: cmpt: bkwd: hld up & bhd: effrt over 2f out: sn drvn: no imp)	2½	**5**	2/1 ^{2}	48	—
1510^{12}	**Tindaya** (PDEvans) **2-9-0** MFenton(4) (prom to ½-wy: sn rdn & wknd: t.o)	10	**6**	20/1	21	—
1645^{5}	**Dawn Patrol** (KWHogg) **2-8-9** JCarroll(5) (s.i.s: led after 1f to 3f out: sn wknd: t.o)	3	**7**	14/1	8	—
				(SP 120.9%)		**7 Rn**

1m 12.61 (0.91) CSF £8.62 TOTE £1.80: £1.30 £2.20 (£4.20) OWNER H R H Prince Fahd Salman (WHATCOMBE) BRED Lodge Park Stud

1411 Central Park (IRE), carrying a summer bloom on his coat, did not have a lot to beat here and, in command from halfway, drew right away for a facile success. (11/10: op 4/6)

Lady From Limerick (IRE), a leggy filly from a winning family, drifted right, possibly due to greenness, when in pursuit of the winner in the latter stages, and was unable to make any impression. She will know more next time. (6/1)

Captain Jones (IRE), smartly into his stride to show ahead for the first furlong, was struggling to keep up soon after halfway, but he did persevere and he is getting to realise what the game is all about. (16/1)
The Groveller, flat to the boards entering the last quarter-mile, was too backward to do himself justice on this occasion, but with plenty of stamina on his dam's side, he could be one for later in the season. (11/1)
Durar, a not over-big, strongly-made colt, who will need a stiffer test of stamina to make his mark, was unable to prove troublesome on this debut and may well need another outing to put an edge on him. (2/1)
822 Tindaya, a most impressive mover, does not possess much in the way of ability if this poor performance is anything to go by, but horses and women do make fools of you. (20/1)

1750 BAILEYS ORIGINAL IRISH CREAM H'CAP (0-70) (3-Y.O) (Class E)
- Abandoned -Course unsafe

1751 ASPECTS BEAUTY H'CAP (0-80) (3-Y.O) (Class D)
- Abandoned -Course unsafe

1752 ZOE'S 21ST BIRTHDAY MAIDEN STKS (3-Y.O+) (Class D)
- Abandoned -Course unsafe

1753 ROSTHERNE LIMITED STKS (0-85) (3-Y.O+) (Class D)
- Abandoned -Course unsafe

T/Plpt: £1.70 (7,731.55 Tckts). T/Qdpt: Not won IM

1286-SOUTHWELL (L-H) (Standard)
Friday June 6th
WEATHER: overcast & warm WIND: mod half against

1754 CHEETAH H'CAP (0-65) (3-Y.O+) (Class F)
2-20 (2-20) **7f (Fibresand)** £2,277.00 (£627.00: £297.00) Stalls: Low GOING: 0.05 sec per fur (STD)

				SP	RR	SF
*860*5	**Princess Efisio (54)** (BAMcMahon) **4-9-3** GDuffield(2) (a.p: led over 1f out: rdn out)	—	**1**	12/1	66	43
*1291**	**Johnnie the Joker (58)** (JPLeigh) **6-9-7b** DeanMcKeown(9) (w ldr: led over 2f out: hdd over 1f out: one pce)	1¼	**2**	8/1 3	67	44
*1291*3	**Bentico (61)** (MrsNMacauley) **8-9-5v**(5) GFaulkner(5) (lw: chsd ldrs: one pce appr fnl f)	1½	**3**	10/1	67	44
*1289*7	**Zain Dancer (42)** (DNicholls) **5-8-5** AlexGreaves(10) (hdwy over 4f out: chal over 1f out: no ex fnl f)	hd	**4**	15/8 1	48	25
1315 15	**Monte Cavo (35)** (MBrittain) **6-7-5**(7) DMernagh(16) (lw: prom tl rdn & btn over 1f out)	1¾	**5**	12/1	37	14
1285 9	**Naughty Pistol (USA) (63)** (PDEvans) **5-9-5b**(7) AMcCarthy(6) (outpcd: brought wd & rdn over 2f out: nvr rchd ldrs)	7	**6**	14/1	49	26
*1082*12	**Sand Star (65)** (DHaydnJones) **5-10-0** DWright(4) (led over 4f: wknd over 1f out)	s.h	**7**	25/1	50	27
1333 3	**Carlton (IRE) (62)** (GLewis) **3-9-1** NDay(7) (lw: sn outpcd: hdwy 2f out: nvr able to chal)	hd	**8**	5/1 2	47	14
1422 13	**Jigsaw Boy (58)** (PGMurphy) **8-9-7** DHarrison(11) (no ch fnl 4f)	nk	**9**	12/1	43	20
*1132*2	**Bold Aristocrat (IRE) (62)** (RHollinshead) **6-9-11** FLynch(14) (nvr trbld ldrs)	½	**10**	14/1	45	22
*1289**	**Sweet Mate (52)** (SRBowring) **5-9-1b** SWebster(13) (b.hind: in tch: effrt over 2f out: sn btn)	s.h	**11**	5/1 2	35	12
*1433*6	**Smart Guest (52)** (DShaw) **5-8-12**(3) OPears(3) (b: b.hind: spd 2f: sn lost pl)	s.h	**12**	14/1	35	12
1315 10	**Finisterre (IRE) (53)** (JJO'Neill) **4-9-2** JCarroll(8) (lw: sn wl bhd: nvr trbld ldrs)	2	**13**	20/1	32	9
*1580*7	**Efipetite (39)** (NBycroft) **4-8-2** RPrice(1) (sn pushed along: n.d)	2	**14**	25/1	13	—
1090 12	**Bison Belting (54)** (JAGlover) **3-8-7** GCarter(12) (chsd ldrs 4f: sn rdn & wknd)	16	**15**	14/1	—	—
1511 15	**Northern Judge (43)** (APJames) **4-8-6** MFenton(15) (w ldrs over 3f)	30	**16**	16/1	—	—
				(SP 156.4%)	**16 Rn**	

1m 31.9 (5.40) CSF £119.50 CT £1,006.80 TOTE £17.50: £2.40 £3.40 £3.00 £1.10 (£320.00) Trio £167.00 OWNER Mr J. D. Graham (TAMWORTH) BRED J. D. Graham
WEIGHT FOR AGE 3yo-10lb
Princess Efisio held the inside throughout and bounced back to her form of last season. (12/1)
1291* Johnnie the Joker ran his race but may be slightly better at a mile these days. (8/1)
1291 Bentico is back in form but has only won once since October 1995. (10/1)
1289 Zain Dancer, over his ideal trip, looked all over the winner early in the straight, but didn't look enthusiastic when asked to win his race. (15/8: op 4/1)
1291 Monte Cavo travelled well enough until looking short of speed at this trip. (12/1)
734 Naughty Pistol (USA), back on her favoured surface, was well beaten but shaped as if she may soon return to form. (14/1)
Smart Guest (14/1: 20/1-12/1)

1755 PUMA CLAIMING STKS (4-Y.O+) (Class F)
2-55 (2-55) **2m (Fibresand)** £2,277.00 (£627.00: £297.00) Stalls: Low GOING: 0.05 sec per fur (STD)

				SP	RR	SF
1452 4	**Sedbergh (USA) (70)** (MrsMReveley) **4-9-5** DHarrison(3) (chsd ldr: led over 4f out: sn rdn clr: eased cl home)	—	**1**	11/10 1	78+	—
1605 8	**Faugeron (50)** (NTinkler) **8-8-10** JCarroll(4) (prom: chsd wnr over 4f out: rdn & no imp fnl 2f)	6	**2**	12/1	62	—
*1579*2	**Cuban Nights (USA) (65)** (BJLlewellyn) **5-9-2** VSlattery(2) (lw: hld up: hdwy 8f out: rdn 4f out: one pce)	1½	**3**	4/1 2	67	—
1232 6	**Needwood Poppy (25)** (BCMorgan) **9-8-3** GCarter(7) (lw: sn wl bhd: r.o fnl 3f: nrst fin)	1	**4**	33/1	53	—
*151*4	**Strike-a-Pose (24)** (BJLlewellyn) **7-8-2**(7) JWilkinson(6) (chsd ldrs 11f)	3	**5**	14/1	56	—
1570 4	**Pharly Dancer (59)** (WWHaigh) **8-8-5b**1(5) GParkin(1) (plld hrd: led: sn clr: hdd & wknd over 4f out)	25	**6**	5/1 3	32	—
	Maddie (WWHaigh) **5-9-1** VHalliday(5) (rangy: lw: sn wl bhd)	dist	**7**	8/1	—	—
*16*12	**Captain Tandy (IRE) (24)** (CSmith) **8-8-10** GDuffield(8) (t.o fnl 10f)	4	**8**	33/1	—	—
				(SP 115.6%)	**8 Rn**	

3m 50.1 (24.10) CSF £15.30 TOTE £1.80: £1.10 £2.50 £1.60 (£8.10) OWNER Mr P. D. Savill (SALTBURN) BRED Mulholland Brothers
WEIGHT FOR AGE 4yo-1lb
OFFICIAL EXPLANATION Pharly Dancer: no explanation offered.
1452 Sedbergh (USA) found a poor race and did the job in good style. (11/10)

Faugeron, on the All-Weather for the first time, seemed to run a much-improved race and will have probably have ruined his handicap mark as a result. (12/1)
1579 Cuban Nights (USA) lacks any turn of foot and these tactics gave him little chance. (4/1: op 5/2)
1232 Needwood Poppy, on her debut on the surface, was totally taken off her feet for a mile and a half. (33/1)
151 Strike-a-Pose, in good form over hurdles of late, would have been considerably better off with the winner in a handicap and has probably run quite well. (14/1)
1570 Pharly Dancer, stepping up in trip, pulled too hard in these first-time blinkers, giving himself no chance of lasting home. Why the trainer failed to say as much when quizzed by the Stewards is a mystery, (5/1)

1756 JAMES LATHAM MIDLAND/CSC FOREST PRODUCTS H'CAP (0-60) (3-Y.O) (Class F)
3-25 (3-29) **1m (Fibresand)** £2,277.00 (£627.00: £297.00) Stalls: Low GOING: 0.05 sec per fur (STD)

				SP	RR	SF
1513^{3}	**Sparky (57)** (MWEasterby) **3-9-0b**(5) GParkin(8) (hdwy 4f out: rdn to ld over 1f out: sn clr: eased nr fin)	—	**1**	$15/2^{3}$	66+	42
1151^{7}	**Muara Bay (39)** (GLewis) **3-7-12**(3)ow1 AWhelan(13) (a.p: led over 2f out: hdd over 1f out: one pce)	4	**2**	$7/2^{1}$	40	15
1513^{5}	**Euroquest (46)** (DNicholls) **3-8-8** DRMcCabe(14) (lw: hdwy over 2f out: nvr nrr)	1½	**3**	14/1	44	20
1429^{2}	**Madam Lucy (47)** (WWHaigh) **3-8-9** ACulhane(9) (lw: bhd: rdn & c wd over 2f out: styd on wl: nrst fin)	1	**4**	$7/1^{2}$	43	19
1284^{5}	**Shaded (IRE) (56)** (JWWatts) **3-9-4** JCarroll(2) (lw: led tl rdn & hdd over 2f out: sn btn)	nk	**5**	$15/2^{3}$	51	27
1465^{9}	**Kustom Kit Klassic (52)** (SRBowring) **3-9-0** SWebster(12) (b: lw: in tch: rdn 3f out: nvr trbld ldrs)	1	**6**	16/1	45	21
1416^{6}	**Purple Maize (50)** (JAkehurst) **3-8-12** CRutter(4) (sn pushed along: hdwy 4f out: wknd over 1f out)	1	**7**	9/1	41	17
1430^{6}	**Robbo (57)** (CWThornton) **3-9-5** DeanMcKeown(1) (prom over 5f)	1¾	**8**	14/1	45	21
1333^{7}	**Why O Six (48)** (RAFahey) **3-8-3b**1(7) RWinston(5) (w ldrs tl wknd over 2f out)	1	**9**	20/1	34	10
600^{5}	**Petula Boy (40)** (SRBowring) **3-8-2** MFenton(16) (prom tl rdn & btn over 2f out)	2	**10**	20/1	22	—
1503^{8}	**Lycius Touch (45)** (AGNewcombe) **3-8-7** RPrice(7) (swtg: prom 4f)	9	**11**	16/1	9	—
1500^{4}	**Racing Heart (45)** (PJMakin) **3-8-7** DHarrison(15) (swtg: stdd s: hld up: n.d)	1	**12**	$15/2^{3}$	7	—
1580^{8}	**Naivasha (59)** (JBerry) **3-9-2**(5) TEDurcan(11) (s.i.s: a bhd)	5	**13**	14/1	11	—
	Koordinaite (38) (WJMusson) **3-8-0** DeclanO'Shea(6) (b: bhd fnl 4f)	2½	**14**	20/1	—	—
1272^{8}	**Hever Golf Charmer (55)** (TJNaughton) **3-9-3** GDuffield(3) (lw: in tch 3f: sn rdn & bhd)	5	**15**	14/1	—	—
1121^{6}	**Mr Music (50)** (KMcAuliffe) **3-8-12v**1 FLynch(10) (sn bhd)	6	**16**	14/1	—	—
				(SP 139.4%)	**16 Rn**	

1m 45.4 (6.40) CSF £34.30 CT £349.96 TOTE £9.20: £2.70 £1.90 £4.20 £1.30 (£53.70) Trio Not won; £206.80 to Epsom Downs 7/6/97
OWNER Abbots Salford Carav Park (SHERIFF HUTTON) BRED Godolphin Management Co Ltd
1513 Sparky moved well to post despite this being his debut on the surface and ran out a ready winner. He looks the sort who could thrive here. (15/2)
Muara Bay, a poor mover, ran much better than he had on the Equitrack and was unfortunate to catch a bit of a tartar in the winner. (7/2)
1513 Euroquest did some good late work but the winner confirmed Carlisle placings. (14/1)
1429 Madam Lucy, scrubbed along and brought wide as she was last time she ran here, only hit her stride when the race was over. (7/1)
1284 Shaded (IRE), with less than a test of stamina than of late, was made plenty use of to little effect. (15/2)
1134 Kustom Kit Klassic, who tried much further last time, wore a tongue-strap and lacked the pace to mount a challenge. (16/1)

1757 LANGLEY MECHANICAL SERVICES MAIDEN H'CAP (0-70) (3-Y.O+ F & M) (Class E)
3-55 (3-56) **1m (Fibresand)** £3,096.25 (£925.00: £442.50: £201.25) Stalls: Low GOING: 0.05 sec per fur (STD)

				SP	RR	SF
1580^{2}	**Molly Music (55)** (GGMargarson) **3-8-7** DBiggs(7) (sn pushed along: hdwy 3f out: led 1f out: rdn & qcknd clr)	—	**1**	$4/1^{1}$	71	28
1470^{8}	**Degree (54)** (SCWilliams) **4-9-3** GCarter(3) (lw: sn pushed along: hdwy 3f out: r.o fnl f: nt trble wnr)	6	**2**	16/1	58	26
1429^{4}	**Phoenix Princess (53)** (BAMcMahon) **3-8-5** GDuffield(9) (trckd ldrs: led over 3f out tl over 2f out: one pce fnl f)	1¾	**3**	$4/1^{1}$	54	11
1580^{4}	**Champagne On Ice (44)** (PDEvans) **3-7-3**(7) AMcCarthy(10) (hdwy 4f out: rdn 2f out: sn btn)	s.h	**4**	$11/2^{2}$	44	1
590^{2}	**Faym (IRE) (66)** (JWharton) **3-9-4** JCarroll(4) (led over 4f: led over 2f out to 1f out: wknd)	5	**5**	$4/1^{1}$	56	13
1221^{10}	**Miami Moon (57)** (CWThornton) **3-8-9** DeanMcKeown(5) (chsd ldrs 5f)	6	**6**	$8/1^{3}$	35	—
1401^{7}	**Just Typical (44)** (NTinkler) **3-7-10** KimTinkler(8) (w ldr 4f)	17	**7**	33/1	—	—
1297^{3}	**Keen Companion (65)** (TJNaughton) **4-9-11**(3) JDSmith(2) (a bhd)	7	**8**	$11/2^{2}$	—	—
1271^{9}	**Glorious Dancer (44)** (JHetherton) **3-7-5**(5) IonaWands(6) (spd over 2f out: sn bhd)	hd	**9**	16/1	—	—
1467^{24}	**Rustic Song (IRE) (33)** (JWharton) **4-7-10** NVarley(1) (lw: s.i.s: a bhd)	2½	**10**	20/1	—	—
				(SP 121.3%)	**10 Rn**	

1m 45.7 (6.70) CSF £68.06 CT £258.61 TOTE £3.20: £1.80 £4.60 £1.20 (£27.40) Trio £69.50 OWNER Mr P. E. Axon (NEWMARKET) BRED D. P. Martin
LONG HANDICAP Champagne On Ice 7-6 Just Typical 7-2 Glorious Dancer 7-8 Rustic Song (IRE) 7-1
WEIGHT FOR AGE 3yo-11lb
1580 Molly Music is game and looks to be thriving, for she could not go the early pace, but the further they went, the better she got, fairly shooting clear in the final furlong. She can win again. (4/1)
28 Degree normally forces the pace, but got left behind on this occasion until her stamina came into play. (16/1)
1429 Phoenix Princess did best of those involved with the fast early pace and, if her early enthusiasm can be tempered, should find a race. (4/1: op 7/1)
1580 Champagne On Ice got going earlier this time but was flat to the boards early in the straight. (11/2)
590 Faym (IRE) set a fast pace and paid the price in the closing stages. Seven looks her trip. (4/1)
Miami Moon sat close to the good early pace but had cracked by the home turn. (8/1)
1297 Keen Companion (11/2: op 3/1)

1758 FARMERS WEEKLY (S) STKS (2-Y.O) (Class F)
4-25 (4-26) **6f (Fibresand)** £1,984.50 (£547.00: £259.50) Stalls: Low GOING: 0.05 sec per fur (STD)

				SP	RR	SF
1330^{4}	**Figawin** (GLewis) **2-8-11** NDay(10) (lw: chsd ldrs: ev ch whn rdn & edgd lft over 1f out: led & veered rt ins fnl f: r.o nr fin)	—	**1**	$11/4^{2}$	59	1
1440^{9}	**Katie's Cracker** (MRChannon) **2-8-7**ow1 RPainter(3) (dwlt: hdwy over 2f out: nrst fin)	1¼	**2**	7/1	52	—
1120^{6}	**Gymcrak Mystery** (GHolmes) **2-8-6** AlexGreaves(11) (b.hind: trckd ldrs: led over 2f out: hdd & one pce ins fnl f)	1½	**3**	11/1	47	—
872^{3}	**Daynabee** (NTinkler) **2-8-6** KimTinkler(5) (lw: led 1f: wknd over 2f out)	2	**4**	14/1	41	—
1370^{6}	**Chika Shan (IRE)** (BSmart) **2-8-6**(5) ADaly(4) (chsd ldrs 4f)	5	**5**	8/1	33	—

1438^{6}	**Goldenacres** (JNeville) **2-8-11** DeanMcKeown(9) (nvr plcd to chal)	nk	**6**	6/1^{3}	32	—
1461^{4}	**Margaret's Dancer** (CSmith) **2-8-11b** GDuffield(2) (lw: nvr trbld ldrs)	2½	**7**	16/1	26	—
1461^{5}	**Averham Star** (DShaw) **2-8-8b^{1}**(3) CTeague(1) (in tch: n.m.r over 3f out: no ch after)	5	**8**	25/1	12	—
1310^{6}	**Risky Whisky** (JBerry) **2-9-3b^{1}** GCarter(8) (dwlt: led after 1f: wknd & hdd over 2f out)	6	**9**	11/8^{1}	2	—
	E B Treasure (NBycroft) **2-8-6** DWright(6) (w'like: scope: bit bkwd: a bhd)	¾	**10**	20/1	—	—
				(SP 136.2%)	**10 Rn**	

1m 21.0 (7.50) CSF £24.82 TOTE £3.80: £1.60 £3.10 £4.20 (£39.90) Trio £33.80 OWNER Highclere Thoroughbred Racing Ltd (EPSOM) BRED Chippenham Lodge Stud

Bt in 7,400gns

OFFICIAL EXPLANATION Risky Whisky: ran too freely as a result of wearing first-time blinkers.

1330 Figawin beat a subsequent winner when fourth at Newcastle, and looked in charge early in the straight after struggling to go the pace, but almost threw this race away by failing to keep straight. Blinkers may help. (11/4)

Katie's Cracker, a half-sister to One For The Pot, threatens to stay further as she was doing all her best work at the finish. (7/1: 5/1-8/1)

Gymcrak Mystery has improved from her debut and she should find a similar race. (11/1: op 7/1)

872 Daynabee, stepped up in trip, lost her position on the home turn but found a couple of those ahead stopping even more quickly in the final furlong. (14/1)

1370 Chika Shan (IRE), a dipped-backed colt, showed speed for half a mile. This was a race where the leaders may have gone too fast early. (8/1)

Goldenacres, nibbled at in the market, was given what can only be described as a peculiar ride, and is worth bearing in mind as he gives the strong impression he is capable of better. (6/1: op 16/1)

1310 Risky Whisky all but bolted in the first-time blinkers and has gone the wrong way since encountering fast ground. (11/8: 4/5-7/4)

1759 LION H'CAP (0-65) (3-Y.O+) (Class F)

4-55 (4-56) **5f (Fibresand)** £2,277.00 (£627.00: £297.00) Stalls: High GOING: 0.05 sec per fur (STD)

				SP	RR	SF
1311^{2}	**Goretski (IRE) (59)** (NTinkler) **4-9-10** DHarrison(8) (prom: led 2f out: sn clr: rdn out)	—	**1**	13/2^{3}	69	50
1602*	**Shadow Jury (65)** (DWChapman) **7-9-13b**(3) 7x OPears(11) (bhd: rdn & hdwy over 2f out: kpt on fnl f)	4	**2**	13/2^{3}	62	43
1627^{4}	**Sotonian (HOL) (44)** (PSFelgate) **4-8-9** DWright(13) (chsd ldrs: outpcd 2f out: kpt on fnl f)	s.h	**3**	9/2^{1}	41	22
1090^{10}	**Sea Ya Maite (49)** (SRBowring) **3-8-7**^{ow1} SWebster(6) (b: w ldrs: rdn over 2f out: no ex ins fnl f)	nk	**4**	20/1	45	18
949^{11}	**Time To Fly (45)** (BWMurray) **4-8-10b** GCarter(7) (w ldrs: ev ch 2f out: one pce)	s.h	**5**	8/1	41	22
779^{7}	**Grand Chapeau (IRE) (52)** (DNicholls) **5-9-3** AlexGreaves(12) (lw: prom: rdn over 1f out: one pce)	hd	**6**	12/1	48	29
1289^{2}	**Silk Cottage (55)** (RMWhitaker) **5-9-6** DeanMcKeown(2) (led 3f)	2	**7**	15/2	44	25
1467*	**Afaan (IRE) (66)** (RFMarvin) **4-9-12**(5) 7x HBastiman(5) (sn rdn & bhd: nvr trbld ldrs)	1½	**8**	11/2^{2}	50	31
1289^{12}	**Bent Raiwand (USA) (36)** (DonEnricoIncisa) **4-8-1** KimTinkler(10) (lw: sn pushed along: bhd fnl 3f)	nk	**9**	33/1	19	—
956^{12}	**Boffy (IRE) (46)** (BPJBaugh) **4-8-6b**(5) IonaWands(4) (lw: bhd tl sme hdwy fnl f)	1	**10**	20/1	26	7
1620^{14}	**Lochon (43)** (MrsNMacauley) **6-8-5b**(3)^{ow1} CTeague(3) (b: rdn 2f out: a bhd)	¾	**11**	20/1	21	1
1666^{11}	**Delrob (49)** (DHaydnJones) **6-8-9b**(5) GFaulkner(1) (w ldr over 2f: edgd lft & sn bhd)	1¼	**12**	8/1	23	4
1250*	**Pleasure Time (63)** (CSmith) **4-10-0b** GDuffield(9) (a bhd)	3	**13**	7/1	27	8
				(SP 131.6%)	**13 Rn**	

60.5 secs (3.50) CSF £46.42 CT £201.57 TOTE £6.00: £1.70 £2.90 £2.10 (£27.90) Trio £47.50 OWNER Mr P. D. Savill (MALTON) BRED Pierre Brichart

WEIGHT FOR AGE 3yo-7lb

1311 Goretski (IRE), having his first taste of All-Weather racing, has been in good form lately and took this in fine style. (13/2)

1602* Shadow Jury stuck to the stands rail, although rather taken off his feet early on, and rallied well in the last quarter-mile. He remains in good form and this is his time of year as he does most of his winning between May and July. (13/2)

1627 Sotonian (HOL), back on the Fibresand which has seen both of his victories to date, at Wolverhampton, ran his second good race of the week and should find another chance before long. (9/2: op 10/1)

Sea Ya Maite, bandaged and with his tongue tied down, is not a typical sprinter on looks, but ran his best race and this could well be his trip. (20/1)

593* Time To Fly faced a stiff task after such a big rise in the weights for his Wolverhampton win two outings ago, but ran fast towards the centre until outpaced towards the finish. (8/1)

779 Grand Chapeau (IRE) having his first look at the All-Weather, ran well for a long way and is capable of finding a race off this sort of mark. (12/1)

T/Plpt: £96.90 (89.41 Tckts). T/Qdpt: £20.90 (21.72 Tckts) Dk

1395-DONCASTER (L-H) (St crse Gd, Gd to frm ptchs, Rnd crse Gd to Firm, Good patches)

Saturday June 7th

WEATHER: sunny periods WIND: mod against

1760 VODAFONE DERBY DAY MAIDEN AUCTION STKS (2-Y.O) (Class E)

2-20 (2-27) **6f** £3,304.25 (£989.00: £474.50: £217.25) Stalls: High GOING minus 0.04 sec per fur (G)

				SP	RR	SF
1328^{5}	**Premium Pursuit** (RAFahey) **2-8-11** ACulhane(2) (mde all far side: kpt on wl fnl 2f)	—	**1**	20/1	81	27
1569^{3}	**Country Garden** (RHannon) **2-8-0**(3) AWhelan(9) (swtchd far side after 1f: chsd ldrs: effrt & ev ch 2f out: no ex fnl f)	1½	**2**	4/1^{1}	69	15
	Starliner (IRE) (MBrittain) **2-8-3** GBardwell(7) (leggy: unf: racd far side: hdwy 2f out: styd on wl)	1¾	**3**	33/1	64	10
1418^{3}	**Mohawk (IRE)** (JLDunlop) **2-8-11** AClark(3) (lw: chsd ldrs far side: effrt 2f out: nt qckn)	nk	**4**	5/1^{2}	72	18
1396^{6}	**Top Floor (IRE)** (NTinkler) **2-8-8** KimTinkler(8) (led centre: kpt on fnl 2f: no imp)	hd	**5**	20/1	68	14
	Dry Lightning (MBell) **2-8-3** MFenton(13) (neat: w ldrs centre tl wknd appr fnl f)	1¼	**6**	11/1	60	6
1510^{9}	**Lord of Love** (TDEasterby) **2-8-5** TWilliams(12) (bhd centre tl r.o fnl 2f)	s.h	**7**	20/1	62	8
1143^{6}	**Alpen Wolf (IRE)** (WRMuir) **2-8-11** BDoyle(19) (racd centre: chsd ldrs: rdn ½-wy: no imp after)	2	**8**	10/1	63	9
1466^{4}	**Ella Falls (IRE)** (TDBarron) **2-7-11**(3) PFessey(20) (lw: hld up stands' side: hdwy ½-wy: sn rdn & no imp)	¾	**9**	6/1^{3}	50	—
938^{4}	**Festival Flyer** (RBoss) **2-8-11** GDuffield(11) (racd centre: sn drvn along: n.d)	hd	**10**	6/1^{3}	60	6
1616^{6}	**Scene (IRE)** (MartynMeade) **2-7-7**(7) RBrisland(18) (swtg: racd centre: chsd ldrs over 4f)	1	**11**	33/1	47	—
1174^{8}	**Harnage (IRE)** (MRChannon) **2-8-8** RPerham(21) (racd stands' side: s.i.s: hdwy ½-wy: n.d)	s.h	**12**	20/1	54	—

				SP	RR	SF
1267^{4}	**Petara (IRE)** (JSWainwright) **2-8-8** MRimmer(6) (chsd ldrs far side 4f)	½	**13**	20/1	53	—
	Catherines Song (CADwyer) **2-7-11**$^{(7)ow1}$ JoHunnam(5) (w'like: b: b.off hind: gd spd far side 4f)	hd	**14**	25/1	49	—
1026^{4}	**Estopped (IRE)** (MRChannon) **2-8-11** JFortune(15) (racd centre: sn outpcd)	1	**15**	9/1	53	—
1418^{5}	**Heavenly Falls (IRE)** (CADwyer) **2-8-5** NVarley(10) (racd centre: hdwy u.p ½-wy: sn wknd)	½	**16**	25/1	46	—
1240^{12}	**No Shame** (JGSmyth-Osbourne) **2-8-0**$^{(3)}$ DO'Donohoe(1) (racd far side: wl bhd tl sme late hdwy)	s.h	**17**	50/1	44	—
1126^{8}	**Sandmoor Tartan** (TDEasterby) **2-8-5**$^{(3)}$ RHavlin(14) (lw: cl up centre over 3f: wknd)	½	**18**	20/1	47	—
	Jasmine Tea (MartynMeade) **2-8-6** FNorton(4) (unf: racd far side: n.d)	1¾	**19**	20/1	41	—
	Eddie Rombo (NTinkler) **2-8-3**$^{(5)}$ IonaWands(16) (w'like: scope: bit bkwd: sn outpcd centre: a bhd)	5	**20**	33/1	29	—
836^{11}	***Latin Bay*** (PWHarris) **2-8-5** NConnorton(17) (Withdrawn not under Starters' orders: bolted bef s)		**W**	33/1	—	—

(SP 147.4%) **20 Rn**

1m 15.67 (4.67) CSF £89.09 TOTE £28.30: £4.90 £1.70 £15.50 (£82.40) Trio £320.00; £405.67 to 9/6/97 OWNER Mr J. C. Parsons (MALTON) BRED Cheveley Park Stud Ltd

1328 Premium Pursuit turned out to be well drawn. He continued his improvement and appreciated the extra distance, and there looks to be more to come. (20/1)

1569 Country Garden was warm beforehand. Wisely switched to the far side, she had her chances but, when the pressure was on, she again failed to come up with the goods. (4/1: 7/2-9/4)

Starliner (IRE), a tall, lean filly, showed promise, picking up ground in useful style, and will be well suited by longer distances later on. (33/1)

1418 Mohawk (IRE), well drawn, had his chances but proved well short of toe when asked a question. (5/1)

1396 Top Floor (IRE) made the mistake of switching towards the centre of the track after the start and was always struggling, but still ran well enough to suggest that he is improving. (20/1)

Dry Lightning put up a decent debut run and should be all the sharper for it. (11/1: 8/1-12/1)

1510 Lord of Love has not much to recommend him on looks, but he ran well and should pick up a race in due course. (20/1)

1143 Alpen Wolf (IRE) ran quite well from a poor draw. (10/1: 7/1-11/1)

1466 Ella Falls (IRE) had no chance being drawn where she was and this effort is best ignored. (6/1)

1761 KONICA EAST DIRECT H'CAP (0-75) (3-Y.O+) (Class D)

2-50 (2-55) **7f** £4,142.50 (£1,240.00: £595.00: £272.50) Stalls: High GOING minus 0.04 sec per fur (G)

				SP	RR	SF
1584^{2}	**Jedi Knight (55)** (MWEasterby) **3-8-1** FNorton(14) (hld up: stdy hdwy: led appr fnl f: rdn & r.o wl)	—	**1**	11/2^{2}	68	40
1511^{4}	**Allinson's Mate (IRE) (64)** (TDBarron) **9-8-13b**$^{(7)}$ KimberleyHart(12) (lw: bhd: hdwy over 2f out: hung lft: r.o: nrst fin)	1¾	**2**	5/1^{1}	73	55
1324^{13}	**Grey Kingdom (62)** (MBrittain) **6-9-4** GBardwell(11) (a cl up: led 2f out tl appr fnl f: kpt on)	¾	**3**	10/1	69	51
1489^{4}	**Suez Tornado (IRE) (61)** (EJAlston) **4-9-3v** ACulhane(6) (lw: in tch: hdwy u.p & ev ch over 1f out: kpt on one pce)	1¾	**4**	7/1^{3}	64	46
1009^{17}	**Jo Maximus (65)** (JGSmyth-Osbourne) **5-9-7** RPerham(13) (b.off hind: led 5f: no ex)	½	**5**	25/1	67	49
1448^{8}	**Hotcake (40)** (MissSEHall) **4-7-10** NCarlisle(7) (in tch: effrt over 2f out: nt pce to chal)	½	**6**	33/1	41	23
1655^{2}	**Legal Issue (IRE) (55)** (WWHaigh) **5-8-6**$^{(5)}$ GParkin(8) (chsd ldrs tl wknd fnl 2f)	2	**7**	11/2^{2}	51	33
974^{9}	**Keston Pond (IRE) (62)** (MrsVAAconley) **7-9-4** MDeering(5) (mid div: rdn over 2f out: edgd lft: nvr able to chal)	3½	**8**	12/1	50	32
1560^{11}	**Oriole (40)** (DonEnricoIncisa) **4-7-10** KimTinkler(2) (chsd ldrs tl outpcd fnl 2f)	2	**9**	25/1	24	6
1385^{7}	**Al Reet (IRE) (57)** (SRBowring) **6-8-13** SWebster(4) (gd spd 4f: sn wknd)	2	**10**	14/1	36	18
1395^{15}	**Halmanerror (63)** (MrsJRRamsden) **7-9-5** JFortune(3) (trckd ldrs tl lost pl over 2f out: n.d after)	nk	**11**	7/1^{3}	42	24
1446^{10}	**Celandine (66)** (AndrewTurnell) **4-9-3**$^{(5)}$ ADaly(15) (swtchd lft after s: spd 4f)	½	**12**	33/1	44	26
	Pine Ridge Lad (IRE) (63) (JLEyre) **7-9-5** RLappin(16) (bit bkwd: b: b.hind: racd alone stands' side: spd 4f)	s.h	**13**	12/1	40	22
	Tickntima (75) (MDHammond) **3-9-7** GDuffield(10) (hld up & a bhd)	¾	**14**	25/1	51	23
1406^{3}	**Look Who's Calling (IRE) (72)** (BAMcMahon) **4-10-0** MWigham(9) (chsd ldrs to ½-wy)	5	**15**	14/1	36	18
	Tawafij (USA) (72) (MDHammond) **8-10-0** AClark(1) (nvr wnt pce)	4	**16**	10/1	27	9

(SP 136.8%) **16 Rn**

1m 28.09 (3.59) CSF £32.22 CT £211.93 TOTE £5.90: £1.30 £1.90 £2.10 £1.90 (£18.80) Trio £71.20 OWNER Mr K. Hodgson (SHERIFF HUTTON) BRED E. J. B. Maude

LONG HANDICAP Oriole 7-6 Hotcake 7-9

WEIGHT FOR AGE 3yo-10lb

1584 Jedi Knight is in top form just now and went really well during the race and, once in front approaching the final furlong, it was always his. (11/2)

1511 Allinson's Mate (IRE) ran his usual game race and finished well, despite tending to go left, and was never quite good enough. (5/1)

929* Grey Kingdom ran a cracker after being hoisted a stone in the weights, and struggled on in the final furlong, despite always being held. (10/1)

1489 Suez Tornado (IRE) is running consistently well at present and, with a bit more help from the Handicapper, he should find his first race in this country. (7/1)

638 Jo Maximus has gained all his three victories at Brighton and this was a much better effort from him. (25/1)

Hotcake ran better this time, and there ought to be a modest race to be found. (33/1)

1762 WORTHINGTON CONDITIONS STKS (3-Y.O+) (Class C)

3-20 (3-21) **1m 2f 60y** £5,302.40 (£1,961.60: £940.80: £384.00: £152.00: £59.20) Stalls: Low GOING minus 0.36 sec per fur (F)

				SP	RR	SF
917a^{7}	**Poseidon** (MRChannon) **3-8-8** JFortune(4) (trckd ldrs: chal over 1f out: rdn to ld wl ins fnl f)	—	**1**	10/1	110	62
1159^{7}	**Yorkshire (IRE)** (PFICole) **3-8-4** GDuffield(3) (plld hrd: led after 2f & hung rt: qcknd over 3f out: hdd & no ex towards fin)	½	**2**	9/4^{2}	105	57
1490^{3}	**Bequeath (110)** (HRACecil) **5-9-10** JLowe(6) (lw: b: hld up: hdwy 4f out: ch 2f out: r.o one pce)	1¼	**3**	9/2^{3}	110	75
1257^{3}	**Premier Bay (98)** (PWHarris) **3-8-1** BDoyle(1) (led 2f: chsd ldr: ev ch 4f out: outpcd fnl 2f)	3	**4**	7/1	96	48
1239*	**Garuda (IRE)** (JLDunlop) **3-8-4** AClark(2) (lw: s.i.s: hld up: effrt & n.m.r over 3f out: r.o one pce)	1½	**5**	15/8^{1}	96	48
	Poddington (96) (RAkehurst) **6-9-3** RPerham(5) (plld hrd early: in tch: hdwy to chal over 3f out: wknd over 2f out)	10	**6**	8/1	81	46

(SP 116.4%) **6 Rn**

2m 8.0 (0.20) CSF £31.20 TOTE £19.20: £4.10 £1.10 (£15.00) OWNER Allevamento La Nuova Sbarra SRL (UPPER LAMBOURN) BRED Mrs W. H. Gibson Fleming

WEIGHT FOR AGE 3yo-13lb

917a Poseidon was stepping up in trip and got it particularly well and, given a smashing ride, proved game under pressure. (10/1)

1159 Yorkshire (IRE) gave his rider problems by pulling hard and then hanging, but he still put up a decent performance, and if he can be sorted out there is obviously better to come. (9/4: 6/4-5/2)
1490 Bequeath had his chances, but was always tending to edge left under pressure and was never doing enough. (9/2)
1257 Premier Bay had previously looked likely to appreciate this trip but, when it came down to it, he proved disappointing in the last couple of furlongs. (7/1)
1239* Garuda (IRE) looked magnificent but was not suited by this messy event on fast ground and failed to offer a threat. This is not his true form. (15/8)
Poddington, very fresh for his seasonal debut, pulled too hard for his own good and ran poorly. (8/1)

1763 SASHA LYONS MEMORIAL H'CAP (0-80) (4-Y.O+) (Class D)

4-15 (4-15) **1m 4f** £6,004.00 (£1,792.00: £856.00: £388.00) Stalls: Low GOING minus 0.36 sec per fur (F)

				SP	RR	SF
1605[3]	**Northern Motto (50)** (JSGoldie) **4-8-3** NVarley(2) (a.p: chal over 2f out: rdn to ld cl home)	—	**1**	13/2[3]	61	43
	Hawker Hunter (USA) (75) (RAkehurst) **6-10-0** GDuffield(1) (swtg: led & sn clr: rdn over 2f out: r.o: jst ct)	nk	**2**	14/1	86	68
552[4]	**Suga Hawk (IRE) (58)** (EJAlston) **5-8-11** JFortune(11) (chsd ldrs: hdwy u.p over 1f out: nt pce to chal)	1¼	**3**	12/1	67	49
1459[10]	**Mawared (IRE) (70)** (JLDunlop) **4-9-9** AClark(5) (b: hld up: hdwy over 3f out: rdn 2f out: styd on: no imp)	3	**4**	7/1	75	57
1427[6]	**Traceability (75)** (SCWilliams) **4-9-11**(3) DGriffiths(3) (lw: trckd clr ldr: effrt & ch over 3f out: outpcd fnl 2f)	4	**5**	8/1	75	57
1562*	**Summerhill Special (IRE) (65)** (DWBarker) **6-9-4** TWilliams(6) (b.nr hind: hld up & bhd: effrt over 3f out: nvr able to chal)	¾	**6**	7/1	64	46
1445[2]	**Kintavi (52)** (TWDonnelly) **7-8-2**(3) PFessey(4) (b: hld up: hdwy 4f out: wknd over 2f out)	¾	**7**	6/1[2]	50	32
1494[6]	**Charter (64)** (WStorey) **6-8-12**(5) GParkin(7) (hld up & bhd: n.d)	¾	**8**	25/1	61	43
1408[7]	**Salska (56)** (AStreeter) **6-8-6**(3) RHavlin(8) (lw: hld up: hdwy 6f out: outpcd fnl 3f)	s.h	**9**	12/1	53	35
1398[2]	**Ledgendry Line (70)** (MrsMReveley) **4-9-9** ACulhane(10) (lw: plld hrd: outpcd 4f out: n.d after)	2	**10**	2/1[1]	64	46
1022[8]	**Blenheim Terrace (60)** (CBBBooth) **4-8-13** KHodgson(9) (swtg: hld up: effrt over 4f out: sn rdn & n.d)	1½	**11**	11/1	52	34
				(SP 131.3%)	**11 Rn**	

2m 32.41 (2.41) CSF £95.48 CT £1,007.76 TOTE £9.60: £4.30 £5.40 £3.40 (£52.50) Trio £449.90; £259.82 to 9/6/97 OWNER Mr D. Callaghan (GLASGOW) BRED Exors of the late Sir Robin McAlpine
OFFICIAL EXPLANATION **Ledgendry Line: the jockey reported that the gelding would not settle and found nothing when let down.**
1605 Northern Motto, from a yard in top form at the moment, stays much further than this and proved very determined under pressure. (13/2)
Hawker Hunter (USA) has changed stables after some disappointing efforts over fences, and the Handicapper has dropped him 15lb since his last Flat run three seasons ago. He got himself stirred up beforehand but ran really well, although he did have things his own way out in front. (14/1)
552 Suga Hawk (IRE) is running consistently well but just lacks that final dash. (12/1)
Mawared (IRE) has yet to win a race and looks a bit of a character, but kept staying on under pressure. (7/1)
986 Traceability looked particularly well and had his chances, but is proving disappointing at the moment and put up little fight. (8/1: op 12/1)
1562* Summerhill Special (IRE) tried to come from behind in this slowly-run event, but always had too much on. (7/1)
1445 Kintavi was not suited by this messy event. (6/1)
1494 Charter is running well and is one to keep in mind. (25/1)
612 Blenheim Terrace (11/1: 8/1-12/1)

1764 ST JOHN AMBULANCE MAIDEN STKS (3-Y.O+) (Class D)

4-45 (4-46) **5f** £3,590.00 (£1,070.00: £510.00: £230.00) Stalls: High GOING minus 0.04 sec per fur (G)

				SP	RR	SF
1406[4]	**Furnish (90)** (BWHills) **3-8-6**(3) JDSmith(7) (lw: trckd ldr: led over 1f out: r.o)	—	**1**	6/4[1]	75	29
1394[3]	**Polish Romance (USA) (79)** (MRStoute) **3-8-9** AClark(6) (mde most tl hdd over 1f out: kpt on same pce)	1¼	**2**	5/2[2]	71	25
1090[2]	**Frederick James** (MJHeaton-Ellis) **3-9-0** GDuffield(3) (chsd ldrs: outpcd ½-wy: kpt on wl fnl f)	1½	**3**	5/2[2]	71	25
1511[13]	**Dona Filipa (33)** (MissLCSiddall) **4-8-13**(3) OPears(5) (hld up: effrt ½-wy: r.o: nrst fin)	1¼	**4**	50/1	41 t	23
	Mischievous Time (ASmith) **3-9-0** NConnorton(1) (leggy: outpcd ½-wy: n.d after)	2½	**5**	25/1	38 t	13
	Harvey's Future (TTClement) **3-8-9**(5) GFaulkner(4) (b: hld up: hdwy after 2f: btn appr fnl f)	hd	**6**	20/1[3]	38 t	13
1604[6]	**Fancy Clancy (29)** (MissLCSiddall) **4-8-9**(7) TSiddall(2) (lw: cl up 3f: sn wknd)	1½	**7**	25/1	28 t	10
				(SP 111.6%)	**7 Rn**	

61.96 secs (3.56) CSF £4.66 TOTE £2.40: £1.80 £1.60 (£1.80) OWNER Mr K. Abdulla (LAMBOURN) BRED Juddmonte Farms
WEIGHT FOR AGE 3yo-7lb
1406 Furnish, taken to post early, takes a strong hold and did just enough to win what looks a very modest race. (6/4)
1394 Polish Romance (USA) is without doubt her own worst enemy. (5/2: 6/4-11/4)
1090 Frederick James found this trip too sharp but was keeping on really well at the end. (5/2: op 4/1)
Dona Filipa is either showing signs of improvement or this was a very bad race, as she was picking up nicely at the end. (50/1)
Mischievous Time never looked happy but was not beaten all that far. (25/1)

1765 'TATTENHAM CORNER' H'CAP (0-80) (4-Y.O+ F & M) (Class D)

5-15 (5-16) **6f** £3,817.50 (£1,140.00: £545.00: £247.50) Stalls: High GOING minus 0.04 sec per fur (G)

				SP	RR	SF
1385[2]	**Almasi (IRE) (62)** (CFWall) **5-8-13** GDuffield(6) (lw: bhd: hdwy over 2f out: r.o u.p to ld wl ins fnl f)	—	**1**	6/5[1]	73	50
1079[10]	**Bollin Dorothy (48)** (TDEasterby) **4-7-13** TWilliams(1) (trckd ldrs: hdwy to ld over 1f out: qcknd: no ex towards fin)	½	**2**	10/1	58	35
1223[B]	**Oatey (64)** (MrsJRRamsden) **4-9-1** JFortune(3) (lw: hld up: hdwy 2f out: r.o: nrst fin)	4	**3**	5/1[2]	63	40
1627[14]	**Stolen Kiss (IRE) (63)** (MWEasterby) **5-8-9b**(5) IonaWands(4) (lw: mde most tl hdd over 1f out: no ex)	2½	**4**	11/1	55	32
1446[3]	**Lunar Mist (75)** (MartynMeade) **4-9-9**(3) RHavlin(7) (lw: w ldrs tl outpcd 2f out: sn btn)	2½	**5**	13/2[3]	61	38
1269[6]	**Antonias Melody (74)** (SRBowring) **4-9-11** SWebster(5) (w ldrs over 3f: sn rdn & btn)	4	**6**	10/1	49	26
1583[10]	**Formidable Liz (58)** (MDHammond) **7-8-9** DaleGibson(8) (effrt ½-wy: sn rdn & hung lft: no imp)	s.h	**7**	12/1	33	10
1332[2]	**Ballard Lady (IRE) (45)** (JSWainwright) **5-7-5b**(5) JBramhill(9) (w ldrs 3f: sn rdn & btn)	2½	**8**	9/1	13	—
385[7]	**Steal 'Em (65)** (ABailey) **4-8-11**(5) GFaulkner(2) (a bhd)	hd	**9**	25/1	33	10
				(SP 123.5%)	**9 Rn**	

1m 14.13 (3.13) CSF £14.80 CT £46.99 TOTE £2.10: £1.50 £2.20 £2.00 (£14.20) Trio £49.20 OWNER The Equema Partnership (NEWMARKET) BRED Newtownbarry House Stud
LONG HANDICAP Ballard Lady (IRE) 7-6
1385 Almasi (IRE), off a fair mark, had to work hard for success but she is in good form at present. (6/5)
901 Bollin Dorothy, from a yard just coming right, put up a decent effort and looks well worth keeping in mind. (10/1)
901 Oatey seems none the worse for her crashing fall last time and this was a useful effort, but in the past she has proved better at the minimum trip. (5/1)

1327 Stolen Kiss (IRE) is both looking and running quite well just now, but is never one to fully rely on. (11/1: op 7/1)
1446 Lunar Mist is proving difficult to win with despite some reasonable efforts, and probably needs a stronger gallop. (13/2)
1269 Antonias Melody was well outpaced from halfway, despite some strong attention. (10/1)
1332 Ballard Lady (IRE) (9/1: op 6/1)

T/Plpt: £520.00 (28.35 Tckts). T/Qdpt: £82.40 (6.24 Tckts) AA

1735-EPSOM (L-H) (Good)
Saturday June 7th
WEATHER: sunny WIND: mod half bhd

1766 VODAC 'DASH' RATED STKS H'CAP (0-105) (Listed) (3-Y.O+) (Class A)
2-00 (2-00) **5f** £27,780.29 (£10,397.70: £5,086.35: £2,189.25: £982.13: £499.28) Stalls: High GOING: 0.00 sec per fur (G)

				SP	RR	SF
1455[5]	**Ya Malak (104)** (DNicholls) **6-9-2** AlexGreaves(10) (lw: a gng wl: a.p: led over 1f out: qcknd: easily)	—	**1**	13/2[3]	120+	88
1590[5]	**Dashing Blue (99)** (IABalding) **4-8-11** LDettori(11) (hdwy over 1f out: r.o ins fnl f)	5	**2**	13/2[3]	99	67
877[7]	**Anotheranniversary (92)** (GLewis) **4-8-4** PaulEddery(13) (b.hind: led over 3f: unable qckn)	½	**3**	12/1	90	58
1158[4]	**Surprise Mission (91)** (MrsJRRamsden) **5-8-3** SSanders(5) (a.p: hrd rdn & ev ch over 1f out: one pce)	1	**4**	6/1[2]	86	54
1112[3]	**Blue Iris (102)** (MAJarvis) **4-9-0** MRoberts(2) (w ldr: ev ch over 1f out: wknd fnl f)	1½	**5**	5/1[1]	92	60
1590[7]	**Speed On (97)** (HCandy) **4-8-9** CRutter(9) (a.p: rdn over 2f out: nt clr run 1f out: one pce)	hd	**6**	12/1	87	55
	Laurel Delight (91) (JBerry) **7-8-3** PRoberts(12) (lw: nvr nr to chal)	½	**7**	16/1	80	48
1158[14]	**Amazing Bay (92)** (IABalding) **4-8-4**ow1 TQuinn(8) (lw: hld up: rdn over 1f out: one pce)	½	**8**	20/1	79	46
	Kumait (USA) (92) (SbinSuroor) **3-7-11** RFfrench(4) (bit bkwd: a bhd)	½	**9**	10/1	77	38
1608[6]	**Dancethenightaway (91)** (BJMeehan) **3-7-10** JQuinn(6) (bhd fnl 3f)	2	**10**	16/1	70	31
1158[12]	**Repertory (92)** (MSSaunders) **4-8-4** PPMurphy(3) (a bhd)	1½	**11**	20/1	66	34
1034[4]	**That Man Again (91)** (SCWilliams) **5-8-3b** GCarter(7) (lw: prom over 3f)	1¼	**12**	10/1	61	29

(SP 112.5%) **12 Rn**

55.17 secs (0.67) CSF £41.63 CT £338.35 TOTE £7.20: £2.40 £2.10 £3.10 (£18.10) Trio £36.60 OWNER Contrac Promotions Ltd (THIRSK) BRED Mrs R. B. Kennard
LONG HANDICAP Laurel Delight 7-11 That Man Again 7-11 Dancethenightaway 7-9
WEIGHT FOR AGE 3yo-7lb
IN-FOCUS: Thunder and lightning produced half an inch of rain during the night and changed the ground to Good.
1455 Ya Malak, who had no luck in running in last week's Temple Stakes, made up for it in no uncertain fashion. Always travelling supremely well, his jockey wisely steered him to the favoured stands' rail and he sprinted right away to win with a ton in hand. The King's Stand Stakes at Royal Ascot is next on the agenda. (13/2)
1590 Dashing Blue, 6lb higher than he has ever won off before, was at the back of the field until running on in the last furlong-and-a-half, only to find the winner home and dry. (13/2)
573 Anotheranniversary ran her best race since her comeback and took the field along until collared at the distance. (12/1)
1158 Surprise Mission, 8lb higher than he has ever won off before, still had every chance approaching the final furlong before tapped for toe.(6/1)
1112 Blue Iris disputed the lead from the start until tiring in the final furlong. She has yet to win a listed event. (5/1)
1034 Speed On, a leading light from the off, was being bustled along from halfway. He failed to get a clear run entering the final furlong and got unbalanced as a result, but it made little difference to his chances. (12/1)

1767 VODAFONE DIOMED STKS (Gp 3) (3-Y.O+) (Class A)
2-30 (2-31) **1m 114y** £32,000.00 (£12,112.50: £5,931.25: £2,706.25) Stalls: Low GOING: 0.00 sec per fur (G)

				SP	RR	SF
1552a*	**Polar Prince (IRE) (110)** (MAJarvis) **4-9-4** RCochrane(1) (a.p: chsd ldr over 2f out: led 1f out: rdn out)	—	**1**	14/1	118	101
1462*	**Faithful Son (USA)** (MRStoute) **3-8-6** MJKinane(6) (lw: hdwy over 2f out: hrd rdn over 1f out: r.o)	½	**2**	9/4[1]	117	88
1490*	**Cap Juluca (IRE) (107)** (RCharlton) **5-9-4** RHughes(2) (led: rdn over 2f out: hdd 1f out: unable qckn)	1¾	**3**	5/1[2]	114	97
1412[2]	**Amid Albadu (USA) (107)** (JLDunlop) **3-8-6** RHills(4) (lw: hld up: rdn 3f out: r.o one pce fnl f)	1	**4**	5/1[2]	112	83
	Almushtarak (IRE) (106) (KMahdi) **4-9-4** RPrice(5) (lw: hdwy over 2f out: hrd rdn over 1f out: one pce)	½	**5**	33/1	111	94
628a[8]	**Kammtarra (USA) (118)** (SbinSuroor) **4-9-4** LDettori(3) (lw: chsd ldr 3f: chsd ldr over 3f out tl over 2f out: sn wknd)	6	**6**	5/1[2]	100	83
1261*	**Prince of My Heart (108)** (BWHills) **4-9-4** MHills(8) (lw: bhd fnl 3f)	7	**7**	16/1	87	70
1541a[5]	**Fantastic Fellow (USA)** (CEBrittain) **3-8-8**ow2 OPeslier(7) (b.off hind: lw: chsd ldr over 5f out tl over 3f out: wknd over 2f out)	1¾	**8**	7/1[3]	85	54
917a[6]	**Hurricane State (USA) (110)** (PWChapple-Hyam) **3-8-9** JReid(9) (lw: hmpd over 5f out: a bhd)	½	**9**	25/1	85	56

(SP 112.6%) **9 Rn**

1m 42.26 (0.26) CSF £40.47 TOTE £17.90: £3.60 £1.50 £1.90 (£35.30) Trio £32.00 OWNER Mrs Christine Stevenson (NEWMARKET) BRED Michael Morrin
WEIGHT FOR AGE 3yo-12lb
1552a* Polar Prince (IRE) gave chase to the leader and, striking the front entering the final furlong, won his first race beyond seven furlongs. (14/1: 10/1-16/1)
1462* Faithful Son (USA) coped well with this jump into Group company, but looked ill-at-ease running down Tattenham Hill. Picking up ground in the straight, he responded to pressure and kept on well but found the line always beating him. He should soon find a similar race. (9/4: op 6/4)
1490* Cap Juluca (IRE) gave a good account of himself as he merrily bowled along in front. He did not look entirely happy on the track in the straight, but was only headed a furlong from home. He should find a Pattern race before long. (5/1)
1412 Amid Albadu (USA) looked in great shape beforehand. He stayed on in the closing stages, but never seriously threatened. A Pattern race can be found for him. (5/1)
Almushtarak (IRE), who has changed stables since last year, looked in fine fettle for this reappearance but, after moving up, had nothing left from the distance. (33/1)
628a Kammtarra (USA) looked extremely well in the paddock, but had been hung out to dry two furlongs from home. (5/1)

1768 LONDON CAR TELEPHONES H'CAP (4-Y.O+) (Class B)
3-00 (3-08) **1m 2f 18y** £31,650.00 (£11,850.00: £5,800.00: £2,500.00: £1,125.00: £575.00) Stalls: Low GOING: 0.00 sec per fur (G)

				SP	RR	SF
1450*	**Champagne Prince (91)** (PWHarris) **4-8-12**(7) CLowther(14) (a.p: led 5f out: rdn out)	—	**1**	15/2[3]	103	79

				SP	RR	SF
1176^{6}	**Star Manager (USA) (84)** (PFICole) **7-8-12** TQuinn(7) (lw: hdwy over 2f out: hrd rdn over 1f out: r.o wl ins fnl f)	½	**2**	16/1	95	71
1459*	**Fahs (USA) (80)** (RAkehurst) **5-8-8** MJKinane(12) (a.p: hrd rdn & ev ch ins fnl f: unable qckn)	½	**3**	9/2 ^{1}	90	66
1308^{9}	**Conspicuous (IRE) (82)** (LGCottrell) **7-8-10** MRoberts(3) (hld up: rdn over 3f out: swtchd rt over 2f out: one pce)	1¼	**4**	14/1	90	66
1456^{6}	**Major Change (94)** (MissGayKelleway) **5-9-8** KFallon(8) (lw: rdn over 2f out: hdwy over 1f out: r.o)	1	**5**	10/1	101	77
987*	**Autumn Cover (79)** (PRHedger) **5-8-2**(5) RFfrench(5) (lw: a.p: rdn 3f out: wknd over 2f out)	3½	**6**	12/1	80	56
1652^{2}	**Tertium (IRE) (79)** (MartynWane) **5-8-7** LDettori(6) (lw: rdn over 2f out: hdwy over 1f out: nvr nrr)	½	**7**	9/1	80	56
1300^{5}	**Bardon Hill Boy (IRE) (85)** (BHanbury) **5-8-13** WRyan(2) (nvr nrr)	4	**8**	25/1	79	55
1016^{4}	**Rockforce (92)** (MRChannon) **5-9-6** RHughes(4) (lw: nvr nr to chal)	4	**9**	7/1 ^{2}	80	56
1157^{5}	**Spirito Libro (USA) (85)** (DJSCosgrove) **4-8-10**(3) MartinDwyer(10) (a bhd)	6	**10**	16/1	63	39
1092^{5}	**Trojan Risk (77)** (GLewis) **4-8-5b¹** JQuinn(11) (b.off hind: lw: bhd fnl 2f)	1½	**11**	9/1	53	29
939*	**The Dilettanti (USA) (96)** (JARToller) **4-9-10** SSanders(1) (led 5f: wknd over 2f out)	1	**12**	12/1	70	46
1456^{11}	**Hunters of Brora (IRE) (91)** (JDBethell) **7-9-5** JReid(13) (hld up: rdn over 3f out: sn wknd)	4	**13**	14/1	59	35
1476^{6}	**Henry The Fifth (95)** (CEBrittain) **4-9-9** OPeslier(9) (w ldr 5f: wknd over 3f out)	6	**14**	33/1	53	29
				(SP 118.8%)	**14 Rn**	

2m 6.94 (2.94) CSF £109.53 CT £553.42 TOTE £6.10: £1.90 £4.30 £2.50 (£69.00) Trio £99.20 OWNER Magnum Force (BERKHAMSTED) BRED Cheveley Park Stud Ltd

1450* Champagne Prince continues to defy the Handicapper. Leading at halfway, he had a tremendous duel with the third but just managed to prevail. (15/2)

1176 Star Manager (USA) is not the easiest of individuals to win with and usually goes best when fresh. He finished in good style and would surely have prevailed with a little further to go. (16/1)

1459* Fahs (USA) has shot up 10lb in the handicap for his recent Sandown victory, but still ran a first-class race. He had a ding-dong battle with the winner, but was just unable to get past. (9/2)

Conspicuous (IRE) chased the leaders but failed to find the necessary turn of foot in the final quarter-mile. He is still high in the handicap. (14/1)

1456 Major Change was doing all his best work in the last furlong-and-a-half. (10/1)

987* Autumn Cover has never won over this trip and had shot his bolt over two furlongs from home. A return to a mile is needed. (12/1)

1769 VODAFONE DERBY STKS (Gp 1) (3-Y.O C & F) (Class A)

3-45 (3-50) **1m 4f 10y** £595,250.00 (£224,325.00: £109,037.50: £48,887.50) Stalls: Centre GOING: 0.00 sec per fur (G)

				SP	RR	SF
1159*	**Benny The Dip (USA) (119)** (JHMGosden) **3-9-0** WRyan(8) (lw: chsd ldr 10f out: led over 4f out: clr over 2f out: all out)	—	**1**	11/1 ^{3}	127	91
1103*	**Silver Patriarch (IRE) (116)** (JLDunlop) **3-9-0** PatEddery(5) (in rr: hrd rdn & hdwy over 2f out: chsd wnr over 1f out: str run fnl f: jst failed)	s.h	**2**	6/1 ^{2}	127	91
$1541a^{3}$	**Romanov (IRE)** (PWChapple-Hyam) **3-9-0** JReid(7) (lw: rdn over 4f out: hdwy over 2f out: hrd rdn over 1f out: r.o one pce)	5	**3**	25/1	120	84
940*	**Entrepreneur (124)** (MRStoute) **3-9-0** MJKinane(13) (lw: mid-div ½-wy: rdn over 3f out: hdwy over 2f out: one pce)	3½	**4**	4/6 ^{1}	116	80
1146*	**The Fly (103)** (BWHills) **3-9-0** RCochrane(3) (nt clr run over 2f out: hdwy over 1f out: nvr nrr)	3	**5**	12/1	112	76
691*	**Fahris (IRE) (113)** (BHanbury) **3-9-0** RHills(10) (b: swtg: a.p: chsd wnr over 3f out tl over 1f out: sn wknd)	1	**6**	12/1	110	74
1173*	**Symonds Inn (105)** (JGFitzGerald) **3-9-0** KFallon(1) (lw: hld up: rdn over 4f out: wknd over 2f out)	4	**7**	33/1	105	69
1159^{3}	**Musalsal (IRE) (113)** (BWHills) **3-9-0** MHills(6) (lw: nvr nr to chal)	3½	**8**	40/1	100	64
1477*	**Bold Demand** (SbinSuroor) **3-9-0** LDettori(2) (lw: prom over 8f)	5	**9**	20/1	94	58
1205a*	**Cloudings (IRE)** (AFabre,France) **3-9-0** OPeslier(14) (w'like: scope: hld up: hrd rdn over 3f out: sn wknd)	12	**10**	12/1	78	42
1553a*	**Single Empire (IRE) (99)** (PWChapple-Hyam) **3-9-0** DHarrison(4) (a.p: rdn 6f out: wkng whn bmpd over 2f out)	1¼	**11**	33/1	76	40
1032*	**Crystal Hearted (109)** (HCandy) **3-9-0** AMcGlone(9) (led over 7f: wknd over 3f out)	3½	**12**	66/1	72	36
1103^{4}	**Papua (106)** (IABalding) **3-9-0** GCarter(11) (swtg: bhd fnl 4f)	5	**13**	150/1	65	29
				(SP 124.8%)	**13 Rn**	

2m 35.77 (1.27) CSF £68.26 TOTE £8.90: £2.30 £2.00 £4.30 (£20.40) Trio £118.60 OWNER Mr Landon Knight (NEWMARKET) BRED Landon Knight

Official Explanation: Entrepreneur was subsequently found to be suffering from a hamstring strain

1159* Benny The Dip (USA) was given a superb ride by Ryan. Despite worries about the trip, Gosden had told Ryan to be positive, and that is exactly what he did. Leading rounding Tattenham Corner, he made his bid for glory and had soon opened up a good five lengths on his rivals. However the distress signals were being sent out in the final furlong, as the runner-up closed fast, and he found the line coming not a stride too soon. This trip is really stretching him to the limit, and it would surely be wise to drop him back to a mile-and-a-quarter, with the Eclipse at Sandown the obvious target. (11/1: 8/1-12/1)

1103* Silver Patriarch (IRE), whose trainer must have been delighted with the half-an-inch of overnight rain, came so close, yet so far. A big, long-striding individual, this course was certainly not to his liking and Eddery was soon nudging him along. Stone cold last running down Tattenham Hill, his stamina really came into play and, absolutely eating up the ground in the final quarter-mile, he would have prevailed in one more stride. The St Leger looks tailor-made for him but, more immediately, the Irish Derby beckons, and he must have an outstanding chance on a course that will suit him much better. (6/1)

1541a Romanov (IRE) ran a fine race especially considering he was poorly just thirteen days ago after finishing third in the Irish 2,000 Guineas. Bustled along rounding Tattenham Corner, he stayed on under pressure for third prize. There is a good Group race to be won with him. (25/1)

940* Entrepreneur looked in tremendous shape in the paddock, and was all the rage in the market. Unfortunately he was a major disappointment. Never going well, and not coming down Tattenham Hill, he began to pick up ground in the straight, but the stick was soon drawn and he was labouring. Kinane reported afterwards that the colt never felt right and would never have won at any distance. This is surely not his true running, and hopefully he will soon bounce back. (4/6: 10/11-evens)

1146* The Fly, a leggy, lightly-made individual, was taking a big step-up in class but acquitted himself well, staying on, having not had the clearest of passages early in the straight (12/1: op 20/1)

691* Fahris (IRE), whose Derby preparation had to be interrupted by a sinus operation last month, found that counting against him. Going in pursuit of the winner early in the straight, he had nothing more to offer when collared below the distance. He can find a Group race before long. (12/1)

1173* Symonds Inn chased the leaders, but the writing was on the wall early in the straight. (33/1)

1159 Musalsal (IRE), who had moved up into midfield after halfway, could never get in a blow at the leaders. (40/1)

1477* Bold Demand was taking a big step-up in class, but was close up until tiring early in the straight. On pulling up, he was found to have lost a shoe. (20/1)

1205a* Cloudings (IRE), a round-bodied colt, had plenty to find on his form so far, and so it proved as he dropped back early in the straight. (12/1)

1553a* Single Empire (IRE), winner of the Italian Derby thirteen days ago, lost fifteen kilos as a result and found this race coming too soon. Bustled along at the top of the hill, he was beginning to back-pedal early in the straight. His jockey reported that he was never travelling as well as he had done in Italy, and he will now have a rest. (33/1)
1032* Crystal Hearted had a lot more to do, but did a good job of pacemaking until collared rounding Tattenham Corner. (66/1)
1103 Papua has had his limitations well exposed this season, and was completely out of his league. (150/1)

1770 TALKLAND CONDITIONS STKS (3-Y.O) (Class B)

4-30 (4-30) **7f** £20,937.00 (£7,833.00: £3,829.00: £1,645.00: £735.00: £371.00) Stalls: Low GOING: 0.00 sec per fur (G)

				SP	RR	SF
940[13]	**Hidden Meadow (115)** (IABalding) **3-9-0** MHills(2) (led 6f out: shkn up over 1f out: comf)	—	**1**	6/5[1]	114+	81
1304*	**Wasp Ranger (USA) (94)** (PFICole) **3-9-0** TQuinn(4) (lw: hld up: rdn over 2f out: chsd wnr over 1f out: no imp)	5	**2**	14/1	103	70
	Moonshine Girl (USA) (102) (MRStoute) **3-8-6** JReid(6) (lw: a.p: chsd wnr over 2f out tl over 1f out: one pce)	1¼	**3**	7/1	92	59
1403*	**Tomba (113)** (BJMeehan) **3-9-9** KDarley(1) (lw: rdn over 2f out: nvr nr to chal)	5	**4**	7/2[2]	97	64
942[18]	**Zaretski (87)** (CEBrittain) **3-9-0** MRoberts(3) (led 1f: wknd over 2f out)	4	**5**	20/1	79	46
940[11]	**Tycoon Todd (USA)** (SbinSuroor) **3-9-0** LDettori(5) (a bhd)	nk	**6**	9/2[3]	79	46

(SP 109.8%) **6 Rn**

1m 21.69 (1.39) CSF £16.85 TOTE £2.20: £1.40 £3.60 (£10.20) OWNER Mr George Strawbridge (KINGSCLERE) BRED I. A. Balding
OFFICIAL EXPLANATION **Hidden Meadow: considering the improvement in form compared with the colts previous run in the 2,000 Guineas, the trainer stated that the colt may have had a throat infection.**
679* Hidden Meadow, who flopped badly in the 2,000 Guineas, bounced back in no uncertain terms and had little more than an exercise gallop as he made virtually all the running. He will now head for the St James's Palace Stakes at Royal Ascot. (6/5: 4/5-5/4)
1304* Wasp Ranger (USA) had more on his plate this time and, although struggling into second place below the distance, had no hope with the winner. (14/1)
Moonshine Girl (USA) looked in good shape for this reappearance and took second place over a quarter-of-a-mile from home, but she was collared for that position below the distance and could only struggle on at one pace. A return to six furlongs might help. (7/1)
1403* Tomba had everything against him here - wrong trip, wrong ground and conceding lumps of weight all round - so it was no surprise he could never make his presence felt. Six furlongs on soft ground is his ideal requirement. (7/2)
508 Zaretski broke best of all, and raced in second place and had shot his bolt two furlongs from home. (20/1)

1771 PAKNET RATED STKS H'CAP (0-105) (4-Y.O+) (Class B)

5-05 (5-06) **1m 4f 10y** £24,113.60 (£9,022.40: £4,411.20: £1,896.00: £848.00: £428.80) Stalls: Centre GOING: 0.00 sec per fur (G)

				SP	RR	SF
1261[6]	**Arabian Story (100)** (LordHuntingdon) **4-8-11** LDettori(3) (b: mde virtually all: clr over 2f out: comf)	—	**1**	3/1[1]	116+	93
1241[4]	**Harbour Dues (103)** (LadyHerries) **4-9-0** PatEddery(1) (lw: hdwy over 3f out: chsd wnr over 2f out: r.o one pce)	3	**2**	8/1[3]	115	92
1325*	**Hoh Express (93)** (IABalding) **5-8-4**ow3 KDarley(6) (lw: rdn over 3f out: hdwy over 1f out: r.o one pce)	8	**3**	6/1[2]	94	68
962[7]	**Artic Courier (89)** (DJSCosgrove) **6-7-9**(5) RFfrench(7) (no hdwy fnl 3f)	7	**4**	20/1	81	58
1450[4]	**Romios (IRE) (90)** (PFICole) **5-8-1** CRutter(4) (hld up: rdn over 2f out: sn wknd)	2½	**5**	6/1[2]	79	56
1176*	**Give Me A Ring (IRE) (95)** (CWThornton) **4-8-6** DeanMcKeown(2) (chsd wnr over 10f out tl over 2f out: sn wknd)	1	**6**	6/1[2]	82	59
	Willie Conquer (89) (RAkehurst) **5-7-11**(3) MartinDwyer(8) (bhd fnl 4f)	7	**7**	6/1[2]	67	44
1476[4]	**Rocky Oasis (USA) (102)** (MRStoute) **4-8-13** OPeslier(5) (lw: hld up: rdn over 3f out: wknd over 2f out)	1¼	**8**	12/1	79	56
	Lombardic (USA) (89) (JABOld) **6-8-0** JQuinn(9) (bit bkwd: prom 8f: t.o)	dist	**9**	10/1	—	—

(SP 114.8%) **9 Rn**

2m 35.1 (0.60) CSF £24.96 CT £122.90 TOTE £3.20: £1.30 £2.10 £2.30 (£8.90) Trio £24.10 OWNER The Queen (WEST ILSLEY) BRED The Queen
LONG HANDICAP Artic Courier 7-9 Willie Conquer 7-13
1261 Arabian Story was racing over a far more suitable trip and, making virtually all the running, forged clear in the straight for a Royal victory on Derby Day. The Northumberland Plate is his next likely target. (3/1)
1241 Harbour Dues looked in great shape beforehand, and ran a fine race despite being 9lb higher than when last seen in a handicap. (8/1)
1325* Hoh Express looked in tremendous shape in the paddock. Bustled along and going nowhere entering the straight, he stayed on to finish a moderate third. (6/1)
789 Artic Courier is not easy to win with and was making little impression in the straight. (20/1)
1450 Romios (IRE) chased the leaders, but the writing was on the wall over two furlongs from home. (6/1)
1176* Give Me A Ring (IRE), 9lb higher than he has ever won off before, found that enough to stop him. (6/1)

1772 VODAPAGE H'CAP (0-100) (3-Y.O+) (Class C)

5-35 (5-38) **6f** £24,053.75 (£7,280.00: £3,552.50: £1,688.75) Stalls: High GOING: 0.00 sec per fur (G)

				SP	RR	SF
1634[3]	**Warning Time (90)** (BJMeehan) **4-9-8** JReid(2) (lw: hdwy over 4f out: led ins fnl f: rdn out)	—	**1**	14/1	101	84
1578[5]	**Kira (83)** (JLEyre) **7-9-1** KFallon(8) (led over 4f out tl ins fnl f: unable qckn)	¾	**2**	14/1	92	75
1034[2]	**Selhurstpark Flyer (IRE) (94)** (JBerry) **6-9-7**(5) PRoberts(12) (b: led over 1f: rdn over 1f out: one pce)	1	**3**	9/2[2]	100	83
	Clan Chief (83) (JRArnold) **4-9-1** DHarrison(5) (lw: hdwy over 2f out: hrd rdn over 1f out: r.o one pce)	1¼	**4**	10/1	86	69
1596[2]	**My Best Valentine (96)** (JWhite) **7-9-9**(5) RFfrench(4) (rdn over 2f out: hdwy over 1f out: r.o)	nk	**5**	9/1	98	81
1107*	**Youdontsay (84)** (TJNaughton) **5-9-2** PatEddery(1) (lw: rdn over 2f out: hdwy over 1f out: nvr nrr)	1	**6**	8/1[3]	84	67
1608*	**Literary Society (USA) (77)** (JARToller) **4-8-9** SSanders(7) (lw: nt clr run over 2f out: swtchd lft: hdwy over 1f out: nvr nrr)	3	**7**	9/1	69	52
1488[2]	**White Emir (80)** (BJMeehan) **4-8-12b** MHills(10) (lw: a.p: rdn over 2f out: wknd over 1f out)	s.h	**8**	12/1	71	54
1468[8]	**For the Present (82)** (TDBarron) **7-9-0** KDarley(11) (bhd fnl 2f)	2	**9**	10/1	68	51
1317[5]	**Marl (85)** (RAkehurst) **4-9-3** TQuinn(6) (bhd fnl 4f)	1½	**10**	9/1	67	50
1259[7]	**Lord Olivier (IRE) (77)** (WJarvis) **7-8-9** LDettori(3) (bhd fnl 2f)	nk	**11**	4/1[1]	58	41
834[4]	**Eastern Prophets (85)** (GLewis) **4-9-3** PaulEddery(9) (swtg: prom over 2f)	3	**12**	14/1	58	41

(SP 125.2%) **12 Rn**

1m 9.48 (1.48) CSF £187.75 CT £959.16 TOTE £29.00: £6.60 £4.80 £1.50 (£171.10) Trio £321.40 OWNER Mr F. C. T. Wilson (UPPER LAMBOURN) BRED F. C. T. Wilson
1634 Warning Time soon in a handy position, managed to get on top inside the final furlong to win his first race since his two-year-old days. The Wokingham at Royal Ascot is his next port of call. (14/1: 10/1-16/1)

1158 Kira was soon at the head of affairs but, collared inside the final furlong, found the winner just too good. (14/1)
1034 Selhurstpark Flyer (IRE), winner of this race last year, was 15lb higher on this occasion, but nevertheless gave a good account of himself. (9/2: op 7/1)
Clan Chief had a good campaign last year, and looks set to do well again this season if this reappearance is anything to go by. He should soon find a race. (10/1)
1596 My Best Valentine stayed on in the last furlong-and-a-half, but found it all over bar the shouting. (9/1: op 6/1)
1107* Youdontsay stayed on in the closing stages, but never threatened to get there in time. (8/1)
1317 Marl (9/1: 6/1-10/1)

T/Jkpt: Not won; £14,065.32 to 9/6/97. T/Plpt: £141.70 (525.23 Tckts). T/Qdpt: £28.10 (97.06 Tckts) AK

1748-HAYDOCK (L-H) (Good to firm, Firm patches, Good fnl bnd)
Saturday June 7th
WEATHER: overcast & thunder showers WIND: str across becoming str against race 4

1773 DOUGLAS RATED STKS H'CAP (0-95) (3-Y.O) (Class C)
2-10 (2-10) **1m 2f 120y** £6,277.80 (£2,350.20: £1,150.10: £495.50: £222.75: £113.65) Stalls: High GOING minus 0.34 sec per fur (GF)

				SP	RR	SF
1458^{6}	**Shadoof (75)** (WRMuir) **3-8-3** TSprake(1) (hld up in rr: hdwy 2f out: chal u.p ins fnl f: bmpd & led nr fin)	—	1	8/1	84	56
*1123**	**Crystal Gold (85)** (MRStoute) **3-8-13** DHolland(5) (led: edgd rt ins fnl f: hrd rdn & hung rt: hdd cl home)	s.h	2	$15/8^{1}$	94	66
1110^{2}	**Sellette (IRE) (78)** (DHaydnJones) **3-8-6** SDrowne(2) (chsd ldrs: effrt & ev ch ins fnl f: hrd rdn: unable qckn)	½	3	8/1	86	58
1175^{7}	**Foot Battalion (IRE) (85)** (RHollinshead) **3-8-13** FLynch(3) (hld up & bhd: hdwy 3f out: rdn & one pce fnl f)	5	4	16/1	86	58
1278^{3}	**Night Mirage (USA) (74)** (MJohnston) **3-8-2** JFanning(8) (trckd ldrs: rdn over 2f out: sn btn)	3	5	15/2	70	42
1271^{2}	**Epworth (80)** (JAGlover) **3-8-8** NDay(4) (lw: prom: chsd ldrs 3f out: hrd rdn & wknd over 1f out)	2½	6	$4/1^{3}$	72	44
966^{6}	**Beryllium (89)** (RHannon) **3-9-3** DaneO'Neill(6) (trckd ldrs over 7f: sn rdn & wknd: eased: t.o)	8	7	16/1	69	41
1416^{2}	**Jack The Lad (IRE) (81)** (JHetherton) **3-8-9** SWhitworth(7) (chsd ldr 7f: rdn & wknd over 2f out: t.o)	s.h	8	$7/2^{2}$	61	33
				(SP 122.8%)		**8 Rn**

2m 12.04 (0.54) CSF £23.03 CT £120.63 TOTE £8.80: £1.80 £1.20 £2.60 (£10.30) OWNER Mrs H. Levy (LAMBOURN) BRED The Sussex Stud
1458 Shadoof came good at the first time of asking over this longer trip, delivering his challenge between horses to gain command in the final strides. (8/1)
1123* Crystal Gold, a strongly-made individual, set out to make it all and for most of the way looked to be in control but, inclined to edge off a true line, possibly due to the strong cross-wind, he bumped the winner close home and would almost certainly have been disqualified even if he had succeeded. (15/8)
1110 Sellette (IRE) did not impress to post but she ran her heart out once again, and fortune must favour her before long. (8/1)
597 Foot Battalion (IRE) did not last out the nine furlongs at Ripon, and though he was ridden to get the trip this time, had reached the end of his tether before the final furlong. (16/1)
1278 Night Mirage (USA) has been competing over longer trips this term, and she found the quickening tempo too much for her entering the last quarter-mile. (15/2)
1271 Epworth should have had no trouble staying this trip, and she remained in the action until fading quickly below the distance. (4/1)
1416 Jack The Lad (IRE) seems to have gone off the boil, for he was a serious threat until fading quickly over two furlongs out. (7/2)

1774 E.B.F. HOLSTEN PILS MAIDEN STKS (2-Y.O) (Class D)
2-40 (2-41) **5f** £3,420.00 (£1,035.00: £505.00: £240.00) Stalls: Low GOING minus 0.34 sec per fur (GF)

				SP	RR	SF
557^{4}	**Rejected** (RHannon) **2-9-0** DaneO'Neill(4) (bit bkwd: hld up: hdwy 2f out: r.o to ld ins fnl f: sn clr)	—	1	$2/1^{2}$	86+	40
1466^{3}	**Sharp Cracker (IRE)** (MJohnston) **2-8-9** JWeaver(6) (stumbled s: led over 3f out tl hdd & outpcd ins fnl f)	4	2	$5/2^{3}$	68	22
1174^{2}	**Happy Days** (DMoffatt) **2-8-11**(3) DarrenMoffatt(5) (led over 1f: swtchd rt over 1f out: sn rdn: nt pce to chal)	½	3	$6/4^{1}$	72	26
	Shamwari Song (JAGlover) **2-9-0** NDay(2) (unf: scope: bit bkwd: s.i.s: a bhd & outpcd)	5	4	8/1	56	10
	Classic Silver (IRE) (WWHaigh) **2-9-0** SWhitworth(3) (w'like: neat: lw: sn pushed along & outpcd)	4	5	20/1	43	—
				(SP 117.8%)		**5 Rn**

61.25 secs (1.75) CSF £7.34 TOTE £2.60: £1.40 £1.50 (£3.10) OWNER Mr T. G. Holdcroft (MARLBOROUGH) BRED J. H. H. Benbow and B. A. McMahon
557 Rejected has been brought along steadily and it would seem to be paying off, for he won this in workmanlike style and there is no reason why he should not continue to progress. (2/1)
1466 Sharp Cracker (IRE) was down on her head leaving the stalls, but soon recovered to force the pace and looked to have everything in trouble until the winner came on the scene. (5/2)
1174 Happy Days stuck on determinedly inside the final furlong but was never promising to get to terms with the principals. A late April foal, she will do better if not rushed and, as she has shown in the past, a longer trip looks a must. (6/4)
Shamwari Song, an unfurnished colt who was not born until May 20th, looks to need time and he was always being taken off his legs. (8/1)

1775 ROTHMANS ROYALS NORTH SOUTH CHALLENGE SERIES H'CAP (0-100) (3-Y.O+) (Class C)
3-15 (3-15) **1m 30y** £7,035.00 (£2,130.00: £1,040.00: £495.00) Stalls: Low GOING minus 0.34 sec per fur (GF)

				SP	RR	SF
1495^{7}	**Band on the Run (82)** (BAMcMahon) **10-9-0** LNewton(3) (hdwy 4f out: rdn 2f out: r.o to ld ins fnl f: hld on gamely)	—	1	$8/1^{3}$	92	62
1495^{4}	**Bollin Frank (69)** (TDEasterby) **5-8-1** LCharnock(10) (led after 1f: rdn 2f out: hdd ins fnl f: rallied cl home)	nk	2	$3/1^{1}$	78	48
1264^{3}	**Pomona (82)** (PJMakin) **4-9-0** DHolland(5) (hmpd after 2f: hdwy & nt clr run 2f out: r.o u.p fnl f)	¾	3	$7/1^{2}$	90	60
1175^{19}	**Irish Accord (USA) (92)** (MrsJRRamsden) **3-8-13** FLynch(2) (lw: hld up: hdwy on ins 4f out: rdn wl over 1f out: nt pce to chal)	½	4	11/1	99	58
1560^{8}	**Impulsive Air (IRE) (65)** (EWeymes) **5-7-11** DaleGibson(1) (lw: led 1f: hrd drvn & ev ch 1f out: unable qckn)	¾	5	20/1	71	41
1450^{12}	**Moving Arrow (93)** (MissSEHall) **6-9-11** DaneO'Neill(7) (swtg: hld up: hdwy 2f out: swtchd rt: kpt on u.p fnl f)	1¼	6	12/1	96	66
1442^{8}	**Q Factor (75)** (DHaydnJones) **5-8-7** SDrowne(8) (trckd ldrs: hrd rdn 2f out: wknd fnl f)	3½	7	12/1	71	41
1392^{7}	**Night Chorus (75)** (BSRothwell) **3-7-3**(7) PDoe(4) (lw: nvr plcd to chal)	½	8	25/1	70	29
947^{13}	**Sandmoor Chambray (80)** (TDEasterby) **6-8-12** JCarroll(9) (hld up: hdwy on ins over 2f out: nt rch ldrs)	1½	9	10/1	72	42
1397^{4}	**Highborn (IRE) (90)** (PSFelgate) **8-9-8** GHind(11) (hld up: hdwy 3f out: rdn & wknd fnl 2f)	1¼	10	10/1	80	50
1583^{6}	**Gulf Shaadi (67)** (EJAlston) **5-7-6**(7) JFowle(6) (prom 5f: sn rdn & wknd: t.o)	11	11	10/1	35	5

				SP	RR	SF
1559[5]	**Master Beveled (75)** (PDEvans) **7-8-7b** JFEgan(12) (b.nr fore: w ldrs tl ½-wy: wknd qckly: t.o)	2½	**12**	7/1 [2]	38	8
738[16]	**Grand Musica (89)** (IABalding) **4-9-7** SWhitworth(13) (lw: dwlt: effrt over 3f out: sn rdn: no imp: t.o)	nk	**13**	14/1	52	22
				(SP 127.4%)	**13 Rn**	

1m 41.43 (0.83) CSF £31.22 CT £176.16 TOTE £9.90: £2.40 £2.00 £2.60 (£17.70) Trio £64.10 OWNER Mr D. J. Allen (TAMWORTH) BRED Mrs J. R. Hine and Miss J. Bunting

LONG HANDICAP Night Chorus 7-5

WEIGHT FOR AGE 3yo-11lb

OFFICIAL EXPLANATION **Sandmoor Chambray: the trainer reported that the gelding, having come out of the race very jarred up, was found to have very sore feet the next morning. Grand Musica: lost a shoe.**

1495 Band on the Run was unable to win a race last year, and looked a shadow of his old self, but he returned to form here with a deserved, hard-fought victory, and there is life in the old dog yet. (8/1)

1495 Bollin Frank, a narrow winner of this race twelve months ago, battled on willingly under a very strong ride, but the winner proved just too good in a spirited set-to to the line. He should not be long in making amends. (3/1)

1264 Pomona performs much better on a sound surface and appeared to be a shade unlucky, for she found all the trouble that was going and yet still failed narrowly. She deserves a change of fortune. (7/1)

555 Irish Accord (USA), pitted against older rivals for the first time, probably adopted the right tactics by staying on the rail, for he has a tendency to hang that way. However, he has yet to prove he stays a mile, and he failed to make the slightest impression once into the final furlong. (11/1)

1560 Impulsive Air (IRE), in the firing line from the break, was being made to work from below the distance and found an extra effort beyond him. He will get it right again one of these days. (20/1)

Moving Arrow, only seems to find his true form in the second part of the year, so this encouraging effort from the top of the handicap is at least a step in the right direction. (12/1)

Q Factor (12/1: op 8/1)

1776 JOHN OF GAUNT STKS (Listed) (3-Y.O+) (Class A)

4-10 (4-10) **7f 30y** £12,965.00 (£3,920.00: £1,910.00: £905.00) Stalls: Low GOING minus 0.34 sec per fur (GF)

				SP	RR	SF
1210[6]	**Decorated Hero (117)** (JHMGosden) **5-9-3** GHind(4) (lw: mde all: qcknd 2f out: r.o wl)	—	**1**	11/8 [1]	118	53
1532a[3]	**Lucayan Prince (USA) (122)** (DRLoder) **4-9-5b** DRMcCabe(6) (lw: chsd wnr thrght: effrt & drvn along appr fnl f: r.o)	1	**2**	15/8 [2]	118	53
713a[4]	**My Branch (110)** (BWHills) **4-8-12** DHolland(3) (chsd ldng pair: rdn over 1f out: nt pce to chal)	3½	**3**	9/4 [3]	103	38
1610[4]	**El Opera (IRE) (91)** (PFICole) **4-8-7** JCarroll(5) (lw: stdd s: effrt & nt clr run over 2f out: sn outpcd)	5	**4**	8/1	87	22
				(SP 118.8%)	**4 Rn**	

1m 29.74 (1.74) CSF £4.42 TOTE £2.20 (£2.10) OWNER Exors of the late Mr Herbert Allen (NEWMARKET) BRED Reg Griffin and Jim McGrath

1210 Decorated Hero would have found this a shade easier than his usual role, leading the Derby winner in his work. (11/8)

1532a Lucayan Prince (USA), an extremely handsome colt, was able to turn the tables on My Branch even on these worse terms, but the winner pinched the race when quickening clear two furlongs out, and his sustained late effort was never going to get him there. He does not win as often as he should. (15/8)

713a My Branch, still to come in her coat, has in the past found her best form in the autumn, and she is certainly worth waiting for. (9/4)

1610 El Opera (IRE) is possibly not quite up to this class, but what little chance she had was snuffed out when she was stopped in her tracks, while trying to creep up the inside, on the approach to the last quarter-mile. (8/1)

1777 HORSEPOWER BY SCANIA MAIDEN STKS (3-Y.O) (Class D)

4-40 (4-40) **1m 30y** £3,647.50 (£1,105.00: £540.00: £257.50) Stalls: Low GOING minus 0.34 sec per fur (GF)

				SP	RR	SF
1589[8]	**Another Night (IRE) (82)** (RHannon) **3-9-0** DaneO'Neill(5) (a.p: led 2f out: drvn clr fnl f: readily)	—	**1**	9/4 [2]	81+	44
935[4]	**Kaziranga (USA)** (LMCumani) **3-8-9** GHind(6) (chsd ldrs: rdn over 1f out: nt pce of wnr)	3½	**2**	3/1 [3]	69	32
1265[4]	**Topton (IRE)** (IABalding) **3-9-0** SWhitworth(2) (lw: a.p: rdn wl over 1f out: r.o one pce)	1¼	**3**	5/1	72	35
1234[7]	**Indian Brave (82)** (MJohnston) **3-9-0** JWeaver(1) (lw: plld hrd: hld up: effrt & drvn 2f out: wknd appr fnl f)	4	**4**	2/1 [1]	64	27
945[4]	**Van Chino** (BAMcMahon) **3-9-0** LNewton(3) (lw: led to 2f out: hrd drvn & wknd over 1f out)	nk	**5**	12/1	63	26
599[12]	**Zagros (IRE)** (TDEasterby) **3-9-0** JCarroll(4) (bkwd: s.s: a in rr)	6	**6**	20/1	51	14
				(SP 118.2%)	**6 Rn**	

1m 43.31 (2.71) CSF £9.24 TOTE £3.40: £1.50 £1.70 (£4.40) OWNER Mr Bob Lalemant (MARLBOROUGH) BRED M. Lambert

Another Night (IRE) opened his account with impressive ease on this step-up to a mile, and though he may not have beaten much, showed what a progressive colt he really is. (9/4)

935 Kaziranga (USA), a daughter of German 1,000 Guineas winner Kazoo, should have benefited from this slightly longer trip, but she does nothing quickly, and is taking time to get the hang of the job. (3/1: op 2/1)

1265 Topton (IRE) had a sounder surface than on his debut last month, and showed much improved form. He is gradually getting the hang of the game. (5/1)

Indian Brave pulled his jockey's arms out in the early stages and, though he had reached a challenging position entering the last quarter-mile, the earlier exertions had taken their toll. (2/1: op 3/1)

945 Van Chino, who coughed a couple of times in the paddock, set the pace until the winner went on and then gradually dropped away. These were new tactics over this longer trip and he is still only learning the ropes. (12/1: op 8/1)

1778 PENNY LANE H'CAP (0-90) (4-Y.O+) (Class C)

5-10 (5-11) **1m 6f** £5,374.50 (£1,626.00: £793.00: £376.50) Stalls: Centre GOING minus 0.34 sec per fur (GF)

				SP	RR	SF
1260[3]	**Samuel Scott (72)** (MCPipe) **4-8-10** DaneO'Neill(2) (mde all: clr 2f out: unchal)	—	**1**	5/2 [1]	87	40
728[10]	**Nanton Point (USA) (75)** (LadyHerries) **5-8-13** TSprake(6) (hld up: effrt & rdn over 2f out: styd on ins fnl f)	4	**2**	7/1	85	38
1413[4]	**Sea Freedom (66)** (GBBalding) **6-8-4v** SDrowne(3) (chsd wnr: rdn over 1f out: styd on same pce)	hd	**3**	11/4 [2]	76	29
1319[9]	**General Assembly (IRE) (90)** (HRACecil) **5-10-0** JCarroll(5) (lw: a chsng ldrs: wnt 2nd appr fnl f: hrd drvn: one pce)	nk	**4**	5/2 [1]	100	53
1400[4]	**Castle Courageous (78)** (LadyHerries) **10-8-9**(7) PDoe(1) (b: dropped rr ½-wy: t.o fnl 3f)	9	**5**	9/1	78	31
1408[10]	**Dancing Cavalier (64)** (RHollinshead) **4-8-2**ow2 FLynch(4) (lw: hld up: hdwy u.p 3f out: wknd over 1f out: t.o)	11	**6**	4/1 [3]	51	2
				(SP 126.3%)	**6 Rn**	

3m 3.17 (4.97) CSF £21.02 TOTE £3.40: £2.00 £5.70 (£15.90) OWNER Richard Green (Fine Paintings) (WELLINGTON) BRED R. Green

1260 Samuel Scott, winning his first race under any Rules, completed a three-timer for his jockey with a very easy all-the-way success. The torrential thunder storm which hit the track just before this race could have made the ground perfect for him. (5/2)

Nanton Point (USA) has struck form at this time of year in the past, and this staying-on performance could indicate that he is about to find his way. (7/1)

1413 Sea Freedom is struggling to come to terms with this step-up in grade, but he is not short on stamina, and he only just lost out in an all-out duel for the runner-up prize. (11/4)
1319 General Assembly (IRE) looks to be a difficult animal to get fit, for he is still carrying plenty of condition even after a couple of runs and, nudged along from halfway, began to stay on in the closing stages without having the speed to get in a blow against the winner. (5/2)

T/Plpt: £63.00 (258.94 Tckts). T/Qdpt: £32.60 (15.94 Tckts) IM

1606-NEWMARKET (R-H) (Good)
Saturday June 7th
WEATHER: fine WIND: mod across

1779 NEWMARKET LADIES' H'CAP (0-60) (4-Y.O+) (Class F)
6-40 (6-42) **1m 4f (July)** £4,597.50 (£1,380.00: £665.00: £307.50) Stalls: Low GOING minus 0.36 sec per fur (F)

				SP	RR	SF
1478^{9}	**Chris's Lad (60)** (BJMeehan) **6-11-7b** MissJAllison(16) (lw: hdwy over 2f out: led ins fnl f: r.o)	—	**1**	9/1	71	57
1599*	**Bellas Gate Boy (49)** (JPearce) **5-10-10** MrsLPearce(8) (hld up: hdwy over 2f out: led over 1f out: hdd ins fnl f: unable qckn)	3½	**2**	7/1^{2}	55	41
1694^{3}	**Acerbus Dulcis (26)** (MCChapman) **6-8-10**(5) MissEFolkes(1) (swtg: in tch: rdn over 2f out: r.o one pce)	2½	**3**	16/1	29	15
	Non Vintage (IRE) (43) (MCChapman) **6-10-4** MrsFNeedham(2) (bit bkwd: swtg: towards rr: hdwy over 1f out: styd on ins fnl f)	s.h	**4**	20/1	46	32
1562^{2}	**Heathyards Rock (64)** (RMMcKellar) **5-11-6**(5) MissRClark(24) (mid div: rdn over 2f out: styd on one pce)	¾	**5**	9/1	66	52
1507^{7}	**Open Affair (47)** (HAkbary) **4-10-3**(5) MissIFoustok(3) (swtg: nvr nrr)	1¼	**6**	16/1	47	33
865^{12}	**Stonecutter (48)** (WRMuir) **4-10-4v**(5) MissSDeburiatte(12) (prom: ev ch 2f out: grad wknd)	hd	**7**	20/1	48	34
	Hancock (30) (JHetherton) **5-9-5** MissPRobson(21) (swtg: nvr nrr)	nk	**8**	25/1	30	16
1452^{7}	**Dashing Invader (USA) (37)** (PWHarris) **4-9-12b^{1}** MissAElsey(5) (dwlt: sn rcvrd: prom tl wknd 2f out)	hd	**9**	20/1	37	23
770^{8}	**Mega Tid (31)** (JRPoulton) **5-9-1**(5) MissJWormall(14) (nvr nrr)	s.h	**10**	50/1	31	17
1632^{11}	**One In The Eye (42)** (JRPoulton) **4-9-12**(5)ow4 MrsCPoulton(25) (a.p: led over 2f out: hdd over 1f out: sn wknd)	½	**11**	25/1	41	23
	Strat's Legacy (39) (DWPArbuthnot) **10-10-0** MrsDArbuthnot(9) (swtg: prom 11f)	1	**12**	16/1	37	23
1515*	**Durgams First (IRE) (46)** (MrsMReveley) **5-10-7** MissDianaJones(7) (swtg: hdwy 4f out: wknd 2f out)	2½	**13**	11/4^{1}	40	26
*407**	**Don't Drop Bombs (USA) (46)** (DTThom) **8-10-7** MissJFeilden(20) (lw: prom tl wknd 3f out)	3	**14**	8/1^{3}	36	22
	Mick's Tycoon (IRE) (25) (TRWatson) **9-8-9**(5) MrsCWatson(23) (nvr bttr than mid div)	nk	**15**	66/1	15	1
955^{10}	**Slapy Dam (47)** (CASmith) **5-10-3**(5) MrsDSmith(22) (mid div tl wknd over 2f out)	nk	**16**	16/1	36	22
1623^{5}	**Rehaab (56)** (DMorris) **4-10-12**(5) MissEJJones(10) (led: hdd over 2f out: sn wknd)	hd	**17**	14/1	45	31
1133^{7}	**Cohiba (39)** (BJCurley) **4-9-9**(5) MrsAStringer(27) (a bhd)	¾	**18**	20/1	27	13
1393^{4}	**Kernof (IRE) (50)** (MDHammond) **4-10-6**(5) MissAJSmith(13) (swtg: bhd fr ½-wy)	nk	**19**	10/1	38	24
1435^{8}	**Contract Bridge (IRE) (49)** (PGMurphy) **4-10-5**(5) MissLGreen(11) (hdwy 4f out: wknd over 2f out)	s.h	**20**	14/1	37	23
1445^{3}	**May King Mayhem (27)** (MrsALMKing) **4-8-11**(5) MissTSpearing(6) (bhd fnl 4f)	1	**21**	14/1	14	—
1424^{9}	**Norsong (40)** (RAkehurst) **5-9-10**(5) MrsKHills(19) (bhd fnl 4f)	1¾	**22**	14/1	24	10
1086^{11}	**Alisura (56)** (DTThom) **4-10-12**(5) MrsDMcHale(18) (lw: a bhd)	s.h	**23**	40/1	40	26
	Lizium (38) (JCFox) **5-9-8**(5) MissSarah-JaneDurman(26) (a bhd)	3	**24**	66/1	18	4
1237^{17}	**Gracious Imp (USA) (28)** (JRJenkins) **4-8-12**(5) MissCTownsley(17) (a bhd)	1¼	**25**	66/1	6	—
	Premier Star (32) (KGWingrove) **7-9-2**(5)ow2 MrsHNoonan(15) (a bhd)	3½	**26**	66/1	6	—
				(SP 166.7%)		**26 Rn**

2m 35.68 (6.68) CSF £74.97 CT £992.90 TOTE £10.10: £2.60 £2.60 £5.30 £4.50 (£31.70) Trio £256.60 OWNER Mrs Susan McCarthy (UPPER LAMBOURN) BRED Tyrian Breeding
Chris's Lad stays further than this and, having hit the front inside the final furlong, proved much too strong for his opponents. (9/1: 8/1-12/1)
1599* Bellas Gate Boy normally runs over a shorter distance, but got the trip well enough. (7/1: op 9/2)
1694 Acerbus Dulcis was never far away, but only had the one speed to offer in the final two furlongs. (16/1)
Non Vintage (IRE) looked in need of this beforehand, but nothing was staying on stronger at the finish. (20/1)
1562 Heathyards Rock was never that far away, but found the big weight tying him down in the final couple of furlongs. (9/1)
595 Open Affair was never nearer than at the finish. (16/1)
1515* Durgams First (IRE) dropped away tamely in the final two furlongs. (11/4)
650 Norsong (14/1: op 8/1)

1780 WALTER EARL (S) STKS (3-Y.O) (Class E)
7-05 (7-07) **1m (July)** £3,882.50 (£1,160.00: £555.00: £252.50) Stalls: Low GOING minus 0.21 sec per fur (GF)

				SP	RR	SF
1373^{7}	**Rumbustious (60)** (RHannon) **3-8-6** PatEddery(5) (hld up: hdwy 2f out: led ins fnl f: r.o)	—	**1**	4/1^{3}	54	21
1464*	**Janglynyve (60)** (SPCWoods) **3-8-11** LDettori(4) (chsd ldrs: ev ch ins fnl f: edgd rt: styd on cl home)	nk	**2**	6/4^{1}	58	25
1448^{5}	**Sun Fairy** (JAGlover) **3-8-2**(7)ow3 TPengkerego(11) (hdwy 2f out: rdn over 1f out: styd on ins fnl f)	hd	**3**	14/1	56	20
1642^{5}	**Miss Barcelona (IRE) (45)** (MJPolglase) **3-8-6** SSanders(2) (led 1f: led again over 2f out: hdd ins fnl f: one pce)	1¼	**4**	16/1	51	18
1587^{15}	**Sandweld (72)** (CADwyer) **3-8-11** NVarley(8) (mid div: hdwy 2f out: rdn over 1f out: one pce)	4	**5**	8/1	48	15
	Fly High (DMorris) **3-8-6** PBloomfield(10) (w'like: rr: sn pushed along: sme hdwy fnl 2f: nvr nrr)	2½	**6**	25/1	38	5
	Radar O'Reilly (RJRWilliams) **3-8-11** RCochrane(1) (chsd ldrs tl wknd over 2f out)	¾	**7**	20/1	41	8
62^{3}	**Petite Danseuse (79)** (CADwyer) **3-8-6** JStack(3) (chsd ldrs tl wknd over 1f out)	hd	**8**	2/1^{2}	36	3
1464^{4}	**Wheildon** (SCWilliams) **3-8-11** KRutter(9) (bhd fnl 3f)	13	**9**	14/1	15	—
	Small Risk (47) (TTClement) **3-7-13**(7) CWebb(13) (a bhd)	4	**10**	16/1	2	—
1316^{14}	**Wintered Out** (GLMoore) **3-8-6** CandyMorris(6) (plld hrd: led after 1f: hdd over 2f out: sn wknd)	¾	**11**	33/1	1	—
935^{9}	**Sang d'Antibes (FR) (62)** (DJSCosgrove) **3-8-6** JQuinn(12) (mid div tl wknd over 2f out)	2	**12**	16/1	—	—
	Dijon (BobJones) **3-8-11** NDay(7) (bhd fr ½-wy: t.o)	28	**13**	20/1	—	—
				(SP 151.7%)		**13 Rn**

1m 43.19 (5.19) CSF £11.84 TOTE £5.00: £1.60 £1.40 £5.70 (£4.00) Trio £71.70 OWNER Mr Christopher Curtis (MARLBOROUGH) BRED Fulling Mill Stud and C. Curtis
No bid
OFFICIAL EXPLANATION **Radar O'Reilly: bumped his head on the stalls and suffered a slight nostril injury. He also ran too freely early on.**
Rumbustious, held up in mid-division, was produced with a well-timed challenge to lead entering the final furlong. (4/1)

1464* Janglynyve did not help her cause by edging right inside the final furlong. (6/4: op 9/4)
1448 Sun Fairy stepped up on her debut and stayed on promisingly inside the final furlong. (14/1)
1642 Miss Barcelona (IRE) cut out much of the running, but only had the one pace to offer in the final furlong. (16/1)
62 Petite Danseuse appeared straight enough beforehand, but she dropped away disappointingly from below the distance, and maybe the race will bring her on. (2/1)

1781 NGK SPARK PLUGS H'CAP (0-80) (3-Y.O) (Class D)

7-35 (7-36) **6f (July)** £4,620.00 (£1,380.00: £660.00: £300.00) Stalls: Low GOING minus 0.21 sec per fur (GF)

				SP	RR	SF
1589^{3}	**Shalstayholy (IRE) (60)** (GLMoore) **3-8-2v** JQuinn(6) (hld up gng wl: hdwy 2f out: led 1f out: r.o)	—	**1**	$5/2^{1}$	71	45
1410^{8}	**Ivory Dawn (65)** (KTIvory) **3-8-4**(3) MartinDwyer(8) (chsd ldrs: ev ch 1f out: hrd rdn ins fnl: unable qckn)	2	**2**	13/2	71	45
968^{7}	**Rosy Outlook (USA) (79)** (IABalding) **3-9-7** LDettori(7) (lw: a.p: ev ch 1f out: one pce)	½	**3**	$9/2^{2}$	83	57
1119^{6}	**Rainbow Rain (USA) (75)** (MJohnston) **3-9-3** MRoberts(11) (lw: trckd ldrs: rdn & outpcd 2f out: rallied ins fnl f: r.o)	½	**4**	$11/2^{3}$	78	52
1573^{6}	**Bold Spring (IRE) (66)** (RHannon) **3-8-8b¹** PatEddery(9) (keen hold: hld up in rr: hdwy 1f out: r.o)	nk	**5**	$11/2^{3}$	68	42
1496^{12}	**Three For A Pound (67)** (JAGlover) **3-8-9** GCarter(2) (prom tl wknd ins fnl f)	½	**6**	12/1	68	42
1439^{6}	**Silver Purse (67)** (APJones) **3-8-9** RPrice(1) (led: hdd 1f out: sn wknd)	1½	**7**	14/1	64	38
1385^{6}	**La Dolce Vita (70)** (TDBarron) **3-8-12** KDarley(5) (prom: ev ch over 1f out: wknd ins fnl f)	½	**8**	10/1	66	40
1115^{10}	**Gresatre (58)** (CADwyer) **3-8-0** NVarley(10) (towards rr: rdn 3f out: sn btn)	4	**9**	16/1	43	17
1650^{7}	**Hype Superior (IRE) (64)** (ABailey) **3-8-6** PaulEddery(3) (a bhd)	s.h	**10**	13/2	49	23
	M T Vessel (55) (JRJenkins) **3-7-11** GBardwell(4) (keen hold: in tch tl wknd 3f out)	9	**11**	33/1	16	—
				(SP 136.5%)	**11 Rn**	

1m 13.73 (1.73) CSF £20.97 CT £71.95 TOTE £4.50: £1.80 £2.20 £1.60 (£18.80) Trio £81.70 OWNER J B R Leisure Ltd (BRIGHTON) BRED Mrs P. Grubb

1589 Shalstayholy (IRE) was always travelling best, and produced a nice turn of foot to win this going away. (5/2)
1141 Ivory Dawn was always to the fore and had every chance. (13/2)
778* Rosy Outlook (USA) ran very well under her big weight. (9/2)
1119 Rainbow Rain (USA) was well outpaced two furlongs out, but nothing was staying on stronger in the final furlong, and a step back up to seven furlongs will definitely suit. (11/2)
1573 Bold Spring (IRE) was very keen in blinkers for the first time, and did not really consent to settle until halfway. He stayed on promisingly in the final furlong, and all is not lost yet. (11/2)
469* Three For A Pound (12/1: 8/1-14/1)
1439 Silver Purse (14/1: 10/1-20/1)
1119 Hype Superior (IRE) (13/2: 9/2-7/1)

1782 BAILEYS IRISH CREAM LIQUER H'CAP (0-90) (3-Y.O+) (Class C)

8-05 (8-06) **1m (July)** £6,004.00 (£1,792.00: £856.00: £388.00) Stalls: Low GOING minus 0.21 sec per fur (GF)

				SP	RR	SF
1308^{6}	**King of Tunes (FR) (77)** (JJSheehan) **5-9-3** RCochrane(8) (lw: hld up: gd hdwy over 1f out: led ins fnl f: r.o wl)	—	**1**	$5/1^{2}$	90	59
1256^{5}	**Wild Sky (IRE) (76)** (MJHeaton-Ellis) **3-8-5** AClark(9) (chsd ldrs: led over 1f out: hdd ins fnl f: one pce)	2½	**2**	7/1	84	42
1442^{3}	**Iamus (82)** (TDBarron) **4-9-8** LDettori(1) (hld up: hdwy & n.m.r over 1f out: swtchd rt: r.o ins fnl f)	½	**3**	7/1	89	58
1458^{5}	**Purchasing Power (IRE) (70)** (NACallaghan) **3-7-13** JQuinn(7) (lw: set stdy pce: hdd over 1f out: one pce)	1	**4**	$6/1^{3}$	75	33
895^{19}	**Admirals Flame (IRE) (77)** (CFWall) **6-9-3** SSanders(4) (swtg: hld up: hdwy & n.m.r appr fnl f: r.o one pce ins fnl f)	1	**5**	12/1	80	49
1305^{4}	**Green Jewel (87)** (RHannon) **3-9-2** DaneO'Neill(6) (chsd ldrs: nt clr run over 1f out: swtchd lft: rdn ins fnl f: one pce)	nk	**6**	$6/1^{3}$	89	47
1389^{2}	**Whittle Rock (75)** (MrsMReveley) **4-9-1** ACulhane(10) (plld hrd: hld up in rr: effrt over 1f out: sn btn)	3	**7**	8/1	71	40
1606^{3}	**Alpine Hideaway (IRE) (76)** (BHanbury) **4-9-2** JStack(3) (keen hold: mid div: rdn 2f out: wknd appr last)	¾	**8**	10/1	71	40
1214^{4}	**Saifan (88)** (DMorris) **8-10-0b** NDay(2) (lw: trckd ldrs: nt clr run over 1f out: nt rcvr)	5	**9**	$2/1^{1}$	73	42
1495^{3}	**Lay The Blame (73)** (MDHammond) **4-8-13** TQuinn(11) (prom tl wknd over 1f out)	1	**10**	12/1	56	25
	Hopeful Bid (IRE) (58) (PHowling) **8-7-12** NCarlisle(13) (bit bkwd: prom tl wknd wl over 1f out)	2	**11**	33/1	37	6
431^{7}	**Lady Godiva (70)** (MJPolglase) **3-7-10**(3) MartinDwyer(5) (in tch: rdn over 2f out: sn wknd)	1	**12**	16/1	47	5
				(SP 148.0%)	**12 Rn**	

1m 40.37 (2.37) CSF £46.45 CT £251.24 TOTE £8.10: £2.60 £3.30 £2.00 (£40.10) Trio £116.70 OWNER Mrs Eileen Sheehan (FINDON) BRED Thierry Storme
WEIGHT FOR AGE 3yo-11lb

895 King of Tunes (FR) won this race, which was run at a muddling pace, with a sharp turn of foot. (5/1)
1256 Wild Sky (IRE) was never that far away, but had no answer to the winner's burst of speed in the final furlong. (7/1)
1442 Iamus was slightly unlucky, for he was making good headway when stopped below the distance. Switched right, he ran on strongly but the winner had flown. (7/1)
1458 Purchasing Power (IRE) set only a moderate pace and was tapped for foot in the final furlong. (6/1)
Admirals Flame (IRE) was another to get slightly hampered below the distance, but this made little difference to his finishing position. (12/1)
1305 Green Jewel was never far away. She was short of room below the distance, but this did not make a lot of difference. (6/1)
1214 Saifan was going well enough when completely stopped in his run over a furlong out, and this race can be forgotten. (2/1: 9/2-7/4)

1783 FRANK BUTTERS MAIDEN STKS (2-Y.O F) (Class D)

8-35 (8-35) **6f (July)** £3,913.25 (£1,166.00: £555.50: £250.25) Stalls: Low GOING minus 0.21 sec per fur (GF)

				SP	RR	SF
	Stayingalive (USA) (PFICole) **2-8-11** TQuinn(6) (w'like: scope: lw: keen hold: a.p: led ins fnl f: r.o wl)	—	**1**	$9/4^{3}$	—	45
1240^{3}	**Tadwiga** (RHannon) **2-8-11** DaneO'Neill(5) (lw: a.p: led 2f out: hdd ins fnl f: unable qckn)	2	**2**	$13/8^{1}$	—	40
	Likely Story (IRE) (JLDunlop) **2-8-11** KDarley(1) (unf: bit bkwd: chsd ldrs: rdn over 1f out: styd on ins fnl f)	1	**3**	16/1	—	37
1321^{W}	**Solo Spirit** (JRJenkins) **2-8-11** GBardwell(3) (unf: pushed along thrght: towards rr tl mod late hdwy)	3	**4**	40/1	—	29
	Migrate (USA) (JHMGosden) **2-8-11** LDettori(7) (unf: scope: bit bkwd: swvd rt s: hld up: rdn 2f out: no hdwy)	1¼	**5**	$2/1^{2}$	—	26
	Aunt Sadie (RCharlton) **2-8-11** PatEddery(2) (w'like: bit bkwd: a bhd)	2	**6**	9/1	—	20
1295^{2}	**High Gain** (PHowling) **2-8-11** PaulEddery(4) (led: hdd 2f out: wknd over 1f out)	3	**7**	16/1	—	12
				(SP 126.4%)	**7 Rn**	

1m 14.33 (2.33) CSF £6.63 TOTE £4.00: £1.80 £1.80 (£3.50) OWNER H R H Prince Fahd Salman (WHATCOMBE) BRED Mr and Mrs John C. Mabee

Stayingalive (USA), a really imposing filly by Gone West, won this in very impressive fashion. She can go on to better things. (9/4)
1240 Tadwiga has learnt from her experience at Newbury and raced much more prominently this time, but she had no answer to the winner's speed in the final furlong. (13/8)
Likely Story (IRE) ran a promising race. Most of her trainer's two-year-olds improve for the run and, if paddock appearance is anything to go by, she will be no different. (16/1)
Solo Spirit was never going the pace, and was never nearer than at the finish. (40/1)
Migrate (USA) was very green in the early stages of the race and will come on for the outing. (2/1)
Aunt Sadie (9/1: 6/1-10/1)

1784 CECIL BOYD ROCHFORT MAIDEN STKS (3-Y.O F) (Class D)

9-05 (9-06) **1m 2f (July)** £4,020.50 (£1,199.00: £572.00: £258.50) Stalls: Low GOING minus 0.36 sec per fur (F)

				SP	RR	SF
1318[3]	**Keyboogie (USA)** (RCharlton) **3-8-11** PatEddery(4) (dwlt: sn rcvrd: chsd ldrs: led over 2f out: rdn ins fnl f: r.o wl)	—	**1**	1/3[1]	83	29
1477[6]	**Graceful Lass** (DRLoder) **3-8-11** KDarley(1) (hld up: hdwy over 3f out: chsd wnr over 1f out: rdn ins fnl f: unable qckn)	2	**2**	12/1	80	26
833[6]	**La Curamalal (IRE)** (GWragg) **3-8-11** MHills(7) (led after 2f: hdd over 2f out: one pce)	3	**3**	9/1[3]	75	21
1415[3]	**City Gambler (72)** (GCBravery) **3-8-11** MRimmer(3) (led 2f: w ldr tl over 2f out: grad wknd)	2½	**4**	14/1	71	17
	Gallant Heights (GCBravery) **3-8-11** NDay(8) (leggy: unf: rdn over 3f out: nvr nrr)	½	**5**	50/1	70	16
	Alpina (USA) (JHMGosden) **3-8-11** LDettori(5) (w'like: bit bkwd: rr: rdn & sme hdwy over 2f out: wknd over 1f out)	1¾	**6**	11/4[2]	67	13
1556a[7]	**Rufalda (IRE)** (LMCumani) **3-8-4(7)** DYoung(6) (chsd ldrs tl wknd over 3f out)	1½	**7**	40/1	65	11
	Shelteez (USA) (MBell) **3-8-6(5)** GFaulkner(2) (leggy: a bhd)	10	**8**	40/1	49	—
				(SP 132.9%)	**8 Rn**	

2m 8.23 (4.63) CSF £8.22 TOTE £1.50: £1.10 £2.20 £2.20 (£4.00) OWNER Mr K. Abdulla (BECKHAMPTON) BRED Juddmonte Farms
1318 Keyboogie (USA) won this ultimately like the odds suggested she would. Always travelling well, she took up the running over two furlongs out, and although Eddery had to shake her up inside the final furlong, she responded well to win going away. She will be even better at a mile-and-a-half. (1/3: op 4/7)
1477 Graceful Lass ran a very promising race. She chased the leader from below the distance and momentarily looked dangerous. She should have no trouble finding a race, possibly over further. (12/1: 6/1-14/1)
La Curamalal (IRE) ran her best race to date, and is now qualified for handicaps. (9/1: 6/1-12/1)
1415 City Gambler cut out much of the running, but was put in her place in the final two furlongs. (14/1: op 33/1)
Gallant Heights was being pushed along some way from home. (50/1)
Alpina (USA) was too backward to do herself justice. (11/4)

T/Plpt: £43.60 (393.23 Tckts). T/Qdpt: £9.80 (80.55 Tckts) SM

1575-WOLVERHAMPTON (L-H) (Standard)

Saturday June 7th

WEATHER: fine WIND: sunny

1785 GIRTH H'CAP (0-60) (3-Y.O) (Class F)

7-00 (7-01) **1m 6f 166y (Fibresand)** £2,277.00 (£627.00: £297.00) Stalls: Low GOING: 0.27 sec per fur (SLW)

				SP	RR	SF
967[8]	**Sipowitz (44)** (CACyzer) **3-8-6(3)** AWhelan(6) (hld up: hdwy u.p 4f out: led wl over 1f out: rdn out)	—	**1**	25/1	47	13
1469[2]	**Alagna (47)** (SCWilliams) **3-8-12** SDrowne(2) (trckd ldrs: ev ch 2f out: sn rdn & nt run on)	1¾	**2**	2/1[2]	48	14
1299[5]	**Sam Peeb (45)** (RAFahey) **3-8-3(7)** RWinston(7) (a.p: plld hrd: led over 5f out: hdd wl over 1f out: no ex)	8	**3**	5/4[1]	37	3
1043[7]	**Warrlin (49)** (CWFairhurst) **3-9-0** LCharnock(8) (lw: prom: jnd ldr 4f out: wknd 2f out)	7	**4**	12/1	34	—
1502[4]	**Moorbird (IRE) (56)** (JLHarris) **3-9-7v** BDoyle(9) (led over 4f: led again 7f out: hdd over 5f out: wknd wl over 2f out)	6	**5**	10/1	34	—
1248[16]	**Kustom Kit Xpres (45)** (SRBowring) **3-8-5(5)** DSweeney(10) (chsd ldrs: lost pl 8f out: effrt over 4f out: sn btn)	1½	**6**	33/1	22	—
1043[12]	**Woodland Nymph (50)** (DJGMurraySmith) **3-9-1** JFEgan(1) (hld up: hdwy over 5f out: wknd 3f out)	hd	**7**	6/1[3]	27	—
1299[9]	**Propellant (55)** (CWThornton) **3-9-6** JFanning(3) (lw: prom over 10f)	dist	**8**	25/1	—	—
1217[6]	**Bella Daniella (33)** (TTClement) **3-7-7(5)ow2** RMullen(5) (prom: led 10f out: hdd 7f out: sn wknd)	dist	**9**	33/1	—	—
156[4]	**Hoh Down (IRE) (46)** (RTJuckes) **3-8-11b** MFenton(4) (b.hind: bit bkwd: s.i.s: a in rr)	8	**10**	33/1	—	—
				(SP 125.4%)	**10 Rn**	

3m 26.7 (19.30) CSF £70.79 CT £106.44 TOTE £34.20: £5.70 £1.50 £1.10 (£106.60) Trio £31.90 OWNER Mr R. M. Cyzer (HORSHAM) BRED C. A. and R. M. Cyzer
LONG HANDICAP Bella Daniella 7-9
Sipowitz, like his namesake, gave supporters of the favourite the blues. After showing nothing on his three previous visits to the racecourse, the combination of taking on handicappers for the first time plus this extended trip, proved ideal. (25/1)
1469 Alagna, for whom it looked a matter of how far turning for home, not for the first time failed to produce when asked. A pair of blinkers might be the answer. (2/1)
1299 Sam Peeb did not do himself any favours by racing very freely. (5/4)
Warrlin (12/1: op 8/1)
1502 Moorbird (IRE) (10/1: 7/1-11/1)

1786 SADDLE CLAIMING STKS (3-Y.O+) (Class F)

7-30 (7-31) **7f (Fibresand)** £2,277.00 (£627.00: £297.00) Stalls: High GOING: 0.27 sec per fur (SLW)

				SP	RR	SF
1754[3]	**Bentico (61)** (MrsNMacauley) **8-9-7v** BDoyle(8) (trckd ldrs: led over 2f out: rdn clr: eased cl home)	—	**1**	9/2[2]	74	46
89[7]	**Ashgore (71)** (JLEyre) **7-8-13** DWright(7) (bit bkwd: prom: drvn along over 2f out: styd on same pce)	6	**2**	4/1[1]	52	24
1291[9]	**Jilly Beveled (36)** (RonaldThompson) **5-8-6** DRMcCabe(6) (dwlt: bhd tl r.o appr fnl f: nvr nrr)	1¼	**3**	33/1	42	14
467[6]	**Sense of Priority (73)** (DNicholls) **8-9-3** AlexGreaves(3) (bit bkwd: hld up: effrt over 2f out: hung lft over 1f out: no imp)	1½	**4**	4/1[1]	50	22
1754[9]	**Jigsaw Boy (58)** (PGMurphy) **8-9-5** SDrowne(4) (sn outpcd: hdwy ½-wy: wknd over 1f out)	5	**5**	9/1	41	13
860[9]	**Loch Style (47)** (RHollinshead) **4-9-3** FLynch(10) (s.i.s: hdwy ½-wy: rdn & wknd 2f out)	1½	**6**	8/1	35	7

				SP	RR	SF
	Thordis (60) (PJMakin) **4-9-11v** DHolland(1) (swtg: led: rdn & hdd over 2f out: sn wknd)	½	**7**	10/1	42	14
1047[5]	**Advance Repro (58)** (JAkehurst) **3-7-12b** LCharnock(2) (chsd ldrs: rdn ½-wy: wknd over 2f out)	4	**8**	15/2	16	—
1292[16]	**Sea Dreams (IRE)** (DMHyde) **6-8-8b[1]**(3) RHavlin(5) (chsd ldrs over 3f)	1	**9**	33/1	17	—
1135[8]	**People Direct (50)** (KMcAuliffe) **4-8-12** JFanning(9) (chsd ldrs tl ½-wy)	2	**10**	7/1[3]	13	—
				(SP 118.5%)	**10 Rn**	

1m 31.6 (6.90) CSF £21.22 TOTE £4.50: £1.70 £2.30 £6.40 (£20.10) Trio Not won; £144.95 to 9/6/97 OWNER Twenty Twenty Racing (MELTON MOWBRAY) BRED Britton House Stud
WEIGHT FOR AGE 3yo-10lb

1754 Bentico, none the worse for his outing the previous day, was gaining his first success since this time last year. (9/2: op 3/1)
89 Ashgore will be all the sharper with this outing under his belt. (4/1)
312* Jilly Beveled, who would have met these on more advantageous terms in a handicap, lost her chance at the start. (33/1)
467 Sense of Priority, a course and distance winner, was coming back after a break. Given a chance early on, he hung when asked for an effort once in line for home, and never looked likely to take a hand in proceedings. (4/1: op 5/2)
687 Loch Style (8/1: tchd 12/1)
Thordis (10/1: op 6/1)
People Direct (7/1: op 12/1)

1787 SURCINGLE MAIDEN STKS (3-Y.O) (Class D)

8-00 (8-04) **7f (Fibresand)** £3,804.85 (£1,136.80: £543.90: £247.45) Stalls: High GOING: 0.27 sec per fur (SLW)

				SP	RR	SF
	Snow Kid (DRLoder) **3-9-0** DRMcCabe(9) (w'like: scope: chsd ldrs: led over 1f out: r.o wl)	—	**1**	10/11[1]	91	53
1394[4]	**Night Express (72)** (BHanbury) **3-9-0** BDoyle(8) (a.p: rdn & ev ch over 1f out: r.o one pce)	5	**2**	20/1	80	42
1265[2]	**Icy Guest (USA)** (PJMakin) **3-8-9** JCarroll(10) (led: rdn & hdd over 1f out: styd on same pce)	¾	**3**	9/1	73	35
1110[3]	**Persevere** (LordHuntingdon) **3-8-4**(5) AimeeCook(7) (prom over 5f)	7	**4**	9/1	57	19
1415[6]	**Swing West (USA)** (PFICole) **3-9-0** CRutter(11) (trckd ldrs: rdn & btn 2f out)	6	**5**	8/1[3]	48	10
1430[8]	**Krabloonik (FR)** (SirMarkPrescott) **3-9-0** GDuffield(4) (nvr plcd to chal)	¾	**6**	16/1	46	8
	Zabriskie (MRStoute) **3-9-0** DHolland(12) (lengthy: s.i.s: sn prom: wknd over 2f out)	2	**7**	3/1[2]	42	4
1409[8]	**Aurora Bay (IRE)** (MBell) **3-8-9** MFenton(5) (b.off hind: outpcd fr ½-wy)	14	**8**	33/1	5	—
1271[6]	**Pharly Star** (DShaw) **3-9-0** JFanning(2) (bit bkwd: sn outpcd)	5	**9**	50/1	—	—
1090[13]	**Blue Cheese** (MrsNMacauley) **3-8-9** SDrowne(6) (b: prom tl ½-wy)	1	**10**	50/1	—	—
778[8]	**Verasica** (RHollinshead) **3-8-9** FLynch(1) (s.i.s: a outpcd & bhd)	12	**11**	50/1	—	—
287[8]	**Bustingoutallover (USA)** (CWThornton) **3-8-9** LCharnock(3) (s.i.s: sn outpcd & bhd)	1	**12**	50/1	—	—
				(SP 129.9%)	**12 Rn**	

1m 30.4 (5.70) CSF £28.28 TOTE £1.90: £1.20 £5.60 £2.10 (£31.10) Trio £39.70 OWNER Mr Ali Saeed (NEWMARKET) BRED Raymond Clive Tooth

Snow Kid, from a yard whose runners here have to be respected, is a good-looking son of Indian Ridge. Travelling well throughout, he lengthened when asked and ran out a very easy winner. (10/11: evens-5/4)
1394 Night Express, a gelding who carries plenty of condition, may well be suited by further. (20/1)
1265 Icy Guest (USA) was always there to be shot at, and just found her male rivals too strong in the closing stages. (9/1: op 5/1)
1110 Persevere, who will stay further in due course, may well do better when tackling handicappers. (9/1: op 5/1)
1297 Krabloonik (FR), dropping back in trip although bred to be suited by further, is now handicapped and no doubt will be placed to advantage. (16/1)

1788 THOROUGHBRED H'CAP (0-100) (3-Y.O+) (Class C)

8-30 (8-30) **1m 1f 79y (Fibresand)** £5,447.45 (£1,625.60: £776.30: £351.65) Stalls: Low GOING: 0.27 sec per fur (SLW)

				SP	RR	SF
1262[6]	**Alsahib (USA) (64)** (WRMuir) **4-8-0** TSprake(5) (hld up: hdwy ½-wy: rdn to ld ins fnl f: styd on strly)	—	**1**	6/1[3]	82	57
*1430**	**Dalliance (IRE) (89)** (MRStoute) **3-8-13** DHolland(2) (chsd ldr: led over 4f out: hdd & unable qckn ins fnl f)	2	**2**	4/5[1]	104	67
*1575**	**Anonym (IRE) (72)** (JLEyre) **5-8-3b**(5) RMullen(6) (hld up: hdwy ½-wy: wknd over 2f out)	15	**3**	11/2[2]	61	36
1154[4]	**Castles Burning (USA) (76)** (CACyzer) **3-8-0** LCharnock(4) (mid div: drvn along ½-wy: wknd over 3f out)	nk	**4**	12/1	64	27
1576[3]	**Rambo Waltzer (82)** (DNicholls) **5-8-13**(5) IonaWands(3) (lost pl after 2f: sn wl bhd: fin lame)	6	**5**	7/1	60	35
1135[5]	**Heathyards Lady (USA) (64)** (RHollinshead) **6-7-11**(3) PFessey(1) (b: s.i.s: sn trckng ldrs: wknd over 3f out)	nk	**6**	12/1	42	17
947[17]	**Censor (88)** (DNicholls) **4-9-10** AlexGreaves(7) (led over 4f: wknd 3f out: t.o)	20	**7**	16/1	32	7
				(SP 119.0%)	**7 Rn**	

2m 1.7 (5.70) CSF £10.84 TOTE £11.10: £3.30 £1.40 (£5.30) OWNER Mr S. Channing-Williams (LAMBOURN) BRED Shadwell Estate Co., Ltd. and Shadwell Farm Inc.
WEIGHT FOR AGE 3yo-12lb
OFFICIAL EXPLANATION Rambo Waltzer: finished lame behind.

1262 Alsahib (USA) handled this surface well and got off the mark in good style. He can follow up. (6/1)
1430* Dalliance (IRE) impressive over this trip here last time, was unfortunate to come up against what appeared a well-handicapped winner. They pulled a long way clear of the rest. (4/5)
1575* Anonym (IRE), raised 4lb for winning an amateur riders' event here last time, was easily shaken off in the final quarter-mile. He may have found this trip beyond him. (11/2: op 7/2)

1789 MARTINGALE (S) STKS (2-Y.O F) (Class G)

9-00 (9-04) **6f (Fibresand)** £1,984.50 (£547.00: £259.50) Stalls: Low GOING: 0.27 sec per fur (SLW)

				SP	RR	SF
1614[7]	**Michelee** (PDEvans) **2-8-9** JFEgan(7) (led 1f: sn lost pl: hdwy ½-wy: led ins fnl f: r.o strly)	—	**1**	16/1	70+	6
1626*	**Edna's Gift (IRE)** (JBerry) **2-8-11**(3) PFessey(8) (hld up: hdwy ½-wy: led over 2f out: hdd & unable qckn ins fnl f)	5	**2**	8/13[1]	62	—
1432[2]	**Jack-N-Jilly (IRE)** (JSMoore) **2-8-6**(3) PPMurphy(5) (prom: outpcd over 2f out: styd on ins fnl f)	3½	**3**	8/1[3]	47	—
1290[3]	**Karenaragon** (RonaldThompson) **2-8-4**(5) GMilligan(4) (bhd tl r.o appr fnl f: nvr nrr)	5	**4**	33/1	34	—
1432[3]	**Sylvan Cloud** (CWFairhurst) **2-8-9** LCharnock(6) (prom over 3f)	1¼	**5**	16/1	31	—
1286[4]	**Gifted Bairn (IRE)** (DNicholls) **2-8-9** AlexGreaves(3) (chsd ldrs: rdn 2f out: sn wknd)	nk	**6**	11/2[2]	30	—
1626[8]	**Step In To The Sun** (RAFahey) **2-8-9b[1]** JCarroll(2) (sn outpcd)	1¼	**7**	16/1	27	—
1444[R]	**Miss Equal** (MCPipe) **2-8-9** TSprake(1) (led after 1f tl over 2f out)	13	**8**	25/1	—	—
	Romantic Secret (RTJuckes) **2-8-9** MFenton(9) (lt-f: dwlt: sn prom: wknd over 2f out)	1½	**9**	33/1	—	—

				SP	RR	SF
1290[2]	***Medina Miss*** (WGMTurner) **2-8-2**(7) DMcGaffin(10) (Withdrawn not under Starter's orders: lame at s)		**W**	8/1[3]	—	—
				(SP 126.9%)		**9 Rn**

1m 19.2 (8.00) CSF £22.07 TOTE £15.40: £1.90 £1.10 £1.70 (£8.00) Trio £33.60 OWNER Mr John Pugh (WELSHPOOL) BRED Llety Stud No bid

Michelee, better for her outing at Hamilton, proved well-suited by this trip. (16/1)
1626* Edna's Gift (IRE) who will stay further, was easily outpointed in the closing stages. (8/13)
1432 Jack-N-Jilly (IRE), consistent at this level, is proving difficult to place. He may enjoy success when the nursery season commences. (8/1: op 5/1)
1290 Karenaragon came from out of the clouds to finish fourth albeit well beaten, and will be better suited when the emphasis is on stamina.(33/1)

1790 BRIDLE APPRENTICE H'CAP (0-65) (3-Y.O+) (Class G)
9-30 (9-32) **6f (Fibresand)** £1,984.50 (£547.00: £259.50) Stalls: Low GOING: 0.27 sec per fur (SLW)

				SP	RR	SF
1289[5]	**Hoh Majestic (IRE) (56)** (RonaldThompson) **4-9-4v**(3) GMilligan(6) (a.p: led ins fnl f: rdn out)	—	**1**	7/2[2]	56	26
1279[10]	**Itsinthepost (63)** (VSoane) **4-9-11**(3) IonaWands(3) (chsd ldrs: rdn & ev ch ins fnl f: no ex nr fin)	1	**2**	7/1	60	30
1613[15]	**Marino Street (44)** (PDEvans) **4-8-4v**(5) AMcCarthy(2) (s.i.s: sn outpcd: hdwy over 1f out: fin wl)	1¼	**3**	8/1	38	8
1428[3]	**River Ensign (38)** (WMBrisbourne) **4-8-3** RMullen(7) (led: rdn & hdd ins fnl f: no ex)	½	**4**	5/1[3]	31	1
1433[11]	**Opening Range (35)** (NEBerry) **6-7-9**(5) RWinston(1) (w ldrs: rdn 2f out: wknd fnl f)	2	**5**	25/1	22	—
1496[2]	**Fine Times (60)** (CWFairhurst) **3-8-12v**(5) TSiddall(4) (b.hind: trckd ldrs: rdn ½-wy: sn lost tch)	6	**6**	7/2[2]	31	—
1676[6]	**Norling (IRE) (45)** (KOCunningham-Brown) **7-8-10** RFfrench(5) (prom to ½-wy)	3	**7**	2/1[1]	8	—
				(SP 121.9%)		**7 Rn**

1m 18.5 (7.30) CSF £27.43 TOTE £4.10: £2.00 £2.70 (£19.20) OWNER Mrs Ronnie Hague (DONCASTER) BRED Ballinacurra Stud
WEIGHT FOR AGE 3yo-8lb

1289 Hoh Majestic (IRE), taken early to post, was given a confident ride and ran out a comfortable winner. (7/2)
Itsinthepost, a course and distance winner, lost nothing in defeat. (7/1: 4/1-8/1)
Marino Street lost her chance at the start, but was coming home best of all. (8/1)
1428 River Ensign, a maiden, showed plenty of dash and was only run out of it in the closing stages. (5/1)
1496 Fine Times (7/2: 2/1-4/1)
1676 Norling (IRE) (2/1: 7/2-7/4)

T/Plpt: £25.30 (347.67 Tckts). T/Qdpt: £5.30 (77.55 Tckts) CR

1383-NOTTINGHAM (L-H) (Good to firm)
Monday June 9th
WEATHER: sunny periods WIND: slt against

1791 E.B.F. MAIDEN STKS (2-Y.O) (Class D)
2-30 (2-31) **5f 13y** £3,494.25 (£1,044.00: £499.50: £227.25) Stalls: High GOING minus 0.32 sec per fur (GF)

				SP	RR	SF
1486[4]	**Cortachy Castle (IRE)** (BJMeehan) **2-9-0** PatEddery(1) (mde all: drew clr & edgd lft fnl f)	—	**1**	4/11[1]	66+	40
	Moontabeh (PTWalwyn) **2-9-0** RHills(2) (neat: cmpt: bkwd: a.p: chsd wnr last 2f: no imp fnl f)	3	**2**	9/2[2]	57	31
	Anita At Dawn (IRE) (BPalling) **2-8-9** TSprake(6) (lt-f: unf: chsd wnr 3f: wknd wl over 1f out)	3½	**3**	16/1	40	14
1026[7]	**Flame Tower (IRE)** (RHannon) **2-9-0** DaneO'Neill(3) (bit bkwd: a chsng ldrs: rdn 2f out: no imp)	s.h	**4**	14/1[3]	45	19
	Boccolino (TDBarron) **2-9-0** KDarley(4) (small: sltly dipped: s.s: effrt 2f out: wknd wl over 1f out)	3	**5**	16/1	36	10
1492[10]	**Ra Ra Rasputin** (BAMcMahon) **2-9-0** LNewton(5) (lw: s.s: a bhd & outpcd)	1¼	**6**	20/1	32	6
1669[7]	**Stephangeorge** (MBrittain) **2-9-0** GBardwell(7) (trckd ldrs: sn pushed along: outpcd fnl 2f)	4	**7**	50/1	19	—
				(SP 116.7%)		**7 Rn**

60.7 secs (1.80) CSF £2.35 TOTE £1.20: £1.20 £1.60 (£1.90) OWNER Mrs E. A. Lerpiniere (UPPER LAMBOURN) BRED Mrs G. Doyle

1486 Cortachy Castle (IRE) did not have a great deal to beat, but he showed his dislike for this firm ground by hanging left when drawing clear inside the last furlong. (4/11: op 4/6)
Moontabeh, a not over-big, stocky colt who could only improve for the run, was poised to challenge at the distance before lack of peak condition began to take its toll. (9/2: 9/4-5/1)
Anita At Dawn (IRE), a lightly-made half-sister to middle-distance winner Thaljanah, shows plenty of knee action, but she was always in the action and only dropped away below the distance. (16/1)
Flame Tower (IRE) still needed this and, bustled along a quarter-mile out, was unable to raise his pace. (14/1: op 8/1)
Boccolino was always at full stretch after losing ground at the start, but the experience will not be lost. (16/1)

1792 RISLEY H'CAP (0-80) (3-Y.O) (Class D)
3-00 (3-00) **5f 13y** £3,518.20 (£1,048.60: £499.80: £225.40) Stalls: High GOING minus 0.32 sec per fur (GF)

				SP	RR	SF
1294[3]	**Lamarita (77)** (JMPEustace) **3-9-7** JTate(4) (hld up: hdwy 2f out: swtchd rt & led appr fnl f: comf)	—	**1**	2/1[1]	83+	45
1644[2]	**Suite Factors (57)** (KRBurke) **3-8-1** PaulEddery(3) (lw: led: hrd rdn & hdd over 1f out: one pce)	1¾	**2**	11/4[2]	58	20
	Barnburgh Boy (75) (TDBarron) **3-9-5** KDarley(2) (h.d.w: swtg: bkwd: dwlt: hdwy ½-wy: kpt on u.p fnl f)	1½	**3**	8/1	71	33
1275[2]	**Mutasawwar (72)** (EALDunlop) **3-9-2** RHills(5) (b: prom: ev ch wl over 1f out: sn rdn: one pce)	nk	**4**	7/2[3]	67	29
1730[10]	**Ice Age (65)** (RJRWilliams) **3-8-6**(3) DGriffiths(1) (prom: effrt & ev ch over 1f out: wknd fnl 200y)	1	**5**	33/1	57	19
1644[3]	**Anokato (66)** (KTIvory) **3-8-7b**(3) MartinDwyer(6) (b: chsd ldrs: rdn ½-wy: sn btn)	1½	**6**	5/1	53	15
				(SP 112.9%)		**6 Rn**

60.8 secs (1.90) CSF £7.17 TOTE £3.60: £1.90 £1.70 (£3.20) OWNER Park Lane Racing / Mrs D A La Trobe (NEWMARKET) BRED Britton House Stud

1294 Lamarita needs to be produced from off the pace and, ridden to perfection, won with quite a bit in hand. (2/1)
1644 Suite Factors had to settle for the runner-up spot once again, but he gave it all he had, and these forceful tactics are sure to pay off one of these days. (11/4)
Barnburgh Boy, a heavy-topped colt, needed the run after being out of action since the autumn. He handled this ground particularly well, and did well to make the frame after being caught flat-footed at the start. He has certainly trained on and should win races. (8/1: 5/1-9/1)
1275 Mutasawwar went with the pace and promised to make a race of it inside the final quarter-mile, but he had no answer when the tempo was stepped-up. (7/2: 3/1-9/2)
Ice Age, a mediocre mover on lively ground, raced in the centre of the track and joined issue over a furlong out but, once the winner set sail for home, he had to admit the quickening pace too much for him. (33/1)

1793 HOLME PIERREPONT CONDITIONS STKS (3-Y.O+) (Class C)
3-30 (3-30) **1m 54y** £4,875.84 (£1,683.04: £805.02: £326.10) Stalls: Low GOING minus 0.32 sec per fur (GF)

				SP	RR	SF
1257^{4}	**Harry Wolton (103)** (HRACecil) **3-8-10** KFallon(3) (hld up: hdwy over 2f out: led ins fnl f: drifted rt: r.o)	—	**1**	$10/11^{1}$	107	44
	Mandilak (USA) (LMCumani) **3-8-10** LDettori(2) (bkwd: led: rn wd ent st: hdd & edgd rt ins fnl f)	1¼	**2**	$3/1^{2}$	105	42
1216^{5}	**Shawaf (USA) (96)** (JLDunlop) **3-8-10** RHills(1) (hld up: effrt 2f out: hrd drvn & one pce fnl f)	3½	**3**	$3/1^{2}$	98	35
1490^{5}	**My Lewicia (IRE) (96)** (PWHarris) **4-8-13** PatEddery(4) (hld up: hdwy to go 2nd 3f out: rdn & wknd fnl 2f)	11	**4**	$7/1^{3}$	68	16
				(SP 114.9%)	**4 Rn**	

1m 43.7 (2.40) CSF £3.93 TOTE £1.60 (£2.20) OWNER Old Road Securities Plc (NEWMARKET) BRED T. D. Holland-Martin
WEIGHT FOR AGE 3yo-11lb

1257 Harry Wolton moved very short to post and certainly won no supporters with his restricted action, but he had the edge in fitness over his only serious rival and, despite drifting almost the entire width of the track inside the final furlong, was well on top at the finish. (10/11: 5/4-4/5)
Mandilak (USA), a strong colt carrying plenty of condition, has never raced round bends before and he had trouble handling the turn for home. Edging right with the winner after being headed inside the last furlong, he is sure to strip fitter for the run, and it would be advisable to wait for the more yielding ground, because he looked ill at ease on this. (3/1: op 7/4)
1216 Shawaf (USA) waited on the leaders and was close enough to pose a threat approaching the final furlong, but he failed to pick up when sent about his work and proved more than a shade disappointing. (3/1)
1490 My Lewicia (IRE) has not really come in her coat yet and, though she moved into second place three furlongs out, the winner knocked her out of her stride when he prepared to deliver his challenge and she dropped away tamely. (7/1)

1794 STANTON BY DALE H'CAP (0-80) (3-Y.O+ F & M) (Class D)
4-00 (4-00) **1m 54y** £3,518.20 (£1,048.60: £499.80: £225.40) Stalls: Low GOING minus 0.32 sec per fur (GF)

				SP	RR	SF
1153^{4}	**Scarlet Crescent (70)** (PTWalwyn) **3-9-1** PatEddery(3) (lw: dropped rr 5f out: hdwy 2f out: led ent fnl f: r.o wl)	—	**1**	$2/1^{2}$	76	25
1268^{14}	**Vanishing Trick (USA) (79)** (HRACecil) **3-9-10** KFallon(2) (bkwd: hld up: hdwy 4f out: sn drvn along: led over 1f out: hdd ent fnl f: one pce)	1¾	**2**	$4/6^{1}$	82	31
1273^{15}	**Charlton Imp (USA) (54)** (RJHodges) **4-8-5**(5) RFfrench(4) (lw: led over 2f: nt clr run & swtchd over 1f out: r.o wl ins fnl f)	¾	**3**	12/1	55	15
958^{15}	**Solfegietto (77)** (MBell) **3-9-8** MFenton(1) (swtg: plld hrd: led over 5f out tl over 1f out: sn btn)	1½	**4**	$9/1^{3}$	75	24
				(SP 111.0%)	**4 Rn**	

1m 46.2 (4.90) CSF £3.52 TOTE £2.40 (£1.10) OWNER Leonard Collins & Mrs P T Walwyn (LAMBOURN) BRED P. J. McCalmont
WEIGHT FOR AGE 3yo-11lb

1153 Scarlet Crescent, much happier back on turf and returning to a mile, won this cosily and looks as if she is thriving at present. (2/1)
Vanishing Trick (USA) is a strong, close-coupled filly, but she looked more like a mare in foal and, off the bridle early in the straight, eventually struck the front briefly, but the race-fit winner took her measure without much difficulty and she could do little about it. (4/6)
554 Charlton Imp (USA) is little better than a plater and, had she not been forced to check and switch approaching the final furlong, she would have definitely secured the runner-up prize. Sure to be happier on a more yielding surface, she seems to be very much on the upgrade. (12/1)
Solfegietto, taken to post steadily, pulled too hard for her own good once in action, and she was at the end of her tether when collared below the distance. She is hardly bred to get this trip, and will need to settle to give herself any chance at all. (9/1: op 5/1)

1795 WOODTHORPE H'CAP (0-70) (3-Y.O+) (Class E)
4-30 (4-31) **1m 6f 15y** £3,200.25 (£957.00: £458.50: £209.25) Stalls: Low GOING minus 0.32 sec per fur (GF)

				SP	RR	SF
1763^{9}	**Salska (56)** (AStreeter) **6-9-3** TSprake(3) (hld up: effrt & rdn over 2f out: styd on to ld last stride)	—	**1**	11/1	67	30
986^{3}	**Tawafek (USA) (60)** (SDow) **4-9-7** JReid(2) (lw: hld up in tch: pushed along 3f out: hdwy to ld wl ins fnl f: hdd post)	s.h	**2**	$11/4^{1}$	71	34
1390^{11}	**Winnebago (46)** (CWThornton) **4-8-7** DeanMcKeown(8) (led: drvn clr 3f out: wknd & hdd wl ins fnl f)	¾	**3**	20/1	56	19
1481^{3}	**Gumair (USA) (67)** (RHannon) **4-10-0** PatEddery(5) (chsd ldr: rdn over 2f out: wknd appr fnl f)	2½	**4**	$5/1^{3}$	74	37
1570^{3}	**Batabanoo (45)** (MrsMReveley) **8-8-6** KDarley(10) (lw: hld up in rr: hdwy 3f out: kpt on u.p ins fnl f)	s.h	**5**	$9/2^{2}$	52	15
1560^{7}	**Advance East (47)** (MDods) **5-8-8** KFallon(9) (hld up: effrt & hrd drvn over 2f out: nvr able to chal)	½	**6**	11/1	54	17
650^{11}	**Brighter Byfaah (IRE) (45)** (NAGraham) **4-8-6** MRimmer(6) (bit bkwd: trckd ldrs tl wknd 3f out)	2½	**7**	14/1	49	12
1232^{7}	**Contrarie (41)** (MJRyan) **4-7-11**(5) RMullen(1) (hld up & bhd: effrt over 2f out: no imp)	1	**8**	14/1	44	7
1654^{5}	**Amiarge (50)** (MBrittain) **7-8-11** GBardwell(7) (chsd ldrs: rdn 4f out: grad wknd)	½	**9**	10/1	52	15
1491^{8}	**Durham (60)** (GLMoore) **6-9-7v** CandyMorris(4) (prom tl rdn & wknd over 3f out)	1¼	**10**	7/1	61	24
				(SP 117.9%)	**10 Rn**	

3m 6.7 (8.20) CSF £38.10 CT £560.50 TOTE £13.30: £2.30 £1.60 £10.20 (£20.10) Trio £328.80; £379.78 to Salisbury 10/6/97 OWNER Mr P. L. Clinton (UTTOXETER) BRED J. A. Haverhals

Salska, making a quick reappearance over a more suitable trip, needed every yard of it and timed her run to perfection. (11/1: 8/1-12/1)
986 Tawafek (USA), made to work soon after entering the straight, has never tackled such a long trip before but, under a forceful ride, he nosed ahead in the shadow of the post before the winner nicked it off him right off the line. He is one of the worst movers in racing but he seemed to act on the ground. (11/4)
Winnebago was not afraid to force the pace at her first attempt at this extended trip, and her supporters must have been counting their money entering the final furlong. However, she had been out on her own for a long time, and her stamina gave out in the last hundred yards. She has still to win a race but, over a trip such as this, her turn cannot be far away. (20/1)
1481 Gumair (USA) had the misfortune of being a maiden carrying top weight in a handicap and, though he gave chase to the long-time leader, he was hard at work some way out and had soon met his match. (5/1)
1570 Batabanoo is getting no younger and he seems to have lost some of his pace, for though he was still staying on at the finish, he could never get within striking range of the principals. (9/2)
1560 Advance East, still struggling to win at this game, was returning to a longer trip, but he failed to stay in the past and twelve furlongs may be as far as he is likely to get. (11/1)

1796 SHERWOOD APPRENTICE LIMITED STKS (0-55) (3-Y.O+) (Class F)
5-00 (5-06) **1m 1f 213y** £2,277.00 (£627.00: £297.00) Stalls: Low GOING minus 0.32 sec per fur (GF)

				SP	RR	SF
1678^{8}	**Blockade (USA) (61)** (MBell) **8-9-2**(3) RMullen(7) (t: hld up in rr: hdwy over 2f out: led wl ins fnl f: comf)	—	**1**	$6/1^{3}$	61+	43

				SP	RR	SF
1632^{5}	**Renata's Prince (IRE) (50)** (KRBurke) **4-9-3** JDSmith(4) (hld up in tch: hdwy 3f out: led ins fnl f: sn hdd: no ex)	1½	**2**	9/2^{2}	57	39
1390^{7}	**Forest Fantasy (55)** (JWharton) **4-8-11**$^{(3)}$ RFfrench(9) (swtg: hld up: hdwy 5f out: led over 1f out tl ins fnl f)	1½	**3**	7/2^{1}	51	33
1568^{12}	**Bold Saint (IRE) (48)** (PWHarris) **3-7-13b^{1}**$^{(5)}$ CLowther(5) (led & sn clr: hdd over 1f out: kpt on u.p)	1¾	**4**	12/1	51	20
1118^{7}	**Monis (IRE) (35)** (RonaldThompson) **6-8-12**$^{(5)}$ GMilligan(1) (trckd ldrs: effrt & rdn 2f out: nt pce to chal)	2	**5**	25/1	48	30
1233^{14}	**Sheilas Dream (50)** (GLMoore) **4-9-0**$^{(5)ow5}$ MBatchelor(2) (bit bkwd: hld up: hdwy & swtchd rt over 3f out: rdn & one pce fnl 2f)	2½	**6**	16/1	46	23
1623^{6}	**Nicola's Princess (48)** (BAMcMahon) **4-8-7**$^{(7)}$ SRighton(6) (chsd ldrs: hrd drvn 2f out: wknd appr fnl f)	2	**7**	12/1	38	20
1384^{11}	**Welsh Mountain (52)** (MJHeaton-Ellis) **4-8-10**$^{(7)}$ JFowle(3) (lw: trckd ldrs: drvn along 3f out: no imp)	1¾	**8**	16/1	38	20
1501^{9}	**Persephone (22)** (JLHarris) **4-8-9b**$^{(5)}$ APolli(12) (chsd ldrs over 7f: sn wknd: t.o)	6	**9**	50/1	26	8
838^{18}	**Suleika Dancer (53)** (SGKnight) **4-9-0** DarrenMoffatt(10) (a in rr: t.o)	2	**10**	25/1	22	4
1441^{2}	**Acquittal (IRE) (41)** (AStreeter) **5-9-3v** RHavlin(11) (a in rr: t.o)	2½	**11**	7/1	21	3
1513*	**Coral Island (58)** (JGFitzGerald) **3-8-3**$^{(3)}$ GParkin(8) (lw: prom tl wknd over 4f out: t.o)	5	**12**	9/2^{2}	15	—
1433^{12}	**Four of Spades (50)** (RJHodges) **6-9-0**$^{(3)}$ AmandaSanders(13) (bkwd: hld up: a bhd: t.o)	4	**13**	20/1	7	—
	Happy Venturer (IRE) (30) (GFierro) **4-8-10**$^{(7)}$ DHayden(14) (Withdrawn not under Starter's orders: bolted bef s & uns rdr)		**W**	50/1	—	—

(SP 128.9%) **13 Rn**

2m 6.6 (4.10) CSF £30.89 TOTE £6.30: £2.50 £1.80 £1.40 (£35.60) Trio £35.20 OWNER Mr A. M. Warrender (NEWMARKET) BRED Patricia C. Warrender

WEIGHT FOR AGE 3yo-13lb

STEWARDS' ENQUIRY Righton susp. 20-21/6/97 (careless riding).

1503* Blockade (USA), suited by such a strongly-run race, adopted the tactics so successful at Yarmouth, and again won with the minimum of fuss. (6/1: op 7/2)

1632 Renata's Prince (IRE) did not stride to post with any freedom, but he was produced to win his race inside the last furlong, and was a shade unfortunate to meet the winner on one of his good days. (9/2)

1390 Forest Fantasy did her best to extend her advantage after leading into the final furlong, but the principals were in full stride by then, and had the legs of her in the dash to the line. (7/2)

Bold Saint (IRE) produced a much-improved performance in his first-time blinkers, but it is doubtful if he will stay much beyond a mile when running so freely and, if he does take a step down in distance, the hint should be taken. (12/1)

687 Monis (IRE) did not fare badly and, when he does return to sprinting, he has more than enough ability to find another opening. (25/1)

Sheilas Dream, still carrying surplus condition, made an effort early in the straight and she could be capable of picking up a small race. (16/1)

1093 Nicola's Princess (12/1: op 8/1)

1513* Coral Island ran very flat, and it is possible he had not fully recovered from the hard race he had when successful at Carlisle. (9/2: op 2/1)

T/Plpt: £49.10 (205.14 Tckts). T/Qdpt: £27.80 (17.35 Tckts) IM

1645-**PONTEFRACT** (L-H) (Good to firm)

Monday June 9th

WEATHER: sunny periods WIND: slt across

1797 JUNE MAIDEN AUCTION STKS (2-Y.O) (Class F)

2-45 (2-49) **5f** £2,682.00 (£752.00: £366.00) Stalls: Low GOING minus 0.31 sec per fur (GF)

				SP	RR	SF
1251^{2}	**Tamerin Bay** (RBoss) **2-8-3** GDuffield(14) (lw: trckd ldrs: led appr fnl f: r.o wl)	—	**1**	5/2^{1}	69	16
1577^{2}	**Tangerine Flyer** (JBerry) **2-8-3**$^{(5)}$ PRoberts(10) (lw: plld hrd: w ldr: effrt 2f out: nt qckn fnl f)	5	**2**	4/1^{2}	58	5
1616^{10}	**Snappy Times** (MDods) **2-8-8** AClark(12) (a chsng ldrs: outpcd 2f out: kpt on towards fin)	1	**3**	50/1	55	2
902^{9}	**Super Rascal** (NPLittmoden) **2-8-5** TGMcLaughlin(6) (prom: outpcd 2f out: kpt on ins fnl f)	s.h	**4**	50/1	52	—
1447^{3}	**Cumbrian Cadet** (TDEasterby) **2-8-8** JCarroll(4) (b.hind: lw: led tl hdd appr fnl f: sn btn)	hd	**5**	5/2^{1}	54	1
1492^{16}	**Velvet Story** (NTinkler) **2-8-8** KimTinkler(1) (outpcd & bhd tl styd on fnl 2f)	2½	**6**	33/1	46	—
	Celtic Comfort (PCHaslam) **2-8-3** LCharnock(3) (w'like: leggy: s.i.s: stdy hdwy over 1f out: nvr plcd to chal)	hd	**7**	33/1	41	—
	Heathyards Sheik (RHollinshead) **2-8-5** FLynch(2) (cmpt: s.i.s: hdwy over 1f out: nvr nr to chal)	¾	**8**	14/1^{3}	41	—
1498^{2}	**Eurofen** (PDEvans) **2-8-3v** JFEgan(11) (bolted gng to s: gd spd 4f)	½	**9**	25/1	37	—
1510^{11}	**Russian Romeo (IRE)** (BAMcMahon) **2-8-2**$^{(3)}$ PFessey(7) (outpcd fr ½-wy)	4	**10**	33/1	26	—
	Mystery Man (PCHaslam) **2-8-6**^{ow1} JFortune(15) (w'like: bkwd: dwlt: n.d)	s.h	**11**	25/1	27	—
	Tina Knows (IRE) (JLEyre) **2-7-12** TWilliams(8) (leggy: unf: mid div: effrt over 2f out: no imp)	½	**12**	16/1	17	—
1616^{4}	**Scotch Time** (RAFahey) **2-8-3b^{1}** FNorton(9) (wnt lft & bmpd s: swvd rt & outpcd)	¾	**13**	16/1	20	—
	Pitchmark (IRE) (EWeymes) **2-7-12** JQuinn(5) (leggy: unf: sn outpcd & bhd)	1	**14**	25/1	12	—
	Mariana (RMWhitaker) **2-8-0** DWright(13) (Withdrawn not under Starter's orders: ref to ent stalls)		**W**	16/1	—	—

(SP 125.7%) **14 Rn**

64.6 secs (2.90) CSF £9.99 TOTE £3.80: £1.60 £1.30 £14.80 (£3.30) Trio £310.60; £306.30 to Salisbury 10/6/97 OWNER Mr P. Asquith (NEWMARKET) BRED G. W. Hampson

1251 Tamerin Bay has certainly improved from his debut and won this in useful style. (5/2)

1577 Tangerine Flyer, a free-running sort, was restrained this time and then failed to pick up late on. On a sharper track he may be better if allowed to use his tremendous early pace. (4/1)

664 Snappy Times, after a poor effort last time, ran well and should stay further. (50/1)

Super Rascal ran a fair race and gave the impression that another furlong should suit. (50/1)

1447 Cumbrian Cadet looked the part but disappointed and, racing on the rail on this well watered ground, may have been at a disadvantage. (5/2)

Velvet Story is improving and should appreciate a bit further. (33/1)

Celtic Comfort had what can only be described as a pipe-opener, and showed plenty of promise. (33/1)

Heathyards Sheik needed this experience-wise and time should see some improvement. (14/1)

1616 Scotch Time, with blinkers on for the first time, took a strong hold going down, and absolutely no interest coming back. (16/1)

1798 DEWSBURY (S) STKS (3-Y.O+) (Class G)

3-15 (3-19) **1m 2f 6y** £2,406.00 (£666.00: £318.00) Stalls: Low GOING minus 0.31 sec per fur (GF)

				SP	RR	SF
1574^{5}	**Anchor Venture (52)** (SPCWoods) **4-9-4** WRyan(5) (lw: trckd ldrs: led over 2f out: rdn out)	—	**1**	3/1^{1}	51	45

				SP	RR	SF
1686^{5}	**Bold Top (40)** (BSRothwell) **5-9-4be** JFEgan(4) (a cl up: led 3f out: sn hdd & outpcd: kpt on wl towards fin)	nk	**2**	10/1	51	45
1603^{5}	**Diamond Crown (IRE) (42)** (MartynWane) **6-9-4** JCarroll(1) (swtg: hld up & bhd: swvd lft 3f out: hdwy 2f out: r.o towards fin)	4	**3**	$7/2^{2}$	44	38
1441^{5}	**River Run (IRE) (46)** (RHollinshead) **5-9-4** FLynch(6) (swtg: in tch: hdwy 4f out: sn chsng ldrs: one pce appr fnl f)	1	**4**	8/1	43	37
843^{9}	**She's Simply Great (IRE) (51)** (JJO'Neill) **4-8-13** RHughes(13) (hld up: n.m.r 3f out: styd on fnl 2f)	2½	**5**	$11/2^{3}$	34	28
1683^{14}	**Persian Sunset (IRE) (35)** (MissJBower) **5-8-10**(3) PFessey(12) (stdd s: hdwy 4f out: sn chsng ldrs: one pce appr fnl f)	1½	**6**	20/1	31	25
1449^{8}	**Digital Option (IRE) (47)** (MrsJRRamsden) **3-8-6**ow1 JFortune(9) (lw: bhd: hmpd 3f out: n.d)	5	**7**	13/2	29	9
1576^{4}	**That Old Feeling (IRE) (70)** (DWChapman) **5-9-4** ACulhane(8) (hld up: effrt over 3f out: rdn & btn 2f out)	1½	**8**	9/1	26	20
1570^{9}	**Paperwork Pete (IRE)** (WStorey) **5-9-4** SWhitworth(7) (hld up & bhd: n.m.r 2f out: nvr nr to chal)	1	**9**	100/1	24	18
	Showstopper (TJEtherington) **3-8-5** LCharnock(3) (leggy: unf: s.i.s: hdwy over 3f out: wknd wl over 1f out)	2½	**10**	25/1	20	1
1464^{6}	**Victory At Hart (43)** (DMorris) **3-8-5** PBloomfield(10) (in tch tl wandered & wknd 2f out)	½	**11**	25/1	19	—
1631^{14}	**Mustard (30)** (ABMulholland) **4-8-13** DWright(11) (led tl hdd & wknd 3f out)	19	**12**	16/1	—	—
1512^{10}	**Lake Aria** (MrsAMNaughton) **4-8-8**(5) JBramhill(2) (chsd ldrs tl wknd 4f out: hmpd 3f out)	16	**13**	100/1	—	—
1287^{7}	**Dino's Mistral (32)** (FHLee) **4-9-4b**1 JWeaver(14) (w ldrs tl wknd qckly 3f out)	3½	**14**	20/1	—	—

(SP 131.2%) **14 Rn**

2m 13.8 (4.20) CSF £31.92 TOTE £3.90: £1.60 £2.80 £1.90 (£15.40) Trio £16.00 OWNER Dr Frank Chao (NEWMARKET) BRED High Point B/stock Ltd & Chao Racing & B/stock Ltd
WEIGHT FOR AGE 3yo-13lb
Bt in 11,000 gns

1574 Anchor Venture, looking very fit, won his first race, but he was fast running out of fuel after looking well on top. (3/1: op 7/1)
1222 Bold Top has yet to win a race but, with a little further to go, he would have rectified that here. (10/1)
1603 Diamond Crown (IRE) is a funny customer who likes things to go just right, and tried to come from way behind. He met with trouble but finished fast to show he is in good form. (7/2)
1441 River Run (IRE) is running quite well at the moment, but just lacks any finishing kick. (8/1)
She's Simply Great (IRE) is difficult to weigh up, but she has ability and was making up a fair amount of ground when it was all too late. (11/2)
Persian Sunset (IRE), dropped out this time, showed a useful turn of foot half-a-mile from home but, once the race was seriously on, she proved disappointing. (20/1)
1576 That Old Feeling (IRE) (9/1: 6/1-10/1)

1799 TAVERN GROUP H'CAP (0-90) (3-Y.O+) (Class C)

3-45 (3-49) **6f** £7,895.00 (£2,360.00: £1,130.00: £515.00) Stalls: Low GOING minus 0.31 sec per fur (GF)

				SP	RR	SF
1561^{9}	**French Grit (IRE) (71)** (MDods) **5-8-9** AClark(6) (hld up & bhd: hdwy 2f out: led ins fnl f: r.o)	—	**1**	14/1	81	54
827^{7}	**Fairy Prince (IRE) (60)** (MrsALMKing) **4-7-5**(7)ow2 RWinston(10) (a chsng ldrs: led ins fnl f: sn hdd: kpt on)	1	**2**	25/1	67	38
1594^{3}	**So Intrepid (IRE) (75)** (JMBradley) **7-8-13** JWeaver(11) (swtg: hld up & bhd: hdwy over 1f out: r.o wl)	hd	**3**	9/1	82	55
1662*	**Ziggy's Dancer (USA) (87)** (EJAlston) **6-9-11** 6x ACulhane(7) (lw: hld up: effrt over 2f out: kpt on: nt pce to chal)	2	**4**	11/1	89	62
1402^{4}	**First Maite (79)** (SRBowring) **4-9-3b** SWebster(5) (lw: a chsng ldrs: effrt 2f out: r.o one pce ins fnl f)	½	**5**	11/1	79	52
1020*	**Fame Again (65)** (MrsJRRamsden) **5-8-3** FLynch(3) (lw: hld up & bhd: hdwy on ins 2f out: nvr able to chal)	¾	**6**	$9/4^{1}$	63	36
1578^{2}	**Cim Bom Bom (IRE) (73)** (MBell) **5-8-11v** JFortune(14) (led tl hdd ins fnl f: no ex)	s.h	**7**	11/1	71	44
863^{13}	**Bollin Harry (70)** (TDEasterby) **5-8-8** JCarroll(1) (lw: chsd ldrs: effrt 2f out: btn whn n.m.r 2f out)	3½	**8**	$5/1^{2}$	59	32
1471^{5}	**Spotted Eagle (70)** (MartynWane) **4-8-5**(3) PFessey(4) (hld up: n.d)	2½	**9**	50/1	52	25
677^{12}	**Saseedo (USA) (90)** (WAO'Gorman) **7-10-0** EmmaO'Gorman(2) (s.i.s: nvr rchd ldrs)	hd	**10**	25/1	72	45
1291^{8}	**Awesome Venture (58)** (MCChapman) **7-7-10** DeclanO'Shea(13) (cl up tl wknd appr fnl f)	2	**11**	100/1	35	8
1254^{2}	**Swino (88)** (PDEvans) **3-9-4** JFEgan(9) (lw: in tch tl wknd over 2f out)	nk	**12**	12/1	64	29
1446^{5}	**Bowlers Boy (64)** (JJQuinn) **4-8-2** JQuinn(12) (hld up: effrt 2f out: sn rdn & btn)	3½	**13**	$6/1^{3}$	31	4
1259^{10}	**Mallia (80)** (TDBarron) **4-9-4** LCharnock(8) (swtg: prom 4f: sddle slipped & eased)	30	**14**	16/1	—	—

(SP 127.6%) **14 Rn**

1m 16.1 (1.10) CSF £311.40 CT £3,031.42 TOTE £18.20: £5.20 £6.70 £3.40 (£241.00) Trio £586.90 OWNER Mr Michael Wilson (DARLINGTON) BRED Miss Aisling O'Connell
LONG HANDICAP Awesome Venture 7-2
WEIGHT FOR AGE 3yo-8lb
OFFICIAL EXPLANATION **Bowlers Boy: ran too freely early on and had no more to give in the closing stages. Mallia: reported that the saddle had slipped during the race. French Grit (IRE): regarding the improvement in form, the trainer reported that the gelding had pulled very hard previously at Ayr, and was fitted with a cross noseband for today's race.**

596* French Grit (IRE), happier in this stronger-run event, was wearing a cross-noseband and, getting everything right, won well. (14/1)
Fairy Prince (IRE), after over six weeks off, came back in top form and deserves to find a race. (25/1)
1594 So Intrepid (IRE) is off a reasonable mark and is obviously in good form, but his effort was just too late on this occasion. (9/1)
1662* Ziggy's Dancer (USA) has not won over this trip for some time, but he seemed to get it well enough. (11/1)
1402 First Maite had his chances throughout, but was short of a change of gear in the closing stages. He appears to have run up to his form. (11/1)
1020* Fame Again, racing up the inner on what may well have been slightly slower ground, never got in a blow and is worth another chance. (9/4)
1578 Cim Bom Bom (IRE) showed tremendous early pace from his outside draw, and this All-Weather specialist is obviously in good heart. (11/1)
596 Bollin Harry was wearing a tongue-strap and never really fired. (5/1)

1800 BOROUGH H'CAP (0-70) (3-Y.O+) (Class E)

4-15 (4-16) **1m 4y** £3,353.00 (£1,004.00: £482.00: £221.00) Stalls: Low GOING minus 0.31 sec per fur (GF)

				SP	RR	SF
1560^{3}	**Bowcliffe (46)** (EJAlston) **6-8-5** JFEgan(16) (lw: hld up & bhd: gd hdwy on outside 2f out: led 1f out: r.o u.p)	—	**1**	$9/1^{3}$	60	35
1631^{3}	**Pleasure Trick (USA) (37)** (DonEnricoIncisa) **6-7-10** KimTinkler(15) (hld up & bhd: gd hdwy on outside over 1f out: r.o towards fin)	nk	**2**	$8/1^{2}$	50	25
1603^{4}	**Kass Alhawa (54)** (DWChapman) **4-8-13** ACulhane(6) (hld up: nt clr run 2f out tl ins fnl f: r.o)	3	**3**	11/1	61	36
1603^{3}	**Dictation (USA) (55)** (JJO'Neill) **5-9-0v**1 RHughes(5) (hld up: stdy hdwy 2f out: rdn & no ex appr fnl f)	3	**4**	10/1	56	31
1463^{9}	**Absolutely Fayre (60)** (VSoane) **6-9-5** GHind(13) (dwlt: hdwy over 2f out: styd on towards fin)	2	**5**	25/1	57	32
1583^{7}	**Forest Robin (65)** (MrsJRRamsden) **4-9-10** JFortune(11) (hld up: hdwy on ins 3f out: rdn & no imp)	s.h	**6**	$4/1^{1}$	62	37

1395^{6} **Oneoftheoldones (39)** (JNorton) **5-7-12** JQuinn(14) (prom: effrt 3f out: one pce) s.h **7** 20/1 36 11
1495^{5} **Gilling Dancer (IRE) (52)** (PCalver) **4-8-11** JCarroll(3) (swtg: hdwy to ld after 1½f: hdd 1f out: sn btn) s.h **8** 12/1 49 24
1513^{4} **Rude Awakening (68)** (CWFairhurst) **3-8-9**$^{(7)}$ TSiddall(9) (lw: hld up: effrt 3f out: n.d after) 2 **9** 12/1 61 25
1631^{6} **Paint It Black (56)** (DNicholls) **4-9-1** AlexGreaves(2) (trckd ldrs tl rdn & wknd 2f out) hd **10** 9/1^{3} 49 24
1472^{3} **Habeta (USA) (37)** (JWWatts) **11-7-10** JLowe(1) (prom tl outpcd & hmpd 3f out: n.d after) ½ **11** 9/1^{3} 29 4
575^{11} **Mutahadeth (62)** (DShaw) **3-8-10** JFanning(8) (b.hind: rr div: rdn 3f out: n.m.r & n.d) hd **12** 14/1 54 18
925^{9} **Generous Present (50)** (JWPayne) **4-8-9** WRyan(7) (chsd ldrs tl wknd fnl 2½f) s.h **13** 12/1 42 17
1560^{13} **King Chestnut (46)** (MDods) **6-8-5** FLynch(10) (s.i.s: n.d) ½ **14** 50/1 37 12
1603* **Power Game (57)** (JBerry) **4-9-2b** SWhitworth(12) (rn wd bnd after 1f: lost tch fnl 3f) ¾ **15** 8/1^{2} 46 21
1436^{6} **Attarikh (IRE) (62)** (MrsALMKing) **4-9-0b**$^{1(7)}$ RWinston(4) (plld hrd: led 1½f: cl up tl wknd over 2f out) 5 **16** 16/1 41 16
(SP 135.8%) **16 Rn**

1m 45.5 (3.10) CSF £79.02 CT £791.18 TOTE £9.00: £1.80 £2.30 £5.10 £2.30 (£46.60) Trio £276.20 OWNER Mr Philip Davies (PRESTON) BRED Lady Matthews
LONG HANDICAP Pleasure Trick (USA) 7-6
WEIGHT FOR AGE 3yo-11lb
1560 Bowcliffe, given a fine ride, got it right this time and the line came just soon enough. (9/1)
1631 Pleasure Trick (USA) did his usual and, like the winner, tried to come from way behind but, in his case, the effort was always a couple of strides too late. (8/1)
1603 Kass Alhawa needs holding up, but met with traffic problems and, despite finishing fast, the effort was always too late. He is obviously extremely well at present. (11/1: 8/1-12/1)
1603 Dictation (USA) had a visor on for the first time and travelled well, but his response when ridden left a little to be desired. (10/1)
Absolutely Fayre finished quite well giving the impression that longer trips should help. (25/1)
1583 Forest Robin did all his racing up the inside on probably slower ground and never got in a blow. (4/1)
1603* Power Game (8/1: 6/1-9/1)

1801 YOUNGSTERS NOVICE STKS (2-Y.O) (Class D)
4-45 (4-45) **6f** £3,243.00 (£918.00: £449.00) Stalls: Low GOING minus 0.31 sec per fur (GF)

SP RR SF
1557^{4} **Aberkeen** (MDods) **2-8-12** DaleGibson(4) (set slow pce tl qcknd over 2f out: r.o wl) — **1** 11/10^{1} 57 —
Panama House (TDEasterby) **2-8-12** LCharnock(1) (w'like: leggy: scope: plld hrd: trckd ldrs: effrt 2f out: kpt on) 1¾ **2** 4/1^{3} 52 —
Captain McCloy (USA) (MrsJRRamsden) **2-8-12** JFortune(3) (w'like: scope: s.s: sn rcvrd & cl up: rdn 2f out: nt qckn fnl f) nk **3** 13/8^{2} 52 —
(SP 105.7%) **3 Rn**

1m 20.8 (5.80) CSF £4.51 TOTE £2.50 (£2.30) OWNER Mr N. A. Riddell (DARLINGTON) BRED Mrs Wendy Jacqueline Muir
1557 Aberkeen made his experience tell and, always in command in what turned out to be a two-and-a-half furlong sprint, found all that was necessary. (11/10)
Panama House was wearing a tongue-strap on his debut, looked likely to benefit from this and ran reasonably, but it was a very messy event. (4/1: op 9/4)
Captain McCloy (USA), a fair sort, was clueless at the start but, because there was no pace on, he soon recovered, but was then tapped for foot in the final sprint. (13/8: evens-7/4)

1802 PONTEFRACT SERIES (ROUND 2) APPRENTICE H'CAP (0-70) (3-Y.O+) (Class F)
5-15 (5-15) **1m 2f 6y** £2,412.00 (£682.00: £336.00) Stalls: Low GOING minus 0.31 sec per fur (GF)

SP RR SF
1268^{6} **Marsh Marigold (57)** (JHetherton) **3-7-11**$^{(5)}$ JennyBenson(8) (dwlt: bhd tl hdwy over 2f out: led ins fnl f: r.o wl) — **1** 9/1 71 33
1472^{10} **Bedazzle (38)** (MBrittain) **6-7-5**$^{(5)}$ DMernagh(3) (hdwy 7f out: sn in tch: kpt on u.p fnl f: no ch w wnr) 5 **2** 16/1 44 19
1631^{13} **Tinklers Folly (57)** (RMWhitaker) **5-8-10**$^{(5)}$ PFredericks(7) (in tch: hdwy to ld 3f out: hdd ins fnl f: kpt on one pce) s.h **3** 33/1 63 38
1145^{10} **Duraid (IRE) (65)** (DenysSmith) **5-9-6**$^{(3)}$ DMcGaffin(9) (lw: trckd ldrs: ev ch 2f out: rdn & no ex appr fnl f) 2½ **4** 9/2^{3} 67 42
1086^{6} **Bubble Wings (FR) (70)** (SPCWoods) **5-10-0** CWebb(1) (bhd: effrt & nt clr run 2f out: hung lft & styd on: n.d) 4 **5** 11/4^{1} 66 41
1268^{8} **In Good Faith (52)** (JJQuinn) **5-8-10** RWinston(5) (lw: hld up: effrt 3f out: rdn & sn btn) 2 **6** 15/2 44 19
1463^{2} **Sandmoor Denim (50)** (SRBowring) **10-8-8** PDoe(6) (lw: in tch tl outpcd fnl 3f) 4 **7** 4/1^{2} 36 11
1424^{10} **Whothehellisharry (41)** (PTDalton) **4-7-8**$^{(5)}$ RBrisland(4) (outpcd over 4f out: sn btn) 4 **8** 16/1 21 —
1576^{2} **Eastleigh (38)** (RHollinshead) **8-7-3**$^{(7)}$ PMQuinn(10) (b.nr hind: set str pce tl hdd & wknd qckly 3f out) 5 **9** 10/1 10 —
1574^{8} **Cascatelle Bleue (IRE) (55)** (MHTompkins) **4-8-8**$^{(5)}$ PClarke(2) (chsd ldrs tl wknd fnl 3f) 6 **10** 16/1 17 —
(SP 116.3%) **10 Rn**

2m 13.5 (3.90) CSF £128.93 CT £4,060.67 TOTE £15.10: £3.10 £3.40 £4.70 (£46.30) Trio £203.70 OWNER Mrs Barbara Sadler (MALTON) BRED R. M. West
LONG HANDICAP Eastleigh 7-5 Bedazzle 7-7
WEIGHT FOR AGE 3yo-13lb
1268 Marsh Marigold, well suited by the very strong pace, came from way behind to win going right away. (9/1: op 5/1)
848 Bedazzle ran a sound race and kept struggling on, but lacks any real turn of foot. (16/1)
Tinklers Folly put in a reasonable performance, but all his wins have been over shorter trips and he looks worth keeping an eye on. (33/1)
686 Duraid (IRE) travelled particularly well, but disappointed when let down. His stable is bang out of form. (9/2)
1086 Bubble Wings (FR) does not look an easy ride and, trying to come from behind, found trouble, tended to hang and never got anywhere near. (11/4: 3/1-2/1)
36 In Good Faith has more ability but was not in a co-operative mood. (15/2: 5/1-8/1)
1576 Eastleigh (10/1: op 6/1)

T/Jkpt: Not won; £18,093.28 to Salisbury 10/6/97. T/Plpt: £1,397.40 (14.2 Tckts). T/Qdpt: £185.80 (4.68 Tckts) AA

1675-WARWICK (L-H) (Good to firm, Firm patches)
Monday June 9th
WEATHER: fine but cloudy WIND: nil

1803 GALLOWS HILL APPRENTICE H'CAP (0-70) (3-Y.O+) (Class E)
6-15 (6-15) **1m 2f 169y** £2,966.25 (£885.00: £422.50: £191.25) Stalls: Low GOING minus 0.39 sec per fur (F)

Form	Horse / details	Dist	Pos	SP	RR	SF
1665^{10}	**Kirov Protege (IRE) (33)** (MrsLCJewell) **5-7-3**(7) DarrenWilliams(1) (a.p: led ins fnl f: r.o)	—	1	33/1	46	17
	Hay Dance (44) (PJHobbs) **6-8-0**(7) RCody-Boutcher(2) (lw: tk keen hold: hdwy 2f out: r.o wl ins fnl f)	nk	2	11/4^{1}	57	28
1384^{10}	**Mazilla (50)** (AStreeter) **5-8-10v**(3) JBramhill(6) (lw: plld hrd: a.p: led over 2f out tl ins fnl f)	1¼	3	4/1^{3}	61	32
1491^{6}	**Tonka (63)** (PJMakin) **5-9-9**(3) DSweeney(5) (tk keen hold in rr: hdwy fnl f: r.o)	3½	4	3/1^{2}	69	40
1431^{3}	**Hill Farm Dancer (53)** (WMBrisbourne) **6-8-11**(5) AnthonyBond(4) (s.s: hdwy 3f out: one pce fnl 2f)	1¼	5	13/2	57	28
1233^{7}	**Printers Quill (48)** (MajorDNChappell) **5-8-8**(3) ADaly(9) (bhd fnl 3f)	6	6	13/2	43	14
	Laazim Afooz (65) (RTPhillips) **4-9-9**(5) AimeeCook(3) (bkwd: plld hrd: led tl hdd over 2f out: sn wknd)	1½	7	10/1	58	29
1624^{4}	**Gold Clipper (47)** (MJRyan) **3-7-10** MBaird(8) (lw: s.s: gd hdwy 6f out: wknd wl over 1f out)	½	8	14/1	39	—
	Asking (33) (JABennett) **5-7-5**(5) IonaWands(7) (b: bkwd: prom tl wknd 3f out)	5	9	50/1	17	—

(SP 119.0%) **9 Rn**

2m 18.4 (4.40) CSF £115.00 CT £424.32 TOTE £81.00: £9.40 £1.40 £1.50 (£36.90) Trio £98.50; £56.89 to 11/6/97 OWNER Mr Richard Dean (SUTTON VALENCE) BRED Irish National Stud Co Ltd
LONG HANDICAP Kirov Protege (IRE) 7-1 Gold Clipper 6-7 Asking 7-7
WEIGHT FOR AGE 3yo-14lb
1507 Kirov Protege (IRE), who has been struggling to find a trip, gave his rider his first winner and his trainer her first success on the Flat. (33/1)
Hay Dance, four times a winner over hurdles last season, may have preferred a stronger-run race. (11/4)
Mazilla, 2lb lower than when completing a hat-trick last August, was very keen in the refitted visor in a moderately-run race. (4/1)
1491 Tonka, again 5lb higher than when winning at Nottingham, did not find the leaders coming back to him because of the lack of early pace. (3/1)
1431 Hill Farm Dancer is not taking advantage of being given a chance by the Handicapper on the turf. (13/2)
Laazim Afooz (10/1: 8/1-12/1)

1804 HAZY DAYS MEDIAN AUCTION MAIDEN STKS (3-Y.O) (Class E)
6-45 (6-46) **1m 2f 169y** £2,992.25 (£893.00: £426.50: £193.25) Stalls: Low GOING minus 0.39 sec per fur (F)

Form	Horse / details	Dist	Pos	SP	RR	SF
1144^{3}	**In Question (83)** (BWHills) **3-9-0** MHills(1) (lw: mde all: rdn clr over 1f out: easily)	—	1	1/2^{1}	79+	43
1477^{9}	**Expialiodoocius** (JRFanshawe) **3-9-0** KFallon(2) (a.p: chsd wnr 3f out: one pce fnl 2f)	6	2	12/1	70	34
1384^{15}	**The Roundsills (54)** (RFJohnsonHoughton) **3-9-0** JReid(7) (prom tl wknd over 2f out)	6	3	25/1	61	25
	Frankie (MHTompkins) **3-9-0** DBiggs(5) (s.i.s: sme hdwy over 2f out: n.d)	nk	4	12/1	61	25
1477^{8}	**Pardan** (BPalling) **3-9-0** TSprake(6) (plld hrd: chsd wnr over 7f: sn wknd)	12	5	8/1^{3}	43	7
	Handley Cross (USA) (IABalding) **3-9-0** SWhitworth(4) (hld up: rdn & hdwy over 3f out: wknd over 2f out)	1¾	6	6/1^{2}	40	4
1499^{10}	**Caribbee Beach (IRE)** (GGMargarson) **3-8-2**(7) JGotobed(3) (plld hrd: dropped rr over 6f out: sn t.o)	dist	7	50/1	—	—

(SP 113.3%) **7 Rn**

2m 17.2 (3.20) CSF £7.14 TOTE £1.40: £1.10 £3.20 (£2.80) OWNER Mr K. Abdulla (LAMBOURN) BRED Juddmonte Farms
1144 In Question made the most of a golden opportunity. (1/2)
Expialiodoocius had finished ten lengths behind the winner on soft ground on his debut. (12/1: 8/1-14/1)
The Roundsills is over two stone inferior to the winner on official ratings. (25/1)
Pardan (8/1: tchd 12/1)

1805 SCOTTISH EQUITABLE/JOCKEYS ASSOCIATION H'CAP (0-80) (3-Y.O+) (Class D)
7-15 (7-16) **1m 4f 115y** £3,518.20 (£1,048.60: £499.80: £225.40) Stalls: Low GOING minus 0.39 sec per fur (F)

Form	Horse / details	Dist	Pos	SP	RR	SF
1592^{9}	**Galapino (59)** (MissGayKelleway) **4-8-9**(5) RMullen(6) (led over 3f: hrd rdn to ld wl over 1f out: drvn out)	—	1	5/1^{2}	64	44
1588^{6}	**Pay Homage (63)** (IABalding) **9-9-4** MHills(8) (lw: hld up: stdy hdwy over 4f out: hrd rdn & r.o wl ins fnl f)	hd	2	8/1	68	48
1491^{3}	**Reaganesque (USA) (50)** (PGMurphy) **5-8-5** KDarley(10) (a.p: led 5f out tl wl over 1f out: nt qckn fnl f)	nk	3	5/2^{1}	55	35
1372^{2}	**Foreign Rule (IRE) (72)** (PWChapple-Hyam) **3-8-10** JReid(4) (hld up: rdn over 6f out: styd on fnl f)	1¾	4	6/1^{3}	74	37
1387^{6}	**Tasik Chini (USA) (70)** (PFICole) **3-8-8** GHind(7) (w ldr: led 9f out to 5f out: one pce fnl 2f)	nk	5	10/1	72	35
1478^{4}	**Casual Water (IRE) (73)** (AGNewcombe) **6-10-0** JQuinn(1) (lw: nvr trbld ldrs)	2	6	13/2	72	52
1478^{11}	**Serious Trust (60)** (MrsLCJewell) **4-9-1** RHughes(5) (bhd fnl 2f)	6	7	12/1	52	32
1478^{10}	**Haroldon (IRE) (70)** (BPalling) **8-9-11** TSprake(3) (b: a bhd)	1	8	25/1	60	40
1169^{3}	**Atlantic Mist (57)** (BRMillman) **4-8-12** KFallon(9) (hld up: hdwy 8f out: hrd rdn over 2f out: wknd wl over 1f out)	3	9	8/1	44	24

(SP 115.7%) **9 Rn**

2m 41.1 (3.60) CSF £40.56 CT £111.83 TOTE £4.60: £1.50 £1.90 £1.10 (£31.10) Trio £26.00 OWNER Mr Nigel Dearman (WHITCOMBE) BRED Dayspring Co Ltd
WEIGHT FOR AGE 3yo-17lb
1036 Galapino bounced back to form off a 2lb lower mark following a disappointing effort last time. (5/1)
1588 Pay Homage, 18lb lower than when last scoring in May 1995, is usually apprentice ridden and also benefited from a longer trip. (8/1)
1491 Reaganesque (USA), 1lb lower than his last win, seems most effective when able to make all. (5/2)
1372 Foreign Rule (IRE) gave the impression he needs an even stiffer test of stamina. (6/1)
1387 Tasik Chini (USA), on the same mark as when winning at Folkestone, was back to a mile-and-a-half. (10/1)
1478 Casual Water (IRE), up 2lb, was 3lb higher than when narrowly winning at Goodwood last August. (13/2)

1806 E.B.F. ROYAL MAIDEN STKS (2-Y.O F) (Class D)
7-45 (7-47) **5f** £3,315.55 (£990.40: £473.70: £215.35) Stalls: Low GOING minus 0.39 sec per fur (F)

Form	Horse / details	Dist	Pos	SP	RR	SF
536^{2}	**Mugello** (APJarvis) **2-8-11** MHills(2) (mde all: rdn clr over 1f out: easily)	—	1	7/2^{1}	77+	53
	Eleonora d'Arborea (BJMeehan) **2-8-11** KDarley(1) (w'like: s.i.s: sn rcvrd: chsd wnr fnl f: no imp)	4	2	7/2^{1}	64	40
1457^{4}	**Really Done It Now (IRE)** (KRBurke) **2-8-11** PaulEddery(7) (chsd wnr: one pce fnl 2f)	3	3	10/1	55	31
1306^{4}	**Be My Wish** (MissGayKelleway) **2-8-11** KFallon(9) (a.p: one pce fnl 2f)	3	4	4/1^{2}	45	21

				SP	RR	SF
1593^{6}	**Mari-Ela (IRE)** (JRArnold) **2-8-11** JQuinn(5) (prom over 2f)	1¼	**5**	16/1	41	17
	Baby's Tiara (IRE) (RAkehurst) **2-8-11** JReid(8) (lt-f: wnt rt s: sme hdwy 2f out: n.d)	hd	**6**	10/1	41	17
1564^{5}	**Cherished (IRE)** (PFICole) **2-8-11** RHughes(4) (nvr nr to chal)	nk	**7**	$5/1^{3}$	40	16
	High Carry (JEBanks) **2-8-11** JStack(10) (w'like: scope: outpcd)	¾	**8**	25/1	37	13
1293^{5}	**Allasella (IRE)** (BPalling) **2-8-11** TSprake(6) (spd over 2f)	½	**9**	10/1	36	12
	Flying Singer (IABalding) **2-8-11** SWhitworth(11) (leggy: lw: outpcd)	1¾	**10**	14/1	30	6
1457^{10}	**Isabella** (TKeddy) **2-8-11** MFenton(3) (prom tl wknd qckly 2f out)	7	**11**	33/1	8	—
				(SP 127.7%)	**11 Rn**	

58.5 secs (0.20 under 2y best) (0.50) CSF £15.63 TOTE £4.00: £1.60 £1.70 £2.50 (£17.10) Trio £36.40 OWNER Mrs A. Jarvis (ASTON UPTHORPE) BRED G. Dudfield

536 Mugello broke the juvenile course record, and her trainer is thinking of a possible tilt at the Queen Mary. (7/2)

Eleonora d'Arborea, a sister to Ortolan and half-sister to Red Embers, was well supported in the ring. Catching a tartar in the winner, there will be other days for her. (7/2)

1457 Really Done It Now (IRE) was not disgraced in a hot race. (10/1)

1306 Be My Wish again showed plenty of speed. (4/1)

1593 Mari-Ela (IRE) may need a stiffer test of stamina. (16/1)

Baby's Tiara (IRE), a 60,000 guineas half-sister to several winners in the States, should be better for the experience. (10/1)

Flying Singer (14/1: op 8/1)

1807 RAINBOW CLAIMING STKS (3-Y.O) (Class F)

8-15 (8-18) **7f** £2,808.30 (£778.80: £372.90) Stalls: Low GOING minus 0.39 sec per fur (F)

				SP	RR	SF
1375^{8}	**Eager To Please (60)** (MissGayKelleway) **3-9-3** KFallon(14) (b.hind: lw: mde all: wnt lft after s: hrd rdn over 1f out: all out)	—	**1**	8/1	65	37
1448^{3}	**Impala (52)** (WGMTurner) **3-8-8**$^{(5)}$ DSweeney(5) (a.p: ev ch fnl f: r.o)	nk	**2**	10/1	60	32
1464^{3}	**Soura (USA) (55)** (PAKelleway) **3-8-7**^{ow1} JReid(10) (lw: sltly hmpd after s: a.p: ev ch over 1f out: nt qckn ins fnl f)	nk	**3**	$7/1^{3}$	54	25
1633^{11}	**Feel A Line (50)** (BJMeehan) **3-8-5b** PaulEddery(4) (hld up: hdwy on ins 3f out: hrd rdn & r.o ins fnl f)	½	**4**	10/1	51	23
1464^{5}	**Hint of Victory (57)** (MBell) **3-9-1** MFenton(9) (lw: chsd ldrs: rdn over 2f out: wknd fnl f)	3	**5**	14/1	54	26
	Phylida (63) (PJMakin) **3-8-3**$^{(3)}$ RHavlin(6) (s.s: hdwy over 3f out: rdn over 2f out: wknd over 1f out)	1¾	**6**	8/1	41	13
1573*	**Docklands Carriage (IRE) (63)** (NTinkler) **3-8-13b** KDarley(3) (lw: chsd ldrs: hrd rdn over 2f out: no hdwy)	½	**7**	$3/1^{1}$	47	19
	Inkwell (AHide) **3-8-7** AMcGlone(7) (hdwy over 3f out: wknd wl over 1f out)	½	**8**	25/1	39	11
1000^{14}	**The Wyandotte Inn (68)** (RHollinshead) **3-8-13** FLynch(8) (a bhd)	2	**9**	$5/1^{2}$	41	13
	Court House (67) (BAMcMahon) **3-8-9** LNewton(12) (a bhd)	½	**10**	8/1	36	8
	Rambo Tango (BRCambidge) **3-8-12** SWhitworth(13) (swtg: bkwd: hld up: a bhd)	2	**11**	66/1	34	6
1247^{8}	**Owdy (24)** (MrsNMacauley) **3-8-2b**$^{(5)}$ AimeeCook(1) (lw: s.s: a bhd)	hd	**12**	66/1	29	1
546^{8}	**Carrie's Fantasy** (AGNewcombe) **3-7-10** JLowe(11) (b.hind: a bhd: t.o)	16	**13**	50/1	—	—
				(SP 121.1%)	**13 Rn**	

1m 27.3 (2.70) CSF £77.52 TOTE £8.10: £2.40 £3.30 £2.30 (£51.90) Trio £97.10 OWNER Miss Jo Crowley (WHITCOMBE) BRED Mrs Sara Hood

1238 Eager To Please survived a Stewards' Enquiry after having quickly come across from his outside draw. He saw the trip out really well, having dropped back to five last time. (8/1)

1448 Impala seemed to settle better having been beaten in a seller last time. (10/1)

1464 Soura (USA) was forced to check briefly when the winner cut across, but it is doubtful if that or 1lb overweight made the difference. (7/1)

1333 Feel A Line, blinkered for his last two outings, appreciated this drop in class but needs to return to a mile. (10/1)

1464 Hint of Victory had finished four-and-a-half lengths behind Soura on identical terms over a mile last time. (14/1)

Phylida seems better on grass than on sand. (8/1)

1808 'NURSERY WOOD' H'CAP (0-70) (3-Y.O+) (Class E)

8-45 (8-46) **2m 20y** £2,940.25 (£877.00: £418.50: £189.25) Stalls: Low GOING minus 0.39 sec per fur (F)

				SP	RR	SF
1424^{5}	**Badawi (FR) (37)** (NMBabbage) **7-7-10** FNorton(1) (mde all: rdn over 1f out: r.o wl)	—	**1**	$9/4^{1}$	45	17
1565^{2}	**Nile Valley (IRE) (64)** (PWChapple-Hyam) **3-7-11**$^{(5)}$ RFfrench(2) (a.p: wnt 2nd 3f out: rdn 2f out: r.o one pce)	1½	**2**	$5/2^{2}$	71	22
1654^{2}	**Romalito (42)** (MBlanshard) **7-8-1** JQuinn(7) (hld up: stdy hdwy 8f out: chsd wnr 4f out to 3f out: sn rdn: one pce)	1	**3**	$9/4^{1}$	48	20
1413^{6}	**Fieldridge (65)** (MPMuggeridge) **8-9-10** JReid(3) (hld up: wknd 3f out)	9	**4**	$6/1^{3}$	62	34
	China Mail (IRE) (45) (JABennett) **5-8-4** TSprake(4) (hld up: rdn over 6f out: a bhd)	1¾	**5**	50/1	40	12
	Jenzsoph (IRE) (44) (PJHobbs) **6-7-10b**$^{(7)ow7}$ RCody-Boutcher(5) (chsd wnr 12f: sn wknd: t.o)	13	**6**	7/1	26	—
				(SP 118.9%)	**6 Rn**	

3m 32.5 (7.00) CSF £8.13 TOTE £3.70: £2.30 £1.90 (£4.40) OWNER Mr Gareth Gregory (CHELTENHAM) BRED Buckram Oak Holdings

LONG HANDICAP Jenzsoph (IRE) 7-3

WEIGHT FOR AGE 3yo-21lb

1424 Badawi (FR) was 5lb better off then when finishing less than four lengths behind Romalito here last month. (9/4)

1565 Nile Valley (IRE) was 1lb lower than when second last time. (5/2)

1654 Romalito could not confirm last month's form with the winner on 5lb better terms. (9/4)

1114 Fieldridge, down 5lb this season, got left for dead on the home turn. (6/1: 8/1-5/1)

Jenzsoph (IRE) (7/1: op 4/1)

T/Plpt: £120.20 (115.14 Tckts). T/Qdpt: £69.90 (12.96 Tckts) KH

1632-WINDSOR (Fig. 8) (Good to firm)
Monday June 9th

All races hand timed

WEATHER: sunny WIND: almost nil

1809 ARISTON DIALOGIC CLAIMING STKS (3-Y.O+) (Class F)

6-30 (6-34) **1m 3f 135y** £2,612.00 (£732.00: £356.00) Stalls: High GOING minus 0.29 sec per fur (GF)

				SP	RR	SF
	Blush (MCPipe) **3-7-11**(3) MartinDwyer(12) (stdd s: hdwy 3f out: led over 1f out: drvn out)	—	**1**	9/2[2]	56	27
1473[7]	**Statajack (IRE) (73)** (DRCElsworth) **9-9-9b** RCochrane(10) (b: stdy hdwy 4f out: ev ch 1f out: hrd rdn: nt qckn)	1¾	**2**	100/30[1]	62	48
1686[4]	**At Liberty (IRE) (67)** (RHannon) **5-9-12b[1]** DaneO'Neill(14) (hdwy & hrd rdn over 2f out: styd on: nt rch 1st 2)	1¾	**3**	6/1	62	48
1642[8]	**Shabanaz (55)** (WRMuir) **12-9-3** PatEddery(17) (rdn 6f out: hdwy fnl 2f: nvr nrr)	2	**4**	5/1[3]	50	36
1574[4]	**Le Grand Gousier (USA) (56)** (RJRWilliams) **3-8-10** GDuffield(3) (a.p: ev ch 2f out: one pce)	s.h	**5**	10/1	58	29
250[4]	**Dark Age (IRE)** (RAkehurst) **4-9-7**(7) DDenby(1) (a.p: led over 3f out: hdd & wknd over 1f out)	¾	**6**	20/1	60	46
340[7]	**Persian Butterfly (50)** (RMStronge) **5-9-2** DRMcCabe(15) (nvr trbld ldrs)	1¼	**7**	33/1	47	33
	Stockbrook (KRBurke) **4-9-7** BDoyle(5) (nvr nr to chal)	13	**8**	25/1	34	20
	Lost Lagoon (USA) (73) (PEccles) **5-9-6** CRutter(16) (dwlt: sn prom: ev ch 3f out: wknd 2f out)	s.h	**9**	7/1	33	19
277[4]	**Buzzby Babe (34)** (AGFoster) **3-7-10** NAdams(4) (nvr trbld ldrs)	3½	**10**	20/1	19	—
1139[14]	**Challenger (IRE) (36)** (JJSheehan) **4-9-3** NCarlisle(2) (lw: hdwy & hrd rdn over 3f out: sn wknd)	½	**11**	50/1	24	10
1229[9]	**On The Wildside (40)** (MRChannon) **4-8-12** RPerham(8) (plld hrd: prom tl wknd 3f out)	14	**12**	33/1	—	—
1133[11]	**Precedency (46)** (KMcAuliffe) **5-9-2v** MRoberts(6) (b: led 5f: rn wd 5f out: wknd 3f out)	2½	**13**	25/1	—	—
	Brume La Voile (JGSmyth-Osbourne) **4-9-9** DHarrison(18) (a bhd)	7	**14**	50/1	—	—
	Tedross (JRPoulton) **6-9-5**(3) AWhelan(7) (2nd tl led over 6f out: hdd & wknd qckly over 3f out)		**15**	50/1	—	—
1142[10]	**Just Flamenco (38)** (MJRyan) **6-9-2** GCarter(13) (a bhd)		**16**	33/1	—	—
	Yo-Mate (26) (THind) **6-9-1**(3) MHenry(11) (Withdrawn not under Starter's orders: bolted bef s: vet's advice)		**W**	25/1	—	—

(SP 129.6%) **16 Rn**

2m 31.1 (5.10) CSF £16.49 TOTE £5.90: £2.70 £1.40 £2.50 (£8.40) Trio £29.60 OWNER Seaborough Manor Ltd (WELLINGTON) BRED R. Barber

WEIGHT FOR AGE 3yo-15lb

Blush, whose only previous outing was when third in a seller last October, proved much too good for this field. Steadied at the start, she came through to lead approaching the final furlong. She can win again in this company and will probably be suited by further. (9/2)

Statajack (IRE) travelled extremely well throughout the race, and moved up menacingly to challenge at the distance. In the final furlong he could not peg back the winner, who may turn out to be well above this grade. (100/30)

1686 At Liberty (IRE), blinkered for the first time, made somewhat laboured headway under hard driving over two furlongs from home. Though he stayed on for third, he never promised to win. (6/1)

1247 Shabanaz was being pushed along before the halfway stage and, though he stayed on in the last two furlongs, he never appeared likely to catch the leaders. (5/1: 3/1-11/2)

1574 Le Grand Gousier (USA), close-up throughout, had every chance but could not quicken in the closing stages. (10/1: 7/1-12/1)

250 Dark Age (IRE) went to the front over three furlongs and, despite his big weight, hung on until weakening approaching the final furlong. (20/1)

1810 PERFECTLY GRILLED NEW WORLD H'CAP (0-70) (3-Y.O F) (Class E)

7-00 (7-02) **5f 217y** £3,078.75 (£930.00: £452.50: £213.75) Stalls: High GOING minus 0.29 sec per fur (GF)

				SP	RR	SF
1580[3]	**Dayrella (49)** (WRMuir) **3-7-12**(3) MartinDwyer(16) (lw: a.p: led ins fnl f: drvn out)	—	**1**	15/2[3]	57	22
1141[3]	**Sally Green (IRE) (65)** (CFWall) **3-9-3** GDuffield(5) (lw: a.p: led over 1f out tl ins fnl f)	¾	**2**	9/1	71	36
1279[4]	**Will To Win (54)** (PGMurphy) **3-8-6** DHarrison(2) (lw: a.p: r.o ins fnl f)	2	**3**	6/1[2]	55	20
1151[10]	**Hever Golf Mover (63)** (TJNaughton) **3-9-1** DHolland(7) (hdwy fnl 2f: nrst fin)	½	**4**	9/1	62	27
1566[12]	**Heavenly Miss (IRE) (65)** (JJBridger) **3-9-3b** RCochrane(10) (led tl wknd over 1f out)	¾	**5**	10/1	62	27
1245[11]	**Lamorna (56)** (MRChannon) **3-8-8** PatEddery(8) (nt clr run over 2f out: hdwy over 1f out: nt rch ldrs)	1¼	**6**	11/2[1]	50	15
1479[4]	**Shifting Time (67)** (IABalding) **3-9-5** LDettori(6) (hrd rdn & no hdwy fnl 2f)	1¾	**7**	11/2[1]	56	21
1458[12]	**Tabasco Jazz (68)** (BJMeehan) **3-9-6b** BDoyle(1) (swtg: prom tl wknd wl over 1f out)	¾	**8**	14/1	55	20
1666[5]	**Robec Girl (IRE) (59)** (KMcAuliffe) **3-8-11v** DRMcCabe(11) (b.hind: swtg: spd over 3f)	s.h	**9**	14/1	46	11
1439[9]	**Strat's Quest (69)** (DWPArbuthnot) **3-9-7** RPrice(13) (bhd fnl 2f)	2	**10**	14/1	51	16
1089[11]	**Royal Emblem (50)** (AGFoster) **3-7-13b[1]**(3) MHenry(3) (plld hrd: prom tl hrd rdn & wknd qckly over 1f out)	s.h	**11**	25/1	32	—
1589[14]	**Chain Reaction (IRE) (63)** (MAJarvis) **3-9-1** MRoberts(14) (b: prom over 2f)	1	**12**	8/1	42	7
1681[6]	**Breffni (IRE) (52)** (RDickin) **3-8-4**[ow1] DaneO'Neill(12) (a bhd)	1	**13**	25/1	28	—
	Curzon Street (67) (HCandy) **3-9-5** CRutter(9) (bhd fnl 2f)	½	**14**	16/1	42	7

(SP 130.6%) **14 Rn**

1m 13.3 (2.80) CSF £72.85 CT £415.95 TOTE £9.20: £3.00 £3.20 £1.80 (£31.90) Trio £13.50 OWNER Dulverton Equine (LAMBOURN) BRED R. B. Warren

1580 Dayrella, whose four previous runs this year were on the All-Weather, was close up throughout and ran on under pressure to lead inside the final furlong. (15/2)

1141 Sally Green (IRE) was soon racing in second place and looked much like the winner when taking up the running approaching the final furlong. She could not quicken when headed in the last hundred yards. (9/1: 6/1-10/1)

1279 Will To Win, always chasing the leaders, looked held below the distance, but ran on inside the final furlong. (6/1)

995 Hever Golf Mover stayed on in the last two furlongs, but could not quite reach the leading trio. (9/1)

1141 Heavenly Miss (IRE) showed good early pace and had most of the field in trouble by halfway. She weakened when headed approaching the final furlong. (10/1: 7/1-12/1)

Lamorna, denied a clear run over two furlongs from home, was never nearer than at the finish. Nonetheless, this was a considerable improvement on her two previous efforts this season and she should pay to follow. (11/2)

945 Tabasco Jazz (14/1: op 8/1)

1666 Robec Girl (IRE) (14/1: 10/1-16/1)

1141* Strat's Quest (14/1: 8/1-16/1)

Chain Reaction (IRE) (8/1: 6/1-9/1)

1811 STRAWBERRY FRIDGE H'CAP (0-80) (3-Y.O+) (Class D)

7-30 (7-31) **1m 2f 7y** £3,681.50 (£1,112.00: £541.00: £255.50) Stalls: High GOING minus 0.29 sec per fur (GF)

				SP	RR	SF
1463^{*}	**Princess Danielle (61)** (WRMuir) **5-8-9** MRoberts(10) (a.p: led 2f out: drvn out)	—	**1**	9/1	73	46
1632^{*}	**Carburton (71)** (JAGlover) **4-9-5** 5x NDay(3) (hdwy 4f out: hrd rdn 3f out: ev ch fnl 2f: r.o)	¾	**2**	$3/1^{1}$	82	55
1588^{*}	**Vola Via (USA) (80)** (IABalding) **4-10-0** LDettori(8) (hdwy 4f out: rdn over 2f out: r.o one pce)	1	**3**	$13/2^{2}$	89	62
1239^{8}	**Wathbat Nashwan (72)** (LMCumani) **3-8-7** PatEddery(14) (lw: chsd ldr: ev ch 2f out: nt qckn)	hd	**4**	$3/1^{1}$	81	41
640^{6}	**Fabulous Mtoto (59)** (MSSaunders) **7-8-7** NCarlisle(13) (lw: a abt same pl)	5	**5**	20/1	60	33
1244^{4}	**Peppers (IRE) (67)** (KRBurke) **4-9-1** BDoyle(11) (lw: no hdwy fnl 3f)	¾	**6**	$8/1^{3}$	67	40
1427^{10}	**Newport Knight (70)** (RAkehurst) **6-9-4** AClark(1) (b: nvr nr to chal)	2	**7**	25/1	67	40
1219^{9}	**Star of Ring (IRE) (65)** (MJHeaton-Ellis) **4-8-13** DHolland(12) (led tl wknd 2f out)	3½	**8**	25/1	56	29
1244^{11}	**Fern's Governor (58)** (WJMusson) **5-8-6** GCarter(4) (nvr trbld ldrs)	s.h	**9**	10/1	49	22
1459^{2}	**Nordansk (55)** (MMadgwick) **8-8-3** NVarley(5) (lw: sme hdwy 5f out: sn rdn & btn)	1¼	**10**	14/1	44	17
1477^{12}	**Bonanza Peak (USA) (66)** (MrsJCecil) **4-9-0** RCochrane(7) (lw: a bhd)	1¼	**11**	16/1	53	26
1215^{7}	**Full Throttle (68)** (MHTompkins) **4-8-13**(3) MHenry(6) (a bhd)	¾	**12**	25/1	54	27
1320^{14}	**Ortelius (74)** (RHannon) **3-8-9** DaneO'Neill(2) (lw: bhd most of wy)	7	**13**	33/1	49	9
1437^{4}	**Atomic Shell (CAN) (70)** (CFWall) **4-9-4** GDuffield(9) (swtg: a bhd)	1¼	**14**	16/1	43	16
				(SP 131.2%)	**14 Rn**	

2m 7.9 (3.00) CSF £33.68 CT £184.76 TOTE £6.90: £2.20 £1.80 £2.70 (£8.80) Trio £10.50 OWNER Mrs Marion Wickham (LAMBOURN) BRED Mrs Wickham

WEIGHT FOR AGE 3yo-13lb

1463* Princess Danielle was soon racing in third place, albeit several lengths behind the two leaders. She came through to strike the front at the two-furlong marker, and ran on bravely under pressure. (9/1)

1632* Carburton improved from the home turn in the centre of the course and, under maximum pressure, moved up to challenge two furlongs out. He always looked held by the winner, but kept battling on to the end. (3/1)

1588* Vola Via (USA) ran a fine race under his big weight. He crept into a challenging position at the two-furlong marker, but ran on at one pace in the closing stages. (13/2)

Wathbat Nashwan, the medium of a gamble and far less experienced than his mainly older rivals, raced in second place. He still had every chance two furlongs out but failed to quicken. He will be better for the race. (3/1)

640 Fabulous Mtoto was in fifth place a long way from the finish and never appeared likely to find the pace to trouble the leaders. (20/1)

1244 Peppers (IRE), in much the same position throughout the last half-mile, could make no headway under pressure. (8/1)

1812 INDESIT VALUE MAIDEN AUCTION STKS (2-Y.O) (Class E)

8-00 (8-02) **5f 217y** £3,257.50 (£985.00: £480.00: £227.50) Stalls: High GOING minus 0.29 sec per fur (GF)

				SP	RR	SF
1109^{4}	**Lord Kintyre** (BRMillman) **2-8-8** BDoyle(1) (a.p: led wl over 1f out: r.o wl)	—	**1**	$6/1^{2}$	80	31
1593^{3}	**Brandon Frank** (IABalding) **2-8-6** PatEddery(22) (hld up: hdwy & ev ch over 1f out: no imp)	2½	**2**	$6/1^{2}$	71	22
	Speedfit Too (IRE) (GGMargarson) **2-8-12** GCarter(4) (w'like: s.s: gd hdwy fnl 2f: nvr nrr)	1¼	**3**	33/1	74	25
648^{4}	**Eleventh Duke (IRE)** (RHannon) **2-8-7** LDettori(18) (lw: hld up: hdwy & ev ch over 1f out: nt qckn)	s.h	**4**	$3/1^{1}$	69	20
	Coolin River (IRE) (KRBurke) **2-8-6** JFEgan(20) (w'like: a.p: r.o one pce fnl 2f)	4	**5**	25/1	57	8
1619^{7}	**Wild Lilly** (MJRyan) **2-7-13** GBardwell(12) (led over 4f)	2	**6**	33/1	45	—
	Shecando (IRE) (CJames) **2-8-3** CRutter(3) (leggy: a.p: edgd rt over 1f out: rdn & nt qckn fnl f)	nk	**7**	33/1	48	—
1163^{7}	**Oisin (IRE)** (MrsPNDutfield) **2-8-6** RPrice(25) (nrst fin)	hd	**8**	33/1	51	2
	Ambitious (JRFanshawe) **2-8-4** DHarrison(17) (unf: chsd ldrs tl wknd 2f out)	1	**9**	$3/1^{1}$	46	—
	Roborant (JLDunlop) **2-8-12** RCochrane(16) (unf: s.s: hdwy fnl 2f: r.o)	nk	**10**	12/1	53	4
	Acid Test (WRMuir) **2-8-11** DaneO'Neill(13) (unf: bit bkwd: prom 3f)	hd	**11**	20/1	52	3
1461^{2}	**The Honorable Lady** (MRChannon) **2-8-0**(3) PPMurphy(23) (nvr trbld ldrs)	1¼	**12**	20/1	41	—
993^{5}	**Blue Desert** (MBell) **2-8-6** MRoberts(5) (nvr bttr than mid div)	s.h	**13**	10/1	44	—
722^{8}	**King Darius (IRE)** (RHannon) **2-8-3**(7) RSmith(21) (outpcd)	¾	**14**	33/1	46	—
1593^{10}	**Clear View** (BJMeehan) **2-8-0**(7) GHannon(14) (gd spd 4f)	s.h	**15**	33/1	42	—
	Persian Venture (BJMeehan) **2-8-10** DHolland(9) (neat: lw: s.s: a bhd)	¾	**16**	33/1	43	—
	Global Risk (CMurray) **2-8-6** PBloomfield(24) (leggy: outpcd)	1¼	**17**	33/1	36	—
	Chief Blade (RAkehurst) **2-8-11** AClark(15) (w'like: outpcd)	nk	**18**	20/1	40	—
	Muja's Magic (IRE) (KTIvory) **2-7-11**(3) MartinDwyer(2) (leggy: a bhd)	1¼	**19**	33/1	26	—
	State Gala (IRE) (MBell) **2-8-2** DRMcCabe(8) (neat: a bhd)	1	**20**	33/1	25	—
1251^{10}	**Won't Forget Me (IRE)** (MHTompkins) **2-8-2**(3) MHenry(7) (a bhd)	1¼	**21**	20/1	25	—
	Toy (IRE) (MRStoute) **2-8-3** GDuffield(6) (leggy: lt-f: prom over 3f)	nk	**22**	$8/1^{3}$	22	—
1635^{11}	**Courtney Gym (IRE)** (MRChannon) **2-8-7** RPerham(11) (a bhd)	1½	**23**	33/1	22	—
	Erika's Young Man (MJHaynes) **2-8-4**(3) AWhelan(19) (unf: a bhd)	5	**24**	33/1	9	—
				(SP 164.7%)	**24 Rn**	

1m 13.1 (2.60) CSF £41.52 TOTE £9.70: £2.40 £2.00 £13.20 (£27.40) Trio Not won; £571.14 to 11/6/97 OWNER Mr M. Calvert (CULLOMPTON) BRED Rowcliffe Stud

1109 Lord Kintyre, all the better for his Bath debut, was travelling well throughout on the heels of the leaders. He quickened to go clear approaching the final furlong and won readily. (6/1)

1593 Brandon Frank had a clear run on the stands rails throughout and moved up to challenge approaching the final furlong. He had every chance but could make no impression on the winner. (6/1: 4/1-7/1)

Speedfit Too (IRE) had the double disadvantage of a slow start and a poor draw. Behind until past halfway, he made good late headway and should certainly be able to win a race. (33/1)

648 Eleventh Duke (IRE) was travelling well on the heels of the leading group from the start and moved up to challenge approaching the final furlong. When put to his best he could not quicken. (3/1)

Coolin River (IRE) made a satisfactory debut. Always chasing the leaders, he kept on well in the closing stages and should be better for the experience. (25/1)

Wild Lilly made the running until weakening approaching the final furlong. (33/1)

Ambitious (3/1: 2/1-7/2)

Roborant (12/1: op 6/1)

993 Blue Desert (10/1: 6/1-12/1)

Toy (IRE) (8/1: 6/1-10/1)

1813 NEW WORLD IMAGE CLASSIC LIMITED STKS (0-80) (3-Y.O+) (Class D)
8-30 (8-30) **1m 67y** £3,428.00 (£1,034.00: £502.00: £236.00) Stalls: High GOING minus 0.29 sec per fur (GF)

				SP	RR	SF
1427[4]	**Moon Blast (79)** (LadyHerries) **3-8-11** RCochrane(5) (mde virtually all: veered lft cl home: all out)	—	**1**	9/2[2]	92	20
934[6]	**Blessed Spirit (78)** (CFWall) **4-9-3** GDuffield(2) (swtg: stdd s: hdwy on bit 2f out: ev ch ins fnl f: no ex nr fin)	hd	**2**	9/2[2]	87	26
1423*	**Compromise (IRE) (79)** (BWHills) **3-8-11** PatEddery(7) (lw: chsd wnr: ev ch 2f out: one pce fnl f)	2	**3**	3/1[1]	88	16
1207[7]	**Kafil (USA) (80)** (MajorWRHern) **3-8-9** RHills(6) (lw: a.p: rdn over 2f out: one pce)	2	**4**	9/2[2]	82	10
	Catch The Lights (80) (MissCJohnsey) **4-9-3** MRoberts(4) (prom tl wknd over 2f out)	2½	**5**	20/1	74	13
1262[10]	**Koathary (USA) (80)** (LGCottrell) **6-9-6** DHolland(3) (b: effrt & rdn 3f out: wknd 2f out)	s.h	**6**	9/2[2]	77	16
1175[11]	**Calypso Lady (IRE) (80)** (RHannon) **3-8-6** DaneO'Neill(1) (a bhd)	s.h	**7**	8/1[3]	74	2

(SP 113.6%) **7 Rn**

1m 47.6 (5.40) CSF £22.31 TOTE £7.10: £3.00 £2.20 (£11.70) OWNER Angmering Park Stud (LITTLEHAMPTON) BRED Lavinia Duchess of Norfolk

WEIGHT FOR AGE 3yo-11lb

1427 Moon Blast, allowed to bowl along in front, settled better then usual. He had to be put to his best in the final two furlongs but, though swerving left near the finish, kept on well to the end. (9/2)

934 Blessed Spirit, dropped out last at the start, made very smooth headway to track the winner from two furlongs out. She was still on the bit when she challenged inside the final furlong but failed to put her head in front. (9/2: op 3/1)

1423* Compromise (IRE) raced in second place. He had every chance two furlongs out but could not quicken with the first two from the distance. (3/1: op 2/1)

Kafil (USA) travelled comfortably on the heels of the leaders until coming under pressure approaching the two-furlong marker. Though he stayed on, he failed to quicken. (9/2: 5/1-8/1)

1262 Koathary (USA) made some headway from the rear of the field under pressure over three furlongs from home, but was a spent force at the two-furlong marker. (9/2)

966 Calypso Lady (IRE) was always behind and never held out any hope. (8/1)

1814 MERLONI DOMESTIC APPLIANCES LIMITED STKS (0-60) (3-Y.O+) (Class F)
9-00 (9-00) **5f 10y** £2,570.00 (£720.00: £350.00) Stalls: High GOING minus 0.29 sec per fur (GF)

				SP	RR	SF
1479*	**Songsheet (69)** (MSSaunders) **4-8-13**(3) PPMurphy(10) (lw: hdwy 2f out: hrd rdn over 1f out: led ins fnl f: r.o)	—	**1**	7/4[1]	71	50
1627[11]	**Mindrace (58)** (KTIvory) **4-8-13v**[1](3) MartinDwyer(6) (a.p: ev ch 1f out: nt qckn)	¾	**2**	25/1	69	48
1479[3]	**Runs in the Family (58)** (GMMcCourt) **5-9-2b** DHarrison(4) (a.p: ev ch 2f out: r.o ins fnl f)	1¾	**3**	8/1	63	42
1566[3]	**Whizz Kid (51)** (JJBridger) **3-8-1**(5) RMullen(5) (rdn along: hdwy fnl 2f: nvr nrr)	nk	**4**	12/1	59	31
1743*	**Polly Golightly (61)** (MBlanshard) **4-9-5b** 3x NAdams(2) (led: edgd lft over 1f out: wknd & hdd ins fnl f)	nk	**5**	100/30[2]	64	43
	Ashkernazy (IRE) (45) (NEBerry) **6-8-13** DaneO'Neill(3) (nvr nrr)	1½	**6**	20/1	53	32
1419[10]	**Mijas (58)** (LMontagueHall) **4-9-2** AClark(9) (prom 3f)	2½	**7**	8/1	49	28
1479[5]	**Pearl Dawn (IRE) (49)** (PCClarke) **7-8-13** JFEgan(1) (lw: a bhd)	1½	**8**	20/1	41	20
57[11]	**Dancing Jack (40)** (JJBridger) **4-9-2** RCochrane(7) (lw: a bhd)	3½	**9**	40/1	33	12
1279[11]	**Dancing Mystery (49)** (EAWheeler) **3-8-4b**[1](5) ADaly(8) (a bhd)	1	**10**	6/1[3]	30	2

(SP 119.4%) **10 Rn**

61.2 secs (1.50) CSF £53.30 TOTE £2.70: £1.10 £4.10 £2.00 (£50.80) Trio £47.90 OWNER Mr M. S. Saunders (WELLS) BRED Lord Matthews

WEIGHT FOR AGE 3yo-7lb

1479* Songsheet, well favoured by the race conditions, made no mistake. She closed on the leaders from two furlongs out and, sustaining her effort, struck the front inside the last furlong. (7/4)

Mindrace, visored for the first time, was always close up. He had every chance but could not quicken with the winner inside the final furlong. (25/1)

1479 Runs in the Family, always in the first three, had every chance and kept on well towards the finish. (8/1: 3/1-9/1)

1566 Whizz Kid was being driven along to go the pace from the start. She stayed on in the last two furlongs but could not reach the leaders. (12/1: 8/1-14/1)

1743* Polly Golightly set a strong gallop. She began to edge to the left approaching the final furlong and soon weakened when headed in the last one hundred and fifty yards. (100/30)

T/Plpt: £53.70 (380.14 Tckts). T/Qdpt: £13.20 (74.3 Tckts) AK/Hn

1466-REDCAR (L-H) (Firm, Good to firm patches)
Tuesday June 10th
WEATHER: overcast WIND: fresh half behind

1815 MAGNUM (S) STKS (2-Y.O) (Class G)
2-00 (2-05) **7f** £2,202.50 (£615.00: £297.50) Stalls: High GOING minus 0.59 sec per fur (F)

				SP	RR	SF
1626[3]	**Huxleen** (WGMTurner) **2-8-1**(5) DSweeney(3) (a cl up: led over 2f out: styd on)	—	**1**	3/1[2]	64	6
1498*	**Arm And A Leg (IRE)** (CADwyer) **2-9-1** JStack(5) (hld up: hdwy & ev ch over 1f out: rdn & no ex)	1¾	**2**	11/8[1]	69	11
1577[9]	**Greenbrook** (WGMTurner) **2-8-11** GDuffield(8) (led over 4f: r.o one pce)	½	**3**	25/1	64	6
	Last Lap (TDEasterby) **2-8-6** DeanMcKeown(1) (leggy: s.s: styd on fnl 2f: nrst fin)	2	**4**	16/1	54	—
1581[4]	**Moss Side Monkey** (JBerry) **2-8-11v**[1] KDarley(2) (s.s: sn in tch: effrt over 2f out: wknd over 1f out)	½	**5**	8/1	58	—
1600[4]	**Sunshine Pet (IRE)** (JJO'Neill) **2-8-6** JCarroll(9) (chsd ldrs 5f: sn rdn & btn)	4	**6**	4/1[3]	44	—
1298[8]	**Toll's Times** (MWEasterby) **2-8-6**(5) GParkin(7) (trckd ldrs tl rdn & wknd 2f out)	3½	**7**	14/1	41	—
1019[7]	**Diamond Steve** (NTinkler) **2-9-1b**[1] KimTinkler(10) (lw: sn pushed along: lost tch fnl 3f)	1¼	**8**	6/1	42	—
948[9]	**Newgate Noblesse** (BWMurray) **2-8-6** VHalliday(4) (prom: rdn ½-wy: sn wknd)	16	**9**	16/1	—	—
1758[2]	**Katie's Cracker** (MRChannon) **2-8-6** JFortune(6) (Withdrawn not under Starter's orders: broke out of stalls & bolted)		**W**	4/1[3]	—	—

(SP 154.8%) **9 Rn**

1m 26.0 (3.00) CSF £8.21 TOTE £4.40: £1.40 £1.10 £6.30 (£3.50) Trio £35.80 OWNER Mrs C. L. Rivenaes (SHERBORNE) BRED Ivar Rivenaes

Bt in 4,800gns

1626 Huxleen was wearing a brush pricker on her near side to stop her hanging left and she did nothing wrong, winning this moderate race convincingly. (3/1)
1498* Arm And A Leg (IRE), trying his longest trip to date, went well for a long way but was then just outstayed. (11/8: 5/4-9/4)
Greenbrook, a stable companion of the winner, had shown nothing previously and this was obviously quite encouraging. (25/1)
Last Lap, a very green newcomer, should improve plenty from the experience. (16/1)
1581 Moss Side Monkey had the visor on instead of blinkers but he still was not co-operating. (8/1)
1600 Sunshine Pet (IRE), taking a big step up in trip, failed to get home. (4/1)
859 Diamond Steve (6/1: op 10/1)

1816 JEROBOAM H'CAP (0-70) (3-Y.O+) (Class E)
2-30 (2-32) **6f** £3,034.75 (£913.00: £441.50: £205.75) Stalls: High GOING minus 0.59 sec per fur (F)

				SP	RR	SF
1395[14]	**Lillibella (45)** (MrsJRRamsden) **4-8-6** JFortune(2) (w ldr: edgd lft ½-wy: led 2f out: r.o u.p)	—	**1**	11/2[3]	54	32
1511[11]	**Kid Ory (41)** (DWChapman) **6-7-11b[1]**(5) KSked(6) (led tl hdd 2f out: kpt on towards fin)	½	**2**	11/2[3]	49	27
1511[6]	**Densben (47)** (DenysSmith) **13-8-8** ACulhane(3) (outpcd & bhd tl styd on wl fnl 2f)	1¼	**3**	8/1	51	29
1613*	**Henry the Hawk (42)** (MDods) **6-7-10**(7) RWinston(1) (b: a chsng ldrs: nt qckn fnl 2f)	1	**4**	11/4[1]	44	22
1613[10]	**Corniche Quest (IRE) (65)** (MRChannon) **4-9-12** JFEgan(9) (chsd ldrs: rdn over 2f out: one pce)	nk	**5**	4/1[2]	66	44
1734[8]	**Millesime (IRE) (52)** (MartynWane) **5-8-13** JCarroll(7) (in tch: rdn ½-wy: no imp)	1½	**6**	8/1	49	27
749[15]	**Crissem (IRE) (65)** (RHollinshead) **4-9-12** FLynch(8) (drvn along over 3f out: sn btn)	2½	**7**	50/1	55	33
1225[11]	**Souperficial (49)** (NTinkler) **6-8-10v** KimTinkler(5) (chsd ldrs: rdn ½-wy: sn wknd)	1¼	**8**	9/1	36	14
	Olifantsfontein (40) (JSWainwright) **9-7-10v**(5) JBramhill(4) (sn drvn along: a bhd)	2½	**9**	66/1	20	—
				(SP 113.1%)		**9 Rn**

1m 10.8 (0.60) CSF £31.82 CT £218.45 TOTE £7.20: £2.10 £1.10 £2.00 (£24.30) Trio £123.70 OWNER Mrs Peter Hastings (THIRSK) BRED Mrs P. Hastings
749 Lillibella, appreciating the drop back in trip, tended to hang left at halfway but did nothing wrong under pressure in the closing stages and the line was always going to come in time. (11/2)
1289 Kid Ory had the blinkers on for the first time and showed good attitude to fight back after looking beaten. It is two seasons since he last won but he should not be written off. (11/2)
1511 Densben, from a yard that can do nothing right at the moment, ran a super race, making fair late progress. (8/1)
1613* Henry the Hawk had his chances but lacked the toe to take them. (11/4)
1584 Corniche Quest (IRE) had a poor draw last time but there were no such excuses here. (4/1)

1817 MANOR CONSTRUCTION CLAIMING STKS (3-Y.O+) (Class F)
3-00 (3-01) **2m 4y** £2,477.50 (£690.00: £332.50) Stalls: Centre GOING minus 0.59 sec per fur (F)

				SP	RR	SF
1648[3]	**Royal Expression (79)** (MrsMReveley) **5-10-0** ACulhane(3) (outpcd & lost tch 5f out: hdwy over 3f out: led wl over 1f out: styd on)	—	**1**	11/10[2]	61	24
	Good Hand (USA) (75) (SEKettlewell) **11-9-10** JFortune(1) (lw: b: in tch: outpcd over 3f out: styd on & ev ch 2f out: nt qckn)	2½	**2**	5/6[1]	55	18
493[11]	**Longcroft (35)** (SEKettlewell) **5-9-4** JStack(4) (led to ½-wy: led over 3f out tl wl over 1f out: sn outpcd)	3	**3**	16/1[3]	46	9
1383[15]	**Jungle Fresh (38)** (JDBethell) **4-9-9** TWilliams(5) (lw: a.p: ch over 2f out: sn outpcd)	10	**4**	66/1	42	4
1654[8]	**Ship's Dancer (28)** (DonEnricoIncisa) **4-9-2b** KimTinkler(2) (sn cl up: led ½-wy tl over 3f out: sn wknd)	13	**5**	66/1	22	—
				(SP 111.0%)		**5 Rn**

3m 33.7 (8.70) CSF £2.12 TOTE £2.80: £1.10 £1.40 (£1.10) OWNER Mr Les De La Haye (SALTBURN) BRED K. Panos
WEIGHT FOR AGE 4yo-1lb
1648 Royal Expression lost all interest at halfway and was soon tailed off but somehow his rider persuaded him to run in the home straight and in the end he did it nicely. He looks one to be wary of. (11/10)
Good Hand (USA) won this last year and looked a picture here but basically they did not go fast enough soon enough for his liking. (5/6)
Longcroft had plenty on here and in the circumstances this was a fair effort. (16/1)
Jungle Fresh, trying his longest trip to date, showed something for the first time but did not appear to last home. (66/1)
Ship's Dancer had only got in the first three once in twenty-one starts previously and was not in danger of improving on that here. (66/1)

1818 EVENING GAZETTE H'CAP (0-70) (3-Y.O+ F & M) (Class E)
3-30 (3-31) **1m** £2,859.25 (£859.00: £414.50: £192.25) Stalls: High GOING minus 0.59 sec per fur (F)

				SP	RR	SF
1135[9]	**Best of All (IRE) (62)** (JBerry) **5-9-10b** KDarley(7) (trckd ldrs: led wl over 1f out: r.o)	—	**1**	6/1[3]	73	56
1097[13]	**Queens Consul (IRE) (66)** (BSRothwell) **7-10-0** MFenton(8) (cl up: led over 4f tl wl over 1f out: one pce)	2½	**2**	9/2[1]	72	55
1683[2]	**Mcgillycuddy Reeks (IRE) (34)** (DonEnricoIncisa) **6-7-10** KimTinkler(11) (sn chsng ldrs: effrt over 3f out: rdn & one pce fnl f)	nk	**3**	5/1[2]	39	22
1390[10]	**Cruz Santa (45)** (TDBarron) **4-8-7** JCarroll(10) (prom: outpcd 3f out: kpt on appr fnl f)	5	**4**	15/2	40	23
1395[11]	**Born A Lady (42)** (MrsVAAconley) **4-8-4** MDeering(6) (chsd ldrs: outpcd over 2f out: sn btn)	3	**5**	14/1	31	14
1788[6]	**Heathyards Lady (USA) (48)** (RHollinshead) **6-8-10** FLynch(4) (b: styd on fnl 3f: n.d)	s.h	**6**	10/1	37	20
	White Hare (50) (MrsMReveley) **4-8-12** ACulhane(9) (bit bkwd: a bhd)	4	**7**	7/1	31	14
1467[17]	**Stolen Music (IRE) (36)** (REBarr) **4-7-5**(7) DMernagh(2) (outpcd & bhd fnl 3f)	9	**8**	25/1	—	—
636[9]	**Celia's Rainbow (35)** (RMWhitaker) **4-7-11**ow1 DWright(3) (led over 4f: sn wknd)	2	**9**	33/1	—	—
1470[6]	**Madison Mist (64)** (MrsJRRamsden) **3-9-1** JFortune(1) (lost tch & eased fnl 3f)	15	**10**	5/1[2]	—	—
				(SP 112.6%)		**10 Rn**

1m 35.2 (0.20) CSF £29.06 CT £130.56 TOTE £5.20: £2.10 £2.30 £1.30 (£11.70) Trio £22.10 OWNER Mr Robert Aird (COCKERHAM) BRED Mrs D. Hutch
LONG HANDICAP Mcgillycuddy Reeks (IRE) 7-6 Celia's Rainbow 7-9
WEIGHT FOR AGE 3yo-11lb
OFFICIAL EXPLANATION **Madison Mist: the jockey reported that the filly had lost her action. The trainer subsequently reported that the filly had lost her off fore plate.**
951 Best of All (IRE), warm and edgy in the preliminaries, did nothing wrong in the race and won well. (6/1)
589 Queens Consul (IRE) has dropped to a really good mark and showed something here and ought to be able to find a suitable race. (9/2)
1683 Mcgillycuddy Reeks (IRE) had her chances but this trip, if anything, was a bit too sharp for her. (5/1)
Cruz Santa ran reasonably and, once her stable strikes form, she will be one to be watched. (15/2)
1289 Born A Lady, from an out of form yard, was left struggling in the last two furlongs. (14/1)
1135 Heathyards Lady (USA) is much better on the All-Weather and never got going here until too late. (10/1)

1819 METHUSALEM MEDIAN AUCTION MAIDEN STKS (2-Y.O) (Class D)

4-00 (4-01) **6f** £3,338.50 (£1,003.00: £484.00: £224.50) Stalls: High GOING minus 0.59 sec per fur (F)

				SP	RR	SF
979[8]	**Cumbrian Caruso** (TDEasterby) **2-9-0** JCarroll(12) (trckd ldrs: hdwy to ld over 1f out: r.o u.p)	—	1	25/1	68	30
993[6]	**Durham Flyer** (TDEasterby) **2-9-0** DeanMcKeown(10) (cl up: led ½-wy tl appr fnl f: kpt on)	½	2	20/1	67	29
	Mountain Song (SirMarkPrescott) **2-9-0** GDuffield(11) (cmpt: scope: a w ldrs: rdn over 1f out: nt qckn towards fin)	s.h	3	8/11[1]	67+	29
	Fundance (MDods) **2-9-0** JFEgan(3) (w'like: bit bkwd: trckd ldrs: chal 1f out: wandered u.p)	½	4	25/1	65	27
	Cocksure (IRE) (JMPEustace) **2-9-0** JTate(8) (cmpt: scope: s.i.s: hdwy ½-wy: rn green: nvr able chal)	5	5	13/2[3]	52	14
971[7]	**Circuiteer (IRE)** (JBerry) **2-9-0** KDarley(2) (led to ½-wy: sn outpcd)	s.h	6	25/1	52	14
	Percy (JFBottomley) **2-9-0** KHodgson(4) (small: cmpt: trckd ldrs tl outpcd fnl 2f)	1½	7	50/1	48	10
1684[6]	**Sealed By Fate (IRE)** (JSWainwright) **2-9-0** MRimmer(13) (s.i.s: n.d)	4	8	5/1[2]	37	—
	Silver Hope (IRE) (RHollinshead) **2-9-0** WRyan(5) (cmpt: bit bkwd: s.s: n.d)	nk	9	25/1	36	—
	Ludere (IRE) (WWHaigh) **2-9-0** LCharnock(9) (cmpt: bit bkwd: s.i.s: nvr wnt pce: kpt on)	1¾	10	50/1	32	—
	Taylor's Pride (TDBarron) **2-8-9** RLappin(6) (neat: scope: unruly in stalls: n.d)	1¾	11	25/1	22	—
1760[15]	**Estopped (IRE)** (MRChannon) **2-9-0** JFortune(7) (unruly in stalls: cl up to ½-wy: wknd qckly)	½	12	20/1	26	—
	Eager Hero (MBrittain) **2-9-0** GBardwell(1) (small: cmpt: rn green: in tch over 3f)	1½	13	25/1	22	—
				(SP 124.4%)	**13 Rn**	

1m 11.5 (1.30) CSF £380.44 TOTE £32.90: £5.80 £2.50 £1.20 (£54.80) Trio £36.10 OWNER Cumbrian Industrials Ltd (MALTON) BRED J. R. M. and Mrs P. Lewis

Cumbrian Caruso appreciated this faster surface and, travelling well, found all that was necessary when ridden and should improve further. (25/1)
993 Durham Flyer is improving and appreciated the trip and no doubt a race or two will be found. (20/1)
Mountain Song, a good-looking sort, appeared green in the paddock and showed a moderate action going down but, judging by the market support, he is well thought of and there should be plenty of improvement once he learns what the game is all about. (8/11: 4/5-evens)
Fundance, a decent sort, ran well but was all over the place when ridden and will obviously improve no end with experience. (25/1)
Cocksure (IRE) took the eye in the paddock but proved green in the race and there should be plenty more to come once he gets his act together. (13/2: 7/1-9/2)
Circuiteer (IRE) is a good-actioned sort but, once off the bit, he lacks any change of gear. (25/1)

1820 SALMANAZAR H'CAP (0-65) (3-Y.O) (Class F)

4-30 (4-33) **1m 2f** £2,722.50 (£760.00: £367.50) Stalls: Low GOING minus 0.59 sec per fur (F)

				SP	RR	SF
1296[6]	**Who's That Man (54)** (SCWilliams) **3-8-10** KDarley(1) (trckd ldrs: squeezed thro to ld wl over 1f out: hld on wl)	—	1	7/1[3]	59	28
*1756**	**Sparky (64)** (MWEasterby) **3-9-1b**(5) 5x GParkin(14) (lw: b: hld up: hdwy whn nt clr run over 1f out: swtchd & qcknd to chal wl over 1f out: no ex nr fin)	nk	2	9/2[2]	69	38
1094[7]	**Touch'n'go (64)** (MJohnston) **3-9-6** JWeaver(4) (led tl hdd wl over 1f out: one pce)	6	3	8/1	59	28
1449[9]	**Kweilo (65)** (JWPayne) **3-9-7** WRyan(13) (lw: hld up & bhd: hdwy over 3f out: ch over 1f out: nt qckn)	nk	4	12/1	59	28
1568[3]	**Flashtalkin' Flood (57)** (CADwyer) **3-8-13** JStack(15) (racd wd: a.p: kpt on one pce fnl 2f)	1	5	7/2[1]	50	19
1390[8]	**Bollero (IRE) (60)** (JBerry) **3-8-11**(5) PRoberts(9) (a chsng ldrs: effrt 3f out: one pce fnl 2f)	1	6	11/1	51	20
1373[11]	**Chorus Song (USA) (59)** (PWChapple-Hyam) **3-8-12**(3) RHavlin(16) (b.nr hind: mid div: kpt on fnl 3f: nt pce to chal)	nk	7	10/1	50	19
825[7]	**Think Again (IRE) (45)** (RCraggs) **3-8-1** LCharnock(5) (a.p: ev ch over 2f out: wknd over 1f out)	¾	8	20/1	35	4
1603[2]	**Barresbo (62)** (CWFairhurst) **3-8-11**(7) TSiddall(10) (mid div: effrt 3f out: no imp)	2	9	11/1	48	17
1683[13]	**Father Eddie (57)** (JJO'Neill) **3-8-13v**1 JFortune(17) (a rr div)	2½	10	33/1	39	8
1333[9]	**Al Ava Consonant (47)** (JDBethell) **3-8-3** TWilliams(3) (bhd: effrt 4f out: n.d)	1½	11	50/1	27	—
1423[15]	**Damanka (IRE) (52)** (MBell) **3-8-8** MFenton(2) (in tch tl wknd fnl 3f)	¾	12	14/1	31	—
1469[13]	**Grovefair Lad (IRE) (46)** (MartynWane) **3-8-2**ow1 FLynch(7) (w ldrs tl wknd over 2f out)	3½	13	14/1	19	—
1582[7]	**Dissington Times (44)** (WMcKeown) **3-7-9**(5) JBramhill(8) (unruly in stalls: sn cl up: wknd fnl 3f)	1¾	14	25/1	14	—
1582[6]	**Kalousion (48)** (TJEtherington) **3-8-4**ow1 JCarroll(11) (a rr div)	9	15	20/1	4	—
1299[14]	**Lady Salome (47)** (JGFitzGerald) **3-8-3** JFanning(12) (racd wd: prom 6f)	5	16	33/1	—	—
1140[7]	**Blue Hopper (57)** (MRChannon) **3-8-13** JFEgan(6) (a bhd: t.o)	27	17	12/1	—	—
				(SP 139.7%)	**17 Rn**	

2m 5.9 (2.30) CSF £37.18 CT £255.70 TOTE £8.50: £1.60 £1.60 £2.30 £3.70 (£34.80) Trio £43.90 OWNER Mr M Jameson And Mr John T Duffy (NEWMARKET) BRED T. P. Milne and M. Jameson

925 Who's That Man failed to act on the soft last time but, well-ridden here, did it in determined style and was staying on particularly strongly at the finish. (7/1)
1756* Sparky travelled well but had traffic problems at a vital stage. However, he still got out in time but, when challenging and looking likely to win, he found the effort just too much for his liking. (9/2: 3/1-5/1)
1094 Touch'n'go, happier at this shorter trip, ran well but always seemed to be finding the ground a bit too lively when the pressure was on in the closing stages. (8/1)
1449 Kweilo had a tongue-strap fitted and ran much better, coming from way behind, but still did not pick up when looking likely to have a chance. (12/1)
1568 Flashtalkin' Flood has ability but, taking a strong hold here, raced very wide, particularly on the home turn. Once he can be straightened out, there should be better to come. (7/2)
1096 Bollero (IRE) jumped off on terms but then failed to pick up at the business end. (11/1)
749 Chorus Song (USA), trying her longest trip to date, looked to be going quite well but then failed to pick up when ridden. (10/1)
Blue Hopper (12/1: op 8/1)

T/Plpt: £18.10 (773.22 Tckts). T/Qdpt: £2.80 (287.58 Tckts) AA

1163-SALISBURY (R-H) (Good to firm)
Tuesday June 10th
All races hand timed.
WEATHER: fine WIND: nil

1821 EDDIE REAVEY MAIDEN AUCTION STKS (I) (2-Y.O F) (Class F)
2-15 (2-17) **6f** £2,602.00 (£722.00: £346.00) Stalls: High GOING minus 0.69 sec per fur (HD)

	Horse	Dist	Pos	SP	RR	SF
	Parisian Lady (IRE) (AGNewcombe) **2-8-0** NVarley(6) (leggy: lw: bhd tl gd hdwy over 1f out: led ins fnl f: r.o wl)	—	1	33/1	80	40
1466^{2}	**Fayrana (IRE)** (JWHills) **2-8-7** MHills(4) (chsd ldr: led 2f out tl ins fnl f)	2½	2	$6/1^{3}$	80	40
	Zizi (IRE) (KRBurke) **2-8-3** JQuinn(2) (small: str: bit bkwd: a.p: ev ch over 1f out: one pce)	3½	3	12/1	67	27
1619^{3}	**Arian Da** (BPalling) **2-8-7** TSprake(8) (led: rdn over 3f out: hdd 2f out: wknd over 1f out)	2½	4	$6/1^{3}$	64	24
1330^{3}	**Bali Dance** (CBBBooth) **2-8-7** LDettori(11) (lw: nvr nr to chal)	nk	5	$7/2^{2}$	64	24
1447^{4}	**Patricia Olive (IRE)** (MHTompkins) **2-8-0**(3) MHenry(10) (prom tl wknd over 1f out)	2	6	$11/4^{1}$	54	14
	Kate Lane (IRE) (MrsPNDutfield) **2-8-2**(5) AimeeCook(12) (unf: nvr nrr)	1¾	7	33/1	54	14
1564^{9}	**Jackies Webb** (BSmart) **2-7-13**(5)ow1 ADaly(5) (lw: chsd ldrs: rdn 3f out: wknd 2f out)	1	8	16/1	48	7
1616^{8}	**Miss Dangerous** (MRChannon) **2-8-4**(3) PPMurphy(3) (a bhd)	¾	9	16/1	49	9
1240^{13}	**Burning Love** (JSMoore) **2-7-11**(3) MartinDwyer(1) (prom over 3f)	¾	10	25/1	40	—
	Mercury Falling (DWPArbuthnot) **2-8-3** SWhitworth(9) (b: unf: s.s: a bhd)	4	11	14/1	32	—
	Dot (RHannon) **2-8-4**ow1 DaneO'Neill(7) (small: a bhd)	3½	12	12/1	24	—
				(SP 121.0%)	**12 Rn**	

1m 12.1 (0.31 under 2y best) (-0.90) CSF £202.57 TOTE £96.70: £14.20 £2.30 £2.30 (£272.10) Trio Not won; £482.69 to Beverley 11/6/97
OWNER Mr Alex Gorrie (BARNSTAPLE) BRED Clinton Investments
IN-FOCUS: **This time compared favourably with the six-furlong handicap.**
Parisian Lady (IRE), a half-sister to bumper winner Mister Gigi, only cost 2,000 gns and surprised connections for the further she went the better she got. (33/1)
1466 Fayrana (IRE) did nothing wrong but had no answer to the winner's strong finish. (6/1: op 4/1)
Zizi (IRE), a half-sister to ten-furlong winner Minimize, was supported in the ring and should come on a bit for the outing. (12/1: 20/1-10/1)
1619 Arian Da, stepping up to six, did not see out the trip on this testing course. (6/1: op 7/2)
1330 Bali Dance was never going to make the long trip from Yorkshire pay off. (7/2)
1447 Patricia Olive (IRE) did not seem to benefit from this extra furlong. (11/4)
Mercury Falling (14/1: tchd 25/1)
Dot (12/1: op 5/1)

1822 CITY BOWL H'CAP (0-80) (3-Y.O+ F & M) (Class D)
2-45 (2-46) **1m 4f** £3,548.00 (£1,064.00: £512.00: £236.00) Stalls: High GOING minus 0.69 sec per fur (HD)

	Horse	Dist	Pos	SP	RR	SF
1435^{3}	**Shalateeno (64)** (BRMillman) **4-9-8** TSprake(7) (plld hrd: mde all: sn clr: rdn over 2f out: all out)	—	1	$13/2^{2}$	68	31
838^{11}	**Dramatic Moment (66)** (JRArnold) **4-9-7**(3) MartinDwyer(6) (lw: hld up: hdwy 3f out: ev ch fnl f: r.o)	hd	2	20/1	70	33
1591^{5}	**Lonely Heart (77)** (DRCElsworth) **3-9-6** RCochrane(3) (lw: hld up: hdwy on ins over 3f out: nt clr run fnl 2f)	1¾	3	$8/1^{3}$	79	27
1420*	**Timissa (IRE) (80)** (LMCumani) **3-9-9** LDettori(4) (lw: a.p: rdn 3f out: one pce)	2½	4	$8/11^{1}$	78	26
1299^{12}	**Lady of The Lake (70)** (JLDunlop) **3-8-13** PatEddery(5) (bhd: rdn over 5f out: nvr nrr)	1½	5	$13/2^{2}$	66	14
60^{6}	**Troia (IRE) (60)** (BSmart) **3-7-12**(5) ADaly(2) (chsd wnr: rdn 5f out: wknd over 2f out)	1¾	6	33/1	54	2
969^{3}	**Viking Dream (IRE) (54)** (JCFox) **5-8-7**(5) RMullen(1) (rdn over 4f out: bhd fnl 3f)	2½	7	14/1	45	8
				(SP 110.0%)	**7 Rn**	

2m 34.1 (3.10) CSF £96.05 TOTE £7.50: £2.90 £3.80 (£23.60) OWNER Mr G. Palmer (CULLOMPTON) BRED Mrs M. Palmer and G. Palmer
WEIGHT FOR AGE 3yo-15lb
1435 Shalateeno took a strong hold as usual but, under a fine ride, held on gamely to the line. (13/2)
Dramatic Moment ran much better than on her previous run for her new trainer. (20/1)
1591 Lonely Heart, trying a longer trip, would probably have made a winning handicap debut with any luck in running. (8/1: 6/1-9/1)
1420* Timissa (IRE) should have been suited by this step up in distance but lacked a turn of foot. (8/11)
1299 Lady of The Lake gave the impression she needs even further. (13/2: 5/1-8/1)

1823 LAVERSTOCK MAIDEN STKS (3-Y.O F) (Class D)
3-15 (3-21) **1m** £3,886.00 (£1,168.00: £564.00: £262.00) Stalls: High GOING minus 0.69 sec per fur (HD)

	Horse	Dist	Pos	SP	RR	SF
	Gift Token (77) (MajorDNChappell) **3-8-11** KFallon(3) (hld up: hdwy over 2f out: led 1f out: drvn out)	—	1	20/1	86	40
1316^{2}	**Blueygreen (85)** (PWChapple-Hyam) **3-8-11** JReid(1) (w ldr: led over 2f out to 1f out: one pce)	3	2	$15/8^{1}$	80	34
1591^{3}	**Kawa-Ib (IRE)** (PTWalwyn) **3-8-11** PatEddery(5) (led over 5f: one pce fnl f)	1¾	3	$2/1^{2}$	77	31
1415^{5}	**Cordate (IRE)** (JHMGosden) **3-8-11** LDettori(13) (lw: a.p: rdn 3f out: one pce fnl 2f)	1	4	$5/1^{3}$	75	29
1030^{9}	**Mystery Hill (USA)** (JHMGosden) **3-8-11** GHind(4) (lw: a.p: one pce fnl 2f)	¾	5	25/1	73	27
	Hidden Agenda (FR) (RCharlton) **3-8-11** TSprake(9) (scope: bhd: rdn over 3f out: nvr nr to chal)	6	6	12/1	61	15
1087^{11}	**My Girl Lucy** (PMitchell) **3-8-8**(3) MHenry(11) (chsd ldrs over 5f)	1¼	7	50/1	59	13
1415^{4}	**Misty Point** (IABalding) **3-8-11** MHills(10) (chsd ldrs over 5f)	2	8	8/1	55	9
1420^{8}	**Magaona (FR)** (RHannon) **3-8-11** DaneO'Neill(8) (hld up mid div: rdn over 3f out: sn wknd)	1	9	50/1	53	7
1316^{9}	**Flying Colours (IRE) (73)** (CJBenstead) **3-8-11** AMcGlone(6) (a bhd)	½	10	33/1	52	6
1297^{5}	**Bellagrana** (MJFetherston-Godley) **3-8-11** DHolland(2) (a bhd)	nk	11	40/1	51	5
	Chili Bouchier (USA) (DMarks) **3-8-8**(3) AWhelan(14) (a bhd: t.o)	13	12	50/1	25	—
	Catherston Lucky (GBBalding) **3-8-11** SDrowne(12) (unf: a bhd: t.o fnl 2f)	16	13	50/1	—	—
	Cherrymentary (KOCunningham-Brown) **3-8-11** BDoyle(7) (Withdrawn not under Starter's orders: ref to ent stalls)		W	50/1	—	—
				(SP 127.4%)	**13 Rn**	

1m 40.0 (0.00) CSF £52.79 TOTE £24.00: £3.40 £1.50 £1.70 (£37.50) Trio £30.10 OWNER Mrs D. Ellis (PULBOROUGH) BRED Miss E. Drax
IN-FOCUS: **This was Major Chappell's first winner from his new base.**
Gift Token appreciated this extra furlong and will now go for the Fern Hill at Ascot on Saturday week. (20/1)
1316 Blueygreen, stepping up to a mile, could not hold the winner in the final furlong. (15/8: 5/4-2/1)
1591 Kawa-Ib (IRE) could not get the better of her market rival let alone the winner. (2/1)

1415 Cordate (IRE) may do better over further. (5/1)
Mystery Hill (USA), trying an extra furlong, might be suited by an even longer distance and is now qualified for handicaps. (25/1)
Hidden Agenda (FR) is bred to require further and ran accordingly. (12/1: op 8/1)

1824 BLANDFORD H'CAP (0-90) (3-Y.O+) (Class C)
3-45 (3-45) **6f** £5,277.00 (£1,596.00: £778.00: £369.00) Stalls: High GOING minus 0.69 sec per fur (HD)

			SP	RR	SF
1317^{9}	**Purple Fling (68)** (LGCottrell) **6-8-8** DHolland(8) (lw: a.p: hrd rdn over 2f out: led ins fnl f: r.o) ......—	**1**	6/1	76	52
1410^{6}	**Delta Soleil (USA) (81)** (PWHarris) **5-9-0**(7) CLowther(7) (w ldr: led over 1f out: edgd lft & hdd ins fnl f) ......nk	**2**	11/2 3	88	64
1317^{2}	**Sir Joey (USA) (84)** (PGMurphy) **8-9-10** KFallon(1) (lw: hld up in rr: hdwy 2f out: sn hrd rdn: hmpd & snatched up nr fin) 1¼	**3**	9/4 1	88	64
1594^{9}	**Faraway Lass (78)** (LordHuntingdon) **4-9-4** DHarrison(5) (s.i.s: sn prom: rdn 3f out: one pce fnl 2f) 1½	**4**	5/1 2	78	54
1402^{8}	**Bajan Rose (77)** (MBlanshard) **5-9-3** RCochrane(3) (led over 4f: one pce) ......½	**5**	12/1	76	52
	Golden Pound (USA) (83) (MissGayKelleway) **5-9-9** DaneO'Neill(4) (b.hind: rdn over 2f out: no hdwy) 1½	**6**	10/1	78	54
1594^{6}	**Mister Jolson (78)** (RJHodges) **8-8-13**(5) RFfrench(6) (nvr trbld ldrs) ......s.h	**7**	11/2 3	72	48
457^{8}	**Robellion (65)** (DWPArbuthnot) **6-8-5v** SWhitworth(2) (a bhd) 3½	**8**	14/1	50	26

(SP 115.9%) **8 Rn**

1m 11.8 (-1.20) CSF £35.79 CT £88.33 TOTE £8.20: £2.00 £2.00 £1.40 (£21.80) OWNER Mr Simon Mounsey (CULLOMPTON) BRED Mrs P. Lewis

403 Purple Fling, dropped 2lb, was 3lb better off than when less than three lengths behind Sir Joey last time at Goodwood. (6/1)
1410 Delta Soleil (USA) has gradually been slipping down the handicap and was suited by this stiff six. (11/2)
1317 Sir Joey (USA) has gone up a total of 4lb for finishing second on his last two runs and found trouble so late on that it is doubtful if his made any difference. (9/4: 6/4-5/2)
Faraway Lass gave notice she is coming to hand. (5/1)
1021 Bajan Rose, down 4lb, is still 3lb higher than when winning at Chester a year ago. (12/1)

1825 SHERBORNE CLAIMING H'CAP (0-60) (3-Y.O+) (Class F)
4-15 (4-16) **1m 4f** £2,994.00 (£834.00: £402.00) Stalls: High GOING minus 0.69 sec per fur (HD)

			SP	RR	SF
1779^{22}	**Norsong (40)** (RAkehurst) **5-8-9** AClark(15) (led after 2f: all out) ......—	**1**	8/1 3	50	14
1632^{10}	**Courageous Knight (42)** (PHayward) **8-8-8**(3) MHenry(4) (hdwy 3f out: hrd rdn & r.o ins fnl f) ......½	**2**	10/1	51	15
1636^{6}	**Rock The Barney (IRE) (40)** (MDIUsher) **8-8-9** DRMcCabe(9) (lw: wl bhd tl rapid hdwy over 2f out: one pce ins fnl f) 1¼	**3**	9/2 2	48	12
1426^{3}	**Chief Predator (USA) (52)** (RHannon) **3-8-6** DaneO'Neill(11) (bhd tl gd hdwy fnl 2f: nrst fin) ......hd	**4**	10/1	60	9
	Two Socks (59) (JSKing) **4-9-9**(5) RFfrench(10) (plld hrd: a.p: ev ch 2f out: one pce) ......s.h	**5**	16/1	67	31
1592^{10}	**High Desire (IRE) (49)** (JRArnold) **4-9-4** DHarrison(8) (hld up: hdwy 4f out: wknd 2f out) 3	**6**	16/1	53	17
1426^{2}	**Ronquista d'Or (51)** (GAHam) **3-8-5** NCarlisle(2) (nvr nrr) ......½	**7**	12/1	54	3
	Shy Paddy (IRE) (38) (KOCunningham-Brown) **5-8-7** BDoyle(3) (prom tl wknd 2f out) ......s.h	**8**	33/1	41	5
1686*	**Sun of Spring (55)** (DWChapman) **7-9-7**(3) 5x PFessey(6) (prom tl wknd 2f out) 1¼	**9**	4/1 1	56	20
1636^{10}	**Blue And Royal (IRE) (42)** (VSoane) **5-8-11** CRutter(13) (a mid div) ......s.h	**10**	33/1	43	7
1636^{12}	**Oscar Rose (41)** (MJBolton) **4-8-10** JQuinn(16) (nvr nr ldrs) 3	**11**	33/1	38	2
1632^{13}	**Country Thatch (44)** (CAHorgan) **4-8-13** PaulEddery(20) (wl bhd tl some late hdwy) 2½	**12**	12/1	38	2
1383^{17}	**Racing Hawk (USA) (43)** (MSSaunders) **5-8-12** RPrice(19) (mid div: rdn 3f out: bhd fnl 2f) ......¾	**13**	33/1	36	—
210^{6}	**Rapid Liner (38)** (RJBaker) **4-8-7**ow2 VSlattery(17) (prom: hrd rdn over 5f out: wknd over 3f out) 1¾	**14**	33/1	28	—
1416^{5}	**Kingsdown Trix (IRE) (55)** (GLMoore) **3-8-9** RPerham(5) (hld up: hdwy 5f out: wknd over 2f out) 2½	**15**	14/1	42	—
1507^{11}	**Blaze of Oak (USA) (36)** (JMBradley) **6-8-5** TSprake(1) (lw: hld up mid div: bhd fnl 3f) 2	**16**	16/1	20	—
1618^{2}	**Nornax Lad (USA) (50)** (MartynMeade) **9-9-5** FNorton(7) (led 2f: rdn over 4f out: wknd over 3f out) 5	**17**	9/1	28	—
1445^{W}	**Prove The Point (IRE) (38)** (MrsPNDutfield) **4-8-2**(5) AimeeCook(12) (a bhd) 1¼	**18**	33/1	14	—
1636^{17}	**Seventh Edition (55)** (PGMurphy) **4-9-10** SDrowne(18) (prom over 8f: t.o) 18	**19**	33/1	7	—
	Thor's Phantom (40) (MDIUsher) **4-8-9** JMarshall(14) (prom 6f: t.o fnl 3f) ......nk	**20**	33/1	—	—

(SP 140.7%) **20 Rn**

2m 34.9 (3.90) CSF £82.10 CT £373.40 TOTE £10.70: £2.60 £5.50 £1.30 £2.50 (£149.60) Trio £387.90 OWNER The Fairy Story Partnership (EPSOM) BRED Deepwood Farm Stud
WEIGHT FOR AGE 3yo-15lb

650 Norsong, making a quick reappearance, was 11lb lower than when winning over an extra quarter-mile here last June. (8/1)
Courageous Knight seemed rejuvenated by this step up in distance. (10/1)
1636 Rock The Barney (IRE) came from an impossible position but not surprisingly could not sustain the run. (9/2: 3/1-5/1)
1426 Chief Predator (USA), 8lb lower than when last in a handicap, was another who found himself with a lot to do. (10/1: op 6/1)
Two Socks ran well on his first run for his new stable. (16/1)
High Desire (IRE), dropped in class, improved considerably on his two previous efforts this season. (16/1)
1426 Ronquista d'Or (12/1: 7/1-14/1)
Country Thatch (12/1: tchd 20/1)
906* Kingsdown Trix (IRE) (14/1: 6/1-16/1)

1826 DORSET H'CAP (0-70) (3-Y.O) (Class E)
4-45 (4-50) **1m** £3,288.25 (£991.00: £480.50: £225.25) Stalls: High GOING minus 0.69 sec per fur (HD)

			SP	RR	SF
1151^{9}	**Chasetown Flyer (USA) (52)** (NEBerry) **3-8-4** BDoyle(3) (a.p: rdn to ld over 1f out: r.o wl) ......—	**1**	33/1	60	25
1568^{6}	**Sand Cay (USA) (62)** (RHannon) **3-9-0** DaneO'Neill(12) (a.p: r.o one pce fnl f) 1½	**2**	14/1	67	32
1164^{10}	**First Chance (IRE) (68)** (DRCElsworth) **3-9-6** RCochrane(11) (lw: a.p: r.o ins fnl f) 1	**3**	25/1	71	36
1633*	**Agent Mulder (61)** (PDCundell) **3-8-13** 6x RPerham(5) (a.p: led 2f out: sn hdd: one pce fnl f) ......s.h	**4**	4/1 1	64	29
1633^{8}	**Jolly Jackson (55)** (RAkehurst) **3-8-7** KFallon(16) (hld up: hdwy over 3f out: r.o one pce fnl f) ......hd	**5**	13/2 3	58	23
1568^{2}	**Warring (62)** (MSSaunders) **3-8-11**(3) PPMurphy(14) (a.p: one pce fnl 2f) ......½	**6**	13/2 3	64	29
1245^{7}	**Sound Appeal (62)** (AGFoster) **3-9-0b** TSprake(13) (gd late hdwy: fin wl) ......s.h	**7**	25/1	64	29
1567^{5}	**Flyaway Hill (FR) (63)** (PWHarris) **3-9-1** AClark(2) (hld up & bhd: hdwy 4f out: rdn over 2f out: one pce) 1¼	**8**	10/1	62	27
1164^{6}	**Hadawah (USA) (62)** (JLDunlop) **3-9-0** PatEddery(17) (nvr nr to chal) 2	**9**	5/1 2	57	22
1245^{13}	**Inclination (69)** (MBlanshard) **3-9-7** JQuinn(10) (led 6f) 1	**10**	33/1	62	27
1474^{5}	**Time Can Tell (66)** (CMurray) **3-9-4** NicolaHowarth(8) (prom over 5f) ......½	**11**	33/1	58	23
1000^{11}	**Oneknight With You (65)** (MJFetherston-Godley) **3-9-3** LDettori(1) (prom tl wknd over 1f out) ......nk	**12**	10/1	57	22

1423^{5}	**Mary Culi (60)** (HCandy) **3-8-12** CRutter(15) (a bhd)	½	**13**	8/1	51	16
1568^{11}	**Aficionado (IRE) (67)** (RJHodges) **3-9-0**$^{(5)}$ RFfrench(18) (a bhd)	½	**14**	25/1	57	22
1485^{6}	**Kanawa (52)** (APJones) **3-8-4** GHind(9) (plld hrd mid div: bhd fnl 2f)	7	**15**	33/1	28	—
1587^{9}	**Ardent (61)** (CJBenstead) **3-8-13** AMcGlone(6) (a bhd)	5	**16**	14/1	27	—
	Sea Mist (IRE) (60) (PGMurphy) **3-8-12** SDrowne(4) (a bhd)	1¼	**17**	33/1	23	—
1568^{4}	**Sun O'Tirol (IRE) (60)** (JRArnold) **3-8-12** DHarrison(7) (prom: rdn & ev ch over 2f out: eased whn btn over 1f out)	½	**18**	20/1	22	—
				(SP 137.0%)	**18 Rn**	

1m 40.9 (0.90) CSF £406.26 CT £10,420.83 TOTE £40.60: £5.90 £5.50 £3.70 £1.90 (£395.10) Trio £674.40; £854.92 to Beverley 11/6/97
OWNER Mr D. W. Smith (UPPER LAMBOURN) BRED Pin Oak Stud

649 Chasetown Flyer (USA), 3lb lower than his last outing on turf, came into his own over this longer distance. (33/1)
1568 Sand Cay (USA), dropped 3lb, was suited by this stiff mile. (14/1)
642 First Chance (IRE) should stay further. (25/1)
1633* Agent Mulder was effectively 9lb higher than when second over course and distance before his win last time. (4/1)
840 Jolly Jackson is on a handy mark having come down nearly a stone this season but seems to require a longer trip. (13/2)
1568 Warring was 4lb higher than when a good second last time. (13/2)
Sound Appeal seems the type to have a mind of her own and took an age to respond to her rider's urgings. (25/1)
Flyaway Hill (FR) (10/1: op 6/1)
1164 Hadawah (USA), given a chance by the handicapper, might do better over an extra quarter-mile. (5/1)
1423 Mary Culi (8/1: tchd 12/1)

1827 EDDIE REAVEY MAIDEN AUCTION STKS (II) (2-Y.O F) (Class E)

5-15 (5-18) **6f** £2,581.00 (£716.00: £343.00) Stalls: High GOING minus 0.69 sec per fur (HD)

				SP	RR	SF
985^{8}	**Lisa's Pride (IRE)** (MissGayKelleway) **2-8-7** KFallon(1) (s.i.s: hrd rdn over 2f out: str run to ld nr fin)	—	**1**	20/1	73	24
828^{2}	**Phone Alex (IRE)** (RHannon) **2-8-7** PatEddery(3) (w ldr: hrd rdn & ev ch fnl f: r.o)	½	**2**	8/13^{1}	72	23
1593^{4}	**Fire Goddess** (JSMoore) **2-7-11**$^{(3)}$ MHenry(7) (led: rdn over 2f out: hdd nr fin)	hd	**3**	13/2^{3}	64	15
1136^{4}	**Elleysanta** (AGNewcombe) **2-8-0** JQuinn(4) (a.p: ev ch ins fnl f: r.o)	hd	**4**	20/1	64	15
999^{7}	**Shalad'or** (BRMillman) **2-8-1**^{ow1} BDoyle(9) (plld hrd: prom tl wknd over 1f out)	4	**5**	50/1	55	5
1480^{2}	**Bermuda Triangle (IRE)** (MJHaynes) **2-7-11**$^{(3)}$ AWhelan(10) (nvr nrr)	1¼	**6**	4/1^{2}	50	1
1163^{8}	**Petaling (IRE)** (BJMeehan) **2-8-7** JReid(11) (prom 3f)	3	**7**	9/1	49	—
	Wind In The Park (MSalaman) **2-7-9**$^{(5)}$ RFfrench(5) (unf: sn outpcd)	2	**8**	50/1	37	—
1425^{10}	**Fleet Lady (IRE)** (MrsPNDutfield) **2-8-3** SDrowne(2) (chsd ldrs 3f)	hd	**9**	66/1	40	—
	Princess Senorita (PEccles) **2-8-0** CRutter(8) (unf: dwlt: outpcd: t.o fnl 3f)	11	**10**	50/1	7	—
	Impish Lady (IRE) (MartynMeade) **2-8-7** FNorton(6) (scope: dwlt: sn t.o)	16	**11**	20/1	—	—
				(SP 126.9%)	**11 Rn**	

1m 13.8 (0.80) CSF £31.05 TOTE £15.80: £3.10 £1.20 £2.40 (£8.20) Trio £33.00 OWNER Mr A. P. Griffin (WHITCOMBE) BRED Weatherfield Ltd

IN-FOCUS: **This was 1.7 seconds slower than the first division.**

Lisa's Pride (IRE) is a half-sister to the sprinter Soba Guest, a mile winner in Spain and a nine furlong winner in Ireland. She really relished this extra furlong and should stay further. (20/1)
828 Phone Alex (IRE) completed a miserable afternoon for favourite backers especially those chasing their losses on the apparent odds-on good thing. (8/13)
1593 Fire Goddess had a hard race in an attempt to keep the edge over the favourite. (13/2: 9/2-7/1)
1136 Elleysanta looked much more at home over this extra furlong. (20/1)
Shalad'or, a half-sister to second-race winner Shalateeno and Shalholme, is going to need to settle better to get six at this stage of her career. (50/1)
1480 Bermuda Triangle (IRE), a half-sister to five-furlong winner The Dream Maker, shaped as though she already needed further. (4/1)

T/Jkpt: Not won; £25,585.74 to Beverley 11/6/97. T/Plpt: £563.70 (35.5 Tckts). T/Qdpt: £8.40 (193.73 Tckts) KH

1682-BEVERLEY (R-H) (Good becoming Soft)
Wednesday June 11th

WEATHER: steady & persistent rain WIND: slt half bhd

1828 POLYGON (HUMBERSIDE) H'CAP (0-70) (3-Y.O+ F & M) (Class E)

2-00 (2-02) **5f** £3,153.25 (£946.00: £455.50: £210.25) Stalls: High GOING minus 0.47 sec per fur (F)

				SP	RR	SF
1602^{3}	**Sunset Harbour (IRE) (40)** (SEKettlewell) **4-7-8**$^{(5)}$ RFfrench(1) (swtchd rt s: sn chsng ldrs: led over 1f out: hld on towards fin)	—	**1**	9/1^{3}	47	21
1734^{7}	**Pathaze (39)** (NBycroft) **4-7-12** LCharnock(12) (chsd ldrs: chal over 1f out: nt qckn nr fin)	s.h	**2**	20/1	46	20
1627^{6}	**Dominelle (50)** (TDEasterby) **5-8-9** JCarroll(6) (racd stands' side: chsd ldrs: styd on wl ins fnl f)	hd	**3**	9/1^{3}	57	31
1419^{3}	**Pharaoh's Joy (57)** (JWPayne) **4-9-2** KDarley(3) (racd stands' side: chsd ldrs: nt qckn appr fnl f)	1¾	**4**	8/1^{2}	58	32
	Premium Gift (58) (CBBBooth) **5-9-3** KHodgson(16) (lw: bhd: hdwy ½-wy: styd on wl fnl f: nt rch ldrs)	hd	**5**	10/1	59	33
1428^{4}	**Amoeba (IRE) (48)** (ABailey) **4-8-7b** DWright(7) (bhd: styd on appr fnl f: nt rch ldrs)	¾	**6**	14/1	46	20
1468^{12}	**Tart and a Half (69)** (JLEyre) **5-9-11v**$^{1(3)}$ OPears(15) (swvd rt s: hdwy ½-wy: sn chsng ldrs: rdn & wknd over 1f out)	s.h	**7**	14/1	67	41
1561^{8}	**Time To Tango (61)** (GMMoore) **4-9-6** JWeaver(9) (led tl over 1f out: grad wknd)	1¾	**8**	8/1^{2}	53	27
1644^{4}	**Caspian Morn (62)** (WGMTurner) **3-8-9**$^{(5)}$ DSweeney(2) (racd stands' side: chsd ldrs tl wknd over 1f out)	1	**9**	20/1	51	18
1667^{3}	**Mystical (54)** (MrsLStubbs) **3-7-13v**$^{(7)}$ JGotobed(11) (w ldr tl wknd over 1f out)	½	**10**	11/1	42	9
1765^{3}	**Oatey (64)** (MrsJRRamsden) **4-9-9** JFortune(14) (lw: chsd ldrs: effrt 2f out: wknd appr fnl f)	hd	**11**	2/1^{1}	51	25
1759^{9}	**Bent Raiwand (USA) (50)** (DonEnricoIncisa) **4-8-9** KimTinkler(17) (sn bhd)	½	**12**	33/1	36	10
883^{18}	**Rotherfield Park (IRE) (40)** (CSmith) **5-7-6**$^{(7)ow3}$ RWinston(4) (racd stands' side: outpcd fr ½-wy)	2½	**13**	33/1	18	—
1573^{10}	**Sarabi (50)** (JPearce) **3-7-13v**$^{(3)}$ MHenry(10) (chsd ldrs over 3f: sn wknd)	2	**14**	20/1	21	—
1627^{12}	**Oh Whataknight (60)** (RMWhitaker) **4-9-5** DeanMcKeown(8) (b: sn bhd)	1	**15**	33/1	28	2
1586^{2}	**Ohnonotagain (40)** (LRLloyd-James) **5-7-13** DaleGibson(13) (sn drvn along & bhd)	2½	**16**	16/1	—	—

1604[3]	**Superfrills (40)** (MissLCSiddall) **4-7-13** TWilliams(5) (racd stands' side: chsd ldrs: edgd rt ½-wy: sn lost pl)	nk	**17**	20/1	—	—
				(SP 140.1%)		**17 Rn**

63.4 secs (1.60) CSF £177.42 CT £1,603.08 TOTE £11.40: £2.40 £3.90 £2.30 £1.90 (£72.70) Trio £430.70; £181.99 to Newbury 12/6/97
OWNER Mr J. Tennant (MIDDLEHAM) BRED Robert J. Thomas
LONG HANDICAP Rotherfield Park (IRE) 7-3
WEIGHT FOR AGE 3yo-7lb
IN-FOCUS: **The going was officially Good to Firm changed to Good after the fourth race but, after persistent and heavy rain in the morning and throughout the afternoon, the jockeys reported the going was Good to Soft for Race 1 and Soft thereafter.**
1602 Sunset Harbour (IRE), on paper worst drawn, was switched to race on the far side and got home by the skin of her teeth. (9/1)
Pathaze has only won once from twenty-six outings but she nearly made it two here. (20/1)
1627 Dominelle, on her toes beforehand, came out best of the five who raced towards the stands' side. (9/1)
1419 Pharaoh's Joy was second best on the stands' side. (8/1)
Premium Gift, on her reappearance, looked in good shape beforehand and ran creditably, sticking on nicely in the final furlong. (10/1)
901 Time To Tango (8/1: 6/1-9/1)
1765 Oatey had much more use made of her than usual and this below-par effort is best overlooked. (2/1)

1829 MORE LEARNING CLAIMING STKS (2-Y.O) (Class F)
2-30 (2-33) **5f** £2,547.50 (£710.00: £342.50) Stalls: High GOING minus 0.47 sec per fur (F)

				SP	RR	SF
1253[3]	**Penniless (IRE)** (NTinkler) **2-8-12** KimTinkler(7) (chsd ldrs: rdn & hung rt over 1f out: styd on wl fnl f: led last 50y)	—	**1**	7/1	73	11
1444[3]	**Sandy Shore** (JWharton) **2-8-12** JCarroll(6) (prom: rdn & outpcd ½-wy: kpt on wl fnl f)	¾	**2**	11/1	71	9
*1432**	**Ellenbrook (IRE)** (JBerry) **2-8-5b**(3) PFessey(11) (led: rdn over 1f out: hdd nr fin)	nk	**3**	3/1 [2]	66	4
1569[5]	**Bow Peep (IRE)** (MWEasterby) **2-8-7**(5) GParkin(8) (sn bhd & pushed along: swtchd outside 2f out: styd on wl fnl f)	1½	**4**	6/1 [3]	65	3
1466[6]	**Inchalong** (MBrittain) **2-8-8** KDarley(3) (in tch: rdn & wl outpcd ½-wy: styd on fnl f)	hd	**5**	9/1	61	—
1391[4]	**Mister Bankes** (WGMTurner) **2-8-10b**[1](7) DMcGaffin(10) (w ldr: rdn & hung rt over 1f out: sn wknd)	1¾	**6**	7/4 [1]	64	2
993[12]	**Hayburner** (MWEasterby) **2-8-13** DaleGibson(2) (s.i.s: bhd: sme hdwy appr fnl f: n.d)	4	**7**	25/1	47	—
1492[13]	**Are Yer There** (MWEasterby) **2-9-3** TLucas(5) (sn outpcd: kpt on appr fnl f: nvr nr ldrs)	1	**8**	25/1	48	—
	Wynbury Flyer (FMurphy) **2-8-4**(5) RFfrench(4) (lt-f: unf: sn bhd)	¾	**9**	20/1	38	—
1600[6]	**Miss Beveled** (MBrittain) **2-7-7v**[1](7) DMernagh(9) (chsd ldrs 3f: sn wknd)	½	**10**	16/1	27	—
	Tancred Times (DWBarker) **2-8-0** TWilliams(1) (lt-f: unf: bit bkwd: unruly s: swvd lft s: sn chsng ldrs: edgd rt & wknd ½-wy)	½	**11**	16/1	25	—
				(SP 130.7%)		**11 Rn**

64.8 secs (3.00) CSF £80.46 TOTE £7.80: £3.00 £2.30 £1.70 (£44.20) Trio £43.80 OWNER Consultco Ltd (MALTON) BRED Clinton Investments
1253 Penniless (IRE) had to be pulled out from behind the two leaders. Once in the clear, she stayed on in determined fashion. (7/1)
1444 Sandy Shore is improving with every outing and there was plenty to like about the way she stuck on here. (11/1)
1432* Ellenbrook (IRE) set a strong gallop but in the rain-softened ground she was worn down near the finish. (3/1: op 2/1)
1569 Bow Peep (IRE) failed completely to go the pace but finished best of all. Despite having shown speed on her debut, she seems to be crying out for six furlongs. (6/1)
1466 Inchalong is another who now finds the minimum trip too sharp. (9/1)
1391 Mister Bankes, fitted with blinkers for the first time, was on his toes beforehand and gave his rider problems, persisting in hanging right. (7/4)
Hayburner stayed on late in the day and needs at least six. (25/1)
Are Yer There showed definite signs of ability and is the type to show in a more favourable light in Nursery company over further later on. (25/1)

1830 ELTHERINGTON H'CAP (0-70) (3-Y.O+) (Class E)
3-00 (3-01) **7f 100y** £3,834.00 (£1,152.00: £556.00: £258.00) Stalls: High GOING minus 0.47 sec per fur (F)

				SP	RR	SF
1496[9]	**Dee Pee Tee Cee (IRE) (46)** (MWEasterby) **3-8-3** TLucas(1) (mde virtually all: swtchd rt after 1f: styd on strly fnl f)	—	**1**	13/2 [2]	60	31
1154[7]	**Duke Valentino (56)** (RHollinshead) **5-9-6**(3) DGriffiths(7) (hld up & bhd: gd hdwy 2f out: styd on same pce ins fnl f: no imp)	2	**2**	25/1	66	47
1687*	**Reinhardt (IRE) (40)** (DNicholls) **4-8-2**(5) IonaWands(11) (sn drvn along: in tch: styd on same pce fnl 2f)	1¾	**3**	13/2 [2]	46	27
1655[5]	**Euro Sceptic (IRE) (42)** (TDEasterby) **5-8-9b** JWeaver(3) (bhd: shkn up over 2f out: styd on wl appr fnl f: nt rch ldrs)	1¼	**4**	7/2 [1]	45	26
1580[10]	**Sandblaster (43)** (JLEyre) **4-8-10** MGallagher(6) (plld hrd: trckd ldrs: rdn over 2f out: wknd over 1f out)	hd	**5**	14/1	46	27
1655[3]	**Oriel Lad (31)** (DonEnricoIncisa) **4-7-12b** KimTinkler(10) (bhd: hdwy on ins over 2f out: nvr nr to chal)	1¼	**6**	12/1	31	12
1677[3]	**Cee-Jay-Ay (46)** (JBerry) **10-8-13** KDarley(12) (s.i.s: sn drvn along: hdwy ½-wy: one pce whn n.m.r over 1f out)	½	**7**	10/1	45	26
1631[7]	**Roseate Lodge (34)** (SEKettlewell) **11-7-8**(7) JennyBenson(8) (mid div: effrt 3f out: hung lft & styd on appr fnl f)	½	**8**	20/1	32	13
1511*	**Shontaine (53)** (MJohnston) **4-9-1**(5) KSked(5) (chsd ldrs: rdn over 2f out: wknd over 1f out)	nk	**9**	7/1 [3]	51	32
1584[4]	**Surf City (50)** (WWHaigh) **4-9-3** LCharnock(14) (lw: chsd ldrs: rdn over 3f out: wknd 2f out)	hd	**10**	10/1	47	28
1674[3]	**Desert Cat (IRE) (57)** (MartynWane) **4-9-10** JCarroll(2) (hdwy & swtchd stands' side over 2f out: n.d)	nk	**11**	11/1	54	35
1511[3]	**Rymer's Rascal (57)** (EJAlston) **5-9-10** ACulhane(13) (lw: trckd ldrs: chal 3f out: edgd lft & wknd over 1f out)	1	**12**	15/2	52	33
1603[11]	**Perilous Plight (49)** (MrsLStubbs) **6-8-11**(5) PRoberts(4) (s.i.s: a bhd: c wd ent st)	6	**13**	25/1	31	12
1433[2]	**Dawalib (USA) (55)** (DHaydnJones) **7-9-8** JFortune(9) (in tch: effrt over 3f out: sn rdn & wknd: p.u & dismntd nr fin)		**P**	9/1	—	—
				(SP 136.5%)		**14 Rn**

1m 33.7 (1.70) CSF £163.69 CT £1,056.47 TOTE £9.30: £2.60 £7.10 £2.40 (£124.20) Trio £543.50 OWNER Early Morning Breakfast Syndicate (SHERIFF HUTTON) BRED Michael and Heather Scott
WEIGHT FOR AGE 3yo-10lb
OFFICIAL EXPLANATION **Euro Sceptic (IRE): rider reported his instructions were to drop the gelding in, as the horse does not like to see too much daylight. However, he was unable to get covered up without losing too much ground. Once in the straight, the gelding had to work his way through a tight field. Dawalib (USA): was distressed.**
1496 Dee Pee Tee Cee (IRE), stepping up in distance and slipping down the weights, was worst drawn, but his jockey showed plenty of enterprise, bouncing him out of the stalls and switching him across to secure the rails position. The way he stayed on when challenged, the full mile will suit him even better. (13/2)

297* Duke Valentino ran his best race on the turf for a long time but he is almost a two stone better horse on the All-Weather. (25/1)
1687* Reinhardt (IRE), who was possibly flattered by his win over five furlongs here a week ago, when the leaders went too fast, on this occasion was under pressure some way from home. Sticking on at the finish, a slight step up in distance might suit him. (13/2)
1655 Euro Sceptic (IRE) was poorly drawn in stall three but the winner was drawn two outside him. A horse who has to be covered up, he was kept wide and when eventually switched inside, he took it in his head to run on. He likes it round here, and there is no doubt he is on a mark from which he can win again when everything goes right. (7/2: 11/2-3/1)
1116 Sandblaster is still a maiden after nineteen outings, but she certainly has the ability to open her account . (14/1)

1831 UNIVERSITY OF LINCOLNSHIRE AND HUMBERSIDE H'CAP (0-80) (3-Y.O+) (Class D)

3-30 (3-33) **1m 1f 207y** £3,470.00 (£1,040.00: £500.00: £230.00) Stalls: High GOING minus 0.08 sec per fur (G)

				SP	RR	SF
1268[7]	**Flying North (IRE) (73)** (MrsMReveley) **4-9-12** ACulhane(3) (hld up: stdy hdwy over 3f out: led over 1f out: sn clr)	—	1	4/1[3]	88	72
1427[11]	**Askern (60)** (DHaydnJones) **6-8-13** LCharnock(5) (s.i.s: hdwy 4f out: led over 2f out tl over 1f out: no ch w wnr)	8	2	11/2	62	46
1463[7]	**Gold Desire (49)** (MBrittain) **7-8-2** JLowe(2) (sn outpcd & pushed along: hdwy over 2f out: one pce)	2½	3	7/2[2]	47	31
1482[10]	**Bandore (IRE) (80)** (DRLoder) **3-9-6** KDarley(4) (trckd ldrs: rdn & wknd over 1f out: eased)	14	4	9/1	56	27
1683*	**Mr Teigh (65)** (MrsJRRamsden) **5-9-4** [5x] JFortune(6) (sn w ldr: styd alone far side: wknd over 2f out: virtually p.u ins fnl f)	12	5	7/4[1]	21	5
1597[3]	**Prospector's Cove (75)** (JPearce) **4-10-0v[1]** MWigham(1) (led tl over 2f out: sn wknd & eased)	1	6	12/1	30	14
				(SP 111.7%)		**6 Rn**

2m 6.9 (3.80) CSF £22.89 TOTE £5.20: £1.80 £2.90 (£21.80) OWNER Dr Glyn Meredith (SALTBURN) BRED P. Henley
WEIGHT FOR AGE 3yo-13lb
OFFICIAL EXPLANATION **Mr Teigh: no explanation offered.**
1268 Flying North (IRE), an in-and-out performer, showed a good turn of foot in what was a moderately-run affair. (4/1)
Askern kicked for home off the bend, but in the end was left for dead by the winner on ground softer than he prefers. (11/2)
1463 Gold Desire looks in the grip of the Handicapper at present. (7/2)
Bandore (IRE), from a 5lb lower mark, wore a tongue strap. He found little under pressure and was eased and presumably had some sort of problem. (9/1: op 6/1)
1683* Mr Teigh was the only one to stay on the far side. The ground was almost certainly much slower than the official going because of the persistent rain on watered ground. This is best overlooked. (7/4)
Prospector's Cove, who was fitted with a visor for the first time, made no appeal at all in the paddock. (12/1: op 8/1)

1832 ERNEST NORRIS MEMORIAL H'CAP (0-85) (3-Y.O+) (Class D)

4-00 (4-00) **1m 3f 216y** £3,444.00 (£1,032.00: £496.00: £228.00) Stalls: High GOING minus 0.08 sec per fur (G)

				SP	RR	SF
1459[8]	**Infatuation (71)** (LadyHerries) **4-9-12** KDarley(1) (hld up: stdy hdwy over 4f out: hung rt & led over 1f out: drvn out)	—	1	9/4[1]	83	—
1660[3]	**Road Racer (IRE) (61)** (MrsJRRamsden) **4-9-2** JFortune(5) (lw: hld up: stdy hdwy over 2f out: effrt over 1f out: sn rdn & no imp)	2½	2	3/1[3]	70	—
1628[2]	**Augustan (55)** (SGollings) **6-8-10** JWeaver(4) (trckd ldrs: kpt on same pce appr fnl f)	nk	3	3/1[3]	63	—
1408*	**Express Gift (54)** (MrsMReveley) **8-8-9** ACulhane(2) (hld up: hdwy over 4f out: sn chsng ldrs: led over 2f out tl over 1f out: sn wl outpcd)	4	4	5/2[2]	57	—
1624[6]	**Swiftway (65)** (KWHogg) **3-8-5** DeanMcKeown(3) (set mod pce: hdd over 2f out: wknd over 1f out)	3	5	16/1	64	—
				(SP 115.2%)		**5 Rn**

2m 52.0 (19.00) CSF £8.96 TOTE £3.10: £1.70 £1.80 (£6.60) OWNER Lady Katharine Phillips (LITTLEHAMPTON) BRED Cheveley Park Stud Ltd
WEIGHT FOR AGE 3yo-15lb
Infatuation, stepping up in distance, has an awkward head carriage, but he did nothing wrong and took this in decisive fashion. (9/4)
1660 Road Racer (IRE) tried hard to get in a blow but in the end the winner proved much too good. (3/1)
1628 Augustan is running right up to his best at present. (3/1)
1408* Express Gift had little chance over this trip in a slowly-run race. (5/2)
445 Swiftway set only a modest pace but his stamina seemed to give out. (16/1)

1833 UNIVERSITY INTERNATIONAL LIMITED STKS (0-70) (3-Y.O+) (Class E)

4-30 (4-31) **1m 100y** £2,812.00 (£841.00: £403.00: £184.00) Stalls: High GOING minus 0.08 sec per fur (G)

				SP	RR	SF
1651[2]	**Neronian (IRE) (70)** (BWHills) **3-8-8** JCarroll(1) (trckd ldrs: rdn to ld over 1f out: styd on wl)	—	1	6/4[1]	77	39
1302[6]	**Get The Point (70)** (RHollinshead) **3-8-8** FLynch(5) (hld up: hdwy over 2f out: kpt on fnl f: no imp)	1¾	2	4/1[2]	74	36
1421[8]	**Freedom Chance (IRE) (70)** (JWHills) **3-8-7(3)** MHenry(4) (trckd ldrs: pushed along over 3f out: one pce fnl 2f)	½	3	4/1[2]	75	37
1495[6]	**Stellar Line (USA) (70)** (MJPolglase) **4-9-7** KDarley(3) (led tl over 1f out: one pce)	½	4	4/1[2]	74	47
1472[13]	**Raed (69)** (MrsASwinbank) **4-9-5** JFortune(2) (trckd ldrs: plld hrd: rdn & outpcd over 1f out: edgd rt & sn wknd)	2½	5	5/1[3]	67	40
				(SP 116.7%)		**5 Rn**

1m 48.9 (4.90) CSF £7.69 TOTE £2.50: £1.60 £2.00 (£4.10) OWNER Sheikh Mohammed (LAMBOURN) BRED Sheikh Mohammed Bin Rashid Al Maktoum
WEIGHT FOR AGE 3yo-11lb
1651 Neronian (IRE) took this modest event mostly contested by disappointing horses in decisive fashion. (6/4: 4/5-15/8)
842 Get The Point, a pottery mover, was probably suited by the rain-softened ground. Given a patient ride, he never came under severe pressure and seemed to be asked to do just enough to secure second spot. (4/1)
535* Freedom Chance (IRE) appeared to run better after two moderate efforts. (4/1: op 7/1)
1495 Stellar Line (USA), who wore a cross-noseband, as usual set the pace. (4/1: 3/1-9/2)
899 Raed pulled very hard and it is hard to know what trip will suit him best. (5/1)

1834 REGIONAL UNIVERSITY MAIDEN STKS (3-Y.O+) (Class D)

5-00 (5-01) **7f 100y** £3,457.00 (£1,036.00: £498.00: £229.00) Stalls: High GOING minus 0.08 sec per fur (G)

				SP	RR	SF
	Prima Verde (LMCumani) **4-9-2** KDarley(6) (b: trckd ldrs: shkn up to ld over 2f out: pushed wl clr over 1f out: eased towards fin)	—	1	5/2[2]	68+	50

				SP	RR	SF
1271^{10}	**Impetus** (JHetherton) **3-8-11** JLowe(7) (b.hind: stdd s: hld up & bhd: hdwy over 1f out: kpt on wl)	8	**2**	33/1	56	28
	Taragona (RHollinshead) **4-9-2** FLynch(4) (sn bhd: hdwy u.p 2f out: styd on ins fnl f)	nk	**3**	20/1	50	32
1630^{6}	**Storyteller (IRE)** (MrsJRRamsden) **3-8-11** JFortune(9) (trckd ldrs: outpcd over 2f out: kpt on fnl f)	2	**4**	$10/1^{3}$	51	23
	Quaint Desire (MBrittain) **4-9-0**(7) DMernagh(5) (leggy: bhd fr ½-wy)	3	**5**	20/1	45	27
1302^{3}	**Round Robin (IRE)** (CWThornton) **3-8-11** DeanMcKeown(1) (lw: trckd ldrs: rdn & hung rt over 2f out: lost pl over 1f out)	1¼	**6**	$4/5^{1}$	42	14
1656^{3}	**Forest Signal** (MBrittain) **3-8-11** JCarroll(8) (led tl over 2f out: wknd fnl f)	1	**7**	14/1	40	12
1686^{8}	**Rush Me Not (IRE)** (MPBielby) **4-9-2**(5) GParkin(2) (outpcd fr ½-wy)	1	**8**	50/1	38	20

(SP 114.3%) **8 Rn**

1m 36.0 (4.00) CSF £74.37 TOTE £3.70: £1.60 £2.80 £2.30 (£63.80) Trio £156.50 OWNER The Lawster Partnership (NEWMARKET) BRED Mrs L. Popely

WEIGHT FOR AGE 3yo-10lb

OFFICIAL EXPLANATION Round Robin (IRE): no explanation offered.

Prima Verde, a heavy-topped filly, had just one previous outing at three. Bandaged in front, she seemed to appreciate the rain-softened ground and, pushed well clear, would have won by at least twelve lengths but for being eased up near the line. Her trainer will be hoping the Handicapper does not take this runaway success too literally because the form is almost certainly very poor. (5/2: op 6/4)

Impetus, who had shown next to nothing on two previous outings, still needs to learn to settle. (33/1)

Taragona, who had just one outing at three, stayed on from off the pace. (20/1)

765 Storyteller (IRE), who was having his mandatory third outing, is not the best of movers. Now qualified for a handicap mark, he should be suited by a step up in distance. (10/1: op 6/1)

Quaint Desire, who looks to have trouble with splints, was having his first ever outing. (20/1)

1302 Round Robin (IRE) was most disappointing, wanting to do nothing but hang under pressure. He must be better than he showed here. (4/5: evens-6/5)

T/Jkpt: Not won; £41,772.82 to Newbury 12/6/97. T/Plpt: £543.70 (26.8 Tckts). T/Qdpt: £56.40 (11.81 Tckts) WG

1613-HAMILTON (R-H) (Good, Good to soft patches)
Wednesday June 11th

WEATHER: overcast, rain last 2 races WIND: almost nil

1835 AKELER DEVELOPMENTS AMATEUR H'CAP (0-75) (3-Y.O+) (Class E)
7-00 (7-05) **5f 4y** £3,273.75 (£990.00: £482.50: £228.75) Stalls: Low GOING minus 0.26 sec per fur (GF)

				SP	RR	SF
1468^{6}	**Squire Corrie (71)** (DWChapman) **5-11-13** MissRClark(2) (swtchd far side: mde all: r.o wl)	—	**1**	20/1	82	64
1410^{4}	**Natural Key (70)** (DHaydnJones) **4-11-12** MissDianaJones(10) (a.p: hdwy 2f out: r.o: nrst fin)	2	**2**	$6/1^{2}$	75	57
1662^{6}	**Insider Trader (62)** (MrsJRRamsden) **6-10-13v**(5) MissERamsden(5) (lw: swtchd far side: chsd ldrs: effrt 2f out: kpt on)	1	**3**	11/1	63	45
1560^{12}	**Mister Westsound (37)** (MissLAPerratt) **5-9-0b**(7) MrDBShaw(7) (s.s: hdwy 2f out: r.o)	nk	**4**	33/1	38	20
1613^{9}	**Sunday Mail Too (IRE) (41)** (MissLAPerratt) **5-9-6**(5) MissBridgetGatehouse(16) (lw: prom: kpt on one pce appr fnl f)	s.h	**5**	14/1	41	23
1613^{3}	**Pallium (IRE) (43)** (DANolan) **9-9-13** MissJAllison(14) (hdwy ½-wy: sn in tch: no imp fnl f)	s.h	**6**	9/1	43	25
1561^{3}	**Just Bob (72)** (SEKettlewell) **8-12-0** MrsDKettlewell(3) (lw: s.i.s: racd centre: nvr rchd ldrs)	1	**7**	12/1	69	51
1613^{14}	**Impish (IRE) (55)** (TJEtherington) **3-10-4** MissAElsey(15) (prom: rdn ½-wy: no imp after)	hd	**8**	$7/1^{3}$	52	27
1613^{11}	**Suedoro (48)** (JSGoldie) **7-9-13**(5)ow8 MrOMcPhail(8) (in tch centre tl outpcd appr fnl f)	1½	**9**	25/1	40	14
1602^{5}	**Johayro (61)** (JSGoldie) **4-11-3** MrRHale(4) (cl up tl wknd appr fnl f)	nk	**10**	20/1	52	34
1311^{8}	**Leading Princess (IRE) (51)** (MissLAPerratt) **6-10-0b**(7)ow1 MissALHutchinson(1) (racd alone stands' side: no ch fr ½-wy)	½	**11**	25/1	40	21
1311^{5}	**King of Show (IRE) (50)** (RAllan) **6-10-1v**(5) MrVLukaniuk(17) (lw: chsd ldrs over 3f)	nk	**12**	10/1	38	20
1572^{5}	**Antithesis (IRE) (48)** (JSHaldane) **4-9-11**(7) MrJAStack(6) (racd centre: n.d)	3½	**13**	25/1	25	7
	Serious Hurry (37) (RMMcKellar) **9-9-2b**(5) MissADeniel(9) (spd 3f: wknd)	1	**14**	50/1	11	—
1613^{8}	**Tropical Beach (60)** (JBerry) **4-11-2** MrsLPearce(13) (sn outpcd & bhd)	4	**15**	$4/1^{1}$	21	3
1604^{7}	**Midas Man (37)** (DANolan) **6-9-0**(7) MrsDWilkinson(11) (s.s: a bhd)	1¾	**16**	200/1	—	—
1613^{6}	**Diet (46)** (MissLAPerratt) **11-9-9v**(7)ow9 MrRayBarrett(12) (sn bhd)	¾	**17**	20/1	—	—

(SP 119.8%) **17 Rn**

61.2 secs (2.90) CSF £109.41 CT £1,326.75 TOTE £22.00: £4.80 £1.40 £2.10 £3.90 (£68.30) Trio £206.30 OWNER Miss N. F. Thesiger (YORK) BRED Whitsbury Manor Stud

LONG HANDICAP Serious Hurry 9-5 Midas Man 8-9 Diet 9-6

WEIGHT FOR AGE 3yo-7lb

1468 Squire Corrie, well handled, showed tremendous speed to get across to the far side and was always in command. (20/1)

1410 Natural Key ran well off a handicap mark higher than she has won off and is obviously in good form. (6/1)

1662 Insider Trader had the visor on for the first time this season and ran well from a poor draw and, like the winner, crossed over to the far side. (11/1: 8/1-12/1)

Mister Westsound is a law unto himself and, after his usual slow start, he raced up the centre of the track and finished like the proverbial train. (33/1)

924 Sunday Mail Too (IRE) looked the part and had a good draw but was never quite good enough to take advantage of it. (14/1: op 8/1)

1613 Pallium (IRE) is running quite well but failed to pick up when ridden from halfway. (9/1: op 6/1)

1561 Just Bob did his usual and gave ground away at the start and, from his draw, that made the task impossible. (12/1)

1311 King of Show (IRE) (10/1: op 6/1)

1836 GLENGOYNE SINGLE HIGHLAND MALT CONDITIONS STKS (3-Y.O+) (Class C)
7-30 (7-30) **1m 1f 36y** £7,018.50 (£2,271.00: £1,110.50) Stalls: High GOING minus 0.26 sec per fur (GF)

				SP	RR	SF
	Riyadian (112) (PFICole) **5-9-4** TQuinn(3) (lw: b.off hind: mde all: pushed clr 3f out: easily)	—	**1**	$1/4^{1}$	112+	70
1739^{7}	**Unconditional Love (IRE) (95)** (MJohnston) **4-8-13** JWeaver(1) (a chsng wnr: rdn & no imp fnl 3f)	6	**2**	$14/1^{3}$	97	55
983*	**Rickenbacker (IRE)** (PWChapple-Hyam) **3-8-7**(3) RHavlin(2) (chsd ldrs: drvn along ½-wy: nvr able to chal)	1¾	**3**	$9/2^{2}$	103?	49

(SP 104.8%) **3 Rn**

1m 55.6 (1.30) CSF £3.54 TOTE £1.20 (£1.90) OWNER H R H Prince Fahd Salman (WHATCOMBE) BRED Newgate Stud Co.

WEIGHT FOR AGE 3yo-12lb

Riyadian was impressive in beating his two rivals and put up a really good time in the conditions. Hopefully he has not got over his niggling problems and will go on from here. (1/4)
Unconditional Love (IRE) put up a good performance but was completely outclassed by the winner, although this should have done her good. (14/1: op 8/1)
983* Rickenbacker (IRE), a winner of a maiden on soft ground last time, found this company a different matter and was struggling a long way from home. (9/2)

1837 SAINTS AND SINNERS CHALLENGE CUP H'CAP (0-85) (3-Y.O+) (Class D)

8-00 (8-01) **1m 65y** £7,035.00 (£2,130.00: £1,040.00: £495.00) Stalls: High GOING minus 0.26 sec per fur (GF)

				SP	RR	SF
1739*	**Philistar (66)** (KRBurke) **4-9-4** 6x TQuinn(5) (hld up: hdwy over 2f out: rdn to ld ins fnl f: hung rt: r.o)	—	**1**	13/8 1	76	42
1615^{2}	**Principal Boy (IRE) (44)** (TJEtherington) **4-7-10** DaleGibson(6) (in tch: hdwy 3f out: chal ins fnl f: kpt on wl)	¾	**2**	6/1 2	53	19
1663^{2}	**Takhlid (USA) (68)** (DWChapman) **6-9-3**(3) PFessey(2) (lw: cl up: led over 3f out tl ins fnl f: no ex)	½	**3**	10/1	76	42
1622^{3}	**Scaraben (75)** (SEKettlewell) **9-9-13** JFortune(4) (bhd: hdwy fnl 2f: nrst fin)	2	**4**	8/1 3	79	45
1082^{5}	**Prime Light (75)** (GWragg) **4-9-13** KDarley(7) (chsd ldrs: effrt 3f out: btn whn hmpd ins fnl f)	1½	**5**	6/1 2	76	42
600^{7}	**Belle Bijou (62)** (MJohnston) **3-8-3** DeanMcKeown(8) (in tch: effrt over 3f out: no imp)	1½	**6**	16/1	60	15
1615^{5}	**Rapid Mover (48)** (DANolan) **10-7-9b**(5)ow4 KSked(10) (led tl hdd over 3f out: grad wknd)	nk	**7**	200/1	25 t	7
1493^{4}	**Ninth Symphony (59)** (PCHaslam) **3-8-0** LCharnock(9) (bhd: effrt 4f out: n.d)	1¾	**8**	50/1	33 t	8
824^{10}	**Celebration Cake (IRE) (72)** (MissLAPerratt) **5-9-10** JWeaver(3) (lw: chsd ldrs tl rdn & btn 1f out)	1¼	**9**	16/1	44 t	30
1427^{12}	**William Wallace (64)** (DHaydnJones) **3-8-5** JCarroll(1) (chsd ldrs tl wknd fnl 2f)	9	**10**	8/1 3	18 t	—

(SP 112.2%) **10 Rn**

1m 48.2 (4.10) CSF £9.81 CT £64.76 TOTE £2.60: £1.30 £1.80 £2.90 (£7.70) Trio £26.20 OWNER Mr Nigel Shields (WANTAGE) BRED John A. Jones Morgan
LONG HANDICAP Rapid Mover 6-6
WEIGHT FOR AGE 3yo-11lb
1739* Philistar carries his head at an angle and tends to hang but is in tremendous form and, coming from off the pace, it is hard to judge how much he has to spare and the handicapper cannot over-punish him. (13/8)
1615 Principal Boy (IRE) is running tremendously well at present but, despite trying hard, met one too good here. (6/1)
1663 Takhlid (USA), a free-runner, is in good heart and is running consistently well just now. (10/1: 8/1-12/1)
1622 Scaraben is running well but is taking time to warm to his task these days. (8/1)
1082 Prime Light is beginning to prove disappointing. (6/1)
239* Belle Bijou, dropped back in trip here, lacked the pace to make any impression. (16/1)
Celebration Cake (IRE) is coming to himself looks wise and just needs a bit of help from the handicapper. (16/1)

1838 HAMILTON ADVERTISER (S) STKS (3-Y.O+) (Class E)

8-30 (8-34) **1m 1f 36y** £3,533.75 (£1,070.00: £522.50: £248.75) Stalls: High GOING minus 0.26 sec per fur (GF)

				SP	RR	SF
544^{9}	**Zorba (64)** (CWThornton) **3-8-4** DeanMcKeown(7) (lw: mde all: pushed clr over 2f out: rdn out)	—	**1**	2/1 1	70	26
1230^{16}	**Trying Times (IRE)** (JBerry) **4-9-2** KDarley(13) (chsd ldrs: wnt 2nd over 3f out: no imp)	8	**2**	4/1 3	56	24
1449^{W}	**Beau Roberto (54)** (MJohnston) **3-8-4b** DaleGibson(10) (a.p: effrt 4f out: r.o one pce)	½	**3**	9/2	55	11
	Just Whistle (MissMKMilligan) **5-8-11** JCarroll(6) (chsd wnr tl wknd fnl 3½f)	2½	**4**	20/1	46	14
667^{5}	**Murron Wallace (46)** (DHaydnJones) **3-7-13** LCharnock(3) (s.i.s: hdwy 5f out: sn chsng ldrs: outpcd fnl 2f)	3	**5**	7/2 2	41	—
1615^{6}	**Sweet Note (IRE) (46)** (MissLAPerratt) **3-7-13** NKennedy(12) (hdwy & prom 4f out: wknd fnl 2f)	8	**6**	20/1	27	—
	Palace River (IRE) (DMoffatt) **9-8-8**(3) DarrenMoffatt(2) (a outpcd & bhd)	4	**7**	16/1	20	—
1731^{5}	**Down Hearted (IRE)** (WTKemp) **3-8-4**(3)ow3 RHavlin(1) (sn outpcd & bhd)	7	**8**	50/1	15	—
	Operatic Dancer (27) (RMMcKellar) **6-8-9**(7) JMcAuley(5) (lw: cl up: c wd st: wknd 4f out)	1	**9**	100/1	11	—
1266^{8}	**Dario's Girl** (DMoffatt) **4-8-8**(3) PFessey(4) (a bhd)	22	**10**	50/1	—	—
1613^{16}	**Ragtime Cowgirl (32)** (DANolan) **4-8-6**(5) KSked(8) (chsd ldrs tl rdn & wknd 4f out)	6	**11**	16/1	—	—
1231^{4}	***One Life To Live (IRE) (48)*** (SEKettlewell) **4-9-2b**[1] JFortune(11) (Withdrawn not under Starter's orders: difference of opinion between trainer and owner)		**W**	4/1 3	—	—

(SP 139.9%) **11 Rn**

1m 59.1 (4.80) CSF £8.92 TOTE £2.60: £1.40 £1.60 £2.20 (£9.70) Trio £14.10 OWNER Mr G. Reed (MIDDLEHAM) BRED B. Freiha
WEIGHT FOR AGE 3yo-12lb
Bt in 7,400gns
417 Zorba has been difficult to win with and left nothing to chance here. Well in command in the last two furlongs, his rider kept him going to win as far as possible. His confidence should have been boosted. (2/1)
Trying Times (IRE), dropped in class, put up a much better effort but looked one-paced. (4/1: 8/1-9/2)
Beau Roberto has a look of something better but his performances continue to disappoint. (9/2)
Just Whistle has been disappointing over hurdles and last ran on the Flat almost two years ago. In the circumstances this was not a bad effort. (20/1)
667 Murron Wallace has ability but gives the impression that she is not really putting it in. (7/2)

1839 WILCON HOMES E.B.F. MAIDEN STKS (2-Y.O) (Class D)

9-00 (9-02) **6f 5y** £3,517.50 (£1,065.00: £520.00: £247.50) Stalls: Low GOING minus 0.01 sec per fur (G)

				SP	RR	SF
1228^{3}	**Crazee Mental** (DHaydnJones) **2-8-9** JCarroll(1) (lw: trckd ldrs: led over 2f out: r.o)	—	**1**	2/1 2	70	26
1607^{7}	**Outsourcing (USA)** (PFICole) **2-9-0** TQuinn(7) (lw: chsd ldrs: ev ch 2f out: nt qckn ins fnl f)	1½	**2**	7/4 1	71	27
684^{5}	**Burnt Yates (IRE)** (MWEasterby) **2-9-0** LCharnock(9) (hld up: effrt ½-wy: styd on: no imp)	4	**3**	5/1 3	60	16
	Buzz (CWThornton) **2-9-0** DeanMcKeown(4) (w'like: bit bkwd: rn green & bhd: hdwy 2f out: hmpd over 1f out: r.o towards fin)	3½	**4**	33/1	51	7
1466^{9}	**Shalyah (IRE)** (MrsJRRamsden) **2-8-9** JFortune(5) (in tch: no imp fr ½-wy)	1¾	**5**	16/1	41	—
	My Lost Love (MJohnston) **2-9-0** JWeaver(3) (w'like: bit bkwd: dwlt: sme hdwy 2f out: n.d)	10	**6**	8/1	20	—
1492^{7}	**Sharp Shooter (IRE)** (MrsJRRamsden) **2-9-0** MDeering(2) (lost tch fr ½-wy)	3½	**7**	25/1	11	—
1328^{9}	**Ngaere Princess** (WTKemp) **2-8-6b**[1](3) PFessey(8) (led & sn clr: hdd over 2f out: sn wknd)	5	**8**	66/1	—	—
1407^{3}	**Llanasa** (JBerry) **2-8-9** KDarley(6) (spd 4f: eased whn btn)	3	**9**	9/1	—	—

(SP 121.6%) **9 Rn**

1m 14.7 (4.70) CSF £5.66 TOTE £3.50: £1.10 £1.30 £2.00 (£4.20) Trio £15.20 OWNER Mr Hugh O'Donnell (PONTYPRIDD) BRED Limestone Stud

1228 Crazee Mental knew her job this time and did it well, responding to pressure in the final furlong. (2/1)
1607 Outsourcing (USA) has obviously improved for his initial run, but he met a useful opponent here and is worth another chance. (7/4: evens-2/1)
684 Burnt Yates (IRE) is learning and looks the type to do well in nurseries. (5/1)
Buzz was coltish in the paddock, but showed plenty of promise after looking extremely green early on, and is one to keep in mind when put over longer trips. (33/1)
Shalyah (IRE) is learning and in time better looks likely. (16/1)
My Lost Love needed this quite badly and, like many from this yard, missed the break and was never able to get anywhere near. (8/1: op 4/1)

1840 TENNENT CALEDONIAN BREWERIES H'CAP (0-80) (3-Y.O+) (Class D)

9-30 (9-31) **1m 5f 9y** £4,123.50 (£1,248.00: £609.00: £289.50) Stalls: High GOING minus 0.01 sec per fur (G)

				SP	RR	SF
1618*	**Lord Advocate (51)** (DANolan) **9-9-0b**(5) 5x KSked(5) (cl up: led 7f out: edgd rt over 2f out: kpt on wl fnl f)....—	1	4/1 2	63	45
1562 4	**Sherqy (IRE) (56)** (SEKettlewell) **5-9-10** JFortune(4) (prom: hdwy on ins whn nt clr run & swtchd over 2f out: styd on: no imp)....2½	2	4/1 2	65	47
1585 4	**Trilby (56)** (GRichards) **4-9-10v1** TQuinn(2) (b: a.p: effrt 4f out: n.m.r over 2f out: one pce)....1½	3	9/2 3	63	45
	Thunderheart (54) (RAllan) **6-9-8** JWeaver(6) (lw: trckd ldrs: ev ch over 3f out: edgd rt & wknd fnl 2½f)....4	4	12/1	56	38
1618 3	**Cois Na Farraige (IRE) (46)** (MissLAPerratt) **4-9-0** KDarley(7) (lw: prom tl wknd fnl 3f)....12	5	4/1 2	34	16
950*	**Silver Pearl (43)** (MrsAMNaughton) **6-8-11** JCarroll(1) (dwlt: effrt 5f out: wknd over 2f out)....24	6	5/2 1	1	—
	Shirlaty (45) (CWThornton) **4-8-13** DeanMcKeown(3) (led tl sddle slipped & hdd 7f out: sn t.o)....dist	7	33/1	—	—
			(SP 117.4%)	**7 Rn**		

2m 55.2 (9.50) CSF £19.28 TOTE £3.20: £1.60 £3.50 (£14.80) OWNER Mrs J. McFadyen-Murray (WISHAW) BRED London Thoroughbred Services Ltd

1618* Lord Advocate, allowed to have his own way, kept picking up the pace in the last half-mile and was always in command. (4/1)
1562 Sherqy (IRE) gives the impression that he has more ability if the key can be found. (4/1: 3/1-9/2)
1585 Trilby was short of room at one stage but is basically short of pace. (9/2: op 3/1)
Thunderheart, who missed all last season, looked big and well here and ran a fair race until running out of fuel in the last two furlongs. (12/1)
1618 Cois Na Farraige (IRE) was 16lb better in with Lord Advocate on their last running but he proved a big disappointment. (4/1)

T/Plpt: £18.40 (721.82 Tckts). T/Qdpt: £7.10 (81.3 Tckts) AA

1779-NEWMARKET (R-H) (Good to soft)

Wednesday June 11th

Race 6: hand timed
WEATHER: overcast, thunderstorm last race WIND: slt across

1841 JUPITER LIMITED STKS (0-75) (3-Y.O+) (Class D)

6-40 (6-40) **1m 6f 175y (July)** £3,557.50 (£1,060.00: £505.00: £227.50) Stalls: High GOING minus 0.11 sec per fur (G)

				SP	RR	SF
1276 5	**Tramline (72)** (MBlanshard) **4-9-10** JQuinn(6) (hld up: hdwy & nt clr run over 2f out: led over 1f out: rdn out)—	1	11/2	88	70
1162 15	**Pike Creek (USA) (75)** (IABalding) **4-9-7** WRyan(5) (chsd ldrs: led 5f out to 4f out: ev ch over 1f out: one pce)....2	2	7/2 2	83	65
1387 4	**Polyphony (USA) (75)** (RCharlton) **3-8-6b1** PatEddery(3) (lw: led to 5f out: led 4f out tl hdd over 1f out)....9	3	3/1 1	78	40
969 2	**Desert Dunes (71)** (NAGraham) **4-9-10** RCochrane(2) (plld hrd: trckd ldrs: lost pl over 4f out: rallied 3f out: btn appr fnl f)....7	4	5/1	69	51
1277 4	**Whirlawhile (USA) (73)** (EALDunlop) **3-8-1**(3) DO'Donohoe(4) (b.hind: hld up: hdwy 5f out: rdn & wknd 2f out)10	5	9/2 3	58	20
789 16	**Chatham Island (72)** (CEBrittain) **9-9-10** BDoyle(1) (b: chsd ldr 9f)....s.h	6	8/1	58	40
			(SP 108.6%)	**6 Rn**		

3m 13.91 (5.41) CSF £21.02 TOTE £12.60: £3.50 £2.30 (£38.30) OWNER H C Promotions Ltd (UPPER LAMBOURN) BRED Juddmonte Farms
WEIGHT FOR AGE 3yo-20lb

1023 Tramline, who now qualifies for a handicap mark, was stepped up to a more appropriate trip and did the job well. Why he didn't take his chance in a handicap rather than meet the runner-up on much worse terms, only connections can know. However, this will ruin his favourable mark and he would be well advised to defy a penalty before being reassessed. (11/2)
881 Pike Creek (USA) looked to stay this trip better than she had in the past, but her lack of any turn of foot continues to cost her races. (7/2: 5/2-4/1)
1387 Polyphony (USA), taken down last, was woken up by the first-time blinkers, but failed to last home. A slight drop in trip should see him back in front. (3/1)
969 Desert Dunes, on his toes and warm beforehand, was rather disappointing and didn't help himself by taking a keen hold. (5/1)
1277 Whirlawhile (USA) races quite keenly and didn't seem to stay this longer trip after briefly looking a threat. (9/2)
Chatham Island, having only his second run since last August, ran way below his best. (8/1: op 5/1)

1842 DAILY TELEGRAPH MAIDEN AUCTION STKS (2-Y.O) (Class D)

7-10 (7-10) **6f (July)** £3,752.50 (£1,120.00: £535.00: £242.50) Stalls: High GOING minus 0.11 sec per fur (G)

				SP	RR	SF
	Arawak Cay (IRE) (DRLoder) **2-8-10** OPeslier(1) (str: scope: lw: mde all: pushed out)....—	1	10/11 1	84+	27
	Linden Heights (LMCumani) **2-8-7** PatEddery(7) (w'like: scope: chsd wnr: no imp appr fnl f: eased nr fin)....2	2	7/1 3	76+	19
	Little Indian (SPCWoods) **2-8-10** WRyan(8) (neat: scope: hdwy over 1f out: r.o ins fnl f)....½	3	20/1	77	20
	Balla d'Aire (IRE) (RBoss) **2-8-7** LDettori(2) (w'like: leggy: chsd ldrs: one pce fnl f)....nk	4	5/1 2	74	17
1577 4	**Ringleader** (PFICole) **2-8-7** JQuinn(4) (chsd ldrs 4f)....1¼	5	11/1	70	13
	Aldwych Arrow (IRE) (MBell) **2-8-7** MRoberts(10) (cmpt: wnt lft s: bhd: r.o appr fnl f: nvr able to chal)....2½	6	20/1	64	7
861 6	**Mamora Bay (IRE)** (MHTompkins) **2-8-5** DBiggs(9) (bkwd: hmpd s: sn prom: edgd lft & wknd appr fnl f)....1¾	7	8/1	57	—
1396 11	**Gift of Gold** (ICampbell) **2-8-5**(5) RMullen(3) (lw: plld hrd: prom 4f)....½	8	50/1	61	4
	Brimstone (IRE) (DRCElsworth) **2-8-7** RCochrane(5) (gd sort: scope: s.i.s: plld hrd: hdwy over 2f out: n.m.r & wknd qckly appr fnl f)....4	9	14/1	47	—
	Dentardia (IRE) (JMPEustace) **2-8-7** JTate(6) (wl grwn: bkwd: sn rdn along: a bhd)....1	10	25/1	44	—
			(SP 123.0%)	**10 Rn**		

1m 16.19 (4.19) CSF £7.29 TOTE £2.00: £1.10 £2.00 £4.20 (£5.80) Trio £53.70 OWNER Lucayan Stud (NEWMARKET) BRED Louis A. Walshe

Arawak Cay (IRE), a half-brother to prolific middle-distance All-Weather winner Persian Conquest, was on his toes and needed two handlers in the parade ring. However, he did nothing wrong in the race and looks certain to improve with racing. (10/11)
Linden Heights, a half-brother to the temperamental Linda's Joy, shows nothing of those characteristics and shaped with considerable promise. (7/1: op 4/1)
Little Indian, a half-brother to Mukaddar, was really motoring in the closing stages and will be better for another furlong. (20/1)
Balla d'Aire (IRE), a wiry newcomer, looked well forward and ran fast to the final furlong. (5/1)
1577 Ringleader kept trying to the line, but looked short of speed in the last couple of furlongs. (11/1: 6/1-12/1)
Aldwych Arrow (IRE), already a gelding, went to post rather keenly and took some settling in the rear early on. He did some late work and will come on for the run. (20/1)
861 Mamora Bay (IRE) (8/1: 4/1-11/1)
Brimstone (IRE) missed the break, probably by design, and made a quite promising move until getting very leg-weary in the closing stages. Still up behind, he has the scope to make into a good-looking colt. (14/1)

1843 NGK SPARK PLUGS H'CAP (0-70) (3-Y.O+ F & M) (Class E)

7-40 (7-41) **7f (July)** £3,947.50 (£1,180.00: £565.00: £257.50) Stalls: High GOING minus 0.11 sec per fur (G)

				SP	RR	SF
1439[4]	**Sharp 'n' Shady (55)** (CFWall) **4-9-7** PatEddery(5) (lw: hld up: hdwy 2f out: led over 1f out: rdn out)	—	**1**	100/30[1]	66	42
1639[4]	**La Chatelaine (42)** (GLewis) **3-7-7**(5) RFfrench(3) (lw: hdwy over 2f out: r.o fnl f: nt rch wnr)	1	**2**	9/1	51	17
1388[7]	**Push A Venture (53)** (SPCWoods) **3-8-9** WRyan(10) (plld hrd: a.p: kpt on fnl f)	2	**3**	14/1	57	23
1395[2]	**Octavia Hill (54)** (PWHarris) **4-9-6b** OPeslier(8) (led: sn clr: hdd over 1f out: rdn: edgd lft & one pce ins fnl f)	hd	**4**	4/1[2]	58	34
1096[17]	**Hajat (52)** (NAGraham) **3-8-8** RCochrane(1) (hld up & bhd: rdn & n.m.r 2f out: r.o fnl f)	2	**5**	20/1	51	17
1248[12]	**Ella Lamees (62)** (WJMusson) **3-9-4** KFallon(9) (hld up: kpt on fnl 2f: nvr able to chal)	6	**6**	10/1	48	14
	Bonsiel (45) (KMahdi) **3-8-1** JQuinn(2) (in tch: rdn 3f out: sn btn)	3	**7**	6/1[3]	24	—
1501[13]	**Bear To Dance (33)** (PHowling) **4-7-8**(5) RMullen(11) (prom: rdn 3f out: wknd appr fnl f)	2	**8**	25/1	7	—
995[7]	**Hurgill Lady (62)** (JWWatts) **3-9-4** LDettori(4) (chsd ldr tl wknd 2f out)	s.h	**9**	9/1	36	2
*1757**	**Molly Music (60)** (GGMargarson) **3-9-2** 5x DBiggs(7) (rdn & hdwy 3f out: wknd over 1f out)	1¾	**10**	15/2	30	—
	Badger Bay (IRE) (60) (CADwyer) **4-9-12** JStack(6) (swtg: plld hrd: trckd ldrs: rdn over 3f out: sn wknd)	3½	**11**	20/1	22	—
				(SP 118.3%)	**11 Rn**	

1m 29.54 (4.54) CSF £30.02 CT £348.86 TOTE £3.20: £1.70 £2.50 £5.60 (£18.00) Trio £28.50 OWNER Mr Walter Grubmuller (NEWMARKET) BRED R. and A. Craddock
WEIGHT FOR AGE 3yo-10lb
1439 Sharp 'n' Shady has the knee action of one who appreciated the rain that fell for most of the day, and broke her duck in good style. (100/30)
1639 La Chatelaine confirmed her recent improvement on much softer ground. (9/1)
1388 Push A Venture, very free to post and early in the race, stayed on surprisingly well. She would certainly win races if she only learnt to settle. (14/1)
1395 Octavia Hill ran freely in front in blinkers and soon held a lead of three or four lengths. Once headed, she did not stop, but hung away from the whip, ruining her place chances. (4/1)
Hajat, brought towards the stands side despite her draw, did some late work once getting a clear run. (20/1)
778 Ella Lamees only stayed on past beaten horses and is beginning to look moderate. (10/1)
Hurgill Lady (9/1: 6/1-10/1)
1757* Molly Music (15/2: 5/1-8/1)

1844 ESSEX CUP H'CAP (0-70) (3-Y.O+) (Class E)

8-10 (8-11) **1m 4f (July)** £4,045.00 (£1,210.00: £580.00: £265.00) Stalls: High GOING minus 0.11 sec per fur (G)

				SP	RR	SF
1491[5]	**Ancient Quest (70)** (NACallaghan) **4-10-0** PaulEddery(3) (a.p: led over 2f out: rdn & hld on wl fnl f)	—	**1**	11/1	81	52
1641[4]	**Yet Again (45)** (MissGayKelleway) **5-8-3** SSanders(6) (in tch: hdwy 4f out: ev ch over 1f out tl unable qckn nr fin)	nk	**2**	6/1[2]	56	27
1393[8]	**Dalwhinnie (60)** (JWharton) **4-9-4** KFallon(2) (swtg: a.p: ev ch 2f out: one pce appr fnl f)	1¼	**3**	14/1	69	40
1779[16]	**Slapy Dam (49)** (CASmith) **5-8-7**vow2 ACulhane(14) (b: b.off hind: chsd ldrs: lost pl 5f out: rdn & kpt on wl fnl 2f)	1½	**4**	25/1	56	25
1118[5]	**Lookingforarainbow (IRE) (64)** (BobJones) **9-9-8** NDay(13) (trckd ldrs: rdn 2f out: nt pce to chal)	3½	**5**	8/1	66	37
1632[7]	**Fairy Knight (69)** (RHannon) **5-9-13** PatEddery(1) (lw: hld up: hdwy 5f out: wknd & eased fnl f)	3	**6**	11/2[1]	67	38
1105[10]	**Moonlight Invader (IRE) (62)** (EALDunlop) **3-8-2**(3) DO'Donohoe(12) (lw: s.i.s: bhd: hdwy 4f out: nvr rchd ldrs)	2	**7**	12/1	58	14
1408[2]	**Swan Hunter (68)** (DJSCosgrove) **4-9-12** MRimmer(11) (plld hrd: chsd ldrs 8f)	10	**8**	8/1	50	21
1093[5]	**What A Fuss (58)** (BHanbury) **4-9-2** WRyan(9) (swtg: led: sn clr: wknd & hdd over 2f out)	1½	**9**	12/1	38	9
1636[9]	**Admirals Secret (USA) (57)** (CFWall) **8-9-1** NCarlisle(10) (bkwd: chsd ldrs 9f)	10	**10**	20/1	24	—
1244[12]	**Formidable Flame (53)** (WJMusson) **4-8-11** RCochrane(5) (hld up & bhd: effrt 3f out: sn btn & eased)	5	**11**	25/1	13	—
1732*	**Cottage Prince (IRE) (50)** (JJQuinn) **4-8-8** 4x LDettori(7) (swtg: chsd ldr tl wknd 4f out: eased whn btn)	16	**12**	13/2[3]	—	—
341[10]	**Venture Connect (65)** (CPEBrooks) **3-8-8** RPerham(15) (rdn 3f out: a bhd)	7	**13**	25/1	—	—
1470[3]	**Dancing Queen (IRE) (67)** (MBell) **3-8-10** MFenton(4) (a bhd)	21	**14**	12/1	—	—
				(SP 119.6%)	**14 Rn**	

2m 36.51 (7.51) CSF £64.89 CT £843.71 TOTE £20.30: £4.50 £2.50 £5.40 (£54.10) Trio £377.10 OWNER Midcourts (NEWMARKET) BRED Patrick Eddery Ltd
WEIGHT FOR AGE 3yo-15lb
OFFICIAL EXPLANATION **Dancing Queen (IRE): was in season.**
1491 Ancient Quest, ridden much closer to the pace this time, proved very game, conceding weight up the final rise. (11/1: 8/1-12/1)
1641 Yet Again looked the winner when mounting his challenge, but could never quite force his head in front and had to give best near the finish. This softer ground seemed to suit him. (6/1)
Dalwhinnie got in a muck sweat beforehand, but has now run her two best races at Newmarket. She has the ability to break her duck. (14/1)
955 Slapy Dam certainly looks a better horse when he can get his toe in. (25/1)
1118 Lookingforarainbow (IRE) runs some of his best races here and is well worth looking out for at this track on faster ground, as he is definitely on a winning mark. (8/1)
1233 Fairy Knight, with cut in the ground again, found this race more competitive than the one he won at Haydock, but would not have been beaten too far but for being eased right down (11/2)
Moonlight Invader (IRE) (12/1: op 8/1)

1845 SPORT OF KINGS TOUR H'CAP (0-80) (3-Y.O+) (Class D)
8-40 (8-41) **1m (July)** £3,817.50 (£1,140.00: £545.00: £247.50) Stalls: High GOING minus 0.11 sec per fur (G)

				SP	RR	SF
1761^{4}	**Suez Tornado (IRE) (61)** (EJAlston) **4-8-13v** JFEgan(2) (chsd ldrs: led over 1f out: rdn clr)	—	**1**	$8/1^{3}$	69	35
1501^{4}	**Gain Line (USA) (54)** (BobJones) **4-8-6** NDay(5) (plld hrd: a.p: kpt on wl fnl f)	3	**2**	12/1	56	22
1436*	**Mo-Addab (IRE) (74)** (ACStewart) **7-9-12** MRoberts(8) (chsd ldrs: rdn over 2f out: ev ch over 1f out: one pce)	nk	**3**	$9/4^{1}$	75	41
1175^{16}	**Smart Spirit (IRE) (69)** (MrsMReveley) **3-8-10** ACulhane(3) (lw: hld up & bhd: hdwy over 1f out: styng on whn nt clr run ins fnl f)	1½	**4**	$11/2^{2}$	67	22
1244^{19}	**Deevee (48)** (CJBenstead) **8-8-0** JLowe(11) (stdd s: hdwy over 2f out: wknd ins fnl f)	½	**5**	12/1	45	11
1427^{7}	**Janie's Boy (71)** (MrsJCecil) **3-8-12** RCochrane(1) (led tl hdd & btn over 1f out)	½	**6**	9/1	67	22
1606^{8}	**Saltando (IRE) (55)** (PatMitchell) **6-8-4v**(3) MartinDwyer(9) (chsd ldr: rdn over 2f out: sn btn)	5	**7**	16/1	41	7
1384^{14}	**Conic Hill (IRE) (44)** (JPearce) **6-7-10** GBardwell(10) (bhd fnl 3f)	3	**8**	33/1	24	—
	Julietta Mia (USA) (72) (WRMuir) **3-8-13** DaneO'Neill(6) (in tch: effrt over 3f out: rdn & wknd 2f out)	1¼	**9**	$8/1^{3}$	50	5
1606^{9}	**Tart (FR) (67)** (JPearce) **4-9-2**(3) CTeague(7) (lw: a bhd)	s.h	**10**	25/1	45	11
1314^{3}	**Right Tune (78)** (BHanbury) **3-9-5** JStack(4) (b: b.nr hind: prom over 5f)	nk	**11**	$8/1^{3}$	55	10

(SP 117.5%) **11 Rn**

1m 43.24 (5.24) CSF £90.91 CT £266.91 TOTE £14.40: £3.70 £3.30 £1.40 (£72.80) Trio £112.50 OWNER Mr John Patrick Barry (PRESTON)
LONG HANDICAP Conic Hill (IRE) 7-7
WEIGHT FOR AGE 3yo-11lb

1761 Suez Tornado (IRE) has been in good form without winning, but thrived on this softer surface, finding a good turn of foot to impress in a poor race. (8/1)
1501 Gain Line (USA) got the trip well, sticking to his guns despite taking a strong hold. (12/1: op 8/1)
1436* Mo-Addab (IRE) likes this ground and tried hard to challenge against the stands rail in the dip, but could not match the winner's turn of foot. (9/4)
998 Smart Spirit (IRE), again dropped right out, really caught the eye in the last furlong and ought to be to winning a race somewhere. (11/2)
Deevee, dropped out at the start and taken to the centre of the course, has done all his winning over a mile, but didn't seem to get home on this occasion. (12/1)
1226* Janie's Boy, dropping in trip, looked a reluctant pacemaker at a sedate pace and this race was not run to suit him. (9/1: 6/1-10/1)
1314 Right Tune (8/1: 6/1-9/1)

1846 VENUS MAIDEN STKS (3-Y.O) (Class D)
9-10 (9-11) **1m 4f (July)** £3,850.00 (£1,150.00: £550.00: £250.00) Stalls: High GOING minus 0.11 sec per fur (G)

				SP	RR	SF
1239^{11}	**Badge of Fame (IRE)** (LMCumani) **3-8-9**(5) RFfrench(8) (in tch: n.m.r over 2f out: rdn & r.o wl to ld nr fin)	—	**1**	16/1	79	36
	Seattle Art (USA) (HRACecil) **3-9-0** KFallon(6) (chsd ldrs: led over 2f out tl hdd & unable qckn nr fin)	nk	**2**	$5/2^{2}$	79	36
	Liffre (IRE) (JHMGosden) **3-8-9** LDettori(5) (hdwy 3f out: ev ch over 1f out: wknd fnl f)	4	**3**	$7/4^{1}$	68	25
	High Intrigue (IRE) (HRACecil) **3-9-0** WRyan(9) (lw: led tl over 2f out: one pce)	4	**4**	$13/2^{3}$	68	25
1023^{10}	**Aboo Hom** (ACStewart) **3-9-0** MRoberts(3) (hld up: rdn & wandered over 2f out: no imp)	5	**5**	16/1	61	18
	Hadidi (66) (DMorley) **3-9-0** GCarter(4) (chsd ldr 10f)	3	**6**	16/1	57	14
	Zerpour (IRE) (LMCumani) **3-8-7**(7) DYoung(7) (w'like: scope: bit bkwd: s.s: hdwy 3f out: nvr able to chal)	1¼	**7**	$13/2^{3}$	56	13
1023^{W}	**Prince Alex (IRE)** (ACStewart) **3-9-0** DHarrison(1) (wl grwn: chsd ldrs: rdn & hung lft over 2f out: sn wknd)	21	**8**	20/1	28	—

(SP 114.0%) **8 Rn**

2m 36.9 (7.90) CSF £50.82 TOTE £17.20: £2.60 £1.50 £1.20 (£24.20) Trio £21.00 OWNER Mr M Tabor & Mrs John Magnier (NEWMARKET)
BRED Gerald W. Leigh
IN-FOCUS: **This race was run in almost total darkness and a particularly heavy thunderstorm began during the race.**
Badge of Fame (IRE) didn't get the clearest of runs towards the stands rail, but this may have had the effect of sheltering from the elements, and he found a good turn of foot to pounce near the line. (16/1)
Seattle Art (USA) looks to have done well over the winter and showed a fine action going down. The fact that he tried so hard into the cloudburst shows his heart is in the right place, and he should soon be winning over a distance of ground. (5/2)
Liffre (IRE), led round by two handlers in the paddock, looked dangerous when mounting her challenge, but the effort quickly petered out. (7/4)
High Intrigue (IRE), a tall colt who has thickened out over the winter, ran a very respectable first race of the year. (13/2: 5/1-8/1)
Aboo Hom hung left then right once he saw daylight, but allowances should be made for terrible conditions. (16/1)
Hadidi, out of the very useful mare, Sesame, herself a sister to Celeric, looked in great shape and the family tend to improve with time. (16/1)
Zerpour (IRE), very slow to start, did look like taking a hand before his efforts took their toll and this half-brother to Zabadi and Zafzala should do better in time. (13/2: op 10/1)

T/Plpt: £75.30 (188.32 Tckts). T/Qdpt: £15.30 (44 Tckts) Dk

1821-SALISBURY (R-H) (Good to firm)
Wednesday June 11th
All races excluding Race 2: hand timed
WEATHER: overcast WIND: almost nil becoming slt across

1847 E.B.F. WHITEPARISH NOVICE STKS (2-Y.O F) (Class D)
2-20 (2-21) **5f** £3,255.50 (£974.00: £467.00: £213.50) Stalls: High GOING minus 0.47 sec per fur (F)

				SP	RR	SF
	Desert Lady (IRE) (RCharlton) **2-8-8** TSprake(6) (str: w'like: chsd ldr: led wl over 1f out: rdn out)	—	**1**	$2/1^{1}$	81+	11
1425^{5}	**Universal Lady** (CJames) **2-8-8** JReid(9) (led over 3f: r.o)	¾	**2**	10/1	79?	9
	Midsummer Night (IRE) (RHannon) **2-8-8** DaneO'Neill(7) (leggy: unf: a.p: rdn over 2f out: r.o wl nr fin)	½	**3**	$4/1^{3}$	77	7
	Kawafil (IRE) (PTWalwyn) **2-8-8** RPrice(5) (neat: lw: bhd: sn pushed along: sme late hdwy: bttr for r)	nk	**4**	10/1	76+	6
	Dodo (IRE) (DRCElsworth) **2-8-8** PatEddery(3) (w'like: scope: bit bkwd: a.p: one pce fnl 2f)	1¼	**5**	$11/4^{2}$	72	2
	Robin Lane (IABalding) **2-8-8** MHills(4) (scope: bit bkwd: nvr trbld ldrs)	4	**6**	10/1	59	—
	Saligo (IRE) (HMorrison) **2-8-8** CRutter(1) (unf: bkwd: s.s: a bhd)	5	**7**	33/1	43	—
	Jonathan's Girl (JJBridger) **2-8-3**(5) ADaly(8) (lengthy: bit bkwd: outpcd)	4	**8**	50/1	30	—

(SP 112.2%) **8 Rn**

62.6 secs (2.60) CSF £20.30 TOTE £3.30: £1.50 £1.60 £1.70 (£7.70) Trio £27.30 OWNER The Thoroughbred Corporation (BECKHAMPTON)
BRED Theo Waddington (UK) Ltd

Desert Lady (IRE), a half-sister to seven-furlong winner Carlton, had to be kept up to her work after looking inexperienced once hitting the front. Described by her trainer as a nice filly, she was a late April foal who seems sure to improve. (2/1: op 5/4)
1425 Universal Lady ran her best race to date and made sure the winner did not have things all her own way. (10/1: op 5/1)
Midsummer Night (IRE), out of a daughter of Vilikaia, gave the impression she already needs six and should soon get off the mark. (4/1)
Kawafil (IRE), another who shaped as though she needed a longer trip, will be better for the experience. (10/1: 6/1-11/1)
Dodo (IRE), a half-sister to Irish winner Hamad, was not knocked about once her chance had gone and should come on for the outing. (11/4: 2/1-4/1)
Robin Lane is bred to need much further than the minimum trip and ran accordingly. (10/1: 6/1-11/1)

1848 AMBER TRUST H'CAP (0-70) (3-Y.O+) (Class E)
2-50 (2-52) **5f** £2,898.25 (£871.00: £420.50: £195.25) Stalls: High GOING minus 0.47 sec per fur (F)

				SP	RR	SF
1514^{2}	**Barranak (IRE) (52)** (GMMcCourt) **5-8-10** CRutter(2) (mde virtually all: edgd rt ins fnl f: r.o wl)	—	**1**	6/1^{2}	62	37
1566^{*}	**Lucky Dip (68)** (DRCElsworth) **3-9-5** JReid(1) (hld up: hdwy over 1f out: hrd rdn & r.o ins fnl f)	2	**2**	6/1^{2}	72	40
834^{9}	**High Domain (IRE) (68)** (JLSpearing) **6-9-12** SDrowne(10) (w ldrs: ev ch 2f out: r.o one pce)	hd	**3**	11/1	71	46
1667^{*}	**Littlestone Rocket (56)** (WRMuir) **3-8-7b** ^{6x} DaneO'Neill(12) (a.p: ev ch over 1f out: one pce)	nk	**4**	10/1	58	26
835^{10}	**Friendly Brave (USA) (70)** (MissGayKelleway) **7-10-0** RHughes(11) (lw: hld up: hdwy & nt clr run over 1f out: bmpd ins fnl f: nt rcvr)	1¼	**5**	7/1^{3}	68	43
1446^{7}	**Macgillycuddy (IRE) (62)** (MrsPNDutfield) **8-9-1b**$^{(5)}$ TEDurcan(3) (nvr nr to chal)	1¼	**6**	14/1	56	31
1514^{3}	**Ned's Bonanza (52)** (MDods) **8-8-10** AClark(9) (hld up: hdwy whn nt clr run over 1f out: swtchd rt & bmpd ins fnl f: nt rcvr)	hd	**7**	3/1^{1}	46	21
1479^{2}	**The Fugative (50)** (PMitchell) **4-8-5**$^{(3)}$ AWhelan(8) (s.i.s: hdwy on ins over 1f out: bdly hmpd ins fnl f: nt rcvr)	1¼	**8**	10/1	40	15
1676^{W}	**Chief's Lady (38)** (JMBradley) **5-7-10** FNorton(7) (prom 3f)	hd	**9**	12/1	28	3
1743^{12}	**Sharp Stock (63)** (RJHodges) **4-9-7** SophieMitchell(4) (w wnr: ev ch 2f out: sn wknd)	1	**10**	20/1	50	25
1620^{11}	**Red Time (50)** (MSSaunders) **4-8-1**$^{(7)}$ ClaireAngell(5) (outpcd)	nk	**11**	33/1	36	11
1279^{17}	**Perchance To Dream (IRE) (52)** (BRMillman) **3-8-3** TSprake(6) (outpcd)	1¾	**12**	33/1	32	—
				(SP 117.6%)	**12 Rn**	

61.1 secs (1.10) CSF £36.96 CT £354.98 TOTE £9.30: £2.50 £1.70 £3.90 (£18.20) Trio £56.70 OWNER Mr Mac Carthy (WANTAGE) BRED M. MacCarthy
LONG HANDICAP Chief's Lady 7-8
WEIGHT FOR AGE 3yo-7lb
1514 Barranak (IRE), who likes to get his toe in, was not inconvenienced by the slight ease in the ground following overnight rain. It has to be said he missed all the congestion on the inside by racing towards the centre of the course. (6/1)
1566* Lucky Dip, making her handicap debut, does seem suited to a stiff five. (6/1)
High Domain (IRE) was racing on ground plenty fast enough for him and one cannot help thinking that the trouble behind helped him reach the prize money. (11/1: 8/1-12/1)
1667* Littlestone Rocket, penalized for only winning a seller, was another who probabaly benefited from the misfortune of others. (10/1)
731 Friendly Brave (USA), down to a mark 3lb lower than when he last won, got no sort of run at all. (7/1)
Macgillycuddy (IRE), five times a winner in Ireland, has not scored since 1994 and likes soft ground, having never won on ground faster than good. (14/1)
1514 Ned's Bonanza, dropped 8lb this season, appeared to be going strongly when encountering all sorts of trouble in running. (3/1)
1479 The Fugative, up 2lb, did not seem to be travelling quite so well as some of the other unlucky horses when nearly put through the rails. (10/1)

1849 BOLLINGER CHAMPAGNE CHALLENGE SERIES GENTLEMEN'S H'CAP (0-70) (3-Y.O+) (Class F)
3-20 (3-20) **6f 212y** £2,882.00 (£866.00: £418.00: £194.00) Stalls: High GOING minus 0.47 sec per fur (F)

				SP	RR	SF
1566^{9}	**Silver Lining (58)** (APJones) **3-10-6**$^{(4)}$ MrJGoldstein(2) (stumbled s: sn rcvrd: led over 1f out: all out)	—	**1**	20/1	69	40
1509^{2}	**Sharp Imp (58)** (RMFlower) **7-11-6b** MrTMcCarthy(3) (hld up & bhd: hdwy 2f out: r.o ins fnl f)	½	**2**	9/2^{1}	68	49
1395^{4}	**Morocco (IRE) (58)** (MRChannon) **8-11-6** MrRThornton(6) (hld up & bhd: hdwy 2f out: r.o ins fnl f)	nk	**3**	6/1^{2}	67	48
1509^{6}	**Justinianus (IRE) (46)** (JJBridger) **5-10-4**$^{(4)ow6}$ MrDBridger(4) (lw: plld hrd: rdn over 2f out: hdd over 1f out: edgd lft ins fnl f: nt qckn)	½	**4**	10/1	54	29
1446^{6}	**White Settler (66)** (RJHodges) **4-12-0** MrJTizzard(7) (hld up & bhd: hdwy over 1f out: r.o one pce fnl f)	1½	**5**	7/1	71	52
1395^{8}	**Pointer (56)** (MrsPNDutfield) **5-11-4** MrLJefford(10) (a.p: ev ch 2f out: wknd over 1f out)	nk	**6**	7/1	60	41
1680^{3}	**Delight of Dawn (43)** (EAWheeler) **5-10-1**$^{(4)}$ MrJDewhurst(9) (lw: reard s: hld up & plld hrd: no hdwy fnl 2f)	1½	**7**	13/2^{3}	43	24
1458^{7}	**Havago (66)** (RHannon) **3-11-4** MrCVigors(12) (lw: prom over 5f)	4	**8**	8/1	57	28
1566^{11}	**Folly Foot Fred (45)** (BRMillman) **3-9-7**$^{(4)}$ MrLBaker(1) (s.s: a bhd)	d.h	**8**	25/1	36	7
1439^{10}	**Calandrella (40)** (GBBalding) **4-10-2** MrKGoble(11) (lw: mid div: rdn over 3f out: sn bhd)	1½	**10**	25/1	28	9
1467^{8}	**Severn Mill (33)** (JMBradley) **6-9-5**$^{(4)ow2}$ MrSDurack(8) (prom over 4f)	5	**11**	33/1	9	—
316^{*}	**Mr Nevermind (IRE) (62)** (GLMoore) **7-11-6**$^{(4)}$ MrIMongan(5) (dwlt: a bhd: t.o)	16	**12**	7/1	2	—
				(SP 118.9%)	**12 Rn**	

1m 29.7 (3.70) CSF £94.94 CT £568.53 TOTE £29.10: £5.30 £2.30 £2.00 (£101.60) Trio £134.10 OWNER The Lambourn Racing Club (EASTBURY) BRED R. Hutt
LONG HANDICAP Severn Mill 9-2
WEIGHT FOR AGE 3yo-10lb
876 Silver Lining, down 6lb, was stepping up to seven and gave his rider his first ever Flat winner, also getting his trainer off the mark on the level for the season. (20/1)
1509 Sharp Imp, up 3lb, seemed to get the trip well enough for one who has recently been a Brighton regular over six but has won there over this trip. (9/2)
1395 Morocco (IRE) again ran well but is the type who likes to do it all on the bridle. (6/1)
1509 Justinianus (IRE), dropped 2lb, looked far more experienced than his rider in the closing stages. (10/1)
1446 White Settler, now only 2lb higher than his previous win, needs at least this trip. (7/1: op 9/2)
834 Pointer is still 5lb higher than the highest mark off which he has won. (7/1)

1850 BISHOPSTONE CONDITIONS STKS (3-Y.O) (Class C)
3-50 (3-50) **1m 6f** £4,636.70 (£1,689.20: £824.60: £353.00: £156.50) Stalls: High GOING minus 0.47 sec per fur (F)

				SP	RR	SF
1242^{2}	**Winter Garden (100)** (LMCumani) **3-9-2** LDettori(1) (lw: mde all: shkn up 2f out: r.o wl)	—	**1**	2/7^{1}	96	—

				SP	RR	SF
	Tycooness (IRE) (MJohnston) **3-8-3** JFanning(5) (lengthy: lw: hld up: hdwy over 4f out: rdn over 2f out: chsd wnr over 1f out: hrd rdn: nt qckn)	1	**2**	10/1^{3}	82	—
1165^{3}	**Fletcher (84)** (HMorrison) **3-8-11** RHughes(3) (hld up: hdwy over 2f out: one pce fnl f)	½	**3**	14/1	89	—
1434^{2}	**Tikopia** (IABalding) **3-8-11** MHills(4) (hld up: chsd wnr over 4f out tl over 1f out: wknd fnl f)	6	**4**	9/2^{2}	82	—
1637^{6}	**Foleys Quest (IRE)** (JSMoore) **3-8-7**^{ow1} JReid(2) (chsd wnr over 9f: wknd 3f out)	6	**5**	50/1	15 t	—

(SP 113.7%) **5 Rn**

3m 10.6 (11.90) CSF £4.19 TOTE £1.30: £1.10 £2.30 (£5.10) OWNER Sheikh Mohammed (NEWMARKET) BRED Darley Stud Management Co Ltd

1242 Winter Garden, described by Dettori as a big baby who only does as much as he wants to, gave the impression he could have found more if required. (2/7: 1/3-1/2)

Tycooness (IRE), a half-sister to Broken Hearted, was inclined to flash her tail when hit with the whip but in fairness she did keep responding to pressure. (10/1: 5/1-12/1)

1165 Fletcher could not sustain his effort in the closing stages. (14/1)

1434 Tikopia appeared not to stay this extra quarter-mile. (9/2)

1851 FONTHILL STUD & SUMMERDOWN STABLES MAIDEN STKS (3-Y.O) (Class D)

4-20 (4-22) **6f 212y** £3,691.00 (£1,108.00: £534.00: £247.00) Stalls: High GOING minus 0.47 sec per fur (F)

				SP	RR	SF
1587^{3}	**Mr Sponge (USA)** (IABalding) **3-9-0** LDettori(3) (w ldr: led over 3f out: rdn out)	—	**1**	8/11^{1}	83	40
1320^{3}	**Khafaaq (78)** (MajorWRHern) **3-9-0** TSprake(9) (led over 3f: wknd ins fnl f)	5	**2**	5/2^{2}	72	29
118^{6}	**Eliza** (LordHuntingdon) **3-8-9** PatEddery(5) (hld up: stdy hdwy over 2f out: one pce fnl f)	1¼	**3**	20/1	64	21
964^{5}	**Verdi (IRE)** (KMcAuliffe) **3-9-0** JReid(4) (rdn 4f out: no hdwy fnl 2f)	2½	**4**	12/1^{3}	63	20
	Meilleur (IRE) (LadyHerries) **3-9-0** MHills(2) (w'like: scope: lw: nvr nrr)	s.h	**5**	12/1^{3}	63	20
	Shades of Love (VSoane) **3-9-0** CRutter(7) (bit bkwd: no hdwy fnl 3f)	5	**6**	66/1	51	8
1167^{9}	**Over The Moon** (MJFetherston-Godley) **3-8-9** FNorton(10) (prom over 4f)	nk	**7**	66/1	46	3
1587^{11}	**Giko** (JRPoulton) **3-9-0** SDrowne(8) (prom tl rdn & wknd over 2f out)	1¼	**8**	16/1	48	5
1394^{5}	**Balladara (IRE)** (RHannon) **3-9-0** DaneO'Neill(1) (lw: s.s: a bhd)	3	**9**	16/1	41	—
1485^{11}	**Kildee Boy** (APJones) **3-9-0** RPrice(6) (lw: prom 4f: wknd qckly: t.o)	15	**10**	66/1	6	—

(SP 122.9%) **10 Rn**

1m 27.7 (1.70) CSF £2.51 TOTE £2.00: £1.30 £1.20 £3.10 (£2.30) Trio £11.20 OWNER Mr Paul Mellon (KINGSCLERE) BRED Michael S. Anderson and Brick Kiln Stud

1587 Mr Sponge (USA) had obviously been laid out by his trainer as a 90th birthday winner for Paul Mellon, one of British racing's greatest supporters. (8/11: 11/10-4/6)

1320 Khafaaq, dropping back from a mile, even found this testing seven beyond him. (5/2: 7/4-7/2)

Eliza, a half-sister to mile winner Waldo, was not given a hard race and may be an interesting proposition now she has qualified for handicaps. (20/1)

964 Verdi (IRE), a half-brother to mile and a half scorer Rahwah, is out of a ten-furlong winner and may do better over further. (12/1: 8/1-14/1)

Meilleur (IRE), related to several winning sprinters, is a half-brother to Lucedeo. (12/1: 5/1-14/1)

1852 BARFORD ST. MARTIN LIMITED STKS (0-85) (3-Y.O+) (Class D)

4-50 (4-50) **1m 1f 209y** £3,574.00 (£1,072.00: £516.00: £238.00) Stalls: High GOING minus 0.47 sec per fur (F)

				SP	RR	SF
1456^{16}	**Lomberto (82)** (VSoane) **4-9-6** CRutter(1) (lw: chsd ldr: rdn over 3f out: led nr fin: all out)	—	**1**	50/1	84	30
1563*	**Scoss (84)** (LMCumani) **3-8-9** PatEddery(2) (lw: led: rdn 2f out: hdd nr fin)	nk	**2**	11/4^{2}	86	19
*491**	**Motet (85)** (GWragg) **3-8-9** MHills(4) (a.p: hrd rdn & ev ch ins fnl f: nt qckn)	nk	**3**	2/1^{1}	85	18
1482^{4}	**Love Has No Pride (USA) (84)** (RHannon) **3-8-7** DaneO'Neill(7) (hld up: hrd rdn over 2f out: one pce)	3	**4**	7/2^{3}	78	11
1747^{4}	**Carlys Quest (64)** (JNeville) **3-8-7** AMcGlone(5) (bhd: outpcd 5f out: styd on fnl 2f: nt rch ldrs)	nk	**5**	50/1	78	11
	Bullfinch (82) (RTPhillips) **4-9-6** RHughes(6) (hld up & plld hrd: rdn 3f out: sn wknd)	9	**6**	14/1	63	9
1261^{7}	**Medieval Lady (85)** (IABalding) **4-9-3** JReid(3) (s.s: t.o fnl 4f)	19	**7**	7/2^{3}	30	—

(SP 115.0%) **7 Rn**

2m 9.9 (4.60) CSF £168.73 TOTE £56.40: £6.50 £1.80 (£104.40) OWNER Mr Saleh Al Homeizi (ASTON ROWANT) BRED C. R. and V. M. Withers

WEIGHT FOR AGE 3yo-13lb

OFFICIAL EXPLANATION **Medieval Lady: had become unsettled in the stalls. Lomberto: regarding the improvement in form, the trainer reported that his previous run was his first outing for eight months, and that it was a much better class of race, as confirmed by the Handicapper.**

Lomberto, fifth in the Horris Hill as a juvenile, disappointed last season and was having his second run for his new stable. (50/1)

1563* Scoss put in a brave attempt to make all. (11/4: 7/4-3/1)

491* Motet found this more competitive than on the sand at Lingfield. (2/1)

1482 Love Has No Pride (USA) could never get to grips with the principals. (7/2)

1747 Carlys Quest would have been much better-off in a handicap. (50/1)

Bullfinch (14/1: 12/1-25/1)

T/Plpt: £24.90 (454.21 Tckts). T/Qdpt: £3.60 (186.34 Tckts) KH

1688-YARMOUTH (L-H) (Firm)
Wednesday June 11th

WEATHER: raining WIND: almost nil

1853 CHARTER H'CAP (0-70) (3-Y.O) (Class E)

2-10 (2-11) **1m 6f 17y** £3,018.25 (£901.00: £430.50: £195.25) Stalls: Low GOING minus 0.57 sec per fur (F)

				SP	RR	SF
1469*	**Aurelian (57)** (MBell) **3-8-10** MFenton(6) (hld up: pushed along & hdwy 4f out: led wl over 1f out: r.o)	—	**1**	9/2^{2}	61	27
1487^{5}	**Ginger Rogers (45)** (DWPArbuthnot) **3-7-12** JQuinn(2) (hld up: rdn over 3f out: nt clr run over 2f out: swtchd rt over 1f out: styd on strly ins fnl f)	¾	**2**	33/1	48	14
1731*	**Eponine (70)** (MRChannon) **3-9-9**^{5x} JFEgan(5) (a.p: rdn over 2f out: kpt on one pce)	½	**3**	9/1	73	39
	Golden Melody (60) (MJHeaton-Ellis) **3-8-13** SSanders(9) (b.hind: hld up: pushed along 8f out: hdwy 3f out: n.m.r 2f out: one pce)	3	**4**	25/1	59	25

1387^{2}	**Jucinda (61)** (JPearce) **3-9-0** BDoyle(1) (sn led: hdd after 4f: hrd rdn over 2f out: one pce)	1	**5**	$5/1^{3}$	59	25
1449^{4}	**Krosno (64)** (SCWilliams) **3-9-3** KFallon(3) (led 9f out: hdd wl over 1f out: wknd ins fnl f)	4	**6**	$7/2^{1}$	58	24
1465^{6}	**As-Is (67)** (MJohnston) **3-9-6** DHolland(4) (lw: prom tl wknd over 1f out)	2½	**7**	$5/1^{3}$	58	24
1282^{2}	**High On Life (68)** (ACStewart) **3-9-7** MRoberts(7) (a bhd)	nk	**8**	11/2	58	24
1502*	**Dawn Summit (56)** (BHanbury) **3-8-9** JStack(10) (lw: led after 4f: hdd 9f out: wknd over 2f out)	5	**9**	12/1	41	7
862^{9}	**Mechilie (43)** (JWPayne) **3-7-10b**^{1} GBardwell(8) (a bhd)	5	**10**	50/1	22	—

(SP 115.6%) **10 Rn**

3m 2.1 (4.10) CSF £129.82 CT £1,165.52 TOTE £7.90: £1.90 £6.40 £2.60 (£91.80) Trio £136.40 OWNER Mr Desmond Fitzgerald (NEWMARKET) BRED D. Fitzgerald
LONG HANDICAP Mechilie 6-11
1469* Aurelian, despite being by a sprinter, has found his niche as a stayer. (9/2: op 7/1)
1487 Ginger Rogers, by Gold Cup winner Gildoran, ran on strongly on her first try over the trip despite not getting the clearest of runs. She can pick up a similar event. (33/1)
1731* Eponine won a claimer last time and ran well under her penalty here. (9/1: op 6/1)
Golden Melody did not have the clearest of runs and this was a promising seasonal debut. (25/1)
1387 Jucinda looked slow in the last two furlongs. (5/1)
1449 Krosno appears not to stay. (7/2)
1282 High On Life (11/2: op 3/1)
1502* Dawn Summit (12/1: op 8/1)

1854 E.B.F. RIVER BURE NOVICE MEDIAN AUCTION STKS (2-Y.O) (Class E)

2-40 (2-40) **6f 3y** £3,210.00 (£960.00: £460.00: £210.00) Stalls: Low GOING minus 0.57 sec per fur (F)

				SP	RR	SF
1251*	**Shawdon** (SirMarkPrescott) **2-9-4** SSanders(2) (lw: mde all: qcknd clr ent fnl f: r.o wl)	—	**1**	$2/7^{1}$	77+	16
	Jus'chillin' (IRE) (CADwyer) **2-8-7** NVarley(5) (w'like: bit bkwd: in tch: hrd rdn ½-wy: kpt on to chse wnr over 1f out: no imp)	4	**2**	$20/1^{3}$	55	—
	Up The Wall (ICampbell) **2-8-12** GBardwell(1) (leggy: unf: outpcd & bhd tl sme hdwy 1f out: kpt on ins fnl f)	3	**3**	25/1	52	—
	Great Melody (IRE) (JMPEustace) **2-8-12** RCochrane(4) (w'like: bit bkwd: chsd wnr tl wknd over 1f out)	3½	**4**	$7/2^{2}$	43	—
1007^{6}	**Fred's In The Know** (CMurray) **2-8-12** NicolaHowarth(3) (in tch tl wknd over 2f out)	3	**5**	33/1	35	—

(SP 111.5%) **5 Rn**

1m 13.7 (2.80) CSF £8.33 TOTE £1.10: £1.10 £3.10 (£3.90) OWNER Mr Cyril Humphris (NEWMARKET) BRED C. Humphris
1251* Shawdon won this as easily as the market suggests. (2/7)
Jus'chillin' (IRE) looked in need of the run and will improve. (20/1)
Up The Wall could not go the early pace. (25/1)
Great Melody (IRE), quite an attractive, stocky sort, will come on for the run. (7/2)

1855 RADIO NORFOLK CONDITIONS STKS (3-Y.O+) (Class C)

3-10 (3-10) **6f 3y** £5,102.14 (£1,763.34: £845.17: £344.35) Stalls: Low GOING minus 0.57 sec per fur (F)

				SP	RR	SF
1590^{8}	**Hattab (IRE) (97)** (PTWalwyn) **3-8-10** DHolland(3) (mde all: set stdy pce: qcknd 2f out: sn clr: easily)	—	**1**	$6/4^{1}$	107+	28
745^{3}	**Venture Capitalist (108)** (DNicholls) **8-9-0** AlexGreaves(4) (plld hrd: chsd wnr: hrd rdn over 1f out: one pce)	7	**2**	$6/4^{1}$	84	13
1403^{7}	**Johnny Staccato (91)** (JMPEustace) **3-8-8** RCochrane(2) (keen hold: chsd ldrs: rdn over 1f out: one pce)	¾	**3**	$3/1^{2}$	84	5
1689^{11}	**Spanish Stripper (USA) (25)** (MCChapman) **6-9-0** DeclanO'Shea(1) (in tch tl wknd over 2f out)	6	**4**	$50/1^{3}$	5 t	—

(SP 107.0%) **4 Rn**

1m 12.2 (1.30) CSF £3.60 TOTE £2.20 (£1.50) OWNER Mr Hamdan Al Maktoum (LAMBOURN) BRED Shadwell Estate Company Limited
WEIGHT FOR AGE 3yo-8lb
1212 Hattab (IRE) was given a canny ride by Holland here, dictating at a steady pace, and the race was over as soon as he quickened up. He was not originally in this race and was only put in after they re-opened the event. This is a good advertisement for the BHB initiative. (6/4)
745 Venture Capitalist pulled too hard and was not suited by the moderate pace. (6/4)
1212 Johnny Staccato had it to do at the weights and did not help his cause by taking a tug. (3/1)

1856 TOLLHOUSE (S) STKS (2-Y.O) (Class G)

3-40 (3-43) **7f 3y** £2,180.50 (£603.00: £287.50) Stalls: Low GOING minus 0.20 sec per fur (GF)

				SP	RR	SF
	Sick As A Parrot (CADwyer) **2-8-11** JStack(6) (unf: bit bkwd: dwlt: sn rcvrd to chse ldrs: led over 1f out: rdn ins fnl f: r.o)	—	**1**	$5/1^{3}$	58	25
1444^{4}	**Lasham** (NACallaghan) **2-9-2** WRyan(4) (stdd s: hld up: hdwy 2f out: chsd wnr ins fnl f: r.o)	1	**2**	$Evens^{1}$	61	28
1370^{3}	**Calliram** (MBlanshard) **2-8-7**ow1 RCochrane(7) (chsd ldrs: led over 2f out: hdd over 1f out: one pce)	1¾	**3**	$4/1^{2}$	48	14
767^{9}	**Tinos Island (IRE)** (MHTompkins) **2-8-6** DBiggs(1) (chsd ldrs: rdn over 1f out: one pce)	2	**4**	33/1	42	9
1370^{4}	**The Hobby Lobby (IRE)** (MRChannon) **2-8-11v**^{1} JQuinn(2) (keen hold: led: hdd over 2f out: wknd over 1f out)	3½	**5**	7/1	39	6
1581^{6}	**Flirtina** (PDEvans) **2-8-6** JFEgan(3) (w ldr tl wknd over 2f out)	2½	**6**	25/1	29	—
	Sparkling Secret (CMurray) **2-8-11** NicolaHowarth(5) (w'like: bit bkwd: a bhd)	½	**7**	25/1	32	—

(SP 109.8%) **7 Rn**

1m 28.8 (4.60) CSF £8.73 TOTE £4.90: £1.30 £1.50 (£4.00) OWNER Mrs Shelley Dwyer (NEWMARKET) BRED Helshaw Grange Farms Ltd, Miss Powner & A. Hampton
No bid
Sick As A Parrot won this despite looking in the paddock as though the race would do him good. (5/1: op 8/1)
1444 Lasham was held up to get the trip. He appeared to get it well enough but had to admit the winner was too strong. (Evens)
1370 Calliram had every chance but could not quicken up in the closing stages. (4/1: 3/1-9/2)
Tinos Island (IRE) hunted up the leaders but, when put under pressure below the distance, could only find the one speed. (33/1)
1370 The Hobby Lobby (IRE) (7/1: op 9/2)

1857 POTTER HEIGHAM H'CAP (0-70) (3-Y.O+) (Class E)

4-10 (4-11) **6f 3y** £2,914.25 (£869.00: £414.50: £187.25) Stalls: Low GOING minus 0.20 sec per fur (GF)

				SP	RR	SF
1279^{16}	**Don Pepe (60)** (RBoss) **6-9-4** KFallon(3) (lw: hld up & bhd: rdn over 1f out: led ins fnl f: r.o)	—	**1**	$13/2^{3}$	71	52
357^{4}	**Prima Silk (70)** (MJRyan) **6-10-0** GCarter(1) (rr: pushed along over 3f out: hdwy over 1f out: ev ch ins fnl f: r.o)	½	**2**	$9/2^{2}$	80	61

			Pos	SP	RR	SF
1671[4]	**Double Oscar (IRE) (49)** (DNicholls) **4-8-7b** AlexGreaves(8) (hld up: hdwy ½-wy: led over 1f out: hdd ins fnl f: unable qckn)	¾	3	9/2[2]	57	38
1419[5]	**Bright Paragon (IRE) (40)** (KTIvory) **8-7-9**(3) MartinDwyer(5) (b: b.hind: w ldr: led over 2f out: hdd over 1f out: one pce)	¾	4	9/2[2]	46	27
1385[10]	**Rambold (60)** (NEBerry) **6-9-4** MRoberts(4) (led: hdd over 2f out: wkng whn n.m.r ins fnl f)	2½	5	5/2[1]	59	40
1666[8]	**Waders Dream (IRE) (47)** (PatMitchell) **8-8-5v** MFenton(2) (outpcd & bhd: sme hdwy over 1f out: nvr nrr)	s.h	6	11/1	46	27
1047[13]	**Hannah's Usher (60)** (CMurray) **5-9-4** NicolaHowarth(6) (chsd ldrs tl wknd over 2f out)	7	7	10/1	40	21
1620[18]	**Invigilate (38)** (MRChannon) **8-7-10v** JQuinn(7) (in tch to ½-wy)	6	8	16/1	2	—

(SP 119.8%) **8 Rn**

1m 13.2 (2.30) CSF £34.18 CT £136.48 TOTE £5.20: £1.50 £1.50 £1.20 (£13.10) OWNER Mrs Elaine Aird (NEWMARKET) BRED Patrick Eddery Ltd

LONG HANDICAP Invigilate 7-9

Don Pepe was held up just behind the leaders and was produced with a well-timed challenge to lead inside the final furlong. (13/2)

357 Prima Silk looked unlikely to take a hand when being scrubbed along before halfway but to her credit kept she kept improving. After having every chance in the final furlong, she just found the winner that bit too strong. (9/2)

1671 Double Oscar (IRE) moved up going well after halfway and looked like scoring when leading below the distance but was worn down in the closing stages. This was his best run for a while. (9/2)

1236* Bright Paragon (IRE) showed his usual early dash but is probably best at five. (9/2)

Rambold cut out much of the running but had no more to give in the final furlong. (5/2)

Waders Dream (IRE) (11/1: op 7/1)

1858 WEATHERBYS ECLIPSE PEDIGREES MAIDEN STKS (3-Y.O F) (Class D)

4-40 (4-41) **7f 3y** £3,581.90 (£1,068.20: £509.60: £230.30) Stalls: Low GOING minus 0.20 sec per fur (GF)

			Pos	SP	RR	SF
1234[4]	**Topatori (IRE) (72)** (MHTompkins) **3-8-11** DBiggs(4) (hld up in tch: swtchd rt over 1f out: str run fnl f to ld nr fin)	—	1	11/4[2]	72	39
	Moon Fairy (JGSmyth-Osbourne) **3-8-11** SSanders(5) (unf: hld up & bhd: hdwy to ld ins fnl f: hdd nr fin)	¾	2	11/1	70	37
1643[2]	**Tithcar** (BHanbury) **3-8-11** MRimmer(2) (led: hdd ins fnl f: unable qckn)	1	3	11/4[2]	68	35
	Sharpwitted (JHMGosden) **3-8-11** GHind(7) (tall: scope: a.p: ev ch ins fnl f: btn whn n.m.r cl home)	½	4	6/4[1]	67	34
1587[13]	**Blazer's Baby** (JRFanshawe) **3-8-11** DHarrison(1) (w ldr: rdn 2f out: wknd over 1f out)	2	5	10/1[3]	62	29
1643[4]	**Cabcharge Glory** (GGMargarson) **3-8-11** GBardwell(3) (bhd fr ½-wy)	13	6	66/1	33	—
1119[16]	**Love Over Gold (30)** (MCChapman) **3-8-11** DeclanO'Shea(6) (s.i.s: plld hrd: sn prom: wknd 3f out: t.o whn fell over 1f out)		F	100/1	—	—

(SP 113.2%) **7 Rn**

1m 27.6 (3.40) CSF £28.41 TOTE £8.50: £1.60 £4.30 (£36.50) OWNER Mr M. P. Bowring (NEWMARKET) BRED Frank Dunne

1234 Topatori (IRE) always appeared to be travelling well. She had to be switched to get a run below the distance but, once starting her move, always looked like getting up. (11/4)

Moon Fairy was supported in the ring and ran really well here. Produced with a well-timed challenge to lead inside the final furlong, she was just worn down close home. She should be able to find a race. (11/1)

1643 Tithcar made a bold bid to make all but could not quicken up in the final furlong. (11/4)

Sharpwitted, a tall, lengthy, beautifully-bred filly by Sadler's Wells out of the Triple Crown winner Oh So Sharp, had every chance but could not find a turn of foot in the final furlong. Connections will be very keen to get a win into her. (6/4: op 4/6)

Blazer's Baby (10/1: 7/1-11/1)

1859 HORNING H'CAP (0-70) (3-Y.O F) (Class E)

5-10 (5-10) **1m 2f 21y** £3,044.25 (£909.00: £434.50: £197.25) Stalls: Low GOING minus 0.57 sec per fur (F)

			Pos	SP	RR	SF
1443[6]	**Top Jem (65)** (MJRyan) **3-9-2** GBardwell(7) (chsd ldrs: rdn over 2f out: led & edgd lft ins fnl f: r.o)	—	1	7/2[2]	71	41
1316[13]	**Cheek To Cheek (57)** (CACyzer) **3-8-8** KFallon(4) (chsd ldrs: rdn over 2f out: ev ch wl ins fnl f: r.o)	s.h	2	12/1	63	33
1694[6]	**Poker Princess (52)** (MBell) **3-8-3** MFenton(6) (a.p: ev ch ins fnl f: unable qckn)	¾	3	8/1	57	27
1474[3]	**Top Shelf (61)** (CEBrittain) **3-8-12** SSanders(5) (lw: led: hdd ins fnl f: one pce)	hd	4	11/2[3]	66	36
1633[3]	**Princess of Hearts (60)** (MCPipe) **3-8-11b** PaulEddery(2) (hld up in rr: hdwy over 2f out: sn rdn: one pce)	1¼	5	9/4[1]	63	33
1624[8]	**Bewitching Lady (49)** (DWPArbuthnot) **3-7-11**(3) MartinDwyer(3) (hld up: rdn over 3f out: wknd 2f out)	3½	6	20/1	46	16
1641[8]	**Princess Topaz (70)** (CACyzer) **3-9-7** GCarter(8) (hld up: effrt over 2f out: no hdwy)	1¾	7	16/1	64	34
	Cambridge Ball (IRE) (67) (MJohnston) **3-9-4** DHolland(10) (chsd ldrs: rdn over 3f out: wknd over 2f out)	¾	8	7/1	60	30
693[10]	**Pat Said No (IRE) (62)** (DJSCosgrove) **3-8-13** MRimmer(1) (hld up: rdn 3f out: sn wknd)	20	10	12/1	23	—

(SP 118.0%) **9 Rn**

2m 9.2 (5.40) CSF £41.71 CT £289.96 TOTE £4.50: £1.50 £3.00 £2.70 (£38.80) Trio £166.30 OWNER Mr John Malpass (NEWMARKET) BRED Malpass Brothers Ltd

STEWARDS' ENQUIRY Bardwell susp. 20-21/6/97 (careless riding).

885 Top Jem raced just behind the leaders. She came under pressure over two furlongs out but, to her credit, kept staying on and got in front inside the final furlong to score a game success. (7/2)

Cheek To Cheek ran easily her best run to date. Like the winner, she came under pressure at the two-furlong pole and stayed on strongly to almost get in front inside the final furlong. She could never quite grab the lead. (12/1)

1694 Poker Princess was to the fore throughout and had every chance. (8/1)

1474 Top Shelf made a brave effort to make all but was just worn down in the final furlong. (11/2: 4/1-6/1)

1633 Princess of Hearts, held up to get the trip, made headway over two furlongs out but soon came under pressure and she had little more to give. (9/4: op 4/1)

Cambridge Ball (IRE) (7/1: op 9/2)

T/Plpt: £518.20 (13.84 Tckts). T/Qdpt: £70.50 (6.25 Tckts) SM

1510-CARLISLE (R-H) (Firm)
Thursday June 12th
WEATHER: overcast WIND: mod half against

1860 WASTWATER MEDIAN AUCTION MAIDEN STKS (2-Y.O) (Class E)
2-20 (2-21) **5f** £2,947.25 (£893.00: £436.50: £208.25) Stalls: High GOING minus 0.39 sec per fur (F)

				SP	RR	SF
1396^{9}	**Wait'n'see** (MWEasterby) **2-9-0** TLucas(9) (lw: trckd ldrs: qcknd to ld over 1f out: edgd lft: r.o wl)	—	**1**	11/4^{2}	77	44
1569^{2}	**Patsy Culsyth** (MJohnston) **2-8-9** DHolland(1) (lw: w ldrs: effrt 2f out: nt pce of wnr)	3	**2**	11/8^{1}	62	29
1569^{12}	**Chikapenny** (MrsLStubbs) **2-8-9** ACulhane(6) (s.i.s: hdwy ½-wy: kpt on wl)	1¼	**3**	14/1	58	25
1749^{7}	**Dawn Patrol** (KWHogg) **2-8-9** LCharnock(2) (led over 3f: grad wknd)	4	**4**	9/1	46	13
	Amington Girl (PDEvans) **2-8-9** JCarroll(5) (leggy: s.s: nrst fin)	3	**5**	20/1	36	3
684^{9}	**Candy Twist** (RonaldThompson) **2-8-9** TWilliams(7) (w ldrs tl wknd over 1f out)	1	**6**	50/1	33	—
1038^{5}	**Flying High (IRE)** (FMurphy) **2-9-0** JFortune(3) (outpcd ½-wy: no imp after)	¾	**7**	16/1	35	2
1492^{9}	**Three Tenners** (JBerry) **2-8-4**(5) TEDurcan(10) (outpcd fr ½-wy: sn bhd)	1¾	**8**	5/1^{3}	25	—
1614^{4}	**Glass River** (PDEvans) **2-9-0** JFEgan(4) (lw: s.i.s: nvr trbld ldrs)	¾	**9**	10/1	27	—

(SP 123.8%) **9 Rn**

61.5 secs (1.30) CSF £6.82 TOTE £2.70: £1.10 £1.60 £4.30 (£2.50) Trio £57.10 OWNER Mr M. W. Easterby (SHERIFF HUTTON) BRED Exors of the late Countess of Durham
OFFICIAL EXPLANATION **Wait'n'see: regarding the improvement in form, the matter was referred to Portman Square as the film of the gelding's last run was not avaliable.**
STEWARDS ENQUIRY: Wait'n'see: regarding the improvement in form, trainer subsequently fined £2,500 under non-triers rule.
1396 Wait'n'see was wearing a tongue-strap and, taken early to post, misbehaved on the way but it was a different matter on the way back as he won particularly well and was heavily supported to do so. (11/4: 11/2-5/2)
1569 Patsy Culsyth did her utmost but the winner was always a class above her. (11/8)
Chikapenny is learning what the game is all about and by the way she finished here, she should pick up a race in due course. (14/1)
1645 Dawn Patrol has the early pace but as yet cannot maintain it. (9/1)
Amington Girl ran well after a very poor start and there would seem to be better to come. (20/1)
Candy Twist showed plenty of speed this time and is obviously learning. (50/1)
1614 Glass River was disappointing here as he never showed anything after a moderate start. This was probably just an off day. (10/1)

1861 BUTTERMERE CLAIMING STKS (3-Y.O+) (Class F)
2-50 (2-51) **5f 207y** £2,542.00 (£712.00: £346.00) Stalls: High GOING minus 0.39 sec per fur (F)

				SP	RR	SF
1613^{5}	**Winter Scout (USA) (53)** (RAFahey) **9-8-6b**(7) RWinston(6) (lw: bhd: hdwy over 2f out: led appr fnl f: edgd rt: r.o)	—	**1**	5/2^{2}	66	23
1786^{4}	**Sense of Priority (59)** (DNicholls) **8-9-1** AlexGreaves(7) (trckd ldrs: disp ld 2f out: sn rdn: no ex fnl f)	2	**2**	9/2^{3}	63	20
1572^{3}	**Donna's Dancer (IRE) (65)** (NTinkler) **3-8-7b** KimTinkler(5) (jnd ldrs after 2f: outpcd whn hmpd ins fnl f: no ex)	1	**3**	11/2	60	9
1514^{10}	**La Volta (49)** (JGFitzGerald) **4-8-8** JFortune(3) (trckd ldrs: effrt over 2f out: r.o one pce)	¾	**4**	8/1	51	8
1127^{8}	**Forecast (39)** (KAMorgan) **4-8-9** DeanMcKeown(2) (b: cl up: led after 2f tl appr fnl f: btn whn hmpd ins fnl f)	2½	**5**	50/1	45	2
1734^{2}	**Skyers Flyer (IRE) (65)** (RonaldThompson) **3-8-6** TWilliams(8) (dwlt: hld up & bhd: hdwy ½-wy: sn rdn: wknd over 1f out)	1¾	**6**	13/8^{1}	46	—
1127^{9}	**Ragazzo (IRE) (29)** (JSWainwright) **7-8-9** LCharnock(4) (lw: led 2f: sn drvn along: wknd fnl 2½f)	6	**7**	66/1	24	—

(SP 114.8%) **7 Rn**

1m 14.9 (3.10) CSF £13.05 TOTE £4.50: £2.40 £2.60 (£11.00) OWNER Mrs S. M. Russell (MALTON) BRED Virginia Kraft Payson
WEIGHT FOR AGE 3yo-8lb No bid
1613 Winter Scout (USA) quickened up well to win this for the second year running. (5/2)
1786 Sense of Priority looked to be going best for much of the trip but just found one too determined when the race was really on. He is however in good heart. (9/2)
1572 Donna's Dancer (IRE) had no excuses this time and, after holding every chance, was looking beaten when the winner crossed him. (11/2: 4/1-7/1)
La Volta, happy to sit on the bridle, did not do a lot once off it. (8/1: 6/1-10/1)
Forecast got into the race this time but, once pressure was applied, he was soon back-pedalling. (50/1)
1734 Skyers Flyer (IRE) has plenty of ability but does not always put it in. (13/8)

1862 CARLISLE GLASS H'CAP (0-80) (3-Y.O+) (Class D)
3-20 (3-20) **7f 214y** £3,582.50 (£1,085.00: £530.00: £252.50) Stalls: High GOING minus 0.39 sec per fur (F)

				SP	RR	SF
1761*	**Jedi Knight (60)** (MWEasterby) **3-8-10**(5) 5x GParkin(2) (plld hrd early: sltly outpcd ½-wy: hdwy on bit to ld ins fnl f: easily)	—	**1**	11/8^{1}	68++	22
1652^{3}	**Pekay (63)** (MJohnston) **4-10-1** 5x DHolland(4) (cl up: slt ld 1f out: sn hdd & no ch w wnr)	1¼	**2**	5/2^{2}	69	34
1560^{10}	**Highspeed (IRE) (57)** (SEKettlewell) **5-9-9** JFortune(3) (hld up & bhd: hdwy 2f out: nrst fin)	¾	**3**	11/1	61	26
1683^{10}	**Bulsara (57)** (CWFairhurst) **5-9-9v**^{1} DeanMcKeown(7) (lw: hld up: effrt 3f out: sn chsng ldrs: kpt on one pce fnl f)	s.h	**4**	9/1	61	26
1631^{8}	**Spanish Verdict (56)** (DenysSmith) **10-9-8** ACulhane(6) (lw: led tl hdd 1f out: sn btn)	1¾	**5**	6/1^{3}	56	21
950^{13}	**Marzocco (30)** (TAKCuthbert) **9-7-5**(5) JBramhill(1) (trckd ldrs: effrt & ch 2f out: wknd fnl f)	1¾	**6**	100/1	27	—
1495^{9}	**Thatched (IRE) (55)** (REBarr) **7-9-4**(3) PFessey(5) (trckd ldrs: effrt over 2f out: wknd fnl f)	s.h	**7**	7/1	52	17

(SP 116.8%) **7 Rn**

1m 41.5 (4.50) CSF £4.74 TOTE £2.20: £1.10 £3.10 (£2.70) OWNER Mr K. Hodgson (SHERIFF HUTTON) BRED E. J. B. Maude
LONG HANDICAP Marzocco 7-2
WEIGHT FOR AGE 3yo-11lb
1761* Jedi Knight is in tremendous form and won pulling several buses here and looked as though he should stay further. (11/8)
1652 Pekay ran a fine race and kept responding to pressure but the winner was in a different league. (5/2)
Highspeed (IRE) put in a promising effort here and was certainly not knocked about and is one to watch. (11/1: 8/1-12/1)
824 Bulsara had a visor on for the first time but this trip was probably on the sharp side. (9/1)
1472 Spanish Verdict loves this ground and this track and despite his years he will find a suitable race once his stable strikes form. (6/1)
Marzocco ran reasonably especially considering he was 8lb out of the handicap. (100/1)

1863 LONGHORN HARDWARE H'CAP (0-70) (3-Y.O) (Class E)

3-50 (3-51) **1m 4f** £2,853.00 (£864.00: £422.00: £201.00) Stalls: High GOING minus 0.39 sec per fur (F)

				SP	RR	SF
1465*	**Scarrots (64)** (SCWilliams) **3-9-6** JFortune(8) (mde all: pushed along 2f out: r.o strly)	—	1	9/4[1]	75	34
1299[4]	**Wildmoor (55)** (JDBethell) **3-8-11** TWilliams(3) (cl up chsng group: hdwy 4f out: ch over 2f out: one pce)	6	2	5/1[3]	58	17
665[4]	**Kingdom Pearl (47)** (MJCamacho) **3-8-3** LCharnock(2) (hdwy over 4f out: styd on: no imp)	1½	3	12/1	48	7
*1579**	**Skelton Sovereign (IRE) (57)** (RHollinshead) **3-8-13** FLynch(1) (s.i.s: bhd tl hdwy over 3f out: no imp)	1½	4	10/1	56	15
1469[12]	**Maremma (40)** (DonEnricoIncisa) **3-7-10** KimTinkler(6) (lw: bhd: sme hdwy 2f out: n.d)	1¾	5	16/1	37	—
1469[5]	**Ziggy's Viola (IRE) (55)** (MrsMReveley) **3-8-11** ACulhane(7) (chsd clr ldrs: rdn over 3f out: wknd wl over 1f out)	2	6	100/30[2]	49	8
1497[9]	**Cochiti (41)** (CWThornton) **3-7-11** DaleGibson(5) (outpcd & lost tch ½-wy: n.d)	1	7	16/1	34	—
1329[4]	**Baby Jane (65)** (BMactaggart) **3-9-7** JCarroll(4) (swtg: w wnr tl wknd fnl 3f)	18	8	9/1	34	—

(SP 109.1%) **8 Rn**

2m 34.7 (5.70) CSF £11.17 CT £86.38 TOTE £2.20: £1.10 £1.60 £4.00 (£14.20) OWNER Mr Bruce Wyatt (NEWMARKET) BRED R. G. Percival
LONG HANDICAP Maremma 7-6

1465* Scarrots loves to dominate and got stronger as the race progressed. (9/4: op 6/4)
1299 Wildmoor, suited by the strong pace, got into it early in the straight but then found the winner far too good. (5/1)
665 Kingdom Pearl does not do anything quickly but does stay. (12/1: op 8/1)
1579* Skelton Sovereign (IRE) is a consistent, albeit moderate performer and the struggle required here was always beyond him. (10/1)
793 Maremma was probably flattered by staying on from off a strong pace. (16/1)
1469 Ziggy's Viola (IRE) chased the tearaway leaders which found her out some way from home. (100/30)

1864 ENNERDALE RATING RELATED MAIDEN STKS (0-60) (3-Y.O) (Class F)

4-20 (4-21) **5f 207y** £2,612.00 (£732.00: £356.00) Stalls: High GOING minus 0.39 sec per fur (F)

				SP	RR	SF
1470[9]	**Court Express (60)** (TJEtherington) **3-9-0** ACulhane(1) (lw: bhd: hdwy ½-wy: led 1f out: r.o)	—	1	8/1	67	23
1638[4]	**Nervous Rex (55)** (WRMuir) **3-8-7**(7) JWilkinson(4) (lw: racd wd: a chsng ldrs: kpt on ins fnl f)	2½	2	11/1	60	16
1687[5]	**Mill End Boy (60)** (MWEasterby) **3-8-9**(5) GParkin(2) (bhd: hdwy to ld wl over 1f out: hdd 1f out: no ex)	1¼	3	11/4[1]	57	13
1080[10]	**Red Romance (46)** (DenysSmith) **3-9-0** LCharnock(6) (cl up: carried lft ½-wy r.o one pce)	hd	4	20/1	57	13
1586[3]	**Rockaroundtheclock (52)** (PDEvans) **3-9-0b** JFEgan(5) (swtg: a in tch: rdn ½-wy: kpt on same pce)	nk	5	6/1[2]	56	12
1496[7]	**Sparkling Harry (53)** (MissLCSiddall) **3-9-0** DeanMcKeown(10) (lw: chsd ldrs: chal 2f out: btn appr fnl f)	3½	6	7/1[3]	46	2
1226[7]	**Heathyards Pearl (USA) (57)** (RHollinshead) **3-8-8**(3) DGriffiths(7) (in tch: effrt & ch 2f out: wknd fnl f)	3½	7	16/1	34	—
667[6]	**Presentiment (58)** (MartynWane) **3-9-0** JCarroll(12) (led over 4f: edgd lft & grad wknd)	1¾	8	14/1	32	—
1467[16]	**Thewrightone (IRE) (35)** (GROldroyd) **3-8-5v**[1](7)ow1 RFarmer(3) (sn outpcd & bhd: n.d)	1	9	50/1	28	—
1573[9]	**Changed To Baileys (IRE) (58)** (JBerry) **3-9-0b** JFortune(9) (s.i.s: hdwy on ins ½-wy: sn wknd)	¾	10	9/1	28	—
1733[4]	**Kippilaw (60)** (MJohnston) **3-8-11** DHolland(11) (spd to ½-wy: sn wknd)	s.h	11	6/1[2]	24	—
1582[5]	**Ohio Royale (48)** (GROldroyd) **3-9-0** MMcAndrew(8) (in tch tl wknd fnl 2f)	1	12	50/1	25	—

(SP 118.4%) **12 Rn**

1m 14.9 (3.10) CSF £83.02 TOTE £11.40: £3.20 £1.90 £1.80 (£67.00) Trio £51.20 OWNER Mr J. Pain (MALTON) BRED J. A. Pain

Court Express, dropping back in trip, looked particularly well and, coming from behind, won going away, suggesting that he should get a bit further. (8/1)
1638 Nervous Rex, from a yard in form, was always racing on the outside of the field and finished up on the stands rails and, to his credit, he was keeping on well. (11/1)
1687 Mill End Boy had his chances here but, once the pressure was on, his limitations were again exposed. (11/4)
Red Romance ran his best race of the season. (20/1)
1586 Rockaroundtheclock was edgy beforehand and had the blinkers back on but was never doing quite enough. (6/1: 7/2-13/2)
1394 Sparkling Harry, who ran quite well with the blinkers on last time, failed to respond to pressure on this occasion without them. (7/1)

1865 CRUMMOCK WATER APPRENTICE H'CAP (0-65) (3-Y.O+) (Class F)

4-55 (4-56) **5f** £2,682.00 (£752.00: £366.00) Stalls: High GOING minus 0.39 sec per fur (F)

				SP	RR	SF
1578[10]	**Ramsey Hope (59)** (CWFairhurst) **4-9-5v**(5) TSiddall(6) (lw: hdwy & hung lft 2f out: led ins fnl f: r.o)	—	1	16/1	65	52
1790[3]	**Marino Street (54)** (PDEvans) **4-9-5** DGriffiths(4) (hdwy & hmpd 2f out: styd on to chal ins fnl f: kpt on towards fin)	nk	2	14/1	59	46
1671[2]	**Featherstone Lane (46)** (MissLCSiddall) **6-8-11** OPears(7) (hdwy ½-wy: ch ins fnl f: nt qckn)	1¾	3	3/1[1]	45	32
1236[5]	**Thick as Thieves (39)** (RonaldThompson) **5-8-4** DarrenMoffatt(2) (chsd clr ldr: ev ch ins fnl f: no ex)	nk	4	13/2	38	25
1627[7]	**Bowcliffe Grange (IRE) (53)** (DWChapman) **5-9-4** PFessey(1) (led & sn clr: racd stands' side: hdd & hung rt ins fnl f)	1	5	12/1	48	35
1828*	**Sunset Harbour (IRE) (47)** (SEKettlewell) **4-8-7**(5) 7x JennyBenson(10) (hdwy ½-wy: chsng ldrs appr fnl f: nt qckn)	¾	6	6/1[3]	40	27
1759[6]	**Grand Chapeau (IRE) (52)** (DNicholls) **5-9-0**(3) IonaWands(5) (wnt lft s: hdwy 2f out: no imp)	¾	7	15/2	43	30
1627[9]	**L A Touch (52)** (JJQuinn) **4-9-0**(3) KSked(3) (lw: hdwy u.p 2f out: hung rt & n.d)	¾	8	12/1	40	27
1620[5]	**Mu-Arrik (31)** (GROldroyd) **9-7-10v** JBramhill(8) (nvr wnt pce)	½	9	12/1	18	5
1594[8]	**Rich Glow (53)** (NBycroft) **6-9-4** PRoberts(9) (lw: outpcd & bhd ½-wy: n.d)	2½	10	11/2[2]	32	19

(SP 115.4%) **10 Rn**

61.6 secs (1.40) CSF £197.70 CT £782.46 TOTE £19.50: £4.90 £2.10 £1.20 (£69.10) Trio £297.20; £301.40 to Sandown 13/6/97 OWNER Mr C. D. Barber-Lomax (MIDDLEHAM) BRED Norton Grove Stud Ltd
LONG HANDICAP Mu-Arrik 7-9
STEWARDS' ENQUIRY Obj. to Ramsey Hope by Griffiths overruled.

348* Ramsey Hope is an All-Weather specialist these days but he does like to come from off a strong pace and was well suited here. (16/1)
1790 Marino Street got messed about by the winner when starting her run, but she still had every chance and kept staying on well and is obviously on good terms with herself. (14/1)
1671 Featherstone Lane did his usual and had his chances but failed to take them. (3/1: tchd 100/1)
1236 Thick as Thieves showed plenty of speed but just lacked that final kick and it is now three seasons since he last won. (13/2)
406 Bowcliffe Grange (IRE) could have his name pencilled in now if there were any four-furlong races, but he can win at this trip when he really comes right. (12/1: 8/1-14/1)
1828* Sunset Harbour (IRE), a winner the previous day, was never firing on this occasion. (6/1)
1311* Rich Glow never showed a thing and seems to save all his best for Ayr. (11/2)

T/Plpt: £67.40 (171.38 Tckts). T/Qdpt: £10.30 (60.53 Tckts) AA

1742-GOODWOOD (R-H) (Good to firm, Good patches becoming Good)
Thursday June 12th
WEATHER: overcast with early drizzle WIND: almost nil

1866 ROOKWOOD MAIDEN STKS (3-Y.O) (Class D)
2-10 (2-11) **1m 2f** £4,012.50 (£1,200.00: £575.00: £262.50) Stalls: High GOING minus 0.01 sec per fur (G)

				SP	RR	SF
1316^{6}	**Khawafi** (EALDunlop) **3-8-6**(3) DO'Donohoe(11) (led 8f out: clr 6f out: unchal)	—	**1**	$9/2^{2}$	79+	56
	Song of Freedom (JHMGosden) **3-9-0** GHind(9) (a.p: chsd wnr over 3f out: r.o one pce)	4	**2**	$5/2^{1}$	78	55
	Alarmist (RCharlton) **3-9-0** TSprake(6) (neat: rdn & hdwy over 3f out: r.o one pce)	hd	**3**	10/1	77	54
1318^{7}	**Dundel (IRE) (80)** (BWHills) **3-8-9** PaulEddery(3) (rdn & hdwy over 2f out: r.o one pce)	nk	**4**	$7/1^{3}$	72	49
	Polenista (JLDunlop) **3-8-9** MRoberts(2) (leggy: lt-f: hdwy over 1f out: one pc: bttr for r)	4	**5**	10/1	66	43
	Flowing Fortune (EALDunlop) **3-9-0** JWeaver(7) (rdn over 2f out: nvr nr to chal)	¾	**6**	10/1	69	46
	Azores (PFICole) **3-8-7**(7) DavidO'Neill(1) (w'like: lw: nvr nrr: bttr for r)	1½	**7**	12/1	67	44
1434^{8}	**Puteri Wentworth** (MissGayKelleway) **3-8-9** SSanders(4) (b.hind: prom over 6f)	1	**8**	50/1	60	37
1420^{3}	**Off The Rails** (HCandy) **3-8-9** CRutter(5) (led 2f: wknd over 2f out)	2½	**9**	12/1	56	33
	City Hall (IRE) (MRStoute) **3-9-0** WRyan(10) (bit bkwd: bhd fnl 7f)	3	**10**	8/1	57	34
1477^{10}	**Tarxien** (KRBurke) **3-9-0** WJO'Connor(12) (bit bkwd: a bhd)	3	**11**	50/1	52	29
	Signed And Sealed (USA) (CACyzer) **3-9-0** AMorris(8) (leggy: scope: a bhd)	11	**12**	33/1	34	11

(SP 119.9%) **12 Rn**

2m 11.26 (4.66) CSF £14.68 TOTE £5.80: £1.80 £1.70 £4.50 (£9.10) Trio £38.30 OWNER Mr Hamdan Al Maktoum (NEWMARKET) BRED Shadwell Estate Company Limited

IN-FOCUS: **This race turned into a meaningless contest as Khawafi was handed the race on a plate by the other jockeys, who all appeared to have fallen asleep until too late.**

1316 Khawafi appreciated the longer trip and was given a superb ride by O'Donohoe who completely outwitted the other eleven jockeys. Soon at the head of affairs, the filly forged clear at the top of the hill, despite not going a tremendous gallop, and the combination was a good five or six lengths clear entering the straight. When the other jockeys at last realised what was going on, the filly was too far clear to be caught. (9/2)

Song of Freedom, a half-brother to the very high-class Singspiel, went in pursuit of the winner of three furlongs from home, but never looked like reeling in that rival. (5/2: 6/4-11/4)

Alarmist, a half-brother to Fox Sparrow, at last realised that the winner had sprouted wings but, although staying on, never threatened to get near that rival. (10/1: 8/1-12/1)

1028 Dundel (IRE), last in two Listed races so far this season, was taking a drop back in class but was still unable to come up with the goods. (7/1)

Polenista, a narrow, lightly-made filly, was given a nice, quiet introduction and improvement can be expected. (10/1: op 6/1)

Flowing Fortune never threatened at any stage. (10/1)

Azores, a medium-sized colt who is a half-brother to Oaks winner Lady Carla, looked fit enough and, given a nice educational ride, should have learnt a lot from this. (12/1)

1867 DARNLEY (S) STKS (2-Y.O) (Class E)
2-40 (2-41) **5f** £3,427.50 (£1,020.00: £485.00: £217.50) Stalls: Low GOING minus 0.01 sec per fur (G)

				SP	RR	SF
1635^{6}	**Ivory's Joy** (KTIvory) **2-8-6b** CScally(4) (b: lw: w ldr: led 2f out: rdn out)	—	**1**	10/1	65	11
1614^{3}	**Sun In The Morning** (BJMeehan) **2-8-11** PaulEddery(2) (led 3f: ev ch ins fnl f: r.o)	½	**2**	$Evens^{1}$	68	14
	Shanthi (PJMakin) **2-8-6** SSanders(5) (leggy: lt-f: s.s: wl bhd 3f: hdwy over 1f out: r.o wl ins fnl f)	1¼	**3**	$4/1^{3}$	59+	5
1675^{8}	**Silent Pride (IRE)** (MDIUsher) **2-8-6** TSprake(3) (a.p: rdn over 2f out: unable qckn)	1¼	**4**	$3/1^{2}$	55	1
	Lady Ralphina (JJBridger) **2-8-1**(5) ADaly(1) (leggy: lt-f: dwlt: a wl bhd)	21	**5**	16/1	—	—

(SP 110.0%) **5 Rn**

61.24 secs (4.54) CSF £18.98 TOTE £10.70: £2.90 £1.40 (£5.90) OWNER Mr K. T. Ivory (RADLETT) BRED David S. Leggate

No bid

1635 Ivory's Joy, with more substance than most of her rivals, looked in good shape beforehand. Disputing the lead until showing narrowly in front a quarter of a mile from home, she was rousted along to keep the runner-up at bay. (10/1)

1614 Sun In The Morning, conceding weight all-round, took the field along. Collared a quarter of a mile from home, she stuck to her task well but was unable to get back in front. (Evens)

Shanthi, a sparely-made filly, would surely have won this, had she not been asleep in the stalls as they opened, costing her a good ten lengths. Her cause appeared absolutely hopeless but she really grasped what was required in the last furlong and a half, and made up a lot of ground. Sure to be a lot wiser for this, she is certainly capable of winning a similar event before long. (4/1)

1295 Silent Pride (IRE) was taking a drop in class but was still unable to reproduce her promising Sandown debut. (3/1)

Lady Ralphina has little substance and no ability if this initial run is anything to go by. (16/1)

1868 BADGER BREWERY H'CAP (0-95) (3-Y.O) (Class C)
3-10 (3-11) **1m 4f** £5,385.00 (£1,605.00: £765.00: £345.00) Stalls: Low GOING minus 0.01 sec per fur (G)

				SP	RR	SF
1416*	**Ciro's Pearl (IRE) (77)** (MHTompkins) **3-9-0** WRyan(5) (lost pl over 5f out: nt clr run over 2f out: rallied over 1f out: led ins fnl f: r.o wl)	—	**1**	$11/2^{3}$	85	48
1258^{3}	**Nightlark (IRE) (82)** (DRLoder) **3-9-5** DRMcCabe(1) (lw: hdwy 7f out: led over 3f out tl over 1f out: ev ch ins fnl f: unable qckn)	1¼	**2**	13/2	88	51
1296^{4}	**Pennys From Heaven (79)** (HCandy) **3-9-2** TQuinn(7) (lw: led over 8f: led over 1f out tl ins fnl f: one pce)	½	**3**	$11/4^{1}$	85	48
1474*	**Protocol (IRE) (77)** (JWHills) **3-9-0** RHughes(4) (lw: hdwy over 5f out: rdn over 2f out: one pce)	1¼	**4**	$9/2^{2}$	81	44
700^{2}	**Ikatania (84)** (JLDunlop) **3-9-7** TSprake(3) (swtg: hdwy & nt clr run on ins 6f out: nt clr run on ins fr 3f out: nt rcvr)	nk	**5**	9/1	88	51
1230^{3}	**Irsal (78)** (ACStewart) **3-9-1** MRoberts(8) (lw: a.p: ev ch over 2f out: wknd over 1f out)	3	**6**	9/1	78	41
1592^{2}	**Heart of Armor (83)** (PFICole) **3-9-6** CRutter(2) (lw: dropped rr 7f out: ralllied over 3f out: ev ch over 2f out: wknd over 1f out)	nk	**7**	7/1	82	45

			Pos	SP	RR	SF
1025⁷	**Davoski (78)** (BWHills) **3-9-1** PaulEddery(6) (swtg: lost pl over 5f out: rallied over 3f out: ev ch over 2f out: sn wknd)	9	**8**	7/1	65	28
				(SP 118.6%)		**8 Rn**

2m 40.79 (7.59) CSF £38.56 CT £109.67 TOTE £6.40: £1.50 £2.50 £1.20 (£22.70) OWNER Mr J. H. Shannon (NEWMARKET) BRED Johnny Kelly

1416* Ciro's Pearl (IRE) appreciated this longer trip and, after losing her pitch at the top of the hill and then finding her way blocked early in the straight, rallied nicely from below the distance to get on top inside the final furlong. (11/2)
1258 Nightlark (IRE) was much happier with this return to better ground. Gaining a slender advantage soon after the bugler called, she was headed below the distance but still had every chance inside the final furlong before the winner went by. She should soon find a race. (13/2: 4/1-7/1)
1296 Pennys From Heaven adopted his usual front-running role but, despite some good efforts in his career to date, lack of acceleration is becoming a bit of a problem. (11/4)
1474* Protocol (IRE), up 4lb for his recent Sandown success, was bustled along over a quarter of a mile from home and, although not having a great deal of room, was tapped for toe from below the distance. (9/2)
700 Ikatania was without a shadow of a doubt the hard-luck story of the race, and had nowhere to go along the inside rail all the way up the straight. (9/1)
1230 Irsal, as at Hamilton last time out, seemed to find this trip a bit too much and, after having every chance over a quarter of a mile from home, had shot his bolt below the distance. (9/1)
568* Davoski (7/1: 9/2-15/2)

1869 EQUITY FINANCIAL COLLECTIONS LIMITED STKS (0-90) (3-Y.O) (Class C)

3-40 (3-41) **1m 1f** £5,336.25 (£1,590.00: £757.50: £341.25) Stalls: High GOING minus 0.01 sec per fur (G)

				SP	RR	SF
958⁵	**Maylane (90)** (ACStewart) **3-8-12** MRoberts(6) (s.s: hdwy over 2f out: led 1f out: comf)	—	**1**	5/1	99+	62
1670²	**Atlantic Desire (IRE) (87)** (MJohnston) **3-8-9** JWeaver(2) (w ldr: led over 2f out to 1f out: unable qckn)	½	**2**	13/8¹	95	58
1782⁶	**Green Jewel (87)** (RHannon) **3-8-11** RHughes(1) (stdy hdwy over 2f out: hrd rdn over 1f out: one pce)	1½	**3**	9/2³	94	57
1173⁴	**Sophomore (88)** (BWHills) **3-8-12** PaulEddery(4) (lw: a.p: rdn over 2f out: wknd over 1f out)	7	**4**	11/4²	83	46
1595⁶	**Rich In Love (IRE) (86)** (CACyzer) **3-8-9** WRyan(5) (led over 6f: wknd over 1f out)	nk	**5**	20/1	80	43
	Zimiri (75) (JARToller) **3-9-0** SSanders(3) (bit bkwd: prom over 6f)	13	**6**	16/1	61?	24
				(SP 110.3%)		**6 Rn**

1m 56.79 (3.79) CSF £11.93 TOTE £5.00: £2.70 £1.40 (£5.00) OWNER Sheikh Ahmed Al Maktoum (NEWMARKET) BRED Sheikh Ahmed Bin Rashid Al Maktoum

958 Maylane, who has proved extremely temperamental on both his previous runs this season, not surprisingly has been gelded since his last outing. That appears to have done the trick for, although sluggish leaving the stalls, he came through to strike the front a furlong from home and comfortably had the measure of his rivals. (5/1)
1670 Atlantic Desire (IRE) disputed the lead until going on over a quarter of a mile from home. Headed a furlong out, she was then put in her place by the winner. She might be worth a try over bit further. (13/8)
1782 Green Jewel crept closer in the straight but, shown the persuader below the distance, failed to find the necessary turn of foot. (9/2)
1173 Sophomore was the paddock pick but he yet again disappointed and had given his all below the distance. He is becoming expensive to follow. (11/4)
1595 Rich In Love (IRE) took the field along but she was collared over a quarter of a mile from home and was soon in trouble. (20/1)
Zimiri was certainly up against it - he was at least 15lb worse off with all his rivals on official adjusted ratings and the only runner without a recent outing under his belt - so it was no surprise when he dropped away approaching the final quarter mile. (16/1)

1870 ALBERT MEDIAN AUCTION MAIDEN STKS (3-Y.O) (Class D)

4-10 (4-10) **7f** £3,590.00 (£1,070.00: £510.00: £230.00) Stalls: High GOING minus 0.01 sec per fur (G)

				SP	RR	SF
1406²	**Geimhriuil (IRE) (83)** (LMCumani) **3-9-0** JWeaver(1) (hld up: qckd to ld over 1f out: comf)	—	**1**	4/9¹	83+	55
1271⁴	**Khalik (IRE)** (EALDunlop) **3-9-0** WRyan(7) (b: led over 5f: unable qckn)	3½	**2**	11/2²	75	47
1477¹⁷	**Olivo (IRE) (79)** (CAHorgan) **3-9-0** PaulEddery(5) (hld up: rdn over 2f out: r.o one pce)	¾	**3**	12/1	73	45
	Monaco (IRE) (LMCumani) **3-9-0** DRMcCabe(4) (w'like: scope: bit bkwd: nt clr run on ins over 1f out: swtchd lft & hdwy over 1f out: r.o one pce)	hd	**4**	14/1	73+	45
991¹¹	**Top of The Green (IRE) (55)** (PJMakin) **3-9-0** SSanders(6) (swtg: a.p: ev ch 2f out: wknd over 1f out)	8	**5**	66/1	55	27
1637⁷	**Reward** (PFICole) **3-9-0** TQuinn(3) (prom 5f)	5	**6**	11/2²	43	15
1406⁵	***Swift Sovereign*** (JHMGosden) **3-9-0** GHind(2) (Withdrawn not under Starter's orders: lame)		**W**	10/1³	—	—
				(SP 124.9%)		**6 Rn**

1m 28.35 (3.55) CSF £3.41 TOTE £1.50: £1.40 £1.90 (£3.10) OWNER Mr M. J. Dawson (NEWMARKET) BRED Miss Suzanne O'Neill

1406 Geimhriuil (IRE) confirmed the promise shown at Haydock recently and proved to be in a different class to his rivals, needing only to be woken up to show a nice turn of foot to lead below the distance. (4/9)
1271 Khalik (IRE) reverted to the front-running role he adopted on his debut but was firmly brushed aside by the winner when collared over a furlong out. (11/2: 4/1-6/1)
Olivo (IRE), sold out of Paul Cole's stable for 22,000gs last Autumn and subsequently gelded, beat only one home on his debut for his new connections recently but ran better here, if failing to produce that vital turn of foot. (12/1: 8/1-12/1)
Monaco (IRE), a round-bodied gelding, did not run badly on this racecourse debut and, after being switched to get a clear run, stayed on nicely in the last furlong and a half. (14/1)
Top of The Green (IRE) was close up until calling it a day below the distance. (66/1)
1637 Reward was close up until tiring two furlongs from home. (11/2)

1871 MORTAR MILL H'CAP (0-85) (3-Y.O+) (Class D)

4-45 (4-46) **2m** £3,427.50 (£1,020.00: £485.00: £217.50) Stalls: High GOING minus 0.01 sec per fur (G)

				SP	RR	SF
1325⁴	**Transom (USA) (80)** (MrsAJPerrett) **6-10-0** TQuinn(2) (in rr tl gd hdwy over 1f out: rdn: led last stride)	—	**1**	7/4¹	87	62
1585²	**Cloud Inspector (IRE) (70)** (MJohnston) **6-9-4** JWeaver(1) (hld up: rdn over 3f out: led over 1f out: hrd rdn: hdd last stride)	hd	**2**	3/1³	77	52
1278⁶	**Mighty Phantom (USA) (69)** (JWHills) **4-9-2** RHughes(5) (led tl over 1f out: one pce)	3½	**3**	11/1	72	46
1778⁵	**Castle Courageous (78)** (LadyHerries) **10-9-12** WRyan(4) (b: chsd ldrs tl over 2f out: one pce)	nk	**4**	10/1	81	56
1778²	**Nanton Point (USA) (75)** (LadyHerries) **5-9-9** JQuinn(3) (hld up: rdn over 2f out: wknd fnl f)	2	**5**	9/4²	76	51
				(SP 109.6%)		**5 Rn**

3m 33.78 (9.78) CSF £6.58 TOTE £2.50: £1.40 £1.70 (£4.00) OWNER Mr Seymour Cohn (PULBOROUGH) BRED E. A. Cox Jnr
WEIGHT FOR AGE 4yo-1lb

1325 Transom (USA) confirmed the promise shown here last month after a lengthy lay-off but appeared to have been set far too much to do as he was a good dozen lengths off the leader in last place entering the straight. However, he made giant strides from below the distance and, throwing down his challenge inside the final furlong, got up in the last couple of strides. (7/4)
1585 Cloud Inspector (IRE) managed to get to the front below the distance but, despite doing little wrong, was caught in the last couple of strides. He should soon pick up his first British victory. (3/1)
Mighty Phantom (USA) took the field along, but she was collared over a furlong out and could then only go up and down in the same place. (11/1)
1400 Castle Courageous is finding old-age catching up with him for, although leniently treated, he was tapped for toe in the final quarter-mile. (10/1: 12/1-8/1)
1778 Nanton Point (USA) chased the leaders but had run out of gas entering the final furlong. (9/4)

T/Plpt: £9.20 (1,419.12 Tckts). T/Qdpt: £6.70 (99.72 Tckts) AK

1486-NEWBURY (L-H) (Good to firm becoming Good)
Thursday June 12th
WEATHER: overcast WIND: slt across

1872 E.B.F. KENNETT MAIDEN STKS (2-Y.O) (Class D)
2-00 (2-02) **6f 8y** £3,863.50 (£1,168.00: £569.00: £269.50) Stalls: High GOING minus 0.21 sec per fur (GF)

				SP	RR	SF
	Mazboon (USA) (EALDunlop) **2-9-0** KFallon(12) (scope: a.p: led over 1f out: r.o wl)	—	**1**	5/1[3]	93	24
	Starmaker (IRE) (PWChapple-Hyam) **2-9-0** PatEddery(14) (w'like: lw: w ldrs: led over 2f out tl over 1f out: r.o)	1½	**2**	3/1[1]	89	20
	Elakik (JLDunlop) **2-9-0** KDarley(15) (gd sort: gd hdwy & wnt lft over 1f out: fin wl)	2½	**3**	12/1	82+	13
	Classic Manoeuvre (USA) (RHannon) **2-9-0** DaneO'Neill(9) (neat: rdn & hdwy over 2f out: nrst fin)	½	**4**	16/1	81	12
	Commander Charlie (IABalding) **2-9-0** RCochrane(13) (w'like: a.p: ev ch over 1f out: nt qckn)	½	**5**	13/2	80	11
	Chief Cashier (GBBalding) **2-9-0** SDrowne(1) (w'like: bit bkwd: wl bhd tl gd hdwy fnl 2f)	1½	**6**	50/1	76	7
	Silver Strand (IRE) (BWHills) **2-8-9** MHills(6) (gd sort: bhd tl r.o fnl f)	hd	**7**	25/1	71	2
1480[U]	**Kennet** (PDCundell) **2-9-0** RPerham(5) (prom tl wknd 2f out)	½	**8**	50/1	74	5
	Free (PFICole) **2-9-0** TQuinn(8) (leggy: scope: w ldrs tl wknd over 1f out)	hd	**9**	4/1[2]	74	5
1425[8]	**Caversfield** (RHannon) **2-8-11**(3) MartinDwyer(16) (led over 3f)	½	**10**	50/1	73	4
	Top Maite (AGFoster) **2-8-11**(3) AWhelan(4) (leggy: a bhd)	1½	**11**	50/1	69	—
	Deterrent (JHMGosden) **2-9-0** LDettori(11) (w'like: bit bkwd: hld up: hdwy & hmpd over 1f out: nt rcvr)	s.h	**12**	15/2	69	—
	Fair Game (IRE) (JLDunlop) **2-9-0** AClark(3) (lengthy: nvr nr to chal)	½	**13**	33/1	67	—
	Sadir (MajorWRHern) **2-9-0** SWhitworth(18) (w'like: chsd ldrs tl wknd over 2f out)	3	**14**	33/1	59	—
	Grinkov (IRE) (HMorrison) **2-9-0** DHarrison(17) (w'like: chsd ldrs tl wknd 2f out)	1¼	**15**	25/1	56	—
	Appyabo (MRChannon) **2-9-0** RPainter(7) (leggy: mid div tl wknd 2f out)	½	**16**	50/1	55	—
	Gunboat Diplomacy (MJFetherston-Godley) **2-9-0** AMcGlone(2) (leggy: unf: a bhd)	s.h	**17**	33/1	54	—
	Shannon's Secret (IRE) (BJMeehan) **2-9-0** BDoyle(10) (gd sort: bkwd: sn bhd)	6	**18**	33/1	39	—
				(SP 129.6%)	**18 Rn**	

1m 15.91 (4.11) CSF £17.58 TOTE £10.50: £2.80 £1.70 £6.50 (£33.70) Trio £73.80 OWNER Mr Hamdan Al Maktoum (NEWMARKET) BRED Streicher Stables
STEWARDS' ENQUIRY Darley susp. 21&23-24/6/97 (careless riding)
Mazboon (USA), an active sort, looked very fit. Always well placed, he took the lead approaching the final furlong and stayed on strongly. (5/1: 4/1-7/1)
Starmaker (IRE), a workmanlike individual, looked very fit. He disputed the lead from the start but, after a gaining a definite advantage approaching the two-furlong marker, was outpaced by the winner at the distance. (3/1: 7/4-7/2)
Elakik, a very good-looking Green Desert, colt, had plenty to do at halfway but came through strongly in the closing stages and is one to follow. (12/1: 6/1-14/1)
Classic Manoeuvre (USA), a neatly-made colt, was being driven along from some way out. He kept staying on but, though running into fourth place, never appeared likely to trouble the leaders. (16/1)
Commander Charlie was always close up and had every chance. He could not quicken under pressure in the final furlong. (13/2)
Chief Cashier looked in need of the race and was toiling in the rear for most of the way. He suddenly realised what was required of him very late and finished in tremendous style. (50/1)
Silver Strand (IRE), the only filly in the field, has plenty of scope and quality. She was behind for a long way but was running on in good style at the finish. (25/1)
Free (4/1: op 6/4)

1873 KINGSCLERE CONDITIONS STKS (2-Y.O) (Class B)
2-30 (2-31) **6f 8y** £6,011.00 (£2,249.00: £1,099.50: £472.50: £211.25: £106.75) Stalls: High GOING minus 0.21 sec per fur (GF)

				SP	RR	SF
1607[2]	**Trans Island** (IABalding) **2-9-0** KDarley(5) (lw: mde all: r.o wl)	—	**1**	2/7[1]	86	20
	Tumbleweed Hero (BJMeehan) **2-8-11** MTebbutt(2) (gd sort: chsd ldrs: r.o ins fnl f: no ch w wnr)	2½	**2**	15/2[2]	76	10
	Huntswood (RHannon) **2-8-11** DaneO'Neill(3) (cmpt: bit bkwd: a.p: rdn over 1f out: r.o one pce)	¾	**3**	10/1	74	8
	Clermont City (IRE) (PWChapple-Hyam) **2-8-11** PatEddery(4) (scope: rdn along in rr: sme hdwy 2f out: sn wknd)	12	**4**	8/1[3]	43	—
1635[10]	**Raazi** (RMStronge) **2-8-9** KFallon(1) (w wnr 3f: wknd qckly)	10	**5**	66/1	14	—
				(SP 111.2%)	**5 Rn**	

1m 16.22 (4.42) CSF £2.93 TOTE £1.30: £1.10 £1.80 (£3.10) OWNER Al Muallim Partnership (KINGSCLERE) BRED Godolphin Management Co Ltd
1607 Trans Island had an easy task. He made all the running and though he had to be pushed along quite vigorously he never looked in danger of defeat. (2/7: op 1/2)
Tumbleweed Hero made a satisfactory debut. Being chased along from halfway, he stayed on to take second place inside the final furlong. He has plenty of scope for improvement. (15/2: 3/1-15/2)
Huntswood took second place soon after halfway but could make no impression on the winner approaching the final furlong. (10/1: 4/1-12/1)
Clermont City (IRE) drifted in the betting and ran very moderately. At the back of the field from the start. he was being chased along vigorously after only a furlong and never held out any hope. (8/1: op 9/4)
Raazi weakened rapidly after disputing the lead to halfway. (66/1)

1874 GEORGE SMITH MEMORIAL RATED STKS H'CAP (0-100) (3-Y.O+) (Class B)

3-00 (3-01) **7f (straight)** £7,579.20 (£2,812.80: £1,356.40: £562.00: £231.00: £98.60) Stalls: High GOING minus 0.21 sec per fur (GF)

				SP	RR	SF
892[19]	**Neuwest (USA) (85)** (RAkehurst) **5-8-10** LDettori(6) (lw: a.p: led over 1f out: comf)	—	**1**	3/1[1]	98+	48
450[6]	**Alamein (USA) (85)** (WJHaggas) **4-8-10** KFallon(5) (gd hdwy fnl 2f: nvr nrr)	3½	**2**	5/1[3]	90	40
1308[11]	**Volley (IRE) (83)** (MajorDNChappell) **4-8-8** DHarrison(2) (chsd ldr: ev ch over 1f out: r.o one pce)	hd	**3**	16/1	88	38
1397[2]	**Persian Fayre (86)** (JBerry) **5-8-11** KDarley(8) (lw: led tl wknd over 1f out)	3½	**4**	3/1[1]	83	33
	Divina Luna (88) (JWHills) **4-8-10**(3) MHenry(1) (bit bkwd: prom tl wknd over 1f out)	2½	**5**	13/2	79	29
	Trailblazer (83) (CWThornton) **3-7-7**(5) RMullen(4) (bit bkwd: in tch tl wknd over 2f out)	8	**6**	16/1	56	—
1309[5]	**Everglades (IRE) (96)** (RCharlton) **9-9-7** PatEddery(3) (swtg: mid div: rdn over 2f out: sn wknd)	½	**7**	9/2[2]	68	18
	Desert Green (FR) (92) (RHannon) **8-9-3** DaneO'Neill(7) (t.o fnl 5f)	dist	**8**	20/1	—	—

(SP 114.7%) **8 Rn**

1m 26.92 (2.82) CSF £16.70 CT £185.87 TOTE £3.30: £1.40 £1.60 £4.20 (£10.30) OWNER Mr P. Green (EPSOM) BRED Robert Bloomer and Sharon L. Bloomer

WEIGHT FOR AGE 3yo-10lb

752 Neuwest (USA), who has changed stables since his last run, tracked the leader on the rails. He went to the front approaching the final furlong and drew clear for a comfortable win. He looks likely to score again. (3/1)

450 Alamein (USA), his trainer's first runner for a while and without the blinkers that he needs. was behind until running on in very good style in the closing stages. He will soon return to form. (5/1)

Volley (IRE) was in second place for most of the way but, after having every chance approaching the final furlong, could not quicken with the winner. (16/1)

1397 Persian Fayre tried to make all the running as usual but soon weakened when headed approaching the final furlong. (3/1)

Divina Luna raced in third place and was still close enough at the two-furlong marker but then began to weaken. (13/2)

1309 Everglades (IRE) needs the ground faster than this and was being chased along soon after halfway. (9/2)

1875 BALLYMACOLL STUD STKS (Listed) (3-Y.O F) (Class A)

3-30 (3-32) **1m 2f 6y** £11,795.00 (£3,560.00: £1,730.00: £815.00) Stalls: Low GOING minus 0.21 sec per fur (GF)

				SP	RR	SF
	Squeak (JHMGosden) **3-8-9** LDettori(3) (lw: prom tl outpcd 3f out: rallied fnl f: led nr fin)	—	**1**	13/2[3]	92	35
1318[2]	**Priena (IRE)** (DRLoder) **3-8-9** KDarley(6) (w ldr: led & qcknd over 3f out: hdd cl home)	½	**2**	3/1[1]	91	34
1168*	**Western Hour (USA) (80)** (PWChapple-Hyam) **3-8-9** KFallon(1) (led tl over 3f out: rallied fnl f: r.o)	nk	**3**	10/1	91	34
1075a[3]	**Viscoumtess Brave (IRE)** (LordHuntingdon) **3-8-9** RCochrane(9) (w'like: bhd tl gd hdwy over 1f out: nt rch ldrs)	1	**4**	10/1	89	32
1318[5]	**Dust Dancer (82)** (JLDunlop) **3-8-9** BDoyle(4) (swtg: outpcd 3f out: rallied fnl f: r.o)	1	**5**	20/1	88	31
890[2]	**Flamboyance (USA)** (JRFanshawe) **3-8-9** DHarrison(7) (lw: hld up: effrt & nt clr run over 2f out: one pce fnl f)	hd	**6**	15/2	87	30
	The Faraway Tree (GWragg) **3-8-9** AClark(8) (bit bkwd: nvr nr to chal)	2	**7**	10/1	84	27
1028[3]	**Apache Star (84)** (GWragg) **3-8-9** MHills(10) (prom tl wknd over 2f out)	s.h	**8**	12/1	84	27
1591*	**Maroulla (IRE)** (MRStoute) **3-8-9** PatEddery(5) (lw: prom tl wknd over 2f out)	1½	**9**	11/2[2]	82	25
1147[9]	**Calypso Grant (IRE) (97)** (PWHarris) **3-8-12** NDay(2) (a bhd)	2	**10**	9/1	82	25

(SP 115.2%) **10 Rn**

2m 9.18 (5.18) CSF £23.62 TOTE £5.10: £1.50 £1.70 £2.80 (£6.30) Trio £46.80 OWNER Lord Hartington (NEWMARKET) BRED Side Hill Stud

Squeak was close up until the tap was turned on approaching the three-furlong marker and then she looked beaten. Eventually finding a clear run, she stayed on in good style to snatch the race in the last fifty yards. (13/2)

1318 Priena (IRE) seemed to have made a winning move when quickening from a slow pace approaching the three-furlong marker but, though she still looked in control inside the final furlong, she was collared in the last fifty yards. (3/1)

1168* Western Hour (USA) set a slow pace until over three furlongs from home where she failed to quicken with the second. After looking beaten she was coming again strongly at the finish. (10/1)

1075a Viscoumtess Brave (IRE), having her first race in England, was behind for most of the way in a slowly-run affair and, in the circumstances did extremely well to reach fourth place. She is one to follow. (10/1: 8/1-12/1)

1318 Dust Dancer was one of several tapped for toe at the three-furlong marker but she stayed on again in the closing stages. (20/1)

890 Flamboyance (USA) appeared to be travelling well for most of the race but was denied a clear run at a crucial stage. When she eventually found daylight in the last furlong, she could do no more. It may pay to ignore this effort. (15/2)

1591* Maroulla (IRE) (11/2: 4/1-6/1)

1876 BUCKLEBURY MAIDEN STKS (3-Y.O) (Class D)

4-00 (4-01) **7f (straight)** £3,863.50 (£1,168.00: £569.00: £269.50) Stalls: High GOING minus 0.21 sec per fur (GF)

				SP	RR	SF
	Hajr (IRE) (EALDunlop) **3-9-0** KFallon(1) (gd sort: bit bkwd: hdwy 3f out: led & edgd rt over 1f out: hdd ins fnl f: sn led again)	—	**1**	7/2[2]	81	30
	Jorrocks (USA) (IABalding) **3-8-11**(3) MartinDwyer(7) (w'like: scope: hdwy 2f out: swtchd lft over 1f out: led ins fnl f: sn hdd)	nk	**2**	8/1	80	29
1265[9]	**Davids Revenge** (MajorDNChappell) **3-9-0** AClark(11) (lw: led: qcknd clr over 3f out: hdd over 1f out)	2½	**3**	25/1	75	24
1587[4]	**Blewbury Hill (IRE)** (RFJohnsonHoughton) **3-9-0** PatEddery(10) (a.p: hmpd & snatched up over 1f out: nt rcvr)	2½	**4**	11/10[1]	69+	18
	Dust (LordHuntingdon) **3-8-9** LDettori(8) (w'like: scope: a.p: r.o one pce fnl 2f)	1¼	**5**	7/1[3]	61	10
	Fife Major (USA) (BWHills) **3-9-0** MHills(5) (lw: a.p: no hdwy fnl 2f)	1½	**6**	10/1	63	12
	Misconduct (GLMoore) **3-8-9** SWhitworth(2) (lengthy: bkwd: nvr nr to chal)	3½	**7**	66/1	50	—
	Zingaro (IRE) (CEBrittain) **3-9-0** BDoyle(4) (lw: prom tl wknd 2f out)	hd	**8**	20/1	54	3
	Posative (MSalaman) **3-8-9** DHarrison(6) (w'like: scope: bhd fnl 3f)	hd	**9**	66/1	49	—
	Gajan (IRE) (JNeville) **3-9-0** MFenton(9) (lengthy: bhd fnl 4f)	11	**10**	66/1	29	—
	How Bizarre (THind) **3-9-0** NDay(3) (lengthy: rdn along in rr: sn t.o)	dist	**11**	66/1	—	—

(SP 117.1%) **11 Rn**

1m 28.41 (4.31) CSF £26.68 TOTE £4.50: £1.70 £2.50 £3.30 (£32.40) Trio £142.60 OWNER Maktoum Al Maktoum (NEWMARKET) BRED Ridgecourt Stud

Hajr (IRE), a very good-looking individual, missed the break but came with a steady run from three furlongs out. He edged right approaching the final furlong causing the favourite to snatch up but ran on to win on merit and has plenty of improvement in him. (7/2: 2/1-4/1)

Jorrocks (USA), a workmanlike gelding with a bit of scope, made ground at the two-furlong marker and, after switching left, snatched the lead for a few strides inside the final furlong. Close home he could do no more but should pay to follow. (8/1: op 5/1)
Davids Revenge showed considerable improvement on his previous effort. He made the running until approaching the final furlong and kept on at one pace. (25/1)
1587 Blewbury Hill (IRE) was always close up. He was challenging but under strong pressure when he had to be snatched up approaching the final furlong. He was certainly unlucky not to have finished closer but the winner would have been too good anyway. (11/10: 5/4-evens)
Dust settled well and came with a run approaching the final furlong but lack of experience told its tale at the finish. She can improve. (7/1: 5/1-8/1)
Fife Major (USA) chased the leaders throughout but could make no headway under pressure in the final quarter-mile. (10/1: 7/1-11/1)

1877 FURLONG CLUB H'CAP (0-85) (3-Y.O) (Class D)

4-30 (4-33) **1m 4f 5y** £3,668.50 (£1,108.00: £539.00: £254.50) Stalls: Low GOING minus 0.21 sec per fur (GF)

				SP	RR	SF
1173^{5}	**Rainwatch (81)** (JLDunlop) **3-9-4** PatEddery(4) (led after 3f tl over 3f out: led 2f out: r.o wl)	—	**1**	3/1^{2}	95	49
1384*	**Travelmate (73)** (JRFanshawe) **3-8-10** DHarrison(7) (lw: hld up: hdwy 3f out: ev ch 1f out: r.o)	1¼	**2**	9/4^{1}	85	39
928^{2}	**Little Acorn (84)** (SCWilliams) **3-9-7** KDarley(5) (swtg: a.p: led over 3f out to 2f out: wknd fnl f)	3	**3**	12/1	92	46
1242^{8}	**Highly Prized (77)** (IABalding) **3-8-11**$^{(3)}$ MartinDwyer(2) (lw: lost pl 7f out: hdwy & hrd rdn 3f out: one pce)	3	**4**	11/1	81	35
1474^{6}	**Palaemon (59)** (GBBalding) **3-7-10v**^{1} NVarley(8) (hrd rdn over 4f out: no rspnse)	9	**5**	12/1	51	5
797^{5}	**Norman Conquest (USA) (75)** (IABalding) **3-8-12** LDettori(9) (lw: led 3f: wknd 3f out)	8	**6**	9/2^{3}	57	11
1297^{4}	**Khayal (USA) (68)** (BWHills) **3-8-5** MHills(6) (a bhd: t.o fnl 2f)	19	**7**	15/2	24	—
1150^{4}	**Spartan Royale (80)** (CEBrittain) **3-9-3** KFallon(3) (lw: a bhd: t.o)	¾	**8**	10/1	35	—
				(SP 118.5%)		**8 Rn**

2m 35.4 (5.40) CSF £9.69 CT £64.24 TOTE £3.70: £1.70 £1.50 £1.50 (£3.60) Trio £13.70 OWNER Hesmonds Stud (ARUNDEL) BRED Hesmonds Stud Ltd
1173 Rainwatch was given a brilliant ride. Inclined to pull in the closing stages, he was allowed to stride on after three furlongs and then slowed the pace down. Headed in the straight, he regained his advantage at the two-furlong marker and stayed on strongly. Still inexperienced, he can on to better things. (3/1)
1384* Travelmate was going extremely well for much of the race and looked a big danger when moving up to challenge at the distance. Though unable to peg back the winner, time may tell he was taking on a useful rival. (9/4)
928 Little Acorn went to the front over three furlongs from home but his stride was shortening approaching the final furlong and he found the leading pair drawing away. (12/1)
967 Highly Prized lost his good early place and, though making ground under strong pressure three furlongs out, could not reach a challenging position. (11/1)
Palaemon, visored for the first time, looked anything but enthusiastic and gave his rider a very hard time. (12/1: 8/1-14/1)
797 Norman Conquest (USA) made the early running but faded disappointingly from the three-furlong marker. (9/2: 3/1-5/1)
1297 Khayal (USA) (15/2: 5/1-8/1)

1878 LEVY BOARD APPRENTICE H'CAP (0-80) (3-Y.O+) (Class E)

5-00 (5-08) **1m (straight)** £3,582.50 (£1,085.00: £530.00: £252.50) Stalls: High GOING minus 0.21 sec per fur (GF)

				SP	RR	SF
1273^{9}	**Ca'd'oro (53)** (GBBalding) **4-8-6** PPMurphy(6) (hdwy over 2f out: swtchd rt over 1f out: led ins fnl f: drvn out)	—	**1**	10/1	63	51
1442^{6}	**Therhea (IRE) (62)** (BRMillman) **4-9-1** AWhelan(4) (lw: a.p: led wl over 1f out: edgd rt & hdd ins fnl f)	1¼	**2**	5/1^{1}	70	58
1739^{17}	**Amber Fort (74)** (DRCElsworth) **4-9-13v** MHenry(2) (stumbled s: hrd rdn 3f out: hdwy 2f out: ev ch 1f out: nt qckn)	1½	**3**	12/1	79	67
1489^{8}	**Eurobox Boy (59)** (APJarvis) **4-8-5**$^{(7)}$ CCarver(7) (a.p: r.o one pce fnl 2f)	2½	**4**	15/2^{2}	59	47
1689*	**Mr Rough (56)** (DMorris) **6-8-4**$^{(5)}$ 6x AEddery(1) (lw: hdwy fnl 2f: nvr nrr)	s.h	**5**	8/1^{3}	55	43
661^{8}	**Tatika (73)** (GWragg) **7-9-7**$^{(5)}$ GMilligan(5) (lw: hdwy over 2f out: ev ch over 1f out: wknd fnl f)	2½	**6**	8/1^{3}	67	55
1442^{9}	**Noble Dane (IRE) (77)** (PWHarris) **3-9-0**$^{(5)}$ CLowther(8) (hdwy & hrd rdn 3f out: wknd 2f out)	¾	**7**	12/1	70	47
	Veni Vidi Vici (IRE) (68) (MJHeaton-Ellis) **4-9-0**$^{(7)}$ JFowle(13) (lw: led over 4f out tl wl over 1f out: wknd)	1¼	**8**	25/1	58	46
1048^{10}	**Sea Spouse (44)** (MBlanshard) **6-7-4**$^{(7)}$ KerryBaker(14) (w ldrs tl wknd 2f out)	1½	**9**	33/1	31	19
1588^{4}	**Absolute Utopia (USA) (55)** (NEBerry) **4-8-8** RHavlin(9) (hrd rdn over 3f out: no rspsnse)	1½	**10**	12/1	39	27
1599^{5}	**Dancing Lawyer (55)** (BJMeehan) **6-8-1**$^{(7)}$ GHannon(11) (nvr nr ldrs)	1¾	**11**	16/1	36	24
1575^{2}	**Waikiki Beach (USA) (67)** (GLMoore) **6-9-1**$^{(5)}$ MBatchelor(15) (b: lw: prom tl hrd rdn & wknd 2f out)	11	**12**	14/1	26	14
1482^{8}	**Scathebury (62)** (KRBurke) **4-8-8**$^{(7)}$ PWright(10) (swtg: hld up: effrt & rdn 2f out: sn wknd)	s.h	**13**	14/1	21	9
	King Parrot (IRE) (55) (LordHuntingdon) **9-8-1**$^{(7)}$ RLake(12) (lw: led over 3f: wknd 3f out)	4	**14**	10/1	6	—
				(SP 117.9%)		**14 Rn**

1m 40.18 (2.18) CSF £52.77 CT £415.56 TOTE £12.10: £2.90 £2.10 £3.60 (£37.20) Trio £153.00 OWNER Miss B. Swire (ANDOVER) BRED Miss B. Swire
WEIGHT FOR AGE 3yo-11lb
1273 Ca'd'oro, patiently ridden, came with a strong run approaching the final furlong and, squeezing through on the rails, ran on to win readily. (10/1: 6/1-11/1)
1442 Therhea (IRE), close up throughout, led below the distance but drifted right and was collared inside the final furlong. (5/1)
1166 Amber Fort went on his nose when the stalls opened and was under pressure a long way out. To his credit he came to have a chance at the distance, but could find no extra in the last furlong. (12/1: op 7/1)
733 Eurobox Boy, close up throughout, ran on at one pace in the final quarter-mile. (15/2)
1689* Mr Rough failed to go the pace but was staying on strongly in the closing stages. (8/1: 6/1-9/1)
363* Tatika came with a good looking run in the centre of the course approaching the two-furlong marker but could not sustain the effort in the final furlong. (8/1: 6/1-9/1)
723 Noble Dane (IRE) (12/1: 7/1-14/1)
1575 Waikiki Beach (USA) (14/1: op 8/1)
King Parrot (IRE) (10/1: op 6/1)

T/Jkpt: £12,373.20 (4.55 Tckts). T/Plpt: £65.80 (298.11 Tckts). T/Qdpt: £14.20 (68.63 Tckts) Hn

1879a (Irish Racing) - See Computer Raceform

0014a-LEOPARDSTOWN (Dublin, Ireland) (L-H) (Good)
Monday June 2nd

1880a SILVER FLASH STKS (Listed) (2-Y.O F)
3-00 (3-03) **6f** IR £12,900.00 (IR £3,700.00: IR £1,700.00: IR £500.00) GOING: 0.07 sec per fur (G)

	Runner	Dist	Pos	SP	RR	SF
	Heeremandi (IRE) (APO'Brien,Ireland) **2-8-11** CRoche (hld up trckng ldrs: smooth hdwy to jn ldr over 1f out: led early fnl f: eased clr: comf)	—	1	2/9[1]	91+	35
	Festival Song (USA) (APO'Brien,Ireland) **2-8-8** JAHeffernan (led & disp ld: led ½-wy: rdn & jnd over 1f out: hdd & no ch w wnr ins fnl f)	3	2	33/1	80	24
	Attractive Crown (USA) (KPrendergast,Ireland) **2-8-8** SCraine (s.s: bhd: r.o wl fnl f: 2nd cl home)	s.h	3	14/1	80	24
	Via Splendida (IRE) (JSBolger,Ireland) **2-8-8** JoannaMorgan (chsd ldrs: fair 4th & rdn ½-wy: no imp 2f out: kpt on fnl f)	1	4	9/1[2]	77	21
	Dress Design (IRE) (JMuldoon,Ireland) **2-8-8** WJSupple (disp ld: 2nd ½-wy: btn wl over 1f out)	3	5	20/1	69	13
	Jeanne D'Arc (DKWeld,Ireland) **2-8-8** MJKinane (s.s: n.d)	5	6	10/1[3]	56	—

(SP 115.3%) **6 Rn**

1m 15.4 (4.70) OWNER Mrs David Nagle (PILTOWN)

Heeremandi (IRE) so impressive at Fairyhouse on her debut, was a class above this opposition. She only had to be shaken up to draw clear inside the last and looks a genuine sort. The Queen Mary Stakes beckons, despite the shorter trip at Ascot. She swished her tail at Fairyhouse and looked a bit highly strung, but was more relaxed here. (2/9)
Festival Song (USA), well beaten at Gowran a couple of days previously on her debut, put up a much improved effort here against her stable companion, being outpaced after making all the running. (33/1)
Attractive Crown (USA) made up an ocean of ground inside the last and will certainly get her turn. (14/1: op 8/1)
Via Splendida (IRE), outpaced from halfway, ran on again inside he last. (9/1: op 6/1)

1881a BALLYOGAN STKS (Gp 3) (3-Y.O+)
3-30 (3-34) **5f** IR £19,500.00 (IR £5,700.00: IR £2,700.00: IR £900.00) GOING: 0.07 sec per fur (G)

	Runner	Dist	Pos	SP	RR	SF
1532a[2]	**Catch The Blues (IRE)** (APO'Brien,Ireland) **5-8-13b** CRoche (hld up trckng ldrs: 3rd over 1f out: rdn & r.o wl to led last 50 yds)	—	1	2/1[1]	117	45
1186a[3]	**Ailleacht (USA)** (JSBolger,Ireland) **5-8-13** KJManning (disp ld: led 2f out: sn rdn: r.o: hdd last 50 yds)	½	2	8/1	115	43
1455[3]	**Bolshoi (IRE)** (JBerry) **5-9-2b** SCraine (hld up: last 2f out: rdn & r.o wl ins fnl f)	¾	3	100/30[2]	116	44
1171[4]	**Averti (IRE)** (WRMuir) **6-8-13** MRoberts (s.s: pushed along on ins over 2f out: nt clr run over 1f out: r.o. ins fnl f)	nk	4	6/1[3]	112	40
1186a[2]	**Check The Band (USA)** (APO'Brien,Ireland) **3-8-9** JAHeffernan (sn disp: 2nd & rdn 1½f out: no ex ins fnl f)	nk	5	10/1	112	35
	Lidanna (DHanley,Ireland) **4-9-3** MJKinane (prom tl wknd over 1f out)	2	6	13/2	109	37
1532a[4]	**Symboli Kildare (IRE)** (JOxx,Ireland) **4-8-13b** JPMurtagh (hld up: rdn 2f out: no imp last 1½f)	3½	7	20/1	94	22

(SP 109.0%) **7 Rn**

60.9 secs (3.40) OWNER Mrs H. M. Keaveney (PILTOWN)

1532a Catch The Blues (IRE) certainly deserved this. Always travelling well on the outer, she ran on well to lead close home. She needs a bit of time early on to settle, and it looks as though the King's Stand will be her Ascot target. She might find that company too hot. (2/1)
1186a Ailleacht (USA) ran her best race of the season, disputing the lead throughout and only going under close home. (8/1)
1455 Bolshoi (IRE), out the backdoor for most of the way, got going too late. (100/30)
1171 Averti (IRE) didn't have much luck in running, but came through late to be nearest at the finish. (6/1)
1186a Check The Band (USA) will derive benefit from this and won't always be the stable's second string. (10/1)

1882a - 1895a (Irish Racing) - See Computer Raceform

1537a-CURRAGH (Newbridge, Ireland) (R-H) (St crse Yielding, Rnd crse Good)
Friday June 6th

1896a GALLINULE STKS (Gp 2) (3-Y.O+)
6-30 (6-32) **1m 2f** IR £32,500.00 (IR £9,500.00: IR £4,500.00: IR £1,500.00) GOING: 0.38 sec per fur (GS)

	Runner	Dist	Pos	SP	RR	SF
	Johan Cruyff (APO'Brien,Ireland) **3-8-9**[ow1] KJManning (sn chsng ldr: 3rd ½-wy: 2nd 4f out: chal early st: led 1½f out: pushed clr ins last)	—	1	8/1[3]	113+	61
	Olympic Majesty (FR) (CO'Brien,Ireland) **3-8-8** WJSupple (led after 3f: rdn & hdd 1½f out: sn no ex: kpt on same pce)	4	2	Evens[1]	106	55
	Mingling Glances (USA) (APO'Brien,Ireland) **3-8-6**[ow1] CRoche (hld up towards rr: 3rd & trckd ldrs 3f out: effrt & nt rch ldrs 1½f out: eased whn btn ins last)	6	3	6/4[2]	94	42
1195a[4]	**Plaza De Toros (USA)** (APO'Brien,Ireland) **3-8-8** PShanahan (sn led 3f: 2nd ½-wy: 4th & rdn st: sn btn: dropped bhd)	25	4	10/1	56	5

(SP 110.2%) **4 Rn**

2m 11.9 (7.90) OWNER Mrs John Magnier (PILTOWN)

IN-FOCUS: **This was possibly the most uncompetitive Group Two event ever run at the Curragh.**
Johan Cruyff, totally unfancied in the betting, had to be stirred up to challenge two furlongs out, but was soon in total command and drew right away over the last furlong. It is difficult to gage his merit, but he will fulfil his Irish Derby engagement. He stays on well and will improve a bit for this. He went up 2lb for this and is now rated 111. (8/1: op 5/1)
Olympic Majesty (FR) went on after three furlongs but gave up the ghost pretty quickly when headed by the winner. At this stage of his career, he would have to be termed a bit of a disappointment. (Evens)
Mingling Glances (USA), rather surprisingly the choice of Roche over her two stable companions, made headway to flatter in second place before the straight, but she cried enough a furlong and a half out and was eased inside the last. (6/4: op Evens)
1195a Plaza De Toros (USA) ran in front early, but had dropped out before the straight and is another with a major question mark regarding his future. (10/1: op 6/1)

1897a - 1908a (Irish Racing) - See Computer Raceform

TABY (Stockholm, Sweden) (L-H) (Good)
Tuesday June 3rd

1909a JOCKEYKLUBBENS JUBILEUMSLOPNING (3-Y.O)
6-50 (6-50) **1m** £21,990.00 (£10,995.00: £5,277.00)

				SP	RR	SF
1358a3	**Hever Golf Glory** (TJNaughton) **3-9-2** PatEddery	—	1		87	—
	Chirac (WNeuroth,Norway) **3-9-2** FJohansson	2	2		83	—
	Little Egypt (SWE) (JTorok,Sweden) **3-9-2** JohnFortune	1½	3		80	—
						12 Rn

1m 35.5 TOTE 2.86Kr: 1.33Kr 1.84Kr 2.45Kr (21.47Kr) OWNER Hever Racing Club (EPSOM) BRED Mrs L. Popely
1358a Hever Golf Glory raced in fourth place before moving up to third entering the straight. Quickening up to take the lead two furlongs out, he ran on well to withstand the challenge of the runner-up.

1910a IBM PC TABY VARSPRINT (Listed) (4-Y.O+)
7-20 (7-32) **6f** £25,619.00 (£6,831.00: £5,124.00: £3,416.00: £1,708.00)

				SP	RR	SF
1721a3	**Hever Golf Rose** (TJNaughton) **6-8-12** PatEddery	—	1		104	—
	Hakiki (IRE) (WNeuroth,Norway) **5-9-2** FJohansson	2	2		103	—
	Troon (RHaugen,Norway) **7-9-2** MSantos	1½	3		99	—
13032	**Tadeo** (MJohnston) **4-9-2** JWeaver (btn approx 5l)		5		—	—
						13 Rn

1m 9.6 TOTE 1.81Kr: 1.24Kr 1.96Kr 1.76Kr (15.37Kr) OWNER Hever Racing Club (EPSOM) BRED Ronald Popely
1721a Hever Golf Rose took the lead just over three furlongs and soon went clear to take this in commanding style. She will soon be on her travels again, as her next target is the Group Three Holstein Trophy at Hamburg on July 5th.
1303 Tadeo had an unfavourable draw being on the wide outside, and was unable to quicken in the final stages.

1728a-SAN SIRO (Milan, Italy) (R-H) (Good)
Wednesday June 4th

1911a PREMIO CRODA ROSSA (3-Y.O)
4-15 (4-20) **1m 4f** £5,786.00 (£2,314.00: £1,388.00)

				SP	RR	SF
	Cholas (EBorromeo,Italy) **3-9-2** MTellini	—	1		—	—
	Gelosia (GVerricelli,Italy) **3-8-13** SDettori	6½	2		—	—
	Nobady Els (IRE) (MLivraghi,Italy) **3-9-2** ACarboni	1¼	3		—	—
	Quirinale (IRE) (LordHuntingdon) **3-9-2** EBotti (btn over 20l)		9		—	—
						9 Rn

2m 35.4 (15.40) TOTE 40L: 14L 35L 53L (442L) OWNER Scuderia Rencati BRED Azienda Agricola Rosati Colarieti
Quirinale (IRE), a son of Slip Anchor, made a very disappointing debut. Always towards the rear of the field, he was never able to get into a challenging position.

BELMONT PARK (New York, USA) (L-H) (Firm)
Saturday June 7th

1912a BELMONT STKS (GRADE 1) (3-Y.O)
10-30 (10-30) **1m 4f (Dirt)** £257,500.00 (£85,833.00: £47,208.00)

				SP	RR	SF
	Touch Gold (USA) (DHofmans,USA) **3-9-0** CMcCarron	—	1		126	—
*1364a**	**Silver Charm (USA)** (BBaffert,USA) **3-9-0** GaryStevens	¾	2		125	—
1364a2	**Free House (USA)** (JGonzalez,USA) **3-9-0** KDesormeaux	1	3		124	—
						7 Rn

2m 28.82 P-M $ 7.30: PL (1-2) $3.30 $3.00 SHOW (1-2-3) $2.60 $2.40 $2.70 OWNER Mr F Stronach & Stonerside Stable BRED Holtsinger Inc & Hill N Dale Farm & Star Stable
Touch Gold (USA) set the early pace, but was soon settled and tracked the leaders for most of the way until getting down to business in the straight. Running on very well in the stretch, he put up a strong performance to overcome the Triple Crown-seeking Silver Charm inside the final seventy-five yards. Described as versatile, strong and still developing, he looks a star of the future.
1364a* Silver Charm (USA) and connections deserve our sympathy. With the race in his grasp, he was swallowed up close home by the very fast-finishing winner, turning his Triple Crown ambitions to ashes.

0811a-MAISONS-LAFFITTE (France) (Very Soft)
Saturday June 7th

1913a PRIX DU LYS (Gp 3) (3-Y.O)
2-25 (2-24) **1m 5f** £24,691.00 (£8,979.00: £4,489.00)

				SP	RR	SF
	Vertical Speed (FR) (AFabre,France) **3-9-2** TJarnet	—	1		109++	—
	Assos (USA) (DSepulchre,France) **3-9-2** CAsmussen	2½	2		106	—
629a4	**Keroub (FR)** (PBary,France) **3-9-2** SGuillot	s.h	3		106	—
						4 Rn

2m 55.0 P-M 1.60F: 1.10F 1.40F OWNER Mr Daniel Wildenstein (CHANTILLY) BRED Allez France Stables
Vertical Speed (FR), coasting throughout, was in second place until taking the lead two furlongs from home, where he stretched out well to win with plenty in hand. He is a very smart colt in the making and he will go on to much better things, possibly over longer. He may be entered in the St Leger and is in the Arc de Triomphe. Something like the Prix Hubert de Chaudenay at the end of July may be his next race, and he is a colt worth following.

Assos (USA), in third place for much of the way, looked outpaced with one-and-a-half furlongs left to run. He did however stay on at the end having met with a little interference a furlong out. He is improving, but is possibly no better than listed class, and may next go for the Prix Berteux.
629a Keroub (FR), held up in last place, began to look dangerous when making a forward move two furlongs out, but he did not want to go through with his challenge and was one-paced in the final furlong. This distance may have been on the long side for him.

1914a PRIX DU CHEMIN DE FER DU NORD (Gp 3) (4-Y.O+)
2-55 (3-03) **1m** £24,691.00 (£8,979.00: £4,489.00)

	Horse	Dist	Pos	SP	RR	SF
	Perim (FR) (GLievre,France) **4-8-11b[1]** GGuignard	—	1		115	—
	Battle Dore (USA) (AFabre,France) **4-8-11** TJarnet	s.h	2		115	—
922a[8]	**Trojan Sea (USA)** (DSmaga,France) **6-8-11** DBoeuf	1½	3		112	—
						9 Rn

1m 38.8 (2.80) P-M 8.90F: 2.20F 1.80F 1.50F (18.20F) OWNER G. Lievre BRED Domaine de Menneval
Perim (FR) ran out a very game winner. Trained by a permit holder near the Swiss border, he has only three stablemates. Leading approaching the final furlong, he hung on gamely to the line. He is very consistent and will probably go on to the Prix Messidor at Deauville in July.
Battle Dore (USA) tried to make every yard of the running, but was passed one out before running on again in the final stages. He would have won in another few strides, and the manner in which he finished suggests a longer trip might be to his advantage. He is another who could end up in the Messidor.
716a Trojan Sea (USA) was held up before making decent progress from two furlongs out and was staying on at the finish. He is always there or thereabouts in Group Three company and was used as a pacemaker for Pilsudski in the Prix Ganay.

1725a-CHANTILLY (France) (R-H) (Soft)
Sunday June 8th

1915a PRIX DE LA JONCHERE (Gp 3) (3-Y.O C & G)
2-00 (1-52) **1m** £24,691.00 (£8,979.00: £4,489.00) GOING minus 0.06 sec per fur (G)

	Horse	Dist	Pos	SP	RR	SF
1358a*	**Kaldou Star** (ELellouche,France) **3-8-11** TThulliez	—	1		107	44
1544a[3]	**Fine Fellow (IRE)** (MmeCHead,France) **3-9-1** FHead	nk	2		110	47
1361a[2]	**Aneysar (IRE)** (AdeRoyerDupre,France) **3-8-11** GMosse	½	3		105	42
						4 Rn

1m 41.0 (4.50) P-M 3.80F: 1.60F 1.40F OWNER Mr J. C. Seroul
Kaldou Star was given a fine ride but was a shade fortunate to have found an opening on the rail coming to the final furlong. He took full advantage and accelerated to win a shade cheekily. He is progressing and seems the sort who could stay further and he is likely to be aimed at the ten-furlong Prix Eugene Adam next time out.
820a Fine Fellow (IRE), trying to make all the running, unfortunately hung left away from the rail under pressure inside the final furlong and may have given the race away. Nevertheless, this was a decent performance and he deserves future success as he is such a game performer.
1361a Aneysar (IRE) took a little time to settle, but given every chance, was unable to quicken inside the final furlong. He may be more effective over a longer trip.

1916a PRIX DE DIANE HERMES (Gp 1) (3-Y.O F)
3-15 (3-19) **1m 2f 110y** £157,127.00 (£62,851.00: £31,425.00: £15,713.00: £7,856.00) GOING minus 0.06 sec per fur (G)

	Horse	Dist	Pos	SP	RR	SF
	Vereva (IRE) (AdeRoyerDupre,France) **3-9-0** GMosse (a cl up: rapid prog to ld over 1f out: r.o wl: easily)	—	1	27/10[2]	121+	93
1203a[6]	**Mousse Glacee (FR)** (JLesbordes,France) **3-9-0** TThulliez (mid div: hmpd over 1f out: styd on strly fnl f)	1½	2	97/10	119	91
1366a*	**Brilliance (FR)** (PBary,France) **3-9-0** SGuillot (a cl up: squeezed whn effrt 1f out: r.o one pce)	2	3	18/10[1]	116	88
1533a[4]	**Ryafan (USA)** (JHMGosden) **3-9-0** LDettori (led tl over 1f out: styd on one pce)	½	4	124/10	115	87
813a[3]	**La Nana (FR)** (DSepulchre,France) **3-9-0** ODoleuze (hld up: prog 2f out: hung rt 1f out: styd on)	nse	5	266/10	115	87
1203a*	**Always Loyal (USA)** (MmeCHead,France) **3-9-0** FHead (cl up thrght: hmpd over 1f out: r.o fnl f)	s.h	6	61/10	115	87
	Golden Arches (FR) (PDemercastel,France) **3-9-0** TGillet (hld up: slt prog 2f out: no ex)	1½	7	341/10	113	85
1202a[4]	**Anna Thea (IRE)** (HBlume,Germany) **3-9-0** THellier (hld up in rr: styd on one pce)	1	8	78/1	111	83
921a*	**Queen Maud (IRE)** (JdeRoualle,France) **3-9-0** CAsmussen (hld up: slt prog 2f out: no ch whn hmpd appr fnl f)	1	9	97/10	109	81
	Palme D'Or (IRE) (AFabre,France) **3-9-0** OPeslier (trckd ldr: hmpd st: dropped out)	½	10	57/10[3]	109	81
1366a[4]	**Darashandeh (IRE)** (AdeRoyerDupre,France) **3-9-0** DBoeuf (mid div: slt effrt st: btn 1f out)	½	11	27/10[2]	108	80
1203a[4]	**Dances With Dreams** (PWChapple-Hyam) **3-9-0** JReid (a cl up: 3rd st: wknd qckly bef fnl f: dropped out)	3	12	311/10	103	75
				(SP 155.8%)		**12 Rn**

2m 8.2 (0.20) P-M 3.70F: 1.60F 2.20F 1.40F (26.70F) OWNER H H Aga Khan (CHANTILLY) BRED H. H. The Aga Khans Studs S C
IN-FOCUS: **For betting purposes Darashandeh (IRE) and Vereva (IRE) were coupled**
Vereva (IRE), a half-sister to Valanour, is endowed with his outstanding turn of foot, and looked in a class of her own. She hacked around the final turn before bursting into the lead over a furlong out and, not subjected to pressure in the final furlong, won with a little in hand. A slight cough delayed her debut so she had three races within a month. She has gone from strength to strength, really looking on the boil at the moment, and connections must decide whether to take advantage of her current form, or to give her a rest before an Arc de Triomphe preparation. They do not seem to be tempted by the Eclipse Stakes for which she would have to be supplemented, but could go for the King George. (27/10)
818a Mousse Glacee (FR) showed her true form, but was unlucky on two occasions in the straight. However, even with a better run, it is doubtful whether she would have beaten the winner. She is much better over this distance and will probably appreciate further. She has further scope for improvement and now heads for the Irish Oaks. (97/10)
1366a* Brilliance (FR) was another to have met with interference in the straight and returned with several superficial cuts on her legs. She would probably have preferred more of a gallop but did not really show the same sparkle as in the Prix Saint-Alary. She will also be going for the Irish Oaks. (18/10)
1533a Ryafan (USA) ran a really game race. Sticking to her guns, she led to the furlong marker but was then one-paced to the line. She has taken a little time to come to hand this season, so should improve for the outing. The Nassau Stakes at Goodwood looks a possible target. (124/10)
1203a Dances With Dreams was well up for most of the way and in third place entering the straight. However, by the furlong marker she was a spent force and dropped out very quickly. Her pilot reported that she did not stay. (311/10)

1917a GRAND PRIX DE CHANTILLY (Gp 2) (4-Y.O+)
4-20 (4-25) **1m 4f** £39,282.00 (£15,713.00: £7,856.00: £3,928.00) GOING minus 0.06 sec per fur (G)

			SP	RR	SF
916a*	**Steward (FR)** (DSepulchre,France) **4-8-11** SGuillot (hld up: effrt 1½f out: led wl ins fnl f: easily) ——	1		120	66
1359a*	**Surgeon** (JdeRoualle,France) **4-8-11** CAsmussen (mid div ent st: prog 1½f out: led briefly ins fnl f: outpcd cl home) ¾	2		119	65
1363a4	**Darazari (IRE)** (AdeRoyerDupre,France) **4-9-0** GMosse (led: effrt 1½f out: hdd fnl 100y: styd on one pce) nk	3		122	68
1363a*	**Flyway (FR)** (ELellouche,France) **4-9-0** TThulliez (in rr: nvr threatened) ¾	4		121	67
1033*	**Royal Court (IRE)** (PWChapple-Hyam) **4-8-11** JReid (prom to 2f out: nt qckn: r.o fnl f) hd	5		118	64
					5 Rn

2m 30.5 (3.70) TOTE 6.00F: 2.50F 2.10F OWNER G. Coude BRED Jean-Charles Coude
916a* Steward (FR), a game and consistent performer, is improving with every race. Connections were worried about the trip beforehand, but he may have been suited by the slowish pace, and was given a good ride, being produced at exactly the right time inside the final furlong. The Grand Prix de Saint-Cloud is a natural target, but this may be bypassed in favour of a tilt at the Grand Prix de Deauville.
Surgeon looked the winner as the field approached the final furlong, but he could not match the speed of the winner in the final one hundred yards. He is much improved this term, and a Group race should come his way. The Prix Maurice de Nieuil next month looks a prime target.
1363a Darazari (IRE) made the running at a very sedate pace early on. He went for the line one-and-a-half out, but was one-paced inside the final furlong. An encouraging effort, he may miss the Grand Prix, but he could still be entered in the King George VI and Queen Elizabeth Diamond Stakes. The best is yet to come from him.
1363a* Flyway (FR) never really got in a blow and could only stay on at the one pace. He was a lucky winner of the Jean de Chaudenay and is really only a Group Three performer. It would not come as a surprise if he was soon campaigning in the States.
1033* Royal Court (IRE) was close to the lead two furlongs from home, but at this point he seemed one-paced, and only ran on again in the closing stages. The ground was too fast for him, in contrast to when he won at Chester previously. He will be a force to be reckoned with whenever the ground is testing.

MULHEIM (Mulheim-Ruhr, Germany) (Soft)
Sunday June 8th

1918a PREIS DER DIANA (Gp 2) (3-Y.O F)
4-20 (4-24) **1m 3f** £75,758.00 (£30,303.00: £15,151.00: £8,333.00)

			SP	RR	SF
1202a*	**Que Belle (USA)** (HRemmert,Germany) **3-9-2** KWoodburn (in tch: str run to ld ins fnl f: drvn out) ——	1		114	—
	Borgia (GER) (BSchutz,Germany) **3-9-2** AStarke (a.p: qcknd to ld 2f out: hdd ins fnl f: kpt on one pce) 1½	2		112	—
1202a14	**Enigma (GER)** (BSchutz,Germany) **3-9-2** WNewnes (last ent st: r.o wl) 5	3		105	—
	Acerbis (GER) (HJentzsch,Germany) **3-9-2** PSchiergen (disp ld: rdn & one pce fnl 2f) ½	4		104	—
921a2	**Tashiriya (IRE)** (AdeRoyerDupre,France) **3-9-2** PCoppin (trckd wnr: rdn & no ex fr 2f out) 2¼	5		101	—
	Panthere (GER) (BSchutz,Germany) **3-9-2** NGrant (disp ld: led 3f out: hdd 2f out: wknd) 7	6		90	—
	Wellesiena (GER) (ALowe,Germany) **3-9-2** TMundry (mid div: sn btn) nk	7		90	—
	Old Queen (GER) (RSuerland,Germany) **3-9-2** AHelfenbein (in rr early: improved ½-wy: btn 4f out:) 7	8		80	—
					8 Rn

2m 25.73 TOTE 18DM: 12DM 15DM 27DM OWNER M & U Stoof BRED Hedgestone Management
Que Belle (USA) completed the classic double in impressive style. Connections would like to give her a rest and have the Arc de Triomphe in mind for her.
Borgia (GER) took the lead with over two furlongs to go but found the winner just too strong.
Enigma (GER), who was last entering the straight, made up a lot of ground to and may be better suited by further.

1911a-SAN SIRO (Milan, Italy) (R-H) (Good)
Sunday June 8th

1919a PREMIO VERZIERE (Listed) (3-Y.O+ F & M)
4-50 (5-19) **1m** £23,142.00 (£10,183.00: £5,554.00: £2,777.00)

			SP	RR	SF
	Karla Wyller (ITY) (MLivraghi,Italy) **4-9-0** ADiNardo ——	1		98	—
1369a3	**Bazelle (FR)** (BGrizzetti,Italy) **4-9-0** MTellini nse	2		98	—
	Woopi Gold (IRE) (MGuarnieri,Italy) **3-8-3** MEsposito 1	3		96	—
	Infiel (Md'Auria,Italy) **4-9-0** MDemuro s.h	4		96	—
13266	**Tsarnista** (JLDunlop) **4-9-0** FJovine nse	5		96	—
					10 Rn

1m 40.5 (10.50) TOTE 91L: 28L 56L 18L (957L) OWNER Scuderia Longobardi BRED SRP
1326 Tsarnista delayed the race as she needed to be led down to the start. When the race eventually got underway, she was always well placed and seemed to have every chance a furlong out, but was unable to progress and lost fourth place in a photo.

1434-CHEPSTOW (L-H) (Good to Firm, firm patches)
Friday June 13th
WEATHER: overcast WIND: nil

1920 ORSINO AMATEUR H'CAP (0-80) (3-Y.O+) (Class G)
6-40 (6-50) **7f 16y** £2,402.00 (£672.00: £326.00) Stalls: High GOING minus 0.36 sec per fur (F)

			SP	RR	SF
1584*	**Stackattack (IRE) (62)** (MrsJRRamsden) **4-10-12**(3) MissERamsden(12) (lw: plld hrd: mde all: clr over 1f out: edgd lft ins fnl f: r.o wl) ——	1	3/1 1	75+	49
16329	**Caudillo (IRE) (60)** (MrsPNDutfield) **4-10-13** MrLJefford(2) (lw: hld up: hdwy over 2f out: chsd wnr over 1f out: no imp) 3½	2	20/1	65	39
16778	**Asterix (45)** (JMBradley) **9-9-9b**(3)ow5 MissVRoberts(3) (hdwy over 1f out: r.o one pce fnl f) 1¾	3	14/1	46	15
17792	**Bellas Gate Boy (49)** (JPearce) **5-10-2** MrsLPearce(9) (lw: s.s: hdwy fnl 2f: nvr nrr) nk	4	3/1 1	49	23

				SP	RR	SF
1473[5]	**Finsbury Flyer (IRE) (57)** (RJHodges) **4-10-10** MrJTizzard(4) (prom: rdn over 2f out: wknd ins fnl f)	3	**5**	6/1[2]	51	25
1599[4]	**Flying Pennant (IRE) (59)** (JMBradley) **4-10-9**(3) MrOMcPhail(11) (prom: rdn over 2f out: wknd fnl f)	¾	**6**	8/1[3]	51	25
1575[4]	**Everset (FR) (52)** (ABailey) **9-10-0**(5)ow6 MissALHutchinson(10) (swtg: s.s: nrst fin)	nk	**7**	20/1	43	11
1320[15]	**Coastguards Hero (52)** (MDIUsher) **4-10-5** MrEJames(1) (swtg: uns rdr & bolted bef s: s.s: nvr nr ldrs)	1½	**8**	16/1	40	14
1599[6]	**Love Legend (40)** (DWPArbuthnot) **12-9-7v** MrsDArbuthnot(8) (prom over 5f)	1¼	**9**	25/1	25	—
1658[9]	**Knobbleeneeze (75)** (MRChannon) **7-12-0v** MrCVigors(5) (prom over 5f)	3½	**10**	9/1	52	26
1565[7]	**First Man (50)** (BJLlewellyn) **3-9-7b[1]** MissEJJones(6) (swtg: s.i.s: sn chsng ldrs: wknd 2f out)	9	**11**	50/1	7	—
879[10]	**Indian Wolf (40)** (BJLlewellyn) **4-9-7** MissMCoombe(7) (bhd fnl 3f)	2½	**12**	50/1	—	—
				(SP 115.2%)	**12 Rn**	

1m 22.8 (3.50) CSF £65.07 CT £663.89 TOTE £3.50: £1.50 £4.70 £2.90 (£48.70) Trio £95.10 OWNER Miss E. L. Ramsden (THIRSK) BRED John Bernard O'Connor

LONG HANDICAP Love Legend 9-0 Asterix 9-3 First Man 8-1 Indian Wolf 8-4

WEIGHT FOR AGE 3yo-10lb

1584* Stackattack (IRE) took advantage of only being put up 2lb for his victory over subsequent dual scorer Jedi Knight at Catterick. (3/1)

1292 Caudillo (IRE), due to go down 3lb, still seems to have connections struggling to find her best trip. (20/1)

1483 Asterix needs a mile nowadays. (14/1)

1779 Bellas Gate Boy, 3lb higher than when winning over this distance at Lingfield, really does find seven the bare minimum. (3/1)

1473 Finsbury Flyer (IRE) may have found this ground too lively. (6/1)

1599 Flying Pennant (IRE), dropped 3lb, was flagging in the closing stages. (8/1)

1921 SECOND SEVERN CROSSING CLAIMING STKS (3-Y.O) (Class F)

7-10 (7-15) **7f 16y** £2,556.00 (£716.00: £348.00) Stalls: High GOING minus 0.36 sec per fur (F)

				SP	RR	SF
1090[9]	**Prospering** (JGSmyth-Osbourne) **3-7-12** JLowe(8) (hdwy over 3f out: rdn over 2f out: led 1f out: r.o)	—	**1**	20/1	54	—
1154[5]	**Effervescence (76)** (RHannon) **3-9-7** RHughes(7) (w ldr: led over 2f out to 1f out: r.o)	½	**2**	9/4[1]	76	18
1568[8]	**Prince of Fortune (49)** (MBlanshard) **3-8-7** NAdams(11) (led over 4f: one pce)	3	**3**	7/1	55	—
1167[12]	**Ginny Wossername (50)** (MartynMeade) **3-8-2b** FNorton(1) (swtg: lw: a.p: one pce fnl 3f)	4	**4**	10/1	41	—
1667[4]	**Blazing Castle (58)** (WGMTurner) **3-8-2**(7) DMcGaffin(4) (wl bhd tl hdwy over 1f out: nvr nrr)	½	**5**	5/1[2]	47	—
1485[8]	**Beveled Crystal** (CJames) **3-8-10** NVarley(9) (prom over 4f)	3½	**6**	33/1	40	—
	Moredun (IRE) (IABalding) **3-8-5** BDoyle(3) (w'like: scope: lw: a bhd)	7	**7**	11/2[3]	19	—
	Nikki Star (CJHill) **3-7-7**(5) APolli(10) (w'like: leggy: dwlt: sn prom: wknd 2f out)	3½	**8**	20/1	4	—
	Just Sidium (CJHill) **3-8-6** RPrice(5) (unf: bkwd: plld hrd: prom centre: rn green: wknd over 2f out)	2½	**9**	20/1	7	—
	Grace (JMBradley) **3-7-11**(7) JFowle(2) (leggy: swvd lft s: hdwy 5f out: wknd over 2f out)	3½	**10**	20/1	—	—
1807[4]	***Feel A Line (50)*** (BJMeehan) **3-8-7b** SWhitworth(6) (Withdrawn not under Starter's orders: spread plate)		**W**	6/1	—	—
				(SP 120.7%)	**10 Rn**	

1m 23.9 (4.60) CSF £46.04 TOTE £17.20: £3.60 £1.10 £2.00 (£25.10) Trio £111.20; £34.46 to 16/6/97 OWNER Mr P. D. Player (TOWCESTER) BRED P. D. Player and A. Miles

Prospering clmd Mr D Cox £3,000

Prospering stepped up considerably on her debut, and will now be trained by Ron Hodges. (20/1)

1154 Effervescence, dropped into a claimer, would have had more to do had this been a handicap, and is still looking for his first victory on grass. (9/4)

1167 Prince of Fortune had pulled too hard when tried over a mile last time. (7/1)

Ginny Wossername was made to look very one-paced. (10/1)

1667 Blazing Castle has yet to prove that he really stays seven. (5/1)

1922 FRIDAY NIGHT MAIDEN STKS (3-Y.O F) (Class D)

7-40 (7-42) **1m 4f 23y** £3,533.50 (£1,063.00: £514.00: £239.50) Stalls: Low GOING minus 0.36 sec per fur (F)

				SP	RR	SF
1234[3]	**Ridaiyma (IRE)** (LMCumani) **3-8-11** JWeaver(2) (lw: a gng wl: wnt 2nd over 3f out: led 2f out: pushed out)	—	**1**	6/4[1]	86	44
1420[2]	**Melodica** (MRStoute) **3-8-11** DHarrison(5) (stdd s: stdy hdwy 6f out: rdn over 3f out: chsd fnl f: no imp)	3½	**2**	4/1[2]	81	39
1646[5]	**Ikhtisar (USA)** (PTWalwyn) **3-8-11** RHughes(3) (chsd ldr: rdn over 3f out: one pce fnl 2f)	3	**3**	20/1	77	35
1477[5]	**Dancing Feather** (BWHills) **3-8-11** MHills(1) (led: hdd 2f out: wknd fnl f)	3	**4**	6/4[1]	73	31
1420[4]	**Jude** (PFICole) **3-8-4**(7) JBosley(4) (last whn rdn 4f out: no response)	1½	**5**	16/1[3]	63 t	30
				(SP 110.6%)	**5 Rn**	

2m 35.9 (3.50) CSF £7.36 TOTE £2.40: £1.10 £1.50 (£2.80) OWNER H H Aga Khan (NEWMARKET) BRED His Highness the Aga Khan's Studs S.C.

IN-FOCUS: **All five fillies were attempting a mile and a half for the first time.**

1234 Ridaiyma (IRE), suited by this step-up in distance, scored with the minimum of fuss. (6/4)

1420 Melodica proved no match for the winner. (4/1: op 5/2)

1646 Ikhtisar (USA) lacked a turn of foot. (20/1)

1477 Dancing Feather did nothing more than set the race up for the winner. (6/4)

1420 Jude lacks substance and it is difficult to see where she goes from here. (16/1)

1923 ROUND COURSE H'CAP (0-80) (3-Y.O+) (Class D)

8-10 (8-11) **1m 2f 36y** £3,579.00 (£1,077.00: £521.00: £243.00) Stalls: Low GOING minus 0.36 sec per fur (F)

				SP	RR	SF
1588[2]	**Anak-Ku (65)** (MissGayKelleway) **4-9-1** JWeaver(1) (mde all: rdn over 2f out: r.o wl)	—	**1**	7/2[3]	78	41
1435[2]	**Roufontaine (75)** (WRMuir) **6-9-11** MHills(2) (lw: hld up: effrt 2f out: chsd wnr fnl f: hrd rdn: r.o)	¾	**2**	2/1[1]	87	50
1414[4]	**Monument (62)** (JSKing) **5-8-12** BDoyle(3) (lw: chsd wnr: hrd rdn & ev ch over 2f out: one pce fnl f)	2½	**3**	11/2	70	33
1739[9]	**Tremplin (USA) (74)** (NACallaghan) **5-9-10** RHughes(5) (plld hrd in rr: rdn over 2f out: one pce)	2½	**4**	11/4[2]	78	41
1559[3]	**Premier Generation (IRE) (70)** (DWPArbuthnot) **4-9-6** SWhitworth(4) (hld up: hdwy 4f out: wknd over 1f out)	5	**5**	6/1	66	29
				(SP 111.9%)	**5 Rn**	

2m 8.9 (3.60) CSF £10.12 TOTE £3.70: £1.50 £1.20 (£3.40) OWNER H R H Sultan Ahmad Shah (WHITCOMBE) BRED John Rose

1588 Anak-Ku seems to have a mind of his own and, after being mounted on the course, would not comply with the instruction to canter in front of the stands before going to post. However, his attitude in the race could not be faulted. (7/2)

1435 Roufontaine found the winner had got first run. (2/1)

1414 Monument was 4lb better off than when finishing three lengths behind the runner-up over course and distance last September. (11/2: 7/2-6/1)

Tremplin (USA), already due to be dropped 2lb, should have benefited from this longer trip. (11/4)

1559 Premier Generation (IRE), 7lb higher than when winning at Newbury, seems at his best on soft ground. (6/1: op 4/1)

1924 E.B.F. NOVICE STKS (2-Y.O) (Class D)
8-40 (8-41) **6f 16y** £3,207.00 (£966.00: £468.00: £219.00) Stalls: High GOING minus 0.36 sec per fur (F)

			Pos	SP	RR	SF
1321[3]	**Indian Missile** (JLDunlop) **2-8-12** BDoyle(1) (chsd ldr: rdn over 1f out: led nr fin)	—	**1**	Evens[1]	70	17
695*	**Blakeset** (RHannon) **2-9-4** RHughes(5) (swtg: led: rdn & edgd lft over 1f out: hdd nr fin)	s.h	**2**	3/1[3]	76	23
1274[3]	**The Rich Man (IRE)** (BWHills) **2-8-12** MHills(3) (lw: s.i.s: hld up: rdn over 1f out: one pce)	3½	**3**	5/2[2]	61	8
	Downclose Duchess (MBlanshard) **2-8-7** JQuinn(4) (small: bkwd: trckd ldrs: wknd over 1f out)	5	**4**	25/1	43	—
	Santa Court (RDickin) **2-8-12** JWeaver(2) (neat: s.s: hdwy 4f out: rdn 2f out: sn wknd)	3½	**5**	20/1	38	—

(SP 112.2%) **5 Rn**

1m 12.6 (3.40) CSF £4.09 TOTE £1.80: £1.30 £1.30 (£2.40) OWNER Mr Khalil Alsayegh (ARUNDEL) BRED Bishop's Down Farm
1321 Indian Missile just got the better of a good battle with the runner-up. (Evens)
695* Blakeset did not mind this extra furlong. (3/1)
1274 The Rich Man (IRE) should have been suited by this longer trip and was a bit disappointing. (5/2)
Downclose Duchess is a half-sister to seven-furlong juvenile scorer Downclose. (25/1)

1925 ALVESTON MAIDEN H'CAP (0-70) (3-Y.O+) (Class E)
9-10 (9-12) **6f 16y** £3,226.50 (£972.00: £471.00: £220.50) Stalls: High GOING minus 0.36 sec per fur (F)

			Pos	SP	RR	SF
1743[2]	**Flying Harold (42)** (MRChannon) **4-8-2**(3) PPMurphy(4) (hld up: gd hdwy to ld over 1f out: edgd lft: r.o wl)	—	**1**	11/4[1]	54	36
1139[13]	**Classic Leader (65)** (ICampbell) **4-10-0v** RPrice(6) (lw: a.p: rdn 1f out: r.o one pce)	2½	**2**	20/1	70	52
649[5]	**Mike's Double (IRE) (49)** (MissGayKelleway) **3-8-4** JFEgan(5) (hld up & plld hrd: hdwy 2f out: r.o one pce ins fnl f)	s.h	**3**	5/1[2]	54	28
1467[4]	**Priory Gardens (IRE) (41)** (JMBradley) **3-7-3**(7) JFowle(13) (led over 4f: one pce)	nk	**4**	15/2[3]	46	20
1849[11]	**Severn Mill (33)** (JMBradley) **6-7-10** JLowe(8) (s.s: hdwy over 1f out: r.o)	1¾	**5**	25/1	33	15
1292[6]	**Saxon Bay (58)** (KOCunningham-Brown) **5-9-7** BDoyle(9) (lw: a.p: ev ch over 1f out: wknd ins fnl f)	nk	**6**	20/1	57	39
1506[7]	**Homestead (53)** (RHannon) **3-8-8** WJO'Connor(11) (nvr nr to chal)	2½	**7**	11/1	46	20
997[6]	**Soda (54)** (JLSpearing) **3-8-9** SDrowne(14) (lw: nvr trbld ldrs)	½	**8**	11/1	45	19
1639[10]	**Sharp Holly (IRE) (38)** (JABennett) **5-8-1** SophieMitchell(7) (swtg: bhd fnl 2f)	nk	**9**	40/1	28	10
1567[10]	**Bairn Atholl (40)** (RJHodges) **4-8-3** NVarley(2) (prom over 3f)	¾	**10**	33/1	28	10
1485[10]	**Dorado Beach (45)** (LGCottrell) **3-8-0** JQuinn(12) (plld hrd early: hdwy over 2f out: wknd over 1f out)	nk	**11**	33/1	33	7
1388[14]	**Alpine Music (IRE) (55)** (JMBradley) **3-8-10** JWeaver(3) (reard st: a bhd)	1½	**12**	25/1	39	13
1375[5]	**Chloe Nicole (USA) (60)** (PFICole) **3-9-1** CRutter(10) (lw: prom over 3f)	1	**13**	15/2[3]	41	15
3[11]	**Parellie (33)** (CJHill) **4-7-10** NAdams(15) (w ldr over 3f: t.o)	10	**14**	33/1	—	—
	Royal Intrusion (37) (RJHodges) **4-8-0** FNorton(1) (swtg: a bhd: t.o fnl 3f)	1¾	**15**	16/1	—	—

(SP 117.9%) **15 Rn**

1m 10.7 (1.50) CSF £58.73 CT £243.79 TOTE £2.90: £1.30 £5.70 £2.50 (£43.60) Trio £49.90 OWNER Mr Malcolm Allen (UPPER LAMBOURN) BRED M. P. Allen
LONG HANDICAP Priory Gardens (IRE) 7-9 Parellie 7-7 Severn Mill 7-3
WEIGHT FOR AGE 3yo-8lb
1743 Flying Harold appreciated this return to six, and was due to go up 6lb tomorrow. (11/4)
Classic Leader, visored for the first time when dropped into a claimer on his last run, was a stone lower than the time before. (20/1)
649 Mike's Double (IRE), dropped 3lb, was without the blinkers this time. (5/1)
1467 Priory Gardens (IRE) had no answer when the winner went for home. (15/2)
Severn Mill, 7lb out of the handicap, was making a quick reappearance but needs to revert to seven. (25/1)
1292 Saxon Bay was trying his luck at sprinting. (20/1)

T/Plpt: £10.30 (1,161.71 Tckts). T/Qdpt: £3.00 (217.56 Tckts) KH

1866-GOODWOOD (R-H) (Good)
Friday June 13th
WEATHER: fine WIND: almost nil

1926 SOUTHERN FM AMATEUR H'CAP (0-70) (3-Y.O+) (Class E)
6-30 (6-31) **1m 1f** £4,110.00 (£1,230.00: £590.00: £270.00) Stalls: High GOING minus 0.12 sec per fur (G)

			Pos	SP	RR	SF
1463[5]	**Shining Example (66)** (PJMakin) **5-11-2**(5) MrLBaker(2) (swtg: a gng wl: hdwy 2f out: led ins fnl f: r.o wl)	—	**1**	11/2[2]	75	57
1748[2]	**Cuban Reef (47)** (WJMusson) **5-10-2** MrTMcCarthy(4) (hdwy 3f out: r.o wl ins fnl f)	1½	**2**	2/1[1]	53	35
1421[7]	**Tribal Peace (IRE) (60)** (BGubby) **5-11-1** MrJRees(6) (rdn & hdwy 2f out: swtchd lft over 1f out: r.o)	nk	**3**	14/1	66	48
1384[2]	**Koraloona (IRE) (49)** (GBBalding) **4-10-4** MrsAPerrett(9) (led 2f: ev ch over 1f out: unable qckn)	1¼	**4**	6/1[3]	53	35
1320[17]	**Warren Knight (52)** (CAHorgan) **4-10-2**(5) MrJGoldstein(10) (lw: a.p: led 2f out tl ins fnl f: one pce)	¾	**5**	25/1	54	36
1632[6]	**Ring the Chief (36)** (MDIUsher) **5-9-0**(5) MrsAUsher(8) (swtg: a.p: one pce fnl 2f)	2	**6**	12/1	35	17
1086[4]	**Mimosa (61)** (SDow) **4-11-2** MrTCuff(11) (rdn & hdwy fnl 2f: nvr nrr)	hd	**7**	12/1	60	42
1748[11]	**Proud Brigadier (IRE) (38)** (MRBosley) **9-9-7** MrsSBosley(13) (b: a.p: ev ch 2f out: wknd fnl f)	½	**8**	33/1	36	18
1689[3]	**Nabjelsedr (40)** (AGNewcombe) **7-9-4**(5)ow1 MrSDurack(7) (b: rdn 3f out: a mid div)	1¼	**9**	6/1[3]	35	16
1748[7]	**Squared Away (47)** (JWPayne) **5-9-11b**(5) MissCLake(5) (lw: prom 6f)	½	**10**	25/1	42	24
1677[13]	**Digpast (IRE) (53)** (JJBridger) **7-10-3b**(5) MrDBridger(3) (s.s: plld hrd: rapid hdwy to ld after 2f: hdd & wknd 2f out)	3½	**11**	33/1	41	23
1639[9]	**Hatta Sunshine (USA) (37)** (GLMoore) **7-9-6v** MrsJMoore(14) (lw: a bhd)	4	**12**	20/1	18	—
1809[11]	**Challenger (IRE) (36)** (JJSheehan) **4-9-0**(5) MissCHannaford(12) (hdwy 3f out: wknd wl over 1f out)	¾	**13**	50/1	16	—
1383[4]	**I'm a Nut Man (37)** (CASmith) **6-9-1**(5) MrsDSmith(1) (b: bhd fnl 7f)	s.h	**14**	16/1	17	—

(SP 125.5%) **14 Rn**

2m 0.25 (7.25) CSF £14.76 CT £142.82 TOTE £6.70: £2.30 £1.60 £3.10 (£5.50) Trio £16.00 OWNER Mr D. M. Ahier (MARLBOROUGH) BRED Stetchworth Park Stud Ltd
1463 Shining Example, back on a winning handicap mark, fully justified his rider's confidence throughout the race. (11/2)
1748 Cuban Reef, currently in-foal to First Trump, is running well at present as so many pregnant mares do. She is even better over another furlong. (2/1)

1123 Tribal Peace (IRE) is inconsistent but is well handicapped at present. He did not get the best of runs, but showed that he can still produce the goods from time to time. (14/1)
1384 Koraloona (IRE), a maiden, has run well enough in her last two races to suggest a small opportunity can be found. (6/1)
Warren Knight has been slipping down the weights thanks to some poor efforts, and now occupies a more realistic position in the handicap. (25/1)
1632 Ring the Chief stays this trip well on turf, but others proved to be quicker as the race reached its climax. (12/1)
1086 Mimosa (12/1: op 8/1)

1927 E.B.F. SUSSEX ENTERPRISE MAIDEN STKS (2-Y.O F) (Class D)
7-00 (7-00) **6f** £3,915.00 (£1,170.00: £560.00: £255.00) Stalls: Low GOING minus 0.12 sec per fur (G)

Form	Horse / details	Dist	Pos	SP	RR	SF
1645^{2}	**Filfilah** (PTWalwyn) **2-8-11** PatEddery(6) (chsd ldr: led over 1f out: rdn out)	—	**1**	5/6^{1}	71+	39
1457^{8}	**Jilted (IRE)** (RHannon) **2-8-8**(3) MartinDwyer(2) (led over 4f: rdn & r.o)	1¼	**2**	14/1	68	36
999^{3}	**Composition** (MAJarvis) **2-8-11** LDettori(7) (swtg: hld up: rdn 2f out: one pce)	1¼	**3**	10/1	64	32
1564^{3}	**Tajmil (IRE)** (MajorWRHern) **2-8-11** TSprake(5) (b: a.p: hrd rdn 2f out: one pce)	hd	**4**	13/2^{3}	64	32
	Chocolate (IRE) (JLDunlop) **2-8-11** TQuinn(8) (w'like: scope: dwlt: hdwy 3f out: one pce fnl 2f)	2½	**5**	3/1^{2}	57	25
1564^{8}	**Phantom Waters** (RFJohnsonHoughton) **2-8-11** SSanders(4) (dwlt: rdn 3f out: no hdwy fnl 2f)	2	**6**	40/1	52	20
	Siena (GER) (MRChannon) **2-8-4**(7) AEddery(1) (leggy: unf: bit bkwd: squeezed & lost pl after 1f: nt rcvr)	7	**7**	25/1	33	1
	Persian Fantasia (JLDunlop) **2-8-11** PaulEddery(9) (neat: dwlt: a bhd)	nk	**8**	25/1	33	1
	Idaho (IRE) (BGubby) **2-8-11** AClark(3) (w'like: rdn over 3f out: a bhd)	5	**9**	50/1	19	—

(SP 120.7%) **9 Rn**

1m 12.98 (3.18) CSF £14.29 TOTE £1.90: £1.10 £3.10 £1.60 (£9.20) Trio £20.00 OWNER Mr Hamdan Al Maktoum (LAMBOURN) BRED Shadwell Estate Company Limited
1645 Filfilah carries condition. Completing a thoroughly professional victory, she looks the sort to win more races. (5/6: evens-11/10)
1293 Jilted (IRE) battled on gamely, appearing to handle the longer trip without difficulty. (14/1: op 6/1)
999 Composition stayed the trip well enough, and was beaten by lack of acceleration rather than any shortfall in stamina. (10/1: op 6/1)
1564 Tajmil (IRE) ran another respectable race, and is capable of winning a maiden as long as ambitions are kept to a realistic level. (13/2: 4/1-7/1)
Chocolate (IRE), a 115,000 guineas newcomer, gave herself a bit to do, and used up her energy getting into the chasing group. (3/1)
Phantom Waters soon recovered from a sluggish start, but she will come into her own over longer trips. (40/1)

1928 EQUITY FINANCIAL COLLECTIONS H'CAP (0-85) (3-Y.O) (Class D)
7-30 (7-30) **1m 2f** £3,785.00 (£1,130.00: £540.00: £245.00) Stalls: High GOING minus 0.12 sec per fur (G)

Form	Horse / details	Dist	Pos	SP	RR	SF
1637^{3}	**Titta Ruffo (80)** (BJMeehan) **3-9-7** PatEddery(2) (rdn 5f out: hdwy 3f out: led over 1f out: r.o wl)	—	**1**	7/2^{3}	90	59
1813*	**Moon Blast (83)** (LadyHerries) **3-9-10** 4x AClark(3) (chsd ldr: led 3f out tl over 1f out: btn whn jinked lft ins fnl f)	1¾	**2**	5/2^{2}	90	59
1508*	**Rhapsody In White (IRE) (76)** (MAJarvis) **3-8-12**(5) RMullen(5) (hld up: rdn over 2f out: 3rd & btn whn sltly hmpd ins fnl f)	1	**3**	10/1	82	51
1458^{11}	**Passiflora (65)** (JLDunlop) **3-8-6** PaulEddery(1) (hrd rdn 2f out: nvr nr to chal)	5	**4**	14/1	63	32
1623*	**Kilshanny (72)** (LMCumani) **3-8-13** 4x LDettori(4) (sn ld: hdd 3f out: wknd over 1f out)	1	**5**	5/4^{1}	68	37

(SP 111.0%) **5 Rn**

2m 11.15 (4.55) CSF £11.53 TOTE £3.90: £1.50 £1.70 (£5.10) OWNER Mr Mario Lanfranchi (UPPER LAMBOURN) BRED C. Wiggins
OFFICIAL EXPLANATION **Kilshanny: no explanation offered.**
1637 Titta Ruffo, niggled along at halfway, but a clear winner in the end, may be more at home on a flatter track. (7/2)
1813* Moon Blast again showed a tendency to edge left towards the finish, and would be helped by a running rail on that side in the closing stages. (5/2)
1508* Rhapsody In White (IRE), not attempting to lead on this occasion, ran with credit considering that the Handicapper had taken no chances. (10/1: 6/1-12/1)
Passiflora is plummeting down the handicap, but never threatened to win here. (14/1: 10/1-16/1)
1623* Kilshanny was dropping back in trip, but that ought not to have been a problem. Her connections could offer no explanation for this disappointing performance. (5/4: op 2/1)

1929 PREBENDAL SCHOOL QUINCENTENNIAL CELEBRATION CLAIMING STKS (3-Y.O) (Class D)
8-00 (8-02) **1m** £3,525.00 (£1,050.00: £500.00: £225.00) Stalls: High GOING minus 0.12 sec per fur (G)

Form	Horse / details	Dist	Pos	SP	RR	SF
1748^{6}	**Merciless Cop (65)** (BJMeehan) **3-8-9** PatEddery(7) (a.p: swtchd lft 2f out: led 1f out: all out)	—	**1**	5/2^{2}	61	38
1416^{4}	**Tulsa (IRE) (50)** (BGubby) **3-8-9** AClark(2) (hld up: led over 2f out to 1f out: hrd rdn: r.o wl)	½	**2**	20/1	60	37
1633^{18}	**My Beloved (IRE) (65)** (RHannon) **3-8-6** DaneO'Neill(6) (hdwy 2f out: hrd rdn & ev ch ins fnl f: r.o)	¾	**3**	3/1^{3}	56	33
1688^{2}	**Matoaka** (RJRWilliams) **3-8-10** LDettori(4) (led 5f: ev ch 1f out: r.o)	nk	**4**	7/4^{1}	59	36
1639^{6}	**Bon Guest (IRE) (54)** (TJNaughton) **3-8-7** SSanders(1) (swtg: hld up rr: hdwy 2f out: hrd rdn over 1f out: one pce)	3	**5**	8/1	50	27
1155^{11}	**Zest (USA) (65)** (MBell) **3-8-6** TQuinn(3) (lw: chsd ldr: led 3f out tl over 2f out: wknd wl over 1f out)	7	**6**	16/1	35	12
1487^{P}	**Hot Shot** (GLMoore) **3-8-5** CandyMorris(5) (hld up: rdn over 2f out: sn wknd)	17	**7**	50/1	—	—

(SP 113.7%) **7 Rn**

1m 41.6 (4.40) CSF £42.51 TOTE £2.90: £1.70 £5.80 (£38.50) OWNER Mr Mario Lanfranchi (UPPER LAMBOURN) BRED G. S. Shropshire
1748 Merciless Cop, well backed to give owner and trainer a quick double and Eddery a treble, was given a swashbuckling ride, which seemed to confirm that the money was down. (5/2)
Tulsa (IRE) was badly in on official figures, but he has been running recently over six furlongs and ten furlongs, and this seemed to be more his trip. (20/1)
1167 My Beloved (IRE) proved that she stays a mile with a sound effort. (3/1)
1688 Matoaka is still a maiden, but she has had only four races, and could not be ruled out in similar company. (7/4)
1639 Bon Guest (IRE), not well in at the weights, would have had more chance in a low-grade handicap. (8/1: 6/1-10/1)
935 Zest (USA), reluctant to race on sand last time, tends to take too strong a hold on turf. This leggy, sparely-made filly looks a bit of handful. (16/1)

1930 WILEY EUROPE MAIDEN STKS (3-Y.O) (Class D)
8-30 (8-30) **1m 4f** £4,115.00 (£1,140.00: £545.00) Stalls: Low GOING minus 0.12 sec per fur (G)

Form	Horse / details	Dist	Pos	SP	RR	SF
1242^{5}	**Catchable (83)** (HRACecil) **3-9-0** KFallon(3) (lw: outpcd in rr: rdn & hdwy 3f out: led over 1f out: r.o wl)	—	**1**	100/30^{2}	89	55

				SP	RR	SF
528[2]	**Dark Green (USA) (92)** (PFICole) **3-9-0** TQuinn(1) (chsd ldr: led after 3f tl over 1f out: unable qckn)	2	**2**	1/3[1]	86	52
1405[4]	**San Glamore Melody (FR)** (JHMGosden) **3-9-0** LDettori(2) (led 3f: rdn 4f out: eased whn btn over 2f out: virtually p.u)	dist	**3**	8/1[3]	—	—
				(SP 109.2%)	**3 Rn**	

2m 38.4 (5.20) CSF £4.75 TOTE £3.80: (£1.30) OWNER Lord Howard de Walden (NEWMARKET) BRED Lord Howard de Walden
1242 Catchable, pushed along from the start, looked better the further he went, winning well in the end, and giving the impression that he would stay a longer trip. (100/30)
528 Dark Green (USA) looked in good shape, but he may have needed the run after a ten-week absence. Nonetheless, his response was still disappointing, and he is surely capable of better. (1/3)
San Glamore Melody (FR), only a few lengths off the other pair at the time, was eased to a canter when Dettori felt his chance had gone, but there was nothing physically wrong with him. (8/1)

1931 AMBROSE HARCOURT'S HEART AND SOUL H'CAP (0-75) (3-Y.O) (Class D)
9-00 (9-00) **6f** £3,882.50 (£1,160.00: £555.00: £252.50) Stalls: Low GOING minus 0.12 sec per fur (G)

				SP	RR	SF
1781[2]	**Ivory Dawn (65)** (KTIvory) **3-8-13**(3) MartinDwyer(8) (b: lw: a.p: led 2f out: rdn out)	—	**1**	7/2[2]	76	47
1661[2]	**C-Harry (IRE) (57)** (RHollinshead) **3-8-8** FLynch(7) (hdwy 2f out: unable qckn fnl f)	2½	**2**	5/2[1]	61	32
1087[6]	**Prince Zando (65)** (CAHorgan) **3-9-2** PaulEddery(3) (dwlt: hdwy 2f out: hrd rdn over 1f out: one pce)	2	**3**	5/1	64	35
1573[5]	**Mon Bruce (60)** (WRMuir) **3-8-11** DaneO'Neill(1) (hld up: hrd rdn over 1f out: one pce)	1¼	**4**	14/1	56	27
1810[6]	**Lamorna (56)** (MRChannon) **3-8-7** TQuinn(6) (a.p: led 3f out to 2f out: one pce)	¾	**5**	9/2[3]	50	21
1666[2]	**Peter Perfect (55)** (GLewis) **3-8-3b**(3) AWhelan(4) (swtg: rdn & no hdwy fnl 2f)	1¾	**6**	7/1	44	15
1810[5]	**Heavenly Miss (IRE) (65)** (JJBridger) **3-8-11**(5) ADaly(2) (lw: led 3f: wknd 2f out)	3½	**7**	14/1	45	16
1644[5]	**Rise 'n Shine (68)** (CACyzer) **3-9-5** LDettori(9) (lw: prom 3f: eased whn btn over 1f out)	15	**8**	10/1	8	—
				(SP 120.6%)	**8 Rn**	

1m 12.78 (2.98) CSF £12.31 CT £40.85 TOTE £5.30: £2.10 £1.40 £3.20 (£5.20) Trio £25.20 OWNER Mr Dean Ivory (RADLETT) BRED Stratford Place Stud
1781 Ivory Dawn was winning for the first time in her eleventh race, but she has put in some excellent efforts this season, and is from a stable in good form. She will win more races now she has got the habit. (7/2)
1661 C-Harry (IRE), due to go up 5lb in the weights, was clearly held in the last furlong, and the Handicapper may have to think again. (5/2)
768 Prince Zando, making a satisfactory handicap debut, tried to come from a fair way back, and can find a race in due course. (5/1)
1573 Mon Bruce is nose-diving down the handicap, but he failed to find any significant response when coming off the bridle. (14/1: op 8/1)
1810 Lamorna, subjected to different tactics this time, did not live up to the promise of her previous run. (9/2)
1666 Peter Perfect still looks a few pounds too high in the handicap. (7/1: op 9/2)

T/Plpt: £87.30 (142.11 Tckts). T/Qdpt: £39.80 (12.11 Tckts) LMc

1473-SANDOWN (R-H) (Good to firm, Straight crse Good patches)
Friday June 13th
WEATHER: warm WIND: almost nil

1932 E.B.F. WEST END MAIDEN STKS (2-Y.O) (Class D)
2-15 (2-16) **5f 6y** £3,160.00 (£955.00: £465.00: £220.00) Stalls: Low GOING minus 0.18 sec per fur (GF)

				SP	RR	SF
	Overture (IRE) (RHannon) **2-9-0** DaneO'Neill(6) (neat: a.p: led over 1f out: drvn out)	—	**1**	3/1[1]	81+	29
	Clef of Silver (WJarvis) **2-9-0** MHills(3) (w'like: bit bkwd: nt clr run 2f out: hdwy over 1f out: ev ch ins fnl f: r.o wl)	hd	**2**	7/2[2]	81+	29
	Take A Turn (MRChannon) **2-8-11**(3) PPMurphy(7) (unf: led 1f: ev ch over 1f out: unable qckn)	4	**3**	20/1	68	16
	Ellway Prince (IABalding) **2-9-0** LDettori(1) (w'like: hld up: rdn over 2f out: nt clr run over 1f out: r.o one pce)	1¼	**4**	3/1[1]	64	12
	Zeppo (IRE) (MJHeaton-Ellis) **2-9-0** SDrowne(9) (str: bit bkwd: hrd rdn & hdwy over 1f out: one pce)	1¼	**5**	20/1	60	8
1251[8]	**Balanita (IRE)** (BPalling) **2-9-0** TSprake(5) (led 4f out tl over 1f out: sn wknd)	hd	**6**	4/1[3]	60	8
1418[10]	**Sky Mountain (IRE)** (GLewis) **2-9-0** PaulEddery(8) (hld up: rdn over 2f out: wknd over 1f out)	½	**7**	20/1	58	6
	Stone of Destiny (BJMeehan) **2-9-0** MTebbutt(10) (str: scope: hdwy over 2f out: wknd over 1f out)	¾	**8**	20/1	56	4
	Vista Alegre (PJMakin) **2-9-0** SSanders(4) (str: scope: bit bkwd: bhd fnl 3f)	2	**9**	16/1	49	—
				(SP 117.2%)	**9 Rn**	

63.08 secs (3.28) CSF £11.79 TOTE £3.60: £1.50 £1.90 £2.20 (£9.20) Trio £65.40 OWNER Mr J. A. Lazzari (MARLBOROUGH) BRED Barronstown Stud
Overture (IRE), whose dam won both the Cherry Hinton and Musidora Stakes, is a half-sister to numerous winners including Irish 1,000 Guineas winner Nicer. Although not very big, this nippy sort knew what was required and, leading over a furlong out, just managed to hold off the very persistent runner-up. (3/1: 9/4-4/1)
Clef of Silver, a medium-sized individual, only just failed to make a winning debut. Not getting the best of runs, he threw down his challenge inside the final furlong, and only just failed. Sure to come on for this, he should soon go one better. (7/2)
Take A Turn, rather weak at present, nevertheless had every chance below the distance. (20/1)
Ellway Prince, a medium-sized colt, did not get the best of runs below the distance, but stayed on up the hill. (3/1)
Zeppo (IRE), a round-bodied colt, looked as though this debut would do him good and, after moving up under pressure below the distance, could then make no further impression. (20/1)
1251 Balanita (IRE), one of only two with the benefit of a run under his belt, was soon at the head of affairs but, collared below the distance, soon dropped away. (4/1: 5/2-9/2)

1933 SBJ GROUP MAIDEN STKS (2-Y.O) (Class D)
2-50 (2-53) **7f 16y** £3,598.75 (£1,090.00: £532.50: £253.75) Stalls: High GOING minus 0.44 sec per fur (F)

				SP	RR	SF
1607[6]	**Muhtathir** (JHMGosden) **2-9-0** GHind(14) (lw: plld hrd: chsd ldr: led 3f out: clr over 1f out: rdn out)	—	**1**	7/1	90	41
	Craigsteel (HRACecil) **2-9-0** KFallon(9) (leggy: a.p: chsd wnr over 2f out: r.o)	½	**2**	11/4[2]	89	40
	Mulahen (DMorley) **2-9-0** JStack(7) (str: scope: bit bkwd: shkn up over 2f out: gd hdwy over 1f out: r.o: bttr for r)	3	**3**	25/1	82+	33
1174[4]	**Monsajem (USA)** (SbinSuroor) **2-9-0** LDettori(12) (lw: a.p: rdn 3f out: unable qckn)	3	**4**	5/2[1]	75	26
1163[5]	**Lincolnshire (USA)** (PFICole) **2-9-0** PatEddery(13) (a.p: rdn over 3f out: one pce)	¾	**5**	6/1[3]	74	25

	Royal Bounty (IRE) (MajorWRHern) **2-8-9** TSprake(2) (leggy: a.p: rdn over 2f out: wknd over 1f out)	2	**6**	33/1	64	15
1619[6]	**Lady Yavanna** (KMcAuliffe) **2-8-9** DaneO'Neill(11) (hld up: rdn over 3f out: sn wknd)	nk	**7**	50/1	63	14
1480[4]	**Master Mac (USA)** (RAkehurst) **2-9-0** SSanders(4) (hld up: rdn over 3f out: wknd 2f out)	1	**8**	25/1	66	17
1263[10]	**Night Vigil (IRE)** (BWHills) **2-9-0** MHills(6) (bit bkwd: nvr nrr)	½	**9**	25/1	65	16
	Eljjanah (USA) (JLDunlop) **2-9-0** GCarter(10) (leggy: s.s: hdwy on ins over 2f out: wknd fnl f)	¾	**10**	13/2	63	14
1163[4]	**Rodinia (USA)** (GLewis) **2-9-0** PaulEddery(15) (led 4f: wknd over 1f out)	2½	**11**	25/1	58	9
	Gay Abandon (KMcAuliffe) **2-8-9** BDoyle(3) (leggy: lt-f: a bhd)	3	**12**	50/1	46	—
	Temper Lad (USA) (JHMGosden) **2-9-0** AMcGlone(8) (scope: rdn 5f out: a bhd)	1¾	**13**	33/1	47	—
1645[9]	**Meadgate's Dreamer (IRE)** (BPalling) **2-8-9** SDrowne(1) (bhd fnl 3f)	1¾	**14**	50/1	38	—
	Iron Mountain (IRE) (NACallaghan) **2-9-0** RHughes(5) (w'like: scope: bkwd: s.s: a bhd)	20	**15**	33/1	—	—

(SP 125.4%) **15 Rn**

1m 30.51 (1.91) CSF £22.64 TOTE £12.70: £3.40 £1.50 £9.50 (£15.70) Trio £63.20 OWNER Mr Hamdan Al Maktoum (NEWMARKET) BRED Shadwell Estate Company Limited

IN-FOCUS: **There was a lot to like about this field in the paddock, and time may tell that this was a very hot maiden - Benny The Dip finished second to Putra in this event last year.**

1607 Muhtathir, a tall, attractive colt, put up a scintillating performance in a hot race. Leading three furlongs from home, he forged clear below the distance, and although the runner-up was closing the gap, he was not going to be overhauled. The Solario Stakes here at the end of August looks on the cards. He will be even better with some cut in the ground, according to his trainer. (7/1)

Craigsteel, a plain, athletic colt, who is a half-brother to Inchrory and Pennycairn, was the subject of encouraging home reports, and comes from a stable that does really well with its two-year-olds here - all three of their juvenile newcomers won here last season, and their five-year juvenile record stands at 43%. He ran on in good style up the hill, to finish well clear of the remainder, if unable to overhaul the winner in time. He looks a ready-made winner. (11/4: op 5/4)

Mulahen, an attractive, good-bodied colt, was not subjected to a hard time, but put in some sterling work in the last furlong-and-a-half to finish a clear third best. Sure to strip a lot fitter for this, he should have no problem opening his account. (25/1)

1174 Monsajem (USA), a tall, attractive individual with bags of scope, looked superb in the paddock, but was rather disappointing, failing to find another gear. This looked a very hot affair, and he should not take long to pick up an ordinary maiden event. (5/2)

1163 Lincolnshire (USA) was taking a step-up in distance, but Eddery was at work on him soon after entering the straight, to no effect. (6/1)

Royal Bounty (IRE), a tall, plain filly, with not much substance, was close up until calling it a day below the distance. (33/1)

Eljjanah (USA) (13/2: 3/1-8/1)

1934 DEVITT INSURANCE SERVICES CUP H'CAP (0-100) (3-Y.O+) (Class C)

3-20 (3-23) **1m 2f 7y** £7,035.00 (£2,130.00: £1,040.00: £495.00) Stalls: High GOING minus 0.44 sec per fur (F)

				SP	RR	SF
1606[2]	**Orsay (76)** (WRMuir) **5-8-11** MRoberts(3) (stdy hdwy over 2f out: led over 1f out: drvn out)	—	**1**	3/1[2]	85	38
1176[3]	**Game Ploy (POL) (89)** (DHaydnJones) **5-9-10** PatEddery(6) (lw: chsd ldr over 10f out: led over 2f out tl over 1f out: ev ch fnl f: r.o wl)	nk	**2**	5/1[3]	98	51
1678[7]	**General Haven (71)** (TJNaughton) **4-8-6** TSprake(4) (a.p: rdn over 3f out: unable qckn)	2½	**3**	25/1	76	29
1414[3]	**Bit on the Side (IRE) (83)** (NEBerry) **8-9-4** SDrowne(5) (dropped rr over 3f out: nt clr run & swtchd lft over 2f out: r.o one pce)	1½	**4**	9/1	85	38
	Puce (82) (LMCumani) **4-9-3** LDettori(7) (hld up: rdn over 3f out: one pace)	nk	**5**	9/4[1]	84	37
1482[3]	**Effectual (87)** (MissGayKelleway) **4-9-8** RHughes(1) (led over 7f: wknd fnl f)	¾	**6**	8/1	88	41
1319[7]	**Male-Ana-Mou (IRE) (88)** (DRCElsworth) **4-9-9** KFallon(8) (swtg: chsd ldr over 1f: rdn 3f out: wknd over 2f out)	3	**7**	7/1	84	37
1660[2]	**Quiet Arch (IRE) (69)** (WRMuir) **4-8-4**ow2 DaneO'Neill(2) (lw: hld up: rdn over 2f out: sn wknd)	3½	**8**	9/1	59	10

(SP 119.9%) **8 Rn**

2m 9.58 (2.88) CSF £17.78 CT £292.89 TOTE £3.80: £1.50 £1.60 £6.40 (£11.90) OWNER Mr D. J. Deer (LAMBOURN) BRED D. J. and Mrs Deer

1606 Orsay appreciated the step-up in trip and, striking the front below the distance, just managed to prevail in a tremendous battle with the second. (3/1)

1176 Game Ploy (POL) likes to hear his feet rattle, and moved to the front over a quarter of a mile from home. Marginally headed by the winner below the distance, he had a tremendous dual with that rival, and only just lost out. All four of his wins to date came last year over a mile-and-a-quarter. (5/1)

1156 General Haven was a leading light from the outset, but never looked like finding the necessary turn of foot in the straight. (25/1)

1414 Bit on the Side (IRE) once again found this trip too sharp, but was staying on up the hill. Given some cut in the ground, and a step-up to a mile-and-a-half, she can find a race. (9/1)

Puce, a plain, weak-looking filly, was being bustled along early in the straight, but failed to find the necessary turn of foot. A step up to a mile-and-a-half is needed. (9/4)

1482 Effectual has been in fine form this year, and took the field along until halfway up the straight. (8/1: 6/1-9/1)

1660 Quiet Arch (IRE) (9/1: 6/1-10/1)

1935 C. GORDON MEDLEN AND SONIA P. COE MEMORIAL H'CAP (0-90) (3-Y.O+) (Class C)

3-55 (3-56) **7f 16y** £5,628.00 (£1,704.00: £832.00: £396.00) Stalls: High GOING minus 0.44 sec per fur (F)

				SP	RR	SF
1243[3]	**Mara River (79)** (IABalding) **3-8-10** MHills(9) (lw: nt clr run on ins & lost pl wl over 1f out: swtchd lft: str run fnl f: led nr fin)	—	**1**	5/1[2]	87	42
1489[11]	**Rakis (IRE) (80)** (MrsLStubbs) **7-9-7** PatEddery(7) (b: lw: rdn over 2f out: gd hdwy fnl f: fin wl)	s.h	**2**	10/1	88	53
1453[7]	**Zelda Zonk (77)** (BJMeehan) **5-9-4** BDoyle(3) (rdn over 2f out: hdwy over 1f out: hrd rdn & ev ch wl ins fnl f: one pce)	½	**3**	14/1	84	49
1512*	**St Blaine (CAN) (84)** (DRLoder) **3-9-1** LDettori(6) (a.p: rdn over 2f out: led 1f out tl hdd nr fin)	nk	**4**	100/30[1]	90	45
1489[12]	**Xenophon of Cunaxa (IRE) (65)** (MJFetherston-Godley) **4-8-6** DaneO'Neill(8) (a.p: rdn over 3f out: one pce)	1¾	**5**	33/1	67	32
1453[6]	**Intisab (87)** (RWArmstrong) **4-10-0** GCarter(2) (rdn over 2f out: hdwy over 1f out: one pce fnl f)	hd	**6**	12/1	89	54
1324[4]	**No Extras (IRE) (64)** (GLMoore) **7-8-5** SWhitworth(1) (swtg: rdn over 2f out: hdwy 1f out: r.o wl)	nk	**7**	5/1[2]	65	30
1154[3]	**Pengamon (78)** (HJCollingridge) **5-9-5** JQuinn(4) (nvr nr to chal)	1½	**8**	16/1	76	41
1214[6]	**Mullitover (85)** (MJHeaton-Ellis) **7-9-12** MRoberts(10) (led: clr over 2f out: hdd 1f out: sn wknd)	1	**9**	10/1	81	46
1589*	**Kaiser Kache (IRE) (83)** (KMcAuliffe) **3-9-0** SSanders(11) (chsd ldr over 5f: eased whn btn fnl f)	4	**10**	7/1[3]	70	25
1489[9]	**Zurs (IRE) (70)** (MissGayKelleway) **4-8-11** KFallon(5) (s.s: a bhd)	4	**11**	10/1	48	13

(SP 119.4%) **11 Rn**

1m 30.09 (1.49) CSF £50.27 CT £617.60 TOTE £6.30: £2.00 £2.10 £2.80 (£28.60) Trio £83.90 OWNER Mr Nigel Harris (KINGSCLERE) BRED Mrs I. A. Balding

WEIGHT FOR AGE 3yo-10lb
IN-FOCUS: This race was run at a very fast pace.
1243 Mara River appreciated the extra furlong, and after losing her pitch early in the final quarter-mile, was still only seventh entering the final furlong. However she produced a whirlwind finish to get up near the line. (5/1)
1264 Rakis (IRE), winner of this race last year, appeared to have no hope of following up as he struggled in midfield in the straight. Still only eighth entering the final furlong, he flew alongside the winner, and failed by only a whisker. All ten of his victories to date have come over this trip. (10/1: 7/1-11/1)
1453 Zelda Zonk, 9lb higher than she has ever won off before, went very close. Making a very determined challenge inside the final furlong, she was about to strike the front in the last fifty yards when the winner and second both flew by. (14/1)
1512* St Blaine (CAN) managed to get to the front a furlong out, but despite doing little wrong, was worried out of it in the closing stages. (100/30)
159 Xenophon of Cunaxa (IRE), never far away, was being pushed along in the straight, but could only go up and down in the same place. (33/1)
1453 Intisab picked up ground below the distance, but was making no further impression in the final furlong. She could do with dropping a few pounds in the handicap. (12/1: 8/1-14/1)
1214 Mullitover (10/1: 7/1-11/1)

1936 NORWEST HOLST CONSTRUCTION MAIDEN STKS (3-Y.O) (Class D)
4-30 (4-40) **1m 2f 7y** £3,647.50 (£1,105.00: £540.00: £257.50) Stalls: High GOING minus 0.44 sec per fur (F)

				SP	RR	SF
931[2]	**Haltarra (USA) (108)** (SbinSuroor) **3-9-0** LDettori(2) (mde all: shkn up over 1f out: comf)	—	**1**	1/5[1]	91+	30
	Russian Ruler (IRE) (APJarvis) **3-9-0** SDrowne(6) (lw: plld hrd: a.p: chsd wnr over 2f out: r.o)	3	**2**	25/1	86	25
	Rolling Stone (LadyHerries) **3-9-0** RCochrane(4) (w'like: scope: stdy hdwy over 1f out: r.o one pce: bttr for r)	6	**3**	33/1	77	16
	Salsee Lad (JRFanshawe) **3-9-0** KFallon(1) (hld up: rdn over 4f out: wknd over 2f out)	3½	**4**	50/1	71	10
	Jandal (CJBenstead) **3-9-0** CRutter(11) (leggy: s.s: hdwy 8f out: rdn over 2f out: wknd wl over 1f out)	2	**5**	66/1	68	7
	Prime Minister (RCharlton) **3-9-0** TSprake(8) (leggy: scope: plld hrd: chsd wnr over 7f: wknd wl over 1f out)	2½	**6**	33/1	64	3
	Sylvan Jubilacion (PMitchell) **3-9-0** GCarter(3) (bhd fnl 5f)	3	**7**	100/1	59	—
	Junction City (USA) (IABalding) **3-9-0** PatEddery(5) (str: scope: lw: s.s: a bhd)	13	**8**	12/1[2]	38	—
1591[6]	***Kristal Bridge*** (PWHarris) **3-8-9** AClark(9) (Withdrawn not under Starter's orders: ref to ent stalls & bolted bef s)		**W**	14/1[3]	—	—
				(SP 111.9%)	**8 Rn**	

2m 10.94 (4.24) CSF £7.16 TOTE £1.20: £1.10 £1.60 £2.00 (£3.20) Trio £15.50 OWNER Godolphin (NEWMARKET) BRED Gainsborough Farm Inc
931 Haltarra (USA), who only just lost out in a listed race on his reappearance, was virtually unbackable, and had little more than an exercise gallop to dispose of this field. (1/5)
Russian Ruler (IRE) looked in good shape for this reappearance, and ran a race full of promise. Although no match for the winner, he moved into second place over a quarter of a mile from home, and pulled well clear of the remainder. He should soon be winning. (25/1)
Rolling Stone, a good-sized individual, was given a very quiet introduction, but caught the eye, staying on to finish a clear third best. Ray Cochrane reported afterwards that he twisted his neck when the colt became over-excited in the stalls, hence the quiet ride, and gave up his ride in the next race. Improvement can be expected. (33/1)
Salsee Lad, who has been gelded since last year, had been hung out to dry over two furlongs from home. (50/1)
Jandal, a tall colt, soon recovered from a tardy start, but had shot his bolt early in the final quarter-mile. (66/1)
Prime Minister, tall, angular colt, who is a half-brother to the very fast Eveningperformance, was fitted with a tongue-strap. Racing keenly in second place, he dropped away over two furlongs from home. (33/1)
Junction City (USA) (12/1: 5/1-14/1)
Kristal Bridge (14/1: 10/1-16/1)

1937 NORWEST HOLST CONSTRUCTION CLAIMING STKS (3-Y.O+) (Class F)
5-00 (5-10) **5f 6y** £2,788.00 (£844.00: £412.00: £196.00) Stalls: Low GOING minus 0.18 sec per fur (GF)

				SP	RR	SF
1772[8]	**White Emir (80)** (BJMeehan) **4-9-7b** PatEddery(4) (lw: hdwy over 1f out: led ins fnl f: rdn out)	—	**1**	4/1[3]	86	51
1676[2]	**Montendre (90)** (RJHodges) **10-9-2** LDettori(1) (lw: a.p: rdn over 1f out: r.o ins fnl f)	nk	**2**	9/2	80	45
1572*	**Palacegate Touch (76)** (JBerry) **7-9-1b**(7) CLowther(3) (lw: led over 3f: unable qckn)	1	**3**	7/2[2]	83	48
1608[3]	**Gone Savage (82)** (WJMusson) **9-9-9** DHolland(5) (hld up: led over 1f out tl ins fnl f: one pce)	½	**4**	5/4[1]	82	47
1848[4]	**Littlestone Rocket (50)** (WRMuir) **3-8-7b** DaneO'Neill(2) (lw: a.p: rdn over 2f out: wknd over 1f out)	4	**5**	14/1	61	19
1220[11]	**Sacred Spirit** (APJarvis) **5-8-13** SDrowne(7) (b: chsd ldr over 3f)	½	**6**	66/1	58	23
				(SP 113.0%)	**6 Rn**	

62.07 secs (2.27) CSF £20.19 TOTE £4.70: £2.10 £2.70 (£9.50) OWNER The Three Bears Racing (UPPER LAMBOURN) BRED G. Dickinson
WEIGHT FOR AGE 3yo-7lb
1488 White Emir looked in good shape beforehand and, picking up ground to lead inside the final furlong, just kept the runner-up at bay to gain his first victory since his two-year-old days. (4/1)
1676 Montendre, with 10lb or more in hand of his rivals on official adjusted ratings, was never far away and, running on inside the final furlong, only just failed. He is on the downgrade, and has won just once since 1993. (9/2)
1572* Palacegate Touch, who has gained six of his last eight victories in this grade, took the field along but, collared below the distance, failed to find another gear. (7/2)
1608 Gone Savage goes particularly well here, where he has won five times. Unfortunately, he travelled so well he struck the front below the distance, which was much too early for him. Headed inside the final furlong, he failed to summon up another gear. In a bigger field, where he can be covered up until later, he should soon regain the winning thread. (5/4)
1848 Littlestone Rocket, making a quick reappearance, was close up until running out of steam below the distance. (14/1)

1938 KINGSWOOD CORPORATE ENTERTAINMENT H'CAP (0-70) (3-Y.O) (Class E)
5-35 (5-38) **1m 3f 91y** £3,306.25 (£1,000.00: £487.50: £231.25) Stalls: High GOING minus 0.44 sec per fur (F)

				SP	RR	SF
1272[6]	**Arriving (60)** (JWHills) **3-9-1** KFallon(8) (hdwy 3f out: led over 2f out: clr over 1f out: r.o wl)	—	**1**	12/1[3]	70	38
1449[6]	**Keepsake (IRE) (46)** (MDIUsher) **3-8-1** RStreet(12) (hdwy over 1f out: chsd wnr fnl f: r.o)	1½	**2**	20/1	54	22
1742[3]	**Padauk (66)** (MJHaynes) **3-9-7** MRoberts(2) (hdwy over 6f out: ev ch over 2f out: unable qckn)	3½	**3**	16/1	69	37
1299[7]	**Laguna Bay (IRE) (58)** (APJarvis) **3-8-13** SDrowne(9) (a.p: rdn over 4f out: one pce)	s.h	**4**	20/1	61	29
1636*	**Dizzy Tilly (62)** (TJNaughton) **3-9-3** 5x DHolland(6) (led 3f: ev ch over 2f out: one pce)	½	**5**	11/4[1]	64	32
1694*	**Zorro (51)** (RMFlower) **3-8-6** GHind(13) (swtg: stdy hdwy whn hmpd over 2f out: nt rcvr)	1¾	**6**	11/4[1]	51	19
1237[15]	**Golden Saddle (USA) (62)** (PFICole) **3-9-3** CRutter(7) (lw: hld up: rdn over 3f out: wknd over 1f out)	2½	**7**	12/1[3]	58	26

1296[3]	**Herbshan Dancer (57)** (BRMillman) **3-8-12** JQuinn(1) (s.s: hdwy & nt clr run on ins over 2f out: one pce)	hd	**8**	9/1[2]	53	21
1168[6]	**Inimitable (64)** (JLDunlop) **3-9-5** GCarter(10) (nvr nr to chal)	1¾	**9**	9/1[2]	58	26
1465[3]	**Persian Blue (65)** (RHannon) **3-9-6** DaneO'Neill(3) (lw: hld up: rdn over 3f out: wknd over 2f out)	4	**10**	9/1[2]	53	21
1624[2]	**Soda Pop (IRE) (60)** (CEBrittain) **3-9-1** MRimmer(4) (a.p: led 4f out tl over 2f out: sn wknd)	¾	**11**	12/1[3]	47	15
1474[7]	**Motcombs Club (53)** (NACallaghan) **3-8-5**(3) DO'Donohoe(11) (lw: bhd fnl 6f)	1¼	**12**	20/1	38	6
1296[5]	**Running Free (IRE) (52)** (MJFetherston-Godley) **3-8-7b** AMcGlone(5) (led over 8f out to 4f out: sn wknd)	8	**13**	33/1	26	—

(SP 129.5%) **13 Rn**

2m 27.16 (3.76) CSF £224.09 CT £3,513.44 TOTE £14.50: £4.20 £14.00 £5.90 (£647.30) Trio £1,036.40; £1,328.39 to York 14/6/97 OWNER Wyck Hall Stud (LAMBOURN) BRED L. H. J. Ward

1272 Arriving appreciated the step-up in distance on this handicap debut, and skipped clear for a decisive victory. (12/1: op 8/1)
1449 Keepsake (IRE) left previous form well behind, and ran on to take second place entering the final furlong. (20/1)
1742 Padauk, a maiden shouldering top weight, had every chance before his lack of acceleration was exposed. (16/1)
952 Laguna Bay (IRE), never far away, was made to look very pedestrian in the straight. (20/1)
1636* Dizzy Tilly, set to rise 3lb in future handicaps, had every chance before plodding on at one pace. (11/4)
1694* Zorro, set to rise 7lb in future handicaps, had no luck in running, as he was badly interfered with as he was beginning to pick up ground. His jockey was extremely tender on him from that point, although the colt was noted staying on, and with a bit more effort would surely have finished third. This run is best ignored. (11/4)
1296 Herbshan Dancer (9/1: 6/1-10/1)
1465 Persian Blue (9/1: 6/1-10/1)
1624 Soda Pop (IRE) (12/1: op 8/1)

T/Jkpt: £7,100.00 (0.3 Tckts); £2,919.26 to York 14/6/97. T/Plpt: £131.40 (134.6 Tckts). T/Qdpt: £12.90 (82.07 Tckts) AK

1754-SOUTHWELL (L-H) (Standard)
Friday June 13th

WEATHER: overcast with showers WIND: slight half behind

1939 MERLIN LAND ROVER DISCOVERY MEDIAN AUCTION MAIDEN STKS (3-Y.O) (Class E)

2-30 (2-31) **1m (Fibresand)** £3,070.25 (£917.00: £438.50: £199.25) Stalls: Low GOING minus 0.40 sec per fur (FST)

				SP	RR	SF
1230[11]	**Canadian Fantasy (70)** (MJohnston) **3-9-0** JWeaver(2) (lw: mde virtually all: hrd rdn & swished tail fnl f: all out)	—	**1**	7/1[3]	77	18
1078[11]	**Cartouche (73)** (SirMarkPrescott) **3-9-0** GDuffield(7) (w wnr: rdn 2f out: sustained chal ins fnl f)	nk	**2**	5/4[1]	76	17
1780[7]	**Radar O'Reilly** (RJRWilliams) **3-8-11**(3) MBaird(9) (bit bkwd: drvn along & outpcd: effrt over 2f out: no imp)	11	**3**	9/1	54	—
1624[9]	**Keen Dancer (69)** (MBell) **3-8-9**(5) GFaulkner(3) (chsd ldrs: rdn 3f out: wknd appr fnl f)	4	**4**	7/2[2]	46	—
1401[4]	**Avanti Blue (50)** (KMcAuliffe) **3-9-0v[1]** WJO'Connor(1) (prom: sn pushed along: lost tch ent st)	15	**5**	20/1	16	—
586[15]	**Pen Friend** (WJHaggas) **3-9-0** GBardwell(6) (sn wl bhd & outpcd: n.d)	½	**6**	12/1	15	—
662[7]	**Our Future (IRE) (60)** (RonaldThompson) **3-9-0** TWilliams(11) (bit bkwd: rdn along ½-wy: sn bhd)	¾	**7**	25/1	14	—
1512[8]	**Spare My Blushes** (BAMcMahon) **3-8-9** LNewton(10) (dwlt: a in rr: t.o)	2½	**8**	33/1	4	—
	Nobby Beach (WRMuir) **3-8-7**(7) JWilkinson(8) (w'like: leggy: bit bkwd: in tch over 4f: sn wknd: t.o)	1½	**9**	14/1	6	—
	Certainty (JRFanshawe) **3-8-9** DHarrison(5) (lengthy: scope: bkwd: s s: a wl bhd: t.o)	16	**10**	8/1	—	—
	Shotley Princess (35) (NBycroft) **3-8-4**(5) JBramhill(4) (h.d.w: s.s: a bhd: t.o)	5	**11**	50/1	—	—

(SP 128.1%) **11 Rn**

1m 43.8 (4.80) CSF £15.56 TOTE £7.60: £1.60 £1.10 £2.70 (£3.70) Trio £36.60 OWNER Julian Clopet and Associates (MIDDLEHAM) BRED Newgate Stud Co

511 Canadian Fantasy, a very poor mover, almost broke his duck when last in action on the All-Weather and, adopting identical tactics, finally got off the mark, despite a lot of tail-swishing when subjected to pressure. (7/1)
874 Cartouche, a bitter disappointment when gambled on at Carlisle last month, looked to have shot his bolt when hard at work below the distance, but with his stamina coming into play, rallied willingly to keep the issue in doubt right to the line. (5/4)
Radar O'Reilly has shown little in his previous races, but he was the subject of inspired support here, and he obviously shows more at home than he has shown on the racecourse. (9/1: op 16/1)
1624 Keen Dancer, having his first outing on the All-Weather, was in trouble before reaching the straight, and he is not yet getting it together. (7/2: 3/1-9/2)
1401 Avanti Blue, still searching for a correct trip, was off the bridle after the first couple of furlongs, and he had been hung out to dry by the time he reached the straight. (20/1)
479 Pen Friend was soon well adrift of the field, and looked to be hating the kickback, but he did stay on in the latter stages, and is capable of better than he has shown so far. (12/1: op 8/1)
Certainty (8/1: op 5/1)

1940 MERLIN RANGE ROVER CLAIMING STKS (4-Y.O+) (Class F)

3-00 (3-00) **1m 6f (Fibresand)** £2,277.00 (£627.00: £297.00) Stalls: High GOING minus 0.40 sec per fur (FST)

				SP	RR	SF
*1288**	**Kalamata (73)** (JAGlover) **5-9-7** NDay(6) (lw: a.p: led over 2f out: hrd rdn fnl f: hld on gamely)	—	**1**	4/5[1]	84	10
*1755**	**Sedbergh (USA) (70)** (MrsMReveley) **4-9-3** DHarrison(8) (a.p: led over 4f out tl over 2f out: hrd rdn & kpt on towards fin)	½	**2**	7/2[2]	79	5
1562[7]	**Mister Aspecto (IRE) (69)** (MJohnston) **4-9-7b** JWeaver(5) (lw: chsd ldr: led over 6f out to 4f out: rdn & outpcd ent st: styd on fnl f)	2	**3**	13/2[3]	81	7
1660[9]	**Evezio Rufo (49)** (NPLittmoden) **5-8-6v**(5)ow2 GFaulkner(1) (wl bhd tl styd on fnl 3f: nvr nrr)	19	**4**	20/1	49	—
1434[9]	**Sheep Stealer** (REPeacock) **9-8-10**(5) JBramhill(2) (lost tch over 7f out: n.d afterwards)	6	**5**	50/1	47	—
1755[2]	**Faugeron (40)** (NTinkler) **8-8-3** LCharnock(9) (trckd ldrs: sn drvn along: lost tch 6f out: t.o)	7	**6**	14/1	27	—
	Liathach (JRFanshawe) **6-9-3** GDuffield(7) (bit bkwd: trckd ldrs to ½-wy: sn wknd: t.o)	29	**7**	10/1	7	—
1413[10]	**Red Whirlwind (50)** (RSimpson) **7-8-5b** MGallagher(3) (slt ld over 7f: sn hrd drvn & wknd: t.o)	17	**8**	50/1	—	—
1417[7]	**Club Elite (24)** (MissAStokell) **5-7-7**(5) APolli(10) (swtg: a wl bhd: t.o)	11	**9**	50/1	—	—
	Needle Knot (IRE) (RonaldThompson) **4-9-7** TWilliams(4) (prom 4f: sn lost pl: t.o p.u 7f out)		**P**	50/1	—	—

(SP 119.5%) **10 Rn**

3m 9.7 (11.70) CSF £3.32 TOTE £1.80: £1.00 £2.00 £2.10 (£2.10) Trio £4.00 OWNER Mr B. H. Farr (WORKSOP) BRED Worksop Manor Stud Farm
No bid

1288* Kalamata completed his hat-trick over course and distance, in just over a month, but he had to battle hard this time to shake off a very persistent rival. (4/5: op evens)
1755* Sedbergh (USA) had a hard set-to with his market rival throughout the final quarter-mile, and he gave it all he had, but once the winner had his head in front, he was in no mood to give best. (7/2)
1562 Mister Aspecto (IRE) could not hold his pitch when the leading pair took one another on entering the straight, but he was back into his stride nearing the finish, and would have been the one to beat with a little further to travel. (13/2)

1941 MERLIN LAND ROVER DEFENDER MEDIAN AUCTION MAIDEN STKS (2-Y.O) (Class F)

3-35 (3-37) **5f (Fibresand)** £2,277.00 (£627.00: £297.00) Stalls: High GOING minus 0.40 sec per fur (FST)

				SP	RR	SF
1306^{5}	**Pure Coincidence** (GLewis) **2-9-0** DHarrison(10) (a.p: led over 1f out: sn clr: impressive)	—	**1**	$9/2^{2}$	77+	23
1263^{3}	**Legs Be Frendly (IRE)** (KMcAuliffe) **2-9-0** WJO'Connor(13) (lw: led after 2f tl rdn & hdd over 1f out: no ch w wnr)	3½	**2**	$5/4^{1}$	66	12
1447^{6}	**Bolero Kid** (MWEasterby) **2-9-0** DaleGibson(14) (prom: outpcd ½-wy: rallied u.p fnl f)	½	**3**	9/1	64	10
1557^{3}	**Peter's Imp (IRE)** (JBerry) **2-8-9**(5) TEDurcan(2) (hmpd s: hdwy far side 2f out: nt rch ldrs)	5	**4**	$11/2^{3}$	48	—
1569^{8}	**Oriel Girl** (PDEvans) **2-8-9** JFEgan(6) (led 2f: rdn 2f out: r.o one pce)	1½	**5**	10/1	38	—
	Red Pepper (IRE) (PHowling) **2-9-0** NCarlisle(5) (w'like: bkwd: swvd lft s: sn chsng ldrs: one pce appr fnl f)	½	**6**	33/1	42	—
460^{5}	**Mill End Quest** (MWEasterby) **2-8-9** TLucas(9) (bit bkwd: outpcd tl r.o ins fnl f)	2	**7**	20/1	30	—
1286^{3}	**Captain Brady (IRE)** (WGMTurner) **2-8-9**(5) DSweeney(12) (prom 3f: sn rdn & outpcd)	hd	**8**	20/1	35	—
1286^{10}	**Liberte Bell (IRE)** (SirMarkPrescott) **2-8-9** GDuffield(3) (s.i.s: nvr on terms)	½	**9**	16/1	29	—
1510^{5}	**Half A Knicker** (RAFahey) **2-8-7**(7) RWinston(7) (w'like: scope: bkwd: nvr plcd to chal)	hd	**10**	13/2	33	—
	Revenge Is Sweet (BAMcMahon) **2-9-0** LNewton(8) (spd 3f)	¾	**11**	20/1	31	—
1286^{9}	**Jen's In The Know** (CMurray) **2-8-9** NicolaHowarth(4) (w ldrs centre: rdn 2f out: sn outpcd)	hd	**12**	33/1	25	—
1228^{8}	**Ellenber** (WMcKeown) **2-9-0** LCharnock(1) (bit bkwd: hmpd s: a outpcd)	½	**13**	33/1	29	—
1581^{7}	**Collacar** (DShaw) **2-8-11**(3) CTeague(11) (swtg: chsd ldrs to ½-wy: sn wknd)	1¼	**14**	33/1	25	—
				(SP 142.4%)	**14 Rn**	

59.3 secs (2.30) CSF £10.59 TOTE £6.40: £1.10 £1.20 £5.70 (£9.60) Trio £74.50 OWNER Mrs Andry Muinos (EPSOM) BRED R. and Mrs Parker
No bid
OFFICIAL EXPLANATION **Half A Knicker: the jockey reported that the colt was unsuited by the surface.**
1306 Pure Coincidence, an attractive son of a very useful racemare, made his first appearance on the sand a winning one with a very impressive display, and he could be set to go places. (9/2: 7/2-6/1)
1263 Legs Be Frendly (IRE), stepping back to the minimum trip, was unable to respond when the winner set sail for home, but he did nothing wrong, and his turn will come. (5/4)
1447 Bolero Kid had the favoured stand side stall, but he lost his pitch at halfway, and it was only his undoubted stamina that enabled him to get so close at the finish. He is crying out for six furlongs plus. (9/1)
1557 Peter's Imp (IRE) did best of those racing from the low-numbered stalls after being impeded at the start, and his luck is due a change. (11/2: 4/1-6/1)
1280 Oriel Girl gave it her best shot on this All-Weather debut, but the principals were too smart for her in the sprint to the line. (10/1)
Red Pepper (IRE) caused problems when he swerved left leaving the start, but remained in the chasing group, until feeling the strain approaching the final furlong. (33/1)

1942 NEW LAND ROVER FREELANDER H'CAP (0-70) (3-Y.O+) (Class E)

4-05 (4-06) **5f (Fibresand)** £2,940.25 (£877.00: £418.50: £189.25) Stalls: High GOING minus 0.40 sec per fur (FST)

				SP	RR	SF
*1759**	**Goretski (IRE) (66)** (NTinkler) **4-9-10** 7x DHarrison(5) (a.p: led over 2f out: rdn out)	—	**1**	$5/2^{1}$	73	43
1765^{4}	**Stolen Kiss (IRE) (63)** (MWEasterby) **5-9-7b** GDuffield(8) (lw: hdwy 2f out: rdn fnl f: fin strly)	hd	**2**	10/1	70	40
1759^{4}	**Sea Ya Maite (48)** (SRBowring) **3-7-13** DaleGibson(6) (b: dwlt: hdwy u.p ½-wy: kpt on towards fin)	nk	**3**	$8/1^{3}$	54	17
	Mullagh Hill Lad (IRE) (66) (BAMcMahon) **4-9-10** LNewton(4) (bkwd: a.p: ev ch over 1f out: one pce fnl f)	1¾	**4**	12/1	66	36
1759^{3}	**Sotonian (HOL) (44)** (PSFelgate) **4-8-2** DWright(7) (lw: led over 2f: rdn & one pce ins fnl f)	1¾	**5**	$7/1^{2}$	39	9
*1428**	**Napier Star (70)** (MrsNMacauley) **4-10-0v** SWebster(2) (lw: wl bhd & outpcd tl r.o appr fnl f)	1¾	**6**	12/1	59	29
905^{5}	**Perfect Brave (62)** (JBalding) **6-9-6** JEdmunds(11) (trckd ldrs stands' side: one pce fnl 2f)	¾	**7**	16/1	49	19
1401^{3}	**Magic Fizz (62)** (TJEtherington) **3-8-13** LCharnock(1) (in tch: rdn & no hdwy fnl 2f)	nk	**8**	14/1	48	11
1375^{9}	**Nampara Bay (50)** (GCBravery) **3-8-1** DRMcCabe(10) (spd 3f: sn lost tch)	4	**9**	$8/1^{3}$	23	—
1402^{3}	**Bee Health Boy (59)** (MWEasterby) **4-9-3b** TLucas(9) (lw: early spd: rdn ½-wy: sn outpcd)	5	**10**	$5/2^{1}$	16	—
1227^{9}	**Morning Star (62)** (WMcKeown) **3-8-13** TWilliams(3) (prom tl ½-wy: sn rdn & outpcd)	4	**11**	33/1	6	—
				(SP 131.8%)	**11 Rn**	

58.07 secs (1.07) CSF £31.67 CT £176.28 TOTE £2.40: £1.80 £2.10 £2.60 (£16.30) Trio £49.70 OWNER Mr P. D. Savill (MALTON) BRED Pierre Brichart
WEIGHT FOR AGE 3yo-7lb
OFFICIAL EXPLANATION **Bee Health Boy: resented the kickback.**
1759* Goretski (IRE), making a quick reappearance, was able to defy a 7lb penalty, but he needed to work to do so, and it is going to get more difficult once he has been reassessed. (5/2)
1765 Stolen Kiss (IRE) gave sure signs that he is back on song with a strong-finishing narrow defeat, and if this race had been over six furlongs, he would have been a clear cut winner. (10/1)
1759 Sea Ya Maite has not won a race yet, but he ran a fine race here after losing ground at the start, and sprinting is his game. (8/1)
Mullagh Hill Lad (IRE) failed to win last year, and he was seeing a racecourse for the first time in over eight months, so this very promising return to action could suggest he is back to something like his best. (12/1)
1759 Sotonian (HOL) looks a picture, and did his best to attack from the front, but the winner also likes to dictate, and that rival proved the stronger when the battle to the line got under way. (7/1)
1428* Napier Star is too consistent to get any help from the handicapper but, racing on the slower far side, she was unable to make her presence felt this time. (12/1: op 8/1)
1151 Nampara Bay (8/1: 6/1-9/1)
1402 Bee Health Boy does need another furlong, but he resented sand being kicked in his face, and was having none of it from halfway. (5/2)

1943 0115 942 4333 FOR THE BEST 4 X 4 X FAR (S) STKS (3-Y.O+) (Class G)

4-40 (4-40) **1m 3f (Fibresand)** £1,984.50 (£547.00: £259.50) Stalls: Low GOING minus 0.40 sec per fur (FST)

				SP	RR	SF
1683^{7}	**Heighth of Fame (65)** (JHetherton) **6-9-7** GDuffield(9) (chsd ldrs: led 2f out: sn wl clr: eased nr fin)	—	**1**	$11/10^{1}$	70+	21

				SP	RR	SF
1222^{7}	**Champagne Warrior (IRE) (54)** (MJCamacho) **4-9-7** LCharnock(6) (a.p: led over 5f out to 2f out: sn rdn & btn)	10	**2**	5/2^{2}	56	7
1579^{6}	**Royal Legend (52)** (JPearce) **5-9-12v** MWigham(2) (trckd ldrs: effrt & rdn 3f out: nvr able chal)	2½	**3**	11/2^{3}	57	8
1618^{4}	**Carol Again (43)** (NBycroft) **5-9-2**(5) DSweeney(5) (s.s: hdwy over 3f out: sn rdn: no imp)	14	**4**	12/1	32	—
1576^{8}	**Medland (IRE) (36)** (BJMcMath) **7-9-7** GBardwell(7) (hld up: effrt 4f out: sn rdn: no imp)	11	**5**	40/1	16	—
1601^{4}	**Philgem (19)** (CWFairhurst) **4-9-7** NKennedy(4) (lw: hld up: a in rr: t.o fnl 4f)	3	**6**	14/1	11	—
	Tovarich (58) (RonaldThompson) **6-9-7v^{1}** TWilliams(8) (swtg: bkwd: led tl ½-wy: sn wknd: t.o)	5	**7**	14/1	4	—
	Eau Secours (FR) (RHarris) **5-9-2** SWebster(1) (bkwd: chsd ldrs 5f: wknd qckly: t.o)	15	**8**	40/1	—	—
	Sandown Sue (TRWatson) **3-8-2** LNewton(3) (leggy: lt-f: unf: dwlt: a bhd: t.o)	23	**9**	40/1	—	—
				(SP 119.9%)	**9 Rn**	

2m 27.5 (7.50) CSF £3.70 TOTE £1.90: £1.00 £2.20 £2.10 (£3.80) Trio £10.90 OWNER Dr W D Mackenzie And Janet Elvans (MALTON) BRED Paul Mellon
WEIGHT FOR AGE 3yo-14lb
Bt in 5,800 gns
1138 Heighth of Fame reserves his best for this surface, but he has done all his winning at slightly longer trips in the past. Pushing the pace, he cruised into the lead soon after straightening up, and from then on the race was as good as over. (11/10)
1222 Champagne Warrior (IRE) got to the front at halfway, and did her best to get away from the winner, but he always had her in his sights, and left her for dead inside the last quarter-mile. (5/2)
1287* Royal Legend opened his account over course and distance last month, but he found this company just too strong for him, and he was never able to deliver a challenge. (11/2)
Tovarich (14/1: 3/1-16/1)

1944 MERLIN LAND ROVER HAYDN ROAD NOTTINGHAM AMATEUR H'CAP (0-65) (3-Y.O+) (Class G)
5-15 (5-17) **7f (Fibresand)** £1,984.50 (£547.00: £259.50) Stalls: Low GOING minus 0.40 sec per fur (FST)

				SP	RR	SF
1575^{7}	**Dream Carrier (IRE) (39)** (REPeacock) **9-9-4**(5) MrsCPeacock(1) (w ldr: qcknd wl over 1f out: sn clr)	—	**1**	16/1	51	33
429^{4}	**Mustang (33)** (CWThornton) **4-8-12b**(5) MrJCrowley(3) (bkwd: slt ld: rdn & hdd wl over 1f out: no ch w wnr)	7	**2**	12/1	29	11
1756^{2}	**Muara Bay (40)** (GLewis) **3-9-0** MissJFeilden(7) (trckd ldrs: effrt & rdn 2f out: kpt on)	¾	**3**	4/1^{1}	34	6
1799^{11}	**Awesome Venture (60)** (MCChapman) **7-10-11**(5) MrNChapman(10) (lw: hdwy on ins over 2f out: sn rdn: r.o one pce)	2	**4**	25/1	50	32
1759^{11}	**Lochon (42)** (MrsNMacauley) **6-9-12v** MrRThornton(2) (sn trckng ldrs: rdn 2f out: nvr able chal)	3	**5**	16/1	25	7
1575^{3}	**Dancing Sioux (62)** (RGuest) **5-10-13**(5) MissZBurkett(5) (b: lw: hld up: effrt over 2f out: nvr nr to chal)	1¼	**6**	5/1^{3}	42	24
1754^{11}	**Sweet Mate (52)** (SRBowring) **5-10-8** MrMHNaughton(4) (b.hind: w ldrs: rdn & outpcd fnl 2f)	nk	**7**	8/1	31	13
1677^{11}	**Montone (IRE) (65)** (JRJenkins) **7-11-7v** DrMMannish(11) (dwlt: nvr nrr)	2	**8**	14/1	40	22
1289^{11}	**Prudent Princess (40)** (AHide) **5-9-10** MissLHide(14) (prom: drvn along ent st: sn outpcd)	½	**9**	20/1	14	—
1560^{9}	**Maurangi (30)** (BWMurray) **6-9-0** MissAElsey(15) (a in rr)	½	**10**	14/1	3	—
1576^{5}	**Pc's Cruiser (IRE) (38)** (NPLittmoden) **5-9-3b**(5) MrJTyler-Morris(6) (s.s: outpcd: a bhd)	½	**11**	14/1	9	—
1575^{5}	**Desert Invader (IRE) (63)** (DWChapman) **6-11-5** MissRClark(16) (prom on outside: swtchd ins ent st: sn lost tch)	hd	**12**	9/2^{2}	34	16
1583^{9}	**Agent (64)** (JLEyre) **4-11-6** MissDianaJones(13) (hld up: a bhd)	1¼	**13**	14/1	32	14
367^{2}	**Recessions Over (34)** (NPLittmoden) **6-8-13**(5) MrVLukaniuk(9) (bkwd: prom 4f: sn wknd: t.o)	10	**14**	7/1	—	—
1613^{2}	**Craigie Boy (34)** (NBycroft) **7-9-4**ow2 MissJAllison(12) (a in rr: t.o)	2½	**15**	9/1	—	—
361^{7}	**Emma's Risk (40)** (RHarris) **3-8-9**(5) MissHWebster(8) (chsd ldrs over 4f out: sn wknd & eased: t.o)	12	**16**	33/1	—	—
				(SP 146.1%)	**16 Rn**	

1m 30.1 (3.60) CSF £208.14 CT £870.71 TOTE £28.00: £5.60 £2.60 £1.90 £3.50 (£153.40) Trio £227.90 OWNER Mr R. E. Peacock (MALMESBURY) BRED Mellon Stud
LONG HANDICAP Muara Bay 8-12 Maurangi 8-13 Emma's Risk 8-9
WEIGHT FOR AGE 3yo-10lb
490 Dream Carrier (IRE) was a standing dish around here a few years ago, and he obviously has not forgotten where the winning post is, for he drew right away inside the distance to supply his jockey with her first ever success. (16/1)
429 Mustang tried his hardest to make all, but the winner kept him company, and with a lack of a recent run taking its toll, he was forced to give best soon after entering the final quarter-mile. He could be worth keeping in mind from now on. (12/1)
1756 Muara Bay struggled with the pace on this return to a shorter trip, and despite staying on, could not muster the speed to get involved. (4/1: 3/1-9/2)
972 Awesome Venture made his run up the inside rail once in line for home, but he was unable to summon the pace to threaten the leading pair. (25/1)
1089 Lochon enjoyed a smooth run up the inside to press the leaders, but lack of stamina caught him out early in the straight, and he could do little more than gallop on the spot. (16/1)
1575 Dancing Sioux attracted market support, but he failed to fire at all, and his finishing position was as close as he could manage. (5/1)
1289* Sweet Mate raced too freely in the early stages, and with nothing in reserve for a final battle, dropped away tamely as lack of stamina proved his undoing. (8/1)
870 Montone (IRE) (14/1: op 8/1)
1575 Desert Invader (IRE) (9/2: 4/1-6/1)
306* Agent (14/1: op 8/1)

T/Plpt: £8.30 (1200.41 Tckts). T/Qdpt: £7.50 (63.89 Tckts) IM

1170-YORK (L-H) (Good to soft)
Friday June 13th
WEATHER: sunny periods WIND: moderate half behind

1945 UNIVERSITY OF YORK NOVICE STKS (2-Y.O F) (Class D)
2-10 (2-12) **6f** £5,238.75 (£1,560.00: £742.50: £333.75) Stalls: High GOING: 0.30 sec per fur (G)

				SP	RR	SF
1440*	**Sapphire Ring** (RCharlton) **2-9-0** KDarley(4) (lw: trckd ldrs: swtchd over 1f out: led ins fnl f: edgd rt: r.o wl)	—	**1**	5/2^{2}	93+	64
1619*	**Lady In Waiting** (PFICole) **2-9-0** TQuinn(1) (w ldrs: led & qcknd over 1f out: hdd ins fnl f: r.o)	½	**2**	evens^{1}	92	63
1407*	**Sea Magic (IRE)** (BWHills) **2-9-0** WRyan(2) (w ldrs: rdn 2f out: not qckn fnl f)	6	**3**	6/1	76	47

				SP	RR	SF
1386*	**Saffron Lane (IRE)** (RHannon) **2-9-0** RPerham(3) (cl up: led ½-wy tl appr fnl f: sn outpcd)	3½	**4**	9/2[3]	66	37
1675[7]	**Malozza** (PDEvans) **2-8-10** ACulhane(5) (swtg: led to ½-wy: sn rdn & btn)	18	**5**	14/1	14	—

(SP 117.7%) **5 Rn**

1m 14.69 (4.19) CSF £5.36 TOTE £3.40: £1.60 £1.30 (£1.90) OWNER The Thoroughbred Corporation (BECKHAMPTON) BRED Mrs Mary Taylor

1440* Sapphire Ring travelled on the bridle, and won really well despite showing signs of inexperience, and better now looks likely. (5/2)

1619* Lady In Waiting was very much on her toes, and sweating slightly in the preliminaries, but she did show a really good action on the way to post. She put up a good effort in the race, but had to admit she had met one too good late on. Nevertheless. she ought to find further success. (evens)

1407* Sea Magic (IRE), who won an iffy contest last time, ran quite well here until the tap was really turned on approaching the final furlong. (6/1)

1386* Saffron Lane (IRE) had her limitations exposed here, and seems to have her problems. (9/2)

1675 Malozza, who was wearing a tongue-strap, looked very lean and was sweating and ran badly. (14/1: 10/1-16/1)

1946 MARKETING WEEK H'CAP (0-100) (3-Y.O+) (Class C)

2-40 (2-40) **5f** £7,570.00 (£2,260.00: £1,080.00: £490.00) Stalls: High GOING: 0.30 sec per fur (G)

				SP	RR	SF
1835*	**Squire Corrie (78)** (DWChapman) **5-8-11**(3) 7x PFessey(11) (chsd ldrs: led 1½f out: styd on wl)	—	**1**	13/2[3]	90	73
1608[4]	**Crofters Ceilidh (83)** (BAMcMahon) **5-9-5** KDarley(7) (chsd ldrs: chal 1½f out: kpt on u.p)	½	**2**	9/2[2]	93	76
1602[2]	**Lady Sheriff (77)** (MWEasterby) **6-8-8b**(5) GParkin(8) (b.nr hind: a chsng ldrs: kpt on fnl 2f: nvr able chal)	3	**3**	7/2[1]	78	61
1627[5]	**Swan At Whalley (65)** (RAFahey) **5-8-1** FNorton(4) (disp ld over 3f: kpt on one pce)	½	**4**	14/1	64	47
744[12]	**Tuscan Dawn (73)** (JBerry) **7-8-4**(5) PRoberts(6) (trckd ldrs: effrt 2f out: nt qckn)	2	**5**	12/1	66	49
1468[13]	**Swynford Dream (82)** (JFBottomley) **4-9-4** WRyan(1) (disp ld over 3f: wknd)	2	**6**	10/1	68	51
1608[7]	**Lago Di Varano (88)** (RMWhitaker) **5-9-10v** JCarroll(10) (outpcd & bhd: sme hdwy 2f out: n.d)	½	**7**	9/2[2]	73	56
1410[12]	**Osomental (87)** (DHaydnJones) **3-9-2** TQuinn(2) (sn drvn along & bhd)	2½	**8**	16/1	64	40
1799[14]	**Mallia (80)** (TDBarron) **4-9-2** JFortune(9) (a outpcd)	2½	**9**	9/1	49	32
	Rushcutter Bay (87) (TTClement) **4-9-4**(5) RMullen(5) (lw: nvr wnt pce)	2½	**10**	25/1	48	31
1034[7]	**Pride of Brixton (83)** (CWThornton) **4-9-5** DeanMcKeown(3) (a outpcd & bhd)	4	**11**	9/1	31	14

(SP 125.1%) **11 Rn**

60.67 secs (2.97) CSF £34.88 CT £112.85 TOTE £7.80: £2.50 £1.90 £1.50 (£20.80) Trio £13.10 OWNER Miss N. F. Thesiger (YORK) BRED Whitsbury Manor Stud

WEIGHT FOR AGE 3yo-7lb

1835* Squire Corrie is in the form of his life and, again poorly drawn, did the business well. (13/2)

1608 Crofters Ceilidh is running well, but she won last season with the blinkers on, and is yet to have them fitted this term. (9/2)

1602 Lady Sheriff could never quite get in a serious blow, despite struggling on, and probably found this testing ground just too much. (7/2)

1627 Swan At Whalley is now behaving himself at the start, and still possesses plenty of speed, which should bring its success. (14/1)

488 Tuscan Dawn ran well after almost two months off, and on ground slower than ideal. (12/1)

1158 Swynford Dream has done all his winning on a faster surface, and this was a decent effort. (10/1)

Mallia ran as though this trip was on the sharp side. (9/1)

Pride of Brixton (9/1: 6/1-10/1)

1947 SHEPHERD EBOR TRIAL RATED STKS H'CAP (0-100) (4-Y.O+) (Class B)

3-10 (3-10) **1m 5f 194y** £9,346.20 (£3,361.20: £1,605.60: £648.00: £249.00) Stalls: Low GOING: 0.70 sec per fur (GS)

				SP	RR	SF
1162[7]	**Purple Splash (88)** (PJMakin) **7-8-12v**(3) RHavlin(3) (hld up: smooth hdwy over 3f out: led wl over 1f out: pushed clr)	—	**1**	9/2[3]	101	79
1176[7]	**Brandon Magic (86)** (IABalding) **4-8-13** KDarley(1) (lw: trckd ldr: led 3f out tl wl over 1f out: no ch w wnr)	3½	**2**	5/1	95	73
1260[2]	**Thaljanah (IRE) (85)** (BSmart) **5-8-12** JFortune(4) (led tl hdd 3f out: sn outpcd)	4	**3**	3/1[2]	89	67
1319[5]	**Benatom (USA) (94)** (HRACecil) **4-9-7** WRyan(2) (trckd ldrs: effrt over 3f out: sn btn)	2½	**4**	6/4[1]	96	74
1478[3]	**Arctic Fancy (USA) (81)** (PWHarris) **4-8-8** TQuinn(5) (s.v.s: hdwy & in tch after 4f: outpcd fnl 4f)	nk	**5**	9/2[3]	82	60

(SP 118.0%) **5 Rn**

3m 6.87 (13.27) CSF £24.83 TOTE £6.80: £2.90 £2.00 (£16.30) OWNER Sir Christopher Walford (MARLBOROUGH) BRED W. and R. Barnett Ltd

1162 Purple Splash had the ground he loves, and stays particularly well, and that was all that was required here. (9/2)

1016 Brandon Magic looked superb, but was taking a big step up in trip, and after travelling well, was just outpointed in the last two furlongs. (5/1)

1260 Thaljanah (IRE), warm and edgy beforehand, proved disappointing once the pressure was on early in the straight. (3/1)

1319 Benatom (USA) did not impress in the paddock, and is probably better on faster ground, and was beaten a long way out here. (6/4)

1478 Arctic Fancy (USA) threw all chances away when giving the opposition a good twenty lengths' start. (9/2)

1948 ANTHONY FAWCETT MEMORIAL SPRINT RATED STKS H'CAP (0-100) (4-Y.O+) (Class B)

3-40 (3-41) **6f** £9,472.20 (£3,499.80: £1,674.90: £679.50: £264.75: £98.85) Stalls: High GOING: 0.30 sec per fur (G)

				SP	RR	SF
1402*	**Tedburrow (95)** (EJAlston) **5-9-2** ACulhane(8) (a gng wl: hdwy to ld 1f out: rdn & r.o wl)	—	**1**	9/2[3]	104	76
1317[3]	**Sea-Deer (86)** (CADwyer) **8-8-7** JFortune(10) (lw: hld up: hdwy ½-wy: chsd wnr fnl f: r.o)	2	**2**	100/30[2]	90	62
1303[3]	**Daawe (USA) (86)** (MrsVAAconley) **6-8-7** MDeering(5) (plld hrd: led after 2½f tl 1½f out: kpt on one pce)	3	**3**	12/1	82	54
1148[5]	**Double Splendour (IRE) (97)** (PSFelgate) **7-9-4** KDarley(2) (trckd ldrs: chal 2f out: sn rdn & nt qckn)	1¼	**4**	3/1[1]	89	61
946[6]	**Royal Mark (IRE) (86)** (TDBarron) **4-8-7** JCarroll(6) (hld up: hdwy 2f out: styd on towards fin)	hd	**5**	12/1	78	50
1824[6]	**Golden Pound (USA) (86)** (MissGayKelleway) **5-8-2**(5) RMullen(3) (b.hind: hld up: effrt over 2f out: sn rdn & nvr able chal)	nk	**6**	14/1	77	49
1303[5]	**Westcourt Magic (95)** (MWEasterby) **4-8-11**(5) GParkin(1) (led 2½f: lost pl ½-wy: kpt on fnl f)	2½	**7**	25/1	80	52
677[11]	**Madly Sharp (100)** (JWWatts) **6-9-7** TQuinn(9) (trckd ldrs: effrt 2f out: r.o one pce)	1	**8**	8/1	82	54
1148[11]	**Hoh Returns (IRE) (88)** (MBell) **4-8-9** MFenton(7) (lw: cl up tl wknd 1f out)	2½	**9**	14/1	63	35
1101[4]	**West Humble (94)** (LadyHerries) **4-9-1** WRyan(4) (spd to ½-wy: sn wl bhd)	30	**10**	5/1	—	—

(SP 126.6%) **10 Rn**

1m 14.0 (3.50) CSF £19.89 CT £165.33 TOTE £5.10: £1.90 £1.60 £2.80 (£8.00) Trio £43.50 OWNER Mr Philip Davies (PRESTON) BRED Lady Matthews

LONG HANDICAP Daawe (USA) 7-10 Golden Pound (USA) 8-4 Royal Mark (IRE) 8-6

OFFICIAL EXPLANATION **West Humble: bolted on the way to the start.**

1402* Tedburrow seems to have really improved this season and, always going best, won most emphatically. (9/2)

1317 Sea-Deer is running really well and deserves to find a race, and is probably better on a slightly faster surface. (100/30)

1303 Daawe (USA) looks in top form, and ran a smashing race from 11lb out of the handicap. (12/1)

1148 Double Splendour (IRE) keeps running well, but has yet to win off a mark as high as this. (3/1)
946 Royal Mark (IRE), from a yard that has yet to strike serious form, he put up a useful effort here over a trip probably just too sharp. (12/1)
Golden Pound (USA) never got into this, but left the impression that he is now coming to hand. (14/1)
1303 Westcourt Magic walked to post this time, then showed some of his old speed, and if he can be sorted out, the ability is still there. (25/1)
1101 West Humble spoiled any chances she had by bolting on the way to post. (5/1: 7/1-9/2)

1949 MARK NICHOLAS MEDIA LIMITED STKS (0-90) (3-Y.O) (Class C)
4-10 (4-11) **1m 3f 195y** £7,050.00 (£2,100.00: £1,000.00: £450.00) Stalls: Low GOING: 0.70 sec per fur (GS)

			SP	RR	SF
1372*	**Montfort (USA) (90)** (PFICole) **3-9-0** TQuinn(3) (lw: led: bit slipped: hdd after 2f: sn lost pl & rdn: hdwy 4f out: led 1½f out: styd on) —	**1**	5/6^{1}	98+	65
775^{4}	**Cybertechnology (88)** (BWHills) **3-8-12** WRyan(2) (trckd ldrs: led 3f out to 1½f out: no ex) 5	**2**	11/4^{2}	89	56
1612^{3}	**Sun Alert (USA) (78)** (MJPolglase) **3-8-9v^{1}** TGMcLaughlin(4) (cl up: rdn over 3f out: sn btn) 10	**3**	11/1	73	40
1242^{6}	**Iechyd-Da (IRE) (89)** (MBell) **3-8-12v^{1}** MFenton(1) (lw: mde most after 2f: hdd 3f out: sn rdn & btn) 20	**4**	7/2^{3}	49	16

(SP 111.8%) **4 Rn**

2m 41.01 (13.21) CSF £3.27 TOTE £1.70: (£1.70) OWNER Sir George Meyrick (WHATCOMBE) BRED Timothy J. Rooney
1372* Montfort (USA) looks an awkward customer, and just wanted to hang back towards the stables early on, causing his bit to slip right through his mouth, and he soon lost all interest in the race, but his rider worked a miracle, and persuaded him to run in the straight. He nevertheless looks one to be wary of. (5/6)
775 Cybertechnology, trying his longest trip to date, found that, combined with the energy-sapping ground, too much late on. (11/4)
1612 Sun Alert (USA) had plenty on here, and was in a visor for the first time, which seemed to have no effect. (11/1)
1242 Iechyd-Da (IRE) had a visor on for the first time, and looked particularly well, but once an effort was required, he soon decided it was not for him. (7/2: 5/2-4/1)

1950 RACING CHANNEL MEDIAN AUCTION MAIDEN STKS (3 & 4-Y.O) (Class E)
4-45 (4-45) **1m 3f 195y** £4,386.00 (£1,308.00: £624.00: £282.00) Stalls: Low GOING: 0.70 sec per fur (GS)

			SP	RR	SF
575^{3}	**Sandbaggedagain (74)** (MWEasterby) **3-8-4**(5) GParkin(3) (lw: a gng wl: led on bit ins fnl f: very cheekily) —	**1**	Evens^{1}	82+	43
1612^{5}	**Vicki Romara (78)** (MJohnston) **3-8-4** JFanning(1) (led: rdn over 2f out: hdd ins fnl f: no ch w wnr) ½	**2**	5/4^{2}	76	37
1497^{8}	**Spick And Span** (CWThornton) **3-8-9** DeanMcKeown(2) (trckd ldrs: effrt over 4f out: one pce) 15	**3**	12/1^{3}	61	22
1405^{5}	**Northern Maestro** (MrsMReveley) **3-8-9** ACulhane(4) (swtg: hld up & bhd: hdwy 4f out: wknd qckly over 4f out) dist	**4**	14/1	—	—

(SP 108.8%) **4 Rn**

2m 43.61 (15.81) CSF £2.32 TOTE £2.10: (£1.20) OWNER Mrs Christopher Hanbury (SHERIFF HUTTON) BRED Mrs A. Scott
575 Sandbaggedagain, taking a big step up in trip, at last did the business, and did it without coming off the bridle. This should have boosted his confidence. (Evens)
1612 Vicki Romara looked ultra-fit, and attempted to make her stamina tell, but the winner made her look very onepaced. (5/4: 4/5-6/4)
Spick And Span, an angular gelding, he looked very slow here once the pace picked up early in the straight. (12/1)
Northern Maestro failed to impress on looks, and ran as though something was wrong. (14/1)

T/Plpt: £84.70 (207.07 Tckts). T/Qdpt: £114.80 (4.51 Tckts) AA

1563-BATH (L-H) (Good to firm)
Saturday June 14th
WEATHER: overcast WIND: slt across

1951 JUNE CLAIMING STKS (3-Y.O+) (Class F)
2-00 (2-02) **1m 2f 46y** £2,570.00 (£720.00: £350.00) Stalls: Low GOING minus 0.51 sec per fur (F)

			SP	RR	SF
1323^{10}	**Brighstone (89)** (DRCElsworth) **4-10-0** AMcGlone(3) (mde all: r.o wl) —	**1**	9/2^{2}	78	50
1592^{8}	**White Plains (IRE) (78)** (MCPipe) **4-10-0** RHughes(4) (a.p: chsd wnr fnl 2f: hrd rdn: no imp) 2½	**2**	8/15^{1}	74	46
1825^{13}	**Racing Hawk (USA) (43)** (MSSaunders) **5-9-4** RPrice(9) (bhd tl hdwy over 1f out: nvr nrr) 10	**3**	20/1	48	20
	Northern Saga (IRE) (37) (CJDrewe) **4-9-4** TSprake(7) (lw: bhd tl hdwy 3f out: one pce fnl 2f) nk	**4**	33/1	48	20
1426^{4}	**Warrior King (IRE) (46)** (MrsPNDutfield) **3-8-1**(3) AWhelan(12) (s.s: bhd tl gd hdwy fnl f: nrst fin) 1¼	**5**	11/1^{3}	45	4
1567^{8}	**Naburn Loch (38)** (DMHyde) **7-8-6**(3) RHavlin(10) (prom tl wknd 2f out) hd	**6**	50/1	37	9
	Sans Pere (NMBabbage) **4-9-0** FNorton(8) (sme hdwy over 3f out: sn rdn: one pce fnl 2f) 1½	**7**	33/1	40	12
1463^{18}	**Eric's Bett (58)** (PGMurphy) **4-9-6** JLowe(6) (prom: rdn 3f out: sn wknd) ½	**8**	16/1	45	17
1620^{16}	**Amnesty Bay (25)** (MDIUsher) **5-8-11** JMarshall(5) (bhd fnl 3f) ½	**9**	50/1	35	7
1576^{7}	**Scottish Park (44)** (MCPipe) **8-8-6**(3) MHenry(11) (a bhd) 2½	**10**	12/1	29	1
	Anotherone to Note (39) (AJChamberlain) **6-8-9**(5) JBramhill(1) (prom: rdn over 4f out: wknd over 2f out) 3½	**11**	50/1	29	1
1591^{8}	**Miss Mezzanine (35)** (EAWheeler) **3-7-7**(7) SCarson(2) (bhd fnl 3f) 3½	**12**	50/1	22	—

(SP 123.8%) **12 Rn**

2m 9.0 (2.50) CSF £6.53 TOTE £4.60: £1.50 £1.10 £4.80 (£2.00) Trio £40.30 OWNER Mrs C. M. Poland (WHITCOMBE) BRED Michael Poland
WEIGHT FOR AGE 3yo-13lb
Brighstone clmd EJLeigh £10,000, White Plains (IRE) clmd Miss RJPatman £10,000
Brighstone, bought out of Henry Cecil's yard for only 2,000 guineas after disappointing last season, was taking a big drop in class. He now goes to Martin Pipe and certainly has the physique to make a jumper. (9/2)
647* White Plains (IRE), back to his best trip, would have been 11lb better off with the winner in a handicap. (8/15)
Racing Hawk (USA) would have been getting over 36lb from the winner had this been a handicap. (20/1)
Northern Saga (IRE) was no less than three stone wrong with the winner based on official ratings. (33/1)
1426 Warrior King (IRE), another with an impossible task at the weights, found this trip inadequate. (11/1)
Naburn Loch was pulled up in a maiden point in April. (50/1)
Scottish Park (12/1: op 8/1)

1952 E.B.F. PUMP ROOM NOVICE STKS (2-Y.O) (Class D)
2-30 (2-33) **5f 11y** £3,181.00 (£958.00: £464.00: £217.00) Stalls: High GOING minus 0.24 sec per fur (GF)

			SP	RR	SF
1635^{2}	**Islamabad** (GLewis) **2-8-12** PaulEddery(2) (b.hind: a.p: chsd ldr over 2f out: led over 1f out: sn clr) —	**1**	5/6^{1}	90	35

				SP	RR	SF
1386[3]	**Gypsy Hill** (DHaydnJones) **2-8-11** SWhitworth(5) (s.s: hdwy wl over 1f out: no ch w wnr)	5	2	8/1[3]	73	18
	Monte Lemos (IRE) (RCharlton) **2-8-12** TSprake(1) (wl grwn: tk keen hold: hdwy over 2f out: chsd wnr over 1f out: edgd lft: one pce)	hd	3	13/8[2]	74	19
1829[6]	**Mister Bankes** (WGMTurner) **2-8-9**(7) DMcGaffin(3) (led over 3f: btn whn n.m.r on ins ins fnl f)	1½	4	14/1	73	18
1504[4]	**Persian Fortune** (WGMTurner) **2-8-4**(5) DSweeney(4) (chsd ldr: rdn 3f out: wknd over 1f out)	3½	5	50/1	55	—
				(SP 112.4%)		**5 Rn**

63.0 secs (2.50) CSF £7.84 TOTE £1.50: £1.20 £1.90 (£4.20) OWNER Mr A. A. Hussain (EPSOM) BRED M. G. T. Stokes
1635 Islamabad would have been heading for Royal Ascot had he not been beaten on his debut. (5/6)
1386 Gypsy Hill still managed to get up for second place, despite being tightened up on the rails near the finish. (8/1: 9/2-9/1)
Monte Lemos (IRE), a half-brother to Gone For A Burton and Secret Combe, disappointed, having reportedly been working well at home. (13/8)
1829 Mister Bankes continues to find things a lot more competitive than at the beginning of the season. (14/1: op 6/1)
1504 Persian Fortune found this a lot different to a seller on the sand at Southwell. (50/1)

1953 BARBARA KNIGHT'S 70TH BIRTHDAY H'CAP (0-80) (4-Y.O+) (Class D)
3-05 (3-05) **2m 1f 34y** £3,442.50 (£1,035.00: £500.00: £232.50) Stalls: High GOING minus 0.51 sec per fur (F)

				SP	RR	SF
1481[2]	**Russian Rose (IRE) (65)** (JARToller) **4-9-6** PaulEddery(7) (hld up: hdwy over 3f out: wnt 2nd over 2f out: hrd rdn to ld 1f out: r.o wl)	—	1	7/2[2]	76	34
1665[2]	**Matthias Mystique (57)** (MissBSanders) **4-8-12** TSprake(4) (hld up: stdy hdwy over 9f out: led 3f out to 1f out: one pce)	3½	2	4/1[3]	65	23
1654[3]	**Paradise Navy (68)** (CREgerton) **8-9-10b** RHughes(5) (lw: hld up: hmpd on ins over 4f out: hdwy over 3f out: rdn over 1f out: one pce)	1½	3	11/4[1]	74	33
1665[5]	**Coleridge (40)** (JJSheehan) **9-7-10b** NVarley(2) (chsd ldr 8f: hrd rdn to ld over 3f out: sn hdd: one pce)	nk	4	9/1	46	5
1636[14]	**Suitor (42)** (SDow) **4-7-11**ow1 FNorton(6) (hld up: hdwy to chse ldr over 9f out: wknd over 4f out)	4	5	20/1	44	1
	Chucklestone (40) (JSKing) **14-7-10** NAdams(1) (bit bkwd: prom tl wknd over 3f out)	1½	6	16/1	41	—
	Fairly Sharp (IRE) (68) (GraemeRoe) **4-9-9** MFenton(8) (led: hdd over 3f out: wknd over 2f out: t.o)	25	7	7/2[2]	46	4
				(SP 111.8%)		**7 Rn**

3m 48.2 (6.80) CSF £15.46 CT £38.02 TOTE £5.10: £2.50 £2.20 (£7.50) OWNER Ash Partnership (WHITSBURY) BRED Edward Keyes
LONG HANDICAP Suitor 7-9 Chucklestone 7-7 Coleridge 7-9
WEIGHT FOR AGE 4yo-1lb
1481 Russian Rose (IRE), down 5lb, was not found wanting on the stamina front over this longer trip. (7/2)
1665 Matthias Mystique, up 2lb, made a bid for glory once in line for home. (4/1)
1654 Paradise Navy, 3lb higher than the highest mark off which he has won, now has a record of just four wins from forty-nine starts, so he is usually one to oppose. (11/4)
1665 Coleridge responded to pressure, but his one pace was never enough. (9/1)
61 Suitor was reverting to a longer trip, having come down 6lb in the ratings on grass. (20/1)
Chucklestone never assumed his favourite front-running position. (16/1)

1954 CHARLCOMBE MAIDEN AUCTION STKS (2-Y.O) (Class E)
3-35 (3-37) **5f 11y** £2,917.75 (£877.00: £423.50: £196.75) Stalls: High GOING minus 0.24 sec per fur (GF)

				SP	RR	SF
1564[2]	**Petarga** (JARToller) **2-8-4** PaulEddery(10) (a.p: rdn over 1f out: led ins fnl f: r.o wl)	—	1	4/5[1]	72	26
850[7]	**Hoh Justice** (IABalding) **2-8-10** SWhitworth(7) (lw: chsd ldrs: outpcd over 2f out: rallied over 1f out: r.o wl ins fnl f)	1¼	2	11/2[2]	74	28
	Quakeress (IRE) (JohnBerry) **2-8-5** MFenton(2) (w'like: bkwd: led tl ins fnl f)	1	3	12/1	66	20
1812[19]	**Muja's Magic (IRE)** (KTIvory) **2-8-0** JLowe(12) (mid div: hdwy over 1f out: r.o)	½	4	25/1	59	13
1760[8]	**Alpen Wolf (IRE)** (WRMuir) **2-8-12** TSprake(4) (a.p: one pce fnl 2f)	s.h	5	7/1[3]	71	25
1593[8]	**Magical Dancer (IRE)** (MrsPNDutfield) **2-8-1**(3) AWhelan(8) (no hdwy fnl 2f)	1¼	6	20/1	59	13
	Kathies Pet (RJHodges) **2-7-10**(5)ow2 AmandaSanders(5) (w'like: bkwd: no hdwy fnl 2f)	1¼	7	40/1	52	4
1425[7]	**Regalo** (DMHyde) **2-8-3**(3)ow2 JDSmith(9) (w ldr: ev ch over 1f out: wknd fnl f)	s.h	8	20/1	57	9
	Praetorian Gold (RHannon) **2-8-1**(7) RSmith(6) (dwlt: a bhd)	s.h	9	10/1	59	13
	Dance To The Beat (MartynMeade) **2-8-1** FNorton(11) (w'like: s.s: a bhd)	1¾	10	20/1	46	—
1486[6]	**Blue Shadow** (RHannon) **2-8-10** RHughes(3) (prom over 3f out: eased whn btn fnl f)	hd	11	8/1	55	9
	Amiasapphire (RJHodges) **2-7-13** NVarley(1) (w'like: bit bkwd: swvd lft s: a bhd: t.o)	15	12	50/1	—	—
				(SP 133.9%)		**12 Rn**

63.1 secs (2.60) CSF £5.36 TOTE £2.00: £1.10 £1.90 £2.60 (£4.80) Trio £32.10 OWNER Mrs R. W. Gore-Andrews (WHITSBURY) BRED Lord Swaythling
1564 Petarga, back to the minimum distance, had no Ascot Cyclone to contend with this time. (4/5)
Hoh Justice is crying out for a longer trip. (11/2)
Quakeress (IRE) is a half-sister to five-furlong scorer Crissem, and a useful nine-furlong winner in Ireland. She will come on for the outing, and would not have to improve much to take a similar event. (12/1)
Muja's Magic (IRE), a half-sister to two winners abroad, fared much better than when making her debut in a big field at Windsor on Monday. (25/1)
1760 Alpen Wolf (IRE) had been tried over six last time. (7/1)
Praetorian Gold (10/1: op 5/1)

1955 BECKFORD TOWER H'CAP (0-85) (3-Y.O+) (Class D)
4-05 (4-06) **1m 5y** £3,488.00 (£1,049.00: £507.00: £236.00) Stalls: Low GOING minus 0.51 sec per fur (F)

				SP	RR	SF
1640[4]	**Confronter (55)** (SDow) **8-8-10**ow2 RHughes(8) (hld up: hdwy over 2f out: squeezed thro on ins to ld ins fnl f: r.o wl)	—	1	7/1	63	31
1568*	**Blue Imperial (FR) (63)** (JWHills) **3-8-4**(3) MHenry(6) (a.p: hrd rdn over 2f out: ev ch ins fnl f: r.o wl)	s.h	2	9/4[1]	71	30
1640*	**Sooty Tern (68)** (JMBradley) **10-9-2**(7) JFowle(2) (lw: chsd ldr: ev ch over 1f out: nt qckn ins fnl f)	1¼	3	6/1[3]	73	43
1739[14]	**Night Wink (USA) (73)** (GLMoore) **5-10-0** SWhitworth(9) (led tl ins fnl f)	½	4	12/1	77	47
1273*	**Vanborough Lad (41)** (MJBolton) **8-7-10** JLowe(4) (hld up & plld hrd: hdwy 2f out: n.m.r & swtchd rt over 1f out: r.o)	½	5	13/2	44	14
998[3]	**Jalb (IRE) (73)** (ACStewart) **3-9-3** PaulEddery(5) (hld up: rdn & swtchd rt over 1f out: no hdwy)	2	6	6/1[3]	72	31
1301[8]	**What Happened Was (76)** (MartynMeade) **3-9-6** FNorton(7) (lw: nvr nr to chal)	½	7	16/1	74	33

				SP	RR	SF
1632[18]	**Noeprob (USA) (55)** (RJHodges) **7-8-5**(5) AmandaSanders(3) (prom over 5f)	1¼	**8**	11/2[2]	51	21
1781[7]	**Silver Purse (63)** (APJones) **3-8-2**(5) DSweeney(1) (lw: bhd tl rdn & hdwy over 2f out: sn wknd)	4	**9**	9/1	51	10

(SP 124.1%) **9 Rn**

1m 40.4 (2.20) CSF £22.76 CT £97.70 TOTE £7.60: £2.00 £1.90 £1.70 (£14.40) Trio £16.50 OWNER Hatfield Ltd (EPSOM) BRED Hamilton Bloodstock (UK) Ltd

LONG HANDICAP Vanborough Lad 7-9

WEIGHT FOR AGE 3yo-11lb

1640 Confronter has steadily been coming down the handicap and just managed to hold on. (7/1)

1568* Blue Imperial (FR), up a further 5lb, did not try to make all this time, but lost nothing in defeat. (9/4)

1640* Sooty Tern had beaten the winner nearly three-and-a-half lengths at Brighton last time on 6lb better terms. (6/1)

291 Night Wink (USA), down to a mark lower than his two wins last summer, showed definite signs of a return to form. (12/1)

1273* Vanborough Lad, raised 3lb, was still just out of the handicap, and did not settle as well as his rider would have liked. (13/2: 9/2-7/1)

998 Jalb (IRE) had only come down a pound. (6/1)

1632 Noeprob (USA) (11/2: 7/2-6/1)

1956 BEDMINSTER LIMITED STKS (0-65) (3-Y.O) (Class F)

4-40 (4-41) **1m 3f 144y** £2,542.00 (£712.00: £346.00) Stalls: Low GOING minus 0.51 sec per fur (F)

				SP	RR	SF
1565*	**Sudest (IRE) (65)** (IABalding) **3-9-1** SWhitworth(5) (chsd ldr: led over 3f out: r.o wl)	—	**1**	3/1[2]	79	45
1747[7]	**Ludo (62)** (RHannon) **3-8-13** RHughes(3) (a.p: r.o one pce fnl 2f)	3½	**2**	5/1	72	38
1277[7]	**Stahr (62)** (HCandy) **3-8-11** NAdams(6) (hld up: hdwy 2f out: r.o ins fnl f)	1	**3**	12/1	69	35
1443[3]	**Farley Mount (65)** (LordHuntingdon) **3-8-11** TSprake(4) (hld up: rdn over 2f out: hdwy over 1f out: r.o)	¾	**4**	5/2[1]	68	34
1853[3]	**Eponine (65)** (MRChannon) **3-8-10** FNorton(8) (a.p: rdn over 3f out: one pce fnl 2f)	nk	**5**	100/30[3]	66	32
1612[4]	**Walkabout (62)** (BWHills) **3-8-11** PaulEddery(7) (led: hdd over 3f out: hrd rdn over 2f out: one pce)	hd	**6**	6/1	67	33
	Prairie Minstrel (USA) (64) (RDickin) **3-8-6**(5) DSweeney(2) (hld up & bhd: gd hdwy over 3f out: wknd over 2f out: t.o)	15	**7**	25/1	47	13
1756[16]	**Mr Music (46)** (KMcAuliffe) **3-8-8**(3) MHenry(1) (rdn over 6f out: dropped rr 4f out: t.o whn eased 2f out)	dist	**8**	33/1	—	—

(SP 122.1%) **8 Rn**

2m 28.6 (1.90) CSF £18.17 TOTE £4.70: £1.50 £1.80 £2.40 (£8.60) OWNER Robert & Elizabeth Hitchins (KINGSCLERE) BRED Airlie Stud

1565* Sudest (IRE), dropping back in trip, sensibly threw down the gauntlet entering the home straight. (3/1)

1624* Ludo, stepping-up in distance, had been given a short break after three quick races. (5/1)

Stahr did better over this longer distance. (12/1)

1443 Farley Mount is another who benefited from a step-up in trip. (5/2)

1853 Eponine, making a quick reappearance, was coming back from a mile and three-quarters. (100/30)

1612 Walkabout was taking a big drop in grade, but still found lack of a turn of foot a problem. (6/1: 3/1-13/2)

1957 LEVY BOARD H'CAP (0-85) (3-Y.O+) (Class D)

5-10 (5-11) **5f 161y** £3,624.50 (£1,091.00: £528.00: £246.50) Stalls: High GOING minus 0.24 sec per fur (GF)

				SP	RR	SF
1468[5]	**Spender (76)** (PWHarris) **8-9-7**(3) MHenry(6) (lw: a.p: led over 1f out: drvn out)	—	**1**	10/1	85	60
541[3]	**Gi La High (63)** (MartynMeade) **4-8-11** FNorton(9) (rdn 3f out: hdwy over 1f out: fin wl)	nk	**2**	8/1	71	46
1848[7]	**Ned's Bonanza (52)** (MDods) **8-8-0** PaulEddery(3) (lw: hld up: rdn over 2f out: hdwy over 1f out: ev ch ins fnl f: nt qckn)	½	**3**	15/8[1]	59	34
1578[9]	**Just Loui (78)** (WGMTurner) **3-8-13**(5) DSweeney(4) (lw: a.p: one pce fnl f)	1¼	**4**	14/1	81	48
1402[10]	**Lord Sky (50)** (ABailey) **6-7-12** NAdams(1) (led tl hdd over 1f out: one pce)	½	**5**	12/1	52	27
1594[5]	**Kildee Lad (74)** (APJones) **7-9-5**(3) JDSmith(5) (hld up: hdwy over 1f out: one pce fnl f)	hd	**6**	5/1[3]	76	51
1225[6]	**Meranti (53)** (JMBradley) **4-7-8**(7) JFowle(2) (lw: stdd s: nvr trbld ldrs)	1¼	**7**	10/1	51	26
1814[2]	**Mindrace (55)** (KTIvory) **4-8-3v** DBiggs(8) (lw: chsd ldr tl rdn & wknd over 2f out)	7	**8**	4/1[2]	34	9
1410[9]	**Depreciate (76)** (CJames) **4-9-10** RHughes(7) (a bhd)	5	**9**	20/1	41	16

(SP 119.9%) **9 Rn**

1m 11.4 (1.90) CSF £82.06 CT £199.76 TOTE £9.20: £2.00 £2.20 £1.20 (£28.70) Trio £43.30 OWNER The Entrepreneurs (BERKHAMSTED) BRED The Mount Coote Partnership

WEIGHT FOR AGE 3yo-8lb

1468 Spender had shown signs of a return to form at Redcar, having found the ground too soft here the time before. (10/1)

541 Gi La High, up 3lb, was coming back after a rest, and again found the post arriving too soon. (8/1)

1848 Ned's Bonanza had no excuses this time, and could never quite manage to poke his head in front. (15/8)

1107 Just Loui was 2lb lower than when fourth at Lingfield. (14/1: op 7/1)

1037 Lord Sky was back on faster ground. (12/1)

1594 Kildee Lad was 2lb lower than when winning here last July. (5/1: 7/2-11/2)

T/Plpt: £13.30 (866.62 Tckts). T/Qdpt: £7.70 (67.96 Tckts) KH

1619-LEICESTER (R-H) (Good, Good to soft patches)

Saturday June 14th

WEATHER: overcast WIND: slight half against

1958 SPORTING BLUE H'CAP (0-80) (3-Y.O) (Class D)

6-45 (6-55) **7f 9y** £4,370.00 (£1,310.00: £630.00: £290.00) Stalls: High GOING: 0.05 sec per fur (G)

				SP	RR	SF
1170[18]	**Pericles (70)** (MJohnston) **3-8-11** JWeaver(3) (trckd ldrs stands' side: rdn to ld wl ins fnl f: r.o)	—	**1**	20/1	80	39
1256[7]	**Pet Express (57)** (PCHaslam) **3-7-5**(7) RWinston(6) (a.p stands' side: led over 1f out tl wl ins fnl f)	½	**2**	20/1	66	25
1005[11]	**With A Will (59)** (HCandy) **3-7-7**(7) NicolaWright(7) (w ldr stands' side: ev ch fnl f: unable qckn)	½	**3**	20/1	67	26
1691[3]	**Song Mist (IRE) (72)** (PFICole) **3-8-13** TQuinn(4) (chsd ldrs stands' side: kpt on u.p ins fnl f: nt pce to chal)	3½	**4**	6/1[2]	72	31
1589[6]	**Cherokee Flight (66)** (SMellor) **3-8-7** JFEgan(14) (led far side after 4f tl rdn & one pce appr fnl f)	¾	**5**	16/1	64	23
	Silca Key Silca (78) (MRChannon) **3-9-5** JFortune(10) (still unf: in tch: effrt over 2f out: wknd appr fnl f)	2½	**6**	20/1	70	29
864[14]	**Mysterium (56)** (NPLittmoden) **3-7-6**(5)ow1 RMullen(5) (prom stands' side over 5f)	2½	**7**	50/1	43	1
1302*	**Raaha (76)** (RWArmstrong) **3-9-3** RPrice(9) (prom 3f: sn drvn along: bhd fr ½-wy)	2½	**8**	3/1[1]	57	16

				SP	RR	SF
1691[8]	**Supreme Maimoon (68)** (MJPolglase) **3-8-9** TGMcLaughlin(15) (in tch: effrt over 3f out: grad wknd)	nk	**9**	33/1	48	7
1238[5]	**Al Masroor (USA) (72)** (JWPayne) **3-8-13** AMcGlone(17) (lw: nvr trbld ldrs)	4	**10**	11/1	43	2
1754[8]	**Carlton (IRE) (62)** (GLewis) **3-8-3** NDay(12) (a bhd)	2	**11**	14/1	29	—
990[11]	**Bubbly (73)** (JLDunlop) **3-9-0** KDarley(13) (chsd ldrs: rdn & wknd 3f out)	nk	**12**	8/1[3]	39	—
1589[9]	**Indian Blaze (65)** (PWHarris) **3-7-13**(7) CLowther(11) (led 4f: wknd over 2f out)	1¾	**13**	16/1	27	—
1589[5]	**Secret Combe (IRE) (80)** (PJMakin) **3-9-4**(3) RHavlin(8) (chsd ldrs far side: rdn wl over 2f out: sn btn)	s.h	**14**	10/1	42	1
1746*	**Big Ben (73)** (RHannon) **3-9-0** DaneO'Neill(16) (trckd ldrs far side 4f: sn lost tch)	s.h	**15**	6/1[2]	35	—
1568[7]	***Swan Island (61)*** (BPalling) **3-8-2b[1]** SDrowne(2) (Withdrawn not under Starter's orders: unruly in stalls)		**W**	14/1	—	—
1170[13]	***Halowing (USA) (77)*** (JGSmyth-Osbourne) **3-9-4** KFallon(1) (Withdrawn not under Starter's orders: broke loose bef s)		**W**	12/1	—	—
				(SP 138.8%)	**15 Rn**	

1m 27.6 (5.00) CSF £324.34 CT £3,887.15 TOTE £38.10: £8.20 £4.10 £13.90 (£174.70) Trio Not won; £273.68 to 16/6/97 OWNER Mr David Abell (MIDDLEHAM) BRED Elsdon Farms
LONG HANDICAP Mysterium 7-5
OFFICIAL EXPLANATION **Raaha: rider reported that the filly never travelled down the hill and might have been unsettled by the delay at the start.**
IN-FOCUS: **Five horses raced on the stands side and the first four were amongst that five.**
Pericles, in no hurry to take on the leaders, responded willingly when sent about his work and, forging through to lead inside the final furlong, won a shade easier than the margin would suggest. (20/1)
372 Pet Express, one of five to race on the stands' side, kicked for home below the distance and battled on gamely when challenged, but the winner proved that bit stronger. (20/1)
With A Will turned in his best performance yet and was only lacking a turn of finishing speed inside the final hundred yards. Now that he is coming to himself, he is worth keeping in mind. (20/1)
1691 Song Mist (IRE) is yet to prove she stays seven furlongs. She rallied inside the distance but she was under pressure to do so, and her lack of pace was evident. (6/1)
1589 Cherokee Flight had more use made of him and he won the race on the far side, but the principals had the race to themselves inside the distance. (16/1)
Silca Key Silca is a badly handicapped filly with only a maiden success to her name, but she ran with credit on this belated seasonal debut and she does seem to have trained on. (20/1)
1302* Raaha opened her account in a poor maiden at Beverley last month, but she looked very lacklustre in herself and her coat, and never really fired. (3/1)
606* Bubbly (8/1: 6/1-10/1)

1959 TIPSTERS TABLE NOVICE MEDIAN AUCTION STKS (2-Y.O) (Class F)
7-15 (7-18) **5f 2y** £2,532.00 (£702.00: £336.00) Stalls: High GOING: 0.05 sec per fur (G)

				SP	RR	SF
1425[4]	**Magic Rainbow** (MBell) **2-8-12** MFenton(1) (swvd lft s: hdwy ½-wy: rdn over 1f out: r.o to ld wl ins fnl f)	—	**1**	85/40[1]	76	10
1614*	**Pierpoint (IRE)** (RAFahey) **2-8-9**(7) RWinston(7) (hdwy wl over 1f out: kpt on u.p ins fnl f)	¾	**2**	13/2	78	12
1161[4]	**Ruzen (IRE)** (BPalling) **2-9-2** TSprake(5) (led & sn clr: rdn & hdd wl ins fnl f)	½	**3**	5/2[2]	76	10
1425[9]	**Desert Native** (RHannon) **2-8-7** DaneO'Neill(6) (sn wl outpcd: effrt over 1f out: nvr nrr)	3½	**4**	11/2	56	—
	Bound To Please (PJMakin) **2-8-12** TQuinn(3) (w'like: scope: bit bkwd: hmpd s: sn chsng ldrs: rdn & wknd over 1f out)	1¼	**5**	4/1[3]	57	—
1480[6]	**Impulse (IRE)** (APJarvis) **2-8-12** KDarley(4) (lw: swvd lft s: sn chsng ldrs: rdn along ½-wy: wknd wl over 1f out)	hd	**6**	10/1	57	—
	God Knows (IRE) (MJFetherston-Godley) **2-8-7** JQuinn(2) (w'like: bkwd: b: sn outpcd: a bhd: t.o)	18	**7**	20/1	—	—
				(SP 123.1%)	**7 Rn**	

63.9 secs (5.40) CSF £16.79 TOTE £3.30: £1.70 £1.90 (£3.90) OWNER Mr P. T. Fenwick (NEWMARKET) BRED R. T. and Mrs Watson
1425 Magic Rainbow again forfeited ground at the start, but he knew more this time and stayed on steadily to gain command nearing the finish. (85/40)
1614* Pierpoint (IRE), set alight inside the last quarter-mile, stuck to his task in the closing stages, but the winner had the legs of him. (13/2)
1161 Ruzen (IRE), very much on his toes and back in his own class, attempted to run his rivals off their legs and, for most of the way, did just that. However, his stride shortened in the final hundred yards and he was worn down close home. (5/2)
Bound To Please, impeded leaving the stalls, was soon bustled along to chase the leaders, but lack of peak condition began to tell approaching the final furlong. (4/1)
1480 Impulse (IRE), hoping for a change of fortune on this return to the minimum trip, swerved violently left as the stalls opened and, soon at full stretch, failed to make any impression. (10/1)

1960 LEICESTER MERCURY STKS (Listed) (4-Y.O+) (Class A)
7-45 (7-46) **1m 3f 183y** £10,441.00 (£3,766.00: £1,808.00: £740.00: £295.00) Stalls: High GOING: 0.05 sec per fur (G)

				SP	RR	SF
1454[3]	**Eva Luna (USA) (111)** (HRACecil) **5-8-13** KFallon(4) (lw: chsd ldr: racd centre st: led 3f out: sn rdn: drew clr appr fnl f)	—	**1**	9/4[2]	123	65
1490[4]	**River North (IRE) (99)** (LadyHerries) **7-8-12** JReid(5) (b: bit bkwd: chsd ldrs: rdn & outpcd over 2f out: styd on fnl f: no ch w wnr)	9	**2**	20/1	110	52
	Sharaf Kabeer (106) (SbinSuroor) **4-9-1** LDettori(2) (bkwd: led to 3f out: rdn over 1f out: kpt on)	hd	**3**	5/1	113	55
1172[6]	**Key to My Heart (IRE) (110)** (MissSEHall) **7-9-1** JWeaver(3) (lw: hld up: brought centre to chse wnr st: rdn wl over 1f out: one pce)	nk	**4**	11/4[3]	112	54
1323[3]	**Medaille Militaire (109)** (JLDunlop) **5-9-1** KDarley(1) (hld up & bhd: hdwy over 3f out: rdn & btn 2f out)	1¼	**5**	15/8[1]	111	53
				(SP 113.6%)	**5 Rn**	

2m 33.8 (5.30) CSF £32.42 TOTE £2.90: £1.40 £3.40 (£32.70) OWNER Mr K. Abdulla (NEWMARKET) BRED Juddmonte Farms
OFFICIAL EXPLANATION **Medaille Militaire: no explanation offerd.**
1454 Eva Luna (USA) was back to something like her best, but she had to work to put her stamp on proceedings, before storming clear impressively. This trip is as short as she needs. (9/4)
1490 River North (IRE), still not the finished article as far as fitness is concerned, was in serious trouble over two furlongs out but, with stamina coming into play, was able to gain the runner-up spot close home. He should continue to progress. (20/1)
Sharaf Kabeer was the most backward of the field on this return to action, but he forced the pace, and was only really shaken off entering the last furlong. A winner over fourteen furlongs, he can soon regain winning ways. (5/1)

1172 Key to My Heart (IRE) followed the winner down the centre of the track from the turn into the straight, but he was being made to work entering the final quarter-mile and failed to pick up sufficiently to pose a serious threat. (11/4)
1323 Medaille Militaire looked very hard-trained and edgy in the preliminaries and his effort to get himself into the action in the straight was very short-lived and, in truth, he was never a factor. Unless something was amiss, this was very much an off-day. (15/8)

1961 PROPERTY GUIDE MEDIAN AUCTION MAIDEN STKS (2-Y.O) (Class D)
8-15 (8-17) **5f 218y** £3,392.00 (£1,016.00: £488.00: £224.00) Stalls: High GOING: 0.05 sec per fur (G)

				SP	RR	SF
1120[3]	**Sweet Reward** (JGSmyth-Osbourne) **2-9-0** KFallon(6) (sn drvn along: hdwy over 2f out: led ent fnl f: pushed clr)	—	**1**	8/1	72	30
	Bold King (JWHills) **2-9-0** MHills(9) (w'like: leggy: s.s: hdwy 2f out: r.o wl fnl f: impr)	3	**2**	12/1	64+	22
	Montano (USA) (PFICole) **2-9-0** TQuinn(8) (w'like: scope: led tl hdd 1f out: r.o one pce)	2½	**3**	4/1[2]	57	15
1480[7]	**Red Maple (USA)** (PFICole) **2-9-0** JFortune(5) (in tch: hdwy 2f out: kpt on ins fnl f)	s.h	**4**	14/1	57	15
	Smart Beau (USA) (RCharlton) **2-9-0** JReid(4) (gd sort: bkwd: dwlt: sn pushed along: nvr nr to chal)	3	**5**	9/2[3]	49	7
1240[5]	**Face-Off** (RHannon) **2-8-9** DaneO'Neill(3) (prom tl rdn & wknd wl over 1f out)	nk	**6**	8/1	43	1
	Refined (IRE) (LMCumani) **2-8-9** LDettori(1) (w'like: scope: bkwd: prom: ev ch 3f out: wknd fnl 2f: t.o)	11	**7**	2/1[1]	14	—
1330[9]	**Blue Anchor** (MrsMReveley) **2-9-0** ACulhane(7) (bit bkwd: a outpcd: t.o)	1½	**8**	50/1	15	—
1286[7]	**Lawful Contract (IRE)** (RHollinshead) **2-9-0** FLynch(10) (prom tl wknd qckly 2f out: t.o)	9	**9**	50/1	—	—
	Khattaff (IRE) (MajorWRHern) **2-9-0** RHills(2) (cmpt: bkwd: prom: hrd rdn & wknd over 2f out: t.o)	2½	**10**	9/1	—	—

(SP 122.0%) **10 Rn**

1m 15.1 (5.10) CSF £94.65 TOTE £8.20: £1.80 £3.20 £1.90 (£51.00) Trio Not won; £144.45 to 16/6/97 OWNER Mr C. S. Tateson (TOWCESTER) BRED C. S. Tateson
1120 Sweet Reward had the longer trip that he needs, and came into his own on meeting the rising ground, after struggling and looking anything but a winner for most of the way. (8/1)
Bold King made a promising racecourse debut after walking out of the stalls, and he should be a different proposition when he tackles a longer trip. (12/1)
Montano (USA), very keen to post, was allowed to tow his rivals along but, on this more yielding ground, he was at the end of his tether when collared. He looks the type to benefit from a faster surface. (4/1)
1263 Red Maple (USA), bred to need further, was staying on promisingly in the latter stages and he looks to have the ability to win races. (14/1)
Smart Beau (USA), an attractive colt who can only improve for the run, was always having trouble with the pace and a longer trip could be the answer. (9/2)
1240 Face-Off pushed the pace and looked a threat, until she beat a retreat under pressure from below the distance. (8/1)
Refined (IRE), a late foal who is a half-sister to winners, was too backward to do herself justice and, after sharing the lead three furlongs out, gradually faded and came home in her own time. (2/1)
Khattaff (IRE) (9/1: 5/1-10/1)

1962 SPORTS MERCURY CONDITIONS STKS (3-Y.O) (Class C)
8-45 (8-46) **1m 3f 183y** £4,726.60 (£1,749.40: £839.70: £343.50: £136.75: £54.05) Stalls: High GOING: 0.05 sec per fur (G)

				SP	RR	SF
1015[4]	**Ghataas (103)** (JLDunlop) **3-9-0** RHills(6) (lw: plld hrd: hld up: hdwy over 2f out: led over 1f out: r.o strly)	—	**1**	100/30[3]	105	39
1146[3]	**Blue River (IRE) (95)** (TGMills) **3-9-0** LDettori(5) (lw: led tl hdd over 1f out: nt pce of wnr fnl f)	2	**2**	9/4[1]	102	36
1762[2]	**Yorkshire (IRE)** (PFICole) **3-9-0** TQuinn(2) (a.p: chal appr fnl f: sn rdn: unable qckn)	¾	**3**	5/2[2]	101	35
1271*	**Darcy** (MRStoute) **3-9-0** KDarley(7) (s.i.s: sn chsng ldrs: rdn & btn wl over 1f out)	1¾	**4**	6/1	99	33
1277*	**River Pilot** (RCharlton) **3-9-0** TSprake(3) (hld up: hdwy ent st: rdn 2f out: sn btn)	2	**5**	8/1	96	30
	Sheer Folly (USA) (PFICole) **3-9-0** JReid(4) (stdd s: effrt & rdn 3f out: no rspnse: t.o)	dist	**6**	14/1	—	—

(SP 114.5%) **6 Rn**

2m 37.9 (9.40) CSF £10.57 TOTE £6.20: £2.20 £1.40 (£6.60) OWNER Mr Hamdan Al Maktoum (ARUNDEL) BRED Shadwell Estate Company Limited
1015 Ghataas, taking a keen tug, was anchored off the pace. He got the better of a set-to to nose ahead approaching the final furlong and, finding extra, forged clear for a comfortable success. (100/30)
1146 Blue River (IRE), a most fluent mover who looked on good terms with himself, did not quite last home on his first attempt at the trip. However, he was pitted against some high-class rivals, and the company may have been too strong. (9/4)
1762 Yorkshire (IRE) settled slightly better over this longer trip, but he was still keen to get on with it and, though he ranged upsides on the run to the final furlong, was found wanting in the race to the finish. Once he gets his act together, he could be as good as his breeding suggests he should be. (5/2)
1271* Darcy, upped in grade over this much longer trip, was throwing out distress signals entering the last quarter-mile and, though he was not beaten far in the end, the company more than the trip could have been the problem. (6/1)
1277* River Pilot moved up smoothly once in line for home and soon had every chance but, when the pace lifted over two furlongs out, he had to admit that, at this stage of his career, he was not up to it. (8/1)

1963 MERCURY RACE NIGHT H'CAP (0-70) (3-Y.O+ F & M) (Class E)
9-15 (9-17) **5f 218y** £3,119.00 (£932.00: £446.00: £203.00) Stalls: High GOING: 0.05 sec per fur (G)

				SP	RR	SF
1446[4]	**Faith Alone (61)** (CFWall) **4-9-5** GDuffield(11) (b: trckd ldrs: led over 1f out: pushed out)	—	**1**	3/1[1]	69	60
1857[2]	**Prima Silk (70)** (MJRyan) **6-10-0** GCarter(14) (hld up: hdwy over 2f out: ev ch over 1f out: no ex fnl f)	1¼	**2**	5/1[2]	75	66
1730[3]	**Gold Edge (54)** (MRChannon) **3-8-4** JFEgan(6) (dwlt: hld up: hdwy 2f out: sn rdn: r.o fnl f)	1¼	**3**	13/2[3]	55	38
1680[5]	**Newlands Corner (59)** (JAkehurst) **4-9-3b** DBiggs(5) (s.i.s: hdwy over 2f out: kpt on u.p fnl f)	½	**4**	9/1	59	50
1680[6]	**Aquatic Queen (50)** (RJWeaver) **3-7-7**(7) RWinston(3) (b.hind: prom: rdn over 1f out: one pce)	s.h	**5**	16/1	50	33
1580[5]	**Patina (50)** (RHollinshead) **3-8-0** JQuinn(12) (lw: s.i.s: hdwy over 2f out: bmpd wl over 1f out: nt pce to chal)	¾	**6**	16/1	48	31
1620[10]	**Tymeera (51)** (BPalling) **4-8-9** TSprake(8) (lw: led 2f: rdn over 1f out: one pce)	¾	**7**	10/1	47	38
1439[3]	**Make Ready (63)** (JNeville) **3-8-13** JReid(7) (chsd ldrs: rdn wl over 1f out: no imp)	1¼	**8**	13/2[3]	56	39
1316[10]	**Senorita Matilda (USA) (70)** (RHannon) **3-9-6** DaneO'Neill(4) (lw: hld up: hdwy stands' side over 3f out: sn rdn: btn over 1f out)	1	**9**	7/1	60	43
1764[4]	**Dona Filipa (38)** (MissLCSiddall) **4-7-10** NCarlisle(1) (chsd ldrs: rdn along over 2f out: sn wknd)	hd	**10**	16/1	28	19
1681[3]	**Brin-Lodge (IRE) (38)** (KSBridgwater) **4-7-5b**[1](5) JBramhill(10) (b.hind: s.i.s: led after 2f tl over 1f out: sn wknd)	1¼	**11**	50/1	24	15
1865[8]	**L A Touch (49)** (JJQuinn) **4-8-7** JFortune(9) (prom 4f)	2½	**12**	16/1	29	20
1734[11]	**Madam Zando (39)** (JBalding) **4-7-11**ow1 DaleGibson(13) (lw: sn pushed along: a outpcd)	1½	**13**	33/1	15	5

				SP	RR	SF
889^{11}	**Silver Jubilee (55)** (BPalling) **3-7-12**(7)ow9 CLowther(2) (bit bkwd: s.s: sn rdn along: a bhd: t.o)	13	**14**	20/1	—	—
				(SP 133.1%)	**14 Rn**	

1m 13.3 (3.30) CSF £17.11 CT £93.57 TOTE £4.20: £2.00 £2.30 £2.70 (£12.80) Trio £37.30 OWNER Mrs R. M. S. Neave (NEWMARKET) BRED J. R. Mitchell
LONG HANDICAP Dona Filipa 7-6 Brin-Lodge (IRE) 7-0 Madam Zando 7-4 Silver Jubilee 7-4
WEIGHT FOR AGE 3yo-8lb
1446 Faith Alone, who is in-foal, returned to form with a readily-gained success and, if the ground remains on the easy side, there is no reason why she cannot follow up. (3/1)
1857 Prima Silk, having her second run in four days, responded to pressure to give herself every chance approaching the final furlong, before the winner proved too sharp. (5/1)
1730 Gold Edge is a trier who invariably makes the frame, and that elusive first success must be near at hand. (13/2)
1680 Newlands Corner won three races in August last season and she may be the type who finds her form at that time of year. (9/1: op 6/1)
1680 Aquatic Queen continues to run well and deserves to find an opening but, as yet, finding her correct trip seems to be the problem for her trainer. (16/1)
1580 Patina, last to exit from the stalls, did not enjoy a trouble-free passage when delivering her challenge, but she does seem to lack pace and this step down to sprinting may not necessarily be the answer. (16/1)

T/Plpt: £1,555.50 (8.95 Tckts). T/Qdpt: £32.70 (29.33 Tckts) IM

1593-**LINGFIELD (L-H) (Turf Good to firm, Good patches, AWT Standard)**
Saturday June 14th

WEATHER: overcast WIND: almost nil

1964 SETTER RATING RELATED MAIDEN APPRENTICE STKS (0-70) (3-Y.O+) (Class F)

6-00 (6-00) **2m (Equitrack)** £2,277.00 (£627.00: £297.00) Stalls: High GOING minus 0.50 sec per fur (FST)

				SP	RR	SF
1260^{5}	**Dark Waters (IRE) (70)** (NAGraham) **4-9-11** GMilligan(2) (mde all: rdn over 2f out: clr over 1f out: unchal)	—	**1**	100/30^{3}	63	28
1809^{5}	**Le Grand Gousier (USA) (56)** (RJRWilliams) **3-8-5** AimeeCook(8) (a.p: chsd wnr fnl 5f: rdn over 2f out: one pce)	5	**2**	3/1^{2}	58	3
1642^{7}	**Hazel (46)** (MissGayKelleway) **5-9-9** JoHunnam(1) (dwlt: sn rcvrd: hdwy over 3f out: rdn 2f out: kpt on one pce)	3	**3**	16/1	52	18
1665^{3}	**Duncombe Hall (38)** (CACyzer) **4-9-4**(7) RSawyer(6) (lw: chsd ldrs: rdn over 2f out: one pce)	1¼	**4**	5/2^{1}	54	19
986^{12}	**Greenwich Fore (66)** (TGMills) **3-8-0**(5) PClarke(5) (rr: rdn 5f out: nvr nrr)	2½	**5**	9/2	51	—
1779^{25}	**Gracious Imp (USA) (28)** (JRJenkins) **4-9-3**(5) SCarson(4) (in tch: rdn 4f out: sn wknd)	10	**6**	40/1	38	3
78^{6}	**Code Red (48)** (JFfitch-Heyes) **4-9-8**(3) MBatchelor(7) (lw: a bhd)	13	**7**	12/1	28	—
	Bright Sapphire (20) (PButler) **11-9-7**(5) TSiddall(3) (bit bkwd: in tch tl wknd 5f out)	7	**8**	33/1	21	—
				(SP 113.8%)	**8 Rn**	

3m 29.37 (8.37) CSF £12.41 TOTE £3.90: £1.40 £1.60 £2.20 (£10.90) OWNER Mr Brian March (NEWMARKET) BRED Ballymacoll Stud Farm Ltd
WEIGHT FOR AGE 3yo-21lb, 4yo-1lb
1260 Dark Waters (IRE), was given a very enterprising ride by his young jockey. Making all the running, he quickened turning for home, and soon had the race sown up. (100/30)
1809 Le Grand Gousier (USA) chased the winner from the top of the hill, but could not make any impression in the straight. (3/1)
417 Hazel was being pushed along some way from home, and could only plug on at the one speed. (16/1)
1665 Duncombe Hall tracked the leaders, but had little to give in the final three furlongs. (5/2)
Greenwich Fore (9/2: op 5/2)

1965 RETRIEVER (S) H'CAP (0-60) (3-Y.O+) (Class G)

6-30 (6-35) **7f** £1,984.50 (£547.00: £259.50) Stalls: High GOING minus 0.31 sec per fur (GF)

				SP	RR	SF
1483^{9}	**Abtaal (49)** (RJHodges) **7-9-3** RPerham(1) (swtchd stands' side: hld up: hdwy 2f out: hrd rdn ins fnl f: led last stride)	—	**1**	14/1	54	36
1642^{6}	**Silver Harrow (52)** (AGNewcombe) **4-9-3**(3) DGriffiths(18) (chsd ldrs: led over 1f out: hdd last stride)	s.h	**2**	10/1	57	39
1599^{10}	**Roy Boy (60)** (CAHorgan) **5-10-0** DHarrison(4) (led far side: ev ch ins fnl f: unable qckn)	1¼	**3**	33/1	62	44
1374^{8}	**Super Park (41)** (JPearce) **5-8-9** AClark(6) (mid div: hdwy 3f out: rdn appr fnl f: kpt on one pce)	nk	**4**	7/1	42	24
1501^{12}	**On The Green (40)** (AHide) **4-8-8v^{1}** GBardwell(15) (chsd ldrs: rdn over 1f out: one pce)	¾	**5**	33/1	40	22
1814^{8}	**Pearl Dawn (IRE) (49)** (PCClarke) **7-9-3** CandyMorris(3) (chsd ldr far side: rdn appr fnl f: one pce)	nk	**6**	20/1	48	30
997^{3}	**Bon Secret (IRE) (41)** (TJNaughton) **5-8-9** SSanders(7) (lw: hld up: rdn over 2f out: hdwy over 1f out: kpt on one pce ins fnl f)	hd	**7**	9/1	40	22
326^{7}	**Shashi (IRE) (60)** (PatMitchell) **5-10-0** PBloomfield(9) (nvr nrr)	hd	**8**	33/1	59	41
1620^{13}	**The Frisky Farmer (47)** (WGMTurner) **4-8-8**(7) DMcGaffin(16) (lw: prom: led over 2f out: hdd over 1f out: sn wknd)	1¼	**9**	14/1	43	25
1878^{11}	**Dancing Lawyer (55)** (BJMeehan) **6-9-9b^{1}** BDoyle(14) (chsd ldrs: rdn over 2f out: grad wknd)	1¼	**10**	9/2^{1}	48	30
1473^{10}	**Ki Chi Saga (USA) (50)** (MMadgwick) **5-9-4** NVarley(11) (dwlt: nvr nrr)	1½	**11**	20/1	39	21
1857^{7}	**Hannah's Usher (60)** (CMurray) **5-10-0** NicolaHowarth(5) (dwlt: hdwy 3f out: rdn 2f out: wknd appr fnl f)	hd	**12**	20/1	49	31
1676^{3}	**Superlao (BEL) (41)** (JJBridger) **5-8-4**(5) ADaly(12) (b.hind: chsd ldrs: rdn over 2f out: wknd wl over 1f out)	2½	**13**	16/1	24	6
1128^{11}	**Bagshot (49)** (GLMoore) **6-9-3v^{1}** CRutter(2) (racd far side: in tch to ½-wy)	1	**14**	11/1	30	12
1689^{5}	**Battle Ground (IRE) (50)** (NACallaghan) **3-8-8** MRoberts(13) (lw: chsd ldrs: rdn over 2f out: sn wknd)	1½	**15**	6/1^{2}	28	—
307^{7}	**Kayzee (IRE) (50)** (SDow) **3-8-8** WRyan(10) (a bhd)	7	**16**	14/1	12	—
319^{2}	**Blushing Grenadier (IRE) (47)** (MJFetherston-Godley) **5-9-1v** DHolland(17) (led: hdd over 2f out: sn wknd)	3	**17**	13/2^{3}	2	—
1639*	**Dark Menace (51)** (EAWheeler) **5-8-12b**(7) SCarson(8) (prom tl wknd over 2f out)	2	**18**	15/2	1	—
				(SP 146.5%)	**18 Rn**	

1m 24.31 (3.11) CSF £147.03 CT £4,294.52 TOTE £22.90: £6.20 £3.50 £5.00 £2.60 (£215.70) Trio Not won; £476.00 to 16/6/97 OWNER Mr P. Slade (SOMERTON)
WEIGHT FOR AGE 3yo-10lb
No bid
1483 Abtaal was given a very enterprising ride. Tacking over to the stands' side from stall one, he made good progress under pressure from below the distance, and got up in the shadow of the post. (14/1: 8/1-16/1)

Silver Harrow looked sure to win when taking it up below the distance, but had no answer to the winner's late thrust. (10/1)
Roy Boy led for the whole way on the far side, but could not quite live with the stands' side group in the final furlong. (33/1)
Super Park made his effort approaching the two pole, but could only plug on at one speed in the final furlong. (7/1)
1599 Dancing Lawyer, tried in blinkers for the first time, cried enough in the final two furlongs. (9/2)
578 Bagshot (11/1: 6/1-12/1)

1966 POINTER H'CAP (0-70) (3-Y.O F) (Class E)

7-00 (7-03) **7f** £3,252.25 (£973.00: £466.50: £213.25) Stalls: High GOING minus 0.31 sec per fur (GF)

				SP	RR	SF
1439[5]	**Tajrebah (USA) (67)** (PTWalwyn) **3-9-7** DHolland(12) (hld up: swtchd lft & hdwy over 2f out: led ins fnl f: r.o wl)	—	**1**	10/1	74	46
1661[6]	**Davis Rock (66)** (WRMuir) **3-9-6** MRoberts(9) (a.p: led over 2f out: hdd ins fnl f: unable qckn)	¾	**2**	10/1	71	43
1248*	**Viva Verdi (IRE) (65)** (JLDunlop) **3-9-5** WRyan(7) (lw: hld up: hdwy over 2f out: hrd rdn ins fnl f: unable qckn)	hd	**3**	3/1[2]	70	42
1781*	**Shalstayholy (IRE) (67)** (GLMoore) **3-9-7v** SWhitworth(10) (lw: a.p: ev ch ins fnl f: one pce)	nk	**4**	7/4[1]	71	43
1089[12]	**Polgwynne (51)** (BSmart) **3-8-0**(5) ADaly(2) (prom: ev ch ent fnl f: one pce)	¾	**5**	16/1	54	26
1651[3]	**Signs And Wonders (67)** (CACyzer) **3-9-4**(3) AWhelan(3) (hld up: hdwy over 1f out: rdn ins fnl f: one pce)	1	**6**	11/2[3]	67	39
1484[4]	**Keen Waters (42)** (JRArnold) **3-7-10** JLowe(1) (hld up: sme hdwy 2f out: rdn over 1f out: wknd fnl f)	2½	**7**	12/1	37	9
1690[6]	**Crackerbox (42)** (CADwyer) **3-7-3**(7) DarrenWilliams(5) (led: hdd over 2f out: sn wknd)	2½	**8**	33/1	31	3
1237[12]	**Kilmeena Lady (56)** (JCFox) **3-8-10** AClark(8) (a bhd)	1	**9**	50/1	43	15
1633[15]	**Java Bay (47)** (MBlanshard) **3-8-1** CRutter(4) (chsd ldrs: rdn over 2f out: wknd over 1f out)	1¼	**10**	33/1	31	3
320[5]	**Hever Golf Lover (IRE) (57)** (TJNaughton) **3-8-11** SSanders(11) (a bhd)	10	**11**	12/1	18	—
	Wrn Princess (55) (BJMeehan) **3-8-9** MTebbutt(6) (plld hrd: prom tl wknd over 2f out)	5	**12**	14/1	5	—

(SP 130.7%) **12 Rn**

1m 23.79 (2.59) CSF £105.29 CT £356.10 TOTE £12.10: £3.30 £2.10 £1.50 (£42.30) Trio £44.40 OWNER Mr Hamdan Al Maktoum (LAMBOURN) BRED Shadwell Farm Inc
LONG HANDICAP Keen Waters 7-8 Crackerbox 7-5
1439 Tajrebah (USA), produced with a well-timed challenge to lead inside the final furlong, won this with a little in hand. (10/1)
1661 Davis Rock was always to the fore, and ran a sound race, continuing the fine run of his trainer. (10/1)
1248* Viva Verdi (IRE) tracked the leaders. She came under pressure from below the distance and, although staying on, could not find the necessary change of pace. (3/1)
1781* Shalstayholy (IRE), raised 7lb for her win last Saturday, found this weighing her down in the final furlong. (7/4)
1484 Keen Waters (12/1: 8/1-14/1)
320 Hever Golf Lover (IRE) (12/1: 9/1-14/1)
Wrn Princess (14/1: 8/1-16/1)

1967 KAY AND CHARLIE PIKE 50TH ANNIVERSARY MAIDEN STKS (3-Y.O+) (Class D)

7-30 (7-33) **6f** £3,773.00 (£1,127.00: £539.00: £245.00) Stalls: High GOING minus 0.31 sec per fur (GF)

				SP	RR	SF
1691[2]	**March Crusader (72)** (BHanbury) **3-8-12** JStack(9) (lw: a.p: led over 2f out: rdn & edgd lft ins fnl f: r.o)	—	**1**	3/1[2]	88	60
1587[7]	**Always On My Mind** (PJMakin) **3-8-7** SSanders(5) (a.p: rdn over 1f out: ev ch & edgd lft ins fnl f: unable qckn)	nk	**2**	11/2	82	54
565[2]	**Malabi (USA)** (JLDunlop) **3-8-12** WRyan(2) (lw: rr: sn pushed along: sme hdwy 2f out: kpt on one pce ins fnl f)	6	**3**	9/4[1]	71	43
1650[3]	**Husun (USA)** (PTWalwyn) **3-8-7** DHolland(7) (chsd ldrs: rdn over 2f out: one pce)	½	**4**	5/1[3]	65	37
1265[6]	**Fur Will Fly (75)** (IABalding) **3-8-7** SWhitworth(1) (sn pushed along towards rr: sme hdwy over 2f out: rdn appr fnl f: one pce)	1	**5**	11/1	62	34
	Ceanothus (IRE) (WJHaggas) **3-8-7** MRoberts(11) (s.i.s: bhd & pushed along: mod hdwy appr fnl f: nvr nrr)	2½	**6**	20/1	56	28
1638[2]	**Goodbye Gatemen (IRE) (70)** (BAPearce) **3-8-12** GBardwell(4) (led: hdd over 2f out: sn wknd)	3½	**7**	14/1	51	23
	Sandy Saddler (SDow) **3-8-12** RPerham(6) (unf: bit bkwd: dwlt: a bhd)	1	**8**	25/1	49	21
1237[16]	**Durable George** (JJBridger) **3-8-7**(5) ADaly(3) (chsd ldrs: rdn over 3f out: sn wknd)	9	**9**	100/1	25	—
792[13]	**Magazine Gap (43)** (PatMitchell) **4-9-1**(5) AmandaSanders(8) (chsd ldrs: rdn 3f out: wknd over 2f out)	s.h	**10**	100/1	24	4
	Tashannah (PRHedger) **4-9-1** NVarley(10) (w'like: bit bkwd: in tch: rdn ½-wy: sn wknd)	1¾	**11**	14/1	15	—

(SP 120.1%) **11 Rn**

1m 9.65 (0.65) CSF £18.12 TOTE £5.60: £1.80 £1.80 £1.80 (£19.00) Trio £19.30 OWNER Maktoum Al Maktoum (NEWMARKET) BRED Gainsborough Stud Management Ltd
WEIGHT FOR AGE 3yo-8lb
1691 March Crusader looked to be travelling well when taking it up over two furlongs out, but did not help his cause by edging to his left when coming under pressure. Luckily for him, the runner-up was doing the same, and he had enough in hand to score. (3/1: op 2/1)
Always On My Mind ran her best race to date, and would have been closer but for edging to her left in the final furlong. (11/2: op 10/1)
565 Malabi (USA) plugged on for third in the closing stages, but looked quite slow. (9/4: 2/1-3/1)
1650 Husun (USA) hunted up the leading pack, but proved very one-paced under pressure. (5/1: op 3/1)
1638 Goodbye Gatemen (IRE) (14/1: 8/1-16/1)
Tashannah (14/1: tchd 7/1)

1968 INFONET H'CAP (0-70) (3-Y.O+) (Class E)

8-00 (8-03) **1m 2f** £3,174.25 (£949.00: £454.50: £207.25) Stalls: High GOING minus 0.31 sec per fur (GF)

				SP	RR	SF
1233[13]	**Zamalek (USA) (40)** (RMFlower) **5-7-12** FNorton(2) (hld up in mid div: hdwy over 2f out: rdn over 1f out: styd on ins fnl f: led cl home)	—	**1**	10/1	49	28
1678[3]	**Sam Rockett (44)** (MissGayKelleway) **4-7-13**(3) AWhelan(7) (a.p: led 2f out: rdn ins fnl f: hdd cl home)	hd	**2**	6/1[3]	53	32
1506[13]	**Sovereign Crest (IRE) (44)** (CAHorgan) **4-8-2** PaulEddery(13) (s.s: rr: gd hdwy on ins over 1f out: styd on ins fnl f)	nk	**3**	14/1	52	31
1459[11]	**Zidac (70)** (PJMakin) **5-10-0** SSanders(5) (b: chsd ldrs: hrd rdn over 1f out: one pce)	1¼	**4**	13/2	76	55
1642[9]	**Harvey White (IRE) (52)** (JPearce) **5-8-10** AClark(4) (hld up: hdwy 2f out: n.m.r over 1f out: swtchd lft: styd on ins fnl f)	¾	**5**	20/1	57	36
1632[3]	**Kristal Breeze (52)** (WRMuir) **5-8-10** MRoberts(8) (trckd ldrs: rdn over 2f out: wknd ins fnl f)	1¼	**6**	9/4[1]	55	34
1632[14]	**Double Rush (IRE) (48)** (TGMills) **5-8-6** GBardwell(3) (hld up: pushed along 4f out: hdwy over 2f out: wknd ins fnl f)	1¼	**7**	9/1	49	28

				SP	RR	SF
	Lavender Della (IRE) (60) (MJFetherston-Godley) **4-9-4** DHolland(11) (nvr nrr)	½	**8**	20/1	60	39
	Debutante Days (64) (ACStewart) **5-9-8** DHarrison(1) (prom: rdn over 3f out: grad wknd)	½	**9**	16/1	64	43
1320[16]	**Moi Canard (49)** (BAPearce) **4-8-2**(5) ADaly(12) (led: hdd 2f out: sn wknd)	¾	**10**	33/1	47	26
1445[12]	**Executive Officer (38)** (RMFlower) **4-7-10** JLowe(10) (a bhd)	¾	**11**	50/1	35	14
1668[2]	**Passage Creeping (IRE) (67)** (SDow) **4-9-11** WRyan(6) (hld up in tch: rdn over 2f out: grad wknd)	½	**12**	4/1[2]	63	42
1779[11]	**One In The Eye (38)** (JRPoulton) **4-7-10** NVarley(9) (chsd ldrs: rdn 4f out: wknd over 2f out)	1¼	**13**	33/1	32	11
				(SP 127.4%)	**13 Rn**	

2m 8.49 (3.79) CSF £63.29 CT £793.56 TOTE £14.40: £3.30 £2.00 £3.70 (£36.50) Trio £171.90 OWNER Rare Stakes Partnership (JEVINGTON) BRED Buckram Oak Farm

LONG HANDICAP Executive Officer 6-11 One In The Eye 7-7

188 Zamalek (USA) started to make headway early in the straight and, coming under pressure below the distance, kept staying on and got up close home. (10/1)

1678 Sam Rockett looked sure to win when leading two out, but was worn down in the last few strides. (6/1)

Sovereign Crest (IRE) was the unlucky horse of the race. He missed the break and was some way in arrears, but made good headway on the inside in the final two furlongs, and was still staying on strongly at the finish. (14/1)

1142 Zidac ran a sound race, but found his big weight beating him in the final furlong. (13/2)

Harvey White (IRE) was slightly unlucky, as he was checked in his run below the distance and, although staying on in the final furlong, could never get to the leaders in time. (20/1)

1632 Kristal Breeze had every chance up the straight, but had no more to give in the final furlong. (9/4)

1969 BEAGLE LIMITED STKS (0-65) (3-Y.O+) (Class F)

8-30 (8-31) **1m (Equitrack)** £2,277.00 (£627.00: £297.00) Stalls: High GOING minus 0.50 sec per fur (FST)

				SP	RR	SF
886[6]	**Pennywell (65)** (RFJohnsonHoughton) **3-8-8** SSanders(6) (a.p: led over 1f out: r.o wl)	—	1	11/4[1]	71	42
*1786**	**Bentico (70)** (MrsNMacauley) **8-9-8v** BDoyle(3) (led: hdd over 2f out: ev ch over 1f out: one pce)	1¾	2	5/1[3]	71	53
1421[6]	**Sweet Supposin (IRE) (64)** (CADwyer) **6-9-10v** DHarrison(1) (hld up in tch: rdn & outpcd over 2f out: kpt on one pce ins last)	1¼	3	9/2[2]	70	52
1606[4]	**Resist the Force (USA) (63)** (CACyzer) **7-9-5**(3) AWhelan(2) (a.p: led over 2f out: hdd over 1f out: no ex ins last)	hd	4	11/4[1]	68	50
1639[13]	**Hawaii Storm (FR) (53)** (DJSffrenchDavis) **9-9-1**(7) KerryBaker(7) (in tch tl outpcd over 4f out)	10	5	16/1	48	30
490[5]	**Invocation (64)** (GLMoore) **10-9-12** AClark(5) (hld up: rdn over 2f out: sn wknd)	2½	6	7/1	47	29
1009[13]	**Into Debt (34)** (JRPoulton) **4-9-3** LeesaLong(4) (s.s: a bhd)	7	7	25/1	24	6
1639[11]	**Rawi (56)** (MissGayKelleway) **4-9-8** DHolland(8) (hld up: rdn over 3f out: sn wknd)	3½	8	8/1	22	4
				(SP 121.5%)	**8 Rn**	

1m 38.27 (0.87) CSF £16.58 TOTE £5.10: £1.60 £1.80 £2.20 (£7.60) OWNER Lady Rothschild (DIDCOT) BRED Lord Rothschild

WEIGHT FOR AGE 3yo-11lb

886 Pennywell was always to the fore and, after leading approaching the final furlong, ran on strongly. (11/4)

1786* Bentico dictated at a steady pace, but could not match the winner's turn of foot in the final furlong. (5/1: 3/1-11/2)

1082 Sweet Supposin (IRE) is better suited by a stronger gallop than this. (9/2)

1606 Resist the Force (USA) was always to the fore but, after having every chance, tired in the final furlong. (11/4)

T/Plpt: £950.90 (12.14 Tckts). T/Qdpt: £16.20 (57.84 Tckts) SM

1932-SANDOWN (R-H) (Good to firm, Rnd cse Firm ptchs, 5f cse Good patches)
Saturday June 14th

WEATHER: overcast WIND: almost nil

1970 E.B.F. PORTMAN SQUARE MAIDEN STKS (2-Y.O F) (Class D)

1-50 (1-50) **5f 6y** £3,208.75 (£970.00: £472.50: £223.75) Stalls: Low GOING minus 0.17 sec per fur (GF)

				SP	RR	SF
	Stop Out (HMorrison) **2-8-11** CRutter(4) (leggy: unf: scope: dwlt: hdwy over 1f out: led ins fnl f: rdn out)	—	1	33/1	79	18
1847[3]	**Midsummer Night (IRE)** (RHannon) **2-8-11** TQuinn(6) (b.hind: a.p: led 3f out tl ins fnl f: r.o)	½	2	7/4[1]	77	16
1486[5]	**Katah** (JHMGosden) **2-8-11** GHind(1) (b.hind: lw: a.p: rdn over 2f out: unable qckn)	1¾	3	7/4[1]	72	11
	Frankie Fair (IRE) (MAJarvis) **2-8-11** MRoberts(5) (scope: lw: a.p: rdn over 2f out: wknd over 1f out)	3	4	12/1	62	1
	Alpha Whisky (GER) (IABalding) **2-8-11** WRyan(7) (leggy: bit bkwd: dwlt: hdwy over 2f out: rdn over 1f out: wknd fnl f)	1	5	8/1[3]	59	—
1240[8]	**Gipsy Moth** (BJMeehan) **2-8-11** MTebbutt(2) (a.p: rdn over 2f out: wknd over 1f out)	1½	6	11/2[2]	54	—
1240[9]	**Respond** (GLMoore) **2-8-11** CandyMorris(3) (led 2f: wknd wl over 1f out)	¾	7	33/1	52	—
				(SP 112.8%)	**7 Rn**	

63.66 secs (3.86) CSF £80.87 TOTE £24.90: £4.90 £1.30 (£49.10) OWNER Sheran Macdonald-Buchanan & Partners (EAST ILSLEY) BRED R. P. Williams

Stop Out, a tall, quite attractive filly with plenty of scope, picked up nicely from below the distance and, leading inside the last, was ridden along to secure victory. (33/1)

1847 Midsummer Night (IRE), an unfurnished filly, looked very fit, and was making a quick reappearance. Soon at the head of affairs, she was passed by the winner inside the final furlong, but to her credit kept on well to the line. She should soon go one better. (7/4)

1486 Katah was never far away, but failed to quicken in the second half of the race. She looks one of the stable's lesser lights. (7/4: 5/4-evens)

Frankie Fair (IRE), quite an attractive, well-proportioned newcomer, with plenty of scope for the future, was close up until tiring below the distance. She can step-up on this before long. (12/1: op 7/1)

Alpha Whisky (GER), a tall filly, did not look fully wound-up, and so it proved for, after making a forward move at halfway, she had come to end of her tether entering the final furlong. (8/1: op 4/1)

Gipsy Moth was close up until calling it a day over a furlong out. (11/2)

1971 PHILIP RING MATURITY CLAIMING STKS (3-Y.O) (Class F)

2-20 (2-24) **1m 2f 7y** £2,710.00 (£820.00: £400.00: £190.00) Stalls: High GOING minus 0.39 sec per fur (F)

				SP	RR	SF
1624[7]	**Double Gold (64)** (BJMeehan) **3-8-5** TQuinn(1) (mde all: clr 2f out: rdn out)	—	1	1/3[1]	58	27

				SP	RR	SF
1825[4]	**Chief Predator (USA) (52)** (RHannon) **3-8-9b[1]** RPerham(2) (lw: chsd wnr over 2f: rdn over 3f out: chsd wnr over 1f out: r.o)	1¾	**2**	6/1[2]	59	28
1506[10]	**Euro Superstar (FR) (40)** (SDow) **3-8-4** SSanders(3) (lw: s.s: rdn 3f out: nvr nr to chal)	8	**3**	20/1[3]	41	10
1820[17]	**Blue Hopper (57)** (MRChannon) **3-8-1v[1](3)ow1** PPMurphy(4) (lw: s.s: plld hrd: hdwy 8f out: chsd wnr over 7f out tl over 1f out: sn wknd)	s.h	**4**	6/1[2]	41	9

(SP 108.3%) **4 Rn**

2m 10.79 (4.09) CSF £2.55 TOTE £1.30: (£1.70) OWNER Mr Michael Edwards (UPPER LAMBOURN) BRED Catridge Farm Stud Ltd
Double Gold clmd Chris Ranson £11,000

1487* Double Gold, officially best-in at the weights, adopted her usual front-running role, and had little problem landing the odds. (1/3)
1825 Chief Predator (USA), 16lb behind the winner on official adjusted ratings, was fitted with blinkers for the first time, but was rather surprisingly taking a drop in distance - he was running on strongly over a mile and a half at Salisbury on Tuesday. He moved into second place approaching the final furlong, but failed to get to the winner. He remains a maiden. (6/1: op 7/2)
Euro Superstar (FR) is a bad performer who continues to show little. (20/1)
Blue Hopper, who has shown little so far this season, pulled his way into second place over seven furlongs from home, but she was collared for that position below the distance, and soon dropped away. (6/1: 7/2-13/2)

1972 JOHNSTONE DOUGLAS H'CAP (0-75) (3-Y.O+) (Class D)

2-55 (2-58) **1m 14y** £3,582.50 (£1,085.00: £530.00: £252.50) Stalls: High GOING minus 0.39 sec per fur (F)

				SP	RR	SF
1422[9]	**Baba Au Rhum (IRE) (60)** (IPWilliams) **5-9-0** AClark(11) (a.p: led 3f out: hrd rdn ins fnl f: r.o wl)	—	**1**	12/1	73	44
1459[12]	**Desert Time (66)** (CAHorgan) **7-9-6** DHolland(12) (rdn & hdwy over 1f out: r.o wl ins fnl f)	2	**2**	25/1	75	46
1745[4]	**Thatchmaster (IRE) (59)** (CAHorgan) **6-8-13** DHarrison(10) (led 5f: rdn over 2f out: unable qckn)	¾	**3**	9/2[1]	67	38
1606[11]	**Soaking (48)** (MDIUsher) **7-8-2** DRMcCabe(2) (rdn over 2f out: hdwy over 1f out: r.o wl ins fnl f)	nk	**4**	25/1	55	26
1743[6]	**Sea Danzig (60)** (JJBridger) **4-8-9(5)** ADaly(6) (lw: a.p: rdn 3f out: one pce)	1¾	**5**	14/1	64	35
895[16]	**Missile Toe (IRE) (58)** (DMorris) **4-8-12** NDay(1) (hld up: rdn over 2f out: one pce)	s.h	**6**	25/1	61	32
1597[4]	**Kailey Senor (USA) (74)** (RWArmstrong) **4-10-0** MRoberts(17) (mid div whn hmpd over 2f out: hdwy fnl f: r.o)	1¼	**7**	10/1	75	46
1506[9]	**Multi Franchise (48)** (RMFlower) **4-8-2** GHind(4) (a.p: ev ch over 2f out: wknd over 1f out)	hd	**8**	33/1	49	20
1459[14]	**Balance of Power (59)** (SDow) **5-8-13** WRyan(5) (hld up: rdn over 2f out: wknd over 1f out)	½	**9**	25/1	59	30
1320[6]	**Superior Force (57)** (MissBSanders) **4-8-11** SSanders(7) (lw: prom over 6f)	1¼	**10**	10/1	54	25
1782[11]	**Hopeful Bid (IRE) (56)** (PHowling) **8-8-10** NCarlisle(8) (rdn over 3f out: a mid div)	2	**11**	50/1	49	20
1633[4]	**Interdream (61)** (RHannon) **3-8-4** RPerham(16) (b.hind: a bhd)	2½	**12**	11/2[2]	49	9
1633[13]	**Broughtons Error (67)** (WJMusson) **3-8-10** JQuinn(3) (a bhd)	hd	**13**	11/1	55	15
1639[5]	**Velvet Jones (42)** (GFHCharles-Jones) **4-7-10** GBardwell(14) (s.s: a bhd)	¾	**14**	8/1	29	—
1000[6]	**Jupiter (IRE) (68)** (GCBravery) **3-8-11** MRimmer(13) (hld up: rdn over 2f out: sn wknd)	4	**15**	7/1[3]	47	7
1459[9]	**Zermatt (IRE) (61)** (MDIUsher) **7-9-1** BDoyle(15) (lw: dwlt: a bhd)	s.h	**16**	14/1	40	11

(SP 125.0%) **16 Rn**

1m 43.48 (2.28) CSF £271.78 CT £1,430.26 TOTE £14.80: £2.50 £9.90 £1.30 £4.10 (£173.60) Trio £354.70 OWNER Mr & Mrs John Poynton (ALVECHURCH) BRED A. Brosnan
WEIGHT FOR AGE 3yo-11lb

1248 Baba Au Rhum (IRE) struck the front three furlongs from home, and with a useful advantage below the distance, was not going to be caught. (12/1)
Desert Time bounced back to form, running on strongly to take second place. He is nicely weighted at present. (25/1)
1745 Thatchmaster (IRE), 7lb higher than when winning a claimer last year, ran another solid race. Taking the field along, he was collared three furlongs from home, and although failing to find another gear, managed to hold on for third prize. (9/2)
403 Soaking, racing at the back of the field, put in some sterling work in the last furlong and a half. (25/1)
1488 Sea Danzig, never far away, was made to look very pedestrian in the straight. He stays this trip, but has gained both his victories to date over seven furlongs. (14/1)
Missile Toe (IRE) chased the leaders, but could could make no impression in the final quarter-mile. He is not easy to win with, having scored just once from twenty-three starts. (25/1)
849 Kailey Senor (USA), well-beaten in three conditions races over a mile-and-a-half so far this season, was taking a drop in distance, and making his handicap debut. He did not do at all badly, considering he was hampered, and ran on nicely in the final furlong. A half-brother to El Gran Senor, this is his trip, and he should be able to find a handicap before long. (10/1: 5/1-12/1)
383 Superior Force (10/1: 7/1-11/1)
1219 Broughtons Error (11/1: 8/1-12/1)

1973 ROTHMANS ROYALS NORTH SOUTH CHALLENGE SERIES H'CAP (0-95) (3-Y.O) (Class C)

3-30 (3-32) **1m 1f** £7,067.50 (£2,140.00: £1,045.00: £497.50) Stalls: High GOING minus 0.39 sec per fur (F)

				SP	RR	SF
	Rudimental (78) (SirMarkPrescott) **3-8-10** SSanders(7) (hld up: led wl over 1f out: rdn out)	—	**1**	5/2[1]	87	53
690[14]	**Sir Talbot (83)** (RHannon) **3-9-1** RPerham(5) (lw: chsd ldr: led over 3f out tl wl over 1f out: ev ch ins fnl f: unable qckn)	1¼	**2**	12/1	90	56
1788[2]	**Dalliance (IRE) (89)** (MRStoute) **3-9-7v[1]** DHolland(2) (rdn over 2f out: hdwy over 1f out: edgd rt ins fnl f: r.o one pce)	hd	**3**	9/2[2]	96	62
1500*	**Our Way (73)** (CEBrittain) **3-8-5** BDoyle(1) (lw: a.p: rdn over 2f out: ev ch over 1f out: one pce)	3	**4**	15/2	74	40
1595[7]	**Brandon Jack (75)** (IABalding) **3-8-7** MRoberts(3) (lw: rdn over 2f out: nvr nr to chal)	5	**5**	8/1	67	33
1264*	**Tal-Y-Llyn (IRE) (80)** (BWHills) **3-8-12** WRyan(4) (lw: rdn 3f out: sme hdwy 2f out: wknd wl over 1f out)	3½	**6**	5/1[3]	66	32
1462[5]	**Manazil (IRE) (84)** (RWArmstrong) **3-9-2** GCarter(8) (lw: rdn over 3f out: sme hdwy 2f out: wknd wl over 1f out)	6	**7**	15/2	60	26
1784[4]	**City Gambler (72)** (GCBravery) **3-8-4** DHarrison(6) (b.off hind: led over 5f: wknd over 1f out)	s.h	**8**	11/1	47	13
1589[10]	**Maladerie (IRE) (75)** (MRChannon) **3-8-4(3)** PPMurphy(9) (lw: prom over 6f)	5	**9**	33/1	42	8

(SP 117.0%) **9 Rn**

1m 54.29 (1.19) CSF £32.09 CT £119.32 TOTE £4.20: £1.80 £3.50 £1.60 (£36.40) Trio £59.40 OWNER Cheveley Park Stud (NEWMARKET) BRED Cheveley Park Stud Ltd

Rudimental, a big boat of a horse, made a winning debut on turf, after an absence of eleven months. Striking the front early in the final quarter-mile, he was ridden along to shake off the attentions of the runner-up in the last half-furlong. He can win again. (5/2)
479* Sir Talbot had more use made of him again, and bounced back to form. Showing in front early in the straight, he was collared by the winner early in the final quarter-mile but, to his credit, stuck to that rival really well until forced to concede defeat in the last one hundred yards. (12/1)
1788 Dalliance (IRE), fitted with a visor for the first time, picked up ground below the distance, and looked as if he might pose a real problem to the winner. However, he then drifted in behind that rival, and failed to find what was required. (9/2: op 3/1)

1500* Our Way, never far away, had every chance below the distance before tapped for toe. (15/2: 5/1-8/1)
Brandon Jack may have been dropped 10lb in the handicap following a string of bad performances so far this season, but he showed no encouragement here. (8/1: 5/1-9/1)
1264* Tal-Y-Llyn (IRE) never threatened, and a brief effort two furlongs from home came to nothing. (5/1)
889* Manazil (IRE) (15/2: 5/1-8/1)
1784 City Gambler (11/1: 8/1-12/1)

1974 BERKELEY SQUARE H'CAP (0-80) (3-Y.O+) (Class D)
4-00 (4-03) **1m 6f** £3,582.50 (£1,085.00: £530.00: £252.50) Stalls: High GOING minus 0.39 sec per fur (F)

				SP	RR	SF
1162^{4}	**Siege Perilous (IRE) (69)** (SCWilliams) **4-9-3** DHolland(8) (a.p: rdn over 2f out: led 1f out: r.o wl)	—	**1**	4/1^{2}	78	34
	Tudor Island (75) (CEBrittain) **8-9-9** BDoyle(7) (b: b.hind: led over 5f: led 6f out to 3f out: led over 1f out: sn hdd: r.o)	½	**2**	8/1	83	39
1114^{4}	**Coh Sho No (56)** (SDow) **4-8-4** SSanders(3) (hld up: hrd rdn over 2f out: unable qckn)	1½	**3**	10/1	63	19
1478^{5}	**Renzo (IRE) (80)** (MrsAJPerrett) **4-10-0b^{1}** AClark(5) (hdwy over 6f out: hrd rdn 2f out: nt run on)	nk	**4**	6/1^{3}	86	42
1434^{4}	**Psicossis (76)** (HRACecil) **4-9-10** WRyan(2) (chsd ldr: led over 8f out to 6f out: led 3f out tl over 1f out: one pce)	s.h	**5**	6/1^{3}	82	38
250^{3}	**Alarico (FR) (65)** (IPWilliams) **4-8-13** GaryStevens(4) (swtg: plld hrd: lost pl over 4f out: r.o one pce fnl f)	nk	**6**	10/1	71	27
1592^{5}	**Taufan Boy (74)** (PWHarris) **4-9-8** NDay(6) (bhd fnl 6f)	3	**7**	7/1	77	33
1125^{5}	**Sharaf (IRE) (54)** (WRMuir) **4-8-2v^{1}** JQuinn(9) (lw: stumbled s: sme hdwy on ins over 1f out: wknd fnl f)	½	**8**	20/1	56	12
1779*	**Chris's Lad (65)** (BJMeehan) **6-8-13b** MTebbutt(1) (a bhd)	nk	**9**	7/2^{1}	67	23
				(SP 117.3%)	**9 Rn**	

3m 5.55 (6.65) CSF £33.29 CT £274.29 TOTE £4.70: £1.70 £2.60 £2.60 (£13.80) Trio £48.50 OWNER Mr S. Demanuele (NEWMARKET) BRED Miss Honora Corridan
IN-FOCUS: **This was a first ride in Britain for ten years for Gary Stevens, one of America's top jockeys.**
1162 Siege Perilous (IRE) deservedly came good after three promising runs this season, leading a furlong out and keeping on just too strongly for the persistent runner-up. (4/1: 3/1-9/2)
Tudor Island made a very pleasing return to action. Making a lot of the running, he was eventually passed by the winner a furlong out but, to his credit, kept on well to the bitter end. Four of his six wins to date have come over this trip. (8/1)
1114 Coh Sho No does nothing more than stay, and needs further than this, for she could only plod on at one pace in the straight. (10/1: 8/1-12/1)
1478 Renzo (IRE), 4lb higher for finishing fifth here recently, was fitted with blinkers for the first time, but still looked thoroughly ungenuine. He refused to put his best foot forward in the straight, despite his rider's urgings, and should be avoided like the plague. (6/1)
1434 Psicossis, done no favours by the Handicapper on this handicap debut, showed in front for a second time three furlongs from home but, collared below the distance, failed to find another gear. (6/1: op 4/1)
250 Alarico (FR), off the course since February, coped with the extra half-mile. Done no favours on the home turn, resulting in him losing his pitch, he stayed on again in the final furlong. (10/1)

1975 LEICESTER SQUARE CONDITIONS STKS (3-Y.O+) (Class C)
4-35 (4-36) **5f 6y** £4,477.40 (£1,676.60: £820.80: £354.00: £159.50: £81.70) Stalls: Low GOING minus 0.17 sec per fur (GF)

				SP	RR	SF
1855^{3}	**Johnny Staccato (91)** (JMPEustace) **3-8-7** JTate(6) (s.i.s: outpcd: gd hdwy fnl f: led nr fin)	—	**1**	14/1	94	37
1721a^{6}	**Crowded Avenue (98)** (PJMakin) **5-9-0** SSanders(7) (hld up: rdn over 1f out: led ins fnl f: hdd nr fin)	nk	**2**	9/4^{1}	93	43
1394*	**Wellspring (IRE)** (DRLoder) **3-8-6** GaryStevens(9) (lw: hld up: rdn over 1f out: r.o one pce)	1½	**3**	5/1^{3}	87	30
1594*	**Kilcullen Lad (IRE) (75)** (PMooney) **3-8-7v** WRyan(2) (lw: a.p: rdn over 1f out: ev ch ins fnl f: one pce)	hd	**4**	12/1	88	31
	Fond Embrace (95) (HCandy) **4-8-9** GCarter(4) (led tl ins fnl f: one pce)	hd	**5**	6/1	83	33
1855^{2}	**Venture Capitalist (108)** (DNicholls) **8-9-0** AlexGreaves(8) (swtg: hdwy over 1f out: hrd rdn: one pce)	½	**6**	4/1^{2}	86	36
506^{8}	**Loving And Giving (83)** (HCandy) **3-8-2** CRutter(5) (no hdwy fnl 2f)	2	**7**	14/1	75	18
1809^{6}	**Dark Age (IRE)** (RAkehurst) **4-8-11**(7) DDenby(1) (lw: s.s: outpcd: nvr nrr)	nk	**8**	50/1	51 t	33
1608^{9}	**Bowden Rose (79)** (MBlanshard) **5-9-1b** JQuinn(3) (a.p: rdn over 2f out: wknd fnl f)	1¾	**9**	12/1	42 t	24
				(SP 112.4%)	**9 Rn**	

62.2 secs (2.40) CSF £40.32 TOTE £19.50: £3.20 £1.60 £2.00 (£40.70) Trio £70.80 OWNER Mr J. C. Smith (NEWMARKET) BRED Bishop's Down Farm
WEIGHT FOR AGE 3yo-7lb
1855 Johnny Staccato, unable to go the early pace, was still only seventh entering the final furlong, but then produced a whirlwind finish up the hill to snatch the spoils near the line. This was his first attempt at five furlongs, and even on this very stiff uphill track, it nearly proved too sharp. (14/1: 10/1-16/1)
1721a Crowded Avenue, with ground and distance in his favour - he has yet to win beyond five furlongs - looked to have made a winning move as he led inside the final furlong, only to be caught near the line. He should soon be winning. (9/4)
1394* Wellspring (IRE), looking in fine shape beforehand, may have won at Pontefract recently, but she was certainly pitched in at the deep end on only her second racecourse appearance. Nevertheless, she acquitted herself well, and stayed on in the final furlong to snatch third prize right on the line. (5/1)
1594* Kilcullen Lad (IRE) may have had a tremendous amount to do at the weights, but he is a really consistent colt, and gave a very good account of himself, still having every chance inside the final furlong before tapped for toe. In less exalted company, he should soon be winning again. (12/1)
Fond Embrace, the only runner without a recent outing under her belt, was not going to hang around, and set the pace until eventually being overhauled inside the final furlong. (6/1)
1855 Venture Capitalist, making a quick reappearance, was 8lb clear on official adjusted ratings, but he has never won over this trip and, after moving up below the distance, could make no further impression. All six of his victories to date have come over six furlongs, and a return to that trip is required. (4/1: op 5/2)
Loving And Giving (14/1: 10/1-20/1)

1976 GROSVENOR SQUARE MAIDEN STKS (3-Y.O) (Class D)
5-05 (5-06) **7f 16y** £3,403.75 (£1,030.00: £502.50: £238.75) Stalls: High GOING minus 0.39 sec per fur (F)

				SP	RR	SF
991^{4}	**Warningford** (JRFanshawe) **3-9-0** DHarrison(1) (a.p: led 2f out: shkn up over 1f out: qcknd ins fnl f: r.o wl)	—	**1**	6/5^{1}	96	40
1737^{6}	**Shawm (88)** (DRLoder) **3-9-0** GaryStevens(5) (lw: a.p: ev ch wl over 1f out: unable qckn)	3	**2**	5/4^{2}	89	33
1499^{4}	**Bint Shihama (USA)** (CEBrittain) **3-8-9** BDoyle(3) (hld up: rdn over 2f out: one pce)	3½	**3**	10/1^{3}	76	20
1690^{2}	**Free As A Bird** (MRChannon) **3-8-6**(3) PPMurphy(6) (hld up: rdn 2f out: wknd 1f out)	5	**4**	20/1	65	9

				SP	RR	SF
	Cold Lazarus (RTPhillips) **3-9-0** GHind(4) (bit bkwd: led 5f: wknd over 1f out)	4	**5**	14/1	61	5
1851^{9}	**Balladara (IRE)** (RHannon) **3-9-0** RPerham(2) (lw: a bhd)	1¼	**6**	66/1	58	2

(SP 111.9%) **6 Rn**

1m 31.02 (2.42) CSF £2.69 TOTE £2.70: £1.40 £1.10 (£2.00) OWNER Barford Bloodstock (NEWMARKET) BRED Mrs C. Handscombe

991 Warningford proved far too good for this field. Leading a quarter-of-a-mile from home, he was woken up, and sprinted away from the runner-up in the final furlong. (6/5)

1737 Shawm, on level terms with the winner entering the final quarter-mile, was then left standing by that rival in the final furlong. A return to a mile would help. (5/4: evens-11/8)

1499 Bint Shihama (USA) needs time to develop, and failed to quicken from below the distance. (10/1: 5/1-12/1)

1690 Free As A Bird was not up to this company, and was left standing inside the distance. (20/1)

Cold Lazarus did not look fully wound up for this reappearance, and so it proved, for after haring into the lead, he was collared a quarter of a mile out, and soon done with. (14/1)

1394 Balladara (IRE), a half-brother to Cool Edge, looked tremendous in the paddock, but unfortunately does not seem to have much ability.(66/1)

T/Plpt: £62.70 (244.23 Tckts). T/Qdpt: £15.40 (63 Tckts) AK

1945-YORK (L-H) (Good to soft, Good patches)
Saturday June 14th

WEATHER: overcast WIND: slight against

1977 MICHAEL SOBELL SILVER TANKARD H'CAP (0-75) (3-Y.O+) (Class D)

2-10 (2-13) **6f** £7,717.50 (£2,340.00: £1,145.00: £547.50) Stalls: High GOING: 0.35 sec per fur (G)

				SP	RR	SF
1761^{3}	**Grey Kingdom (62)** (MBrittain) **6-8-8**(7) DMernagh(9) (cl up stands' side: led over 1f out: r.o)	—	**1**	16/1	73	49
1759^{8}	**Afaan (IRE) (63)** (RFMarvin) **4-9-2v^{1}** TGMcLaughlin(19) (cl up stands' side: led 2f out: hdd over 1f out: kpt on)	1½	**2**	33/1	70	46
1594^{2}	**Thwaab (66)** (FWatson) **5-9-5v** KFallon(21) (bhd & drvn along: hdwy stands' side ½-wy: kpt on: nrst fin)	¾	**3**	7/1^{2}	71	47
1609^{9}	**The Gay Fox (75)** (BAMcMahon) **3-9-6** GDuffield(23) (prom stands' side: hdwy 2f out: kpt on wl)	½	**4**	25/1	79	47
1035^{5}	**Erupt (65)** (GBBalding) **4-9-4v** MHills(18) (swtg: hdwy stands' side ½-wy: kpt on fnl f)	3	**5**	12/1	61	37
1734^{3}	**Brecongill Lad (66)** (MissSEHall) **5-9-5** KDarley(14) (chsd ldrs stands' side tl wknd over 1f out)	hd	**6**	14/1	61	37
1835^{7}	**Just Bob (72)** (SEKettlewell) **8-9-4**(7) JennyBenson(6) (lw: hdwy centre over 2f out: nvr able to chal)	½	**7**	25/1	66	42
1170^{12}	**Baritone (74)** (JWWatts) **3-9-5b^{1}** JReid(22) (outpcd tl styd on u.p fnl f)	s.h	**8**	20/1	68	36
1799^{3}	**So Intrepid (IRE) (75)** (JMBradley) **7-10-0** PatEddery(4) (racd far side: chsd ldrs: hdwy over 2f out: no ch w stands' side)	1¼	**9**	8/1^{3}	66	42
1662^{5}	**U-No-Harry (IRE) (64)** (RHollinshead) **4-9-3** FLynch(7) (lw: chsd ldrs centre: nt qckn fnl 2f)	1	**10**	16/1	52	28
1765^{6}	**Antonias Melody (70)** (SRBowring) **4-9-9** SWebster(17) (cl up stands' side over 4f)	nk	**11**	33/1	57	33
1468*	**Blessingindisguise (64)** (MWEasterby) **4-9-3b** TLucas(20) (led stands' side 4f: wknd)	s.h	**12**	10/1	51	27
1488^{6}	**Bayin (USA) (64)** (MDIUsher) **8-9-3** RStreet(12) (lw: s.i.s: hld up: hdwy ½-wy: n.d)	hd	**13**	16/1	51	27
1627*	**Benzoe (IRE) (72)** (MrsJRRamsden) **7-9-11** JFortune(1) (s.s: racd far side: hdwy 2f out: nvr rchd ldrs)	1¼	**14**	6/1^{1}	55	31
1561^{7}	**Don't Care (IRE) (67)** (MissLAPerratt) **6-9-1b**(5) TEDurcan(8) (cl up centre 4f)	hd	**15**	33/1	50	26
1505^{3}	**Gwespyr (60)** (RHannon) **4-8-13** DaneO'Neill(15) (racd stands' side: n.d)	hd	**16**	16/1	43	19
1761^{11}	**Halmanerror (63)** (MrsJRRamsden) **7-9-2** MGallagher(10) (racd centre: outpcd fr ½-wy)	hd	**17**	20/1	46	22
1468^{3}	**Antarctic Storm (60)** (RAFahey) **4-8-13** ACulhane(5) (chsd ldrs centre over 3f)	2½	**18**	33/1	36	12
1583^{8}	**Jo Mell (74)** (TDEasterby) **4-9-13** LCharnock(11) (s.s: swtchd far side: effrt ½-wy: no imp)	1¼	**19**	14/1	47	23
1734^{9}	**Foist (67)** (MWEasterby) **5-9-1**(5) GParkin(16) (s.i.s: a outpcd & bhd)	¾	**20**	8/1^{3}	38	14
1662^{3}	**The Wad (61)** (DNicholls) **4-9-0** JWeaver(2) (led & clr far side tl wknd qckly 2f out)	6	**21**	14/1	16	—
1225^{21}	**Mr Speaker (IRE) (63)** (CFWall) **4-9-2** LDettori(13) (sn bhd)	3	**22**	16/1	10	—
443^{11}	**Mansab (USA) (66)** (PGMurphy) **4-9-5** SDrowne(3) (chsd ldrs far side to ½-wy: wknd qckly)	11	**23**	12/1	—	—

(SP 151.9%) **23 Rn**

1m 16.14 (5.64) CSF £474.41 CT £3,732.38 TOTE £27.60: £4.50 £12.50 £2.30 £8.10 (£552.50) Trio £1,566.00; £904.36 to 16/6/97 OWNER Mr M. Brittain (WARTHILL) BRED Northgate Lodge Stud Ltd

WEIGHT FOR AGE 3yo-8lb

OFFICIAL EXPLANATION **Mansab (USA): the trainer reported that the gelding struck into himself. Jo Mell: was found to be lame on its off hind the next morning.**

1761 Grey Kingdom has improved all season and this was a tremendous effort, and he was nicely in command by the finish. (16/1)

1467* Afaan (IRE), who disappointed on sand over the minimum trip last time, was back to his best and stuck to his task well when obviously second best. (33/1)

1594 Thwaab came from way off the pace to run another fine race, and will surely pick up a decent race this season. (7/1: 10/1-6/1)

1000* The Gay Fox looks the type ideally suited to a really stiff six furlongs, and was sticking to his task well in the closing stages. (25/1)

1035 Erupt had the visor on for the first time this season and got worked-up in the preliminaries, but still ran quite well, staying on, albeit in vain. (12/1)

1734 Brecongill Lad, without any headgear this time, had his chances but declined the struggle late on. (14/1)

1835 Just Bob is both looking and running well at present. (25/1)

930 Baritone had blinkers on for the first time and ran as though another furlong was needed, but he is probably his own worst enemy. (20/1)

1799 So Intrepid (IRE) won the race up the far side but he had no chance with the stands' side group, and this was probably a very good effort. (8/1)

1978 LEONARD SAINER E.B.F. STKS (2-Y.O) (Class D)

2-40 (2-41) **6f** £4,260.00 (£1,290.00: £630.00: £300.00) Stalls: High GOING: 0.35 sec per fur (G)

				SP	RR	SF
	Carbon (DMorley) **2-9-0** LDettori(6) (w'like: scope: hld up: hdwy & swtchd over 1f out: qcknd to ld ins fnl f)	—	**1**	7/1^{3}	75+	30
1657^{2}	**Iris May** (JBerry) **2-8-4**(5) TEDurcan(4) (s.i.s: sn rcvrd & hmpd: led after 2½f tl ins fnl f: no ex)	1¼	**2**	8/1	67	22
1510^{3}	**Lakeland Pride (IRE)** (PDEvans) **2-9-0** JFEgan(3) (led 2½f: chsd ldrs: kpt on towards fin)	¾	**3**	16/1	70	25
	Success And Glory (IRE) (HRACecil) **2-9-0** KFallon(2) (neat: unf: chsd ldrs: drvn along ½-wy: r.o one pce)	½	**4**	5/6^{1}	68	23
1744^{2}	**Bemsha Swing (IRE)** (RHannon) **2-9-0** PatEddery(5) (lw: w ldrs tl wknd fnl 2f)	2½	**5**	9/4^{2}	62	17
	Naked Oat (BSmart) **2-9-0** JReid(1) (cmpt: bit bkwd: s.i.s: n.d)	1¾	**6**	20/1	57	12

(SP 119.6%) **6 Rn**

1m 17.4 (6.90) CSF £55.93 TOTE £6.70: £2.00 £2.80 (£17.20) OWNER Lord Hartington (NEWMARKET) BRED Side Hill Stud

Carbon would have been unlucky had he been beaten, as he had trouble in getting a run, and then, probably through greenness, carried his head rather high. (7/1)
1657 Iris May ran well in a race where things did not really go her way, and she should not be long in going one better. (8/1)
1510 Lakeland Pride (IRE) is improving all the time and gave the distinct impression that further will suit. (16/1)
Success And Glory (IRE) came with a big reputation but was never going in the race, and it was only his rider's determination that got him so close. He is probably worth a chance on faster ground. (5/6)
1744 Bemsha Swing (IRE) looked well enough but ran moderately, giving up when the race was really on in the last couple of furlongs. This was not his true form. (9/4)
Naked Oat needed this and, after a tardy start, never made any impression. He was not beaten that far and can only improve. (20/1)

1979 CADOGAN SILVER SALVER H'CAP (0-90) (3-Y.O+) (Class C)
3-10 (3-12) **1m 205y** £10,942.50 (£3,315.00: £1,620.00: £772.50) Stalls: Low GOING: 0.35 sec per fur (G)

			SP	RR	SF
678^{6}	**Dreams End (77)** (PBowen) **9-9-2** KFallon(7) (lw: bhd: hdwy 3f out: rdn to ld ins fnl f: r.o) ....—	**1**	3/1^{1}	87	72
1878^{4}	**Eurobox Boy (59)** (APJarvis) **4-7-12** DWright(10) (cl up: led 3½f out tl ins fnl f: kpt on one pce) 1¾	**2**	14/1	66	51
1775^{9}	**Sandmoor Chambray (79)** (TDEasterby) **6-9-4** JCarroll(11) (a chsng ldrs: rdn 3f out: kpt on: nt pce to chal) ..¾	**3**	7/1^{2}	85	70
1300^{3}	**High Premium (84)** (RAFahey) **9-9-2**(7) RWinston(1) (chsd ldrs: effrt over 3f out: nt qckn appr fnl f) ....hd	**4**	15/2^{3}	89	74
1837^{3}	**Takhlid (USA) (68)** (DWChapman) **6-8-7** ACulhane(15) (swtg: plld hrd: hdwy 3f out: ev ch 2f out: no ex fnl f) hd	**5**	14/1	73	58
1775^{12}	**Master Beveled (73)** (PDEvans) **7-8-12** JFEgan(13) (b.nr fore: bhd: rdn & swtchd ins over 3f out: gd hdwy 2f out: nt qckn ins fnl f) ....d.h	**5**	12/1	78	63
	Jameel Asmar (80) (CREgerton) **5-9-5** JFortune(16) (s.s: nrst fin) 5	**7**	20/1	76	61
1442^{7}	**Wakeel (USA) (77)** (SDow) **5-9-2** JReid(4) (in tch tl outpcd fnl 3f) ....nk	**8**	12/1	73	58
1262*	**Phonetic (76)** (GBBalding) **4-9-1** SDrowne(2) (lw: in tch tl outpcd fnl 2f) 1½	**9**	7/1^{2}	69	54
1615^{4}	**Nobby Barnes (57)** (DonEnricoIncisa) **8-7-10** KimTinkler(12) (s.i.s: effrt 4f out: sme late hdwy) 2½	**10**	50/1	46	31
1268^{5}	**Mels Baby (IRE) (76)** (JLEyre) **4-9-1** TWilliams(9) (lw: prom: rdn over 3f out: grad wknd fnl 2f) 2½	**11**	9/1	60	45
1800^{10}	**Paint It Black (57)** (DNicholls) **4-7-5**(5) IonaWands(14) (mid div: rdn over 3f out: sn btn) 1¼	**12**	25/1	39	24
56^{8}	**Rebel County (IRE) (89)** (ABailey) **4-10-0** DaneO'Neill(5) (n.d) 1	**13**	25/1	69	54
1775*	**Band on the Run (85)** (BAMcMahon) **10-9-10** LNewton(8) (a chsng ldrs: effrt over 3f out: wknd fnl 2f) ....hd	**14**	9/1	65	50
1266^{7}	**Mbulwa (60)** (RAFahey) **11-7-13** LCharnock(3) (led tl hdd 3½f out: wknd 2f out) 5	**15**	33/1	31	16
1788^{7}	**Censor (85)** (DNicholls) **4-9-10** KDarley(6) (lw: prom tl wknd over 3f out) 3½	**16**	20/1	50	35
			(SP 132.6%)		**16 Rn**

1m 55.15 (6.15) CSF £44.41 CT £269.45 TOTE £3.60: £1.30 £4.90 £2.50 £1.60 (£50.80) Trio £180.30 OWNER Mr T. G. Price (HAVERFORD-WEST) BRED Hascombe and Valiant Studs
LONG HANDICAP Paint It Black 7-9 Nobby Barnes 6-7
678 Dreams End loves to come from off the pace and, once he started his run over three furlongs out, he was always going to win this, and looked to have a bit in hand. (3/1)
1878 Eurobox Boy likes to be in the firing line, and ran a sound race to show he keeps his form well. (14/1)
444 Sandmoor Chambray was trying to win this for the second year running and, despite being 6lb higher, had his chances, but was short of the necessary change of gear. (7/1)
1300 High Premium does not seem to know how to run a bad race, and this was another game effort. (15/2)
1837 Takhlid (USA) got himself in a state beforehand sweating quite badly, and was again inclined to race too freely, which certainly did not help his cause. (14/1)
1559 Master Beveled was without the blinkers he has been wearing of late, and this time he had the going he needs but, taking time to find his stride, never really got in a blow. (12/1)
Jameel Asmar missed all last season and would prefer a longer trip but, after a slow start, did quite well. (20/1)

1980 WILLIAM HILL TROPHY H'CAP (0-105) (3-Y.O) (Class B)
3-40 (3-42) **6f** £35,109.00 (£10,647.00: £5,211.00: £2,493.00) Stalls: High GOING: 0.35 sec per fur (G)

			SP	RR	SF
1737^{5}	**Return of Amin (71)** (JDBethell) **3-7-7**(3) PFessey(7) (mid div: hdwy 2f out: r.o to ld wl ins fnl f) ....—	**1**	11/1	84	51
1254^{7}	**Double Action (86)** (TDEasterby) **3-8-11** KFallon(13) (bhd: rdn over 2f out: hdwy over 1f out: r.o wl towards fin) ....nk	**2**	14/1	98	65
1158^{3}	**Bishops Court (96)** (MrsJRRamsden) **3-9-7** JFortune(5) (lw: hld up: smooth hdwy ½-wy: led ins fnl f: sn hrd rdn: hdd & nt qckn towards fin) 1¼	**3**	11/2^{2}	105	72
1609^{3}	**Sharp Hat (92)** (RHannon) **3-9-3** DaneO'Neill(4) (swtg: chsd ldrs: led wl over 1f out tl ins fnl f: kpt on) 1½	**4**	9/1	97	64
1634^{2}	**Yorkie George (87)** (LMCumani) **3-8-12** LDettori(15) (lw: bhd: gd hdwy over 2f out: ch appr fnl f: no ex) 2½	**5**	9/4^{1}	85	52
1673*	**Prince Dome (IRE) (81)** (MartynWane) **3-8-6** 7x JCarroll(9) (lw: w ldrs: rdn 2f out: kpt on one pce) ....¾	**6**	20/1	77	44
1673^{4}	**Double-J (IRE) (84)** (KMcAuliffe) **3-8-9** WJO'Connor(18) (bhd: hdwy over 1f out: styd on) ....nk	**7**	20/1	79	46
1629^{3}	**Style Dancer (IRE) (74)** (RMWhitaker) **3-7-10**(3)ow2 MartinDwyer(8) (swtg: hdwy ½-wy: rdn & no imp) ....nk	**8**	25/1	69	34
1170^{6}	**Silent Miracle (IRE) (77)** (MBell) **3-7-11**(5) RMullen(16) (led: rdn & hung lft 2f out: sn hdd & grad wknd) ....s.h	**9**	14/1	72	39
1170^{10}	**For Your Eyes Only (87)** (TDEasterby) **3-8-12** JFEgan(14) (bhd & nt clr run after 2f: sme late hdwy) 1	**10**	33/1	79	46
1737^{4}	**Restless Spirit (USA) (86)** (MJohnston) **3-8-11** JWeaver(2) (lw: effrt ½-wy: no imp) 1½	**11**	9/1	74	41
1254^{8}	**Brutal Fantasy (IRE) (85)** (JLEyre) **3-8-10** RLappin(1) (lw: cl up over 4f) 2½	**12**	33/1	66	33
784^{2}	**Select Choice (IRE) (82)** (APJarvis) **3-8-7**ow1 JReid(11) (spd 4f) 1½	**13**	25/1	59	25
1254*	**Treasure Touch (IRE) (90)** (DNicholls) **3-8-10**(5) IonaWands(19) (in tch: outpcd ½-wy: n.d after) 2½	**14**	12/1	61	28
1610^{8}	**Dayville (USA) (86)** (JBerry) **3-8-11** KDarley(3) (sn outpcd & bhd) ....nk	**15**	25/1	56	23
1609^{6}	**Cadeaux Cher (88)** (BWHills) **3-8-13** MHills(10) (b: a outpcd & bhd) 5	**16**	20/1	44	11
1770^{5}	**Zaretski (87)** (CEBrittain) **3-8-12** RHills(12) (gd spd 4f: wknd) 3	**17**	25/1	35	2
1634*	**Triple Hay (96)** (RHannon) **3-9-7** 7x PatEddery(6) (bhd: hdwy u.p 2f out: sn wknd) 3	**18**	6/1^{3}	36	3
877^{9}	**Vax Star (96)** (JLSpearing) **3-9-7** SDrowne(17) (cl up tl rdn & btn 2f out) ....¾	**19**	33/1	34	1
			(SP 148.3%)		**19 Rn**

1m 14.68 (4.18) CSF £150.51 CT £907.91 TOTE £18.70: £2.80 £4.00 £2.50 £2.20 (£164.10) Trio £572.30 OWNER Sheikh Amin Dahlawi (MID-DLEHAM) BRED Al Dahlawi Stud Co Ltd
LONG HANDICAP Prince Dome (IRE) 8-2 Return of Amin 7-5
1737 Return of Amin has been promising to do something like this all season and, getting everything right, thoroughly deserved it. (11/1)
1018 Double Action just went flat at a vital stage entering the last two furlongs and his rider then galvanised him into action, but the line was always going to come too soon. He will nevertheless be one to be reckoned with this season, and should get a bit further. (14/1)
1158 Bishops Court did well to come over from his low draw, and looked likely to trot up for much of the trip, but he just failed to see it out this time. He is probably best at the minimum distance. (11/2: 4/1-6/1)

1609 Sharp Hat is a free-runner who did remarkably well from his low draw and is proving ultra-consistent this year. (9/1)
1634 Yorkie George likes cut in the ground but, after making up a tremendous amount of ground from halfway, he reached the end of his tether with a furlong left. (9/4)
1673* Prince Dome (IRE) is probably better on a faster surface, and this was a really good effort. (20/1)
1673 Double-J (IRE) ran as though another furlong might well help. (20/1)
1629 Style Dancer (IRE) ran over seven furlongs last time, and left the impression that another furlong may well have seen him with a chance. (25/1)
For Your Eyes Only was messed about in the first half of the race, and then was not given a hard time when obviously beaten. He should improve for the run. (33/1)

1981 QUEEN MOTHER'S CUP LADIES' H'CAP (0-95) (3-Y.O+) (Class C)

4-15 (4-16) **1m 3f 195y** £10,845.00 (£3,285.00: £1,605.00: £765.00) Stalls: Low GOING: 0.35 sec per fur (G)

				SP	RR	SF
1162^{5}	**Raffles Rooster (66)** (AGNewcombe) **5-9-2** MissERamsden(5) (swtg: trckd ldrs: hdwy on bit to ld appr fnl f: shkn up & r.o wl)	—	**1**	$5/1^{2}$	80	57
1329*	**Shaffishayes (66)** (MrsMReveley) **5-9-2** MrsSBosley(2) (hld up: hdwy on bit 3f out: ev ch 1f out: r.o: nt pce of wnr)	3	**2**	11/1	76	53
1398^{5}	**Temptress (70)** (JohnHarris) **4-9-6** MissTSpearing(9) (lw: bhd: pushed along 7f out: styd on fnl 3f: nrst fin)	4	**3**	16/1	75	52
1016*	**Break the Rules (84)** (MCPipe) **5-10-6** MrsAPerrett(13) (lw: bhd: rdn & hdwy 4f out: nvr able to chal)	s.h	**4**	$7/2^{1}$	89	66
1398*	**Veridian (73)** (PWHarris) **4-9-9** MissAElsey(3) (cl up: led ent st: hdd appr fnl f: one pce)	1	**5**	8/1	76	53
1268^{2}	**Leviticus (IRE) (76)** (TPTate) **3-8-11** MissADeniel(7) (chsd ldrs: effrt 3f out: one pce)	nk	**6**	8/1	79	41
1763^{8}	**Charter (62)** (WStorey) **6-8-12** MrsCFord(14) (bhd: hdwy 3f out: edgd lft & n.d)	1½	**7**	33/1	63	40
1840^{2}	**Sherqy (IRE) (60)** (SEKettlewell) **5-8-10** MrsCWilliams(6) (bhd: hdwy u.p 3f out: nvr rchd ldrs)	5	**8**	16/1	54	31
1482*	**Danish Rhapsody (IRE) (85)** (LadyHerries) **4-10-7** MrsMCowdrey(12) (lw: hdwy 6f out: sn chsng ldrs: wknd fnl 2f)	½	**9**	$5/1^{2}$	78	55
100^{6}	**Celestial Choir (90)** (JLEyre) **7-10-12** MissDianaJones(4) (outpcd & lost pl 8f out: n.d)	¾	**10**	12/1	82	59
1660^{7}	**Rasayel (USA) (75)** (PDEvans) **7-9-11**ow1 MissKChilton(10) (racd wd: led tl hdd ent st: sn wknd)	5	**11**	16/1	61	37
1427^{3}	**Nosey Native (61)** (JPearce) **4-8-11** MrsLPearce(8) (chsd ldrs: ch 3f out: wknd wl over 1f out)	6	**12**	$15/2^{3}$	39	16
1145^{7}	**Hazard a Guess (IRE) (82)** (DNicholls) **7-10-4** MissJAllison(11) (hld up & bhd: hdwy appr st: wknd 3f out)	4	**13**	11/1	54	31
1176^{9}	**Story Line (92)** (DWPArbuthnot) **4-11-0** MrsDArbuthnot(1) (lost tch fnl 4f)	½	**14**	25/1	64	41

(SP 138.3%) **14 Rn**

2m 38.28 (10.48) CSF £62.86 CT £798.82 TOTE £6.90: £1.60 £3.70 £6.90 (£47.20) Trio £646.50 OWNER Mr Mark Leatham (BARNSTAPLE) BRED G. Strawbridge & London Thoroughbred Services Ltd
LONG HANDICAP Sherqy (IRE) 8-6
WEIGHT FOR AGE 3yo-15lb
1162 Raffles Rooster, given a smashing ride, was well-suited by the strong pace and won in really useful style. (5/1: op 8/1)
1329* Shaffishayes is in particularly good form at present, but met one far too good. (11/1)
1398 Temptress was surprisingly dropped out, and then took an age to get going and never had a chance. (16/1)
1016* Break the Rules, stepping-up in trip, was always finding the effort just too much. (7/2)
1398* Veridian, who is probably not an easy ride, ran well and is obviously on pretty good terms with himself. (8/1)
1268 Leviticus (IRE), trying his longest trip to date, ran reasonably but failed to pick up when asked a serious question. (8/1: 6/1-9/1)
1763 Charter has ability but, when asked to stretch, was always inclined to hang. (33/1)

1982 DANIEL PRENN ROYAL YORKSHIRE RATED STKS H'CAP (0-100) (3-Y.O) (Class B)

4-45 (4-46) **1m 2f 85y** £9,251.40 (£3,462.60: £1,693.80: £729.00: £327.00: £166.20) Stalls: Low GOING: 0.35 sec per fur (G)

				SP	RR	SF
1762^{4}	**Premier Bay (95)** (PWHarris) **3-9-3b¹** JReid(3) (mde all: kpt on wl fnl 3f)	—	**1**	10/1	103	71
966*	**Union Town (IRE) (99)** (SirMarkPrescott) **3-9-7** GDuffield(4) (lw: cl up: chal 3f out: sn rdn: no ex ins fnl f)	1¼	**2**	5/1	105	73
1399^{4}	**Lawahik (98)** (DMorley) **3-9-6** RHills(6) (lw: trckd ldrs: smooth hdwy to chal 3f out: rdn 2f out: nt run on)	2½	**3**	$3/1^{3}$	100	68
1773^{8}	**Jack The Lad (IRE) (82)** (JHetherton) **3-8-4** LCharnock(2) (chsd ldrs: outpcd over 3f out: no imp after)	4	**4**	9/1	78	46
1611*	**The Prince (95)** (GWragg) **3-9-3** MHills(5) (lw: hld up: effrt over 3f out: hung lft: no imp)	¾	**5**	$9/4^{1}$	90	58
	Al Azhar (92) (IABalding) **3-9-0** PatEddery(1) (bit bkwd: hld up: effrt 4f out: sn btn)	17	**6**	$5/2^{2}$	61	29

(SP 120.1%) **6 Rn**

2m 16.52 (7.52) CSF £55.93 TOTE £15.70: £3.30 £2.70 (£32.10) OWNER Prime Cartel (BERKHAMSTED) BRED Pendley Farm
LONG HANDICAP Jack The Lad (IRE) 8-3
OFFICIAL EXPLANATION **Al Azhar: might have injured his back on the way to the start. The Prince: the trainer reported that, according to the jockey, the colt had choked during the race.**
1762 Premier Bay had blinkers on for the first time and they worked the oracle. (10/1)
966* Union Town (IRE) had a real battle with the winner from early in the straight, and this easier ground probably found him out late on. (5/1)
1399 Lawahik had the ground he likes but, after looking likely to trot up, his response when ridden was, to say the least, very disappointing. (3/1)
1773 Jack The Lad (IRE) ran quite well in this company, but was found wanting for speed in the last half-mile. (9/1)
1611* The Prince was disappointing as, when an effort was required, all he wanted to do was hang. Something was probably wrong. (9/4)
Al Azhar looked really good last year, but this was most disappointing as he showed nothing, and something was obviously amiss. (5/2)

1983 CHARLES HENRY MEMORIAL MAIDEN STKS (3-Y.O) (Class D)

5-15 (5-15) **7f 202y** £5,420.00 (£1,640.00: £800.00: £380.00) Stalls: Low GOING: 0.35 sec per fur (G)

				SP	RR	SF
1415^{2}	**Illusion** (MRStoute) **3-9-0** JReid(3) (lw: trckd ldr: led over 2f out: shkn up & r.o fnl f: comf)	—	**1**	$4/5^{1}$	88+	43
1650^{2}	**Present Chance (80)** (BAMcMahon) **3-9-0** LNewton(1) (hld up: hdwy 3f out: chal 2f out: wknd ins fnl f)	5	**2**	15/2	78	33
1512^{3}	**Sharbadarid (IRE)** (LMCumani) **3-9-0** LDettori(4) (led tl hdd over 2f out: sn outpcd)	4	**3**	$100/30^{2}$	70	25
1030^{2}	**Radiancy (IRE)** (JPLeigh) **3-8-9** DeanMcKeown(2) (prom: hdwy & ev ch over 2f out: sn rdn & wknd)	2½	**4**	$7/2^{3}$	60	15

(SP 112.6%) **4 Rn**

1m 45.08 (8.08) CSF £6.79 TOTE £1.80: (£6.40) OWNER Cheveley Park Stud (NEWMARKET) BRED W. and R. Barnett Ltd
1415 Illusion, unlucky last time, had a nice confidence-booster and it should have taught him plenty. (4/5: 8/11-10/1)
1650 Present Chance, trying a much longer trip, ran a useful race but just failed to see it out and seven furlongs may well be ideal. (15/2)
1512 Sharbadarid (IRE) ran a shade better on this easier surface, but there is still plenty more needed. (100/30)
1030 Radiancy (IRE) had her chances but she seriously ran out of fuel approaching the final furlong. (7/2)

T/Jkpt: Not won; £10,437.61 to 16/6/97. T/Plpt: £5,496.80 (9.28 Tckts). T/Qdpt: £147.30 (21.09 Tckts) AA

1638-BRIGHTON (L-H) (Firm)
Monday June 16th
WEATHER: sunny WIND: mod bhd

1984 MONTPELIER (S) STKS (2-Y.O) (Class G)
2-15 (2-16) **5f 213y** £1,984.50 (£547.00: £259.50) Stalls: Low GOING minus 0.57 sec per fur (F)

Form	Horse		Pos	SP	RR	SF
1263[8]	**Kim's Brave** (BJMeehan) **2-8-11** TQuinn(5) (bit bkwd: a.p: bmpd 3f out: rdn over 1f out: led ins fnl f: r.o wl)	—	1	8/11[1]	61	11
1789[W]	**Medina Miss** (WGMTurner) **2-8-1**(5) DSweeney(7) (w ldr: led over 3f out tl over 1f out: r.o one pce)	2½	2	8/1	49	—
	Private Seal (GLMoore) **2-8-11** CandyMorris(2) (leggy: unf: a.p: led over 1f out tl ins fnl f: one pce)	nk	3	4/1[2]	54	4
530[5]	**Casa Rosa** (RHannon) **2-8-6** DaneO'Neill(3) (rdn & no hdwy fnl 2f)	2½	4	10/1	42	—
	Lake Wobegone (IRE) (JohnBerry) **2-8-11** MFenton(1) (leggy: led over 2f: wknd over 1f out)	12	5	15/2[3]	15	—
	Sweet Senorita (MMadgwick) **2-8-6** NVarley(6) (leggy: bit bkwd: rn wd st: a bhd)	4	6	25/1	—	—
				(SP 113.7%)		**6 Rn**

1m 9.6 (2.40) CSF £7.00 TOTE £1.80: £1.10 £3.10 (£3.70) OWNER Mr J. K. Sim (UPPER LAMBOURN) BRED C. R. Mason
Bt in 8,500gns, Casa Rosa sold 600gns to a purchaser in the Isle Of Wight.
Kim's Brave still did not look fully fit, but nevertheless went off odds-on favourite and, never far away, launched his challenge from below the distance. He managed to get on top inside the final furlong and soon put daylight between himself and his rivals. (8/11)
1290 Medina Miss, a lightly-made filly, was in front by halfway. Collared below the distance, she was soon back in third place but, struggling on, managed to regain the runner-up berth. (8/1: op 4/1)
Private Seal proved rather colty and troublesome in the paddock on this racecourse debut. Nevertheless, he went on below the distance before overhauled inside the final furlong. (4/1)
530 Casa Rosa, given an eleven-week break, was making little impression on the principals in the final quarter-mile. (10/1: op 9/4)
Lake Wobegone (IRE), quite a tall colt with more to like about him than the others in the field, was sent off in front. Collared over three furlongs from home, he grimly tried to hold on, but had come to the end of his tether below the distance. (15/2: 10/1-11/2)

1985 LEWES LIMITED STKS (0-60) (3-Y.O+) (Class F)
2-45 (2-48) **1m 1f 209y** £2,277.00 (£627.00: £297.00) Stalls: High GOING minus 0.57 sec per fur (F)

Form	Horse		Pos	SP	RR	SF
1837*	**Philistar (76)** (KRBurke) **4-9-11** BDoyle(2) (stdy hdwy 4f out: led over 1f out: pushed out)	—	1	8/11[1]	76	47
	Double Eight (IRE) (60) (BWHills) **3-8-4** AClark(7) (swtg: hld up: chsd ldr over 4f out: led over 2f out tl over 1f out: unable qckn)	2½	2	10/1	63	22
1641[6]	**Oberons Boy (IRE) (58)** (SDow) **4-9-5** TQuinn(6) (lw: hld up: rdn over 1f out: r.o one pce)	s.h	3	7/1[3]	66	37
1459[13]	**Clouds Hill (FR) (57)** (RHannon) **4-9-5v**[1] DaneO'Neill(4) (chsd ldr: led 7f out: clr over 4f out: hdd over 2f out: wknd over 1f out)	4	4	16/1	60	31
1859[5]	**Princess of Hearts (63)** (MCPipe) **3-8-6b** GDuffield(3) (a bhd)	8	5	7/2[2]	46	5
1506[6]	**Hannalou (FR) (55)** (TGMills) **4-9-2** JReid(5) (bhd fnl 3f)	13	6	8/1	23	—
1796[10]	**Suleika Dancer (53)** (SGKnight) **4-8-11**(5) GFaulkner(1) (led 3f: wknd over 4f out)	5	7	50/1	15	—
				(SP 120.7%)		**7 Rn**

1m 59.9 (1.60) CSF £9.76 TOTE £2.20: £1.20 £6.00 (£21.00) OWNER Mr Nigel Shields (WANTAGE) BRED John A. Jones Morgan
WEIGHT FOR AGE 3yo-12lb
1837* Philistar, with 6lb or more in hand of his rivals on official adjusted ratings, continues in a rich vein of form, and had little problem landing his fourth race of the month. (8/11)
Double Eight (IRE), the only runner without a recent outing under her belt, ran her best race to date. Sent to the front over a quarter-of-a-mile from home, she was firmly put in her place when collared below the distance. (10/1: 7/1-12/1)
1427 Oberons Boy (IRE) stayed on from below the distance and failed by only a whisker to take second prize. He is not easy to win with and has now scored just once from twenty-six starts. (7/1)
Clouds Hill (FR) showed his first sign of form this season. In front seven furlongs from home, he forged clear at the top of the hill, but he was headed before the quarter-mile point, and had run out of gas below the distance. He remains a maiden. (16/1)

1986 OPERATIC SOCIETY CHALLENGE CUP MEDIAN AUCTION MAIDEN STKS (3 & 4-Y.O) (Class F)
3-15 (3-16) **1m 3f 196y** £2,461.80 (£679.80: £323.40) Stalls: High GOING minus 0.57 sec per fur (F)

Form	Horse		Pos	SP	RR	SF
1296[7]	**Tommy Tortoise (67)** (MissGayKelleway) **3-8-10** SSanders(6) (lw: hld up: rdn over 4f out: edgd lft & led over 1f out: edgd lft ins fnl f: r.o wl)	—	1	7/2[2]	70	25
1563[3]	**Little Miss Rocker (70)** (IABalding) **3-8-5** TQuinn(2) (a.p: led over 5f out tl over 1f out: 2nd & btn whn nt clr run ins fnl f)	1¾	2	11/10[1]	63	18
773[8]	**Shilling (IRE)** (ACStewart) **3-8-5** DHarrison(4) (hld up: rdn whn bmpd over 1f out: 3rd & btn whn hmpd on ins ins fnl f)	2½	3	8/1	59	14
1592[6]	**Walk On By (68)** (RHannon) **3-8-10** DaneO'Neill(1) (led over 6f: rdn over 2f out: 3rd & btn whn nt clr run over 1f out)	1¾	4	5/1[3]	62	17
1502[2]	**Zafarelli** (JRJenkins) **3-8-10** JReid(3) (prom over 8f)	1¾	5	12/1	60	15
1276[10]	**Mystic Strand** (WGMTurner) **4-9-0**(5) DSweeney(5) (a bhd)	14	6	16/1	36	5
				(SP 111.2%)		**6 Rn**

2m 31.1 (3.50) CSF £6.94 TOTE £4.00: £1.40 £1.20 (£4.60) OWNER Mr Tommy Staunton (WHITCOMBE) BRED R. E. A. Bott (Wigmore Street) Ltd
WEIGHT FOR AGE 3yo-14lb
1140 Tommy Tortoise was certainly the paddock pick. Despite drifting left on the camber, he led below the distance but, continuing to drift inside the final furlong, caused a knock-on effect. However, he was the best horse on the day and was quite rightly allowed to keep the race after a Stewards' enquiry. (7/2)
1563 Little Miss Rocker, a tall filly, was taking another step-up in distance. Bustled to the front at the top of the hill, she was collared below the distance and was held in second place when done no favours by the hanging winner inside the final furlong. (11/10: evens-6/5)
Shilling (IRE), a tall, plain filly, was beginning to get going when involved in scrimmaging below the distance. She was grimly trying to stay on, but would not have troubled the winner, when hampered along the inside rail inside the final furlong. (8/1)
1592 Walk On By attempted to make all the running. Collared over five furlongs from home, he looked to be labouring when done no favours below the distance. (5/1: op 9/4)
1502 Zafarelli was having his first run for his new stable, but had been hung out to dry over three furlongs from home. (12/1)

1987 HAILSHAM H'CAP (0-70) (3-Y.O+ F & M) (Class E)
3-45 (3-46) **7f 214y** £2,888.25 (£861.00: £410.50: £185.25) Stalls: Low GOING minus 0.57 sec per fur (F)

			SP	RR	SF
1373[4]	**Whispered Melody (53)** (RAkehurst) **4-8-11** AClark(5) (a.p: chsd ldr 5f out: led over 3f out: clr 2f out: r.o wl)—	**1**	100/30[3]	64	23
1739[8]	**Sylvan Princess (70)** (DJSCosgrove) **4-9-7**(7) CLowther(3) (s.s: rdn & hdwy over 2f out: r.o one pce)..............3	**2**	3/1[2]	75	34
1668[4]	**Queen's Insignia (USA) (53)** (PFICole) **4-8-11b[1]** TQuinn(1) (led over 4f: rdn over 2f out: one pce)..............1¼	**3**	11/4[1]	56	15
1373[W]	**Good News (IRE) (65)** (MMadgwick) **3-8-13** RPerham(2) (lw: rdn over 4f out: hdwy over 1f out: r.o one pce) hd	**4**	6/1	67	16
1484[2]	**Ladybower (IRE) (38)** (JRPoulton) **5-7-10** NVarley(7) (chsd ldr 3f: wknd over 2f out)..............4	**5**	12/1	32	—
1508[2]	**Fable (55)** (JARToller) **3-8-3** SSanders(6) (lw: s.s: a bhd)..............3	**6**	12/1	43	—
1567[7]	**Mashkorah (USA) (56)** (RHannon) **3-8-4** DaneO'Neill(4) (5th whn j.path over 5f out: bhd fnl 5f)..............3	**7**	14/1	38	—

(SP 111.1%) **7 Rn**

1m 33.4 (2.10) CSF £11.77 TOTE £4.00: £1.70 £1.80 (£5.80) OWNER Mr D. J. Hillyard (EPSOM) BRED Pendley Farm
LONG HANDICAP Ladybower (IRE) 7-2
WEIGHT FOR AGE 3yo-10lb

1373 Whispered Melody struck the front over three furlongs from home and, rigorously rousted along, forged clear to lose her maiden tag. (100/30)
1219 Sylvan Princess likes to hear her feet rattle but, despite staying on to take second place in the closing stages, was unable to trouble the winner. She could do with a slight drop in the handicap. (3/1)
1668 Queen's Insignia (USA), fitted with blinkers for the first time, was reverting back to a more suitable trip. Attempting to make all the running, she was collared over three furlongs from home and then failed to find another gear. (11/4)
1008* Good News (IRE) failed to repeat the form she showed here last month, but did struggle on from below the distance, only just failing to take third prize. (6/1)
1484 Ladybower (IRE), 8lb out of the handicap, had been hung out to dry over a quarter-of-a-mile from home. (12/1)
1508 Fable (12/1: 6/1-14/1)
Mashkorah (USA) (14/1: 7/1-16/1)

1988 COLDEAN MAIDEN H'CAP (0-70) (3-Y.O) (Class E)
4-15 (4-15) **6f 209y** £3,174.25 (£949.00: £454.50: £207.25) Stalls: Low GOING minus 0.57 sec per fur (F)

			SP	RR	SF
1921[W]	**Feel A Line (45)** (BJMeehan) **3-7-10b**(3)ow2 MartinDwyer(8) (hdwy over 3f out: led 1f out: edgd lft ins fnl f: r.o wl)..............—	**1**	11/2	54	27
1810[14]	**Curzon Street (67)** (HCandy) **3-9-7** CRutter(2) (led over 5f out to 1f out: 2nd & btn whn n.m.r on ins ins fnl f)1¾	**2**	12/1	72	47
1781[5]	**Bold Spring (IRE) (63)** (RHannon) **3-9-3** DaneO'Neill(5) (hdwy over 3f out: hrd rdn over 2f out: r.o one pce) 1¼	**3**	9/4[1]	65	40
1012[6]	**Fan of Vent-Axia (45)** (DJSCosgrove) **3-7-10**(3) MBaird(9) (rdn over 3f out: hdwy over 1f out: r.o wl ins fnl f) s.h	**4**	12/1	47	22
1633[9]	**Linden's Lad (IRE) (53)** (JRJenkins) **3-8-7** JReid(1) (bmpd s: hdwy 5f out: rdn over 2f out: one pce)..............1¼	**5**	5/1[3]	52	27
1780[4]	**Miss Barcelona (IRE) (45)** (MJPolglase) **3-7-8**(5) RMullen(6) (b.nr hind: a.p: rdn over 2f out: wknd over 1f out)..............½	**6**	10/1	43	18
1483[2]	**Ar Hyd Y Knos (46)** (GLMoore) **3-8-0** JQuinn(4) (led over 1f: rdn over 2f out: wknd over 1f out)..............3	**7**	9/2[2]	37	12
1467[25]	**Canton Ron (45)** (CADwyer) **3-7-13** NVarley(3) (lw: hld up: rdn 4f out: wknd 2f out)..............4	**8**	16/1	27	2
1458[15]	**Saltimbanco (58)** (RAkehurst) **3-8-5**(7) DDenby(7) (lw: bhd fnl 5f)..............4	**9**	12/1	31	6

(SP 119.1%) **9 Rn**

1m 20.6 (0.60) CSF £64.52 CT £176.72 TOTE £6.70: £1.90 £2.10 £1.10 (£37.10) Trio £33.00 OWNER Mr J. S. Gutkin (UPPER LAMBOURN) BRED W. R. Jones

1807 Feel A Line, who edged closer at halfway, struck the front entering the final furlong and, although drifting left, doing the runner-up no favours, was already in command. (11/2: 7/2-6/1)
Curzon Street ran her best race since her Lingfield debut last year. Soon at the head of affairs, she was caught entering the final furlong and was already booked for second place when slightly tightened up by the winner soon afterwards. (12/1: 8/1-14/1)
1781 Bold Spring (IRE), who inched closer at halfway, struggled on for third. He remains a maiden after fourteen attempts and is becoming very disappointing. (9/4)
Fan of Vent-Axia, 9lb lower than at the beginning of the season, ran on in the last furlong and a half, only just failing to take third prize. (12/1:op 20/1)
Linden's Lad (IRE), soon in a handy position, was made to look very pedestrian in the final quarter-mile. He is a very poor performer who has yet to make the frame. (5/1)
1780 Miss Barcelona (IRE) is extremely exposed and appears a lost cause, having now failed to get off the mark after twenty-four attempts. (10/1: 6/1-11/1)
1483 Ar Hyd Y Knos (9/2: 5/2-5/1)

1989 HANNINGTONS OF BRIGHTON H'CAP (0-80) (3-Y.O) (Class D)
4-45 (4-47) **5f 213y** £3,518.20 (£1,048.60: £499.80: £225.40) Stalls: Low GOING minus 0.57 sec per fur (F)

			SP	RR	SF
995[3]	**Levelled (68)** (MRChannon) **3-8-8**(3) PPMurphy(3) (lw: swtchd lft 2f out: hdwy on ins over 1f out: hrd rdn: last last strides)..............—	**1**	9/2[2]	75	30
1644*	**Tear White (IRE) (67)** (TGMills) **3-8-7**(3) AWhelan(8) (led: rdn fnl f: hdd last strides)..............nk	**2**	4/1[1]	73	28
1374[13]	**Marengo (68)** (JAkehurst) **3-8-11** SSanders(4) (lw: a.p: hrd rdn over 1f out: ev ch wl ins fnl f: r.o)..............s.h	**3**	8/1	74	29
1638*	**Third Party (68)** (SDow) **3-8-11** JReid(6) (bmpd s: chsd ldr over 4f out tl over 2f out: wknd over 1f out)..............5	**4**	4/1[1]	61	16
1957[4]	**Just Loui (78)** (WGMTurner) **3-9-2**(5) DSweeney(7) (chsd ldr tl hmpd on ins over 4f out: wknd over 2f out)......3	**5**	5/1[3]	63	18
1661[5]	**Farewell My Love (IRE) (66)** (PFICole) **3-8-9v[1]** TQuinn(2) (b.off fore: bmpd s: a bhd)..............1½	**6**	4/1[1]	47	2
94*	**Masterstroke (69)** (BJMeehan) **3-8-5**(7) GHannon(1) (bit bkwd: bhd fnl 4f)..............4	**7**	8/1	39	—
765[8]	**Geordie Lad (55)** (JABennett) **3-7-12v[1]** NVarley(5) (b: bhd fnl 3f)..............9	**8**	33/1	1	—

(SP 120.0%) **8 Rn**

1m 8.2 (1.00) CSF £21.96 CT £130.63 TOTE £5.20: £1.60 £2.20 £2.90 (£21.30) OWNER Maygain Ltd (UPPER LAMBOURN) BRED J. F. Watson
STEWARDS' ENQUIRY Whelan susp. 25-29/6/97 (careless riding).

995 Levelled was rather surprisingly switched over to the rails by Murphy, when he would have been much better advised going for a gap towards the outside. Nevertheless, he picked up ground below the distance and, responding to pressure, got in front in the last few strides. (9/2: op 3/1)
1644* Tear White (IRE) is getting used to this course and attempted to make all the running. It looked as if he was holding on below the distance but he was worried out of it in the last few strides. His jockey was later suspended for five days for careless riding over an incident at the top of the hill, where he tightened up another rival. (4/1)

1012 Marengo has proved himself to be a very tricky customer, but this was one of his better days. With his jockey desperately trying to launch a challenge, the colt did not look completely happy with the situation but, nevertheless, did little wrong. (8/1)
1638* Third Party had more on her plate and, after showing in second place for much of the way, had shot her bolt below the distance. (4/1: 3/1-9/2)
1957 Just Loui found his exertions on Saturday taking their toll, and was waving the white flag over two furlongs from home. This run is best ignored but he has yet to win on grass. (5/1)
94* Masterstroke (8/1: op 9/2)

T/Plpt: £11.70 (1,027.67 Tckts). T/Qdpt: £9.30 (65.66 Tckts) AK

1600-MUSSELBURGH (R-H) (Good)
Monday June 16th
WEATHER: Sunny WIND: slt bhd

1990 E.B.F. MEDIAN AUCTION MAIDEN STKS (2-Y.O F) (Class F)
2-00 (2-00) **5f** £2,705.00 (£815.00: £395.00: £185.00) Stalls: High GOING minus 0.14 sec per fur (G)

				SP	RR	SF
1569^{4}	**Its All Relative** (JBerry) **2-8-11** KDarley(4) (lw: led after 1f: styd on strly fnl 2f)	—	1	$8/11^{1}$	75	33
1255^{2}	**Carambo** (JLEyre) **2-8-11** RLappin(2) (lw: cl up: rdn 2f out: nt qckn)	1¾	2	$13/8^{2}$	69	27
1941^{5}	**Oriel Girl** (PDEvans) **2-8-11** JFEgan(3) (a chsng ldrs: rdn 2f out: no ex fnl f)	1½	3	$8/1^{3}$	65	23
1280^{3}	**Crafty Pet (IRE)** (RAFahey) **2-8-11** ACulhane(1) (cl up tl rdn & wknd 2f out)	12	4	16/1	26	—
1839^{8}	**Ngaere Princess** (WTKemp) **2-8-11b** JCarroll(5) (led 1f: wknd qckly ½-wy)	6	5	100/1	7	—

(SP 114.0%) **5 Rn**

60.6 secs (2.90) CSF £2.08 TOTE £2.00: £1.10 £1.10 (£1.40) OWNER Mr R. Leah (COCKERHAM) BRED R. Leah
1569 Its All Relative, a useful-looking sort, had the edge from a long way out and won tidily. (8/11)
1255 Carambo had her usual two handlers in the paddock, but behaved well and ran another fair race, and will obviously find her mark. (13/8)
1941 Oriel Girl has been disappointing of late, but this was a much better effort. (8/1: op 5/1)
1280 Crafty Pet (IRE) had the disadvantage of racing on the outside of the field, but this was still a poor effort. (16/1)
Ngaere Princess, ridden with more restraint this time, showed little. (100/1)

1991 WIMPEY HOMES JUBILEE RATING RELATED MAIDEN STKS (0-60) (3-Y.O+) (Class F)
2-30 (2-30) **1m 16y** £2,582.50 (£720.00: £347.50) Stalls: High GOING minus 0.14 sec per fur (G)

				SP	RR	SF
1757^{2}	**Degree (60)** (SCWilliams) **4-9-4** JFEgan(2) (lw: a.p: led wl over 1f out: hung lft: drvn out)	—	1	$2/1^{1}$	59	44
	Beano Script (60) (JHanson) **4-9-7** ACulhane(6) (lw: bhd: hdwy 3f out: hung bdly lft: ev ch 1f out: kpt on u.p)	1	2	$100/30^{3}$	60	45
1756^{15}	**Hever Golf Charmer (49)** (TJNaughton) **3-8-11** JWeaver(4) (hdwy ½-wy: styd on u.p fnl 2f: nvr able to chal)	¾	3	7/1	59	34
1506^{12}	**Time of Night (USA) (58)** (RGuest) **4-9-4b¹** PBloomfield(3) (lw: led & sn clr: hdd wl over 1f out: sn btn)	1¾	4	$9/4^{2}$	52	37
1733^{5}	**Hong Kong Express (IRE) (50)** (JBerry) **3-8-8b** KDarley(1) (chsd ldr: rdn over 3f out: sn wknd)	7	5	10/1	38	13

(SP 108.8%) **5 Rn**

1m 43.6 (4.60) CSF £7.92 TOTE £4.30: £1.40 £1.30 (£8.30) OWNER Mr D. A. Shekells (NEWMARKET) BRED Juddmonte Farms
WEIGHT FOR AGE 3yo-10lb
STEWARDS' ENQUIRY Egan susp. 25-26/6/97 (excessive use of whip)
1757 Degree broke her duck at last but, in doing so, had a very hard race and hung badly left under vigorous driving. (2/1)
Beano Script, the pick on looks, appeared to be travelling best halfway up the straight, but then proved clueless and hung badly left, throwing his chance away. (100/30)
Hever Golf Charmer is learning and was staying on, but this was not a very good event. (7/1)
1503 Time of Night (USA) had the blinkers on for the first time and probably raced too freely. (9/4)
1733 Hong Kong Express (IRE) was trying her longest trip to date, and it did not appear to help at all. (10/1: op 5/1)

1992 WIMPEY HOMES EDINBURGH GOLD CUP H'CAP (0-75) (3-Y.O+) (Class D)
3-00 (3-00) **1m 4f 31y** £5,608.00 (£1,684.00: £812.00: £376.00) Stalls: High GOING minus 0.14 sec per fur (G)

				SP	RR	SF
1660^{5}	**Ambidextrous (IRE) (47)** (EJAlston) **5-8-0**ow2 JFEgan(6) (lw: a.p: rdn to ld over 2f out: hung bdly lft: styd on wl)	—	1	$5/2^{2}$	59	40
1748^{5}	**Westminster (IRE) (60)** (MHTompkins) **5-8-13v** KDarley(4) (lw: hld up: hdwy 3f out: sn rdn: styd on: nt pce to chal)	3	2	$5/1^{3}$	68	51
1313^{2}	**Manful (75)** (MissLAPerratt) **5-10-0b** NKennedy(5) (lw: chsd ldr: effrt over 3f out: one pce fnl 2f)	2½	3	9/1	80	63
1601*	**Latvian (57)** (RAllan) **10-8-10** JWeaver(3) (hld up: swtchd stands' side & effrt over 3f out: rdn & no imp)	1½	4	10/1	60	43
1559^{4}	**Keep Battling (48)** (JSGoldie) **7-7-12**(3) PFessey(2) (hld up & bhd: effrt over 3f out: nvr able to chal)	nk	5	6/1	50	33
1515^{2}	**The Butterwick Kid (60)** (RAFahey) **4-8-6**(7) RWinston(1) (trckd ldrs: effrt over 2f out: one pce)	s.h	6	$13/8^{1}$	62	45
1281^{5}	**Jubran (USA) (45)** (JLEyre) **11-7-12** TWilliams(7) (lw: led & sn clr: hdd over 2f out: sn wknd)	8	7	20/1	37	20

(SP 121.5%) **7 Rn**

2m 38.6 (5.10) CSF £15.33 TOTE £4.00: £1.30 £3.50 (£10.70) OWNER Mrs Carol McPhail (PRESTON) BRED Saeed Manana
1660 Ambidextrous (IRE) kept tabs on the leaders for a change and led some way out but, despite hanging badly under pressure, he was never in danger. (5/2)
1748 Westminster (IRE) likes to come from behind and needs a strong pace and, despite staying on, was never quite good enough, but does look as though he is coming to hand. (5/1)
1313 Manful looks particularly well at the moment and this was not a bad effort. (9/1: 6/1-10/1)
1601* Latvian ran reasonably but was never fully co-operating. (10/1)
1559 Keep Battling is the one horse in this yard who is not really firing at the moment. (6/1)
1515 The Butterwick Kid looks to have lost his edge for the time being. (13/8)

1993 WIMPEY HOMES FANFARE CLAIMING STKS (3-Y.O+) (Class F)
3-30 (3-31) **7f 30y** £2,635.00 (£735.00: £355.00) Stalls: High GOING minus 0.14 sec per fur (G)

				SP	RR	SF
1631^{9}	**Broctune Gold (65)** (MrsMReveley) **6-9-10** ACulhane(4) (mde all: qcknd clr over 2f out: comf)	—	1	$11/10^{1}$	62+	41
1878^{13}	**Scathebury (62)** (KRBurke) **4-9-12** JFEgan(5) (hld up: effrt ½-wy: styd on fnl 2f: no ch w wnr)	4	2	$7/2^{3}$	55	34
1289^{15}	**Lady Silk (33)** (MissJFCraze) **6-8-13** SWebster(3) (in tch: outpcd 3f out: kpt on fnl f)	2½	3	33/1	36	15

				SP	RR	SF
1389^{7}	**Miletrian City (40)** (JBerry) **4-8-11b**(3) PFessey(6) (bhd: styd on fnl 3f: n.d)	½	**4**	16/1	36	15
1835^{13}	**Antithesis (IRE) (48)** (JSHaldane) **4-8-11** JCarroll(7) (b.hind: hld up: hdwy 4f out: sn chsng ldrs: wknd appr fnl f)	2	**5**	16/1	29	8
1835^{17}	**Diet (33)** (MissLAPerratt) **11-8-12v** JWeaver(1) (cl up tl wknd fnl 3f)	7	**6**	25/1	14	—
1674^{5}	**Genuine John (IRE) (62)** (JParkes) **4-9-3**(3) RHavlin(2) (b: chsd wnr to ½-wy: sn rdn & wknd)	2½	**7**	5/2 ²	17	—
1802^{10}	**Cascatelle Bleue (IRE) (55)** (MHTompkins) **4-8-9v¹** KDarley(8) (prom tl rdn & wknd fnl 3f)	¾	**8**	10/1	4	—
				(SP 126.1%)		**8 Rn**

1m 30.7 (4.70) CSF £5.60 TOTE £2.10: £1.10 £1.60 £5.20 (£3.50) OWNER Mrs M. B. Thwaites (SALTBURN) BRED A. J. Poulton (Epping) Ltd

1285 Broctune Gold is at his best when allowed to dominate, and was always far too good for these. (11/10: 6/4-evens)

1139* Scathebury, after a couple of poor efforts, put in a better run but had no chance with the winner, despite staying on. (7/2)

203 Lady Silk has not been running well lately but, under a determined ride, did make some late ground and obviously has more ability if she can be persuaded. (33/1)

526 Miletrian City is showing signs of coming to form but is never one to rely on. (16/1)

1572 Antithesis (IRE) showed a good turn of speed halfway through the race, but then failed to get home over this longer trip. (16/1)

1674 Genuine John (IRE) (5/2: 2/1-3/1)

Cascatelle Bleue (IRE) (10/1: 7/1-12/1)

1994 WIMPEY HOMES OPTIMA H'CAP (0-70) (3-Y.O+) (Class E)

4-00 (4-01) **1m 16y** £3,571.00 (£1,078.00: £524.00: £247.00) Stalls: High GOING minus 0.14 sec per fur (G)

				SP	RR	SF
1818*	**Best of All (IRE) (67)** (JBerry) **5-10-2b** 5x KDarley(3) (bhd: hdwy 3f out: styd on wl to ld wl ins fnl f)	—	**1**	13/2 ²	80	59
1862*	**Jedi Knight (65)** (MWEasterby) **3-8-13**(5) 5x GParkin(4) (outpcd appr st: hdwy 3f out: led appr fnl f: nt qckn towards fin)	1½	**2**	4/6 ¹	75	44
1830^{4}	**Euro Sceptic (IRE) (43)** (TDEasterby) **5-8-3b**(3)ow1 RHavlin(2) (lw: cl up: led over 2f out tl appr fnl f: one pce)	2	**3**	9/1	49	27
1862^{7}	**Thatched (IRE) (55)** (REBarr) **7-8-13**(5) KSked(7) (chsd ldrs: hdwy & ev ch over 1f out: no ex)	1½	**4**	25/1	58	37
1384^{4}	**Riccarton (50)** (PCalver) **4-8-13** JCarroll(1) (dwlt: hdwy 3f out: sn hrd rdn & no imp)	2	**5**	10/1	49	28
1442^{4}	**Broughton's Pride (IRE) (53)** (JLEyre) **6-9-2** MGallagher(5) (chsd ldrs tl wknd fnl 2f)	4	**6**	8/1 ³	44	23
1472^{11}	**Imperial Or Metric (IRE) (64)** (RAFahey) **3-8-10b¹**(7) RWinston(6) (led tl hdd & wknd over 2f out)	3½	**7**	33/1	48	17
				(SP 110.3%)		**7 Rn**

1m 43.2 (4.20) CSF £9.52 TOTE £6.30: £2.40 £1.30 (£3.10) OWNER Mr Robert Aird (COCKERHAM) BRED Mrs D. Hutch

WEIGHT FOR AGE 3yo-10lb

1818* Best of All (IRE) is in really good form and proved most determined under pressure to take this. (13/2: 5/1-8/1)

1862* Jedi Knight looked all at sea on this track, and should be forgiven this lapse. (4/6)

1830 Euro Sceptic (IRE) looked particularly well and has ability, but gives the impression that he is not fully co-operating. (9/1: op 6/1)

824* Thatched (IRE) is a difficult sort to weigh up but, basically, he saves his best for Carlisle. (25/1)

1384 Riccarton has the ability to win but, as yet, lacks the inclination. (10/1: op 6/1)

1442 Broughton's Pride (IRE) (8/1: 6/1-10/1)

958 Imperial Or Metric (IRE) was tried with blinkers, but they had absolutely no effect. (33/1)

1995 WIMPEY HOMES PAGEANT H'CAP (0-70) (3-Y.O) (Class E)

4-30 (4-31) **5f** £3,148.50 (£948.00: £459.00: £214.50) Stalls: High GOING minus 0.14 sec per fur (G)

				SP	RR	SF
1730*	**William's Well (51)** (MWEasterby) **3-8-2b** DaleGibson(4) (lw: in tch: hdwy & hung lft appr fnl f: sn led: hung rt & r.o u.p)	—	**1**	7/2 ¹	59	35
1566^{4}	**College Princess (46)** (SCWilliams) **3-7-4**(7) DarrenWilliams(8) (a chsng ldrs: kpt on fnl 2f)	1½	**2**	14/1	49	25
1681*	**Nopalea (70)** (TJNaughton) **3-9-2**(5) TEDurcan(2) (lw: bhd: hdwy ½-wy: nt clr run & swtchd over 1f out: nrst fin)	¾	**3**	7/2 ¹	71	47
1730^{2}	**Tinker's Surprise (IRE) (52)** (JBalding) **3-8-3** TWilliams(9) (led early: led 2f out tl hdd 1f out: no ex)	1	**4**	10/1	50	26
1792^{2}	**Suite Factors (61)** (KRBurke) **3-8-7**(5) GParkin(6) (chsd ldrs: outpcd ½-wy: kpt on: no imp)	1½	**5**	13/2 ³	54	30
1835^{8}	**Impish (IRE) (53)** (TJEtherington) **3-8-4** MGallagher(7) (dwlt: hdwy ½-wy: no imp)	s.h	**6**	10/1	46	22
1127^{15}	**Keen To Please (51)** (DenysSmith) **3-7-11**(5) IonaWands(3) (chsd ldrs: effrt 2f out: hmpd appr fnl f: no imp)	2	**7**	14/1	37	13
1730^{5}	**Northern Sal (55)** (MissLAPerratt) **3-8-1**(5) KSked(11) (chsd ldrs: rdn whn hmpd appr fnl f: wknd)	1¼	**8**	12/1	37	13
1604*	**Toronto (57)** (JBerry) **3-8-5b**(3) PFessey(10) (sn led tl hdd 2f out: sn wknd)	1	**9**	9/2 ²	36	12
	Miss St Kitts (45) (JSGoldie) **3-7-3**(7) JMcAuley(1) (nvr wnt pce)	hd	**10**	20/1	24	—
	Tazibari (63) (DMoffatt) **3-8-11**(3) DarrenMoffatt(5) (sn outpcd & bhd)	7	**11**	20/1	19	—
				(SP 124.7%)		**11 Rn**

60.0 secs (2.30) CSF £53.51 CT £173.31 TOTE £5.50: £2.00 £2.50 £3.00 (£51.60) Trio £160.60 OWNER Mr K. Hodgson (SHERIFF HUTTON) BRED M. W. Easterby and K. Hodgson

LONG HANDICAP Miss St Kitts 7-7

1730* William's Well responded to pressure but, in doing so, wandered about badly and seems quite a hard ride. (7/2: op 2/1)

1566 College Princess does not look much in the paddock, but is running well at the moment and another furlong might help. (14/1)

1681* Nopalea had a good draw, but her come-from-behind style of racing proved her undoing, as she was always struggling for a clear run. (7/2)

1730 Tinker's Surprise (IRE) keeps running well but is just short of that finishing dash. (10/1)

1792 Suite Factors normally likes to make it, but he was never quick enough on this occasion. (13/2)

1223 Impish (IRE) cannot afford to give away ground at the start on a track as sharp as this. (10/1)

779 Keen To Please was running reasonably when she got murdered approaching the final furlong. (14/1)

1730 Northern Sal (12/1: op 8/1)

1996 WIMPEY HOMES FRESCO APPRENTICE H'CAP (0-60) (3-Y.O+) (Class G)

5-00 (5-02) **1m 6f** £2,388.00 (£668.00: £324.00) Stalls: High GOING minus 0.14 sec per fur (G)

				SP	RR	SF
1118^{3}	**Forgie (IRE) (58)** (PCalver) **4-9-12** DarrenMoffatt(6) (a.p: rdn to ld ins fnl f: styd on wl)	—	**1**	5/1 ³	70	—
1605*	**Hasta la Vista (47)** (MWEasterby) **7-8-12b**(3) GParkin(12) (lw: led tl hdd over 2f out: rallied to disp ld ins fnl f: sn hdd: kpt on wl)	½	**2**	2/1 ¹	58	—
1623^{3}	**Afon Alwen (59)** (SCWilliams) **4-9-6**(7) DarrenWilliams(4) (hld up: gd hdwy 4f out: led over 2f out tl ins fnl f: no ex)	1	**3**	11/4 ²	69	—
1785^{4}	**Warrlin (59)** (CWFairhurst) **3-8-3**(7) TSiddall(11) (in tch: effrt 3f out: r.o one pce)	5	**4**	25/1	64	—
1574^{7}	**Finestatetobein (31)** (FWatson) **4-7-13** PFessey(9) (lw: prom: effrt 4f out: rdn & one pce)	½	**5**	20/1	35	—

1605^{4}	**Recluse (28)** (WTKemp) **6-7-3b**(7) PBradley(10) (lw: cl up tl wknd 3f out)	5	**6**	25/1	26	—
	Valiant Dash (28) (JSGoldie) **11-7-3**(7) JMcAuley(2) (chsd ldrs tl outpcd 6f out: n.d after)	2½	**7**	20/1	23	—
1585^{6}	**Penny Peppermint (28)** (REBarr) **5-7-3**(7) NPollard(3) (hdwy ½-wy: outpcd ent st: sn btn)	1	**8**	33/1	22	—
1732^{4}	**Zamhareer (USA) (45)** (WStorey) **6-8-8v**(5) IonaWands(1) (lw: racd wd: pushed along most of wy: prom tl outpcd fnl 4f)	2	**9**	$5/1^{3}$	37	—
1281^{11}	**Dunrowan (50)** (MrsMReveley) **4-9-1**(3) SCopp(7) (lw: hld up & bhd: hdwy 4f out: hrd rdn & wknd fnl 2f)	hd	**10**	25/1	42	—
	Ijab (CAN) (35) (JParkes) **7-8-3b**ow2 RHavlin(5) (b: chsd ldrs tl wknd fnl 3f)	1½	**11**	9/1	25	—
1601^{10}	**She's A Winner (IRE) (37)** (PMonteith) **4-8-0**(5) KSked(8) (bhd most of wy)	3	**12**	33/1	24	—
				(SP 130.3%)	**12 Rn**	

3m 8.1 CSF £14.22 CT £32.42 TOTE £5.70: £2.20 £1.20 £1.90 (£7.20) Trio £9.70 OWNER Mrs Janis MacPherson (RIPON) BRED Stilvi Compania Financiera And Roncon Ltd.

LONG HANDICAP Valiant Dash 7-5 Penny Peppermint 7-8 Recluse 7-4

WEIGHT FOR AGE 3yo-17lb

1118 Forgie (IRE) stays well and showed fine courage to get the better of a most determined opponent. (5/1: 4/1-6/1)

1605* Hasta la Vista seems to relish a battle but had to admit defeat, although he does look particularly well at the moment. (2/1)

1623 Afon Alwen, stepping-up in trip, got to the front too soon and then failed to last home. More patient tactics are needed. (11/4)

Warrlin seems short of any turn of foot and was just marking time all the way up the straight. (25/1)

Finestatetobein showed her first real signs of form and is beginning to come to herself looks-wise. (20/1)

1605 Recluse again took the eye in the paddock, but his performance left something to be desired. (25/1)

1732 Zamhareer (USA) won his two races over two miles last season, and seems to have lost his dash at the moment as he was off the bridle throughout. (5/1: 4/1-6/1)

Ijab (CAN) (9/1: 7/1-12/1)

T/Plpt: £33.20 (315.6 Tckts). T/Qdpt: £5.70 (131.57 Tckts) AA

1797-PONTEFRACT (L-H) (Good, Good to firm patches)
Monday June 16th

WEATHER: fine WIND: almost nil

1997 TATTERSALLS MAIDEN AUCTION STKS (2-Y.O F) (Class E)

6-45 (6-48) **6f** £3,347.00 (£1,016.00: £498.00: £239.00) Stalls: Low GOING minus 0.11 sec per fur (G)

				SP	RR	SF
	Risky Girl (MJHeaton-Ellis) **2-8-0** JLowe(9) (leggy: unf: mde virtually all: hld on wl towards fin)	—	**1**	16/1	66	9
1616^{2}	**Demolition Jo** (PDEvans) **2-8-1** JFEgan(10) (chsd ldrs on ins: nt clr run over 2f out: ev ch fnl f: r.o u.p)	hd	**2**	$9/4^{1}$	67	10
1564^{6}	**Aspen (IRE)** (RHannon) **2-8-5** GCarter(12) (trckd ldrs: rdn & edgd lft over 1f out: nt qckn nr fin)	½	**3**	$5/1^{2}$	69	12
	Delciana (IRE) (PWHarris) **2-8-6** KDarley(6) (neat: chsd ldrs: nt qckn appr fnl f)	1¾	**4**	$11/2^{3}$	66	9
1253^{11}	**Miss Main Street (IRE)** (JJQuinn) **2-8-1** DWright(17) (hdwy on outside over 2f out: edgd lft & styd on wl fnl f)	s.h	**5**	33/1	61	4
1760^{17}	**No Shame** (JGSmyth-Osbourne) **2-8-4** TSprake(8) (sn drvn along: outpcd ½-wy: styd on fnl f)	2½	**6**	20/1	57	—
	Good On Yer (SEKettlewell) **2-8-1** JFanning(11) (cmpt: hld up: hdwy 2f out: kpt on wl fnl f)	½	**7**	25/1	53	—
	Mary Lou (IRE) (MRChannon) **2-7-13**(7)ow4 AEddery(2) (leggy: bhd & drvn along: hdwy on outside over 2f out: styd on towards fin)	3	**8**	16/1	50	—
1466^{5}	**Flower O'Cannie (IRE)** (MWEasterby) **2-8-5** TLucas(13) (trckd ldrs: effrt 2f out: grad wknd)	1	**9**	10/1	46	—
1569^{7}	**Sing For Me (IRE)** (RHollinshead) **2-7-13** NCarlisle(5) (chsd ldrs: ev ch over 1f out: sn wknd)	nk	**10**	20/1	39	—
	Parlez Moi d'Amour (IRE) (CWThornton) **2-8-0** DRMcCabe(16) (unf: scope: bit bkwd: s.s: bhd: hdwy on outside 2f out: nvr nr ldrs)	½	**11**	14/1	39	—
1137^{3}	**Beechwood Quest (IRE)** (BSRothwell) **2-7-13be** LCharnock(15) (chsd ldrs: drvn along ½-wy: lost pl 2f out)	1¾	**12**	16/1	33	—
	Torianna (USA) (JBerry) **2-8-4** JCarroll(7) (leggy: unf: scope: w ldrs: wkng whn hmpd over 1f out)	2	**13**	8/1	33	—
1645^{4}	**Townville Cee Cee** (JSWainwright) **2-7-9**(5) JBramhill(3) (w ldrs: rdn & wandered over 1f out: sn wknd)	d.h	**14**	9/1	22	—
	Dahlidya (MJPolglase) **2-8-1** JTate(14) (neat: unruly in stalls: s.s: a bhd)	2½	**14**	20/1	23	—
	Lilian Marks (IRE) (BJMeehan) **2-8-3**ow1 DeanMcKeown(4) (leggy: unf: w ldrs tl wknd over 2f out)	1¼	**16**	12/1	22	—
1577^{7}	**Stravsea** (BPJBaugh) **2-8-0** GBardwell(1) (in tch tl lost pl ½-wy: sn bhd)	½	**17**	33/1	18	—
				(SP 149.0%)	**17 Rn**	

1m 20.1 (5.10) CSF £53.00 TOTE £24.10: £4.60 £1.30 £1.90 (£47.00) Trio £150.30; £25.41 to 18/6/97 OWNER Mr F. J. Sainsbury (WROUGHTON) BRED J. Salmon

Risky Girl, who is on the leg at present, showed a high action going down. She proved very willing but, in truth, the race was not much better than a seller. (16/1)

1616 Demolition Jo, very keen going to post, did not have the best of runs on the inner. Probably racing on the slower ground in the straight, try as hard as she might, she could not force her head in front. (9/4)

Aspen (IRE) showed the benefit of her initial outing and should have further improvement in her. (5/1)

Delciana (IRE), a sharp type, showed a quick action. She gave a good account of herself and should come on for the run. (11/2: op 3/1)

Miss Main Street (IRE), who showed plenty of knee action going down, was on paper worst drawn but, probably racing on the faster ground on the wide outside, she finished in pleasing fashion. (33/1)

No Shame struggled to go the pace and needs seven. (20/1)

Good On Yer, who showed plenty of knee action going down, ran a pleasing first race. (25/1)

Mary Lou (IRE), on the leg at present, did not seem to have much idea but showed ability, staying on at the line. (16/1)

Parlez Moi d'Amour (IRE), green and backward, showed some promise after missing the break. (14/1)

Torianna (USA) (8/1: 5/1-10/1)

1998 BEECH (S) STKS (3-Y.O) (Class G)

7-15 (7-17) **1m 4y** £2,448.00 (£678.00: £324.00) Stalls: Low GOING minus 0.11 sec per fur (G)

				SP	RR	SF
1807^{10}	**Court House (67)** (BAMcMahon) **3-9-0** LNewton(12) (hld up: hdwy over 2f out: led 1f out: sn clr)	—	**1**	9/1	66	19
1780^{3}	**Sun Fairy** (JAGlover) **3-8-9** GCarter(10) (hdwy over 2f out: styd on fnl f: no imp)	2½	**2**	$9/4^{1}$	56	9
168^{10}	**Silent Valley (46)** (MissLCSiddall) **3-8-9** DeanMcKeown(5) (bhd: hdwy over 2f out: hung lft & styd on ins fnl f)	hd	**3**	12/1	56	9
	Macari (BPJBaugh) **3-9-0** ACulhane(1) (chsd ldrs: drvn along over 3f out: one pce)	2	**4**	33/1	57	10
1780^{6}	**Fly High** (DMorris) **3-8-9** PBloomfield(11) (chsd ldrs: effrt over 2f out: kpt on same pce appr fnl f)	d.h	**4**	$3/1^{2}$	52	5

748^{10} **Dance Melody (43)** (GROldroyd) **3-8-9** LCharnock(8) (swtg: chsd ldrs: drvn along over 2f out: wknd over 1f out) ....4 **6** 25/1 44 —
1312^{4} **Italian Symphony (IRE) (57)** (PDEvans) **3-9-0** JFEgan(9) (hld up: nt clr run & swtchd rt over 1f out: sn rdn & no imp) ....1¼ **7** 14/1 46 —
Hatimena (JGFitzGerald) **3-8-9** MRoberts(3) (str: bkwd: rn green: sn bhd & pushed along: sme hdwy over 1f out: n.d) ....1¾ **8** 8/1 38 —
1756^{10} **Petula Boy (35)** (SRBowring) **3-9-0** SWebster(7) (sn bhd & drvn along) ....¾ **9** 25/1 41 —
1428^{9} **Terry's Rose (53)** (RHollinshead) **3-8-9** KDarley(4) (plld hrd: led: hdd whn slipped, stumbled & hit rail 1f out).½ **10** 11/1 35 —
Juicy Ting (62) (PCHaslam) **3-9-0** JWeaver(6) (lw: w ldrs tl wknd over 1f out) ....5 **11** $4/1^{3}$ 30 —
462^{5} **Crosby Nod (54)** (EWeymes) **3-9-0** JCarroll(13) (in tch: drvn along 3f out: sn wl outpcd) ....2½ **12** 12/1 25 —
1426^{5} **Greenacres Goddess** (TWall) **3-8-4**(5) JBramhill(2) (hdwy on ins & nt clr run over 2f out: sn wknd) ....2 **13** 20/1 16 —
(SP 142.7%) **13 Rn**

1m 49.7 (7.30) CSF £31.09 TOTE £12.90: £2.90 £2.00 £6.80 (£22.60) Trio £169.30; £100.21 to 18/6/97 OWNER Mr J. R. Smith (TAMWORTH) BRED W. F. Macauley
Sold A Mann 3,000gns

Court House, who is not an easy ride, sped through on the outside and was probably racing on the faster ground. Significantly, connections let him go cheaply at the auction. (9/1)
1780 Sun Fairy is now qualified for a handicap mark, and will be suited by a slight step-up in distance. (9/4)
84 Silent Valley would have been meeting the winner on 16lb better terms in a handicap. (12/1)
Macari showed very little in three outings as a juvenile. (33/1)
Fly High, well supported in the market, finished closer to Sun Fairy than she had done first time at Newmarket. (3/1: op 5/1)
1312 Italian Symphony (IRE) looked to be full of running on the inner but, when switched to get a run, he said no thank you. (14/1: op 8/1)
Juicy Ting looked really fit and well on his reappearance and attracted plenty of market support, but he dropped right away once in line for home. (4/1)

1999 LANDBRIDGE SHIPPING H'CAP (0-75) (3-Y.O) (Class D)

7-45 (7-46) **1m 2f 6y** £5,344.50 (£1,596.00: £763.00: £346.50) Stalls: Low GOING minus 0.11 sec per fur (G)

SP RR SF

1392^{2} **Honourable (72)** (JWWatts) **3-9-4** JCarroll(9) (hld up: stdy hdwy over 4f out: led over 2f out: sn drvn wl clr: eased towards fin) ....— **1** $4/1^{2}$ 82 52
1392^{6} **Bally Souza (IRE) (75)** (MJohnston) **3-9-7** JWeaver(4) (lw: trckd ldrs: rdn & hung lft over 1f out: kpt on: no ch w wnr) 5 **2** 10/1 77 47
1636^{13} **Sadler's Blaze (IRE) (55)** (PWHarris) **3-8-1b¹** GCarter(8) (sn chsng ldrs: led 3f out: sn hdd: one pce) ....½ **3** 14/1 56 26
1802^{*} **Marsh Marigold (57)** (JHetherton) **3-7-10**(7) JennyBenson(1) (s.v.s: bhd tl styd on fnl 3f: nvr nr to chal) ....2½ **4** $11/2^{3}$ 54 24
1129^{5} **Diamond Eyre (52)** (JLEyre) **3-7-12** DWright(6) (a chsng ldrs: drvn along over 4f out: wknd appr fnl f) 3 **5** 8/1 44 14
1820^{2} **Sparky (59)** (MWEasterby) **3-8-5b** TLucas(7) (b: hld up: hdwy over 4f out: rdn over 2f out: wknd over 1f out).nk **6** $7/4^{1}$ 51 21
900^{15} **Kingdom Emperor (50)** (MJCamacho) **3-7-10v¹** LCharnock(3) (hld up & plld hrd: effrt over 3f out: sn lost pl & eased) ....18 **7** 14/1 13 —
1390^{15} **Lindrick Lady (IRE) (70)** (BSRothwell) **3-9-2** JFEgan(2) (led to 3f out: sn lost pl & eased) 1½ **8** 12/1 31 1
1416^{3} **Soden (IRE) (68)** (TGMills) **3-9-0** GBardwell(5) (swtg: chsd ldrs: drvn along ½-wy: lost pl 3f out: eased) ....2½ **9** 9/1 25 —
(SP 123.0%) **9 Rn**

2m 15.0 (5.40) CSF £42.38 CT £478.84 TOTE £5.30: £1.90 £2.90 £3.70 (£20.40) Trio £109.10 OWNER Sheikh Mohammed (RICHMOND) BRED Darley Stud Management Co Ltd

1392 Honourable proved well suited by the step-up in distance and, sweeping round the outside on the final turn, would have won by at least ten lengths but for being eased. Connections will no doubt be keen to turn him out soon under a penalty. (4/1)
1392 Bally Souza (IRE) on paper was closely matched with the winner on their running here last time, but it proved a very one-sided contest.(10/1)
Sadler's Blaze (IRE), in blinkers for the first time, made the best of his way home. (14/1)
1802* Marsh Marigold, from the same mark as that from which she won here, lost her chance leaving the stalls. She would have only finished second at best. (11/2)
1129 Diamond Eyre was very edgy beforehand. (8/1)
1820 Sparky had a good chance on paper, 5lb lower than Redcar, but he was in trouble some way from home and his action left something to be desired. (7/4)

2000 PONTEFRACT CUP H'CAP (0-70) (4-Y.O+) (Class E)

8-15 (8-16) **2m 1f 216y** £3,915.00 (£1,170.00: £560.00: £255.00) Stalls: Centre GOING minus 0.11 sec per fur (G)

SP RR SF

1605^{5} **Tancred Mischief (38)** (DWBarker) **6-7-3**(7) JennyBenson(3) (bhd: nt clr run over 2f out and 1f out: swtchd outside: fin wl to ld last 30y) ....— **1** 14/1 45 9
1654^{*} **Hullbank (67)** (WWHaigh) **7-9-11** ACulhane(5) (hld up: stdy hdwy 3f out: led on bit 1f out: hdd & nt qckn nr fin) ....1½ **2** $4/1^{1}$ 73 37
1654^{4} **Sushi Bar (IRE) (38)** (MrsMReveley) **6-7-10** NCarlisle(11) (bhd: effrt 3f out: n.m.r & hung lft over 1f out: styd on same pce) ....1¾ **3** $13/2^{3}$ 42 6
1497^{7} **Euphoric Illusion (46)** (MrsSJSmith) **6-8-4** DeanMcKeown(7) (s.i.s: sn trckng ldrs: effrt 3f out: n.m.r over 1f out: styd on same pce) 1¼ **4** 14/1 49 13
1100^{9} **Gymcrak Cyrano (IRE) (39)** (NChamberlain) **8-7-11**ow1 NKennedy(1) (trckd ldrs: smooth hdwy to ld over 3f out: hdd 1f out: one pce) 2 **5** 33/1 40 3
1133^{5} **Another Quarter (IRE) (48)** (MCChapman) **4-8-5** MRoberts(12) (b: hld up: hdwy over 4f out: sn chsng ldrs: outpcd 2f out: kpt on fnl f) 1¼ **6** 33/1 48 11
1779^{8} **Hancock (39)** (JHetherton) **5-7-4**(7)ow1 JFowle(13) (sn trckng ldrs: led 12f out to 10f out: one pce fnl 2f) 1¾ **7** 12/1 38 1
846^{7} **Alwarqa (58)** (MartynWane) **4-9-1** JCarroll(16) (bhd: hdwy over 3f out: sn chsng ldrs: one pce fnl 2f) 1 **8** 12/1 56 19
1817^{3} **Longcroft (41)** (SEKettlewell) **5-7-13**ow3 JFEgan(15) (trckd ldrs: drvn along ½-wy: outpcd fnl 3f) ....1 **9** 10/1 38 —
1585^{5} **Arian Spirit (IRE) (45)** (JLEyre) **6-8-3** RLappin(14) (s.s: bhd: drvn along 6f out: some hdwy 2f out: n.d) ....nk **10** 8/1 42 6
1585^{3} **Marsayas (IRE) (56)** (MJCamacho) **4-8-13** LCharnock(4) (trckd ldrs: ev ch tl wknd over 1f out: eased) ....3 **11** $9/2^{2}$ 50 13
1796^{5} **Monis (IRE) (38)** (RonaldThompson) **6-7-5**(5) JBramhill(8) (sn chsng ldrs: drvn along over 4f out: lost pl over 2f out) ....12 **12** 33/1 21 —
1494^{8} **Highflying (70)** (GMMoore) **11-10-0** JTate(9) (trckd ldrs: led 10f out tl over 3f out: wknd appr fnl f) 5 **13** 15/2 49 13

669^{6}	**Hunting Ground (42)** (BPJBaugh) **9-7-7**$^{(7)ow4}$ RWinston(2) (b: b.hind: led: sddle slipped: hdd after 6f: rn wd & lost pl 8f out: sn t.o: virtually p.u)	dist	**14**	50/1	—	—
				(SP 123.0%)	**14 Rn**	

4m 7.1 (15.10) CSF £62.86 CT £378.50 TOTE £19.10: £3.60 £2.90 £1.80 (£154.50) Trio £105.60 OWNER Mr D. W. Barker (RICHMOND) BRED W. G. Barker

LONG HANDICAP Gymcrak Cyrano (IRE) 7-4 Longcroft 7-7 Hancock 7-2 Tancred Mischief 7-2 Monis (IRE) 7-7 Sushi Bar (IRE) 7-9 Hunting Ground 7-2

WEIGHT FOR AGE 4yo-1lb

1605 Tancred Mischief, who likes to come from behind, was 8lb out of the handicap. Trapped in on the inner and with nowhere to go, when pulled to the wide outside she flew. Almost certainly racing on the faster ground, she got up near the line. (14/1: tchd 25/1)

1654* Hullbank, from a 4lb higher mark, came through on the bridle to show ahead a furlong out but had no answer to the winner's whirlwind finish. (4/1)

1654 Sushi Bar (IRE), 6lb better off with Hullbank compared to Beverley, tends to find his own trouble and is not the strongest of finishers. (13/2)

Euphoric Illusion, placed in two bumpers, seemed to lack the speed to get himself out of trouble. He looks a potential hurdler. (14/1: op 8/1)

Gymcrak Cyrano (IRE), 6lb out of the handicap and carrying 1lb overweight, moved up on the bridle to take charge but, in the final-furlong dash, proved very one-paced. (33/1)

1585 Marsayas (IRE), under pressure a long way from home, was eased when his chance had gone. (9/2: op 3/1)

2001 CEDAR LIMITED STKS (0-65) (3-Y.O+) (Class F)

8-45 (8-46) **5f** £2,500.00 (£700.00: £340.00) Stalls: Low GOING minus 0.11 sec per fur (G)

				SP	RR	SF
1602^{8}	**Royal Dome (IRE) (65)** (MartynWane) **5-9-3** JCarroll(9) (lw: trckd ldrs: effrt over 1f out: r.o u.p to ld ins fnl f: jst hld on)	—	**1**	11/1	67	47
1799^{13}	**Bowlers Boy (64)** (JJQuinn) **4-9-3** JFEgan(2) (trckd ldr: led over 1f out tl ins fnl f: kpt on wl)	hd	**2**	7/2^{2}	67	47
1599^{7}	**River Tern (65)** (JMBradley) **4-9-6** JWeaver(3) (s.i.s: hdwy ½-wy: rdn & nt qckn appr fnl f)	3	**3**	12/1	60	40
1816^{5}	**Corniche Quest (IRE) (63)** (MRChannon) **4-8-13**$^{(7)}$ AEddery(7) (sn bhd: hdwy 2f out: styd on fnl f)	nk	**4**	10/1	59	39
1835^{15}	**Tropical Beach (58)** (JBerry) **4-8-12**$^{(5)}$ PRoberts(10) (sn outpcd & pushed along: hdwy over 2f out: nvr rchd ldrs)	2½	**5**	12/1	48	28
1401*	**Alamode (65)** (JGSmyth-Osbourne) **3-8-11** TSprake(8) (lw: trckd ldrs: effrt 2f out: sn outpcd)	½	**6**	11/2^{3}	47	21
1828^{11}	**Oatey (62)** (MrsJRRamsden) **4-9-0** ACulhane(6) (lw: hld up: effrt over 2f out: nvr nr to chal)	½	**7**	6/1	42	22
1734^{5}	**Just Dissident (IRE) (57)** (RMWhitaker) **5-9-3** DeanMcKeown(5) (lw: unruly in stalls: led tl over 1f out: sn wknd)	1	**8**	10/1	42	22
1730^{4}	**Lunar Music (48)** (RonaldThompson) **3-8-8** TWilliams(1) (hld up: outpcd fr ½-wy)	1	**9**	20/1	36	10
1681^{2}	**Blue Lamp (USA) (63)** (MAJarvis) **3-8-8** MRoberts(4) (lw: chsd ldrs: rdn over 2f out: sn wknd)	nk	**10**	3/1^{1}	35	9
				(SP 123.6%)	**10 Rn**	

64.5 secs (2.80) CSF £47.75 TOTE £17.00: £3.10 £1.60 £2.80 (£15.60) Trio £144.20 OWNER Mr G. W. Jones (RICHMOND) BRED Michael F. Fogarty

WEIGHT FOR AGE 3yo-6lb

OFFICIAL EXPLANATION Blue Lamp (USA): no explanation offered.

Royal Dome (IRE), who has never won before July before, came right back to his best but, at the line, it was a desperate thing. (11/1: 8/1-12/1)

1446 Bowlers Boy, an in-and-out performer, probably ran up to his best. (7/2)

1385 River Tern, happier over this trip, again swished his tail violently under pressure. (12/1)

1816 Corniche Quest (IRE) would have been 5lb better off with the winner in a handicap. (10/1)

1613 Tropical Beach put a poor effort at Hamilton behind him, and would have been meeting the winner on 7lb better terms if this had been a handicap. (12/1)

1401* Alamode still lacks experience. (11/2)

1828 Oatey (6/1: op 7/2)

1681 Blue Lamp (USA) ran poorly, dropping right away once in line for home. There was no obvious excuse. (3/1)

2002 WALNUT H'CAP (0-70) (3-Y.O+) (Class E)

9-15 (9-17) **6f** £3,353.00 (£1,004.00: £482.00: £221.00) Stalls: Low GOING minus 0.11 sec per fur (G)

				SP	RR	SF
1333^{4}	**King Uno (43)** (MrsJRRamsden) **3-8-0v** JFanning(13) (dwlt: hdwy u.p ½-wy: styd on wl appr fnl f: led last strides)	—	**1**	7/1^{2}	52	21
1957^{7}	**Meranti (53)** (JMBradley) **4-9-3** JWeaver(10) (w ldr: led over 2f out: sn drvn clr: jst ct)	hd	**2**	5/1^{1}	62	38
1680*	**Twin Creeks (61)** (VSoane) **6-9-11** CRutter(1) (lw: trckd ldrs: styd on wl fnl f)	¾	**3**	9/1	68	44
1816^{2}	**Kid Ory (41)** (DWChapman) **6-8-5b** ACulhane(7) (unruly in stalls: mde most tl over 2f out: kpt on same pce appr fnl f)	nk	**4**	7/1^{2}	47	23
1734*	**Napoleon Star (IRE) (52)** (SRBowring) **6-9-2b** SWebster(3) (hdwy u.p over 2f out: n.m.r: styd on wl fnl f)	1¼	**5**	7/1^{2}	55	31
1514^{7}	**Sing With the Band (46)** (BAMcMahon) **6-8-10** LNewton(15) (lw: hdwy over 2f out: styd on fnl f)	¾	**6**	12/1	47	23
1655^{4}	**Dispol Diamond (51)** (GROldroyd) **4-9-1** KDarley(9) (swtg: mid div: sn drvn along: kpt on appr fnl f)	2	**7**	12/1	46	22
1315^{16}	**Be Warned (57)** (MDods) **6-9-7b** JFEgan(2) (hdwy over 2f out: kpt on fnl f: n.d)	1¼	**8**	8/1^{3}	49	25
1580^{6}	**Legend of Aragon (50)** (JAGlover) **3-8-7v**^{1} GCarter(5) (hld up: hdwy over 2f out: eased ins fnl f)	nk	**9**	16/1	41	10
1691^{4}	**A Breeze (65)** (DMorris) **3-9-8** NDay(8) (sn drvn along: nvr wnt pce)	1¼	**10**	11/1	53	22
1496^{15}	**Colonel's Pride (56)** (RMWhitaker) **3-8-13** DeanMcKeown(4) (hld up: stdy hdwy over 1f out: nvr nr ldrs)	¾	**11**	50/1	42	11
1446^{8}	**Beldray Park (IRE) (52)** (MrsALMKing) **4-9-2** TSprake(12) (chsd ldrs tl lost pl 2f out)	s.h	**12**	25/1	38	14
1496*	**Swift (62)** (MJPolglase) **3-9-5** MRoberts(11) (lw: w ldrs tl wknd over 1f out)	½	**13**	8/1^{3}	46	15
1816^{4}	**Henry the Hawk (45)** (MDods) **6-8-4**$^{(5)}$ SCopp(14) (b: w ldrs tl wknd 2f out)	1¾	**14**	8/1^{3}	25	1
1676^{7}	**Culsyth Flyer (50)** (PJBevan) **6-9-0** NCarlisle(6) (s.i.s: sn bhd: t.o ½-wy)	dist	**15**	50/1	—	—
				(SP 134.9%)	**15 Rn**	

1m 19.2 (4.20) CSF £42.18 CT £314.41 TOTE £13.00: £3.30 £2.90 £3.30 (£32.50) Trio £89.30 OWNER J & M Leisure Ltd (THIRSK) BRED M. J. Simmonds

WEIGHT FOR AGE 3yo-7lb

1333 King Uno, who has tumbled down the weights, came from some way off the pace after missing the break. Almost certainly racing on the better ground, he got up in the final strides. (7/1: 5/1-8/1)

1225 Meranti, 10lb higher in the weights compared with when he won his first race at Nottingham in April, looked home and dry when kicking four lengths clear off the bend. Sticking to the inner, he was almost certainly racing on the slower ground and, treading water in the closing stages, was just caught. (5/1)

1680* Twin Creeks, drawn one, raced keenly but he kept on in good style. This was probably a good effort from a poor draw, and he is better suited by seven furlongs or even a mile. (9/1)
1816 Kid Ory, having his fiftieth race, became very upset in the stalls and, in the circumstances, acquitted himself well. (7/1)
1734* Napoleon Star (IRE) did not have a lot of room, but he was already under pressure and it was basically his lack of pace that got him into bother. He might be worth a try over seven. (7/1)
394 Sing With the Band took the eye beforehand and has done all her winning over five. (12/1)
863 Be Warned (8/1: op 12/1)
Colonel's Pride, a keen, going sort, hinted that there may be slightly better to come. (50/1)

T/Plpt: £501.70 (35.09 Tckts). T/Qdpt: £193.80 (4.35 Tckts) WG

1809-WINDSOR (Fig. 8) (Good to firm)
Monday June 16th
WEATHER: overcast WIND: almost nil

2003 BOWRING MARSH & MCLENNAN (S) STKS (2-Y.O) (Class G)
6-30 (6-31) **5f 10y** £2,388.00 (£668.00: £324.00) Stalls: Low GOING minus 0.10 sec per fur (G)

				SP	RR	SF
1635^{9}	**Mislead (IRE)** (JSMoore) **2-8-6** MFenton(2) (hdwy 2f out: led wl ins fnl f: drvn out)	—	**1**	14/1	57	24
	Kolby (ABailey) **2-8-11b^{1}** KFallon(13) (w'like: a.p: led wl over 1f out: hdd wl ins fnl f)	nk	**2**	15/8 ^{1}	61	28
	Fast Franc (IRE) (BJMeehan) **2-8-11** PatEddery(11) (w'like: a.p: ev ch 1f out: nt qckn)	1½	**3**	7/2 ^{2}	56	23
902^{10}	**Rosewood Lady (IRE)** (KRBurke) **2-8-6** BDoyle(8) (a.p: one pce fnl 2f)	2	**4**	14/1	45	12
1438^{5}	**Dixie Crossroads** (RHannon) **2-8-6** DaneO'Neill(6) (chsd ldrs: swtchd rt over 1f out: one pce)	4	**5**	6/1 ^{3}	32	—
	Lady Almitra (CJHill) **2-8-6** DHarrison(14) (unf: bit bkwd: a.p: no hdwy fnl 2f)	3½	**6**	20/1	21	—
1635^{8}	**Hugger-Mugger** (JRArnold) **2-8-6b$^{(5)}$** ADaly(1) (spd over 3f)	nk	**7**	20/1	25	—
1444^{7}	**Fleur-de-Lys** (WJMusson) **2-8-6** AMcGlone(3) (s.s: nrst fin)	½	**8**	12/1	19	—
	Lionels Lucky Lady (JSMoore) **2-8-3$^{(3)}$** MHenry(12) (lt-f: nvr bttr than mid div)	s.h	**9**	25/1	19	—
	Bradbury Falls (IRE) (DJSCosgrove) **2-8-6** JQuinn(5) (neat: bit bkwd: nvr nr ldrs)	1½	**10**	14/1	14	—
	Just For Tina (CJHill) **2-8-6** NAdams(9) (w'like: bit bkwd: s.s: a bhd)	1¼	**11**	8/1	10	—
1564^{13}	**Lamoura** (RBrotherton) **2-8-6** RPrice(10) (led over 3f: wknd qckly: t.o)	13	**12**	33/1	—	—
1425^{14}	**Liberalis** (GFHCharles-Jones) **2-8-3$^{(3)}$** DO'Donohoe(4) (wl bhd fnl 3f: t.o)	16	**13**	33/1	—	—
	Eastwell Minstrel (RCurtis) **2-8-8$^{(3)}$** MBaird(7) (w'like: s.s: a t.o)	dist	**14**	33/1	—	—
				(SP 132.3%)	**14 Rn**	

63.2 secs (3.50) CSF £37.55 TOTE £43.20: £6.10 £1.50 £1.70 (£116.10) Trio £60.80 OWNER Mr P. Henley (HUNGERFORD) BRED Peter Henley Jnr
Bt in 6,000 gns. Fast Franc (IRE) clmd SCWilliams £6,000
Mislead (IRE) came with a steady run in the last two furlongs and ran on to beat a poor field narrowly. (14/1: op 8/1)
Kolby, blinkered for this his debut, was always close up. After striking the front under maximum pressure below the distance, he could not quite hold the winner. (15/8)
Fast Franc (IRE) looked very fit and was close up all the way. After having every chance, he could find no extra, and was claimed for 6,000 guineas after the race. (7/2: 5/2-4/1)
592 Rosewood Lady (IRE), always chasing the leaders, ran on at one pace in the final quarter-mile. (14/1: op 7/1)
1438 Dixie Crossroads has already had three chances and looked as if she would need plenty more here. Though never far behind the leaders, she could not quicken when required. (6/1: 5/2-13/2)
Lady Almitra made a satisfactory debut, always chasing up the leaders. She will be better for the experience and can win a seller. (20/1)
1019 Fleur-de-Lys (12/1: op 8/1)
Bradbury Falls (IRE) (14/1: 8/1-16/1)
Just For Tina (8/1: 4/1-9/1)

2004 NEWTON INVESTMENT MANAGEMENT H'CAP (0-70) (3-Y.O+) (Class E)
7-00 (7-01) **1m 67y** £3,176.25 (£960.00: £467.50: £221.25) Stalls: Low GOING minus 0.10 sec per fur (G)

				SP	RR	SF
1826^{*}	**Chasetown Flyer (USA) (58)** (NEBerry) **3-8-12** ^{6x} BDoyle(9) (hdwy & hrd rdn over 2f out: led wl ins fnl f: all out)	—	**1**	9/1 ^{3}	70	42
1677^{2}	**Samara Song (50)** (IPWilliams) **4-9-0** KFallon(16) (a.p: led wl over 1f out: hdd & nt qckn wl ins fnl f)	1	**2**	5/1 ^{1}	60	42
1955^{5}	**Vanborough Lad (40)** (MJBolton) **8-8-1$^{(3)}$** MHenry(3) (hdwy 3f out: ev ch 1f out: nt qckn)	½	**3**	12/1	49	31
1849^{7}	**Delight of Dawn (47)** (EAWheeler) **5-8-6$^{(5)}$** ADaly(11) (hdwy on ins over 2f out: r.o one pce)	1½	**4**	12/1	53	35
1568^{5}	**Brave Envoy (62)** (MJHeaton-Ellis) **3-9-2** SDrowne(13) (lw: hdwy & rdn 3f out: styd on: nt rch ldrs)	5	**5**	14/1	59	31
1955^{8}	**Noeprob (USA) (55)** (RJHodges) **7-9-5** RPerham(12) (nvr nrr)	¾	**6**	12/1	50	32
1747^{3}	**Regal Reprimand (66)** (GLewis) **3-9-6** PaulEddery(17) (b.hind: led tl wknd wl over 1f out)	4	**7**	11/2 ^{2}	53	25
1501^{6}	**Jibereen (58)** (PHowling) **5-9-8** SWhitworth(8) (b: lw: nvr nr to chal)	¾	**8**	16/1	44	26
1155^{8}	**Quarterstaff (65)** (CFWall) **3-9-5** GDuffield(4) (lw: bhd tl styd on fnl 2f)	s.h	**9**	12/1	51	23
1878^{9}	**Sea Spouse (44)** (MBlanshard) **6-8-8** NAdams(14) (chsd ldr tl wknd 2f out)	5	**10**	20/1	20	2
1633^{2}	**Chingachgook (62)** (PWHarris) **3-9-2** PatEddery(18) (chsd ldrs: btn whn hmpd wl over 1f out)	s.h	**11**	11/2 ^{2}	38	10
1141^{22}	**Batsman (55)** (WJMusson) **3-8-9** GHind(1) (lw: prom tl wknd over 3f out)	5	**12**	33/1	22	—
1765^{9}	**Steal 'Em (60)** (ABailey) **4-9-10** AMcGlone(5) (b: a bhd)	hd	**13**	33/1	26	8
1796^{13}	**Four of Spades (50)** (RJHodges) **6-8-9v$^{(5)}$** AmandaSanders(6) (prom tl wknd 3f out)	1½	**14**	33/1	13	—
	Sakharov (56) (BPalling) **8-9-6** DHarrison(2) (b: bhd fnl 3f)	1¼	**15**	25/1	17	—
1680^{9}	**Rosenkavalier (IRE) (54)** (LGCottrell) **3-8-8** JQuinn(10) (a bhd)	1¾	**16**	33/1	12	—
1238^{12}	**Keen Alert (70)** (MBell) **3-9-10** MFenton(15) (a bhd)	2½	**17**	25/1	23	—
1155^{9}	**Yanavanavano (IRE) (50)** (GLewis) **3-8-1$^{(3)}$** MBaird(7) (s.s: a t.o)	dist	**18**	20/1	—	—
				(SP 129.7%)	**18 Rn**	

1m 46.9 (4.70) CSF £45.79 CT £519.28 TOTE £12.50: £2.50 £1.30 £2.50 £2.50 (£34.60) Trio £62.50 OWNER Mr D. W. Smith (UPPER LAMBOURN) BRED Pin Oak Stud
WEIGHT FOR AGE 3yo-10lb
1826* Chasetown Flyer (USA) came with a run from the junction and, given a very hard race, went to the front well inside the final furlong. (9/1: 6/1-10/1)

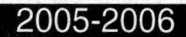

1677 Samara Song, always close up and travelling well, looked like winning when taking up the running below the distance, but was collared inside the last half-furlong. (5/1)
1955 Vanborough Lad, making a quick reappearance after running fifth on Saturday, moved up to challenge and dispute the lead below the distance. After having every chance he could not quicken near the finish. (12/1)
1680 Delight of Dawn found a good run on the inside from a long way back but could not quite reach the leaders. (12/1)
1568 Brave Envoy came under strong pressure three furlongs out but, though he kept staying on, he never appeared likely to catch the leaders. (14/1: op 8/1)
1632 Noeprob (USA), who had run very poorly at Bath two days earlier, was ridden with more restraint this time and was running on well at the finish. With the same tactics, she can win if reverting to selling company. (12/1: 7/1-14/1)
1747 Regal Reprimand, dropped in distance, set a strong pace but was quickly beaten when headed below the distance. (11/2: 4/1-6/1)
Quarterstaff (12/1: 7/1-14/1)
1633 Chingachgook (11/2: 4/1-6/1)

2005 EL CAMINO RESOURCES H'CAP (0-80) (3-Y.O) (Class D)

7-30 (7-31) **1m 2f 7y** £3,662.00 (£1,106.00: £538.00: £254.00) Stalls: Low GOING minus 0.10 sec per fur (G)

				SP	RR	SF
1637^{5}	**Contentment (IRE) (69)** (JWHills) **3-8-10** RHills(7) (lw: hdwy over 2f out: led & wnt rt wl over 1f out: r.o wl)	—	**1**	7/1	83	45
1499^{6}	**Real Estate (70)** (CFWall) **3-8-11** GDuffield(4) (lw: hdwy 3f out: led 2f out: sn hdd: nt qckn)	2½	**2**	6/1^{2}	80	42
1637^{2}	**Mystic Ridge (81)** (DRCElsworth) **3-9-8** RHughes(6) (lw: a.p: led 3f out: hrd rdn & hdd 2f out: one pce)	10	**3**	13/2^{3}	75	37
1256^{3}	**Just Grand (IRE) (76)** (MJohnston) **3-9-3** JReid(1) (lw: hdwy fnl 2f: nvr nrr)	¾	**4**	6/1^{2}	69	31
1820*	**Who's That Man (59)** (SCWilliams) **3-7-11**$^{(3)}$ 5x MHenry(10) (a.p: one pce fnl 2f)	s.h	**5**	6/1^{2}	52	14
1316^{7}	**Anchored In Love (75)** (RCharlton) **3-9-2** PatEddery(11) (lw: led after 3f to 3f out: sn wknd)	8	**6**	11/2^{1}	55	17
1144^{4}	**Northern Touch (72)** (SCWilliams) **3-8-13** SDrowne(9) (no hdwy fnl 3f)	2	**7**	14/1	49	11
	Harmony Hall (73) (JRFanshawe) **3-9-0** DHarrison(2) (hdwy & hrd rdn over 2f out: wknd over 1f out)	s.h	**8**	13/2^{3}	50	12
1009^{15}	**Irish Fiction (IRE) (55)** (DJSCosgrove) **3-7-7**$^{(3)}$ MBaird(5) (lw: hdwy & hrd rdn over 2f out: sn wknd)	1½	**9**	20/1	29	—
1811^{13}	**Ortelius (74)** (RHannon) **3-9-1v^{1}** DaneO'Neill(3) (lw: led 3f: wknd 3f out)	10	**10**	25/1	32	—
1679^{3}	**Tycoon Girl (IRE) (77)** (BJMeehan) **3-9-4b^{1}** MTebbutt(8) (plld hrd: prom tl wknd 3f out)	6	**11**	16/1	26	—
				(SP 118.6%)	**11 Rn**	

2m 10.0 (5.10) CSF £44.70 CT £264.36 TOTE £9.60: £2.30 £2.50 £1.80 (£44.10) Trio £151.20 OWNER Mr C. R. Nelson (LAMBOURN) BRED Baronrath Stud Ltd
LONG HANDICAP Irish Fiction (IRE) 7-7
1637 Contentment (IRE), travelling very strongly throughout, made smooth headway over two furlongs from home. When sent to the front below the distance, he readily drew clear although drifting slightly to the right. (7/1)
1499 Real Estate showed considerable improvement on his three previous efforts. He went to the front two furlongs out and, though soon headed, drew right away from the remainder. (6/1)
1637 Mystic Ridge, on his handicap debut, took up the running three furlongs out. Soon hard ridden, he had no chance with the first two but kept on well for third place. (13/2)
1256 Just Grand (IRE) was at the back of the field until staying on under pressure in the final quarter-mile. (6/1)
1820* Who's That Man, always on the heels of the leaders, could make no headway in the closing stages. (6/1)
992 Anchored In Love, running in her first handicap, went to the front after three furlongs but soon weakened when headed at the three furlong marker. (11/2: 7/2-6/1)
1144 Northern Touch (14/1: op 8/1)
Harmony Hall (13/2: 4/1-7/1)

2006 TOTE CREDIT SPRINT H'CAP (0-75) (3-Y.O+) (Class D)

8-00 (8-03) **5f 217y** £5,680.00 (£1,720.00: £840.00: £400.00) Stalls: Low GOING minus 0.10 sec per fur (G)

				SP	RR	SF
1488^{3}	**Rififi (58)** (RIngram) **4-8-11** SWhitworth(1) (b: lw: wl bhd tl gd hdwy 2f out: r.o to ld wl ins fnl f)	—	**1**	20/1	67	40
1799^{2}	**Fairy Prince (IRE) (58)** (MrsALMKing) **4-8-11** KFallon(22) (hdwy over 2f out: led over 1f out tl wl ins fnl f)	nk	**2**	11/2^{2}	66	39
1743^{3}	**Willow Dale (IRE) (68)** (DRCElsworth) **4-9-7** TQuinn(21) (hdwy over 1f out: r.o ins fnl f)	¾	**3**	12/1^{3}	74	47
752^{4}	**Kings Harmony (IRE) (72)** (PJMakin) **4-9-11** SSanders(11) (a.p: ev ch 1f out: nt qckn)	1¾	**4**	20/1	74	47
21^{2}	**Never Think Twice (63)** (KTIvory) **4-9-2v** CScally(15) (b: gd hdwy over 1f out: nrst fin)	1¼	**5**	25/1	61	34
1509^{10}	**Pride of Hayling (IRE) (59)** (PRHedger) **6-8-12** SDrowne(14) (a.p: hrd rdn & one pce fnl 2f)	¾	**6**	25/1	55	28
1294^{6}	**V I P Charlie (70)** (JRJenkins) **3-8-13**$^{(3)}$ AWhelan(18) (lw: hdwy fnl 2f: nvr nrr)	½	**7**	5/1^{1}	65	31
1489^{13}	**Sovereigns Court (61)** (LGCottrell) **4-9-0** DHolland(10) (nvr plcd to chal)	½	**8**	20/1	55	28
1599^{3}	**Apollo Red (73)** (GLMoore) **8-9-12** CandyMorris(2) (swtg: led over 4f: eased whn btn ins fnl f)	½	**9**	20/1	65	38
1385^{5}	**Alfahaal (IRE) (55)** (RFJohnsonHoughton) **4-8-8** PatEddery(8) (prom over 3f)	1¼	**10**	12/1^{3}	44	17
1761^{5}	**Jo Maximus (60)** (JGSmyth-Osbourne) **5-8-13** RPerham(20) (prom 4f)	s.h	**11**	16/1	49	22
1489^{7}	**Victory Team (IRE) (75)** (GBBalding) **5-10-0** RHughes(12) (hdwy 2f out: nt rch ldrs)	nk	**12**	25/1	63	36
1666*	**Rockcracker (IRE) (57)** (GGMargarson) **5-8-7b**$^{(3)}$ MHenry(4) (nvr bttr than mid div)	1¾	**13**	16/1	40	13
1250^{13}	**General Sir Peter (IRE) (59)** (NACallaghan) **5-8-7**$^{(5)}$ AmandaSanders(6) (prom 3f)	s.h	**14**	20/1	42	15
1141^{15}	**Hype Energy (65)** (GLewis) **3-8-11** PaulEddery(13) (nvr trbld ldrs)	1	**15**	20/1	45	11
1662^{4}	**Beau Venture (USA) (65)** (BPalling) **9-9-4** DHarrison(19) (w ldr tl wknd 2f out)	1¾	**16**	20/1	41	14
	Rock Symphony (74) (WJHaggas) **7-9-13** MHills(23) (hld up: hdwy 2f out: sn wknd)	hd	**17**	16/1	50	23
1680^{4}	**Speedy Classic (USA) (58)** (MJHeaton-Ellis) **8-8-11** AClark(17) (prom 3f)	½	**18**	12/1^{3}	32	5
1743^{11}	**Scissor Ridge (67)** (JJBridger) **5-9-6** JQuinn(7) (early spd: sn bhd)	nk	**19**	33/1	40	13
1790^{7}	**Norling (IRE) (43)** (KOCunningham-Brown) **7-7-7**$^{(3)}$ MBaird(3) (spd 4f)	nk	**20**	50/1	16	—
1509*	**Ivory's Grab Hire (68)** (KTIvory) **4-9-4b**$^{(3)}$ MartinDwyer(16) (prom 4f)	nk	**21**	12/1^{3}	40	13
1225^{15}	**Shining Cloud (66)** (MBell) **4-9-5** MFenton(5) (prom 3f)	s.h	**22**	20/1	38	11
	Belzao (57) (THind) **4-8-10** JReid(9) (a bhd)	8	**23**	33/1	7	—
				(SP 137.9%)	**23 Rn**	

1m 13.8 (3.30) CSF £101.97 CT £1,335.39 TOTE £41.80: £6.20 £1.70 £2.30 £4.50 (£128.20) Trio £559.60 OWNER Brooknight Guarding Ltd (EPSOM) BRED Milton Park Stud Partnership
LONG HANDICAP Norling (IRE) 7-6
WEIGHT FOR AGE 3yo-7lb
1488 Rififi, last away from the number one stall, was brought right across behind his field. He made rapid headway from the two-furlong marker and ran on to strike the front well inside the final furlong. (20/1)

1799 Fairy Prince (IRE) came with a strong run to take the lead approaching the final furlong, but could not quite hold the late challenge of the winner. (11/2)
1743 Willow Dale (IRE) continues to knock at the door. She improved below the distance but, though running on inside the last furlong, could not find quite enough. (12/1)
752 Kings Harmony (IRE) was always close up. He disputed the lead from the two-furlong marker until unable to quicken inside the distance. (20/1)
21 Never Think Twice came with a good late run on the stands' rails but could not quite reach the leaders. (25/1)
Pride of Hayling (IRE) chased the leaders throughout and, hard ridden in the final quarter-mile, kept on at one pace. (25/1)
1294 V I P Charlie ran on in the last two furlongs under pressure, but was too late to trouble the leaders. (5/1: op 5/2)
1385 Alfahaal (IRE) (12/1: 8/1-14/1)
1509* Ivory's Grab Hire (12/1: 8/1-14/1)

2007 STEAMSHIP MUTUAL CONDITIONS STKS (2-Y.O) (Class C)

8-30 (8-31) **5f 10y** £4,422.50 (£1,610.00: £785.00: £335.00: £147.50) Stalls: Low GOING minus 0.10 sec per fur (G)

				SP	RR	SF
1684[4]	**Prince Foley** (WGMTurner) **2-8-12**(7) DMcGaffin(5) (swtchd lft 2f out: led over 1f out: drvn out)	—	**1**	15/8[2]	89	36
1295[3]	**Summer Deal (USA)** (PFICole) **2-8-6** TQuinn(1) (w ldrs: ev ch whn n.m.r over 1f out: swtchd lft & r.o ins fnl f)	1	**2**	100/30[3]	73	20
	Hoh Navigator (IRE) (MBell) **2-8-8** MFenton(3) (w'like: bit bkwd: w ldr: ev ch over 1f out: edgd lft: r.o)	nk	**3**	6/1	74	21
1873[3]	**Huntswood** (RHannon) **2-8-11** PatEddery(4) (led over 3f: r.o one pce)	nk	**4**	7/4[1]	76	23
1418[8]	**Pianist (IRE)** (GLewis) **2-8-11** PaulEddery(2) (a bhd: rdn along: wknd 2f out: t.o)	17	**5**	20/1	22	—
				(SP 113.3%)		**5 Rn**

63.2 secs (3.50) CSF £7.98 TOTE £2.90: £1.70 £1.60 (£3.30) OWNER Foley Steelstock (SHERBORNE) BRED Ian Slocock
1684 Prince Foley, switched to the centre of the course two furlongs out, soon came through to take the lead and ran on gamely under pressure. (15/8)
1295 Summer Deal (USA) disputed the lead from the start, but was squeezed for room at the distance. When switched to the left, she ran on again but it was too late. (100/30)
Hoh Navigator (IRE), a workmanlike sort, looked just in need of the race. Disputing the lead from the start, he had every chance but was inclined to edge left under pressure in the closing stages. (6/1)
1873 Huntswood, running over a shorter trip, tried to lead all the way but was outpaced approaching the final furlong. (7/4)
Pianist (IRE) was always struggling to go the pace and was tailed off from two furlongs out. (20/1)

2008 BAILEYS ORIGINAL IRISH CREAM MAIDEN STKS (3-Y.O+) (Class D)

9-00 (9-06) **1m 2f 7y** £3,779.00 (£1,142.00: £556.00: £263.00) Stalls: Low GOING minus 0.10 sec per fur (G)

				SP	RR	SF
	Ismaros (HRACecil) **3-8-12** KFallon(22) (scope: bit bkwd: rapid hdwy over 1f out: str run to ld cl home)	—	**1**	7/1	78	38
	Silence Reigns (MRStoute) **3-8-12** PaulEddery(25) (w'like: bit bkwd: hdwy 2f out: led ins fnl f tl nr fin)	nk	**2**	14/1	78	38
	True Glory (IRE) (JHMGosden) **3-8-7** GHind(7) (lw: hdwy over 2f out: ev ch ins fnl f: r.o)	¾	**3**	7/2[2]	71	31
	Bright Heritage (IRE) (95) (DRLoder) **4-9-10** PatEddery(4) (lw: led tl wknd ins fnl f)	½	**4**	5/2[1]	76	48
511[4]	**Classic Jenny (IRE)** (ICampbell) **4-9-5** RHughes(14) (hdwy fnl 2f: nvr nrr)	¾	**5**	50/1	69	41
	Lookout (BWHills) **3-8-7** MHills(18) (lw: chsd ldr tl wknd over 1f out)	2	**6**	5/1[3]	66	26
1420[6]	**Top** (JRFanshawe) **3-8-7** DHarrison(13) (a.p: no hdwy fnl 3f)	1¾	**7**	20/1	63	23
	Tribal Moon (IRE) (LadyHerries) **4-9-3**(7) PDoe(19) (a.p: ev ch over 1f out: wknd ins fnl f)	2½	**8**	66/1	64	36
	Magic Lahr (GER) (IABalding) **4-9-7**(3) MartinDwyer(20) (str: bit bkwd: prom tl wknd 2f out)	½	**9**	33/1	64	36
1563[4]	**Limelight** (JARToller) **3-8-7** SSanders(24) (nrst fin)	½	**10**	20/1	58	18
1477[13]	**Capsoff (IRE)** (GAHubbard) **4-9-5** AClark(3) (prom tl wknd over 2f out)	¾	**11**	66/1	57	29
	Young Marcius (USA) (PFICole) **3-8-12** TQuinn(15) (w'like: nvr trbld ldrs)	hd	**12**	16/1	61	21
	Back Row (LMCumani) **3-8-7** BDoyle(8) (neat: bit bkwd: nvr nr ldrs)	nk	**13**	20/1	56	16
1784[7]	**Rufalda (IRE)** (LMCumani) **3-8-0**(7) DYoung(6) (nvr on terms)	nk	**14**	50/1	56	16
1804[4]	**Frankie** (MHTompkins) **3-8-12** DBiggs(21) (nvr nr ldrs)	3	**15**	33/1	56	16
	Mukdar (USA) (MajorWRHern) **3-8-12** RHills(9) (w'like: bit bkwd: nvr nr to chal)	¾	**16**	10/1	55	15
1637[10]	**Silvery** (JARToller) **3-8-4**(3) AWhelan(1) (a bhd)	1½	**17**	50/1	47	7
1637[12]	**Shirazan (IRE)** (LMCumani) **3-8-12** DHolland(2) (lw: prom tl wknd qckly over 1f out)	7	**18**	16/1	41	1
	Abbey Theatre (IRE) (MSalaman) **3-8-12** SWhitworth(16) (leggy: unf: a bhd)	2	**19**	50/1	38	—
1809[15]	**Tedross** (JRPoulton) **6-9-10** SDrowne(11) (prom tl wknd over 2f out)	1	**20**	66/1	36	8
1292[10]	**Switch To Senate** (DJSCosgrove) **3-8-12** MRimmer(23) (a bhd)	s.h	**21**	66/1	36	—
1682[7]	**Snow Carnival** (LadyHerries) **4-9-10** GDuffield(17) (a bhd)	1½	**22**	50/1	34	6
1784[8]	**Shelteez (USA)** (MBell) **3-8-0**(7) DMulhall(12) (a bhd)	9	**23**	50/1	14	—
255[8]	**Triple Challenge** (GLMoore) **3-8-7** CandyMorris(5) (a bhd: t.o)	20	**24**	66/1	—	—
	Dunabrattin (DTThom) **4-9-10** JReid(10) (Withdrawn not under Starter's orders)		**W**	50/1	—	—
				(SP 148.8%)		**24 Rn**

2m 11.2 (6.30) CSF £96.00 TOTE £6.40: £2.90 £6.00 £2.00 (£40.60) Trio £79.20 OWNER Mr L. Marinopoulos (NEWMARKET) BRED Stilvi Compania Financiera S A
WEIGHT FOR AGE 3yo-12lb
Ismaros looked just in need of the race. The task appeared hopeless at the two-furlong marker, but he came with a most impressive late surge to snatch the race close home. He has plenty of scope and is an exciting prospect. (7/1: 2/1-8/1)
Silence Reigns, a useful sort like the winner, looked just in need of it. He made ground two furlongs out and collared the leader inside the final furlong, only to be run out of it near the finish. (14/1: 7/1-16/1)
True Glory (IRE) came with a steady run in the centre of the course from two-and-a-half furlongs out but, after having every chance inside the last furlong, could not find quite enough. There are plenty of races to be picked up with her. (7/2: 4/1-5/2)
Bright Heritage (IRE), having his first outing for almost two years, may have set off too fast. Although he appeared to have the race in safe keeping approaching the final furlong, he tied up in the last hundred and fifty yards. He can leave this running far behind. (5/2: 6/4-3/1)
511 Classic Jenny (IRE) stayed on well in the last two furlongs, but just too late to trouble the leaders. (50/1)
Lookout raced in second place until weakening approaching the final furlong. Time may tell she was running against some very useful rivals. (5/1: tchd 8/1)
Mukdar (USA) (10/1: 3/1-12/1)

T/Jkpt: Not won; £13,736.56 to Royal Ascot 17/6/97. T/Plpt: £183.30 (105.28 Tckts). T/Qdpt: £38.20 (22.14 Tckts) Hn

0890-ROYAL ASCOT (R-H) (Good, Good to firm patches)
Tuesday June 17th
WEATHER: v.warm WIND: almost nil

2009 QUEEN ANNE STKS (Gp 2) (3-Y.O+) (Class A)
2-30 (2-32) **1m (straight)** £65,080.00 (£24,454.00: £11,827.00: £5,239.00) Stalls: Low GOING minus 0.24 sec per fur (GF)

				SP	RR	SF
	Allied Forces (USA) (SbinSuroor) **4-9-5** LDettori(11) (lw: hdwy over 3f out: led over 1f out: rdn out)	—	**1**	10/1	129	87
1476[3]	**Centre Stalls (IRE) (116)** (RFJohnsonHoughton) **4-9-2** TQuinn(4) (lw: hdwy over 2f out: hrd rdn over 1f out: ev ch ins fnl f: r.o wl)	nk	**2**	11/1	125	83
1210[2]	**Ali-Royal (IRE) (120)** (HRACecil) **4-9-2** KFallon(2) (swtg: nt clr run 3f out: swtchd rt & stumbled over 2f out: hrd rdn & hdwy over 1f out: r.o one pce)	1¼	**3**	9/4[1]	123	81
1598*	**Nwaamis (USA) (110)** (JLDunlop) **5-9-2** RHills(9) (lw: a.p: led over 2f out tl over 1f out: one pce)	1¼	**4**	11/1	120	78
1554a[2]	**Wixim (USA) (118)** (RCharlton) **4-9-5** PatEddery(3) (b.hind: hld up: n.m.r 2f out: rdn wl over 1f out: one pce)	nk	**5**	11/2[3]	123	81
1210[8]	**Bin Rosie (116)** (DRLoder) **5-9-2b** KDarley(7) (hld up: rdn over 3f out: one pce)	hd	**6**	16/1	120	78
1210[9]	**Beauchamp King (112)** (JLDunlop) **4-9-2** JReid(10) (lw: hdwy over 2f out: wknd over 1f out)	3	**7**	50/1	114	72
1323[5]	**Amrak Ajeeb (IRE) (107)** (BHanbury) **5-9-2** MRimmer(1) (lw: rdn over 4f out: nvr nr to chal)	½	**8**	20/1	113	71
852[7]	**Restructure (IRE) (114)** (MrsJCecil) **5-9-2** RCochrane(5) (led over 5f: wknd wl over 1f out)	nk	**9**	20/1	112	70
1770*	**Hidden Meadow (115)** (IABalding) **3-8-6** MHills(8) (lw: prom over 6f)	3	**10**	5/1[2]	106	54
1728a*	**Gothenberg (IRE) (115)** (MJohnston) **4-9-5** JWeaver(6) (lw: prom 4f)	1	**11**	20/1	107	65

(SP 110.7%) **11 Rn**

1m 39.72 (-0.28) CSF £92.02 TOTE £7.90: £2.10 £3.20 £1.60 (£67.00) Trio £50.70 OWNER Godolphin (NEWMARKET) BRED Buckram Oak Farm
WEIGHT FOR AGE 3yo-10lb

Allied Forces (USA), a very useful juvenile for Henry Cecil in 1995, was trained in America last year, where he won four of his nine races. Wintered in Dubai, he has been working well on the gallops since his return, but looked to have something to do compared with official ratings. Nevertheless, he moved to the front below the distance, and kept the runner-up at bay, to give Godolphin their first British Group winner of the season. He will now go for the Sussex Stakes. (10/1)
1476 Centre Stalls (IRE) appreciated the return to a mile, and ran the race of his life. Throwing down his challenge in the last furlong, he made sure the winner did not have things his own way. He will win a Group race according to his trainer. (11/1: 8/1-12/1)
1210 Ali-Royal (IRE) did not have the best of luck and, after switching to get a clear run, then stumbled. Nevertheless, he picked up ground under pressure but, having got into third place, was making no further impression on the front two in the last seventy-five yards. Another Group victory should not be far away. (9/4)
1598* Nwaamis (USA), a winner of two conditions races this season, had far more on his plate, but acquitted himself really well, showing in front over a quarter-of-a-mile from home before being headed by the winner. (11/1: 8/1-12/1)
1554a Wixim (USA), who was heavily bandaged behind, failed to find a turn of foot when asked in the last quarter-mile. Although all three of his wins have been on fast ground, he would prefer more cut, according to his trainer. (11/2)
830 Bin Rosie chased the leaders, but could make little impact when the race began in earnest. (16/1)
1770* Hidden Meadow, whose trainer rates him as good as Selkirk, ran here in preference to the St James's Palace Stakes. Noted to have an injury above his nearside eye, he showed up until dropping tamely away well over a furlong from home. He is better than this, and maybe this run came too quickly after his Epsom victory ten days earlier. He is well worth another chance. (5/1)

2010 PRINCE OF WALES'S STKS (Gp 2) (3-Y.O+) (Class A)
3-05 (3-06) **1m 2f** £67,312.00 (£25,309.60: £12,254.80: £5,443.60) Stalls: High GOING minus 0.24 sec per fur (GF)

				SP	RR	SF
1476*	**Bosra Sham (USA) (131)** (HRACecil) **4-9-5** KFallon(1) (lw: hld up: qcknd to ld 2f out: clr over 1f out: v.impressive)	—	**1**	4/11[1]	131	95
	Alhaarth (IRE) (SbinSuroor) **4-9-6** LDettori(4) (led 8f: unable qckn)	8	**2**	10/1[3]	119	83
720a*	**London News (SAF)** (BWHills) **5-9-8** DJWhyte(5) (gd sort: chsd ldr over 2f: rdn over 2f out: sn wknd)	5	**3**	10/1[3]	113	77
1210[3]	**Even Top (IRE) (122)** (MHTompkins) **4-9-3** TQuinn(2) (lw: w ldr over 7f out tl over 2f out: sn wknd)	½	**4**	13/2[2]	107	71
1542a[4]	**Acharne (110)** (CEBrittain) **4-9-3** BDoyle(3) (lw: s.s: a bhd)	½	**5**	66/1	107	71
1326[4]	**Balalaika (102)** (LMCumani) **4-9-0** JReid(7) (sme hdwy on ins wl over 1f out: sn wknd)	hd	**6**	25/1	103?	67

(SP 110.2%) **6 Rn**

2m 4.16 (-1.34) CSF £4.31 TOTE £1.50: £1.10 £2.00 (£3.10) OWNER Mr Wafic Said (NEWMARKET) BRED Gerald W. Leigh
1476* Bosra Sham (USA) treated this field with contempt, putting up a scintillating performance. Effortlessly moving to the front, she shot clear in a matter of strides. She looks almost invincible at present, and surely needs only to turn up at Sandown to land the Eclipse. (4/11)
Alhaarth (IRE), who has spent the winter in Dubai, did not live up to expectations last year, but made a pleasing reappearance for his new stable. Taking the field along, he was firmly put in his place by the winner, but still finished well clear of the remainder. (10/1)
720a* London News (SAF), a very attractive individual, who is the best ten-furlong horse in South Africa, has won ten of his eighteen races, including the £220,000 Queen Elizabeth II Cup in Hong Kong. He has been given time to get acclimatised since arriving at Barry Hills' five weeks ago, but he can never have met one as good as Bosra Sham, and was left standing in the straight. (10/1)
1210 Even Top (IRE) was returning to a more suitable trip, but was rather disappointing. After moving up to dispute the lead in Swinley Bottom, he was left for dead early in the straight. (13/2: 4/1-7/1)
1542a Acharne is not in this league. (66/1)
1326 Balalaika was more at home over this trip, but found the opposition too hot. (25/1)

2011 ST JAMES'S PALACE STKS (Gp 1) (3-Y.O C & F) (Class A)
3-45 (3-48) **1m (round)** £134,680.00 (£50,394.00: £24,197.00: £10,529.00) Stalls: High GOING minus 0.24 sec per fur (GF)

				SP	RR	SF
1725a*	**Starborough (119)** (DRLoder) **3-9-0** LDettori(5) (lw: mde all: hrd rdn over 1f out: r.o wl)	—	**1**	11/2[3]	124	96
1544a*	**Air Express (IRE) (116)** (CEBrittain) **3-9-0** BDoyle(8) (a.p: chsd wnr over 2f out: hrd rdn over 1f out: r.o)	1	**2**	20/1	122	94
1204a*	**Daylami (IRE)** (AdeRoyerDupre,France) **3-9-0** GMosse(7) (lt-f: rdn over 3f out: bmpd over 2f out: hdwy over 1f out: unable qckn)	4	**3**	7/2[2]	114	86
1541a*	**Desert King (IRE)** (APO'Brien,Ireland) **3-9-0** CRoche(3) (h.d.w: nvr gng wl: hrd rdn & hdwy over 1f out: one pce)	½	**4**	2/1[1]	113	85
940[3]	**Poteen (USA) (119)** (LMCumani) **3-9-0** PatEddery(2) (lw: bmpd over 2f out: nvr nr to chal)	2	**5**	7/2[2]	109	81
737[4]	**In Command (IRE) (117)** (BWHills) **3-9-0** MHills(4) (hdwy over 3f out: nt clr run & swtchd lft over 2f out: wknd over 1f out)	5	**6**	25/1	99	71

1307^{2} **Running Stag (USA) (107)** (PMitchell) **3-9-0** KFallon(6) (lw: chsd wnr 2f: rdn over 3f out: wknd over 1f out) .1½ **7** 66/1 96 68
1725a^{2} **Mamalik (USA)** (JHMGosden) **3-9-0** RHills(1) (chsd wnr 6f out tl over 2f out: sn wknd) 16 **8** 11/1 64 36
(SP 111.6%) **8 Rn**

1m 39.18 (-1.62) CSF £88.92 TOTE £4.90: £1.10 £3.10 £1.60 (£33.30) OWNER Sheikh Mohammed (NEWMARKET) BRED Sheikh Mohammed Bin Rashid Al Maktoum

1725a* Starborough was given a masterly ride by Dettori, who set a very brisk pace. Given a few cracks of the whip over a furlong out, he kept up the gallop to hold off the runner-up. (11/2)
1544a* Air Express (IRE), winner of both the Italian and German 2,000 Guineas, ran a tremendous race. He desperately tried to make a race of it with the winner, and although unable to master that rival, finished well clear of the remainder. The Group One Prix Jacques le Marois at Deauville is his primary target. (20/1)
1204a* Daylami (IRE), winner of the French 2,000 Guineas, was rather disappointing, but has not run on ground quite this lively before. Involved in a barging match early in the straight, he struggled into third place, but had no hope of reeling-in the front two. A step-up in trip now looks likely. (7/2: op 9/4)
1541a* Desert King (IRE), winner of the Irish 2,000 Guineas, was extremely disappointing and was never travelling. Roche was at work for most of the trip and, although struggling on into fourth place, he never posed a threat. He is much better than this, and this effort is best ignored. (2/1)
940 Poteen (USA) failed to sparkle and, engaged in a barging match with Daylami early in the straight, never threatened. (7/2)
737 In Command (IRE), who was found to be coughing after his disappointing reappearance in the Greenham Stakes, did not have the clearest of runs early in the straight but it made little difference. (25/1)
1307 Running Stag (USA), rather colty beforehand, had a stiff task but nevertheless showed up well, eventually tiring inside the final quarter-mile. (66/1)
1725a Mamalik (USA) was very disappointing. Having shown in second place for much of the trip, he dropped away tamely early in the straight. This was surely not his true form, but it transpired he had been struck into. (11/1: 8/1-12/1)

2012 COVENTRY STKS (Gp 3) (2-Y.O) (Class A)

4-20 (4-22) **6f** £26,920.00 (£10,196.00: £4,998.00: £2,286.00) Stalls: Low GOING minus 0.24 sec per fur (GF)

SP RR SF

1531a^{7} **Harbour Master (FR)** (APO'Brien,Ireland) **2-8-12b^{1}** CRoche(3) (leggy: rdn over 3f out: hdwy over 1f out: str run to ld wl ins fnl f: r.o wl) ....— **1** 16/1 97 71
1396* **Desert Prince (IRE)** (DRLoder) **2-8-12** OPeslier(2) (lw: a.p: n.m.r over 2f out: rdn wl over 1f out: ev ch wl ins fnl f: unable qckn) ....1½ **2** 3/1^{1} 93 67
1744* **Bold Fact (USA)** (HRACecil) **2-8-12** KFallon(10) (lw: a.p: led 2f out: hung bdly rt over 1f out: hdd wl ins fnl f: nt rcvr) ....½ **3** 7/1^{3} 92+ 66
1306* **Diligence (IRE)** (PFICole) **2-8-12** TQuinn(11) (a.p: hrd rdn over 1f out: one pce) 2½ **4** 10/1 85 59
1396^{2} **Hayil (USA)** (DMorley) **2-8-12** MHills(8) (a.p: led 3f out to 2f out: wknd fnl f) 1½ **5** 12/1 81 55
1321* **Shadow of Doubt (IRE)** (PWChapple-Hyam) **2-8-12** JReid(4) (no hdwy fnl 2f) ....½ **6** 7/1^{3} 80 54
1812^{3} **Speedfit Too (IRE)** (GGMargarson) **2-8-12** GCarter(12) (outpcd: hdwy over 1f out: nvr nrr) 2 **7** 100/1 74 48
1480* **Swift Alliance** (RAkehurst) **2-8-12** DHarrison(1) (rdn over 3f out: nvr nr to chal) ....nk **8** 33/1 74 48
893^{5} **Hickory (IRE)** (MJHaynes) **2-8-12** RCochrane(14) (nvr nrr) 4 **9** 100/1 63 37
1684^{2} **Rusty Babe (IRE)** (JJQuinn) **2-8-12** MJKinane(6) (rdn over 3f out: sme hdwy over 1f out: sn wknd) ....¾ **10** 20/1 61 35
1411* **Chips (IRE)** (DRCElsworth) **2-8-12v^{1}** RHughes(5) (led 3f) 1½ **11** 8/1 57 31
1475^{5} **Blueridge Dancer (IRE)** (BJMeehan) **2-8-12** MTebbutt(15) (hld up: rdn over 2f out: wknd over 1f out) ....½ **12** 16/1 56 30
1263* **Bold Edge** (RHannon) **2-8-12** PatEddery(13) (swtg: prom over 3f) ....1¾ **13** 4/1^{2} 51 25
1486^{2} **Hadid (USA)** (BWHills) **2-8-12** RHills(7) (hld up: rdn over 2f out: sn wknd) 2 **14** 14/1 46 20
1391^{2} **Out Like Magic** (PDEvans) **2-8-7** JFEgan(9) (a bhd) 1¼ **15** 50/1 37 11
(SP 128.0%) **15 Rn**

1m 14.45 (0.45) CSF £59.64 TOTE £26.90: £6.10 £2.20 £2.70 (£74.20) Trio £162.50 OWNER Mrs John Magnier (PILTOWN) BRED Haras de Bernesq

1531a Harbour Master (FR), who made a winning debut at the Curragh in April only to flop on a return visit last month, was tried in blinkers to overcome his inexperience and sharpen him up. It certainly worked and, eating up ground from below the distance, stormed through to lead in the closing stages, to give Aidan O'Brien his first Flat-race victory in Britain. The stable has a wealth of two-year-old talent, and this colt is rated a couple of lengths behind King of Kings. (16/1)
1396* Desert Prince (IRE) well-regarded by his stable, was never far away and looked likely to take full advantage of the erratic course taken by Bold Fact. However, just as he was about to strike the front, the winner swept by. He should not take long to return to the winner's enclosure. (3/1)
1744* Bold Fact (USA) should have won this. Leading a quarter-of-a-mile from home, he looked set for victory, but drifted across the track to the far rail despite all Fallon's attempts to keep him straight. Not surprisingly he was collared in the closing stages. Losses are only lent. (7/1: 5/1-8/1)
1306* Diligence (IRE), a laid-back individual, was always to the fore but, under pressure below the distance, failed to find the necessary turn of foot. (10/1)
1396 Hayil (USA) moved to the front at halfway, but he was collared at the two pole, and had come to the end of his tether in the final furlong. (12/1)
1321* Shadow of Doubt (IRE) raced behind the leaders, but was making little impression in the final quarter-mile. (7/1)

2013 BRITANNIA H'CAP (0-105) (3-Y.O C & G) (Class B)

4-55 (4-57) **1m (straight)** £30,480.00 (£9,240.00: £4,520.00: £2,160.00) Stalls: Low GOING minus 0.24 sec per fur (GF)

SP RR SF

1741^{4} **Fly To The Stars (100)** (MJohnston) **3-9-3** OPeslier(14) (hdwy 2f out: led over 1f out: r.o wl) ....— **1** 20/1 111 83
1221* **Komi (94)** (MRStoute) **3-8-11** JReid(5) (hdwy over 1f out: r.o wl ins fnl f) 1½ **2** 12/1 102 74
1595^{11} **Rapier (85)** (RHannon) **3-8-2**ow1 DaneO'Neill(3) (a.p: led 2f out tl over 1f out: unable qckn) ....s.h **3** 50/1 93 64
1175^{14} **Tigrello (85)** (GLewis) **3-8-2** PaulEddery(24) (racd far side: hdwy over 1f out: ev ch ins fnl f: r.o one pce) ....hd **4** 50/1 93 65
1305^{3} **Just Nick (83)** (WRMuir) **3-7-11**(3) MartinDwyer(18) (lw: racd far side: hdwy 2f out: ev ch ins fnl f: one pce) 1 **5** 25/1 89 61
1658^{2} **Nomore Mr Niceguy (91)** (EJAlston) **3-8-8** JFEgan(1) (a.p: rdn over 2f out: one pce) ....s.h **6** 33/1 97 69
1658^{11} **Teofilio (IRE) (94)** (DRLoder) **3-8-11** MJKinane(8) (lw: hdwy 2f out: hrd rdn over 1f out: one pce) ....½ **7** 20/1 99 71
1682* **Asef Alhind (83)** (BHanbury) **3-8-0** RHills(9) (lw: led 6f: one pce) ....nk **8** 25/1 87 59
1404^{6} **Amyas (IRE) (95)** (BWHills) **3-8-12** MHills(10) (rdn over 2f out: hdwy fnl f: r.o) 1 **9** 25/1 97 69
1175^{17} **Bold Oriental (IRE) (85)** (NACallaghan) **3-8-2** SDrowne(23) (racd far side: hdwy over 2f out: rdn over 1f out: one pce) ....hd **10** 33/1 87 59
597^{2} **Handsome Ridge (104)** (JHMGosden) **3-9-7** GaryStevens(26) (lw: racd far side: nvr nr to chal) ....½ **11** 16/1 105 77
1412^{5} **Nigrasine (100)** (JLEyre) **3-9-3** DeanMcKeown(19) (racd far side: a.p: rdn over 2f out: one pce) ....nk **12** 50/1 100 72
675^{7} **Redwing (90)** (JLDunlop) **3-8-7** KDarley(12) (s.s: nvr nrr) ....¾ **13** 10/1^{3} 89 61
1412^{4} **Swiss Law (103)** (SbinSuroor) **3-9-6** LDettori(2) (lw: prom over 5f) ....nk **14** 9/1^{2} 101 73

				SP	RR	SF
1175[3]	**Over To You (USA) (83)** (EALDunlop) **3-8-0** TSprake(20) (racd far side: hdwy over 1f out: r.o)	¾	**15**	16/1	80	52
1737[3]	**Sharp Temper (85)** (BWHills) **3-8-2** GCarter(15) (nvr nrr)	1¼	**16**	20/1	79	51
1404[2]	**Future Perfect (85)** (PFICole) **3-8-2** CRutter(11) (hld up: rdn over 2f out: wknd over 1f out)	nk	**17**	25/1	79	51
1656*	**Generous Libra (93)** (DRLoder) **3-8-10** PatEddery(25) (racd far side: a.p: hrd rdn over 1f out: sn wknd)	1	**18**	7/1[1]	85	57
1307[6]	**Further Outlook (USA) (95)** (MrsAJPerrett) **3-8-12** KFallon(22) (racd far side: prom over 6f)	1	**19**	40/1	85	57
1404*	**Alezal (96)** (WJarvis) **3-8-13** SSanders(28) (racd far side: prom over 5f)	nk	**20**	11/1	85	57
1770[2]	**Wasp Ranger (USA) (96)** (PFICole) **3-8-13** TQuinn(13) (lw: hld up: rdn over 2f out: eased whn btn ins fnl f)	½	**21**	20/1	84	56
1775[4]	**Irish Accord (USA) (92)** (MrsJRRamsden) **3-8-9** JFortune(16) (lw: racd far side: a bhd)	1¾	**22**	16/1	76	48
1688*	**Bevier (79)** (CEBrittain) **3-7-5**(5) RMullen(27) (racd far side: bhd fnl 2f)	2½	**23**	50/1	58	30
1935[10]	**Kaiser Kache (IRE) (85)** (KMcAuliffe) **3-8-2**ow2 BDoyle(21) (lw: racd far side: prom over 5f)	1½	**24**	50/1	61	31
1238[3]	**Praeditus (80)** (RHannon) **3-7-11** GBardwell(4) (lw: prom over 5f)	nk	**25**	50/1	56	28
645*	**China Red (USA) (90)** (JWHills) **3-8-7** AClark(7) (prom over 5f)	2	**26**	33/1	62	34
1404[3]	**Caviar Royale (IRE) (96)** (TDBarron) **3-8-13** DHarrison(6) (prom over 6f)	4	**27**	50/1	60	32
1175[15]	**Kennemara Star (IRE) (79)** (JLDunlop) **3-7-10** JQuinn(17) (racd far side: a bhd)	5	**28**	7/1[1]	33	5
				(SP 137.2%)	**28 Rn**	

1m 39.95 (-0.05) CSF £193.77 CT £10,356.60 TOTE £28.50: £6.00 £3.10 £27.10 £23.30 (£228.30) Trio Not won; £9,210.00 to Royal Ascot 18/6/97 OWNER Mr P. D. Savill (MIDDLEHAM) BRED Bishop's Down Farm
LONG HANDICAP Bevier 7-7 Kennemara Star (IRE) 7-8
OFFICIAL EXPLANATION **Kennemara Star (IRE): no explanation offered, other than the going may have been too firm.**
1741 Fly To The Stars, reverting back to a mile, came through to lead below the distance and, given a few cracks of the whip, responded really well to hold on. (20/1)
1221* Komi, one of the most inexperienced in the field, really found his feet and ran on really strongly in the closing stages, but the line was always coming too soon. A step-up in distance would certainly be in his favour. (12/1)
853 Rapier, who was virtually unrideable at Lingfield last time out, gave a much better account of himself, and showed with a narrow advantage entering the last quarter-mile. He failed to find another gear when headed. (50/1)
1004* Tigrello, one of thirteen who elected to race on the far side, picked up ground from below the distance but, despite coming out best of that group, was unable to master his rivals on the stands' side. (50/1)
1305 Just Nick came through to lead the far-side group below the distance, but did not have overall control. He failed to find another gear when collared inside the final furlong. (25/1)
1658 Nomore Mr Niceguy, the most experienced in the line-up, was never far way, but failed to find that vital turn of foot. (33/1)
675 Redwing (10/1: 7/1-12/1)
1175 Kennemara Star (IRE) (7/1: 9/2-8/1)

2014 ASCOT STKS H'CAP (0-95) (4-Y.O+) (Class C)
5-30 (5-35) **2m 4f** £30,090.00 (£9,120.00: £4,460.00: £2,130.00) Stalls: High GOING minus 0.24 sec per fur (GF)

				SP	RR	SF
1778[3]	**Sea Freedom (65)** (GBBalding) **6-8-3v** SDrowne(24) (lw: lost pl over 12f out: rallied over 3f out: led ins fnl f: r.o wl)	—	**1**	20/1	77	55
1400[6]	**Shirley Sue (70)** (MJohnston) **4-8-6** RHills(2) (rdn & hdwy over 2f out: r.o wl ins fnl f)	½	**2**	20/1	82	58
1478*	**Arcady (60)** (JLHarris) **4-7-5**(5) RMullen(22) (b: lost pl over 12f out: hdwy & nt clr run on ins over 2f out: swtchd lft: r.o wl ins fnl f)	s.h	**3**	25/1	72	48
	Tamarpour (USA) (61) (MCPipe) **10-7-10b**(3)ow1 MHenry(6) (b: rdn over 5f out: gd hdwy over 1f out: r.o wl ins fnl f)	s.h	**4**	25/1	73	50
1413*	**Shining Dancer (65)** (SDow) **5-8-3** JFEgan(20) (lw: hrd rdn & hdwy over 2f out: r.o)	1	**5**	12/1[3]	76	54
1665[6]	**Pleasureland (IRE) (60)** (RCurtis) **4-7-7**(3) MBaird(7) (gd hdwy over 7f out: led 5f out tl over 1f out: one pce)	hd	**6**	40/1	71	47
1477[16]	**Burn Out (62)** (JPearce) **5-8-0** GBardwell(23) (nt clr run over 6f out: rdn over 5f out: gd hdwy over 1f out: r.o wl)	hd	**7**	20/1	73	51
1871[5]	**Nanton Point (USA) (74)** (LadyHerries) **5-8-12** JQuinn(18) (lw: hld up: rdn over 5f out: led over 1f out tl ins fnl f: one pce)	nk	**8**	16/1	84	62
1763*	**Northern Motto (60)** (JSGoldie) **4-7-10** NVarley(19) (a.p: rdn over 3f out: wknd fnl f)	5	**9**	50/1	66	42
1698a[5]	**Miltonfield (86)** (JEMulhern,Ireland) **8-9-5**(5) TEDurcan(11) (lw: hdwy fnl 2f: nvr nrr)	3	**10**	12/1[3]	90	68
1408[3]	**General Mouktar (58)** (MCPipe) **7-7-7**(3) PFessey(12) (nvr nr to chal)	1	**11**	25/1	61	39
1413[7]	**Northern Fleet (75)** (MrsAJPerrett) **4-8-11** PatEddery(9) (a.p: led 6f out to 5f out: ev ch over 1f out: wknd fnl f)	1½	**12**	14/1	77	53
1693[2]	**Chabrol (CAN) (67)** (RHarris) **4-7-12**(5)ow5 ADaly(15) (lw: led to 6f out: wknd over 2f out)	2	**13**	33/1	67	38
1413[2]	**Inchcailloch (IRE) (85)** (JSKing) **8-9-9** PaulEddery(10) (lw: rdn & hdwy over 4f out: wknd 2f out)	3	**14**	9/2[1]	83	61
1665[7]	**Spring Marathon (USA) (60)** (MrsPNDutfield) **7-7-7**(5) AimeeCook(4) (nvr nrr)	1½	**15**	66/1	57	35
1400[5]	**Etterby Park (USA) (79)** (MJohnston) **4-9-1** JWeaver(14) (prom tl wknd 5f out)	¾	**16**	20/1	75	51
1478[13]	**Academy House (IRE) (70)** (RAkehurst) **4-8-6** TQuinn(13) (swtg: sme hdwy on ins over 2f out: sn wknd)	6	**17**	16/1	61	37
1478[2]	**Burnt Offering (72)** (CEBrittain) **4-8-8** BDoyle(3) (hdwy 16f out: wknd over 4f out)	5	**18**	16/1	59	35
	Major Dundee (IRE) (74) (MCPipe) **4-8-10v** RHughes(8) (bhd fnl 4f)	11	**19**	14/1	53	29
1478[7]	**Midyan Blue (IRE) (70)** (JMPEustace) **7-8-8** RCochrane(25) (prom tl wknd 6f out)	3½	**20**	25/1	46	24
1413[3]	**Grand Cru (68)** (JCullinan) **6-8-6** MJKinane(16) (lw: hdwy over 5f out: wknd over 4f out)	s.h	**21**	14/1	44	22
1260[8]	**Shadirwan (IRE) (68)** (RAkehurst) **6-8-6** AClark(17) (prom tl wknd over 5f out)	6	**22**	20/1	39	17
1162[6]	**Totem Dancer (76)** (JLEyre) **4-8-12** OPeslier(5) (hdwy over 6f out: wknd over 4f out)	12	**23**	14/1	37	13
1672[3]	**Great Oration (IRE) (59)** (FWatson) **8-7-11** FNorton(21) (bhd fnl 7f)	10	**24**	20/1	12	—
1648*	**Nigel's Lad (IRE) (80)** (PCHaslam) **5-8-13**(5) GFaulkner(1) (lw: prom tl wknd 7f out: t.o)	25	**25**	10/1[2]	13	—
				(SP 139.8%)	**25 Rn**	

4m 23.57 (3.57) CSF £337.83 CT £8,816.72 TOTE £27.40: £5.50 £4.40 £12.90 £7.40 (£222.70) Trio £7,801.60; £9,889.38 to Royal Ascot 18/6/97 OWNER Miss B. Swire (ANDOVER) BRED Stetchworth Park Stud Ltd
LONG HANDICAP Pleasureland (IRE) 7-5 Arcady 7-6 General Mouktar 7-8 Northern Motto 7-4
WEIGHT FOR AGE 4yo-2lb
1778 Sea Freedom relished this marathon trip as acceleration is not his strong-suit. Taking closer order turning for home, he eventually got on top inside the final furlong and held on by the skin of his teeth, to give his trainer and jockey their first Royal Ascot winner. (20/1)
1400 Shirley Sue left a disappointing run at Doncaster well behind. Picking up ground in the straight, she ran on really strongly, and may well have prevailed with a little further to go. (20/1)
1478* Arcady was just beginning to pick up ground when finding his way blocked early in the straight. Switched left to get a clear run, she sprouted wings inside the final furlong and only just failed. (25/1)
Tamarpour (USA), who has not run on the Flat since August 1995, went into overdrive in the final quarter-mile, and finished best of all. (25/1)

1413* Shining Dancer, under pressure as she began to make headway early in the straight, kept on really well to finish right on the heels of the principals. (12/1)
1665 Pleasureland (IRE) showed himself to be a real stayer over hurdles last winter, and thoroughly enjoyed this marathon trip. Moving through to lead five furlongs out, he was eventually collared below the distance and tapped for toe. (40/1)
1871 Nanton Point (USA) gave a good account of himself, and moved to the front below the distance. However, in a tremendous finish, he was worried out of it inside the last. A pleased Lady Herries intends to aim him for the Cesarewitch. (16/1)
1413 Inchcailloch (IRE) was very disappointing. His jockey tried to get him closer approaching the straight, but he never really got to the principals, and punters knew their fate early in the straight. (9/2)
1162 Totem Dancer (14/1: 10/1-16/1)

T/Jkpt: Not won; £46,284.88 to Royal Ascot 18/6/97. T/Plpt: £1,124.20 (112.85 Tckts). T/Qdpt: £532.90 (8.46 Tckts) AK

1626-THIRSK (L-H) (Good)
Tuesday June 17th
WEATHER: sunny periods WIND: slt half against

2015 GROSVENOR CASINOS LEEDS H'CAP (0-80) (3-Y.O+) (Class D)
2-15 (2-16) **1m 4f** £3,626.00 (£1,088.00: £524.00: £242.00) Stalls: High GOING minus 0.51 sec per fur (F)

				SP	RR	SF
1628*	**Tessajoe (75)** (MJCamacho) **5-9-13** LCharnock(1) (b.hind: a.p: hdwy to ld over 1f out: r.o)	—	**1**	6/1 2	85	50
*1431*5	**Canton Venture (76)** (SPCWoods) **5-10-0** DBiggs(8) (mde most tl hdd over 1f out: kpt on wl)	1	**2**	12/1	85	50
16283	**Daira (58)** (JDBethell) **4-8-10** DHolland(11) (in tch: hdwy 3f out: styd on fnl f: nrst fin)	s.h	**3**	8/1	67	32
15153	**In the Money (IRE) (51)** (RHollinshead) **8-8-3** FLynch(4) (bhd: hdwy ent st: styd on fnl 2f: nrst fin)	¾	**4**	7/1 3	59	24
	Crystal Falls (IRE) (75) (JJO'Neill) **4-9-13** GDuffield(7) (trckd ldrs: effrt 3f out: kpt on one pce)	hd	**5**	25/1	83	48
18323	**Augustan (56)** (SGollings) **6-8-8** ACulhane(10) (rr div tl styd on fnl 2f: nt pce to chal)	1¾	**6**	9/1	61	26
13014	**Saddlers' Hope (72)** (JRFanshawe) **3-8-10** NDay(6) (lw: prom tl wknd fnl 2½f)	nk	**7**	12/1	77	28
14816	**Opera Buff (IRE) (68)** (MissGayKelleway) **6-9-3**(3) AWhelan(3) (lw: bhd: effrt u.p 3f out: nvr rchd ldrs)	3	**8**	11/1	69	34
1678*	**Mad Militant (IRE) (63)** (AStreeter) **8-8-12**(3) RHavlin(5) (lw: bhd: effrt 3f out: nvr rchd ldrs)	1¼	**9**	6/1 2	62	27
1950*	**Sandbaggedagain (79)** (MWEasterby) **3-8-12**(5) 5x GParkin(2) (b.nr hind: hld up: hdwy on outside 3f out: sn rdn: hung lft & btn)	2½	**10**	4/1 1	75	26
*337*3	**Premier (78)** (MJohnston) **3-9-2** JFanning(9) (lw: chsd ldrs tl wknd fnl 3f)	10	**11**	16/1	60	11
	Exactly (IRE) (70) (JLEyre) **4-9-8** TWilliams(12) (b.hind: disp ld 4f: chsd ldr tl wknd qckly over 2f out)	1¼	**12**	16/1	51	16
				(SP 121.5%)	**12 Rn**	

2m 33.6 (2.90) CSF £71.10 CT £537.31 TOTE £6.70: £2.50 £3.20 £1.80 (£36.60) Trio £185.30 OWNER Riley Partnership (MALTON) BRED A. and Mrs Rhodes
WEIGHT FOR AGE 3yo-14lb
1628* Tessajoe is in top from and, always going well, gained his third course win without much difficulty. (6/1)
1431 Canton Venture is off a 6lb higher mark than he has previously won off, but he is obviously in really good heart and kept fighting back. (12/1)
1628 Daira has the ability but is not the most reliable of characters, but she was keeping on well and is obviously in good form. (8/1)
1515 In the Money (IRE) put in a better effort this time and was staying on well at the end. (7/1)
Crystal Falls (IRE) ran well after well over a year off and ought to improve for the outing. (25/1)
1832 Augustan is basically short of toe and needs a flat-out gallop. (9/1)
1301 Saddlers' Hope (12/1: op 8/1)
1950* Sandbaggedagain had to struggle this time, and showed his true colours by hanging once under pressure. (4/1)

2016 GROSVENOR CASINOS NORTH EAST REGION (S) STKS (2-Y.O) (Class G)
2-50 (2-54) **6f** £2,442.50 (£680.00: £327.50) Stalls: High GOING minus 0.51 sec per fur (F)

				SP	RR	SF
182911	**Tancred Times** (DWBarker) **2-8-6** TWilliams(13) (chsd ldrs: led 2f out: r.o)	—	**1**	33/1	64	—
18295	**Inchalong** (MBrittain) **2-8-6** JCarroll(2) (a.p: ev ch over 1f out: kpt on wl)	1	**2**	5/1 2	61	—
14384	**Tremonnow** (JMBradley) **2-8-6** LCharnock(16) (a chsng ldrs: kpt on fnl f)	1	**3**	5/1 2	59	—
*1758**	**Figawin** (GLewis) **2-9-4** NDay(18) (a chsng ldrs: kpt on one pce fnl 2f)	½	**4**	7/1	69	—
16002	**Newhargen (IRE)** (PDEvans) **2-8-11** GDuffield(17) (led tl hdd 2f out: kpt on same pce)	½	**5**	12/1	61	—
18157	**Toll's Times** (MWEasterby) **2-8-6**(5) GParkin(11) (drvn along & hdwy after 2f: kpt on: nvr able to chal)	1¾	**6**	33/1	56	—
*1789*2	**Edna's Gift (IRE)** (JBerry) **2-8-6**(7) CLowther(5) (prom: hung lft over 2f out: r.o one pce)	½	**7**	6/1 3	57	—
12987	**Adrenalin** (MrsJRRamsden) **2-8-11** ACulhane(10) (s.s & swtchd rt s: hdwy ½-wy: no imp)	½	**8**	25/1	54	—
15813	**Hopefully** (MRChannon) **2-8-6** RPerham(7) (a.p: outpcd over 2f out: no imp after)	¾	**9**	11/1	47	—
	Son of Skelton (JWharton) **2-8-11** JFanning(1) (leggy: scope: s.i.s: stdy hdwy over 1f out: nvr nr to chal)	nk	**10**	50/1	51+	—
15812	**Final Claim** (JGFitzGerald) **2-8-11** DHolland(12) (b: lw: chsd ldrs: outpcd ½-wy: sn btn)	3	**11**	3/1 1	43	—
16145	**Docklands Dispatch (IRE)** (NTinkler) **2-8-8**(3) PMcCabe(8) (a bhd)	hd	**12**	12/1	43	—
181913	**Eager Hero** (MBrittain) **2-8-4**(7) DMernagh(9) (sn outpcd & bhd)	nk	**13**	100/1	42	—
16264	**Dispol Lass** (PCalver) **2-8-3**(3) DarrenMoffatt(15) (chsd ldrs 4f: wknd)	2	**14**	20/1	32	—
*1290*5	**General Joey** (MDods) **2-8-8**(3) CTeague(14) (lw: s.s: a bhd)	2	**15**	100/1	31	—
18156	**Sunshine Pet (IRE)** (JJO'Neill) **2-8-6b1** RLappin(4) (nvr wnt pce)	2	**16**	50/1	21	—
12537	**Sixth Avenue (IRE)** (RMWhitaker) **2-8-3**(3) RHavlin(6) (a bhd)	7	**17**	20/1	2	—
				(SP 134.0%)	**17 Rn**	

1m 13.6 (3.90) CSF £179.11 TOTE £58.90: £8.40 £3.00 £2.30 (£305.10) Trio £329.60; £417.83 to Ascot 18/6/97 OWNER The Ebor Partnership (RICHMOND) BRED W. L. Barker
No bid
Tancred Times is obviously a bit of a character as she showed last time, but she also showed she has plenty of ability when in the mood. (33/1)
1829 Inchalong put in a tremendous effort from a very poor draw, and will surely find a suitable event before long. (5/1)
1438 Tremonnow found this trip on this track too sharp and will find a race in due course. (5/1)
1758* Figawin took a strong hold on the way down, and that certainly did not help his cause. (7/1: 9/2-8/1)
1600 Newhargen (IRE) again had his chances, but was then found wanting when the pressure was on in the last couple of furlongs. (12/1)
743 Toll's Times was off the bridle throughout, but to his credit he kept on, albeit in vain. (33/1)
Son of Skelton, poorly drawn here, caught the eye making steady late progress and looks worth keeping an eye on. (50/1)

2017 GROSVENOR CASINOS SCARBOROUGH LADIES' H'CAP (0-70) (3-Y.O) (Class G)

3-25 (3-26) **6f** £2,390.00 (£665.00: £320.00) Stalls: High GOING minus 0.51 sec per fur (F)

				SP	RR	SF
1925^{4}	**Priory Gardens (IRE) (40)** (JMBradley) **3-9-6**(4) MissADeniel(12) (chsd ldrs: led appr fnl f: edgd lft & r.o)	—	1	$6/1^{2}$	53	17
1673^{6}	**Two On The Bridge (65)** (DenysSmith) **3-11-7** MissRClark(11) (led tl hdd appr fnl f: styd on same pce)	3	2	$7/1^{3}$	70	34
1514*	**Mungo Park (57)** (MrsJRRamsden) **3-10-9**(4) MissERamsden(10) (lw: s.i.s: hdwy ½-wy: sn rdn & nt pce to chal)	1½	3	$6/5^{1}$	58	22
1673^{5}	**Rum Lad (56)** (JJQuinn) **3-10-12** MissAElsey(1) (cl up: rdn ½-wy: r.o one pce)	nk	4	10/1	56	20
1781^{9}	**Gresatre (54)** (CADwyer) **3-10-10v^{1}** MissJAllison(3) (s.i.s: bhd tl styd on appr fnl f)	1	5	16/1	52	16
1733^{3}	**Captain Carparts (55)** (JLEyre) **3-10-11v** MissDianaJones(7) (chsd ldrs tl rdn & btn over 1f out)	nk	6	12/1	52	16
1650^{5}	**Prince of Parkes (64)** (JBerry) **3-11-6b^{1}** MrsLPearce(8) (sn chsng ldrs: rdn & btn over 1f out)	½	7	10/1	59	23
1730^{11}	**Alisadara (40)** (NBycroft) **3-9-6**(4) MrsCWilliams(4) (some hdwy 2f out: nvr rchd ldrs)	6	8	20/1	19	—
1790^{6}	**Fine Times (60)** (CWFairhurst) **3-11-2v** MrsSBosley(6) (b.hind: a outpcd)	nk	9	11/1	39	3
1392^{9}	**Paldost (45)** (MDHammond) **3-9-8**(7) MissAJSmith(2) (outpcd & lost tch fr ½-wy)	nk	10	100/1	23	—
1820^{8}	**Think Again (IRE) (45)** (RCraggs) **3-9-8**(7) MissNicolaCraggs(5) (rdn ½-wy: sn lost pl)	nk	11	20/1	22	—
785^{16}	**Tom Pladdey (42)** (RBastiman) **3-9-5**(7) MissRBastiman(9) (sn chsng ldrs: sn drvn along: wknd qckly wl over 1f out)	5	12	66/1	6	—
				(SP 124.3%)	**12 Rn**	

1m 13.1 (3.40) CSF £44.21 CT £77.84 TOTE £7.80: £2.00 £2.10 £1.30 (£17.20) Trio £12.50 OWNER Mr Gwilym Fry (CHEPSTOW) BRED Sean Madigan

1925 Priory Gardens (IRE) was well drawn and well handled and did it nicely, and he looks to be improving. (6/1)
1673 Two On The Bridge, from a yard yet to have a winner this season, put up a good performance but was easily picked off late on. (7/1)
1514* Mungo Park looks a difficult ride and was never quite doing enough when it mattered. (6/5)
1673 Rum Lad ran well from his low draw. (10/1: 8/1-12/1)
581 Gresatre, who has been very disappointing, was tried in a visor and did not seem to be co-operating for much of the race, but then ran on when it was all over. (16/1)
1733 Captain Carparts has yet to win a race and he was struggling for speed a long way out. (12/1: op 7/1)
1496 Fine Times (11/1: 8/1-12/1)

2018 GROSVENOR CASINOS HUDDERSFIELD MEDIAN AUCTION MAIDEN STKS (I) (2-Y.O) (Class F)

4-00 (4-06) **7f** £2,320.00 (£645.00: £310.00) Stalls: Low GOING minus 0.51 sec per fur (F)

				SP	RR	SF
1744^{4}	**Carry The Flag** (PFICole) **2-9-0** ACulhane(8) (trckd ldrs: led 2f out: pushed clr: easily)	—	1	$4/9^{1}$	62+	35
1440^{8}	**Bobbydazzle** (DrJDScargill) **2-8-6**(3) DGriffiths(6) (uns rdr & bolted 2f bef s: bhd: rn wd appr st: hdwy 2f out: r.o towards fin)	2½	2	25/1	51	24
1760^{13}	**Petara (IRE)** (JSWainwright) **2-9-0** RLappin(7) (mid div: styd on fnl 3f: no imp)	1½	3	25/1	53	26
	Danzig Flyer (IRE) (PWHarris) **2-9-0** GDuffield(9) (w'like: a chsng ldrs: one pce fnl 2f)	5	4	14/1	41	14
1391^{5}	**High Money** (GLewis) **2-9-0** NDay(1) (w ldr: led 3f out to 2f out: wknd)	¾	5	$12/1^{3}$	40	13
	Semi Circle (TDEasterby) **2-8-6**(3) RHavlin(3) (leggy: scope: chsd ldrs tl wknd fnl 2f)	5	6	33/1	23	—
	Hope Value (TDEasterby) **2-9-0** LCharnock(4) (leggy: scope: drvn along ent st: nvr trbld ldrs)	1¾	7	25/1	24	—
1749^{3}	**Captain Jones (IRE)** (BJMeehan) **2-9-0** WJO'Connor(2) (lw: led tl hdd 3f out: wknd fnl 2f)	1	8	$5/1^{2}$	22	—
684^{8}	**Donna's Double** (NTinkler) **2-9-0** KimTinkler(11) (chsd ldrs tl st: sn wknd)	1¼	9	33/1	19	—
1829^{8}	**Are Yer There** (MWEasterby) **2-8-9**(5) GParkin(10) (lost tch fr ½-wy)	½	10	25/1	18	—
1286^{5}	**Monopoly (IRE)** (MJohnston) **2-9-0** JFanning(5) (s.i.s: hdwy on outside appr st: sn wknd)	14	11	25/1	—	—
				(SP 125.4%)	**11 Rn**	

1m 26.7 (1.80) CSF £20.98 TOTE £1.50: £1.10 £5.90 £3.70 (£21.60) Trio £235.00; £182.06 to Ascot 18/6/97 OWNER Mr Athos Christodoulou (WHATCOMBE) BRED A. Christodoulou

1744 Carry The Flag had a simple task and did it really well, and this should have done his confidence no end of good. (4/9)
Bobbydazzle gave problems before the start and did not look the easiest of rides but, judging from the way she finished, there is plenty of ability there. (25/1)
1267 Petara (IRE) ran reasonably but looks short of toe. (25/1)
Danzig Flyer (IRE) put up a reasonable first effort and looks likely to benefit from it. (14/1)
1391 High Money gave all sorts of problems in the paddock and, after racing freely, he gave up two furlongs out. (12/1: op 8/1)
Semi Circle put up a reasonable first effort and should improve in due course. (33/1)

2019 GROSVENOR CASINOS NEWCASTLE H'CAP (0-70) (3-Y.O+) (Class E)

4-35 (4-38) **7f** £3,335.25 (£1,002.00: £483.50: £224.25) Stalls: Low GOING minus 0.51 sec per fur (F)

				SP	RR	SF
1584^{5}	**Castel Rosselo (57)** (ICampbell) **7-9-8** RPrice(5) (trckd ldrs: led over 1f out: pushed out)	—	1	$7/2^{1}$	71	53
1639^{8}	**Mr Cube (IRE) (48)** (JMBradley) **7-8-6b**(7) CLowther(4) (chsd ldrs: rdn over 2f out: styd on ins fnl f)	1¾	2	14/1	58	40
1631^{5}	**Terdad (USA) (59)** (TDBarron) **4-9-3b^{1}**(7) KimberleyHart(3) (sn chsng ldrs: led over 4f out tl over 1f out: kpt on same pce)	hd	3	12/1	69	51
1733*	**High Spirits (IRE) (54)** (TDEasterby) **3-8-10b** LCharnock(12) (hld up: hdwy over 2f out: edgd lft & styd on)	2	4	$6/1^{3}$	59	32
1655*	**Java Red (IRE) (47)** (JGFitzGerald) **5-8-7**(5) GParkin(1) (lw: s.i.s: hdwy & nt clr run over 2f out: styd on fnl f)	¾	5	11/1	51	33
1458^{3}	**Rotor Man (IRE) (64)** (JDBethell) **3-9-6** DHolland(6) (led tl over 4f out: outpcd fnl 2f)	1½	6	12/1	64	37
1830*	**Dee Pee Tee Cee (IRE) (53)** (MWEasterby) **3-8-9** 7x TLucas(2) (lw: chsd ldrs: hmpd over 4f out: wknd 2f out)	½	7	$9/2^{2}$	52	25
1800^{4}	**Dictation (USA) (55)** (JJO'Neill) **5-9-6** MFenton(8) (hld up & bhd: hdwy 2f out: kpt on: nvr rchd ldrs)	nk	8	16/1	53	35
1560^{6}	**Brandonville (57)** (NTinkler) **4-9-8** KimTinkler(15) (bhd tl styd on u.p fnl 2f)	nk	9	12/1	55	37
1020^{21}	**Axeman (IRE) (50)** (MartynWane) **5-9-1** JCarroll(14) (s.s: wl bhd tl styd on fnl 2f)	1¼	10	100/1	45	27
1248^{10}	**Ochos Rios (IRE) (59)** (BSRothwell) **6-9-3**(7) RWinston(9) (in tch: c wd ent st: hung rt & grad wknd fnl 2f)	3	11	9/1	47	29
946^{8}	**The Barnsley Belle (IRE) (48)** (JLEyre) **4-8-13** TWilliams(13) (bhd & c wd 3f out: n.d)	1¾	12	14/1	32	14
1650^{8}	**Maydoro (54)** (MDods) **4-9-5** RLappin(10) (hld up: a in rr)	¾	13	50/1	36	18
1501^{5}	**Godmersham Park (58)** (PSFelgate) **5-9-9** GDuffield(7) (chsd ldrs: effrt over 2f out: sn wknd)	2	14	16/1	36	18
1944^{12}	**Desert Invader (IRE) (53)** (DWChapman) **6-9-4** ACulhane(11) (rr div: c wd ent st: n.d)	nk	15	20/1	30	12
1631^{15}	**Bernard Seven (IRE) (48)** (MDods) **5-8-13b** MDeering(16) (racd wd: chsd ldrs tl lost pl 3f out)	1¾	16	50/1	21	3
				(SP 130.9%)	**16 Rn**	

1m 25.8 (0.90) CSF £52.50 CT £392.15 TOTE £5.10: £1.20 £3.60 £3.20 £2.30 (£43.60) Trio £321.90 OWNER Mr T. J. Dawson (NEWMARKET) BRED Hascombe and Valiant Studs

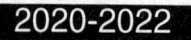

WEIGHT FOR AGE 3yo-9lb
1584 Castel Rosselo made up for his misfortune at Catterick, and could be named the winner some way from home. (7/2)
1506 Mr Cube (IRE) put his poor effort last time behind him. (14/1)
1631 Terdad (USA), in blinkers for the first time, was ridden with plenty of dash. (12/1)
1733* High Spirits (IRE), an excitable type, was almost certainly flattered by his Catterick success. (6/1)
1655* Java Red (IRE), from a 3lb higher mark, missed the break slightly and then met trouble halfway up the straight. It was basically his lack of speed that was his undoing and he is best on a stiffer track. (11/1: 8/1-12/1)
1830* Dee Pee Tee Cee (IRE) was unable to dominate, and his cause was not helped when knocked sideways turning out of the back straight. (9/2: op 3/1)

2020 GROSVENOR CASINOS SHEFFIELD MAIDEN STKS (3-Y.O) (Class D)
5-10 (5-11) **7f** £3,730.00 (£1,120.00: £540.00: £250.00) Stalls: Low GOING minus 0.51 sec per fur (F)

				SP	RR	SF
	Karawan (JHMGosden) **3-8-9** JCarroll(4) (lw: trckd ldrs: led over 4f out: shkn up & styd on strly fnl 2f: readily)	—	1	9/4[2]	70+	30
1787[7]	**Zabriskie** (MRStoute) **3-9-0** DHolland(6) (chsd ldrs: rdn & hung lft over 1f out: no ch w wnr)	2½	2	5/1[3]	69	29
	Wishing Stone (USA) (EALDunlop) **3-8-6**(3) DO'Donohoe(8) (neat: bit bkwd: hld up: hdwy over 2f out: sn rdn: rn green: styd on wl fnl f)	1¼	3	6/5[1]	61	21
	Shoshaloza (USA) (PRWebber) **3-8-9** RPerham(11) (neat: trckd ldrs: one pce whn hmpd over 1f out)	3	4	10/1	55	15
845[12]	**Gablesea (60)** (BPJBaugh) **3-9-0** ACulhane(12) (hld up: hdwy on outside over 2f out: nvr nr to chal)	2½	5	16/1	54	14
	Nordico Melody (IRE) (MrsSJSmith) **3-8-11**(3) OPears(3) (in tch: one pce fnl 2f)	½	6	50/1	53	13
	General Hastie (CWThornton) **3-9-0** TWilliams(7) (cmpt: bit bkwd: led tl over 4f out: sn drvn along: wknd over 1f out)	3	7	50/1	46	6
	Fortune's Way (IRE) (JWharton) **3-8-9** JFanning(1) (cmpt: bkwd: sme hdwy over 2f out: nvr nr ldrs)	½	8	25/1	40	—
1271[7]	**Heubach Boy** (MrsASwinbank) **3-9-0** GDuffield(10) (lw: sn bhd)	4	9	50/1	36	—
1497[10]	**Avro Avian** (MJCamacho) **3-8-9** LCharnock(5) (sn outpcd & bhd)	¾	10	50/1	29	—
1512[7]	**Imperial Line (IRE)** (ABMulholland) **3-9-0** WJO'Connor(9) (b: trckd ldrs: effrt over 2f out: sn lost pl)	1	11	200/1	32	—

(SP 120.1%) **11 Rn**

1m 26.7 (1.80) CSF £12.63 TOTE £3.30: £1.10 £2.10 £1.10 (£6.40) Trio £2.20 OWNER Mr Hamdan Al Maktoum (NEWMARKET) BRED S. Niarchos
Karawan looked outstanding in the paddock and took this in fine style. She is sure to go on to better things. (9/4)
Zabriskie, a moderate mover, hung in behind the winner and flashed his tail. He is obviously one to have reservations about. (5/1)
Wishing Stone (USA), who looked in need of the outing, showed a pronounced knee action going to post. Settled off the pace, when asked to join issue she ran green, but there was a lot to like about the way she was staying on in the closing stages. She should be a different proposition next time. (6/5: op 4/5)
Shoshaloza (USA) ran creditably but she was just starting to tire when knocked sideways by the runner-up. (10/1)
503 Gablesea, having his first outing for fifty-two days, was dropped in at the start. It is just possible that he will turn out to be a sprinter. (16/1)

2021 'RIEN NE VA PLUS' H'CAP (0-80) (3-Y.O+ F & M) (Class D)
5-40 (5-40) **1m** £3,600.00 (£1,080.00: £520.00: £240.00) Stalls: Low GOING minus 0.51 sec per fur (F)

				SP	RR	SF
1628[5]	**Cashmere Lady (65)** (JLEyre) **5-9-8**(3) OPears(6) (lw: mde all: shkn up 2f out: rdn & styd on wl)	—	1	11/4[2]	76	50
1845[11]	**Right Tune (78)** (BHanbury) **3-10-0** JStack(3) (lw: trckd ldrs: effrt ½-wy: chsd wnr appr fnl f: edgd lft & no imp)	3½	2	6/1[3]	82	46
1754[6]	**Naughty Pistol (USA) (54)** (PDEvans) **5-8-11b**(3) AWhelan(1) (outpcd & pushed along ½-wy: edgd rt & styd on u.p fnl 2f)	4	3	16/1	50	24
1674[2]	**Dispol Gem (64)** (PCalver) **4-9-10** GDuffield(8) (lw: trckd ldrs: chal over 2f out: sn rdn: one pce)	¾	4	6/4[1]	59	33
1818[6]	**Heathyards Lady (USA) (48)** (RHollinshead) **6-8-8** FLynch(2) (b: dwlt: hld up: hdwy over 2f out: sn rdn: nvr nr to chal)	3½	5	7/1	36	10
1757[6]	**Miami Moon (48)** (CWThornton) **3-7-12** LCharnock(4) (chsd ldrs: drvn along ½-wy: outpcd fnl 3f)	¾	6	25/1	34	—
	Kissel (65) (SEKettlewell) **5-9-4**(7) JennyBenson(7) (w ldrs tl lost pl over 2f out)	s.h	7	20/1	51	25
1820[6]	**Bollero (IRE) (60)** (JBerry) **3-8-5**(5) PRoberts(5) (hld up: effrt over 3f out: sn wknd)	hd	8	6/1[3]	46	10

(SP 122.2%) **8 Rn**

1m 38.1 (1.60) CSF £19.43 CT £212.17 TOTE £4.30: £1.20 £1.80 £3.10 (£12.60) OWNER Mrs Sybil Howe (HAMBLETON) BRED J. L. Eyre
WEIGHT FOR AGE 3yo-10lb
1628 Cashmere Lady, dropping back in distance, was given a lovely ride, settling well in front. Ridden this way, a mile-and-a-quarter will be no problem. (11/4)
1314 Right Tune ran easily her best so far this year, even though she proved no match. (6/1)
1754 Naughty Pistol (USA), hard at way some from home, seems suited by the step-up to a mile. (16/1)
1674 Dispol Gem, 6lb higher than when she won at Redcar two outings ago, showed a desperate action going to post. (6/4)

2022 GROSVENOR CASINOS HUDDERSFIELD MEDIAN AUCTION MAIDEN STKS (II) (2-Y.O) (Class F)
6-10 (6-12) **7f** £2,302.50 (£640.00: £307.50) Stalls: Low GOING minus 0.51 sec per fur (F)

				SP	RR	SF
1819[3]	**Mountain Song** (SirMarkPrescott) **2-9-0** GDuffield(2) (mde all: clr over 2f out: v.easily)	—	1	4/6[1]	71+	31
	Rioja (TPTate) **2-9-0** NConnorton(3) (w'like: unf: sn trckng wnr: kpt on fnl 2f: no imp)	6	2	14/1	57	17
	Simply Gifted (TDEasterby) **2-9-0** LCharnock(1) (leggy: bit bkwd: s.i.s: sn trckng ldrs: hmpd ½-wy: styd on one pce)	3	3	12/1[3]	50	10
1510[10]	**The Cannie Rover** (MWEasterby) **2-9-0** TLucas(8) (hld up: hdwy over 2f out: styd on fnl f)	½	4	20/1	49	9
	Watkins (FMurphy) **2-9-0** JStack(10) (cmpt: bit bkwd: sn outpcd & bhd: hdwy over 1f out: styd on wl towards fin)	1½	5	50/1	46	6
1396[12]	**On The Mat** (JJO'Neill) **2-9-0** JCarroll(5) (sn outpcd & bhd: some hdwy 2f out: n.d)	½	6	50/1	45	5
1744[6]	**Cut Diamond** (PFICole) **2-9-0** DHolland(4) (hmpd ½-wy: nt clr run over 2f out: n.d after)	¾	7	5/2[2]	43	3
1267[9]	**Dancing Em** (TDEasterby) **2-8-9** TWilliams(11) (chsd ldrs: drvn along ½-wy: wknd over 2f out)	hd	8	25/1	38	—
1577[6]	**Angie Minor** (JWharton) **2-8-9** JFanning(9) (hld up: sn bhd)	13	9	50/1	8	—
1577[10]	**Red Risk** (PWHarris) **2-9-0** WJO'Connor(6) (chsd ldrs: edgd rt & wknd over 2f out)	nk	10	50/1	12	—
	Pollyteknick (NPLittmoden) **2-8-9** TGMcLaughlin(7) (lt-f: sn bhd)	3½	11	20/1	—	—

(SP 124.1%) **11 Rn**

1m 27.1 (2.20) CSF £11.80 TOTE £1.50: £1.20 £2.50 £2.70 (£23.70) Trio £329.90; £162.67 to Ascot 18/6/97 OWNER Eclipse Thoroughbreds (NEWMARKET) BRED Mrs R. D. Peacock

1819 Mountain Song, who has a long stride, proved a different proposition with his initial outing under his belt and proved a different class to this lot. He should enjoy further success. (4/6: 10/11-evens)
Rioja, who has a powerful action, was always going to finish clear second best. (14/1)
Simply Gifted, who is on the leg, has plenty of knee action. After missing the break slightly, he raced keenly and, after being hampered, kept on creditably. (12/1: tchd 20/1)
1120 The Cannie Rover, who has a round action, is now qualified for a nursery mark. A mile will suit him. (20/1)
Watkins, who showed plenty of knee going down, came from out of the clouds on the wide outside in the closing stages. Very inexperienced, and bred for stamina on his dam's side, this son of King's Signet will need at least a mile. (50/1)
1744 Cut Diamond, who showed a very scratchy action, met trouble twice but it almost certainly made little difference to his finishing position. (5/2: 11/10-11/4)

T/Plpt: £48.80 (287.32 Tckts). T/Qdpt: £3.10 (293.66 Tckts) AA/WG

2009-ROYAL ASCOT (R-H) (Good to firm)
Wednesday June 18th
WEATHER: overcast WIND: slight against

2023 JERSEY STKS (Gp 3) (3-Y.O) (Class A)
2-30 (2-33) **7f** £34,700.00 (£13,147.50: £6,448.75: £2,953.75) Stalls: Low GOING minus 0.19 sec per fur (GF)

				SP	RR	SF
1412*	**Among Men (USA)** (MRStoute) **3-8-13** MJKinane(13) (lw: a.p: edgd lft fr ½-wy: rdn 2f out: r.o to ld wl ins fnl f)	—	**1**	4/1[1]	118	89
	Kahal (SbinSuroor) **3-8-10** LDettori(2) (a chsng ldrs stands' side: led appr fnl f: hrd rdn & hdd towards fin)	½	**2**	5/1[2]	114	85
1265*	**Hornbeam (103)** (JRJenkins) **3-8-10** RCochrane(12) (hdwy over 2f out: hrd rdn & r.o wl ins fnl f)	2½	**3**	66/1	108	79
1305*	**Captain Collins (IRE) (100)** (PWChapple-Hyam) **3-8-10** JReid(21) (chsd ldrs centre: rdn wl over 1f out: kpt on)	½	**4**	14/1	107+	78
1610*	**Nightbird (IRE) (116)** (SbinSuroor) **3-8-10** JWeaver(14) (swtg: racd centre: led tl ent fnl f: rdn & no ex)	¾	**5**	10/1	105+	76
1541a[9]	**Peartree House (IRE) (100)** (WRMuir) **3-8-10** MRoberts(11) (b.hind: hld up: hdwy wl over 1f out: nrst fin)	¾	**6**	50/1	104	75
1326[8]	**Supercal (99)** (DRCElsworth) **3-8-10** DHolland(1) (swtg: bhd: rdn & edgd rt over 2f out: nvr nrr)	nk	**7**	50/1	103	74
1170*	**Tayseer (USA) (97)** (EALDunlop) **3-8-10** WRyan(19) (lw: hdwy fnl 2f: nt rch ldrs)	2½	**8**	9/1[3]	97	68
1212[5]	**Omaha City (IRE) (99)** (BGubby) **3-8-10** AClark(3) (hld up: hdwy over 1f out: nvr nrr)	¾	**9**	66/1	96	67
1544a[11]	**Groom's Gordon (FR) (100)** (JLDunlop) **3-8-10b[1]** TQuinn(6) (chsd ldrs stands' side over 4f)	¾	**10**	50/1	94	65
	Wind Cheetah (USA) (108) (MRStoute) **3-8-10** GaryStevens(10) (swtg: chsd ldrs over 4f)	¾	**11**	33/1	92	63
1533a[8]	**Via Verbano (IRE)** (JSBolger,Ireland) **3-8-7** SCraine(17) (lt-f: a outpcd)	1¼	**12**	20/1	86	57
1216[4]	**Tumbleweed Pearl (97)** (BJMeehan) **3-8-7** BDoyle(15) (bhd: effrt & nt clr run over 2f out: nt rcvr)	3½	**13**	50/1	78	49
1403[2]	**Man Howa (IRE) (100)** (LMCumani) **3-8-10** PatEddery(16) (hrd rdn over 2f out: sn btn)	1¼	**14**	16/1	78	49
1587*	**Shaheen (USA) (93)** (HRACecil) **3-8-10** KFallon(7) (lw: hld up: effrt & rdn over 2f out: no imp)	1	**15**	10/1	76	47
1307[5]	**Indiscreet (CAN) (100)** (DRLoder) **3-8-10** OPeslier(4) (lw: led stands' side to ½-wy: sn rdn & fdd)	¾	**16**	20/1	74	45
1216*	**Andreyev (IRE) (108)** (RHannon) **3-8-13** RHughes(18) (lw: a in rr: rdn over 2f out: no rspnse)	3	**17**	20/1	71	42
1551a[4]	**Cryhavoc (93)** (JRArnold) **3-8-10** SSanders(9) (prom over 4f: sn rdn & wknd)	1¾	**18**	66/1	64	35
1621*	**Meshhed (USA) (101)** (BHanbury) **3-8-7** RHills(8) (w ldrs early: sn lost pl)	1½	**19**	10/1	57	28
1587[2]	**Satin Stone (USA)** (JHMGosden) **3-8-10** GHind(20) (swtg: racd centre: j.path ½-wy: sn bhd: t.o)	8	**20**	33/1	42	13
				(SP 119.0%)	**20 Rn**	

1m 26.66 (-0.54) CSF £16.58 TOTE £4.90: £2.20 £1.70 £11.10 (£7.50) Trio £270.70 OWNER Mr M Tabor & Mrs John Magnier (NEWMARKET) BRED Gail Beitz & Gainsborough Farm
IN-FOCUS: On the straight course the stands side always appeared to have the advantage and the draw did make a difference.
1412* Among Men (USA) goes from strength to strength, and even this step down to seven furlongs was not enough to prevent him from maintaining his impressive winning record. (4/1)
Kahal, fifth in the Dewhurst on his previous appearance on a racecourse in the autumn, has since changed stables. Looking magnificent but sure to benefit from the run, he proved a real tough nut to crack, and he should win his share of good races. (5/1)
1265* Hornbeam looked ill at ease cantering to post and took a long time to find top gear, but he finished in fine style, and a mile is well within his capacity. (66/1)
1305* Captain Collins (IRE) failed to maintain his winning sequence, but he ran possibly his best race yet and he too gives the impression that a slightly longer trip would not come amiss. (14/1)
1610* Nightbird (IRE), sweating and a bit on edge in the preliminaries, would have won this had she been drawn on the stands' side, for she led her rivals a merry dance on her own out in the centre of the track, until finding demands too much for her inside the final furlong. She will not be long in regaining the winning thread. (10/1)
1541a Peartree House (IRE) has not got the speed to succeed at this trip in such hot company and he was only finding his stride when the race was as good as over. (50/1)
1101* Supercal was doing some sterling work in the closing stages, but she was unable to hold her stands' side pitch, and gradually drifted out towards the centre of the track when delivering her challenge. (50/1)
1170* Tayseer (USA) (9/1: 6/1-10/1)
1621* Meshhed (USA) (10/1: 8/1-12/1)

2024 QUEEN MARY STKS (Gp 3) (2-Y.O F) (Class A)
3-05 (3-07) **5f** £27,040.00 (£10,242.00: £5,021.00: £2,297.00) Stalls: Low GOING minus 0.19 sec per fur (GF)

				SP	RR	SF
1475[3]	**Nadwah (USA)** (PTWalwyn) **2-8-8** RHills(1) (lw: stdd s: hdwy ½-wy: rdn to ld ins fnl f: drifted rt)	—	**1**	10/1	97	57
1839*	**Crazee Mental** (DHaydnJones) **2-8-8** JCarroll(13) (hld up: hdwy over 2f out: hung bdly lft & led appr fnl f: hdd fnl 100y)	s.h	**2**	50/1	97	57
1013*	**Daunting Lady (IRE)** (RHannon) **2-8-8** PatEddery(2) (a chsng ldrs: rdn 2f out: bdly hmpd over 1f out: nt rcvr)	3	**3**	4/1[2]	87+	47
1735[4]	**Banningham Blade** (KTIvory) **2-8-8** MartinDwyer(15) (a.p: hrd rdn over 2f out: one pce fnl f)	s.h	**4**	33/1	87	47
1653[2]	**Forest Treasure (IRE)** (JBerry) **2-8-8** GCarter(16) (b.hind: led tl hdd & hmpd over 1f out)	s.h	**5**	25/1	87	47
1880a*	**Heeremandi (IRE)** (APO'Brien,Ireland) **2-8-8** CRoche(5) (scope: lw: chsd ldrs: drvn along ½-wy: nt pce to chal)	½	**6**	7/4[1]	85	45
1149[3]	**Child Prodigy (IRE)** (JWWatts) **2-8-8** JReid(9) (a.p: rdn over 2f out: hmpd over 1f out: one pce)	1¾	**7**	20/1	80	40
1564*	**Ascot Cyclone (USA)** (BWHills) **2-8-8** MHills(10) (chsd ldrs: effrt & nt cl run over 2f out: outpcd appr fnl f)	1½	**8**	8/1[3]	75	35

				SP	RR	SF
1486*	**Compradore** (MBlanshard) **2-8-8** JQuinn(18) (prom: sltly hmpd over 1f out: sn btn)	1¼	**9**	33/1	71	31
1806*	**Mugello** (APJarvis) **2-8-8** KFallon(12) (lw: outpcd tl styd on appr fnl f)	½	**10**	12/1	69	29
1653[7]	**Folklore** (DRLoder) **2-8-8** KDarley(17) (chsd ldrs: wkng whn nt clr run over 1f out)	nk	**11**	33/1	68	28
1653[6]	**Heavenly Abstone** (PDEvans) **2-8-8v** JFEgan(3) (bhd: rdn over 2f out: no imp)	nk	**12**	50/1	67	27
1211[2]	**Pacifica** (RBoss) **2-8-8** LDettori(6) (outpcd fr ½-wy)	hd	**13**	12/1	67	27
1653[5]	**Kilcora (IRE)** (CADwyer) **2-8-8** DHarrison(8) (mid div: hrd drvn 2f out: sn btn)	½	**14**	40/1	66	26
1653*	**Filey Brigg** (WTKemp) **2-8-8** JFortune(4) (a bhd & outpcd)	2½	**15**	50/1	58	18
1211[5]	**Bodfaridistinction (IRE)** (ABailey) **2-8-8** OPeslier(14) (outpcd)	1¼	**16**	50/1	54	14
1806[2]	**Eleonora d'Arborea** (BJMeehan) **2-8-8** MJKinane(11) (outpcd fr ½-wy)	2	**17**	40/1	47	7
1457[6]	**Jay Gee (IRE)** (GGMargarson) **2-8-8** GBardwell(7) (spd 3f: wknd qckly: t.o)	6	**18**	100/1	28	—

(SP 123.1%) **18 Rn**

61.39 secs (1.19) CSF £409.44 TOTE £11.30: £3.00 £10.10 £1.30 (£1364.40) Trio £524.30 OWNER Mr Hamdan Al Maktoum (LAMBOURN) BRED Shadwell Farm Inc

STEWARDS' ENQUIRY Carroll susp. 27-28/6/97 (careless riding).

1475 Nadwah (USA) likes to do it the hard way and was not afraid to give her rivals a start, but she drifted almost the whole width of the track after taking control two hundred yards out and, in the end, found the line arriving not a stride too soon. (10/1)

1839* Crazee Mental caused havoc when bursting through to lead approaching the final furlong, and then went the other way after the winner had taken her measure. However, she kept staying on and must have been something to bet on when winning her previous race over an extra furlong at Hamilton. (50/1)

1013* Daunting Lady (IRE), always at full stretch to keep tabs on the leaders, was poised to challenge when stopped in her tracks by the antics of the runner-up approaching the last furlong, and was unable to recover her momentum. She should not be long in making amends. (4/1: 3/1-9/2)

1735 Banningham Blade was unable to confirm her form with the winner and, although she was slightly knocked out of her stride entering the final furlong, this performance was a shade below her best. (33/1)

1653 Forest Treasure (IRE) adopted new tactics this time and set a strong pace, but she had just been collared when Crazee Mental almost knocked her over entering the final furlong, and she had no chance at all of recovering. (25/1)

1880a* Heeremandi (IRE) could not handle this step down to the minimum trip on such lively ground, and was never in a position to deliver a challenge. (7/4)

1564* Ascot Cyclone (USA) (8/1: 6/1-10/1)

2025 CORONATION STKS (Gp 1) (3-Y.O F) (Class A)

3-45 (3-47) **1m (round)** £121,199.99 (£45,303.75: £21,714.38: £9,406.88) Stalls: High GOING minus 0.19 sec per fur (GF)

				SP	RR	SF
960[13]	**Rebecca Sharp (94)** (GWragg) **3-9-0** MHills(3) (hld up: hdwy to ld over 1f out: hrd rdn: r.o wl)	—	**1**	25/1	119	71
960[5]	**Ocean Ridge (USA) (111)** (SbinSuroor) **3-9-0** GaryStevens(6) (lw: a.p: ev ch 2f out: rallied u.p towards fin)	¾	**2**	16/1	118	70
960*	**Sleepytime (IRE) (122)** (HRACecil) **3-9-0** KFallon(4) (lw: a.p: effrt & n.m.r wl over 1f out: sn rdn: unable qckn)	2	**3**	5/6[1]	114	66
1533a*	**Classic Park** (APO'Brien,Ireland) **3-9-0** SCraine(2) (lw: hld up & bhd: effrt & drvn over 2f out: nrst fin)	1½	**4**	4/1[2]	111	63
960[8]	**Khassah (111)** (JHMGosden) **3-9-0** RHills(1) (lw: led tl over 1f out: rdn & one pce fnl f)	hd	**5**	8/1	110	62
960[10]	**Moonlight Paradise (USA) (113)** (SbinSuroor) **3-9-0** LDettori(5) (dwlt: hld up in rr: drvn along 3f out: no imp fnl 2f)	4	**6**	6/1[3]	102	54

(SP 109.7%) **6 Rn**

1m 42.04 (1.24) CSF £274.12 TOTE £14.70: £3.50 £4.20 (£72.10) OWNER Mr A. E. Oppenheimer (NEWMARKET) BRED Hascombe and Valiant Studs

OFFICIAL EXPLANATION **Rebecca Sharp: regarding the improvement in form, the trainer could offer no explanation for her poor run last time out in the 1,000 Guineas, but did state that she had become unsettled before the parade.**

960 Rebecca Sharp looked out of her class when finishing behind four of today's rivals in the 1,000 Guineas, but she put matters right today with a hard-fought success and, once again, a three-year-old filly has made a fool of the form book. (25/1)

960 Ocean Ridge (USA) runs better when she is allowed to remain in the firing line and, coming back for more at the finish, made sure the winner knew she had been in a race. (16/1)

960* Sleepytime (IRE) may have found the lively ground and the sedate pace all against her. She was tightened up below the distance, but she did not really fire this time and was a shadow of the high-class filly we saw at Newmarket. (5/6)

1533a* Classic Park needs cut in the ground but she did not have that here and, in the circumstances, probably ran as well as could be expected. (4/1)

960 Khassah ran a brave race from the front and she only lost out inside the distance. These tactics will certainly pay off for her one of these days. (8/1)

960 Moonlight Paradise (USA) has been highly-tried in both her outings this term, but she has failed to fire in either of them and, unless there is a reason, one would question whether she has trained on. (6/1)

2026 ROYAL HUNT CUP H'CAP (3-Y.O+) (Class B)

4-20 (4-24) **1m (straight)** £59,200.20 (£22,051.80: £10,700.90: £4,509.50: £1,929.75: £897.85) Stalls: Low GOING minus 0.19 sec per fur (GF)

				SP	RR	SF
1176[12]	**Red Robbo (CAN) (88)** (RAkehurst) **4-8-6** OPeslier(17) (a.p stands' side: rdn to ld ins fnl f: all out)	—	**1**	16/1	102	73
1085[2]	**Crown Court (USA) (89)** (LMCumani) **4-8-7** PatEddery(16) (b: lw: overall ldr tl hdd ins fnl f: hrd rdn: kpt on)	¾	**2**	12/1[3]	102	73
1214[3]	**Cadeaux Tryst (100)** (EALDunlop) **5-9-4** RHills(2) (b: hld up: hdwy over 1f out: fin wl)	¾	**3**	33/1	111	82
1324[2]	**Dancing Image (87)** (IABalding) **4-8-5** LDettori(3) (hld up: hdwy 2f out: rdn appr fnl f: r.o)	hd	**4**	9/1[1]	98	69
1456[12]	**Hal's Pal (96)** (DRLoder) **4-9-0** KDarley(26) (hld up: hdwy u.p appr fnl f: nvr nrr)	nk	**5**	33/1	106+	77
1323[7]	**Lonely Leader (IRE) (102)** (RHannon) **4-9-6** DaneO'Neill(30) (lw: racd far side: hdwy 3f out: led over 1f out tl wl ins fnl f)	½	**6**	25/1	111	82
981[2]	**Ramooz (USA) (106)** (BHanbury) **4-9-10** WRyan(5) (b: lw: hdwy 3f out: rdn over 1f out: nt pce to chal)	1½	**7**	33/1	112	83
1456[4]	**Crumpton Hill (IRE) (90)** (NAGraham) **5-8-8** RCochrane(4) (hld up: hdwy wl over 1f out: nrst fin)	s.h	**8**	12/1[3]	96	67
1745[3]	**Forza Figlio (88)** (MissGayKelleway) **4-8-6** SSanders(6) (a.p: rdn & one pce appr fnl f)	s.h	**9**	33/1	94	65
1450[7]	**Najm Mubeen (IRE) (93)** (ACStewart) **4-8-11** MRoberts(8) (chsd ldrs stands' side: rdn & one pce appr fnl f)	1¼	**10**	40/1	97	68
1308[7]	**Law Commission (91)** (DRCElsworth) **7-8-9** DHolland(11) (hdwy u.p 2f out: nvr nrr)	hd	**11**	50/1	94	65
1397[3]	**Mawingo (IRE) (82)** (GWragg) **4-8-0** JQuinn(27) (lw: bhd far side: hdwy wl over 1f out: nvr nrr)	1¾	**12**	12/1[3]	82	53
1768[7]	**Tertium (IRE) (81)** (MartynWane) **5-7-10**(3)ow1 AWhelan(18) (prom far side tl rdn & wknd over 1f out)	s.h	**13**	25/1	81	51
738*	**Hawksley Hill (IRE) (98)** (MrsJRRamsden) **4-9-2** JFortune(22) (hdwy u.p wl over 1f out: nt rch ldrs)	nk	**14**	11/1[2]	97	68
1456[14]	**Kayvee (98)** (MrsAJPerrett) **8-9-2** AClark(23) (nvr nrr)	nk	**15**	33/1	97	68
1782*	**King of Tunes (FR) (84)** (JJSheehan) **5-8-2** 7x SDrowne(31) (racd far side: rdn over 2f out: n.d)	nk	**16**	33/1	82	53
1456[5]	**Another Time (86)** (SPCWoods) **5-8-4** DBiggs(13) (a in rr)	½	**17**	33/1	83	54

				SP	RR	SF
1775[3]	**Pomona (82)** (PJMakin) **4-8-0** DRMcCabe(15) (lw: a in rr)	nk	**18**	40/1	78	49
1308*	**Gold Spats (USA) (94)** (MRStoute) **4-8-12** JReid(21) (prom far side: rdn 2f out: sn btn)	2½	**19**	12/1[3]	85	56
1979*	**Dreams End (84)** (PBowen) **9-8-2** 7x GCarter(9) (a in rr)	¾	**20**	20/1	74	45
1160[12]	**Celestial Key (USA) (100)** (MJohnston) **7-9-4** JWeaver(28) (chsd ldrs far side over 5f)	nk	**21**	50/1	89	60
1782[3]	**Iamus (82)** (TDBarron) **4-7-9**(5) RMullen(19) (lw: no ch whn hmpd over 1f out)	½	**22**	50/1	70	41
1262[9]	**Yalta (IRE) (83)** (RCharlton) **4-8-1** TSprake(24) (a bhd)	hd	**23**	20/1	71	42
738[5]	**Sky Dome (IRE) (86)** (MHTompkins) **4-8-1**(3) MHenry(32) (lw: prom far side: ev ch 2f out: sn wknd)	¾	**24**	25/1	73	44
1456[2]	**Bold Words (CAN) (104)** (EALDunlop) **3-8-12** KFallon(7) (lw: prom stands' side tl wknd over 2f out)	nk	**25**	12/1[3]	90	51
1456[8]	**General Academy (IRE) (98)** (PAKelleway) **4-9-2** DHarrison(20) (prom far side 5f)	½	**26**	50/1	83	54
1308[5]	**Arterxerxes (82)** (MJHeaton-Ellis) **4-8-0** JLowe(25) (lw: led far side tl hdd & wknd over 1f out)	nk	**27**	66/1	66	37
892*	**Tregaron (USA) (103)** (RAkehurst) **6-9-7** TQuinn(14) (lw: chsd ldrs far side over 5f: eased whn btn)	2	**28**	12/1[3]	83	54
1300[2]	**Kala Sunrise (88)** (CSmith) **4-8-6** JFEgan(10) (lw: bhd fnl 3f)	nk	**29**	50/1	68	39
	Gates (USA) (90) (DKWeld,Ireland) **4-8-8** MJKinane(1) (prom stands' side over 4f)	1¼	**30**	25/1	67	38
1317[19]	**Varnishing Day (IRE) (85)** (PWChapple-Hyam) **5-8-0**(3) DO'Donohoe(12) (chsd ldr stands' side to ½-wy: rdn & edgd rt: sn wknd: t.o)	10	**31**	66/1	42	13
1782[9]	**Saifan (88)** (DMorris) **8-8-6b** NDay(29) (lw: racd far side: a in rr: t.o)	5	**32**	33/1	35	6
				(SP 136.5%)	**32 Rn**	

1m 40.3 (0.30) CSF £141.89 CT £5,689.78 TOTE £26.10: £5.20 £2.90 £8.10 £1.40 (£254.80) Trio £6,083.20 OWNER Lucayan Stud (EPSOM) BRED Richard D. Maynard

WEIGHT FOR AGE 3yo-10lb

Red Robbo (CAN), always with the pace on the stands' side, found extra when shaken-up and, after striking the front just inside the final furlong, was in no mood to give best. (16/1)

1085 Crown Court (USA) made his way over to the stands' side and had most of his rivals in trouble two furlongs out, but the winner had kept him in his sights, and had the legs of him in the battle to the line. Still comparatively lightly-raced, there is a decent handicap in him. (12/1)

1214 Cadeaux Tryst, denied a clear passage when about to make his move, just had to sit and suffer until the gap presented itself but, when it did eventually arrive, the principals had gone beyond recall. Compensation awaits. (33/1)

1324 Dancing Image took time to pick up when given the office, and he was only into his stride late in the final furlong. He does give the impression that another furlong could be made to measure. (9/1)

661* Hal's Pal did a lot of running in the latter stages to win the race on the far side, but the stands' side-principals had got away. There was no disgrace in this. (33/1)

987 Lonely Leader (IRE) headed the far side group below the distance and soon opened up a clear lead on that side, but his weight was beginning to take its toll and, without being able to reach the principals, he was outstayed by Hal's Pal nearing the finish. (25/1)

981 Ramooz (USA), back in his own class, promised to get into the action entering the last furlong but, on ground plenty fast enough for him, could not find the speed to carry him through. (33/1)

1456 Crumpton Hill (IRE), staying on late in the day to finish a close-up eighth, is giving notice that he is about to find his form. (12/1)

2027 QUEEN'S VASE STKS (Gp 3) (3-Y.O) (Class A)

4-55 (4-55) **2m 45y** £32,450.00 (£12,285.00: £6,017.50: £2,747.50) Stalls: High GOING minus 0.19 sec per fur (GF)

				SP	RR	SF
1150[2]	**Windsor Castle (96)** (PFICole) **3-8-11b1** TQuinn(12) (chsd ldrs: led ins fnl f: styd on strly)	—	**1**	9/2[2]	107	69
1612*	**Three Cheers (IRE) (80)** (JHMGosden) **3-8-11v** LDettori(9) (lw: hld up: hdwy & nt clr run over 2f out: rallied appr fnl f: fin wl)	nk	**2**	8/1[3]	107	69
1738[8]	**Book At Bedtime (IRE) (95)** (CACyzer) **3-8-8** KFallon(4) (hld up & bhd: hdwy on ins & nt clr run 3f out: styd on fnl f)	2	**3**	12/1	102+	64
1850*	**Winter Garden (100)** (LMCumani) **3-8-11** PatEddery(8) (lw: hld up: hdwy on outside over 2f out: led ent fnl f: sn hdd: rdn & no ex)	½	**4**	9/2[2]	104	66
	Public Purse (USA) (AFabre,France) **3-8-11** OPeslier(1) (b: leggy: scope: hld up: hdwy to ld over 2f out: hdd over 1f out: one pce)	1	**5**	4/1[1]	103	65
1850[3]	**Fletcher (84)** (HMorrison) **3-8-11** RHughes(7) (hld up: hdwy over 1f out: styd on)	1¾	**6**	40/1	102	64
1150*	**Flirting Around (USA) (89)** (MRStoute) **3-8-11** JReid(10) (lw: prom: rdn & one pce fnl 2f)	1½	**7**	9/1	100	62
1647[3]	**Sausalito Bay (87)** (IABalding) **3-8-11** RCochrane(5) (lw: trckd ldrs: hrd drvn over 2f out: styd on same pce)	3	**8**	20/1	97	59
1218*	**Assured Gamble** (CEBrittain) **3-8-11** BDoyle(6) (lw: led tl hdd over 2f out: sn hrd rdn: wknd over 1f out)	1¼	**9**	16/1	96	58
1307[3]	**Shii-Take (105)** (RAkehurst) **3-8-11** AClark(2) (lw: bhd: sme hdwy whn nt clr run over 2f out)	1	**10**	9/1	95	57
1553a[11]	**State Fair (106)** (BWHills) **3-8-11** MHills(11) (w ldr tl rdn & wkng whn hmpd on ins over 1f out: t.o)	17	**11**	12/1	78	40
				(SP 115.9%)	**11 Rn**	

3m 29.48 (2.28) CSF £36.27 TOTE £6.00: £2.10 £1.70 £3.30 (£17.60) Trio £90.70 OWNER H R H Prince Fahd Salman (WHATCOMBE) BRED Newgate Stud Co

IN-FOCUS: **None of these had ever been asked to tackle such an extended trip before.**

1150 Windsor Castle needed to show that he does possess the necessary stamina in a spirited duel throughout the final quarter-mile but, in the end, the line arrived just in time. (9/2)

1612* Three Cheers (IRE) did not enjoy the run of the race in the closing stages, otherwise it is more than possible that he would have won. (8/1)

1738 Book At Bedtime (IRE), trying for an almost non-existent passage through on the inside from the turn for home, never once shirked the issue and she deserves reward. (12/1)

1850* Winter Garden produced a telling burst of speed to show ahead briefly passing the furlong marker but the winner worried him out of it and his stamina appeared to be sapping close home. (9/2: 3/1-5/1)

Public Purse (USA), a challenger from France taking a big step up in class and distance, worked hard to force his head in front soon after entering the straight, but the challenges came in thick and fast on the run to the final furlong, and his stamina appeared to desert him. (4/1: 3/1-9/2)

1850 Fletcher crept up from the rear once in line for home but, despite staying on, could not reach the leaders. (40/1)

1553a State Fair (12/1: 8/1-14/1)

2028 BESSBOROUGH H'CAP (0-105) (3-Y.O+) (Class B)

5-30 (5-31) **1m 4f** £29,180.00 (£8,840.00: £4,320.00: £2,060.00) Stalls: High GOING minus 0.19 sec per fur (GF)

				SP	RR	SF
1145[5]	**Zaralaska (90)** (LMCumani) **6-8-13** PatEddery(4) (lw: hld up: gd hdwy 2f out: swtchd rt & led 1f out: r.o strly)	—	**1**	8/1[3]	104+	70
1597[2]	**Nabhaan (IRE) (100)** (DMorley) **4-9-9** RHills(13) (hld up & bhd: hdwy over 2f out: ev ch ent fnl f: nt pce of wnr)	2½	**2**	14/1	111	77
1771[7]	**Willie Conquer (88)** (RAkehurst) **5-8-11** AClark(3) (hld up: hdwy 2f out: ev ch 1f out: unable qckn)	1	**3**	14/1	97	63
1169*	**Mazurek (78)** (MCPipe) **4-8-1** PaulEddery(14) (lw: led 3f: led over 3f out tl over 1f out: one pce)	2½	**4**	13/2[2]	84	50
1685[2]	**Tykeyvor (IRE) (88)** (LadyHerries) **7-8-11** GaryStevens(9) (lw: a.p: ev ch over 1f out: one pce)	nk	**5**	10/1	94	60

				SP	RR	SF
1325[3]	**Humourless (94)** (LMCumani) **4-9-3** LDettori(5) (b.hind: led after 3f tl over 3f out: ld over 1f out: sn hdd: one pce)	hd	**6**	6/1[1]	100	66
1771[3]	**Hoh Express (90)** (IABalding) **5-8-13** MHills(20) (lw: hld up: hdwy fnl f: nvr nrr)	½	**7**	14/1	95	61
1319[6]	**Rokeby Bowl (90)** (IABalding) **5-8-10**(3) MartinDwyer(10) (lw: styd on fnl 2f: nvr nrr)	s.h	**8**	20/1	95	61
789[5]	**Wild Rita (81)** (WRMuir) **5-8-4** DaneO'Neill(7) (lw: bhd: hdwy over 2f out: nt rchd ldrs)	hd	**9**	25/1	86	52
1268[3]	**Docklands Limo (81)** (BJMcMath) **4-8-4** GBardwell(16) (b.off hind: bhd: hrd drvn 3f out: no imp)	½	**10**	33/1	85	51
	Oops Pettie (86) (MrsJCecil) **4-8-9** RCochrane(15) (swtg: nvr trbld ldrs)	hd	**11**	11/1	90	56
1431[2]	**Ground Game (87)** (DRLoder) **4-8-10** OPeslier(17) (lw: nvr plcd to chal)	nk	**12**	16/1	90	56
	Better Offer (IRE) (105) (MrsAJPerrett) **5-10-0** MJKinane(18) (hld up: a bhd)	1¼	**13**	16/1	107	73
1685*	**Far Ahead (84)** (JLEyre) **5-8-7** RLappin(6) (a mid div)	1	**14**	25/1	84	50
1456[7]	**Kuala Lipis (USA) (95)** (PFICole) **4-9-4** TQuinn(2) (chsd ldrs: hrd drvn 2f out: eased whn btn & n.m.r appr fnl f)	1¾	**15**	25/1	93	59
1768[9]	**Rockforce (92)** (MRChannon) **5-9-1** RHughes(12) (chsd ldrs tl rdn & wknd wl over 1f out)	2	**16**	25/1	87	53
	Filial (IRE) (80) (BJMeehan) **4-8-3** BDoyle(19) (lw: prom tl wknd fnl 2f)	2	**17**	33/1	73	39
1145[4]	**Berlin Blue (80)** (JWWatts) **4-8-3** JCarroll(1) (lw: hld up: hdwy 7f out: wknd over 2f out)	nk	**18**	20/1	72	38
1176[5]	**Wahiba Sands (95)** (JLDunlop) **4-9-4** KDarley(8) (hld up in rr: hrd drvn ent st: no imp)	3½	**19**	9/1	83	49

(SP 128.7%) **19 Rn**

2m 31.76 (1.76) CSF £95.98 CT £1,430.99 TOTE £8.00: £1.90 £4.50 £4.00 £1.90 (£123.90) Trio £853.80 OWNER Fittocks Stud (NEWMARKET) BRED Fittocks Stud Ltd

1145 Zaralaska caught the eyes of the stewards when finishing a never-nearer fifth at York last month and, with stronger handling and a slightly longer trip, he delivered the goods in fine style with a runaway victory, after having trouble obtaining a clear run inside the last quarter-mile. (8/1)
1597 Nabhaan (IRE) looked as though he had timed his run to perfection when joining forces a furlong out but the winner, with the rail to race against, soon showed him a clear pair of heels. (14/1)
Willie Conquer produced his best form in the latter part of the year last year but showed his turn is near at hand with a very promising effort, and he is one to keep in mind. (14/1)
1169* Mazurek gave a good account of himself on this step up in class and he did not fail for the want of trying. He is certainly at the right end of the handicap. (13/2)
1685 Tykeyvor (IRE), winner of this race twelve months ago, had 10lb more to carry this time and, though he remained in the action all the way, he was found wanting when the race to the line really developed. (10/1)
1325 Humourless again gave it his best shot, but a turn of finishing speed was missing when the final battle developed. (6/1)
1771 Hoh Express may have had trouble finding a way through, but his customary late flourish did not reach a crescendo until the race was as good as over. (14/1)

T/Jkpt: Not won; £86,261.65 to Ascot 19/6/97. T/Plpt: £4,566.30 (30.59 Tckts). T/Qdpt: £789.60 (7.46 Tckts) IM

1835-HAMILTON (R-H) (Good to soft, Good patches)
Wednesday June 18th
WEATHER: overcast & raining WIND: almost nil

2029 RUTHERGLEN LIMITED STKS (0-60) (3-Y.O) (Class F)
2-10 (2-10) **1m 65y** £2,402.00 (£672.00: £326.00) Stalls: High GOING minus 0.25 sec per fur (GF)

				SP	RR	SF
1756[13]	**Naivasha (60)** (JBerry) **3-8-5**(3) PFessey(5) (mde most: clr after 1f: rdn over 2f out: jst lasted)	—	**1**	10/1[3]	57	20
1756[8]	**Robbo (54)** (CWThornton) **3-8-11** DeanMcKeown(4) (lw: a chsng wnr: kpt on u.p fnl 2f: nrst fin)	nk	**2**	7/1[2]	59	22
1622[10]	**Bluebell Miss (58)** (MJRyan) **3-8-5**(3) MBaird(1) (lw: chsd ldrs: effrt 4f out: styd on wl fnl f)	nk	**3**	7/1[2]	56	19
1994[2]	**Jedi Knight (60)** (MWEasterby) **3-8-12**(5) GParkin(3) (lw: plld hrd: lost pl appr st: hdwy u.p 3f out: swtchd outside: styd on towards fin)	s.h	**4**	2/5[1]	65	28
1838[6]	**Sweet Note (IRE) (42)** (MissLAPerratt) **3-8-3**(5) TEDurcan(2) (in tch: outpcd 4f out: no imp)	8	**5**	66/1	40	3

(SP 107.0%) **5 Rn**

1m 49.6 (5.50) CSF £59.32 TOTE £7.80: £4.50 £2.10 (£14.10) OWNER Mrs Joy Hobby (COCKERHAM) BRED J. A. E. Hobby
OFFICIAL EXPLANATION **Jedi Knight: no explanation offered, other than that the gelding was having his fourth race in ten days.**
1044 Naivasha, in a race where no one wanted to make it, took advantage of this and stole a clear lead after a furlong which proved decisive. (10/1: op 5/1)
1430 Robbo, having his first run on turf, put up a reasonable performance and was staying on well at the end. (7/1)
Bluebell Miss looked in good condition and ran her best race for some time. (7/1)
1994 Jedi Knight beat himself here by pulling hard and then suddenly dropping everything and losing touch. This moody customer was staying on well at the finish. As he has shown when things go his way, he is useful. (2/5)
952 Sweet Note (IRE) ran poorly in what was a messy race. (66/1)

2030 SUNDAY MAIL (QUALIFIER) H'CAP (0-70) (3-Y.O+) (Class E)
2-45 (2-45) **1m 1f 36y** £3,485.00 (£1,055.00: £515.00: £245.00) Stalls: High GOING minus 0.25 sec per fur (GF)

				SP	RR	SF
1837[2]	**Principal Boy (IRE) (44)** (TJEtherington) **4-8-2** DaleGibson(5) (lw: hld up: hdwy 3f out: rdn to ld appr fnl f: r.o)	—	**1**	5/2[1]	53	39
1838[W]	**One Life To Live (IRE) (49)** (SEKettlewell) **4-8-2b**(5)ow1 GParkin(8) (trckd ldrs: effrt 3f out: ev ch ins fnl f: kpt on u.p)	nk	**2**	14/1	58	43
1472[5]	**Leif the Lucky (USA) (57)** (MissSEHall) **8-8-12**(3) OPears(7) (hld up: effrt 3f out: sn chsng ldrs: rdn & no imp fnl 2f)	4	**3**	100/30[2]	59	45
1624[11]	**Double Flight (67)** (MJohnston) **3-8-9**(5) KSked(3) (cl up: led 4f out: qcknd clr 3f out: hung lft & hdd appr fnl f: sn btn)	2	**4**	15/2	65	40
1748[B]	**Hutchies Lady (38)** (RMMcKellar) **5-7-7b**(3) PFessey(6) (b.hind: sn bhd: effrt 4f out: n.d)	8	**5**	16/1	22	8
1243[12]	**Biff-Em (IRE) (70)** (MissLAPerratt) **3-8-12**(5) TEDurcan(4) (led tl hdd 4f out: wknd 3f out)	9	**6**	25/1	38	13
1007	**Out on a Promise (IRE) (70)** (LLungo) **5-10-0** DeanMcKeown(2) (chsd ldrs tl rdn & btn over 3f out)	3	**7**	8/1	33	19
1831[2]	**Askern (60)** (DHaydnJones) **6-9-4** ACulhane(9) (lw: trckd ldrs: ev ch over 3f out: sn rdn & wknd qckly)	20	**8**	7/2[3]	—	—

(SP 113.1%) **8 Rn**

1m 57.5 (3.20) CSF £34.54 CT £106.52 TOTE £2.80: £1.10 £3.60 £1.10 (£28.10) Trio £30.40 OWNER Mr Chris Moreno (MALTON) BRED Mrs M. Mansergh
LONG HANDICAP Hutchies Lady 7-7

WEIGHT FOR AGE 3yo-11lb
OFFICIAL EXPLANATION **Askern: was found to be suffering from a heart irregularity.**
1837 Principal Boy (IRE) has now run his last four races on this track, winning twice and finishing second on two occasions, and this was another game performance. (5/2)
1231 One Life To Live (IRE) put up a useful performance with the blinkers on here and certainly has the ability to pick up a race. (14/1)
1472 Leif the Lucky (USA) travelled well yet again but when it came down to a struggle he was found wanting as usual. (100/30)
1270 Double Flight, looking ultra-fit, helped force the pace but, inclined to hang when ridden, he was well short of speed at this trip. (15/2)
1231 Hutchies Lady is not really co-operating at the moment. (16/1)
Biff-Em (IRE), taking a step up in trip, still looked as though he would be all the better for the race and either blew up or did not stay or a combination of both. (25/1)
1831 Askern is a funny customer and ran one of his bad races here but he does look well at the moment and is likely to do better at any time. (7/2)

2031 DRUMLOCH (QUALIFIER) CLAIMING STKS (2-Y.O) (Class F)

3-20 (3-20) **5f 4y** £2,514.00 (£704.00: £342.00) Stalls: Low GOING minus 0.50 sec per fur (F)

				SP	RR	SF
1829[3]	**Ellenbrook (IRE)** (JBerry) **2-8-7b**[(3)] PFessey(2) (mde all: kpt on wl fnl 2f)	—	1	5/4[1]	65	26
1821[6]	**Patricia Olive (IRE)** (MHTompkins) **2-8-12** DaleGibson(1) (lw: chsd wnr thrght: hung rt u.p fnl 2f: no imp)	3	2	5/2[2]	57	18
1019*	**Mighty Sure (IRE)** (MWEasterby) **2-8-11**[(5)] GParkin(4) (b.hind: lw: a chsng ldrs: sn drvn along: nvr able to chal)	1	3	3/1[3]	58	19
1815[8]	**Diamond Steve** (NTinkler) **2-8-5v** KimTinkler(3) (bmpd s: sn outpcd & wl bhd)	10	4	16/1	15	—
				(SP 103.9%)		**4 Rn**

59.8 secs (1.50) CSF £3.83 TOTE £1.60: (£2.60) OWNER Mr J. K. Brown (COCKERHAM) BRED M. Bourke
1829 Ellenbrook (IRE), out like a flash, got the best ground on the far rails and the race was never in doubt. (5/4: evens-10/1)
1821 Patricia Olive (IRE) had her chances but just wanted to hang when ridden and may well need a pair of blinkers. (5/2)
1019* Mighty Sure (IRE) was always being taken off her legs here. (3/1)
859 Diamond Steve took a bump leaving the stalls and was completely outpaced throughout the race. (16/1)

2032 LOCH STRIVEN (S) STKS (3-Y.O+) (Class G)

3-55 (3-55) **5f 4y** £2,274.00 (£639.00: £312.00) Stalls: Low GOING minus 0.50 sec per fur (F)

				SP	RR	SF
1671*	**Palacegate Jack (IRE) (60)** (JBerry) **6-9-4b**[(5)] TEDurcan(5) (lw: racd far side: mde all: sn clr: unchal)	—	1	11/8[1]	61	36
1861[3]	**Donna's Dancer (IRE) (65)** (NTinkler) **3-8-11b** KimTinkler(4) (racd far side: sn outpcd & bhd: styd on wl fnl f)	3½	2	9/4[2]	44	13
1835[11]	**Leading Princess (IRE) (50)** (MissLAPerratt) **6-9-4b** NKennedy(3) (lw: led stands' side: rdn 2f out: no ch w wnr)	1¼	3	4/1[3]	41	16
1993[6]	**Diet (33)** (MissLAPerratt) **11-8-10v**[(7)] MSemple(6) (lw: chsd wnr far side: sn outpcd: lost tch fr ½-wy)	2	4	50/1	34	9
1604[4]	**My Saltarello (IRE) (46)** (ABMulholland) **3-8-6b**[(5)] GParkin(1) (lw: cl up stands' side: no ch fr ½-wy)	¾	5	9/1	31	—
1835[16]	**Midas Man (25)** (DANolan) **6-9-3** VHalliday(2) (racd stands' side: n.d)	10	6	100/1	—	—
				(SP 105.8%)		**6 Rn**

59.9 secs (1.60) CSF £3.69 TOTE £2.00: £1.30 £1.10 (£1.90) OWNER Mr William Burns (COCKERHAM) BRED Brendan and Sheila Powell
WEIGHT FOR AGE 3yo-6lb
Bt in 4,400gns
1671* Palacegate Jack (IRE) had far too much speed for this bunch and, gaining the best ground on the far rails, was never going to be caught. (11/8: op evens)
1861 Donna's Dancer (IRE) found the scorching early pace way beyond him but he was picking up ground when it was all over. (9/4)
956* Leading Princess (IRE) tried the impossible racing up the stands' side and was always fighting a lost cause. (4/1)
1613 Diet tried to take the winner on but this old stager hasn't the pace any more. (50/1)
1604 My Saltarello (IRE) had no chance racing up the stands' side. (9/1)

2033 ROTARY INTERNATIONAL CONVENTION-GLASGOW H'CAP (0-80) (3-Y.O+) (Class D)

4-30 (4-30) **6f 5y** £3,533.75 (£1,070.00: £522.50: £248.75) Stalls: Low GOING minus 0.50 sec per fur (F)

				SP	RR	SF
1835[4]	**Mister Westsound (46)** (MissLAPerratt) **5-7-10b** NKennedy(6) (lw: s.s: hdwy 2f out: r.o to ld ins fnl f)	—	1	14/1	55	13
1835[2]	**Natural Key (70)** (DHaydnJones) **4-9-6** ACulhane(8) (a chsng ldrs: hdwy u.p over 1f out: styd on wl)	1½	2	7/4[1]	75	33
1835[9]	**Suedoro (46)** (JSGoldie) **7-7-7**[(3)] PFessey(2) (cl up: ev ch over 1f out: kpt on same pce)	½	3	20/1	50	8
1613[12]	**Another Nightmare (IRE) (46)** (RMMcKellar) **5-7-3**[(7)] JMcAuley(9) (led tl hdd & wknd ins fnl f)	2	4	25/1	44	2
953[6]	**Bold Street (IRE) (58)** (GMMoore) **7-8-3b**[(5)] GParkin(7) (in tch: outpcd 2f out: kpt on fnl f)	nk	5	8/1[3]	56	14
1830[9]	**Shontaine (53)** (MJohnston) **4-8-3** DeanMcKeown(3) (lw: chsd ldrs: outpcd over 2f out: styd on fnl f)	nk	6	10/1	50	8
1835[6]	**Pallium (IRE) (50)** (DANolan) **9-7-9**[(5)ow4] KSked(5) (chsd ldrs over 4f: wknd)	1½	7	12/1	43	—
1561[4]	**Garnock Valley (78)** (JBerry) **7-9-9b**[(5)] TEDurcan(4) (nvr rchd ldrs)	¾	8	3/1[2]	69	27
1944[15]	**Craigie Boy (46)** (NBycroft) **7-7-10b** DaleGibson(1) (lw: effrt ½-wy: sn btn)	5	9	10/1	24	—
				(SP 113.6%)		**9 Rn**

1m 11.8 (1.80) CSF £34.84 CT £463.10 TOTE £10.60: £1.30 £1.30 £5.80 (£9.70) Trio £35.00 OWNER David Sutherland-Ian Hay (AYR) BRED Red House Stud
LONG HANDICAP Another Nightmare (IRE) 7-0 Mister Westsound 7-1 Pallium (IRE) 7-9 Suedoro 7-1 Craigie Boy 7-4
1835 Mister Westsound looked superb and, after his usual tardy start, produced a tremendous run to settle it. He is worth following whilst in this mood. (14/1)
1835 Natural Key is running well at the moment but, despite responding to pressure, was never good enough. (7/4: 5/4-2/1)
Suedoro showed her first signs of form this season here and will obviously pick up a race or two. (20/1)
1227 Another Nightmare (IRE) likes cut in the ground and is coming to form. (25/1)
Bold Street (IRE) is showing signs of ability. (8/1)
1511* Shontaine probably just found this trip too sharp. (10/1: op 4/1)
1835 Pallium (IRE) (12/1: 6/1-14/1)

2034 SOUTH LANARKSHIRE H'CAP (0-70) (4-Y.O+) (Class E)

5-05 (5-06) **1m 5f 9y** £3,046.00 (£922.00: £450.00: £214.00) Stalls: High GOING minus 0.25 sec per fur (GF)

				SP	RR	SF
1996[2]	**Hasta la Vista (47)** (MWEasterby) **7-8-11b**[(5)] GParkin(2) (lw: led tl hdd over 4f out: rallied to ld wl ins fnl f)	—	1	11/2[3]	60	39

1840[3] **Trilby (56)** (GRichards) **4-9-6v**(5) TEDurcan(4) (lw: trckd ldrs: led over 4f out & qcknd: rdn 2f out: hdd & no ex wl ins f fnl) 1¼ **2** 8/1 68 47
1693[3] **Tissue of Lies (USA) (59)** (MJohnston) **4-10-0** DeanMcKeown(6) (lw: chsd ldrs: rdn 4f out: styd on one pce)2½ **3** 6/1 67 46
1039[6] **Philmist (45)** (MissLAPerratt) **5-9-0b** NKennedy(9) (bhd: effrt 4f out: styd on: nvr rchd ldrs) 8 **4** 14/1 44 23
1840* **Lord Advocate (50)** (DANolan) **9-9-0b**(5) 4x KSked(7) (lw: chsd ldrs: outpcd 6f out: hdwy 4f out: no imp) 1 **5** 5/1 2 47 26
1491[2] **Golden Hadeer (55)** (MJRyan) **6-9-7**(3) MBaird(1) (sn pushed along to chse ldrs: chal 7f out: outpcd over 3f out: grad wknd) 1 **6** 7/4 1 51 30
Monaco Gold (IRE) (41) (MrsMReveley) **5-8-10** ACulhane(5) (swtg: prom tl wknd fnl 4f) 5 **7** 14/1 31 10
1605[9] **Ballet de Cour (32)** (TJEtherington) **4-8-1v1** DaleGibson(8) (outpcd 5f out: a in rr) ....¾ **8** 25/1 21 —
Fox Sparrow (55) (NTinkler) **7-9-10b** KimTinkler(3) (a bhd) 1¼ **9** 40/1 43 22
(SP 113.4%) **9 Rn**

2m 52.6 (6.90) CSF £43.51 CT £246.62 TOTE £8.00: £2.80 £4.40 £1.10 (£17.20) Trio £43.50 OWNER Mr K. Hodgson (SHERIFF HUTTON) BRED Clanville Lodge Stud

1996 Hasta la Vista really needs a bit further than this but there was a really strong pace on her and after looking beaten he rallied splendidly. (11/2: 4/1-6/1)

1840 Trilby was going by far the best when kicking on early in the straight but it seems she had done too much too soon and was just worried out of it. Nevertheless she is in fine form. (8/1)

1693 Tissue of Lies (USA) had his chances but lacked the pace to ever take them. (6/1)

1039 Philmist keeps running reasonably but just lacks pace to really get into these strongly-run events. (14/1)

1840* Lord Advocate found this far too competitive for him and was treading water from a long way out. (5/1: 11/4-11/2)

1491 Golden Hadeer had been running his socks off for some time and was wisely not over-punished when beaten here. (7/4)

T/Plpt: £264.10 (23.63 Tckts). T/Qdpt: £16.80 (26.59 Tckts) AA

1791-NOTTINGHAM (L-H) (Good, Good to soft patches)
Wednesday June 18th

WEATHER: overcast WIND: almost nil

2035 SHADWELL STUD SERIES APPRENTICE H'CAP (0-70) (3-Y.O+) (Class F)

6-50 (6-50) **1m 6f 15y** £2,854.50 (£792.00: £379.50) Stalls: Low GOING minus 0.20 sec per fur (GF)

SP RR SF

1778[6] **Dancing Cavalier (59)** (RHollinshead) **4-9-1**(5) PFredericks(8) (b.off hind: lw: hld up: hdwy 4f out: led over 2f out: sn qcknd clr) ....— **1** 7/1 71 46
Needwood Epic (48) (BCMorgan) **4-8-2**(7) DHayden(4) (a.p: ev ch over 2f out: edgd rt over 1f out: kpt on) 7 **2** 25/1 52 27
Early Peace (IRE) (49) (MDods) **5-8-10** SCopp(5) (hdwy 4f out: rdn & edgd lft over 1f out: r.o) ....hd **3** 16/1 53 28
1296[8] **Wesley's Lad (IRE) (58)** (JNeville) **3-8-2** PPMurphy(7) (s.i.s: sn chsng ldrs: one pce fnl 3f) 1½ **4** 20/1 60 18
1570* **Rose of Glenn (45)** (BPalling) **6-8-6** ADaly(1) (plld hrd: chsd ldrs: rdn & hld whn hmpd over 1f out: no ch after) 3 **5** 9/1 44 19
1408[5] **Turgenev (IRE) (65)** (RBastiman) **8-9-12b** HBastiman(3) (hdwy 8f out: ev ch over 2f out: wkng whn n.m.r 1f out) ....½ **6** 4/1 3 63 38
888[13] **Sheriff (56)** (JWHills) **6-8-10**(7) SamDickerson(10) (lw: rn wd after 2f: bhd fnl 6f) 1 **7** 10/1 53 28
1685[4] **Spa Lane (53)** (MPBielby) **4-9-0** DSweeney(2) (led 2f: led 7f out tl hdd & wknd over 2f out) ....½ **8** 7/2 2 50 25
My Rossini (49) (PJBevan) **8-8-10** DDenby(6) (bit bkwd: led after 2f: hdd 7f out: sn wknd) 2½ **9** 8/1 43 18
1465[2] **Mystic Quest (IRE) (67)** (KMcAuliffe) **3-8-6**(5) TField(9) (hdwy 8f out: ev ch 4f out: wknd 2f out) 9 **10** 11/4 1 51 9
(SP 126.1%) **10 Rn**

3m 6.0 (7.50) CSF £160.05 CT £2,487.12 TOTE £7.90: £2.60 £7.40 £5.30 (£179.70) Trio Not won; £112.72 to 20/6/97 OWNER The Three R's (UPPER LONGDON) BRED A. P. Hume

WEIGHT FOR AGE 3yo-17lb

OFFICIAL EXPLANATION Mystic Quest: no explanation offered.

888 Dancing Cavalier, suited by the fast early pace, bounced back to his early season form with an impressive success. (7/1)

Needwood Epic is lightly-made and probably does not take a lot of getting ready. She was on a 17lb lower mark that at the start of last season and may find a small handicap. (25/1)

Early Peace (IRE), towards the rear for the first mile, made his move on the outside but was tending to drift left-handed as the competitors for second place got in each other's way going to the furlong pole. (16/1)

Wesley's Lad (IRE), stepping up in trip, still looked short of pace. (20/1)

1570* Rose of Glenn would not have won but was still in the scrap for second place when made the meat in the sandwich. (9/1: 6/1-10/1)

1408 Turgenev (IRE) made a bold bid early in the straight but his lack of any change of gear saw his chance gradually recede. (4/1: op 9/4)

1465 Mystic Quest (IRE), going up in trip, may well have not stayed but had had three hard races in succession this season. (11/4)

2036 KPMG PASAS H'CAP (0-70) (3-Y.O+) (Class E)

7-20 (7-22) **1m 54y** £3,382.25 (£1,013.00: £486.50: £223.25) Stalls: Low GOING minus 0.20 sec per fur (GF)

SP RR SF

1878[2] **Therhea (IRE) (62)** (BRMillman) **4-9-5**(3) AWhelan(3) (b.off hind: lw: sn chsng ldrs: n.m.r over 2f out: squeezed thro: led ins fnl f: rdn out) ....— **1** 3/1 1 71 55
1473[9] **Lynton Lad (67)** (CPEBrooks) **5-9-13** RPerham(2) (led after 2f: hdd ins fnl f: unable qckn) 2½ **2** 20/1 71 55
*1754** **Princess Efisio (60)** (BAMcMahon) **4-9-6** JFEgan(10) (swtg: chsd ldrs: rdn 4f out: one pce appr fnl f) ....nk **3** 13/2 3 64 48
1489[6] **Ben Gunn (65)** (PTWalwyn) **5-9-11** RPrice(12) (lw: chsd ldrs: rdn 2f out: one pce) ....nk **4** 11/2 2 68 52
1463[11] **Lucky Begonia (IRE) (52)** (WJMusson) **4-8-12** MRimmer(18) (bhd: hdwy 3f out: r.o wl fnl f) 1¼ **5** 16/1 53 37
1463[8] **Classic Ballet (FR) (55)** (RGuest) **4-9-1** WJO'Connor(14) (chsd ldrs: ev ch over 2f out: btn appr fnl f) ....½ **6** 14/1 55 39
947[10] **Karinska (55)** (MCChapman) **7-9-1** FNorton(11) (hdwy 4f out: one pce appr fnl f) ....nk **7** 14/1 54 38
1495[11] **Up in Flames (IRE) (60)** (SRBowring) **6-9-6** SWebster(5) (in tch: n.m.r & swtchd 2f out: sn rdn & btn) 4 **8** 20/1 51 35
1800[15] **Power Game (57)** (JBerry) **4-9-3b** GCarter(17) (in tch: no imp fnl 3f) 2 **9** 9/1 44 28
Young Dalesman (58) (AStreeter) **4-9-4** LNewton(7) (bit bkwd: nvr trbld ldrs) 3 **10** 20/1 40 24
1660[6] **Scenicris (IRE) (59)** (RHollinshead) **4-8-12**(7) PFredericks(4) (nvr nr to chal) ....s.h **11** 9/1 40 24
763[14] **Mybotye (62)** (RBastiman) **4-9-3**(5) HBastiman(1) (nvr trbld ldrs) ....hd **12** 16/1 43 27
1754[7] **Sand Star (60)** (DHaydnJones) **5-9-6** JQuinn(8) (plld hrd: chsd ldrs over 6f) 1¾ **13** 14/1 38 22
1588[9] **Flotilla (70)** (SMellor) **3-9-6** MWigham(13) (a bhd) ....hd **14** 16/1 48 22
1097[19] **Bon Luck (IRE) (67)** (JABennett) **5-9-13** TSprake(16) (nvr nr ldrs) 2 **15** 20/1 41 25

				SP	RR	SF
1207^{12}	**The Negotiator (68)** (MJHeaton-Ellis) **3-9-4** SDrowne(15) (w ldrs: rn wd over 4f out: wknd 3f out)	nk	**16**	7/1	41	15
1677^{5}	**Kingchip Boy (59)** (MJRyan) **8-9-0v**(5) RMullen(6) (led 2f: wknd qckly wl over 1f out)	2½	**17**	8/1	27	11
1225^{16}	**Royal South (IRE) (65)** (PSFelgate) **4-9-8**(3) PMcCabe(9) (s.s: rn wd over 4f out: a bhd)	12	**18**	16/1	10	—

(SP 159.9%) **18 Rn**

1m 44.8 (3.50) CSF £82.77 CT £385.63 TOTE £4.30: £1.40 £9.40 £3.10 £1.90 (£84.80) Trio £152.20 OWNER Ray Gudge, Colin Lew Calvert (CULLOMPTON) BRED Mrs W. Hanson

WEIGHT FOR AGE 3yo-10lb

1878 Therhea (IRE) showed plenty of courage to squeeze through a narrow gap and re-couped last week's losses in tenacious style. (3/1)
1219 Lynton Lad, taken on by two rivals early on, soon got on top and was only caught near the finish. This is the way to ride him. (20/1)
1754* Princess Efisio got warm and moved down poorly but ran well and appears to get this trip. (13/2)
1489 Ben Gunn ran his best ever race beyond seven furlongs. (11/2)
Lucky Begonia (IRE), dropped in trip, found the fast early pace had taken its toll on those who raced more prominently and finished to considerable effect. (16/1)
Classic Ballet (FR), another taking a step down in trip, was made plenty of use of but was clearly getting nowhere in the closing stages. (14/1)
1677 Kingchip Boy (8/1: 6/1-9/1)

2037 TATTERSALLS MAIDEN AUCTION STKS (2-Y.O) (Class E)

7-50 (7-52) **5f 13y** £3,148.25 (£941.00: £450.50: £205.25) Stalls: High GOING minus 0.20 sec per fur (GF)

				SP	RR	SF
1564^{12}	**Tempus Fugit** (BRMillman) **2-8-0** TSprake(2) (racd far side: mde all: rdn out)	—	**1**	25/1	77	26
1735^{6}	**Conectis (IRE)** (DJSCosgrove) **2-8-1** GCarter(1) (chsd wnr far side: rdn over 1f out: r.o: nt rch wnr)	½	**2**	$5/2^{1}$	76	25
	Italian Rose (WJMusson) **2-7-13** JQuinn(15) (leggy: dwlt: hdwy over 1f out: r.o wl ins fnl f)	3	**3**	16/1	65	14
1749^{4}	**The Groveller** (PDEvans) **2-8-7** JFEgan(8) (lw: hdwy over 2f out: no imp ins fnl f)	1	**4**	$5/1^{2}$	70	19
	The Limping Cat (IRE) (BCMorgan) **2-8-8** LNewton(12) (neat: w'like: a.p: one pce appr fnl f)	½	**5**	8/1	69	18
1797^{2}	**Tangerine Flyer** (JBerry) **2-8-2**(5) PRoberts(16) (led stands' side: one pce appr fnl f)	½	**6**	$5/2^{1}$	67	16
1812^{11}	**Acid Test** (WRMuir) **2-8-11** FLynch(9) (s.i.s: hdwy 2f out: sn rdn & edgd lft: no imp)	1¾	**7**	16/1	65	14
1669^{3}	**Jacobina** (TDBarron) **2-8-2** JTate(13) (b.hind: nvr trbld ldrs)	s.h	**8**	14/1	56	5
1569^{U}	**Scolding** (KAMorgan) **2-8-0** FNorton(10) (b: s.i.s: nvr nrr)	½	**9**	25/1	52	1
	Double Power (LRLloyd-James) **2-7-13** NAdams(3) (unf: bit bkwd: s.i.s: racd far side: a bhd)	1¾	**10**	16/1	46	—
1791^{4}	**Flame Tower (IRE)** (RHannon) **2-8-6** WJO'Connor(11) (lw: prom 3f)	¾	**11**	8/1	50	—
	Cape Hope (RBoss) **2-8-6** GDuffield(7) (w'like: unf: spd 3f)	6	**12**	$11/2^{3}$	31	—
1626^{2}	**Sans Rivale** (BJMeehan) **2-8-1** CRutter(5) (prom over 3f)	½	**13**	9/1	25	—
1174^{9}	**Julies Jewel (IRE)** (MCChapman) **2-8-7** SDrowne(6) (spd over 2f)	3	**14**	25/1	21	—
	Ashangem (BobJones) **2-8-6** NDay(4) (lt-f: unf: sn bhd)	2	**15**	10/1	14	—

(SP 166.4%) **15 Rn**

61.4 secs (2.50) CSF £105.71 TOTE £75.50: £11.60 £1.80 £6.70 (£376.20) Trio £145.40; £184.38 to 20/6/97 OWNER The Keepers (CULLOMPTON) BRED A. and Mrs Rhodes

Tempus Fugit left her Bath debut behind, breaking smartly and heading straight for the far rail. Showing terrific speed to go three lengths clear, she was coming to the end of her tether but never likely to be caught. (25/1)
893 Conectis (IRE), back in her own class, is finding it hard to break her duck although five does seems a little too sharp. (5/2: op 6/4)
Italian Rose, a leggy, rather likeable half-sister to a couple of winning sprinters, missed the break but finished strongly and should find a race despite her bargain basement purchase price. (16/1)
1749 The Groveller did some good work towards the centre of the track but probably found this trip too sharp. (5/1)
The Limping Cat (IRE), a smallish, stocky, sprint-bred newcomer, showed plenty of pace towards the stands' rail. (8/1: op 20/1)
1797 Tangerine Flyer, with the rails draw, tried to make all against the fence, but the two racing on the opposite rail had him in trouble some way from home. (5/2)
Cape Hope (11/2: 3/1-6/1)
1626 Sans Rivale (9/1: 4/1-10/1)

2038 E.B.F. NOVICE STKS (2-Y.O) (Class D)

8-20 (8-23) **6f 15y** £3,978.10 (£1,190.80: £571.40: £261.70) Stalls: High GOING minus 0.20 sec per fur (GF)

				SP	RR	SF
	Tracking (HRACecil) **2-8-12** KFallon(5) (wl grwn: chsd ldr: pushed along 3f out: led over 1f out: sn drew clr: comf)	—	**1**	$2/7^{1}$	79+	33
1997^{2}	**Demolition Jo** (PDEvans) **2-8-7v**[1] JFEgan(3) (led over 4f: sn rdn & unable qckn)	2½	**2**	$5/1^{2}$	67	21
1564^{7}	**Make Believe** (RCharlton) **2-8-7** TSprake(6) (chsd ldrs: rdn over 1f out: one pce)	4	**3**	$9/1^{3}$	57	11
1806^{7}	**Cherished (IRE)** (PFICole) **2-8-7** TQuinn(1) (chsd ldrs: no imp appr fnl f)	½	**4**	10/1	56	10
	Chayanee's Arena (IRE) (AGNewcombe) **2-8-7** SDrowne(4) (lt-f: unf: a bhd)	4	**5**	16/1	45	—

(SP 119.4%) **5 Rn**

1m 14.8 (3.30) CSF £2.52 TOTE £1.40: £1.10 £1.60 (£1.90) OWNER Buckram Oak Holdings (NEWMARKET) BRED Buckram Thoroughbred Enterprises Inc

Tracking, whose half-brother was sold cheaply out of the yard unraced last year, shows a deal more promise. Rather green and noisy in the paddock, as one might expect from a colt making his debut against four fillies, he got fractious in the stalls as the debutante in the next berth gave a lot of trouble. He looked to be struggling at halfway but Fallon wisely switched him to the stands' rail, the field having drifted towards the centre and, once he hit his stride, he won in decent style. If his temperament holds up, he should prove useful. (2/7)
1997 Demolition Jo is very sparely-made and may not have a lot of improvement in her but deserves to find a race as she had these at full stretch by halfway, again edging left away from the stands rail which made the favourite's task a lot easier. (5/1: op 3/1)
Make Believe reversed Bath form with Cherished but had to work hard in the last furlong and a half to do so. (9/1: 6/1-10/1)
1564 Cherished (IRE) was not given an unduly hard time when it became obvious she could not go with the principals. (10/1: op 6/1)
Chayanee's Arena (IRE) gave a lot of trouble at the start and appeared short of pace once the stalls opened. (16/1)

2039 BURTON JOYCE (S) H'CAP (0-60) (3-Y.O+) (Class G)

8-50 (8-52) **1m 1f 213y** £1,984.50 (£547.00: £259.50) Stalls: Low GOING minus 0.20 sec per fur (GF)

				SP	RR	SF
1798^{3}	**Diamond Crown (IRE) (42)** (MartynWane) **6-8-12** KFallon(2) (hld up: hdwy over 2f out: led wl ins fnl f: rdn out)	—	**1**	$5/2^{1}$	51	14
1441*	**Arzani (USA) (52)** (DJSCosgrove) **6-9-8** MRimmer(7) (b: hld up: hdwy over 2f out: ev ch ins fnl f: unable qckn nr fin)	½	**2**	$11/2^{2}$	60	23
1445^{7}	**Spring Campaign (IRE) (48)** (MCPipe) **4-9-4v**[1] TQuinn(14) (chsd ldrs: led ins fnl f: sn hdd & unable qckn)	1¾	**3**	12/1	53	16

1825^{6}	**High Desire (IRE) (49)** (JRArnold) **4-9-2**(3) MartinDwyer(13) (in tch: hdwy 2f out: n.m.r over 1f out: r.o wl ins fnl f)	nk	**4**	8/1	54	17
1574^{10}	**Opera Fan (IRE) (41)** (KAMorgan) **5-8-11** JQuinn(16) (lw: chsd ldr: ev ch ins fnl f: one pce nr fin)	hd	**5**	12/1	46	9
1802^{8}	**Whothehellisharry (41)** (PTDalton) **4-8-8**(3) PMcCabe(1) (lw: led: clr over 5f out: wknd & hdd ins fnl f)	1¼	**6**	25/1	44	7
1951^{3}	**Racing Hawk (USA) (43)** (MSSaunders) **5-8-13** RPrice(10) (chsd ldrs: rdn 2f out: r.o nr fin)	hd	**7**	10/1	46	9
1809^{13}	**Precedency (46)** (KMcAuliffe) **5-9-2** JFEgan(6) (lw: rdn & hdwy 3f out: swtchd rt & r.o wl fnl f)	¾	**8**	25/1	47	10
1622^{5}	**Moneghetti (40)** (JLHarris) **6-8-10** GDuffield(9) (in tch: plld out over 1f out: rdn & no imp)	1½	**9**	14/1	39	2
1093^{15}	**Lila Pedigo (IRE) (54)** (MissJFCraze) **4-9-7**(3) OPears(15) (lw: nvr trbld ldrs)	1½	**10**	20/1	51	14
	Suile Mor (47) (BRMillman) **5-9-3** TSprake(17) (hdwy over 3f out: wknd over 2f out)	hd	**11**	16/1	43	6
	Big Pat (50) (JGMO'Shea) **8-9-1**(5) RMullen(11) (b: n.d)	4	**12**	12/1	40	3
1507^{4}	**Aquavita (50)** (RHannon) **3-8-8** WJO'Connor(4) (plld hrd: chsd ldrs 7f)	hd	**13**	10/1	40	—
1802^{7}	**Sandmoor Denim (50)** (SRBowring) **10-9-6** SWebster(8) (hld up: effrt 3f out: no imp)	3	**14**	6/1 ^{3}	35	—
1798^{4}	**River Run (IRE) (46)** (RHollinshead) **5-9-2** FLynch(12) (lw: rdn 3f out: sn bhd)	3½	**15**	10/1	25	—
	Foreign Judgement (USA) (44) (WJMusson) **4-9-0** BDoyle(5) (rdn 5f out: a bhd)	s.h	**16**	16/1	23	—
1780^{9}	**Wheildon (50)** (SCWilliams) **3-8-8** SDrowne(18) (b.nr hind: chsd ldrs 5f)	9	**17**	10/1	15	—

(SP 159.7%) **17 Rn**

2m 10.7 (8.20) CSF £18.29 CT £157.65 TOTE £3.20: £1.20 £2.20 £4.30 £2.20 (£11.30) Trio £100.90 OWNER Mr J. M. Pickup (RICHMOND) BRED Dene Investments N V
WEIGHT FOR AGE 3yo-12lb
No bid
1798 Diamond Crown (IRE), produced on the wide outside, got a clear run as a consequence, quickening in fine style to snatch the spoils in the closing stages. (5/2: op 6/1)
1441* Arzani (USA) made his move on the inside of the winner and could never quite force his head in front. He remains a threat in this class. (11/2: 4/1-6/1)
Spring Campaign (IRE) tore off after the clear leaders and finally wore them down inside the final furlong, only for the first two to sweep by as if he was running through treacle within a couple of strides. (12/1)
1825 High Desire (IRE), dropped in trip, went for an ambitious run up the inside approaching the final furlong and finished quite strongly once through the gap. (8/1)
Opera Fan (IRE), in second place from the off, moved upsides in the final furlong but the tank was empty when the finishers appeared. (12/1)
1222 Whothehellisharry set off at a rate of knots and strung the field out but could not quite last home. Such tactics will surely see him break his duck in a similar race. (25/1)
Big Pat (12/1: 6/1-14/1)
1463 Sandmoor Denim (6/1: op 4/1)

2040 OLD LENTON H'CAP (0-70) (3-Y.O F) (Class E)

9-20 (9-22) **1m 54y** £3,096.25 (£925.00: £442.50: £201.25) Stalls: Low GOING minus 0.20 sec per fur (GF)

				SP	RR	SF
1747^{6}	**Saffron Rose (63)** (MBlanshard) **3-9-5** JQuinn(6) (lw: plld hrd: chsd ldrs: led 4f out: clr over 2f out: rdn & hld on wl fnl f)	—	**1**	6/1 ^{3}	76	28
1500^{2}	**Calamander (IRE) (63)** (WRMuir) **3-9-5** KFallon(13) (lw: trckd ldrs: rdn over 2f out: wnt 2nd over 1f out: nt rch wnr)	2½	**2**	5/2 ^{1}	71	23
1757^{3}	**Phoenix Princess (49)** (BAMcMahon) **3-8-5** GDuffield(7) (lw: rdn 3f out: hdwy over 1f out: r.o)	2½	**3**	9/1	52	4
1633^{7}	**Daintree (IRE) (55)** (HJCollingridge) **3-8-11** MRimmer(10) (b.hind: lw: plld hrd: a.p: one pce appr fnl f)	1½	**4**	11/1	55	7
1622^{2}	**Rochea (51)** (MrsNMacauley) **3-8-7** BDoyle(8) (hdwy over 2f out: r.o fnl f)	nk	**5**	6/1 ^{3}	51	3
983^{3}	**Welcome Home (65)** (PTDalton) **3-9-7** JFEgan(9) (led 2f: one pce fnl 3f)	¾	**6**	11/1	63	15
1642^{4}	**Native Princess (IRE) (50)** (BWHills) **3-8-6** GCarter(2) (in tch: rdn 3f out: no hdwy)	1½	**7**	10/1	45	—
1780*	**Rumbustious (60)** (RHannon) **3-9-2b**[1] WJO'Connor(3) (chsd ldrs: hmpd 4f out: sn btn)	1	**8**	4/1 ^{2}	54	6
1757^{9}	**Glorious Dancer (40)** (JHetherton) **3-7-10** NAdams(5) (dwlt: n.d)	s.h	**9**	25/1	33	—
1139^{11}	**Schisandra (40)** (MJFetherston-Godley) **3-7-10b**[1] FNorton(12) (stdd s: nvr nr to chal)	½	**10**	25/1	32	—
1297^{6}	**Tetris (IRE) (60)** (CFWall) **3-9-2** NCarlisle(4) (lw: hld up: nvr nr ldrs)	¾	**11**	10/1	51	3
1785^{6}	**Kustom Kit Xpres (51)** (SRBowring) **3-8-7**ow1 SWebster(11) (plld hrd: led after 2f: hdd 4f out: hmpd & wknd 3f out)	¾	**12**	25/1	41	—
1421^{3}	**Enchanting Eve (61)** (CNAllen) **3-9-0**(3) MartinDwyer(1) (prom 4f)	7	**13**	11/1	37	—

(SP 141.9%) **13 Rn**

1m 47.3 (6.00) CSF £22.88 CT £139.35 TOTE £6.10: £2.90 £1.70 £2.20 (£8.40) Trio £33.70 OWNER The Lower Bowden II Syndicate (UPPER LAMBOURN) BRED The Duke of Marlborough
LONG HANDICAP Glorious Dancer 7-7
1164 Saffron Rose took a fierce hold and her rider bit the bullet and kicked hard for home early in the straight, quickly stealing enough lead to last home. (6/1)
1500 Calamander (IRE) stalked the leaders but was rather caught by surprise when the winner kicked and could never make up the leeway. She should soon get off the mark. (5/2)
1757 Phoenix Princess, back on turf, settled better this time but then took an awful lot of waking up only beginning to close in the last couple of furlongs. (9/1)
Daintree (IRE), a moderate mover, took a keen hold and could do little more in the closing stages. (11/1: op 7/1)
1622 Rochea, who is proving hard to place, was again doing her best work at the finish. (6/1)
983 Welcome Home, a good mover, broke well but soon lost the lead. The way she keeps plugging away suggests she might be worth a try front running over further. (11/1)
1780* Rumbustious (4/1: 3/1-9/2)
1297 Tetris (IRE) (10/1: op 5/1)

T/Plpt: £222.40 (48.7 Tckts). T/Qdpt: £8.40 (81.71 Tckts) Dk

1492-RIPON (R-H) (Good)
Wednesday June 18th
WEATHER: overcast, rain last 2 races WIND: almost nil

2041 NORTHALLERTON APPRENTICE (S) H'CAP (0-60) (3-Y.O+) (Class F)
7-00 (7-00) **1m** £2,873.30 (£808.80: £395.90) Stalls: High GOING minus 0.47 sec per fur (F)

				SP	RR	SF
1683^{8}	**Prime Partner (33)** (TDEasterby) **4-8-6**$^{(3)}$ RWinston(13) (trckd ldrs: led over 1f out: edgd lft: styd on)	—	**1**	6/1^{2}	43	34
1802^{2}	**Bedazzle (35)** (MBrittain) **6-8-6**$^{(5)}$ DMernagh(10) (trckd ldrs: ev ch 2f out: nt qckn ins fnl f)	½	**2**	3/1^{1}	44	35
1639^{12}	**Chalky Dancer (30)** (HJCollingridge) **5-8-6** JWilkinson(7) (a chsng ldrs: led over 3f tl over 1f out: one pce)	3	**3**	7/1^{3}	33	24
1820^{13}	**Grovefair Lad (IRE) (45)** (MartynWane) **3-8-8**$^{(3)}$ PDoe(2) (lw: bhd: hrd rdn over 2f out: styd on wl fnl f)	3	**4**	16/1	42	23
1388^{5}	**Flagstaff (USA) (38)** (KRBurke) **4-8-7v**$^{(7)}$ PWright(12) (s.i.s: rn wd ent st: styd on fnl 2f)	hd	**5**	15/2	35	26
1603^{12}	**Special-K (48)** (EWeymes) **5-9-5**$^{(5)}$ TSiddall(1) (bhd tl styd on fnl 3f)	hd	**6**	15/2	45	36
687^{12}	**Harry's Treat (42)** (JLEyre) **5-8-13**$^{(5)}$ SBuckley(16) (chsd ldrs tl wknd 2f out)	½	**7**	14/1	38	29
526^{8}	**Intrepid Fort (20)** (BWMurray) **8-7-5**$^{(5)}$ CCogan(4) (bhd: rn wd ent st: styd on fnl 2f)	1½	**8**	33/1	13	4
1441^{16}	**Polar Refrain (35)** (JNorton) **4-8-6b**$^{(5)}$ JennyBenson(14) (s.i.s: hdwy 3f out: nvr nr ldrs)	¾	**9**	12/1	26	17
1312^{3}	**Nukud (USA) (23)** (GROldroyd) **5-7-8**$^{(5)}$ NPollard(9) (nvr bttr than mid div)	2	**10**	33/1	10	1
1694^{9}	**Bad News (25)** (JMBradley) **5-8-1** AimeeCook(15) (t: lost pl 6f out: n.d after)	4	**11**	16/1	4	—
1639^{2}	**Okay Baby (IRE) (26)** (JMBradley) **5-8-2** JoHunnam(8) (bhd: hdwy over 3f out: sn wknd)	½	**12**	6/1^{2}	4	—
796^{10}	**Noble Canonire (34)** (DShaw) **5-8-5b**$^{(5)}$ SRighton(5) (swtg: s.s: a bhd)	3	**13**	20/1	6	—
1576^{11}	**Guy's Gamble (34)** (JWharton) **4-8-10b**^{1} KimberleyHart(6) (lw: chsd ldrs: rn wd ent st: lost pl over 3f out)	4	**14**	20/1	—	—
1441^{18}	**Our Tom (30)** (JWharton) **5-8-3v**$^{1(3)}$ VictoriaAppleby(17) (racd keenly: led tl over 3f out: sn bhd)	9	**15**	33/1	—	—

(SP 134.1%) **15 Rn**

1m 40.3 (2.10) CSF £23.10 CT £125.55 TOTE £9.50: £2.70 £1.90 £3.70 (£29.30) Trio £26.30 OWNER Mr Peter Bourke (MALTON) BRED P. and Mrs Venner
WEIGHT FOR AGE 3yo-10lb
No bid

1388 Prime Partner, who apparently did not stay a mile and a quarter last time, was well handled by his promising young rider. He was getting off the mark at the seventeenth attempt which underlines the poor class of this event, even by selling race standards. (6/1)
1802 Bedazzle, who has only won once from forty-four starts, never gave up trying. (3/1)
1388 Chalky Dancer is still a maiden after twenty-one outings and rarely runs twice alike. (7/1)
900 Grovefair Lad (IRE), who looked well beforehand, turned in a better effort. (16/1)
1388 Flagstaff (USA) did as well as could be expected, considering he missed the break slightly and ran wide on the bend. (15/2)
Special-K hinted at a return to form. (15/2)

2042 COVERDALE NOVICE MEDIAN AUCTION STKS (2-Y.O) (Class E)
7-30 (7-30) **5f** £2,765.25 (£837.00: £408.50: £194.25) Stalls: Low GOING minus 0.47 sec per fur (F)

				SP	RR	SF
1854*	**Shawdon** (SirMarkPrescott) **2-9-10** SSanders(3) (lw: led over 1f: rdn to ld over 1f out: hld on wl)	—	**1**	4/9^{1}	80	21
	D'Marti (CBBBooth) **2-8-7** KHodgson(6) (w'like: unf: scope: sn pushed along: hdwy ½-wy: ev ch ins fnl f: r.o)	¾	**2**	7/1^{3}	61	2
1797^{W}	**Mariana** (RMWhitaker) **2-8-7** DeanMcKeown(4) (leggy: s.i.s: hdwy ½-wy: rn green: kpt on wl fnl f)	¾	**3**	16/1	58	—
948*	**Katy Thomas** (JBerry) **2-8-10**$^{(3)}$ PFessey(1) (chsd ldr: led over 3f out tl hdd & wknd over 1f out)	3	**4**	9/2^{2}	55	—
	Dispol Emerald (SEKettlewell) **2-8-7** ACulhane(7) (lt-f: unf: trckd ldrs tl rdn & wknd over 1f out)	5	**5**	33/1	33	—
	Cherokee Charlie (RCraggs) **2-8-12** JLowe(5) (cmpt: bkwd: s.s: a wl bhd)	5	**6**	50/1	22	—
	Vogue Imperial (IRE) (PCHaslam) **2-8-12** LCharnock(2) (w'like: bit bkwd: s.i.s: sn rdn along & wl bhd)	7	**7**	20/1	—	—

(SP 115.5%) **7 Rn**

60.5 secs (2.70) CSF £3.95 TOTE £1.50: £1.30 £4.80 (£5.10) OWNER Mr Cyril Humphris (NEWMARKET) BRED C. Humphris

1854* Shawdon, very free going to post, was conceding 11lb and more away all-round. Not very big to be shouldering such a big weight, his heart is certainly in the right place. (4/9)
D'Marti looked more than fit enough to do herself justice first time. Slightly at sea on the undulating track, she took time to get into full stride but, almost upsides inside the last, pushed the winner all the way to the line. (7/1)
Mariana missed the break and ran a bit green. Taking time to get going, she was putting in all her best work in the final furlong. (16/1)
948* Katy Thomas, who showed a round action going down, took on the winner but cried enough coming to the final furlong. (9/2)
Dispol Emerald, a plain filly, was too keen for her own good. (33/1)

2043 PRICE WATERHOUSE H'CAP (0-85) (3-Y.O+) (Class D)
8-00 (8-00) **1m 2f** £3,485.00 (£1,055.00: £515.00: £245.00) Stalls: High GOING minus 0.47 sec per fur (F)

				SP	RR	SF
1668*	**Opalette (69)** (LadyHerries) **4-9-7** DHarrison(4) (lw: trckd ldrs: led 3f out: styd on u.p: hld on wl)	—	**1**	13/8^{1}	77	41
1782^{10}	**Lay The Blame (72)** (MDHammond) **4-9-10** ACulhane(7) (trckd ldrs: a gng wl: effrt over 2f out: chal over 1f out: nt qckn wl ins fnl f)	½	**2**	9/1	79	43
1831^{3}	**Gold Desire (49)** (MBrittain) **7-8-1** JLowe(9) (trckd ldrs: styd on same pce fnl f)	¾	**3**	7/1	55	19
1313^{6}	**Sing And Dance (47)** (EWeymes) **4-7-6**$^{(7)ow3}$ RWinston(5) (hld up: hdwy on outside 5f out: sn pushed along: one pce fnl 2f)	3½	**4**	20/1	47	8
699^{8}	**Foxes Tail (76)** (MissSEHall) **3-8-11**$^{(5)}$ GParkin(1) (trckd ldrs: effrt over 3f out: sn outpcd: hung lft & kpt on fnl f)	nk	**5**	5/1^{2}	76	28
1296^{10}	**Cee-N-K (IRE) (71)** (MJohnston) **3-8-11** JWeaver(8) (led to 3f out: wknd over 1f out)	1¾	**6**	8/1	68	20
509^{8}	**Don Sebastian (75)** (WJHaggas) **3-9-1** SSanders(2) (hld up: effrt over 3f out: sn chsng ldrs: wknd over 1f out)	1	**7**	11/2^{3}	71	23
	Ghostly Apparition (48) (JohnUpson) **4-8-0** LCharnock(3) (bit bkwd: hld up: drvn along & outpcd over 4f out: hung rt: n.d)	7	**8**	33/1	32	—
1097^{16}	**No Cliches (68)** (DNicholls) **4-9-6** AlexGreaves(6) (trckd ldrs tl lost pl over 2f out: eased)	7	**9**	14/1	41	5

(SP 118.1%) **9 Rn**

2m 6.7 (3.20) CSF £16.45 CT £76.74 TOTE £2.50: £1.30 £2.50 £1.90 (£8.70) Trio £50.00 OWNER Angmering Park Stud (LITTLEHAMPTON)
BRED Lavinia Duchess Of Norfolk
LONG HANDICAP Sing And Dance 7-7
WEIGHT FOR AGE 3yo-12lb

1668* Opalette, who looked outstandingly well, defied a 4lb hike in the weights. She proved very willing but, in the end, there was nothing at all to spare. (13/8)
1495 Lay The Blame, who continually swished his tail in the paddock, proved suited by the step up in distance. In a moderately-run race, he moved up on the bridle to challenge but, in the end, the winner proved too determined. (9/1)
1831 Gold Desire is firmly in the grip of the Handicapper at present. (7/1)
1313 Sing And Dance, who was found to have a heart irregularity when tailed off at Ayr, ran as well as could be expected from 3lb out of the handicap. She seems to have nothing in the way of finishing speed. (20/1)
Foxes Tail, who needed the outing, gave his apprentice rider problems. He has plenty of ability but is not one to totally rely on. (5/1)
634 Cee-N-K (IRE) showed a poor action going down. His stamina seemed to give out and he is probably best at a mile on the All-Weather surfaces. (8/1)
388 Don Sebastian, having his first outing for eighty-one days, showed a scratchy action going down. From a stable that has clearly had problems, he ran a satisfactory comeback race. (11/2: 4/1-6/1)

2044 NORMAN WELLS MEMORIAL CHALLENGE TROPHY H'CAP (0-95) (3-Y.O) (Class C)

8-30 (8-31) **6f** £6,302.25 (£1,908.00: £931.50: £443.25) Stalls: Low GOING minus 0.47 sec per fur (F)

				SP	RR	SF
1980[2]	**Double Action (86)** (TDEasterby) **3-9-7** LCharnock(2) (trckd ldrs: chal over 1f out: rdn to ld ins fnl f: drvn out)	—	1	6/4[1]	94	38
1661[3]	**Bayford Thrust (76)** (JBerry) **3-8-8**(3) PFessey(1) (b: b.hind: led tl ins fnl f: r.o same pce)	1¾	2	9/1	79	23
1980[12]	**Brutal Fantasy (IRE) (85)** (JLEyre) **3-9-6** MGallagher(5) (s.i.s: sn chsng ldrs: nt qckn fnl 2f)	3	3	14/1	80	24
1460[3]	**Soviet Leader (86)** (RGuest) **3-9-7** PBloomfield(7) (trckd ldrs on outside: drvn along ½-wy: kpt on same pce appr fnl f)	1	4	11/2[2]	79	23
1792[3]	**Barnburgh Boy (75)** (TDBarron) **3-8-10** DHarrison(8) (s.s: wl bhd tl styd on wl fnl 2f)	½	5	12/1	66	10
	Gaelic Storm (80) (MJohnston) **3-9-1** JWeaver(3) (dwlt s: sn chsng ldrs: wknd & eased over 1f out)	5	6	7/1[3]	58	2
1673[8]	**Express Girl (61)** (DMoffatt) **3-7-7**(3) DarrenMoffatt(6) (w ldrs: rdn ½-wy: wkng whn n.m.r 2f out)	1¾	7	20/1	34	—
1305[6]	**Broad River (USA) (82)** (EALDunlop) **3-9-0**(3) DO'Donohoe(9) (swvd rt s: nvr wnt pce)	3	8	8/1	47	—
1561[5]	**The Lambton Worm (80)** (DenysSmith) **3-9-1b1** ACulhane(10) (w ldrs: rdn & hung bdly lft 2f out: sn wknd)	hd	9	12/1	45	—
1225[23]	**Denton Lad (69)** (JWWatts) **3-8-4** NConnorton(4) (w ldrs tl wknd over 2f out)	2½	10	16/1	27	—
				(SP 121.7%)	**10 Rn**	

1m 12.4 (1.90) CSF £15.43 CT £134.89 TOTE £2.10: £1.40 £2.00 £3.60 (£4.60) Trio £98.80 OWNER Mr C. H. Stevens (MALTON) BRED Whitsbury Manor Stud
LONG HANDICAP Express Girl 7-9
1980 Double Action, due to go up in the weights 5lb after a sterling effort at York, had to struggle to overcome the pacesetter, but in the end did it in workmanlike style. (6/4: evens-13/8)
1661 Bayford Thrust has come down 12lb in the weights this year. Not very big, he has plenty of speed but had to give best inside the last. (9/1)
1254 Brutal Fantasy (IRE) was poorly drawn when behind Double Action at York four days earlier. (14/1)
1460 Soviet Leader, a fair type making his handicap debut, was not helped by racing up the centre. He looks to have been pitched in a trifle high in the weights. (11/2: 6/1-9/1)
1792 Barnburgh Boy, still carrying plenty of condition, lost a fair bit of ground at the start but was staying on in good style at the finish. (12/1)
Gaelic Storm, making a belated reappearance, showed plenty of knee action going down. After missing the break, he showed plenty of toe and was eased as soon as he began to tire. (7/1)

2045 MIDDLEHAM MAIDEN STKS (3-Y.O) (Class D)

9-00 (9-02) **1m** £3,501.25 (£1,060.00: £517.50: £246.25) Stalls: High GOING minus 0.47 sec per fur (F)

				SP	RR	SF
1611[4]	**Vain Tempest** (PWChapple-Hyam) **3-8-11**(3) RHavlin(11) (lw: uns rdr leaving paddock: chsd ldrs: led 2f out: rdn & swvd lft 1f out: styd on)	—	1	10/11[1]	86	40
1041[2]	**No Grousing (IRE)** (PCHaslam) **3-9-0** LCharnock(9) (trckd ldrs: effrt over 2f out: edgd rt & nt qckn fnl f)	1¾	2	12/1	83	37
1499[9]	**River Tweed** (JHMGosden) **3-8-9** JWeaver(2) (stdd s: hdwy & swtchd ins over 3f out: nt clr run & swtchd lft 2f out: kpt on wl appr fnl f)	1¾	3	25/1	74	28
727[14]	**Magic Hill** (JHMGosden) **3-8-9** GHind(7) (chsd ldrs: effrt over 2f out: styd on one pce)	1¼	4	14/1	72	26
1437[3]	**Fayik** (MRStoute) **3-9-0** DHarrison(8) (led to 2f out: one pce)	2½	5	6/1[3]	72	26
1239[6]	**Dina Line (USA)** (MBell) **3-8-9** MFenton(4) (bit bkwd: sn in tch: hdwy on outside & prom whn bmpd 2f out: kpt on same pce)	2½	6	10/1	62	16
1221[4]	**Zaahir (IRE) (76)** (BWHills) **3-8-11**(3) JDSmith(5) (lw: b.hind: chsd ldrs: drvn along over 3f out: outpcd fnl 2f)	4	7	9/2[2]	59	13
	Ingleborough (DMoffatt) **3-8-11**(3) DarrenMoffatt(12) (chsd ldrs tl rdn & lost pl over 3f out)	5	8	50/1	49	3
	Mill Orchid (JBerry) **3-8-6**(3) PFessey(1) (leggy: lt-f: s.i.s: a bhd)	1½	9	33/1	41	—
1671[7]	**Petaz** (MWEasterby) **3-8-4**(5) GParkin(6) (a in rr)	2½	10	50/1	36	—
1041[3]	**Tipperary Sunset (IRE)** (JJQuinn) **3-9-0** DaleGibson(3) (chsd ldrs: outpcd 4f out: sn lost pl)	¾	11	25/1	39	—
	Indian Affair (WWHaigh) **3-8-9** ACulhane(10) (rangy: unf: s.s: rn green & a wl bhd)	10	12	50/1	14	—
				(SP 124.8%)	**12 Rn**	

1m 40.1 (1.90) CSF £12.75 TOTE £2.10: £1.30 £1.70 £3.30 (£8.00) Trio £57.40 OWNER H R H Princess Michael of Kent (MARLBOROUGH) BRED HRH Princess Michael of Kent
1611 Vain Tempest unseated his rider when brought out onto the course and clearly has a bit of temperament about him. After hitting the front, he veered badly left but was always doing more than enough. (10/11)
1041 No Grousing (IRE) will be done no favours by the Handicapper after this effort. (12/1)
River Tweed, taken to post early and dropped in at the start, clearly possesses a fair bit of ability but is also something of a madam. Switched wide to get a run, she was by no means knocked about. (25/1)
Magic Hill, a small, strongly-made filly, has further improvement in her. (14/1)
1437 Fayik, who showed plenty of knee action going down, lacks anything in the way of finishing speed and might be worth a try over further. (6/1: op 4/1)
Dina Line (USA), who carries condition, showed a poor action going down. She ran creditably and can do better in due course. (10/1: 6/1-11/1)
1221 Zaahir (IRE) (9/2: op 5/2)

2046 LEYBURN MAIDEN STKS (3-Y.O+) (Class D)

9-30 (9-46) **1m 4f 60y** £3,566.25 (£1,080.00: £527.50: £251.25) Stalls: Low GOING minus 0.47 sec per fur (F)

				SP	RR	SF
1130[2]	**Mumaris (USA) (90)** (ACStewart) **3-8-10** MRoberts(11) (lw: trckd ldr: led 3f out: styd on strly fnl f)	—	1	2/1[1]	81	5

1612^{2}	**Awesome Wells (IRE)** (HRACecil) **3-8-10** JLowe(1) (hld up: effrt over 3f out: sn chsng ldrs: styd on same pce fnl f)	1½	**2**	5/1^{3}	79	3
1497^{3}	**Kayfiyah (IRE)** (DMorley) **3-8-5** MFenton(3) (hdwy over 3f out: sn chsng ldrs: kpt on same pce appr fnl f)	nk	**3**	16/1	74	—
1477^{4}	**Machiavelli** (HRACecil) **3-8-10** AMcGlone(14) (lw: trckd ldrs: led over 4f out to 3f out: kpt on one pce)	1¼	**4**	11/4^{2}	77	1
1405^{2}	**Vrennan** (JRFanshawe) **3-8-5** DHarrison(6) (trckd ldrs: drvn along 4f out: wknd over 1f out)	3½	**5**	14/1	68	—
1784^{6}	**Alpina (USA)** (JHMGosden) **3-8-5** GHind(15) (a in tch: drvn along & one pce fnl 3f)	¾	**6**	10/1	67	—
	Jazz Track (IRE) (PWChapple-Hyam) **3-8-7**(3) RHavlin(5) (w'like: bit bkwd: s.i.s: bhd & drvn along: styd on fnl 3f)	nk	**7**	12/1	71	—
	Sefton Blake (MGMeagher) **3-8-10** DaleGibson(19) (w'like: unf: s.i.s: bhd tl styd on fnl 3f)	3	**8**	66/1	65	—
1512^{5}	**Sabu** (JIACharlton) **5-9-7**(3) DarrenMoffatt(9) (reluctant to go to s: hld up & plld hrd: bhd: hrd rdn & styd on fnl 2f)	hd	**9**	33/1	64	2
732^{3}	**Surtsey** (MJohnston) **3-8-10** JWeaver(10) (led tl over 4f out: wknd over 2f out)	nk	**10**	14/1	64	—
	Doubly Sharp (USA) (MJohnston) **3-8-10** JFanning(18) (w'like: bit bkwd: unruly in stalls: in tch tl lost pl over 2f out)	1	**11**	25/1	63	—
967^{6}	**Hoh Explorer (IRE)** (DWBarker) **3-8-10** TWilliams(7) (hld up: hdwy over 3f out: grad wknd)	nk	**12**	33/1	62	—
	Summer Thyme (JBerry) **3-8-2**(3) PFessey(16) (lt-f: unf: trckd ldrs tl lost pl 3f out)	3	**13**	33/1	53	—
1230^{9}	**Tam O'Shanter** (CWThornton) **3-8-10** DeanMcKeown(8) (trckd ldrs: hung rt & outpcd fnl 3f)	nk	**14**	50/1	58	—
1558^{4}	**Ardarroch Prince** (MrsMReveley) **6-9-10** ACulhane(17) (unruly s: a wl bhd)	17	**15**	20/1	36	—
1497^{11}	**Notary** (JWWatts) **3-8-10** NConnorton(4) (in tch tl lost pl 4f out: eased & sn bhd)	17	**16**	25/1	14	—
1834^{5}	**Quaint Desire** (MBrittain) **4-9-3**(7) DMernagh(2) (s.i.s: hung lft & racd wd: rn v.wd ent st)	2½	**17**	50/1	11	—
	Golden Glory (MBrittain) **4-9-5**(5) GParkin(13) (rangy: unf: unruly & uns rdr bef s: s.i.s: a bhd)	8	**18**	50/1	—	—
	Prince Moshar (SGollings) **3-8-10** SSanders(12) (Withdrawn not under Starter's orders: unruly & ref to ent stalls)		**W**	66/1	—	—
				(SP 142.8%)	**18 Rn**	

2m 41.7 (8.20) CSF £11.84 TOTE £3.00: £1.60 £1.80 £5.90 (£7.30) Trio £199.80 OWNER Mr Hamdan Al Maktoum (NEWMARKET) BRED Shadwell Farm Inc

WEIGHT FOR AGE 3yo-14lb

1130 Mumaris (USA), who was suited by the step up in distance, in the end took an event run in near-darkness after the delay in ready fashion. (2/1)

1612 Awesome Wells (IRE), dropped back in distance, proved keen early on in a race that was run at a snail's pace in the dark. Sticking on strongly in the final furlong, a truly-run mile and a half should see him off the mark. (5/1)

1497 Kayfiyah (IRE) is improving with every outing and there should be better to come. (16/1)

1477 Machiavelli, suited by the extra distance, carried his head high under pressure. (11/4)

1405 Vrennan, who is not very big, showed a good action going down and, by no means knocked about, she needs one more outing to qualify for a handicap mark. (14/1)

1784 Alpina (USA), who was still carrying condition, raced with her head up in the air in the closing stages. (10/1: op 6/1)

Jazz Track (IRE), a backward-looking newcomer, showed ability after missing the break and taking a long time to get into full stride. (12/1: op 6/1)

Sefton Blake, a keen type, was dropped in at the start. Sticking on nicely in the final two furlongs, there should be better to come. (66/1)

T/Plpt: £10.70 (998.28 Tckts). T/Qdpt: £3.70 (170.81 Tckts) WG

1785-WOLVERHAMPTON (L-H) (Standard)

Wednesday June 18th

WEATHER: overcast WIND: almost nil

2047 E.B.F. ASTON MAIDEN STKS (2-Y.O) (Class D)

2-20 (2-22) **6f (Fibresand)** £3,773.00 (£1,127.00: £539.00: £245.00) Stalls: Low GOING: 0.07 sec per fur (STD)

				SP	RR	SF
	Calchas (IRE) (SirMarkPrescott) **2-9-0** GDuffield(3) (w'like: disp ld after 1f: led over 1f out: pushed clr)	—	**1**	7/2^{2}	88+	39
684^{4}	**Bernardo Bellotto (IRE)** (MBell) **2-9-0** MFenton(5) (led 1f: chsd ldrs: rdn & outpcd appr fnl f)	6	**2**	4/1^{3}	72	23
1797^{4}	**Super Rascal** (NPLittmoden) **2-9-0** TGMcLaughlin(9) (lw: a.p: rdn 2f out: kpt on)	1½	**3**	6/1	68	19
1616^{3}	**Just Another Time** (JBerry) **2-8-7**(7) CLowther(1) (disp ld after 1f tl rdn & wknd over 1f out)	½	**4**	9/1	67	18
1657^{6}	**Chasetown Cailin** (RHollinshead) **2-8-9** FLynch(4) (a mid div: rdn & no imp fnl 2f)	1¼	**5**	11/1	58	9
1791^{6}	**Ra Ra Rasputin** (BAMcMahon) **2-9-0** LNewton(6) (dwlt: sn pushed along: a bhd)	6	**6**	33/1	47	—
1396^{7}	**The Thruster** (MajorWRHern) **2-9-0** SWhitworth(8) (mid div: drvn along over 2f out: no imp)	d.h	**6**	15/8^{1}	47	—
1657^{4}	**Great Lyth Lass (IRE)** (PDEvans) **2-8-9** LCharnock(10) (in tch tl rdn & wknd over 2f out)	8	**8**	6/1	21	—
1267^{11}	**Summer River (IRE)** (CMurray) **2-9-0v^{1}** NicolaHowarth(7) (a bhd)	5	**9**	33/1	13	—
1267^{12}	**Ragford (IRE)** (JMPEustace) **2-9-0b^{1}** JTate(2) (mid div: rdn & btn over 2f out: eased)	9	**10**	33/1	—	—
				(SP 132.7%)	**10 Rn**	

1m 15.8 (4.60) CSF £18.79 TOTE £11.00: £2.10 £2.60 £1.10 (£13.00) Trio £42.60 OWNER Sheikh Ahmed bin Saeed Al Maktoum (NEWMARKET) BRED Sheikh Ahmed bin Saeed al Maktoum

Calchas (IRE), the stable pick of five five-day entries, won this with the minimum of fuss. He looks sure to improve for the run and can go on to better things. (7/2: 5/2-9/2)

684 Bernardo Bellotto (IRE) had all his other rivals well held, but was comprehensively put in his place by the newcomer. (4/1: op 2/1)

1797 Super Rascal found himself tapped for speed turning for home, but stuck gamely to his task. (6/1: 8/1-5/1)

1616 Just Another Time battled for the lead, but had come to the end of his tether below the distance. (9/1: op 6/1)

1657 Chasetown Cailin (11/1: 8/1-12/1)

1396 The Thruster was never able to reach a challenging position. With his dam winning between one mile and a mile-and-a-half, he may need further before opening his account. (15/8: 3/1-7/4)

1657 Great Lyth Lass (IRE) (6/1: op 7/2)

2048 COPPICE CLAIMING STKS (4-Y.O+) (Class F)

2-55 (2-56) **2m 46y (Fibresand)** £2,277.00 (£627.00: £297.00) Stalls: Low GOING: 0.07 sec per fur (STD)

				SP	RR	SF
1570^{6}	**Petoskin (72)** (JPearce) **5-8-13** MWigham(5) (lw: a.p: led over 4f out: hdd over 1f out: shkn up to ld cl home)	—	**1**	6/5^{1}	69	20

1122* **Castle Secret (48)** (DBurchell) **11-8-7** RPrice(3) (b.nr hind: lw: chsd ldrs: led after 2f: hdd over 4f out: sn rdn: led over 1f out: hdd last stride)	s.h	**2**	5/1	63	14
1940^{3} **Mister Aspecto (IRE) (69)** (MJohnston) **4-9-9b** JFanning(2) (lw: led 2f: styd cl up: rdn over 2f out: one pce fnl f)	5	**3**	5/2^{2}	74	25
1755^{3} **Cuban Nights (USA) (53)** (BJLlewellyn) **5-8-6**(5) JBramhill(1) (reard leaving stalls: rdn 7f out: lost tch over 5f out: t.o)	dist	**4**	4/1^{3}	—	—
139^{8} **Awestruck (32)** (BPreece) **7-8-7b** VSlattery(4) (chsd ldrs tl rdn & wknd ½-wy: t.o)	dist	**5**	50/1	—	—

(SP 112.7%) **5 Rn**

3m 44.4 (17.40) CSF £7.26 TOTE £2.20: £1.10 £2.70 (£3.60) OWNER Mrs Jean Routledge (NEWMARKET) BRED James Wigan

1570 Petoskin was confidently ridden to land his fourth course win. His jockey remained very cool when narrowly headed entering the final furlong, applying only minimum pressure to put his head in front in the final strides. (6/5)

1122* Castle Secret put up a gritty performance having regained the lead early in the straight. He fought tooth and nail to hang on to it, but he was denied right on the line. (5/1)

1940 Mister Aspecto (IRE), stepped-up in trip, seemed to cope well enough but was anchored by his weight in the closing stages. (5/2)

1755 Cuban Nights (USA), having put up a respectable performance in a similar race over course and distance two months ago, ran a shocker. This run is best forgotten. (4/1)

2049 WOODLAND H'CAP (0-70) (3-Y.O+ F & M) (Class E)

3-30 (3-30) **1m 4f (Fibresand)** £2,836.25 (£845.00: £402.50: £181.25) Stalls: Low GOING: 0.07 sec per fur (STD)

			SP	RR	SF
1387^{8} **Goodwood Lass (IRE) (65)** (JLDunlop) **3-8-13** GDuffield(4) (trckd ldr: led over 4f out: clr appr fnl f: styd on)	—	**1**	7/2^{2}	73	32
1796^{7} **Nicola's Princess (49)** (BAMcMahon) **4-8-11** LNewton(5) (lw: hdwy 5f out: rdn 3f out: kpt on fnl f)	8	**2**	5/1^{3}	46	19
1686^{3} **Needwood Nutkin (34)** (BCMorgan) **4-7-10** LCharnock(3) (lw: led over 7f: chsd wnr: outpcd wl over 1f out)	1	**3**	10/1	30	3
1414^{16} **Antiguan Jane (64)** (RWArmstrong) **4-9-12** RPrice(2) (chsd ldrs: rdn 5f out: sn btn)	11	**4**	16/1	45	18
1785^{7} **Woodland Nymph (50)** (DJGMurraySmith) **3-7-12** NAdams(1) (in tch: pushed along 1/2-wy: sn wknd)	6	**5**	5/1^{3}	23	—
1156^{9} **Willie Rushton (55)** (GLMoore) **4-9-3** SWhitworth(6) (b: b.hind: rdn & lost tch 5f out: t.o)	9	**6**	5/1^{3}	16	—
1981^{11} **Rasayel (USA) (55)** (PDEvans) **7-9-0**(3) DGriffiths(7) (hld up & bhd: rdn 5f out: no rspnse: t.o)	2½	**7**	3/1^{1}	13	—

(SP 112.2%) **7 Rn**

2m 43.4 (10.90) CSF £18.52 TOTE £3.60: £2.00 £2.80 (£10.00) OWNER Goodwood Racehorse Owners Group(Two) Ltd (ARUNDEL) BRED Floors Farming and Side Hill Stud

LONG HANDICAP Needwood Nutkin 7-8

WEIGHT FOR AGE 3yo-14lb

OFFICIAL EXPLANATION **Rasayel (USA): was never travelling and lost her action at the begining of the back straight on the final circuit.**

Goodwood Lass (IRE) moved well to post and found this company much more to her liking, forging clear in the home straight. (7/2)

1093 Nicola's Princess stuck on gamely to claim second near the finish, but the winner was home and hosed. (5/1: 3/1-11/2)

1686 Needwood Nutkin kept tabs on the winner until left standing early in the straight. (10/1)

Willie Rushton (5/1: 3/1-6/1)

1278 Rasayel (USA), never going at any stage, was last throughout. This was confirmed at the subsequent enquiry and the jockey added that the horse lost his action at the beginning of the back straight. (3/1: op 2/1)

2050 FOREST H'CAP (0-80) (3-Y.O+) (Class D)

4-05 (4-05) **5f (Fibresand)** £3,518.20 (£1,048.60: £499.80: £225.40) Stalls: Low GOING: 0.07 sec per fur (STD)

			SP	RR	SF
1743^{7} **Malibu Man (69)** (EAWheeler) **5-9-2**(5) ADaly(8) (mde all: clr over 2f out: unchal)	—	**1**	9/2	83	44
1627^{8} **Manolo (FR) (63)** (JBerry) **4-9-1b** GDuffield(6) (chsd wnr: rdn & no imp fnl 2f)	5	**2**	2/1^{1}	61	22
1942^{6} **Napier Star (70)** (MrsNMacauley) **4-9-8v** SWebster(1) (hmpd after 1f: bhd tl styd on wl fr 2f out: nvr nrr)	s.h	**3**	10/1	68	29
1759^{7} **Silk Cottage (55)** (RMWhitaker) **5-8-4**(3) RHavlin(5) (hdwy over 3f out: rdn & one pce appr fnl f)	2	**4**	12/1	46	7
1759^{2} **Shadow Jury (62)** (DWChapman) **7-9-0b** LCharnock(7) (chsd ldrs: rdn & one pce fr over 1f out)	nk	**5**	3/1^{2}	53	14
1957^{2} **Gi La High (67)** (MartynMeade) **4-9-5** FNorton(3) (a mid div)	5	**6**	4/1^{3}	42	3
1572^{7} **Captain Sinbad (44)** (KSBridgwater) **5-7-5v^{1}**(5) JBramhill(4) (prom over 3f)	2	**7**	20/1	12	—
1780^{8} **Petite Danseuse (79)** (CADwyer) **3-9-11** KRutter(2) (a bhd)	s.h	**8**	12/1	47	2
1814^{7} **Mijas (76)** (LMontagueHall) **4-10-0** FLynch(9) (bhd fr ½-wy)	1¾	**9**	12/1	38	—
1661^{8} **Weet Ees Girl (IRE) (63)** (PDEvans) **3-8-6**(3)ow3 DGriffiths(10) (outpcd)	9	**10**	14/1	—	—

(SP 140.1%) **10 Rn**

62.8 secs (3.90) CSF £15.55 CT £92.72 TOTE £6.90: £3.10 £1.90 £2.40 (£22.90) Trio £138.90; £70.46 to Ascot 19/6/97 OWNER Church Racing Partnership (PANGBOURNE) BRED Mrs M. Chubb

LONG HANDICAP Captain Sinbad 6-5

WEIGHT FOR AGE 3yo-6lb

1743 Malibu Man broke well and had the race won by halfway. He is useful in this class when he can dominate. (9/2)

1627 Manolo (FR), well supported to make a successful All-Weather debut, was left standing by the winner. (2/1: op 5/1)

1942 Napier Star had to be snatched up on the first bend and lost a fair bit of ground. She did very well to get so close under the circumstances. (10/1: op 6/1)

1289 Silk Cottage never had the pace to get anywhere near the winner. (12/1: op 7/1)

1759 Shadow Jury (3/1: 2/1-7/2)

1957 Gi La High (4/1: op 9/4)

1780 Petite Danseuse (12/1: op 8/1)

2051 SPINNEY (S) STKS (2-Y.O) (Class G)

4-40 (4-40) **5f (Fibresand)** £1,984.50 (£547.00: £259.50) Stalls: Low GOING: 0.07 sec per fur (STD)

			SP	RR	SF
1758^{9} **Risky Whisky** (JBerry) **2-8-9b**(7) CLowther(6) (lw: chsd ldr: rdn to chal appr fnl f: led cl home)	—	**1**	7/2^{2}	64	—
1789^{6} **Gifted Bairn (IRE)** (DNicholls) **2-8-6** AMcGlone(4) (led: rdn & jnd over 1f out: hdd & no ex nr fin)	hd	**2**	11/2	54	—
1600^{5} **I'm Not Sure** (JBerry) **2-8-6** NAdams(2) (lw: chsd ldrs: ev ch over 1f out: rdn & unable qckn)	2½	**3**	20/1	46	—
Glenstal Lad (RHollinshead) **2-8-8**(3) DGriffiths(5) (neat: s.i.s: kpt on fnl 2f: n.d)	¾	**4**	25/1	48	—
1941^{14} **Collacar** (DShaw) **2-8-8**(3) CTeague(1) (lw: in tch: rdn & one pce fr over 1f out)	1¾	**5**	33/1	43	—
1867^{4} **Silent Pride (IRE)** (MDIUsher) **2-8-6** JMarshall(7) (lw: prom to ½-wy)	1¼	**6**	8/1	34	—

				SP	RR	SF
1867^{2}	**Sun In The Morning** (BJMeehan) **2-8-11b^{1}** MTebbutt(3) (lw: hdwy over 3f out: rdn & wknd over 1f out)	2½	**7**	6/4^{1}	31	—
1797^{9}	**Eurofen** (PDEvans) **2-8-11** GDuffield(8) (sn drvn along: bhd fnl 3f)	6	**8**	4/1^{3}	12	—
				(SP 120.3%)		**8 Rn**

65.5 secs (6.60) CSF £21.55 TOTE £8.80: £2.50 £1.40 £6.70 (£12.10) OWNER Mr J. Berry (COCKERHAM) BRED Roldvale Ltd
No bid

1758 Risky Whisky, evidently more used to the blinkers this time, and suited by the return to the minimum trip, just got up in the last few strides. (7/2: op 2/1)

1286 Gifted Bairn (IRE) attempted to make all and it was only in the dying strides that she was thwarted. She can find a similar race over this trip. (11/2: op 3/1)

1600 I'm Not Sure put in her best run to date, although she seems pushed to get even the minimum trip at the moment. (20/1)

Glenstal Lad made a reasonable debut, staying on in the closing stages without ever threatening the principals. An extra furlong should not go amiss. (25/1)

1867 Silent Pride (IRE) (8/1: 5/1-9/1)

1867 Sun In The Morning, tried in blinkers for the first time, dropped away quite tamely early in the straight. (6/4: 4/5-7/4)

1498 Eurofen (4/1: op 6/1)

2052 COVERT H'CAP (0-70) (3-Y.O) (Class E)

5-15 (5-15) **1m 1f 79y (Fibresand)** £2,836.25 (£845.00: £402.50: £181.25) Stalls: Low GOING: 0.07 sec per fur (STD)

				SP	RR	SF
1929*	**Merciless Cop (68)** (BJMeehan) **3-9-5** 5x MTebbutt(7) (a.p: led 1f out: rdn out)	—	**1**	7/2^{3}	76	35
*1939**	**Canadian Fantasy (75)** (MJohnston) **3-9-12** 5x JFanning(4) (lw: led 1f: chsd ldr tl outpcd over 1f out: rdn & kpt on fnl f)	1½	**2**	5/2^{2}	80	39
1429^{3}	**Royal Roulette (57)** (SPCWoods) **3-8-8** FLynch(6) (bhd tl styd on fr 2f out: r.o)	hd	**3**	10/1	62	21
1787^{6}	**Krabloonik (FR) (56)** (SirMarkPrescott) **3-8-7** GDuffield(3) (lw: plld hrd: led after 1f tl rdn & hdd over 1f out: one pce)	1	**4**	2/1^{1}	60	19
1646^{6}	**Tellion (70)** (MajorWRHern) **3-9-7** SWhitworth(2) (chsd ldrs tl rdn & wknd 2f out)	6	**5**	7/1	63	22
1757^{4}	**Champagne On Ice (45)** (PDEvans) **3-7-10** NAdams(5) (b.hind: hdwy over 4f out: rdn 3f out: sn btn)	7	**6**	14/1	26	—
1513^{6}	**Weet And See (67)** (RHollinshead) **3-9-1**(3) DGriffiths(1) (bhd fnl 4f: t.o)	23	**7**	7/1	9	—
				(SP 124.9%)		**7 Rn**

2m 4.5 (8.50) CSF £13.00 TOTE £5.30: £10.10 £1.10 (£9.10) OWNER Mr Mario Lanfranchi (UPPER LAMBOURN) BRED G. S. Shropshire
LONG HANDICAP Champagne On Ice 7-9

1929* Merciless Cop showed no ill effects of his hard race less than a week ago, and responded well all the way to the line. (7/2)

1939* Canadian Fantasy put in a renewed effort in the final furlong after losing his pitch turning for home. He seems in fine fettle at the moment. (5/2: 2/1-3/1)

1429 Royal Roulette made up a lot of ground with a run up the inside in the final quarter-mile. She was visored when winning early in the year. (10/1)

1787 Krabloonik (FR) again made things hard for himself by refusing to settle, and had no more to give at the business end of the race. (2/1)

1646 Tellion, struggling from some way out, looks very one-paced. (7/1)

1757 Champagne On Ice raced with his tongue tied down and was beaten before the home turn. This completed a miserable day for his yard's five runners. (14/1: 8/1-16/1)

1513 Weet And See (7/1: 3/1-8/1)

T/Plpt: £388.50 (15.46 Tckts). T/Qdpt: £100.60 (3.69 Tckts) J

2023-ROYAL ASCOT (R-H) (Good)

Thursday June 19th

Race 6: poor visibility
WEATHER: Continuous rain WIND: moderate across

2053 RIBBLESDALE STKS (Gp 2) (3-Y.O F) (Class A)

2-30 (2-33) **1m 4f** £69,568.00 (£26,174.40: £12,687.20: £5,650.40) Stalls: Low GOING minus 0.08 sec per fur (G)

				SP	RR	SF
1738^{4}	**Yashmak (USA) (114)** (HRACecil) **3-8-8** KFallon(2) (sn chsng ldrs: led over 3f out: sn drvn clr: v.impressive)	—	**1**	7/2^{2}	114+	65
	Akdariya (IRE) (JOxx,Ireland) **3-8-8** JPMurtagh(6) (angular: hld up & bhd: hdwy over 3f out: chsd wnr wl over 1f out: no imp)	9	**2**	9/1	102	53
1738^{3}	**Crown of Light (98)** (MRStoute) **3-8-8** LDettori(9) (sn led & hung lft: hdd over 8f out: rdn over 2f out: one pce)	3½	**3**	100/30^{1}	97	48
1646^{4}	**Alcalali (USA) (80)** (PAKelleway) **3-8-8** JReid(3) (hld up: snatched up 5f out: effrt over 3f out: no hdwy fnl 2f)	nk	**4**	66/1	97	48
1540a^{2}	**Sublime Beauty (USA)** (JSBolger,Ireland) **3-8-8b** MJKinane(5) (neat: chsd ldrs: rdn over 2f out: one pce)	1¾	**5**	25/1	95	46
1209^{2}	**Tempting Prospect (100)** (LordHuntingdon) **3-8-8** DHarrison(1) (lw: bmpd after 2f: chsd ldrs tl outpcd over 2f out)	½	**6**	7/1	94	45
1738^{11}	**Siyadah (USA) (102)** (SbinSuroor) **3-8-8** OPeslier(7) (lw: sn pushed along: a in rr)	4	**7**	14/1	89	40
1318*	**Maid of Camelot (95)** (RCharlton) **3-8-8** PatEddery(4) (n.m.r & lost pl after 2f: hdwy 5f out: hrd drvn over 3f out: hung rt: sn btn)	4	**8**	6/1^{3}	83	34
960^{9}	**Sarayir (USA) (104)** (MajorWRHern) **3-8-8** RHills(8) (led over 8f out tl over 3f out: sn rdn & wknd)	7	**9**	8/1	74	25
				(SP 105.2%)		**9 Rn**

2m 33.21 (3.21) CSF £26.52 TOTE £3.70: £1.40 £2.80 £1.40 (£20.40) Trio £11.90 OWNER Mr K. Abdulla (NEWMARKET) BRED Juddmonte Farms

1738 Yashmak (USA) upheld the Oaks form on this rain-sodden ground with a very impressive runaway victory, and she is obviously more at home on such galloping tracks as this. (7/2: 5/2-4/1)

Akdariya (IRE) kept up her trainer's record of having trained the runner-up in this race for the third time in four years, but she came here with only a maiden success to her name so connections have every right to be delighted at her progress. (9/1: op 6/1)

1738 Crown of Light had a half length in hand of the winner on her Oaks running but, with more use made of her, she could do little more than gallop on the spot for the final quarter-mile. (100/30: 9/4-7/2)

1646 Alcalali (USA) did not enjoy the best of luck in running on this step up to twelve furlongs, but she showed plenty of promise and that initial success is surely within her grasp. (66/1)

1540a Sublime Beauty (USA), a challenger from Ireland who has been running consistently well without a win to her name this term, was feeling the strain turning in and, once the winner kicked clear, she must have wondered what had hit her. (25/1)
1209 Tempting Prospect had a rear view of the winner over a slightly shorter trip last month and, from the entrance to the straight, she was always finding the increasing tempo too much for her. (7/1)

2054 NORFOLK STKS (Gp 3) (2-Y.O) (Class A)

3-05 (3-05) **5f** £25,240.00 (£9,552.00: £4,676.00: £2,132.00) Stalls: High GOING minus 0.08 sec per fur (G)

				SP	RR	SF
1675*	**Tippitt Boy** (KMcAuliffe) **2-8-12** JReid(2) (hld up: hdwy wl over 1f out: led ins fnl f: all out)	—	**1**	33/1	100	50
1531a[2]	**Hopping Higgins (IRE)** (APO'Brien,Ireland) **2-8-7** MJKinane(3) (scope: lw: led tl ins fnl f: rallied u.p cl home)	s.h	**2**	4/1 [2]	95	45
1842*	**Arawak Cay (IRE)** (DRLoder) **2-8-12** OPeslier(6) (a chsng ldrs: rdn over 1f out: r.o)	1¼	**3**	6/1 [3]	96	46
1161*	**Bodyguard** (PFICole) **2-8-12** TQuinn(1) (plld hrd: hld up: effrt on ins 2f out: bdly hmpd appr fnl f: nt rcvr)	1	**4**	5/2 [1]	93+	43
1475*	**Pool Music** (RHannon) **2-8-12** RHughes(4) (lw: chsd ldrs: rdn whn bdly hmpd appr fnl f: nt rcvr)	1¼	**5**	5/2 [1]	89+	39
1774*	**Rejected** (RHannon) **2-8-12** DaneO'Neill(5) (w ldr 3f: wkng whn rdn & edgd lft appr fnl f: sn wknd)	6	**6**	8/1	69	19
				(SP 105.5%)	**6 Rn**	

62.57 secs (2.37) CSF £126.39 TOTE £14.10: £3.80 £1.90 (£43.60) OWNER Highgrove Developments Ltd (LAMBOURN) BRED Cheveley Park Stud Ltd

1675* Tippitt Boy caused a major success as the rank outsider in the field but he showed the right battling qualities in the sprint to the line and he is obviously better than his previous form suggests. (33/1)
1531a Hopping Higgins (IRE) has plenty of speed and she fought back gamely after being headed, but the winner had come fresh on the scene and was able to find just enough to repel her bid. (4/1)
1842* Arawak Cay (IRE) could have found this race coming plenty soon enough after winning on his debut nine days ago, but he coped adequately with this step down to the minimum trip and there are many prizes to be won with him. (6/1)
1161* Bodyguard, restrained under a fearsome hold, elected to make his move on the inside rail and he was still looking for an opening when he was almost put over the rails approaching the final furlong and was lucky to remain on his feet. He would have taken all the beating. (5/2)
1475* Pool Music, content to wait on the leaders, became the meat in the sandwich approaching the final furlong and what chance he had soon disappeared. (5/2)
1774* Rejected had the lead for three furlongs, but he was struggling to hold his pitch when he hung badly left under pressure approaching the final furlong and faded quickly. (8/1)

2055 GOLD CUP STKS (Gp 1) (4-Y.O+) (Class A)

3-45 (3-47) **2m 4f** £113,556.00 (£42,789.80: £20,794.90: £9,319.30) Stalls: Low GOING: 0.03 sec per fur (G)

				SP	RR	SF
1454[2]	**Celeric (117)** (DMorley) **5-9-2** PatEddery(2) (hld up in rr: hdwy 3f out: shkn up to ld wl ins fnl f)	—	**1**	11/2 [2]	127	79
1172[9]	**Classic Cliche (IRE)** (SbinSuroor) **5-9-2** LDettori(10) (lw: hld up: hdwy 5f out: led 2f out tl wl ins fnl f)	¾	**2**	6/1 [3]	126	78
1033[6]	**Election Day (IRE) (110)** (MRStoute) **5-9-2v** MJKinane(13) (lw: trckd ldrs: rdn 2f out: styd on wl ins fnl f)	1	**3**	25/1	126	78
1454[5]	**Heron Island (IRE) (111)** (PWChapple-Hyam) **4-9-0** JReid(11) (hld up in rr: hdwy over 2f out: sn rdn: styd on)	5	**4**	33/1	122	72
1172[4]	**Samraan (USA) (114)** (JLDunlop) **4-9-0** TQuinn(1) (hld up: hdwy 4f out: rdn & btn appr fnl f)	9	**5**	10/1	114	64
	Double Eclipse (IRE) (113) (MJohnston) **5-9-2** MRoberts(4) (trckd ldrs: led over 4f out to 2f out: sn rdn & wknd)	hd	**6**	14/1	114	66
1319*	**Jiyush (106)** (EALDunlop) **4-9-0** RHills(12) (hld up: hdwy on ins 4f out: rdn whn hmpd over 2f out: nt rcvr)	3½	**7**	20/1	112	62
891[8]	**Double Trigger (IRE) (121)** (MJohnston) **6-9-2b[1]** JWeaver(7) (led 4f: hrd rdn & wknd over 1f out)	4	**8**	9/1	108	60
1033[3]	**Moonax (IRE) (114)** (BWHills) **6-9-2** MHills(6) (sn pushed along: a in rr)	7	**9**	16/1	103	55
1548a*	**Camp David (GER)** (AWohler,Germany) **7-9-2** ABoschert(5) (lw: hld up in rr: btn whn bdly hmpd 3f out: t.o)	10	**10**	25/1	95	47
1365a[6]	**Nononito (FR)** (JLesbordes,France) **6-9-2** GMosse(8) (chsd ldrs: hrd drvn & wknd 4f out: t.o)	5	**11**	15/2	91	43
1454*	**Persian Punch (IRE) (110)** (DRCElsworth) **4-9-0** RCochrane(3) (hld up: hdwy 8f out: rdn whn nt clr run over 2f out: t.o)	½	**12**	9/2 [1]	90	40
1365a[2]	**Grey Shot (110)** (IABalding) **5-9-2** OPeslier(9) (lw: led after 4f tl over 4f out: wknd over 2f out: t.o)	1	**13**	12/1	90	42
				(SP 114.3%)	**13 Rn**	

4m 26.19 (6.19) CSF £31.56 TOTE £5.30: £2.00 £1.90 £5.00 (£9.70) Trio £125.30 OWNER Mr Christopher Spence (NEWMARKET) BRED Chieveley Manor Enterprises
WEIGHT FOR AGE 4yo-2lb

1454 Celeric, in conditions more suitable to Cheltenham in March, warmed the cockles of the heart with this scintillating performance at his first attempt at such an extended trip under a ride that must class with some of the finest ever seen. (11/2)
1172 Classic Cliche (IRE) adopted the tactics that were successful in this race last year and his supporters must have been on good terms with themselves when he struck the front two furlongs out but, hard as he tried, the winner proved too good for him in the run to the line. This performance at least shows that his lacklustre effort at York last month was too bad to be true. (6/1: op 4/1)
1033 Election Day (IRE) ran a fine race on his first attempt at the trip and he was still battling hard at the finish. It could be wise to keep him for stamina-sapping tests for stamina seems to be his strong suit. (25/1)
1454 Heron Island (IRE), patiently ridden at this first try over such an extended trip, responded when set alight into the straight, but his run had come to an end below the distance and he was unable to give the principals much cause for concern. (33/1)
1172 Samraan (USA) has always lost out in his confrontations with the winner and, in this instance, it would seem lack of stamina was the problem. (10/1: 7/1-11/1)
Double Eclipse (IRE) performs well when fresh but he had a thirteen month absence from the racecourse to overcome this time and the fact that he only called enough passing the quarter mile marker, is a sure sign that he has lost none of his ability. (14/1)
1454* Persian Punch (IRE), 5lb worse off with the winner than when finishing three quarters of a length to the good on their most recent clash, was hard at work and going nowhere when short of room entering the straight. (9/2)

2056 CORK AND ORRERY STKS (Gp 3) (3-Y.O+) (Class A)

4-20 (4-25) **6f** £34,850.00 (£13,205.00: £6,477.50: £2,967.50) Stalls: High GOING: 0.03 sec per fur (G)

				SP	RR	SF
1171*	**Royal Applause (117)** (BWHills) **4-9-3** MHills(16) (lw: mde all far side: clr whn hung lft wl ins fnl f)	—	**1**	11/2 [1]	121	86
1609*	**Blue Goblin (USA) (108)** (LMCumani) **3-8-6** GaryStevens(4) (hld up stands' side: hdwy to ld 1f out: hrd rdn: r.o)	1½	**2**	13/2 [2]	113	71
1881a*	**Catch The Blues (IRE)** (APO'Brien,Ireland) **5-9-0v** CRoche(21) (hdwy far side over 2f out: rdn over 1f out: r.o)	s.h	**3**	12/1	114	79
1720a*	**Monaassib (111)** (EALDunlop) **6-9-3** DO'Donohoe(7) (w ldrs stands' side: rdn over 1f out: one pce)	1½	**4**	11/1	113	78

	Indian Rocket (JLDunlop) **3-9-0** RHills(19) (b: swtg: chsd ldrs: rdn wl over 1f out: kpt on wl fnl f)	nk	**5**	33/1	116	74
1455^{4}	**Royale Figurine (IRE) (107)** (MJFetherston-Godley) **6-8-10** DHolland(5) (hld up & bhd: gd hdwy appr fnl f: nrst fin)	hd	**6**	14/1	105	70
1171^{3}	**Blue Duster (USA) (116)** (SbinSuroor) **4-8-10** LDettori(14) (chsd ldrs: rdn over 1f out: one pce)	nk	**7**	$13/2^{2}$	104	69
1767^{5}	**Almushtarak (IRE) (106)** (KMahdi) **4-8-13** RPrice(11) (lw: chsd ldrs stands' side: rdn over 2f out: wknd fnl f)	nk	**8**	50/1	106	71
$1720a^{3}$	**Easy Dollar (106)** (BGubby) **5-8-13b** AClark(1) (prom stands' side tl rdn & outpcd appr fnl f)	¾	**9**	25/1	104	69
1948*	**Tedburrow (95)** (EJAlston) **5-8-13** ACulhane(15) (hld up in rr: hdwy wl over 1f out: nvr nrr)	nk	**10**	25/1	103	68
1776^{2}	**Lucayan Prince (USA) (119)** (DRLoder) **4-9-3b** OPeslier(17) (dwlt: effrt over 2f out: sn rdn: nt pce to chal)	¾	**11**	$9/1^{3}$	105	70
1609^{2}	**Connemara (IRE) (103)** (CADwyer) **3-8-3** DHarrison(2) (swtg: chsd ldrs stands' side over 4f)	2	**12**	25/1	93	51
745*	**Soviet State (USA) (108)** (PWChapple-Hyam) **3-8-6** JReid(13) (lw: nvr plcd to chal)	1	**13**	33/1	93	51
1455^{7}	**Farhana (110)** (WJarvis) **4-8-10** PatEddery(25) (lw: hdwy ½-wy far side: effrt 2f out: rdn & wknd appr fnl f)	½	**14**	14/1	89	54
1596^{4}	**Jayannpee (107)** (IABalding) **6-8-13** MartinDwyer(23) (chsd ldrs far side 4f)	1¼	**15**	33/1	89	54
1210^{10}	**Cayman Kai (IRE) (110)** (RHannon) **4-8-13** RHughes(18) (lw: a mid div)	nk	**16**	33/1	88	53
1532a*	**Burden Of Proof (IRE)** (CO'Brien,Ireland) **5-9-3** JPMurtagh(20) (lw: a bhd & outpcd)	s.h	**17**	16/1	92	57
1596*	**Cyrano's Lad (IRE) (103)** (CADwyer) **8-8-13** KFallon(22) (chsd wnr: hrd drvn 2f out: wknd qckly appr fnl f)	2	**18**	33/1	83	48
	China Girl (IRE) (92) (PWChapple-Hyam) **3-8-3** DJWhyte(24) (lw: a bhd far side)	3½	**19**	50/1	70	28
$1198a^{3}$	**Theano (IRE)** (APO'Brien,Ireland) **4-8-10** TQuinn(9) (chsd ldrs stands' side 4f)	½	**20**	33/1	69	34
1770^{3}	**Moonshine Girl (USA) (102)** (MRStoute) **3-8-3** WRyan(10) (outpcd)	1¼	**21**	33/1	66	24
1598^{3}	**Russian Music (103)** (MissGayKelleway) **4-8-13** JWeaver(12) (lw: led stands' side over 3f: sn wknd)	½	**22**	40/1	67	32
$1881a^{2}$	**Ailleacht (USA)** (JSBolger,Ireland) **5-8-10** MJKinane(8) (lw: sn lost pl & bhd)	2	**23**	25/1	59	24
				(SP 129.6%)		**23 Rn**

1m 15.33 (1.33) CSF £30.25 TOTE £4.70: £2.00 £2.60 £5.20 (£13.00) Trio £112.00 OWNER Maktoum Al Maktoum (LAMBOURN) BRED Gainsborough Stud Management Ltd

WEIGHT FOR AGE 3yo-7lb

1171* Royal Applause is certainly at the top of his form this year and, with the speed to burn off several useful rivals, his forceful tactics are really paying off. The July Cup at Newmarket and the Breeders' Cup Sprint in the autumn have been pencilled in as possible objectives. (11/2)

1609* Blue Goblin (USA), covered up on the stands side, quickened up to take command on that side entering the final furlong and he did look set to score but the winner, racing wide of him, had stolen too much of a lead. (13/2)

1881a* Catch The Blues (IRE) finished strongly on the far side of the track but she had mistimed her run and had allowed the winner to get away. This was a very decent performance and she still retains her zest for the game. (12/1)

1720a* Monaassib lost his unbeaten record for this season but he went down fighting and, as he is at his best in the early part of the year, maybe this is a sign that he is just going off the boil. (11/1: 8/1-12/1)

Indian Rocket enjoyed a very rewarding first season and this extremely promising return to action would suggest that he is still as good as ever. (33/1)

1455 Royale Figurine (IRE), doing all her best work in the closing stages, failed to go out on a winning note here but all is not lost yet as she tries again tomorrow over the minimum trip in the King's Stand Stakes. (14/1)

1171 Blue Duster (USA), very free to post, did her best to make her presence felt but she was off the bridle approaching the final furlong, and lacked the pace to deliver a challenge. (13/2)

1767 Almushtarak (IRE), narrowly beaten in the Jersey Stakes at this meeting last year, has since changed stables and was returning to sprinting. Tracking the leaders on the stands side, he only got shaken off inside the distance and is worth keeping in mind. (50/1)

2057 CHESHAM STKS (Listed) (2-Y.O) (Class A)

4-55 (4-56) 7f £24,053.75 (£7,280.00: £3,552.50: £1,688.75) Stalls: High GOING: 0.03 sec per fur (G)

				SP	RR	SF
1749*	**Central Park (IRE)** (PFICole) **2-9-0** LDettori(6) (a.p: led over 2f out: hrd rdn: r.o strly fnl f)	—	**1**	$7/1^{3}$	97	70
1607*	**Cape Verdi (IRE)** (PWChapple-Hyam) **2-8-9** JReid(11) (hld up: hdwy on bit over 2f out: jnd wnr appr fnl f: sn rdn: unable qckn)	1½	**2**	$2/1^{1}$	89	62
1174^{3}	**Wales** (PFICole) **2-8-12** TQuinn(2) (hld up: stdy hdwy ½-wy: rdn 2f out: nt pce of ldrs)	4	**3**	12/1	82	55
1872^{4}	**Classic Manoeuvre (USA)** (RHannon) **2-8-12** DaneO'Neill(4) (lw: hld up: hdwy u.p 2f out: styd on wl ins fnl f)	½	**4**	25/1	81	54
	Saints Be Praised (USA) (DRLoder) **2-8-12** OPeslier(12) (str: scope: lw: hld up: hdwy over 2f out: one pce fnl f)	1¼	**5**	20/1	78	51
1263^{2}	**Anvil (USA)** (GLewis) **2-8-12** GaryStevens(8) (lw: prom tl wknd over 1f out)	3½	**6**	25/1	70	43
1240^{2}	**Ajig Dancer** (MRChannon) **2-8-7** RPerham(7) (plld hrd: chsd ldrs tl wknd wl over 1f out)	8	**7**	10/1	47	20
1192a*	**Sideman (IRE)** (APO'Brien,Ireland) **2-9-0** CRoche(1) (scope: prom over 5f: sn rdn & wknd)	¾	**8**	$7/2^{2}$	52	25
1692^{4}	**Rebalza (IRE)** (JMPEustace) **2-8-12** RCochrane(10) (a bhd)	2½	**9**	50/1	45	18
1263^{4}	**Exbourne's Wish (USA)** (BWHills) **2-8-12** MHills(5) (led tl over 2f out: sn wknd)	nk	**10**	14/1	44	17
1149*	**Balance The Books** (RHannon) **2-8-9** PatEddery(9) (chsd ldrs over 4f: sn wknd: t.o)	6	**11**	10/1	27	—
	Alazan (DMHyde) **2-8-12** MJKinane(3) (w'like: scope: lw: s.v.s: a t.o)	14	**12**	50/1	—	—
				(SP 117.0%)		**12 Rn**

1m 29.84 (2.64) CSF £18.04 TOTE £4.70: £1.40 £1.30 £3.30 (£5.10) Trio £24.40 OWNER H R H Prince Fahd Salman (WHATCOMBE) BRED Lodge Park Stud

OFFICIAL EXPLANATION **Sideman (IRE): no explanation offered.**

1749* Central Park (IRE), a very progressive colt, proved much too strong for his rivals over this longer trip and he does look a star in the making. (7/1: 10/1-5/1)

1607* Cape Verdi (IRE) cruised through to join the winner below the distance and briefly looked to be well in control, but she found the colt in no mood to give best and it was she who cracked once shown the persuader. (2/1: 8/11-9/4)

1174 Wales has still not come to himself and, though he did stay on under pressure, could not muster the speed to reach the leading pair. He has time on his side. (12/1)

1872 Classic Manoeuvre (USA), making a quick reappearance, responded to firm driving in the latter stages and he should not remain a maiden for long. (25/1)

Saints Be Praised (USA), a strongly-made colt who will be all the better for the race, showed plenty of promise and will soon improve on this. (20/1)

1263 Anvil (USA) ran a bit too free, pushing the pace, and he was at the end of his tether before reaching the final furlong. (25/1)

1192a* Sideman (IRE) would have hit the bookmakers hard if he had succeeded, for he was backed to take a fortune out of the ring but could not fulfil the promise he has shown back home in Ireland, and was throwing out distress signals on the approach to the final furlong. (7/2)

2058 KING GEORGE V H'CAP (0-105) (3-Y.O) (Class B)

5-30 (5-32) **1m 4f** £29,180.00 (£8,840.00: £4,320.00: £2,060.00) Stalls: Low GOING: 0.03 sec per fur (G)

				SP	RR	SF
1405*	**Heritage (82)** (JHMGosden) **3-8-6** LDettori(14) (lw: hld up & bhd: hdwy on ins & nt clr run over 2f out: swtchd lft: str run to ld ins fnl f)	—	**1**	15/2[2]	96	64
1497[2]	**Taunt (85)** (DMorley) **3-8-9** GCarter(10) (hld up: hdwy over 3f out: led over 1f out tl hdd & no ex ins fnl f)	1	**2**	16/1	98	66
1868*	**Ciro's Pearl (IRE) (81)** (MHTompkins) **3-8-2**(3) 4x MHenry(6) (a.p: hrd drvn 2f out: styd on one pce fnl f)	3½	**3**	14/1	89	57
1331*	**Memorise (USA) (85)** (HRACecil) **3-8-9** KFallon(1) (hld up: hdwy 2f out: hrd rdn & r.o wl fnl f)	hd	**4**	10/1	93	61
1434*	**Prairie Falcon (IRE) (89)** (BWHills) **3-8-13** GaryStevens(7) (a.p: ev ch 2f out: rdn & wknd fnl f)	3½	**5**	16/1	92	60
1435*	**Star Precision (92)** (GBBalding) **3-9-2** SDrowne(20) (lw: hld up in tch: effrt over 2f out: sn rdn: wknd appr fnl f)	1¼	**6**	7/1[1]	94	62
1747[2]	**Party Romance (USA) (86)** (BHanbury) **3-8-10** WRyan(13) (lw: chsd ldr: led 3f out tl over 1f out: wknd fnl f)	2½	**7**	16/1	84	52
1741[2]	**Supply And Demand (97)** (GLMoore) **3-9-7** TQuinn(15) (hld up & bhd: hdwy u.p 2f out: nvr nrr)	1½	**8**	16/1	93	61
1647[2]	**Southerly Wind (87)** (MrsJRRamsden) **3-8-11** JFortune(17) (lw: hld up: rdn & hdwy over 2f out: nt rch ldrs)	¾	**9**	9/1[3]	82	50
1742*	**Generous Gift (97)** (EALDunlop) **3-9-4**(3) DO'Donohoe(16) (lw: chsd ldrs tl wknd over 1f out)	¾	**10**	16/1	91	59
966[2]	**Ginzbourg (87)** (JLDunlop) **3-8-11** TSprake(12) (lw: hld up: hdwy over 5f out: rdn ent st: sn wknd)	3	**11**	20/1	77	45
1595*	**Henley (USA) (87)** (DRLoder) **3-8-11** DRMcCabe(19) (lw: led to 3f out: hrd rdn & wknd appr fnl f)	5	**12**	12/1	71	39
1595[3]	**Maradi (IRE) (77)** (MBell) **3-7-10**(5) RMullen(2) (lw: racd wd: sme hdwy whn hmpd wl over 1f out)	2	**13**	33/1	58	26
1647[5]	**Zinzari (FR) (85)** (DRLoder) **3-8-9** KDarley(8) (lw: mid div whn hmpd 2f out)	2½	**14**	12/1	63	31
1399[7]	**Salamah (87)** (RCharlton) **3-8-11** OPeslier(4) (lw: s.s: sn rdn: hdwy 5f out: wkng whn hmpd 2f out)	hd	**15**	10/1	64	32
1025[5]	**Mister Pink (90)** (RFJohnsonHoughton) **3-9-0** JReid(18) (a bhd)	5	**16**	33/1	61	29
1025[6]	**Burundi (IRE) (75)** (PWChapple-Hyam) **3-7-13** NAdams(5) (a in rr)	2	**17**	25/1	43	11
1130*	**Banbury (USA) (95)** (JWWatts) **3-9-5** PatEddery(3) (lw: chsd ldrs: rdn over 3f out: sn wknd)	1½	**18**	15/2[2]	61	29
1747[8]	**Behind The Scenes (75)** (CACyzer) **3-7-13** JLowe(9) (lw: a bhd)	1½	**19**	40/1	39	7
1474[2]	**Madame Chinnery (80)** (JMPEustace) **3-8-4** JTate(11) (bhd whn nt clr run 3f out: t.o)	29	**20**	20/1	5	—

(SP 137.4%) **20 Rn**

2m 34.33 (4.33) CSF £112.86 CT £1,556.61 TOTE £6.10: £1.50 £6.40 £3.80 £2.40 (£111.00) Trio £854.00 OWNER Highclere Thoroughbred Racing Ltd (NEWMARKET) BRED Mrs C. R. Philipson

1405* Heritage, with more patient tactics employed, landed the gamble readily and, as he is a son of prolific race-mare Misty Halo, this could be the start of something good. (15/2)

1497 Taunt made up a deal of ground inside the last half-mile and looked the likely winner when forging ahead at the distance but the winner saw the trip out better and he had to admit he had met one too good. His turn is just round the corner. (16/1)

1868* Ciro's Pearl (IRE) performed with credit on this step up in class and, though outpaced inside the final furlong, she certainly gave it her best shot. (14/1)

1331* Memorise (USA) did not begin to make progress until straightened up for home and, though he did stay on, could not quite reach the leaders. (10/1)

1434* Prairie Falcon (IRE), a winner at this trip taking on handicappers for the first time, was in with every chance until fading out in the latter stages. He will certainly win more races. (16/1)

1435* Star Precision was unable to maintain her winning sequence but she has climbed up the handicap now, and was never able to land a serious blow. (7/1)

1647 Southerly Wind should have been in his element over this trip, but he did not find his stride until far too late and the ever-softening ground may have had something to do with it. (9/1)

1399 Salamah (10/1: 8/1-12/1)

T/Jkpt: £113,036.90 (0.09 Tckts); £144,878.32 to Ascot 20/6/97. T/Plpt: £222.20 (658.79 Tckts). T/Qdpt: £19.50 (423.8 Tckts) IM

2041-RIPON (R-H) (Good)
Thursday June 19th

WEATHER: overcast with some rain WIND: fresh behind

2059 MASHAM MEDIAN AUCTION MAIDEN STKS (3-Y.O) (Class E)

2-10 (2-15) **1m 2f** £2,843.25 (£861.00: £420.50: £200.25) Stalls: High GOING minus 0.38 sec per fur (F)

				SP	RR	SF
1512[2]	**Raivue** (EWeymes) **3-9-0** GHind(4) (lw: trckd ldrs: led over 2f out: styd on)	—	**1**	6/1[3]	77	37
1630[3]	**Billy Nomaite** (MrsSJSmith) **3-8-11**(3) OPears(12) (led tl hdd over 2f out: kpt on same pce)	2½	**2**	12/1	73	33
1497[6]	**Northern Flash** (FMurphy) **3-9-0** DeanMcKeown(7) (a in tch: hdwy & ev ch over 1f out: rdn & one pce)	½	**3**	8/1	72	32
1870[4]	**Monaco (IRE)** (LMCumani) **3-9-0** BDoyle(6) (lw: trckd ldrs: effrt 3f out: one pce)	1¼	**4**	2/1[1]	70	30
1563[2]	**Miss Riviera Rose (72)** (GWragg) **3-8-4**(5) GMilligan(11) (chsd ldrs: effrt 3f out: hung lft & one pce)	1¼	**5**	9/4[2]	63	23
	Pemberley (IRE) (WJHaggas) **3-9-0** SSanders(9) (w'like: dwlt: plld hrd & hdwy after 2f: effrt & hung rt 3f out: sn btn)	13	**6**	11/1	47	7
1646[10]	**Classical Dance (IRE)** (MrsMReveley) **3-9-0** DaleGibson(8) (a bhd)	8	**7**	100/1	35	—
124[12]	**Eternal Host (IRE) (40)** (RHollinshead) **3-8-11**(3) DGriffiths(2) (a bhd)	nk	**8**	66/1	34	—
	Russian Aspect (MWEasterby) **3-8-9**(5) GParkin(5) (bkwd: a bhd)	1¾	**9**	33/1	31	—
1939[10]	**Certainty** (JRFanshawe) **3-8-9** NVarley(10) (cl up tl rdn & wknd qckly 3f out)	6	**10**	25/1	17	—
	Kosevo (IRE) (MGMeagher) **3-9-0** JCarroll(1) (cl up tl wknd over 3f out)	5	**11**	66/1	14	—
1798[10]	**Showstopper** (TJEtherington) **3-9-0** JStack(3) (s.i.s: a wl bhd)	14	**12**	100/1	—	—

(SP 117.3%) **12 Rn**

2m 7.3 (3.80) CSF £64.42 TOTE £6.80: £1.80 £2.10 £1.60 (£20.50) Trio £70.80 OWNER Mrs A. Birkett (MIDDLEHAM) BRED Lady Sutton

1512 Raivue, a big, strong sort, travelled on the bridle and then stayed on well when asked the question, suggesting that he should get further. (6/1)

1630 Billy Nomaite put up a decent show here and should pick up a race in due course, and he looks the type to do well at the National Hunt game. (12/1)

1497 Northern Flash, a plain-looking individual, ran much better this time but he does seem short of a turn of foot. (8/1: op 33/1)

1870 Monaco (IRE), steeping up three furlongs in trip, had his chances but looked very one-paced. (2/1: op 11/10)

1563 Miss Riviera Rose would certainly find no supporters on looks as she is small and light-framed but she has ability, and seemed to get unbalanced on this occasion. (9/4)

Pemberley (IRE) has plenty to learn and, once he settles, there should be some improvement. (11/1: op 7/1)

2060 RICHMOND CONDITIONS STKS (2-Y.O) (Class C)

2-45 (2-46) **6f** £4,204.64 (£1,573.76: £769.88: £331.40: £148.70: £75.62) Stalls: Low GOING minus 0.38 sec per fur (F)

				SP	RR	SF
1298*	**Royal Dream** (JBerry) **2-8-3**(3) PFessey(6) (mde all: hung rt fr ½-wy: kpt on wl)	—	**1**	4/1[3]	73	31
1819*	**Cumbrian Caruso** (TDEasterby) **2-9-1** JCarroll(3) (lw: a chsng ldrs: effrt over 2f out: styd on: nt pce of wnr)	2½	**2**	2/1[2]	75	33
1418*	**Deki (USA)** (DMorley) **2-9-1** JStack(2) (cl up: rdn 2f out: r.o one pce)	½	**3**	11/8[1]	74	32
1267[10]	**Grand Estate** (TDEasterby) **2-8-11** DeanMcKeown(4) (hung rt most of wy: in tch tl outpcd fnl 2f)	6	**4**	9/1	54	12
1801*	**Aberkeen** (MDods) **2-9-1** DaleGibson(5) (chsd ldrs tl rdn & btn 2f out)	½	**5**	10/1	57	15
1819[8]	**Sealed By Fate (IRE)** (JSWainwright) **2-8-11** SSanders(1) (lw: in tch tl outpcd fr ½-wy)	½	**6**	25/1	51	9
				(SP 118.4%)	**6 Rn**	

1m 12.4 (1.90) CSF £12.13 TOTE £3.80: £1.90 £1.80 (£5.20) OWNER Mrs B. A. Matthews (COCKERHAM) BRED P. J. and Mrs Sands

1298* Royal Dream, taking quite a step up in class, showed she is on the upgrade and, if she can be cured of hanging, there is obviously more to come. (4/1)

1819* Cumbrian Caruso put up a decent effort and kept struggling on but always found the winner too quick. (2/1)

1418* Deki (USA) went particularly well in the first half of the race but then failed to pick up when ridden, and this would seem to be as good as he is. (11/8)

1267 Grand Estate has more ability but was giving his rider problems throughout by hanging. (9/1: 6/1-10/1)

1801* Aberkeen won a messy race last time and had his limitations exposed here. (10/1: 7/1-14/1)

1684 Sealed By Fate (IRE) was never quick enough to make an impression here, but did not run too badly. (25/1)

2061 RACING CHANNEL H'CAP (0-80) (3-Y.O+) (Class D)

3-20 (3-21) **5f** £3,501.25 (£1,060.00: £517.50: £246.25) Stalls: Low GOING minus 0.38 sec per fur (F)

				SP	RR	SF
1977[12]	**Blessingindisguise (64)** (MWEasterby) **4-9-0b**(5) GParkin(14) (mde all: kpt on fnl f)	—	**1**	9/1	73	56
1666[4]	**Mousehole (69)** (RGuest) **5-9-10** PBloomfield(9) (drvn along thrght: in tch: kpt on wl fnl f)	½	**2**	13/2[2]	76	59
1828[7]	**Tart and a Half (69)** (JLEyre) **5-9-7**(3) OPears(2) (lw: trckd ldrs: squeezed thro ent fnl f: r.o)	hd	**3**	9/1	76	59
1627[10]	**Chemcast (68)** (JLEyre) **4-9-9b** MGallagher(1) (lw: cl up: effrt 2f out: nt qckn fnl f)	2	**4**	10/1	69	52
1671[3]	**Here Comes a Star (46)** (JMCarr) **9-8-1** NKennedy(5) (lw: hdwy u.p ½-wy: styd on: nvr able to chal)	1¾	**5**	16/1	41	24
1627[15]	**Kalar (50)** (DWChapman) **8-8-2b**(3) PFessey(4) (a chsng ldrs: no ex fnl f)	hd	**6**	11/1	45	28
1835[3]	**Insider Trader (61)** (MrsJRRamsden) **6-9-2v** JCarroll(6) (lw: effrt ½-wy: edgd rt: nvr able to chal)	½	**7**	11/4[1]	54	37
1687[6]	**Good To Talk (44)** (TDEasterby) **4-7-6**(7)ow3 RWinston(10) (gd spd 4f)	nk	**8**	20/1	36	16
1828[8]	**Time To Tango (61)** (GMMoore) **4-9-2** JFEgan(12) (s.i.s: hdwy ½-wy: sn btn)	2½	**9**	16/1	45	28
545[9]	**Tutu Sixtysix (41)** (DonEnricoIncisa) **6-7-10** KimTinkler(3) (nvr wnt pce)	¾	**10**	100/1	23	6
1848[3]	**High Domain (IRE) (68)** (JLSpearing) **6-9-9** SSanders(11) (in tch tl wknd fnl 2f)	3	**11**	7/1[3]	40	23
1627[13]	**Allwight Then (IRE) (51)** (TDBarron) **6-8-6** RLappin(13) (cl up over 3f: wknd)	1½	**12**	14/1	18	1
*1433**	**Theatre Magic (46)** (DShaw) **4-8-1** TWilliams(7) (lw: b: s.i.s: n.d)	¾	**13**	13/2[2]	11	—
1765[7]	**Formidable Liz (54)** (MDHammond) **7-8-9** DaleGibson(8) (sn outpcd & bhd)	3	**14**	20/1	9	—
				(SP 132.2%)	**14 Rn**	

58.6 secs (0.80) CSF £65.46 CT £532.59 TOTE £10.70: £3.50 £2.80 £2.60 (£96.90) Trio £554.50 OWNER Mr A. G. Black (SHERIFF HUTTON) BRED Mrs A. Meller

LONG HANDICAP Tutu Sixtysix 6-7 Good To Talk 7-9

OFFICIAL EXPLANATION Insider Trader: hung right from the outset.

1468* Blessingindisguise, despite being poorly drawn, won well and was always going to hang on. (9/1: 11/2-10/1)

1666 Mousehole seemed better in blinkers last year and was off the bridle for much of the way on this occasion, and only ran on when it was all over. (13/2)

1468 Tart and a Half, who has blistering speed, was ridden with restraint. She finished well and there is surely a race to be picked up. (9/1)

494* Chemcast showed his customary speed, ran pretty well and is now dropping down to a decent mark. (10/1)

1671 Here Comes a Star looks superb and is beginning to show signs of form. (16/1)

1269 Kalar ran reasonably and is dropping to a mark he can win off. (11/1)

1835 Insider Trader had the strong pace here that he really likes but, inclined to hang from the word go, failed to get in a blow. This effort is best ignored. (11/4)

Allwight Then (IRE) (14/1: 20/1-12/1)

1433* Theatre Magic (13/2: op 10/1)

2062 R.L. DAVISON & TORCH MOTOR POLICIES AT LLOYD'S H'CAP (0-90) (3-Y.O) (Class C)

3-55 (3-56) **1m** £5,810.00 (£1,760.00: £860.00: £410.00) Stalls: High GOING minus 0.38 sec per fur (F)

				SP	RR	SF
1958[10]	**Al Masroor (USA) (72)** (JWPayne) **3-8-7** DeanMcKeown(3) (a.p: rdn to ld 1f out: styd on wl)	—	**1**	20/1	81	49
1297*	**Green Power (82)** (JRFanshawe) **3-9-3** NVarley(1) (lw: mid div: gd hdwy over 3f out: ev ch 2f out: kpt on wl u.p)	¾	**2**	9/2[2]	90	58
1737[10]	**Plan For Profit (IRE) (80)** (MJohnston) **3-9-1** BDoyle(14) (outpcd & bhd tl hdwy 3f out: styd on wl towards fin)	½	**3**	10/1	87	55
1513[2]	**Jack Flush (IRE) (66)** (BSRothwell) **3-8-1** TWilliams(12) (b.nr fore: b.off hind: a cl up: nt qckn fnl 2f)	1¼	**4**	11/1	70	38
1670[3]	**Boater (74)** (DMorley) **3-8-9** MFenton(10) (led tl hdd 1f out: no ex)	hd	**5**	8/1[3]	78	46
1811[4]	**Wathbat Nashwan (72)** (LMCumani) **3-8-7** SSanders(6) (bmpd appr st: hdwy 3f out: nvr able to chal)	1½	**6**	11/4[1]	73	41
1017[12]	**Hawait (IRE) (86)** (BWHills) **3-9-4**(3) JDSmith(2) (trckd ldrs: effrt 3f out: one pce fnl 2f)	hd	**7**	11/1	87	55
1773[4]	**Foot Battalion (IRE) (83)** (RHollinshead) **3-9-1**(3) DGriffiths(13) (nvr rchd ldrs)	8	**8**	10/1	68	36
1243[6]	**Samsung Spirit (76)** (EWeymes) **3-8-11** GHind(7) (prom tl grad wknd fnl 3f)	1	**9**	20/1	59	27
1399[10]	**Greenaway Bay (USA) (85)** (GWragg) **3-9-6** PaulEddery(15) (lw: mid div: effrt over 3f out: sn rdn: eased whn btn fnl f)	1	**10**	8/1[3]	66	34
1810[10]	**Strat's Quest (69)** (DWPArbuthnot) **3-8-4** SWhitworth(9) (a rr div)	s.h	**11**	25/1	50	18
1496[14]	**Gipsy Princess (64)** (MWEasterby) **3-7-13** DaleGibson(5) (b: a rr div)	1½	**12**	25/1	42	10
1170[19]	**Jay-Owe-Two (IRE) (77)** (RMWhitaker) **3-8-7**(5) GParkin(11) (hld up & bhd: nvr nr to chal)	3	**13**	20/1	49	17
1794[2]	**Vanishing Trick (USA) (79)** (HRACecil) **3-9-0** AMcGlone(8) (plld hrd early: lost pl & bmpd appr st: n.d after)	2½	**14**	8/1[3]	46	14

			SP	RR	SF
	Maraud (75) (JLSpearing) **3-8-10** JFEgan(4) (cl up tl wknd over 3f out)........4	**15**	33/1	34	2
			(SP 137.9%)		**15 Rn**

1m 39.3 (1.10) CSF £102.86 CT £944.82 TOTE £48.60: £10.60 £2.50 £2.60 (£137.60) Trio £251.50 OWNER Al Muallim Partnership (NEWMARKET) BRED Angus MacLean and Mike Simpson

OFFICIAL EXPLANATION **Al Masroor (USA): regarding the improvement in form, the trainer reported that the colt had failed to handle the downhill part of the course last time, and that he is a stuffy horse who benefited from having had a run only five days earlier.**

1238 Al Masroor (USA), trying his longest trip to date, was always going within himself and did the job nicely, giving the impression that there is more to come. (20/1)

1297* Green Power likes easy ground and stays this trip particularly well and, judging from the way he was keeping on, there is more to come. (9/2)

1458* Plan For Profit (IRE), trying a longer trip, came too late. This strong finisher is obviously improving and will get further yet. (10/1)

1513 Jack Flush (IRE) is in good form and ran well again but just found this company too good late on. (11/1)

1670 Boater did his usual and tried to gallop the opposition into the ground but he had run himself out with a furlong left. (8/1)

1811 Wathbat Nashwan was always finding this trip on the sharp side and failed to offer a threat. (11/4)

1017 Hawait (IRE) ran reasonably under top weight and also considering that he had been off the track for over six weeks. (11/1)

2063 BEAUMONTS INSURANCE LADIES' DERBY H'CAP (0-70) (3-Y.O+) (Class E)

4-30 (4-31) **1m 4f 60y** £2,908.25 (£881.00: £430.50: £205.25) Stalls: Low GOING minus 0.38 sec per fur (F)

			SP	RR	SF
1763⁶	**Summerhill Special (IRE) (65)** (DWBarker) **6-11-7** MissERamsden(2) (lw: b.nr hind: a.p: led over 3f out: qcknd clr: eased fnl f: fin 1st: disq: plcd last)........	**1d**	6/1 2	74+	55
1981 12	**Nosey Native (61)** (JPearce) **4-11-3** MrsLPearce(1) (wl bhd: hdwy over 3f out: r.o wl fnl f: nrst fin: fin 2nd: 5l: awrdd r)........5	**1**	8/1	64	45
848 18	**High Low (USA) (45)** (MDHammond) **9-9-11**(4) MissAJSmith(4) (hmpd after s: in tch: kpt on fnl 2f: no imp: fin 3rd: btn 5l & ½l: plcd 2nd)........½	**2**	20/1	40	21
1424⁷	**Stalled (IRE) (50)** (PTWalwyn) **7-10-6** MarchionessBlandford(6) (lw: bhd tl styd on fnl 4f: nvr rchd ldrs: fin 4th, 1½l: plcd 3rd)........1½	**3**	11/1	43	24
1832⁴	**Express Gift (54)** (MrsMReveley) **8-10-10** MrsSBosley(5) (hmpd after s: rr div: c wd & effrt 3f out: no imp: fin 5th: 2½l: plcd 4th)........2½	**4**	9/2 1	44	25
1779⁵	**Heathyards Rock (64)** (RMMcKellar) **5-11-6** MrsCWilliams(9) (bhd: hdwy 4f out: nr clr run over 1f out: swtchd & no imp: fin 6th, ½l: plcd 5th)........½	**5**	8/1	53	34
1683⁵	**Hawkish (USA) (50)** (DMorley) **8-10-6** MissDianaJones(11) (a in tch: rdn over 3f out: one pce: fin 7th, plcd 6th)........1¾	**6**	6/1 2	37	18
1601²	**Indonesian (IRE) (50)** (PCalver) **5-10-6** MrsFNeedham(8) (in tch: hdwy over 3f out: wknd 2f out: fin 8th, plcd 7th)........1½	**7**	10/1	35	16
1748*	**Mowlaie (55)** (DWChapman) **6-10-11** MissRClark(13) (cl up: led 6½f out tl over 3f out: wknd: fin 9th, plcd 8th)........4	**8**	13/2 3	35	16
1748⁹	**Phanan (33)** (REPeacock) **11-9-3** MrsCPeacock(12) (chsd ldrs tl wknd fnl 3½f: fin 10th, plcd 9th)........3½	**9**	33/1	8	—
	Kimberley Boy (37) (MrsMReveley) **7-9-3**(4) MissJEastwood(10) (b.hind: led tl hdd 6½f out: wknd 4f out: fin 11th, plcd 10th)........10	**10**	33/1	—	—
	Muhtadi (IRE) (64) (LadyHerries) **4-11-6** MrsMCowdrey(7) (lw: hmpd after s: a wl bhd: fin 12th, plcd 11th)....17	**11**	7/1	4	—
1818⁸	**Stolen Music (IRE) (36)** (REBarr) **4-9-6** MissAElsey(3) (n.d: fin 13th, plcd 12th)........nk	**12**	100/1	—	—
			(SP 123.9%)		**13 Rn**

2m 40.6 (7.10) CSF £151.11 CT £1,623.43 TOTE £6.00: £2.20 £8.40 £3.00 (£119.10) Trio £292.30; £210.03 to Ascot 20/6/97 OWNER Mr Jeff Pearce (NEWMARKET) BRED Lady Jennifer Green

STEWARDS' ENQUIRY Ramsden susp. 28/6-2/7/97 (irresponsible riding).

1763 Summerhill Special (IRE) absolutely trotted up but was disqualified for irresponsible riding when hampering three rivals leaving the stalls, which would seem extremely harsh considering this was an amateur event and she won so easily. (6/1)

1427 Nosey Native, given a lot to do, made up a tremendous amount of ground in the last three furlongs but never had a chance with the very easy winner and, later, was very fortunate to get the race in the Stewards' room. (8/1)

High Low (USA) has been running well over hurdles and this was another fair effort and he is clearly in good heart. (20/1)

1424 Stalled (IRE) looks well but runs when in the mood but was never doing things fast enough here. (11/1)

1832 Express Gift took a bump at the start and then failed to make any impression, but he still has his chances if good enough. (9/2)

1779 Heathyards Rock would have been a good bit closer if he had not been stopped in his run approaching the last furlong. (8/1)

2064 LEVY BOARD H'CAP (0-80) (3-Y.O) (Class D)

5-05 (5-10) **1m 4f 60y** £3,436.25 (£1,040.00: £507.50: £241.25) Stalls: Low GOING minus 0.38 sec per fur (F)

			SP	RR	SF
1470*	**Heart of Gold (IRE) (79)** (MissSEHall) **3-9-6** AMcGlone(3) (lw: chsd ldrs: pushed along after 4f: led 4f out: styd on strly)........—	**1**	11/4 2	93	49
1470²	**Klondike Charger (USA) (74)** (BWHills) **3-8-12**(3) JDSmith(4) (in tch: hdwy to chse wnr 4f out: hung rt 2f out: no imp)........10	**2**	11/2 3	75	31
1414 13	**Supreme Sound (73)** (PWHarris) **3-9-0** SSanders(2) (chsd ldrs: rdn 4f out: sn wl outpcd)........5	**3**	14/1	67	23
1649²	**Stakis Casinos Boy (IRE) (80)** (MJohnston) **3-9-7** BDoyle(5) (lw: sn outpcd & bhd: hdwy over 3f out: hung rt & n.d)........12	**4**	11/4 2	59	15
1469³	**Monarch's Pursuit (55)** (TDEasterby) **3-7-7v1**(3) PFessey(6) (lw: w ldr: led 6f out to 4f out: sn wknd)........5	**5**	12/1	27	—
1863*	**Scarrots (69)** (SCWilliams) **3-8-10** 5x JFEgan(7) (lw: set str pce tl hdd 6f out: sn wknd)........nk	**6**	5/2 1	41	—
			(SP 111.6%)		**6 Rn**

2m 37.3 (3.80) CSF £16.06 TOTE £3.90: £1.30 £2.30 (£10.60) OWNER Mr C. Platts (MIDDLEHAM) BRED Miss Fiona Meehan

LONG HANDICAP Monarch's Pursuit 7-8

1470* Heart of Gold (IRE) improved again at this longer trip and really appreciated the extremely strong pace to win going right away. He will get further yet. (11/4)

1470 Klondike Charger (USA) tried to give the winner a race in the last half-mile but tended to hang under pressure and was eventually eased when well beaten in the last furlong. (11/2)

Supreme Sound had his chances but looked one-paced when ridden in the straight. (14/1)

1649 Stakis Casinos Boy (IRE) looked particularly well but always found the pace here far too strong and then hung when put under serious pressure in the home straight. (11/4)

1469 Monarch's Pursuit raced too freely in the visor here and was done with a long way from home. (12/1: 6/1-14/1)

1863* Scarrots did not like being taken on in the lead and threw in the towel entering the straight. (5/2)

2065 BEDALE LIMITED STKS (0-70) (4-Y.O+) (Class E)
5-40 (5-41) **1m 2f** £2,765.25 (£837.00: £408.50: £194.25) Stalls: High GOING minus 0.38 sec per fur (F)

			SP	RR	SF
1923*	**Anak-Ku (65)** (MissGayKelleway) **4-9-1** SSanders(8) (mde all: hld on wl) —	1	9/2 3	81	38
1811 2	**Carburton (69)** (JAGlover) **4-8-13** NDay(1) (a.p: slipped ent st: hdwy & ev ch over 1f out: styd on towards fin) s.h	2	4/5 1	79	36
1481 5	**Florentino (IRE) (65)** (BWHills) **4-8-8**(3) JDSmith(5) (reard s: sn rcvrd & prom: ev ch 2f out: r.o one pce) ¾	3	4/1 2	76	33
1739 11	**Toujours Riviera (70)** (JPearce) **7-8-8**(3) CTeague(6) (plld hrd: bhd: stdy hdwy on ins 4f out: rdn over 2f out: sn btn) 8	4	8/1	63	20
1686 2	**Golden Thunderbolt (FR) (69)** (NTinkler) **4-8-13** DeanMcKeown(2) (in tch: effrt over 3f out: btn over 2f out) 3½	5	10/1	59	16
1221 8	**Mr Montague (IRE) (58)** (TWDonnelly) **5-8-8**(3) PFessey(7) (cl up tl wknd fnl 3f) 1¼	6	50/1	55	12
	Some Horse (IRE) (70) (MGMeagher) **4-8-11** JCarroll(3) (hld up: effrt 4f out: btn over 2f out) 1¾	7	12/1	53	10
1230 7	**Get A Life (50)** (JO'Reilly) **4-8-8** JO'Reilly(4) (hdwy & prom whn slipped ent st: wknd 4f out) 23	8	100/1	13	—
			(SP 124.6%)		**8 Rn**

2m 7.2 (3.70) CSF £8.48 TOTE £5.20: £1.80 £1.20 £2.20 (£3.30) OWNER H R H Sultan Ahmad Shah (WHITCOMBE) BRED John Rose
1923* Anak-Ku is a game sort and refused to give in here but he did have a hard race. (9/2)
1811 Carburton slipped badly on the home turn and, but for that, would surely have won. (4/5: tchd evens)
1481 Florentino (IRE), very edgy in the stalls, then reared up as they opened and obviously has temperament problems, but he certainly has plenty of ability when things go right, and this was not a bad effort. (4/1)
1471 Toujours Riviera spent most of the race pulling his rider's arms out and then failed to quicken when ridden. (8/1: op 5/1)
1686 Golden Thunderbolt (FR) ran reasonably but was always short of speed when the race really began in the last three furlongs. (10/1: op 5/1)
Mr Montague (IRE) showed his first signs of form here. (50/1)

T/Plpt: £4,839.70 (2.53 Tckts). T/Qdpt: £427.30 (1.93 Tckts) AA

1939-SOUTHWELL (L-H) (Standard)
Thursday June 19th
WEATHER: showers WIND: slight half against

2066 JAK POINTS MAIDEN AUCTION STKS (2-Y.O F) (Class F)
2-20 (2-21) **5f (Fibresand)** £2,277.00 (£627.00: £297.00) Stalls: High GOING: 0.18 sec per fur (SLW)

			SP	RR	SF
	Socket Set (BAMcMahon) **2-8-7** LNewton(5) (w'like: w ldrs: led over 1f out: r.o wl) —	1	5/2 1	73+	35
1492 4	**Happy Days Again (IRE)** (JWharton) **2-8-7** JQuinn(2) (w ldrs: rdn over 1f out: no imp) 1½	2	3/1 2	68	30
	Opopmil (IRE) (TDEasterby) **2-8-7** FNorton(1) (w'like: bit bkwd: sn wl outpcd: hdwy ½-wy: edgd rt & styd on appr fnl f) 3½	3	8/1	57+	19
1829 4	**Bow Peep (IRE)** (MWEasterby) **2-8-4b1** LCharnock(11) (w ldrs: rdn 2f out: edgd lft: kpt on same pce) 2½	4	9/2 3	46	8
828 12	**Blarney Park** (CADwyer) **2-7-9**(5) RFfrench(3) (in tch: drvn along ½-wy: sn outpcd) 5	5	12/1	26	—
1126 3	**Miss Puci** (JBerry) **2-8-4** GDuffield(4) (w ldrs: rdn & egdd lft ½-wy: sn wknd) nk	6	3/1 2	29	—
1941 12	**Jen's In The Know** (CMurray) **2-8-2** NicolaHowarth(8) (led tl hdd & wknd over 1f out) ¾	7	25/1	25	—
1657 7	**Gorgeous** (NPLittmoden) **2-7-9**(5) IonaWands(7) (s.i.s: bhd tl sme late hdwy) nk	8	8/1	22	—
1492 15	**Cinder Hills** (MWEasterby) **2-8-4** TLucas(9) (dwlt: a outpcd) nk	9	14/1	25	—
	Tilburg (MrsNMacauley) **2-8-7**ow7 SWebster(6) (leggy: b.nr hind: in tch: outpcd ½-wy: sn lost pl) 1	10	20/1	25	—
902 13	**Ruths Gem (IRE)** (DTThom) **2-8-0** NCarlisle(12) (sn outpcd & bhd) 3	11	25/1	8	—
750 8	**Katies Treat (IRE)** (DTThom) **2-8-2** CRutter(10) (sn bhd) 1½	12	33/1	5	—
			(SP 148.7%)		**12 Rn**

61.1 secs (4.10) CSF £11.62 TOTE £6.80: £1.30 £2.10 £5.30 (£11.10) Trio £96.10; £74.52 to Royal Ascot 20/6/97 OWNER Mr J. C. Fretwell (TAMWORTH) BRED Mrs J. McMahon
Socket Set, a fair sort, had clearly been taught her job judging by the market support. Always travelling nicely, she took this modest event with the minimum of fuss. (5/2)
1492 Happy Days Again (IRE) matched strides with the leaders on the far side but once the winner was given the office, it was over in a matter of strides. (3/1)
Opopmil (IRE), a fair sort, looked on the backward side. Very green going down, she was soon behind but did show promise, sticking on strongly coming to the final furlong. She might need another outing to teach her her job. (8/1: 6/1-10/1)
1829 Bow Peep (IRE), tried in blinkers this time, showed plenty of speed but, under pressure, tended to edge left towards the centre. (9/2)
1126 Miss Puci matched strides with the leaders but, under pressure, edged left. (3/1)

2067 MARCRIST CLAIMING STKS (3-Y.O+) (Class F)
2-55 (2-55) **1m 3f (Fibresand)** £2,277.00 (£627.00: £297.00) Stalls: Low GOING: 0.18 sec per fur (SLW)

			SP	RR	SF
1507 3	**Private Fixture (IRE) (38)** (DMarks) **6-9-6** GDuffield(6) (chsd ldrs: styd on u.p appr fnl f: hung lft: led nr fin) —	1	8/1	73	55
	Anyar Reem (63) (DShaw) **6-9-8b1** JFanning(1) (b: led: kpt on u.p fnl 3f: hdd nr fin) ½	2	5/1 2	74	56
1943 2	**Champagne Warrior (IRE) (54)** (MJCamacho) **4-9-0** LCharnock(4) (blind off eye: lw: trckd ldrs: effrt 3f out: kpt on same pce appr fnl f: eased nr fin) 4	3	11/8 1	61	43
1636 8	**Zatopek (50)** (JCullinan) **5-9-4** VSlattery(7) (hdwy u.p over 5f out: wknd 3f out) 10	4	7/1	50	32
1943 3	**Royal Legend (52)** (JPearce) **5-9-4v** MWigham(2) (trckd ldrs: rdn over 4f out: lost pl 3f out) 5	5	11/2 3	43	25
1689 15	**Safa Dancer (34)** (BAMcMahon) **4-8-11** LNewton(8) (in tch: pushed along 6f out: wknd 3f out) 8	6	25/1	24	6
605 8	**Mystical Island** (CACyzer) **3-8-7**(3) AWhelan(5) (sn outpcd: rdn 8f out: sn wl bhd: t.o 3f out) 18	7	16/1	10	—
668 4	**Bold Habit (42)** (JPearce) **12-9-2** GBardwell(3) (s.i.s: sn wl bhd: t.o 3f out: virtually p.u) dist	8	11/1	—	—
			(SP 115.8%)		**8 Rn**

2m 28.8 (8.80) CSF £43.82 TOTE £7.30: £2.20 £1.30 £1.10 (£19.60) OWNER Mr John Jackson (UPPER LAMBOURN) BRED Maurice and Jeremiah Sheahan
WEIGHT FOR AGE 3yo-13lb
1507 Private Fixture (IRE), who has not won for four years, would have been meeting the favourite on 22lb better terms in a handicap. He showed a poor action going down, but his rider was in no mood to accept defeat and he gained the day near the line. (8/1: op 5/1)

Anyar Reem, having his first outing for three years, was heavily bandaged in front and wore a tongue-strap. Setting out to gallop his rivals into submission, he was only worn down near the line. (5/1: op 8/1)
1943 Champagne Warrior (IRE) travelled smoothly but, suddenly under pressure on the turn in, could pull out no more. (11/8: evens-6/4)
1287 Zatopek is still a maiden after twenty-five starts and is likely to remain so for a good while yet. (7/1: 5/1-8/1)
1943 Royal Legend does not look in love with the game anymore. (11/2)

2068 IDEAL STANDARD H'CAP (0-65) (3-Y.O) (Class F)
3-30 (3-30) **1m 4f (Fibresand)** £2,277.00 (£627.00: £297.00) Stalls: Low GOING: 0.18 sec per fur (SLW)

Form	Horse	Dist	Pos	SP	RR	SF
1140[18]	**Big Bang (61)** (MBlanshard) **3-9-3** JQuinn(8) (hdwy u.p 4f out: styd on to ld jst ins fnl f: all out)	—	1	10/1	68	24
1465[10]	**Bonne Ville (60)** (BPalling) **3-9-2** GDuffield(9) (sn chsng ldrs: drvn along over 4f out: styd on wl towards fin)	nk	2	5/1[3]	67	23
1756[6]	**Kustom Kit Klassic (47)** (SRBowring) **3-7-12**(5) KSked(5) (b: hdwy 7f out: chal over 2f out: nt qckn ins fnl f)	nk	3	12/1	53	9
1625[6]	**Sarbaron (IRE) (65)** (PWHarris) **3-9-0**(7) CLowther(7) (chsd ldrs: led over 4f out tl jst ins fnl f: one pce)	½	4	8/1	71	27
*1785**	**Sipowitz (46)** (CACyzer) **3-7-13**(3) AWhelan(3) (sn pushed along: chsd ldrs tl lost pl over 4f out: kpt on appr fnl f)	8	5	3/1[2]	41	—
1863[3]	**Kingdom Pearl (47)** (MJCamacho) **3-8-3** LCharnock(6) (led to 9f out: led over 5f out tl over 4f out: wknd 2f out: eased)	19	6	13/2	17	—
1785[2]	**Alagna (47)** (SCWilliams) **3-8-3** FLynch(1) (led 9f out tl over 5f out: lost pl over 4f out: eased)	3½	7	2/1[1]	12	—
1863[7]	**Cochiti (41)** (CWThornton) **3-7-11** FNorton(4) (sn bhd & drvn along: t.o 3f out)	7	8	16/1	—	—
1785[9]	**Bella Daniella (40)** (TTClement) **3-7-5**(5) IonaWands(2) (sn drvn along & bhd: t.o 4f out)	1¾	9	33/1	—	—

(SP 125.1%) **9 Rn**

2m 47.1 (14.10) CSF £58.54 CT £573.23 TOTE £14.00: £2.20 £2.60 £1.80 (£20.20) Trio £65.40 OWNER Mr Gregory West (UPPER LAMBOURN) BRED J. Hamilton
LONG HANDICAP Bella Daniella 7-0
OFFICIAL EXPLANATION **Alagna: no explanation offered.**
417* Big Bang, who had run poorly on his three previous outings since winning a maiden at Wolverhampton, stuck on in persistent fashion to force his head in front inside the last. This looked a particularly weak handicap. He might prove an easier ride if fitted with blinkers. (10/1: op 6/1)
1043 Bonne Ville, tailed off on the grass last time, only really found her stride inside the last and would have made it with a little further to go. (5/1)
1756 Kustom Kit Klassic proved well suited by this step up in distance. (12/1)
842 Sarbaron (IRE) looked to have been given plenty of weight on his handicap debut. A big boat of a horse, he made the best of his way home but was never going quick enough to last out. (8/1)
1785* Sipowitz, who won over a mile six last time from a 2lb lower mark, could not go the pace and was struggling badly half a mile from home. (3/1)
1785 Alagna, who looked very fit, dropped right out with over half a mile to go and her rider allowed her to coast in. (2/1)

2069 JACKSON BUILDING CENTRES LIMITED STKS (0-65) (3-Y.O+) (Class F)
4-05 (4-06) **6f (Fibresand)** £2,600.40 (£719.40: £343.20) Stalls: Low GOING: 0.18 sec per fur (SLW)

Form	Horse	Dist	Pos	SP	RR	SF
1754[10]	**Bold Aristocrat (IRE) (60)** (RHollinshead) **6-9-5** FLynch(1) (lw: hdwy on ins ½-wy: led over 1f out: hld on towards fin)	—	1	10/1	74	55
1942[2]	**Stolen Kiss (IRE) (60)** (MWEasterby) **5-8-13b** GDuffield(4) (trckd ldrs gng wl: chal over 1f out: sn rdn: nt qckn towards fin)	nk	2	7/4[1]	67	48
1761[10]	**Al Reet (IRE) (50)** (SRBowring) **6-8-8**(5) KSked(2) (led tl over 1f out: one pce)	2½	3	16/1	61	42
1790[2]	**Itsinthepost (64)** (VSoane) **4-8-8**(5) IonaWands(6) (lw: sn outpcd & drvn along: hdwy over 2f out: nvr rchd ldrs)	2½	4	5/1[3]	54	35
1944[4]	**Awesome Venture (60)** (MCChapman) **7-9-2** FNorton(7) (chsd ldrs: drvn along ½-wy: outpcd appr fnl f)	4	5	16/1	46	27
382[5]	**Deeply Vale (IRE) (62)** (GLMoore) **6-9-2** CRutter(5) (sn pushed along: hdwy & swtchd rt 2f out: no imp)	1	6	12/1	44	25
1781[6]	**Three For A Pound (64)** (JAGlover) **3-8-12b**[1] LCharnock(10) (racd wd: hdwy to chse ldrs ½-wy: wknd & eased over 1f out)	¾	7	3/1[2]	45	19
1761[8]	**Keston Pond (IRE) (56)** (MrsVAAconley) **7-9-2** MDeering(3) (dwlt: sme hdwy 2f out: n.d)	¾	8	6/1	40	21
*1790**	**Hoh Majestic (IRE) (60)** (RonaldThompson) **4-9-0v**(5) GMilligan(9) (racd wd: wl bhd fnl 2f)	12	9	9/1	11	—
303[2]	**Newington Butts (IRE) (48)** (KMcAuliffe) **7-8-13e** JQuinn(8) (b.nr hind: chsd ldrs tl lost pl 2f out: eased)	12	10	16/1	—	—

(SP 136.7%) **10 Rn**

1m 18.1 (4.60) CSF £29.93 TOTE £11.30: £3.10 £1.90 £2.90 (£19.60) Trio £80.30 OWNER Mrs J. Hughes (UPPER LONGDON) BRED Scarteen Stud
WEIGHT FOR AGE 3yo-7lb
1132 Bold Aristocrat (IRE) had a dream run up the inner and, in the end, showed more resolution on the day than the runner-up. (10/1: 8/1-12/1)
1942 Stolen Kiss (IRE), easily best in on official figures, tracked the leaders travelling smoothly but, when popped the question, she flashed her tail and did not put it all in. She has only won twice from thirty-eight starts and it is easy to see why. (7/4)
1385 Al Reet (IRE), who set the pace, turned in her best performance since winning a handicap in Ireland in November 1995. (16/1)
1790 Itsinthepost struggled to go the pace and, though sticking on, was never going to take a hand. (5/1)
1944 Awesome Venture found this trip too sharp. (16/1)
241 Deeply Vale (IRE) (12/1: 7/1-14/1)
1790* Hoh Majestic (IRE) (9/1: op 5/1)

2070 ARMITAGE SHANKS APPRENTICE (S) H'CAP (0-60) (3-Y.O+) (Class G)
4-40 (4-41) **7f (Fibresand)** £2,007.50 (£570.00: £282.50) Stalls: Low GOING: 0.18 sec per fur (SLW)

Form	Horse	Dist	Pos	SP	RR	SF
1926[6]	**Ring the Chief (33)** (MDIUsher) **5-8-4** GHannon(3) (led: clr over 2f out: jst hld on)	—	1	4/1[1]	45	25
1855[4]	**Spanish Stripper (USA) (25)** (MCChapman) **6-7-10** SCarson(7) (a chsng ldrs: wnt 2nd over 1f out: styd on wl towards fin)	nk	2	14/1	36	16
	Arrasas Lady (25) (JRPoulton) **7-7-10** JFowle(15) (b: mid div: hdwy over 2f out: kpt on one pce fnl f)	7	3	33/1	20	—
1944[11]	**Pc's Cruiser (IRE) (38)** (NPLittmoden) **5-8-4v**(5) KPierrepont(4) (s.s: bhd: gd hdwy on outside over 2f out: edgd lft: nvr nr to chal)	3	4	7/1	27	7
1620[9]	**Astral Invader (IRE) (32)** (MSSaunders) **5-8-3** KerryBaker(5) (chsd ldrs tl wknd over 1f out)	nk	5	7/1	20	—
1802[9]	**Eastleigh (53)** (RHollinshead) **8-9-5**(5) LisaWatson(6) (bhd: hdwy on outside over 2f out: edgd lft: hung rt fnl f: nvr nr ldrs)	1	6	10/1	39	19
1009[4]	**Rocky Waters (USA) (39)** (MDIUsher) **8-8-10v** RCody-Boutcher(2) (chsd ldrs tl wknd 2f out)	1¾	7	6/1[3]	21	1

				SP	RR	SF
1115[4]	**Soviet Lady (IRE) (45)** (JLEyre) **3-8-7** SBuckley(8) (bhd: sme hdwy 2f out: n.d)	5	**8**	5/1[2]	15	—
1483[8]	**First Gold (49)** (JWharton) **8-9-6** TSiddall(10) (bhd: sme hdwy over 2f out: n.d)	s.h	**9**	8/1	19	—
1848[11]	**Red Time (38)** (MSSaunders) **4-8-9** ClaireAngell(1) (nvr bttr than mid div)	¾	**10**	20/1	6	—
1441[15]	**Persian Dawn (39)** (RTPhillips) **4-8-5**(5) NicolaWright(12) (bhd & c wd ent st: n.d)	1½	**11**	20/1	4	—
951[11]	**Magic Melody (42)** (JLSpearing) **4-8-13** SRighton(11) (mid div: effrt on outside over 2f out: sn wknd)	¾	**12**	25/1	5	—
	Mrs Keen (34) (PButler) **4-8-5** NPollard(13) (hmpd s: a bhd)	7	**13**	33/1	—	—
873[10]	**Julia's Relative (52)** (RonaldThompson) **3-9-0b** DMernagh(14) (swvd lft s: hdwy ½-wy: wknd over 2f out)	9	**14**	12/1	—	—
1757[10]	**Rustic Song (IRE) (25)** (JWharton) **4-7-10b**[1] PBradley(9) (chsd ldrs tl wknd 2f out)	1¼	**15**	33/1	—	—

(SP 132.7%) **15 Rn**

1m 33.3 (6.80) CSF £57.11 CT £1,561.26 TOTE £8.00: £3.50 £1.90 £76.80 (£15.40) Trio Not won; £192.11 to Royal Ascot 20/6/97 OWNER Mr G. A. Summers (WANTAGE) BRED Mrs Trisha Dunbar
LONG HANDICAP Arrasas Lady 7-1 Rustic Song (IRE) 7-5
WEIGHT FOR AGE 3yo-9lb
Bt in 3,800gns
1926 Ring the Chief, only 3lb higher than when he recorded his only previous victory here in February, shot clear off the turn and, well handled, just lasted home. (4/1)
772 Spanish Stripper (USA) has only won once in fifty-one outings but he almost made it two here on one of his better days. (14/1)
Arrasas Lady was having her first outing on the Flat for 677 days and was 9lb out of the handicap. (33/1)
1576 Pc's Cruiser (IRE) is his own worst enemy. Giving away plenty of ground at the start and running wide on the turn, all he did was go left under pressure for the boy. (7/1)
484* Astral Invader (IRE) is better suited by turf. (7/1)
1576 Eastleigh, as usual, was difficult to load and came wide off the bend. Edging left, he hung back right in the final furlong and ended up where he began in the centre. He really needs a mile. (10/1)
577* Julia's Relative (12/1: op 8/1)

2071 BARLOW WARMASTYLE H'CAP (0-70) (3-Y.O+) (Class E)

5-15 (5-16) **1m (Fibresand)** £3,382.25 (£1,013.00: £486.50: £223.25) Stalls: Low GOING: 0.18 sec per fur (SLW)

				SP	RR	SF
1754[2]	**Johnnie the Joker (61)** (JPLeigh) **6-9-0b**(5) DSweeney(2) (mde virtually all: clr over 1f out: r.o wl)	—	**1**	7/2[2]	74	54
1473[4]	**Jona Holley (43)** (GLMoore) **4-8-1** CRutter(8) (bhd & pushed along: styd on fnl 2f: no ch w wnr)	6	**2**	6/1	44	24
1800[12]	**Mutahadeth (66)** (DShaw) **3-9-0** JFanning(12) (b.hind: racd wd: chsd ldrs: edgd lft & kpt on same pce fnl 2f)	¾	**3**	9/1	66	36
1463[6]	**Mercury (IRE) (48)** (JAGlover) **4-8-6b**[1] GDuffield(3) (sn trckng ldrs: wnt 2nd over 2f out: rdn & wknd over 1f out)	nk	**4**	9/4[1]	47	27
864[19]	**Holders Hill (IRE) (60)** (MGMeagher) **5-9-1**(3) AWhelan(6) (chsd ldrs: outpcd over 4f out: swtchd rt over 1f out: kpt on)	1¼	**5**	16/1	56	36
1576[6]	**Chadleigh Lane (USA) (62)** (ABMulholland) **5-9-1v**(5) GFaulkner(7) (racd wd: bhd: hdwy whn hmpd over 1f out: nvr nr to chal)	1¾	**6**	14/1	55	35
1802[6]	**In Good Faith (57)** (JJQuinn) **5-8-10**(5) RFfrench(9) (racd wd: chsd ldrs tl lost pl over 2f out: kpt on appr fnl f)	1¾	**7**	10/1	46	26
653[9]	**Manabar (43)** (MJPolglase) **5-7-10**(5) IonaWands(1) (in tch to ½-wy: sn lost pl)	3½	**8**	16/1	25	5
908[11]	**Bronhallow (39)** (MrsBarbaraWaring) **4-7-11** FNorton(11) (b.hind: chsd ldrs tl over 2f out: wkng whn hmpd over 1f out)	8	**9**	40/1	5	—
1500[7]	**Singforyoursupper (50)** (GGMargarson) **3-7-12** GBardwell(5) (v.unruly & uns rdr gng to s: sn bhd & drvn along: racd wd)	1½	**10**	25/1	13	—
	Racing Brenda (70) (BCMorgan) **6-10-0** CHodgson(4) (chsd ldrs tl lost pl 3f out: hmpd over 1f out)	4	**11**	20/1	25	5
	Slievenamon (53) (JEBanks) **4-8-11** JQuinn(10) (lw: chsd ldrs: drvn along ½-wy: n.m.r over 2f out: wkng whn hmpd over 1f out: eased)	11	**12**	9/2[3]	—	—

(SP 134.0%) **12 Rn**

1m 45.3 (6.30) CSF £25.68 CT £175.50 TOTE £4.40: £2.30 £5.20 £2.80 (£22.00) Trio £79.20 OWNER Miss M. Carrington-Smith (GAINSBOROUGH) BRED Miss M. Carrington-Smith
WEIGHT FOR AGE 3yo-10lb
STEWARDS' ENQUIRY Whelan susp. 30/6-3/7/97 (careless riding).
1754 Johnnie the Joker has now won five of his eight races here and, well suited by a mile nowadays, had this won with over a furlong left to go. (7/2: 3/1-9/2)
1473 Jona Holley, having his first outing since being claimed, stayed on late in the day and will be suited by further and give in the ground on turf. (6/1: op 4/1)
513 Mutahadeth showed a return to form on his favourite surface after two poor efforts on turf. (9/1: op 6/1)
1463 Mercury (IRE), 8lb better off with Johnnie the Joker and with blinkers on for the first time, moved up into second looking a real danger once in line for home but, under pressure, to be truthful he did not find a lot. (9/4)
28 Holders Hill (IRE), running over a trip short of his best, was switched violently right over a furlong out, causing a chain reaction. (16/1)

T/Plpt: £573.50 (13.98 Tckts). T/Qdpt: £61.60 (9.77 Tckts) WG

2072a - 2077a (Irish Racing) - See Computer Raceform

0065a-LEOPARDSTOWN (Dublin, Ireland) (L-H) (Yielding to soft)
Wednesday June 11th

2078a BALLYCORUS STKS (Gp 3) (3-Y.O+)

7-00 (7-04) **7f** IR £19,500.00 (IR £5,700.00: IR £2,700.00: IR £900.00) GOING: 0.45 sec per fur (GS)

				SP	RR	SF
1719a[3]	**Wizard King** (SirMarkPrescott) **6-9-9** GDuffield (hld up: towards rr early: wnt 3rd bef ½-wy: cld st: led under 2f out: drvn clr: r.o wl)	—	**1**	2/1[2]	119+	37
713a*	**Cool Edge (IRE)** (MHTompkins) **6-9-9** MJKinane (cl up: disp ld bef ½-wy: led st: hdd under 2f out: rdn & no ex: kpt on: no ch w wnr)	4	**2**	5/2[3]	110	28
	Crown Regent (IRE) (APO'Brien,Ireland) **3-8-9** CRoche (led: hdd st: 3rd, rdn & btn 2f out: kpt on same pce)	3	**3**	5/4[1]	99	7
	Gaultier Gale (IRE) (DHanley,Ireland) **3-8-9** WJSmith (2nd briefly early: 4th & rdn st: nt trble ldrs over 1½f out: kpt on same pce)	nk	**4**	25/1	98	6

1541a7 **Mosconi (IRE)** (JSBolger,Ireland) **3-8-9** KJManning (hld up: last st: sn rdn & effrt: btn over 1½f out: eased) ....20 **5** 12/1 53 —
(SP 117.9%) **5 Rn**

1m 34.1 (9.10) OWNER Sh Ahmed Bin Saeed Al Maktoum (NEWMARKET) BRED Sheikh Mohammed bin Rashid al Maktoum
1719a Wizard King notched up his fifth Irish win and has only been beaten on two visits! With waiting tactics adopted this time, he was an improving second on the outer well before the straight and, despite being carried wide, quickly assumed command for what was eventually a very easy win. He seems better than ever. (2/1)
713a* Cool Edge (IRE), always close up, disputed the lead before the straight but, running wide, had absolutely nothing in the way of the winners turn of foot. (5/2: op 6/4)
Crown Regent (IRE), a surprise favourite, found his limitations rather harshly exposed and was beaten from the turn in. (5/4: op 9/4)
Gaultier Gale (IRE) ran well enough to suggest he will get through a nice handicap. (25/1)
1541a Mosconi (IRE) seems to have left his smart two-year-old form well behind him. (12/1: op 8/1)

2079a GLENCAIRN STKS (Listed) (4-Y.O+)
7-30 (7-33) **1m 1f** IR £12,900.00 (IR £3,700.00: IR £1,700.00: IR £500.00) GOING: 0.45 sec per fur (GS)

				SP	RR	SF
1058a3	**Tout A Coup (IRE)** (GACusack,Ireland) **4-8-11** PJSmullen (mde all: kpt on u.p whn chal fnl f)	—	**1**	8/1	103+	19
1198a3	**Theano (IRE)** (APO'Brien,Ireland) **4-8-6** JAHeffernan (hld up in tch: 4th st: sn chal: 2nd & ev ch over 1½f out: kpt on u.p ins last: no ex)	½	**2**	4/1 2	97	13
	Rithab (JMuldoon,Ireland) **4-8-6b** WJSupple (hld up: 5th ½-wy: chsd ldrs st: swtchd to outside to chal over 1f out: r.o u.p ins last)	s.h	**3**	20/1	97	13
1058a2	**Raiyoun (IRE)** (JOxx,Ireland) **4-8-10**ow1 JPMurtagh (rn 3rd: hld up: 2nd & chal over 2f out: 3rd & no ex over 1f out)	1½	**4**	8/11 1	98	13
1062a4	**Orange Grouse (IRE)** (LBrowne,Ireland) **4-8-6** JPSpencer (hld up towards rr: cld st: 6th & no imp 1½f out: kpt on same pce)	4½	**5**	20/1	86	2
	Inchacooley (IRE) (MBrassil,Ireland) **5-8-6** PShanahan (6th ½-wy: rdn & no imp over 1½f out: kpt on same pce)	hd	**6**	25/1	86	2
1532a5	**Ger's Royale (IRE)** (PJFlynn,Ireland) **6-9-0** MJKinane (sn chsng ldr: 3rd & effrt over 2f out: btn wl over 1f out: wknd)	½	**7**	5/1 3	93	9

(SP 119.0%) **7 Rn**

2m 3.2 (12.70) OWNER Edmund Loder (NAAS) BRED E. J. Loder
1058a Tout A Coup (IRE) made all the running and quite comfortably reversed previous Curragh form with Raiyoun, ten lengths in front of her on their last encounter. She came wide entering the straight, and despite edging right close home, there was never any question about the result being changed in the subsequent Stewards' Enquiry. (8/1)
1198a Theano (IRE) held up and taking a strong hold, got into a challenging position early in the straight and had every chance. She was slightly inconvenienced by the winner in the last few strides but not enough to have got the race. (4/1: op 2/1)
Rithab is only a handicapper and ran her best race ever. She might have got her nose in front if her run had started earlier. (20/1)
1058a Raiyoun (IRE) proved a real disappointment, looking very one paced over the last furlong and a half. (8/11)
1062a Orange Grouse (IRE) gave them plenty of start, but ran on in the straight and certainly wasn't disgraced. (20/1)

2080a (Irish Racing) - See Computer Raceform

2081a EAGLE STAR FOUR IN A ROW STKS (3-Y.O+)
8-30 (8-30) **1m 4f** IR £4,110.00 (IR £930.00: IR £390.00: IR £210.00) GOING: 0.45 sec per fur (GS)

				SP	RR	SF
1540a*	**Dr Johnson (USA)** (CO'Brien,Ireland) **3-9-4** CRoche (rn 3rd: rdn & chsd ldrs over 3f out: 2nd & chal st: led early fnl f: rdn & styd on strly)	—	**1**	4/6 1	109	37
809a2	**Zafarabad (IRE)** (JOxx,Ireland) **3-9-1** JPMurtagh (rn 2nd: disp ld 4f out: led over 3f out: jnd under 2f out: rdn & hdd early fnl f: s.o: no ex)	1	**2**	9/4 2	105	33
	Gordi (USA) (DKWeld,Ireland) **4-10-5** MJKinane (hld up: rn 4th: kpt on st: nvr nr to chal)	15	**3**	5/1 3	88	31
	Apache Chief (IRE) (JCHayden,Ireland) **3-8-10** WJSupple (plld hrd: towards rr: n.d: kpt on)	4½	**4**	33/1	74	2
	Nordic Project (IRE) (JSBolger,Ireland) **3-9-1** KJManning (led: jnd 4f out: hdd over 3f out: 3rd & btn over 2f out: eased)	2½	**5**	8/1	75	3

(SP 121.5%) **5 Rn**

2m 45.2 (15.20) OWNER M. V. O'Brien
1540a* Dr Johnson (USA) earned his tilt at the Irish Derby after a sustained tussle with the runner-up in the straight. He got in front just inside the last furlong and battled on bravely. He might prefer faster ground and the trainer believes a stronger pace would suit. (4/6)
809a Zafarabad (IRE) took over three and a half furlongs out, but found the winner two strong inside the last. (9/4: op 6/4)
Gordi (USA) was never put into the race despite staying on slightly over the last quarter-mile. (5/1)
Nordic Project (IRE) (8/1: op 5/1)

2082a - 2095a (Irish Racing) - See Computer Raceform

1913a-MAISONS-LAFFITTE (France) (Soft)
Friday June 13th

2096a PRIX DE DRAVEIL H'CAP (4-Y.O+)
4-50 (4-51) **5f 110y** £5,612.00

				SP	RR	SF
	Arctic Starry (FR) (RCrepon,France) **5-9-11b** AJunk	—	**1**		83+	—
	Stitched Up (IRE) (France) **8-8-3** SCoffigny	2	**2**		55	—
	Navajo (France) **11-7-10** SFargeat	½	**3**		47	—
14198	**Village Native (FR)** (KOCunningham-Brown) **4-8-9** FSanchez (btn over 8l)		**12**		—	—

19 Rn

65.8 secs (2.30) P-M 4.60F: 2.40F 2.70F 4.90F (23.80F) OWNER Ecurie Hippoline
1327 Village Native (FR), whose connections raided similar events last season and found little reward, was beaten quite comprehensively. He is very average and will have to find more to win an event like this.

1544a-COLOGNE (Germany) (R-H) (Heavy)
Sunday June 15th

2097a OPPENHEIM-COLONIA-UNION-RENNEN (Gp 2) (3-Y.O)
3-40 (3-48) **1m 3f** £45,455.00 (£18,182.00: £9,091.00: £4,545.00)

	Horse	Dist	Pos	SP	RR	SF
1545a²	**Caitano** (BSchutz,Germany) **3-9-2** AStarke	—	1		112	—
	San Suru (GER) (PRau,Germany) **3-9-2** TMundry	3½	2		107	—
	Saugerties (USA) (HJentzsch,Germany) **3-9-2** PSchiergen	1½	3		105	—
	Widar (ALowe,Germany) **3-9-2** EvanDeKeera	nk	4		104	—
	Mojito (GER) (ALowe,Germany) **3-9-2** ASuborics	½	5		104	—
1544a⁴	**Icemoon (GER)** (HBlume,Germany) **3-9-2** THellier	3½	6		99	—
1544a⁵	**Eden Rock (GER)** (BSchutz,Germany) **3-9-2** NGrant	2	7		96	—
1544a⁶	**Happy Change (GER)** (AWohler,Germany) **3-9-2** GCarter	2½	8		92	—
	Baroon (AWohler,Germany) **3-9-2** ABoschert	7	9		82	—
1544a⁷	**Fan (GER)** (AWohler,Germany) **3-9-2** WRyan	6	10		73	—
	Uno Sobotica (GER) (ALowe,Germany) **3-9-2** KWoodburn	¾	11		72	—
	Mann o Mann (GER) (NSauer,Germany) **3-9-2** BRussell	3½	12		67	—

12 Rn

2m 24.04 (14.04) TOTE 37DM: 17DM 33DM 44DM OWNER Stall Blauer Reiter
Caitano, who was disqualified and placed second last time out, gained compensation here, justifying favouritism and running out an impressive winner. He may now to go for Deutsches Derby, and has already been installed as favourite.
San Suru (GER) put up a bold show against the impressive winner, and should find a similar event when not up against one so good.

1919a-SAN SIRO (Milan, Italy) (R-H) (Good)
Sunday June 15th

2098a PREMIO BIMBI (2-Y.O)
2-50 (2-55) **6f** £13,500.00

	Horse	Dist	Pos	SP	RR	SF
	Slaney Squire (IRE) (GColleo,Italy) **2-9-1** MLatorre	—	1		—	—
	Rambo Rally (GPacciati,Italy) **2-8-12** GUda	4	2		—	—
	Blu Carillon (IRE) (OPessi,Italy) **2-8-12** LDettori	1	3		—	—
	Frond (LMCumani) **2-8-8** GaryStevens (btn approx 8½l)		5		—	—

5 Rn

1m 10.9 (0.20 under 2y best) (2.90) TOTE 20L: 15L 24L (74L) OWNER Scuderia Andy Capp BRED Dr F. Castelfranchi
Frond dropped out steadily having raced up with the pace to halfway. A well-bred filly, she will be better for the experience.

2099a PREMIO LEGNANO (Gp 3) (3-Y.O+ F & M)
3-50 (4-14) **1m 4f** £51,251.00 (£23,492.00: £13,090.00: £6,545.00)

	Horse	Dist	Pos	SP	RR	SF
932⁹	**Tulipa (USA)** (SbinSuroor) **4-9-6** PatEddery	—	1		112	—
1157*	**Papering (IRE)** (LMCumani) **4-9-6** LDettori	nk	2		112	—
1368a³	**Sopran Mariduff** (RRossini,Italy) **3-8-5** JReid	4½	3		106	—
1199a³	**Reine Wells (IRE)** (PBary,France) **4-9-6** SGuillot	3¾	4		101	—
	Anno Luce (JHMGosden) **4-9-6** GaryStevens	3¾	5		96	—
	Robereva (IRE) (APecorano,Italy) **4-9-6** CColombi	11	6		81	—

6 Rn

2m 26.7 (6.70) TOTE 11L: 15L 11L (22L) OWNER Godolphin (NEWMARKET) BRED Fares Farm Inc
Tulipa (USA) was given an enterprising ride. Settling well in front, she quickened up in the straight and, battling on stoutly, just had enough in reserve to hold the runner-up.
1157* Papering (IRE) was caught slightly flat-footed when the winner went for home. Only half a length down entering the final furlong, she was always being held. The Lancashire Oaks is her next target.
Anno Luce dropped away tamely having tracked the winner into the straight. Formerly trained in Germany and having her first start for Gosden, she is capable of much better.

2100a GRAN PREMIO DI MILANO (Gp 1) (3-Y.O+)
4-20 (4-55) **1m 4f** £251,481.00 (£128,826.00: £75,599.00: £37,799.00)

	Horse	Dist	Pos	SP	RR	SF
	Shantou (USA) (JHMGosden) **4-9-7** LDettori (mid div: hdwy to ld over 2f out: edgd rt 1f out: drvn out)	—	1		128	—
1549a*	**Luso** (CEBrittain) **5-9-7** GaryStevens (led to ½-wy: rdn 2f out: sltly hmpd 1f out: styd on)	1¼	2		126	—
1542a³	**Taipan (IRE)** (JLDunlop) **5-9-7** PatEddery (hld up in rr: hdwy over 2f out: styd on wl fnl f: nrst fin)	½	3		126	—
922a⁵	**Strategic Choice (USA)** (PFICole) **6-9-7** TQuinn (prom: led 6f out tl over 2f out: one pce)	1	4		124	—
1549a²	**Toto le Moko (IRE)** (AVerdesi,Italy) **4-9-7** GPucciatti (in rr: n.d)	8½	5		113	—
1724a³	**Needle Gun (IRE)** (CEBrittain) **7-9-7** BDoyle (prom: rdn & wknd 3f out)	3½	6		108	—

6 Rn

2m 26.0 (6.00) TOTE 15L: 12L 18L (26L) OWNER Sheikh Mohammed (NEWMARKET) BRED Darley Stud Management Inc
Shantou (USA) was keen early on, but Dettori soon had him settled in fourth place. Coming on the outside to hit the front over two furlongs out, he quickened up well to go over a length clear, but hung right at the distance and needed to be driven out. This was a sound effort on ground which was some way faster than the official 'good'. He would be better with some cut and the King George is one of his options.
1549a* Luso posted his usual game effort. Making the running to halfway, he took up the chase when Shantou went on in the final quarter-mile. Although slightly hampered by the winner a furlong out, he was beaten on merit.
1542a Taipan (IRE) put up a cracking performance and looks more than capable of breaking his Group-race duck when he finds soft ground. Switched off in the rear, he stayed on strongly in the final two and a half furlongs and was finishing best of all.
922a Strategic Choice (USA) took up the running before the home turn, but could only plug on at the same pace when headed by the winner. These are his ideal conditions so he was a little disappointing.

1724a Needle Gun (IRE) was third into the straight but dropped away soon after. On the go since running in Dubai in early April, he looks in need of a rest.

2101a PREMIO TONY BIN (3-Y.O)
4-50 (5-30) **1m 2f** £9,642.00 (£4,243.00: £2,314.00)

				SP	RR	SF
1555a*	**Barba Papa (IRE)** (LMCumani) **3-9-2** LDettori	—	**1**		108	—
1399^{5}	**Passi d'Orlando (IRE)** (JLDunlop) **3-8-12** PatEddery	nk	**2**		104	—
1069a^{2}	**Sunny Sample (IRE)** (BGrizzetti,Italy) **3-8-12** GForte	2¾	**3**		99	—
						6 Rn

2m 2.1 (8.10) TOTE 16L: 13L 17L (33L) OWNER Giocri (NEWMARKET) BRED Rathasker Stud
1555a* Barba Papa (IRE) made all and kept on with real determination under pressure in the closing stages. Cumani will now look for a handicap for him.
1399 Passi d'Orlando (IRE) was in second place throughout but was never quite able to peg back the winner.

2102a PREMIO BERSAGLIO H'CAP (3-Y.O+)
5-20 (6-05) **6f** £32,785.00 (£14,425.00: £7,868.00)

				SP	RR	SF
	Pappa Reale (RBrogi,Italy) **4-8-8** GBietolini	—	**1**		99	—
1201a*	**Armando Carpio** (ARenzoni,Italy) **4-9-1** JacquelineFreda	nse	**2**		106	—
1552a^{2}	**How Long** (LMCumani) **4-9-0** LDettori	hd	**3**		105	—
						10 Rn

1m 8.5 (0.50) TOTE 78L: 17L 18L 12L (239L) OWNER Scuderia Archi Romani
1552a How Long was right in the firing line from the off, but was just outbattled in the last fifty yards. Although odds-on, this was a highly respectable effort as the winner broke the track record, and the runner-up was a Group Three winner on his previous start.

2053-ROYAL ASCOT (R-H) (Races 1&2 Good, Gd to sft ptches, Races 3&4 Good to soft, Races 5&6 Soft)
Friday June 20th
WEATHER: raining WIND: almost nil

2103 WINDSOR CASTLE STKS (2-Y.O) (Class B)
2-30 (2-31) **5f** £19,773.00 (£7,407.00: £3,628.50: £1,567.50: £708.75: £365.25) Stalls: Low GOING minus 0.05 sec per fur (G)

				SP	RR	SF
1619^{2}	**Asfurah (USA)** (SbinSuroor) **2-8-6** RHills(8) (lw: w ldr: led over 3f out tl over 1f out: led wl ins fnl f: r.o wl)	—	**1**	7/1^{2}	96	56
1791*	**Cortachy Castle (IRE)** (BJMeehan) **2-8-13** PatEddery(11) (lw: led over 1f: led over 1f out tl wl ins fnl f: r.o wl)	nk	**2**	11/2^{1}	102	62
1109^{6}	**Aurigny** (SDow) **2-8-8** TQuinn(12) (hld up: rdn over 1f out: unable qckn fnl f)	1¾	**3**	40/1	91	51
1812*	**Lord Kintyre** (BRMillman) **2-8-11** BDoyle(9) (lw: hld up: rdn over 1f out: one pce)	s.h	**4**	14/1	94	54
1635*	**Alfiglia** (PJMakin) **2-8-8** SSanders(1) (rdn over 2f out: hdwy over 1f out: r.o)	1¼	**5**	15/2^{3}	87	47
1310^{2}	**One Singer** (MJohnston) **2-8-11** MHills(2) (a.p: rdn over 2f out: one pce)	1	**6**	11/1	87	47
1391^{3}	**Classy Cleo (IRE)** (RHannon) **2-8-8** MRoberts(5) (swtg: a.p: hrd rdn over 1f out: sn wknd)	1½	**7**	16/1	79	39
1510*	**Minetta** (MBell) **2-8-6** MFenton(15) (hdwy over 2f out: wknd over 1f out)	2½	**8**	33/1	69	29
1669^{2}	**Shegardi** (DRLoder) **2-8-11** GaryStevens(6) (hld up: rdn over 2f out: wknd over 1f out)	½	**9**	7/1^{2}	73	33
1593*	**Contrary Mary** (GLewis) **2-8-6** MJKinane(4) (swtg: hld up: rdn over 1f out: wkng whn hung bdly rt fnl f)	2½	**10**	7/1^{2}	60	20
	Quiz Show (RHannon) **2-8-3** DaneO'Neill(14) (w'like: scope: bit bkwd: s.s: a wl bhd)	3	**11**	20/1	47	7
1310^{3}	**Vice Presidential** (TJEtherington) **2-8-11** JReid(7) (hld up: rdn over 2f out: sn wknd)	3	**12**	20/1	46	6
	Wandering Wolf (RHannon) **2-8-8** OPeslier(13) (lw: s.s: a wl bhd)	2	**13**	10/1	36	—
1653^{4}	**Lady Moll** (RBoss) **2-8-6** KFallon(10) (bhd fnl 3f)	5	**14**	20/1	18	—
				(SP 114.3%)		**14 Rn**

62.03 secs (1.83) CSF £35.73 TOTE £7.90: £3.20 £2.00 £13.60 (£26.30) Trio £365.70 OWNER Godolphin (NEWMARKET) BRED Shadwell Farm Inc
1619 Asfurah (USA) put up a very gritty display. Disputing the lead from the start, she had a tremendous battle with the runner-up in the final quarter-mile and, although Hills dropped his whip in the last one hundred yards, the combination managed to get up near the finish to give Godolphin their first two-year-old winner of the season. She will now step up to six furlongs. (7/1)
1791* Cortachy Castle (IRE), well regarded at home, seemed well suited by the underfoot conditions and ran a very big race. Disputing the lead from the start, he had a narrow advantage over the winner from below the distance but was just worried out of it in the closing stages. He is entered in a lot of the big races and should not take long to return to the winner's enclosure. (11/2)
1109 Aurigny, who came back with a throat infection after her poor run at Bath last time out, ran a sound race and was right on the heels of the front two entering the final furlong before tapped for toe. (40/1)
1812* Lord Kintyre did not run badly and chased the leaders if failing to find the necessary turn of foot from below the distance. (14/1)
1635* Alfiglia stayed on well in the last furlong and a half but never looked like getting to the principals in time. (15/2)
1310 One Singer had the rain-softened ground to contend with and, although never far away, never looked like finding another gear in the final quarter-mile. He is probably better on a sounder surface. (11/1)
Wandering Wolf (10/1: op 6/1)

2104 HARDWICKE STKS (Gp 2) (4-Y.O+) (Class A)
3-05 (3-05) **1m 4f** £74,510.99 (£28,007.55: £13,553.78: £6,012.68) Stalls: High GOING: 0.09 sec per fur (G)

				SP	RR	SF
1476^{2}	**Predappio** (SbinSuroor) **4-8-12** GaryStevens(7) (lw: hdwy 8f out: chsd ldr over 7f out: led over 3f out tl over 1f out: hrd rdn: led ins fnl f: r.o wl)	—	**1**	6/1^{2}	131	90
922a^{3}	**Pilsudski (IRE) (126)** (MRStoute) **5-9-0** MJKinane(3) (lw: hdwy over 3f out: led over 1f out tl ins fnl f: unable qckn)	½	**2**	2/1^{1}	132	91
1172^{3}	**Whitewater Affair (113)** (MRStoute) **4-8-6** OPeslier(9) (lw: a.p: rdn over 2f out: one pce)	2½	**3**	12/1	121	80
1917a^{5}	**Royal Court (IRE) (114)** (PWChapple-Hyam) **4-8-9** JReid(10) (rdn 5f out: hdwy over 1f out: one pce)	3½	**4**	14/1	119	78

				SP	RR	SF
1736^{4}	**Ela-Aristokrati (IRE) (114)** (MHTompkins) **5-8-9** RCochrane(4) (lw: s.s: rdn over 2f out: nvr nr to chal)	1	**5**	20/1	118	77
1736^{2}	**Dushyantor (USA) (120)** (HRACecil) **4-8-12** WRyan(6) (lw: no hdwy fnl 3f)	½	**6**	8/1	120	79
1323^{2}	**King Alex (110)** (RCharlton) **4-8-9** PatEddery(8) (chsd ldr over 4f: rdn over 2f out: wknd over 1f out)	1¾	**7**	$6/1^{2}$	115	74
$1365a^{7}$	**Mongol Warrior (USA)** (LordHuntingdon) **4-8-12** DHarrison(5) (a bhd)	13	**8**	33/1	101	60
	Lady Carla (122) (HRACecil) **4-8-11** KFallon(2) (a.p: rdn over 5f out: 6th & wkng whn nt clr run & snatched up 3f out)	1	**9**	$7/1^{3}$	98	57
$1363a^{3}$	**Busy Flight (116)** (BWHills) **4-8-9** MHills(1) (lw: led over 8f)	8	**10**	11/1	86	45
				(SP 115.9%)		**10 Rn**

2m 32.14 (2.14) CSF £16.58 TOTE £6.60: £2.10 £1.50 £2.60 (£5.00) Trio £25.90 OWNER Godolphin (NEWMARKET) BRED Sheikh Mohammed bin Rashid al Maktoum

1476 Predappio, who made such an encouraging reappearance behind Bosra Sham at Sandown recently, certainly had things in his favour here, a step up to a mile and a half and some cut in the ground. Sent to the front over three furlongs from home, he looked destined for second place when headed by the runner-up below the distance but he showed real grit and determination to battle his way back into the front in the last one hundred yards and give his jockey his first winner in Britain. A return trip for the King George VI and Queen Elizabeth Diamond Stakes looks likely especially if there is some give underfoot. (6/1: 7/2-13/2)

922a Pilsudski (IRE) appreciated the return to a mile and a half and the easy ground and looked set for victory as he moved up to lead below the distance. However, he had not bargained on such a tenacious rival and was worried out of it inside the final furlong. Compensation awaits. (2/1)

1172 Whitewater Affair, who goes well with some cut in the ground, was always close up but failed to find that vital turn of foot in the short home straight. (12/1)

1917a Royal Court (IRE) loves the mud and could well have done with more rain. Bustled along at least five furlongs from home, he picked up ground below the distance but could then make no further impression. (14/1: 10/1-16/1)

1736 Ela-Aristokrati (IRE) found this company on this ground too hot and, although struggling on in the closing stages, never posed a threat. He is capable of winning a Pattern race but it will probably come in Listed or Group Three company. (20/1)

1736 Dushyantor (USA) does lack acceleration at this kind of level and that was once again demonstrated here, for when the real race began in earnest turning for home, he was left for dead. (8/1: 6/1-9/1)

1323 King Alex had the ground and distance in his favour but was rather disappointing for, after playing a leading role, he had shot his bolt in the final quarter-mile. (6/1)

Lady Carla, so impressive in last year's Oaks, has been off the course with vertebrae problems since flopping in the Irish Oaks over eleven months ago. Looking fit for this return, she raced in a handy position but Fallon was already bustling her along over five furlongs from home and she was already back-pedalling when done no favours turning into the straight. Fallon reported afterwards that she gave him a fantastic ride but did not like the soft ground. (7/1)

1363a Busy Flight once again showed this soft ground is not for him and, after setting the pace, dropped tamely away when collared over three furlongs from home. A return to a sounder surface is required. (11/1)

2105 WOKINGHAM H'CAP (0-110) (3-Y.O+) (Class B)

3-45 (3-47) **6f** £48,013.40 (£17,870.60: £8,660.30: £3,636.50: £1,543.25: £705.95) Stalls: Low GOING: 0.09 sec per fur (G)

				SP	RR	SF
1772^{3}	**Selhurstpark Flyer (IRE) (94)** (JBerry) **6-8-9**(5) PRoberts(5) (b: a.p: led over 2f out tl over 1f out: hrd rdn: led wl ins fnl f: r.o wl)	—	**1**	25/1	111	88
1317^{7}	**Danetime (IRE) (91)** (NACallaghan) **3-8-4** GaryStevens(19) (swtchd lft 5f out: hrd rdn over 1f out: rapid hdwy fnl f: fin wl)	hd	**2**	$7/1^{1}$	108+	78
1148*	**Bollin Joanne (101)** (TDEasterby) **4-9-7** KFallon(4) (lw: a.p: hrd rdn over 1f out: led ins fnl f: sn hdd: unable qckn)	1	**3**	12/1	115	92
1317*	**Oggi (86)** (PJMakin) **6-8-6** RCochrane(16) (a.p: led over 1f out tl ins fnl f: one pce)	½	**4**	$10/1^{3}$	99	76
1772*	**Warning Time (98)** (BJMeehan) **4-9-4** 8x JReid(7) (rdn over 2f out: hdwy over 1f out: r.o)	nk	**5**	33/1	110	87
1590^{4}	**To the Roof (IRE) (105)** (PWHarris) **5-9-4**(7) CLowther(23) (led over 3f: hrd rdn over 1f out: one pce)	1½	**6**	33/1	113	90
1148^{9}	**King of Peru (96)** (NPLittmoden) **4-9-2** WRyan(11) (hdwy over 1f out: r.o)	1	**7**	66/1	101	78
1610^{3}	**Wildwood Flower (97)** (RHannon) **4-9-3** DaneO'Neill(14) (hdwy over 1f out: r.o)	¾	**8**	20/1	100	77
	Best Before Dawn (IRE) (95) (APO'Brien,Ireland) **6-9-1** 5x CRoche(3) (a.p: rdn over 1f out: one pce)	hd	**9**	$9/1^{2}$	98	75
1317^{6}	**Double Bounce (89)** (PJMakin) **7-8-9** DHolland(17) (hdwy & nt clr run over 1f out: nvr nrr)	s.h	**10**	12/1	92	69
1160^{2}	**Prince Babar (101)** (JEBanks) **6-9-2**(5) RMullen(8) (lw: prom over 3f)	hd	**11**	14/1	104	81
1148^{6}	**Cretan Gift (95)** (NPLittmoden) **6-9-1b** TGMcLaughlin(29) (hdwy over 2f out: hrd rdn over 1f out: wknd fnl f)	nk	**12**	66/1	97	74
1598^{2}	**Tumbleweed Ridge (94)** (BJMeehan) **4-9-0** PatEddery(10) (s.s: nvr nrr)	nk	**13**	11/1	95	72
1658*	**Albert The Bear (92)** (JBerry) **4-8-7**(5) 8x TEDurcan(21) (prom 4f)	nk	**14**	33/1	92	69
1948^{2}	**Sea-Deer (86)** (CADwyer) **8-8-6** AMcGlone(24) (prom over 4f)	s.h	**15**	20/1	86	63
1160^{10}	**Patsy Grimes (92)** (JSMoore) **7-8-12** RHughes(12) (lw: a mid div)	½	**16**	66/1	91	68
1874^{2}	**Alamein (USA) (85)** (WJHaggas) **4-8-5b** TQuinn(13) (a mid div)	3	**17**	16/1	76	53
892^{6}	**Emerging Market (99)** (JLDunlop) **5-9-5** KDarley(25) (rdn over 2f out: hdwy over 1f out: wknd fnl f)	nk	**18**	20/1	89	66
1596^{5}	**Hello Mister (91)** (TEPowell) **6-8-8**(3) PMcCabe(2) (lw: s.s: nvr nrr)	¾	**19**	33/1	79	56
942*	**Perryston View (85)** (PCalver) **5-8-5** MJKinane(26) (lw: a mid div)	hd	**20**	12/1	73	50
1148^{3}	**World Premier (99)** (CEBrittain) **4-9-5** BDoyle(20) (lw: bhd fnl 2f)	3½	**21**	25/1	77	54
1462^{3}	**Royal Aty (IRE) (106)** (PAKelleway) **3-9-5** DHarrison(9) (prom 4f)	nk	**22**	50/1	84	54
980^{6}	**Astrac (IRE) (105)** (MissGayKelleway) **6-9-11** SSanders(28) (lw: mid div over 4f)	s.h	**23**	25/1	82	59
1946^{10}	**Rushcutter Bay (89)** (TTClement) **4-8-4v**(5)ow2 GFaulkner(22) (prom 4f)	1¼	**24**	66/1	63	38
*1578**	**Bold Effort (FR) (87)** (KOCunningham-Brown) **5-8-7b** 5x MRoberts(15) (mid div over 4f)	¾	**25**	25/1	59	36
1772^{6}	**Youdontsay (84)** (TJNaughton) **5-7-13**(5) RFfrench(6) (lw: prom over 3f)	nk	**26**	25/1	55	32
1766^{11}	**Repertory (92)** (MSSaunders) **4-8-9**(3) PPMurphy(1) (s.s: a bhd)	s.h	**27**	66/1	63	40
1446*	**Mr Bergerac (IRE) (85)** (BPalling) **6-8-5** 5x TSprake(18) (bhd fnl 2f)	2	**28**	33/1	51	28
1634^{4}	**Paris Babe (88)** (DMorris) **5-8-8** NDay(27) (a bhd)	1	**29**	40/1	51	28
1948^{9}	**Hoh Returns (IRE) (88)** (MBell) **4-8-8v¹** MFenton(30) (bhd fnl 3f)	13	**30**	50/1	17	—
				(SP 137.6%)		**30 Rn**

1m 15.31 (1.31) CSF £148.05 CT £2,077.72 TOTE £31.90: £6.00 £3.10 £2.90 £1.80 (£313.30) Trio £943.50 OWNER Mr Chris Deuters (COCKERHAM) BRED Gay O'Callaghan

WEIGHT FOR AGE 3yo-7lb

STEWARDS' ENQUIRY Stevens susp.29 & 30/6/97 (excessive use of whip).

1772 Selhurstpark Flyer (IRE) goes well for his young rider and, although the combination were narrowly headed below the distance, they fought back well to regain the advantage in the closing stages. (25/1)

930 Danetime (IRE) bounced back to form. He appeared to have been set an impossible task, as he was still out the back below the distance, but came with a whirlwind finish in the final furlong and would surely have prevailed in a couple more strides. Stevens was later handed a two-day ban for excessive use of the whip. As for Danetime, he is a winner without a penalty. (7/1)
1148* Bollin Joanne lost absolutely nothing in defeat. A leading player throughout, she had just managed to get to the front inside the final furlong when passed by the winner. She has done all her winning at six furlongs. (12/1)
1317* Oggi, a stone higher than at the beginning of the season, was never far away and made his bid for glory below the distance. Collared inside the final furlong, he failed to find another gear. He has gained all six of his wins to date over six furlongs. (10/1)
1772* Warning Time had no easy task with an 8lb penalty for his recent Epsom win but nevertheless stayed on well in the last furlong and a half if finding the line always coming too soon. (33/1)
1590 To the Roof (IRE) has been running well in Listed and Group Three company recently so it is hardly surprising he has risen in the handicap. Despite being a stone higher than when last successful, he still gave a very good account of himself and took the field along until over two furlongs from home. Responding to pressure, he failed to find another gear but nevertheless struggled on. (33/1)
961 King of Peru stayed on in the last furlong and a half but it was all too late. His last victory came over seven furlongs and a return to that trip may be in his favour. (66/1)

2106 KING'S STAND STKS (Gp 2) (3-Y.O+) (Class A)

4-20 (4-21) **5f** £73,512.00 (£27,624.60: £13,362.30: £5,921.10) Stalls: Low GOING: 0.30 sec per fur (G)

				SP	RR	SF
1721a^{4}	**Don't Worry Me (IRE)** (GHenrot,France) **5-8-13** OPeslier(4) (swtg: hdwy over 1f out: led ins fnl f: r.o wl)	—	**1**	33/1	120	94
1721a*	**Titus Livius (FR)** (JEPease,France) **4-9-2** CAsmussen(2) (lw: rdn 2f out: swtchd lft over 1f out: gd hdwy fnl f: fin wl)	nk	**2**	7/1^{1}	122	96
1910a*	**Hever Golf Rose (111)** (TJNaughton) **6-8-13** PatEddery(3) (lw: a.p: hrd rdn over 1f out: ev ch ins fnl f: unable qckn)	1	**3**	7/1^{1}	116	90
1881a^{4}	**Averti (IRE) (107)** (WRMuir) **6-9-2** KFallon(8) (lw: hld up: rdn over 2f out: r.o one pce)	1	**4**	33/1	116	90
1455^{8}	**Easycall (118)** (BJMeehan) **3-8-10** MTebbutt(11) (bmpd s: a.p: hrd rdn & ev ch over 1f out: one pce)	¾	**5**	11/1	113	81
	Struggler (112) (DRLoder) **5-9-2** KDarley(15) (bit bkwd: bmpd s: a.p: hrd rdn over 1f out: one pce)	½	**6**	16/1	112	86
1590^{3}	**Rambling Bear (109)** (MBlanshard) **4-9-2** RCochrane(1) (lw: s.s: rdn & hdwy over 1f out: nt clr run ins fnl f: one pce)	s.h	**7**	12/1	112	86
1881a^{3}	**Bolshoi (IRE) (106)** (JBerry) **5-9-2b** MJKinane(17) (rdn & hdwy over 1f out: one pce)	hd	**8**	10/1^{3}	111	85
1455*	**Croft Pool (107)** (JAGlover) **6-9-2** GCarter(14) (lw: rdn over 2f out: hdwy over 1f out: nvr nrr)	nk	**9**	16/1	110	84
1766*	**Ya Malak (95)** (DNicholls) **6-9-2** AlexGreaves(13) (lw: a.p: led over 2f out tl ins fnl f: sn wknd)	½	**10**	8/1^{2}	109	83
941*	**Deep Finesse (113)** (MAJarvis) **3-8-10b** MRoberts(5) (rdn over 2f out: hdwy & nt clr run 1f out: nvr nrr)	1¼	**11**	12/1	105	73
1590^{2}	**Compton Place (112)** (JARToller) **3-8-10** SSanders(7) (led over 2f: hrd rdn over 1f out: wknd fnl f)	hd	**12**	12/1	104	72
792*	**Cathedral (IRE) (98)** (BJMeehan) **3-8-10** TQuinn(9) (lw: wnt rt s: w ldr over 2f: hrd rdn over 1f out: wknd fnl f)	¾	**13**	20/1	102	70
1881a^{5}	**Check The Band (USA)** (APO'Brien,Ireland) **3-8-10b** CRoche(12) (hdwy over 1f out: wknd fnl f)	s.h	**14**	20/1	102	70
1590*	**Almaty (IRE)** (JHMGosden) **4-9-2** GaryStevens(16) (lw: a.p: ev ch over 1f out: eased whn btn fnl f)	¾	**15**	7/1^{1}	99	73
1590^{6}	**Brave Edge (105)** (RHannon) **6-9-2** DaneO'Neill(18) (a bhd)	nk	**16**	33/1	98	72
2056^{6}	**Royale Figurine (IRE) (107)** (MJFetherston-Godley) **6-8-13** DHolland(6) (lw: bhd fnl 2f)	½	**17**	20/1	94	68
1455^{6}	**Sylva Paradise (IRE) (106)** (CEBrittain) **4-9-2** DJWhyte(10) (hmpd s: bhd fnl 2f)	3	**18**	66/1	87	61

(SP 125.5%) **18 Rn**

61.95 secs (1.75) CSF £218.69 TOTE £21.90: £5.10 £2.20 £1.70 (£38.70) Trio £50.20 OWNER Mr J. F. Gribomont BRED Irish National Stud Co Ltd
WEIGHT FOR AGE 3yo-6lb
1721a Don't Worry Me (IRE), who finished one and a half lengths behind the runner-up at Chantilly last time out, just managed to reverse the form and give her trainer the biggest the win of his career. Coming through to lead inside the final furlong, she found the line only just coming in time. (33/1)
1721a* Titus Livius (FR) had it all to do at the back of the field a quarter of a mile from home and, once his jockey got a run from him in the final furlong, the colt came flying through and would surely have prevailed in a couple more strides. (7/1)
1910a* Hever Golf Rose ran yet another tremendous race. In the front line throughout, she probably got her head in front for a few strides inside the final furlong before the winner went by. She has now won over £600,000 in prizemoney and will now head for the Group Three Holstein Trophy at Hamburg in Germany, a race she won in 1995 and finished second in last year. (7/1)
1881a Averti (IRE) gave a good account of himself. Chasing the leaders, he was being bustled along at halfway but, to his credit, stayed on nicely in the closing stages. (33/1)
Easycall ran much better here and had every chance below the distance before tapped for toe. (11/1)
Struggler had a stiff task on this reappearance and did not look fully wound up. Nevertheless, he was never far away and kept plodding on in the final quarter-mile. (16/1)
1590 Rambling Bear did not have a penalty to shoulder here. Picking up ground from below the distance, he did not get the best of runs inside the final furlong but it made little difference to his chances. A return to six furlongs would surely help. (12/1)
1766* Ya Malak (8/1: 6/1-9/1)
1590 Compton Place (12/1: op 8/1)
1590* Almaty (IRE) found this rain all against him and reportedly lost a shoe, so in the circumstances did not do badly. Still in with every chance below the distance, he then tired and his jockey eased him considerably in the final furlong when all chance had evaporated. He is a very useful performer and back on a fast surface he will not take long to regain the winning thread. (7/1: 9/2-8/1)

2107 KING EDWARD VII STKS (Gp 2) (3-Y.O C & G) (Class A)

4-55 (5-02) **1m 4f** £73,384.00 (£27,637.20: £13,418.60: £6,000.20) Stalls: High GOING: 0.30 sec per fur (G)

				SP	RR	SF
1159^{4}	**Kingfisher Mill (USA) (112)** (MrsJCecil) **3-8-8** PatEddery(2) (lw: mde all: clr wl over 1f out: r.o wl)	—	**1**	9/4^{1}	123	61
788*	**Palio Sky (102)** (JLDunlop) **3-8-8** MJKinane(1) (lw: a.p: chsd wnr fnl 2f: no imp)	8	**2**	9/2^{3}	112	50
1553a^{D}	**Musical Dancer (USA) (105)** (EALDunlop) **3-8-8** KFallon(3) (n.m.r 2f out: nvr nr to chal)	1½	**3**	13/2	110	48
1553a^{3}	**Panama City (USA) (107)** (PWChapple-Hyam) **3-8-8** JReid(6) (chsd wnr 10f: wknd over 1f out)	3½	**4**	5/2^{2}	106	44
1276*	**Solo Mio (IRE) (98)** (BWHills) **3-8-8** MHills(4) (lw: hld up: rdn 3f out: wknd over 2f out)	3	**5**	9/2^{3}	102	40

(SP 109.0%) **5 Rn**

2m 38.36 (8.36) CSF £11.05 TOTE £2.50: £1.40 £2.40 (£6.80) OWNER Lord Howard de Walden (NEWMARKET) BRED Lord Howard de Walden
1159 Kingfisher Mill (USA) is certainly going the right way and, making all the running, forged clear in the final quarter-mile for a very convincing victory. Described as a big baby by his trainer, he is very tough but very lazy according to Eddery, who believes this is his optimum trip. The King George VI and Queen Elizabeth Diamond Stakes is a possibility. (9/4)
788* Palio Sky struggled into second place a quarter of a mile from home but had no hope with the winner. (9/2: 3/1-5/1)

1553a Musical Dancer (USA), who disgraced himself in the Italian Derby, struggled on in the straight without ever threatening to get into it. (13/2)
1553a Panama City (USA), who has won in this ground, raced in second place, but he was collared for that position two furlongs from home and soon capitulated. (5/2)
1276* Solo Mio (IRE) took closer order from Swinley Bottom but had been hung out to dry early in the straight. (9/2: op 7/1)

2108 QUEEN ALEXANDRA STKS (4-Y.O+) (Class B)

5-30 (5-36) **2m 6f 34y** £19,164.00 (£7,176.00: £3,513.00: £1,515.00: £682.50: £349.50) Stalls: High GOING: 0.30 sec per fur (G)

Form	Horse / details	Dist	Pos	SP	RR	SF
1027^{4}	**Canon Can (USA) (97)** (HRACecil) **4-9-1** KFallon(10) (lw: bdly hmpd 7f out: gd hdwy 3f out: led 2f out: all out)	—	**1**	8/1	106	62
1027^{5}	**Old Rouvel (USA) (98)** (DJGMurraySmith) **6-9-0** MJKinane(6) (nt clr run 7f out: hdwy over 3f out: edgd rt 2f out: ev ch fnl 2f: r.o)	nk	**2**	13/2^{2}	105	61
	Daraydan (IRE) (102) (MCPipe) **5-9-0** RHughes(9) (a.p: led over 5f out to 2f out: sn wknd)	27	**3**	11/2^{1}	85	41
	Cuff Link (IRE) (104) (MajorWRHern) **7-9-0** PaulEddery(13) (hdwy over 5f out: chsd ldr over 3f out tl over 2f out: wkng whn n.m.r 2f out)	1½	**4**	10/1	84	40
1252^{3}	**Aardwolf (50)** (CPEBrooks) **6-9-0v^{1}** TQuinn(11) (a.p: led over 8f out tl over 5f out: wknd 3f out)	3	**5**	16/1	82	38
2014^{14}	**Inchcailloch (IRE) (85)** (JSKing) **8-9-0** GCarter(1) (rdn & hdwy over 5f out: wknd over 3f out)	20	**6**	20/1	68	24
	Pleasure Shared (IRE) (PJHobbs) **9-9-0** GaryStevens(14) (bit bkwd: s.s & sddle slipped: sn wl bhd: mod late hdwy: t.o)	dist	**7**	16/1	—	—
1778^{4}	**General Assembly (IRE) (90)** (HRACecil) **5-9-0** WRyan(8) (lw: prom tl wknd 7f out: t.o)	1¾	**8**	10/1	—	—
1491*	**Premier Night (81)** (SDow) **4-8-7** JReid(2) (bhd fnl 7f: t.o)	3	**9**	25/1	—	—
	Speed to Lead (IRE) (87) (MissGayKelleway) **5-8-9** PatEddery(3) (lw: led tl over 8f out: wknd 6f out: t.o)	1½	**10**	7/1^{3}	—	—
	French Holly (USA) (FMurphy) **6-9-0** RCochrane(4) (lw: bhd fnl 7f: t.o)	1	**11**	12/1	—	—
1319^{2}	**Bahamian Sunshine (USA) (96)** (RAkehurst) **6-9-0** OPeslier(7) (rdn 12f out: bhd fnl 8f: t.o fnl 7f)	25	**12**	11/2^{1}	—	—
	Nazmi (IRE) (PO'Leary,Ireland) **5-9-0** CRoche(5) (dwlt: a bhd: t.o fnl 8f)	½	**13**	33/1	—	—

(SP 116.9%) **13 Rn**

5m 7.37 (17.37) CSF £51.39 TOTE £9.40: £3.70 £2.80 £2.60 (£43.50) Trio £84.20 OWNER Canon (Anglia) O A Ltd (NEWMARKET) BRED Elkay Stables

1027 Canon Can (USA) was lame after working on Tuesday having trodden on a shoe and reportedly having had part of a hoof cut away, which makes this performance even more commendable. In the race itself, he also appeared to have no luck for he was badly hampered as the field swung out of Swinley Bottom and moved over to the outside rail. Making significant headway turning for home, he struck the front a quarter of a mile out and, in a tremendous battle with the runner-up, just prevailed. He will need a good rest to get over this energy-sapping run. (8/1: 6/1-9/1)
1027 Old Rouvel (USA) looked as if this might be his day as he threw down a very determined challenge in the final quarter-mile. However, getting his head in front is a real problem for him and, although doing nothing wrong, he just failed. He is notoriously difficult to win with and his record now stands at two wins from twenty-two starts. (13/2)
Daraydan (IRE), winner of three Novice Hurdles this winter, was having his first run on the Flat since last August. Moving to the front over five furlongs from home, he was collared a quarter of a mile out and soon tired in these very testing conditions. (11/2)
Cuff Link (IRE), winner of this race in 1994 and 1995, missed last year's event after being cast in his box two days before the race. Making his first appearance since, although he reportedly went well in a racecourse gallop at Newbury two weeks ago, he was not helped by the soft ground but still ran well. Moving up to take second place over three furlongs from home, he was collared for that position early in the straight and then tired. He has done all his winning on a fast surface. (10/1)
1252 Aardwolf certainly had a severe test here and moved to the front running into Swinley Bottom. Collared over five furlongs from home, he was out on his feet three furlongs from the finish. (16/1)
2014 Inchcailloch (IRE), who disappointed in the Ascot Stakes on Tuesday, was rousted along to take closer order over five furlongs from home but his exertions on Tuesday had taken their toll over three furlongs from home. (20/1)

T/Jkpt: Not won; £242,983.62 to Ascot 21/6/97. T/Plpt: £212.60 (670.54 Tckts). T/Qdpt: £47.50 (149.23 Tckts) AK/IM

1557-AYR (L-H) (Good)
Friday June 20th

WEATHER: overcast WIND: slt against

2109 AYR APPRENTICE (S) H'CAP (0-60) (3-Y.O+) (Class G)

2-10 (2-11) **1m** £2,374.00 (£664.00: £322.00) Stalls: Low GOING minus 0.14 sec per fur (G)

Form	Horse / details	Dist	Pos	SP	RR	SF
1560^{2}	**Running Green (58)** (DMoffatt) **6-9-9v**(5) TSiddall(6) (b: a.p: qcknd to ld ins fnl f: all out)	—	**1**	7/2^{1}	68	47
1993^{4}	**Miletrian City (40)** (JBerry) **4-8-5b**(5) SBuckley(11) (lw: in tch: hdwy & swtchd over 1f out: r.o wl towards fin)	hd	**2**	9/1	50	29
2033^{6}	**Shontaine (53)** (MJohnston) **4-9-9** KSked(5) (chsd ldrs: led over 2f out tl ins fnl f: no ex)	1½	**3**	6/1^{3}	60	39
1944^{10}	**Maurangi (29)** (BWMurray) **6-7-13** KimberleyHart(1) (rr div: hdwy 3f out: styd on: nvr able to chal)	1¾	**4**	9/1	32	11
1613^{4}	**Seconds Away (32)** (JSGoldie) **6-7-11**(5) JMcAuley(10) (lw: bhd: brought wd st: r.o fnl 2f)	1¾	**5**	10/1	32	11
1849^{3}	**Morocco (IRE) (58)** (MRChannon) **8-10-0** AEddery(9) (bhd: hdwy 3f out: nvr rchd ldrs)	1¼	**6**	5/1^{2}	55	34
1754^{14}	**Efipetite (30)** (NBycroft) **4-8-0** IonaWands(3) (led tl hdd & wknd over 2f out)	5	**7**	33/1	17	—
1291^{7}	**David James' Girl (37)** (ABailey) **5-8-2**(5) JennyBenson(2) (b: bhd: hdwy 3f out: no imp fnl 2f)	2½	**8**	12/1	19	—
1631^{10}	**Silent System (IRE) (26)** (DWChapman) **4-7-5b^{1}**(5) PBradley(7) (s.i.s: outpcd & bhd tl styd on fnl f)	¾	**9**	12/1	7	—
1993^{8}	**Cascatelle Bleue (IRE) (55)** (MHTompkins) **4-9-6v**(5) PClarke(12) (chsd ldrs tl wknd 3f out)	4	**10**	25/1	28	7
1467^{10}	**Fisiostar (33)** (MDods) **4-7-12b**(5)ow3 PFredericks(4) (prom tl wknd 2f out)	½	**11**	10/1	5	—
1838^{11}	**Ragtime Cowgirl (30)** (DANolan) **4-7-9**(5) NPollard(8) (chsd ldrs tl wknd over 3f out)	3½	**12**	33/1	—	—

(SP 116.5%) **12 Rn**

1m 42.58 (5.18) CSF £30.82 CT £167.52 TOTE £4.10: £1.30 £4.10 £2.40 (£22.30) Trio £24.80 OWNER Die-Hard Racing Club (CARTMEL)
BRED Mount Coote Stud
LONG HANDICAP Silent System (IRE) 7-7
No bid
1560 Running Green, who is running consistently well at present, always looked likely to win this but in the end the line came just in time. (7/2)
1993 Miletrian City is fast coming to hand and, in another stride, this would have been his. (9/1)
2033 Shontaine has never won over quite this far and, despite a gallant effort, the trip just proved beyond him. (6/1: op 4/1)
1128 Maurangi has not won for three seasons but he did show some signs of coming back to form here. (9/1)
1613 Seconds Away ran reasonably but he was never in danger of losing his maiden tag. (10/1)

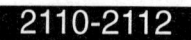

1849 Morocco (IRE) runs when in the mood and was never fully co-operating this time. (5/1: 3/1-11/2)

2110 BELLEISLE MEDIAN AUCTION MAIDEN STKS (2-Y.O) (Class E)

2-45 (2-47) **6f** £3,054.25 (£919.00: £444.50: £207.25) Stalls: High GOING minus 0.14 sec per fur (G)

				SP	RR	SF
	Aix En Provence (USA) (MJohnston) **2-9-0** JWeaver(1) (w'like: leggy:scope: trckd ldrs: qcknd to ld wl over 1f out: shkn up & sn clr)	—	1	3/1[1]	85+	35
1328[4]	**Prix Star** (CWFairhurst) **2-9-0** LCharnock(2) (lw: w ldr: effrt 2f out: r.o: nt pce of wnr)	3½	2	3/1[1]	76	26
1819[4]	**Fundance** (MDods) **2-9-0** DaleGibson(7) (lw: hld up: effrt & swtchd 2f out: edgd lft & nt qckn)	1¼	3	4/1[2]	72	22
1669[6]	**Inshallah** (MartinTodhunter) **2-8-9** NConnorton(5) (nt clr run to ½-wy: swtchd & styd on steadily appr fnl f)	1¼	4	20/1[3]	64+	14
1510[6]	**Quiz Master** (EWeymes) **2-9-0** GHind(3) (led over 4f: sn rdn & btn)	¾	5	3/1[1]	67	17
	Thorntoun Belle (IRE) (JSGoldie) **2-8-6**(3) PFessey(8) (unf: sn outpcd & bhd)	4	6	33/1	51	1
	Globe Raider (JJO'Neill) **2-9-0** ACulhane(4) (unf: scope: chsd ldrs over 3f: sn outpcd)	3½	7	50/1	47	—
	Durgams Delight (IRE) (BWMurray) **2-8-9** VHalliday(6) (leggy: unf: bit bkwd: unruly leaving paddock: swvd lft s & uns rdr)		U	50/1	—	—

(SP 106.6%) **8 Rn**

1m 13.38 (3.58) CSF £9.37 TOTE £2.20: £1.50 £1.60 £1.30 (£4.80) OWNER Featherstone, Bird (MIDDLEHAM) BRED Albatroz, Schumer & Schwartz

Aix En Provence (USA), a very fit-looking newcomer, went really well during the race and settled it in a few strides approaching the final furlong. The opposition may not have been much but the way he beat them had to be admired. (3/1: 2/1-4/1)

1328 Prix Star went well on the bridle but proved a shade disappointing off it and only ran on when passed by the winner. (3/1)

1819 Fundance still did not look fully wound up and again showed signs of greenness, and obviously has more to give when he realises what the game is about. (4/1)

1669 Inshallah was running into the back of another runner for the first half of the race and was then given a sympathetic ride. Some irmprovement looks likely. (20/1)

1510 Quiz Master failed to impress on looks and ran moderately and seems to be going the wrong way at the moment. (3/1: 5/2-4/1)

Thorntoun Belle (IRE) looked as though she had done plenty of work but she failed to show any sparkle. (33/1)

2111 BEN H'CAP (0-85) (4-Y.O+) (Class D)

3-20 (3-21) **5f** £3,473.50 (£1,048.00: £509.00: £239.50) Stalls: High GOING minus 0.14 sec per fur (G)

				SP	RR	SF
1946*	**Squire Corrie (78)** (DWChapman) **5-9-7**[7x] ACulhane(2) (lw: trckd ldr: led 2f out: pushed out)	—	1	6/4[1]	88	46
1766[12]	**That Man Again (85)** (SCWilliams) **5-10-0** JWeaver(9) (lw: a chsng ldrs: rdn 2f out: edgd lft: r.o)	1	2	7/1[2]	92	50
1865[10]	**Rich Glow (53)** (NBycroft) **6-7-10** LCharnock(5) (lw: bhd: hdwy whn nt clr run & swtchd 1f out: r.o ins fnl f)	hd	3	8/1[3]	60	18
2033[8]	**Garnock Valley (78)** (JBerry) **7-9-7b** GHind(4) (sn outpcd & bhd: hdwy over 1f out: styng on whn hmpd ins fnl f: fin 5th: 1¼l: plcd 4th)	2	4	11/1	78	36
1835[10]	**Johayro (61)** (JSGoldie) **4-7-11**(7) JMcAuley(3) (led 3f: edgd lft u.p & nt qckn: fin 4th: 2l: plcd 5th)	1¼	5	20/1	57	15
2033[7]	**Pallium (IRE) (57)** (DANolan) **9-7-9**(5)ow4 KSked(7) (spd 3f: rdn & one pce)	¾	6	25/1	51	5
1766[7]	**Laurel Delight (85)** (JBerry) **7-9-9**(5) SCopp(1) (prom tl outpcd fnl 2f)	nk	7	8/1[3]	78	36
1865*	**Ramsey Hope (59)** (CWFairhurst) **4-8-2v** NKennedy(6) (lw: chsd ldrs tl outpcd after 2f: n.d after)	¾	8	7/1[2]	49	7
2032[3]	**Leading Princess (IRE) (53)** (MissLAPerratt) **6-7-7b**(3) PFessey(8) (chsd ldrs: rdn ½-wy: sn btn)	1¾	9	25/1	38	—

(SP 108.0%) **9 Rn**

59.64 secs (2.64) CSF £9.42 CT £47.82 TOTE £2.10: £1.20 £2.20 £1.80 (£8.60) Trio £36.50 OWNER Miss N. F. Thesiger (YORK) BRED Whitsbury Manor Stud

LONG HANDICAP Pallium (IRE) 7-2 Leading Princess (IRE) 7-7

STEWARDS' ENQUIRY McAuley susp. 29/6/97 (careless riding).

1946* Squire Corrie gets better with each run and was always in command here. (6/4: evens-13/8)

1034 That Man Again ran moderately albeit in a hot race last time when wearing blinkers. He was without them again here and tended to hang in the closing stages. (7/1)

1865 Rich Glow, back on his favourite track, ran really well and, but for being hampered, would have been a good bit closer. (8/1)

1561 Garnock Valley, completely outpaced early on, then picked up well in the closings stages only to run into trouble. Given soft ground, he could be well worth keeping in mind. (11/1: 7/1-12/1)

1835 Pallium (IRE) keeps running reasonably but, up with the pace these days, he used to be at his best when dropped out. (25/1)

2112 E.B.F. MAIDEN STKS (2-Y.O) (Class D)

3-55 (3-56) **7f** £3,649.00 (£1,102.00: £536.00: £253.00) Stalls: Low GOING minus 0.14 sec per fur (G)

				SP	RR	SF
1510[2]	**Winsome George** (CWFairhurst) **2-9-0** NKennedy(3) (hld up: hmpd & outpcd ½-wy: qcknd to ld ins fnl f: r.o wl)	—	1	5/1[2]	77	20
1396[10]	**Hogaif (IRE)** (JHMGosden) **2-9-0** GHind(4) (cl up: led over 2f out tl ins fnl f: nt qckn)	3	2	5/1[2]	70	13
1978[3]	**Lakeland Pride (IRE)** (PDEvans) **2-9-0** JFEgan(6) (lw: hld up: hdwy on outside ent st: ev ch 2f out: kpt on u.p)	s.h	3	8/1[3]	70	13
	Love Academy (MJohnston) **2-9-0** JWeaver(5) (wl grwn: lw: trckd ldrs: ev ch 2f out: hrd drvn appr fnl f: no ex)	4	4	1/2[1]	61+	4
1873[4]	**Clermont City (IRE)** (PWChapple-Hyam) **2-8-11**(3) RHavlin(1) (led tl hdd over 2f out: sn wknd)	4	5	16/1	52	—
	Crosby Don (EWeymes) **2-9-0** LCharnock(2) (w'like: scope: bit bkwd: s.i.s: shkn up & sn chsng ldrs: wknd over 2f out)	6	6	66/1	38	—

(SP 118.5%) **6 Rn**

1m 30.12 (5.72) CSF £28.41 TOTE £6.40: £2.40 £2.30 (£16.00) OWNER Mr C. D. Barber-Lomax (MIDDLEHAM) BRED Blue Blood Investments

1510 Winsome George has been crying out for this trip and won this in tremenous style. He will appreciate further yet. (5/1)

Hogaif (IRE) looked fit and showed a fair bit of improvement this time, and a run-of-the-mill event should come his way. (5/1: op 3/1)

1978 Lakeland Pride (IRE) was always having to race wide but still had his chances and did keep struggling on. (8/1)

Love Academy is a big sort who came with a reputation to match but, after looking to be going well, he failed to produce anything when ridden. There is obviously more ability there is he can be persuaded. (1/2)

1873 Clermont City (IRE) helped set the race up but looked very slow when tackled approaching the last quarter-mile. (16/1)

Crosby Don is a useful-looking sort but was badly in need of this and blew up. (66/1)

2113 DALMILLING H'CAP (0-85) (3-Y.O) (Class D)

4-30 (4-30) **1m 1f** £3,610.00 (£1,090.00: £530.00: £250.00) Stalls: Low GOING minus 0.14 sec per fur (G)

Last	Horse / details	Dist	Pos	SP	RR	SF
1301[2]	**Can Can Lady (77)** (MJohnston) **3-8-13** JWeaver(3) (trckd ldr: led wl over 1f out: shkn up & r.o wl)	—	1	100/30[3]	87	58
1146[8]	**Stone Flower (USA) (83)** (PWChapple-Hyam) **3-9-2**(3) RHavlin(4) (led: qcknd over 3f out: hdd wl over 1f out: kpt on)	2	2	11/1	89	60
1833*	**Neronian (IRE) (71)** (BWHills) **3-8-4**(3) 5x JDSmith(6) (lw: hld up: effrt over 3f out: styd on: no imp)	5	3	3/1[2]	69	40
1670[4]	**Brave Montgomerie (81)** (MissLAPerratt) **3-9-3** ACulhane(5) (hld up & bhd: effrt over 3f out: nvr able to chal)	¾	4	9/1	77	48
1582[3]	**Mystique Air (IRE) (70)** (EWeymes) **3-8-6** LCharnock(1) (prom tl outpcd fnl 2½f)	4	5	16/1	59	30
741[6]	**Minersville (USA) (85)** (JHMGosden) **3-9-7** GHind(2) (hdwy to trck ldrs 6f out: rdn & wl outpcd fnl 3f)	6	6	7/4[1]	63	34

(SP 108.7%) **6 Rn**

1m 53.56 (1.69 under best) (3.06) CSF £30.98 TOTE £4.30: £2.20 £2.60 (£18.90) OWNER Mr A. W. Robinson (MIDDLEHAM) BRED Godolphin Management Co Ltd

1301 Can Can Lady is a tough and consistent sort and, once she hit the front, she was always finding plenty. (100/30)
507 Stone Flower (USA), a rather edgy filly, was allowed to stride on here and to give her credit she did respond to pressure when passed. (11/1: 5/1-12/1)
1833* Neronian (IRE) had his limitations exposed this time and looked well short of pace. (3/1: 2/1-7/2)
1670 Brave Montgomerie was given a lot to do and never got in a blow, and is worth another chance. (9/1)
1582 Mystique Air (IRE) failed to impress on looks and, trying her longest trip to date, ran moderately, stopping quickly in the last two furlongs. (16/1)
524* Minersville (USA), on looks, would have picked this lot up and carried them, but his performance was moderate to say the least and he looks to have lost the thread for the time being. (7/4)

2114 AYR BEACH MAIDEN H'CAP (0-70) (3-Y.O+) (Class E)

5-05 (5-05) **1m 5f 13y** £2,956.75 (£889.00: £429.50: £199.75) Stalls: Low GOING minus 0.14 sec per fur (G)

Last	Horse / details	Dist	Pos	SP	RR	SF
1763[10]	**Ledgendry Line (70)** (MrsMReveley) **4-10-0** ACulhane(5) (hld up & bhd: stdy hdwy over 2f out: led ins fnl f: comf)	—	1	5/2[1]	83	46
1795[3]	**Winnebago (46)** (CWThornton) **4-8-4** GHind(1) (led & sn clr: stdd appr st: qcknd over 3f out: hdd & no ch w wnr ins fnl f)	3	2	3/1[2]	55	18
1574[3]	**Indigo Dawn (54)** (MJohnston) **3-7-11** LCharnock(6) (chsd ldr tl outpcd ent st: kpt on wl fnl 2f)	2	3	5/1[3]	61	9
1795[6]	**Advance East (47)** (MDods) **5-8-5** JFEgan(4) (hld up & bhd: hdwy to chse ldr ent st: hrd drvn 2f out: sn btn)	1½	4	12/1	52	15
1042[5]	**Fanadiyr (IRE) (40)** (JSGoldie) **5-7-9**(3) PFessey(3) (sn trckng ldrs: effrt ent st: sn btn)	3½	5	20/1	41	4
1742[2]	**Autumn Time (IRE) (65)** (PWChapple-Hyam) **3-8-5**(3) RHavlin(2) (chsd ldrs: outpcd 7f out: wknd over 3f out)	3	6	3/1[2]	62	10
1511[14]	**Rattle (42)** (DANolan) **4-7-9**(5)ow4 KSked(7) (effrt appr st: rdn & wknd 3f out)	nk	7	100/1	39?	—

(SP 108.7%) **7 Rn**

2m 53.82 (9.02) CSF £8.33 TOTE £3.50: £2.90 £1.80 (£8.10) OWNER The Home & Away Partnership (SALTBURN) BRED W. R. Lewis
LONG HANDICAP Rattle 6-11
WEIGHT FOR AGE 3yo-15lb

1398 Ledgendry Line, much better suited by the strong pace here, came from behind. Kept on the bridle, he did it nicely to show that when things go his way, he is quite useful. (5/2)
1795 Winnebago was given a cracking ride but, despite this, found the winner in a different league. He deserves to pick up a race. (3/1)
1574 Indigo Dawn, not the easiest of rides, was trying her longest trip to date here and ran as though she will get further. (5/1)
1795 Advance East likes to do it all on the bridle and, once he came off it approaching the last quarter-mile, he soon gave up. (12/1)
Fanadiyr (IRE) had little form to recommend him and, once the race began in the home straight, he soon dropped away. (20/1)
1742 Autumn Time (IRE) ran a stinker and was beaten before the home turn and was obviously out of sorts. (3/1: 7/4-100/30)

T/Plpt: £77.20 (102.81 Tckts). T/Qdpt: £18.30 (25.91 Tckts) AA

1926-GOODWOOD (R-H) (St crse Soft, Rnd crse Good to soft)

Friday June 20th

WEATHER: unsettled WIND: fresh half against

2115 BROOKLANDS ANNIVERSARY APPRENTICE H'CAP (0-70) (3-Y.O+) (Class E)

6-30 (6-31) **6f** £4,012.50 (£1,200.00: £575.00: £262.50) Stalls: Low GOING: 0.18 sec per fur (G)

Last	Horse / details	Dist	Pos	SP	RR	SF
1483[13]	**Arnie (IRE) (38)** (JRPoulton) **5-7-5b**[1](5) RBrisland(2) (racd stands side: rdn & lost pl over 3f out: rallied over 1f out: str run to ld wl ins fnl f)	—	1	33/1	48	30
1849[4]	**Justinianus (IRE) (44)** (JJBridger) **5-7-11**(5)ow4 DavidO'Neill(4) (chsd ldr: swtchd lft over 1f out: led ins fnl f: sn hdd)	1¼	2	4/1[2]	51	29
1505*	**Stand Tall (60)** (LadyHerries) **5-8-13**(5) PDoe(13) (hld up: hdwy over 2f out: ev ch over 1f out: nt qckn ins fnl f)	1¼	3	7/2[1]	63	45
1594[7]	**Half Tone (55)** (RMFlower) **5-8-10b**(3) GMilligan(10) (hld up: hdwy over 1f out: r.o ins fnl f)	½	4	9/2[3]	57	39
1509[7]	**Tachycardia (39)** (RJO'Sullivan) **5-7-6**(5)ow1 SCarson(5) (led: clr over 2f out: hdd ins fnl f)	nk	5	14/1	40	21
1925[6]	**Saxon Bay (58)** (KOCunningham-Brown) **5-9-2** TEDurcan(12) (hld up: hdwy over 1f out: one pce fnl f)	1¾	6	16/1	55	37
1969[6]	**Invocation (55)** (GLMoore) **10-8-13** GayeHarwood(9) (hld up: hdwy 2f out: wknd ins fnl f)	1¼	7	14/1	48	30
855[11]	**Primelta (48)** (RAkehurst) **4-8-1**(5) PFitzsimons(3) (prom over 3f)	s.h	8	14/1	41	23
1848[5]	**Friendly Brave (USA) (70)** (MissGayKelleway) **7-10-0** RMullen(6) (hld up: hrd rdn & hdwy over 1f out: wknd fnl f)	nk	9	9/2[3]	62	44
1620*	**Mister Raider (49)** (EAWheeler) **5-8-7b** ADaly(7) (hld up: rdn over 1f out: wknd fnl f)	1	10	8/1	39	21
1920[8]	**Coastguards Hero (52)** (MDIUsher) **4-8-3**(7) JBosley(14) (s.s: a bhd: t.o)	19	11	20/1	—	—

(SP 123.3%) **11 Rn**

1m 14.42 (4.62) CSF £153.66 CT £561.08 TOTE £35.20: £8.50 £1.30 £1.40 (£56.70) Trio £83.70 OWNER Mr Mike Culling (LEWES) BRED St Simon Foundation
LONG HANDICAP Tachycardia 7-6 Arnie (IRE) 6-12

OFFICIAL EXPLANATION Arnie (IRE): regarding the improvement in form compared with the gelding's previous performance, the trainer reported that the gelding benefited from the softer surface and from the first-time blinkers.

855 Arnie (IRE) found the combination of first-time blinkers and racing under the stands' rails doing the trick. Who knows, he might even be back. (33/1)
1849 Justinianus (IRE), dropped 6lb, was due to go back up 6lb tomorrow. (4/1)
1505* Stand Tall, dropping back from seven, found the soft ground putting more of an emphasis on stamina. (7/2)
1419 Half Tone would probably have preferred faster ground. (9/2)
339 Tachycardia, 4lb out of the handicap, could not quite last home in the rain-softened going. (14/1: 12/1-20/1)
1925 Saxon Bay was due to come down 7lb in future handicaps. (16/1)
490 Invocation (14/1: op 8/1)
1848 Friendly Brave (USA) (9/2: op 3/1)

2116 LUFTHANSA CARGO MAIDEN STKS (3-Y.O+) (Class D)
7-00 (7-02) **1m 1f** £3,687.50 (£1,100.00: £525.00: £237.50) Stalls: High GOING: 0.34 sec per fur (G)

				SP	RR	SF
1591[2]	**Doyella (IRE) (84)** (DRLoder) **3-8-7** KDarley(3) (lw: mde all: clr over 2f out: easily)	—	1	8/13[1]	79+	39
	Viburnum (AGFoster) **3-8-7** TSprake(6) (lengthy: bhd: rdn over 3f out: styd on fnl 2f: no ch w wnr)	10	2	14/1	61	21
1499[3]	**Blowing Away (IRE)** (MHTompkins) **3-8-7** DBiggs(4) (s.i.s: sn prom: chsd wnr fnl 6f: no imp fnl 3f)	½	3	11/4[2]	60	20
2008[22]	**Snow Carnival** (LadyHerries) **4-9-9** GDuffield(2) (chsd wnr 3f: rdn 5f out: wknd fnl f)	7	4	10/1[3]	53	24
2008[20]	**Tedross** (JRPoulton) **6-9-6**(3) AWhelan(7) (lw: prom over 5f: t.o)	23	5	33/1	12	—
	Ishmael (GLMoore) **4-9-9** AClark(8) (w'like: s.s: t.o fnl 4f)	dist	6	20/1	—	—
				(SP 112.0%)		**6 Rn**

2m 1.95 (8.95) CSF £10.19 TOTE £1.80: £1.30 £2.30 (£5.90) OWNER Mr Saeed Manana (NEWMARKET) BRED Alan Dargan
WEIGHT FOR AGE 3yo-11lb
1591 Doyella (IRE), described as a good galloper, revelled in the soft going. (8/13: 4/9-4/6)
Viburnum, out of an unraced sister to useful stayer Warm Feeling, found the ground putting the emphasis on stamina in the later stages over this inadequate trip. (14/1)
1499 Blowing Away (IRE) got very tired in the testing ground and just lost second place. (11/4)
Snow Carnival was another to become leg-weary in the stamina-sapping going. (10/1)

2117 OMEGA DYNAMIC H'CAP (0-85) (3-Y.O+) (Class D)
7-30 (7-35) **1m** £5,872.50 (£1,755.00: £840.00: £382.50) Stalls: High GOING: 0.34 sec per fur (G)

				SP	RR	SF
1878*	**Ca'd'oro (53)** (GBBalding) **4-7-10** NVarley(8) (hld up: pushed along & hdwy over 4f out: led over 1f out: rdn out)	—	1	7/4[1]	65	47
1442[10]	**Artful Dane (IRE) (76)** (MJHeaton-Ellis) **5-9-5v** AClark(4) (a.p: led & edgd rt 2f out: hdd over 1f out: nt qckn)	1½	2	10/1	85	67
1622[4]	**The Executor (64)** (RJO'Sullivan) **7-8-7** SSanders(2) (hld up: hdwy over 1f out: styd on fnl f)	6	3	10/1	61	43
791[10]	**Proud Monk (65)** (GLMoore) **4-8-5v**(3) AWhelan(9) (hld up: nt clr run on ins & swtchd lft over 2f out: no hdwy)	1¼	4	10/1	60	42
841[7]	**Nichol Fifty (72)** (MHTompkins) **3-8-5** DBiggs(5) (nvr trbld ldrs)	1	5	14/1	65	37
1016[8]	**Stone Ridge (IRE) (83)** (RHannon) **5-9-12** DaneO'Neill(7) (lw: a.p: led wl over 2f out: sn hdd: wknd over 1f out)	1¼	6	4/1[2]	73	55
1682[4]	**Tassili (IRE) (70)** (LadyHerries) **4-8-13** KDarley(10) (plld hrd: prom over 5f)	9	7	7/1[3]	42	24
1739[18]	**Orange Place (IRE) (77)** (TJNaughton) **6-9-6** TQuinn(1) (led over 5f: wknd qckly: t.o)	24	8	4/1[2]	1	—
1598[5]	**Rock Falcon (IRE) (85)** (LadyHerries) **4-9-9**(5) GMilligan(3) (unruly bef s: ref to r: tk no part)		R	11/1	—	—
				(SP 131.1%)		**9 Rn**

1m 43.19 (5.99) CSF £22.91 CT £143.37 TOTE £3.30: £1.50 £3.10 £2.00 (£17.30) Trio £195.60 OWNER Miss B. Swire (ANDOVER) BRED Miss B. Swire
WEIGHT FOR AGE 3yo-10lb
1878* Ca'd'oro just managed to beat the Handicapper, being due to be raised 7lb tomorrow for last week's Newbury win. (7/4)
1166 Artful Dane (IRE) came up against a well-handicapped rival. (10/1: op 6/1)
1622 The Executor was staying on at the death. (10/1)
Proud Monk did not mind the give in the ground but could not take advantage of being dropped 8lb. (10/1)
Nichol Fifty is stoutly-bred and it was rather surprising to see him being dropped back from a mile and a quarter. (14/1: 7/1-16/1)
832 Stone Ridge (IRE) had dropped to a mark 4lb lower than when winning last season's Lincoln on this sort of ground. (4/1: 7/2-11/2)

2118 RAC CENTENARY H'CAP (0-80) (4-Y.O+) (Class D)
8-00 (8-04) **1m 2f** £5,726.25 (£1,710.00: £817.50: £371.25) Stalls: High GOING: 0.34 sec per fur (G)

				SP	RR	SF
1926[4]	**Koraloona (IRE) (49)** (GBBalding) **4-7-13** TSprake(13) (a.p: nt clr run 3f out: led ins fnl f: r.o wl)	—	1	5/1[2]	58	32
1414[11]	**Edan Heights (74)** (SDow) **5-9-5**(5) ADaly(9) (a.p: led ins fnl f: sn hdd: nt qckn)	1½	2	15/2	81	55
1683[4]	**Grand Splendour (70)** (LadyHerries) **4-9-6** DHolland(1) (hld up & bhd: rdn 3f out: hdwy over 1f out: r.o ins fnl f)	½	3	4/1[1]	76	50
1768[11]	**Trojan Risk (72)** (GLewis) **4-9-5**(3) AWhelan(2) (s.i.s: plld hrd: sn prom: led over 2f out tl ins fnl f)	1¾	4	11/1	75	49
657[10]	**Kedwick (IRE) (61)** (PRHedger) **8-8-11b** DBiggs(6) (b: s.s: hld up: stdy hdwy 3f out: hung rt fnl 2f: one pce)	nk	5	5/1[2]	64	38
1822[2]	**Dramatic Moment (66)** (JRArnold) **4-8-13**(3) MartinDwyer(4) (nvr nrr)	2½	6	6/1[3]	65	39
987[13]	**Hardy Dancer (72)** (GLMoore) **5-9-8** SSanders(3) (lw: hld up: hrd rdn over 2f out: btn whn carried rt ins fnl f)	hd	7	12/1	70	44
1588[5]	**Mutadarra (IRE) (64)** (WJMusson) **4-9-0** BDoyle(12) (plld hrd: a bhd)	½	8	11/1	62	36
1934[3]	**General Haven (70)** (TJNaughton) **4-9-6** TQuinn(10) (set slow pce: qcknd 5f out: hdd over 2f out: wknd over 1f out: eased whn btn)	2	9	6/1[3]	64	38
	Mazirah (46) (RCurtis) **6-7-10** NAdams(5) (s.s: a bhd)	2	10	25/1	37	11
1811[10]	**Nordansk (55)** (MMadgwick) **8-8-5** NVarley(8) (s.s: hdwy 7f out: wknd over 3f out)	nk	11	10/1	46	20
				(SP 131.0%)		**11 Rn**

2m 16.51 (9.91) CSF £43.46 CT £158.44 TOTE £7.00: £1.90 £2.20 £2.30 (£31.50) Trio £153.00 OWNER Mr Bernard Keay (ANDOVER) BRED Eaton Farms Inc, Red Bull Stable and Joe Hernon
LONG HANDICAP Mazirah 7-1
1926 Koraloona (IRE) has been knocking at the door and did not mind the return to ten furlongs in soft ground. (5/1)
Edan Heights, down 2lb, relished the give in the ground but the big weight concession proved too much. (15/2)
1683 Grand Splendour seems worth another try at a mile and a half. (4/1: 3/1-9/2)
591 Trojan Risk, dropped 5lb, had disappointed when tried in blinkers last time. (11/1: 7/1-12/1)
476* Kedwick (IRE) was 8lb higher than when winning at Folkestone in March and looked a difficult ride. (5/1: op 3/1)

1822 Dramatic Moment did not appear suited by this shorter trip in a slowly-run race although the ground conditions were totally different to last week's good effort at Salisbury. (6/1)
521 Hardy Dancer (12/1: op 8/1)
1588 Mutadarra (IRE) (11/1: 8/1-12/1)

2119 DAILY TELEGRAPH H'CAP (0-85) (3-Y.O+ F & M) (Class D)
8-30 (8-32) **7f** £5,433.75 (£1,620.00: £772.50: £348.75) Stalls: High GOING: 0.34 sec per fur (G)

				SP	RR	SF
*1580**	**Tea Party (USA) (59)** (KOCunningham-Brown) **4-8-9b**$^{(3)}$ MartinDwyer(2) (a.p: led over 2f out: jst hld on)	—	1	8/1	68	40
1662^{2}	**Palo Blanco (75)** (GLMoore) **6-10-0** CandyMorris(5) (hld up & plld hrd: rdn 3f out: hdwy 2f out: r.o wl ins fnl f: jst failed)	s.h	2	15/2	84	56
1737^{12}	**Song of Skye (79)** (TJNaughton) **3-9-9** DHolland(1) (hld up: rdn 3f out: hdwy over 1f out: ev ch whn edgd rt ins fnl f: r.o)	½	3	8/1	87	50
1453*	**Out Line (62)** (MMadgwick) **5-9-1** NVarley(7) (hld up: rdn 4f out: hdwy 2f out: one pce fnl f)	1¾	4	$5/1^{2}$	66	38
1640^{2}	**Kentucky Fall (FR) (66)** (LadyHerries) **4-9-5** AClark(6) (plld hrd: prom: ev ch over 2f out: wknd over 1f out)	4	5	$6/1^{3}$	61	33
1690*	**Eurolink Profile (77)** (LMCumani) **3-9-7** KDarley(3) (hld up: hdwy over 2f out: ev ch over 1f out: wknd ins fnl f)	¾	6	$2/1^{1}$	70	33
1640^{3}	**Sis Garden (55)** (JCullinan) **4-8-5v**$^{1(3)}$ DO'Donohoe(4) (led over 4f: eased whn btn fnl f)	14	7	$5/1^{2}$	16	—
				(SP 114.9%)	**7 Rn**	

1m 31.93 (7.13) CSF £59.29 TOTE £9.80: £3.30 £2.80 (£47.80) OWNER Mr A. J. Richards (STOCKBRIDGE) BRED W. S. Farish and Bayard Sharp
WEIGHT FOR AGE 3yo-9lb
1580* Tea Party (USA), 3lb lower than when successful at Wolverhampton last time, was suited by the give underfoot and held on by a whisker. (8/1)
1662 Palo Blanco, stepping up to seven, did not mind the underfoot conditions but found the post arriving a fraction too soon. (15/2)
1453 Song of Skye (8/1: op 5/1)
1453* Out Line was running off a mark 4lb higher than at Sandown. (5/1: 7/2-11/2)
1640 Kentucky Fall (FR) took a strong hold and the soft ground was also not in her favour. (6/1: 4/1-13/2)
1690* Eurolink Profile,m due to go down 3lb tomorrow, found these ground conditions totally different to Yarmouth. (2/1: 6/4-9/4)
1640 Sis Garden (5/1: op 8/1)

2120 LUFTHANSA BEST ALL CARGO CARRIER LIMITED STKS (0-80) (3-Y.O+) (Class D)
9-00 (9-01) **1m 2f** £3,557.50 (£1,060.00: £505.00: £227.50) Stalls: High GOING: 0.34 sec per fur (G)

				SP	RR	SF
1811^{3}	**Vola Via (USA) (80)** (IABalding) **4-9-3**$^{(3)}$ MartinDwyer(3) (lw: led over 7f: led & edgd lft over 1f out: r.o wl)	—	1	$4/1^{3}$	90	47
1973*	**Rudimental (78)** (SirMarkPrescott) **3-8-10** GDuffield(1) (wnt 2nd 6f out: led wl over 2f out tl over 1f out: hrd rdn: one pce)	3½	2	$5/6^{1}$	86	31
1443*	**Henry's Mother (79)** (MRChannon) **3-8-7** TQuinn(4) (lw: chsd wnr 4f: one pce fnl 2f)	¾	3	$3/1^{2}$	82	27
991^{8}	**Shaddad (USA) (80)** (JLDunlop) **3-8-8** KDarley(2) (lw: a bhd: t.o fnl 4f)	dist	4	7/1	—	—
				(SP 112.0%)	**4 Rn**	

2m 17.14 (10.54) CSF £7.48 TOTE £4.50: (£2.30) OWNER Mr G. M. Smart (KINGSCLERE) BRED Hurstland Farm Inc.
WEIGHT FOR AGE 3yo-12lb
1811 Vola Via (USA) handles all sorts of ground and was well ridden when wanting to lean on the runner-up. (4/1)
1973* Rudimental seemed set to score when taking it up and should have acted on the soft ground having won at Wolverhampton. (5/6)
1443* Henry's Mother, a sister to Rockforce, was trying an extra quarter-mile and could never quite make her presence felt. (3/1)

T/Plpt: £109.20 (136.04 Tckts). T/Qdpt: £92.30 (7.17 Tckts) KH

1841-**NEWMARKET (R-H) (Good to soft)**
Friday June 20th
WEATHER: overcast, rain race 2 WIND: mod against

2121 BUGATTI APPRENTICE H'CAP (0-70) (3-Y.O+) (Class E)
6-45 (6-47) **1m (July)** £3,696.25 (£1,120.00: £547.50: £261.25) Stalls: High GOING: 0.14 sec per fur (G)

				SP	RR	SF
1754^{5}	**Monte Cavo (35)** (MBrittain) **6-7-5**$^{(5)}$ DMernagh(7) (chsd ldrs: led over 1f out: sn rdn clr)	—	1	12/1	51	20
1843^{2}	**La Chatelaine (45)** (GLewis) **3-7-10** RFfrench(9) (hld up: hdwy 4f out: rdn 3f out: outpcd appr fnl f)	8	2	$2/1^{1}$	45	4
1845^{2}	**Gain Line (USA) (54)** (BobJones) **4-8-8**$^{(7)}$ DYoung(12) (plld hrd: prom: led over 3f out tl over 1f out: sn btn)	hd	3	$4/1^{2}$	54	23
1951^{9}	**Amnesty Bay (35)** (MDIUsher) **5-7-5**$^{(5)}$ JFowle(13) (hld up: rdn & hdwy 2f out: nvr able to chal)	2	4	25/1	31	—
1803*	**Kirov Protege (IRE) (35)** (MrsLCJewell) **5-7-5**$^{(5)}$ ^{5x} DarrenWilliams(11) (bhd: rdn 3f out: styd on: nvr rchd ldrs)	1	5	8/1	29	—
	Secret Ballot (IRE) (60) (KMahdi) **3-8-8**$^{(3)}$ DDenby(4) (lw: w ldrs over 4f)	1½	6	14/1	51	10
1501^{2}	**Mezzoramio (47)** (KAMorgan) **5-8-5v**$^{(3)}$ JoHunnam(6) (led 2f: led 4f out: sn hdd: wknd over 1f out)	1½	7	$9/2^{3}$	35	4
1689^{4}	**Hadadabble (36)** (PatMitchell) **4-7-11** AmandaSanders(8) (nvr trbld ldrs)	s.h	8	16/1	24	—
1796^{9}	**Persephone (35)** (JLHarris) **4-7-7b**$^{(3)}$ APolli(5) (chsd ldrs: rdn & edgd lft 3f out: sn wknd)	1½	9	33/1	20	—
340^{9}	**Mediate (IRE) (41)** (AHide) **5-7-11v**$^{(5)ow2}$ JGotobed(2) (lw: rdn 2f out: nvr nr ldrs)	nk	10	16/1	25	—
951^{5}	**Chairmans Choice (60)** (APJarvis) **7-9-0**$^{(7)}$ CDavies(1) (s.s: swtchd rt: led after 2f to 4f out: wknd qckly)	dist	11	10/1	—	—
322^{5}	***Rash Gift (55)*** (LordHuntingdon) **4-8-13**$^{(3)}$ AimeeCook(14) (Withdrawn not under Starter's orders: late arrival of jockey)		W	7/1	—	—
1587^{16}	***Loganlea (IRE) (59)*** (WJMusson) **3-8-10** DSweeney(3) (Withdrawn not under Starter's orders: late arrival of jockey)		W	14/1	—	—
1220^{14}	***Cross of Valour (65)*** (PHowling) **4-9-12** PRoberts(10) (Withdrawn not under Starter's orders: late arrival of jockey)		W	20/1	—	—
				(SP 148.6%)	**11 Rn**	

1m 45.16 (7.16) CSF £34.98 CT £111.65 TOTE £14.60: £3.50 £1.60 £1.70 (£9.50) Trio £16.70 OWNER Mr M. Brittain (WARTHILL) BRED Sheikh Mohammed bin Rashid al Maktoum
LONG HANDICAP La Chatelaine 7-7 Persephone 6-11 Monte Cavo 7-5 Kirov Protege (IRE) 6-13 Amnesty Bay 7-0

WEIGHT FOR AGE 3yo-10lb
1754 Monte Cavo, having failed twice previously on a similar surface, certainly handled it on this occasion and broke his duck in emphatic style. (12/1: op 8/1)
1843 La Chatelaine again ran soundly but the extra furlong and the fact that she was out of the handicap didn't help. (2/1)
1845 Gain Line (USA) took his usual strong hold and was flagging towards the finish. (4/1)
Amnesty Bay, whose only win came over course and distance two years ago, never looked like following up despite staying on. (25/1)
1803* Kirov Protege (IRE), taking a considerable drop in trip from his recent win, was never going to close in time. (8/1)
Secret Ballot (IRE) looked ready for this handicap debut, but doesn't seem to last home with these tactics. (14/1)

2122 BUGATTI INTERNATIONAL RALLY H'CAP (0-90) (3-Y.O+) (Class C)
7-15 (7-19) **1m 4f (July)** £5,900.00 (£1,760.00: £840.00: £380.00) Stalls: High GOING: 0.14 sec per fur (G)

	Horse	Dist	Pos	SP	RR	SF
1877^{2}	**Travelmate (73)** (JRFanshawe) **3-8-4** DHarrison(3) (lw: prom: led 2f out: rdn out)	—	**1**	$5/2^{1}$	83	44
1325^{8}	**My Learned Friend (75)** (AHide) **6-9-6** AMcGlone(9) (trckd ldrs: rdn over 1f out: r.o wl fnl f: nt rch wnr)	nk	**2**	12/1	85	60
1414^{5}	**Sofyaan (USA) (78)** (LadyHerries) **4-9-9** RCochrane(13) (hld up & plld hrd: nt clr run 2f out: hdwy over 1f out: r.o ins fnl f)	½	**3**	$9/2^{2}$	87	62
1646*	**Life of Riley (85)** (GLewis) **3-9-2** PaulEddery(10) (b: prom: rdn & ev ch 2f out: one pce fnl f)	1½	**4**	13/2	92	53
1215^{8}	**Magic Combination (IRE) (70)** (BJCurley) **4-9-1** WRyan(2) (lw: hld up: stdy hdwy 2f out: r.o nr fin)	1½	**5**	16/1	75	50
1844^{3}	**Dalwhinnie (60)** (JWharton) **4-8-5** RHills(6) (hld up: hdwy over 5f out: one pce fnl 2f)	1¼	**6**	11/1	63	38
1398^{6}	**Classic Find (USA) (76)** (ICampbell) **4-9-7** RPrice(8) (b: plld hrd: chsd ldrs tl rdn 3f out: wknd fnl f)	1	**7**	16/1	78	53
1981^{3}	**Temptress (70)** (JohnHarris) **4-8-10**(5) RFfrench(4) (hld up: effrt over 2f out: no imp)	hd	**8**	8/1	72	47
1459^{6}	**Mattimeo (IRE) (70)** (APJarvis) **4-9-1** SDrowne(5) (chsd ldrs tl rdn & btn 3f out)	9	**9**	8/1	60	35
1430^{3}	**Raise A Prince (FR) (72)** (JWHills) **4-9-3** MHills(1) (a bhd)	1¾	**10**	16/1	60	35
1782^{12}	**Lady Godiva (67)** (MJPolglase) **3-7-12** JQuinn(7) (lw: led tl hdd & wknd 2f out)	6	**11**	25/1	47	8
1260^{6}	**Al's Alibi (74)** (WRMuir) **4-9-5** KFallon(11) (lw: w ldr over 9f)	1	**12**	$11/2^{3}$	52	27
1768^{8}	***Bardon Hill Boy (IRE) (83)*** (BHanbury) **5-10-0** JStack(12) (Withdrawn not under Starter's orders: late arrival of jockey)		**W**		—	—
				(SP 135.2%)		**12 Rn**

2m 37.26 (8.26) CSF £37.66 CT £131.36 TOTE £4.40: £1.90 £3.10 £2.30 (£19.00) Trio £87.40 OWNER Barford Bloodstock II (NEWMARKET) BRED London Thoroughbred Services Ltd
WEIGHT FOR AGE 3yo-14lb
1877 Travelmate due to go up 3lb, is on the up, but had to struggle late in the day after looking all over the winner. Ten furlongs may be his trip. (5/2: 2/1-3/1)
962 My Learned Friend, unlucky to be eliminated from the Bessborough at the overnight stage, a race in which he finished second last year, found the rain against him and that made the difference between defeat and victory. He is certainly on a winning mark at present. (12/1: op 6/1)
1414 Sofyaan (USA) had anything but a trouble-free passage, but fairly flew up the stands rail once in the clear and is surely going to win a race or two off this sort of mark. (9/2: op 7/1)
1646* Life of Riley, a likeable sort, didn't look out of his depth in this grade and, being by Caerleon, is likely to do better on faster ground. (13/2: 3/1-7/1)
442 Magic Combination (IRE) caught the eye in the closing stages but, in fairness to the connections, appeared to be struggling to handle the rain-softened ground. (16/1)
1844 Dalwhinnie, ridden from the back after a slightly tardly start, could never get into the race this time. (11/1: 8/1-12/1)

2123 NGK SPARK PLUGS MAIDEN STKS (2-Y.O) (Class D)
7-45 (7-45) **6f (July)** £4,092.00 (£1,221.00: £583.00: £264.00) Stalls: High GOING: 0.14 sec per fur (G)

	Horse	Dist	Pos	SP	RR	SF
	Marksman (IRE) (LMCumani) **2-9-0** PatEddery(4) (w'like: bit bkwd: trckd ldrs: led 1f out: sn pushed clr: comf)	—	**1**	$5/2^{2}$	77+	53
	Hill Magic (DRCElsworth) **2-9-0** RCochrane(3) (w'like: scope: bit bkwd: s.i.s: hdwy over 2f out: ev ch over 1f out: r.o)	3	**2**	16/1	69	45
	Hujoom (IRE) (JLDunlop) **2-9-0** WRyan(1) (unf: chsd ldrs: kpt on ins fnl f)	½	**3**	5/1	68	44
1692^{2}	**Mishraak (IRE)** (RWArmstrong) **2-9-0** RHills(2) (led 5f: sn btn)	¾	**4**	$6/4^{1}$	66	42
	Docksider (USA) (JWHills) **2-9-0** MHills(5) (leggy: scope: dwlt: sn pushed along: bhd fnl 2f)	13	**5**	$4/1^{3}$	31	7
1645^{12}	**Dooze (IRE)** (JHMGosden) **2-8-9** AGarth(6) (chsd ldr over 3f: sn rdn & bhd)	7	**6**	14/1	7	—
				(SP 117.8%)		**6 Rn**

1m 16.06 (4.06) CSF £35.77 TOTE £2.80: £1.30 £4.70 (£17.30) OWNER Mr G. P. D. Milne (NEWMARKET) BRED Jeremy Hill
Marksman (IRE), the first foal of an unraced dam, was carrying a fair bit of condition but clearly has plenty of ability, doing the job in excellent style. Sure to stay further, he is expected to take in another small race before stepping up in class. (5/2)
Hill Magic, whose half-sister Formidable Lass is little more than a plater, is going to prove a great deal better than that on this evidence. Burly and slow to break, he came with a promising run on the outside but once it was clear that he could not get to the winner, he was eased in the final strides. Just what this form is worth is anybody's guess, but he should win a race. (16/1)
Hujoom (IRE), a half-brother to Fortune Cay and Lifewatch Vision, looked green beforehand but did well in the race over a trip likely to prove some way short of his best. (5/1: 5/2-6/1)
1692 Mishraak (IRE) let down the Yarmouth form, going out like a damp squib once headed. (6/4: 5/4-9/4)
Docksider (USA), a tall, really attractive newcomer, is a half-brother to Scarpetta who went close to winning a Newbury maiden for the yard last season. Very keen going to post, he was caught flat-footed as the stalls opened and this is probably best ignored. (4/1: op 8/1)
Dooze (IRE) again faded quickly in the second half of the race having shown some speed, and is going to need more time and a longer trip judged on her pedigree. (14/1: op 6/1)

2124 VISION EXPRESS H'CAP (0-95) (3-Y.O+) (Class C)
8-15 (8-15) **7f (July)** £6,316.00 (£1,888.00: £904.00: £412.00) Stalls: High GOING: 0.14 sec per fur (G)

	Horse	Dist	Pos	SP	RR	SF
1166^{D}	**Elfland (IRE) (81)** (LadyHerries) **6-9-2** RCochrane(6) (swtg: hld up: nt clr run & squeezed thro 2f out: led ins fnl f: rdn out)	—	**1**	$11/2^{3}$	90	73
1775^{10}	**Highborn (IRE) (89)** (PSFelgate) **8-9-10** WRyan(8) (hmpd s: hld up: hdwy over 1f out: r.o wl ins fnl f)	1½	**2**	12/1	95	78
1977*	**Grey Kingdom (67)** (MBrittain) **6-7-9**(7) 5x DMernagh(5) (wnt rt s: prom: led 3f out tl hdd & one pce ins fnl f)	nk	**3**	$4/1^{2}$	72	55
1935^{2}	**Rakis (IRE) (80)** (MrsLStubbs) **7-9-1** PatEddery(11) (b: chsd ldrs: lost pl 3f out: rallied appr fnl f: r.o)	6	**4**	$7/2^{1}$	71	54
1410^{14}	**Unshaken (80)** (JRFanshawe) **3-8-6** MHills(4) (chsd ldrs: rdn whn sltly hmpd 2f out: no ch after)	6	**5**	25/1	58	32

				SP	RR	SF
1456^{15}	**Welton Arsenal (92)** (KBishop) **5-9-8**$^{(5)}$ RFfrench(9) (lw: plld hrd: prom 5f)	s.h	**6**	7/1	69	52
1655^{6}	**Mountgate (68)** (MPBielby) **5-8-3** DRMcCabe(3) (s.i.s: hdwy 3f out: wknd fnl f)	½	**7**	12/1	44	27
1935^{8}	**Pengamon (78)** (HJCollingridge) **5-8-13** JQuinn(7) (chsd ldrs tl wknd over 1f out)	¾	**8**	14/1	53	36
1739^{16}	**Sandabar (77)** (MRStoute) **4-8-12** KFallon(2) (lw: hld up: hdwy over 3f out: rdn & wknd appr fnl f)	2½	**9**	11/2^{3}	46	29
	Present Generation (80) (RGuest) **4-9-1** PBloomfield(1) (bit bkwd: hld up: effrt 3f out: nvr trbld ldrs)	2	**10**	14/1	44	27
1745^{8}	**Civil Liberty (87)** (GLewis) **4-9-8** PaulEddery(10) (led 4f)	9	**11**	14/1	31	14
				(SP 124.7%)		**11 Rn**

1m 28.29 (3.29) CSF £67.63 CT £274.35 TOTE £5.40: £2.30 £4.40 £1.90 (£72.10) Trio £78.80 OWNER The High Flying Partnership (LITTLEHAMPTON) BRED A. Tarry
WEIGHT FOR AGE 3yo-9lb
1166 Elfland (IRE) has had an injury-blighted career but has returned in great form and, despite being in a real lather, took this in good style, showing plenty of courage to force his way through after looking unlikely to get a run. (11/2: 4/1-6/1)
1397 Highborn (IRE) looked on good terms with himself and took the eye going down. Forced to wait for a gap to appear against the stands rail, he fairly flew once he got through but the winner was all but home by then. There are still races in this genuine veteran. (12/1: 6/1-14/1)
1977* Grey Kingdom, off his highest ever mark, was found out by the stiff seven, given the conditions. (4/1: op 6/1)
1935 Rakis (IRE) must be considered slightly unlucky, as being shuffled back through the field was not entirely of his own making. (7/2)
Unshaken was having his first run beyond six furlongs and is worth another try at the trip, in the circumstances. (25/1)
1214* Welton Arsenal looked magnificent but raced far too keenly and ruined his chance. (7/1)
1655 Mountgate (12/1: op 7/1)
1154 Pengamon (14/1: 10/1-16/1)
Civil Liberty (14/1: 8/1-16/1)

2125 LONDON EXECUTIVE AVIATION CLAIMING STKS (3-Y.O) (Class D)

8-45 (8-45) **1m (July)** £4,175.00 (£1,250.00: £600.00: £275.00) Stalls: High GOING: 0.14 sec per fur (G)

				SP	RR	SF
1493*	**Ultra Boy (75)** (PCHaslam) **3-9-3**$^{(5)}$ RFfrench(5) (lw: led after 1f: rdn & hdd ins fnl f: led again nr fin)	—	**1**	9/4^{1}	80	47
1484^{5}	**Jukebox Jive (49)** (CADwyer) **3-7-6**$^{(7)}$ DarrenWilliams(4) (trckd ldrs: rdn to ld ins fnl f: edgd lft & ct nr fin)	s.h	**2**	14/1	57	24
1826^{11}	**Time Can Tell (66)** (CMurray) **3-8-10b^{1}** JQuinn(8) (plld hrd: led 1f: one pce ins fnl f)	1¾	**3**	9/2^{2}	64	31
1638^{5}	**Distinctive Dream (IRE) (43)** (KTIvory) **3-8-7b**^{ow1} RCochrane(1) (prom: pushed along 3f out: kpt on fnl f)	2½	**4**	20/1	56	22
2017^{5}	**Gresatre (54)** (CADwyer) **3-8-10** DHarrison(9) (lw: hld up: hdwy 3f out: wknd ins fnl f)	2	**5**	14/1	55	22
1681^{5}	**Millpet (54)** (RGuest) **3-8-9** PBloomfield(10) (chsd ldrs tl rdn & wknd wl over 1f out)	3½	**6**	16/1	47	14
1921^{2}	**Effervescence (76)** (RHannon) **3-9-8** PatEddery(3) (hld up & plld hrd: rdn over 2f out: no imp)	3½	**7**	9/4^{1}	53	20
1688^{3}	**Nicker** (WJarvis) **3-9-2** WRyan(7) (b.hind: rdn over 2f out: a bhd)	hd	**8**	6/1^{3}	47	14
1638^{6}	**Hot News** (JRJenkins) **3-8-4** SDrowne(6) (b.hind: lw: plld hrd: trckd ldrs tl wknd 3f out)	½	**9**	25/1	34	1
				(SP 121.8%)		**9 Rn**

1m 44.84 (6.84) CSF £37.03 TOTE £2.90: £1.40 £3.30 £1.50 (£24.30) Trio £41.20 OWNER Pet Express (W&R) Ltd (MIDDLEHAM) BRED Cheveley Park Stud Ltd
OFFICIAL EXPLANATION **Effervescence: the jockey reported that the colt was labouring from three furlongs out and would not pick up on the ground.**
1493* Ultra Boy is probably not at his best with so much cut in the ground, but running straight and true along the stand's rail, won him the day. (9/4)
602 Jukebox Jive, stepping up in trip, looked to have taken the winner's measure inside the final furlong but, crucially hung away from her pilot's whip, handing the advantage back right on the line. This was her first encounter with the rain-softened ground and she should soon be winning in this grade. (14/1)
1474 Time Can Tell, on his toes in first-time blinkers, took a bit of settling early on but stuck on to the line, unsurprisingly as he has been racing over further. (9/2: op 7/1)
871 Distinctive Dream (IRE) got this trip well and shaped as if he may stay further still, despite his speedy sire. (20/1)
2017 Gresatre again briefly flattered to deceive but may not last a mile in any case. (14/1)
1681 Millpet, stepping up from the minimum trip, didn't last home. (16/1)
1921 Effervescence looked at sea on the loose, rain-softened ground. (9/4: 9/4-7/2)
1688 Nicker (6/1: op 7/2)

2126 GAZELEY MAIDEN STKS (3-Y.O) (Class D)

9-15 (9-16) **1m 2f (July)** £4,378.00 (£1,309.00: £627.00: £286.00) Stalls: High GOING: 0.14 sec per fur (G)

				SP	RR	SF
1611^{2}	**Bombazine (IRE)** (LMCumani) **3-8-9** PatEddery(10) (a.p: ev ch 2f out: led ins fnl f: drvn out)	—	**1**	Evens^{1}	88	39
	Light Programme (HRACecil) **3-9-0** WRyan(11) (w'like: scope: bit bkwd: dwlt: hld up: hdwy 3f out: ev ch 2f out: r.o wl ins fnl f: jst failed)	hd	**2**	5/1^{2}	93	44
847^{5}	**Monitor** (HRACecil) **3-9-0** KFallon(6) (a.p: ev ch 2f out: led 1f out: sn hdd: no ex nr fin)	nk	**3**	5/1^{2}	92	43
	Dovedon Star (PAKelleway) **3-8-9** DJWhyte(7) (leggy: unf: bit bkwd: s.i.s: rdn 3f out: hdwy over 1f out: fin wl)	1	**4**	33/1	86	37
1130^{4}	**Mengaab (USA)** (JHMGosden) **3-9-0** AMcGlone(4) (w ldr: led 2f out to 1f out: one pce)	3	**5**	6/1^{3}	86	37
1276^{3}	**Legendary Lover (IRE)** (RCharlton) **3-9-0** PaulEddery(9) (lw: led 8f: one pce)	nk	**6**	10/1	86	37
676^{8}	**Bedouin Honda** (CEBrittain) **3-9-0** WJO'Connor(8) (chsd ldrs tl rdn & btn over 2f out)	5	**7**	20/1	78	29
350^{4}	**Bogan (IRE)** (LordHuntingdon) **3-9-0** DHarrison(12) (lw: prom 7f)	5	**8**	33/1	70	21
	Veuve Clicquot (RWArmstrong) **3-8-9** RPrice(5) (unf: scope: bit bkwd: a bhd)	nk	**9**	20/1	64	15
1409^{10}	**Colour Key (USA)** (DRCElsworth) **3-9-0** RCochrane(1) (stdd s: hld up & plld hrd: effrt 3f out: no imp)	3	**10**	33/1	64	15
				(SP 125.1%)		**10 Rn**

2m 11.66 (8.06) CSF £5.86 TOTE £2.20: £1.20 £1.80 £2.10 (£4.50) Trio £9.00 OWNER Mr Gerald Leigh (NEWMARKET) BRED Gerald W. Leigh
1611 Bombazine (IRE) came on for her first run, but will certainly know she has been in a race as she really had to battle her heart out to prevail. (Evens)
Light Programme, well supported despite being the apparent second string, lost this by wandering going into the Dip. Really hitting his stride on meeting the rising ground, he looks sure to win races. (5/1: 5/1-11/4)
847 Monitor becomes that rare animal, a useful Cecil maiden after three runs, and the great man should place him to advantage before long, with handicap options now open to him. (5/1: 3/1-13/2)
Dovedon Star, a half-sister to Two Left Feet, finished in great style and looks likely to take after another relative, Star Performer, who won over two miles. (33/1)
1130 Mengaab (USA), beaten in a very hot maiden this time, lacks a turn of foot but will find an ordinary race. (6/1)
1276 Legendary Lover (IRE) set a steady pace but could not quicken as well as the principals and probably needs a stiffer test. (10/1: 8/1-12/1)

350 Bogan (IRE), being by Caerleon, is worth a try on faster ground. (33/1)

T/Plpt: £114.30 (158.16 Tckts). T/Qdpt: £18.60 (39.12 Tckts) Dk

1815-REDCAR (L-H) (Good, Good to firm patches)
Friday June 20th
WEATHER: overcast WIND: mod half bhd

2127 INGS MAIDEN STKS (2-Y.O) (Class D)
2-20 (2-21) **5f** £3,367.75 (£1,012.00: £488.50: £226.75) Stalls: Centre GOING minus 0.28 sec per fur (GF)

	Horse / details	Dist	Pos	SP	RR	SF
	Ouaisne (RGuest) **2-9-0** PBloomfield(1) (w'like: cmpt: mde all: clr over 1f out: easily)	—	1	12/1	86+	44
1267[7]	**Dangerman (IRE)** (MWEasterby) **2-9-0** TLucas(3) (sn bhd: shkn up & hdwy over 1f out: r.o strly towards fin)	5	2	10/1 3	70+	28
	Boulevard Rouge (USA) (MJohnston) **2-8-9** DeanMcKeown(4) (leggy: scope: bit bkwd: s.i.s: sn chsng ldrs: rdn & outpcd ½-wy: styd on fnl f)	½	3	11/4 2	63	21
1797[5]	**Cumbrian Cadet** (TDEasterby) **2-9-0** JCarroll(7) (lw: chsd ldrs: kpt on same pce fnl 2f)	½	4	6/4 1	67	25
1228[5]	**Junior Muffin (IRE)** (JBerry) **2-9-0** JFanning(8) (chsd ldrs: rdn ½-wy: wknd over 1f out)	1¾	5	11/4 2	61	19
	Smart Prince (JJQuinn) **2-9-0** JLowe(5) (neat: sn trckng ldrs: outpcd ½-wy: sn lost pl)	3½	6	20/1	50	8
1860[7]	**Flying High (IRE)** (FMurphy) **2-9-0** JTate(9) (sn outpcd & bhd)	2	7	25/1	44	2
	Lunchtime Girl (JDBethell) **2-8-9** TWilliams(2) (lengthy: unf: bkwd: swvd rt s: sn chsng ldrs: rdn & outpcd ½-wy: hung lft & sn lost pl)	1¼	8	25/1	35	—
	Walworth Wizard (MDods) **2-9-0** SWhitworth(6) (leggy: unf: s.s: a bhd)	3	9	20/1	30	—

(SP 127.3%) **9 Rn**

59.2 secs (1.70) CSF £114.27 TOTE £9.30: £2.20 £3.80 £1.50 (£101.80) Trio Not won; £145.61 to Ascot 21/6/97 OWNER Matthews Breeding and Racing (NEWMARKET) BRED Matthews Breeding and Racing Ltd

Ouaisne, a close-coupled attractive colt, showed a good action going down. He clearly knew his job and had his race won some way from home. He is useful. (12/1)

1267 Dangerman (IRE), who showed a choppy action going down, had another educational outing. His rider picked up his whip but only waved it and never hit him. Staying in really strongly at the line, he will be an interesting proposition in Nurseries over six and seven furlongs later on. (10/1)

Boulevard Rouge (USA) looked in need of the outing and showed definite signs of inexperience. The outing will have taught her a lot. (11/4)

1797 Cumbrian Cadet, who looked very well in himself, had no excuse and this is probably as good as he is. (6/4: op 3/1)

1228 Junior Muffin (IRE) looked very fit indeed. (11/4: 2/1-3/1)

2128 NEWTON CLAIMING STKS (3-Y.O+) (Class F)
2-55 (2-56) **1m 2f** £2,553.00 (£708.00: £339.00) Stalls: Low GOING minus 0.28 sec per fur (GF)

	Horse / details	Dist	Pos	SP	RR	SF
1838*	**Zorba (64)** (CWThornton) **3-9-1** DeanMcKeown(7) (lw: mde all: readily)	—	1	9/4 1	75	35
898[2]	**My Millie (48)** (DWBarker) **4-8-12** TWilliams(2) (trckd ldrs: wnt 2nd 3f out: rdn over 1f out: hung lft: no ch w wnr)	5	2	100/30 2	52	24
1689[6]	**Guesstimation (USA) (58)** (JPearce) **8-9-2**(3) CTeague(5) (b.hind: hld up: hdwy over 2f out: sn rdn & hung lft: kpt on: nvr nr ldrs)	6	3	9/4 1	49	21
1756[4]	**Madam Lucy (47)** (WWHaigh) **3-7-7**(5) JBramhill(1) (chsd ldrs: sn pushed along: one pce fnl 3f)	3	4	5/1 3	36	—
1472[9]	**Major Mouse (45)** (WWHaigh) **9-8-13** MWigham(3) (hld up: effrt over 3f out: no imp)	7	5	9/1	27	—
1798[9]	**Paperwork Pete (IRE)** (WStorey) **5-9-1** SWhitworth(8) (chsd ldrs: outpcd 4f out: sn lost pl)	11	6	16/1	12	—
1798[12]	**Mustard (25)** (ABMulholland) **4-9-0** DWright(6) (trckd wnr: rdn over 3f out: wknd over 2f out)	1	7	25/1	9	—
	Kirkham (MrsVAAconley) **3-9-1** MDeering(4) (leggy: hld up & plld hrd: bhd fnl 4f)	1½	8	20/1	20	—

(SP 125.8%) **8 Rn**

2m 8.7 (5.10) CSF £10.30 TOTE £3.20: £1.10 £1.20 £1.10 (£4.20) OWNER Mr G. Reed (MIDDLEHAM) BRED B. Freiha
WEIGHT FOR AGE 3yo-12lb
Zorba clmd JHetherton £10,000

OFFICIAL EXPLANATION **Paperwork Pete (IRE): gurgled.**

1838* Zorba, allowed to set his own pace, always had the situation well under control. (9/4: 6/4-5/2)

898 My Millie, having her first race for seven weeks, moved up within striking range of the winner three furlongs out. Pulled out to make her challenge over a furlong out, her rider had his whip in his right hand and she again dived left in behind the winner. She would not have troubled him in any case. (100/30)

1689 Guesstimation (USA) was not suited by the modest pace at which the race was run and, under pressure, all he could do was hang left and keep on at the one pace. (9/4)

1756 Madam Lucy is very onepaced but still ran her best race so far on grass. (5/1: op 3/1)

415 Major Mouse is not firing at present. (9/1: 6/1-10/1)

2129 FULL MOON H'CAP (0-90) (3-Y.O+) (Class C)
3-30 (3-31) **6f** £5,231.25 (£1,575.00: £762.50: £356.25) Stalls: Centre GOING minus 0.28 sec per fur (GF)

	Horse / details	Dist	Pos	SP	RR	SF
1948[3]	**Daawe (USA) (75)** (MrsVAAconley) **6-9-6** MDeering(4) (lw: trckd ldrs: led over 1f out: rdn & wnt lft ins fnl f: r.o)	—	1	4/1 1	84	70
	Saint Express (79) (MrsMReveley) **7-9-10** DeanMcKeown(6) (led tl over 1f out: kpt on wl)	1½	2	14/1	84	70
1942[10]	**Bee Health Boy (67)** (MWEasterby) **4-8-7b**(5) GParkin(10) (a chsng ldrs: styd on wl ins fnl f)	1	3	13/2	69	55
1799[8]	**Bollin Harry (70)** (TDEasterby) **5-9-1** JCarroll(9) (chsd ldrs: styd on same pce fnl 2f)	¾	4	9/1	70	56
1824[2]	**Delta Soleil (USA) (81)** (PWHarris) **5-9-12** MRimmer(3) (trckd ldrs: ev ch 2f out: kpt on same pce)	nk	5	5/1 3	81	67
1977[14]	**Benzoe (IRE) (72)** (MrsJRRamsden) **7-9-3** MWigham(2) (lw: s.s: bhd tl hdwy on stands' side over 1f out: nvr rchd ldrs)	½	6	9/2 2	70	56
1772[9]	**For the Present (80)** (TDBarron) **7-9-11** RLappin(7) (chsd ldrs: rdn & outpcd 2f out: styd on fnl f)	nk	7	6/1	77	63
1830[3]	**Reinhardt (IRE) (51)** (DNicholls) **4-7-3**(7) JoanneDavies(8) (sn bhd: wnt lft 2f out: kpt on fnl f)	1¾	8	10/1	44	30
1799*	**French Grit (IRE) (78)** (MDods) **5-9-9** 7x SWhitworth(1) (hld up: hdwy 2f out: eased ins fnl f)	1¾	9	13/2	66	52
1799[9]	**Spotted Eagle (70)** (MartynWane) **4-9-1** DWright(5) (in tch: rdn ½-wy: lost pl over 1f out)	3	10	25/1	50	36

(SP 125.4%) **10 Rn**

1m 10.9 (0.70) CSF £60.04 CT £343.36 TOTE £3.60: £1.50 £3.30 £2.60 (£31.90) Trio £29.00 OWNER Mrs Andrea Mallinson (WESTOW) BRED Gainsborough Farm W.C.

LONG HANDICAP Reinhardt (IRE) 7-6
1948 Daawe (USA), who was out of the handicap at York, was in effect 11lb better in here and scored decisively despite going badly left inside the last. (4/1)
Saint Express, who has slipped down the weights, showed all his old speed and kept going right to the bitter end. (14/1: 8/1-16/1)
1942 Bee Health Boy ran really well racing towards the stands' side. (13/2)
1799 Bollin Harry, who again wore a tongue-strap, kept on much better this time. (9/1)
1824 Delta Soleil (USA) ran well under top weight but is better over seven. (5/1)
1627* Benzoe (IRE), as usual, gave away an appreciable amount of ground at the start. (9/2)
744 For the Present did not take the eye in the paddock but ran creditably and is on the way back. (6/1)
1830 Reinhardt (IRE) (10/1: op 9/2)

2130 K M GROUP SERVICES H'CAP (0-80) (3-Y.O) (Class D)
4-05 (4-07) **7f** £3,886.00 (£1,168.00: £564.00: £262.00) Stalls: Centre GOING minus 0.28 sec per fur (GF)

			SP	RR	SF
2002 13	**Swift (62)** (MJPolglase) **3-8-3** JTate(9) (dwtl: hdwy ½-wy: rdn to ld jst ins fnl f: r.o wl) ....—	**1**	7/1	72	39
1472 14	**Pension Fund (66)** (MWEasterby) **3-8-7** TLucas(4) (lw: trckd ldrs: outpcd 2f out: styd on wl fnl f) 2	**2**	9/2 3	71	38
1333 2	**Rock Island Line (IRE) (71)** (JBerry) **3-8-12** JFanning(1) (trckd ldrs: led ½-wy tl over 1f out: unable qckn).....nk	**3**	11/4 1	76	43
1781 8	**La Dolce Vita (66)** (TDBarron) **3-8-7** RLappin(10) (hld up & plld hrd: effrt & nt clr run 2f out: r.o fnl f).......nk	**4**	7/1	70	37
1958 2	**Pet Express (57)** (PCHaslam) **3-7-5**(7) RWinston(2) (lw: w ldrs: led over 1f out tl jst ins fnl f: wknd nr fin).......¾	**5**	7/2 2	59	26
1764 3	**Frederick James (75)** (MJHeaton-Ellis) **3-9-2** JCarroll(7) (chsd ldrs: drvn along ½-wy: wknd over 1f out)......1¼	**6**	5/1	75	42
1496 10	**Tarradale (55)** (CBBBooth) **3-7-10** JLowe(8) (drvn along ½-wy: sme hdwy 2f out: nvr nr to chal).......1¾	**7**	20/1	51	18
1629 4	**Grate Times (70)** (EWeymes) **3-8-8b**(3) MHenry(6) (led to ½-wy: sn rdn: hung rt & lost pl 2f out).......3½	**8**	12/1	58	25
1096 16	**Noirie (57)** (MBrittain) **3-7-12**ow2 TWilliams(11) (chsd ldrs: hrd rdn ½-wy: sn lost pl).......¾	**9**	25/1	43	8
1037 11	**Tribal Mischief (62)** (DMoffatt) **3-8-0**(3) DarrenMoffatt(3) (s.i.s: a bhd: hrd rdn ½-wy).......4	**10**	20/1	39	6

(SP 129.8%) **10 Rn**

1m 25.1 (2.10) CSF £38.31 CT £105.56 TOTE £14.50: £4.00 £1.60 £1.40 (£38.80) Trio £48.80 OWNER Gen Sir Geoffrey Howlett (NEWMARKET) BRED Mrs Amschel Rothschild
STEWARDS' ENQUIRY Moffatt susp. 29-30/6/97 (improper use of whip).
1496* Swift, a grand type of horse, appreciated the really good ground. It looked a good deal softer than good to firm and, in the end, he did it in good style. (7/1)
699 Pension Fund has slipped down the weights and is now 9lb lower than when he won a competitive Nursery at York in August. Looking in tremendous shape, he finished strongly after being tapped for foot. A stiffer track or an easy mile will suit him better and he is certainly on a winning mark again now. (9/2: 4/1-5/2)
1333 Rock Island Line (IRE), 4lb higher and a furlong down in trip, took it up travelling strongly at halfway but could find no extra in the final furlong. (11/4)
1385 La Dolce Vita, running over possibly her best trip, did well to finish so close considering she met trouble when starting her effort. (7/1)
1958 Pet Express faded near the line after showing ahead over a furlong out. Six furlongs is probably his optimum trip. (7/2)
1764 Frederick James, who had plenty on at the weights, wore a tongue-strap. (5/1)

2131 STAITHES MAIDEN STKS (3-Y.O+) (Class D)
4-40 (4-42) **1m 6f 19y** £3,639.00 (£1,092.00: £526.00: £243.00) Stalls: Centre GOING minus 0.28 sec per fur (GF)

			SP	RR	SF
1230 6	**Media Star (USA)** (JHMGosden) **4-9-7v1** JCarroll(1) (lw: mde virtually all: clr 4f out: eased towards fin).......—	**1**	5/1 2	62+	41
1930 3	**San Glamore Melody (FR)** (JHMGosden) **3-8-4** JLowe(6) (lw: reluctant to go to s: hld up & plld hrd: drvn along 7f out: hrd rdn & wnt 2nd 3f out: no ch w wnr).......11	**2**	6/1 3	50	12
1258 7	**Stoned Imaculate (IRE)** (FMurphy) **3-8-0**ow1 JFanning(3) (sn trckng ldrs: rdn over 4f out: one pce).......½	**3**	20/1	45	6
1866 7	**Azores** (PFICole) **3-8-4** CRutter(4) (w wnr: rn wd bnd after 2f: drvn along over 5f out: one pce).......1½	**4**	5/6 1	47	9
	Genereux (SMellor) **4-9-7** MWigham(5) (sn drvn along: hdwy to chse ldrs after 3f: sn rdn: outpcd 5f out: eased over 1f out).......24	**5**	14/1	20	—
	Landler (JNorton) **4-9-4**(3) OPears(2) (chsd ldrs: sn drvn along: outpcd 5f out: eased 2f out).......14	**6**	6/1 3	4	—
	Annaletta (JPearce) **3-7-13** TWilliams(7) (Withdrawn not under Starter's orders: v.unruly & ref to ent stalls).....	**W**	12/1	—	—

(SP 118.9%) **6 Rn**

3m 6.8 (7.50) CSF £28.94 TOTE £3.50: £3.30 £3.20 (£8.90) OWNER Mr K. Abdulla (NEWMARKET) BRED Juddmonte Farms
WEIGHT FOR AGE 3yo-17lb
1230 Media Star (USA), who had misbehaved beforehand on his two previous outings, was much more settled here in a visor for the first time. Rousted along in the early stages and pulling well clear once in line for home, he would have had at least fifteen lengths to spare over some disappointing rivals but for being eased near the line. Unfortunately the handicapper will take no chances with him. (5/1)
1930 San Glamore Melody (FR) was reluctant to go to the post. After taking a keen grip early on, he had to be really rousted along to take second place three furlongs out. If this is the best he can do he is very moderate indeed. (6/1)
Stoned Imaculate (IRE) ran better than on her debut. (20/1)
1866 Azores, a half-brother to Lady Carla, made no appeal in the paddock. Ducking out on the first bend, he was left behind turning in and proved woefully one-paced. (5/6)
Genereux, having his first outing since a two-year-old, showed a moderate action going down and was eased off late in the day. (14/1)
Landler, who won a National Hunt Flat race at Doncaster in March, was soon hard at work and left behind turning in. His rider called it a day two furlongs out. (6/1)
Annaletta (12/1: op 8/1)

2132 GRIBDALE RATING RELATED MAIDEN STKS (0-65) (3-Y.O) (Class F)
5-15 (5-16) **1m 3f** £2,448.00 (£678.00: £324.00) Stalls: Low GOING minus 0.28 sec per fur (GF)

			SP	RR	SF
1742 5	**Gee Bee Boy (65)** (APJarvis) **3-9-0** DWright(1) (hld up & plld hrd: effrt over 4f out: rdn over 2f out: styd on to ld over 1f out).......—	**1**	11/4 1	74	31
1624 12	**Pointe Fine (FR) (60)** (JWHills) **3-8-8**(3) MHenry(7) (effrt on outside over 3f out: styd on ins fnl f).......4	**2**	7/1	65	22
1470 4	**Quest For Best (USA) (65)** (JHMGosden) **3-8-11v** JCarroll(2) (trckd ldrs: led 4f out tl over 1f out: one pce)....¾	**3**	4/1 2	64	21
1820 4	**Kweilo (65)** (JWPayne) **3-9-0** DeanMcKeown(8) (hld up: hdwy on ins over 3f out: n.m.r: rdn & fnd nil over 1f out).......8	**4**	9/2 3	56	13
1322 4	**Sandystones (65)** (NAGraham) **3-8-11** JLowe(4) (trckd ldrs: drvn along over 4f out: wknd 2f out).......1¾	**5**	5/1	50	7
1115 5	**Broadgate Flyer (IRE) (50)** (MrsLStubbs) **3-9-0** MRimmer(6) (chsd ldrs: drvn along 4f out: lost pl over 2f out).1	**6**	20/1	52	9

1938[7] **Golden Saddle (USA) (62)** (PFICole) **3-9-0** CRutter(5) (chsd ldrs: rdn 4f out: sn lost pl: eased)......................21 **7** 9/2[3] 21 —
1470[5] **Allied Academy (64)** (SCWilliams) **3-9-0** JTate(3) (led to 4f out: sn wknd: virtually p.u)................................dist **8** 6/1 — —
(SP 131.2%) **8 Rn**

2m 23.2 (6.20) CSF £24.53 TOTE £3.60: £2.00 £2.40 £2.30 (£13.80) OWNER Grant & Bowman Ltd (ASTON UPTHORPE) BRED Miss S. E. Jarvis

1742 Gee Bee Boy took some settling in the early stages. With it all to do straightening up, in the end he did it in good style. The handicapper should not be too harsh on him and a follow up is very much on the cards. (11/4)
1121 Pointe Fine (FR), always inclined to edge left, stayed on in the last and certainly gets the trip. (7/1)
1470 Quest For Best (USA), a temperamental filly, went for home half a mile out but she never looked that enthusiastic. (4/1)
1820 Kweilo again wore a tongue-strap. Shut in on the inside when he saw daylight, he found nothing at all. (9/2)
1322 Sandystones was in trouble early in the straight. (5/1)
Golden Saddle (USA), who did not impress with his action going down, wore a tongue-strap. Suddenly coming under pressure turning in, he dropped right away and his rider soon called it a day. (9/2)

T/Plpt: £102.70 (86.45 Tckts). T/Qdpt: £15.80 (49.15 Tckts) WG

2103-ASCOT (R-H) (Soft)
Saturday June 21st
WEATHER: sunny WIND: almost nil

2133 LONDON CLUBS FERN HILL RATED STKS H'CAP (0-105) (Listed) (3-Y.O F) (Class A)
2-00 (2-00) **1m (straight)** £12,578.80 (£4,709.20: £2,304.60: £993.00: £446.50: £227.90) Stalls: Low GOING: 0.22 sec per fur (G)

SP RR SF

958* **Brave Kris (IRE) (90)** (LMCumani) **3-9-0** LDettori(2) (stdd s: rdn & hdwy over 1f out: led ins fnl f: r.o wl) ....— **1** 5/1[1] 102 56
1453[3] **Dancing Drop (97)** (RHannon) **3-9-7** DaneO'Neill(5) (hdwy over 2f out: led over 1f out tl ins fnl f: unable qckn)..2½ **2** 14/1 104 58
1869[2] **Atlantic Desire (IRE) (88)** (MJohnston) **3-8-12** JWeaver(7) (led over 6f: one pce)..3 **3** 9/1[3] 89 43
1175[4] **Kalinka (IRE) (86)** (PFICole) **3-8-10** TQuinn(9) (nt clr run over 2f out: hdwy & nt clr run over 1f out: r.o ins fnl f)..½ **4** 7/1[2] 86 40
1740[7] **Marie Dora (FR) (83)** (IABalding) **3-8-7** SWhitworth(3) (nt clr run over 2f out: swtchd rt & hdwy over 1f out: nvr nrr)..2½ **5** 14/1 78 32
1740[5] **Baked Alaska (95)** (ACStewart) **3-9-5** MRoberts(4) (hld up: rdn over 3f out: wknd fnl f) 1½ **6** 10/1 87 41
1238[13] **Summer Queen (83)** (SPCWoods) **3-8-7** WRyan(6) (hdwy 2f out: wknd fnl f) 2 **7** 40/1 71 25
1304[2] **Selfish (90)** (HRACecil) **3-9-0** KFallon(11) (lw: prom over 6f)..1¾ **8** 5/1[1] 75 29
1823* **Gift Token (92)** (MajorDNChappell) **3-9-2** JReid(10) (lw: prom over 5f)..2 **9** 12/1 73 27
1875[6] **Flamboyance (USA) (90)** (JRFanshawe) **3-9-0** MHills(12) (prom over 6f)..nk **10** 10/1 70 24
1146[13] **Marathon Maid (85)** (RAFahey) **3-8-9b1** JQuinn(13) (a bhd) ....½ **11** 33/1 64 18
1453[4] **Alpine Time (IRE) (86)** (DRLoder) **3-8-10** PatEddery(1) (prom over 5f)..4 **12** 9/1[3] 57 11
(SP 110.4%) **12 Rn**

1m 45.93 (5.93) CSF £64.55 CT £531.55 TOTE £4.30: £1.80 £3.90 £2.90 (£30.10) Trio £69.10 OWNER Mr Robert Smith (NEWMARKET) BRED Clare Dore Ltd
LONG HANDICAP Summer Queen 8-3

958* Brave Kris (IRE), an excitable filly according to her trainer, was given a peach of a ride by Dettori, who switched her off nicely at the back of the field, and then produced her with a lovely run to get up in the last one hundred yards. (5/1)
1453 Dancing Drop coped with both the step-up in distance and the very soft ground - her two wins to date have come over six furlongs on a fast surface. Gaining the upper hand below the distance, she grimly made her way for home, but was unable to cope with the winner inside the final furlong. (14/1: 8/1-16/1)
1869 Atlantic Desire (IRE) took the field along but, collared over a furlong out, could then only struggle on at one pace. A step-up in trip may help. (9/1)
1175 Kalinka (IRE) did not have a trouble-free passage, and had nowhere to go on a couple of occasions before running on below the distance, only just failing to take third prize. She has shown herself to be an awkward customer in the past. (7/1)
1409* Marie Dora (FR) did not have the best of runs at the back of the field. Switched below the distance, she stayed on, but by then it was all too late. (14/1)
1740 Baked Alaska chased the leaders, but her jockey was hard at work on her soon after halfway and she eventually tired inside the distance. (10/1: 8/1-12/1)
1304 Selfish was very surprisingly running here, considering she has given clear indication on her last two outings that this trip is stretching her to the limit, and on this occasion she had soft ground to contend with. It therefore came as no surprise to see her tire below the distance. (5/1)
1823* Gift Token (12/1: 8/1-14/1)
1875 Flamboyance (USA) (10/1: op 6/1)
1453 Alpine Time (IRE) (9/1: 6/1-10/1)

2134 PALAN H'CAP (0-105) (3-Y.O) (Class B)
2-30 (2-32) **5f** £14,720.00 (£4,460.00: £2,180.00: £1,040.00) Stalls: Low GOING: 0.22 sec per fur (G)

SP RR SF

1980[6] **Prince Dome (IRE) (80)** (MartynWane) **3-7-12**(3) AWhelan(9) (a.p: rdn over 2f out: led 1f out: drvn out) ....— **1** 25/1 93 65
1980[3] **Bishops Court (98)** (MrsJRRamsden) **3-9-5** JFortune(6) (lw: hdwy over 1f out: ev ch ins fnl f: r.o) ....nk **2** 9/4[1] 110 82
1609[4] **Plaisir d'Amour (IRE) (81)** (NACallaghan) **3-7-11**(5) RFfrench(13) (rdn over 2f out: hdwy over 1f out: r.o ins fnl f)..4 **3** 14/1 80 52
1609[5] **Polish Warrior (IRE) (84)** (TDBarron) **3-8-5b1** TSprake(10) (led to 1f out: unable qckn)................................s.h **4** 10/1[3] 83 55
1294[11] **Mangus (IRE) (77)** (KOCunningham-Brown) **3-7-9**(3) DarrenMoffatt(16) (a.p: hrd rdn over 1f out: one pce) .....½ **5** 33/1 75 47
1737[16] **Rudi's Pet (IRE) (85)** (RHannon) **3-8-6b1** DaneO'Neill(12) (a.p: hrd rdn over 1f out: one pce) ....½ **6** 33/1 81 53
988[5] **Caerfilly Dancer (91)** (RAkehurst) **3-8-12** TQuinn(14) (hdwy over 2f out: rdn over 1f out: one pce) 1¼ **7** 20/1 83 55
1294[2] **Chili Concerto (86)** (PJMakin) **3-8-7** SSanders(19) (a.p: hrd rdn over 1f out: wknd fnl f) 1 **8** 14/1 75 47
1403[6] **Myrmidon (92)** (MrsLStubbs) **3-8-13** KFallon(4) (rdn & hdwy over 1f out: one pce) ....½ **9** 14/1 79 51
1766[10] **Dancethenightaway (88)** (BJMeehan) **3-8-9** PatEddery(7) (a mid div)..1 **10** 11/1 72 44
968[10] **Darb Alola (USA) (97)** (MRStoute) **3-9-4** JReid(5) (hld up: rdn over 2f out: wknd over 1f out) ....½ **11** 20/1 79 51
1799[12] **Swino (86)** (PDEvans) **3-8-7v1** JFEgan(17) (hdwy over 1f out: wknd fnl f)..nk **12** 25/1 67 39

				SP	RR	SF
1931*	**Ivory Dawn (77)** (KTIvory) **3-7-9**(3)ow2 MartinDwyer(18) (hdwy over 2f out: edgd lft 2f out: wknd fnl f)	1¾	**13**	20/1	53	23
1018^{4}	**Sabina (86)** (IABalding) **3-8-7** LDettori(2) (lw: mid div & no ch whn nt clr run on ins over 1f out)	1¼	**14**	6/1^{2}	58	30
1571*	**Bramble Bear (75)** (MBlanshard) **3-7-10** JQuinn(3) (bhd fnl 3f)	5	**15**	14/1	31	3
1275*	**Cauda Equina (77)** (MRChannon) **3-7-12** CRutter(11) (bmpd s: bhd fnl 2f)	nk	**16**	20/1	32	4
1975^{4}	**Kilcullen Lad (IRE) (87)** (PMooney) **3-8-8** WJO'Connor(15) (hdwy over 2f out: hmpd 2f out: sn wknd)	nk	**17**	25/1	41	13
2044^{4}	**Soviet Leader (86)** (RGuest) **3-8-7** PaulEddery(8) (b.hind: prom tl wknd & hmpd over 2f out)	1¼	**18**	20/1	36	8
				(SP 130.4%)		**18 Rn**

62.53 secs (2.33) CSF £68.40 CT £831.42 TOTE £57.30: £11.30 £1.50 £5.00 £2.60 (£91.60) Trio £524.40 OWNER Mr G. W. Jones (RICHMOND) BRED Airlie Stud

LONG HANDICAP Bramble Bear 7-7 Ivory Dawn 7-8

1980 Prince Dome (IRE), whose two wins to date have come on a fast surface, coped with the soft ground, although his trainer admitted he would not have wanted anymore rain. A leading player from the outset, he struck the front a furlong out and, although the runner-up looked like taking him soon afterwards, he kept pulling out a bit more to give Wane his biggest winner to date. He is still improving according to his trainer, and the drop from six furlongs to five furlongs made all the difference. (25/1)

1980 Bishops Court had both trip and going in his favour, so it was no surprise to see him all the rage in the market. He looked all set to land the odds as he launched his challenge inside the final furlong, but he had met a real tartar and was unable to get by. (9/4: 2/1-3/1)

1609 Plaisir d'Amour (IRE) found the drop to the minimum trip too sharp for her and, although running on in the last furlong-and-a-half to snatch third prize, found the first two had already flown. A return to six furlongs is required. (14/1: 10/1-20/1)

1609 Polish Warrior (IRE) took the field along but, collared a furlong from home, was then left standing. (10/1: op 6/1)

1018 Mangus (IRE), a leading player from the outset, never looked like quickening up in the final quarter-mile. (33/1)

501 Rudi's Pet (IRE) has been falling in the handicap and was back over a more suitable trip. Consequently he ran better, and was never far away if tapped for toe in the last two furlongs. (33/1)

1294 Chili Concerto (14/1: op 8/1)

1403 Myrmidon (14/1: 12/1-20/1)

2135 MILCARS CONDITIONS STKS (3-Y.O) (Class B)

3-00 (3-01) **1m 4f** £9,340.87 (£3,406.50: £1,665.75: £716.25: £320.63) Stalls: High GOING: 0.22 sec per fur (G)

				SP	RR	SF
1399*	**Falak (USA) (108)** (MajorWRHern) **3-9-5** RHills(3) (hld up: led 2f out: drvn out)	—	**1**	7/2^{3}	112	57
1159^{5}	**Monza (USA) (108)** (PWChapple-Hyam) **3-8-11** JReid(5) (led over 5f: led over 2f out: sn hdd: hrd rdn & ev ch ins fnl f: r.o wl)	hd	**2**	3/1^{2}	104	49
1307^{4}	**Conon Falls (IRE) (104)** (JHMGosden) **3-8-11** LDettori(1) (lw: chsd ldr: led over 6f out tl over 2f out: unable qckn)	5	**3**	7/4^{1}	97	42
1762*	**Poseidon** (MRChannon) **3-9-5** JFortune(2) (hld up: slipped & lost pl over 4f out: nt rcvr)	12	**4**	12/1	89	34
1962^{2}	**Blue River (IRE) (95)** (TGMills) **3-8-11** TQuinn(4) (bhd fnl 3f)	14	**5**	6/1	63	8
				(SP 105.6%)		**5 Rn**

2m 39.51 (9.51) CSF £11.77 TOTE £4.70: £2.00 £1.70 (£5.20) OWNER Mr Hamdan Al Maktoum (LAMBOURN) BRED Shadwell Farm Inc

1399* Falak (USA) saw out this longer trip in very testing conditions. He had no easy task with an 8lb penalty but, easing his way to the front a quarter-of-a-mile out, he showed real battling qualities to keep the very persistent runner-up at bay. The soft ground appeared to be no problem to him. (7/2)

1159 Monza (USA) enjoyed the soft ground and longer trip and put up a fine battling display. Having been collared by the winner, he refused to lie down and, battling his heart out, only just failed to get back up. His trainer will look for a small Listed race for him, but admitted it may well have to be on the continent. (3/1)

1307 Conon Falls (IRE) had the ground in his favour, but seems to lack a vital turn of foot even over this longer trip. Dettori tried to make a race of it as he moved the colt to the front soon after Swinley Bottom, but he was collared early in the straight and then tapped for toe. (7/4)

1762* Poseidon had not been asked any sort of question when losing his hind legs soon after the path just over half-a-mile from home. Losing ground and his action as a result, it was no surprise he could never get back into it. (12/1)

1962 Blue River (IRE) ran no race at all, and this ground may have been far too soft for his liking. (6/1)

2136 LADBROKE H'CAP (0-105) (4-Y.O+) (Class B)

3-35 (3-35) **1m 2f** £21,885.00 (£6,630.00: £3,240.00: £1,545.00) Stalls: High GOING: 0.22 sec per fur (G)

				SP	RR	SF
1160^{4}	**Winter Romance (100)** (EALDunlop) **4-9-9** MHills(2) (lw: hld up: chsd ldr 2f out: led over 1f out: drvn out)	—	**1**	9/2^{1}	114	73
1768^{4}	**Conspicuous (IRE) (81)** (LGCottrell) **7-8-4** MRoberts(13) (bhd whn nt clr run over 4f out: hdwy over 2f out: ev ch ins fnl f: r.o wl)	s.h	**2**	9/1	95	54
2028^{10}	**Docklands Limo (81)** (BJMcMath) **4-8-4** DHarrison(11) (a.p: led over 2f out tl over 1f out: unable qckn)	2	**3**	25/1	92	51
1771^{5}	**Romios (IRE) (90)** (PFICole) **5-8-13** TQuinn(1) (hdwy & edgd rt over 2f out: rdn over 1f out: one pce)	3½	**4**	10/1	95	54
1934^{2}	**Game Ploy (POL) (92)** (DHaydnJones) **5-9-1** PatEddery(7) (hdwy over 2f out: rdn over 1f out: wknd fnl f)	2	**5**	7/1^{2}	94	53
1768^{2}	**Star Manager (USA) (86)** (PFICole) **7-8-9** CRutter(15) (hld up: rdn over 2f out: sn wknd)	6	**6**	9/1	78	37
1979^{5}	**Master Beveled (76)** (PDEvans) **7-7-13**ow3 JFEgan(16) (b.nr fore: nvr nr to chal)	2	**7**	10/1	65	21
1414^{9}	**Arctiid (USA) (89)** (JHMGosden) **4-8-12** LDettori(18) (chsd ldr 8f: wknd over 1f out)	½	**8**	8/1^{3}	77	36
1261^{8}	**Wilcuma (105)** (PJMakin) **6-10-0** JFortune(8) (a bhd)	2	**9**	12/1	90	49
1160^{6}	**Musick House (IRE) (93)** (PWChapple-Hyam) **4-9-2b** JReid(4) (led over 7f)	½	**10**	16/1	77	36
1450^{10}	**Remaadi Sun (82)** (MDIUsher) **5-8-5** RStreet(3) (a bhd)	s.h	**11**	25/1	66	25
1768^{14}	**Henry The Fifth (89)** (CEBrittain) **4-8-12** WRyan(12) (bhd fnl 3f)	19	**12**	33/1	43	2
1559*	**Wafir (IRE) (85)** (PCalver) **5-8-5**(3) DarrenMoffatt(6) (lw: 9th whn hmpd & fell over 2f out)		**F**	7/1^{2}	—	—
				(SP 116.7%)		**13 Rn**

2m 11.97 (6.47) CSF £38.39 CT £829.99 TOTE £5.70: £2.20 £2.60 £5.50 (£19.70) Trio £178.80 OWNER Maktoum Al Maktoum (NEWMARKET) BRED Gainsborough Stud Management Ltd.

1160 Winter Romance had the soft ground he needs - he has not had it since winning in the mud at Haydock in May 1996 - and duly obliged. Coping well with the longer trip, he struck the front approaching the final furlong but, with the runner-up finishing really well, would surely have been passed in a few more strides. (9/2)

1768 Conspicuous (IRE) ran a tremendous race. Picking up ground early in the straight, he threw down the gauntlet inside the final furlong and would surely have prevailed in a couple more strides. He is a winner without a penalty. (9/1)

1268 Docklands Limo, who cut little ice in the Bessborough Handicap at the Royal Meeting on Wednesday, appreciated the return to a mile-and-a-quarter. Sent on early in the straight, he was collared approaching the final furlong and then tapped for toe. (25/1)

1771 Romios (IRE) has won twice on this ground. Drifting right as he picked up ground early in the straight, he failed to quicken from below the distance. (10/1)

1934 Game Ploy (POL), 11lb higher than he has ever won off, found the ground all against him and, after taking closer order early in the straight, was out on his feet inside the final furlong. (7/1)
1768 Star Manager (USA) is not easy to win with and is currently 5lb higher than he has ever won off. (9/1: 7/1-12/1)
Arctiid (USA) (8/1: 6/1-9/1)
1261 Wilcuma (12/1: op 8/1)

2137 TRIUMVIRATE LIMITED STKS (0-90) (3-Y.O) (Class C)
4-10 (4-10) **1m (round)** £6,272.00 (£2,348.00: £1,149.00: £495.00: £222.50: £113.50) Stalls: High GOING: 0.22 sec per fur (G)

	Horse	Dist	Pos	SP	RR	SF
963[3]	**Right Wing (IRE) (89)** (MajorWRHern) **3-8-11** TSprake(3) (squeezed out & dropped rr over 6f out: hdwy 2f out: led over 1f out: edgd rt ins fnl f: r.o wl)	—	**1**	6/1[3]	95	67
1146[11]	**Sugarfoot (90)** (NTinkler) **3-8-11** WRyan(2) (hdwy 2f out: chsd wnr over 1f out: r.o one pce)	¾	**2**	20/1	94	66
1399[8]	**Lord Eurolink (IRE) (90)** (JLDunlop) **3-8-13** LDettori(8) (rdn over 2f out: hdwy over 1f out: r.o one pce)	1½	**3**	7/1	93	65
723[8]	**Maftool (82)** (JHMGosden) **3-8-13** RHills(9) (lw: hdwy over 1f out: hrd rdn: one pce)	2½	**4**	12/1	88	60
1777*	**Another Night (IRE) (88)** (RHannon) **3-8-13** DaneO'Neill(7) (s.s: hdwy to chse ldr over 6f out: led 2f out tl over 1f out: sn wknd)	½	**5**	14/1	87	59
776[2]	**Courtship (88)** (HRACecil) **3-8-11** KFallon(6) (lw: a.p: rdn over 2f out: wknd over 1f out)	2½	**6**	11/2[2]	80	52
1406*	**Sweet Contralto (85)** (DRLoder) **3-8-10** PatEddery(1) (prom over 5f)	2	**7**	2/1[1]	75	47
1741[6]	**Strathmore Clear (89)** (GLewis) **3-9-1** PaulEddery(4) (led 6f)	3½	**8**	14/1	73	45
1110*	**Irish Light (USA) (85)** (MRStoute) **3-8-10** JReid(5) (prom over 6f)	1½	**9**	11/2[2]	65	37
				(SP 116.7%)		**9 Rn**

1m 45.4 (4.60) CSF £105.46 TOTE £7.70: £2.30 £3.10 £2.00 (£72.60) Trio £215.60 OWNER Lord Chelsea (LAMBOURN) BRED Tarworth Bloodstock Investments Ltd and J. J. Melk
963 Right Wing (IRE) coped well with the testing ground. Striking the front below the distance, he drifted right inside the final furlong but, despite this and his rider dropping his whip, the combination was not going to be caught. (6/1: 4/1-13/2)
957 Sugarfoot came through to take second place below the distance but, despite staying on, was unable to seriously threaten the winner. He did not like the soft ground according to his trainer. (20/1)
1023* Lord Eurolink (IRE) who appeared not to stay a mile-and-a-quarter last time out, appreciated the drop in distance, and stayed on in the last furlong and a half to take third prize. (7/1)
463* Maftool picked up ground nicely below the distance, but once pressure was applied, did not find as much as was first expected. (12/1)
1777* Another Night (IRE) had more on his plate here. Striking the front early in the straight, he was soon headed and beaten. (14/1: 10/1-16/1)
776 Courtship was close up until calling it a day below the distance. (11/2: 4/1-6/1)
1406* Sweet Contralto (2/1: op 3/1)
1741 Strathmore Clear (14/1: 8/1-16/1)
1110* Irish Light (USA) (11/2: 4/1-6/1)

2138 E.B.F. NOVICE STKS (2-Y.O F) (Class D)
4-40 (4-41) **6f** £5,550.00 (£1,680.00: £820.00: £390.00) Stalls: Low GOING: 0.22 sec per fur (G)

	Horse	Dist	Pos	SP	RR	SF
1664*	**Ffestiniog (IRE)** (PFICole) **2-9-3** TQuinn(2) (mde all: rdn out)	—	**1**	3/1[1]	81	49
	Forum (CEBrittain) **2-8-11** BDoyle(5) (leggy: scope: s.s: stdy hdwy 2f out: rdn over 1f out: r.o)	1¾	**2**	12/1	70	38
1827[3]	**Fire Goddess** (JSMoore) **2-8-11** WJO'Connor(10) (hld up: rdn over 1f out: unable qckn)	2½	**3**	16/1	64	32
	Next Round (IRE) (MBell) **2-8-11** MFenton(8) (lt-f: rdn & hdwy over 1f out: r.o)	nk	**4**	14/1	63	31
1564[4]	**Mighty Magic** (MrsPNDutfield) **2-8-11** SSanders(11) (lw: hdwy over 2f out: rdn over 1f out: one pce)	1¾	**5**	12/1	58	26
897*	**Days of Grace** (MartynMeade) **2-9-1** FNorton(9) (a.p: rdn over 2f out: wknd fnl f)	2½	**6**	12/1	56	24
	Dancing Icon (IRE) (RHannon) **2-8-11** RHughes(3) (unf: scope: hld up: n.m.r on ins over 4f out: nt clr run over 2f out: wknd over 1f out)	nk	**7**	5/1[3]	51	19
	Surpresa Cara (GLewis) **2-8-11** PaulEddery(1) (scope: bit bkwd: s.s: a bhd)	¾	**8**	10/1	49	17
1954[4]	**Muja's Magic (IRE)** (KTIvory) **2-8-8**(3) MartinDwyer(7) (prom over 4f)	2	**9**	14/1	43	11
1295[5]	**Angelique** (MJHaynes) **2-8-11** JReid(4) (lw: bhd fnl 3f)	nk	**10**	14/1	43	11
1827*	**Lisa's Pride (IRE)** (MissGayKelleway) **2-8-13** KFallon(6) (lw: hld up: rdn over 2f out: sn wknd)	16	**11**	9/2[2]	2	—
				(SP 117.9%)		**11 Rn**

1m 19.17 (5.17) CSF £37.16 TOTE £2.90: £1.50 £4.20 £4.00 (£34.20) Trio £108.20 OWNER Elite Racing Club (WHATCOMBE) BRED Theo Waddington
1664* Ffestiniog (IRE), who has been working well since her Folkestone victory, is certainly going the right way and once again made every post a winning one, being rousted along to keep her rivals at bay. She is now likely to be upped in class, probably to listed company. (3/1)
Forum, a tall filly with plenty of room for development, made a very pleasing debut. Creeping closer a quarter-of-a-mile from home, she ran on nicely in the closing stages to finish a very promising second. She is very good according to her trainer, who hopes to run her in some of the top fillies' races over seven furlongs or a mile. She should soon be winning. (12/1: 6/1-14/1)
1827 Fire Goddess chased the leaders but, asked for her effort in the last furlong-and-a-half, failed to find the necessary turn of foot. (16/1)
Next Round (IRE), a lightly-made individual, put in some nice work in the last furlong-and-a-half, only just failing to take third prize. (14/1: 8/1-16/1)
1564 Mighty Magic took closer order soon after halfway, but never looked like quickening up from below the distance. (12/1: op 20/1)
897* Days of Grace was close up until tiring inside the final furlong. (12/1: op 7/1)
Dancing Icon (IRE), quite a lengthy filly who needs time to develop, did not have the best of runs, but had shot her bolt below the distance. (5/1: 3/1-11/2)
Surpresa Cara (10/1: 5/1-12/1)

2139 CHURCHILL H'CAP (0-80) (3-Y.O+) (Class D)
5-10 (5-10) **2m 45y** £5,836.00 (£1,768.00: £864.00: £412.00) Stalls: High GOING: 0.22 sec per fur (G)

	Horse	Dist	Pos	SP	RR	SF
1413[8]	**Bolivar (IRE) (65)** (RAkehurst) **5-8-13b** TQuinn(17) (led 2f: hrd rdn over 1f out: led wl ins fnl f: r.o wl)	—	**1**	6/1[2]	77	59
1387*	**Right Man (68)** (GLewis) **3-7-5**(5) RFfrench(7) (lw: rdn & hdwy over 2f out: r.o wl ins fnl f)	½	**2**	11/4[1]	80	42
735[14]	**Shaft of Light (78)** (LordHuntingdon) **5-9-12** LDettori(15) (lw: led over 14f out tl over 9f out: led 3f out tl wl ins fnl f: unable qckn)	½	**3**	10/1	89	71
1956*	**Sudest (IRE) (70)** (IABalding) **3-7-9**(3)ow1 MartinDwyer(1) (lw: rdn & hdwy over 2f out: swtchd rt over 1f out: r.o)	1½	**4**	10/1	80	41
1648[2]	**Diego (67)** (CEBrittain) **4-9-1** DJWhyte(12) (hld up: rdn over 2f out: one pce)	5	**5**	16/1	72	54
1413[5]	**Bridie's Pride (48)** (GAHam) **6-7-3**(7) JFowle(16) (a.p: ev ch over 2f out: wknd over 1f out)	nk	**6**	50/1	52	34
1494[4]	**French Ivy (USA) (63)** (FMurphy) **10-8-11** KFallon(14) (b: nvr nr to chal)	¾	**7**	7/1[3]	67	49

1795[2] **Tawafek (USA) (65)** (SDow) **4-8-13** JReid(9) (nvr nrr) 3 **8** 12/1 66 48
1665[11] **Veronica Franco (48)** (RIngram) **4-7-10** NAdams(4) (s.s: hdwy over 2f out: wknd over 1f out)....5 **9** 50/1 44 26
1092[6] **Palamon (USA) (75)** (PEccles) **4-9-9** JFortune(8) (lw: hld up: rdn over 2f out: sn wknd: t.o)....18 **10** 33/1 53 35
1678[4] **Sandy Floss (IRE) (70)** (RHBuckler) **4-9-4** PatEddery(10) (b: hld up: rdn over 5f out: wknd over 2f out: t.o)...29 **11** 14/1 19 1
650[12] **Requested (50)** (MDIUsher) **10-7-12v[1]** DRMcCabe(13) (s.s: a bhd: t.o) ....12 **12** 40/1 — —
1778* **Samuel Scott (77)** (MCPipe) **4-9-11** DaneO'Neill(5) (lw: a.p: led over 9f out to 3f out: wkng whn broke down & p.u over 1f out: dead).... **P** 6/1[2] — —
1133[2] **High Five (IRE) (48)** (RIngram) **7-7-10** JQuinn(11) (b: lw: bhd fnl 7f: t.o whn p.u over 2f out: dismntd).... **P** 8/1 — —
(SP 126.6%) **14 Rn**

3m 38.67 (11.47) CSF £21.44 CT £156.09 TOTE £6.60: £2.00 £2.00 £2.40 (£9.40) Trio £55.60 OWNER BEL Leisure Ltd (EPSOM) BRED A. Hanahoe
LONG HANDICAP Bridie's Pride 7-5 Veronica Franco 7-6 Right Man 7-8
WEIGHT FOR AGE 3yo-20lb

Bolivar (IRE), whose trainer was concerned that the gelding would not handle the soft ground, had no problems with it. A leading light from the off, he responded to pressure to get up in the last fifty yards. It takes a lot of work to get him fit, Akehurst later revealed. (6/1)
1387* Right Man had no problems with this longer trip. Put to sleep off the pace, he picked up ground in the straight and, running on strongly, only just failed in a tight finish. (11/4)
Shaft of Light ran much better and, after showing in front early on, regained the advantage turning for home. Grimly trying to fend off his rivals, he was eventually worried out of it in the closing stages. (10/1)
1956* Sudest (IRE) continues in fine form and seemed to cope with the soft ground on this occasion. Weaving his way through the pack in the straight, he finished right on the heels of the principals. (10/1: op 6/1)
1648 Diego chased the leaders, but was making little impression on the principals in the straight. (16/1)
1413 Bridie's Pride was close up until calling it a day below the distance. (50/1)
1795 Tawafek (USA) (12/1: op 8/1)

T/Jkpt: £335,618.20 (0.46 Tckts); £255,258.93 to 23/6/97. T/Plpt: £185.40 (603.17 Tckts). T/Qdpt: £64.30 (49.1 Tckts) AK

2109-**AYR (L-H) (Good)**
Saturday June 21st
WEATHER: overcast & heavy showers WIND: mod bhd

2140 SEAFIELD NOVICE AUCTION STKS (2-Y.O) (Class E)
2-15 (2-16) **5f** £2,781.25 (£835.00: £402.50: £186.25) Stalls: High GOING minus 0.14 sec per fur (G)

SP RR SF
1729* **Baby Grand (IRE)** (TDBarron) **2-8-5**(7) KimberleyHart(3) (mde most: rdn 2f out: hld on wl)....— **1** 100/30[3] 80 40
1760* **Premium Pursuit** (RAFahey) **2-9-4** ACulhane(1) (a cl up: kpt on wl fnl 2f)....½ **2** 3/1[2] 84 44
1729[2] **Always Lucky** (JBerry) **2-8-4**(3) PFessey(4) (lw: disp ld 3f: rdn & one pce)....2½ **3** 5/2[1] 65 25
Barrelbio (IRE) (JJO'Neill) **2-8-5** GDuffield(5) (cmpt: s.s: bhd tl styd on fnl f)....4 **4** 50/1 51 11
897[4] **Rhinefield Beauty (IRE)** (JSGoldie) **2-8-0** TWilliams(2) (s.i.s: sn trckng ldrs: effrt 2f out: no rspnse: fin lame)1½ **5** 3/1[2] 41 1
(SP 103.6%) **5 Rn**

59.5 secs (2.50) CSF £10.79 TOTE £3.30: £1.30 £1.90 (£8.20) OWNER Mrs D. E. Sharp (THIRSK) BRED Rathbarry Stud
OFFICIAL EXPLANATION **Rhinefield Beauty (IRE): returned lame on her off-fore.**
1729* Baby Grand (IRE) has plenty of early pace and is tough and genuine, and refused to be beaten. (100/30: 9/4-7/2)
1760* Premium Pursuit, who ideally needs further, put in a useful effort in the circumstances. (3/1)
1729 Always Lucky, from a yard in top form, looked particularly well and had the speed to take the winner on but, when it came down to a fight, it was a different matter. (5/2)
Barrelbio (IRE), a handy type, has plenty to learn but he was picking up at the end, and there would seem to be some ability there. (50/1)
897 Rhinefield Beauty (IRE) ran moderately, dropping tamely away in the last two furlongs, and was later found to be lame. (3/1)

2141 GOLF EVENTS H'CAP (0-90) (3-Y.O) (Class C)
2-45 (2-47) **5f** £5,312.50 (£1,600.00: £1,136.75: £1,136.75) Stalls: High GOING minus 0.14 sec per fur (G)

SP RR SF
1673[7] **Nifty Norman (72)** (JBerry) **3-8-2**(5) TEDurcan(6) (cl up: led ½-wy: r.o)....— **1** 5/1 79 30
1764* **Furnish (86)** (BWHills) **3-9-7** DHolland(3) (a cl up: rdn 2f out: kpt on)....1¼ **2** 7/2[3] 89 40
1980[9] **Silent Miracle (IRE) (75)** (MBell) **3-8-10** ACulhane(5) (lw: led to ½-wy: rdn & r.o one pce)....1¼ **3** 9/4[1] 74 25
1673[3] **Night Flight (78)** (JJO'Neill) **3-8-13** GDuffield(4) (lw: dwlt: sn chsng ldrs: rdn 2f out: kpt on towards fin)....d.h **3** 3/1[2] 81 32
1989* **Levelled (75)** (MRChannon) **3-8-7**(3) 7x PPMurphy(1) (chsd ldrs: rdn 2f out: grad wknd)....4 **5** 7/1 61 12
Martine (69) (ABailey) **3-7-13**(5) IonaWands(2) (nvr wnt pce)....1 **6** 20/1 52 3
(SP 111.9%) **6 Rn**

59.79 secs (2.79) CSF £20.41 TOTE £6.00: £2.70 £2.00 (£10.20) OWNER Mrs Norma Peebles (COCKERHAM) BRED Mrs Norma Peebles
1673 Nifty Norman, given a chance by the Handicapper, appreciated the rain that fell during the afternoon and bounced back to form in good style. (5/1)
1764* Furnish looked to have plenty on, but ran a fair race and, by the look of things, should stay a bit further. (7/2)
1170 Silent Miracle (IRE) had her chances but, when the pressure was on, she lacked the speed over this trip. (9/4)
1673 Night Flight was always finding this trip a bit on the sharp side, but he was battling on well at the end. (3/1)
1989* Levelled showed up well but his penalty seemed to anchor him in the last two furlongs. (7/1)
Martine, having her first run of the season, was always finding things happening too quickly at this trip. (20/1)

2142 TENNENT CALEDONIAN BREWERIES TROPHY RATED STKS H'CAP (0-90) (3-Y.O+) (Class C)
3-15 (3-16) **1m 7f** £6,239.15 (£2,275.40: £1,112.70: £478.50: £214.25) Stalls: Low GOING minus 0.14 sec per fur (G)

SP RR SF
1804* **In Question (83)** (BWHills) **3-9-3** DHolland(2) (lw: mde all: qcknd clr over 2f out: hung lft & styd on wl)....— **1** 9/4[1] 95 17
1242[3] **Percy Isle (IRE) (84)** (MRStoute) **3-9-4** GDuffield(1) (trckd wnr: effrt over 3f out: r.o one pce)....6 **2** 5/2[2] 90 12
Go With The Wind (64) (JSGoldie) **4-8-12**(5) RMullen(3) (hld up: effrt 4f out: styd on: no imp)....5 **3** 10/1 64 5
1408[4] **Secret Service (IRE) (70)** (CWThornton) **5-9-9** DeanMcKeown(5) (chsd ldrs: rdn appr st: btn over 2f out)....2 **4** 7/2[3] 68 9
1224[4] **Dirab (75)** (TDBarron) **4-10-0** LCharnock(4) (lw: prom: rdn 5f out: btn over 3f out)....9 **5** 5/1 64 5
(SP 107.3%) **5 Rn**

3m 24.81 (14.11) CSF £7.01 TOTE £3.00: £1.30 £1.90 (£1.80) OWNER Mr K. Abdulla (LAMBOURN) BRED Juddmonte Farms

WEIGHT FOR AGE 3yo-19lb
1804* In Question appreciated the big step-up in distance and, by the look of things, there is better to come and he should stay further yet. (9/4: 6/4-5/2)
1242 Percy Isle (IRE) looks a real stayer and he has a laid-back attitude, but found this winner far too good. (5/2)
Go With The Wind ran reasonably but was never doing enough to make any impression on the front pair. (10/1)
1408 Secret Service (IRE) did not look quite right and ran moderately, being beaten early in the straight. This is certainly not his true form. (7/2)
1224 Dirab ran no sort of race and this effort is best forgotten. (5/1)

2143 ROMAN WARRIOR SHIELD MAIDEN STKS (3-Y.O+) (Class D)

3-45 (3-47) **7f** £3,434.50 (£1,036.00: £503.00: £236.50) Stalls: Low GOING minus 0.14 sec per fur (G)

				SP	RR	SF
1866^{4}	**Dundel (IRE) (80)** (BWHills) **3-8-7** DHolland(4) (lw: trckd ldrs: led 2f out: rdn & r.o wl)	—	**1**	11/4^{2}	80	23
1643^{3}	**Literary (80)** (JHMGosden) **3-8-7** GHind(3) (led tl hdd 2f out: one pce)	5	**2**	3/1^{3}	69	12
	Native Rhythm (IRE) (PWChapple-Hyam) **3-8-4**(3) RHavlin(5) (lw: a chsng ldrs: effrt 3f out: styd on same pce)	1½	**3**	6/4^{1}	65	8
1090^{6}	**Ocker (IRE) (71)** (MHTompkins) **3-8-12** DaleGibson(8) (chsd ldrs: c wd st: sn rdn & no imp)	3½	**4**	5/1	62	5
983^{12}	**Bernie's Star (IRE)** (NBycroft) **3-8-12** LCharnock(1) (sn outpcd & bhd)	16	**5**	100/1	26	—
	Fizzy Boy (IRE) (PMonteith) **4-9-4**(3) PFessey(6) (prom to st: sn lost pl)	2½	**6**	100/1	20	—
1798^{13}	**Lake Aria** (MrsAMNaughton) **4-8-11**(5) JBramhill(2) (chsd ldrs tl outpcd appr st: sn t.o)	10	**7**	150/1	—	—
	Ballantrae Boy (RMMcKellar) **3-8-12** GDuffield(7) (b: b.hind: s.s: sn wl t.o)	dist	**8**	50/1	—	—
				(SP 112.9%)	**8 Rn**	

1m 29.29 (4.89) CSF £10.11 TOTE £3.70: £1.60 £1.10 £1.30 (£3.30) OWNER Sheikh Mohammed (LAMBOURN) BRED Sheikh Mohammed Bin Rashid Al Maktoum
WEIGHT FOR AGE 3yo-9lb
1866 Dundel (IRE), a lean filly, dropped back in trip, got it right and won in useful style. (11/4: 2/1-3/1)
1643 Literary, an edgy sort, was taken to post early and attempted to make all, but was well out-pointed in the last couple of furlongs. (3/1)
Native Rhythm (IRE) looked fit for her seasonal debut but was a bit on edge, and was never doing enough when ridden early in the straight. (6/4)
1090 Ocker (IRE) was always having to race wide to get in a challenge, and his lack of pace was well exposed in the final three furlongs. (5/1)
Bernie's Star (IRE) has plenty to learn yet. (100/1)

2144 ARRAN H'CAP (0-70) (3-Y.O+) (Class E)

4-15 (4-20) **7f** £3,093.25 (£931.00: £450.50: £210.25) Stalls: Low GOING minus 0.14 sec per fur (G)

				SP	RR	SF
2033*	**Mister Westsound (42)** (MissLAPerratt) **5-8-2b** 6x NKennedy(13) (lw: s.i.s: hdwy on outside over 2f out: led ins fnl f: comf)	—	**1**	6/1^{3}	55+	20
2019^{8}	**Dictation (USA) (54)** (JJO'Neill) **5-9-0** GDuffield(12) (lw: a.p: styd on u.p fnl f)	2½	**2**	20/1	61	26
2033^{3}	**Suedoro (39)** (JSGoldie) **7-7-8**(5) JBramhill(10) (lw: in tch: effrt over 2f out: styd on fnl f)	1¼	**3**	16/1	43	8
1658^{7}	**Myttons Mistake (56)** (ABailey) **4-8-11**(5) IonaWands(9) (a.p: led over 2f out tl ins fnl f: one pce)	½	**4**	12/1	59	24
1613^{7}	**Termon (38)** (MissLAPerratt) **4-7-12** NCarlisle(5) (hld up: effrt 3f out: n.m.r: styd on ins fnl f)	nk	**5**	14/1	41	6
1285^{7}	**Nkapen Rocks (SPA) (53)** (CaptJWilson) **4-8-10**(3) PFessey(4) (stdd s: bhd tl styd on wl fnl 2f)	nk	**6**	20/1	55	20
1505^{2}	**Statoyork (63)** (BWHills) **4-9-9** DHolland(7) (bhd: effrt & nt clr run 2f out: hdwy over 1f out: no ex ins fnl f)	s.h	**7**	4/1^{2}	65	30
1603^{9}	**Miss Pigalle (37)** (MissLAPerratt) **6-7-11** LCharnock(3) (chsd ldrs tl wknd over 1f out)	1¾	**8**	16/1	35	—
1631^{11}	**Stephensons Rocket (49)** (RAFahey) **6-8-9** GHind(11) (in tch: effrt over 2f out: sn btn)	1½	**9**	20/1	43	8
1632^{21}	**Sweet Ciseaux (IRE) (37)** (MJHeaton-Ellis) **4-7-11**ow1 DaleGibson(8) (lw: chsd ldrs tl wknd fnl 2f)	2½	**10**	12/1	26	—
1800^{2}	**Pleasure Trick (USA) (41)** (DonEnricoIncisa) **6-8-1** KimTinkler(2) (a bhd)	s.h	**11**	9/1	30	—
1315^{2}	**Superpride (57)** (MrsMReveley) **5-9-3** ACulhane(1) (lw: led tl hdd over 2f out: sn btn)	¾	**12**	3/1^{1}	44	9
477^{10}	**Greatest (66)** (MissGayKelleway) **6-9-7b**(5) RMullen(6) (cl up tl wknd wl over 2f out)	9	**13**	12/1	32	—
				(SP 125.1%)	**13 Rn**	

1m 29.1 (4.70) CSF £116.64 CT £1,095.00 TOTE £7.90: £1.90 £2.40 £5.30 (£133.00) Trio £278.90; £117.86 to 23/6/97 OWNER David Sutherland-Ian Hay (AYR) BRED Red House Stud
LONG HANDICAP Sweet Ciseaux (IRE) 7-9
2033* Mister Westsound gained his first win over this trip in some style and is flying at present. (6/1)
1800 Dictation (USA) is a most frustrating character as he keeps running well without success, but the ability is obviously there if the key can be found. (20/1)
2033 Suedoro is running into form and is worth keeping an eye on. (16/1)
371 Myttons Mistake has not won for two years, but he is in good form just now. (12/1)
1613 Termon is running reasonably and there could be a race to be found for her. (14/1)
1285 Nkapen Rocks (SPA) has plenty of ability but rarely puts it in, although he was finishing strongly this time. (20/1)
1505 Statoyork (4/1: 3/1-9/2)
538 Sweet Ciseaux (IRE) (12/1: op 8/1)
1800 Pleasure Trick (USA) (9/1: 6/1-10/1)
403 Greatest (12/1: op 6/1)

2145 DOONFOOT H'CAP (0-60) (3-Y.O+) (Class F)

4-50 (4-51) **1m 2f 192y** £2,864.00 (£804.00: £392.00) Stalls: Low GOING minus 0.14 sec per fur (G)

				SP	RR	SF
1992^{2}	**Westminster (IRE) (60)** (MHTompkins) **5-9-7v**(7) PClarke(4) (hld up & bhd: hdwy on bit 3f out: led appr fnl f: shkn up & r.o)	—	**1**	4/1^{2}	74	43
1601^{8}	**Bruz (29)** (LLungo) **6-7-11**ow1 DaleGibson(9) (bhd: hdwy 3f out: chsd wnr fnl f: styd on wl)	4	**2**	33/1	37	5
1943^{6}	**Philgem (36)** (CWFairhurst) **4-8-4** NKennedy(16) (hld up & bhd: hdwy appr st: disp ld 2f out: hdd appr fnl f: kpt on)	4	**3**	9/1^{3}	38	7
1748^{10}	**Forzair (50)** (JJO'Neill) **5-9-4v^{1}** DeanMcKeown(7) (lw: in tch tl hmpd & lost pl 6f out: styd on u.p fnl 3f: nrst fin)	4	**4**	33/1	46	15
	Thisonesforalice (38) (JSGoldie) **9-7-13**(7)ow3 AEddery(11) (hld up: hdwy to disp ld 2f out: hdd appr fnl f: wknd)	2	**5**	50/1	31	—
1232^{9}	**Vintage Taittinger (IRE) (32)** (JSGoldie) **5-7-11**(3) PFessey(14) (lw: chsd ldrs: rdn appr st: outpcd fnl 3f)	7	**6**	4/1^{2}	15	—
1463^{4}	**Snowy Mantle (39)** (JDBethell) **4-8-7** TWilliams(8) (lw: trckd ldrs: gng wl: led 3f out to 2f out: rdn & fnd nil)	¾	**7**	3/1^{1}	21	—

955[8]	**Shamokin (32)** (FWatson) **5-7-7**(7)ow2 KimberleyHart(3) (w ldrs tl wknd fnl 3½f)	5	**8**	16/1	7	—
1469[14]	**Bout (41)** (RMMcKellar) **3-7-3**(7) JMcAuley(13) (b.nr hind: prom: outpcd appr st: sn btn)	1¼	**9**	33/1	14	—
1333[10]	**Emily-Jayne (41)** (MrsMReveley) **3-7-5**(5) IonaWands(1) (outpcd 7f out: n.d after)	1½	**10**	33/1	12	—
1943[4]	**Carol Again (28)** (NBycroft) **5-7-10b[1]** LCharnock(5) (trckd ldrs: chal appr st: wknd fnl 2½f)	1½	**11**	33/1	—	—
1818[3]	**Mcgillycuddy Reeks (IRE) (38)** (DonEnricoIncisa) **6-8-6** KimTinkler(6) (led tl hdd 3f out: sn rdn & btn)	1½	**12**	14/1	4	—
1837[7]	**Rapid Mover (32)** (DANolan) **10-7-9b**(5)ow4 KSked(12) (chsd ldrs tl wknd qckly appr st)	3½	**13**	25/1	—	—
1840[6]	**Silver Pearl (40)** (MrsAMNaughton) **6-8-3**(5) JBramhill(15) (b: chsd ldrs tl wknd fnl 3f)	4	**14**	10/1	—	—
	Chanson d'Amour (IRE) (42) (MissLAPerratt) **3-7-11** NCarlisle(2) (lw: a bhd: t.o)	dist	**15**	50/1	—	—

(SP 119.1%) **15 Rn**

2m 23.64 (7.74) CSF £127.19 CT £1,026.78 TOTE £3.90: £1.50 £8.50 £2.40 (£473.70) Trio £239.60; £141.75 to 23/6/97 OWNER Mr Michael Jenkins (NEWMARKET) BRED Ballymacarney Stud

LONG HANDICAP Emily-Jayne 7-9 Bruz 7-9 Rapid Mover 7-8 Carol Again 7-7 Bout 7-4

WEIGHT FOR AGE 3yo-13lb

1992 Westminster (IRE), given a most patient ride, came sailing through on the bridle and, racing up the stands' side, trotted up. (4/1)

1229 Bruz, like the winner, came wide and late, but was never anything like good enough. (33/1)

1601 Philgem ran a fair race and is keeping her form really well this year. (9/1: 6/1-10/1)

1579 Forzair, in a visor for the first time, was messed about by weakening horses on the home turn but, given some strong assistance, stayed on steadily. (33/1)

Thisonesforalice, having his first run for over a year, put up a decent performance and his stable is certainly in good form. (50/1)

Vintage Taittinger (IRE) has been winning over hurdles, but found this trip on the sharp side. (4/1)

1463 Snowy Mantle travelled as though this was hers for the taking but, when it came down to a struggle in the last two furlongs, she was extremely disappointing. (3/1)

1618 Carol Again had blinkers on for the first time and raced far too freely. (33/1)

950* Silver Pearl (10/1: 7/1-12/1)

T/Plpt: £160.90 (72.98 Tckts). T/Qdpt: £80.40 (7.25 Tckts) AA

1964-LINGFIELD (L-H) (Turf Good, AWT Standard)
Saturday June 21st

WEATHER: unsettled WIND: fresh half bhd

2146 TAIWAN AMATEUR H'CAP (0-70) (3-Y.O+) (Class F)

6-15 (6-19) **1m 3f 106y** £2,277.00 (£627.00: £297.00) GOING minus 0.28 sec per fur (GF)

				SP	RR	SF
1507*	**Manileno (51)** (MCPipe) **3-9-8** MrJGoldstein(9) (lw: mde all: rdn over 2f out: clr over 1f out: easily)	—	**1**	11/8[1]	61+	16
1463[13]	**Benjamins Law (45)** (JAPickering) **6-9-10**(5) MrVLukaniuk(6) (hld up: hdwy 5f out: chsd wnr over 1f out: no imp)	3½	**2**	8/1[2]	50	18
	Grand Applause (IRE) (40) (MSalaman) **7-9-5**(5) MrSRutherford(2) (hld up: stdy hdwy over 4f out: styd on fnl 2f)	3½	**3**	20/1	40	8
1748[P]	**Gold Blade (65)** (JPearce) **8-11-7** MrsLPearce(5) (hld up & bhd: gd hdwy 5f out: one pce fnl 2f)	nk	**4**	8/1[2]	65	33
770[5]	**Nails Tails (36)** (SDow) **4-9-6** MrTCuff(1) (lw: lost pl 6f out: rallied 2f out: styd on fnl f)	1¼	**5**	8/1[2]	34	2
1779[14]	**Don't Drop Bombs (USA) (46)** (DTThom) **8-10-2v** MissJFeilden(3) (chsd wnr tl wknd over 1f out)	1	**6**	10/1[3]	43	11
1663[5]	**Spectacle Jim (43)** (BAPearce) **8-9-8**(5)ow7 MrsKHills(8) (b: lw: prom 8f)	1½	**7**	50/1	38	—
1779[12]	**Strat's Legacy (39)** (DWPArbuthnot) **10-9-9** MrsDArbuthnot(13) (nvr trbld ldrs)	3	**8**	12/1	29	—
1445[5]	**Spiral Flyer (IRE) (35)** (MDIUsher) **4-9-0**(5)ow5 MrsAUsher(10) (bhd fnl 4f)	3½	**9**	14/1	21	—
1779[10]	**Mega Tid (32)** (JRPoulton) **5-8-11**(5)ow1 MissJWormall(12) (chsd ldrs tl rdn & wknd 3f out)	3	**10**	33/1	13	—
1944[8]	**Montone (IRE) (60)** (JRJenkins) **7-11-2** DrMMannish(7) (a bhd)	1½	**11**	20/1	39	7
1138[5]	**Burning Cost (40)** (REPeacock) **7-9-5**(5)ow10 MrsCPeacock(11) (racd wd: prom over 8f: t.o)	9	**12**	50/1	7	—
607[13]	**Sussex Gorse (39)** (JELong) **6-9-4b**(5)ow9 MrTWaters(4) (plld hrd: a bhd)	9	**13**	100/1	—	—

(SP 116.3%) **13 Rn**

2m 34.66 (9.96) CSF £9.89 CT £141.23 TOTE £2.50: £1.90 £2.60 £3.80 (£8.70) Trio £20.80 OWNER Mr Stuart Mercer (WELLINGTON) BRED Mrs C. Ashworth and C. Barber-Lomax

LONG HANDICAP Burning Cost 8-9 Sussex Gorse 7-13

WEIGHT FOR AGE 3yo-13lb

1507* Manileno had little difficulty defying a 6lb hike in the ratings. (11/8)

1233 Benjamins Law seemed to stay this longer distance well enough, and simply met one too good. (8/1)

Grand Applause (IRE), still a maiden, made a respectable comeback and should benefit from a stiffer test of stamina. (20/1)

384 Gold Blade, down to a mark 2lb lower than when he last won, was reported to have got unbalanced on the uneven ground at Haydock last time. (8/1: op 5/1)

770 Nails Tails got going too late to get back into the picture. (8/1)

407* Don't Drop Bombs (USA) has won twice over a mile-and-a-half on the Equitrack, but seems more effective over shorter distances these days. (10/1)

Strat's Legacy (12/1: op 8/1)

2147 TATTERSALLS MAIDEN AUCTION STKS (2-Y.O) (Class E)

6-45 (6-45) **5f** £2,914.25 (£869.00: £414.50: £187.25) Stalls: High GOING minus 0.28 sec per fur (GF)

				SP	RR	SF
1827[2]	**Phone Alex (IRE)** (RHannon) **2-8-2** DaneO'Neill(5) (a.p: rdn to ld over 1f out: r.o wl)	—	**1**	2/1[1]	72	20
1569[10]	**Sweet Rosie (IRE)** (RBoss) **2-8-0** JQuinn(7) (a.p: hrd rdn & r.o ins fnl f)	1¾	**2**	33/1	64	12
1970[4]	**Frankie Fair (IRE)** (MAJarvis) **2-8-3** MRoberts(1) (led over 3f: one pce)	1¾	**3**	2/1[1]	62	10
1664[3]	**Muftuffenuf** (PRWebber) **2-8-3** DHarrison(2) (s.i.s: hdwy 3f out: ev ch over 1f out: edgd rt: wknd fnl f)	2	**4**	7/1[2]	55	3
	Relate (MartynMeade) **2-8-4** FNorton(3) (w'like: s.s: outpcd: hdwy fnl 2f: nt rch ldrs)	1½	**5**	15/2[3]	52	—
	Marahill Lad (PHowling) **2-8-12** PaulEddery(4) (w'like: w ldrs 3f)	4	**6**	14/1	47	—
1812[6]	**Wild Lilly** (MJRyan) **2-7-10**(3) MBaird(6) (hdwy 3f out: wknd wl over 1f out)	5	**7**	12/1	18	—

(SP 108.2%) **7 Rn**

59.47 secs (2.47) CSF £57.00 TOTE £2.50: £1.40 £4.80 (£16.60) OWNER J B R Leisure Ltd (MARLBOROUGH) BRED E. Moloney

1827 Phone Alex (IRE), despite dropping back to a pretty easy five, was well on top in the end. (2/1: op evens)

902 Sweet Rosie (IRE), closely related to a mile juvenile winner, is crying out for a longer trip. (33/1)

1970 Frankie Fair (IRE) was a bit disappointing and did nothing more than give the winner a nice lead. (2/1)
1664 Muftuffenuf was trying her luck at the minimum distance. (7/1: 3/1-15/2)
Relate, a half-sister to Marsh Marigold, seemed likely to finish out with the washing and will know more next time. (15/2: 10/1-6/1)
Marahill Lad is a half-brother to stayer and winning hurdler Puff Puff, Nellie's Gamble and Mykindofmusic. (14/1: 10/1-16/1)
1812 Wild Lilly (12/1: op 6/1)

2148 VINES OF SEVENOAKS H'CAP (0-70) (3-Y.O+) (Class E)

7-15 (7-16) **5f** £3,174.25 (£949.00: £454.50: £207.25) Stalls: High GOING minus 0.28 sec per fur (GF)

				SP	RR	SF
1848*	**Barranak (IRE) (60)** (GMMcCourt) **5-9-4** CRutter(6) (lw: chsd ldr: rdn to ld last stride)	—	**1**	3/1[1]	65	48
1814[5]	**Polly Golightly (65)** (MBlanshard) **4-9-9b** NAdams(5) (led tl hdd last stride)	s.h	**2**	9/2[3]	70	53
1633[16]	**Village Pub (FR) (47)** (KOCunningham-Brown) **3-7-8b**(5) RFfrench(9) (a.p: r.o ins fnl f)	½	**3**	16/1	50	27
1792[5]	**Ice Age (60)** (RJRWilliams) **3-8-12** KFallon(8) (lw: hld up: rdn & hdwy over 1f out: nt qckn ins fnl f)	nk	**4**	6/1	62	39
1814*	**Songsheet (69)** (MSSaunders) **4-9-10**(3) PPMurphy(1) (lw: hld up: rdn & hdwy over 1f out: nt qckn ins fnl f)	s.h	**5**	9/2[3]	71	54
1848[10]	**Sharp Stock (59)** (RJHodges) **4-9-3** SDrowne(10) (swtg: prom: outpcd 2f out: rallied nr fin)	1	**6**	7/1	58	41
1857[4]	**Bright Paragon (IRE) (40)** (KTIvory) **8-7-9**(3)ow1 MartinDwyer(3) (b.hind: chsd ldrs: rdn over 2f out: wknd ins fnl f)	2½	**7**	4/1[2]	31	13
1743[9]	**Sweet Magic (65)** (PHowling) **6-9-9b[1]** PaulEddery(2) (hld up mid div: wknd over 1f out)	9	**8**	25/1	27	10
1620[19]	**Mazzarello (IRE) (38)** (RIngram) **7-7-7v**(3) MBaird(4) (squeezed out s: racd wd: outpcd)	3	**9**	50/1	—	—
				(SP 119.8%)	**9 Rn**	

58.67 secs (1.67) CSF £15.86 CT £172.17 TOTE £4.80: £1.60 £1.60 £2.70 (£11.90) Trio £65.70 OWNER Mr Mac Carthy (WANTAGE) BRED M. MacCarthy
LONG HANDICAP Mazzarello (IRE) 7-2
WEIGHT FOR AGE 3yo-6lb
1848* Barranak (IRE) again benefited from overnight rain, easing the ground. At the top of his form, he defied an 8lb rise in the ratings with the help of the stands' rails in the closing stages. (3/1)
1814 Polly Golightly had gone up a stone since finishing second prior to her two wins. Racing towards the centre of the course, one cannot help thinking she would have held on had she been nearer the stands' side. (9/2: op 3/1)
Village Pub (FR) seems more effective sprinting and probably ran his best race to date. (16/1)
1792 Ice Age, who has dropped no less than 25lb this season, appeared to be coming to take a hand but got frozen out in the closing stages. (6/1)
1814* Songsheet, up 7lb for her two victories, was 7lb worse off with the runner-up than when beating her about three lengths last time. (9/2: 3/1-5/1)
1327 Sharp Stock, dropped 4lb, may be worth a try at six. (7/1)

2149 JARDINE INSURANCE SERVICES LIMITED STKS (0-70) (3-Y.O) (Class E)

7-45 (7-45) **7f** £2,966.25 (£885.00: £422.50: £191.25) Stalls: High GOING minus 0.28 sec per fur (GF)

				SP	RR	SF
1741[9]	**Mr Paradise (IRE) (67)** (TJNaughton) **3-8-11**(3) JDSmith(5) (lw: hld up: rdn & hdwy over 2f out: r.o to ld last stride)	—	**1**	8/1	79	51
1958*	**Pericles (77)** (MJohnston) **3-9-0** JWeaver(3) (lw: a.p: carried lft & led over 1f out: hdd last stride)	s.h	**2**	9/4[1]	79	51
1826[10]	**Inclination (65)** (MBlanshard) **3-8-8** JQuinn(4) (lw: w ldr over 4f: r.o one pce)	2½	**3**	10/1	67	39
1787[2]	**Night Express (70)** (BHanbury) **3-8-11** WRyan(6) (led: rdn 2f out: edgd lft & hdd over 1f out: one pce)	1¼	**4**	100/30[3]	67	39
1966*	**Tajrebah (USA) (70)** (PTWalwyn) **3-8-11** RHills(2) (hld up: rdn over 2f out: nvr nr to chal)	1	**5**	11/4[2]	65	37
341[4]	**Daring Flight (USA) (70)** (LordHuntingdon) **3-8-11** DHarrison(1) (bhd fnl 2f: t.o)	29	**6**	7/1	—	—
				(SP 113.2%)	**6 Rn**	

1m 23.06 (1.86) CSF £24.38 TOTE £10.20: £2.70 £2.00 (£11.50) OWNER Mr G. E. Archer (EPSOM) BRED Airlie Stud
1651* Mr Paradise (IRE), highly tried over a mile-and-a-quarter at Epsom, needed every yard of this seven and had the favoured stands' rails. (8/1: 6/1-9/1)
1958* Pericles was favoured by race conditions having now been raised to 77 in this 0-70. Carried into the centre of the course, he was the second horse of the evening to be touched off by a rival under the stands' rail. (9/4)
840 Inclination, dropping back from a mile, might be better suited to a stiffer seven. (10/1)
1787 Night Express did not help his cause by coming off a true line. (100/30)
1966* Tajrebah (USA) did not have ground conditions so fast as last week. (11/4)

2150 MARK WILLSON 18TH BIRTHDAY H'CAP (0-60) (3-Y.O+) (Class F)

8-15 (8-16) **1m 1f** £3,085.50 (£858.00: £412.50) Stalls: Low GOING minus 0.28 sec per fur (GF)

				SP	RR	SF
1968[5]	**Harvey White (IRE) (52)** (JPearce) **5-9-7** CRutter(8) (lw: hdwy over 2f out: led ins fnl f: all out)	—	**1**	9/1	61	23
1844[9]	**What A Fuss (55)** (BHanbury) **4-9-10** WRyan(12) (a.p: led over 1f out tl ins fnl f: r.o wl)	s.h	**2**	11/1	64	26
1796[2]	**Renata's Prince (IRE) (50)** (KRBurke) **4-9-5** KFallon(2) (a.p: led 2f out: sn hdd: nt qckn)	1¼	**3**	9/4[1]	57	19
1968*	**Zamalek (USA) (43)** (RMFlower) **5-8-12** FNorton(1) (a.p: hrd rdn 2f out: one pce)	1¼	**4**	11/2[2]	48	10
	Your Most Welcome (56) (DJSffrenchDavis) **6-9-6**(5) RFfrench(7) (hld up: sn bhd: hdwy fnl 2f: too much to do)	½	**5**	20/1	60	22
1968[3]	**Sovereign Crest (IRE) (46)** (CAHorgan) **4-9-1** PaulEddery(4) (s.s: gd hdwy on ins over 2f out: wknd over 1f out)	5	**6**	13/2[3]	41	3
1503[5]	**Law Dancer (IRE) (51)** (TGMills) **4-9-6** RHills(3) (s.s: nvr nrr)	1½	**7**	12/1	43	5
1660[4]	**Queens Stroller (IRE) (44)** (REPeacock) **6-8-13** DHarrison(14) (prom: ev ch over 2f out: wknd over 1f out)	nk	**8**	12/1	36	—
1642*	**Roman Reel (USA) (52)** (GLMoore) **6-9-7** MWigham(13) (lw: prom tl hrd rdn & wknd over 2f out)	2	**9**	14/1	40	2
1794[3]	**Charlton Imp (USA) (52)** (RJHodges) **4-9-7** SDrowne(11) (led 7f: wknd wl over 1f out)	1½	**10**	14/1	37	—
1968[10]	**Moi Canard (46)** (BAPearce) **4-8-10**(5) ADaly(9) (bhd fnl 3f)	3	**11**	40/1	26	—
1606[5]	**Errant (50)** (DJSCosgrove) **5-9-5** JQuinn(5) (b: a bhd)	2½	**12**	12/1	26	—
				(SP 121.4%)	**12 Rn**	

1m 57.16 (6.66) CSF £97.14 CT £279.14 TOTE £9.10: £2.80 £3.60 £1.70 (£54.30) Trio £123.40 OWNER The Harvey White Partnership (NEWMARKET) BRED Mrs C. L. Weld
1968 Harvey White (IRE) had no traffic problems to contend with this time, but had to give his all over this slightly shorter trip. (9/1)
1093 What A Fuss, dropping back in distance, bounced back to form having slipped a total of 5lb down the weights. (11/1)
1796 Renata's Prince (IRE) again ran well, having gone for home a little earlier over this slightly shorter trip. (9/4)
1968* Zamalek (USA) was 3lb worse off with the winner than when beaten three lengths over an extra furlong here a week ago. (11/2: 4/1-6/1)

Your Most Welcome made an eyecatching reappearance, having been dropped out by her rider. (20/1)
1968 Sovereign Crest (IRE) is an habitual slow starter. (13/2: 9/2-7/1)
1794 Charlton Imp (USA) (14/1: 10/1-16/1)

2151 BEIJING MAIDEN H'CAP (0-65) (3-Y.O) (Class F)

8-45 (8-49) **1m (Equitrack)** £2,277.00 (£627.00: £297.00) Stalls: Low GOING minus 0.50 sec per fur (FST)

				SP	RR	SF
1633^{5}	**Around Fore Alliss (65)** (TGMills) **3-9-7** KFallon(6) (hld up & bhd: hdwy 3f out: led over 1f out: drvn out)	—	1	$9/2^{2}$	75	44
1633^{17}	**Welcome Heights (40)** (MJFetherston-Godley) **3-7-5**(5) RFfrench(4) (hld up: hdwy 2f out: r.o wl ins fnl f: nt rch wnr)	1½	2	33/1	47	16
1633^{10}	**Kristopher (60)** (JWHills) **3-9-2** RHills(11) (a.p: led over 2f out tl over 1f out: one pce)	1¾	3	11/1	64	33
1589^{11}	**Bapsford (50)** (GLMoore) **3-8-6** RPerham(8) (lw: hld up: hdwy 2f out: sn rdn: hung lft over 1f out: one pce)	2	4	$6/1^{3}$	50	19
1988^{8}	**Canton Ron (52)** (CADwyer) **3-8-8** DHarrison(7) (prom: led 3f out: sn hdd: wknd over 1f out)	1½	5	25/1	49	18
1690^{5}	**Go For Green (62)** (DrJDScargill) **3-9-1**(3) DGriffiths(9) (lw: bhd tl hdwy over 2f out: wknd over 1f out)	3	6	8/1	53	22
1642^{10}	**Leg Beforum (IRE) (54)** (LMontagueHall) **3-8-10** JWeaver(12) (nvr nr to chal)	2½	7	16/1	40	9
1843^{3}	**Push A Venture (49)** (SPCWoods) **3-8-5** WRyan(2) (prom: led over 3f out: sn hdd: wknd wl over 1f out)	1¼	8	$2/1^{1}$	32	1
1164^{14}	**Dr Woodstock (49)** (MartynMeade) **3-8-5** FNorton(3) (lw: prom 4f)	½	9	33/1	31	—
1691^{5}	**Castle Ashby Jack (60)** (PHowling) **3-9-2b** PaulEddery(5) (prom 5f)	1¼	10	14/1	40	9
1730^{13}	**Formidable Spirit (40)** (MJHeaton-Ellis) **3-7-10v** JQuinn(1) (led over 4f: sn wknd)	3½	11	33/1	13	—
1826^{6}	**Warring (62)** (MSSaunders) **3-9-1**(3) PPMurphy(10) (a bhd: t.o)	10	12	15/2	15	—
				(SP 122.2%)	**12 Rn**	

1m 39.31 (1.91) CSF £141.99 CT £1,419.68 TOTE £4.60: £1.50 £7.70 £2.90 (£100.30) Trio £98.40 OWNER John Humphreys (Turf Accountants) Ltd (EPSOM) BRED Mrs Mary Taylor and Miss Dorothy Fleming
LONG HANDICAP Formidable Spirit 7-6
1633 Around Fore Alliss, proven on this surface, was 3lb higher than when shaping well at Windsor last time. (9/2)
Welcome Heights showed a marked improvement on his sand debut off a mark 8lb lower than when finishing well behind the winner at Windsor. (33/1)
Kristopher, yet another who ran at Windsor, was 7lb better off with Around Fore Alliss having been beaten only three lengths. (11/1: op 7/1)
Bapsford was 8lb lower than his previous run on the sand. Supported in the ring on this step-up to a mile, he proved a difficult ride in the short home straight. (6/1: 10/1-9/2)
Canton Ron did not see out this longer trip. (25/1)
1690 Go For Green seemed to find this mile beyond her on her All-Weather debut. (8/1)
1843 Push A Venture (2/1: 6/4-9/4)
1826 Warring (15/2: 5/1-8/1)

T/Plpt: £64.30 (250.71 Tckts). T/Qdpt: £26.50 (32.25 Tckts) KH

2127-REDCAR (L-H) (Good, Good to firm patches)
Saturday June 21st
WEATHER: showers WIND: slt hlf bhd

2152 'HAND TO ROUF' LADIES' MAIDEN H'CAP (0-70) (3-Y.O+) (Class G)

2-10 (2-11) **1m** £2,216.50 (£619.00: £299.50) Stalls: Centre GOING minus 0.34 sec per fur (GF)

				SP	RR	SF
1800^{3}	**Kass Alhawa (53)** (DWChapman) **4-10-9** MissRClark(10) (hld up gng wl: shkn up to ld jst ins fnl f: hrd rdn: all out)	—	1	$3/1^{1}$	64	46
2019^{3}	**Terdad (USA) (59)** (TDBarron) **4-10-11**(4) MissMKeuthen(2) (swtg: trckd ldrs: led over 1f out tl jst ins fnl f: nt qckn nr fin)	nk	2	$9/2^{3}$	69	51
1800^{6}	**Forest Robin (65)** (MrsJRRamsden) **4-11-3v¹**(4) MissERamsden(11) (lw: trckd ldrs: led 3f out tl over 1f out: one pce)	5	3	11/2	65	47
1689^{2}	**Clytha Hill Lad (34)** (JMBradley) **6-9-0**(4) MissADeniel(4) (b: led to 3f out: edgd lft: kpt on appr fnl f)	2	4	$7/2^{2}$	30	12
1787^{5}	**Swing West (USA) (67)** (PFICole) **3-10-9**(4) MissSHiggins(8) (lw: chsd ldrs: outpcd over 2f out: edgd lft & kpt on fnl f)	s.h	5	5/1	63	35
	Miss Alice (42) (CSmith) **3-8-12**(4) MrsMMorris(5) (w ldrs tl wknd over 2f out)	10	6	16/1	18	—
2041^{8}	**Intrepid Fort (30)** (BWMurray) **8-9-0b** MrsSBosley(3) (jnd ldrs after 2f: edgd lft & lost pl over 2f out)	2½	7	33/1	1	—
1495^{12}	**Midday Cowboy (USA) (50)** (MDHammond) **4-9-13**(7) MissAJSmith(6) (in tch: effrt over 2f out: sn wknd)	6	8	25/1	9	—
463^{7}	**Born On The Wild (44)** (SEKettlewell) **4-10-0** MrsDKettlewell(9) (trckd ldrs tl lost pl ½-wy)	nk	9	25/1	3	—
1694^{11}	**African Sun (IRE) (43)** (MCChapman) **4-9-6**(7) MissEFolkes(7) (sn drvn along: bhd fr ½-wy)	s.h	10	16/1	2	—
	Golden Fish (38) (EJAlston) **5-9-4**(4) MrsCWilliams(1) (in tch: rdn & lost pl ½-wy: sn bhd)	13	11	33/1	—	—
				(SP 122.8%)	**11 Rn**	

1m 39.3 (4.30) CSF £15.32 CT £66.67 TOTE £4.00: £1.20 £2.00 £2.00 (£9.50) Trio £15.60 OWNER Mr J. B. Wilcox (YORK) BRED L. H. J. Ward
LONG HANDICAP Intrepid Fort 8-4
WEIGHT FOR AGE 3yo-10lb
1800 Kass Alhawa was given a well-judged ride. After coming there on the bridle, he seemed in two minds whether to go through with his effort, but his rider made his mind up for him. (3/1)
2019 Terdad (USA), with the blinkers left off, was warm beforehand but on this occasion battled back. (9/2)
1800 Forest Robin, in a visor for the first time, is still a maiden after twenty-four attempts. The Handicapper seems slow to show him any mercy. (11/2)
1689 Clytha Hill Lad was racing from a 5lb higher mark. (7/2)
1415 Swing West (USA), on his handicap debut, might appreciate a step-up in distance. (5/1)

2153 'BOTTLE AND A HALF' (S) STKS (2-Y.O) (Class G)

2-40 (2-42) **7f** £2,272.50 (£635.00: £307.50) Stalls: Centre GOING minus 0.34 sec per fur (GF)

				SP	RR	SF
1310^{7}	**Linnetsong** (GROldroyd) **2-8-6v¹** KHodgson(2) (chsd ldrs: styd on to ld jst ins fnl f: hld on wl)	—	1	33/1	62	16
1815^{3}	**Greenbrook** (WGMTurner) **2-8-6**(5) DSweeney(3) (led: edgd rt & hdd jst ins fnl f: kpt on wl)	1½	2	$7/2^{3}$	64	18

1812[12] **The Honorable Lady** (MRChannon) **2-8-6** AClark(11) (swvd rt s: sn pushed along & outpcd: hdwy ½-wy: nt qckn fnl f)........3 **3** 5/2[1] 52 6
927[4] **Captain Bliss** (NTinkler) **2-8-11b** FLynch(9) (a chsng ldrs: one pce fnl 2f)........1¼ **4** 4/1 54 8
1941[13] **Ellenber** (WMcKeown) **2-8-11** NDay(7) (chsd ldrs: hrd rdn over 2f out: sn outpcd)........1¾ **5** 33/1 50 4
1829[7] **Hayburner** (MWEasterby) **2-8-11** TLucas(4) (trckd ldrs: rdn over 2f out: sn outpcd: edgd rt)........2 **6** 11/2 45 —
1815[4] **Last Lap** (TDEasterby) **2-8-6** JCarroll(1) (drvn along & outpcd ½-wy: sme hdwy over 1f out: n.d)........4 **7** 3/1[2] 31 —
1447[12] **Behind The Veil** (MrsMReveley) **2-8-3**(5)ow2 SCopp(10) (sn outpcd & drvn along: bhd fr ½-wy)........4 **8** 14/1 24 —
1789[5] **Sylvan Cloud** (CWFairhurst) **2-8-6b[1]** GCarter(6) (w ldrs tl lost pl over 3f out)........1 **9** 14/1 20 —
Lady So Bold (MrsLStubbs) **2-8-6** DWright(8) (leggy: unf: s.i.s: bhd fr ½-wy)........½ **10** 12/1 19 —
1581[8] **Flash d'Or (IRE)** (MWEasterby) **2-8-7b[1]**(5) GParkin(5) (s.s: hrd rdn & edgd rt ½-wy: sn wl bhd)........19 **11** 8/1 — —
(SP 149.2%) **11 Rn**

1m 26.9 (3.90) CSF £166.88 TOTE £91.60: £11.30 £2.20 £1.50 (£52.40) Trio £171.30; £217.26 to 23/6/97 OWNER Mr Robert Cook (YORK) BRED M. J. and Mrs E. Cowie
No bid
IN-FOCUS: **This was Kevin Hodgson's first winner since his return to the saddle this season, after an absence of six years. He has over two hundred and fifty career wins to his credit.**
Linnetsong, tailed off last in her two previous outings in better company, wore a visor for the first time. Even by selling race standards, this was probably a poor contest. (33/1)
1815 Greenbrook made the running, and this is probably as good as he is. (7/2)
1461 The Honorable Lady was soon hard at work, and the step-up in distance can have done her no harm. (5/2)
743 Captain Bliss, on his toes beforehand, seems to be on the downgrade. (4/1)
Ellenber was running in a seller for the first time. (33/1)
1829 Hayburner, up in distance, showed no improvement and did not keep straight. (11/2)
1815 Last Lap finished further behind Greenbrook than she had done here last time. (3/1)
1432 Sylvan Cloud (14/1: 10/1-16/1)
Lady So Bold (12/1: 8/1-14/1)
1253 Flash d'Or (IRE) (8/1: 6/1-9/1)

2154 TEES COMPONENTS H'CAP (0-60) (3-Y.O+) (Class F)
3-10 (3-18) **1m 6f 19y** £2,868.00 (£798.00: £384.00) Stalls: Low GOING minus 0.34 sec per fur (GF)

SP RR SF
1140[5] **Classic Line (59)** (JLDunlop) **3-9-0** GCarter(9) (prom early: bhd & pushed along 10f out: swtchd outside & gd hdwy over 2f out: styd on strly: edgd lft: led nr fin)........— **1** 9/2[2] 69 30
1825[9] **Sun of Spring (50)** (DWChapman) **7-9-3**(5) GParkin(14) (in tch: hdwy to ld 2f out: hdd nr fin)........1½ **2** 14/1 58 36
1605[2] **Charity Crusader (36)** (MrsMReveley) **6-8-3b**(5)ow2 SCopp(5) (lw: s.i.s: bhd tl hdwy over 3f out: styd on same pce fnl f)........¾ **3** 11/2[3] 43 19
1452[3] **Highfield Fizz (38)** (CWFairhurst) **5-8-10** JCarroll(10) (b.off hind: hld up & bhd: hdwy over 3f out: nt qckn appr fnl f)........1 **4** 8/1 44 22
1515[4] **Anchorena (45)** (DWBarker) **5-9-3** FLynch(12) (unruly s: bhd: hdwy 3f out: edgd lft: nvr nr to chal)........1¼ **5** 14/1 50 28
1779[9] **Dashing Invader (USA) (37)** (PWHarris) **4-8-6b**(3) MHenry(2) (unruly s: set str pce: hdd 3f out: one pce)........1¾ **6** 11/1 40 18
1641[3] **Almuhtaram (56)** (GLewis) **5-10-0b** AClark(15) (sn bhd: hdwy on outside over 3f out: nvr nr ldrs)........4 **7** 10/1 54 32
*1940** **Kalamata (48)** (JAGlover) **5-9-6** NDay(8) (chsd ldrs: rdn to ld 3f out: hung lft & hdd 2f out: grad wknd)........hd **8** 4/1[1] 46 24
1654[6] **Junior Ben (IRE) (32)** (MESowersby) **5-7-11**(7) CLowther(13) (trckd ldrs tl wknd 2f out)........5 **9** 20/1 25 3
2000[5] **Gymcrak Cyrano (IRE) (32)** (NChamberlain) **8-8-4** NVarley(3) (chsd ldrs: sn pushed along: outpcd fnl 3f)........2 **10** 14/1 22 —
2000[3] **Sushi Bar (IRE) (37)** (MrsMReveley) **6-8-9** JFanning(1) (bhd: hdwy u.p over 3f out: sn wknd)........3 **11** 7/1 24 2
1844[12] **Cottage Prince (IRE) (51)** (JJQuinn) **4-9-9** JLowe(7) (bhd: hdwy & pushed along over 5f out: lost pl over 2f out: eased)........1¼ **12** 12/1 37 15
Our Main Man (44) (RMWhitaker) **7-8-13**(3) OPears(11) (bit bkwd: hdwy 7f out: sn prom: lost pl over 3f out)....7 **13** 33/1 22 —
2000[6] **Another Quarter (IRE) (48)** (MCChapman) **4-8-13**(7) VictoriaAppleby(6) (b: rel to s: chsd ldrs: rdn over 5f out: lost pl over 4f out)........4 **14** 25/1 21 —
1445[6] **Nawaji (USA) (35)** (WRMuir) **4-8-7** SophieMitchell(4) (bhd: lost tch over 4f out: p.u over 2f out: sddle slipped)... **P** 16/1 — —
(SP 139.7%) **15 Rn**

3m 6.8 (7.50) CSF £69.34 CT £348.33 TOTE £4.00: £2.10 £5.00 £2.40 (£50.50) Trio £144.50 OWNER Eurostrait Ltd (ARUNDEL) BRED Eurostrait Ltd
WEIGHT FOR AGE 3yo-17lb
1140 Classic Line, whose Windsor form has worked out really well, proved suited by the extra two furlongs and, by the way she ran, two miles will be no problem. Hard at work and with only the puller-up behind her turning in, she suddenly decided to run halfway up the straight, and came from out of the clouds to get up near the line. (9/2: op 5/2)
1686* Sun of Spring had the prize whipped from under his nose in the shadow of the post. (14/1)
1605 Charity Crusader took plenty of stoking up before he decided to stay on. (11/2)
1452 Highfield Fizz came from off the pace in a strongly-run race. (8/1)
1515 Anchorena, who has her share of temperament, would have preferred faster ground. (14/1)
1452 Dashing Invader (USA), with the blinkers on again, took some loading into the stalls. Setting a very strong pace, he kept going surprisingly well. He is still a maiden after fifteen outings, but surely there is an opening for him. (11/1)
1940* Kalamata, who is about a stone better on the All-Weather, hung under pressure and did not look happy in his work. (4/1)

2155 VAUX GOLD TANKARD H'CAP (0-90) (3-Y.O+) (Class C)
3-40 (3-46) **1m 2f** £10,260.00 (£3,105.00: £1,515.00: £720.00) Stalls: Low GOING minus 0.34 sec per fur (GF)

SP RR SF
1595[4] **Hen Harrier (89)** (JLDunlop) **3-9-3** GCarter(1) (hld up: stdy hdwy 6f out: rdn over 2f out: led over 1f out: hld on towards fin)........— **1** 5/1[2] 98 46
1450[5] **Billy Bushwacker (88)** (MrsMReveley) **6-9-9**(5) SCopp(9) (hld up: hdwy on ins 3f out: nt clr run over 1f out: ev ch ins fnl f: nt qckn nr fin)........nk **2** 5/1[2] 97 57
1660* **Bay of Islands (81)** (DMorris) **5-9-7** NDay(2) (lw: chsd ldrs: rdn & lost pl over 3f out: hdwy over 1f out: styd on wl nr fin)........¾ **3** 5/1[2] 88 48
1979[3] **Sandmoor Chambray (79)** (TDEasterby) **6-9-5** JCarroll(5) (lw: trckd ldrs: rdn to ld over 2f out: edgd lft & hdd over 1f out: no ex)........¾ **4** 13/2[3] 85 45
1979[2] **Eurobox Boy (61)** (APJarvis) **4-8-1** DWright(3) (sn chsng ldrs: rdn over 3f out: styd on same pce appr fnl f)...¾ **5** 7/1 66 26
1325[7] **Slip Jig (IRE) (72)** (KRBurke) **4-8-7**(5) DSweeney(7) (hld up: hdwy over 3f out: n.m.r 2f out: kpt on)........3 **6** 16/1 72 32

Form	Runner	Btn	Pos	SP	RR	SF
1773[5]	**Night Mirage (USA) (72)** (MJohnston) **3-8-0b[1]** JFanning(8) (led: clr 5f out: hdd over 2f out: wknd over 1f out)	3½	7	16/1	67	15
1979[11]	**Mels Baby (IRE) (75)** (JLEyre) **4-9-1** MGallagher(6) (hld up: hdwy u.p 4f out: lost pl 2f out)	5	8	10/1	62	22
1773[2]	**Crystal Gold (88)** (MRStoute) **3-8-13**(3) MHenry(4) (lw: trckd ldrs: drvn along 4f out: wknd over 1f out: eased)	9	9	5/2[1]	60	8

(SP 125.3%) **9 Rn**

2m 7.0 (3.40) CSF £30.08 CT £124.99 TOTE £6.10: £2.20 £1.20 £2.00 (£11.80) Trio £33.90 OWNER Sir Thomas Pilkington (ARUNDEL) BRED Mrs Rebecca Philipps
WEIGHT FOR AGE 3yo-12lb
OFFICIAL EXPLANATION Crystal Gold: no explanation offered.
1595 Hen Harrier, as usual on her toes beforehand, was 7lb higher in the weights than when winning at Ripon two outings ago. (5/1)
1450 Billy Bushwacker, who has not won for over two years, ran out of room coming to the final furlong but, after having every chance, he seemed to be out-battled near the line. (5/1)
1660* Bay of Islands, up 6lb in the weights, dropped right out early in the straight. Staying on really strongly at the finish, he will be suited by a step-up in distance. (5/1)
1979 Sandmoor Chambray rolled off a true line, getting in Billy Bushwacker's way. This trip seemed to stretch his stamina to the very limit. (13/2)
1979 Eurobox Boy, who has done all his winning over a mile, seemed to stay alright. (7/1)
1773 Crystal Gold, in trouble once in line for home, dropped right out over a furlong out, and connections could offer no reason why. (5/2)

2156 'TOP MIX' MAIDEN STKS (3-Y.O+) (Class D)

4-15 (4-16) **1m** £3,691.00 (£1,108.00: £534.00: £247.00) Stalls: Centre GOING minus 0.34 sec per fur (GF)

Form	Runner	Btn	Pos	SP	RR	SF
1499[2]	**Muhtafel** (JLDunlop) **3-8-11** GCarter(7) (lw: trckd ldrs: led over 3f out: pushed out)	—	1	6/4[2]	87	30
1630[2]	**Dantesque (IRE) (82)** (GWragg) **4-9-7** AClark(8) (lw: trckd ldrs: chal 3f out: nt qckn wl ins fnl f)	nk	2	5/4[1]	86	39
	Sweet Fortune (USA) (MRStoute) **3-8-11** FLynch(10) (tall: trckd ldrs: ev ch 3f out: sn rdn: edgd lft & grad wknd)	13	3	5/1[3]	60	3
1258[6]	**Gymcrak Gorjos** (GHolmes) **3-8-6** TLucas(1) (b.hind: in tch: outpcd ½-wy: kpt on fnl f)	4	4	33/1	47	—
2046[17]	**Quaint Desire** (MBrittain) **4-9-0**(7) DMernagh(6) (s.s: sn wl bhd: sme late hdwy)	7	5	66/1	38	—
	Hanajir (IRE) (CWThornton) **3-8-6** JLowe(9) (unf: s.i.s: sme hdwy ½-wy: eased 2f out)	2½	6	20/1	28	—
2046[18]	**Golden Glory** (MBrittain) **4-9-7** DWright(3) (sn wl outpcd & bhd)	hd	7	66/1	33	—
1448[7]	**Frugal** (BWMurray) **4-9-7** VHalliday(4) (in tch: rdn ½-wy: sn lost pl)	½	8	100/1	32	—
2046[9]	**Sabu** (JIACharlton) **5-9-7** JCarroll(11) (in tch: drvn along ½-wy: hung lft & sn wl outpcd)	3½	9	25/1	25	—
2045[10]	**Petaz** (MWEasterby) **3-8-2**(5)ow1 GParkin(2) (led tl over 3f out: wknd over 2f out)	6	10	66/1	9	—
1787[12]	**Bustingoutallover (USA)** (CWThornton) **3-8-6** RPrice(5) (s.i.s: sn trckng ldrs: lost pl over 3f out: eased)	22	11	66/1	—	—

(SP 119.6%) **11 Rn**

1m 38.5 (3.50) CSF £3.24 TOTE £2.60: £1.10 £1.10 £2.00 (£1.50) Trio £1.60 OWNER Mr Hamdan Al Maktoum (ARUNDEL) BRED Shadwell Estate Company Limited
WEIGHT FOR AGE 3yo-10lb
1499 Muhtafel, a grand big type, was suited by the galloping flat track. His rider never had to get really serious with him and he will be an interesting proposition in handicap company. (6/4: evens-13/8)
1630 Dantesque (IRE), already rated 82, never gave up trying despite looking as if something was hurting him in the tight finish. (5/4)
Sweet Fortune (USA), very colty beforehand, tended to edge in behind the first two and ran as if needing the outing. (5/1: op 3/1)
Gymcrak Gorjos was having her third run and now qualifies for a handicap mark. Putting in her best work at the finish, she will be suited by further. (33/1)
1834 Quaint Desire kept straight this time after running very wide on the home turn at Ripon three days earlier. (66/1)

2157 'DOUBLE CARPET' RATING RELATED MAIDEN STKS (0-70) (3-Y.O+) (Class E)

4-45 (4-45) **6f** £2,781.25 (£835.00: £402.50: £186.25) Stalls: Centre GOING minus 0.34 sec per fur (GF)

Form	Runner	Btn	Pos	SP	RR	SF
1687[4]	**Midnight Shift (IRE) (69)** (RGuest) **3-8-11** PBloomfield(2) (w ldrs: led over 2f tl over 1f out: styd on u.p to ld nr fin)	—	1	11/4[1]	74	31
1687[2]	**Archello (IRE) (67)** (GROldroyd) **3-8-6**(5) GParkin(1) (trckd ldrs: led over 1f out: sn rdn & edgd rt: hdd nr fin)	nk	2	3/1[2]	73	30
2017[2]	**Two On The Bridge (65)** (DenysSmith) **3-8-7**(7) CLowther(4) (led: hung lft & hdd over 2f out: styd on same pce)	2½	3	4/1[3]	70	27
792[6]	**Marylebone (IRE) (70)** (JBerry) **3-9-0b[1]** GCarter(3) (chsd ldrs: rdn & outpcd ½-wy: kpt on fnl f)	2½	4	4/1[3]	63	20
1925[2]	**Classic Leader (64)** (ICampbell) **4-9-7v** RPrice(5) (sn drvn along: wandered u.p: nt keen)	1¼	5	9/2	60	24
998[8]	**Wagga Moon (IRE) (63)** (JJO'Neill) **3-9-0v[1]** JCarroll(6) (racd stands side: chsd ldrs tl wknd over 1f out)	1¾	6	11/1	55	12

(SP 118.2%) **6 Rn**

1m 12.7 (2.50) CSF £11.03 TOTE £4.30: £1.70 £2.10 (£4.30) OWNER Mr C. J. Mills (NEWMARKET) BRED A. Steigenberger
WEIGHT FOR AGE 3yo-7lb
1687 Midnight Shift (IRE), much happier over six, reversed Beverley placings with the runner-up. (11/4)
1687 Archello (IRE) was only worn down near the finish. She certainly seemed to stay the six alright. (3/1)
2017 Two On The Bridge, who continually swished her tail in the paddock, hung under pressure. (4/1)
792 Marylebone (IRE), tried in blinkers, showed no improvement and is basically a disappointing type. (4/1)
1925 Classic Leader wanted nothing to do with it. (9/2)
634 Wagga Moon (IRE), tried in a visor, was isolated on the stands' side rail. (11/1)

2158 'LONG-UN' H'CAP (0-70) (3-Y.O) (Class E)

5-15 (5-15) **1m 1f** £2,898.25 (£871.00: £420.50: £195.25) Stalls: Low GOING minus 0.34 sec per fur (GF)

Form	Runner	Btn	Pos	SP	RR	SF
2019[7]	**Dee Pee Tee Cee (IRE) (54)** (MWEasterby) **3-8-5** TLucas(1) (trckd ldrs: rdn over 2f out: led over 1f out: r.o wl towards fin)	—	1	6/4[1]	64	19
1999[4]	**Marsh Marigold (65)** (JHetherton) **3-8-9**(7) JennyBenson(4) (dwlt s: hdwy & swtchd outside 3f out: ev ch over 1f out: not qckn)	2½	2	13/2	71	26
1004[6]	**Hulal (60)** (ACStewart) **3-8-11** JCarroll(6) (lw: led tl over 1f out: kpt on sme pce)	2	3	6/1	62	17
1833[3]	**Freedom Chance (IRE) (70)** (JWHills) **3-9-4**(3) MHenry(7) (lw: chsd ldr: rdn over 4f out: one pce fnl 2f)	1	4	7/2[2]	70	25
1284[3]	**Polarize (55)** (TDBarron) **3-8-6** GCarter(3) (hld up: hdwy over 3f out: sn rdn: nvr rch ldrs)	½	5	6/1	54	9
1796[12]	**Coral Island (58)** (JGFitzGerald) **3-8-4**(5) GParkin(5) (lw: drvn along over 5f out: outpcd over 3f out: styd on fnl 2f)	1½	6	5/1[3]	55	10
	Il Principe (IRE) (45) (JohnBerry) **3-7-10** NVarley(2) (in tch: rdn over 4f out: lost pl 3f out)	12	7	25/1	20	—

889^{10} **Midnight Romance (48)** (APJarvis) **3-7-13** DWright(8) (chsd ldrs: rdn over 4f out: wknd over 2f out) ....4 **8** 12/1 16 —
(SP 132.3%) **8 Rn**

1m 55.5 (4.80) CSF £13.59 CT £49.93 TOTE £2.30: £1.30 £1.80 £1.30 (£10.40) OWNER Early Morning Breakfast Syndicate (SHERIFF HUTTON) BRED Michael and Heather Scott

LONG HANDICAP Il Principe (IRE) 7-7

2019 Dee Pee Tee Cee (IRE) was backed as if defeat was out of the question but, though he made hard work of it, he was right on top at the finish. This trip suited him much better than the seven at Thirsk four days earlier. (6/4)
1999 Marsh Marigold ran well considering she was racing from an 8lb higher mark than at Pontefract. (13/2)
1004 Hulal seems to have been pitched in several pounds too high on his handicap debut. (6/1)
1833 Freedom Chance (IRE) was hard at work a long way from home. (7/2)
1284 Polarize had the blinkers left off. (6/1)
1796 Coral Island has run two very flat races since his win at Carlisle. (5/1: op 3/1)

T/Plpt: £48.00 (314.14 Tckts). T/Qdpt: £12.60 (62 Tckts) WG

2047-WOLVERHAMPTON (L-H) (Standard)
Saturday June 21st

WEATHER: continuous rain WIND: mod half bhd

IN-FOCUS: **After the heavy rain in the past few days, the course was subject to an inspection with water lying in places. Though the meeting survived, the floodlights were not working and the final race was run in semi-darkness.**

2159 WALSALL MAIDEN H'CAP (0-65) (3-Y.O) (Class F)
7-00 (7-01) **1m 1f 79y (Fibresand)** £2,277.00 (£627.00: £297.00) Stalls: Low GOING minus 0.39 sec per fur (FST)

			SP	RR	SF
1624^{10} **Grand Hotel (IRE) (47)** (PWHarris) **3-8-3** BDoyle(4) (led after 2f: hrd rdn wl over 1f out: r.o wl)	—	**1**	6/1^{3}	53	24
1803^{8} **Gold Clipper (40)** (MJRyan) **3-7-3**(7) AMcCarthy(9) (lw: hdwy ½-wy: jnd wnr over 1f out: hrd rdn: unable qckn)	½	**2**	7/1	45	16
1998^{9} **Petula Boy (40)** (SRBowring) **3-7-3**(7) PDoe(3) (dwlt: hdwy over 2f out: rdn & edgd rt over 1f out: nt pce to chal)	5	**3**	25/1	37	8
1859^{3} **Poker Princess (52)** (MBell) **3-8-8** MFenton(6) (hld up in tch: effrt over 2f out: rdn & carried rt over 1f out: no imp)	2½	**4**	2/1^{1}	44	15
1119^{14} **Gadroon (41)** (PCHaslam) **3-7-4**(7)ow1 RWinston(8) (hdwy 5f out: rdn over 3f out: grad wknd)	13	**5**	10/1	11	—
1387^{9} **Mogul (65)** (NAGraham) **3-9-7** AMcGlone(1) (prom to ½-wy: sn rdn & lost tch)	nk	**6**	3/1^{2}	35	2
Moor Hall Princess (41) (NMBabbage) **3-7-6**(5)ow1 AimeeCook(5) (nt grwn: bkwd: led 2f: rdn & wknd 3f out: eased whn btn fnl f: t.o)	7	**7**	16/1	—	—
1388^{17} **Spanish Warrior (55)** (JWHills) **3-8-11** MRimmer(7) (lw: prom: hrd drvn 3f out: sn wknd: t.o)	nk	**8**	10/1	12	—

(SP 113.0%) **8 Rn**

1m 59.8 (3.80) CSF £41.81 CT £879.68 TOTE £6.10: £1.10 £2.00 £4.90 (£22.10) Trio £87.80 OWNER New Friends (BERKHAMSTED) BRED Canice M. Farrell Jnr

LONG HANDICAP Gold Clipper 7-3 Moor Hall Princess 7-6 Petula Boy 7-5

Grand Hotel (IRE), a strongly-made colt from a winning family, came good at the first time of asking on the All-Weather and, though the company was not great, he showed more resolution in an all-out duel to the line. (6/1)
1624 Gold Clipper, some way ahead of the winner when they met earlier in the month, looked to be going best when he ranged upsides below the distance but, in a real slog to the finish, could never quite gain command. (7/1)
600 Petula Boy has got the ability to win a small race, but as yet appears to have no trip. (25/1)
1859 Poker Princess handles this surface well but she lacks stamina, and the fact that she was carried right approaching the final furlong had no bearing on the final outcome. (2/1)
868 Spanish Warrior (10/1: op 5/1)

2160 WILLENHALL CLAIMING STKS (3-Y.O+) (Class F)
7-30 (7-31) **1m 100y (Fibresand)** £2,277.00 (£627.00: £297.00) Stalls: Low GOING minus 0.39 sec per fur (FST)

			SP	RR	SF
1786^{10} **People Direct (46)** (KMcAuliffe) **4-8-10** JFEgan(8) (sn pushed along: mde all: clr fr ½-wy: unchal)	—	**1**	8/1	56	35
1929^{5} **Bon Guest (IRE) (58)** (TJNaughton) **3-8-11** SSanders(6) (lw: hdwy ½-wy: wnt 2nd wl over 1f out: no imp on wnr)	6	**2**	100/30^{2}	56	25
1433^{9} **Dragonjoy (56)** (NPLittmoden) **4-9-0v**(7) DMcGaffin(3) (chsd wnr 5f out tl wl over 1f out: nvr able to chal)	2½	**3**	7/2^{3}	51	30
1473^{8} **Arcatura (60)** (CJames) **5-8-10**(3) CTeague(9) (swtg: hld up: hdwy over 2f out: kpt on u.p ins fnl f)	nk	**4**	5/1	42	21
1606^{10} **Doctor Bravious (IRE) (65)** (MBell) **4-9-4v**(5) GFaulkner(5) (lw: hdwy 5f out: hrd drvn over 2f out: no imp)	2½	**5**	3/1^{1}	48	27
1634^{8} **Rivers Magic (72)** (JJBridger) **4-9-9** SophieMitchell(1) (bit bkwd: chsd wnr 3f: rdn & wknd over 2f out)	3	**6**	10/1	42	21
Mill Dancer (IRE) (35) (JGMO'Shea) **5-7-13**(7) RWinston(4) (bit bkwd: rdn after 2f: lost tch ½-wy: t.o)	17	**7**	25/1	—	—
Blue Havana (GraemeRoe) **5-9-0** MFenton(2) (trckd ldrs 5f: sn wknd: t.o)	13	**8**	25/1	—	—

(SP 114.9%) **8 Rn**

1m 47.9 (2.90) CSF £31.88 TOTE £8.00: £2.00 £1.50 £1.30 (£12.60) Trio £24.40 OWNER Mr Peter Barclay (LAMBOURN) BRED James Thom and Sons and Peter Orr

WEIGHT FOR AGE 3yo-10lb

People Direct clmd RSalter £4,000

OFFICIAL EXPLANATION **People Direct: regarding the improved form, the filly was reported to be unreliable and to need to dominate.**

People Direct, bustled along to force the pace, was never on the bridle, but she responded to a strong ride and was beyond recall from halfway. (8/1)
1929 Bon Guest (IRE) moved into second place soon after straightening up but, hard as he tried, failed to make any inroads on the winner. (100/30)
1093 Arcatura finds this trip not quite far enough and, though he stayed on in the closing stages, was never going to get there in time. (5/1: op 3/1)
895 Doctor Bravious (IRE), winner of his only race over course and distance eighteen months ago, does not show a lot of enthusiasm for the game, and a course of hurdling might change his attitude. (3/1: 2/1-100/30)

2161 ROTHMANS ROYALS NORTH SOUTH CHALLENGE SERIES H'CAP (0-95) (3-Y.O+) (Class C)
8-00 (8-01) **1m 100y (Fibresand)** £5,257.65 (£1,567.20: £747.10: £337.05) Stalls: Low GOING minus 0.39 sec per fur (FST)

			SP	RR	SF
2021* **Cashmere Lady (82)** (JLEyre) **5-9-0**(3) 6x OPears(3) (mde all: clr 2f out: drvn out)	—	**1**	6/1	95	62

Form	Horse	Pos	SP	RR	SF
1969[2]	**Bentico (67)** (MrsNMacauley) **8-8-2v**ow1 BDoyle(4) (chsd wnr most of wy: hrd rdn 2f out: no imp) 5	**2**	7/1	71	37
1111[3]	**Broughtons Turmoil (70)** (BRMillman) **8-8-2**(3) AWhelan(2) (lw: hld up in tch: effrt 2f out: sn rdn: one pce appr fnl f) .....nk	**3**	4/1[3]	73	40
*1048**	**Water Garden (77)** (GWragg) **3-8-2**ow1 AClark(6) (dwlt: hdwy on ins 4f out: sn pushed along: nvr rchd ldrs) 7	**4**	11/4[2]	67	23
1456[9]	**Concer Un (93)** (SCWilliams) **5-10-0** JFortune(5) (b: prom: hrd drvn over 3f out: sn btn) 1	**5**	7/1	81	48
*1788**	**Alsahib (USA) (78)** (WRMuir) **4-8-13** TSprake(7) (lw: trckd ldrs: hrd drvn 3f out: no imp) ....¾	**6**	5/2[1]	64	31
2061[13]	**Theatre Magic (70)** (DShaw) **4-8-5** JFanning(1) (b: hld up: effrt on outside over 4f out: sn rdn & wknd: t.o)....16	**7**	11/1	26	—
			(SP 122.9%)		**7 Rn**

1m 45.8 (0.80) CSF £45.94 TOTE £7.60: £2.90 £2.50 (£12.20) OWNER Mrs Sybil Howe (HAMBLETON) BRED J. L. Eyre
WEIGHT FOR AGE 3yo-10lb
STEWARDS' ENQUIRY Whelan susp. 4-5&7-8/7/97 (excessive use of whip). Millman fined £115 (failure to give adequate instructions to rider).

2021* Cashmere Lady, winning her second race of the week, goes extremely well for this boy and she had the prize safely under wraps from a long way out. (6/1)

1969 Bentico ran his usual game race but he was always playing second fiddle to the winner, and was unable to make any impression. (7/1)

1111 Broughtons Turmoil, having his first run on the All-Weather for eleven months, looked assured of the runner-up prize approaching the final furlong, but stamina deserted him inside the last one hundred yards. (4/1)

1048* Water Garden, trying a slightly longer trip, was never travelling at any stage and her supporters soon knew their fate. (11/4: 2/1-3/1)

677 Concer Un has been pitted against much stronger opposition in recent races, and he tried hard to keep tabs on the winner, but the concession of 14lb was taking its toll at the end of the end of the back straight, and his measure had been taken. (7/1)

1788* Alsahib (USA), the only one to attract significant support in the ring, was always making hard work of it and it must be said he ran a bit flat. (5/2: op 5/1)

2162 DUDLEY H'CAP (0-85) (3-Y.O+) (Class D)

8-25 (8-29) **6f** **(Fibresand)** £3,613.75 (£1,078.00: £514.50: £232.75) Stalls: Low GOING minus 0.39 sec per fur (FST)

Form	Horse	Pos	SP	RR	SF
1662[7]	**The Happy Fox (IRE) (81)** (BAMcMahon) **5-9-12b** LNewton(2) (lw: a.p: led 2f out: clr fnl f: r.o wl) ....—	**1**	10/1	90	44
1113*	**Intiaash (IRE) (69)** (DHaydnJones) **5-9-0** JCarroll(1) (lw: dwlt: bhd tl gd hdwy 2f out: r.o fnl f: nt rch wnr)......2½	**2**	4/1[1]	71	25
2050[3]	**Napier Star (67)** (MrsNMacauley) **4-8-12v** BDoyle(9) (lw: bhd tl gd hdwy appr fnl f: fin wl) ....hd	**3**	8/1	69	23
1957[9]	**Depreciate (71)** (CJames) **4-9-2** JFEgan(10) (a.p: rdn over 1f out: kpt on: nt pce to chal).....................nk	**4**	16/1	72	26
1578[3]	**Robo Magic (USA) (83)** (LMontagueHall) **5-10-0** FLynch(3) (b: led over 4f out to 2f out: sn rdn & outpcd) 1	**5**	6/1[3]	82	36
1799[5]	**First Maite (80)** (SRBowring) **4-9-11b** SWebster(8) (hdwy 3f out: hrd rdn over 1f out: kpt on one pce)...........s.h	**6**	7/1	79	33
1920[7]	**Everset (FR) (65)** (ABailey) **9-8-10** DWright(4) (b: lw: outpcd) 1¼	**7**	20/1	60	14
1402[5]	**Broadstairs Beauty (IRE) (76)** (DShaw) **7-9-4**(3) CTeague(6) (b: b.hind: spd 4f).....................2½	**8**	6/1[3]	65	19
253[6]	**Pageboy (78)** (PCHaslam) **8-9-9** JFortune(5) (bit bkwd: led over 1f: rdn over 2f out: sn btn) ....½	**9**	12/1	65	19
1320[13]	**Oberon's Dart (IRE) (72)** (PJMakin) **4-9-3** SSanders(11) (lw: outpcd: a bhd: t.o).....................12	**10**	14/1	27	—
1963[2]	**Prima Silk (77)** (MJRyan) **6-9-8** AClark(12) (in tch: rdn & outpcd ½-wy: t.o).....................hd	**11**	5/1[2]	32	—
			(SP 122.9%)		**11 Rn**

1m 13.5 (2.30) CSF £47.46 CT £323.25 TOTE £11.90: £2.40 £1.40 £2.60 (£26.30) Trio £96.80 OWNER Mr G. Whitaker (TAMWORTH) BRED Abbey Lodge Stud

1578 The Happy Fox (IRE) adopted a more positive approach on this return to six furlongs and, kicking for home from the turn into the straight, won comfortably. This was his first success beyond the minimum trip, but it will almost certainly not be his last. (10/1)

1113* Intiaash (IRE), sluggish leaving the start, did a lot of running to fill the runner-up spot but the winner had got away, and she always had too much to do. (4/1)

2050 Napier Star adopted the same tactics on this step-up to six furlongs and finished like a train but, in this class, her effort was always going to be too late. (8/1)

1021 Depreciate has not won a race since his two-year-old days, but he showed enough on this All-Weather debut to suggest that a return to form is imminent. (16/1)

1578 Robo Magic (USA) adopted unfamiliar tactics on this occasion, but it backfired somewhat, for the finishing kick was not there when it was most needed. (6/1)

1799 First Maite failed to get in a blow despite running on, and may have found the conditions more testing than he wished. (7/1)

2163 OSWESTRY (S) STKS (2-Y.O) (Class G)

8-55 (8-56) **6f** **(Fibresand)** £1,984.50 (£547.00: £259.50) Stalls: Low GOING minus 0.39 sec per fur (FST)

Form	Horse	Pos	SP	RR	SF
*1789**	**Michelee** (PDEvans) **2-8-11** JFEgan(6) (chsd ldrs: shkn up to ld appr fnl f: sn clr) ....—	**1**	4/7[1]	65+	1
1789[3]	**Jack-N-Jilly (IRE)** (JSMoore) **2-8-3**(3) MHenry(3) (a.p: rdn over 2f out: kpt on ins fnl f: no ch w wnr)................5	**2**	7/1[3]	47	—
1984[2]	**Medina Miss** (WGMTurner) **2-8-1**(5) DSweeney(4) (led tl hdd over 1f out: sn hrd rdn: one pce).....................1	**3**	3/1[2]	44	—
1847[8]	**Jonathan's Girl** (JJBridger) **2-8-6** SophieMitchell(5) (bit bkwd: hdwy 3f out: rdn & hung lft appr fnl f: no imp)..3	**4**	12/1	36	—
1827[11]	**Impish Lady (IRE)** (MartynMeade) **2-7-13**(7) RBrisland(2) (reard s: a bhd & outpcd: t.o) 13	**5**	16/1	1	—
1286[11]	**Risknowt Getnowt** (TWall) **2-8-11b[1]** SSanders(1) (sn pushed along: chsd ldrs to ½-wy: sn outpcd: t.o) 2½	**6**	20/1	—	—
			(SP 119.5%)		**6 Rn**

1m 15.8 (4.60) CSF £5.68 TOTE £1.60: £1.30 £2.40 (£4.50) OWNER Mr John Pugh (WELSHPOOL) BRED Llety Stud
Bt in 5,200gns

1789* Michelee followed up her success over course and distance earlier in the month with another impressive performance, but she proved rather costly to retain, and could now be set for a step-up in grade. (4/7)

1789 Jack-N-Jilly (IRE), 11lb better off for a beating of over eight lengths a fortnight ago, had little hope of turning the tables with the winner. (7/1: op 4/1)

1984 Medina Miss tried hard to gallop the opposition into the ground, but she was always a sitting duck and was well outpaced when the winner set sail for home. (3/1)

2164 CODSALL H'CAP (0-65) (3-Y.O+) (Class F)

9-25 (9-28) **1m 4f** **(Fibresand)** £2,277.00 (£627.00: £297.00) Stalls: Low GOING minus 0.39 sec per fur (FST)

Form	Horse	Pos	SP	RR	SF
1636[3]	**State Approval (62)** (PEccles) **4-9-7**(5) GFaulkner(1) (mde all: clr over 2f out: unchal) ....—	**1**	9/2[2]	80	62
857[2]	**Wildfire (SWI) (51)** (RAkehurst) **6-9-1** SSanders(2) (b: chsd wnr thrght: rdn 3f out: sn outpcd) 15	**2**	11/2[3]	49	31
1463[12]	**African-Pard (IRE) (45)** (DHaydnJones) **5-8-9** AClark(8) (lw: hld up: hdwy 4f out: styd on u.p ins fnl f).............5	**3**	10/1	36	18
1233[U]	**Fresh Fruit Daily (50)** (PAKelleway) **5-9-0** DBiggs(3) (a chsng ldrs: rdn wl over 2f out: no imp).....................4	**4**	9/2[2]	36	18
	Sommersby (IRE) (48) (MrsNMacauley) **6-8-12** BDoyle(5) (b: bit bkwd: in tch: effrt over 3f out: wknd fnl 2f)....8	**5**	20/1	23	5
1281[7]	**General Glow (49)** (PDEvans) **4-8-13** JFEgan(4) (trckd ldrs: pushed along 6f out: sn btn) ....nk	**6**	12/1	24	6

				SP	RR	SF
1732[3]	**Course Fishing (33)** (BAMcMahon) **6-7-11** JLowe(10) (bit bkwd: mid div: effrt 4f out: sn hrd drvn: btn fnl 3f)	.hd	**7**	7/2 [1]	8	—
1779[7]	**Stonecutter (57)** (WRMuir) **4-9-7v** SophieMitchell(9) (hld up: hdwy on ins 5f out: rdn & wknd wl over 2f out)	...7	**8**	20/1	23	5
1641[7]	**Urgent Reply (USA) (56)** (CADwyer) **4-9-6** JCarroll(7) (chsd ldrs: drvn along 4f out: sn btn)	s.h	**9**	14/1	21	3
2015[4]	**In the Money (IRE) (58)** (RHollinshead) **8-9-8** FLynch(6) (sn drvn along: a in rr)	s.h	**10**	6/1	23	5
516[12]	**River Captain (USA) (58)** (DJGMurraySmith) **4-9-8** SWhitworth(11) (bit bkwd: a bhd: t.o fnl 4f)	28	**11**	16/1	—	—

(SP 127.1%) **11 Rn**

2m 35.0 (2.50) CSF £29.36 CT £220.88 TOTE £6.50: £1.90 £2.10 £4.10 (£28.20) Trio £87.90 OWNER The Claddagh Ring Partnership (LAMBOURN) BRED Collin Stud and The Pharly Syndicate

1636 State Approval is not over-big but his heart is in the right place and, bowling along in front in the very gloomy conditions, made it look all so easy after shaking off the runner-up on the home turn. (9/2)

857 Wildfire (SWI), the only one able to make a race of it, was being made to work fully three furlongs out, and he had to admit he had met one too good. (11/2)

360 African-Pard (IRE) is finding it difficult to open his account, but he is not short in the stamina stakes and will get it right one of these days. (10/1)

1125* Fresh Fruit Daily tracked the leading pair and kept battling on, but she was fighting a lost cause before reaching the end of the back straight. (9/2)

General Glow (12/1: op 6/1)

1732 Course Fishing did not relish this soggy surface, and was never in a position to cause concern. Still looking to have something left to work on, a return to the turf could bring about improvement. (7/2: op 6/1)

1106 Urgent Reply (USA) (14/1: op 6/1)

T/Plpt: £833.50 (18.4 Tckts). T/Qdpt: £43.00 (25.35 Tckts) IM

1990-MUSSELBURGH (R-H) (Good to soft)
Monday June 23rd

WEATHER: overcast WIND: almost nil

2165 CRAIGLEITH CLAIMING STKS (2-Y.O) (Class E)

2-30 (2-30) **5f** £2,786.25 (£840.00: £407.50: £191.25) Stalls: High GOING minus 0.08 sec per fur (G)

				SP	RR	SF
2031*	**Ellenbrook (IRE)** (JBerry) **2-8-3b**(3) PFessey(1) (mde all: drvn along ½-wy: styd on)	—	**1**	4/9 [1]	64	14
1614[2]	**Makahu Don** (WTKemp) **2-8-7** JCarroll(2) (outpcd tl hdwy over 1f out: r.o)	1½	**2**	5/1 [3]	60	10
1990[3]	**Oriel Girl** (PDEvans) **2-8-4** LCharnock(4) (lw: chsd wnr tl rdn & btn appr fnl f)	3	**3**	4/1 [2]	48	—
1961[8]	**Blue Anchor** (MrsMReveley) **2-9-7** ACulhane(3) (a outpcd & bhd)	3	**4**	66/1	55	5

(SP 107.4%) **4 Rn**

61.8 secs (4.10) CSF £2.77 TOTE £1.30 (£1.80) OWNER Mr J. K. Brown (COCKERHAM) BRED M. Bourke

2031* Ellenbrook (IRE) always had too much pace for this opposition, but she needed to be rousted along to put it beyond doubt. (4/9)

1614 Makahu Don ran as though another furlong would have seen him the comfortable winner. (5/1: op 3/1)

1990 Oriel Girl is really coming to herself looks-wise, and showed good speed until tiring late on. (4/1: op 5/2)

Blue Anchor was being taken off his legs, but he still finished within sight of the leaders for the first time, and over further better is likely. (66/1)

2166 YVONNE MURRAY M.B.E. H'CAP (0-70) (3-Y.O+) (Class E)

3-00 (3-00) **2m** £2,900.00 (£875.00: £425.00: £200.00) Stalls: High GOING: 0.10 sec per fur (G)

				SP	RR	SF
2034[2]	**Trilby (54)** (GRichards) **4-9-4v**(5) TEDurcan(3) (a.gng wl: led far side over 2f out: pushed along & r.o wl)	—	**1**	3/1 [2]	68	—
2034*	**Hasta la Vista (51)** (MWEasterby) **7-9-1b**(5) 4x GParkin(4) (lw: led tl hdd over 2f out: r.o one pce)	7	**2**	3/1 [2]	58	—
1996[9]	**Zamhareer (USA) (45)** (WStorey) **6-8-9**(5) IonaWands(7) (chsd ldrs: pushed along appr st: one pce fnl 3f)	9	**3**	8/1	43	—
	Sarasota Storm (55) (MBell) **5-9-10** MFenton(1) (hld up: hdwy to ld stands' side over 2f out: no ch w ldrs far side)	4	**4**	11/4 [1]	49	—
1840[4]	**Thunderheart (50)** (RAllan) **6-9-5** ACulhane(6) (chsd ldrs: swtchd stands' side ent st: btn over 2f out)	7	**5**	5/1 [3]	37	—
	Fret (USA) (40) (JSWainwright) **7-8-4**(5) JBramhill(2) (pushed along 7f out: racd stands' side st: n.d)	7	**6**	50/1	20	—
1785[8]	**Propellant (56)** (CWThornton) **3-8-5**ow1 DeanMcKeown(5) (a bhd: racd stands' side st)	1¼	**7**	50/1	35	—

(SP 108.4%) **7 Rn**

3m 37.6 CSF £10.06 TOTE £4.00: £1.90 £1.70 (£3.70) OWNER Mrs B. C. Finch (PENRITH) BRED Newgate Stud Co

WEIGHT FOR AGE 3yo-20lb

2034 Trilby, ridden with more restraint this time, won particularly well. (3/1)

2034* Hasta la Vista set the race up for the winner and was well tapped for foot in the closing stages. (3/1: op 2/1)

1996 Zamhareer (USA) ran a shade better, but he was again left wanting a long way from home. (8/1)

Sarasota Storm, unbeaten on this track previously, did not look fully wound up and crossed over to the stands' side entering the straight. He beat his three opponents on that side but was completely outpointed by the three racing up the far side. (11/4)

1840 Thunderheart was a top of the ground performer three years ago and these conditions were just a shade too testing for him. (5/1)

2167 HADDINGTON RATING RELATED MAIDEN STKS (0-65) (3-Y.O+) (Class F)

3-30 (3-33) **5f** £2,598.00 (£728.00: £354.00) Stalls: High GOING minus 0.08 sec per fur (G)

				SP	RR	SF
1733[8]	**Blazing Imp (USA) (40)** (MrsJJordan) **4-9-3** MFenton(3) (chsd ldrs: led ins fnl f: all out)	—	**1**	33/1	58	45
2017[7]	**Prince of Parkes (64)** (JBerry) **3-8-6b**(5) PRoberts(4) (chsd ldr: rdn to ld ins fnl f: sn hdd: rallied towards fin)	hd	**2**	7/2 [2]	58	39
2061[8]	**Good To Talk (40)** (TDEasterby) **4-9-3b** JCarroll(2) (led tl hdd ins fnl f: no ex)	2	**3**	5/1 [3]	51	38
1828[10]	**Mystical (51)** (MrsLStubbs) **3-8-8v** ACulhane(8) (lw: s.i.s: hdwy 2f out: nrst fin)	½	**4**	6/1	47	28
1963[3]	**Gold Edge (53)** (MRChannon) **3-8-8** NKennedy(7) (hdwy after 1½f: sn chsng ldrs: edgd rt & no ex appr fnl f)	3½	**5**	9/4 [1]	36	17
1828[17]	**Superfrills (35)** (MissLCSiddall) **4-9-0** DeanMcKeown(9) (lw: racd centre: in tch: rdn ½-wy: no imp)	2½	**6**	16/1	28	15
1864[4]	**Red Romance (50)** (DenysSmith) **3-8-11** LCharnock(5) (in tch tl outpcd fnl 2f)	6	**7**	7/1	11	—
1764[7]	**Fancy Clancy (34)** (MissLCSiddall) **4-8-7**(7) TSiddall(1) (nvr wnt pce)	1	**8**	33/1	5	—
1681[4]	**Astral Crown (IRE) (33)** (JBerry) **3-8-5b**(3) PFessey(10) (b.hind: s.i.s: n.d)	5	**9**	20/1	—	—

1375^{10}	**Eaton Park (IRE) (51)** (MissGayKelleway) **3-8-13**^{ow2} RHughes(6) (spd to ½-wy: sn btn & eased)	9	**10**	8/1	—	—
				(SP 124.1%)		**10 Rn**

60.5 secs (2.80) CSF £138.72 TOTE £69.00: £8.80 £1.80 £1.70 (£363.40) Trio £187.50 OWNER Mrs J. Jordan (YARM) BRED Halsall Investments Inc.
WEIGHT FOR AGE 3yo-6lb
OFFICIAL EXPLANATION **Blazing Imp (USA): regarding the improved form, the trainer's representative reported that this was the gelding's first run from the yard, and that he had run too freely and failed to stay last time.**
Blazing Imp (USA) did not have a lot to recommend him but he showed fine determination to win this, and it was certainly no fluke. (33/1)
1650 Prince of Parkes had a golden opportunity, but yet again he failed to take it. (7/2)
1687 Good To Talk has plenty of speed but, when it comes down to a struggle, he is certainly lacking in that department. (5/1)
1667 Mystical looked particularly well and, after a poor start, only got going when it was too late. (6/1)
1963 Gold Edge has plenty of ability but all she wanted to do was hang when the pressure was applied. (9/4: 6/4-5/2)
1604 Superfrills was always racing on the outside of the field, and may have done better had she stuck to the far side. (16/1)
Eaton Park (IRE) spoilt all his chances by pulling extremely hard going to post. (8/1: op 5/1)

2168 LINLITHGOW NOVICE AUCTION STKS (2-Y.O) (Class E)
4-00 (4-00) **7f 30y** £2,770.00 (£835.00: £405.00: £190.00) Stalls: High GOING: 0.10 sec per fur (G)

				SP	RR	SF
1839^{4}	**Buzz** (CWThornton) **2-8-12** DeanMcKeown(6) (lw: hld up: effrt over 2f out: rdn to ld wl ins fnl f)	—	**1**	15/8^{2}	77+	—
1616*	**Jacmar (IRE)** (MissLAPerratt) **2-8-10** NKennedy(1) (lw: trckd ldrs: led over 2f out: r.o: hdd & no ex towards fin)	1	**2**	6/4^{1}	73	—
1669^{8}	**Deeceebee** (WStorey) **2-8-3**$^{(3)}$ PFessey(3) (trckd ldr: ev ch over 2f out: nt qckn fnl f)	1¾	**3**	20/1	65	—
1819^{2}	**Durham Flyer** (TDEasterby) **2-8-9** JCarroll(4) (led: qcknd ent st: hdd over 2f out: one pce)	nk	**4**	7/2^{3}	67	—
1760^{7}	**Lord of Love** (TDEasterby) **2-8-6** LCharnock(2) (in tch tl outpcd fnl 3f)	5	**5**	10/1	53	—
1038^{6}	**Cosmic Case** (JSGoldie) **2-8-1** TWilliams(5) (nvr trbld ldrs)	5	**6**	50/1	37	—
				(SP 112.8%)		**6 Rn**

1m 35.3 (9.30) CSF £4.67 TOTE £3.20: £1.40 £1.10 (£1.30) OWNER Mr G. Reed (MIDDLEHAM) BRED I. W. T. and Mrs Loftus
1839 Buzz confirmed his promise of last time and, despite the steady early pace, did it nicely. There is certainly better to come. (15/8: 11/8-9/4)
1616* Jacmar (IRE) again took the eye in the paddock and should have been suited by the trip and the ground, but he just met one too good. (6/4)
Deeceebee improved considerably for this step-up in trip, and there is obviously a race to be picked up with him. (20/1)
1819 Durham Flyer tried to pinch this by quickening early in the straight, but was well tapped for speed in the last two furlongs and is probably better on faster ground. (7/2)
1760 Lord of Love looks one likely to do better in nurseries. (10/1: 8/1-12/1)
1038 Cosmic Case failed to show anything positive. (50/1)

2169 WALLYFORD H'CAP (0-65) (3-Y.O) (Class F)
4-30 (4-35) **7f 30y** £2,724.00 (£764.00: £372.00) Stalls: High GOING: 0.10 sec per fur (G)

				SP	RR	SF
2019^{4}	**High Spirits (IRE) (54)** (TDEasterby) **3-8-13b** LCharnock(1) (in tch: rdn to ld over 1f out: r.o)	—	**1**	7/2^{1}	71	29
1820^{9}	**Barresbo (60)** (CWFairhurst) **3-8-12**$^{(7)}$ TSiddall(5) (cl up: led over 2f out tl over 1f out: nt qckn)	3	**2**	11/2^{3}	70	28
1496^{11}	**Anetta (54)** (MissSEHall) **3-8-13** ACulhane(4) (bhd: hdwy over 3f out: chsng ldrs over 1f out: no ex)	2½	**3**	6/1	59	17
1810^{4}	**Hever Golf Mover (62)** (TJNaughton) **3-9-7** JCarroll(9) (chsd ldrs: effrt 3f out: r.o one pce)	hd	**4**	13/2	66	24
2017^{10}	**Paldost (45)** (MDHammond) **3-8-4** DaleGibson(7) (lw: chsd ldrs: disp ld 4f out tl over 2f out: rdn & grad wknd)	1¾	**5**	50/1	46	4
1467^{7}	**Hi Mujtahid (IRE) (42)** (SEKettlewell) **3-8-1**^{ow2} JFEgan(3) (lw: in tch: effrt 4f out: sn rdn: btn over 2f out)	4	**6**	5/1^{2}	34	—
1807*	**Eager To Please (60)** (MissGayKelleway) **3-9-5b** RHughes(2) (b.hind: led tl hdd over 2f out: sn wknd)	1	**7**	7/2^{1}	49	7
1864^{3}	**Mill End Boy (55)** (MWEasterby) **3-8-9**$^{(5)}$ GParkin(8) (plld hrd: trckd ldrs: effrt over 3f out: btn over 2f out)	5	**8**	9/1	33	—
1995^{10}	**Miss St Kitts (42)** (JSGoldie) **3-8-1** TWilliams(6) (plld hrd: bhd: effrt 3f out: n.d)	6	**9**	33/1	7	—
				(SP 119.0%)		**9 Rn**

1m 32.6 (6.60) CSF £21.71 CT £104.10 TOTE £3.60: £1.80 £1.50 £3.00 (£7.70) Trio £50.40 OWNER Mrs J. B. Mountifield (MALTON) BRED Sean Twomey
OFFICIAL EXPLANATION **Eager To Please: was not suited by the ground.**
2019 High Spirits (IRE) obviously appreciates cut in the ground and won this really well, finishing strongly. (7/2)
1603 Barresbo is running well and, round about this trip, deserves to pick up a race. (11/2)
Anetta does not look an easy ride but did run a shade better this time. (6/1)
1810 Hever Golf Mover had her chances but lacked the pace to take them. (13/2: 7/2-7/1)
1041 Paldost ran his best race to date and is coming to himself looks-wise. (50/1)
1467 Hi Mujtahid (IRE) proved disappointing when asked for an effort early in the straight. (5/1)
1864 Mill End Boy spent all his energy pulling his rider's arms out. (9/1: op 5/1)

2170 ORMISTON H'CAP (0-65) (3-Y.O+) (Class F)
5-00 (5-00) **1m 4f 31y** £2,612.00 (£732.00: £356.00) Stalls: High GOING: 0.10 sec per fur (G)

				SP	RR	SF
1779^{19}	**Kernof (IRE) (50)** (MDHammond) **4-9-7** JCarroll(8) (a.p: effrt 2f out: r.o u.p to ld wl ins fnl f)	—	**1**	11/2^{2}	59	41
1844^{2}	**Yet Again (47)** (MissGayKelleway) **5-9-4** RHughes(5) (in tch: hdwy to ld over 1f out: r.o u.p: hdd wl ins fnl f: rallied)	hd	**2**	8/11^{1}	56	38
1992^{4}	**Latvian (57)** (RAllan) **10-10-0v** JFEgan(6) (led tl hdd 2f out: one pce)	2	**3**	10/1	63	45
1686^{7}	**Eden Dancer (40)** (MrsMReveley) **5-8-11** ACulhane(3) (bhd: rdn 3f out: styd on: no imp)	4	**4**	20/1	41	23
1732^{2}	**Majal (IRE) (52)** (JSWainwright) **8-9-9** DeanMcKeown(1) (lw: hld up: hdwy to ld 2f out: hung bdly rt: sn hdd & wknd)	1¼	**5**	8/1^{3}	51	33
	Ibn Masirah (54) (MrsMReveley) **3-8-6**$^{(5)}$ SCopp(2) (nvr trbld ldrs)	2½	**6**	33/1	50	18
955^{13}	**Breydon (44)** (PMonteith) **4-8-10**$^{(5)}$ JBramhill(4) (chsd ldrs tl wknd fnl 2½f)	hd	**7**	20/1	40	22
1229^{16}	**Mystic Times (35)** (BMactaggart) **4-8-3**$^{(3)}$ PFessey(9) (cl up tl wknd 3f out)	4	**8**	33/1	26	8
1731^{4}	**Zanabay (48)** (WStorey) **3-8-5** TWilliams(7) (unruly leaving paddock: plld hrd: a bhd)	8	**9**	10/1	28	—
				(SP 118.0%)		**9 Rn**

2m 44.5 (11.00) CSF £8.81 CT £35.34 TOTE £7.60: £2.00 £1.30 £1.90 (£5.90) Trio £24.60 OWNER Mr J. M. Gahan (MIDDLEHAM) BRED David Wallace
WEIGHT FOR AGE 3yo-14lb
1393 Kernof (IRE), given a fine ride, was produced with a run to settle it late on. (11/2: 4/1-6/1)

1844 Yet Again is better on the faster surface, but put up a good performance and this consistent sort is not done with. (8/11: evens-4/6)
1992 Latvian ran much better this time when allowed to bowl along in front, but he was always tending to hang when the pressure was on and was worried out of it in the last two furlongs. (10/1)
Eden Dancer ran quite well, staying on in the closing stages, and seems to be gradually coming to hand. (20/1)
1732 Majal (IRE) looked particularly well, but threw all chance away by hanging badly right when asked a question. (8/1)
Ibn Masirah, suited by the step-up in trip, was noted making a little late headway. (33/1)

T/Plpt: £41.50 (294.98 Tckts). T/Qdpt: £12.40 (68.3 Tckts) AA

2035-NOTTINGHAM (L-H) (Soft)
Monday June 23rd
WEATHER: cloudy with rain WIND: almost nil becoming mod bhd

2171 SUN CHEMICAL (S) H'CAP (0-60) (3-Y.O) (Class G)
2-15 (2-16) **1m 54y** £2,513.70 (£698.20: £335.10) Stalls: Low GOING: 0.09 sec per fur (G)

				SP	RR	SF
1820^{5}	**Flashtalkin' Flood (57)** (CADwyer) **3-9-7** WRyan(12) (chsd ldrs: led over 2f out: sn clr: comf)	—	**1**	$2/1^{1}$	76+	44
1689^{9}	**Cimmerian (50)** (MJohnston) **3-9-0** JWeaver(15) (lw: chsd ldrs: rdn 2f out: r.o ins fnl f: no ch w wnr)	4	**2**	14/1	61	29
1988*	**Feel A Line (49)** (BJMeehan) **3-8-13b** 6x MTebbutt(7) (lw: a.p: chsd wnr over 2f out: hrd rdn & edgd lft appr fnl f: one pce)	3	**3**	10/1	54	22
1921^{3}	**Prince of Fortune (49)** (MBlanshard) **3-8-13** NAdams(4) (hdwy on ins over 3f out: nt clr run over 2f out: swtchd: r.o one pce)	2	**4**	12/1	51	19
1965^{15}	**Battle Ground (IRE) (48)** (NACallaghan) **3-8-12** PatEddery(2) (hld up: hdwy fnl 2f: nvr nrr)	4	**5**	10/1	42	10
1689^{7}	**Misterton (39)** (JAGlover) **3-8-3b** GCarter(3) (bhd: hdwy 2f out: nvr nrr)	1¼	**6**	16/1	30	—
1661^{7}	**Joyful Joy (39)** (BPJBaugh) **3-8-3** NCarlisle(8) (b.off hind: swtg: hld up: hdwy 3f out: sn rdn: wknd over 1f out)	½	**7**	33/1	29	—
1167^{5}	**Circle of Magic (52)** (PJMakin) **3-9-2** SSanders(13) (swtg: hld up: hdwy 3f out: wknd over 1f out)	1½	**8**	10/1	40	8
1272^{14}	**Seamus (43)** (CJHill) **3-8-7** JQuinn(11) (swtg: nvr nr to chal)	1½	**9**	20/1	28	—
2017^{8}	**Alisadara (41)** (NBycroft) **3-8-5**ow1 SDrowne(18) (hdwy 3f out: wknd wl over 1f out)	1¾	**10**	25/1	22	—
2040^{12}	**Kustom Kit Xpres (50)** (SRBowring) **3-9-0** SWebster(17) (nvr bttr than mid div)	½	**11**	25/1	30	—
1998^{4}	**Macari (45)** (BPJBaugh) **3-8-9** RPerham(9) (prom: rdn 3f out: sn wknd)	¾	**12**	10/1	24	—
193^{8}	**Gymcrak Watermill (IRE) (40)** (GHolmes) **3-8-4** JStack(16) (b.hind: a in rr)	4	**13**	33/1	11	—
1584^{6}	**Bali-Pet (45)** (JParkes) **3-8-9b**ow1 JReid(1) (prom tl rdn & wknd over 2f out: t.o)	5	**14**	$15/2^{2}$	6	—
2040^{7}	**Native Princess (IRE) (50)** (BWHills) **3-9-0b¹** MHills(14) (led over 5f: grad wknd: t.o)	s.h	**15**	$9/1^{3}$	11	—
1105^{13}	**Craven Hill (IRE) (44)** (NAGraham) **3-8-8b¹** AMcGlone(6) (rel to r: a bhd: t.o)	6	**16**	16/1	—	—
1998^{12}	**Crosby Nod (54)** (EWeymes) **3-9-4** LDettori(10) (lw: mid div: eased whn btn fnl 2f: t.o)	5	**17**	14/1	—	—
				(SP 142.6%)	**17 Rn**	

1m 48.2 (6.90) CSF £33.55 CT £252.32 TOTE £3.00: £1.10 £6.60 £2.40 £2.80 (£38.00) Trio £41.00 OWNER Richard Flood Bloodstock Ltd (NEWMARKET) BRED Mrs Alison Roberts
Bt in 8,400gns

1820 Flashtalkin' Flood proved a class apart on the step down to selling company, and did not need to get serious to defy top weight, but connections had to pay dearly to retain him and it is doubtful if he will remain in this class. (2/1)
Cimmerian showed improved form without ever promising to overturn the favourite, but at least she does seem to be getting it together. (14/1)
1988* Feel A Line sat closer to the pace than he did when successful over a slightly shorter trip at Brighton, and again drifted left when put under pressure, but his ability to get the mile ridden this way must be very much in doubt. (10/1)
1921 Prince of Fortune finished some way behind the winner over this trip last month and, though he was forced to switch inside the final quarter-mile, it did not appear to have any bearing on the final outcome. (12/1)
1689 Battle Ground (IRE), ridden with restraint, was gradually getting closer in the latter stages without ever threatening to take a hand in proceedings. (10/1: op 6/1)
Misterton stayed on to reach his final placing and he is slowly but surely getting it together. It would seem he could need possibly another half-mile before he really succeeds. (16/1)
1167 Circle of Magic (10/1: op 6/1)
462 Crosby Nod (14/1: 10/1-16/1)

2172 NOTTINGHAM EVENING POST MAIDEN STKS (I) (3-Y.O+) (Class D)
2-45 (2-45) **1m 54y** £2,801.90 (£828.20: £389.60: £170.30) Stalls: Low GOING: 0.09 sec per fur (G)

				SP	RR	SF
	Mithali (BWHills) **4-9-7** RHills(2) (mde all: rdn clr over 1f out: easily)	—	**1**	$8/1^{3}$	85+	38
1582^{2}	**Yabint El Sultan (73)** (BAMcMahon) **3-8-6** LNewton(7) (lw: hld up: hdwy 3f out: r.o ins fnl f: no ch w wnr)	3½	**2**	$11/2^{2}$	73	16
1876^{2}	**Jorrocks (USA)** (IABalding) **3-8-11** PatEddery(4) (lw: hld up: chsd wnr 3f out tl ins fnl f)	2½	**3**	$4/7^{1}$	73	16
	She's A Cracker (MrsNMacauley) **3-8-6** DHarrison(8) (hdwy fnl 2f: nt rch ldrs)	5	**4**	66/1	59	2
	Chloe's Anchor (WAO'Gorman) **4-9-2** JReid(3) (bit bkwd: plld hrd: hld up in tch: effrt & rdn 3f out: no hdwy fnl 2f)	1½	**5**	10/1	56	9
	Desert Warrior (IRE) (KMahdi) **3-8-8**(3) DO'Donohoe(10) (lw: plld hrd: sn chsng ldrs: wknd 2f out)	2½	**6**	14/1	56	—
	Rise Above (IRE) (THind) **3-8-6** AClark(9) (unf: scope: prom: pushed along 3f out: sn outpcd)	3	**7**	40/1	45	—
	Kailey Goddess (USA) (RWArmstrong) **4-9-7** RPrice(1) (chsd ldrs tl wknd over 2f out)	½	**8**	10/1	49	2
	Crompton Lights (DJSCosgrove) **3-8-11** MRimmer(5) (leggy: dwlt: wl bhd fnl 4f)	nk	**9**	20/1	49	—
2008^{23}	**Shelteez (USA)** (MBell) **3-7-13**(7) NicolaCole(6) (dwlt: a wl bhd: t.o fr ½-wy)	4	**10**	33/1	36	—
				(SP 126.6%)	**10 Rn**	

1m 48.8 (7.50) CSF £49.54 TOTE £8.60: £1.60 £1.50 £1.10 (£19.00) Trio £4.50 OWNER Mr Hamdan Al Maktoum (LAMBOURN) BRED Shadwell Estate Company Limited
WEIGHT FOR AGE 3yo-10lb

Mithali, a choicely-bred colt who has been given time to develop, made his first appearance in this country a winning one with a very smooth success and, though he may not have had much to beat, he looks set to go places. (8/1: op 4/1)
1582 Yabint El Sultan, making her move once in line for home, stuck to the task willingly and she seems to need at least a mile. (11/2)
1876 Jorrocks (USA) had much softer ground to contend with this time and a slightly longer trip and, struggling to reach the winner from below the distance, gradually weakened towards the finish. (4/7)

She's A Cracker will eventually need a stiffer test of stamina and, though she stayed on steadily in the latter stages on her seasonal debut, she was never a factor. (66/1)
Chloe's Anchor needed the run and the experience and she did not fare badly after taking a keen tug until past halfway. (10/1: op 5/1)
Desert Warrior (IRE), who has changed stables since last season, looked well tuned-up for this first outing since the autumn, but he refused to settle and had run himself out entering the last quarter-mile. (14/1: 8/1-16/1)
Kailey Goddess (USA) (10/1: op 5/1)

2173 NOTTINGHAM EVENING POST MAIDEN STKS (II) (3-Y.O+) (Class D)

3-15 (3-17) **1m 54y** £2,770.05 (£818.40: £384.70: £167.85) Stalls: Low GOING: 0.09 sec per fur (G)

				SP	RR	SF
1322^{6}	**Liquid Gold (IRE)** (WAO'Gorman) **3-8-6**$^{(5)}$ RFfrench(6) (a.p: led ins fnl f: pushed out)	—	1	7/2^{3}	62	24
	Karakia (IRE) (JHMGosden) **3-8-6** LDettori(1) (unf: scope: bit bkwd: dwlt: sn chsng ldrs: rdn over 2f out: ev ch 1f out: unable qckn)	1¼	2	3/1^{2}	55	17
	Windy Treat (USA) (EALDunlop) **3-8-8**$^{(3)}$ DO'Donohoe(8) (w'like: scope: lw: s.v.s: hdwy over 3f out: hrd drvn over 1f out: kpt on wl)	3	3	9/4^{1}	54	16
1851^{6}	**Shades of Love** (VSoane) **3-8-11** CRutter(3) (led tl ins fnl f: rdn & no ex)	1¼	4	16/1	51	13
1807^{11}	**Rambo Tango** (BRCambidge) **3-8-11** NAdams(5) (swtg: hld up & bhd: styd on appr fnl f: nvr nrr)	4	5	66/1	44	6
1876^{10}	**Gajan (IRE)** (JNeville) **3-8-11** SDrowne(7) (hld up mid div: wknd over 1f out)	¾	6	100/1	42	4
	Awassi (IRE) (KMahdi) **4-9-7** PatEddery(2) (bkwd: prom: ev ch over 2f out: wknd & eased appr fnl f)	7	7	7/2^{3}	29	1
	Rockie The Jester (JPLeigh) **3-8-11** JWeaver(9) (lengthy: bkwd: s.s: a bhd)	1¾	8	50/1	25	—
	Enavius (IRE) (MBell) **3-8-11** DHarrison(4) (w ldr: rdn over 3f out: sn wknd: t.o)	12	9	14/1	2	—
				(SP 117.2%)	**9 Rn**	

1m 49.3 (8.00) CSF £13.37 TOTE £6.30: £1.80 £1.40 £1.20 (£5.90) Trio £3.40 OWNER Mr N. S. Yong (NEWMARKET) BRED Rowanstown Stud
WEIGHT FOR AGE 3yo-10lb
1322 Liquid Gold (IRE), an impressive-looking individual who was colty in the preliminaries, picked up willingly when sent about his business and, in the end, won a shade cosily. He still leaves the impression there is something more to work on. (7/2)
Karakia (IRE), a newcomer with plenty of scope about her, can only improve with this run under her belt, and she should have little trouble making the grade. (3/1: 2/1-7/2)
Windy Treat (USA), a full-brother to a couple of winners, looked the business and, if he had not lost all of fifteen lengths at the start, he would probably have come home on his own. (9/4: 5/4-5/2)
Shades of Love knew what was needed and set out to make it all, but the leading pair were waiting to pounce, and he was found wanting in the last two hundred yards. (16/1)
Rambo Tango showed much improved form on this occasion and stayed on well inside the distance, but it is doubtful if he is really up to this class. (66/1)
Awassi (IRE), an attractive ex-Irish colt who is a very poor mover, joined issue three furlongs out and posed a threat until feeling the strain below the distance. Eased considerably once beaten, he will soon leave this form behind. (7/2)
Enavius (IRE) (14/1: op 8/1)

2174 SUN CHEMICAL H'CAP (0-70) (3-Y.O+) (Class E)

3-45 (3-46) **1m 1f 213y** £3,486.25 (£1,045.00: £502.50: £231.25) Stalls: Low GOING: 0.09 sec per fur (G)

				SP	RR	SF
1693^{4}	**Tonnerre (52)** (BAMcMahon) **5-9-4** LNewton(2) (lw: a.p: led 3f out: clr over 1f out: r.o wl)	—	1	16/1	65	15
1383*	**Hill Farm Blues (55)** (WMBrisbourne) **4-9-7** AGarth(8) (a.p: chsd wnr over 2f out: kpt on wl fnl f)	1½	2	9/1	66	16
1968^{6}	**Kristal Breeze (52)** (WRMuir) **5-9-4** JReid(11) (lw: a.p: rdn & one pce fnl 2f)	1¾	3	7/1^{3}	60	10
2071^{9}	**Bronhallow (39)** (MrsBarbaraWaring) **4-8-5v**^{1} SDrowne(6) (b.hind: hld up in tch: hdwy over 3f out: nt pce to chal)	3	4	50/1	42	—
1803^{3}	**Mazilla (50)** (AStreeter) **5-8-13v**$^{(3)}$ RHavlin(17) (lw: hdwy on ins over 3f out: one pce fnl 2f)	¾	5	6/1^{2}	52	2
2152^{10}	**African Sun (IRE) (43)** (MCChapman) **4-8-9** RPerham(5) (swtg: hld up: hdwy & rdn over 1f out: nvr nrr)	1¼	6	20/1	43	—
1803^{4}	**Tonka (58)** (PJMakin) **5-9-10** DHarrison(1) (hld up & bhd: effrt over 2f out: rdn over 1f out: too much to do)	nk	7	100/30^{1}	57	7
1796^{3}	**Forest Fantasy (53)** (JWharton) **4-9-5** LDettori(13) (hld up: hdwy over 3f out: wknd fnl 2f)	2	8	6/1^{2}	49	—
1852^{5}	**Carlys Quest (69)** (JNeville) **3-9-9** AMcGlone(3) (lw: dwlt: nvr nrr)	1	9	16/1	64	2
843^{3}	**Yuppy Girl (IRE) (40)** (CaptJWilson) **4-8-1**$^{(5)}$ RFfrench(9) (a in rr)	2½	10	16/1	30	—
1694^{2}	**Zahran (IRE) (37)** (JMBradley) **6-7-12**$^{(5)ow3}$ ADaly(14) (led 1f: sn lost pl: n.d after)	hd	11	10/1	27	—
1779^{18}	**Cohiba (39)** (BJCurley) **4-8-5** JFanning(7) (a bhd)	3	12	14/1	25	—
1845^{7}	**Saltando (IRE) (53)** (PatMitchell) **6-9-2**$^{(3)}$ DO'Donohoe(10) (lw: s.i.s: effrt 4f out: sn rdn & wknd: t.o)	9	13	16/1	24	—
1800^{14}	**King Chestnut (37)** (MDods) **6-8-3**^{ow1} AClark(4) (lw: plld hrd: hld up: bhd fnl 3f: t.o)	2½	14	25/1	4	—
1800^{5}	**Absolutely Fayre (54)** (VSoane) **6-9-6** CRutter(12) (plld hrd: prom tl wknd over 2f out: t.o)	1¾	15	10/1	18	—
1463^{16}	**Gulf of Siam (50)** (JMackie) **4-9-2b**^{1} JQuinn(15) (dwlt: led after 1f to 3f out: sn wknd: t.o)	21	16	25/1	—	—
				(SP 136.9%)	**16 Rn**	

2m 14.2 (11.70) CSF £150.78 CT £1,040.57 TOTE £21.00: £4.20 £3.30 £2.00 £17.40 (£136.20) Trio £871.90 OWNER Mr Ian Guise (TAMWORTH) BRED Mrs Amanda Skiffington
WEIGHT FOR AGE 3yo-12lb
1693 Tonnerre had the ground he requires but he was taking a big step down in distance. Pushing the pace until taking command three furlongs out, he quickened the tempo to draw clear below the distance and, though the runner-up kept plugging away, he won with a fair bit in hand. (16/1)
1383* Hill Farm Blues turned in a very genuine performance on this step-up in class, and battled away right to the end. She is worth keeping in mind while she is at her peak. (9/1)
1968 Kristal Breeze can handle soft ground and she tried hard to get into the action throughout the final quarter-mile but, with the principals keeping up the gallop, she lacked the speed to carry it through. (7/1)
Bronhallow showed more urgency in his first-time visor, and it would seem all is not lost yet. (50/1)
1803 Mazilla crept through on the inside rail early in the straight, but a turn of speed was missing when she was asked for her effort, and she is not yet firing this term. (6/1)
1024 African Sun (IRE), making a quick reappearance, stayed on well in the closing stages and gives the impression that there is a race in him if he could be relied on. (20/1)
1803 Tonka took time to respond when ridden early in the straight, and he was only finding top gear when the race was all but over. He is the sort to make a fool of jockeys when in this mood. (100/30)

2175 HARLAND SIMON CLAIMING STKS (4-Y.O+) (Class F)
4-15 (4-15) **2m 9y** £2,600.40 (£719.40: £343.20) Stalls: Low GOING: 0.09 sec per fur (G)

Form	Horse	Dist	Pos	SP	RR	SF
1452[6]	**Brodessa (52)** (MrsMReveley) **11-8-5** AMcGlone(3) (trckd ldrs: led over 3f out: styd on strly)	—	**1**	3/1[3]	54	14
1844[8]	**Swan Hunter (68)** (DJSCosgrove) **4-9-9** MRimmer(8) (lw: hld up: hdwy 9f out: chsd wnr appr fnl f: no imp)	4	**2**	5/2[2]	68	28
2035[5]	**Rose of Glenn (45)** (BPalling) **6-8-9** JQuinn(2) (a chsng ldrs: rdn & ev ch over 2f out: kpt on one pce)	4	**3**	14/1	50	10
1665[8]	**Ginka (28)** (JWMullins) **6-8-7**ow1 VSlattery(10) (sn wl bhd & t.o: rdn & styd on fnl 2f)	9	**4**	20/1	39	—
2000[9]	**Longcroft (35)** (SEKettlewell) **5-8-1**(5) RFfrench(11) (lost pl 7f out: rallied over 2f out: nt rch ldrs)	hd	**5**	7/1	38	—
1940[2]	**Sedbergh (USA) (68)** (MrsMReveley) **4-9-9** DHarrison(4) (lw: led tl hdd over 3f out: sn wknd: t.o)	17	**6**	2/1[1]	38	—
1940[7]	**Liathach** (JRFanshawe) **6-8-5** GDuffield(9) (w ldr tl wknd over 3f out: t.o)	2½	**7**	14/1	18	—
1809[W]	**Yo-Mate (26)** (THind) **6-8-11** AClark(1) (hld up: bhd fnl 4f: t.o)	5	**8**	50/1	19	—
1779[23]	**Alisura (56)** (DTThom) **4-7-13**(7) DarrenWilliams(5) (lw: hld up: hdwy ½-wy: wknd over 4f out: t.o)	1¼	**9**	20/1	12	—
1570[7]	**Bobby's Dream (35)** (MHTompkins) **5-7-7v**1(7) JSavage(6) (hld up: effrt 6f out: sn wknd: t.o)	2½	**10**	20/1	4	—

(SP 129.0%) **10 Rn**

3m 40.0 (17.00) CSF £10.70 TOTE £4.70: £1.60 £1.40 £3.00 (£7.10) Trio £29.90 OWNER Mr R. W. S. Jevon (SALTBURN) BRED B. Fairs
Sedbergh (USA) clmd Mrs V C Ward £9,000

1452 Brodessa has done all his winning on firm ground including this event twelve months ago but, after taking charge soon after straightening up, there was only ever going to be one winner. (3/1: 2/1-100/30)

1408 Swan Hunter, trying his luck over a longer trip, went after the winner approaching the final furlong but, with the pace never dropping, he found the concession of so much weight beyond him. (5/2)

2035 Rose of Glenn did pose a threat halfway up the straight, but she is not at her best on such testing ground, and had to admit the leading pair too strong for her. (14/1)

603 Ginka runs as if she needs all of three miles, for she was well adrift and hard at work until deciding to run on when it was all too late. (20/1)

1817 Longcroft, a springer in the market, was inclined to run her race in snatches and, after losing her place inside the final mile, was unable to get back into it. (7/1: op 20/1)

1940 Sedbergh (USA) has won on the All-Weather but not on ground as soft as he encountered here, and he stopped to nothing after being collared early in the straight. He was claimed for £9,000 and will now operate from a different yard. (2/1)

Liathach (14/1: 8/1-16/1)

2176 E.B.F. MAIDEN STKS (2-Y.O) (Class D)
4-45 (4-48) **6f 15y** £3,728.50 (£1,114.00: £533.00: £242.50) Stalls: High GOING: 0.09 sec per fur (G)

Form	Horse	Dist	Pos	SP	RR	SF
1791[3]	**Anita At Dawn (IRE)** (BPalling) **2-8-9** TSprake(2) (w ldr: led over 1f out: r.o wl)	—	**1**	20/1	72	33
1829[2]	**Sandy Shore** (JWharton) **2-8-4**(5) RFfrench(8) (chsd ldrs: outpcd ½-wy: rallied u.p appr fnl f: r.o)	½	**2**	12/1	71	32
1924[3]	**The Rich Man (IRE)** (BWHills) **2-9-0** MHills(1) (lw: led: rdn 2f out: hdd over 1f out: kpt on u.p)	hd	**3**	9/2[3]	75	36
	Rico Suave (IRE) (SirMarkPrescott) **2-9-0** GDuffield(6) (str: scope: bit bkwd: sn pushed along: hdwy over 1f out: nrst fin)	nk	**4**	10/1	75+	36
1744[5]	**Middle Temple** (EALDunlop) **2-8-11**(3) DO'Donohoe(9) (chsd ldrs: rdn ½-wy: no hdwy)	3½	**5**	7/2[2]	65	26
	Simlet (WJarvis) **2-9-0** JReid(3) (small: bkwd: swvd lft s: nvr nrr)	1¼	**6**	9/1	62+	23
	O'Kelly (DEN) (RGuest) **2-8-9** JQuinn(4) (lt-f: unf: sn outpcd: a bhd)	1¼	**7**	16/1	54	15
1941[6]	**Red Pepper (IRE)** (PHowling) **2-9-0** SDrowne(10) (prom over 3f)	3	**8**	16/1	51	12
	Chaska (MJohnston) **2-8-9** JWeaver(5) (lengthy: unf: s.s: a bhd & outpcd)	5	**9**	12/1	33	—
1692[3]	**Moothyeb (USA)** (SbinSuroor) **2-9-0** LDettori(7) (prom: drvn along ½-wy: wknd 2f out: eased whn no ch fnl f)	2½	**10**	7/4[1]	31	—

(SP 127.8%) **10 Rn**

1m 16.4 (4.90) CSF £236.13 TOTE £18.60: £3.30 £2.30 £1.80 (£66.30) Trio £37.70 OWNER Merthyr Motor Auctions (COWBRIDGE) BRED Humphrey Okeke

1791 Anita At Dawn (IRE) came into her own on this more suitable ground over an extra furlong and won a shade more easily than the margin suggests. (20/1)

1829 Sandy Shore is progressing in the right direction and it can only be a matter of time before she does strike it lucky. (12/1)

1924 The Rich Man (IRE) had a battle royal with the winner and looked done for when robbed of the lead approaching the last furlong, but he was coming back for more in the dying strides and his turn will come. (9/2)

Rico Suave (IRE), who has been gelded and looked far from fully wound-up, was finding his feet in the closing stages and this was a very promising debut. (10/1: op 6/1)

1744 Middle Temple, bustled along soon after halfway, kept staying on without having the speed to mount a challenge. (7/2: op 9/4)

Simlet, a smallish colt whose dam won over extreme distances, lost ground by swerving as the stalls opened and was taken off his legs all the way. He might be worth remembering when the mile nurseries arrive. (9/1)

Chaska (12/1: 8/1-14/1)

1692 Moothyeb (USA) looked very starey in his coat and, if he has spent the winter in Dubai, it could be a sign that he thinks it is time to prepare for the colder weather to arrive. Never really travelling, he was not unduly punished when all chance had gone and he will live to fight another day. (7/4: 6/4-9/4)

2177 MILES 33 H'CAP (0-60) (3-Y.O+) (Class F)
5-15 (5-16) **6f 15y** £3,224.10 (£897.60: £432.30) Stalls: High GOING: 0.09 sec per fur (G)

Form	Horse	Dist	Pos	SP	RR	SF
1734[4]	**Superbit (60)** (BAMcMahon) **5-10-0** LNewton(10) (racd centre: mde all: clr over 1f out: comf)	—	**1**	12/1	70	49
1963[5]	**Aquatic Queen (48)** (RJWeaver) **3-8-2**(7) RWinston(3) (b.hind: a.p: rdn to chse wnr wl over 1f out: r.o)	2	**2**	8/1[2]	53	25
1965[8]	**Shashi (IRE) (56)** (PatMitchell) **5-9-10** RLappin(4) (hdwy over 1f out: fin wl)	1	**3**	25/1	58	37
1816[8]	**Souperficial (46)** (NTinkler) **6-9-0v** KimTinkler(13) (s.s: hdwy over 2f out: r.o one pce fnl f)	nk	**4**	16/1	47	26
1572[4]	**Southern Dominion (45)** (MissJFCraze) **5-8-13** SWebster(12) (b.hind: prom: rdn ½-wy: kpt on wl ins fnl f)	1½	**5**	16/1	42	21
1944[2]	**Mustang (48)** (CWThornton) **4-9-2b** MTebbutt(20) (prom stands' side: hrd rdn & one pce fnl 2f)	s.h	**6**	12/1	45	24
1748[12]	**Best Kept Secret (45)** (LJBarratt) **6-8-13b** SDrowne(14) (hdwy over 1f out: nrst fin)	hd	**7**	33/1	42	21
2006[14]	**General Sir Peter (IRE) (59)** (NACallaghan) **5-9-8**(5) AmandaSanders(15) (lw: s.s: bhd: rdn & hdwy 2f out: nvr nrr)	¾	**8**	14/1	54	33
1655[8]	**Martindale (IRE) (45)** (JHanson) **4-8-13** EJohnson(17) (prom over 4f)	2	**9**	14/1	35	14
1944[7]	**Sweet Mate (52)** (SRBowring) **5-8-13b**(7) FBoyle(5) (b.hind: no hdwy fnl 2f)	¾	**10**	14/1	40	19
1620[6]	**Petraco (IRE) (52)** (NASmith) **9-9-6** MRimmer(8) (nvr trbld ldrs)	s.h	**11**	14/1	40	19
1089[2]	**Nellie North (49)** (GMMcCourt) **4-9-3b** JQuinn(19) (prom stands' side 4f)	hd	**12**	3/1[1]	36	15

				SP	RR	SF
1586[4]	**Carreamia (53)** (JLEyre) **4-9-4**(3) OPears(7) (drvn along ½-wy: a bhd)	1¾	**13**	14/1	36	15
1661[4]	**Municipal Girl (IRE) (54)** (BPalling) **3-9-1** TSprake(18) (led stands' side: hrd drvn 2f out: sn outpcd)	6	**14**	12/1	21	—
1471[6]	**Prominent (55)** (MrsVAAconley) **3-9-2** MDeering(9) (lw: sn outpcd)	5	**15**	33/1	9	—
972[7]	**Super Rocky (54)** (RBastiman) **8-9-3**(5) HBastiman(1) (prom: rdn 3f out: sn lost tch)	1¾	**16**	33/1	3	—
1666[14]	**Deerly (53)** (RDickin) **4-9-7** JWeaver(11) (spd over 3f)	3½	**17**	8/1[2]	—	—
1843[11]	**Badger Bay (IRE) (57)** (CADwyer) **4-9-11** NVarley(6) (outpcd)	2½	**18**	33/1	—	—
*421**	**Amy Leigh (IRE) (52)** (CaptJWilson) **4-8-13b**(7) AngelaHartley(2) (chsd wnr centre tl wknd qckly wl over 1f out)	3	**19**	12/1	—	—
1135[13]	**Lachesis (48)** (DShaw) **4-8-13b**(3) CTeague(16) (lw: outpcd)	2½	**20**	10/1[3]	—	—
				(SP 147.8%)	**20 Rn**	

1m 16.5 (5.00) CSF £107.99 CT £2,265.82 TOTE £13.50: £2.70 £2.00 £10.80 £3.00 (£74.10) Trio £560.70; £173.76 to Warwick 24/6/97
OWNER Mr Neville Smith (TAMWORTH) BRED A. D. Bottomley
WEIGHT FOR AGE 3yo-7lb

1734 Superbit defied top weight with a very game all-the-way success and, with his stable on a high at present, there is nothing to say he will not follow up. (12/1)

1963 Aquatic Queen is certainly knocking at the door and, though the winner always had her measure, she never stopped trying and she is ready to lose her maiden tag. (8/1)

286 Shashi (IRE) has been tried over seven furlongs, and the way she was staying on from off the pace one would be right in thinking that is the trip she needs. (25/1)

1098 Souperficial recovered from a tardy start and ran his best race this season. If he could be relied to run two races alike, he would be worth waiting for. (16/1)

1572 Southern Dominion looks to be a hard ride and he appeared to be in trouble at halfway, but he kept pulling out more under pressure, and was still running on at the finish. (16/1)

1944 Mustang should have been suited by the more testing ground, but he was racing on the slower stands' side, and his measure had been taken some way out. (12/1: 8/1-14/1)

Best Kept Secret, brought back to sprinting, was running on best of all in the closing stages and, if he returns to selling company, the hint should be taken. (33/1)

1089 Nellie North showed up with the stands' side leaders, but was flat to the boards two furlongs out and she quickly threw in the towel. (3/1: op 9/2)

1661 Municipal Girl (IRE) (12/1: op 8/1)

883 Lachesis (10/1: 8/1-12/1)

T/Jkpt: £357,519.10 (0.1 Tckts); £453,193.30. T/Plpt: £44.90 (1,097.84 Tckts). T/Qdpt: £37.10 (27.09 Tckts) IM

2003-WINDSOR (Fig. 8) (Soft, Good to soft patches)
Monday June 23rd
WEATHER: sunny WIND: almost nil

2178 DELTA AIRLINES H'CAP (0-70) (3-Y.O F) (Class E)
6-40 (6-40) **1m 2f 7y** £2,882.25 (£873.00: £426.50: £203.25) Stalls: High GOING: 0.20 sec per fur (G)

				SP	RR	SF
790[3]	**Seattle Swing (70)** (JHMGosden) **3-9-7** LDettori(5) (a.p: led 4f out: comf)	—	**1**	100/30[1]	77+	35
1859*	**Top Jem (67)** (MJRyan) **3-9-4** GBardwell(4) (hdwy 3f out: chsd wnr fnl 2f: one pce)	1¾	**2**	100/30[1]	71	29
1568[9]	**Misty Rain (67)** (BWHills) **3-9-1**(3) JDSmith(1) (hdwy 3f out: hrd rdn 2f out: one pce)	4	**3**	12/1	65	23
1500[8]	**River of Fortune (IRE) (58)** (MHTompkins) **3-8-6**(3) MHenry(2) (lw: hdwy 3f out: one pce fnl 2f)	6	**4**	7/1[3]	46	4
1110[13]	**Isca Maiden (45)** (PHayward) **3-7-3**(7) PDoe(7) (no hdwy fnl 3f)	2½	**5**	50/1	29	—
1809*	**Blush (60)** (MCPipe) **3-8-8**(3) MartinDwyer(9) (prom tl wknd over 2f out)	4	**6**	7/2[2]	38	—
1637[8]	**Sweetchildofmine (64)** (HAkbary) **3-9-1** TQuinn(8) (chsd ldrs 3f out: sn wknd)	4	**7**	15/2	36	—
1820[12]	**Damanka (IRE) (49)** (MBell) **3-8-0**ow2 JTate(6) (a bhd)	1	**8**	20/1	19	—
1574[9]	**Showcase (54)** (JWHills) **3-8-5** PatEddery(3) (b.nr hind: led 6f: wknd over 2f out)	10	**9**	12/1	8	—
				(SP 114.7%)	**9 Rn**	

2m 15.7 (10.80) CSF £13.23 CT £106.05 TOTE £3.50: £1.40 £1.90 £3.10 (£6.00) Trio £36.10 OWNER Cheveley Park Stud (NEWMARKET)
BRED Cheveley Park Stud Ltd
LONG HANDICAP Isca Maiden 7-5

790 Seattle Swing was soon racing in second place. She was allowed to stride into the lead four furlongs from home and won with plenty in hand. (100/30)

1859* Top Jem moved easily enough into second place approaching the two-furlong marker, but was unable to cause the winner any anxiety. (100/30: 2/1-7/2)

1121 Misty Rain moved up in the centre of the course three furlongs from home and, soon under hard driving, kept on at one pace. (12/1: op 7/1)

River of Fortune (IRE) made a forward move three furlongs out but was making no impression on the leaders from the two-furlong marker. (7/1: 9/2-8/1)

Isca Maiden, always in mid-division, could make no headway in the closing stages. (50/1)

1809* Blush, dropped in distance, was ill-suited by the modest early pace and could not quicken when the tap was turned on from three furlongs out. (7/2)

Showcase (12/1: 8/1-14/1)

2179 PERPETUAL H'CAP (0-70) (3-Y.O+) (Class E)
7-10 (7-12) **5f 217y** £2,965.00 (£895.00: £435.00: £205.00) Stalls: High GOING: 0.01 sec per fur (G)

				SP	RR	SF
2006[3]	**Willow Dale (IRE) (68)** (DRCElsworth) **4-9-12** TQuinn(6) (a.p: led over 2f out: r.o wl)	—	**1**	6/1[1]	80	51
2006[5]	**Never Think Twice (63)** (KTIvory) **4-9-4v**(3) MartinDwyer(3) (b: hdwy fnl 2f: nvr nrr)	5	**2**	8/1	62	33
1509[5]	**Sizzling (59)** (RHannon) **5-9-3** DaneO'Neill(1) (a.p: hrd rdn & one pce fnl 2f)	2	**3**	14/1	52	23
1963[8]	**Make Ready (62)** (JNeville) **3-8-10**(3) DO'Donohoe(4) (a.p: r.o one pce fnl 2f)	1	**4**	14/1	53	17
1963*	**Faith Alone (68)** (CFWall) **4-9-12** GDuffield(10) (b: a.p: ev ch 2f out: one pce)	1	**5**	6/1[1]	56	27
1925*	**Flying Harold (49)** (MRChannon) **4-8-4**(3) PPMurphy(8) (nvr nr to chal)	1	**6**	7/1[2]	34	5
	Press Again (41) (PHayward) **5-7-10**(3)ow3 MHenry(14) (no hdwy fnl 3f)	3	**7**	50/1	18	—
1965[17]	**Blushing Grenadier (IRE) (41)** (MJFetherston-Godley) **5-7-10v**(3)ow1 AWhelan(12) (chsd ldr over 3f: sn wknd)	1¼	**8**	15/2[3]	15	—
1966[12]	**Wrn Princess (48)** (BJMeehan) **3-7-13** CRutter(7) (nvr bttr than mid div)	1½	**9**	25/1	18	—

1810*	**Dayrella (56)** (WRMuir) **3-8-7** JReid(13) (lw: spd 4f)	s.h	**10**	7/1 ^{2}	26	—
1743^{4}	**Walk the Beat (61)** (MartynMeade) **7-9-5** RPerham(9) (nvr nr ldrs)	3	**11**	14/1	23	—
2006*	**Rififi (65)** (RIngram) **4-9-9** 7x SWhitworth(2) (b: lw: a bhd)	1¾	**12**	6/1 ^{1}	22	—
1225^{24}	**Double Matt (IRE) (70)** (MrsPSly) **5-10-0** NCarlisle(11) (a bhd)	8	**13**	50/1	6	—
1814^{10}	**Dancing Mystery (47)** (EAWheeler) **3-7-5b**(7) SCarson(5) (led over 3f)	nk	**14**	33/1	—	—

(SP 121.4%) **14 Rn**

1m 14.7 (4.20) CSF £47.52 CT £594.49 TOTE £5.80: £2.10 £2.50 £5.70 (£25.90) Trio £139.90 OWNER Michael Jackson Bloodstock Ltd (WHITCOMBE) BRED Shunya Seki

LONG HANDICAP Press Again 7-9

WEIGHT FOR AGE 3yo-7lb

2006 Willow Dale (IRE) went to the front soon after halfway and, coming clear approaching the final furlong, won readily. (6/1)

2006 Never Think Twice was under pressure a long way out but, though staying on in the last two furlongs to take second place, was never near the winner. (8/1: 6/1-10/1)

1509 Sizzling showed good speed throughout, and stayed on at one pace under hard driving in the final quarter-mile. (14/1: 10/1-16/1)

1439 Make Ready led the far-side group for a long way but, hard ridden, could not quicken in the last two furlongs. (14/1: 10/1-16/1)

1963* Faith Alone, tucked in behind the leaders on the stands' rails, moved up to have every chance two furlongs out, but could find no extra under pressure. (6/1)

1810* Dayrella (7/1: 6/1-15/1)

1743 Walk the Beat (14/1: 10/1-16/1)

2180 CHEVELEY PARK STUD CONDITIONS STKS (3-Y.O+) (Class C)

7-40 (7-40) **1m 2f 7y** £4,659.17 (£1,712.30: £836.15: £358.25: £159.13) Stalls: High GOING: 0.20 sec per fur (G)

				SP	RR	SF
1738^{7}	**Bint Baladee (98)** (SbinSuroor) **3-8-5** LDettori(5) (lw: hld up in rr: hdwy 2f out: led ins fnl f: r.o wl)	—	**1**	9/4 ^{2}	99	34
1793^{2}	**Mandilak (USA) (100)** (LMCumani) **3-8-10** PatEddery(3) (chsd ldr: led 3f out: hrd rdn 2f out: hdd ins fnl f)	1	**2**	5/4 ^{1}	102	37
1962^{4}	**Darcy (96)** (MRStoute) **3-8-10** JReid(1) (lw: hld up: effrt & ev ch over 1f out: one pce)	¾	**3**	9/1	101	36
1477^{15}	**Joli's Son** (MJHaynes) **4-9-4** SWhitworth(6) (a.p: ev ch over 2f out: wknd over 1f out)	7	**4**	66/1	51 t	33
1261^{2}	**Wijara (IRE) (100)** (RHannon) **5-9-4** DaneO'Neill(4) (lw: led: racd alone stands' side st: hdd 3f out: sn wknd)	4	**5**	7/2 ^{3}	45 t	27

(SP 108.9%) **5 Rn**

2m 13.8 (8.90) CSF £4.86 TOTE £2.70: £1.50 £1.50 (£2.30) OWNER Godolphin (NEWMARKET) BRED Gainsborough Stud Management Ltd

WEIGHT FOR AGE 3yo-12lb

1738 Bint Baladee, dropping back in distance having run in the Oaks, was settled in last place. She moved up smoothly two furlongs out, and quickened well when given the office. (9/4)

1793 Mandilak (USA) raced in second place until leading three furlongs out. Hard ridden at the two-furlong marker, he battled on but could not quicken with the winner inside the last furlong. He appeared suited by this longer trip. (5/4)

1962 Darcy tracked the leaders and, after having every chance approaching the final furlong, failed to quicken under pressure. (9/1: 6/1-10/1)

Joli's Son looked a big danger when moving up to dispute the lead, but his effort petered out approaching the final furlong. (66/1)

1261 Wijara (IRE) made the running. He ploughed a lone furrow down the stands' rails in the straight, but was easily outpaced from three furlongs out. (7/2: 9/4-4/1)

2181 E.B.F. REALLY USEFUL MEDIAN AUCTION MAIDEN STKS (2-Y.O) (Class D)

8-10 (8-13) **5f 217y** £3,615.00 (£1,095.00: £535.00: £255.00) Stalls: High GOING: 0.01 sec per fur (G)

				SP	RR	SF
1480^{10}	**Ben Rinnes** (RFJohnsonHoughton) **2-8-9**(5) ADaly(6) (a.p: led 2f out: r.o wl)	—	**1**	50/1	84	42
	Merlin's Ring (IABalding) **2-9-0** SWhitworth(13) (unf: hdwy over 2f out: chsd wnr fnl f: no imp)	2½	**2**	20/1	77	35
	Da Boss (WRMuir) **2-9-0** JReid(16) (w'like: scope: lw: prom 3f: rallied over 1f out: fin wl)	¾	**3**	8/1 ^{2}	75	33
1664^{2}	**First Dance** (RHannon) **2-8-9** MHills(19) (hdwy 2f out: one pce fnl f)	s.h	**4**	7/1 ^{1}	70	28
1251^{7}	**Hiding Place** (MBell) **2-8-9** MFenton(17) (hdwy over 1f out: nvr nrr)	2	**5**	20/1	65	23
1819^{5}	**Cocksure (IRE)** (JMPEustace) **2-9-0** JTate(2) (led 4f: r.o one pce)	hd	**6**	12/1	70	28
1783^{6}	**Aunt Sadie** (RCharlton) **2-8-9** TSprake(23) (bit bkwd: mid div: styd on fnl f)	hd	**7**	10/1 ^{3}	64	22
1842^{5}	**Ringleader** (PFICole) **2-8-11**(3) AWhelan(22) (nvr nr to chal)	1½	**8**	14/1	65	23
1932^{5}	**Zeppo (IRE)** (MJHeaton-Ellis) **2-9-0** SDrowne(5) (no hdwy fnl 2f)	1¼	**9**	14/1	62	20
1872^{18}	**Shannon's Secret (IRE)** (BJMeehan) **2-9-0** MTebbutt(3) (bit bkwd: nvr trbld ldrs)	1½	**10**	33/1	58	16
1806^{6}	**Baby's Tiara (IRE)** (RAkehurst) **2-8-9** AClark(14) (prom 4f)	¾	**11**	16/1	51	9
	Technician (IRE) (MAJarvis) **2-9-0** GDuffield(25) (scope: prom over 3f)	1½	**12**	33/1	52	10
	Taste of Success (PWHarris) **2-8-11**(3) MHenry(20) (str: bkwd: nvr bttr than mid div)	¾	**13**	33/1	50	8
1959^{5}	**Bound To Please** (PJMakin) **2-9-0** SSanders(24) (prom 4f)	nk	**14**	14/1	49	7
1961^{10}	**Khattaff (IRE)** (MajorWRHern) **2-9-0** JWeaver(10) (nvr bttr than mid div)	2½	**15**	20/1	42	—
	Recognition (WJarvis) **2-9-0** LDettori(21) (str: scope: bit bkwd: bhd tl hdwy over 1f out: nvr on terms)	1½	**16**	10/1 ^{3}	38	—
2022^{7}	**Cut Diamond** (PFICole) **2-9-0** TQuinn(11) (lw: rdn along: bhd fnl 3f)	hd	**17**	10/1 ^{3}	38	—
	American Cousin (BJMeehan) **2-8-7**(7) GHannon(4) (w'like: scope: a bhd)	hd	**18**	25/1	38	—
1812^{10}	**Roborant** (JLDunlop) **2-9-0** PatEddery(9) (nvr nr ldrs)	1¼	**19**	8/1 ^{2}	35	—
1321^{8}	**Argumentative** (SDow) **2-9-0** RPerham(15) (prom over 3f)	nk	**20**	12/1	34	—
1959^{4}	**Desert Native** (RHannon) **2-8-9** DaneO'Neill(8) (bhd fnl 2f)	2	**21**	10/1 ^{3}	23	—
1293^{7}	**Ready Fontaine** (JNeville) **2-9-0** AMcGlone(12) (a bhd)	½	**22**	40/1	27	—
1806^{8}	**High Carry** (JEBanks) **2-8-9** JStack(18) (a bhd)	6	**23**	50/1	6	—
	Highland Lord (MJFetherston-Godley) **2-9-0** CRutter(7) (w'like: bkwd: s.s: a wl bhd)	2	**24**	33/1	6	—
	Red Head And Dotty (BJMcMath) **2-8-9** GBardwell(1) (w'like: bkwd: a bhd)	6	**25**	50/1	—	—
	Allaton (IRE) (MrsPSly) **2-9-0** NCarlisle(26) (str: bit bkwd: prom 3f: wknd qckly)	¾	**26**	50/1	—	—

(SP 152.5%) **26 Rn**

1m 14.5 (4.00) CSF £831.00 TOTE £97.40: £19.30 £8.10 £3.50 (£2,409.20; £1,526.98 to 25/6/97) Trio Not won; £676.61 to 25/6/97 OWNER Mr Anthony Pye-Jeary (DIDCOT) BRED Sir David Wills

Ben Rinnes put his two previous modest efforts far behind. Always well-placed, he took the lead two furlongs out and stayed on strongly. (50/1)

Merlin's Ring made a promising first appearance. He improved from two furlongs out, but could make no impression on the winner. He should soon go one better. (20/1)

Da Boss failed to hold a good early place, but rallied in fine style approaching the final furlong and finished strongly. He has plenty of scope and should pay to follow. (8/1: 10/1-5/1)

1664 First Dance made ground two furlongs out but, though staying on, never appeared likely to get in a serious blow. (7/1)

1251 Hiding Place began to run on when it was all too late. (20/1)

1819 Cocksure (IRE) made much of the running, and kept on at one pace when headed two furlongs from home. (12/1)
Aunt Sadie, always in the chasing group, did not really find her stride until too late. A longer distance should help. (10/1)
1842 Ringleader (14/1: 10/1-16/1)
Recognition was at the back of the field until making some headway approaching the final furlong. He did not have a hard race and may be capable of improvement. (10/1: 6/1-12/1)
2022 Cut Diamond (10/1: op 6/1)
Roborant (8/1: op 5/1)
Argumentative (12/1: 20/1-33/1)
Desert Native (10/1: 7/1-12/1)

2182 JACOBS HOLDINGS H'CAP (0-70) (3-Y.O) (Class E)

8-40 (8-41) **1m 3f 135y** £2,883.75 (£870.00: £422.50: £198.75) Stalls: High GOING: 0.20 sec per fur (G)

				SP	RR	SF
2005[2]	**Real Estate (70)** (CFWall) **3-9-7** GDuffield(1) (lw: a.p: led 3f out tl ins fnl f: led last strides: all out)	—	**1**	7/4[1]	80	48
1694[4]	**Mardrew (61)** (RHarris) **3-8-7**(5) ADaly(8) (lw: hdwy 3f out: led ins fnl f: edgd lft: hdd last strides)	hd	**2**	6/1[2]	71	39
1938[8]	**Herbshan Dancer (57)** (BRMillman) **3-8-8** TSprake(2) (b.hind: lw: hdwy 4f out: w wnr 3f out tl wknd ins fnl f)	2½	**3**	7/1[3]	63	31
1938[2]	**Keepsake (IRE) (50)** (MDIUsher) **3-8-1** RStreet(3) (hdwy 4f out: wknd over 2f out)	15	**4**	6/1[2]	36	4
1474[9]	**Here's To Howie (USA) (69)** (RHannon) **3-9-6** DaneO'Neill(6) (prom tl wknd over 2f out)	1¼	**5**	16/1	53	21
886[8]	**Baubigny (USA) (67)** (MRChannon) **3-9-1**(3) PPMurphy(5) (lw: nvr nr to chal)	2	**6**	12/1	48	16
1568[10]	**Certain Magic (54)** (WRMuir) **3-8-5** AClark(10) (lw: nvr trbld ldrs)	1¼	**7**	14/1	34	2
900[14]	**Mister Jay (48)** (PTWalwyn) **3-7-10**(3)ow2 MHenry(9) (lw: wl bhd fnl 3f)	8	**8**	20/1	17	—
1805[5]	**Tasik Chini (USA) (70)** (PFICole) **3-9-7b** TQuinn(7) (chsd ldr: led 4f out tl wknd 3f out)	3½	**9**	7/1[3]	34	2
1277[10]	**Gore Hill (45)** (MBlanshard) **3-7-10** NAdams(4) (wl bhd fnl 4f: t.o)	16	**10**	40/1	—	—
1237[13]	**Sequoia Prince (CAN) (52)** (MBell) **3-8-3** MFenton(11) (lw: led tl wknd qckly 4f out: t.o)	9	**11**	20/1	—	—
				(SP 122.1%)	**11 Rn**	

2m 36.6 (10.60) CSF £11.28 CT £57.59 TOTE £2.80: £1.40 £1.90 £2.10 (£6.80) Trio £18.90 OWNER Mr N. Ahamad (NEWMARKET) BRED Bishop's Down Farm
LONG HANDICAP Gore Hill 7-3
STEWARDS' ENQUIRY Daly susp. 2-3/7/97 (excessive use of whip).
2005 Real Estate is steadily improving. He struck the front three furlongs out and battled back well when headed inside the final furlong. (7/4)
1694 Mardrew made smooth headway four furlongs out. His challenge was delayed until inside the final furlong where he took a narrow advantage, but he edged to the left and was caught in the last few strides. (6/1: op 4/1)
1296 Herbshan Dancer moved up to dispute the lead early in the straight but, after having every chance, weakened inside the final furlong. (7/1)
1938 Keepsake (IRE) made a forward move from the back of the field four furlongs from home, but weakened approaching the two-furlong marker. (6/1)
641* Here's To Howie (USA) chased the leaders but floundered in the soft going with well over two furlongs still to race. (16/1)
431 Baubigny (USA) (12/1: 8/1-14/1)
837 Certain Magic (14/1: op 8/1)

2183 ANIMAL HEALTH TRUST/YOUTH CLUBS UK MAIDEN STKS (3-Y.O) (Class D)

9-10 (9-11) **1m 67y** £3,642.50 (£1,100.00: £535.00: £252.50) Stalls: High GOING: 0.20 sec per fur (G)

				SP	RR	SF
1773[3]	**Sellette (IRE) (80)** (DHaydnJones) **3-8-9** SDrowne(4) (lw: a.p: led over 2f out: r.o wl)	—	**1**	3/1[1]	79	29
	Lawz (IRE) (CJBenstead) **3-9-0** GDuffield(2) (leggy: scope: gd hdwy 5f out: ev ch 3f out tl wknd ins fnl f)	2	**2**	20/1	80	30
1437[5]	**Danzas** (RCharlton) **3-9-0** TSprake(12) (hdwy over 2f out: styd on: nrst fin)	¾	**3**	12/1	79	29
2020[2]	**Zabriskie** (MRStoute) **3-9-0** JReid(7) (a.p: ev ch over 1f out: wknd fnl f)	6	**4**	4/1[2]	67	17
	Isabella Gonzaga (JLDunlop) **3-8-9** AClark(9) (unf: scope: bit bkwd: hdwy 3f out: one pce fnl 2f)	3	**5**	20/1	56	6
1823[5]	**Mystery Hill (USA) (78)** (JHMGosden) **3-8-9** LDettori(1) (lw: chsd ldrs: no hdwy fnl 2f)	nk	**6**	6/1	56	6
1876[6]	**Fife Major (USA)** (BWHills) **3-9-0** MHills(15) (lw: led tl over 2f out: one pce)	1¾	**7**	14/1	57	7
	Russian Olive (LMCumani) **3-8-9** JWeaver(11) (prom tl wknd over 1f out)	1½	**8**	9/2[3]	50	—
	Poleaxe (MrsJCecil) **3-8-6**(3) MartinDwyer(8) (leggy: s.s: hdwy over 2f out: nvr nr to chal)	¾	**9**	15/2	48	—
693[12]	**Wonderboy (IRE)** (RAkehurst) **3-9-0** TQuinn(6) (lw: bhd fnl 3f)	¾	**10**	25/1	52	2
	Borrador (RCurtis) **3-9-0** NAdams(10) (unf: s.s: a bhd)	6	**11**	50/1	40	—
1088[6]	**Balfour Lady** (JARToller) **3-8-9** SSanders(3) (prom tl wknd 3f out)	s.h	**12**	16/1	35	—
1858[6]	**Cabcharge Glory** (GGMargarson) **3-8-9** GBardwell(13) (lw: bhd whn hmpd 6f out: nvr on terms)	2½	**13**	33/1	30	—
1787[8]	**Aurora Bay (IRE)** (MBell) **3-8-9** MFenton(14) (a bhd: t.o)	25	**14**	33/1	—	—
	Petsong (VSoane) **3-9-0** CRutter(5) (w ldr tl wknd over 3f out: t.o)	1	**15**	50/1	—	—
				(SP 132.6%)	**15 Rn**	

1m 50.5 (8.30) CSF £68.29 TOTE £3.70: £1.30 £6.70 £4.70 (£118.40) Trio £36.50 OWNER Mrs Judy Mihalop (PONTYPRIDD) BRED Duncan A. McGregor
1773 Sellette (IRE) was always close-up. She struck the front over two furlongs from home and, after a sharp struggle with the runner-up, came clear inside the final furlong. (3/1)
Lawz (IRE), a very tall colt, made a most encouraging debut. He moved up rapidly to join the leaders early in the straight and, after having every chance, did not weaken until inside the final furlong. He should certainly be capable of improvement. (20/1)
1437 Danzas made a forward move over three furlongs out but, though staying on, was never going to get there in time. He is on the upgrade. (12/1)
2020 Zabriskie, always close up, drew almost level with the winner approaching the final furlong, only to weaken in the last hundred and fifty yards. (4/1)
Isabella Gonzaga, unfurnished as yet, made a promising first appearance. She improved three furlongs out and, though she lacked the pace of the placed horses, was staying on to the finish. She will be better over a longer trip. (20/1)
1823 Mystery Hill (USA) chased the leaders throughout, but could make no headway under pressure in the final quarter-mile. (6/1: 3/1-13/2)
1876 Fife Major (USA) (14/1: op 7/1)
Russian Olive ran rather better than her final position would suggest. She was hunting up the leaders until tiring approaching the final furlong, and should come on for this, her first appearance of the season. (9/2: 5/2-5/1)
Poleaxe (15/2: 7/1-12/1)

T/Plpt: £957.10 (23.68 Tckts). T/Qdpt: £109.30 (8.89 Tckts) AK/Hn

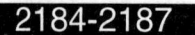

1853-YARMOUTH (L-H) (Good)

Monday June 23rd

WEATHER: fine WIND: mod bhd

2184 TOTE PLACE ONLY MAIDEN STKS (3-Y.O F) (Class D)

6-25 (6-26) **1m 3y** £3,932.25 (£1,176.00: £563.50: £257.25) Stalls: Low GOING minus 0.53 sec per fur (F)

				SP	RR	SF
833[7]	**Alifandango (IRE)** (ACStewart) **3-8-11** MRoberts(2) (chsd ldrs: outpcd 4f out: rallied appr fnl f: r.o to ld nr fin)	—	1	12/1	77	21
1976[3]	**Bint Shihama (USA)** (CEBrittain) **3-8-11** BDoyle(3) (lw: w ldr: led 4f out: clr ins fnl f: ct nr fin)	hd	2	13/8[1]	77	21
1823[4]	**Cordate (IRE)** (JHMGosden) **3-8-11** WRyan(5) (lw: chsd ldrs: pushed along 3f out: one pce ins fnl f)	1¾	3	3/1[2]	73	17
1646[8]	**Love Venture** (SPCWoods) **3-8-11** WJO'Connor(6) (prom: rdn 2f out: one pce)	3	4	33/1	67	11
	Ajeebah (IRE) (WJHaggas) **3-8-11** NDay(1) (leggy: scope: prom 5f: sn rdn & btn)	5	5	20/1	57	1
1858[4]	**Sharpwitted** (JHMGosden) **3-8-11** GHind(4) (prom 4f: rdn over 2f out: btn whn eased ins fnl f)	½	6	3/1[2]	56+	—
1587[10]	**Pointelle** (AHide) **3-8-11** DBiggs(7) (hld up: rdn 3f out: no imp)	1¼	7	20/1	54	—
606[2]	**E Sharp (USA)** (WJHaggas) **3-8-11** RCochrane(8) (reard s: hld up & plld hrd: hdwy 2f out: btn appr fnl f)	1¼	8	8/1[3]	51	—
	Epsilon (NAGraham) **3-8-11** PaulEddery(9) (a bhd)	24	9	33/1	3	—

(SP 122.3%) **9 Rn**

1m 39.0 (3.00) CSF £29.79 TOTE £14.90: £2.40 £1.20 £2.20 (£17.90) Trio £14.20 OWNER Mr M. J. Rees (NEWMARKET) BRED Humphrey Okeke

Alifandango (IRE), dropped in trip after running respectably over ten furlongs, was outpaced at halfway and did not see much daylight until the distance. Once in the clear, she found a nice turn of foot to snatch the race out of the fire. Handicaps over further would seem to offer her an interesting future. (12/1)

1976 Bint Shihama (USA) looked sure to win entering the final furlong but tended to idle in front, allowing the winner to pounce on the line. (13/8)

1823 Cordate (IRE), rather keen going to post, looked to lack pace in the final furlong after appearing a threat. (3/1)

1304 Love Venture ran a little better and ought to get ten furlongs in time. (33/1)

Ajeebah (IRE), a well-made newcomer who looked to just need the race, should come on for the run. (20/1)

1858 Sharpwitted never looked like living up to her pedigree and connections will do well to find a race for her. (3/1: op 6/4)

2185 TOTE JACKPOT LIMITED STKS (0-90) (3-Y.O+) (Class C)

6-55 (6-55) **6f 3y** £5,115.30 (£1,523.40: £725.20: £326.10) Stalls: Low GOING minus 0.53 sec per fur (F)

				SP	RR	SF
2105[15]	**Sea-Deer (86)** (CADwyer) **8-9-4** RCochrane(3) (trckd ldrs: rdn to ld ins fnl f)	—	1	4/5[1]	93	43
	Shamanic (82) (SPCWoods) **5-9-4** WRyan(2) (hld up: hdwy over 1f out: r.o wl ins fnl f)	1¼	2	10/1	90	40
1609[10]	**Paddy Lad (IRE) (90)** (RGuest) **3-8-11** PBloomfield(1) (led: rdn & qcknd over 2f out: hdd ins fnl f: one pce)	½	3	4/1[3]	88	31
1609[8]	**Snap Crackle Pop (IRE) (88)** (RFJohnsonHoughton) **3-8-8** PaulEddery(4) (w ldr: rdn over 2f out: ev ch 1f out: one pce)	nk	4	3/1[2]	85	28

(SP 109.6%) **4 Rn**

1m 11.9 (1.00) CSF £8.08 TOTE £1.90 (£5.10) OWNER Mr M. M. Foulger (NEWMARKET) BRED Stetchworth Park Stud Ltd

WEIGHT FOR AGE 3yo-7lb

1948 Sea-Deer has been going up the handicap without winning, but was the only one of these in form and will not have done much for his mark by taking this on worse terms than he would have met a couple of these in handicaps. (4/5: 5/4-4/6)

Shamanic, having his first run for a new yard, looked well forward and took a keen hold. He finished strongly to beat a couple of rivals on worse terms than he would meet them in handicaps. (10/1: 7/1-11/1)

968 Paddy Lad (IRE) had to dictate the pace somewhat reluctantly, but had no other obvious excuse. (4/1: 9/4-9/2)

988 Snap Crackle Pop (IRE) looked to have been well placed but could not get to the front and found little in the final sprint. (3/1: 7/4-7/2)

2186 TOTE PLACEPOT (S) STKS (2-Y.O) (Class G)

7-25 (7-28) **5f 43y** £2,238.00 (£618.00: £294.00) Stalls: Low GOING minus 0.53 sec per fur (F)

				SP	RR	SF
1760[14]	**Catherines Song** (CADwyer) **2-8-6** DHolland(1) (b.off hind: lw: a.p: led ins fnl f: pushed out)	—	1	2/1[1]	66	23
1867*	**Ivory's Joy** (KTIvory) **2-8-11b** CScally(6) (b: b.hind: lw: led after 1f: hdd ins fnl f: unable qckn)	2	2	4/1[2]	65	22
2003[3]	**Fast Franc (IRE)** (SCWilliams) **2-8-11** GCarter(3) (dwlt: sn chsng ldrs: pushed along after 2f: kpt on: nt pce to chal)	3	3	2/1[1]	56	13
2016[9]	**Hopefully** (MRChannon) **2-8-6** BDoyle(4) (led 1f: prom tl rdn & btn 2f out)	¾	4	9/2[3]	48	5
1251[13]	**Angry Albert** (CSmith) **2-8-11** WRyan(2) (dwlt: a bhd)	3½	5	25/1	43	—
2051[8]	**Eurofen** (PDEvans) **2-8-11v** NDay(5) (lw: sn bhd)	15	6	14/1	—	—

(SP 115.4%) **6 Rn**

62.4 secs (1.40) CSF £9.94 TOTE £2.90: £1.80 £1.90 (£9.60) OWNER The Select Newmarket Partnership (NEWMARKET) BRED Matthews Breeding and Racing Ltd

Bt in 5,000gns

Catherines Song, whose full-sister Arasong won over course and distance two years ago, is very much sprint-bred and picked up nicely although still a little on the green side. She may prove slightly better than the average plater. (2/1: tchd 3/1)

1867* Ivory's Joy again looked in terrific shape and had a good try at making most, although she could not respond when the winner challenged. She looks sure to find another ordinary seller. (4/1: 9/4-9/2)

2003 Fast Franc (IRE), making his debut for the yard just seven days after being claimed on his debut, missed the break slightly and was always playing catch up. He looks sure to stay another furlong. (2/1)

1581 Hopefully is minute and her best chance of winning may have already passed, but her pedigree suggests she ought to stay much further. (9/2)

Angry Albert, a full-brother to the very moderate Tom Pladdey, seems of similar ability. (25/1)

1498 Eurofen (14/1: 6/1-16/1)

2187 TOTE BOOKMAKERS H'CAP (0-80) (3-Y.O+) (Class D)

7-55 (7-55) **1m 2f 21y** £3,557.50 (£1,060.00: £505.00: £227.50) Stalls: Low GOING minus 0.33 sec per fur (GF)

				SP	RR	SF
1747*	**American Whisper (68)** (PWHarris) **3-7-12**(7) CLowther(2) (lw: trckd ldrs: led over 2f out: clr over 1f out: pushed out)	—	1	7/2[1]	81	34

1972^{6}	**Missile Toe (IRE) (57)** (DMorris) **4-8-6** NDay(9) (hld up: hdwy over 3f out: tried to squeeze thro & hmpd over 1f out: edgd rt & r.o wl ins fnl f) 3½	2	7/1	65	30
1414^{10}	**Polar Champ (79)** (SPCWoods) **4-10-0** WRyan(1) (led: rdn & hdd over 2f out: kpt on same pce) ....hd	3	8/1	86	51
1796^{*}	**Blockade (USA) (60)** (MBell) **8-8-4**(5) RMullen(7) (t: hld up: rdn & hdwy over 3f out: r.o wl fnl f) ....s.h	4	$7/2^{1}$	67	32
1831^{6}	**Prospector's Cove (70)** (JPearce) **4-9-5** GHind(5) (chsd ldrs: rdn over 2f out: no ex fnl f) 1½	5	16/1	75	40
1811^{11}	**Bonanza Peak (USA) (63)** (MrsJCecil) **4-8-12** RCochrane(4) (lw: hld up: nt clr run on ins over 3f out tl plld out appr fnl f: btn whn hmpd ins fnl f: fin 7th, 2l: plcd 6th) 4½	6	$5/1^{2}$	61	26
1972^{7}	**Kailey Senor (USA) (73)** (RWArmstrong) **4-9-8** MRoberts(8) (prom 6f: fin 8th, plcd 7th) 1½	7	$5/1^{2}$	68	33
1679^{4}	**Michael Venture (75)** (SPCWoods) **3-8-12** DBiggs(6) (plld hrd: prom 5f: sn wl bhd: fin 9th, plcd 8th) ....dist	8	33/1	—	—
1588^{W}	**North Reef (IRE) (73)** (JPearce) **6-9-8** MWigham(3) (swtg: chsd ldr: pushed along 5f out: bmpd & veered lft over 1f out: btn whn hmpd ins fnl f: fin 6th, btn 2½l: disq)	D	$11/2^{3}$	74	39

(SP 125.6%) **9 Rn**

2m 7.3 (3.50) CSF £28.83 CT £175.45 TOTE £5.20: £1.60 £2.70 £2.60 (£17.20) Trio £46.30 OWNER The Confederates (BERKHAMSTED) BRED Cambremont Ltd Partnership

WEIGHT FOR AGE 3yo-12lb

STEWARDS' ENQUIRY Wigham susp. 2-5, 7-12 & 14-15/7/97 (intentional interference).

1747* American Whisper, back on good ground for the first time since his two-year-old debut, looked to relish it and, given a good aggressive ride by his young pilot, came home in good style clear of the trouble in behind. (7/2: 5/2-4/1)

1972 Missile Toe (IRE), stepping up to ten furlongs for the first time, was held up to get the trip and got it well. Three furlongs from home Day began to look for a run but was in the process of committing to an almost non-existent gap when forced back in. Rolling around as a result, the Stewards took the view that he was unbalanced when pushing his assailant aside inside the final furlong. A cynic might have seen it as Day 2 Wigham 1. (7/1)

974* Polar Champ, dropped in class, was outpaced by the winner early in the straight and could do nothing about it. (8/1)

1796* Blockade (USA) found those in front not stopping when he made his move, and would probably have liked a stronger early pace. (7/2)

1831 Prospector's Cove, on the heels of the leaders on the inside, did not see a lot of daylight but gave the impression that he could have done little more even if he had. (16/1)

Bonanza Peak (USA), an attractive colt, is a poor mover. Buried away on the inside, he saw no daylight at all and, when switched off the rails, was a sufferer in the spat between Missile Toe and North Reef. He looks the sort who ought to win off this sort of mark. (5/1)

1427* North Reef (IRE) got warm and was taken down steadily. He was already being pushed along when Missile Toe looked to be going for the narrowest of gaps on his inner. Wigham took action to keep his rival in but, given that it all happened in a split second, his actions may have been instinctive, although clearly intentional. The jockey's ban may now seem a little harsh, but the camera patrol film looked pretty damning when viewed in slow motion. (11/2)

2188 TOTE CREDIT MAIDEN STKS (3-Y.O) (Class D)

8-25 (8-26) **1m 6f 17y** £3,826.90 (£1,058.40: £504.70) Stalls: High GOING minus 0.33 sec per fur (GF)

			SP	RR	SF
1949^{3}	**Sun Alert (USA) (74)** (MJPolglase) **3-8-9** TGMcLaughlin(3) (lw: trckd ldr: rdn & hung rt over 3f out: led 2f out: edgd lft: r.o) ....—	1	$4/1^{2}$	76	27
1846^{2}	**Seattle Art (USA)** (HRACecil) **3-9-0** WRyan(1) (lw: led over 12f: one pce) 2	2	$1/4^{1}$	79	30
833^{9}	**Divinity** (CEBrittain) **3-8-9** BDoyle(2) (hld up: effrt 3f out: sn rdn & btn) 3	3	$8/1^{3}$	70?	21

(SP 111.1%) **3 Rn**

3m 5.2 (7.20) CSF £5.45 TOTE £5.60 (£1.30) OWNER Mr K. S. Lee (NEWMARKET) BRED Juddmonte Farms

1949 Sun Alert (USA), the only one proven over the trip, looked in two minds when initially let down, but eventually got her act together and strode on well in the last furlong to cause an upset. (4/1: 3/1-9/2)

1846 Seattle Art (USA), stepping up in trip, looked to lack gears at the end of a steadily-run race rather than not stay. (1/4)

Divinity, stepped up half-a-mile for this first run since April, never left last place. (8/1)

2189 TOTE DUAL FORECAST H'CAP (0-70) (3-Y.O) (Class E)

8-55 (8-56) **1m 6f 17y** £3,044.25 (£909.00: £434.50: £197.25) Stalls: High GOING minus 0.33 sec per fur (GF)

			SP	RR	SF
1853^{2}	**Ginger Rogers (47)** (DWPArbuthnot) **3-7-13** JQuinn(7) (a.p: led 3f out: rdn & hld on wl fnl f) ....—	1	$9/2^{3}$	54	18
1649^{6}	**French Mist (69)** (CEBrittain) **3-9-7** BDoyle(4) (lw: chsd ldrs: rdn over 2f out: ev ch ins fnl f: unable qckn) ....¾	2	14/1	75	39
1986^{*}	**Tommy Tortoise (71)** (MissGayKelleway) **3-9-9** 4x RCochrane(1) (lw: hdwy over 2f out: r.o fnl f) ....nk	3	$4/1^{2}$	77	41
1853^{*}	**Aurelian (60)** (MBell) **3-8-7**(5) GFaulkner(6) (hdwy 4f out: one pce fnl f) 1	4	$4/1^{2}$	65	29
1846^{6}	**Hadidi (64)** (DMorley) **3-9-2** RHills(8) (hld up: hdwy 8f out: shkn up over 2f out: styd on same pce) 1½	5	5/1	67	31
1853^{4}	**Golden Melody (58)** (MJHeaton-Ellis) **3-8-10v**1 DHolland(3) (led after 2f: rdn & hdd 3f out: n.m.r & wknd wl over 1f out) 2½	6	9/1	58	22
1853^{5}	**Jucinda (61)** (JPearce) **3-8-13** GHind(2) (led 2f: rdn & btn over 3f out) 1½	7	10/1	59	23
1637^{11}	**Sixties Melody (50)** (RBoss) **3-8-2**ow1 MRoberts(5) (lw: nvr nr to chal) 1¼	8	16/1	47	10
1574^{*}	**Fullopep (65)** (MrsMReveley) **3-9-3** DHarrison(10) (lw: hld up: hdwy over 3f out: rdn & btn 2f out) 5	9	$3/1^{1}$	56	20
1853^{9}	**Dawn Summit (56)** (BHanbury) **3-8-1**(7) CLowther(9) (chsd ldrs 10f: no imp) ....½	10	20/1	47	11

(SP 136.3%) **10 Rn**

3m 5.2 (7.20) CSF £70.46 CT £265.61 TOTE £5.70: £1.10 £4.30 £1.30 (£46.00) Trio £48.60 OWNER Mr W. H. Ponsonby (COMPTON) BRED R. Barber

1853 Ginger Rogers, made more use of this time, clearly has more stamina than speed but her heart is in the right place. She will stay further still and is at the right end of the handicap. (9/2: op 5/2)

1649 French Mist, back over this trip after two tries over shorter, looked a threat on the inside in the last two furlongs but, with little racing room, was outbattled by the winner. The head-on showed that she had caused little if any interference to Golden Melody, an incident over which an enquiry was held. (14/1)

1986* Tommy Tortoise looks an out-and-out stayer. (4/1: 5/1-8/1)

1853* Aurelian could not confirm course and distance form with the winner. (4/1)

1846 Hadidi travelled well for much of the race, but did not pick up as well as might have been expected. He should not be written off yet. (5/1)

1853 Golden Melody, visored for the first time, was on the retreat when dropping back sharply when short of room on the inside. She was hardly interfered with at all and may be one to be a little wary of. (9/1: op 6/1)

1853 Jucinda (10/1: 5/1-12/1)

T/Plpt: £446.20 (28.65 Tckts). T/Qdpt: £149.60 (5.08 Tckts) Dk

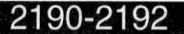

2146-LINGFIELD (L-H) (Turf Good, AW Standard)
Tuesday June 24th
WEATHER: sunny WIND: almost nil

2190 LONDON COLLEGE OF BEAUTY THERAPY MAIDEN STKS (3-Y.O) (Class D)
2-30 (2-32) **1m 2f** £3,645.60 (£1,087.80: £519.40: £235.20) Stalls: Low GOING minus 0.12 sec per fur (G)

				SP	RR	SF
1477³	**Hachiyah (IRE) (87)** (DMorley) **3-8-9** RHills(1) (a.p: led over 2f out: clr over 1f out: comf)	—	**1**	15/8²	86+	32
1738⁹	**Imperial Scholar (IRE) (100)** (JMPEustace) **3-8-9** JTate(7) (lw: hdwy over 2f out: hrd rdn over 1f out: chsd wnr ins fnl f: r.o one pce)	3½	**2**	11/8¹	80	26
1678²	**Dawam Allail (IRE) (75)** (MAJarvis) **3-9-0** PatEddery(6) (a.p: chsd wnr over 2f out tl ins fnl f: one pce)	2½	**3**	11/2³	81	27
963¹⁵	**Shahboor (USA)** (MRStoute) **3-9-0** JReid(8) (hdwy over 2f out: wknd over 1f out)	2	**4**	8/1	78	24
1742⁴	**Action Stations** (CACyzer) **3-9-0** JWeaver(5) (led 1f: ev ch 3f out: rdn over 2f out: sn wknd)	13	**5**	20/1	57	3
	Lancashire Knight (SDow) **3-9-0** WRyan(3) (led 9f out tl over 2f out: sn wknd)	1¼	**6**	66/1	55	1
1742⁶	**Across The Water** (CACyzer) **3-8-6**(3) AWhelan(4) (bhd fnl 3f)	15	**7**	40/1	26	—
742¹⁵	**Interregnum** (AGFoster) **3-8-9** RPerham(2) (a bhd)	6	**8**	100/1	17	—

(SP 113.1%) **8 Rn**

2m 11.16 (6.46) CSF £4.21 TOTE £2.90: £1.30 £1.10 £1.20 (£2.10) OWNER Mr Hamdan Al Maktoum (NEWMARKET) BRED SHADWELL ESTATE COMPANY LIMITED

1477 Hachiyah (IRE) made no mistake here, cruising into the lead over two furlongs out and scooting clear to win with plenty in hand. (15/8)

1738 Imperial Scholar (IRE), who has been unsuccessfully competing in races like the Nell Gwyn Stakes and the Oaks, showed that just because she has been running in those type of events, does not mean she is a good thing in an ordinary maiden such as this. Unable to cope with the winner, she had a real battle for second place in the final quarter-mile and just managed to prevail. (11/8)

1678 Dawam Allail (IRE) lack of acceleration was once again there for all to see, and he was collared for the runner-up berth inside the final furlong. (11/2: 4/1-6/1)

Shahboor (USA) had less on his plate this time and showed his first sign of ability, taking closer order in the straight before tiring below the distance. (8/1: tchd 12/1)

2191 CROWHURST (S) STKS (2-Y.O) (Class G)
3-00 (3-01) **6f** £1,984.50 (£547.00: £259.50) Stalls: High GOING minus 0.12 sec per fur (G)

				SP	RR	SF
1760¹⁶	**Heavenly Falls (IRE)** (CADwyer) **2-8-8**(3) DO'Donohoe(3) (hld up: nt clr run 4f out: hrd rdn over 1f out: led nr fin)	—	**1**	4/1³	64	18
2003⁴	**Rosewood Lady (IRE)** (KRBurke) **2-8-6** BDoyle(5) (led: hrd rdn over 1f out: hdd nr fin)	s.h	**2**	5/1	59	13
1760¹²	**Harnage (IRE)** (MRChannon) **2-8-8**(3) PPMurphy(2) (hld up: hrd rdn over 1f out: one pce ins fnl f)	1	**3**	3/1²	61	15
1856³	**Calliram** (MBlanshard) **2-8-3**(3) MartinDwyer(1) (a.p: chsd ldr 3f out to 1f out: wknd)	3	**4**	15/2	48	2
*1124*⁷	**Slim Prior** (KRBurke) **2-8-11** RPerham(7) (bit bkwd: w ldr 3f: wknd over 1f out)	2½	**5**	33/1	47	1
	Inner Key (APJones) **2-8-8**(3) JDSmith(4) (leggy: dwlt: a bhd)	2	**6**	33/1	41	—
1854³	**Up The Wall** (ICampbell) **2-8-11** PatEddery(6) (lw: nt clr run 4f out: swtchd lft & rdn over 3f out: sme hdwy 2f out: wknd over 1f out)	½	**7**	9/4¹	40	—
*1758*⁵	**Chika Shan (IRE)** (BSmart) **2-8-8**(3) PMcCabe(8) (bhd fnl 3f)	½	**8**	33/1	39	—

(SP 113.0%) **8 Rn**

1m 13.66 (4.66) CSF £21.31 TOTE £6.10: £1.40 £1.20 £2.30 (£15.50) OWNER Mr M. E. Hall (NEWMARKET) BRED Mrs Aine O'Farrell
Bt in 4,000gns. Up The Wall clmd Terry Connors £5,750

1418 Heavenly Falls (IRE) appreciated the drop in class but he certainly struggled, and it took some very stern riding from the saddle to get him up near the finish. (4/1: op 6/1)

2003 Rosewood Lady (IRE), who almost won on her debut, again just lost out. Attempting to make all the running, she responded well to pressure and looked likely to keep the winner at bay until passed in the last few strides. (5/1)

Harnage (IRE) was taking a drop in class and ran his best race to date. On level terms with the winner below the distance, he remained on the heels of the first two in the final furlong, if failing to find that vital turn of foot. (3/1)

1856 Calliram moved into second place at halfway but had little left in the locker when collared. (15/2: 5/1-8/1)

Slim Prior was carrying condition for this first run in six weeks, and dropped away below the distance. (33/1)

1854 Up The Wall (9/4: op 6/4)

2192 MARIE POWER 40TH BIRTHDAY H'CAP (0-80) (3-Y.O) (Class D)
3-30 (3-32) **6f** £3,836.70 (£1,146.60: £548.80: £249.90) Stalls: High GOING minus 0.12 sec per fur (G)

				SP	RR	SF
1958⁶	**Silca Key Silca (78)** (MRChannon) **3-9-4**(3) PPMurphy(6) (chsd ldr 5f out: led over 1f out: r.o wl)	—	**1**	11/2³	93	66
2044²	**Bayford Thrust (76)** (JBerry) **3-9-2**(3) PFessey(1) (b.hind: led over 4f: unable qckn)	6	**2**	100/30²	75	48
1966⁴	**Shalstayholy (IRE) (67)** (GLMoore) **3-8-10v** SWhitworth(3) (lw: bmpd over 5f out: swtchd rt: hdwy over 3f out: rdn over 2f out: one pce)	3	**3**	3/1¹	58	31
1807⁹	**The Wyandotte Inn (65)** (MrsNMacauley) **3-8-3**(5) AmandaSanders(7) (lost pl 4f out: no hdwy fnl 2f)	3	**4**	20/1	48	21
*1787*³	**Icy Guest (USA) (73)** (PJMakin) **3-9-2** PatEddery(9) (prom 3f)	1½	**5**	3/1¹	52	25
1167⁷	**Parijazz (IRE) (60)** (MartynMeade) **3-7-10**(7) RBrisland(8) (reard s: nvr nr to chal)	3	**6**	16/1	31	4
1237¹⁴	**Chakra (61)** (SDow) **3-8-4**ow1 RPerham(2) (a bhd)	4	**7**	50/1	21	—
882⁶	**Gunners Glory (63)** (BJMeehan) **3-8-6b** BDoyle(4) (lw: bmpd over 5f out: prom over 3f)	½	**8**	12/1	22	—
*1155*⁴	**Noble Investment (70)** (JMPEustace) **3-8-13b** JTate(5) (lw: bhd fnl 3f)	16	**9**	25/1	—	—

(SP 112.6%) **9 Rn**

1m 10.92 (1.92) CSF £20.93 CT £58.55 TOTE £7.30: £1.70 £1.40 £1.60 (£10.90) Trio £5.20 OWNER Mr Tim Corby (UPPER LAMBOURN) BRED Alan Gibson

1958 Silca Key Silca appreciated the drop in distance - seven furlongs seemed to be beyond her at Leicester on her reappearance - and, striking the front over a furlong out, was rousted along to forge clear. (11/2)

2044 Bayford Thrust, 12lb lower than at the beginning of the season, took the field along but, collared by the winner approaching the final furlong, was firmly put in his place. (100/30: 9/4-7/2)

1966 Shalstayholy (IRE) continues to give a good account of herself, but failed to find a turn of foot in the final quarter-mile. The Handicapper appears to have her measure at present. (3/1)

634 The Wyandotte Inn found this all happening too quickly for him. A return to seven furlongs is required. (20/1)

1787 Icy Guest (USA) found the drop in distance all against her and was getting left behind from halfway. A return to seven furlongs is needed. (3/1)
882 Gunners Glory (12/1: op 8/1)

2193 HENRY STREETER LIMITED STKS (0-70) (3-Y.O+) (Class E)
4-00 (4-00) **1m (Equitrack)** £2,784.25 (£829.00: £394.50: £177.25) Stalls: High GOING minus 0.54 sec per fur (FST)

				SP	RR	SF
2161^{2}	**Bentico (66)** (MrsNMacauley) **8-9-7v** BDoyle(4) (led 1f: led over 3f out: clr over 1f out: comf)	—	**1**	Evens^{1}	79	61
2150^{7}	**Law Dancer (IRE) (66)** (TGMills) **4-9-5** PatEddery(2) (lw: hld up: chsd wnr over 2f out: unable qckn)	8	**2**	4/1^{3}	61	43
2040^{13}	**Enchanting Eve (68)** (CNAllen) **3-8-7**(3) MartinDwyer(3) (lw: led 7f out tl over 3f out: wknd over 2f out)	6	**3**	15/8^{2}	50	22
1967^{10}	**Magazine Gap (51)** (PatMitchell) **4-9-0**(5) AmandaSanders(1) (lw: hld up: rdn wl over 1f out: sn wknd)	¾	**4**	50/1	48	30
				(SP 106.7%)		**4 Rn**

1m 37.32 (-0.08) CSF £4.71 TOTE £1.90: (£2.00) OWNER Twenty Twenty Racing (MELTON MOWBRAY) BRED Britton House Stud
WEIGHT FOR AGE 3yo-10lb
2161 Bentico, making a quick reappearance, had a nice saunter round, leading over three furlongs from home and scooting clear in the straight to win with plenty in hand. (Evens)
1503 Law Dancer (IRE), making a quick reappearance, was taking a drop in distance and, although moving into second place over two furlongs out, had no hope with the winner. Both his wins to date have come on the Wolverhampton Fibresand over a mile-and-a-quarter. (4/1)
1421 Enchanting Eve was very disappointing and, once headed over three furlongs from home, the writing was on the wall. (15/8)

2194 KNIGHT FRANK H'CAP (0-80) (3-Y.O F) (Class D)
4-30 (4-31) **1m 3f 106y** £3,422.65 (£1,019.20: £485.10: £218.05) Stalls: Low GOING minus 0.12 sec per fur (G)

				SP	RR	SF
1784^{2}	**Graceful Lass (80)** (DRLoder) **3-9-7** PatEddery(3) (b.nr hind: hld up: led over 2f out: clr over 1f out: comf)	—	**1**	13/8^{1}	92+	54
1938*	**Arriving (67)** (JWHills) **3-8-8** RHills(4) (hdwy 3f out: chsd wnr over 2f out: no imp)	1¼	**2**	13/8^{1}	77	39
1258^{4}	**Georgia Venture (74)** (SPCWoods) **3-9-1** WRyan(1) (dropped rr 4f out: r.o one pce fnl 2f)	1¼	**3**	11/1^{3}	83	45
1999^{2}	**Bally Souza (IRE) (75)** (MJohnston) **3-9-2** JWeaver(2) (lw: led 9f: one pce)	½	**4**	6/1^{2}	83	45
1859^{2}	**Cheek To Cheek (58)** (CACyzer) **3-7-10**(3) AWhelan(5) (lw: w ldr: ev ch over 2f out: sn wknd)	10	**5**	6/1^{2}	52	14
				(SP 113.1%)		**5 Rn**

2m 30.69 (5.99) CSF £4.14 TOTE £2.60: £1.50 £1.20 (£2.00) OWNER Mr A. M. Budgett (NEWMARKET) BRED Kirtlington Stud Ltd
1784 Graceful Lass appreciated the step-up in trip and, leading over two furlongs from home, forged clear for a decisive victory. (13/8)
1938* Arriving moved into second place early in the straight, but she was unable to make a race of it with the winner. (13/8)
1258 Georgia Venture had dropped back to last place running down the hill, but struggled on again in the final quarter-mile. (11/1: 8/1-14/1)
1999 Bally Souza (IRE) was taking a step-up in distance, but despite this she took the field along. She had nothing left when headed, but may be worth another try at the trip using less forceful tactics. (6/1: 4/1-13/2)
1859 Cheek To Cheek found this trip too far for, after having every chance a quarter-of-a-mile from home, then stopped as if shot. (6/1: 4/1-13/2)

2195 SCHATUNOWSKI BROOKS APPRENTICE H'CAP (0-70) (3-Y.O+) (Class F)
5-00 (5-02) **1m 2f** £2,410.50 (£678.00: £331.50) Stalls: High GOING minus 0.12 sec per fur (G)

				SP	RR	SF
1629^{5}	**Absolute Liberty (USA) (65)** (SPCWoods) **3-9-2** GMilligan(8) (mde virtually all: rdn out)	—	**1**	6/1	74	38
2121^{W}	**Rash Gift (55)** (LordHuntingdon) **4-9-4** AimeeCook(4) (a.p: shkn up over 1f out: r.o one pce)	1	**2**	15/2	62	38
2121^{5}	**Kirov Protege (IRE) (36)** (MrsLCJewell) **5-7-8**(5) DarrenWilliams(3) (lw: wnt prom & ev ch over 2f out: one pce)	hd	**3**	3/1^{2}	43	19
2041^{5}	**Flagstaff (USA) (38)** (KRBurke) **4-7-12**(3) RWinston(2) (hdwy on ins over 3f out: rdn over 2f out: one pce)	1¾	**4**	4/1^{3}	42	18
1811^{6}	**Peppers (IRE) (65)** (KRBurke) **4-9-9**(5) EmilyJoyce(5) (lw: s.s: hdwy over 1f out: edgd lft: r.o)	s.h	**5**	5/2^{1}	69	45
1011^{10}	**Another Fiddle (IRE) (40)** (JELong) **7-7-12**(5) RBrisland(7) (b: b.hind: dwlt: bhd fnl 5f)	9	**6**	33/1	30	6
2150^{9}	**Roman Reel (USA) (52)** (GLMoore) **6-8-8**(7) CherylBone(6) (lw: sttd s: hdwy over 8f out: wknd over 3f out)	1¾	**7**	13/2	39	15
				(SP 115.9%)		**7 Rn**

2m 11.31 (6.61) CSF £45.72 CT £147.13 TOTE £8.50: £2.50 £2.70 (£11.90) OWNER Mr S. P. C. Woods (NEWMARKET) BRED Charles Weston
WEIGHT FOR AGE 3yo-12lb
1629 Absolute Liberty (USA) had the most proficient jockey aboard and that made all the difference. Making virtually all the running, he was strongly tackled in the straight, but was not going to be denied. (6/1)
Rash Gift, given a four-month break, was never far away. Her jockey was not very strong on her, but she stayed on in the final furlong to snatch second prize right on the line. (15/2)
2121 Kirov Protege (IRE) was making a quick reappearance after finding a mile too sharp at Newmarket on Friday. Looking a serious threat to the winner in the straight, he was tapped for toe from below the distance. (3/1)
2041 Flagstaff (USA) nipped along the inside rail entering the straight but, despite all his rider's efforts, failed to find another gear. He remains a maiden after twenty-two attempts. (4/1)
1811 Peppers (IRE) received no assistance from the saddle. The filly picked up ground below the distance, but her jockey then gave her a rather feeble whack of the whip and she drifted slightly left as a result. Nevertheless, the combination struggled on to be nearest at the line. (5/2)

T/Plpt: £78.90 (212.01 Tckts). T/Qdpt: £25.20 (33.38 Tckts) AK

1803-WARWICK (L-H) (Good, Good to soft patches)
Tuesday June 24th
WEATHER: cloudy WIND: mod bhd

2196 RAYNSFORD NOVICE AUCTION STKS (2-Y.O) (Class E)
2-15 (2-17) **7f** £3,226.25 (£965.00: £462.50: £211.25) Stalls: Low GOING minus 0.04 sec per fur (G)

				SP	RR	SF
1251^{3}	**Opposition Leader** (BWHills) **2-8-12** DHolland(15) (racd wd: a.p: led over 1f out: r.o wl)	—	**1**	4/1^{2}	78	40
1675^{4}	**Signatory** (RHannon) **2-8-9** DaneO'Neill(13) (led tl edgd rt & hdd over 1f out: one pce)	2	**2**	8/1	70	32
1954^{2}	**Hoh Justice** (IABalding) **2-8-12** LDettori(2) (a.p: rdn over 1f out: one pce)	1¼	**3**	2/1^{1}	71	33
1438*	**Island Girl (IRE)** (DWPArbuthnot) **2-8-6** TQuinn(12) (racd wd: a.p: one pce fnl 2f)	1¼	**4**	9/1	62	24
1760^{6}	**Dry Lightning** (MBell) **2-8-4** MFenton(9) (bit bkwd: prom tl rdn & wknd over 2f out)	hd	**5**	5/1^{3}	60	22

Form	Runner	Dist	Pos	SP	RR	SF
1812[16]	**Persian Venture** (BJMeehan) **2-8-12** MTebbutt(14) (racd wd: prom tl rdn & wkng whn sltly hmpd over 1f out)	1½	**6**	20/1	64	26
	Howies Choice (IRE) (KMcAuliffe) **2-8-12** JFEgan(5) (leggy: lt-f: s.s: nvr nrr)	2	**7**	20/1	60	22
1510[8]	**Catch The Rainbow** (JGSmyth-Osbourne) **2-8-4** TSprake(8) (prom over 3f)	hd	**8**	16/1	51	13
1812[8]	**Oisin (IRE)** (MrsPNDutfield) **2-8-6** RPrice(4) (rdn 3f out: bhd fnl 2f)	hd	**9**	33/1	53	15
1577[3]	**Gralmano (IRE)** (NPLittmoden) **2-8-6** TGMcLaughlin(1) (a bhd)	3½	**10**	10/1	45	7
1675[5]	**Donegal Sean** (KMcAuliffe) **2-8-12** DRMcCabe(3) (prom over 3f)	1¾	**11**	20/1	47	9
1842[10]	**Dentardia (IRE)** (JMPEustace) **2-8-12** MRimmer(7) (bit bkwd: a bhd)	4	**12**	25/1	38	—
	La Vizelle (IRE) (RGuest) **2-8-1** JQuinn(11) (leggy: lt-f: unf: hld up mid div: bhd fnl 2f)	6	**13**	50/1	13	—
1760[W]	**Latin Bay** (PWHarris) **2-8-6** AClark(10) (s.i.s: a bhd: t.o)	7	**14**	33/1	2	—

(SP 132.1%) **14 Rn**

1m 29.1 (4.50) CSF £33.28 TOTE £5.40: £1.40 £3.50 £1.20 (£17.50) Trio £7.60 OWNER Mr Stephen Crown (LAMBOURN) BRED Cheveley Park Stud Ltd

1251 Opposition Leader appeared as if he had just been newly elected over this extra furlong. (4/1: op 5/2)

1675 Signatory showed considerable improvement over this longer trip, and can soon go one better in a similar event. (8/1: 6/1-10/1)

1954 Hoh Justice got the step-up in distance, but could not deliver the goods. (2/1: 11/8-9/4)

1438* Island Girl (IRE) was not disgraced in this higher grade and seemed to get the trip well enough. (9/1)

1760 Dry Lightning, a half-sister to three winners, should now be approaching her peak. (5/1)

Persian Venture is a half-brother to Clued Up. (20/1)

2197 GREENACRES H'CAP (0-70) (3-Y.O+ F & M) (Class E)

2-45 (2-56) **5f** £3,330.25 (£997.00: £478.50: £219.25) Stalls: Low GOING minus 0.21 sec per fur (GF)

Form	Runner	Dist	Pos	SP	RR	SF
1814[3]	**Runs in the Family (57)** (GMMcCourt) **5-9-3b** DHarrison(1) (w ldr: rdn 2f out: led over 1f out: sn clr: eased nr fin)	—	**1**	7/2[1]	66	48
1925[10]	**Bairn Atholl (36)** (RJHodges) **4-7-10** NAdams(2) (chsd ldrs: rdn 2f out: r.o ins fnl f: nt trble wnr)	2½	**2**	33/1	37	19
1865[6]	**Sunset Harbour (IRE) (45)** (SEKettlewell) **4-8-0**(5) RFfrench(5) (lw: chsd ldrs: r.o ins fnl f)	nk	**3**	7/1[3]	45	27
1743[5]	**Sally Slade (68)** (CACyzer) **5-10-0** GDuffield(8) (hdwy stands' side over 1f out: r.o)	s.h	**4**	11/2[2]	68	50
1479[8]	**Another Batchworth (66)** (EAWheeler) **5-9-7b**(5) ADaly(3) (lw: led over 3f: wknd ins fnl f)	1¾	**5**	12/1	60	42
1848[9]	**Chief's Lady (42)** (JMBradley) **5-8-2**ow4 JFEgan(11) (chsd ldrs: no hdwy fnl 2f)	1	**6**	16/1	33	11
1963[7]	**Tymeera (48)** (BPalling) **4-8-8** TSprake(4) (sn outpcd: nvr nrr)	nk	**7**	7/1[3]	38	20
1977[11]	**Antonias Melody (68)** (SRBowring) **4-10-0b** SWebster(15) (racd wd: spd 3f)	1½	**8**	8/1	53	35
2019[13]	**Maydoro (54)** (MDods) **4-9-0** AClark(9) (lw: s.s: a bhd)	4	**9**	33/1	27	9
1963[11]	**Brin-Lodge (IRE) (36)** (KSBridgwater) **4-7-5b**(5) JBramhill(14) (b.hind: racd wd: spd 3f)	¾	**10**	66/1	6	—
956[14]	**Forzara (47)** (JLSpearing) **4-8-7** SDrowne(7) (racd wd: spd 3f)	1¼	**11**	14/1	13	—
1810[7]	**Shifting Time (65)** (IABalding) **3-9-5** LDettori(6) (lw: chsd ldrs over 2f)	2½	**12**	8/1	23	—
1810[13]	**Breffni (IRE) (44)** (RDickin) **3-7-12** JQuinn(13) (bolted bef s: reard stalls: a bhd)	4	**13**	25/1	—	—
345[7]	**Whisper Low (IRE) (50)** (RHollinshead) **3-8-4** FLynch(10) (bkwd: outpcd)	3	**14**	33/1	—	—

(SP 119.2%) **14 Rn**

60.0 secs (2.00) CSF £126.28 CT £556.69 TOTE £4.20: £1.60 £25.30 £1.90 (£161.80) Trio £539.80 OWNER Mr Geoffrey Greenwood (WANTAGE) BRED Mr and Mrs J. K. S. Cresswell

LONG HANDICAP Bairn Atholl 7-9 Brin-Lodge (IRE) 7-2

WEIGHT FOR AGE 3yo-6lb

1814 Runs in the Family was the only horse able to go with the furious pace set by Another Batchworth. (7/2)

Bairn Atholl, dropped 4lb, was just out of the handicap and ran easily her best race to date on this first venture over the minimum distance. (33/1)

1865 Sunset Harbour (IRE) was 5lb higher than when winning at Beverley. (7/1)

1743 Sally Slade, dropped 3lb, finished with a flourish under the stands' rails and seems to be coming to hand. (11/2)

1479 Another Batchworth failed to get home after setting a blistering pace, and needs to come down a few pounds. (12/1)

1620 Chief's Lady was on the same mark as when just pipped in a Leicester seller over six. (16/1)

Forzara (14/1: 10/1-16/1)

1479 Shifting Time (8/1: op 9/2)

2198 SYD MERCER MEMORIAL H'CAP (0-80) (3-Y.O+) (Class D)

3-15 (3-19) **1m 6f 194y** £3,677.45 (£1,097.60: £524.30: £237.65) Stalls: Low GOING minus 0.04 sec per fur (G)

Form	Runner	Dist	Pos	SP	RR	SF
2035*	**Dancing Cavalier (59)** (RHollinshead) **4-8-3**(7) PFredericks(13) (hld up & bhd: hdwy over 4f out: carried rt 2f out: edgd lft fnl f: led last stride)	—	**1**	2/1[1]	68	44
1592[4]	**Silently (77)** (JSKing) **5-9-9**(5) RFfrench(1) (lw: a.p: led 1f out: hdd last stride)	s.h	**2**	12/1	86	62
2034[6]	**Golden Hadeer (55)** (MJRyan) **6-8-6** AClark(7) (led 11f out tl over 7f out: led over 3f out to 1f out: one pce)	1¾	**3**	8/1[2]	62	38
1808*	**Badawi (FR) (45)** (NMBabbage) **7-7-10** FNorton(10) (a.p: rdn over 3f out: one pce fnl 2f)	2½	**4**	8/1[2]	49	25
1795*	**Salska (61)** (AStreeter) **6-8-12** TSprake(3) (hld up in rr: hdwy 3f out: nt rch ldrs)	½	**5**	8/1[2]	65	41
1422[18]	**Lime Street Blues (IRE) (65)** (TKeddy) **6-9-2** MFenton(11) (bkwd: prom: hung rt 2f out: sn wknd)	8	**6**	50/1	60	36
1974[3]	**Coh Sho No (54)** (SDow) **4-8-5** TQuinn(9) (racd wd: prom: led over 7f out tl over 3f out: wknd 2f out)	1¼	**7**	11/1	48	24
1953[3]	**Paradise Navy (67)** (CREgerton) **8-9-4b** RHughes(4) (lw: s.i.s: hld up: hdwy 5f out: wknd over 3f out)	7	**8**	10/1[3]	53	29
1808[3]	**Romalito (45)** (MBlanshard) **7-7-10** JQuinn(2) (a bhd: t.o)	8	**9**	12/1	23	—
1592[7]	**Credit Squeeze (63)** (RFJohnsonHoughton) **7-9-0** MRoberts(6) (b: bkwd: a bhd: t.o)	3	**10**	14/1	38	14
1387[10]	**Sad Mad Bad (USA) (74)** (MJohnston) **3-8-6** WJO'Connor(5) (lw: led over 3f: wknd 8f out: t.o)	4	**11**	16/1	44	1
1805[6]	**Casual Water (IRE) (70)** (AGNewcombe) **6-9-7** SDrowne(12) (hld up: a bhd: t.o)	2	**12**	8/1[2]	38	14

(SP 125.1%) **12 Rn**

3m 18.9 (8.90) CSF £27.33 CT £157.36 TOTE £2.60: £1.50 £3.10 £3.50 (£31.70) Trio £97.00 OWNER The Three R's (UPPER LONGDON) BRED A. P. Hume

LONG HANDICAP Badawi (FR) 7-8

WEIGHT FOR AGE 3yo-19lb

2035* Dancing Cavalier, unpenalised for last week's win, is described by his trainer as a tough sort who thrives on racing. (2/1)

1592 Silently, just pipped by the well-handicapped winner, deserves to go one better. (12/1: 9/1-14/1)

2034 Golden Hadeer is now 18lb higher than the first of his three turf wins this season, and 8lb higher than for the last of those victories. (8/1)

1808* Badawi (FR), up 8lb, was still 2lb wrong in the handicap. (8/1)

1795* Salska was 5lb higher for her win at Nottingham. (8/1)

1808 Romalito (12/1: op 7/1)

1805 Casual Water (IRE) (8/1: 6/1-9/1)

2199 BLACKBRAKE PLANTATION MAIDEN H'CAP (0-60) (3-Y.O+) (Class F)
3-45 (3-45) **1m 4f 115y** £3,039.30 (£844.80: £405.90) Stalls: Low GOING minus 0.04 sec per fur (G)

				SP	RR	SF
1445[4]	**Schnozzle (IRE) (44)** (KSBridgwater) **6-8-12** TSprake(10) (a.p: led over 1f out: r.o)	—	1	6/1[3]	58	40
1393[6]	**Passing Strangers (USA) (52)** (PWHarris) **4-8-13**(7) CLowther(4) (lw: chsd ldr: led over 2f out tl over 1f out: r.o)	¾	2	10/1	65	47
1968[8]	**Lavender Della (IRE) (60)** (MJFetherston-Godley) **4-10-0** DHolland(2) (hld up & bhd: gd hdwy 3f out: edgd lft wl over 1f out: r.o one pce)	5	3	12/1	67	49
2114[4]	**Advance East (46)** (MDods) **5-9-0** AClark(5) (hld up & bhd: hdwy over 2f out: rdn over 1f out: one pce)	3½	4	12/1	48	30
838[4]	**Aztec Flyer (USA) (49)** (CEBrittain) **4-9-3** MRoberts(1) (hld up: rdn over 3f out: wknd 2f out)	9	5	7/1	40	22
1809[7]	**Persian Butterfly (49)** (RMStronge) **5-9-3** DRMcCabe(7) (hld up: hdwy 6f out: btn whn nt clr run wl over 1f out)	hd	6	20/1	40	22
1968[2]	**Sam Rockett (46)** (MissGayKelleway) **4-9-0** TQuinn(11) (led: hdd over 2f out: sn wknd)	2	7	5/2[1]	34	16
1617[2]	**Jean Pierre (52)** (JPearce) **4-9-6** LDettori(8) (hld up: hdwy over 4f out: wknd wl over 1f out)	8	8	5/1[2]	30	12
1632[22]	**Impetuous Lady (USA) (40)** (WJMusson) **4-8-8** JQuinn(3) (hld up mid div: bhd fnl 4f)	6	9	16/1	10	—
2049[5]	**Woodland Nymph (55)** (DJGMurraySmith) **3-8-8v[1]** DHarrison(13) (hdwy 7f out: rdn & wknd 3f out)	1¼	10	20/1	24	—
1276[9]	**Light Reflections (55)** (PGMurphy) **4-9-9** SDrowne(6) (prom over 8f: t.o)	20	11	12/1	—	—
1822[6]	**Troia (IRE) (56)** (BSmart) **3-8-9** SSanders(12) (lw: prom over 6f: t.o)	1¼	12	16/1	—	—
1636[16]	**Victor Blum (USA) (43)** (CAHorgan) **4-8-11** PaulEddery(9) (prom over 8f: t.o)	20	13	16/1	—	—
				(SP 131.4%)	**13 Rn**	

2m 45.8 (8.30) CSF £65.42 CT £656.63 TOTE £5.60: £1.60 £3.10 £5.10 (£37.00) Trio £160.70 OWNER Wiilsford Racing Incorporated (LAPWORTH) BRED Rathbarry Stud and Miss S. Ryan

WEIGHT FOR AGE 3yo-15lb

1445 Schnozzle (IRE), dropped 4lb, showed why he had been backed last time but, after travelling well, did not find an awful lot when striking the front. (6/1)

1393 Passing Strangers (USA) bounced back to form, having come down 6lb this season after a couple of disappointing efforts. (10/1)

Lavender Della (IRE) has yet to prove she really stays this distance, having possibly made up ground too quickly. (12/1)

2114 Advance East, making a quick reappearance, was going nowhere when slightly involved in some scrimmaging early in the home straight. (12/1)

838 Aztec Flyer (USA) is beginning to look like a horse with no trip. (7/1)

1617 Jean Pierre (5/1: op 3/1)

2200 GAVESTON (S) STKS (3-Y.O+) (Class G)
4-15 (4-15) **1m 2f 169y** £1,984.50 (£547.00: £259.50) Stalls: Low GOING minus 0.04 sec per fur (G)

				SP	RR	SF
2128[3]	**Guesstimation (USA) (58)** (JPearce) **8-9-7** LDettori(3) (hld up: hdwy on ins 3f out: plld out over 1f out: rdn to ld last strides)	—	1	13/8[1]	61	28
2029[3]	**Bluebell Miss (58)** (MJRyan) **3-8-3** GBardwell(4) (hld up: hdwy over 2f out: led ins fnl f: hrd rdn & hdd last strides)	hd	2	3/1[2]	56	10
1683[11]	**Runic Symbol (37)** (MBlanshard) **6-9-7** JQuinn(8) (hld up & bhd: gd hdwy 2f out: r.o ins fnl f)	2	3	12/1	58	25
2019[16]	**Bernard Seven (IRE) (48)** (MDods) **5-9-7b** AClark(7) (hld up & plld hrd: hdwy 5f out: led over 2f out: clr over 1f out: hdd ins fnl f: wknd)	3½	4	14/1	53	20
1798[11]	**Victory At Hart (40)** (DMorris) **3-8-8** PBloomfield(9) (led 1f: edgd rt bnd over 2f out: sn wknd)	8	5	33/1	41	—
2039[8]	**Precedency (46)** (KMcAuliffe) **5-9-7** JFEgan(6) (hld up mid div: bhd fnl 2f)	2	6	12/1	38	5
	Real Fire (IRE) (45) (MGMeagher) **3-8-8** DaneO'Neill(13) (prom tl wknd over 2f out)	¾	7	25/1	37	—
1951[6]	**Naburn Loch (33)** (DMHyde) **7-8-13**(3) RHavlin(5) (a.p: led over 3f out tl over 2f out: sn wknd)	¾	8	33/1	31	—
1825[18]	**Prove The Point (IRE) (35)** (MrsPNDutfield) **4-9-2b[1]** RPrice(1) (plld hrd: led after 1f: hdd over 3f out: wknd qckly over 2f out: t.o)	12	9	50/1	13	—
	Woodlands Energy (26) (PAPritchard) **6-9-2** NAdams(11) (s.s: sn rcvrd: rdn over 6f out: sn bhd: t.o)	6	10	100/1	4	—
1570[2]	**Risky Rose (42)** (RHollinshead) **5-8-13**(3) DGriffiths(2) (hld up: bhd tl b.d bnd over 2f out)		B	4/1[3]	—	—
2005[9]	**Irish Fiction (IRE) (52)** (DJSCosgrove) **3-8-8v[1]** MRimmer(12) (prom: 5th whn hmpd & fell bnd over 2f out: dead)		F	14/1	—	—
486[6]	**Rosalee Royale** (JohnBerry) **5-9-2** MFenton(10) (bit bkwd: bhd tl hmpd & uns rdr bnd over 2f out)		U	50/1	—	—
				(SP 126.5%)	**13 Rn**	

2m 24.0 (10.00) CSF £5.86 TOTE £2.60: £1.10 £1.50 £3.20 (£5.00) Trio £35.50 OWNER The Exclusive Two Partnership (NEWMARKET) BRED Oak Crest Farm

WEIGHT FOR AGE 3yo-13lb

No bid

IN-FOCUS: **This race was marred by a pile-up on the home turn.**

2128 Guesstimation (USA), back into a seller, would have had a stiffer task had this been a handicap. (13/8: 5/4-2/1)

2029 Bluebell Miss, dropped in grade, was another well in at the weights. (3/1)

1384 Runic Symbol, descending into selling company, would have been better off with the first two in a handicap. (12/1)

213 Bernard Seven (IRE), upped in trip and dropped in class, failed to last home after refusing to settle. (14/1)

2201 UGLY BRIDGE H'CAP (0-80) (3-Y.O+) (Class D)
4-45 (4-53) **1m** £3,741.15 (£1,117.20: £534.10: £242.55) Stalls: Low GOING minus 0.04 sec per fur (G)

				SP	RR	SF
1489[3]	**Sharp Rebuff (79)** (PJMakin) **6-10-0** SSanders(2) (a.p: led ins fnl f: drvn out)	—	1	6/1[2]	89	54
1878[8]	**Veni Vidi Vici (IRE) (64)** (MJHeaton-Ellis) **4-8-13** SDrowne(5) (hld up & bhd: hdwy over 2f out: ev ch 1f out: nt qckn)	1½	2	9/1	71	36
1775[7]	**Q Factor (73)** (DHaydnJones) **5-9-8** JCarroll(13) (a.p: led over 1f out tl ins fnl f)	2½	3	15/2	75	40
1658[8]	**Sualtach (IRE) (70)** (RHollinshead) **4-9-5** LDettori(6) (hld up: hdwy over 1f out: nvr nrr)	¾	4	8/1	71	36
	Helios (62) (DJGMurraySmith) **9-8-4**(7) CLowther(1) (bit bkwd: led over 6f: wknd fnl f)	nk	5	20/1	62	27
1606[6]	**Wild Palm (68)** (WAO'Gorman) **5-9-3b** DHolland(3) (lw: hld up & plld hrd: nt clr run over 2f out: hdwy fnl f: r.o)	2½	6	8/1	63	28
1955[3]	**Sooty Tern (68)** (JMBradley) **10-8-12**(5) RFfrench(10) (prom over 5f)	1¾	7	10/1	59	24
1955*	**Confronter (58)** (SDow) **8-8-7** MRoberts(9) (nvr trbld ldrs)	2½	8	7/1[3]	44	9

2036[18] **Royal South (IRE) (65)** (PSFelgate) **4-9-0** GHind(14) (s.s: plld hrd: sn prom: wknd 2f out)....1¼ **9** 25/1 49 14
Desert Lynx (IRE) (68) (TRWatson) **4-9-3** TQuinn(11) (plld hrd: prom: ev ch over 2f out: sn wknd)....1¾ **10** 16/1 48 13
Colins Choice (62) (JLSpearing) **3-7-10**(5) IonaWands(7) (a bhd)....½ **11** 33/1 41 —
1782[5] **Admirals Flame (IRE) (76)** (CFWall) **6-9-11** GDuffield(4) (b: hld up: a bhd)....1½ **12** 4/1[1] 52 17
1958[5] **Cherokee Flight (64)** (SMellor) **3-8-3** JFEgan(12) (chsd ldrs tl wknd 2f out)....4 **13** 14/1 32 —
(SP 124.0%) **13 Rn**

1m 41.6 (5.20) CSF £54.74 CT £396.08 TOTE £8.00: £2.90 £1.60 £3.20 (£33.30) Trio £82.50 OWNER Mr D. M. Ahier (MARLBOROUGH) BRED Farmers Hill and Fitzroy Studs
WEIGHT FOR AGE 3yo-10lb
1489 Sharp Rebuff put up a solid performance on this return to his best trip. (6/1)
Veni Vidi Vici (IRE), dropped 4lb, came with a well-timed run and his turn is near. (9/1)
Q Factor would not have minded softer ground, having slipped to a mark 2lb lower than when she last won. (15/2: 5/1-8/1)
1035 Sualtach (IRE), dropped 7lb this season, is another who would have appreciated more give underfoot. (8/1)
Helios, who has changed stables, should be sharper for the outing. (20/1)
1606 Wild Palm, down 2lb, gave the impression he could be finding his form. (8/1)
1782 Admirals Flame (IRE) (4/1: op 5/2)

T/Jkpt: £5,644.40 (110.63 Tckts). T/Plpt: £127.10 (653.24 Tckts). T/Qdpt: £39.50 (34.69 Tckts) KH

1860-CARLISLE (R-H) (Firm, Good to firm patches becoming Good)
Wednesday June 25th
WEATHER: raining WIND: mod half bhd

2202 E.B.F. CROWTHER HOMES MAIDEN STKS (2-Y.O) (Class D)
2-15 (2-15) **5f 207y** £3,647.50 (£1,105.00: £540.00: £257.50) Stalls: Centre GOING minus 0.45 sec per fur (F)

SP RR SF

Eloquent (SirMarkPrescott) **2-8-9** GDuffield(6) (w'like: leggy: sn pushed along: sn w ldrs: led ½-wy: styd on wl towards fin)....— **1** 4/6[1] 78+ 22
1801[2] **Panama House** (TDEasterby) **2-9-0** LCharnock(3) (chsd ldrs: rdn to chal ins fnl f: nt qckn)....¾ **2** 9/1[3] 81 25
Empire Park (MJohnston) **2-9-0** JWeaver(1) (wl grwn: rn green & sn outpcd: hdwy over 1f out: styd on towards fin)....2½ **3** 12/1 74+ 18
1645[7] **Elsinore (IRE)** (MrsJRRamsden) **2-8-9** JFortune(8) (trckd ldrs: shkn up & kpt on fnl f)....½ **4** 14/1 68 12
1839[3] **Burnt Yates (IRE)** (MWEasterby) **2-9-0** TLucas(2) (lw: led to ½-wy: wkng whn n.m.r ent fnl f)....½ **5** 11/4[2] 72 16
Watchman (TPTate) **2-9-0** NConnorton(5) (w'like: leggy: scope: bit bkwd: w ldrs tl wknd 2f out: eased)....8 **6** 50/1 50 —
Two Williams (MWEasterby) **2-9-0** DaleGibson(9) (w'like: str: bit bkwd: s.i.s: hdwy ½-wy: wknd & eased over 1f out)....1¼ **7** 20/1 47 —
2042[6] **Cherokee Charlie** (RCraggs) **2-9-0** DeanMcKeown(10) (bit bkwd: s.s: hdwy & hung bdly lft after 2f: sn lost pl)....nk **8** 50/1 46 —
Dougs Dream (IRE) (MrsASwinbank) **2-8-9** NDay(4) (w'like: s.i.s: sn drvn along & wl bhd)....¾ **9** 25/1 39 —
(SP 123.6%) **9 Rn**

1m 14.3 (2.50) CSF £7.93 TOTE £1.70: £1.10 £1.60 £2.90 (£5.60) Trio £17.00 OWNER Cheveley Park Stud (NEWMARKET) BRED Cheveley Park Stud Ltd
Eloquent, a likeable filly, ran green and had to be rousted along to get to the head of affairs. In the end she scored tidily. Clearly useful, a step up to seven will be no problem. (4/6: op 6/4)
1801 Panama House again wore a tongue-strap. Challenging inside the last, he flashed his tail and in the end the winner proved much too strong. (9/1: op 6/1)
Empire Park has plenty of size and scope. He showed a fair bit of knee action going down and, after being outpaced and running green, he was putting in some pleasing work at the finish. He probably needs seven already and is sure to improve and make his mark. (12/1: op 7/1)
1645 Elsinore (IRE), an excitable type, took time to settle. Her fourth place here will qualify her for a handicap mark with one more educational outing her belt. (14/1)
1839 Burnt Yates (IRE) possibly found the ground too fast and was fading when tightened up inside the last. (11/4)
Watchman proved keen in the early stages. In need of the race, his rider was very kind on him. He will probably need at least one more outing before he is ready to do himself justice. (50/1)

2203 BBC RADIO CUMBRIA (S) STKS (3-Y.O+) (Class G)
2-45 (2-45) **5f 207y** £2,398.50 (£671.00: £325.50) Stalls: Centre GOING minus 0.45 sec per fur (F)

SP RR SF

1864[2] **Nervous Rex (55)** (WRMuir) **3-8-5**(7) JWilkinson(15) (hmpd on ins after ½-wy: gd hdwy & swtchd lft over 1f out: qcknd to ld ins fnl f: edgd rt & sn clr)....— **1** 5/1[3] 61 35
1079[8] **Needle Match (48)** (JJO'Neill) **4-9-10** JCarroll(6) (lw: hld up: effrt & n.m.r over 2f out: ev ch ins fnl f: edgd lft & nt qckn)....2½ **2** 12/1 59 40
1676[4] **Ultra Beet (64)** (PCHaslam) **5-9-10b** JWeaver(14) (lw: led tl ins fnl f)....1¾ **3** 9/2[2] 55 36
2017[9] **Fine Times (60)** (CWFairhurst) **3-8-12v** DeanMcKeown(10) (b.off hind: sn chsng ldrs: kpt on one pce fnl 2f) 1¼ **4** 9/1 46 20
2061[5] **Here Comes a Star (46)** (JMCarr) **9-9-5** ACulhane(4) (lw: hdwy over 2f out: ev ch ins fnl f: no ex)....nk **5** 8/1 45 26
1835[12] **King of Show (IRE) (46)** (RAllan) **6-9-0v**(5) RFfrench(11) (bhd: hdwy on outside over 1f out: styd on towards fin)....1 **6** 16/1 43 24
Mr Fortywinks (IRE) (62) (JLEyre) **3-8-12** FLynch(3) (unruly in paddock: s.i.s: bhd tl styd on appr fnl f)....nk **7** 11/1 42 16
2044[7] **Express Girl (60)** (DMoffatt) **3-8-4**(3) DarrenMoffatt(7) (chsd ldrs tl rdn & lost pl ½-wy: styd on appr fnl f)....1¾ **8** 8/1 32 6
1998[10] **Terry's Rose (53)** (RHollinshead) **3-8-7** KDarley(12) (chsd ldrs: rdn & nt clr run on ins over 2f out: no imp whn hmpd over 1f out)....1¾ **9** 8/1 28 2
1865[2] **Marino Street (58)** (PDEvans) **4-9-0** JFortune(2) (chsd ldrs: rdn ½-wy: sn wl outpcd)....2 **10** 7/2[1] 22 3
304[9] **Imp Express (IRE) (40)** (GMMoore) **4-9-5** NCarlisle(1) (chsd ldrs tl wknd over 1f out)....1½ **11** 16/1 23 4
1430[10] **Shark (IRE)** (KAMorgan) **4-9-2**(3) OPears(8) (chsd ldrs: lost pl over 2f out)....s.h **12** 33/1 23 4
1428[10] **Little Papoose (33)** (BAMcMahon) **4-9-0** LNewton(9) (chsd ldrs: hung rt & wknd 2f out)....¾ **13** 33/1 16 —
1861[5] **Forecast (39)** (KAMorgan) **4-9-5** DaleGibson(5) (b: sn bhd)....nk **14** 16/1 20 1

896[23]	**Wild Prospect (23)** (ABailey) **9-9-5** LCharnock(13) (a bhd)	1¾	**15**	33/1	15	—
				(SP 142.9%)		**15 Rn**

1m 13.5 (1.70) CSF £68.87 TOTE £5.40: £1.70 £4.50 £2.10 (£54.00) Trio £154.10 OWNER Mr Michael Payton (LAMBOURN) BRED Hellwood Stud Farm
WEIGHT FOR AGE 3yo-7lb
Bt in 4,100gns
1864 Nervous Rex is well named. Short of room on the inner, he eventually made his way to the wide outside but, after hitting the front, he dived right as he shot clear. (5/1)
610 Needle Match, having his first outing for seven weeks, was without the blinkers. After meeting trouble, he had every chance but was left for dead by the winner in the closing stages. (12/1)
1676 Ultra Beet ran well and presumably needed the outing at Warwick last time, his first for eight weeks. (9/2)
1496 Fine Times ran much better after two poor efforts. (9/1)
2061 Here Comes a Star saw a lot of daylight on the outside. (8/1)

2204 EDMUNDSON ELECTRICAL H'CAP (0-80) (3-Y.O+) (Class D)
3-15 (3-16) **6f 206y** £3,533.75 (£1,070.00: £522.50: £248.75) Stalls: High GOING minus 0.45 sec per fur (F)

				SP	RR	SF
1861*	**Winter Scout (USA) (57)** (RAFahey) **9-8-6**(7) RWinston(9) (lw: trckd ldrs: edged rt & led over 1f out: hld on wl towards fin)	—	**1**	11/2	67	31
2019[2]	**Mr Cube (IRE) (48)** (JMBradley) **7-7-13b**(5) RFfrench(1) (hld up: lost pl 3f out: styng on whn hmpd over 1f out: kpt on wl towards fin)	½	**2**	4/1[2]	57	21
1761[2]	**Allinson's Mate (IRE) (68)** (TDBarron) **9-9-5b**(5) KimberleyHart(3) (lw: trckd ldrs: styng on u.p whn wnt rt just ins fnl f)	nk	**3**	5/1[3]	76	40
1994[3]	**Euro Sceptic (IRE) (42)** (TDEasterby) **5-7-12** LCharnock(7) (lw: hld up: effrt over 2f out: hung rt & n.m.r over 1f out: kpt on same pce)	½	**4**	7/2[1]	49	13
1816[7]	**Crissem (IRE) (62)** (RHollinshead) **4-9-4** FLynch(10) (trckd ldrs: effrt over 3f out: styd on one pce appr fnl f)	¾	**5**	25/1	67	31
1830[12]	**Rymer's Rascal (57)** (EJAlston) **5-8-13** ACulhane(5) (lw: trckd ldrs: led over 2f out tl over 1f out: kpt on same pce)	s.h	**6**	8/1	62	26
1830[6]	**Oriel Lad (40)** (DonEnricoIncisa) **4-7-10b** KimTinkler(2) (hld up: outpaced over 3f out: styd on fnl 2f)	1¾	**7**	16/1	41	5
1631[12]	**Welcome Lu (41)** (JLHarris) **4-7-11**ow1 DaleGibson(8) (led tl over 3f out: wknd & eased over 1f out)	6	**8**	10/1	28	—
	Fonzy (66) (MrsSJSmith) **3-8-10**(3) OPears(4) (unruly s: w ldr: led over 3f out tl over 2f out: wknd & eased over 1f out)	1½	**9**	20/1	50	5
1830[7]	**Cee-Jay-Ay (47)** (JBerry) **10-8-0**(3) PFessey(6) (s.s: reluctant to r: hdwy u.p 5f out: wknd over 2f out)	½	**10**	8/1	30	—
				(SP 120.1%)		**10 Rn**

1m 28.3 (2.60) CSF £26.13 CT £111.37 TOTE £6.80: £2.80 £1.60 £1.40 (£18.00) Trio £21.10 OWNER Mrs S. M. Russell (MALTON) BRED Virginia Kraft Payson
LONG HANDICAP Oriel Lad 7-8
WEIGHT FOR AGE 3yo-9lb
1861* Winter Scout (USA), who looked particularly well, was recording his first success over seven. (11/2)
2019 Mr Cube (IRE) was probably the worst sufferer in what was a very rough race run at a modest pace to halfway. (4/1)
1761 Allinson's Mate (IRE), 10lb higher than when successful at Doncaster three outings ago, suddenly ducked right just inside the last but recovered to be staying on again at the line. (5/1)
1994 Euro Sceptic (IRE), who is hard to win with, ran into some trouble but it was basically of his own making. He persisted in hanging right under pressure. (7/2)
Crissem (IRE), who has only had five outings since winning as a two-year-old at Haydock, has hopefully put her problems behind her. (25/1)
Welcome Lu (10/1: op 20/1)

2205 CROWTHER HOMES CARLISLE BELL H'CAP (0-80) (3-Y.O+) (Class D)
3-45 (3-48) **7f 214y** £7,490.00 (£2,270.00: £1,110.00: £530.00) Stalls: High GOING minus 0.45 sec per fur (F)

				SP	RR	SF
1781[4]	**Rainbow Rain (USA) (73)** (MJohnston) **3-9-1** MRoberts(11) (lw: hld up & plld hrd: effrt over 3f out: nt clr run over 1f out: swtchd outside & fin wl to ld last strides)	—	**1**	6/1[2]	81	41
1775[2]	**Bollin Frank (71)** (TDEasterby) **5-9-9** LCharnock(7) (lw: trckd ldrs: led over 1f out tl nr fin)	¾	**2**	5/1[1]	78	48
1858*	**Topatori (IRE) (72)** (MHTompkins) **3-9-0** DBiggs(2) (trckd ldrs: ev ch over 1f out: nt qckn wl ins fnl f)	s.h	**3**	9/1	78	38
1994[4]	**Thatched (IRE) (54)** (REBarr) **7-8-6** DeanMcKeown(8) (hld up: effrt over 2f out: styd on fnl f)	1½	**4**	16/1	57	27
1800*	**Bowcliffe (51)** (EJAlston) **6-8-3** GDuffield(3) (lw: hld up: smooth hdwy over 2f out: nr clr run over 1f out: kpt on same pce)	½	**5**	8/1[3]	53	23
1471[2]	**Quilling (75)** (MDods) **5-9-10**(3) CTeague(12) (trckd ldrs: plld hrd: hmpd & lost pl after 2f: hdwy on ins over 1f out: fell sn after line: dead)	nk	**6**	16/1	77	47
1739[10]	**Pride of Pendle (67)** (MartynWane) **8-9-5** JCarroll(14) (sltly hmpd s: bhd: swtchd outside & styd on wl last 150 yards)	s.h	**7**	8/1[3]	69	39
1800[8]	**Gilling Dancer (IRE) (51)** (PCalver) **4-8-0**(3) DarrenMoffatt(1) (mid div: hdwy over 2f out: sn rdn & no imp)	1¾	**8**	25/1	49	19
2043[2]	**Lay The Blame (72)** (MDHammond) **4-9-10** ACulhane(9) (lw: bhd & drvn along over 3f out: kpt on appr fnl f: n.d)	hd	**9**	10/1	70	40
1862[4]	**Bulsara (56)** (CWFairhurst) **5-8-5**(3) PFessey(13) (chsd ldrs: drvn along over 3f out: sn wl outpcd)	1¼	**10**	12/1	52	22
1833[5]	**Raed (67)** (MrsASwinbank) **4-9-5** NDay(5) (led tl hdd & wknd over 1f out)	1¼	**11**	16/1	60	30
1862[5]	**Spanish Verdict (54)** (DenysSmith) **10-7-13**(7) CLowther(6) (lw: chsd ldrs tl wknd over 1f out)	s.h	**12**	12/1	47	17
1652*	**Murphy's Gold (IRE) (52)** (RAFahey) **6-7-11**(7) RWinston(10) (hld up & plld hrd: effrt over 2f out: sn wknd)	1	**13**	5/1[1]	43	13
1472[16]	**Talented Ting (IRE) (47)** (PCHaslam) **8-7-8**(5) RFfrench(15) (swvd lft s: a bhd)	3½	**14**	16/1	31	1
1584[7]	**King Athelstan (USA) (59)** (BAMcMahon) **9-8-4**(7) SRighton(4) (hld up: hdwy over 3f out: sn wknd)	nk	**15**	16/1	42	12
				(SP 137.6%)		**15 Rn**

1m 39.0 (2.00) CSF £37.51 CT £270.54 TOTE £6.90: £1.90 £2.80 £2.90 (£17.90) Trio £140.90 OWNER Maktoum Al Maktoum (MIDDLEHAM) BRED Louise I. Humphrey, Pierce & Pierce & G. Watts Hum
WEIGHT FOR AGE 3yo-10lb
OFFICIAL EXPLANATION Murphy's Gold (IRE): slipped on the bend and lost a shoe.
IN-FOCUS: This completed a full set for Michael Roberts, eleven times Champion Jockey in his native South Africa. He has now ridden a winner on all thirty-seven British Flat tracks since his first success at Ayr in April 1978.

1781 Rainbow Rain (USA), stepping up to a mile for the first time, proved well suited by it. Keen early on, he had to be switched wide to get a run, but finished with a real flourish to get up near the line. On the evidence of this, an even longer trip may suit him, and there are surely more races to be won with this grand type. (6/1)
1775 Bollin Frank, on a 2lb higher mark, had the prize whipped from under his nose. (5/1)
1858* Topatori (IRE) probably ran her best race yet, underlining the revival in her stable's fortunes. (9/1)
1994 Thatched (IRE) was running from a 3lb higher mark than he has ever won off. (16/1)
1800* Bowcliffe, as usual, travelled smoothly after meeting trouble. He found the 5lb rise in the weights too much to handle. (8/1)
1471 Quilling, a real character and a winner of four races, was sadly fatally injured. (16/1)
1472 Pride of Pendle, just 1lb higher than when successful in a competitive handicap at Ayr in September, ran easily her best race yet for her new trainer, and she is one to keep an eye on form now on. (8/1)
1652* Murphy's Gold (IRE) dropped right out after refusing to settle. (5/1)

2206 C.G. TRUCK H'CAP (0-70) (3-Y.O) (Class E)

4-15 (4-31) **5f 207y** £3,063.90 (£928.20: £453.60: £216.30) Stalls: Centre GOING minus 0.36 sec per fur (F)

				SP	RR	SF
1864*	**Court Express (63)** (TJEtherington) **3-9-5** ACulhane(1) (sn bhd & pushed along: hdwy over 2f out: rdn to ld ins fnl f: r.o wl)	—	**1**	5/2[2]	74	47
1730[9]	**Bold Brief (51)** (DenysSmith) **3-8-7** LCharnock(5) (trckd ldrs: led 2f out tl ins fnl f: r.o same pce)	1½	**2**	6/1	58	31
1691[7]	**Tailwind (65)** (WRMuir) **3-9-7** MRoberts(2) (chsd ldrs: hung rt ½-wy: sn outpcd)	4	**3**	5/1[3]	61	34
2002[9]	**Legend of Aragon (50)** (JAGlover) **3-8-6** GDuffield(6) (sn pushed along: nvr nr to chal)	¾	**4**	9/1	44	17
1691[6]	**Royal Cascade (IRE) (55)** (BAMcMahon) **3-8-11** LNewton(8) (s.i.s: sn drvn along & chsng ldrs: wknd 2f out)	s.h	**5**	10/1	49	22
2017*	**Priory Gardens (IRE) (47)** (JMBradley) **3-7-12**(5) 7x RFfrench(7) (led to 2f out: wknd over 1f out)	1¼	**6**	5/4[1]	38	11
				(SP 123.1%)	**6 Rn**	

1m 13.7 (1.90) CSF £17.84 CT £66.93 TOTE £3.10: £1.70 £3.10 (£20.10) OWNER Mr J. Pain (MALTON) BRED J. A. Pain
1864* Court Express ran an almost identical race to last time and, in the end, scored decisively. (5/2)
1496 Bold Brief, with the blinkers left off, made the best of the way home but, in the end, the winner proved much too strong. (6/1)
1451* Tailwind gave his rider no co-operation, wanting to do nothing but hang. (5/1: op 3/1)
1580 Legend of Aragon had no headgear on this time. (9/1)
1691 Royal Cascade (IRE) seems better suited by the All-Weather surfaces. (10/1: op 5/1)
2017* Priory Gardens (IRE), who was well drawn at Thirsk, ran a poor race even considering that he was shouldering a 7lb penalty. (5/4)

2207 KLOCKNER MOELLER MAIDEN H'CAP (0-60) (3-Y.O+) (Class F)

4-45 (4-54) **2m 1f 52y** £2,654.00 (£744.00: £362.00) Stalls: High GOING minus 0.36 sec per fur (F)

				SP	RR	SF
865[11]	**Black Ice Boy (IRE) (28)** (RBastiman) **6-8-10b** DeanMcKeown(2) (mde all: styd on fnl 2f: hld on wl)	—	**1**	33/1	37	—
1469[6]	**Arisaig (IRE) (53)** (PCalver) **3-8-12**(3) DarrenMoffatt(3) (mid div: drvn along over 4f out: styd on fnl 2f: nt rch wnr)	½	**2**	11/2[1]	62	5
1996[8]	**Penny Peppermint (26)** (REBarr) **5-8-8** JCarroll(8) (s.i.s: bhd: hdwy on outside over 2f out: styd on fnl f)	3	**3**	20/1	32	—
2000[7]	**Hancock (30)** (JHetherton) **5-8-7**(5) RFfrench(6) (lw: prom: outpcd over 3f out: hung rt: kpt on)	2½	**4**	11/2[1]	33	—
1469[8]	**Ocean Breeze (40)** (JSWainwright) **3-7-11**(5) JBramhill(7) (hdwy 11f out: rdn & one pce fnl 3f)	hd	**5**	14/1	43	—
262[2]	**Old Hush Wing (IRE) (45)** (PCHaslam) **4-9-13** JFortune(15) (chsd ldrs: drvn along 9f out: outpcd fnl 3f)	2½	**6**	7/1[3]	46	9
1996[4]	**Warrlin (59)** (CWFairhurst) **3-9-0**(7) TSiddall(11) (hld up: hdwy 10f out: rdn over 3f out: nvr nr to chal)	3	**7**	7/1[3]	57	—
1779[15]	**Mick's Tycoon (IRE) (25)** (TRWatson) **9-8-7** GDuffield(12) (bhd: reminders after 1f: sme hdwy 2f out: n.d)	¾	**8**	20/1	23	—
1817[5]	**Ship's Dancer (28)** (DonEnricoIncisa) **4-8-10b** KimTinkler(4) (bhd: sme hdwy 2f out: n.d)	5	**9**	20/1	21	—
	Cuillin Caper (25) (TRWatson) **5-8-7** TWilliams(9) (trckd ldrs: ev ch & rdn over 2f out: wknd qckly over 1f out)	¾	**10**	10/1	17	—
2000[4]	**Euphoric Illusion (46)** (MrsSJSmith) **6-9-11**(3) OPears(13) (bolted gng to s: hdwy 10f out: sn rdn: lost pl 3f out)	hd	**11**	11/2[1]	38	1
2145[2]	**Bruz (27)** (LLungo) **6-8-9** DaleGibson(10) (bhd: hdwy over 4f out: sn wknd & eased)	4	**12**	6/1[2]	15	—
1996[7]	**Valiant Dash (23)** (JSGoldie) **11-7-12**(7) JMcAuley(1) (chsd ldrs: drvn along & outpcd 8f out: sn lost pl)	1¼	**13**	14/1	10	—
1785[5]	**Moorbird (IRE) (50)** (JLHarris) **3-8-9b**(3) PFessey(14) (chsd ldrs to ½-wy: sn lost pl)	6	**14**	10/1	32	—
1838[7]	**Palace River (IRE) (37)** (DMoffatt) **9-9-5** LCharnock(5) (p.u after 6f: dead)		**P**	14/1	—	—
				(SP 140.8%)	**15 Rn**	

3m 52.2 (15.20) CSF £207.85 CT £3,515.28 TOTE £132.50: £12.10 £1.90 £8.20 (£499.60) Trio Not won; £483.66 to Salisbury 26/6/97
OWNER Mrs Judith Marshall (WETHERBY) BRED Swettenham Stud and Barronstown Stud
WEIGHT FOR AGE 3yo-20lb
Black Ice Boy (IRE), who was tailed off first time, was given an enterprising ride in this low-grade maiden handicap. All he does is stay and his trainer reckons he has only just got over the virus. (33/1)
1469 Arisaig (IRE), 3lb higher and stepping-up in distance, stuck to his guns in determined fashion, but was never going to reel in the winner. (11/2)
Penny Peppermint returned from the wilderness. (20/1)
Hancock gave his rider problems, persisting in hanging into the fence. (11/2)
Ocean Breeze is woefully one-paced. (14/1)
262 Old Hush Wing (IRE) was having his first outing since finishing fourth over hurdles in February. (7/1)
2000 Euphoric Illusion, top weight yet rated only forty-six on the official scale, proved headstrong going down and over-shot the start. Hard at work at the halfway mark, he dropped right out turning in. (11/2)

2208 CROWTHER HOMES BURGH BARONY RACES GENTLEMEN'S LIMITED STKS (0-60) (3-Y.O+) (Class F)

5-15 (5-19) **1m 4f** £2,430.00 (£680.00: £330.00) Stalls: High GOING minus 0.36 sec per fur (F)

				SP	RR	SF
1981[8]	**Sherqy (IRE) (56)** (SEKettlewell) **5-11-0** MrABalding(1) (lw: hld up: hdwy on bit 2f out: led ins fnl f: smoothly)	—	**1**	Evens[1]	47	38
*1943**	**Heighth of Fame (43)** (JHetherton) **6-11-2**(4)ow4 MrJByrne(7) (led: hung lft over 3f out: hdd ins fnl f: no ch w wnr)	1½	**2**	9/2[3]	51	38
	Able Player (USA) (25) (KJDrewry) **10-10-10**(4) MrKDrewry(3) (chsd ldrs: drvn along over 4f out: one pce fnl 2f)	4	**3**	16/1	40	31
1840[5]	**Cois Na Farraige (IRE) (55)** (MissLAPerratt) **4-11-0** MrRHale(6) (trckd ldrs: rdn & outpcd over 2f out: edgd lft: kpt on fnl f)	2½	**4**	9/1	36	27

2170[2] **Yet Again (47)** (MissGayKelleway) **5-11-8** MrTMcCarthy(4) (trckd ldrs: effrt & hung rt 2f out: wknd over 1f out) ....nk **5** 2/1[2] 44 35
1654[9] **So Keen (42)** (ABailey) **4-10-10**(4) MrDBShaw(2) (unruly: hld up: hdwy over 2f out: sn rdn & wknd)....2½ **6** 14/1 33 24
1467[14] **Interaction (31)** (RCraggs) **3-9-10**(4) MrOMcPhail(5) (chsd ldr: drvn along over 3f out: wknd over 1f out: eased) 3 **7** 25/1 29 6
(SP 127.9%) **7 Rn**

2m 37.6 (8.60) CSF £6.79 TOTE £2.60: £1.20 £1.90 (£8.50) OWNER Miss N. F. Thesiger (MIDDLEHAM) BRED Shadwell Estate Company Limited
WEIGHT FOR AGE 3yo-14lb
1840 Sherqy (IRE) looked to have been found a good opportunity, and took this in smooth fashion under a well-judged ride. (Evens)
1943* Heighth of Fame forced the pace but, in the end, the winner proved much too good. He is much more effective on the All-Weather. (9/2)
Able Player (USA), making a return to Flat action after a lengthy absence, won a low-grade handicap hurdle at Huntingdon in April. He did not lack encouragement from the saddle. (16/1)
1840 Cois Na Farraige (IRE) ran much better than he had at Hamilton. (9/1)
2170 Yet Again was having his second outing in three days, and he looked far from enthusiastic about it. (2/1)
So Keen, dropping in distance, gave his rider problems. (14/1)

T/Jkpt: Not won; £5,749.62 to Salisbury 26/6/97. T/Plpt: £216.70 (103.54 Tckts). T/Qdpt: £70.10 (14.89 Tckts) WG

1657-CHESTER (L-H) (Soft, Heavy patches becoming Heavy)
Wednesday June 25th
All Races - hand timed due to a technical fault
WEATHER: rain WIND: nil

2209 YELLOW LABEL CLAIMING STKS (3-Y.O+) (Class D)
6-50 (6-51) **1m 2f 75y** £3,493.00 (£1,054.00: £512.00: £241.00) Stalls: High GOING: 0.70 sec per fur (GS)

SP RR SF
1981[4] **Break the Rules (84)** (MCPipe) **5-9-12** KDarley(2) (hld up: hdwy over 3f out: rdn to ld over 1f out: sn clr) ....— **1** 2/5[1] 76 53
2049[2] **Nicola's Princess (44)** (BAMcMahon) **4-8-13** MWigham(4) (lw: w ldr over 7f: hrd drvn 2f out: kpt on fnl f: no ch w wnr) 7 **2** 16/1 52 29
1782[7] **Whittle Rock (72)** (MrsMReveley) **4-9-7** ACulhane(3) (lw: stdd s: hdwy 3f out: rdn 2f out: no imp) ....3½ **3** 9/2[2] 55 32
2004[13] **Steal 'Em (60)** (ABailey) **4-8-9v**[1](5) PRoberts(5) (mde most tl rdn & hdd over 1f out: wknd qckly) 7 **4** 20/1 37 14
1834[3] **Taragona** (RHollinshead) **4-8-10** FLynch(1) (lw: hld up: drvn along & lost tch over 3f out: t.o) ....9 **5** 10/1[3] 19 —
Thenorthernplayboy (IRE) (TWall) **4-8-13b**[1](3) DGriffiths(6) (bkwd: lost tch over 4f out: t.o) ....dist **6** 50/1 — —
(SP 111.3%) **6 Rn**

2m 23.2 (14.50) CSF £7.83 TOTE £1.40: £1.30 £2.60 (£5.30) OWNER Mr A. J. Lomas (WELLINGTON) BRED Cleaboy Farms Co
Break The Rules clmd GMcCreedy-Smith £15,000
IN-FOCUS: **The continous rain throughout the evening, which got heavier as time progressed, made conditions almost unraceable for the last two races, and there will have to be a doubt about the strength of the form.**
1981 Break the Rules, twice a winner here in the past, had to be bustled along to take command entering the straight but, once in front, the rest was easy. (2/5)
2049 Nicola's Princess was struggling to hold her pitch as the pace lifted on the approach to the straight but, with stamina coming into play, she stayed on again in the latter stages without having the speed to trouble the winner. (16/1)
1389 Whittle Rock can cope with testing ground but her stamina is suspect and she was in trouble on the turn for home. (9/2: op 3/1)
Steal 'Em did her best to make all but she had company for most of the way and she was down to a walk after being collared early in the straight. (20/1)
1834 Taragona (10/1: 8/1-12/1)

2210 LA GRANDE DAME ROSE H'CAP (0-85) (3-Y.O+ F & M) (Class D)
7-20 (7-21) **1m 4f 66y** £3,473.50 (£1,048.00: £509.00: £239.50) Stalls: Low GOING: 0.70 sec per fur (GS)

SP RR SF
1562[3] **Kathryn's Pet (60)** (MrsMReveley) **4-8-11** ACulhane(2) (lw: set slow pce: mde all: qcknd clr 3f out: hld on nr fin) ....— **1** 5/2[1] 70 41
1973[7] **Manazil (IRE) (81)** (RWArmstrong) **3-9-4** RPrice(6) (a.p: rdn over 3f out: r.o wl towards fin) 1¼ **2** 11/1 89 46
2049[7] **Rasayel (USA) (73)** (PDEvans) **7-9-5**(5) RFfrench(1) (chsd ldrs tl dropped rr 5f out: rallied u.p 2f out: styd on) 3 **3** 7/1 78 49
436[5] **Toi Toi (IRE) (73)** (DWPArbuthnot) **3-8-10** SWhitworth(3) (b.hind: bkwd: hld up: pushed along 6f out: hrd rdn over 2f out: no imp) ....4 **4** 100/30[2] 72 29
1923[2] **Roufontaine (77)** (WRMuir) **6-10-0** MRoberts(4) (lw: s.s: hdwy over 4f out: wknd 3f out: t.o) ....12 **5** 4/1[3] 61 32
764* **Dominant Duchess (80)** (JWHills) **3-9-3** AClark(5) (swtg: sn chsng wnr: rdn & wknd over 3f out: t.o) ....3½ **6** 4/1[3] 59 16
(SP 112.5%) **6 Rn**

2m 53.2 (17.00) CSF £26.69 TOTE £2.60: £1.40 £4.80 (£17.70) OWNER Mr Bill Brown (SALTBURN) BRED N. J. Dent
WEIGHT FOR AGE 3yo-14lb
OFFICIAL EXPLANATION **Roufontaine: could not handle the very soft ground.**
1562 Kathryn's Pet made up for an unlucky run at Ayr with a fine tactical ride but she was getting very leg-weary inside the last furlong and the winning post arrived plenty soon enough. (5/2)
889* Manazil (IRE) had more use made of her in these testing conditions, and the way she stayed on after looking in trouble out in the country would suggest that stamina could be her strong suit. (11/1: 7/1-12/1)
2049 Rasayel (USA) has won on the All-Weather but she did not relish these conditions and it was only her undoubted stamina that enabled her to make the frame. (7/1)
Toi Toi (IRE), taking on handicappers for the first time, was not fully tuned up after a three month break and though she should be in her element at this sort of trip was unable to get herself into it. (100/30)

2211 LE PRIX DE LA GRANDE DAME RATED STKS H'CAP (0-100) (3-Y.O+) (Class B)
7-50 (7-52) **6f 18y** £9,655.60 (£3,600.40: £1,750.20: £741.00: £320.50: £152.30) Stalls: Low GOING: 0.70 sec per fur (GS)

SP RR SF
1317[8] **Charlie Sillett (84)** (BWHills) **5-8-4**(3) JDSmith(1) (hdwy over 2f out: led 1f out: r.o wl) ....— **1** 6/1[3] 94 66

				SP	RR	SF
1948[7]	**Westcourt Magic (90)** (MWEasterby) **4-8-13** MWigham(7) (chsd ldrs: rdn over 1f out: kpt on wl ins fnl f)	1½	2	20/1	96	68
1658[5]	**Gadge (84)** (ABailey) **6-8-7** DWright(6) (w ldr: led over 3f out to 1f out: hrd rdn & no ex fnl f)	1¾	3	5/1[2]	85	57
1799[4]	**Ziggy's Dancer (USA) (85)** (EJAlston) **6-8-8** RLappin(2) (hdwy on ins over 1f out: nt rch ldrs)	2½	4	8/1	80	52
2105*	**Selhurstpark Flyer (IRE) (97)** (JBerry) **6-9-1**(5) 3x PRoberts(3) (b: lw: slt ld over 2f: rdn & ev ch over 1f out: wknd fnl f)	8	5	15/8[1]	71	43
1634[5]	**Blues Queen (86)** (MRChannon) **3-7-13**(3)ow2 PPMurphy(5) (chsd ldrs 4f: sn wknd)	3½	6	25/1	51	14
671[7]	**My Melody Parkes (98)** (JBerry) **4-9-7** KDarley(8) (bit bkwd: s.i.s: a bhd & outpcd)	hd	7	16/1	62	34
1948[8]	**Madly Sharp (95)** (JWWatts) **6-9-4** GDuffield(12) (hdwy over 2f out: sn hrd drvn: no imp)	¾	8	12/1	57	29
2134[12]	**Swino (86)** (PDEvans) **3-7-11**(5) RFfrench(10) (sn drvn along: a bhd & outpcd)	½	9	16/1	47	12
1948[10]	**West Humble (92)** (LadyHerries) **4-9-1** AClark(4) (outpcd: effrt ½-wy: no imp)	¾	10	16/1	51	23
1608[10]	**Taoiste (85)** (RWArmstrong) **4-8-8** RPrice(9) (effrt ½-wy: rdn & wknd 2f out: t.o)	9	11	33/1	20	—
1910a[5]	**Tadeo (95)** (MJohnston) **4-9-4** MRoberts(11) (b: chsd ldrs 3f: wknd qckly: t.o)		12	9/1	—	—

(SP 123.7%) **12 Rn**

1m 19.4 (6.10) CSF £115.24 CT £605.71 TOTE £6.30: £1.40 £7.30 £2.10 (£78.00) Trio £306.90 OWNER Mr John Sillett (LAMBOURN) BRED J. Sillett

LONG HANDICAP Gadge 8-5 Charlie Sillett 8-3

WEIGHT FOR AGE 3yo-7lb

Charlie Sillett, who had everything in his favour here and was well suited by the fast-run race, swooped to conquer entering the final furlong for a very smooth success. (6/1)

1948 Westcourt Magic has been out of sorts for quite some time and he has done all his winning on a sound surface, but he was back to something like his old self here and when conditions suit he could return to form. (20/1)

1658 Gadge eventually won the battle of the front runners but they had gone off at a suicidal pace and he was at the end of his tether once headed. (5/1)

1799 Ziggy's Dancer (USA) knows this track well, and though he may be better over the minimum trip nowadays he stuck to the rails and battled on to be nearest at the finish. (8/1)

2105* Selhurstpark Flyer (IRE) had probably not fully recovered from his hard-fought success at Royal Ascot six days ago, and his attempt to concede 10lb in a spirited duel with Gadge for supremacy obviously took its toll and he was legless on reaching the final furlong. (15/8)

1634 Blues Queen held her pitch behind the tearaway leading pair for the best part of half a mile before the exertions in the ground began to tell. (25/1)

Madly Sharp (12/1: op 8/1)

1910a Tadeo (9/1: op 6/1)

2212 WIDOW NOVICE STKS (2-Y.O) (Class D)

8-20 (8-22) **5f 16y** £3,454.00 (£1,042.00: £506.00: £238.00) Stalls: Low GOING: 0.70 sec per fur (GS)

				SP	RR	SF
1657[3]	**Jimmy Too** (BAMcMahon) **2-8-12** MWigham(7) (trckd ldrs: pushed along ½-wy: gd hdwy to ld fnl 50y)	—	1	13/2	66	37
1675[2]	**Sandside** (JBerry) **2-9-1**(3) PFessey(2) (lw: led tl wl ins fnl f)	½	2	9/4[1]	70	41
*1941**	**Pure Coincidence** (GLewis) **2-9-0** AClark(6) (lw: a.p: ev ch 1f out: wknd qckly fnl 150y)	7	3	3/1[2]	44	15
	Phantom Ring (ABailey) **2-8-7** MRoberts(4) (cmpt: bkwd: outpcd tl r.o ins fnl f)	2	4	12/1	31	2
	Super Snip (ABailey) **2-8-12** KDarley(1) (w'like: scope: bkwd: s.v.s: outpcd tl r.o ins fnl f)	½	5	7/1	35	6
1657[8]	**Dernier Croise (FR)** (BJMeehan) **2-8-12** MTebbutt(3) (w ldrs: rdn 2f out: wknd qckly)	1¼	6	100/30[3]	31	2

(SP 112.4%) **6 Rn**

67.3 secs (7.10) CSF £19.63 TOTE £6.80: £2.00 £1.80 (£6.50) OWNER Mr J. D. Graham (TAMWORTH) BRED J. D. Graham

1657 Jimmy Too, making hard work of it from halfway, still had all of five lengths to make up passing the furlong marker but, with the leaders down to a walk, he stuck on under strong driving to forge ahead nearing the line. (13/2)

1675 Sandside, returning to the minimum trip, looked to have the situation under control once she had shaken off Pure Coincidence, but try as he might the conditions sapped his reserves and he was forced to give best. (9/4)

1941* Pure Coincidence failed to live up to his earlier billing but he gave it all he had and had every chance until hitting a brick wall halfway through the last furlong. (3/1: op 2/1)

Phantom Ring, a choppy mover from a good winning family, found the early pace too much for her but she was picking up in the closing stages and will be all the wiser for the experience. (12/1: op 5/1)

2213 PONSARDIN MAIDEN STKS (3-Y.O) (Class D)

8-50 (8-50) **1m 5f 89y** £3,680.00 (£1,030.00: £500.00) Stalls: Low GOING: 1.15 sec per fur (S)

				SP	RR	SF
1846[4]	**High Intrigue (IRE)** (HRACecil) **3-9-0** AMcGlone(3) (lw: mde virtually all: clr over 3f out: drvn out)	—	1	2/9[1]	68	—
1469[7]	**Spondulicks (IRE) (50)** (BPJBaugh) **3-9-0** GHind(2) (lw: chsd ldrs: rdn 5f out: grad lost tch)	18	2	4/1[2]	47	—
2059[8]	**Eternal Host (IRE) (40)** (RHollinshead) **3-8-11**(3) DGriffiths(1) (s.s: a bhd: t.o fnl 6f)	dist	3	16/1[3]	—	—

(SP 107.7%) **3 Rn**

3m 26.0 (36.00) CSF £1.35 TOTE £1.20 (£1.30) OWNER Mrs E. A. Harris (NEWMARKET) BRED Airlie Stud

1846 High Intrigue (IRE), a very attractive colt, was faced with this simple task to get off the mark but his jockey never took things for granted and kept him up to his work right to the line. (2/9: 1/6-1/4)

1094 Spondulicks (IRE) did his best to make a race of it but he was being driven along in earnest five furlongs out and his measure had been taken. (4/1)

2214 RICH RESERVE H'CAP (0-80) (3-Y.O) (Class D)

9-20 (9-23) **7f 2y** £3,590.50 (£1,084.00: £527.00: £248.50) Stalls: Low GOING: 1.15 sec per fur (S)

				SP	RR	SF
1582*	**Woodbeck (78)** (JAGlover) **3-9-7** NDay(10) (lw: racd wd: chsd ldrs: led over 2f out: rdn clr fnl f)	—	1	8/1	86	51
1663[4]	**Muscatana (64)** (BWHills) **3-8-4**(3) JDSmith(7) (lw: racd ins: a.p: ev ch over 1f out: one pce ins fnl f)	3	2	12/1	65	30
2130[3]	**Rock Island Line (IRE) (71)** (JBerry) **3-8-9**(5) PRoberts(9) (s.s: hdwy over 2f out: rdn & one pce fnl f)	1¼	3	7/2[1]	69	34
	Nominator Lad (76) (BAMcMahon) **3-9-5** MWigham(2) (h.d.w: bkwd: hld up in rr: hdwy 3f out: styd on one pce appr fnl f)	3	4	14/1	68	33
1977[8]	**Baritone (71)** (JWWatts) **3-8-11**(3) PFessey(6) (lw: chsd ldrs tl rdn & wknd wl over 1f out)	6	5	7/1	49	14
1658[12]	**I Can't Remember (75)** (PDEvans) **3-8-13**(5) RFfrench(4) (lost pl ½-wy: sn bhd: t.o)	9	6	7/2[1]	32	—
1966[2]	**Davis Rock (67)** (WRMuir) **3-8-10** MRoberts(5) (lw: hld up: hdwy on ins over 2f out: eased whn btn appr fnl f: t.o)	3½	7	6/1[3]	16	—

1845[6] **Janie's Boy (70)** (MrsJCecil) **3-8-13** GDuffield(3) (lw: led over 1f: hrd drvn ½-wy: sn wknd: t.o) 9	**8**	4/1[2]	—	—
2020[5] **Gablesea (60)** (BPJBaugh) **3-8-3** GHind(8) (led over 5f out tl over 2f out: wknd qckly t.o) 12	**9**	25/1	—	—
		(SP 120.5%)	**9 Rn**	

1m 37.8 (12.60) CSF £93.33 CT £366.52 TOTE £10.80: £2.90 £5.40 £1.60 (£106.80) Trio £98.30 OWNER Mr B. H. Farr (WORKSOP) BRED Worksop Manor Stud Farm

1582* Woodbeck turned in a fine weight-carrying performance in ever-worsening conditions and, picking her ground on the wide outside, stayed on far too strongly for her rivals. (8/1: op 5/1)

873 Muscatana, in contrast to the winner, took the inside route. She was upsides entering the final furlong, but once pressure was applied she had nothing more to give. (12/1: op 8/1)

2130 Rock Island Line (IRE) was the hard luck story of the race for he gave away considerable ground with a slow start and yet still performed well. (7/2)

Nominator Lad gor very colty following a filly round the paddock, but ran well considering he was carrying so much condition. With his stable in unstoppable form, he is worth bearing in mind. (14/1)

1977 Baritone (7/1: op 7/2)

T/Plpt: £66.50 (264.48 Tckts). T/Qdpt: £13.20 (57.86 Tckts) IM

1766-**EPSOM (L-H) (Good to soft)**
Wednesday June 25th
WEATHER: overcast & damp WIND: mod across

2215 E.B.F. NOVICE STKS (2-Y.O) (Class D)
6-40 (6-42) **7f** £3,111.25 (£940.00: £457.50: £216.25) Stalls: Low GOING: 0.18 sec per fur (G)

		SP	RR	SF
*2047** **Calchas (IRE)** (SirMarkPrescott) **2-9-4** SSanders(4) (lw: chsd ldr: led 4f out: qcknd 2f out: easily) ....—	**1**	Evens[1]	81+	31
1924* **Indian Missile** (JLDunlop) **2-9-4** RHills(1) (lw: hld up: rdn over 3f out: chsd wnr ins fnl f: no imp) 5	**2**	100/30[3]	70	20
1932* **Overture (IRE)** (RHannon) **2-9-4** DaneO'Neill(2) (led 3f: rdn 3f out: wknd over 1f out) 3	**3**	3/1[2]	63	13
1267[5] **Wathbat Lion** (MAJarvis) **2-8-12** WRyan(3) (lw: rdn 3f out: nvr nr to chal) 1	**4**	8/1	54	4
1321[7] **Basic Style** (NACallaghan) **2-8-12** RHughes(5) (bhd fnl 4f) 2	**5**	66/1	50	—
		(SP 110.7%)	**5 Rn**	

1m 27.28 (6.98) CSF £4.30 TOTE £2.30: £1.10 £2.40 (£3.10) OWNER Sheikh Ahmed bin Saeed Al Maktoum (NEWMARKET) BRED Sheikh Ahmed bin Saeed al Maktoum

IN-FOCUS: Although only five runners, they looked a nice lot in the paddock and this race should not be under-estimated.

2047* Calchas (IRE), having his first run on grass after hacking up on the All-Weather at Wolverhampton last week, put up a very polished display, gaining a slender advantage rounding Tattenham Corner and breezing clear in the straight to win with a ton in hand. The rain-softened ground was no problem and he looks sure to go on to better things. (Evens)

1924* Indian Missile looked very well in the paddock but, although eventually winning the battle for second place inside the final furlong, was no match for the winner. (100/30)

1932* Overture (IRE) found the step-up from five to seven furlongs on this rain-softened ground too much. In front until nearly halfway, he was looking very leg-weary from below the distance, and was caught for the runner-up berth inside the final furlong. A drop in distance is needed. (3/1)

1267 Wathbat Lion looked in fine shape beforehand, but could never summon up the necessary turn of foot to get in a blow. (8/1)

2216 EVENING STANDARD H'CAP (0-80) (3-Y.O+) (Class D)
7-10 (7-19) **7f** £3,501.25 (£1,060.00: £517.50: £246.25) Stalls: Low GOING: 0.18 sec per fur (G)

		SP	RR	SF
1782[4] **Purchasing Power (IRE) (70)** (NACallaghan) **3-8-9** PatEddery(12) (lw: chsd ldr: led 3f out: rdn out) ....—	**1**	7/2[1]	78	42
2002[3] **Twin Creeks (61)** (VSoane) **6-8-9** CRutter(6) (lw: a.p: rdn over 2f out: unable qckn ins fnl f) 1½	**2**	11/1	66	39
1958[W] **Halowing (USA) (77)** (JGSmyth-Osbourne) **3-9-2** SSanders(10) (lw: a.p: rdn over 2f out: one pce) 2½	**3**	20/1	76	40
1963[4] **Newlands Corner (57)** (JAkehurst) **4-8-5b** DaneO'Neill(4) (lw: hrd rdn & hdwy over 1f out: r.o one pce) ....nk	**4**	11/1	55	28
1640[6] **Fionn de Cool (IRE) (64)** (RAkehurst) **6-8-12** TQuinn(8) (lw: hdwy 5f out: rdn over 2f out: wkng whn hung lft ins fnl f) ....¾	**5**	8/1	61	34
2006[8] **Sovereigns Court (61)** (LGCottrell) **4-8-9** DHolland(9) (lw: rdn over 2f out: hdwy over 1f out: one pce) ....½	**6**	5/1[2]	56	29
2006[12] **Victory Team (IRE) (75)** (GBBalding) **5-9-9** RHughes(3) (hdwy over 1f out: one pce) ....hd	**7**	25/1	70	43
2036[17] **Kingchip Boy (59)** (MJRyan) **8-8-7b** GCarter(13) (b: nvr nrr) 3	**8**	16/1	47	20
1935[11] **Zurs (IRE) (64)** (MissGayKelleway) **4-8-7**(5) RMullen(14) (s.s: nvr nrr) ....nk	**9**	12/1	52	25
1676[5] **Hard to Figure (80)** (RJHodges) **11-10-0** SDrowne(11) (lw: bhd fnl 3f) ....hd	**10**	16/1	67	40
1666[10] **Ed's Folly (IRE) (57)** (SDow) **4-8-5** JQuinn(7) (lw: led 4f: wknd over 1f out) ....nk	**11**	16/1	44	17
1658[4] **Stoppes Brow (77)** (GLMoore) **5-9-8v**(3) DO'Donohoe(1) (s.s: sme hdwy 2f out: wknd over 1f out) ....¾	**12**	11/2[3]	62	35
942[29] **Kind of Light (74)** (RGuest) **4-9-8** PBloomfield(5) (prom over 4f) 1	**13**	25/1	57	30
		(SP 119.8%)	**13 Rn**	

1m 25.69 (5.39) CSF £38.05 CT £633.32 TOTE £3.50: £2.00 £3.10 £6.90 (£17.70) Trio £128.60 OWNER Mr M Tabor & Mrs John Magnier (NEWMARKET) BRED Barronstown Stud and Roncon Ltd

WEIGHT FOR AGE 3yo-9lb

1782 Purchasing Power (IRE) was well-suited by the rain-softened ground. (7/2)

2002 Twin Creeks appreciated the return to seven furlongs. Never far away, he was only about a length down on the winner entering the final furlong, but failed to find that vital turn of foot. (11/1: 7/1-12/1)

853 Halowing (USA), who has dropped 11lb in the handicap since the beginning of the season, ran her best race of the campaign so far, playing an active role until tapped for toe in the final quarter-mile. (20/1)

1963 Newlands Corner, under pressure to pick up ground below the distance, struggled on and only just failed to take third prize. She has done all her winning on fast ground over six furlongs. (11/1)

1640 Fionn de Cool (IRE) is extremely difficult to win with. Soon in a handy position, he was already beaten when giving his rider steering problems inside the final furlong as he tried to hang left on the camber. One victory from forty-four starts says it all. (8/1: 5/1-9/1)

Sovereigns Court began a forward move below the distance, but could make no further impression inside the final furlong. He remains a maiden. (5/1)

2217 GALA STKS (Listed) (3-Y.O+) (Class A)
7-40 (7-42) **1m 2f 18y** £11,943.00 (£3,378.00: £1,649.00) Stalls: Low GOING: 0.18 sec per fur (G)

				SP	RR	SF
1767[3]	**Cap Juluca (IRE) (109)** (RCharlton) **5-9-4** RHughes(4) (lw: mde all: rdn out)	—	1	9/4[3]	114	33
1767[4]	**Amid Albadu (USA) (107)** (JLDunlop) **3-8-6** RHills(3) (lw: chsd wnr: rdn over 2f out: unable qckn)	1¼	2	6/4[1]	112	19
1740[2]	**Charlotte Corday (107)** (GWragg) **4-8-13** MHills(2) (hld up: rdn over 2f out: one pce)	5	3	15/8[2]	99	18

(SP 105.6%) **3 Rn**

2m 14.38 (10.38) CSF £5.11 TOTE £2.50 (£1.60) OWNER Mr Martin Myers (BECKHAMPTON) BRED Mrs N. Myers
WEIGHT FOR AGE 3yo-12lb

1767 Cap Juluca (IRE), who had his tongue tied for the first time, had gained all his six previous wins on a fast surface, but he appeared to have no problems with this rain-softened ground. Making it all, he carried his head awkwardly in the straight as he had done at the last meeting, but proved too good for the runner-up. He will remain in this class or Group Three company. (9/4: op 5/4)
1767 Amid Albadu (USA), a length behind the winner in the Group Three Diomed Stakes here on Derby day, was meeting that rival on identical terms. Looking extremely well beforehand, he was always just being held. (6/4)
1740 Charlotte Corday failed to cope with this rain-softened ground. (15/8)

2218 UBS H'CAP (0-75) (3-Y.O+) (Class D)
8-10 (8-13) **1m 4f 10y** £3,517.50 (£1,065.00: £520.00: £247.50) Stalls: Centre GOING: 0.18 sec per fur (G)

				SP	RR	SF
1844*	**Ancient Quest (73)** (NACallaghan) **4-10-0** PaulEddery(3) (stdy hdwy over 6f out: led 3f out: clr over 1f out: easily)	—	1	9/2[2]	88+	58
*1431**	**Glow Forum (52)** (LMontagueHall) **6-8-4**(3) DO'Donohoe(7) (stdy hdwy 8f out: led over 5f out to 3f out: hrd rdn over 2f out: unable qckn)	9	2	4/1[1]	55	25
1825[2]	**Courageous Knight (45)** (PHayward) **8-7-11**(3) MHenry(4) (dropped rr 7f out: rdn over 3f out: r.o one pce fnl f)	3	3	20/1	44	14
1968[7]	**Double Rush (IRE) (46)** (TGMills) **5-8-1** JQuinn(6) (swtg: rdn & hdwy over 2f out: one pce)	1	4	16/1	44	14
1985[3]	**Oberons Boy (IRE) (58)** (SDow) **4-8-13** WRyan(5) (lw: lost pl over 6f out: shkn up over 3f out: n.m.r over 2f out & over 1f out: swtchd lft: one pce)	½	5	14/1	55	25
1809[2]	**Statajack (IRE) (64)** (DRCElsworth) **9-9-5b** PatEddery(1) (b: nvr nr to chal)	½	6	7/1	60	30
1971[2]	**Chief Predator (USA) (55)** (RHannon) **3-7-10b** GBardwell(9) (lw: prom over 9f)	5	7	12/1	45	1
1641*	**Mr Browning (USA) (67)** (RAkehurst) **6-9-8b** TQuinn(10) (led over 6f: wknd over 2f out)	13	8	11/2[3]	40	10
1974[6]	**Alarico (FR) (62)** (IPWilliams) **4-9-3** RHughes(2) (chsd ldr over 3f: wknd over 2f out)	4	9	11/2[3]	29	—
1809[3]	***At Liberty (IRE) (65)*** (RHannon) **5-9-6b** DaneO'Neill(8) (Withdrawn not under Starter's orders: lame at s)		W	16/1	—	—

(SP 112.3%) **9 Rn**

2m 44.8 (10.30) CSF £17.85 CT £239.78 TOTE £7.80: £2.00 £1.60 £4.20 (£8.90) Trio £63.50 OWNER Midcourts (NEWMARKET) BRED Patrick Eddery Ltd
LONG HANDICAP Chief Predator (USA) 7-7
WEIGHT FOR AGE 3yo-14lb

1844* Ancient Quest was in his element on this rain-softened ground. Gaining a narrow advantage early in the straight, he was shaken up and shot clear below the distance to win with a ton in hand. If the rain continues, a quick hat-trick could be well be on the cards. (9/2)
1431* Glow Forum has been in sparkling form on the All-Weather so far this year and gave a good account of herself on this return to grass. (4/1: 9/2-3/1)
1825 Courageous Knight looked far from likely to get into the prize-money as he dropped back to last place seven furlongs from home. Still out with the washing entering the straight, he struggled on in the final furlong past tired rivals to take third prize. (20/1)
1421 Double Rush (IRE), taking a step-up in distance, was then only treading water in the final quarter-mile. (16/1)
1985 Oberons Boy (IRE) did not have the run of the race. Losing his pitch and failing to handle Tattenham Hill, he was towards the back of the field entering the straight, and then did not get the best of runs. His jockey was far from hard on him, and the combination never looked like getting back into it. (14/1)
1641* Mr Browning (USA) (11/2: 7/2-6/1)

2219 EPSOM & EWELL HERALD CONDITIONS STKS (3-Y.O F) (Class C)
8-40 (8-40) **1m 114y** £4,990.00 (£1,615.00: £790.00) Stalls: Low GOING: 0.18 sec per fur (G)

				SP	RR	SF
	Dragonada (USA) (100) (HRACecil) **3-8-12** WRyan(3) (lw: chsd ldr: led 3f out: rdn over 1f out: edgd lft ins fnl f: r.o wl)	—	1	6/4[1]	108	33
1621[2]	**Natalia Bay (IRE) (94)** (PFICole) **3-8-8** TQuinn(1) (led over 5f: unable qckn fnl 2f)	2½	2	9/4[3]	99	24
1621[3]	**Star Profile (IRE)** (SbinSuroor) **3-9-0v**[1] PatEddery(2) (lw: hld up: rdn over 3f out: sn wknd)	20	3	15/8[2]	68	—

(SP 105.6%) **3 Rn**

1m 50.04 (8.04) CSF £4.31 TOTE £2.50 (£2.40) OWNER Niarchos Family (NEWMARKET) BRED Flaxman Holdings Ltd
OFFICIAL EXPLANATION Star Profile (IRE): gurgled all the way up the straight.

Dragonada (USA) made a pleasing return to action, leading three furlongs from home and being bustled along from below the distance to dispose of the runner-up. (6/4)
1621 Natalia Bay (IRE), taking a step-up in trip, took the field along. Narrowly headed three furlongs from home, she was brushed aside by the winner in the final quarter-mile. (9/4)
1621 Star Profile (IRE), fitted with a visor for the first time, finished a head behind Natalia Bay on the same terms at Leicester last time out, but she flopped badly in the ground, and her jockey later reported that she gurgled up the straight. (15/8)

2220 PRINCE'S STAND H'CAP (0-80) (3-Y.O+) (Class D)
9-10 (9-10) **6f** £3,338.75 (£1,010.00: £492.50: £233.75) Stalls: High GOING: 0.18 sec per fur (G)

				SP	RR	SF
1848[8]	**The Fugative (50)** (PMitchell) **4-8-2** SSanders(6) (hld up: rdn over 2f out: led ins fnl f: r.o wl)	—	1	5/1[3]	62	49
1989[3]	**Marengo (68)** (JAkehurst) **3-8-13** DHolland(7) (lw: w ldr: styd far side st: led over 3f out: hdd ins fnl f: unable qckn)	3½	2	6/1	71	51
2115[2]	**Justinianus (IRE) (46)** (JJBridger) **5-7-12** GBardwell(9) (lw: led over 2f: rdn over 3f out: one pce)	s.h	3	7/2[1]	49	36
1634[6]	**Sharp Pearl (76)** (PRWebber) **4-10-0b** RHughes(1) (lw: outpcd: hdwy over 1f out: r.o)	1	4	14/1	76	63
1957[6]	**Kildee Lad (72)** (APJones) **7-9-10** TSprake(4) (lw: hld up: rdn over 2f out: one pce)	2½	5	5/1[3]	65	52
2006[21]	**Ivory's Grab Hire (69)** (KTIvory) **4-9-4b**(3) MartinDwyer(8) (hld up: rdn over 3f out: wknd 2f out)	2½	6	7/1	56	43
2006[17]	**Rock Symphony (74)** (WJHaggas) **7-9-12** MHills(2) (lw: a bhd)	nk	7	14/1	60	47

1141[21]	**Papita (IRE) (70)** (SDow) **3-9-1** WRyan(3) (a wl bhd)	10	**8**	12/1	29	9
1989[2]	**Tear White (IRE) (67)** (TGMills) **3-8-12** TQuinn(5) (lw: hld up: rdn over 2f out: sn wknd)	13	**9**	9/2 [2]	—	—
				(SP 121.5%)	**9 Rn**	

1m 11.6 (3.60) CSF £33.72 CT £110.57 TOTE £7.80: £1.90 £2.90 £1.70 (£34.20) Trio £43.50 OWNER Mr J. A. Redmond (EPSOM) BRED J. A. Redmond
WEIGHT FOR AGE 3yo-7lb
1848 The Fugative chased the leaders. Leading the stands' side group below the distance, she gained overall control inside the final furlong and kept on well to lose her maiden tag. (5/1: 3/1-6/1)
1989 Marengo was given an enterprising ride by Holland, who elected to stay on the far rails. He was the only horse to do so all evening, resulting in him racing on virgin ground compared with the other runners who were racing on the churned-up ground on the stands' side. He appeared to be in front over three furlongs from home and was probably not overhauled until inside the final furlong. (6/1)
2115 Justinianus (IRE) ran another sound race, but he lacks acceleration and that was again evident here. (7/2)
1113 Sharp Pearl, who has changed stables since his last run, got stuck in the mud and, unable to go the pace, was only staying on from below the distance. Both wins to date have come on fast ground. (14/1: 10/1-20/1)
1509* Ivory's Grab Hire (7/1: 5/1-8/1)

T/Plpt: £129.30 (128.54 Tckts). T/Qdpt: £36.10 (17.5 Tckts) AK

2029-**HAMILTON** (R-H) (Soft)
Wednesday June 25th
WEATHER: overcast WIND: almost nil

2221 SCOTTISH RIFLES SERIES (ROUND 4) APPRENTICE H'CAP (0-65) (3-Y.O+) (Class F)
7-00 (7-13) **5f 4y** £2,738.00 (£768.00: £374.00) Stalls: High GOING: 0.15 sec per fur (G)

				SP	RR	SF
2109[12]	**Ragtime Cowgirl (33)** (DANolan) **4-7-5**(7)ow2 NPollard(11) (mde all: kpt on wl fnl f)	—	**1**	6/1	29	11
2069[2]	**Stolen Kiss (IRE) (60)** (MWEasterby) **5-9-8b**(3) GParkin(10) (lw: wnt 3½f after false s: chsd ldr: rdn 2f out: hung lft ins fnl f: no ex)	3	**2**	2/5 [1]	46	30
2032[4]	**Diet (33)** (MissLAPerratt) **11-7-5v**(7) JennyBenson(1) (wnt 3½f after false s: racd centre: outpcd ½-wy: kpt on fnl f)	2	**3**	10/1	13	—
2032[6]	**Midas Man (32)** (DANolan) **6-7-4b**1(7)ow1 PBradley(2) (wnt 3½f after false s: sn outpcd & bhd)	11	**4**	50/1	—	—
2050[2]	**Manolo (FR) (63)** (JBerry) **4-9-9**(5) CLowther(7) (lw: wnt 3½f after false s: outpcd & bhd fr ½-wy)	6	**5**	3/1 [3]	—	—
1835[5]	***Sunday Mail Too (IRE) (38)*** (MissLAPerratt) **5-7-12**(5) IonaWands(4) (Withdrawn not under Starter's orders: passed post after false s)		**W**	11/1	—	—
2033[4]	***Another Nightmare (IRE) (36)*** (RMMcKellar) **5-7-8**(7) JMcAuley(3) (Withdrawn not under Starter's orders: passed post after false s)		**W**	6/1	—	—
1942*	***Goretski (IRE) (60)*** (NTinkler) **4-9-4**(7) PFredericks(9) (Withdrawn not under Starter's orders: passed post after false s)		**W**	2/1 [2]	—	—
1995[6]	***Impish (IRE) (52)*** (TJEtherington) **3-8-8**(3) JBramhill(6) (Withdrawn not under Starter's orders: passed post after false s)		**W**	7/1	—	—
2002[4]	***Kid Ory (44)*** (DWChapman) **6-8-6b**(3) DSweeney(5) (Withdrawn not under Starter's orders: passed post after false s)		**W**	12/1	—	—
	Aye Ready (35) (DANolan) **4-7-9**(5)ow4 KSked(8) (Withdrawn not under Starter's orders: bolted bef s: veterinary advice)		**W**	100/1	—	—
				(SP 121.7%)	**5 Rn**	

63.3 secs (5.00) CSF £9.18 TOTE £13.20: £1.80 £1.40 (£3.20) Trio £2.10 OWNER Mrs J. McFadyen-Murray (WISHAW) BRED D. G. Mason
LONG HANDICAP Ragtime Cowgirl 7-9 Midas Man 6-13 Aye Ready 7-4
WEIGHT FOR AGE 3yo-6lb
IN-FOCUS: Stall number eleven (a different set to the others) failed to open. The Starter did not appear to notice for a while and when he eventually flagged, the recall man was walking off the track. He did return and try to do his job, but the runners were already going past him. This caused five runners to complete the course, four to pull up approaching the final furlong and one lucky soul, Ragtime Cowgirl, was left in the traps. In the re-run, only the winner started from the correct stall.
1037 Ragtime Cowgirl had an advantage over the rest as her stall did not open first time. Making full use of her luck and her good draw, she did it determinedly, albeit in a time two seconds slower than the first 'race'. (6/1: tchd 33/1)
2069 Stolen Kiss (IRE) expended a lot of energy in the first running of this event and, after holding every chance in the race proper, found the struggle beyond her, but she is not the most genuine of characters. (2/5: 1/3-5/1)
2032 Diet ran well considering it was his second race of the night, and was keeping on at the end in what appeared the slower ground. (10/1: op 20/1)
Midas Man had blinkers on for the first time and, wearing his usual tongue-strap, did not show anything in either running of the race. (50/1)
2050 Manolo (FR) was obviously upset by the whole farcical proceedings and ran no sort of race. (3/1: op 6/1)
1942* Goretski (IRE) won the original running of this in good style, and in a two-second faster time than the eventual winner. (2/1)

2222 HAMILTON PARK (QUALIFIER) MAIDEN AUCTION STKS (2-Y.O F) (Class E)
7-30 (7-44) **6f 5y** £3,225.00 (£975.00: £475.00: £225.00) Stalls: High GOING: 0.15 sec per fur (G)

				SP	RR	SF
1997[9]	**Flower O'Cannie (IRE)** (MWEasterby) **2-8-2**(5)ow1 GParkin(2) (unruly & led to post: trckd ldrs: rdn to ld ins fnl f: kpt on)	—	**1**	12/1	69	37
1978[2]	**Iris May** (JBerry) **2-8-3**(5) TEDurcan(5) (b.hind: led: rdn 2f out: hdd & no ex ins fnl f)	1¼	**2**	1/2 [1]	67	36
1569[6]	**Frisky Lady** (TDEasterby) **2-8-3** LCharnock(4) (a chsng ldrs: rdn ½-wy: btn 1½f out)	4	**3**	7/1 [3]	51	20
1616[5]	**Marske Machine** (NTinkler) **2-8-2** DaleGibson(1) (prom tl rdn & wknd 2f out)	5	**4**	14/1	37	6
1997[8]	**Mary Lou (IRE)** (MRChannon) **2-8-3** JCarroll(3) (chsd ldrs tl wknd fnl 2f)	2½	**5**	13/2 [2]	31	—
				(SP 106.9%)	**5 Rn**	

1m 14.7 (4.70) CSF £16.38 TOTE £10.80: £2.70 £1.10 (£5.80) OWNER Mrs E. Rhind (SHERIFF HUTTON) BRED Rathasker Stud

1466 Flower O'Cannie (IRE) gave problems in the paddock and eventually had to be led all the way to the start but she then showed plenty of ability and won the race in good style. (12/1: op 8/1)
1978 Iris May had the form and the draw but when the pressure was on she either got stuck in the mud or did not relish the struggle. (1/2)
1569 Frisky Lady travelled well, but once off the bit she was a shade disappointing. (7/1)
1616 Marske Machine behaved better this time but her performance left plenty to be desired. (14/1)

2223 STRATHCLYDE H'CAP (0-90) (3-Y.O+) (Class C)

8-00 (8-04) **1m 1f 36y** £5,828.00 (£1,648.00: £804.00) Stalls: High GOING: 0.15 sec per fur (G)

				SP	RR	SF
1837^{4}	**Scaraben (72)** (SEKettlewell) **9-9-9** JFortune(2) (hld up: effrt over 2f out: rdn to ld cl home)	—	1	5/4^{1}	80	43
	Western General (73) (MissMKMilligan) **6-9-10** JWeaver(3) (led: qcknd over 3f out: r.o u.p: jst ct)	hd	2	100/30^{3}	81	44
2030*	**Principal Boy (IRE) (50)** (TJEtherington) **4-8-1** ^{5x} DaleGibson(1) (trckd ldr: chal over 2f out: no ex wl ins fnl f)	¾	3	13/8^{2}	57	20
				(SP 105.6%)	**3 Rn**	

2m 3.0 (8.70) CSF £4.52 TOTE £2.40 (£4.50) OWNER Mr J. Tennant (MIDDLEHAM) BRED Burton Agnes Stud Co Ltd
1837 Scaraben, in a messy race, was given a most determined ride and did just enough. (5/4)
Western General, against two opponents who needed holding up, was bound to have the run of the race, but despite a valiant attempt he was just touched off. (100/30)
2030* Principal Boy (IRE) likes the ground and the track but is pretty high in the weights just now and that, coupled with some recent hard races, just found him out. (13/8: 11/10-7/4)

2224 CAMERONIANS H'CAP (0-80) (3-Y.O) (Class D)

8-30 (8-30) **1m 3f 16y** £3,403.75 (£1,030.00: £502.50: £238.75) Stalls: High GOING: 0.15 sec per fur (G)

				SP	RR	SF
1449*	**Fantail (73)** (MHTompkins) **3-9-7** DBiggs(1) (chsd ldrs: pushed along over 4f out: rdn over 2f out: styd on to ld ins fnl f)	—	1	6/4^{1}	83	51
1863^{8}	**Baby Jane (60)** (BMactaggart) **3-8-8** DeanMcKeown(4) (led tl hdd ins fnl f: kpt on)	1½	2	14/1	68	36
1837^{6}	**Belle Bijou (58)** (MJohnston) **3-8-6** JWeaver(2) (chsd ldr: effrt over 3f out: wl outpcd fnl 2f)	6	3	4/1^{3}	57	25
1230^{4}	**Rare Talent (73)** (MRChannon) **3-9-7** JCarroll(5) (hld up: effrt over 3f out: sn rdn & btn)	5	4	7/2^{2}	65	33
1837^{8}	**Ninth Symphony (54)** (PCHaslam) **3-8-2** LCharnock(3) (hld up: effrt over 4f out: sn rdn & btn)	10	5	8/1	32	—
				(SP 100.0%)	**5 Rn**	

2m 28.5 (9.10) CSF £15.61 TOTE £2.30: £1.80 £4.10 (£5.80) OWNER Pamela, Lady Nelson of Stafford (NEWMARKET) BRED Skyline Racing Limited
1449* Fantail, on soft ground for the first time here, took some riding but kept responding to pressure and won as though he will appreciate further. (6/4)
1329 Baby Jane is dropping down the handicap and ran much better this time, taking well to this soft surface. (14/1: 8/1-16/1)
1837 Belle Bijou ran reasonably and is slipping down to a fair mark. (4/1: 3/1-9/2)
1230 Rare Talent did not seem to act on this soft ground. (7/2)

2225 HYNDFORD CLAIMING STKS (3-Y.O+) (Class D)

9-00 (9-01) **1m 4f 17y** £3,371.25 (£1,020.00: £497.50: £236.25) Stalls: High GOING: 0.15 sec per fur (G)

				SP	RR	SF
2034^{7}	**Monaco Gold (IRE) (41)** (MrsMReveley) **5-8-10**(5) SCopp(5) (led after 5f: kpt on wl fnl 3f)	—	1	16/1	69	51
1817*	**Royal Expression (79)** (MrsMReveley) **5-9-8** JFortune(4) (lw: bhd: drvn along over 3f out: styd on fnl f: nrst fin)	2½	2	5/2^{3}	73	55
1956^{5}	**Eponine (70)** (MRChannon) **3-8-3**ow1 JCarroll(7) (led 5f: chsd wnr: effrt & ch over 2f out: btn appr fnl f)	1	3	7/4^{1}	66	33
1674^{4}	**Sun Mark (IRE) (62)** (MrsASwinbank) **6-9-5** JWeaver(1) (lw: chsd ldrs: effrt over 2f out: one pce)	1	4	2/1^{2}	67	49
1996^{12}	***She's A Winner (IRE) (37)*** (PMonteith) **4-8-5b^{1}**(5) JBramhill(2) (Withdrawn not under Starter's orders: ref to ent stalls)		W	50/1	—	—
				(SP 106.1%)	**4 Rn**	

2m 41.1 (9.10) CSF £44.64 TOTE £16.10: £4.60 (£10.60) OWNER Mr D. McGonagle (SALTBURN) BRED Miss M. Tucker
WEIGHT FOR AGE 3yo-14lb
Royal Expression clmd Mrs PA Pugh £10,000
OFFICIAL EXPLANATION **Monaco Gold (IRE): regarding the improvement in form, the trainer's representative stated that prior to his previous run, the gelding had been off course for some nine months and that he had blown up.**
Monaco Gold (IRE), is a very edgy individual who had the run of the race and basically pinched it. (16/1)
1817* Royal Expression normally likes further and faster ground but is also moody and only ran when it was all over here. (5/2)
1956 Eponine looked to have a real chance here and raced up with the pace but proved disappointing when the pressure was on. Perhaps this soft ground did not suit her. (7/4)

2226 STONEHOUSE MAIDEN H'CAP (0-65) (3-Y.O+) (Class F)

9-30 (9-31) **1m 65y** £2,682.00 (£752.00: £366.00) Stalls: High GOING: 0.15 sec per fur (G)

				SP	RR	SF
1838^{2}	**Trying Times (IRE) (50)** (JBerry) **4-9-4**(5) TEDurcan(5) (lw: a.p: rdn to ld ins fnl f: r.o)	—	1	9/4^{1}	60	40
848^{W}	**Katie Komaite (39)** (CaptJWilson) **4-8-12** JFortune(4) (a.p: hdwy & ev ch 1f out: r.o one pce)	2	2	8/1	45	25
2159^{5}	**Gadroon (40)** (PCHaslam) **3-8-3** LCharnock(1) (led: qcknd 5f out: rdn 3f out: edgd lft: hdd & no ex ins fnl f)	½	3	14/1	45	15
2109^{9}	**Silent System (IRE) (23)** (DWChapman) **4-7-5b**(5) IonaWands(10) (lw: in tch: outpcd & lost pl 5f out: r.o fnl 2f)	nk	4	14/1	28	8
2041^{4}	**Grovefair Lad (IRE) (43)** (MartynWane) **3-7-13**(7) JMcAuley(7) (bhd tl styd on fnl 3f)	2½	5	5/1^{2}	43	13
1950^{4}	**Northern Maestro (35)** (MrsMReveley) **3-7-12** DaleGibson(9) (hld up & bhd: hdwy 3f out: nvr nr to chal)	6	6	10/1	23	—
1837^{10}	**William Wallace (60)** (DHaydnJones) **3-9-9v^{1}** JCarroll(3) (chsd ldrs: chal 5f out: rdn 3f out: wandered & wknd fnl 2f)	¾	7	5/1^{2}	47	17
2145^{15}	**Chanson d'Amour (IRE) (42)** (MissLAPerratt) **3-7-12**(7) CLowther(11) (chsd ldrs tl outpcd fnl 4f)	nk	8	33/1	28	—
1820^{15}	**Kalousion (42)** (TJEtherington) **3-8-5** MGallagher(8) (cl up tl wknd 5f out)	1½	9	16/1	25	—
1630^{4}	**General Monty (55)** (TDBarron) **5-9-7**(7) VictoriaAppleby(2) (bhd: brought wd & effrt 5f out: n.d)	½	10	7/1^{3}	37	17
2029^{5}	**Sweet Note (IRE) (37)** (MissLAPerratt) **3-8-0** NKennedy(6) (a bhd)	3	11	16/1	14	—
				(SP 124.8%)	**11 Rn**	

1m 52.3 (8.20) CSF £20.53 CT £199.77 TOTE £3.10: £1.90 £2.40 £6.10 (£11.00) Trio £189.00 OWNER Mrs Chris Deuters (COCKERHAM) BRED Gainsborough Stud Management Ltd

WEIGHT FOR AGE 3yo-10lb
1838 Trying Times (IRE) has really got his act together and, pushed out, stayed this trip in really good style. (9/4)
Katie Komaite likes the ground and had her chances but under serious pressure, she did not look all that co-operative. (8/1)
Gadroon, who had shown nothing previously, put up a much-improved performance under an enterprising ride. (14/1)
1631 Silent System (IRE) looked well and certainly has ability if he can be fully persuaded to use it. (14/1)
2041 Grovefair Lad (IRE) is an edgy customer who takes time to get going and only ran on when it was all over on this occasion. (5/1)
1950 Northern Maestro, patiently ridden, never got into it despite staying on. (10/1: op 12//1)
1630 General Monty (7/1: 5/1-8/1)

T/Plpt: £620.90 (16.69 Tckts). T/Qdpt: £400.00 (0.6 Tckts); £216.25 to 27/6/97 AA

1847-SALISBURY (R-H) (Good to soft)
Wednesday June 25th
WEATHER: unsettled WIND: nil

2227 E.B.F. WEYHILL MAIDEN STKS (2-Y.O F) (Class D)
2-30 (2-32) **5f** £3,626.00 (£1,088.00: £524.00: £242.00) Stalls: High GOING: 0.23 sec per fur (G)

				SP	RR	SF
1847^{4}	**Kawafil (IRE)** (PTWalwyn) **2-8-11** RHills(1) (a.p: led over 1f out: swvd lft ins fnl f: r.o wl)	—	**1**	11/4 ^{1}	94+	41
	Perfect Harmony (IRE) (BJMeehan) **2-8-11** MTebbutt(4) (str: bit bkwd: chsd ldrs: hrd rdn over 1f out: r.o ins fnl f: no ch w wnr)	5	**2**	16/1	78	25
	Kenkan (IRE) (PFICole) **2-8-11** TQuinn(7) (cmpt: led over 3f: one pce)	1¼	**3**	4/1 ^{3}	74	21
1847^{5}	**Dodo (IRE)** (DRCElsworth) **2-8-11** PatEddery(8) (prom: rdn over 3f out: wknd over 1f out)	¾	**4**	3/1 ^{2}	72	19
	Gaily Mill (IABalding) **2-8-8**(3) MartinDwyer(3) (lengthy: scope: bit bkwd: wnt lft s: no hdwy fnl 2f)	½	**5**	12/1	70	17
	To Love With Love (WJarvis) **2-8-11** JReid(6) (w'like: prom over 3f)	2	**6**	12/1	64	11
	Captivating (IRE) (RHannon) **2-8-11** DaneO'Neill(11) (lt-f: chsd ldrs: rdn & wknd over 2f out)	¾	**7**	10/1	61	8
	Frolicking (JLDunlop) **2-8-11** WRyan(5) (unf: dwlt: a bhd)	1¾	**8**	12/1	56	3
	Floral Park (GBBalding) **2-8-8**(7)ow4 FTynan(2) (leggy: lt-f: s.s: a bhd)	9	**9**	33/1	31	—
1806^{9}	**Allasella (IRE)** (BPalling) **2-8-11** TSprake(9) (prom over 2f)	1½	**10**	12/1	22	—
1564^{10}	**Francesca's Folly** (JWHills) **2-8-11** MHills(10) (dwlt: sn t.o)	19	**11**	33/1	—	—
				(SP 123.3%)	**11 Rn**	

64.41 secs (4.41) CSF £46.77 TOTE £3.20: £1.40 £3.50 £4.60 (£51.20) Trio £72.20 OWNER Mr Hamdan Al Maktoum (LAMBOURN) BRED Shadwell Estate Company Limited
1847 Kawafil (IRE), with the rain-softened ground putting the emphasis on stamina, did this in good style despite ducking left in the closing stages. She is going the right way. (11/4)
Perfect Harmony (IRE) is a half-sister to National Stakes winner Amaretto Bay. She will already need six furlongs on better ground, and will not have to improve much to get off the mark. (16/1)
Kenkan (IRE), a sister to Song Mist and half-sister to Highland Rhapsody, had been reported to have been working well at home. Friendless in the market probably due to the change in the going, she showed plenty of speed and could take some catching on a faster surface. (4/1: op 6/4)
1847 Dodo (IRE) had finished only just over a length behind the winner on her debut on much quicker ground. (3/1)
Gaily Mill is a half-sister to mile-and-three-quarter winner Arrastra and the stable's winning three-year-old Mara River. She will come into her own over longer distances. (12/1: op 8/1)
To Love With Love, a half-sister to Love Returned and Allyana, shaped well until getting bogged down in the soggy going. (12/1)
Captivating (IRE) (10/1: op 6/1)
Frolicking (12/1: op 7/1)

2228 MARTIN CLAIMING STKS (3-Y.O+) (Class F)
3-00 (3-08) **1m** £2,826.00 (£786.00: £378.00) Stalls: High GOING: 0.23 sec per fur (G)

				SP	RR	SF
1292^{8}	**Cape Pigeon (USA) (65)** (LGCottrell) **12-8-12v** DHolland(8) (lw: w ldr: led on bit over 2f out: rdn out)	—	**1**	7/1	72	36
	Young Duke (IRE) (75) (MrsSDWilliams) **9-9-5** LDettori(7) (b: hld up mid div: hdwy over 2f out: chsd wnr over 1f out: no imp)	6	**2**	3/1 ^{1}	67	31
2070^{11}	**Persian Dawn (39)** (RTPhillips) **4-8-7** RPerham(12) (hld up: hdwy over 2f out: sn hrd rdn: one pce)	2	**3**	50/1	51	15
2160^{6}	**Rivers Magic (72)** (JJBridger) **4-9-2**(5) ADaly(9) (swtg: hld up & bhd: hdwy over 2f out: nvr nrr)	¾	**4**	12/1	64	28
1929^{4}	**Matoaka (66)** (RJRWilliams) **3-8-7** JQuinn(10) (lw: hld up: hdwy over 2f out: hrd rdn over 1f out: one pce)	s.h	**5**	6/1 ^{3}	59	13
1971^{3}	**Euro Superstar (FR) (37)** (SDow) **3-8-5** TQuinn(5) (no hdwy fnl 2f)	½	**6**	20/1	38 t	10
	Baba Sadhu (PJMakin) **3-8-9** SSanders(1) (w'like: prom: lost pl 4f out: styd on fnl f)	nk	**7**	12/1	42 t	14
1951^{10}	**Scottish Park (40)** (MCPipe) **8-8-4**(3) MHenry(6) (nvr trbld ldrs)	2½	**8**	12/1	25 t	7
1484^{9}	**Jaazim (37)** (MMadgwick) **7-9-2** WRyan(17) (prom over 5f)	nk	**9**	25/1	33 t	15
1086^{8}	**Shanghai Lil (28)** (MJFetherston-Godley) **5-8-9** JReid(13) (n.d)	1½	**10**	33/1	23 t	5
	Pampasa (FR) (CJames) **3-8-0** CRutter(11) (a bhd)	6	**11**	25/1	12 t	—
1005^{16}	**Fairly Sure (IRE) (40)** (NEBerry) **4-8-0**(7) DDenby(14) (led: hrd rdn & hdd over 2f out: sn wknd)	½	**12**	50/1	8 t	—
197^{7}	**Green Golightly (USA) (40)** (RMFlower) **6-8-12** FNorton(3) (plld hrd: prom 5f)	5	**13**	25/1	3 t	—
1414^{12}	**Golden Ace (IRE) (86)** (RHannon) **4-9-10** DaneO'Neill(16) (lw: prom tl rdn & wknd over 2f out)	hd	**14**	100/30 ^{2}	15 t	—
2039^{6}	**Whothehellisharry (38)** (PTDalton) **4-8-12**(3) PMcCabe(15) (a bhd: t.o)	7	**15**	50/1	—	—
	Tarian (USA) (NMLampard) **5-8-5**(7) RCody-Boutcher(4) (Withdrawn not under Starter's orders: ref to ent stalls)		**W**	33/1	—	—
				(SP 126.0%)	**15 Rn**	

1m 47.92 (7.92) CSF £23.77 TOTE £7.50: £2.50 £2.00 £10.80 (£9.10) Trio £602.20; £8.48 to Salisbury 26/6/97 OWNER Mr E Gadsden and Mrs M Fairburn (CULLOMPTON) BRED Ashwood Thoroughbreds, Inc.
WEIGHT FOR AGE 3yo-10lb
Cape Pigeon (USA), who has had the cough since making his seasonal debut, had not scored on this sort of ground since recording his first ever win at Lingfield in the heavy six years ago. (7/1)
Young Duke (IRE) was not disgraced, considering he has never won on ground worse than good to firm. (3/1)
Persian Dawn ran easily her best race of the season. (50/1)
Rivers Magic was given a lot to do, having made all when winning on this ground at Haydock last July. (12/1)
1929 Matoaka could not quicken up in this yielding going. (6/1)
Baba Sadhu (12/1: op 7/1)

2229 MARGADALE CONDITIONS STKS (3-Y.O) (Class C)

3-30 (3-32) **6f 212y** £4,561.00 (£1,699.00: £824.50: £347.50: £148.75: £69.25) Stalls: High GOING: 0.23 sec per fur (G)

Form	Horse	Dist	Pos	SP	RR	SF
*1787**	**Snow Kid** (DRLoder) **3-9-0** PatEddery(5) (mde virtually all: clr over 1f out: easily)	—	**1**	5/2[1]	102+	57
768*	**Peppiatt** (RAkehurst) **3-8-10** TQuinn(1) (hdwy over 2f out: chsd wnr over 1f out: no imp)	7	**2**	7/1[3]	82	37
1851*	**Mr Sponge (USA)** (IABalding) **3-9-0** LDettori(6) (lw: a.p: rdn over 2f out: one pce)	1¼	**3**	5/2[1]	83	38
1876*	**Hajr (IRE)** (EALDunlop) **3-8-11**(3) DO'Donohoe(7) (s.s: hdwy over 4f out: one pce fnl 2f)	hd	**4**	5/1[2]	83	38
1823[12]	**Chili Bouchier (USA)** (DMarks) **3-8-5** SSanders(3) (rdn over 3f out: sn wl bhd)	10	**5**	100/1	51	6
1415*	**Byzantium** (LordHuntingdon) **3-9-0** DHarrison(2) (lw: prom over 3f)	1	**6**	5/1[2]	58	13
	Hanan (USA) (PAKelleway) **3-8-5** DJWhyte(4) (w wnr: n.m.r over 3f out: wknd over 2f out)	4	**7**	8/1	39	—

(SP 115.1%) **7 Rn**

1m 31.09 (5.09) CSF £19.45 TOTE £3.10: £1.20 £5.20 (£10.20) OWNER Mr Ali Saeed (NEWMARKET) BRED Raymond Clive Tooth

1787* Snow Kid, a progressive sort, relished the ground, and Eddery reported that he should be up to winning at least a Group Three in the soft. (5/2)

768* Peppiatt proved no match for a winner who looks decidedly useful in this sort of ground. (7/1: 8/1-12/1)

1851* Mr Sponge (USA) found underfoot conditions totally different to his course and distance win a fortnight ago. (5/2)

1876* Hajr (IRE) is a 250,000 guineas half-brother to French 1,000 Guineas winner Danseuse du Soir, and good performers Dana Springs and Don Corleone. Really bred to require further, he probably also wants better ground. (5/1: op 3/1)

1415* Byzantium, dropping back to seven, appeared all at sea in the soft ground. (5/1)

Hanan (USA) (8/1: 5/1-9/1)

2230 GIBBS MEW BIBURY CUP H'CAP (0-95) (3-Y.O) (Class C)

4-00 (4-02) **1m 4f** £5,572.50 (£1,680.00: £815.00: £382.50) Stalls: High GOING: 0.23 sec per fur (G)

Form	Horse	Dist	Pos	SP	RR	SF
1877*	**Rainwatch (90)** (JLDunlop) **3-9-7** PatEddery(4) (mde all: rdn & edgd rt over 2f out: r.o wl)	—	**1**	2/1[1]	103	44
1868[7]	**Heart of Armor (82)** (PFICole) **3-8-13** TQuinn(6) (a.p: hrd rdn 3f out: swtchd rt over 1f out: no imp)	7	**2**	6/1[3]	86	27
1270[3]	**Spy Knoll (76)** (MRStoute) **3-8-7**[ow1] JReid(5) (lw: hdwy 6f out: ev ch 3f out: sn rdn: one pce)	½	**3**	6/1[3]	79	19
1852[3]	**Motet (83)** (GWragg) **3-9-0** MHills(10) (hld up & bhd: hdwy 5f out: outpcd over 2f out: styd on ins fnl f)	2	**4**	8/1	83	24
1437[7]	**Deep Water (USA) (74)** (PFICole) **3-7-12**(7)[ow2] DavidO'Neill(8) (plld hrd: prom tl wknd wl over 1f out)	½	**5**	20/1	74	13
1679[2]	**Tom Tailor (GER) (82)** (DRCElsworth) **3-8-13** TSprake(9) (prom tl rdn & wknd over 3f out)	1¾	**6**	7/2[2]	79	20
966[4]	**Northern Sun (85)** (TGMills) **3-9-2** WRyan(11) (hdwy 4f out: wknd 2f out)	nk	**7**	14/1	82	23
1868[4]	**Protocol (IRE) (76)** (JWHills) **3-8-7** RHills(3) (hld up: hdwy 4f out: wknd wl over 1f out)	3½	**8**	8/1	68	9
1649[3]	**Nordic Crest (IRE) (74)** (PWHarris) **3-8-5** JQuinn(2) (bhd fnl 5f: t.o)	10	**9**	8/1	53	—
*1846**	***Badge of Fame (IRE) (85)*** (LMCumani) **3-9-2** LDettori(7) (Withdrawn not under Starter's orders: uns rdr bef s: rdr injured)		**W**	6/1[3]	—	—

(SP 143.2%) **9 Rn**

2m 42.94 (11.94) CSF £15.28 CT £62.52 TOTE £3.40: £1.50 £2.30 £2.00 (£13.90) Trio £16.00 OWNER Hesmonds Stud (ARUNDEL) BRED Hesmonds Stud Ltd

1877* Rainwatch, up 9lb, handled the ground conditions well and was a most appropriately-named winner on a very wet day. Subsequently described by his trainer as no superstar, he thinks he could be suited by an extra quarter-mile. (2/1: 9/4-7/2)

1592 Heart of Armor was still 5lb higher then when he scored in similar conditions at Windsor last month. (6/1)

1270 Spy Knoll travelled well until finding disappointingly little once coming under pressure. (6/1)

1852 Motet had softer ground to contend with for this step-up in distance on his handicap debut. (8/1: 6/1-10/1)

1437 Deep Water (USA) is not one who readily accepts restraint. (20/1)

1679 Tom Tailor (GER), 10lb higher than when third in a nursery on his final outing last season, had no excuses on account of the ground this time. (7/2)

1649 Nordic Crest (IRE) (8/1: 6/1-11/1)

1846* Badge of Fame (IRE) (6/1: 4/1-13/2)

2231 SHREWTON RATING RELATED MAIDEN LIMITED STKS (0-65) (3-Y.O) (Class F)

4-30 (4-32) **6f 212y** £2,721.00 (£756.00: £363.00) Stalls: High GOING: 0.23 sec per fur (G)

Form	Horse	Dist	Pos	SP	RR	SF
1587[6]	**Dulcinea (61)** (IABalding) **3-8-11** DHarrison(7) (hld up: hdwy over 2f out: led over 1f out: rdn out)	—	**1**	5/1[2]	70	40
1925[3]	**Mike's Double (IRE) (48)** (MissGayKelleway) **3-9-0** JQuinn(6) (hld up & bhd: nt clr run, swtchd rt & hdwy over 1f out: r.o ins fnl f)	1½	**2**	11/2[3]	70	40
1851[8]	**Giko (65)** (JRPoulton) **3-9-0** SDrowne(10) (a.p: led & edgd lft 2f out: hdd over 1f out: one pce)	hd	**3**	14/1	69	39
2040[6]	**Welcome Home (65)** (PTDalton) **3-8-11** SSanders(4) (led: rdn & hdd 2f out: one pce)	2	**4**	10/1	62	32
1826[2]	**Sand Cay (USA) (64)** (RHannon) **3-9-0** DaneO'Neill(5) (a.p: one pce fnl 2f)	½	**5**	5/1[2]	64	34
1931[3]	**Prince Zando (64)** (CAHorgan) **3-9-0** PaulEddery(2) (prom tl wknd over 1f out)	8	**6**	6/1	45	15
1848[12]	**Perchance To Dream (IRE) (47)** (BRMillman) **3-8-11** TSprake(3) (a bhd)	3½	**7**	33/1	34	4
1976[4]	**Free As A Bird (65)** (MRChannon) **3-8-11** PatEddery(1) (w ldr 4f: sn wknd)	2	**8**	4/1[1]	30	—
1967[9]	**Durable George (43)** (JJBridger) **3-8-9**(5) ADaly(8) (plld hrd: a bhd)	hd	**9**	33/1	32	2
792[14]	**Hoh Dancer (64)** (IABalding) **3-8-8**(3) MartinDwyer(9) (prom: put hd in air & wknd qckly over 2f out: t.o)	17	**10**	11/1	—	—

(SP 113.0%) **10 Rn**

1m 32.33 (6.33) CSF £28.71 TOTE £6.50: £2.40 £1.80 £3.00 (£16.80) Trio £57.40 OWNER Miss K. Rausing (KINGSCLERE) BRED Miss K. Rausing

1587 Dulcinea, dropped in grade, came into her own on this rain-softened ground. (5/1: op 5/2)

1925 Mike's Double (IRE) was supported in the ring over this longer trip. He may have been a little unlucky because by the time he found daylight, the winner had got first run. (11/2)

1087 Giko seems at his best with give in the ground. (14/1: op 8/1)

2040 Welcome Home was dropping back to seven on the right type of going. (10/1)

1826 Sand Cay (USA), back to seven, found the ground putting the emphasis on stamina, but the problem was he could not quicken in it. (5/1: op 3/1)

1931 Prince Zando does not stay seven in ground as soft as this. (6/1: op 7/2)

656 Hoh Dancer (11/1: 8/1-12/1)

2232 ALDERHOLT SPRINT H'CAP (0-85) (3-Y.O+) (Class D)
5-00 (5-01) **5f** £3,743.00 (£1,124.00: £542.00: £251.00) Stalls: High GOING: 0.23 sec per fur (G)

				SP	RR	SF
1937*	**White Emir (80)** (BJMeehan) **4-9-9b** PatEddery(5) (lw: stdd s: hld up in rr: swtchd rt 1f out: str run to ld nr fin)	—	1	9/2 1	86	68
1849 6	**Pointer (55)** (MrsPNDutfield) **5-7-7**(5) AimeeCook(8) (a.p: led wl ins fnl f: hdd nr fin)	nk	2	5/1 2	60	42
2115 4	**Half Tone (55)** (RMFlower) **5-7-9b**(3) MartinDwyer(7) (a.p: ev ch ins fnl f: nt qckn)	¾	3	9/2 1	58	40
1824 5	**Bajan Rose (76)** (MBlanshard) **5-9-5b1** JQuinn(1) (led tl rdn & hdd wl ins fnl f)	1¼	4	9/2 1	75	57
1824 7	**Mister Jolson (77)** (RJHodges) **8-9-6** SDrowne(4) (lw: a.p: n.m.r over 1f out: one pce)	hd	5	11/2 3	75	57
1948 6	**Golden Pound (USA) (83)** (MissGayKelleway) **5-9-12** DaneO'Neill(2) (b.hind: a.p: rdn 2f out: one pce)	½	6	8/1	80	62
1848 6	**Macgillycuddy (IRE) (59)** (MrsPNDutfield) **8-8-2b** TSprake(3) (prom: rdn over 2f out: one pce)	nk	7	10/1	55	37
1824 8	**Robellion (63)** (DWPArbuthnot) **6-8-6v** DHarrison(9) (prom tl wknd qckly over 1f out)	10	8	12/1	27	9

(SP 114.5%) **8 Rn**

63.43 secs (3.43) CSF £24.61 CT £96.62 TOTE £4.40: £1.90 £1.50 £1.50 (£17.60) Trio £19.80 OWNER The Three Bears Racing (UPPER LAMBOURN) BRED G. Dickinson

1937* White Emir has been transformed by waiting tactics and, under a masterly ride by Eddery, it was timed to perfection. (9/2)
1849 Pointer seems to need the ground as soft as this to be effective over this minimum trip. (5/1)
2115 Half Tone again showed he can handle soft ground. (9/2: 4/1-6/1)
1824 Bajan Rose was certainly sharpened up by the blinkers, but could not quite last home in the testing conditions. (9/2)
1594 Mister Jolson, 2lb higher than when winning this race last year, should not be considered unlucky. (11/2: 7/2-6/1)
1948 Golden Pound (USA) again had the ground slower than he prefers. (8/1: 6/1-9/1)
405 Robellion (12/1: 8/1-14/1)

T/Plpt: £115.50 (162.03 Tckts). T/Qdpt: £73.40 (14.62 Tckts) KH

2202-CARLISLE (R-H) (Good, Good to soft back st)
Thursday June 26th
WEATHER: overcast WIND: strong half behind

2233 CUMREW (S) STKS (2-Y.O) (Class G)
2-15 (2-16) **5f** £2,174.50 (£607.00: £293.50) Stalls: High GOING minus 0.69 sec per fur (HD)

				SP	RR	SF
*2051**	**Risky Whisky** (JBerry) **2-9-1b**(3) PFessey(8) (mde all: qcknd ½-wy: styd on u.p)	—	1	9/4 1	70	12
1797 6	**Velvet Story** (NTinkler) **2-8-11** KimTinkler(6) (lw: sn drvn along: hdwy 2f out: r.o: nrst fin)	2½	2	6/1	55	—
1860 5	**Amington Girl** (PDEvans) **2-8-6** JFortune(3) (a chsng ldrs: rdn 2f out: r.o one pce)	¾	3	5/2 2	48	—
2016 15	**General Joey** (MDods) **2-8-11b** SWebster(2) (chsd ldrs tl rdn & wl outpcd fnl 2f)	3½	4	33/1	41	—
1557 6	**Up The Clarets (IRE)** (JJO'Neill) **2-8-11** KDarley(5) (spd over 3f: wknd)	1¼	5	5/1 3	37	—
2016 6	**Toll's Times** (MWEasterby) **2-8-11b** TLucas(7) (chsd ldrs tl wknd wl over 1f out)	5	6	6/1	21	—
1758 10	**E B Treasure** (NBycroft) **2-8-6** LCharnock(1) (hung bdly lft & no ch fr ½-wy)	9	7	50/1	—	—
2153 11	**Flash d'Or (IRE)** (MWEasterby) **2-8-8**(5) GParkin(4) (reard s & s.s: nt rcvr)	22	8	16/1	—	—

(SP 115.4%) **8 Rn**

62.3 secs (2.10) CSF £15.08 TOTE £2.70: £1.30 £1.50 £1.40 (£5.10) OWNER Mr J. Berry (COCKERHAM) BRED Roldvale Ltd
No bid. Velvet Story clmd DMaloney £5,750

2051* Risky Whisky always had too much toe for this lot but he did need to be kept up to his work all the way home. (9/4: 13/8-5/2)
1797 Velvet Story spoilt his chances because of lack of early pace but he does finish well and will surely find success. (6/1)
1860 Amington Girl did not impress in the paddock this time but still ran pretty well and there is obviously a race or two to be found. (5/2)
1290 General Joey jumped off on terms for a change but then failed to pick up late on. (33/1)
Up The Clarets (IRE) is rather like the football team he is named after and has not impressed for some time. (5/1)
2016 Toll's Times gives the impression that he has the ability but does not seem to use it. (6/1)

2234 PLAYGROUP LUNCHEON CLUB MEDIAN AUCTION MAIDEN STKS (3 & 4-Y.O) (Class E)
2-45 (2-46) **5f 207y** £2,853.00 (£864.00: £422.00: £201.00) Stalls: Centre GOING minus 0.69 sec per fur (HD)

				SP	RR	SF
1587 5	**Compatibility (IRE) (81)** (JHMGosden) **3-9-0** GHind(3) (lw: trckd ldrs: led 1½f out: qcknd: easily)	—	1	4/9 1	83++	19
2113 5	**Mystique Air (IRE) (70)** (EWeymes) **3-8-9** JWeaver(6) (led tl hdd 1½f out: no ch w wnr)	2½	2	3/1 2	71	7
2109 11	**Fisiostar (30)** (MDods) **4-9-4b**(3) CTeague(5) (cl up: rdn over 2f out: one pce)	nk	3	50/1	37 t	19
1451 9	**Running Bear** (MissSEHall) **3-9-0** JCarroll(2) (stdd s: hdwy 2f out: nvr plcd to chal)	3½	4	7/1 3	27 t	2
	La Perdoma (MissMKMilligan) **3-8-9** ACulhane(7) (leggy: s.s: hdwy ½-wy: sn wknd)	11	5	33/1	—	—
	Chief's Spirit (GMMoore) **3-9-0** JTate(4) (leggy: bit bkwd: dwlt: a outpcd & bhd)	7	6	14/1	—	—

(SP 118.3%) **6 Rn**

1m 13.5 (1.70) CSF £2.16 TOTE £1.40: £1.10 £1.20 (£1.50) OWNER Sheikh Mohammed (NEWMARKET) BRED Mrs K. Osthus
WEIGHT FOR AGE 3yo-7lb

1587 Compatibility (IRE) has had easy races already and, in this moderate event, he beat this lot on the bridle and, no doubt, his confidence will have been boosted no end. (4/9: 1/3-1/2)
2113 Mystique Air (IRE), dropped back in trip, ran better but had no chance with the easy winner. (3/1)
896 Fisiostar had no chance here on the book but did run reasonably well. (50/1)
Running Bear went to post far too fast and just seemed to have an educational, and this is best forgotten as he will do better. (7/1)
La Perdoma gave many lengths away at the start but did show a little during the race. (33/1)

2235 LADBROKES LUCKY CHOICE H'CAP (0-70) (3-Y.O) (Class E)
3-15 (3-16) **5f** £2,856.25 (£865.00: £422.50: £201.25) Stalls: High GOING minus 0.69 sec per fur (HD)

				SP	RR	SF
2017 4	**Rum Lad (56)** (JJQuinn) **3-9-6** JLowe(6) (hdwy ½-wy: rdn to ld wl ins fnl f: eased towards fin)	—	1	7/2 2	67	43
1995*	**William's Well (58)** (MWEasterby) **3-9-3b**(5) 7x GParkin(5) (lw: cl up: rdn to ld ins fnl f: sn hdd & nt qckn)	¾	2	6/4 1	67	43
1730 6	**Star of The Road (47)** (JMCarr) **3-8-11** ACulhane(4) (in tch: hdwy ½-wy: ev ch over 1f out: nt qckn)	2½	3	9/1	48	24
783 9	**Melbourne Princess (52)** (RMWhitaker) **3-9-2** DeanMcKeown(7) (led tl hdd & no ex ins fnl f)	1½	4	8/1 3	48	24

1995^{9}	**Toronto (57)** (JBerry) **3-9-4b**(3) PFessey(8) (chsd ldrs: effrt ½-wy: btn over 1f out)	½	**5**	9/1	51	27
2167^{7}	**Red Romance (50)** (DenysSmith) **3-9-0** LCharnock(3) (spd over 3f: wknd)	3	**6**	10/1	35	11
1467^{19}	**Bellarula (47)** (MDods) **3-8-11** SWebster(1) (sn pushed along: no imp fr ½-wy)	1¼	**7**	20/1	28	4
1864^{7}	**Heathyards Pearl (USA) (52)** (RHollinshead) **3-8-13**(3) DGriffiths(2) (outpcd & bhd fr ½-wy)	½	**8**	33/1	31	7

(SP 110.1%) **8 Rn**

60.4 secs (0.20) CSF £7.64 CT £33.79 TOTE £4.80: £1.20 £1.20 £1.70 (£4.00) OWNER Mr B. Shaw (MALTON) BRED Mrs M. Shaw

2017 Rum Lad came from off the pace and did it well to win a shade cosily. (7/2)

1995* William's Well ran his usual game race and kept responding to pressure but was well held late on. (6/4)

1496 Star of The Road has ability but, as yet, does not see it out, and may well do better as he strengthens. (9/1)

Melbourne Princess has bags of early speed but keeps failing to last home. (8/1)

1604* Toronto has ability but is a difficult customer to win with. (9/1)

1864 Red Romance is from a yard that can do little right at present. (10/1)

2236 UCB FILMS CUMBERLAND PLATE H'CAP (0-80) (3-Y.O+) (Class D)

3-45 (3-47) **1m 4f** £7,002.50 (£2,120.00: £1,035.00: £492.50) Stalls: High GOING minus 0.39 sec per fur (F)

				SP	RR	SF
2005^{4}	**Just Grand (IRE) (76)** (MJohnston) **3-9-1** JWeaver(2) (hld up: rdn 3f out: hdwy to ld wl over 1f out: r.o wl)	—	**1**	7/1	86	35
1617^{3}	**Campaspe (58)** (JGFitzGerald) **5-8-11** JFortune(4) (lw: trckd ldrs: ev ch 2f out: nt pce of wnr)	3½	**2**	11/2 3	63	26
1748^{8}	**Rex Mundi (61)** (PDEvans) **5-9-0** JCarroll(9) (disp ld tl hdd over 3f out: led again 2f out: sn hdd & one pce)	½	**3**	14/1	66	29
1779^{13}	**Durgams First (IRE) (51)** (MrsMReveley) **5-8-4**ow3 ACulhane(1) (lw: hld up: hdwy 6f out: sn chsng ldrs: rdn & one pce fnl 2f)	¾	**4**	8/1	55	15
1763^{3}	**Suga Hawk (IRE) (58)** (EJAlston) **5-8-11** GHind(3) (cl up: led over 3f out to 2f out: wknd)	2	**5**	6/1	59	22
1491^{9}	**Warning Reef (70)** (PEccles) **4-9-9h** DeanMcKeown(6) (bhd: sme hdwy u.p 2f out: n.d)	hd	**6**	33/1	71	34
2015^{5}	**Crystal Falls (IRE) (75)** (JJO'Neill) **4-10-0** KDarley(8) (cl up tl rdn & wknd fnl 3f)	1¼	**7**	10/1	74	37
2145*	**Westminster (IRE) (65)** (MHTompkins) **5-8-11v**(7) 5x PClarke(7) (lw: hld up & bhd: effrt & c wd 3f out: sn rdn & btn)	3	**8**	3/1 1	60	23
1672^{4}	**Ballpoint (70)** (GMMoore) **4-9-4**(5) GParkin(5) (disp ld tl hdd & wknd over 3f out)	19	**9**	7/2 2	40	3

(SP 119.2%) **9 Rn**

2m 33.9 (4.90) CSF £42.54 CT £485.64 TOTE £6.60: £3.30 £1.80 £3.70 (£36.20) Trio £74.50 OWNER Maktoum Al Maktoum (MIDDLEHAM) BRED Gainsborough Stud Management Ltd

WEIGHT FOR AGE 3yo-14lb

OFFICIAL EXPLANATION **Ballpoint: no explanation offered.**

2005 Just Grand (IRE) has been messing about over inadequate trips and, once he found his stride here, he won particularly well. He looks likely to get further. (7/1)

1617 Campaspe, back to form here after a disappointing effort last time, kept responding to pressure but lacked any turn of foot to trouble the winner and seemed to need further. (11/2)

Rex Mundi does not do anything quickly but does respond to pressure and was always short of speed in the closing stages. (14/1)

1779 Durgams First (IRE) looks well but was just tapped for speed in the closing stages, and gives the impression these days that longer trips suit him better. (8/1)

1763 Suga Hawk (IRE) again had his chances but, when the battle was on, he was found wanting. (6/1)

777 Warning Reef has yet to win a race and this trip in certainly short of his best. (33/1)

2015 Crystal Falls (IRE) is coming to himself looks-wise and should not be written off yet. (10/1)

2145* Westminster (IRE) showed his true colours here and wanted nothing to do with it when ridden early in the straight. He obviously needs a flat-out gallop and everything going his way. (3/1)

2237 RED MILLS IRISH HORSEFEEDS LADIES' H'CAP (0-65) (3-Y.O+) (Class G)

4-15 (4-19) **6f 206y** £2,444.00 (£684.00: £332.00) Stalls: High GOING minus 0.39 sec per fur (F)

				SP	RR	SF
1830^{8}	**Roseate Lodge (32)** (SEKettlewell) **11-10-0** MrsDKettlewell(5) (hld up: stdy hdwy 2f out: shkn up ins fnl f: qcknd to ld nr fin)	—	**1**	14/1	42	30
2002*	**King Uno (48)** (MrsJRRamsden) **3-10-2v**(5) 5x MissERamsden(12) (cl up: led 3f out tl ct cl home)	½	**2**	7/2 1	57	36
1862^{6}	**Marzocco (25)** (TAKCuthbert) **9-9-2**(5)ow3 MissHCuthbert(4) (w ldrs: outpcd over 2f out: kpt on fnl f)	2	**3**	25/1	29	14
2041*	**Prime Partner (33)** (TDEasterby) **4-9-10**(5) MissADeniel(8) (hld up: hdwy to chal 2f out: wknd ins fnl f)	¾	**4**	13/2	36	24
1733^{7}	**Belbay Star (33)** (JLEyre) **4-10-1** MissDianaJones(2) (a chsng ldrs: effrt over 2f out: nt qckn)	¾	**5**	16/1	34	22
2169^{6}	**Hi Mujtahid (IRE) (40)** (SEKettlewell) **3-9-13** MrsSBosley(10) (lw: in tch: effrt over 2f out: one pce)	hd	**6**	25/1	41	20
2109^{8}	**David James' Girl (37)** (ABailey) **5-10-0v**1(5) MissBridgetGatehouse(13) (b: led tl hdd 3f out: grad wknd)	½	**7**	20/1	36	24
2004^{4}	**Delight of Dawn (47)** (EAWheeler) **5-11-1** MrsLPearce(6) (lw: hld up & bhd: effrt over 2f out: nvr nrr)	s.h	**8**	11/2 3	46	34
2109^{2}	**Miletrian City (40)** (JBerry) **4-10-3b**(5) MissVMarshall(11) (lw: mid div: rdn over 2f out: kpt on one pce)	hd	**9**	9/1	39	27
2152*	**Kass Alhawa (58)** (DWChapman) **4-11-12** 5x MissRClark(9) (lw: hld up & bhd: effrt over 2f out: nvr rchd ldrs)	½	**10**	5/1 2	56	44
2144^{3}	**Suedoro (39)** (JSGoldie) **7-10-7** MissPRobson(1) (cl up tl wknd over 2f out)	4	**11**	9/1	28	16
2205^{13}	**Murphy's Gold (IRE) (52)** (RAFahey) **6-11-1**(5) MrsCWilliams(3) (lw: hld up & bhd: effrt 3f out: n.d)	11	**12**	9/1	15	3
1467^{5}	**Manhattan Diamond (46)** (ABailey) **3-10-0b**(5) MissALHutchinson(7) (dwlt: hdwy to chse ldrs ½-wy: wknd 2f out)	2½	**13**	16/1	4	—

(SP 128.5%) **13 Rn**

1m 30.0 (4.30) CSF £59.85 CT £1,190.52 TOTE £18.00: £3.40 £1.80 £11.60 (£30.90) Trio £524.20; £339.66 to Folkestone 27/6/97 OWNER Mr Jon Firth (MIDDLEHAM) BRED Barrettstown Stud Farms Ltd

WEIGHT FOR AGE 3yo-9lb

1631 Roseate Lodge has obviously come right in a big way as he spent most of the race on the bridle and, patiently ridden, produced a good burst to settle it close home. (14/1)

2002* King Uno looked to have done everything right but was then just touched off. (7/2)

1862 Marzocco is running well at the moment and is likely to appreciate a bit further. (25/1)

2041* Prime Partner, who has won over further, looked a tricky customer here as he quickened splendidly to challenge early in the straight, only to stop as though shot late on. (13/2)

1467 Belbay Star keeps running as though she may well get further. (16/1)

2169 Hi Mujtahid (IRE) ran better this time and there seems to be ability there. (25/1)

2004 Delight of Dawn tried to come from behind but there was no real pace on for a change and his task was always impossible. (11/2)

2152* Kass Alhawa had an impossible task, trying to come from way off the pace. (5/1)

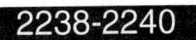

2238 RAYOPHANE H'CAP (0-70) (3-Y.O) (Class E)

4-45 (4-49) **7f 214y** £2,913.75 (£882.00: £430.50: £204.75) Stalls: High GOING minus 0.39 sec per fur (F)

				SP	RR	SF
2017^{6}	**Captain Carparts (55)** (JLEyre) **3-8-7** TWilliams(3) (mde all: hld on wl)	—	**1**	16/1	64	11
2130^{2}	**Pension Fund (66)** (MWEasterby) **3-9-4** TLucas(4) (lw: prom: hdwy 3f out: disp ld ins fnl f: edgd rt & no ex)	nk	**2**	10/11 ^{1}	74	21
2029^{2}	**Robbo (54)** (CWThornton) **3-8-6b¹** DeanMcKeown(6) (chsd ldrs: hrd drvn 3f out: one pce)	5	**3**	5/1 ^{2}	52	—
1999^{5}	**Diamond Eyre (52)** (JLEyre) **3-8-4** RLappin(1) (hld up & bhd: effrt & c wd 3f out: nvr able to chal)	nk	**4**	10/1	50	—
1834^{4}	**Storyteller (IRE) (56)** (MrsJRRamsden) **3-8-8** JFortune(5) (chsd ldrs: pushed along 3f out: wknd fnl 2f)	9	**5**	13/2 ^{3}	36	—
1833^{2}	**Get The Point (69)** (RHollinshead) **3-9-7** FLynch(2) (lw: hld up: effrt 3f out: sn rdn & no imp)	3½	**6**	5/1 ^{2}	42	—
				(SP 114.0%)	**6 Rn**	

1m 41.8 (4.80) CSF £29.41 TOTE £15.70: £4.90 £1.20 (£21.60) OWNER Mrs Caroline Page (HAMBLETON) BRED H. Jackson and L. Ayre

2017 Captain Carparts appreciated this longer trip and showed fine battling qualities to hold on. (16/1)

2130 Pension Fund always looked likely to win this but, when it came down to a struggle, he just wanted to hang right and failed to go through with it. (10/11: evens-4/5)

2029 Robbo had blinkers on this time and they did not have the desired effect. (5/1)

1999 Diamond Eyre, settled off the pace, struggled on when ridden but was never doing anything like enough. (10/1)

1834 Storyteller (IRE) does not as yet look quite right and was beaten some way out. (13/2)

1833 Get The Point has more ability but was not co-operating this time. (5/1: op 8/1)

2239 WALTON LIMITED STKS (0-60) (3-Y.O+) (Class F)

5-15 (5-18) **7f 214y** £2,598.00 (£728.00: £354.00) Stalls: High GOING minus 0.39 sec per fur (F)

				SP	RR	SF
2158*	**Dee Pee Tee Cee (IRE) (54)** (MWEasterby) **3-8-13** TLucas(2) (chsd ldrs: rdn 2f out: r.o gamely to ld wl ins fnl f)	—	**1**	5/2 ^{2}	71	24
2144^{12}	**Superpride (57)** (MrsMReveley) **5-9-5** ACulhane(1) (lw: led: qcknd 3f out: hdd & no ex wl ins fnl f)	¾	**2**	14/1	66	29
1826^{8}	**Flyaway Hill (FR) (60)** (PWHarris) **3-8-6** KDarley(4) (outpcd & bhd 3f out: hdwy u.p 2f out: nvr able to chal)	4	**3**	5/2 ^{2}	55	8
1991^{2}	**Beano Script (60)** (JHanson) **4-9-5** DaleGibson(6) (chsd ldrs: outpcd & edgd lft over 2f out: kpt on)	¾	**4**	9/1 ^{3}	56	19
2036^{9}	**Power Game (55)** (JBerry) **4-9-4b**(5) TEDurcan(7) (hld up & bhd: hdwy ½-wy: rdn & no imp fnl 2f)	nk	**5**	12/1	59	22
1089^{17}	**Move Smartly (IRE) (48)** (MrsLStubbs) **7-9-5** JWeaver(3) (lw: in tch: effrt on outside over 3f out: sn outpcd)	6	**6**	33/1	43	6
1862^{3}	**Highspeed (IRE) (57)** (SEKettlewell) **5-9-5** JFortune(5) (chsd ldrs: rdn 3f out: sn btn)	7	**7**	9/4 ^{1}	29	—
				(SP 115.2%)	**7 Rn**	

1m 41.1 (4.10) CSF £32.88 TOTE £3.30: £1.90 £3.90 (£20.60) OWNER Early Morning Breakfast Syndicate (SHERIFF HUTTON) BRED Michael and Heather Scott

WEIGHT FOR AGE 3yo-10lb

2158* Dee Pee Tee Cee (IRE) is obviously game and stays particularly well, but he did have his second consecutive hard race here. (5/2)

1315 Superpride, taken last and very steadily to post as usual, then tried to pinch this when quickening three furlongs out but this trip, on this track, was probably just too much. (14/1)

Flyaway Hill (FR) got completely out-paced at halfway but was struggling on as though a bit further may well help. (5/2)

1991 Beano Script had his chances but his rider had to concentrate on keeping him straight, and he was left behind in the last couple of furlongs. (9/1)

1603* Power Game had plenty on here and did not run too badly. (12/1)

896 Move Smartly (IRE) was without the visor he has worn lately and he failed to make any impression, but was not over-punished and should be all the better for it. (33/1)

1862 Highspeed (IRE) ran a stinker and something was obviously wrong with him. (9/4)

T/Plpt: £21.80 (872.07 Tckts). T/Qdpt: £18.00 (60.88 Tckts) AA

2227-SALISBURY (R-H) (Soft)

Thursday June 26th

Race 2: flip-start; Race 6: hand-timed

WEATHER: raining WIND: strong half against

2240 SOUTHAMPTON CLAIMING STKS (2-Y.O) (Class F)

2-00 (2-01) **6f 212y** £2,553.00 (£708.00: £339.00) Stalls: Low GOING: 0.29 sec per fur (G)

				SP	RR	SF
1330*	**Lord Smith** (WGMTurner) **2-8-3**(7)ow2 DMcGaffin(2) (lw: chsd ldr: led 2f out: edgd rt over 1f out: rdn out)	—	**1**	7/4 ^{1}	71	15
1797^{7}	**Celtic Comfort** (PCHaslam) **2-8-8**(3) MHenry(8) (bhd: rdn 4f out: hdwy over 1f out: styd on wl ins fnl f)	hd	**2**	9/2 ^{3}	72	18
1461*	**Who Nose (IRE)** (BJMeehan) **2-8-10b** MTebbutt(9) (lw: hld up: rdn over 2f out: ev ch whn hung rt ins fnl f: one pce)	2	**3**	5/1	66	12
2016^{4}	**Figawin** (GLewis) **2-8-4** PaulEddery(5) (lw: led 5f: wknd over 2f out)	6	**4**	4/1 ^{2}	46	—
1758^{6}	**Goldenacres** (JNeville) **2-8-4** SDrowne(1) (lw: bhd fnl 3f)	6	**5**	10/1	33	—
1760^{19}	**Jasmine Tea** (MartynMeade) **2-7-13** FNorton(4) (lw: bhd fnl 4f)	¾	**6**	20/1	26	—
1675^{R}	**Distinctly Lillie (IRE)** (JSMoore) **2-8-5** AClark(3) (dwlt: a bhd)	8	**7**	16/1	14	—
1607^{11}	**Dancing Al** (JSMoore) **2-9-1** NAdams(7) (prom over 3f)	2½	**8**	11/1	18	—
				(SP 119.3%)	**8 Rn**	

1m 34.95 (8.95) CSF £9.45 TOTE £2.60: £1.10 £1.80 £1.90 (£5.20) Trio £6.30 OWNER Mrs M. S. Teversham (SHERBORNE) BRED Mrs M. S. Teversham

Lord Smith clmd DPipe £9,000

1330* Lord Smith, again up in distance, held on well in testing conditions and now goes to Martin Pipe. (7/4)

1797 Celtic Comfort, a brother to a winner in Italy and a half-brother to Daring King, is certainly going the right way and can take a similar event. (9/2: 3/1-5/1)

1461* Who Nose (IRE) seemed to handle the soft ground well enough, but did not help his cause by edging into the centre of the course in the closing stages. (5/1)

2016 Figawin did not see out the trip in the very soft ground. (4/1)

2241 HERBERT AND GWEN BLAGRAVE MEMORIAL CONDITIONS STKS (3-Y.O+) (Class C)
2-30 (2-30) **1m 6f** £5,276.50 (£1,699.00: £824.50) GOING: 0.29 sec per fur (G)

				SP	RR	SF
1949*	**Montfort (USA) (94)** (PFICole) **3-8-13** TQuinn(2) (lw: chsd ldrs: led 5f out: clr 2f out: easily)	—	**1**	$1/2^{1}$	112+	9
	Lettyfak (FR) (IPWilliams) **3-8-9** PatEddery(1) (w'like: scope: led 9f: eased whn btn fnl 2f)	8	**2**	$4/1^{2}$	99	—
	Smart Play (USA) (95) (LordHuntingdon) **4-9-6** JReid(4) (bit bkwd: hld up: rdn over 2f out: no hdwy)	1	**3**	$4/1^{2}$	92	6
				(SP 106.7%)	**3 Rn**	

3m 18.78 (20.08) CSF £2.47 TOTE £1.50 (£1.60) OWNER Sir George Meyrick (WHATCOMBE) BRED Timothy J. Rooney
WEIGHT FOR AGE 3yo-17lb

1949* Montfort (USA) will probably now be freshened up for a tilt at the Melrose Handicap at York's Ebor meeting. (1/2: op 1/3)
Lettyfak (FR) was an eleven-furlong soft-ground winner in the French provinces for Andre Fabre. Despite accepting the situation in the final quarter-mile, he still held on for second. (4/1)
Smart Play (USA), who has changed stables, did not appear to handle the testing ground and could not get past the second, despite his rival being eased from the quarter-mile marker. (4/1: op 5/2)

2242 NOEL CANNON MEMORIAL TROPHY H'CAP (0-100) (3-Y.O+) (Class C)
3-00 (3-01) **1m** £5,507.50 (£1,660.00: £805.00: £377.50) Stalls: Low GOING: 0.29 sec per fur (G)

				SP	RR	SF
1739^{13}	**Cinema Paradiso (91)** (PFICole) **3-8-13** TQuinn(1) (w ldr: rallied ins fnl f: led last strides)	—	**1**	$6/1^{3}$	97	32
1813^{6}	**Koathary (USA) (78)** (LGCottrell) **6-8-10** DHolland(5) (lw: a.p: led over 2f out: hrd rdn fnl f: hdd last strides)	nk	**2**	$3/1^{1}$	83	28
1979^{8}	**Wakeel (USA) (75)** (SDow) **5-8-2**(5) ADaly(8) (lw: s.s: hld up in rr: hdwy over 1f out: r.o one pce fnl f)	2	**3**	$3/1^{1}$	76	21
1793^{4}	**My Lewicia (IRE) (92)** (PWHarris) **4-9-3**(7) CLowther(7) (lw: hld up: rdn over 3f out: hdwy over 1f out: r.o one pce fnl f)	nk	**4**	10/1	93	38
1741^{5}	**Chief Monarch (87)** (BSmart) **3-8-9** SSanders(10) (lw: prom tl wknd wl over 1f out)	16	**5**	13/2	56	—
	Strazo (IRE) (93) (LadyHerries) **4-9-11** JReid(2) (led over 5f)	2½	**6**	$11/2^{2}$	57	2
2026^{11}	**Law Commission (91)** (DRCElsworth) **7-9-9** PatEddery(9) (hld up: hdwy 4f out: wknd wl over 1f out)	1¼	**7**	$6/1^{3}$	52	—
				(SP 116.4%)	**7 Rn**	

1m 48.83 (8.83) CSF £22.85 CT £59.22 TOTE £6.70: £3.00 £2.20 (£14.00) Trio £15.60 OWNER Mr Christopher Wright (WHATCOMBE) BRED Barrettstown Stud Farms Ltd
WEIGHT FOR AGE 3yo-10lb

1170 Cinema Paradiso, dropped 4lb, was ridden closer to the pace this time and had the help of the stands rails in a finish of tired horses. (6/1)
1813 Koathary (USA), who won on yielding ground last season, looked set to score until unable to withstand the winner's renewed effort. (3/1)
1442 Wakeel (USA), down 2lb, started joint-favourite, having won in the heavy at Cagnes-Sur-Mer. (3/1)
1793 My Lewicia (IRE) had registered her only win in good-to-soft ground at Kempton. (10/1)
1308 Law Commission (6/1: op 4/1)

2243 CHAMPAGNE AUCTION STKS (2-Y.O) (Class B)
3-30 (3-32) **6f 212y** £9,843.00 (£3,687.00: £1,806.00: £780.00: £352.50: £181.50) Stalls: Low GOING: 0.29 sec per fur (G)

				SP	RR	SF
2022*	**Mountain Song** (SirMarkPrescott) **2-8-12** GDuffield(18) (a gng wl: led 3f out: clr over 1f out: easily)	—	**1**	$2/1^{1}$	94+	25
1941^{2}	**Legs Be Frendly (IRE)** (KMcAuliffe) **2-8-8** JReid(4) (lw: a.p: rdn over 2f out: chsd wnr fnl f: no imp)	8	**2**	8/1	72	3
1411^{7}	**Timekeeper (USA)** (MBell) **2-8-11** MFenton(15) (a.p: rdn over 2f out: one pce)	½	**3**	12/1	74	5
1396^{4}	**Herminius (IRE)** (JLDunlop) **2-8-12** PatEddery(2) (a.p: rdn over 2f out: one pce)	2½	**4**	$11/4^{2}$	69	—
	Daring News (RHannon) **2-8-5** RPerham(10) (str: scope: lw: many positions: rdn over 2f out: hdwy wl over 1f out: eased whn btn fnl f: bttr for r)	1	**5**	20/1	59+	—
1396^{5}	**Saddlers' Roe (IRE)** (BWHills) **2-8-8** MHills(8) (lw: nvr nr to chal)	7	**6**	$13/2^{3}$	46	—
	Titan (SDow) **2-8-2**ow1 SSanders(3) (str: scope: s.s: nvr nrr)	¾	**7**	33/1	39	—
822^{8}	**Black Jet** (NPLittmoden) **2-8-4** RFfrench(17) (nvr nr ldrs)	5	**8**	33/1	29	—
1797*	**Tamerin Bay** (RBoss) **2-8-4** WRyan(13) (led 4f: wknd over 1f out)	1¾	**9**	10/1	25	—
1411^{5}	**Fiveo'clock Shadow (IRE)** (BJMeehan) **2-8-4** TQuinn(6) (prom 5f)	5	**10**	12/1	14	—
	Lauren's Lad (GLewis) **2-8-4** CRutter(5) (neat: s.s: a bhd)	nk	**11**	20/1	13	—
	Annie Hall (MartynMeade) **2-8-0** FNorton(7) (w'like: a bhd)	2	**12**	33/1	4	—
2003*	**Mislead (IRE)** (JSMoore) **2-7-13** NAdams(11) (lw: a bhd)	nk	**13**	14/1	3	—
	Imperator (IRE) (LadyHerries) **2-8-5** AClark(12) (w'like: s.s: a bhd: t.o fnl 3f)	23	**14**	20/1	—	—
				(SP 138.7%)	**14 Rn**	

1m 34.2 (8.20) CSF £18.76 TOTE £3.40: £1.50 £2.20 £5.50 (£10.80) Trio £58.00 OWNER Eclipse Thoroughbreds (NEWMARKET) BRED Mrs R. D. Peacock

2022* Mountain Song, a brother to Raindancing, apparently surprised his trainer by the way he took to the conditions. The intention is to go for a Listed race in Milan prior to the Solario Stakes at Sandown. (2/1)
1941 Legs Be Frendly (IRE) had already showed he could handle plenty of give underfoot but caught a tartar in the winner. (8/1)
822* Timekeeper (USA) showed plenty of stamina over this extra furlong on soft ground, but was still only playing for the places. (12/1: 8/1-14/1)
1396 Herminius (IRE) deserves another chance on better ground. (11/4)
Daring News, a brother to Red Hot Risk, did not have the best of days for making his racecourse debut and seems sure to improve. (20/1)
1396 Saddlers' Roe (IRE), a half-brother to Tony's Fen, is out of a half-sister to Carroll House. Given the conditions, this run is probably best forgotten. (13/2: 7/2-7/1)
Titan, a half-brother to three winners, is likely to do better in due course. (33/1)
1797* Tamerin Bay (10/1: op 5/1)
2003* Mislead (IRE) (14/1: 10/1-16/1)

2244 DEVERILL H'CAP (0-70) (3-Y.O+ F & M) (Class E)
4-00 (4-01) **6f** £3,210.25 (£967.00: £468.50: £219.25) Stalls: Low GOING: 0.29 sec per fur (G)

				SP	RR	SF
1765*	**Almasi (IRE) (68)** (CFWall) **5-9-12** GDuffield(8) (lw: hld up & bhd: gd hdwy over 1f out: rdn to ld wl ins fnl f: r.o)	—	**1**	$7/2^{2}$	78	60
1920^{2}	**Caudillo (IRE) (57)** (MrsPNDutfield) **4-8-10**(5) AimeeCook(16) (lw: hdwy over 2f out: led over 1f out tl wl ins fnl f: r.o)	hd	**2**	14/1	67	49
1965^{13}	**Superlao (BEL) (38)** (JJBridger) **5-7-3**(7) PDoe(9) (a.p: led 2f out tl over 1f out: one pce)	3½	**3**	14/1	38	20

1439[14]	**Tinker Osmaston (58)** (RJHodges) **6-9-2** JQuinn(2) (hld up & plld hrd: hdwy 2f out: one pce fnl f)	1¾	**4**	7/1	54	36
1921[6]	**Beveled Crystal (50)** (CJames) **3-8-1** CRutter(14) (hld up mid div: no hdwy fnl 2f)	1¾	**5**	25/1	41	16
2001[4]	**Corniche Quest (IRE) (63)** (MRChannon) **4-9-4**(3) PPMurphy(12) (lw: hld up: hdwy over 2f out: hrd rdn over 1f out: one pce)	1¾	**6**	6/1[3]	49	31
1849[10]	**Calandrella (38)** (GBBalding) **4-7-10** NAdams(13) (led over 1f: wknd over 2f out)	3	**7**	33/1	16	—
1810[3]	**Will To Win (54)** (PGMurphy) **3-8-5** DHarrison(3) (lw: hld up: rdn over 2f out: eased whn btn fnl f)	½	**8**	5/2[1]	31	6
2177[3]	**Shashi (IRE) (56)** (PatMitchell) **5-8-9**(5) AmandaSanders(10) (b.hind: bhd fnl 2f)	1	**9**	10/1	30	12
1925[11]	**Dorado Beach (45)** (LGCottrell) **3-7-10** NCarlisle(4) (s.s: a bhd)	½	**10**	33/1	18	—
1810[11]	**Royal Emblem (46)** (AGFoster) **3-7-6b**(5)ow1 RFfrench(17) (lw: led over 4f out to 2f out: sn wknd)	nk	**11**	33/1	18	—
1780[10]	**Small Risk (48)** (TTClement) **3-7-10v**[1](3)ow3 MartinDwyer(6) (prom 3f)	5	**12**	33/1	7	—
1989[4]	**Third Party (68)** (SDow) **3-9-5** TQuinn(1) (bhd fnl 3f)	2½	**13**	10/1	20	—
				(SP 124.7%)		**13 Rn**

1m 18.35 (5.35) CSF £46.68 CT £576.23 TOTE £5.00: £2.30 £4.10 £4.20 (£46.00) Trio £232.30 OWNER The Equema Partnership (NEWMARKET) BRED Newtownbarry House Stud
LONG HANDICAP Calandrella 7-6 Royal Emblem 7-9 Small Risk 7-8 Dorado Beach 7-5
WEIGHT FOR AGE 3yo-7lb
1765* Almasi (IRE), raised 6lb, came from last to first in the final quarter-mile. (7/2: 5/2-4/1)
1920 Caudillo (IRE) found the testing ground helping on this drop back to six. (14/1: 10/1-16/1)
1676 Superlao (BEL), down 3lb, was by no means friendless in the market but would probably have preferred a sounder surface. (14/1)
1113 Tinker Osmaston was 7lb lower than her last win on good-to-soft at Chepstow in October 1995. (7/1)
Beveled Crystal was having her first run on soft ground on this handicap debut. (25/1)
2001 Corniche Quest (IRE) did not mind the easy ground but was already due to go down 1lb. (6/1)

2245 CARNARVON CHALLENGE CUP AMATEUR H'CAP (0-70) (3-Y.O) (Class F)
4-30 (4-36) **1m** £2,798.00 (£778.00: £374.00) Stalls: Low GOING: 0.29 sec per fur (G)

				SP	RR	SF
1633[6]	**Righty Ho (57)** (PTWalwyn) **3-11-6** MissSSamworth(3) (a.p: led over 4f out: jst hld on)	—	**1**	6/1[3]	68	33
1826[5]	**Jolly Jackson (54)** (RAkehurst) **3-11-3** MrKGoble(2) (hld up: rdn & hdwy over 2f out: r.o ins fnl f)	nk	**2**	7/2[2]	64	29
2151[2]	**Welcome Heights (40)** (MJFetherston-Godley) **3-10-3** MrsDArbuthnot(1) (a.p: ev ch 2f out: one pce)	4	**3**	6/1[3]	42	7
1807[8]	**Inkwell (39)** (AHide) **3-10-2** MrLBaker(11) (hld up: rdn over 2f out: one pce)	1¾	**4**	12/1	38	3
1465[11]	**Yangtze (IRE) (45)** (BRMillman) **3-10-8b** MrRThornton(12) (lw: a.p: rdn over 3f out: one pce fnl 2f)	1½	**5**	14/1	41	6
*2052**	**Merciless Cop (70)** (BJMeehan) **3-12-5** 5x MissJAllison(8) (s.s: hdwy over 4f out: hrd rdn over 2f out: sn wknd)	2½	**6**	5/2[1]	61	26
1951[5]	**Warrior King (IRE) (43)** (MrsPNDutfield) **3-10-6** MrLJefford(10) (lw: trckd ldrs: rdn over 3f out: wknd 2f out)	3	**7**	8/1	28	—
1487[6]	**Arthur's Seat (52)** (LordHuntingdon) **3-11-1** MrsMCowdrey(5) (lw: led over 3f: sn wknd)	6	**8**	10/1	25	—
1668[6]	**Forget To Remindme (51)** (JSMoore) **3-11-0** MrsSMoore(4) (lw: bhd fnl 3f: t.o)	15	**9**	12/1	—	—
				(SP 121.6%)		**9 Rn**

1m 52.2 (12.20) CSF £26.30 CT £113.83 TOTE £7.50: £2.20 £1.70 £1.50 (£15.00) Trio £27.30 OWNER Mr Eric Perry (LAMBOURN) BRED B. J. Warren
1392 Righty Ho had made his debut in similar conditions at Windsor last August. (6/1)
1826 Jolly Jackson found the testing ground putting the emphasis on stamina and would have prevailed with a little further to travel. (7/2)
2151 Welcome Heights is in good form and finished much closer to the winner than he had two outings ago at Windsor. (6/1: op 4/1)
Inkwell, no shorter than 25/1 on his three previous starts, did not look a blot on the handicap. (12/1)
Yangtze (IRE) was dropping back considerably in distance, having been tried in blinkers last time. (14/1)
2052* Merciless Cop had to shoulder an awful lot of weight for this sort of ground. (5/2: 2/1-100/30)
1951 Warrior King (IRE) (8/1: op 12/1)
1167* Forget To Remindme (12/1: op 8/1)

2246 ALINGTON MAIDEN H'CAP (0-65) (3-Y.O+) (Class F)
5-00 (5-01) **1m 1f 209y** £3,078.00 (£858.00: £414.00) Stalls: Low GOING: 0.29 sec per fur (G)

				SP	RR	SF
1938[9]	**Inimitable (60)** (JLDunlop) **3-8-11** PatEddery(14) (mde all: edgd lft 1f out: all out)	—	**1**	11/4[1]	68	36
1779[21]	**May King Mayhem (33)** (MrsALMKing) **4-7-10** JQuinn(9) (lw: bhd: hrd rdn over 3f out: hdwy over 1f out: ev ch ins fnl f: r.o)	nk	**2**	20/1	41	21
1968[13]	**One In The Eye (34)** (JRPoulton) **4-7-11** NVarley(2) (gd hdwy over 1f out: one pce ins fnl f)	3	**3**	16/1	37	17
1826[7]	**Sound Appeal (62)** (AGFoster) **3-8-13b** TSprake(12) (a.p: one pce fnl 2f)	¾	**4**	7/1[3]	64	32
2039[4]	**High Desire (IRE) (45)** (JRArnold) **4-8-5**(3) MartinDwyer(6) (a.p: no hdwy fnl 3f)	3½	**5**	9/2[2]	41	21
1803[9]	**Asking (33)** (JABennett) **5-7-10** NAdams(5) (b: prom: ev ch over 2f out: wknd over 1f out)	d.h	**6**	33/1	27	7
1985[4]	**Clouds Hill (FR) (57)** (RHannon) **4-9-6v** DaneO'Neill(18) (prom tl wknd over 1f out)	1	**6**	14/1	51	31
1505[4]	**Manikato (USA) (65)** (DJSCosgrove) **3-8-9v**(7) CLowther(10) (lw: s.i.s: hdwy over 3f out: wknd over 2f out)	7	**8**	7/1[3]	48	16
1968[11]	**Executive Officer (33)** (RMFlower) **4-7-10b**[1] FNorton(1) (bhd fnl 3f)	1¾	**9**	33/1	13	—
1757[8]	**Keen Companion (65)** (TJNaughton) **4-9-11**(3) JDSmith(16) (prom tl rdn & wknd 3f out:)	1	**10**	11/1	44	24
2193[4]	**Magazine Gap (43)** (PatMitchell) **4-8-1**(5) AmandaSanders(3) (lw: a bhd)	hd	**11**	33/1	21	1
2121[8]	**Hadadabble (37)** (PatMitchell) **4-7-11**(3)ow3 MHenry(11) (a bhd)	6	**12**	16/1	6	—
1677[6]	**Myosotis (46)** (PJMakin) **3-7-6b**(5)ow1 RFfrench(4) (a bhd)	1½	**13**	12/1	12	—
1276[11]	**Canadian Jive (44)** (DWPArbuthnot) **4-8-7** SWhitworth(7) (a bhd: t.o)	13	**14**	33/1	—	—
1796[4]	**Bold Saint (IRE) (46)** (PWHarris) **3-7-6b**(5) RMullen(15) (lw: bhd fnl 4f: t.o)	10	**15**	9/1	—	—
				(SP 130.8%)		**15 Rn**

2m 15.59 (10.29) CSF £63.99 CT £704.45 TOTE £3.40: £1.70 £4.30 £5.40 (£82.50) Trio £386.70; £168.85 to Folkestone 27/6/97 OWNER Aylesfield Farms Stud Ltd (ARUNDEL) BRED Aylesfield Farms Stud
LONG HANDICAP May King Mayhem 7-4 Myosotis 7-7 Asking 7-2 Executive Officer 7-2
WEIGHT FOR AGE 3yo-12lb
1168 Inimitable, dropped 4lb, needed a strong ride from Eddery to hold on. (11/4)
1445 May King Mayhem, 6lb out of the handicap, could not peg back the winner, having been under pressure from a long way out. (20/1)
587 One In The Eye, down 4lb, could not sustain a promising-looking run. (16/1)
1826 Sound Appeal had a longer trip this time but the soft ground was probably not in her favour. (7/1)
2039 High Desire (IRE), dropped 4lb, is due to go back up the same amount in future handicaps. (9/2)
Asking seemed to act on the going but stamina in these conditions proved a problem. (33/1)

1985 Clouds Hill (FR), dropped 7lb, is set to go down a further 4lb. Certainly sharpened up by the visor, he did not last home in this ground. (14/1)
1297 Keen Companion (11/1: 7/1-12/1)

T/Jkpt: £6,285.10 (1.5 Tckts). T/Plpt: £88.20 (287.71 Tckts). T/Qdpt: £28.50 (48.58 Tckts) KH

2247a - 2266a (Irish Racing) - See Computer Raceform

0029a-GOWRAN PARK (Kilkenny, Ireland) (R-H) (Good to yielding)
Sunday June 22nd

2267a VICTOR MCCALMONT MEMORIAL STKS (Listed) (3-Y.O+ F & M)
4-00 (4-01) **1m 4f** IR £9,825.00 (IR £2,775.00: IR £1,275.00: IR £375.00)

	Horse / details	Dist	Pos	SP	RR	SF
1540a3	**Token Gesture (IRE)** (DKWeld,Ireland) **3-8-12** MJKinane (hld up in tch: 4th & trckd ldrs st: led under 2f out: rdn & r.o.)	—	1	6/1 3	113	—
1698a*	**French Ballerina (IRE)** (PJFlynn,Ireland) **4-9-10** JAHeffernan (hld up: cl up: 3rd ½-wy: 2nd over 4f out: led 2½f out: hdd under 2f out: rdn & no ex over 1f out: kpt on)	2	2	11/10 1	108	—
1366a7	**Family Tradition (IRE)** (APO'Brien,Ireland) **3-8-10** CRoche (towards rr: cld early st: 6th over 1½f out: 3rd & nt rch ldrs ins last: kpt on)	2	3	10/1	106	—
1533a3	**Caiseal Ros (IRE)** (JSBolger,Ireland) **3-8-8ow1** KJManning (rn 3rd early: 4th ½-wy: 6th & rdn st: chsd ldrs: no imp 1½f out: kpt on same pce)	3½	4	6/1 3	99	—
	Aliya (IRE) (JOxx,Ireland) **3-8-8ow1** JPMurtagh (cl up: 2nd ½-wy: led over 4f out: hdd 2½f out: 4th, rdn & nt qckn over 1½f out: kpt on same pce)	2	5	4/1 2	96	—
	Rossmore Girl (IRE) (PJFlynn,Ireland) **4-9-7** SCraine (hld up: 7th ½-wy: wnt 3rd st: chsd ldrs 2f out: nt trble ldrs 1½f out: kpt on same pce)	2½	6	12/1	92	—
	Meglio Che Posso (IRE) (WPMullins,Ireland) **6-9-7** DJCasey (6th ½-wy: 7th st: rdn & chsd ldrs st: nt rch ldrs over 1½f out: kpt on same pce)	½	7	25/1	91	—
	Red Affair (IRE) (JOxx,Ireland) **3-8-7** PJSmullen (towards rr: 9th & sme hdwy st: 7th, rdn & nt trble ldrs 1½f out: kpt on same pce)	1	8	25/1	90	—
	Charita (IRE) (JGBurns,Ireland) **3-8-7** NGMcCullagh (8th ½-wy & st: rdn & no imp over 1½f out)	3	9	25/1	86	—
809a8	**Moon Flower (IRE)** (APO'Brien,Ireland) **3-8-7** PShanahan (towards rr: n.d)	15	10	25/1	66	—
1698a8	**Mount Row** (CCollins,Ireland) **4-9-7** WJSmith (led & disp ld: hdd over 4f out: rdn & wknd early st)	8	11	25/1	55	—

(SP 132.2%) **11 Rn**

2m 41.6 OWNER Moyglare Stud Farm (CURRAGH)
1540a Token Gesture (IRE) maintains her rate of improvement with by far her best performance yet. Coming wide into the straight, she got the better of the runner-up well over a furlong out and will now take her chance in the Irish Oaks. She went up 5lb for this to 112. (6/1: op 7/2)
1698a* French Ballerina (IRE), forced to miss Ascot because she was in season, showed herself to be very vulnerable to a filly with a turn of foot. She definitely needs further now. (11/10: op 7/4)
1366a Family Tradition (IRE), totally friendless in the market, came from off the pace to challenge on the inner over a furlong out, but is not yet at her peak. (10/1)
1533a Caiseal Ros (IRE) rather let down the form of the Irish 1,000 Guineas with this display, she was being pushed along shortly after halfway and just plodded on at one pace. (6/1: op 4/1)
Aliya (IRE) found this transition from maiden to listed company, a bit too stiff for her at this stage. (4/1)
Rossmore Girl (IRE) (12/1: op 8/1)

1915a-CHANTILLY (France) (R-H) (Very Soft)
Monday June 16th

2268a PRIX LA FLECHE (Listed) (2-Y.O)
2-20 (2-22) **5f 110y** £15,713.00 (£5,387.00: £4,040.00: £2,694.00)

	Horse / details	Dist	Pos	SP	RR	SF
	Scenery (IRE) (AFabre,France) **2-9-2** OPeslier	—	1		—	—
	Zelding (IRE) (France) **2-8-13** CHanotel	nk	2		—	—
	Saralea (FR) (France) **2-8-13** DBoeuf	2	3		—	—
16578	**Dernier Croise (FR)** (BJMeehan) **2-9-2** MTebbutt	hd	4		—	—

8 Rn

67.9 secs (5.40) P-M 2.10F: 1.40F 2.50F 1.30F (31.40F) OWNER Sheikh Mohammed (CHANTILLY) BRED Sheikh Mohammed
Dernier Croise (FR) was well up for much of the way and, battling on gamely to the line, only lost third place close home.

2096a-MAISONS-LAFFITTE (France) (Good to soft)
Tuesday June 17th

2269a PRIX DU CARROUSSEL (Listed) (4-Y.O+)
3-20 (3-22) **1m 7f** £15,713.00 (£5,387.00: £4,040.00)

	Horse / details	Dist	Pos	SP	RR	SF
1365a3	**Philanthrop (FR)** (J-PGallorini,France) **5-9-1** TGillet	—	1		116	—
1359a2	**Yokohama (USA)** (France) **6-8-12** FHead	2	2		111	—
	Poltarf (USA) (JHMGosden) **6-8-12** GHind	hd	3		111	—

8 Rn

3m 16.9 (2.40) P-M 3.40F: 1.30F 1.50F 3.40F (5.20F) OWNER J. Menuisier BRED S. Niarchos
Poltarf (USA) was given every possible chance, but lacked the speed to go with the winner and the runner-up in the straight. He did run on again in the final furlong.

1719a-LONGCHAMP (Paris, France) (R-H) (Very Soft)
Thursday June 19th

2270a LA COUPE (Gp 3) (4-Y.O+)
3-35 (3-32) **1m 2f** £24,691.00 (£8,979.00: £4,489.00)

				SP	RR	SF
	For Valour (USA) (AFabre,France) **4-8-11** TGillet	—	1		118	—
916a3	**Si Seductor (USA)** (AFabre,France) **4-8-11** TJarnet	1½	2		116	—
922a6	**Bulington (FR)** (H-APantall,France) **5-8-11** CAsmussen	s.h	3		116	—
1359a3	**Tamure (IRE)** (JHMGosden) **5-8-11** DBoeuf (btn approx 4½l)		5		111	—
						8 Rn

2m 9.3 (9.30) P-M 32.00F: 3.90F 2.00F 1.30F (49.20F) OWNER Mr A. J. Richards (CHANTILLY) BRED Ewar Stud Farms
For Valour (USA) came with a storming late run to lead inside the final furlong. He won this race in most impressive style and looks as if he could stay further, so may be allowed to take his chance in the Group Two Maurice de Nieuil at Maisons-Laffitte at the end of July.
916a Si Seductor (USA) moved smoothly into the lead halfway up the straight and looked to have this race sewn up, but he could not resist the final late burst of his stablemate. He is just below Group standard.
Bulington (FR) needs better ground to show his best. He was not given a hard race but had every chance, and will now go to Vichy in an attempt to win a second Grand Prix.
1359a Tamure (IRE) led from the start, but was a beaten force soon after entering the straight. This was a disappointing performance and he is yet to recapture his form.

1199a-LYON PARILLY (Lyon, France) (Soft)
Saturday June 21st

2271a GRAND PRIX DE LYON (Listed) (3-Y.O+)
3-25 (3-25) **1m 4f** £22,447.00 (£8,081.00: £6,061.00)

				SP	RR	SF
	L'Africain Bleu (FR) (MmeCHead,France) **4-9-2** ODoleuze	—	1		115	—
1597*	**Taufan's Melody** (LadyHerries) **6-9-5** GMilligan	2½	2		115	—
	Trait De Genie (FR) (France) **5-9-9** AStarke	2½	3		115	—
						8 Rn

2m 31.8 P-M 3.00F: 2.10F 2.50F 3.80F (14.10F) OWNER Wertheimer Brothers (CHANTILLY)
1597* Taufan's Melody put in a game effort, trying to catch the winner who made every yard of the running. He stayed on one-paced to take second place and was not given a hard race. He may now go for the Grand Prix de Vichy.

DORTMUND (Germany) (R-H) (Good)
Sunday June 22nd

2272a GROSSER PREIS DER DORTMUNDER WIRTSCHAFT (Gp 3) (3-Y.O+)
3-30 (3-33) **1m 1f** £27,462.00 (£10,985.00: £5,492.00)

				SP	RR	SF
	Kalatos (GER) (AWohler,Germany) **5-9-2** WRyan	—	1		116	—
1544a2	**Is Tirol (IRE)** (MHofer,Germany) **3-8-3** ASuborics	½	2		113	—
1728a2	**Zero Problemo (IRE)** (BSchutz,Germany) **4-9-2** AStarke	½	3		114	—
						11 Rn

1m 47.2 TOTE 163DM: 23DM 11DM 12DM OWNER R & D Mitzlaff BRED Frau R & D Mitzlaff
Kalatos (GER) caused quite a surprise here. Making all the running under a forceful ride by Ryan, he looked in danger of being caught by the favourite over a furlong out, but the combination battled on well and was not going to give in.
Is Tirol (IRE), second to Air Express in the German 2,000 Guineas, loomed up looking dangerous over a furlong out, but appeared not to stay this extra furlong.
Zero Problemo (IRE) came with a challenge on the inner, but was given little room by the winner and should soon be able to gain compensation.

2270a-LONGCHAMP (Paris, France) (R-H) (Holding)
Sunday June 22nd

2273a PRIX DE LA PORTE MAILLOT (Gp 3) (3-Y.O)
1-35 (1-34) **7f** £24,691.00 (£8,979.00: £4,489.00) GOING: 0.29 sec per fur (G)

				SP	RR	SF
	Occupandiste (IRE) (MmeCHead,France) **4-8-13** ODoleuze	—	1		113	96
	Vernoy (USA) (AFabre,France) **3-8-7** OPeslier	½	2		115	89
	Whenby (USA) (MmeCHead,France) **4-8-13** FHead	2	3		107	90
1720a5	**Diffident (FR)** (SbinSuroor) **5-9-2** LDettori		6		—	—
1719a4	**Craigievar** (JRFanshawe) **3-8-7** DHarrison		8		—	—
						8 Rn

1m 21.2 (2.20) P-M 3.90F: 2.50F 2.50F 2.90F (23.40F) OWNER Wertheimer Brothers (CHANTILLY) BRED J. Wertheimer & Frere
Occupandiste (IRE) made every yard of the running in this Group Three event and held on gamely to the line. She thrives on a testing surface and may even go on to better things. She has plenty of speed and could now be aimed at the Prix de Ris-Orangis at Deauville and, if all goes well, another target could be the Prix Maurice de Gheest at the same track in August.
Vernoy (USA) had many lengths to make up with a furlong left to run, but, cutting down the winner, would have won in another ten yards. He may also be aimed at the Ris-Orangis.
Whenby (USA) finished well and was putting in her best work at the finish. The distance was a little short and she is not quite up to Group standard.
1720a Diffident (FR) was given every chance but was a spent force by the furlong marker. He is another who would be better suited by a firmer track.
1719a Craigievar was soon in the leading group, but was beaten by the furlong marker before dropping back to last place.

2274a GRAND PRIX DE PARIS (Gp 1) (3-Y.O C & F)
2-45 (2-48) **1m 2f** £134,680.00 (£53,872.00: £26,936.00: £13,468.00) GOING: 0.29 sec per fur (G)

			SP	RR	SF
1726a*	**Peintre Celebre (USA)** (AFabre,France) **3-9-2** OPeslier (mid div: 2nd st: led 1½ out: pushed out: easily).....—	**1**		122+	54
1726a^{5}	**Ithaki (IRE)** (JEPease,France) **3-9-2** CAsmussen (trckd wnr: 5th st: effrt fr 2f out: styd on one pce)................2	**2**		119	51
1726a^{6}	**Shaka** (J-CRouget,France) **3-9-2** J-RDubosc (in rr: 4th st: r.o fr 2f out: one pce cl home)................................1	**3**		117	49
1070a^{3}	**Alekos (USA)** (CLaffon-Parias,France) **3-9-2** DBoeuf (hld up: effrt fr 2f out: one pce)..5	**4**		109	41
1541a^{11}	**Royal Amaretto (IRE)** (BJMeehan) **3-9-2** MTebbutt (a cl up: led bef st tl 1½f out: wknd qckly)......................2½	**5**		105	37
1205a^{2}	**Zenith Rose (FR)** (PLenogue,France) **3-9-2** SGuillot (prom: 3rd st: sn btn)..s.h	**6**		105	37
	Super Cub (USA) (AFabre,France) **3-9-2** TJarnet (led fr s tl 4f out: last st: t.o) 20	**7**		73	5

7 Rn

2m 8.4 (8.40) P-M 1.40F: 1.10F 2.10F OWNER Mr D. Wildenstein (CHANTILLY) BRED Allez France Stables

1726a* Peintre Celebre (USA) won this race with plenty in hand, but he was not so spectacular on this occasion and that was due to the testing ground. Racing behind the leaders, he moved smoothly into the lead a furlong and a half out and then was just ridden out with hands and heels and, considering these conditions, this was a decent performance. After the race his connections announced the King George at Ascot as the colt's next target but this was changed twenty-four hours later. Instead he will now take a rest until the autumn when he will be prepared for the Arc de Triomphe via the Prix Niel. A son of Nureyev, he is still improving and will take all the beating in the Arc, but it is a shame he misses the King George as the track would have been perfect for him.

1070a Ithaki (IRE) tracked the winner for most of the way, but could not match the winner's speed early in the straight. An improving sort, he will now be put aside until the autumn when the Arc might be fitted into his programme.

1070a* Shaka was given every chance and would have been second if ridden for that place. Instead connections decided to take on the winner, resulting in him fading inside the final furlong. He will now be given a deserved rest.

1070a Alekos (USA) was held up for a late run and put his best work in at the finish. He is not really up to this class, but he could now be prepared for the Arlington Million.

1541a Royal Amaretto (IRE) raced close to the lead which he took before the straight. He hung on until one and a half furlongs from home before dropping back quickly. He will have a rest and then be aimed at a Group Three event, but connections still have their eyes on the St Leger and the Prix Royal-Oak

2275a PRIX DE MALLERET (Gp 2) (3-Y.O F)
3-20 (3-25) **1m 4f** £33,670.00 (£13,468.00: £6,734.00: £3,367.00) GOING: 0.29 sec per fur (G)

			SP	RR	SF
1360a^{2}	**Silver Fun (FR)** (MmeCHead,France) **3-8-9** ODoleuze (mde all: gd spd 1½f out: swished tail u.p: r.o wl) .....—	**1**		107	18
	Tenuous (PBary,France) **3-8-9** SGuillot (prom: led briefly st: one pce cl home) 2½	**2**		104	15
1722a^{2}	**Kassana (IRE)** (AdeRoyerDupre,France) **3-8-9** GMosse (hld up: effrt 2f out: styd on one pce fnl f)..................2	**3**		101	12
	Leros (FR) (DSepulchre,France) **3-8-9** CAsmussen (hld up: 4th st: styd on one pce fnl 1½f) ....¾	**4**		100	11
1722a*	**Legend Maker (IRE)** (AFabre,France) **3-8-9** TJarnet (a cl up: hrd rdn 2f out: wknd fnl f)...............................nk	**5**		100	11
	Yvecrique (FR) (J-PGauvin,France) **3-8-9** RJuteau (cl up: last pl & wl btn st) 20	**6**		73	—

6 Rn

2m 40.7 (14.70) P-M 13.30F: 5.40F 2.70F OWNER Wertheimer Brothers (CHANTILLY)

1360a Silver Fun (FR) was taken quickly to the front and never lost the lead. She was just headed by the runner-up in the straight, but then found another gear and was going away at the finish. She bled in her previous race which explains a below-par performance, finishing behind several of the rivals she met here. She is highly-rated and will be given a break before preparing for the Prix Vermeille in September.

Tenuous looked like the winner halfway up the straight, but she did not stretch out in the final furlong. She was given every chance and might be better suited to ground of a less holding nature.

1722a Kassana (IRE) had every chance on this occasion, but never looked like reaching the lead. She stayed on one-paced in the final furlong and was a disappointing favourite.

Leros (FR) was not seen with a chance until the straight. She ran on but is not quite up to this class.

1663-FOLKESTONE (R-H) (Soft)
Friday June 27th
WEATHER: unsettled WIND: fresh across

2276 CHANNEL (S) STKS (2-Y.O) (Class G)
2-10 (2-10) **5f** £2,070.00 (£570.00: £270.00) Stalls: Low GOING: 0.29 sec per fur (G)

			SP	RR	SF
2186^{3}	**Fast Franc (IRE)** (SCWilliams) **2-8-11** TSprake(2) (lw: mde all: clr over 1f out: comf) ....—	**1**	1/2 1	55+	33
	Just A Stroll (JSMoore) **2-8-8**(3) PPMurphy(1) (neat: outpcd early: hdwy over 1f out: styd on ins fnl f) 3½	**2**	4/1 2	44?	22
1827^{8}	**Wind In The Park** (MSalaman) **2-8-6** SWhitworth(3) (w ldr tl wknd over 2f out)...8	**3**	9/2 3	13	—
1564^{14}	**Silvazine** (DJSffrenchDavis) **2-8-6** RPrice(4) (a bhd) 12	**4**	12/1	—	—

(SP 112.5%) **4 Rn**

62.67 secs (5.07) CSF £2.83 TOTE £1.40: (£2.00) OWNER Mr J. W. Lovitt (NEWMARKET) BRED Richard Evans
No bid

2186 Fast Franc (IRE) put his previous experience to good use here. (1/2: op 1/3)

Just A Stroll got the hang of things late on, and kept on nicely in the closing stages. (4/1)

Wind In The Park showed pace to halfway. (9/2: op 3/1)

2277 STONE STREET H'CAP (0-80) (3-Y.O+) (Class D)
2-40 (2-41) **5f** £3,622.50 (£1,080.00: £515.00: £232.50) Stalls: Low GOING: 0.29 sec per fur (G)

			SP	RR	SF
2220*	**The Fugative (57)** (PMitchell) **4-8-13** 7x SSanders(2) (chsd ldr: led 2f out: hrd rdn ins fnl f: r.o wl).................—	**1**	6/5 1	66	—
1967^{7}	**Goodbye Gatemen (IRE) (68)** (BAPearce) **3-9-1**(3) MartinDwyer(1) (led: hdd 2f out: hrd rdn over 1f out: styd on one pce ins fnl f)..1¼	**2**	10/1	73	—
2197^{4}	**Sally Slade (68)** (CACyzer) **5-9-10** MRoberts(3) (trckd ldrs: ev ch ent fnl f: one pce) ....¾	**3**	2/1 2	71	4
1666^{3}	**Texas Cowgirl (IRE) (57)** (HVanderdussen,Belgium) **7-8-13b** SMaertens(4) (rr effrt over 1f out: one pce) 1	**4**	3/1 3	56	—

(SP 112.9%) **4 Rn**

64.9 secs (7.30) CSF £11.15 TOTE £2.30: (£7.00) OWNER Mr J. A. Redmond (EPSOM) BRED J. A. Redmond
WEIGHT FOR AGE 3yo-6lb

IN-FOCUS: This race was over two seconds slower than the first race and, in that race, all four horses tacked over to the far side, whereas in the other two races on the straight course they stayed on the stands side. That probably explains the difference in times.
2220* The Fugative won her second race in forty-eight hours here, defying her penalty in the gamest style. (6/5)
1638 Goodbye Gatemen (IRE), trying five furlongs today, showed plenty of pace and kept on in the closing stages. (10/1: 6/1-11/1)
2197 Sally Slade had her chance, but only had the one speed to offer in the final furlong. (2/1)
1666 Texas Cowgirl (IRE) made a brief move below the distance, but was soon beaten. (3/1)

2278 HYTHE FESTIVAL MAIDEN STKS (3-Y.O) (Class D)

3-10 (3-12) **6f** £3,785.00 (£1,130.00: £540.00: £245.00) Stalls: Low GOING: 0.29 sec per fur (G)

				SP	RR	SF
	Fiametta (CEBrittain) **3-8-9** BDoyle(4) (leggy: hld up in tch: led over 1f out: rdn ins fnl f: r.o)	—	**1**	$15/2^{3}$	80	5
935^{2}	**Fonteyn** (ACStewart) **3-8-9** MRoberts(3) (led: hdd over 3f out: sltly outpcd over 2f out: rallied & nt clr run over 1f out: str run & ev ch wl ins fnl f: r.o)	nk	**2**	$2/1^{2}$	79	4
1237^{2}	**Flourishing Way (78)** (RCharlton) **3-8-9** TSprake(7) (prom: led 2f out: hdd over 1f out: one pce)	4	**3**	$4/6^{1}$	69	—
	Hever Golf Rocket (TJNaughton) **3-9-0** SSanders(1) (str: bit bkwd: dwlt: hdwy over 2f out: wknd over 1f out)	4	**4**	25/1	63	—
2125^{9}	**Hot News** (JRJenkins) **3-8-7**(7) SCarson(6) (b.hind: led over 3f out: hdd 2f out: sn wknd)	12	**5**	100/1	31	—
1851^{10}	**Kildee Boy** (APJones) **3-9-0** RPrice(2) (sn outpcd)	hd	**6**	100/1	31	—
1415^{8}	**Secret Strength** (LadyHerries) **3-9-0** AClark(5) (in tch tl wknd over 2f out)	14	**7**	25/1	—	—
				(SP 114.8%)		**7 Rn**

1m 18.3 (8.10) CSF £20.84 TOTE £11.10: £3.30 £1.10 (£12.30) OWNER Mr B. H. Voak (NEWMARKET) BRED Rockwell Bloodstock
Fiametta took it up travelling well below the distance, but had to be ridden out to score. (15/2: 6/1-10/1)
935 Fonteyn was slightly unlucky. She led early, and after being headed over three furlongs out, was staying on again below the distance when short of room. Once clear in the final furlong, she stayed on strongly but found the winner too strong. (2/1)
1237 Flourishing Way was disappointing. She had every chance, leading two furlongs out, but was soon put in her place. (4/6)
Hever Golf Rocket, quite an imposing type in the paddock, can improve from this. (25/1)

2279 ROMNEY MARSH H'CAP (0-65) (3-Y.O+) (Class F)

3-40 (3-40) **1m 4f** £3,131.70 (£871.20: £419.10) Stalls: Low GOING: 0.64 sec per fur (GS)

				SP	RR	SF
1732^{6}	**Arif (IRE) (35)** (BJCurley) **5-7-10**(3) MartinDwyer(13) (mde all: rdn & edgd lft ins fnl f: r.o)	—	**1**	14/1	46	28
1417^{6}	**Dutch Dyane (33)** (GPEnright) **4-7-4**(7)ow1 PDoe(11) (a.p: chsd wnr over 2f out: rdn & hung lft ins fnl f: unable qckn)	1¼	**2**	33/1	42	23
1636^{2}	**Nothing Doing (IRE) (42)** (WJMusson) **8-8-6** JQuinn(7) (hld up in tch: rdn 2f out: r.o one pce)	nk	**3**	$3/1^{2}$	51	33
2118^{10}	**Mazirah (37)** (RCurtis) **6-8-1** JLowe(3) (rr: rdn & hdwy 2f out: r.o ins fnl f)	1½	**4**	12/1	44	26
1844^{10}	**Admirals Secret (USA) (52)** (CFWall) **8-9-2** TSprake(12) (lw: mid div: rdn over 2f out: kpt on one pce ins fnl f)	¾	**5**	8/1	58	40
1431^{4}	**Premier Dance (49)** (DHaydnJones) **10-8-13** AClark(6) (swtg: hld up: hdwy over 2f out: keeping on one pce whn nt clr run over 1f out)	1¾	**6**	$6/1^{3}$	53	35
2164^{2}	**Wildfire (SWI) (48)** (RAkehurst) **6-8-12** SSanders(4) (b: prom: chsd wnr 5f out tl over 2f out: wknd wl over 1f out)	9	**7**	$15/8^{1}$	40	22
1805^{7}	**Serious Trust (58)** (MrsLCJewell) **4-9-1**(7) DarrenWilliams(5) (lw: mid div tl wknd 2f out)	¾	**8**	14/1	49	31
1465^{8}	**Hippios (55)** (SDow) **3-7-12**(7)ow9 DSalt(10) (a bhd)	10	**9**	33/1	32	—
2067^{4}	**Zatopek (43)** (JCullinan) **5-8-4**(3) DO'Donohoe(8) (a bhd)	12	**10**	11/1	4	—
2049^{4}	**Antiguan Jane (64)** (RWArmstrong) **4-10-0b1** MRoberts(9) (chsd wnr tl wknd qckly 5f out)	16	**11**	12/1	4	—
1964^{6}	**Gracious Imp (USA) (36)** (JRJenkins) **4-7-7**(7)ow4 SCarson(1) (dwlt: a bhd)	5	**12**	33/1	—	—
				(SP 131.1%)		**12 Rn**

2m 47.4 (16.20) CSF £396.59 CT £1,609.63 TOTE £19.20: £4.40 £9.90 £1.30 (£195.60) Trio £430.40 OWNER Mr P. Byrne (NEWMARKET)
BRED T. J. Rooney
LONG HANDICAP Hippios 7-4 Dutch Dyane 7-2 Gracious Imp (USA) 7-6
WEIGHT FOR AGE 3yo-14lb
OFFICIAL EXPLANATION Arif (IRE): regarding the apparent improvement in form, the trainer's representative reported that the gelding needed his previous race which was his first for the yard, and was also suited by today's softer ground and slower early pace.
1732 Arif (IRE), unusually for a winner from this stable, did not appear to be supported in the market. Connections reported that he was suited by the rain-softened ground. (14/1: 6/1-16/1)
Dutch Dyane ran her best race to date, keeping on well in the final two furlongs despite hanging to her left. She is from a family who appreciate soft ground, and this may well be the key. (33/1)
1636 Nothing Doing (IRE) appeared to have every chance. (3/1)
Mazirah kept on from the rear in the closing stages, but never threatened the principals. (12/1: op 8/1)
1636 Admirals Secret (USA) (8/1: 6/1-9/1)
2164 Wildfire (SWI) was disappointing, being beaten before the home turn. (15/8: 3/1-7/4)
2067 Zatopek (11/1: 8/1-12/1)

2280 ARGLES & COURT SOLICITORS H'CAP (0-90) (3-Y.O+ F & M) (Class C)

4-10 (4-10) **6f 189y** £5,559.25 (£1,669.00: £804.50: £372.25) Stalls: Low GOING: 0.64 sec per fur (GS)

				SP	RR	SF
2201^{3}	**Q Factor (73)** (DHaydnJones) **5-9-1** AClark(4) (chsd ldr: pushed along 3f out: led over 1f out: edgd rt 1f out: sn clr: eased nr fin)	—	**1**	$13/8^{1}$	86+	59
1397*	**Waypoint (82)** (RCharlton) **4-9-10** TSprake(3) (hld up: rdn 2f out: one pce)	5	**2**	$100/30^{3}$	83	56
2119^{2}	**Palo Blanco (75)** (GLMoore) **6-9-3** CandyMorris(2) (hld up: rdn over 1f out: one pce)	s.h	**3**	$11/4^{2}$	76	49
1935^{4}	**St Blaine (CAN) (85)** (DRLoder) **3-9-4** DRMcCabe(1) (lw: led: hdd over 1f out: bit short of room 1f out: one pce)	s.h	**4**	$100/30^{3}$	86	50
				(SP 110.9%)		**4 Rn**

1m 29.0 (7.60) CSF £6.69 TOTE £2.80: (£5.00) OWNER Mr H. G. Collis (PONTYPRIDD) BRED A. Sofroniou and H. Collis
WEIGHT FOR AGE 3yo-9lb
2201 Q Factor, appreciating the rain-softened ground, ran out an emphatic winner, having looked momentarily in trouble before the home turn. (13/8)
1397* Waypoint plugged on at the one speed in the final two furlongs, but found her weight slowing her down. (100/30: 2/1-7/2)
2119 Palo Blanco appeared to have very chance. (11/4)
1935 St Blaine (CAN) probably did not appreciate the rain-softened ground. (100/30: 9/4-7/2)

2281 SHEPWAY H'CAP (0-70) (3-Y.O+) (Class E)

4-40 (4-41) **1m 1f 149y** £3,288.60 (£982.80: £470.40: £214.20) Stalls: Low GOING: 0.64 sec per fur (GS)

				SP	RR	SF
1139^{7}	**Bold Faith (45)** (WJMusson) **4-9-3** JQuinn(4) (b: hld up: hdwy 4f out: led ent fnl f: r.o)	—	**1**	11/4^{1}	57	26
1632^{4}	**Bakers Daughter (56)** (JRArnold) **5-9-11**$^{(3)}$ MartinDwyer(5) (a.p: chal strly & ev ch thrght fnl f: r.o)	s.h	**2**	3/1^{2}	68	37
1668^{5}	**Isis Honda (IRE) (59)** (CEBrittain) **3-9-5** BDoyle(7) (led 2f: remained prom: nt clr run 1f out: rallied ins fnl f: r.o)	1	**3**	8/1	69	26
1677*	**Lorins Gold (34)** (AndrewTurnell) **7-8-6** TSprake(12) (led after 2f: hdd ent fnl f: one pce)	1¼	**4**	8/1	42	11
1139^{3}	**Mad Alex (50)** (MJHaynes) **4-9-8** MRoberts(8) (chsd ldrs tl wknd over 2f out)	5	**5**	11/2	50	19
1694^{5}	**Golden Touch (USA) (56)** (DJSCosgrove) **5-10-0** SSanders(9) (hld up: hrd rdn over 2f out: no hdwy)	¾	**6**	10/1	55	24
1580^{11}	**La Spagna (28)** (MDIUsher) **6-8-0** DRMcCabe(10) (a bhd)	11	**7**	33/1	9	—
1484^{7}	**Barbrallen (30)** (MrsLCJewell) **5-8-2** SophieMitchell(11) (a bhd)	1¼	**8**	33/1	8	—
2195^{3}	**Kirov Protege (IRE) (36)** (MrsLCJewell) **5-8-1**$^{(7)}$ DarrenWilliams(6) (bhd fnl 4f)	hd	**9**	9/2^{3}	14	—
1929^{2}	**Tulsa (IRE) (63)** (BGubby) **3-9-9** AClark(2) (racd wd: mid div tl wknd 3f out)	3	**10**	8/1	36	—
1958^{9}	**Supreme Maimoon (60)** (MJPolglase) **3-9-6** TGMcLaughlin(1) (racd wd: in tch tl wknd wl over 2f out)	¾	**11**	12/1	32	—
				(SP 141.2%)	**11 Rn**	

2m 12.8 (15.10) CSF £12.63 CT £62.10 TOTE £4.80: £2.30 £2.20 £1.80 (£16.40) Trio £50.20 OWNER Jumbo Ltd (NEWMARKET) BRED Juddmonte Farms

WEIGHT FOR AGE 3yo-12lb

213 Bold Faith, very well supported from 8/1 to 11/4 favourite in the ring, and racing in a handicap for the first time, showed much-improved form to score. (11/4)

1632 Bakers Daughter tried her heart out here, and just lost out on the nod. (3/1)

1668 Isis Honda (IRE) was always to the fore, and did not have much luck when short of room entering the final furlong. To her credit she rallied strongly, but the damage was done. (8/1)

1677* Lorins Gold cut out much of the running, but only had the one pace to offer in the final furlong. (8/1)

T/Plpt: £229.50 (43.52 Tckts). T/Qdpt: £64.20 (12.06 Tckts) SM

2115-GOODWOOD (R-H) (St crse Soft, Rnd crse Good to soft)

Friday June 27th

Race 6: poor visibility

WEATHER: gloomy with late drizzle WIND: mod half against

2282 MIDSUMMER APPRENTICE H'CAP (0-80) (4-Y.O+) (Class E)

6-40 (6-40) **7f** £3,915.00 (£1,170.00: £560.00: £255.00) Stalls: High GOING: 0.32 sec per fur (G)

				SP	RR	SF
1878^{3}	**Amber Fort (74)** (DRCElsworth) **4-9-10v** RMullen(7) (hld up: led over 1f out: hrd rdn & edgd lft ins fnl f: r.o wl)	—	**1**	2/1^{1}	83	50
2109^{6}	**Morocco (IRE) (59)** (MRChannon) **8-8-6**$^{(3)}$ AEddery(6) (lw: hld up: rdn over 1f out: ev ch ins fnl f: unable qckn)	¾	**2**	6/1^{3}	66	33
1972^{5}	**Sea Danzig (59)** (JJBridger) **4-8-9** ADaly(4) (lw: led over 5f: one pce)	2½	**3**	13/2	61	28
1754^{16}	**Northern Judge (46)** (APJames) **4-7-5b**$^{(5)}$ RBrisland(3) (lw: chsd ldr 2f: ev ch over 1f out: one pce)	1	**4**	25/1	45	12
1849^{5}	**White Settler (65)** (RJHodges) **4-9-1** RFfrench(2) (rdn over 2f out: hdwy over 1f out: one pce)	hd	**5**	6/1^{3}	64	31
1926^{11}	**Digpast (IRE) (46)** (JJBridger) **7-7-5b**$^{(5)}$ PDoe(5) (lw: s.s: hdwy over 5f out: chsd ldr 5f out tl over 2f out: hrd rdn over 1f out: one pce)	hd	**6**	25/1	45	12
2115^{3}	**Stand Tall (60)** (LadyHerries) **5-8-7**$^{(3)}$ GMilligan(1) (b.hind: stdy hdwy over 1f out: sn wknd)	3½	**7**	7/2^{2}	51	18
1965*	**Abtaal (52)** (RJHodges) **7-7-13**$^{(3)}$ DDenby(8) (lw: hdwy 2f out: wknd over 1f out)	3	**8**	7/1	36	3
				(SP 117.7%)	**8 Rn**	

1m 31.9 (7.10) CSF £13.77 CT £58.93 TOTE £3.60: £1.10 £1.30 £1.90 (£7.90) OWNER The Caledonian Racing Society (WHITCOMBE) BRED Campbell Stud

LONG HANDICAP Digpast (IRE) 7-7 Northern Judge 7-1

STEWARDS' ENQUIRY Mullen susp 7/7/97 (careless riding).

1878 Amber Fort enjoys these underfoot conditions, and eased his way to the front below the distance. Given a few reminders, he did drift to his left inside the final furlong, but was not going to be denied. (2/1)

2109 Morocco (IRE) left his poor run at Ayr last Friday well behind. Throwing down his challenge in the final quarter-mile, he still had every chance early inside the final furlong before the winner asserted. (6/1)

1972 Sea Danzig, reverting back to the trip he has gained both his victories over, took the field along but, collared approaching the final furlong, failed to find another gear. (13/2)

1003 Northern Judge ran his best race so far this season. A leading light throughout, his inexperienced rider looked round twice in the straight to see where the opposition was, but the combination was tapped for toe in the final furlong. (25/1)

1849 White Settler, racing at the back of the field, made a forward move below the distance, but could then make no further impression. (6/1)

380 Digpast (IRE) is not very reliable, and as usual lost ground at the start. He soon came through to show in second place but, collared for that position over a quarter of a mile from home, could then only go up and down in the same place. (25/1)

2115 Stand Tall found this trip in these testing conditions too much for him and, after moving up sweetly below the distance, soon capitulated. (7/2)

1965* Abtaal (7/1: 5/1-8/1)

2283 FINDON (S) STKS (2-Y.O) (Class E)

7-10 (7-10) **6f** £5,287.50 (£1,575.00: £750.00: £337.50) Stalls: Low GOING: 0.32 sec per fur (G)

				SP	RR	SF
2186^{2}	**Ivory's Joy** (KTIvory) **2-8-6**$^{(5)}$ RFfrench(4) (b: b.hind: mde all: clr over 1f out: pushed out)	—	**1**	3/1^{2}	73	25
2191^{2}	**Rosewood Lady (IRE)** (KRBurke) **2-8-6** CRutter(2) (hld up: chsd wnr over 3f out: rdn over 2f out: no imp)	3½	**2**	3/1^{2}	59	11
1867^{3}	**Shanthi** (PJMakin) **2-8-6** SSanders(1) (hld up: rdn over 2f out: one pce)	½	**3**	4/5^{1}	57	9
	River Frontier (IRE) (MDIUsher) **2-8-6** RPrice(3) (neat: bit bkwd: chsd wnr over 2f: wknd over 2f out)	17	**4**	10/1^{3}	12	—
				(SP 114.6%)	**4 Rn**	

1m 16.64 (6.84) CSF £11.24 TOTE £3.20: (£5.00) OWNER Mr K. T. Ivory (RADLETT) BRED David S. Leggate

No bid

2186 Ivory's Joy is turning into quite a useful little plater, and despite having run just four days ago, disposed of these rivals with the minimum of fuss. Connections must have been delighted she did not attract a bid at the subsequent auction. (3/1)

2191 Rosewood Lady (IRE), who had a hard race at Lingfield on Tuesday, moved into second place just before halfway, but try as she might, had no hope with the winner. (3/1)
1867 Shanthi, less than two lengths behind the winner here on her debut earlier this month, when she lost a good ten lengths at the start, was very disappointing and, bustled along over a quarter of a mile from home, never looked like producing that vital turn of foot. Maybe the soft ground was not to her liking. (4/5: tchd evens)
River Frontier (IRE), looking as though the run would do her good, raced in second place in the first half of the race, but was soon in trouble. (10/1: op 6/1)

2284 DINAH SHERIDAN H'CAP (0-90) (3-Y.O+) (Class C)

7-40 (7-40) **1m 6f** £5,433.75 (£1,620.00: £772.50: £348.75) Stalls: High GOING: 0.32 sec per fur (G)

				SP	RR	SF
1270[2]	**Thornby Park (78)** (JLDunlop) **3-8-4** TSprake(5) (b: lw: hld up: chsd ldr over 8f out: led over 3f out: shkn up over 1f out: comf)	—	**1**	15/8[1]	92+	24
1258*	**Milly of The Vally (84)** (HRACecil) **3-8-10** WRyan(1) (lw: chsd ldr over 5f: rdn over 2f out: chsd wnr over 1f out: unable qckn)	1¾	**2**	2/1[2]	96+	28
1947[2]	**Brandon Magic (85)** (IABalding) **4-10-0** TQuinn(6) (lw: hdwy over 3f out: chsd wnr over 2f out tl over 1f out: wknd fnl f)	3	**3**	7/2[3]	94	43
1841*	**Tramline (82)** (MBlanshard) **4-9-11** JQuinn(2) (a bhd)	5	**4**	4/1	85	34
1795[10]	**Durham (55)** (GLMoore) **6-7-12v** CRutter(4) (led tl over 3f out: wknd over 2f out)	2½	**5**	20/1	55	4
				(SP 115.1%)		**5 Rn**

3m 15.15 (16.15) CSF £5.78 TOTE £3.30: £1.90 £1.40 (£3.30) OWNER Appleby Lodge Stud (ARUNDEL) BRED G. W. Mills and Sons
WEIGHT FOR AGE 3yo-17lb
1270 Thornby Park was well suited by the longer trip, and put up a polished display, leading early in the straight, and needing only to be shaken up to pull away from below the distance. (15/8)
1258* Milly of The Vally is a real stayer, and was well suited by this longer trip and the mud. Rousted along in the straight, she struggled into second place below the distance, but had no hope with the winner. (2/1)
1947 Brandon Magic goes well with some cut, but this trip, in this ground, appeared to stretch him to the limit. Having moved onto the heels of the winner over a quarter of a mile from home, he was collared for the runner-up berth below the distance, and then tired inside the final furlong. (7/2)
1841* Tramline ran a lifeless race, and never threatened to get into it. (4/1: op 5/2)
Durham again ran poorly, and after dictating matters from the front, tamely dropped away once caught early in the straight. In four runs so far this season, he has managed to beat just two horses. (20/1)

2285 WEATHERBYS BANKING SERVICES H'CAP (0-80) (3-Y.O+) (Class D)

8-10 (8-11) **1m 1f** £4,542.00 (£1,356.00: £648.00: £294.00) Stalls: High GOING: 0.32 sec per fur (G)

				SP	RR	SF
1973[5]	**Brandon Jack (70)** (IABalding) **3-8-7** MRoberts(7) (lw: hdwy over 2f out: led over 1f out: drvn out)	—	**1**	5/1[3]	78	41
1249*	**Island Sanctuary (IRE) (76)** (PJMakin) **3-8-13** SSanders(4) (lw: hld up: rdn over 3f out: ev ch fnl f: r.o wl)	hd	**2**	4/1[2]	84	47
	Dead Aim (IRE) (75) (IABalding) **3-8-12** BDoyle(6) (lw: dwlt: rdn over 3f out: hdwy over 1f out: r.o one pce)	2	**3**	8/1	79	42
1926[3]	**Tribal Peace (IRE) (61)** (BGubby) **5-8-9** AClark(9) (lw: hld up: rdn over 5f out: one pce fnl 2f)	½	**4**	4/1[2]	64	38
1878[12]	**Waikiki Beach (USA) (64)** (GLMoore) **6-8-12** SWhitworth(5) (lw: led over 7f)	19	**5**	16/1	34	8
1926[7]	**Mimosa (60)** (SDow) **4-8-8** WRyan(2) (s.i.s: nvr nrr)	1¾	**6**	12/1	27	1
2113*	**Can Can Lady (83)** (MJohnston) **3-9-6** 6x JReid(8) (lw: bhd fnl 4f)	1¾	**7**	3/1[1]	46	9
2122[11]	**Lady Godiva (67)** (MJPolglase) **3-8-4** JQuinn(1) (chsd ldr 8f out: ev ch over 2f out: wknd over 1f out)	9	**8**	33/1	14	—
1975[8]	**Dark Age (IRE) (80)** (RAkehurst) **4-10-0** TQuinn(10) (lw: chsd ldr 1f: wknd over 4f out: t.o)	25	**9**	14/1	—	—
				(SP 116.0%)		**9 Rn**

2m 1.56 (8.56) CSF £23.16 CT £143.78 TOTE £6.10: £2.00 £1.90 £3.30 (£29.40) Trio £140.90 OWNER Mr R. P. B. Michaelson (KINGSCLERE) BRED Highclere Stud Ltd
WEIGHT FOR AGE 3yo-11lb
1973 Brandon Jack, dropped another 5lb after yet another poor run at Sandown recently, bounced back to form on this soft ground. Gaining a very slender advantage approaching the final furlong, he had a tremendous battle with the runner-up, and just managed to prevail. (5/1)
1249* Island Sanctuary (IRE) only just failed to complete the hat-trick. Throwing down his challenge below the distance, he may well have got his head in front for a few strides inside the final furlong, but found the winner just a little bit too strong. (4/1: op 5/2)
Dead Aim (IRE) made a very pleasing reappearance over this longer trip. Racing at the back of the field, he stayed on under pressure to finish a very promising third. (8/1: 5/1-9/1)
1926 Tribal Peace (IRE), off the bridle well before halfway, could only go up and down in the same place in the final quarter-mile. (4/1: 3/1-9/2)
1575 Waikiki Beach (USA) took the field along, but when he was eventually overhauled below the distance he had nothing more to offer. A drop in class and a return to the All-Weather is needed. (16/1)
1809 Dark Age (IRE) (14/1: op 6/1)

2286 E.B.F. SUPERIOR NOVICE STKS (2-Y.O) (Class D)

8-40 (8-40) **6f** £5,047.25 (£1,508.00: £721.50: £328.25) Stalls: Low GOING: 0.32 sec per fur (G)

				SP	RR	SF
2037[2]	**Conectis (IRE)** (DJSCosgrove) **2-8-8**ow1 JReid(3) (mde all: drvn out)	—	**1**	11/2[3]	77	23
1872[5]	**Commander Charlie** (IABalding) **2-8-12** TQuinn(2) (lw: hld up: chsd wnr over 2f out: ev ch 1f out: unable qckn)	½	**2**	3/1[2]	80	27
1872[3]	**Elakik** (JLDunlop) **2-8-12** RHills(6) (lw: plld hrd: hld up: rdn over 2f out: ev ch 1f out: one pce)	¾	**3**	4/5[1]	78	25
1675[6]	**Ballet Rambert** (MJHeaton-Ellis) **2-8-8**(5) RFfrench(5) (chsd wnr over 3f: wknd over 1f out)	2	**4**	10/1	73	20
	Piped Aboard (IRE) (JLDunlop) **2-8-12** TSprake(7) (w'like: scope: a bhd)	4	**5**	10/1	62	9
				(SP 114.1%)		**5 Rn**

1m 16.58 (6.78) CSF £20.60 TOTE £6.10: £1.90 £2.10 (£8.80) OWNER Camelot Racing (NEWMARKET) BRED Golden Vale Stud
2037 Conectis (IRE), the most experienced runner in the field, was outclassed by her rivals on looks in the paddock, but it was a totally different story in the race itself, as she made all the running, and responded to pressure to keep her two persistent rivals at bay. (11/2: 4/1-6/1)
1872 Commander Charlie looked in fine shape beforehand, and reversed form with the third - he had finished a length behind that rival on their debuts at Newbury recently. Moving into second place soon after halfway, he was one of three almost in line entering the final furlong before tapped for toe. (3/1: op 2/1)
1872 Elakik was rather disappointing. Taking a keen hold, and tending to hang during the race, he was busted along over a quarter of a mile from home, but was certainly close enough if good enough entering the final furlong before tapped for toe. (4/5: tchd evens)

1675 Ballet Rambert, in second place until past halfway, had shot her bolt below the distance. (10/1: 7/1-11/1)
Piped Aboard (IRE), a half-brother to several winners, never threatened to get into it. (10/1: op 6/1)

2287 CRAVEN MEDIAN AUCTION MAIDEN STKS (3-Y.O) (Class D)

9-10 (9-12) **1m 2f** £3,850.00 (£1,150.00: £550.00: £250.00) Stalls: High GOING: 0.32 sec per fur (G)

Form	Horse	Dist	Pos	SP	RR	SF
958^{9}	**Nawasib (IRE) (84)** (JLDunlop) **3-8-9** BDoyle(5) (hld up: rdn over 3f out: str run to ld wl ins fnl f: r.o wl)	—	**1**	$7/2^{2}$	78	38
1850^{4}	**Tikopia (84)** (IABalding) **3-9-0** SWhitworth(9) (lw: hld up: led over 3f out: hrd rdn over 1f out: hdd wl ins fnl f: unable qckn)	1½	**2**	$7/2^{2}$	81	41
1866^{3}	**Alarmist** (RCharlton) **3-9-0** TSprake(8) (hdwy over 4f out: chsd ldr over 2f out tl ins fnl f: r.o one pce)	¾	**3**	$9/4^{1}$	79	39
1322^{5}	**Chandler's Hall** (MJHeaton-Ellis) **3-9-0** AClark(3) (lw: led over 1f: rdn over 3f out: wknd over 2f out)	15	**4**	12/1	55	15
1423^{10}	**Imperial Glen (IRE)** (MDIUsher) **3-8-9** RPrice(10) (lw: led over 8f out tl over 3f out: wknd over 2f out)	10	**5**	50/1	34	—
	My Roland (IRE) (JFfitch-Heyes) **3-9-0** MRoberts(7) (w'like: scope: hdwy 7f out: wknd over 5f out)	2	**6**	16/1	36	—
	Dazzling Stone (LadyHerries) **3-8-9**(5) GMilligan(2) (bit bkwd: a bhd)	8	**7**	7/1	23	—
	Darapour (IRE) (LMCumani) **3-8-9**(5) RFfrench(4) (w'like: scope: s.s: a wl bhd)	7	**8**	$11/2^{3}$	12	—

(SP 118.6%) **8 Rn**

2m 16.77 (10.17) CSF £15.41 TOTE £4.70: £1.80 £1.20 £1.50 (£12.00) Trio £4.30 OWNER Prince A. A. Faisal (ARUNDEL) BRED Nawara Stud Co Ltd

Nawasib (IRE) appreciated the step up in trip. Outpaced as the real race developed entering the straight, she looked booked for third place below the distance, but then found another gear, and came flying through to snatch the spoils in the closing stages. (7/2: op 9/4)
1850 Tikopia, taking a drop in distance, made his bid for glory as the bugler called entering the straight. Under pressure below the distance, it looked as if he was holding on, until the late flourish of the winner caught him out in the closing stages. (7/2: 3/1-9/2)
1866 Alarmist took closer order running down the hill, and came through to take second place over a quarter of a mile from home. Grimly trying to get on terms with the leader, he was unable to cope with the winner when that rival went sailing by inside the final furlong. (9/4)
1322 Chandler's Hall was close up until left for dead over two furlongs from home. (12/1)
Imperial Glen (IRE) was soon at the head of affairs, but she was collared early in the straight, and was soon in trouble. (50/1)
Darapour (IRE) (11/2: 5/2-6/1)

T/Plpt: £181.80 (74.52 Tckts). T/Qdpt: £25.90 (38.78 Tckts) AK

1669-NEWCASTLE (L-H) (Good)

Friday June 27th

WEATHER: overcast, rain last two races WIND: str half against

2288 YORKSHIRE-TYNE TEES TELEVISION (S) STKS (2-Y.O) (Class E)

6-15 (6-20) **6f** £7,262.50 (£2,200.00: £1,075.00: £512.50) Stalls: High GOING: 0.20 sec per fur (G)

Form	Horse	Dist	Pos	SP	RR	SF
2016^{2}	**Inchalong** (MBrittain) **2-8-6** GCarter(9) (lw: dwlt: sn chsng ldrs: led over 1f out: hld on wl towards fin)	—	**1**	12/1	61	20
971^{5}	**Erro Codigo** (MrsJRRamsden) **2-8-11** JFortune(3) (swtchd rt & hdwy 4f out: chsd wnr appr fnl f: kpt on wl u.p)	½	**2**	$4/1^{2}$	65	24
1821^{5}	**Bali Dance** (CBBBooth) **2-8-6** KHodgson(16) (sn drvn along: hdwy ½-wy: styd on fnl f)	1¾	**3**	$7/2^{1}$	55	14
2165^{2}	**Makahu Don** (WTKemp) **2-8-11** GDuffield(14) (trckd ldrs: effrt & hung lft 2f out: one pce)	3	**4**	$5/1^{3}$	52	11
1645^{6}	**Bint Nadia** (JDBethell) **2-8-6** DHolland(6) (bhd & drvn along: styd on fnl 2f)	nk	**5**	11/2	46	5
1760^{9}	**Ella Falls (IRE)** (TDBarron) **2-8-6** RLappin(13) (lw: dwlt: hdwy ½-wy. nvr nr to chal)	½	**6**	13/2	45	4
1997^{12}	**Beechwood Quest (IRE)** (BSRothwell) **2-8-6** LCharnock(5) (w ldrs: led over 2f out: hdd & wknd over 1f out)	1¼	**7**	25/1	42	1
1267^{13}	**Wee Christy (IRE)** (WMcKeown) **2-8-11** NDay(8) (s.i.s: wl bhd tl styd on fnl 2f)	¾	**8**	33/1	45	4
697^{7}	**Castle Friend** (PCHaslam) **2-8-4**(7) CLowther(1) (bit bkwd: s.s: sn drvn along: sme hdwy ½-wy: wknd over 1f out)	1½	**9**	25/1	41	—
2153^{6}	**Hayburner** (MWEasterby) **2-8-11** TLucas(11) (trckd ldrs tl wknd 2f out)	1½	**10**	20/1	37	—
1819^{6}	**Circuiteer (IRE)** (JBerry) **2-8-11b**[1] DMcKeown(7) (led tl over 2f out: sn wknd)	hd	**11**	12/1	36	—
	Peaceful Reign (MrsJRRamsden) **2-8-11** AMunro(4) (str: compact: bit bkwd: chsd ldrs 2f: sn wknd)	3	**12**	16/1	28	—
	Rockswain (IRE) (PCHaslam) **2-8-4**(7) PGoode(12) (compact: dwlt: a bhd: sn drvn along)	1½	**13**	33/1	24	—
	Shirleys Girl (IRE) (WStorey) **2-8-6** NKennedy(15) (leggy: unf: s.i.s: sn wl bhd)	24	**14**	33/1	—	—
*2016**	***Tancred Times*** (DWBarker) **2-8-6** TWilliams(10) (Withdrawn not under Starter's orders: v.unruly & ref to ent stalls)		**W**	10/1	—	—

(SP 139.2%) **14 Rn**

1m 17.77 (6.27) CSF £52.01 TOTE £10.30: £2.10 £2.30 £1.70 (£24.20) Trio £46.80 OWNER Northgate Lodge Partnerships (WARTHILL) BRED R. B. Warren
No bid

2016 Inchalong gained a well-deserved, overdue first victory in this valuable seller, which considering the prize money resulted in a disappointing field. (12/1: op 8/1)
971 Erro Codigo was switched towards the stands side to overcome his low draw. Always making hard work of it, he was never going to quite overhaul the winner. (4/1)
1821 Bali Dance was putting in her best work at the finish. (7/2)
2165 Makahu Don proved suited by the step up to six, but gave her rider problems by persistently hanging. (5/1)
1645 Bint Nadia is an excitable type, but does not lack some ability. (11/2)
1819 Circuiteer (IRE) (12/1: op 8/1)

2289 NORTHERN ROCK SAVE THE CHILDREN FUND GOSFORTH PARK CUP H'CAP (0-105) (3-Y.O+) (Class B)

6-45 (6-48) **5f** £14,265.00 (£4,320.00: £2,110.00: £1,005.00) Stalls: High GOING: 0.20 sec per fur (G)

Form	Horse	Dist	Pos	SP	RR	SF
1468^{2}	**Moon Strike (FR) (83)** (HAkbary) **7-8-7** AMunro(2) (chsd ldrs: led ins fnl f: jst hld on)	—	**1**	$5/1^{1}$	100	61
2061*	**Blessingindisguise (72)** (MWEasterby) **4-7-10b** 7x LCharnock(4) (w ldr: led 2f out: hdd ins fnl f: styd on wl)	s.h	**2**	10/1	89	50
1766^{4}	**Surprise Mission (89)** (MrsJRRamsden) **5-8-13** JFortune(6) (lw: hld up gng wl: swtchd rt ½-wy: nt clr run over 1f out: kpt on wl)	2½	**3**	$5/1^{1}$	98	59
1946^{3}	**Lady Sheriff (77)** (MWEasterby) **6-7-12b**(3) PFessey(3) (lw: s.i.s: bhd tl hdwy 2f out: nvr nr to chal)	1¾	**4**	10/1	80	41

2129[2]	**Saint Express (80)** (MrsMReveley) **7-8-4**ow1 ACulhane(8) (hld up & bhd: hdwy whn nt clr run 1f out: styd on towards fin)	nk	**5**	13/2	82	42
2211[4]	**Ziggy's Dancer (USA) (85)** (EJAlston) **6-8-9** RLappin(9) (sn bhd: hmpd ½-wy & over 1f out: kpt on)	¾	**6**	11/1	85	46
1402[6]	**Lord High Admiral (CAN) (81)** (MJHeaton-Ellis) **9-8-5v** RPerham(10) (led to 2f out: wknd fnl f)	½	**7**	6/1[3]	79	40
1269*	**Canovas Heart (86)** (BobJones) **8-8-10** NDay(11) (trckd ldrs tl wknd over 1f out)	nk	**8**	11/2[2]	83	44
1608[11]	**Ansellman (80)** (JBerry) **7-8-4b** GCarter(7) (outpcd whn hmpd ½-wy: n.d after)	1	**9**	14/1	74	35
1772[2]	**Kira (85)** (JLEyre) **7-8-2**(7) SBuckley(12) (b: sn drvn along: chsd ldrs tl wknd over 1f out)	2½	**10**	12/1	71	32
1721a[8]	**Passion For Life (104)** (GLewis) **4-10-0** DHarrison(1) (racd wd: chsd ldrs: drvn along ½-wy: sn lost pl)	6	**11**	14/1	71	32
1946[6]	**Swynford Dream (79)** (JFBottomley) **4-8-3** GDuffield(5) (lw: unruly in stalls: w ldrs tl wknd over 1f out)	hd	**12**	20/1	46	7

(SP 128.6%) **12 Rn**

61.17 secs (2.77) CSF £54.86 CT £250.57 TOTE £8.00: £3.00 £3.00 £2.90 (£75.20) Trio £150.30 OWNER Mr A. Foustok (NEWMARKET) BRED Haras de Manneville in France

LONG HANDICAP Blessingindisguise 7-2

STEWARDS' ENQUIRY Fortune susp. 7-9/7/97 (careless riding).

1468 Moon Strike (FR) was meeting the runner-up on 10lb better terms compared to Redcar. He did just enough to give Alan Munro a winner on his first day back here. (5/1)

2061* Blessingindisguise is in the form of his life at present, and after being headed, battled back well, just failing to get back up in what turned out to be a two-horse finish. (10/1)

1766 Surprise Mission, 6lb higher than Chester, seemed determined to overcome get as near to the stands'-side rail as possible, and as a result managed to hamper Ziggy's Dancer twice. His rider was later suspended. (5/1)

1946 Lady Sheriff came from off the pace after missing the break. (10/1)

2129 Saint Express, who was making hard work of it some way from home, and met trouble at one stage, is possibly better over six and on faster ground these days. (13/2)

2211 Ziggy's Dancer (USA), a five-furlong specialist, was interfered with twice by Surprise Mission, and in the circumstances did well to finish as close as he did. (11/1)

1402 Lord High Admiral (CAN), who is slipping down the weights, is sure to pop up again when everything goes his own way. He likes to dominate. (6/1)

1269* Canovas Heart was racing from an 8lb higher mark than at Ripon. (11/2)

2290 STEPHEN EASTEN DOBSON PEACOCK H'CAP (0-85) (3-Y.O+) (Class D)

7-30 (7-30) **1m (round)** £7,360.00 (£2,230.00: £1,090.00: £520.00) Stalls: Low GOING: 0.05 sec per fur (G)

				SP	RR	SF
1802[4]	**Duraid (IRE) (64)** (DenysSmith) **5-8-3**(7) CLowther(4) (sn trckng ldrs: hmpd appr st: nt clr run 2f out: swtchd rt over 1f out: qcknd to ld wl ins fnl f)	—	**1**	16/1	79	41
2062*	**Al Masroor (USA) (74)** (JWPayne) **3-8-10** 5x DeanMcKeown(1) (lw: trckd ldrs: led over 1f out tl wl ins fnl f)	1½	**2**	6/1[2]	86	38
892[18]	**Master Charter (80)** (MrsJRRamsden) **5-9-12** AMunro(6) (s.s: stdy hdwy over 2f out: hmpd over 1f out: kpt on same pce)	2	**3**	25/1	88	50
1845*	**Suez Tornado (IRE) (68)** (EJAlston) **4-9-0v** ACulhane(10) (lw: hld up & bhd: effrt on outside over 3f out: styd on appr fnl f)	1	**4**	9/1	74	36
1175[6]	**Share Delight (IRE) (80)** (BWHills) **3-9-2** AMcGlone(12) (lw: hld up & plld hrd: effrt over 2f out: styd on same pce)	nk	**5**	10/1	85	37
2013[4]	**Tigrello (85)** (GLewis) **3-9-7** DHarrison(5) (chsd ldrs: pushed along over 3f out: outpcd appr fnl f)	4	**6**	11/4[1]	82	34
1384[8]	**Winston (56)** (JDBethell) **4-7-13**(3) PFessey(8) (trckd ldrs: effrt over 2f out: wkng whn bmpd over 1f out)	1	**7**	16/1	51	13
1775[5]	**Impulsive Air (IRE) (64)** (EWeymes) **5-8-10** DaleGibson(2) (lw: chsd ldrs: drvn along over 3f out: wknd over 1f out)	1	**8**	14/1	57	19
2062[4]	**Jack Flush (IRE) (66)** (BSRothwell) **3-8-2** LCharnock(11) (b.nr fore: chsd ldr: wknd over 1f out)	nk	**9**	11/1	59	11
1979[15]	**Mbulwa (56)** (RAFahey) **11-8-2** GCarter(3) (led tl over 1f out: wknd fnl f)	nk	**10**	25/1	48	10
2062[3]	**Plan For Profit (IRE) (80)** (MJohnston) **3-9-2** DHolland(13) (bhd: hdwy on ins over 2f out: nt clr run over 1f out & ins fnl f: nt rcvr)	¾	**11**	7/1[3]	71	23
1560*	**Somerton Boy (IRE) (73)** (PCalver) **7-9-5** GDuffield(9) (lw: hld up: effrt over 2f out: hung bdly lft & eased)	15	**12**	7/1[3]	34	—
1631*	**Gulliver (73)** (MrsJRRamsden) **4-9-5** JFortune(7) (b.off fore: dwlt: effrt over 2f out: virtually p.u over 1f out: lame)	20	**13**	15/2	—	—

(SP 131.3%) **13 Rn**

1m 44.7 (5.70) CSF £109.05 CT £2,231.82 TOTE £23.20: £4.20 £2.80 £6.60 (£74.80) Trio £250.80 OWNER Mr A. Suddes (BISHOP AUCKLAND) BRED Hussein Hurami

WEIGHT FOR AGE 3yo-10lb

1802 Duraid (IRE), dropped back to a mile, finally came good, but he certainly seemed to have luck on his side in the stewards' room. The boy switched him right off the rail, hampering Master Charter and Winston. Finishing with a flourish, he led and went clear near the line. It is hard to believe the same panel of stewards that threw out Epic Stand here allowed him to keep the race, deeming the interference accidental, which it was clearly not. The boy must have known that in the tightly-packed field such a manoeuvre would cause interference. (16/1)

2062* Al Masroor (USA), only 2lb higher in the weights despite the penalty, made the best of his way home, escaping any problems behind, but he was mown down by the winner near the line. (6/1: 4/1-13/2)

Master Charter, having his first outing for two months, travelled strongly. After being knocked out of his stride by the winner, he kept on all the way to the line under his big weight. (25/1)

1845* Suez Tornado (IRE) was racing from a 7lb higher mark in a much more competitive event. (9/1)

1175 Share Delight (IRE), who as usual wore a tongue-strap, was very keen going to post. (10/1)

2013 Tigrello, who had his tongue tied down, is not very big, and he never looked like posing a serious threat. (11/4: 4/1-5/2)

2062 Plan For Profit (IRE), trying for an ambitious run up the inner, was completely stopped coming to the final furlong, and with no way out his rider called it a day inside the last. The impression was that he would have finished third at worst. (7/1)

1631* Gulliver, heavily bandaged on his off-fore, was in trouble some way out, and after virtually being pulled up, was dismounted after the line. (15/2)

2291 HAMLET EXTRA MILD CIGARS H'CAP (0-90) (3-Y.O+) (Class C)

8-00 (8-00) **1m 4f 93y** £5,962.50 (£1,800.00: £875.00: £412.50) Stalls: Low GOING: 0.05 sec per fur (G)

				SP	RR	SF
1625*	**Kilma (USA) (84)** (LMCumani) **3-9-10** KDarley(1) (trckd ldrs: chal over 1f out: led last strides)	—	**1**	4/1[3]	94	62
2064*	**Heart of Gold (IRE) (83)** (MissSEHall) **3-9-9** 4x AMcGlone(6) (trckd ldr: led over 3f out to nr fin)	s.h	**2**	100/30[2]	93	61
1999*	**Honourable (76)** (JWWatts) **3-9-2** 4x GDuffield(3) (hld up: effrt & nt clr run 3f out tl over 1f out: styd on same pce fnl f)	2	**3**	5/4[1]	83	51

2114*	**Ledgendry Line (74)** (MrsMReveley) **4-10-0** 4x ACulhane(4) (lw: hld up: hdwy on ins over 2f out: nt clr run: several positions: nvr nr to chal)	5	**4**	9/1	75	57
2132*	**Gee Bee Boy (69)** (APJarvis) **3-8-9** 4x DWright(5) (lw: unruly in stalls: hld up: effrt on outside over 3f out: edgd lft: qcknd over 1f out)	4	**5**	10/1	65	33
2014[9]	**Northern Motto (54)** (JSGoldie) **4-8-8** NVarley(7) (trckd ldrs: drvn along over 4f out: wknd over 1f out)	s.h	**6**	10/1	50	32
1654[7]	**Regal Eagle (63)** (MDHammond) **4-9-3** DHolland(2) (led tl over 3f out: wknd over 2f out: eased)	10	**7**	33/1	46	28

(SP 118.6%) **7 Rn**

2m 45.3 (7.80) CSF £17.05 TOTE £3.80: £2.30 £1.90 (£5.70) OWNER Sheikh Ahmed Al Maktoum (NEWMARKET) BRED Heronwood Farm Inc
WEIGHT FOR AGE 3yo-14lb

1625* Kilma (USA), having only her third ever outing, carried her head high and swished her tail, but rider did brilliantly to force her head in front in the final strides. To be fair to her, she is still inexperienced. (4/1)

2064* Heart of Gold (IRE), racing over a shorter trip and with the early pace not strong, took it up turning in, and quickly went for home. Giving his all, he had to give best on the line. Developing physically all the time, he can do nothing but improve further. (100/30)

1999* Honourable, stepping up two furlongs in trip, found all the trouble going. When he did get clear coming to the final furlong, he stuck on, but to be honest, was never going to find sufficient to reach the first two. It is possible he is better-suited by a strongly-run race over a mile and a quarter. (5/4)

2114* Ledgendry Line, under a 4lb penalty, was ridden from off the pace in a moderately-run race. After looking for an opening, instead of coming to the outside his rider switched him to the inner, and asked him to do just enough to finish fourth. He is better than he showed here. (9/1: op 6/1)

2132* Gee Bee Boy found this much tougher. Making his effort on the outer once in line for home, he tended to edge left, posing problems for Honourable on his inner. (10/1: op 5/1)

2292 GO EVENING RACING WITH THE DAILY TELEGRAPH LIMITED STKS (0-90) (3-Y.O+) (Class C)

8-30 (8-30) **1m 2f 32y** £5,022.00 (£1,521.00: £743.00: £354.00) Stalls: High GOING: 0.05 sec per fur (G)

				SP	RR	SF
2133[3]	**Atlantic Desire (IRE) (88)** (MJohnston) **3-8-6** DHolland(1) (lw: mde all: pushed clr 2f out: styd on wl)	—	**1**	7/4 1	96	41
2155[2]	**Billy Bushwacker (88)** (MrsMReveley) **6-9-7** ACulhane(5) (lw: hld up: effrt over 2f out: sn chsng wnr: no imp)	2½	**2**	5/2 2	95	52
1981[10]	**Celestial Choir (89)** (JLEyre) **7-9-1**(3) OPears(2) (trckd ldrs: pushed along 5f out: outpcd fnl 2f)	7	**3**	10/1	81	38
1637*	**Arctic Owl (85)** (JRFanshawe) **3-8-11** DHarrison(4) (sn trckng ldrs: effrt 3f out: sn hrd drvn: wknd 1f out)	2½	**4**	3/1 3	82	27
1949[2]	**Cybertechnology (86)** (BWHills) **3-8-9** AMcGlone(3) (trckd ldrs: pushed along over 3f out: lost pl over 2f out: eased)	22	**5**	5/1	45	—

(SP 115.7%) **5 Rn**

2m 13.5 (6.80) CSF £6.24 TOTE £2.70: £1.30 £2.00 (£2.70) OWNER Atlantic Racing Ltd (MIDDLEHAM) BRED Hamwood Stud
WEIGHT FOR AGE 3yo-12lb

2133 Atlantic Desire (IRE) was racing over a mile and a quarter for the first time since two. Given an intelligent ride, she stepped up the gallop to show in a clear lead two furlongs from home and, kept up to her work, was never in any danger. (7/4)

2155 Billy Bushwacker went in pursuit of the winner two furlongs from home, but he was never doing anything like enough to trouble her. (5/2)

100 Celestial Choir, best in on official figures, ran better than at York last time, but still seems off the boil at present. (10/1)

1637* Arctic Owl, an immature type, travelled strongly but, asked to improve once in line for home, seemed to lose his action altogether a furlong out. He is far from the finished article yet. (3/1)

1949 Cybertechnology ran very poorly indeed. (5/1: 7/2-11/2)

2293 STANLEY RACING (FOR THE WILLIAM EDWIN NEESHAM TROPHY) H'CAP (0-75) (4-Y.O+) (Class D)

9-00 (9-00) **1m 2f 32y** £4,162.50 (£1,260.00: £615.00: £292.50) Stalls: High GOING: 0.05 sec per fur (G)

				SP	RR	SF
2122[9]	**Mattimeo (IRE) (70)** (APJarvis) **4-9-9** KDarley(7) (lw: trckd ldrs: nt clr run on ins & swtchd rt over 1f out: r.o wl to ld nr fin: readily)	—	**1**	8/1	81	44
1313[5]	**Opulent (71)** (MrsMReveley) **6-9-10** ACulhane(5) (trckd ldrs: led over 3f out: sn clr: wknd & hdd wl ins fnl f)	1	**2**	12/1	80	43
2043[4]	**Sing And Dance (44)** (EWeymes) **4-7-11**ow1 DaleGibson(2) (trckd ldrs: wl outpcd over 3f out: styd on appr fnl f)	2	**3**	16/1	50	12
2043[3]	**Gold Desire (48)** (MBrittain) **7-8-1** GCarter(8) (trckd ldrs: drvn along over 3f out: one pce)	1½	**4**	9/4 2	52	15
1450[8]	**Gymcrak Premiere (74)** (GHolmes) **9-9-13** DHarrison(9) (b.hind: hld up: hdwy 2f out: nvr nr to chal)	1½	**5**	8/1	76	39
1992[7]	**Jubran (USA) (45)** (JLEyre) **11-7-12** DWright(4) (hld up: drvn along 3f out: no imp)	¾	**6**	25/1	45	8
1992[5]	**Keep Battling (48)** (JSGoldie) **7-8-1** TWilliams(6) (hld up & plld hrd: hdwy over 3f out: sn chsng ldrs: wknd appr fnl f)	s.h	**7**	16/1	48	11
1832[2]	**Road Racer (IRE) (62)** (MrsJRRamsden) **4-9-1** JFortune(3) (hld up: hdwy ½-wy: effrt & nt clr run over 2f out: n.d after)	¾	**8**	2/1 1	61	24
1992[3]	**Manful (75)** (MissLAPerratt) **5-10-0b** NKennedy(1) (led tl over 3f out: wknd over 1f out: eased)	1	**9**	7/1 3	73	36

(SP 122.1%) **9 Rn**

2m 15.2 (8.50) CSF £94.54 CT £1,381.70 TOTE £12.70: £2.50 £1.90 £3.40 (£68.30) Trio £127.60 OWNER Mrs Monica Keogh (ASTON UPTHORPE) BRED W. J. Byrne
LONG HANDICAP Sing And Dance 7-8

1459 Mattimeo (IRE), who apparently found conditions too testing last time, was given a very cool ride. With nowhere to go, Darley sat and waited until he could switch to the outer. Once there, his mount quickened up nicely and was back on the bridle at the line. There was no doubt Mattimeo can win again from this sort of mark. (8/1)

1313 Opulent, racing with his tongue tied down, took it up turning for home and, quickly stepping up what had been a moderate pace, showed four lengths clear. Treading water inside the last, he was caught near the line. He presumably has some sort of wind problem. (12/1)

2043 Sing And Dance, carrying 3lb more than her intended handicap mark, was caught completely flat-footed when Opulent injected some pace into the race turning in. Staying on at the finish, she might be worth a try over further. (16/1)

2043 Gold Desire, who is weighted up to the hilt, ran his usual sound race. (9/4: tchd 7/2)

1450 Gymcrak Premiere, only 2lb higher than when successful first time at Beverley four outings ago, would probably have appreciated faster ground. (8/1: 6/1-9/1)

1832 Road Racer (IRE), trying for an ambitious run through horses in what turned out to be a half-mile sprint, ran completely out of room, and his rider soon called it a day. (2/1)

T/Plpt: £1,607.20 (12.09 Tckts). T/Qdpt: £330.00 (2.96 Tckts) WG

2121-NEWMARKET (R-H) (Soft)
Friday June 27th
WEATHER: heavy rain WIND: mod half behind

2294 LARK CLAIMING STKS (3-Y.O) (Class D)
2-00 (2-05) **1m 2f (July)** £3,492.50 (£1,040.00: £495.00: £222.50) Stalls: High GOING: 0.56 sec per fur (GS)

				SP	RR	SF
1780[2]	**Janglynyve (60)** (SPCWoods) **3-7-13**(5) RFfrench(3) (trckd ldr: led over 1f out: rdn out)	—	**1**	15/8[2]	67	29
*1429**	**Going For Broke (68)** (PCHaslam) **3-8-8**(5) GFaulkner(2) (led over 8f: unable qckn)	2½	**2**	6/5[1]	72	34
2008[21]	**Switch To Senate** (DJSCosgrove) **3-8-3** JStack(5) (chsd ldrs: rdn 3f out: no imp)	25	**3**	50/1	22	—
1929[3]	**My Beloved (IRE) (59)** (RHannon) **3-8-10** PatEddery(1) (lw: hld up: hdwy 7f out: rdn over 4f out: sn btn)	15	**4**	7/2[3]	5	—
				(SP 104.4%)	**4 Rn**	

2m 16.54 (12.94) CSF £3.82 TOTE £2.50: (£1.50) OWNER The Storm Again Syndicate (NEWMARKET) BRED S. J. Mear
Janglynyve clmd FSainsbury £8,000. Going For Broke clmd DCosgrove £10,000.
IN-FOCUS: **With the rain having fallen all day, racing took place in some of the worst conditions seen at Headquarters in recent years.**
1780 Janglynyve loved the ground but had to show real battling qualities to get the trip in the conditions. (15/8)
1429* Going For Broke tried hard to make all for a four-timer and did not fail for the want of trying. (6/5: evens-10/11)
Switch To Senate handled the ground but could not go with the first two in the closing stages. (50/1)
1929 My Beloved (IRE) has quite a low action and, pulled to the centre of the track early in the straight, was soon clearly getting stuck in the mud. (7/2: 5/2-4/1)

2295 E.B.F. EQUITY FINANCIAL COLLECTIONS MAIDEN STKS (2-Y.O) (Class D)
2-30 (2-31) **6f (July)** £4,163.50 (£1,243.00: £594.00: £269.50) Stalls: Centre GOING: 0.21 sec per fur (G)

				SP	RR	SF
1842[2]	**Linden Heights** (LMCumani) **2-9-0** PatEddery(3) (lw: mde all: rdn & hld on wl fnl f)	—	**1**	10/11[1]	83	46
1872[12]	**Deterrent** (JHMGosden) **2-9-0** LDettori(7) (a.p: ev ch 1f out: unable qckn ins fnl f)	2½	**2**	9/2[3]	76	39
	Setteen (MAJarvis) **2-9-0** WRyan(5) (neat: scope: hld up: hdwy over 1f out: r.o wl ins fnl f)	1¼	**3**	100/30[2]	73+	36
	Mushraaf (JLDunlop) **2-9-0** RHills(4) (w'like: scope: a.p: effrt over 2f out: btn over 1f out)	1¼	**4**	7/1	70	33
	Mantles Star (GLewis) **2-9-0** PaulEddery(8) (w'like: in tch: rdn over 1f out: kpt on fnl f)	3	**5**	16/1	62	25
	Beware (RWArmstrong) **2-9-0** GCarter(6) (w'like: scope: in tch: rdn over 2f out: no imp appr fnl f)	2½	**6**	16/1	55	18
	Kite (MBell) **2-8-9** MFenton(1) (cmpt: a bhd)	5	**7**	20/1	37	—
697[9]	**Imbackagain (IRE)** (PCHaslam) **2-9-0** DeanMcKeown(2) (prom over 3f)	½	**8**	33/1	40	3
				(SP 125.6%)	**8 Rn**	

1m 17.0 (5.00) CSF £5.77 TOTE £2.30: £1.30 £1.60 £1.10 (£2.70) OWNER Mr H. C. Chung (NEWMARKET) BRED Mrs Susan Field
1842 Linden Heights, taken down steadily, showed a fine attitude when seriously put to work and should continue to progress. (10/11: 6/4-10/11)
Deterrent, a quite narrow but attractive sort who can still be made fitter, left his unlucky debut run behind and should have little trouble being placed to advantage. (9/2: op 3/1)
Setteen, a good-moving half-brother to Can Can Lady, was doing his best work towards the finish and should stay another furlong. (100/30: 7/4-7/2)
Mushraaf, an expensive half-brother to Cunning, shaped as if the race was very much needed and should come on a lot for it. (7/1)
Mantles Star, a half-brother to some diverse performers, most notably Compton Place and Quakers Field, is still a little on the leg and finished as though he will stay further. (16/1)
Kite, a strongly-made newcomer, was cheaply bought and showed no immediate promise. (20/1)

2296 ORWELL RATED STKS H'CAP (0-90) (3-Y.O+) (Class C)
3-00 (3-02) **1m 2f (July)** £5,110.20 (£1,891.80: £908.40: £372.00: £148.50: £59.10) Stalls: High GOING: 0.56 sec per fur (GS)

				SP	RR	SF
1404[5]	**Sky Commander (USA) (86)** (MRStoute) **3-8-10** LDettori(9) (hdwy over 4f out: rdn over 2f out: styd on to ld nr fin)	—	**1**	9/2[2]	96	56
1852*	**Lomberto (83)** (VSoane) **4-9-5** CRutter(6) (lw: w ldr: led ins fnl f: hdd & unable qckn nr fin)	s.h	**2**	12/1	93	65
1763[5]	**Traceability (72)** (SCWilliams) **4-8-8** JReid(3) (led over 9f: one pce)	1¼	**3**	5/1[3]	80	52
2122[W]	**Bardon Hill Boy (IRE) (83)** (BHanbury) **5-9-5** JStack(5) (hdwy over 1f out: r.o)	1¼	**4**	10/1	89	61
2013[10]	**Bold Oriental (IRE) (85)** (NACallaghan) **3-8-9** SDrowne(7) (hld up: n.m.r over 2f out: swtchd & hdwy appr fnl f: rdn & r.o)	1	**5**	11/2	89	49
1320[4]	**Judicial Supremacy (80)** (JRFanshawe) **3-7-13**(5) RFfrench(2) (prom 8f)	2½	**6**	9/2[2]	80	40
1852[2]	**Scoss (84)** (LMCumani) **3-8-8** PatEddery(10) (plld hrd: prom: rdn over 2f out: sn wknd)	3½	**7**	7/2[1]	79	39
738[14]	**Secret Aly (CAN) (85)** (CEBrittain) **7-9-7** TQuinn(1) (lw: hdwy over 5f out: rdn & wknd 3f out)	19	**8**	16/1	49	21
				(SP 113.3%)	**8 Rn**	

2m 13.85 (10.25) CSF £49.82 CT £252.65 TOTE £4.80: £1.50 £2.60 £1.90 (£43.50) Trio £59.40 OWNER Maktoum Al Maktoum (NEWMARKET) BRED Heronwood Farm Inc
WEIGHT FOR AGE 3yo-12lb
OFFICIAL EXPLANATION **Scoss: was unsuited by the ground.**
1404 Sky Commander (USA), brought up the centre of the course, probably did not have the best of the ground, but loves to get his toe in and showed great resolution to force his head in front where it matters. (9/2)
1852* Lomberto, for whom the desperate ground held no terrors, has clearly been rejuvenated by the new yard. (12/1: op 5/1)
1763 Traceability has never run in ground anything like as testing but seemed to handle it, and this represents a return to somewhere near his best form. (5/1: op 10/1)
1300 Bardon Hill Boy (IRE) was not suited by the leaders playing cat and mouse and his stamina came into play too late. (10/1)
990 Bold Oriental (IRE) was proven on the ground and over the trip but, combined, they represented the stiffest test of stamina he had ever faced. Put to sleep at the back, he was denied clear passage at a vital time. (11/2)
1320 Judicial Supremacy found the conditions very testing for a step up in trip and was on the retreat towards the finish. (9/2)

2297 CAM H'CAP (0-80) (3-Y.O+) (Class D)
3-30 (3-30) **1m 4f (July)** £7,197.50 (£2,180.00: £1,065.00: £507.50) Stalls: High GOING: 0.56 sec per fur (GS)

				SP	RR	SF
1981[2]	**Shaffishayes (68)** (MrsMReveley) **5-9-7** DeanMcKeown(5) (hld up: hdwy to ld over 2f out: sn rdn: hld on wl fnl f)	—	**1**	7/4[1]	76	46
	Rusk (73) (JPearce) **4-9-12** MWigham(2) (lw: hld up: hdwy over 2f out: rdn & r.o fnl f: nt rch wnr)	½	**2**	7/1	80	50

1678[6]	**Isitoff (72)** (SCWilliams) **4-9-11** JReid(4) (lw: a.p: led over 3f out tl over 2f out: sn btn)	13	**3**	7/1	62	32
1841[5]	**Whirlawhile (USA) (70)** (EALDunlop) **3-8-9** MHills(3) (b.hind: hld up: hdwy 7f out: wknd 3f out)	12	**4**	11/2[3]	44	—
1685[3]	**Eagle Canyon (IRE) (71)** (BHanbury) **4-9-10** JStack(6) (a.p: led 5f out tl hdd & wknd 3f out)	5	**5**	7/2[2]	38	8
1844[11]	**Formidable Flame (48)** (WJMusson) **4-8-1** GCarter(1) (led 4f: wknd 5f out)	14	**6**	25/1	—	—
1434[5]	**Mardi Gras (IRE) (76)** (JLDunlop) **3-9-1b[1]** TQuinn(7) (b.nr fore: plld hrd: led after 4f: hdd 5f out: sn wknd)	14	**7**	13/2	6	—

(SP 116.2%) **7 Rn**

2m 44.5 (15.50) CSF £13.95 TOTE £2.50: £1.50 £3.10 (£8.60) OWNER Mr P. Davidson-Brown (SALTBURN) BRED W. G. Barker
WEIGHT FOR AGE 3yo-14lb

1981 Shaffishayes has had the habit in the past of going to post too keenly, but was taken down early this time and did the job in good style. (7/4)
Rusk had run well fresh in the past and looked ready for this belated seasonal debut. He stayed on in terrific style towards the finish, without ever looking like getting there in time. (7/1: op 9/2)
1678 Isitoff, untried on the surface, seemed to handle it well enough but his stamina was giving out late on. (7/1)
1841 Whirlawhile (USA), dropped in trip, failed to last home any better and is becoming disappointing. (11/2: 3/1-6/1)
1685 Eagle Canyon (IRE) was made plenty of use of, but the testing ground found him out. (7/2)
Formidable Flame, adopting new tactics, was the first beaten. (25/1)
1434 Mardi Gras (IRE) took a suicidal hold in first-time blinkers and paid the penalty. (13/2)

2298 GIRDLESTONE PUMPS H'CAP (0-85) (3-Y.O) (Class D)
4-00 (4-01) **5f (July)** £4,503.00 (£1,344.00: £642.00: £291.00) Stalls: Centre GOING: 0.21 sec per fur (G)

				SP	RR	SF
1977[4]	**The Gay Fox (74)** (BAMcMahon) **3-8-10** TQuinn(1) (w ldrs: led on bit over 2f out: rdn 1f out: r.o wl)	—	**1**	7/4[1]	82	59
2134[13]	**Ivory Dawn (73)** (KTIvory) **3-8-4**(5) GFaulkner(3) (b.hind: hld up: hdwy 2f out: ev ch 1f out: unable qckn)	1¾	**2**	4/1[2]	75	52
1792*	**Lamarita (85)** (JMPEustace) **3-9-7** JTate(2) (hld up: hdwy over 2f out: wknd ins fnl f)	2	**3**	4/1[2]	81	58
2148[4]	**Ice Age (61)** (RJRWilliams) **3-7-6**(5)ow1 RFfrench(6) (w ldr: ev ch over 1f out: sn btn)	1¼	**4**	4/1[2]	53	29
1608[8]	**Nor-Do-I (79)** (JMPEustace) **3-9-1** PBloomfield(5) (prom 2f)	14	**5**	8/1[3]	26	3
1781[11]	**M T Vessel (60)** (JRJenkins) **3-7-10** GBardwell(4) (sn pushed along: led over 2f: sn wknd)	15	**6**	33/1	—	—

(SP 110.4%) **6 Rn**

61.62 secs (3.12) CSF £7.91 TOTE £2.00: £1.30 £1.90 (£2.90) OWNER Mr G. Whitaker (TAMWORTH) BRED Cheveley Park Stud Ltd
LONG HANDICAP M T Vessel 7-1

1977 The Gay Fox, dropped in trip, was made plenty of use of in the testing conditions and stayed on strongly towards the finish. (7/4: 3/1-6/4)
1931* Ivory Dawn, with the draw giving her a chance this time, threw down a determined challenge in the Dip but did not stay on quite as well as the winner. (4/1)
1792* Lamarita was another proven on the ground, but a promising effort against the far rail was petering out near the finish. (4/1: op 7/4)
2148 Ice Age seems best at the minimum trip and ran fast in the centre of the course, until found out by the rising ground. (4/1: op 5/2)
Nor-Do-I, with the blinkers left off again, was out of contention by halfway but may be worth noting when they are re-applied. (8/1)
M T Vessel, bustled along to lead after a few strides, looked all at sea on the ground. (33/1)

2299 BURE CONDITIONS STKS (3-Y.O+ F & M) (Class C)
4-30 (4-30) **6f (July)** £4,503.00 (£1,677.00: £813.50: £342.50: £146.25: £67.75) Stalls: Centre GOING: 0.21 sec per fur (G)

				SP	RR	SF
1021*	**Bint Albaadiya (USA)** (MRStoute) **3-8-11** JReid(1) (lw: hld up: hdwy over 2f out: led over 1f out: rdn out)	—	**1**	15/8[2]	107	75
1975[3]	**Wellspring (IRE)** (DRLoder) **3-8-7** LDettori(4) (hld up: hdwy 2f out: chsd wnr fnl f: kpt on)	2½	**2**	7/2[3]	96	64
2105[8]	**Wildwood Flower (97)** (RHannon) **4-8-10** DaneO'Neill(3) (w ldrs: ev ch over 1f out: wknd ins fnl f)	2	**3**	7/4[1]	87	62
1590[9]	**Jennelle (93)** (CADwyer) **3-8-2**(7) JoHunnam(2) (b.nr fore: w ldr: rdn over 2f out: wknd over 1f out)	nk	**4**	16/1	92	60
1946[2]	**Crofters Ceilidh (88)** (BAMcMahon) **5-8-10** TQuinn(5) (led over 4f)	¾	**5**	6/1	84	59

(SP 113.5%) **5 Rn**

1m 14.74 (2.74) CSF £8.28 TOTE £3.10: £1.60 £1.60 (£4.10) OWNER Sheikh Ahmed Al Maktoum (NEWMARKET) BRED Swettenham Stud
WEIGHT FOR AGE 3yo-7lb

1021* Bint Albaadiya (USA) maintained her unbeaten record in good style, coping with softer ground and the step up in class. (15/8: 4/5-2/1)
1975 Wellspring (IRE) has a low action and looked to be hating the ground and so, in the circumstances, ran an excellent race to get so close without being unduly punished. (7/2)
1610 Wildwood Flower, another with an action better-suited to faster ground, finally gave best inside the final furlong. (7/4)
877 Jennelle goes on the ground but this was her first run beyond the minimum trip and she lost her place rapidly on meeting the rising ground, before getting a second wind to almost snatch third place. (16/1)
1946 Crofters Ceilidh, having her first run beyond five furlongs for a couple of years, was taken on from the start and failed to see the trip out in the conditions. (6/1)

T/Jkpt: £298.40 (23.79 Tckts). T/Plpt: £58.60 (376.92 Tckts). T/Qdpt: £14.10 (98.41 Tckts) Dk

2159-WOLVERHAMPTON (L-H) (Standard)
Friday June 27th
WEATHER: overcast but dry WIND: str half against

2300 WILLOW MEDIAN AUCTION MAIDEN STKS (3 & 4-Y.O) (Class F)
2-20 (2-21) **5f (Fibresand)** £2,277.00 (£627.00: £297.00) Stalls: Low GOING minus 0.38 sec per fur (FST)

				SP	RR	SF
	Pizzicato (RJRWilliams) **3-8-5**(3) DGriffiths(9) (w'like: scope: hdwy 2f out: led ins fnl f: r.o wl)	—	**1**	6/1	58	12
2151[10]	**Castle Ashby Jack (60)** (PHowling) **3-8-13b** FNorton(5) (b.hind: a.p: rdn to chal 1f out: unable qckn)	1¼	**2**	2/1[1]	59	13
1921[9]	**Just Sidium** (CJHill) **3-8-3**(5) DSweeney(3) (led over 1f: led 2f out tl ins fnl f)	3	**3**	20/1	44	—
2148[3]	**Village Pub (FR) (47)** (KOCunningham-Brown) **3-8-13b** FLynch(6) (lw: prom: racd wd & rdn 2f out: no imp)	2½	**4**	5/1[3]	41	—
	Nesbet (BRCambidge) **3-8-13** NAdams(4) (nt grwn: nvr nr to chal)	1¾	**5**	20/1	36	—
2197[10]	**Brin-Lodge (IRE) (40)** (KSBridgwater) **4-8-9b**(5) JBramhill(2) (b.hind: drvn to ld over 3f out: hdd 2f out: rdn & btn appr fnl f)	¾	**6**	11/1	28	—
1437[8]	**Blue Calvine** (CJHill) **3-8-10**(3) RHavlin(10) (outpcd)	1¼	**7**	20/1	29	—
2020[8]	**Fortune's Way (IRE)** (JWharton) **3-8-8** KDarley(1) (b: bit bkwd: chsd ldrs to ½-wy: sn rdn & outpcd)	½	**8**	14/1	23	—
1966[8]	**Crackerbox (41)** (CADwyer) **3-8-8** JFEgan(8) (outpcd)	2	**9**	11/1	16	—

1876⁷ **Misconduct** (GLMoore) **3-8-8** MTebbutt(7) (bkwd: s.i.s: racd wd: a outpcd)....½ **10** 4/1 2 15 —
(SP 121.9%) **10 Rn**

61.8 secs (2.90) CSF £17.03 TOTE £5.80: £1.90 £1.10 £7.00 (£26.90) Trio £72.20 OWNER Mr Richard Morris Jr (NEWMARKET) BRED Bolton Grange

WEIGHT FOR AGE 3yo-6lb

Pizzicato, a scopey half-sister to two winners, with still a bit left to work on, did not have a lot to beat on her racecourse debut, and accomplished it with the minimum of fuss. (6/1)

1691 Castle Ashby Jack, brought back to sprinting, has had more than enough chances without success, and punters are beginning to despair of him. (2/1)

Just Sidium improved on her debut earlier in the month, and was only forced to give best as lack of peak fitness caught up with her. (20/1)

2148 Village Pub (FR) is certainly not as good as he looks, and it is possible he is better on turf. (5/1)

Nesbet only beat one home in his two outings last season, so at least this was a step in the right direction. (20/1)

1681 Brin-Lodge (IRE) is of little account, but she did show up with the pace until finding the demands too great approaching the final furlong. (11/1)

1690 Crackerbox (11/1: 8/1-12/1)

2301 POPLAR CLAIMING STKS (3-Y.O+) (Class G)

2-50 (2-52) **1m 4f (Fibresand)** £2,277.00 (£627.00: £297.00) Stalls: Low GOING minus 0.38 sec per fur (FST)

			SP	RR	SF
310a13 **Twilight Sleep (USA)** (LordHuntingdon) **5-9-13** KDarley(11) (a.p: led over 3f out: sn clr: comf)	—	**1**	4/1 2	77+	36
1863⁴ **Skelton Sovereign (IRE) (60)** (RHollinshead) **3-8-7** FLynch(2) (hld up: hdwy over 3f out: chsd wnr fnl 2f: no imp)	4	**2**	11/2	66	11
1445¹⁵ **Jump The Lights (64)** (SPCWoods) **4-9-9** WJO'Connor(3) (hld up: effrt & rdn 3f out: styd on ins fnl f)	8	**3**	8/1	57	16
1503³ **Esperto (52)** (JPearce) **4-9-2**(3) CTeague(4) (bit bkwd: hld up in tch: effrt 3f out: sn rdn: no imp)	1¼	**4**	4/1 2	51	10
1825⁷ **Ronquista d'Or (51)** (GAHam) **3-8-2**(7) JFowle(9) (bhd: hdwy 3f out: styd on u.p appr fnl f)	1¼	**5**	12/1	54	—
2063⁵ **Heathyards Rock (64)** (RMMcKellar) **5-9-10**(3) PFessey(10) (lw: trckd ldrs: rdn over 2f out: sn btn)	2½	**6**	5/1 3	54	13
*1943*⁷ **Tovarich (50)** (RonaldThompson) **6-9-4b**(5) JBramhill(7) (bit bkwd: led over 8f: sn hrd drvn & wknd)	1¼	**7**	33/1	49	8
1809¹⁴ **Brume La Voile** (JGSmyth-Osbourne) **4-9-5** JFEgan(1) (bit bkwd: chsd ldrs tl rdn & wknd 3f out: t.o)	9	**8**	33/1	33	—
1951⁷ **Sans Pere** (NMBabbage) **4-9-1** VSlattery(6) (lw: in tch: rdn 7f out: sn wknd: t.o)	11	**9**	20/1	14	—
2174² **Hill Farm Blues (51)** (WMBrisbourne) **4-9-8** AGarth(8) (b.off hind: s.v.s: hdwy after 3f: hrd drvn & lost pl 5f out: t.o)	3	**10**	3/1 1	17	—
1567⁹ **Inchella** (APJones) **4-8-10** NAdams(5) (a bhd: t.o)	20	**11**	25/1	—	—
Eau Benite (NEBerry) **6-9-3** MTebbutt(12) (prom tl ½-wy: sn lost tch: t.o)	7	**12**	25/1	—	—

(SP 134.2%) **12 Rn**

2m 39.4 (6.90) CSF £25.92 TOTE £5.40: £3.10 £2.30 £2.70 (£20.00) Trio £37.80 OWNER The Queen (WEST ILSLEY) BRED The Queen

WEIGHT FOR AGE 3yo-14lb

Twilight Sleep (USA) clmd DPipe snr £9,000. Jump The Lights clmd ETWay £7,000

310a Twilight Sleep (USA) won his maiden three years ago, and has not had much racing since. Produced fit and well for this debut on the All-Weather, he kicked on at the end of the back straight and, soon clear, proved a class apart. (4/1)

1863 Skelton Sovereign (IRE) made an effort to give chase to the winner before reaching the straight, but hard as he tried, was unable to make any further impression. (11/2: 4/1-6/1)

908 Jump The Lights, a half brother to Path of Peace, scored his only success over course and distance in the spring of last year, and has not done much since, but he did stay on from some way off the pace here and is worth another try over an extended trip. (8/1)

1503 Esperto was unable to transfer his consistent form from the turf to this surface, but he was having his first try at the trip, and it is more than possible he did not quite see it out. (4/1: op 9/4)

1426 Ronquista d'Or has shown some promise in his most recent outings on the turf, but he still remains a maiden, and his final placing was as close as he could manage here. (12/1: op 8/1)

2063 Heathyards Rock, still struggling to make his mark for his new stable, is probably better when not so much use is made of him. (5/1)

2174 Hill Farm Blues made up too much ground too soon after losing many lengths at the start, and she was in serious trouble soon after halfway. (3/1)

2302 STAR ENGINEERING AMATEUR H'CAP (0-70) (4-Y.O+) (Class E)

3-20 (3-21) **1m 100y (Fibresand)** £3,070.25 (£917.00: £438.50: £199.25) Stalls: Low GOING minus 0.38 sec per fur (FST)

			SP	RR	SF
*2071** **Johnnie the Joker (67)** (JPLeigh) **6-11-4b** 6x MissDianaJones(5) (mde all: shkn up over 1f out: r.o wl)	—	**1**	3/1 1	77	58
1292¹² **Failed To Hit (47)** (NPLittmoden) **4-9-5b1**(7) MrJTyler-Morris(8) (plld hrd: a.p: chal over 1f out: unable qckn fnl f)	1¾	**2**	25/1	54	35
*1944** **Dream Carrier (IRE) (49)** (REPeacock) **9-9-9**(5) MrsCPeacock(2) (chsd wnr: styd ins: r.o one pce appr fnl f)	2½	**3**	6/1	51	32
*2162*⁷ **Everset (FR) (65)** (ABailey) **9-10-9**(7) MissALHutchinson(4) (b: trckd ldrs: effrt over 2f out: nt pce to chal)	1¾	**4**	5/1 3	64	45
1666⁹ **Indian Serenade (40)** (RSimpson) **6-9-2**(3) MrsJMoore(10) (hld up: effrt 3f out: nt rch ldrs)	6	**5**	33/1	27	8
1979⁵ **Takhlid (USA) (70)** (DWChapman) **6-11-7** MissRClark(13) (nvr nr to chal)	½	**6**	5/1 3	56	37
1677⁷ **Wentbridge Lad (IRE) (55)** (PDEvans) **7-10-1**(5) MrWMcLaughlin(3) (nvr bttr than mid div)	3	**7**	14/1	36	17
2041¹³ **Noble Canonire (39)** (DShaw) **5-8-13**(5) MrsMMorris(6) (trckd ldrs over 5f)	1¼	**8**	14/1	17	—
*1754*¹² **Smart Guest (50)** (DShaw) **5-9-10**(5) MissVMarshall(11) (b: b.hind: hdwy 5f out: wknd over 2f out)	1¾	**9**	14/1	25	6
1920⁴ **Bellas Gate Boy (40)** (JPearce) **5-9-5** MrsLPearce(7) (s.v.s: a bhd)	nk	**10**	9/2 2	14	—
1748S **Clued Up (47)** (PDEvans) **4-9-7v**(5)ow1 MrAEvans(9) (a in rr)	nk	**11**	12/1	21	1
*1575*⁸ **Breezed Well (43)** (KGWingrove) **11-9-3**(5)ow8 MrsHNoonan(12) (a in rr)	1	**12**	40/1	15	—
1677⁹ **Haydown (IRE) (35)** (MRBosley) **5-8-11**(3) MrsSBosley(1) (prom to ½-wy: sn rdn & wknd: t.o)	23	**13**	25/1	—	—

(SP 131.6%) **13 Rn**

1m 49.1 (4.10) CSF £88.09 CT £430.03 TOTE £3.60: £1.60 £4.20 £2.90 (£61.90) Trio £285.80; £88.59 to Newcastle 28/6/97 OWNER Miss M. Carrington-Smith (GAINSBOROUGH) BRED Miss M. Carrington-Smith

LONG HANDICAP Breezed Well 8-9 Haydown (IRE) 8-9

2071* Johnnie the Joker, always calling the tune, answered his rider's every call when she shook him up below the distance, and he is at the top of his form just now. (3/1)

857 Failed To Hit, taking a keen tug, and always in the action, did pose a threat approaching the final furlong, but once the winner found extra there was nothing he could do about it. He would seem to be getting his act together, and a repeat could see him in the winner's enclosure. (25/1)

1944* Dream Carrier (IRE) was unable to adopt front-running tactics, but he was always thereabouts, if unable to increase his work-rate in the battle to the finish. (6/1)

1575 Everset (FR), the subject of quite a gamble, probably had too much use made of him over this, a trip at which he has yet to score, for he was close enough entering the final furlong, before finding an extra effort beyond him. (5/1)
Indian Serenade, held up to get the trip, did make some late progress, but far too late to cause concern. (33/1)
1979 Takhlid (USA) had the beating of the winner on their last coming-together, but he lay too far out of his ground this time, and was never able to land a blow. (5/1)
1422 Clued Up (12/1: op 8/1)

2303 SILVER BIRCH H'CAP (0-90) (3-Y.O) (Class C)
3-50 (3-50) **7f (Fibresand)** £5,494.90 (£1,640.20: £783.60: £355.30) Stalls: High GOING minus 0.38 sec per fur (FST)

				SP	RR	SF
2149[2]	**Pericles (80)** (MJohnston) **3-9-2**(3) KMChin(1) (mde all: rdn & edgd lft ins fnl f: hld on)	—	**1**	8/1	86	31
2192[4]	**The Wyandotte Inn (80)** (MrsNMacauley) **3-9-0**(5) AmandaSanders(3) (lw: trckd ldrs: outpcd 3f out: rallied fnl f: fin wl)	½	**2**	16/1	85	30
*1969**	**Pennywell (65)** (RFJohnsonHoughton) **3-8-4** JFEgan(2) (lw: chsd wnr: rdn & ev ch over 1f out: no ex fnl f)	nk	**3**	5/2[1]	69	14
1583*	**Rechullin (82)** (DRLoder) **3-9-7** KDarley(7) (chsd ldrs: effrt & rdn wl over 1f out: nvr able to chal)	1	**4**	7/2[2]	84	29
1843[10]	**Molly Music (65)** (GGMargarson) **3-8-1**(3) MHenry(6) (lw: bhd & outpcd tl r.o wl appr fnl f)	1¾	**5**	10/1	63	8
1583[2]	**Nant Y Gamer (FR) (82)** (JBerry) **3-9-2**(5) TEDurcan(4) (lw: a chsng ldrs: remained ins: rdn wl over 1f out: grad wknd)	¾	**6**	8/1	78	23
2149*	**Mr Paradise (IRE) (73)** (TJNaughton) **3-8-9**(3) 6x JDSmith(8) (lw: outpcd & a bhd)	4	**7**	5/1[3]	60	5
1983[2]	**Present Chance (80)** (BAMcMahon) **3-9-5** LNewton(5) (lw: prom: ev ch 2f out: sn hrd drvn: wknd fnl f)	4	**8**	5/1[3]	58	3
				(SP 121.3%)	**8 Rn**	

1m 28.2 (3.50) CSF £117.27 CT £332.89 TOTE £11.80: £2.60 £3.20 £1.30 (£59.50) OWNER Mr David Abell (MIDDLEHAM) BRED Elsdon Farms

OFFICIAL EXPLANATION **Mr Paradise (IRE): appeared to be unsuited by seven furlongs on this track.**
2149 Pericles adopted the tactics that were successful on his previous appearance on the sand, and despite showing signs of tying up inside the last furlong, held on gamely to the line. (8/1)
2192 The Wyandotte Inn, struggling to hold on at the end of the back straight, found fresh reserves once in line for home and, finishing strongly, only just failed to peg back the winner. He is certainly ready to strike again. (16/1)
1969* Pennywell looked likely to land the gamble when almost upsides on straightening up, but she does appear to find this trip a bit on the sharp side, and could never quite summon the pace to strike the front. (5/2: op 5/1)
1583* Rechullin, looking a bit wintry in her coat, after the cold snap that has been evident this past week, was always poised to challenge, but when the question was popped she lacked the speed to go through with her run. (7/2: 5/2-4/1)
1757* Molly Music, taken off her legs for all of five furlongs, did well to get so close at the finish, without ever promising to reach the principals. (10/1)
1583 Nant Y Gamer (FR) remained on the slower inside rail, and pressed the leaders until getting outpaced approaching the final furlong. (8/1: op 5/1)
1983 Present Chance (5/1: 4/1-6/1)

2304 BEECH (S) STKS (2-Y.O) (Class G)
4-20 (4-20) **7f (Fibresand)** £1,984.50 (£547.00: £259.50) Stalls: High GOING minus 0.38 sec per fur (FST)

				SP	RR	SF
1432[4]	**Rock From The Sun** (WGMTurner) **2-8-1**(5) DSweeney(7) (led after 1f: clr 2f out: unchal)	—	**1**	5/1[2]	56	—
2051[6]	**Silent Pride (IRE)** (MDIUsher) **2-8-6** JMarshall(5) (chsd ldrs: wnt 2nd over 2f out: sn rdn: no imp)	5	**2**	7/1[3]	45	—
2051[4]	**Glenstal Lad** (RHollinshead) **2-8-8**(3) DGriffiths(2) (led 1f: outpcd ½-wy: sme late hdwy: n.d)	5	**3**	evens[1]	38	—
1789[4]	**Karenaragon** (RonaldThompson) **2-8-7e**ow1 WJO'Connor(6) (prom: rdn & outpcd over 2f out: sn btn)	hd	**4**	5/1[2]	34	—
1213[6]	**Talaheart** (CNAllen) **2-8-3b**1(3) JDSmith(4) (a bhd & outpcd: t.o)	15	**5**	7/1[3]	—	—
	Remember Frimley (CJHill) **2-8-6** NAdams(3) (leggy: lt-f: s.s: effrt & drvn ½-wy: rn green & wknd 2f out: t.o)	8	**6**	8/1	—	—
				(SP 119.4%)	**6 Rn**	

1m 31.4 CSF £36.82 TOTE £6.60: £4.70 £2.70 (£16.00) OWNER Mascalls Stud (SHERBORNE) BRED Mascalls Stud
No bid
1432 Rock From The Sun is not ideally bred for stamina, but she put her previous experience to good use, and slipped her field turning into the straight. (5/1: 7/2-11/2)
1867 Silent Pride (IRE) moved into second place on the home turn, but her lack of stamina soon took its toll, and she could do little more than plug on at the one pace. (7/1: op 9/2)
2051 Glenstal Lad, not much bigger than a pony, still looked very wintry in his coat, and after getting outpaced at halfway, was never going to get back into it. (evens)
1789 Karenaragon would seem to need all of this trip, but as yet she is not furnished to her frame, and had been shaken off on the home turn. (5/1)
1213 Talaheart (7/1: op 4/1)
Remember Frimley (8/1: 6/1-10/1)

2305 OAK H'CAP (0-65) (3-Y.O+) (Class F)
4-50 (4-51) **6f (Fibresand)** £2,277.00 (£627.00: £297.00) Stalls: Low GOING minus 0.38 sec per fur (FST)

				SP	RR	SF
2019[15]	**Desert Invader (IRE) (63)** (DWChapman) **6-9-8**(5) DSweeney(1) (led after 2f: rdn over 1f out: r.o strly)	—	**1**	13/2[2]	76	34
1790[5]	**Opening Range (32)** (NEBerry) **6-7-3**(7) PBradley(10) (led after 1f: sn hdd: sustained chal fnl f: nt rch wnr)	1½	**2**	16/1	41	—
590[7]	**Qualitair Silver (47)** (JFBottomley) **3-8-4** NCarlisle(8) (bit bkwd: trckd ldrs: hrd drvn wl over 1f out: kpt on)	3½	**3**	16/1	47	—
1514[12]	**Soaked (33)** (DWChapman) **4-7-6b**1(5) IonaWands(4) (s.s: hdwy to chse wnr ½-wy: wknd appr fnl f)	½	**4**	12/1	31	—
1730[7]	**Corinchili (56)** (GGMargarson) **3-8-10**(3) MHenry(12) (chsd ldrs: effrt & rdn 2f out: drifted lft ins fnl f: one pce)	hd	**5**	11/1	54	5
2203[10]	**Marino Street (44)** (PDEvans) **4-8-8v** JFEgan(5) (led 1f: hrd drvn over 2f out: sn btn)	1½	**6**	9/1	38	—
*2070**	**Ring the Chief (33)** (MDIUsher) **5-7-6**(5) JBramhill(11) (outpcd & bhd tl sme late hdwy)	hd	**7**	4/1[1]	27	—
1942[8]	**Magic Fizz (58)** (TJEtherington) **3-9-1** MTebbutt(6) (lw: sn drvn along & outpcd)	2½	**8**	9/1	45	—
1944[5]	**Lochon (36)** (MrsNMacauley) **6-8-0v** NAdams(2) (outpcd: a bhd)	1½	**9**	20/1	19	—
2069[9]	**Hoh Majestic (IRE) (60)** (RonaldThompson) **4-9-5v**(5) PRoberts(9) (spd over 3f)	2½	**10**	4/1[1]	37	—
1566[7]	**Sparkling Edge (59)** (CADwyer) **3-8-13**(3) JDSmith(7) (prom 4f: sn rdn & wknd)	2	**11**	7/1[3]	30	—

1245[14]	**Impy Fox (IRE) (56)** (PMooney) **3-8-13** WJO'Connor(3) (bit bkwd: outpcd: a bhd)	s.h	**12**	12/1	27	—
				(SP 126.1%)		**12 Rn**

1m 14.4 (3.20) CSF £102.63 CT £1,500.70 TOTE £10.30: £2.90 £6.10 £3.50 (£635.50) Trio £332.20; £280.78 to Newcastle 28/6/97 OWNER Mr David Chapman (YORK) BRED Gainsborough Stud Management Ltd

LONG HANDICAP Opening Range 7-9

WEIGHT FOR AGE 3yo-7lb

1575 Desert Invader (IRE) has a heart as big as himself and, given a grand ride, was always going too well for his pursuers. (13/2)

Opening Range put in a determined last-furlong challenge, but the winner was in full flight by then, and she could not quicken sufficiently to get to terms. Still to get off the mark, her turn is long overdue. (16/1)

399 Qualitair Silver, very free to post, did look as though she would benefit from this first run in almost three months, but she was staying on doggedly at the finish, and if lowered in class could find that elusive opening. (16/1)

423 Soaked has a habit of missing the break, but he recovered to join his stable-mate two furlongs out, before the earlier exertions took their toll. (12/1)

1428 Corinchili, trying her luck at this slightly longer trip, pressed the leaders until fading under pressure approaching the last furlong. (11/1)

1865 Marino Street, from a stable right out of form at the present time, was at full stretch and in trouble before reaching the home straight. (9/1: op 6/1)

2070* Ring the Chief has only ever won at seven furlongs, and he was always finding the pace too strong for him on this occasion. (4/1)

T/Plpt: £1,531.50 (8.11 Tckts). T/Qdpt: £722.40 (1.16 Tckts) IM

1951-BATH (L-H) (Good)
Saturday June 28th

WEATHER: overcast WIND: almost nil

2306 WESTON MAIDEN AUCTION STKS (2-Y.O) (Class E)

2-15 (2-19) **5f 161y** £3,171.25 (£955.00: £462.50: £216.25) Stalls: High GOING minus 0.13 sec per fur (G)

				SP	RR	SF
1812[2]	**Brandon Frank** (IABalding) **2-8-6** SWhitworth(2) (lw: a.p: led over 1f out: drvn out)	—	**1**	3/1[1]	79	23
	Regal Revolution (PTWalwyn) **2-7-13** JLowe(11) (w'like: gd hdwy over 1f out: r.o wl ins fnl f)	1¼	**2**	12/1	69+	13
1847[2]	**Universal Lady** (CJames) **2-7-13** DRMcCabe(10) (a.p: ev ch over 1f out: r.o ins fnl f)	½	**3**	4/1[2]	67	11
1827[4]	**Elleysanta** (AGNewcombe) **2-8-0**ow1 JFEgan(5) (w ldr: led 2f out tl over 1f out: one pce)	1½	**4**	5/1[3]	64	7
1954[10]	**Dance To The Beat** (MartynMeade) **2-8-1** FNorton(16) (prom: c wd st: one pce fnl 2f)	¾	**5**	40/1	63	7
	Deva Lady (MRChannon) **2-8-4**ow1 RPerham(15) (lengthy: hmpd over 3f out: hdwy over 1f out: nrst fin)	½	**6**	20/1	64	7
1812[14]	**King Darius (IRE)** (RHannon) **2-8-8** WJO'Connor(1) (chsd ldrs: no hdwy fnl 2f)	nk	**7**	25/1	68	12
1812[7]	**Shecando (IRE)** (CJames) **2-8-1** CRutter(12) (chsd ldrs: no hdwy fnl 2f)	1¼	**8**	20/1	57	1
1486[10]	**Water Force** (GBBalding) **2-8-11** RPrice(3) (lw: s.s: nvr nrr)	¾	**9**	50/1	65	9
2037[7]	**Acid Test** (WRMuir) **2-8-4**(7) JWilkinson(9) (lw: prom 3f)	½	**10**	20/1	64	8
	Roi de Danse (JWHills) **2-8-8** JReid(8) (scope: led over 3f: wknd over 1f out)	1½	**11**	4/1[2]	56	—
1997[16]	**Lilian Marks (IRE)** (BJMeehan) **2-8-4**ow3 PaulEddery(6) (a bhd)	1¾	**12**	33/1	48	—
1847[7]	**Saligo (IRE)** (HMorrison) **2-7-13** NAdams(14) (a bhd)	¾	**13**	40/1	41	—
1797[10]	**Russian Romeo (IRE)** (BAMcMahon) **2-8-6** LNewton(4) (chsd ldrs 3f)	4	**14**	40/1	36	—
1954[12]	**Amiasapphire** (RJHodges) **2-7-13**(3)ow3 PPMurphy(13) (a bhd)	½	**15**	66/1	31	—
	Magni Momenti (RHannon) **2-8-1** DBiggs(7) (w'like: b.hind: a bhd)	7	**16**	25/1	10	—
				(SP 125.0%)		**16 Rn**

1m 13.5 (4.00) CSF £32.86 TOTE £3.60: £1.40 £2.90 £1.70 (£28.10) Trio £22.40 OWNER Stamford Bridge Partnership (KINGSCLERE) BRED Miss J. A. Challen

1812 Brandon Frank has certainly improved since stepping up from the minimum distance. (3/1: 2/1-100/30)

Regal Revolution, a half-sister to mile and ten-furlong winner Diego, finished in the style of a ready-made future winner over a longer trip. (12/1: 6/1-14/1)

1847 Universal Lady kept on over this extended five and seems ready to tackle the full extra furlong. (4/1)

1827 Elleysanta was taking a slight step up in grade. (5/1)

Dance To The Beat, a half-sister to a winner over a mile and three-quarters, improved considerably on her debut and should not be inconvenienced by further. (40/1)

Deva Lady, a half-sister to seven furlong juvenile scorer Story Line and mile winner Party Line, is out of a mare who won over a mile as a two-year-old. Sure to benefit from a longer distance, she is one to keep an eye on. (20/1)

Roi de Danse (4/1: op 6/1)

2307 STAYERS (S) H'CAP (0-60) (3-Y.O+) (Class F)

2-50 (2-51) **2m 1f 34y** £2,556.00 (£716.00: £348.00) Stalls: High GOING minus 0.13 sec per fur (G)

				SP	RR	SF
	Selmeston (IRE) (40) (SCWilliams) **5-8-13** JReid(2) (bit bkwd: chsd ldr: led over 2f out: sn hdd: led over 1f out: drvn out)	—	**1**	9/1	48	15
2146[9]	**Spiral Flyer (IRE) (30)** (MDIUsher) **4-8-3** CRutter(4) (hld up: hdwy 4f out: led 2f out tl over 1f out: r.o)	½	**2**	33/1	38	5
1825[17]	**Nornax Lad (USA) (51)** (MartynMeade) **9-9-3b**(7) RBrisland(7) (lw: hld up & bhd: hdwy 5f out: one pce fnl 2f)	5	**3**	8/1[3]	54	21
2146[3]	**Grand Applause (IRE) (40)** (MSalaman) **7-8-13** SWhitworth(9) (hld up: hdwy over 3f out: wknd 2f out)	7	**4**	3/1[1]	36	3
	Excelled (IRE) (35) (CJDrewe) **8-8-8** AClark(6) (nvr nr ldrs)	6	**5**	33/1	26	—
2035[4]	**Wesley's Lad (IRE) (55)** (JNeville) **3-8-5**(3) PPMurphy(11) (hld up mid div: no hdwy fnl 3f)	hd	**6**	3/1[1]	46	—
2039[7]	**Racing Hawk (USA) (40)** (MSSaunders) **5-8-13** RPrice(3) (hld up & plld hrd: lost pl 8f out: n.d after)	13	**7**	10/1	19	—
1825[14]	**Rapid Liner (34)** (RJBaker) **4-8-7**ow1 VSlattery(10) (rdn over 6f out: bhd fnl 4f)	hd	**8**	33/1	12	—
1809[10]	**Buzzby Babe (43)** (AGFoster) **3-7-10** NAdams(1) (hld up: hdwy on ins 8f out: nt clr run & lost pl 5f out: nt rcvr)	½	**9**	20/1	21	—
1825[11]	**Oscar Rose (34)** (MJBolton) **4-8-2**(5) GMilligan(8) (prom tl stirrup broke 2f out: sn wknd)	6	**10**	20/1	6	—
1601[5]	**Carol's Dream (USA) (55)** (JWHills) **5-10-0** PaulEddery(5) (lw: led tl hdd over 2f out: wknd qckly: t.o)	22	**11**	6/1[2]	7	—
				(SP 112.8%)		**11 Rn**

3m 57.6 (16.20) CSF £247.64 CT £2,218.90 TOTE £10.50: £2.30 £2.60 £3.80 (£66.90) Trio £212.70 OWNER Mr Chris Wright (NEWMARKET) BRED St Simon Foundation

LONG HANDICAP Buzzby Babe 7-1

WEIGHT FOR AGE 3yo-20lb

No bid

OFFICIAL EXPLANATION Oscar Rose: the rider reported that the pin in his left stirrup came loose from the leather, causing him to lose the stirrup at the one furlong marker, preventing him from riding the gelding out to the line.

Selmeston (IRE) proved good enough, despite looking in need of this first run for a year. (9/1)
1445 Spiral Flyer (IRE), down 5lb, showed the step up from a mile and a half held no terrors for her. (33/1)
1618 Nornax Lad (USA) has won over two mile five furlongs over hurdles but seems to prefer faster ground. (8/1: op 5/1)
2146 Grand Applause (IRE) appeared to find this extended two miles beyond him. (3/1)
1601 Carol's Dream (USA) (6/1: op 4/1)

2308 LITTLE SOMERFORD LIMITED STKS (0-70) (3-Y.O+) (Class E)

3-20 (3-20) **5f 161y** £2,956.75 (£889.00: £429.50: £199.75) Stalls: High GOING minus 0.13 sec per fur (G)

				SP	RR	SF
1977^{13}	**Bayin (USA) (62)** (MDIUsher) **8-9-0** RStreet(6) (hld up in rr: gd hdwy over 1f out: led wl ins fnl f: r.o wl)	—	**1**	10/1	71	48
2115^{9}	**Friendly Brave (USA) (68)** (MissGayKelleway) **7-9-0** AClark(7) (hld up: pushed along over 3f out: hdwy 2f out: ev ch 1f out: nt qckn)	1¾	**2**	7/1	66	43
1942^{4}	**Mullagh Hill Lad (IRE) (45)** (BAMcMahon) **4-9-0** LNewton(4) (a.p: led ins fnl f: sn hdd: nt qckn)	½	**3**	10/1	65	42
1594^{4}	**Indian Relative (70)** (RGuest) **4-8-11** GHind(2) (hld up: hdwy on ins over 2f out: sn rdn: ev ch 1f out: one pce)	nk	**4**	$2/1^{1}$	61	38
2061^{11}	**High Domain (IRE) (70)** (JLSpearing) **6-9-0** PaulEddery(1) (led: rdn over 2f out: hdd ins fnl f)	2	**5**	$6/1^{3}$	58	35
1848^{2}	**Lucky Dip (70)** (DRCElsworth) **3-8-7** JReid(3) (w ldr tl wknd over 1f out)	½	**6**	$11/4^{2}$	57	27
2148^{5}	**Songsheet (69)** (MSSaunders) **4-9-0**(3) PPMurphy(5) (trckd ldrs: ev ch over 1f out: wknd ins fn f)	¾	**7**	8/1	58	35
				(SP 116.1%)		**7 Rn**

1m 12.2 (2.70) CSF £70.90 TOTE £11.50: £3.90 £3.40 (£41.00) OWNER Mr Trevor Barker (WANTAGE) BRED David V. Hall
WEIGHT FOR AGE 3yo-7lb

1488 Bayin (USA), dropped out at the start as usual, came from last to first in typical style. (10/1: op 11/2)
1848 Friendly Brave (USA) had probably found the ground too soft at Goodwood last week. (7/1: 5/1-8/1)
1942 Mullagh Hill Lad (IRE) would have been much better off in a handicap and can soon find a suitable opportunity. (10/1)
1594 Indian Relative, well in at the weights, has registered both her previous wins on firm ground. (2/1)
1848 High Domain (IRE) has won over six but his other four victories have been at the bare minimum. (6/1)
1848 Lucky Dip seemed to find this extended five beyond her best. (11/4)
2148 Songsheet (8/1: 5/1-9/1)

2309 ROTHMANS ROYALS NORTH SOUTH CHALLENGE SERIES H'CAP (0-90) (3-Y.O) (Class C)

3-55 (3-56) **1m 5y** £6,110.25 (£1,842.00: £893.50: £419.25) Stalls: Low GOING minus 0.13 sec per fur (G)

				SP	RR	SF
1935*	**Mara River (82)** (IABalding) **3-9-4** SWhitworth(6) (lw: trckd ldrs: hrd rdn to ld ins fnl f: all out)	—	**1**	$5/2^{2}$	90	37
1955^{7}	**What Happened Was (72)** (MartynMeade) **3-8-8** FNorton(3) (hld up & bhd: gd hdwy over 2f out: ev ch fnl f: r.o wl)	nk	**2**	25/1	79	26
1437*	**Stilett (IRE) (83)** (LMCumani) **3-9-5** GHind(5) (led tl hdd ins fnl f: r.o)	s.h	**3**	$15/8^{1}$	90	37
2043^{7}	**Don Sebastian (73)** (WJHaggas) **3-8-9** CRutter(7) (lw: hld up: hdwy over 2f out: rdn over 1f out: one pce)	3	**4**	9/1	74	21
1663^{3}	**Kewarra (73)** (BRMillman) **3-8-9** JReid(1) (plld hrd: a.p: one pce fnl 2f)	s.h	**5**	$7/1^{3}$	74	21
723^{10}	**Faringdon Future (80)** (BWHills) **3-9-2** PaulEddery(9) (swtg: chsd ldr: wknd over 1f out)	½	**6**	16/1	80	27
1611^{5}	**Supremism (75)** (CEBrittain) **3-8-11** WJO'Connor(4) (lw: hld up: hdwy over 2f out: wknd over 1f out)	5	**7**	12/1	65	12
1962^{6}	**Sheer Folly (USA) (85)** (PFICole) **3-9-7** JFEgan(2) (hld up in rr: c wd & hdwy 2f out: wknd wl over 1f out)	2	**8**	14/1	71	18
1869^{6}	**Zimiri (75)** (JARToller) **3-8-11** AClark(8) (plld hrd: prom tl wknd qckly over 2f out: t.o)	18	**9**	16/1	25	—
				(SP 115.8%)		**9 Rn**

1m 43.6 (5.40) CSF £56.20 CT £129.11 TOTE £3.60: £1.30 £3.00 £1.60 (£31.60) Trio £21.60 OWNER Mr Nigel Harris (KINGSCLERE) BRED Mrs I. A. Balding

1935* Mara River, raised 3lb, was up another furlong and had to dig deep over this stiffish mile. (5/2)
What Happened Was, down 15lb this season after a couple of poor runs in the soft, very nearly made the Handicapper pay. (25/1)
1437* Stilett (IRE), adopting different tactics on this handicap debut, kept on willingly to the end. Out of an Irish mile and a half winner, there seems no reason why he should not stay further. (15/8)
2043 Don Sebastian, probably not helped by the drying ground, comes from a stable which is showing signs of coming out of the doldrums. (9/1: op 6/1)
1663 Kewarra may have settled better in a stronger-run race. (7/1)
Faringdon Future has still to prove he stays a mile. (16/1)
Sheer Folly (USA) (14/1: 8/1-16/1)

2310 CLAVERTON CLAIMING H'CAP (0-70) (3-Y.O+) (Class E)

4-30 (4-32) **1m 5y** £3,307.75 (£997.00: £483.50: £226.75) Stalls: Low GOING minus 0.13 sec per fur (G)

				SP	RR	SF
194^{8}	**Mislemani (IRE) (47)** (AGNewcombe) **7-9-5** RPrice(5) (lw: swtchd rt & gd hdwy wl over 1f out: led ins fnl f: r.o wl)	—	**1**	25/1	60	41
2071^{2}	**Jona Holley (43)** (GLMoore) **4-9-1** CRutter(13) (gd hdwy over 1f out: ev ch ins fnl f: r.o)	nk	**2**	$7/1^{3}$	55	36
2004^{3}	**Vanborough Lad (41)** (MJBolton) **8-8-13** JReid(12) (a.p: ev ch 1f out: nt qckn)	2	**3**	$5/2^{1}$	49	30
2004^{6}	**Noeprob (USA) (52)** (RJHodges) **7-9-10** RPerham(16) (led tl ins fnl f)	½	**4**	$9/2^{2}$	59	40
1640^{8}	**Cats Bottom (51)** (AGNewcombe) **5-9-6**(3) PPMurphy(3) (hdwy over 2f out: r.o one pce fnl f)	1½	**5**	14/1	55	36
2067^{6}	**Safa Dancer (28)** (BAMcMahon) **4-8-0**ow3 LNewton(11) (hld up: hdwy over 2f out: ev ch over 1f out: wknd ins fnl f)	hd	**6**	20/1	32	10
2228^{10}	**Shanghai Lil (28)** (MJFetherston-Godley) **5-7-7**(7) RBrisland(1) (prom tl wknd over 1f out)	1¼	**7**	20/1	30	11
2040^{8}	**Rumbustious (56)** (RHannon) **3-9-4** WJO'Connor(15) (nvr trbld ldrs)	3½	**8**	10/1	51	22
1689^{12}	**Return To Brighton (32)** (JMBradley) **5-7-13**(5) ADaly(10) (nvr rchd ldrs)	d.h	**8**	25/1	27	8
1951^{8}	**Eric's Bett (50)** (PGMurphy) **4-9-8** JLowe(7) (n.d)	3½	**10**	14/1	38	19
1969^{5}	**Hawaii Storm (FR) (30)** (DJSffrenchDavis) **9-7-9**(7) KerryBaker(8) (s.s: nvr nr ldrs)	½	**11**	25/1	17	—
1965^{11}	**Ki Chi Saga (USA) (44)** (MMadgwick) **5-8-9**(7) DMcGaffin(9) (lw: n.d)	1	**12**	33/1	29	10
1951^{11}	**Anotherone to Note (36)** (AJChamberlain) **6-8-8** DBiggs(17) (chsd ldrs tl wknd 2f out)	¾	**13**	50/1	19	—
1988^{4}	**Fan of Vent-Axia (42)** (DJSCosgrove) **3-8-4v** AClark(2) (prom: rdn over 3f out: wknd over 2f out)	s.h	**14**	10/1	25	—
1509^{8}	**Smiling Bess (41)** (JSKing) **4-8-13** PaulEddery(18) (swtg: chsd ldr tl wknd over 2f out)	1½	**15**	40/1	21	2

				SP	RR	SF
1921[4]	**Ginny Wossername (43)** (MartynMeade) **3-8-5** FNorton(6) (lw: a bhd)	1½	**16**	16/1	20	—
2121[4]	**Amnesty Bay (25)** (MDIUsher) **5-7-11v** JMarshall(14) (a bhd)	nk	**17**	11/1	2	—
1925[12]	**Alpine Music (IRE) (50)** (JMBradley) **3-8-12** VSlattery(4) (rdn & hdwy over 3f out: wknd over 2f out)	nk	**18**	50/1	26	—

(SP 135.3%) **18 Rn**

1m 43.2 (5.00) CSF £175.11 CT £578.03 TOTE £47.20: £8.20 £2.40 £1.40 £2.00 (£188.30) Trio £168.70 OWNER Mrs Pamela Cann (BARNSTAPLE) BRED Gainsborough Stud Management Ltd
WEIGHT FOR AGE 3yo-10lb
91 Mislemani (IRE), having his first outing for five months, sprang a surprise off a mark 6lb lower than when he last ran on the turf. (25/1)
2071 Jona Holley got going even later than the winner but had no excuses. (7/1)
2004 Vanborough Lad continues in good form but this was not going to be his day. (5/2)
2004 Noeprob (USA) was 7lb better off than the third than when beaten a neck here last month. (9/2)
870 Cats Bottom, down 2lb, ran her best race for a while. (14/1)
Safa Dancer, reverting to a mile, came with a dangerous-looking run and might even be worth a try at seven. (20/1)
1780* Rumbustious (10/1: 6/1-12/1)
Eric's Bett (14/1: 16/1-25/1)
2121 Amnesty Bay (11/1: 8/1-12/1)

2311 ST JOHN AMBULANCE MAIDEN STKS (3-Y.O+) (Class D)

5-00 (5-03) **1m 3f 144y** £3,692.75 (£1,112.00: £538.50: £251.75) Stalls: Low GOING minus 0.13 sec per fur (G)

				SP	RR	SF
725[4]	**Pentad (USA)** (RCharlton) **3-8-10** PaulEddery(5) (lw: a.p: led over 2f out: rdn out)	—	**1**	7/4[2]	88	60
1165[4]	**Royal Crown (IRE)** (PWChapple-Hyam) **3-8-10** JReid(10) (a.p: ev ch over 2f out: r.o one pce fnl f)	1½	**2**	11/2[3]	86	58
676[15]	**Shadiann (IRE)** (LMCumani) **3-8-10** GHind(3) (a.p: r.o one pce fnl 2f)	1½	**3**	11/1	84	56
	Sir Ricky (USA) (RCharlton) **3-8-10** WJO'Connor(4) (bit bkwd: hld up: hdwy 5f out: nvr nr to chal)	4	**4**	16/1	78	50
1930[2]	**Dark Green (USA) (89)** (PFICole) **3-8-10** CRutter(8) (led: hdd over 2f out: wknd fnl f)	1½	**5**	6/4[1]	76	48
1477[14]	**Height of Heights (IRE)** (LadyHerries) **4-9-5**(5) GMilligan(11) (sme hdwy over 3f out: nvr nr ldrs)	8	**6**	14/1	65	51
	Ajcombe (IRE) (LadyHerries) **4-9-10** AClark(9) (bkwd: s.s: a bhd: t.o)	21	**7**	25/1	37	23
2008[19]	**Abbey Theatre (IRE)** (MSalaman) **3-8-10** LNewton(7) (a bhd: t.o)	3	**8**	66/1	32	4
969[7]	**Western Playboy (62)** (RJBaker) **5-9-10** VSlattery(2) (hld up mid div: bhd fnl 4f: t.o)	hd	**9**	66/1	32	18
	Dewi Sant (DBurchell) **3-8-10** RPrice(1) (lengthy: s.s: a bhd: t.o)	26	**10**	50/1	—	—
1004[8]	**Jay-Em-Bee** (JMBradley) **4-9-10** JLowe(12) (a bhd: t.o fnl 3f)	21	**11**	66/1	—	—

(SP 122.9%) **11 Rn**

2m 30.2 (3.50) CSF £11.31 TOTE £3.00: £1.50 £1.30 £2.20 (£5.90) Trio £7.20 OWNER Mr K. Abdulla (BECKHAMPTON) BRED George A. Smith and W. E. Johnston
WEIGHT FOR AGE 3yo-14lb
IN-FOCUS: **With the ground improving to good before racing, this was the only event where the runners elected to come down the stands side.**
725 Pentad (USA) fulfilled the promise of his debut and always appeared in control in the final quarter mile. (7/4)
1165 Royal Crown (IRE) was always just playing second fiddle. (11/2: 4/1-6/1)
Shadiann (IRE) is out of an Irish mile and a half winner who is a half-sister to Prix Vermeille winner Sharaya. Not unnecessarily knocked about, he is definitely on the upgrade. (11/1: 6/1-12/1)
Sir Ricky (USA), a 200,000gs colt, is out of a six-furlong winner in Japan who is a sister to Intrepidity. A stable companion of the winner, he should soon leave this form behind. (16/1)
1930 Dark Green (USA) was soon taking the field along at a good pace, but found himself doing nothing more than setting the race up for others. (6/4: 5/4-9/4)
1106 Height of Heights (IRE) (14/1: 10/1-20/1)

T/Plpt: £297.80 (43.27 Tckts). T/Qdpt: £50.30 (14.85 Tckts) KH

1760-DONCASTER (L-H) (Good to soft, Soft patches)

Saturday June 28th

WEATHER: overcast with showers WIND: almost nil

2312 E.B.F. LONSDALE MAIDEN STKS (2-Y.O F) (Class D)

6-50 (6-51) **7f** £3,327.00 (£996.00: £478.00: £219.00) Stalls: High GOING: 0.22 sec per fur (G)

				SP	RR	SF
	Bahr (BWHills) **2-8-11** DHolland(6) (neat: in tch: shkn up 3f out: led wl over 1f out: r.o wl)	—	**1**	8/1[3]	97+	56
	Dazilyn Lady (USA) (PWHarris) **2-8-11** KDarley(1) (unf: scope: trckd ldrs: chal 2f out: sn rdn & nt pce of wnr)	8	**2**	8/1[3]	79	38
	Light Step (USA) (HRACecil) **2-8-11** WRyan(7) (neat: mde most over 5f: sn btn)	1	**3**	5/2[2]	76	35
1783[5]	**Migrate (USA)** (JHMGosden) **2-8-11** LDettori(2) (cl up: rdn over 2f out: sn btn)	8	**4**	10/11[1]	58	17
1847[6]	**Robin Lane** (IABalding) **2-8-11** PatEddery(3) (prom tl wknd over 2f out)	9	**5**	11/1	38	—
1091[2]	**Positive Air** (BAMcMahon) **2-8-11** JFortune(4) (outpcd 3f out: sn bhd)	1¾	**6**	16/1	34	—
1440[10]	**Ghorapani (IRE)** (MrsNMacauley) **2-8-11** BDoyle(5) (disp ld to ½-wy: sn rdn & btn)	2	**7**	50/1	29	—

(SP 119.4%) **7 Rn**

1m 29.32 (4.82) CSF £65.23 TOTE £11.10: £4.70 £2.30 (£38.20) OWNER Mr Bassam Freiha (LAMBOURN) BRED Sheikh Mohammed bin Rashid al Maktoum
Bahr is neither very big, nor robust, but she can certainly go, and once shaken up, she answered in splendid style to win going right away. (8/1)
Dazilyn Lady (USA) travelled pretty well, but then failed to match the winner when the pace increased, but she did look the type to benefit from this. (8/1)
Light Step (USA), a handy little filly, she certainly looked fit, but after leading, she was made to look very pedestrian in the last furlong and a half. (5/2: op 11/8)
1783 Migrate (USA) looked to be going well, but then disappointed when ridden, and gives the impression that she has more ability, but may be her own worst enemy, and she is inclined to get a bit warm beforehand. (10/11: 6/4-4/5)
1847 Robin Lane, taking a step up in trip, this lightly made sort proved most disappointing. (11/1)
1091 Positive Air, trying a longer trip, ran too bad to be true. (16/1)

2313 BAILEYS ORIGINAL IRISH CREAM MAIDEN H'CAP (0-70) (3-Y.O+) (Class E)
7-20 (7-23) **6f** £4,370.00 (£1,310.00: £630.00: £290.00) Stalls: High GOING: 0.42 sec per fur (GS)

				SP	RR	SF
	Muhandam (IRE) (65) (BobJones) **4-9-7**(7) CLowther(21) (chsd ldrs: led 1½f out: styd on wl)	—	**1**	20/1	72	51
1467[2]	**Gay Breeze (37)** (PSFelgate) **4-8-0** DWright(15) (lw: led tl hdd 1½f out: no ex)	1½	**2**	8/1	40	19
1401[5]	**Miss Peregrine (49)** (RGuest) **3-8-5** MRoberts(20) (w ldrs tl outpcd over 2f out: kpt on u.p fnl f)	nk	**3**	16/1	51	23
2177[13]	**Carreamia (53)** (JLEyre) **4-8-13**(3) OPears(19) (hdwy over 2f out: styd on wl towards fin)	nk	**4**	20/1	54	33
1864[8]	**Presentiment (54)** (MartynWane) **3-8-10** DHolland(1) (chsd ldr far side: kpt on wl fnl 2f)	1¼	**5**	16/1	52	24
1864[6]	**Sparkling Harry (53)** (MissLCSiddall) **3-8-9b** KDarley(9) (racd far side: outpcd: hdwy u.p over 2f out: nrst fin)	nk	**6**	14/1	50	22
2019[6]	**Rotor Man (IRE) (62)** (JDBethell) **3-9-4b[1]** JWeaver(4) (led far side: rdn 2f out: nt qckn)	2	**7**	8/1	54	26
1942[3]	**Sea Ya Maite (48)** (SRBowring) **3-8-4** DaleGibson(13) (b: s.i.s: sme late hdwy)	nk	**8**	7/1[2]	39	11
2152[3]	**Forest Robin (62)** (MrsJRRamsden) **4-9-11v** JFortune(14) (lw: s.i.s: styd on u.p fnl 2f: n.d)	hd	**9**	11/2[1]	53	32
1800[16]	**Attarikh (IRE) (57)** (MrsALMKing) **4-9-6b** TSprake(5) (lw: chsd ldrs far side tl wknd fnl 2f)	¾	**10**	20/1	46	25
1828[12]	**Bent Raiwand (USA) (45)** (DonEnricoIncisa) **4-8-8** KimTinkler(8) (racd far side: prom tl wknd 2 ½f)	¾	**11**	33/1	32	11
1573[8]	**Falls O'Moness (IRE) (63)** (KRBurke) **3-9-5** DRMcCabe(17) (lw: sn drvn along: sme hdwy 3f out: n.d)	2½	**12**	16/1	43	15
	Play The Tune (50) (NMBabbage) **4-8-13** BDoyle(2) (chsd ldrs far side: effrt over 2f out: sn btn)	hd	**13**	20/1	30	9
1834[7]	**Forest Signal (65)** (MBrittain) **3-9-0**(7) DMernagh(7) (racd far side: in tch tl wknd fnl 2f)	nk	**14**	25/1	44	16
2157[5]	**Classic Leader (63)** (ICampbell) **4-9-12v** SDrowne(6) (racd far side: sn outpcd)	¾	**15**	16/1	40	19
2130[7]	**Tarradale (50)** (CBBBooth) **3-8-6** KHodgson(11) (in tch: outpcd ½-wy: no imp after)	s.h	**16**	25/1	27	—
1650[4]	**Midyan Queen (63)** (RHollinshead) **3-9-5** FLynch(10) (racd far side: outpcd fr ½-wy)	s.h	**17**	10/1	40	12
1451[6]	**Onemoretime (45)** (BWMurray) **3-8-1** MDeering(22) (b.hind: outpcd ½-wy: sn bhd)	1¼	**18**	33/1	19	—
1780[5]	**Sandweld (49)** (CADwyer) **3-8-5**ow1 PatEddery(16) (lw: shkn up ½-wy: n.d)	2	**19**	8/1	17	—
1582[4]	**In Good Nick (63)** (MWEasterby) **3-9-5b** TLucas(18) (lw: spd 3f: wknd qckly)	s.h	**20**	15/2[3]	31	3
2002[11]	**Colonel's Pride (51)** (RMWhitaker) **3-8-7** VHalliday(12) (prom over 3f)	2	**21**	25/1	14	—
1656[5]	**Chief Connections (50)** (MPBielby) **4-8-13** ACulhane(3) (racd far side: sn bhd)	7	**22**	25/1	—	—

(SP 152.6%) **22 Rn**

1m 17.79 (6.79) CSF £168.01 CT £2,486.31 TOTE £42.90: £6.90 £2.40 £5.00 £5.00 (£164.60) Trio £488.30; £144.43 to 30/6/97 OWNER Mr C. G. Davey (NEWMARKET) BRED Gay O'Callaghan

WEIGHT FOR AGE 3yo-7lb

OFFICIAL EXPLANATION **Sandweld: the trainer reported that the colt was suffering from a respiratory problem.**

Muhandam (IRE) took the eye beforehand, and showed fine determination to take this rather moderate event. (20/1)

1467 Gay Breeze put in another decent effort, and will surely find a similar event within his capabilities. (8/1)

1401 Miss Peregrine, although stepping up a furlong in trip, again left the impression that a bit further would help. (16/1)

1586 Carreamia was picking up ground in pleasing style in the closing stages, and should appreciate further. (20/1)

667 Presentiment, racing on what turned out to be the unfavoured side of the track, finished well to win that race, but failed to trouble the stands side group. (16/1)

1864 Sparkling Harry has shown ability before, and finished with quite a flourish here, but far too late. He was again fitted with the blinkers here, which seemed to improve him. (14/1)

1458 Rotor Man (IRE) had blinkers on for the first time, and blazed a trail up the far side, only to run out of fuel approaching the last furlong. (8/1)

1942 Sea Ya Maite is both looking and running well at the moment, and is worth keeping in mind, especially on the All-Weather. (7/1)

2314 WESTSIDE MAGAZINE GROUP CONDITIONS STKS (2-Y.O) (Class C)
7-50 (7-51) **5f** £4,477.20 (£1,654.80: £792.40: £322.00: £126.00: £47.60) Stalls: High GOING: 0.42 sec per fur (GS)

				SP	RR	SF
	Princess Natalie (TDBarron) **2-8-6** KDarley(2) (w'like: scope: trckd ldrs: qcknd to ld appr fnl f: r.o)	—	**1**	8/1	79+	35
1847*	**Desert Lady (IRE)** (RCharlton) **2-8-10** PatEddery(3) (w ldrs: led 1½f out: sn hdd & outpcd: kpt on towards fin)	½	**2**	5/4[1]	81	37
2042[2]	**D'Marti** (CBBBooth) **2-8-6** KHodgson(4) (lw: outpcd & bhd: hdwy 2f out: r.o)	½	**3**	6/1[3]	76	32
1657*	**Yorkies Boy** (BAMcMahon) **2-9-1** JFortune(1) (lw: led 3½f: rdn & no ex)	2½	**4**	13/2	77	33
1961[3]	**Montano (USA)** (PFICole) **2-8-11** TQuinn(7) (lw: w ldrs: rdn ½-wy: sn outpcd)	3	**5**	3/1[2]	63	19
2042[4]	**Katy Thomas** (JBerry) **2-8-5**(3) PFessey(6) (sn outpcd & wl bhd)	12	**6**	9/1	22	—

(SP 118.2%) **6 Rn**

63.75 secs (5.35) CSF £18.02 TOTE £10.80: £2.80 £1.60 (£11.10) OWNER Burke's 5th Family Settlement (THIRSK) BRED Cheveley Park Stud Ltd

Princess Natalie, a decent-looking newcomer, travelled on the bridle, and produced a useful turn of foot to settle it. There looks to be more to come. (8/1: 6/1-9/1)

1847* Desert Lady (IRE) raced upsides the leaders with her rider giving the impression that the race was hers for the taking, but the winner surprised her for toe entering the final furlong, and despite a valiant effort, the chance had gone. (5/4)

2042 D'Marti again finished strongly, and it would seem that another furlong will bring her success. (6/1)

1657* Yorkies Boy has previously been at his best on faster ground, and was left struggling here approaching the final furlong. (13/2)

1961 Montano (USA) showed speed, but never looked happy on this easy surface, and dropped tamely away in the last couple of furlongs. (3/1)

2042 Katy Thomas ran no sort of race here, and something was obviously amiss. (9/1)

2315 YORKSHIRE-TYNE TEES TELEVISION MAIDEN STKS (3-Y.O+) (Class D)
8-20 (8-22) **1m 2f 60y** £4,240.00 (£1,270.00: £610.00: £280.00) Stalls: Low GOING: 0.42 sec per fur (GS)

				SP	RR	SF
1023[3]	**Military (USA)** (HRACecil) **3-8-11** WRyan(11) (lw: mde all: all out)	—	**1**	5/1[2]	92	56
2008[3]	**True Glory (IRE)** (JHMGosden) **3-8-6** LDettori(9) (a.p: effrt over 2f out: hdwy over 1f out: r.o towards fin)	hd	**2**	3/1[1]	87	51
1558[2]	**Colour Code** (MrsASwinbank) **5-9-9** SSanders(8) (hld up: hdwy over 2f out: n.m.r: swtchd over 1f out: r.o wl: too much to do)	2½	**3**	5/1[2]	88	64
1682[2]	**Coretta (IRE)** (LMCumani) **3-8-6** PatEddery(13) (lw: chsd ldrs tl outpcd fnl 2f: eased ins fnl f)	6	**4**	3/1[1]	74	38
2008[6]	**Lookout** (BWHills) **3-8-6** DHolland(5) (mid div: effrt over 2f out: styd on towards fin)	1¼	**5**	10/1[3]	72	36
1282[3]	**In The Genes** (JLEyre) **3-8-11** MGallagher(2) (bit bkwd: in tch: kpt on fnl 3f: no imp)	nk	**6**	33/1	76	40
	Alakdar (CAN) (ACStewart) **3-8-11** GCarter(15) (wl grwn: scope: bkwd: chsd ldrs tl wknd over 2f out: eased whn btn)	2	**7**	12/1	73	37
1846[8]	**Prince Alex (IRE)** (ACStewart) **3-8-11** MRoberts(10) (bit bkwd: hld up & bhd: hdwy 4f out: styd on wl)	½	**8**	25/1	72	36
1823[6]	**Hidden Agenda (FR)** (RCharlton) **3-8-6** TSprake(3) (lw: bhd: hdwy 4f out: shkn up & n.d)	2	**9**	16/1	64	28

Form	Horse	Dist	Pos	SP	RR	SF
2008[16]	**Mukdar (USA)** (MajorWRHern) **3-8-11** BDoyle(6) (nvr bttr than mid div)	5	**10**	14/1	61	25
2008[9]	**Magic Lahr (GER)** (IABalding) **4-9-6**(3) MartinDwyer(1) (bit bkwd: nvr trbld ldrs)	½	**11**	25/1	61	37
	Es Go (RBastiman) **4-9-4**(5) HBastiman(17) (bkwd: s.i.s: hld up & bhd: nvr nr to chal)	2½	**12**	50/1	57	33
	Murchan Tyne (IRE) (EJAlston) **4-9-4** SDrowne(16) (s.i.s: n.d)	hd	**13**	50/1	52	28
1950[3]	**Spick And Span** (CWThornton) **3-8-11** DeanMcKeown(12) (lw: hld up & bhd: nvr nr to chal)	s.h	**14**	66/1	57	21
1877[6]	**Norman Conquest (USA) (73)** (IABalding) **3-8-11** KDarley(7) (prom tl wknd fnl 4f)	1	**15**	25/1	55	19
1936[4]	**Salsee Lad** (JRFanshawe) **3-8-11** DHarrison(14) (prom tl wknd fnl 4f)	7	**16**	25/1	44	8
2059[7]	**Classical Dance (IRE)** (MrsMReveley) **3-8-11** ACulhane(18) (shkn up 7f out: a bhd)	4	**17**	50/1	38	2
2143[5]	**Bernie's Star (IRE)** (NBycroft) **3-8-11** LCharnock(4) (s.i.s: a bhd)	8	**18**	100/1	25	—
				(SP 139.4%)	**18 Rn**	

2m 17.1 (9.30) CSF £19.55 TOTE £5.70: £2.20 £2.00 £2.00 (£8.70) Trio £9.80 OWNER The Thoroughbred Corporation (NEWMARKET) BRED Morven Stud Ltd

WEIGHT FOR AGE 3yo-12lb

1023 Military (USA), who looks the type that would excite many a national hunt trainer, appreciated this trip. Made plenty of use of, he just managed to get home in front. (5/1: 7/2-11/2)

2008 True Glory (IRE) is learning, but took time to find her stride here, and just failed to make it. There is obviously a race or two in her. (3/1)

1558 Colour Code gave the impression that had he been ridden with more dash, he might well have won this. (5/1: 4/1-6/1)

1682 Coretta (IRE) looked fit, and had her chances, but this lightly-made filly was well held late on, and was then wisely not overpunished. (3/1)

2008 Lookout looks likely to stay further, and was really getting the hang of things in the last three furlongs. (10/1: op 6/1)

1282 In The Genes ran well in this company, and there obviously a race to be won with her. (33/1)

Alakdar (CAN), a really nice sort, needed this, and ran well until blowing up in the straight, from which point he was eased a good bit. (12/1: op 8/1)

Prince Alex (IRE) took the eye in the paddock, and also in the race, running on from the back of the field in the closing stages. (25/1)

Es Go needed this, and never got into it, but left the impression that there is ability there. (50/1)

2316 CASTLE WORKING MENS CLUB STAYERS' H'CAP (0-80) (4-Y.O+) (Class D)

8-50 (8-52) **1m 6f 132y** £3,980.00 (£1,190.00: £570.00: £260.00) Stalls: Low GOING: 0.42 sec per fur (GS)

Form	Horse	Dist	Pos	SP	RR	SF
1795[9]	**Amiarge (45)** (MBrittain) **7-7-13** GBardwell(6) (chsd ldrs: led wl over 4f out: styd on wl)	—	**1**	20/1	58	19
2035[8]	**Spa Lane (50)** (MPBielby) **4-8-4** DRMcCabe(9) (dwlt: bhd tl hdwy 3f out: hung lft: styd on: nrst fin)	2	**2**	16/1	61	22
1636[7]	**Compass Pointer (50)** (JMPEustace) **4-8-1**(3) MartinDwyer(8) (bhd: hdwy to ld after 4f: hdd wl over 4f out: r.o one pce)	hd	**3**	10/1	61	22
1981[7]	**Charter (62)** (WStorey) **6-9-2** GCarter(4) (lw: prom: pushed along 6f out: hdwy 4f out: hung lft 2f out: nt qckn)	4	**4**	9/2[2]	68	29
2035[6]	**Turgenev (IRE) (60)** (RBastiman) **8-9-0b** DeanMcKeown(10) (dwlt: hdwy after 6f: wnt prom 4f out: rdn, hung lft & nt qckn fnl 3f)	nk	**5**	4/1[1]	66	27
2063[D]	**Summerhill Special (IRE) (70)** (DWBarker) **6-9-10** WRyan(7) (lw: trckd ldrs: outpcd 4f out: no imp after)	17	**6**	11/2[3]	57	18
2198*	**Dancing Cavalier (73)** (RHollinshead) **4-9-6**(7) 4x PFredericks(5) (lw: b.off hind: hld up: effrt over 4f out: n.d)	12	**7**	13/2	47	8
1974[7]	**Taufan Boy (70)** (PWHarris) **4-9-10** LDettori(2) (led 4f: chsd ldr tl wknd 3f out: eased whn btn fnl 2f)	1¼	**8**	11/2[3]	43	4
2034[3]	**Tissue of Lies (USA) (59)** (MJohnston) **4-8-13** JWeaver(3) (chsd ldrs tl wknd 5f out)	4	**9**	13/2	28	—
2015[6]	**Augustan (56)** (SGollings) **6-8-10** PatEddery(1) (lw: lost tch after 4f: n.d after)	17	**10**	7/1	6	—
				(SP 127.9%)	**10 Rn**	

3m 21.72 (18.12) CSF £297.86 CT £3,096.03 TOTE £24.70: £5.80 £5.50 £3.10 (£319.80) Trio £413.40; £116.47 to 30/6/97 OWNER Miss Debi Woods (WARTHILL) BRED Follies Partnership

1654 Amiarge certainly stays further and, made plenty of use of, took command a long way out and was never going to stop. (20/1)

1685 Spa Lane seems at his best when ridden from behind, but on this occasion he was always having just too much to do. (16/1)

1408 Compass Pointer, restrained early on, took charge after four furlongs. Although headed early in the straight, he does stay, but was always then short of toe. (10/1)

1981 Charter had his chances, but again tended to hang left when asked a serious question, and was never doing enough. (9/2)

2035 Turgenev (IRE), happy on this soft ground, seemed to go to his left when ridden in the straight, and was never doing enough. (4/1)

2063 Summerhill Special (IRE) was obviously not in the mood this time, and who could blame her after getting disqualified after winning easily last time out. (11/2)

2198* Dancing Cavalier obviously found this one too many races, and was never happy. (13/2)

2317 GO RACING IN YORKSHIRE H'CAP (0-70) (3-Y.O+ F & M) (Class E)

9-20 (9-23) **7f** £3,356.25 (£1,005.00: £482.50: £221.25) Stalls: High GOING: 0.42 sec per fur (GS)

Form	Horse	Dist	Pos	SP	RR	SF
2069[3]	**Al Reet (IRE) (50)** (SRBowring) **6-9-0** DeanMcKeown(12) (trckd ldrs: hdwy to ld jst ins fnl f: r.o)	—	**1**	9/1[3]	59	41
2019[12]	**The Barnsley Belle (IRE) (42)** (JLEyre) **4-8-6** MGallagher(2) (cl up: led wl over 2f out tl ins fnl f: kpt on)	1¼	**2**	16/1	48	30
1843*	**Sharp 'n' Shady (60)** (CFWall) **4-9-10** SSanders(9) (lw: trckd ldrs: hdwy over 2f out: hrd rdn & ch ins fnl f: nt qckn)	½	**3**	9/4[1]	65	47
1965[5]	**On The Green (38)** (AHide) **4-8-2v** GBardwell(4) (hdwy ½-wy: sn rdn: styd on fnl 2f: nt pce to chal)	½	**4**	20/1	42	24
2062[12]	**Gipsy Princess (61)** (MWEasterby) **3-9-2** TLucas(13) (chsd ldrs: effrt 2f out: nt qckn)	2	**5**	20/1	60	33
2130[4]	**La Dolce Vita (68)** (TDBarron) **3-9-9** RLappin(8) (swtg: hld up & bhd: effrt & n.m.r over 2f out: hdwy over 1f out: nvr able to chal)	hd	**6**	10/1	67	40
1584[3]	**Komlucky (50)** (ABMulholland) **5-8-9v**(5) GFaulkner(11) (led tl hdd wl over 2f out: grad wknd)	¾	**7**	9/1[3]	47	29
2002[6]	**Sing With the Band (44)** (BAMcMahon) **6-8-8** JFortune(15) (lw: plld hrd: prom: effrt over 2f out: nt qckn)	½	**8**	9/1[3]	40	22
2002[7]	**Dispol Diamond (49)** (GROldroyd) **4-8-13** KDarley(1) (hld up: effrt over 2f out: nt clr run & no imp after)	3	**9**	9/1[3]	38	20
929[11]	**Gormire (40)** (JHetherton) **4-8-4b[1]** NKennedy(7) (dwlt: hld up: effrt 3f out: sn btn)	½	**10**	25/1	28	10
1993[3]	**Lady Silk (33)** (MissJFCraze) **6-7-11** TWilliams(6) (lw: bhd: hdwy on outside over 2f out: n.d)	2½	**11**	14/1	16	—
2109[7]	**Efipetite (32)** (NBycroft) **4-7-10** LCharnock(14) (spd over 4f: sn btn)	2	**12**	33/1	10	—
1680[8]	**Perfect Poppy (59)** (JRFanshawe) **3-9-0** DHarrison(10) (chsd ldrs 4f: sn wknd)	½	**13**	8/1[2]	36	9
1963[6]	**Patina (48)** (RHollinshead) **3-8-3** JQuinn(5) (chsd ldrs tl wknd over 2f out)	8	**14**	12/1	7	—
				(SP 127.5%)	**14 Rn**	

1m 32.23 (7.73) CSF £132.70 CT £416.39 TOTE £10.90: £2.90 £2.40 £2.10 (£37.10) Trio £93.80 OWNER The Gemini Partnership 4 (EDWIN-STOWE) BRED D. Cordell-Lavarack

LONG HANDICAP Efipetite 7-3

WEIGHT FOR AGE 3yo-9lb

2069 Al Reet (IRE), who showed last time that she was coming to hand, did the business in good style here. (9/1)
579* The Barnsley Belle (IRE) looks on good terms with herself at the moment, but despite a gallant effort, she was never quite good enough. (16/1)
1843* Sharp 'n' Shady travelled quite well, and had her chances, but then failed to pick up when put under serious pressure. (9/4)
On The Green was always having to struggle to get into it, and lacked the pace to really make her presence felt, despite staying on. She looks particularly well at the moment, and is running into form. (20/1)
Gipsy Princess showed her first signs of encouragement this season. (20/1)
2130 La Dolce Vita, a warm and edgy individual, appeared a shade unlucky, but she might well turn out to be her own worst enemy. (10/1)

T/Plpt: £7,985.40 (2.52 Tckts). T/Qdpt: £164.40 (8.43 Tckts) AA

2190-LINGFIELD (L-H) (Turf Soft, AWT Standard)
Saturday June 28th
WEATHER: overcast WIND: almost nil

2318 GALLAGHER GROUP APPRENTICE H'CAP (0-70) (3-Y.O+) (Class F)
6-35 (6-35) **1m 3f 106y** £2,368.00 (£673.00: £334.00) Stalls: High GOING: 0.44 sec per fur (GS)

				SP	RR	SF
2218[2]	**Glow Forum (52)** (LMontagueHall) **6-8-6**(7) DHayden(4) (b: chsd ldr 10f out tl over 2f out: rdn: led ins fnl f: r.o wl)	—	**1**	4/5 [1]	60	34
1153[6]	**Rising Dough (IRE) (63)** (GLMoore) **5-9-5**(5) TField(5) (plld hrd: hdwy on ins over 3f out: led over 2f out: hrd rdn over 1f out: hdd ins fnl f: unable qckn)	1¼	**2**	11/2 [3]	69	43
1641[2]	**Colour Counsellor (37)** (RMFlower) **4-7-7b**(5) JFowle(3) (lw: led 9f: one pce)	1¼	**3**	12/1	42	16
2146[5]	**Nails Tails (44)** (SDow) **4-7-9**(10)ow9 DSalt(2) (hld up: rdn over 2f out: one pce)	1¼	**4**	6/1	47	12
2160[2]	**Bon Guest (IRE) (53)** (TJNaughton) **3-7-7**(8) RachaelMoody(1) (lw: no hdwy fnl 3f)	1	**5**	5/1 [2]	54	15

(SP 109.6%) **5 Rn**

2m 38.89 (14.19) CSF £5.06 TOTE £1.60: £1.30 £1.70 (£4.00) OWNER Miss J D Anstee & Partners (EPSOM) BRED Forum Bloodstock Ltd
LONG HANDICAP Nails Tails 7-6
WEIGHT FOR AGE 3yo-13lb

2218 Glow Forum, runner-up at Epsom on Wednesday evening, again showed her liking for some cut. She appeared to be in trouble as the runner-up went for home over a quarter of a mile out, but her rider remained calm, and the combination managed to get in front in the last one hundred yards. (4/5: op evens)
1153 Rising Dough (IRE), who has shown a real liking for this track in the mud over hurdles, had conditions to suit and slipped through to lead over a quarter of a mile from home. It looked as if he would prevail, but despite his rider doing nothing wrong, the combination was overhauled in the last one hundred yards. (11/2: 4/1-13/2)
1641 Colour Counsellor took the field along but, collared over a quarter of a mile from home, could only go up and down in the same place. Both his wins to date have come in sellers. (12/1: 7/1-14/1)
2146 Nails Tails chased the leaders, but never threatened to find another gear in the straight. (6/1)
2160 Bon Guest (IRE) was taking a big step up in distance, but he received little assistance from the saddle, and was making no impression in the straight. (5/1)

2319 LUMIS COLOUR CLAIMING STKS (3-Y.O) (Class F)
7-05 (7-07) **7f (Equitrack)** £2,669.70 (£739.20: £353.10) Stalls: Low GOING minus 0.50 sec per fur (FST)

				SP	RR	SF
1958[15]	**Big Ben (70)** (RHannon) **3-9-6** DaneO'Neill(9) (chsd ldr over 1f: chsd ldr over 2f out: led over 1f out: r.o wl)	—	**1**	6/1 [3]	80	50
1989[5]	**Just Loui (88)** (WGMTurner) **3-8-9**(7) DMcGaffin(7) (lw: chsd ldr over 5f out: led over 3f out tl over 1f out: unable qckn)	2	**2**	13/8 [1]	71	41
362[4]	**Misty Cay (IRE) (56)** (SDow) **3-8-3** JTate(5) (rdn over 4f out: hdwy over 1f out: r.o ins fnl f)	1¼	**3**	8/1	56	26
1509[12]	**Without Friends (IRE) (60)** (JFfitch-Heyes) **3-8-12** GDuffield(2) (rdn over 4f out: hdwy over 1f out: r.o one pce)	1½	**4**	14/1	61	31
1689[13]	**Paddy Hurry (38)** (NACallaghan) **3-8-2b** JFEgan(12) (rdn thrght: chsd ldrs: one pce fnl 3f)	1	**5**	25/1	49	19
1807[5]	**Hint of Victory (65)** (MBell) **3-8-10b**[1] MFenton(1) (lw: s.s: hdwy over 1f out: nvr nrr)	¾	**6**	13/2	55	25
1746[2]	**Hever Golf Charger (IRE) (59)** (TJNaughton) **3-8-12b** RPerham(11) (led over 3f: wknd over 1f out)	2½	**7**	8/1	51	21
1988[7]	**Ar Hyd Y Knos (46)** (GLMoore) **3-8-7** SWhitworth(10) (s.s: a bhd)	8	**8**	16/1	28	—
1989[7]	**Masterstroke (70)** (BJMeehan) **3-8-5**(7) GHannon(6) (hld up: shkn up 3f out: sn wknd)	3	**9**	11/2 [2]	26	—
1929[7]	**Hot Shot** (GLMoore) **3-8-2** CandyMorris(8) (hld up: rdn over 3f out: sn wknd)	½	**10**	50/1	15	—
	Rae Un Soleil (JFfitch-Heyes) **3-7-8**(5) RMullen(4) (leggy: s.s: a wl bhd)	3	**11**	50/1	5	—

(SP 123.6%) **11 Rn**

1m 25.39 (0.99) CSF £15.29 TOTE £7.10: £2.00 £2.80 £1.30 (£7.50) Trio £24.70 OWNER Lady Davis (MARLBOROUGH) BRED Mrs M. Lingwood
Just Loui clmd NShields £10,000, Ar Hyd Y Knos clmd DBaker £8,000

1746* Big Ben was trying the All-Weather for the first time, but seemed perfectly at home on it, sweeping into the lead below the distance, and soon asserting. (6/1: 5/1-8/1)
1989 Just Loui was returning to the All-Weather, where he has gained all five of his victories to date. Sent on at halfway, he ran rather wide coming into the straight and, soon headed, failed to find another gear. With a more experienced rider on board, and a drop back to six furlongs, he can find another race on sand. (13/8)
237 Misty Cay (IRE), given a four-month break, was putting in all her best work in the last furlong and a half. A return to a mile might help. (8/1)
1008 Without Friends (IRE) is an exposed plater, but did stay on in the short home straight to be nearest at the line. (14/1)
Paddy Hurry is a poor performer and, rousted along for much of the trip, was made to look very pedestrian in the second half of the race. (25/1)
1807 Hint of Victory, fitted with blinkers for the first time, gave little encouragement, and was only struggling on past beaten horses. (13/2: 9/2-7/1)
1746 Hever Golf Charger (IRE) (8/1: 6/1-9/1)
94* Masterstroke (11/2: 7/2-13/2)

2320 E.B.F. WIMPEY HOMES MAIDEN STKS (2-Y.O) (Class D)
7-35 (7-37) **5f** £3,315.55 (£990.40: £473.70: £215.35) Stalls: High GOING: 0.14 sec per fur (G)

				SP	RR	SF
1744[8]	**Batswing** (MartynMeade) **2-9-0b**[1] FNorton(11) (mde all: clr over 1f out: r.o wl)	—	**1**	20/1	66+	41

				SP	RR	SF
504[4]	**Halmahera (IRE)** (IABalding) **2-9-0** SWhitworth(5) (hld up: rdn over 2f out: unable qckn)	2	**2**	9/2[2]	60	35
1791[2]	**Moontabeh** (PTWalwyn) **2-9-0** RHills(8) (lw: chsd wnr: rdn over 2f out: one pce)	s.h	**3**	11/10[1]	59	34
	Centre Court (RHannon) **2-8-9** DaneO'Neill(12) (neat: bit bkwd: s.s: hdwy over 1f out: wknd fnl f)	3½	**4**	13/2[3]	43	18
1933[15]	**Iron Mountain (IRE)** (NACallaghan) **2-8-7b[1]**(7) DMcGaffin(3) (bit bkwd: dwlt: hdwy over 3f out: rdn over 2f out: wknd fnl f)	2	**5**	25/1	42	17
1984[3]	**Private Seal** (GLMoore) **2-9-0** CandyMorris(4) (prom 3f)	s.h	**6**	20/1	42	17
	Facile Tigre (SDow) **2-8-11**(3) DO'Donohoe(10) (w'like: bkwd: s.s: rdn over 2f out: swtchd rt over 1f out: nt clr run on ins ins fnl f: nvr nrr)	s.h	**7**	16/1	42	17
1255[7]	**Night People** (WJarvis) **2-9-0** EmmaO'Gorman(7) (lw: nvr nr to chal)	1¼	**8**	20/1	38	13
1842[6]	**Aldwych Arrow (IRE)** (MBell) **2-9-0** MFenton(2) (lw: outpcd)	1	**9**	16/1	34	9
	Silver Joy (KMcAuliffe) **2-8-9** JFEgan(6) (unf: prom over 3f)	1¾	**10**	25/1	24	—
	Mystery Guest (IRE) (SirMarkPrescott) **2-9-0** GDuffield(1) (w'like: scope: bit bkwd: bhd fnl 2f)	1¼	**11**	7/1	25	—
1932[7]	**Sky Mountain (IRE)** (GLewis) **2-9-0** RPerham(9) (a bhd)	½	**12**	25/1	23	—
				(SP 129.2%)		**12 Rn**

60.96 secs (3.96) CSF £98.06 TOTE £13.60: £3.00 £1.80 £1.10 (£26.00) Trio £17.10 OWNER Mr Richard Withers (MALMESBURY) BRED C. R. and V. M. Withers

1492 Batswing was a revelation in the first-time blinkers and, making all the running, forged clear from below the distance for a decisive victory. (20/1)

504 Halmahera (IRE), off the track for three months, had a ding-dong battle for second place in the final furlong, and although just winning that battle, had no hope of challenging the winner. (9/2)

1791 Moontabeh, the paddock pick, raced in second place. However, his jockey was concerned from halfway and, unable to contain the winner, was caught for the runner-up berth right on the line. He can find a race when stepped up in distance. (11/10)

Centre Court was carrying condition for this debut and, after taking closer order below the distance, tired in the final furlong, as lack of peak fitness took its toll. (13/2: 4/1-7/1)

Iron Mountain (IRE), an attractive individual, still did not look fully fit, but nevertheless left his Sandown debut well behind, taking closer order over three furlongs from home before tiring inside the distance. (25/1)

1984 Private Seal had far more on his plate here, and had been hung out to dry two furlongs from home. (20/1)

Mystery Guest (IRE) (7/1: 3/1-8/1)

2321 MER CAR POLISH H'CAP (0-70) (3-Y.O+) (Class E)

8-05 (8-05) **5f** £3,096.25 (£925.00: £442.50: £201.25) Stalls: High GOING: 0.14 sec per fur (G)

				SP	RR	SF
2244[3]	**Superlao (BEL) (38)** (JJBridger) **5-7-3**(7) PDoe(2) (a.p: led over 1f out: r.o wl)	—	**1**	7/1	47	29
2148*	**Barranak (IRE) (64)** (GMMcCourt) **5-9-8** CRutter(4) (led over 3f: unable qckn)	1¼	**2**	4/1[2]	69	51
2232[3]	**Half Tone (54)** (RMFlower) **5-8-12b** DaneO'Neill(1) (lw: outpcd: hdwy over 1f out: one pce)	1¾	**3**	11/4[1]	53	35
2115[5]	**Tachycardia (40)** (RJO'Sullivan) **5-7-5**(7)ow2 SCarson(8) (a.p: swtchd lft 2f out: rdn over 1f out: one pce)	hd	**4**	8/1	39	19
1223[9]	**Master of Passion (70)** (JMPEustace) **8-10-0b** JTate(6) (hdwy 4f out: ev ch 2f out: wknd over 1f out)	nk	**5**	14/1	68	50
1814[4]	**Whizz Kid (51)** (JJBridger) **3-7-12**(5) ADaly(5) (nvr nr to chal)	1¼	**6**	12/1	45	21
2061[2]	**Mousehole (72)** (RGuest) **5-10-2** PBloomfield(7) (outpcd)	1½	**7**	9/2[3]	61	43
1236[12]	**Secret Miss (38)** (APJones) **5-7-10** NAdams(3) (lw: bhd fnl 3f)	12	**8**	13/2	—	—
				(SP 116.2%)		**8 Rn**

60.64 secs (3.64) CSF £32.47 CT £87.70 TOTE £11.00: £2.20 £2.00 £1.70 (£44.10) OWNER Mr J. F. Walls (LIPHOOK) BRED Haras Flying Horse

LONG HANDICAP Tachycardia 7-8 Secret Miss 7-6

WEIGHT FOR AGE 3yo-6lb

2244 Superlao (BEL), third at Salisbury on Thursday, gained her first victory in this country. Never far away, she grabbed the initiative below the distance, and kept on far too strongly for her rivals, much to the delight of her jockey, who did a Frankie Dettori in the last few yards, holding his arm high and waving it around. (7/1)

2148* Barranak (IRE) failed in his bid to complete the hat-trick. Dictating matters from the front, he was collared below the distance, and failed to find another gear. (4/1: 5/2-9/2)

2232 Half Tone, making a quick reappearance, picked up ground below the distance, but was making no further impression in the final furlong. All six of his victories to date have come over five furlongs. (11/4)

2115 Tachycardia, switched off the rails to get a clear run a quarter of a mile from home, never looked like finding that vital turn of foot. (8/1)

53 Master of Passion is finding old age against him these days, but did not run badly here, having every chance a quarter of a mile from home, before younger rivals had his measure. (14/1: 10/1-16/1)

1814 Whizz Kid is only plating-class, and could never get into it. (12/1: 8/1-14/1)

760 Secret Miss (13/2: 10/1-6/1)

2322 MOOR ENVELOPES (S) H'CAP (0-60) (3-Y.O+) (Class G)

8-35 (8-36) **1m 5f (Equitrack)** £2,219.70 (£614.20: £293.10) Stalls: Low GOING minus 0.50 sec per fur (FST)

				SP	RR	SF
1222[5]	**Bedouin Prince (USA) (36)** (MrsLStubbs) **10-9-0** JFEgan(6) (b: hld up: chsd ldr over 4f out: led over 2f out: clr wl over 1f out: r.o wl)	—	**1**	5/2[2]	52	33
1417[4]	**Illegally Yours (38)** (LMontagueHall) **4-8-13**(3) DO'Donohoe(4) (s.i.s: hdwy 8f out: rdn over 4f out: chsd wnr ins fnl f: no imp)	8	**2**	11/2	44	25
106[7]	**Turrill House (21)** (WJMusson) **5-7-13**ow1 CRutter(7) (lw: s.s: hdwy over 5f out: one pce fnl 4f)	3½	**3**	5/1[3]	23	3
1417[3]	**Lucy Tufty (28)** (JPearce) **6-8-6** GHind(5) (chsd ldr: led 5f out tl over 2f out: wknd over 1f out)	nk	**4**	11/2	30	11
*1417**	**Carrolls Marc (IRE) (46)** (CMurray) **9-9-10** GDuffield(8) (b.hind: hld up: rdn over 4f out: one pce)	4	**5**	2/1[1]	43	24
2146[7]	**Spectacle Jim (29)** (BAPearce) **8-8-2**(5) ADaly(2) (b: led 8f)	24	**6**	16/1	—	—
2160[7]	**Mill Dancer (IRE) (35)** (JGMO'Shea) **5-8-13** DaneO'Neill(3) (prom over 5f)	10	**7**	25/1	—	—
				(SP 119.1%)		**7 Rn**

2m 46.1 (4.10) CSF £16.13 CT £59.55 TOTE £3.40: £2.10 £1.90 (£13.30) OWNER Mr Tim Dean (WARTHILL) BRED Kinderhill Select Bloodstock

No bid

1222 Bedouin Prince (USA) cruised into the lead over a quarter of a mile from home, and sprinted away in the short straight to gain his first victory in nearly four and a half years in this bad race. (5/2)

1417 Illegally Yours is very exposed. Taking closer order a mile from home, she was certainly tapped for toe in the last half-mile, but did struggle on for second place inside the final furlong. She remains a maiden. (11/2: 4/1-7/1)

Turrill House, who has shown little on the Flat, but did win a selling handicap hurdle in the spring, took closer order over five furlongs from home, but was made to look woefully one-paced in the last half-mile. (5/1)
1417 Lucy Tufty went on five furlongs from home. Collared over a quarter of a mile out, she was tired in the straight, but held on to second place until inside the final furlong. (11/2: 7/2-6/1)
1417* Carrolls Marc (IRE) was made to look extremely pedestrian in the last half-mile. (2/1)

2323 MANSTON MEDIAN AUCTION MAIDEN STKS (3-Y.O) (Class F)
9-05 (9-05) **1m 1f** £2,277.00 (£627.00: £297.00) Stalls: Low GOING: 0.44 sec per fur (GS)

				SP	RR	SF
1939[2]	**Cartouche (66)** (SirMarkPrescott) **3-9-0** GDuffield(5) (led over 6f: hrd rdn over 1f out: led ins fnl f: drvn out)	—	**1**	9/4[2]	75	18
1939[3]	**Radar O'Reilly (58)** (RJRWilliams) **3-9-0** GHind(2) (plld hrd: chsd ldr: led over 2f out: hrd rdn over 1f out: hdd ins fnl f: unable qckn)	¾	**2**	8/1	74	17
2059[4]	**Monaco (IRE)** (LMCumani) **3-9-0** JReid(1) (lw: hld up: rdn over 2f out: one pce)	2½	**3**	4/5[1]	69	12
1986[4]	**Walk On By (68)** (RHannon) **3-9-0** DaneO'Neill(3) (lost pl 4f out: no hdwy fnl 3f)	3	**4**	6/1[3]	64	7
	Ewar Snowflake (KOCunningham-Brown) **3-8-9** RPerham(4) (unf: scope: a in rr: t.o)	dist	**5**	33/1	—	—

(SP 114.7%) **5 Rn**

2m 3.4 (12.90) CSF £17.80 TOTE £3.20: £1.20 £2.90 (£24.50) OWNER Lady Fairhaven (NEWMARKET) BRED Lord Fairhaven
1939 Cartouche set the pace but, headed over a quarter of a mile from home, looked set for second place. However, his jockey got down to some serious work, and the combination struggled back to the front inside the final furlong. (9/4)
1939 Radar O'Reilly was very well supported in the market, but refused to settle in the early stages. Nevertheless, he appeared to have made a winning move as he gained control over a quarter of a mile from home, but the winner proved a real thorn in his side, and he was worried out of it inside the last one hundred yards. (8/1)
2059 Monaco (IRE) chased the leaders, but was made to look extremely one-paced in the straight. (4/5)
1986 Walk On By completely lost his pitch running down the hill, and was making no impression in the straight. (6/1: op 4/1)

T/Plpt: £27.90 (483.22 Tckts). T/Qdpt: £11.50 (63.31 Tckts) AK

2288-NEWCASTLE (L-H) (Heavy)
Saturday June 28th
WEATHER: raining WIND: str half against

2324 E.B.F. JAMAR LINER AGENCIES MAIDEN STKS (2-Y.O) (Class D)
2-10 (2-11) **6f** £3,615.00 (£1,095.00: £535.00: £255.00) Stalls: High GOING: 0.62 sec per fur (GS)

				SP	RR	SF
2168[3]	**Deeceebee** (WStorey) **2-9-0** JQuinn(3) (mde all: r.o strly fnl f: rdn out)	—	**1**	11/2[2]	74	28
1932[2]	**Clef of Silver** (WJarvis) **2-9-0** TQuinn(4) (reard s: sn trckng ldrs: effrt over 2f out: rdn & wnt 2nd over 1f out: wknd ins fnl f)	6	**2**	5/6[1]	58	12
	Tearaway (JWWatts) **2-9-0** NConnorton(2) (leggy: b: chsd ldrs: outpcd over 2f out: styd on appr fnl f)	1¼	**3**	10/1	55	9
2060[4]	**Grand Estate** (TDEasterby) **2-9-0** KDarley(9) (trckd ldrs: ev ch over 2f out: kpt on same pce)	hd	**4**	15/2[3]	54	8
	First Frame (JLEyre) **2-8-11**(3) OPears(5) (leggy: s.i.s: stdy hdwy over 2f out: wknd over 1f out)	6	**5**	16/1	38	—
2047[3]	**Super Rascal** (NPLittmoden) **2-9-0** AMunro(11) (w ldrs: hung lft over 2f out: grad wknd)	2	**6**	11/1	33	—
1492[14]	**Reach For A Star** (CWThornton) **2-9-0** DeanMcKeown(6) (trckd ldrs tl wknd over 2f out)	hd	**7**	20/1	33	—
	Jockweiler (IRE) (MrsJRRamsden) **2-9-0** JFortune(8) (neat: hld up & plld hrd: trckd ldrs tl lost pl over 2f out)	4	**8**	11/1	22	—
	Danzino (IRE) (APJarvis) **2-9-0** SDrowne(1) (cmpt: chsd ldrs: rdn & lost pl ½-wy)	7	**9**	9/1	4	—
	Miss Pugh (CWFairhurst) **2-8-9** RLappin(10) (lt-f: unf: s.i.s: hmpd after 2f: sn wl bhd)	½	**10**	25/1	—	—

(SP 131.9%) **10 Rn**

1m 20.28 (8.78) CSF £10.83 TOTE £6.10: £1.20 £1.10 £3.50 (£3.80) Trio £33.30 OWNER Mr D. C. Batey (CONSETT) BRED Maristow Farms Partnership
2168 Deeceebee has big feet, ideal for testing ground such as this and, well supported in the market, his rider left nothing to chance. (11/2: 12/1-5/1)
1932 Clef of Silver reared leaving the stalls. On the winner's quarters over a furlong out, he soon came under pressure, and his stride shortened markedly in the last one hundred yards. On ground such as this, he seemed to run out of stamina. (5/6: 4/5-6/5)
Tearaway, a poor mover, was tapped for foot when the race began in earnest soon after halfway, but recovered to be staying on at the finish. He was almost certainly suited by the rain-soaked ground. (10/1)
2060 Grand Estate looked a real danger soon after halfway, but in the ground gradually tired. He now seems to be coming to hand and is qualified for a nursery mark. (15/2)
First Frame shaped by no means badly on his debut. (16/1)
2047 Super Rascal wanted to do nothing but hang left. (11/1)
Jockweiler (IRE) (11/1: 8/1-12/1)

2325 JOURNAL 'GOOD MORNING' H'CAP (0-100) (3-Y.O+) (Class C)
2-45 (2-46) **7f** £13,030.00 (£3,940.00: £1,920.00: £910.00) Stalls: High GOING: 0.68 sec per fur (GS)

				SP	RR	SF
1977[19]	**Jo Mell (73)** (TDEasterby) **4-8-11** LCharnock(4) (chsd ldrs: led over 2f out: drvn out)	—	**1**	8/1[3]	86	68
2026[13]	**Tertium (IRE) (79)** (MartynWane) **5-9-3** AMunro(13) (lw: s.i.s: hld up & bhd: edgd lft fr ½-wy: styd on fnl f)	3½	**2**	14/1	84	66
1980[5]	**Yorkie George (94)** (LMCumani) **3-9-9** KDarley(7) (chsd ldrs: outpcd over 2f out: styd on ins fnl f)	½	**3**	11/4[1]	98	71
1737[2]	**Gee Bee Dream (82)** (APJarvis) **3-8-11** SDrowne(1) (racd far side: a chsng ldrs: styd on same pce fnl 2f)	1¼	**4**	10/1	83	56
1629*	**Weetman's Weigh (IRE) (80)** (RHollinshead) **4-9-1**(3) DGriffiths(15) (hdwy over 2f out: sn chsng ldrs: nt qckn appr fnl f)	nk	**5**	10/1	80	62
1737[7]	**Jeffrey Anotherred (93)** (KMcAuliffe) **3-9-8** MRoberts(14) (trckd ldrs: kpt on same pce fnl 2f)	1½	**6**	12/1	90	63
1874[4]	**Persian Fayre (85)** (JBerry) **5-9-4**(5) TEDurcan(2) (racd far side: led tl over 2f out: wknd fnl f)	3½	**7**	14/1	74	56
1980[11]	**Restless Spirit (USA) (87)** (MJohnston) **3-9-2** BDoyle(8) (chsd ldrs: drvn along & outpcd ½-wy: n.d)	14	**8**	14/1	44	17
1495[P]	**Mouche (80)** (MrsJRRamsden) **3-8-9** JFortune(11) (hld up: drvn along ½-wy: n.d)	¾	**9**	25/1	35	8
1583[5]	**Royal Ceilidh (IRE) (75)** (DenysSmith) **4-8-13** FLynch(12) (chsd ldrs: drvn along 3f out: sn wknd)	½	**10**	25/1	29	11
2204[3]	**Allinson's Mate (IRE) (68)** (TDBarron) **9-7-13b**(7) RWinston(16) (racd stands' side: sn bhd)	1½	**11**	16/1	19	1
1658[10]	**Iblis (IRE) (82)** (GWragg) **5-9-6** SSanders(3) (racd far side: chsd ldrs: rdn ½-wy: wknd over 2f out)	½	**12**	12/1	32	14
1782[8]	**Alpine Hideaway (IRE) (75)** (BHanbury) **4-8-13** AMcGlone(10) (hdwy over 2f out: sn rdn: n.d)	¾	**13**	20/1	23	5

1874^{5} **Divina Luna (86)** (JWHills) **4-9-7**$^{(3)}$ MHenry(5) (chsd ldrs: drvn along ½-wy: lost pl over 2f out) ....¾ **14** 25/1 32 14
1920* **Stackattack (IRE) (67)** (MrsJRRamsden) **4-8-5** JQuinn(6) (trckd ldrs: drvn along ½-wy: hung lft & sn lost pl) 1½ **15** 7/1^{2} 10 —
1973^{6} **Tal-Y-Llyn (IRE) (77)** (BWHills) **3-8-6** GCarter(9) (lw: chsd ldrs: drvn along & lost pl 3f out) ....7 **16** 9/1 4 —
(SP 136.0%) **16 Rn**

1m 31.52 (7.02) CSF £112.01 CT £376.30 TOTE £10.80: £2.20 £3.00 £1.60 £2.70 (£96.40) Trio £110.30 OWNER C H Newton Jnr Ltd (MALTON) BRED D.B. Lamplough
WEIGHT FOR AGE 3yo-9lb
1583 Jo Mell, third in this race last year, had apparently injured his back leaving the stalls at York on his previous start. Revelling in the ground, he ran out a decisive winner. (8/1)
1652 Tertium (IRE) edged left from halfway, and ended up racing on the favoured far side. He stuck on really well inside the last, and looked to be back on song. (14/1)
1980 Yorkie George, 7lb higher than at York, stuck on inside the last, after being tapped for foot at one stage. He certainly stayed this trip well. (11/4)
1737 Gee Bee Dream, 2lb higher in the weights, ran well on the favoured far side. (10/1)
1629* Weetman's Weigh (IRE), 7lb higher in the weights than when winning a handicap at Thirsk three outings ago, moved up looking a real danger, but in the final furlong could only keep on at the same pace. The handicapper looks to have his measure now. (10/1)
1017 Jeffrey Anotherred was suited by the heavy overnight rain. (12/1)
1874 Persian Fayre made the running on the far side, but got leg-weary entering the last. (14/1)
1920* Stackattack (IRE) (7/1: op 4/1)

2326 TOTE BOOKMAKERS SPRINT TROPHY H'CAP (0-95) (3-Y.O+) (Class C)
3-15 (3-16) **6f** £13,615.00 (£4,120.00: £2,010.00: £955.00) Stalls: High GOING: 0.74 sec per fur (S)

SP RR SF
2105^{12} **Cretan Gift (93)** (NPLittmoden) **6-9-7b**$^{(5)}$ PRoberts(4) (lw: chsd ldrs: styd on wl to ld last 50y) ....— **1** 16/1 102 79
1980* **Return of Amin (81)** (JDBethell) **3-8-4**$^{(3)}$ PFessey(6) (lw: trckd ldr: led over 2f out: hdd wl ins fnl f) ....nk **2** 6/1^{3} 89 59
2124^{3} **Grey Kingdom (69)** (MBrittain) **6-7-9**$^{(7)}$ DMernagh(15) (w ldrs: nt qckn ins fnl f) ....hd **3** 16/1 77 54
2044^{9} **The Lambton Worm (78)** (DenysSmith) **3-8-4**ow1 FLynch(8) (a chsng ldrs: rdn ½-wy: kpt on same pce) 3½ **4** 25/1 77 46
2211^{3} **Gadge (82)** (ABailey) **6-8-8**$^{(7)}$ CLowther(1) (led tl over 2f out: wknd over 1f out)..1¾ **5** 5/1^{2} 76 53
2129^{3} **Bee Health Boy (67)** (MWEasterby) **4-8-0b** DaleGibson(3) (w ldrs: rdn over 2f out: kpt on one pce)..............hd **6** 10/1 61 38
2111^{4} **Garnock Valley (76)** (JBerry) **7-8-9b** GCarter(13) (hdwy u.p over 2f out: kpt on: nvr rchd ldrs).......................s.h **7** 9/1 70 47
2105^{28} **Mr Bergerac (IRE) (82)** (BPalling) **6-9-1** TSprake(10) (hdwy over 2f out: sn rdn: nvr nr to chal) 1½ **8** 25/1 72 49
1948^{4} **Double Splendour (IRE) (95)** (PSFelgate) **7-10-0** KDarley(5) (hld up: hdwy 2f out: kpt on: nvr rchd ldrs) ....½ **9** 10/1 83 60
1980^{10} **For Your Eyes Only (83)** (TDEasterby) **3-8-9** AMunro(19) (racd stands side: bhd: styd on wl appr fnl)............¾ **10** 16/1 69 39
2129* **Daawe (USA) (82)** (MrsVAAconley) **6-9-1** MDeering(12) (hld up & bhd) ....¾ **11** 11/1 66 43
1583^{3} **Magic Mill (IRE) (80)** (JLEyre) **4-8-13v**[1] JFortune(2) (trckd ldrs tl wknd over 2f out)...................................nk **12** 20/1 63 40
2129^{4} **Bollin Harry (68)** (TDEasterby) **5-8-1** LCharnock(16) (w ldrs tl wknd over 1f out) 1½ **13** 12/1 47 24
2141^{3} **Night Flight (77)** (JJO'Neill) **3-8-3** AMcGlone(11) (in tch: rdn ½-wy: grad wknd)..1½ **14** 25/1 52 22
1874^{6} **Trailblazer (80)** (CWThornton) **3-8-6** DeanMcKeown(7) (mid div: rdn ½-wy: sn btn) ....¾ **15** 33/1 53 23
2211* **Charlie Sillett (87)** (BWHills) **5-9-3**$^{(3)}$ 7x JDSmith(17) (hld up & bhd: effrt over 2f out: n.d) ....1¾ **16** 4/1^{1} 56 33
1946^{9} **Mallia (77)** (TDBarron) **4-8-10** RLappin(9) (bhd fr ½-wy) 5 **17** 16/1 32 9
1967* **March Crusader (82)** (BHanbury) **3-8-8** MRoberts(14) (lw: s.i.s: a bhd) ....s.h **18** 14/1 37 7
1948^{5} ***Royal Mark (IRE) (84)*** (TDBarron) **4-9-3** TQuinn(18) (Withdrawn not under Starter's orders) .... **W** — —
(SP 144.6%) **18 Rn**

1m 18.12 (6.62) CSF £109.52 CT £1,536.96 TOTE £31.00: £5.50 £1.80 £2.80 £10.80 (£165.80) Trio £655.10 OWNER Mr T. Clarke (WOLVERHAMPTON) BRED Hesmonds Stud Ltd
WEIGHT FOR AGE 3yo-7lb
OFFICIAL EXPLANATION **Charlie Sillett: no explanation offered.**
1148 Cretan Gift, 20lb higher than when he last won a handicap on turf at Redcar in November, lacked nothing on the score of gameness. (16/1)
1980* Return of Amin, 10lb higher in the weights, was only worn down near the line. (6/1)
2124 Grey Kingdom, happier over this stiff six, came off third best in a tight three-way battle. (16/1)
1561 The Lambton Worm is slowly but surely coming down the weights. Under pressure a long way out, to his credit he kept on all the way to the line. (25/1)
2211 Gadge gets no respite. (5/1)
2129 Bee Health Boy found this company a fraction too tough. (10/1)
2111 Garnock Valley, with the ground in his favour, was doing some solid work in the final quarter-mile. (9/1)
1948 Double Splendour (IRE) ran as if on the verge of recovering his best form. (10/1: op 6/1)
1980 For Your Eyes Only, down 4lb, raced widest of all. Staying on really well at the finish, he looks to be on the way back. (16/1)
2211* Charlie Sillett, drawn towards the stands side, was settled early on. Trying to improve soon after halfway, he was having his second race in three days, and never looked like picking up. (4/1)

2327 'NEWCASTLE BROWN ALE' NORTHUMBERLAND PLATE H'CAP (3-Y.O+) (Class B)
3-50 (3-51) **2m 19y** £72,546.00 (£27,114.00: £13,232.00: £5,660.00: £2,505.00: £1,243.00) Stalls: High GOING: 0.80 sec per fur (S)

SP RR SF
2027* **Windsor Castle (104)** (PFICole) **3-8-10b** 8x TQuinn(20) (lw: chsd ldrs: drvn along over 4f out: styd on wl to ld wl ins fnl f)...— **1** 10/1 118 60
1548a^{2} **Sweetness Herself (98)** (MJRyan) **4-9-7**$^{(3)}$ MBaird(3) (trckd ldrs: led over 3f out tl wl ins fnl f) ....1 **2** 15/2^{3} 111 73
1224* **Onefourseven (74)** (JLEyre) **4-8-0** TWilliams(14) (hdwy 10f out: drvn along 5f out: n.m.r over 2f out: styd on wl appr fnl f)...1½ **3** 20/1 86 48
1974* **Siege Perilous (IRE) (73)** (SCWilliams) **4-7-13**ow1 3x TSprake(12) (lw: chsd ldrs: drvn along 5f out: hung lft over 2f out: one pce) 4 **4** 10/1 81 42
1027* **Top Cees (95)** (MrsJRRamsden) **7-9-7** JFortune(6) (hld up: hdwy over 3f out: rdn 2f out: kpt on: nvr nr to chal) ....5 **5** 5/2^{1} 98 60
2027^{7} **Flirting Around (USA) (91)** (MRStoute) **3-7-6**$^{(5)}$ow1 RFfrench(8) (lw: led to 10f out: chsd ldrs tl outpcd fnl 2f) ..2 **6** 6/1^{2} 92 33
2014^{18} **Burnt Offering (72)** (CEBrittain) **4-7-12** DaleGibson(17) (hld up & bhd: hdwy 3f out: kpt on: nvr rchd ldrs) .....hd **7** 50/1 73 35
1672^{5} **Opaque (70)** (WStorey) **5-7-7**$^{(3)}$ PFessey(2) (bhd: hdwy over 3f out: nvr nr ldrs)..s.h **8** 10/1 70 32
Lallans (IRE) (97) (MJohnston) **4-9-9** BDoyle(11) (lw: bhd: hdwy 7f out: rdn over 3f out: sn wknd)....................5 **9** 33/1 93 55
1947^{3} **Thaljanah (IRE) (85)** (BSmart) **5-8-11** SSanders(1) (chsd ldrs tl wknd 3f out) 5 **10** 20/1 76 38
1947^{5} **Arctic Fancy (USA) (81)** (PWHarris) **4-8-0**$^{(7)}$ CLowther(18) (lw: hld up: hdwy 10f out: prom 4f out: sn wknd)...5 **11** 33/1 67 29
1672^{2} **Noufari (FR) (70)** (RHollinshead) **6-7-10** NCarlisle(13) (bhd: hdwy u.p 6f out: n.d)..½ **12** 40/1 55 17

				SP	RR	SF
1400^{3}	**Go Britannia (86)** (DRLoder) **4-8-12** KDarley(4) (lw: hld up: hdwy 5f out: sn drvn along: lost pl over 3f out) ..1¾	**13**		16/1	69	31
2014^{16}	**Etterby Park (USA) (82)** (MJohnston) **4-8-5**$^{(3)ow3}$ KMChin(7) (bhd: hdwy 10f out: drvn along 5f out: n.d) 1¾	**14**		25/1	64	23
2142^{5}	**Dirab (75)** (TDBarron) **4-8-1** LCharnock(16) (lw: bhd: drvn along 5f out: n.d) 3½	**15**		20/1	53	15
1947^{4}	**Benatom (USA) (94)** (HRACecil) **4-9-6v^{1}** AMcGlone(19) (trckd ldrs: led 10f out tl over 3f out: wknd)......2½	**16**		25/1	70	32
2108^{2}	**Old Rouvel (USA) (98)** (DJGMurraySmith) **6-9-10** MRoberts(15) (lw: racd wd: hdwy 10f out: lost pl over 3f out) ......nk	**17**		14/1	73	35
1871*	**Transom (USA) (83)** (MrsAJPerrett) **6-8-9** ^{3x} JQuinn(5) (in tch: rdn 8f out: t.o 4f out: virtually p.u) ......dist	**18**		9/1	—	—

(SP 136.7%) **18 Rn**

3m 45.35 (19.85) CSF £74.33 CT £1,401.41 TOTE £10.50: £3.10 £1.90 £3.60 £2.30 (£60.60) Trio £456.20 OWNER H R H Prince Fahd Salman (WHATCOMBE) BRED Newgate Stud Co
LONG HANDICAP Noufari (FR) 6-13 Opaque 7-9 Flirting Around (USA) 7-9
WEIGHT FOR AGE 3yo-20lb

2027* Windsor Castle must be very tough, because this came just ten days after his hard race at Royal Ascot. Making light of the ground, he stuck on relentlessly to get the better of the runner-up in the final hundred yards. He is only the third three-year-old to win the Pitmen's Derby this century. (10/1: op 6/1)
1548a Sweetness Herself, 22lb higher than when she won her last handicap at Doncaster in November, set sail for home coming off the turn, and ran her heart out, but near the line had to give best. (15/2)
1224* Onefourseven, 6lb higher tended to make his own trouble, but after being switched he was staying on best of all at the line. (20/1)
1974* Siege Perilous (IRE) tended to hang under pressure and got in the way of Onefourseven. (10/1)
1027* Top Cees, 8lb higher, and suited by the ground, started a heavily-backed favourite, but was given plenty to do. After making his move off the bend, he was flat out two furlongs out, and never looked like taking a hand. (5/2)
1150* Flirting Around (USA), who defeated Windsor Castle narrowly at York in May, was meeting him on considerably better terms, but he had no excuse here. (6/1: 5/1-8/1)
1672 Opaque ran much better on this totally different ground. (10/1)
1400 Etterby Park (USA), unlike Chester, was settled towards the rear. (25/1)
1871* Transom (USA) ran as if something was amiss, being under pressure at halfway, and was virtually pulled up once in line for home. (9/1)

2328 UK LAND ESTATES TROPHY H'CAP (0-95) (3-Y.O) (Class C)

4-20 (4-22) **1m 2f 32y** £7,555.00 (£2,290.00: £1,120.00: £535.00) Stalls: High GOING: 0.86 sec per fur (S)

			SP	RR	SF
2178^{2}	**Top Jem (70)** (MJRyan) **3-7-10** GBardwell(8) (chsd ldrs: led over 3f out: clr 2f out: drvn out) ......—	**1**	6/1^{2}	85	49
1773^{6}	**Epworth (78)** (JAGlover) **3-8-4** GCarter(7) (hld up: effrt over 3f out: chsd wnr fnl 2f: no imp)......5	**2**	9/1	85	49
1649^{5}	**Ibin St James (71)** (JDBethell) **3-7-8b**$^{(3)}$ PFessey(3) (chsd ldrs: drvn along 6f out: one pce fnl 2f)......6	**3**	16/1	69	33
1595^{5}	**Bali Paradise (USA) (95)** (PFICole) **3-9-7** TQuinn(2) (w ldrs tl wknd over 2f out)......8	**4**	9/1	80	44
524^{5}	**Sioux (79)** (CWThornton) **3-8-5** DeanMcKeown(9) (hld up: effrt over 3f out: n.m.r over 1f out: nvr nr ldrs)......3	**5**	10/1	59	23
2043^{5}	**Foxes Tail (75)** (MissSEHall) **3-8-1** LCharnock(10) (trckd ldrs: rdn over 3f out: hung lft: wknd 2f out) 1	**6**	9/1	54	18
2137^{4}	**Maftool (85)** (JHMGosden) **3-8-11** AMcGlone(5) (trckd ldrs: effrt over 3f out: sn wknd)......7	**7**	2/1^{1}	53	17
2128*	**Zorba (74)** (JHetherton) **3-8-0** NKennedy(1) (led tl over 3f out: wknd over 2f out) 2	**8**	12/1	39	3
2062^{8}	**Foot Battalion (IRE) (80)** (RHollinshead) **3-8-6** FLynch(4) (s.i.s: bhd & drvn along over 4f out: n.d) ......¾	**9**	16/1	43	7
2005*	**Contentment (IRE) (79)** (JWHills) **3-8-2**$^{(3)}$ MHenry(11) (hld up: effrt over 3f out: sn wknd)......2	**10**	7/1^{3}	39	3
2015^{10}	**Sandbaggedagain (80)** (MWEasterby) **3-8-1**$^{(5)ow1}$ GParkin(12) (racd wd: plld hrd: effrt over 3f out: sn lost pl)½	**11**	9/1	39	2
1741^{8}	**Aerleon Pete (IRE) (78)** (MRStoute) **3-8-4** KDarley(6) (hld up: drvn along over 4f out: n.d)......3	**12**	6/1^{2}	33	—

(SP 143.0%) **12 Rn**

2m 19.5 (12.80) CSF £65.76 CT £805.06 TOTE £6.80: £2.00 £4.00 £3.50 (£40.30) Trio £140.10 OWNER Mr John Malpass (NEWMARKET) BRED Malpass Brothers Ltd
LONG HANDICAP Top Jem 7-7

2178 Top Jem, who is very much on the up, took advantage of a favourable handicap mark and, after hitting the front, her rider left nothing to chance. (6/1)
1773 Epworth went in pursuit of the winner two out, but was never making any impression. (9/1)
1649 Ibin St James, hard at work at halfway, proved woefully one-paced. (16/1)
1595 Bali Paradise (USA) had a lot to do under top weight, giving 10lb or more all around in this ground. (9/1)
524 Sioux, on her handicap debut, and having her first outing since March, did not shape at all badly, and should improve for the race. (10/1)
2043 Foxes Tail yet again gave his rider problems. (9/1)
2137 Maftool, who had run so well when he had plenty on his plate at Ascot a week earlier, was disappointing here, coming under pressure once in line for home, and soon dropping right out. He is a lot better than he showed here. (2/1: op 4/1)
2015 Sandbaggedagain (9/1: 6/1-10/1)

2329 COLONEL PORTER BROWN ALE CHIPCHASE STKS (Listed) (3-Y.O+) (Class A)

4-50 (4-52) **6f** £12,718.00 (£4,762.00: £2,331.00: £1,005.00: £452.50: £231.50) Stalls: High GOING: 0.92 sec per fur (S)

			SP	RR	SF
1770^{4}	**Tomba (113)** (BJMeehan) **3-8-12** MTebbutt(9) (lw: trckd ldrs: qcknd to ld 2f out: rdn clr) ......—	**1**	5/4^{1}	121	78
	Azizzi (CREgerton) **5-9-1** TQuinn(3) (lw: led to 2f out: kpt on same pce: no ch w wnr)......5	**2**	12/1	104	68
2106^{7}	**Rambling Bear (108)** (MBlanshard) **4-9-7** MRoberts(7) (lw: hld up: effrt over 2f out: kpt on one pce fnl f)......½	**3**	7/2^{3}	108	72
2105^{7}	**King of Peru (96)** (NPLittmoden) **4-9-1** TGMcLaughlin(4) (lw: trckd ldrs: ev ch 2f out: nt qckn appr fnl f)......1¼	**4**	9/1	99	63
1171^{9}	**Carranita (IRE) (106)** (BPalling) **7-9-0** TSprake(5) (chsd ldrs: effrt over 2f out: wknd over 1f out)......¾	**5**	5/2^{2}	96	60

(SP 112.9%) **5 Rn**

1m 18.35 (6.85) CSF £15.20 TOTE £1.90: £1.20 £2.30 (£6.40) Trio £5.90 OWNER Mr J. R. Good (UPPER LAMBOURN) BRED Mrs P. Good
WEIGHT FOR AGE 3yo-7lb

1770 Tomba is ideally suited by six furlongs and soft ground, and he had this won in a matter of strides. (5/4: evens-11/8)
Azizzi, having his first run for over a year, showed bags of early speed. (12/1: 8/1-14/1)
2106 Rambling Bear had a stiff task under a 6lb penalty. (7/2)
2105 King of Peru ran a pleasing race for his new trainer. (9/1)
961 Carranita (IRE) having her first outing for forty-four days, ran as if in need of the outing. (5/2)

2330 PATTERSON FORD MAIDEN STKS (3-Y.O+) (Class D)

5-20 (5-21) **1m 3y (straight)** £5,158.50 (£1,563.00: £764.00: £364.50) Stalls: Centre GOING: 0.98 sec per fur (S)

			SP	RR	SF
	Ganga (IRE) (WJarvis) **3-8-7** SSanders(1) (lw: leggy: unf: s.i.s: smooth hdwy over 3f out: led on bit over 1f out: sn qcknd wl clr: eased towards fin) ......—	**1**	6/1	81+	49

				SP	RR	SF
2059^{3}	**Northern Flash** (FMurphy) **3-8-12** DeanMcKeown(7) (w ldr: kpt on appr fnl f: no ch w wnr)	7	**2**	$4/1^{3}$	72	40
	Desert Track (JHMGosden) **3-8-12** AMcGlone(4) (lw: trckd ldrs: drvn along & outpcd over 3f out: kpt on one pce appr fnl f)	5	**3**	$evens^{1}$	62	30
2045^{6}	**Dina Line (USA)** (MBell) **3-8-2**$^{(5)}$ GFaulkner(9) (lw: led tl over 1f out: sn wknd)	7	**4**	8/1	43	11
	Teulada (USA) (LMCumani) **3-8-7** KDarley(8) (sn chsng ldrs: rn green & pushed along ½-wy: sn bhd)	14	**5**	$7/2^{2}$	15	—
	Bold Appeal (IRE) (WStorey) **5-9-8** GCarter(5) (trckd ldrs tl lost pl ½-wy: sn bhd & eased)	30	**6**	20/1	—	—

(SP 122.4%) **6 Rn**

1m 50.6 (12.00) CSF £29.67 TOTE £6.60: £2.10 £1.30 (£20.70) Trio £23.20 OWNER Cuadra Africa (NEWMARKET) BRED Cambremont Ltd Partnership

WEIGHT FOR AGE 3yo-10lb

Ganga (IRE), who had one outing behind Reams Of Verse at two, revelled in the ground, and proved much too good for this lot. But for being eased right up, she would have won by an even wider margin. (6/1)

2059 Northern Flash kept on under pressure to finish second best, but this will not have done his handicap mark any good. (4/1: 7/1-7/2)

Desert Track, who showed plenty of promise on his only outing at two, was flat out and getting outpaced at halfway. Perhaps the ground was against him. (evens)

2045 Dina Line (USA) made the running, but fell in a heap over a furlong out. (8/1: op 4/1)

Teulada (USA) made no appeal in the paddock, and running very green, was out with the washing from halfway. (7/2: op 7/4)

T/Jkpt: Not won; £8,725.27 to Doncaster 29/6/97. T/Plpt: £347.80 (147.19 Tckts). T/Qdpt: £94.50 (23.06 Tckts) WG

2294-NEWMARKET (R-H) (Soft)
Saturday June 28th

WEATHER: fine WIND: slt across

2331 DOM RUINART CHAMPAGNE H'CAP (0-90) (3-Y.O+ F & M) (Class C)

2-00 (2-02) **1m (July)** £6,018.75 (£1,800.00: £862.50: £393.75) Stalls: Low GOING minus 0.04 sec per fur (G)

				SP	RR	SF
1834*	**Prima Verde (75)** (LMCumani) **4-9-3** LDettori(6) (b.nr fore: a.p: rdn 2f out: led ins fnl f: r.o)	—	**1**	$5/2^{1}$	84	26
1935^{6}	**Intisab (85)** (RWArmstrong) **4-9-13** RHills(2) (prom: lost pl 3f out: rdn & r.o strly ins fnl f)	nk	**2**	20/1	93	35
1737^{11}	**Sleepless (84)** (NAGraham) **3-9-2** DHolland(4) (hld up: rdn 2f out: styd on wl fnl f)	½	**3**	$7/2^{2}$	91	23
1589^{2}	**Undercover Agent (IRE) (83)** (JLDunlop) **3-9-1** PatEddery(5) (hld up & plld hrd: sltly hmpd over 4f out: plld out over 1f out: r.o wl)	hd	**4**	$5/1^{3}$	90	22
688^{6}	**Telemania (IRE) (82)** (WJHaggas) **3-9-0** MHills(8) (swtg: led over 7f: one pce)	nk	**5**	10/1	89	21
1813^{2}	**Blessed Spirit (78)** (CFWall) **4-9-6** GDuffield(11) (lw: hld up & plld hrd: hdwy & n.m.r over 1f out: swtchd & hmpd ins fnl f: fin wl)	½	**6**	6/1	84	26
1973^{4}	**Our Way (73)** (CEBrittain) **3-8-0**$^{(5)}$ RMullen(9) (chsd ldrs: rdn 2f out: btn fnl f)	¾	**7**	20/1	77	9
1794*	**Scarlet Crescent (72)** (PTWalwyn) **3-8-4** JStack(3) (plld hrd: chsd ldrs: rdn over 2f out: wkng whn n.m.r wl ins fnl f)	2	**8**	14/1	72	4
1845^{10}	**Tart (FR) (64)** (JPearce) **4-8-6** NDay(1) (lw: a bhd)	½	**9**	33/1	63	5
1811^{9}	**Fern's Governor (56)** (WJMusson) **5-7-12** NVarley(10) (in tch tl stumbled & uns rdr 5f out)		**U**	12/1	—	—

(SP 117.7%) **10 Rn**

1m 45.13 (7.13) CSF £53.64 CT £163.24 TOTE £3.00: £1.70 £6.20 £1.10 (£33.40) Trio £61.70 OWNER The Lawster Partnership (NEWMARKET) BRED Mrs L. Popely

WEIGHT FOR AGE 3yo-10lb

1834* Prima Verde, in her first handicap, was kept close to the pace and had time to respond when the pace quickened approaching the final quarter-mile. She took her time to get on top, but is lightly raced and should have more improvement in her. (5/2)

1935 Intisab tracked the leader but then lost her place as the tempo began to increase. Finally asked for her effort on meeting the rising ground she fairly flew, but could not get up in time. (20/1)

1245* Sleepless was some way off the pace when the race proper began and, although she gradually closed all the way to the line, she was never doing enough. (7/2)

1589 Undercover Agent (IRE) took some settling at the slow early pace and, by the time she pulled to the outside and began her challenge, all the principals were quickening. (5/1)

688 Telemania (IRE) got warm and moved keenly to post, but was able to dictate matters from the start. Only worn down by the winner inside the final furlong, there were a few hard luck stories in behind. (10/1: 7/1-12/1)

1813 Blessed Spirit took a deal of holding early on and, not for the first time in her life, found plenty of trouble at the business end. She needs to be produced late and such tactics would have been easier to execute in a more truly-run race. (6/1)

1794* Scarlet Crescent (14/1: 10/1-20/1)

933 Fern's Governor (12/1: 10/1-20/1)

2332 BLOMBERG CLAIMING STKS (3-Y.O) (Class D)

2-30 (2-31) **1m (July)** £4,077.50 (£1,220.00: £585.00: £267.50) Stalls: Low GOING minus 0.04 sec per fur (G)

				SP	RR	SF
2125^{2}	**Jukebox Jive (49)** (CADwyer) **3-7-6**$^{(7)}$ DarrenWilliams(5) (lw: hdwy over 2f out: led 1f out: edgd lft: rdn clr nr fin)	—	**1**	$6/1^{3}$	64	26
2159^{4}	**Poker Princess (52)** (MBell) **3-7-8**$^{(5)}$ RMullen(9) (trckd ldrs: ev ch 2f out: led over 1f out: sn hdd: wknd nr fin)	2½	**2**	10/1	59	21
1988^{6}	**Miss Barcelona (IRE) (45)** (MJPolglase) **3-7-8**$^{(5)}$ JBramhill(3) (swtg: prom: rdn 3f out: r.o fnl f)	3½	**3**	25/1	52	14
1484^{11}	**Wing of A Prayer (49)** (WJarvis) **3-8-4** DaneO'Neill(11) (hld up: rdn 3f out: styd on fnl f)	1¼	**4**	20/1	55	17
1017^{11}	**Test The Water (IRE) (88)** (RHannon) **3-9-10** PatEddery(4) (rdn & hdwy 2f out: n.m.r 1f out: no imp & eased)	s.h	**5**	$2/1^{1}$	74	36
2040^{3}	**Phoenix Princess (49)** (BAMcMahon) **3-8-3** GDuffield(8) (plld hrd: w ldr: led over 3f out tl over 1f out: sn wknd)	1¼	**6**	12/1	51	13
	Jilly Woo (DRCElsworth) **3-7-6**$^{(7)}$ JFowle(7) (dwlt: nvr trbld ldrs)	1¼	**7**	20/1	44	6
2125^{4}	**Distinctive Dream (IRE) (43)** (KTIvory) **3-8-5b**$^{(3)}$ MartinDwyer(12) (stdd s: hld up: hdwy 5f out: rdn & wknd appr fnl f)	4	**8**	16/1	45	7
1858^{5}	**Blazer's Baby** (JRFanshawe) **3-7-13** NVarley(1) (in tch: rdn over 3f out: no imp)	1¼	**9**	9/1	34	—
*225**	**Spaniard's Mount (69)** (MHTompkins) **3-9-2v** RHills(6) (lw: plld hrd: sn led: wknd & hdd over 3f out)	6	**10**	$4/1^{2}$	39	1

2121^{W} **Loganlea (IRE) (59)** (WJMusson) **3-8-3** JStack(10) (prom tl wknd 3f out)..........10 **11** 10/1 6 —
Prince de Loir (DJSCosgrove) **3-9-0** WRyan(2) (Withdrawn not under Starter's orders) .... **W** 33/1 — —
(SP 125.7%) **11 Rn**

1m 43.4 (5.40) CSF £59.67 TOTE £6.80: £1.80 £3.70 £4.10 (£26.20) Trio £90.00 OWNER North End Partnership (NEWMARKET) BRED Mrs T. C. Griffiths

Jukebox Jive clmd MSharky £6,000

2125 Jukebox Jive was helped by the placing of the stalls on the far side as, once in front, she again came off a true line. (6/1)

2159 Poker Princess, dropped in trip, tried to make her stamina tell in the last two furlongs but, after appearing more intimidated than hampered by the winner, gave up in the closing stages. (10/1: 7/1-11/1)

1988 Miss Barcelona (IRE) had never raced on ground this soft but seemed to handle it. (25/1)

606 Wing of A Prayer, stepping up in distance, did enough in the last furlong to suggest that he stays. (20/1)

723 Test The Water (IRE), who won a competitive Ascot nursery last season, was taking a big drop in class. Never travelling all that well, forward progress was hampered by interference and the situation was accepted. Not a great mover, if he retains any ability he should be able to win in this grade. (2/1)

2040 Phoenix Princess again took a strong hold, which prevented her from lasting home in the rain-softened ground. (12/1)

1409 Loganlea (IRE) (10/1: 7/1-12/1)

2333 NGK SPARK PLUGS FRED ARCHER STKS (Listed) (4-Y.O+) (Class A)

3-00 (3-02) **1m 4f (July)** £10,807.80 (£3,731.80: £1,785.90: £724.50) Stalls: High GOING minus 0.04 sec per fur (G)

SP RR SF

1454^{6} **Kutta (107)** (RWArmstrong) **5-8-11** RHills(1) (lw: trckd ldr: led 2f out: rdn out)..........— **1** $11/10^{1}$ 120 57
1771^{2} **Harbour Dues (106)** (LadyHerries) **4-8-11** PatEddery(3) (lw: hld up: hdwy 5f out: rdn 3f out: kpt on fnl f: nt pce to chal)..........4 **2** $7/4^{2}$ 115 52
$2099a^{5}$ **Anno Luce** (JHMGosden) **4-8-12v[1]** LDettori(2) (led: rdn over 3f out: hdd 2f out: sn btn)..........6 **3** $9/2^{3}$ 108 45
1960^{2} **River North (IRE) (99)** (LadyHerries) **7-8-11** OPeslier(4) (b: chsd ldrs: no imp fnl 3f)..........8 **4** 9/1 96 33
(SP 112.2%) **4 Rn**

2m 34.2 (5.20) CSF £3.18 TOTE £2.00: (£1.80) OWNER Mr Hamdan Al Maktoum (NEWMARKET) BRED Shadwell Estate Company Limited

1454 Kutta was beginning to look a hard horse to win with, but had an outstanding chance on the book, and Hills did not mess about once he decided it was time to go. (11/10)

1771 Harbour Dues seemed happy to allow the winner first run and was never going to close the gap in time. (7/4)

2099a Anno Luce, making her debut in this country, ran a little better in a first-time visor. She is going to be hard to place here and her future may well lie in foreign Group races. (9/2: 3/1-5/1)

1960 River North (IRE), once the emphasis was switched to speed, was left toiling. (9/1: op 6/1)

2334 VAN GEEST CRITERION STKS (Gp 3) (3-Y.O+) (Class A)

3-30 (3-30) **7f (July)** £20,928.00 (£7,752.00: £3,726.00: £1,530.00: £615.00: £249.00) Stalls: Low GOING minus 0.04 sec per fur (G)

SP RR SF

2026^{7} **Ramooz (USA) (106)** (BHanbury) **4-9-2** WRyan(1) (b: hld up: hdwy 3f out: n.m.r 2f out: rdn & r.o wl to ld nr fin)..........— **1** $11/4^{1}$ 114 66
2056^{8} **Almushtarak (IRE) (106)** (KMahdi) **4-9-2** PatEddery(8) (in tch: hdwy 2f out: led ins fnl f: hrd rdn & ct nr fin)...hd **2** 7/1 114 66
2023^{11} **Wind Cheetah (USA) (108)** (MRStoute) **3-8-7** MHills(7) (lw: a.p: ev ch over 2f out: led over 1f out tl ins fnl f: unable qckn)..........½ **3** 12/1 113 56
1776^{3} **My Branch (105)** (BWHills) **4-8-13** DHolland(9) (hld up: hdwy 2f out: r.o wl ins fnl f)..........nk **4** $5/1^{3}$ 109 61
2023^{8} **Tayseer (USA) (97)** (EALDunlop) **3-8-7** JWeaver(10) (hld up: rdn 2f out: kpt on: nvr rchd ldrs)..........2½ **5** $5/1^{3}$ 106 49
1455^{10} **Abou Zouz (USA) (113)** (DRLoder) **3-8-7** OPeslier(4) (lw: trckd ldrs: rdn over 2f out: no imp)..........1¾ **6** 8/1 102 45
Queen's Pageant (82) (JLSpearing) **3-8-4** DaneO'Neill(3) (lw: chsd ldr: ev ch over 2f out tl wknd fnl f)..........2 **7** 40/1 95 38
2105^{21} **World Premier (99)** (CEBrittain) **4-9-2** RHills(2) (led: hdd over 1f out: sn wknd)..........2 **8** 20/1 93 45
2023^{7} **Supercal (99)** (DRCElsworth) **3-8-4** GDuffield(5) (chsd ldrs tl rdn & btn 2f out)..........½ **9** $4/1^{2}$ 89 32
(SP 118.5%) **9 Rn**

1m 27.59 (2.59) CSF £21.28 TOTE £3.40: £1.30 £2.10 £2.70 (£11.70) Trio £129.00 OWNER Mr Hilal Salem (NEWMARKET) BRED Gainsborough Stud Management Ltd

WEIGHT FOR AGE 3yo-9lb

2026 Ramooz (USA) does seem best over seven and, handling this sticky ground better than might have been expected, showed tremendous courage to force his way to the front after having anything but a trouble-free passage along the far rail. (11/4)

2056 Almushtarak (IRE) looked in really good shape and ran right to his best over what is probably his ideal trip. (7/1: 5/1-8/1)

Wind Cheetah (USA), with his tongue tied down this time, was taken to post last but still proved a little keen. Finally showing that he has ability to match his looks, he was finally worried out of it in the dying strides. (12/1: 10/1-16/1)

1776 My Branch, taken down early, finished strongly to run another sound race on ground softer than she is used to. (5/1: op 3/1)

1170* Tayseer (USA), held up in rear, could not quicken on this ground and never landed a blow. He was entered in the Britannia at Ascot and set to get weight from the winner Fly To The Stars, a horse he had beaten at level weights last year, so the handicap option would still have been open to him, but this run will not help his mark. (5/1)

Abou Zouz (USA) did not pick up well enough to land a blow once ridden along and can still be made fitter. (8/1)

2335 LADBROKE EMPRESS STKS (Listed) (2-Y.O F) (Class A)

4-05 (4-05) **6f (July)** £8,873.20 (£3,278.80: £1,569.40: £637.00: £248.50: £93.10) Stalls: Low GOING minus 0.04 sec per fur (G)

SP RR SF

1945^{2} **Lady In Waiting** (PFICole) **2-8-11** LDettori(5) (lw: hld up: hdwy 2f out: rdn to ld ins fnl f)..........— **1** $5/2^{2}$ 92 54
1645* **Land of Dreams** (MJohnston) **2-8-11** JWeaver(7) (hld up: hdwy to ld over 1f out: qcknd & edgd lft: hdd & no ex ins fnl f)..........1¾ **2** $5/2^{2}$ 87 49
1213* **Silent Tribute (IRE)** (MBell) **2-8-11** MFenton(4) (prom: rdn 2f out: kpt on wl fnl f)..........½ **3** 16/1 86 48
1945* **Sapphire Ring** (RCharlton) **2-8-11** PatEddery(6) (lw: stdd s: hld up & plld hrd: rdn over 1f out: no imp)..........2½ **4** $2/1^{1}$ 79 41
2024^{17} **Eleonora d'Arborea** (BJMeehan) **2-8-8** OPeslier(3) (plld hrd: prom 3f)..........2½ **5** 33/1 70? 32
2024^{4} **Banningham Blade** (KTIvory) **2-8-13** MartinDwyer(2) (led 1f: led 2f out: sn hdd: wknd fnl f)..........nk **6** $15/2^{3}$ 74 36
*2066** **Socket Set** (BAMcMahon) **2-8-8** GDuffield(1) (led after 1f to 2f out: wknd appr fnl f)..........7 **7** 16/1 50 12
(SP 116.9%) **7 Rn**

1m 14.74 (2.74) CSF £8.75 TOTE £3.60: £1.90 £2.30 (£7.00) OWNER Pegasus Racing Ltd (WHATCOMBE) BRED Mrs J. Haigh

1945 Lady In Waiting takes a good hold and, with the benefit of hindsight, was probably made too much use of at York last time. Produced last, she did the job in great style. (5/2)

1645* Land of Dreams, who got a little warm and doesn't yet look the finished article, showed a great turn of foot to go a couple of lengths to the good but, changing her legs in the Dip where the ground was at its deepest, lost her action and was pegged back by the winner. Still green, she pricked her ears when going clear and is best forgiven this first reverse. (5/2: 6/4-3/1)
1213* Silent Tribute (IRE), given time to recover from a debut that is working out solidly, lacked the turn of foot of the first two but stayed on really stoutly to the line. (16/1)
1945* Sapphire Ring, who had beaten the winner at York last time, has a very good action and may not have run to her best on the sticky surface. Whatever the reason, she was clearly in trouble below the distance. (2/1)
1806 Eleonora d'Arborea has run up light with racing and, after taking a strong hold, was no match for the principals in the last couple of furlongs. (33/1)
2024 Banningham Blade, trying six for the second time, but this time on testing ground, was found wanting for stamina after running her usual good race. (15/2)

2336 KRIS MAIDEN STKS (2-Y.O) (Class D)

4-35 (4-38) **7f (July)** £4,056.25 (£1,210.00: £577.50: £261.25) Stalls: Low GOING minus 0.04 sec per fur (G)

				SP	RR	SF
	The Glow-Worm (IRE) (BWHills) **2-9-0** MHills(7) (cmpt: scope: a.p: led ins fnl f: pushed out)	—	**1**	25/1	73	30
	Matata (IRE) (NACallaghan) **2-8-9** GDuffield(4) (gd sort: neat: lw: in tch: hdwy over 1f out: ev ch ins fnl f: unable to qckn nr fin)	¾	**2**	50/1	66	23
1933[10]	**Eljjanah (USA)** (JLDunlop) **2-9-0** RHills(3) (lw: hld up: rdn over 1f out: r.o wl ins fnl f)	hd	**3**	16/1	71	28
1293[3]	**Al's Fella (IRE)** (PFICole) **2-9-0** DHolland(10) (racd alone centre: disp ld tl led wl over 2f out: hdd & one pce ins fnl f)	hd	**4**	16/1	71	28
	Radar (IRE) (MAJarvis) **2-9-0** DaneO'Neill(1) (w'like: scope: trckd ldrs: outpcd 2f out: r.o strly ins fnl f)	½	**5**	33/1	70	27
	Exit To Somewhere (IRE) (HRACecil) **2-9-0** WRyan(6) (cmpt: trckd ldrs: rdn & btn whn nt clr run ins fnl f)	1¼	**6**	4/7[1]	67	24
	Pay On Red (USA) (PFICole) **2-9-0** PatEddery(8) (gd sort: lw: led over 4f: wknd over 1f out)	3½	**7**	9/2[2]	59	16
	Laffah (USA) (JHMGosden) **2-9-0** LDettori(2) (gd sort: bkwd: rdn 3f out: nvr nr ldrs)	2½	**8**	9/1[3]	53	10
	Prince Batshoof (MBell) **2-9-0** MFenton(5) (cmpt: bkwd: s.i.s: a bhd)	4	**9**	33/1	44	1
	Fantasy Night (IRE) (JLDunlop) **2-9-0** OPeslier(9) (gd sort: bkwd: prom tl wknd 3f out)	¾	**10**	33/1	42	—
				(SP 118.2%)	**10 Rn**	

1m 30.52 (5.52) CSF £787.87 TOTE £20.70: £3.10 £6.40 £2.80 (£125.50) Trio £510.50; £589.65 to Doncaster 29/6/97 OWNER Mrs J. M. Corbett (LAMBOURN) BRED Dr J. Ryan and Rozelle Bloodstock
The Glow-Worm (IRE), quite keen going down, was always in the first three and held on in a driving finish. This looked a very decent bunch on looks but the fact they finished in such a heap must question the value of the form. (25/1)
Matata (IRE) flashed her tail in the paddock but stuck on strongly when finding her stride, and looks sure to stay further. (50/1)
Eljjanah (USA) left his debut run behind, staying on in fine style on meeting the rising ground. Better ground should see more improvement. (16/1)
1293 Al's Fella (IRE), quite keen to post, ploughed a lone furrow up the centre of the track for much of the race. Only caught inside the final furlong, he should find a race. (16/1)
Radar (IRE) looked well in his coat and showed a good action going down, but paddock inspection showed he would come on a lot for the run. Left behind going into the Dip, he flashed his tail when hit with the whip but really responded, staying on strongly towards the finish. Normal improvement should see him in the winner's enclosure. (33/1)
Exit To Somewhere (IRE) had two handlers in the paddock and was taken down steadily. Clearly expected to run a great deal better than he did, this half brother to Ivan Luis should not be written off. (4/7)
Pay On Red (USA) ran as if needing the race more than it appeared. (9/2: 6/1-4/1)
Laffah (USA) (9/1: 7/1-12/1)
Prince Batshoof, a half brother to Supply And Demand, looked to badly need the run, and will leave this form behind in time. (33/1)

2337 EQUINE FERTILITY UNIT/ANIMAL HEALTH TRUST APPRENTICE H'CAP (0-70) (3-Y.O+) (Class E)

5-05 (5-05) **7f (July)** £3,517.50 (£1,065.00: £520.00: £247.50) Stalls: Low GOING minus 0.04 sec per fur (G)

				SP	RR	SF
2004[8]	**Jibereen (53)** (PHowling) **5-8-10**(3) RMullen(1) (lw: b: hld up: plld out & rdn 1f out: qcknd to ld ins fnl f)	—	**1**	5/1[3]	62	47
2121[6]	**Secret Ballot (IRE) (55)** (KMahdi) **3-8-6** DO'Donohoe(4) (h.d.w: in tch: hdwy 4f out: rdn & led over 1f out: hdd & one pce ins fnl f)	1¾	**2**	8/1	60	36
2216*	**Purchasing Power (IRE) (76)** (NACallaghan) **3-9-13** 6x RHavlin(3) (lw: led over 2f: ev ch over 1f out: one pce)	4	**3**	8/11[1]	72	48
1935[5]	**Xenophon of Cunaxa (IRE) (63)** (MJFetherston-Godley) **4-9-6**(3) DSweeney(2) (w ldrs: led over 4f out: hdd & wknd over 1f out)	1½	**4**	9/2[2]	55	40
2121[W]	**Cross of Valour (65)** (PHowling) **4-9-11** MartinDwyer(5) (prom 4f: sn bhd)	15	**5**	20/1	23	8
				(SP 108.6%)	**5 Rn**	

1m 28.99 (3.99) CSF £34.51 TOTE £5.20: £1.60 £2.00 (£21.00) OWNER Mr Liam Sheridan (NEWMARKET) BRED Mrs J. Everitt
WEIGHT FOR AGE 3yo-9lb
1501 Jibereen had plummeted down the handicap being 17lb lower than for his last win on the All-Weather and 16lb lower than when giving Declan Murphy a comeback winner the last time he won on turf. He produced a good turn of foot to seal matters and certainly has a chance of finding more races given his current mark. (5/1)
2121 Secret Ballot (IRE), a good mover, is thriving and, ridden with a little more restraint, looked a winner until done for foot. He had a hard race and may remember this. (8/1: op 5/1)
2216* Purchasing Power (IRE) could not dominate but kept plugging away and continues to run well. (8/11: 1/2-4/5)
1935 Xenophon of Cunaxa (IRE), taken down early, was still rather keen and is not giving himself a chance of lasting home at the moment. (9/2)
Cross of Valour always seemed better over six in any case, but has completely lost the plot since changing stables. (20/1)

T/Plpt: £742.80 (38.91 Tckts). T/Qdpt: £102.30 (13.34 Tckts) Dk

2312-DONCASTER (L-H) (Good to soft, Good patches)
Sunday June 29th
WEATHER: overcast WIND: slt half bhd

2338 DONCASTER 'MILESTONE RIDE' CONDITIONS STKS (3-Y.O+) (Class C)
2-00 (2-02) **1m (straight)** £4,948.12 (£1,807.50: £886.25: £383.75: £174.38) Stalls: High GOING: 0.30 sec per fur (G)

				SP	RR	SF
	Lord of Men (JHMGosden) **4-9-1** GHind(4) (hld up: hdwy ½-wy: led over 2f out: shkn up & r.o fnl f)	—	**1**	7/4[1]	105	69
2026[29]	**Kala Sunrise (88)** (CSmith) **4-9-1** JFortune(3) (trckd ldrs: effrt over 2f out: ch over 1f out: no ex)	4	**2**	25/1	97	61
2009[8]	**Amrak Ajeeb (IRE) (107)** (BHanbury) **5-9-1** RHills(1) (lw: cl up: led ½-wy: hdd & hung lft over 2f out: sn btn)	4	**3**	7/4[1]	89	53
1740[3]	**Out West (USA) (102)** (HRACecil) **3-8-10** WRyan(5) (lw: prom tl rdn & btn 3f out)	16	**4**	7/2[2]	62	16
2101a*	**Barba Papa (IRE)** (LMCumani) **3-8-12**(5) RFfrench(2) (led to ½-wy: sn rdn & btn)	8	**5**	6/1[3]	53	7

(SP 113.1%) **5 Rn**

1m 42.5 (5.30) CSF £33.57 TOTE £3.00: £1.60 £2.60 (£24.40) OWNER Sheikh Mohammed (NEWMARKET) BRED Sheikh Mohammed bin Rashid al Maktoum
WEIGHT FOR AGE 3yo-10lb

Lord of Men, returning here after twenty months off with a broken pelvis, failed to impress in the paddock but there was little wrong with his racing performance, as he travelled well and picked up when asked, despite the odd flash of the tail. (7/4)
1300 Kala Sunrise appeared to run way above himself here but there are plenty of ifs about the form and it should certainly not be taken literally. (25/1)
1323 Amrak Ajeeb (IRE), normally held up, was ridden up with the pace this time and, once in front, all he wanted to do was hang and this is certainly not the way to ride him. (7/4)
1740 Out West (USA), a lean filly, racing with cut in the ground for the first time, never looked happy and was left struggling soon after halfway. (7/2: 5/2-4/1)
2101a* Barba Papa (IRE) had his limitations exposed a long way out. (6/1)

2339 '50 YEARS OF TIMEFORM' H'CAP (0-90) (3-Y.O+) (Class C)
2-30 (2-31) **5f** £5,408.75 (£1,640.00: £802.50: £383.75) Stalls: High GOING: 0.30 sec per fur (G)

				SP	RR	SF
1946[4]	**Swan At Whalley (63)** (RAFahey) **5-7-12**(7) RWinston(5) (chsd ldrs: led appr fnl f: styd on u.p)	—	**1**	14/1	76	49
2111*	**Squire Corrie (85)** (DWChapman) **5-9-13** ACulhane(2) (lw: chsd ldrs: hrd rdn & ch appr fnl f: nt qckn)	2	**2**	6/1[2]	92	65
2134[4]	**Polish Warrior (IRE) (83)** (TDBarron) **3-9-5b** WRyan(6) (lw: a chsng ldrs: hdwy u.p 2f out: btn appr fnl f)	¾	**3**	6/1[2]	87	54
*2050**	**Malibu Man (72)** (EAWheeler) **5-8-9**(5) ADaly(1) (lw: led tl hdd appr fnl f: sn btn)	½	**4**	10/1[3]	75	48
1937[3]	**Palacegate Touch (77)** (JBerry) **7-8-12b**(7) CLowther(9) (lw: outpcd tl styd on u.p fnl 2f: nrst fin)	nk	**5**	12/1	79	52
2162[8]	**Broadstairs Beauty (IRE) (72)** (DShaw) **7-8-11b**(3) CTeague(4) (b: drvn along ½-wy: kpt on: no imp)	1	**6**	12/1	70	43
1946[7]	**Lago Di Varano (86)** (RMWhitaker) **5-10-0** DeanMcKeown(7) (outpcd & bhd: hdwy over 1f out: nvr rchd ldrs)	½	**7**	10/1[3]	83	56
2129[6]	**Benzoe (IRE) (70)** (MrsJRRamsden) **7-8-12** JFortune(10) (bhd: sme hdwy 2f out: n.d)	1	**8**	6/1[2]	64	37
2197[8]	**Antonias Melody (68)** (SRBowring) **4-8-10b** SWebster(3) (sn drvn along: nvr bttr than mid div)	2	**9**	33/1	55	28
1977[6]	**Brecongill Lad (65)** (MissSEHall) **5-8-2v**(5) RFfrench(12) (racd stands' side: sn outpcd & bhd)	½	**10**	12/1	51	24
1828[5]	**Premium Gift (58)** (CBBBooth) **5-8-0** GCarter(11) (lw: racd stands' side: effrt ½-wy: a bhd)	2	**11**	5/1[1]	37	10
2148[2]	**Polly Golightly (67)** (MBlanshard) **4-8-9b** NAdams(8) (spd stands' side 3f: wknd qckly)	½	**12**	11/1	45	18

(SP 118.7%) **12 Rn**

62.24 secs (3.84) CSF £87.31 CT £518.64 TOTE £17.70: £3.50 £3.10 £2.10 (£113.40) Trio £200.00 OWNER Mr Kevin Ainsworth (MALTON) BRED R. L. Cox
WEIGHT FOR AGE 3yo-6lb
OFFICIAL EXPLANATION **Premium Gift: had bled from the nose.**

1946 Swan At Whalley is in top form at present and was able to go the very strong pace, seeing it out most determinedly. (14/1)
2111* Squire Corrie is looking better with every run and he again ran his heart out, but did have his first really hard race for a while. (6/1)
2134 Polish Warrior (IRE) looked magnificent and has plenty of speed but he was never quite doing enough when ridden. Once the key is found, he should go on improving. (6/1)
2050* Malibu Man is probably better on a faster surface but still showed blistering speed here, only to run out of fuel late on. (10/1)
1937 Palacegate Touch was drawn away from the strong pace and took time to get going, but he did finish well to show he is still in good heart. (12/1)
1223 Broadstairs Beauty (IRE), for once in his life, could not live with the pace but he did struggle on, albeit in vain. (12/1)
1158 Lago Di Varano, the winner of this last year, was completely taken off his legs this time and, although staying on, never had a hope. (10/1)
1828 Premium Gift, an extremely unlucky loser in this last season, was gambled on to make amends but, as it turned out, she was poorly drawn and never ran any sort of race. It transpired she had broken a blood-vessel. (5/1: op 8/1)

2340 MAIL ON SUNDAY MILE (QUALIFIER) H'CAP (0-80) (3-Y.O+) (Class D)
3-00 (3-03) **1m (round)** £7,717.50 (£2,340.00: £1,145.00: £547.50) Stalls: High GOING: 0.30 sec per fur (G)

				SP	RR	SF
2205[7]	**Pride of Pendle (67)** (MartynWane) **8-9-0**(3) MartinDwyer(13) (hld up: hdwy over 2f out: led ins fnl f: r.o)	—	**1**	12/1	77	59
*2161**	**Cashmere Lady (72)** (JLEyre) **5-9-5**(3) OPears(7) (lw: a.p: led wl over 1f out tl ins fnl f: kpt on same pce)	1¼	**2**	5/1[1]	80	62
1845[3]	**Mo-Addab (IRE) (74)** (ACStewart) **7-9-10** SWhitworth(2) (swtg: chsd ldrs: ev ch over 1f out: kpt on)	nk	**3**	13/2[2]	81	63
1831[5]	**Mr Teigh (68)** (MrsJRRamsden) **5-9-4** JFortune(4) (in tch: hdwy to chal wl over 1f out: shkn up & nt qckn)	2½	**4**	9/1	70	52
1788[3]	**Anonym (IRE) (63)** (JLEyre) **5-8-13** TWilliams(10) (bhd: effrt ½-wy: styd on fnl 2f: nrst fin)	1½	**5**	14/1	62	44
1878[7]	**Noble Dane (IRE) (74)** (PWHarris) **3-8-7b**1(7) CLowther(9) (led & sn clr: hdd wl over 1f out: no ex)	1½	**6**	10/1	70	42
2238[2]	**Pension Fund (69)** (MWEasterby) **3-8-9** TLucas(5) (bhd: rdn 3f out: n.d)	2	**7**	9/1	61	33
1245[2]	**Trading Aces (75)** (MBell) **3-9-1v** MFenton(12) (chsd ldrs tl grad wknd fnl 2½f)	¾	**8**	7/1[3]	65	37
2036[8]	**Up in Flames (IRE) (55)** (SRBowring) **6-8-5** DaleGibson(6) (prom tl rdn & wknd fnl 3f)	s.h	**9**	14/1	45	27
1800[7]	**Oneoftheoldones (46)** (JNorton) **5-7-7**(3) PFessey(14) (bhd: rdn ½-wy: n.d)	1½	**10**	25/1	33	15
1972[16]	**Zermatt (IRE) (56)** (MDIUsher) **7-8-6** JCarroll(3) (outpcd ½-wy: n.d afterwards)	9	**11**	25/1	25	7
1813[3]	**Compromise (IRE) (79)** (BWHills) **3-9-2**(3) JDSmith(8) (lw: reard s: s.s: nt rcvr)	27	**12**	7/1[3]	—	—
2062[13]	**Jay-Owe-Two (IRE) (75)** (RMWhitaker) **3-9-1** DeanMcKeown(11) (swtg: reard s: s.v.s: nt rcvr)	½	**13**	33/1	—	—
	Star of Gold (73) (CREgerton) **5-9-9** WRyan(1) (lw: chsd clr ldr 3f: wknd rapidly: sn t.o)	16	**14**	20/1	—	—

(SP 120.5%) **14 Rn**

1m 44.86 (6.46) CSF £61.69 CT £407.92 TOTE £11.30: £2.60 £2.20 £2.70 (£29.20) Trio £106.90 OWNER Mrs Linda Miller (RICHMOND) BRED James Simpson

LONG HANDICAP Oneoftheoldones 7-0
WEIGHT FOR AGE 3yo-10lb
2205 Pride of Pendle came back to form here in real style and looks one to keep on the right side of. (12/1)
2161* Cashmere Lady looked superb and did her best, but the winner was always too strong. Nevertheless, she is in tremendous heart. (5/1)
1845 Mo-Addab (IRE) got very warm beforehand as he often does and he still had his chances and kept responding to pressure, but was never quite good enough. (13/2)
1831 Mr Teigh looked to be travelling particularly well halfway up the straight but then failed to pick up when asked, and probably needs further. (9/1)
1788 Anonym (IRE) has been in top form on the All-Weather and this was not a bad effort, as he was gradually picking up all the way up the straight. (14/1)
723 Noble Dane (IRE) had the blinkers on for the first time and they certainly woke her up, but she had run herself out over a furlong from home. (10/1)
1813 Compromise (IRE) was on his hind legs as the stalls opened and that was all chance gone. (7/1)

2341 LUCKY CHOICE H'CAP (0-105) (3-Y.O+) (Class B)

3-35 (3-37) **1m 2f 60y** £12,544.00 (£4,696.00: £2,298.00: £990.00: £445.00: £227.00) Stalls: Low GOING: 0.30 sec per fur (G)

				SP	RR	SF
	Present Arms (USA) (88) (PFICole) **4-9-3** JFortune(5) (lw: trckd ldrs: led wl over 1f out: shkn up & r.o)	—	**1**	11/1	98	65
2028^{16}	**Rockforce (91)** (MRChannon) **5-9-3**(3) PPMurphy(1) (hld up: hdwy on ins 4f out: sn trckng ldrs: kpt on wl fnl f)	1¾	**2**	$13/2^{3}$	98	65
1647*	**Pinchincha (FR) (84)** (DMorris) **3-8-1**ow3 NDay(9) (bhd: shkn up 4f out: hdwy 2f out: kpt on: nt pce to chal)	1	**3**	$11/4^{1}$	90	42
2155^{4}	**Sandmoor Chambray (79)** (TDEasterby) **6-8-8b** JCarroll(2) (cl up: led wl over 3f out tl wl over 1f out: wknd ins fnl f)	5	**4**	$13/2^{3}$	77	44
2026^{26}	**General Academy (IRE) (95)** (PAKelleway) **4-9-10** SWhitworth(4) (bhd: rdn over 4f out: styd on fnl 2f: n.d)	4	**5**	25/1	87	54
1775^{6}	**Moving Arrow (91)** (MissSEHall) **6-9-6** WRyan(3) (hld up & bhd: effrt ent st: n.d)	4	**6**	7/1	77	44
2118^{2}	**Edan Heights (76)** (SDow) **5-8-2**(3) DO'Donohoe(7) (cl up: ev ch 3f out: wknd 2f out)	¾	**7**	$11/2^{2}$	60	27
1741^{10}	**River's Source (USA) (85)** (BWHills) **3-8-2b**[1] AClark(8) (in tch: rdn over 3f out: sn btn)	nk	**8**	8/1	69	24
597^{4}	**Waiting Game (IRE) (95)** (DRLoder) **3-8-12** DRMcCabe(6) (led tl hdd wl over 3f out: sn btn & eased)	dist	**9**	7/1	—	—
				(SP 117.0%)	**9 Rn**	

2m 15.43 (7.63) CSF £74.11 CT £232.23 TOTE £10.20: £3.10 £2.00 £1.60 (£53.10) Trio £63.60 OWNER H R H Prince Fahd Salman (WHATCOMBE) BRED Tri-Star Stable
WEIGHT FOR AGE 3yo-12lb
Present Arms (USA) looked particularly well for his seasonal debut here and, travelling on the bridle, was never going to be beaten. He looks likely to improve as he goes over longer trips. (11/1)
1016 Rockforce travels well in his races but was in a bit of a pocket most of the way up the straight here and then, despite running on, was always well second best. His style of running suggests he should get a bit further. (13/2)
1647* Pinchincha (FR) needed two lads in the paddock and was very edgy but he was as game as they come in the race. He kept responding to pressure all the way up the straight but was never quite up to the task. (11/4)
2155 Sandmoor Chambray keeps running consistently well but just needs a bit of help from the Handicapper. (13/2)
General Academy (IRE) does not as yet look quite right but, after being behind, he did respond to pressure in the closing stages to show that he still has ability. (25/1)
1775 Moving Arrow has plenty of ability when things go right but it was not his day this time and he showed little. (7/1)

2342 DAVID SCOTT & CO (PATTERN MAKERS) 1997 EURO-AMERICAN CHALLENGE INVITATION AMATEUR H'CAP (0-70) (3-Y.O+) (Class E)

4-20 (4-22) **1m 2f 60y** £3,501.25 (£1,060.00: £517.50: £246.25) Stalls: Low GOING: 0.30 sec per fur (G)

				SP	RR	SF
2067^{2}	**Anyar Reem (63)** (DShaw) **6-11-10b** MrCBonner(7) (b: trckd ldrs: rdn to ld ins fnl f: styd on wl)	—	**1**	8/1	75	60
2030^{3}	**Leif the Lucky (USA) (55)** (MissSEHall) **8-11-2** MrRBellocq(9) (plld hrd: trckd ldrs: led ent st: hdd ins fnl f: no ex)	2½	**2**	$9/2^{2}$	63	48
1315^{7}	**Sagebrush Rollor (52)** (JWWatts) **9-10-13** MrEHennau(3) (lw: hld up: hdwy 4f out: ev ch 1f out: nt qckn)	s.h	**3**	12/1	60	45
1449^{3}	**Madison Welcome (IRE) (64)** (MrsJRRamsden) **3-10-13** MissEJohnsonHoughton(5) (bhd: effrt 4f out: styd on: no imp)	3	**4**	$11/2^{3}$	67	40
2030^{2}	**One Life To Live (IRE) (52)** (SEKettlewell) **4-10-13v**[1] MrTSchmeer(4) (trckd ldrs: effrt over 2f out: sn rdn & btn)	4	**5**	$7/2^{1}$	49	34
2145^{5}	**Thisonesforalice (35)** (JSGoldie) **9-9-10** MissBRoesch(1) (chsd ldrs tl rdn & outpcd fnl 3f)	3	**6**	25/1	28	13
1452^{5}	**Lord Hastie (USA) (42)** (CWThornton) **9-10-3b** MrGSmith(6) (s.s: n.d)	1¾	**7**	13/2	32	17
461^{18}	**Newbridge Boy (52)** (MGMeagher) **4-10-13** RevSKennedy(10) (led tl hdd ent st: rdn & wknd 4f out)	25	**8**	14/1	3	—
1944^{13}	**Agent (53)** (JLEyre) **4-11-0** MrsEVanOrshoven(2) (lw: cl up tl wknd fnl 4f)	9	**9**	11/1	—	—
1689^{10}	**Mubariz (IRE) (35)** (CSmith) **5-9-10** MissBPatterson(8) (t: a bhd: t.o)	dist	**10**	20/1	—	—
				(SP 111.5%)	**10 Rn**	

2m 20.27 (12.47) CSF £38.11 CT £383.33 TOTE £7.40: £2.10 £1.30 £3.40 (£15.60) Trio £64.40 OWNER Mr Paul Murphy (NEWARK) BRED Miss K. Rausing and Mrs S. M. Rogers
LONG HANDICAP Thisonesforalice 9-8
WEIGHT FOR AGE 3yo-12lb
2067 Anyar Reem was fitted with all the aids and, well-handled, was produced to take it as the opposition tired. (8/1)
2030 Leif the Lucky (USA) is a tricky customer but he enjoyed this and, taking charge entering the straight, ran his best race for a while, only to cry enough when it really mattered. (9/2)
1315 Sagebrush Roller was full of himself here and almost bolted going to post. He ran his best race for a long time over this extra distance, but he just failed to pick up when it was needed. (12/1)
1449 Madison Welcome (IRE) was staying on at the end, suggesting that further should suit. (11/2: op 7/2)
2030 One Life To Live (IRE) had the visor on instead of blinkers and looked to be going well, but failed to respond when ridden and, most likely, needs stronger handling. (7/2)
2145 Thisonesforalice had his chances but failed to see it out. (25/1)
1452 Lord Hastie (USA) did not run too badly after a very slow start. (13/2)

2343 E.B.F. HALSALL ELECTRICAL NOVICE STKS (2-Y.O) (Class D)
4-50 (4-50) **6f** £3,485.00 (£1,055.00: £515.00: £245.00) Stalls: High GOING: 0.30 sec per fur (G)

	Horse		Pos	SP	RR	SF
	Tajasur (IRE) (JLDunlop) **2-8-12** RHills(4) (gd sort: trckd ldrs: led on bit ent fnl f: rn green: jst hld on)	—	1	2/1 1	79+	40
1267*	**Alconleigh** (MJohnston) **2-9-4** JCarroll(1) (led tl hdd ins fnl f: rallied)	hd	2	2/1 1	85	46
	Shifting (CWThornton) **2-8-7** DeanMcKeown(2) (neat: scope: hld up: effrt & outpcd 2f out: kpt on: n.d)	3½	3	8/1 2	64	25
1978*	**Carbon** (DMorley) **2-9-4** GCarter(3) (plld hrd: trckd ldr: effrt over 1f out: sn btn)	s.h	4	2/1 1	75	36
				(SP 111.1%)		**4 Rn**

1m 16.79 (5.79) CSF £5.84 TOTE £2.70: (£3.30) OWNER Mr Hamdan Al Maktoum (ARUNDEL) BRED Tommy Burns
Tajasur (IRE) looked the pick in the paddock and for most of the race looked likely to trot up but, running green, only just lasted home. However, he was certainly not given a hard time and should improve a fair deal for the experience. (2/1)
1267* Alconleigh is improving, both physically and performance-wise, and this was a cracking effort. (2/1)
Shifting looked likely to benefit from this and never got in a blow, but did show enough to give plenty of hope for the future. (8/1: op 14/1)
1978* Carbon spoiled his chances by pulling far too hard and this is best ignored. (2/1)

T/Jkpt: Not won; £14,795.82 to Windsor 30/6/97. T/Plpt: £411.20 (58.65 Tckts). T/Qdpt: £60.70 (23.7 Tckts) AA

2282-GOODWOOD (R-H) (Good to soft, Soft patches)
Sunday June 29th
WEATHER: overcast WIND: almost nil

2344 BOLLINGER CHAMPAGNE CHALLENGE SERIES GENTLEMEN'S H'CAP (0-70) (3-Y.O+) (Class E)
2-15 (2-15) **1m 4f** £3,550.00 (£1,075.00: £525.00: £250.00) Stalls: Low GOING: 0.15 sec per fur (G)

	Horse		Pos	SP	RR	SF
2118*	**Koraloona (IRE) (54)** (GBBalding) **4-10-12** MrLJefford(6) (a.p: led over 2f out: drvn out)	—	1	11/4 1	62	31
	Warm Spell (57) (GLMoore) **7-10-11v1(4)** MrIMongan(4) (b: bit bkwd: hld up: ev ch fnl 2f: r.o)	hd	2	13/2	65	34
1632 19	**Dauphin (IRE) (44)** (WJMusson) **4-10-2** MrTMcCarthy(1) (hld up: rdn over 2f out: r.o one pce)	2	3	7/1	49	18
1844 6	**Fairy Knight (69)** (RHannon) **5-11-13** MrCVigors(2) (lw: hld up: rdn over 2f out: one pce)	3½	4	4/1 3	70	39
2318 4	**Nails Tails (35)** (SDow) **4-9-7** MrTCuff(3) (led over 9f)	nk	5	12/1	35	4
1748 3	**Farringdon Hill (70)** (JHMGosden) **6-11-10(4)** MrCRanson(7) (b.hind: w ldr over 9f: eased whn btn fnl f)	20	6	100/30 2	44	13
	Java Shrine (USA) (58) (AJChamberlain) **6-10-12(4)** MrSCarroll(5) (bit bkwd: bhd fnl 6f)	18	7	40/1	8	—
				(SP 105.7%)		**7 Rn**

2m 49.18 (15.98) CSF £16.02 TOTE £3.50: £1.90 £2.80 (£10.40) OWNER Mr Bernard Keay (ANDOVER) BRED Eaton Farms Inc, Red Bull Stable and Joe Hernon
LONG HANDICAP Nails Tails 9-3
2118* Koraloona (IRE), successful here in similar conditions nine days ago, coped well with the longer trip. Leading over a quarter of a mile from home, he had a tremendous battle-royal with the runner-up, but just managed to keep that rival at bay. He wants plenty of rain according to his trainer. (11/4)
Warm Spell, without a run since finishing second over hurdles at Kempton last October, was carrying condition but he loves this ground and made a very pleasing reappearance. Throwing down a very determined challenge in the final quarter-mile, he may have got his head in front for a couple of strides inside the final furlong, but was just unable to get the better of the winner. (13/2: 9/2-7/1)
1001* Dauphin (IRE) chased the leaders but, despite staying on, was unable to get on terms with the front two. (7/1)
1844 Fairy Knight, tucked in behind the front rank in the straight, failed to quicken when his rider asked him for his effort. (4/1)
2318 Nails Tails, who finished fourth at Lingfield less than twenty-two hours earlier, took the field along but, collared over a quarter of a mile from home, found his earlier exertions taking their toll. (12/1: op 8/1)
1748 Farringdon Hill was back over a more suitable trip but both his victories to date have come on fast ground, and these underfoot conditions were not to his liking. (100/30)

2345 MILESTONE RIDE CONDITIONS STKS (3-Y.O+) (Class B)
2-50 (2-50) **1m 1f** £13,478.00 (£4,718.00: £2,309.00: £995.00) Stalls: High GOING: 0.15 sec per fur (G)

	Horse		Pos	SP	RR	SF
2013 11	**Handsome Ridge (104)** (JHMGosden) **3-8-6**ow1 JReid(3) (hld up: chsd ldr 2f out: led ins fnl f: pushed out)	—	1	11/10 1	110	52
1032 2	**Barnum Sands (103)** (JLDunlop) **3-8-9** KDarley(1) (lw: led: rdn over 1f out: hdd ins fnl f: r.o)	nk	2	9/2 3	113	56
1982 2	**Union Town (IRE) (102)** (SirMarkPrescott) **3-8-7** GDuffield(2) (swtg: chsd ldr over 6f out tl over 3f out: wknd over 2f out)	10	3	3/1 2	93	36
931 4	**Desert Horizon (100)** (JHMGosden) **3-8-5** AMcGlone(4) (b: lw: chsd ldr over 2f: chsd ldr over 3f out to 2f out: wknd over 1f out)	½	4	6/1	90	33
				(SP 105.1%)		**4 Rn**

1m 58.63 (5.63) CSF £5.28 TOTE £2.10: (£3.10) OWNER Platt Promotions Ltd (NEWMARKET) BRED Mrs Willa Harford
597 Handsome Ridge appreciated the underfoot conditions and put up a tidy performance. Easing his way into second place a quarter of a mile from home, he was shaken up and, although only gaining a narrow advantage inside the final furlong, always had the measure of his rival. (11/10)
1032 Barnum Sands ran much better here. Taking the field along, he was marginally collared inside the final furlong and, although failing by only a neck, was always playing second fiddle to the winner. A step up in trip would suit. (9/2: 3/1-5/1)
1982 Union Town (IRE) again showed that this soft ground is not for him. Off the bridle well before halfway, he was going in reverse over two furlongs from home. He has done all his winning on a fast surface. (3/1)
931 Desert Horizon, who had a bad infection in his foot after his last run back at the beginning of May, looked in good shape for this return. Showing in second place as the bugler called entering the straight, he was collared for that position two furlongs from home and was soon in trouble. (6/1: 4/1-7/1)

2346 MAIL ON SUNDAY MILE (QUALIFIER) H'CAP (0-90) (3-Y.O+) (Class C)
3-20 (3-22) **1m** £14,655.00 (£4,440.00: £2,170.00: £1,035.00) Stalls: High GOING: 0.15 sec per fur (G)

	Horse		Pos	SP	RR	SF
1935 7	**No Extras (IRE) (62)** (GLMoore) **7-8-1** JQuinn(13) (plld hrd: a.p: rdn over 1f out: led ins fnl f: drvn out)	—	1	7/1	73	58
2036*	**Therhea (IRE) (69)** (BRMillman) **4-8-8** TSprake(7) (lw: hdwy & nt clr run over 2f out: nt clr run over 1f out: ev ch ins fnl f: r.o)	½	2	9/1	79	64
250 2	**Brilliant Red (89)** (PRHedger) **4-10-0** GDuffield(12) (led: hrd rdn over 1f out: hdd ins fnl f: unable qckn)	1¾	3	25/1	96	81

1739[2]	**Sweet Wilhelmina (68)** (LordHuntingdon) **4-8-7** DHarrison(9) (hld up: ev ch over 1f out: wknd fnl f)	4	**4**	7/2[1]	67	52
2117[6]	**Stone Ridge (IRE) (81)** (RHannon) **5-9-6b** DaneO'Neill(6) (chsd ldr over 5f: wknd over 1f out)	nk	**5**	16/1	79	64
1745[2]	**Sue's Return (78)** (APJarvis) **5-9-3** DHolland(11) (hld up: rdn 3f out: one pce)	1	**6**	7/1	74	59
2117*	**Ca'd'oro (60)** (GBBalding) **4-7-13** NVarley(3) (lw: hld up: rdn over 2f out: wknd 1f out)	¾	**7**	9/2[2]	54	39
2124[10]	**Present Generation (78)** (RGuest) **4-9-3** SSanders(10) (lw: nvr nrr)	2	**8**	25/1	68	53
1870*	**Geimhriuil (IRE) (83)** (LMCumani) **3-8-12** KDarley(2) (lw: hld up: rdn over 2f out: wknd over 1f out)	nk	**9**	5/1[3]	73	48
1308[10]	**Capilano Princess (80)** (DHaydnJones) **4-9-5** SDrowne(1) (sme hdwy over 2f out: wknd over 1f out)	1¼	**10**	25/1	67	52
1739[12]	**La Modiste (68)** (MissGayKelleway) **4-8-2**(5) RMullen(4) (a bhd)	6	**11**	25/1	43	28
1588[7]	**Press On Nicky (69)** (WRMuir) **4-8-8** MRoberts(5) (lw: a bhd)	3½	**12**	20/1	37	22
1979[13]	**Rebel County (IRE) (87)** (ABailey) **4-9-12** DWright(14) (lw: a bhd)	3	**13**	25/1	49	34
				(SP 121.9%)	**13 Rn**	

1m 41.09 (3.89) CSF £56.87 CT £1,335.29 TOTE £10.50: £2.50 £4.30 £4.60 (£68.10) Trio £495.40 OWNER Mr K. Higson (BRIGHTON) BRED R. J. Cullen

WEIGHT FOR AGE 3yo-10lb

1324 No Extras (IRE) has fallen in the handicap and took full advantage of it here, after a couple of encouraging runs recently. Taking a keen hold, he raced up with the pace and, responding to pressure, got up inside the final furlong. (7/1)

2036* Therhea (IRE), 7lb higher than when winning at Nottingham, did not have the best of runs in the straight, but he nevertheless came to have every chance inside the final furlong before the winner pulled out a bit extra. (9/1: 6/1-10/1)

250 Brilliant Red made a very pleasing reappearance after a four-month absence and attempted to make all the running. Responding to pressure, he was only worried out of it inside the final furlong. (25/1)

1739 Sweet Wilhelmina travelled well during the race and looked all over the winner as she loomed up alongside the leader over a quarter of a mile from home. However, when let down below the distance, the response was rather disappointing and she tired in the final furlong. She tired badly in soft ground at Newbury last month and it does appear that she cannot get home when conditions are testing. A return to the winner's enclosure looks likely when the fast ground returns. (7/2)

2117 Stone Ridge (IRE) raced in second place until over two furlongs from home and had come to the end of his tether below the distance. All three of his wins to date have come over a mile. (16/1)

1745 Sue's Return was being bustled along early in the straight but was made to look very pedestrian. (7/1)

1870* Geimhriuil (IRE) (5/1: 3/1-11/2)

2347 LUCKY CHOICE STEWARDS CUP TRIAL H'CAP (0-90) (3-Y.O+) (Class C)

3-50 (3-51) **6f** £11,283.75 (£3,420.00: £1,672.50: £798.75) Stalls: Low GOING: 0.15 sec per fur (G)

				SP	RR	SF
1673[2]	**Always Alight (72)** (KRBurke) **3-8-5** JQuinn(9) (lw: hdwy over 1f out: led wl ins fnl f: drvn out)	—	**1**	11/2[3]	80	49
2134[6]	**Rudi's Pet (IRE) (82)** (RHannon) **3-9-1b** DaneO'Neill(3) (a.p: led over 3f out: rdn over 1f out: hdd wl ins fnl f: r.o)	nk	**2**	14/1	89	58
1977[9]	**So Intrepid (IRE) (75)** (JMBradley) **7-9-1** GDuffield(6) (lw: nt clr run 2f out: hdwy over 1f out: ev ch wl ins fnl f: r.o)	s.h	**3**	13/2	82	58
1824[3]	**Sir Joey (USA) (84)** (PGMurphy) **8-9-10** SDrowne(7) (rdn over 2f out: hdwy over 1f out: wknd fnl f)	6	**4**	9/2[2]	75	51
1977[5]	**Erupt (64)** (GBBalding) **4-8-4** SSanders(2) (a.p: rdn over 2f out: wknd fnl f)	2	**5**	7/1	50	26
1876[4]	**Blewbury Hill (IRE) (77)** (RFJohnsonHoughton) **3-8-10** JReid(5) (lw: hld up: rdn over 2f out: wknd fnl f)	2½	**6**	7/1	56	25
2192*	**Silca Key Silca (85)** (MRChannon) **3-9-4** 7x KDarley(1) (prom over 4f)	1¼	**7**	3/1[1]	61	30
2115[7]	**Invocation (57)** (GLMoore) **10-7-6**(5)ow1 RMullen(8) (lw: virtually ref to r: a wl bhd)	10	**8**	33/1	6	—
1946[8]	**Osomental (83)** (DHaydnJones) **3-9-2v** DHolland(4) (led over 2f: wkng whn n.m.r 2f out)	5	**9**	20/1	19	—
				(SP 111.3%)	**9 Rn**	

1m 13.53 (3.73) CSF £67.49 CT £452.40 TOTE £5.40: £1.50 £2.80 £1.90 (£47.20) Trio £182.40 OWNER Mr M. Nelmes-Crocker (WANTAGE) BRED Bylon Farmers Ltd

LONG HANDICAP Invocation 7-7

WEIGHT FOR AGE 3yo-7lb

1673 Always Alight looked in good shape beforehand and was brought with a well-timed run to get up in the closing stages. He is not entered in the Stewards' Cup but has the Ayr Gold Cup as the long-term plan. (11/2)

2134 Rudi's Pet (IRE) went on just before halfway but, despite grimly trying to hold on, was worried out of it in the last fifty yards. (14/1: 8/1-16/1)

1977 So Intrepid (IRE) picked up ground below the distance and was one of three fighting for the advantage in the closing stages, before just losing out. (13/2: 9/2-7/1)

1824 Sir Joey (USA) made his effort below the distance but had nothing left to offer in the final furlong. (9/2)

1977 Erupt was close up until tiring in the final furlong. He has not won since his juvenile days. (7/1: 5/1-15/2)

1876 Blewbury Hill (IRE), taking a drop in distance for this handicap debut, chased the leaders but had nothing left in the locker in the final furlong. (7/1: 5/1-15/2)

2192* Silca Key Silca failed to handle the soft ground and, pushed along from halfway, eventually tired below the distance. (3/1)

2348 TRIUMVIRATE LIMITED STKS (0-90) (3-Y.O+) (Class C)

4-25 (4-25) **1m 4f** £6,491.00 (£2,271.00: £1,110.50: £477.50) Stalls: Low GOING: 0.15 sec per fur (G)

				SP	RR	SF
1875[5]	**Dust Dancer (88)** (JLDunlop) **3-8-7** JReid(1) (chsd ldr: led over 2f out: comf)	—	**1**	3/1[3]	100+	47
2136[4]	**Romios (IRE) (90)** (PFICole) **5-9-10** CRutter(2) (lw: hld up: chsd wnr 2f out: edgt rt over 1f out: no imp)	6	**2**	6/1	95	56
2028[7]	**Hoh Express (90)** (IABalding) **5-9-10** KDarley(3) (hld up: rdn over 2f out: one pce)	2	**3**	2/1[2]	92	53
2046*	**Mumaris (USA) (90)** (ACStewart) **3-8-10** MRoberts(4) (lw: led over 9f)	6	**4**	7/4[1]	84	31
				(SP 109.0%)	**4 Rn**	

2m 41.85 (8.65) CSF £16.19 TOTE £3.10: (£6.30) OWNER Hesmonds Stud (ARUNDEL) BRED Hesmonds Stud Ltd

WEIGHT FOR AGE 3yo-14lb

OFFICIAL EXPLANATION Mumaris (IRE): no explanation offered.

1875 Dust Dancer seems to have found her right trip and, cruising into the lead over a quarter of a mile from home, sprinted away inside the distance to win with plenty in hand. (3/1)

2136 Romios (IRE) moved into second place a quarter of a mile out, but he drifted in behind the winner and failed to contain that rival. (6/1: 4/1-13/2)

2028 Hoh Express was asked for his effort over two furlongs from home but failed to find the necessary response. (2/1)

2046* Mumaris (USA) had more on his plate here and, taking the field along, tamely dropped away when collared over two furlongs from home. (7/4)

2349 SCULPTURE AT GOODWOOD MEDIAN AUCTION MAIDEN STKS (2-Y.O) (Class D)
5-00 (5-00) **7f** £3,598.75 (£1,090.00: £532.50: £253.75) Stalls: High GOING: 0.15 sec per fur (G)

				SP	RR	SF
1933[8]	**Master Mac (USA)** (RAkehurst) **2-9-0** SSanders(2) (chsd ldr: hrd rdn over 1f out: led wl ins fnl f: r.o wl)	—	**1**	7/1	75	35
2047[2]	**Bernardo Bellotto (IRE)** (MBell) **2-9-0** DHarrison(5) (lw: led: hrd rdn over 1f out: hdd wl ins fnl f: r.o)	nk	**2**	5/1[2]	74	34
1970[7]	**Respond** (GLMoore) **2-8-9** CandyMorris(7) (lw: hld up: rdn over 2f out: unable qckn fnl f)	¾	**3**	25/1	68	28
1933[5]	**Lincolnshire (USA)** (PFICole) **2-9-0** JReid(4) (hld up: rdn over 2f out: one pce)	½	**4**	11/2[3]	72	32
1978[6]	**Naked Oat** (BSmart) **2-9-0** MTebbutt(6) (lw: nvr nr to chal)	2½	**5**	12/1	66	26
1927[5]	**Chocolate (IRE)** (JLDunlop) **2-8-9** KDarley(3) (lw: hld up: rdn over 2f out: wknd fnl f)	1	**6**	5/2[1]	59	19
1927[2]	**Jilted (IRE)** (RHannon) **2-8-9** DaneO'Neill(1) (lw: a.p: rdn over 2f out: wknd over 1f out)	3	**7**	5/2[1]	52	12
				(SP 113.2%)	**7 Rn**	

1m 31.24 (6.44) CSF £36.84 TOTE £8.20: £3.00 £2.60 (£21.50) OWNER Mr Charles Parker (EPSOM) BRED Joe Lee

1480 Master Mac (USA) left his poor run at Sandown well behind. Responding to pressure below the distance, he got up in the closing stages to give Reg Akehurst a rare two-year-old winner. (7/1)

2047 Bernardo Bellotto (IRE) was well suited by the step up in trip and attempted to make all the running. Gamely responding to pressure, he was only worried out of it in the closing stages. He has now finished second in four of his five races and richly deserves a change of luck. (5/1: 4/1-13/2)

Respond ran her best race to date over this longer trip and was snapping at the heels of the first two in the final furlong, if just failing to find that vital turn of foot. (25/1)

1933 Lincolnshire (USA), who went down very freely to post, once again had his lack of acceleration exposed. (11/2: op 3/1)

1978 Naked Oat, at the back of the field, never threatened to get into it. (12/1: 10/1-16/1)

1927 Chocolate (IRE) chased the leaders but melted away in the final furlong. (5/2)

1927 Jilted (IRE) appeared to find this longer trip beyond her and, after racing in close contention, tired below the distance. (5/2: op 6/4)

T/Plpt: £9,933.80 (1.89 Tckts). T/Qdpt: £429.60 (2.5 Tckts) AK

2165-**MUSSELBURGH (R-H) (Good to soft)**
Monday June 30th
WEATHER: overcast WIND: slt across

2350 EVENING NEWS APPRENTICE H'CAP (0-60) (3-Y.O+) (Class G)
6-55 (6-56) **2m** £2,144.00 (£609.00: £302.00) Stalls: High GOING: 0.08 sec per fur (G)

				SP	RR	SF
2145[6]	**Vintage Taittinger (IRE) (27)** (JSGoldie) **5-7-13** JMcAuley(2) (lw: chsd ldrs: led 6f out: hld on wl u.p fnl 2f)	—	**1**	7/1	38	—
2166*	**Trilby (59)** (GRichards) **4-9-12v**(5) 5x DHayden(1) (trckd ldrs: effrt ent st: ev ch 2f out: edgd rt & nt qckn)	2	**2**	11/8[1]	68	—
2175*	**Brodessa (57)** (MrsMReveley) **11-10-1** 5x PFredericks(6) (lw: hld up: effrt ent st: chsng ldrs & hpmd 3f out: styd on)	1¼	**3**	5/1[2]	65	—
2000*	**Tancred Mischief (40)** (DWBarker) **6-8-12** CarolynBales(7) (hld up & bhd: outpcd appr st: styd on wl towards fin)	3½	**4**	6/1	44	—
2000[10]	**Arian Spirit (IRE) (40)** (JLEyre) **6-8-12** SBuckley(5) (lw: hld up: effrt 5f out: styd on: no imp)	s.h	**5**	11/2[3]	44	—
1996[6]	**Recluse (24)** (WTKemp) **6-7-10b** PBradley(4) (lw: chsd ldrs tl outpcd fnl 4f)	3	**6**	33/1	25	—
	Dallai (IRE) (33) (GPKelly) **6-8-0**(5) JoanneDavies(3) (bkwd: led tl hdd 6f out: wknd qckly 4f out: t.o)	dist	**7**	100/1	—	—
				(SP 104.9%)	**7 Rn**	

3m 40.9 CSF £13.01 TOTE £7.20: £3.60 £1.50 (£6.60) OWNER Die-Hard Racing Club (GLASGOW) BRED Carrigbeg Stud Co Ltd

LONG HANDICAP Recluse 7-8

2145 Vintage Taittinger (IRE), much happier over this longer trip, proved far too gutsy for the runner-up. (7/1: op 4/1)

2166* Trilby went well for much of the trip but, when an effort was required in the straight, he tended to hang right and failed to come up with the goods. (11/8)

2175* Brodessa is in really good heart at present and put up a fair performance, but did not have the best of runs early in the straight. However, he kept responding to pressure. (5/1)

2000* Tancred Mischief needs a stronger gallop than was set here, and could never get going in time. (6/1: op 4/1)

Arian Spirit (IRE) is coming to herself looks-wise and, although never making an impression, she should not be written off yet. (11/2: op 10/1)

1996 Recluse had her chances but looked very slow when the pace was on in the last four furlongs. (33/1)

2351 CREDIT LYONNAIS LAING LIMITED STKS (0-50) (3-Y.O+) (Class F)
7-25 (7-26) **1m 4f 31y** £2,757.50 (£770.00: £372.50) Stalls: High GOING: 0.08 sec per fur (G)

				SP	RR	SF
2154[2]	**Sun of Spring (54)** (DWChapman) **7-9-6**(3) PFessey(4) (hld up: hdwy 4f out: led over 1f out tl wl ins fnl f: rallied to ld nr fin)	—	**1**	5/4[2]	61	40
1230[12]	**Wellcome Inn (50)** (JO'Reilly) **3-8-7** JO'Reilly(1) (trckd ldr after 2f: led over 3f tl over 1f out: led wl ins fnl f: jst ct)	s.h	**2**	7/1[3]	59	24
1992*	**Ambidextrous (IRE) (55)** (EJAlston) **5-9-2**(7) PFredericks(2) (lw: hld up: hdwy 4f out: disp ld 2f out: no ex ins fnl f)	1¾	**3**	10/11[1]	59	38
1820[14]	**Dissington Times (39)** (WMcKeown) **3-8-7b**[1] ACulhane(3) (unruly s: led tl hdd over 3f out: sn btn)	14	**4**	50/1	38	3
				(SP 111.3%)	**4 Rn**	

2m 44.8 (11.30) CSF £8.65 TOTE £2.80: (£7.80) OWNER Mr S. B. Clark (YORK) BRED R. H. Cowell

WEIGHT FOR AGE 3yo-14lb

2154 Sun of Spring is a game sort and, in this messy race, that won the day. (5/4)

558 Wellcome Inn attracted some fair support at big prices and almost brought off a touch, and this quite attractive sort should find a race in due course. (7/1: 10/1-13/2)

1992* Ambidextrous (IRE) had his chances but basically he needs a stronger pace than was set here. (10/11: 4/5-evens)

Dissington Times, in blinkers for the first time, looked a bit of a monkey both in the stalls and in the race, and was easily picked off in the straight. (50/1)

2352 EVENING NEWS H'CAP (0-80) (3-Y.O+) (Class D)

7-55 (7-57) **1m 6f** £3,517.50 (£1,065.00: £520.00: £247.50) Stalls: High GOING: 0.08 sec per fur (G)

				SP	RR	SF
1996*	**Forgie (IRE) (64)** (PCalver) **4-9-10** KDarley(6) (mde most: kpt on wl u.p fnl 2f)	—	1	2/1 1	74	—
2154 3	**Charity Crusader (39)** (MrsMReveley) **6-7-13** DaleGibson(4) (trckd ldrs: rdn over 4f out: chsd wnr fnl 1½f: no imp)	2	2	3/1 2	47	—
471 6	**Love Me Do (USA) (64)** (MJohnston) **3-8-4**(3) KMChin(1) (disp ld to ½-wy: ev ch tl outpcd fnl 2f)	3½	3	12/1	68	—
2142 3	**Go With The Wind (64)** (JSGoldie) **4-9-10** ACulhane(7) (hld up & bhd: raced stands' side st: sme hdwy 2f out: n.d)	2½	4	5/1 3	65	—
2035 3	**Early Peace (IRE) (49)** (MDods) **5-8-9** JFEgan(5) (lw: trckd ldrs: effrt over 3f out: wknd fnl 2f)	4	5	5/1 3	45	—
2170 7	**Breydon (44)** (PMonteith) **4-7-13**(5) JBramhill(3) (cl up tl rdn & btn wl over 2f out)	10	6	16/1	29	—
2143 6	**Fizzy Boy (IRE) (41)** (PMonteith) **4-7-12**(3) PFessey(2) (hld up: effrt ent st: racd stands' side & sn wl bhd)	28	7	100/1	—	—
				(SP 106.2%)		**7 Rn**

3m 11.1 CSF £6.23 TOTE £2.60: £1.50 £1.50 (£3.50) OWNER Mrs Janis MacPherson (RIPON) BRED Stilvi Compania Financiera And Roncon Ltd.

WEIGHT FOR AGE 3yo-17lb

1996* Forgie (IRE), well-handled, was made plenty of use of and, once stepping up the pace early in the straight, he always had too much courage for the runner-up. (2/1)
2154 Charity Crusader was always well enough placed if good enough, but he was never doing enough when it mattered. He certainly has the ability to win a race, but needs things to go just right. (3/1)
471 Love Me Do (USA) raced with the winner but, when the pressure was on in the straight, there was little more to come. (12/1: op 8/1)
2142 Go With The Wind tried to come from off the pace and gave further ground away by coming over to the stands' side. He was never doing enough to get anywhere near. (5/1)
2035 Early Peace (IRE) was a shade disappointing this time and seems to be having problems in finding a correct trip. (5/1)

2353 LAING & CRUICKSHANK INVESTMENT MANAGEMENT RATING RELATED MAIDEN STKS (0-65) (3-Y.O+) (Class F)

8-25 (8-25) **7f 30y** £2,617.50 (£730.00: £352.50) Stalls: High GOING: 0.08 sec per fur (G)

				SP	RR	SF
2152 2	**Terdad (USA) (62)** (TDBarron) **4-9-6** KDarley(4) (lw: trckd ldrs: led over 2f out: rdn & r.o wl)	—	1	10/11 1	70	37
1967 6	**Ceanothus (IRE) (65)** (WJHaggas) **3-8-8** JFortune(3) (lw: prom: outpcd ½-wy: styd on fnl 2f: no ch w wnr)	5	2	2/1 2	56	14
2125 6	**Millpet (51)** (RGuest) **3-8-8** PBloomfield(5) (s.i.s: hdwy ½-wy: no imp fnl 2f)	4	3	16/1	47	5
2151 3	**Kristopher (58)** (JWHills) **3-8-11** DeanMcKeown(2) (cl up tl rdn & btn 2f out)	6	4	5/1 3	36	—
1733 2	**Serape (45)** (MrsLStubbs) **4-9-3** JFEgan(1) (b: lw: led tl hdd over 2f out: sn btn)	1¼	5	20/1	31	—
				(SP 113.0%)		**5 Rn**

1m 32.3 (6.30) CSF £2.82 TOTE £1.60: £1.10 £3.60 (£2.40) OWNER Burke's 5th Family Settlement (THIRSK) BRED Gainsborough Farm Inc

WEIGHT FOR AGE 3yo-9lb

2152 Terdad (USA), from a yard just striking real form, looked particularly well and, once sent on approaching the final quarter-mile, his rider left nothing to chance. (10/11)
Ceanothus (IRE) took the eye in the paddock and moved well to post, but she was tapped for toe at a vital stage and could never recover. (2/1)
2125 Millpet has ability but does not quite come up with the goods, and finding her ideal distance is proving a problem. (16/1)
2151 Kristopher seems to go well on the bridle but does not do a lot off it. (5/1)
1733 Serape is an in-and-out performer who was not co-operating this time. (20/1)

2354 NFU MUTUAL (S) H'CAP (0-60) (3-Y.O) (Class F)

8-55 (8-56) **5f** £2,722.50 (£760.00: £367.50) Stalls: High GOING: 0.08 sec per fur (G)

				SP	RR	SF
2167 4	**Mystical (51)** (MrsLStubbs) **3-9-0v** ACulhane(10) (lw: hdwy ½-wy: led 1f out: shkn up & r.o strly)	—	1	6/1 3	64	39
1467 13	**Hiltons Executive (IRE) (39)** (EJAlston) **3-8-2**ow3 JFEgan(11) (cl up: led ½-wy tl hdd 1f out: sn outpcd)	5	2	12/1	36	8
1995 2	**College Princess (47)** (SCWilliams) **3-8-10** KDarley(6) (cl up stands' side: nt qckn fnl f)	1¾	3	3/1 1	38	13
	Flo's Choice (IRE) (48) (JO'Reilly) **3-8-11** JO'Reilly(4) (s.i.s: styd on fr ½-wy: nrst fin)	2½	4	33/1	31	6
1604 5	**La Doyenne (IRE) (46)** (CBBBooth) **3-8-9** KHodgson(1) (cl up stands' side: rdn ½-wy: edgd rt & nt qckn)	½	5	7/1	28	3
2017 12	**Tom Pladdey (37)** (RBastiman) **3-8-0b**1 DaleGibson(8) (outpcd & bhd tl sme late hdwy)	½	6	12/1	17	—
1995 7	**Keen To Please (48)** (DenysSmith) **3-8-11** JFortune(9) (lw: cl up tl wknd fnl 2f)	¾	7	9/2 2	26	1
2235 4	**Melbourne Princess (52)** (RMWhitaker) **3-9-1** DeanMcKeown(12) (led to ½-wy: sn wknd)	8	8	6/1 3	4	—
2169 9	**Miss St Kitts (41)** (JSGoldie) **3-7-13**(5) JBramhill(5) (sn outpcd: bhd fr ½-wy)	1¼	9	25/1	—	—
2167 9	**Astral Crown (IRE) (33)** (JBerry) **3-7-10b** LCharnock(7) (b.hind: spd to ½-wy: sn wknd)	nk	10	25/1	—	—
1942 11	**Morning Star (58)** (WMcKeown) **3-9-2**(5) KSked(2) (sn outpcd & bhd)	1	11	25/1	2	—
2235 5	**Toronto (55)** (JBerry) **3-9-1b**(3) PFessey(3) (stumbled & uns rdr s)		U	6/1 3	—	—
				(SP 128.4%)		**12 Rn**

61.5 secs (3.80) CSF £71.71 CT £246.68 TOTE £5.30: £1.80 £2.90 £1.70 (£24.70) Trio £98.50 OWNER Consultco Ltd (WARTHILL) BRED Stud-On-The-Chart

Bt in 4,100gns

2167 Mystical really showed what she can do and, coming from off the pace, won in tremendous style and is obviously in top form. (6/1)
Hiltons Executive (IRE) showed plenty of toe but was completely outclassed by the winner in the closing stages. (12/1)
1995 College Princess had her chances but her limitations were well exposed when the pressure was on. (3/1)
Flo's Choice (IRE) did not have the best of starts but showed a glimmer of ability, staying on at the end. (33/1)
1604 La Doyenne (IRE) went strongly to post but, on the way back, all she wanted to do was hang right. (7/1)
Tom Pladdey had blinkers on for the first time and they did not have the desired effect, although he was struggling on when it was all over. (12/1: 8/1-14/1)

2355 XEROX BUSINESS SERVICES H'CAP (0-70) (3-Y.O+) (Class E)

9-25 (9-25) **1m 16y** £2,802.50 (£845.00: £410.00: £192.50) Stalls: High GOING: 0.08 sec per fur (G)

				SP	RR	SF
1830 5	**Sandblaster (39)** (JLEyre) **4-7-11** DWright(1) (chsd ldr: rdn to ld 1½f out: r.o)	—	1	9/2 3	52	34
1994*	**Best of All (IRE) (73)** (JBerry) **5-10-3b** KDarley(6) (lw: a chsng ldrs: rdn & ev ch ins fnl f: nt qckn)	2½	2	5/2 2	81	63
1993*	**Broctune Gold (65)** (MrsMReveley) **6-9-9** ACulhane(2) (lw: led tl hdd 1½f out: no ex u.p)	½	3	2/1 1	72	54

				SP	RR	SF
2144[8]	**Miss Pigalle (38)** (MissLAPerratt) **6-7-10** NKennedy(5) (lw: prom: outpcd 3f out: kpt on appr fnl f: no imp)	2½	**4**	11/1	40	22
2221[3]	**Diet (38)** (MissLAPerratt) **11-7-7v**(3) PFessey(4) (lw: bhd: effrt ½-wy: n.d)	6	**5**	33/1	28	10
1583[4]	**Chinour (IRE) (51)** (EJAlston) **9-8-9** JFEgan(3) (chsd ldrs tl wknd fnl 2½f)	1¾	**6**	9/2 [3]	38	20

(SP 109.5%) **6 Rn**

1m 44.4 (5.40) CSF £13.94 TOTE £5.20: £2.00 £1.90 (£8.20) OWNER Mr Graham Wood (HAMBLETON) BRED B. Burrough
LONG HANDICAP Miss Pigalle 7-8 Diet 7-5

1830 Sandblaster won her first race and did it well, suggesting that, at last, the penny has dropped. (9/2)
1994* Best of All (IRE), off her highest mark to date, ran well but just found one too strong. (5/2)
1993* Broctune Gold did his usual and blazed off in front, but he could never shake the opposition off and was out-battled in the last furlong-and-a-half. (2/1)
1285* Miss Pigalle ran reasonably but without looking likely to really get into it, and obviously has more ability if she can be persuaded. (11/1)
2221 Diet did not try to lay up with the pace this time, probably because of the extended trip, and these tactics certainly did not work. (33/1)
1583 Chinour (IRE) runs when in the mood, and he probably saw too much daylight too soon on this occasion. (9/2)

T/Plpt: £32.00 (428.64 Tckts). T/Qdpt: £5.00 (163.54 Tckts) AA

1997-PONTEFRACT (L-H) (Soft, Heavy patches)
Monday June 30th

WEATHER: raining WIND: moderate half behind

2356 RACING CHANNEL MAIDEN AUCTION STKS (I) (2-Y.O) (Class D)

2-45 (2-47) **5f** £2,721.25 (£820.00: £397.50: £186.25) Stalls: High GOING: 0.51 sec per fur (GS)

				SP	RR	SF
	Suivez La Trace (RAFahey) **2-8-7** JCarroll(4) (w'like: cmpt: lw: chsd ldrs: pshd along ½-wy: led over 1f out: r.o wl)	—	**1**	6/1 [3]	80+	40
1213[5]	**Mysticism** (CEBrittain) **2-7-12** DaleGibson(2) (w ldr: led over 2f out tl over 1f out: nt qckn)	2½	**2**	5/1 [2]	63	23
2227[2]	**Perfect Harmony (IRE)** (BJMeehan) **2-7-11**(3) MartinDwyer(1) (chsd ldrs: rdn along ½-wy: wandered over 1f out: kpt on same pce)	3	**3**	7/4 [1]	55	15
2127[2]	**Dangerman (IRE)** (MWEasterby) **2-8-5** TLucas(3) (lw: drvn along & outpcd ½-wy: hdwy over 1f out: kpt on towards fin)	1½	**4**	13/2	56	16
	Dancing Rio (IRE) (PCHaslam) **2-8-3** LCharnock(5) (cmpt: bit bkwd: sn outpcd: swvd rt over 1f out: kpt on)	1	**5**	12/1	50	10
	Perfect Peach (JBerry) **2-7-13**(3) PFessey(9) (w'like: leggy: bit bkwd: led tl over 2f out: wknd over 1f out)	½	**6**	7/1	48+	8
1760[20]	**Eddie Rombo** (NTinkler) **2-8-5** KDarley(6) (sn outpcd)	½	**7**	25/1	49	9
1774[4]	**Shamwari Song** (JAGlover) **2-8-3** NDay(8) (sn outpcd)	½	**8**	11/1	46	6
2140[4]	**Barrelbio (IRE)** (JJO'Neill) **2-8-4**ow1 ACulhane(7) (hld up & a bhd)	½	**9**	8/1	45	4

(SP 124.1%) **9 Rn**

67.4 secs (5.70) CSF £35.46 TOTE £7.90: £1.90 £2.30 £1.10 (£24.20) Trio £23.10 OWNER Clayton Bigley Partnership Ltd (MALTON) BRED J. S. A. and Mrs Shorthouse

Suivez La Trace, a likeable colt who is not very big but well put together, looked well in the paddock and certainly knew his job. (6/1: 10/1-11/2)
1213 Mysticism, who is not very big, showed plenty of toe but, in the end, found the winner much too good. (5/1)
2227 Perfect Harmony (IRE), making a quick reappearance, did not seem to appreciate racing away from the inside rail. Because of the ground, the stalls were placed on the outside and the horses raced towards the stands' side rail. Under pressure, she seemed to lose her way. (7/4: 5/4-15/8)
2127 Dangerman (IRE), keen going to post, gave a problem or two in the stalls. After being outpaced, he was staying on at the finish and looks a likely type for a nursery over six or seven furlongs. (13/2)
Dancing Rio (IRE), who has a pronounced round action, looked on the backward side and swerved violently right coming to the final furlong. (12/1: op 8/1)
Perfect Peach, a decent sort, looked in need of the outing. She showed bags of toe but tired coming to the final furlong. The outing should bring her on a good deal. (7/1)

2357 SMEATON (S) H'CAP (0-60) (3-Y.O) (Class G)

3-15 (3-17) **1m 4f 8y** £2,574.00 (£714.00: £342.00) Stalls: Low GOING: 0.51 sec per fur (GS)

				SP	RR	SF
862[13]	**Captain Flint (40)** (ASmith) **3-7-12**(7) RWinston(3) (sn trckng ldrs: led 3f out: drvn clr fnl f)	—	**1**	20/1	56	6
1798[7]	**Digital Option (IRE) (42)** (MrsJRRamsden) **3-8-7** JFortune(6) (hld up: hdwy on wd outside over 2f out: kpt on fnl f: no ch w wnr)	15	**2**	11/2 [2]	38	—
2207[5]	**Ocean Breeze (40)** (JSWainwright) **3-8-0b[1]**(5) JBramhill(4) (bhd & pushed along: reminders after 2f: hdwy ½-wy: chal over 2f out: one pce)	1½	**3**	4/1 [1]	34	—
1502[3]	**Fortune Hopper (56)** (JPearce) **3-9-7** GBardwell(2) (sn pushed along: hdwy to chse ldrs over 3f out: wknd over 1f out)	16	**4**	4/1 [1]	29	—
2200[7]	**Real Fire (IRE) (45)** (MGMeagher) **3-8-10** JFEgan(8) (hdwy 8f out: chsd ldrs tl wknd over 2f out)	s.h	**5**	9/1	18	—
1449[10]	**Fearless Sioux (45)** (CWThornton) **3-8-10** DeanMcKeown(1) (chsd ldrs tl lost pl over 2f out)	8	**6**	6/1 [3]	7	—
2068[9]	**Bella Daniella (31)** (TTClement) **3-7-7**(3) PFessey(10) (trckd ldrs tl wknd 3f out)	9	**7**	33/1	—	—
2171[6]	**Misterton (39)** (JAGlover) **3-8-4b** GCarter(7) (led to 3f out: sn wknd)	1¼	**8**	4/1 [1]	—	—
1229[14]	**Ballydinero (IRE) (46)** (CaptJWilson) **3-8-11** ACulhane(9) (hdwy ½-wy: wknd qckly 5f out: sn virtually p.u)	dist	**9**	12/1	—	—
2039[17]	**Wheildon (46)** (SCWilliams) **3-8-11b[1]** KDarley(5) (chsd ldrs: drvn along ½-wy: wknd over 4f out: sn t.o)	5	**10**	13/2	—	—

(SP 128.4%) **10 Rn**

2m 53.6 (19.30) CSF £126.27 CT £502.98 TOTE £27.60: £7.50 £2.20 £1.10 (£106.10) Trio £67.80 OWNER Mrs G. Wood (BEVERLEY) BRED F. Haydon
LONG HANDICAP Bella Daniella 7-9
No bid

IN-FOCUS: **After heavy morning rain, the stalls over five and six furlongs were placed on the outside. The majority of the runners stayed wide and ended up on the stands' side rail where the best ground seemed to be.**
Captain Flint certainly came into his own in these testing conditions, and his young rider left nothing to chance, driving him right out. (20/1)
Digital Option (IRE) has slipped down the ratings and, stepping-up in distance, made his effort on the wide outside in search of the better ground but, in the final furlong, the winner ran right away from him. (11/2: 7/2-6/1)
2207 Ocean Breeze, a proven stayer fitted with blinkers for the first time, came in for plenty of market support. Soon under pressure after having every chance and sticking to the far side in the straight, he proved woefully one-paced. (4/1: op 7/1)

1502 Fortune Hopper was soon being rousted along. (4/1: 3/1-9/2)
Real Fire (IRE) seemed to run out of stamina over this trip and on this ground. (9/1)
609 Fearless Sioux was getting nowhere on the turn for home. (6/1: op 4/1)
1464 Wheildon (13/2: 4/1-7/1)

2358 DELACY H'CAP (0-90) (3-Y.O+ F & M) (Class C)

3-45 (3-48) **6f** £6,004.00 (£1,792.00: £856.00: £388.00) Stalls: High GOING: 0.51 sec per fur (GS)

				SP	RR	SF
1501[15]	**Watch The Fire (60)** (JEBanks) **4-7-12**(5) RMullen(3) (s.s: hdwy over 2f out: qcknd to ld 1f out: edgd lft: hld on wl)	—	**1**	16/1	66	48
1799[6]	**Fame Again (64)** (MrsJRRamsden) **5-8-7** JFortune(1) (trckd ldrs going wl: chal 1f out: edgd lft & nt qckn nr fin)	½	**2**	4/6[1]	69	51
968[12]	**Lady Diesis (USA) (88)** (BWHills) **3-9-7**(3) JDSmith(4) (trckd ldrs: led 2f out to 1f out: sn wknd)	5	**3**	7/1[3]	79	54
2061[14]	**Formidable Liz (53)** (MDHammond) **7-7-10** DaleGibson(5) (led: drvn along ½-wy: hdd 2f out: wknd fnl f)	4	**4**	9/1	34	16
1967[4]	**Husun (USA) (74)** (PTWalwyn) **3-8-10** RHills(2) (trckd ldrs: effrt over 2f out: sn wknd & eased)	10	**5**	4/1[2]	28	3
				(SP 108.4%)		**5 Rn**

1m 21.0 (6.00) CSF £24.76 TOTE £10.60: £3.30 £1.10 (£10.30) OWNER Mr E. Carter (NEWMARKET) BRED Red House Stud
LONG HANDICAP Formidable Liz 7-7
WEIGHT FOR AGE 3yo-7lb
Watch The Fire gave a problem or two at the stalls and came out awkwardly, forfeiting three lengths. Given time to find her stride, she came through on the bridle to show ahead a furlong out but, edging left and with her young rider using his whip in his right hand, she contributed to the favourite going across the course. (16/1)
1799 Fame Again, 10lb higher in the weights compared with when she won first time this year at Nottingham three outings earlier, has shown she likes this ground. She came there like the winner, on the bridle, but, pushed slightly left and, more importantly, tending to edge left by herself, she did not find as much as seemed likely and was held near the line. (4/6)
Lady Diesis (USA) seemed to appreciate the ground, but was left for dead by the first two in the final furlong. (7/1)
Formidable Liz, 3lb out of the weights, made the running but tired in this ground in the final furlong. (9/1)
1967 Husun (USA) did not seem to relish the testing conditions and was allowed to come home in her own time. (4/1)

2359 SPINDRIFTER CONDITIONS STKS (2-Y.O) (Class C)

4-15 (4-15) **6f** £4,410.69 (£1,651.30: £808.15: £348.25: £156.63: £79.98) Stalls: High GOING: 0.51 sec per fur (GS)

				SP	RR	SF
2176[3]	**The Rich Man (IRE)** (BWHills) **2-8-10** MHills(4) (led to 2f out: hrd rdn & rallied to ld last 50y)	—	**1**	11/4[2]	75	46
2060[2]	**Cumbrian Caruso** (TDEasterby) **2-9-2** JCarroll(5) (lw: unruly in stalls: trckd ldr: smooth hdwy to ld 2f out: hdd wl ins fnl f: no ex)	½	**2**	9/2	80	51
	Legend of Love (JAGlover) **2-8-7** NDay(6) (w'like: trckd ldrs: r.o fnl f: will improve)	3	**3**	16/1	63+	34
2012[15]	**Out Like Magic** (PDEvans) **2-8-11** JFEgan(2) (trckd ldrs: effrt over 2f out: outpcd appr fnl f)	1½	**4**	7/2[3]	63	34
1961*	**Sweet Reward** (JGSmyth-Osbourne) **2-9-2** DHarrison(1) (hld up: effrt over 2f out: sn rdn & hung lft: nvr able to chal)	nk	**5**	9/4[1]	67	38
	Western Lord (CSmith) **2-8-7** JTate(3) (leggy: bit bkwd: s.i.s: a outpcd & bhd: eased over 1f out)	28	**6**	25/1	—	—
				(SP 107.6%)		**6 Rn**

1m 21.7 (6.70) CSF £12.70 TOTE £2.80: £1.80 £2.20 (£9.20) OWNER Marston Stud (LAMBOURN) BRED Lady Richard Wellesley and Grange Nominees
2176 The Rich Man (IRE) responded to severe pressure to get back up near the line. He seems to be improving with his races and he will be suited by a step-up to seven. (11/4: op 7/4)
2060 Cumbrian Caruso became upset in the stalls. Travelling smoothly, he took the advantage off the bend and went a length up but, possibly floundering in the ground, was worn down near the line. (9/2)
Legend of Love has plenty of substance. Tracking the leaders travelling smoothly, he ran on in promising fashion under a considerate ride. There looks to be plenty of improvement in him. (16/1)
1391 Out Like Magic is fully exposed and is going backwards, if anything. (7/2)
1961* Sweet Reward, who looked very fit indeed, would not settle and, when asked to join issue, hung left. He probably wants a truly-run seven. (9/4)

2360 WRAGBY MAIDEN STKS (3 Y.O) (Class D)

4-45 (4-48) **1m 2f 6y** £3,696.25 (£1,120.00: £547.50: £261.25) Stalls: Low GOING: 0.51 sec per fur (GS)

				SP	RR	SF
2008[2]	**Silence Reigns** (MRStoute) **3-9-0** KDarley(2) (trckd ldrs gng wl: led on bit over 1f out: v.easily)	—	**1**	8/13[1]	79++	11
2008[7]	**Top** (JRFanshawe) **3-8-9** DHarrison(3) (led after 2f tl over 1f out: no ch w wnr)	1¾	**2**	9/1[3]	71	3
	Understudy (RHollinshead) **3-8-9** FLynch(1) (swtg: hld up: jnd ldrs 5f out: rdn over 2f out: styd on same pce)	1¼	**3**	12/1	31 t	1
	Passionelle (BWHills) **3-8-9** MHills(7) (led after 1f: hdd 8f out: drvn along & outpcd 3f out: kpt on appr fnl f)	5	**4**	5/1[2]	23 t	—
	Glittering (USA) (CEBrittain) **3-9-0** WJO'Connor(4) (w'like: str: led 1f: trckd ldrs: drvn along & outpcd 3f out: sn wknd)	¾	**5**	10/1	27 t	—
	The Orraman (IRE) (JJO'Neill) **3-9-0** JFortune(5) (in tch: drvn along over 3f out: sn lost pl)	11	**6**	40/1	10 t	—
	Who Dealt (RHollinshead) **3-8-6**(3) DGriffiths(6) (rangy: unf: bit bkwd: stdd s: hld up & plld hrd: bhd fnl 4f: t.o)	dist	**7**	40/1	—	—
				(SP 110.2%)		**7 Rn**

2m 26.3 (16.70) CSF £5.87 TOTE £1.80: £1.10 £2.10 (£4.20) OWNER Cheveley Park Stud (NEWMARKET) BRED Cheveley Park Stud Ltd
2008 Silence Reigns, who showed a markedly round action going down, was never out of third gear. It will be interesting to see what mark the Handicapper gives him with one more outing. (8/13)
Top, loaded into the stalls with the help of a Monty Roberts type blanket, went on after two furlongs but the pace she set was not strong. Continually swishing her tail, the winner was simply toying with her. (9/1)
Understudy, who ran in the provinces in France at two, showed plenty of knee action going down. Moving up onto the heels of the first two turning in, she was soon flat-out and only able to keep on at the one pace. (12/1)
Passionelle, a narrow type, was quite keen going to post but in the race she ran green. Sticking on again coming to the final furlong, she should have some improvement in her, especially with a stiffer test. (5/1: op 3/1)
Glittering (USA) was green and colty in the paddock. (10/1: 8/1-12/1)

2361 RACING CHANNEL MAIDEN AUCTION STKS (II) (2-Y.O) (Class D)
5-15 (5-17) **5f** £2,705.00 (£815.00: £395.00: £185.00) Stalls: High GOING: 0.51 sec per fur (GS)

				SP	RR	SF
1492[8]	**Marton Moss (SWE)** (TDEasterby) **2-8-7** KDarley(7) (trckd ldrs gng wl: led on bit 1f out: drvn out)	—	1	6/1[3]	75+	39
2202[7]	**Two Williams** (MWEasterby) **2-8-7** TLucas(8) (trckd ldrs: stdy hdwy over 1f out: fin wl: nvr plcd to chal)	2½	2	16/1	67+	31
1669[4]	**Rich Choice** (JDBethell) **2-8-0** TWilliams(4) (led to 1f out: wknd towards fin)	1	3	7/2[1]	57	21
1510[7]	**Whacker-Do (IRE)** (RHollinshead) **2-8-3** JCarroll(1) (chsd ldrs: rdn over 2f out: nt qckn appr fnl f)	nk	4	13/2	59	23
1492[5]	**Tom Dougal** (CSmith) **2-8-3** JTate(6) (hdwy over 2f out: kpt on one pce over 1f out)	hd	5	6/1[3]	59	23
	Naviasky (IRE) (MrsJRRamsden) **2-8-5** JFortune(9) (w'like: str: s.i.s: hdwy 2f out: styd on fnl f)	½	6	13/2	59+	23
	Wilton (JHetherton) **2-8-5** DHarrison(5) (cmpt: unf: drvn along & outpcd ½-wy)	4	7	10/1	46	10
1447[7]	**King of Dance** (BSRothwell) **2-8-7** WJO'Connor(3) (chsd ldrs: rdn over 2f out: hung lft & wknd over 1f out)	1¼	8	5/1[2]	44	8
	Full Moon (PDEvans) **2-8-3** JFEgan(2) (cmpt: unf: sn outpcd & bhd)	2½	9	16/1	32	—

(SP 115.0%) **9 Rn**

67.5 secs (5.80) CSF £86.23 TOTE £8.70: £3.60 £2.20 £1.90 (£32.20) Trio £207.40 OWNER Mr T. H. Bennett (MALTON) BRED Mrs M. Campbell Andenaes

1492 Marton Moss (SWE) still looks far from the finished article but certainly has an engine. He has a round action and was well suited by the rain-soaked ground but, after taking it up on the bridle, he had to be pushed right out. (6/1)
Two Williams certainly caught the eye. After doing just enough to finish second, he will be a very interesting proposition in a nursery over six or seven furlongs with one more outing under his belt. (16/1)
1669 Rich Choice was very keen indeed going to post. Doing too much in the race, she faded towards the finish. (7/2: op 2/1)
Whacker-Do (IRE), hard at work someway out, stuck to his guns and will be suited by six. (13/2)
1492 Tom Dougal seems to be improving a little bit with each outing. (6/1)
Naviasky (IRE), who carried plenty of condition, ran a pleasing first race and can do better, especially over further. (13/2: 4/1-7/1)

2362 PONTEFRACT SERIES (ROUND 3) APPRENTICE H'CAP (0-70) (3-Y.O+) (Class F)
5-45 (5-45) **1m 2f 6y** £2,364.50 (£672.00: £333.50) Stalls: Low GOING: 0.51 sec per fur (GS)

				SP	RR	SF
898[3]	**Cashmirie (32)** (JLEyre) **5-7-10** PDoe(3) (racd wd: chsd ldrs: led over 4f out: hung lft & clr 2f out: drvn out)	—	1	5/1[3]	42	4
2154[9]	**Junior Ben (IRE) (32)** (MESowersby) **5-7-5**(5) NPollard(2) (hld up: hdwy over 3f out: styd on sme pce appr fnl f: no imp)	3½	2	6/1	36	—
2158[2]	**Marsh Marigold (67)** (JHetherton) **3-9-0**(5) JennyBenson(5) (racd wd: hld up: hdwy over 3f out: rdn & kpt on same pce appr fnl f)	2	3	7/4[1]	68	18
2041[2]	**Bedazzle (38)** (MBrittain) **6-7-13**(3) DMernagh(6) (lw: trckd ldrs: rdn over 2f out: one pce)	2	4	4/1[2]	36	—
2226[4]	**Silent System (IRE) (32)** (DWChapman) **4-7-10** RWinston(4) (trckd ldrs: drvn along over 3f out: wknd over 2f out)	16	5	5/1[3]	5	—
	First Bite (IRE) (60) (MDHammond) **5-9-10** NHorrocks(1) (led tl over 4f out: wknd over 2f out)	8	6	14/1	20	—

(SP 110.6%) **6 Rn**

2m 24.9 (15.30) CSF £29.70 TOTE £6.50: £2.30 £2.00 (£21.20) OWNER Mr Ernest Spencer (HAMBLETON) BRED G. E. Peace
LONG HANDICAP Junior Ben (IRE) 7-7 Cashmirie 7-8 Silent System (IRE) 6-12
WEIGHT FOR AGE 3yo-12lb

898 Cashmirie, one of two to race wide, was clear when she hung badly left turning in and ended up on the far rail. Keeping up the gallop, she was never in any danger. (5/1)
1393 Junior Ben (IRE), dropped back in distance and held up, made his effort rounding the home turn but was never doing enough to get in a blow at the winner. (6/1)
2158 Marsh Marigold, like the winner, raced wide down the side straight. Up another 2lb in the weights compared with Redcar, she looks well in the grip of the Handicapper now. (7/4)
2041 Bedazzle has only won once from forty-five starts and it is not hard to see why. (4/1)
2226 Silent System (IRE) pulled hard early and then did anything but keep a straight line in the home straight. He is proving disappointing and is probably temperamental. (5/1)

T/Plpt: £38.20 (420.95 Tckts). T/Qdpt: £7.00 (109.58 Tckts) WG

2066-SOUTHWELL (L-H) (Standard)
Monday June 30th
WEATHER: raining WIND: mod bhd

2363 E.B.F. PUTNEY MAIDEN STKS (2-Y.O) (Class D)
2-30 (2-30) **7f (Fibresand)** £3,468.25 (£1,036.00: £495.50: £225.25) Stalls: High GOING minus 0.48 sec per fur (FST)

				SP	RR	SF
1267[2]	**Prose (IRE)** (RHannon) **2-9-0** DaneO'Neill(3) (a.p: led over 2f out: clr appr fnl f)	—	1	4/1[2]	82	21
2176[4]	**Rico Suave (IRE)** (SirMarkPrescott) **2-9-0** GDuffield(4) (lw: trckd ldrs: pshd along ½-wy: rdn 2f out: nt pce of wnr)	7	2	8/11[1]	66	5
1684[7]	**Falkenberg (FR)** (MJohnston) **2-9-0** JWeaver(1) (lw: led tl over 2f out: rdn & one pce appr fnl f)	1½	3	12/1	63	2
1933[9]	**Night Vigil (IRE)** (BWHills) **2-9-0** MHills(6) (lw: hld up: effrt 3f out: rdn & swtchd lft over 1f out: no imp)	3½	4	8/1	55	—
1760[4]	**Mohawk (IRE)** (JLDunlop) **2-9-0** TSprake(2) (lw: prom: hrd rdn over 2f out: sn btn)	5	5	6/1[3]	43	—
1854[2]	**Jus'chillin' (IRE)** (CADwyer) **2-8-9** NVarley(5) (b: sn pushed along: hung rt: a in rr)	5	6	10/1	27	—
1933[14]	**Meadgate's Dreamer (IRE)** (BPalling) **2-8-9** SDrowne(7) (a bhd: t.o fnl 2f)	5	7	50/1	15	—

(SP 122.0%) **7 Rn**

1m 29.9 (3.40) CSF £7.24 TOTE £5.10: £1.50 £1.10 (£2.90) OWNER Highclere Thoroughbred Racing Ltd (MARLBOROUGH) BRED P. J. B. O'Callaghan

1267 Prose (IRE), well suited by this step-up in trip, made his first appearance on the sand a winning one with a very smoothly-gained success, and there is no reason why he should not continue to progress. (4/1)
2176 Rico Suave (IRE) could have found this race coming far too soon after his promising debut a week ago and, off the bridle at halfway, was never going to trouble the winner. (8/11: evens-11/10)
1228 Falkenberg (FR), taking a big step-up in distance, attempted to do it from the front but, once the winner had taken his measure, he could do little more than stay on at the one pace. (12/1: op 8/1)

Night Vigil (IRE), a well-grown colt who carries plenty of condition, was unable to make his presence felt, but he is now getting to know what is needed and he can soon make his mark. (8/1: tchd 12/1)
1760 Mohawk (IRE) (6/1: op 4/1)

2364 HAMPSTEAD APPRENTICE CLAIMING STKS (3-Y.O) (Class G)
3-00 (3-00) **1m 3f (Fibresand)** £1,984.50 (£547.00: £259.50) Stalls: High GOING minus 0.48 sec per fur (FST)

				SP	RR	SF
1513^{7}	**Mirror Four Sport (60)** (MJohnston) **3-7-5**$^{(7)}$ NPollard(4) (set str pce: mde all: clr 3f out: unchal)	—	1	$4/7^{1}$	58+	3
1958^{7}	**Mysterium (55)** (NPLittmoden) **3-8-8**$^{(7)}$ KPierrepont(6) (hld up: hdwy to chse wnr over 2f out: no imp)	10	2	$9/2^{2}$	61	6
2171^{14}	**Bali-Pet (55)** (JParkes) **3-8-0**$^{(3)}$ DSweeney(5) (hld up: hdwy 6f out: rdn 3f out: sn btn)	9	3	$6/1^{3}$	35	—
2159^{3}	**Petula Boy (33)** (SRBowring) **3-8-4**$^{(7)}$ FBoyle(3) (dropped rr ½-wy: effrt over 2f out: nt rch ldrs)	1½	4	8/1	41	—
1858^{F}	**Love Over Gold (20)** (MCChapman) **3-7-12**$^{(3)ow3}$ AmandaSanders(2) (lw: b.nr hind: dwlt: plld hrd: sn prom: rdn & wknd over 4f out: t.o)	30	5	50/1	—	—
2128^{8}	**Kirkham** (MrsVAAconley) **3-8-12**$^{(5)}$ GMilligan(1) (bit bkwd: chsd ldrs: rdn over 3f out: sn wknd: t.o)	5	6	33/1	—	—

(SP 112.1%) **6 Rn**

2m 26.1 (6.10) CSF £3.23 TOTE £2.10: £1.10 £2.10 (£3.10) OWNER Mark Johnston Racing Ltd (MIDDLEHAM) BRED T. Young
Mirror Four Sport clmd J. Clarke £3,000
1229 Mirror Four Sport made sure the emphasis would be on stamina by setting a brisk pace and, forging clear before reaching the straight, came home at her leisure. (4/7)
368 Mysterium came from off the pace to chase up the winner soon after straightening up, but the weight concession proved a big stumbling block and he was unable to pose a threat. (9/2: op 3/1)
1584 Bali-Pet, well suppported in the ring, had moved into a challenging position at the end of the back straight, but he was soon being rowed along and stamina appeared to desert him. (6/1: op 10/1)

2365 WESTMINSTER H'CAP (0-70) (3-Y.O+) (Class E)
3-30 (3-30) **1m 4f (Fibresand)** £2,888.25 (£861.00: £410.50: £185.25) Stalls: High GOING minus 0.48 sec per fur (FST)

				SP	RR	SF
2154^{13}	**Our Main Man (50)** (RMWhitaker) **7-8-4**$^{(5)}$ GParkin(4) (hld up: hdwy 3f out: led over 1f out: comf)	—	1	20/1	63+	18
2048^{3}	**Mister Aspecto (IRE) (69)** (MJohnston) **4-10-0v** JWeaver(2) (lw: led tl over 1f out: sn hrd rdn: one pce)	3½	2	$9/2^{2}$	77	32
*2068**	**Big Bang (64)** (MBlanshard) **3-8-9** JQuinn(1) (trckd ldrs: effrt & rdn over 2f out: styd on same pce)	¾	3	$5/1^{3}$	71	12
1683^{6}	**Kilnamartyra Girl (46)** (JParkes) **7-8-0**$^{(5)}$ DSweeney(9) (hld up in rr: hdwy 4f out: nt rch ldrs)	5	4	6/1	47	2
1409^{9}	**Wontcostalotbut (55)** (MJWilkinson) **3-8-0** NAdams(7) (chsd ldrs: hrd drvn 3f out: sn wknd)	7	5	16/1	46	—
753^{4}	**English Invader (58)** (CADwyer) **6-9-3** NVarley(3) (lw: s.i.s: a bhd)	3½	6	11/2	45	—
2164^{5}	**Sommersby (IRE) (48)** (MrsNMacauley) **6-8-7** SSanders(5) (b: bit bkwd: chsd ldr tl rdn & wknd 2f out)	hd	7	14/1	35	—
1287^{5}	**Shuttlecock (38)** (DWChapman) **6-7-11** DWright(8) (chsd ldrs over 7f: sn wknd: t.o)	8	8	12/1	14	—
*2049**	**Goodwood Lass (IRE) (75)** (JLDunlop) **3-9-6** GDuffield(6) (prom: rdn & lost pl 5f out: t.o)	9	9	$3/1^{1}$	39	—

(SP 114.5%) **9 Rn**

2m 38.9 (5.90) CSF £97.22 CT £482.36 TOTE £25.60: £4.70 £2.00 £2.70 (£67.40) Trio £105.80 OWNER Mr Christopher Cooke (LEEDS) BRED Pinfold Stud and Farms Ltd
WEIGHT FOR AGE 3yo-14lb
OFFICIAL EXPLANATION **Goodwood Lass (IRE): resented the kickback.**
Our Main Man, given a very confident ride, cruised through to take command below the distance and won with any amount in hand. A strong individual who still looked as though the run would improve him, he failed to win a race last season but if this is anything to go by he could be in for a rewarding time this term. (20/1)
2048 Mister Aspecto (IRE), prepared to force the pace even with top weight, comfortably had the measure of the remainder of his rivals until the winner appeared on the scene and spoiled the party. (9/2)
2068* Big Bang had to admit older rivals too strong for him in the latter stages but he gave his best shot and was not disgraced in this company. (5/1)
1390 Kilnamartyra Girl ran no race at all and though she has won on this surface she probably prefers the Turf. (6/1)
2049* Goodwood Lass (IRE) (3/1: op 6/4)

2366 EAST MIDLANDS ELECTRICITY (NOTTINGHAM) HEATWISE H'CAP (0-60) (3-Y.O+) (Class F)
4-00 (4-02) **6f (Fibresand)** £2,277.00 (£627.00: £297.00) Stalls: High GOING minus 0.48 sec per fur (FST)

				SP	RR	SF
1759^{5}	**Time To Fly (42)** (BWMurray) **4-8-5b**$^{(5)}$ DSweeney(1) (led after 1f: clr ½-wy: hrd rdn fnl f: hld on wl)	—	1	7/1	52	39
1786^{7}	**Thordis (55)** (PJMakin) **4-9-9** SSanders(3) (a.p: str chal u.p fnl f: r.o)	½	2	$11/2^{2}$	64	51
2061^{10}	**Tutu Sixtysix (28)** (DonEnricoIncisa) **6-7-10** KimTinkler(6) (bhd & outpcd: rdn 2f out: kpt on appr fnl f)	6	3	25/1	21	8
2050^{4}	**Silk Cottage (52)** (RMWhitaker) **5-9-3**$^{(3)}$ OPears(9) (lw: hld up: effrt over 2f out: sn rdn: nt rch ldrs)	½	4	$13/2^{3}$	43	30
1620^{12}	**Ticka Ticka Timing (33)** (BWMurray) **4-8-1** MDeering(8) (lw: led 1f: hrd rdn over 1f out: one pce)	¾	5	33/1	22	9
2109^{3}	**Shontaine (58)** (MJohnston) **4-9-12** JWeaver(2) (bhd: hdwy over 2f out: eased whn btn over 1f out)	1¼	6	$7/2^{1}$	44	31
1650^{6}	**Komaseph (54)** (RFMarvin) **5-9-8** TGMcLaughlin(10) (lw: nvr nr to chal)	¾	7	$11/2^{2}$	38	25
2305^{3}	**Qualitair Silver (47)** (JFBottomley) **3-8-8** NCarlisle(5) (dwlt: a bhd)	5	8	8/1	18	—
1942^{7}	**Perfect Brave (58)** (JBalding) **6-9-12** JEdmunds(7) (trckd ldrs: rdn along over 2f out: sn btn & eased)	3½	9	10/1	19	6
1925^{8}	**Soda (53)** (JLSpearing) **3-9-0b** SDrowne(4) (lw: sn drvn along: a in rr)	2½	10	7/1	8	—

(SP 118.3%) **10 Rn**

1m 14.7 (1.20) CSF £41.88 CT £853.67 TOTE £7.60: £2.70 £1.90 £3.40 (£11.70) Trio £123.80 OWNER Mr B. Murray (MALTON) BRED Miss N. A. Harrod
WEIGHT FOR AGE 3yo-7lb
1759 Time To Fly had gained a healthy lead at halfway and always looked to be in control but he was trying this trip for the first time and in the end the post arrived not a stride too soon. (7/1: op 9/2)
Thordis, without the visor and returning to sprinting, delivered a determined last-furlong challenge but the winner, in receipt of 17lb, had pinched too much start and he was never going to get there. A return to a more suitable seven furlongs could see him back to winning ways. (11/2)
332 Tutu Sixtysix, four times successful at the minimum trip several years ago, stuck on doggedly in the latter stages and it is possible she still has the ability to pick up another small race. (25/1)
2050 Silk Cottage, struggling to hold his pitch on the home turn, did stay on inside the distance but the leading pair had got away and he lacked the speed to make much impact. (13/2)
Ticka Ticka Timing, winner of a seller over course and distance two years ago but lightly raced since, showed something of a return to form and if lowered in class she could be worth supporting. (33/1)

2109 Shontaine, much better over longer trips nowadays, tried to get himself into the action soon after entering the straight but he lacked the speed to do so and the position was accepted. (7/2)
1650 Komaseph (11/2: 7/1-9/2)

2367 DOCKLANDS (S) STKS (2-Y.O F) (Class G)

4-30 (4-33) **5f (Fibresand)** £1,984.50 (£547.00: £259.50) Stalls: High GOING minus 0.48 sec per fur (FST)

				SP	RR	SF
	Chinaider (IRE) (JJO'Neill) **2-8-8** JQuinn(7) (w'like: scope: bit bkwd: bhd: hdwy over 2f out: led ins fnl f: edgd lft: comf)	—	**1**	10/1	65+	10
1758[4]	**Daynabee** (NTinkler) **2-8-8** KimTinkler(4) (a.p: drvn along wl over 1f out: unable qckn fnl f)	1¾	**2**	8/1	59	4
2051[3]	**I'm Not Sure** (JBerry) **2-8-8** NAdams(1) (a.p: led ½-wy tl hdd & no ex ins fnl f)	1¾	**3**	7/1[3]	54	—
	Touchanova (AHide) **2-8-3**(5) GMilligan(2) (lt-f: bkwd: s.s: outpcd & bhd: hdwy wl over 1f out: r.o)	½	**4**	8/1	52	—
1758[3]	**Gymcrak Mystery** (GHolmes) **2-8-8** JStack(6) (led over 2f: rdn wl over 1f out: one pce)	1½	**5**	5/2[1]	47	—
767[2]	**Miss Scooter** (APJones) **2-8-8** SDrowne(8) (chsd ldrs over 2f: sn rdn & outpcd)	8	**6**	5/1[2]	22	—
2233[8]	**Flash d'Or (IRE)** (MWEasterby) **2-8-9**(5) GParkin(5) (sn chsd along: outpcd fr ½-wy: t.o)	6	**7**	10/1	9	—
	Verdant Express (WGMTurner) **2-8-3**(5) DSweeney(9) (leggy: lt-f: bit bkwd: swvd rt s: racd alone: a bhd & outpcd)	3	**8**	5/1[2]	—	—
1290[6]	**Wideyedbushytailed** (MrsNMacauley) **2-8-3**(5) PRoberts(3) (lw: sn drvn along: outpcd fr ½-wy: t.o)	3½	**9**	25/1	—	—

(SP 118.7%) **9 Rn**

59.4 secs (2.40) CSF £81.23 TOTE £9.10: £1.40 £2.30 £2.60 (£55.80) Trio £96.20 OWNER Mr E. A. Brook (PENRITH) BRED James McMullan
No bid

Chinaider (IRE), a scopey newcomer not ideally-bred for speed, made progress down the centre of the track and, despite showing signs of greenness once in front, won going away. (10/1)
1758 Daynabee, stepping back to the minimum trip, turned the tables on the favourite but the winner proved far superior to her in the sprint to the line. (8/1: op 4/1)
2051 I'm Not Sure is not yet lasting home on this surface and it might be worth giving her a chance of the Turf. (7/1: op 4/1)
Touchanova, looking far from fully wound up for this racecourse debut, showed promise after forfeiting ground at the start and in this class she looks a ready-made winner. (8/1: op 14/1)
1758 Gymcrak Mystery got the best of the break but may have done too much too soon for she was in trouble below the distance and her measure had been taken. (5/2: 7/4-11/4)
767 Miss Scooter (5/1: op 5/2)
1253 Flash d'Or (IRE) (10/1: op 25/1)

2368 CHELSEA H'CAP (0-60) (3-Y.O+) (Class F)

5-00 (5-01) **1m (Fibresand)** £2,277.00 (£627.00: £297.00) Stalls: High GOING minus 0.48 sec per fur (FST)

				SP	RR	SF
2121*	**Monte Cavo (41)** (MBrittain) **6-8-9** GBardwell(11) (hdwy u.p 2f out: r.o to ld fnl 100y)	—	**1**	9/2[1]	54	26
*2160**	**People Direct (46)** (NPLittmoden) **4-9-0** RLappin(8) (lw: led: clr ½-wy: wknd & hdd wl ins fnl f)	1¾	**2**	9/2[1]	56	28
1384[12]	**Saratoga Red (USA) (57)** (WAO'Gorman) **3-9-1b[1]** EmmaO'Gorman(4) (bit bkwd: effrt & rdn 3f out: kpt on ins fnl f)	1½	**3**	7/1[3]	64	26
2177[6]	**Mustang (35)** (CWThornton) **4-8-3b** JQuinn(3) (a.p: hrd rdn 2f out: r.o one pce)	1¼	**4**	6/1[2]	39	11
2039[14]	**Sandmoor Denim (42)** (SRBowring) **10-8-3**(7) FBoyle(9) (in tch: hdwy over 2f out: kpt on u.p)	2½	**5**	10/1	41	13
2004[15]	**Sakharov (54)** (BPalling) **8-9-8** GDuffield(5) (b: bkwd: hld up: effrt on ins ent st: styd on one pce ent fnl f)	hd	**6**	14/1	53	25
2158[5]	**Polarize (53)** (TDBarron) **3-8-11** GHind(16) (chsd ldrs: rdn 2f out: nt pce to chal)	1	**7**	8/1	50	12
2144[11]	**Pleasure Trick (USA) (55)** (DonEnricoIncisa) **6-9-9** KimTinkler(12) (hdwy over 2f out: sn rdn: nt rch ldrs)	3	**8**	10/1	46	18
2317[12]	**Efipetite (33)** (NBycroft) **4-7-12**(3) MBaird(13) (hdwy on outside 3f out: nvr nr to chal)	4	**9**	33/1	16	—
2302[8]	**Noble Canonire (39)** (DShaw) **5-8-7** JFanning(1) (b.hind: a in rr)	4	**10**	25/1	14	—
2069[5]	**Awesome Venture (57)** (MCChapman) **7-9-11** AMcGlone(10) (b.off hind: mid div: hrd drvn 3f out: no imp)	s.h	**11**	12/1	32	4
2070[12]	**Magic Melody (34)** (JLSpearing) **4-8-2b[1]** FNorton(6) (prom over 5f)	2½	**12**	33/1	4	—
1467[21]	**Only Josh (IRE) (57)** (MrsVAAconley) **3-9-1** MDeering(2) (chsd ldrs over 4f: sn lost tch)	½	**13**	25/1	26	—
513[4]	**Loxley's Girl (IRE) (40)** (HAkbary) **3-7-12** NVarley(15) (b: bkwd: chsd ldr to ½-wy: grad wknd: t.o)	8	**14**	16/1	—	—
1603[13]	**Samspet (42)** (RAFahey) **3-8-0** NAdams(7) (prom tl wknd over 3f out: t.o)	¾	**15**	7/1[3]	—	—
1826[15]	**Kanawa (50)** (APJones) **3-8-3**(5) DSweeney(14) (swtg: s.s: a bhd: t.o)	30	**16**	33/1	—	—

(SP 141.7%) **16 Rn**

1m 41.9 (2.90) CSF £23.82 CT £144.90 TOTE £3.20: £1.70 £3.50 £1.90 £2.50 (£7.70) Trio £81.30 OWNER Mr Mel Brittain (WARTHILL) BRED Sheikh Mohammed bin Rashid al Maktoum
WEIGHT FOR AGE 3yo-10lb

2121* Monte Cavo, from a stable in top form, landed the spoils on this return to the sand but his prospects looked bleak turning in and had the long-time leader not weakened it is doubtful if he would have made it. (9/2: op 3/1)
2160* People Direct is not the easiest to peg back when she blazes a trail but she was taking a step up in class this time and was down to a walk inside the last furlong. (9/2)
412 Saratoga Red (USA), a strongly-made colt who will always carry lots of condition, was woken up by the application of blinkers. He does look to be too much of a handful for the girl and it would be interesting to see if one of the top male riders could get to the bottom of him. (7/1: 12/1-20/1)
2177 Mustang, always in the chasing group, was hard at work entering the last quarter-mile and he could not muster the speed to mount a challenge. (6/1)
1463 Sandmoor Denim was beginning to find his stride in the closing stages but, over a trip that could be on the short side now, was never in a position to cause concern. (10/1)
Sakharov, who has never won beyond seven furlongs, still needed this so this running-on performance was probably better than it appears. (14/1)
2158 Polarize, taking on older rivals this time, was never far away but, hard at work early in the straight, could not find the pace to prove a serious threat. He is running well and there is another race to be won. (8/1)

T/Plpt: £65.30 (193.86 Tckts). T/Qdpt: £48.80 (14.68 Tckts) IM

2178-WINDSOR (Fig. 8) (Good to soft, Soft patches)
Monday June 30th
WEATHER: overcast WIND: almost nil

2369 MARK H'CAP (0-70) (3-Y.O+) (Class E)
6-40 (6-41) **1m 67y** £3,160.00 (£955.00: £465.00: £220.00) Stalls: High GOING: 0.36 sec per fur (GS)

				SP	RR	SF
1987^{3}	**Queen's Insignia (USA) (53)** (PFICole) **4-8-12** TQuinn(4) (a.p: led over 1f out: rdn out)	—	**1**	10/1	64	46
2036^{4}	**Ben Gunn (65)** (PTWalwyn) **5-9-10** PatEddery(3) (lw: rdn & hdwy over 2f out: r.o)	1½	**2**	7/1^{2}	73	55
2310^{3}	**Vanborough Lad (41)** (MJBolton) **8-7-11**(3) MHenry(16) (hdwy over 1f out: r.o wl ins fnl f)	nk	**3**	7/1^{2}	49	31
1506^{8}	**Shouldbegrey (40)** (WRMuir) **4-7-13v** DRMcCabe(11) (rdn over 2f out: hdwy over 1f out: r.o)	3½	**4**	16/1	41	23
*2193**	**Bentico (55)** (MrsNMacauley) **8-9-0v** 5x BDoyle(10) (b: a.p: hrd rdn over 2f out: unable qckn)	1¼	**5**	12/1	53	35
1920^{5}	**Finsbury Flyer (IRE) (55)** (RJHodges) **4-8-9**(5) RFfrench(13) (rdn over 3f out: hdwy over 1f out: nvr nrr)	2½	**6**	13/2^{1}	49	31
1670^{7}	**Silver Secret (69)** (MJHeaton-Ellis) **3-9-4** SWhitworth(6) (lw: hdwy 5f out: rdn over 3f out: wknd fnl f)	3	**7**	20/1	57	29
1987*	**Whispered Melody (59)** (RAkehurst) **4-9-4** AClark(7) (a.p: led tl over 3f out to over 1f out: sn wknd)	¾	**8**	13/2^{1}	45	27
	Battleship Bruce (64) (PBowen) **5-9-9** MFenton(18) (led over 6f out to 3f out: sn wknd)	½	**9**	20/1	49	31
1810^{12}	**Chain Reaction (IRE) (60)** (MAJarvis) **3-8-9** JReid(8) (b: led over 1f: hrd rdn 2f out: sn wknd)	1¾	**10**	16/1	42	14
2070^{7}	**Rocky Waters (USA) (41)** (MDIUsher) **8-7-7v**(7)ow4 SCarson(15) (b.hind: hld up: rdn 2f out: wknd over 1f out)	hd	**11**	20/1	23	1
1993^{2}	**Scathebury (57)** (KRBurke) **4-9-2** DHolland(12) (hdwy over 1f out: wknd fnl f)	hd	**12**	8/1^{3}	39	21
1826^{18}	**Sun O'Tirol (IRE) (60)** (JRArnold) **3-8-6**(3) MartinDwyer(14) (prom over 4f)	1¼	**13**	33/1	39	11
1505^{7}	**Tayovullin (IRE) (66)** (HMorrison) **3-9-1** CRutter(1) (b.hind: lw: hdwy over 2f out: wknd over 1f out)	½	**14**	16/1	44	16
2164^{9}	**Urgent Reply (USA) (56)** (CADwyer) **4-8-12**(3) DO'Donohoe(5) (bhd fnl 3f)	¾	**15**	12/1	33	15
	Cabcharge Blue (60) (TJNaughton) **5-8-12**(7) RachaelMoody(2) (a bhd)	1¼	**16**	50/1	34	16
2310^{12}	**Ki Chi Saga (USA) (44)** (MMadgwick) **5-8-3** TSprake(9) (lw: a bhd)	½	**17**	25/1	17	—
1048^{15}	**Square Deal (FR) (52)** (SRBowring) **6-8-11** SWebster(17) (b: 8th whn hmpd on ins 6f out: bhd fnl 4f)	26	**18**	20/1	—	—

(SP 132.7%) **18 Rn**

1m 50.3 (8.10) CSF £69.66 CT £511.60 TOTE £10.40: £2.10 £2.00 £2.20 £3.30 (£42.20) Trio £56.30 OWNER Mr W. H. Ponsonby (WHATCOMBE) BRED Stephen E. Johnson and Mrs Johnson
LONG HANDICAP Rocky Waters (USA) 7-6
WEIGHT FOR AGE 3yo-10lb

1987 Queen's Insignia (USA) moved to the front below the distance and, rousted along, kept on well to gain her first victory since September 1995. (10/1)
2036 Ben Gunn has never won over this trip but he made significant progress over a quarter of a mile from home and kept on well for second prize. (7/1)
2310 Vanborough Lad, making a quick reappearance, put in some good work in the last furlong and a half but was unable to get there in time. (7/1)
1273 Shouldbegrey, bustled along over a quarter of a mile from home, stayed on from below the distance but failed to get to the principals in time. (16/1)
2193* Bentico, in fine form on the All-Weather recently, was never far away but, try as he might, failed to quicken in the final quarter-mile. (12/1)
1920 Finsbury Flyer (IRE) began to pick up ground below the distance but he had a tendency to hang left in the final furlong and failed to get to the principals. Both his wins to date have come in claimers and a drop in class would help. (13/2: 4/1-7/1)
1993 Scathebury (8/1: op 5/1)
1106 Urgent Reply (USA) (12/1: 7/1-14/1)

2370 SLOUGH ESTATES NOVICE AUCTION STKS (2-Y.O) (Class D)
7-10 (7-11) **5f 10y** £3,127.50 (£945.00: £460.00: £217.50) Stalls: High GOING: 0.06 sec per fur (G)

				SP	RR	SF
	Ella (IRE) (LordHuntingdon) **2-7-11**(5) AimeeCook(7) (neat: hld up: chsd ldr 1f out: led wl ins fnl f: r.o wl)	—	**1**	16/1	85+	50
2037*	**Tempus Fugit** (BRMillman) **2-8-5** BDoyle(9) (led: rdn & hung lft 1f out: hdd wl ins fnl f: unable qckn)	1¼	**2**	6/1^{3}	84	49
2103^{3}	**Aurigny** (SDow) **2-8-7** TQuinn(5) (s.s & carried rt s: rdn & hdwy over 1f out: hung lft fnl f: r.o)	1¼	**3**	6/5^{1}	82	47
1084^{3}	**Whisky Mack (IRE)** (RHannon) **2-8-7** DaneO'Neill(8) (lw: rdn over 2f out: hdwy over 1f out: nvr nrr)	3½	**4**	5/1^{2}	71	36
1635^{3}	**Fast Tempo (IRE)** (BPalling) **2-8-7** TSprake(3) (chsd ldr to 1f out: sn wknd)	hd	**5**	8/1	71	36
1842^{9}	**Brimstone (IRE)** (DRCElsworth) **2-8-7** PaulEddery(1) (hld up: rdn over 2f out: sn wknd)	1¼	**6**	14/1	67	32
	Wolfhunt (PJMakin) **2-8-10** SSanders(2) (cmpt: hdwy 2f out: wknd over 1f out)	½	**7**	14/1	68	33
1952^{4}	**Mister Bankes** (WGMTurner) **2-8-3**(7) DMcGaffin(6) (lw: hld up: rdn over 2f out: sn wknd)	1	**8**	10/1	65	30
1970^{6}	**Gipsy Moth** (BJMeehan) **2-7-13**(3) MartinDwyer(4) (swvd rt s: bhd fnl 2f)	3	**9**	20/1	47	12

(SP 120.6%) **9 Rn**

62.2 secs (2.50) CSF £103.05 TOTE £24.10: £3.50 £1.80 £1.20 (£83.70) Trio £29.00 OWNER Coriolan Partnership (WEST ILSLEY) BRED Rocklow Stud

Ella (IRE) did not particularly take the eye in the paddock, being rather sparely-made and dull in her coat, but it proved a different story in the race itself and, moving into second place entering the final furlong, she got on top in the closing stages. (16/1)
2037* Tempus Fugit attempted to make all the running. Drifting over to the rail in the final furlong, she did little wrong but was worried out of it in the closing stages. (6/1)
2103 Aurigny, who has not had a great deal of time to recover from her Royal Ascot exertions, was done no favours at the start. Picking up ground below the distance, she gave Quinn some problems as she continually tried to hang but, nevertheless, kept on to the line, if not looking likely to overhaul the front two. (6/5: evens-11/8)
1084 Whisky Mack (IRE), who has been gelded since his last outing seven and a half weeks ago, was led round by two handlers in the paddock. Racing off the pace, he stayed on from below the distance to be nearest at the line. (5/1)
1635 Fast Tempo (IRE) found the soft ground putting more of an emphasis on stamina and, after racing in second place, had nothing more to offer when collared for that position a furlong out. A return to a fast surface would be in her favour. (8/1: op 9/2)
1842 Brimstone (IRE) (14/1: op 8/1)
Wolfhunt (14/1: 5/1-16/1)
1952 Mister Bankes (10/1: 7/1-11/1)

2371 SUNLEY CONDITIONS STKS (2-Y.O F) (Class C)

7-40 (7-41) **5f 217y** £4,356.40 (£1,627.60: £793.80: £339.00: £149.50: £73.70) Stalls: High GOING: 0.06 sec per fur (G)

				SP	RR	SF
1211[3]	**Hoh Chi Min** (MBell) **2-8-12** JReid(5) (hld up: stumbled over 3f out: rdn 2f out: led last strides)	—	1	9/4[1]	80	32
2103[7]	**Classy Cleo (IRE)** (RHannon) **2-8-12** PatEddery(6) (led over 4f out: hrd rdn fnl f: hdd last strides)	nk	2	4/1[2]	79	31
1653[8]	**Sada** (MajorWRHern) **2-8-8** TSprake(2) (hld up: rdn over 1f out: ev ch ins fnl f: one pce)	1¼	3	5/1[3]	72	24
1952[2]	**Gypsy Hill** (DHaydnJones) **2-8-10** SDrowne(7) (lw: s.s: rdn & hdwy over 2f out: one pce)	½	4	5/1[3]	73	25
1806[10]	**Flying Singer** (IABalding) **2-8-5**(3) MartinDwyer(3) (stumbled over 3f out: lost pl 2f out: r.o one pce fnl f)	2	5	25/1	65	17
2007[2]	**Summer Deal (USA)** (PFICole) **2-8-8** TQuinn(1) (led over 1f: rdn over 2f out: wknd over 1f out)	1¾	6	4/1[2]	61	13
	Blueberry (SDow) **2-8-5** SSanders(4) (scope: s.s: a bhd)	5	7	20/1	44	—

(SP 112.7%) **7 Rn**

1m 15.4 (4.90) CSF £10.10 TOTE £3.30: £1.80 £2.10 (£4.10) OWNER Mr D. F. Allport (NEWMARKET) BRED Christian Marner

1211 Hoh Chi Min handles these conditions well and was given a fine ride by Reid, for the situation did not look brilliant below the distance as she had a couple of lengths to make up on the leader and did not appear to be going well. However, her jockey coaxed one last spurt out of her inside the final furlong and managed to get her up with a couple of strides to go. (9/4: 6/4-5/2)

1391 Classy Cleo (IRE), the most experienced runner in the field, was soon at the head of affairs and looked likely to hold on, only to be caught by the winner in the last couple of strides. Compensation awaits. (4/1: op 2/1)

1653 Sada launched her challenge in the final quarter-mile and was still battling for honours inside the final furlong, before tapped for toe. (5/1)

1952 Gypsy Hill once again lost ground at the start but, after picking up ground soon after halfway, could then make no further impression. (5/1)

Flying Singer got outpaced a quarter of a mile from home but did struggle on again when it was all over. (25/1)

2007 Summer Deal (USA) broke best of all but she was soon passed and tamely dropped away below the distance. (4/1: 3/1-9/2)

2372 WILLIAM HILL ACTION LINE H'CAP (0-70) (3-Y.O+) (Class E)

8-10 (8-11) **5f 217y** £3,160.00 (£955.00: £465.00: £220.00) Stalls: High GOING: 0.06 sec per fur (G)

				SP	RR	SF
2244[4]	**Tinker Osmaston (58)** (RJHodges) **6-9-3** JQuinn(2) (hld up: led over 1f out: drvn out)	—	1	15/2[3]	70	52
2179[2]	**Never Think Twice (61)** (KTIvory) **4-9-3v**(3) MartinDwyer(3) (b: s.s: rdn over 2f out: hdwy over 1f out: edgd lft ins fnl f: r.o)	1	2	7/2[1]	70	52
1666[W]	**Denbrae (IRE) (68)** (DJGMurraySmith) **5-9-6**(7) CLowther(12) (rdn over 2f out: hdwy over 1f out: unable qckn)	4	3	12/1	67	49
2096a[12]	**Village Native (FR) (58)** (KOCunningham-Brown) **4-9-3b** JReid(1) (led over 4f)	½	4	10/1	55	37
2130*	**Swift (69)** (MJPolglase) **3-9-7** PatEddery(6) (a.p: rdn over 2f out: ev ch over 1f out: sn wknd)	3½	5	7/2[1]	57	32
1743[8]	**Divine Miss-P (60)** (APJarvis) **4-9-5** DHolland(5) (lw: rdn over 3f: no hdwy fnl 2f)	½	6	11/1	47	29
2002[5]	**Napoleon Star (IRE) (51)** (SRBowring) **6-8-10b** SWebster(9) (lw: lost pl 4f out: r.o one pce fnl f)	2	7	7/1[2]	32	14
	Imposing Time (67) (MissGayKelleway) **6-9-12** SSanders(4) (swtg: prom over 4f)	1¼	8	16/1	45	27
649[13]	**Forgotten Times (USA) (65)** (TMJones) **3-9-3** NCarlisle(7) (prom over 2f)	7	9	20/1	24	—
1966[9]	**Kilmeena Lady (46)** (JCFox) **3-7-7**(5) RMullen(10) (s.s: a bhd)	¾	10	33/1	3	—
1756[7]	**Purple Maize (51)** (JAkehurst) **3-7-12b**[1](5)ow5 ADaly(11) (a bhd)	3	11	20/1	—	—
2062[11]	**Strat's Quest (66)** (DWPArbuthnot) **3-9-4** SWhitworth(8) (lw: bhd fnl 3f)	3	12	8/1	7	—

(SP 123.3%) **12 Rn**

1m 14.3 (3.80) CSF £31.33 CT £300.22 TOTE £8.90: £2.40 £1.40 £4.60 (£16.00) Trio £72.60 OWNER Mr John Luff (SOMERTON) BRED Mrs R. D. Peacock

WEIGHT FOR AGE 3yo-7lb

2244 Tinker Osmaston, making a quick reappearance, failed to score last year but she has fallen in the handicap as a result and took advantage of that here, leading approaching the final furlong, and responding well to pressure. (15/2)

2179 Never Think Twice made his move below the distance and, despite drifting in behind the winner, kept on well to the line. (7/2)

520 Denbrae (IRE) began to pick up ground on the outside of the field below the distance but was unable to reel in the front two in the final furlong. All three of his wins to date have come over six furlongs. (12/1: 7/1-14/1)

2096a Village Native (FR) took the field along but, collared approaching the final furlong, soon had bellows to mend. (10/1)

2130* Swift had every chance below the distance before tiring. (7/2)

1141* Strat's Quest (8/1: op 5/1)

2373 T B W A H'CAP (0-75) (3-Y.O+) (Class D)

8-40 (8-40) **1m 3f 135y** £3,623.00 (£1,094.00: £532.00: £251.00) Stalls: High GOING: 0.36 sec per fur (GS)

				SP	RR	SF
838*	**Kinnescash (IRE) (59)** (PBowen) **4-8-12** MFenton(9) (chsd ldr: led 7f out: clr 4f out: pushed out)	—	1	4/1[3]	73	42
2139[10]	**Palamon (USA) (70)** (PEccles) **4-9-4**(5) GFaulkner(1) (lw: rdn over 2f out: hdwy to chse wnr over 1f out: r.o one pce)	2	2	33/1	81	50
1434[7]	**Alhosaam (72)** (MajorWRHern) **3-8-11** TSprake(8) (lw: hld up: rdn 3f out: edgd lft over 1f out: r.o one pce)	nk	3	100/30[2]	83	38
2218*	**Ancient Quest (80)** (NACallaghan) **4-10-5** 5x PaulEddery(4) (a.p: rdn 3f out: bmpd over 1f out: one pce)	¾	4	11/4[1]	90	59
2182[3]	**Herbshan Dancer (57)** (BRMillman) **3-7-10** JQuinn(5) (lw: hrd rdn & hdwy over 1f out: wknd fnl f)	5	5	10/1	60	15
1805[8]	**Haroldon (IRE) (65)** (BPalling) **8-9-4** DaneO'Neill(3) (b: hdwy over 3f out: rdn over 2f out: wknd over 1f out)	1¼	6	40/1	66	35
2174[3]	**Kristal Breeze (52)** (WRMuir) **5-8-5** AClark(6) (lw: bhd fnl 3f)	1½	7	9/1	51	20
1169[14]	**Astral Weeks (IRE) (53)** (MJBolton) **6-8-3**(3) MHenry(10) (bhd fnl 3f)	2	8	50/1	49	18
1923[3]	**Monument (61)** (JSKing) **5-8-9**(5) RFfrench(7) (led over 4f: wknd over 2f out)	5	9	12/1	51	20
1811[7]	**Newport Knight (68)** (RAkehurst) **6-9-7** TQuinn(11) (hdwy over 2f out: wknd over 1f out)	3½	10	8/1	53	22

(SP 115.0%) **10 Rn**

2m 38.1 (12.10) CSF £114.81 CT £442.53 TOTE £4.70: £1.60 £8.10 £2.10 (£159.10) Trio £449.30 OWNER Mr D. R. James (HAVERFORD-WEST) BRED Frank Barry

WEIGHT FOR AGE 3yo-14lb

838* Kinnescash (IRE), winner of three races over hurdles recently, carried on the good work here. Sent on seven furlongs from home, he forged clear early in the straight and, shaken up, never looked like being caught. (4/1: 5/2-9/2)

Palamon (USA) ran much better here and came through to take second place below the distance, if unable to reel in the winner. (33/1)

1434 Alhosaam, fitted with a cross-noseband for this handicap debut, ran his best race to date. Chasing the leaders, he drifted slightly left below the distance, doing Ancient Quest no favours, but nevertheless stayed on, only just failing to win the battle for second prize. (100/30)

2218* Ancient Quest, looking for a quick hat-trick on ground he likes, found his welter burden the stumbling block and, although never far away, failed to quicken under his massive weight in the final quarter mile. (11/4)

2182 Herbshan Dancer made an effort from the back of the field below the distance but had come to the end of his tether in the final furlong. (10/1)

1923 Monument (12/1: 8/1-14/1)
Newport Knight (8/1: 6/1-9/1)

2374 E D S DEFENCE LIMITED STKS (0-65) (3-Y.O+) (Class F)

9-10 (9-13) **1m 2f 7y** £2,612.00 (£732.00: £356.00) Stalls: High GOING: 0.36 sec per fur (GS)

Form	Horse	Dist	Pos	SP	RR	SF
1938^{5}	**Dizzy Tilly (65)** (TJNaughton) **3-8-6** DHolland(11) (led 8f out to 3f out: hrd rdn over 2f out: led over 1f out: r.o wl)	—	**1**	$9/2^{2}$	72	34
2117^{3}	**The Executor (64)** (RJO'Sullivan) **7-9-5** JQuinn(9) (rdn & hdwy 2f out: chsd wnr over 1f out: unable qckn)	3	**2**	8/1	68	42
2161^{6}	**Alsahib (USA) (65)** (WRMuir) **4-9-7** JReid(7) (rdn over 2f out: hdwy over 1f out: r.o)	2	**3**	9/1	67	41
2068^{4}	**Sarbaron (IRE) (65)** (PWHarris) **3-8-0**(7) CLowther(5) (lw: led 2f: hrd rdn over 2f out: one pce)	hd	**4**	20/1	65	27
1939^{4}	**Keen Dancer (65)** (MBell) **3-8-7** MFenton(3) (lw: hdwy to ld 3f out: hdd over 1f out: sn wknd)	2	**5**	16/1	62	24
1956^{2}	**Ludo (62)** (RHannon) **3-8-9** DaneO'Neill(10) (rdn 5f out: hdwy over 1f out: nvr nrr)	1½	**6**	$13/2^{3}$	61	23
2008^{10}	**Limelight (62)** (JARToller) **3-8-4** SSanders(1) (nvr nr to chal)	1¼	**7**	10/1	54	16
369^{2}	**Whispering Dawn (65)** (CPEBrooks) **4-8-13**(3) PPMurphy(4) (b.hind: s.s: nvr nrr)	2	**8**	12/1	51	25
2117^{4}	**Proud Monk (63)** (GLMoore) **4-9-5v** SWhitworth(12) (plld hrd: prom 8f)	½	**9**	9/1	53	27
2245^{6}	**Merciless Cop (65)** (BJMeehan) **3-8-11** MTebbutt(8) (hld up: rdn over 2f out: wknd over 1f out)	nk	**10**	$13/2^{3}$	57	19
	Ellway Lady (IRE) (64) (IABalding) **3-8-1**(3) MartinDwyer(6) (hld up: stumbled over 3f out: rdn over 2f out: sn wknd)	3	**11**	20/1	45	7
1877^{7}	**Khayal (USA) (65)** (BWHills) **3-8-7** PatEddery(2) (prom over 7f)	nk	**12**	$4/1^{1}$	48	10
				(SP 128.1%)		**12 Rn**

2m 15.6 (10.70) CSF £40.27 TOTE £4.40: £1.90 £1.80 £2.70 (£18.00) Trio £42.00 OWNER Mrs S. Leech (EPSOM) BRED Dandy's Farm
WEIGHT FOR AGE 3yo-12lb
1938 Dizzy Tilly was collared for the lead three furlongs from home but, refusing to lie down, got back in front again below the distance and kept on really well. (9/2: op 3/1)
2117 The Executor may have had two recent runs under his belt but he was still carrying condition. Nevertheless, he came through to take second place approaching the final furlong, if unable to get on terms with the winner. (8/1)
2161 Alsahib (USA) began to pick up ground below the distance but, despite running on, found the winner already home and dry. He has yet to win on grass. (9/1)
2068 Sarbaron (IRE), the early leader, came under pressure over a quarter of a mile from home but could only go up and down in the same place. (20/1)
1939 Keen Dancer moved through to lead three furlongs from home but he was collared below the distance and had nothing more to offer. He remains a maiden. (16/1)
1956 Ludo stayed on in the last furlong and a half but, by then, the game was up. (13/2: 4/1-7/1)
1563 Limelight (10/1: 7/1-12/1)
2117 Proud Monk (9/1: 14/1-8/1)
2245 Merciless Cop (13/2: 7/2-7/1)

T/Jkpt: Not won; £22,831.66 to Chepstow 1/7/97. T/Plpt: £64.50 (444.12 Tckts). T/Qdpt: £14.90 (90.51 Tckts) AK

1920-CHEPSTOW (L-H) (Good to soft)
Tuesday July 1st
WEATHER: showers WIND: nil

2375 BOLLINGER CHAMPAGNE CHALLENGE SERIES GENTLEMEN'S H'CAP (0-70) (3-Y.O+) (Class G)

2-00 (2-01) **1m 14y** £2,374.00 (£664.00: £322.00) Stalls: High GOING: 0.31 sec per fur (G)

Form	Horse	Dist	Pos	SP	RR	SF
2302^{11}	**Clued Up (50)** (PDEvans) **4-10-4v**(4) MrAEvans(8) (hld up: hdwy 3f out: led wl over 1f out: r.o wl)	—	**1**	8/1	63	46
2039^{11}	**Suile Mor (47)** (BRMillman) **5-10-5** MrLJefford(5) (w ldr: ev ch 2f out: one pce)	3½	**2**	14/1	53	36
2201^{5}	**Helios (62)** (DJGMurraySmith) **9-11-6** MrTMcCarthy(6) (lw: a.p: led 4f out tl wl over 1f out: one pce)	1¼	**3**	$4/1^{3}$	66	49
72^{2}	**Nordic Breeze (IRE) (69)** (MCPipe) **5-11-13** MrAFarrant(7) (lw: hld up: rdn & r.o one pce fnl 2f)	¾	**4**	$7/2^{2}$	71	54
1926^{8}	**Proud Brigadier (IRE) (46)** (MRBosley) **9-10-0**(4)ow10 MrSJEdwards(2) (nvr nr to chal)	3	**5**	25/1	42	15
1920^{3}	**Asterix (40)** (JMBradley) **9-9-8b**(4)ow1 MrOMcPhail(4) (b: plld hrd: prom tl wknd 2f out)	2	**6**	7/1	32	14
	Moultazim (USA) (35) (MrsSDWilliams) **7-9-3**(4) MrVLukaniuk(10) (prom over 5f)	3½	**7**	33/1	20	3
1926^{*}	**Shining Example (70)** (PJMakin) **5-11-10**(4) MrLBaker(1) (hld up in rr: nt clr run & swtchd lft over 3f out: n.d)	1¼	**8**	$3/1^{1}$	53	36
	Super Serenade (52) (GBBalding) **8-10-6**(4)ow2 MrJThatcher(3) (prom over 5f)	4	**9**	10/1	27	8
1663^{6}	**Sarum (35)** (JELong) **11-9-3**(4) MrTWaters(9) (b: led 4f: wknd over 2f out: t.o)	10	**10**	40/1	—	—
				(SP 115.8%)		**10 Rn**

1m 40.4 (9.20) CSF £99.60 CT £469.13 TOTE £9.40: £1.80 £3.20 £1.30 (£86.80) Trio £89.50 OWNER Mrs E. J. Williams (WELSHPOOL) BRED C. R. and V. M. Withers
LONG HANDICAP Moultazim (USA) 9-5
1422 Clued Up was 4lb higher than when winning another race in this series on soft ground at Hamilton in May. (8/1)
Suile Mor was sharper for the run at Nottingham. (14/1)
2201 Helios handles all types of ground but his best form is on a fast surface. (4/1)
72 Nordic Breeze (IRE) shaped as if he needs further than a mile these days. (7/2)
1920 Asterix has never scored on ground worse than good. (7/1)

2376 SUMMER (S) STKS (3-Y.O) (Class G)

2-30 (2-31) **1m 14y** £2,234.00 (£624.00: £302.00) Stalls: High GOING: 0.31 sec per fur (G)

Form	Horse	Dist	Pos	SP	RR	SF
2021^{8}	**Bollero (IRE) (56)** (JBerry) **3-8-6**(3) PFessey(6) (mde all: rdn over 3f out: edgd lft over 2f out: r.o wl)	—	**1**	$5/2^{2}$	59	19
2245^{7}	**Warrior King (IRE) (43)** (MrsPNDutfield) **3-8-9**(5) AimeeCook(4) (hld up: hdwy over 3f out: r.o one pce fnl 2f)	4	**2**	$13/2^{3}$	56	16
1989^{6}	**Farewell My Love (IRE) (64)** (PFICole) **3-8-9** KDarley(8) (a.p: rdn over 3f out: one pce fnl 2f)	nk	**3**	$11/10^{1}$	51	11
1966^{10}	**Java Bay (47)** (MBlanshard) **3-8-9** JQuinn(3) (nvr trbld ldrs)	5	**4**	14/1	41	1
1921^{10}	**Grace** (JMBradley) **3-8-9** SDrowne(7) (hld up: hdwy over 3f out: wknd over 2f out)	11	**5**	20/1	19	—
2159^{8}	**Spanish Warrior (50)** (JWHills) **3-9-0** NAdams(2) (lw: rdn over 4f out: bhd fnl 3f: t.o)	14	**6**	12/1	—	—

1963[14]	**Silver Jubilee (35)** (BPalling) **3-8-9** TSprake(5) (prom over 4f: t.o)	¾	**7**	20/1	—	—
				(SP 113.4%)		**7 Rn**

1m 40.6 (9.40) CSF £16.99 TOTE £3.60: £1.90 £2.50 (£9.60) OWNER Mr Ian Bolland (COCKERHAM) BRED Mrs G. Donnelly
No bid
1820 Bollero (IRE), described as a bit of a madam at home, took advantage of a drop in class. (5/2)
1951 Warrior King (IRE), descending to selling company, got the better of the separate battle for second. (13/2: op 3/1)
1661 Farewell My Love (IRE), tried in a visor last time, does not mind this ground but it put more of an emphasis on stamina on this step up to a mile. (11/10: 4/5-5/4)
Java Bay was having her first run in a seller. (14/1)
868 Spanish Warrior (12/1: op 6/1)

2377 STEWARDS TRIAL H'CAP (0-100) (3-Y.O+) (Class C)
3-00 (3-04) **5f 16y** £5,377.50 (£1,620.00: £785.00: £367.50) Stalls: High GOING: 0.31 sec per fur (G)

				SP	RR	SF
2347[3]	**So Intrepid (IRE) (75)** (JMBradley) **7-8-10** SDrowne(5) (hld up: hdwy 2f out: led ins fnl f: drvn out)	—	**1**	7/1[3]	83	45
2197*	**Runs in the Family (64)** (GMMcCourt) **5-7-8b**(5) 7x RMullen(12) (led: hdd & edgd lft ins fnl f: r.o)	½	**2**	11/2[1]	70	32
1765[5]	**Lunar Mist (73)** (MartynMeade) **4-8-1**(7) RBrisland(2) (hdwy over 2f out: ev ch over 1f out: r.o)	nk	**3**	14/1	79	41
2134[16]	**Cauda Equina (75)** (MRChannon) **3-8-2**(3) PPMurphy(13) (bhd tl gd hdwy fnl f: nvr nrr)	1¼	**4**	14/1	77	34
2289[9]	**Ansellman (80)** (JBerry) **7-8-12b**(3) PFessey(11) (b: a.p: one pce fnl f)	hd	**5**	11/1	81	43
1975[5]	**Fond Embrace (93)** (HCandy) **4-10-0** GCarter(8) (chsd ldr: ev ch 1f out: wknd ins fnl f)	nk	**6**	10/1	93	55
2232[5]	**Mister Jolson (77)** (RJHodges) **8-8-12** LDettori(3) (lw: hdwy over 1f out: styng on whn nt clr run wl ins fnl f)	s.h	**7**	10/1	77	39
2211[2]	**Westcourt Magic (90)** (MWEasterby) **4-9-11** KDarley(4) (hld up: hdwy fnl f: nt rch ldrs)	½	**8**	6/1[2]	89	51
2105[27]	**Repertory (89)** (MSSaunders) **4-9-10** RPrice(10) (hld up: hdwy over 2f out: wknd over 1f out)	¾	**9**	25/1	85	47
2134[9]	**Myrmidon (88)** (MrsLStubbs) **3-9-4b[1]** JFEgan(1) (s.i.s: a bhd)	1¾	**10**	10/1	79	36
2162[2]	**Intiaash (IRE) (80)** (DHaydnJones) **5-9-1** JReid(9) (lw: bhd fnl 2f)	1¼	**11**	6/1[2]	67	29
2232[4]	**Bajan Rose (75)** (MBlanshard) **5-8-10b** JQuinn(7) (a bhd)	1¼	**12**	10/1	58	20
2134[5]	**Mangus (IRE) (75)** (KOCunningham-Brown) **3-8-2**(3) MartinDwyer(6) (prom: rdn over 2f out: wknd wl over 1f out)	2½	**13**	16/1	50	7
				(SP 124.2%)		**13 Rn**

61.4 secs (4.40) CSF £42.94 CT £508.35 TOTE £8.10: £2.60 £2.10 £6.30 (£17.60) Trio £85.10 OWNER Mr E. A. Hayward (CHEPSTOW) BRED Crest Stud Ltd
WEIGHT FOR AGE 3yo-5lb
2347 So Intrepid (IRE), considered unlucky by his trainer at Goodwood two days ago, will be aimed at a return to Sussex for the Stewards' Cup. (7/1)
2197* Runs in the Family does not mind this sort of going but one cannot help feeling it takes the edge of her speed. (11/2: 4/1-6/1)
1765 Lunar Mist had been dropped 2lb after disappointing last time. (14/1)
1275* Cauda Equina was down 2lb after being bumped at the start in another competitive event at Ascot last time. (14/1)
1402 Ansellman was 5lb higher than when winning this race last season. (11/1)
1975 Fond Embrace ran very well until anchored by her big weight. (10/1)
2232 Mister Jolson needs a stiffer course over the minimum trip nowadays. (10/1)
2211 Westcourt Magic did not seem suited to waiting tactics. (6/1)

2378 BREAM CLAIMING STKS (2-Y.O) (Class F)
3-30 (3-36) **6f 16y** £2,512.50 (£700.00: £337.50) Stalls: High GOING: 0.31 sec per fur (G)

				SP	RR	SF
2306[7]	**King Darius (IRE)** (RHannon) **2-9-0** DaneO'Neill(1) (lw: pushed along 4f out: hdwy 2f out: led over 1f out: rdn out)	—	**1**	9/4[1]	74	25
1952[5]	**Persian Fortune** (WGMTurner) **2-7-7**(7) SCarson(2) (led: hdd over 1f out: one pce)	2	**2**	9/2[2]	55	6
2016[7]	**Edna's Gift (IRE)** (JBerry) **2-7-13**(3) PFessey(3) (w ldr: rdn & ev ch 2f out: wknd over 1f out)	6	**3**	9/4[1]	41	—
447[10]	**Satis (IRE)** (MRChannon) **2-8-3**(3) PPMurphy(6) (trckd ldr: one pce fnl f)	nk	**4**	6/1[3]	44	—
648[10]	**Bellow (IRE)** (HMorrison) **2-9-0** CRutter(4) (racd alone stands' side: bhd fnl 2f)	1¼	**5**	10/1	49	—
	The Imposter (IRE) (DJGMurraySmith) **2-8-4**(7) CLowther(5) (w'like: s.i.s: outpcd)	5	**6**	10/1	33	—
	Hi Rudolf (AJChamberlain) **2-8-3** DBiggs(7) (unf: outpcd: t.o)	26	**7**	33/1	—	—
				(SP 115.1%)		**7 Rn**

1m 16.2 (7.00) CSF £11.84 TOTE £2.90: £1.70 £2.40 (£5.40) OWNER Mr John Perry (MARLBOROUGH) BRED Dr Jim Moore
King Darius (IRE), making a quick reappearance, benefited from a drop in grade. (9/4)
1952 Persian Fortune relished the give in the ground. (9/2)
1789 Edna's Gift (IRE) has been running in sellers. (9/4)
Satis (IRE), who presumably has had her training problems, does not look anything special. (6/1)
Bellow (IRE) was racing on ground that had already been chewed up. (10/1: 6/1-12/1)
The Imposter (IRE) (10/1: 7/1-12/1)

2379 WORTHINGTON DRAUGHT BITTER MAIDEN STKS (3-Y.O) (Class D)
4-00 (4-02) **1m 2f 36y** £3,738.25 (£1,126.00: £545.50: £255.25) Stalls: Low GOING: 0.45 sec per fur (GS)

				SP	RR	SF
	Kaliana (IRE) (LMCumani) **3-8-9** JReid(5) (neat: hld up: hdwy over 4f out: led over 1f out: pushed out)	—	**1**	7/2[2]	87	58
	Masharik (IRE) (MajorWRHern) **3-8-9** RHills(2) (unf: s.i.s: hld up: rdn & n.m.r over 2f out: nt clr run over 1f out: swtchd rt & r.o ins fnl f)	3½	**2**	5/1[3]	82	53
2126[5]	**Mengaab (USA) (82)** (JHMGosden) **3-9-0** LDettori(1) (chsd ldr: led over 3f out: rdn over 2f out: hdd over 1f out: one pce)	s.h	**3**	2/1[1]	86	57
1591[7]	**Polska Princess (GER)** (LordHuntingdon) **3-8-9** KDarley(3) (prom: rdn 3f out: wknd 2f out)	12	**4**	10/1	63	34
1868[3]	**Pennys From Heaven (79)** (HCandy) **3-9-0** CRutter(6) (led: rdn & hdd over 3f out: wknd over 2f out)	5	**5**	2/1[1]	60	31
2173[6]	**Gajan (IRE)** (JNeville) **3-9-0** SDrowne(4) (a bhd: t.o fnl 5f)	11	**6**	50/1	42	13
				(SP 116.6%)		**6 Rn**

2m 14.3 (9.00) CSF £19.94 TOTE £4.70: £1.80 £2.70 (£11.00) OWNER H H Aga Khan (NEWMARKET) BRED His Highness the Aga Khan's Studs S.C.
Kaliana (IRE), a half-sister to Kahyasi, certainly showed she could handle yielding going. (7/2: 5/2-4/1)
Masharik (IRE), a half-sister to Ibn Bey and Roseate Tern, did not get the run of the race but already seemed to need further, even on ground like this. (5/1: 7/2-6/1)

2126 Mengaab (USA) is proving disappointing. (2/1: op 5/4)
Polska Princess (GER) (10/1: op 6/1)

2380 MIDDLE LODGE H'CAP (0-85) (3-Y.O F) (Class D)

4-30 (4-32) **1m 2f 36y** £3,647.25 (£1,098.00: £531.50: £248.25) Stalls: Low GOING: 0.45 sec per fur (GS)

Form	Horse	Dist	Pos	SP	RR	SF
1437^{2}	**Cugina (73)** (GBBalding) **3-8-9** RPrice(3) (plld hrd early: hdwy over 3f out: led wl over 1f out: rdn & edgd lft ins fnl f: r.o wl)	—	**1**	$9/1^{3}$	81	52
2210^{4}	**Toi Toi (IRE) (73)** (DWPArbuthnot) **3-8-9** SWhitworth(5) (hld up: hdwy over 3f out: ev ch over 2f out: r.o one pce fnl f)	2	**2**	16/1	78	49
1875^{8}	**Apache Star (84)** (GWragg) **3-9-6** MHills(8) (a.p: rdn over 3f out: led over 2f out tl wl over 1f out: btn whn hmpd & snatched up ins fnl f)	2	**3**	$6/1^{2}$	86	57
2178*	**Seattle Swing (75)** (JHMGosden) **3-8-11** ^{5x} LDettori(2) (a.p: rdn over 2f out: one pce)	1	**4**	$5/4^{1}$	75	46
2116*	**Doyella (IRE) (85)** (DRLoder) **3-9-7** KDarley(6) (lw: led over 7f: wknd over 1f out)	2½	**5**	$6/1^{2}$	81	52
1567^{4}	**Nubile (68)** (BWHills) **3-8-4** DHolland(7) (s.s: sn rcvrd: wknd over 2f out)	9	**6**	$9/1^{3}$	50	21
1587^{8}	**Atnab (USA) (60)** (PTWalwyn) **3-7-10** JQuinn(1) (hld up in rr: wl bhd fnl 3f)	1	**7**	$6/1^{2}$	41	12
1813^{7}	**Calypso Lady (IRE) (77)** (RHannon) **3-8-13** DaneO'Neill(4) (lw: prom: rdn over 3f out: wknd over 2f out)	½	**8**	20/1	57	28

(SP 117.9%) **8 Rn**

2m 15.0 (9.70) CSF £127.65 CT £854.10 TOTE £9.60: £2.50 £3.10 £1.60 (£68.10) OWNER Miss B. Swire (ANDOVER) BRED Miss B. Swire
LONG HANDICAP Atnab (USA) 7-8
STEWARDS' ENQUIRY Price susp.10-12/7/97(careless riding)
1437 Cugina, travelling strongly when striking the front, crossed to the fence after her rider went for his whip, resulting in him picking up a three-day ban for careless riding. (9/1)
2210 Toi Toi (IRE) had been tried over a mile and a half on her handicap debut. (16/1)
1028 Apache Star was taking a drop in class. (6/1)
2178* Seattle Swing failed to pick up when the chips were down. (5/4)
2116* Doyella (IRE) had a lot more to do here than at Goodwood last time. (6/1)
1567 Nubile (9/1: 6/1-10/1)

2381 LIONS LODGE H'CAP (0-70) (3-Y.O+) (Class E)

5-00 (5-00) **2m 2f** £2,800.75 (£841.00: £405.50: £187.75) Stalls: Low GOING: 0.45 sec per fur (GS)

Form	Horse	Dist	Pos	SP	RR	SF
2131*	**Media Star (USA) (70)** (JHMGosden) **4-10-0v** LDettori(6) (hld up: hdwy 8f out: led wl over 2f out: sn clr: rdn out)	—	**1**	$2/1^{1}$	88	61
2139^{6}	**Bridie's Pride (46)** (GAHam) **6-7-11**(7) JFowle(7) (led: hdd wl over 2f out: no ch w wnr)	7	**2**	$9/2^{3}$	58	31
2014^{11}	**General Mouktar (56)** (MCPipe) **7-9-0** DHolland(1) (hld up: hdwy 6f out: rdn over 4f out: sn wknd)	17	**3**	$7/2^{2}$	53	26
1825^{8}	**Shy Paddy (IRE) (41)** (KOCunningham-Brown) **5-7-10**(3)ow3 MartinDwyer(4) (hld up: hdwy over 7f out: wknd 4f out)	4	**4**	20/1	34	4
2014^{15}	**Spring Marathon (USA) (55)** (MrsPNDutfield) **7-8-8**(5) AimeeCook(3) (bhd fnl 5f)	2	**5**	20/1	46	19
2139^{11}	**Sandy Floss (IRE) (68)** (RHBuckler) **4-9-5**(7) CLowther(2) (w ldr: rdn & wknd over 5f out)	29	**6**	14/1	34	7
1795^{4}	**Gumair (USA) (67)** (RHannon) **4-9-11** JReid(5) (bhd fnl 6f: t.o)	dist	**7**	5/1	—	—

(SP 106.6%) **7 Rn**

4m 9.6 (19.60) CSF £8.69 TOTE £2.60: £1.70 £2.10 (£4.70) OWNER Mr K. Abdulla (NEWMARKET) BRED Juddmonte Farms
LONG HANDICAP Shy Paddy (IRE) 7-6
2131* Media Star (USA) defied a welter burden, especially in this ground, in an uncompetitive event. (2/1: 6/4-9/4)
2139 Bridie's Pride was probably not helped by being taken on for the lead. (9/2)
1408 General Mouktar has not won on the Flat for nearly four years and has yet to prove he really stays this sort of distance. (7/2)
1795 Gumair (USA) (5/1: op 3/1)

T/Jkpt: £32,472.30 (1 Tckts). T/Plpt: £1,404.80 (16.56 Tckts). T/Qdpt: £105.90 (15.03 Tckts) KH

2221-HAMILTON (R-H) (Soft)

Tuesday July 1st

WEATHER: overcast WIND: almost nil

2382 ROSEBANK AMATEUR H'CAP (0-65) (3-Y.O+) (Class F)

2-15 (2-15) **5f 4y** £2,458.00 (£688.00: £334.00) Stalls: Low GOING minus 0.02 sec per fur (G)

Form	Horse	Dist	Pos	SP	RR	SF
2221W	**Another Nightmare (IRE) (41)** (RMMcKellar) **5-9-12**(4) MrsCWilliams(3) (sn led: racd far side after 1f: clr 2f out: kpt on)	—	**1**	$6/1^{3}$	52	35
2111^{6}	**Pallium (IRE) (45)** (DANolan) **9-10-6b** MissDianaJones(5) (a chsng ldrs: kpt on fnl f)	1½	**2**	15/2	51	34
2001^{5}	**Tropical Beach (55)** (JBerry) **4-11-2b** MrsLPearce(2) (sn outpcd & bhd: hdwy over 1f out: styd on wl towards fin)	½	**3**	$7/2^{2}$	60	43
386^{9}	**Marjorie Rose (IRE) (60)** (ABailey) **4-11-0**(7) MissALHutchinson(8) (a chsng ldrs: kpt on fnl 2f: nt pce to chal)	2½	**4**	12/1	57	40
2221W	**Kid Ory (43)** (DWChapman) **6-10-4b** MissRClark(9) (led early: cl up tl rdn & btn over 1f out)	1	**5**	$3/1^{1}$	37	20
2221W	**Sunday Mail Too (IRE) (38)** (MissLAPerratt) **5-9-6**(7) MrDBShaw(4) (lw: racd centre: nvr wnt pce)	2½	**6**	9/1	24	7
2030^{6}	**Biff-Em (IRE) (65)** (MissLAPerratt) **3-11-7** MrRHale(7) (chsd ldrs 3f: wknd)	2½	**7**	10/1	43	21
480^{7}	**Southern Rule (25)** (PMooney) **10-8-7b**(7) MissLMcIntosh(6) (t: outpcd ½-wy: sn bhd)	nk	**8**	7/1	2	—
2221W	**Aye Ready (37)** (DANolan) **4-9-5**(7)ow12 MissDCarter(1) (lw: s.i.s: racd centre: a outpcd & bhd)	9	**9**	100/1	—	—

(SP 113.5%) **9 Rn**

62.8 secs (4.50) CSF £44.88 CT £164.03 TOTE £5.30: £1.70 £2.80 £1.10 (£22.20) Trio £18.40 OWNER GM Engineering (LESMAHAGOW)
BRED John J. Ryan
WEIGHT FOR AGE 3yo-5lb
2033 Another Nightmare (IRE) had the speed to get over to the favoured far rails and, clear just after halfway, she loves the soft ground and was never going to stop. (6/1: op 4/1)
2111 Pallium (IRE) ran another fair race and was keeping on in pleasing style. (15/2)
2001 Tropical Beach gave signs of coming back to form here and finished pretty well. (7/2)

318 Marjorie Rose (IRE), having her first run since early March, ran well and should be all the better for it. (12/1)
2002 Kid Ory, who ran really well in the false-start race last week, was disappointing this time but he certainly has more ability if he can be persuaded. (3/1)
1835 Sunday Mail Too (IRE) was always racing in the slower ground and never had a hope. (9/1)

2383 KIRKMUIRHILL (QUALIFIER) (S) STKS (2-Y.O) (Class F)
2-45 (2-47) **6f 5y** £2,598.00 (£728.00: £354.00) Stalls: Low GOING: 0.08 sec per fur (G)

				SP	RR	SF
2276*	**Fast Franc (IRE)** (SCWilliams) **2-9-3** 6x JWeaver(8) (mde all: kpt on strly fnl 2f)	—	1	6/4 1	70+	19
	Ribble Assembly (RAFahey) **2-8-11** JCarroll(7) (w'like: unruly s: dwlt: sn rcvrd: chsd ldrs: rdn 2f out: kpt on one pce)	2½	2	4/1 2	57	6
2153^{5}	**Ellenber** (WMcKeown) **2-8-11b^{1}** LCharnock(3) (outpcd tl hdwy 2f out: styd on wl)	¾	3	16/1	55	4
2191^{3}	**Harnage (IRE)** (MRChannon) **2-8-11** JFortune(2) (in tch: styd on u.p fnl f: nvr able to chal)	½	4	4/1 2	54	3
1815^{5}	**Moss Side Monkey** (JBerry) **2-8-6**(5) TEDurcan(6) (lw: chsd ldrs tl rdn & btn appr fnl f)	2	5	8/1 3	49	—
	Anniemitchellslass (DMoffatt) **2-8-3**(3) DarrenMoffatt(4) (lt-f: sn outpcd & wl bhd: styd on fnl 2f)	hd	6	25/1	44	—
993^{11}	**Just Nobby** (NTinkler) **2-8-11b^{1}** KimTinkler(5) (chsd ldrs over 4f: wknd)	3	7	33/1	41	—
2233^{5}	**Up The Clarets (IRE)** (JJO'Neill) **2-8-11b^{1}** MFenton(1) (racd centre: a outpcd & bhd)	3	8	12/1	33	—
2153^{8}	**Behind The Veil** (MrsMReveley) **2-8-6** ACulhane(9) (prom tl ½-wy: sn lost pl)	4	9	33/1	17	—
				(SP 114.4%)	**9 Rn**	

1m 16.3 (6.30) CSF £6.53 TOTE £2.50: £1.10 £1.20 £2.60 (£3.10) Trio £23.40 OWNER Mr J. W. Lovitt (NEWMARKET) BRED Richard Evans
Bt in 7,000gns
2276* Fast Franc (IRE) made his experience tell and won in useful style, giving the impression that he can step up in class. (6/4)
Ribble Assembly took the eye in the paddock but gave problems in the stalls and then missed the kick. However, he still ran particularly well and, if his temperament can be sorted out, there is obviously better to come. (4/1)
2153 Ellenber had blinkers on for the first time but it took a while for the penny to drop, and the race was almost over when he ran on. (16/1)
2191 Harnage (IRE) did not impress on looks and was never going well enough to make a serious impression. (4/1: 3/1-9/2)
1815 Moss Side Monkey has the looks but it seems to be his attitude that is the problem at the moment. (8/1)
Anniemitchellslass was pretty fit on her debut here but proved very slow early on and, despite finishing quite well, never had a hope. It would appear she needs further. (25/1)
2233 Up The Clarets (IRE) (12/1: op 8/1)

2384 CELTIC PATRON DAY LIMITED STKS (0-50) (3-Y.O+) (Class F)
3-15 (3-16) **6f 5y** £2,570.00 (£720.00: £350.00) Stalls: Low GOING: 0.08 sec per fur (G)

				SP	RR	SF
2177^{4}	**Souperficial (46)** (NTinkler) **6-9-2v** KimTinkler(7) (bhd: hdwy 2f out: led ins fnl f: r.o)	—	1	9/1	52	34
2144^{9}	**Stephensons Rocket (46)** (RAFahey) **6-8-9**(7) RWinston(8) (chsd ldrs: chal 1f out: kpt on)	1	2	9/2 1	49	31
2111^{9}	**Leading Princess (IRE) (48)** (MissLAPerratt) **6-9-2b** JWeaver(11) (led tl hdd ins fnl f: no ex)	½	3	9/2 1	48	30
2179^{6}	**Flying Harold (49)** (MRChannon) **4-9-5** JFortune(5) (in tch: rdn ½-wy: styd on fnl f: nrst fin)	1¼	4	8/1	48	30
2317^{7}	**Komlucky (50)** (ABMulholland) **5-8-11v**(5) TEDurcan(2) (chsd ldrs: ev ch over 1f out: sn btn)	3	5	15/2 3	37	19
2177^{12}	**Nellie North (49)** (GMMcCourt) **4-8-6v**(7) AEddery(4) (lw: chsd ldrs: rdn 2f out: one pce)	½	6	6/1 2	32	14
1865^{9}	**Mu-Arrik (29)** (GROldroyd) **9-8-9v**(7) RFarmer(9) (bmpd s: nvr wnt pce)	2½	7	66/1	29	11
2203^{2}	**Needle Match (48)** (JJO'Neill) **4-9-8** JCarroll(1) (bhd: hdwy ½-wy: rdn 2f out: sn wknd)	13	8	10/1	—	—
2033^{9}	**Craigie Boy (40)** (NBycroft) **7-8-11b**(5) PRoberts(3) (lw: a outpcd & bhd)	nk	9	14/1	—	—
610^{18}	**Six for Luck (46)** (DANolan) **5-9-2** VHalliday(6) (cl up 4f: wknd qckly)	½	10	16/1	—	—
2237^{11}	**Suedoro (45)** (JSGoldie) **7-8-8**(5) JBramhill(10) (lw: bmpd s: sddle slipped: chsd ldrs tl uns rdr 2f out)		U	8/1	—	—
				(SP 117.8%)	**11 Rn**	

1m 15.1 (5.10) CSF £44.89 TOTE £9.80: £2.90 £1.30 £2.30 (£17.30) Trio £30.30 OWNER Mrs Christine Cawley (MALTON) BRED C. L. Loyd
2177 Souperficial, coming from off the pace and racing in what was probably the slower ground, finished well to win for the first time on a soft surface. (9/1)
1079 Stephensons Rocket got the favoured ground up the far rails and ran his best race for a while but he just failed to do enough when it mattered. (9/2)
2032 Leading Princess (IRE) has the speed and the ability but does not often put it to full use, although this was her best effort for a while. (9/2)
1925* Flying Harold won his only race on a faster surface and, in the circumstances, this was not a bad effort. (8/1)
1584 Komlucky is in good heart but this was just short of her ideal trip. (15/2)
2177 Nellie North looked pretty well but was always struggling in the soft conditions. (6/1)
2144 Suedoro took a hefty bump leaving the stalls and this probably caused her saddle to slip. She then ran pretty well, until unshipping her rider just after halfway. (8/1)

2385 SUNDAY MAIL (QUALIFIER) H'CAP (0-75) (3-Y.O+) (Class D)
3-45 (3-46) **1m 1f 36y** £3,436.25 (£1,040.00: £507.50: £241.25) Stalls: High GOING: 0.08 sec per fur (G)

				SP	RR	SF
2052^{2}	**Canadian Fantasy (74)** (MJohnston) **3-9-5** JWeaver(8) (lw: led 3f: cl up: led 3½f out: sn hdd: led wl ins fnl f: all out)	—	1	7/2 3	82	38
2223^{2}	**Western General (73)** (MissMKMilligan) **6-9-7**(7) NHorrocks(9) (lw: hld up: smooth hdwy to chal 3f out: hung lft 2f out: r.o fnl f: jst failed)	s.h	2	7/1	81	47
	Sarmatian (USA) (71) (MDHammond) **6-9-12** JFortune(7) (lw: trckd ldrs: led 3f out tl wl ins fnl f: one pce)	¾	3	3/1 2	78	44
1979^{10}	**Nobby Barnes (41)** (DonEnricoIncisa) **8-7-10** KimTinkler(3) (bhd: hdwy 2f out: styd on wl towards fin)	nk	4	20/1	47	13
2223^{3}	**Principal Boy (IRE) (48)** (TJEtherington) **4-8-3** DaleGibson(5) (a.p: rdn & ev ch over 1f out: no ex)	½	5	11/4 1	53	19
2144^{5}	**Termon (42)** (MissLAPerratt) **4-7-11**ow1 NKennedy(6) (lw: bhd: sme hdwy 3f out: nvr rchd ldrs)	5	6	10/1	39	4
2145^{13}	**Rapid Mover (45)** (DANolan) **10-7-9b**(5)ow4 KSked(4) (led after 3f tl 3½f out: wknd)	3½	7	66/1	35	—
2030^{5}	**Hutchies Lady (41)** (RMMcKellar) **5-7-3**(7) JMcAuley(2) (b.hind: chsd ldrs tl wknd fnl 3f)	6	8	16/1	21	—
1798^{8}	**That Old Feeling (IRE) (50)** (DWChapman) **5-8-5** ACulhane(1) (in tch c wd st: wknd fnl 4f)	dist	9	20/1	—	—
				(SP 112.4%)	**9 Rn**	

2m 2.5 (8.20) CSF £24.12 CT £72.63 TOTE £4.20: £2.00 £2.40 £1.40 (£10.90) Trio £25.20 OWNER Julian Clopet and Associates (MIDDLE-HAM) BRED Newgate Stud Co
LONG HANDICAP Termon 7-4 Rapid Mover 6-9 Hutchies Lady 7-3 Nobby Barnes 7-9
WEIGHT FOR AGE 3yo-10lb
2052 Canadian Fantasy, who looked particularly well, won his first race on turf here and showed fine courage to do so. (7/2)

2223 Western General looks magnificent at present and, had he not got unbalanced at a vital stage, he could well have won this. He really does deserve a change of luck. (7/1: op 7/2)
Sarmatian (USA), fit from hurdling, put up a decent show but was just out-battled late on. (3/1)
1615 Nobby Barnes likes to come from off the pace but, despite finishing quite well, the effort was again too late. (20/1)
2223 Principal Boy (IRE) does not know how to run a bad race on this ground and track but he just failed to quicken enough late on. (11/4)
2144 Termon looks in tremendous condition but was 6lb out of the handicap and, with another 1lb overweight, she failed to make an impression. (10/1)

2386 RIVER CLYDE CLAIMING STKS (3-Y.O+) (Class F)
4-15 (4-15) **1m 3f 16y** £2,444.00 (£684.00: £332.00) Stalls: High GOING: 0.08 sec per fur (G)

				SP	RR	SF
2225*	**Monaco Gold (IRE) (40)** (MrsMReveley) **5-8-13** DWright(6) (chsd ldr: led over 4f out: styd on wl)	—	1	2/1[1]	46	32
2021[6]	**Miami Moon (44)** (CWThornton) **3-8-2** DaleGibson(3) (bhd: racd centre: styd on wl fnl 3f: nrst fin)	1¾	2	12/1	45	19
2145[3]	**Philgem (31)** (CWFairhurst) **4-8-8** NKennedy(8) (bhd: hdwy 3f out: styd on: nvr able to chal)	4	3	9/2[3]	33	19
1570[8]	**Craigary (30)** (MrsASwinbank) **6-8-13b** JFortune(2) (lw: led tl hdd over 4f out: hrd rdn & one pce)	3½	4	20/1	33	19
	Dancing Cormorant (PMonteith) **4-9-8**(5) JBramhill(7) (chsd ldrs: effrt over 3f out: one pce)	2	5	50/1	44	30
1731[2]	**Aunt Daphne** (BAMcMahon) **3-8-0** LCharnock(4) (chsd ldrs tl wknd fnl 3f)	6	6	6/1	20	—
2226*	**Trying Times (IRE) (50)** (JBerry) **4-9-8**(5) TEDurcan(1) (lw: t: hdwy 6f out: sn in tch: outpcd fnl 3f)	4	7	4/1[2]	29	15
	Cittern (56) (MrsMReveley) **7-9-5** ACulhane(9) (chsd ldrs: pushed along over 4f out: sn wknd)	1¾	8	8/1	19	5
1838[10]	**Dario's Girl (30)** (DMoffatt) **4-8-7**(3) DarrenMoffatt(5) (a bhd)	10	9	50/1	—	—
				(SP 113.3%)		**9 Rn**

2m 29.4 (10.00) CSF £24.70 TOTE £3.00: £1.10 £2.60 £1.50 (£30.60) Trio £42.10 OWNER Mr D. McGonagle (SALTBURN) BRED Miss M. Tucker
WEIGHT FOR AGE 3yo-12lb
2225* Monaco Gold (IRE) is on really good terms with himself and won this particularly well. (2/1)
1757 Miami Moon, trying her longest trip to date, was staying on splendidly and seems to be getting her act together. (12/1)
2145 Philgem keeps running well but he is never quite doing enough when it matters. (9/2)
Craigary was given a most forceful ride and this would seem as good as he is. (20/1)
Dancing Cormorant missed all last season and was carrying bags of condition here but ran really well, only to blow up in the last furlong and a half. (50/1)
1731 Aunt Daphne was disappointing this time and probably found the ground too testing. (6/1: op 7/2)
2226* Trying Times (IRE), who has been tubed this season, was stepping up in trip here and ran disappointingly. (4/1)
Cittern (8/1: op 5/1)

2387 CAMPSIE FELL H'CAP (0-70) (3-Y.O) (Class E)
4-45 (4-45) **1m 4f 17y** £2,791.25 (£845.00: £412.50: £196.25) Stalls: High GOING: 0.08 sec per fur (G)

				SP	RR	SF
1863[2]	**Wildmoor (55)** (JDBethell) **3-8-7** TWilliams(3) (lw: bhd: hdwy 4f out: styd on to ld cl home)	—	1	3/1[2]	62	22
2224[3]	**Belle Bijou (58)** (MJohnston) **3-8-7**(3) KMChin(2) (chsd ldrs: led over 2f out: rdn & wandered over 1f out: hdd & nt qckn towards fin)	¾	2	12/1	64	24
1617*	**Quezon City (57)** (MJCamacho) **3-8-9** LCharnock(5) (lw: cl up: led wl over 4f out tl over 2f out: sn outpcd)	5	3	11/10[1]	56	16
1863[5]	**Maremma (44)** (DonEnricoIncisa) **3-7-10** KimTinkler(6) (bhd: hdwy over 4f out: styd on: nvr rchd ldrs)	½	4	16/1	43	3
2046[10]	**Surtsey (69)** (MJohnston) **3-9-7** JWeaver(4) (lw: bhd: c wd & effrt st: rdn & no rspnse: t.o)	dist	5	100/30[3]	—	—
1939[11]	**Shotley Princess (45)** (NBycroft) **3-7-11**ow1 NKennedy(1) (led tl hdd wl over 4f out: sn wknd: t.o)	5	6	100/1	—	—
				(SP 110.3%)		**6 Rn**

2m 43.7 (11.70) CSF £30.95 TOTE £3.70: £1.30 £2.50 (£8.70) OWNER Stonehouse Racing (MIDDLEHAM) BRED C. J. Hill
LONG HANDICAP Maremma 7-2 Shotley Princess 6-10
1863 Wildmoor, who stays well, got the fast pace required and saw it out most determinedly. (3/1)
2224 Belle Bijou looked to have won this when kicking on halfway up the straight but, as she tired, she started to wander about and was just out-stayed. (12/1: 8/1-14/1)
1617* Quezon City looked extremely fit but these testing conditions found him out in the last couple of furlongs. (11/10: op evens)
1863 Maremma certainly does not do anything quickly but she was staying on at the end. (16/1)
732 Surtsey looked really well but showed no enthusiasm at all in the race. (100/30)

T/Plpt: £55.90 (326.67 Tckts). T/Qdpt: £18.50 (68.73 Tckts) AA

2215-EPSOM (L-H) (Soft, Good to soft patches)
Wednesday July 2nd
WEATHER: overcast & cold, rain from race 4 WIND: fresh across

2388 E.B.F. TATTENHAM MAIDEN STKS (2-Y.O) (Class D)
6-20 (6-21) **6f** £3,273.75 (£990.00: £482.50: £228.75) Stalls: High GOING: 0.13 sec per fur (G)

				SP	RR	SF
	Toblersong (RAkehurst) **2-9-0** TQuinn(3) (w'like: scope: a.p: chsd ldr over 2f out: rdn over 1f out: led ins fnl f: r.o wl)	—	1	4/1[3]	77+	45
	High Sheriff (IRE) (WJHaggas) **2-9-0** SSanders(4) (unf: scope: chsd ldr: led over 2f out tl ins fnl f: r.o)	½	2	11/1	76+	44
2181[18]	**American Cousin** (BJMeehan) **2-9-0** MTebbutt(7) (lw: rdn over 3f out: hdwy over 1f out: unable qckn)	10	3	25/1	49	17
2320[5]	**Iron Mountain (IRE)** (NACallaghan) **2-9-0** WRyan(5) (lw: wl bhd 4f: stdy hdwy over 1f out: nvr nrr)	½	4	10/1	48	16
2320[11]	**Mystery Guest (IRE)** (SirMarkPrescott) **2-9-0** GDuffield(10) (lw: shkn up over 2f out: nvr nr to chal)	s.h	5	8/1	48	16
1932[6]	**Balanita (IRE)** (BPalling) **2-9-0** TSprake(2) (lw: led over 3f)	1¼	6	7/2[2]	44	12
2181[20]	**Argumentative** (SDow) **2-9-0** RPerham(1) (stdd s: wl bhd 4f: stdy hdwy over 1f out: nt clr run ins fnl f: nvr nrr)	1	7	25/1	42	10
	Lucky Double (RHannon) **2-9-0** PatEddery(9) (cmpt: prom over 2f)	2	8	2/1[1]	36	4
472[8]	**Miss Skye (IRE)** (TJNaughton) **2-8-9** PaulEddery(8) (b.hind: bit bkwd: prom over 4f)	½	9	33/1	30	—
2163[4]	**Jonathan's Girl** (JJBridger) **2-8-6**(3) MartinDwyer(6) (a bhd)	7	10	33/1	11	—
				(SP 117.7%)		**10 Rn**

1m 12.36 (4.36) CSF £40.98 TOTE £6.10: £1.80 £2.10 £3.30 (£68.80) Trio £169.60 OWNER The Fairy Story Partnership (EPSOM) BRED Deepwood Farm Stud

Toblersong, a plain, strongly-made colt who is a half-brother to several winners, made a very pleasing debut. Moving into second place over a quarter of a mile from home, he was woken up below the distance and gained the upper hand inside the final furlong. (4/1: 3/1-9/2)
High Sheriff (IRE), who was entered for the Derby, has subsequently been gelded. Although needing time to develop, he made a very pleasing debut and moved to the front over a quarter of a mile from home. Although the winner proved too good for him inside the final furlong, he still finished well clear of the remainder. He should soon go one better. (11/1: 7/1-12/1)
American Cousin failed to come down Tattenham Hill. Nevertheless, he picked up ground below the distance to take third place but had no hope of reeling in the front two. (25/1)
2320 Iron Mountain (IRE) was making a quick reappearance and was given a quiet ride. Well behind the leaders, his jockey was not hard on him but the combination stayed on in eyecatching style to finish fourth. A good-looking individual with plenty of substance, he is now qualified for Nurseries and looks one to keep an eye on. (10/1)
Mystery Guest (IRE), making a quick reappearance, was shaken up over a quarter of a mile from home but never really looked like getting involved. A good-looking individual, his future probably lies in Nurseries. (8/1: 6/1-10/1)
1932 Balanita (IRE) took the field along but he failed to handle Tattenham Corner and was soon headed and in trouble. (7/2)
Argumentative, who finished last on his debut and twentieth on his second start, raced up with the pace on those occasions but this time he was steadied at the back of the field. His jockey was certainly not hard on him but the combination gradually crept closer from below the distance until meeting traffic problems inside the final furlong. He is now qualified for Nurseries and it would be no surprise to see improvement from him. (25/1)

2389 GUARDIAN PROPERTIES MAIDEN STKS (3-Y.O F) (Class D)
6-50 (6-53) **1m 2f 18y** £3,468.75 (£1,050.00: £512.50: £243.75) Stalls: Low GOING: 0.13 sec per fur (G)

				SP	RR	SF
	Spartan Girl (IRE) (LordHuntingdon) **3-8-11** DHarrison(1) (swtg: a.p: chsd ldr over 3f out: led over 2f out: hrd rdn over 1f out: r.o wl)	—	**1**	7/1	86	38
978^{3}	**Manuetti (IRE)** (EALDunlop) **3-8-11** RHughes(2) (led over 7f: unable qckn)	2	**2**	8/1	83	35
2126^{4}	**Dovedon Star** (PAKelleway) **3-8-6**(5) RMullen(7) (lw: hdwy over 3f out: rdn over 2f out: one pce)	2½	**3**	$15/8^{1}$	79	31
1591^{4}	**Elbaaha (83)** (MAJarvis) **3-8-11** WRyan(3) (hld up: rdn over 3f out: one pce)	hd	**4**	$5/1^{2}$	79	31
2046^{6}	**Alpina (USA)** (JHMGosden) **3-8-11** GHind(4) (prom over 6f)	16	**5**	16/1	53	5
1322^{8}	**Dazla's Double** (RRowe) **3-8-11** TQuinn(6) (s.s: hdwy over 3f out: wknd over 2f out)	4	**6**	50/1	47	—
1322^{2}	**Rocky Dance (FR)** (APJarvis) **3-8-11** DHolland(8) (lw: a bhd)	1¼	**7**	6/1	45	—
1646^{W}	**Hope Chest** (DRLoder) **3-8-11** PatEddery(5) (lw: chsd ldr over 6f)	nk	**8**	$11/2^{3}$	45	—

(SP 112.6%) **8 Rn**

2m 12.48 (8.48) CSF £53.69 TOTE £8.40: £1.90 £2.40 £1.50 (£37.20) OWNER Lord Weinstock (WEST ILSLEY) BRED Ballymacoll Stud Farm Ltd

Spartan Girl (IRE), a lightly-made filly who does not appear to take much getting fit, looked well beforehand but was rather warm on a cold night. Moving to the front over a quarter of a mile from home, she was given a few reminders to wake her up below the distance but soon disposed of the runner-up for a cosy success. (7/1: 9/2-8/1)
978 Manuetti (IRE), who has been moved from the Saeed bin Suroor stable since her last start, took the field along but she was collared over a quarter of a mile from home and was no match for the winner from below the distance. (8/1)
2126 Dovedon Star began a forward move as the field panned over to the stands' side but she was soon being bustled along and was only fighting for third prize. She will probably do better over further. (15/8)
1591 Elbaaha had an extra furlong and soft ground this time, putting less of an emphasis on acceleration, but that still did not stop her looking very one-paced in the straight. (5/1)
2046 Alpina (USA) looked big and well in the preliminaries. Given considerate handling, she was close up until dropping away rounding Tattenham Corner. She is now qualified for handicaps and looks one to note with interest. (16/1)
1372 Hope Chest (11/2: 4/1-6/1)

2390 NABS H'CAP (0-95) (3-Y.O+) (Class C)
7-20 (7-22) **7f** £5,272.25 (£1,598.00: £781.50: £373.25) Stalls: Low GOING: 0.13 sec per fur (G)

				SP	RR	SF
2326^{3}	**Grey Kingdom (69)** (MBrittain) **6-8-0**(7) DMernagh(1) (a.p: led over 3f out: swtchd stands' side over 2f out: drvn out)	—	**1**	$3/1^{1}$	78	32
1658^{6}	**Chickawicka (IRE) (90)** (BPalling) **6-9-9**(5) DSweeney(6) (hdwy over 2f out: ev ch fnl 2f: r.o wl)	nk	**2**	9/1	98	52
2119*	**Tea Party (USA) (61)** (KOCunningham-Brown) **4-7-10b**(3) MartinDwyer(8) (lw: hdwy over 4f out: c stands' side & lost pl over 3f out: rallied over 1f out: r.o)	1¾	**3**	$5/1^{2}$	65	19
2036^{2}	**Lynton Lad (68)** (CPEBrooks) **5-8-6b** RPerham(10) (a.p: led 5f out tl over 3f out: c stands' side st: rdn over 2f out: one pce)	1	**4**	$8/1^{3}$	70	24
2069^{6}	**Deeply Vale (IRE) (66)** (GLMoore) **6-8-4** SWhitworth(11) (hld up: c stands' side st: rdn over 2f out: wknd over 1f out)	5	**5**	20/1	57	11
2124^{8}	**Pengamon (70)** (HJCollingridge) **5-8-8** JQuinn(4) (nvr nr to chal)	7	**6**	12/1	45	—
2220^{8}	**Papita (IRE) (70)** (SDow) **3-7-9**(5) RFfrench(7) (a bhd)	1	**7**	33/1	42	—
2124^{11}	**Civil Liberty (83)** (GLewis) **4-9-7** PaulEddery(2) (bhd fnl 2f)	1	**8**	25/1	53	7
1737^{17}	**Zaima (IRE) (89)** (JLDunlop) **3-9-5** PatEddery(9) (lw: prom over 5f)	¾	**9**	$3/1^{1}$	57	3
2228^{4}	**Rivers Magic (72)** (JJBridger) **4-8-10** DHarrison(3) (led 2f: wknd over 2f out)	7	**10**	20/1	24	—
2117^{R}	**Rock Falcon (IRE) (85)** (LadyHerries) **4-9-9v**[1] RHughes(5) (ref to r: t.n.p)		**R**	25/1	—	—

(SP 115.6%) **11 Rn**

1m 26.02 (5.72) CSF £25.39 CT £121.01 TOTE £4.20: £1.30 £2.50 £1.90 (£14.70) Trio £14.50 OWNER Mr Mel Brittain (WARTHILL) BRED Northgate Lodge Stud Ltd
WEIGHT FOR AGE 3yo-8lb
OFFICIAL EXPLANATION **Zaima (IRE): failed to handle the track.**
2326 Grey Kingdom made the long journey from the north pay off. Gaining control entering the straight, he was switched over to the stands' side in search of the better ground over a quarter of a mile from home and, responding to pressure, just held off the runner-up who was racing in the centre of the track. (3/1)
1658 Chickawicka (IRE), 8lb higher than when winning this race last year, elected to come down the centre of the course in the straight. Throwing down a determined challenge in the final quarter-mile, he gave his all and only just failed. (9/1: 7/1-11/1)
2119* Tea Party (USA) is in good form at present and was suited by the underfoot conditions. Tracking over to the stands' side in the straight, she soon lost her place but did stay on again from below the distance to take third prize. (5/1)
2036 Lynton Lad, a leading player from the outset, came over to the stands' side in the straight but failed to find another gear. (8/1: 6/1-9/1)
241 Deeply Vale (IRE), having his first run of the season on grass, was another who elected to come over to the stands' side but had shot his bolt below the distance. (20/1)
1154 Pengamon (12/1: op 8/1)

1305 Zaima (IRE) did not look at all happy coming down Tattenham Hill and was off the bridle. Nevertheless, she held on until stopping as if shot below the distance. (3/1)

2391 ALLIED DUNBAR H'CAP (0-85) (3-Y.O+) (Class D)

7-50 (7-55) **1m 4f 10y** £4,182.00 (£1,266.00: £618.00: £294.00) Stalls: Centre GOING: 0.27 sec per fur (G)

			SP	RR	SF
1169^{8}	**Tappeto (70)** (HCandy) **5-9-0** CRutter(1) (hld up: chsd ldr over 2f out: led ins fnl f: rdn out).........—	**1**	10/1	80	48
1877^{3}	**Little Acorn (83)** (SCWilliams) **3-9-0** DaneO'Neill(8) (led: clr 7f out: rdn over 2f out: hdd ins fnl f: r.o).........½	**2**	$4/1^{2}$	92	47
2218^{6}	**Statajack (IRE) (64)** (DRCElsworth) **9-8-8b** TQuinn(2) (b: hdwy 3f out: rdn 2f out: unable qckn).........4	**3**	7/1	68	36
1771^{4}	**Artic Courier (84)** (DJSCosgrove) **6-10-0** RHughes(9) (hld up: rdn 2f out: one pce).........2	**4**	7/1	85	53
2242^{3}	**Wakeel (USA) (75)** (SDow) **5-9-5** SSanders(3) (swtchd lft over 2f out: rdn & hdwy over 1f out: one pce).......s.h	**5**	$6/1^{3}$	76	44
1928^{3}	**Rhapsody In White (IRE) (76)** (MAJarvis) **3-8-2**(5) RMullen(5) (bhd fnl 3f).........8	**6**	9/1	67	22
1592*	**Roisin Clover (69)** (RRowe) **6-8-13** WRyan(4) (b: lw: a bhd).........hd	**7**	7/1	60	28
1868^{5}	**Ikatania (84)** (JLDunlop) **3-9-1** PatEddery(6) (lw: chsd ldr over 9f).........1¾	**8**	$7/2^{1}$	72	27
			(SP 113.1%)	**8 Rn**	

2m 45.43 (10.93) CSF £44.24 CT £273.21 TOTE £17.20: £3.30 £1.30 £1.60 (£34.20) Trio £82.30 OWNER Mrs David Blackburn (WANTAGE) BRED Mrs D. Blackburn

WEIGHT FOR AGE 3yo-13lb

1022 Tappeto, who flopped last time out, bounced back to form here. Joining the leader in the final quarter-mile, he got on top inside the final furlong. (10/1)

1877 Little Acorn was given a lovely ride by O'Neill. Setting an extremely moderate early pace, the combination forged clear in the last mile and had a very useful advantage running down Tattenham Hill. Bustled along in the straight, he was joined by the winner in the final quarter-mile and, although flashing his tail, only gave best inside the final furlong. (4/1)

1809 Statajack (IRE) is a tricky customer and, although taking closer order early in the straight, failed to contain the front two in the final quarter-mile. (7/1: 5/1-8/1)

1771 Artic Courier, 4lb higher than when winning this race last year, chased the leaders but never looked like quickening up in the straight. He has done all his winning on a fast surface. (7/1: 5/1-8/1)

2242 Wakeel (USA) acts in the mud but, after picking up ground on the outside of the field below the distance, could then only go up and down in the same place. Life is proving very hard for him and he has yet to win a handicap. (6/1)

1928 Rhapsody In White (IRE) was taking a step up in distance but was in trouble early in the straight. The soft ground may well have been to blame. (9/1)

1592* Roisin Clover hated the ground and was always at the back. She loves to hear her feet rattle. (7/1)

2392 ALAN COWING RETIREMENT CLAIMING STKS (3-Y.O) (Class E)

8-20 (8-23) **1m 114y** £2,791.25 (£845.00: £412.50: £196.25) Stalls: Low GOING: 0.27 sec per fur (G)

			SP	RR	SF
1807^{2}	**Impala (53)** (WGMTurner) **3-8-11**(5) DSweeney(9) (lw: a.p: led over 1f out: r.o wl).........—	**1**	$11/2^{3}$	70	42
2309^{4}	**Don Sebastian (73)** (WJHaggas) **3-9-3b¹** CRutter(3) (hdwy over 2f out: hrd rdn: chsd wnr over 1f out: r.o one pce).........2	**2**	$6/4^{1}$	67	39
1503^{7}	**Bobbitt (50)** (WJarvis) **3-8-4** DaneO'Neill(5) (hdwy over 3f out: hrd rdn over 2f out: one pce).........1	**3**	16/1	52	24
2332^{3}	**Miss Barcelona (IRE) (43)** (MJPolglase) **3-7-11**(5) JBramhill(1) (led: rdn over 2f out: hdd over 1f out: sn wknd)5	**4**	6/1	41	13
2125^{7}	**Effervescence (70)** (RHannon) **3-9-2** PatEddery(7) (lw: chsd ldr 7f).........3½	**5**	$5/1^{2}$	48	20
2059^{6}	**Pemberley (IRE)** (WJHaggas) **3-9-2** SSanders(4) (lw: s.s: a bhd).........2	**6**	7/1	45	17
	Moontalk (MJHaynes) **3-7-11**(3) MartinDwyer(6) (leggy: s.s: a bhd).........4	**7**	14/1	21	—
2004^{18}	**Yanavanavano (IRE) (40)** (GLewis) **3-8-11** PaulEddery(2) (prom 4f: t.o whn fell ins fnl f).........	**F**	33/1	—	—
			(SP 114.3%)	**8 Rn**	

1m 50.19 (8.19) CSF £12.89 TOTE £5.60: £1.70 £1.40 £2.20 (£6.00) Trio £18.30 OWNER Mrs C. A. Scott (SHERBORNE) BRED W. G. M. Turner

1807 Impala seemed to relish the underfoot conditions and, gaining control below the distance, soon asserted for a cosy success. (11/2: 4/1-6/1)

2309 Don Sebastian, making a quick reappearance, was best in on the official adjusted ratings. Fitted with blinkers for the first time, he struggled into second place below the distance but failed to find that vital turn of foot to seriously trouble the winner. (6/4)

864 Bobbitt was taking a drop in class and ran better as a result, taking closer order entering the straight before tapped for toe in the final quarter-mile. (16/1)

2332 Miss Barcelona (IRE) took the field along but she was collared below the distance and soon had bellows to mend. To say she is exposed is something of an understatement. (6/1)

2125 Effervescence, whose connections reported last time out that the colt did not like the soft ground, was bizarrely running here considering the advance going for this meeting was soft. It therefore came as absolutely no surprise when he dropped away below the distance. (5/1)

2059 Pemberley (IRE) (7/1: 5/1-8/1)

Moontalk (14/1: 10/1-16/1)

2393 CHANTILLY H'CAP (0-85) (3-Y.O+) (Class D)

8-50 (8-51) **6f** £3,355.00 (£1,015.00: £495.00: £235.00) Stalls: High GOING: 0.27 sec per fur (G)

			SP	RR	SF
2134^{3}	**Plaisir d'Amour (IRE) (80)** (NACallaghan) **3-9-1**(5) RFfrench(1) (outpcd: hdwy over 1f out: str run to ld last stride).........—	**1**	$11/4^{1}$	88	65
2105^{25}	**Bold Effort (FR) (82)** (KOCunningham-Brown) **5-9-11b**(3) MartinDwyer(7) (a.p: edgd lft 2f out: led & edgd lft 1f out: hrd rdn: hdd last stride).........s.h	**2**	6/1	90	73
2179*	**Willow Dale (IRE) (75)** (DRCElsworth) **4-9-7** 6x TQuinn(5) (hdwy 3f out: n.m.r & swtchd rt over 1f out: r.o ins fnl f).........1¾	**3**	$11/4^{1}$	78	61
2232^{6}	**Golden Pound (USA) (81)** (MissGayKelleway) **5-9-13** DaneO'Neill(4) (hdwy 3f out: led 2f out to 1f out: one pce).........1½	**4**	$9/2^{2}$	80	63
2220^{3}	**Justinianus (IRE) (50)** (JJBridger) **5-7-3**(7) PDoe(3) (chsd ldr over 2f: 5th & btn whn hmpd 2f out).........1	**5**	9/1	47	30
2220^{2}	**Marengo (70)** (JAkehurst) **3-8-10** DHolland(6) (led 4f: 3rd & btn whn squeezed out 1f out).........1¾	**6**	$11/2^{3}$	62	39
			(SP 111.2%)	**6 Rn**	

1m 12.25 (4.25) CSF £17.34 TOTE £3.40: £2.00 £3.00 (£17.20) OWNER Mr M Tabor & Mrs John Magnier (NEWMARKET) BRED L. K. and K. McCreery

LONG HANDICAP Justinianus (IRE) 7-6

WEIGHT FOR AGE 3yo-6lb

2134 Plaisir d'Amour (IRE) nearly got caught out by this very fast six furlongs but luckily for her the soft ground made it a bit more of a test. In last place and going nowhere in the straight, she began to find her feet from below the distance and came with a real rattle to get up in the last couple of strides under a fine ride. (11/4: 2/1-3/1)
1578* Bold Effort (FR) is not very consistent but ran a fine race here. Despite drifting left on the camber in the straight, he gained control a furlong out, but although doing nothing wrong was caught in the last couple of strides. (6/1: op 4/1)
2179* Willow Dale (IRE) is holding her form very well indeed. Switched to the outside to get a clear run below the distance, she looked tapped for toe but got her second wind in the closing stages. (11/4)
2232 Golden Pound (USA) moved to the front a quarter of a mile from home but, collared a furlong out, was then left for dead. Both his wins to date have come on fast ground. (9/2)
2220 Justinianus (IRE), in second place early, was already struggling when hampered a quarter of a mile from home. (9/1)
2220 Marengo took the field along but he was collared a quarter of a mile out and was already held when squeezed for room entering the final furlong. (11/2)

T/Plpt: £270.90 (88.96 Tckts). T/Qdpt: £15.90 (118.12 Tckts) AK

2276-FOLKESTONE (R-H) (Soft)
Wednesday July 2nd
WEATHER: unsettled WIND: fresh across

2394 E.B.F. ROMNEY MARSH MAIDEN STKS (2-Y.O F) (Class D)
2-30 (2-31) **6f 189y** £3,694.10 (£1,104.80: £529.40: £241.70) Stalls: Low GOING: 0.18 sec per fur (G)

				SP	RR	SF
2138[4]	**Next Round (IRE)** (MBell) **2-8-11** MFenton(4) (led 1f: remained prom: led over 1f out: r.o)	—	**1**	9/4[2]	75	10
1440[7]	**Flow By** (JLDunlop) **2-8-11** TSprake(9) (lw: hld up: hdwy over 2f out: styd on strly ins fnl f)	1¼	**2**	9/2[3]	72	7
	Fawning (MBlanshard) **2-8-11** JQuinn(5) (leggy: bit bkwd: hld up: hdwy 2f out: rdn over 1f out: r.o)	4	**3**	25/1	63	—
	Campari (IRE) (MAJarvis) **2-8-11** SSanders(8) (unf: bit bkwd: in tch: rdn 2f out: one pce)	½	**4**	12/1	62	—
1440[3]	**Latin Nexus (USA)** (PFICole) **2-8-11** TQuinn(1) (lw: led after 1f: hdd over 1f out: wknd ent fnl f)	2½	**5**	2/1[1]	56	—
	Jazz Singer (RHannon) **2-8-11** DaneO'Neill(6) (neat: bit bkwd: nvr nrr)	nk	**6**	10/1	55	—
	Suellajoy (BSmart) **2-8-11** MTebbutt(2) (w'like: bit bkwd: nvr nrr)	1¼	**7**	25/1	52	—
	Elba Magic (IRE) (HJCollingridge) **2-8-11** VSmith(3) (w'like: bit bkwd: c wd st: nvr on terms)	3	**8**	10/1	45	—
1927[7]	**Siena (GER)** (MRChannon) **2-8-11** CandyMorris(12) (chsd ldrs tl wknd over 2f out)	3	**9**	33/1	38	—
1933[12]	**Gay Abandon** (KMcAuliffe) **2-8-11** JFEgan(11) (bhd fnl 3f)	4	**10**	25/1	29	—
1664[6]	**After Dawn (IRE)** (MrsPNDutfield) **2-8-11** SWhitworth(7) (a bhd)	3	**11**	25/1	22	—
	Little Emily (CEBrittain) **2-8-11** WJO'Connor(10) (leggy: bit bkwd: prom: rdn over 3f out: wknd over 2f out)	5	**12**	10/1	10	—

(SP 135.6%) **12 Rn**

1m 29.7 (8.30) CSF £13.07 TOTE £3.20: £1.30 £2.90 £13.30 (£11.50) Trio £260.60; £88.12 to Haydock 3/7/97 OWNER Deln Ltd (NEWMARKET) BRED Deln Ltd
2138 Next Round (IRE) had run promisingly on her debut at Ascot and fulfilled that promise here. Never far away, she led below the distance and saw it out well. (9/4)
1440 Flow By looked well beforehand. She started to make headway early in the straight and stayed on strongly inside the final furlong. She is improving. (9/2: 4/1-7/1)
Fawning put up a promising performance here, making steady headway in the final two furlongs. She can be made fitter and should pick up a small race. (25/1)
Campari (IRE) ran quite promisingly here considering the race was needed. (12/1: 8/1-14/1)
1440 Latin Nexus (USA) was a bit disappointing. She cut out a lot of the running but, headed below the distance, was soon beaten. (2/1: 7/4-11/4)
Jazz Singer is an unprepossessing-looking filly but nonetheless showed promise for the future here. (10/1: op 4/1)
Elba Magic (IRE) (10/1: 20/1-8/1)
Little Emily (10/1: 6/1-12/1)

2395 WOODCHURCH H'CAP (0-65) (3-Y.O+) (Class F)
3-00 (3-03) **6f 189y** £2,277.00 (£627.00: £297.00) Stalls: Low GOING: 0.18 sec per fur (G)

				SP	RR	SF
2069[4]	**Itsinthepost (48)** (VSoane) **4-8-11** CRutter(13) (hld up mid div: pushed along 3f out: hdwy 2f out: led ins fnl f: r.o)	—	**1**	16/1	63	27
2004[10]	**Sea Spouse (34)** (MBlanshard) **6-7-11** NAdams(16) (lw: led: rdn & hung lft over 1f out: edgd rt ins fnl f: hdd & unable qckn)	2	**2**	10/1	44	8
2019*	**Castel Rosselo (61)** (ICampbell) **7-9-10** RPrice(6) (lw: chsd ldrs: rdn over 1f out: one pce)	2	**3**	5/2[1]	67	31
1958[3]	**With A Will (61)** (HCandy) **3-8-9**(7) NicolaWright(4) (lw: chsd ldrs: rdn over 1f out: kpt on ins fnl f)	nk	**4**	10/1	66	22
284[11]	**Prince Zizim (35)** (CADwyer) **4-7-12** JQuinn(15) (hld up towards rr: hdwy 2f out: styng on one pce whn n.m.r wl ins fnl f)	½	**5**	33/1	39	3
1849[8]	**Havago (63)** (RHannon) **3-9-4** DaneO'Neill(8) (chsd ldr: rdn over 1f out: wknd ins fnl f)	s.h	**6**	8/1	67	23
601[8]	**River Seine (FR) (45)** (SGKnight) **5-8-8** SSanders(3) (mid div: rdn over 2f out: kpt on one pce ins fnl f)	nk	**7**	25/1	48	12
1483[12]	**Shermood (33)** (KTIvory) **4-7-5**(5) RFfrench(2) (b.hind: dwlt: hld up in rr: hdwy over 1f out: nvr nrr)	nk	**8**	25/1	35	—
2179[8]	**Blushing Grenadier (IRE) (40)** (MJFetherston-Godley) **5-8-0**(3) MartinDwyer(5) (hdwy over 3f out: rdn over 2f out: grad wknd)	1½	**9**	9/1	39	3
	Court Minstrel (51) (RAkehurst) **8-9-0** TQuinn(12) (a bhd)	1¾	**10**	13/2[3]	46	10
1987[5]	**Ladybower (IRE) (33)** (JRPoulton) **5-7-10** NVarley(14) (chsd ldrs tl wknd 2f out)	5	**11**	20/1	16	—
1958[13]	**Indian Blaze (59)** (PWHarris) **3-9-0b**[1] DHolland(10) (in tch: rdn over 2f out: sn wknd)	1½	**12**	12/1	39	—
2036[12]	**Mybotye (57)** (RBastiman) **4-9-1b**[1](5) HBastiman(9) (keen hold: hdwy 5f out: hrd rdn 2f out: sn wknd)	7	**13**	9/2[2]	20	—
2281[8]	**Barbrallen (34)** (MrsLCJewell) **5-7-4**(7)ow1 DarrenWilliams(1) (a bhd)	5	**14**	33/1	—	—
1830[P]	**Dawalib (USA) (55)** (DHaydnJones) **7-9-4** AClark(11) (lw: bhd fnl 4f)	12	**15**	12/1	—	—
1804[7]	**Caribbee Beach (IRE) (44)** (GGMargarson) **3-7-10**(3)ow3 MHenry(7) (a bhd)	11	**16**	50/1	—	—

(SP 140.9%) **16 Rn**

1m 28.2 (6.80) CSF £164.77 CT £527.08 TOTE £22.40: £3.00 £2.10 £1.30 £3.70 (£59.80) Trio £115.60 OWNER First Class Four Seasons (ASTON ROWANT) BRED Roldvale Ltd
LONG HANDICAP Ladybower (IRE) 7-5 Shermood 7-2 Barbrallen 7-7 Caribbee Beach (IRE) 7-9
WEIGHT FOR AGE 3yo-8lb

2069 Itsinthepost was held up in the middle of the field. She made good headway early in the straight and stayed on strongly to lead inside the last and win going away. (16/1)
376 Sea Spouse made a bold bid to make all but did not help his cause by hanging to his left approaching the last. (10/1: op 6/1)
2019* Castel Rosselo had every chance but found his weight beating him in the final furlong or so. (5/2)
1958 With A Will was never far away and kept on for pressure in the final furlong. (10/1)
Prince Zizim was unlucky not to be closer. He was making headway on the inside in the final furlong when virtually running into the back of the third. But for this he would have been fighting out the minor places. (33/1)
Court Minstrel (13/2: 11/4-7/1)
571 Mybotye (9/2: op 8/1)

2396 HAMSTREET (S) STKS (2-Y.O) (Class G)
3-30 (3-30) **5f** £1,984.50 (£547.00: £259.50) Stalls: Low GOING: 0.18 sec per fur (G)

			SP	RR	SF
2003[14]	**Eastwell Minstrel** (RCurtis) **2-8-11** JLowe(1) (dwlt: bdly outpcd & wl bhd: hdwy over 1f out: rdn & hung rt ins fnl f: str run to ld cl home) ....—	**1**	8/1[3]	65	—
2367[8]	**Verdant Express** (WGMTurner) **2-8-1**(5) DSweeney(4) (led: clr over 1f out: rdn & edgd rt ins fnl f: hdd cl home) ....½	**2**	3/1[2]	58	—
2003[10]	**Bradbury Falls (IRE)** (DJSCosgrove) **2-8-6** JQuinn(2) (chsd ldr to ½-wy: rdn 2f out: one pce) ....¾	**3**	3/1[2]	56	—
2163[2]	**Jack-N-Jilly (IRE)** (JSMoore) **2-8-3**(3) MHenry(3) (chsd ldr ½-wy to 1f out: wknd ins fnl f) 3	**4**	11/10[1]	46	—
			(SP 108.7%)		**4 Rn**

65.8 secs (8.20) CSF £26.89 TOTE £7.50: (£12.80) OWNER Eastwell Manor Racing (LAMBOURN) BRED Letts Green Farm Ltd
No bid
Eastwell Minstrel ran an extraordinary race to win this. He looked thoroughly reluctant for three-fifths of the journey but, picking up his bit approaching the final furlong, produced a strong challenge inside the last to get up close home. (8/1)
Verdant Express looked sure to win when clear over one furlong out but her stride shortened inside the last and she was collared late on. (3/1: op 7/4)
Bradbury Falls (IRE) was never that far away but came under pressure two furlongs out and only had the one pace to give. (3/1: op 6/1)
2163 Jack-N-Jilly (IRE) was very disappointing, being hard ridden fully two furlongs from home, and had very little more to offer. (11/10: op 1/2)

2397 LEAS H'CAP (0-70) (3-Y.O) (Class E)
4-00 (4-01) **1m 7f 92y** £3,122.25 (£933.00: £446.50: £203.25) Stalls: Low GOING: 0.18 sec per fur (G)

			SP	RR	SF
1986[5]	**Zafarelli (54)** (JRJenkins) **3-8-5** SSanders(12) (hld up: hdwy 6f out: chsd ldr 3f out: led gng wl over 1f out: rdn out ins fnl f) ....—	**1**	10/1	63	33
1465[7]	**Nick of Time (60)** (JLDunlop) **3-8-11** TQuinn(13) (hld up in tch: rdn over 2f out: styd on to chse wnr ins fnl f: r.o) 2	**2**	7/1	67	37
1623[7]	**Cadbury Castle (45)** (MBlanshard) **3-7-10** JQuinn(11) (a.p: led 6f out: hdd over 1f out: one pce) 3½	**3**	20/1	48	18
1938[12]	**Motcombs Club (48)** (NACallaghan) **3-7-8**(5) RFfrench(10) (hld up mid div: hdwy over 2f out: sn hrd rdn: styd on ins fnl f) 4	**4**	6/1[3]	47	17
2068[7]	**Alagna (50)** (SCWilliams) **3-7-8**(7) DarrenWilliams(7) (hld up: hdwy ½-wy: wknd 2f out) 15	**5**	10/1	34	4
1387[3]	**Bisquet-de-Bouche (50)** (RDickin) **3-8-1** CRutter(5) (hld up in tch: rdn over 3f out: wknd over 2f out) 8	**6**	11/2[2]	25	—
2068[5]	**Sipowitz (46)** (CACyzer) **3-7-6**(5)ow1 RMullen(1) (a in rr: lost tch 6f out) 1	**7**	6/1[3]	20	—
2279[9]	**Hippios (49)** (SDow) **3-7-7b**[1](7)ow4 DSalt(4) (hdwy 6f out: wknd over 2f out) ....½	**8**	33/1	23	—
1808[2]	**Nile Valley (IRE) (68)** (PWChapple-Hyam) **3-9-5** DHarrison(8) (prom: chsd ldr 6f out to 3f out: wknd over 2f out) 5	**9**	4/1[1]	37	7
2225[3]	**Eponine (72)** (MRChannon) **3-9-9** JFEgan(6) (chsd ldrs tl wknd 3f out) 8	**10**	6/1[3]	32	2
1168[14]	**Bint Rosie (47)** (MJFetherston-Godley) **3-7-9**(3) MartinDwyer(2) (sltly hmpd 9f out: a bhd: t.o) 21	**11**	25/1	—	—
1565[6]	**Foxford Lad (45)** (TMJones) **3-7-10b**[1] NAdams(3) (led: hdd 6f out: sn wknd: t.o) 17	**12**	50/1	—	—
1443[10]	**Flying Esprit (48)** (GGMargarson) **3-7-10b**[1](3)ow3 MHenry(9) (a bhd: t.o fnl 7f) ....dist	**13**	50/1	—	—
			(SP 124.4%)		**13 Rn**

3m 31.9 (13.90) CSF £70.72 CT £1,273.65 TOTE £12.00: £3.30 £2.50 £5.40 (£38.10) Trio £256.10 OWNER Mr R. M. Ellis (ROYSTON) BRED Miss K. RAUSING
LONG HANDICAP Sipowitz 7-9 Hippios 7-5 Foxford Lad 6-13 Flying Esprit 6-7
1986 Zafarelli won this in good fashion and has obviously found its niche as a stayer. (10/1: 8/1-12/1)
842 Nick of Time stayed on well in the final two furlongs and is sure to pick up a similar event soon. (7/1)
Cadbury Castle ran her best race for a long time here and in this sort of form can pick up a small staying event. (20/1)
Motcombs Club was well supported in the ring but was never put in the race with much of a chance. He did stay on in the final two furlongs and obviously stays. (6/1: 12/1-5/1)
2068 Sipowitz (6/1: op 7/2)
1808 Nile Valley (IRE) ran disappointingly here and probably did not like the ground. (4/1)
2225 Eponine (6/1: 4/1-13/2)

2398 SHADDOXHURST H'CAP (0-65) (3-Y.O+) (Class F)
4-30 (4-31) **1m 4f** £2,277.00 (£627.00: £297.00) Stalls: Low GOING: 0.18 sec per fur (G)

			SP	RR	SF
1956[3]	**Stahr (59)** (HCandy) **3-8-12b**[1] CRutter(12) (mde virtually all: rdn over 1f out: r.o wl) ....—	**1**	17/2	71	28
2174[4]	**Bronhallow (32)** (MrsBarbaraWaring) **4-7-12v** FNorton(7) (a.p: chsd wnr 2f out: hrd rdn appr last: one pce) 4	**2**	10/1	39	9
2318*	**Glow Forum (52)** (LMontagueHall) **6-9-4** DHolland(5) (hld up mid div: hdwy over 2f out: hrd rdn over 1f out: r.o) ....nk	**3**	7/2[1]	58	28
1244[16]	**Fourdaned (IRE) (55)** (SDow) **4-9-7** RPerham(13) (hld up: hdwy 2f out: nvr plcd to chal) 1½	**4**	25/1	59	29
2246[2]	**May King Mayhem (33)** (MrsALMKing) **4-7-6**(7)ow3 RWinston(6) (hld up: hdwy over 2f out: sn rdn: kpt on one pce ins fnl f) ....¾	**5**	5/1[2]	36	3
2246[6]	**Asking (30)** (JABennett) **5-7-3**(7) PDoe(11) (prom tl wknd over 1f out) ....½	**6**	33/1	33	3
2279[3]	**Nothing Doing (IRE) (42)** (WJMusson) **8-8-8** JQuinn(3) (lw: hld up: effrt 3f out: sn btn) 14	**7**	9/1	26	—
1999[3]	**Sadler's Blaze (IRE) (54)** (PWHarris) **3-8-7v**[1] AClark(8) (s.s: sn rdn & prom: wknd over 2f out) 3	**8**	12/1	34	—
2174[7]	**Tonka (58)** (PJMakin) **5-9-10** DHarrison(10) (lw: hld up: hdwy ½-wy: wknd 3f out) 4	**9**	7/2[1]	33	3

				SP	RR	SF
2182^{7}	**Certain Magic (54)** (WRMuir) **3-8-4**(3) MartinDwyer(9) (in tch tl wknd over 5f out)	1¼	**10**	16/1	27	—
1859^{4}	**Top Shelf (61)** (CEBrittain) **3-9-0** WJO'Connor(4) (prom tl wknd over 2f out)	½	**11**	$7/1^{3}$	33	—
1964^{4}	**Duncombe Hall (40)** (CACyzer) **4-8-6** GDuffield(1) (a bhd)	3½	**12**	11/1	8	—
1277^{8}	**Happy Medium (IRE) (56)** (GPEnright) **4-9-3**(5) RFfrench(2) (a bhd: t.o fnl 5f)	11	**13**	33/1	9	—

(SP 134.9%) **13 Rn**

2m 43.8 (12.60) CSF £92.14 CT £334.67 TOTE £10.60: £3.50 £3.10 £1.50 (£70.80) Trio £140.60 OWNER Mrs David Blackburn (WANTAGE) BRED Mrs M. J. Blackburn

LONG HANDICAP May King Mayhem 7-7 Asking 7-5

WEIGHT FOR AGE 3yo-13lb

1956 Stahr made nearly all of the running and ran on strongly in the final furlong to score impressively. (17/2: 6/1-9/1)
2174 Bronhallow chased the winner all the way up the straight but could never quite get on terms. (10/1: 8/1-12/1)
2318* Glow Forum tried to take closer order before the home turn but did not pick up very quickly. She was staying on strongly at the end and may need further on turf to be seen at her best. (7/2)
544 Fourdaned (IRE) was never put in the race with a chance but was noted staying on very strongly in the final furlong under anything but a forceful ride. (25/1)
2246 May King Mayhem made his move before the home turn and plugged on up the straight without ever looking like getting on terms. (5/1)
2174 Tonka was disappointing here, dropping away tamely in the final three furlongs. (7/2)
1859 Top Shelf (7/1: 5/1-8/1)

2399 TENTERDEN H'CAP (0-60) (3-Y.O+) (Class F)

5-00 (5-00) **1m 1f 149y** £3,201.00 (£891.00: £429.00) Stalls: Low GOING: 0.18 sec per fur (G)

				SP	RR	SF
2310^{2}	**Jona Holley (43)** (GLMoore) **4-8-11** CRutter(15) (a.p: led over 1f out: r.o)	—	**1**	$100/30^{1}$	56	13
2150^{2}	**What A Fuss (58)** (BHanbury) **4-9-7**(5) RMullen(10) (hld up bhd ldrs: hdwy to chse wnr appr fnl f: sn rdn: one pce)	3	**2**	$11/2^{3}$	66	23
2171^{5}	**Battle Ground (IRE) (48)** (NACallaghan) **3-8-0**(5) RFfrench(14) (chsd ldrs: rdn 2f out: kpt on one pce ins last)	nk	**3**	11/1	56	2
2039^{2}	**Arzani (USA) (55)** (DJSCosgrove) **6-9-9** RHughes(1) (hld up: hdwy on ins over 2f out: swtchd lft & rdn over 1f out: one pce)	2½	**4**	7/1	58	15
2150^{4}	**Zamalek (USA) (43)** (RMFlower) **5-8-11** DaneO'Neill(9) (led: hdd over 1f out: wknd ins last)	½	**5**	8/1	46	3
2200^{3}	**Runic Symbol (37)** (MBlanshard) **6-8-5** JQuinn(12) (mid div: rdn over 2f out: one pce)	1½	**6**	9/1	37	—
1568^{W}	**Doyenne (48)** (GLewis) **3-8-5** NAdams(6) (dwlt: a bhd)	13	**7**	16/1	27	—
2195^{4}	**Flagstaff (USA) (34)** (KRBurke) **4-7-9**(7) RWinston(2) (in tch: rdn over 2f out: sn wknd)	½	**8**	12/1	12	—
1986^{6}	**Mystic Strand (52)** (WGMTurner) **4-9-1**(5) DSweeney(3) (dwlt: a bhd)	3	**9**	33/1	25	—
1985^{7}	**Suleika Dancer (40)** (SGKnight) **4-8-8b¹** MFenton(13) (a bhd)	s.h	**10**	33/1	13	—
1001^{18}	**Baranov (IRE) (57)** (DJGMurraySmith) **4-9-11** DHarrison(4) (a bhd)	5	**11**	25/1	22	—
1991*	**Degree (60)** (SCWilliams) **4-10-0** JFEgan(5) (chsd ldrs tl wknd qckly over 2f out: t.o)	14	**12**	10/1	1	—
*2159**	**Grand Hotel (IRE) (47)** (PWHarris) **3-8-4** FNorton(7) (chsd ldrs tl rdn & wknd 3f out: t.o)	10	**13**	$9/2^{2}$	—	—
574^{19}	**Khabar (50)** (RBastiman) **4-8-13**(5) HBastiman(11) (prom tl wknd qckly over 2f out: t.o)	1¼	**14**	25/1	—	—

(SP 134.8%) **14 Rn**

2m 9.3 (11.60) CSF £21.20 CT £179.61 TOTE £4.30: £2.00 £2.20 £4.00 (£12.20) Trio £76.20 OWNER Joe Bates (Bloodstock) Ltd (BRIGHTON) BRED I. A. Balding

WEIGHT FOR AGE 3yo-11lb

2310 Jona Holley was always well positioned and, after leading below the distance, ran on strongly to score and give his rider a big-priced treble. (100/30)
2150 What A Fuss travelled nicely behind the leaders. He chased the winner below the distance but only had the one pace inside the final furlong. He gave the impression here that he would be worth a try dropping back at a mile. (11/2)
2171 Battle Ground (IRE) was never far away and kept on gamely for pressure in the final two furlongs. (11/1)
2039 Arzani (USA) was held up in the rear. He made a move early in the straight but, once let down, only had the one speed to give. (7/1: 9/2-15/2)
2150 Zamalek (USA) attempted to make all the running but, after being headed over one furlong out, had little extra to offer. (8/1)
2200 Runic Symbol (9/1: 6/1-10/1)
2195 Flagstaff (USA) (12/1: 8/1-14/1)
1991* Degree (10/1: op 6/1)

T/Jkpt: Not wcn; £4,857.94 to Haydock 3/7/97. T/Plpt: £5,771.40 (4.4 Tckts). T/Qdpt: £567.60 (2.66 Tckts) SM

2152-REDCAR (L-H) - Wednesday July 2nd

2400 Abandoned-Waterlogged

2184-YARMOUTH (L-H) (Good to soft)

Wednesday July 2nd

WEATHER: rain first 2 races WIND: fresh half against

2406 E.D.P. BEST FOR SPORT APPRENTICE LIMITED STKS (0-70) (3-Y.O+) (Class G)

6-35 (6-37) **5f 43y** £2,259.00 (£624.00: £297.00) Stalls: Low GOING: 0.11 sec per fur (G)

				SP	RR	SF
2308^{7}	**Songsheet (69)** (MSSaunders) **4-9-2** PPMurphy(6) (lw: racd centre: mde virtually all: clr appr fnl f)	—	**1**	$2/1^{3}$	78	41
1780^{12}	**Sang d'Antibes (FR) (56)** (DJSCosgrove) **3-7-12**(7) SGaillard(4) (hld up in rr: r.o appr fnl f: nvr nrr)	6	**2**	14/1	54	12
2006^{22}	**Shining Cloud (63)** (MBell) **4-8-7**(3) GFaulkner(1) (lw: w ldrs: rdn 2f out: sn outpcd)	1¾	**3**	$13/8^{1}$	48	11
2298^{4}	**Ice Age (60)** (RJRWilliams) **3-8-8** DGriffiths(3) (disp ld 3f: sn rdn & outpcd)	1	**4**	$7/4^{2}$	48	6
1843^{8}	**Bear To Dance (26)** (PHowling) **4-8-10** DO'Donohoe(2) (swtg: chsd ldrs to ½-wy: sn rdn & wknd)	1¼	**5**	20/1	41	4
1385^{12}	***Royal Blackbird (60)*** (JEBanks) **3-8-0**(5) CLowther(5) (Withdrawn not under Starter's orders: unruly & spread plate bef s)		**W**	11/4	—	—

(SP 145.9%) **5 Rn**

65.2 secs (4.20) CSF £24.57 TOTE £3.00: £1.20 £4.40 (£23.80) OWNER Mr M. S. Saunders (WELLS) BRED Lord Matthews

WEIGHT FOR AGE 3yo-5lb

2148 Songsheet had gone off the boil a bit of late, but she bounced back to form here with more use made of her, and handed her rivals a thorough thrashing. (2/1: 2/1-7/2)
584 Sang d'Antibes (FR) found things happening far too quickly on this return to sprinting, but she was beginning to find her stride when it was all too late. (14/1: 14/1-33/1)
942 Shining Cloud does most of his racing over a slightly longer trip and, though she did go with the pace, was the first of the leaders to crack and her measure had been taken below the distance. (13/8: 6/4-5/2)
2298 Ice Age, fighting for the lead until past halfway, had done too much too soon and he was left floundering from below the distance. (7/4: 6/4-7/2)
Royal Blackbird (11/4: 4/1-5/2)

2407 E.D.P. BEST FOR JOBS (S) STKS (3-Y.O) (Class G)
7-05 (7-05) **7f 3y** £2,364.00 (£654.00: £312.00) Stalls: Low GOING: 0.11 sec per fur (G)

			SP	RR	SF
2171³	**Feel A Line (49)** (BJMeehan) **3-9-5b** JReid(4) (hld up: hdwy 2f out: led ins fnl f: r.o wl) ....—	1	7/2¹	66	47
2332⁸	**Distinctive Dream (IRE) (45)** (KTIvory) **3-9-0b** CScally(5) (a.p: led over 4f out tl hdd & no ex ins fnl f)....3	2	9/1	54	35
417³	**Windborn (49)** (CNAllen) **3-8-9** LDettori(3) (bit bkwd: chsd ldrs: effrt & ev ch appr fnl f: sn hrd rdn: one pce) ...3	3	4/1²	42	23
1167³	**Last Chance (63)** (DJSCosgrove) **3-9-0** GCarter(1) (led 3f: hrd drvn over 1f out: sn btn)....2½	4	7/2¹	42	23
1500⁹	**Fontcaudette (IRE) (47)** (JEBanks) **3-8-2**(7) CLowther(6) (lw: prom: drvn along 3f out: grad wknd)....½	5	20/1	36	17
1998⁴	**Fly High** (DMorris) **3-8-9** PBloomfield(9) (chsd ldrs 4f: sn rdn & wknd)....7	6	11/2³	20	1
1441¹⁹	**Sidney The Kidney (56)** (MJRyan) **3-8-6**(3) MBaird(8) (bhd fnl 3f: t.o)....9	7	4/1²	—	—
1483¹⁴	**Jingoist (IRE) (48)** (JLHarris) **3-8-9b** BDoyle(7) (hrd drvn ½-wy: a bhd: t.o)....3	8	20/1	—	—
	Double-E-I-B-A (DJSCosgrove) **3-9-0** JStack(2) (bkwd: a bhd: t.o)....12	9	33/1	—	—
			(SP 122.3%)		**9 Rn**

1m 29.7 (5.50) CSF £33.63 TOTE £4.80: £1.60 £3.50 £1.30 (£23.00) Trio £44.30 OWNER Mr J. S. Gutkin (UPPER LAMBOURN) BRED W. R. Jones
No bid
2171 Feel A Line made smooth headway two furlongs out and, gaining command two hundred yards out, quickly put his stamp on proceedings. (7/2)
2125 Distinctive Dream (IRE), in the firing line from the break, was unable to respond when the winner was let loose and had soon met his match. (9/1)
417 Windborn has had plenty of opportunities but she is still struggling to open her account and she was once again found wanting for a turn of speed when the whips were cracking. (4/1)
1167 Last Chance helped force the pace but he was hard at work inside the distance and, on this ground, failed to last home. (7/2)
Fontcaudette (IRE) ran up to her best on this step down to selling company but she was making hard work of it from some way out and her ability is somewhat limited. (20/1)
1998 Fly High (11/2: 4/1-6/1)

2408 EASTERN DAILY PRESS H'CAP (0-75) (3-Y.O+) (Class D)
7-35 (7-36) **1m 3y** £4,077.50 (£1,220.00: £585.00: £267.50) Stalls: Low GOING: 0.11 sec per fur (G)

			SP	RR	SF
887¹²	**Polish Rhythm (IRE) (60)** (GAHubbard) **4-8-13**(3) DO'Donohoe(4) (bit bkwd: mde all: pushed clr 2f out: styd on wl)....—	1	33/1	69	40
2201²	**Veni Vidi Vici (IRE) (64)** (MJHeaton-Ellis) **4-9-6** SDrowne(2) (lw: hld up: hdwy over 2f out: hrd rdn & unable qckn fnl f)....2½	2	2/1¹	68	39
	Silk St John (74) (MJRyan) **3-9-7** GCarter(3) (bkwd: hld up: hdwy 3f out: hrd rdn appr fnl f: one pce)....½	3	9/2²	77	39
1427⁹	**Kalinini (USA) (75)** (LMCumani) **3-9-8** LDettori(5) (lw: stdd s: hdwy 2f out: shkn up appr fnl f: nt pce to chal)1¼	4	9/2²	76	38
2036⁷	**Karinska (51)** (MCChapman) **7-8-0**(7) SCarson(8) (chsd ldrs: rdn along ½-wy: rallied 2f out: one pce appr fnl f)....2	5	11/1	48	19
2124⁵	**Unshaken (75)** (JRFanshawe) **3-9-8v¹** MHills(1) (chsd ldrs: effrt 3f out: sn rdn: wknd ins fnl f)....2½	6	14/1	67	29
1878⁵	**Mr Rough (55)** (DMorris) **6-8-11** NDay(6) (prom tl rdn & eased wl over 1f out)....7	7	8/1³	33	4
2004¹¹	**Chingachgook (61)** (PWHarris) **3-8-8** KFallon(7) (prom: drvn along over 2f out: sn wknd)....2½	8	11/1	34	—
1837⁵	**Prime Light (72)** (GWragg) **4-9-9**(5) GMilligan(10) (hld up: hdwy 3f out: rdn & wknd fnl 2f: t.o)....9	9	10/1	27	—
990¹⁴	**Doc Ryan's (75)** (MJRyan) **3-9-5**(3) MBaird(9) (lw: chsd ldrs over 5f: sn lost tch: t.o)....1	10	10/1	28	—
			(SP 125.3%)		**10 Rn**

1m 42.6 (6.60) CSF £96.79 CT £336.03 TOTE £59.80: £7.90 £1.30 £1.20 (£128.00) Trio £330.00; £102.28 to 4/7/97 OWNER Mr G. A. Hubbard (WOODBRIDGE) BRED M. Maguire
WEIGHT FOR AGE 3yo-9lb
Polish Rhythm (IRE) attacked from the front on this step down to a mile and, quickening the tempo to gain a valuable cushion entering the final quarter-mile, stayed on far too strongly for the favourite. (33/1)
2201 Veni Vidi Vici (IRE) did pose a serious threat when delivering his challenge passing the furlong marker but the winner was not done with and she found more to repel his bid. (2/1)
Silk St John, tackling a slightly longer trip on this seasonal debut, ran a race full of promise and, with this run to put an edge on him, should be able to find an opening. (9/2)
533 Kalinini (USA) performed at this trip in his first season and restrained in the rear, looked to be given too much to do. In truth, he was only finding his stride inside the distance and, on such a flat track, he does seem to need a stiffer test. (9/2)
Karinska, off the bridle at halfway, renewed her effort in the latter stages but could not muster the pace to get serious. (11/1)
2124 Unshaken acts on this ground and was in hot pursuit of the leaders all the way but lack of stamina appeared to be his problem once inside the final furlong. (14/1)
1633 Chingachgook (11/1: 7/1-12/1)
1837 Prime Light (10/1: 8/1-12/1)

2409 E.D.P. BIG NEWS MAIDEN STKS (2-Y.O) (Class D)
8-05 (8-06) **6f 3y** £3,743.15 (£1,119.20: £536.10: £244.55) Stalls: Low GOING: 0.11 sec per fur (G)

			SP	RR	SF
	Greenlander (CEBrittain) **2-9-0** LDettori(2) (neat: cmpt: bit bkwd: hld up: hdwy over 2f out: led ent fnl f: sn clr)....—	1	100/30²	84+	8

	Horse	Dist	Pos	SP	RR	SF
	Althib (IRE) (MRStoute) **2-9-0** RHills(6) (str: scope: bit bkwd: led tl hdd appr fnl f: sn outpcd)	3	2	5/6[1]	76	—
	Wuxi Venture (SPCWoods) **2-9-0** DBiggs(3) (cmpt: bkwd: s.s: hdwy 2f out: kpt on ins fnl f)	5	3	9/2[3]	63	—
	Teepee (IRE) (WJarvis) **2-8-9** JReid(1) (lengthy: unf: bit bkwd: s.i.s: plld hrd: sn prom: wknd wl ins fnl f)	½	4	7/1	56	—
	Fen Warrior (WJHaggas) **2-9-0** KFallon(4) (leggy: unf: racd keenly: prom tl hrd drvn & wknd wl over 1f out)	3½	5	14/1	52	—
2147[6]	**Marahill Lad** (PHowling) **2-9-0** SDrowne(5) (hld up: hrd drvn over 2f out: no imp)	2	6	25/1	47	—

(SP 118.8%) **6 Rn**

1m 18.1 (7.20) CSF £6.39 TOTE £4.50: £1.90 £1.10 (£2.30) OWNER Sheikh Marwan Al Maktoum (NEWMARKET) BRED Sheikh Marwan al Maktoum

Greenlander, whose dam was twice a winner at two miles in a limited number of runs, looked far from the finished article in the paddock but he let his class do the talking once in action and he does look a very promising recruit. (100/30)

Althib (IRE), a strongly-made colt who will strip much fitter for the run, set out to make all but, once the winner was sent about his work, was swiftly put in his place. A sounder surface could also be to his advantage. (5/6: 4/5-5/4)

Wuxi Venture, a compact colt who is a poor mover in his slower paces, did well to make the frame after losing ground at the start. He was beaten quite some way and not too much can be read into this debut. (9/2: 5/2-9/2)

Teepee (IRE) has still got a bit of strengthening up to do and she will be all the better for the run. She was a bit too keen for her own good and had run herself into the ground before reaching the last furlong. (7/1: 5/1-8/1)

Fen Warrior, who has been gelded, raced keenly and pressed the leader until tying up below the distance. (14/1)

2410 E.D.P. WHAT'S ON MAIDEN STKS (3-Y.O+) (Class D)

8-35 (8-38) **1m 3f 101y** £3,932.25 (£1,176.00: £563.50: £257.25) Stalls: Low GOING: 0.11 sec per fur (G)

	Horse	Dist	Pos	SP	RR	SF
1625[2]	**Purist (89)** (MRStoute) **3-8-12** JReid(3) (lw: sn led: clr 2f out: r.o wl)	—	1	6/4[1]	70	40
1846[3]	**Liffre (IRE)** (JHMGosden) **3-8-7** LDettori(4) (a.p: effrt on ins 2f out: swtchd rt appr fnl f: kpt on: no ch w wnr)	2½	2	5/1[3]	62	32
2008[11]	**Capsoff (IRE)** (GAHubbard) **4-9-5** PBloomfield(7) (lw: chsd ldrs: hrd drvn & lost pl 3f out: styd on wl ins fnl f)	1¼	3	50/1	60	42
1846[5]	**Aboo Hom** (ACStewart) **3-8-12** GCarter(10) (lw: hld up in rr: hdwy & swtchd rt over 1f out: fin wl)	s.h	4	20/1	65	35
2046[3]	**Kayfiyah (IRE) (80)** (DMorley) **3-8-7** RHills(8) (hld up: plld hrd: hdwy over 3f out: chsd wnr 2f out tl 1f out: wknd ins fnl f)	1¾	5	7/1	57	27
	Bina Gardens (HRACecil) **3-8-7** KFallon(9) (w'like: leggy: bit bkwd: a chsng ldrs: rdn over 2f out: wknd ins fnl f)	1¾	6	7/4[2]	55	25
1434[6]	**Yak Alfaraj** (MRStoute) **3-8-12** KBradshaw(2) (lw: hld up: pushed along 3f out: no imp)	1	7	33/1	58	28
2188[3]	**Divinity** (CEBrittain) **3-8-7** BDoyle(6) (swtg: prom over 8f)	8	8	20/1	42	12
2172[9]	**Crompton Lights** (DJSCosgrove) **3-8-5**(7) SGaillard(1) (bit bkwd: a wl bhd: t.o)	5	9	66/1	40	10
	Crystal Hills (IRE) (JHMGosden) **3-8-12** AGarth(12) (bkwd: hld up in rr: drvn along over 4f out: no imp: t.o)	3½	10	25/1	35	5
1809[8]	**Stockbrook** (KRBurke) **4-9-10** SDrowne(11) (bkwd: bhd: rdn 4f out: t.o)	14	11	66/1	16	—

(SP 126.8%) **11 Rn**

2m 31.0 (9.20) CSF £9.05 TOTE £2.70: £1.30 £1.90 £4.90 (£6.20) Trio £352.50; £104.27 to 4/7/97 OWNER Mr R. Barnett (NEWMARKET) BRED W. and R. Barnett Ltd

WEIGHT FOR AGE 3yo-12lb

1625 Purist had the easier ground that he requires and, making sure there was going to be no hanging about, was always calling the tune and broke his duck readily. He should go on to better things. (6/4)

1846 Liffre (IRE), never far away, was going nowhere when she attempted to make a move up the inside rail but she did stay on well once switched to the outside approaching the final furlong and she is gaining experience all the time. (5/1)

Capsoff (IRE), inclined to run her race in snatches, stayed on really well inside the final furlong and stamina could be her strong suit. (50/1)

1846 Aboo Hom, a fine-looking son of an Italian Oaks winner, still learning the ropes, was given plenty to do. Making good progress from off the pace inside the last quarter-mile, he finished strongly and could now be finding his way. (20/1)

2046 Kayfiyah (IRE) looked set to take the measure of the winner when delivering her challenge approaching the final furlong but she was being matched stride for stride and was run out of the prizes nearing the line. She is continuing to progress and her turn will come. (7/1)

Bina Gardens, bred to compete at the highest level, is not a lot to look at in this early stage of her career but she would have learned much from this debut and should benefit considerably when she is racing on a more sounder surface. (7/4)

2411 E.D.P. BEST FOR CLASSIFIEDS H'CAP (0-75) (3-Y.O+) (Class D)

9-05 (9-05) **1m 6f 17y** £4,542.00 (£1,356.00: £648.00: £294.00) GOING: 0.11 sec per fur (G)

	Horse	Dist	Pos	SP	RR	SF
2316[3]	**Compass Pointer (50)** (JMPEustace) **4-8-4** JTate(9) (hld up: in tch: effrt over 2f out: styd on u.p to ld wl ins fnl f)	—	1	5/1[2]	60	17
2230[3]	**Spy Knoll (75)** (MRStoute) **3-9-0** JReid(7) (lw: a.p: led over 4f out: hrd rdn: ct cl home)	hd	2	11/4[1]	85	27
1252[7]	**Children's Choice (IRE) (48)** (WJMusson) **6-8-2** AMcGlone(10) (hld up in rr: hdwy over 2f out: nt clr run ent fnl f: r.o wl towards fin)	½	3	20/1	57	14
1693*	**Charnwood Jack (USA) (65)** (ICampbell) **4-9-5** RPrice(1) (trckd ldrs: effrt 3f out: ev ch over 1f out: rdn & no ex)	1	4	9/1	73	30
1795[8]	**Contrarie (42)** (MJRyan) **4-7-7**(3) MBaird(8) (hld up: hdwy 8f out: rdn & wknd appr fnl f)	5	5	11/2[3]	45	2
2189[2]	**French Mist (69)** (SDow) **3-8-8** BDoyle(5) (lw: hld up: hdwy 3f out: rdn & wknd ins fnl f)	1	6	5/1[2]	70	12
2175[2]	**Swan Hunter (68)** (DJSCosgrove) **4-9-8** GCarter(6) (lw: hld up: effrt & rdn 3f out: nt rch ldrs)	3	7	7/1	66	23
2064[3]	**Supreme Sound (68)** (PWHarris) **3-8-7** KFallon(2) (lw: led 10f: rdn & wknd 2f out: t.o)	11	8	10/1	53	—
2174[6]	**African Sun (IRE) (47)** (MCChapman) **4-7-8**(7)ow5 SCarson(4) (a bhd: t.o)	7	9	33/1	25	—
1841[6]	**Chatham Island (70)** (CEBrittain) **9-9-10** LDettori(11) (hld up: a bhd: t.o)	3	10	10/1	44	1
	Bellroi (IRE) (48) (MHTompkins) **6-8-2** DBiggs(3) (bkwd: chsd ldrs: rdn over 3f out: sn wknd: t.o)	9	11	25/1	12	—

(SP 127.6%) **11 Rn**

3m 12.5 (14.50) CSF £18.65 CT £246.62 TOTE £5.40: £2.50 £1.10 £3.50 (£13.40) Trio £49.80 OWNER Park Lane Racing (NEWMARKET) BRED The Hon. Miss Pearl Lawson Johnston

LONG HANDICAP African Sun (IRE) 7-8 Contrarie 7-6

WEIGHT FOR AGE 3yo-15lb

2316 Compass Pointer was the business on this rain-softened ground and, ridden with restraint, timed his effort to perfection. (5/1)

2230 Spy Knoll, a good-looking colt, kicked for home form the turn into the straight and always seemed to have the edge but the concession of 10lb turned the tables against him in the dying strides. Fortune will favour him before long. (11/4)

Children's Choice (IRE) may well have been an unlucky loser for she had to search for an opening approaching the final furlong and when it did appear the race was all but over. Her turn is near at hand. (20/1)

1693* Charnwood Jack (USA) opened his account over course and distance last month but he was stepping up in grade this time and his determined late effort just failed to materialise. (9/1)
1232 Contrarie took closer order before halfway and was on the heels of the leaders from the entrance to the straight but her effort petered out below the distance. (11/2)
2189 French Mist did not quite last home on this rain-softened ground after looking likely to get into it inside the distance. That elusive first success is just around the corner. (5/1)

T/Plpt: £24.70 (735.56 Tckts). T/Qdpt: £4.90 (296.77 Tckts) IM

1729-CATTERICK (L-H) (Soft, Good to soft patches, Heavy patches home bnd)
Thursday July 3rd
WEATHER: overcast WIND: almost nil

2412 SAINT-CLOUD (S) STKS (2-Y.O) (Class G)
2-20 (2-23) **5f** £2,302.50 (£640.00: £307.50) Stalls: Low GOING: 0.29 sec per fur (G)

				SP	RR	SF
2165[3]	**Oriel Girl** (PDEvans) **2-8-6v[1]** JFEgan(15) (lw: led stands' side: led overall ins fnl f: r.o u.p)	—	1	7/4[1]	65	24
2288[7]	**Beechwood Quest (IRE)** (BSRothwell) **2-8-6be** LCharnock(4) (led far side: clr ½-wy: hdd ins fnl f: kpt on)	1¾	2	6/1[3]	59	18
2288[10]	**Hayburner** (MWEasterby) **2-8-11** TLucas(14) (prom stands' side: rdn ½-wy: kpt on: no imp)	6	3	14/1	45	4
2186[5]	**Angry Albert** (CSmith) **2-8-4v[1](7)** CLowther(11) (lw: outpcd tl styd on fnl 2f)	2	4	12/1	39	—
1860[6]	**Candy Twist** (RonaldThompson) **2-8-1(5)** JBramhill(7) (a chsng ldrs: rdn & no imp fr ½-wy)	½	5	20/1	32	—
2042[5]	**Dispol Emerald** (SEKettlewell) **2-8-6** JFortune(13) (w wnr stands' side tl wknd fnl 2f)	5	6	5/1[2]	16	—
767[7]	**Sea Imp (IRE)** (MartynMeade) **2-7-13(7)** RBrisland(2) (chsd ldrs far side to ½-wy: sn outpcd)	½	7	8/1	15	—
1124[5]	**Wilfred Sherman (IRE)** (JBerry) **2-8-8(3)** PFessey(12) (lw: s.i.s: bhd tl sme late hdwy)	1	8	8/1	16	—
2233[7]	**E B Treasure** (NBycroft) **2-8-6** DHolland(10) (nvr trbld ldrs)	2½	9	66/1	3	—
1791[5]	**Boccolino** (TDBarron) **2-8-11** RLappin(1) (chsd ldrs centre 3f: wknd)	3	10	5/1[2]	—	—
1124[8]	**Sharp Pet** (DMcCain) **2-8-6b[1]** GDuffield(3) (bolted 3f gng to post: n.d)	1½	11	66/1	—	—
2288[14]	**Shirleys Girl (IRE)** (WStorey) **2-8-6** NKennedy(8) (s.i.s: a bhd)	1¾	12	50/1	—	—
2233[4]	**General Joey** (MDods) **2-8-6b(5)** PRoberts(6) (cl up far side 3f: sn wknd)	hd	13	25/1	—	—
				(SP 134.1%)	**13 Rn**	

63.0 secs (5.30) CSF £12.66 TOTE £2.70: £1.40 £2.30 £4.20 (£20.90) Trio £131.00 OWNER Mr D. Maloney (WELSHPOOL) BRED Mrs F. A. Veasey
No bid
OFFICIAL EXPLANATION **Hayburner: was later found to have sore shins.**
2165 Oriel Girl had the necessary high draw for soft ground and, in a visor for the first time, did it well. Now she has broken her duck, she should go on. (7/4)
1137 Beechwood Quest (IRE) ran a super race up the far side, showing blistering speed, and a similar event would seem to be on the cards. (6/1)
2153 Hayburner has a poor action and does not do anything quickly but was responding to pressure in the latter half of the race. (14/1)
2186 Angry Albert had a visor on for the first time and, although struggling on in the closing stages, he never gave any signs of hope. (12/1)
1860 Candy Twist showed speed but was always struggling in this soft ground and dropped out from halfway. (20/1)
2042 Dispol Emerald had the speed to race with the winner but she still needed this and blew up some way out. (5/1: 4/1-6/1)
648 Sea Imp (IRE) (8/1: 6/1-9/1)
1791 Boccolino (5/1: 7/2-11/2)

2413 'TURMERIC' H'CAP (0-70) (3-Y.O+) (Class E)
2-50 (2-50) **1m 7f 177y** £2,940.25 (£877.00: £418.50: £189.25) Stalls: Low GOING: 0.71 sec per fur (S)

				SP	RR	SF
2166[2]	**Hasta la Vista (52)** (MWEasterby) **7-9-10b** LDettori(6) (set slow pce: qcknd 3f out: r.o wl fnl 2f)	—	1	11/8[1]	61	16
2350[4]	**Tancred Mischief (40)** (DWBarker) **6-8-5(7)** JennyBenson(5) (s.i.s: plld hrd & sn trckng ldrs: ev ch 2f out: r.o)	1½	2	4/1[3]	48	3
1100[18]	**Gymcrak Tiger (IRE) (50)** (GHolmes) **7-9-8b** JFortune(2) (b.hind: lw: plld hrd: a.p: effrt 4f out: one pce fnl 2f)	2½	3	20/1	55	10
2166[3]	**Zamhareer (USA) (43)** (WStorey) **6-8-10(5)** IonaWands(4) (lw: prom: outpcd 5f out: hdwy 3f out: styd on: nt pce to chal)	1	4	5/1	47	2
2154[10]	**Gymcrak Cyrano (IRE) (32)** (NChamberlain) **8-8-4** NKennedy(3) (s.i.s: hld up & bhd: effrt 4f out: sn rdn: nvr able chal)	1	5	8/1	35	—
2236[4]	**Durgams First (IRE) (48)** (MrsMReveley) **5-8-13(7)** CLowther(1) (lw: plld hrd: sn trckng ldr: wknd 3f out)	20	6	7/2[2]	31	—
	Karaylar (IRE) (44) (WStorey) **5-9-2** JFanning(7) (b: bit bkwd: prom tl outpcd 4f out: wknd qckly)	dist	7	50/1	—	—
				(SP 118.8%)	**7 Rn**	

3m 52.1 (30.10) CSF £7.06 TOTE £1.80: £1.10 £2.60 (£4.60) OWNER Mr K. Hodgson (SHERIFF HUTTON) BRED Clanville Lodge Stud
2166 Hasta la Vista had things all his own way and, given a fine ride, was always doing too much for these rivals. (11/8)
2350 Tancred Mischief ran well considering there was no pace on, and she is obviously in really good heart. (4/1)
Gymcrak Tiger (IRE) would have preferred a much stronger gallop and ran well in the circumstances. (20/1)
2166 Zamhareer (USA) needs a stronger pace and has made it in the past, so it is mystifying why he did not here. (5/1: op 8/1)
2000 Gymcrak Cyrano (IRE) tried to come from behind in a messy race, but did not have the required turn of foot and needs a stronger gallop. (8/1)
2236 Durgams First (IRE), who prefers faster ground, because of the snail's pace set in the race spent much of the time pulling his rider's arms out. This is best ignored. (7/2)

2414 CHANTILLY RATING RELATED MAIDEN STKS (0-60) (3-Y.O) (Class F)
3-20 (3-20) **1m 5f 175y** £2,511.00 (£696.00: £333.00) Stalls: Low GOING: 0.71 sec per fur (S)

				SP	RR	SF
1168[9]	**Itatinga (USA) (60)** (MRStoute) **3-8-11** GDuffield(2) (lw: led after 4f: qkcnd 6f out: styd on strly fnl 2f)	—	1	2/1[2]	68+	10
2132[3]	**Quest For Best (USA) (60)** (JHMGosden) **3-8-11v** LDettori(3) (hld up: hdwy to chal over 2f out: sn rdn: fnd nil)	8	2	11/4[3]	59	1
2351[2]	**Wellcome Inn (50)** (JO'Reilly) **3-9-0** JO'Reilly(4) (lw: hld up: hdwy 7f out: outpcd appr st: styd on fnl 2f)	2	3	11/2	59	1

				SP	RR	SF
1956[6]	**Walkabout (58)** (BWHills) **3-9-0** DHolland(1) (led 4f: chsd wnr: drvn along 5f out: wknd fnl 3f)	7	**4**	7/4[1]	51	—

(SP 111.7%) **4 Rn**

3m 21.1 (25.10) CSF £7.19 TOTE £2.50: (£2.90) OWNER Sheikh Mohammed (NEWMARKET) BRED Darley Stud Management Inc

Itatinga (USA), taking a big step up in trip, looked green at times but she gradually realised what was required. Getting stronger as the race progressed, she looked pretty useful in the end. (2/1)
2132 Quest For Best (USA) went well when tracking the leaders but, once she was asked for a real effort early in the straight, she soon took the easy way out and downed tools immediately. (11/4)
2351 Wellcome Inn ran well without offering a threat and there is obviously a race to be picked up in due course. (11/2: 4/1-6/1)
1956 Walkabout seemed all at sea on this soft ground. (7/4)

2415 LONGCHAMP H'CAP (0-75) (3-Y.O) (Class D)

3-50 (3-58) **7f** £4,003.00 (£1,204.00: £582.00: £271.00) Stalls: Low GOING: 0.71 sec per fur (S)

				SP	RR	SF
2069[7]	**Three For A Pound (63)** (JAGlover) **3-8-9** JFortune(1) (trckd ldrs: effrt 2f out: r.o u.p to ld nr fin)	—	**1**	7/1	72	46
2158[3]	**Hulal (60)** (ACStewart) **3-8-6** JCarroll(3) (cl up: led over 2f out: hdd & no ex towards fin)	s.h	**2**	7/1	69	43
2237[6]	**Hi Mujtahid (IRE) (50)** (SEKettlewell) **3-7-10** NKennedy(13) (led tl hdd over 2f out: kpt on same pce)	3½	**3**	50/1	51	25
2143[2]	**Literary (75)** (JHMGosden) **3-9-7** LDettori(8) (bhd: effrt appr st: nrst fin)	¾	**4**	5/1[3]	74	48
2214[5]	**Baritone (71)** (JWWatts) **3-9-3** GDuffield(7) (lw: chsd ldrs: effrt ent st: one pce fnl 2f)	1½	**5**	9/1	67	41
2151[9]	**Dr Woodstock (50)** (MartynMeade) **3-7-3**(7) RBrisland(10) (s.i.s: hdwy & prom ½-wy: one pce fnl 2f)	¾	**6**	50/1	44	18
2169*	**High Spirits (IRE) (58)** (TDEasterby) **3-8-4b** 6x LCharnock(9) (lw: chsd ldrs: sn pushed along: outpcd fnl 2f)	7	**7**	11/4[1]	36	10
2130[8]	**Grate Times (65)** (EWeymes) **3-8-11** DaleGibson(2) (nvr trbld ldrs)	8	**8**	11/1	25	—
2214[2]	**Muscatana (64)** (BWHills) **3-8-10** DHolland(11) (effrt appr st: n.d)	¾	**9**	9/2[2]	22	—
2157[6]	**Wagga Moon (IRE) (60)** (JJO'Neill) **3-7-13b**[1](7) CLowther(12) (w ldrs 5f: wknd)	hd	**10**	25/1	18	—
2059[9]	**Russian Aspect (58)** (MWEasterby) **3-8-4**ow2 TLucas(6) (sn outpcd & bhd)	1¼	**11**	33/1	12	—
1333[11]	**Treasure Hill (IRE) (50)** (DWChapman) **3-7-7**(3) PFessey(4) (uns rdr & bolted bef s: s.i.s: outpcd & bhd: hmpd ent st: n.d)	6	**12**	25/1	—	—
1995[11]	**Tazibari (58)** (DMoffatt) **3-8-4** JFEgan(5) (b.nr hind: prom 3f: sn bhd)	16	**13**	20/1	—	—

(SP 124.2%) **13 Rn**

1m 32.5 (8.90) CSF £48.58 CT £2,162.66 TOTE £12.10: £2.60 £1.90 £8.50 (£39.30) Trio £503.90; £645.85 to Warwick 4/7/97 OWNER Hyde Sporting Promotions Ltd (WORKSOP) BRED Roldvale Ltd

LONG HANDICAP Hi Mujtahid (IRE) 7-0 Treasure Hill (IRE) 7-6 Dr Woodstock 7-2

469* Three For A Pound likes this track, is game and, responding to some strong driving, pinched it on the line. (7/1)
2158 Hulal, dropped back in trip, looked to have this won but was just touched off by a more determined rival. (7/1)
2237 Hi Mujtahid (IRE) ran his best race to date from 10lb out of the handicap. (50/1)
2143 Literary, ridden from behind this time, could never get in a blow, despite staying on. The ability is there. (5/1)
1977 Baritone looks the part and has the ability but is not putting his heart into it. (9/1: op 14/1)
Dr Woodstock seems to have ability and is gradually learning. (50/1)
2169* High Spirits (IRE) was never on the bridle on this occasion and something would seem to be wrong with him. (11/4)

2416 DEAUVILLE LIMITED STKS (0-65) (4-Y.O+) (Class F)

4-20 (4-24) **7f** £2,511.00 (£696.00: £333.00) Stalls: Low GOING: 0.71 sec per fur (S)

				SP	RR	SF
2317[3]	**Sharp 'n' Shady (60)** (CFWall) **4-8-11** GDuffield(6) (chsd ldrs: outpcd appr st: styd on u.p to ld wl ins fnl f)	—	**1**	9/4[1]	65	45
1761[7]	**Legal Issue (IRE) (55)** (WWHaigh) **5-8-11** RLappin(5) (s.i.s: sn rcvrd & chsng ldrs: led ins fnl f: hdd & nt qckn towards fin)	¾	**2**	9/1	63	43
2021[7]	**Kissel (62)** (SEKettlewell) **5-8-8** JFortune(2) (chsd ldrs: led wl over 1f out tl ins fnl f: no ex)	1¼	**3**	12/1	57	37
2353*	**Terdad (USA) (62)** (TDBarron) **4-9-0** 3x JCarroll(3) (lw: chsd ldrs: ev ch 2f out: wknd fnl f)	3	**4**	4/1[3]	57	37
2144[7]	**Statoyork (61)** (BWHills) **4-8-11** DHolland(1) (led tl hdd wl over 1f out: sn btn & sltly hmpd)	5	**5**	4/1[3]	42	22
1745[7]	**Dummer Golf Time (62)** (LordHuntingdon) **4-8-11v** LDettori(7) (prom: rdn ½-wy: sn outpcd)	5	**6**	7/2[2]	31	11
1828[16]	**Ohnonotagain (33)** (LRLloyd-James) **5-8-8** KimTinkler(4) (lw: outpcd ½-wy: a bhd)	4	**7**	66/1	19	—

(SP 112.2%) **7 Rn**

1m 32.8 (9.20) CSF £20.49 TOTE £3.20: £1.40 £2.00 (£6.60) OWNER Mr Walter Grubmuller (NEWMARKET) BRED R. and A. Craddock

2317 Sharp 'n' Shady got the strong gallop she needs here and kept responding to pressure and, in the end, won nicely. (9/4)
1655 Legal Issue (IRE) likes this track and ran well and seems to be coming to hand. (9/1: 6/1-10/1)
Kissel showed her first real signs of form in this country and is obviously getting her act together. (12/1)
2353* Terdad (USA) could never gain the initiative this time and finally gave up entering the last furlong. (4/1)
1505 Statoyork went off at a rate of knots and the soft ground found him out in the straight. (4/1)
Dummer Golf Time has done most of his running on a much faster surface and, never happy here, was given an easy time when beaten. (7/2)

2417 AUTEUIL H'CAP (0-70) (3-Y.O) (Class E)

4-50 (4-51) **5f 212y** £2,940.25 (£877.00: £418.50: £189.25) Stalls: High GOING: 0.71 sec per fur (S)

				SP	RR	SF
2235*	**Rum Lad (62)** (JJQuinn) **3-9-5** 7x JLowe(4) (lw: chsd ldrs: rdn to ld wl over 1f out: r.o wl fnl f)	—	**1**	4/1[3]	75	41
2235[2]	**William's Well (58)** (MWEasterby) **3-9-1b** LDettori(5) (lw: led tl hdd wl over 1f out: rallied ent fnl f: nt qckn towards fin)	1½	**2**	3/1[2]	67	33
2237[2]	**King Uno (48)** (MrsJRRamsden) **3-8-5v** JFortune(1) (lw: trckd ldrs: effrt 1½f out: nt qckn)	2½	**3**	2/1[1]	50	16
2177[15]	**Prominent (55)** (MrsVAAconley) **3-8-12** MDeering(7) (bhd: sme hdwy u.p 2f out: no imp)	3½	**4**	50/1	48	14
2157[3]	**Two On The Bridge (64)** (DenysSmith) **3-9-0**(7) CLowther(2) (chsd ldrs: rdn ½-wy: one pce afer)	2	**5**	4/1[3]	52	18
2167[2]	**Prince of Parkes (61)** (JBerry) **3-8-13b**(5) PRoberts(6) (w ldr tl rdn & wknd fnl 2½f)	nk	**6**	7/1	48	14
2032[2]	**Donna's Dancer (IRE) (56)** (NTinkler) **3-8-13b** KimTinkler(3) (lw: sn outpcd & bhd)	4	**7**	10/1	32	—

(SP 121.9%) **7 Rn**

1m 19.5 (8.60) CSF £16.29 TOTE £6.40: £3.30 £1.60 (£9.80) OWNER Mr B. Shaw (MALTON) BRED Mrs M. Shaw

2235* Rum Lad is in tremendous form and, once again, he responded to pressure in game style to win really well. (4/1: 3/1-9/2)
2235 William's Well had no excuses here and was just beaten by a more determined rival. (3/1)
2237 King Uno travelled well but was a shade disappointing when asked a question. Nevertheless, he looks the sort that will always pick up a race or two. (2/1: op 3/1)
701 Prominent put in his best run for his new stable here and seems to be coming to hand. (50/1)
2157 Two On The Bridge again had his chances but failed to pick up when ridden. (4/1: 3/1-9/2)

2167 Prince of Parkes is proving difficult to win with. (7/1)
2032 Donna's Dancer (IRE) (10/1: op 6/1)

T/Plpt: £427.80 (30.04 Tckts). T/Qdpt: £80.90 (7.26 Tckts) AA

1773-HAYDOCK (L-H) (Good to soft)
Thursday July 3rd
WEATHER: fine WIND: nil

2418 HALEWOOD APPRENTICE H'CAP (0-70) (3-Y.O+) (Class E)
2-10 (2-10) **7f 30y** £2,948.75 (£890.00: £432.50: £203.75) Stalls: Low GOING: 0.04 sec per fur (G)

				SP	RR	SF
2019^{9}	**Brandonville (56)** (NTinkler) **4-9-4**(5) RStudholme(7) (plld hrd: led over 3f: led over 1f out: r.o wl)	—	1	10/1	66	52
1765^{8}	**Ballard Lady (IRE) (40)** (JSWainwright) **5-8-4**(3) PDoe(5) (lw: a.p: led over 3f out: rdn & hung bdly lft 2f out: hdd over 1f out: one pce)	1¾	2	11/2^{2}	46	32
2237^{4}	**Prime Partner (37)** (TDEasterby) **4-8-4** RWinston(9) (lw: plld hrd: chsd ldr tl racd alone far side st: rdn & ev ch whn edgd rt 1f out: one pce)	1¼	3	7/1	40	26
2244^{2}	**Caudillo (IRE) (57)** (MrsPNDutfield) **4-9-7**(3) DMcGaffin(4) (hld up: hdwy 3f out: ev ch whn carried lft over 1f out: nt rcvr)	s.h	4	11/4^{1}	60	46
2144^{6}	**Nkapen Rocks (SPA) (51)** (CaptJWilson) **4-9-4** KSked(6) (lw: chsd ldrs: ev ch whn hung bdly lft over 1f out: nt rcvr)	2½	5	13/2^{3}	49	35
2161^{7}	**Theatre Magic (42)** (DShaw) **4-8-4**(5) SRighton(2) (lw: hdwy 3f out: ev ch whn carried lft over 1f out: nt rcvr)	½	6	14/1	38	24
1828^{6}	**Amoeba (IRE) (46)** (ABailey) **4-8-8b**(5) RCody-Boutcher(1) (lw: hld up & plld hrd: hdwy over 3f out: ev ch 2f out: wknd over 1f out)	1¼	7	8/1	40	26
2021^{5}	**Heathyards Lady (USA) (44)** (RHollinshead) **6-8-6**(5) PFredericks(8) (b: prom over 4f)	7	8	16/1	22	8
2282^{4}	**Northern Judge (37)** (APJames) **4-8-4b** GMilligan(3) (a bhd: t.o)	20	9	13/2^{3}	—	—
				(SP 114.0%)	**9 Rn**	

1m 33.05 (5.05) CSF £57.45 CT £378.66 TOTE £14.30: £2.70 £1.40 £1.50 (£32.20) Trio £56.10 OWNER Mr Philip Grundy (MALTON) BRED Cheveley Park Stud Ltd
IN-FOCUS: **There were plenty of hard luck stories here and the form should be treated with caution.**
1560 Brandonville, 4lb higher than when scoring at Ayr in May, missed all the trouble in a very messy race, being the only horse who stayed near the stands' rails. (10/1)
1332 Ballard Lady (IRE), 5lb higher than when winning this race last year, was one of the instigators of the traffic problems and gave away more ground than her margin of defeat. (11/2)
2237 Prime Partner, 4lb higher than when winning a seller at Ripon, stayed in splendid isolation on the far side until coming off the fence as everything bar the winner drifted towards him. (7/1)
2244 Caudillo (IRE), due to go up 5lb in future handicaps, had an unlucky run in trying to beat the handicapper. (11/4)
2144 Nkapen Rocks (SPA), down 2lb, caused his own downfall but may have been distracted by the antics of the runner-up. (13/2)
1433* Theatre Magic, rated two stone lower than on the sand, was another of the hard luck stories. (14/1)
1428 Amoeba (IRE) (8/1: op 12/1)

2419 SUMMER (S) STKS (2-Y.O) (Class F)
2-40 (2-41) **6f** £2,542.00 (£712.00: £346.00) Stalls: High GOING: 0.04 sec per fur (G)

				SP	RR	SF
1860^{8}	**Three Tenners** (JBerry) **2-8-6** KDarley(5) (lw: hmpd s: rdn & hdwy 2f out: r.o to ld wl ins fnl f)	—	1	6/1^{3}	68	16
1997^{17}	**Stravsea** (BPJBaugh) **2-8-6** NCarlisle(6) (wnt lft s: led tl hdd wl ins fnl f)	¾	2	33/1	66	14
2018^{7}	**Hope Value** (TDEasterby) **2-8-11b^{1}** DeanMcKeown(2) (s.s: hrd rdn & hdwy over 1f out: r.o ins fnl f)	1½	3	9/1	67	15
2003^{2}	**Kolby** (ABailey) **2-8-11b** DWright(8) (lw: w ldr: ev ch 2f out: wknd over 1f out)	5	4	4/6^{1}	54	2
2191^{5}	**Slim Prior** (KRBurke) **2-8-11** BDoyle(3) (prom tl wknd over 1f out)	2½	5	16/1	47	—
2153^{9}	**Sylvan Cloud** (CWFairhurst) **2-8-3v^{1}**(3) DarrenMoffatt(1) (prom: rdn over 2f out: wknd wl over 1f out)	6	6	20/1	26	—
1749^{6}	**Tindaya** (PDEvans) **2-8-11** DaneO'Neill(7) (rdn 4f out: sn bhd)	¾	7	11/2^{2}	29	—
				(SP 113.3%)	**7 Rn**	

1m 17.34 (5.64) CSF £134.44 TOTE £4.00: £1.40 £8.30 (£55.20) OWNER Mr N. J. Wilson (COCKERHAM) BRED Mrs J. M. Berry
No bid
Three Tenners, dropped into a seller, was trying an extra furlong after disappointing on firm ground last time. (6/1)
Stravsea did the winner no favours leaving the stalls and gave the impression she wanted to go left-handed throughout the race. (33/1)
Hope Value, a half-brother to Mhemeanles, was tried in blinkers having made his debut over seven. (9/1: op 6/1)
2003 Kolby, up in trip, would not have won at five and may need faster ground. (4/6)

2420 HEUBACH MAIDEN STKS (3-Y.O) (Class D)
3-10 (3-12) **7f 30y** £3,965.75 (£1,196.00: £580.50: £272.75) Stalls: Low GOING: 0.04 sec per fur (G)

				SP	RR	SF
1611^{6}	**Sheltering Sky (IRE)** (JLDunlop) **3-9-0** KDarley(12) (a.p: led wl over 1f out: drvn out)	—	1	3/1^{2}	90	64
1851^{2}	**Khafaaq (78)** (MajorWRHern) **3-9-0** TSprake(5) (lw: a.p: rdn over 2f out: r.o one pce fnl f)	1½	2	2/1^{1}	87	61
1423^{6}	**Summerosa (USA) (85)** (PWChapple-Hyam) **3-8-6**(3) RHavlin(13) (b.nr fore: lw: led 5f out tl wl over 1f out: wknd ins fnl f)	3	3	4/1^{3}	75	49
	Bushwhacker (CREgerton) **3-9-0** RHughes(11) (w'like: dwlt: hdwy 3f out: one pce fnl 2f)	6	4	20/1	67	41
2183^{9}	**Poleaxe** (MrsJCecil) **3-8-9** JTate(3) (led 2f: wknd 2f out)	6	5	13/2	48	22
1866^{11}	**Tarxien** (KRBurke) **3-9-0** BDoyle(10) (nvr nr to chal)	nk	6	50/1	52	26
	Bustopher Jones (CREgerton) **3-9-0** DaneO'Neill(2) (rangy: s.s: nvr trbld ldrs)	2½	7	20/1	47	21
2045^{8}	**Ingleborough** (DMoffatt) **3-8-11**(3) DarrenMoffatt(14) (chsd ldrs 4f)	2	8	33/1	42	16
	Perfect Bear (MrsSJSmith) **3-8-11**(3) OPears(6) (prom over 3f)	1¼	9	50/1	39	13
84^{7}	**Danehill Princess (IRE) (66)** (RHollinshead) **3-8-6**(3) DGriffiths(8) (lw: bhd fnl 3f)	s.h	10	25/1	34	8
	Beau Tudor (IRE) (MissLCSiddall) **3-8-7**(7) TSiddall(7) (rangy: dwlt: a bhd)	7	11	50/1	24	—
	Madge's Pet (GBarnett) **3-8-9** NCarlisle(9) (w'like: bhd fnl 3f)	2½	12	50/1	13	—
1787^{9}	**Pharly Star** (DShaw) **3-8-11**(3) CTeague(4) (a bhd)	1¼	13	50/1	15	—

2020[7] **General Hastie** (CWThornton) **3-9-0** DeanMcKeown(1) (b.hind: dwlt: a bhd) ... hd	**14**	25/1	15	—
		(SP 121.6%)	**14 Rn**	

1m 31.28 (3.28) CSF £7.65 TOTE £3.70: £1.70 £1.60 £1.30 (£5.30) Trio £3.70 OWNER Mr Victor Behrens (Susa Racing) (ARUNDEL) BRED Miss K. Rausing

IN-FOCUS: This was a strongly-run race.

1611 Sheltering Sky (IRE), dropping back from a mile, had been considered too big to run as a two-year-old. (3/1: op 7/4)
1851 Khafaaq is certainly finding it difficult to lose his maiden tag. (2/1)
1423 Summerosa (USA) eventually paid the penalty for taking the field along at a break-neck gallop. (4/1)
Bushwhacker, a half-brother to six-furlong winner Failed to Hit, was one of the few to show some promise for the future. (20/1)
Poleaxe, out of an unraced half-sister to Kris, Diesis and Keen, paid the penalty for attempting to go the strong pace after losing the early lead. (13/2)

2421 WEATHERBYS INSURANCE SERVICES H'CAP (0-80) (3-Y.O+ F & M) (Class D)

3-40 (3-41) **1m 3f 200y** £3,579.00 (£1,077.00: £521.00: £243.00) Stalls: High GOING: 0.04 sec per fur (G)

		SP	RR	SF
1968[9] **Debutante Days (64)** (ACStewart) **5-9-10** RHughes(2) (a.p: nt clr run & swtchd lft to ld 1f out: r.o wl) ... —	**1**	8/1[3]	79	51
2195[5] **Peppers (IRE) (65)** (KRBurke) **4-9-11** BDoyle(1) (lw: hld up: hdwy 2f out: r.o one pce fnl f) ... 1¾	**2**	5/1[2]	78	50
2194[4] **Bally Souza (IRE) (74)** (MJohnston) **3-9-7** JWeaver(5) (lw: chsd ldrs: led wl over 2f out: hdd 1f out: one pce) .¾	**3**	5/1[2]	86	45
2210* **Kathryn's Pet (65)** (MrsMReveley) **4-9-11** 5x ACulhane(6) (hld up: stdy hdwy 9f out: ev ch over 1f out: wknd fnl f) ... 5	**4**	9/4[1]	70	42
2122[6] **Dalwhinnie (59)** (JWharton) **4-9-5** KDarley(3) (swtg: led over 9f: wknd 1f out) ... ½	**5**	5/1[2]	63	35
2058[20] **Madame Chinnery (79)** (JMPEustace) **3-9-12** JTate(4) (hld up: rdn over 3f out: eased whn btn fnl 2f) ... dist	**6**	5/1[2]	—	—
		(SP 108.5%)	**6 Rn**	

2m 38.31 (8.91) CSF £39.26 TOTE £8.60: £2.10 £2.30 (£20.40) OWNER Mrs Shirley Brasher (NEWMARKET) BRED Lady McAlpine
WEIGHT FOR AGE 3yo-13lb

OFFICIAL EXPLANATION **Madame Chinnery: lost her action.**

Debutante Days bounced back to form and might be the sort who enjoys being messed about a bit in a race. (8/1)
2195 Peppers (IRE) was stepping up in distance in an attempt to secure that elusive first victory. (5/1)
2194 Bally Souza (IRE), taking on older horses for the first time, was already set to go down 1lb. (5/1)
2210* Kathryn's Pet was carrying 1lb more than she was set to carry in future handicaps. (9/4)
2122 Dalwhinnie was already set to drop 4lb on Saturday. (5/1)
1474 Madame Chinnery was reported by her rider to have lost her action. (5/1)

2422 ECCLES H'CAP (0-80) (3-Y.O+) (Class D)

4-10 (4-19) **6f** £3,738.25 (£1,126.00: £545.50: £255.25) Stalls: High GOING: 0.04 sec per fur (G)

		SP	RR	SF
2201[10] **Desert Lynx (IRE) (68)** (TRWatson) **4-9-5** RHughes(13) (hld up: hdwy whn nt clr run over 1f out: swtchd lft: led ins fnl f: r.o wl) ... —	**1**	16/1	76	49
1765[2] **Bollin Dorothy (51)** (TDEasterby) **4-8-2** TWilliams(5) (hld up: rdn & hdwy 2f out: ev ch 1f out: nt qckn) ... 2	**2**	6/1[3]	54	27
2326[6] **Bee Health Boy (67)** (MWEasterby) **4-8-13b**(5) GParkin(10) (a.p: n.m.r wl over 1f out: squeezed thro ins fnl f: r.o) ... hd	**3**	11/2[2]	69	42
863[8] **Safio (63)** (ABailey) **4-9-0** DWright(8) (led tl ins fnl f) ... 1½	**4**	9/1	61	34
2204[5] **Crissem (IRE) (62)** (RHollinshead) **4-8-13** FLynch(6) (lw: s.s: hdwy fnl f: nvr nrr) ... hd	**5**	20/1	60	33
2232[7] **Macgillycuddy (IRE) (59)** (MrsPNDutfield) **8-8-5b**(5) TEDurcan(2) (rdn over 4f out: hdwy over 1f out: one pce fnl f) ... hd	**6**	25/1	57	30
1977[17] **Halmanerror (61)** (MrsJRRamsden) **7-8-12** DeanMcKeown(11) (prom tl wknd over 1f out) ... 1¼	**7**	14/1	56	29
835[13] **Maiteamia (72)** (SRBowring) **4-9-9b** SWebster(7) (b.off hind: prom: wkng whn sltly hmpd 1f out) ... 3½	**8**	16/1	57	30
2130[6] **Frederick James (75)** (MJHeaton-Ellis) **3-9-6** SWhitworth(3) (bhd: sme hdwy whn nt clr run over 1f out: n.d) .. 2	**9**	16/1	55	22
1977[20] **Foist (65)** (MWEasterby) **5-9-2** KDarley(4) (hld up: rdn over 2f out: wknd over 1f out) ... 1½	**10**	7/1	41	14
2326[7] **Garnock Valley (76)** (JBerry) **7-9-13b** GCarter(12) (lw: outpcd) ... 1½	**11**	7/2[1]	48	21
2162[4] **Depreciate (71)** (CJames) **4-9-8** CRutter(1) (prom 4f) ... 1¾	**12**	16/1	38	11
2372[8] **Imposing Time (67)** (MissGayKelleway) **6-9-4** JWeaver(9) (b: prom: rdn over 2f out: sn wknd) ... 2	**13**	14/1	29	2
		(SP 119.9%)	**13 Rn**	

1m 15.8 (4.10) CSF £99.66 CT £571.73 TOTE £22.30: £4.60 £2.10 £2.00 (£205.70) Trio £175.00 OWNER Mrs R. T. Watson (FORD) BRED Mr and Mrs Dare Wigan
WEIGHT FOR AGE 3yo-6lb

Desert Lynx (IRE) settled much better than on her seasonal debut and was subsequently described by her trainer to have had everything in her favour today. (16/1)
1765 Bollin Dorothy, raised 3lb for her good second at Doncaster, was already due to go up another 2lb because Almasi has scored again. (6/1)
2326 Bee Health Boy, due to drop 2lb at the weekend, would have given the winner more to think about with a trouble-free run and was unlucky not to finish second. (11/2)
835 Safio, down 3lb, ran well after a break and may have preferred slightly better ground. (9/1)
2204 Crissem (IRE), set to go down 3lb in future handicaps, was hampered by a slow start and has yet to really find the right trip. (20/1)
1848 Macgillycuddy (IRE) continues to slip down the ratings and was already due to descend a further 3lb. (25/1)

2423 HOUGHTON GREEN H'CAP (0-80) (3-Y.O) (Class D)

4-40 (4-42) **1m 6f** £3,556.25 (£1,070.00: £517.50: £241.25) Stalls: Centre GOING: 0.04 sec per fur (G)

		SP	RR	SF
1805[4] **Foreign Rule (IRE) (72)** (PWChapple-Hyam) **3-8-12**(3) RHavlin(3) (rdn over 5f out: hdwy to ld over 3f out: all out) ... —	**1**	11/2[3]	83	24
2284* **Thornby Park (82)** (JLDunlop) **3-9-11** 4x TSprake(6) (hld up: hdwy 5f out: rdn over 2f out: ev ch over 1f out: nt qckn) ... 1¼	**2**	8/11[1]	92	33
1922[3] **Ikhtisar (USA) (70)** (PTWalwyn) **3-8-13** RHughes(4) (led 1f: outpcd over 3f out: styd on fnl 2f) ... ¾	**3**	15/2	79	20
2301[2] **Skelton Sovereign (IRE) (54)** (RHollinshead) **3-7-6**(5) RFfrench(2) (hld up in rr: rdn over 4f out: styd on fnl 2f: n.d) ... 2	**4**	12/1	60	1
2207[7] **Warrlin (59)** (CWFairhurst) **3-8-2**ow1 GCarter(5) (led after 1f: hdd over 6f out: wknd 5f out) ... 6	**5**	25/1	59	—

Form	Horse	Dist	Pos	SP	RR	SF
1491[4]	**Brand New Dance (75)** (DWPArbuthnot) **3-9-4** SWhitworth(1) (plld hrd: led over 6f out tl over 3f out: sn wknd)	5	**6**	5/1[2]	69	10
				(SP 113.2%)	**6 Rn**	

3m 12.22 (14.02) CSF £9.26 TOTE £6.30: £2.10 £1.20 (£3.50) OWNER Mr R. E. Sangster (MARLBOROUGH) BRED Dr M. Marchetti
1805 Foreign Rule (IRE) managed to see off the hot-pot favourite over this longer distance. (11/2)
2284* Thornby Park would have had to carry a further 4lb had the handicapper had his way. (8/11)
1922 Ikhtisar (USA) may need even further to offset her lack of speed. (15/2)
2301 Skelton Sovereign (IRE) showed how well she stays but had more to do in this company. (12/1)

T/Jkpt: Not won; £11,387.97 to Warwick 4/7/97. T/Plpt: £443.00 (45.71 Tckts). T/Qdpt: £15.50 (102.09 Tckts) KH

2406-YARMOUTH (L-H) (Good to soft)
Thursday July 3rd
WEATHER: overcast WIND: str half against

2424 FRED ARMSTRONG H'CAP (0-70) (3-Y.O+) (Class E)
2-00 (2-03) **6f 3y** £3,278.25 (£981.00: £470.50: £215.25) Stalls: Low GOING: 0.25 sec per fur (G)

Form	Horse	Dist	Pos	SP	RR	SF
2179[5]	**Faith Alone (68)** (CFWall) **4-9-9**(5) RMullen(2) (lw: trckd ldrs: squeezed thr to ld 200y out: sprinted clr)	—	**1**	11/2[3]	78+	60
1857*	**Don Pepe (64)** (RBoss) **6-9-10** KFallon(6) (lw: chsd ldrs: rdn to chal 1f out: nt pce of wnr)	4	**2**	4/1[2]	63	45
2201[6]	**Wild Palm (68)** (WAO'Gorman) **5-10-0v** EmmaO'Gorman(3) (lw: chsd ldrs: outpcd wl over 1f out: styd on strly ins fnl f)	hd	**3**	8/1	67	49
2372[2]	**Never Think Twice (61)** (KTIvory) **4-9-4b**(3) MartinDwyer(1) (b: led to 2f out: ev ch ent fnl f: unable qckn)	¾	**4**	3/1[1]	58	40
2162[10]	**Oberon's Dart (IRE) (68)** (PJMakin) **4-10-0** SSanders(5) (a.p: led 2f out tl hdd & one pce ins fnl f)	3	**5**	16/1	57	39
2070[5]	**Astral Invader (IRE) (41)** (MSSaunders) **5-8-1** JQuinn(7) (chsd ldrs: rdn over 1f out: one pce)	¾	**6**	7/1	28	10
1666[13]	**Shavinsky (52)** (PHowling) **4-8-12** DHarrison(8) (lw: bhd: effrt & rdn 2f out: no imp)	1½	**7**	20/1	35	17
2115*	**Arnie (IRE) (44)** (JRPoulton) **5-7-13b**(5) AimeeCook(9) (a in rr)	1½	**8**	8/1	23	5
1620[20]	**Sharp Return (55)** (MJRyan) **3-8-9** NDay(10) (lw: bhd: hrd drvn 2f out: t.o)	13	**9**	25/1	—	—
	Eternally Grateful (40) (KTIvory) **4-7-7**(7)ow4 SCarson(4) (s.s: a bhd & outpcd: t.o)	3	**10**	50/1	—	—
				(SP 111.6%)	**10 Rn**	

1m 16.0 (5.10) CSF £23.51 CT £154.75 TOTE £6.40: £2.40 £1.80 £1.50 (£18.20) Trio £34.10 OWNER Mrs R. M. S. Neave (NEWMARKET) BRED J. R. Mitchell
LONG HANDICAP Eternally Grateful 7-9
WEIGHT FOR AGE 3yo-6lb
2179 Faith Alone, always travelling cosily in behind the leaders, came between horses to lead just inside the final furlong and stormed clear for another very easy success. (11/2: op 7/2)
1857* Don Pepe enjoys himself at the seaside and he came to win his race entering the final furlong but the winner had the legs of him over this trip. (4/1)
2201 Wild Palm has been running over longer trips and he looked beaten when outpaced below the distance, but he found fresh reserves in the final two hundred yards and finished strongly. He is knocking at the door. (8/1: 6/1-9/1)
2372 Never Think Twice, a very poor mover, should have had the beating of the winner on Windsor runnings, but he adopted more forceful tactics on this occasion and they obviously did not suit. (3/1)
Oberon's Dart (IRE) gained command passing the quarter-mile pole and did his best to hold on but, at this shorter trip, he was swamped for speed in the sprint to the line. (16/1)
2070 Astral Invader (IRE), taking a step up in class, showed signs of a return to form and he is worth keeping in mind. (7/1: 12/1-6/1)

2425 DUNSTON (S) STKS (2-Y.O) (Class G)
2-30 (2-31) **6f 3y** £2,406.00 (£666.00: £318.00) Stalls: Low GOING: 0.25 sec per fur (G)

Form	Horse	Dist	Pos	SP	RR	SF
2243[10]	**Fiveo'clock Shadow (IRE)** (BJMeehan) **2-8-11** MTebbutt(10) (a.p: led over 1f out: sn clr: eased nr fin)	—	**1**	11/8[1]	63+	21
2153[4]	**Captain Bliss** (NTinkler) **2-8-11b** PatEddery(7) (led: sn clr: hdd over 1f out: hrd rdn: sn outpcd)	2½	**2**	7/1[3]	56	14
1819[12]	**Estopped (IRE)** (MRChannon) **2-8-8**(3) PPMurphy(9) (hld up: hdwy over 2f out: r.o wl ins fnl f)	s.h	**3**	15/2	56	14
	Tender Doll (IRE) (CADwyer) **2-7-13**(7) JoHunnam(6) (leggy: lt-f: bit bkwd: bhd: hdwy over 1f out: nrst fin)	1¾	**4**	10/1	47	5
2016[5]	**Newhargen (IRE)** (PDEvans) **2-8-11b** KFallon(1) (a.p: ev ch over 1f out: rdn & wknd fnl f)	½	**5**	9/2[2]	50	8
1091[8]	**Jaybee Silver** (MHTompkins) **2-8-6** DBiggs(2) (s.s: bhd tl r.o appr fnl f)	1½	**6**	16/1	41	—
1854[5]	**Fred's In The Know** (CMurray) **2-8-11** JQuinn(4) (a bhd: rdn along ½-wy: no imp)	3	**7**	25/1	38	—
2196[13]	**La Vizelle (IRE)** (RGuest) **2-8-6** PBloomfield(3) (bit bkwd: trckd ldrs over 4f: sn wknd)	4	**8**	12/1	23	—
2066[12]	**Katies Treat (IRE)** (DTThom) **2-8-6** DHarrison(11) (a in rr: t.o)	7	**9**	33/1	4	—
2066[11]	**Ruths Gem (IRE)** (DTThom) **2-8-6** WRyan(8) (lw: chsd ldrs over 3f: sn lost tch: t.o)	2	**10**	33/1	—	—
				(SP 116.9%)	**10 Rn**	

1m 17.7 (6.80) CSF £10.20 TOTE £2.40: £1.10 £1.40 £2.90 (£6.20) Trio £17.40 OWNER Mrs D. E. Blackshaw (UPPER LAMBOURN) BRED Seamus Kelly
Bt in 11,000 gns
1411 Fiveo'clock Shadow (IRE), lowered to selling company, won this in a common canter. He proved very costly to retain and it is doubtful if he competes at this level again. (11/8)
2153 Captain Bliss set a telling gallop and never once stopped trying after being headed, but the winner was toying with him inside the distance. (7/1)
1026 Estopped (IRE) should be well suited by a step up in distance for he stayed on really well in the latter stages and only just failed to secure the runner-up prize. (15/2: 5/1-8/1)
Tender Doll (IRE), a rather lightly-made debutante, was getting to realise what was needed in the closing stages and there are races to be won in this grade. (10/1: op 6/1)
2016 Newhargen (IRE) continues to run well but he is short of the necessary speed at the business end and it could be worth giving him a try at a longer trip. (9/2)
Jaybee Silver again lost ground at the start, but she did stay on in the latter stages and is gaining experience all the time. (16/1)

2426 HEMSBY CONDITIONS STKS (3-Y.O+) (Class C)
3-00 (3-00) **7f 3y** £5,188.49 (£1,921.50: £923.25: £378.75: £151.88: £61.13) Stalls: Low GOING: 0.25 sec per fur (G)

Form	Horse	Dist	Pos	SP	RR	SF
2229*	**Snow Kid** (DRLoder) **3-8-12** PatEddery(4) (lw: mde all: qckd over 2f out: rdn clr fnl f)	—	**1**	4/5[1]	116	70

1460²	**Imroz (USA) (100)** (HRACecil) **3-8-1** AMcGlone(3) (a.p: rdn to chal over 1f out: hrd drvn & one pce fnl f)	2½	2	100/30²	99	53
2106¹⁷	**Royale Figurine (IRE) (106)** (MJFetherston-Godley) **6-9-3** WRyan(6) (prom: rdn & outpcd over 2f out: kpt on u.p fnl f)	1¾	3	11/2³	103	65
691⁶	**Shock Value (IRE) (102)** (MRStoute) **3-8-6** KFallon(1) (hld up & bhd: gd hdwy over 2f out: rdn & wknd ins fnl f)	s.h	4	9/1	100	54
1170⁹	**Fun Galore (USA) (99)** (BWHills) **3-8-6** MHills(5) (bit bkwd: hld up: effrt 2f out: sn hrd drvn: no imp)	5	5	14/1	89	43
	Hakkaniyah (90) (DMorley) **3-8-1** RHills(2) (chsd ldrs 5f: sn lost tch: t.o)	15	6	33/1	50	4

(SP 113.6%) **6 Rn**

1m 28.2 (4.00) CSF £3.48 TOTE £1.90: £1.30 £1.40 (£2.40) OWNER Mr Ali Saeed (NEWMARKET) BRED Raymond Clive Tooth
WEIGHT FOR AGE 3yo-8lb

2229* Snow Kid retained his unbeaten record in this better-class event with an impressive all-the-way win. He he is now going to try his luck in a Group Three event in France in ten days' time, ground permitting. (4/5)

1460 Imroz (USA), back over a more suitable trip, did her best to get to terms on the approach to the final furlong but the winner was much too strong for her and her head came up. She could have a mind of her own. (100/30: 7/4-7/2)

2056 Royale Figurine (IRE), attempting a new trip in an effort to finish her career on a high, did give it her best shot which, on the day, was just not good enough. (11/2: 4/1-6/1)

691 Shock Value (IRE), brought back to seven furlongs, produced a good burst of speed to pose a threat below the distance, but he had been out of action for ten weeks and it began to tell as the tempo lifted. (9/1)

1170 Fun Galore (USA) (14/1: 10/1-16/1)

2427 LODDON H'CAP (0-80) (3-Y.O+ F & M) (Class D)

3-30 (3-30) **7f 3y** £3,868.55 (£1,156.40: £553.70: £252.35) Stalls: Low GOING: 0.25 sec per fur (G)

				SP	RR	SF
2408⁵	**Karinska (51)** (MCChapman) **7-8-2**(7) SCarson(3) (hld up: hdwy over 2f out: led appr fnl f: r.o wl)	—	1	7/2³	55	32
1647⁴	**Listed Account (USA) (74)** (LMCumani) **3-9-10** PatEddery(4) (chsd ldr: drvn along 2f out: led over 1f out: sn hdd: hrd rdn: unable qckn)	1¾	2	11/10¹	74	43
2192⁵	**Icy Guest (USA) (73)** (PJMakin) **3-9-9** SSanders(2) (led tl hdd over 1f out: sn rdn: one pce)	3	3	7/4²	66	35
1823⁷	**My Girl Lucy (63)** (PMitchell) **3-8-10**(3) MHenry(1) (chsd ldrs: rdn & outpcd over 3f out: styd on wl towards fin)	hd	4	16/1	56	25

(SP 112.1%) **4 Rn**

1m 31.1 (6.90) CSF £7.42 TOTE £4.20: (£3.00) OWNER Mr Geoff Whiting (MARKET RASEN) BRED Sheikh Mohammed bin Rashid al Maktoum
WEIGHT FOR AGE 3yo-8lb

2408 Karinska, unplaced over a mile the previous day, caused quite an upset with a well-deserved, clear-cut success. It may well have been her finale as she is expecting twins to Rock City. (7/2)

1647 Listed Account (USA) has not produced the goods as yet, though he did look the winner when poking his head in front briefly, before the winner did him for a turn of speed. (11/10: 4/5-11/8)

2192 Icy Guest (USA) forced the pace but she was always a sitting duck and had little in reserve once collared. (7/4)

My Girl Lucy dropped to the rear and was hard ridden three furlongs out, but she kept persevering and was pegging back the leaders inside the final furlong. (16/1)

2428 CATFIELD CLAIMING STKS (3-Y.O+) (Class F)

4-00 (4-00) **1m 3y** £2,669.70 (£739.20: £353.10) Stalls: Low GOING: 0.25 sec per fur (G)

				SP	RR	SF
2332¹⁰	**Spaniard's Mount (69)** (MHTompkins) **3-8-8**(3) MHenry(6) (lw: trckd ldrs: pushed along 3f out: led appr fnl f: rdn clr)	—	1	7/2²	70	32
1622*	**Trojan Hero (SAF)** (MrsMReveley) **6-9-9** KFallon(10) (a.p: led wl over 1f out: hdd ent fnl f: sn rdn: one pce)	2½	2	Evens¹	68	39
1139¹⁸	**Hever Golf Eagle (30)** (TJNaughton) **4-8-13** SSanders(8) (a.p: effrt & ev ch 1f out: rdn & unable qckn)	hd	3	14/1	58	29
1938¹¹	**Soda Pop (IRE) (60)** (CEBrittain) **3-8-9** WRyan(2) (hld up: outpcd 2f out: styd on wl appr fnl f)	2	4	5/1³	59	21
2070²	**Spanish Stripper (USA) (25)** (MCChapman) **6-8-6**(7) SCarson(7) (racd keenly: led tl hdd & wknd wl over 1f out)	6	5	14/1	42	13
	Tyrolean Dancer (IRE) (56) (SPCWoods) **3-8-4** DBiggs(4) (lt-f: unf: b.off hind: a in rr: t.o)	12	6	14/1	18	—
2059¹⁰	**Certainty** (JRFanshawe) **3-8-4** DHarrison(1) (bhd: effrt & rdn 3f out: sn wknd: t.o)	¾	7	33/1	16	—
1944⁹	**Prudent Princess (40)** (AHide) **5-8-5v** GBardwell(3) (lw: s.s: a in rr: t.o)	s.h	8	25/1	8	—
2337⁵	**Cross of Valour (65)** (PHowling) **4-8-12** JQuinn(11) (bhd: rdn over 3f out: no rspnse: t.o)	½	9	25/1	14	—

(SP 119.5%) **9 Rn**

1m 44.1 (8.10) CSF £6.81 TOTE £4.70: £1.10 £1.10 £4.00 (£5.20) Trio £20.20 OWNER Mr B. Schmidt-Bodner (NEWMARKET) BRED Whitsbury Manor Stud
WEIGHT FOR AGE 3yo-9lb

225* Spaniard's Mount acts well on this easier ground. Lowered in company, he threw down his challenge approaching the final furlong and was pushed out for a comfortable win. (7/2: 5/2-4/1)

1622* Trojan Hero (SAF), rather surprisingly not opting for a step up in class after winning a similar race a month ago, looked all over the winner below the distance but, once the winner appeared on the scene, the weight concession took its toll. (Evens)

338* Hever Golf Eagle came back much better than he went to post and he was always a live threat, but he was unable to find anything extra in the battle to the line. (14/1)

1624 Soda Pop (IRE) found this trip inadequate and he was only finding his stride when the race was as good as over. (5/1: op 3/1)

2070 Spanish Stripper (USA) raced very keenly and had run himself into the ground soon after passing the quarter-mile marker. (14/1)

Tyrolean Dancer (IRE) (14/1: 8/1-16/1)

2429 E.B.F. HAPPISBURGH NOVICE STKS (2-Y.O) (Class D)

4-30 (4-31) **7f 3y** £3,720.00 (£1,110.00: £530.00: £240.00) Stalls: Low GOING: 0.25 sec per fur (G)

				SP	RR	SF
1872*	**Mazboon (USA)** (EALDunlop) **2-9-4** RHills(5) (lw: led tl over 1f out: hrd rdn to ld ins fnl f: r.o)	—	1	4/9¹	88	44
1466*	**Behold** (JRFanshawe) **2-8-11** DHarrison(3) (s.i.s: sn prom: shkn up to ld over 1f out: hung lft: hdd ins fnl f: r.o)	½	2	11/2²	80	36
	Lone Piper (CEBrittain) **2-8-12** WRyan(2) (neat: hld up: & bhd: hdwy over 1f out: r.o wl towards fin)	½	3	13/2³	80	36
1984*	**Kim's Brave** (BJMeehan) **2-8-12** MTebbutt(4) (lw: chsd wnr: rdn over 2f out: kpt on one pce ins fnl f)	½	4	25/1	79	35

				SP	RR	SF
2243^{3}	**Timekeeper (USA)** (MBell) **2-8-13**(5) RMullen(1) (lw: hld up: hdwy 2f out: rdn & one pce appr fnl f)	1	**5**	9/1	82	38
				(SP 111.8%)		**5 Rn**

1m 30.8 (6.60) CSF £3.19 TOTE £1.40: £1.10 £1.90 (£2.40) OWNER Mr Hamdan Al Maktoum (NEWMARKET) BRED Streicher Stables

1872* Mazboon (USA) did not find this as straightforward as it appeared on paper and he had to work hard to regain the advantage, but he does at least show that he has the right commitment. (4/9)

1466* Behold had more to do this time and she may well have succeeded, had she not hung both left and right when put under pressure. She is clearly useful. (11/2: 5/2-6/1)

Lone Piper did not impress with his action to post but he turned in a very sound debut and he can improve on this. (13/2: 4/1-9/1)

1984* Kim's Brave, happy to be given a lead, was made to work over two furlongs out but he stuck to his task and was suited by this trip. (25/1)

2243 Timekeeper (USA) posed a live threat when putting in his bid over a furlong out but, with the tempo being maintained, failed to find a turn of finishing speed. (9/1: 5/1-10/1)

2430 HICKLING LADIES' H'CAP (0-70) (3-Y.O+) (Class G)

5-00 (5-00) **1m 2f 21y** £2,322.00 (£642.00: £306.00) Stalls: Low GOING minus 0.03 sec per fur (G)

				SP	RR	SF
1623^{4}	**Calendula (60)** (DMorley) **4-10-11** MissJAllison(1) (hld up & bhd: hdwy over 3f out: led over 2f out: all out)	—	**1**	5/1^{3}	70	51
1926^{10}	**Squared Away (45)** (JWPayne) **5-9-5b**(5) MissCLake(9) (hld up in rr: hdwy 3f out: ev ch ins fnl f: r.o)	½	**2**	12/1	54	35
1798*	**Anchor Venture (50)** (SPCWoods) **4-9-10**(5) MissDMcHale(3) (trckd ldrs: ev ch ins fnl f: unable qckn)	1¼	**3**	10/1	57	38
2302^{10}	**Bellas Gate Boy (49)** (JPearce) **5-10-0** MrsLPearce(4) (s.i.s: hld up: hdwy over 2f out: r.o wl ins fnl f)	¾	**4**	7/2^{1}	55	36
2187^{4}	**Blockade (USA) (60)** (MBell) **8-10-6**(5) MrsGBell(5) (t: hld up: c stands' side st: ev ch 2f out: no ex ins fnl f)	3½	**5**	4/1^{2}	61	42
1663*	**Marjaana (IRE) (70)** (PTWalwyn) **4-11-2**(5) MissSSamworth(7) (led tl over 2f out: sn rdn: r.o one pce)	nk	**6**	13/2	70	51
1779^{3}	**Acerbus Dulcis (35)** (MCChapman) **6-9-0** MrsSBosley(2) (chsd ldr: rdn over 2f out: wknd ins fnl f)	nk	**7**	20/1	35	16
2279*	**Arif (IRE) (40)** (BJCurley) **5-9-0**(5) 5x MrsAStringer(8) (prom over 7f)	2½	**8**	11/2	36	17
1383^{5}	**Captain Marmalade (44)** (DTThom) **8-9-4**(5)ow1 MissFBurke(10) (b: a in rr)	¾	**9**	12/1	38	18
1218^{4}	**Not Forgotten (USA) (68)** (PAKelleway) **3-10-3**(5) MissALHutchinson(6) (lw: mid div: pushed along over 5f out: wknd 3f out: t.o)	6	**10**	20/1	53	23
				(SP 121.6%)		**10 Rn**

2m 12.2 (8.40) CSF £60.32 CT £528.57 TOTE £6.30: £1.50 £4.00 £2.80 (£46.80) Trio £454.50; £230.50 to Warwick 4/7/97 OWNER Mr Christopher Spence (NEWMARKET) BRED Chieveley Manor Enterprises

LONG HANDICAP Acerbus Dulcis 8-8

WEIGHT FOR AGE 3yo-11lb

1623 Calendula, winning for the first time on turf, and over a shorter trip, needed to pull out all the stops in the final hundred yards. (5/1)

1422 Squared Away ran by far his best race under a very competent ride, but the winner had taken first run and was not going to give away her advantage. (12/1: 8/1-14/1)

1798* Anchor Venture is in good form, but he may have found this trip a bit on the sharp side on such a flat track. (10/1)

1920 Bellas Gate Boy did miss the beat at the start but it did not cost him much ground. Delivering a determined last-furlong challenge, he just lacked the pace to get to terms. (7/2)

2187 Blockade (USA), the only one who elected to come over to the stands side from the turn into the straight, was certainly on terms two furlongs out and he may have got to the front but, with lack of company, he could only plug on at the one pace in the race to the line. (4/1)

1663* Marjaana (IRE) has been in fine form on much faster ground and she ran up to her mark here, but the weight concession to all her rivals must have been a stumbling block in the closing stages. (13/2)

1779 Acerbus Dulcis was in the firing line with every chance, until feeling the strain inside the final furlong. (20/1)

2279* Arif (IRE) (11/2: op 3/1)

T/Plpt: £32.70 (391.62 Tckts). T/Qdpt: £10.20 (69.57 Tckts) IM

2431a - 2438a (Irish Racing) - See Computer Raceform

1895a-CURRAGH (Newbridge, Ireland) (R-H) (Yielding)
Friday June 27th

2439a GOFFS £100,000 CHALLENGE (2-Y.O)

7-30 (7-33) **6f 63y** IR £59,000.00 (IR £19,000.00: IR £9,000.00: IR £4,000.00)

				SP	RR	SF
1783^{2}	**Tadwiga** (RHannon) **2-8-9** PatEddery (cl up: 3rd ½-wy: led & rdn 2f out: r.o u.p)	—	**1**	7/4^{1}	83+	37
1480^{8}	**Soft Touch (IRE)** (MissGayKelleway) **2-8-9** NGMcCullagh (chsd ldrs: hdwy ½-wy: 4th & chal 2f out: 2nd u.p & no ex 1½f out: kpt on)	2	**2**	14/1	78	32
	Prospectus (IRE) (JSBolger,Ireland) **2-9-0** KJManning (cl up: 4th ½-wy: 2nd & ev ch 2f out: 3rd & no ex over 1f out)	5½	**3**	16/1	69	23
1328^{2}	**Occhi Verdi (IRE)** (MJohnston) **2-8-9** JWeaver (led 4f: 3rd u.p 1½f out: sn no ex)	s.h	**4**	7/1	64	18
	Munasib (IRE) (DHanley,Ireland) **2-9-0** WJSmith (towards rr: rdn & hdwy ½-wy: 5th u.p 1½f out: kpt on: no imp)	hd	**5**	25/1	69	23
	Retention (IRE) (KPrendergast,Ireland) **2-9-0b**^{1} SCraine (chsd ldrs: rdn over 2f out: 6th & nt trble ldrs over 1f out: kpt on)	s.h	**6**	10/1	68	22
	George (IRE) (MHalford,Ireland) **2-9-0** PShanahan (dwlt: towards rr early: rdn & hdwy 2f out: kpt on ins last: nrst fin)	1½	**7**	8/1	65	19
1932^{3}	**Take A Turn** (MRChannon) **2-9-0** RHughes (in tch: 5th & trckd ldrs ½-wy: 6th, rdn & nt rch ldrs 1½f out: kpt on)	½	**8**	10/1	63	17
1531a^{5}	**Magical Baba (IRE)** (PatrickPrendergast,Ireland) **2-9-0b**^{1} MJKinane (prom: 2nd ½-wy: btn & wknd 2f out)	4½	**9**	13/2^{3}	52	6
1228*	**Colours To Gold (IRE)** (RAFahey) **2-8-9** CRoche (chsd ldrs: 6th ½-wy: rdn & btn 2f out)	½	**10**	6/1^{2}	46	—
	To The Skies (USA) (JGBurns,Ireland) **2-8-9** PJSmullen (towards rr: n.d fr ½-wy)	15	**11**	16/1	7	—
	Sun Lion (IRE) (CO'Brien,Ireland) **2-9-0b**^{1} JPMurtagh (n.d)	¾	**12**	16/1	11	—
				(SP 133.9%)		**12 Rn**

1m 18.8 (4.30) OWNER Stonethorn Stud Farms Ltd (MARLBOROUGH) BRED Stonethorn Stud Farms Ltd

1783 Tadwiga had, on paper, something in hand of these, and was always in control once she had hit the front. (7/4)

750 Soft Touch (IRE) posed the only threat to the winner over the last furlong and a half, but could never throw down a serious challenge. (14/1)
Prospectus (IRE), always chasing the leaders, stayed on best close home to just earn third place. (16/1)
1328 Occhi Verdi (IRE) came out very fast and led until being headed by the winner. (7/1: op 7/2)
Munasib (IRE), a slow starter, showed considerable improvement on his first run. (25/1)
George (IRE) (8/1: op 5/1)
1932 Take A Turn dropped right away from halfway. (10/1: op 6/1)
1531a Magical Baba (IRE) (13/2: op 3/1)
1228* Colours To Gold (IRE) showed early speed but was done with from halfway. (6/1: op 7/2)

2440a (Irish Racing) - See Computer Raceform

2441a CHAPMANS (KILDARE) VOLVO H'CAP (0-105) (3-Y.O+)
8-30 (8-30) **1m** IR £13,000.00 (IR £3,800.00: IR £1,800.00: IR £600.00) GOING: 0.01 sec per fur (G)

				SP	RR	SF
	Vivo (IRE) (JOxx,Ireland) **4-9-8** JPMurtagh (hld up in tch: chal over 2f out: rdn & edgd rt 1½f out: sn disp ld: led early fnl f: r.o u.p)	—	**1**	7/4[1]	107	34
	The Bower (IRE) (CCollins,Ireland) **8-9-2b**(8) PMDonohue (led & disp ld: rdn 2f out: hdd early fnl f: no ex u.p: kpt on)	¾	**2**	12/1	108	35
2079a[6]	**Inchacooley (IRE)** (MBrassil,Ireland) **5-8-11** PShanahan (towards rr: hld up: clsd fr 3f out: 4th & chal over 1f out: 3rd & no ex u.p ins last: kpt on)	1	**3**	14/1	93	20
1979[4]	**High Premium** (RAFahey) **9-8-2**(6) RWinston (cl up: 3rd ½-wy: 7th, rdn & no ex over 1f out: kpt on fnl f)	hd	**4**	9/1	89	16
	Quws (KPrendergast,Ireland) **3-9-2** SCraine (hld up: hdwy 3f out: chsd ldrs whn n.m.r 1½f out: kpt on ins last: nrst fin)	½	**5**	8/1[3]	106	23
	Graduated (IRE) (JSBolger,Ireland) **5-8-10** KJManning (hld up: 5th ½-wy: chal over 2f out: 2nd & rdn 1½f out: no ex ins last)	nk	**6**	12/1	90	17
2267a[7]	**Meglio Che Posso (IRE)** (WPMullins,Ireland) **6-8-9** CRoche (mid div: chsd ldrs 2f out: 6th & no ex over 1f out: kpt on)	1	**7**	12/1	87	14
1058a[5]	**Wray (IRE)** (LBrowne,Ireland) **5-8-7**(6) JPSpencer (hld up: chsd ldrs over 2f out: nt rch ldrs over 1f out: kpt on ins last)	hd	**8**	7/1[2]	91	18
807a[4]	**Beautiful Fire (IRE)** (DKWeld,Ireland) **3-9-2** MJKinane (hld up: towards rr ½-wy: hdwy 2f out: 9th & nt trble ldrs over 1f out: kpt on)	s.h	**9**	10/1	103	20
	Eternal Joy (APO'Brien,Ireland) **3-8-1** JAHeffernan (in tch: 4th ½-wy: rdn & no ex whn hmpd 1½f out: no imp 1f out: kpt on same pce)	1½	**10**	8/1[3]	85	2
	Stylish Allure (USA) (DKWeld,Ireland) **4-8-8b**(6) DPMcDonogh (chsd ldrs: lost tch after ½-wy: rdn & n.d 2f out)	7	**11**	20/1	74	1
	Soviet Dreamer (LeeBowles,Ireland) **4-7-10** JMorgan (2nd & disp ld: rdn & wknd fr 3f out: sn n.d)	8	**12**	25/1	40	—

(SP 128.5%) **12 Rn**

1m 42.0 (7.00) OWNER Rusy Shroff (CURRABEG)
Vivo (IRE), an easy winner at Cork on his reappearance, had a theoretical 2lb in hand here. He edged right a furlong and a half out, but was in command once he hit the front at the furlong marker. With a rise of 4lb, he would still look a good proposition for another one of these, possibly the Golden Pages at Leopardstown. (7/4)
The Bower (IRE), despite a couple of below par efforts this season, showed here he retains his enthusiasm, and this is undoubtedly his favourite track. (12/1)
Inchacooley (IRE) ran on well over the last furlong after being switched out. (14/1: op 8/1)
1979 High Premium got the break on the inner to challenge from two and a half furlongs out and got his head in front at one stage. He found things a bit warm inside the last, but was far from disgraced. (9/1: op 6/1)
Graduated (IRE) (12/1: op 6/1)
Meglio Che Posso (IRE) (12/1: op 8/1)
807a Beautiful Fire (IRE) (10/1: op 6/1)
NR

2442a - 2445a (Irish Racing) - See Computer Raceform

2436a-CURRAGH (Newbridge, Ireland) (R-H) (Yielding)
Saturday June 28th

2446a INDEPENDENT NEWSPAPERS PRETTY POLLY STKS (Gp 2) (3-Y.O+ F & M)
4-00 (4-02) **1m 2f** IR £36,000.00 (IR £11,400.00: IR £5,400.00: IR £1,800.00) GOING: 0.10 sec per fur (G)

				SP	RR	SF
1542a*	**Dance Design (IRE)** (DKWeld,Ireland) **4-10-0** MJKinane (mde all: qcknd clr 2f out: r.o: easily)	—	**1**	4/9[1]	113+	70
1062a[3]	**Chania (IRE)** (JOxx,Ireland) **3-8-9**ow1 JPMurtagh (rn 2nd briefly early: 4th ½-wy: 5th & chsd ldrs st: hdwy over 2f out: wnt mod 2nd 2f out: kpt on: no ch w wnr)	2½	**2**	13/2[2]	102	46
2267a[4]	**Caiseal Ros (IRE)** (JSBolger,Ireland) **3-8-9**ow1 KJManning (cl up: 2nd after 3f: rdn & chsd wnr st: nt trble wnr over 2f out: 3rd u.p 1½f out: one pce)	4½	**3**	8/1[3]	95	39
1784*	**Keyboogie (USA)** (RCharlton) **3-8-8** PShanahan (dwlt: hld up: 5th ½-wy: wnt 3rd st: 2nd, rdn & chsd wnr 1½f out: one pce: no imp)	½	**4**	8/1[3]	93	38
2079a*	**Tout A Coup (IRE)** (GACusack,Ireland) **4-9-6** PJSmullen (cl up: 3rd ½-wy: rdn bef st: 4th & btn over 2f out)	1½	**5**	10/1	91	48
1698a[3]	**Sadlers Home (IRE)** (JSBolger,Ireland) **3-8-8b** SCraine (a same pl: rdn & no imp 2f out)	3½	**6**	33/1	85	30

(SP 116.8%) **6 Rn**

2m 9.0 (5.00) OWNER Moyglare Stud Farm (CURRAGH)
1542a* Dance Design (IRE) has been cleverly placed this season and took another nice prize with the minimum of fuss. She made all the running as usual, and was clearly enjoying herself entering the straight with Kinane able to ease her before the line. It looks as though she will travel later this season, with Arlington and the Beverly D Stakes, the main target. (4/9)
1062a Chania (IRE) proved difficult to settle early. Fifth into the straight, she was in futile pursuit of the winner from a furlong out, and is rather flattered by her proximity at the finish (13/2: op 4/1)
2267a Caiseal Ros (IRE) again failed to live up to her 1,000 Guineas form. Second into the straight, she was soon under pressure and found only one pace. (8/1)

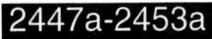

1784* Keyboogie (USA), waited with, made a promising move on the outside running into the straight, and went second briefly two furlongs out, but that was the extent of her effort and she dropped away tamely. (8/1)
2079a* Tout A Coup (IRE), friendless in the market, kept in touch until running down the hill into the straight, and dropping away. (10/1: op 6/1)

2447a E.B.F. SUMMER H'CAP (0-105) (3-Y.O+ F & M)
4-30 (4-32) **7f** IR £22,750.00 (IR £6,650.00: IR £3,150.00: IR £1,050.00) GOING: 0.10 sec per fur (G)

Form	Horse	Btn	Pos	SP	RR	SF
	Realt Dhun Eibhir (JGBurns,Ireland) **4-8-0b**^{ow2} NGMcCullagh (in tch: effrt over 2f out: 2nd & chal 1½f out: rdn & r.o. to ld last 50 yds)	—	1	16/1	81	35
	Vintage Escape (IRE) (JGBurns,Ireland) **4-7-11b**^{1} GForte (cl up: led 2½f out: hdd last 50 yds)	1	2	16/1	76	32
	Bold Tycoon (IRE) (JSBolger,Ireland) **3-8-8**^{ow1} KJManning (prom: 3rd, rdn & ev ch 2f out: no ex u.p 1f out: kpt on)	2½	3	12/1	90	36
2079a^{5}	**Orange Grouse (IRE)** (LBrowne,Ireland) **4-9-7** SCraine (hld up in tch: rdn & chsd ldrs 2f out: 4th u.p & no ex 1f out: kpt on)	1½	4	10/1	91	47
	Ministerial Model (IRE) (APO'Brien,Ireland) **3-9-3** CRoche (hld up: towards rr: hdwy 2f out: 5th 1f out: kpt on: nt rch ldrs)	1	5	9/2^{2}	93	40
	More Risk (IRE) (JGCoogan,Ireland) **4-7-13b**$^{(2)}$ EAhern (chsd ldrs: came across to stands' rail ½-wy: rdn over 2f out: kpt on)	s.h	6	16/1	68	24
	Archway Belle (IRE) (PJFlynn,Ireland) **4-7-10** JoannaMorgan (in tch: 5th & effrt 1½f out: no ex: kpt on)	1	7	16/1	61	17
2105^{16}	**Patsy Grimes** (JSMoore) **7-9-10** RHughes (chsd ldrs: 7th & rdn over 2f out: nt trble ldrs over 1f out: kpt on ins last)	¾	8	10/1	87	43
1186a^{4}	**Trickery (IRE)** (ALeahy,Ireland) **3-7-13**$^{(6)}$ ^{6x} DPMcDonogh (in tch: rdn over 2f out: nt trble ldrs over 1f out)	½	9	10/1	76	23
	Karatisa (IRE) (JOxx,Ireland) **3-9-5** JPMurtagh (led & disp ld: hdd over 2f out: sn wknd: lame)	4	10	7/4^{1}	81	28
1062a^{5}	**Velvet Appeal (IRE)** (MHalford,Ireland) **3-8-11** WJSupple (stmbld first f: towards rr: no imp last 2f)	½	11	8/1^{3}	72	19
	Trapped (IRE) (PJFlynn,Ireland) **3-8-9** MJKinane (dwlt: hld up: effrt over 2f out: sn no imp)	1½	12	12/1	66	13
				(SP 131.8%)		**12 Rn**

1m 27.9 (4.90) OWNER Liam Creane (CURRAGH)
Realt Dhun Eibhir found this trip a bit more suitable and come wide and late to get the better of her stable companion. (16/1)
Vintage Escape (IRE) went into the lead three furlongs out and looked to have stolen the race, before being thwarted close home. (16/1)
Bold Tycoon (IRE) looked rather one-paced inside the last. (12/1: op 7/1)
Ministerial Model (IRE) (9/2: op 3/1)
452 Patsy Grimes, tracking the leaders to halfway, was finding things a bit of a struggle from three furlongs out. (10/1)
1062a Velvet Appeal (IRE) (8/1: op 5/1)
NR

2448a - 2450a (Irish Racing) - See Computer Raceform

2443a-CURRAGH (Newbridge, Ireland) (R-H) (Yielding)
Sunday June 29th

2451a ARTHUR GUINNESS RAILWAY STKS (Gp 3) (2-Y.O)
2-00 (2-01) **6f** IR £18,000.00 (IR £5,700.00: IR £2,700.00: IR £900.00) GOING: 0.10 sec per fur (G)

Form	Horse	Btn	Pos	SP	RR	SF
1538a*	**King Of Kings (IRE)** (APO'Brien,Ireland) **2-8-10** CRoche (hld up: rn 3rd: trckd ldrs: shkn up over 2f out: swtchd rt to chal: led ins last: comf)	—	1	2/9^{1}	107+	53
1475^{4}	**Danyross (IRE)** (APO'Brien,Ireland) **2-8-7** JAHeffernan (led & disp ld: hdd ins last: kpt on: no ex)	1	2	14/1	101	47
1531a^{3}	**Dixie Dynamo (USA)** (CCollins,Ireland) **2-8-10** PShanahan (2nd & disp ld: rdn & no ex over 1f out: nt qckn with ldrs)	5	3	7/1^{2}	91	37
1880a^{2}	**Festival Song (USA)** (APO'Brien,Ireland) **2-8-7** LDettori (towards rr: 4th, rdn & nt trble ldrs 1½f out: kpt on)	nk	4	14/1	87	33
1538a^{4}	**Bismarck (IRE)** (DKWeld,Ireland) **2-8-10** MJKinane (towards rr: n.d)	8	5	12/1^{3}	69	15
				(SP 115.3%)		**5 Rn**

1m 14.0 (3.50) OWNER Mrs John Magnier (PILTOWN)
1538a* King Of Kings (IRE) got himself a bit warm down at the start and certainly knows a bit more about what the game entails. The idea was to relax him in the race, but he had to be ridden to get the better of his stable companion from a furlong out and was certainly not as impressive as on his debut. Having said that, he appeared to have any amount in hand, and looks like facing another easy task in a Group Three on Oaks day. (2/9)
1475 Danyross (IRE) popped out in front to make the running, and it was amusing to see her rider having a look behind to ascertain the proximity of the winner with two furlongs left to race. She is useful in her own right and the stable opinion is that her Sandown run was below par. (14/1)
1531a Dixie Dynamo (USA) ran second to two furlongs out but could only run on at the one pace. (7/1)
1880a Festival Song (USA) stayed on nicely from the rear, without ever looking a possibility. (14/1)
Bismarck (IRE) (12/1: op 8/1)

2452a (Irish Racing) - See Computer Raceform

2453a BUDWEISER AMERICAN BOWL INTERNATIONAL STKS (Gp 2) (3-Y.O+)
3-15 (3-15) **1m (New)** IR £30,000.00 (IR £9,500.00: IR £4,500.00: IR £1,500.00) GOING: 0.10 sec per fur (G)

Form	Horse	Btn	Pos	SP	RR	SF
2010^{2}	**Alhaarth (IRE)** (SbinSuroor) **4-9-11** LDettori (rn 2nd: chal early st: led jst ins last: rdn & r.o.)	—	1	Evens^{1}	128	75
2009^{11}	**Gothenberg (IRE)** (MJohnston) **4-9-11** JWeaver (led: rdn & jnd over 1½f out: hdd jst ins last: kpt on u.p: no ex)	1	2	9/1	126	73
1767*	**Polar Prince (IRE)** (MAJarvis) **4-9-5** OPeslier (hld up towards rr: cld on ins st: 4th & nt rch ldrs 1f out: kpt on ins last: 3rd cl home)	nk	3	6/1^{3}	119	66
2009^{5}	**Wixim (USA)** (RCharlton) **4-9-11** PatEddery (hld up towards rr: 4th & cld st: chal to disp ld over 1½f out: ev ch: no ex ins last)	nk	4	3/1^{2}	125	72
2010^{3}	**London News (SAF)** (BWHills) **4-10-0** MHills (rn 3rd: pushed along & chsd ldrs ½-wy: 5th & btn over 2f out)	4	5	6/1^{3}	120	67
				(SP 113.6%)		**5 Rn**

1m 39.0 (4.00) OWNER Godolphin (NEWMARKET) BRED Shadwell Estate Company Limited

2010 Alhaarth (IRE) allowed the runner-up to do the donkey work, and his challenge from two furlongs out only got serious when he led with just under a furlong to race. He quickened up well and will come on for this. (Evens)
1728a* Gothenberg (IRE), back on his favourite racecourse and with ground to suit, left his Ascot run well behind. Cut in the ground is certainly essential for him. (9/1)
1767* Polar Prince (IRE), settled at the rear, ran on with some purpose late on, and one might feel that an earlier move would have been interesting. (6/1: op 4/1)
2009 Wixim (USA) had to be switched out to challenge and looked a real possibility with just over a furlong left to race, but he couldn't quicken and lost third place close home. (3/1)
2010 London News (SAF) managed to reproduce his Ascot form with the winner to the pound, but was absolutely no threat over the last furlong and a half, having turned into the straight in third place. (6/1: op 7/2)

2454a BUDWEISER IRISH DERBY STKS (Gp 1) (3-Y.O C & F)
4-00 (4-03) **1m 4f** IR £398,200.00 (IR £135,700.00: IR £65,700.00: IR £23,700.00) GOING: 0.10 sec per fur (G)

				SP	RR	SF
2011[4]	**Desert King (IRE)** (APO'Brien,Ireland) **3-9-0** CRoche (hld up: 8th 4f out: clsd st: 5th & chal 2f out: led jst ins last: r.o)	—	**1**	11/2[3]	124	69
2081a*	**Dr Johnson (USA)** (CO'Brien,Ireland) **3-9-0** JPMurtagh (hld up in tch: 5th 4f out: chal over 2f out: led over 1½f out: rdn & drifted rt: hdd u.p jst ins last: r.o)	1	**2**	12/1	123	68
1204a[2]	**Loup Sauvage (USA)** (AFabre,France) **3-9-0** OPeslier (towards rr: hld up: hdwy st: 4th & rdn 2f out: 3rd & effrt 1½f out: nt rch ldrs early fnl f: r.o)	s.h	**3**	8/1	123	68
1896a*	**Johan Cruyff** (APO'Brien,Ireland) **3-9-0** JAHeffernan (hld up in tch: 4th ½-wy: 3rd & trckd ldr st: sn disp ld: led briefly 2f out: 4th, rdn & nt qckn over 1f out: kpt on same pce)	7	**4**	12/1	113	58
1769[2]	**Silver Patriarch (IRE)** (JLDunlop) **3-9-0** PatEddery (sn chsng ldr & disp ld: pushed along ½-wy: led st: sn jnd: hdd 2f out: sn btn & wknd: lame)	5	**5**	5/4[1]	107d	52
1541a[2]	**Verglas (IRE)** (KPrendergast,Ireland) **3-9-0** WJSupple (towards rr: hdwy bef st: 7th & rdn 2f out: no imp: kpt on same pce)	hd	**6**	33/1	107	52
1726a[11]	**Casey Tibbs (IRE)** (DKWeld,Ireland) **3-9-0** PShanahan (hld up towards rr: sme hdwy bef st: 8th & rdn 2f out: kpt on same pce: no imp)	1	**7**	33/1	105	50
1533a[2]	**Strawberry Roan (IRE)** (APO'Brien,Ireland) **3-8-11** LDettori (in tch: 6th 4f out: chsd ldrs wknd st: sn n.d)	10	**8**	5/1[2]	89	34
1769[5]	**The Fly** (BWHills) **3-9-0** MHills (led & disp ld: hdd st: 6th & btn 2f out)	3	**9**	11/1	88	33
2267a*	**Token Gesture (IRE)** (DKWeld,Ireland) **3-8-11** MJKinane (cl up: hld up: 3rd & trckd ldrs 4f out: 4th, rdn & wknd st: sn btn: eased)	4½	**10**	16/1	79	24
				(SP 123.1%)		**10 Rn**

2m 32.5 (5.50) OWNER Mr M. Tabor (PILTOWN)
2011 Desert King (IRE) put his Ascot performance well behind him here. Niggled along in Roche's inimitable fashion turning into the straight, he threw down his challenge two furlongs out and was always travelling best of the principals from that point, and led just inside the last furlong. He is worth more than the length verdict, but although providing conclusive proof that he does stay a mile and a half, there would have to be the thought that ten furlongs would be his optimum. He has a number of possibilities from here on, but a return to Ascot for the King George might be pushing things a bit too far. (11/2)
2081a* Dr Johnson (USA) justified his trainer's faith in him and continued his improvement (up 11lb for this run) with a very solid performance. He got to the front two furlongs out, but just could not match the winner's power thrust. (12/1)
1204a Loup Sauvage (USA), out the back early, came through between horses a furlong and half out, and ran on well to be nearest at the line. (8/1)
1896a* Johan Cruyff was just totally outpaced over the last furlong and a half. (12/1)
1769 Silver Patriarch (IRE) never looked happy disputing the lead on the outside of The Fly. He managed to get his head in front on the turn in, but dropped away very quickly from the two furlong marker. A variety of excuses included 'slightly lame' and 'respiratory tract infection', but this was not his Epsom running at all. (5/4)
1541a Verglas (IRE), held up to get the trip, kept on in the straight but was never a possibility. (33/1)
1195a Casey Tibbs (IRE) didn't have much use made of him, but his jockey subsequently said that he did not stay. (33/1)
1533a Strawberry Roan (IRE) showed no sparkle at all and never got into a position to deliver any sort of challenge. (5/1)
1769 The Fly led and disputed running a bit freely, and dropped right out in the straight. (11/1)
2267a* Token Gesture (IRE) close up until dropping away before the straight, was subsequently disclosed as having a respiratory tract infection. (16/1)

2455a (Irish Racing) - See Computer Raceform

2456a WATERFORD CRYSTAL WORLD SPORTS CURRAGH CUP (Gp 3) (3-Y.O+)
5-30 (5-30) **1m 6f** IR £6,850.00 (IR £1,550.00: IR £650.00: IR £350.00) GOING: 0.10 sec per fur (G)

				SP	RR	SF
1454[7]	**Orchestra Stall** (JLDunlop) **5-9-13** PatEddery (hld up: wnt 4th over 4f out: trckd ldrs st: opening & chal 2f out: led 1½f out: drvn clr: r.o: eased nr fin)	—	**1**	9/2[3]	113+	52
2081a[2]	**Zafarabad (IRE)** (JOxx,Ireland) **3-8-8**ow1 JPMurtagh (sn chsng ldr: chal st: led over 2f out: rdn & sn hdd: edgd lft: 3rd & nt qckn 1½f out: kpt on same pce)	5	**2**	15/8[2]	105	26
1698a[2]	**Damancher** (CRoche,Ireland) **5-9-10** CRoche (in tch: 4th ½-wy: 5th, rdn & chsd ldrs st: nt rch ldrs 1½f out: styd on ins last)	¾	**3**	12/1	103	42
2081a[3]	**Gordi (USA)** (DKWeld,Ireland) **4-9-13** MJKinane (sn led: hdd briefly over 2f out: rallied to ld again: hdd 1½f out: nt qckn w wnr: kpt on same pce)	3	**4**	5/1	103	42
2267a[2]	**French Ballerina (IRE)** (PJFlynn,Ireland) **4-9-7** JAHeffernan (cl up: mostly 3rd: rdn to chal st: 3rd & no ex 2f out: 4th & one pce 1½f out)	3	**5**	7/4[1]	94	33
1896a[4]	**Plaza De Toros (USA)** (APO'Brien,Ireland) **3-8-7b**[1] WJSupple (dwlt: hld up towards rr: 6th & rdn early st: no imp over 1½f out)	10	**6**	16/1	85	7
	Premier Project (IRE) (JSBolger,Ireland) **5-9-10** KJManning (dwlt: hld up towards rr: rdn & n.d st: eased)	dist	**7**	20/1	—	—
				(SP 124.3%)		**7 Rn**

3m 4.5 (11.50) OWNER D. Sieff (ARUNDEL) BRED Alan Gibson
1454 Orchestra Stall left his recent Sandown effort behind him here, putting in an impressive performance. After going to the front a furlong and a half out, he was eased near the finish and this was a very solid effort by an improving individual. (9/2)
2081a Zafarabad (IRE), whose 1lb overweight made absolutely no difference, was totally outpaced by the winner, but this was a fair effort by a three-year-old and he certainly stays this trip. (15/8)
1698a Damancher ran a bit above himself and will be harder to place in future, as he has gone up 3lb for this effort. (12/1: op 7/1)

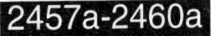

2081a Gordi (USA) showed that he is on his was back, only weakening inside the last furlong. Melbourne could be a possible for him. (5/1)
2267a French Ballerina (IRE) was struggling to mount a challenge on the outer from two and a half furlongs out, but this was a below-par day for her. (7/4: op 4/5) NR

2268a-CHANTILLY (France) (R-H) (Holding)
Friday June 27th

2457a PRIX DE SAINT-PATRICK (Listed) (3-Y.O C & G)
3-20 (3-19) **1m** £15,713.00 (£5,387.00: £4,040.00)

				SP	RR	SF
	Night Player (IRE) (RCollet,France) **3-8-11** DBoeuf	—	1		107?	—
	Kepster (USA) (ELellouche,France) **3-8-11** TThulliez	5	2		97	—
	Mateyev (USA) (MmeCHead,France) **3-8-11b¹** ODoleuze	¾	3		96	—
1909a*	**Hever Golf Glory** (TJNaughton) **3-8-11** CAsmussen (btn approx 20l)		6		—	—
						6 Rn

1m 42.5 (6.00) P-M 12.30F: 6.90F 4.4OF OWNER Mr R. C. Strauss (CHANTILLY) BRED Kilfrush Stud Ltd
1909a* Hever Golf Glory ran way below his best form. He was never really in the hunt and eventually finished last, beaten over twenty lengths. His trainer thought that the extremely testing ground, which he was racing on for the first time, did not suit him. This effort is best forgotten.

HAMBURG (Germany) (R-H) (Soft)
Saturday June 28th

2458a DEUTSCHER HEROLD-PREIS (Gp 3) (3-Y.O+ F & M)
3-43 (3-45) **1m 3f** £32,576.00 (£13,636.00: £6,818.00)

				SP	RR	SF
1916a⁸	**Anna Thea (IRE)** (HBlume,Germany) **3-8-7** TMundry	—	1		107	—
1918a³	**Enigma (GER)** (BSchutz,Germany) **3-8-5** AStarke	s.h	2		105	—
	Wala (GER) (AWohler,Germany) **3-8-7** ABoschert	4	3		101	—
						6 Rn

2m 26.9 (11.40) TOTE 39DM: 25DM 24DM OWNER Gestut Rottgen
Anna Thea (IRE) hit the front a furlong and a half out, and held on bravely to keep the fast-finishing runner-up at bay close home.
1918a Enigma (GER) was running on very well in the closing stages, but could not overhaul the winner.

2458a-HAMBURG (Germany) (R-H) (Soft)
Sunday June 29th

2459a IDEE HANSA-PREIS (Gp 2) (3-Y.O+)
3-25 (3-26) **1m 3f** £53,030.00 (£32,576.00: £13,636.00: £6,818.00: £3,788.00)

				SP	RR	SF
1724a*	**Oxalagu (GER)** (BSchutz,Germany) **5-9-6** AStarke (trckd ldr tl led 1½f out: r.o wl)	—	1		118	—
1724a⁷	**Surako (GER)** (HJentzsch,Germany) **4-9-4** PSchiergen (prom: hrd rdn & ev ch 1f out: r.o one pce)	¾	2		115	—
2104⁸	**Mongol Warrior (USA)** (LordHuntingdon) **4-9-6** KWoodburn (led tl 1½f out: outpcd tl rallied cl home)	hd	3		117	—
1073a⁵	**Protektor (GER)** (ALowe,Germany) **8-9-6** ASuborics (a in tch: cl up st: kpt on fnl 2f)	¾	4		116	—
	Bad Bertrich Again (IRE) (ALowe,Germany) **4-9-6** GBocskai (hld up: kpt on one pce fnl 2f)	3	5		111	—
	Sir Warren (IRE) (HBlume,Germany) **4-9-2** THellier (rr st: nvr able to chal)	2	6		104	—
	Turbo Drive (BSchutz,Germany) **3-8-1** NGrant (rr st: bhd fnl 2f)	¾	7		101	—
						7 Rn

2m 26.7 (11.20) TOTE 21DM: 11DM 14DM 14DM (74DM) OWNER Gestut Rietberg
1365a Mongol Warrior (USA) dominated the lead and set a steady pace until he was headed one and a half furlongs out. He was then outpaced, but rallied in the closing stages, only just missing out on second place. He would have preferred the ground even softer.

1546a-SAINT-CLOUD (France) (L-H) (Very Soft)
Sunday June 29th

2460a GRAND PRIX DE SAINT-CLOUD (Gp 1) (3-Y.O+ C & F)
2-45 (2-45) **1m 4f** £134,680.00 (£53,872.00: £26,936.00: £13,468.00)

				SP	RR	SF
922a*	**Helissio (FR)** (ELellouche,France) **4-9-9** CAsmussen (set gd pce & mde all: drew clr: impressive)	—	1	1/10¹	133+	—
1362a*	**Magellano (USA)** (AFabre,France) **3-8-8** TGillet (niggled along early: last st: prog fr 2f out: r.o: no ch w wnr)	5	2	92/10	125	—
1836*	**Riyadian** (PFICole) **5-9-9** TQuinn (racd 3rd tl st: sn rdn: onepcd)	2	3	85/10³	124	—
1917a³	**Darazari (IRE)** (AdeRoyerDupre,France) **4-9-9** GMosse (2nd fr s tl st: fnd nil whn hrd rdn: drppd out fnl f)	4	4	74/10²	118	—
				(SP 123.1%)		**4 Rn**

2m 29.5 (0.20) P-M 1.10F OWNER Mr Enrique Sarasola BRED Ecurie Skymarc Farm
922a* Helissio (FR), looking magnificent in the paddock, put up a mighty performance and ridiculed his three rivals. He led from pillar to post and was given a few inches of rein at the furlong marker where he had already wrapped everything up. Although this was his first race for two months since he went down with a cough, he looked better than ever and went extremely well for his new partner. Although the ground was testing, he ran a very decent time. It will take a good horse to beat him in his next likely target, the King George VI and Queen Elizabeth Diamond Stakes. A second attempt at the Arc is in his programme and he may be warmed up for that by a run over a mile in the Prix du Moulin de Longchamp. (1/10)
1362a* Magellano (USA) found the early pace a bit hot but stuck to his guns nevertheless. Keeping in touch, he found another gear in the straight where he ran on well without ever bothering the winner. This was a decent effort from a three-year-old, and he stays well for a son of Miswaki. Very much on the upgrade, he could now be aimed at the Prix Maurice de Nieuil later on in the month at Maisons-Laffitte. (92/10)
1836* Riyadian was given every chance, but he had run out of steam by the straight, and proved a little disappointing. He is not an easy horse to train and no plans will be made until he returns home, but he could be tried over a shorter distance next time out. (85/10)

1917a Darazari (IRE) was a little nervous before the race and not too keen to enter the stalls. Well up and given every chance, he threw in the towel early in the straight. He has not always shown his best at this track, and would probably prefer a firmer surface. He may try for a repeat win in the Prix Maurice de Nieuil. (74/10)

2098a-SAN SIRO (Milan, Italy) (R-H) (Heavy)
Sunday June 29th

2461a PREMIO TREBBIA MAIDEN (3-Y.O F)
3-15 (4-00) **1m 2f** £5,786.00

				SP	RR	SF
	Kenmist (LMCumani) **3-8-11** FJovine	—	**1**		95	—
	Hobean (VCaruso,Italy) **3-8-11** MEsposito	3¼	**2**		90	—
1367a[3]	**Kaberlaba (ITY)** (Ld'Auria,Italy) **3-9-0** GForte	1¼	**3**		91	—

11 Rn

2m 12.0 (18.00) TOTE 53L: 23L 36L 26L (378L) OWNER Sagittario SRL (NEWMARKET) BRED Azienda Agricola Il Tiglio di Amelia Prevedello

Kenmist, raced in mid-division, made headway on the outside to lead one and a half furlongs out and, pushed out, won easily.

2462a GRAN PREMIO D'ITALIA (Listed) (3-Y.O)
4-05 (5-00) **1m 2f** £38,570.00 (£16,971.00: £9,257.00)

				SP	RR	SF
1741*	**Jaunty Jack** (LMCumani) **3-9-2** FJovine	—	**1**		107	—
1553a[7]	**Honey Colour (IRE)** (ACalchetti,Italy) **3-9-2** OFancera	1½	**2**		105	—
1553a[12]	**Yavlensky (IRE)** (JLDunlop) **3-9-2** BDoyle	2½	**3**		101	—
2101a[2]	**Passi d'Orlando (IRE)** (JLDunlop) **3-9-2** GForte (btn approx 15½l)		**5**		—	—

6 Rn

2m 11.2 (17.20) TOTE 16L: 13L 21L (50L) OWNER Allevamento Gialloblu (NEWMARKET) BRED Fonthill Stud

1741* Jaunty Jack, racing in third, made smooth headway to take the lead over two furlongs out and ran on well.

1553a Yavlensky (IRE) led until being headed over two furlongs out, and could only run on at the one pace.

2101a Passi d'Orlando (IRE) tracked the leader for seven furlongs and soon weakened.

1828-BEVERLEY (R-H) (Heavy)
Friday July 4th
Races 2, 4 & 5: flip start
WEATHER: fine & sunny WIND: slt half bhd

2463 FERGUSON FAWSITT ARMS (S) H'CAP (0-60) (3-Y.O+) (Class F)
6-50 (6-55) **7f 100y** £2,847.00 (£792.00: £381.00) Stalls: High GOING: 0.77 sec per fur (S)

				SP	RR	SF
2041[6]	**Special-K (44)** (EWeymes) **5-8-12**(7) TSiddall(12) (uns rdr gng to s: sn prom: effrt over 2f out: led ins fnl f: jst hld on)	—	**1**	11/1	55	31
2368[15]	**Samspet (42)** (RAFahey) **3-8-9** DeanMcKeown(14) (led tl over 1f out: styd on wl towards fin)	½	**2**	10/1	52	20
2418[3]	**Prime Partner (37)** (TDEasterby) **4-8-5**(7) RWinston(15) (trckd ldrs: led over 1f out tl ins fnl f: wknd towards fin)	1½	**3**	5/1[2]	44	20
2019[5]	**Java Red (IRE) (45)** (JGFitzGerald) **5-9-6b** KFallon(8) (sn bhd & drvn along: styd on fnl 2f: nt rch ldrs)	1¼	**4**	3/1[1]	49	25
2302[9]	**Smart Guest (50)** (DShaw) **5-9-8**(3) OPears(4) (b: trckd ldrs: effrt 2f out: one pce)	3	**5**	20/1	48	24
2204[7]	**Oriel Lad (38)** (DonEnricoIncisa) **4-8-13b** KimTinkler(2) (hld up: hdwy over 4f out: rdn over 1f out: nvr nr to chal)	1¼	**6**	16/1	33	9
2206[4]	**Legend of Aragon (48)** (JAGlover) **3-8-8v**(7) TPengkerego(5) (chsd ldrs: effrt 2f out: grad wknd)	2	**7**	10/1	39	7
2070[9]	**First Gold (39)** (JWharton) **8-9-0** JQuinn(10) (s.i.s: bhd tl styd on fnl 2f)	3½	**8**	10/1	22	—
1786[3]	**Jilly Beveled (34)** (RonaldThompson) **5-8-6**(3) PFessey(7) (bhd: sme hdwy 2f out: n.d)	¾	**9**	12/1	16	—
2033[5]	**Bold Street (IRE) (53)** (GMMoore) **7-10-0b** NCarlisle(6) (lw: a bhd)	¾	**10**	10/1	33	9
2366[6]	**Shontaine (53)** (MJohnston) **4-10-0** JWeaver(11) (lw: chsd ldrs: rdn 2f out: sn wknd)	2½	**11**	6/1[3]	28	4
1818[5]	**Born A Lady (39)** (MrsVAAconley) **4-9-0** MDeering(9) (hld up: a bhd)	¾	**12**	12/1	12	—
1816[9]	**Olifantsfontein (35)** (JSWainwright) **9-8-10v** RLappin(13) (b: sn drvn along: chsd ldrs tl lost pl over 2f out)	1¾	**13**	20/1	4	—
1250[12]	**Klipspinger (43)** (BSRothwell) **4-9-4be** JFortune(1) (a bhd: sn drvn along)	7	**14**	14/1	—	—

(SP 138.1%) **14 Rn**

1m 44.4 (12.40) CSF £121.84 CT £436.85 TOTE £8.70: £2.60 £4.80 £2.40 (£127.10) Trio £149.20 OWNER Mr G. Falshaw (MIDDLEHAM)
BRED Patrick Diamond
WEIGHT FOR AGE 3yo-8lb
No bid

2041 Special-K, dropped 4lb after Ripon, gave her rider a problem or two going to the start but in the race she proved most willing, though at the end there was not an ounce to spare. (11/1: 7/1-12/1)

1284 Samspet put two poor runs behind him and, after being headed, he rallied near the line. (10/1: 14/1-9/1)

2418 Prime Partner, having his second outing in two days, raced keenly, and after taking it up on the rain-sodden ground his stamina seemed to give out towards the finish. (5/1)

2019 Java Red (IRE), with the blinkers back on, was always making hard work of it on this ground. (3/1)

Smart Guest ran easily his best race since changing stables. (20/1)

2464 BOLLINGER CHAMPAGNE CHALLENGE SERIES GENTLEMEN'S H'CAP (0-70) (3-Y.O+) (Class E)
7-20 (7-20) **1m 3f 216y** £3,197.00 (£956.00: £458.00: £209.00) GOING: 0.77 sec per fur (S)

				SP	RR	SF
1233[8]	**Lalindi (IRE) (68)** (ACStewart) **6-11-10b**(4) MrCRanson(3) (led after 1f: clr over 3f out: racd alone far side: wknd ins fnl f: all out)	—	**1**	9/4[1]	80?	25
2236[3]	**Rex Mundi (61)** (PDEvans) **5-11-3**(4) MrAEvans(2) (trckd ldr: rdn over 2f out: styd on ins fnl f)	1¼	**2**	9/4[1]	71	16

				SP	RR	SF
1805[2]	**Pay Homage (66)** (IABalding) **9-11-12** MrABalding(1) (lw: hld up: hdwy over 2f out: sn rdn & hung rt: wknd over 1f out)	8	**3**	5/2[2]	66	11
1811[12]	**Full Throttle (66)** (MHTompkins) **4-11-8**(4) MrCBHills(4) (led 1f: chsd ldrs tl wknd 2f out: eased)	16	**4**	7/2[3]	44	—
				(SP 112.3%)	**4 Rn**	

2m 59.8 (26.80) CSF £7.13 TOTE £2.90 (£3.40) OWNER Mr Christopher Ranson (NEWMARKET) BRED Hascombe and Valiant Studs
Lalindi (IRE), 4lb lower in the weights than when she last won at Haydock a year ago, had the blinkers back on. The only one to stick to the better ground on the far side rail in the home straight, she got home with nothing all to spare to give her rider his first winner in Britain for twenty years. (9/4)
2236 Rex Mundi came out best of the three who came up the unfavoured stands' side. Despite the ground being softer than he prefers, he stuck on in most genuine fashion. (9/4)
1805 Pay Homage, who is hard to win with these days, floundered badly in the ground. (5/2)
Full Throttle is out of form and is not suited by a soft surface. (7/2)

2465 WILLIAM JACKSON'S H'CAP (0-85) (4-Y.O+) (Class D)
7-50 (7-50) **1m 100y** £5,466.75 (£1,644.00: £794.50: £369.75) Stalls: High GOING: 0.77 sec per fur (S)

				SP	RR	SF
2293[2]	**Opulent (71)** (MrsMReveley) **6-10-0** JWeaver(9) (trckd ldr: styd far side & led 3f out: hung bdly lft 1f out: hld on towards fin)	—	**1**	5/1[2]	85	41
1422[11]	**Night of Glass (55)** (JLEyre) **4-8-12v** MGallagher(8) (b: chsd ldrs: styd far side: ev ch & hrd rdn ins fnl f: nt qckn nr fin)	hd	**2**	9/1	69	25
2239[2]	**Superpride (56)** (MrsMReveley) **5-8-13** ACulhane(1) (led to 3f out: hung bdly rt: kpt on same pce appr fnl f)	2½	**3**	7/1	65	21
1745[6]	**Duello (69)** (MBlanshard) **6-9-12** JQuinn(2) (trckd ldrs: lost pl over 3f out: styd on appr fnl f)	3½	**4**	6/1[3]	72	28
2290[7]	**Winston (56)** (JDBethell) **4-8-10**(3) PFessey(5) (hld up: effrt over 3f out: nvr nr to chal)	7	**5**	10/1	45	1
2205[2]	**Bollin Frank (71)** (TDEasterby) **5-10-0** KFallon(6) (lw: chsd ldrs: effrt over 2f out: sn wknd)	1½	**6**	6/4[1]	57	13
1830[2]	**Duke Valentino (58)** (RHollinshead) **5-8-12**(3) DGriffiths(7) (hld up: effrt over 3f out: sn bhd & eased)	28	**7**	8/1	—	—
2205[4]	**Thatched (IRE) (53)** (REBarr) **7-8-10** DeanMcKeown(3) (hld up: hdwy over 4f out: lost pl over 3f out: eased)	¾	**8**	8/1	—	—
				(SP 124.8%)	**8 Rn**	

1m 57.8 (13.80) CSF £48.49 CT £299.98 TOTE £5.90: £1.90 £3.40 £2.00 (£41.00) Trio £96.00 OWNER Mrs Eileen Hawkey (SALTBURN) BRED Bloomsbury Stud
2293 Opulent, who again wore a tongue-strap, was suited by the drop back in distance. Sticking to the far side, he hung badly left under pressure and in the end did only just enough. (5/1)
866 Night of Glass, a light-framed individual, was given a much more patient ride. The only one to remain on the best ground on the far side throughout in the home straight, he might be flattered by this. (9/1)
2239 Superpride, a headstrong sort, was as usual taken to post early. Brought wide off the bend, in the end he hung badly right and crossed over with the winner, his stable companion. (7/1)
1745 Duello did best of those who were brought to race on the stands' side. The going was probably even worse there which makes the jockeys' tactics throughout the night difficult to understand. (6/1)
2205 Bollin Frank has won on easy ground but he found these conditions all too much for him. (6/4)

2466 WELLBEING NOVICE STKS (2-Y.O) (Class D)
8-20 (8-20) **5f** £3,210.00 (£960.00: £460.00: £210.00) GOING: 0.77 sec per fur (S)

				SP	RR	SF
1492*	**Princely Heir (IRE)** (MJohnston) **2-9-4** JWeaver(4) (mde all: clr far side over 1f out: edgd lft: styd on strly)	—	**1**	5/4[1]	101+	59
1729[3]	**Branston Berry (IRE)** (JLEyre) **2-8-11** RLappin(1) (swtg: racd stands' side: a chsng wnr: rdn over 1f out: kpt on)	9	**2**	3/1[3]	65	23
2037[12]	**Cape Hope** (RBoss) **2-8-12** KFallon(5) (sn outpcd: hdwy over 1f out: nvr nr to chal)	2½	**3**	7/1	58	16
2212[2]	**Sandside** (JBerry) **2-9-1**(3) PFessey(3) (chsd ldrs: sn drvn along: wknd 2f out: eased towards fin)	10	**4**	5/2[2]	32	—
				(SP 110.5%)	**4 Rn**	

68.3 secs (6.50) CSF £4.91 TOTE £1.90 (£2.90) OWNER Maktoum Al Maktoum (MIDDLEHAM) BRED Gainsborough Stud Management Ltd
1492* Princely Heir (IRE), cool and calm beforehand, proved much too good for this lot and is clearly useful at least. (5/4)
1729 Branston Berry (IRE), very much on her toes and edgy beforehand, was taken to post early. Brought to race up the unfavoured stands' side, she proved no match at all for the winner but still came out second best. (3/1)
Cape Hope was soon being taken off his feet. (7/1)
2212 Sandside, edgy beforehand, ran very poorly even considering the conditions and his rider gave up soon after halfway. (5/2)

2467 JACKSONS FAMILY FOODSTORE MAIDEN STKS (2-Y.O) (Class D)
8-50 (8-51) **5f** £3,673.25 (£1,106.00: £535.50: £250.25) GOING: 0.77 sec per fur (S)

				SP	RR	SF
2361[2]	**Two Williams** (MWEasterby) **2-9-0** TLucas(8) (wl away: mde all on far side: clr over 1f out: easily)	—	**1**	7/1	76+	41
2066[3]	**Opopmil (IRE)** (TDEasterby) **2-8-9** WJO'Connor(1) (chsd ldrs: kpt on appr fnl f: no ch w wnr)	8	**2**	9/1	58	10
	Requestor (JGFitzGerald) **2-9-0** KFallon(10) (cmpt: hdwy ½-wy: styd on fnl f)	s.h	**3**	5/2[1]	63+	15
2110[5]	**Quiz Master** (EWeymes) **2-9-0** JQuinn(16) (hdwy ½-wy: sn chsng ldrs: kpt on same pce: nvr nr to chal)	3	**4**	11/2[3]	54	6
979[5]	**Kettlesing (IRE)** (MWEasterby) **2-8-9b** JWeaver(3) (bhd: hdwy ½-wy: hung lft & styd on appr fnl f)	½	**5**	8/1	47	—
	Nuclear Debate (USA) (MrsJRRamsden) **2-9-0** JFortune(7) (w'like: bit bkwd: mid div: styd on fnl 2f: nvr nr ldrs)	s.h	**6**	11/1	52	4
1819[7]	**Percy** (JFBottomley) **2-9-0** NCarlisle(14) (chsd ldrs: edgd rt & wknd over 1f out)	1¼	**7**	20/1	48	—
2181[12]	**Technician (IRE)** (MAJarvis) **2-9-0** MFenton(9) (chsd ldrs 3f: sn wknd)	3½	**8**	9/1	37	—
	Colonel Custer (CWThornton) **2-9-0** DeanMcKeown(11) (unf: scope: s.i.s: bhd tl sme hdwy 2f out)	1¼	**9**	33/1	33	—
2127[6]	**Smart Prince** (JJQuinn) **2-9-0** TWilliams(6) (chsd ldrs tl wknd 2f out)	2½	**10**	20/1	25	—
	Hoyland Common (IRE) (NTinkler) **2-8-9** KimTinkler(5) (outpcd fr ½-wy)	1½	**11**	20/1	15	—
	Itsnotyetnamed (ASmith) **2-9-0** RLappin(2) (leggy: unf: sn outpcd & bhd)	4	**12**	33/1	7	—
2127[8]	**Lunchtime Girl** (JDBethell) **2-8-9** DHolland(13) (a in rr)	2½	**13**	20/1	—	—
1645[3]	**First Village (IRE)** (JBerry) **2-8-6**(3) PFessey(12) (lw: w.r.s: a bhd)	4	**14**	9/2[2]	—	—
	Catfoot Lane (WGMTurner) **2-8-9** ACulhane(4) (leggy: lt-f: unf: swtg: unruly s: s.i.s: a wl bhd: t.o)	18	**15**	14/1	—	—
				(SP 145.7%)	**15 Rn**	

69.2 secs (7.40) CSF £69.27 TOTE £7.50: £3.20 £4.80 £1.10 (£38.70) Trio £119.80 OWNER Mr W. L. Caley (SHERIFF HUTTON) BRED W. L. Caley

IN-FOCUS: Due to the state of the ground three of the races were started with the flip start tape. There was a really ragged start to this event, the winner got a flyer and First Village whipped round and lost all chance.
2361 Two Williams, who has wind problems according to his trainer, got a flyer from the tape start and scored with plenty in hand. To the naked eye the winning margin looked about half the Judge's official version. (7/1)
2066 Opopmil (IRE), drawn one, raced towards the stands' side. The ground was almost certainly better on the far side. (9/1)
Requestor, a fair sort, is from a stable not renowned for first time out two-year-old winners. He showed promise, sticking on nicely at the finish, and should have plenty of improvement in him. (5/2)
2110 Quiz Master on his toes beforehand, has run up a shade light. (11/2)
979 Kettlesing (IRE) was again staying on at the finish and looks capable of better in time. (8/1)
Nuclear Debate (USA), a fair sort, picked up nicely late in the day and can do a fair bit better. (11/1)
1645 First Village (IRE), who was very weak in the market, turned right round when the tape was released and she had no chance from the word go. (9/2: 9/4-5/1)

2468 SANCTON H'CAP (0-70) (3-Y.O F) (Class E)
9-20 (9-21) **1m 1f 207y** £2,966.25 (£885.00: £422.50: £191.25) Stalls: High GOING: 0.77 sec per fur (S)

				SP	RR	SF
1999^{8}	**Lindrick Lady (IRE) (67)** (BSRothwell) **3-9-7** JFortune(1) (mde all: rdn over 2f out: wknd towards fin: jst hld on)	—	1	$7/2^{2}$	75	46
2149^{3}	**Inclination (60)** (MBlanshard) **3-9-0** JQuinn(2) (chsd ldrs: rdn 2f out: styd on towards fin)	½	2	6/1	67	38
1985^{2}	**Double Eight (IRE) (60)** (BWHills) **3-9-0** DHolland(4) (chsd ldrs: rdn & edgd lft over 2f out: styd on wl towards fin)	hd	3	$5/1^{3}$	67	38
2362^{3}	**Marsh Marigold (67)** (JHetherton) **3-9-7** KFallon(7) (hld up: hdwy on outside over 4f out: rdn 2f out: sn btn & eased)	22	4	$3/1^{1}$	39	10
2178^{4}	**River of Fortune (IRE) (58)** (MHTompkins) **3-8-9**(3) MHenry(9) (trckd ldrs tl lost pl over 3f out)	nk	5	7/1	29	—
1844^{14}	**Dancing Queen (IRE) (62)** (MBell) **3-9-2** MFenton(8) (hld up: effrt over 3f out: sn wknd)	14	6	7/1	11	—
2387^{6}	**Shotley Princess (42)** (NBycroft) **3-7-7**(3) PFessey(6) (stdd s: hld up: jnd ldr 6f out: wknd over 4f out)	4	7	33/1	—	—
26^{3}	**Lochlass (IRE) (64)** (SPCWoods) **3-9-4** WJO'Connor(5) (chsd ldrs tl lost pl over 3f out)	11	8	10/1	—	—
2040^{9}	**Glorious Dancer (43)** (JHetherton) **3-7-11**ow1 NCarlisle(3) (in tch tl lost pl 4f out)	2½	9	25/1	—	—

(SP 119.1%) **9 Rn**

2m 18.0 (14.90) CSF £23.46 CT £96.96 TOTE £4.40: £1.50 £1.90 £1.80 (£21.10) Trio £20.50 OWNER Mr S. P. Hudson (MALTON) BRED F. D. McAuley
LONG HANDICAP Shotley Princess 6-12 Glorious Dancer 6-13
1390 Lindrick Lady (IRE), back on her favourite stamping ground and with the ground to suit, was only 2lb higher than when she won here two outings ago. She proved very willing but was leg weary near the line and, in the end, the post came just in time. This was a race in which only the first four ever seriously entered the contest. (7/2)
2149 Inclination, a very narrow type, was stepping up three furlongs in trip. She proved well suited by it and, after taking an age to get into full stride, was fast cutting down the winner at the line. (6/1)
1985 Double Eight (IRE) seemed to be suited by this soft ground. (5/1: op 100/30)
2362 Marsh Marigold, unlike the first three home, came wide off the bend, strange tactics considering the results earlier in the night. On the heels of the leaders two furlongs from home, she soon became very tired and was eased up. (3/1)

T/Plpt: £781.70 (18.03 Tckts). T/Qdpt: £35.40 (22.9 Tckts) WG

2382-HAMILTON (R-H) (Good to Soft)
Friday July 4th
WEATHER: sunny WIND: mod across

2469 TILNEY PORTFOLIO LADIES' H'CAP (0-75) (3-Y.O+) (Class F)
6-40 (6-40) **1m 3f 16y** £2,794.00 (£784.00: £382.00) Stalls: High GOING minus 0.25 sec per fur (GF)

				SP	RR	SF
2034^{4}	**Philmist (40)** (MissLAPerratt) **5-10-0b** MissAElsey(5) (hdwy 7f out: led appr fnl f: styd on)	—	1	15/2	46	35
2342^{4}	**Madison Welcome (IRE) (64)** (MrsJRRamsden) **3-10-8**(4) MissERamsden(10) (lw: outpcd & bhd: hdwy 2f out: r.o wl towards fin)	¾	2	$5/1^{2}$	69	46
2063^{3}	**Stalled (IRE) (50)** (PTWalwyn) **7-10-6**(4) MarchionessBlandford(7) (lw: bhd: hdwy 5f out: chsng ldrs over 2f out: kpt on towards fin)	nk	3	12/1	55	44
2351*	**Sun of Spring (59)** (DWChapman) **7-11-5** 5x MissRClark(4) (lw: chsd ldrs: led over 2f out tl over 1f out: one pce)	nk	4	$6/1^{3}$	63	52
2063^{2}	**High Low (USA) (45)** (MDHammond) **9-9-12**(7) MrsAHammond(1) (lw: chsd ldr: led 3f out: sn hdd & one pce)	1	5	9/1	48	37
2352^{3}	**Love Me Do (USA) (64)** (MJohnston) **3-10-8**(4) MrsCWilliams(8) (lw: a.p: effrt 4f out: one pce)	1¾	6	8/1	64	41
2034^{5}	**Lord Advocate (54)** (DANolan) **9-10-7b**(7) MissDCarter(6) (chsd ldrs: ev ch 3f out: one pce appr fnl f)	nk	7	7/1	54	43
2063*	**Nosey Native (61)** (JPearce) **4-11-7** MrsLPearce(3) (bhd: hdwy 4f out: no imp fnl 2f)	¾	8	$7/2^{1}$	60	49
2385^{8}	**Hutchies Lady (35)** (RMMcKellar) **5-9-2**(7)ow1 MissHCuthbert(9) (b.hind: bhd: sme hdwy 5f out: sn btn)	8	9	66/1	22	10
2385^{7}	**Rapid Mover (26)** (DANolan) **10-9-0b** MrsSBosley(2) (led tl hdd 3f out: sn wknd)	6	10	12/1	4	—

(SP 115.4%) **10 Rn**

2m 27.4 (8.00) CSF £40.38 CT £407.65 TOTE £10.50: £2.70 £1.80 £2.10 (£23.70) Trio £45.00 OWNER Mr C. D. Barber-Lomax (AYR) BRED Mrs M. Morley
WEIGHT FOR AGE 3yo-12lb
2034 Philmist has been given a chance by the handicapper, and got the fast pace she required, doing just enough in the end to gain her first success on turf. (15/2)
2342 Madison Welcome (IRE) never got going until very late and then finished like the proverbial train, and in another couple of strides he would have won. (5/1)
2063 Stalled (IRE) stays further and likes strongly-run races, but this funny customer was never doing things soon enough this time. He looks particularly well at present. (12/1: op 8/1)
2351* Sun of Spring looked magnificent and ran his heart out but was just tapped for foot in the closing stages. (6/1)
2063 High Low (USA) tried to pick the best ground up the far rails but a lack of a change of gear was again exposed. (9/1: op 6/1)
2352 Love Me Do (USA) seemed short of any turn of foot. (8/1: op 5/1)

2034 Lord Advocate (7/1: op 7/2)
2063* Nosey Native failed to impress on looks and ran disappointingly. (7/2)

2470 FOUR SEASONS HEALTH AND BEAUTY CLINIC CLAIMING STKS (3-Y.O+) (Class D)
7-10 (7-14) **1m 1f 36y** £3,696.25 (£1,120.00: £547.50: £261.25) Stalls: High GOING minus 0.25 sec per fur (GF)

				SP	RR	SF
1951[2]	**White Plains (IRE) (78)** (KRBurke) **4-9-5**(7) CLowther(4) (mde most: kpt on wl fnl f)	—	1	2/1[2]	87	22
2223*	**Scaraben (72)** (SEKettlewell) **9-9-7** JStack(1) (lw: sn trckng wnr: effrt 3f out: disp ld appr fnl f: rdn & no ex)	1	2	4/9[1]	80	15
2114[7]	**Rattle (25)** (DANolan) **4-8-10**(5) KSked(2) (a bhd)	13	3	50/1	5 t	—
	Ribbonletta (MissLAPerratt) **3-8-0** NKennedy(5) (unf: unruly s: dwlt: a bhd)	12	4	33/1[3]	—	—
2221[4]	**Midas Man (20)** (DANolan) **6-8-8b**(7) PBradley(3) (cl up tl wknd fnl 3½f)	8	5	66/1	—	—

(SP 109.0%) **5 Rn**

2m 2.2 (7.90) CSF £2.92 TOTE £3.40: £1.50 £1.00 (£1.10) OWNER Mr Nigel Shields (WANTAGE) BRED Howard Kaskel
WEIGHT FOR AGE 3yo-10lb
1951 White Plains (IRE) had only one serious rival here and proved too tough for him when the pressure was on. (2/1)
2223* Scaraben gave his usual problems before the start and then raced with every chance, but if anything he saw too much daylight too soon and decided it was not for him. (4/9: op 4/6)
Rattle has yet to show anything positive this season. (50/1)
Ribbonletta, a lightly-made sort, looked a handful before the start and then showed nothing in the race. (33/1)

2471 PRECON BLOCK LIMITED STKS (0-55) (3-Y.O+) (Class F)
7-40 (7-40) **1m 65y** £2,542.00 (£712.00: £346.00) Stalls: High GOING minus 0.25 sec per fur (GF)

				SP	RR	SF
1732[5]	**Lapu-Lapu (54)** (MJCamacho) **4-9-1** LCharnock(1) (lw: trckd ldr: led over 3f out: rdn & r.o wl fnl 2f)	—	1	9/4[2]	61	25
2036[6]	**Classic Ballet (FR) (52)** (RGuest) **4-9-1** GDuffield(2) (trckd ldrs: hdwy over 3f out: sn chsng wnr & rdn: kpt on towards fin)	¾	2	11/8[1]	60	24
2239[5]	**Power Game (55)** (JBerry) **4-9-3b**(5) TEDurcan(3) (trckd ldrs: effrt 3f out: rdn & btn wl over 1f out)	6	3	3/1[3]	55	19
2071[6]	**Chadleigh Lane (USA) (52)** (ABMulholland) **5-8-13v**(7) CLowther(4) (led tl hdd over 3f out: sn outpcd)	2	4	10/1	49?	13

(SP 107.0%) **4 Rn**

1m 49.8 (5.70) CSF £5.14 TOTE £2.70 (£2.80) OWNER Mr Dunstan French (MALTON) BRED Mrs S. Camacho
1732 Lapu-Lapu, the pick on looks, did it well and looks in top form. (9/4)
2036 Classic Ballet (FR) looks a difficult customer to win with and gives the impression that she is suited by further, and also has more ability if she can be persuaded. (11/8)
2239 Power Game likes things to go all his way and had his chances here but found this opposition much too strong. (3/1: 2/1-7/2)
1576 Chadleigh Lane (USA) has only ever won on sand and never looked likely to lose that record here. (10/1: 4/1-11/1)

2472 TOTE BOOKMAKERS H'CAP (0-85) (3-Y.O+) (Class D)
8-10 (8-10) **6f 5y** £5,831.00 (£1,763.00: £859.00: £407.00) Stalls: High GOING minus 0.25 sec per fur (GF)

				SP	RR	SF
2339[5]	**Palacegate Touch (77)** (JBerry) **7-9-5b**(7) CLowther(5) (s.i.s: sn trckng ldrs: led over 2f out: hung bdly lft: kpt on wl)	—	1	4/1[3]	84	52
2144*	**Mister Westsound (51)** (MissLAPerratt) **5-8-0b** NKennedy(1) (lw: dwlt: hdwy 2f out: ev ch ins fnl f: r.o)	1¼	2	9/4[1]	55	23
2384[3]	**Leading Princess (IRE) (51)** (MissLAPerratt) **6-7-9b**(5)ow3 KSked(2) (lw: cl up: effrt over 2f out: hung bdly lft: kpt on)	nk	3	7/1	54	19
2326[4]	**The Lambton Worm (77)** (DenysSmith) **3-9-6** LCharnock(4) (lw: chsd ldrs: effrt over 2f out: nt qckn)	3½	4	100/30[2]	71	33
2382*	**Another Nightmare (IRE) (47)** (RMMcKellar) **5-7-10** 6x JLowe(3) (led tl hdd over 2f out: no ex)	½	5	4/1[3]	39	7
2355[5]	**Diet (47)** (MissLAPerratt) **11-7-3v**(7) JMcAuley(6) (lw: sn outpcd & bhd)	11	6	50/1	10	—

(SP 108.3%) **6 Rn**

1m 12.5 (2.50) CSF £11.32 TOTE £5.80: £2.50 £2.00 (£4.70) OWNER Laurel (Leisure) Ltd (COCKERHAM) BRED The Woodhaven Stud
LONG HANDICAP Diet 6-10
WEIGHT FOR AGE 3yo-6lb
2339 Palacegate Touch did his best to throw this away by hanging all the way across the track but this old character was then always doing enough. (4/1)
2144* Mister Westsound produced his usual late burst but on this occasion he was never quite finding enough. (9/4)
2384 Leading Princess (IRE) is a real character these days and she hung badly left here, following the winner, but still ran pretty well and obviously had plenty more ability. (7/1)
2326 The Lambton Worm looks in great condition but as yet this season he has not struck form, although he is coming on slowly but surely. (100/30)
2382* Another Nightmare (IRE) could never get away from her field this time and was comfortably picked off. (4/1)
2355 Diet looks well enough but this old stager is not doing it at the moment. (50/1)

2473 E.B.F. MEDIAN AUCTION MAIDEN STKS (2-Y.O) (Class E)
8-40 (8-41) **5f 4y** £3,225.00 (£975.00: £475.00: £225.00) Stalls: High GOING minus 0.25 sec per fur (GF)

				SP	RR	SF
2110[2]	**Prix Star** (CWFairhurst) **2-9-0v**[1] LCharnock(5) (lw: mde all: drvn out)	—	1	2/1[1]	76	21
2439a[8]	**Take A Turn** (MRChannon) **2-9-0** RPerham(8) (a chsng wnr: ev ch over 1f out: kpt on)	½	2	11/2	74	19
2066[6]	**Miss Puci** (JBerry) **2-8-2**(7) CLowther(2) (a chsng ldrs: kpt on fnl 2f)	2½	3	16/1	61	6
	Friar Tuck (MissLAPerratt) **2-9-0** NKennedy(7) (w'like: scope: bit bkwd: s.s: hdwy ½-wy: kpt on wl)	½	4	14/1	65+	10
2202[5]	**Burnt Yates (IRE)** (MWEasterby) **2-9-0** DaleGibson(3) (chsd ldrs tl outpcd appr fnl f)	2½	5	100/30[2]	57	2
	Oare Kite (PTWalwyn) **2-8-9** JLowe(4) (w'like: leggy: scope: lw: dwlt: sn outpcd & bhd: styd on fnl f)	hd	6	7/2[3]	52	—
1941[9]	**Liberte Bell (IRE)** (SirMarkPrescott) **2-8-9** GDuffield(9) (prom tl outpcd fnl 2f)	hd	7	25/1	51	—
	Nebuchadnezzar (JJO'Neill) **2-8-9**(5) TEDurcan(1) (w'like: bit bkwd: s.i.s: a outpcd & bhd)	2½	8	25/1	48	—

(SP 114.3%) **8 Rn**

61.6 secs (3.30) CSF £12.30 TOTE £2.30: £1.10 £1.70 £5.00 (£6.90) Trio £33.70 OWNER Mr M. J. Grace (MIDDLEHAM) BRED M. J. and Mrs Grace
2110 Prix Star had the visor on for the first time and, given a superb ride, did just enough. It will be interesting to see if they work twice. (2/1)
2439a Take A Turn is learning and he was keeping on particularly well at the end. (11/2)
2066 Miss Puci ran well and by the way she stayed on she should get further. (16/1)
Friar Tuck not surprisingly needed this, but is a useful-looking type and showed plenty of promise after a very poor start. (14/1)

2202 Burnt Yates (IRE) gives the impression that time will see better from him. (100/30)
Oare Kite took the eye in the paddock but proved clueless early on in the race and it was all over when she decided to run on. There is obviously much better to come when she gets the hang of things. (7/2)
Liberte Bell (IRE) looks the type who is taking her time to get fit and will do better in due course. (25/1)

2474 RAGE OF BOTHWELL MAIDEN H'CAP (0-65) (3-Y.O+) (Class E)

9-10 (9-12) **1m 5f 9y** £2,668.00 (£748.00: £364.00) Stalls: High GOING minus 0.25 sec per fur (GF)

Form	Horse / details	Dist	Pos	SP	RR	SF
2114[3]	**Indigo Dawn (55)** (MJohnston) **3-9-5**(3) KMChin(4) (lw: chsd ldrs tl outpcd & lost pl appr st: hdwy over 2f out: led 1f out: styd on wl)	—	1	2/1[2]	66	28
2046[14]	**Tam O'Shanter (55)** (CWThornton) **3-9-8** JFanning(1) (unruly s: led 5f: cl up: led 3f out tl hdd 1f out: kpt on)	2	2	8/1	64	26
2020[9]	**Heubach Boy (47)** (MrsASwinbank) **3-9-0** GDuffield(2) (lw: hdwy 8f out: sn chsng ldrs & drvn along: ev ch 2f out: r.o one pce)	hd	3	4/1[3]	55	17
1844[7]	**Moonlight Invader (IRE) (57)** (EALDunlop) **3-9-10** JStack(5) (lw: trckd ldrs: rdn over 4f out: ch over 1f out: one pce)	2	4	7/4[1]	63	25
1463[15]	**In A Tizzy (31)** (ABMulholland) **4-8-7**(5) IonaWands(6) (led after 5f tl hdd 3f out: wknd 2f out)	6	5	10/1	30	6

(SP 109.9%) **5 Rn**

2m 55.5 (9.80) CSF £15.26 TOTE £2.20: £1.50 £3.40 (£6.90) OWNER Greenland Park Ltd (MIDDLEHAM) BRED Lahama Ltd
WEIGHT FOR AGE 3yo-14lb

2114 Indigo Dawn just stays. After looking to have no chance early in the straight, her stamina came into play and she won going away. (2/1)
Tam O'Shanter was a real handful before the start but she ran quite well despite carrying her head at an angle and certainly stays well enough. (8/1)
Heubach Boy, making his handicap debut, was gambled on but seemed in trouble a long way out and it took a lot of persistence from his rider to keep him in the race with a chance. (4/1: op 5/2)
Moonlight Invader (IRE) keeps trying longer trips but it seems that it is his attitude that needs sorting out. (7/4)
1118 In A Tizzy has never been any closer than fourth on the Flat and she found it all too much here with two furlongs left. She does not seem to stay. (10/1)

T/Plpt: £33.40 (366.85 Tckts). T/Qdpt: £11.30 (45.56 Tckts) AA

2418-HAYDOCK (L-H) (Good)

Friday July 4th

WEATHER: sunny periods WIND: slt half against

2475 FRANK WOOTTON H'CAP (0-85) (4-Y.O+) (Class D)

7-00 (7-00) **1m 6f** £3,488.00 (£1,049.00: £507.00: £236.00) Stalls: Centre GOING minus 0.10 sec per fur (G)

Form	Horse / details	Dist	Pos	SP	RR	SF
2316[5]	**Turgenev (IRE) (60)** (RBastiman) **8-8-7** PatEddery(3) (chsd clr ldng pair: disp ld over 1f out: shkn up to ld nr fin)	—	1	3/1[2]	71	40
1871[2]	**Cloud Inspector (IRE) (72)** (MJohnston) **6-9-5** BDoyle(1) (lw: chsd ldr: led 2f out: hrd rdn & hdd nr fin)	hd	2	4/1	83	52
2122[7]	**Classic Find (USA) (73)** (ICampbell) **4-9-6** AMackay(5) (b: lw: hld up: hdwy 3f out: hrd rdn & one pce appr fnl f)	6	3	16/1	77	46
2218[5]	**Oberons Boy (IRE) (58)** (SDow) **4-8-5** JFEgan(4) (lw: hld up: hdwy 3f out: rdn & nt clr run over 2f out: one pce)	1½	4	14/1	60	29
2063[4]	**Express Gift (54)** (MrsMReveley) **8-7-12**(3) DarrenMoffatt(6) (lw: hld up: hdwy over 3f out: rdn & wknd 2f out)	6	5	7/2[3]	50	19
1497[5]	**Well Armed (IRE) (65)** (JJO'Neill) **6-8-12b[1]** JCarroll(2) (lw: set str pce: hung rt 3f out: hdd & wknd fnl 2f)	1¾	6	16/1	59	28
2028[18]	**Berlin Blue (77)** (JWWatts) **4-9-10** LDettori(7) (hld up mid div: lost pl ent st: hrd rdn 3f out: no rspnse)	1	7	11/4[1]	69	38

(SP 112.3%) **7 Rn**

3m 5.95 (7.75) CSF £13.49 TOTE £2.80: £1.60 £2.20 (£6.50) OWNER Mrs Bridget Tranmer (WETHERBY) BRED Paolo Tomei

2316 Turgenev (IRE), back on his favourite track and with the right man on top, was coaxed to do just enough to get the better of a very persistent challenger. (3/1)
1871 Cloud Inspector (IRE) has not enjoyed the best of fortunes since he came to this country and once again was forced to give best in the dying strides. He certainly did nothing wrong and an overdue success is near at hand. (4/1)
1398 Classic Find (USA), very much on his toes and racing with his tongue tied down, turned in an encouraging performance and he is ready to strike. (16/1)
2218 Oberons Boy (IRE), continuing his step up in distance, was denied a clear run when poised to challenge entering the last quarter-mile and when he did find room the task was always beyond him. He must not be written off yet. (14/1)
2063 Express Gift finished four lengths ahead of the winner when they last met, but with an 8lb turnaround in the weighs and a certain Mr Eddery to contend with, he never got in a blow this time. (7/2)
1497 Well Armed (IRE) set a very brisk pace and if he had had eight or ten flights in front of him it may have been a different matter. Edging into the centre of the track from the home turn, he had shot his bolt once collared. (16/1)

2476 ASPECTS BEAUTY CONDITIONS STKS (3-Y.O+) (Class C)

7-30 (7-30) **6f** £5,112.00 (£1,908.00: £929.00: £395.00: £172.50: £83.50) Stalls: High GOING minus 0.10 sec per fur (G)

Form	Horse / details	Dist	Pos	SP	RR	SF
1462[2]	**Za-Im (102)** (BWHills) **3-8-9** RHills(4) (w ldr: led ins fnl f: r.o wl)	—	1	11/4[1]	110	47
1596[6]	**Indian Spark (102)** (WGMTurner) **3-8-4**(5) DSweeney(1) (lw: mde most tl hdd ins fnl f)	1	2	15/2	107	44
2056[16]	**Cayman Kai (IRE) (106)** (RHannon) **4-9-1** RHughes(6) (lw: stdd s: hdwy & rdn 2f out: kpt on: nt pce to chal)	1¾	3	7/2[3]	103	46
2056[15]	**Jayannpee (105)** (IABalding) **6-9-1** LDettori(2) (lw: trckd ldrs: effrt & rdn wl over 1f out: one pce)	hd	4	100/30[2]	102	45
1578[6]	**Zuhair (86)** (DMcCain) **4-9-1** JCarroll(3) (b: chsd ldrs: rdn 2f out: sn btn)	2½	5	25/1	96	39
1101[5]	**Prends Ca (IRE) (90)** (WRMuir) **4-8-10** PatEddery(7) (hld up: effrt 2f out: sn rdn: no imp)	hd	6	15/2	91	34
	Domulla (103) (RAkehurst) **7-9-1** SSanders(5) (chsd ldrs over 3f: outpcd fnl 2f: t.o)	13	7	7/1	61	4

(SP 111.8%) **7 Rn**

1m 14.42 (2.72) CSF £20.59 TOTE £3.50: £2.20 £2.50 (£15.30) OWNER Mr Hamdan Al Maktoum (LAMBOURN) BRED Shadwell Estate Company Limited
WEIGHT FOR AGE 3yo-6lb

1462 Za-Im, stepping back to sprinting for the first time this season, proved too strong for the long-time leader inside the final furlong and won with a shade in hand. (11/4)
1596 Indian Spark is not the easiest to pass when he is allowed to blaze the trail and he did not go down without a fight this time, but the winner had the legs of him when it mattered. (15/2)
980 Cayman Kai (IRE), still carrying plenty of condition, probably benefits from a seventh furlong now and his sustained last-furlong dash was never quite going to get him there. (7/2)
1596 Jayannpee came down the centre of the track and always had a few lengths to make up on the principals. Responding to pressure, he kept battling away but a turn of finishing speed was the one thing that was missing. (100/30)
1410 Zuhair did his very best to hold his pitch in the chasing group but the tempo never dropped and he was in trouble from below the distance. (25/1)
1101 Prends Ca (IRE), returning to sprinting, was unable to get in a blow against the leaders and it is possible she does need at least seven furlongs nowadays. (15/2)

2477 GOLDWELL (HAIR/COSMETICS) MAIDEN AUCTION STKS (2-Y.O) (Class D)

8-00 (8-04) **6f** £4,034.00 (£1,217.00: £591.00: £278.00) Stalls: High GOING minus 0.10 sec per fur (G)

				SP	RR	SF
1842[3]	**Little Indian** (SPCWoods) **2-8-8** WRyan(10) (lw: chsd ldrs: rdn 1f out: r.o to ld fnl 50y)	—	**1**	15/8[1]	89	33
1675[3]	**Lido (IRE)** (BWHills) **2-8-6** RHills(4) (lw: a.p: led over 1f out tl hdd wl ins fnl f)	1	**2**	7/2[2]	84	28
	Bodfari Pride (IRE) (ABailey) **2-8-6** SSanders(8) (wl grwn: bit bkwd: outpcd: hdwy wl over 1f out: r.o ins fnl f)	6	**3**	16/1	68	12
2037[4]	**The Groveller** (PDEvans) **2-8-6** JFEgan(5) (hdwy ½-wy: rdn 2f out: r.o one pce)	¾	**4**	14/1	66	10
	Maggice (RHollinshead) **2-7-12** DWright(15) (lt-f: unf: s.s: hdwy & swtchd rt over 2f out: r.o)	3	**5**	33/1	50	—
1619[4]	**Saint Ann (USA)** (MJohnston) **2-8-6** BDoyle(6) (w ldrs: led over 2f out tl over 1f out: wknd fnl f)	s.h	**6**	9/2[3]	58	2
2110[3]	**Fundance** (MDods) **2-8-8** JReid(11) (w ldrs: ev ch over 1f out: sn rdn & outpcd)	½	**7**	8/1	59	3
	Golden Strategy (IRE) (RHannon) **2-8-11** RHughes(12) (cmpt: bit bkwd: sn chsng ldrs: btn whn hmpd & snatched up ins fnl)	¾	**8**	14/1	60	4
	Lesley's Adventure (IRE) (CaptJWilson) **2-7-12** CRutter(9) (lt-f: bkwd: dwlt: effrt & carried lft 3f out: n.d)	2	**9**	40/1	42	—
2022[6]	**On The Mat** (JJO'Neill) **2-8-6** JCarroll(3) (lw: chsd ldrs 4f)	¾	**10**	33/1	48	—
1645[8]	**Spice Girl** (PDEvans) **2-8-1** LNewton(7) (trckd ldrs: rdn 2f out: no imp)	1¾	**11**	20/1	38	—
	Cool Mystery (ABMulholland) **2-8-3** SDrowne(2) (w'like: scope: bkwd: prom over 4f)	2	**12**	50/1	35	—
1510[14]	**Hey Up Mate (IRE)** (JBerry) **2-8-6b[1]** KDarley(13) (led over 3f: wknd qckly: t.o)	5	**13**	25/1	24	—
	Double Appeal (IRE) (CaptJWilson) **2-7-5(7)** AngelaHartley(1) (w'like: scope: bit bkwd: s.s: a wl outpcd)	3½	**14**	50/1	7	—
				(SP 126.4%)	**14 Rn**	

1m 15.4 (3.70) CSF £7.15 TOTE £2.70: £1.30 £2.20 £4.90 (£4.90) Trio £37.20 OWNER Mr G. V. Wright (NEWMARKET) BRED M. S. Anderson
1842 Little Indian, strongly supported in the offices throughout the day after such a promising debut at Headquarters, did look to be held passing the furlong pole but the further he went the stronger he got and, swooping to lead late on, won going away. He does look a useful colt. (15/8)
1675 Lido (IRE) kicked on into the final furlong and looked to have stolen a march but the winner swooped to conquer nearing the finish and he must have wondered what had hit him. He is going the right way and there are races to be won. (7/2: op 9/4)
Bodfari Pride (IRE), a well-grown colt who does look to need time, ran a very encouraging race on this debut and the experience is sure to stand him in good stead. (16/1)
2037 The Groveller is a trier but he does lack a bit of pace and he was never going well enough to make his presence felt. (14/1)
Maggice, an unfurnished half-sister to three winners, did extremely well to reach her finishing position after a tardy start and she will be well worth keeping in mind. (33/1)
1619 Saint Ann (USA) knew much more this time and showed plenty of pace to share the lead, but she may have done too much too soon for she was a spent force inside the last furlong. (9/2)
Golden Strategy (IRE), colty in the paddock after following a filly round, still has plenty left to work on. Tracking the leaders, he was just beginning to feel the pinch when he became the meat in the sandwich and had to be checked two hundred yards out. (14/1: 10/1-16/1)

2478 BIRCHLEY RATED STKS H'CAP (0-95) (3-Y.O+) (Class C)

8-30 (8-32) **7f 30y** £8,027.24 (£2,995.16: £1,457.58: £618.90: £269.45: £129.67) Stalls: Low GOING minus 0.10 sec per fur (G)

				SP	RR	SF
2325*	**Jo Mell (78)** (TDEasterby) **4-8-7** 3x JCarroll(2) (mde all: qcknd clr wl over 1f out: unchal)	—	**1**	7/2[1]	91	51
2013[18]	**Generous Libra (93)** (DRLoder) **3-9-0** PatEddery(6) (lw: plld hrd: hld up in rr: hdwy on ins 2f out: r.o fnl f: no ch w wnr)	4	**2**	9/2[2]	97	49
1980[7]	**Double-J (IRE) (81)** (KMcAuliffe) **3-8-2** JFEgan(4) (a.p: hrd rdn over 1f out: kpt on same pce)	¾	**3**	25/1	83	35
2325[5]	**Weetman's Weigh (IRE) (80)** (RHollinshead) **4-8-9** LDettori(3) (hld up: nt clr run over 2f out: swtchd rt wl over 1f out: sn rdn: no imp)	¾	**4**	5/1[3]	81	41
2105[14]	**Albert The Bear (90)** (JBerry) **4-9-5** KDarley(9) (hld up mid div: hdwy over 2f out: sn rdn: nt pce to chal)	2	**5**	11/1	86	46
1979[14]	**Band on the Run (85)** (BAMcMahon) **10-9-0** LNewton(7) (hld up: effrt over 2f out: sn rdn: no imp)	¾	**6**	10/1	80	40
1397[6]	**Pleading (92)** (HCandy) **4-9-7** CRutter(1) (lw: s.s: hdwy over 2f out: nvr plcd to chal)	1¼	**7**	8/1	84	44
1264[5]	**My Valentina (82)** (BWHills) **3-8-3** RHills(10) (hld up: hdwy on outside over 2f out: nt rch ldrs)	4	**8**	16/1	65	17
2290[11]	**Plan For Profit (IRE) (82)** (MJohnston) **3-8-3** BDoyle(5) (prom over 4f: sn wknd)	½	**9**	11/1	64	16
2280*	**Q Factor (78)** (DHaydnJones) **5-8-7** 3x SDrowne(8) (prom: rdn along 3f out: sn wknd: t.o)	6	**10**	11/2	46	6
				(SP 119.1%)	**10 Rn**	

1m 30.84 (2.84) CSF £17.70 CT £314.23 TOTE £4.10: £1.60 £2.10 £5.00 (£11.00) Trio £133.30 OWNER C H Newton Jnr Ltd (MALTON) BRED D.B. Lamplough
LONG HANDICAP Jo Mell 8-2 Q Factor 8-2
WEIGHT FOR AGE 3yo-8lb
2325* Jo Mell, at the top of his form at present, was able to defy a small penalty with an all the way, clear-cut success, and in this mood further success awaits. (7/2)
1656* Generous Libra had his full share of weight for one so short on experience but he does look a progressive colt and we have not seen the best of him yet. (9/2)
1980 Double-J (IRE) won his maiden at the minimum trip twelve months ago and as yet he has to prove himself at this trip. He pushed the pace and kept on under strong pressure to suggest another success in beckoning. (25/1)
2325 Weetman's Weigh (IRE) was trapped on the inside when he should have been making his effort and when he did switch to find racing space was unable to pick up sufficiently to deliver a challenge. It is doubtful if he had been able to trouble the winner even with a clear run. (5/1)
1658* Albert The Bear, settled just off the pace, did not find the expected response when let down and was never a serious factor. (11/1)

1775* Band on the Run found this step back to seven furlongs catching him out and he was unable to quicken enough to mount a challenge. (10/1)

2479 BAILEYS ORIGINAL IRISH CREAM CLAIMING STKS (3-Y.O+) (Class E)

9-00 (9-01) **1m 3f 200y** £2,835.00 (£855.00: £415.00: £195.00) Stalls: Low GOING minus 0.10 sec per fur (G)

				SP	RR	SF
1215[6]	**Welsh Mill (IRE) (78)** (MrsMReveley) **8-10-0** KDarley(4) (lw: hld up: hdwy ½-wy: rdn to ld appr fnl f: hung lft: all out)	—	1	4/7[1]	73	42
2145[4]	**Forzair (45)** (JJO'Neill) **5-9-4** JCarroll(1) (lw: mde most tl rdn & hdd 1f out: rallied nr fin)	nk	2	10/1[3]	63	32
1809[4]	**Shabanaz (53)** (WRMuir) **12-9-0** JReid(5) (lw: a.p: drvn along 2f out: r.o one pce)	5	3	7/2[2]	52	21
	Single Man (IRE) (FHLee) **4-9-10** CRutter(2) (trckd ldrs: hrd drvn & wknd 3f out)	10	4	25/1	48	17
	Tycoon Ted (WMBrisbourne) **4-9-6** JFEgan(6) (b: bkwd: s.s: a bhd: t.o fr ½-wy)	18	5	33/1	20	—
2039[12]	**Big Pat (50)** (JGMO'Shea) **8-9-2** VSlattery(3) (b: bit bkwd: dwlt: sn w ldr: rdn & wknd over 2f out: t.o)	2½	6	10/1[3]	13	—

(SP 110.8%) **6 Rn**

2m 38.54 (9.14) CSF £6.59 TOTE £1.60: £1.30 £3.10 (£3.80) OWNER Mr D. S. Hall (SALTBURN) BRED Ballymacoll Stud Farm Ltd

1215 Welsh Mill (IRE) was in two minds about going through with his effort after poking his head in front entering the final furlong and Darley had to get serious to enable him to land the spoils. (4/7)

2145 Forzair ran in a visor on his previous outing but it was left off this time. With three wins to his name, all gained on the All-Weather, he did his best to run his rivals into the ground and he stuck on willingly after being headed. He is capable of winning on turf. (10/1)

1809 Shabanaz has yet to succeed at this trip and, with age catching up with him, his opportunities in future will be limited. (7/2)

2480 ELLESMERE H'CAP (0-70) (3-Y.O+) (Class E)

9-30 (9-31) **5f** £3,078.75 (£930.00: £452.50: £213.75) Stalls: High GOING minus 0.10 sec per fur (G)

				SP	RR	SF
2289[2]	**Blessingindisguise (70)** (MWEasterby) **4-9-9b**[(5)] GParkin(5) (lw: mde virtually all: qcknd clr 1f out: eased & hld on cl home)	—	1	11/10[1]	77+	63
2111[3]	**Rich Glow (53)** (NBycroft) **6-8-11** KDarley(6) (lw: outpcd ½-wy: swtchd rt 2f out: str run wl ins fnl f)	hd	2	6/1[3]	60	46
2177*	**Superbit (67)** (BAMcMahon) **5-9-11** [7x] LNewton(7) (lw: w wnr: rdn 2f out: rallied cl home)	½	3	5/1[2]	72	58
	My Abbey (50) (ABailey) **8-8-8** SSanders(2) (a.p: rdn over 1f out: r.o wl)	½	4	20/1	54	40
2366[9]	**Perfect Brave (55)** (JBalding) **6-8-13** JEdmunds(8) (lw: a chsng ldrs: effrt appr fnl f: r.o)	½	5	25/1	57	43
1743[10]	**John O'Dreams (43)** (MrsALMKing) **12-8-1** CRutter(9) (b: lw: s.s: bhd: hdwy & nt clr run 1f out: nt rcvr)	½	6	14/1	43	29
1311[6]	**Cross The Border (57)** (DNicholls) **4-9-1** AlexGreaves(4) (bhd: rdn wl over 1f out: styng on whn nt clr run jst ins fnl f)	1¾	7	8/1	52	38
159[8]	**Panther (IRE) (69)** (PDEvans) **7-9-13** JFEgan(3) (swtchd rt s: a bhd & outpcd)	1	8	16/1	61	47
2167[3]	**Good To Talk (40)** (TDEasterby) **4-7-12b** FNorton(1) (outpcd)	1½	9	8/1	27	13

(SP 122.0%) **9 Rn**

61.87 secs (2.37) CSF £8.02 CT £24.09 TOTE £1.90: £1.20 £1.50 £1.90 (£5.20) Trio £5.50 OWNER Mr A. G. Black (SHERIFF HUTTON) BRED Mrs A. Meller

2289 Blessingindisguise, given an almost over-confident ride, was a length and a half to the good entering the final furlong but, with success seemingly assured, his jockey eased him close home and in the end the line arrived only just in time. (11/10)

2111 Rich Glow found all the trouble that was going and he looked sure to finish in the pack but he produced a telling burst of speed inside the final one hundred yards and was only half a stride down at the line. (6/1)

2177* Superbit is on good terms with himself and rallied in fine style towards the finish after always looking to be coming off second best in his duel with the winner. (5/1)

My Abbey, reappearing after an absence of 659 days, looked well tuned up and was mounted on the track. Never far away, she ran her race out to the finish and she has lost none of her ability. (20/1)

905 Perfect Brave has probably tired of the All-Weather and he ran a fine race in defeat. He is weighted to win again but may require another furlong. (25/1)

1083 John O'Dreams, last to leave the stalls, had a nightmare run when trying to find a way through and even at his advanced age there could still be a race or two in him. (14/1)

1311 Cross The Border (8/1: op 5/1)

2167 Good To Talk (8/1: op 14/1)

T/Plpt: £11.70 (1,803.15 Tckts). T/Qdpt: £3.20 (377.14 Tckts) IM

1970-SANDOWN (R-H) (Good to soft, Good patches round crse)

Friday July 4th

WEATHER: overcast WIND: almost nil

2481 KPMG H'CAP (0-70) (3-Y.O) (Class E)

2-00 (2-02) **5f 6y** £3,550.00 (£1,075.00: £525.00: £250.00) Stalls: High GOING: 0.11 sec per fur (G)

				SP	RR	SF
1810[2]	**Sally Green (IRE) (68)** (CFWall) **3-9-5** LDettori(9) (hld up: chsd ldr over 2f out: led over 1f out: rdn out)	—	1	2/1[1]	74	36
2071[10]	**Singforyoursupper (45)** (GGMargarson) **3-7-10** GBardwell(10) (lw: led 1f: led 3f out tl over 1f out: unable qckn)	1½	2	13/2[3]	46	8
1995[3]	**Nopalea (70)** (TJNaughton) **3-9-7** PatEddery(7) (b.off fore: lw: rdn & hdwy over 1f out: one pce)	3½	3	3/1[2]	60	22
2006[15]	**Hype Energy (62)** (GLewis) **3-8-13** AClark(8) (rdn thrght: lost pl over 3f out: r.o one pce fnl f)	1¼	4	9/1	48	10
2179[14]	**Dancing Mystery (49)** (EAWheeler) **3-7-7**[(7)ow2] SCarson(5) (plld hrd: hdwy over 1f out: one pce)	s.h	5	33/1	35	—
2192[8]	**Gunners Glory (63)** (BJMeehan) **3-9-0b** BDoyle(6) (dropped rr over 3f out: n.m.r over 1f out: nvr nr to chal)	½	6	16/1	47	9
2321[6]	**Whizz Kid (51)** (JJBridger) **3-7-11**[(5)] RMullen(1) (prom over 3f)	2½	7	12/1	27	—
2298[6]	**M T Vessel (51)** (JRJenkins) **3-8-2b**[1] GCarter(4) (led 4f out to 3f out: wknd over 1f out)	5	8	33/1	12	—
2231[9]	**Durable George (52)** (JJBridger) **3-7-12**[(5)ow7] ADaly(2) (lw: prom over 3f)	3	9	50/1	3	—
	Royal Orchid (IRE) (66) (RHannon) **3-9-3** DaneO'Neill(3) (b.hind: lw: a bhd)	1¼	10	16/1	13	—

(SP 109.0%) **10 Rn**

64.35 secs (4.55) CSF £12.43 CT £29.93 TOTE £2.10: £1.30 £1.60 £1.90 (£6.40) Trio £4.80 OWNER Mr K. V. Stenborg (NEWMARKET) BRED Mrs C. A. Moore

LONG HANDICAP Durable George 7-8 Singforyoursupper 7-8

IN-FOCUS: This race yet again illustrated that it is absolutely imperative to have a high draw when the stalls are on the far side and the ground is riding soft.
1810 Sally Green (IRE), led round by two handlers in the paddock, looked very well beforehand but spoilt her appearance by getting rather warm. Blessed with a high draw, she cruised into the lead approaching the final furlong and was rousted along to assert her authority and win a very poor handicap by Sandown standards. (2/1)
Singforyoursupper appreciated the drop in distance and soft ground and, combined with the best draw of all, bounced back to form. Making the vast majority of the running, she was collared approaching the final furlong and, although put in her place by the winner, still finished well clear of the remainder. (13/2)
1995 Nopalea is proving very consistent but, after struggling through to take third place in the final furlong, had no hope of getting to the front two. (3/1)
652 Hype Energy, who had shown nothing in three previous runs this season, ran better here. Off the bridle virtually throughout, she soon lost her early position but did struggle on again in the closing stages. (9/1: 6/1-10/1)
Dancing Mystery, who took a keen hold early on, moved up below the distance but could then make no further impression. (33/1)
882 Gunners Glory has been very disappointing this season and, not surprisingly, is set to fall 7lb in future handicaps. Dropping back to last place over three furlongs from home, he never threatened to get into it. His best run so far this season came in a seller and a return to that class looks the answer. (16/1)
2321 Whizz Kid (12/1: op 7/1)

2482 PILLAR PROPERTY INVESTMENTS CONDITIONS STKS (2-Y.O) (Class C)
2-35 (2-35) **7f 16y** £4,611.90 (£1,613.90: £789.45: £339.75) Stalls: High GOING: 0.11 sec per fur (G)

				SP	RR	SF
1933*	**Muhtathir** (JHMGosden) **2-9-1** RHills(3) (lw: mde all: clr over 1f out: easily)	—	1	1/2 1	105+	65
2057 4	**Classic Manoeuvre (USA)** (RHannon) **2-8-11** PatEddery(1) (lw: chsd wnr 1f: rdn over 2f out: chsd wnr over 2f out: no imp)	9	2	15/8 2	81	41
	Celestial Bay (IRE) (AGFoster) **2-8-3** BDoyle(2) (leggy: dwlt: plld hrd: chsd wnr 6f out tl over 2f out: eased whn btn fnl f)	5	3	25/1 3	61	21
1812 24	**Erika's Young Man** (MJHaynes) **2-8-8**(3) MHenry(4) (a bhd: t.o)	30	4	100/1	2	—
				(SP 106.3%)		**4 Rn**

1m 32.39 (3.79) CSF £1.45 TOTE £1.50 (£1.10) OWNER Mr Hamdan Al Maktoum (NEWMARKET) BRED Shadwell Estate Company Limited
1933* Muhtathir won over this course and distance last month when his trainer reported that he would be even better with some cut. Looking magnificent in the paddock although half asleep, he had little more than an exercise gallop as he annihilated the opposition. He has a tremendous amount of scope and looks a very useful individual. A return visit for the Solario Stakes at the end of August looks on the cards and he must have a seriously good chance especially if there is some give underfoot. (1/2)
2057 Classic Manoeuvre (USA) had a real battle for second place in the straight and, although eventually winning, had absolutely no hope with the winner. (15/8)
Celestial Bay (IRE), a tall, sparely-made filly, was certainly given no easy task on this debut but acquitted herself well. Soon racing in second place, she had a real battle for that position in the straight but eventually had to concede defeat from below the distance. (25/1)

2483 E D & F MAN H'CAP (0-80) (3-Y.O+) (Class D)
3-10 (3-11) **1m 3f 91y** £3,647.50 (£1,105.00: £540.00: £257.50) Stalls: High GOING: 0.11 sec per fur (G)

				SP	RR	SF
2122 5	**Magic Combination (IRE) (69)** (BJCurley) **4-9-3** WRyan(8) (led tl over 1f out: rdn: led wl ins fnl f: r.o wl)	—	1	11/2	78	50
1923 5	**Premier Generation (IRE) (68)** (DWPArbuthnot) **4-9-2** DHolland(5) (swtg: hdwy over 2f out: led over 1f out tl wl ins fnl f: r.o)	nk	2	11/2	77	49
1459 3	**Typhoon Eight (IRE) (70)** (RWArmstrong) **5-9-4** GCarter(7) (hld up: n.m.r & swtchd lft over 2f out: r.o ins fnl f)	2	3	11/2	76	48
1825 3	**Rock The Barney (IRE) (49)** (MDIUsher) **8-7-6**(5)ow1 RMullen(3) (lw: s.s: hdwy over 2f out: hrd rdn over 1f out: unable qckn)	1¼	4	10/1	53	24
1763 2	**Hawker Hunter (USA) (78)** (RAkehurst) **6-9-12** TQuinn(4) (lw: chsd ldr over 9f)	2½	5	2/1 1	79	51
2118 6	**Dramatic Moment (66)** (JRArnold) **4-9-0** PatEddery(6) (prom 9f)	s.h	6	10/1	66	38
1208 4	**Royal Seaton (74)** (MrsPNDutfield) **8-9-5**(3) RHavlin(9) (lw: hld up: rdn over 2f out: sn wknd)	nk	7	10/1	74	46
2122 8	**Temptress (68)** (JohnHarris) **4-9-2** LDettori(1) (hld up: rdn over 2f out: wknd over 1f out)	1¼	8	4/1 3	66	38
2122 3	***Sofyaan (USA) (80)*** *(LadyHerries)* ***4-10-0*** *RCochrane(2) (Withdrawn not under Starter's orders: bolted bef s)*		W	7/2 2	—	—
				(SP 149.0%)		**8 Rn**

2m 31.89 (8.49) CSF £36.21 CT £166.16 TOTE £9.00: £2.30 £1.50 £2.10 (£18.40) Trio £121.00 OWNER Mrs B. J. Curley (NEWMARKET)
LONG HANDICAP Rock The Barney (IRE) 7-3
2122 Magic Combination (IRE) confirmed the promise shown at Newmarket recently under a fine ride from Ryan. Bowling along in front, he was marginally headed below the distance but, with his jockey doing little more than shaking him up, the combination managed to get back in front again in the closing stages. (11/2)
1923 Premier Generation (IRE) is at his best with some give underfoot and appeared to have made a winning move as he gained a narrow advantage below the distance. Unfortunately for him, the winner refused to lie down and he was passed in the closing stages. (11/2)
1459 Typhoon Eight (IRE) appreciated the step up in distance and, after switching left to get a clear run over a quarter of a mile from home, stayed on up the hill to take third prize inside the final furlong. (11/2)
1825 Rock The Barney (IRE) has yet to win on ground worse than good and, after making a forward move from the back of the field over a quarter of a mile from home, could only go up and down in the same place from below the distance. (10/1)
1763 Hawker Hunter (USA) was most disappointing after his encouraging reappearance at Doncaster last month. Racing in second place, he was being vigorously ridden along over a quarter of a mile out but the writing was soon on the wall. (2/1)
2118 Dramatic Moment once again showed that soft ground is not for her and had been hung out to dry over a quarter of a mile from home. (10/1: 8/1-12/1)

2484 WATES CENTENARY DRAGON STKS (Listed) (2-Y.O) (Class A)
3-40 (3-47) **5f 6y** £10,158.50 (£2,856.00: £1,395.50) Stalls: High GOING: 0.11 sec per fur (G)

				SP	RR	SF
2054 4	**Bodyguard** (PFICole) **2-9-3** TQuinn(1) (lw: chsd ldr: led over 1f out: rdn out)	—	1	6/5 2	103	16
2024 3	**Daunting Lady (IRE)** (RHannon) **2-8-12** PatEddery(2) (lw: led over 3f: hrd rdn & ev ch fnl f: r.o)	nk	2	Evens 1	97	10
2370 3	**Aurigny** (SDow) **2-8-10** WRyan(3) (hld up: rdn over 1f out: wknd fnl f)	5	3	7/1 3	79	—
				(SP 108.0%)		**3 Rn**

65.53 secs (5.73) CSF £2.54 TOTE £1.80 (£1.40) OWNER H R H Prince Fahd Salman (WHATCOMBE) BRED M. Rapp

2054 Bodyguard, who had no luck in running in the Norfolk Stakes at Royal Ascot, regained the winning thread here. Stalking his market rival, he gained a narrow advantage approaching the final furlong and, with Quinn not resorting to the whip but just vigorously riding him along, just managed to keep the very persistent runner-up at bay. The Richmond Stakes at the big Goodwood meeting is his next port of call. (6/5: 5/4-evens)
2024 Daunting Lady (IRE), who spread a plate and had to be re-shod down at the start, set a very moderate pace until quickening things up from halfway. Marginally headed approaching the final furlong, she refused to give way and, in a tremendous battle with the winner, only just lost out. She should soon regain the winning thread. (Evens)
2370 Aurigny, making a quick reappearance, was on the heels of the front two a furlong from home before tiring. (7/1: 6/1-10/1)

2485 CORPORATE SERVICES GROUP H'CAP (0-75) (3-Y.O+) (Class D)
4-10 (4-14) **1m 14y** £3,615.00 (£1,095.00: £535.00: £255.00) Stalls: High GOING: 0.11 sec per fur (G)

				SP	RR	SF
2150^{3}	**Renata's Prince (IRE) (51)** (KRBurke) **4-8-5** LDettori(7) (swtchd lft 3f out: hdwy over 2f out: led over 1f out: edgd rt ins fnl f: r.o wl)	—	**1**	$5/1^{2}$	62	48
2346^{2}	**Therhea (IRE) (69)** (BRMillman) **4-9-9** BDoyle(3) (lw: hld up: nt clr run on ins over 2f out tl over 1f out: swtchd lft: unable qckn ins fnl f)	1¼	**2**	$11/8^{1}$	78	64
2187^{7}	**Kailey Senor (USA) (73)** (RWArmstrong) **4-9-13** RPrice(8) (lw: rdn over 3f out: hdwy over 1f out: r.o one pce)	3½	**3**	12/1	75	61
1972*	**Baba Au Rhum (IRE) (66)** (IPWilliams) **5-9-6** AClark(6) (plld hrd: hld up: chsd ldr over 2f out: led wl over 1f out: sn hdd: wknd ins fnl f)	½	**4**	$11/2^{3}$	67	53
1968^{4}	**Zidac (70)** (PJMakin) **5-9-10** PatEddery(5) (lw: chsd ldrs over 5f: wknd over 1f out)	1¼	**5**	10/1	68	54
2216^{5}	**Fionn de Cool (IRE) (64)** (RAkehurst) **6-9-4** TQuinn(1) (led over 6f)	¾	**6**	9/1	61	47
	Comanche Companion (59) (TJNaughton) **7-8-13** DaneO'Neill(4) (a bhd)	2½	**7**	10/1	51	37
2115^{11}	**Coastguards Hero (47)** (MDIUsher) **4-8-1** JMarshall(2) (swtg: prom 5f)	5	**8**	50/1	29	15

(SP 112.0%) **8 Rn**

1m 46.31 (5.11) CSF £10.68 CT £68.54 TOTE £4.10: £1.30 £1.20 £3.00 (£4.00) OWNER Mr P. Sweeting (WANTAGE) BRED John Harrington
2150 Renata's Prince (IRE) came with a nice run to strike the front below the distance and, despite drifting right in the closing stages, kept on for a cosy success. (5/1)
2346 Therhea (IRE), set to rise 4lb in future handicaps, again encountered traffic problems. Boxed in with nowhere to go along the inside rail, his jockey eventually managed to switch him left and get a clear run below the distance but the winner had got first run on him and he was unable to peg that rival back. (11/8)
1972 Kailey Senor (USA) was back over his ideal trip and, bustled along in the straight, stayed on from below the distance to snatch third prize. (12/1)
1972* Baba Au Rhum (IRE), who has been raised 6lb for his win here three weeks ago, poked his head in front early in the final quarter-mile but, no sooner had he got there, than he was passed by the winner. (11/2: 4/1-6/1)
1968 Zidac was not helped by the drop in distance and, after racing in second place until over two furlongs from home, was left for dead from below the distance. Both his wins to date have come over a mile and a quarter. (10/1)
2216 Fionn de Cool (IRE) was not going to hang around and set a brisk pace but, once collared below the distance, the writing was soon on the wall. His record now stands at one win from forty-five starts. (9/1: op 5/1)
Comanche Companion (10/1: 6/1-11/1)

2486 QUEEN SQUARE MAIDEN STKS (3 & 4-Y.O) (Class D)
4-40 (4-44) **1m 6f** £3,533.75 (£1,070.00: £522.50: £248.75) Stalls: High GOING: 0.11 sec per fur (G)

				SP	RR	SF
2027^{3}	**Book At Bedtime (IRE) (95)** (CACyzer) **3-8-6** LDettori(2) (mde all: clr 2f out: easily)	—	**1**	$1/6^{1}$	85+	29
2046^{5}	**Vrennan** (JRFanshawe) **3-8-6** PatEddery(3) (chsd wnr 2f: chsd wnr 7f out: rdn 3f out: eased whn btn ins fnl f)	7	**2**	$8/1^{2}$	77	21
1938^{3}	**Padauk (64)** (MJHaynes) **3-8-11** TQuinn(5) (lw: hld up: rdn 3f out: wknd over 2f out)	11	**3**	$14/1^{3}$	69	13
1239^{4}	**Final Stage (IRE)** (PWChapple-Hyam) **3-8-8**(3) RHavlin(4) (lw: rdn over 8f out: a bhd)	3	**4**	20/1	66	10
2126^{9}	**Veuve Clicquot** (RWArmstrong) **3-8-6** RPrice(1) (lw: chsd wnr 12f out to 7f out: rdn over 3f out: wknd over 2f out)	2½	**5**	50/1	58	2

(SP 110.2%) **5 Rn**

3m 11.45 (12.55) CSF £2.00 TOTE £1.20: £1.10 £1.90 (£1.70) OWNER Mr R. M. Cyzer (HORSHAM) BRED Sheikh Mohammed Bin Rashid Al Maktoum
2027 Book At Bedtime (IRE), who has been competing at the very highest level recently, had a straightforward task in this poor event and had little more than an exercise gallop. (1/6: op 1/4)
2046 Vrennan moved into second place at halfway but she had no hope with the winner and her jockey eased her down when all chance had evaporated inside the final furlong. (8/1: 6/1-10/1)
1938 Padauk was taking a step up in distance but had been hung out to dry approaching the final quarter-mile. (14/1: 8/1-16/1)
1239 Final Stage (IRE), off the bridle early in the back straight, is short on ability and is certainly one of the stable's third division horses. (20/1)
Veuve Clicquot, in second place in the first half of the race, was going in reverse approaching the final quarter-mile. (50/1)

T/Plpt: £25.70 (726.38 Tckts). T/Qdpt: £19.90 (36.31 Tckts) AK

2196-WARWICK (L-H) (Soft)
Friday July 4th
WEATHER: overcast WIND: almost nil

2487 BIG APPLE MAIDEN H'CAP (0-65) (3-Y.O+) (Class F)
2-15 (2-20) **1m 2f 169y** £2,277.00 (£627.00: £297.00) Stalls: Low GOING: 0.27 sec per fur (G)

				SP	RR	SF
886^{13}	**Come Together (58)** (DWPArbuthnot) **3-8-9** SWhitworth(17) (racd wd: lost pl 7f out: hdwy 4f out: led over 1f out: drvn out)	—	**1**	33/1	67	25
2152^{5}	**Swing West (USA) (63)** (PFICole) **3-9-0** CRutter(18) (racd wd: led after 2f: hdd over 1f out: nt qckn)	2½	**2**	8/1	68	26
1087^{5}	**Mowjood (USA) (62)** (MRStoute) **3-8-13** JReid(4) (lw: rdn & hdwy over 3f out: r.o ins fnl f)	s.h	**3**	$3/1^{1}$	67+	25
2281^{3}	**Isis Honda (IRE) (59)** (CEBrittain) **3-8-10** WJO'Connor(11) (a.p: one pce fnl f)	1½	**4**	15/2	62	20
2008^{8}	**Tribal Moon (IRE) (65)** (LadyHerries) **4-9-7**(7) PDoe(8) (hdwy over 2f out: wknd fnl f)	3	**5**	$6/1^{2}$	64	34
2208^{6}	**So Keen (44)** (ABailey) **4-8-2**(5)ow2 PRoberts(10) (hdwy 4f out: wknd over 1f out)	4	**6**	25/1	37	5
482^{8}	**Indian Nectar (50)** (RBrotherton) **4-8-13** SDrowne(19) (racd wd: prom tl wknd over 1f out)	nk	**7**	50/1	42	12

				SP	RR	SF
1986[2]	**Little Miss Rocker (68)** (IABalding) **3-9-2**(3) MartinDwyer(3) (hld up: rdn 4f out: wknd 3f out)	3	**8**	7/1[3]	56	14
1991[3]	**Hever Golf Charmer (58)** (TJNaughton) **3-8-9** TSprake(16) (lw: n.d)	1	**9**	20/1	44	2
13[6]	**Chocolate Ice (59)** (RJO'Sullivan) **4-9-8** ACulhane(14) (prom: rdn 6f out: wknd 2f out: eased whn btn fnl f)	¾	**10**	20/1	44	14
1938[13]	**Running Free (IRE) (50)** (MJFetherston-Godley) **3-8-1** FNorton(7) (prom over 5f)	2½	**11**	33/1	31	—
1623[8]	**Misellina (FR) (50)** (JSMoore) **3-8-1** JFEgan(6) (lw: dwlt: nvr nr ldrs)	3½	**12**	66/1	26	—
2174[10]	**Yuppy Girl (IRE) (40)** (CaptJWilson) **4-7-12**(5) RFfrench(5) (s.s: a bhd)	3	**13**	20/1	12	—
	Such Presence (48) (KSBridgwater) **3-7-13** JBramhill(15) (b: rdn 7f out: bhd fnl 4f)	9	**14**	66/1	6	—
926[3]	**Baaheth (USA) (62)** (SCWilliams) **3-8-6**(7) DarrenWilliams(9) (a bhd)	2½	**15**	33/1	17	—
2068[3]	**Kustom Kit Klassic (48)** (SRBowring) **3-7-13** DWright(1) (b: bhd fnl 4f)	½	**16**	16/1	2	—
1804[2]	**Expialiodoocius (63)** (JRFanshawe) **3-9-0** KFallon(13) (hdwy 4f out: rdn over 2f out: sn wknd)	4	**17**	7/1[3]	11	—
1646[9]	**Straffan Gold (USA) (55)** (GWragg) **3-8-6** JQuinn(12) (a bhd)	9	**18**	20/1	—	—
2039[16]	**Foreign Judgement (USA) (38)** (WJMusson) **4-8-1** DRMcCabe(20) (b: dwlt: a bhd)	6	**19**	66/1	—	—
1230[13]	**Banneret (USA) (54)** (JO'Reilly) **4-9-3** VHalliday(2) (bit bkwd: led 2f: wknd qckly 5f out: t.o)	dist	**20**	25/1	—	—
				(SP 135.0%)	**20 Rn**	

2m 26.2 (12.20) CSF £245.49 CT £968.34 TOTE £35.00: £6.30 £3.50 £1.70 £1.30 (£295.20) Trio Not won; £813.52 to Sandown 5/7/97
OWNER Mr Christopher Wright (COMPTON) BRED Snailwell Stud Co Ltd
WEIGHT FOR AGE 3yo-12lb
IN-FOCUS: The stands' side was the place to be in the home straight throughout the afternoon.
Come Together, down 6lb, was trying a longer trip. She relished the soft ground, having finished fifth when pulling too hard in the only race run on the day the jockeys considered the course unsafe at Haydock last year. (33/1)
2152 Swing West (USA), dropped 4lb, was also stepping up from a mile and seemed suited to the give underfoot. (8/1)
1087 Mowjood (USA), having his first run on soft going, was attempting an extra half-mile and certainly did not find stamina a problem, only just failing to snatch second place. (3/1)
2281 Isis Honda (IRE) handles all sorts of ground but keeps finding one or two too good for her. (15/2)
Tribal Moon (IRE) was bought for only 900 gns last year and gelded prior to making his seasonal debut last month. (6/1: 4/1-7/1)
2208 So Keen, still struggling to find the right trip, had been dropped 5lb and was due to go down a further 2lb tomorrow. (25/1)

2488 JOHN CATTELL'S FINAL FURLONG OF FREEDOM (S) H'CAP (0-60) (3-Y.O+) (Class G)

2-50 (2-55) **1m** £2,925.30 (£815.80: £393.90) Stalls: Low GOING: 0.27 sec per fur (G)

				SP	RR	SF
1292[4]	**Queen of Shannon (IRE) (49)** (AWCarroll) **9-9-3**(7) RStudholme(15) (s.s: gd hdwy over 1f out: led ins fnl f: rdn out)	—	**1**	7/1[2]	67	41
2039[9]	**Moneghetti (37)** (JLHarris) **6-8-7**(5) RFfrench(17) (chsd ldr: led over 3f out tl ins fnl f)	5	**2**	14/1	45	19
1576[10]	**My Handsome Prince (34)** (PJBevan) **5-8-9** NCarlisle(13) (lw: s.s: sn rcvrd: r.o one pce fnl f)	2½	**3**	20/1	37	11
2109[4]	**Maurangi (26)** (BWMurray) **6-8-1**ow1 MDeering(11) (a.p: hmpd & swtchd lft 2f out: edgd rt fnl f: r.o one pce)	1½	**4**	10/1	26	—
1483[10]	**Sweet Seventeen (30)** (HJCollingridge) **4-8-5** DianaWeeden(19) (hdwy over 1f out: r.o)	nk	**5**	33/1	29	3
1095[6]	**Foolish Flutter (IRE) (37)** (RBastiman) **3-8-3b** JFEgan(2) (hdwy over 1f out: nvr nrr)	2	**6**	20/1	32	—
1506[3]	**Gold Lance (USA) (48)** (RJO'Sullivan) **4-9-9** SSanders(1) (hld up: hdwy over 4f out: one pce fnl 2f)	½	**7**	7/1[2]	42	16
2177[7]	**Best Kept Secret (45)** (LJBarratt) **6-9-6** SDrowne(18) (rdn 3f out: no hdwy fnl 2f)	¾	**8**	10/1	38	12
2368[5]	**Sandmoor Denim (49)** (SRBowring) **10-9-3**(7) FBoyle(12) (b: racd alone far side st: no hdwy fnl 2f)	1¼	**9**	8/1[3]	39	13
2226[2]	**Katie Komaite (39)** (CaptJWilson) **4-9-0** KFallon(9) (prom 6f)	1¼	**10**	6/1[1]	27	1
2310[7]	**Shanghai Lil (28)** (MJFetherston-Godley) **5-8-3** FNorton(16) (n.d)	s.h	**11**	16/1	16	—
2070[6]	**Eastleigh (33)** (RHollinshead) **8-8-8** FLynch(14) (b.hind: chsd ldrs 6f)	1¼	**12**	20/1	18	—
224[6]	**Little Pilgrim (32)** (TMJones) **4-8-7** RPerham(5) (prom 6f)	½	**13**	50/1	16	—
2310[6]	**Safa Dancer (25)** (BAMcMahon) **4-8-0** LNewton(7) (a bhd)	1	**14**	16/1	7	—
2237[7]	**David James' Girl (32)** (ABailey) **5-8-7** AMackay(8) (b: a bhd)	nk	**15**	20/1	14	—
2228[8]	**Scottish Park (40)** (MCPipe) **8-8-12b**(3) MartinDwyer(10) (chsd ldrs over 5f)	¾	**16**	14/1	20	—
2160[4]	**Arcatura (48)** (CJames) **5-9-9** CRutter(3) (bhd fnl 3f)	3½	**17**	11/1	21	—
1467[18]	**Commin' Up (50)** (MissMERowland) **4-9-11** NAdams(20) (racd wd: led over 4f: wknd 2f out)	4	**18**	20/1	15	—
2150[10]	**Charlton Imp (USA) (50)** (RJHodges) **4-9-11** JQuinn(4) (a bhd)	9	**19**	12/1	—	—
1473[11]	**Spirit of Sport (30)** (AGNewcombe) **4-8-5b** JBramhill(6) (swtg: chsd ldrs tl hmpd & fell over 3f out)		**F**	25/1	—	—
				(SP 142.3%)	**20 Rn**	

1m 45.0 (8.60) CSF £93.69 CT £1,788.84 TOTE £9.40: £2.50 £4.40 £5.80 £2.40 (£61.70) Trio £867.40 OWNER J Wigmore Racing Partnership (WORCESTER) BRED George Killoughery
WEIGHT FOR AGE 3yo-9lb
No bid
1292 Queen of Shannon (IRE) had worn a visor when taking in a similar event off a 5lb lower mark at Windsor last August. (7/1)
1622 Moneghetti, down 3lb, had no answer to the winner in the final two hundred yards. (14/1)
1266 My Handsome Prince, back to a mile, was 3lb lower than when in a handicap two outings ago. (20/1)
2109 Maurangi had been given a real chance by the handicapper being 4lb lower than at Ayr. (10/1)
Sweet Seventeen, 10lb lower than when last in a handicap, ran better than her finishing position suggests, having raced on slower ground up the centre in the straight. (33/1)
Foolish Flutter (IRE), who has slipped down the ratings, found this shorter distance inadequate. (20/1)
1794 Charlton Imp (USA) (12/1: op 8/1)

2489 PYMENTS CLAIMING STKS (2-Y.O) (Class F)

3-25 (3-41) **7f** £2,554.20 (£706.20: £336.60) Stalls: Low GOING: 0.27 sec per fur (G)

				SP	RR	SF
2240*	**Lord Smith** (MCPipe) **2-9-4**(3) MartinDwyer(4) (mde all: rdn clr fnl f)	—	**1**	11/8[1]	67	34
1827[7]	**Petaling (IRE)** (BJMeehan) **2-8-12** MTebbutt(1) (a.p: chsd wnr 3f out: rdn over 1f out: no imp)	4	**2**	10/1	49	16
*2163**	**Michelee** (PDEvans) **2-9-2** JFEgan(6) (lw: chsd wnr: rdn over 3f out: wknd 2f out)	6	**3**	7/4[2]	39	6
2227[9]	**Floral Park** (GBBalding) **2-8-4** SDrowne(5) (s.s: nvr nr ldrs)	1½	**4**	33/1	24	—
2240[4]	**Figawin** (GLewis) **2-8-7** DHarrison(2) (lw: hld up & plld hrd: hdwy over 3f out: wknd wl over 1f out)	1½	**5**	7/2[3]	23	—
*1815**	***Huxleen*** (WGMTurner) **2-8-5**(7) DMcGaffin(3) (Withdrawn not under Starter's orders: v unruly bef s)		**W**	15/2	—	—
				(SP 124.5%)	**5 Rn**	

1m 32.5 (7.90) CSF £13.94 TOTE £1.80: £1.10 £3.80 (£12.60) OWNER Mr A. J. Lomas (WELLINGTON) BRED Mrs M. S. Teversham
2240* Lord Smith had handled much worse conditions at Salisbury last time. (11/8)
Petaling (IRE) was encountering soft ground for the first time on this drop in class. (10/1)

2163* Michelee had her two wins in Wolverhampton sellers put into perspective over this extra furlong. (7/4: 13/8-5/2)
2240 Figawin confirmed he does not stay seven in this sort of ground. (7/2)

2490 HELLER INVEST IN SUCCESS TROPHY H'CAP (0-70) (3-Y.O+) (Class E)
3-55 (4-02) **1m 6f 194y** £3,174.25 (£949.00: £454.50: £207.25) Stalls: Low GOING: 0.27 sec per fur (G)

				SP	RR	SF
2146*	**Manileno (57)** (MCPipe) **3-7-11**(3) MartinDwyer(4) (mde all: rdn over 1f out: r.o wl)	—	**1**	Evens[1]	71++	17
2014[13]	**Chabrol (CAN) (62)** (RHarris) **4-9-8** SSanders(5) (lw: racd wd: chsd wnr over 4f out: ev ch over 1f out: one pce)	5	**2**	7/1	71	34
2139[8]	**Tawafek (USA) (65)** (SDow) **4-9-11** JReid(3) (prom: wnt wd over 7f out: one pce fnl 2f)	2	**3**	5/1[2]	72	35
1825[5]	**Two Socks (59)** (JSKing) **4-9-0**(5) RFfrench(1) (lw: chsd wnr over 11f: styd far side st: sn wknd)	15	**4**	6/1[3]	49+	12
1844[4]	**Slapy Dam (50)** (CASmith) **5-8-10v** ACulhane(6) (lw: bhd fnl 4f: t.o)	22	**5**	8/1	17	—
2284[5]	**Durham (55)** (GLMoore) **6-9-1v** SWhitworth(2) (hld up: wnt wd over 7f out: bhd fnl 4f: t.o)	4	**6**	16/1	17	—

(SP 110.4%) **6 Rn**

3m 27.1 (17.10) CSF £7.53 TOTE £1.80: £1.60 £2.60 (£5.30) OWNER Mr Stuart Mercer (WELLINGTON) BRED Mrs C. Ashworth and C. Barber-Lomax
WEIGHT FOR AGE 3yo-17lb
2146* Manileno, up another 6lb, found no problem with either the soft ground or longer distance. (Evens)
1693 Chabrol (CAN) tried hard to make a race of it but is probably more effective on a sounder surface. (7/1)
1795 Tawafek (USA) is another who seems better suited to faster ground. (5/1)
1825 Two Socks made the mistake of staying on the inside in the home straight. (6/1)

2491 STARS AND STRIPES MAIDEN STKS (3-Y.O+) (Class D)
4-25 (4-30) **6f** £4,378.15 (£1,313.20: £632.10: £291.55) Stalls: Low GOING: 0.27 sec per fur (G)

				SP	RR	SF
1967[2]	**Always On My Mind (76)** (PJMakin) **3-8-8** SSanders(9) (lw: led over 1f: led over 1f out: sn clr: comf)	—	**1**	3/1[2]	84+	29
2173[7]	**Awassi (IRE)** (KMahdi) **4-9-2**(3) DO'Donohoe(12) (hdwy 2f out: r.o fnl f: no ch w wnr)	4	**2**	16/1	78+	29
1141[9]	**Savona (IRE) (71)** (PJMakin) **3-8-8** MHills(8) (lw: s.s: hdwy 3f out: one pce fnl f)	3	**3**	10/1	65	10
	Bacchus (ACStewart) **3-8-13** DHarrison(13) (scope: bit bkwd: s.s: hdwy over 3f out: rdn over 1f out: one pce)	2	**4**	5/2[1]	65	10
2183[12]	**Balfour Lady** (JARToller) **3-8-8** WJO'Connor(3) (nvr nrr)	4	**5**	25/1	49	—
2229[7]	**Hanan (USA)** (PAKelleway) **3-8-8** JFEgan(11) (prom: hrd rdn 3f out: wknd wl over 1f out)	1	**6**	14/1	47	—
2244[7]	**Calandrella (34)** (GBBalding) **4-8-11**(3) PPMurphy(5) (nvr nr to chal)	1¾	**7**	66/1	42	—
2300[10]	**Misconduct** (GLMoore) **3-8-8** SWhitworth(4) (sn bhd)	1	**8**	33/1	39	—
2278[3]	**Flourishing Way (78)** (RCharlton) **3-8-8b[1]** TSprake(6) (led over 4f out tl over 1f out: wknd qckly)	nk	**9**	9/2[3]	39	—
1851[3]	**Eliza (70)** (LordHuntingdon) **3-8-8** JReid(1) (chsd ldr tl wknd 2f out)	1¼	**10**	9/1	35	—
	Beaucatcher (IRE) (MJHeaton-Ellis) **3-8-8** SDrowne(7) (lengthy: scope: bkwd: a bhd)	5	**11**	25/1	22	—
215[9]	**Silent Symphony** (MrsSDWilliams) **5-8-11**(3) CTeague(10) (bkwd: prom over 2f out: t.o)	10	**12**	66/1	—	—
	Catria (IRE) (75) (JHMGosden) **3-8-8** AGarth(2) (bhd fnl 3f: t.o)	3½	**13**	9/1	—	—

(SP 127.0%) **13 Rn**

1m 18.2 (6.20) CSF £47.04 TOTE £3.60: £1.60 £3.90 £2.80 (£52.20) Trio £161.10 OWNER Mascalls Stud (MARLBOROUGH) BRED Mascalls Stud Farm
WEIGHT FOR AGE 3yo-6lb
1967 Always On My Mind acted well on this easier ground. (3/1)
2173 Awassi (IRE), a 75,000 gns yearling, was bought for only 750 gns by his present connections. He does not look a bad buy especially when considering he did not appear suited to this drop back to sprinting. (16/1)
Savona (IRE) could make no impression on her stable companion. (10/1)
Bacchus, who played up in the paddock, was very green leaving the stalls and should be better for the experience. (5/2)
1088 Balfour Lady was trying her luck at sprinting but is bred to need further. (25/1)
Hanan (USA), thought good enough to run in the Prix Robert Papin last year, is bred to require much further and probably also needs some better ground. (14/1)
Catria (IRE) (9/1: 6/1-10/1)

2492 WHITE HOUSE MAIDEN STKS (3-Y.O+) (Class D)
4-55 (4-57) **1m** £4,441.85 (£1,332.80: £641.90: £296.45) GOING: 0.27 sec per fur (G)

				SP	RR	SF
645[3]	**Speculator (IRE)** (WJHaggas) **3-8-12** MHills(15) (a.p: led over 1f out: r.o wl)	—	**1**	3/1[1]	93	55
2190[3]	**Dawam Allail (IRE) (75)** (MAJarvis) **3-8-12** SSanders(18) (lw: led tl over 1f out: one pce)	2½	**2**	7/1	88	50
1813[4]	**Kafil (USA) (76)** (MajorWRHern) **3-8-12** TSprake(17) (a.p: one pce fnl 2f)	5	**3**	9/2[3]	78	40
1587[14]	**Sahara River (USA)** (RCharlton) **3-8-7** DHarrison(12) (hdwy 4f out: hrd rdn 3f out: one pce)	3	**4**	4/1[2]	67	29
	Crown of Thorns (USA) (JHMGosden) **3-8-12** AGarth(5) (w'like: unf: lw: s.s: hdwy 3f out: one pce fnl 2f)	4	**5**	8/1	64	26
2172[6]	**Desert Warrior (IRE)** (KMahdi) **3-8-9**(3) DO'Donohoe(11) (lw: s.s: hdwy wl over 1f out: nt rch ldrs)	2	**6**	16/1	60	22
2315[11]	**Magic Lahr (GER)** (IABalding) **4-9-4**(3) MartinDwyer(10) (stdy hdwy fnl 2f: r.o)	nk	**7**	33/1	59	30
1409[4]	**Massyar Seventeen** (HJCollingridge) **3-8-12** DianaWeeden(7) (bit bkwd: nvr nr ldrs)	5	**8**	20/1	49	11
2173[8]	**Rockie The Jester** (JPLeigh) **3-8-9**(3) CTeague(2) (n.d)	7	**9**	50/1	35	—
2059[11]	**Kosevo (IRE)** (MGMeagher) **3-8-12** MFenton(13) (w ldr: rdn over 3f out: sn wknd)	1¼	**10**	50/1	33	—
1976[5]	**Cold Lazarus** (RTPhillips) **3-8-12** JReid(8) (bhd fnl 3f)	½	**11**	20/1	32	—
	Minster Star (JLSpearing) **3-8-7** NVarley(1) (w'like: a bhd)	2½	**12**	66/1	22	—
841[15]	**Charcol** (JEBanks) **4-8-11**(5) PRoberts(6) (b.off hind: dwlt: a bhd)	3½	**13**	66/1	15	—
	Classic Form (IRE) (ICampbell) **4-9-2** SDrowne(9) (a bhd)	8	**14**	20/1	—	—
	Baleriena (BEL) (JMPlasschaert,Belgium) **4-9-5**ow3 MKeogh(3) (lengthy: prom over 3f)	¾	**15**	7/1	—	—
1823[13]	**Catherston Lucky** (GBBalding) **3-8-4**(3) PPMurphy(4) (a bhd)	3½	**16**	66/1	—	—
	Milton Abbot (MSSaunders) **4-9-7** JFEgan(14) (unf: bkwd: a bhd: t.o)	dist	**17**	66/1	—	—

(SP 132.3%) **17 Rn**

1m 42.5 (6.10) CSF £22.15 TOTE £3.50: £2.00 £1.60 £2.40 (£5.90) Trio £10.00 OWNER Highclere Thoroughbred Racing Ltd (NEWMARKET) BRED Airlie Stud
WEIGHT FOR AGE 3yo-9lb
645 Speculator (IRE), a half-brother to Dewhurst winner and 2,000 Guineas third Huntingdale, handled the conditions and ended a one hundred day drought for his stable. (3/1)
2190 Dawam Allail (IRE) reverted to front-running tactics on this drop back to a mile. (7/1)

1813 Kafil (USA) could not quicken up in this soft ground. (9/2: 3/1-5/1)
Sahara River (USA) was another devoid of finishing speed in the soft going. (4/1)
Crown of Thorns (USA) is the first foal of a mare who finished second in both the Fillies' Mile and the Rockfel as a two-year-old. (8/1: op 9/2)
2172 Desert Warrior (IRE) showed a little promise and is at least qualified for handicaps. (16/1)
Magic Lahr (GER), dropping back to a mile, is another who will now get a handicap mark and may be worth bearing in mind on better ground when reverting to further. (33/1)
Baleriena (BEL) (7/1: 8/1-12/1)

T/Jkpt: Not won; £17,583.03 to Sandown 5/7/97. T/Plpt: £74.60 (289.37 Tckts). T/Qdpt: £8.70 (146 Tckts) KH

2463-BEVERLEY (R-H) (Heavy)
Saturday July 5th
Races 4, 5 & 6: flip start
WEATHER: overcast WIND: almost nil

2493 PAUL TEAGUE AND LARA KING (S) STKS (2-Y.O) (Class F)
2-00 (2-04) **7f 100y** £2,889.00 (£804.00: £387.00) Stalls: High GOING: 0.61 sec per fur (GS)

Form	Horse	Dist	Pos	SP	RR	SF
2153[2]	**Greenbrook** (WGMTurner) **2-8-6**(5) DSweeney(5) (mde all: clr 2f out: jst hld on)	—	1	7/4[1]	64	33
2016[10]	**Son of Skelton** (JWharton) **2-8-11** FLynch(10) (chsd ldrs: styd on wl ins fnl f: jst failed)	hd	2	5/1	64	33
2022[8]	**Dancing Em** (TDEasterby) **2-8-6** TWilliams(11) (a chsng ldrs: one pce fnl 2f)	9	3	8/1	40	9
2153[7]	**Last Lap** (TDEasterby) **2-8-6** DeanMcKeown(9) (chsd ldrs: one pce fnl 2f)	nk	4	7/1	39	8
1815[W]	**Katie's Cracker** (MRChannon) **2-8-7**ow1 RPainter(6) (swtg: chsd ldrs tl wknd over 1f out)	6	5	11/4[2]	27	—
2018[9]	**Donna's Double** (NTinkler) **2-8-11** KimTinkler(3) (racd wd: in tch: outpcd over 3f out: kpt on fnl 2f)	2	6	16/1	27	—
2031[4]	**Diamond Steve** (NTinkler) **2-8-13v**(5) IonaWands(12) (sn bhd: sme hdwy 2f out: n.d)	2½	7	12/1	28	—
1819[10]	**Ludere (IRE)** (WWHaigh) **2-8-11** RLappin(7) (chsd ldrs tl wknd over 3f out)	1½	8	10/1	18	—
2018[10]	**Are Yer There** (MWEasterby) **2-8-11** JLowe(4) (racd wd: chsd ldrs tl outpcd 3f out: n.d after)	¾	9	20/1	17	—
1569[13]	**Musical Pet (IRE)** (JLEyre) **2-8-6** MGallagher(8) (drvn along ½-wy: a in rr)	2½	10	14/1	6	—
1626[5]	**Dutch Patriarch** (MWEasterby) **2-8-3**(5)ow2 GParkin(1) (s.i.s: a wl bhd)	3½	11	9/1	1	—
2153[10]	**Lady So Bold** (MrsLStubbs) **2-8-6** DWright(15) (s.i.s: a bhd)	nk	12	20/1	—	—
	Disco Tex (MWEasterby) **2-8-11** TLucas(13) (leggy: scope: s.i.s: a bhd)	3½	13	14/1	—	—
1758[7]	**Margaret's Dancer** (CSmith) **2-8-8**(3) DO'Donohoe(2) (racd wd: a bhd: c stands' side: t.o)	28	14	20/1	—	—
2288[5]	***Bint Nadia*** (JDBethell) **2-8-6** MFenton(14) (Withdrawn not under Starter's orders: sweated up bdly & became distressed in paddock)		W	7/2[3]	—	—
				(SP 185.8%)	**14 Rn**	

1m 42.3 (10.30) CSF £14.16 TOTE £2.80: £1.50 £3.70 £2.60 (£14.40) Trio £68.80 OWNER Mrs L. P. Green (SHERBORNE) BRED B. E. Green
No bid
2153 Greenbrook seemed to appreciated this softer ground and, after taking a decisive lead halfway up the straight, the post came just in time. (7/4)
2016 Son of Skelton confirmed the promise shown on his debut. Taking time to get into full stride, he would have made it in two more strides. (5/1)
Dancing Em was left behind by the first two in the final quarter-mile. (8/1)
2153 Last Lap finished even further behind Greenbrook this time. (7/1)
1758 Katie's Cracker, withdrawn at the start last time, again gave problems. Awash with sweat, she was going up and down in the same place with over a furlong to go. (11/4)

2494 HULL MITSUBISHI CENTRE LADIES' H'CAP (0-80) (3-Y.O+) (Class F)
2-30 (2-30) **1m 1f 207y** £2,630.00 (£730.00: £350.00) Stalls: High GOING: 0.61 sec per fur (GS)

Form	Horse	Dist	Pos	SP	RR	SF
2302[12]	**Breezed Well (43)** (KGWingrove) **11-9-1**(4) MrsHNoonan(5) (trckd ldr: led over 5f out: clr 3f out: drvn out)	—	1	16/1[3]	57	29
2146[4]	**Gold Blade (60)** (JPearce) **8-10-8** MrsLPearce(4) (trckd ldrs: rdn over 2f out: styd on fnl f: no imp)	5	2	5/2[2]	66	38
1981[6]	**Leviticus (IRE) (76)** (TPTate) **3-10-9**(4) MissADeniel(1) (lw: led tl over 5f out: rdn over 1f out: one pce)	1½	3	5/2[2]	80	41
2118[3]	**Grand Splendour (71)** (LadyHerries) **4-11-5** MrsMCowdrey(2) (lw: hld up: effrt over 3f out: sn rdn: hung rt & wknd: eased)	dist	4	11/10[1]	—	—
				(SP 110.6%)	**4 Rn**	

2m 18.3 (15.20) CSF £48.22 TOTE £17.40 (£15.20) OWNER Mrs H. Noonan (NEWMARKET) BRED Mrs F. Gilsenan
WEIGHT FOR AGE 3yo-11lb
OFFICIAL EXPLANATION Grand Splendour: was unsuited by the ground.
Breezed Well had not won for three and a half years. Belying his age, he showed in a clear lead early in the straight and, kept up to the gallop, recorded his fifth success on his one hundred and seventh outing. (16/1)
2146 Gold Blade was 7lb lower in the weights than when he last won at Catterick eleven months ago. The ground was a bit sticky for him and he could never raise his gallop sufficiently to get near the winner. (5/2)
1981 Leviticus (IRE) seems to have nothing in the way of finishing speed. (5/2)
2118 Grand Splendour, who took a tug early on, gave her rider problems hanging into the fence and, left well behind once in line for home, was allowed to come home in her own time. (11/10: evens-6/5)

2495 MILLERS MILE H'CAP (0-85) (3-Y.O) (Class D)
3-00 (3-00) **1m 100y** £5,082.00 (£1,536.00: £748.00: £354.00) Stalls: High GOING: 0.61 sec per fur (GS)

Form	Horse	Dist	Pos	SP	RR	SF
2239*	**Dee Pee Tee Cee (IRE) (62)** (MWEasterby) **3-7-12** JLowe(4) (lw: mde all: rdn over 2f out: styd on strly fnl f)	—	1	11/4[2]	80	38
1087[4]	**Gharib (USA) (72)** (ACStewart) **3-8-8** TWilliams(6) (b.hind: trckd ldrs: chal over 2f out: rdn over 1f out: nt qckn)	6	2	4/1[3]	79	37
2172[2]	**Yabint El Sultan (70)** (BAMcMahon) **3-8-6** LNewton(1) (trckd ldrs: effrt 3f out: kpt on one pce)	2½	3	9/2	72	30
1775[8]	**Night Chorus (70)** (BSRothwell) **3-8-6** MFenton(2) (hld up & plld hrd: effrt over 3f out: one pce)	5	4	8/1	63	21
1249[5]	**Petite Risk (60)** (KWHogg) **3-7-10** NKennedy(7) (hld up: effrt over 3f out: sn wknd)	3½	5	14/1	46	4
	Lord Discord (63) (TDEasterby) **3-7-13** DWright(5) (chsd ldrs: drvn along 4f out: sn outpcd)	nk	6	12/1	48	6

				SP	RR	SF
2330*	**Ganga (IRE) (85)** (WJarvis) **3-9-4**(3) DO'Donohoe(3) (hld up & plld hrd: effrt over 3f out: hung rt & sn wknd)	4	**7**	7/4[1]	63	21
				(SP 126.7%)	**7 Rn**	

1m 53.8 (9.80) CSF £14.83 TOTE £3.60: £1.80 £3.90 (£14.20) OWNER Early Morning Breakfast Syndicate (SHERIFF HUTTON) BRED Michael and Heather Scott
LONG HANDICAP Petite Risk 7-5
OFFICIAL EXPLANATION **Ganga (IRE): the rider reported that the filly felt flat and could not handle the sticky ground.**
2239* Dee Pee Tee Cee (IRE) made it four wins from his last five starts. 16lb higher than when his winning run kicked off here last month, he got the favoured rail position and, although looking likely to be swamped at one stage, eventually came right away in the final furlong. He is a very tough individual. (11/4: 2/1-3/1)
1087 Gharib (USA), who had had three mandatory runs beforehand, loomed up looking sure to win coming to the final quarter-mile but, under pressure, found the winner much too strong in the final furlong. He would probably appreciate better ground and further. (4/1)
2172 Yabint El Sultan kept on at the same pace under pressure. The handicapper looks to have pitched her in a few pounds too high. (9/2)
1249 Night Chorus would not settle in the early stages. (8/1)
1249 Petite Risk was 5lb out of the handicap. (14/1)
2330* Ganga (IRE) looked to have been given plenty to do on her debut in handicap company. Pulling hard early on, when she was asked for an effort at halfway all she wanted to do was hang right. (7/4)

2496 B.B.C. RADIO HUMBERSIDE MAIDEN STKS (3-Y.O+) (Class D)
3-30 (3-33) **5f** £4,237.00 (£1,276.00: £618.00: £289.00) GOING: 0.61 sec per fur (GS)

				SP	RR	SF
	Mary Magdalene (MBell) **3-8-9** MFenton(12) (trckd ldrs: led ½-wy: pushed clr over 1f out)	—	**1**	7/2[2]	67	44
1781[10]	**Hype Superior (IRE) (60)** (ABailey) **3-9-0** DWright(6) (hdwy ½-wy: styd on ins fnl f: no ch w wnr)	6	**2**	10/1[3]	53	30
1963[10]	**Dona Filipa (33)** (MissLCSiddall) **4-9-0** DeanMcKeown(5) (sn chsng ldrs: styd on same pce fnl 2f)	½	**3**	25/1	46	28
2157[2]	**Archello (IRE) (67)** (GROldroyd) **3-8-4v[1]**(5) GParkin(2) (a chsng ldrs: kpt on same pce fr ½-wy)	1½	**4**	3/1[1]	41	18
2303[8]	**Present Chance (80)** (BAMcMahon) **3-9-0** LNewton(7) (lw: chsd ldrs: rdn ½-wy: wknd over 1f out)	5	**5**	3/1[1]	30	7
1764[5]	**Mischievous Time** (ASmith) **3-9-0** RLappin(1) (racd stands' side: chsd ldrs tl wknd over 1f out)	2	**6**	11/1	24	1
2167[8]	**Fancy Clancy (34)** (MissLCSiddall) **4-8-7**(7) TSiddall(10) (prom early: outpcd fr ½-wy)	8	**7**	25/1	—	—
2001[10]	**Blue Lamp (USA) (63)** (MAJarvis) **3-8-9b[1]** FLynch(13) (swtg: led to ½-wy: wknd over 1f out: sddle slipped: eased)	6	**8**	7/2[2]	—	—
	Okra (JDBethell) **3-8-6**(3) RHavlin(8) (lengthy: unf: bit bkwd: sn outpcd)	1½	**9**	16/1	—	—
	Just Blink (IRE) (SCWilliams) **4-8-11**(3) DO'Donohoe(9) (s.s: a wl bhd)	1¼	**10**	11/1	—	—
	Easy Nomi (KWHogg) **7-9-5** MGallagher(4) (s.i.s: a wl bhd)	1¼	**11**	33/1	—	—
423[7]	**Seanchai (IRE) (26)** (PSFelgate) **4-9-5** JFanning(3) (racd stands' side: edgd rt & lost pl ½-wy)	nk	**12**	25/1	—	—
1764[6]	***Harvey's Future*** (TTClement) **3-8-9**(5) GFaulkner(11) (Withdrawn not under Starter's orders: lame at s)		**W**	16/1	—	—
				(SP 146.4%)	**12 Rn**	

67.9 secs (6.10) CSF £41.02 TOTE £5.00: £1.60 £5.20 £4.80 (£80.30) Trio Not won; £282.46 to 7/7/97 OWNER Lord Lloyd-Webber (NEWMARKET) BRED Watership Down Stud
WEIGHT FOR AGE 3yo-5lb
OFFICIAL EXPLANATION **Blue Lamp (USA): the saddle slipped in the closing stages.**
Mary Magdalene, who has plenty of size and scope, showed promise in one outing at two. Showing a fair bit of knee action going down, she raced on the favoured far side and had only to be kept up to her work to pull clear. A half-sister to Roger the Butler, she looks a fair prospect. (7/2)
1119 Hype Superior (IRE), who has been facing stiff tasks in handicaps, stayed on to finish second best but the winner was totally different class. (10/1)
1764 Dona Filipa was officially drawn five but seemed to start in double figures on the far side in the flip start. She was beaten off a handicap mark of only 38 last time which emphasises the low class of this sprint maiden. (25/1)
2157 Archello (IRE) was tried in a visor but to no great effect. (3/1)
1983 Present Chance was being run off his legs at halfway. He does not look a five-furlong horse. (3/1: 7/4-100/30)
1764 Mischievous Time was one of two to race on the almost certainly unfavoured stands' side. (11/1: 20/1-10/1)
2001 Blue Lamp (USA), in blinkers for the first time, got warm and did not appeal on looks. Racing on the best ground, she showed plenty of toe but found little and, her saddle having slipped, she was eased right up near the line. (7/2)
Just Blink (IRE) (11/1: 6/1-12/1)

2497 RACING CHANNEL H'CAP (0-80) (3-Y.O+) (Class D)
4-00 (4-00) **5f** £3,730.00 (£1,120.00: £540.00: £250.00) GOING: 0.61 sec per fur (GS)

				SP	RR	SF
2001[2]	**Bowlers Boy (66)** (JJQuinn) **4-9-1** NConnorton(9) (lw: trckd ldrs: rdn to ld wl ins fnl f)	—	**1**	4/1[2]	74	56
2289[4]	**Lady Sheriff (75)** (MWEasterby) **6-9-10b** TLucas(5) (lw: trckd ldr: led over 1f out: hdd last 75 yards)	¾	**2**	2/1[1]	81	63
1734[10]	**Camionneur (IRE) (47)** (TDEasterby) **4-7-10b** DWright(1) (s.i.s: hdwy u.p ½-wy: styd on same pce appr fnl f)	4	**3**	6/1	40	22
2372[7]	**Napoleon Star (IRE) (53)** (SRBowring) **6-8-2**ow2 LNewton(10) (sn outpcd: styd on appr fnl f)	½	**4**	8/1	44	24
2308[5]	**High Domain (IRE) (68)** (JLSpearing) **6-9-3** DeanMcKeown(7) (lw: led tl hdd & wknd over 1f out)	3½	**5**	5/1[3]	48	30
2061[3]	**Tart and a Half (72)** (JLEyre) **5-9-2v**(5) GParkin(2) (chsd ldrs: rdn ½-wy: wknd over 1f out)	½	**6**	6/1	50	32
2050[5]	**Shadow Jury (64)** (DWChapman) **7-8-8b**(5) DSweeney(8) (trckd ldrs tl grad wknd fnl 2f)	6	**7**	13/2	23	5
2384[9]	**Craigie Boy (47)** (NBycroft) **7-7-10v** NKennedy(6) (s.i.s: sme hdwy on outside over 3f out: n.d)	2	**8**	11/1	—	—
2366[3]	**Tutu Sixtysix (47)** (DonEnricoIncisa) **6-7-10** KimTinkler(4) (sn outpcd & bhd: rdn & hung rt ½-wy)	5	**9**	25/1	—	—
				(SP 135.2%)	**9 Rn**	

67.5 secs (5.70) CSF £13.55 CT £49.58 TOTE £5.40: £2.10 £1.20 £3.50 (£7.50) Trio £57.30 OWNER Bowlers Racing (MALTON) BRED Roldvale Ltd
LONG HANDICAP Craigie Boy 7-3 Tutu Sixtysix 6-3
STEWARDS' ENQUIRY Wright, Newton & Mckeown fined £120 each (failure to ride to draw)
2001 Bowlers Boy was well handled and was persuaded to do just enough. (4/1)
2289 Lady Sheriff took over looking all over a winner one a half furlongs out but had to give best near the line. (2/1: op 9/2)
1734 Camionneur (IRE), drawn one, appeared to start in midfield. Given a month's rest, he put his very disappointing effort on his previous start behind him. (6/1: op 4/1)
2002 Napoleon Star (IRE), who was drawn ten, seemed to elect to start near the unfavoured stands' side. Soon hard at work, he was staying on at the finish and must be worth a try over six. (8/1)
2308 High Domain (IRE), who was drawn seven of the ten, appeared to jump off right on the favoured far side. Breaking smartly, he made the running but dropped away tamely coming to the final furlong. (5/1)
2061 Tart and a Half, from a 3lb higher mark, almost certainly found the ground too soft. (6/1)

2498 BLAIR JACOBS H'CAP (0-70) (3-Y.O+) (Class E)
4-30 (4-33) **2m 35y** £3,062.25 (£918.00: £441.50: £203.25) GOING: 0.61 sec per fur (GS)

				SP	RR	SF
2207*	**Black Ice Boy (IRE) (32)** (RBastiman) **6-8-0b**$^{(5)}$ DSweeney(4) (sn led: clr 6f out: unchal)........	—	1	6/1	43	7
	Memorable (30) (KWHogg) **6-8-3** RLappin(6) (w wnr: drvn along 9f out: kpt on one pce)........	12	2	14/1	29	—
2154*	**Classic Line (65)** (JLDunlop) **3-9-2**$^{(3)}$ DO'Donohoe(3) (chsd ldrs: drvn along & outpcd 10f out: rdn 8f out: hdwy 6f out: nvr nr to chal)........	3	3	4/5^{1}	61	6
2316*	**Amiarge (51)** (MBrittain) **7-9-10** DWright(5) (led early: chsd ldrs: pushed along 10f out: wknd 3f out: eased)	dist	4	7/2^{2}	—	—
1252^{6}	**Kinoko (48)** (KWHogg) **9-9-7** DeanMcKeown(2) (lw: trckd ldrs: drvn along 11f out: lost pl 8f out: t.o 5f out)..	dist	5	11/2^{3}	—	—
	Sophie Lockett (40) (KWHogg) **4-8-13** FLynch(1) (swtg: sn bhd: sme hdwy 7f out: sn lost pl: t.o 5f out)........	6	6	25/1	—	—
				(SP 118.0%)	**6 Rn**	

3m 58.0 (27.50) CSF £71.77 TOTE £6.40: £2.30 £4.40 (£35.60) OWNER Mrs Judith Marshall (WETHERBY) BRED Swettenham Stud and Barronstown Stud

WEIGHT FOR AGE 3yo-19lb

2207* Black Ice Boy (IRE), up 6lb and in a more competitive handicap, had his rivals strung out like washing setting out on to the final circuit and, clear three-quarters of a mile from home, kept up the gallop in relentless fashion. Clearly all he does is stay. (6/1)

Memorable, absent from the Flat for 659 days, was a winning hurdler two seasons ago. Despite carrying condition, he raced upsides the winner but, left behind at halfway, did enough to finish second. (14/1)

2154* Classic Line certainly looked to have her fair share of temperament here. Sulking a circuit from home, she was hard ridden at halfway and, though keeping on sufficiently well to finish third, never looked to be putting her heart into the game. (4/5)

2316* Amiarge, who is not very big to be carrying such a big weight, was racing off a 6lb higher mark. Dropping right out three furlongs from home, he was virtually pulled up. (7/2)

632* Kinoko looked much better than usual in the paddock but ran poorly, being under pressure with over a circuit to go and soon dropping right out. (11/2)

2499 JEREMY BUXTON AND JUDI MURDEN NOVICE STKS (2-Y.O) (Class D)
5-00 (5-06) **7f 100y** £3,723.50 (£1,118.00: £539.00: £249.50) Stalls: High GOING: 0.61 sec per fur (GS)

				SP	RR	SF
2222*	**Flower O'Cannie (IRE)** (MWEasterby) **2-8-6**$^{(5)}$ GParkin(1) (swtg: w ldrs: led 1f out: drvn out)........	—	1	7/2^{2}	89?	46
1872^{2}	**Starmaker (IRE)** (PWChapple-Hyam) **2-8-9**$^{(3)}$ RHavlin(6) (w ldrs: led 3f out: rdn over 1f out: sn hdd & nt qckn)........	2½	2	8/15^{1}	85	42
2202^{6}	**Watchman** (TPTate) **2-8-12** NConnorton(4) (sn outpcd: nt clr run over 1f out: swtchd outside & styd on)......	18	3	12/1	46	3
2153*	**Linnetsong** (GROldroyd) **2-8-7v** KHodgson(3) (sn outpcd & pushed along: rdn & hung rt 3f out: n.d)........	5	4	12/1	30	—
2112^{6}	**Crosby Don** (EWeymes) **2-8-12** DeanMcKeown(7) (swtg: dwlt: sn chsng ldrs: wknd over 1f out)........	8	5	16/1	18	—
594^{10}	**Prince Nicholas** (KWHogg) **2-8-12** FLynch(2) (sn pushed along: hdwy u.p ½-wy: sn lost pl)........	4	6	20/1	10	—
2018^{3}	**Petara (IRE)** (JSWainwright) **2-8-12** RLappin(5) (led tl 3f out: hung rt & wknd qckly over 1f out)........	4	7	8/1^{3}	1	—
				(SP 124.6%)	**7 Rn**	

1m 41.1 (9.10) CSF £5.82 TOTE £5.00: £1.80 £1.10 (£2.40) OWNER Mrs E. Rhind (SHERIFF HUTTON) BRED Rathasker Stud

2222* Flower O'Cannie (IRE), on edge and sweating in the paddock, behaved herself comparatively well on the way to the start this time and in the race did nothing wrong, getting on top of the uneasy favourite in the final furlong. (7/2)

1872 Starmaker (IRE), on his toes beforehand, did not impress on looks. Pushed to the front three furlongs out and racing on the favoured inside, he still found the winner much too good. (8/15: 4/11-4/7)

2202 Watchman struggled to go the pace, keeping on to finish a poor third. He still lacks experience and is not fully fit yet. (12/1)

2153* Linnetsong, another on her toes beforehand, wanted to do nothing but hang under pressure. (12/1)

2112 Crosby Don, sweating beforehand, missed the break and found little under pressure. (16/1)

T/Plpt: £8,435.40 (1.4 Tckts). T/Qdpt: £474.10 (1.39 Tckts) WG

2233-CARLISLE (R-H) (Good, Good to soft patches)
Saturday July 5th
WEATHER: sunny WIND: almost nil

2500 GILSLAND NOVICE AUCTION STKS (2-Y.O) (Class F)
6-40 (6-43) **5f 207y** £2,752.00 (£772.00: £376.00) Stalls: Centre GOING minus 0.36 sec per fur (F)

				SP	RR	SF
2240^{2}	**Celtic Comfort** (PCHaslam) **2-8-5** LCharnock(6) (chsd ldrs: sn pushed along: styd on to ld ins fnl f)........	—	1	4/1^{2}	72	6
2060^{5}	**Aberkeen** (MDods) **2-9-2** DaleGibson(13) (chsd ldrs: chal ins fnl f: kpt on)........	nk	2	16/1	82	16
2024^{12}	**Heavenly Abstone** (PDEvans) **2-8-12v** JFEgan(2) (lw: cl up: led wl over 2f out tl ins fnl: no ex)........	1½	3	2/1^{1}	74	8
2168^{5}	**Lord of Love** (TDEasterby) **2-8-8** JCarroll(9) (chsd ldrs: outpcd ½-wy: kpt on fnl f)........	nk	4	16/1	69	3
	Fashion Victim (THCaldwell) **2-8-5**$^{(7)}$ CLowther(5) (w'like: bit bkwd: s.i.s: hdwy over 2f out: styd on towards fin)........	1½	5	50/1	69	3
861^{7}	**Cool Secret** (ABMulholland) **2-8-5**$^{(7)}$ PBradley(11) (s.i.s: hdwy 2f out: styd on wl)........	1	6	20/1	67	1
2202^{9}	**Dougs Dream (IRE)** (MrsASwinbank) **2-7-7**$^{(7)}$ RWinston(1) (sn pushed along & bhd: sme late hdwy)........	4	7	66/1	44	—
1581*	**Pigeon** (DWBarker) **2-8-2** TWilliams(3) (unruly s: chsd ldrs: hrd rdn ½-wy: sn wknd)........	3½	8	16/1	36	—
1997*	**Risky Girl** (MJHeaton-Ellis) **2-8-9** JLowe(4) (dwlt: drvn along & sn in tch: outpcd fnl 2½f)........	hd	9	5/1^{3}	43	—
	Petite Tache (NChamberlain) **2-7-9**$^{(5)}$ KSked(8) (neat: bkwd: nvr trbld ldrs)........	hd	10	66/1	34	—
	Saint Albert (PTWalwyn) **2-8-8** RPrice(12) (w'like: scope: bit bkwd: prom to ½-wy: sn rdn & wknd)........	½	11	5/1^{3}	41	—
2110^{7}	**Globe Raider** (JJO'Neill) **2-8-4**$^{(5)ow4}$ TEDurcan(7) (led over 3f: wknd qckly appr fnl f)........	nk	12	100/1	41	—
2018^{6}	**Semi Circle** (TDEasterby) **2-7-11**$^{(3)}$ DarrenMoffatt(10) (dwlt: a bhd)........	¾	13	66/1	30	—
				(SP 116.5%)	**13 Rn**	

1m 15.8 (4.00) CSF £55.55 TOTE £4.00: £1.20 £3.50 £1.30 (£25.10) Trio £143.20 OWNER Mr A. P. Brookes (MIDDLEHAM) BRED Frank Sheridan

OFFICIAL EXPLANATION Risky Girl: became very upset at the start and, as a result, ran disappointingly.

2240 Celtic Comfort certainly stays further as he showed last time and he needed plenty of help from the saddle but, once in front, galloped on stoutly. (4/1)

2060 Aberkeen came back to form here and showed a good attitude under pressure, but the winner had his measure in the closing stages. (16/1)
1653 Heavenly Abstone was having her ninth run of the season here. She looked well and soon showed plenty of enthusiasm but was plain and simply not good enough. (2/1)
2168 Lord of Love ran in what was a hot race last time at Musselburgh and showed here that his turn will come in due course. (16/1)
Fashion Victim, who looks likely to need further, ran well and was staying on splendidly at the end. (50/1)
861 Cool Secret, after over two months off, again showed ability, picking up well after a poor start. (20/1)
1581* Pigeon had temperament problems at the start and that is obviously affecting her performance. (16/1)
1997* Risky Girl got upset by the horse in the next stall and ran no sort of race and should be forgiven this. (5/1)

2501 MACMILLAN NURSES CLAIMING STKS (3-Y.O+) (Class E)

7-10 (7-11) **6f 206y** £2,905.00 (£880.00: £430.00: £205.00) Stalls: High GOING minus 0.36 sec per fur (F)

				SP	RR	SF
2376*	**Bollero (IRE) (56)** (JBerry) **3-8-2**(7) CLowther(1) (lw: mde most: hld on wl)	—	**1**	5/2^{1}	62	30
2204*	**Winter Scout (USA) (57)** (RAFahey) **9-9-1**(7) RWinston(8) (lw: in tch: hdwy 3f out: sn rdn: chsng ldrs ent fnl f: r.o wl)	hd	**2**	5/2^{1}	67	43
1830^{10}	**Surf City (50)** (WWHaigh) **4-9-2** LCharnock(3) (chsd ldrs: ev ch over 1f out: nt qckn)	2½	**3**	7/1^{3}	55	31
1471^{7}	**Move With Edes (65)** (WGMTurner) **5-9-3**(5) TEDurcan(2) (lw: chsd wnr: disp ld over 2f out: wknd fnl f)	hd	**4**	7/2^{2}	61	37
1998^{7}	**Italian Symphony (IRE) (50)** (PDEvans) **3-8-8** JFEgan(7) (chsd ldrs tl wknd fnl 2f)	8	**5**	12/1	36	4
	Chalice (MrsASwinbank) **4-8-9** RPrice(6) (hdwy 4f out: sn chsng ldrs & rdn: wknd fnl 2½f)	7	**6**	12/1	13	—
	No Problem Jac (JJO'Neill) **4-9-7** JCarroll(4) (s.i.s: a outpcd & bhd)	8	**7**	33/1	7	—
	The Vale (IRE) (RMMcKellar) **5-9-8** JLowe(5) (dwlt: a wl bhd)	8	**8**	200/1	—	—

(SP 110.7%) **8 Rn**

1m 28.7 (3.00) CSF £7.41 TOTE £2.70: £1.20 £1.60 £2.60 (£3.50) OWNER Mr Ian Bolland (COCKERHAM) BRED Mrs G. Donnelly
WEIGHT FOR AGE 3yo-8lb
2376* Bollero (IRE) has really been sorted out by forcing the pace and she certainly stays further and proved most persistent. (5/2)
2204* Winter Scout (USA) is in tremendous form this season and, in another couple of strides, he would have made it three in a row. (5/2: 7/4-3/1)
1584 Surf City looked to have plenty on here but put up a useful performance and, although still a maiden after sixteen starts, there is certainly ability there. (7/1)
1085 Move With Edes trotted up in this race last year and this was by far his best effort this season. (7/2)
1998 Italian Symphony (IRE) has changed stables but, as yet, his attitude is the same. (12/1)

2502 TINDALE H'CAP (0-60) (3-Y.O+) (Class F)

7-40 (7-42) **7f 214y** £3,074.00 (£864.00: £422.00) Stalls: High GOING minus 0.36 sec per fur (F)

				SP	RR	SF
2205^{5}	**Bowcliffe (51)** (EJAlston) **6-9-9** JFortune(9) (lw: hld up: hdwy on bit 2f out: led ent fnl f: shkn up & r.o)	—	**1**	4/1^{1}	68	43
2204^{4}	**Euro Sceptic (IRE) (41)** (TDEasterby) **5-8-6b**(7) RWinston(15) (trckd ldrs: nt clr run 3f out to 2f out: sn hrd drvn: kpt on towards fin)	4	**2**	5/1^{2}	50	25
2145^{7}	**Snowy Mantle (39)** (JDBethell) **4-8-8**(3) PFessey(16) (lw: cl up: led over 3f out tl ins fnl f: hdd ent fnl f: wknd)	1	**3**	11/2^{3}	46	21
2021^{3}	**Naughty Pistol (USA) (52)** (PDEvans) **5-9-10b** JFEgan(5) (mid div: c wd st: styd on u.p: nrst fin)	1	**4**	14/1	57	32
2293^{3}	**Sing And Dance (43)** (EWeymes) **4-9-1** DaleGibson(1) (hdwy 3f out: kpt on: nvr able to chal)	2½	**5**	10/1	43	18
2362^{5}	**Silent System (IRE) (24)** (DWChapman) **4-7-3**(7) PBradley(2) (chsd ldrs: c wd st: rdn & one pce)	1¼	**6**	33/1	21	—
1603^{7}	**Charisse Dancer (45)** (CWThornton) **4-9-3** DeanMcKeown(3) (rr div: efft & nt clr run over 2f out: styd on towards fin)	3½	**7**	10/1	35	10
2342^{9}	**Agent (49)** (JLEyre) **4-9-4**(3) OPears(13) (trckd ldrs: outpcd 2f out: no imp after)	½	**8**	20/1	38	13
1798^{5}	**She's Simply Great (IRE) (46)** (JJO'Neill) **4-8-13**(5) TEDurcan(6) (mid div: hdwy 2f out: no imp)	¾	**9**	20/1	34	9
2170^{8}	**Mystic Times (30)** (BMactaggart) **4-7-11**(5) KSked(17) (w ldrs tl wknd fnl 2½f)	1¼	**10**	25/1	15	—
1390^{12}	**Petit Flora (37)** (GHolmes) **5-8-4**(5) GParkin(10) (b.hind: in tch tl wknd fnl 2f)	1¾	**11**	33/1	19	—
2355*	**Sandblaster (45)** (JLEyre) **4-9-3** 6x DWright(11) (dwlt: hdwy ½-wy: sn wknd)	s.h	**12**	5/1^{2}	27	2
2145^{9}	**Bout (35)** (RMMcKellar) **3-7-12** JLowe(12) (outpcd & bhd fr ½-wy)	8	**13**	66/1	1	—
1451^{8}	**Makati (33)** (MJCamacho) **3-7-10** LCharnock(14) (s.i.s: nvr nr to chal)	3	**14**	14/1	—	—
2041^{10}	**Nukud (USA) (29)** (GROldroyd) **5-7-8v**(7)ow5 DMernagh(7) (a bhd)	4	**15**	66/1	—	—
2071^{11}	**Racing Brenda (45)** (BCMorgan) **6-9-3** JCarroll(18) (led tl hdd & wknd over 3f out)	1	**16**	33/1	—	—
1044^{14}	**Hio Nod (35)** (MJCamacho) **3-7-12** TWilliams(8) (outpcd ½-wy: sn bhd)	3	**17**	66/1	—	—

(SP 126.9%) **17 Rn**

1m 40.3 (3.30) CSF £19.64 CT £108.16 TOTE £5.20: £1.70 £1.60 £1.70 £4.10 (£10.50) Trio £33.20 OWNER Mr Philip Davies (PRESTON) BRED Lady Matthews
LONG HANDICAP Nukud (USA) 7-6 Silent System (IRE) 7-8
WEIGHT FOR AGE 3yo-9lb
2205 Bowcliffe has been a revelation this season and, travelling particularly well here, there were never any doubts about the result. (4/1)
2204 Euro Sceptic (IRE) took a strong hold but was then denied a clear run at a vital stage, but the winner always looked too good for him anyway. (5/1)
2145 Snowy Mantle, dropped back in trip, sailed along on the bridle until the pressure was applied, from which point she found absolutely nothing. (11/2)
2021 Naughty Pistol (USA) has not won for some time and this trip is two furlongs further than she has ever been successful over but, judging from the way she finished, she certainly stays. (14/1)
2293 Sing And Dance is still searching for her first win and this trip was always proving too sharp. (10/1)
2362 Silent System (IRE) is a frustrating character who is not giving it his best shot. (33/1)
Charisse Dancer would have been a fair bit closer had she seen any sort of daylight early in the straight and she looks to be improving. (10/1)

2503 TALKIN TARN H'CAP (0-70) (3-Y.O+) (Class E)

8-10 (8-10) **1m 4f** £2,931.00 (£888.00: £434.00: £207.00) Stalls: High GOING minus 0.36 sec per fur (F)

				SP	RR	SF
2398^{5}	**May King Mayhem (36)** (MrsALMKing) **4-7-13** TWilliams(12) (lw: sn pushed along: hdwy 6f out: led wl over 2f out: r.o strly)	—	**1**	8/1	53	33
2236^{5}	**Suga Hawk (IRE) (57)** (EJAlston) **5-9-6** JFEgan(9) (a chsng ldrs: one pce fnl 2f)	10	**2**	13/2^{3}	61	41

				SP	RR	SF
2030[7]	**Out on a Promise (IRE) (65)** (LLungo) **5-10-0** DaleGibson(6) (rr div: hdwy 3f out: styd on: nrst fin)	1¾	**3**	20/1	66	46
2015[3]	**Daira (59)** (JDBethell) **4-9-5**(3) PFessey(11) (rr div: hdwy u.p over 3f out: nvr rchd ldrs)	4	**4**	100/30[2]	55	35
2208*	**Sherqy (IRE) (56)** (SEKettlewell) **5-9-5** JFortune(4) (lw: hld up: hdwy over 3f out: wnt 3rd 2f out: sn btn)	¾	**5**	5/2[1]	51	31
2293[6]	**Jubran (USA) (40)** (JLEyre) **11-8-3** DWright(5) (hdwy 5f out: sn prom: wknd fnl 2½f)	2½	**6**	14/1	32	12
2049[3]	**Needwood Nutkin (33)** (BCMorgan) **4-7-10** LCharnock(8) (led tl hdd wl over 2f out: sn btn)	2½	**7**	14/1	21	1
2342[7]	**Lord Hastie (USA) (42)** (CWThornton) **9-8-5b** DeanMcKeown(1) (lw: wnt prom 7f out: rdn 3f out: sn wknd)	1	**8**	7/1	29	9
2063[7]	**Indonesian (IRE) (50)** (PCalver) **5-8-10**(3) DarrenMoffatt(10) (in tch: effrt 4f out: outpcd fnl 2f)	3	**9**	14/1	33	13
2226[9]	**Kalousion (50)** (TJEtherington) **3-7-9b**[1](5)ow4 KSked(7) (chsd ldrs tl outpcd & lost pl 6f out)	9	**10**	66/1	21	—
2156[9]	**Sabu (64)** (JIACharlton) **5-9-13** JCarroll(3) (cl up tl wknd fnl 3½f)	10	**11**	20/1	22	2
2145[14]	**Silver Pearl (35)** (MrsAMNaughton) **6-7-12** JLowe(2) (b: drvn along 7f out: bhd fnl 4f)	7	**12**	10/1	—	—
				(SP 128.7%)	**12 Rn**	

2m 32.3 (3.30) CSF £57.62 CT £949.76 TOTE £8.10: £2.10 £3.40 £5.80 (£47.30) Trio £230.60; £152.67 to Windsor 7/7/97 OWNER Mr S. J. Harrison (STRATFORD-UPON-AVON) BRED P. D. and Mrs Player
LONG HANDICAP Needwood Nutkin 7-9 Kalousion 7-0
WEIGHT FOR AGE 3yo-13lb
2398 May King Mayhem won his first race here and in some style and it would appear that all he does is stay. (8/1)
2236 Suga Hawk (IRE) raced with every chance throughout but was made to look very one-paced yet again when the pressure was on. (13/2)
Out on a Promise (IRE), ridden from behind this time, was picking up ground nicely in the closing stages, suggesting that he is in good heart. (20/1)
2015 Daira had an obvious chance here but she failed to come up with the goods. (100/30)
2208* Sherqy (IRE), patiently ridden, found this far too competitive in the last two furlongs and the situation had to be accepted. (5/2)
1281 Jubran (USA) had a chance this time but proved disappointing under pressure. (14/1)
2342 Lord Hastie (USA) keeps slipping down the handicap but his performances are getting worse. (7/1)

2504 BRAMPTON H'CAP (0-70) (3-Y.O+) (Class E)

8-40 (8-41) **5f** £3,087.00 (£936.00: £458.00: £219.00) Stalls: High GOING minus 0.36 sec per fur (F)

				SP	RR	SF
2382[3]	**Tropical Beach (55)** (JBerry) **4-8-9b**(5) TEDurcan(6) (chsd ldrs: led ½-wy: rdn & r.o)	—	**1**	5/1	67	51
2206[2]	**Bold Brief (51)** (DenysSmith) **3-7-12**(7) CLowther(5) (prom: hdwy ½-wy: kpt on u.p: nt pce of wnr)	1¼	**2**	6/1	59	38
2017[3]	**Mungo Park (57)** (MrsJRRamsden) **3-8-11** JFortune(8) (hld up: hdwy on bit 2f out: rdn over 1f out: hung lft & nt run on)	s.h	**3**	5/2[1]	65	44
1977[7]	**Just Bob (69)** (SEKettlewell) **8-9-7**(7) JennyBenson(2) (lw: bhd: effrt ½-wy: r.o towards fin)	1¾	**4**	7/2[2]	71	55
2221[2]	**Stolen Kiss (IRE) (60)** (MWEasterby) **5-9-5b** DaleGibson(3) (disp ld to ½-wy: rdn & grad wknd)	1¼	**5**	4/1[3]	58	42
2221[W]	**Impish (IRE) (50)** (TJEtherington) **3-8-4** LCharnock(4) (disp ld to ½-wy: wknd appr fnl f)	½	**6**	15/2	47	26
2203[3]	**Ultra Beet (60)** (PCHaslam) **5-8-12v**(7) PGoode(1) (chsd ldrs to ½-wy: hung rt & wknd)	1	**7**	20/1	53	37
	Hamilton Gold (44) (MGMeagher) **4-8-3** JCarroll(7) (chsd ldrs: chal ½-wy: sn rdn & wknd)	5	**8**	40/1	21	5
				(SP 120.7%)	**8 Rn**	

61.2 secs (1.00) CSF £33.64 CT £85.71 TOTE £5.40: £1.40 £2.10 £1.90 (£15.80) OWNER Mr Jim Unsworth (COCKERHAM) BRED P. Balding
WEIGHT FOR AGE 3yo-5lb
2382 Tropical Beach has really been woken up with the blinkers back on and, in front a long way out for him, he was never going to be caught. (5/1)
2206 Bold Brief ran another fair race but was always just finding this trip too sharp. (6/1)
2017 Mungo Park went well for much of the trip but, once an effort was needed in the final furlong, his head went up and he wanted none of it. (5/2)
1977 Just Bob never got going until too late and should certainly not be written off yet. (7/2)
2221 Stolen Kiss (IRE) went well until an effort was required. (4/1)
1995 Impish (IRE) is slipping back down the handicap but does seem better when the ground is softer. (15/2)

2505 GELTSDALE LIMITED STKS (0-65) (3-Y.O+) (Class F)

9-10 (9-10) **5f 207y** £2,486.00 (£696.00: £338.00) Stalls: Centre GOING minus 0.36 sec per fur (F)

				SP	RR	SF
2358*	**Watch The Fire (60)** (JEBanks) **4-8-9**(7) CLowther(2) (hld up & bhd: nt clr run & swtchd over 1f out: swtchd again ins fnl f: r.o wl to ld nr fin)	—	**1**	2/1[1]	63	26
2206*	**Court Express (67)** (TJEtherington) **3-9-2** JCarroll(6) (lw: trckd ldrs: rdn to ld 1½f out: r.o: jst ct)	s.h	**2**	9/4[2]	69	26
2415[10]	**Wagga Moon (IRE) (60)** (JJO'Neill) **3-8-10** LCharnock(3) (a cl up: rdn 2f out: kpt on)	½	**3**	40/1	62	19
1573[4]	**Cairn Dhu (58)** (DWBarker) **3-8-13** TWilliams(5) (led: qcknd over 2f out: hdd 1½f out: no ex)	2½	**4**	12/1[3]	58	15
2313[10]	**Attarikh (IRE) (53)** (MrsALMKing) **4-9-2b** JFortune(1) (hld up: effrt over 2f out: sme late hdwy)	nk	**5**	14/1	54	17
1561[2]	**Amron (63)** (JBerry) **10-9-0**(5) TEDurcan(4) (chsd ldrs tl outpcd appr fnl f)	1	**6**	2/1[1]	54	17
				(SP 114.2%)	**6 Rn**	

1m 15.0 (3.20) CSF £6.43 TOTE £2.50: £1.80 £1.50 (£3.30) OWNER Mr E. Carter (NEWMARKET) BRED Red House Stud
WEIGHT FOR AGE 3yo-6lb
2358* Watch The Fire likes to come from off the pace but had trouble getting a run and then showed a super turn of foot to make it. There would seem to be more to come. (2/1)
2206* Court Express is in tremendous form and he tried all he could here but, had he won it, it would have been an injustice. (9/4)
2157 Wagga Moon (IRE) was tried unsuccessfully with blinkers two days earlier and ran much better this time without them. (40/1)
1573 Cairn Dhu ran a deal better here after a lay-off and may well be coming back to form. (12/1)
Attarikh (IRE) ran his best race for his new connections and, judging by the way he finished, he may well need a bit further. (14/1)
1561 Amron likes to come from behind off a flat-out pace, and saw too much daylight too soon on this occasion. (2/1)

T/Plpt: £30.80 (459.48 Tckts). T/Qdpt: £13.90 (50.99 Tckts) AA

2375-CHEPSTOW (L-H) (Good to Soft)

Saturday July 5th

WEATHER: Fine WIND: almost nil

2506 STARLING MAIDEN STKS (3-Y.O F) (Class D)

2-25 (2-28) **7f 16y** £3,806.50 (£1,147.00: £556.00: £260.50) Stalls: High GOING: 0.13 sec per fur (G)

				SP	RR	SF
2184[2]	**Bint Shihama (USA) (78)** (CEBrittain) **3-8-11** WJO'Connor(2) (a.p: led ins fnl f: r.o wl)	—	**1**	5/2[1]	77	9
	Quibbling (HCandy) **3-8-11** NAdams(10) (dwlt: gd hdwy 1f out: r.o wl ins fnl f)	1	**2**	14/1	75	7
	Made Bold (HCandy) **3-8-11** AMunro(3) (bhd tl gd hdwy 1f out: r.o wl ins fnl f)	½	**3**	6/1[3]	74	6
2020[4]	**Shoshaloza (USA)** (PRWebber) **3-8-11** RPerham(6) (prom: outpcd wl over 1f out: styd on fnl f)	¾	**4**	12/1	72	4
2376[5]	**Grace** (JMBradley) **3-8-11** SDrowne(7) (s.i.s: hdwy over 3f out: led over 2f out: faltered & hdd ins fnl f: wknd)	3½	**5**	25/1	64	—
2143[3]	**Native Rhythm (IRE)** (PWChapple-Hyam) **3-8-11** SWhitworth(9) (lw: trckd ldrs: wknd over 2f out)	5	**6**	5/1[2]	53	—
	Spirit Lady (JSKing) **3-8-11** DBiggs(1) (leggy: s.s: a bhd)	3	**7**	25/1	46	—
1823[8]	**Misty Point** (IABalding) **3-8-8(3)** DGriffiths(5) (lw: hdwy over 3f out: rdn & wknd over 2f out)	1½	**8**	7/1	43	—
2045[3]	**River Tweed** (JHMGosden) **3-8-11** AMcGlone(4) (led over 4f: sn wknd)	s.h	**9**	5/1[2]	42	—
1563[6]	**My Jess** (SGKnight) **3-8-11** VSlattery(8) (chsd ldrs tl rdn over 4f out: bhd fnl 2f: t.o)	17	**10**	40/1	4	—

(SP 113.2%) **10 Rn**

1m 27.2 (7.90) CSF £35.02 TOTE £2.40: £1.50 £3.70 £2.80 (£15.00) Trio £29.10 OWNER Mr Mohamed Obaida (NEWMARKET) BRED Gainsborough Farm Inc

2184 Bint Shihama (USA), out of a sister to Sayyedati, struck the front later this time over this shorter trip. (5/2: 2/1-3/1)

Quibbling, a half-sister to Exemption and Exclusion, is crying out for a longer trip and should soon get off the mark. (14/1: 10/1-16/1)

Made Bold seems to be going the right way and a step up in distance should help. (6/1: op 4/1)

2020 Shoshaloza (USA) is a well-bred filly, being out of a half-sister to a Lancashire Oaks winner and a Flying Childers winner. She is yet another who shaped as if she needs further. (12/1)

Grace was backed at long odds despite being beaten in a seller here earlier in the week. She looked like landing a tickle until tying up in the closing stages, and is obviously better than her previous form suggests. (25/1)

2143 Native Rhythm (IRE) is bred to need at least a mile but did not run like it here. (5/1)

2507 W.A. BLYTH 60TH ANNIVERSARY H'CAP (0-80) (3-Y.O+ F & M) (Class D)

2-55 (2-58) **1m 2f 36y** £3,556.25 (£1,070.00: £517.50: £241.25) Stalls: Low GOING: 0.13 sec per fur (G)

				SP	RR	SF
2346[10]	**Capilano Princess (78)** (DHaydnJones) **4-10-0** SDrowne(4) (hld up: hdwy over 2f out: led over 1f out: r.o)	—	**1**	9/1	87	66
1822*	**Shalateeno (66)** (BRMillman) **4-9-2** AMunro(1) (led: hdd over 1f out: r.o)	nk	**2**	7/2[2]	75	54
2328*	**Top Jem (77)** (MJRyan) **3-9-2** GBardwell(5) (hld up: hdwy over 4f out: rdn over 2f out: wknd fnl f)	6	**3**	6/4[1]	76	44
1822[3]	**Lonely Heart (77)** (DRCElsworth) **3-8-13(3)** DGriffiths(3) (lw: prom tl wknd wl over 1f out)	5	**4**	4/1[3]	68	36
2150[8]	**Queens Stroller (IRE) (46)** (REPeacock) **6-7-10v[1]** FNorton(6) (hld up: rdn over 3f out: wknd 2f out)	3	**5**	20/1	33	12
2059[5]	**Miss Riviera Rose (70)** (GWragg) **3-8-9** SWhitworth(2) (prom over 6f: t.o)	24	**6**	5/1	19	—

(SP 113.7%) **6 Rn**

2m 12.3 (7.00) CSF £37.05 TOTE £15.40: £3.40 £1.90 (£15.80) OWNER Mr H. G. Collis (PONTYPRIDD) BRED Mrs O. M. Collis

LONG HANDICAP Queens Stroller (IRE) 7-6

WEIGHT FOR AGE 3yo-11lb

OFFICIAL EXPLANATION Miss Riviera Rose: finished distressed.

IN-FOCUS: A slowly-run race in which many of the runners pulled hard.

1092* Capilano Princess, down 2lb, appreciated the return to this trip having been beaten over a mile at Goodwood on her last two starts. (9/1)

1822* Shalateeno, up 2lb, was not allowed to go off as quickly as she wanted which stood her in good stead at the business end over this shorter distance. (7/2)

2328* Top Jem, raised 7lb, did not have ground conditions so testing this time but it is possible that her Newcastle win may have taken the edge off her. (6/4)

1822 Lonely Heart was 2lb better off with the runner-up than when beaten two lengths when unlucky in running over a quarter of a mile further at Salisbury. (4/1)

1660 Queens Stroller (IRE), 4lb out of the handicap, was visored for the first time having disappointed when tried in blinkers once last year. (20/1)

2059 Miss Riviera Rose (5/1: op 8/1)

2508 ROTHMANS ROYALS NORTH SOUTH CHALLENGE SERIES H'CAP (0-85) (3-Y.O+) (Class D)

3-25 (3-28) **1m 14y** £4,354.00 (£1,312.00: £636.00: £298.00) Stalls: High GOING: 0.13 sec per fur (G)

				SP	RR	SF
2340[11]	**Zermatt (IRE) (50)** (MDIUsher) **7-7-10** NAdams(9) (mde all: rdn over 3f out: clr 2f out: r.o wl)	—	**1**	16/1	63	14
2346*	**No Extras (IRE) (67)** (GLMoore) **7-8-13** SWhitworth(6) (hld up & plld hrd: hdwy over 2f out: chsd wnr over 1f out: rdn & r.o ins fnl f)	2	**2**	5/2[1]	76	27
2242[2]	**Koathary (USA) (80)** (LGCottrell) **6-9-9(3)** DGriffiths(3) (hld up & bhd: hdwy over 3f out: wknd over 1f out)	11	**3**	7/2[3]	67	18
1979[9]	**Phonetic (74)** (GBBalding) **4-9-6** SDrowne(1) (nvr nr to chal)	¾	**4**	100/30[2]	60	11
1458[10]	**Orontes (USA) (72)** (RHannon) **3-8-9** WJO'Connor(7) (chsd wnr: rdn over 3f out: wknd over 2f out)	½	**5**	12/1	57	—
2021[2]	**Right Tune (78)** (BHanbury) **3-9-1** JStack(5) (a bhd)	8	**6**	13/2	47	—
933[16]	**Serendipity (FR) (76)** (BRMillman) **4-9-8** AMunro(2) (lw: plld hrd: prom 6f)	1¾	**7**	8/1	41	—
1920[6]	**Flying Pennant (IRE) (57)** (JMBradley) **4-8-3** GBardwell(4) (a bhd)	2	**8**	12/1	18	—
2282[5]	***White Settler (63)*** (RJHodges) **4-8-9** FNorton(8) (Withdrawn not under starter's orders:- non-arrival)		**W**	8/1	—	—

(SP 119.6%) **8 Rn**

1m 38.4 (7.20) CSF £53.50 CT £165.59 TOTE £13.10: £2.80 £1.50 £2.00 (£21.30) Trio £32.40 OWNER Mrs M. P. Pearson (WANTAGE) BRED Ivan W. Allan and K. C. Choo

WEIGHT FOR AGE 3yo-9lb

Zermatt (IRE) stole this race having slipped to a mark 17lb lower than winning over a mile and a quarter on similar ground at Kempton in May last year. (16/1)

2346* No Extras (IRE), up 5lb, found the winner had slipped the field and Whitworth got caught napping by the tactics. (5/2)

2242 Koathary (USA), raised 2lb for his narrow defeat last time, is 10lb higher than when completing a hat-trick last season, and no less than 25lb up on the first of those wins. (7/2)

1262* Phonetic might need further unless the ground is really testing. (100/30)

Orontes (USA), dropped 10lb this season, does not seem suited to cut in the ground. (12/1)

2021 Right Tune appears more on song on a sounder surface. (13/2)
Serendipity (FR), a real springer in the market, ran much too freely but has slipped down the ratings and was apparently considered ready to strike. (8/1: op 25/1)

2509 E.B.F. MEDIAN AUCTION MAIDEN STKS (2-Y.O) (Class F)

3-55 (4-02) **6f 16y** £3,037.50 (£850.00: £412.50) Stalls: High GOING: 0.13 sec per fur (G)

				SP	RR	SF
2320[2]	**Halmahera (IRE)** (IABalding) **2-9-0** SWhitworth(13) (hld up: hdwy over 2f out: led ins fnl f: r.o wl)	—	**1**	6/4[1]	71	35
1961[2]	**Bold King** (JWHills) **2-8-11**(3) MHenry(9) (a.p: led over 1f out tl ins fnl f)	2	**2**	100/30[2]	66	30
1480[3]	**Striding King** (MRChannon) **2-9-0** RPerham(1) (led over 4f: wknd fnl f)	7	**3**	8/1[3]	47	11
2306[9]	**Water Force** (GBBalding) **2-8-11**(3) DGriffiths(8) (prom tl wknd over 1f out)	s.h	**4**	20/1	47	11
1924[5]	**Santa Court** (RDickin) **2-9-0** AMcGlone(11) (s.s: hdwy over 3f out: one pce fnl 2f)	3½	**5**	25/1	38	2
1872[11]	**Top Maite** (AGFoster) **2-9-0** AMunro(4) (no hdwy fnl 2f)	nk	**6**	20/1	37	1
1924[4]	**Downclose Duchess** (MBlanshard) **2-8-9** NAdams(12) (nvr trbld ldrs)	1¾	**7**	16/1	28	—
	Mystagogue (RHannon) **2-9-0** DBiggs(7) (neat: dwlt: sme hdwy over 2f out: n.d)	1	**8**	12/1	30	—
	Petane (IRE) (JRArnold) **2-9-0** GBardwell(2) (neat: dwlt: nvr nrr)	¾	**9**	50/1	28	—
	Tui (KMcAuliffe) **2-8-9** SDrowne(14) (lt-f: a bhd)	½	**10**	25/1	22	—
2016[3]	**Tremonnow** (JMBradley) **2-8-9** VSlattery(10) (a bhd)	1¼	**11**	14/1	18	—
2022[10]	**Red Risk** (PWHarris) **2-9-0** FNorton(3) (prom over 3f)	1	**12**	66/1	21	—
	Riley (RCharlton) **2-9-0** WJO'Connor(5) (cmpt: prom: wkng whn hung lft over 1f out)	hd	**13**	8/1[3]	20	—
	Ginnieshope (SGKnight) **2-8-9** NVarley(6) (w'like: prom: rdn over 3f out: sn wknd: t.o)	7	**14**	66/1	—	—
				(SP 127.7%)	**14 Rn**	

1m 14.4 (5.20) CSF £5.41 TOTE £2.40: £1.30 £1.70 £3.50 (£3.10) Trio £6.70 OWNER Robert & Elizabeth Hitchins (KINGSCLERE) BRED Mrs John McEnery
2320 Halmahera (IRE) had shown he could handle give underfoot last time and came into his own on this step up to six. (6/4)
1961 Bold King, a half-brother to seven-furlong juvenile winner Spanish Luck, beat the others easily enough and should not be hard to place. (100/30)
1480 Striding King either needs less use made of him or a return to five at the moment. (8/1)
Water Force, out of a maiden half-sister to Cambridgeshire winner Quinlan Terry, ran his best race to date, but was in trouble when the tap was fully turned on. (20/1)
Santa Court, a brother to a winner in Belgium, again lost ground at the start. (25/1)
Mystagogue (12/1: op 5/1)
Riley (8/1: 4/1-10/1)

2510 CHAFFINCH MAIDEN H'CAP (0-65) (3-Y.O) (Class F)

4-25 (4-35) **6f 16y** £2,862.50 (£800.00: £387.50) Stalls: High GOING: 0.13 sec per fur (G)

				SP	RR	SF
2245[3]	**Welcome Heights (40)** (MJFetherston-Godley) **3-7-10** FNorton(10) (hld up: nt clr run over 2f out: hdwy over 1f out: led ins fnl f: r.o wl)	—	**1**	12/1	50	21
2167[5]	**Gold Edge (52)** (MRChannon) **3-8-8** RPerham(11) (hdwy over 1f out: hung lft & r.o ins fnl f)	2½	**2**	9/1	55	26
2231[3]	**Giko (65)** (JRPoulton) **3-9-7** SDrowne(9) (lw: a.p: r.o one pce fnl 2f)	1¾	**3**	12/1	64	35
2313[5]	**Presentiment (53)** (MartynWane) **3-8-6**(3) JDSmith(4) (hdwy over 1f out: nvr nrr)	hd	**4**	8/1[3]	52	23
2149[4]	**Night Express (65)** (BHanbury) **3-9-7** JStack(8) (a.p: led on bit 2f out: edgd lft over 1f out: hdd ins fnl f)	hd	**5**	4/1[1]	63	34
2310[18]	**Alpine Music (IRE) (42)** (JMBradley) **3-7-5b**[1](7) JFowle(15) (lw: prom 4f)	3½	**6**	33/1	31	2
1265[5]	**Oxbane (65)** (HCandy) **3-9-7** SWhitworth(5) (prom: eased whn btn fnl f)	2½	**7**	8/1[3]	48	19
2231[2]	**Mike's Double (IRE) (65)** (MissGayKelleway) **3-9-0**(7) AngelaGallimore(16) (lw: prom: ev ch 2f out: wknd over 1f out)	nk	**8**	5/1[2]	47	18
2366[10]	**Soda (47)** (JLSpearing) **3-8-3b** NVarley(3) (prom: rdn 3f out: eased whn btn 1f out)	½	**9**	20/1	27	—
1843[5]	**Hajat (46)** (NAGraham) **3-8-2** AMcGlone(13) (prom over 3f)	1¼	**10**	8/1[3]	23	—
1423[9]	**Agift (63)** (RFJohnsonHoughton) **3-9-5** NAdams(14) (prom over 3f)	3	**11**	25/1	32	3
1976[6]	**Balladara (IRE) (59)** (RHannon) **3-8-8**(7) RSmith(1) (a bhd)	hd	**12**	16/1	28	—
1988[3]	**Bold Spring (IRE) (63)** (RHannon) **3-9-5v** DBiggs(12) (lw: led 4f: wknd qckly)	nk	**13**	10/1	31	2
1315[18]	**Zalotto (IRE) (52)** (TJEtherington) **3-8-8** WJO'Connor(6) (a bhd: t.o)		**14**	20/1	—	—
2184[8]	***E Sharp (USA) (57)*** (WJHaggas) **3-8-13** GBardwell(7) (Withdrawn not under Starter's orders: horse came out under front of stall)		**W**	12/1	—	—
				(SP 134.4%)	**14 Rn**	

1m 14.2 (5.00) CSF £100.78 CT £1,072.70 TOTE £21.60: £3.90 £2.10 £5.00 (£54.00) Trio £413.80; £139.91 to Windsor 7/7/97 OWNER The Most Welcome Partnership (EAST ILSLEY) BRED R. E. A. Bott (Wigmore Street) Ltd
LONG HANDICAP Welcome Heights 7-8
2245 Welcome Heights found the drop back to sprinting doing the trick and, 2lb wrong at the weights here, might still be ahead of the handicapper next time. (12/1)
2167 Gold Edge has had plenty of chances and briefly hung fire in the last two hundred yards just as the winner was in full flight. (9/1)
2231 Giko was dropping back to six for this handicap debut. (12/1)
2313 Presentiment appears to need a return to a longer trip. (8/1)
2149 Night Express, back to six, again showed a tendency to go left-handed under pressure. (4/1)
Alpine Music (IRE) was reverting to sprinting on this first run in blinkers. (33/1)
1843 Hajat (8/1: 5/1-10/1)

2511 SWALLOW MAIDEN H'CAP (0-65) (3-Y.O+) (Class F)

4-55 (5-06) **2m 2f** £2,635.00 (£735.00: £355.00) Stalls: Low GOING: 0.13 sec per fur (G)

				SP	RR	SF
2381[2]	**Bridie's Pride (46)** (GAHam) **6-8-4**(7) JFowle(9) (led after 3f: rdn over 3f out: hdd 2f out: led 1f out: hung rt ins fnl f: r.o)	—	**1**	7/2[2]	56	38
2411[5]	**Contrarie (38)** (MJRyan) **4-8-3** DBiggs(1) (hld up mid div: hdwy 10f out: led 2f out to 1f out: one pce)	3½	**2**	5/1	45	27
2307[2]	**Spiral Flyer (IRE) (31)** (MDIUsher) **4-7-10** JMarshall(6) (hld up: hdwy over 5f out: rdn 4f out: wknd over 2f out)	16	**3**	7/1	24	6

2322[3]	**Turrill House (31)** (WJMusson) **5-7-10** FNorton(10) (bhd tl styd on fnl 3f: nvr nr ldrs)	7	**4**	10/1	17	—
	Trust Deed (USA) (31) (SGKnight) **9-7-5b**(5) APolli(8) (hdwy 9f out: wknd over 5f out)	7	**5**	50/1	11	—
2301[5]	**Ronquista d'Or (52)** (GAHam) **3-7-10** NVarley(5) (bhd tl sme hdwy over 5f out: n.d)	13	**6**	10/1	21	—
1808[5]	**China Mail (IRE) (40)** (JABennett) **5-8-5** NAdams(3) (prom: rdn over 12f out: wknd over 5f out)	2	**7**	25/1	7	—
2014[6]	**Pleasureland (IRE) (60)** (RCurtis) **4-9-11** GBardwell(2) (hld up mid div: rdn 10f out: sn lost pl: t.o)	dist	**8**	4/1 3	—	—
2131[2]	**San Glamore Melody (FR) (56)** (JHMGosden) **3-8-0v**[1] AMcGlone(4) (plld hrd early: prom tl wknd over 4f out: t.o)	15	**9**	3/1 1	—	—
2301[8]	**Brume La Voile (45)** (JGSmyth-Osbourne) **4-8-10** WJO'Connor(7) (led 3f: wknd 10f out: t.o)	dist	**10**	40/1	—	—

(SP 122.8%) **10 Rn**

4m 5.6 (15.60) CSF £20.46 CT £109.97 TOTE £5.50: £1.70 £2.10 £1.80 (£16.10) Trio £40.30 OWNER Mr K. C. White (AXBRIDGE) BRED Mrs A. Meller
LONG HANDICAP Ronquista d'Or 7-9 Turrill House 7-7 Trust Deed (USA) 6-13
WEIGHT FOR AGE 3yo-21lb
2381 Bridie's Pride stays all day and had nothing of the calibre of Media Star to contend with this time. (7/2)
2411 Contrarie, down 4lb, had her rider looking round for dangers prior to taking it up, but in the end she got outstayed by the winner. (5/1)
2307 Spiral Flyer (IRE) found this race more strongly-run than the seller at Bath last time. (7/1)
2322 Turrill House (10/1: 7/1-12/1)
2301 Ronquista d'Or (10/1: op 20/1)

T/Plpt: £137.00 (92.58 Tckts). T/Qdpt: £17.70 (46.38 Tckts) KH

2475-HAYDOCK (L-H) (Good)
Saturday July 5th
WEATHER: sunny & warm WIND: mod half against

2512 SHADWELL STUD SERIES APPRENTICE H'CAP (0-80) (3-Y.O+) (Class E)
2-35 (2-36) **1m 2f 120y** £3,109.50 (£936.00: £453.00: £211.50) Stalls: Low GOING minus 0.14 sec per fur (G)

				SP	RR	SF
2062[6]	**Wathbat Nashwan (72)** (LMCumani) **3-9-0** RFfrench(6) (led 1f: led wl over 1f out: r.o wl)	—	**1**	100/30 2	83	53
2351[3]	**Ambidextrous (IRE) (55)** (EJAlston) **5-8-9** CLowther(7) (lw: hld up: hdwy over 2f out: sn rdn: kpt on)	¾	**2**	12/1	65	47
2373*	**Kinnescash (IRE) (64)** (PBowen) **4-9-4** 5x ADaly(4) (a.p: rdn 3f out: r.o one pce)	1½	**3**	7/4 1	72	54
2342[2]	**Leif the Lucky (USA) (55)** (MissSEHall) **8-8-9** PRoberts(8) (lw: chsd ldrs: outpcd 2f out: styd on ins fnl f)	1¼	**4**	5/1 3	61	43
1923[4]	**Tremplin (USA) (70)** (NACallaghan) **5-9-10** TEDurcan(1) (s.s: hdwy 4f out: rdn & one pce appr fnl f)	1½	**5**	8/1	73	55
	Suivez (51) (MrsNMacauley) **7-8-5** RMullen(3) (b: a in rr)	3	**6**	25/1	50	32
2058[17]	**Burundi (IRE) (72)** (PWChapple-Hyam) **3-9-0v**[1] RWinston(2) (led after 1f tl hdd & wknd wl over 1f out)	1¼	**7**	10/1	69	39
2374[3]	**Alsahib (USA) (65)** (WRMuir) **4-9-5** JWilkinson(5) (hld up in tch: rdn 3f out: sn btn)	3	**8**	12/1	57	39

(SP 115.5%) **8 Rn**

2m 15.93 (4.43) CSF £38.73 CT £82.75 TOTE £4.30: £1.60 £1.80 £1.30 (£40.40) OWNER Sheikh Ahmed Al Maktoum (NEWMARKET) BRED Sheikh Ahmed Bin Rashid Al Maktoum
WEIGHT FOR AGE 3yo-12lb
2062 Wathbat Nashwan, a grand stamp of horse who would not be out of place in the Triumph Hurdle at Cheltenham, appreciated having more use made of him and, back over this more suitable trip, won a shade cleverly. (100/30)
2351 Ambidextrous (IRE) finds this trip a bit on the sharp side and he was only finding his stride when the race was all but over. (12/1)
2373* Kinnescash (IRE) has stepped up in the weights with his recent good run and, with the drying ground probably not in his favour, did not fail for the want of trying but the principals proved too strong for him. (7/4)
2342 Leif the Lucky (USA), much better when he can get his toe in, was tapped for speed when the tempo picked up entering the last quarter-mile but he renewed his challenge inside the distance and is due a change of fortune. (5/1)
1923 Tremplin (USA) is not really big enough to carry top weight and, missing the break probably by choice, could not muster the pace to deliver a serious challenge. (8/1)
1025 Burundi (IRE) ran a bit too free in his first-time visor and tied up rather quickly after losing the advantage. (10/1)
2374 Alsahib (USA) (12/1: op 8/1)

2513 LETHEBY & CHRISTOPHER LANCASHIRE OAKS STKS (Gp 3) (3-Y.O+ F & M) (Class A)
3-05 (3-06) **1m 3f 200y** £20,440.00 (£7,712.00: £3,756.00: £1,692.00) Stalls: Low GOING minus 0.14 sec per fur (G)

				SP	RR	SF
1875*	**Squeak** (JHMGosden) **3-8-4** GHind(2) (lw: hld up & bhd: rdn over 3f out: hdwy over 2f out: led ins fnl f: all out)	—	**1**	9/2 3	108	52
2099a*	**Tulipa (USA)** (SbinSuroor) **4-9-8** PatEddery(6) (lw: led tl hdd ins fnl f: rallied gamely u.p: jst failed)	s.h	**2**	5/2 2	113	70
1738[10]	**Attitre (FR) (102)** (CEBrittain) **3-8-5**ow1 JFortune(7) (hld up: hdwy wl over 1f out: rdn & unable qckn fnl f)	1¼	**3**	11/1	107	50
2058[6]	**Star Precision (92)** (GBBalding) **3-8-4** RPrice(3) (a.p: rdn wl over 1f out: r.o one pce)	½	**4**	11/1	106	50
1199a*	**Camporese (IRE)** (PWChapple-Hyam) **4-9-6** JReid(5) (trckd ldrs: drvn along over 3f out: styd on one pce)	½	**5**	2/1 1	108	65
2053[8]	**Maid of Camelot (95)** (RCharlton) **3-8-4b**[1] TSprake(8) (lw: plld hrd: hld up: effrt 2f out: nt clr run: nvr able to chal)	s.h	**6**	8/1	105	49
934[5]	**Woodren (USA) (78)** (RGuest) **4-9-3** JCarroll(1) (chsd ldrs: ev ch 3f out: rdn 2f out: sn btn)	3½	**7**	33/1	100	57
2053[4]	**Alcalali (USA) (95)** (PAKelleway) **3-8-4** RHills(4) (hld up: hdwy 3f out: nt clr run wl over 1f out: no imp)	2½	**8**	16/1	97	41

(SP 116.7%) **8 Rn**

2m 33.12 (3.72) CSF £15.08 TOTE £4.40: £1.40 £1.40 £2.50 (£5.60) OWNER Lord Hartington (NEWMARKET) BRED Side Hill Stud
WEIGHT FOR AGE 3yo-13lb
1875* Squeak retained her unbeaten record with a very gutsy performance against some older rivals and, though she only just lasted home, this was her first ever attempt at the trip. (9/2: op 3/1)
2099a* Tulipa (USA), proven in Group company and over the trip, fought back so strongly in the closing stages that she was in front a stride past the line. (5/2)
1738 Attitre (FR) has been very highly tried of late and, adopting more patient tactics, did threaten danger entering the final furlong. With the leaders showing no signs of stopping, she just could not get to terms. (11/1)
2058 Star Precision turned in a very pleasing display on this step up to Group company and connections have every reason to be delighted with her progress. (11/1)

1199a* Camporese (IRE) did not stand out in the paddock and, not relishing this ever-drying ground, performed some way below her best. She has proved she is much better than this and this can be classed as an off day. (2/1)
1318* Maid of Camelot, inclined to take a keen hold in her first-time blinkers, did not enjoy the run of the race when delivering her challenge but it did appear lack of pace was the main problem. (8/1)

2514 LETHEBY & CHRISTOPHER OLD NEWTON CUP H'CAP (0-110) (3-Y.O+) (Class B)

3-35 (3-37) **1m 3f 200y** £36,800.00 (£11,150.00: £5,450.00: £2,600.00) Stalls: Low GOING minus 0.14 sec per fur (G)

				SP	RR	SF
2028*	**Zaralaska (103)** (LMCumani) **6-9-8** PatEddery(13) (hld up in tch: smooth hdwy 3f out: led on bit over 1f out: rdn & r.o wl)	—	**1**	5/1[2]	113++	82
2122[2]	**My Learned Friend (78)** (AHide) **6-7-6**(5) RMullen(4) (lw: hld up: hdwy 3f out: rdn & r.o wl ins fnl f)	1½	**2**	12/1	86	55
1981*	**Raffles Rooster (77)** (AGNewcombe) **5-7-3**(7) RWinston(16) (a.p: rdn over 1f out: kpt on wl nr fin)	nk	**3**	10/1	85	54
2028[2]	**Nabhaan (IRE) (105)** (DMorley) **4-9-10** RHills(11) (lw: hld up: hdwy 3f out: ev ch wl over 1f out: unable qckn)	s.h	**4**	12/1	113	82
2026[20]	**Dreams End (83)** (PBowen) **9-7-11**(5) ADaly(5) (hld up & bhd: effrt & hmpd ½-wy out: rallied u.p wl over 1f out)	½	**5**	10/1	90	59
2028[8]	**Rokeby Bowl (90)** (IABalding) **5-8-9** JReid(15) (lw: chsd ldrs: effrt 2f out: kpt on u.p ins fnl f)	hd	**6**	20/1	97	66
2058*	**Heritage (92)** (JHMGosden) **3-7-9**(3) MartinDwyer(6) (lw: hld up in rr: hdwy 2f out: rdn & one pce fnl f)	¾	**7**	5/2[1]	98	54
2015*	**Tessajoe (79)** (MJCamacho) **5-7-12** LCharnock(8) (b.nr hind: lw: a.p: led over 2f out tl over 1f out: rdn & wknd fnl f)	2	**8**	20/1	82	51
2028[4]	**Mazurek (78)** (MCPipe) **4-7-6**(5) RFfrench(7) (hld up: hdwy ½-wy: rdn 3f out: sn btn)	4	**9**	10/1	76	45
1242*	**Cyrian (IRE) (90)** (PFICole) **3-7-10** JQuinn(12) (lw: s.s: sn prom: led over 3f out tl over 2f out: sn wknd)	nk	**10**	8/1[3]	87	43
1208*	**Whitechapel (USA) (84)** (LordHuntingdon) **9-8-3** TQuinn(10) (trckd ldrs: pushed along ent st: wknd 2f out)	2	**11**	8/1[3]	79	48
2028[9]	**Wild Rita (81)** (WRMuir) **5-8-0** TSprake(1) (prom: wkng whn hmpd over 3f out)	nk	**12**	25/1	75	44
2136[11]	**Remaadi Sun (80)** (MDIUsher) **5-7-13** RStreet(3) (a in rr)	nk	**13**	33/1	74	43
2292[3]	**Celestial Choir (86)** (JLEyre) **7-8-5** JFortune(9) (lw: hld up in rr: rdn over 2f out: no rspnse)	2½	**14**	25/1	76	45
2341[2]	**Rockforce (93)** (MRChannon) **5-8-9**(3) PPMurphy(2) (trckd ldrs: wkng whn nt clr run over 2f out)	2½	**15**	16/1	80	49
2027[9]	**Assured Gamble (90)** (CEBrittain) **3-7-10** DaleGibson(14) (led tl hdd over 3f out: sn wknd: t.o)	9	**16**	33/1	65	21

(SP 139.1%) **16 Rn**

2m 31.28 (1.88) CSF £61.34 CT £560.84 TOTE £6.90: £2.30 £2.00 £2.00 £3.40 (£79.00) Trio £416.90 OWNER Fittocks Stud (NEWMARKET) BRED Fittocks Stud Ltd
LONG HANDICAP Raffles Rooster 7-9 Cyrian (IRE) 7-7 Assured Gamble 7-8
WEIGHT FOR AGE 3yo-13lb
2028* Zaralaska enjoyed a more trouble-free passage than he did at Royal Ascot and, even with the 13lb rise in the weights, still demolished a competitive field with the utmost ease. He is certainly a class act. (5/1)
2122 My Learned Friend ran out of his skin to finish a worthy runner-up in such a high-class event and, if he appears again before the handicapper steps in, compensation would be just reward. (12/1)
1981* Raffles Rooster has improved out of all recognition this season and this very brave performance has got to be his best yet. (10/1)
2028 Nabhaan (IRE) enjoyed an 8lb pull in the weights with the winner for the two and a half lengths defeat at Royal Ascot but it counted for nothing when the race began in earnest and he was comprehensively outpointed once again. He is running consistently well under big weights and he deserves the rub of the green. (12/1)
1979* Dreams End had a nightmare run from the time he tried to make progress but he kept battling away and, if his attentions are switched back to hurdles for the forthcoming Galway Festival in Ireland, he will be the one they all have to beat. (10/1)
1319 Rokeby Bowl, reported to have found trouble behind the winner at Royal Ascot, did not have a great deal of chance of turning the tables here, but he put in a spirited late rally and he should be capable of winning at this trip. (20/1)
2058* Heritage is not so effective on this more lively surface and, as the race was run, always seemed to have too much to do. A determined rally approaching the final furlong was never going to succeed. (5/2)
2015* Tessajoe appeared to be out of his league here but he was only shaken off inside the last furlong and he is thriving this term. (20/1)
1242* Cyrian (IRE) had the break he needed to recover from his exertions at Newbury but he took charge after losing ground at the start and did eventually poke his nose in front. In this class he was unable to maintain it and was going in reverse before reaching the final furlong. This was another big step up for him and, if he remains in his own age group, he should soon recover his form. (8/1)

2515 HAYDOCK PARK JULY TROPHY STKS (Listed) (3-Y.O C & G) (Class A)

4-10 (4-11) **1m 3f 200y** £12,250.00 (£3,700.00: £1,800.00: £850.00) Stalls: Low GOING minus 0.14 sec per fur (G)

				SP	RR	SF
1553a[5]	**Ivan Luis (FR) (105)** (MBell) **3-8-10** TQuinn(3) (a.p: outpcd 2f out: rallied to ld ins fnl f: r.o wl)	—	**1**	5/1[3]	107	49
2107[3]	**Musical Dancer (USA) (105)** (EALDunlop) **3-8-10** RHughes(5) (plld hrd: hld up: led wl over 1f out tl hdd & no ex ins fnl f)	1¾	**2**	5/1[3]	105	47
1762[5]	**Garuda (IRE) (97)** (JLDunlop) **3-8-10** TSprake(4) (lw: s.s: plld hrd: hdwy 3f out: sn ev ch: rdn & one pce fnl f)	½	**3**	9/1	104	46
2180[2]	**Mandilak (USA) (100)** (LMCumani) **3-8-10** PatEddery(2) (hld up & bhd: pushed along 3f out: swtchd wd & hdwy 2f out: sn rdn: unable qckn)	1¼	**4**	4/1[2]	102	44
2135[2]	**Monza (USA) (106)** (PWChapple-Hyam) **3-8-10** JReid(1) (lw: led tl over 3f out: wknd over 1f out)	1¼	**5**	15/8[1]	101	43
1769[9]	**Bold Demand (99)** (SbinSuroor) **3-8-10** RHills(6) (lw: chsd ldr: led over 3f out tl wl over 1f out: nt clr run & wknd ins fnl f)	nk	**6**	5/1[3]	100	42

(SP 114.8%) **6 Rn**

2m 34.43 (5.03) CSF £27.49 TOTE £6.10: £2.20 £2.10 (£10.10) OWNER Mr Luciano Gaucci (NEWMARKET) BRED Rodrigo Investments
1553a Ivan Luis (FR) has competed at the highest level and this first Listed victory was not coming out of turn. He holds a St Leger engagement but his immediate target could be the Gordon Stakes at Goodwood later this month. (5/1)
2107 Musical Dancer (USA) finished ahead of the winner before being disqualified after finishing fifth in the Italian Derby in May and he did look the likely winner when gaining command inside the last quarter-mile but Ivan Luis found the better turn of foot under a determined ride and had the legs of him on the run to the line. (5/1)
1762 Garuda (IRE) did not give himself a chance of staying this trip with his tearaway tactics and once he does learn to settle he could be up with the best. (9/1)
2180 Mandilak (USA), thrown in at the deep end here, was struggling to stay in touch early in the straight. With stamina coming into play, he did stay on after being switched but failed to summon up the pace to get to terms. (4/1)
2135 Monza (USA), one of many from this yard not really firing at present, adopted forceful tactics, but he was being made to work entering the final quarter-mile and his measure had been taken. (15/8)

1769 Bold Demand, an also-ran in the Derby, travelled whilst being given a lead. He tried to extend his lead once in front but he did appear to be fighting a lost cause when short of room inside the last furlong. (5/1)

2516 E.B.F. BELLCHARM CITROEN NOVICE STKS (2-Y.O F) (Class D)

4-45 (4-46) **6f** £3,738.25 (£1,126.00: £545.50: £255.25) Stalls: High GOING: 0.12 sec per fur (G)

				SP	RR	SF
	Woodland Melody (USA) (PWChapple-Hyam) **2-8-8** JReid(5) (lengthy: scope: s.i.s: sn pushed along: gd hdwy to ld wl ins fnl f)	—	**1**	11/2	83	44
1783[3]	**Likely Story (IRE)** (JLDunlop) **2-8-8** TQuinn(2) (chsd ldrs: led 2f out tl wl ins fnl f)	¾	**2**	11/4[1]	81	42
	Robeena (CNAllen) **2-8-5**(3) MartinDwyer(4) (neat: bkwd: hld up: swtchd lft & hdwy 2f out: ev ch 1f out: unable qckn)	1	**3**	16/1	78	39
1945[3]	**Sea Magic (IRE)** (BWHills) **2-9-0** PatEddery(1) (chsd ldrs: rdn ½-wy: ev ch over 1f out: btn whn nt clr run ins fnl f)	3	**4**	9/2[3]	76	37
	Rewardia (IRE) (PDEvans) **2-8-8** JFortune(7) (lt-f: unf: dwlt: hdwy 2f out: sn rdn: nt rch ldrs)	6	**5**	20/1	54	15
*1045**	**Piccolo Cativo** (CaptJWilson) **2-8-3**(7) AngelaHartley(9) (spd 4f)	3½	**6**	20/1	47	8
2057[11]	**Balance The Books** (RHannon) **2-9-0** RHughes(10) (led tl hdd 2f out: sn rdn & wknd)	2½	**7**	4/1[2]	44	5
2212[4]	**Phantom Ring** (ABailey) **2-8-3**(5) PRoberts(8) (bit bkwd: disp ld 4f: sn rdn & outpcd)	¾	**8**	16/1	36	—
2060*	**Royal Dream** (JBerry) **2-9-1**(3) PFessey(6) (lw: w ldrs over 4f: sn wknd)	nk	**9**	7/1	46	7
	Caroline's Pet (IRE) (ABailey) **2-8-8** AMackay(3) (lt-f: bkwd: s.s: a bhd & outpcd: t.o)	9	**10**	25/1	12	—

(SP 117.9%) **10 Rn**

1m 15.87 (4.17) CSF £18.77 TOTE £6.80: £2.30 £1.70 £2.00 (£6.70) Trio £114.40 OWNER Mr R. E. Sangster (MARLBOROUGH) BRED Seahorse Investments

Woodland Melody (USA), a 75,000gns yearling from a winning family, took a long time to grasp what was needed after losing ground at the start. Once the penny dropped, she quickened up impressively to win going away and she can only improve with experience. (11/2: 3/1-6/1)
1783 Likely Story (IRE) looked to hold all the aces entering the last furlong but the picture changed once the winner found her stride and she had met her match close home. Losses should be recovered with interest. (11/4)
Robeena, reported to have been showing up well on the gallops, did look as though she would strip fitter for the run. Running on strongly after being switched, she does look a sure-fire future winner. (16/1)
1945 Sea Magic (IRE) has only ever run on more yielding ground and, though she joined issue below the distance, did appear to be held when squeezed for room just inside the final furlong. (9/2)

2517 B T RACEPAGER COCK O'THE NORTH H'CAP (0-100) (3-Y.O) (Class C)

5-20 (5-20) **6f** £5,322.50 (£1,610.00: £785.00: £372.50) Stalls: High GOING: 0.12 sec per fur (G)

				SP	RR	SF
2013[12]	**Nigrasine (99)** (JLEyre) **3-9-3**(3) OPears(9) (lw: mde all: hrd drvn fnl f: hld on gamely)	—	**1**	5/1[3]	109	75
2325[8]	**Restless Spirit (USA) (85)** (MJohnston) **3-8-3**(3) KMChin(1) (chsd ldrs: jnd wnr over 1f out: rdn & hung rt: r.o)	hd	**2**	12/1	95	61
2234*	**Compatibility (IRE) (81)** (JHMGosden) **3-8-2** GHind(3) (lw: trckd ldrs: effrt over 1f out: kpt on u.p towards fin)	1½	**3**	9/2[2]	87	53
1609[12]	**Granny's Pet (100)** (PFICole) **3-9-7b1** TQuinn(6) (swtchd rt s: hld up: hdwy 2f out: rdn whn nt clr run appr fnl f)	1¾	**4**	6/1	101	67
2211[6]	**Blues Queen (81)** (MRChannon) **3-7-13**(3)ow1 PPMurphy(8) (prom tl lost pl over 2f out: rallying whn nt clr run appr fnl f)	s.h	**5**	16/1	82	47
1294[4]	**Ellens Lad (IRE) (86)** (RHannon) **3-8-7**ow1 JReid(5) (nvr nr to chal)	1¾	**6**	8/1	82	47
2214[3]	**Rock Island Line (IRE) (75)** (JBerry) **3-7-7**(3) PFessey(2) (prom: rdn & carried rt appr fnl f: nt rcvr)	hd	**7**	15/2	71	37
	Just Visiting (92) (CaptJWilson) **3-8-13** JFortune(4) (lw: trckd ldrs 4f)	2½	**8**	25/1	81	47
2141[2]	**Furnish (86)** (BWHills) **3-8-7** PatEddery(7) (prom tl drvn along & wknd over 2f out)	6	**9**	5/2[1]	59	25

(SP 118.0%) **9 Rn**

1m 14.5 (2.80) CSF £58.40 CT £266.88 TOTE £6.50: £1.50 £3.20 £2.80 (£54.20) Trio £361.70 OWNER Mr M. Gleason (HAMBLETON) BRED Lady Jennifer Green

LONG HANDICAP Rock Island Line (IRE) 7-6

OFFICIAL EXPLANATION Furnish: the jockey reported that the filly would not settle and ran too freely in the early stages.
1412 Nigrasine, prepared to force the pace on this return to sprinting, showed the right attitude under strong pressure and held on grimly all the way to the line. (5/1)
1737 Restless Spirit (USA), a strongly-made colt who carries plenty of condition, was drawn on the outside. He was upsides striving for the lead when he hung badly right under pressure approaching the final furlong and, causing major trouble, may well have had to pay for it if he had got the verdict. (12/1: op 8/1)
2234* Compatibility (IRE), in his first handicap, did not find top gear until well inside the final furlong and he does seem to need a stiffer test of stamina. (9/2: 5/2-5/1)
1403 Granny's Pet had the blinds on for the first time and was taken to post very steadily. Patiently ridden, he was making his effort between horses but he looked to be struggling with the pace when he was denied a clear run approaching the final furlong and his chance had gone. (6/1)
2211 Blues Queen looked to have shot her bolt when losing her pitch soon after halfway, but she was putting in a renewed effort when suffering a knock-on effect approaching the final furlong and that ruined whatever chance she had. (16/1)
1294 Ellens Lad (IRE) did not impress to post and was never able to get himself into the action. (8/1: op 5/1)
2214 Rock Island Line (IRE) was still in with every chance when he was knocked out of his stride approaching the final furlong and had little chance of regaining his momentum. (15/2)
2141 Furnish faded very quickly after showing plenty of speed until past halfway, and her jockey reported she would not settle and eventually ran herself out. (5/2)

T/Plpt: £195.10 (173.25 Tckts). T/Qdpt: £71.70 (16.32 Tckts) IM

2171-NOTTINGHAM (L-H) (Soft, Heavy patches)
Saturday July 5th
WEATHER: fine WIND: slt half against

2518 'FAMILY NIGHT' (S) H'CAP (0-60) (3-Y.O+) (Class G)
6-50 (6-50) **1m 6f 15y** £1,984.50 (£547.00: £259.50) Stalls: Low GOING minus 0.09 sec per fur (G)

				SP	RR	SF
2430^{8}	**Arif (IRE) (35)** (BJCurley) **5-9-5** JFanning(4) (led 1f: led wl over 2f out: rdn & hld on fnl f)	—	1	9/4^{1}	47	38
2175^{7}	**Liathach (28)** (JRFanshawe) **6-8-12** TSprake(9) (sn w ldrs: led 6f out tl wl over 2f out: ev ch fnl f: unable qckn nr fin)	s.h	2	10/1	40	31
2307^{6}	**Wesley's Lad (IRE) (55)** (JNeville) **3-9-5**(5) RFfrench(5) (lw: hld up: hdwy over 4f out: kpt on appr fnl f: nt pce to chal)	8	3	11/2	58	34
2034^{8}	**Ballet de Cour (25)** (TJEtherington) **4-8-9v** NCarlisle(3) (lw: chsd ldrs: rdn & one pce fnl 3f)	6	4	9/2^{3}	21	12
1118^{10}	**Dramatic Pass (IRE) (20)** (MCChapman) **8-7-11**(7) SCarson(1) (hdwy & nt clr run over 5f out: rdn & edgd rt over 3f out: sn btn)	3	5	50/1	13	4
2322^{4}	**Lucy Tufty (38)** (JPearce) **6-9-5**(3) CTeague(10) (hdwy 8f out: rdn over 3f out: wknd 2f out)	2	6	7/2^{2}	28	19
2281^{7}	**La Spagna (27)** (MDIUsher) **6-8-11** DRMcCabe(2) (lw: bhd: hdwy 4f out: rdn 2f out: nvr able to chal)	2	7	20/1	15	6
	Kindred Greeting (29) (JO'Reilly) **5-8-13b** JO'Reilly(6) (b: b.hind: bit bkwd: trckd ldrs over 10f)	20	8	10/1	—	—
1940^{9}	**Club Elite (23)** (MissAStokell) **5-8-7v** JQuinn(8) (t.o fnl 5f)	dist	9	50/1	—	—
	Junction Twentytwo (30) (DJWintle) **7-9-0** MFenton(7) (lw: led after 1f: hdd 6f out: sn t.o)	dist	10	25/1	—	—
				(SP 117.3%)	**10 Rn**	

3m 8.9 (10.40) CSF £23.13 CT £101.41 TOTE £3.90: £2.40 £1.80 £1.80 (£27.70) Trio £44.70 OWNER Mr P. Byrne (NEWMARKET) BRED T. J. Rooney
WEIGHT FOR AGE 3yo-15lb
No bid
2279* Arif (IRE), wearing a tongue-strap as he often has in the past, proved game in a dour struggle. (9/4)
Liathach, a half-brother to the useful Ardkinglass amongst others, is very lightly-made and rather lengthy but, wearing a tongue-strap for the first time, showed a fair bit of improvement and enough to suggest a similar contest will come his way. (10/1: 7/1-11/1)
2035 Wesley's Lad (IRE) lacks pace and could not give these so much start despite staying on. (11/2: 4/1-6/1)
1229 Ballet de Cour is proving hard to place and did not look a total enthusiast in the last couple of furlongs. (9/2: op 3/1)
Dramatic Pass (IRE), after running once in three and a quarter years, has now had six races in seven weeks, this being his best effort. (50/1)
2322 Lucy Tufty, who won over hurdles five weeks ago, did not quite see out the trip on such testing ground. (7/2)
Kindred Greeting (10/1: 6/1-11/1)

2519 FRIAR TUCK MAIDEN AUCTION STKS (2-Y.O F) (Class E)
7-20 (7-20) **6f 15y** £3,486.25 (£1,045.00: £502.50: £231.25) Stalls: Low GOING minus 0.09 sec per fur (G)

				SP	RR	SF
1872^{7}	**Silver Strand (IRE)** (BWHills) **2-8-0** GCarter(7) (b.hind: a.p: led 2f out: clr over 1f out: rdn out)	—	1	Evens^{1}	71	—
	Constant Attention (PFICole) **2-8-8** TQuinn(6) (leggy: lt-f: sn pushed along: in tch: effrt over 2f out: chsd wnr ins fnl f: r.o)	1¾	2	11/4^{2}	74	—
	Zena (WJarvis) **2-7-13**(5) RFfrench(4) (neat: s.s: hdwy 2f out: r.o ins fnl f)	4	3	8/1	60	—
	Chameli (MrsLStubbs) **2-8-0** TSprake(2) (lengthy: bit bkwd: rn green early: in tch: kpt on fnl f)	½	4	25/1	55	—
1447^{11}	**Moy (IRE)** (MBrittain) **2-8-0** NCarlisle(1) (b: led 4f: wknd ins fnl f)	s.h	5	20/1	54	—
	General Klaire (BAMcMahon) **2-8-4** JQuinn(5) (leggy: scope: w ldrs 4f)	8	6	13/2^{3}	37	—
	Lanara (MrsNMacauley) **2-8-3**ow3 RLappin(3) (unf: scope: s.i.s: sn wl bhd)	27	7	33/1	—	—
				(SP 112.7%)	**7 Rn**	

1m 18.4 (6.90) CSF £3.35 TOTE £1.90: £1.30 £1.50 (£2.10) OWNER Miss Susan McIntyre (LAMBOURN) BRED Patrick Hayes
1872 Silver Strand (IRE) isn't over-big and had acquired bandages behind since her debut, but was able to come away from some very modest rivals when required. (Evens)
Constant Attention isn't much to look at but has quite a speedy pedigree. Never travelling in the race, she only really got going near the finish and ought to stay seven. Her useful half-sister Self Assured did not like soft ground, so all is not lost yet. (11/4: 2/1-9/2)
Zena, a half-sister to last week's Gosforth Park Cup winner Moon Strike, lacks inches but stayed on quite pleasingly after a poor start. (8/1)
Chameli, whose half-brother Hurgill Dancer won over a mile and a half at Ripon earlier in the season, looked well in his coat without appearing fully fit and ought to improve in time. (25/1)
971 Moy (IRE) settled much better in front but her proximity must cast doubt on the form. (20/1)
General Klaire, a tall, quite attractive individual, shaped with some promise but it may be worth noting that his half-brother Silver Button failed to progress. (13/2)

2520 SHERIFF OF NOTTINGHAM MEDIAN AUCTION MAIDEN STKS (2-Y.O) (Class F)
7-50 (7-52) **5f 13y** £2,277.00 (£627.00: £297.00) Stalls: Low GOING minus 0.09 sec per fur (G)

				SP	RR	SF
1492^{12}	**Welcome Sunset** (JWharton) **2-8-9**(5) RFfrench(4) (s.i.s: hdwy 2f out: led ins fnl f: rdn out)	—	1	8/1^{3}	84	14
	Facsimile (CaptJWilson) **2-8-9** KFallon(7) (lt-f: hdwy 2f out: led over 1f out: sn rdn: hdd & one pce ins fnl f)	2½	2	100/30^{2}	71	1
1635^{5}	**Bandbox (IRE)** (SMellor) **2-9-0** JQuinn(6) (lw: bhd: nt clr run 2f out: plld out over 1f out: r.o ins fnl f)	3	3	9/4^{1}	67	—
2306^{14}	**Russian Romeo (IRE)** (BAMcMahon) **2-9-0v^{1}** LNewton(2) (led 2f: kpt on fnl f)	s.h	4	12/1	66	—
	Mountain Magic (DJSffrenchDavis) **2-8-9** TQuinn(5) (w'like: unf: chsd ldrs over 3f)	1½	5	9/4^{1}	57	—
2181^{26}	**Allaton (IRE)** (MrsPSly) **2-9-0** NCarlisle(1) (w ldr: led 3f out tl hdd & wknd over 1f out)	5	6	33/1	46	—
2066^{10}	**Tilburg** (MrsNMacauley) **2-8-9** MFenton(3) (lw: w ldrs: ev ch whn rdn & wandered 2f out: sn wknd)	10	7	25/1	9	—
				(SP 110.2%)	**7 Rn**	

63.5 secs (4.60) CSF £29.29 TOTE £10.90: £2.90 £1.60 (£15.00) OWNER Mr John Goddard (MELTON MOWBRAY) BRED J. Goddard and J. Steel
STEWARDS' ENQUIRY Newton susp. 14-16/7/97 (excessive use of whip).
Welcome Sunset, much fitter this time, got worked up once installed and again missed the break. Closing rapidly by the far rail passing the furlong pole, he soon took charge. A big, rangy individual, there is speed on the dam's side of his pedigree but he should stay another furlong. (8/1: 6/1-9/1)

Facsimile, a sister of the stable's useful juvenile of 1996 Just Visiting, is quite tall but lightly-made and showed enough to suggest she can win a juvenile race or two despite giving trouble at the start. (100/30)
1635 Bandbox (IRE), noisy in the paddock and quite keen going down, didn't get the run of the race but looks anything but an easy ride. Another furlong may give him the time to get his act together. (9/4: 5/4-5/2)
Russian Romeo (IRE) tried to lead in a first-time visor but didn't last long. There is stamina in his pedigree and his chance, if one can be found, will probably be in a poor nursery over further. (12/1: 8/1-14/1)
Mountain Magic, rather keen going down, has quite a speedy pedigree but didn't show an awful lot. (9/4: op 4/1)
Allaton (IRE), a tall, weak-looking gelding, again tied up quickly in the closing stages. (33/1)

2521 NOTTINGHAM EVENING POST MAIDEN H'CAP (0-70) (3-Y.O+) (Class E)

8-20 (8-21) **1m 1f 213y** £3,694.25 (£1,109.00: £534.50: £247.25) Stalls: Low GOING minus 0.09 sec per fur (G)

				SP	RR	SF
2122[10]	**Raise A Prince (FR) (69)** (JWHills) **4-9-11v[1](3)** MHenry(14) (plld hrd: led 6f out: clr over 4f out: rdn 2f out: jst hld on)	—	**1**	12/1	75	31
2155[7]	**Night Mirage (USA) (69)** (MJohnston) **3-9-3** JFanning(10) (w ldrs: rdn over 2f out: r.o fnl f: nt rch wnr)	½	**2**	6/1	74	19
1694[10]	**Select Star (IRE) (60)** (APJarvis) **3-8-8** SDrowne(3) (b.hind: hdwy 5f out: outpcd 3f out: r.o wl fnl f)	½	**3**	20/1	64	9
2052[5]	**Tellion (68)** (MajorWRHern) **3-9-2** TSprake(6) (lw: in tch: hdwy over 4f out: r.o wl ins fnl f)	½	**4**	12/1	72	17
2238[3]	**Robbo (57)** (CWThornton) **3-8-5b** SSanders(12) (lw: chsd ldrs: one pce fnl f)	1	**5**	9/1	59	4
2199[8]	**Jean Pierre (50)** (JPearce) **4-8-9** KFallon(11) (lw: hld up & bhd: hdwy over 3f out: n.m.r & no imp fnl f)	½	**6**	5/1[3]	51	7
1955[6]	**Jalb (IRE) (69)** (ACStewart) **3-9-3** SWhitworth(5) (lw: hdwy 4f out: kpt on fnl f: nt pce to chal)	¾	**7**	9/2[2]	69	14
1956[7]	**Prairie Minstrel (USA) (58)** (RDickin) **3-8-6** ACulhane(2) (plld hrd: prom: chsd wnr over 2f out: rdn over 1f out: wknd ins fnl f)	1¾	**8**	33/1	55	—
1237[11]	**Perlethorpe (60)** (MBell) **3-8-8** MFenton(4) (hdwy 2f out: n.m.r fnl f: nvr nrr)	nk	**9**	12/1	57	2
1579[5]	**Slightly Special (IRE) (37)** (DTThom) **5-7-10** JQuinn(9) (b: dropped rr 6f out: nvr plcd to chal)	s.h	**10**	20/1	34	—
2005[7]	**Northern Touch (68)** (SCWilliams) **3-8-9**(7) DarrenWilliams(7) (led 1f: wknd over 3f out)	3	**11**	12/1	60	5
2364[4]	**Petula Boy (49)** (SRBowring) **3-7-6**(5)ow1 RFfrench(1) (hld up: hdwy 7f out: wknd 3f out)	2½	**12**	33/1	37	—
2052[4]	**Krabloonik (FR) (59)** (SirMarkPrescott) **3-8-7** GDuffield(8) (lw: hld up: hdwy 4f out: wknd over 2f out)	5	**13**	4/1[1]	39	—
2036[10]	**Young Dalesman (50)** (AStreeter) **4-8-9** LNewton(13) (led after 1f to 6f out: wknd 4f out)	9	**14**	20/1	15	—
				(SP 130.1%)		**14 Rn**

2m 11.5 (9.00) CSF £75.69 CT £1,341.34 TOTE £14.50: £3.50 £2.40 £7.40 (£29.40) Trio £228.60; £170.65 to 7/7/97 OWNER Mr George Tong (LAMBOURN) BRED S. Niarchos
LONG HANDICAP Petula Boy 6-9 Slightly Special (IRE) 7-8
WEIGHT FOR AGE 3yo-11lb
1430 Raise A Prince (FR), not for the first time, was racing with his tongue tied down. Refusing to settle in the first time visor, his pilot wisely gave up trying to hold him once in front, and he had just enough in the tank to last home. (12/1: op 8/1)
1773 Night Mirage (USA) looked beaten when the tempo quickened early in the straight but found her stamina coming into play at the finish. (6/1)
Select Star (IRE), heavily bandaged behind, bandages which appeared to come loose during the race, was outpaced as the tempo increased, only to close rapidly nearing the end. He doesn't seem an easy ride. (20/1)
2052 Tellion took a long time to make any impression on the leaders but was another closing fast in the final furlong. A half-brother to Kalko and Meltemison, he should make an interesting hurdler in time. (12/1: op 8/1)
2238 Robbo, stepping up in trip, could do little in the final furlong. (9/1)
1617 Jean Pierre, back over what seems his best trip, looked to have been given a chance by the Handicapper, but made very heavy weather of making progress towards the inside. He remains a maiden. (5/1)

2522 'FUN FOR ALL THE FAMILY' LIMITED STKS (0-55) (3-Y.O) (Class F)

8-50 (8-50) **1m 1f 213y** £2,277.00 (£627.00: £297.00) Stalls: Low GOING minus 0.09 sec per fur (G)

				SP	RR	SF
2337[2]	**Secret Ballot (IRE) (55)** (KMahdi) **3-8-11**(3) DO'Donohoe(3) (lw: in tch: rdn & hdwy 3f out: led over 1f out: sn clr: comf)	—	**1**	11/4[2]	68+	5
2008[17]	**Silvery (48)** (JARToller) **3-8-11** SSanders(2) (hdwy over 3f out: kpt on fnl f)	1¾	**2**	16/1	62	—
2332[2]	**Poker Princess (52)** (MBell) **3-8-6**(5) RMullen(4) (w ldr: led wl over 1f out: sn hdd & one pce)	¾	**3**	5/2[1]	61	—
1998[2]	**Sun Fairy (49)** (JAGlover) **3-8-11** GCarter(5) (hld up & bhd: rdn 3f out: r.o: nvr able to chal)	5	**4**	7/2[3]	53	—
2071[3]	**Mutahadeth (55)** (DShaw) **3-9-2** JFanning(9) (stumbled after 2f: in tch: rdn 3f out: no imp)	3	**5**	7/1	53	—
1430[9]	**Tezaab (55)** (BHanbury) **3-9-0** JStack(8) (hld up & bhd: rdn over 3f out: nvr nrr)	2	**6**	12/1	48	—
1096[7]	**Don't Worry Mike (52)** (FHLee) **3-9-0** ACulhane(7) (lw: plld hrd: lost pl 5f out: n.d afterwards)	¾	**7**	12/1	47	—
2152[6]	**Miss Alice (38)** (CSmith) **3-8-11** JTate(6) (lw: led: rdn over 2f out: hdd & wknd wl over 1f out)	½	**8**	40/1	43	—
2159[2]	**Gold Clipper (33)** (MJRyan) **3-8-11**(3) MBaird(1) (lw: plld hrd: prom tl rdn & wknd over 3f out)	6	**9**	12/1	36	—
				(SP 121.4%)		**9 Rn**

2m 13.3 (10.80) CSF £44.13 TOTE £3.60: £1.40 £3.30 £1.40 (£70.30) Trio £115.00 OWNER Mr Waleed Al-Mutawa (NEWMARKET) BRED Godolphin Management Co Ltd
2337 Secret Ballot (IRE) clearly takes his racing well and this step up in trip suited him despite a speedy pedigree, although the moderate early pace may have aided his cause. (11/4)
Silvery, taking a big drop in class, is a good mover and has found her level. (16/1)
2332 Poker Princess does seem something of a weak finisher, whatever the trip. (5/2)
1998 Sun Fairy was held up to get the trip but such a muddling early pace didn't help, for when the pace quickened she was not placed to respond. She is worth another chance. (7/2)
2071 Mutahadeth another poorly placed when the dash for the line began, failed to make any ground at all. (7/1)
1155 Tezaab well in arrears when the tempo increased, just stayed on past beaten horses. (12/1: op 8/1)
2159 Gold Clipper (12/1: 8/1-14/1)

2523 BBC RADIO NOTTINGHAM H'CAP (0-70) (3-Y.O) (Class E)

9-20 (9-21) **1m 54y** £3,564.25 (£1,069.00: £514.50: £237.25) Stalls: Low GOING minus 0.09 sec per fur (G)

				SP	RR	SF
2040*	**Saffron Rose (70)** (MBlanshard) **3-9-7** JQuinn(12) (lw: trckd ldrs: led over 2f out: rdn over 1f out: drew clr ins fnl f)	—	**1**	3/1[2]	79	34

1988⁵	**Linden's Lad (IRE) (50)** (JRJenkins) **3-8-1v¹** GCarter(3) (plld hrd: in tch: rdn 2f out: r.o wl fnl f) 1½	**2**	8/1	56	11
	Star Turn (IRE) (60) (MBell) **3-8-11** MFenton(13) (led over 2f: led over 3f out tl over 2f out: one pce ins fnl f)s.h	**3**	11/1	66	21
2036¹⁶	**The Negotiator (63)** (MJHeaton-Ellis) **3-9-0** SDrowne(5) (hld up & plld hrd: hdwy 2f out: r.o fnl f) ....¾	**4**	11/1	68	23
2231⁴	**Welcome Home (58)** (PTDalton) **3-8-9** SSanders(7) (plld hrd: chsd ldrs: rdn 2f out: wknd ins fnl f) 6	**5**	11/2³	51	6
1757⁵	**Faym (IRE) (64)** (JWharton) **3-8-10**(5) RFfrench(2) (plld hrd: prom over 5f out) 2½	**6**	10/1	52	7
1496¹⁶	**Redspet (49)** (SRBowring) **3-7-7**(7)ow4 FBoyle(11) (plld hrd: w ldr: led over 5f out tl over 3f out: sn btn) 3½	**7**	50/1	30	—
2036¹⁴	**Flotilla (62)** (SMellor) **3-8-13** RPerham(10) (lw: bhd fnl 5f) 3	**8**	20/1	37	—
2171⁷	**Joyful Joy (45)** (BPJBaugh) **3-7-5**(5) IonaWands(6) (lw: effrt over 2f out: nvr trbld ldrs) ....½	**9**	50/1	20	—
1994⁷	**Imperial Or Metric (IRE) (56)** (RAFahey) **3-8-7** ACulhane(4) (b: in tch: rdn 3f out: sn btn) 3	**10**	7/1	25	—
*2151**	**Around Fore Alliss (65)** (TGMills) **3-9-2** KFallon(8) (lw: w ldrs: hrd rdn 3f out: sn wknd & eased) 5	**11**	5/2¹	24	—
874¹³	**Superapparos (48)** (SRBowring) **3-7-8**(5)ow3 RMullen(1) (a bhd) 3	**12**	50/1	1	—
			(SP 129.0%)	**12 Rn**	

1m 47.8 (6.50) CSF £26.93 CT £226.67 TOTE £4.10: £1.70 £2.60 £3.10 (£50.30) Trio £201.30; £51.05 to 7/7/97 OWNER The Lower Bowden II Syndicate (UPPER LAMBOURN) BRED The Duke of Marlborough

LONG HANDICAP Joyful Joy 6-12 Redspet 6-9 Superapparos 7-5

2040* Saffron Rose, held on to a bit longer this time, repeated her recent course and distance victory, coming away near the finish after looking in some danger. (3/1)

1988 Linden's Lad (IRE) gives the odd flash of the tail but was very free both going down and in the early stages, in a first-time visor. To his credit, he stuck to his task approaching the final furlong, but whether the headgear will work as well again is anybody's guess. (8/1: op 5/1)

Star Turn (IRE) was pretty headstrong going down and stepping up in trip on his seasonal debut, so this run suggests she may find a similar race. (11/1: 8/1-12/1)

790 The Negotiator takes a fierce grip, but at least was able to be held up on this occasion and came home quite well. He looks as though further would suit him if only he would learn to settle. (11/1: 8/1-12/1)

2231 Welcome Home gave some trouble at the start but couldn't get to the head of affairs and had done her running in the final furlong. (11/2: 4/1-6/1)

1757 Faym (IRE) moved down moderately on this turf debut but ran well enough. (10/1)

1994 Imperial Or Metric (IRE) (7/1: op 16/1)

2151* Around Fore Alliss, taken quietly to post after the others, was giving his rider problems on the home turn. Upsides the leaders early in the straight, he failed to respond to some sharp reminders and the situation was accepted. (5/2: op 4/1)

T/Plpt: £292.10 (47.7 Tckts). T/Qdpt: £291.10 (2.71 Tckts) Dk

2481-SANDOWN (R-H) (Good to soft, Good patches)
Saturday July 5th
WEATHER: warm WIND: almost nil

2524 E.B.F. PADDOCK MAIDEN STKS (2-Y.O) (Class D)
2-15 (2-19) **7f 16y** £3,533.75 (£1,070.00: £522.50: £248.75) Stalls: High GOING: 0.05 sec per fur (G)

			SP	RR	SF
	Almutawakel (SbinSuroor) **2-9-0** LDettori(3) (w'like: scope: lw: a.p: chsd ldr over 1f out: led ins fnl f: pushed out) ....—	**1**	9/4²	85+	49
	Ray's Folly (IRE) (MAJarvis) **2-9-0** RCochrane(9) (w'like: scope: led tl ins fnl f: r.o) ....nk	**2**	33/1	84	48
	Marran (IRE) (JLDunlop) **2-9-0** MJKinane(5) (w'like: rdn over 2f out: hdwy over 1f out: r.o) 3	**3**	14/1	78	42
1933³	**Mulahen** (DMorley) **2-9-0** GCarter(4) (lw: chsd ldr over 5f: unable qckn) ....nk	**4**	2/1¹	77	41
	Nautical Star (JWHills) **2-9-0** MHills(7) (w'like: scope: lw: rdn over 2f out: hdwy fnl f: r.o) ....s.h	**5**	16/1	77	41
2181³	**Da Boss** (WRMuir) **2-9-0** DaneO'Neill(10) (a.p: rdn over 2f out: one pce) ....¾	**6**	11/2³	75	39
	Due South (EALDunlop) **2-8-9** KFallon(2) (neat: s.s: rdn over 2f out: nvr nr to chal) 3	**7**	11/1	63	27
	Petruchio (IRE) (MajorDNChappell) **2-9-0** AClark(8) (str: scope: bit bkwd: hld up: rdn over 3f out: wknd over 1f out) 2	**8**	40/1	64	28
1240¹⁰	**Primavera** (MJHaynes) **2-8-9** WRyan(6) (a bhd) 1¾	**9**	66/1	55	19
	Circus (CEBrittain) **2-9-0** BDoyle(1) (str: scope: bit bkwd: s.s: a bhd) ....¾	**10**	25/1	58	22
			(SP 111.1%)	**10 Rn**	

1m 33.29 (4.69) CSF £71.32 TOTE £3.60: £1.50 £2.90 £3.20 (£20.10) Trio £62.50 OWNER Godolphin (NEWMARKET) BRED Shadwell Estate Company Limited

IN-FOCUS: **This looked a quality field in the paddock, and time may tell that this was a hot maiden.**

Almutawakel, a good-bodied individual, with plenty of scope, knew what was required, as he needed only to be shaken up to lead inside the last furlong. More will be heard of him. (9/4: 2/1-100/30)

Ray's Folly (IRE), an attractive colt with plenty of scope, made a very pleasing start to his career. Attempting to make all the running, he was only passed inside the last furlong, and kept on well to the line. He should have no problem going one better. (33/1)

Marran (IRE), a half-brother to Khamaseen and Azzilfi, had less scope than many in this field, but nevertheless grasped the hang of things in the last furlong-and-a-half, and stayed on to snatch third prize. He should soon find a race. (14/1: 5/1-16/1)

1933 Mulahen, who made a pleasing debut here three weeks ago behind Muhtathir, looked in very good shape in the paddock, but failed to find that vital turn of foot in the last quarter-mile. He has plenty of scope, and should soon pick up an ordinary maiden. (2/1)

Nautical Star, an attractive newcomer, was rather noisy in the paddock. Only grasping what was required in the last furlong, he nevertheless stayed on and only just missed out on the prizemoney. He will have learnt a lot from this. (16/1)

2181 Da Boss, one of only three in the field with racecourse experience, was never far away, but failed to quicken in the final quarter-mile. (11/2)

Due South (11/1: 6/1-12/1)

2525 KINGSTON RATED STKS H'CAP (0-100) (3-Y.O+) (Class B)
2-45 (2-51) **1m 14y** £9,355.80 (£3,502.20: £1,713.60: £738.00: £331.50: £168.90) Stalls: High GOING: 0.05 sec per fur (G)

			SP	RR	SF
1450⁹	**Clan Ben (IRE) (91)** (HRACecil) **5-8-12** KFallon(2) (lw: rdn 6f out: hdwy over 1f out: led ins fnl f: r.o wl) ....—	**1**	10/1	100	69
1456¹⁰	**Aunty Jane (95)** (JLDunlop) **4-9-2** KDarley(5) (lw: a.p: rdn over 3f out: led over 1f out tl ins fnl f: unable qckn) 1¾	**2**	16/1	101	70
1462⁶	**Mukaddar (USA) (96)** (CJBenstead) **3-8-8** GDuffield(1) (lw: chsd ldr 7f out: rdn over 2f out: ev ch 1f out: one pce) ....¾	**3**	25/1	100	60

1739[3]	**Star Talent (USA) (88)** (IABalding) **6-8-9** RCochrane(4) (lw: hdwy over 1f out: r.o one pce)	nk	**4**	11/2[3]	91	60
2026[5]	**Hal's Pal (97)** (DRLoder) **4-9-4** LDettori(6) (lw: rdn over 2f out: hdwy over 1f out: r.o)	nk	**5**	4/1[2]	100	69
2201*	**Sharp Rebuff (86)** (PJMakin) **6-8-7** SSanders(10) (a.p: nt clr run on ins over 2f out & over 1f out: wknd fnl f)	2½	**6**	7/1	84	53
1973[3]	**Dalliance (IRE) (92)** (MRStoute) **3-8-4v** WRyan(9) (led over 6f: btn whn n.m.r on ins, ins fnl f)	2	**7**	9/1	86	46
2026[15]	**Kayvee (95)** (MrsAJPerrett) **8-9-2** AClark(8) (hdwy over 2f out: wknd over 1f out)	1½	**8**	20/1	86	55
1976*	**Warningford (93)** (JRFanshawe) **3-8-5** DHarrison(3) (hdwy over 2f out: wknd over 1f out)	16	**9**	3/1[1]	52	12
	Prince of India (100) (LordHuntingdon) **5-9-7** MJKinane(7) (a bhd: p.u over 5f out: dismntd)		**P**	25/1	—	—
				(SP 110.3%)		**10 Rn**

1m 44.35 (3.15) CSF £130.06 CT £3,296.08 TOTE £10.10: £2.30 £2.80 £5.50 (£58.90) Trio £421.60 OWNER Angus Dundee Plc (NEWMARKET) BRED T. Hillman

WEIGHT FOR AGE 3yo-9lb

OFFICIAL EXPLANATION **Warningford: no explanation offered. Clan Ben (IRE): regarding the improvement in form, the Handicapper reported that the horse was running off a 2lb lower mark here than on his previous outing, and over a two furlong shorter distance. He added his three previous wins had all been over one mile.**

1176 Clan Ben (IRE) appreciated the return to a mile. Soon off the bridle, he picked up ground from below the distance and swept into the lead inside the last to win his first handicap. (10/1)

Aunty Jane put up a good display. Gaining control below the distance, she was unable to cope with the winner's challenge. She should soon open her account for her new stable. (16/1)

Mukaddar (USA), who had beaten just two home in three races this term, left that form well behind over this longer trip, having every chance entering the final furlong before tapped for toe. (25/1)

1739 Star Talent (USA), as usual, was put to sleep at the back of the field. He did not encounter traffic problems this time but, despite staying on, never threatened to land a serious blow. (11/2)

2026 Hal's Pal, racing at the back of the field, made late headway but never threatened to get into it. All three of his wins have been on Wolverhampton's Fibresand. (4/1)

2201* Sharp Rebuff, 7lb higher for his recent Warwick success, failed to get the best of runs along the inside rail in the straight but, when he saw daylight, he tired inside the last. (7/1: 5/1-15/2)

2526 SANDOWN PARK SPRINT STKS (Listed) (3-Y.O+) (Class A)

3-20 (3-22) **5f 6y** £11,522.50 (£3,490.00: £1,705.00: £812.50) Stalls: High GOING: 0.05 sec per fur (G)

				SP	RR	SF
2106[10]	**Ya Malak (113)** (DNicholls) **6-9-7** AlexGreaves(12) (lw: nt clr run over 2f out: stdy hdwy over 1f out: rdn fnl f: led nr fin)	—	**1**	11/2[2]	117	77
2106[6]	**Struggler (112)** (DRLoder) **5-9-3** LDettori(11) (a.p: rdn over 2f out: led ins fnl f: hdd nr fin)	nk	**2**	7/2[1]	112	72
2106[13]	**Cathedral (IRE) (98)** (BJMeehan) **3-8-12** JWeaver(1) (outpcd: gd hdwy over 1f out: r.o one pce)	2½	**3**	33/1	104+	59
679[8]	**Proud Native (IRE) (112)** (APJarvis) **3-8-12** MJKinane(13) (lw: rdn over 2f out: hdwy over 1f out: one pce)	½	**4**	12/1	103	58
2105[6]	**To the Roof (IRE) (105)** (PWHarris) **5-9-3** MHills(14) (lw: led to 1f out: sn wknd)	hd	**5**	7/2[1]	102	62
2056[10]	**Tedburrow (102)** (EJAlston) **5-9-3** ACulhane(9) (outpcd: hdwy over 1f out: nvr nrr)	s.h	**6**	11/1	102	62
2023[9]	**Omaha City (IRE) (95)** (BGubby) **3-8-12** AClark(2) (rdn over 2f out: hdwy over 1f out: one pce)	1¼	**7**	40/1	98	53
	Eveningperformance (116) (HCandy) **6-9-5** CRutter(3) (chsd ldrs over 3f)	1¼	**8**	11/1	96	56
2277[3]	**Sally Slade (67)** (CACyzer) **5-8-12** GDuffield(8) (outpcd)	1¼	**9**	100/1	85	45
2106[16]	**Brave Edge (106)** (RHannon) **6-9-3** DaneO'Neill(5) (spd over 3f)	s.h	**10**	20/1	90	50
2106[8]	**Bolshoi (IRE) (106)** (JBerry) **5-9-3b** KDarley(4) (lw: a.p: rdn over 2f out: wknd fnl f)	s.h	**11**	10/1[3]	90	50
2106[18]	**Sylva Paradise (IRE) (103)** (CEBrittain) **4-9-3** BDoyle(10) (bhd fnl 2f)	s.h	**12**	20/1	90	50
2105[23]	**Astrac (IRE) (103)** (MissGayKelleway) **6-9-7b[1]** KFallon(6) (spd over 3f)	4	**13**	20/1	81	41
1975*	**Johnny Staccato (93)** (JMPEustace) **3-8-12** JTate(7) (squeezed out s: a bhd: virtually p.u fnl 2f: sddle slipped)	dist	**14**	20/1	—	—
				(SP 118.7%)		**14 Rn**

61.69 secs (1.89) CSF £20.25 TOTE £5.60: £2.60 £1.80 £3.90 (£7.40) Trio £184.20 OWNER Contrac Promotions Ltd (THIRSK) BRED Mrs R. B. Kennard

WEIGHT FOR AGE 3yo-5lb

OFFICIAL EXPLANATION **Johnny Staccato: saddle slipped after one furlong.**

1766* Ya Malak once again showed that he is extremely useful when things go his way - he saw too much daylight at Royal Ascot last time. Blessed with a good draw, he was given a lovely ride by Alex Greaves, who covered him up in the middle of the pack. Making his run from below the distance, he got up in the closing stages. He will go to Chester before running in the Group Three King George Stakes at Goodwood. (11/2: 4/1-6/1)

2106 Struggler showed the benefit of his run at Royal Ascot, and managed to get to the front early in the last furlong. Almost immediately challenged by the winner, he was only worried out of it in the closing stages. (7/2)

792* Cathedral (IRE) did not appear to have a prayer from his low draw, which makes this performance most commendable. Unable to go the early pace, he made giant strides below the distance, and stayed on for third. (33/1)

Proud Native (IRE) did not find the drop to five furlongs in his favour and, after beginning a forward move below the distance, made no further impression in the final furlong. (12/1)

2105 To the Roof (IRE) had the best draw of all, and tried to make that tell as he took the field along until collared a furlong out. (7/2)

1948* Tedburrow did not have an easy task, but stayed on to be nearest at the line. (11/1)

Eveningperformance (11/1: 8/1-12/1)

1881a Bolshoi (IRE) (10/1: 8/1-12/1)

2527 CORAL-ECLIPSE STKS (Gp 1) (3-Y.O+) (Class A)

4-05 (4-08) **1m 2f 7y** £145,440.00 (£54,272.00: £25,936.00: £11,152.00) Stalls: High GOING: 0.05 sec per fur (G)

				SP	RR	SF
2104[2]	**Pilsudski (IRE) (126)** (MRStoute) **5-9-7** MJKinane(1) (lw: led 1f: led 2f out: drvn out)	—	**1**	11/2[2]	132	63
1769*	**Benny The Dip (USA) (124)** (JHMGosden) **3-8-10** WRyan(2) (lw: led 9f out to 2f out: rdn: r.o ins fnl f)	1¼	**2**	6/1[3]	130	50
2010*	**Bosra Sham (USA) (131)** (HRACecil) **4-9-4** KFallon(4) (swtg: hld up: nt clr run on ins over 2f out: swtchd lft & rdn: r.o)	s.h	**3**	4/7[1]	127+	58
2009*	**Allied Forces (USA)** (SbinSuroor) **4-9-7** LDettori(5) (swtg: hld up: rdn over 2f out: r.o one pce)	3½	**4**	16/1	124	55
1554a*	**Sasuru (119)** (GWragg) **4-9-7** MHills(3) (b: hld up: rdn over 2f out: sn wknd)	5	**5**	8/1	116	47
				(SP 110.3%)		**5 Rn**

2m 12.51 (5.81) CSF £31.88 TOTE £6.10: £1.90 £1.80 (£16.50) OWNER Lord Weinstock (NEWMARKET) BRED Ballymacoll Stud Co

WEIGHT FOR AGE 3yo-11lb

IN-FOCUS: A race in which the repercussions and media furore following the defeat of the favourite took much of the credit away from a fine performance by the winner, given an enterprising ride by Michael Kinane.
2104 Pilsudski (IRE), whose connections believe was beaten by lack of peak fitness in the soft ground at Royal Ascot, put up a tremendous display. Gaining control at the quarter-mile pole, he responded well to pressure to keep the challengers at bay. He will probably run in the King George at Ascot, then have a break before a second attempt at the Arc. (11/2: 7/2-6/1)
1769* Benny The Dip (USA), who has had a small problem since the Derby according to his trainer, was wisely returning to possibly his best trip. Instructed to set a slow pace, Ryan carried out his instructions to the letter. Winding up the pace in the straight, although he could not resist the winner's challenge, he was fighting back inside the final furlong. The Juddmonte International at York is his next target, with the Breeders' Cup his long-term objective. (6/1)
2010* Bosra Sham (USA), described by Henry Cecil as the best he has trained, was disappointing. The slow pace and a crucial piece of mis-judgement by Fallon cost her the race, as an abortive attempt to get a run up the inside possibly cost her more than the distance by which she was beaten. She is better suited by being able to quicken off a fast pace, and this race is best forgotten. (4/7)
2009* Allied Forces (USA), awash with sweat beforehand, was found wanting in this company over a trip beyond his best. Held up in last place, he was unable to mount an effective challenge. A return to a mile is on the cards. (16/1)
1554a* Sasuru has shown himself to be a classy performer, but found this company too hot, and was soon in trouble once the race began in earnest. Further success awaits in lesser company. (8/1)

2528 WIMBLEDON H'CAP (0-100) (3-Y.O+) (Class C)

4-40 (4-41) **1m 2f 7y** £11,040.00 (£3,345.00: £1,635.00: £780.00) Stalls: High GOING: 0.05 sec per fur (G)

Form	Horse	Dist	Pos	SP	RR	SF
2118^{4}	**Trojan Risk (71)** (GLewis) **4-8-4** PaulEddery(1) (lw: stdy hdwy 2f out: swtchd lft over 1f out: led ins fnl f: drvn out)	—	1	16/1	82	45
1234*	**Patriot Games (IRE) (82)** (MRStoute) **3-8-4** WRyan(3) (nt clr run over 2f out: hdwy over 1f out: r.o wl ins fnl f)	1	2	$11/2^{2}$	91	43
1659^{2}	**Night Watch (USA) (92)** (IABalding) **4-9-11** LDettori(13) (b: lw: led: rdn over 1f out: hdd ins fnl f: unable qckn)	hd	3	16/1	101	64
1934*	**Orsay (80)** (WRMuir) **5-8-13** KFallon(2) (lw: hdwy over 2f out: rdn over 1f out: r.o)	nk	4	$5/1^{1}$	89	52
1831*	**Flying North (IRE) (80)** (MrsMReveley) **4-8-13** ACulhane(10) (hdwy on ins 3f out: rdn over 2f out: one pce)	1¾	5	10/1	86	49
2209*	**Break the Rules (84)** (DNicholls) **5-9-3** AlexGreaves(4) (swtchd rt over 2f out: hdwy over 1f out: nvr nrr)	½	6	9/1	89	52
1985*	**Philistar (76)** (KRBurke) **4-8-9** BDoyle(14) (plld hrd: a.p: chsd ldr over 2f out to 1f out: one pce)	s.h	7	9/1	81	44
	Gone for a Burton (IRE) (84) (PJMakin) **7-9-3** SSanders(5) (nt clr run over 2f out: hdwy & bmpd over 1f out: swtchd rt: one pce fnl f)	¾	8	20/1	88	51
2013^{8}	**Asef Alhind (83)** (BHanbury) **3-8-5** MHills(8) (plld hrd: prom over 7f)	1¼	9	$8/1^{3}$	85	37
2136^{2}	**Conspicuous (IRE) (84)** (LGCottrell) **7-9-3** KDarley(6) (lw: hld up: rdn over 2f out: wknd over 1f out)	½	10	$11/2^{2}$	85	48
2028^{5}	**Tykeyvor (IRE) (88)** (LadyHerries) **7-9-7** GDuffield(7) (bhd fnl 2f)	2	11	12/1	86	49
1981^{14}	**Story Line (86)** (DWPArbuthnot) **4-9-5** DHarrison(9) (lw: prom over 7f)	2	12	50/1	81	44
2242^{6}	**Strazo (IRE) (90)** (LadyHerries) **4-9-9** RCochrane(11) (chsd ldr over 7f: wknd wl over 1f out)	¾	13	20/1	84	47
2285^{9}	**Dark Age (IRE) (70)** (RAkehurst) **4-8-3** AClark(12) (lw: prom over 7f)	hd	14	33/1	63	26
				(SP 121.5%)	**14 Rn**	

2m 12.73 (6.03) CSF £89.72 CT £1,332.73 TOTE £20.60: £3.40 £2.10 £3.80 (£80.10) Trio £417.70 OWNER Mr Jim McCarthy (EPSOM) BRED Roldvale Ltd
WEIGHT FOR AGE 3yo-11lb
2118 Trojan Risk looked in good shape beforehand, and came with a good run to lead inside the last. (16/1)
1234* Patriot Games (IRE) appreciated the slightly longer trip, but did not have the best of runs. With not a great deal of room, the winner had first run, and was not for catching. (11/2: 7/2-6/1)
1659 Night Watch (USA), all the better for his recent run after a lay-off, attempted to make all, and was not overhauled until inside the last. This was a good effort, and he deserves to win soon. (16/1)
1934* Orsay began to pick up ground over a quarter-of-a-mile from home, and looked a serious threat below the distance. Despite staying on, he proved no match for the winner. (5/1)
1831* Flying North (IRE), 7lb higher for his Beverley win last month, found the weight increase telling here, for after poking up the inner early in the straight, he could make no further impression. (10/1)
2209* Break the Rules, having his first run for his new stable, has been in sparkling form this season but, despite staying on, never threat-ened to get into it. (9/1)
1682* Asef Alhind (8/1: 6/1-9/1)

2529 VICTORIA AMATEUR TURF CLUB H'CAP (0-95) (3-Y.O+) (Class C)

5-15 (5-18) **5f 6y** £5,810.00 (£1,760.00: £860.00: £410.00) Stalls: High GOING: 0.05 sec per fur (G)

Form	Horse	Dist	Pos	SP	RR	SF
1772^{5}	**My Best Valentine (95)** (VSoane) **7-10-0** RCochrane(6) (lw: gd hdwy over 1f out: qcknd to ld ins fnl f: comf)	—	1	20/1	108	74
2111^{2}	**That Man Again (85)** (SCWilliams) **5-9-4** KDarley(10) (lw: led: rdn over 2f out: hdd ins fnl f: unable qckn)	2½	2	$11/2^{2}$	90	56
	Music Gold (IRE) (92) (WAO'Gorman) **4-9-11b** DHarrison(7) (rdn & hdwy over 1f out: r.o ins fnl f)	½	3	50/1	96	62
2321^{2}	**Barranak (IRE) (65)** (GMMcCourt) **5-7-9**(3) MBaird(12) (hld up: rdn over 2f out: r.o ins fnl f)	nk	4	$8/1^{3}$	68	34
1772^{4}	**Clan Chief (83)** (JRArnold) **4-9-2** AClark(9) (w ldr: rdn over 2f out: ev ch ins fnl f: sn wknd)	¾	5	$5/1^{1}$	83	49
2289^{6}	**Ziggy's Dancer (USA) (84)** (EJAlston) **6-9-3** KFallon(8) (rdn 3f out: hdwy over 1f out: nvr nrr)	nk	6	10/1	83	49
1937^{4}	**Gone Savage (80)** (WJMusson) **9-8-13** LDettori(2) (rdn over 1f out: hdwy fnl f: nvr nrr)	¾	7	$11/2^{2}$	77	43
2232*	**White Emir (84)** (BJMeehan) **4-9-3b** BDoyle(11) (swtg: hdwy over 1f out: wknd fnl f)	½	8	$11/2^{2}$	79	45
942^{12}	**Galine (82)** (WAO'Gorman) **4-9-1** EmmaO'Gorman(13) (swtg: hld up: rdn over 2f out: wknd over 1f out)	½	9	10/1	76	42
2006^{19}	**Scissor Ridge (63)** (JJBridger) **5-7-3**(7) PDoe(1) (swtg: a bhd)	2	10	50/1	50	16
2347^{2}	**Rudi's Pet (IRE) (84)** (RHannon) **3-8-12b** DaneO'Neill(4) (lw: prom over 3f)	hd	11	12/1	71	32
1766^{6}	**Speed On (95)** (HCandy) **4-10-0** CRutter(5) (lw: prom over 3f)	2	12	20/1	76	42
1317^{10}	**Akalim (65)** (LGCottrell) **4-7-7**(5)ow1 AimeeCook(3) (prom tl wknd & hmpd over 1f out)	¾	13	33/1	43	8
				(SP 116.2%)	**13 Rn**	

62.28 secs (2.48) CSF £107.56 CT £4,876.76 TOTE £18.40: £3.50 £2.20 £12.00 (£48.80) Trio £389.80 OWNER The Valentines (ASTON ROWANT) BRED Ridgecourt Stud
WEIGHT FOR AGE 3yo-5lb
1772 My Best Valentine, who has done all his winning at around seven furlongs, had no problem with the drop in distance, and put up a tremendous performance from his draw, slicing through the opposition to lead inside the last. He will now run in the Stewards' Cup at Goodwood, for which he escapes a penalty. (20/1)

2111 That Man Again merrily bowled along in front until put in his place by the winner in the last furlong. Although he has not scored for nearly two years, he has returned to form this season, and should soon be winning. (11/2)
Music Gold (IRE) made a pleasing seasonal debut, running on nicely in the last furlong-and-a half to take third place. (50/1)
2321 Barranak (IRE), put up a pound for finishing second to Superlao at Lingfield last week, chased the leaders, but never got in a serious blow. He is nevertheless in good form at present. (8/1: 6/1-9/1)
1772 Clan Chief ran a sound race, disputing the lead until tiring inside the last. He should soon find a suitable opportunity. (5/1)
2289 Ziggy's Dancer (USA), off the bridle from before halfway, struggled on from below the distance without ever threatening. (10/1)
1937 Gone Savage, put to sleep at the back of the field, found his stride far too late. (11/2)
2347 Rudi's Pet (IRE) (12/1: op 8/1)

2530 SPINAL INJURIES ASSOCIATION H'CAP (0-85) (3-Y.O+) (Class D)

5-45 (5-46) **2m 78y** £5,160.00 (£1,560.00: £760.00: £360.00) Stalls: High GOING: 0.05 sec per fur (G)

				SP	RR	SF
2139^{2}	**Right Man (74)** (GLewis) **3-8-5** PaulEddery(7) (stdy hdwy over 3f out: led over 2f out: clr over 1f out: r.o wl)	—	1	15/8^{1}	91+	51
975*	**Ramike (IRE) (80)** (MJohnston) **3-8-11** JWeaver(5) (lw: hld up: led over 7f out tl over 6f out: rdn over 3f out: ev ch over 2f out: unable qckn)	10	2	10/1	87	47
1027^{12}	**Bowcliffe Court (IRE) (77)** (RAkehurst) **5-9-13** SSanders(8) (lw: hld up: rdn over 3f out: ev ch over 2f out: one pce)	½	3	11/2^{3}	84	63
2014^{8}	**Nanton Point (USA) (74)** (LadyHerries) **5-9-10** RCochrane(2) (led 9f: led over 6f out tl over 2f out: one pce)	4	4	13/2	77	56
2225^{2}	**Royal Expression (78)** (FJordan) **5-10-0** KDarley(1) (nvr nr to chal)	8	5	20/1	73	52
2014^{21}	**Grand Cru (65)** (JCullinan) **6-9-1** WRyan(6) (lw: a bhd)	½	6	14/1	60	39
1974^{9}	**Chris's Lad (57)** (BJMeehan) **6-8-7b** BDoyle(3) (lw: prom tl over 2f out: wknd)	½	7	4/1^{2}	51	30
*1964**	**Dark Waters (IRE) (70)** (NAGraham) **4-9-6** LDettori(4) (prom over 12f: virtually p.u fnl 3f: t.o)	dist	8	8/1	—	—
				(SP 115.1%)	**8 Rn**	

3m 40.85 (8.85) CSF £20.32 CT £80.78 TOTE £2.70: £1.30 £2.30 £2.00 (£8.40) OWNER Mr G. V. Wright (EPSOM) BRED A. C. Birkle
WEIGHT FOR AGE 3yo-19lb
2139 Right Man put up a tremendous performance, as he eased his way into the lead before shooting clear for a decisive victory. (15/8)
975* Ramike (IRE) suffered his first defeat of the season, before left for dead by the winner. (10/1: 8/1-12/1)
1027 Bowcliffe Court (IRE), one of four in line early in the straight, had no answer once the winner quickened. (11/2)
2014 Nanton Point (USA) made the majority of the running, but was only fighting for minor honours once collared. (13/2)
2225 Royal Expression had the right trip, but the ground was against him, and he was at the back of the field until plodding on past beaten rivals. (20/1)
1413 Grand Cru needs a bog, and was always languishing at the back of the field. (14/1: 8/1-16/1)

T/Jkpt: Not won; £36,487.15 to 7/7/97. T/Plpt: £4,953.70 (11.23 Tckts). T/Qdpt: £228.00 (12.11 Tckts) AK

2306-BATH (L-H) (Good)
Monday July 7th
WEATHER: Fine WIND: almost nil

2531 KNOCKDOWN (S) H'CAP (0-60) (3-Y.O+) (Class G)

2-00 (2-00) **1m 5f 22y** £2,360.00 (£660.00: £320.00) Stalls: Low GOING minus 0.39 sec per fur (F)

				SP	RR	SF
202^{3}	**Royal Circus (37)** (IPWilliams) **8-9-0** KFallon(1) (swtg: mde virtually all: rdn over 2f out: all out)	—	1	7/1^{3}	49	30
*2067**	**Private Fixture (IRE) (38)** (DMarks) **6-9-1** GDuffield(7) (w wnr: rdn & ev ch fnl 2f: r.o)	hd	2	4/1^{1}	50	31
2307^{5}	**Excelled (IRE) (30)** (CJDrewe) **8-8-7** TSprake(10) (bit bkwd: hld up: rdn & hdwy 3f out: one pce fnl 2f)	5	3	16/1	36	17
2307^{3}	**Nornax Lad (USA) (47)** (MartynMeade) **9-9-3b(7)** RBrisland(2) (swtg: plld hrd: prom tl wknd over 2f out)	3	4	10/1	49	30
2357^{4}	**Fortune Hopper (56)** (JPearce) **3-9-2(3)** CTeague(4) (nvr trbld ldrs)	2½	5	12/1	55	22
2189^{10}	**Dawn Summit (50)** (BHanbury) **3-8-13** JStack(13) (hld up & plld hrd: hdwy over 4f out: wknd 3f out)	1½	6	10/1	47	14
1287^{10}	**Gunner B Special (33)** (JNeville) **4-8-7(3)** DO'Donohoe(6) (s.s: nvr nr ldrs)	¾	7	33/1	29	10
1507^{10}	**Bresil (USA) (22)** (JJBridger) **8-7-10(3)** MHenry(8) (hld up: hdwy 4f out: wknd 3f out)	½	8	25/1	18	—
2175^{3}	**Rose of Glenn (45)** (BPalling) **6-9-1(7)** CLowther(3) (prom 9f: sddle slipped)	½	9	8/1	40	21
2128^{6}	**Paperwork Pete (IRE) (30)** (WStorey) **5-8-7** SWhitworth(12) (a bhd)	1¼	10	7/1^{3}	24	5
771^{9}	**Riscatto (USA) (53)** (WRMuir) **3-9-2** JReid(9) (bit bkwd: prom over 9f)	2	11	11/2^{2}	44	11
	Perfect Bertie (IRE) (36) (NMBabbage) **5-8-8(5)** RFfrench(5) (bkwd: plld hrd: sddle slipped: hdwy over 5f out: wknd over 3f out)	1¾	12	10/1	25	6
2301^{11}	**Inchella (30)** (APJones) **4-8-7** NAdams(11) (a bhd: t.o)	24	13	33/1	—	—
				(SP 122.1%)	**13 Rn**	

2m 51.9 (6.20) CSF £32.05 CT £402.05 TOTE £8.10: £2.40 £1.80 £3.50 (£12.90) Trio £57.00 OWNER Mr P. W. Hiatt (ALVECHURCH) BRED Snailwell Stud Co Ltd
WEIGHT FOR AGE 3yo-14lb
No bid
OFFICIAL EXPLANATION **Rose of Glenn: saddle slipped. Perfect Bertie (IRE): saddle slipped.**
202 Royal Circus held on gamely off a mark 2lb lower than when last winning on grass nearly three years ago. (7/1)
2067* Private Fixture (IRE) has certainly improved for the step up to this sort of trip. (4/1)
Excelled (IRE) seemed better suited to this type of distance. (16/1)
2307 Nornax Lad (USA), dropped 4lb, ran too freely. (10/1)
2357 Fortune Hopper (12/1: op 8/1)
1502* Dawn Summit refused to settle on this drop into a seller. (10/1: 8/1-12/1)
2175 Rose of Glenn (8/1: op 4/1)
Paperwork Pete (IRE) (7/1: op 14/1)
582* Riscatto (USA) (11/2: 4/1-6/1)

2532 LIMPLEY STOKE MAIDEN STKS (I) (3-Y.O) (Class D)

2-30 (2-35) **1m 2f 46y** £3,101.25 (£930.00: £447.50: £206.25) Stalls: Low GOING minus 0.39 sec per fur (F)

				SP	RR	SF
	Meteor Strike (USA) (MrsAJPerrett) **3-9-0** PatEddery(4) (wl grwn: bit bkwd: mde all: rdn over 1f out: r.o wl)	—	1	10/1	81	41
	Livius (IRE) (MajorDNChappell) **3-9-0** MHills(7) (w'like: str: swtg: hld up: hdwy over 2f out: r.o ins fnl f)	½	2	20/1	80	40
2183[3]	**Danzas** (RCharlton) **3-9-0** TSprake(5) (lw: swtg: hld up: rdn & hdwy over 2f out: r.o one pce fnl f)	½	3	10/11[1]	79	39
	Marsul (USA) (JHMGosden) **3-9-0** RHills(1) (h.d.w: bit bkwd: prom tl rdn & wknd 2f out)	5	4	9/1[3]	72	32
1625[4]	**Arletty** (HRACecil) **3-8-9** KFallon(11) (lw: w wnr: ev ch over 2f out: wknd over 1f out)	¾	5	5/1[2]	65	25
1276[7]	**Woody's Boy (IRE)** (MJHeaton-Ellis) **3-9-0** SDrowne(2) (bit bkwd: no hdwy fnl 3f)	1¼	6	33/1	69	29
2287[7]	**Dazzling Stone** (LadyHerries) **3-9-0** RCochrane(8) (swtg: prom over 7f)	7	7	16/1	58	18
	Miss Kemble (BWHills) **3-8-9** GCarter(9) (unf: scope: s.s: a bhd)	nk	8	14/1	52	12
1508[4]	**Aegean** (RHannon) **3-9-0** DaneO'Neill(3) (hld up mid div: bhd fnl 3f: t.o)	22	9	12/1	23	—
	Negative (MSalaman) **3-8-9** SWhitworth(6) (lt-f: unf: bit bkwd: unruly s: s.i.s: a bhd: t.o)	½	10	100/1	17	—
	Daniel's Mascot (AGNewcombe) **3-9-0** TQuinn(10) (leggy: lt-f: unf: a bhd: t.o)	20	11	33/1	—	—
				(SP 120.0%)		**11 Rn**

2m 9.7 (3.20) CSF £177.29 TOTE £8.80: £2.40 £2.80 £1.10 (£104.50) Trio £118.70 OWNER Mr K. Abdulla (PULBOROUGH) BRED Juddmonte Farms

Meteor Strike (USA) is a rather imposing individual who showed the right sort of attitude and seems sure to come on for the run. (10/1)
Livius (IRE), a half-brother to a German Derby winner, made a promising debut and should not be inconvenienced by a mile and a half. (20/1)
2183 Danzas, stepping up from a mile, was very uneasy in the market, admittedly having opened at a very short price. (10/11)
Marsul (USA) should at least be sharper for the outing. (9/1)
1625 Arletty, a half-sister to Ascot Gold Cup winner Paean and top miler Shavian, is at least now qualified for handicaps. (5/1)
Woody's Boy (IRE) is a half-brother to hurdler Kierchem and a five-furlong juvenile winner who went on to stay a mile and a half. (33/1)
Miss Kemble (14/1: 8/1-20/1)

2533 RACING CHANNEL H'CAP (0-80) (3-Y.O+) (Class D)

3-00 (3-07) **1m 2f 46y** £3,738.25 (£1,126.00: £545.50: £255.25) Stalls: Low GOING minus 0.39 sec per fur (F)

				SP	RR	SF
2301[10]	**Hill Farm Blues (58)** (WMBrisbourne) **4-8-6** AGarth(5) (s.s: gd hdwy over 2f out: led ins fnl f: r.o wl)	—	1	14/1	69	46
2065*	**Anak-Ku (73)** (MissGayKelleway) **4-9-2**(5) RFfrench(4) (lw: led tl ins fnl f)	3	2	11/2	79	56
2210[3]	**Rasayel (USA) (72)** (PDEvans) **7-9-6** JFEgan(3) (hld up: rdn & hdwy 4f out: one pce fnl 2f)	¾	3	10/1	77	54
2030[8]	**Askern (60)** (DHaydnJones) **6-8-8** AMackay(7) (hld up: hdwy fnl 2f: nt rch ldrs)	1¼	4	16/1	63	40
1102[4]	**Go For Salt (USA) (78)** (MRStoute) **3-9-1** KFallon(9) (hld up: hdwy over 2f out: ev ch over 1f out: wknd ins fnl f)	nk	5	7/2[1]	81	47
1811[5]	**Fabulous Mtoto (57)** (MSSaunders) **7-8-5** RPrice(10) (hld up: hdwy 3f out: one pce fnl 2f)	½	6	12/1	59	36
2310*	**Mislemani (IRE) (51)** (AGNewcombe) **7-7-10**(3) MartinDwyer(1) (plld hrd: sn prom: wknd over 2f out)	3½	7	5/1[3]	47	24
2028[17]	**Filial (IRE) (80)** (BJMeehan) **4-9-7**(7) GHannon(2) (bhd fnl 3f)	5	8	14/1	69	46
1811[8]	**Star of Ring (IRE) (63)** (MJHeaton-Ellis) **4-8-11** SDrowne(8) (prom: rdn & wknd 2f out)	6	9	16/1	42	19
1972[3]	**Thatchmaster (IRE) (59)** (CAHorgan) **6-8-7** PaulEddery(6) (chsd ldr: rdn over 4f out: wknd over 2f out)	3	10	9/2[2]	34	11
				(SP 114.3%)		**10 Rn**

2m 8.1 (1.60) CSF £79.56 CT £739.31 TOTE £20.90: £4.00 £2.00 £2.30 (£54.80) Trio £85.40 OWNER Mr Dennis Newton (NESSCLIFFE) BRED D. Newton

WEIGHT FOR AGE 3yo-11lb

2301 Hill Farm Blues has improved for the change of stables this season and was 9lb higher than when winning a seller on her reappearance. (14/1: 10/1-16/1)
2065* Anak-Ku continues in fine form, having been raised 8lb for his two victories last month. (11/2: 3/1-6/1)
2210 Rasayel (USA) is finding things difficult off a mark 7lb higher than when winning a Ladies' race at Nottingham. (10/1)
2030 Askern was apparently suffering from a heart irregularity when disappointing last time. (16/1)
1102 Go For Salt (USA), thought good enough to contest the Lingfield Oaks Trial, came up empty after being well in the shake-up. (7/2: op 9/4)
1811 Fabulous Mtoto is still 8lb higher than the second of his wins last summer, and 16lb up on the first. (12/1)
Filial (IRE) (14/1: 10/1-16/1)

2534 E.B.F. EVERSHOT MAIDEN STKS (2-Y.O) (Class D)

3-30 (3-32) **5f 161y** £3,517.50 (£1,065.00: £520.00: £247.50) Stalls: High GOING minus 0.39 sec per fur (F)

				SP	RR	SF
2123[2]	**Hill Magic** (DRCElsworth) **2-9-0** RCochrane(15) (hld up: hdwy 2f out: led ins fnl f: r.o wl)	—	1	7/2[2]	77	30
2181[7]	**Aunt Sadie** (RCharlton) **2-8-9** TSprake(11) (a.p: hrd rdn & ev ch over 1f out: r.o one pce ins fnl f)	1	2	9/1	69	22
1970[5]	**Alpha Whisky (GER)** (IABalding) **2-8-9** JReid(14) (plld hrd: a.p: ev ch over 1f out: one pce)	1½	3	10/1	65	18
2306[6]	**Deva Lady** (MRChannon) **2-8-9** RPerham(8) (a.p: led over 2f out tl ins fnl f)	hd	4	10/1	65	18
2227[8]	**Frolicking** (JLDunlop) **2-8-9** GCarter(12) (hdwy over 2f out: r.o ins fnl f)	1¾	5	14/1	60	13
	Defiance (BWHills) **2-9-0** MHills(7) (lengthy: unf: bit bkwd: hdwy over 1f out: r.o: bttr for r)	½	6	8/1	64	17
1744[3]	**Night Flyer** (JWHills) **2-9-0** KFallon(1) (swtg: prom: led 3f out: sn hdd: wknd over 1f out)	1¼	7	3/1[1]	60	13
2227[10]	**Allasella (IRE)** (BPalling) **2-8-9** DHarrison(3) (swtg: chsd ldrs over 3f)	2	8	33/1	49	2
	Storm Cry (USA) (MajorDNChappell) **2-9-0** RHills(4) (leggy: lt-f: unf: s.s: a bhd)	3½	9	14/1	45	—
	Tightrope (SirMarkPrescott) **2-9-0** GDuffield(13) (w'like: leggy: s.s: a bhd)	1¼	10	5/1[3]	41	—
1235[5]	**Corsecan** (SDow) **2-8-11**(3) DO'Donohoe(10) (stdd s: a bhd)	1¾	11	50/1	36	—
	Second Sun (JJBridger) **2-8-11**(3) MHenry(6) (lt-f: unf: swtg: led over 2f: wknd over 2f out)	4	12	50/1	25	—
	Belle de Montfort (JLSpearing) **2-8-9** SDrowne(9) (small: lt-f: w ldrs tl wknd over 2f out)	3	13	33/1	12	—
	I Cried For You (IRE) (RHannon) **2-9-0** PatEddery(5) (leggy: lt-f: s.s: a bhd)	5	14	8/1	3	—
				(SP 137.4%)		**14 Rn**

1m 12.0 (2.50) CSF £36.76 TOTE £5.00: £1.90 £3.20 £3.30 (£26.90) Trio £69.10 OWNER Michael Jackson Bloodstock Ltd (WHITCOMBE) BRED Mrs M. Fairbairn and E. Gadsden

2123 Hill Magic came with a nicely-timed run for a workmanlike win. (7/2)
2181 Aunt Sadie, a half-sister to five-furlong two-year-old winner Eye Shadow and mile winner Gushing, again showed that stamina is not a problem. (9/1)

1970 Alpha Whisky (GER), a half-sister to good middle-distance handicapper Smart Blade, is out of a winner over a mile and three quarters. Seeing a bit too much daylight on the outside early on, she will do better when tackling a longer trip. (10/1)
2306 Deva Lady made more use of her stamina this time. (10/1)
Frolicking, a half-sister to a German two-year-old who scored over five furlongs and a mile, shaped as though a longer distance would not come amiss. (14/1: 10/1-16/1)
Defiance, a half-brother to six and seven-furlong winner Waypoint, is out of a mare who scored three times at the minimum, including a Group Three. Showing plenty of promise for the future, he will soon leave this form behind. (8/1: 6/1-9/1)
1744 Night Flyer, a 60,000gs first foal of an unraced half-sister to Polish Patriot, sweated up on a warm day and was disappointing. (3/1)
I Cried For You (IRE) (8/1: op 5/1)

2535 ACTON TURVILLE MAIDEN H'CAP (0-75) (3-Y.O+) (Class D)
4-00 (4-01) **2m 1f 34y** £3,465.25 (£1,042.00: £503.50: £234.25) Stalls: High GOING minus 0.39 sec per fur (F)

				SP	RR	SF
1822[5]	**Lady of The Lake (67)** (JLDunlop) **3-9-1** PatEddery(5) (mde all: qcknd 7f out: rdn over 3f out: clr over 2f out: r.o wl)	—	**1**	3/1[2]	79	32
2316[4]	**Charter (61)** (WStorey) **6-10-0** GCarter(2) (hld up: rdn over 4f out: chsd wnr over 2f out: no imp)	7	**2**	5/2[1]	67	39
2307[10]	**Oscar Rose (30)** (MJBolton) **4-7-6**(5)ow1 RFfrench(4) (hld up: lost pl 7f out: rallied over 3f out: one pce fnl 2f)	2	**3**	20/1	34	5
2189[6]	**Golden Melody (57)** (MJHeaton-Ellis) **3-8-5v** SDrowne(3) (sn chsng wnr: one pce fnl 3f)	1½	**4**	8/1	59	12
2178[9]	**Showcase (51)** (JWHills) **3-7-10**(3)ow3 MHenry(7) (b.nr hind: plld hrd in rr: t.o fnl 3f)	25	**5**	20/1	30	—
888[10]	**Northern Drums (55)** (NMBabbage) **4-9-8** KFallon(6) (lw: swtg: bhd: hrd rdn & sme hdwy 3f out: eased whn btn over 1f out)	1½	**6**	4/1[3]	33	5
1964[2]	**Le Grand Gousier (USA) (56)** (RJRWilliams) **3-8-4** GDuffield(1) (prom: hrd rdn over 3f out: wknd over 2f out: eased whn btn fnl f)	¾	**7**	4/1[3]	33	—
				(SP 114.2%)		**7 Rn**

3m 49.6 (8.20) CSF £9.95 TOTE £3.10: £1.70 £4.40 (£6.00) OWNER Capt J. Macdonald-Buchanan (ARUNDEL) BRED The Lavington Stud
LONG HANDICAP Showcase 7-9
WEIGHT FOR AGE 3yo-19lb
1822 Lady of The Lake, down 3lb, came into her own over this longer distance and was certainly ridden as if stamina was not going to be a problem. (3/1)
2316 Charter, dropped 9lb this season, remains a maiden on the Flat having won a Worcester bumper two years ago. (5/2)
Oscar Rose, dropped a stone this season, could not collar the runner-up let alone bother the winner. (20/1)
2189 Golden Melody, trying a marathon trip, looked devoid of finishing pace. (8/1)

2536 SALTFORD APPRENTICE H'CAP (0-65) (3-Y.O+) (Class G)
4-30 (4-33) **5f 11y** £2,175.50 (£618.00: £306.50) Stalls: High GOING minus 0.39 sec per fur (F)

				SP	RR	SF
2221[W]	**Goretski (IRE) (60)** (NTinkler) **4-9-11**(3) PFredericks(15) (chsd ldr: led ins fnl f: comf)	—	**1**	2/1[1]	71+	51
2148[7]	**Bright Paragon (IRE) (39)** (KTIvory) **8-8-2**(5) SCarson(1) (b.hind: a.p: r.o ins fnl f)	2½	**2**	15/2[3]	42	22
	Tommy Tempest (35) (REPeacock) **8-7-12**(5) RBrisland(10) (led tl ins fnl f)	hd	**3**	33/1	38	18
	Moving Up (IRE) (38) (TEPowell) **4-8-1**(5) RCody-Boutcher(8) (rdn & hdwy over 2f out: r.o one pce fnl f)	nk	**4**	50/1	40	20
2179[4]	**Make Ready (59)** (JNeville) **3-9-3**(5) PBradley(12) (a chsng ldrs: hrd rdn over 2f out: r.o one pce fnl f)	hd	**5**	6/1[2]	61	36
1759[12]	**Delrob (38)** (DHaydnJones) **6-7-10v**(10)ow2 JoeleneRichards(5) (swtg: nvr nr to chal)	1¼	**6**	16/1	36	14
2305[6]	**Marino Street (56)** (PDEvans) **4-9-5v**(5) GHannon(3) (nvr nr to chal)	s.h	**7**	12/1	53	33
2197[2]	**Bairn Atholl (36)** (RJHodges) **4-8-4** DMcGaffin(6) (nvr trbld ldrs)	¾	**8**	6/1[2]	31	11
2424[6]	**Astral Invader (IRE) (41)** (MSSaunders) **5-8-9** AngelaGallimore(14) (rdn over 2f out: no hdwy)	1¾	**9**	10/1	31	11
1814[6]	**Ashkernazy (IRE) (45)** (NEBerry) **6-8-8**(5) KerryBaker(7) (spd over 2f)	½	**10**	12/1	33	13
1931[8]	**Rise 'n Shine (60)** (CACyzer) **3-9-4**(5) DarrenWilliams(13) (prom over 2f)	4	**11**	16/1	35	10
2197[11]	**Forzara (44)** (JLSpearing) **4-8-9**(3) SRighton(4) (plld hrd: a bhd)	½	**12**	20/1	18	—
1814[9]	**Dancing Jack (38)** (JJBridger) **4-8-6** PDoe(9) (s.s: a bhd)	½	**13**	50/1	10	—
2510[9]	**Soda (47)** (JLSpearing) **3-8-7**(3) PClarke(16) (a bhd)	1½	**14**	25/1	14	—
1676[8]	**Mister Sean (IRE) (28)** (JMBradley) **4-7-5b**(5) JFowle(2) (b.hind: swtg: s.s: a bhd: t.o)	8	**15**	50/1	—	—
2197[6]	***Chief's Lady (38)*** (JMBradley) **5-7-13**(7) JBosley(11) (Withdrawn not under Starter's orders: uns rdr bef s: jockey inj.)		**W**	16/1	—	—
				(SP 133.2%)		**15 Rn**

62.2 secs (1.70) CSF £15.18 CT £371.34 TOTE £2.80: £1.50 £3.00 £9.10 (£12.50) Trio £132.00 OWNER Mr P. D. Savill (MALTON) BRED Pierre Brichart
LONG HANDICAP Mister Sean (IRE) 7-7
WEIGHT FOR AGE 3yo-5lb
2221 Goretski (IRE), although 6lb higher than when winning at Hamilton in May, has since scored twice at Southwell and was 6lb lower than the second of those wins. (2/1)
1857 Bright Paragon (IRE) was 3lb higher than when landing a Lingfield seller in May. (15/2)
Tommy Tempest, 5lb lower than when last on grass, ran a cracker on this first run for eleven months. (33/1)
Moving Up (IRE) was something of a revelation having been campaigned between a mile and thirteen furlongs as a three-year-old. (50/1)
2179 Make Ready was probably not really suited by this drop back to five. (6/1: tchd 9/1)
1428 Delrob has slipped to a mark that is 13lb lower than her only previous win on the turf two years ago. (16/1)
2305 Marino Street (12/1: 7/1-14/1)

2537 LIMPLEY STOKE MAIDEN STKS (II) (3-Y.O) (Class D)
5-00 (5-01) **1m 2f 46y** £3,078.50 (£923.00: £444.00: £204.50) Stalls: Low GOING minus 0.39 sec per fur (F)

				SP	RR	SF
2287[8]	**Darapour (IRE)** (LMCumani) **3-8-9**(5) RFfrench(8) (hld up: hdwy over 4f out: rdn over 3f out: r.o to ld wl ins fnl f)	—	**1**	16/1	81+	48
1028[4]	**Desert Beauty (IRE)** (MRStoute) **3-8-9** JReid(5) (bit bkwd: led over 2f: led over 1f out tl wl ins fnl f)	¾	**2**	4/7[1]	75	42
1868[6]	**Irsal (75)** (ACStewart) **3-9-0** RHills(2) (led 8f out tl over 1f out: one pce)	1¼	**3**	8/1	78	45
833[10]	**Silankka** (MRChannon) **3-8-9** RPerham(3) (bit bkwd: hld up & bhd: hdwy on ins 2f out: r.o ins fnl f)	2½	**4**	33/1	69	36

	Devilish Charm (USA) (MrsAJPerrett) **3-9-0** PatEddery(1) (w'like: bkwd: s.s: hdwy 2f out: swtchd rt over 1f out: one pce fnl f)	s.h	**5**	14/1	74	41
2190^{2}	**Imperial Scholar (IRE) (94)** (JMPEustace) **3-8-9** RCochrane(9) (prom: rdn over 2f out: wknd over 1f out)	hd	**6**	7/2^{2}	69	36
1637^{4}	**Juggler** (LordHuntingdon) **3-9-0** DHarrison(4) (hld up: hdwy over 3f out: wknd over 1f out: eased whn btn)	4	**7**	6/1^{3}	67	34
2311^{8}	**Abbey Theatre (IRE)** (MSalaman) **3-8-7**(7) SCarson(7) (hld up mid div: bhd fnl 3f: t.o)	19	**8**	100/1	38	5
2311^{10}	**Dewi Sant** (DBurchell) **3-9-0** VSlattery(6) (bit bkwd: prom tl wknd over 2f out: t.o)	¾	**9**	100/1	37	4
1322^{9}	**Halavadream** (MJBolton) **3-9-0** GDuffield(10) (a bhd: t.o fnl 3f)	dist	**10**	100/1	—	—

(SP 129.7%) **10 Rn**

2m 8.9 (2.40) CSF £26.28 TOTE £18.40: £4.00 £1.10 £2.70 (£22.40) Trio £31.40 OWNER H H Aga Khan (NEWMARKET) BRED His Highness the Aga Khan's Studs S.C.

Darapour (IRE) is out of a mare who won over a mile and a half in France and is closely related to Darshaan. Stepping up out of all recognition on his debut, he gave the impression he might well stay further. (16/1)

1028 Desert Beauty (IRE), a well-bred half-sister to Election Day, was very much the meeting's talking horse having been all at sea in the soft ground in the Cheshire Oaks last time. (4/7)

1868 Irsal forced the pace on this return to ten furlongs. (8/1: 6/1-10/1)

Silankka, a half-sister to Helios and Storm Dust, did not run as a juvenile having split a pastern. A longer trip might help. (33/1)

Devilish Charm (USA) was not disgraced and will strip fitter for the outing. (14/1: 8/1-16/1)

2190 Imperial Scholar (IRE), although managing to beat three home in the Oaks, has yet to prove she is effective at a mile and a quarter. (7/2)

1637 Juggler (6/1: op 3/1)

T/Plpt: £54.80 (309.12 Tckts). T/Qdpt: £20.70 (49.96 Tckts) KH

2350-**MUSSELBURGH** (R-H) (Good)
Monday July 7th

WEATHER: Sunny WIND: almost nil

2538 E.B.F. PRESTONPANS MEDIAN AUCTION MAIDEN STKS (2-Y.O) (Class E)

2-15 (2-15) **5f** £2,916.25 (£880.00: £427.50: £201.25) Stalls: High GOING minus 0.34 sec per fur (GF)

				SP	RR	SF
1941^{7}	**Mill End Quest** (MWEasterby) **2-8-9** TLucas(3) (lw: cl up: led ½-wy: rdn & r.o)	—	**1**	6/1	66	—
2127^{4}	**Cumbrian Cadet** (TDEasterby) **2-9-0b^{1}** JCarroll(5) (lw: a chsng ldrs: ev ch 2f out: r.o one pce)	2½	**2**	11/2^{3}	63	—
1860^{3}	**Chikapenny** (MrsLStubbs) **2-8-9b^{1}** JWeaver(2) (lw: bhd: hdwy ½-wy: ch appr fnl f: no ex)	s.h	**3**	7/1	58	—
1136^{2}	**Charlies Lad (IRE)** (RGuest) **2-9-0** PBloomfield(7) (chsd ldrs: rdn 2f out: nt qckn)	2½	**4**	3/1^{2}	55	—
	Essandess (IRE) (JLEyre) **2-8-9** RLappin(6) (lt-f: dwlt: styd on fnl 2f: nrst fin)	2	**5**	14/1	43	—
2127^{9}	**Walworth Wizard** (MDods) **2-9-0** DaleGibson(1) (sn outpcd & bhd: sme hdwy ½-wy: n.d)	1½	**6**	100/1	44	—
2037^{6}	**Tangerine Flyer** (JBerry) **2-9-0** KDarley(4) (led to ½-wy: sn btn)	hd	**7**	7/4^{1}	43	—
1990^{5}	**Ngaere Princess** (WTKemp) **2-8-6b**(3) PFessey(8) (in tch to ½-wy: sn wl bhd)	10	**8**	200/1	6	—

(SP 111.7%) **8 Rn**

62.0 secs (4.30) CSF £33.56 TOTE £6.30: £1.30 £1.50 £2.80 (£25.00) OWNER Mr W. T. Allgood (SHERIFF HUTTON) BRED Mrs D. Hammerson

460 Mill End Quest, well supported, got the favoured stands' rails and, given a fine ride, was always too strong for the rest. She looks likely to stay further. (6/1)

2127 Cumbrian Cadet had blinkers on for the first time and had his chances but was well second best in the closing stages. (11/2: op 3/1)

1860 Chikapenny was tried in blinkers this time and went pretty well, but once a real effort was required in the last two furlongs she was slightly disappointing. (7/1)

1136 Charlies Lad (IRE) had his chances again but failed to respond to pressure. (3/1)

Essandess (IRE) is not very big or robust but, after a poor start, she did show some ability. (14/1: op 8/1)

Walworth Wizard is short of any real pace. (100/1)

2037 Tangerine Flyer, a good-actioned sort, has plenty of pace but for some reason is not seeing it out at the moment. (7/4)

2539 ASA INTERNATIONAL (S) H'CAP (0-60) (3-Y.O+) (Class F)

2-45 (2-45) **2m** £2,472.00 (£692.00: £336.00) Stalls: High GOING minus 0.34 sec per fur (GF)

				SP	RR	SF
2154^{11}	**Sushi Bar (IRE) (36)** (MrsMReveley) **6-8-11** KDarley(5) (lw: trckd ldrs: nt clr run 3f out: swtchd appr fnl f: led ins fnl f: r.o)	—	**1**	7/2^{2}	46	—
2207^{13}	**Valiant Dash (21)** (JSGoldie) **11-7-7**(3) PFessey(4) (cl up: led after 6f to 5f out: led over 2f out tl ins fnl f: nt qckn)	1½	**2**	20/1	30	—
1996^{11}	**Ijab (CAN) (33)** (JParkes) **7-8-8** GBardwell(8) (b: chsd ldrs: sltly hmpd appr st & lost pl: hdwy over 2f out: styd on u.p)	1¾	**3**	7/1^{3}	40	—
2352^{5}	**Early Peace (IRE) (49)** (MDods) **5-9-10b^{1}** JWeaver(2) (bhd: hdwy over 2f out: chsng ldrs appr fnl f: no imp after)	½	**4**	20/1	55	—
2413^{4}	**Zamhareer (USA) (40)** (WStorey) **6-9-1** JFanning(1) (bhd: hdwy ½-wy: chsng ldrs 2f out: btn appr fnl f)	hd	**5**	7/2^{2}	46	—
2307*	**Selmeston (IRE) (42)** (SCWilliams) **5-9-3** JCarroll(6) (trckd ldrs: led 5f out tl over 2f out: wknd over 1f out)	3	**6**	7/4^{1}	45	—
	Flash of Realm (FR) (48) (PMonteith) **11-9-6**(3) OPears(7) (in tch tl outpcd fnl 3f)	13	**7**	66/1	38	—
2175^{10}	**Bobby's Dream (30)** (MHTompkins) **5-8-5** DBiggs(9) (lw: in tch: effrt ent st: wknd fnl 2½f)	2	**8**	20/1	18	—
1615^{7}	**Comic's Future (USA) (30)** (JJO'Neill) **4-8-5b** MFenton(3) (swtg: led 6f: wknd qckly 6f out: sn t.o)	dist	**9**	50/1	—	—

(SP 111.0%) **9 Rn**

3m 32.7 CSF £62.82 CT £405.38 TOTE £4.20: £1.60 £2.70 £1.90 (£51.70) Trio £75.10 OWNER Mr P. D. Savill (SALTBURN) BRED Scarteen Stud

LONG HANDICAP Valiant Dash 7-7

Bt in 6,000 gns

2000 Sushi Bar (IRE) looked magnificent and, had he got a run sooner, would have won far more easily. (7/2)

Valiant Dash ran his best race on the Flat for a long time. (20/1)

Ijab (CAN) is a moody sort, and getting messed about on the home turn did not help his cause. (7/1)

2352 Early Peace (IRE), tried in blinkers this time, gave the impression that he was not really putting his heart into it. (20/1)

2413 Zamhareer (USA) has lost his way this season and this was another moderate effort. (7/2)

2307* Selmeston (IRE) looked to be travelling well enough when in front turning for home but, when ridden, he proved disappointing. (7/4)

2540 LE GARCON D'OR H'CAP (0-60) (3-Y.O+) (Class F)

3-15 (3-19) **5f** £3,078.75 (£930.00: £452.50: £213.75) Stalls: High GOING minus 0.34 sec per fur (GF)

				SP	RR	SF
1816*	**Lillibella (50)** (MrsJRRamsden) **4-9-1**$^{(3)}$ OPears(2) (lw: mde most: r.o wl fnl f)	—	1	5/1^{1}	57	25
2382^{2}	**Pallium (IRE) (45)** (DANolan) **9-8-8b**$^{(5)}$ KSked(4) (a chsng ldrs: ev ch ins fnl f: r.o)	½	2	6/1^{2}	50	18
2177^{5}	**Southern Dominion (44)** (MissJFCraze) **5-8-12b** SWebster(1) (lw: w ldrs stands side: nt qckn appr fnl f)	2½	3	9/1	41	9
2384^{10}	**Six for Luck (46)** (DANolan) **5-9-0** VHalliday(3) (drvn along & a chsng ldrs: nt qckn appr fnl f)	nk	4	50/1	42	10
2197^{9}	**Maydoro (47)** (MDods) **4-9-1** DaleGibson(7) (outpcd & bhd tl styd on u.p fnl 2f)	nk	5	100/1	43	11
2197^{3}	**Sunset Harbour (IRE) (45)** (SEKettlewell) **4-8-8**$^{(5)}$ GParkin(17) (lw: prom far side: kpt on fnl 2f: nvr able to chal)	½	6	6/1^{2}	39	7
2167*	**Blazing Imp (USA) (51)** (MrsJJordan) **4-9-5** MFenton(16) (bhd: hdwy ½-wy: racd far side & nvr trbld ldrs)	nk	7	10/1	44	12
1861^{2}	**Sense of Priority (57)** (DNicholls) **8-9-11** AlexGreaves(8) (bhd: nt clr run 2f out: nvr nr to chal)	1¼	8	16/1	46	14
1687^{3}	**Young Ben (IRE) (36)** (JSWainwright) **5-8-4b** RLappin(13) (b: chsd ldrs tl hung lft & wknd fr ½-wy)	½	9	25/1	23	—
1671^{6}	**Rennyholme (46)** (ABMulholland) **6-9-0** NKennedy(9) (sme hdwy u.p ½-wy: no imp)	nk	10	16/1	32	—
1667^{2}	**Bashful Brave (52)** (BPJBaugh) **6-9-1v**$^{1(5)}$ PRoberts(11) (lw: sn outpcd)	4	11	16/1	26	—
1602^{7}	**Ready Teddy (IRE) (40)** (MissLAPerratt) **4-8-8** JWeaver(10) (spd to ½-wy)	s.h	12	10/1	13	—
	Mystique Smile (39) (JSGoldie) **4-8-4**$^{(3)}$ PFessey(6) (swtg: chsd ldrs to ½-wy)	nk	13	20/1	11	—
2354^{U}	**Toronto (54)** (JBerry) **3-9-3b** KDarley(14) (chsd ldrs far side 3f: wknd qckly)	1½	14	14/1	22	—
1604^{8}	**Lord Cornelious (29)** (DANolan) **4-7-4**$^{(7)ow1}$ NPollard(12) (s.i.s: a bhd)	½	15	200/1	—	—
2480^{9}	**Good To Talk (43)** (TDEasterby) **4-8-11b** JCarroll(5) (spd 3f: wknd qckly)	3	16	12/1	—	—
2061^{6}	**Kalar (48)** (DWChapman) **8-9-2b** ACulhane(15) (led far side tl wknd fr ½-wy & eased)	4	17	8/1^{3}	—	—
				(SP 128.6%)	**17 Rn**	

60.5 secs (2.80) CSF £31.02 CT £202.31 TOTE £7.30: £1.50 £1.80 £4.00 £5.00 (£29.00) Trio £32.50 OWNER Mrs Peter Hastings (THIRSK) BRED Mrs P. Hastings

LONG HANDICAP Lord Cornelious 7-2

WEIGHT FOR AGE 3yo-5lb

1816* Lillibella had the draw and, although dropping back in trip, had the speed and always had the edge. (5/1)

2382 Pallium (IRE), well drawn, did his best but was never quite good enough. (6/1)

2177 Southern Dominion made full use of his good draw but his limitations were well exposed in the last furlong and a half. (9/1)

Six for Luck kept responding to pressure but was never good enough to seriously get into it. (50/1)

Maydoro was completely taken off her legs until picking up ground in the closing stages and looked likely to need further. (100/1)

2197 Sunset Harbour (IRE) came out best of those drawn high and this was not a bad effort. (6/1)

2167* Blazing Imp (USA) ran well from a bad draw to show his win here a couple of weeks ago was no fluke. (10/1)

1861 Sense of Priority showed enough to suggest that he remains in good heart. (16/1)

1311 Ready Teddy (IRE) (10/1: 8/1-12/1)

2167 Good To Talk (12/1: 10/1-16/1)

2541 ASA INTERNATIONAL H'CAP (0-65) (3-Y.O+ F & M) (Class F)

3-45 (3-45) **1m 4f 31y** £2,818.75 (£850.00: £412.50: £193.75) Stalls: High GOING minus 0.34 sec per fur (GF)

				SP	RR	SF
2365^{4}	**Kilnamartyra Girl (38)** (JParkes) **7-8-12** GBardwell(2) (trckd ldrs: effrt over 2f out: hrd rdn fnl f: led nr fin)	—	1	2/1^{1}	48	30
1390^{16}	**Portite Sophie (38)** (MBrittain) **6-8-12** KDarley(5) (led: qcknd 3f out: r.o wl: jst ct)	nk	2	8/1	48	30
2065^{8}	**Get A Life (50)** (JO'Reilly) **4-9-10** JCarroll(4) (trckd ldr: effrt 3f out: one pce appr fnl f)	4	3	13/2	54	36
2386^{3}	**Philgem (31)** (CWFairhurst) **4-8-5b**^{1} NKennedy(3) (lw: trckd ldrs: effrt 3f out: rdn & no imp)	6	4	3/1^{2}	27	9
2221*	**Ragtime Cowgirl (39)** (DANolan) **4-8-8**$^{(5)}$ KSked(1) (hld up: effrt ent st: no imp)	1¾	5	13/2	33	15
1996^{10}	**Dunrowan (45)** (MrsMReveley) **4-9-5** ACulhane(6) (lw: hld up: effrt 4f out: btn & eased over 2f out)	dist	6	4/1^{3}	—	—
				(SP 116.1%)	**6 Rn**	

2m 39.6 (6.10) CSF £17.56 TOTE £2.20: £1.20 £2.90 (£7.30) OWNER Mr P. J. Cronin (MALTON) BRED F. R. Colley

2365 Kilnamartyra Girl is not the easiest of rides but, given some strong assistance here, she ran on to snatch it. (2/1)

1229 Portite Sophie, given an intelligent ride, looked to have pinched it but just failed to last home. (8/1: op 5/1)

558 Get A Life ran her best race to date and just needs a bit of help from the handicapper. (13/2)

2386 Philgem, in blinkers for the first time, failed to have any effect when the pressure was applied. (3/1)

2221* Ragtime Cowgirl, who does stay quite well, has been running over much shorter distances recently and not surprisingly ran very freely here and failed to make an impression. (13/2)

Dunrowan ran as though she has a problem. (4/1)

2542 EAST LOTHIAN COUNCIL CLAIMING STKS (3-Y.O+) (Class F)

4-15 (4-15) **7f 30y** £2,867.50 (£865.00: £420.00: £197.50) Stalls: High GOING minus 0.34 sec per fur (GF)

				SP	RR	SF
2355^{3}	**Broctune Gold (65)** (MrsMReveley) **6-9-10** ACulhane(4) (lw: mde all: drvn out)	—	1	1/2^{1}	68	27
1857^{3}	**Double Oscar (IRE) (48)** (DNicholls) **4-9-3b** AlexGreaves(6) (hld up: smooth hdwy & ev ch over 1f out: rdn & nt qckn)	2½	2	7/2^{2}	55	14
2239^{6}	**Move Smartly (IRE) (44)** (MrsLStubbs) **7-8-10v**$^{(5)}$ PRoberts(1) (rr div: hdwy u.p 2f out: nvr able to chal)	hd	3	16/1	53	12
2234^{3}	**Fisiostar (37)** (MDods) **4-9-1b** JCarroll(2) (chsd ldrs: rdn ½-wy: one pce)	8	4	20/1	35	—
721^{20}	**Knave (42)** (PMonteith) **4-8-4**$^{(7)}$ RWinston(5) (rr div: effrt ent st: n.d)	1¾	5	66/1	27	—
2317^{11}	**Lady Silk (33)** (MissJFCraze) **6-8-12** SWebster(3) (nvr wnt pce)	1	6	25/1	26	—
1238^{14}	**Mirror Four Life (IRE) (73)** (MHTompkins) **3-8-8** DBiggs(7) (chsd wnr: sltly hmpd appr st: wknd fnl 2½f)	10	7	8/1^{3}	8	—
				(SP 116.0%)	**7 Rn**	

1m 30.6 (4.60) CSF £2.34 TOTE £1.70: £1.10 £2.10 (£1.60) OWNER Mrs M. B. Thwaites (SALTBURN) BRED A. J. Poulton (Epping) Ltd

WEIGHT FOR AGE 3yo-8lb

2355 Broctune Gold was never allowed things all his own way here but he was nevertheless always just doing enough. (1/2)

1857 Double Oscar (IRE) looked to be going best when improving halfway up the straight but, when an effort was required in the final furlong, he failed to pick up. (7/2)

2239 Move Smartly (IRE) always had to work hard to improve and was never finding enough late on. (16/1)

2234 Fisiostar came under pressure at halfway and was then never doing anything like enough. (20/1)
496 Knave has yet to show anything positive this year. (66/1)
Mirror Four Life (IRE) showed good speed to take the winner on but got chopped off on the home turn and was soon fighting a lost cause. (8/1)

2543 MILL HILL H'CAP (0-65) (3-Y.O+) (Class F)
4-45 (4-46) **1m 16y** £3,030.00 (£915.00: £445.00: £210.00) Stalls: High GOING minus 0.34 sec per fur (GF)

				SP	RR	SF
2495*	**Dee Pee Tee Cee (IRE) (67)** (MWEasterby) **3-9-13** 5x TLucas(5) (lw: mde all: edgd rt 2f out: r.o wl fnl f: eased cl home)	—	**1**	6/4[1]	80+	52
2237[10]	**Kass Alhawa (57)** (DWChapman) **4-9-12** ACulhane(2) (trckd ldrs: hdwy & ev ch 1f out: r.o: nt pce of wnr)	½	**2**	7/1	69	50
2029*	**Naivasha (56)** (JBerry) **3-8-11**(5) TEDurcan(4) (chsd wnr: effrt 3f out: one pce appr fnl f)	3½	**3**	14/1	61	33
2502[10]	**Mystic Times (31)** (BMactaggart) **4-7-9**(5)ow1 KSked(7) (lw: rr div: effrt ent st: styd on: nt pce to chal)	1¼	**4**	40/1	34	14
2317[2]	**The Barnsley Belle (IRE) (43)** (JLEyre) **4-8-12** MGallagher(6) (lw: chsd ldrs: rdn 3f out: one pce)	1¾	**5**	11/2[2]	42	23
2129[8]	**Reinhardt (IRE) (47)** (DNicholls) **4-9-2** AlexGreaves(11) (hld up & bhd: hdwy over 2f out: nvr plcd to chal)	hd	**6**	13/2[3]	46	27
2169[2]	**Barresbo (60)** (CWFairhurst) **3-8-13**(7) TSiddall(3) (bhd: effrt 3f out: nvr rchd ldrs)	1	**7**	8/1	57	29
2384[U]	**Suedoro (45)** (JSGoldie) **7-8-11**(3) PFessey(10) (bhd: hdwy 3f out: no imp)	½	**8**	20/1	41	22
2385[6]	**Termon (35)** (MissLAPerratt) **4-8-4** NKennedy(8) (lw: bhd: effrt ½-wy: n.d)	1½	**9**	13/2[3]	28	9
2174[14]	**King Chestnut (30)** (MDods) **6-7-13** DaleGibson(1) (chsd ldrs tl wknd over 2f out)	½	**10**	11/1	22	3
2226[8]	**Chanson d'Amour (IRE) (36)** (MissLAPerratt) **3-7-3**(7) JMcAuley(12) (in tch tl wknd fnl 3f)	nk	**11**	100/1	27	—

(SP 128.9%) **11 Rn**

1m 42.0 (3.00) CSF £12.84 CT £111.50 TOTE £2.40: £1.10 £7.00 £2.30 (£21.20) Trio £25.40 OWNER Early Morning Breakfast Syndicate (SHERIFF HUTTON) BRED Michael and Heather Scott
WEIGHT FOR AGE 3yo-9lb
2495* Dee Pee Tee Cee (IRE) is thriving on her racing and, flying out of the stalls, always had the edge and won a shade cheekily. (6/4)
2237 Kass Alhawa, as usual, travelled well, but when it came down to a struggle was always second best. (7/1)
2029* Naivasha ran quite well and kept trying hard but was never good enough in the last couple of furlongs. (14/1: op 8/1)
Mystic Times ran her best race of the season and looks to be coming to hand, and is certainly well-enough handicapped. (40/1)
2317 The Barnsley Belle (IRE) keeps running quite well but has yet to win on turf. (11/2: 3/1-6/1)
1830 Reinhardt (IRE), a winner over the minimum trip, was dropped out and ran well enough to suggest that there is better to come. (13/2)
2384 Suedoro looks well and is one to watch when put back to sprinting. (20/1)

T/Plpt: £125.70 (107.06 Tckts). T/Qdpt: £8.20 (135.19 Tckts) AA

2059-RIPON (R-H) (Good)
Monday July 7th
WEATHER: fine & sunny WIND: almost nil

2544 FISHERGATE (S) STKS (3-Y.O+) (Class F)
7-00 (7-01) **1m 2f** £2,730.50 (£768.00: £375.50) Stalls: High GOING minus 0.40 sec per fur (F)

				SP	RR	SF
2225[4]	**Sun Mark (IRE) (62)** (MrsASwinbank) **6-9-12** SSanders(10) (mde virtually all: hld on wl towards fin)	—	**1**	9/2[3]	61	41
2200*	**Guesstimation (USA) (57)** (JPearce) **8-9-9**(3) CTeague(9) (hdwy over 3f out: ev ch ins fnl f: nt qckn nr fin)	hd	**2**	3/1[1]	61	41
2200[4]	**Bernard Seven (IRE) (30)** (MDods) **5-9-7b** FLynch(6) (trckd ldrs: effrt over 2f out: kpt on one pce)	4	**3**	10/1	49	29
2428[5]	**Spanish Stripper (USA) (25)** (MCChapman) **6-9-0**(7) VictoriaAppleby(13) (swtg: hld up & plld hrd: hdwy over 2f out: styd on fnl f)	hd	**4**	14/1	49	29
2128[2]	**My Millie (50)** (DWBarker) **4-9-2** TWilliams(12) (trckd ldrs: chal on ins whn n.m.r 2f out: sn rdn: one pce)	¾	**5**	7/2[2]	43	23
2130[10]	**Tribal Mischief (55)** (DMoffatt) **3-8-5** JQuinn(18) (trckd ldrs: effrt on ins over 2f out: one pce)	2½	**6**	12/1	39	8
2128[5]	**Major Mouse (43)** (WWHaigh) **9-9-7** RLappin(7) (sn trckng ldrs: effrt over 2f out: no imp)	nk	**7**	14/1	44	24
595[14]	**Irish Oasis (IRE) (37)** (BSRothwell) **4-9-7** MFenton(1) (hdwy on outside whn hmpd over 4f out: sn chsng ldrs: wknd over 2f out)	1¼	**8**	25/1	42	22
2039*	**Diamond Crown (IRE) (46)** (MartynWane) **6-9-12** WJO'Connor(14) (trckd ldrs: effrt & hung lft over 2f out: wkng whn n.m.r over 1f out)	1¾	**9**	6/1	44	24
	Dunston Bill (GBarnett) **3-8-10** DeanMcKeown(2) (unf: bit bkwd: unruly in stalls: dwlt: a bhd)	3	**10**	25/1	34	3
1998[11]	**Juicy Ting (57)** (PCHaslam) **3-8-3**(7) PGoode(5) (jnd wnr over 6f out: edgd lft & lost pl over 2f out)	nk	**11**	11/1	34	3
1247[9]	**Dispol Prince (20)** (GROldroyd) **4-9-0**(7) RFarmer(17) (bhd whn stumbled over 5f out: sn t.o)	28	**12**	50/1	—	—
	Qualitair Beauty (MissLCSiddall) **4-8-13**(3) OPears(3) (bhd: t.o 4f out)	1	**13**	33/1	—	—
	Lena's Pride (GBarnett) **4-9-2** LCharnock(4) (s.i.s: a bhd: t.o 4f out)	5	**14**	33/1	—	—
1998[8]	**Hatimena** (JGFitzGerald) **3-8-5** JFanning(11) (swtg: plld hrd: trckd ldrs tl rn wd & lost pl ent st: sn bhd: t.o)	3½	**15**	10/1	—	—

(SP 142.8%) **15 Rn**

2m 8.0 (4.50) CSF £19.19 TOTE £4.30: £1.90 £1.90 £4.10 (£9.00) Trio £47.00 OWNER Scotnorth Racing Ltd (RICHMOND) BRED Matt Carr
WEIGHT FOR AGE 3yo-11lb
No bid
1674 Sun Mark (IRE) was allowed to dictate his own pace and he found just enough to hang on. (9/2: op 5/2)
2200* Guesstimation (USA) came there to have every chance inside the last but he could not find quite enough to overhaul the winner. He would have preferred a stronger gallop from the outset. (3/1)
2200 Bernard Seven (IRE) would have been meeting the winner on 27lb better terms in a handicap. He has not won for a long time and did not look that enthusiastic in his work. (10/1)
2428 Spanish Stripper (USA), who has only won once in fifty-four outings, made no appeal beforehand. Ridden to get the trip, he did surprisingly well, considering he would have been receiving 32lb from the winner in a handicap. (14/1)
2128 My Millie, who looked very fit indeed, tried for a run up the inside of the winner two furlongs out but there was never a lot of room although, when the gap did come, she did not find an awful lot. (7/2)
Tribal Mischief, whose two previous victories have been recorded over five furlongs, seemed to stay the trip. (12/1)
1998 Juicy Ting (11/1: 8/1-12/1)

2545 SKELLGATE MAIDEN AUCTION STKS (2-Y.O F) (Class F)

7-25 (7-27) **5f** £2,825.70 (£795.20: £389.10) Stalls: High GOING minus 0.40 sec per fur (F)

				SP	RR	SF
2066^{2}	**Happy Days Again (IRE)** (JWharton) **2-8-6** JCarroll(4) (mde all: jst hld on)	—	**1**	4/1^{1}	77	30
	Prime Hand (WJHaggas) **2-8-8** FLynch(3) (w'like: hdwy ½-wy: styd on wl ins fnl f: jst failed)	hd	**2**	5/1^{2}	79+	32
1821^{3}	**Zizi (IRE)** (KRBurke) **2-8-3** JQuinn(5) (lw: chsd ldrs: nt qckn appr fnl f)	2	**3**	5/1^{2}	67	20
	Lets Be Fair (JHanson) **2-8-8** EJohnson(18) (w'like: bit bkwd: w ldrs on outside tl grad wknd fnl f: improve)	4	**4**	33/1	60+	13
	Rare Indigo (JBerry) **2-8-5** KDarley(7) (cmpt: w ldrs: rdn & hung rt over 1f out: sn wknd)	¾	**5**	7/1	54	7
2140^{5}	**Rhinefield Beauty (IRE)** (JSGoldie) **2-8-1** TWilliams(6) (mid div: kpt on fnl 2f: nvr nr to chal)	¾	**6**	25/1	48	1
1253^{5}	**Leather And Scrim (IRE)** (DNicholls) **2-7-10**(5) IonaWands(1) (chsd ldrs tl grad wknd fnl 2f)	1¾	**7**	25/1	42	—
2042^{3}	**Mariana** (RMWhitaker) **2-8-4** DeanMcKeown(11) (chsd ldrs: drvn along ½-wy: no imp)	½	**8**	11/2^{3}	44	—
1760^{3}	**Starliner (IRE)** (MBrittain) **2-8-8** GBardwell(16) (a in tch: drvn along ½-wy: sn outpcd)	nk	**9**	10/1	47	—
2037^{3}	**Italian Rose** (WJMusson) **2-7-11**(3) MBaird(13) (b.nr hind: w ldrs: rdn 2f out: sn wknd)	s.h	**10**	4/1^{1}	38	—
1137^{7}	**Maedaley** (PCHaslam) **2-8-2** LCharnock(2) (outpcd fr ½-wy)	¾	**11**	25/1	38	—
	Premium Princess (JJQuinn) **2-8-1** DRMcCabe(14) (lengthy: s.s: bhd tl sme late hdwy)	hd	**12**	9/1	37	—
	Miss Eliminator (MWEasterby) **2-8-2** JTate(15) (lengthy: unf: bit bkwd: s.i.s: a bhd)	1½	**13**	20/1	33	—
1569^{11}	**Blitz** (MWEasterby) **2-8-0**(5)ow4 DSweeney(10) (outpcd fr ½-wy)	3½	**14**	20/1	25	—
2412^{12}	**Shirleys Girl (IRE)** (WStorey) **2-8-3** JFanning(17) (sn outpcd)	s.h	**15**	50/1	23	—
2147^{2}	**Sweet Rosie (IRE)** (RBoss) **2-8-2** SSanders(8) (chsd ldrs tl wknd over 2f out)	s.h	**16**	12/1	21	—
	Woodlands Pride (IRE) (MCChapman) **2-7-13**(3) DarrenMoffatt(9) (leggy: unf: a outpcd & bhd)	1¼	**17**	50/1	17	—
2051^{2}	**Gifted Bairn (IRE)** (DNicholls) **2-8-7**ow1 WJO'Connor(12) (reard s: a bhd)	2½	**18**	14/1	14	—

(SP 162.6%) **18 Rn**

59.3 secs (1.50) CSF £26.59 TOTE £5.90: £1.70 £2.50 £2.70 (£21.40) Trio £68.90 OWNER Mrs S. M. Moore (MELTON MOWBRAY) BRED William Flood

2066 Happy Days Again (IRE) had experience which enabled her to hang on by the skin of her teeth. (4/1)

Prime Hand, a likeable filly, took time to get going. Putting in some solid work inside the last, she needed two more strides. She will be suited by six furlongs and is sure to go one better. (5/1)

1821 Zizi (IRE), who looked really well beforehand, is better suited by six. (5/1)

Lets Be Fair, drawn eighteen of eighteen, looked in need of the outing and showed definite signs of inexperience going down. She showed bags of toe on the wide outside and was by no means knocked about. (33/1)

Rare Indigo, who showed a scratchy action going down, hung right as she tired after showing good speed. (7/1)

2140 Rhinefield Beauty (IRE) is now qualified for a nursery mark. (25/1)

1253 Leather And Scrim (IRE), absent for fifty-one days and having her third run, showed plenty of toe and was by no means knocked about. (25/1)

2042 Mariana failed to improve on her first effort. (11/2)

1760 Starliner (IRE) (10/1: 8/1-12/1)

2037 Italian Rose ran disappointingly. (4/1)

Premium Princess, who looked backward, showed some ability after a slow break. (9/1)

2546 LISHMAN SIDWELL CAMPBELL & PRICE H'CAP (0-70) (3-Y.O+) (Class E)

7-55 (7-58) **1m** £3,077.25 (£933.00: £456.50: £218.25) Stalls: High GOING minus 0.40 sec per fur (F)

				SP	RR	SF
2021^{4}	**Dispol Gem (64)** (PCalver) **4-9-10** KDarley(17) (chsd ldrs: led 1f out: hld on wl)	—	**1**	9/1^{3}	74	62
2418^{5}	**Nkapen Rocks (SPA) (51)** (CaptJWilson) **4-8-11** JWeaver(1) (trckd ldrs: ev ch 1f out: nt qckn)	¾	**2**	14/1	60	48
	Fancy A Fortune (IRE) (60) (DNicholls) **3-8-11** AlexGreaves(20) (lw: led to 1f out: kpt on)	¾	**3**	14/1	67	46
2290^{8}	**Impulsive Air (IRE) (62)** (EWeymes) **5-9-8** JQuinn(19) (chsd ldrs: effrt over 2f out: kpt on same pce appr fnl f)	¾	**4**	7/1^{1}	68	56
2385^{4}	**Nobby Barnes (40)** (DonEnricoIncisa) **8-8-0** KimTinkler(14) (bhd: hdwy on ins over 2f out: nt clr run: styd on fnl f)	1	**5**	14/1	44	32
1495^{10}	**Flag Fen (USA) (56)** (JParkes) **6-9-2** WJO'Connor(16) (a chsng ldrs: one pce fnl 2f)	¾	**6**	12/1	58	46
2029^{4}	**Jedi Knight (68)** (MWEasterby) **3-9-0**(5) GParkin(8) (trckd ldrs: nt qckn fnl 2f)	½	**7**	7/1^{1}	69	48
2205^{12}	**Spanish Verdict (51)** (DenysSmith) **10-8-8**(3) CTeague(10) (in tch: hmpd & lost pl over 5f out: hdwy over 3f out: nvr nr to chal)	1¼	**8**	11/1	50	38
2313^{9}	**Forest Robin (60)** (MrsJRRamsden) **4-8-13**(7) ClaireWest(9) (prom: drvn along 2f out: sn outpcd)	s.h	**9**	14/1	58	46
2282^{2}	**Morocco (IRE) (60)** (MRChannon) **8-8-13**(7) AEddery(6) (hld up: hdwy & nt clr run over 2f out: kpt on fnl f)	1½	**10**	7/1^{1}	55	43
2201^{9}	**Royal South (IRE) (60)** (PSFelgate) **4-9-6** JTate(7) (hdwy over 5f out: sn chsng ldrs: wknd 2f out)	¾	**11**	20/1	54	42
2239^{4}	**Beano Script (60)** (JHanson) **4-9-6** EJohnson(2) (hld up & bhd: stdy hdwy on outside 2f out: nvr plcd to chal)	¾	**12**	16/1	52	40
2036^{11}	**Scenicris (IRE) (56)** (RHollinshead) **4-8-13**(3) DGriffiths(15) (hld up: effrt over 3f out: no imp: eased fnl f)	7	**13**	20/1	34	22
2340^{9}	**Up in Flames (IRE) (52)** (SRBowring) **6-8-12** JCarroll(13) (trckd ldrs: plld hrd: lost pl 3f out: eased)	2½	**14**	16/1	25	13
2505^{4}	**Cairn Dhu (58)** (DWBarker) **3-8-6**(3) DarrenMoffatt(4) (s.i.s: a bhd)	nk	**15**	25/1	31	10
2238*	**Captain Carparts (59)** (JLEyre) **3-8-10** TWilliams(18) (w ldrs: rdn over 3f out: wknd over 2f out)	½	**16**	15/2^{2}	31	10
2313^{22}	**Chief Connections (44)** (MPBielby) **4-8-4** SSanders(12) (unruly s: a bhd)	nk	**17**	100/1	15	3
2130^{5}	**Pet Express (60)** (PCHaslam) **3-8-11** LCharnock(3) (hld up: a in rr)	2½	**18**	20/1	26	5
	Darling Clover (68) (RBastiman) **5-9-9**(5) HBastiman(11) (b.hind: a bhd)	½	**19**	20/1	33	21
2313^{14}	**Forest Signal (62)** (MBrittain) **3-8-6**(7) DMernagh(5) (drvn along & outpcd 4f out: sn bhd)	8	**20**	25/1	11	—

(SP 141.5%) **20 Rn**

1m 39.5 (1.30) CSF £121.90 CT £1,689.31 TOTE £9.70: £2.10 £3.20 £7.40 £2.70 (£111.20) Trio £412.10 OWNER Mr W. B. Imison (RIPON) BRED R. S. A. Urquhart

WEIGHT FOR AGE 3yo-9lb

2021 Dispol Gem, well drawn and suited by the strong gallop, did just enough and held on in willing fashion. (9/1)

2418 Nkapen Rocks (SPA), taken to post early, became on edge down at the start. Worst drawn, he ran really well and it is hard to see how he is still a maiden after nineteen attempts. (14/1)

Fancy A Fortune (IRE), gelded and having his first run for David Nicholls, looked outstandingly well beforehand. Racing freely, he set the pace and kept going when headed. He has slipped right down the weights and will be interesting next time. (14/1)

1775 Impulsive Air (IRE), well supported in the market and well drawn, ran one of his better races. (7/1)

2385 Nobby Barnes has a losing run stretching back fifty-four races here but, when everything goes his way, there is no doubt that he is capable of adding to his record from this sort of mark. (14/1)
1266* Flag Fen (USA), who tends to hang right, was kept right against the running rail. (12/1)
2029 Jedi Knight was 13lb higher in the weights than when he won at Doncaster four outings ago. (7/1)
2152 Forest Robin (14/1: 10/1-16/1)
2282 Morocco (IRE), held up to get the trip, met trouble in running. (7/1)
2238* Captain Carparts (15/2: 5/1-8/1)

2547 TAYLOR WOODROW H'CAP (0-80) (3-Y.O) (Class D)

8-25 (8-26) **6f** £4,380.00 (£1,320.00: £640.00: £300.00) Stalls: High GOING minus 0.40 sec per fur (F)

				SP	RR	SF
2377^{4}	**Cauda Equina (75)** (MRChannon) **3-9-4** ACulhane(7) (hdwy over 3f out: effrt on ins over 2f out: led jst ins fnl f: hrd rdn & r.o)	—	**1**	7/1	82	35
1980^{8}	**Style Dancer (IRE) (72)** (RMWhitaker) **3-9-1v^{1}** DeanMcKeown(11) (led tl ins fnl f: kpt on same pce)	¾	**2**	8/1	77	30
2192^{2}	**Bayford Thrust (76)** (JBerry) **3-9-2**(3) PFessey(2) (b: b.hind: swtg: chsd ldrs: ev ch over 1f out: r.o same pce)	1	**3**	$7/2^{1}$	78	31
2044^{5}	**Barnburgh Boy (73)** (TDBarron) **3-9-2** SSanders(1) (s.s: hdwy over 2f out: kpt on fnl f)	2½	**4**	$11/2^{3}$	69	22
1781^{3}	**Rosy Outlook (USA) (78)** (IABalding) **3-9-7** KDarley(5) (chsd ldrs: rdn & hung rt 2f out: sn wknd)	3	**5**	$4/1^{2}$	66	19
2417^{2}	**William's Well (60)** (MWEasterby) **3-8-3b** DaleGibson(4) (lw: chsd ldrs: rdn over 1f out: sn outpcd)	nk	**6**	$4/1^{2}$	47	—
2203^{4}	**Fine Times (53)** (CWFairhurst) **3-7-10v** LCharnock(6) (b.off hind: in tch: rdn & edgd lft ½-wy: sn wknd)	3½	**7**	11/1	31	—
2298^{5}	**Nor-Do-I (73)** (JMPEustace) **3-9-2b** JTate(10) (w ldrs tl over 2f out: nt run on)	nk	**8**	14/1	50	3
	Tom Mi Dah (63) (MDHammond) **3-8-6** JCarroll(8) (s.i.s: a bhd)	hd	**9**	25/1	40	—
1250^{17}	**Loch-Hurn Lady (59)** (KWHogg) **3-8-2** JQuinn(3) (sn outpcd & bhd)	¾	**10**	20/1	34	—
2044^{10}	**Denton Lad (66)** (JWWatts) **3-8-9** NConnorton(9) (lw: stumbled s: sn w ldrs: edgd rt & lost pl over 2f out)	1½	**11**	16/1	37	—
				(SP 130.7%)	**11 Rn**	

1m 12.8 (2.30) CSF £63.07 CT £221.80 TOTE £8.30: £2.70 £2.50 £1.50 (£64.90) Trio £34.20 OWNER Mr Michael Foy (UPPER LAMBOURN) BRED R. P. Williams
IN-FOCUS: **Due to the heavy rain the previous week which left a soft patch on the stands' side between the five and six furlong markers, the stalls were placed on the far side.**
2377 Cauda Equina, ridden to get the trip, stuck on under strong pressure and held on grimly near the line. (7/1)
1980 Style Dancer (IRE), from stall eleven, had the best of the draw. With the visor back on, made the running and, keeping on under strong pressure, was just held at bay. (8/1)
2192 Bayford Thrust, a speedy type, was awash with sweat beforehand but it did not stop him coming in for heavy market support. As it turned out, he was poorly drawn but probably ran up to the best he is capable of now. (7/2: op 7/1)
2044 Barnburgh Boy again gave away more ground at the start than what he was eventually beaten by. (11/2)
1781 Rosy Outlook (USA) gave her rider problems, persisting in hanging right and ending up on the far rail. (4/1)
2417 William's Well, 2lb higher in the weights, is possibly better over the minimum trip. (4/1: 3/1-9/2)

2548 BONDGATE H'CAP (0-80) (3-Y.O) (Class D)

8-55 (8-56) **1m 4f 60y** £4,146.00 (£1,248.00: £604.00: £282.00) Stalls: Low GOING minus 0.40 sec per fur (F)

				SP	RR	SF
2182*	**Real Estate (75)** (CFWall) **3-9-5** SSanders(4) (lw: trckd ldrs: led on bit over 2f out: pushed clr 1f out: eased towards fin)	—	**1**	$4/6^{1}$	83	39
1832^{5}	**Swiftway (61)** (KWHogg) **3-8-5** DeanMcKeown(5) (led tl over 2f out: kpt on: no ch w wnr)	4	**2**	12/1	64	20
2046^{12}	**Hoh Explorer (IRE) (64)** (DWBarker) **3-8-8** TWilliams(1) (wnt prom 9f out: pushed along ½-wy: hrd rdn over 3f out: wandered: styd on one pce)	3	**3**	$9/1^{3}$	63	19
2058^{13}	**Maradi (IRE) (77)** (MBell) **3-9-7** MFenton(3) (hld up: hdwy over 3f out: effrt over 2f out: styd on one pce: eased nr fin)	hd	**4**	$9/4^{2}$	76	32
2130^{9}	**Noirie (52)** (MBrittain) **3-7-10** GBardwell(6) (trckd ldrs: drvn along & lost pl 6f out: kpt on fnl 2f)	nk	**5**	16/1	50?	6
				(SP 114.3%)	**5 Rn**	

2m 38.4 (4.90) CSF £9.62 TOTE £1.60: £1.20 £2.60 (£5.90) OWNER Mr N. Ahamad (NEWMARKET) BRED Bishop's Down Farm
LONG HANDICAP Noirie 7-6
2182* Real Estate, who looked outstanding in the paddock, took this with the minimum of fuss and will win better events than this. (4/6)
1832 Swiftway, allowed to set his own pace, was swept aside by the winner. (12/1)
Hoh Explorer (IRE), who looked to have plenty on at the weights for this first outing in handicap company, looks a funny individual. (9/1)
1595 Maradi (IRE) would have held on for third place but for being eased near the line. (9/4: op 6/4)
463 Noirie, who has been campaigned over a variety of distances this year, was 4lb out of the handicap. Dropping right out on the home turn, he was keeping on at the finish under strong driving. He might be worth a try over a mile and a half. (16/1)

2549 KIRKGATE MAIDEN STKS (3-Y.O+) (Class D)

9-25 (9-28) **1m** £3,436.25 (£1,040.00: £507.50: £241.25) Stalls: Low GOING minus 0.40 sec per fur (F)

				SP	RR	SF
1976^{2}	**Shawm (88)** (DRLoder) **3-8-12** KDarley(4) (lw: trckd ldr: lft in ld 5f out: sn clr: easily)	—	**1**	$8/15^{1}$	61+	4
204^{6}	**Weet A Bit (IRE) (40)** (RHollinshead) **3-8-9**(3) DGriffiths(3) (trckd ldrs: kpt on u.p fnl 2f: no ch w wnr)	3½	**2**	25/1	54	—
	Serious Account (USA) (JLEyre) **4-9-7** MGallagher(6) (trckd ldrs: effrt over 2f out: styd on same pce)	s.h	**3**	$12/1^{3}$	54	6
2156^{6}	**Hanajir (IRE)** (CWThornton) **3-8-7** DeanMcKeown(2) (hld up: hdwy over 2f out: shkn up & kpt on: nvr nr to chal)	¾	**4**	25/1	47	—
	Domino Style (MJCamacho) **3-8-7** LCharnock(8) (bit bkwd: trckd ldrs: wnt 2nd over 4f out: one pce fnl 2f)	1	**5**	25/1	45	—
2330^{6}	**Bold Appeal (IRE)** (WStorey) **5-9-7** JFanning(9) (stdd s: hld up: hmpd over 4f out: kpt on fnl 2f: nvr nr ldrs)	1½	**6**	66/1	47	—
2156^{7}	**Golden Glory** (MBrittain) **4-9-0**(7) DMernagh(5) (s.i.s: hdwy over 4f out: one pce)	2	**7**	66/1	43	—
2315^{12}	**Es Go** (RBastiman) **4-9-2**(5) HBastiman(1) (hld up: hmpd over 4f out: kpt on fnl 2f: n.d)	½	**8**	66/1	42	—
2173^{3}	**Windy Treat (USA)** (EALDunlop) **3-8-12** JWeaver(7) (rel to go to s: unruly s: led: rel to r & hdd 5f out: nt keen: virtually p.u)	dist	**9**	$9/4^{2}$	—	—
				(SP 119.7%)	**9 Rn**	

1m 44.3 (6.10) CSF £22.71 TOTE £1.80: £1.10 £2.70 £1.70 (£13.70) Trio £32.30 OWNER Sheikh Mohammed (NEWMARKET) BRED Sheikh Mohammed Bin Rashid Al Maktoum

WEIGHT FOR AGE 3yo-9lb
OFFICIAL EXPLANATION **Windy Treat (USA): the jockey reported that the gelding tried to pull up on the turn into the straight and refused to race thereafter.**
1976 Shawm had his tongue tied down on this occasion. With his only serious rival downing tools, he was never out of second gear to account for this lot. (8/15)
Weet A Bit (IRE) seemed to appreciate the step up in distance. (25/1)
Serious Account (USA), who had just one outing at three for Henry Cecil, lacks scope and is a keen going type. (12/1: 6/1-14/1)
Hanajir (IRE), having only her second outing, wore a tongue-strap. Showing plenty of knee action going down, she does possess some ability. (25/1)
Domino Style, having her third outing, looked burly. She was by no means disgraced and has improvement in her. (25/1)
2173 Windy Treat (USA), who showed plenty of ability after a slow start first time, showed his true colours here. Reluctant to go down to the start, he then gave problems being loaded. Jumping off in front, when he turned in at the five-furlong marker he put the brakes on and wanted no part at all with the game. (9/4)

T/Plpt: £43.00 (458.78 Tckts). T/Qdpt: £13.10 (67.75 Tckts) WG

2369-WINDSOR (Fig. 8) (Good)
Monday July 7th
WEATHER: humid WIND: almost nil

2550 CARE IN THE COMMUNITY H'CAP (0-70) (3-Y.O+) (Class E)
6-40 (6-41) **1m 2f 7y** £3,062.50 (£925.00: £450.00: £212.50) Stalls: High GOING minus 0.15 sec per fur (GF)

				SP	RR	SF
2373^{6}	**Haroldon (IRE) (65)** (BPalling) **8-9-9** DaneO'Neill(11) (b: swtg: gd hdwy on ins 2f out: led ins fnl f: r.o wl)	—	**1**	20/1	74	54
2150^{5}	**Your Most Welcome (56)** (DJSffrenchDavis) **6-9-0** GCarter(10) (a.p: ev ch fnl 2f: r.o)	½	**2**	7/1	64	44
1811*	**Princess Danielle (65)** (WRMuir) **5-9-6**(3) MartinDwyer(2) (a.p: led over 1f out tl ins fnl f)	s.h	**3**	11/4 ^{1}	73	53
1926^{2}	**Cuban Reef (50)** (WJMusson) **5-8-8** KFallon(3) (reard up s: hdwy over 3f out: hrd rdn over 1f out: nt qckn)	1¾	**4**	5/1 ^{2}	55	35
2285^{4}	**Tribal Peace (IRE) (61)** (BGubby) **5-9-5** JStack(13) (a.p: ev ch 2f out: wknd fnl f)	2½	**5**	10/1	62	42
1484^{13}	**Fancy Design (IRE) (39)** (PMitchell) **4-7-6**(5)ow1 AimeeCook(9) (b.off hind: lw: plld hrd: chsd ldr: led over 5f out tl over 1f out)	nk	**6**	50/1	40	19
2187^{5}	**Prospector's Cove (68)** (JPearce) **4-9-12** GHind(6) (nvr nrr)	s.h	**7**	14/1	69	49
2218^{4}	**Double Rush (IRE) (46)** (TGMills) **5-8-4**ow2 TQuinn(8) (swtg: no hdwy fnl 3f)	1	**8**	13/2 ^{3}	45	23
1427^{8}	**Well Drawn (65)** (HCandy) **4-9-9** CRutter(5) (led over 4f: wknd 2f out)	10	**9**	12/1	48	28
1154^{8}	**Tuigamala (38)** (RIngram) **6-7-10** NAdams(4) (lw: wl bhd fnl 4f)	1	**10**	33/1	20	—
2190^{6}	**Lancashire Knight (57)** (SDow) **3-8-4** JFEgan(12) (prom tl wknd 2f out)	½	**11**	33/1	38	7
403^{9}	**Camphar (38)** (RMFlower) **4-7-10** JLowe(1) (b: swtg: plld hrd: prom 6f: wknd qckly: t.o)	dist	**12**	50/1	—	—
1424^{8}	**Soojama (IRE) (57)** (RMFlower) **7-9-1b** SDrowne(7) (swtg: ref to r: t.n.p)		**R**	10/1	—	—

(SP 116.3%) **13 Rn**

2m 10.0 (5.10) CSF £132.06 CT £465.61 TOTE £31.10: £6.10 £1.80 £1.70 (£46.70) Trio £102.70 OWNER Lamb Brook Associates (COWBRIDGE) BRED Owen Bourke in Ireland
LONG HANDICAP Camphar 7-9 Fancy Design (IRE) 7-3
WEIGHT FOR AGE 3yo-11lb
Haroldon (IRE), very warm before the race and taken down to the start early, came with a daring run from well behind on the inside. He struck the front one hundred yards from home and won readily. (20/1)
2150 Your Most Welcome, always close up, drew level two furlongs out but could not quicken close home. (7/1: op 9/2)
1811* Princess Danielle appeared to be travelling well on the heels of the leaders but, after going to the front approaching the final furlong, could not quicken when headed. (11/4)
1926 Cuban Reef lost several lengths by rearing up at the start and, in the circumstances, did well to get into contention below the distance. She could find no extra in the last furlong. (5/1)
2285 Tribal Peace (IRE), close up all the way, had every chance but lacked the final turn of foot. (10/1)
134 Fancy Design (IRE) pulled hard in second place and went to the front approaching halfway. She was not collared until approaching the final furlong and may be capable of winning a race from her lowly mark. (50/1)
2187 Prospector's Cove (14/1: 8/1-16/1)
Well Drawn (12/1: op 8/1)
1424 Soojama (IRE) refused to come out of the stalls and declined to take any part. (10/1)

2551 CADOGAN GROUP LIMITED STKS (0-80) (3-Y.O+) (Class D)
7-10 (7-10) **1m 3f 135y** £3,291.50 (£992.00: £481.00: £225.50) Stalls: High GOING minus 0.15 sec per fur (GF)

				SP	RR	SF
1145^{12}	**Jazz King (74)** (MissGayKelleway) **4-9-6** JReid(1) (lw: mde all: drvn out)	—	**1**	13/2	90	62
2210^{6}	**Dominant Duchess (77)** (JWHills) **3-8-8** KFallon(3) (stdd s: hdwy 3f out: ev ch 1f out: nt qckn: sddle slipped)	2	**2**	11/4 ^{2}	88	47
2328^{2}	**Epworth (79)** (JAGlover) **3-8-4** GCarter(2) (lw: a.p: ev ch 2f out: wknd fnl f)	3	**3**	2/1 ^{1}	80	39
1869^{5}	**Rich In Love (IRE) (80)** (CACyzer) **3-7-13**(5) RFfrench(4) (prom tl wknd over 1f out)	4	**4**	7/1	75	34
1852^{4}	**Love Has No Pride (USA) (79)** (RHannon) **3-8-7** DaneO'Neill(5) (dropped rr 5f out: no ch after)	8	**5**	7/2 ^{3}	67	26

(SP 108.1%) **5 Rn**

2m 30.3 (4.30) CSF £21.24 TOTE £6.60: £2.10 £1.90 (£8.40) OWNER Whitcombe Manor Racing Stables Ltd (WHITCOMBE) BRED Casterbridge Stud and Brook Stud Ltd
WEIGHT FOR AGE 3yo-13lb
Jazz King made all the running and battled on well to beat a poor field. (13/2)
764* Dominant Duchess, steadied at the start, came with a steady run to challenge entering the final furlong but was being held near the finish. It transpired that her saddle had slipped. (11/4)
2328 Epworth, trying a longer trip, looked much like winning when moving up to join Jazz King at the two-furlong marker but, when pressure was applied, she faded. (2/1)
1869 Rich In Love (IRE), in second place to halfway, had shot her bolt approaching the final furlong. (7/1: 5/1-8/1)
1852 Love Has No Pride (USA) dropped back last five furlongs out and was no danger thereafter. (7/2: op 9/4)

2552 A O N GROUP LTD H'CAP (0-70) (3-Y.O+) (Class E)
7-40 (7-42) **1m 67y** £3,030.00 (£915.00: £445.00: £210.00) Stalls: High GOING minus 0.15 sec per fur (GF)

				SP	RR	SF
1262[12]	**Whatever's Right (IRE) (63)** (MDIUsher) **8-9-8** KFallon(8) (swtg: gd hdwy 2f out: hrd rdn to ld cl home: all out)	—	**1**	10/1	73	47
2237[8]	**Delight of Dawn (45)** (EAWheeler) **5-7-13**(5) ADaly(15) (gd hdwy 2f out: led ins fnl f tl nr fin)	nk	**2**	15/2[3]	54	28
2004*	**Chasetown Flyer (USA) (62)** (NEBerry) **3-8-12** JReid(4) (hdwy 2f out: r.o ins fnl f)	1½	**3**	11/2[2]	69	34
1972[8]	**Multi Franchise (45)** (RMFlower) **4-8-4** GHind(17) (a.p: r.o one pce fnl 2f)	½	**4**	12/1	51	25
2246[6]	**Clouds Hill (FR) (52)** (RHannon) **4-8-11v** DaneO'Neill(9) (bhd whn hmpd 6f out: gd hdwy fnl 2f)	1½	**5**	14/1	55	29
2285[8]	**Lady Godiva (62)** (MJPolglase) **3-8-12** TGMcLaughlin(1) (led tl wknd ins fnl f)	nk	**6**	33/1	64	29
2369[4]	**Shouldbegrey (40)** (WRMuir) **4-7-10**(3) MartinDwyer(16) (lw: hmpd 6f out: hdwy fnl 2f: nt rch ldrs)	s.h	**7**	9/1	42	16
1640[7]	**Paddy's Rice (57)** (MBlanshard) **6-9-2** FNorton(7) (swtg: in tch tl wknd over 2f out)	1¼	**8**	14/1	57	31
1796[8]	**Welsh Mountain (46)** (MJHeaton-Ellis) **4-8-5** SWhitworth(5) (hdwy on ins 3f out: hmpd whn 1f out: one pce)	1¼	**9**	25/1	43	17
2347[8]	**Invocation (53)** (GLMoore) **10-8-12** CandyMorris(14) (lw: chsd ldr 5f: wknd 2f out)	2½	**10**	25/1	45	19
1566[8]	**Cambridge Blue (USA) (62)** (GLewis) **3-8-12** PaulEddery(11) (bdly hmpd 6f out: no ch after)	2	**11**	10/1	51	16
2310[4]	**Noeprob (USA) (52)** (RJHodges) **7-8-11** TQuinn(10) (bdly hmpd 6f out: hdwy 3f out: eased whn btn over 1f out)	1¼	**12**	5/1[1]	38	12
2369[13]	**Sun O'Tirol (IRE) (60)** (JRArnold) **3-8-10b[1]** CRutter(12) (prom tl wknd over 2f out)	2½	**13**	33/1	41	6
1849*	**Silver Lining (60)** (APJones) **3-8-10** SDrowne(3) (bhd fnl 3f)	nk	**14**	9/1	41	6
2374[8]	**Whispering Dawn (65)** (CPEBrooks) **4-9-7**(3) PPMurphy(18) (b.hind: mid div whn bdly hmpd 6f out: no ch after)	nk	**15**	14/1	45	19
1297[14]	**Haydn James (USA) (70)** (PWHarris) **3-8-13b[1]**(7) CLowther(6) (lw: bhd most of wy)	½	**16**	20/1	49	14
2281[10]	**Tulsa (IRE) (58)** (BGubby) **3-8-8** JStack(2) (wl bhd fnl 3f)	7	**17**	16/1	24	—
				(SP 133.9%)	**17 Rn**	

1m 46.9 (4.70) CSF £77.71 CT £445.73 TOTE £18.00: £3.00 £2.00 £1.60 £3.90 (£74.90) Trio £160.80 OWNER Mr M. S. C. Thurgood (WANTAGE) BRED Rockville House Stud
WEIGHT FOR AGE 3yo-9lb
STEWARDS' ENQUIRY Fallon susp. 16-17/7/97 (excessive use of whip).
143 Whatever's Right (IRE) came from a fair way back to snatch the race in the last few strides. He was absolutely flat-out. (10/1)
2237 Delight of Dawn came with a good run inside the final furlong, only to be collared near the line. (15/2)
2004* Chasetown Flyer (USA) stayed on under pressure from midfield in the last two furlongs but just too late to catch the leaders. (11/2)
Multi Franchise, always on the premises, ran on at one pace in the final quarter-mile. (12/1)
2246 Clouds Hill (FR) was at the back of the field when hampered six furlongs out and, in the circumstances, did extremely well to reach fifth place. (14/1)
Lady Godiva tried to make all the running and was not collared until inside the final furlong. (33/1)
964 Cambridge Blue (USA) was hampered at the six-furlong marker which seriously affected his chance. (10/1: op 6/1)
2310 Noeprob (USA) was also hampered six furlongs out and this finishing position can be forgotten. (5/1)
369 Whispering Dawn was another badly hampered at the six-furlong marker and this final placing can be ignored. (14/1)

2553 SUNLEY MAIDEN STKS (2-Y.O) (Class D)
8-10 (8-12) **5f 10y** £3,436.25 (£1,040.00: £507.50: £241.25) Stalls: High GOING minus 0.29 sec per fur (GF)

				SP	RR	SF
2320[4]	**Centre Court** (RHannon) **2-8-9** DaneO'Neill(7) (led after 1f: clr fnl 2f: comf)	—	**1**	4/1[2]	76+	35
564[2]	**Loch Laird** (MMadgwick) **2-9-0** JReid(2) (led 1f: a.p: nt qckn fnl f)	2½	**2**	6/1[3]	73	32
	Little Fizz (BJMeehan) **2-8-9** MTebbutt(1) (neat: bit bkwd: a.p: r.o one pce fnl 2f)	½	**3**	20/1	67	26
1492[3]	**Leofric** (MJPolglase) **2-9-0** TGMcLaughlin(12) (dwlt: hdwy fnl 2f: nvr nrr)	2	**4**	8/1	65	24
	Sampower Lady (WJMusson) **2-8-9** KFallon(4) (w'like: a.p: no hdwy fnl 2f)	1½	**5**	16/1	55	14
	Bala (HMorrison) **2-8-9** CRutter(8) (unf: scope: nvr nrr)	1½	**6**	14/1	51	10
	Katyushka (IRE) (MajorDNChappell) **2-8-9** GCarter(5) (neat: bit bkwd: s.s: hdwy 2f out: nt rch ldrs)	s.h	**7**	9/1	51	10
	Tom (LordHuntingdon) **2-9-0** LDettori(3) (w'like: bkwd: chsd ldrs: rdn over 2f out: sn wknd)	2	**8**	5/2[1]	49	8
	Glamorgan (IRE) (CADwyer) **2-9-0** KRutter(9) (leggy: bit bkwd: stumbled bdly s: rdn & hdwy over 2f out: nvr nr ldrs)	1	**9**	20/1	46	5
	Wallflower (SirMarkPrescott) **2-8-9** GDuffield(10) (unf: scope: prom over 2f)	½	**10**	13/2	39	—
1251[11]	**Filgrave (IRE)** (CADwyer) **2-9-0** WRyan(6) (a bhd)	½	**11**	33/1	43	2
	Pippas Pride (IRE) (MJFetherston-Godley) **2-9-0** DHarrison(13) (str: scope: a bhd)	4	**12**	20/1	30	—
				(SP 127.1%)	**12 Rn**	

61.7 secs (2.00) CSF £26.34 TOTE £5.90: £2.50 £1.90 £5.80 (£7.80) Trio £135.80 OWNER Mrs David Sieff (MARLBOROUGH) BRED The Overbury Stud
2320 Centre Court, in the lead after a furlong, was clear below the distance and won with plenty in hand. (4/1: 3/1-5/1)
564 Loch Laird, off the course since his debut in April, led for the first furlong. He remained close up but was no match for the winner in the final quarter-mile. (6/1: 4/1-8/1)
Little Fizz, a sharp sort, made an encouraging debut. Close up all the way, she could not quicken under pressure in the closing stages. (20/1)
1492 Leofric lost a few lengths at the start but stayed on in the last two furlongs without troubling the leaders. (8/1: 5/1-10/1)
Sampower Lady, a useful-looking sort, chased the leaders throughout and is capable of improvement with this experience behind her. (16/1)
Bala was one of those towards the back of the field for much of the way but was going at the finish. (14/1: 7/1-16/1)
Katyushka (IRE), a small filly, lost many lengths at the start and, in the circumstances, did quite well to finish seventh. (9/1: op 3/1)
Tom (5/2: 7/4-11/4)
Wallflower completely lost her place just before halfway and the position was quickly accepted. She may be much better than this. (13/2: 3/1-7/1)

2554 ROYAL WINDSOR RACECOURSE H'CAP (0-70) (3-Y.O) (Class E)
8-40 (8-41) **5f 217y** £3,046.25 (£920.00: £447.50: £211.25) Stalls: High GOING minus 0.29 sec per fur (GF)

				SP	RR	SF
2407[2]	**Distinctive Dream (IRE) (45)** (KTIvory) **3-7-10b**(3) MartinDwyer(8) (b: hdwy 2f out: led 1f out: edgd rt: all out)	—	**1**	12/1	56	32
2004[12]	**Batsman (50)** (WJMusson) **3-8-4** DHarrison(15) (swtg: gd hdwy fnl 2f: nvr nrr)	1¼	**2**	33/1	58	34
2244[8]	**Will To Win (52)** (PGMurphy) **3-8-6** SDrowne(14) (lw: gd hdwy on ins over 1f out: nt qckn ins fnl f)	s.h	**3**	10/1	60	36

				SP	RR	SF
2203*	**Nervous Rex (55)** (WRMuir) **3-8-2**(7) JWilkinson(5) (a.p: led 2f out to 1f out: nt qckn)	nk	**4**	8/1^{3}	62	38
2372^{9}	**Forgotten Times (USA) (65)** (TMJones) **3-9-5** NCarlisle(21) (hdwy over 2f out: ev ch 1f out: nt qckn)	¾	**5**	20/1	70	46
1925^{7}	**Homestead (48)** (RHannon) **3-8-2**ow1 PaulEddery(13) (nrst fin)	½	**6**	25/1	51	26
2317^{14}	**Patina (45)** (RHollinshead) **3-7-8**(5) RFfrench(20) (bhd whn hmpd over 3f out: gd late hdwy)	1¾	**7**	16/1	44	20
1843^{7}	**Bonsiel (48)** (KMahdi) **3-8-2**ow3 RPrice(11) (swtg: led 4f)	1½	**8**	16/1	43	16
1931^{7}	**Heavenly Miss (IRE) (60)** (JJBridger) **3-9-0** RCochrane(10) (prom over 4f)	nk	**9**	14/1	54	30
1876^{3}	**Davids Revenge (67)** (MajorDNChappell) **3-9-7** GCarter(3) (spd 4f)	nk	**10**	13/2^{2}	60	36
2006^{7}	**V I P Charlie (67)** (JRJenkins) **3-9-7** SWhitworth(12) (lw: nvr bttr than mid div)	½	**11**	4/1^{1}	59	35
2192^{7}	**Chakra (49)** (SDow) **3-8-3** JFEgan(18) (hdwy on ins & hrd rdn 2f out: sn wknd)	hd	**12**	33/1	41	17
2184^{7}	**Pointelle (57)** (AHide) **3-8-11** AMcGlone(4) (spd 4f)	1¼	**13**	16/1	45	21
1849^{8}	**Folly Foot Fred (42)** (BRMillman) **3-7-10** FNorton(1) (lw: spd 4f)	s.h	**14**	25/1	30	6
2319^{7}	**Hever Golf Charger (IRE) (59)** (TJNaughton) **3-8-13** TSprake(17) (nvr on terms)	¾	**15**	16/1	45	21
2300^{9}	**Crackerbox (42)** (CADwyer) **3-7-3**(7) DarrenWilliams(2) (outpcd)	¾	**16**	33/1	26	2
2179^{10}	**Dayrella (56)** (WRMuir) **3-8-10** JReid(7) (lw: bhd fnl 2f)	nk	**17**	10/1	39	15
1810^{8}	**Tabasco Jazz (64)** (BJMeehan) **3-9-4** MTebbutt(6) (swtg: bhd fnl 3f)	2	**18**	16/1	42	18
2151^{11}	**Formidable Spirit (42)** (MJHeaton-Ellis) **3-7-10** JLowe(19) (prom 4f)	2½	**19**	33/1	13	—
341^{8}	**Ron's Round (45)** (CADwyer) **3-7-13** NVarley(16) (lw: a bhd)	1¼	**20**	25/1	13	—
2406^{W}	**Royal Blackbird (60)** (JEBanks) **3-8-7**(7) CLowther(9) (a bhd: t.o)	20	**21**	14/1	—	—
				(SP 141.1%)		**21 Rn**

1m 12.4 (1.90) CSF £359.77 CT £3,805.97 TOTE £14.80: £2.70 £12.60 £2.20 £1.80 (£538.00) Trio £1,229.20 OWNER Mr K. T. Ivory (RADLETT) BRED Peter Kehoe

LONG HANDICAP Formidable Spirit 6-13 Folly Foot Fred 7-7 Crackerbox 7-0

2407 Distinctive Dream (IRE) came with a strong run from the two-furlong marker and, striking the front entering the final furlong, won under hard driving despite drifting to the right. (12/1)

Batsman had an enormous amount to do at the two-furlong marker but finished in tremendous style to snatch second place on the line. (33/1)

1810 Will To Win found a clear run on the stands' rails and came with a promising challenge entering the final furlong. Close home she could not quite sustain it. (10/1)

2203* Nervous Rex took a narrow lead at the two-furlong marker and kept on when headed entering the final furlong. (8/1)

339* Forgotten Times (USA) moved up to draw level below the distance but could find no extra inside the last furlong. (20/1)

1963 Patina was quite badly hampered and snatched up on the inside over three furlongs from home when at the back of the field and did extremely well to reach seventh place. (16/1)

2006 V I P Charlie, the medium of a gamble, was never near the leaders at any stage. (4/1: 7/1-7/2)

Royal Blackbird (14/1: 10/1-16/1)

2555 ST JOHN AMBULANCE MAIDEN STKS (3-Y.O F) (Class D)

9-10 (9-11) **1m 67y** £3,603.50 (£1,088.00: £529.00: £249.50) Stalls: High GOING minus 0.15 sec per fur (GF)

				SP	RR	SF
2020^{3}	**Wishing Stone (USA)** (EALDunlop) **3-8-11** KFallon(11) (a.p: rdn 1f out: styd on to ld cl home)	—	**1**	6/4^{1}	64	25
1105^{8}	**Slipstream Star** (IABalding) **3-8-8**(3) MartinDwyer(3) (swtg: plld hrd: led tl nr fin)	nk	**2**	33/1	63	24
2173^{2}	**Karakia (IRE)** (JHMGosden) **3-8-11** LDettori(4) (a.p: rdn over 3f out: ev ch fnl f: no ex)	hd	**3**	7/4^{2}	63	24
2330^{5}	**Teulada (USA)** (LMCumani) **3-8-6**(5) RFfrench(12) (a.p: one pce fnl 2f)	3	**4**	16/1	57	18
	Peace And Quiet (IABalding) **3-8-11** SWhitworth(8) (leggy: unf: hdwy 3f out: rdn & one pce fnl 2f)	2	**5**	12/1	54	15
2183^{5}	**Isabella Gonzaga** (JLDunlop) **3-8-11** TSprake(6) (hdwy & hrd rdn 3f out: one pce fnl 2f)	nk	**6**	10/1^{3}	53	14
2231^{7}	**Perchance To Dream (IRE) (42)** (BRMillman) **3-8-11** SDrowne(5) (chsd ldr over 5f: wknd over 1f out)	1½	**7**	66/1	50	11
2172^{4}	**She's A Cracker** (MrsNMacauley) **3-8-11** DHarrison(9) (swtg: dwlt: nvr nr ldrs)	½	**8**	14/1	49	10
	Shalverton (IRE) (WRMuir) **3-8-11** JReid(10) (w'like: scope: bit bkwd: a bhd: checked 6f out)	1½	**9**	20/1	46	7
	Broughtons Lure (IRE) (WJMusson) **3-8-11** RCochrane(7) (w'like: a bhd)	2	**10**	33/1	42	3
	Just Dickens (RIngram) **3-8-11** AMcGlone(2) (w'like: b.off hind: dwlt: a bhd)	1	**11**	33/1	41	2
2287^{5}	**Imperial Glen (IRE)** (MDIUsher) **3-8-11** JMarshall(1) (prom tl wknd 4f out)	2½	**12**	50/1	36	—
				(SP 122.7%)		**12 Rn**

1m 48.2 (6.00) CSF £63.17 TOTE £3.20: £1.10 £6.90 £1.60 (£105.70) Trio £39.60 OWNER Maktoum Al Maktoum (NEWMARKET) BRED Gainsborough Farm Inc

2020 Wishing Stone (USA) settled in sixth place well on terms with the leaders. She stayed on under pressure to snatch the race in the last few strides. (6/4: 11/10-7/4)

Slipstream Star took a strong hold in the lead but had many of her rivals in trouble fully three furlongs from home. She still looked likely to succeed entering the final furlong only to be collared near the line. Her turn is near at hand. (33/1)

2173 Karakia (IRE), having only her second race, showed distinct signs of greenness. Always close up, she came under pressure with more than three furlongs to race and did not appear to realise what was required. She was grasping the idea in the last furlong and improvement can be expected. (7/4)

2330 Teulada (USA), always hunting up the leaders, ran on at one pace under pressure in the last two furlongs. (16/1)

Peace And Quiet tried to come with a run near the inside over two furlongs from home but, though staying on, could not land a blow. (12/1: 7/1-14/1)

2183 Isabella Gonzaga was being driven along some way from the finish but, though running on at the one pace, never threatened to trouble the leaders. (10/1: op 5/1)

T/Jkpt: Not won; £50,182.87 to Newmarket 8/7/97. T/Plpt: £67.20 (369.59 Tckts). T/Qdpt: £9.40 (136.16 Tckts) AK/Hn

2331-NEWMARKET (R-H) (Good)

Tuesday July 8th

WEATHER: warm & sunny WIND: slt against

2556 STRUTT & PARKER MAIDEN STKS (I) (2-Y.O) (Class D)

2-05 (2-05) **7f (July)** £4,753.00 (£1,414.00: £672.00: £301.00) Stalls: High GOING minus 0.40 sec per fur (F)

				SP	RR	SF
1933^{2}	**Craigsteel** (HRACecil) **2-9-0** KFallon(6) (mde all: rdn clr over 2f out: hld on wl fnl f)	—	**1**	5/4^{1}	96	47

Victory Note (USA) (PWChapple-Hyam) **2-9-0** JReid(3) (w'like: leggy: b: b.hind: a.p: ev ch over 1f out: unable qckn)	2½	**2**	4/1[3]	90+	41
Indimaaj (JLDunlop) **2-9-0** MJKinane(4) (w'like: sn pushed along: hdwy over 1f out: styd on wl ins fnl f)	6	**3**	25/1	77+	28
Rainbow High (BWHills) **2-9-0** MHills(7) (w'like: scope: bit bkwd: dwlt: sn chsng ldrs: one pce fnl 2f)	nk	**4**	12/1	76	27
Arkadian Hero (USA) (LMCumani) **2-9-0** PatEddery(10) (wl grwn: bkwd: chsd wnr over 4f)	hd	**5**	100/30[2]	76+	27
Surprise Present (IRE) (RHannon) **2-9-0** RHughes(2) (gd sort: prom tl wknd wl over 1f out)	8	**6**	14/1	57	8
Maazoom (IRE) (JHMGosden) **2-9-0** LDettori(5) (swtg: scope: s.i.s: nvr nr ldrs)	4	**7**	20/1	48	—
River Beat (IRE) (MHTompkins) **2-9-0** RCochrane(9) (w'like: bit bkwd: nvr nr to chal)	hd	**8**	50/1	48	—
Court Shareef (RDickin) **2-9-0** MRoberts(11) (neat: plld hrd: a bhd)	½	**9**	66/1	47	—

(SP 113.9%) **9 Rn**

1m 26.56 (1.56) CSF £5.46 TOTE £2.10: £1.10 £1.70 £2.70 (£5.10) Trio £49.30 OWNER Sir David Wills (NEWMARKET) BRED Sir David Wills

1933 Craigsteel, given an aggressive ride, proved willing and able in the final furlong and is quoted between 33/1 and 20/1 for the 2,000 Guineas. (5/4)

Victory Note (USA), a good-looking half-brother to Dance So Suite, got a little colty beforehand and was rather keen going down but was the only one to give the winner a stern test and will win races. (4/1: 3/1-9/2)

Indimaaj, rather keen to post, is bred to get middle distances in time and was towards the rear for much of the race. His stamina came into play late in the day and he came home strongly. He should not be too hard to place, probably over further. (25/1)

Rainbow High did not really take the eye in the paddock and looked as if he would be better for the run but shaped quite well. (12/1: 7/1-16/1)

Arkadian Hero (USA), a tall, imposing half-brother to Masnun, ran really well until lack of a run found him out. He looks sure to do better in future. (100/30)

Surprise Present (IRE) looked fit enough and was in the thick of the action until tying up in the final furlong. (14/1)

2557 H & K COMMISSIONS H'CAP (0-80) (3-Y.O+) (Class D)

2-35 (2-36) **1m (July)** £8,285.00 (£2,480.00: £1,190.00: £545.00) Stalls: High GOING minus 0.40 sec per fur (F)

				SP	RR	SF
2369[2]	**Ben Gunn (65)** (PTWalwyn) **5-8-13** RCochrane(11) (hld up: effrt & nt clr run over 2f out: hdwy over 1f out: str run to ld nr fin)	—	**1**	14/1	79	65
2013[28]	**Kennemara Star (IRE) (77)** (JLDunlop) **3-9-2** PatEddery(13) (hld up: hdwy over 2f out: rdn to ld wl ins fnl f: ct nr fin)	hd	**2**	6/1[2]	91	68
2290[4]	**Suez Tornado (IRE) (68)** (EJAlston) **4-8-11v**(5) TEDurcan(14) (in tch: gd hdwy to ld over 1f out: hdd & no ex wl ins fnl f)	nk	**3**	16/1	81	67
2065[4]	**Toujours Riviera (68)** (JPearce) **7-9-2** JWeaver(18) (chsd ldr: led wl over 1f out: sn hdd & one pce)	1½	**4**	20/1	78	64
2331[U]	**Fern's Governor (56)** (WJMusson) **5-8-4** GCarter(16) (hdwy over 4f out: swtchd lft over 1f out: kpt on same pce)	1¾	**5**	20/1	63	49
2372[5]	**Swift (67)** (MJPolglase) **3-8-6** JTate(12) (swtg: hdwy over 2f out: hmpd over 1f out: one pce)	3½	**6**	25/1	67	44
2337*	**Jibereen (56)** (PHowling) **5-8-4** PaulEddery(8) (lw: hld up: hdwy & nt clr run over 1f out: nvr rchd ldrs)	nk	**7**	20/1	55	41
2340[3]	**Mo-Addab (IRE) (74)** (ACStewart) **7-9-8** LDettori(7) (swtg: chsd ldrs: rdn whn hmpd over 1f out: no ch after)	nk	**8**	10/1[3]	73	59
2340*	**Pride of Pendle (71)** (MartynWane) **8-9-5** KFallon(15) (sn pushed along: hdwy over 1f out: hmpd: nvr rchd ldrs)	½	**9**	10/1[3]	69	55
2205*	**Rainbow Rain (USA) (78)** (MJohnston) **3-9-3** MRoberts(20) (prom: rdn over 2f out: sn btn)	2½	**10**	6/1[2]	71	48
2309[2]	**What Happened Was (74)** (MartynMeade) **3-8-13** FNorton(9) (b: b.hind: in tch 4f)	1½	**11**	16/1	64	41
1606*	**Family Man (80)** (JRFanshawe) **4-10-0** DHarrison(3) (hld up: hdwy over 3f out: rdn whn hmpd over 1f out: eased whn btn ins fnl f)	½	**12**	5/1[1]	69	55
1761[12]	**Celandine (60)** (AndrewTurnell) **4-8-3**(5) ADaly(10) (lw: led: sn clr: hdd & wknd wl over 1f out)	2	**13**	66/1	45	31
2005[8]	**Harmony Hall (70)** (JRFanshawe) **3-8-9** TQuinn(17) (b: b.hind: swtg: prom: wkng whn bmpd over 1f out)	nk	**14**	33/1	54	31
2044[8]	**Broad River (USA) (79)** (EALDunlop) **3-9-4** MJKinane(19) (lw: plld hrd: effrt 3f out: nvr nr ldrs)	2	**15**	16/1	59	36
2346[5]	**Stone Ridge (IRE) (80)** (RHannon) **5-9-11b**(3) MartinDwyer(1) (lw: chsd ldrs tl rdn & wknd over 1f out)	nk	**16**	33/1	59	45
1987[2]	**Sylvan Princess (70)** (DJSCosgrove) **4-8-11**(7) CLowther(6) (prom 5f)	5	**17**	20/1	39	25
2346[8]	**Present Generation (75)** (RGuest) **4-9-9** SSanders(5) (in tch over 5f)	nk	**18**	20/1	44	30
	Persica (75) (KMahdi) **4-9-9** RHills(4) (s.i.s: rdn over 3f out: a bhd)	1½	**19**	40/1	41	27
2161[3]	**Broughtons Turmoil (76)** (BRMillman) **8-9-10** JReid(2) (swtg: chsd ldrs over 5f)	1¼	**20**	16/1	39	25

(SP 131.1%) **20 Rn**

1m 37.98 (-0.02) CSF £79.57 CT £1,285.77 TOTE £14.80: £2.80 £1.90 £4.10 £4.90 (£53.60) Trio £675.10 OWNER Mr Michael White (LAMBOURN) BRED Michael White and Peter Walwyn

WEIGHT FOR AGE 3yo-9lb

2369 Ben Gunn came of age over the trip but the signs looked anything but promising below the distance with a wall of horses in front of him. However, a sideways manoeuvre by Fern's Governor left a gap on the rails for him and he quickened in terrific style to get up on the line. (14/1)

1175 Kennemara Star (IRE) got a little warm beforehand and was keen going down but was travelling supremely well when pulled to the outside to begin his move. Finding a good turn of foot, it still took him time to get on top and he was unfortunate to be deprived of victory on the line. With a turn of foot like this, he gives the impression that a top handicap over nine or ten furlongs could come his way in time. (6/1)

2290 Suez Tornado (IRE) would seem to have taken to the track and ran a cracker. This was his best ever performance and he should soon be winning again. (16/1)

2065 Toujours Riviera, with trip and ground ideal, bowled along in second place to the distance. Once in front, he did little to help his jockey. He is on a losing run but retains his ability if the key can be found. (20/1)

933 Fern's Governor has never won below ten furlongs and, although staying on, did look likely to get there when causing all sorts of trouble in the Dip. (20/1)

2372 Swift, a poor mover, was making little impression when a bump in the Dip sealed his fate. (25/1)

2337* Jibereen went to post really well but had a little trouble getting daylight and, by the time he got through, the leaders were beyond recall and he was not knocked about. (20/1)

2340 Mo-Addab (IRE) would have finished a little closer with a clear run but does seem to lack the turn of foot that so often lands handicaps of this type. (10/1)

2340* Pride of Pendle, having bounced back to form on softer ground last time, was never travelling nearly as well on this quicker surface. (10/1)

1606* Family Man, who did not impress in his coat, did find trouble but was already going to struggle to get near the leaders. It is hard to believe this is the same horse who won over the other course and he deserves another chance. (5/1)

2558 CHARLES HEIDSIECK CHAMPAGNE CHERRY HINTON STKS (Gp 2) (2-Y.O F) (Class A)

3-05 (3-06) **6f (July)** £23,198.00 (£8,582.00: £4,116.00: £1,680.00: £665.00: £259.00) Stalls: High GOING minus 0.40 sec per fur (F)

				SP	RR	SF
2103*	**Asfurah (USA)** (SbinSuroor) **2-8-9** LDettori(6) (lw: mde most: rdn & hld on gamely fnl f)	—	**1**	9/2 ^{2}	96	57
2024^{2}	**Crazee Mental** (DHaydnJones) **2-8-9** JCarroll(4) (lw: dwlt: hdwy 2f out: ev ch fnl f: edgd lft & unable qckn)	1	**2**	8/1	93	54
2024^{5}	**Forest Treasure (IRE)** (JBerry) **2-8-9** GCarter(9) (b: outpcd 3f out: rallied appr fnl f: r.o wl nr fin)	1½	**3**	16/1	89	50
$2451a^{2}$	**Danyross (IRE)** (APO'Brien,Ireland) **2-8-9** MJKinane(10) (w wnr: no ex appr fnl f)	nk	**4**	8/1	89	50
2286*	**Conectis (IRE)** (DJSCosgrove) **2-8-9** JReid(8) (hld up: hdwy over 1f out: r.o)	nk	**5**	50/1	88?	49
2138^{2}	**Forum** (CEBrittain) **2-8-9** MRoberts(12) (outpcd: plld out & rdn over 2f out: styd on wl fnl f)	¾	**6**	20/1	86	47
1783*	**Stayingalive (USA)** (PFICole) **2-8-9** TQuinn(5) (lw: chsd ldrs: sltly outpcd whn hmpd over 1f out: styd on wl fnl f)	nk	**7**	9/4 ^{1}	85	46
1174*	**Belladera (IRE)** (NTinkler) **2-8-9** RCochrane(11) (bhd tl styd on fnl 2f)	½	**8**	50/1	84	45
2335^{2}	**Land of Dreams** (MJohnston) **2-8-9** JWeaver(3) (trckd ldrs: chal 2f out: wknd over 1f out)	¾	**9**	5/1 ^{3}	82	43
2057^{7}	**Ajig Dancer** (MRChannon) **2-8-9** RPerham(7) (chsd ldrs 3f)	2	**10**	40/1	76	37
651*	**Rising of The Moon (IRE)** (RHannon) **2-8-9** PatEddery(2) (sn rdn along: bhd fnl 2f)	6	**11**	16/1	60	21
2227*	**Kawafil (IRE)** (PTWalwyn) **2-8-9** RHills(1) (chsd ldrs tl hung bdly lft 2f out: nt rcvr)	1¼	**12**	14/1	57	18
				(SP 117.4%)		**12 Rn**

1m 12.22 (0.22) CSF £35.22 TOTE £4.10: £1.80 £2.20 £4.50 (£11.80) Trio £88.30 OWNER Godolphin (NEWMARKET) BRED Shadwell Farm Inc

2103* Asfurah (USA) again showed heart aplenty for, having disputed the lead with Danyross for most of the race, she dug deep to hold the runner-up. The field finished in such a heap that the value of the form is questionable, but she may well go for the Princess Margaret now. (9/2)
2024 Crazee Mental again gave the impression that she has more speed than steering for a winning chance was forfeited by hanging first left and then drifting right in the final furlong. (8/1: op 5/1)
2024 Forest Treasure (IRE) may have been stepping up a furlong in trip but this run had all the hallmarks of a horse running over a trip short of her best. Outpaced at a vital stage, she came home in great style on meeting the rising ground and looks to have a future over seven furlongs. (16/1)
2451a Danyross (IRE) did not exactly burst the King of Kings bubble but did put their recent meeting into perspective, running a similar sort of race. (8/1: 5/1-9/1)
2286* Conectis (IRE) took six tries to break her duck, but it has to be said that she ran a fine race in this company. She has since been sold to race in America. (50/1)
2138 Forum, who could probably have done with a win under her belt before stepping up to this level, was taken off her feet until staying on strongly towards the finish. She does need further. (20/1)
1783* Stayingalive (USA), whose win here last month has hardly been franked, was being taken off her feet when stopped for a stride or two but got going again nearing the finish. She may need a seventh furlong. (9/4)
2335 Land of Dreams was a bitter disappointment, stopping again once meeting the rising ground. She may have a problem rather than a lack of stamina. (5/1)

2559 PRINCESS OF WALES'S STKS (Gp 2) (3-Y.O+) (Class A)

3-40 (3-44) **1m 4f (July)** £32,908.00 (£12,172.00: £5,836.00: £2,380.00: £940.00: £364.00) Stalls: High GOING minus 0.40 sec per fur (F)

				SP	RR	SF
2100a*	**Shantou (USA) (123)** (JHMGosden) **4-9-7** LDettori(7) (lw: trckd ldrs: ev ch over 1f out: rdn to ld nr fin)	—	**1**	11/4 ^{2}	129	71
	Swain (IRE) (SbinSuroor) **5-9-7** MJKinane(5) (lw: trckd ldr: led over 3f out: hrd rdn fnl f: hdd nr fin)	hd	**2**	15/8 ^{1}	129	71
$2100a^{3}$	**Taipan (IRE) (120)** (JLDunlop) **5-9-2** TQuinn(4) (lw: hdwy 6f out: one pce fnl f)	4	**3**	10/1	119	61
2104^{5}	**Ela-Aristokrati (IRE) (114)** (MHTompkins) **5-9-2** RCochrane(6) (hld up gng wl: effrt over 2f out: no imp)	2½	**4**	25/1	115	57
2055*	**Celeric (117)** (DMorley) **5-9-7** PatEddery(1) (lw: hld up: effrt & outpcd over 3f out: styd on wl fnl f)	1	**5**	13/2 ^{3}	119	61
2104^{6}	**Dushyantor (USA) (120)** (HRACecil) **4-9-5** KFallon(2) (led: qcknd 4f out: sn hdd: one pce appr fnl f)	½	**6**	8/1	116	58
2104^{9}	**Lady Carla (122)** (HRACecil) **4-9-4** WRyan(3) (chsd ldrs: rdn 4f out: wknd 2f out)	6	**7**	10/1	107	49
				(SP 107.9%)		**7 Rn**

2m 29.16 (0.16) CSF £6.65 TOTE £2.70: £1.70 £1.70 (£3.00) OWNER Sheikh Mohammed (NEWMARKET) BRED Darley Stud Management Inc

2100a* Shantou (USA) found the ground just easy enough and moved magnificently to post. He always looked likely to wear down the runner-up once he began his challenge but it took time due to his rival's persistence. (11/4)
Swain (IRE) impressed most paddock judges as being forward enough but got warm by the time the horses left the paddock and was in a muck sweat at the start. Striking for home early, the winner joined him in the Dip and looked to have his measure but Kinane was in no mood to give up and the combination battled on gallantly to the line. This can hardly be described as a prep race. (15/8)
2100a Taipan (IRE) failed to reverse recent San Siro form with the winner on 5lb better terms but ran his best race in this country, although two class acts proved too quick for him in the final furlong. (10/1)
2104 Ela-Aristokrati (IRE) does seem to need holding up, but such tactics often backfire in Group races due to the steady early pace many are run at and this was no exception. (25/1)
2055* Celeric, held up in a steadily-run race over at least half a mile short of his best, ran as well as could have been hoped. (13/2: 7/2-7/1)
2104 Dushyantor (USA), waited with in front, does lack a turn of foot and, hard as he tried in the last half-mile, he was a sitting duck. (8/1)
2104 Lady Carla, with no soft ground to contend with this time, moved down well but, after looking a threat as the pace quickened, was quickly in trouble. (10/1: 8/1-12/1)

2560 NGK SPARK PLUGS RATED STKS H'CAP (0-100) (3-Y.O) (Class B)

4-10 (4-11) **6f (July)** £7,814.40 (£2,889.60: £1,384.80: £564.00: £222.00: £85.20) Stalls: High GOING minus 0.40 sec per fur (F)

				SP	RR	SF
2105^{2}	**Danetime (IRE) (97)** (NACallaghan) **3-9-7** PatEddery(1) (lw: lw: hld up: swtchd & qcknd to ld over 1f out: shkn up & r.o wl)	—	**1**	13/8 ^{1}	113+	73
1650*	**Elnadim (USA) (93)** (JLDunlop) **3-9-3** RHills(10) (lw: lw: hld up: hdwy ½-wy: chal 2f out: r.o one pce)	2	**2**	5/1 ^{2}	104	64
2134^{18}	**Soviet Leader (83)** (RGuest) **3-8-2**(5) RFfrench(3) (trckd ldrs: led over 2f out tl over 1f out: one pce)	¾	**3**	20/1	92	52
2044*	**Double Action (95)** (TDEasterby) **3-9-5** KFallon(11) (lw: lw: bhd: drvn along over 2f out: edgd lft: hdwy over 1f out: styd on)	nk	**4**	13/2	103	63
2347^{7}	**Silca Key Silca (88)** (MRChannon) **3-8-9**(3) PPMurphy(6) (led tl hdd over 2f out: sn btn)	3½	**5**	11/1	87	47
2326^{2}	**Return of Amin (84)** (JDBethell) **3-8-5**(3) PFessey(7) (chsd ldrs tl outpcd 2f out: sn btn)	½	**6**	10/1	81	41

				SP	RR	SF
2299^{4}	**Jennelle (91)** (CADwyer) **3-8-8**$^{(7)}$ JoHunnam(2) (outpcd & bhd fr ½-wy)	2	**7**	33/1	83	43
2298*	**The Gay Fox (83)** (BAMcMahon) **3-8-7** TQuinn(4) (chsd ldrs 4f: sn rdn & btn)	½	**8**	14/1	74	34
1609^{11}	**Alumisiyah (USA) (83)** (RWArmstrong) **3-8-7** GCarter(5) (spd over 3f: sn wknd)	1¼	**9**	20/1	70	30
2134*	**Prince Dome (IRE) (86)** (MartynWane) **3-8-10** MJKinane(8) (chsd ldrs: rdn over 2f out: wknd wl over 1f out)	nk	**10**	11/2^{3}	72	32
				(SP 120.0%)	**10 Rn**	

1m 11.88 (-0.12) CSF £8.82 CT £113.69 TOTE £2.60: £1.40 £2.00 £5.60 (£7.10) Trio £109.90 OWNER Mr M Tabor & Mrs John Magnier (NEWMARKET) BRED Holborn Trust Co
LONG HANDICAP The Gay Fox 8-5 Alumisiyah (USA) 8-6
2105 Danetime (IRE), 6lb higher than at Ascot, missed all the trouble here switching round the outside of the field and, judging from the way he won, he is ready to take on better company. (13/8)
1650* Elnadim (USA) put in a useful effort here against what appears to be a class rival but, despite responding to pressure, he was always short of speed. (5/1)
2044 Soviet Leader put in his best effort in handicap company here and is obviously getting the hang of things. (20/1)
2044* Double Action has not the best of actions and tends to hang left. However, he certainly has an engine and does respond to pressure, and he will always be one to be reckoned with in big handicaps. (13/2)
2347 Silca Key Silca ran quite well but found this company too hot in the last couple of furlongs. (11/1)
2326 Return of Amin is going up in the weights and was on drying ground but he still ran well here and is obviously in good heart. (10/1)
2134* Prince Dome (IRE) ran badly and was obviously not himself on this occasion. (11/2: 4/1-6/1)

2561 EQUITY FINANCIAL COLLECTIONS RATED STKS H'CAP (0-100) (3-Y.O F) (Class B)

4-45 (4-45) **7f (July)** £7,897.92 (£2,921.28: £1,400.64: £571.20: £225.60: £87.36) Stalls: High GOING minus 0.40 sec per fur (F)

				SP	RR	SF
1147^{8}	**Noisette (93)** (JHMGosden) **3-8-7** LDettori(10) (hld up & bhd: stdy hdwy over 2f out: qcknd to ld ins fnl f: cleverly)	—	**1**	5/1^{2}	100+	61
2393*	**Plaisir d'Amour (IRE) (86)** (NACallaghan) **3-7-9**$^{(5)}$ ^{3x} RFfrench(9) (hld up: hmpd & lost pl over 2f out: hdwy over 1f out: r.o)	1¼	**2**	4/1^{1}	90	51
1453^{2}	**Arruhan (IRE) (86)** (PTWalwyn) **3-8-0** RHills(3) (lw: hld up: hdwy 3f out: ev ch ins fnl f: nt qckn)	hd	**3**	7/1^{3}	90	51
2303^{4}	**Rechullin (86)** (DRLoder) **3-7-11**$^{(3)}$ MHenry(7) (chsd ldrs: led 2f out tl ins fnl f: no ex)	hd	**4**	16/1	90	51
2133^{5}	**Marie Dora (FR) (86)** (IABalding) **3-7-11**$^{(3)}$ MartinDwyer(5) (chsd ldrs: led wl over 2f out: hdd 2f out: grad wknd)	4	**5**	10/1	81	42
1326^{9}	**Blane Water (USA) (92)** (JRFanshawe) **3-8-6** DHarrison(11) (hld up: hmpd over 2f out & over 1f out: styd on towards fin)	¾	**6**	25/1	85	46
2280^{4}	**St Blaine (CAN) (86)** (DRLoder) **3-8-0b^{1}** DRMcCabe(8) (in tch tl rdn & wandered 2f out: sn btn)	hd	**7**	10/1	79	40
2133^{2}	**Dancing Drop (100)** (RHannon) **3-9-0** DaneO'Neill(4) (prom tl outpcd fnl 2f)	hd	**8**	4/1^{1}	92	53
1610^{6}	**Conspiracy (100)** (JLDunlop) **3-9-0** TQuinn(2) (rr div: effrt over 2f out: sn btn)	nk	**9**	20/1	92	53
2185^{4}	**Snap Crackle Pop (IRE) (87)** (RFJohnsonHoughton) **3-8-1**^{ow1} PaulEddery(6) (cl up: rdn over 2f out: wknd wl over 1f out)	4	**10**	16/1	70	30
2133^{6}	**Baked Alaska (93)** (ACStewart) **3-8-7v^{1}** MRoberts(1) (lw: plld hrd: led over 4f: wknd qckly)	1	**11**	12/1	73	34
				(SP 115.4%)	**11 Rn**	

1m 24.75 (-0.25) CSF £22.55 CT £129.37 TOTE £3.90: £1.40 £1.80 £2.30 (£9.40) Trio £28.90 OWNER Sheikh Mohammed (NEWMARKET) BRED Sheikh Mohammed Bin Rashid Al Maktoum
LONG HANDICAP Plaisir d'Amour (IRE) 7-8 St Blaine (CAN) 7-13 Marie Dora (FR) 7-11 Rechullin 7-10 Snap Crackle Pop (IRE) 7-13 Arruhan (IRE) 7-12
1147 Noisette, dropped back in trip, was given a lovely ride and hardly knew she was in a race and, coming from virtually last to first, had something in hand. Her confidence should now be sky-high. (5/1)
2393* Plaisir d'Amour (IRE) was always struggling for both pace and room but she did keep responding to pressure, only to find the winner in a different league. (4/1)
1453 Arruhan (IRE) seems difficult to win with but she certainly has ability and likes to come from off the pace, but just lacks that vital kick at the finish. (7/1: 5/1-8/1)
2303 Rechullin was 4lb out of the handicap and stepping up in class and, in the circumstances, ran a useful race. (16/1)
2133 Marie Dora (FR), a winner over further, was obviously being well tapped for foot when the pace was really on here. (10/1)
507 Blane Water (USA) was trying to come from behind when she met with interference in the last two furlongs, and always had an impossible task, but this was not a bad effort. (25/1)
2280 St Blaine (CAN) had blinkers on for the first time and did not seem to like it at all. (10/1: 8/1-12/1)
2133 Baked Alaska, in a visor for the first time, got lit up by them and ran herself into the ground soon after halfway. (12/1)

2562 STRUTT & PARKER MAIDEN STKS (II) (2-Y.O) (Class D)

5-15 (5-18) **7f (July)** £4,753.00 (£1,414.00: £672.00: £301.00) Stalls: High GOING minus 0.40 sec per fur (F)

				SP	RR	SF
	Haami (USA) (JLDunlop) **2-9-0** RHills(6) (gd sort: unf: hld up & bhd: shkn up & qcknd to ld wl over 1f out: r.o wl)	—	**1**	Evens^{1}	90++	26
	Opera King (USA) (SbinSuroor) **2-9-0** LDettori(3) (gd sort: bit bkwd: unruly s: cl up: chal over 2f out: r.o: nt pce of wnr)	2	**2**	3/1^{2}	85	21
	Trident (USA) (MRStoute) **2-9-0** DHarrison(7) (gd sort: trckd ldrs: rdn 2f out: n.m.r: r.o towards fin)	nk	**3**	11/1	85+	21
1839^{2}	**Outsourcing (USA)** (PFICole) **2-9-0** TQuinn(9) (trckd ldrs: led 3f out tl wl over 1f out: one pce)	3½	**4**	11/1	77	13
2057^{5}	**Saints Be Praised (USA)** (DRLoder) **2-9-0** MJKinane(5) (chsd ldrs: effrt over 2f out: wknd fnl f)	1¾	**5**	11/2^{3}	73	9
2018^{2}	**Bobbydazzle** (DrJDScargill) **2-8-6**$^{(3)}$ DGriffiths(10) (plld hrd: bhd: hdwy 2f out: hmpd over 1f out: nrst fin)	1¾	**6**	33/1	64	—
	Tensile (IRE) (LMCumani) **2-8-9**$^{(5)}$ RFfrench(2) (gd sort: neat: dwlt: hld up & bhd: outpcd 3f out: r.o wl fnl f)	hd	**7**	25/1	69+	5
2306^{5}	**Dance To The Beat** (MartynMeade) **2-8-9** FNorton(8) (lw: led 4f: grad wknd)	s.h	**8**	50/1	63	—
	Thrashing (CEBrittain) **2-9-0** WRyan(4) (cmpt: bit bkwd: chsd ldrs tl wknd 2f out)	1¼	**9**	33/1	66	2
	Dil (BHanbury) **2-9-0** JStack(1) (wl grwn: bkwd: plld hrd: bhd fr ½-wy)	½	**10**	25/1	64	—
				(SP 122.6%)	**10 Rn**	

1m 28.35 (3.35) CSF £3.68 TOTE £2.10: £1.50 £1.40 £2.30 (£3.00) Trio £12.10 OWNER Mr Hamdan Al Maktoum (ARUNDEL) BRED Shadwell Farm Inc
Haami (USA), a really nice sort, showed a terrific action going down and, given plenty to do, produced an enviable turn of foot to settle it. There would seem to be plenty more to come. (Evens)
Opera King (USA) was so unruly in the stalls that he managed to completely turn round and had to be taken out and reloaded and, in the

circumstances, ran a cracking race. If his temperament can be mastered, there is obviously better to come. (3/1: tchd 9/2)
Trident (USA), a useful type, showed plenty of promise and, by the way he was keeping on, it should not be long before he does better. (11/1: 6/1-12/1)
1839 Outsourcing (USA) put his experience to full use but he was again out-classed in the closing stages. A drop in class should help boost his confidence. (11/1: 8/1-12/1)
2057 Saints Be Praised (USA) came here with an obvious chance but proved disappointing in the closing stages. (11/2: 3/1-6/1)
2018 Bobbydazzle, upped in class, ran well without getting into it and is one to keep an eye on. (33/1)
Tensile (IRE), held up in this slowly-run event, then got completely outpaced just after halfway but he certainly caught the eye, finishing well. Better looks likely. (25/1)

2563 SOHAM H'CAP (0-80) (3-Y.O+) (Class D)

5-45 (5-47) **5f (July)** £5,390.00 (£1,610.00: £770.00: £350.00) Stalls: High GOING minus 0.40 sec per fur (F)

				SP	RR	SF
2529[7]	**Gone Savage (80)** (WJMusson) **9-10-0** RCochrane(17) (hdwy stands' side over 2f out: r.o u.p to ld last stride)	—	**1**	10/1	85	53
2221[5]	**Manolo (FR) (63)** (JBerry) **4-8-4b**(7) CLowther(13) (cl up stands' side: led wl over 1f out tl ct post)	s.h	**2**	16/1	68	36
1772[7]	**Literary Society (USA) (77)** (JARToller) **4-9-11** SSanders(12) (lw: racd stands' side: chsd ldrs: chal ins fnl f: r.o)	s.h	**3**	10/1	82	50
2393[3]	**Willow Dale (IRE) (77)** (DRCElsworth) **4-9-11** TQuinn(9) (b.nr hind: hdwy far side 2f out: hrd rdn & ev ch ins fnl f: kpt on)	½	**4**	14/1	80	48
2001*	**Royal Dome (IRE) (67)** (MartynWane) **5-9-1** KFallon(5) (cl up far side: rdn 2f out: kpt on u.p fnl f)	s.h	**5**	7/1[1]	70	38
2141[3]	**Silent Miracle (IRE) (75)** (MBell) **3-9-4** MFenton(4) (lw: racd far side: hdwy ½-wy: led 2f out tl ins fnl f)	s.h	**6**	12/1	78	41
1957[3]	**Ned's Bonanza (55)** (MDods) **8-8-3b**[1ow1] MRoberts(16) (bhd stands' side: hdwy 2f out: styd on towards fin)	¾	**7**	8/1[2]	55	22
2480[2]	**Rich Glow (53)** (NBycroft) **6-8-1** GCarter(14) (bhd stands' side: hdwy u.p 2f out: nvr rchd ldrs)	nk	**8**	11/1	52	20
1942[5]	**Sotonian (HOL) (48)** (PSFelgate) **4-7-5**(5) RFfrench(11) (disp ld stands' side 2f: ev ch tl btn appr fnl f)	hd	**9**	33/1	47	15
2406*	**Songsheet (68)** (MSSaunders) **4-9-2** JReid(6) (racd far side: rdn 2f out: styd on: n.d)	1¼	**10**	10/1	63	31
2162[9]	**Pageboy (67)** (PCHaslam) **8-9-1** JWeaver(8) (cl up far side tl outpcd over 1f out: kpt on ins fnl f)	s.h	**11**	20/1	62	30
2141[5]	**Levelled (71)** (MRChannon) **3-8-11**(3) PPMurphy(7) (racd far side: outpcd tl styd on appr fnl f)	hd	**12**	33/1	66	29
2339*	**Swan At Whalley (70)** (RAFahey) **5-8-11**(7) RWinston(10) (led stands' side over 3f: wknd)	1¼	**13**	9/1[3]	61	29
2377[3]	**Lunar Mist (73)** (MartynMeade) **4-9-0**(7) RBrisland(18) (racd stands' side: outpcd over 2f out: n.d after)	nk	**14**	12/1	63	31
2177[8]	**General Sir Peter (IRE) (57)** (NACallaghan) **5-8-0b**[1](5) AmandaSanders(15) (lw: outpcd & bhd stands' side: n.d)	s.h	**15**	33/1	47	15
2220[6]	**Ivory's Grab Hire (67)** (KTIvory) **4-8-12b**(3) MartinDwyer(2) (led far side 3f: wknd)	½	**16**	33/1	55	23
1119[3]	**At Large (IRE) (78)** (JRFanshawe) **3-9-7** DHarrison(1) (chsd ldrs far side: rdn & wknd 2f out)	4	**17**	12/1	53	16
	Awasha (IRE) (64) (KMahdi) **5-8-12** LDettori(3) (dwlt: racd far side: a bhd)	6	**18**	14/1	20	—
				(SP 128.0%)	**18 Rn**	

59.9 secs (1.40) CSF £143.50 CT £1,500.09 TOTE £11.70: £2.80 £3.80 £2.60 £3.10 (£91.40) Trio £606.90 OWNER The Square Table (NEWMARKET) BRED Mrs C. F. Van Straubenzee and R. Mead
LONG HANDICAP Sotonian (HOL) 7-4
WEIGHT FOR AGE 3yo-5lb

2529 Gone Savage came from off the pace as usual and produced a devastating late burst to win off his highest mark to date. (10/1)
2221 Manolo (FR) had the blinkers back on after racing without them last time and was back to his best here but, despite a valiant effort, was just touched off. (16/1)
1608* Literary Society (USA) ran his heart out and kept responding to pressure but could never quite find enough to make it. (10/1)
2393 Willow Dale (IRE) looks a real character and produced a terrific run on the far side but then she just failed to maintain it when it mattered. (14/1)
2001* Royal Dome (IRE) was off the bit someway out but, to give him credit, he kept responding to some very strong driving, albeit in vain. (7/1)
2141 Silent Miracle (IRE) showed a useful turn of foot just after halfway but then failed to maintain it late on. She seems to have more ability than she cares to show at times. (12/1)
1957 Ned's Bonanza was finishing well, suggesting that he is in good heart at present. (8/1)
2480 Rich Glow only got going when it was too late but does look on good terms with himself and, if he returns to Ayr, he is well worth keeping in mind. (11/1: 8/1-12/1)
253 Pageboy ran as though this trip is short of his best these days. (20/1)

T/Jkpt: £13,363.10 (4.16 Tckts). T/Plpt: £44.60 (1,077.86 Tckts). T/Qdpt: £10.40 (223.71 Tckts) Dk/AA

2356-PONTEFRACT (L-H) (Good)

Tuesday July 8th

WEATHER: warm and sunny WIND: almost nil becoming mod against

2564 HYDE SPORTING PROMOTIONS LADIES' H'CAP (0-60) (3-Y.O+) (Class F)

2-20 (2-22) **1m 2f 6y** £3,366.00 (£1,008.00: £484.00: £222.00) Stalls: Low GOING minus 0.42 sec per fur (F)

				SP	RR	SF
2362*	**Cashmirie (30)** (JLEyre) **5-9-5** MissDianaJones(11) (hld up: hdwy 5f out: led over 2f out: sn clr)	—	**1**	11/4[1]	44	32
2146[2]	**Benjamins Law (45)** (JAPickering) **6-9-13**(7) MissEGeorge(7) (chsd ldr: ev ch over 2f out: sn rdn: nt pce of wnr)	2½	**2**	16/1	55	43
1798[2]	**Bold Top (44)** (BSRothwell) **5-10-5be** MissAElsey(1) (dwlt: hdwy 4f out: styd on wl ins fnl f)	1¼	**3**	10/1	52	40
2386[4]	**Craigary (30)** (MrsASwinbank) **6-9-0**(5) MissJWormall(8) (hld up: hdwy 4f out: styd on appr fnl f)	½	**4**	33/1	37	25
2488[4]	**Maurangi (25)** (BWMurray) **6-8-11b**(3) MrsSBosley(3) (hld up: hdwy 3f out: styd on appr fnl f)	½	**5**	14/1	31	19
2344[2]	**Warm Spell (60)** (GLMoore) **7-11-4v**(3) MrsJMoore(9) (b: trckd ldrs: effrt wl over 2f out: wknd over 1f out)	5	**6**	11/1	58	46
1683[3]	**Essayeffsee (55)** (MrsMReveley) **8-10-9**(7) MissJEastwood(15) (lw: chsd ldrs over 6f: grad wknd)	1¾	**7**	9/1	51	39
2332*	**Jukebox Jive (57)** (HAkbary) **3-10-2**(5) MissIFoustok(16) (s.i.s: bhd tl sme late hdwy)	s.h	**8**	14/1	53	30
2430[4]	**Bellas Gate Boy (49)** (JPearce) **5-10-10** MrsLPearce(17) (s.s: bhd: drvn along 4f out: styd on fnl 2f)	¾	**9**	7/1[2]	43	31
1785[3]	**Sam Peeb (36)** (RAFahey) **3-8-9**(5) MissADeniel(6) (nvr bttr than mid div)	3½	**10**	16/1	25	2

1281[4]	**Teejay'n'aitch (IRE) (31)** (JSGoldie) **5-9-6**ow1 MissPRobson(13) (chsd ldrs tl wknd wl over 1f out)....2½	**11**	10/1	16	3
2039[10]	**Lila Pedigo (IRE) (51)** (MissJFCraze) **4-10-12** MissRClark(14) (bhd: effrt 4f out: no imp)....1	**12**	33/1	34	22
2502[6]	**Silent System (IRE) (35)** (DWChapman) **4-9-3**(7)ow10 MissHCuthbert(5) (chsd ldrs 7f: wknd qckly)....4	**13**	33/1	12	—
2152[8]	**Midday Cowboy (USA) (40)** (MDHammond) **4-10-1** MissEJohnsonHoughton(12) (lw: led tl over 2f out: wknd qckly: t.o)....6	**14**	50/1	7	—
2357[2]	**Digital Option (IRE) (42)** (MrsJRRamsden) **3-9-1**(5) MissERamsden(10) (swtg: hld up: effrt 3f out: wknd fnl 2f: t.o)....1¼	**15**	8/1[3]	7	—
	Hobbs Choice (45) (GMMoore) **4-10-1**(5) MrsCWilliams(18) (bkwd: a bhd: t.o)....1¾	**16**	50/1	8	—
			(SP 124.6%)	**16 Rn**	

2m 14.6 (5.00) CSF £45.75 CT £366.31 TOTE £3.50: £1.40 £3.20 £2.80 £6.40 (£46.30) Trio £370.10; £109.49 to Newmarket 9/7/97 OWNER Mr Ernest Spencer (HAMBLETON) BRED G. E. Peace
LONG HANDICAP Silent System (IRE) 8-11
WEIGHT FOR AGE 3yo-11lb

2362* Cashmirie, at home on all types of ground, followed up her recent win over course and distance with another comfortably-gained success, and proved a very popular winner to bring up the half-century for the very competent Diana Jones. (11/4)
2146 Benjamins Law has only ever won on the All-Weather but he ran a fine race here, if finding the winner much too good for him. (16/1)
1798 Bold Top is running well and, though he has been labelled, there is a race waiting to be picked up. (10/1)
2386 Craigary settled much better without the blinkers but, over this shorter trip, could not muster the pace to mount a challenge, despite staying on strongly nearing the finish. (33/1)
2488 Maurangi crept closer on the approach to the straight and kept plugging on, but he is unproven over this trip and lacked anything like the speed to pose a threat. (14/1)
2344 Warm Spell could have found this race coming plenty soon enough but, with neither the ground or the trip in his favour, he probably performed as well as could be expected. (11/1)

2565 DIANNE NURSERY H'CAP (2-Y.O) (Class E)

2-50 (2-52) **6f** £3,535.00 (£1,060.00: £510.00: £235.00) Stalls: Low GOING minus 0.42 sec per fur (F)

			SP	RR	SF
1927[3]	**Composition** (MAJarvis) **2-9-3** FLynch(6) (hld up: hdwy over 2f out: swtchd rt & r.o strly to ld nr fin)....—	**1**	5/1[2]	83	22
2243[2]	**Legs Be Frendly (IRE)** (KMcAuliffe) **2-9-7** JFEgan(2) (a.p: led 3f out: clr over 1f out: rdn & ct cl home)....¾	**2**	7/1	85	24
2037[8]	**Jacobina** (TDBarron) **2-8-8** KDarley(10) (b.hind: swtg: outpcd & pushed along tl styd on appr fnl f)....2½	**3**	14/1	65	4
2288[2]	**Erro Codigo** (MrsJRRamsden) **2-8-9** AMunro(1) (w ldrs: swtchd rt over 2f out: kpt on one pce: fin 4th, 1l: disq: plcd last)....	**4d**	4/1[1]	64	—
1806[5]	**Mari-Ela (IRE)** (JRArnold) **2-8-5** JQuinn(3) (outpcd tl styd on fnl 2f: fin 5th, 1l & s.h: plcd 4th)....1	**4**	16/1	60	1
2191*	**Heavenly Falls (IRE)** (CADwyer) **2-8-4** NVarley(4) (nvr nrr: fin 6th, 2l: plcd 5th)....2	**5**	11/1	53	—
2031[3]	**Mighty Sure (IRE)** (MWEasterby) **2-8-3**(3) GParkin(5) (led to ½-wy: rdn whn hmpd 2f out: fin 7th, 1½l: plcd 6th)....1½	**6**	8/1	51	—
1959[6]	**Impulse (IRE)** (APJarvis) **2-8-6**(7) CCarver(7) (swtg: swvd lft s: bhd tl sme hdwy fnl 2f: fin 8th, s.h: plcd 7th) s.h	**7**	20/1	62	—
2165[4]	**Blue Anchor** (MrsMReveley) **2-7-13** DaleGibson(9) (sn outpcd: a bhd: fin 9th, 3½l: plcd 8th)....3½	**8**	11/1	35	—
1990[2]	**Carambo** (JLEyre) **2-8-13** RLappin(12) (lw: chsd ldrs: wkng whn hmpd 2f out: fin 10th, 4l: plcd 9th)....4	**9**	13/2[3]	38	—
2312[6]	**Positive Air** (BAMcMahon) **2-8-7** GDuffield(11) (chsd ldrs over 3f: fin 11th, 5l: plcd 10th)....5	**10**	16/1	19	—
1616[9]	**Five of Spades (IRE)** (RAFahey) **2-8-12** ACulhane(14) (chsd ldrs: wkng whn hmpd 2f out: sn t.o: fin 12th, 6l: plcd 11th)....6	**11**	9/1	8	—
1797[3]	**Snappy Times** (MDods) **2-8-11** AClark(8) (b.nr hind: s.i.s: a bhd: t.o: fin 13th, 2l: plcd 12th)....2	**12**	33/1	1	—
			(SP 126.4%)	**13 Rn**	

1m 18.5 (3.50) CSF £38.77 CT £449.19 TOTE £5.70: £2.00 £1.90 £6.00 (£11.50) Trio £269.90 OWNER Mr Saeed Manana (NEWMARKET) BRED R. Burton
STEWARDS' ENQUIRY Munro susp. 17-19 & 21-22/7/97 (irresponsible riding)

1927 Composition found this stiff six furlongs ideal and, though she had to search for an opening, when it did come she produced all that was required and won going away. She will be even better when tackling seven furlongs or more. (5/1)
2243 Legs Be Frendly (IRE) gave the impression cantering to post that he was feeling the ground, but he ran up to his mark on the return journey and he has not run a bad race yet. (7/1)
1669 Jacobina, having her first run beyond the minimum trip, took a lot of driving to find top gear but she weaved her way through promisingly in the closing stages, and is grasping what is required. (14/1)
1806 Mari-Ela (IRE), making progress from off the pace, was still galloping on at the finish and she should find her way now that she is trying slightly longer trips. (16/1)
2191* Heavenly Falls (IRE) had much more to do than when successful in a seller last time and his final placing was as close as he could manage. (11/1)
2288 Erro Codigo, in the firing line from the break, caused problems when switched right entering the straight and, though he stayed on to finish fourth, he was disqualified and placed last after a Stewards' enquiry. (4/1)

2566 BRADLEY MAIDEN STKS (3-Y.O+) (Class D)

3-25 (3-29) **1m 2f 6y** £3,647.50 (£1,105.00: £540.00: £257.50) Stalls: Low GOING minus 0.42 sec per fur (F)

			SP	RR	SF
1866[2]	**Song of Freedom** (JHMGosden) **3-8-10** GHind(7) (chsd ldrs: swtchd rt over 1f out: led ins fnl f: r.o)....—	**1**	11/2[3]	88	45
2156[2]	**Dantesque (IRE) (82)** (GWragg) **4-9-7** AClark(13) (hld up in tch: effrt over 2f out: unable qckn ins fnl f)....1¼	**2**	5/1[2]	86	54
	Ghillies Ball (RCharlton) **3-8-10** TSprake(10) (rangy: sn pushed along: hdwy ½-wy: styd on wl ins fnl f)....2½	**3**	16/1	82	39
1846[7]	**Zerpour (IRE)** (LMCumani) **3-8-3**(7) DYoung(3) (hld up: stdy hdwy over 2f out: styd on wl fnl f)....nk	**4**	25/1	82+	39
2008[4]	**Bright Heritage (IRE) (90)** (DRLoder) **4-9-7** KDarley(9) (plld hrd: trckd ldrs: led over 2f out tl ins fnl f)....1¼	**5**	9/4[1]	80	48
	Midnight Watch (USA) (HRACecil) **3-8-10** AMcGlone(5) (unruly s: trckd ldrs tl wknd ins fnl f)....nk	**6**	5/1[2]	79	36
	J B Quick (PWChapple-Hyam) **3-8-7**(3) RHavlin(4) (wl grwn: bkwd: prom tl outpcd over 2f out)....2	**7**	13/2	76	33
	Stormy Story (USA) (JHMGosden) **3-8-10** GDuffield(12) (w'like: str: bkwd: bhd: drvn along 3f out: no imp)....4	**8**	25/1	70	27
1936[2]	**Russian Ruler (IRE) (86)** (APJarvis) **3-8-10** SDrowne(11) (led tl hdd & wknd 2f out)....hd	**9**	8/1	69	26
2126[8]	**Bogan (IRE)** (LordHuntingdon) **3-8-10** AMunro(8) (outpcd fr ½-wy)....¾	**10**	50/1	68	25
2046[8]	**Sefton Blake** (MGMeagher) **3-8-10** DaleGibson(2) (plld hrd: hld up: a bhd)....4	**11**	50/1	62	19
2360[3]	**Understudy** (RHollinshead) **3-8-5** FLynch(6) (hdwy ½-wy: drvn along 3f out: sn lost pl)....7	**12**	20/1	46	3

2172^{8}	**Kailey Goddess (USA)** (RWArmstrong) **4-9-7** JQuinn(1) (hld up: a bhd)	¾	**13**	33/1	49	17

(SP 129.1%) **13 Rn**

2m 11.7 (2.10) CSF £30.60 TOTE £5.90: £2.20 £1.70 £4.30 (£9.00) Trio £104.30 OWNER Sheikh Mohammed (NEWMARKET) BRED Sheikh Mohammed Bin Rashid Al Maktoum

WEIGHT FOR AGE 3yo-11lb

OFFICIAL EXPLANATION **Zerpour (IRE): the stewards enquired into the running of Zerpour. The jockey stated that his instructions were to settle the colt in third or fourth in the early stages and produce him with an effort from about three furlongs out. But the colt was slowly away and, taken back by other horses early on, he was unable to maintain the position he wanted. The colt did however pick up well and make up some ground after turning for home.**

1866 Song of Freedom, pulled wide to deliver his challenge, lengthened up to gain command two hundred yards out and, once in front, there was only gong to be one winner. (11/2: 7/2-6/1)

2156 Dantesque (IRE) should have been ideally suited by this step up to ten furlongs, but he was short of the necessary speed when the battle to the line developed. He was far from fluent with his action to post. (5/1: 7/2-11/2)

Ghillies Ball, a gelded half-brother to two winners who looked sure to benefit from the run, was really finding his stride in the closing stages and he should have little trouble winning races. (16/1)

1846 Zerpour (IRE), given a very patient ride over this slightly shorter trip, was staying on steadily once in line for home and he is getting to understand what it is all about. (25/1)

2008 Bright Heritage (IRE) looked to be well in control when leading the charge into the straight but, as so often in these all-aged events, the youngsters with the advantage of a weight allowance had his measure in the dash to the line. (9/4)

Midnight Watch (USA) has not really done well since last year and he still looks more like a filly than a colt. However, he did look well tuned up and remained in the action until fading inside the final furlong. (5/1: 3/1-6/1)

J B Quick, a strongly-made colt, far from fully wound up, pushed the pace until feeling the strain and calling enough once in line for home. (13/2)

2567 ST. GILES H'CAP (0-80) (3-Y.O+) (Class D)

3-55 (3-59) **6f** £5,572.00 (£1,666.00: £798.00: £364.00) Stalls: Low GOING minus 0.42 sec per fur (F)

				SP	RR	SF
1799^{7}	**Cim Bom Bom (IRE) (71)** (MBell) **5-9-3v**$^{(5)}$ GFaulkner(4) (lw: a.p: led over 2f out: sn qcknd clr: comf)	—	**1**	4/1^{2}	81	57
2497*	**Bowlers Boy (73)** (JJQuinn) **4-9-7**$^{(3)}$ ^{7x} GParkin(9) (a.p: rdn & kpt on fnl f: no ch w wnr)	4	**2**	6/1^{3}	72	48
1170^{17}	**Colway Ritz (75)** (JWWatts) **3-9-6** GDuffield(7) (a chsng ldrs: rdn & kpt on ins fnl f)	½	**3**	33/1	73	43
*2162**	**The Happy Fox (IRE) (74)** (BAMcMahon) **5-9-4b**$^{(7)}$ SRighton(1) (led tl over 2f out: sn rdn: one pce)	½	**4**	9/1	71	47
2019^{11}	**Ochos Rios (IRE) (57)** (BSRothwell) **6-8-8** FLynch(6) (hdwy over 2f out: kpt on wl ins fnl f)	½	**5**	20/1	52	28
2384*	**Souperficial (52)** (NTinkler) **6-8-3v** ^{7x} KimTinkler(3) (s.i.s: hdwy 2f out: r.o wl appr fnl f)	2½	**6**	8/1	41	17
2358^{4}	**Formidable Liz (50)** (MDHammond) **7-8-1** JQuinn(2) (trckd ldrs tl wknd appr fnl f)	½	**7**	14/1	37	13
2358^{2}	**Fame Again (64)** (MrsJRRamsden) **5-9-1** AMunro(11) (lw: hld up: hdwy over 2f out: nvr nr to chal)	2½	**8**	3/1^{1}	45	21
2216^{10}	**Hard to Figure (75)** (RJHodges) **11-9-12** SDrowne(13) (bhd: sme hdwy appr fnl f: nvr nrr)	nk	**9**	20/1	55	31
2162^{11}	**Prima Silk (72)** (MJRyan) **6-9-9** AClark(12) (a bhd & outpcd)	6	**10**	12/1	36	12
2141^{6}	**Martine (67)** (ABailey) **3-8-12** DWright(14) (a bhd)	2½	**11**	33/1	24	—
610^{8}	**Lunch Party (49)** (DNicholls) **5-8-0** DaleGibson(10) (chsd ldrs over 3f)	1¼	**12**	33/1	3	—
2422^{8}	**Maiteamia (72)** (SRBowring) **4-9-9b** SWebster(5) (b.off hind: trckd ldrs tl wknd 2f out)	nk	**13**	14/1	25	1
1754^{4}	**Zain Dancer (46)** (DNicholls) **5-7-11**^{ow1} NKennedy(8) (swtg: sn pushed along: a outpcd)	hd	**14**	20/1	—	—
*2305**	**Desert Invader (IRE) (45)** (DWChapman) **6-7-7**$^{(3)}$ MBaird(15) (racd wd: bhd fr ½-wy: t.o)	7	**15**	16/1	—	—

(SP 130.4%) **15 Rn**

1m 16.1 (1.10) CSF £25.31 CT £656.65 TOTE £6.60: £3.40 £2.30 £8.80 (£28.80) Trio £348.90 OWNER Mr Yucel Birol (NEWMARKET) BRED Tarworth Bloodstock Investments Ltd and J.J. Melk

WEIGHT FOR AGE 3yo-6lb

1799 Cim Bom Bom (IRE), content to be given a lead until past halfway, quickened away impressively once given his head and the contest was soon as good as over. He is becoming something of a course specialist round here. (4/1: op 6/1)

2497* Bowlers Boy, another who shines at this track, was fighting a lost cause from the turn into the straight but he kept battling away and will find easier opportunities. (6/1)

792 Colway Ritz still having trouble finding a correct trip, turned in his best display yet and a repeat could see him getting off the mark. (33/1)

2162* The Happy Fox (IRE), taken to post fairly steadily, soon had the majority of his rivals in trouble by setting a very strong pace, but this played into the hands of the winner and he was left grasping at straws once that rival set sail for home. (9/1)

1020 Ochos Rios (IRE) has not won at this trip since his two-year-old days and does the majority of his racing at longer trips now, but he showed here that he retains plenty of ability on his day. (20/1)

2384* Souperficial was far from disgraced on this step up in class but was unable to get close enough to cause concern. (8/1)

2358 Formidable Liz is usually at her best at this time of year and this pleasing effort would suggest she is approaching her peak. (14/1)

2358 Fame Again has trouble finding the speed to win at this trip when the ground rides so lively and, in this instance, she was always at full stretch in an attempt to keep tabs on the principals. (3/1)

2568 TANSHELF MAIDEN STKS (3-Y.O+) (Class D)

4-25 (4-27) **1m 4f 8y** £3,615.00 (£1,095.00: £535.00: £255.00) Stalls: Low GOING minus 0.42 sec per fur (F)

				SP	RR	SF
2046^{4}	**Machiavelli (85)** (HRACecil) **3-8-8** AMcGlone(4) (a.p: led over 1f out: rdn & hld on towards fin)	—	**1**	9/2^{3}	93	38
1868^{2}	**Nightlark (IRE) (83)** (DRLoder) **3-8-3** KDarley(2) (lw: trckd ldrs: n.m.r over 2f out: styd on u.p towards fin)	hd	**2**	11/8^{1}	88	33
2311^{2}	**Royal Crown (IRE) (85)** (PWChapple-Hyam) **3-8-5**$^{(3)}$ RHavlin(3) (sn pushed along in tch: styd on one pce fnl 2f)	3	**3**	7/2^{2}	89	34
2126^{6}	**Legendary Lover (IRE) (82)** (RCharlton) **3-8-8** TSprake(10) (trckd ldr: led over 2f out tl over 1f out: wknd fnl f)	3½	**4**	9/1	84	29
2008^{14}	**Rufalda (IRE)** (LMCumani) **3-7-10**$^{(7)}$ DYoung(9) (hld up & bhd: hdwy over 2f out: styd on)	2	**5**	25/1	77	22
2360^{4}	**Passionelle** (BWHills) **3-8-3** AClark(11) (wnt prom ½-wy: sn pushed along: wknd 3f out)	12	**6**	14/1	61	6
2410^{3}	**Capsoff (IRE)** (GAHubbard) **4-8-13**$^{(3)}$ DO'Donohoe(5) (led tl hdd over 2f out: sn rdn & btn)	1½	**7**	16/1	59	17
1239^{5}	**Rear Window** (LordHuntingdon) **3-8-8** AMunro(6) (sn drvn along: lost pl 7f out: t.o)	15	**8**	20/1	44	—
2116^{2}	**Viburnum** (AGFoster) **3-8-3** GDuffield(7) (swtg: racd keenly: trckd ldrs over 4f: sn wknd: t.o)	¾	**9**	14/1	38	—
1939^{8}	**Spare My Blushes** (BAMcMahon) **3-8-3** LNewton(1) (a wl bhd: t.o)	hd	**10**	100/1	38	—
	Meadow Blue (40) (MissLCSiddall) **4-8-9**$^{(7)}$ TSiddall(8) (swtg: hld up: outpcd fnl 5f: t.o)	2	**11**	66/1	35	—

(SP 122.8%) **11 Rn**

2m 37.6 (3.30) CSF £10.27 TOTE £5.00: £1.70 £1.10 £1.60 (£4.70) Trio £5.40 OWNER H R H Prince Fahd Salman (NEWMARKET) BRED Coral's Farm and Stud

WEIGHT FOR AGE 3yo-13lb
2046 Machiavelli kicked for home below the distance but the filly proved a thorn in his side inside the final furlong, and he needed to pull out all the stops to hold her at bay. (9/2)
1868 Nightlark (IRE) is finding it increasingly difficult to get winning brackets by her name and she did not enjoy the smoothest of passages entering the straight, but she was only half a stride down at the line and fortune must favour her before long. (11/8: 2/1-5/4)
2311 Royal Crown (IRE) looks to be quite a hard ride and, off the bridle most of the way, never really threatened to quicken up enough to trouble the principals. (7/2: 5/2-4/1)
2126 Legendary Lover (IRE), attempting a longer trip, is a heavy-topped colt who hits the ground hard and, as such, he is almost sure to need more yielding ground and was well out-paced after losing the lead below the distance. (9/1)
1556a Rufalda (IRE), much better suited by this stiffer test of stamina, showed her first glimpse of form and she could be coming to herself. (25/1)
2360 Passionelle did not fare badly on her debut on soft ground, but conditions were not in her favour this time and she had become detached before reaching the home straight. (14/1: op 8/1)

2569 KING RICHARD III H'CAP (0-70) (3-Y.O+ F & M) (Class E)

5-00 (5-01) **1m 4y** £3,353.00 (£1,004.00: £482.00: £221.00) Stalls: Low GOING minus 0.42 sec per fur (F)

			SP	RR	SF
2145[12]	**Mcgillycuddy Reeks (IRE) (38)** (DonEnricoIncisa) **6-7-12** KimTinkler(3) (hld up: hdwy 4f out: led appr fnl f: sn clr) ....—	**1**	20/1	51	18
2317*	**Al Reet (IRE) (53)** (SRBowring) **6-8-13** DeanMcKeown(4) (chsd ldrs: hrd rdn & nt qckn appr fnl f) 3½	**2**	13/2	59	26
1994[6]	**Broughton's Pride (IRE) (52)** (JLEyre) **6-8-5**(7) SBuckley(2) (a chsng ldrs: ev ch over 1f out: one pce ins fnl f) 1¼	**3**	14/1	56	23
2408*	**Polish Rhythm (IRE) (66)** (GAHubbard) **4-9-9**(3) 6x DO'Donohoe(6) (chsd ldr: ev ch over 1f out: no ex nr fin) hd	**4**	5/1 [2]	69	36
1971*	**Double Gold (64)** (MBell) **3-9-1** AMunro(13) (led tl over 1f out: wknd nr fin) 4	**5**	13/2	59	17
2183[8]	**Russian Olive (67)** (LMCumani) **3-9-4** KDarley(8) (hld up: hdwy over 3f out: sn pushed along: nt rch ldrs)....s.h	**6**	4/1 [1]	62	20
1998[3]	**Silent Valley (46)** (MissLCSiddall) **3-7-8**(3) DarrenMoffatt(11) (s.i.s: bhd tl styd on appr fnl f) 2½	**7**	20/1	36	—
2171[2]	**Cimmerian (50)** (MESowersby) **3-7-10**(5) KSked(7) (a bhd) ....nk	**8**	10/1	40	—
2177[18]	**Badger Bay (IRE) (53)** (CADwyer) **4-8-13** NVarley(9) (in tch: drvn along over 3f out: wknd wl over 1f out) 1½	**9**	33/1	40	7
	Catwalk Girl (38) (RAFahey) **4-7-12** DWright(1) (b: bkwd: trckd ldrs 5f: sn outpcd) ....½	**10**	20/1	24	—
2209[3]	**Whittle Rock (68)** (MrsMReveley) **4-10-0** ACulhane(5) (lw: stdd s: effrt over 3f out: eased whn btn appr fnl f).½	**11**	6/1 [3]	53	20
1818[7]	**White Hare (47)** (MrsMReveley) **4-8-7** DaleGibson(12) (bhd & drvn along fr ½-wy: t.o) 11	**12**	14/1	10	—
2468[7]	**Shotley Princess (46)** (NBycroft) **3-7-11**ow1 NKennedy(10) (swtg: a bhd: t.o) 23	**13**	100/1	—	—
			(SP 118.3%)		**13 Rn**

1m 45.7 (3.30) CSF £124.27 CT £1,146.12 TOTE £17.20: £4.50 £2.10 £2.90 (£67.80) Trio £438.30; £246.97 to Newmarket 9/7/97 OWNER Don Enrico Incisa (MIDDLEHAM) BRED Noel Sweeney
LONG HANDICAP Shotley Princess 6-9
WEIGHT FOR AGE 3yo-9lb
1818 Mcgillycuddy Reeks (IRE) has been running well enough to win a race of this description and, swooping into the lead approaching the final furlong, very quickly put the issue beyond doubt. (20/1)
2317* Al Reet (IRE) has not, as yet, won beyond seven furlongs and she also needs more cut in the ground than she had here, so this effort was probably better than it seems. (13/2)
1442 Broughton's Pride (IRE), challenging for the lead when the winner beat her to the punch, could do little more than stay on at the one pace. (14/1)
2408* Polish Rhythm (IRE), fighting for the lead from the break, may have shown in front briefly approaching the final furlong but her penalty was beginning to take its toll and she had given her all nearing the line. (5/1)
1971* Double Gold, a confirmed front-runner who has been winning over ten furlongs this season, forced the pace until the winner went by and than found herself tapped for toe. (13/2)
2183 Russian Olive had it all to do taking on handicappers for the first time and her attempt to get herself into the action approaching the straight came to little. (4/1)

2570 MONKHILL LIMITED STKS (0-70) (3-Y.O+) (Class E)

5-30 (5-31) **1m 2f 6y** £2,788.00 (£844.00: £412.00: £196.00) Stalls: Low GOING minus 0.42 sec per fur (F)

			SP	RR	SF
2065[3]	**Florentino (IRE) (67)** (BWHills) **4-9-7** AMunro(2) (b: hld up in tch: rdn to ld over 1f out: r.o wl) ....—	**1**	11/4 [3]	80	42
2117[5]	**Nichol Fifty (70)** (MHTompkins) **3-8-10** DBiggs(7) (chsd ldrs: led 2f out: sn hdd: rdn & unable qckn fnl f)......1½	**2**	5/2 [2]	78	29
2118[7]	**Hardy Dancer (69)** (GLMoore) **5-9-7v1** AClark(4) (trckd ldrs: pushed along over 2f out: outpcd appr fnl f) 4	**3**	12/1	71	33
1845[4]	**Smart Spirit (IRE) (68)** (MrsMReveley) **3-8-7** ACulhane(6) (hld up: effrt & nt clr run 2f out: nvr able chal) 3½	**4**	2/1 [1]	63	14
2291[5]	**Gee Bee Boy (69)** (APJarvis) **3-8-12** KDarley(3) (led to 2f out: sn rdn & outpcd) ....½	**5**	8/1	67	18
2187[8]	**Michael Venture (67)** (SPCWoods) **3-8-10** WJO'Connor(5) (w ldr: rdn 2f out: sn wknd) 6	**6**	25/1	55	6
219[4]	**Maradata (IRE) (63)** (RHollinshead) **5-9-4** FLynch(1) (s.s: hld up in rr: effrt on outside over 2f out: no imp) ...1½	**7**	25/1	50	12
			(SP 115.1%)		**7 Rn**

2m 13.5 (3.90) CSF £9.31 TOTE £3.20: £1.60 £2.30 (£5.10) OWNER Lady Harrison (LAMBOURN) BRED Fluorocarbon Bloodstock
WEIGHT FOR AGE 3yo-11lb
2065 Florentino (IRE), not winning out of turn, worked hard to lead below the distance and, even then, had to find extra to keep his head in front to the finish. (11/4)
2117 Nichol Fifty is very lightly-raced and, in performing so well here, gave notice that he has the ability to pay his way. (5/2)
521 Hardy Dancer, waiting on the leaders in his first-time visor, was being made to work turning in and did not possess the speed to mount a challenge. (12/1: op 7/1)
1845 Smart Spirit (IRE) should have been thereabouts but she found trouble in running, even in this small field, and was never able to deliver a challenge. (2/1)
2291 Gee Bee Boy, forced to adopt more forceful tactics on this step down in trip, did not have a lot more to give once headed and had shot his bolt below the distance. (8/1)

T/Plpt: £186.80 (109.3 Tckts). T/Qdpt: £24.00 (50.43 Tckts) IM

2388-EPSOM (L-H) (Good to soft, Soft patches, becoming Good to soft)
Wednesday July 9th
WEATHER: fine WIND: almost nil

2571 E.B.F. LORD'S TAVERNERS CHARITY MEDIAN AUCTION MAIDEN STKS (2-Y.O) (Class E)
6-30 (6-31) **6f** £3,322.50 (£1,005.00: £490.00: £232.50) Stalls: High GOING: 0.10 sec per fur (G)

			SP	RR	SF
1557[2] **Lend A Hand** (MJohnston) **2-9-0** JWeaver(5) (lw: hdwy 2f out: r.o to ld last strides)	—	**1**	2/1 [1]	75	40
2349[2] **Bernardo Bellotto (IRE)** (MBell) **2-9-0** TQuinn(7) (led: hrd rdn fnl f: hdd last strides)	nk	**2**	9/4 [2]	74	39
2388[3] **American Cousin** (BJMeehan) **2-9-0** MTebbutt(3) (a.p: r.o one pce fnl 2f)	6	**3**	10/1	58	23
1812[5] **Coolin River (IRE)** (KRBurke) **2-9-0** JFEgan(9) (a.p: hmpd over 3f out: ev ch over 1f out: wknd fnl f)	4	**4**	8/1	48	13
Lilanita (BPalling) **2-8-9** TSprake(2) (neat: s.s: sn prom: rdn & wknd over 1f out)	½	**5**	20/1	41	6
2007[5] **Pianist (IRE)** (GLewis) **2-9-0** AClark(1) (nvr nr to chal)	hd	**6**	33/1	46	11
1235[3] **Ron's Pet** (RHannon) **2-9-0** DaneO'Neill(6) (a bhd)	2½	**7**	4/1 [3]	39	4
Ok John (IRE) (JAkehurst) **2-9-0** SSanders(4) (w'like: chsd ldr tl rn wd & jumped path over 3f out: nt rcvr)	8	**8**	11/1	18	—
2181[22] **Ready Fontaine** (JNeville) **2-9-0** AMcGlone(8) (outpcd: a wl bhd)	12	**9**	33/1	—	—

(SP 123.3%) **9 Rn**

1m 12.55 (4.55) CSF £6.50 TOTE £2.70: £1.30 £1.30 £2.90 (£2.20) Trio £10.40 OWNER Maktoum Al Maktoum (MIDDLEHAM) BRED Gainsborough Stud Management Ltd

OFFICIAL EXPLANATION Ron's Pet: unsuited by the track.

1557 Lend A Hand was not the fastest away nor did he enjoy the clearest of runs but the gap appeared when it mattered most and he quickened to snatch the race in the final strides. A more galloping course would probably suit him better. (2/1: op evens)

2349 Bernardo Bellotto (IRE) made the running and appeared to be in control at the two-furlong marker. Hard ridden in the final furlong, he could not quite hold the winner. (9/4)

2388 American Cousin chased the leaders and ran on at one pace in the final quarter-mile. (10/1: 7/1-11/1)

1812 Coolin River (IRE) was hampered as one of his rivals made for the stands' rails over three furlongs from home but he remained in contention until weakening in the final furlong. (8/1: 5/1-9/1)

Lilanita, a sharp sort, missed the break but showed the pace to go up with the leaders after one hundred yards. She weakened under pressure approaching the final furlong but should be able to win a race. (20/1)

Ok John (IRE) raced in second place. His rider was bringing him wide when he tried to jump a path over three furlongs from home and lost all impetus. (11/1: 10/1-16/1)

2572 PHILIPS LIGHTING MAIDEN STKS (3-Y.O) (Class D)
7-00 (7-02) **1m 4f 10y** £3,485.00 (£1,055.00: £515.00: £245.00) Stalls: Centre GOING: 0.10 sec per fur (G)

			SP	RR	SF
2058[2] **Taunt (91)** (DMorley) **3-9-0** PatEddery(3) (a gng wl: led on bit over 1f out: v.easily)	—	**1**	1/10 [1]	85+	38
1088[7] **Such Boldness** (RAkehurst) **3-9-0** SSanders(4) (led tl over 1f out: no ch w wnr)	4	**2**	33/1 [3]	80	33
725[15] **Darien** (RCharlton) **3-9-0** TSprake(2) (pushed along in rr: one pce fnl 3f)	4	**3**	14/1 [2]	74	27
2046[11] **Doubly Sharp (USA)** (MJohnston) **3-9-0** JWeaver(5) (chsd ldrs: rdn 5f out: wknd 3f out: t.o)	17	**4**	14/1 [2]	52	5

(SP 107.2%) **4 Rn**

2m 44.95 (10.45) CSF £5.07 TOTE £1.10: (£3.40) OWNER Lord Hartington (NEWMARKET) BRED Side Hill Stud

2058 Taunt, cruising over this poor opposition throughout, led on the bridle approaching the final furlong and won with any amount in hand. (1/10)

Such Boldness tried to make all the running but, though easily second best, had no chance with the winner. (33/1)

Darien was being pushed along at the back of the field for most of the way and, though he made some headway in the straight, he was never on terms. (14/1)

Doubly Sharp (USA) began to feel the strain fully five furlongs from home and was well in rear in the straight. (14/1: op 5/1)

2573 ANDREX H'CAP (0-70) (3-Y.O+) (Class E)
7-30 (7-37) **7f** £3,761.25 (£1,140.00: £557.50: £266.25) Stalls: Low GOING: 0.10 sec per fur (G)

			SP	RR	SF
2204[2] **Mr Cube (IRE) (49)** (JMBradley) **7-8-2b**(7) CLowther(6) (hld up: nt clr run over 2f out: led over 1f out: sn clr)	—	**1**	6/1	65	38
2282[3] **Sea Danzig (57)** (JJBridger) **4-9-3** DHarrison(5) (w ldr: led over 2f out tl over 1f out)	4	**2**	11/2 [3]	64	37
2237* **Roseate Lodge (36)** (SEKettlewell) **11-7-3**(7) JennyBenson(10) (hld up in rr: gd hdwy fnl 2f: nrst fin)	2	**3**	12/1	38	11
1972[9] **Balance of Power (56)** (SDow) **5-9-2** SSanders(1) (hdwy 2f out: one pce fnl f)	nk	**4**	8/1	58	31
2121[2] **La Chatelaine (44)** (GLewis) **3-7-7**(3) PFessey(3) (bhd tl effrt on ins & nt clr run over 2f out: fin wl)	nk	**5**	5/1 [2]	45	10
2216[2] **Twin Creeks (63)** (VSoane) **6-9-9** CRutter(13) (chsd ldrs: rdn over 1f out: nt qckn)	¾	**6**	11/2 [3]	62	35
2281[11] **Supreme Maimoon (53)** (MJPolglase) **3-8-5** TGMcLaughlin(11) (prom tl wknd over 1f out)	3	**7**	15/2	45	10
2282[8] **Abtaal (52)** (RJHodges) **7-8-7**(5) AmandaSanders(12) (bhd tl sme hdwy over 2f out: sn wknd)	4	**8**	16/1	35	8
1985[6] **Hannalou (FR) (50)** (TGMills) **4-8-10** TQuinn(4) (led tl wknd over 2f out)	½	**9**	12/1	32	5
2144[13] **Greatest (60)** (MissGayKelleway) **6-9-6b** DHolland(15) (w ldrs tl wknd 2f out)	½	**10**	12/1	41	14
1167[15] **Cheval Roc (56)** (RHannon) **3-8-8** DaneO'Neill(9) (prom tl wknd 2f out)	3	**11**	16/1	30	—
*2179[12] **Rififi (64)** (RIngram) **4-9-10** PatEddery(2) (Withdrawn not under Starter's orders: veterinary advice)*		**W**	4/1 [1]	—	—

(SP 139.4%) **11 Rn**

1m 25.48 (5.18) CSF £30.12 CT £200.24 TOTE £4.90: £1.60 £1.90 £3.80 (£11.30) Trio £83.80 OWNER Mr R. Miles (CHEPSTOW) BRED Lyonstown Stud

WEIGHT FOR AGE 3yo-8lb

2204 Mr Cube (IRE) overcame difficulties, being denied a clear run more than once in the straight. However, he quickened to strike the front approaching the final furlong and quickly raced clear. (6/1)

2282 Sea Danzig disputed the lead until gaining a slight advantage over two furlongs from home. He was quickly outpaced at the distance but kept on well for second. (11/2: 4/1-13/2)

2237* Roseate Lodge was in last place for much of the way but came bursting through the middle of the pack to snatch third on the line. (12/1)

639 Balance of Power came from the back of the field to try to challenge approaching the final furlong but, though staying on, he could not reach the leaders. (8/1: op 12/1)

2121 La Chatelaine, at the back of the field on the inside from the start, had a dreadful run in the straight and in the circumstances did well to reach her final position. (5/1)

2216 Twin Creeks probably found the overnight rain against him and, though he was close enough on the outside in the home straight, he failed to quicken. (11/2: 4/1-6/1)
403 Greatest (12/1: 8/1-14/1)

2574 EVENING STANDARD H'CAP (0-90) (3-Y.O+) (Class C)

8-00 (8-06) **1m 2f 18y** £5,408.75 (£1,640.00: £802.50: £383.75) Stalls: Low GOING: 0.10 sec per fur (G)

				SP	RR	SF
2318^{2}	**Rising Dough (IRE) (65)** (GLMoore) **5-8-4** AClark(12) (hdwy on ins 2f out: nt clr run over 1f out & ins fnl f: qcknd to ld last strides)	—	**1**	7/1	76	46
2190*	**Hachiyah (IRE) (87)** (DMorley) **3-9-1** RHills(11) (a.p: led over 2f out tl fnl strides)	nk	**2**	3/1^{1}	98	57
2296^{3}	**Traceability (72)** (SCWilliams) **4-8-11** JReid(9) (a.p: ev ch 1f out: nt qckn)	1½	**3**	5/1^{2}	80	50
2120*	**Vola Via (USA) (83)** (IABalding) **4-9-5**$^{(3)}$ MartinDwyer(8) (hdwy 5f out: ev ch 2f out: nt qckn)	s.h	**4**	6/1^{3}	91	61
1951*	**Brighstone (89)** (MCPipe) **4-10-0** AMcGlone(4) (lw: chsd ldr: led over 4f out tl over 2f out: wknd fnl f)	8	**5**	14/1	84	54
2341^{7}	**Edan Heights (76)** (SDow) **5-9-1** SSanders(3) (in rr tl hdwy over 2f out: nvr nr to chal)	2½	**6**	12/1	67	37
2230^{6}	**Tom Tailor (GER) (80)** (DRCElsworth) **3-8-3**$^{(5)}$ RMullen(1) (prom tl rdn & wknd over 3f out)	1¼	**7**	10/1	69	28
2230^{7}	**Northern Sun (84)** (TGMills) **3-8-12** TQuinn(7) (a bhd)	2	**8**	16/1	70	29
2058^{11}	**Ginzbourg (87)** (JLDunlop) **3-9-1** PatEddery(6) (effrt & rdn over 2f out: nvr nr ldrs)	1¼	**9**	13/2	71	30
2137^{5}	**Another Night (IRE) (87)** (RHannon) **3-9-1** DaneO'Neill(2) (prom tl wknd 3f out)	1¼	**10**	9/1	69	28
2058^{12}	**Henley (USA) (87)** (DRLoder) **3-9-1** DRMcCabe(13) (lw: led over 5f: wkng whn jumped path over 3f out: t.o)	30	**11**	8/1	22	—
				(SP 132.2%)	**11 Rn**	

2m 10.33 (6.33) CSF £29.15 CT £113.28 TOTE £10.10: £2.20 £1.70 £2.10 (£23.30) Trio £34.00 OWNER Mr Bryan Pennick (BRIGHTON) BRED David John Brown
WEIGHT FOR AGE 3yo-11lb
2318 Rising Dough (IRE) put up a remarkable performance. He was coming to challenge when badly hampered approaching the final furlong and again had a poor run inside the distance. In the nick of time a gap appeared and he quickened to snatch the race. (7/1)
2190* Hachiyah (IRE), well placed throughout, went to the front over two furlongs from home but was soon being driven along and could not quite hold the winner. (3/1)
2296 Traceability had every chance but could not quicken in the final furlong. (5/1)
2120* Vola Via (USA) took closer order approaching Tattenham Corner and, though having every chance, could not quicken in the closing stages. (6/1)
1951* Brighstone raced in second place until leading approaching the straight. Headed over two furlongs out, he did not weaken until the final furlong. (14/1)
2118 Edan Heights was at the back of the field until coming with a run on the outside in the straight but never threatened to catch the leaders. (12/1)
2137 Another Night (IRE) (9/1: 6/1-10/1)

2575 H H & S CLAIMING STKS (3-Y.O+) (Class E)

8-30 (8-31) **6f** £3,241.25 (£980.00: £477.50: £226.25) Stalls: High GOING: 0.10 sec per fur (G)

				SP	RR	SF
2105^{29}	**Paris Babe (83)** (DMorris) **5-9-3** NDay(4) (a.p: led over 2f out: r.o wl)	—	**1**	3/1^{2}	80+	47
1931^{6}	**Peter Perfect (53)** (GLewis) **3-8-6b** PaulEddery(5) (a.p: r.o one pce fnl 2f)	3½	**2**	6/1	66	27
1937^{2}	**Montendre (81)** (RJHodges) **10-8-10** JReid(3) (lw: rdn 3f out: hdwy over 1f out: nt qckn fnl f)	1½	**3**	5/6^{1}	60	27
1965^{9}	**The Frisky Farmer (45)** (WGMTurner) **4-8-3**$^{(5)}$ DSweeney(6) (led over 3f)	2	**4**	25/1	52	19
685^{4}	**Gopi (65)** (RHannon) **3-7-10** JQuinn(7) (plld hrd: w ldrs tl wknd 2f out)	2	**5**	9/2^{3}	41	2
378^{5}	**Seretse's Nephew (50)** (MJPolglase) **3-8-0**$^{(3)}$ MartinDwyer(2) (prom over 3f: t.o)	15	**6**	33/1	8	—
1967^{11}	**Tashannah** (PRHedger) **4-8-0**$^{(5)}$ RFfrench(1) (wl bhd fnl 4f: t.o)	5	**7**	50/1	—	—
				(SP 120.8%)	**7 Rn**	

1m 12.24 (4.24) CSF £20.08 TOTE £5.50: £2.70 £1.80 (£17.10) OWNER Mrs Susan Parry (NEWMARKET) BRED I. W. Parry
WEIGHT FOR AGE 3yo-6lb
1634 Paris Babe, always going well, went to the front over two furlongs from home and won readily. (3/1: 6/4-100/30)
1931 Peter Perfect, close up all the way, was not match for the winner in the final quarter-mile. (6/1)
1937 Montendre, for whom the overnight rain should have been ideal, was never travelling. Hard at work three furlongs out, he came with a run below the distance but could not sustain it in the last furlong. (5/6: evens-11/10)
1509 The Frisky Farmer made the running but was quickly beaten when headed approaching the two-furlong marker. (25/1)
685 Gopi pulled hard with the leader but weakened rapidly when the chips were down. (9/2)

2576 SPORTSGUIDE NEW HORIZONS MINIBUS H'CAP (0-80) (3-Y.O+) (Class D)

9-00 (9-02) **1m 114y** £3,403.75 (£1,030.00: £502.50: £238.75) Stalls: Low GOING: 0.10 sec per fur (G)

				SP	RR	SF
2201^{7}	**Sooty Tern (67)** (JMBradley) **10-9-4**$^{(5)}$ RFfrench(1) (mde virtually all: pushed out)	—	**1**	15/2	74	40
2485*	**Renata's Prince (IRE) (56)** (KRBurke) **4-8-12** ^{5x} KFallon(3) (chsd ldrs: effrt 2f out: ev ch & hrd rdn fnl f: r.o)	hd	**2**	6/5^{1}	63	29
2369^{8}	**Whispered Melody (59)** (RAkehurst) **4-9-1** TQuinn(6) (plld hrd: a.p: ev ch over 1f out: wknd ins fnl f)	4	**3**	5/1^{2}	58	24
2174^{15}	**Absolutely Fayre (51)** (VSoane) **6-8-7** CRutter(7) (in rr tl hdwy 3f out: nvr nr to chal)	4	**4**	20/1	43	9
2030^{4}	**Double Flight (65)** (MJohnston) **3-8-11** JWeaver(4) (a bhd)	2½	**5**	6/1^{3}	52	8
1955^{4}	**Night Wink (USA) (72)** (GLMoore) **5-10-0** SWhitworth(5) (w wnr tl wknd qckly over 2f out)	2½	**6**	13/2	54	20
363^{8}	**Blue Flyer (IRE) (72)** (RIngram) **4-10-0b** AMcGlone(2) (prom tl wknd 4f out: t.o)	15	**7**	12/1	26	—
				(SP 114.0%)	**7 Rn**	

1m 49.69 (7.69) CSF £15.38 TOTE £8.30: £3.10 £1.70 (£5.90) OWNER Mr J. M. Bradley (CHEPSTOW) BRED Sheikh Mohammed bin Rashid al Maktoum
WEIGHT FOR AGE 3yo-10lb
1955 Sooty Tern made all the running. Despite the narrowness of his win, he needed only to be pushed along in the last furlong to hold off the hard-ridden favourite. (15/2: 5/1-8/1)
2485* Renata's Prince (IRE), never far behind the leaders, was driven up on the outside in the straight but, despite having every chance, never appeared likely to put his head in front. (6/5)

1987* Whispered Melody pulled very hard in the early stages and in the circumstances did well to be in with every chance at the distance. She weakened inside the last furlong. (5/1)
1800 Absolutely Fayre was dropped out last and, though making some headway in the straight, was never on terms. (20/1)
2030 Double Flight continues to disappoint and was always behind. (6/1)
1955 Night Wink (USA) went with the winner but weakened rapidly with over two furlongs still to race. (13/2: 4/1-7/1)
121* Blue Flyer (IRE) (12/1: 8/1-14/1)

T/Plpt: £85.60 (213.71 Tckts). T/Qdpt: £45.00 (19.94 Tckts) Hn

2394-FOLKESTONE (R-H) (St crse Good, Rnd crse Good to firm, Good patches)
Wednesday July 9th
WEATHER: warm WIND: slt half against

2577 BRIDGE (S) H'CAP (0-60) (3-Y.O+) (Class G)
2-20 (2-21) **1m 1f 149y** £1,984.50 (£547.00: £259.50) Stalls: Low GOING minus 0.28 sec per fur (GF)

			SP	RR	SF
2399^{3} **Battle Ground (IRE) (45)** (NACallaghan) **3-8-6** SDrowne(5) (lw: hld up: led over 1f out: rdn out)	—	**1**	11/2 ^{2}	57	19
2200^{2} **Bluebell Miss (58)** (MJRyan) **3-9-2**(3) MBaird(8) (hrd rdn & hdwy over 1f out: r.o wl ins fnl f)	1	**2**	8/1 ^{3}	68	30
1825^{12} **Country Thatch (36)** (CAHorgan) **4-8-8** DHolland(3) (rdn 5f out: hdwy over 1f out: r.o wl ins fnl f)	hd	**3**	10/1	46	19
2301^{4} **Esperto (52)** (JPearce) **4-9-10** GBardwell(10) (hld up: rdn 4f out: r.o one pce fnl 2f)	1½	**4**	5/1 ^{1}	60	33
2041^{3} **Chalky Dancer (30)** (HJCollingridge) **5-8-2** DaleGibson(13) (a.p: rdn over 2f out: one pce)	1¼	**5**	10/1	36	9
1633^{14} **Bold Et Noir (44)** (WJarvis) **3-8-5** NDay(6) (hld up: rdn 3f out: wkng whn nt clr run 2f out)	1¼	**6**	16/1	48	10
1636^{4} **Sapphire Son (IRE) (44)** (PCClarke) **5-9-2** NAdams(2) (a.p: rdn over 2f out: wknd over 1f out)	hd	**7**	12/1	47	20
1373^{13} **Harlequin Walk (IRE) (36)** (RJO'Sullivan) **6-8-8** SSanders(7) (led tl over 1f out: sn wknd)	½	**8**	11/2 ^{2}	39	12
1926^{12} **Hatta Sunshine (USA) (34)** (GLMoore) **7-8-3**(3) AWhelan(4) (lw: dwlt: nvr nr to chal)	¾	**9**	14/1	35	8
2228^{6} **Euro Superstar (FR) (37)** (SDow) **3-7-7**(5) RMullen(15) (w ldr tl over 1f out: sn wknd)	nk	**10**	20/1	38	—
2039^{13} **Aquavita (48)** (RHannon) **3-8-9** DaneO'Neill(11) (a bhd)	1	**11**	12/1	47	9
2195^{6} **Another Fiddle (IRE) (33)** (JELong) **7-8-0**(5) GMilligan(1) (b: b.hind: dwlt: a bhd)	1½	**12**	25/1	30	3
2375^{5} **Proud Brigadier (IRE) (36)** (MRBosley) **9-8-8** DRMcCabe(9) (dwlt: stdy hdwy over 1f out: eased whn btn ins fnl f)	1	**13**	20/1	31	4
1779^{17} **Rehaab (52)** (DMorris) **4-9-5**(5) GFaulkner(14) (bhd fnl 2f)	1¾	**14**	9/1	44	17
2294^{3} **Switch To Senate (42)** (DJSCosgrove) **3-8-3** GCarter(12) (a bhd)	29	**15**	16/1	—	—

(SP 133.9%) **15 Rn**

2m 3.5 (5.80) CSF £48.53 CT £414.83 TOTE £6.80: £2.80 £3.10 £3.70 (£13.10) Trio £168.50 OWNER Mr N. A. Callaghan (NEWMARKET)
BRED Gay O'Callaghan
WEIGHT FOR AGE 3yo-11lb
No bid

2399 Battle Ground (IRE) swept into the lead approaching the final furlong and was ridden along to lose his maiden tag at the sixteenth attempt. (11/2)
2200 Bluebell Miss ran a good race considering she is at her best with some cut. Finally picking up ground below the distance, she ran on really strongly to snatch second prize but found the line always coming too soon. (8/1: op 4/1)
Country Thatch, dropped 19lb since the beginning of the season, appreciated the drop in class and ran his best race to date, staying on in really good style in the last furlong and a half and only just losing out for second prize. (10/1)
2301 Esperto chased the leaders but his jockey was hard at work on him running down the hill. He did struggle on in the straight but was noted carrying his head rather high and awkwardly. (5/1)
2041 Chalky Dancer was never far away but was made to look extremely onepaced in the straight. He is very inconsistent and remains a maiden after twenty-two attempts. (10/1)
Bold Et Noir, who had shown nothing in four previous outings, has consequently fallen 8lb in the handicap and was taking a drop in class. He showed his first sign of ability here but was feeling the pinch when chopped for room early in the home straight. (16/1)
1507 Aquavita (12/1: op 8/1)
1273 Proud Brigadier (IRE) was given an interesting ride for, after making steady progress under considerate handling from below the distance, he had just got on to the heels of the principals although not with a great deal of room in which to manoeuvre when his jockey decided to ease him down. He certainly ran better than his final placing suggests but it is worth remembering he has not won for three years. (20/1)

2578 COWDREY NURSERY H'CAP (2-Y.O) (Class E)
2-50 (2-50) **5f** £2,940.25 (£877.00: £418.50: £189.25) Stalls: Low GOING minus 0.08 sec per fur (G)

			SP	RR	SF
2123^{4} **Mishraak (IRE)** (RWArmstrong) **2-9-7** GCarter(1) (mde all: pushed out)	—	**1**	7/4 ^{1}	92	42
2243^{13} **Mislead (IRE)** (JSMoore) **2-8-2**(3) MHenry(4) (lw: a.p: rdn over 2f out: ev ch wl over 1f out: unable qckn)	2½	**2**	12/1	68	18
1293^{10} **Swanmore Lady (IRE)** (SCWilliams) **2-7-6**(5)ow1 RMullen(7) (lw: a.p: rdn over 2f out: ev ch wl over 1f out: one pce)	1¼	**3**	20/1	56	5
2186* **Catherines Song** (CADwyer) **2-8-9** DHolland(6) (b.off hind: a.p: rdn over 2f out: ev ch wl over 1f out: one pce)	1	**4**	9/4 ^{2}	65	15
2138^{9} **Muja's Magic (IRE)** (KTIvory) **2-8-2**(3) MartinDwyer(5) (rdn & no hdwy fnl 2f)	1¼	**5**	7/1 ^{3}	57	7
1293^{4} **Bliss (IRE)** (MrsPNDutfield) **2-8-3**(3) AWhelan(3) (bmpd s: bhd fnl 2f)	1¾	**6**	20/1	52	2
1457^{7} **Summer Day Blues (IRE)** (CMurray) **2-8-6** PBloomfield(2) (b: lw: bhd fnl 2f)	2½	**7**	16/1	44	—
2138^{11} **Lisa's Pride (IRE)** (MissGayKelleway) **2-9-6** SSanders(8) (lw: hld up: rdn over 2f out: sn wknd)	1½	**8**	9/1	53	3

(SP 112.7%) **8 Rn**

60.8 secs (3.20) CSF £21.26 CT £281.27 TOTE £3.10: £1.40 £2.20 £4.00 (£12.90) OWNER Mr Hamdan Al Maktoum (NEWMARKET) BRED Scuderia Dello Zodiaco

2123 Mishraak (IRE) appreciated the return to five furlongs and had absolutely no problems under top weight on this handicap debut in minor company. Making every post a winning one he needed only to be shaken up to assert his authority from below the distance. (7/4)
2003* Mislead (IRE) looked in fine shape beforehand and was never far away. One of four almost in line early in the final quarter-mile, she won the battle for second prize but had no hope with the winner. (12/1: op 8/1)
767 Swanmore Lady (IRE) had every chance early in the final quarter-mile before tapped for toe. (20/1)
2186* Catherines Song, bustled along from halfway, was nevertheless one of four almost in line early in the final quarter-mile before tapped for toe. (9/4)

1954 Muja's Magic (IRE) chased the leaders but never looked like quickening up in the second half of the race. (7/1)

2579 ST LAWRENCE MAIDEN AUCTION STKS (2-Y.O) (Class F)

3-25 (3-26) **6f** £2,277.00 (£627.00: £297.00) Stalls: Low GOING minus 0.08 sec per fur (G)

				SP	RR	SF
2306[2]	**Regal Revolution** (PTWalwyn) **2-7-12** JLowe(9) (mde all: comf)	—	**1**	4/9[1]	59+	16
1569[9]	**Shannon (IRE)** (CADwyer) **2-7-10**(5) RMullen(2) (bmpd s: outpcd: swtchd rt & hdwy wl over 1f out: chsd wnr ins fnl f: unable qckn)	3½	**2**	25/1	53	10
	Roisin Splendour (IRE) (SDow) **2-8-5** SSanders(1) (w'like: chsd wnr: rdn over 2f out: swtchd rt over 1f out: one pce)	1½	**3**	12/1[3]	53	10
1812[21]	**Won't Forget Me (IRE)** (MHTompkins) **2-8-6v[1]** DBiggs(4) (a.p: rdn over 3f out: one pce)	1¾	**4**	20/1	49	6
	High Jinks (BSmart) **2-8-10** DHarrison(7) (str: scope: bit bkwd: s.s: outpcd: hdwy over 1f out: wknd fnl f)	2	**5**	12/1[3]	48	5
	Best Attempt (JNeville) **2-8-10** SDrowne(8) (w'like: prom over 4f)	5	**6**	14/1	34	—
	Fung Shui (IRE) (RHannon) **2-8-10** DaneO'Neill(3) (str: scope: bit bkwd: a bhd)	3	**7**	6/1[2]	26	—
	Marimbo (IRE) (CMurray) **2-8-3** NicolaHowarth(6) (neat: bit bkwd: prom tl wknd & bmpd wl over 1f out)	8	**8**	25/1	—	—
	Risque (MrsAJBowlby) **2-8-10** CandyMorris(5) (w'like: bit bkwd: bhd fnl 3f)	7	**9**	33/1	—	—
				(SP 121.0%)	**9 Rn**	

1m 14.5 (4.30) CSF £20.13 TOTE £1.40: £1.10 £4.40 £2.20 (£13.30) Trio £44.00 OWNER Mr S. W. E. J. Slack (LAMBOURN) BRED T. R. Lock

2306 Regal Revolution had no problems confirming the promise shown on her debut and, making all the running, surged clear from below the distance for a comfortable success. (4/9)

Shannon (IRE), unable to go the early pace, was switched right and began to pick up ground early in the final quarter-mile. She came through to win the battle for second prize inside the final furlong but had no hope with the winner. (25/1)

Roisin Splendour (IRE), quite an attractive filly, made a pleasing debut. Giving chase to the winner, she was switched off the rails below the distance but then failed to find another gear and was caught for second place inside the final furlong. (12/1: op 7/1)

Won't Forget Me (IRE) ran his best race to date and was close up if tapped for toe in the final quarter-mile. (20/1)

High Jinks, a well-made colt, looked as though this debut was needed. Unable to go the early pace, he picked up ground below the distance but then found lack of peak fitness taking its toll in the final furlong. He probably needs further already. (12/1: 10/1-16/1)

Best Attempt, a medium-sized colt, showed up well until tiring below the distance. (14/1: 10/1-16/1)

2580 GODFREY EVANS MEDIAN AUCTION MAIDEN STKS (3 & 4-Y.O) (Class E)

3-55 (3-59) **6f** £2,966.25 (£885.00: £422.50: £191.25) Stalls: Low GOING minus 0.08 sec per fur (G)

				SP	RR	SF
2278[4]	**Hever Golf Rocket** (TJNaughton) **3-8-12** DaneO'Neill(7) (hmpd s: a.p: hrd rdn over 1f out: led ins fnl f: r.o wl)	—	**1**	10/1	63	40
970[7]	**Taffs Well** (RAkehurst) **4-9-4** SSanders(4) (led: hrd rdn over 1f out: hdd ins fnl f: r.o wl)	s.h	**2**	7/1	63	46
2278[2]	**Fonteyn (83)** (ACStewart) **3-8-7** SWhitworth(3) (a.p: rdn over 2f out: ev ch over 1f out: r.o wl: sddle slipped)	s.h	**3**	11/10[1]	58	35
	Turners Way (SDow) **3-8-12** JFEgan(1) (str: scope: bkwd: outpcd: nvr nr to chal)	5	**4**	33/1	49	26
1980[13]	**Select Choice (IRE) (80)** (APJarvis) **3-8-12** SDrowne(8) (swvd lft s: w ldr 4f)	1¼	**5**	9/2[3]	46	23
1972[14]	**Velvet Jones (39)** (GFHCharles-Jones) **4-8-11**(7) CharlotteCox(6) (hmpd s: a bhd)	s.h	**6**	50/1	46	29
	Severity (WJHaggas) **3-8-12** DHolland(5) (w'like: bmpd s: outpcd)	2	**7**	4/1[2]	41	18
	Forward Miss (CJBenstead) **3-8-7** JLowe(2) (outpcd)	9	**8**	40/1	12	—
				(SP 114.7%)	**8 Rn**	

1m 13.7 (3.50) CSF £68.82 TOTE £12.60: £1.80 £2.90 £1.10 (£24.40) OWNER Hever Racing Club (EPSOM) BRED Mrs L. Popely

WEIGHT FOR AGE 3yo-6lb

OFFICIAL EXPLANATION **Fonteyn: the saddle slipped at the two furlong marker.**

2278 Hever Golf Rocket, eight lengths behind Fonteyn on his debut here twelve days ago, reversed the form on this occasion. Never far away, he was shown the persuader below the distance and managed to grab a narrow advantage inside the final furlong and held on well. (10/1)

Taffs Well, sent off favourite for his debut at the beginning of May, finished a well-beaten seventh on that occasion but was a different proposition here. Attempting to make all the running, he was narrowly collared inside the final furlong but, refusing to give way, only just failed to get back up. He should soon find a suitable opportunity. (7/1)

2278 Fonteyn again had no luck in running. Always close up, she delivered her challenge in the final quarter-mile but unfortunately her saddle slipped right back, although her jockey did wonders to get a run out of her and the combination only just failed. She deserves a change of luck. (11/10: evens-7/4)

Turners Way, a well-made colt, was carrying a lot of surplus flesh and, unable to go the pace, never threatened to get into it despite struggling on in the closing stages. (33/1)

784 Select Choice (IRE), a tall, plain gelding, was completely out of his depth last time out but disputed the lead on this occasion until tiring in the final quarter-mile. He has run some good races in maidens but is now becoming extremely frustrating. (9/2: op 3/1)

2581 SANDGATE MOTORS SKODA FELICIA H'CAP (0-70) (3-Y.O+) (Class E)

4-30 (4-32) **5f** £3,018.25 (£901.00: £430.50: £195.25) Stalls: Low GOING minus 0.08 sec per fur (G)

				SP	RR	SF
2277*	**The Fugative (61)** (PMitchell) **4-9-2**(3) AWhelan(9) (lw: hdwy to ld 1f out: rdn out)	—	**1**	5/1[2]	72	52
2321[7]	**Mousehole (70)** (RGuest) **5-10-0** PBloomfield(3) (a.p: rdn over 3f out: ev ch 1f out: r.o one pce)	1½	**2**	5/1[2]	76	56
1937[5]	**Littlestone Rocket (58)** (WRMuir) **3-8-11b** DaneO'Neill(6) (lw: hdwy over 2f out: rdn over 1f out: one pce)	1½	**3**	10/1	59	34
2220[9]	**Tear White (IRE) (68)** (TGMills) **3-9-7** DHolland(4) (lw: led to 1f out: one pce)	s.h	**4**	12/1	69	44
2526[9]	**Sally Slade (67)** (CACyzer) **5-9-11** WJO'Connor(2) (rdn over 2f out: nvr nr to chal)	1	**5**	5/1[2]	65	45
2220[5]	**Kildee Lad (69)** (APJones) **7-9-13** SDrowne(7) (lw: a.p: hrd rdn over 1f out: one pce)	s.h	**6**	13/2[3]	67	47
2308[2]	**Friendly Brave (USA) (66)** (MissGayKelleway) **7-9-10** SSanders(8) (lw: nt clr run over 1f out: hdwy & nt clr run 1f out: eased whn btn wl ins fnl f)	nk	**7**	4/1[1]	63	43
2321*	**Superlao (BEL) (44)** (JJBridger) **5-7-9**(7) PDoe(5) (w ldr over 3f)	3	**8**	8/1	31	11
2372[4]	**Village Native (FR) (58)** (KOCunningham-Brown) **4-8-13b**(3) MartinDwyer(1) (prom over 3f)	3	**9**	7/1	36	16
				(SP 123.7%)	**9 Rn**	

60.1 secs (2.50) CSF £29.67 CT £228.32 TOTE £5.10: £2.10 £1.90 £3.10 (£20.00) Trio £117.50 OWNER Mr J. A. Redmond (EPSOM) BRED J. A. Redmond

WEIGHT FOR AGE 3yo-5lb

2277* The Fugative continues in fine form and, coming through to lead a furlong out, was ridden along to complete the hat-trick. (5/1: 3/1-6/1)

2061 Mousehole, unsuited by the soft ground last time out, was never far away. Certainly close enough if good enough entering the final furlong, he won the battle for second prize but was unable to cope with the winner. (5/1)
1937 Littlestone Rocket took closer order at halfway but then failed to find another gear. (10/1)
1989 Tear White (IRE) was much happier with this return to a sound surface and took the field along until collared a furlong out. (12/1)
2277 Sally Slade, making a quick reappearance, could never get in a serious blow. (5/1)
1957 Kildee Lad, 7lb lower than when last successful, looked in fine shape and was close up until tapped for toe in the final quarter-mile. (13/2)

2582 LESLIE AMES MEMORIAL H'CAP (0-70) (3-Y.O+ F & M) (Class E)
5-05 (5-05) **1m 4f** £2,966.25 (£885.00: £422.50: £191.25) Stalls: Low GOING minus 0.28 sec per fur (GF)

Form	Horse	Dist	Pos	SP	RR	SF
2373^{7}	**Kristal Breeze (52)** (WRMuir) **5-9-2** WJO'Connor(4) (lw: hdwy over 3f out: led over 1f out: comf)	—	1	13/2	61+	41
1668^{3}	**Mono Lady (IRE) (55)** (DHaydnJones) **4-9-5b** AMackay(3) (hdwy & nt clr run over 2f out: chsd wnr ins fnl f: unable qckn)	1½	2	6/1	62	42
2331^{9}	**Tart (FR) (60)** (JPearce) **4-9-10** NDay(1) (hdwy over 3f out: rdn over 2f out: chsd wnr over 1f out tl ins fnl f: one pce)	2½	3	6/1	64	44
2374*	**Dizzy Tilly (70)** (TJNaughton) **3-9-7** 5x DHolland(8) (led 10f out to 7f out: led 5f out tl over 1f out: sn wknd)	2	4	$5/1^{3}$	71	38
1938^{4}	**Laguna Bay (IRE) (56)** (APJarvis) **3-8-7** SDrowne(2) (hld up: rdn over 2f out: wknd over 1f out)	3½	5	$9/2^{2}$	52	19
2414*	**Itatinga (USA) (65)** (MRStoute) **3-9-2** 5x DHarrison(5) (chsd ldr over 9f out: led 7f out to 5f out: ev ch 2f out: wknd over 1f out)	7	6	$2/1^{1}$	52	19
2279^{11}	**Antiguan Jane (64)** (RWArmstrong) **4-10-0b** GCarter(6) (led 2f: wknd over 3f out)	5	7	20/1	44	24
2365^{5}	**Wontcostalotbut (55)** (MJWilkinson) **3-8-6** SWhitworth(7) (prom over 7f)	3½	8	33/1	31	—

(SP 117.8%) **8 Rn**

2m 36.7 (5.50) CSF £42.15 CT £226.82 TOTE £9.50: £1.60 £2.00 £1.50 (£26.50) OWNER Mr S. Lamb (LAMBOURN) BRED R. and Mrs Heathcote
WEIGHT FOR AGE 3yo-13lb
2174 Kristal Breeze crept closer running down the hill and, striking the front approaching the final furlong, shot clear for a decisive victory. (13/2)
1668 Mono Lady (IRE), who went down extremely early to the start, appreciated the return to a longer trip. Taking closer order turning for home, she struggled into second place inside the final furlong but had no hope with the winner. (6/1)
Tart (FR), 10lb lower than at the beginning of the turf season, appreciated the return to a longer distance. Taking closer order running down the hill, she moved into second place below the distance but she had no hope with the winner and was collared for the runner-up berth inside the final furlong. (6/1)
2374* Dizzy Tilly, soon at the head of affairs, made the vast majority of the running until put in her place when collared below the distance. (5/1)
1938 Laguna Bay (IRE) chased the leaders and appeared to be going well running down the hill but she ran out of steam below the distance. (9/2)
2414* Itatinga (USA), in second place for the majority of the final circuit, did not handle the home turn at all well and had been seen off below the distance. (2/1: 5/4-5/2)

T/Plpt: £70.30 (180.68 Tckts). T/Qdpt: £16.60 (46.07 Tckts) AK

2556-NEWMARKET (R-H) (Good to firm, Good fnl 6f)
Wednesday July 9th
WEATHER: warm and sunny WIND: moderate against

2583 MORE O'FERRALL MAIDEN STKS (3-Y.O) (Class D)
2-05 (2-06) **1m 2f (July)** £5,481.00 (£1,638.00: £784.00: £357.00) Stalls: High GOING minus 0.29 sec per fur (GF)

Form	Horse	Dist	Pos	SP	RR	SF
2126^{2}	**Light Programme** (HRACecil) **3-9-0** KFallon(1) (lw: a.p: rdn over 3f out: led wl over 1f out: hld on wl ins fnl f)	—	1	$Evens^{1}$	93	60
	Marilaya (IRE) (LMCumani) **3-8-9** KDarley(12) (neat: scope: trckd ldrs: effrt over 2f out: ev ch fnl f: unable qckn nr fin)	hd	2	25/1	88	55
	Ricardo (RCharlton) **3-9-0** TSprake(5) (gd sort: lw: chsd ldrs: r.o wl fnl f)	2½	3	50/1	89	56
2389^{3}	**Dovedon Star** (PAKelleway) **3-8-9** JWeaver(8) (plld hrd: prom: pushed along & outpcd 4f out: styd on fnl f)	hd	4	16/1	84	51
	Saafeya (IRE) (JHMGosden) **3-8-9** LDettori(3) (w ldr: led over 3f out: hdd wl over 1f out: btn fnl f)	nk	5	$2/1^{2}$	83	50
	Shaska (JHMGosden) **3-8-9** GHind(6) (w'like: leggy: hld up & plld hrd: hdwy over 3f out: wknd fnl f)	¾	6	16/1	82	49
683^{12}	**Water Flower** (JRFanshawe) **3-8-9** MHills(9) (lw: in tch: rdn 3f out: no imp appr fnl f)	2½	7	50/1	78	45
	Pradesh (JHMGosden) **3-8-9** AGarth(4) (gd sort: nvr nrr)	4	8	33/1	72	39
2332^{W}	**Prince de Loir** (DJSCosgrove) **3-9-0** WRyan(11) (nvr nr to chal)	3	9	66/1	72?	39
1866^{5}	**Polenista** (JLDunlop) **3-8-9** TQuinn(2) (plld hrd: effrt 4f out: nvr nr ldrs)	nk	10	14/1	66?	33
	Dr Martens (IRE) (LMCumani) **3-9-0** PatEddery(7) (cmpt: scope: s.i.s: sn trckng ldrs: wknd 3f out)	3	11	20/1	67?	34
1646^{2}	**Robban Hendi (USA)** (MAJarvis) **3-9-0** RCochrane(10) (lw: led: rdn & hdd over 3f out: sn wknd)	4	12	$9/1^{3}$	60?	27

(SP 128.7%) **12 Rn**

2m 5.35 (1.75) CSF £38.79 TOTE £1.90: £1.10 £6.60 £6.50 (£24.30) Trio £306.80 OWNER Mr K. Abdulla (NEWMARKET) BRED Juddmonte Farms
2126 Light Programme, a good mover, got off the mark but didn't make the job look easy and the ride he was given in the final furlong saw Fallon at his very best, straightening his mount without losing any momentum. (Evens)
Marilaya (IRE), a smallish filly making her debut, travelled well throughout, but was just worried out of it by a more experienced rival after looking the winner in the Dip. She should be able to go one better. (25/1)
Ricardo, a tall, very attractive colt, had two handlers and was noisy and colty in the parade ring. Quite keen going down, he was never far away and stuck to his task well. (50/1)
2389 Dovedon Star ran a very similar race to her debut, getting outpaced before staying on well and, now handicapped, improvement ought to be forthcoming over further. (16/1)

Saafeya (IRE), off since last October, was a bit of a tail-swisher in the preliminaries and went down keenly. She stopped quickly after travelling sweetly in front, and should be better for this. (2/1)
Shaska a tall, attractive newcomer, is very closely related to Halling, being out of the same dam by Diesis's full brother Kris. Unfortunately, having shaped well, she proved all but unrideable in the final furlong as her head went in the air. If her problem can be solved, she has the make and shape of a certain winner. (16/1)
1866 Polenista (14/1: 6/1-16/1)
Dr Martens (IRE), a poor mover, couldn't handle the slight drop into the Dip at all, and his pilot concentrated on holding him together. (20/1)
1646 Robban Hendi (USA) (9/1: 4/1-10/1)

2584 TNT INTERNATIONAL AVIATION JULY STKS (Gp 3) (2-Y.O C & G) (Class A)
2-35 (2-35) **6f (July)** £15,924.00 (£5,916.00: £2,858.00: £1,190.00: £495.00: £217.00) Stalls: Low GOING minus 0.29 sec per fur (GF)

				SP	RR	SF
2012[3]	**Bold Fact (USA)** (HRACecil) **2-8-10** KFallon(6) (lw: hld up & plld hrd: hdwy to ld & veered rt over 1f out: r.o wl)	—	**1**	Evens[1]	102	61
2295*	**Linden Heights** (LMCumani) **2-8-10** PatEddery(1) (plld hrd: trckd ldrs: nt clr run 2f out: ev ch over 1f out: outpcd ins fnl f)	2	**2**	7/1[3]	97	56
2054[5]	**Pool Music** (RHannon) **2-8-13** RHughes(8) (lw: in tch: hmpd over 1f out: kpt on fnl f)	2	**3**	11/2[2]	94	53
2012[12]	**Blueridge Dancer (IRE)** (BJMeehan) **2-8-10b[1]** KDarley(2) (led tl over 1f out: one pce)	1¼	**4**	33/1	88	47
2054*	**Tippitt Boy** (KMcAuliffe) **2-9-1** JReid(7) (hld up: nt clr run over 2f out: nvr able to chal)	1½	**5**	16/1	89	48
2012[8]	**Swift Alliance** (RAkehurst) **2-8-10** TQuinn(5) (chsd ldrs 4f)	5	**6**	25/1	71	30
2110*	**Aix En Provence (USA)** (MJohnston) **2-8-10** JWeaver(4) (chsd ldrs 4f)	½	**7**	16/1	69	28
2215*	**Calchas (IRE)** (SirMarkPrescott) **2-8-10** GDuffield(3) (chsd ldrs 4f: sn rdn & btn)	2½	**8**	11/2[2]	63	22
				(SP 111.8%)	**8 Rn**	

1m 12.64 (0.64) CSF £7.38 TOTE £1.80: £1.10 £1.70 £2.00 (£5.50) OWNER Mr K. Abdulla (NEWMARKET) BRED Juddmonte Farms
2012 Bold Fact (USA) repeated his Ascot antics but, with the July course split in two, this is a much narrower track and he quickened in great style once meeting the near rail. He would be a very exciting two-year-old if only he had been born with a sense of direction. (Evens)
2295* Linden Heights, rather keen to post this time, made his pilot's life tricky by racing keenly on the heels of Blueridge Dancer. Eventually getting a run up that one's inside, he did nothing wrong in beating the main group, but lacks the pace of the winner. (7/1: 5/1-8/1)
2054 Pool Music was slightly impeded when the winner cruised up on his inside and promptly hung across him, but then battled on well. (11/2)
1475 Blueridge Dancer (IRE), in first-time blinkers, was taken down steadily after the others. He raced keenly in front but was always edging away from the far rail, eventually letting the runner-up through. (33/1)
2054* Tippitt Boy, very free to post, got none too clear a run, but never looked like following up his Ascot shock. (16/1)
1480* Swift Alliance chased the leaders to the Dip and was eased down in the last half furlong. (25/1)
2110* Aix En Provence (USA) may have got tightened up for a stride or two in the Dip, but the writing was already on the wall. (16/1)
2215* Calchas (IRE) (11/2: 4/1-6/1)

2585 INFLITE ENGINEERING DUKE OF CAMBRIDGE H'CAP (0-105) (3-Y.O) (Class B)
3-10 (3-12) **1m 2f (July)** £19,820.00 (£5,960.00: £2,880.00: £1,340.00) Stalls: High GOING minus 0.29 sec per fur (GF)

				SP	RR	SF
2058[4]	**Memorise (USA) (86)** (HRACecil) **3-8-12** KFallon(12) (a.p: led 3f out: rdn & hld on gamely fnl f)	—	**1**	5/1[1]	95	66
1869*	**Maylane (95)** (ACStewart) **3-9-7** MRoberts(7) (lw: rel to r: sn t.o: hdwy 6f out: ev ch fnl f: unable qckn nr fin)	hd	**2**	10/1	104	75
741[8]	**Mersey Beat (87)** (GLMoore) **3-8-13** AClark(5) (bhd: hdwy 3f out: one pce ins fnl f)	1	**3**	33/1	94	65
2013[9]	**Amyas (IRE) (95)** (BWHills) **3-9-7** MHills(15) (lw: hld up: hdwy 2f out: nt clr run over 1f out: r.o wl ins fnl f)	s.h	**4**	11/1	102	73
1553a[9]	**Stanton Harcourt (USA) (93)** (JLDunlop) **3-9-5** PatEddery(6) (hld up: plld out & hdwy wl over 1f out: r.o)	nk	**5**	10/1	100	71
2210[2]	**Manazil (IRE) (81)** (RWArmstrong) **3-8-7** RHills(9) (lw: hdwy over 2f out: one pce fnl f)	d.h	**6**	20/1	87	58
2296[5]	**Bold Oriental (IRE) (83)** (NACallaghan) **3-8-9** LDettori(3) (hld up: hdwy 2f out: nt pce to chal)	nk	**6**	10/1	89	60
2292*	**Atlantic Desire (IRE) (90)** (MJohnston) **3-9-2** JWeaver(11) (prom: ev ch 3f out tl wknd appr fnl f)	3	**8**	8/1[3]	91	62
1088[3]	**Regal Thunder (USA) (73)** (MRStoute) **3-7-13** JQuinn(2) (lw: hld up: hdwy 4f out: ev ch 3f out: wknd appr fnl f)	½	**9**	6/1[2]	74	45
1875[2]	**Priena (IRE) (93)** (DRLoder) **3-9-5** KDarley(14) (trckd ldrs: no imp fnl 2f)	½	**10**	6/1[2]	93	64
2013[15]	**Over To You (USA) (83)** (EALDunlop) **3-8-9** JReid(1) (hld up: hdwy & ev ch 3f out: wknd over 1f out)	½	**11**	12/1	82	53
2328[9]	**Foot Battalion (IRE) (78)** (RHollinshead) **3-7-13**(5) RFfrench(8) (in tch over 7f)	7	**12**	33/1	66	37
2058[7]	**Party Romance (USA) (86)** (BHanbury) **3-8-12** WRyan(4) (led 8f out tl hdd & wknd 3f out)	nk	**13**	16/1	73	44
1962[5]	**River Pilot (92)** (RCharlton) **3-9-4** TSprake(16) (lw: plld hrd: w ldr: wknd over 3f out)	½	**14**	25/1	79	50
2013[23]	**Bevier (76)** (CEBrittain) **3-8-2** AMunro(13) (b: plld hrd: trckd ldrs 7f)	3	**15**	50/1	58	29
2242*	**Cinema Paradiso (94)** (PFICole) **3-9-6** TQuinn(10) (led 2f: wknd over 4f out)	s.h	**16**	16/1	76	47
				(SP 127.9%)	**16 Rn**	

2m 4.37 (0.77) CSF £49.32 CT £1,407.25 TOTE £6.20: £1.70 £2.70 £9.70 £4.40 (£30.70) Trio £613.80 OWNER Mr K. Abdulla (NEWMARKET) BRED Juddmonte Farms
OFFICIAL EXPLANATION Maylane: lost a shoe.
2058 Memorise (USA), with plenty of pace on, was ridden sensibly close to the pace and made best use of his stamina in a driving finish. (5/1: 7/1-9/2)
1869* Maylane confirmed himself a most able rogue by almost overcoming the ten or twelve lengths his reluctance gave away in the first furlong. (10/1: 7/1-11/1)
365 Mersey Beat showed that he acts on turf as well as the All-Weather surfaces. A half-brother to the likes of Karinga Bay and Roll A Dollar, good handicaps can be found, probably over a longer trip. (33/1)
1404 Amyas (IRE), well supported in the morning exchanges, got warm beforehand but came home in fine style. (11/1: 8/1-12/1)
1553a Stanton Harcourt (USA) moved down well and was buried away until pulled to the outside. Although he stayed on, the leaders were not for catching. (10/1)
2210 Manazil (IRE), dropped in trip, stayed on strongly to be close at the distance but could then find no more and will surely be better over further. (20/1)
2296 Bold Oriental (IRE) finds this class of race a bit rich for his turn of foot. His wins have come in 0-80 and 0-85 races. (10/1)
1088 Regal Thunder (USA) looked to have sneaked a decent handicap mark, having run in three seven-furlong maidens, but proved very keen going down and, with plenty of speed on the dam's side of his pedigree, may not be a natural stayer. (6/1)
1747 Party Romance (USA), taken down early, gave trouble at the start and some tough races seem to have left their mark for the present. (16/1)

2586 AMCOR FALMOUTH STKS (Gp 2) (3-Y.O+ F & M) (Class A)

3-40 (3-40) **1m (July)** £33,662.00 (£12,458.00: £5,979.00: £2,445.00: £972.50: £383.50) Stalls: Low GOING minus 0.29 sec per fur (GF)

				SP	RR	SF
1916a[4]	**Ryafan (USA)** (JHMGosden) **3-8-6** PatEddery(3) (chsd ldrs: rdn over 1f out: styd on wl to ld ins fnl f)	—	**1**	4/1[3]	120	62
2025[2]	**Ocean Ridge (USA) (111)** (SbinSuroor) **3-8-6** LDettori(6) (lw: w ldr tl led 5f out: rdn & hdd ins fnl f: no ex)	¾	**2**	7/4[1]	119	61
2056[20]	**Theano (IRE)** (APO'Brien,Ireland) **4-9-1** TQuinn(2) (hld up: hdwy & n.m.r over 1f out: nt pce to chal)	6	**3**	8/1	107	58
2219*	**Dragonada (USA) (100)** (HRACecil) **3-8-6** KFallon(1) (chsd ldrs: outpcd wl over 1f out: rdn & kpt on wl fnl f)	2	**4**	11/2	103	45
2025[5]	**Khassah (111)** (JHMGosden) **3-8-6** RHills(4) (hld up: rdn over 1f out: no imp)	s.h	**5**	16/1	102	44
2025*	**Rebecca Sharp (94)** (GWragg) **3-8-12** MHills(7) (lw: hld up: hdwy over 2f out: sn rdn & btn)	1½	**6**	3/1[2]	105	47
2217[3]	**Charlotte Corday (107)** (GWragg) **4-9-1** AClark(5) (led 3f: rdn & wknd 2f out)	12	**7**	25/1	75	26

(SP 117.6%) **7 Rn**

1m 38.43 (0.43) CSF £10.91 TOTE £5.30: £2.30 £1.30 (£4.70) OWNER Mr K. Abdulla (NEWMARKET) BRED Juddmonte Farms
WEIGHT FOR AGE 3yo-9lb

IN-FOCUS: **Kieren Fallon answered his critics in the best possible fashion, winning two races he probably should have lost and scoring on a horse who seemed intent on going sideways. His ride for fourth place in this race showed that his biggest strength is his strength.**

1916a Ryafan (USA), with stamina no worry, kept plugging away and really found her stride on meeting the rising ground after appearing well held in the Dip. (4/1)

2025 Ocean Ridge (USA) took a good hold both going down and in the race but was not striding out completely and looked to edge left most of the time. Looking certain to win in the Dip, being in front and on the bridle, once asked to repel the winner she found very little. It is possible the ground had gone just too quick for her. (7/4)

2079a Theano (IRE), very impressive in a Curragh sprint handicap on soft ground last time, found this altogether different but still ran well. (8/1: 5/1-9/1)

2219* Dragonada (USA) looked well held in the Dip but Fallon would not give up and she forced her head up for some valuable black type right on the line. (11/2)

2025 Khassah travelled well enough but does not totally impress with her attitude. (16/1)

2025* Rebecca Sharp, having run a stinker in the 1,000 Guineas, repeated the process here and seems a very hard filly to predict. (3/1)

2217 Charlotte Corday would just about have earned a place in this field on merit, but was used as a pacemaker for her stable companion. (25/1)

2587 ELLESMERE (S) STKS (2-Y.O) (Class E)

4-15 (4-17) **7f (July)** £5,150.00 (£1,550.00: £750.00: £350.00) Stalls: Low GOING minus 0.29 sec per fur (GF)

				SP	RR	SF
2378[5]	**Bellow (IRE)** (HMorrison) **2-8-11** RHughes(6) (mde all: clr over 2f out: pushed out)	—	**1**	20/1	78	36
1856*	**Sick As A Parrot** (CADwyer) **2-8-8**(3) DO'Donohoe(13) (hdwy 4f out: chsd wnr wl over 1f out: no imp)	3	**2**	3/1[1]	71	29
2288[3]	**Bali Dance** (CBBBooth) **2-8-11** KHodgson(10) (lw: in tch: rdn & outpcd 3f out: kpt on appr fnl f)	1½	**3**	4/1[2]	68	26
2419*	**Three Tenners** (JBerry) **2-9-2b[1]** KDarley(11) (sn chsng ldrs: pushed along over 3f out: one pce fnl f)	2	**4**	7/1	68	26
2295[7]	**Kite** (MBell) **2-8-6** MFenton(3) (prom tl btn appr fnl f)	1½	**5**	7/1	55	13
2016[12]	**Docklands Dispatch (IRE)** (NTinkler) **2-8-11** RCochrane(5) (prom: rdn over 2f out: sn btn)	1¼	**6**	20/1	57	15
2306[12]	**Lilian Marks (IRE)** (BJMeehan) **2-8-6** MTebbutt(2) (chsd ldrs tl rdn & wknd 2f out)	2	**7**	20/1	47	5
2493[14]	**Margaret's Dancer** (CSmith) **2-9-2b** GDuffield(7) (hrd rdn over 2f out: n.d)	2½	**8**	40/1	52	10
1821[12]	**Dot** (RHannon) **2-8-6** PatEddery(4) (a bhd)	2	**9**	12/1	37	—
	Lookingforlove Del (IRE) (NACallaghan) **2-8-6** MRoberts(8) (w'like: leggy: s.s: a bhd)	1¾	**10**	14/1	33	—
2425[8]	**La Vizelle (IRE)** (RGuest) **2-8-1b[1]**(5) RFfrench(1) (prom 4f)	1¾	**11**	33/1	29	—
2031[2]	**Patricia Olive (IRE)** (MHTompkins) **2-8-6v[1]** TQuinn(12) (trckd ldrs tl wknd over 1f out)	hd	**12**	11/2[3]	29	—
	Our Dad's Lad (SCWilliams) **2-9-7** AMunro(9) (cmpt: bhd fnl 2f)	s.h	**13**	20/1	44	2

(SP 124.2%) **13 Rn**

1m 28.01 (3.01) CSF £69.55 TOTE £28.30: £5.70 £1.80 £1.60 (£79.00) Trio £163.10 OWNER Capt J Macdonald-Buchanan & Partners (EAST ILSLEY) BRED Mrs Jacqueline Donnelly
Bt in 11,500gns

2378 Bellow (IRE), gelded since his debut, has finally got his act together and was always in total control, despite the odd flash of the tail. (20/1)

1856* Sick As A Parrot, again among the last away, had to work hard to go second, by which time the winner was long gone. (3/1)

2288 Bali Dance stayed on over this extra furlong but was never doing anything quickly. (4/1: 3/1-9/2)

2419* Three Tenners, close enough with two furlongs left, was at the end of her tether in the final furlong. (7/1: op 9/2)

2295 Kite, a moderate mover, chased the winner against the far rail until fading on meeting the rising ground. (7/1)

1614 Docklands Dispatch (IRE) was again disappointing as he does not look the sort to win in this grade. (20/1)

Dot (12/1: 7/1-14/1)

Lookingforlove Del (IRE) (14/1: 5/1-16/1)

La Vizelle (IRE), blinkered for the first time, looked like boiling over both on the way down and early in the race. (33/1)

2031 Patricia Olive (IRE), quite keen to post in a first-time visor, looked to find the aid a hindrance in the heat of battle. (11/2)

2588 E.B.F. NGK SPARK PLUGS NOVICE STKS (2-Y.O) (Class D)

4-45 (4-45) **6f (July)** £5,663.00 (£1,694.00: £812.00: £371.00) Stalls: Low GOING minus 0.29 sec per fur (GF)

				SP	RR	SF
	Daggers Drawn (USA) (HRACecil) **2-8-12** KFallon(3) (gd sort: bit bkwd: in tch: pushed along 3f out: styd on to ld 1f out: sn clr)	—	**1**	4/11[1]	93++	53
2295[2]	**Deterrent** (JHMGosden) **2-8-12** LDettori(8) (lw: a.p: led over 1f out: sn hdd & outpcd)	4	**2**	7/2[2]	82	42
	Krispy Knight (JWHills) **2-8-12** MHills(1) (w'like: scope: bhd: hdwy over 1f out: r.o ins fnl f)	1½	**3**	33/1	78	38
2425*	**Fiveo'clock Shadow (IRE)** (BJMeehan) **2-8-12** MTebbutt(10) (led over 4f: kpt on)	nk	**4**	33/1	78	38
	Long Siege (IRE) (DRLoder) **2-8-12** KDarley(6) (wl grwn: bkwd: chsd ldr 4f: wknd appr fnl f)	2	**5**	33/1	72	32
	Bahamian Melody (USA) (DRLoder) **2-8-12** TQuinn(4) (gd sort: hld up: effrt & plld out 2f out: nt trbld ldrs)	3	**6**	16/1[3]	64	24
	Above Board (BWHills) **2-8-12** RHills(5) (cmpt: scope: bkwd: hld up: rdn over 2f out: no imp)	1½	**7**	33/1	60	20
1744[9]	**Eastwell Hall** (RCurtis) **2-8-12** MRoberts(9) (a bhd)	2	**8**	100/1	55	15

				SP	RR	SF
2196[11]	**Donegal Sean** (KMcAuliffe) **2-8-12** AMunro(7) (bhd fnl 2f)	3	**9**	100/1	47	7

(SP 115.2%) **9 Rn**

1m 13.35 (1.35) CSF £1.56 TOTE £1.40: £1.10 £1.10 £3.50 (£1.60) Trio £11.90 OWNER Cliveden Stud (NEWMARKET) BRED Cliveden Stud

Daggers Drawn (USA), whose dam is a half-sister to Madame Dubois, has a tall reputation but also one for being laid back. He demonstrated this by moving to post alarmingly poorly and early in the race needed to be scrubbed along but, once he realised this was for real, he fairly shot clear of his rivals in impressive style. He already needs further and is a very interesting prospect indeed. (4/11)

2295 Deterrent is no mug as he showed when second to the July Stakes runner-up last time, but he was comprehensively out-kicked here. (7/2: 5/2-4/1)

Krispy Knight hardly looked ready and so to finish so strongly bodes well for the future. (33/1)

2425* Fiveo'clock Shadow (IRE), taking a big step back up in class, ran a very respectable race. (33/1)

Long Siege (IRE), a tall, eye-catching attractive half-brother to Sapieha, looked badly in need of the race but showed a fine action going to post. Only blowing up in the Dip, he looks sure to improve a great deal for this. (33/1)

Bahamian Melody (USA), a fit-looking quality colt, although rather narrow and on the leg for some judges, didn't show an awful lot. (16/1)

2589 REG DAY MEMORIAL H'CAP (0-95) (3-Y.O+) (Class C)

5-20 (5-21) **2m 24y (July)** £6,472.00 (£1,936.00: £928.00: £424.00) Stalls: High GOING minus 0.29 sec per fur (GF)

				SP	RR	SF
2381*	**Media Star (USA) (74)** (JHMGosden) **4-9-4v** 4x LDettori(14) (hld up: hdwy 4f out: led wl over 1f out: r.o strly fnl f)	—	**1**	2/1 1	86	61
1953*	**Russian Rose (IRE) (70)** (JARToller) **4-9-0** PaulEddery(10) (hld up: hdwy 3f out: ev ch over 1f out: unable qckn fnl f)	¾	**2**	16/1	81	56
2475[2]	**Cloud Inspector (IRE) (72)** (MJohnston) **6-8-13**(3) KMChin(11) (lw: chsd ldrs: outpcd over 2f out: kpt on wl fnl f)	2	**3**	14/1	81	56
2014[3]	**Arcady (60)** (JLHarris) **4-7-13**(5) RFfrench(2) (b: w ldrs: led 4f out: hdd wl over 1f out: one pce)	2½	**4**	6/1 3	67	42
2188*	**Sun Alert (USA) (78)** (MJPolglase) **3-7-10**(7) DarrenWilliams(15) (swtg: hld up: hdwy over 1f out: edgd lft & btn fnl f)	4	**5**	40/1	81	37
2000[8]	**Alwarqa (53)** (MartynWane) **4-7-11** FNorton(12) (lw: hld up: rdn 4f out: hdwy over 1f out: nvr rchd ldrs)	1½	**6**	40/1	54	29
732*	**Regait (85)** (MAJarvis) **3-8-10** RCochrane(4) (lw: trckd ldrs: rdn 4f out: btn appr fnl f)	s.h	**7**	10/1	86	42
2058[16]	**Mister Pink (88)** (RFJohnsonHoughton) **3-8-13** GDuffield(6) (hld up: effrt 5f out: btn over 2f out)	5	**8**	33/1	84	40
2198[6]	**Lime Street Blues (IRE) (60)** (TKeddy) **6-8-4** NCarlisle(5) (prom: ev ch 4f out: wknd 2f out)	2	**9**	66/1	54	29
2284[4]	**Tramline (80)** (MBlanshard) **4-9-10** JQuinn(8) (lw: nvr nr to chal)	s.h	**10**	20/1	74	49
2014[12]	**Northern Fleet (71)** (MrsAJPerrett) **4-9-1b**[1] PatEddery(13) (w ldrs tl wknd wl over 2f out)	5	**11**	13/2	60	35
2142*	**In Question (90)** (BWHills) **3-9-1** MHills(3) (led 12f: sn wknd)	7	**12**	5/1 2	72	28
2014[7]	**Burn Out (63)** (JPearce) **5-8-7v**[1] GBardwell(9) (rdn over 4f out: a bhd)	½	**13**	14/1	45	20
2316[2]	**Spa Lane (53)** (MPBielby) **4-7-8**(3) MBaird(7) (hld up: hdwy 7f out: ev ch 4f out: wknd over 2f out)	8	**14**	40/1	27	2

(SP 122.4%) **14 Rn**

3m 26.55 (3.55) CSF £34.20 CT £343.86 TOTE £2.60: £1.60 £3.30 £3.30 (£34.30) Trio £74.00 OWNER Mr K. Abdulla (NEWMARKET) BRED Juddmonte Farms

WEIGHT FOR AGE 3yo-19lb

IN-FOCUS: This win completed a five-timer for owner Khalid Abdulla.

2381* Media Star (USA), a revelation since the visor has been fitted, is a stayer on the up and won in great style. He remains one to keep on the right side of. (2/1)

1953* Russian Rose (IRE) restrained after the first couple of furlongs, came with a great turn of speed on the outside to challenge, but the winner had too much for her. She looks to have good speed for a stayer and should soon be winning again. (16/1)

2475 Cloud Inspector (IRE), beaten in tight finishes in all three runs this year, lacks a change of gear and was taken off his feet at a vital time. (14/1: 8/1-16/1)

2014 Arcady, dropping in trip, did her best to force the pace but, once collared, had no more to give. (6/1)

2188* Sun Alert (USA), whose lack of pace almost got her into trouble passing the two-furlong pole, couldn't quicken. (40/1)

Alwarqa, who twice won off a higher mark last year, failed to shine after a miserable time over hurdles, but this did seem a little better. (40/1)

732* Regait took a keen grip on Newmarket's wide open spaces going down, and certainly didn't seem to last home. (10/1: 8/1-12/1)

2142* In Question, taken down first, was unable to dominate so effectively in this much bigger field and does give the impression that he needs to get his toe in. (5/1: 4/1-6/1)

T/Jkpt: £7,100.00 (0.3 Tckts); £6,645.74 to Newmarket 10/7/97. T/Plpt: £10.50 (3,915.34 Tckts). T/Qdpt: £7.80 (181.79 Tckts) Dk

2318-LINGFIELD (L-H) (Turf Good to firm, AW Standard)

Thursday July 10th

WEATHER: warm WIND: slt across

2590 SAXONBURY H'CAP (0-85) (3-Y.O+) (Class D)

1-50 (1-52) **5f** £3,785.00 (£1,130.00: £540.00: £245.00) Stalls: High GOING minus 0.28 sec per fur (GF)

				SP	RR	SF
1975[9]	**Bowden Rose (78)** (MBlanshard) **5-9-8b**(3) PPMurphy(5) (stdy hdwy over 2f out: hrd rdn over 1f out: led ins fnl f: r.o wl)	—	**1**	12/1	88	70
1946[5]	**Tuscan Dawn (70)** (JBerry) **7-8-12**(5) PRoberts(8) (a.p: rdn over 2f out: ev ch ins fnl f: unable qckn)	1	**2**	5/1 2	77	59
2339[4]	**Malibu Man (71)** (EAWheeler) **5-8-13**(5) ADaly(4) (lw: led tl ins fnl f: one pce)	¾	**3**	9/2 1	75	57
2372*	**Tinker Osmaston (65)** (RJHodges) **6-8-12** 7x SDrowne(1) (a.p: rdn over 2f out: one pce)	1¼	**4**	12/1	65	47
2326[18]	**March Crusader (80)** (BHanbury) **3-9-8** WRyan(6) (lw: s.s: hrd rdn & hdwy 1f out: one pce)	1	**5**	6/1 3	77	54
1792[6]	**Anokato (66)** (KTIvory) **3-8-8** CScally(7) (b: nvr nr to chal)	1½	**6**	20/1	58	35
2377[2]	**Runs in the Family (65)** (GMMcCourt) **5-8-12b** DHarrison(2) (w ldr over 3f)	½	**7**	9/2 1	56	38
2134[17]	**Kilcullen Lad (IRE) (84)** (PMooney) **3-9-12v** DRMcCabe(3) (lw: stdy hdwy over 2f out: eased whn btn & stumbled ins fnl f)	1½	**8**	9/1	70	47
1419[7]	**Dande Flyer (62)** (DWPArbuthnot) **4-8-9v** SWhitworth(10) (s.s: a wl bhd)	2½	**9**	9/2 1	40	22

(SP 115.6%) **9 Rn**

57.76 secs (0.76) CSF £64.59 CT £289.06 TOTE £12.20: £3.50 £2.70 £1.70 (£20.00) Trio £32.00 OWNER G H S Bailey & N C D Hall (UPPER LAMBOURN) BRED E. A. Badger

WEIGHT FOR AGE 3yo-5lb
OFFICIAL EXPLANATION **Dande Flyer: Rider reported that the colt became fractious at the start, dwelt and lost his chance as a result. Kilcullen Lad (IRE): tried to hang badly right in the latter stages.**
1608 Bowden Rose bounced back to form. Creeping closer from halfway, she was given a few cracks with the whip and came through to assert her authority inside the final furlong. (12/1: op 8/1)
1946 Tuscan Dawn, 4lb lower than when last successful, was never far away and had every chance inside the final furlong, before the winner went by. He has done all his winning at this trip. (5/1)
2339 Malibu Man is a really speedy individual and, once again, set out to make it all under the favoured stands rails but, collared inside the final furlong, then failed to find another gear. (9/2)
2372* Tinker Osmaston found her 7lb penalty telling and, although always close up, failed to find the necessary turn of foot in the final quarter mile. (12/1)
1967* March Crusader proved unruly in the stalls and, when they did open, lost ground. Making headway on the outside of the field a furlong from home, he could then make no further progress. This trip was probably too sharp for him and a return to six furlongs would help. (6/1)
1644 Anokato never threatened to get into it. (20/1)
1975 Kilcullen Lad (IRE) has been murdered by the handicapper after an excellent run at Sandown two outings ago in a conditions event. He was given a very interesting ride on this occasion, steadily creeping closer at halfway with his jockey having an extremely tight hold on him. There did appear to be something slightly wrong with the horse below the distance as his jockey failed to ride him at all and McCabe eased him right down in the final furlong. He later reported that the colt tried to hang badly right in the latter stages. This is certainly not his true running and, sure to be dropped a few pounds as a result, he should soon bounce back into the winner's enclosure. (9/1)
473 Dande Flyer lost all chance with an extremely slow start and his jockey did not persevere. (9/2)

2591 MAPLETON MAIDEN STKS (3-Y.O) (Class D)
2-25 (2-30) **7f 140y** £4,110.00 (£1,230.00: £590.00: £270.00) Stalls: High GOING minus 0.28 sec per fur (GF)

				SP	RR	SF
	Jawhari (JLDunlop) **3-9-0** GCarter(6) (stdy hdwy over 2f out: led over 1f out: shkn up: r.o wl)	—	**1**	Evens^{1}	86	56
1297^{8}	**Northern Angel (IRE)** (MrsJCecil) **3-9-0** GHind(10) (lw: hdwy 2f out: hrd rdn over 1f out: r.o ins fnl f)	1½	**2**	40/1	83	53
2133^{8}	**Selfish (90)** (HRACecil) **3-8-9** WRyan(13) (lw: a.p: swtchd lft 3f out: rdn 2f out: swtchd rt: ev ch over 1f out: unable qckn)	hd	**3**	7/4^{2}	78	48
	Silver Kristal (RAkehurst) **3-8-9** SWhitworth(3) (bit bkwd: a.p: rdn 2f out: ev ch over 1f out: one pce)	nk	**4**	8/1^{3}	77	47
686^{3}	**Red Guard (79)** (GWragg) **3-9-0** AClark(2) (hld up: rdn over 2f out: ev ch over 1f out: one pce)	s.h	**5**	14/1	82	52
2183^{2}	**Lawz (IRE)** (CJBenstead) **3-9-0** AMcGlone(1) (lw: a.p: led 3f out to over 1f out: sn wknd)	5	**6**	12/1	71	41
1851^{5}	**Meilleur (IRE)** (LadyHerries) **3-9-0** PaulEddery(8) (nvr nr to chal)	8	**7**	20/1	55	25
1637^{13}	**Forestry** (JGSmyth-Osbourne) **3-9-0** DHarrison(5) (prom over 5f)	2½	**8**	66/1	49	19
2183^{11}	**Borrador** (RCurtis) **3-9-0** JLowe(4) (a bhd)	nk	**9**	66/1	49	19
2392^{6}	**Pemberley (IRE)** (WJHaggas) **3-8-11**(3) MHenry(9) (s.s: a bhd)	1¾	**10**	50/1	45	15
1265^{8}	**Churchill's Shadow (IRE)** (BAPearce) **3-8-11**(3) MartinDwyer(7) (lw: led over 4f)	1	**11**	66/1	43	13
964^{9}	**Falcon Ridge** (JCFox) **3-9-0** SDrowne(11) (lw: a bhd)	5	**12**	66/1	33	3
1939^{9}	**Nobby Beach** (WRMuir) **3-9-0** WJO'Connor(12) (a bhd)	¾	**13**	50/1	31	1

(SP 128.9%) **13 Rn**

1m 30.56 (1.56) CSF £61.41 TOTE £2.40: £1.20 £11.40 £1.10 (£68.20) Trio £50.90 OWNER Mr Hamdan Al Maktoum (ARUNDEL) BRED James Wigan
IN-FOCUS: **This looked quite a decent maiden, especially by Lingfield's standards.**
Jawhari, well backed in the market for this seasonal debut, did not let his supporters down and had little problem as he cruised through to lead a furlong and a half out, and needed only to be shaken up to assert for a cosy success. (Evens)
Northern Angel (IRE) looked in tremendous shape in the paddock and was far happier with this fast ground. Making headway a quarter of a mile out, he responded to pressure and ran on in the closing stages to snatch second place in the last couple of strides. He should soon find a race. (40/1)
2133 Selfish, racing over a trip just short of a mile, continues to be campaigned over a distance beyond her best. Racing against the rails, she was eased off them three furlongs from home to get a clear run but was then switched back early in the final quarter-mile. One of several with every chance below the distance, she was then tapped for toe. If connections would only drop her back to seven furlongs, they would surely reap the rewards. (7/4: 6/4-9/4)
Silver Kristal did not look fully fit for this reappearance but still showed a great deal of promise, having every chance below the distance before tapped for toe. With this run under her belt and possibly over a bit further, she should soon open her account. (8/1)
686 Red Guard, who has been gelded since his last run nearly three months ago, was taking a drop in distance. Nevertheless, he had every chance below the distance before failing to find another gear. He should soon be winning. (14/1: 8/1-16/1)
2183 Lawz (IRE) went on three furlongs from home but, collared below the distance, soon had bellows to mend. (12/1: op 4/1)

2592 VENNER SHIPLEY GOLDEN JUBILEE H'CAP (0-70) (3-Y.O+) (Class E)
2-55 (2-57) **1m 6f** £3,174.25 (£949.00: £454.50: £207.25) Stalls: Low GOING minus 0.28 sec per fur (GF)

				SP	RR	SF
2139^{5}	**Diego (65)** (CEBrittain) **4-9-12** WJO'Connor(7) (a.p: rdn over 2f out: led wl over 1f out: r.o wl)	—	**1**	6/1^{3}	75	53
1477^{18}	**Moon Colony (64)** (LadyHerries) **4-9-11** WRyan(13) (led tl wl over 1f out: unable qckn)	2½	**2**	16/1	71	49
1805^{3}	**Reaganesque (USA) (52)** (PGMurphy) **5-8-13** SDrowne(6) (lw: a.p: rdn over 2f out: one pce)	2	**3**	5/1^{2}	57	35
2490^{6}	**Durham (52)** (GLMoore) **6-8-13v** SWhitworth(2) (rdn over 5f out: hdwy over 1f out: r.o)	1	**4**	8/1	56	34
2154^{7}	**Almuhtaram (53)** (GLewis) **5-9-0b** PaulEddery(10) (a.p: chsd ldr over 11f out tl over 2f out: one pce)	nk	**5**	7/1	56	34
2146^{8}	**Strat's Legacy (38)** (DWPArbuthnot) **10-7-10**(3)ow3 MHenry(8) (rdn over 3f out: hdwy over 1f out: r.o)	nk	**6**	20/1	41	16
2183^{10}	**Wonderboy (IRE) (58)** (RAkehurst) **3-8-4**ow1 DHarrison(12) (lw: rdn & no hdwy fnl 3f)	1	**7**	10/1	60	22
2279^{8}	**Serious Trust (54)** (MrsLCJewell) **4-8-8**(7) DarrenWilliams(11) (hdwy 8f out: rdn 6f out: wknd over 2f out)	10	**8**	20/1	45	23
402^{5}	**Wottashambles (39)** (LMontagueHall) **6-8-0** NVarley(3) (8th whn nt clr run & bdly hmpd over 7f out: nt rcvr)	7	**9**	15/2	22	—
2398^{12}	**Duncombe Hall (40)** (CACyzer) **4-7-12**(3) MartinDwyer(1) (bhd fnl 5f)	½	**10**	12/1	22	—
	Charming Admiral (IRE) (61) (CFWall) **4-9-8** WLord(9) (a bhd: hmpd over 7f out: t.o fnl 6f)	11	**11**	10/1	30	8
	Prerogative (47) (GLMoore) **7-8-5**(3) JDSmith(14) (a bhd: hmpd over 7f out: t.o fnl 6f)	8	**12**	25/1	7	—
1953^{2}	**Matthias Mystique (57)** (MissBSanders) **4-9-4** AClark(4) (6th whn nt clr run, stumbled & fell over 7f out: dead)		**F**	9/1	—	—
2411^{3}	**Children's Choice (IRE) (48)** (WJMusson) **6-8-9** AMcGlone(5) (bhd tl hmpd & uns rdr over 7f out)		**U**	9/2^{1}	—	—

(SP 139.6%) **14 Rn**

3m 4.37 (6.07) CSF £102.07 CT £497.62 TOTE £6.90: £2.10 £3.40 £3.30 (£101.30) Trio £80.60 OWNER Mr C. E. Brittain (NEWMARKET) BRED T. R. Lock

LONG HANDICAP Strat's Legacy 7-9
WEIGHT FOR AGE 3yo-15lb
2139 Diego, never far away, struck the front early in the final quarter-mile and kept up the gallop to win his first handicap. (6/1)
1277 Moon Colony ran his best race since coming over from France. Attempting to make every post a winning one, he was collared early in the final-quarter mile and, although no match for the winner, held on well for second prize. (16/1)
1805 Reaganesque (USA), a leading player throughout, never looked like quickening up in the straight. (5/1)
2284 Durham, who has managed to beat just two home in five previous runs this season, actually beat quite a few on this occasion as he consented to run on from below the distance to take fourth place. He is not one to trust. (8/1)
1641 Almuhtaram, who has been falling in the handicap, moved into second place setting out on the final circuit but he was collared for that position over two furlongs from home, and could then only go up and down in the same place. (7/1)
Strat's Legacy is finding old age against him but did stay on in the closing stages. He has not one for two years. (20/1)
Charming Admiral (IRE) (10/1: 7/1-12/1)

2593 CRAWLEY DOWN GROUP H'CAP (0-80) (3-Y.O+ F & M) (Class D)
3-30 (3-33) **1m 1f** £3,460.00 (£1,030.00: £490.00: £220.00) Stalls: Low GOING minus 0.28 sec per fur (GF)

				SP	RR	SF
2508[6]	**Right Tune (78)** (BHanbury) **3-9-10** WRyan(6) (lw: chsd ldr: led over 2f out: drvn out)	—	**1**	4/1[3]	84	17
2036[5]	**Lucky Begonia (IRE) (50)** (WJMusson) **4-8-6** AMcGlone(2) (hld up: rdn over 2f out: r.o ins fnl f)	1¼	**2**	5/2[2]	54	—
1689[8]	**Square Mile Miss (IRE) (40)** (PHowling) **4-7-10** JLowe(1) (b: lw: led over 6f: unable qckn)	s.h	**3**	13/2	44	—
1802[5]	**Bubble Wings (FR) (69)** (SPCWoods) **5-9-11** WJO'Connor(4) (lw: rdn over 2f out: hdwy fnl f: r.o)	½	**4**	15/8[1]	72	15
2178[3]	**Misty Rain (65)** (BWHills) **3-8-8**(3) JDSmith(3) (bhd fnl 5f)	6	**5**	6/1	57	—
				(SP 111.0%)	**5 Rn**	

1m 58.22 (7.72) CSF £13.10 TOTE £4.80: £2.30 £1.50 (£7.00) OWNER Mr Abdullah Ali (NEWMARKET) BRED Gainsborough Stud Management Ltd
WEIGHT FOR AGE 3yo-10lb
2508 Right Tune, who beat Entrepreneur last year, appreciated this return to a fast surface, leading over a quarter of a mile from home and responding to pressure to keep her rivals at bay. This is her ground. (4/1)
2036 Lucky Begonia (IRE) appreciated the return to a slightly longer trip. Appearing to be going nowhere in third place early in the straight, she then found her feet in the final furlong and ran on to snatch second prize. A little bit further would help. (5/2)
687 Square Mile Miss (IRE) attempted to make all the running but, collared over a quarter of a mile from home, failed to find another gear. (13/2)
1802 Bubble Wings (FR), put to sleep at the back of the field, was asked for an effort early in the straight but there was little forthcoming. She did run on in the closing stages but, by then, it was all far too late. She looks one to leave alone. (15/8: 11/10-9/4)
2178 Misty Rain (6/1: 3/1-13/2)

2594 SLAUGHTON LIMITED STKS (0-85) (3-Y.O+) (Class D)
4-00 (4-02) **1m 2f** £3,804.85 (£1,136.80: £543.90: £247.45) Stalls: Low GOING minus 0.28 sec per fur (GF)

				SP	RR	SF
1981[9]	**Danish Rhapsody (IRE) (85)** (LadyHerries) **4-9-8** PaulEddery(3) (mde all: hrd rdn fnl f: r.o wl)	—	**1**	11/2[3]	102	68
989*	**Zalitzine (USA) (85)** (MRStoute) **3-8-8** DHarrison(2) (lw: stdy hdwy over 6f out: chsd wnr 3f out: ev ch fnl f: r.o)	hd	**2**	5/6[1]	99	54
	Myrtlebank (85) (HRACecil) **3-8-6** WRyan(5) (lw: hdwy on ins over 3f out: rdn over 2f out: unable qckn)	7	**3**	5/1[2]	86	41
2187[3]	**Polar Champ (78)** (SPCWoods) **4-9-3**(5) GFaulkner(6) (stdy hdwy over 6f out: wknd over 3f out)	6	**4**	12/1	81	47
1679*	**Happy Go Lucky (85)** (RJO'Sullivan) **3-8-8** SWhitworth(4) (chsd wnr 7f)	2	**5**	7/1	75	30
2113[6]	**Minersville (USA) (85)** (JHMGosden) **3-8-11v**[1] GHind(1) (lw: rel to r: a bhd)	9	**6**	10/1	63	18
				(SP 115.9%)	**6 Rn**	

2m 6.59 (1.89) CSF £10.06 TOTE £6.80: £2.30 £1.10 (£3.60) OWNER Mr Chris Hardy (LITTLEHAMPTON) BRED Grangemore Stud
WEIGHT FOR AGE 3yo-11lb
1482* Danish Rhapsody (IRE) made every post a winning one and, although looking likely to be passed by the favourite in the last furlong and a half, he refused to give way and battled on well. (11/2)
989* Zalitzine (USA) cruised through into second place early in the straight and looked certain to pick off the leader as she drew alongside that rival below the distance. However, that rival had other ideas and, although she gave her all, just failed to get by. (5/6)
Myrtlebank made up ground along the inside rail entering the straight but was then made to look very pedestrian. (5/1: 7/2-11/2)
2187 Polar Champ had been hung out to dry as soon as they had entered the straight. (12/1: 8/1-14/1)
1679* Happy Go Lucky raced in second place but, collared for that position three furlongs from home, had soon shot her bolt. (7/1)
2113 Minersville (USA) has completely lost his way since his promising reappearance and looks one to be completely wary of, if this run is anything to go by. (10/1: 6/1-12/1)

2595 BIRCHGROVE MEDIAN AUCTION MAIDEN STKS (2-Y.O) (Class F)
4-35 (4-38) **7f (Equitrack)** £2,277.00 (£627.00: £297.00) Stalls: Low GOING minus 0.58 sec per fur (FST)

				SP	RR	SF
2295[5]	**Mantles Star** (GLewis) **2-9-0** PaulEddery(5) (a.p: led 3f out: all out)	—	**1**	11/10[1]	74	29
2018[4]	**Danzig Flyer (IRE)** (PWHarris) **2-8-11**(3) MHenry(4) (hld up: rdn over 2f out: fin wl)	nk	**2**	8/1	73	28
2349[3]	**Respond** (GLMoore) **2-8-9** WRyan(6) (hld up: chsd wnr over 2f out: rdn wl over 1f out: r.o wl ins fnl f)	s.h	**3**	3/1[2]	68	23
1267[8]	**Highbury Legend** (BobJones) **2-9-0** GCarter(1) (lw: s.s: wl bhd over 5f: nvr nrr)	11	**4**	33/1	48	3
2196[2]	**Signatory** (RHannon) **2-9-0** WJO'Connor(7) (lw: led 4f: wknd over 2f out)	1½	**5**	7/2[3]	45	—
2018[8]	**Captain Jones (IRE)** (BJMeehan) **2-8-11**(3) MartinDwyer(2) (chsd ldr 6f out tl over 3f out: sn wknd)	11	**6**	20/1	20	—
1084[7]	**Solway Lass (IRE)** (PEccles) **2-8-9** DHarrison(3) (lw: a bhd: t.o fnl 5f)	26	**7**	33/1	—	—
				(SP 116.6%)	**7 Rn**	

1m 26.24 (1.84) CSF £10.29 TOTE £2.70: £1.30 £3.10 (£8.50) OWNER Mr David Barker (EPSOM) BRED Castle Farm Stud
2295 Mantles Star moved to the front three furlongs from home and appeared to have the race nicely in the bag below the distance. Unfortunately he started to tie up in the closing stages and, with the second and third really flying, found the line only just saving him. (11/10)
2018 Danzig Flyer (IRE) chased the leaders but appeared to be going nowhere in third place entering the straight. However, he found his feet in no uncertain terms in the final furlong and, absolutely flying, would surely have prevailed in a couple more strides. (8/1: 6/1-9/1)
2349 Respond moved into second place over a quarter of a mile from home and, with the winner tying up in the closing stages, ran on really strongly. (3/1)
Highbury Legend lost plenty of ground at the start and was soon tailed off. He did struggle on in the closing stages but never had a hope of

getting into it. (33/1)
2196 Signatory set the pace but he was collared three furlongs from home and soon in trouble. (7/2: 2/1-4/1)

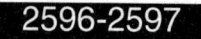

T/Plpt: £55.50 (191.61 Tckts). T/Qdpt: £30.70 (19.64 Tckts) AK

2583-NEWMARKET (R-H) (Good to firm, Good fnl 6f)
Thursday July 10th
WEATHER: sunny WIND: slight against

2596 BAHRAIN STKS (Listed) (3-Y.O) (Class A)
2-05 (2-05) **1m 6f 175y (July)** £10,285.80 (£3,802.20: £1,821.10: £740.50: £290.25: £110.15) Stalls: High GOING minus 0.38 sec per fur (F)

			SP	RR	SF
2027[2]	**Three Cheers (IRE) (104)** (JHMGosden) **3-8-10v** LDettori(4) (hld up: shkn up & hdwy 4f out: led over 2f out: hld on wl) ....—	1	9/4[1]	103	74
2027[4]	**Winter Garden (100)** (LMCumani) **3-8-10** JReid(6) (lw: hld up & bhd: smooth hdwy 3f out: chal on bit appr fnl f: rdn & wandered: kpt on towards fin).......nk	2	100/30[2]	103	74
2486*	**Book At Bedtime (IRE) (98)** (CACyzer) **3-8-5** TQuinn(8) (hmpd after 1f: chsd ldrs: effrt 3f out: one pce fnl 2f).5	3	7/2[3]	92	63
2027[11]	**State Fair (105)** (BWHills) **3-9-1** MHills(3) (lw: hld up: hdwy 6f out: chsng ldrs 3f out: one pce appr fnl f) 2	4	33/1	100	71
2027[6]	**Fletcher (96)** (HMorrison) **3-8-10** RHughes(5) (hld up & bhd: stdy hdwy 4f out: effrt 2f out: rdn & one pce) .....¾	5	40/1	94	65
1930*	**Catchable (84)** (HRACecil) **3-8-10** KFallon(2) (lw: a.p: led over 4f out tl over 2f out: sn rdn & btn) 4	6	16/1	90	61
1230*	**One For Baileys (82)** (MJohnston) **3-8-10** JWeaver(1) (prom tl rdn & wknd over 3f out).......9	7	25/1	80	51
2230*	**Rainwatch (102)** (JLDunlop) **3-8-10** PatEddery(7) (cl up: led 9f out tl over 4f out: sn wknd) 6	8	4/1	74	45
2241[2]	**Lettyfak (FR)** (IPWilliams) **3-8-10** OPeslier(9) (led: hmpd after 1f: hdd 9f out: wknd qckly 5f out: t.o) ....dist	9	100/1	—	—

(SP 112.2%) **9 Rn**

3m 6.68 (-1.82) CSF £8.45 TOTE £2.70: £1.10 £1.50 £1.60 (£4.60) Trio £4.20 OWNER Sheikh Mohammed (NEWMARKET) BRED Sheikh Mohammed Bin Rashid Al Maktoum

2027 Three Cheers (IRE) stays particularly well and, although he needed rousting along some way out, he proved too game for the runner-up when a real fight was on. (9/4)
2027 Winter Garden, who gave the impression that he did not stay at Ascot last time, showed his true colours here and, after looking odds on to win it, then threw it away by hanging. A pair of blinkers might be the answer. (100/30)
2486* Book At Bedtime (IRE) got hampered in the early stages but, otherwise, had no excuses as she had every chance and rather spoilt them herself by tending to hang left. (7/2)
1553a State Fair, who dropped out at Ascot after getting hampered, had his chances here but had given his best over a furlong out. (33/1)
2027 Fletcher spends much of his races on the bridle but, once off it, there is not usually that much to come. (40/1)
1930* Catchable, taking a step up in trip, was made plenty of use of and had his limitations well exposed some way from home, and the very strong pace here might well have contributed some way to this. (16/1)
2230* Rainwatch forced the pace and probably went too fast and stopped a long way out. (4/1)

2597 CHIPPENHAM LODGE STUD MAIDEN STKS (2-Y.O) (Class D)
2-35 (2-36) **6f (July)** £6,472.00 (£1,936.00: £928.00: £424.00) Stalls: Low GOING minus 0.38 sec per fur (F)

			SP	RR	SF
	Embassy (DRLoder) **2-8-11** PatEddery(8) (cmpt: chsd ldrs: shkn up to ld wl over 1f out: r.o wl).......—	1	10/11[1]	85	36
	Expect To Shine (BWHills) **2-8-11** MHills(9) (neat: lw: hdwy ½-wy: effrt 2f out: rdn & r.o wl fnl f) 1¼	2	20/1	82	33
	Zelanda (IRE) (JHMGosden) **2-8-11** AGarth(13) (neat: scope: chsd ldrs: chal 2f out: nt qckn fnl f).......¾	3	50/1	80	31
	Elsurur (USA) (SbinSuroor) **2-8-11** LDettori(1) (gd sort: cl up: chal 2f out: sn rdn: no ex ins fnl f).......1	4	100/30[2]	77	28
	Midnight Line (USA) (HRACecil) **2-8-11** KFallon(4) (w'like: scope: chsd ldrs: rdn over 2f out: r.o one pce).....1	5	9/1	74	25
	Babanina (CEBrittain) **2-8-11** MRoberts(2) (cmpt: scope: led over 4f: wknd appr fnl f).......1¼	6	33/1	71	22
	Obsessed (MRStoute) **2-8-11** JReid(14) (leggy: scope: hld up & bhd: hdwy 2f out: hmpd 1½f out: nvr nr to chal) ....½	7	8/1[3]	70	21
	Cosmic Countess (IRE) (MAJarvis) **2-8-11** RCochrane(10) (cmpt: lw: s.i.s: hdwy ½-wy: no imp) 1¼	8	33/1	66	17
2181[11]	**Baby's Tiara (IRE)** (RAkehurst) **2-8-11** TQuinn(5) (pushed along ½-wy: nvr trbld ldrs).......¾	9	50/1	64	15
	Pre Catelan (MBell) **2-8-11** MFenton(6) (w'like: leggy: cl up 4f: wknd).......2	10	50/1	59	10
	Optimistic (MHTompkins) **2-8-11** DBiggs(11) (neat: bhd: outpcd ½-wy: sme hdwy whn nt clr run ent fnl f)...s.h	11	50/1	59	10
	Gandoura (USA) (JHMGosden) **2-8-11** RHills(7) (w'like: a bhd).......2	12	20/1	54	5
	Queen's Hat (BHanbury) **2-8-11** OPeslier(3) (gd sort: bit bkwd: prom 4f: wknd qckly).......nk	13	33/1	53	4

(SP 122.8%) **13 Rn**

1m 14.0 (2.00) CSF £26.08 TOTE £2.00: £1.30 £3.80 £8.50 (£22.40) Trio £166.70 OWNER Sheikh Mohammed (NEWMARKET) BRED Sheikh Mohammed bin Rashid al Maktoum

Embassy came with a big reputation and justified it in good style, looking as though there is plenty more to come with experience. (10/11: evens-5/4)
Expect To Shine took a while to realise what was needed but she certainly responded to pressure as the race progressed and finished in useful style. She did go a bit freely to post and ought to have learnt plenty from this outing. (20/1)
Zelanda (IRE) shaped well and looks the type to benefit from the run. (50/1)
Elsurur (USA), wearing a tongue-strap, had her chances but, after responding to pressure, was wisely not over-punished when beaten in the closing stages. (100/30)
Midnight Line (USA), a fair sort, found this trip a bit on the sharp side and, after getting outpaced, was sticking on well at the finish. (9/1: op 9/2)
Babanina, looking as though this was needed, ran well until blowing up late on. There should be plenty more to come from her. (33/1)
Obsessed, given a lot to do in this slowly-run event, then met with trouble and by no means had a hard race and is one to watch. (8/1: op 9/2)
Cosmic Countess (IRE) needs to learn to settle and there should be something better to come. (33/1)

2598 LADBROKE BUNBURY CUP H'CAP (0-105) (3-Y.O+) (Class B)

3-05 (3-08) **7f (July)** £23,200.00 (£7,000.00: £3,400.00: £1,600.00) Stalls: Low GOING minus 0.38 sec per fur (F)

Form	Horse	Dist	Pos	SP	RR	SF
2105^{13}	**Tumbleweed Ridge (94)** (BJMeehan) **4-9-6b** MTebbutt(19) (lw: racd stands' side: a.p: rdn to ld ins fnl f: r.o wl)	—	**1**	20/1	107	74
2102a^{3}	**How Long (102)** (LMCumani) **4-10-0** LDettori(3) (hld up: hdwy 3f out: chal 1f out: nt qckn)	3	**2**	16/1	108	75
2124*	**Elfland (IRE) (88)** (LadyHerries) **6-9-0** RCochrane(8) (lw: hdwy ½-wy: led 1½f out tl ins fnl f: no ex)	¾	**3**	10/1^{3}	92	59
2334^{5}	**Tayseer (USA) (100)** (EALDunlop) **3-9-4** KFallon(18) (lw: chsd ldr stands' side: rdn over 2f out: hung lft: kpt on wl towards fin)	¾	**4**	11/1	103	62
2326*	**Cretan Gift (98)** (NPLittmoden) **6-9-10b** JWeaver(16) (racd stands' side: hdwy over 2f out: hung lft: styd on: nrst fin)	nk	**5**	33/1	100	67
2105^{11}	**Prince Babar (100)** (JEBanks) **6-9-7**(5) RMullen(10) (prom: effrt over 2f out: nt qckn appr fnl f)	¾	**6**	10/1^{3}	100	67
2334^{8}	**World Premier (97)** (CEBrittain) **4-9-9** OPeslier(20) (led stands' side 5f: grad wknd)	¾	**7**	16/1	96	63
1578^{7}	**Master Boots (98)** (DRLoder) **4-9-3**(7) CLowther(2) (hdwy u.p 3f out: styd on: nvr nrr)	s.h	**8**	50/1	97	64
2026^{2}	**Crown Court (USA) (93)** (LMCumani) **4-9-5** PatEddery(9) (lw: b: chsd ldrs: effrt over 2f out: nt qckn)	hd	**9**	7/2^{1}	91	58
2026^{8}	**Crumpton Hill (IRE) (92)** (NAGraham) **5-9-4** MRoberts(1) (chsd ldrs: rdn over 2f out: no imp)	½	**10**	15/2^{2}	89	56
2242^{7}	**Law Commission (89)** (DRCElsworth) **7-9-1** DaneO'Neill(7) (effrt ½-wy: sn rdn & no imp)	½	**11**	25/1	85	52
2105^{10}	**Double Bounce (88)** (PJMakin) **7-9-0** DHolland(15) (b: hld up: effrt over 2f out: nvr able to chal)	nk	**12**	20/1	83	50
2161^{5}	**Concer Un (93)** (SCWilliams) **5-9-5** AMunro(4) (b: led tl hdd & wknd 1½f out)	1	**13**	33/1	86	53
2124^{6}	**Welton Arsenal (92)** (KBishop) **5-8-13**(5) RFfrench(12) (effrt 3f out: n.d)	5	**14**	33/1	74	41
2329^{2}	**Azizzi (98)** (CREgerton) **5-9-10** RHughes(6) (chsd ldrs: chal over 2f out: wknd 1f out)	nk	**15**	25/1	79	46
2105^{18}	**Emerging Market (98)** (JLDunlop) **5-9-10** KDarley(14) (b: hld up: hdwy 3f out: sn chsng ldrs: wknd over 1f out)	¾	**16**	14/1	77	44
1799^{10}	**Saseedo (USA) (87)** (WAO'Gorman) **7-8-13b^{1}** EmmaO'Gorman(13) (swtg: s.s: a bhd)	7	**17**	25/1	50	17
1874*	**Neuwest (USA) (94)** (RAkehurst) **5-9-6** TQuinn(11) (b.nr hind: chsd ldrs over 4f: eased whn btn)	¾	**18**	10/1^{3}	56	23
2124^{2}	**Highborn (IRE) (92)** (PSFelgate) **8-9-1**(3) DO'Donohoe(5) (cl up 4f: wknd qckly & eased)	19	**19**	16/1	10	—
1326^{5}	**Jafn (95)** (BHanbury) **3-8-13** RHills(17) (lw: racd stands' side: hung bdly lft over 2f out: sn wknd & eased)	1¾	**20**	12/1	9	—
				(SP 133.4%)	**20 Rn**	

1m 24.86 (-0.14) CSF £275.00 CT £3,172.36 TOTE £16.10: £3.70 £3.60 £2.80 £3.30 (£135.00) Trio £806.20 OWNER The Tumbleweed Partnership (UPPER LAMBOURN) BRED R. A. Dalton

WEIGHT FOR AGE 3yo-8lb

OFFICIAL EXPLANATION **Neuwest (USA): no explanation offered.**

1598 Tumbleweed Ridge, who made up a lot of ground last time after a poor start, had a good draw here and got everything right for once, doing it well. (20/1)

2102a How Long has been in tremendous form this year, albeit without winning. This was another super effort off a high mark and he deserves a change of luck. (16/1)

2124* Elfland (IRE) is in tremendous form at present and put in another great effort here off his highest mark. (10/1)

2334 Tayseer (USA) looked to have plenty on here but ran really well and, by the way he was keeping on, he should get a bit further. (11/1)

2326* Cretan Gift is certainly tough and, although never looking likely to win this, he kept responding to pressure and was still making ground at the finish. (33/1)

1160 Prince Babar keeps running well under big weights but the task was always just too stiff. (10/1)

1148 World Premier tried to make all up what appeared the faster side but he was in trouble some way out, and was well short of pace in the last couple of furlongs, despite struggling on. (16/1)

Master Boots took time to get going but he was keeping on really well at the end and either wants further, or softer ground. (50/1)

2026 Crown Court (USA) looked magnificent and had his chances but lacked a change of gear at this trip. (7/2: 6/1-3/1)

1317 Double Bounce spent the early part of the race swinging off the bit and then failed to pick up sufficiently when asked a question, and is yet to strike any real form this season. (20/1)

1874* Neuwest (USA) (10/1: 7/1-12/1)

2599 DARLEY JULY CUP STKS (Gp 1) (3-Y.O+) (Class A)

3-40 (3-41) **6f (July)** £92,270.00 (£34,130.00: £16,365.00: £6,675.00: £2,637.50: £1,022.50) Stalls: Low GOING minus 0.38 sec per fur (F)

Form	Horse	Dist	Pos	SP	RR	SF
2106^{12}	**Compton Place (111)** (JARToller) **3-8-13** SSanders(1) (lw: hld up: hdwy over 2f out: led 1½f out: r.o wl u.p)	—	**1**	50/1	128	64
2056*	**Royal Applause (117)** (BWHills) **4-9-5** MHills(7) (lw: racd centre: a w ldrs: kpt on u.p fnl f)	1¾	**2**	11/10^{1}	123	65
2056^{5}	**Indian Rocket** (JLDunlop) **3-8-13** RHills(6) (b: led to ½-wy: edgd rt & kpt on u.p)	3	**3**	9/1	115	51
1204a^{6}	**Bahamian Bounty (119)** (SbinSuroor) **3-8-13** LDettori(4) (lw: a chsng ldrs centre: effrt over 2f out: r.o one pce)	hd	**4**	9/2^{2}	115	51
	Coastal Bluff (110) (TDBarron) **5-9-5** KDarley(2) (b.hind: cl up: led ½-wy tl 1½f out: edgd rt & grad wknd)	1¼	**5**	10/1	112	54
2106^{5}	**Easycall (118)** (BJMeehan) **3-8-13** MTebbutt(8) (racd centre: effrt over 2f out: sn rdn & nvr able to chal)	nk	**6**	33/1	111	47
2329^{3}	**Rambling Bear (108)** (MBlanshard) **4-9-5** RCochrane(5) (chsd ldrs tl edgd rt & outpcd fnl 2f)	½	**7**	50/1	110	52
2056^{2}	**Blue Goblin (USA)** (LMCumani) **3-8-13** PatEddery(3) (outpcd ½-wy: n.d after)	3½	**8**	6/1^{3}	100	36
2056^{11}	**Lucayan Prince (USA) (119)** (DRLoder) **4-9-5** OPeslier(9) (lw: racd centre: prom tl outpcd fr ½-wy)	2½	**9**	12/1	94	36
				(SP 113.7%)	**9 Rn**	

1m 12.1 (0.10) CSF £94.92 TOTE £65.00: £7.70 £1.10 £1.90 (£68.50) Trio £135.30 OWNER Duke of Devonshire (WHITSBURY) BRED R. J. Turner

WEIGHT FOR AGE 3yo-6lb

OFFICIAL EXPLANATION **Compton Place: Regarding the improved form, the trainer reported that the colt had found the ground too soft last time, and had settled better here.**

Blue Goblin (USA): Became upset in the stalls.

1590 Compton Place looked absolutely magnificent and, ridden with restraint this time, did everything that was required. His jockey left nothing to chance and drove him all the way to the line. (50/1)

2056* Royal Applause likes to be out in front but was tapped for speed approaching the final furlong and, although battling back, was always second best and probably needs even more use making of him. (11/10)

2056 Indian Rocket went freely to post and came back in similar fashion and there is obviously more ability there when things go his way. (9/1)

1204a Bahamian Bounty dropped back to what appeared his best trip, went well until an effort was required in the last two furlongs, at which point his response was a shade disappointing. (9/2: 7/1-4/1)

Coastal Bluff, making his long-awaited seasonal debut, ran well until the lack of a run told approaching the final furlong and he will no doubt do better before long. (10/1)
2106 Easycall was always struggling to make any progress and, when he did stay on, it was all too late. (33/1)
2329 Rambling Bear found this company too hot when the pace was really on. (50/1)
2056 Blue Goblin (USA) did not run his race this time and something was obviously wrong. (6/1)
1776 Lucayan Prince (USA) had the blinkers left off this time and there was absolutely no improvement for that. (12/1: 8/1-16/1)

2600 WEATHERBYS SUPERLATIVE STKS (Listed) (2-Y.O) (Class A)
4-10 (4-10) **7f** **(July)** £9,581.60 (£3,309.60: £1,584.80: £644.00) Stalls: Low GOING minus 0.38 sec per fur (F)

				SP	RR	SF
1692*	**Baltic State (USA)** (HRACecil) **2-9-0** KFallon(3) (trckd ldr: hdwy to chal wl over 1f out: hrd rdn to ld wl ins fnl f)	—	**1**	8/11[1]	98	44
2335[3]	**Silent Tribute (IRE)** (MBell) **2-8-9** MFenton(4) (led: qcknd 2f out: hdd wl ins fnl f: rallied)	hd	**2**	5/1[3]	93	39
2054[3]	**Arawak Cay (IRE)** (DRLoder) **2-9-0** OPeslier(2) (lw: hld up: effrt over 2f out: styd on u.p: nvr able to chal)	¾	**3**	100/30[2]	96	42
2024[8]	**Ascot Cyclone (USA)** (BWHills) **2-8-9** MHills(1) (hld up: effrt over 2f out: edgd lft & sn btn)	7	**4**	8/1	75	21
				(SP 108.7%)	**4 Rn**	

1m 26.96 (1.96) CSF £4.30 TOTE £1.60: (£2.90) OWNER Mr K. Abdulla (NEWMARKET) BRED Juddmonte Farms
1692* Baltic State (USA) needed all Fallon's considerable strength in this messy race and that was the difference between defeat and victory. (8/11)
2335 Silent Tribute (IRE) tried to pinch this by quickening off a steady pace and it all but worked. (5/1)
2054 Arawak Cay (IRE) tracked the two principals but, when the pace was really on in the last two furlongs, had always just been set too stiff a task to make it. (100/30)
1564* Ascot Cyclone (USA) was in trouble once the pace was stepped up entering the last two furlongs and just seemed to want to hang left. (8/1: op 5/1)

2601 AMCOR H'CAP (0-95) (3-Y.O) (Class C)
4-45 (4-46) **1m** **(July)** £8,740.00 (£2,620.00: £1,260.00: £580.00) Stalls: Low GOING minus 0.38 sec per fur (F)

				SP	RR	SF
2309[3]	**Stilett (IRE) (85)** (LMCumani) **3-8-11** LDettori(12) (hld up: hdwy 3f out: led over 1f out: r.o)	—	**1**	8/1[3]	96	46
1314[4]	**Zoom Up (IRE) (82)** (MJHeaton-Ellis) **3-8-8** SSanders(15) (lw: hdwy 3f out: chal over 1f out: hung lft & styd on)	1½	**2**	33/1	90	40
1399[9]	**Attitude (86)** (HCandy) **3-8-12** CRutter(7) (effrt ½-wy: hdwy 2f out: sn chsng ldrs: styd on u.p)	1½	**3**	16/1	91	41
2214*	**Woodbeck (83)** (JAGlover) **3-8-9** NDay(9) (bhd: hdwy 3f out: hmpd over 1f out: styd on wl towards fin)	nk	**4**	9/1	87	37
1966[6]	**Signs And Wonders (72)** (CACyzer) **3-7-7**(5)ow2 RFfrench(10) (effrt & nt clr run over 3f out: swtchd rt: hmpd wl over 1f out: styd on wl towards fin)	½	**5**	20/1	75	23
2328[4]	**Bali Paradise (USA) (93)** (PFICole) **3-9-5** TQuinn(11) (prom: outpcd over 2f out: kpt on wl towards fin)	hd	**6**	9/1	96	46
2120[2]	**Rudimental (83)** (SirMarkPrescott) **3-8-9** GDuffield(5) (lw: cl up: led 3f out tl over 1f out: wknd)	hd	**7**	7/2[1]	86	36
2013[3]	**Rapier (87)** (RHannon) **3-8-13** DaneO'Neill(8) (hdwy over 3f out: n.m.r & r.o one pce)	¾	**8**	9/1	89	39
2045*	**Vain Tempest (85)** (PWChapple-Hyam) **3-8-11** JReid(3) (prom tl outpcd fnl 2½f)	½	**9**	5/1[2]	86	36
2013[27]	**Caviar Royale (IRE) (95)** (TDBarron) **3-9-7** JCarroll(2) (lw: hld up & bhd: nvr plcd to chal)	2	**10**	33/1	92	42
2062[10]	**Greenaway Bay (USA) (82)** (GWragg) **3-8-8** MHills(1) (lw: effrt over 2f out: n.d)	4	**11**	16/1	71	21
	Poker School (IRE) (87) (NACallaghan) **3-8-13** PatEddery(14) (bhd: effrt on outside 3f out: sn btn)	4	**12**	9/1	68	18
2133[12]	**Alpine Time (IRE) (85)** (DRLoder) **3-8-11** KDarley(13) (prom: rdn 3f out: sn wknd)	3	**13**	25/1	60	10
2137[6]	**Courtship (87)** (HRACecil) **3-8-13** KFallon(6) (cl up: led 4f out: sn lost pl)	1	**14**	9/1	60	10
1773[7]	**Beryllium (82)** (RHannon) **3-8-8** RHills(4) (led 4f: sn wknd)	19	**15**	33/1	17	—
				(SP 129.2%)	**15 Rn**	

1m 39.8 (1.80) CSF £245.77 CT £3,807.87 TOTE £8.00: £2.80 £7.30 £4.70 (£211.90) Trio £415.30 OWNER Scuderia Rencati Srl (NEWMARKET) BRED James M. Egan
LONG HANDICAP Signs And Wonders 7-7
2309 Stilett (IRE) is improving steadily with every run and has a good attitude that should bring further success. (8/1)
1314 Zoom Up (IRE), who disappointed last time on soft, ran much better here but, tending to hang under pressure, was never good enough to seriously trouble the winner. (33/1)
Attitude was always having to work to improve but he kept struggling on and should get further. (16/1)
2214* Woodbeck took time to get into her stride and, when she finally did, she was hampered and, in the end, did really well to finish so close. She is in tremendous form. (9/1)
1651 Signs And Wonders looks a difficult ride but certainly found all the trouble going here and did well to finish so close. (20/1)
2328 Bali Paradise (USA) probably needs more use making of him over this trip and got outpaced at a vital stage, but was keeping on particularly well as the line approached. (9/1)
2120 Rudimental looked well enough and had his chances but was done for speed in the closing stages. (7/2)
2045* Vain Tempest (5/1: 3/1-11/2)
747 Caviar Royale (IRE) never got into this but showed enough to suggest that a further drop down the handicap would make him very interesting. (33/1)
2137 Courtship (9/1: 6/1-10/1)

T/Jkpt: Not won; £17,244.99 to York 11/7/97. T/Plpt: £200.10 (221.87 Tckts). T/Qdpt: £71.20 (25.14 Tckts) AA

2363-SOUTHWELL (L-H) (Standard)
Thursday July 10th
WEATHER: fine WIND: slight half against

2602 ALFRISTON H'CAP (0-65) (3-Y.O+ F & M) (Class F)
2-15 (2-16) **1m** **(Fibresand)** £2,277.00 (£627.00: £297.00) Stalls: Low GOING: 0.05 sec per fur (STD)

				SP	RR	SF
2332[6]	**Phoenix Princess (49)** (BAMcMahon) **3-8-5**(7) SRighton(12) (chsd ldrs: styd on to ld last 75 yards)	—	**1**	10/1	56	32
976[6]	**Kalimat (64)** (WJarvis) **3-9-13** JQuinn(11) (lw: sn trckng ldrs: led over 4f out tl ins fnl f)	1¼	**2**	5/1[1]	69	45

2070[3]	**Arrasas Lady (24)** (JRPoulton) **7-7-3**(7) JFowle(10) (racd wd: a chsng ldrs: styd on same pce fnl 2f)......5	**3**	16/1	19	4
2502[7]	**Charisse Dancer (45)** (CWThornton) **4-9-3** DeanMcKeown(8) (sn outpcd: rdn ½-wy: styd on appr fnl f)........1¼	**4**	8/1[3]	37	22
2246[12]	**Hadadabble (29)** (PatMitchell) **4-8-1**[ow1] TSprake(13) (a chsng ldrs: kpt on one pce fnl 2f)......1	**5**	14/1	19	3
1818[4]	**Cruz Santa (42)** (TDBarron) **4-9-0** RLappin(15) (racd wd: sn in tch: one pce fnl 3f)......¾	**6**	6/1[2]	31	16
2366[8]	**Qualitair Silver (45)** (JFBottomley) **3-8-8** LCharnock(6) (b.hind: w ldrs: wknd 2f out)......5	**7**	12/1	24	—
1443[5]	**Twin Time (65)** (MJHeaton-Ellis) **3-10-0** RPerham(16) (led tl over 4f out: wknd 2f out)......1	**8**	6/1[2]	42	18
2177[20]	**Lachesis (32)** (DShaw) **4-8-4** JFanning(14) (trckd ldrs tl lost pl 3f out)......6	**9**	16/1	—	—
2488[18]	**Commin' Up (42)** (MissMERowland) **4-9-0** NAdams(9) (in tch tl lost pl over 3f out)......3	**10**	16/1	1	—
2313[11]	**Bent Raiwand (USA) (31)** (DonEnricoIncisa) **4-8-3** KimTinkler(1) (hld up: sme hdwy over 2f out: sn wknd)...1½	**11**	25/1	—	—
1998[6]	**Dance Melody (39)** (GROldroyd) **3-8-2**[ow3] AMackay(2) (sn outpcd & drvn along)......½	**12**	33/1	—	—
1798[6]	**Persian Sunset (IRE) (35)** (GWoodward) **5-8-7** LNewton(5) (sn bhd)......2	**13**	33/1	—	—
1796[6]	**Sheilas Dream (48)** (GLMoore) **4-9-6v[1]** CandyMorris(3) (sn bhd & drvn along)......3	**14**	8/1[3]	—	—
2158[8]	**Midnight Romance (43)** (APJarvis) **3-8-6** DWright(7) (racd wd: sn bhd & drvn along)......½	**15**	20/1	—	—
2523[7]	**Redspet (36)** (SRBowring) **3-7-6**(7)[ow3] FBoyle(4) (in tch tl lost pl 3f out)......4	**16**	20/1	—	—
			(SP 127.8%)		**16 Rn**

1m 45.8 (6.80) CSF £52.79 CT £748.52 TOTE £8.90: £2.70 £1.70 £3.80 £2.50 (£22.60) Trio £136.20; £76.76 to York 11/7/97 OWNER Mr R. Thornhill (TAMWORTH) BRED G. Revitt

LONG HANDICAP Arrasas Lady 7-6 Redspet 7-7

WEIGHT FOR AGE 3yo-9lb

2332 Phoenix Princess, who ran too free for her own good last time, was well handled by the boy who looks a promising 7lb claimer. (10/1)

976 Kalimat, tailed off on turf on her previous outing two months ago, handled this surface alright and was only run out of it inside the last. (5/1)

2070 Arrasas Lady, who chose to race wide, showed her vastly-improved effort last time was no fluke. (16/1)

2502 Charisse Dancer, under pressure a long way from home, was staying on when it was all over and will be suited by a step up in distance. (8/1)

1689 Hadadabble has only managed one placing from twenty-nine starts. (14/1)

1818 Cruz Santa was by no means disgraced, considering she had to race wide from her high draw. (6/1)

1443 Twin Time (6/1: 8/1-12/1)

2603 LULLINGTON CLAIMING STKS (3-Y.O+) (Class F)

2-45 (2-45) **7f (Fibresand)** £2,277.00 (£627.00: £297.00) Stalls: Low GOING: 0.05 sec per fur (STD)

			SP	RR	SF
2325[13]	**Alpine Hideaway (IRE) (73)** (BHanbury) **4-9-10** JStack(9) (trckd ldrs gng wl: led over 1f out: drvn out)......—	**1**	15/2[3]	72	52
2377[11]	**Intiaash (IRE) (69)** (DHaydnJones) **5-8-12**(7) JoeleneRichards(4) (lw: s.i.s: bhd: gd hdwy over 2f out: ev ch ins fnl f: nt qckn)......1¼	**2**	10/1	64	44
*2069**	**Bold Aristocrat (IRE) (69)** (RHollinshead) **6-9-3** FLynch(16) (lw: chsd ldrs tl lost pl ½-wy: hdwy on outside over 2f out: hung lft: styd on wl)......1½	**3**	15/2[3]	59	39
2418[6]	**Theatre Magic (68)** (DShaw) **4-9-6** JFanning(10) (trckd ldrs: ev ch over 1f out: kpt on same pce)......1	**4**	13/2[2]	59	39
2070[4]	**Pc's Cruiser (IRE) (33)** (NPLittmoden) **5-8-10v** TGMcLaughlin(1) (lw: s.s: wl bhd: hdwy on outside over 2f out: hung lft: kpt on: nt rch ldrs)......1	**5**	16/1	47	27
2280[3]	**Palo Blanco (77)** (GLMoore) **6-9-5** CandyMorris(7) (trckd ldrs: led over 2f out tl over 1f out: sn wknd)......¾	**6**	7/2[1]	54	34
2463[9]	**Jilly Beveled (36)** (RonaldThompson) **5-8-1**(5) DSweeney(12) (chsd ldrs tl outpcd fnl 2f)......hd	**7**	25/1	41	21
2368[6]	**Sakharov (54)** (BPalling) **8-8-12** TSprake(11) (b: a in tch: rdn over 2f out: no imp)......3½	**8**	12/1	39	19
1786[2]	**Ashgore (68)** (JLEyre) **7-8-12** DWright(6) (bhd & drvn along: n.d)......¾	**9**	8/1	38	18
1787[10]	**Blue Cheese** (MrsNMacauley) **3-8-7** NAdams(15) (sn bhd)......1¾	**10**	50/1	37	9
2002[8]	**Be Warned (76)** (MDods) **6-9-6b** DaleGibson(13) (drvn along ½-wy: n.d)......½	**11**	12/1	40	20
2177[10]	**Sweet Mate (52)** (SRBowring) **5-9-0v[1]** SWebster(2) (b.hind: led tl over 2f out: sn wknd)......1¼	**12**	16/1	32	12
2228[14]	**Golden Ace (IRE) (83)** (RHannon) **4-9-10** RPerham(14) (lw: chsd ldrs tl lost pl 2f out: hung lft & eased)......2½	**13**	11/1	36	16
2020[6]	**Nordico Melody (IRE)** (MrsSJSmith) **3-8-12** OPears(8) (chsd ldrs tl lost pl over 2f out)......6	**14**	16/1	18	—
2496[11]	**Easy Nomi** (KWHogg) **7-9-0** MGallagher(3) (s.s: a wl bhd)......23	**15**	50/1	—	—
			(SP 128.4%)		**15 Rn**

1m 31.6 (5.10) CSF £76.98 TOTE £7.70: £3.10 £4.70 £3.10 (£94.10) Trio £65.60 OWNER Miss Mary Breslin (NEWMARKET) BRED Roseberry Ltd

WEIGHT FOR AGE 3yo-8lb

OFFICIAL EXPLANATION Golden Ace (IRE): hung badly left in the closing stages.

1606 Alpine Hideaway (IRE), having his first outing on sand, handled the surface well and, after travelling comfortably, had only to be kept up to his work. (15/2: op 9/2)

2162 Intiaash (IRE), who gave away ground in the early stages, got almost upsides inside the last and certainly seemed to stay the trip alright. (10/1)

2069* Bold Aristocrat (IRE) can be relied on to give a good account of himself round here. (15/2)

2418 Theatre Magic ran much better after three poor efforts. (13/2)

2070 Pc's Cruiser (IRE), who would have been meeting the winner on two stone better terms in a handicap, ran an amazing race over a trip short of his best. Giving away many lengths at the start, he came on the wide outside turning in but was staying on in good style at the end. (16/1)

2280 Palo Blanco, on her All-Weather debut, travelled strongly but, on this deep surface, seemed to run out of stamina. (7/2)

1261 Golden Ace (IRE) (11/1: 8/1-12/1)

2604 HILTON MEDIAN AUCTION MAIDEN STKS (2-Y.O) (Class F)

3-20 (3-22) **6f (Fibresand)** £2,277.00 (£627.00: £297.00) Stalls: Low GOING: 0.05 sec per fur (STD)

			SP	RR	SF
2467[9]	**Colonel Custer** (CWThornton) **2-9-0** DeanMcKeown(1) (unruly s: w ldrs: rdn to ld over 1f out: styd on wl towards fin)......—	**1**	3/1[2]	76	28
2037[11]	**Flame Tower (IRE)** (RHannon) **2-9-0** RPerham(9) (lw: swtchd lft s: led tl over 1f out: nt qckn ins fnl f)......1¼	**2**	4/1[3]	73	25
2147[3]	**Frankie Fair (IRE)** (MAJarvis) **2-8-9** FLynch(8) (chsd ldrs: effrt 2f out: kpt on same pce)......2	**3**	6/4[1]	62	14
2243[8]	**Black Jet** (NPLittmoden) **2-8-9**(5) DSweeney(4) (hdwy ½-wy: sn rdn: no imp)......2½	**4**	25/1	61	13
	Miss Bananas (TTBill) **2-8-9** TGMcLaughlin(2) (neat: s.i.s: bhd tl sme hdwy fnl 2f)......¾	**5**	25/1	54	6
2419[3]	**Hope Value** (TDEasterby) **2-9-0** LCharnock(7) (sn chsng ldrs: drvn along ½-wy: sn wl outpcd)......3½	**6**	8/1	49	1
	Tamburello (IRE) (JBerry) **2-8-6**(3) PFessey(5) (leggy: scope: bit bkwd: outpcd ½-wy: sn bhd)......5	**7**	9/1	31	—

1961[9] **Lawful Contract (IRE)** (RHollinshead) **2-8-11**(3) DGriffiths(6) (hld up & plld hrd: bhd fr ½-wy)........................19 **8** 33/1 — —
(SP 116.7%) **8 Rn**

1m 19.0 (5.50) CSF £14.07 TOTE £4.00: £1.30 £2.90 £1.10 (£13.10) Trio £5.00 OWNER Mr Guy Reed (MIDDLEHAM) BRED G. Reed

Colonel Custer gave a problem or two at the start but, once underway, did everything right and proved most willing. Very stoutly bred, seven furlongs or a mile will be needed on turf. (3/1: 5/1-5/2)

1791 Flame Tower (IRE) was switched left in the early stages to negate the worst draw. After a good tussle, he had to give best in the final seventy-five yards. (4/1: 5/2-11/2)

2147 Frankie Fair (IRE) raced quite keenly but, after having every chance, could find no more. (6/4: evens-13/8)

Black Jet, a tall individual, was flat-out and making no impression at halfway. (25/1)

Miss Bananas, who is not very big, ran a satisfactory first race. (25/1)

2419 Hope Value (8/1: op 9/2)

Tamburello (IRE) (9/1: op 5/1)

2605 SNELSTON H'CAP (0-70) (3-Y.O) (Class E)

3-50 (3-51) **6f (Fibresand)** £2,810.25 (£837.00: £398.50: £179.25) Stalls: Low GOING: 0.05 sec per fur (STD)

			SP	RR	SF
2313[8]	**Sea Ya Maite (52)** (SRBowring) **3-8-5** DaleGibson(2) (b: trckd ldrs: shkn up to ld 1f out: sn clr: jst hld on).....—	**1**	3/1[2]	62	33
2510[14]	**Zalotto (IRE) (54)** (TJEtherington) **3-8-7b**[1ow2] ACulhane(3) (swtg: sn drvn along & bhd: hdwy on outside over 2f out: hung lft: fin wl)....¾	**2**	20/1	62	31
2206[3]	**Tailwind (63)** (WRMuir) **3-9-2** TSprake(6) (chsd ldrs: led over 1f out: sn hdd & wknd)....3	**3**	9/2[3]	63	34
*2319**	**Big Ben (68)** (RHannon) **3-9-7** RPerham(7) (lw: chsd ldrs: ev ch over 1f out: sn wknd)....nk	**4**	13/8[1]	67	38
2300[4]	**Village Pub (FR) (45)** (KOCunningham-Brown) **3-7-12b** JQuinn(5) (sn trckng ldrs: wknd 2f out)....4	**5**	7/1	34	5
649[3]	**Master Foley (62)** (NPLittmoden) **3-9-1** TGMcLaughlin(1) (led tl over 1f out: sn wknd)....8	**6**	7/1	29	—
2204[9]	**Fonzy (64)** (MrsSJSmith) **3-9-3** OPears(4) (chsd ldrs tl wknd 2f out)....6	**7**	10/1	15	—

(SP 120.1%) **7 Rn**

1m 18.0 (4.50) CSF £54.04 TOTE £6.80: £2.50 £10.90 (£63.80) OWNER Mr S. R. Bowring (EDWINSTOWE) BRED S. R. Bowring

2313 Sea Ya Maite, a particularly tall individual, has given problems in the stalls in the past but, on this occasion, he did absolutely nothing wrong. After travelling strongly and quickening to go three lengths clear, in the end he just held on. Now that he has broken his duck, further success should follow on this surface. (3/1: 9/4-7/2)

1315 Zalotto (IRE), awash with sweat beforehand and with blinkers on for the first time, seemed reluctant to take hold of his bit. With a lot to do turning in, despite hanging left he finished fast. He does not lack ability but is clearly not one to trust implicitly. (20/1)

2206 Tailwind showed ahead for a few strides but was soon left for dead by the winner. (9/2)

2319* Big Ben was worst drawn. (13/8)

649 Master Foley was having his first outing for three months. (7/1)

2606 SELMESTON (S) STKS (2-Y.O) (Class G)

4-20 (4-21) **5f (Fibresand)** £1,984.50 (£547.00: £259.50) Stalls: High GOING: 0.05 sec per fur (STD)

			SP	RR	SF
2412[2]	**Beechwood Quest (IRE)** (BSRothwell) **2-8-6be** LCharnock(2) (mde all: clr ½-wy: drvn out)....—	**1**	7/4[1]	75	30
2367[2]	**Daynabee** (NTinkler) **2-8-6** KimTinkler(1) (a chsng wnr: kpt on fnl 2f: no imp)....5	**2**	7/1	59	14
*2367**	**Chinaider (IRE)** (JJO'Neill) **2-8-11** JQuinn(10) (lw: w ldrs stands's side: rdn ½-wy: hung lft: kpt on same pce: sddle slipped)....2½	**3**	15/8[2]	56	11
2520[4]	**Russian Romeo (IRE)** (BAMcMahon) **2-8-11v** LNewton(4) (chsd ldrs: rdn ½-wy: sn outpcd)....4	**4**	11/2[3]	43	—
872[4]	**Off And Running** (JBerry) **2-8-8**(3) PFessey(8) (s.i.s: sn drvn along & outpcd: hung lft ½-wy: n.d)....1½	**5**	8/1	38	—
2022[11]	**Pollyteknick** (NPLittmoden) **2-8-1**(5) DSweeney(9) (leggy: bit bkwd: w ldr stands' side tl wknd 2f out)....4	**6**	33/1	21	—
	Pride of Bryn (DenysSmith) **2-8-6** ACulhane(5) (s.i.s: sn pushed along: nvr wnt pce)....3½	**7**	33/1	9	—
2396[3]	**Bradbury Falls (IRE)** (DJSCosgrove) **2-8-6** JStack(7) (sn wl outpcd)....3	**8**	14/1	—	—
2304[4]	**Karenaragon** (RonaldThompson) **2-8-6** TWilliams(6) (sn wl outpcd)....3	**9**	33/1	—	—

(SP 125.6%) **9 Rn**

60.7 secs (3.70) CSF £14.89 TOTE £2.80: £1.60 £1.80 £1.10 (£7.70) Trio £5.70 OWNER Mr Walter Bulmer (MALTON) BRED W. J. Murphy and T. J. Newman

Bt in 3,000gns

OFFICIAL EXPLANATION **Chinaider (IRE): saddle slipped.**

2412 Beechwood Quest (IRE) has speed to burn and showed these rivals a clean pair of heels from the halfway mark. (7/4)

2367 Daynabee chased the winner up the centre throughout. (7/1: 9/2-15/2)

2367* Chinaider (IRE), 5lb worse off with Daynabee who she beat two lengths here on her debut, raced upsides the leaders on the stands side. Hanging left under pressure at halfway, her saddle slipped. She would not have beaten the winner under any circumstances. (15/8)

2520 Russian Romeo (IRE), soon flat-out, was left trailing from halfway. (11/2)

872 Off And Running, a tall and weak-looking sort, missed the break slightly and showed a difficult head carriage. He seems to have inherited very little of either his sire or dam's ability. (8/1)

2607 ARLINGTON H'CAP (0-65) (3-Y.O+) (Class F)

4-55 (4-56) **1m 6f (Fibresand)** £2,277.00 (£627.00: £297.00) Stalls: High GOING: 0.05 sec per fur (STD)

			SP	RR	SF
2154[6]	**Dashing Invader (USA) (35)** (PWHarris) **4-7-12b** FNorton(1) (mde all: clr 3f out: hrd rdn & styd on wl: eased nr fin)....—	**1**	7/2[3]	50+	9
2381[4]	**Shy Paddy (IRE) (40)** (KOCunningham-Brown) **5-8-3** JQuinn(8) (in tch: hrd rdn 4f out: styd on one pce)....15	**2**	14/1	38	—
2208[2]	**Heighth of Fame (65)** (JHetherton) **6-10-0** OPears(4) (lw: chsd ldrs: wnt 2nd 4f out: no imp)....1	**3**	100/30[2]	62	21
1100[13]	**Top Prize (35)** (MBrittain) **9-7-12v** GBardwell(5) (bhd & pushed along: sme hdwy on outside over 2f out: nvr nr ldrs)....10	**4**	6/1	20	—
2068[2]	**Bonne Ville (62)** (BPalling) **3-8-10** TSprake(7) (in tch: drvn along 9f out: wknd over 3f out)....6	**5**	3/1[1]	40	—
	Swordking (IRE) (36) (JLHarris) **8-7-10b**[1](3) PFessey(3) (chsd ldrs: pushed along 9f out: sn lost pl)....22	**6**	12/1	—	—
2539[4]	**Early Peace (IRE) (49)** (MDods) **5-8-12b** DaleGibson(2) (sn pushed along & bhd: sme hdwy 6f out: wknd over 4f out)....8	**7**	13/2	—	—
2182[8]	**Mister Jay (48)** (KAMorgan) **3-7-10v**[1] NAdams(6) (sn trckng wnr: rdn & wknd 6f out)....1¼	**8**	16/1	—	—

2498[6]	**Sophie Lockett (40)** (KWHogg) **4-8-3** RLappin(9) (sn bhd & pushed along: t.o 6f out)	dist	9	50/1	—	—	
						(SP 120.1%)	**9 Rn**

3m 12.0 (14.00) CSF £48.57 CT £164.66 TOTE £8.40: £3.30 £2.90 £1.20 (£36.70) Trio £78.30 OWNER The Mutineers (BERKHAMSTED)
BRED Airdrie Partnership
LONG HANDICAP Mister Jay 7-4
WEIGHT FOR AGE 3yo-15lb
2154 Dashing Invader (USA), blinkered on his All-Weather debut, made this a real test of stamina. Driven a long way clear turning in, he would have won by twenty lengths but for being eased up near the line. Connections will be keen to turn him out under a penalty. (7/2)
Shy Paddy (IRE), who has not won for over two years, staged something of a revival. (14/1)
2208 Heighth of Fame was unable to dominate in the way he likes. (100/30)
543 Top Prize was soon in trouble. (6/1)
2068 Bonne Ville (3/1: 2/1-100/30)

T/Plpt: £73.50 (128.86 Tckts). T/Qdpt: £9.50 (74.08 Tckts) WG

2608a - 2636a (Irish Racing) - See Computer Raceform

2459a-HAMBURG (Germany) (R-H) (Soft)
Tuesday July 1st

2637a HOLSTEN PILSNER FREUNDSCHAFTS-RENNEN MAIDEN (2-Y.O F)
4-00 (4-01) **7f** £3,788.00

				SP	RR	SF
	Princess Mona (GER) (HBlume,Germany) **2-8-12** THellier	—	1		—	—
	Wiscalina (GER) (BSchutz,Germany) **2-8-12** AStarke	3½	2		—	—
	Well Set (IRE) (FrauEMader,Germany) **2-9-2** LMader	1¼	3		—	—
1723a[3]	**Supermodel (GER)** (MRChannon) **2-9-0** KWoodburn (btn 19¼l)		5		—	—
						7 Rn

1m 27.3 TOTE 43DM: 19DM 18DM 18DM (276DM) OWNER Gestut Rottgen BRED Gestut Rottgen
1723a Supermodel (GER) was sent off one of the favourites, but was back-pedalling before halfway and may not have handled the ground..

2638a BOSCH-TELECOM-PREIS (Listed) (4-Y.O+)
6-45 (6-50) **2m** £18,939.00

				SP	RR	SF
	Diktys (GER) (HBlume,Germany) **5-9-0** THellier	—	1		113	—
	Fancy Heights (BSchutz,Germany) **4-7-13** ABrockhausen	1¼	2		97	—
	Ballet Prince (IRE) (SJensen,Denmark) **7-8-3** ABest	1¾	3		99	—
1548a[3]	**Lord Jim (IRE)** (LordHuntingdon) **5-9-0** DHarrison (btn approx 10l)		8		—	—
						10 Rn

3m 32.89 TOTE 16DM: 16DM 27DM 32DM (285DM) OWNER Stall Kaiserberg BRED Getsut Rottgen
1548a Lord Jim (IRE) put up a rather mulish display. Unable to get to the front, he was forced up to dispute the lead with half a mile to run, but was never really travelling and dropped away quickly in the final furlong and a half.

DEAUVILLE (France) (R-H) (Very Soft)
Saturday July 5th

2639a PRIX DU BOIS (Gp 3) (2-Y.O)
3-10 (3-14) **5f** £24,691.00 (£8,979.00: £4,489.00)

				SP	RR	SF
2268a[2]	**Zelding (IRE)** (RCollet,France) **2-8-8** TJarnet	—	1		105	—
2103[2]	**Cortachy Castle (IRE)** (BJMeehan) **2-8-11** MTebbutt	2	2		102	—
	Charge D'Affaires (AdeRoyerDupre,France) **2-8-11** GMosse	hd	3		101	—
2127*	**Ouaisne** (RGuest) **2-8-11** DHolland	1½	4		97	—
						7 Rn

60.5 secs (4.00) P-M 4.80F: 2.60F 3.50F OWNER Mr R. C. Strauss (CHANTILLY)
2103 Cortachy Castle (IRE), who appreciates these conditions, put in another bold display, pleasing connections in the process. He may be stepped up a furlong next time with the Prix de Cabourg in August and the Heinz '57' Phoenix Stakes likely targets.
2127* Ouaisne probably found the ground against him and was struggling when hampered over a furlong out. He was staying on though at the finish, and his jockey stated that he would prefer further.

2637a-HAMBURG (Germany) (R-H) (Soft)
Saturday July 5th

2640a HOLSTEN-TROPHY (Gp 3) (3-Y.O+)
3-43 (3-47) **6f** £45,455.00 (£18,182.00: £9,091.00: £4,545.00)

				SP	RR	SF
	Global Player (FrauEMader,Germany) **4-9-3** AStarke	—	1		119	—

				SP	RR	SF
	Fifire (GER) (PPietsch,Germany) **5-9-3** VJakolev	2½	**2**		112	—
	Nautiker (GER) (PRemmert,Germany) **6-9-3** ASuborics	hd	**3**		112	—
2106[3]	**Hever Golf Rose** (TJNaughton) **6-9-1** CAsmussen	¾	**4**		108	—

11 Rn

1m 10.95 (1.45) TOTE 215DM: 54DM 130DM 90DM (5,916DM) OWNER H. Greis BRED Harro U Cloppenburg

2106 Hever Golf Rose broke well from her poor draw and moved into the lead after two furlongs. However, Asmussen reported that he was not happy with her at the halfway mark, and she could only keep on at the same pace when headed a furlong and a half from home. Connections were mystified, but suggested that the rough and patchy ground may have contributed to her poor performance.

2640a-HAMBURG (Germany) (R-H) (Good)
Sunday July 6th

2641a MOET & CHANDON CUP (Listed) (3-Y.O)
12-40 (12-46) **1m 4f** £16,667.00 (£6,667.00: £3,371.00)

				SP	RR	SF
	Maceo (GER) (HJentzsch,Germany) **3-9-2** PSchiergen	—	**1**		111	—
2135[4]	**Poseidon** (MRChannon) **3-9-2** TQuinn	¾	**2**		110	—
	River Foyle (USA) (NLindgren,Sweden) **3-8-12** THellier	hd	**3**		106	—

11 Rn

2m 33.29 (5.29) TOTE 48DM: 20DM 19DM 31DM (192DM) OWNER Gestut Fahrhof BRED Gestut Fahrhof

2135 Poseidon was brought with a well-timed run approaching the furlong pole, but the winner was always finding that little bit extra and he eventually only just held on for second.

2642a BMW DEUTSCHES DERBY (Gp 1) (3-Y.O C & F)
3-50 (3-59) **1m 4f** £173,863.00 (£57,954.00: £34,772.00: £17,386.00: £5,795.00)

				SP	RR	SF
1918a[2]	**Borgia (GER)** (BSchutz,Germany) **3-8-12** OPeslier (mid div: hdwy & 5th st: led ins fnl f: rdn & hung rt: drvn out)	—	**1**		116	—
2097a[9]	**Baroon** (AWohler,Germany) **3-9-2** KFallon (a.p: led appr fnl f: hrd rdn & hung rt: ct ins fnl f: r.o wl)	nk	**2**		120	—
2097a[8]	**Happy Change (GER)** (AWohler,Germany) **3-9-2** WRyan (a.p: led over 3f out tl appr fnl f: r.o one pce)	2½	**3**		116	—
2097a*	**Caitano** (BSchutz,Germany) **3-9-2** AStarke (a.p: hrd rdn & ev ch wl over 1f out: r.o one pce)	1¾	**4**		114	—
2456a[2]	**Zafarabad (IRE)** (JOxx,Ireland) **3-9-2** JPMurtagh (gd hdwy on outside 4f out: one pce fnl f)	3	**5**		110	—
920a[2]	**Baleno (GER)** (BSchutz,Germany) **3-9-2** KDarley (bhd tl gd hdwy over 3f out: styd on fnl 2f)	2	**6**		107	—
	Penalty (GER) (UOstmann,Germany) **3-9-2b[1]** GBocskai (in rr ½-wy: prog fnl 3f: nvr nrr)	¾	**7**		106	—
2097a[4]	**Widar** (ALowe,Germany) **3-9-2** PVanDeKeere (a mid div)	nk	**8**		106	—
	Ferrari (GER) (PLautner,Germany) **3-9-2** WNewnes (unruly s: hld up in rr: no prog)	2½	**9**		103	—
1962[3]	**Yorkshire (IRE)** (PFICole) **3-9-2b[1]** TQuinn (plld hrd: led after 2f tl over 3f out: 2nd st: sn wknd)	1¾	**10**		100	—
2097a[6]	**Icemoon (GER)** (HBlume,Germany) **3-9-2** THellier (a in rr)	1	**11**		99	—
2135[3]	**Conon Falls (IRE)** (JHMGosden) **3-9-2** LDettori (in rr: prog whn hmpd over 3f out: nt recover)	nse	**12**		99	—
2097a[5]	**Mojito (GER)** (ALowe,Germany) **3-9-2** PJohnson (led 2f: prom tl wknd over 4f out)	½	**13**		98	—
	Irish Stainy (IRE) (AWohler,Germany) **3-9-2b[1]** ABoschert (prom: 7th st: sn wknd)	½	**14**		98	—
2097a[2]	**San Suru (GER)** (PRau,Germany) **3-9-2** TMundry (n.d)	nk	**16**		97	—
2272a[2]	**Is Tirol (IRE)** (MHofer,Germany) **3-9-2** ASuborics (hld up: a in rr)	3	**17**		93	—
2097a[3]	**Saugerties (USA)** (HJentzsch,Germany) **3-9-2** PSchiergen (prom to 8f)	4	**18**		88	—
1545a[4]	**Asolo (GER)** (BSchutz,Germany) **3-9-2b[1]** DBoeuf (bhd fnl 3f)	½	**19**		87	—
1544a[9]	**Abou Lahab** (MHofer,Germany) **3-9-2b[1]** KWoodburn (a in rr)	1½	**20**		85	—

(SP 100.0%) **20 Rn**

2m 31.0 (3.00) TOTE 83DM: 29DM 79DM 97DM (2,759DM) OWNER Gestut Ammerland BRED Gestut Ammerland

1918a Borgia (GER) benefitted from a tremendous ride by Peslier. Never really on the bridle, she came with a strong run to lead with one hundred and fifty yards to run and held on despite hanging. Still green, she was a fine second to Que Belle in the German Oaks on her previous start, and both fillies look capable of success outside Germany.

2456a Zafarabad (IRE) was close enough turning into the straight, but found things happening a little too quickly thereafter. He lacks a turn of foot, but is very genuine and would prefer softer ground.

1962 Yorkshire (IRE) pulled his way to the front after two furlongs and stayed at the head of affairs until three furlongs from home. He has yet to run in a race with a really strong pace, but looks one to avoid until he becomes more tractable.

2135 Conon Falls (IRE) was starting to make a little ground from the rear when he was stopped in his tracks and lost all chance beginning the turn for home.

AGNANO (Naples, Italy) (R-H) (Good)
Sunday July 6th

2643a GRAN PREMIO CITTA DI NAPOLI (Gp 3) (3-Y.O+)
9-50 (9-50) **1m 2f** £30,852.00 (£13,577.00: £7,406.00)

				SP	RR	SF
1728a[6]	**Ravier (ITY)** (EBorromeo,Italy) **6-9-2** MEsposito	—	**1**		114	—
931*	**Sandstone (IRE)** (JLDunlop) **3-8-5** FJovine	¾	**2**		—	—
	Hondero (GER) (BOlsson,Germany) **7-9-2** OFancera	hd	**3**		—	—

10 Rn

2m 1.8 TOTE 53L: 19L 15L 27L (64L) OWNER Razza Dormello Olgiata

931* Sandstone (IRE), held up in the rear, stayed on stoutly up the long home straight, but never looked like getting there in time.

2461a-SAN SIRO (Milan, Italy) (R-H) (Soft)
Sunday July 6th

2644a PREMIO PRIMI PASSI (Gp 3) (2-Y.O)
4-20 (4-32) **6f** £30,857.00

			Pos	SP	RR	SF
	Della Scala (IRE) (BGrizzetti,Italy) **2-8-11** GForte	—	**1**		—	—
	That's The Way (BGrizzetti,Italy) **2-8-8** MTellini	3¾	**2**		—	—
2098a*	**Slaney Squire (IRE)** (GColleo,Italy) **2-8-11** MLatorre	s.nk	**3**		—	—
2042*	**Shawdon** (SirMarkPrescott) **2-8-11** GDuffield (btn almost 11l)		**6**		—	—
						7 Rn

1m 14.3 (6.30) TOTE 34L: 20L 35L (161L) OWNER B. Grizzetti BRED Az Agr Il Tiglio de Amelia Prevedello

2042* Shawdon led to halfway before dropping right out in the final furlong and a half. He has disappointed on soft ground once before, and this run may be best forgotten.

2506-CHEPSTOW (L-H) (Good to firm)
Friday July 11th
WEATHER: fine WIND: nil

2645 STRAIGHT MILE H'CAP (0-80) (3-Y.O) (Class D)
6-40 (6-41) **1m 14y** £3,852.00 (£1,161.00: £563.00: £264.00) Stalls: High GOING minus 0.32 sec per fur (GF)

			Pos	SP	RR	SF
2395[4]	**With A Will (61)** (HCandy) **3-8-1**(7) SarahJackson(11) (mde all: jst hld on)	—	**1**	14/1	72	26
2368[3]	**Saratoga Red (USA) (58)** (WAO'Gorman) **3-8-5b** EmmaO'Gorman(10) (a.p: ev ch fnl f: r.o wl)	s.h	**2**	7/1[3]	69	23
2309[5]	**Kewarra (70)** (BRMillman) **3-9-3** TSprake(4) (lw: hld up: hdwy 3f out: ev ch over 1f out: nt qckn)	1¾	**3**	9/1	77	31
2369[7]	**Silver Secret (69)** (MJHeaton-Ellis) **3-9-2** SWhitworth(5) (s.s: plld hrd: sn rcvrd: ev ch over 1f out: one pce)	¾	**4**	16/1	75	29
2557[11]	**What Happened Was (74)** (MartynMeade) **3-9-7** FNorton(8) (nvr nr to chal)	1¼	**5**	10/1	78	32
1567[2]	**Tangshan (CAN) (70)** (MRStoute) **3-9-3** SSanders(2) (swtg: hld up: rdn 3f out: no hdwy fnl 2f)	2	**6**	9/4[1]	70	24
2005[11]	**Tycoon Girl (IRE) (73)** (BJMeehan) **3-9-6** MTebbutt(7) (hld up: hdwy 3f out: wknd over 1f out)	2½	**7**	25/1	68	22
2245[2]	**Jolly Jackson (56)** (RAkehurst) **3-8-3** NCarlisle(1) (lw: bhd fnl 2f)	4	**8**	11/2[2]	43	—
2325[16]	**Tal-Y-Llyn (IRE) (74)** (BWHills) **3-9-7** DHolland(3) (prom over 5f)	8	**9**	12/1	45	—
2062[15]	**Maraud (73)** (JLSpearing) **3-9-6** DRMcCabe(6) (w wnr 5f: sn wknd)	8	**10**	33/1	28	—
2319[3]	**Misty Cay (IRE) (60)** (SDow) **3-8-7** JTate(9) (hung bdly lft over 3f out: a bhd: reins broke)	3	**11**	11/1	9	—
				(SP 113.1%)		**11 Rn**

1m 34.7 (3.50) CSF £95.18 CT £861.89 TOTE £16.30: £3.50 £2.40 £2.70 (£40.30) Trio £115.60 OWNER Mr Henry Candy (WANTAGE) BRED Henry Candy

OFFICIAL EXPLANATION **Misty Cay (IRE): reins had snapped.**

2395 With A Will, reverting to a mile, was the first ride in public for his rider, and not surprisingly the gelding did most of the work. (14/1)

2368 Saratoga Red (USA) confirmed his improvement for the application of blinkers, this time on grass. (7/1: 5/1-8/1)

2309 Kewarra settled better on this occasion off a 3lb lower mark. (9/1)

Silver Secret, due to go down 4lb tomorrow, stepped up on his two previous efforts this season, and seems to be finding his form. (16/1)

2309 What Happened Was, making a quick reappearance, was again 2lb higher than when second at Bath. (10/1)

1567 Tangshan (CAN) sweated up quite badly on an admittedly warm evening, and again apparently did not settle as well as her rider would have liked. (9/4)

2245 Jolly Jackson (11/2: 4/1-6/1)

1973 Tal-Y-Llyn (IRE) (12/1: op 8/1)

2646 EVENING (S) H'CAP (0-60) (3-Y.O+) (Class G)
7-10 (7-15) **1m 14y** £2,626.00 (£736.00: £358.00) Stalls: High GOING minus 0.32 sec per fur (GF)

			Pos	SP	RR	SF
2488[7]	**Gold Lance (USA) (48)** (RJO'Sullivan) **4-9-7** SWhitworth(8) (hdwy 2f out: led ins fnl f: r.o wl)	—	**1**	12/1	59	41
2415[6]	**Dr Woodstock (42)** (MartynMeade) **3-8-6** FNorton(10) (a.p: led 2f out tl ins fnl f: r.o)	¾	**2**	20/1	52	25
2344[7]	**Java Shrine (USA) (53)** (AJChamberlain) **6-9-5**(7) RCody-Boutcher(11) (lw: hdwy over 2f out: ev ch 1f out: nt qckn)	½	**3**	50/1	62	44
2174[11]	**Zahran (IRE) (34)** (JMBradley) **6-8-0**(7) JFowle(15) (hdwy over 2f out: ev ch 1f out: one pce)	1	**4**	11/1	41	23
2171[8]	**Circle of Magic (48)** (PJMakin) **3-8-12b[1]** SSanders(7) (swtg: hdwy over 1f out: r.o)	¾	**5**	20/1	53	26
2152[4]	**Clytha Hill Lad (33)** (JMBradley) **6-8-6** DMcCabe(16) (b: nvr nr to chal)	hd	**6**	9/1	38	20
2488[19]	**Charlton Imp (USA) (50)** (RJHodges) **4-9-2b[1]**(7) DHayden(13) (lw: plld hrd: led: edgd lft & hdd 2f out: sn wknd)	2½	**7**	25/1	50	32
1951[4]	**Northern Saga (IRE) (40)** (CJDrewe) **4-8-8**(5) DSweeney(17) (w ldrs over 5f)	1¾	**8**	16/1	36	18
2375[6]	**Asterix (39)** (JMBradley) **9-8-12b** NCarlisle(2) (b: nvr trbld ldrs)	½	**9**	9/1	34	16
2552[7]	**Shouldbegrey (40)** (WRMuir) **4-8-13** JReid(14) (lw: prom over 5f)	4	**10**	5/1[1]	28	10
2488[2]	**Moneghetti (37)** (JLHarris) **6-8-7**(3) GParkin(4) (n.d)	½	**11**	8/1[3]	24	6
2369[6]	**Finsbury Flyer (IRE) (55)** (RJHodges) **4-9-11**(3) PPMurphy(5) (n.d)	½	**12**	14/1	41	23
2375[2]	**Suile Mor (47)** (BRMillman) **5-9-6** TSprake(3) (lw: bhd fnl 2f)	1¼	**13**	7/1[2]	30	12
2395[9]	**Blushing Grenadier (IRE) (37)** (MJFetherston-Godley) **5-8-10v** DHolland(6) (prom 5f)	1¼	**14**	20/1	18	—
2399[8]	**Flagstaff (USA) (34)** (KRBurke) **4-8-7** JTate(12) (a bhd)	s.h	**15**	16/1	14	—
2004[16]	**Rosenkavalier (IRE) (46)** (LGCottrell) **3-8-10b[1]** MFenton(18) (bhd fnl 3f)	1	**16**	16/1	25	—
2228[3]	**Persian Dawn (34)** (RTPhillips) **4-8-7** MTebbutt(19) (prom 5f)	8	**17**	20/1	—	—
2302[5]	**Indian Serenade (32)** (RSimpson) **6-8-0**(5) AmandaSanders(20) (swtg: bolted bef s: t.o)	22	**18**	50/1	—	—
1926[9]	**Nabjelsedr (38)** (AGNewcombe) **7-8-11** SDrowne(1) (ref to r: t.n.p)		**R**	10/1	—	—
				(SP 136.5%)		**19 Rn**

1m 34.4 (3.20) CSF £227.90 CT £10,116.12 TOTE £23.20: £4.80 £5.40 £18.30 £2.50 (£200.80) Trio Not won; £533.64 to 14/7/97 OWNER Mrs Barbara Marchant (WHITCOMBE) BRED Societe Aland

WEIGHT FOR AGE 3yo-9lb
No bid
1506 Gold Lance (USA) had not run too badly from what turned out to be a bad draw at Warwick a week ago. (12/1)
2415 Dr Woodstock was stepping up to a mile for this return to selling company. (20/1)
Java Shrine (USA), down 5lb, was reverting to a seller, and coming back from a mile and a half. (50/1)
1694 Zahran (IRE) appreciated the faster ground, and being back in this lower grade. (11/1: 8/1-12/1)
1167 Circle of Magic could not take advantage of a 4lb lower mark. (20/1)
2152 Clytha Hill Lad was still 4lb higher than his good second at Yarmouth. (9/1)
2369 Finsbury Flyer (IRE) (14/1: op 8/1)
2375 Suile Mor (7/1: 5/1-8/1)

2647 REGAL RATED STKS H'CAP (0-95) (3-Y.O) (Class C)
7-40 (7-40) **1m 4f 23y** £7,235.60 (£2,184.80: £1,062.40: £501.20) Stalls: Low GOING minus 0.32 sec per fur (GF)

				SP	RR	SF
2194*	**Graceful Lass (86)** (DRLoder) **3-9-6** PatEddery(4) (hld up: hdwy to ld 4f out: rdn out)	—	1	9/4 1	90	60
2027 8	**Sausalito Bay (87)** (IABalding) **3-9-7** SWhitworth(3) (hld up: hdwy 4f out: r.o ins fnl f)	1¾	2	7/1	89	59
1207 6	**Snow Partridge (USA) (82)** (PFICole) **3-9-2** TQuinn(1) (plld hrd: a.p: chsd wnr 4f out: one pce fnl 2f)	½	3	5/1 3	83	53
2058 3	**Ciro's Pearl (IRE) (82)** (MHTompkins) **3-8-13**(3) MHenry(2) (plld hrd: led after 3f: hdd 4f out: one pce fnl 2f)	1¾	4	9/4 1	81	51
2236*	**Just Grand (IRE) (83)** (MJohnston) **3-9-3** JReid(5) (lw: led 3f: wknd over 2f out)	3	5	3/1 2	78	48

(SP 115.7%) **5 Rn**

2m 35.1 (2.70) CSF £16.83 TOTE £2.60: £1.50 £2.50 (£9.50) OWNER Mr A. M. Budgett (NEWMARKET) BRED Kirtlington Stud Ltd
2194* Graceful Lass, up 6lb, looked in control some way out, and just had to be kept up to her work in the closing stages. (9/4)
1647 Sausalito Bay could have found two miles beyond him when highly tried in the Queen's Vase last time. (7/1)
1207 Snow Partridge (USA) was suited by this extra half mile on his handicap debut. (5/1)
2058 Ciro's Pearl (IRE), only up 1lb for her good third at Ascot, ran much too freely here. (9/4)
2236* Just Grand (IRE) had to contend with a 7lb hike in the weights in this tougher race. (3/1)

2648 E.B.F. FLEUR DE LYS NOVICE STKS (2-Y.O) (Class D)
8-10 (8-10) **5f 16y** £3,142.00 (£946.00: £458.00: £214.00) Stalls: High GOING minus 0.32 sec per fur (GF)

				SP	RR	SF
2024 10	**Mugello** (APJarvis) **2-8-13** SDrowne(3) (led 1f: led 2f out: r.o wl)	—	1	7/4 2	94	37
2370 2	**Tempus Fugit** (BRMillman) **2-8-11** TSprake(1) (led 4f out to 1f out: one pce)	2½	2	3/1 3	84	27
2103 5	**Alfiglia** (PJMakin) **2-8-13** SSanders(4) (swtg: pushed along over 3f: hrd rdn & hdwy over 1f out: one pce fnl f)	1½	3	6/4 1	81	24
2138 6	**Days of Grace** (MartynMeade) **2-8-11** JReid(2) (swtg: hld up: a bhd)	4	4	9/1	67	10

(SP 111.4%) **4 Rn**

58.8 secs (1.80) CSF £6.71 TOTE £2.60: (£3.90) OWNER Mrs Ann Jarvis (ASTON UPTHORPE) BRED G. Dudfield
1806* Mugello cut little ice in the Queen Mary, but proved her record-breaking run at Warwick was no fluke. (7/4)
2370 Tempus Fugit was by no means disgraced in a hot little contest. (3/1)
2103 Alfiglia, whose sire has a stamina index of nearly a mile and a half, is finding things happening too quickly over the minimum trip now. (6/4)
2138 Days of Grace had plenty on her plate here. (9/1)

2649 UNIVERSITY AND LITERARY CLUB LIMITED STKS (0-85) (3-Y.O+) (Class D)
8-40 (8-41) **6f 16y** £3,556.25 (£1,070.00: £517.50: £241.25) Stalls: High GOING minus 0.32 sec per fur (GF)

				SP	RR	SF
1980 15	**Dayville (USA) (84)** (JBerry) **3-8-8** DHolland(3) (mde all: rdn over 2f out: r.o wl)	—	1	7/1 3	92	45
1085 3	**Chewit (84)** (GLMoore) **5-9-0** CandyMorris(6) (a.p: ev ch over 1f out: one pce)	2½	2	7/2 1	85	44
2326 8	**Mr Bergerac (IRE) (80)** (BPalling) **6-9-3** TSprake(9) (lw: a.p: r.o ins fnl f)	nk	3	11/2 2	88	47
2393 4	**Golden Pound (USA) (80)** (MissGayKelleway) **5-9-0** JReid(7) (b.hind: swtg: hld up: nt clr run over 2f out: hdwy fnl f: r.o)	1¼	4	7/2 1	81	40
2105 26	**Youdontsay (81)** (TJNaughton) **5-9-0** DaneO'Neill(2) (lw: no hdwy fnl 2f)	¾	5	7/1 3	79	38
2185 2	**Shamanic (84)** (SPCWoods) **5-9-0** TQuinn(1) (plld hrd in rr: hdwy over 2f out: wknd over 1f out)	2½	6	7/2 1	73	32
726 16	**Kilvine (83)** (WJHaggas) **4-9-0** SDrowne(8) (a bhd)	5	7	14/1	60	19
	Mumkin (82) (TThomsonJones) **3-8-8** SSanders(5) (chsd wnr tl wknd over 2f out)	2½	8	20/1	53	6

(SP 118.5%) **8 Rn**

1m 10.5 (1.30) CSF £29.99 TOTE £11.10: £2.40 £1.80 £1.80 (£16.50) Trio £31.80 OWNER Mr T G & Mrs M E Holdcroft (COCKERHAM) BRED Juddmonte Farms
WEIGHT FOR AGE 3yo-6lb
1112 Dayville (USA), walked the last three furlongs to the start, had been highly tried since making a successful seasonal debut. (7/1: 5/1-8/1)
1085 Chewit ran well on this return to sprinting. (7/2)
1446* Mr Bergerac (IRE) would have been 7lb better off with the first two, had this been a handicap. (11/2)
2393 Golden Pound (USA) was another who had a bit to do at the weights. (7/2)
1772 Youdontsay does not seem the most consistent of animals, but has had plenty to do since her Lingfield win. (7/1)
2185 Shamanic pulled like a train, and this run is best forgotten. (7/2: 5/2-4/1)

2650 SUNSET APPRENTICE H'CAP (0-70) (3-Y.O+) (Class G)
9-10 (9-10) **1m 4f 23y** £2,253.00 (£633.00: £309.00) Stalls: Low GOING minus 0.32 sec per fur (GF)

				SP	RR	SF
2398 3	**Glow Forum (56)** (LMontagueHall) **6-8-13**(5) DHayden(3) (hld up: led 3f out: hung rt fnl f: r.o)	—	1	7/2 1	65	41
	Supermick (36) (WRMuir) **6-7-12** KimberleyHart(4) (lw: hld up: hdwy 5f out: ev ch over 1f out: r.o)	¾	2	12/1	44	20
2015 8	**Opera Buff (IRE) (65)** (MissGayKelleway) **6-9-13** JWilkinson(5) (hdwy on ins over 2f out: r.o ins fnl f)	¾	3	9/2 2	72	48
2158 4	**Freedom Chance (IRE) (69)** (JWHills) **3-8-11**(7) SamDickerson(8) (led 5f: led over 3f out: sn hdd: ev ch whn carried rt ins fnl f: nt rcvr)	s.h	4	14/1	76	39
	Meg's Memory (IRE) (55) (AStreeter) **4-9-0**(3) TSiddall(1) (bhd tl gd hdwy over 1f out: nvr nrr)	½	5	14/1	61	37
2236 8	**Westminster (IRE) (64)** (MHTompkins) **5-9-5v**(7) JSavage(2) (dwlt: hdwy over 3f out: one pce fnl f)	s.h	6	6/1 3	70	46
2521 3	**Select Star (IRE) (60)** (APJarvis) **3-8-4**(5) CCarver(10) (b.hind: no hdwy fnl 3f)	2	7	9/1	64	27

2398^{2}	**Bronhallow (36)** (MrsBarbaraWaring) **4-7-7b**$^{1(5)}$ JFowle(6) (lw: plld hrd: chsd ldr: led 7f out tl over 3f out: sn wknd)	6	**8**	13/2	32	8
1805^{9}	**Atlantic Mist (55)** (BRMillman) **4-9-0**$^{(3)}$ RStudholme(7) (trckd ldrs: wknd over 2f out)	6	**9**	8/1	43	19
	Turn To Stone (IRE) (48) (JNeville) **3-7-11** APolli(9) (lw: bhd whn wandered bdly over 2f out)	hd	**10**	16/1	36	—
				(SP 116.0%)	**10 Rn**	

2m 37.8 (5.40) CSF £42.27 CT £175.58 TOTE £3.50: £1.50 £3.10 £2.50 (£32.70) Trio £37.00 OWNER Miss J D Anstee & Partners (EPSOM) BRED Forum Bloodstock Ltd

WEIGHT FOR AGE 3yo-13lb

2398 Glow Forum, up 4lb, was due to go down 2lb, and the fact that her rider had his whip in his right hand held him in good stead in the inevitable enquiry. (7/2)

Supermick, last seen out over hurdles in February, looked straight enough and ran accordingly. (12/1)

1371* Opera Buff (IRE), down 3lb, had one of his better days on grass. (9/2)

2158 Freedom Chance (IRE) was desperately unlucky not to finish in the money. (14/1: op 8/1)

Meg's Memory (IRE) overcame a long absence to win first time out off this mark last season, and finished up running over two miles. It will be interesting to see if she reverts to further next time. (14/1)

2236 Westminster (IRE) was 4lb higher than when winning at Ayr. (6/1: 3/1-13/2)

2398 Bronhallow (13/2: op 4/1)

1169 Atlantic Mist (8/1: 6/1-9/1)

T/Plpt: £1,026.80 (12.42 Tckts). T/Qdpt: £22.20 (26.57 Tckts) KH

2209-CHESTER (L-H) (Good to firm)
Friday July 11th

WEATHER: sunny & v.warm WIND: alm nil

2651 TARPORLEY APPRENTICE H'CAP (0-70) (3-Y.O+) (Class F)
6-30 (6-32) **7f 122y** £2,848.25 (£866.00: £425.50: £205.25) Stalls: Low GOING minus 0.46 sec per fur (F)

				SP	RR	SF
2144^{4}	**Myttons Mistake (53)** (ABailey) **4-8-11** RFfrench(3) (in tch: hdwy 3f out: led ent fnl f: rdn out)	—	**1**	5/2^{1}	64	40
1965^{2}	**Silver Harrow (55)** (AGNewcombe) **4-8-13** DGriffiths(7) (chsd clr ldr: led over 1f out: sn hdd & kpt on u.p)	1	**2**	13/2^{3}	64	40
2418^{2}	**Ballard Lady (IRE) (40)** (JSWainwright) **5-7-7**$^{(5)}$ PDoe(14) (a.p: hrd rdn & ev ch 1f out: unable qckn)	2	**3**	7/1	45	21
2302^{3}	**Dream Carrier (IRE) (42)** (REPeacock) **9-7-7**$^{(7)}$ RBrisland(12) (lw: sn pushed along: hdwy over 2f out: nvr nrr)	½	**4**	12/1	46	22
2488^{8}	**Best Kept Secret (44)** (LJBarratt) **6-8-2v** FLynch(2) (chsd ldrs: effrt & rdn 2f out: kpt on one pce)	2½	**5**	16/1	42	18
2543^{6}	**Reinhardt (IRE) (47)** (DNicholls) **4-8-2v**$^{1(3)}$ RMullen(13) (bhd: effrt u.p 2f out: nt rch ldrs)	nk	**6**	7/1	45	21
2226^{10}	**General Monty (50)** (TDBarron) **5-8-3**$^{(5)}$ VictoriaAppleby(6) (s.i.s: a bhd & outpcd)	2½	**7**	14/1	42	18
2209^{4}	**Steal 'Em (53)** (ABailey) **4-8-8v**$^{(3)}$ PRoberts(11) (set str pce: sn clr: wknd & hdd appr fnl f)	1¼	**8**	12/1	43	19
2204^{10}	**Cee-Jay-Ay (44)** (JBerry) **10-7-13**$^{(3)}$ IonaWands(9) (dwlt: a in rr)	1¾	**9**	6/1^{2}	30	6
1315^{13}	**Magic Lake (45)** (EJAlston) **4-7-10**$^{(7)ow7}$ MelanieWorden(4) (outpcd: a bhd)	2½	**10**	20/1	26	—
2488^{15}	**David James' Girl (38)** (ABailey) **5-7-3b**$^{1(7)}$ JennyBenson(8) (b: lw: outpcd)	hd	**11**	20/1	19	—
2214^{9}	**Gablesea (57)** (BPJBaugh) **3-7-13**$^{(7)ow2}$ PClarke(5) (hdwy 4f out: wknd over 2f out)	¾	**12**	16/1	36	1
2480^{8}	***Panther (IRE) (69)*** (PDEvans) **7-9-13v** OPears(10) (Withdrawn not under Starter's orders: jockey late)		**W**	14/1	—	—
2488^{3}	***My Handsome Prince (38)*** (PJBevan) **5-7-5**$^{(5)}$ DDenby(1) (Withdrawn not under Starter's orders: jockey late)		**W**	12/1	—	—
				(SP 138.9%)	**12 Rn**	

1m 33.63 (1.63) CSF £17.47 CT £95.75 TOTE £3.00: £1.40 £2.10 £3.30 (£10.00) Trio £42.20 OWNER Mr Gordon Mytton (TARPORLEY) BRED R. S. A. Urquhart

LONG HANDICAP David James' Girl 7-4 Magic Lake 7-7 My Handsome Prince 7-6

WEIGHT FOR AGE 3yo-9lb

2144 Myttons Mistake, winning for the first time in two years, benefited from a very confident ride and, produced at the right time, won a shade cleverly. (5/2)

1965 Silver Harrow, beaten in a seller on his previous outing, showed much-improved form here, and he is certainly knocking at the door. (13/2)

2418 Ballard Lady (IRE) found this rapidly-drying ground much too lively, and though she gave of her best, it was just not good enough when the sprint to the line really developed. (7/1)

2302 Dream Carrier (IRE) struggled with the pace on this lively ground, and though he did persevere right to the end, his final placing was as close as he could get. (12/1)

2177 Best Kept Secret has only ever won at sprint distances, and his effort to get himself into the action in the latter stages was never quite going to materialise. (16/1)

2543 Reinhardt (IRE), always being taken along far too fast, was never able to give his supporters much hope. (7/1)

2209 Steal 'Em, successful at this meeting twelve months ago, set a very strong pace, and held a clear lead until tying up and dropping away very quickly once collared. (12/1)

2652 TARVIN LIMITED STKS (0-70) (3-Y.O+) (Class E)
7-00 (7-00) **1m 4f 66y** £3,767.50 (£1,135.00: £550.00: £257.50) Stalls: Low GOING minus 0.46 sec per fur (F)

				SP	RR	SF
2570^{2}	**Nichol Fifty (70)** (MHTompkins) **3-8-7** DBiggs(5) (lw: stumbled s: hdwy 7f out: str run fnl f to ld cl home)	—	**1**	7/1	73	44
2155^{6}	**Slip Jig (IRE) (70)** (KRBurke) **4-9-6** JQuinn(2) (b.nr fore: lw: chsd ldrs: rdn to ld over 1f out: ct last stride)	s.h	**2**	6/1^{3}	73	57
2194^{2}	**Arriving (67)** (JWHills) **3-8-6** KFallon(7) (trckd ldrs: led over 3f out tl rdn & hdd over 1f out: one pce)	2½	**3**	2/1^{1}	69	40
2503^{2}	**Suga Hawk (IRE) (57)** (EJAlston) **5-9-8** JFEgan(4) (hld up: hdwy & drvn 3f out: styd on ins fnl f)	1¼	**4**	14/1	70	54
2316^{6}	**Summerhill Special (IRE) (70)** (DWBarker) **6-9-7** KDarley(3) (b.nr hind: lw: a.p: hrd rdn over 2f out: wknd fnl f)	1¾	**5**	13/2	67	51
2315^{5}	**Lookout (68)** (BWHills) **3-8-5**^{ow1} MHills(8) (led 9f: rdn & wknd wl over 1f out)	4	**6**	11/4^{2}	59	29
2209^{2}	**Nicola's Princess (49)** (BAMcMahon) **4-8-12**$^{(5)}$ RFfrench(1) (lw: hld up & bhd: hdwy 4f out: wknd over 2f out)	5	**7**	12/1	51	35
2213^{2}	**Spondulicks (IRE) (50)** (BPJBaugh) **3-8-2**$^{(5)}$ PRoberts(6) (swtg: prom tl rdn & wknd over 3f out: t.o)	12	**8**	25/1	39	10
				(SP 118.3%)	**8 Rn**	

2m 38.01 (1.81) CSF £45.49 TOTE £8.30: £2.80 £2.60 £1.40 (£68.90) OWNER Mr Lloyd Bedack (NEWMARKET) BRED Sheikh Mohammed Obaid Al Maktoum

WEIGHT FOR AGE 3yo-13lb

2570 Nichol Fifty, well suited by this step up in trip, went one better than he did earlier in the week, though it was only in the dying strides that he finally made it. (7/1: 5/1-8/1)

1036 Slip Jig (IRE) responded to pressure to nose ahead below the distance, and he opened up a two-length lead entering the final furlong, but the strong, late challenge of the winner proved just too much. This was a promising effort, and he should be given a chance to make amends. (6/1)

2194 Arriving gave the impression going to post that she was ill-at-ease on the ground, but she held the call entering the straight, only to be left behind in the battle to the finish. (2/1)

2503 Suga Hawk (IRE) could not go the pace, and though he was staying on in the closing stages, was never a factor. (14/1)

2316 Summerhill Special (IRE), very keen both to the start and in the race, only succeeded in beating herself. (13/2)

2315 Lookout should be well suited to an extended trip, and she was prepared to force the pace, but she was soon in trouble after being headed, and faded rather quickly. The experience should not be lost. (11/4)

2653 BREITLING WATCHES AND WALTONS OF CHESTER H'CAP (0-90) (3-Y.O+) (Class C)

7-30 (7-30) **1m 4f 66y** £6,089.00 (£1,832.00: £886.00: £413.00) Stalls: Low GOING minus 0.46 sec per fur (F)

				SP	RR	SF
1981[5]	**Veridian (73)** (PWHarris) **4-9-1** KFallon(4) (stdd s: hdwy 4f out: shkn up to ld ins fnl f: sn clr)	—	1	7/2[2]	86	52
*2301**	**Twilight Sleep (USA) (77)** (MCPipe) **5-9-5** KDarley(2) (chsd ldr: led over 3f out tl ins fnl f)	3	2	6/1[3]	86	52
2296[4]	**Bardon Hill Boy (IRE) (82)** (BHanbury) **5-9-10** JStack(6) (lw: a.p: jnd ldr 2f out: hrd drvn over 1f out: one pce fnl f)	½	3	8/1	90	56
2483[W]	**Sofyaan (USA) (80)** (LadyHerries) **4-9-8** RCochrane(3) (stdd s: hld up: hdwy 3f out: one pce appr fnl f)	1¼	4	3/1[1]	87	53
2297[2]	**Rusk (75)** (JPearce) **4-9-3** LDettori(7) (lw: hld up & bhd: hdwy over 2f out: nt pce to chal)	1½	5	3/1[1]	80	46
2533[3]	**Rasayel (USA) (72)** (PDEvans) **7-9-0** JFEgan(8) (hld up: effrt over 3f out: sn outpcd: t.o)	13	6	10/1	60	26
2297[5]	**Eagle Canyon (IRE) (71)** (BHanbury) **4-8-13** MHills(1) (led: clr after 4f: hdd over 3f out: eased whn btn fnl 2f: t.o)	1	7	9/1	58	24
				(SP 116.7%)		**7 Rn**

2m 37.84 (1.64) CSF £23.11 CT £143.45 TOTE £5.10: £2.60 £2.10 (£20.60) OWNER Mrs P. W. Harris (BERKHAMSTED) BRED A. L. Penfold and H. Lascelles

1981 Veridian won a tactical race readily, and as long as he can be produced late, he has a good turn of speed which should ensure further success. (7/2)

2301* Twilight Sleep (USA) ran by far his best race yet on this first run since changing stables, and though he is rather high in the handicap, he is fresher than most at this stage of the season. (6/1)

2296 Bardon Hill Boy (IRE), from a stable in form, moved to post very poorly indeed, but he ran a fine race in defeat, and was only shaken off entering the final furlong. He has not yet won a race beyond ten furlongs. (8/1: op 5/1)

2122 Sofyaan (USA), led to post, raced very freely under restraint, and though he was poised to challenge from some way out, was found wanting for a turn of speed when popped the question. He is his own worst enemy. (3/1)

2297 Rusk is rather high in the handicap for a maiden, and it is possible he was not so much at home on this faster ground, for his attempt to get into the action on the approach to the straight never really came to much. (3/1)

2654 RETAIL ADVERTISING SERVICES MAIDEN STKS (3-Y.O+ F & M) (Class D)

8-00 (8-00) **7f 122y** £4,068.00 (£1,224.00: £592.00: £276.00) Stalls: Low GOING minus 0.46 sec per fur (F)

				SP	RR	SF
2495[3]	**Yabint El Sultan (70)** (BAMcMahon) **3-8-12** MRoberts(2) (hld up: hdwy 2f out: led jst ins fnl f: r.o wl)	—	1	9/1	65	39
	Villarica (IRE) (PWChapple-Hyam) **3-8-12** KFallon(5) (s.i.s: bhd: drvn along 3f out: hdwy on outside over 1f out: fin wl)	¾	2	11/2[3]	63	37
1316[12]	**Sceptre Lady (IRE) (85)** (BWHills) **3-8-12** MHills(4) (chsd ldr: drvn along to ld appr fnl f: sn hdd: kpt on u.p)	s.h	3	11/2[3]	63	37
1621[5]	**Chinaberry** (CEBrittain) **3-8-12** KDarley(3) (trckd ldrs: pushed along 4f out: hdwy 2f out: ev ch appr fnl f: rn green: unable qckn)	1	4	5/1[2]	61	35
	Hopesay (83) (JHMGosden) **3-8-12** LDettori(1) (lw: led: rdn & hdd appr fnl f: eased whn btn)	3½	5	8/11[1]	54	28
				(SP 115.3%)		**5 Rn**

1m 33.82 (1.82) CSF £50.00 TOTE £8.60: £2.00 £1.70 (£26.40) OWNER G S D Imports Ltd (TAMWORTH) BRED J. H. H. Benbow and B. A. McMahon

2495 Yabint El Sultan was not winning out of turn and, under a polished ride, swooped through to gain command in the final two hundred yards. (9/1)

Villarica (IRE), whose only previous outing was ten months ago, looked straight enough in condition, but she does not look the ideal type for such a sharp track, so in the circumstances this was a better-than-average performance, and she seems to have what it takes. (11/2: op 7/2)

1030 Sceptre Lady (IRE) came out slightly better on her previous clash with the winner, and she looked to have control when forging ahead entering the final furlong, but in an all-out battle to the line, she was tapped for toe. (11/2: op 7/2)

1621 Chinaberry, struggling to stay in touch half a mile from home, did eventually give herself a live chance approaching the final furlong, but she looked as green as grass under pressure, and she could be a slow learner. (5/1)

Hopesay looked well tuned up for this belated seasonal debut, and travelled smoothly in the lead, but when push came to shove approaching the final furlong, she was soon feeling the strain, and the position was accepted. She should find a suitable opening before long. (8/11: evens-11/10)

2655 KIDSONS IMPEY H'CAP (0-95) (3-Y.O) (Class C)

8-30 (8-31) **5f 16y** £5,894.00 (£1,772.00: £856.00: £398.00) Stalls: Low GOING minus 0.46 sec per fur (F)

				SP	RR	SF
2560[8]	**The Gay Fox (81)** (BAMcMahon) **3-8-8** MRoberts(2) (b: trckd ldrs: nudged along ½-wy: led ins fnl f: r.o)	—	1	7/1	89	49
2339[3]	**Polish Warrior (IRE) (83)** (TDBarron) **3-8-10b** KDarley(4) (w ldr: led ½-wy tl hdd & no ex ins fnl f)	¾	2	3/1[1]	89	49
2211[9]	**Swino (82)** (PDEvans) **3-8-9v** JFEgan(6) (lw: sn pushed along & outpcd: r.o appr fnl f: nt rch ldrs)	5	3	14/1	72	32
2134[15]	**Bramble Bear (72)** (MBlanshard) **3-7-13** JQuinn(5) (sme late hdwy: nvr gng pce of ldrs)	1	4	8/1	59	19
2134[11]	**Darb Alola (USA) (94)** (MRStoute) **3-9-7** FLynch(3) (lw: s.i.s: hdwy 2f out: sn hrd rdn: nvr nr to chal)	nk	5	10/1	80	40
2044[3]	**Brutal Fantasy (IRE) (83)** (JLEyre) **3-8-10** RLappin(1) (b.hind: sn led: hdd over 2f out: wknd 1f out)	½	6	6/1[3]	67	27
2134[8]	**Chili Concerto (84)** (PJMakin) **3-8-11** RCochrane(8) (swtg: chsd ldrs 3f: sn rdn & outpcd: t.o)	6	7	6/1[3]	49	9
2141*	**Nifty Norman (77)** (JBerry) **3-7-11**(7) CLowther(9) (outpcd: a in rr: t.o)	5	8	4/1[2]	27	—
				(SP 112.9%)		**8 Rn**

60.46 secs (0.26) CSF £25.11 CT £261.63 TOTE £7.50: £1.90 £1.60 £3.00 (£12.70) Trio £37.60 OWNER Mr G. Whitaker (TAMWORTH) BRED Cheveley Park Stud Ltd

STEWARDS' ENQUIRY Lappin susp. 21-26/7/97 (failure to secure best possible placing).
2298* The Gay Fox, having his second outing of the week, and returning to the minimum trip, was going nowhere at halfway but, finding extra once straightened up for home, was able to gain his revenge on the favourite. (7/1)
2339 Polish Warrior (IRE), a heavy-topped individual, was far from happy in the prevailing conditions, and though he did appear to have the measure of his rivals approaching the final furlong, was outbattled in a dash to the line. He will return to form when there is a bit of cut in the ground. (3/1: op 2/1)
1254 Swino, off the bridle from the start, was never nearer than at the finish. (14/1)
1571* Bramble Bear was taken off her legs all the way. (8/1)
656* Darb Alola (USA), trotted to the start, could not afford to miss a beat as the stalls opened, and he was always struggling in vain to recover. (10/1)
2044 Brutal Fantasy (IRE), with the best of the draw, was soon having a head-to-head with the favourite, but he was coming out second best in that duel before reaching the straight, as the earlier exertions took their toll. (6/1)

2656 FARNDON CONDITIONS STKS (3-Y.O+) (Class B)

9-00 (9-02) **1m 2f 75y** £8,342.09 (£3,123.90: £1,529.45: £659.75: £297.38: £152.43) Stalls: High GOING minus 0.46 sec per fur (F)

	Horse		Pos	SP	RR	SF
	Bright Water (108) (HRACecil) **4-9-2** KFallon(2) (bit bkwd: hld up: pushed along 5f out: hdwy & rn wd ent st: led 1f out: r.o wl)	—	**1**	5/2 2	100	59
1659*	**Maralinga (IRE) (97)** (LadyHerries) **5-9-6** PaulEddery(6) (led to 1f out: rallied u.p: btn fnl 100y)	2	**2**	6/1	101	60
1982*	**Premier Bay (101)** (PWHarris) **3-8-5** JQuinn(3) (a.p: rdn 3f out: kpt on one pce)	2	**3**	15/2	94	42
1257*	**Catienus (USA) (112)** (MRStoute) **3-8-11** KDarley(4) (chsd ldr tl rdn & btn appr fnl f)	s.h	**4**	9/4 1	100	48
2010 5	**Acharne (110)** (CEBrittain) **4-9-2** MRoberts(1) (lw: plld hrd: prom tl wknd wl over 1f out)	8	**5**	3/1 3	81	40
2315 13	**Murchan Tyne (IRE)** (EJAlston) **4-8-11** JFEgan(5) (a bhd & outpcd: t.o fnl 4f)	9	**6**	33/1	62	21

(SP 113.3%) **6 Rn**

2m 9.24 (0.54) CSF £16.19 TOTE £3.10: £2.00 £2.20 (£10.80) OWNER Mr K. Abdulla (NEWMARKET) BRED Juddmonte Farms
WEIGHT FOR AGE 3yo-11lb
Bright Water, a drifter in the market, no doubt due to his burly paddock appearance, looked to be one of the first beaten when bustled along out in the country, and he had still all of half a dozen lengths to make up three furlongs out. However, with the leaders coming back, he struck the front entering the final furlong, and pulled away for quite a comfortable success. (5/2: 7/4-11/4)
1659* Maralinga (IRE) attempted to repeat his previous all-the-way win here last month, and he did not go down without a fight, but the early pace had been rather hectic, and it took its toll. (6/1)
1982* Premier Bay, a big, strong colt, ill-at-ease on this ever-firming ground, ran well, and if he suffers no ill effects, should not be long in scoring again. (15/2)
1257* Catienus (USA), attempting a longer trip, which should not be a problem, had done all his winning when there has been plenty of cut in the ground, and that was more than likely the cause of this reverse here. (9/4)
2010 Acharne should have been the one to beat here, but he took a fearsome hold, and had run himself out on the home turn. This performance can safely be forgotten. (3/1)

T/Plpt: £350.60 (55.4 Tckts). T/Qdpt: £84.10 (10.56 Tckts) IM

2469-HAMILTON (R-H) (Good to firm, Firm patches)
Friday July 11th

WEATHER: sunny & v.warm WIND: alm nil

2657 'JUDGE' AMATEUR H'CAP (0-65) (3-Y.O+) (Class F)

6-50 (6-50) **5f 4y** £2,640.00 (£740.00: £360.00) Stalls: Low GOING minus 0.56 sec per fur (F)

	Horse		Pos	SP	RR	SF
2540 2	**Pallium (IRE) (45)** (DANolan) **9-10-8b** MrRHale(9) (lw: a chsng ldrs: led ins fnl f: drvn out)	—	**1**	4/1 1	53	35
2237 5	**Belbay Star (31)** (JLEyre) **4-9-8b1** MissDianaJones(10) (led tl hdd ins fnl f: kpt on)	¾	**2**	10/1	37	19
2543 8	**Suedoro (45)** (JSGoldie) **7-10-3(5)** MrOMcPhail(3) (a chsng ldrs centre: hmpd appr fnl f: kpt on wl towards fin)	s.h	**3**	16/1	50	32
2472 5	**Another Nightmare (IRE) (46)** (RMMcKellar) **5-10-4(5)** 5x MrsCWilliams(8) (a cl up: nt qckn ins fnl f)	1½	**4**	9/1	47	29
2540 4	**Six for Luck (46)** (DANolan) **5-10-2(7)** MissDCarter(5) (a chsng ldrs: rdn & one pce fnl 2f)	½	**5**	20/1	45	27
2384 2	**Stephensons Rocket (46)** (RAFahey) **6-10-2(7)** MrCRussell(1) (lw: chsd ldrs centre: one pce appr fnl f)	hd	**6**	5/1 3	45	27
2382 6	**Sunday Mail Too (IRE) (38)** (MissLAPerratt) **5-9-8(7)** MrDBShaw(4) (in tch: rdn & hung rt ½-wy: no imp)	s.h	**7**	20/1	37	19
2061 7	**Insider Trader (60)** (MrsJRRamsden) **6-11-4b(5)** MissERamsden(6) (racd centre: hdwy 2f out: styng on whn n.m.r ins fnl f)	¾	**8**	4/1 1	56	38
2032*	**Palacegate Jack (IRE) (65)** (JBerry) **6-12-0b** MissRClark(2) (lw: w ldrs centre: hung rt appr fnl f & sn wknd)	2	**9**	9/2 2	55	37
2540 15	**Lord Cornelious (30)** (DANolan) **4-9-0(7)** MrsDWilkinson(7) (s.i.s: a outpcd & bhd)	3	**10**	200/1	10	—

(SP 109.8%) **10 Rn**

60.4 secs (2.10) CSF £36.88 CT £493.85 TOTE £5.60: £1.90 £3.10 £4.00 (£19.50) Trio £94.30 OWNER Mrs J. McFadyen-Murray (WISHAW) BRED North Ridge Farm Inc
LONG HANDICAP Lord Cornelious 8-11
2540 Pallium (IRE) made full use of the fastest strip, which despite the drying ground was still on the far rails, and he responded gamely to pressure to gain a well-deserved win. (4/1)
2237 Belbay Star had blinkers on for the first time, and was very much on her toes and looked very lean. However, she did try hard but just found one too determined late on. (10/1)
2543 Suedoro has won all her races over six furlongs, but appeared unlucky here, getting stopped at a vital stage, and is obviously in good heart. (16/1)
2472 Another Nightmare (IRE) had her chances, but is 5lb higher than when she previously won, and although she can go on a fast surface, she is definitely better with real cut. (9/1: 6/1-10/1)
2540 Six for Luck keeps running reasonably, but is not really doing enough when it matters. (20/1)
2384 Stephensons Rocket last won three seasons ago, and that tells its own story. (5/1)
2061 Insider Trader needs the strongest possible handling, and also never saw much daylight here. (4/1)

2658 SCOTTISHPOWER CLASSIC NURSERY H'CAP (2-Y.O) (Class D)
7-20 (7-20) **5f 4y** £3,653.30 (£1,105.40: £539.20: £256.10) Stalls: Low GOING minus 0.56 sec per fur (F)

				SP	RR	SF
1959[2]	**Pierpoint (IRE)** (RAFahey) **2-8-2**(7) RWinston(1) (lw: sn bhd: swtchd rt ½-wy: r.o u.p to ld wl ins fnl f)	—	1	11/4[2]	78	17
2288*	**Inchalong** (MBrittain) **2-7-10** GBardwell(5) (cl up: led wl over 1f out: hdd wl ins fnl f: r.o)	½	2	11/4[2]	63	2
893[4]	**Miquelon** (RHollinshead) **2-9-5**(7) PFredericks(2) (lw: chsd ldrs: sn drvn along: styd on towards fin)	1¾	3	9/4[1]	88	27
2016[14]	**Dispol Lass** (PCalver) **2-7-7**(3) DarrenMoffatt(4) (lw: led early: cl up 3f: sn outpcd)	5	4	50/1	42	—
2233*	**Risky Whisky** (JBerry) **2-8-1b**(3) PFessey(3) (sn led: hdd wl over 1f out: sn btn)	½	5	3/1[3]	48	—
				(SP 111.1%)	**5 Rn**	

60.0 secs (1.70) CSF £9.77 TOTE £3.90: £1.80 £1.30 (£5.50) OWNER Mr R. A. Fahey (MALTON) BRED Mrs C. L. Weld

1959 Pierpoint (IRE) likes the track, and goes on the ground. He is suited by a strong pace, and responded well to pressure. (11/4: 2/1-3/1)
2288* Inchalong is thriving, and ran a game race, but she did not help her chances by going freely to post. (11/4)
893 Miquelon has not been out for some ten weeks, and ran really well, giving the impression that he will be suited by further. (9/4)
1626 Dispol Lass, almost two stone out of the handicap, both looked and ran pretty well. (50/1)
2233* Risky Whisky found this ground in this company too fast. (3/1)

2659 FIELD & LAWN MARQUEES (S) STKS (3-Y.O+) (Class G)
7-50 (7-50) **6f 5y** £2,346.00 (£656.00: £318.00) Stalls: Low GOING minus 0.56 sec per fur (F)

				SP	RR	SF
2169[5]	**Paldost (37)** (MDHammond) **3-8-11** DaleGibson(10) (chsd ldrs: led appr fnl f: all out)	—	1	33/1	55	30
2542[4]	**Fisiostar (37)** (MDods) **4-9-3b** JCarroll(3) (a chsng ldrs: disp ld appr fnl f: sn hdd: kpt on wl)	½	2	33/1	54	35
2472[3]	**Leading Princess (IRE) (48)** (MissLAPerratt) **6-9-4b** JFortune(8) (cl up: hrd drvn over 2f out: r.o one pce)	2½	3	7/2[2]	48	29
2463[11]	**Shontaine (53)** (MJohnston) **4-9-6**(3) KMChin(1) (racd stands' side: outpcd tl styd on wl fnl 2f)	1¾	4	6/1[3]	48	29
2313[4]	**Carreamia (53)** (JLEyre) **4-8-12** MGallagher(4) (sn outpcd: styd on fnl f: nrst fin)	hd	5	7/2[2]	37	18
2501*	**Bollero (IRE) (56)** (JBerry) **3-8-9**(3) PFessey(11) (lw: led tl hdd & wknd appr fnl f)	¾	6	7/4[1]	41	16
2002[14]	**Henry the Hawk (45)** (MDods) **6-8-12**(5) SCopp(2) (b: swtg: racd centre: outpcd ½-wy: nvr trbld ldrs)	3	7	10/1	32	13
956[13]	**True Ballad (37)** (JSGoldie) **5-9-3** ACulhane(9) (hld up & bhd: n.d)	3	8	25/1	24	5
2472[6]	**Diet (33)** (MissLAPerratt) **11-9-0v**(3) DarrenMoffatt(6) (nvr wnt pce)	1	9	33/1	22	3
2382[9]	**Aye Ready (25)** (DANolan) **4-9-3** VHalliday(5) (dwlt: a bhd stands' side: t.o)	dist	10	200/1	—	—
2541[5]	**Ragtime Cowgirl (39)** (DANolan) **4-8-7**(5) KSked(7) (sn outpcd & bhd)	1½	11	25/1	—	—
				(SP 121.2%)	**11 Rn**	

1m 11.2 (1.20) CSF £739.97 TOTE £65.80: £8.70 £4.70 £2.20 (£241.60) Trio £264.00 OWNER Mr S. T. Brankin (MIDDLEHAM) BRED Micky Hammond Racing Ltd and S. Branklin
WEIGHT FOR AGE 3yo-6lb
No bid

2169 Paldost got the favoured far side, continued his improvement, and showed a good attitude under pressure. (33/1)
2542 Fisiostar is an in-and-out performer, who again showed that when in the mood he has the ability. (33/1)
2472 Leading Princess (IRE) did not look quite as well as usual, but still ran a useful race. (7/2)
2366 Shontaine raced up the stands rails which seemed a massive disadvantage, and in the circumstances did really well. He is one to keep in mind for similar events. (6/1)
2313 Carreamia struggles with the early pace, and either needs a pair of blinkers or further. (7/2)
2501* Bollero (IRE), although dropping back in trip, still managed to force the pace, but the effort of seeing off some pretty quick horses tapped all reserves approaching the last furlong. (7/4)
1816 Henry the Hawk (10/1: 6/1-12/1)

2660 'HAMILTON PARK SUNDAY MAIL SERIES' FINAL H'CAP (3-Y.O+) (Class B)
8-20 (8-20) **1m 1f 36y** £8,905.00 (£2,695.00: £1,315.00: £625.00) Stalls: High GOING minus 0.56 sec per fur (F)

				SP	RR	SF
2533[4]	**Askern (60)** (DHaydnJones) **6-9-1** AMackay(14) (lw: chsd ldr after 2f: led over 2f out: hld on wl)	—	1	3/1[1]	69	44
2546[5]	**Nobby Barnes (41)** (DonEnricoIncisa) **8-7-10** KimTinkler(2) (dwlt: hdwy 3f out: swtchd lft: r.o wl fnl f)	½	2	12/1	49	24
*2368**	**Monte Cavo (50)** (MBrittain) **6-8-5** 5x GBardwell(1) (in tch: styd on u.p fnl 2f: nrst fin)	nk	3	7/1[3]	58	33
2355[2]	**Best of All (IRE) (73)** (JBerry) **5-10-0b** ACulhane(7) (hdwy ½-wy: n.m.r over 1f out: styd on wl fnl f)	½	4	10/1	80	55
2362[4]	**Bedazzle (41)** (MBrittain) **6-7-3**(7) DMernagh(13) (lw: hdwy 4f out: chsng ldrs 2f out: r.o one pce)	2½	5	25/1	43	18
1862[2]	**Pekay (64)** (MJohnston) **4-9-2**(3) DarrenMoffatt(16) (chsd ldrs: rdn over 2f out: grad wknd)	¾	6	11/2[2]	65	40
2385[3]	**Sarmatian (USA) (71)** (MDHammond) **6-9-5**(7) NHorrocks(10) (lw: led tl hdd over 2f out: rdn & btn over 1f out)	s.h	7	8/1	72	47
2293[4]	**Gold Desire (49)** (MBrittain) **7-8-4** JCarroll(5) (lw: chsd ldrs tl wknd over 1f out)	2½	8	14/1	46	21
2342[5]	**One Life To Live (IRE) (52)** (SEKettlewell) **4-8-7** JFortune(11) (in tch: effrt over 3f out: sn btn)	3	9	11/1	43	18
2470[3]	**Rattle (45)** (DANolan) **4-7-9**(5)ow4 KSked(15) (prom tl wknd fnl 3f)	3	10	100/1	31	2
2385[5]	**Principal Boy (IRE) (49)** (TJEtherington) **4-8-4** DaleGibson(6) (bhd: effrt over 4f out: n.d)	½	11	12/1	34	9
2469[10]	**Rapid Mover (42)** (DANolan) **10-7-4**(7)ow1 NPollard(9) (n.d)	½	12	100/1	26	—
2385*	**Canadian Fantasy (79)** (MJohnston) **3-9-7**(3) 5x KMChin(8) (sn bhd)	s.h	13	9/1	63	28
2469[9]	**Hutchies Lady (41)** (RMMcKellar) **5-7-3**(7) JMcAuley(12) (b. hind: a bhd)	nk	14	100/1	25	—
2385[2]	**Western General (73)** (MissMKMilligan) **6-9-11**(3) PFessey(3) (lw: in tch tl outpcd fr ½-wy: sn bhd)	4	15	10/1	50	25
				(SP 129.4%)	**15 Rn**	

1m 55.5 (1.20) CSF £40.10 CT £225.96 TOTE £3.40: £1.70 £1.80 £3.00 (£17.30) Trio £80.80 OWNER Mr Hugh O'Donnell (PONTYPRIDD) BRED Highclere Stud Ltd
LONG HANDICAP Bedazzle 7-7 Nobby Barnes 7-9 Rattle 6-8 Hutchies Lady 7-3 Rapid Mover 6-9
WEIGHT FOR AGE 3yo-10lb

2533 Askern is certainly useful when in the mood and everything was right on this occasion. Well handicapped, he did it in good style. (3/1)
2546 Nobby Barnes, set a lot to do as usual, came sailing through when it was just too late. It is three years since he last won, but he is knocking at the door. (12/1)
2368* Monte Cavo, despite shooting up the weights, showed he is in top form and kept battling al the way to the line. (7/1)
2355 Best of All (IRE) came from off the pace and had a few problems in running but certainly finished quite well. (10/1)
2362 Bedazzle has only ever won once but put up a useful effort here and looks particularly well. (25/1)
1862 Pekay had his chances but was short of pace at the business end. (11/2)

2385 Sarmatian (USA) attempted to make it all, but seemed to go too fast too soon and was picked off with ease. (8/1)
2293 Gold Desire looked well but found things happening too quickly over this shorter trip. (14/1)
2342 One Life To Live (IRE) had no headgear on this time and ran moderately. (11/1)

2661 SCOTTISHPOWER TROPHY CLAIMING STKS (3-Y.O+) (Class D)

8-50 (8-50) **1m 4f 17y** £3,403.75 (£1,030.00: £502.50: £238.75) Stalls: High GOING minus 0.56 sec per fur (F)

			SP	RR	SF
2369[15]	**Urgent Reply (USA) (56)** (CADwyer) **4-9-4** JCarroll(3) (lw: mde all: qcknd over 2f out: r.o) ....—	1	5/2[2]	58	22
2170[3]	**Latvian (57)** (RAllan) **10-9-4v** JFortune(7) (lw: a chsng wnr: rdn & hung rt over 2f out: styd on towards fin)...1½	2	Evens[1]	56	20
2208[4]	**Cois Na Farraige (IRE) (46)** (MissLAPerratt) **4-9-3**(3) PFessey(4) (chsd ldrs: effrt 3f out: r.o one pce) 1	3	6/1[3]	57	21
	Havana Heights (IRE) (40) (JLEyre) **4-9-0** MGallagher(5) (hdwy 5f out: rdn over 2f out: nvr able to chal)......2½	4	10/1	47	11
	School of Science (22) (DANolan) **7-8-11**(5) KSked(2) (in tch: outpcd over 3f out: no imp after)....2½	5	100/1	28 t	10
2470[4]	**Ribbonletta** (MissLAPerratt) **3-7-5**(7) DMernagh(6) (dwlt: bhd: hung lft & racd stands' side fnl 3f: n.d) 3½	6	50/1	18 t	—
2539[7]	**Flash of Realm (FR) (48)** (PMonteith) **11-8-8**(7) RWinston(1) (lw: prom tl outpcd fnl 3½f) 4	7	20/1	17 t	—
			(SP 109.7%)		**7 Rn**

2m 37.6 (5.60) CSF £4.42 TOTE £3.40: £1.90 £1.40 (£2.90) OWNER Mr S. Aitken (NEWMARKET) BRED Clovelly Farms
WEIGHT FOR AGE 3yo-13lb
1106 Urgent Reply (USA) looked superb and had too much courage for the runner-up. (5/2)
2170 Latvian had plenty of chances, but was always tending to hang when ridden and, despite keeping on, was never doing enough. (Evens)
2208 Cois Na Farraige (IRE) has ability but gives the impression that he is never quite giving it his best shot. (6/1)
Havana Heights (IRE) ran a reasonable first race of the season, but never looked likely to offer a threat. (10/1: 8/1-12/1)
School of Science is still a maiden after seventeen attempts and there is no real sign of him doing anything about that. (100/1)
2470 Ribbonletta ran a shade better but was again edgy in the stalls and looked very lean. There is plenty more needed. (50/1)

2662 JOE PUNTER MAIDEN H'CAP (0-60) (3-Y.O+) (Class F)

9-20 (9-21) **1m 5f 9y** £2,780.00 (£780.00: £380.00) Stalls: High GOING minus 0.56 sec per fur (F)

			SP	RR	SF
2207[6]	**Old Hush Wing (IRE) (40)** (PCHaslam) **4-8-10** JFortune(8) (swtg: chsd ldrs: rdn to ld appr fnl f: styd on) ......—	1	13/2	50	27
	Lagan (39) (KAMorgan) **4-8-2**(7) RWinston(2) (swtg: set str pace tl hdd appr fnl f: no ex)....4	2	13/2	44	21
2518[4]	**Ballet de Cour (26)** (TJEtherington) **4-7-7b**(3) PFessey(7) (bhd: hdwy over 2f out: styd on wl: nrst fin) ....¾	3	20/1	30	7
2387[4]	**Maremma (40)** (DonEnricoIncisa) **3-7-10** KimTinkler(3) (dwlt: hdwy over 2f out: nvr rchd ldrs) 1½	4	16/1	42	5
2386[2]	**Miami Moon (44)** (CWThornton) **3-8-0** DaleGibson(1) (trckd ldrs: effrt 3f out: rdn & btn 2f out) 3½	5	3/1[2]	42	5
2008[15]	**Frankie (54)** (MHTompkins) **3-8-10** JCarroll(6) (lw: chsd ldrs: rdn over 3f out: wknd fnl 2f) 5	6	4/1[3]	46	9
1838[9]	**Operatic Dancer (27)** (RMMcKellar) **6-7-4**(7) JMcAuley(9) (outpcd & lost tch fnl 4f)....2½	7	100/1	16	—
	Cool Grey (40) (JJO'Neill) **3-7-10** GBardwell(5) (chsd ldr 6f: wknd rapidly tl t.o)....dist	8	20/1	—	—
2046[15]	***Ardarroch Prince (57)*** (MrsMReveley) **6-9-13** ACulhane(4) (lw: Withdrawn not under Starter's orders: ref to ent stalls)....	W	9/4[1]	—	—
			(SP 118.8%)		**8 Rn**

2m 49.6 (3.90) CSF £23.01 CT £246.62 TOTE £6.00: £1.80 £1.70 £2.30 (£32.00) Trio £36.60 OWNER Mr John Blakey (MIDDLEHAM) BRED Lodge Park Stud
LONG HANDICAP Ballet de Cour 7-9 Cool Grey 7-8 Maremma 7-6
WEIGHT FOR AGE 3yo-14lb
2207 Old Hush Wing (IRE), despite getting very warm beforehand, proved to be a determined stayer and got better as the race progressed. (13/2: 5/1-8/1)
Lagan was absolutely dripping with sweat beforehand and then tried to gallop his rivals into the ground, but was comfortably picked off. (13/2: 3/1-7/1)
2518 Ballet de Cour showed he has a little ability by staying on when it was all over. (20/1)
2387 Maremma, as usual for this yard, missed the break and, although making some late ground, never had a hope. (16/1)
2386 Miami Moon was disappointing here, failing to get home after racing too freely. Something was obviously not quite right with her. (3/1)
Frankie, first time in a handicap and over his longest trip to date, proved a big disappointment. (4/1: 3/1-9/2)

T/Plpt: £263.80 (47.07 Tckts). T/Qdpt: £29.50 (28.16 Tckts) AA

2590-LINGFIELD (L-H) (Good to firm, Firm patches, AWT Standard)
Friday July 11th

WEATHER: hot WIND: almost nil

2663 STOCKBROKER CLAIMING STKS (3-Y.O+) (Class F)

2-30 (2-33) **5f (Equitrack)** £2,277.00 (£627.00: £297.00) Stalls: High GOING minus 0.58 sec per fur (FST)

			SP	RR	SF
2603[2]	**Intiaash (IRE) (69)** (DHaydnJones) **5-9-2**(3) MartinDwyer(6) (outpcd: hdwy over 1f out: str run to ld nr fin).....—	1	5/1	75	38
2377[5]	**Ansellman (83)** (JBerry) **7-9-1b**(5) TEDurcan(4) (w ldr: led 2f out: hrd rdn fnl f: hdd nr fin)....½	2	9/4[1]	74	37
2115[10]	**Mister Raider (54)** (EAWheeler) **5-8-11b**(5) ADaly(8) (swtg: outpcd: hdwy over 1f out: r.o wl ins fnl f)....1¾	3	16/1	65	28
2308[6]	**Lucky Dip (68)** (DRCElsworth) **3-8-4** CRutter(2) (a.p: hrd rdn over 1f out: one pce) 1½	4	4/1[3]	53	11
2319[2]	**Just Loui (85)** (KRBurke) **3-9-5** SWhitworth(3) (lw: led 3f: wknd over 1f out) 1¾	5	3/1[2]	62	20
2481[9]	**Durable George (41)** (JJBridger) **3-8-0**(3) MHenry(1) (lw: hld up: rdn over 2f out: sn wknd)....4	6	50/1	34	—
2228[13]	**Green Golightly (USA) (31)** (RMFlower) **6-8-6v**[1] DaneO'Neill(7) (bhd fnl 4f)....¾	7	33/1	29	—
2407[4]	**Last Chance (63)** (DJSCosgrove) **3-8-3**(7)ow3 SGaillard(5) (lw: a bhd) 3½	8	16/1	27	—
			(SP 109.1%)		**8 Rn**

59.09 secs (0.89) CSF £13.72 TOTE £6.90: £1.40 £1.40 £3.40 (£8.20) OWNER Mr Howard Thomas (PONTYPRIDD) BRED Shadwell Estate Company Limited
WEIGHT FOR AGE 3yo-5lb
2603 Intiaash (IRE), who finished second at Southwell the day before, went one better here, but the signs did not look good in the first half of the race, as she got completely outpaced. However, she really found her feet from below the distance, and came with a useful rattle to snatch the spoils in the closing stages. (5/1)

2377 Ansellman was very favourably weighted here and, despite doing little wrong, he was unable to withstand the winner near the finish. All seven of his wins have come at this trip, and if remaining in this grade, he should soon be winning. (9/4)
1620* Mister Raider, awash with sweat beforehand, has gained three of his four victories on the Equitrack, but had no easy task at the weights. Unable to go the pace, he was putting in some good work in the last furlong and a half. (16/1)
2308 Lucky Dip coped well with this surface. Never far away, she railed well into the straight, saving valuable ground, but failed to find the necessary turn of foot from below the distance. (4/1)
2319 Just Loui was rather disappointing. Setting the pace, he took a very wide course, and then tamely dropped away from below the distance. All five of his victories have come on the All-Weather, and if remaining in this grade, and returning to six furlongs, he should soon add to his tally. (3/1)

2664 CASQUET (S) STKS (2-Y.O) (Class G)

3-00 (3-01) **6f** £1,984.50 (£547.00: £259.50) Stalls: High GOING minus 0.46 sec per fur (F)

				SP	RR	SF
2306^{10}	**Acid Test** (WRMuir) **2-8-8**(3) MartinDwyer(5) (a.p: led over 1f out: hrd rdn: r.o wl)	—	1	3/1^{2}	63	11
	Little Tumbler (IRE) (SWoodman) **2-8-6** NDay(1) (neat: a.p: rdn over 2f out: ev ch ins fnl f: r.o wl)	hd	2	11/1	58	6
2378^{6}	**The Imposter (IRE)** (DJGMurraySmith) **2-8-11** SWhitworth(10) (hld up: rdn over 2f out: unable qckn)	2½	3	10/1	56	4
2425^{4}	**Tender Doll (IRE)** (CADwyer) **2-7-13**(7) JoHunnam(7) (hrd rdn over 2f out: hdwy over 1f out: r.o one pce)	nk	4	5/2^{1}	50	—
2191^{4}	**Calliram** (MBlanshard) **2-8-6** NAdams(12) (led over 4f: wknd fnl f)	¾	5	6/1	48	—
2191^{6}	**Inner Key** (APJones) **2-8-8**(3) JDSmith(8) (rdn over 3f out: nvr nr to chal)	5	6	14/1	40	—
1812^{17}	**Global Risk** (CMurray) **2-8-11** PBloomfield(4) (lw: a bhd)	1½	7	20/1	36	—
1984^{6}	**Sweet Senorita** (MMadgwick) **2-8-6** NVarley(9) (a bhd)	1	8	12/1	28	—
2383^{4}	**Harnage (IRE)** (MRChannon) **2-8-11** RHughes(3) (prom over 3f)	½	9	4/1^{3}	32	—
2367^{9}	**Wideyedbushytailed** (MrsNMacauley) **2-8-6v¹** DianaWeeden(2) (swtg: bhd fnl 4f: t.o)	dist	10	20/1	—	—
				(SP 129.2%)	**10 Rn**	

1m 12.2 (3.20) CSF £37.18 TOTE £3.60: £1.50 £3.00 £2.20 (£96.80) Trio £100.30 OWNER Mr A J de V Patrick (LAMBOURN) BRED Cranford Stud
No bid
Acid Test appreciated the drop in class and, leading approaching the final furlong, responded to pressure, and just managed to hold off the persistent runner-up. (3/1)
Little Tumbler (IRE), who cost a mere 1,500 Irish guineas, does not have much substance, but still made a very pleasing debut, having every chance inside the final furlong, and only just losing out. (11/1)
The Imposter (IRE) ran much better than at Chepstow on his debut last week, and chased the leaders, if failing to quicken in the final quarter-mile. (10/1: 7/1-11/1)
2425 Tender Doll (IRE), going nowhere at halfway, stayed on from below the distance, but was never going to get there in time. Another furlong may well be the answer. (5/2)
2191 Calliram is beginning to look pretty exposed in this company, as after setting the pace, she was collared approaching the final furlong, and soon done with. (6/1: 4/1-7/1)
Inner Key, who unseated his rider just as the runners began to leave the paddock, never threatened to get into it. (14/1: 8/1-20/1)
2383 Harnage (IRE) (4/1: 3/1-9/2)

2665 AL AMEAD H'CAP (0-70) (3-Y.O+ F & M) (Class E)

3-30 (3-31) **6f** £3,460.25 (£1,037.00: £498.50: £229.25) Stalls: High GOING minus 0.46 sec per fur (F)

				SP	RR	SF
2119^{4}	**Out Line (61)** (MMadgwick) **5-9-8** NVarley(13) (lw: rdn thrght: outpcd: hdwy on ins over 1f out: led ins fnl f: r.o wl)	—	1	8/1	70	50
1963^{9}	**Senorita Matilda (USA) (67)** (RHannon) **3-9-8** DaneO'Neill(1) (hdwy over 1f out: r.o one pce ins fnl f)	1¾	2	12/1	71	45
2214^{7}	**Davis Rock (66)** (WRMuir) **3-9-4**(3) MartinDwyer(12) (a.p: rdn over 2f out: ev ch ins fnl f: unable qckn)	hd	3	7/1	70	44
2321^{4}	**Tachycardia (36)** (RJO'Sullivan) **5-7-11** JLowe(15) (led tl ins fnl f: one pce)	1	4	11/2^{2}	37	17
1828^{4}	**Pharaoh's Joy (57)** (JWPayne) **4-9-4** RHughes(9) (n.m.r 2f out: hdwy over 1f out: one pce fnl f)	nk	5	5/1^{1}	58	38
1479^{6}	**College Night (IRE) (42)** (SCWilliams) **5-8-0**(3) MHenry(6) (a.p: rdn over 2f out: one pce)	¾	6	9/1	41	21
2115^{8}	**Primelta (46)** (RAkehurst) **4-8-7** WRyan(5) (a.p: rdn over 2f out: one pce)	¾	7	20/1	43	23
2157*	**Midnight Shift (IRE) (69)** (RGuest) **3-9-10** PBloomfield(8) (hdwy over 1f out: eased whn btn ins fnl f)	1	8	13/2	63	37
2554^{5}	**Forgotten Times (USA) (65)** (TMJones) **3-9-1**(5) ADaly(7) (swtg: hdwy over 1f out: wknd fnl f)	nk	9	12/1	58	32
1666^{12}	**May Queen Megan (49)** (MrsALMKing) **4-8-10** GDuffield(14) (hld up: rdn over 3f out: wknd over 1f out)	½	10	20/1	41	21
1955^{9}	**Silver Purse (60)** (APJones) **3-8-12**(3) JDSmith(10) (lw: rdn 3f out: bhd fnl 2f)	¾	11	14/1	50	24
1988^{2}	**Curzon Street (67)** (HCandy) **3-9-8** CRutter(3) (prom over 3f)	½	12	6/1^{3}	56	30
2244^{5}	**Beveled Crystal (47)** (CJames) **3-8-2** NAdams(11) (a bhd)	1½	13	14/1	32	6
				(SP 131.5%)	**13 Rn**	

1m 10.1 (1.10) CSF £100.95 CT £679.92 TOTE £11.20: £3.70 £6.80 £2.50 (£149.30) Trio £156.00 OWNER Miss D. M. Green (DENMEAD) BRED Miss D. M. Green
WEIGHT FOR AGE 3yo-6lb
2119 Out Line nearly got caught out by this drop in distance. Bustled along virtually throughout, she luckily found an opening along the inside rail from below the distance, and swept into the lead inside the final furlong. (8/1)
Senorita Matilda (USA) ran much better here. Picking up ground below the distance, she stayed on for second place, but failed to trouble the winner. (12/1)
1966 Davis Rock, who flopped in the mud last time out, was much happier with this return to a fast surface. Never far away, she may well have got her head in front for a few strides around the furlong marker, but was unable to cope with the winner in the last one hundred yards. (7/1: 5/1-15/2)
2321 Tachycardia was not going to hang around, and set off in front but, collared inside the final furlong, failed to find another gear. (11/2)
1828 Pharaoh's Joy picked up ground below the distance, but was making no further impression in the final furlong. (5/1)
1374 College Night (IRE) was always close up, but could only go up and down in the same place in the final quarter-mile. She is not easy to win with, and has now won just once from twenty nine starts. (9/1)

2666 RYDON GROUP LIMITED STKS (0-90) (3-Y.O+) (Class C)

4-00 (4-00) **7f 140y** £5,447.45 (£1,625.60: £776.30: £351.65) Stalls: High GOING minus 0.46 sec per fur (F)

				SP	RR	SF
2346^{3}	**Brilliant Red (90)** (PRHedger) **4-9-5** GDuffield(1) (a.p: led wl over 1f out tl ins fnl f: hrd rdn: led last strides)	—	1	7/4^{1}	89	53

2026^{12}	**Mawingo (IRE) (81)** (GWragg) **4-9-5** RHughes(3) (b: lw: hld up: hrd rdn over 1f out: led ins fnl f: hdd last strides)	s.h	**2**	3/1^{2}	89	53
2124^{4}	**Rakis (IRE) (82)** (MrsLStubbs) **7-9-8** DaneO'Neill(2) (hld up: rdn over 2f out: one pce)	2	**3**	11/2^{3}	88	52
2478^{5}	**Albert The Bear (90)** (JBerry) **4-9-6**$^{(5)}$ TEDurcan(6) (hld up: rdn over 2f out: one pce)	hd	**4**	7/1	91	55
2013^{26}	**China Red (USA) (88)** (JWHills) **3-8-10**$^{(3)}$ MHenry(5) (led 6f)	½	**5**	15/2	86	41
2136^{12}	**Henry The Fifth (84)** (CEBrittain) **4-9-5b** WRyan(4) (prom over 2f: t.o)	dist	**6**	14/1	—	—

(SP 107.7%) **6 Rn**

1m 29.88 (0.88) CSF £5.88 TOTE £2.30: £1.60 £1.50 (£6.00) OWNER Mrs M. J. George (CHICHESTER) BRED Newgate Stud Co
WEIGHT FOR AGE 3yo-9lb

2346 Brilliant Red was best in at the weights - he was rated 90 in a 0-90 race. Having a tremendous ding-dong battle with the runner-up in the final quarter-mile, he just managed to win the war. (7/4)

1397 Mawingo (IRE) threw down a dangerous-looking challenge in the final quarter-mile, and in a tremendous battle-royal with the winner, only just lost out. A return to a mile would help. (3/1)

2124 Rakis (IRE) chased the leaders but failed to quicken in the final quarter-mile. All ten of his victories have come at seven furlongs. (11/2)

2478 Albert The Bear chased the leaders, but could only go up and down in the same place in the last two furlongs. He goes particularly well around Chester, where he has gained three of his six victories. (7/1: 5/1-8/1)

645* China Red (USA), out of his depth at Royal Ascot last time out, set the pace but, collared below the distance, soon had bellows to mend. (15/2: 5/1-8/1)

2667 JOHN F. MITCHELL MEMORIAL H'CAP (0-70) (3-Y.O) (Class E)

4-30 (4-31) **1m 3f 106y** £3,252.25 (£973.00: £466.50: £213.25) Stalls: High GOING minus 0.46 sec per fur (F)

				SP	RR	SF
1853^{6}	**Krosno (63)** (SCWilliams) **3-8-11**$^{(3)}$ RHavlin(1) (lw: mde all: clr 7f out: unchal)	—	**1**	8/1	75	45
1859^{6}	**Bewitching Lady (46)** (DWPArbuthnot) **3-7-8**$^{(3)ow1}$ MartinDwyer(4) (swtg: hdwy on ins over 3f out: chsd wnr over 2f out: no imp)	3½	**2**	20/1	53	22
2487^{2}	**Swing West (USA) (63)** (PFICole) **3-9-0** CRutter(9) (hdwy over 6f out: rdn over 2f out: one pce)	½	**3**	7/1	69	39
1939^{6}	**Pen Friend (45)** (WJHaggas) **3-7-10** JLowe(7) (a.p: rn wd st: rdn over 2f out: one pce)	3	**4**	16/1	47	17
2224^{4}	**Rare Talent (69)** (MRChannon) **3-9-6** RHughes(5) (bhd whn rn wd st: nvr nr to chal)	7	**5**	14/1	62	32
2182^{2}	**Mardrew (65)** (RHarris) **3-8-11**$^{(5)}$ ADaly(12) (no hdwy fnl 3f)	¾	**6**	8/1	56	26
1988^{9}	**Saltimbanco (48)** (RAkehurst) **3-7-13** NVarley(13) (swtg: nvr nrr)	nk	**7**	8/1	39	9
2323*	**Cartouche (70)** (SirMarkPrescott) **3-9-7** GDuffield(10) (lw: a.p: chsd wnr over 6f out tl over 2f out: sn wknd)	1¼	**8**	13/2^{3}	59	29
1936^{7}	**Sylvan Jubilacion (60)** (PMitchell) **3-8-6**$^{(5)ow6}$ TEDurcan(6) (a bhd)	1¼	**9**	33/1	48	12
	Frost King (60) (MissBSanders) **3-8-11** CandyMorris(11) (bhd fnl 3f)	2½	**10**	33/1	44	14
2374^{6}	**Ludo (62)** (RHannon) **3-8-13** DaneO'Neill(2) (a bhd)	2½	**11**	12/1	43	13
1956^{4}	**Farley Mount (60)** (LordHuntingdon) **3-8-11** WRyan(3) (lw: prom over 4f)	¾	**12**	11/2^{2}	40	10
1938^{6}	**Zorro (58)** (RMFlower) **3-8-9** RPerham(8) (hdwy 7f out: rn wd st: wknd 3f out)	1½	**13**	3/1^{1}	35	5

(SP 130.4%) **13 Rn**

2m 27.12 (2.42) CSF £155.64 CT £1,093.09 TOTE £9.70: £2.00 £5.20 £2.40 (£153.40) Trio £397.20; £447.55 to York 12/7/97 OWNER The Cherry Pickers Syndicate (NEWMARKET) BRED Sheikh Mohammed Bin Rashid Al Maktoum
LONG HANDICAP Pen Friend 7-8

1853 Krosno was much happier with the return to a shorter distance, having failed to stay a mile-and-three-quarters last time out. Given an enterprising ride, he made all the running, and forging clear in the back straight, won unchallenged. His jockey was very easy on him in the closing stages, and the official distance is no true reflection of his superiority. (8/1)

748 Bewitching Lady, who has been dropped 20lb since her handicap debut last October, ran much better here. Struggling into second place over two furlongs from home, she had no hope of reeling in the winner, and is rather flattered to finish so close. (20/1)

2487 Swing West (USA), set to rise 2lb in future handicaps, took closer order before halfway, but was made to look very pedestrian in the straight. (7/1: 5/1-8/1)

1939 Pen Friend appreciated the longer trip on this handicap debut. Never far away, he ran very wide entering the straight, and could then only plod on in his own time. (16/1)

2224 Rare Talent, who did not seem happy on soft ground on his last two starts, raced at the back of the field until making moderate late headway. (14/1)

2182 Mardrew was making no impression on the principals in the straight. (8/1: 6/1-9/1)

Saltimbanco (8/1: op 12/1)

2323* Cartouche (13/2: 4/1-7/1)

1956 Farley Mount (11/2: 4/1-6/1)

2668 JULY H'CAP (0-70) (3-Y.O+) (Class E)

5-00 (5-02) **1m 2f (Equitrack)** £3,070.25 (£917.00: £438.50: £199.25) Stalls: Low GOING minus 0.58 sec per fur (FST)

				SP	RR	SF
2346^{11}	**La Modiste (62)** (MissGayKelleway) **4-9-6** RHughes(2) (a.p: led over 2f out: clr over 1f out: r.o wl)	—	**1**	13/2^{2}	69	47
1371^{10}	**Count Tony (65)** (SPCWoods) **3-8-12** WRyan(4) (lw: hdwy over 4f out: rdn 2f out: chsd wnr fnl f: r.o wl)	½	**2**	14/1	71	38
1969^{3}	**Sweet Supposin (IRE) (65)** (CADwyer) **6-9-4v**$^{(5)}$ TEDurcan(1) (hdwy over 4f out: hrd rdn over 1f out: one pce)	3	**3**	13/2^{2}	66	44
2281^{2}	**Bakers Daughter (46)** (JRArnold) **5-8-1**$^{(3)}$ MartinDwyer(5) (swtg: led 3f: rdn over 2f out: one pce)	½	**4**	2/1^{1}	47	25
2174^{5}	**Mazilla (50)** (AStreeter) **5-8-5v**$^{(3)}$ RHavlin(8) (hld up: rdn over 2f out: sn wknd)	3	**5**	8/1^{3}	46	24
2193^{2}	**Law Dancer (IRE) (60)** (TGMills) **4-9-4** GDuffield(12) (swtg: hdwy 7f out: rdn over 2f out: wknd over 1f out)	¾	**6**	12/1	55	33
1588^{3}	**Piquant (60)** (LordHuntingdon) **10-8-13**$^{(5)}$ AimeeCook(11) (nvr nrr)	1½	**7**	13/2^{2}	52	30
2246^{9}	**Executive Officer (38)** (RMFlower) **4-7-10b** JLowe(13) (s.s: nvr nrr)	3	**8**	50/1	25	3
2365^{7}	**Sommersby (IRE) (48)** (MrsNMacauley) **6-8-6b**^{1} DaneO'Neill(6) (b: chsd ldr: led 7f out tl over 2f out: sn wknd)	2	**9**	25/1	32	10
1825^{15}	**Kingsdown Trix (IRE) (64)** (GLMoore) **3-8-11** RPerham(3) (swtg: a bhd)	nk	**10**	11/1	48	15
2557^{17}	**Sylvan Princess (70)** (DJSCosgrove) **4-9-7**$^{(7)}$ SGaillard(10) (a bhd)	4	**11**	12/1	47	25
660^{13}	**Subtle Touch (IRE) (44)** (TTClement) **6-8-2** NVarley(9) (bit bkwd: bhd fnl 5f)	6	**12**	50/1	12	—
1474^{8}	**The Green Grey (53)** (WRMuir) **3-8-0** CRutter(7) (prom over 5f)		**13**	14/1	—	—

(SP 129.3%) **13 Rn**

2m 5.56 (1.26) CSF £91.94 CT £577.67 TOTE £11.20: £3.30 £2.10 £2.00 (£82.10) Trio £226.00 OWNER Mr John Purcell (WHITCOMBE) BRED G. R. Smith (Thriplow) Ltd
LONG HANDICAP Executive Officer 7-0
WEIGHT FOR AGE 3yo-11lb

1473* La Modiste moved to the front over a quarter of a mile from home, and forging clear in the straight, was not going to be caught in time. (13/2)
976 Count Tony took closer order at halfway. Moving into second place entering the final furlong, he ran on strongly, but failed to get there in time. (14/1)
1969 Sweet Supposin (IRE) is not the easiest of horses to get on with, but gradually crept closer from halfway. Asked for his effort below the distance, he then failed to find what was required. He goes extremely well for Frankie Dettori. (13/2: 9/2-7/1)
2281 Bakers Daughter, the early leader, remained close up, but was tapped for toe in the short home straight. (2/1)
2174 Mazilla chased the leaders, but had been hung out to dry turning for home. (8/1)
2193 Law Dancer (IRE), back at the trip over which he has gained both his successes, took closer order seven furlongs from home, but had been hung out to dry early in the short straight. (12/1)
1588 Piquant (13/2: 9/2-7/1)
906* Kingsdown Trix (IRE) (11/1: 8/1-12/1)

T/Plpt: £1,528.40 (7.72 Tckts). T/Qdpt: £562.10 (1.17 Tckts) AK

2300-WOLVERHAMPTON (L-H) (Standard)
Friday July 11th
WEATHER: fine & warm WIND: alm nil

2669 STARBUCK MEDIAN AUCTION MAIDEN STKS (3-Y.O) (Class F)
2-20 (2-20) **6f (Fibresand)** £2,277.00 (£627.00: £297.00) Stalls: Low GOING: 0.03 sec per fur (STD)

	Runner	Dist	Pos	SP	RR	SF
1302^{5}	**Broadway Melody** (APJarvis) **3-8-9** DHolland(1) (s.i.s: sn w ldrs: led over 2f out: clr whn rdn & edgd rt ins fnl f)	—	**1**	10/1	61	14
2300^{2}	**Castle Ashby Jack (60)** (PHowling) **3-9-0b** FNorton(7) (b.hind: hdwy 3f out: chsd wnr over 1f out: edgd lft & no ex)	3	**2**	2/1 2	58	11
2510^{13}	**Bold Spring (IRE) (74)** (RHannon) **3-9-0** SSanders(4) (sn pushed along: chsd ldrs: no imp fnl 2f)	2½	**3**	6/5 1	51	4
2151^{5}	**Canton Ron (48)** (CADwyer) **3-9-0b** TGMcLaughlin(6) (lw: sn outpcd: kpt on appr fnl f: nt pce to chal)	1½	**4**	10/1	47	—
2313^{12}	**Falls O'Moness (IRE) (60)** (KRBurke) **3-8-9v¹** JQuinn(3) (swtg: plld hrd: led after 1f: hdd over 2f out: wknd over 1f out)	¾	**5**	9/1 3	40	—
2300^{5}	**Nesbet (41)** (BRCambidge) **3-9-0** DWright(2) (lw: led 1f: wknd over 2f out)	4	**6**	9/1 3	35	—
181^{13}	**Flood's Hot Stuff (32)** (NPLittmoden) **3-8-2**(7) KPierrepont(5) (a bhd)	5	**7**	33/1	16	—

(SP 119.9%) **7 Rn**

1m 17.1 (5.90) CSF £29.51 TOTE £12.30: £1.80 £1.40 (£25.40) OWNER Mrs Ann Jarvis (ASTON UPTHORPE) BRED Miss S. E. Jarvis
Broadway Melody, in a much easier grade this time, was in charge in the straight despite showing signs of greenness. (10/1)
2300 Castle Ashby Jack found little off the bridle once the chance was there. (2/1: op 5/4)
1988 Bold Spring (IRE), having his first run on this surface, looked to be hating it on the way down. Scrubbed along from the start, he was never going well enough to take a hand, despite staying on. (6/5)
2151 Canton Ron, off his feet early, stayed on in the straight and would have been meeting the two immediately in front of him on very much better terms in a handicap. (10/1)
1245 Falls O'Moness (IRE), making her debut on the surface, got warm in the first-time visor and, pulling from the off, gave herself little chance of lasting home. (9/1)
2300 Nesbet, nibbled at at fancy price, showed early speed but was fading on the home turn. (9/1)

2670 CANTON APPRENTICE CLAIMING LIMITED STKS (0-60) (3-Y.O) (Class G)
2-50 (2-50) **1m 1f 79y (Fibresand)** £2,007.50 (£570.00: £282.50) Stalls: Low GOING: 0.03 sec per fur (STD)

	Runner	Dist	Pos	SP	RR	SF
2128^{4}	**Madam Lucy (47)** (WWHaigh) **3-7-13**(5)ow4 SCarson(4) (lw: trckd ldrs: led over 2f out: rdn out)	—	**1**	2/1 1	56	21
2318^{5}	**Bon Guest (IRE) (58)** (TJNaughton) **3-8-10**(5) RachaelMoody(3) (hld up: hdwy 5f out: chsd wnr over 1f out: no ex)	½	**2**	5/1 2	66	35
2364^{2}	**Mysterium (55)** (NPLittmoden) **3-8-8**(7) KPierrepont(2) (chsd ldr: ev ch over 2f out: one pce appr fnl f)	5	**3**	5/1 2	58	27
2487^{16}	**Kustom Kit Klassic (48)** (SRBowring) **3-8-10b¹**(3) JFowle(6) (b: dwlt: sn prom: wknd 2f out)	9	**4**	10/1	40	9
2151^{4}	**Bapsford (50)** (GLMoore) **3-8-6**(5) TField(7) (lw: in tch 5f)	1¼	**5**	13/2	36	5
2171^{12}	**Macari (48)** (BPJBaugh) **3-8-6**(3) PClarke(5) (plld hrd: outpcd after 2f: n.d after)	nk	**6**	16/1	34	3
2364^{3}	**Bali-Pet (55)** (JParkes) **3-8-5b** TSiddall(9) (lw: led tl over 2f out: sn wknd)	3½	**7**	6/1 3	24	—
2245^{9}	**Forget To Remindme (48)** (JSMoore) **3-8-1b¹**(7) PaulCleary(1) (chsd ldrs 5f: sn wknd)	4	**8**	10/1	20	—
	Dunston Gold (42) (BPreece) **3-8-0**(5) DHayden(8) (sn wl bhd)	20	**9**	33/1	—	—

(SP 121.3%) **9 Rn**

2m 4.2 (8.20) CSF £11.64 TOTE £3.50: £2.20 £1.60 £1.50 (£7.40) Trio £8.10 OWNER Mr A. K. Smeaton (MALTON) BRED A. K. Smeaton
Bon Guest (IRE) clmd Mr G. Roberts £8,000. Madam Lucy clmd Mr A. Higgins £2,000
2128 Madam Lucy, dropped in to be claimed for just £2,000, made good use of bottom weight and does seem to try. (2/1)
2318 Bon Guest (IRE), a moderate mover, looked a big danger turning in, but the pilot took some time to switch her whip and her mount just stayed on. (5/1: op 3/1)
2364 Mysterium, dropping in trip, was made plenty of use of but proved short of pace in the straight. (5/1)
2068 Kustom Kit Klassic, dropped in trip and with the blinkers fitted, didn't seem to last home. (10/1: op 6/1)
2151 Bapsford, up in trip and on a fresh surface, didn't last to the straight. (13/2)
1998 Macari took a strong hold but lost his place on the sharp bend past the winning post and never looked like recovering.. (16/1)
1167* Forget To Remindme (10/1: op 6/1)

2671 PHOENIX LIMITED STKS (0-65) (3-Y.O+) (Class F)
3-20 (3-21) **7f (Fibresand)** £2,277.00 (£627.00: £297.00) Stalls: High GOING: 0.03 sec per fur (STD)

	Runner	Dist	Pos	SP	RR	SF
2395*	**Itsinthepost (64)** (VSoane) **4-9-4** FNorton(5) (lw: a.p: chsd ldr appr fnl f: rdn & r.o to ld wl ins fnl f)	—	**1**	5/1 2	70	52
1385^{14}	**Mythical (64)** (SirMarkPrescott) **3-8-7** SSanders(10) (chsd ldrs: led 3f out: wknd & hdd wl ins fnl f)	¾	**2**	7/1	65	39
2183^{7}	**Fife Major (USA) (63)** (BWHills) **3-8-10** DHolland(2) (lw: trckd ldr: rdn over 1f out: styd on wl ins fnl f)	½	**3**	8/1	67	41
2424^{3}	**Wild Palm (63)** (WAO'Gorman) **5-9-4v** EmmaO'Gorman(4) (lw: dwlt: rdn & hdwy 3f out: nt pce to chal)	3½	**4**	9/4 1	59	41
2502^{4}	**Naughty Pistol (USA) (59)** (PDEvans) **5-9-1b** JFEgan(8) (lw: hdwy 3f out: nvr rchd ldrs)	5	**5**	6/1 3	45	27
2201^{13}	**Cherokee Flight (62)** (SMellor) **3-8-10** JQuinn(6) (lw: prom: rdn 3f out: wknd over 1f out)	¾	**6**	14/1	46	20

				SP	RR	SF
1828[9]	**Caspian Morn (58)** (WGMTurner) **3-8-2**(5) DSweeney(1) (led 4f: wknd wl over 1f out)	6	**7**	16/1	29	3
2160[3]	**Dragonjoy (56)** (NPLittmoden) **4-9-7v** RLappin(12) (a bhd)	1¼	**8**	12/1	32	14
2201[11]	**Colins Choice (62)** (JLSpearing) **3-8-7** DRMcCabe(11) (a bhd)	1¼	**9**	16/1	24	—
2418[8]	**Heathyards Lady (USA) (61)** (RHollinshead) **6-9-1** FLynch(7) (b: s.s: a bhd)	hd	**10**	10/1	23	5
1977[16]	**Gwespyr (60)** (RHannon) **4-8-11**(7) RSmith(3) (b.nr fore: chsd ldrs 4f)	5	**11**	11/1	15	—
				(SP 128.9%)	**11 Rn**	

1m 29.1 (4.40) CSF £40.29 TOTE £4.70: £1.70 £2.80 £2.90 (£9.70) Trio £155.70; £46.07 to York 12/7/97 OWNER First Class Four Seasons (ASTON ROWANT) BRED Roldvale Ltd
WEIGHT FOR AGE 3yo-8lb
2395* Itsinthepost finished strongly after all seemed lost and threatens to stay further. (5/1)
1121 Mythical possibly needed this after seven weeks off for, clear into the final furlong, she tied up in the final strides. (7/1)
1876 Fife Major (USA), an attractive type to be on this sort of mark, did seem to find this trip too sharp. (8/1)
2424 Wild Palm seems at his best on turf, preferably with a bit of cut. (9/4)
2502 Naughty Pistol (USA), yet to score in a dozen attempts this year, was always making hard work of getting near the leaders. (6/1: op 7/2)
1958 Cherokee Flight made a respectable All-Weather debut, only dropping away on straightening up. (14/1: 8/1-16/1)
1818 Heathyards Lady (USA) (10/1: op 6/1)
1505 Gwespyr (11/1: 7/1-12/1)

2672 JOHNSTON H'CAP (0-85) (3-Y.O+) (Class D)
3-50 (3-50) **1m 100y (Fibresand)** £3,454.50 (£1,029.00: £490.00: £220.50) Stalls: Low GOING: 0.03 sec per fur (STD)

				SP	RR	SF
2368[2]	**People Direct (46)** (NPLittmoden) **4-7-10** JQuinn(3) (lw: mde all: clr over 3f out: rdn out)	—	**1**	9/2[2]	57	33
2465[7]	**Duke Valentino (78)** (RHollinshead) **5-9-11**(3) DGriffiths(10) (lw: hdwy 4f out: kpt on ins fnl f)	5	**2**	12/1	80	56
*2302**	**Johnnie the Joker (73)** (JPLeigh) **6-9-4b**(5) DSweeney(8) (chsd wnr 8f: no imp)	½	**3**	9/2[2]	74	50
2155[5]	**Eurobox Boy (59)** (APJarvis) **4-8-9** DHolland(9) (chsd ldrs: no hdwy fnl 3f)	2	**4**	5/1[3]	56	32
1788[4]	**Castles Burning (USA) (74)** (CACyzer) **3-9-1** DWright(1) (chsd ldrs tl wknd 2f out)	2	**5**	20/1	67	34
2303[5]	**Molly Music (62)** (GGMargarson) **3-8-3** DBiggs(4) (bhd: hdwy 3f out: btn over 1f out)	5	**6**	10/1	46	13
887[8]	**Tallulah Belle (67)** (NPLittmoden) **4-9-3** TGMcLaughlin(7) (bhd: effrt over 2f out: nvr able chal)	4	**7**	12/1	43	19
2137[7]	**Sweet Contralto (81)** (DRLoder) **3-9-8** DRMcCabe(5) (chsd ldrs over 4f: eased whn btn)	20	**8**	5/2[1]	19	—
1082[11]	**Farmost (70)** (SirMarkPrescott) **4-9-6** SSanders(6) (s.i.s: a bhd)	15	**9**	5/1[3]	—	—
				(SP 127.5%)	**9 Rn**	

1m 50.3 (5.30) CSF £57.43 CT £245.79 TOTE £3.80: £1.10 £3.20 £1.60 (£46.50) Trio £28.10 OWNER Mr J. R. Salter (WOLVERHAMPTON) BRED James Thom and Sons and Peter Orr
WEIGHT FOR AGE 3yo-9lb
OFFICIAL EXPLANATION Sweet Contralto: was never travelling and did not appear to like the kickback.
2368 People Direct, whose last two wins had also come over this course and distance, has a mind of her own and dislodged her pilot coming onto the track. She has to dominate to run her race and had galloped the opposition into the ground approaching the final furlong. (9/2)
1830 Duke Valentino returned to his best surface and to form, sticking on well from the back in the closing stages. (12/1: op 6/1)
2302* Johnnie the Joker, in good form from the front of late, simply could not get to the front with the winner in opposition. (9/2: op 3/1)
2155 Eurobox Boy, very consistent on turf this year, ran a better second race on this surface without threatening to take a hand. (5/1: op 3/1)
1154 Castles Burning (USA), ridden more prominently this time, chased the two tearaway leaders and had run himself out by the home turn. (20/1)
2303 Molly Music is probably suited by this trip but seems to be feeling the effects of some tough races recently. (10/1)
796* Tallulah Belle (12/1: op 8/1)
1406* Sweet Contralto (5/2: 4/1-2/1)

2673 MARIANA (S) STKS (3, 4 & 5-Y.O) (Class G)
4-20 (4-20) **1m 4f (Fibresand)** £1,984.50 (£547.00: £259.50) Stalls: Low GOING: 0.03 sec per fur (STD)

				SP	RR	SF
2399[9]	**Mystic Strand (52)** (WGMTurner) **4-8-9**(5) DSweeney(6) (lw: trckd ldrs: led over 2f out: rdn & r.o wl fnl f)	—	**1**	4/1[2]	42	20
2577[4]	**Esperto (50)** (JPearce) **4-9-7**(3) CTeague(4) (hld up & plld hrd: hdwy over 5f out: chsd wnr 2f out: sn rdn: unable qckn fnl f)	2½	**2**	2/5[1]	49	27
2357[9]	**Ballydinero (IRE) (40)** (CaptJWilson) **3-7-13b**[1](7) AngelaHartley(3) (led after 3f tl over 2f out: sn wknd)	15	**3**	8/1[3]	24	—
	Raw Deal (BPreece) **4-9-0** VSlattery(2) (chsd ldrs over 7f: sn btn)	11	**4**	12/1	4	—
	Dunston Star (IRE) (BPreece) **4-9-5** DWright(1) (led 3f: wknd qckly 6f out)	dist	**5**	25/1	—	—
				(SP 114.1%)	**5 Rn**	

2m 45.0 (12.50) CSF £5.77 TOTE £3.00: £1.10 £1.10 (£1.50) OWNER Mr David Bell (SHERBORNE) BRED David P. Bell
WEIGHT FOR AGE 3yo-13lb
No bid
754 Mystic Strand, not really bred for this trip, cruised to the front and her pilot hung on to her as long as possible even though in front. As the favourite loomed up entering the final furlong, he asked for a final effort and the filly responded well. Just when will Sweeney get the credit he deserves. (4/1)
2577 Esperto, having his second run of the week, pulled too hard for his own good, ruining an easy-looking chance. (2/5)
Ballydinero (IRE), made more use of in first-time blinkers, could not last home, even in this grade. (8/1)
Raw Deal, a small filly, has not made any impression over hurdles or on the Flat. (12/1)
Dunston Star (IRE) showed speed for half a mile when last seen, and repeated the process on this seasonal debut. (25/1)

2674 HOWLAND H'CAP (0-65) (3-Y.O+ F & M) (Class F)
4-50 (4-50) **5f (Fibresand)** £2,277.00 (£627.00: £297.00) Stalls: Low GOING: 0.03 sec per fur (STD)

				SP	RR	SF
2305[2]	**Opening Range (35)** (NEBerry) **6-7-10**(7) PBradley(4) (disp ld tl led ins fnl f: drvn out)	—	**1**	7/2[2]	40	4
2177[19]	**Amy Leigh (IRE) (57)** (CaptJWilson) **4-9-4b**(7) AngelaHartley(7) (disp ld tl ins fnl f: one pce)	nk	**2**	11/2	61	25
2382[4]	**Marjorie Rose (IRE) (60)** (ABailey) **4-10-0** DWright(6) (b.hind: chsd ldrs: r.o ins fnl f)	s.h	**3**	2/1[1]	64	28
2536[7]	**Marino Street (41)** (PDEvans) **4-8-9b** JFEgan(2) (lw: sn outpcd: styd on appr fnl f)	4	**4**	5/1[3]	32	—
1790[4]	**River Ensign (37)** (WMBrisbourne) **4-8-5** JQuinn(5) (chsd ldrs: no imp fnl 2f)	2½	**5**	7/2[2]	20	—
2143[7]	**Lake Aria (30)** (MrsAMNaughton) **4-7-5**(7)ow2 JFowle(3) (lw: sn bhd)	3	**6**	33/1	4	—
1428[8]	**Hi Hoh (IRE) (38)** (NPLittmoden) **4-8-6**ow2 TGMcLaughlin(1) (bit bkwd: chsd ldrs over 3f)	3	**7**	16/1	2	—
				(SP 118.7%)	**7 Rn**	

64.1 secs (5.20) CSF £21.99 TOTE £5.30: £2.00 £5.50 (£10.50) OWNER In The Purple Racing (UPPER LAMBOURN) BRED Miss E. Drax

2305 Opening Range confirmed the improvement of his latest run and this may be his best trip for, having gone almost a length up inside the final furlong, he was being pegged back at the finish. (7/2)
421* Amy Leigh (IRE), kept wide of her rivals, ran her race but found the concession of 22lb just beyond her. (11/2: 3/1-6/1)
2382 Marjorie Rose (IRE), dropping to the minimum trip for the first time in a while on the All Weather, struggled to close on the two leaders, but was making rapid strides in the last fifty yards. Six is her trip on this surface. (2/1)
2305 Marino Street, outpaced early as usual, lacked the pace to get into it and one win and twelve places in thirty-six starts says it all. (5/1: 3/1-11/2)
1790 River Ensign, taken to post early, couldn't quite go with the leaders back over the minimum trip. (7/2)
Lake Aria, taking a big drop in trip, didn't know what had hit her. (33/1)

T/Plpt: £10.20 (688.98 Tckts). T/Qdpt: £8.20 (56.73 Tckts) Dk

1977-YORK (L-H) (Good, Good to firm in places)
Friday July 11th
WEATHER: fine & sunny WIND: slt half bhd

2675 NAPOLEONS RACING H'CAP (0-100) (3-Y.O+) (Class C)
2-10 (2-12) **5f** £7,895.00 (£2,360.00: £1,130.00: £515.00) Stalls: Low GOING minus 0.35 sec per fur (F)

Runner	Dist	Pos	SP	RR	SF
1766^{2} **Dashing Blue (99)** (IABalding) **4-10-0** LDettori(14) (lw: racd centre: hld up: smooth hdwy over 1f out: qcknd to ld ins fnl f: r.o wl)	—	**1**	8/1	109	67
2299^{5} **Crofters Ceilidh (88)** (BAMcMahon) **5-9-3** JReid(12) (racd centre: chsd ldrs: led over 1f out tl ins fnl f: nt qckn)	1	**2**	14/1	95	53
1608^{2} **Twice as Sharp (92)** (PWHarris) **5-9-0**(7) CLowther(4) (racd far side: trckd ldrs: ev ch 1f out: nt qckn)	nk	**3**	7/1^{2}	98	56
2497^{2} **Lady Sheriff (75)** (MWEasterby) **6-8-4b** TLucas(7) (lw: racd far side: w ldrs: kpt on same pce fnl f)	1½	**4**	15/2^{3}	76	34
2339^{2} **Squire Corrie (86)** (DWChapman) **5-9-1** ACulhane(9) (lw: racd centre: w ldrs: led over 1f out: sn hdd: no ex)	.1	**5**	8/1	84	42
2529^{2} **That Man Again (85)** (SCWilliams) **5-9-0** KDarley(2) (racd far side: chsd ldrs: outpcd appr fnl f)	1½	**6**	7/1^{2}	78	36
1158^{11} **Stuffed (81)** (MWEasterby) **5-8-7**(3) GParkin(11) (lw: racd centre: hld up: hdwy ½-wy: outpcd appr fnl f)	½	**7**	10/1	72	30
2339^{7} **Lago Di Varano (84)** (RMWhitaker) **5-8-13v** DeanMcKeown(1) (b.hind: racd far side: sn outpcd: styd on appr fnl f)	s.h	**8**	14/1	75	33
2129^{7} **For the Present (79)** (TDBarron) **7-8-8** JCarroll(13) (racd centre: sn drvn along: chsd ldrs over 3f: sn lost pl)	nk	**9**	16/1	69	27
1975^{2} **Crowded Avenue (97)** (PJMakin) **5-9-12** PatEddery(8) (swtg: racd far side: trckd ldrs: effrt over 1f out: rdn & hung lft: sn wknd)	nk	**10**	5/1^{1}	86	44
2289^{10} **Kira (83)** (JLEyre) **7-8-12** OPears(5) (b: racd far side: sn pushed along: prom tl lost pl ½-wy)	hd	**11**	12/1	72	30
2211^{12} **Tadeo (95)** (MJohnston) **4-9-10** MRoberts(6) (racd far side: led tl hdd & wknd over 1f out)	½	**12**	20/1	82	40
2061^{4} **Chemcast (69)** (JLEyre) **4-7-5b**(7)ow2 RWinston(10) (racd centre: w ldrs tl wknd ½-wy)	2	**13**	33/1	50	6
2185* **Sea-Deer (87)** (CADwyer) **8-9-2** KFallon(3) (racd far side: sn outpcd: eased fnl f)	3½	**14**	7/1^{2}	57	15

(SP 131.9%) **14 Rn**

58.5 secs (0.80) CSF £115.14 CT £794.69 TOTE £6.60: £2.60 £4.20 £2.50 (£94.00) Trio £183.40 OWNER Mrs Duncan Allen (KINGSCLERE) BRED Mrs I. A. Balding
1766 Dashing Blue, very keen to post, was skillfully settled off the pace. One of six to race up the centre, in the end he took this in ready fashion. (8/1)
2299 Crofters Ceilidh, with the headgear still left off, is running really well at present. (14/1)
1608 Twice as Sharp was 9lb higher than when he scored here in a similar event in May. He came out best of the far side group. (7/1)
2497 Lady Sheriff is in the form of her life at present. (15/2)
2339 Squire Corrie, who has shot up the weights, was run out of it in the final furlong. (8/1)
2529 That Man Again lacked the pace to get in front in this company. (7/1)
1975 Crowded Avenue boiled up beforehand. Travelling strongly as usual, off the bit he hung left and found little. (5/1)

2676 WWAV NORTH RATED STKS H'CAP (0-100) (3-Y.O+) (Class B)
2-40 (2-41) **1m 3f 195y** £9,942.00 (£3,678.00: £1,764.00: £720.00: £285.00: £111.00) Stalls: Low GOING minus 0.35 sec per fur (F)

Runner	Dist	Pos	SP	RR	SF
1741^{3} **Dream of Nurmi (84)** (DRLoder) **3-7-9**(5) RFfrench(7) (w ldr: led over 2f out: styd on wl u.p fnl f)	—	**1**	11/2^{2}	94	42
2514^{13} **Remaadi Sun (80)** (MDIUsher) **5-8-9** RStreet(6) (hld up: hdwy on ins 6f out: ev ch over 1f out: nt qckn ins fnl f)	1¼	**2**	25/1	88	49
2139^{3} **Shaft of Light (83)** (LordHuntingdon) **5-8-12** LDettori(3) (lw: led tl over 2f out: kpt on one pce)	3½	**3**	4/1^{1}	87	48
2291^{2} **Heart of Gold (IRE) (90)** (MissSEHall) **3-8-6** AMcGlone(2) (trckd ldrs: pushed along 3f out: n.m.r & hung lft 2f out: kpt on same pce)	1¾	**4**	8/1	91	39
782^{3} **Mithak (USA) (89)** (BWHills) **3-8-5**ow1 MHills(8) (trckd ldrs: drvn along & outpcd over 3f out: styd on fnl f)	1	**5**	11/2^{2}	89	36
1982^{3} **Lawahik (98)** (DMorley) **3-9-0** GCarter(1) (trckd ldrs: drvn along over 3f out: edgd rt 2f out: wknd appr fnl f)	2	**6**	12/1	95	43
2341* **Present Arms (USA) (94)** (PFICole) **4-9-9** TQuinn(11) (lw: hdwy & pushed along ½-wy: rdn 3f out: edgd lft: nvr nr to chal)	1½	**7**	4/1^{1}	89	50
2155* **Hen Harrier (92)** (JLDunlop) **3-8-8** JReid(5) (hld up & plld hrd: hdwy on ins 3f out: no imp whn hmpd over 1f out)	2½	**8**	7/1^{3}	84	32
2296^{2} **Lomberto (85)** (VSoane) **4-9-0** RCochrane(9) (sn pushed along: rdn & edgd lft over 1f out: n.d)	½	**9**	10/1	76	37
2293^{9} **Manful (80)** (MissLAPerratt) **5-8-9b** NKennedy(13) (sn pushed along: nvr wnt pce)	1	**10**	33/1	70	31
2028^{14} **Far Ahead (84)** (JLEyre) **5-8-13** OPears(12) (sn pushed along: lost pl over 3f out: eased: t.o)	20	**11**	20/1	47	8
2284^{3} **Brandon Magic (85)** (IABalding) **4-9-0** KDarley(10) (mid div: hdwy u.p 4f out: sn lost pl & eased: t.o)	9	**12**	12/1	36	—

(SP 130.4%) **12 Rn**

2m 29.96 (2.16) CSF £135.92 CT £576.54 TOTE £6.40: £2.00 £4.00 £1.60 (£50.40) Trio £74.20 OWNER Mr Chris Brasher (NEWMARKET) BRED Miss J. Chaplin
LONG HANDICAP Manful 8-3
WEIGHT FOR AGE 3yo-13lb
1741 Dream of Nurmi proved well suited by the step up in distance and, well handled, held on in determined fashion. (11/2)
1145 Remaadi Sun extended his losing sequence to seventeen, but it is surely just a question of time before he gets his head in front again. Making ground on the inner on the home turn, he was upsides with his ears pricked over a furlong out, but in the end the winning combination proved too strong. (25/1)

2139 Shaft of Light set only a modest pace. Quickening up off the bend, at the business end the first two had far too much speed for him. He really needs two miles. (4/1)
2291 Heart of Gold (IRE) still looks far from the finished object. Hanging left and meeting some trouble, he should improve as he gets stronger. (8/1)
782 Mithak (USA), absent since running poorly at Catterick seventy-nine days ago, was badly tapped for foot when the pace was stepped up once in line for home. Staying on in determined fashion at the finish, he looks a stayer, and is capable of better. (11/2)
1982 Lawahik possibly did not appreciate this fast ground. (12/1)
2341* Present Arms (USA) edged left under pressure as if feeling the ground, which was very fast after a hot week. (4/1)
2155* Hen Harrier, who again made little appeal in the paddock, was not making much impression when she was chopped for room on the inner a furlong and a half out. (7/1)

2677 SINGAPORE SUMMER STKS (Listed) (3-Y.O+ F & M) (Class A)

3-10 (3-11) **6f** £14,490.00 (£4,320.00: £2,060.00: £930.00) Stalls: Low GOING minus 0.35 sec per fur (F)

				SP	RR	SF
2299*	**Bint Albaadiya (USA) (104)** (MRStoute) **3-8-8** JReid(1) (trckd ldrs: pushed along & outpcd ½-wy: styd on strly appr fnl f: led nr fin)	—	**1**	4/1^{3}	116	49
2105^{3}	**Bollin Joanne (103)** (TDEasterby) **4-9-0** KFallon(6) (lw: b: trckd ldrs: led & hung lft over 2f out: sn clr: hdd nr fin)	nk	**2**	7/2^{2}	115	54
2056^{12}	**Connemara (IRE) (103)** (CADwyer) **3-8-8** DHarrison(4) (sn outpcd: hdwy u.p over 2f out: styd on fnl f)	4	**3**	11/1	105	38
2023^{5}	**Nightbird (IRE) (116)** (SbinSuroor) **3-8-12** LDettori(2) (trckd ldrs: ev ch over 2f out: wknd fnl f)	2	**4**	11/10^{1}	103	36
2056^{19}	**China Girl (IRE) (90)** (PWChapple-Hyam) **3-8-8** PatEddery(3) (led: clr ½-wy: hdd over 2f out: wknd over 1f out)	¾	**5**	20/1	97	30
1610^{2}	**Elegant Warning (IRE) (108)** (BWHills) **3-8-12** MHills(5) (dwlt s: sn pushed along: nvr wnt pce)	4	**6**	8/1	91	24
2299^{2}	**Wellspring (IRE) (94)** (DRLoder) **3-8-8** KDarley(8) (sn pushed along: nvr wnt pce)	½	**7**	16/1	85	18
2334^{7}	**Queen's Pageant (90)** (JLSpearing) **3-8-8** SDrowne(7) (hld up: effrt ½-wy: lost pl over 2f out: eased)	10	**8**	50/1	59	—
				(SP 121.9%)	**8 Rn**	

1m 11.45 (0.95) CSF £18.05 TOTE £4.80: £1.60 £1.20 £3.10 (£7.10) OWNER Sheikh Ahmed Al Maktoum (NEWMARKET) BRED Swettenham Stud

WEIGHT FOR AGE 3yo-6lb

2299* Bint Albaadiya (USA), who showed plenty of knee action going down, struggled badly to keep up at halfway. Making up four lengths in the final furlong, she led near the line, and will be much better suited by seven. (4/1)
2105 Bollin Joanne took it up soon after halfway and, despite hanging left, was soon driven four lengths clear but, treading water inside the last, she was just shaded out of it. More patient tactics and easier ground would have helped. (7/2)
1609 Connemara (IRE) stuck on in determined fashion, but the first two left her for dead. (11/1)
2023 Nightbird (IRE), who looked very fit indeed, was crowded by the winner soon after halfway, but that was no excuse. (11/10)
China Girl (IRE) set a fierce gallop and was soon clear. She only weakened in the final furlong and possibly still needed the outing. (20/1)
1610 Elegant Warning (IRE) boiled over beforehand, and had two handlers in the paddock. (8/1)

2678 HEARTHSTEAD HOMES H'CAP (0-90) (3-Y.O+) (Class C)

3-40 (3-43) **7f 202y** £8,350.00 (£2,500.00: £1,200.00: £550.00) Stalls: Low GOING minus 0.35 sec per fur (F)

				SP	RR	SF
2478*	**Jo Mell (85)** (TDEasterby) **4-9-11** 5x LCharnock(7) (lw: trckd ldrs: led over 2f out: styd on strly: readily)	—	**1**	3/1^{1}	98	80
2485^{2}	**Therhea (IRE) (73)** (BRMillman) **4-8-10**(3) AWhelan(5) (in tch: hdwy to chse wnr over 2f out: no imp)	1½	**2**	9/1^{3}	83	65
2557^{9}	**Pride of Pendle (71)** (MartynWane) **8-8-11** KFallon(9) (hld up: hdwy over 2f out: styd on wl fnl f)	2	**3**	9/1^{3}	77	59
2478^{6}	**Band on the Run (85)** (BAMcMahon) **10-9-11** MRoberts(1) (sn drvn along: sn in tch: kpt on same pce fnl 2f)	1½	**4**	16/1	88	70
2026^{18}	**Pomona (82)** (PJMakin) **4-9-8** PatEddery(3) (bhd: hdwy over 3f out: hung lft: nvr nr to chal)	1¼	**5**	10/1	82	64
2341^{4}	**Sandmoor Chambray (79)** (TDEasterby) **6-9-5b** JCarroll(8) (bhd: styd on u.p fnl 2f: nvr nr to chal)	1	**6**	10/1	77	59
2341^{6}	**Moving Arrow (88)** (MissSEHall) **6-10-0** JWeaver(14) (trckd ldrs: rdn 4f out: one pce fnl 2f)	2	**7**	16/1	82	64
2026^{22}	**Iamus (82)** (TDBarron) **4-9-8** KDarley(2) (bhd: hdwy on outside over 3f out: nvr nrr)	1	**8**	20/1	74	56
2340^{2}	**Cashmere Lady (73)** (JLEyre) **5-8-13** OPears(11) (mid div: shkn up over 2f out: n.d)	1¾	**9**	10/1	62	44
2290*	**Duraid (IRE) (72)** (DenysSmith) **5-8-5**(7) CLowther(6) (lw: chsd ldrs: effrt over 2f out: wknd over 1f out)	hd	**10**	6/1^{2}	61	43
2328^{8}	**Zorba (70)** (JHetherton) **3-8-1** NKennedy(4) (w ldr tl wknd over 2f out)	¾	**11**	33/1	57	30
2026^{27}	**Arterxerxes (80)** (MJHeaton-Ellis) **4-9-6** SDrowne(12) (mde most tl over 2f out: wknd)	2	**12**	20/1	63	45
1166^{3}	**Mihriz (IRE) (62)** (RAkehurst) **5-8-2**ow1 DHarrison(10) (a in rr)	2½	**13**	6/1^{2}	40	21
2326^{15}	**Trailblazer (76)** (CWThornton) **3-8-7** DeanMcKeown(13) (mid div: drvn along & lost pl 3f out: virtually p.u)	23	**14**	33/1	8	—
				(SP 128.0%)	**14 Rn**	

1m 36.99 (-0.01) CSF £28.12 CT £209.55 TOTE £4.20: £2.30 £2.50 £2.00 (£24.70) Trio £33.90 OWNER C H Newton Jnr Ltd (MALTON) BRED D.B. Lamplough

WEIGHT FOR AGE 3yo-9lb

2478* Jo Mell, 12lb higher than when successful at Newcastle, took this in tremendous fashion despite the ground having dried out considerably. (3/1)
2485 Therhea (IRE), from a 4lb higher mark, stuck on gamely, but on this ground was never going to find enough to get in a blow at the winner. (9/1)
2557 Pride of Pendle, having her second outing in three days, probably ran up to her best. (9/1)
2478 Band on the Run is tremendously game and enthusiastic, even at ten, but the handicapper has his measure now. (16/1)
1775 Pomona wanted to do nothing but hang on this fast ground. (10/1)
2341 Sandmoor Chambray is finding it hard to get his head in front. (10/1)
2290* Duraid (IRE), from an 8lb higher mark, was a major disappointment. He certainly seems to have two ways of running. (6/1)

2679 FOSS CONDITIONS STKS (3-Y.O+) (Class B)

4-10 (4-11) **7f 202y** £9,010.00 (£3,340.00: £1,607.50: £662.50: £268.75: £111.25) Stalls: Low GOING minus 0.35 sec per fur (F)

				SP	RR	SF
2009^{3}	**Ali-Royal (IRE) (120)** (HRACecil) **4-9-7** KFallon(1) (trckd ldrs: rdn to ld over 1f out: r.o wl)	—	**1**	9/4^{2}	123	78
	Weet-A-Minute (IRE) (97) (RHollinshead) **4-9-1** TQuinn(5) (hld up: effrt 3f out: styd on fnl f: no imp)	2½	**2**	50/1	112	67
2009^{9}	**Restructure (IRE) (110)** (MrsJCecil) **5-9-1** PatEddery(3) (lw: led tl over 1f out: kpt on same pce)	2	**3**	8/1^{3}	108	63
2023^{2}	**Kahal (113)** (SbinSuroor) **3-8-6** LDettori(6) (lw: trckd ldr: ev ch tl rdn over 1f out: wknd ins fnl f)	2	**4**	4/7^{1}	104	50

				SP	RR	SF
	General Song (IRE) (KMcAuliffe) **3-8-7**^{ow1} JReid(2) (effrt 4f out: sn lost pl & bhd)	22	**5**	33/1	60	5
2338^{2}	**Kala Sunrise (88)** (CSmith) **4-9-1** JFortune(4) (trckd ldrs: effrt over 3f out: lost pl & eased 2f out: dismntd)	14	**6**	33/1	31	—
				(SP 113.4%)	**6 Rn**	

1m 36.83 (-0.17) CSF £73.62 TOTE £2.70: £1.50 £4.20 (£33.70) OWNER Greenbay Stables Ltd (NEWMARKET) BRED C. H. WACKER III
WEIGHT FOR AGE 3yo-9lb

2009 Ali-Royal (IRE) made light of a 6lb penalty, sticking on and racing with plenty of enthusiasm. (9/4)

Weet-A-Minute (IRE), having his first outing for eight months, and making a belated reappearance, ran really well, considering he would have met the winner on 17lb better terms in a handicap. In addition, he is also better over further. (50/1)

Restructure (IRE) has now finished behind Ali-Royal on each of his four outings this term. (8/1)

2023 Kahal has possibly outgrown his own strength. After travelling strongly he fell in a heap inside the last, and is the type to do better at four. (4/7)

General Song (IRE), out of his class, had two handlers in the paddock. (33/1)

2338 Kala Sunrise, whose jockey was looking down at his hind legs soon after halfway, was virtually pulled up and dismounted after the line. (33/1)

2680 EQUITY FINANCIAL COLLECTIONS MAIDEN STKS (2-Y.O) (Class D)

4-40 (4-41) **6f 214y** £6,316.00 (£1,888.00: £904.00: £412.00) Stalls: High GOING minus 0.35 sec per fur (F)

				SP	RR	SF
	Sharp Play (MJohnston) **2-9-0** DMcKeown(8) (w'like: unf: scope: chsd ldrs: shkn up to ld 2f out: styd on wl fnl f)	—	**1**	16/1	80+	39
	Mowbray (USA) (PFICole) **2-9-0** TQuinn(10) (w'like: strong: w ldr: n.m.r over 2f out: kpt on wl fnl f)	3½	**2**	13/2	72	31
1978^{4}	**Success And Glory (IRE)** (HRACecil) **2-9-0** KFallon(1) (led: rdn & hung rt over 2f out: sn hdd: one pce)	1½	**3**	11/4^{2}	69	28
	Mihnah (IRE) (DMorley) **2-8-9** GCarter(2) (tall: sn trckng ldrs: kpt on wl fnl f: improve)	s.h	**4**	14/1	63+	22
2336^{7}	**Pay On Red (USA)** (PFICole) **2-9-0** JReid(3) (sn pushed along: outpcd ½-wy: kpt on appr fnl f)	4	**5**	9/1	59	18
1801^{3}	**Captain McCloy (USA)** (MrsJRRamsden) **2-9-0** JFortune(6) (s.i.s: outpcd & bhd ½-wy: n.d)	5	**6**	20/1	48	7
	Rabah (JLDunlop) **2-9-0** PatEddery(9) (w'like: chsd ldrs: sn drvn along: rdn & outpcd ½-wy: sn wknd)	s.h	**7**	7/4^{1}	48	7
1607^{5}	**Mumtaaz** (SbinSuroor) **2-9-0** LDettori(4) (lw: trckd ldrs: rdn over 2f out: sn wknd)	2½	**8**	3/1^{3}	42	1
	Red Cascade (IRE) (BWHills) **2-8-9** MHills(7) (leggy: scope: unruly in stalls: s.s: hdwy ½-wy: sn wknd & eased)	hd	**9**	14/1	37	—
	Lambrini Lad (IRE) (ABailey) **2-9-0** SDrowne(5) (w'like: scope: uns rdr bef s: sn outpcd & rdn along)	6	**10**	33/1	28	—
				(SP 138.3%)	**10 Rn**	

1m 25.47 (2.47) CSF £124.91 TOTE £28.80: £3.40 £2.70 £1.40 (£80.00) Trio £147.40 OWNER Mrs I. Bird (MIDDLEHAM) BRED Bloomsbury Stud

Sharp Play looks to have plenty of physical improvement in him. Noisy and colty in the paddock, in end he took this in decisive fashion. In truth it did not look a strong maiden race by York standards. (16/1)

Mowbray (USA), a stocky individual, was driven along to race upsides but was left for dead by the winner in the final furlong. (13/2)

1978 Success And Glory (IRE) apparently had an interrupted journey here on his debut. Rousted along to make the running, he hung and looked unhappy under pressure. More give underfoot might help. (11/4)

Mihnah (IRE), an immature filly, was by no means knocked about. With a tougher introduction, she could probably have finished second, and she should improve and win races. (14/1)

2336 Pay On Red (USA), who has plenty of size and scope, looks a stayer who needs a mile already. (9/1: 12/1-8/1)

1801 Captain McCloy (USA), who showed plenty of knee action going down, stuck on late in the day after a sluggish start. He needs one more outing to qualify for a nursery mark. (20/1)

Rabah came here with quite a reputation. Noisy in the paddock, he showed a good action going down but, in real trouble at halfway, soon dropped right out. Presumably he is capable of a good deal better. (7/4)

1607 Mumtaaz looked very fit, but after travelling strongly to halfway, found very little. (3/1: op 2/1)

T/Jkpt: Not won; £32,454.35 to York 12/7/97. T/Plpt: £287.40 (165.12 Tckts). T/Qdpt: £14.70 (144.26 Tckts) WG

2651-CHESTER (L-H) (Good to firm)

Saturday July 12th

WEATHER: overcast WIND: mod half bhd becoming fresh half bhd

2681 BROXTON NURSERY H'CAP (2-Y.O) (Class D)

2-10 (2-12) **7f 2y** £3,761.00 (£1,133.00: £549.00: £257.00) Stalls: Low GOING minus 0.46 sec per fur (F)

				SP	RR	SF
2489*	**Lord Smith** (MCPipe) **2-8-12**$^{(3)}$ PFessey(1) (mde all: clr 1f out: hld on cl home)	—	**1**	5/2^{1}	75	28
2359^{4}	**Out Like Magic** (PDEvans) **2-9-7** JFEgan(9) (trckd ldrs: effrt 3f out: rdn appr fnl f: fin wl)	½	**2**	10/1	80	33
2500^{4}	**Lord of Love** (TDEasterby) **2-8-11** DeanMcKeown(6) (chsd ldrs: rdn & c wd st: r.o one pce)	6	**3**	11/1	56	9
2604^{2}	**Flame Tower (IRE)** (RHannon) **2-8-5** PaulEddery(2) (chsd wnr over 5f: sn rdn & wknd)	1¼	**4**	8/1	47	—
1735^{7}	**Narrogin (USA)** (MRChannon) **2-9-1v^{1}** JFortune(10) (dwlt: hdwy over 2f out: sn rdn: nt rch ldrs)	s.h	**5**	10/1	57	10
1815^{2}	**Arm And A Leg (IRE)** (CADwyer) **2-8-1**$^{(5)}$ RMullen(3) (sn drvn along: a outpcd)	1½	**6**	9/1	45	—
1961^{4}	**Red Maple (USA)** (PFICole) **2-9-1** FNorton(8) (b.hind: swtg: outpcd: a in rr)	4	**7**	13/2^{3}	45	—
2383*	**Fast Franc (IRE)** (SCWilliams) **2-8-2**$^{(7)}$ DarrenWilliams(4) (prom: rdn over 2f out: wknd wl over 1f out)	1½	**8**	9/2^{2}	35	—
2196^{10}	**Gralmano (IRE)** (NPLittmoden) **2-8-1** DaleGibson(5) (outpcd: a bhd)	½	**9**	25/1	26	—
2378^{3}	**Edna's Gift (IRE)** (JBerry) **2-7-4**$^{(7)}$ PBradley(7) (hmpd sn after s: hdwy ½-wy: rdn 2f out: sn wknd)	hd	**10**	14/1	22	—
				(SP 118.2%)	**10 Rn**	

1m 28.04 (2.84) CSF £26.66 CT £221.02 TOTE £2.90: £1.60 £3.60 £4.00 (£21.90) Trio £62.30 OWNER Mr A. J. Lomas (WELLINGTON) BRED Mrs M. S. Teversham

2489* Lord Smith showed what a versatile individual he really is, with another smooth, all-the-way success on ground much faster than he has tackled before. (5/2)

2359 Out Like Magic was back in her own company in this first handicap, and she performed extremely well under top weight to fail narrowly. She is not built to carry weight, but she has a heart as big as herself. (10/1)

2500 Lord of Love, coming wide off the home turn when trying to deliver his challenge, could only stay on at the one pace, but this is more his trip, and he will get it right one of these days. (11/1: 8/1-12/1)

2604 Flame Tower (IRE), having his second hard race in three days, was finding demands too much for him once straightened up for home. (8/1)
965 Narrogin (USA), sluggish leaving the stalls in his first-time visor, tried hard to recover the lost ground starting the home turn, but could not summon the pace to get serious. (10/1: 6/1-11/1)
1815 Arm And A Leg (IRE) has been competing in sellers in his most recent outings, and found this company on this sharp track too smart for him. (9/1)

2682 CHESTER SUMMER H'CAP (0-80) (3-Y.O+) (Class D)

2-45 (2-46) **1m 7f 195y** £5,832.50 (£1,760.00: £855.00: £402.50) Stalls: Low GOING minus 0.46 sec per fur (F)

				SP	RR	SF
2464[2]	**Rex Mundi (61)** (PDEvans) **5-9-2** JFEgan(4) (chsd ldrs: led over 2f out tl over 1f out: rallied u.p to ld cl home)	—	**1**	8/1	72	26
1224[3]	**Here Comes Herbie (59)** (WStorey) **5-8-11**(3) PFessey(3) (hld up in rr: hdwy 5f out: rdn to ld over 1f out: ct nr fin)	s.h	**2**	11/2[3]	70	24
2014[24]	**Great Oration (IRE) (59)** (FWatson) **8-9-0** JFortune(8) (hld up & bhd: hdwy over 3f out: hrd rdn appr fnl f: fin wl)	½	**3**	8/1	69	23
2350[2]	**Trilby (58)** (GRichards) **4-8-8v**(5) PRoberts(1) (hld up: dropped rr 7f out: swtchd outside over 2f out: styd on strly)	½	**4**	3/1[1]	68	22
2530[2]	**Ramike (IRE) (80)** (MJohnston) **3-9-2** DeanMcKeown(6) (prom: rdn 4f out: sn outpcd: styd on again appr fnl f)	3	**5**	4/1[2]	87	22
2316[7]	**Dancing Cavalier (69)** (RHollinshead) **4-9-3**(7) PFredericks(5) (swtg: hld up: effrt over 3f out: sn hrd rdn: styd on ins fnl f)	5	**6**	12/1	71	25
2381[3]	**General Mouktar (52)** (MCPipe) **7-8-7** PaulEddery(9) (trckd ldrs: rdn over 4f out: sn wknd)	2½	**7**	8/1	51	5
2291[6]	**Northern Motto (53)** (JSGoldie) **4-8-8** NVarley(11) (chsd ldrs: ev ch over 2f out: wknd over 1f out)	1¾	**8**	9/1	51	5
	Bold Elect (52) (EJAlston) **9-8-4**(3) DGriffiths(10) (bkwd: led tl over 2f out: sn rdn & wknd)	nk	**9**	16/1	49	3
2207[11]	**Euphoric Illusion (42)** (MrsSJSmith) **6-7-11** DaleGibson(2) (a bhd: t.o fnl 4f)	15	**10**	25/1	24	—
2236[6]	**Warning Reef (66)** (PEccles) **4-9-7** TGMcLaughlin(7) (a in rr: t.o fnl 4f)	18	**11**	20/1	30	—

(SP 125.9%) **11 Rn**

3m 30.85 (7.95) CSF £50.47 CT £344.32 TOTE £9.60: £2.70 £1.70 £2.50 (£27.50) Trio £88.60 OWNER Mr J. W. Littler (WELSHPOOL) BRED J. W. Littler
WEIGHT FOR AGE 3yo-19lb
2464 Rex Mundi came into his own on this step-up to an extended trip, and the way he battled to regain command close home would suggest he has been crying out for a true test of stamina. (8/1)
1224 Here Comes Herbie, a proven stayer, looked as though he was set to record another success when striking the front below the distance, but had reckoned without the fight-back from the winner, and was touched off right on the line. (11/2)
1672 Great Oration (IRE), 15lb higher than when successful in this event last year, was doing all his best work late on, and he may well have made it in another couple of strides. (8/1)
2350 Trilby, the only one anyone wanted to be on, was getting nowhere when stuck on the inside rail, but she picked up in fine style once switched to the outside, and must be counted an unlucky loser. (3/1: op 7/1)
2530 Ramike (IRE) has been enjoying a rewarding season, but he was none too happy on this track and, after getting outpaced at a crucial time, had little hope of getting back into it. (4/1)

2683 CITY WALL CONDITIONS STKS (3-Y.O+) (Class B)

3-15 (3-17) **5f 16y** £15,535.00 (£5,815.00: £2,845.00: £1,225.00: £550.00: £280.00) Stalls: Low GOING minus 0.46 sec per fur (F)

				SP	RR	SF
2526[6]	**Tedburrow (102)** (EJAlston) **5-9-0** DGriffiths(1) (bhd: hdwy on ins 2f out: led over 1f out: drvn clr)	—	**1**	10/1	106	64
2134[2]	**Bishops Court (102)** (MrsJRRamsden) **3-8-9** JFortune(4) (lw: a.p: ev ch ent fnl f: unable qckn)	1¾	**2**	9/4[1]	101	54
2529[6]	**Ziggy's Dancer (USA) (84)** (EJAlston) **6-9-0** JFEgan(8) (chsd ldrs: outpcd 2f out: swtchd ins: fin wl)	nk	**3**	16/1	100	58
2526*	**Ya Malak (113)** (DNicholls) **6-9-8** AlexGreaves(5) (lw: led ½-wy tl over 1f out: rdn & no ex fnl f)	s.h	**4**	7/2[3]	107	65
2526[11]	**Bolshoi (IRE) (106)** (JBerry) **5-9-2b** EmmaO'Gorman(2) (lw: s.i.s: hdwy & nt clr run ent st: swtchd lft: fin wl)	s.h	**5**	9/1	101	59
2329[4]	**King of Peru (94)** (NPLittmoden) **4-9-0** TGMcLaughlin(6) (lw: sn pushed along: rdn & r.o wl ins fnl f)	¾	**6**	33/1	97	55
2526[2]	**Struggler (112)** (DRLoder) **5-9-0** RHughes(7) (lw: a outpcd)	3½	**7**	3/1[2]	86	44
1766[5]	**Blue Iris (100)** (MAJarvis) **4-8-9** PaulEddery(9) (lw: spd 3f: btn whn bmpd over 1f out)	3½	**8**	8/1	70	28
1980[19]	**Vax Star (92)** (JLSpearing) **3-8-4b[1]** DeanMcKeown(3) (led over 2f: rdn whn stumbled ent st: sn lost pl)	6	**9**	25/1	51	4

(SP 120.9%) **9 Rn**

59.93 secs (-0.27) CSF £31.34 TOTE £11.60: £2.20 £1.40 £2.20 (£18.10) Trio £59.50 OWNER Mr Philip Davies (PRESTON) BRED Lady Matthews
WEIGHT FOR AGE 3yo-5lb
2526 Tedburrow, in a race which lived up to its high billing, enjoyed a charmed run through towards the inside rail and, finding extra after striking the front, won in the style of a most improved performer. (10/1)
2134 Bishops Court needs another furlong when the ground rides as fast as it did here, and it is to his credit that he was able to get himself in with a chance second to none on the approach to the final furlong. He is certainly not enjoying the best of fortune. (9/4)
2529 Ziggy's Dancer (USA) goes well round here, but he had it all to do in this company, and was never going to reach his stable companion after getting tapped for speed approaching the straight. (16/1)
2526* Ya Malak seems to produce his best when coming from off the pace but, on this occasion, he showed ahead at halfway before getting tapped for finishing speed. There is no disgrace in his attempt to concede weight all round. (7/2)
1881a Bolshoi (IRE) has done all his winning on a straight sprint track, and he seemed to lose all chance when taking time to find his stride. Encountering problems in running, he produced a tremendous turn of speed after being switched to the inside, and there is no doubting he still retains all his ability. (9/1)
2329 King of Peru does not possess the speed to win at this trip in such hot company, but he was into his stride inside the final furlong, and it might be wise to take a drop in class. (33/1)

2684 E.B.F. MAIDEN STKS (2-Y.O) (Class D)

3-50 (3-50) **5f 16y** £4,224.00 (£1,272.00: £616.00: £288.00) Stalls: Low GOING minus 0.46 sec per fur (F)

				SP	RR	SF
2007[4]	**Huntswood** (RHannon) **2-9-0** RHughes(4) (mde all: qcknd clr ent fnl f: comf)	—	**1**	15/8[2]	80+	33
2473[2]	**Take A Turn** (MRChannon) **2-9-0** JFortune(2) (w wnr: rdn 2f out: r.o one pce)	2	**2**	7/4[1]	74	27

	Farndon Princess (RHollinshead) **2-8-9** PaulEddery(1) (sltly dipped: unf: s.s: hdwy ½-wy: r.o one pce appr fnl f)	1¾	**3**	7/1	63	16
	Time To Time (TDEasterby) **2-8-9** DeanMcKeown(6) (w'like: scope: bkwd: s.i.s: outpcd tl r.o ins fnl f)	2½	**4**	12/1	55	8
2066^{5}	**Blarney Park** (CADwyer) **2-8-9** NVarley(3) (chsd ldrs: pushed along ½-wy: outpcd appr fnl f)	s.h	**5**	20/1	55	8
2047^{4}	**Just Another Time** (JBerry) **2-8-9**(5) PRoberts(5) (lw: prom tl rdn & outpcd appr fnl f)	½	**6**	9/2^{3}	59	12

(SP 114.3%) **6 Rn**

61.81 secs (1.61) CSF £5.22 TOTE £3.00: £2.10 £1.50 (£2.70) OWNER Mrs D. F. Cock (MARLBOROUGH) BRED Patrick Eddery Ltd

2007 Huntswood did not have a lot to beat, and he achieved it with the minimum of fuss. It could do wonders for his confidence. (15/8: evens-2/1)

2473 Take A Turn did his best to make a race of it, but he was a bit out of his class against a potentially useful winner. (7/4)

Farndon Princess, slightly dipped and very unfurnished, needs time to develop, and as she obviously has ability, it could be the making of her. (7/1)

Time To Time, a filly with plenty of scope, did not stride out with any freedom to post. Taken off her legs for over three furlongs, she did well in the end to finish as close as she did. (12/1)

2047 Just Another Time (9/2: op 3/1)

2685 WATERGATE STREET GALLERY CONDITIONS STKS (2-Y.O) (Class C)

4-25 (4-26) **6f 18y** £5,170.00 (£1,930.00: £940.00: £400.00: £175.00: £85.00) Stalls: Low GOING minus 0.46 sec per fur (F)

				SP	RR	SF
1952*	**Islamabad** (GLewis) **2-9-1** PaulEddery(3) (b.hind: hld up & bhd: hdwy to ld 1f out: sn clr: v.easily)	—	**1**	8/11^{1}	88+	29
2500^{3}	**Heavenly Abstone** (PDEvans) **2-8-10v** JFEgan(4) (a.p: rdn 2f out: kpt on: no ch w wnr)	1¾	**2**	10/1	78	19
2212*	**Jimmy Too** (BAMcMahon) **2-9-1** JFortune(2) (lw: sn drvn along in rr: outpcd 2f out: r.o strly ins fnl f)	nk	**3**	7/2^{2}	83	24
697^{5}	**Somosierra (IRE)** (JBerry) **2-8-6**(5) PRoberts(1) (bit bkwd: led over 1f: rdn whn nt clr run wl over 1f out)	1	**4**	14/1	76	17
2361*	**Marton Moss (SWE)** (TDEasterby) **2-9-1** DeanMcKeown(5) (trckd ldrs on outside: rdn wl over 1f out: one pce)	1½	**5**	9/1^{3}	76	17
2324*	**Deeceebee** (WStorey) **2-8-12**(3) PFessey(6) (led over 4f out to 1f out: wknd fnl f)	½	**6**	10/1	75	16

(SP 115.0%) **6 Rn**

1m 15.65 (2.35) CSF £8.84 TOTE £1.70: £1.30 £2.80 (£5.30) OWNER Mr A. A. Hussain (EPSOM) BRED M. G. T. Stokes

1952* Islamabad, restrained as long as possible on this step-up to six furlongs, overcame problems in running, and quite simply outclassed the opposition. Highly regarded, he is certainly above average. (8/11: 4/6-evens)

2500 Heavenly Abstone tries hard, and gives it her best shot every time, but this winner does look a class individual, and there was no disgrace in having to give best to him. (10/1: op 6/1)

2212* Jimmy Too takes a long time to warm up, and as such always has it all to do, but the sixth furlong came to his aid this time, and he can go on improving. (7/2)

697 Somosierra (IRE) is not being rushed, and he is gradually getting the hang of things. (14/1)

2361* Marton Moss (SWE) struggled with the pace on this much livelier surface, and could never hold out much hope for his supporters. (9/1: op 5/1)

2324* Deeceebee did his share of the pacemaking, but was unable to hold on when the tempo lifted, and this fast ground is not for him. (10/1: op 6/1)

2686 CHESHIRE YEOMANRY H'CAP (0-80) (3-Y.O+) (Class D)

4-55 (4-55) **1m 2f 75y** £4,250.00 (£1,280.00: £620.00: £290.00) Stalls: High GOING minus 0.46 sec per fur (F)

				SP	RR	SF
2512^{2}	**Ambidextrous (IRE) (58)** (EJAlston) **5-8-10** JFEgan(7) (lw: chsd ldrs: effrt & rdn over 1f out: r.o to ld post)	—	**1**	11/4^{1}	64	13
2293^{7}	**Keep Battling (46)** (JSGoldie) **7-7-9**(3) PFessey(5) (hld up & bhd: gd hdwy over 2f out: led over 1f out: edgd rt u.p & hdd last stride)	s.h	**2**	10/1	52	1
2015^{9}	**Mad Militant (IRE) (63)** (AStreeter) **8-8-12**(3) RHavlin(6) (a chsng ldrs: ev ch 1f out: rdn & unable qckn)	1½	**3**	9/2^{2}	67	16
2293^{5}	**Gymcrak Premiere (72)** (GHolmes) **9-9-10v** JFortune(2) (lw: a.p: rdn wl over 1f out: nt pce to chal)	¾	**4**	5/1^{3}	74	23
2285*	**Brandon Jack (75)** (IABalding) **3-9-2** PaulEddery(4) (lw: hld up: effrt over 2f out: rdn & one pce fnl f)	hd	**5**	11/4^{1}	77	15
2174*	**Tonnerre (59)** (BAMcMahon) **5-8-4**(7) SRighton(1) (w ldr: led 3f out tl over 1f out: wknd ins fnl f)	1	**6**	5/1^{3}	60	9
2152^{11}	**Golden Fish (44)** (EJAlston) **5-7-3**(7) PBradley(3) (bkwd: led over 7f: wknd wl over 1f out: t.o)	12	**7**	25/1	26	—

(SP 117.8%) **7 Rn**

2m 14.53 (5.83) CSF £29.93 TOTE £2.70: £1.40 £3.20 (£20.90) OWNER Mrs Carol McPhail (PRESTON) BRED Saeed Manana

LONG HANDICAP Golden Fish 6-13

WEIGHT FOR AGE 3yo-11lb

2512 Ambidextrous (IRE), a very genuine colt who responds to pressure, needed to show his true colours to land the spoils right on the line. This was his first success at this slightly shorter trip. (11/4)

1992 Keep Battling had both the ground and the trip he needs, and he was produced to win his race approaching the final furlong. However, he drifted right under strong pressure close home and, to the surprise of many, came out second best in the photo. He should be given the chance to make amends. (10/1)

1678* Mad Militant (IRE) looked the chief danger to the runner-up entering the final furlong, but he was unable to raise his pace under pressure, and the winner swooped to beat them both. (9/2)

2293 Gymcrak Premiere travelled comfortably, and was always in a challenging position but, once off the bridle soon after straightening up, was unable to go though with his effort. (5/1)

2285* Brandon Jack is not so effective on such lively ground, and it is very doubtful if he truly gets this trip. (11/4)

2174* Tonnerre helped force the pace, but he likes to get his toe in, and was fighting a lost cause entering the final furlong. (5/1)

T/Plpt: £44.80 (508.96 Tckts). T/Qdpt: £10.20 (99.38 Tckts) IM

2663-LINGFIELD (L-H) (Good to firm, Firm patches)

Saturday July 12th

WEATHER: hot WIND: almost nil

2687 NATASHA GLYNNE MAIDEN STKS (3-Y.O+) (Class D)

2-20 (2-22) **1m 1f** £4,503.00 (£1,344.00: £642.00: £291.00) Stalls: Low GOING minus 0.52 sec per fur (F)

				SP	RR	SF
	Labeq (IRE) (PTWalwyn) **3-8-11** RHills(9) (led over 7f out: clr over 2f out: easily)	—	**1**	5/1	91+	19

	Rumuz (IRE) (EALDunlop) **3-8-7**ow1 JReid(4) (neat: led over 1f: chsd wnr fnl 3f: no imp)	7	**2**	7/2 2	75	2
	Versatility (RFJohnsonHoughton) **4-9-2** SSanders(1) (hdwy over 2f out: r.o one pce)	4	**3**	66/1	66	4
	Ninth Chord (JHMGosden) **3-8-11** PatEddery(7) (b.hind: hdwy over 7f out: chsd wnr 4f out to 3f out: wknd 2f out)	3	**4**	6/5 1	66	—
2360 5	**Glittering (USA)** (CEBrittain) **3-8-11** BDoyle(6) (bhd fnl 6f)	9	**5**	25/1	50	—
	Max's Magic (USA) (GLMoore) **4-9-7** SWhitworth(3) (bkwd: bhd fnl 5f)	13	**6**	66/1	27	—
2046 13	**Summer Thyme** (JBerry) **3-8-1**(5) TEDurcan(2) (bhd fnl 6f)	hd	**7**	100/1	22	—
	Bicton Park (KCComerford) **3-8-6**(5) GFaulkner(8) (rrd s: a wl bhd)	1	**8**	50/1	25	—
	Elaysha (USA) (HRACecil) **3-8-6** WRyan(5) (w'like: lw: hdwy over 6f out: wknd over 3f out)	13	**9**	9/2 3	—	—
				(SP 112.3%)		**9 Rn**

1m 54.35 (3.85) CSF £19.64 TOTE £6.10: £1.50 £2.50 £4.50 (£21.40) Trio £177.10; £127.23 to 14/7/97 OWNER Mr Hamdan Al Maktoum (LAMBOURN) BRED Shadwell Estate Company Limited
WEIGHT FOR AGE 3yo-10lb

Labeq (IRE), a big, deep-girthed individual, was soon at the head of affairs, and had no problems forging clear in the straight to win what looked a very bad maiden doing handsprings. (5/1: 7/2-11/2)
Rumuz (IRE), a plain filly with not a great deal of substance, broke best of all but was soon racing in second place. She was briefly headed for that position turning for home, but had no hope with the winner in the straight. (7/2)
Versatility, a sparely-made filly, came out of a moderate-looking pack over a quarter-of-a-mile from home, and struggled on to finish third. (66/1)
Ninth Chord, a big boat of a horse, was very colty in the paddock. Soon racing in a handy position, he showed briefly in front turning for home, but he was out on his feet with two furlongs to go. (6/5: 8/11-11/8)
Elaysha (USA) (9/2: op 9/4)

2688 E.B.F. SURREY NOVICE STKS (2-Y.O) (Class D)
2-55 (2-59) **7f** £4,854.00 (£1,452.00: £696.00: £318.00) Stalls: High GOING minus 0.52 sec per fur (F)

				SP	RR	SF
	Cerisette (IRE) (CEBrittain) **2-8-7** BDoyle(5) (unf: led over 4f out: pushed out)	—	**1**	20/1	85	36
	Mahboob (IRE) (DMorley) **2-8-12** RHills(2) (w'like: scope: dwlt: hld up: swtchd rt over 2f out: chsd wnr wl over 1f out: no imp)	3½	**2**	7/1 3	82	33
	Murmoon (BHanbury) **2-8-12** WRyan(1) (w'like: scope: bit bkwd: hdwy over 2f out: rdn wl over 1f out: one pce)	3	**3**	14/1	75	26
	Wildcat (IRE) (RHannon) **2-8-12** JReid(8) (w'like: s.s: shkn up over 2f out: stdy hdwy fnl f: nvr nrr: bttr for r)	2½	**4**	10/1	69+	20
2243 4	**Herminius (IRE)** (JLDunlop) **2-8-12** PatEddery(3) (lw: a.p: rdn over 3f out: wknd over 1f out)	hd	**5**	11/10 1	69	20
	Three Angels (IRE) (MHTompkins) **2-8-12** DBiggs(9) (w'like: scope: bit bkwd: rdn & swtchd lft over 3f out: nvr nr to chal)	1¼	**6**	40/1	66	17
	Tarashaan (SirMarkPrescott) **2-8-12** SSanders(6) (w'like: scope: bit bkwd: uns rdr & bolted bef s: s.s: a bhd)	1½	**7**	16/1	63	14
2286 4	**Ballet Rambert** (MJHeaton-Ellis) **2-8-8**(5) RFfrench(7) (led over 2f: wkng whn hmpd on ins over 2f out)	hd	**8**	14/1	64	15
2196*	**Opposition Leader** (BWHills) **2-9-2** DHolland(4) (prom 5f)	½	**9**	4/1 2	66	17
				(SP 115.6%)		**9 Rn**

1m 22.1 (0.90) CSF £139.06 TOTE £20.70: £3.00 £1.80 £4.30 (£95.10) Trio £371.20; £109.80 to 14/7/97 OWNER Sheikh Marwan Al Maktoum (NEWMARKET) BRED Sheikh Marwan al Maktoum

Cerisette (IRE), quite a lengthy, plain filly, who needs time to develop, nevertheless made a very pleasing debut, leading over half-a-mile from home, and needing only to be nudged along to pull away from below the distance. (20/1)
Mahboob (IRE), whose dam won the Italian One Thousand Guineas and Oaks, is quite a tall colt with plenty of substance. Switched to the rails, doing the weakening Ballet Rambert no favours, he moved into second place well over a furlong out, and although managing to pull clear of the remainder, had no hope with the winner. This was a pleasing debut, and he should soon find a small race. (7/1: 3/1-8/1)
Murmoon, a good-sized individual, looked as though the run was needed. (14/1: op 7/1)
Wildcat (IRE), quite a tall gelding, was given a nice introduction. He was noted inching closer in the final furlong, and is sure to come on for this. (10/1)
2243 Herminius (IRE) again disappointed, and this time there was no excuse about soft ground. (11/10)
Three Angels (IRE), a plain colt with plenty of substance, did not impress in his coat, and never threatened to get into it. (40/1)
2286 Ballet Rambert (14/1: op 8/1)
2196* Opposition Leader (4/1: 3/1-5/1)

2689 RUINART CHAMPAGNE NURSERY H'CAP (2-Y.O) (Class C)
3-25 (3-26) **6f** £5,900.00 (£1,760.00: £840.00: £380.00) Stalls: High GOING minus 0.52 sec per fur (F)

				SP	RR	SF
2349*	**Master Mac (USA)** (RAkehurst) **2-9-1** SSanders(8) (lw: chsd ldr: rdn over 2f out: led ins fnl f: r.o wl)	—	**1**	6/1 3	81	36
2283*	**Ivory's Joy** (KTIvory) **2-7-13**(5) RFfrench(6) (b: b.hind: lw: led: hrd rdn & hung lft over 1f out: hdd ins fnl f: unable qckn)	1¼	**2**	5/1 2	67	22
1842 7	**Mamora Bay (IRE)** (MHTompkins) **2-8-6** DBiggs(10) (lw: rdn over 4f out: hdwy fnl f: r.o wl)	nk	**3**	8/1	68	23
2196 3	**Hoh Justice** (IABalding) **2-8-12** SWhitworth(9) (rdn over 3f out: hdwy on ins over 1f out: r.o ins fnl f)	s.h	**4**	7/1	74	29
1959*	**Magic Rainbow** (MBell) **2-9-0** MFenton(3) (s.s & swtchd rt: nvr nr to chal)	3	**5**	7/2 1	68	23
*1577**	**Oh Never Again (IRE)** (MJohnston) **2-9-4** DHolland(7) (a.p: rdn over 3f out: wknd over 1f out)	s.h	**6**	9/1	72	27
1872 10	**Caversfield** (RHannon) **2-8-11** PatEddery(4) (lw: a.p: rdn over 2f out: wknd fnl f)	¾	**7**	16/1	63	18
2196 4	**Island Girl (IRE)** (DWPArbuthnot) **2-8-4** BDoyle(5) (bhd fnl 2f)	nk	**8**	14/1	55	10
2181*	**Ben Rinnes** (RFJohnsonHoughton) **2-9-2**(5) ADaly(1) (lw: bhd fnl 3f)	7	**9**	12/1	53	8
2306 4	**Elleysanta** (AGNewcombe) **2-8-9** JReid(2) (bhd fnl 3f)	7	**10**	15/2	23	—
				(SP 118.8%)		**10 Rn**

1m 10.22 (1.22) CSF £33.53 CT £223.55 TOTE £5.30: £2.20 £1.80 £3.10 (£15.30) Trio £124.30 OWNER Mr Charles Parker (EPSOM) BRED Joe Lee

2349* Master Mac (USA) coped well with the drop back to six furlongs. Racing in second place, he was rousted along approaching the final quarter-mile, and managed to get on top inside the final furlong. (6/1: 4/1-13/2)
2283* Ivory's Joy put up a tremendous performance in this much better-class race. Bowling along in front, she hung left under pressure below the distance, and may well have been feeling this fast ground. Collared inside the final furlong, she nevertheless managed to hold on for second prize. (5/1)

861 Mamora Bay (IRE) was soon being bustled along at the back of the field, and for much of the trip appeared to be going absolutely nowhere. He eventually found his feet inside the distance, and running on strongly, would have snatched second place in a few more strides. (8/1)
2196 Hoh Justice, bustled along before halfway, picked up ground along the inside rail below the distance, and staying on, only just missed out on third prize. A return to seven furlongs would probably help. (7/1)
1959* Magic Rainbow is having a real problem breaking on level terms as the stalls open, and for the third time in three outings, he lost ground at the start. On this occasion it proved crucial, for he could never get into it as a result. (7/2)
1577* Oh Never Again (IRE) played an active role until coming to the end of his tether approaching the final furlong. (9/1)
2181* Ben Rinnes (12/1: 8/1-14/1)

2690 DAILY MAIL CLASSIFIED SILVER TROPHY RATED STKS H'CAP (0-105) (Listed) (3-Y.O+) (Class A)

4-00 (4-01) **7f 140y** £12,590.40 (£4,713.60: £2,306.80: £994.00: £447.00: £228.20) Stalls: High GOING minus 0.52 sec per fur (F)

				SP	RR	SF
2026^{3}	**Cadeaux Tryst (102)** (EALDunlop) **5-9-6** RHills(5) (b: a.p: rdn 2f out: led ins fnl f: r.o wl)	—	1	3/1^{2}	112	65
2026^{28}	**Tregaron (USA) (103)** (RAkehurst) **6-9-7** SSanders(4) (lw: rdn 2f out: hdwy over 1f out: r.o)	2	2	6/1^{3}	109	62
2525^{4}	**Star Talent (USA) (89)** (IABalding) **6-8-7** SWhitworth(7) (swtg: stdy hdwy on ins 2f out: ev ch ins fnl f: unable qckn)	nk	3	13/2	94	47
2056^{22}	**Russian Music (100)** (MissGayKelleway) **4-9-4** RFfrench(6) (led tl ins fnl f: sn wknd)	1	4	12/1	103	56
2325^{14}	**Divina Luna (89)** (JWHills) **4-8-7** DHolland(8) (a.p: rdn over 2f out: one pce)	1¼	5	33/1	90	43
2133*	**Brave Kris (IRE) (100)** (LMCumani) **3-8-9** PatEddery(3) (plld hrd: hdwy over 6f out: chsd ldr 6f out tl over 2f out: sn wknd)	8	6	7/4^{1}	84	28
2056^{21}	**Moonshine Girl (USA) (98)** (MRStoute) **3-8-7** JReid(1) (lw: a bhd)	1¼	7	16/1	79	23
1919a^{5}	**Tsarnista (93)** (JLDunlop) **4-8-11b^{1}** WRyan(2) (swtg: hld up: rdn over 2f out: sn wknd)	1	8	14/1	72	25
				(SP 112.2%)	**8 Rn**	

1m 28.48 (-0.52) CSF £18.63 CT £96.46 TOTE £3.40: £1.20 £2.20 £1.60 (£8.20) OWNER Maktoum Al Maktoum (NEWMARKET) BRED Gainsborough Stud Management Ltd
LONG HANDICAP Divina Luna 8-1 Star Talent (USA) 8-6
WEIGHT FOR AGE 3yo-9lb
OFFICIAL EXPLANATION Brave Kris (IRE): bolted going to post and ran too freely in the race.
2026 Cadeaux Tryst, a leading player throughout, was woken up in the final quarter-mile, and managed to get to the front inside the final furlong. (3/1)
892* Tregaron (USA), a massive 34lb higher than when winning his first race last year, left his Royal Hunt Cup run well behind. Picking up ground below the distance, he ran on to snatch second prize, but was unable to get on terms with the winner. This is his ground. (6/1)
2525 Star Talent (USA) put up a tremendous performance and, easing his way into contention in the final quarter-mile, had every chance inside the last two hundred yards, before tapped for toe. (13/2)
1598 Russian Music gave a very good account of himself and, bowling along in front, looked as if he might prevail a quarter-of-a-mile from home. He was eventually collared inside the final furlong, and had little left in the locker. (12/1)
1874 Divina Luna, 6lb out of the handicap, failed to cope with the mud last time out, but was never far away on this occasion. (33/1)
2133* Brave Kris (IRE), very excitable beforehand, and free going to post, had boiled over by the time they set off. Eddery's attempts to settle her at the back of the field proved futile, as she soon pulled her way into second place. Collared for that position before the quarter-mile pole, she was quickly done with. This run is best forgotten, but she needs to learn to calm down. (7/4)
1919a Tsarnista (14/1: op 7/1)

2691 ROTHMANS ROYALS NORTH SOUTH CHALLENGE SERIES H'CAP (0-90) (3-Y.O) (Class C)

4-35 (4-36) **7f** £7,700.00 (£2,300.00: £1,100.00: £500.00) Stalls: High GOING minus 0.52 sec per fur (F)

				SP	RR	SF
2229^{2}	**Peppiatt (80)** (RAkehurst) **3-8-11** SSanders(5) (lw: a.p: rdn over 2f out: led 1f out: r.o wl)	—	1	4/1^{1}	85	60
1737^{8}	**Impulsif (USA) (71)** (DJSffrenchDavis) **3-8-2** MFenton(13) (led: rdn over 2f out: hdd 1f out: unable qckn)	1½	2	12/1	73	48
2298^{2}	**Ivory Dawn (78)** (KTIvory) **3-8-4**(5)ow3 GFaulkner(7) (hld up: rdn over 3f out: one pce fnl f)	nk	3	16/1	79	51
2119^{6}	**Eurolink Profile (74)** (LMCumani) **3-8-0**(5) RFfrench(12) (rdn over 2f out: hdwy over 1f out: one pce)	½	4	11/2	74	49
2325^{4}	**Gee Bee Dream (80)** (APJarvis) **3-8-11** WRyan(9) (lw: rdn over 3f out: hdwy over 1f out: nvr nrr)	1½	5	5/1^{3}	76	51
2013^{13}	**Redwing (90)** (JLDunlop) **3-9-7** PatEddery(4) (swtg: stdy hdwy over 3f out: hrd rdn over 1f out: wknd fnl f)	1½	6	9/2^{2}	83	58
2205^{3}	**Topatori (IRE) (73)** (MHTompkins) **3-8-4** DBiggs(10) (lw: prom over 5f)	1	7	6/1	64	39
2303^{6}	**Nant Y Gamer (FR) (82)** (JBerry) **3-8-8**(5) TEDurcan(6) (prom over 4f)	1½	8	16/1	69	44
2013^{25}	**Praeditus (80)** (RHannon) **3-8-11** JReid(8) (prom over 4f)	1½	9	14/1	64	39
2185^{3}	**Paddy Lad (IRE) (86)** (RGuest) **3-9-3** PBloomfield(2) (bhd fnl 3f)	1¼	10	16/1	67	42
2554^{11}	**V I P Charlie (72)** (JRJenkins) **3-7-12**(5)ow5 ADaly(3) (swtg: bhd fnl 2f)	nk	11	14/1	52	22
2426^{6}	**Hakkaniyah (85)** (DMorley) **3-9-2** RHills(1) (prom over 3f)	13	12	16/1	36	11
694^{14}	**Aegean Sound (75)** (KTIvory) **3-8-6** DHolland(11) (b.hind: bhd fnl 4f)	hd	13	33/1	25	—
				(SP 132.0%)	**13 Rn**	

1m 20.42 (-0.78) CSF £54.10 CT £688.85 TOTE £3.80: £2.20 £3.70 £3.90 (£62.40) Trio £415.00 OWNER Mr Kevin Reddington (EPSOM) BRED D. A. and Mrs Hicks
2229 Peppiatt may have had little experience on his side - this was only his third run - but he did not let that stop him. Gaining control a furlong out, he was rousted along to assert his authority. (4/1: 5/2-9/)
Impulsif (USA) ran by far his best race of the season, taking the field along until passed by the winner a furlong from home. (12/1)
2298 Ivory Dawn, returning to seven furlongs, chased the leaders. Bustled along from halfway, he was on the heels of the principals entering the final furlong, before tapped for toe. (16/1)
2119 Eurolink Profile was happier with the return to a sounder surface but, after moving up below the distance, he failed to find another gear. (11/2)
2325 Gee Bee Dream, out with the washing and going nowhere at halfway, stayed on from below the distance, but found it all over bar the shouting. She might be worth a try at a mile. (5/1)
675 Redwing, who was done no favours by the Handicapper, took closer order on the outside of the field, but had shot his bolt in the final furlong. (9/2)
1238 Praeditus (14/1: 10/1-16/1)

2692 WHITES' WEDDING MAIDEN STKS (3-Y.O+) (Class D)
5-05 (5-10) **1m 6f** £4,056.25 (£1,210.00: £577.50: £261.25) Stalls: High GOING minus 0.52 sec per fur (F)

Form	Horse / details	Dist	Pos	SP	RR	SF
1922^{2}	**Melodica (75)** (MRStoute) **3-8-5** JReid(5) (mde all: rdn out)	—	**1**	9/4^{1}	83	21
2410^{10}	**Crystal Hills (IRE)** (JHMGosden) **3-8-10** AGarth(8) (hdwy 6f out: chsd wnr wl over 1f out: r.o)	1½	**2**	10/1	86	24
2188^{2}	**Seattle Art (USA) (84)** (HRACecil) **3-8-10** WRyan(1) (chsd wnr over 11f out tl wl over 1f out: sn wknd)	8	**3**	3/1^{2}	77	15
1239^{7}	**Coble (76)** (BWHills) **3-8-10** DHolland(6) (a.p: rdn over 3f out: sn wknd)	15	**4**	4/1	60	—
	Ultimate Smoothie (MCPipe) **5-9-11** PatEddery(9) (nvr nrr)	4	**5**	7/2^{3}	55	8
	Arctic Triumph (MBradstock) **6-9-4**(7) RStudholme(2) (s.s: bhd fnl 6f: t.o)	7	**6**	50/1	47	—
2311^{7}	**Ajcombe (IRE)** (LadyHerries) **4-9-6**(5) GMilligan(7) (bit bkwd: a bhd: t.o fnl 6f)	13	**7**	50/1	33	—
	Byhookorbycrook (IRE) (KCComerford) **5-9-1**(5) GFaulkner(4) (plld hrd: chsd wnr over 2f: wknd 8f out: t.o fnl 7f)	dist	**8**	50/1	—	—

(SP 113.0%) **8 Rn**

3m 3.36 (5.06) CSF £22.78 TOTE £3.80: £1.40 £3.50 £1.30 (£11.90) Trio £8.70 OWNER Sheikh Mohammed (NEWMARKET) BRED Sheikh Mohammed Bin Rashid Al Maktoum

WEIGHT FOR AGE 3yo-15lb

1922 Melodica, a tall filly, appreciated the step-up in distance, for she has shown acceleration is not her strong suit. Making all the running, she looked to have things nicely in control in the final quarter-mile but, with the runner-up plodding on, needed to be rousted along to win a bad race. (9/4)

Crystal Hills (IRE), a big individual, appreciated this longer trip, for he is not blessed with acceleration. Struggling into second place well over a furlong from home, he was gradually clawing back the winner's advantage, but was unable to get there in time. He is certainly one of the stable's lesser lights. (10/1: 8/1-14/1)

2188 Seattle Art (USA) was soon racing in second place but, collared for that position well over a furlong from home, he had little left to offer. Maybe a return to an easier surface would help. (3/1: 5/4-7/2)

683 Coble failed to see out this much longer trip, and was out on his feet in the straight. (4/1: op 9/4)

Ultimate Smoothie (7/2: op 10/1)

T/Plpt: £1,501.30 (9.78 Tckts). T/Qdpt: £18.60 (49.87 Tckts) AK

2240-SALISBURY (R-H) (Good to firm, Firm patches)
Saturday July 12th
WEATHER: fine WIND: almost nil

2693 E.B.F. QUEENPOT MAIDEN STKS (I) (2-Y.O) (Class D)
2-15 (2-17) **6f 212y** £3,405.00 (£1,020.00: £490.00: £225.00) GOING minus 0.45 sec per fur (F)

Form	Horse / details	Dist	Pos	SP	RR	SF
	Fakhr (USA) (JLDunlop) **2-9-0** GCarter(9) (w'like: scope: dwlt: pushed along over 3f out: gd hdwy over 1f out: str run to ld wl ins fnl f)	—	**1**	2/1^{1}	91++	34
1933^{6}	**Royal Bounty (IRE)** (MajorWRHern) **2-8-9** TSprake(12) (plld hrd early: hdwy over 2f out: led wl over 1f out tl wl ins fnl f)	¾	**2**	11/2^{3}	84	27
	Chattan (BWHills) **2-8-11**(3) JDSmith(6) (unf: scope: bit bkwd: plld hrd: a.p: led over 2f out tl wl over 1f out: wknd ins fnl f)	5	**3**	10/1	78+	21
1486^{9}	**Santone (IRE)** (RHannon) **2-8-11**(3) MartinDwyer(10) (hld up mid div: hdwy over 2f out: rdn over 1f out: r.o one pce)	¾	**4**	33/1	76	19
	Close Up (IRE) (JLDunlop) **2-9-0** GHind(3) (w'like: bit bkwd: bhd: pushed along over 3f out: hdwy over 1f out: r.o)	1¼	**5**	14/1	73	16
2336^{4}	**Al's Fella (IRE)** (PFICole) **2-9-0** RPerham(5) (prom: ev ch over 2f out: wknd over 1f out)	hd	**6**	5/1^{2}	73	16
2243^{5}	**Daring News** (RHannon) **2-9-0** DaneO'Neill(14) (prom over 4f)	nk	**7**	9/1	72	15
	Zuryaf (IRE) (BJMeehan) **2-9-0** MTebbutt(13) (w'like: bit bkwd: nvr nrr)	3½	**8**	16/1	64	7
1954^{6}	**Magical Dancer (IRE)** (MrsPNDutfield) **2-8-4**(5) AimeeCook(11) (plld hrd mid div: bhd fnl 2f)	s.h	**9**	50/1	59	2
2057^{6}	**Anvil (USA)** (GLewis) **2-9-0** WJO'Connor(1) (led over 4f: wknd wl over 1f out)	¾	**10**	5/1^{2}	62	5
	Balaclava (IRE) (EALDunlop) **2-8-11**(3) DO'Donohoe(7) (leggy: bit bkwd: a bhd)	2	**11**	14/1	58	1
	Cage Aux Folles (IRE) (JWHills) **2-8-11**(3) MHenry(8) (w'like: bit bkwd: mid div: rdn over 3f out: bhd fnl 2f)	hd	**12**	20/1	58	1
	Minjara (APJones) **2-9-0** AMcGlone(2) (w'like: bit bkwd: bhd fnl 2f)	4	**13**	66/1	48	—
2489^{4}	**Floral Park** (GBBalding) **2-8-9** SDrowne(4) (s.s: a bhd)	½	**14**	50/1	42	—

(SP 133.5%) **14 Rn**

1m 28.41 (2.41) CSF £12.63 TOTE £4.00: £2.70 £1.80 £3.10 (£11.00) Trio £50.10 OWNER Mr Hamdan Al Maktoum (ARUNDEL) BRED Shadwell Farm Inc

Fakhr (USA), a well-bred half-brother to Siyadah, had to come from well off the pace and won in the style of a useful recruit. Plenty more will be heard of this Derby entry. (2/1)

1933 Royal Bounty (IRE), a half-sister to Boss Lady and Helen's Bower, has plenty of stamina in her pedigree and will not always meet one so smart. (11/2)

Chattan is the first foal of a mare from the family of Nonoalco who won over seven furlongs and a mile in Ireland. With the combination running too freely and lack of a previous outing telling in the closing stages, he seems sure to improve. (10/1: op 6/1)

Santone (IRE), a 28,000 guineas foal, stepped up on his debut and would appear to be going the right way. (33/1)

Close Up (IRE) is a 60,000 guineas half-brother to five-furlong juvenile winner Blue Movie. A stable companion of the winner, he will be better for the experience. (14/1: op 6/1)

2336 Al's Fella (IRE), whose two previous runs were on soft ground, may not have handled this faster surface. (5/1: 9/2-8/1)

2243 Daring News (9/1: 6/1-10/1)

2694 FELSTEAD LIMITED STKS (0-65) (3-Y.O+) (Class F)
2-50 (2-50) **1m 6f** £2,616.00 (£726.00: £348.00) GOING minus 0.45 sec per fur (F)

Form	Horse / details	Dist	Pos	SP	RR	SF
2490^{3}	**Tawafek (USA) (63)** (SDow) **4-9-6** RPerham(5) (a.p: rdn over 4f out: nt clr run over 2f out: led 1f out: rdn out)	—	**1**	11/4^{2}	74	14

1871[3]	**Mighty Phantom (USA) (65)** (JWHills) **4-9-0**(3) MHenry(2) (wnt 2nd 8f out: rdn over 4f out: led over 1f out: sn hdd: nt qckn)	1¼	2	11/4[2]	70	10
2218[9]	**Alarico (FR) (62)** (IPWilliams) **4-9-8** TSprake(1) (set slow pce tl qcknd after 4f: hdd over 1f out: r.o one pce)	1	3	9/1	73	13
2411[4]	**Charnwood Jack (USA) (65)** (ICampbell) **4-9-8** SDrowne(6) (hld up & plld hrd: bhd fnl 2f)	11	4	2/1[1]	61	1
1641[5]	**Prince Danzig (IRE) (63)** (DJGMurraySmith) **6-9-6** DaneO'Neill(4) (hld up: rdn over 4f out: sn bhd)	3½	5	6/1[3]	55	—
2311[9]	**Western Playboy (54)** (RJBaker) **5-9-6** VSlattery(3) (hld up: rdn over 4f out: sn wl bhd)	6	6	40/1	48?	—
				(SP 113.4%)		**6 Rn**

3m 8.85 (10.15) CSF £9.96 TOTE £3.90: £1.80 £1.80 (£4.90) OWNER Mr Terry Shepherd (EPSOM) BRED Jayeff B Stables
2490 Tawafek (USA) appreciated this faster ground and looked the likely winner some way from home, provided he got a split. (11/4)
1871 Mighty Phantom (USA) would have been 5lb worse off with the winner in a handicap. (11/4: 13/8-3/1)
1974 Alarico (FR) probably failed to handle the yielding ground at Epsom last time. (9/1: 5/1-10/1)
2411 Charnwood Jack (USA), with the first half-mile run at a slow pace, took a fierce hold. (2/1: op 3/1)

2695 GIBBS MEW H'CAP (0-80) (3-Y.O) (Class D)

3-20 (3-20) **1m** £4,796.00 (£1,448.00: £704.00: £332.00) Stalls: High GOING minus 0.45 sec per fur (F)

				SP	RR	SF
723[3]	**Sword Arm (75)** (RCharlton) **3-9-5** TSprake(2) (a.p: led over 2f out: hrd rdn ins fnl f: r.o wl)	—	1	11/2[3]	85	47
2231*	**Dulcinea (60)** (IABalding) **3-8-1**(3) MartinDwyer(12) (lw: hld up mid div: hdwy to chse wnr over 2f out: ev ch ins fnl f: r.o)	nk	2	100/30[1]	69	31
1144[12]	**Begorrat (IRE) (74)** (BJMeehan) **3-9-4** MTebbutt(9) (bhd tl hdwy 3f out: sn rdn: one pce fnl 2f)	4	3	20/1	75	37
1782[2]	**Wild Sky (IRE) (77)** (MJHeaton-Ellis) **3-9-7** SDrowne(7) (lw: hld up: hdwy 3f out: wknd over 1f out)	3	4	4/1[2]	72	34
2231[5]	**Sand Cay (USA) (64)** (RHannon) **3-8-5**(3) DO'Donohoe(10) (plld hrd: prom over 5f)	13	5	8/1	33	—
2183[6]	**Mystery Hill (USA) (74)** (JHMGosden) **3-9-4v[1]** GHind(1) (led over 5f: wknd qckly)	¾	6	6/1	42	4
1249[8]	**Heart Full of Soul (77)** (PFICole) **3-9-2b**(5) DSweeney(3) (prom 4f)	4	7	12/1	37	5
2151[12]	**Warring (62)** (MSSaunders) **3-8-3**(3) MHenry(5) (swtg: hld up: effrt 3f out: sn btn)	nk	8	14/1	21	—
2178[5]	**Isca Maiden (52)** (PHayward) **3-7-3**(7) RBrisland(4) (prom tl wknd qckly over 3f out)	hd	9	50/1	11	—
1870[3]	**Olivo (IRE) (70)** (CAHorgan) **3-9-0** AMcGlone(6) (a bhd)	3½	10	7/1	22	—
	Triple Term (73) (JGSmyth-Osbourne) **3-9-3** WJO'Connor(8) (bhd fnl 4f: t.o)	14	11	20/1	—	—
				(SP 122.2%)		**11 Rn**

1m 41.99 (1.99) CSF £22.41 CT £327.71 TOTE £5.40: £1.90 £1.80 £6.40 (£11.80) Trio £219.90; £204.43 to 14/7/97 OWNER Mr A. E. Oppenheimer (BECKHAMPTON) BRED Hascombe and Valiant Studs
LONG HANDICAP Isca Maiden 6-12
723 Sword Arm, without the visor this time, seems to go well when fresh and held on gamely in the last one hundred and fifty yards. (11/2)
2231* Dulcinea seems to handle all types of ground, and did not mind this return to a mile. (100/30)
795 Begorrat (IRE), down 4lb, was reverting back to a mile after a two-month break. (20/1)
1782 Wild Sky (IRE), although a model of consistency, remains a maiden and may have found this ground a bit lively. (4/1)
2231 Sand Cay (USA), up 2lb, proved difficult to settle and was disappointing. (8/1: 6/1-10/1)
2183 Mystery Hill (USA) went off like a scalded cat in the first-time visor. (6/1)
Heart Full of Soul (12/1: 8/1-14/1)
1826 Warring (14/1: op 8/1)

2696 CRESTED LARK AMATEUR H'CAP (0-70) (3-Y.O+) (Class F)

3-55 (3-56) **1m 4f** £2,952.00 (£822.00: £396.00) Stalls: Low GOING minus 0.45 sec per fur (F)

				SP	RR	SF
2198[10]	**Credit Squeeze (58)** (RFJohnsonHoughton) **7-10-9** MissEJohnsonHoughton(9) (b: led after 2f: r.o wl)	—	1	20/1	69	24
2398[4]	**Fourdaned (IRE) (55)** (SDow) **4-10-6** MrTCuff(2) (lw: bhd: gd hdwy over 2f out: rdn & hung rt over 1f out: r.o)	¾	2	6/1[2]	65	20
1491[7]	**Rising Spray (70)** (CAHorgan) **6-11-7** MrRThornton(1) (bhd tl hdwy over 3f out: rdn over 1f out: one pce)	2	3	9/1[3]	77	32
2469[4]	**Sun of Spring (57)** (DWChapman) **7-10-8** MissRClark(4) (lw: plld hrd: a.p: r.o one pce fnl 2f)	1	4	10/1	63	18
2218[3]	**Courageous Knight (44)** (PHayward) **8-9-9** MrsSBosley(11) (mid div: styd on fnl 2f: nt rch ldrs)	s.h	5	10/1	50	5
2464[3]	**Pay Homage (66)** (IABalding) **9-11-3** MrABalding(12) (hdwy after 3f: lost pl 3f out: rallied over 1f out: styd on ins fnl f)	1	6	10/1	71	26
2014*	**Sea Freedom (68)** (GBBalding) **6-11-5v** MrLJefford(10) (b: prom: rdn over 3f out: styd on ins fnl f)	¾	7	6/1[2]	72	27
2533[6]	**Fabulous Mtoto (57)** (MSSaunders) **7-10-8** MrKGoble(3) (lw: hld up & plld hrd: hdwy 3f out: wknd over 1f out)	hd	8	12/1	61	16
2164[8]	**Stonecutter (48)** (PJMakin) **4-9-8**(5) MissSDeburiatte(13) (hdwy over 4f out: wknd over 3f out)	s.h	9	25/1	51	6
2530[7]	**Chris's Lad (57)** (BJMeehan) **6-10-8b** MissJAllison(15) (lw: sltly hmpd & swtchd lft 3f out: a bhd)	1¼	10	9/2[1]	59	14
2469[8]	**Nosey Native (61)** (JPearce) **4-10-12** MrsLPearce(14) (nt clr run & swtchd lft 3f out: a bhd)	2	11	10/1	60	15
2391[3]	**Statajack (IRE) (62)** (DRCElsworth) **9-10-8b**(5) MrNMoran(5) (b: plld hrd: prom tl wknd wl over 1f out)	1¼	12	9/1[3]	59	14
1169[9]	**Nikita's Star (IRE) (61)** (DJGMurraySmith) **4-10-12** MrTMcCarthy(8) (lw: hld up mid div: bhd fnl 3f)	7	13	20/1	49	4
2146[12]	**Burning Cost (45)** (REPeacock) **7-9-5**(5)ow10 MrsCPeacock(7) (hld up & plld hrd: plld out & hdwy 5f out: rdn & wknd over 3f out)	¾	14	66/1	32	—
411[8]	**Royal Acclaim (35)** (KRBurke) **12-8-9**(5) MissRJPatman(6) (plld hrd: led 2f: wknd 4f out)	1½	15	50/1	20	—
				(SP 127.6%)		**15 Rn**

2m 40.38 (9.38) CSF £124.50 CT £1,089.14 TOTE £23.00: £6.10 £3.10 £2.90 (£118.40) Trio £456.30; £199.26 to 14/7/97 OWNER Mr R. C. Naylor (DIDCOT) BRED Home Stud Ltd
LONG HANDICAP Burning Cost 8-4 Royal Acclaim 8-5
Credit Squeeze, down 5lb, was 11lb lower than when winning over course and distance in May 1995. Walked down to the start before the others, the Stewards were told the gelding failed to stay a mile and seven at Warwick last time. (20/1)
2398 Fourdaned (IRE) has certainly improved for the change of stable, but displayed a very awkward head carriage and, although well handled, gave the impression he could have won had he put his best foot forward. (6/1)
969* Rising Spray, although down 2lb, was still up 26lb for four wins in the last twelve months. (9/1: op 11/2)
2469 Sun of Spring, 2lb lower than when running under a penalty last time, gave another good account of himself, especially considering he did not settle as well as his rider would have liked. (10/1)
2218 Courageous Knight again showed a liking for this sort of trip. (10/1: 8/1-12/1)
2464 Pay Homage lost his position at a vital stage. (10/1)
2014* Sea Freedom, only penalised 3lb for his Ascot Stakes victory, not surprisingly found this distance inadequate. (6/1)
2533 Fabulous Mtoto (12/1: 8/1-14/1)

2697 MYROBELLA NOVICE AUCTION STKS (2-Y.O) (Class F)

4-30 (4-30) **6f** £2,847.00 (£792.00: £381.00) Stalls: High GOING minus 0.45 sec per fur (F)

Form	Horse / details	Dist	Pos	SP	RR	SF
1821*	**Parisian Lady (IRE)** (AGNewcombe) **2-8-5** GHind(3) (lw: mde all: clr 2f out: easily)	—	**1**	$7/4^{1}$	93+	41
2519*	**Silver Strand (IRE)** (BWHills) **2-8-7**(3) JDSmith(10) (a.p: rdn over 2f out: r.o ins fnl f: no ch w wnr)	9	**2**	$9/2^{3}$	74	22
2516^{3}	**Robeena** (CNAllen) **2-8-1**(3) MartinDwyer(1) (hdwy over 2f out: sn chsng wnr: no imp)	2	**3**	$3/1^{2}$	63	11
2196^{9}	**Oisin (IRE)** (MrsPNDutfield) **2-8-4**(5) DSweeney(9) (a.p: pushed along 4f out: one pce fnl 2f)	2	**4**	50/1	62	10
2240^{3}	**Who Nose (IRE)** (BJMeehan) **2-8-13b** MTebbutt(6) (lw: plld hrd early: bhd tl sme hdwy over 1f out: n.d)	nk	**5**	10/1	66	14
884^{5}	**Blushing Victoria** (MartynMeade) **2-8-5**(7) RBrisland(8) (rdn 3f out: no hdwy)	1½	**6**	20/1	61	9
1812^{4}	**Eleventh Duke (IRE)** (RHannon) **2-8-12** DaneO'Neill(7) (prom tl wknd qckly wl over 1f out)	1½	**7**	10/1	57	5
2394^{11}	**After Dawn (IRE)** (MrsPNDutfield) **2-7-13**(5) AimeeCook(5) (a bhd)	1	**8**	50/1	46	—
2243^{9}	**Tamerin Bay** (RBoss) **2-8-10** TSprake(4) (chsd wnr 4f: sn wknd)	2½	**9**	6/1	45	—
				(SP 120.7%)	**9 Rn**	

1m 13.83 (0.83) CSF £9.48 TOTE £3.50: £1.40 £2.30 £1.50 (£11.40) Trio £4.80 OWNER Mr Alex Gorrie (BARNSTAPLE) BRED Clinton Investments

1821* Parisian Lady (IRE) certainly did not go unbacked this time and, proving her debut win to be no fluke, fairly bolted up. (7/4: 9/4-7/2)

2519* Silver Strand (IRE) got the better of the separate battle for the runner-up spot. (9/2: op 5/2)

2516 Robeena is the first foal of a maiden from the family of Mark of Esteem. (3/1)

Oisin (IRE) is a half-brother to Ochos Rios. (50/1)

2240 Who Nose (IRE) (10/1: tchd 16/1)

2698 OWEN TUDOR H'CAP (0-70) (3-Y.O+) (Class E)

5-00 (5-01) **6f** £3,210.25 (£967.00: £468.50: £219.25) Stalls: High GOING minus 0.45 sec per fur (F)

Form	Horse / details	Dist	Pos	SP	RR	SF
2002^{2}	**Meranti (56)** (JMBradley) **4-9-1** TSprake(2) (hld up: led over 1f out: all out)	—	**1**	$7/1^{3}$	66	39
2347^{5}	**Erupt (61)** (GBBalding) **4-9-6** AMcGlone(12) (hdwy over 1f out: r.o wl ins fnl f)	nk	**2**	10/1	70	43
2508^{W}	**White Settler (63)** (RJHodges) **4-9-5**(3) MartinDwyer(9) (hdwy over 1f out: r.o ins fnl f)	1	**3**	14/1	70	43
2006^{2}	**Fairy Prince (IRE) (61)** (MrsALMKing) **4-9-3**(3) MHenry(7) (a.p: led over 2f out tl over 1f out: eased cl home)	hd	**4**	$5/1^{1}$	67	40
2581^{7}	**Friendly Brave (USA) (66)** (MissGayKelleway) **7-9-11** WJO'Connor(16) (lw: a.p: one pce fnl 2f)	1½	**5**	$6/1^{2}$	68	41
2232^{8}	**Robellion (56)** (DWPArbuthnot) **6-8-10v**(5) DSweeney(3) (hdwy 2f out: one pce fnl f)	½	**6**	20/1	57	30
2232^{2}	**Pointer (57)** (MrsPNDutfield) **5-8-11**(5) AimeeCook(11) (bhd whn hmpd over 2f out: hdwy fnl f: r.o)	¾	**7**	$6/1^{2}$	56	29
1977^{22}	**Mr Speaker (IRE) (61)** (CFWall) **4-9-6** GHind(1) (no hdwy fnl 2f)	d.h	**8**	25/1	60	33
2006^{13}	**Rockcracker (IRE) (55)** (GGMargarson) **5-9-0** GCarter(8) (nvr nr to chal)	¾	**8**	16/1	52	25
2529^{10}	**Scissor Ridge (61)** (JJBridger) **5-8-13**(7) PDoe(15) (led over 3f: wknd over 1f out)	nk	**10**	16/1	57	30
2418^{4}	**Caudillo (IRE) (62)** (MrsPNDutfield) **4-9-0**(7) DMcGaffin(4) (a bhd)	1¼	**11**	10/1	55	28
2179^{3}	**Sizzling (57)** (RHannon) **5-9-2** DaneO'Neill(13) (bhd fnl 2f)	½	**12**	$7/1^{3}$	49	22
2006^{6}	**Pride of Hayling (IRE) (56)** (PRHedger) **6-9-1** SDrowne(14) (mid div whn bdly hmpd over 2f out: nt rcvr)	nk	**13**	10/1	47+	20
1089^{16}	**Mellors (IRE) (55)** (MJHeaton-Ellis) **4-8-7**(7) JFowle(6) (prom over 3f out)	3	**14**	25/1	38	11
1599^{9}	**Sharp 'n Smart (65)** (BSmart) **5-9-10b**1 MTebbutt(10) (w ldr tl wknd qckly over 2f out)	3	**15**	20/1	40	13
				(SP 133.2%)	**15 Rn**	

1m 14.72 (1.72) CSF £71.88 CT £917.40 TOTE £7.80: £2.90 £3.30 £5.50 (£44.20) Trio £412.80; £174.46 to 14/7/97 OWNER Mr John Wallis (CHEPSTOW) BRED K. Birkinshaw

2002 Meranti, raised 3lb, acts on this sort of ground and travelled well just in behind the front rank, although he had to dig deep in the end. (7/1)

2347 Erupt, down 3lb, finished with a flourish and showed he does not need soft ground to be seen at his best. (10/1)

2282 White Settler has slipped to a mark 1lb lower than when losing his maiden tag a year ago, and a return to seven could pay dividends. (14/1)

2006 Fairy Prince (IRE), up 3lb for his good effort last time, is 7lb higher than when registering his only win on fast ground at Carlisle just over a year ago. (5/1)

2308 Friendly Brave (USA) has been given a chance by the Handicapper, and was 7lb lower than when he last scored nearly a year ago. He is not so effective over such a stiff six. (6/1)

405 Robellion has slipped to a mark 12lb lower than when winning at Newmarket last August. (20/1)

2699 E.B.F. QUEENPOT MAIDEN STKS (II) (2-Y.O) (Class D)

5-30 (5-33) **6f 212y** £3,405.00 (£1,020.00: £490.00: £225.00) Stalls: High GOING minus 0.45 sec per fur (F)

Form	Horse / details	Dist	Pos	SP	RR	SF
2123^{5}	**Docksider (USA)** (JWHills) **2-8-11**(3) MHenry(8) (led 5f out: clr over 2f out: r.o wl)	—	**1**	10/1	87	33
	Night Shot (IABalding) **2-8-11**(3) MartinDwyer(5) (neat: bit bkwd: hld up: hdwy whn bdly hmpd 2f out: r.o fnl f)	6	**2**	8/1	73+	19
	Beneventus (MajorWRHern) **2-9-0** TSprake(12) (w'like: bit bkwd: led 2f: one pce fnl 2f)	1¼	**3**	12/1	70	16
1174^{6}	**After The Rain** (BWHills) **2-8-11**(3) JDSmith(4) (lw: hld up mid div: hdwy whn bdly hmpd 2f out: r.o ins fnl f)	s.h	**4**	$6/1^{3}$	70+	16
1821^{7}	**Kate Lane (IRE)** (MrsPNDutfield) **2-8-4**(5) AimeeCook(13) (chsd ldrs: swtchd lft & hung lft 2f out: one pce)	½	**5**	66/1	64	10
	Lift The Offer (IRE) (RHannon) **2-9-0** DaneO'Neill(3) (unf: scope: lw: hld up: hdwy over 1f out: r.o one pce fnl f)	½	**6**	$4/1^{2}$	68	14
2336^{8}	**Laffah (USA)** (JHMGosden) **2-9-0** GHind(11) (bhd tl hdwy fnl 2f: nrst fin)	1¼	**7**	11/1	65	11
2038^{5}	**Chayanee's Arena (IRE)** (AGNewcombe) **2-8-6**(3) PPMurphy(7) (nvr nrr)	s.h	**8**	66/1	60	6
	Green Jacket (JLDunlop) **2-9-0** GCarter(9) (unf: scope: bit bkwd: nvr nrr)	1¼	**9**	8/1	62	8
1927^{6}	**Phantom Waters** (RFJohnsonHoughton) **2-8-6**(3) DO'Donohoe(1) (bhd fnl 3f)	3½	**10**	40/1	49	—
2349^{5}	**Naked Oat** (BSmart) **2-9-0** MTebbutt(6) (prom: hrd rdn & wknd over 2f out)	2½	**11**	20/1	48	—
	Desert Arrow (USA) (SbinSuroor) **2-9-0** AMcGlone(10) (w'like: scope: lw: prom: rdn 3f out: sn wknd)	9	**12**	$7/4^{1}$	28	—
828^{15}	**Shalabella (IRE)** (MRChannon) **2-8-9** CandyMorris(2) (bhd fnl 3f)	2½	**13**	66/1	17	—
				(SP 129.7%)	**13 Rn**	

1m 28.52 (2.52) CSF £84.34 TOTE £14.70: £4.30 £3.20 £2.90 (£82.10) Trio £200.90 OWNER Mr Freddy Bienstock (LAMBOURN) BRED Airlie Stud

2123 Docksider (USA), well backed on soft ground at Newmarket on his debut, was a totally different proposition on this surface and had already flown when the trouble occurred at the quarter-mile pole. He would appear to have a bright future. (10/1: 8/1-12/1)

Night Shot, a half-brother to Grey Shot and Sight 'n Sound, would have finished closer but would not have beaten the winner even with a trouble-free run. This was a most satisfactory start to his career. (8/1: 5/1-10/1)
Beneventus, a 20,000 guineas yearling, is the second foal of a seven furlong and mile winner. (12/1: 8/1-14/1)
1174 After The Rain was murdered entering the final quarter-mile, and each-way backers can consider themselves desperately unlucky. He is probably ready to tackle a mile. (6/1)
Kate Lane (IRE), a half-sister to five-furlong juvenile winners Racketeer and Vail Star, caused plenty of problems for those trying to come from behind. (66/1)
Lift The Offer (IRE) is a half-brother to ten-furlong winner Timissa, and a mile-and-a-half winner in Ireland. (4/1)
Green Jacket (8/1: 9/2-9/1)
Desert Arrow (USA) (7/4: 5/4-9/4)

T/Plpt: £178.70 (76.58 Tckts). T/Qdpt: £67.60 (7.8 Tckts) KH

2487-**WARWICK** (L-H) (Good to firm)
Saturday July 12th
WEATHER: warm & sunny WIND: almost nil

2700 NICK KNIGHT MAIDEN AUCTION STKS (2-Y.O F) (Class F)
6-30 (6-36) **7f** £2,785.20 (£772.20: £369.60) Stalls: Low GOING minus 0.34 sec per fur (GF)

				SP	RR	SF
1821^{2}	**Fayrana (IRE)** (JWHills) **2-8-7** NAdams(8) (mde all: rdn fnl f: hld on wl nr fin)	—	1	6/5^{1}	80	27
2306^{3}	**Universal Lady** (CJames) **2-8-1** CRutter(10) (chsd ldrs: effrt over 1f out: r.o ins fnl f: jst failed)	hd	2	9/2^{3}	74	21
1997^{10}	**Sing For Me (IRE)** (RHollinshead) **2-8-1** NCarlisle(1) (in tch: styd on same pce fnl 2f)	5	3	33/1	62	9
1774^{2}	**Sharp Cracker (IRE)** (MJohnston) **2-8-4**(3) PMcCabe(5) (lw: in tch: no hdwy fnl 2f)	2½	4	100/30^{2}	63	10
2509^{11}	**Tremonnow** (JMBradley) **2-8-1** TWilliams(7) (chsd wnr: rdn over 1f out: sn wknd)	¾	5	12/1	55	2
1827^{5}	**Shalad'or** (BRMillman) **2-7-12**(3) MBaird(2) (plld hrd: prom: wkng whn n.m.r over 2f out)	1½	6	16/1	52	—
	Fanti Dancer (IRE) (BJMeehan) **2-8-0**(7) GHannon(12) (w'like: leggy: lw: s.i.s: nvr nr ldrs)	3	7	20/1	51	—
	Jato Dancer (IRE) (MRChannon) **2-8-7** RPerham(6) (leggy: unf: bkwd: in tch 4f)	1	8	16/1	48	—
	Ruby Bear (WMBrisbourne) **2-7-10**(5) RMullen(11) (leggy: bkwd: b.hind: sn pushed along & bhd)	4	9	50/1	33	—
	Theme Tune (DrJDScargill) **2-8-7** JTate(13) (lt-f: unf: s.v.s: a bhd)	s.h	10	20/1	39	—
1959^{7}	**God Knows (IRE)** (MJFetherston-Godley) **2-8-4** FNorton(3) (b.hind: s i.s: a bhd)	2½	11	50/1	30	—
	Lavernock Lady (JJQuinn) **2-7-11**(7) RWinston(9) (unf: bit bkwd: dwlt: a bhd)	2	12	33/1	26	—
2306^{15}	***Amiasapphire*** (RJHodges) **2-8-2**ow1 JStack(4) (Withdrawn not under Starter's orders: wnt down in stalls)		W	50/1	—	—
				(SP 127.5%)	**12 Rn**	

1m 27.7 (3.10) CSF £6.02 TOTE £2.40: £1.30 £1.50 £6.80 (£4.30) Trio £87.30 OWNER Racegoers Club Owners Group (1997) (LAMBOURN)
BRED John McEnery
1821 Fayrana (IRE), whose Salisbury form is working out, just made it home over this extra furlong. (6/5: 6/4-evens)
2306 Universal Lady, a good mover, handled the step-up in trip and clawed back most of the winner's advantage in the final furlong. (9/2: op 3/1)
Sing For Me (IRE), cheaply bought, took quite a keen hold early on, but kept plugging away in the straight without making up much ground. She seemed to get the trip well. (33/1)
1774 Sharp Cracker (IRE) was rather disappointing, but the step-up in trip did not look to be the problem alone. (100/30: 3/1-9/2)
2016 Tremonnow ought to stay this trip in time, but did not last home with so much use made of her. (12/1)
1827 Shalad'or, on her toes and keen, both going down and in the race, did not get much daylight on the inside and proved a difficult ride. (16/1)

2701 ANDY MOLES (S) H'CAP (0-60) (3-Y.O+) (Class G)
7-00 (7-00) **1m 2f 169y** £2,910.00 (£810.00: £390.00) Stalls: Low GOING minus 0.34 sec per fur (GF)

				SP	RR	SF
2399^{4}	**Arzani (USA) (54)** (DJSCosgrove) **6-9-11** RHughes(1) (b: a gng wl: trckd ldrs: led over 1f out: cleverly)	—	1	3/1^{1}	65	33
2488^{6}	**Foolish Flutter (IRE) (39)** (RBastiman) **3-7-5**(7)ow2 RWinston(5) (lw: hld up & plld hrd: n.m.r fr 5f out: swtchd & hdwy over 1f out: fin wl)	½	2	10/1	49	3
2399^{6}	**Runic Symbol (35)** (MBlanshard) **6-8-6** JQuinn(6) (lw: hld up: hdwy over 4f out: nt clr run 3f out: swtchd rt 2f out: one pce fnl f)	1½	3	7/2^{2}	43	11
2228^{15}	**Whothehellisharry (36)** (PTDalton) **4-8-4**(3) PMcCabe(4) (trckd ldrs: n.m.r 2f out: rdn & kpt on fnl f)	s.h	4	14/1	44	12
	Dubai Dolly (IRE) (25) (JWMullins) **4-7-10** NVarley(3) (bhd: c wd & hdwy over 3f out: wknd fnl f)	7	5	33/1	23	—
1785^{10}	**Hoh Down (IRE) (48)** (RTJuckes) **3-8-7**ow2 VSlattery(2) (lw: led 9f out tl over 1f out: sn wknd)	7	6	33/1	35	—
1796^{11}	**Acquittal (IRE) (41)** (AStreeter) **5-8-12v** SSanders(10) (lw: prom: ev ch over 2f out: wknd & eased over 1f out)	¾	7	5/1^{3}	27	—
2039^{5}	**Opera Fan (IRE) (40)** (KAMorgan) **5-8-11** DeanMcKeown(9) (led over 1f: pushed along 4f out: sn wknd)	½	8	8/1	25	—
1445^{8}	**Tocco Jewel (25)** (MJRyan) **7-7-7**(3) MBaird(7) (plld hrd: in tch: effrt 4f out: rdn over 2f out: sn btn)	½	9	20/1	10	—
2226^{5}	**Grovefair Lad (IRE) (42)** (MartynWane) **3-7-12**(3)ow3 AWhelan(8) (stdd s: a bhd)	¾	10	5/1^{3}	25	—
				(SP 118.1%)	**10 Rn**	

2m 20.5 (6.50) CSF £30.62 CT £99.25 TOTE £4.70: £2.20 £2.00 £1.70 (£25.50) Trio £67.30 OWNER Mr D. J. S. Cosgrove (NEWMARKET)
BRED Eaton and Thorne and Robert N. Clay
LONG HANDICAP Foolish Flutter (IRE) 7-6 Tocco Jewel 7-5 Dubai Dolly (IRE) 7-5
WEIGHT FOR AGE 3yo-12lb
No bid
2399 Arzani (USA) was conceding 13lb and more all round, but class told and, after being shaken up and sent clear inside the final furlong, he was eased down near the line. (3/1)
2488 Foolish Flutter (IRE) got none too clear a run, particularly early in the home straight but, once seeing daylight, finished to good effect. A similar race should not be too hard to find as the winner is better than a plater. (10/1)
2200 Runic Symbol seemed to run way above himself in a non-handicap seller here two outings ago, but again showed that he makes poor use of his ability once battle commences. (7/2)
2039 Whothehellisharry weighted to beat the winner on their Nottingham meeting, did not look so good not being able to dominate. (14/1)
Dubai Dolly (IRE), an ex-Irish filly who has shown a glimmer of hope over hurdles recently, might have done better but for making rapid strides around the outside on the home turn, forfeiting many lengths in the process. (33/1)

156 Hoh Down (IRE), back on turf for the first time since her debut, had headgear left off but did not seem to last out the trip. Despite her pedigree, a mile may be her distance. (33/1)

2702 WATCH SECURITY H'CAP (0-70) (3-Y.O+) (Class E)

7-30 (7-30) **1m 6f 194y** £3,200.25 (£957.00: £458.50: £209.25) Stalls: Low GOING minus 0.34 sec per fur (GF)

				SP	RR	SF
2474*	**Indigo Dawn (55)** (MJohnston) **3-7-12** NAdams(3) (lw: a.p: led 4f out: clr over 1f out: rdn & hld on fnl f)	—	**1**	11/2^{3}	65	29
1507^{2}	**Hillswick (36)** (JSKing) **6-7-5**(5) APolli(8) (prom: led over 8f out: hdd 4f out: rallied appr fnl f: nt rch wnr)	½	**2**	16/1	46	27
2503*	**May King Mayhem (46)** (MrsALMKing) **4-8-6** TWilliams(1) (chsd ldrs: pushed along & lost pl 9f out: rallied 4f out: r.o appr fnl f)	1¾	**3**	5/1^{2}	54	35
2199*	**Schnozzle (IRE) (50)** (KSBridgwater) **6-8-10** TQuinn(4) (lw: chsd ldrs: rdn over 2f out: kpt on)	½	**4**	4/1^{1}	57	38
2531*	**Royal Circus (42)** (IPWilliams) **8-7-11**(5) 5x RFfrench(7) (led 6f: btn whn n.m.r ins fnl f)	1¼	**5**	7/1	48	29
2198^{8}	**Paradise Navy (67)** (CREgerton) **8-9-13b** RHughes(2) (lw: hld up: hdwy 4f out: rdn 2f out: no imp)	2	**6**	10/1	71	52
2198^{5}	**Salska (61)** (AStreeter) **6-9-4**(3) RHavlin(6) (dwlt: hdwy 7f out: no imp fnl 3f)	4	**7**	7/1	60	41
2166^{4}	**Sarasota Storm (55)** (MBell) **5-9-1** MFenton(5) (dwlt: hdwy 8f out: wknd 4f out)	2	**8**	13/2	52	33
	Topaglow (IRE) (40) (PTDalton) **4-8-0** NVarley(10) (in tch 9f)	2	**9**	40/1	35	16
2198^{9}	**Romalito (45)** (MBlanshard) **7-8-5** JQuinn(12) (chsd ldrs 8f)	1¾	**10**	14/1	38	19
	Chicago's Best (37) (KCComerford) **10-7-11**ow1 NCarlisle(11) (prom 7f)	4	**11**	66/1	26	6
2397^{6}	**Bisquet-de-Bouche (55)** (RDickin) **3-7-5**(7)ow2 RWinston(9) (chsd ldrs tl wknd 4f out)	3	**12**	14/1	41	3
				(SP 122.6%)	**12 Rn**	

3m 15.3 (5.30) CSF £85.15 CT £435.24 TOTE £6.20: £2.00 £5.60 £2.40 (£64.90) Trio £114.90 OWNER Greenland Park Ltd (MIDDLEHAM) BRED Laharna Ltd

LONG HANDICAP Hillswick 7-3 Chicago's Best 6-8 Bisquet-de-Bouche 7-7

WEIGHT FOR AGE 3yo-17lb

2474* Indigo Dawn, whose half-sister Shirley Sue thrived over a distance of ground around this time last year, seems a similar type although she looks an awkward ride, threatening to throw this away late in the day. (11/2: 5/2-6/1)

1507 Hillswick, the form of whose Brighton race is working out surprisingly well, seemed further improved by this step-up in trip, as he was coming back for more at the finish. (16/1)

2503* May King Mayhem was badly outpaced on the downhill run into the back straight on what is quite a fast track, and is well worth another try over this sort of trip. (5/1: 7/2-6/1)

2199* Schnozzle (IRE), stepped up in trip, did not seem quite so effective. (4/1)

2531* Royal Circus, on a higher mark than he has ever won off, was unable to dominate this time. (7/1)

1953 Paradise Navy looked to have an outstanding chance despite being a couple of pounds higher than his last victory but, as usual, once he came off the bridle, his chance was gone. (10/1)

2703 HOLSTEN PILS H'CAP (0-70) (3-Y.O+) (Class E)

8-00 (8-07) **5f** £3,018.25 (£901.00: £430.50: £195.25) Stalls: Low GOING minus 0.44 sec per fur (F)

				SP	RR	SF
2001^{3}	**River Tern (63)** (JMBradley) **4-9-4**(5) RFfrench(5) (lw: hdwy over 2f out: r.o to ld wl ins fnl f)	—	**1**	8/1	70	51
2006^{16}	**Beau Venture (USA) (64)** (BPalling) **9-9-5**(5) DSweeney(2) (mde most: hdd & unable qckn wl ins fnl f)	1	**2**	10/1	68	49
2148^{6}	**Sharp Stock (57)** (RJHodges) **4-9-3** JQuinn(6) (w ldrs: ev ch over 1f out: one pce)	½	**3**	20/1	59	40
2563^{9}	**Sotonian (HOL) (42)** (PSFelgate) **4-7-11**(5) APolli(7) (stumbled s: w ldr: rdn 2f out: no ex)	nk	**4**	13/2^{2}	43	24
2581*	**The Fugative (68)** (PMitchell) **4-9-11**(3) 7x AWhelan(9) (lw: s.s: wl bhd 3f: nvr rchd ldrs)	2½	**5**	11/4^{1}	61+	42
1572^{6}	**Windrush Boy (47)** (MRBosley) **7-8-7** CRutter(10) (hld up: hdwy 2f out: nvr rchd ldrs)	1½	**6**	14/1	35	16
2050^{7}	**Captain Sinbad (47)** (KSBridgwater) **5-8-7b** VSlattery(8) (w ldr over 3f)	3½	**7**	33/1	24	5
2510^{5}	**Night Express (63)** (BHanbury) **3-9-4** JStack(1) (lw: prom over 3f)	hd	**8**	7/1^{3}	40	16
1401^{6}	**Ioulios (41)** (JEBanks) **3-7-10** JQuinn(11) (lw: plld hrd: sn outpcd)	½	**9**	14/1	16	—
2308^{3}	**Mullagh Hill Lad (IRE) (52)** (BAMcMahon) **4-8-12b** SSanders(3) (s.i.s: in tch whn p.u wl over 1f out)		**P**	11/4^{1}	—	—
				(SP 120.4%)	**10 Rn**	

59.0 secs (1.00) CSF £79.97 CT £1,418.54 TOTE £9.30: £2.50 £2.80 £3.20 (£112.70) Trio £100.50 OWNER Mr M. B. Carver (CHEPSTOW) BRED Bearstone Stud

LONG HANDICAP Ioulios 7-9

WEIGHT FOR AGE 3yo-5lb

OFFICIAL EXPLANATION **Mullagh Hill Lad (IRE): was lame on his off hind.**

2001 River Tern broke better than he has often done in the past, and was produced between horses entering the final furlong. (8/1)

1662 Beau Venture (USA) fought off his rivals for the lead by the final furlong courtesy of having the inside rail, but had no answer when the winner pounced. (10/1)

2148 Sharp Stock, keen and on his toes beforehand, disputed the lead but could not sustain the effort from the distance. (20/1)

1942 Sotonian (HOL), down on his nose as the stalls opened, amazingly lost little ground if any, and only cracked below the distance. (13/2)

2581* The Fugative did remarkably well considering she missed the break, and remains in the form of her life. (11/4)

1572 Windrush Boy did not seem favoured by racing wide, as all the action was against the far rail. He is worth keeping an eye on as he has won in August for each of the last three seasons, ridden by Aimee Cook on each occasion. (14/1)

2308 Mullagh Hill Lad (IRE) appeared to lose his footing on the home turn and was pulled up soon afterwards. (11/4: 7/2-9/4)

2704 HBG HIGGS & HILL MAIDEN STKS (3-Y.O+) (Class D)

8-30 (8-33) **7f** £3,900.40 (£1,166.20: £558.60: £254.80) Stalls: Low GOING minus 0.34 sec per fur (GF)

				SP	RR	SF
2156^{3}	**Sweet Fortune (USA)** (MRStoute) **3-8-13** JReid(3) (hdwy 4f out: led ins fnl f: pushed clr)	—	**1**	11/4^{2}	90+	38
2172^{3}	**Jorrocks (USA)** (IABalding) **3-8-10**(3) MartinDwyer(7) (lw: a.p: led over 1f out: hdd & unable qckn ins fnl f)	3	**2**	4/1^{3}	83	31
2491^{2}	**Awassi (IRE)** (KMahdi) **4-9-4**(3) DO'Donohoe(2) (lw: s.i.s: hdwy 4f out: rdn 2f out: nvr rchd ldrs)	3½	**3**	9/1	75	31
2566^{13}	**Kailey Goddess (USA)** (RWArmstrong) **4-9-7** JQuinn(1) (lw: chsd ldrs: no hdwy fnl 2f)	1¾	**4**	33/1	71	27
2506^{4}	**Shoshaloza (USA)** (PRWebber) **3-8-8** RPerham(8) (r.o fnl 2f: nrst fin)	s.h	**5**	9/1	66	14
2491^{11}	**Beaucatcher (IRE)** (MJHeaton-Ellis) **3-8-8** SDrowne(12) (disp ld tl led over 2f out: hdd & wknd over 1f out)	1½	**6**	40/1	63	11
	Flying Flip (BCMorgan) **3-8-8** DeanMcKeown(10) (unf: scope: lw: nvr trbld ldrs)	½	**7**	50/1	62	10
1638^{3}	**Las Vistas** (HJCollingridge) **3-8-8** NAdams(5) (chsd ldrs 5f)	2	**8**	25/1	57	5

				SP	RR	SF
2506[3]	**Made Bold** (HCandy) **3-8-8** CRutter(9) (sn pushed along: wl bhd tl sme hdwy over 2f out: nvr nr ldrs)	2½	**9**	5/2[1]	51	—
1967[3]	**Malabi (USA)** (JLDunlop) **3-8-13** TQuinn(11) (hld up: effrt 2f out: nvr plcd to chal)	½	**10**	9/2	55	3
2183[15]	**Petsong** (VSoane) **3-8-13** SSanders(13) (in tch over 4f)	19	**11**	66/1	12	—
2420[12]	**Madge's Pet** (GBarnett) **3-8-8** NCarlisle(4) (dwlt: stumbled 4f out: a bhd)	1	**12**	66/1	4	—
576[8]	**Badrinath (IRE)** (HJCollingridge) **3-8-13** MFenton(6) (swtg: led over 4f: wknd qckly)	19	**13**	100/1	—	—

(SP 128.6%) **13 Rn**

1m 27.2 (2.60) CSF £13.71 TOTE £4.40: £1.60 £1.70 £3.70 (£7.90) Trio £50.20 OWNER Maktoum Al Maktoum (NEWMARKET) BRED S. D. Brilie

WEIGHT FOR AGE 3yo-8lb

2156 Sweet Fortune (USA) came on a ton from his first effort and will be a most interesting prospect in handicaps over further. He was unable to race last year due to a knee problem. (11/4)

2172 Jorrocks (USA), dropping back in trip and on faster ground, ran his race this time but had met one far too good. (4/1: op 5/2)

2491 Awassi (IRE), colty beforehand, was probably steadied at the start but lost quite a lot of ground. He does not seem to respond well to being restrained over this longer trip and, with his dam being a half-sister to Colmore Row and Note Book, he seems to want to use his speed. (9/1: 5/1-10/1)

Kailey Goddess (USA) is a half-sister to the very useful 1989 two-year-old Cordoba, and seemed to appreciate this drop back in trip. (33/1)

2506 Shoshaloza (USA) could make little impact and may need further. (9/1: 6/1-10/1)

Beaucatcher (IRE), keen going down, had learnt a lot from her debut but did not last home. She is not without hope. (40/1)

2506 Made Bold, totally taken off her feet on this faster ground, looks sure to improve over further, and will now get a handicap mark. (5/2)

1967 Malabi (USA), ridden for a turn of foot, does not seem to possess much of one. Now he can be handicapped, his trainer may step him up in trip, but his pedigree does not suggest he ought to stay much further. (9/2)

2705 DOMINIC OSTLER H'CAP (0-80) (3-Y.O F) (Class D)

9-00 (9-02) **7f** £4,123.35 (£1,234.80: £592.90: £271.95) Stalls: Low GOING minus 0.34 sec per fur (GF)

				SP	RR	SF
2313[17]	**Midyan Queen (60)** (RHollinshead) **3-8-3** FLynch(8) (hld up: hdwy over 1f out: rdn & r.o wl to ld nr fin)	—	**1**	20/1	66	19
1958[14]	**Secret Combe (IRE) (78)** (PJMakin) **3-9-4**(3) RHavlin(9) (lw: hdwy over 2f out: led 1f out tl ct nr fin)	½	**2**	14/1	83	36
1458[8]	**Caribbean Star (73)** (MRStoute) **3-9-2** JReid(11) (lw: chsd ldrs: pushed along 3f out: styd on wl ins fnl f)	nk	**3**	11/2[3]	77	30
2554[18]	**Tabasco Jazz (64)** (BJMeehan) **3-8-0**(7) GHannon(6) (led over 4f: one pce fnl f)	½	**4**	25/1	67	20
2216[3]	**Halowing (USA) (75)** (JGSmyth-Osbourne) **3-8-13**(5) DSweeney(2) (lw: bhd: hdwy 2f out: nvr able to chal)	2	**5**	5/1[2]	74	27
2231[8]	**Free As A Bird (63)** (MRChannon) **3-8-6** RPerham(12) (hdwy 2f out: no ex appr fnl f)	½	**6**	16/1	60	13
1485*	**Farley Green (70)** (HCandy) **3-8-13** CRutter(10) (swtg: prom: rdn 2f out: btn whn eased fnl f)	2½	**7**	4/1[1]	62	15
1958[4]	**Song Mist (IRE) (72)** (PFICole) **3-9-1** TQuinn(5) (lw: chsd ldrs: rdn 2f out: wknd fnl f)	3½	**8**	4/1[1]	56	9
2427[4]	**My Girl Lucy (58)** (PMitchell) **3-7-12**(3) AWhelan(1) (a bhd)	2½	**9**	25/1	36	—
	Briska (IRE) (74) (RAkehurst) **3-9-3** SSanders(4) (w ldr: led over 2f out: hdd 1f out: wknd)	½	**10**	7/1	51	4
2179[9]	**Wrn Princess (54)** (BJMeehan) **3-7-8**(3)ow1 MartinDwyer(7) (dwlt: hdwy 5f out: wknd 3f out)	6	**11**	33/1	17	—
1921*	**Prospering (53)** (RJHodges) **3-7-10** JQuinn(3) (in tch: nt clr run & lost pl over 3f out: no ch after)	1	**12**	6/1	14	—

(SP 126.8%) **12 Rn**

1m 28.1 (3.50) CSF £255.26 CT £1,617.10 TOTE £34.60: £6.70 £4.00 £1.70 (£104.20) Trio £212.10; £271.96 to 14/7/97 OWNER Mrs Charles Lockhart (UPPER LONGDON) BRED Mrs C. A. R. Lockhart

LONG HANDICAP Wrn Princess 7-0 Prospering 7-5

1650 Midyan Queen, trying seven furlongs on fast ground for the first time, produced a good turn of foot towards the centre of the course to pounce late. (20/1)

1589 Secret Combe (IRE), down a little in the handicap, was quite keen when taken steadily down, but ran her race when asked to do the job in the straight, and should find a similar race. (14/1: op 7/1)

958 Caribbean Star can pull, but was settled if anything, too well on this occasion, and took a lot of getting going. When in this mood another furlong would help. (11/2)

945 Tabasco Jazz, keen going down, was able to lead for the first time since finishing second at Thirsk in May, and ran much better as a consequence. (25/1)

2216 Halowing (USA), certainly ought to be able to find a race off this sort of mark, but finding her trip is a problem, as she seems to need further on this evidence, but has failed to stay a mile in the past. (5/1: op 3/1)

1976 Free As A Bird, restrained on this occasion, made her move on the outside at the same time as the winner, but could not find such a telling turn of foot. (16/1)

1485* Farley Green was quite warm and was not knocked about once her chance had gone. She is probably better than this. (4/1)

1958 Song Mist (IRE) seems to struggle to stay a seventh furlong. (4/1)

Briska (IRE) (7/1: 5/1-15/2)

1921* Prospering had not played her hand when knocked right back at halfway, and is worth keeping in mind, as the Handicapper seems to have taken quite a lenient view of her claiming win. (6/1)

T/Plpt: £1,139.70 (13.11 Tckts). T/Qdpt: £327.30 (2.38 Tckts) Dk

2675-YORK (L-H) (Good, Good to firm patches)

Saturday July 12th

WEATHER: sunny & warm WIND: slt across

2706 JERVAULX MEDIAN AUCTION MAIDEN STKS (2-Y.O) (Class E)

2-00 (2-01) **6f** £4,110.00 (£1,230.00: £590.00: £270.00) Stalls: Low GOING minus 0.40 sec per fur (F)

				SP	RR	SF
2181[2]	**Merlin's Ring** (IABalding) **2-9-0** LDettori(12) (lw: a.p: shkn up over 2f out: led 1f out: r.o: comf)	—	**1**	11/8[1]	77+	35
2467[3]	**Requestor** (JGFitzGerald) **2-9-0** KFallon(5) (lw: trckd ldrs: rdn to ld over 1f out: sn hdd: nt pce of wnr)	1¼	**2**	5/2[2]	74	32
	Up At The Top (IRE) (BWHills) **2-8-9** MHills(3) (leggy: scope: chsd ldrs: outpcd 2f out: r.o wl towards fin)	1½	**3**	10/1	65+	23
2196[7]	**Howies Choice (IRE)** (KMcAuliffe) **2-9-0** GDuffield(8) (led after 1f tl over 1f out: no ex)	2½	**4**	20/1	63	21
	Statua (IRE) (PJMakin) **2-8-9** RCochrane(15) (neat: unf: bhd: hdwy ½-wy: kpt on wl)	1½	**5**	12/1	54	12
2361[6]	**Naviasky (IRE)** (MrsJRRamsden) **2-9-0** MDeering(6) (hld up & bhd: sme hdwy 2f out: kpt on wl towards fin)	½	**6**	20/1	58+	16
1797[8]	**Heathyards Sheik** (RHollinshead) **2-9-0** FLynch(11) (chsd ldrs tl wknd appr fnl f)	½	**7**	25/1	56	14

2306[11]	**Roi de Danse** (JWHills) **2-9-0** AMunro(1) (led early: chsd ldrs tl wknd fnl 2f)	3	**8**	16/1	48	6
2202[3]	**Empire Park** (MJohnston) **2-9-0** MRoberts(2) (sn led: hdd after 1f: wknd fnl 2f)	2	**9**	6/1[3]	43	1
2467[7]	**Percy** (JFBottomley) **2-9-0** NCarlisle(4) (chsd ldrs 4f: wknd)	3	**10**	33/1	35	—
1839[7]	**Sharp Shooter (IRE)** (MrsJRRamsden) **2-9-0** OPears(14) (pushed along ½-wy: nvr nr to chal)	½	**11**	25/1	34	—
	Smooth Princess (IRE) (JGFitzGerald) **2-8-9** JQuinn(13) (w'like: scope: bkwd: plld hrd: n.d)	3½	**12**	33/1	19	—
	Dekelsmary (JBalding) **2-8-9** JEdmunds(10) (w'like: bit bkwd: s.i.s: plld hrd: hdwy ½-wy: sn wknd)	1	**13**	50/1	17	—
	Wedding Band (RHannon) **2-8-9** DHarrison(9) (neat: scope: bit bkwd: dwlt: shkn up ½-wy: a bhd)	3½	**14**	12/1	7	—

(SP 140.4%) **14 Rn**

1m 12.53 (2.03) CSF £4.73 TOTE £2.10: £1.40 £1.50 £2.10 (£3.00) Trio £13.40 OWNER Mrs Richard Plummer & Partners (KINGSCLERE) BRED Mrs A. Plummer

OFFICIAL EXPLANATION **Naviasky (IRE): regarding the running and riding of the gelding, the jockey reported that he had been instructed to give the gelding a chance, keep hold of his head and not seek recourse to the whip. He added that he was outpaced early and the horse had taken his time to find his feet.**

2181 Merlin's Ring took time to warm up but, once he found his stride, he won most authoritatively and looks likely to appreciate a bit further. (11/8)

2467 Requestor improved from his first run but was outclassed in the closing stages. He still should not be hard to place to advantage. (5/2)

Up At The Top (IRE) ran particularly well and, judging from the way she finished, longer trips are going to see better from her. (10/1)

Howies Choice (IRE) showed plenty of toe this time and is obviously learning. (20/1)

Statua (IRE) put in a useful first effort, making up ground in good style from halfway, and looks sure to improve. (12/1)

2361 Naviasky (IRE), suited by this step-up in trip, was given a most sympathetic ride but finished nicely and ought to have learnt plenty, and in due course will do a deal better, probably over further yet. (20/1)

2202 Empire Park still looked as though this was needed and ran well. There is better to come. (6/1: op 4/1)

Wedding Band looks a decent type, although in need of it, but she failed to show anything in the race. (12/1)

2707 EXCLUSIVE CAFE BAR AT WAKEFIELD CONDITIONS STKS (2-Y.O) (Class B)

2-35 (2-35) **6f 214y** £6,658.00 (£2,298.00: £1,099.00: £445.00) Stalls: High GOING minus 0.40 sec per fur (F)

				SP	RR	SF
2038*	**Tracking** (HRACecil) **2-9-0** KFallon(5) (lw: trckd ldrs: outpcd 2f out: rdn to ld 1f out: wandered: styd on)	—	**1**	4/6[1]	82	36
*2363**	**Prose (IRE)** (RHannon) **2-9-0** LDettori(1) (led tl hdd 1f out: rallied)	hd	**2**	7/2[2]	82	36
2336*	**The Glow-Worm (IRE)** (BWHills) **2-9-0** MHills(4) (lw: chsd wnr: rdn 2f out: r.o one pce)	1½	**3**	9/2[3]	78	32
2112*	**Winsome George** (CWFairhurst) **2-9-0** NKennedy(2) (trckd ldrs: wl outpcd over 2f out: swtchd ins fnl f: r.o wl towards fin)	½	**4**	12/1	77	31

(SP 108.1%) **4 Rn**

1m 25.4 (2.40) CSF £2.98 TOTE £1.60: (£1.80) OWNER Buckram Oak Holdings (NEWMARKET) BRED Buckram Thoroughbred Enterprises Inc

2038* Tracking was again very noisy in the paddock, but he did what was required, despite running green. He gave the impression that, if he would fully concentrate, there is better yet to come. (4/6)

2363* Prose (IRE) is thriving as he tries these longer distances. He kept battling back, and will stay further yet. (7/2)

2336* The Glow-Worm (IRE) on much faster ground this time, ran well and this would seem to be as good as he is. (9/2: op 3/1)

2112* Winsome George needed a stronger pace and, had there been another half-furlong, he would definitely have won. He is without doubt a useful performer, but this will have snookered a good handicap mark. (12/1)

2708 JOHN SMITH'S BITTER H'CAP (0-90) (3-Y.O+) (Class C)

3-10 (3-12) **6f 214y** £6,368.00 (£1,904.00: £912.00: £416.00) Stalls: High GOING minus 0.40 sec per fur (F)

				SP	RR	SF
2325[15]	**Stackattack (IRE) (67)** (MrsJRRamsden) **4-8-7** FLynch(8) (lw: trckd ldrs: led wl over 1f out: r.o)	—	**1**	9/2[1]	79	53
2340[5]	**Anonym (IRE) (61)** (JLEyre) **5-8-1b** TWilliams(10) (lw: chsd ldrs: rdn over 2f out: kpt on wl)	1½	**2**	16/1	70	44
2496[5]	**Present Chance (77)** (BAMcMahon) **3-8-9** MRoberts(2) (in tch: outpcd ½-wy: hdwy u.p 2f out: r.o towards fin)	s.h	**3**	20/1	85	51
2390*	**Grey Kingdom (75)** (MBrittain) **6-8-8**(7) DMernagh(1) (led tl hdd wl over 1f out: kpt on same pce)	nk	**4**	7/1[2]	83	57
2013[22]	**Irish Accord (USA) (90)** (MrsJRRamsden) **3-9-8** AMunro(7) (lw: bhd: hdwy over 2f out: nrst fin)	¾	**5**	9/1	96	62
2325[2]	**Tertium (IRE) (80)** (MartynWane) **5-9-3**(3) AWhelan(16) (lw: chsd ldrs: outpcd over 2f out: styd on fnl f)	2½	**6**	8/1[3]	80	54
2302[6]	**Takhlid (USA) (68)** (DWChapman) **6-8-8** ACulhane(9) (cl up over 5f: wknd u.p)	¾	**7**	12/1	67	41
2201[4]	**Sualtach (IRE) (70)** (RHollinshead) **4-8-10** KFallon(18) (lw: bhd: hdwy ½-wy: nvr rchd ldrs)	s.h	**8**	16/1	69	43
2129[5]	**Delta Soleil (USA) (83)** (PWHarris) **5-9-2**(7) CLowther(11) (in tch: effrt ½-wy: no imp)	1¾	**9**	12/1	77	51
2326[W]	**Royal Mark (IRE) (84)** (TDBarron) **4-9-10** JCarroll(5) (bhd: effrt & n.m.r 2f out: nvr nr to chal)	nk	**10**	7/1[2]	78	52
2325[9]	**Mouche (75)** (MrsJRRamsden) **3-8-7** DHarrison(14) (hld up: pushed along ½-wy: no imp)	4	**11**	20/1	60	26
2501[2]	**Winter Scout (USA) (60)** (RAFahey) **9-7-7b**(7) RWinston(13) (racd wd: rdn & no imp fr ½-wy)	nk	**12**	12/1	44	18
*2303**	**Pericles (77)** (MJohnston) **3-8-6**(3) KMChin(3) (lw: chsd ldrs tl wknd fnl 2f)	1¾	**13**	9/1	57	23
2422[2]	**Bollin Dorothy (56)** (TDEasterby) **4-7-10** LCharnock(12) (outpcd fr ½-wy)	¾	**14**	16/1	34	8
1935[3]	**Zelda Zonk (78)** (BJMeehan) **5-9-4** TQuinn(15) (bhd: hdwy ½-wy: sn wknd)	14	**15**	12/1	24	—
2347[9]	**Osomental (79)** (DHaydnJones) **3-8-11** AMackay(4) (bhd fr ½-wy)	8	**16**	33/1	7	—
2325[7]	***Persian Fayre (83)*** (JBerry) **5-9-9** KDarley(17) (Withdrawn not under Starter's orders: veterinary advice)		**W**	14/1	—	—

(SP 141.8%) **16 Rn**

1m 23.42 (0.42) CSF £79.34 CT £1,309.39 TOTE £4.40: £1.40 £3.90 £5.50 £1.40 (£71.70) Trio £893.60 OWNER Miss E. L. Ramsden (THIRSK) BRED John Bernard O'Connor

LONG HANDICAP Bollin Dorothy 7-6

WEIGHT FOR AGE 3yo-8lb

1920* Stackattack (IRE), back on the fast ground he loves, made no mistake and won nicely. (9/2)

2340 Anonym (IRE) looks tremendously well and keeps running his heart out, and deserves a change of luck. (16/1)

2496 Present Chance is proving difficult to win with and to find his ideal trip, but kept responding to pressure in good style. (20/1)

2390* Grey Kingdom keeps going up the weights, but also keeps improving and had the draw to suit his style of running but, on this faster surface, was just done for toe. (7/1)

1775 Irish Accord (USA) ran as though longer trips are what he needs, and he is certainly very well at present. (9/1)

2325 Tertium (IRE) was poorly drawn and always found things happening too quickly at this trip, but he did try hard this time. (8/1)

1948 Royal Mark (IRE) tried to come from behind, but had no luck at all in running and this is best ignored. (7/1)

2709 FOSTER'S SILVER CUP RATED STKS H'CAP (0-105) (Listed) (4-Y.O+) (Class A)

3-40 (3-46) **1m 5f 194y** £12,838.40 (£4,745.60: £2,272.80: £924.00: £362.00: £137.20) Stalls: Low GOING minus 0.40 sec per fur (F)

				SP	RR	SF
2327^{16}	**Benatom (USA) (91)** (HRACecil) **4-8-7** KFallon(1) (lw: a.p: hdwy 4f out: rdn to ld ins fnl f: r.o)	—	1	4/1	103	43
2028^{3}	**Willie Conquer (91)** (RAkehurst) **5-8-7** TQuinn(6) (trckd ldrs: hdwy whn nt clr run 2f out: swtchd 1f out: r.o: nt pce of wnr)	1½	2	2/1^{1}	101	41
2108^{4}	**Cuff Link (IRE) (94)** (MajorWRHern) **7-8-10** RCochrane(8) (cl up: led 9f out tl ins fnl f: no ex)	¾	3	12/1	103	43
1241^{2}	**Further Flight (102)** (BWHills) **11-9-4** MHills(4) (b.hind: hld up: hdwy 4f out: rdn over 2f out: nt pce to chal)	2½	4	11/4^{2}	109	49
1319^{4}	**Snow Princess (IRE) (96)** (LordHuntingdon) **5-8-12** DHarrison(9) (chsd ldrs: wnt 2nd 7f out: wknd fnl 3f)	9	5	4/1	92	32
2028^{13}	**Better Offer (IRE) (105)** (MrsAJPerrett) **5-9-7** JQuinn(7) (hld up: hdwy 4f out: sn rdn: wknd fnl 3f)	8	6	10/1	92	32
	Mattawan (91) (MJohnston) **4-8-7** KMChin(3) (led 5f: chsd ldr tl wknd 4f out)	8	7	12/1	69	9
2269a^{3}	***Poltarf (USA) (100)*** (JHMGosden) **6-9-2** LDettori(2) (Withdrawn not under Starter's orders: veterinary advice)		W	7/2^{3}	—	—
				(SP 146.7%)	**7 Rn**	

2m 56.37 (2.77) CSF £12.67 CT £85.10 TOTE £6.10: £2.20 £1.80 (£7.10) Trio £34.90 OWNER Mr T. F. Harris (NEWMARKET) BRED J. S. Meredith

LONG HANDICAP Benatom (USA) 8-6 Mattawan 8-6

1947 Benatom (USA), back on the ground he likes, was back to form and had his mind made up for him. (4/1)

2028 Willie Conquer got into trouble trying to get up the inner but it is doubtful whether he would have beaten the winner anyway and, hopefully, his rider will not get quite as much criticism as Fallon the previous week. (2/1)

2108 Cuff Link (IRE), who has an abundance of stamina, tried to force the pace, but was done for speed late on. (12/1)

1241 Further Flight never really got on terms but was not over-punished, and his rider missed his next mount as he was not feeling well. (11/4)

1319 Snow Princess (IRE) has lost her form for the moment and was beaten some way out. (4/1)

Better Offer (IRE) goes well on the bridle but is high in the handicap at present, and did not find much once off it. (10/1)

2710 38TH JOHN SMITH'S MAGNET CUP H'CAP (0-110) (3-Y.O+) (Class B)

4-15 (4-27) **1m 2f 85y** £62,755.50 (£18,894.00: £9,147.00: £4,273.50) Stalls: Low GOING minus 0.40 sec per fur (F)

				SP	RR	SF
	Pasternak (85) (SirMarkPrescott) **4-8-3** GDuffield(1) (lw: trckd ldrs: led ins fnl f: rdn & r.o wl)	—	1	13/2^{2}	95++	57
2026^{10}	**Najm Mubeen (IRE) (92)** (ACStewart) **4-8-10** MRoberts(19) (hld up bhd: hdwy on outside 3f out: hung bdly lft fnl 2f: r.o wl)	½	2	16/1	101	63
2136^{5}	**Game Ploy (POL) (92)** (DHaydnJones) **5-8-10** RCochrane(5) (bhd: nt clr run over 3f out to 2f out: r.o wl)	nk	3	12/1	101	63
2136^{6}	**Star Manager (USA) (86)** (PFICole) **7-8-4** AMackay(8) (hdwy 5f out: styd on wl u.p: hmpd wl ins fnl f)	1	4	20/1	93	55
2296^{8}	**Secret Aly (CAN) (85)** (CEBrittain) **7-8-3** JCarroll(3) (led tl hdd & wknd ins fnl f)	1¼	5	25/1	90	52
2058^{9}	**Southerly Wind (89)** (MrsJRRamsden) **3-7-10** LCharnock(2) (lw: a.p: effrt & swtchd 2f out: hrd rdn over 1f out: btn whn bdly hmpd fnl f)	1	6	8/1^{3}	93	44
2028^{19}	**Wahiba Sands (95)** (JLDunlop) **4-8-13** KDarley(11) (bhd: nt clr run 3f out tl appr fnl f: fin fast)	nk	7	16/1	98	60
2155^{3}	**Bay of Islands (83)** (DMorris) **5-8-1**ow2 NDay(7) (in tch: rdn 4f out: one pce appr fnl f)	½	8	14/1	86	46
1767^{7}	**Prince of My Heart (105)** (BWHills) **4-9-2**(7) CLowther(15) (bhd: effrt 4f out: nrst fin)	1½	9	25/1	105	67
2028^{15}	**Kuala Lipis (USA) (95)** (PFICole) **4-8-13** TQuinn(20) (a chsng ldrs: rdn 3f out: kpt on: btn whn hmpd ins fnl f)	½	10	16/1	94	56
2013^{2}	**Komi (94)** (MRStoute) **3-8-1** FLynch(17) (lw: bhd: effrt on outside 3f out: n.d)	s.h	11	4/1^{1}	93	44
2026^{17}	**Another Time (86)** (SPCWoods) **5-8-4** AMunro(13) (bhd: n.m.r 3f out: styd on)	hd	12	25/1	85	47
2136^{F}	**Wafir (IRE) (85)** (PCalver) **5-8-0**(3) DarrenMoffatt(16) (lw: bhd: effrt whn nt clr run 3f out: n.d)	¾	13	20/1	83	45
1979^{7}	**Jameel Asmar (83)** (CREgerton) **5-7-12**(3)ow3 AWhelan(12) (bhd: styd on fnl 3f: n.d)	hd	14	20/1	81	40
1960^{4}	**Key to My Heart (IRE) (110)** (MissSEHall) **7-10-0** DHarrison(9) (b: cl up tl wknd appr fnl f)	s.h	15	16/1	108	70
1323^{9}	**Ball Gown (95)** (DTThom) **7-8-13** DRMcCabe(4) (bhd: nt clr run 3f out: n.d)	nk	16	25/1	92	54
2528^{4}	**Orsay (80)** (WRMuir) **5-7-12** JLowe(10) (hdwy 4f out: sn hrd drvn: wknd fnl 2f)	3	17	14/1	73	35
1208^{2}	**Sharp Consul (IRE) (83)** (HCandy) **5-8-1** CRutter(14) (lw: a bhd)	6	18	12/1	67	29
2028^{6}	**Humourless (94)** (LMCumani) **4-8-12** LDettori(6) (b.hind: lw: chsd ldrs tl wknd fnl 4f)	2	19	4/1^{1}	74	36
1768^{3}	**Fahs (USA) (81)** (RAkehurst) **5-7-13** JQuinn(21) (in tch tl wknd fnl 3f)	6	20	10/1	52	14
1768^{5}	**Major Change (93)** (MissGayKelleway) **5-8-11** KFallon(18) (prom tl wknd fnl 3½f)	2½	21	20/1	60	22
				(SP 160.2%)	**21 Rn**	

2m 8.8 (-0.20) CSF £111.63 CT £1,186.11 TOTE £8.60: £3.10 £5.60 £3.20 £5.60 (£337.70) Trio £2,316.00 OWNER Mr Graham Rock (NEWMARKET) BRED Hesmonds Stud Ltd

LONG HANDICAP Southerly Wind 7-8

WEIGHT FOR AGE 3yo-11lb

Pasternak had connections worried about the fast ground but it proved no problem, and he was always travelling well and won nicely. It would appear he is still going the right way. (13/2: 3/1-7/1)

1450 Najm Mubeen (IRE), dropped out this time, showed just what a frustrating character he is by hanging violently in the last two furlongs, and did remarkably well to finish so close. (16/1)

2136 Game Ploy (POL) came from way behind and got a good run up the inner, but the effort was always too late and he needed a stronger gallop. (12/1)

2136 Star Manager (USA) took a strong hold going to post and then made up a lot of ground in the last half-mile, and being slightly hampered made no difference. (20/1)

521 Secret Aly (CAN) normally likes to come from behind, but he set the pace and was picked off late on. (25/1)

2058 Southerly Wind had his chances and tried hard, but was well beaten when getting knocked sideways in the closing stages. (8/1)

1176 Wahiba Sands had no luck at all in running but finished like the proverbial train, leaving the impression that, had he seen daylight, he would have been in the shake-up. (16/1)

1261* Prince of My Heart was not suited by the steady pace, had trouble in running and did well in the end. (25/1)

1456 Another Time has a poor action but had no luck at all, and would have been a good deal closer. (25/1)

1157 Ball Gown never got a run and this is best forgotten. (25/1)

2028 Humourless weakened in the last half-mile, and was handicapped by his bandages getting loose. (4/1: op 7/1)

2711 NEWCASTLE BROWN ALE H'CAP (0-90) (3-Y.O+) (Class C)
4-45 (4-57) **6f** £6,628.00 (£1,984.00: £952.00: £436.00) Stalls: Low GOING minus 0.40 sec per fur (F)

				SP	RR	SF
1824^{4}	**Faraway Lass (77)** (LordHuntingdon) **4-9-1** DHarrison(8) (chsd ldrs: led wl over 1f out: hld on wl)	—	**1**	14/1	86	58
2339^{8}	**Benzoe (IRE) (68)** (MrsJRRamsden) **7-8-6** JFanning(15) (hld up: stdy hdwy ½-wy: chal ins fnl f: no ex nr fin)	hd	**2**	12/1	77	49
2476^{5}	**Zuhair (90)** (DMcCain) **4-10-0** JCarroll(14) (b: w ldrs: kpt on u.p fnl 2f)	1¾	**3**	33/1	94	66
2105^{4}	**Oggi (87)** (PJMakin) **6-9-11** RCochrane(2) (lw: trckd ldrs: effrt & ev ch 2f out: nt qckn)	1¼	**4**	4/1^{1}	88	60
2326^{11}	**Daawe (USA) (82)** (MrsVAAconley) **6-9-6** MDeering(21) (lw: led over 4f: r.o one pce)	½	**5**	14/1	81	53
2308*	**Bayin (USA) (67)** (MDIUsher) **8-8-5** RStreet(13) (hld up & bhd: effrt ½-wy: r.o: nrst fin)	1¼	**6**	8/1^{2}	63	35
1141^{6}	**Marsad (IRE) (73)** (RAkehurst) **3-8-5** TQuinn(9) (swtg: prom: rdn ½-wy: no imp)	s.h	**7**	11/1	69	35
2567^{10}	**Prima Silk (72)** (MJRyan) **6-8-10** GBardwell(17) (rdn ½-wy: styd on wl: nrst fin)	hd	**8**	33/1	68	40
2326^{17}	**Mallia (71)** (TDBarron) **4-8-9b^{1}** KDarley(11) (effrt ½-wy: sn hrd rdn & no imp)	½	**9**	16/1	65	37
2472^{2}	**Mister Westsound (58)** (MissLAPerratt) **5-7-10b** NKennedy(19) (lw: dwlt: bhd tl sme late hdwy)	1	**10**	33/1	50	22
2547^{2}	**Style Dancer (IRE) (71)** (RMWhitaker) **3-8-3** AMunro(10) (drvn along ½-wy: nvr trbld ldrs)	1¼	**11**	16/1	59	25
2289^{5}	**Saint Express (80)** (MrsMReveley) **7-9-4** ACulhane(22) (lw: cl up tl rdn & btn over 1f out)	1¼	**12**	12/1	65	37
2422^{3}	**Bee Health Boy (67)** (MWEasterby) **4-8-2b$^{(3)}$** GParkin(6) (disp ld early: cl up & wknd fnl 2f)	nk	**13**	16/1	51	23
1777^{5}	**Van Chino (70)** (BAMcMahon) **3-8-2** MRoberts(16) (prom over 4f)	1¼	**14**	25/1	51	17
1977^{10}	**U-No-Harry (IRE) (63)** (RHollinshead) **4-8-1** FLynch(1) (in tch 4f)	1¾	**15**	16/1	39	11
2422^{7}	**Halmanerror (58)** (MrsJRRamsden) **7-7-10** JQuinn(4) (effrt ½-wy: sn rdn & btn)	¾	**16**	20/1	32	4
2422^{10}	**Foist (62)** (MWEasterby) **5-8-0** LCharnock(7) (sn outpcd & bhd)	½	**17**	20/1	35	7
2417*	**Rum Lad (70)** (JJQuinn) **3-8-2** JLowe(5) (sn bhd)	½	**18**	10/1	42	8
2472*	**Palacegate Touch (81)** (JBerry) **7-8-12b$^{(7)}$** CLowther(3) (cl up 4f: wknd)	1	**19**	14/1	50	22
1977^{3}	**Thwaab (66)** (FWatson) **5-8-1v$^{(3)}$** AWhelan(12) (lw: chsd ldrs 4f: wknd)	nk	**20**	9/1^{3}	34	6
2033^{2}	**Natural Key (70)** (DHaydnJones) **4-8-8** AMackay(20) (outpcd & lost tch fr ½-wy)	½	**21**	20/1	37	9
				(SP 144.4%)	**21 Rn**	

1m 10.96 (0.46) CSF £165.97 CT £5,054.24 TOTE £17.00: £2.90 £4.00 £20.90 £1.70 (£122.50) Trio £1,781.70; £1,279.85 to 14/7/97 OWNER Mr J. Rose (WEST ILSLEY) BRED John Rose

LONG HANDICAP Mister Westsound 7-3

WEIGHT FOR AGE 3yo-6lb

1824 Faraway Lass looks in tremendous heart again this year and showed fine courage to hold on. (14/1)

2129 Benzoe (IRE) was produced with a beautifully-timed run, but failed to see it out and needs Jimmy Fortune at his strongest to persuade him. (12/1)

2476 Zuhair is high in the handicap, but is running particularly well and this was another sound effort. (33/1)

2105 Oggi went well for a long way but just failed to pick up when ridden and may just be at his best on easier ground. (4/1)

2129* Daawe (USA) ran his usual game race but was just tapped for speed late on. (14/1)

2308* Bayin (USA), dropped out as usual, finished fast but always had too much to do. He is nevertheless in really good form at present. (8/1)

1963 Prima Silk finished well here to show signs of coming back to form. (33/1)

1946 Mallia had blinkers on for the first time but with no positive effect. (16/1)

2472 Mister Westsound, 7lb out of the handicap, gave too much ground away at the start but still looks extremely well. (33/1)

2712 FISHERGATE NURSERY H'CAP (2-Y.O) (Class C)
5-15 (5-25) **5f** £5,580.00 (£1,665.00: £795.00: £360.00) Stalls: Low GOING minus 0.40 sec per fur (F)

				SP	RR	SF
2335^{7}	**Socket Set** (BAMcMahon) **2-9-5** MRoberts(3) (mde all: r.o wl fnl f)	—	**1**	7/2^{3}	82	33
2356^{2}	**Mysticism** (CEBrittain) **2-8-12** LDettori(6) (dwlt: gd hdwy to chal ins fnl f: no ex u.p)	¾	**2**	3/1^{1}	73	24
2324^{4}	**Grand Estate** (TDEasterby) **2-8-3**^{ow1} KDarley(1) (trckd ldrs: swtchd over 1f out: rdn & nt run on)	3	**3**	100/30^{2}	54	4
1684^{5}	**Hirst Bridge (IRE)** (MWEasterby) **2-9-5b^{1}** TLucas(2) (unruly s: s.i.s: effrt 3f out: sn rdn & no imp)	2½	**4**	8/1	62	13
2140*	**Baby Grand (IRE)** (TDBarron) **2-9-2**$^{(5)}$ KimberleyHart(7) (cl up tl rdn & wknd appr fnl f)	nk	**5**	100/30^{2}	63	14
1829*	**Penniless (IRE)** (NTinkler) **2-8-11** KimTinkler(5) (sn chsng ldrs: rdn & btn appr fnl f)	3	**6**	8/1	43	—
2016^{8}	**Adrenalin** (MrsJRRamsden) **2-7-10** LCharnock(4) (cl up 3f: sn outpcd)	1¾	**7**	12/1	23	—
				(SP 123.3%)	**7 Rn**	

59.74 secs (2.04) CSF £14.55 TOTE £5.00: £2.50 £1.90 (£7.30) OWNER Mr J. C. Fretwell (TAMWORTH) BRED Mrs J. McMahon

2066* Socket Set has plenty of speed and has the courage to match. (7/2)

2356 Mysticism has the ability but failed to come up with the goods when the chips were down. (3/1: 5/1-11/4)

2324 Grand Estate looked likely to win this for a long way but, once asked for an effort, he failed to do a tap. (100/30)

1684 Hirst Bridge (IRE) had blinkers on and seemed unsettled by them, and was never doing enough. (8/1: 6/1-9/1)

2140* Baby Grand (IRE) looked to have plenty on here and was done with someway out. (100/30)

1829* Penniless (IRE) had her limitations exposed once the pace was seriously on. (8/1)

1298 Adrenalin (12/1: op 8/1)

T/Jkpt: £25,321.40 (1.4 Tckts). T/Plpt: £81.50 (779.43 Tckts). T/Qdpt: £67.80 (41.02 Tckts) AA

2140-AYR (L-H) (Good to firm)
Monday July 14th
WEATHER: sunny periods WIND: mod across

2713 E.B.F. MAIDEN STKS (2-Y.O) (Class D)
2-15 (2-17) **6f** £3,571.00 (£1,078.00: £524.00: £247.00) Stalls: High GOING minus 0.26 sec per fur (GF)

				SP	RR	SF
2024^{7}	**Child Prodigy (IRE)** (JWWatts) **2-8-9** JCarroll(2) (lw: mde most: all out)	—	**1**	10/11^{1}	80	27
1310^{4}	**Selkirk Rose (IRE)** (MissLAPerratt) **2-8-9** KDarley(4) (lw: plld hrd: hdwy 2f out: r.o u.p fnl f: jst failed)	hd	**2**	10/1	80	27
2127^{3}	**Boulevard Rouge (USA)** (MJohnston) **2-8-9** JWeaver(5) (lw: cl up: effrt 2f out: nt qckn fnl f)	1¼	**3**	8/1	76	23
1839^{5}	**Shalyah (IRE)** (MrsJRRamsden) **2-8-9** JFortune(8) (trckd ldrs: nt qckn fnl 2f)	5	**4**	25/1	63	10

				SP	RR	SF
2343[3]	**Shifting** (CWThornton) **2-8-9** DeanMcKeown(7) (lw: hld up: effrt ½-wy: sn outpcd: styd on towards fin)	1½	**5**	6/1 [3]	59	6
	Miss Vivien (MissLAPerratt) **2-8-9** NKennedy(6) (w'like: scope: bit bkwd: sn wl bhd: stdy hdwy fnl 2f: nvr plcd to chal)	1½	**6**	50/1	55+	2
1774[3]	**Happy Days** (DMoffatt) **2-8-11**(3) DarrenMoffatt(3) (lw: chsd ldrs: rdn 2f out: sn wknd)	¾	**7**	9/2 [2]	58	5
1557[5]	**Pleasant Dreams** (DenysSmith) **2-8-9** FLynch(1) (spd over 3f: sn wknd)	¾	**8**	33/1	51	—

(SP 113.8%) **8 Rn**

1m 12.9 (3.10) CSF £10.04 TOTE £1.60: £1.10 £2.20 £1.60 (£10.50) OWNER Mr R. E. Sangster (RICHMOND) BRED Mrs E. M. Burke

1149 Child Prodigy (IRE) took the eye in the paddock and managed to break her duck this time, but it was a desperate affair in the end. (10/11: 8/11-evens)

1310 Selkirk Rose (IRE) did not help her chances by pulling hard in the early stages, but she picked up well when asked a question and is obviously improving fast. (10/1)

2127 Boulevard Rouge (USA) is learning quickly and put up a useful effort, and would probably have finished a good bit closer had her rider not dropped his whip. (8/1: 6/1-9/1)

1839 Shalyah (IRE) is coming to hand and, by finishing fourth here, is now qualified for nurseries. (25/1)

2343 Shifting has given the impression on both runs that longer distances will see improvement in her. (6/1)

Miss Vivien looked in need of this and just had a very quiet run, but showed ability and should now improve a good deal. (50/1)

2714 CRAIGIE STAND NURSERY H'CAP (2-Y.O) (Class D)

2-45 (2-46) **7f** £3,512.50 (£1,060.00: £515.00: £242.50) Stalls: Low GOING minus 0.26 sec per fur (GF)

				SP	RR	SF
2359*	**The Rich Man (IRE)** (BWHills) **2-9-0** MHills(7) (lw: trckd ldrs: led 2f out: shkn up & r.o wl fnl f)	—	**1**	11/8 [1]	86+	25
2168[2]	**Jacmar (IRE)** (MissLAPerratt) **2-9-0** JFortune(3) (lw: hld up: hdwy ent st: effrt 2f out: r.o: no ch w wnr)	3	**2**	7/2 [2]	79	18
2499*	**Flower O'Cannie (IRE)** (MWEasterby) **2-9-4**(3) GParkin(1) (hld up: effrt over 2f out: styd on fnl f: no imp)	½	**3**	5/1 [3]	85	24
2222[4]	**Marske Machine** (NTinkler) **2-7-10** NKennedy(2) (lw: bhd: gd hdwy over 2f out: no ex appr fnl f)	1¾	**4**	20/1	56	—
2363[3]	**Falkenberg (FR)** (MJohnston) **2-8-9** JWeaver(5) (led tl hdd 2f out: wknd appr fnl f)	1¾	**5**	10/1	65	4
2383[3]	**Ellenber** (WMcKeown) **2-7-10** LCharnock(6) (chsd ldrs tl wknd fnl 2f)	1¾	**6**	25/1	48	—
2288[4]	**Makahu Don** (WTKemp) **2-7-7b**[1](3) PFessey(4) (trckd ldrs tl wknd 2f out)	19	**7**	8/1	5	—

(SP 109.8%) **7 Rn**

1m 28.82 (4.42) CSF £5.15 TOTE £2.00: £1.70 £1.10 (£2.10) OWNER Marston Stud (LAMBOURN) BRED Lady Richard Wellesley and Grange Nominees

2359* The Rich Man (IRE) certainly appreciated this trip and got stronger as the race progressed. He is improving all the time and there looks to be a decent prize in store. (11/8)

2168 Jacmar (IRE) has not the best of actions for this fast ground but he still ran well, only to be outclassed late on. (7/2)

2499* Flower O'Cannie (IRE) gave plenty of problems in the paddock but then behaved well going to post. However, in the race, she was always short of both pace and room, and only ran when it was too late. The ground was probably a bit too lively. (5/1)

2222 Marske Machine looks well and has ability but is a real handful. (20/1)

2363 Falkenberg (FR) seems high enough in the weights at the moment. (10/1: op 6/1)

2383 Ellenber was 5lb out of the handicap and did not have the blinkers on this time. (25/1)

2288 Makahu Don had blinkers on for the first time and they had an adverse effect. (8/1)

2715 PRINCESS ROYAL STAND H'CAP (0-70) (3-Y.O) (Class E)

3-15 (3-15) **7f** £2,900.00 (£875.00: £425.00: £200.00) Stalls: Low GOING minus 0.26 sec per fur (GF)

				SP	RR	SF
1931[2]	**C-Harry (IRE) (60)** (RHollinshead) **3-8-12** FLynch(11) (hld up: hdwy over 2f out: led ins fnl f: r.o)	—	**1**	100/30 [2]	70	26
2415[3]	**Hi Mujtahid (IRE) (44)** (SEKettlewell) **3-7-10** NKennedy(10) (led tl hdd ins fnl f: r.o)	½	**2**	9/2 [3]	53	9
1838[3]	**Beau Roberto (49)** (JSGoldie) **3-8-1** TWilliams(7) (chsd ldrs: outpcd 2f out: styd on wl towards fin)	s.h	**3**	12/1	58	14
2238[5]	**Storyteller (IRE) (54)** (MrsJRRamsden) **3-8-6v**[1] JFortune(9) (cl up: effrt 2f out: nt qckn)	2½	**4**	12/1	57	13
2415[13]	**Tazibari (48)** (DMoffatt) **3-7-11**(3) DarrenMoffatt(5) (bhd: hdwy over 2f out: r.o: nrst fin)	s.h	**5**	33/1	51	7
2543[3]	**Naivasha (56)** (JBerry) **3-8-5**(3) PFessey(8) (rr div: effrt over 2f out: nt clr run 1f out: styd on)	½	**6**	10/1	58	14
2505[3]	**Wagga Moon (IRE) (59)** (JJO'Neill) **3-8-11** LCharnock(2) (lw: chsd ldrs: ev ch 3f out: one pce fnl 2f)	nk	**7**	8/1	60	16
2340[7]	**Pension Fund (69)** (MWEasterby) **3-9-7b**[1] TLucas(6) (lw: plld hrd: a.p: effrt 2f out: sn btn)	2½	**8**	5/2 [1]	64	20
2382[7]	**Biff-Em (IRE) (61)** (MissLAPerratt) **3-8-13** JWeaver(1) (swtg: stdd s: sme hdwy ent st: n.d)	1¼	**9**	20/1	54	10
2543[11]	**Chanson d'Amour (IRE) (44)** (MissLAPerratt) **3-7-3v**(7) JMcAuley(3) (rdn 3f out: a bhd)	1	**10**	100/1	34	—
2171[10]	**Alisadara (46)** (NBycroft) **3-7-5**(7)ow2 RWinston(4) (sn prom: c wd st: wknd fnl 2½f)	14	**11**	50/1	4	—

(SP 116.1%) **11 Rn**

1m 28.57 (4.17) CSF £16.32 CT £145.52 TOTE £4.00: £1.70 £2.20 £2.60 (£16.90) Trio £32.20 OWNER Mr D. Coppenhall (UPPER LONGDON) BRED Dan O'Loughlin

LONG HANDICAP Chanson d'Amour (IRE) 7-2 Alisadara 6-13

STEWARDS' ENQUIRY McAuley susp. 23-24/7/97 (improper use of whip).

1931 C-Harry (IRE) has been finding it difficult to win on turf but there was nothing wrong with this performance, despite being inclined to pull up once in front. He obviously needs bringing as late as possible. (100/30)

2415 Hi Mujtahid (IRE) is running consistently well just now and deserves to find a race, and seems to go on any ground. (9/2)

1838 Beau Roberto ran well, only to find this trip too short. He looks to be going the right way for his new stable. (12/1)

2238 Storyteller (IRE) is steadily coming right and this was a better effort. (12/1: 6/1-14/1)

Tazibari, ridden from behind this time, showed her first signs of form this season and finished well. She is obviously coming right. (33/1)

2543 Naivasha never had much luck in running and was staying on particularly well at the end. She is still on good terms with herself. (10/1: 8/1-12/1)

2505 Wagga Moon (IRE) looked well and had plenty of chances, but failed to come up with the goods when the pressure was applied. (8/1)

2238 Pension Fund, well-fancied in the blinkers for the first time, pulled far too hard and beat himself. (5/2)

2716 CAMERON LODGE (S) STKS (3-Y.O+) (Class F)

3-45 (3-47) **1m 2f 192y** £2,472.00 (£692.00: £336.00) Stalls: Low GOING minus 0.26 sec per fur (GF)

				SP	RR	SF
2544[2]	**Guesstimation (USA) (57)** (JPearce) **8-9-2**(3) CTeague(8) (lw: b.nr fore: hld up: hdwy 3f out: led 1½f out: shkn up & qcknd)	—	**1**	11/10 [1]	47	40
2386[7]	**Trying Times (IRE) (53)** (JBerry) **4-9-7**(5) TEDurcan(6) (t: a.p: chal over 1f out: kpt on: no ch w wnr)	3½	**2**	8/1 [3]	49	42

2342[6]	**Thisonesforalice (33)** (JSGoldie) **9-9-5** TWilliams(11) (bhd: hdwy over 2f out: styd on wl towards fin)	hd	3	40/1	42	35
2543[4]	**Mystic Times (26)** (BMactaggart) **4-8-9**(5) KSked(3) (lw: chsd ldrs: disp ld over 2f out: one pce appr fnl f)	2	4	20/1	34	27
2544[9]	**Diamond Crown (IRE) (46)** (MartynWane) **6-9-2**(3) AWhelan(7) (hld up & bhd: effrt & n.m.r over 2f out: styd on fnl f)	nk	5	8/1[3]	38	31
2145[8]	**Shamokin (25)** (FWatson) **5-9-2**(3) PFessey(9) (cl up: led over 3f out tl hdd & wknd 1½f out)	1½	6	50/1	36	29
2170[5]	**Majal (IRE) (52)** (JSWainwright) **8-9-5** DeanMcKeown(10) (b: cl up: disp ld over 2f out tl wknd wl over 1f out)	3½	7	7/2[2]	31	24
2542[5]	**Knave (42)** (PMonteith) **4-8-12**(7) RWinston(5) (nvr bttr than mid div)	4	8	25/1	25	18
2237[9]	**Miletrian City (43)** (MissLAPerratt) **4-9-5b** JWeaver(1) (lw: led tl hdd & wknd over 3f out)	14	9	16/1	5	—
2352[7]	**Fizzy Boy (IRE) (34)** (PMonteith) **4-9-5** OPears(4) (in tch to st: sn bhd)	10	10	100/1	—	—
2661[6]	***Ribbonletta*** (MissLAPerratt) **3-8-2** NKennedy(2) (swtg: Withdrawn not under Starter's orders: ref to ent stalls)		W	66/1	—	—
				(SP 113.4%)	**10 Rn**	

2m 21.57 (5.67) CSF £8.59 TOTE £1.80: £1.20 £2.10 £3.70 (£5.20) Trio £31.40 OWNER The Exclusive Two Partnership (NEWMARKET) BRED Oak Crest Farm
WEIGHT FOR AGE 3yo-12lb
Bt in 5,100 gns
2544 Guesstimation (USA) is a character who has plenty of ability but, given a really good ride, was always far too good for this lot. (11/10)
2386 Trying Times (IRE) ran much better after a poor effort last time, but was well out-pointed by the winner in the closing stages. (8/1: 6/1-9/1)
2342 Thisonesforalice had plenty on and, when in the mood, has the ability, but was always far too late when he decided to run. (40/1)
2543 Mystic Times, poorly in here, ran well and is in particularly good form at the moment. (20/1)
2039* Diamond Crown (IRE) likes to come from behind and needs things to go just right, and they never did. (8/1)
689 Shamokin keeps showing bits of ability but is basically disappointing. (50/1)
2109 Miletrian City is normally better over a shorter trip and in blinkers. (16/1)

2717 WESTERN HOUSE H'CAP (0-90) (3-Y.O+) (Class C)

4-15 (4-16) **5f** £5,121.00 (£1,548.00: £754.00: £357.00) Stalls: High GOING minus 0.26 sec per fur (GF)

				SP	RR	SF
2480*	**Blessingindisguise (76)** (MWEasterby) **4-9-4b** TLucas(2) (lw: mde most: rdn & r.o wl appr fnl f: eased towards fin)	—	1	7/2[1]	86+	68
2480[7]	**Cross The Border (54)** (DNicholls) **4-7-10** LCharnock(6) (lw: chsd ldrs: ev ch over 1f out: sn rdn & nt qckn)	¾	2	7/2[1]	62	44
2563[8]	**Rich Glow (54)** (NBycroft) **6-7-10** NKennedy(7) (lw: bhd: several positions: swtchd outside & r.o wl fnl f)	¾	3	5/1[2]	59	41
2563[2]	**Manolo (FR) (63)** (JBerry) **4-8-2b**(3) PFessey(5) (dwlt: hdwy 2f out: kpt on wl)	nk	4	7/1	67	49
2563[5]	**Royal Dome (IRE) (67)** (MartynWane) **5-8-6**(3) AWhelan(1) (lw: chsd ldrs: rdn ½-wy: no imp)	¾	5	6/1[3]	69	51
2111[5]	**Johayro (59)** (JSGoldie) **4-7-8**(7) RWinston(4) (cl up tl wknd over 1f out)	5	6	20/1	45	27
2675[5]	**Squire Corrie (86)** (DWChapman) **5-10-0v** ACulhane(9) (chsd ldrs tl outpcd appr fnl f)	hd	7	7/1	72	54
1977[15]	**Don't Care (IRE) (65)** (MissLAPerratt) **6-8-2b**(5) TEDurcan(8) (nvr wnt pce)	½	8	33/1	49	31
2504[4]	**Just Bob (67)** (SEKettlewell) **8-8-9** JFortune(3) (lw: s.i.s: sn wl bhd: n.d)	1¼	9	7/1	47	29
				(SP 120.6%)	**9 Rn**	

57.65 secs (0.65) CSF £14.81 CT £57.24 TOTE £4.30: £2.00 £2.60 £1.40 (£9.40) Trio £22.70 OWNER Mr A. G. Black (SHERIFF HUTTON) BRED Mrs A. Meller
LONG HANDICAP Rich Glow 7-9
2480* Blessingindisguise is proving ultra-consistent this year and, responding to pressure, always had too much courage for the runner-up. (7/2)
1311 Cross The Border had the ground he likes and the money was certainly on. He had his chances but proved a shade disappointing when ridden. The ability is there if the key can be found. (7/2)
2563 Rich Glow was not given the best of rides, finding all sorts of trouble, and should be noted if returning to this track next weekend. (5/1)
2563 Manolo (FR) gave the rest too much start but still ran well and is obviously in really good heart. (7/1)
2563 Royal Dome (IRE) had a hard race last time and was probably still feeling that. (6/1)
1602 Johayro could never get the lead in this fast-run event and finally had to give up approaching the last furlong. (20/1)
2675 Squire Corrie had the visor on, and it had no real effect. (7/1)

2718 BREATH OF FRESH AYR LIMITED STKS (0-70) (3-Y.O+) (Class E)

4-45 (4-46) **1m 5f 13y** £3,078.75 (£930.00: £452.50: £213.75) Stalls: Low GOING minus 0.26 sec per fur (GF)

				SP	RR	SF
2327[12]	**Noufari (FR) (68)** (RHollinshead) **6-9-8** FLynch(2) (mde all: kpt on wl fnl 2f)	—	1	3/1[2]	80	38
2570*	**Florentino (IRE) (67)** (BWHills) **4-9-10** MHills(1) (b: hld up: hdwy 7f out: chsng wnr 3f out: ev ch over 1f out: no ex u.p)	1	2	4/5[1]	81	39
2198[11]	**Sad Mad Bad (USA) (70)** (MrsMReveley) **3-8-8** KDarley(3) (lw: outpcd 7f out: n.d after)	14	3	10/1	62	6
2142[4]	**Secret Service (IRE) (70)** (CWThornton) **5-9-8b**[1] DeanMcKeown(4) (chsd wnr tl rdn & btn 3f out)	nk	4	7/2[3]	61	19
				(SP 111.9%)	**4 Rn**	

2m 52.52 (7.72) CSF £5.58 TOTE £3.80: (£2.60) OWNER Mr Ed Weetman (UPPER LONGDON) BRED His Highness The Aga Khans Studs S.C. in France
WEIGHT FOR AGE 3yo-14lb
1672 Noufari (FR), given a most positive ride as he stays a deal further, showed the right attitude to gain his first win on turf. (3/1)
2570* Florentino (IRE) ought to have stayed this trip but, when it came down to a fight, he was just found wanting. (4/5)
975 Sad Mad Bad (USA) was in trouble a long way out and was never a danger. (10/1: 8/1-12/1)
2142 Secret Service (IRE) had the blinkers on for the first time and they certainly did not work. (7/2)

T/Plpt: £42.30 (381.39 Tckts). T/Qdpt: £36.10 (18.78 Tckts) AA

2577-FOLKESTONE (R-H) (Good to firm)

Monday July 14th

Race 3: Flag Start
WEATHER: fine WIND: fresh across

2719 HURST GREEN MAIDEN AUCTION STKS (2-Y.O) (Class F)

2-00 (2-07) **6f 189y** £2,277.00 (£627.00: £297.00) Stalls: Low GOING minus 0.33 sec per fur (GF)

			SP	RR	SF
1760^{2}	**Country Garden** (RHannon) **2-8-5** RPerham(2) (lw: hld up: hdwy gng wl over 2f out: led 1f out: r.o)............—	**1**	13/8^{1}	69	18
2243^{7}	**Titan** (SDow) **2-8-8** SSanders(7) (sn led: hdd 1f out: unable qckn) 1¼	**2**	6/1	69	18
	Anna (CEBrittain) **2-8-4** BDoyle(5) (w'like: scope: hld up bhd ldrs: rdn over 2f out: styd on wl ins fnl f)...........½	**3**	7/2^{2}	64	13
1872^{16}	**Appyabo** (MRChannon) **2-8-6**(3) PPMurphy(4) (lw: chsd ldrs: rdn over 1f out: one pce)...........2½	**4**	12/1	63	12
2196^{14}	**Latin Bay** (PWHarris) **2-8-0**(7) CLowther(8) (w ldr tl wknd 2f out)...........3½	**5**	50/1	53	2
1827^{6}	**Bermuda Triangle (IRE)** (MJHaynes) **2-7-10**(3) MartinDwyer(3) (b.hind: lw: a bhd) 2	**6**	5/1^{3}	40	—
2240^{7}	**Distinctly Lillie (IRE)** (JSMoore) **2-8-3**^{ow1} JFEgan(6) (chsd ldrs tl wknd over 2f out)...........2	**7**	40/1	40	—
2565^{4}	**Mari-Ela (IRE)** (JRArnold) **2-8-2** JQuinn(1) (bhd fnl 4f)...........3	**8**	9/1	32	—

(SP 113.4%) **8 Rn**

1m 25.0 (3.60) CSF £10.68 TOTE £2.40: £1.10 £1.40 £1.90 (£6.20) OWNER Lord Carnarvon (MARLBOROUGH) BRED Highclere Stud Ltd

1760 Country Garden was always going well and was not hard pressed to score. (13/8)
2243 Titan ran really well and obviously appreciated the faster ground. (6/1)
Anna, a strong, attractive filly with lots of scope, ran a very promising race on her debut. Pushed along and green before the home turn, she found her stride late on and finished best of all. Bred to stay further, she will improve and have no trouble finding a race. (7/2)
Appyabo improved on her debut and is going the right way. (12/1)
1827 Bermuda Triangle (IRE) (5/1: op 3/1)
2565 Mari-Ela (IRE) (9/1: op 6/1)

2720 E.B.F. ASHFORD MAIDEN STKS (2-Y.O) (Class D)

2-30 (2-33) **6f** £3,673.00 (£1,099.00: £527.00: £241.00) Stalls: Low GOING minus 0.33 sec per fur (GF)

			SP	RR	SF
2320^{3}	**Moontabeh** (PTWalwyn) **2-9-0** JFEgan(3) (lw: mde all: rdn over 1f out: r.o) ....—	**1**	10/11^{1}	77	33
2562^{10}	**Dil** (BHanbury) **2-9-0** JStack(2) (chsd wnr: rdn over 1f out: unable qckn)...........2	**2**	8/1	72	28
	Achilles (RAkehurst) **2-9-0** MTebbutt(13) (unf: mid div: pushed along 3f out: styd on ins fnl f) ....½	**3**	25/1	70	26
2181^{13}	**Taste of Success** (PWHarris) **2-8-7**(7) CLowther(14) (pushed along in rr over 4f out: hdwy over 1f out: styd on ins fnl f)...........2	**4**	25/1	65	21
2534^{7}	**Night Flyer** (JWHills) **2-8-11**(3) MHenry(10) (swtg: hld up towards rr: hdwy over 1f out: styd on ins fnl f)........hd	**5**	12/1	65	21
	Jarrayan (MajorWRHern) **2-8-9** AMcGlone(6) (unf: b.hind: chsd ldrs: rdn over 1f out: wknd ins fnl f)...........nk	**6**	12/1	59	15
2018^{5}	**High Money** (GLewis) **2-9-0** PaulEddery(12) (chsd ldrs: rdn over 1f out: wknd ins fnl f) ....½	**7**	16/1	63	19
	Maginot (USA) (DRLoder) **2-8-11**(3) PMcCabe(8) (unf: bit bkwd: hld up in mid div: shkn up over 1f out: eased ins fnl f)...........3	**8**	7/1^{3}	55	11
2534^{10}	**Tightrope** (SirMarkPrescott) **2-9-0** GDuffield(4) (dwlt: nvr plcd to chal) 1½	**9**	7/1^{3}	51	7
	Chikal (BPalling) **2-9-0** TSprake(5) (unf: mid div: rdn over 2f out: sn wknd)...........¾	**10**	33/1	49	5
2320^{7}	**Facile Tigre** (SDow) **2-9-0** WRyan(7) (chsd ldrs tl wknd qckly over 1f out) 1¼	**11**	11/2^{2}	45	1
	Zimzie (MJHaynes) **2-9-0** SSanders(1) (neat: bit bkwd: a bhd) 2	**12**	33/1	40	—
	Captive Fact (USA) (MrsAJPerrett) **2-9-0** JQuinn(9) (w'like: bit bkwd: dwlt: a bhd) ....s.h	**13**	10/1	40	—
	Premier Jet (MMadgwick) **2-8-9** NVarley(11) (w'like: bit bkwd: a bhd)...........8	**14**	33/1	14	—

(SP 150.8%) **14 Rn**

1m 12.8 (2.60) CSF £11.18 TOTE £2.10: £1.20 £1.60 £5.60 (£6.40) Trio £197.10; £66.65 to Beverley 15/7/97 OWNER Mr Hamdan Al Maktoum (LAMBOURN) BRED Gainsborough Stud Management Ltd

2320 Moontabeh broke smartly and always had the legs of his rivals. (10/11: op 2/1)
Dil ran a really sound race, but connections felt he did not handle the undulations and would have given the winner more of a race on a flatter course. (8/1)
Achilles stayed on promisingly in the final two furlongs and can pick up a small race, especially over further. (25/1)
Taste of Success could not go the early pace, but did stay on. (25/1)
2534 Night Flyer was never really put in the race, and could be seen in a better light now he is qualified for nurseries. (12/1)
Jarrayan ran quite well until weakening in the final furlong. (12/1: op 4/1)
Maginot (USA) ran better than his finishing position suggests. He was given quite an easy time in the final two furlongs when it was obvious he could not pick up the leaders, and will improve considerably on this. (7/1: 5/2-10/1)
Tightrope left the distinct impression that better is to come. (7/1: 4/1-8/1)
Facile Tigre (11/2: 4/1-6/1)

2721 WESTENHANGER H'CAP (0-65) (3-Y.O+) (Class F)

3-00 (3-12) **6f** £2,277.00 (£627.00: £297.00) Stalls: Low GOING minus 0.33 sec per fur (GF)

			SP	RR	SF
2542^{2}	**Double Oscar (IRE) (48)** (DNicholls) **4-8-12b** AlexGreaves(2) (hld up: a gng wl: led on bit over 1f out: sn clr: easily) ....—	**1**	2/1^{1}	67+	—
1969^{4}	**Resist the Force (USA) (55)** (CACyzer) **7-9-0**(5) RFfrench(4) (led: hdd over 1f out: one pce)...........7	**2**	5/1^{2}	55	—
1640^{5}	**Barbason (64)** (GLMoore) **5-10-0** CandyMorris(7) (mid div: sn pushed along: hrd rdn over 2f out: hdwy appr fnl f: r.o)...........1	**3**	5/1^{2}	62	—
2197^{7}	**Tymeera (46)** (BPalling) **4-8-10** TSprake(3) (prom: rdn & outpcd ½-wy: rallied appr fnl f: one pce)...........½	**4**	12/1	42	—
	Supreme Thought (57) (LGCottrell) **5-9-7** SSanders(1) (prom: rdn over 1f out: grad wknd) 1½	**5**	14/1	49	—
2206^{6}	**Priory Gardens (IRE) (45)** (JMBradley) **3-8-3** GDuffield(5) (prom tl rdn & outpcd fnl 2f) 1½	**6**	12/1	33	—
1857^{6}	**Waders Dream (IRE) (43)** (PatMitchell) **8-8-7v** MFenton(14) (nvr nrr) 1¼	**7**	12/1	28	—
1925^{5}	**Severn Mill (32)** (JMBradley) **6-7-3**(7) DarrenWilliams(15) (a bhd)...........2	**8**	20/1	12	—
2382^{5}	**Kid Ory (43)** (DWChapman) **6-8-7b** DWright(10) (prom tl wknd over 1f out)...........½	**9**	15/2^{3}	21	—
772^{9}	**Summerville Wood (65)** (PMooney) **3-9-9b** WJO'Connor(8) (mid div: hrd rdn over 2f out: sn btn: fin lame) 2	**10**	12/1	38	—

2228[9]	**Jaazim (32)** (MMadgwick) **7-7-10** NVarley(13) (in tch on outside tl wknd 2f out)	3	**11**	14/1	—	—
2424[8]	**Arnie (IRE) (44)** (JRPoulton) **5-8-1b**(7) RBrisland(11) (a bhd)	1½	**12**	20/1	5	—
2554[8]	***Bonsiel (45)*** (KMahdi) **3-8-0**(3) MartinDwyer(9) (Withdrawn not under Starter's orders: injured in stalls: dead)		**W**	20/1	—	—
				(SP 136.8%)	**12 Rn**	

1m 9.4 (-0.80) CSF £11.87 CT £44.04 TOTE £2.70: £1.20 £2.50 £2.00 (£5.00) Trio £43.80 OWNER Trilby Racing (THIRSK) BRED Tasia Limited
LONG HANDICAP Severn Mill 7-4 Jaazim 7-9
WEIGHT FOR AGE 3yo-6lb
OFFICIAL EXPLANATION **Summerville Wood: finished lame.**
IN-FOCUS: Due to the accident in the stalls, the race was run over a shorter distance than advertised, resulting in a very fast time.
2542 Double Oscar (IRE) landed a gamble in some style. Always going supremely well, he took it up below the distance and scooted clear for a very easy success. (2/1: op 9/2)
1969 Resist the Force (USA) tried to make all but was smothered for pace in the final furlong or so. (5/1)
1640 Barbason was never really going the pace but, to his credit, he did stay on in the closing stages. He needs further. (5/1: op 5/2)
1003 Tymeera lost a prominent position at halfway and, although rallying approaching the final furlong, never threatened to get back on terms. (12/1)
Supreme Thought (14/1: 10/1-16/1)
2382 Kid Ory (15/2: 9/2-8/1)

2722 BROADSTAIRS LIMITED STKS (0-65) (3-Y.O+) (Class F)
3-30 (3-37) **1m 1f 149y** £2,808.30 (£778.80: £372.90) Stalls: Low GOING minus 0.33 sec per fur (GF)

				SP	RR	SF
2004[7]	**Regal Reprimand (65)** (GLewis) **3-8-8** PaulEddery(2) (chsd ldr ½-wy: led ins fnl f: pushed out)	—	**1**	7/2[2]	73	18
	Marytavy (64) (SirMarkPrescott) **3-8-5** GDuffield(8) (lw: led: hdd ins fnl f: unable qckn)	1¼	**2**	15/8[1]	68	13
1859[7]	**Princess Topaz (65)** (CACyzer) **3-8-5** SSanders(5) (hld up in tch: hrd rdn over 1f out: r.o ins fnl f)	nk	**3**	8/1	67	12
2522*	**Secret Ballot (IRE) (62)** (KMahdi) **3-8-5**(5) RFfrench(1) (b: lw: hld up: rdn over 2f out: styd on one pce ins fnl f)	3	**4**	7/2[2]	68	13
2374[2]	**The Executor (64)** (RJO'Sullivan) **7-9-5** JQuinn(4) (hld up: hdwy over 2f out: hrd rdn over 1f out: wknd ins fnl f)	¾	**5**	9/2[3]	64	20
2246[8]	**Manikato (USA) (62)** (DJSCosgrove) **3-8-8** CRutter(6) (lw: b.hind: rr: rdn 2f out: sn btn)	11	**6**	8/1	46	—
362[6]	**Be True (57)** (GLMoore) **3-8-8** CandyMorris(7) (chsd ldrs tl wknd over 2f out)	2	**7**	25/1	43	—
1804[5]	**Pardan (56)** (BPalling) **3-8-8** TSprake(3) (hld up: hdwy 3f out: wknd 2f out)	¾	**8**	25/1	42	—
				(SP 127.3%)	**8 Rn**	

2m 3.4 (5.70) CSF £10.84 TOTE £4.80: £1.20 £1.60 £4.00 (£8.80) OWNER The Voice Group Ltd (EPSOM) BRED Godolphin Management Co Ltd
WEIGHT FOR AGE 3yo-11lb
2004 Regal Reprimand was always travelling nicely, and his rider did not have to get serious to score. (7/2: 5/2-4/1)
Marytavy has grown into quite a nice-looking filly and ran a good race on her seasonal debut, making a lot of the running before being beaten for a turn of foot in the final furlong. Her shrewd connections should have no trouble finding a similar event. (15/8: 2/1-3/1)
887 Princess Topaz was never that far away and stayed on for pressure in the final furlong. (8/1)
2522* Secret Ballot (IRE) appeared to find the ground a bit too lively. (7/2: 7/4-4/1)
2374 The Executor made her bid early in the straight but soon cried enough. (9/2: 3/1-11/2)
1505 Manikato (USA) (8/1: 3/1-9/1)

2723 SEDLESCOMBE CLAIMING LIMITED STKS (0-55) (I) (3-Y.O+) (Class F)
4-00 (4-01) **6f 189y** £1,927.00 (£527.00: £247.00) Stalls: Low GOING minus 0.33 sec per fur (GF)

				SP	RR	SF
2244[9]	**Shashi (IRE) (55)** (PatMitchell) **5-8-11** PBloomfield(10) (chsd ldrs: rdn over 1f out: led wl ins fnl f: r.o)	—	**1**	11/2[3]	47	37
2488[13]	**Little Pilgrim (25)** (TMJones) **4-8-12** AMcGlone(6) (hld up: in rr: gd hdwy appr fnl f: fin wl)	nk	**2**	20/1	47	37
	Super Scravels (45) (KMahdi) **3-8-6**(5) RFfrench(1) (rr: gd hdwy & nt clr run over 1f out: swtchd lft: str run fnl f: fin wl)	½	**3**	10/1	53	35
2171[4]	**Prince of Fortune (47)** (MBlanshard) **3-8-6** NAdams(13) (sn led: hdd wl ins fnl f: one pce)	nk	**4**	6/1	47	29
2573[8]	**Abtaal (52)** (RJHodges) **7-8-12** RPerham(5) (dwlt: hld up: hdwy 2f out: rdn over 1f out: kpt on one pce ins fnl f)	½	**5**	11/1	44	34
2407*	**Feel A Line (51)** (BJMeehan) **3-9-0b** MTebbutt(11) (chsd ldrs: rdn over 1f out: one pce)	1½	**6**	7/4[1]	51	33
579[14]	**Jubilee Scholar (IRE) (45)** (GLMoore) **4-9-0** CandyMorris(7) (hld up: hdwy over 2f out: rdn over 1f out: one pce)	1	**7**	10/1	40	30
2310[15]	**Smiling Bess (33)** (JSKing) **4-8-11** PaulEddery(9) (prom tl wknd appr fnl f)	nk	**8**	25/1	37	27
2542[3]	**Move Smartly (IRE) (44)** (MrsLStubbs) **7-8-9v**(5) PRoberts(4) (nvr nrr)	½	**9**	8/1	39	29
1979[12]	**Paint It Black (54)** (DNicholls) **4-9-6b** AlexGreaves(8) (prom tl wknd appr fnl f)	hd	**10**	7/2[2]	44	34
1484[6]	**Komodo (USA) (24)** (JELong) **5-8-8** LeesaLong(3) (mid div tl wknd 2f out: hung bdly lft ins fnl f)	9	**11**	20/1	11	1
2395[11]	**Ladybower (IRE) (28)** (JRPoulton) **5-8-8** NVarley(2) (bhd fnl 4f)	2½	**12**	12/1	6	—
1236[15]	**Hever Golf Stormer (IRE) (50)** (BAPearce) **3-7-13**(7) CLowther(12) (bhd fnl 4f)	1¼	**13**	12/1	9	—
				(SP 154.6%)	**13 Rn**	

1m 23.9 (2.50) CSF £128.47 TOTE £6.10: £2.10 £12.60 £6.20 (£80.80) Trio £267.40; £267.40 to Beverley 15/7/97 OWNER Mrs Anna Sanders (NEWMARKET) BRED Sheikh Mohammed bin Rashid al Maktoum
WEIGHT FOR AGE 3yo-8lb
2177 Shashi (IRE) was never far away and, after taking it up approaching the final furlong, held on well. (11/2)
Little Pilgrim came from a long way back and was running on very strongly at the finish. (20/1)
Super Scravels was the unlucky horse here. She was making headway when stopped in her tracks below the distance. Switched left, she rallied strongly and none was finishing better, but she could never reach the principals. She must have gone close with a clear run. (10/1)
2171 Prince of Fortune made a bold effort to make all but had no more to give in the final furlong. (6/1: op 4/1)
512 Jubilee Scholar (IRE) (10/1: 8/1-12/1)
1631 Paint It Black raced prominently before dropping away approaching the final furlong. (7/2: 5/2-4/1)

2724 SEDLESCOMBE CLAIMING LIMITED STKS (0-55) (II) (3-Y.O+) (Class F)

4-30 (4-33) **6f 189y** £1,927.00 (£527.00: £247.00) Stalls: Low GOING minus 0.33 sec per fur (GF)

				SP	RR	SF
1969^{8}	**Rawi (50)** (MissGayKelleway) **4-8-11b**(5) RFfrench(6) (a.p: led appr fnl f: r.o)	—	1	6/1	52	29
1680^{10}	**Lancashire Legend (51)** (SDow) **4-9-0** JFEgan(1) (swtchd rt after 1f: hld up: hdwy over 2f out: ev ch wl ins fnl f: r.o)	nk	2	$5/1^{2}$	49	26
1965^{6}	**Pearl Dawn (IRE) (46)** (PCClarke) **7-8-9** MFenton(5) (hld up in rr: hdwy 2f out: rdn over 1f out: r.o)	1¾	3	$5/1^{2}$	40	17
2041^{12}	**Okay Baby (IRE) (26)** (JMBradley) **5-8-7** TSprake(3) (chsd ldrs: rdn over 1f out: ev ch ins fnl f: one pce)	s.h	4	12/1	38	15
2395^{8}	**Shermood (25)** (KTIvory) **4-8-5** SSanders(7) (mid div: rdn 2f out: kpt on one pce)	1¾	5	14/1	32	9
2332^{7}	**Jilly Woo (47)** (DRCElsworth) **3-7-4**(7) JFowle(10) (rr: rdn 2f out: styd on ins fnl f: nvr nrr)	2½	6	$11/2^{3}$	26	—
2310^{11}	**Hawaii Storm (FR) (24)** (DJSffrenchDavis) **9-8-3**(7) KerryBaker(13) (rr: c wd st: rdn over 2f out: kpt on one pce)	¾	7	33/1	29	6
2244^{10}	**Dorado Beach (40)** (LGCottrell) **3-8-9v**^{1} NCarlisle(12) (led: hdd appr fnl f: sn wknd)	1½	8	33/1	33	2
2407^{3}	**Windborn (44)** (CNAllen) **3-7-13** JQuinn(4) (mid div: rdn over 2f out: wknd over 1f out)	nk	9	$7/2^{1}$	22	—
2342^{10}	**Mubariz (IRE) (35)** (CSmith) **5-8-8** GDuffield(9) (sltly hmpd after 1f: a bhd)	2½	10	33/1	17	—
	Princess Renata (IRE) (45) (PatMitchell) **4-8-9** AMunro(11) (plld hrd: prom: wkng whn hmpd over 2f out: sn lost tch)	hd	11	50/1	18	—
2353^{5}	**Serape (38)** (MrsLStubbs) **4-8-9** DWright(2) (dwlt: sn in tch: rdn 3f out: wknd over 2f out)	nk	12	9/1	18	—
2313^{19}	**Sandweld (48)** (CADwyer) **3-8-2** NVarley(8) (chsd ldrs: wkng whn hmpd over 2f out: sn lost tch)	2	13	7/1	14	—

(SP 132.9%) **13 Rn**

1m 25.0 (3.60) CSF £36.01 TOTE £8.80: £4.10 £1.80 £2.20 (£19.60) Trio £30.00 OWNER Mr Chris Wilkinson (WHITCOMBE) BRED D. G. Mason

WEIGHT FOR AGE 3yo-8lb

STEWARDS' ENQUIRY Egan susp. 23-26/7/97 (careless riding).

383 Rawi was never far away. He led approaching the final furlong and saw it out well for pressure. (6/1: 4/1-7/1)

1374 Lancashire Legend was switched sharply right from his outside stall after a furlong, a manoeuvre which later cost his rider a suspension. Making headway approaching the straight, he came to have every chance inside the final furlong but could not quite get his head in front. (5/1: 4/1-6/1)

1479 Pearl Dawn (IRE) is a tricky customer but appeared to run her race. Held up towards the rear, she made headway early in the straight and, although staying on, never really looked like reaching the principals. (5/1)

1639 Okay Baby (IRE) had her chance entering the final furlong but could not find a change of gear. (12/1: op 8/1)

Jilly Woo (11/2: 6/1-10/1)

2407 Windborn was disappointing, dropping away halfway up the straight. She probably wants it softer. (7/2: 3/1-5/1)

2353 Serape (9/1: 16/1-8/1)

Sandweld (7/1: op 7/2)

2725 ROBERTSBRIDGE H'CAP (0-70) (3-Y.O) (Class E)

5-00 (5-01) **1m 4f** £3,018.25 (£901.00: £430.50: £195.25) Stalls: Low GOING minus 0.33 sec per fur (GF)

				SP	RR	SF
2398*	**Stahr (67)** (HCandy) **3-9-6b** CRutter(4) (mde virtually all: drvn along fnl 3f: r.o)	—	1	$5/4^{1}$	74	35
1592^{11}	**Trooper (65)** (RAkehurst) **3-9-4** SSanders(2) (hld up in tch: rdn 4f out: r.o ins fnl f)	nk	2	$7/2^{3}$	72	33
2521^{4}	**Tellion (68)** (MajorWRHern) **3-9-7** TSprake(3) (chsd wnr: ev ch ins fnl f: one pce)	1¼	3	$100/30^{2}$	73	34
2521^{9}	**Perlethorpe (58)** (MBell) **3-8-11** MFenton(6) (chsd ldrs: rdn 5f out: wknd over 1f out)	2	4	10/1	60	21
2182^{4}	**Keepsake (IRE) (50)** (MDIUsher) **3-8-3** RStreet(1) (hld up: rdn 2f out: sn wknd)	3½	5	4/1	48	9

(SP 118.8%) **5 Rn**

2m 37.7 (6.50) CSF £6.07 TOTE £1.80: £2.40 £1.10 (£5.20) OWNER Mrs David Blackburn (WANTAGE) BRED Mrs M. J. Blackburn

2398* Stahr was given a tremendous ride by Rutter, being ridden and pushed along throughout the final three furlongs, both he and the horse just would not give in. (5/4)

Trooper looked a difficult ride, coming under pressure four furlongs out. He finally picked up approaching the final furlong and ran on well. (7/2: 5/2-4/1)

2521 Tellion had every chance but just could not find a change of pace. (100/30: 7/4-7/2)

485 Perlethorpe (10/1: 5/1-14/1)

2182 Keepsake (IRE) (4/1: 5/1-3/1)

2726 LEVY BOARD MAIDEN APPRENTICE STKS (3-Y.O+) (Class F)

5-30 (5-30) **1m 4f** £2,577.30 (£712.80: £339.90) GOING minus 0.33 sec per fur (GF)

				SP	RR	SF
842^{3}	**King Kato (88)** (MrsAJPerrett) **4-9-4**(3) GayeHarwood(2) (chsd ldr 5f out: pushed along 3f out: led over 1f out: eased nr fin)	—	1	$5/6^{1}$	83+	45
1784^{3}	**La Curamalal (IRE) (76)** (GWragg) **3-8-3** GMilligan(1) (hld up: rdn over 2f out: styd on to chse wnr ins fnl: r.o)	1¼	2	$7/4^{2}$	76	25
2411^{6}	**French Mist (72)** (SDow) **3-7-10**(7) DSalt(3) (led: hdd over 1f out: one pce)	3	3	$7/1^{3}$	72	21
2487^{5}	**Tribal Moon (IRE) (65)** (LadyHerries) **4-9-4**(3) PDoe(4) (chsd ldr 7f: wknd 3f out)	10	4	10/1	64	26

(SP 112.5%) **4 Rn**

2m 36.2 (5.00) CSF £2.48 TOTE £1.50: (£1.20) OWNER Mrs Jenny Ells (PULBOROUGH) BRED D. Macrae

WEIGHT FOR AGE 3yo-13lb

842 King Kato ultimately won this like his price suggested he would. He had to be rousted along before the home turn but, leading below the distance, was well on top at the finish. The further he goes, the better he appears to be. (5/6)

1784 La Curamalal (IRE) ran a sound enough race but is flattered by the winning margin. (7/4)

2411 French Mist set a strong pace but had no more to give from below the distance. (7/1)

2487 Tribal Moon (IRE) was not a factor in the final three furlongs. (10/1: 6/1-12/1)

T/Jkpt: £7,100.00 (0.4 Tckts); £2,105.83 to Beverley 15/7/97. T/Plpt: £80.20 (206.96 Tckts). T/Qdpt: £60.90 (12.72 Tckts) SM

2550-WINDSOR (Fig. 8) (Good to firm)
Monday July 14th
WEATHER: warm WIND: almost nil

2727 IKM NETWORK COMMUNICATIONS (S) STKS (3 & 4-Y.O) (Class G)
6-30 (6-31) **1m 3f 135y** £2,146.50 (£599.00: £289.50) Stalls: High GOING minus 0.22 sec per fur (GF)

				SP	RR	SF
2380^{6}	**Nubile (63)** (BWHills) **3-8-5** DHolland(4) (lw: carried wd 6f out: hdwy 3f out: styd on to ld last strides)	—	1	$11/8^{1}$	52	26
2535^{7}	**Le Grand Gousier (USA) (56)** (RJRWilliams) **3-8-10** RCochrane(10) (lw: led: hrd rdn over 3f out: hdd fnl strides)	hd	2	$9/2^{2}$	57	31
2487^{11}	**Running Free (IRE) (45)** (MJFetherston-Godley) **3-8-10** DaneO'Neill(1) (chsd ldr: ev ch fnl f: r.o)	½	3	33/1	56	30
2376^{2}	**Warrior King (IRE) (43)** (MrsPNDutfield) **3-8-5**(5) AimeeCook(9) (hdwy fnl 2f: nrst fin)	2½	4	9/1	53	27
2602^{14}	**Sheilas Dream (48)** (GLMoore) **4-9-4** CandyMorris(8) (a.p: no hdwy fnl 3f)	1½	5	20/1	46	33
2390^{10}	**Rivers Magic (60)** (JJBridger) **4-9-6**(3) MHenry(6) (swtg: nvr nr to chal)	4	6	20/1	45	32
2531^{11}	**Riscatto (USA) (53)** (WRMuir) **3-9-1** KFallon(3) (lw: hrd rdn over 3f out: no rspnse)	2½	7	$11/2^{3}$	47	21
2531^{5}	**Fortune Hopper (52)** (JPearce) **3-8-10** GBardwell(2) (chsd ldrs: ev ch 3f out: sn wknd)	nk	8	10/1	41	15
2322^{2}	**Illegally Yours (38)** (LMontagueHall) **4-8-11**(7) CLowther(7) (hdwy 7f out: wknd over 3f out)	hd	9	16/1	36	23
	Flying Angel (ABarrow) **3-8-5** NAdams(5) (w'like: a bhd: t.o)	dist	10	20/1	—	—
				(SP 117.9%)	**10 Rn**	

2m 32.8 (6.80) CSF £6.34 TOTE £2.80: £1.20 £2.10 £3.50 (£4.50) Trio £35.80 OWNER Mr J. Hanson (LAMBOURN) BRED Glebe Stud
WEIGHT FOR AGE 3yo-13lb
Nubile sold WMusson 8,000gns. Warrior King (IRE) clmd North End Partners.

1567 Nubile, carried wide at halfway, made headway in the straight but was flat out to beat some modest rivals. It was not until the final strides that she forced her head in front. (11/8: evens-6/4)
1964 Le Grand Gousier (USA), dropped in trip, set out to make all the running. He came under pressure more than three furlongs from home and, though appearing likely to be caught some way out, it was not until the last few strides that he was finally collared. (9/2: 3/1-5/1)
1296 Running Free (IRE) was in second place for much of the way. He still had every chance entering the last furlong but could not find quite enough. (33/1)
2376 Warrior King (IRE) stayed on late but was never on terms with the leading trio. (9/1)
1796 Sheilas Dream, always chasing the leaders, could make no headway under pressure in the straight. (20/1)
582* Riscatto (USA) (11/2: 7/2-6/1)
2357 Fortune Hopper (10/1: 6/1-12/1)

2728 E.B.F. JUNE MAIDEN STKS (2-Y.O F) (Class D)
7-00 (7-10) **5f 217y** £3,647.50 (£1,105.00: £540.00: £257.50) Stalls: High GOING minus 0.60 sec per fur (F)

				SP	RR	SF
	Miss Zafonic (FR) (RHannon) **2-8-11** PatEddery(17) (scope: rdn over 2f out: hdwy over 1f out: qcknd to ld ins fnl f)	—	1	$7/2^{1}$	86+	35
2227^{4}	**Dodo (IRE)** (DRCElsworth) **2-8-11** KFallon(10) (hmpd s: sn prom: ev ch fnl f: r.o)	¾	2	$8/1^{2}$	84	33
2024^{18}	**Jay Gee (IRE)** (GGMargarson) **2-8-11** DBiggs(9) (wnt rt s: a.p: r.o one pce fnl 2f)	3½	3	25/1	75	24
2371^{3}	**Sada** (MajorWRHern) **2-8-11** GCarter(14) (a.p: led over 2f out tl over 1f out: nt qckn)	nk	4	$7/2^{1}$	74	23
	Robsart (IRE) (JRFanshawe) **2-8-11** DHarrison(3) (neat: hdwy 2f out: styd on: nrst fin)	¾	5	12/1	72+	21
	Jungle Story (IRE) (PTWalwyn) **2-8-11** RCochrane(7) (leggy: unf: bit bkwd: s.s: stdy hdwy 2f out: r.o)	3	6	$9/1^{3}$	64+	13
2370^{9}	**Gipsy Moth** (BJMeehan) **2-8-11** MTebbutt(5) (w ldrs: led over 1f out: hdd & wknd ins fnl f)	½	7	50/1	63	12
	Blue Zola (IRE) (MBell) **2-8-11** TQuinn(2) (neat: nvr nrr)	hd	8	14/1	62	11
2138^{5}	**Mighty Magic** (MrsPNDutfield) **2-8-8**(3) RHavlin(13) (a.p: no hdwy fnl 2f)	2	9	14/1	57	6
	Chlo-Jo (AGFoster) **2-8-11** DHolland(11) (neat: bit bkwd: nvr bttr than mid div)	1¼	10	50/1	54	3
	Sunley Seeker (MRChannon) **2-8-11** RPerham(22) (neat: nvr on terms)	s.h	11	33/1	53	2
	Runaround (SDow) **2-8-11** JFEgan(18) (str: bit bkwd: s.s: nvr nr ldrs)	nk	12	50/1	53	2
	Pinup (GLewis) **2-8-11** PaulEddery(20) (neat: a bhd)	1¼	13	20/1	49	—
2371^{7}	**Blueberry** (SDow) **2-8-11** DaneO'Neill(8) (a bhd)	nk	14	25/1	48	—
2312^{7}	**Ghorapani (IRE)** (MrsNMacauley) **2-8-11v¹** BDoyle(16) (b: led over 3f)	hd	15	50/1	48	—
2123^{6}	**Dooze (IRE)** (JHMGosden) **2-8-11v¹** LDettori(21) (w ldrs tl wknd over 2f out)	nk	16	10/1	47	—
1321^{6}	**Sassy (IRE)** (APJarvis) **2-8-11** SDrowne(19) (a bhd)	nk	17	50/1	47	—
	Risada (IRE) (DRLoder) **2-8-8**(3) PMcCabe(6) (neat: a bhd)	2	18	12/1	41	—
	Safabee (MJHaynes) **2-8-11** GBardwell(12) (unf: s.s: a wl bhd)	2½	19	50/1	35	—
836^{15}	**Secret Tango** (APJones) **2-8-11** RPrice(15) (lw: prom over 3f)	1½	20	50/1	31	—
	Princess Deya (DrJDScargill) **2-8-11** JTate(4) (neat: bit bkwd: s.s: a t.o)	dist	21	50/1	—	—
				(SP 134.4%)	**21 Rn**	

1m 11.2 (0.70) CSF £27.09 TOTE £4.10: £1.90 £2.50 £7.00 (£12.80) Trio £274.60 OWNER Midcourts (MARLBOROUGH) BRED Pat Eddery and Terrence-Charles Ellis

Miss Zafonic (FR) has plenty of scope for improvement and made an impressive debut. She was being pushed along in mid-division soon after halfway, but produced a sustained effort to lead inside the final furlong, and won readily. The time of the race was good, and she can be expected to go on to better things. (7/2)
2227 Dodo (IRE), suited by the longer trip and faster ground, was soon well placed, despite being hampered at the start. She had every chance entering the final furlong but could not quicken with the winner. (8/1: 6/1-10/1)
1457 Jay Gee (IRE) dived to the right at the start but was soon well placed. She kept on at one pace under pressure in the last two furlongs. (25/1)
2371 Sada, close-up from the start, went to the front over two furlongs from home but could find no extra when headed approaching the final furlong. (7/2: 5/2-9/2)
Robsart (IRE), in mid-division to halfway, began to stay on from the two-furlong marker but could not quite reach the leaders. She will stay further in due course. (12/1: 5/1-14/1)
Jungle Story (IRE) completely missed the break but made significant headway two furlongs out without threatening to trouble the leaders. Considerable improvement can be expected. (9/1: 5/1-10/1)
2138 Mighty Magic (14/1: 6/1-16/1)
2123 Dooze (IRE) (10/1: 7/1-14/1)
Risada (IRE) (12/1: 5/1-14/1)

2729 CROWN RECRUITMENT & TRAINING RATED STKS H'CAP (0-95) (3-Y.O+) (Class C)

7-30 (7-33) **1m 2f 7y** £4,737.45 (£1,772.14: £866.07: £371.85: £165.93: £83.56) Stalls: High GOING minus 0.22 sec per fur (GF)

	Horse	Dist	Pos	SP	RR	SF
1973[2]	**Sir Talbot (85)** (RHannon) **3-8-0** JQuinn(8) (mde all: r.o wl)	—	**1**	5/1[3]	95	44
2013[17]	**Future Perfect (85)** (PFICole) **3-8-0** CRutter(7) (lw: a.p: chsd wnr & ev ch fnl 3f: nt qckn)	1½	**2**	6/1	93	42
1768[12]	**The Dilettanti (USA) (95)** (JARToller) **4-9-7** SSanders(4) (chsd wnr: hrd rdn over 3f out: r.o one pce)	3	**3**	5/1[3]	98	58
787[10]	**Dance So Suite (89)** (PFICole) **5-9-1** TQuinn(1) (lw: hdwy 4f out: one pce fnl 3f)	1½	**4**	12/1	89	49
	Grief (IRE) (83) (DRCElsworth) **4-8-9** RCochrane(3) (b: bhd tl r.o steadily fnl 2f)	2	**5**	16/1	80	40
2026[23]	**Yalta (IRE) (81)** (RCharlton) **4-8-7** PatEddery(10) (hld up in rr: hdwy 3f out: rdn 2f out: nt qckn)	hd	**6**	11/4[1]	78	38
2528[6]	**Break the Rules (84)** (DNicholls) **5-8-10** AlexGreaves(5) (nvr nr to chal)	hd	**7**	9/2[2]	81	41
2341[8]	**River's Source (USA) (83)** (BWHills) **3-7-7**(5) RFfrench(9) (prom tl wknd 3f out)	1¾	**8**	8/1	77	26
2133[9]	**Gift Token (90)** (MajorDNChappell) **3-8-5** GCarter(2) (lw: prom tl wknd 3f out)	¾	**9**	16/1	83	32

(SP 123.0%) **9 Rn**

2m 7.8 (2.90) CSF £34.18 CT £148.29 TOTE £6.10: £1.80 £1.90 £2.10 (£23.10) Trio £41.90 OWNER Mrs F. Percy-Davis (MARLBOROUGH) BRED Mrs W. H. Gibson Fleming

WEIGHT FOR AGE 3yo-11lb

1973 Sir Talbot made all the running. Keeping on strongly, he had his rivals in trouble a long way out and never appeared likely to be caught. (5/1)

1404 Future Perfect, always one of the leaders, was sent in pursuit of the winner from the three-furlong marker but, despite having every chance, could not peg him back. (6/1: op 4/1)

939* The Dilettanti (USA) showed his Epsom running to be all wrong. In second place until he came under pressure over three furlongs out, he kept on without finding the pace to challenge. (5/1)

Dance So Suite loomed up on the outside three furlongs out, but proved one-paced in the final quarter-mile. He is probably just coming to hand. (12/1: op 8/1)

Grief (IRE), having his first outing on the Flat for nine months, was at the back of the field until running on in fine style in the closing stages. Considerable improvement can be expected. (16/1)

Yalta (IRE) was held up in last place but did not settle properly. He made ground readily enough three furlongs out but, under pressure at the two-furlong marker, found disappointingly little. (11/4: 2/1-3/1)

2730 ORBIS SECURITY SYSTEMS H'CAP (0-70) (3-Y.O+ F & M) (Class E)

8-00 (8-01) **1m 67y** £3,062.50 (£925.00: £450.00: £212.50) Stalls: High GOING minus 0.22 sec per fur (GF)

	Horse	Dist	Pos	SP	RR	SF
2485[7]	**Comanche Companion (57)** (TJNaughton) **7-9-8** PatEddery(11) (lw: led tl over 1f out: led ins fnl f: r.o wl)	—	**1**	9/1	69	50
2550[6]	**Fancy Design (IRE) (33)** (PMitchell) **4-7-7**(5)ow2 AimeeCook(5) (lw: hld up: hdwy 3f out: ev ch over 1f out: nt qckn)	1½	**2**	16/1	42	21
2040[2]	**Calamander (IRE) (65)** (WRMuir) **3-9-7** DaneO'Neill(13) (lw: chsd wnr: led over 1f out tl ins fnl f)	1	**3**	15/2[3]	72	44
1826[3]	**First Chance (IRE) (68)** (DRCElsworth) **3-9-10** RCochrane(1) (lw: rapid hdwy 2f out: one pce fnl f)	2	**4**	12/1	71	43
2369*	**Queen's Insignia (USA) (57)** (PFICole) **4-9-8** TQuinn(7) (a.p: one pce fnl 2f)	3	**5**	5/1[1]	55	36
2390[7]	**Papita (IRE) (63)** (SDow) **3-9-5** JFEgan(6) (hdwy fnl 2f: nvr nrr)	2	**6**	12/1	57	29
2555[7]	**Perchance To Dream (IRE) (46)** (BRMillman) **3-8-2**ow4 SDrowne(8) (prom tl wknd 2f out)	s.h	**7**	16/1	40	8
2199[9]	**Impetuous Lady (USA) (35)** (WJMusson) **4-8-0** JQuinn(10) (nvr bttr than mid div)	1½	**8**	20/1	26	7
2310[5]	**Cats Bottom (47)** (AGNewcombe) **5-8-12** RPrice(4) (wl bhd tl hdwy 2f out: nvr nr to chal)	nk	**9**	10/1	37	18
2416*	**Sharp 'n' Shady (60)** (CFWall) **4-9-11** GDuffield(15) (hdwy & rdn over 2f out: wknd over 1f out)	nk	**10**	13/2[2]	50	31
2119[7]	**Sis Garden (54)** (JCullinan) **4-9-0**(5) RFfrench(9) (nrst fin)	1	**11**	14/1	42	23
2317[4]	**On The Green (37)** (AHide) **4-8-2v** GBardwell(16) (plld hrd: nvr nr ldrs)	5	**12**	14/1	15	—
1239[13]	**Mighty Flow (52)** (MrsPNDutfield) **3-8-5**(3) RHavlin(14) (prom tl wknd 3f out)	¾	**13**	25/1	29	1
2491[7]	**Calandrella (33)** (GBBalding) **4-7-12** NVarley(17) (a bhd)	2	**14**	33/1	6	—
2491[5]	**Balfour Lady (55)** (JARToller) **3-8-11** SSanders(12) (prom tl wknd 3f out)	2	**15**	11/1	24	—
1483[5]	**Don't Forget Shoka (IRE) (40)** (JSMoore) **3-7-10** NAdams(2) (prom tl wknd over 3f out)	7	**16**	33/1	—	—
2424[10]	**Eternally Grateful (35)** (KTIvory) **4-7-9**(5) RMullen(3) (a bhd)	3	**17**	33/1	—	—

(SP 127.1%) **17 Rn**

1m 46.1 (3.90) CSF £128.81 CT £1,077.15 TOTE £10.80: £2.50 £3.50 £1.70 £2.70 (£153.40) Trio £366.10 OWNER Hever Racing Club (EPSOM) BRED The National Stud

LONG HANDICAP Don't Forget Shoka (IRE) 7-6

WEIGHT FOR AGE 3yo-9lb

Comanche Companion came right back to her best with a fine win. She made the running and, after looking beaten when headed below the distance, regained the advantage inside the final furlong. (9/1)

2550 Fancy Design (IRE) raced in mid-field and moved up very smoothly to challenge approaching the final furlong. When put to her best, she could not peg back the winner. (16/1)

2040 Calamander (IRE) raced in second place until leading approaching the final furlong. She could not hold the winner's renewed challenge. (15/2)

1826 First Chance (IRE), with the worst draw, was at the back of the field until making rapid headway at the two-furlong marker. Having reached fourth place at the distance, she could make no further progress. (12/1)

2369* Queen's Insignia (USA), always in the leading group, ran on at one pace under pressure in the final quarter-mile. (5/1)

506 Papita (IRE) was towards the back of the field until running on well in the last two furlongs. (12/1)

2731 FINANCIAL TIMES MAGAZINE MAIDEN STKS (3-Y.O) (Class D)

8-30 (8-32) **1m 2f 7y** £3,662.00 (£1,106.00: £538.00: £254.00) Stalls: High GOING minus 0.22 sec per fur (GF)

	Horse	Dist	Pos	SP	RR	SF
2379[2]	**Masharik (IRE)** (MajorWRHern) **3-8-9** RCochrane(5) (hmpd s: sn prom: led over 2f out: r.o wl)	—	**1**	9/4[1]	85	40
	Kayf Tara (MRStoute) **3-9-0** KFallon(11) (str: scope: bit bkwd: rdn 3f out: swtchd lft & hdwy 2f out: r.o ins fnl f)	2	**2**	9/2[3]	87	42
	Kamanev (IRE) (MRStoute) **3-9-0** DHolland(16) (leggy: scope: lw: gd hdwy over 1f out: r.o ins fnl f)	1¼	**3**	14/1	85	40
2379[3]	**Mengaab (USA) (82)** (JHMGosden) **3-9-0v**[1] LDettori(15) (a.p: ev ch over 1f out: nt qckn)	¾	**4**	4/1[2]	84	39

2131^{4}	**Azores** (PFICole) **3-9-0** TQuinn(10) (led tl over 2f out: r.o one pce)	2	**5**	16/1	80	35
1936^{W}	**Kristal Bridge** (PWHarris) **3-8-2**$^{(7)}$ CLowther(7) (w ldr: ev ch over 1f out: wknd fnl f)	nk	**6**	9/1	75	30
	Moran (RFJohnsonHoughton) **3-9-0** SSanders(17) (str: scope: bkwd: stdy hdwy 2f out: nvr nr to chal)	2	**7**	25/1	77	32
2287^{3}	**Alarmist** (RCharlton) **3-9-0** TSprake(8) (prom tl wknd over 1f out)	½	**8**	6/1	76	31
2389^{7}	**Rocky Dance (FR)** (APJarvis) **3-8-9** SDrowne(6) (lw: gd hdwy 3f out: wknd over 1f out)	11	**9**	25/1	53	8
2287^{6}	**My Roland (IRE)** (JFfitch-Heyes) **3-9-0** DHarrison(2) (lw: nvr bttr than mid div)	3	**10**	50/1	54	9
1823^{10}	**Flying Colours (IRE) (70)** (CJBenstead) **3-8-9** AMcGlone(3) (lw: a bhd)	¾	**11**	33/1	47	2
2315^{8}	**Prince Alex (IRE)** (ACStewart) **3-9-0** MRoberts(1) (a bhd: rn v.wd 6f out)	hd	**12**	16/1	52	7
	Shailendra (IRE) (JHMGosden) **3-8-9** GHind(14) (str: scope: bkwd: nvr on terms)	5	**13**	20/1	39	—
	Fully Booked (JWHills) **3-8-6**$^{(3)}$ MHenry(4) (prom tl wknd 3f out)	3½	**14**	50/1	34	—
2410^{9}	**Crompton Lights** (DJSCosgrove) **3-8-7**$^{(7)}$ SGaillard(13) (a bhd)	6	**15**	66/1	29	—
	Kalmoojid (CJHill) **3-9-0** DaneO'Neill(12) (leggy: bit bkwd: a bhd: hmpd 6f out)	9	**16**	33/1	15	—
				(SP 135.4%)		**16 Rn**

2m 9.4 (4.50) CSF £11.36 TOTE £3.40: £1.40 £2.10 £4.10 (£7.40) Trio £27.00 OWNER Mr Hamdan Al Maktoum (LAMBOURN) BRED Shadwell Estate Company Limited

2379 Masharik (IRE), although hampered at the start, was soon travelling well on the heels of the leaders. She went to the front over two furlongs from home and stayed on strongly. (9/4)

Kayf Tara, a tall, attractive colt, improved from mid-division on the inside three furlongs out. Switched to the centre of the course, he ran on strongly but did not unduly trouble the winner. (9/2: 7/4-5/1)

Kamanev (IRE), a quality colt with plenty of scope, improved quickly approaching the final furlong. Though staying on, he did not trouble the winner but should find it easier to win races. (14/1: op 6/1)

2379 Mengaab (USA), visored for the first time, was close-up throughout but, after having every chance, could find no extra in the last furlong. (4/1)

2131 Azores, given a positive ride, tried to make all the running and kept on at one pace when headed over two furlongs from home. (16/1)

Kristal Bridge disputed the lead from the start, and did not weaken until the final furlong. (9/1)

Moran, a deep-girthed individual, made an encouraging debut. He improved at the two-furlong marker but, though staying on, could not quite find the pace to trouble the leaders. Improvement can be expected. (25/1)

2287 Alarmist (6/1: 3/1-7/1)

2732 RAFFLES NIGHTCLUB AND PIPER CHAMPAGNE H'CAP (0-60) (3-Y.O+) (Class F)

9-00 (9-03) **5f 10y** £2,897.50 (£810.00: £392.50) Stalls: High GOING minus 0.60 sec per fur (F)

				SP	RR	SF
2536^{3}	**Tommy Tempest (36)** (REPeacock) **8-8-4**^{ow1} SSanders(6) (mde all: r.o wl)	—	**1**	9/1^{3}	48	30
2481^{5}	**Dancing Mystery (41)** (EAWheeler) **3-8-4** TSprake(10) (a.p: r.o wl ins fnl f)	½	**2**	10/1	51	29
2384^{6}	**Nellie North (45)** (GMMcCourt) **4-8-13** DHarrison(5) (lw: w ldrs: rdn over 2f out: r.o)	hd	**3**	11/1	55	38
1957^{8}	**Mindrace (59)** (KTIvory) **4-9-13** CScally(14) (a.p: r.o ins fnl f)	nk	**4**	8/1^{2}	68	51
2536^{10}	**Ashkernazy (IRE) (45)** (NEBerry) **6-8-13** RPerham(17) (a.p: ev ch 1f out: nt qckn)	½	**5**	10/1	53	36
2406^{4}	**Ice Age (56)** (RJRWilliams) **3-9-5** RCochrane(12) (s.s: hdwy whn nt clr run over 1f out & ins fnl f: unlucky)	½	**6**	8/1^{2}	62	40
2496^{3}	**Dona Filipa (39)** (MissLCSiddall) **4-8-7** KFallon(2) (lw: nrst fin)	1	**7**	12/1	42	25
2162^{3}	**Napier Star (45)** (MrsNMacauley) **4-8-13v** BDoyle(15) (lw: prom over 2f)	nk	**8**	10/1	47	30
2481^{7}	**Whizz Kid (47)** (JJBridger) **3-8-7**$^{(3)}$ MHenry(4) (nrst fin)	hd	**9**	14/1	49	27
2581^{3}	**Littlestone Rocket (58)** (WRMuir) **3-9-7b** DaneO'Neill(13) (prom 3f)	2½	**10**	8/1^{2}	52	30
2162^{5}	**Robo Magic (USA) (44)** (LMontagueHall) **5-8-5**$^{(7)}$ CLowther(8) (b: mid div: rdn over 2f out: no hdwy)	3	**11**	11/2^{1}	28	11
2536^{2}	**Bright Paragon (IRE) (39)** (KTIvory) **8-8-0**$^{(7)}$ SCarson(1) (b: b.hind: hrd rdn over 2f out: no rspnse)	½	**12**	9/1^{3}	22	5
520^{12}	**Step On Degas (58)** (MJFetherston-Godley) **4-9-7**$^{(5)}$ RFfrench(3) (a bhd)	hd	**13**	12/1	40	23
2278^{6}	**Kildee Boy (44)** (APJones) **3-8-7** RPrice(7) (lw: s.s: a bhd)	4	**14**	33/1	14	—
	Double Or Bust (29) (CJHill) **4-7-6b**$^{1(5)ow1}$ RMullen(9) (swtg: a bhd)	1¼	**15**	33/1	—	—
1644^{7}	**Bestelina (47)** (DJSCosgrove) **3-8-10** GCarter(11) (lw: a bhd)	½	**16**	25/1	11	—
				(SP 136.1%)		**16 Rn**

60.2 secs (0.50) CSF £96.24 CT £946.48 TOTE £14.10: £2.70 £2.50 £2.80 £3.00 (£119.50) Trio £417.20 OWNER Mr R. E. Peacock (MALMESBURY) BRED D. J. Wood

WEIGHT FOR AGE 3yo-5lb

2536 Tommy Tempest gamely held off a whole host of challengers in the last two furlongs. (9/1: 6/1-10/1)

2481 Dancing Mystery, though never far behind the leaders, did not really find his stride until too late. He snatched second place near the line. (10/1)

2384 Nellie North was soon racing in second place and under pressure at halfway. She kept on well but could not peg back the winner. (11/1: 8/1-12/1)

1814 Mindrace, close up throughout, kept on well under pressure in the closing stages under his big weight. (8/1)

Ashkernazy (IRE), fast away on the rails, did not quite have the pace to hold her position and had to be switched to challenge. She kept on well to the end. (10/1)

2406 Ice Age was very unlucky. After a slow start, he was making rapid headway when denied a clear run twice in the last furlong-and-a-half. In the circumstances, he did extremely well to finish so close. (8/1)

2321 Whizz Kid (14/1: op 8/1)

2162 Robo Magic (USA), the medium of a gamble, proved disappointing. Under pressure in mid-field at halfway, there was never any hope. (11/2)

325 Step On Degas (12/1: 8/1-14/1)

T/Plpt: £236.10 (101.52 Tckts). T/Qdpt: £65.20 (23.1 Tckts) AK/Hn

2493-BEVERLEY (R-H) (Good to firm)
Tuesday July 15th
WEATHER: overcast & v.warm WIND: fresh across

2733 MITSUBISHI APPRENTICE H'CAP (0-65) (3-Y.O) (Class F)
2-00 (2-01) **1m 100y** £3,111.00 (£933.00: £449.00: £207.00) Stalls: High GOING minus 0.35 sec per fur (F)

Form	Horse / details	Dist	Pos	SP	RR	SF
2415[7]	**High Spirits (IRE) (59)** (TDEasterby) **3-9-3b**(3) TEDurcan(1) (bhd: hdwy over 3f out: r.o wl to ld wl ins fnl f)	—	1	6/1[2]	71	44
1624[5]	**Sharp Deed (IRE) (54)** (PJMakin) **3-9-1** RHavlin(13) (a chsng ldrs: styd on to ld wl ins fnl f: sn hdd & nt qckn)	½	2	9/1	65	38
2317[5]	**Gipsy Princess (59)** (MWEasterby) **3-9-3**(3) GParkin(11) (led 2f: cl up: led over 2f out tl wl ins fnl f: no ex)	1¾	3	9/2[1]	67	40
2523[3]	**Star Turn (IRE) (60)** (MBell) **3-9-4**(3) RMullen(14) (lw: bhd: hdwy ent st: prom & rdn over 2f out: wandered u.p & one pce)	5	4	9/2[1]	58	31
2045[11]	**Tipperary Sunset (IRE) (45)** (JJQuinn) **3-8-1**(5) DMernagh(12) (lw: hdwy 3f out: hung lft: styd on: no imp)	2	5	14/1	40	13
2463[2]	**Samspet (44)** (RAFahey) **3-8-0**(5) RWinston(7) (led after 2f: c stands' side st: hdd over 2f out: grad wknd)	3	6	7/1[3]	33	6
2392[4]	**Miss Barcelona (IRE) (45)** (MJPolglase) **3-8-1**(5) DarrenWilliams(4) (chsd ldrs tl outpcd fnl 2½f)	s.h	7	14/1	34	7
2569[7]	**Silent Valley (46)** (MissLCSiddall) **3-8-2**(5) TSiddall(10) (lw: sn wl bhd: c wd st: sme late hdwy)	1	8	20/1	33	6
2495[5]	**Petite Risk (55)** (KWHogg) **3-9-2** FLynch(9) (pushed along & hdwy ent st: btn 2f out)	5	9	14/1	32	5
2173[5]	**Rambo Tango (53)** (BRCambidge) **3-8-9**(5) IonaWands(2) (swtg: sn pushed along: in tch 5f)	¾	10	33/1	29	2
	Freedom of Troy (50) (JLEyre) **3-8-6**(5) SBuckley(3) (s.i.s: n.d)	hd	11	25/1	26	—
2040[5]	**Rochea (49)** (MrsNMacauley) **3-8-7**(3) PRoberts(5) (b.nr hind: sn bhd & drvn along: n.d)	1½	12	11/1	22	—
642[4]	**Mendoza (56)** (DJGMurraySmith) **3-9-3** PFessey(6) (in tch to st: sn bhd)	2½	13	10/1	24	—
2547[10]	**Loch-Hurn Lady (59)** (KWHogg) **3-9-1**(5) PBradley(8) (chsd ldrs tl wknd fnl 2f)	nk	14	25/1	27	—

(SP 126.0%) **14 Rn**

1m 47.3 (3.30) CSF £53.93 CT £256.37 TOTE £7.90: £2.80 £3.30 £1.80 (£64.00) Trio £54.80 OWNER Mrs J. B. Mountifield (MALTON) BRED Sean Twomey

2415 High Spirits (IRE), who apparently did not like the soft ground last time (although he won with give previously), acted well on this faster surface and, although given plenty to do, won in good style. (6/1)
1624 Sharp Deed (IRE), who seemed not to stay last time, was dropped back in trip and had no excuses, but was tapped for toe in the closing stages. (9/1)
2317 Gipsy Princess put in her second decent run on the trot, and is obviously in good heart if the right race can be found. (9/2: op 3/1)
2523 Star Turn (IRE) keeps running reasonably and gives the impression that, if he can be persuaded, there is more there. (9/2)
1041 Tipperary Sunset (IRE) is coming to himself looks-wise and, despite getting unbalanced under pressure, this was not a bad effort. (14/1)
2463 Samspet made the mistake of crossing over to the stands' side early in the straight, and threw away all chance. (7/1)

2734 BOSCH CLAIMING STKS (3-Y.O) (Class E)
2-30 (2-31) **7f 100y** £3,208.50 (£963.00: £464.00: £214.50) Stalls: High GOING minus 0.35 sec per fur (F)

Form	Horse / details	Dist	Pos	SP	RR	SF
1661*	**Caution (80)** (MrsJRRamsden) **3-8-6** JFortune(4) (lw: trckd ldrs: effrt over 2f out: led ins fnl f: rdn & r.o wl)	—	1	10/11[1]	67+	44
2659[6]	**Bollero (IRE) (56)** (JBerry) **3-8-1**(3) PFessey(2) (led & sn clr: hdd ins fnl f: r.o)	1½	2	5/1[3]	62	39
1861[6]	**Skyers Flyer (IRE) (67)** (RonaldThompson) **3-8-2** TWilliams(6) (swtg: hld up: hdwy 3f out: btn wl over 1f out)	8	3	9/2[2]	43	20
2496[6]	**Mischievous Time** (ASmith) **3-8-7** RLappin(1) (chsd clr ldr: hdwy u.p 3f out: btn wl over 1f out)	4	4	16/1	39	16
2050[8]	**Petite Danseuse (72)** (CADwyer) **3-8-0**(3) DO'Donohoe(5) (hld up: nvr trbld ldrs)	¾	5	5/1[3]	33	10
	Newtons Corner (IRE) (DNicholls) **3-8-11** AlexGreaves(3) (w'like: leggy: bit bkwd: hld up: outpcd 3f out: sn bhd)	18	6	20/1	3	—

(SP 114.5%) **6 Rn**

1m 33.7 (1.70) CSF £5.63 TOTE £2.10: £1.30 £2.10 (£3.80) OWNER L C and A E Sigsworth (THIRSK) BRED L. C. and Mrs A. E. Sigsworth
Caution clmd Ian Thomas £12,000

1661* Caution only had one serious opponent and beat her really well. She has a really good attitude and was subsequently claimed. (10/11: evens-6/5)
2659 Bollero (IRE) made this a good gallop but, despite a valiant effort, met one far too good in the winner. She is keeping her form well. (5/1)
1861 Skyers Flyer (IRE) is a funny customer who has ability when things go right, but she was off the bit too far out this time. (9/2)
2496 Mischievous Time was dropped in class and upped in trip and there was no real encouragement. (16/1)
1780 Petite Danseuse could never get into this and was not given a hard time. (5/1)
Newtons Corner (IRE) needed this, his first outing, and had to be led part of the way to the start. He then blew up a long way out. (20/1)

2735 COMET H'CAP (0-90) (3-Y.O) (Class C)
3-00 (3-01) **7f 100y** £5,442.50 (£1,640.00: £795.00: £372.50) Stalls: High GOING minus 0.35 sec per fur (F)

Form	Horse / details	Dist	Pos	SP	RR	SF
2043[6]	**Cee-N-K (IRE) (69)** (MJohnston) **3-8-4** BDoyle(6) (lw: a.p: rdn to ld ins fnl f: edgd lft: styd on)	—	1	9/1	81	36
2062[7]	**Hawait (IRE) (86)** (BWHills) **3-9-7** KFallon(2) (hld up: effrt over 2f out: n.m.r: styd on u.p: nrst fin)	½	2	5/2[1]	97	52
2415*	**Three For A Pound (66)** (JAGlover) **3-8-1** GCarter(7) (lw: trckd ldrs: nt clr run 3f out tl ins fnl f: kpt on)	1¼	3	5/1	74	29
2125*	**Ultra Boy (75)** (PCHaslam) **3-8-10** JFortune(4) (led tl hdd ins fnl f: no ex)	½	4	9/2[3]	82	37
2557[10]	**Rainbow Rain (USA) (78)** (MJohnston) **3-8-13** MRoberts(3) (trckd ldrs: rdn over 2f out: sn btn)	4	5	3/1[2]	77	32
2552[6]	**Lady Godiva (62)** (MJPolglase) **3-7-11** JQuinn(5) (swtg: chsd ldrs: chal 3f out: wknd over 1f out)	1¼	6	13/2	58	13
2340[13]	**Jay-Owe-Two (IRE) (75)** (RMWhitaker) **3-8-10** DeanMcKeown(1) (effrt ½-wy: sn rdn & btn)	½	7	16/1	70	25
2417[4]	**Prominent (65)** (MrsVAAconley) **3-8-0b**[1ow4] MDeering(8) (plld hrd: bhd: rdn & wandered bdly 2f out: n.d)	1½	8	33/1	57?	8

(SP 120.6%) **8 Rn**

1m 34.2 (2.20) CSF £30.66 CT £119.93 TOTE £13.20: £3.70 £1.40 £1.60 (£26.20) OWNER Cotterill & Kimberley (MIDDLEHAM) BRED Swettenham Stud
LONG HANDICAP Prominent 7-1

2043 Cee-N-K (IRE) was in a messy race full of iffy characters, and he produced all that was necessary. (9/1)
2062 Hawait (IRE) had slight problems in finding a clear run and then stayed on under pressure, but was inclined to carry his head to one side and left the impression that he is not really giving it his best shot. (5/2)

2415* Three For A Pound, who probably prefers easier ground, got himself shut in, but for which he may well have won. (5/1)
2125* Ultra Boy, having his first run in handicap company for a while, did his usual and blazed a trail, but was comfortably picked off late on. (9/2)
2205* Rainbow Rain (USA) probably saw too much daylight too soon on this occasion. (3/1)
2552 Lady Godiva, who would win no prizes on looks, could never dominate and finally cried enough with over a furlong left. (13/2)
699 Jay-Owe-Two (IRE) got himself in a state beforehand and seems to have lost his way for the time being. (16/1)
2417 Prominent, in blinkers for the first time, was 9lb out of the handicap and, to make things worse, put up another 4lb overweight, and he looked most ungenerous. (33/1)

2736 ORANGE MAIDEN AUCTION STKS (I) (2-Y.O) (Class E)

3-30 (3-33) **5f** £2,906.25 (£870.00: £417.50: £191.25) Stalls: High GOING minus 0.35 sec per fur (F)

				SP	RR	SF
2500^{5}	**Fashion Victim** (THCaldwell) **2-8-7** ACulhane(8) (chsd ldrs: rdn to ld 1f out: r.o)	—	**1**	7/1	69	19
	Gildersleve (JWWatts) **2-7-9**(3) PFessey(11) (neat: lw: hld up: effrt ½-wy: sn clr run: r.o wl fnl f)	nk	**2**	7/1	59+	9
2545^{13}	**Miss Eliminator** (MWEasterby) **2-7-12** DaleGibson(3) (dwlt: hdwy to chse ldrs ½-wy: nt clr run over 1f out: styd on u.p)	2½	**3**	12/1	51	1
2467^{4}	**Quiz Master** (EWeymes) **2-8-7** JQuinn(5) (a cl up: one pce fnl f)	1¾	**4**	$5/1^{2}$	54	4
1860^{2}	**Patsy Culsyth** (MJohnston) **2-8-2** BDoyle(6) (lw: cl up: led 2f out to 1f out: sn outpcd)	½	**5**	$2/1^{1}$	48	—
2361^{7}	**Wilton** (JHetherton) **2-8-7** DHarrison(4) (spd over 3f: wknd)	1¾	**6**	14/1	47	—
2467^{11}	**Hoyland Common (IRE)** (NTinkler) **2-7-12** LCharnock(10) (chsd ldrs: outpcd 2f out: no imp after)	3	**7**	25/1	29	—
1645^{10}	**Brookhouse Lady (IRE)** (RHollinshead) **2-7-12** NCarlisle(1) (outpcd ½-wy: n.d)	¾	**8**	$6/1^{3}$	26	—
2042^{7}	**Vogue Imperial (IRE)** (PCHaslam) **2-8-7** JFortune(7) (bit bkwd: effrt ½-wy: hung lft: sn btn)	3	**9**	20/1	26	—
1797^{12}	**Tina Knows (IRE)** (JLEyre) **2-7-12** DWright(9) (led 3f: sn btn)	½	**10**	20/1	15	—
2565^{12}	**Snappy Times** (MDods) **2-8-7b** TWilliams(2) (b.hind: s.i.s: hdwy ½-wy: wandered u.p & sn btn)	14	**11**	20/1	—	—

(SP 121.8%) **11 Rn**

64.6 secs (2.80) CSF £49.01 TOTE £8.20: £2.10 £2.50 £3.80 (£35.10) Trio £318.80; £238.04 to Sandown 16/7/97 OWNER Mr R. S. G. Jones (WARRINGTON) BRED Theakston Stud
2500 Fashion Victim jumped out on terms this time and, despite the shorter trip, did it well. There would seem to be improvement yet over further. (7/1)
Gildersleve looked very fit for this debut but she failed to make full use of her draw early on, and found trouble aplenty, but for which she would certainly have won. (7/1)
Miss Eliminator is obviously improving and was keeping on nicely at the finish. (12/1: op 8/1)
2467 Quiz Master had his chances but, yet again, failed to come up with the goods when ridden. (5/1)
1860 Patsy Culsyth has had plenty of chances and has fluffed all of them. (2/1)
Wilton showed some toe this time and seemed better suited by this faster ground. (14/1)

2737 SONY H'CAP (0-70) (3-Y.O+) (Class E)

4-00 (4-00) **2m 35y** £3,231.25 (£970.00: £467.50: £216.25) Stalls: High GOING minus 0.35 sec per fur (F)

				SP	RR	SF
2350^{5}	**Arian Spirit (IRE) (34)** (JLEyre) **6-7-11** TWilliams(8) (lw: a.p: effrt 7f out: rdn to ld 2f out: drvn out)	—	**1**	$4/1^{1}$	45	14
2154^{4}	**Highfield Fizz (40)** (CWFairhurst) **5-8-3** LCharnock(7) (b.off hind: hld up: hdwy 6f out: chal 1f out: styd on wl)	nk	**2**	10/1	51	20
1795^{5}	**Batabanoo (45)** (MrsMReveley) **8-8-8** KDarley(9) (hld up: hdwy & prom ½-wy: effrt over 2f out: styd on: nvr able to chal)	¾	**3**	9/1	55	24
2469^{6}	**Love Me Do (USA) (62)** (MJohnston) **3-8-6** JWeaver(2) (a cl up: led 3f out to 2f out: one pce)	¾	**4**	12/1	71	21
2413*	**Hasta la Vista (55)** (MWEasterby) **7-9-4b** KFallon(11) (lw: mde most tl hdd 3f out: sn outpcd)	6	**5**	$4/1^{1}$	58	27
2498*	**Black Ice Boy (IRE) (42)** (RBastiman) **6-8-5b** DeanMcKeown(1) (swtg: w ldr tl wknd fnl 3f)	5	**6**	$9/2^{2}$	40	9
2207^{9}	**Ship's Dancer (33)** (DonEnricoIncisa) **4-7-10b** KimTinkler(6) (bhd: sme hdwy 4f out: n.d)	7	**7**	50/1	24	—
2413^{2}	**Tancred Mischief (40)** (DWBarker) **6-7-10**(7) JennyBenson(10) (hld up: effrt appr st: n.d)	hd	**8**	$11/2^{3}$	31	—
	Can She Can Can (33) (CSmith) **5-7-10** FNorton(3) (prom tl wknd 7f out)	12	**9**	33/1	12	—
1224^{8}	**Rushen Raider (65)** (KWHogg) **5-10-0** FLynch(4) (trckd ldrs: outpcd 5f out: sn wknd & eased)	1¼	**10**	8/1	31	—
2607^{4}	**Top Prize (33)** (MBrittain) **9-7-10v** GBardwell(5) (sn pushed along: lost tch fr ½-wy)	6	**11**	33/1	—	—

(SP 119.3%) **11 Rn**

3m 39.3 (8.80) CSF £40.79 CT £314.58 TOTE £4.00: £1.60 £3.60 £1.80 (£26.40) Trio £60.60 OWNER Mr Martin West (HAMBLETON) BRED M. Ervine in Ireland
LONG HANDICAP Can She Can Can 7-4 Ship's Dancer 7-0 Top Prize 7-7
WEIGHT FOR AGE 3yo-19lb
2350 Arian Spirit (IRE) was so well handicapped she had to win this, but it was never easy. Nevertheless, it should have boosted her confidence. (4/1)
2154 Highfield Fizz likes to come from off the pace and had the race set up but, despite a gallant effort, just met one too good. She is obviously in good heart. (10/1)
1795 Batabanoo ran a fair race after five weeks off and should be all the better for it. (9/1)
2469 Love Me Do (USA) seemed to stay this trip well enough, but was again lacking in pace when it mattered. (12/1)
2413* Hasta la Vista still looked well enough, but he has not won off a mark as high this on turf and that, coupled with recent hard races, probably took the edge off him. (4/1)
2498* Black Ice Boy (IRE) has shot up the weights and could never dominate, and that found him out early in the straight. (9/2)

2738 TOSHIBA H'CAP (0-60) (3-Y.O+) (Class F)

4-30 (4-34) **5f** £3,731.75 (£1,124.00: £544.50: £254.75) Stalls: High GOING minus 0.35 sec per fur (F)

				SP	RR	SF
2540^{9}	**Young Ben (IRE) (38)** (JSWainwright) **5-8-3b**(3)ow2 GParkin(12) (b.hind: mde most: jst hld on)	—	**1**	33/1	49	30
2540^{10}	**Rennyholme (46)** (ABMulholland) **6-9-0** MRoberts(18) (bhd & hmpd ½-wy: hdwy over 1f out: swtchd & r.o wl towards fin)	nk	**2**	16/1	56	39
2504^{5}	**Stolen Kiss (IRE) (57)** (MWEasterby) **5-9-11b** KFallon(17) (lw: a chsng ldrs: hdwy over 1f out: nt qckn ins fnl f)	1¼	**3**	$6/1^{2}$	63	46
2167^{6}	**Superfrills (35)** (MissLCSiddall) **4-8-3** DHarrison(1) (a chsng ldrs: nt qckn fnl f)	2½	**4**	25/1	33	16
2563^{7}	**Ned's Bonanza (54)** (MDods) **8-9-8b** FLynch(19) (lw: chsd ldrs: effrt 2f out: nvr able to chal)	s.h	**5**	$5/2^{1}$	52	35
2497^{3}	**Camionneur (IRE) (46)** (TDEasterby) **4-9-0b** LCharnock(2) (hdwy ½-wy: rdn & styd on: nvr able to chal)	½	**6**	14/1	42	25

				SP	RR	SF
2001[8]	**Just Dissident (IRE) (57)** (RMWhitaker) **5-9-11** DeanMcKeown(6) (lw: disp ld to ½-wy: wknd appr fnl f)	1	**7**	16/1	50	33
1603[14]	**Answers-To-Thomas (38)** (JMJefferson) **4-8-6** JFortune(9) (chsd ldrs tl rdn & btn over 1f out)	½	**8**	50/1	30	13
2203[5]	**Here Comes a Star (44)** (JMCarr) **9-8-12** KDarley(15) (lw: bhd: hdwy whn nt clr run 1f out: n.d)	¾	**9**	14/1	33	16
2504[7]	**Ultra Beet (57)** (PCHaslam) **5-9-11** JWeaver(20) (spd 3f: grad wknd)	s.h	**10**	14/1	46	29
1995[4]	**Tinker's Surprise (IRE) (50)** (JBalding) **3-8-13** JEdmunds(14) (nvr nr to chal)	½	**11**	12/1	37	15
2177[16]	**Super Rocky (50)** (RBastiman) **8-8-13**(5) HBastiman(13) (bhd: hdwy ½-wy: nt clr run: styd on fnl f)	¾	**12**	20/1	35	18
1828[3]	**Dominelle (54)** (TDEasterby) **5-9-8** JCarroll(8) (chsd ldrs: rdn 2f out: wknd)	¾	**13**	9/1 [3]	37	20
2497[4]	**Napoleon Star (IRE) (50)** (SRBowring) **6-9-4v[1]** DaleGibson(16) (sn outpcd & bhd)	s.h	**14**	10/1	32	15
2504*	**Tropical Beach (60)** (JBerry) **4-9-9b**(5) TEDurcan(4) (outpcd fr ½-wy)	1¼	**15**	10/1	38	21
1005[17]	**Skelton Countess (IRE) (45)** (RHollinshead) **4-8-10**(3) DGriffiths(11) (nvr wnt pce)	1¼	**16**	33/1	19	2
2481[2]	**Singforyoursupper (46)** (GGMargarson) **3-8-9** GBardwell(3) (bhd & rdn ½-wy: n.d)	hd	**17**	14/1	20	—
2305[4]	**Soaked (46)** (DWChapman) **4-9-0b** ACulhane(7) (dwlt: a wl bhd)	3½	**18**	33/1	9	—
	Bright Gold (55) (ASmith) **3-9-4b[1]** RLappin(5) (a bhd)	4	**19**	25/1	5	—
1223[U]	**Present 'n Correct (48)** (CBBBooth) **4-9-2** GCarter(10) (dwlt: a wl bhd)	3½	**20**	16/1	—	—
				(SP 146.3%)	**20 Rn**	

63.8 secs (2.00) CSF £491.41 CT £3,314.17 TOTE £63.70: £10.80 £4.40 £1.50 £10.50 (£450.80) Trio £1,594.20; £898.19 to Sandown 16/7/97 OWNER Mr F. Wood (MALTON) BRED George Halford

WEIGHT FOR AGE 3yo-5lb

1687 Young Ben (IRE) had the toe to get clear of trouble and that made all the difference. (33/1)

1514 Rennyholme should have won this, but found all sorts of trouble and then flew when it was too late. (16/1)

2504 Stolen Kiss (IRE) did her usual and failed to take the opportunity when it was there. (6/1)

2167 Superfrills ran an incredible race from the worst draw, and obviously has ability if she can be persuaded. (25/1)

2563 Ned's Bonanza looked to have everything in his favour, but this old character managed to get it wrong. (5/2)

2497 Camionneur (IRE) ran well from a poor draw but is never one to rely on. (14/1)

2739 ORANGE MAIDEN AUCTION STKS (II) (2-Y.O) (Class E)

5-00 (5-02) **5f** £2,883.50 (£863.00: £414.00: £189.50) Stalls: High GOING minus 0.35 sec per fur (F)

				SP	RR	SF
2545[4]	**Lets Be Fair** (JHanson) **2-8-2** EJohnson(8) (mde all: clr 2f out: easily)	—	**1**	Evens [1]	91+	31
2538[2]	**Cumbrian Cadet** (TDEasterby) **2-8-7** KFallon(4) (hdwy ½-wy: styd on: no ch w wnr)	9	**2**	100/30 [2]	67	7
1941[10]	**Half A Knicker** (RAFahey) **2-8-3** JCarroll(1) (bhd: hdwy appr fnl f: styd on wl towards fin)	1½	**3**	12/1	58	—
1136[8]	**Life Sentence** (JGSmyth-Osbourne) **2-8-7** DHarrison(9) (s.i.s: hdwy & swtchd 2f out: styd on)	nk	**4**	25/1	61	1
2519[5]	**Moy (IRE)** (MBrittain) **2-7-12** GBardwell(10) (w ldr 3f: wknd)	1	**5**	20/1	49	—
	Rio (IRE) (JBerry) **2-8-3** KDarley(2) (lengthy: unf: bit bkwd: chsd ldrs tl rdn & btn appr fnl f)	½	**6**	13/2 [3]	53	—
2037[9]	**Scolding** (KAMorgan) **2-7-12** FNorton(5) (gd spd over 3f: wknd)	½	**7**	16/1	46	—
2545[12]	**Premium Princess** (JJQuinn) **2-7-12** JLowe(3) (bit bkwd: bhd: nt clr run 1½f out: n.d)	½	**8**	10/1	44	—
1774[5]	**Classic Silver (IRE)** (WWHaigh) **2-8-7** RLappin(6) (nvr trbld ldrs)	nk	**9**	33/1	53	—
1684[8]	**Dibola** (JSWainwright) **2-8-7** LCharnock(7) (chsd ldrs: sn drvn along: wknd fnl 2f)	3	**10**	33/1	43	—
				(SP 123.6%)	**10 Rn**	

63.5 secs (1.70) CSF £4.03 TOTE £2.20: £1.10 £1.70 £2.10 (£3.90) Trio £11.20 OWNER Mr J. Hanson (WETHERBY) BRED Bearstone Stud

IN-FOCUS: **This was veteran rider Ernie Johnson's first winner for three seasons, and trainer Jack Hanson's first of the year.**

2545 Lets Be Fair confirmed her previous promise in some style and absolutely trotted up. The opposition may have been very moderate but the way in which she dealt with them had to impress. (Evens)

2538 Cumbrian Cadet ran reasonably but never had a hope with the winner, and may be better with cut in the ground. (100/30)

1510 Half A Knicker finished to some purpose and, in doing so, qualified for nurseries, and looks likely to need further. (12/1)

Life Sentence seems to be improving and stayed on particularly well. (25/1)

2519 Moy (IRE) has the toe but, as yet, does not see it out. (20/1)

Rio (IRE), just needing this, showed enough to suggest there is improvement in him. (13/2: 4/1-7/1)

2545 Premium Princess still looked in need of this and never got into it, but was not knocked about and looks likely to improve with time. (10/1)

T/Jkpt: Not won; £6,349.42 to Sandown 16/7/97. T/Plpt: £599.80 (38.22 Tckts). T/Qdpt: £614.10 (2.74 Tckts) AA

1984-BRIGHTON (L-H) (Firm)

Tuesday July 15th

Races 1, 2, 3 & 6: visibility v.poor

WEATHER: sea fret WIND: mod half against

2740 E.B.F. KEMP TOWN MAIDEN STKS (2-Y.O) (Class D)

2-15 (2-15) **5f 213y** £3,292.75 (£982.00: £468.50: £211.75) Stalls: Low GOING minus 0.25 sec per fur (GF)

				SP	RR	SF
938[5]	**Distinct Vintage (IRE)** (RHannon) **2-9-0** RHughes(2) (mde all: clr over 1f out: easily)	—	**1**	9/4 [2]	78+	13
2388[5]	**Mystery Guest (IRE)** (SirMarkPrescott) **2-9-0** GDuffield(6) (lw: hld up: shkn up over 1f out: unable qckn)	8	**2**	6/1	57	—
2320[12]	**Sky Mountain (IRE)** (GLewis) **2-8-11**(3) AWhelan(3) (lw: chsd wnr 2f: lost pl over 2f out: one pce)	nk	**3**	33/1	56	—
2371[5]	**Flying Singer** (IABalding) **2-8-9** SWhitworth(4) (lw: hld up: rdn over 3f out: btn whn n.m.r fnl f)	nk	**4**	4/1 [3]	28	—
2553[3]	**Little Fizz** (BJMeehan) **2-8-9** MTebbutt(5) (chsd wnr 4f out: ev ch over 2f out: hung lft & wknd over 1f out)	1¼	**5**	2/1 [1]	25	—
1664[4]	**Mrs Middle** (NACallaghan) **2-8-9** SDrowne(1) (hld up: rdn over 2f out: 3rd & btn whn hmpd on ins over 1f out)	1¼	**6**	6/1	21	—
				(SP 115.6%)	**6 Rn**	

1m 11.5 (4.30) CSF £15.05 TOTE £2.90: £1.10 £2.40 (£9.20) OWNER Mr E. C. Nagell-Erichsen (MARLBOROUGH) BRED K. and Mrs Cullen

938 Distinct Vintage (IRE) scooted up in this low-grade event, making every post a winning one and forging clear from below the distance to win with a ton in hand. (9/4: 3/1-2/1)

2388 Mystery Guest (IRE), a good-bodied individual, was once again not subjected to a hard time and, although having absolutely no chance with the winner, eventually managed to take second. With three runs under his belt, he is now qualified for nurseries and his very shrewd trainer will surely know where to place him to best effect. (6/1: op 4/1)

Sky Mountain (IRE), a deep-girthed colt whose physique is not ideal for this very tricky course, lost his position before halfway and was then made to look extremely one-paced. (33/1)

2371 Flying Singer is crying out for further and that was again demonstrated here. She was grimly trying to stay on when finding her way blocked in the final furlong, but for which she may have finished second. (4/1: 3/1-9/2)
2553 Little Fizz moved into second place half-a-mile from home but she tired and hung left below the distance. (2/1: 6/4-9/4)
1664 Mrs Middle chased the leaders, but was being made to look extremely pedestrian when hampered along the inside rail below the distance. (6/1: 7/2-13/2)

2741 STEINE CLAIMING STKS (2-Y.O) (Class F)
2-45 (2-47) **6f 209y** £2,277.00 (£627.00: £297.00) Stalls: Low GOING minus 0.25 sec per fur (GF)

				SP	RR	SF
1418^{U}	**Bettron** (RHannon) **2-9-3** DaneO'Neill(6) (lw: s.s & hmpd s: hdwy & n.m.r on ins 2f out: nt clr run on ins over 1f out: swtchd rt 1f out: hrd rdn: led nr fin)	—	**1**	100/30^{2}	71+	16
2320^{6}	**Private Seal** (GLMoore) **2-9-2** GDuffield(4) (a.p: led 2f out: hrd rdn over 1f out: hdd nr fin)	hd	**2**	15/8^{1}	70	15
2378^{2}	**Persian Fortune** (WGMTurner) **2-8-1**$^{(5)}$ DSweeney(5) (a.p: rdn over 2f out: one pce)	4	**3**	13/2	51	—
2196^{6}	**Persian Venture** (BJMeehan) **2-9-7** MTebbutt(7) (rdn over 2f out: hdwy over 1f out: nvr nrr)	2	**4**	5/1^{3}	61	6
2191^{8}	**Chika Shan (IRE)** (BSmart) **2-7-10**$^{(5)}$ RFfrench(1) (led 5f: wknd over 1f out)	nk	**5**	33/1	40	—
	Jilvarra (WGMTurner) **2-8-1**$^{(7)}$ DMcGaffin(8) (leggy: s.s: swvd lft s: nvr nr to chal)	3	**6**	25/1	40	—
2425^{3}	**Estopped (IRE)** (MRChannon) **2-8-13** TQuinn(3) (prom over 5f)	½	**7**	5/1^{3}	44	—
2003^{7}	**Hugger-Mugger** (JRArnold) **2-8-0b**$^{(3)}$ AWhelan(2) (chsd ldr over 4f)	9	**8**	33/1	14	—
2240^{5}	**Goldenacres** (JNeville) **2-8-2b**^{1ow1} SDrowne(9) (a bhd: t.o whn p.u ins fnl f: dismntd)		**P**	12/1	—	—
				(SP 121.9%)	**9 Rn**	

1m 25.2 (5.20) CSF £9.54 TOTE £6.80: £2.60 £1.10 £1.90 (£17.10) Trio £13.90 OWNER Mr R. Gander (MARLBOROUGH) BRED R. A. Gander
Bettron did extremely well considering he had no luck in running. After a tardy start, he was hampered by the erratic course of Jilvarra and lost considerable ground. Nevertheless, he was beginning to inch closer along the inside rail when failing to get a clear run below the distance. Switched right entering the final furlong, he responded to pressure and wore down the leader near the line. (100/30: 3/1-5/1)
2320 Private Seal, who advertised his claims to being a stallion in the paddock, struck the front two furlongs from home and looked to be holding his rivals, only to be worried out of it near the line. (15/8)
2378 Persian Fortune, who proved troublesome when mounted in the paddock, was never far away but found nothing extra in the final quarter-mile. (13/2: 7/2-7/1)
2196 Persian Venture, taking a drop in class but having to concede weight all-round, stayed on without ever threatening to get into it. (5/1: 5/2-11/2)
1758 Chika Shan (IRE) set the pace but, collared two furlongs from home, soon folded. He is a poor plater. (33/1)
1758 Goldenacres (12/1: 8/1-14/1)

2742 WATERHALL MEDIAN AUCTION MAIDEN STKS (3-Y.O) (Class E)
3-15 (3-15) **6f 209y** £3,372.00 (£813.00) Stalls: Low GOING minus 0.25 sec per fur (GF)

				SP	RR	SF
2323^{2}	**Radar O'Reilly (68)** (RJRWilliams) **3-9-0** GDuffield(4) (mde all: clr over 1f out: easily)	—	**1**	1/2^{1}	74+	19
1485^{5}	**Sifwa** (DCO'Brien) **3-8-9** SSanders(3) (lw: hld up: rdn 3f out: chsd wnr fnl 2f: no imp)	12	**2**	7/1^{3}	41	—
2481^{10}	**Royal Orchid (IRE) (63)** (RHannon) **3-8-9** DaneO'Neill(2) (b.hind: lw: chsd wnr 5f: p.u over 1f out: lame)		**P**	5/2^{2}	—	—
				(SP 107.7%)	**3 Rn**	

1m 24.7 (4.70) CSF £3.67 TOTE £1.50: (£2.40) OWNER Mr Harry Ormesher (NEWMARKET) BRED M. H. D. Madden and Partners
2323 Radar O'Reilly gained a bloodless victory and, with the second favourite going lame, needed to do little more than gallop around. (1/2)
1485 Sifwa had absolutely no hope with the winner. She is very moderate. (7/1: op 4/1)

2743 ERIC SIMMS MEMORIAL H'CAP (0-80) (3-Y.O+) (Class D)
3-45 (3-46) **7f 214y** £3,613.75 (£1,078.00: £514.50: £232.75) Stalls: Low GOING minus 0.25 sec per fur (GF)

				SP	RR	SF
2576*	**Sooty Tern (73)** (JMBradley) **10-9-2**$^{(5)}$ 6x RFfrench(8) (hdwy over 2f out: led ins fnl f: rdn out)	—	**1**	9/2^{2}	81	38
2216^{7}	**Victory Team (IRE) (72)** (GBBalding) **5-9-6** RHughes(3) (s.s: stdy hdwy over 1f out: hrd rdn fnl f: r.o)	1	**2**	5/1^{3}	78	35
2121^{11}	**Chairmans Choice (55)** (APJarvis) **7-8-3** SDrowne(2) (chsd ldr: led over 2f out: hrd rdn over 1f out: hdd ins fnl f: unable qckn)	¾	**3**	12/1	60	17
2201^{8}	**Confronter (58)** (SDow) **8-8-6** JFEgan(5) (lw: hld up: rdn over 2f out: one pce)	2½	**4**	6/1	58	15
1639^{7}	**Fort Knox (IRE) (51)** (RMFlower) **6-7-10b**$^{(3)}$ MBaird(7) (s.s: nvr nr to chal)	1¼	**5**	6/1	48	5
2576^{6}	**Night Wink (USA) (72)** (GLMoore) **5-9-6** SWhitworth(6) (lw: prom over 5f)	1	**6**	11/4^{1}	67	24
2006^{9}	**Apollo Red (72)** (GLMoore) **8-9-6** CandyMorris(1) (led over 5f: wknd fnl f)	s.h	**7**	11/1	67	24
1264^{4}	**Manaloj (USA) (76)** (RHannon) **4-9-3**$^{(7)}$ RSmith(4) (prom over 6f)	s.h	**8**	12/1	71	28
				(SP 113.8%)	**8 Rn**	

1m 35.4 (4.10) CSF £24.49 CT £228.75 TOTE £4.40: £1.70 £2.00 £1.50 (£17.90) OWNER Mr J. M. Bradley (CHEPSTOW) BRED Sheikh Mohammed bin Rashid al Maktoum
2576* Sooty Tern continues to defy his age and, despite racing off a mark 6lb higher than he has ever won off before, came through to strike the front inside the final furlong. (9/2: op 3/1)
946 Victory Team (IRE) needs to be held up until as late as possible and that is exactly what Hughes tried to do. Sitting pretty with a double handful, he appeared to be absolutely hacking but, asked for his effort below the distance, did not find as much as first appeared likely and, although running on, was not going to get to the winner in time. (5/1)
951 Chairmans Choice was unable to contain the winner inside the final furlong. (12/1: 8/1-14/1)
1955* Confronter chased the leaders, but was made to look very pedestrian in the final quarter-mile. (6/1)
1506 Fort Knox (IRE) never threatened to get into it and has not won on turf for nearly two years. (6/1)
2576 Night Wink (USA), winner of this race last year, was close up until calling it a day over two furlongs from home. (11/4)
1599 Apollo Red (11/1: 9/2-12/1)

2744 FRIEND-JAMES MEMORIAL LIMITED STKS (0-60) (3-Y.O+) (Class F)
4-15 (4-16) **1m 3f 196y** £2,277.00 (£627.00: £297.00) Stalls: High GOING minus 0.25 sec per fur (GF)

				SP	RR	SF
2468^{3}	**Double Eight (IRE) (60)** (BWHills) **3-8-4** DHolland(5) (mde all: clr over 1f out: pushed out)	—	**1**	5/2^{2}	69	25

Form	Horse / Details	Dist	Pos	SP	RR	SF
2194[5]	**Cheek To Cheek (58)** (CACyzer) **3-8-4** TQuinn(2) (lw: hld up: chsd wnr over 2f out: hrd rdn over 1f out: no imp)	2½	**2**	5/1	66	22
1844[5]	**Lookingforarainbow (IRE) (60)** (BobJones) **9-9-6** NDay(3) (hld up: hrd rdn over 1f out: one pce)	1¼	**3**	6/4[1]	67	36
2178[6]	**Blush (60)** (MCPipe) **3-7-13**(7) CLowther(6) (chsd wnr over 9f: 4th & btn whn n.m.r 2f out)	8	**4**	7/2[3]	55	11
2246[11]	**Magazine Gap (38)** (PatMitchell) **4-9-1**(5) AmandaSanders(4) (lw: hdwy 4f out: wknd over 3f out: t.o)	dist	**5**	25/1	—	—

(SP 111.3%) **5 Rn**

2m 34.1 (6.50) CSF £13.54 TOTE £2.40: £1.80 £2.00 (£6.30) OWNER Mr R. W. Miller (LAMBOURN) BRED Gay O'Callaghan
WEIGHT FOR AGE 3yo-13lb

2468 Double Eight (IRE) made every post a winning one, and forged clear for a cosy success. (5/2: 7/4-11/4)
2194 Cheek To Cheek had no chance with the winner, but just managed to win a tremendous battle for second prize. (5/1: 3/1-11/2)
1844 Lookingforarainbow (IRE) had a much simpler task this time, and the ground in his favour, but he was unable to take advantage of it, only fighting for second place in the final quarter-mile. He has not won for over two years. (6/4)
2178 Blush was well-suited by the return to this trip but not by the moderate early pace. (7/2: 3/1-9/2)

2745 HANNINGTONS OF BRIGHTON H'CAP (0-70) (3-Y.O+) (Class E)

4-45 (4-46) **6f 209y** £3,252.25 (£973.00: £466.50: £213.25) Stalls: Low GOING minus 0.25 sec per fur (GF)

Form	Horse / Details	Dist	Pos	SP	RR	SF
2721[3]	**Barbason (64)** (GLMoore) **5-9-12** CandyMorris(12) (lw: hdwy over 2f out: led 1f out: r.o wl)	—	**1**	4/1[1]	74	56
2282[7]	**Stand Tall (60)** (LadyHerries) **5-9-8** GDuffield(7) (b.hind: hld up: nt clr run over 2f out: rdn: r.o wl ins fnl f)	½	**2**	9/1	69	51
1843[4]	**Octavia Hill (52)** (PWHarris) **4-8-7b**(7) CLowther(11) (rdn over 3f out: hdwy over 1f out: r.o wl ins fnl f)	s.h	**3**	10/1	61	43
2552[4]	**Multi Franchise (45)** (RMFlower) **4-8-7** GHind(8) (led over 1f: led over 2f out tl over 1f out: unable qckn)	¾	**4**	14/1	52	34
1849[2]	**Sharp Imp (59)** (RMFlower) **7-9-7b** DaneO'Neill(6) (a.p: led over 1f out: sn hdd: one pce)	1¼	**5**	8/1[3]	63	45
2724[3]	**Pearl Dawn (IRE) (46)** (PCClarke) **7-8-8** SWhitworth(14) (nt clr run 2f out tl over 1f out: gd hdwy fnl f: r.o wl)	½	**6**	14/1	49	31
1374[12]	**Crystal Heights (FR) (63)** (RJO'Sullivan) **9-9-11** SSanders(9) (b: rdn over 2f out: hdwy 1f out: nvr nrr)	nk	**7**	12/1	65	47
2485[8]	**Coastguards Hero (42)** (MDIUsher) **4-8-4** AMcGlone(5) (rdn over 2f out: nt clr run over 1f out: nvr nrr)	¾	**8**	33/1	43	25
2573*	**Mr Cube (IRE) (55)** (JMBradley) **7-8-12b**(5) 6x RFfrench(1) (nvr nr to chal)	s.h	**9**	4/1[1]	55	37
2372[6]	**Divine Miss-P (56)** (APJarvis) **4-9-4** SDrowne(10) (prom over 5f)	3	**10**	25/1	50	32
2310[14]	**Fan of Vent-Axia (42)** (DJSCosgrove) **3-7-7**(3) MBaird(13) (a bhd)	2	**11**	20/1	31	5
2510[7]	**Oxbane (63)** (HCandy) **3-9-3** CRutter(4) (prom over 4f: mid div & btn whn hmpd over 1f out)	1¼	**12**	14/1	49	23
2197[12]	**Shifting Time (60)** (IABalding) **3-9-0** DHolland(15) (lw: a bhd)	3½	**13**	20/1	38	12
1965[18]	**Dark Menace (49)** (EAWheeler) **5-8-4b**(7) SCarson(3) (led over 5f out tl over 2f out: wkng whn bmpd on ins over 1f out)	8	**14**	16/1	9	—
2573[4]	**Balance of Power (56)** (SDow) **5-9-4** TQuinn(2) (lost pl 5f out: mid div & nt clr run whn fell over 1f out: dead)	...	**F**	6/1[2]	—	—

(SP 134.4%) **15 Rn**

1m 22.5 (2.50) CSF £39.08 CT £330.32 TOTE £4.90: £1.80 £3.70 £3.60 (£25.80) Trio £273.50 OWNER Mr F. L. Hill (BRIGHTON) BRED Sheikh Mohammed bin Rashid al Maktoum
LONG HANDICAP Fan of Vent-Axia 7-8
WEIGHT FOR AGE 3yo-8lb
STEWARDS' ENQUIRY Duffield susp 24-26 & 28/7/97 (careless riding).

2721 Barbason, third at Folkestone over an inadequate six furlongs the day before, showed no ill effects and, coming through to lead a furlong out, soon asserted to win his sixth race of the year. (4/1)
2282 Stand Tall had nowhere to go over a quarter of a mile from home but, when an opening did appear, he ran on really strongly to snatch second prize. His jockey was rather harshly handed a four-day ban for careless riding over an incident which had nothing to do with the fall of Balance of Power. (9/1)
1843 Octavia Hill, bustled along and going nowhere at halfway, found her feet from below the distance and, running on in tremendous style, only just failed to take second prize. (10/1: 8/1-12/1)
2552 Multi Franchise showed in front for the second time before the quarter-mile pole but, collared below the distance, failed to find another gear. (14/1: 10/1-16/1)
1849 Sharp Imp is a come-from-behind specialist, so it was very surprising to see him racing up with the pace. He had just managed to poke his head in front when the winner went by. (8/1)
2724 Pearl Dawn (IRE) at the back of the field when done no favours in the melee below the distance, sprouted wings in the final furlong but found the line always coming too soon. She has yet to win a handicap. (14/1)
879 Crystal Heights (FR) (12/1: 8/1-14/1)

T/Plpt: £228.30 (69.31 Tckts). T/Qdpt: £49.40 (25.58 Tckts) AK

2740-BRIGHTON (L-H) (Firm)
Wednesday July 16th

WEATHER: overcast WIND: slight against

2746 OVINGDEAN MEDIAN AUCTION MAIDEN STKS (2-Y.O F) (Class F)

6-20 (6-20) **5f 59y** £2,277.00 (£627.00: £297.00) Stalls: Low GOING minus 0.30 sec per fur (GF)

Form	Horse / Details	Dist	Pos	SP	RR	SF
1783[7]	**High Gain** (PHowling) **2-8-11** PaulEddery(3) (lw: rdn & lost pl over 3f out: squeezed thro over 2f out: led over 1f out: drvn out)	—	**1**	2/1[2]	72	23
	Aegean Dawn (RHannon) **2-8-11** DaneO'Neill(5) (lengthy: unf: lw: dwlt: sn pushed along: hdwy 2f out: ev ch 1f out: r.o)	nk	**2**	7/4[1]	71	22
2283[3]	**Shanthi** (PJMakin) **2-8-11** DHolland(2) (hld up: nt clr run on ins over 2f out: swtchd rt: r.o ins fnl f)	4	**3**	4/1[3]	59	10
2037[13]	**Sans Rivale** (BJMeehan) **2-8-11** BDoyle(6) (chsd ldr: led over 2f out tl over 1f out: wknd fnl f)	1½	**4**	11/1	54	5
2367[6]	**Miss Scooter** (APJones) **2-8-11** TSprake(4) (lw: s.i.s: sn rcvrd: wknd over 1f out)	3½	**5**	20/1	44	—
	Green Dolphin (WGMTurner) **2-8-6**(5) DSweeney(1) (small: lt-f: bit bkwd: led over 2f: sn wknd: t.o)	15	**6**	14/1	—	—

(SP 109.5%) **6 Rn**

62.8 secs (2.80) CSF £5.06 TOTE £2.10: £1.10 £1.60 (£3.50) OWNER Red Kite Racing (NEWMARKET) BRED Bearstone Stud

1295 High Gain, back at the level at which she made her debut, did not come down the hill all that well, but responded to pressure despite some tail swishing. (2/1)
Aegean Dawn, a half-sister to a bumper and hurdle winner in Ireland, looked green early on. (7/4)
2283 Shanthi was the unlucky horse of the race, and looked to be going well when eventually forced to switch right around the field. (4/1)
1626 Sans Rivale seems to need a return to selling company. (11/1: op 5/1)
767 Miss Scooter was stepping up from sellers. (20/1)
Green Dolphin (14/1: 10/1-16/1)

2747 HANGLETON MAIDEN H'CAP (0-70) (3-Y.O+) (Class E)

6-50 (6-50) **5f 213y** £2,966.25 (£885.00: £422.50: £191.25) Stalls: Low GOING minus 0.30 sec per fur (GF)

				SP	RR	SF
2665^{2}	**Senorita Matilda (USA) (67)** (RHannon) **3-10-0** DaneO'Neill(2) (a.p: led over 1f out: comf)	—	**1**	$15/8^{1}$	78	42
2125^{8}	**Nicker (63)** (WJarvis) **3-9-10** WRyan(7) (lw: outpcd: swtchd rt & hdwy over 1f out: r.o ins fnl f: nt trble wnr)	1¾	**2**	14/1	69	33
2216^{11}	**Ed's Folly (IRE) (57)** (SDow) **4-9-9** RPerham(1) (led 5f out tl over 1f out: nt qckn)	1¼	**3**	$9/2^{3}$	60	29
2510^{2}	**Gold Edge (52)** (MRChannon) **3-8-10**(3) PPMurphy(3) (chsd ldrs: sltly hmpd over 4f out: one pce fnl 2f)	1¼	**4**	$3/1^{2}$	52	16
2496^{8}	**Blue Lamp (USA) (63)** (MAJarvis) **3-9-10b** MRoberts(9) (swtg: a.p: rdn & ev ch 2f out: wknd fnl f)	1½	**5**	7/1	59	23
2406^{2}	**Sang d'Antibes (FR) (52)** (DJSCosgrove) **3-8-13** MRimmer(6) (hmpd s: hdwy on ins 2f out: eased whn btn fnl f)	1¾	**6**	12/1	43	7
2244^{11}	**Royal Emblem (41)** (AGFoster) **3-8-2b**ow1 TSprake(10) (no hdwy fnl 3f)	¾	**7**	33/1	30	—
2554^{19}	**Formidable Spirit (35)** (MJHeaton-Ellis) **3-7-10v** NAdams(4) (lw: led 1f: wknd over 1f out)	1¼	**8**	33/1	21	—
2368^{16}	**Kanawa (47)** (APJones) **3-8-5**(3) JDSmith(5) (wnt rt s: hmpd over 4f out: nt rcvr)	2½	**9**	33/1	26	—
1508^{3}	**Barbury Ballad (IRE) (40)** (MJHeaton-Ellis) **3-7-10**(5) RFfrench(8) (lw: a bhd)	3	**10**	14/1	11	—
				(SP 120.3%)	**10 Rn**	

1m 10.1 (2.90) CSF £28.94 CT £97.64 TOTE £2.50: £2.10 £4.40 £1.30 (£12.60) Trio £44.20 OWNER Mr J. C. Smith (MARLBOROUGH) BRED Swettenham Stud
LONG HANDICAP Formidable Spirit 7-6
WEIGHT FOR AGE 3yo-5lb
2665 Senorita Matilda (USA) made no mistake from a much more favourable draw than when a good second at Lingfield last time. (15/8)
1688 Nicker, whose last two outings have been over a mile, proved difficult to pull out up the camber and found the winner home and dry. (14/1: op 7/1)
1446 Ed's Folly (IRE) probably found seven on yielding ground beyond him last time. (9/2: op 7/1)
2510 Gold Edge had finished four and a half lengths in front of the winner at Leicester but, unlike her rival, she has not progressed. (3/1)
2496 Blue Lamp (USA) appears more effective at the minimum trip. (7/1: 5/1-15/2)
2406 Sang d'Antibes (FR), back up to six, did not have luck on her side on this handicap debut. (12/1: 7/1-14/1)
1508 Barbury Ballad (IRE) (14/1: 12/1-25/1)

2748 WHITE HAWK (S) STKS (3-Y.O+) (Class G)

7-20 (7-21) **7f 214y** £1,984.50 (£547.00: £259.50) Stalls: Low GOING minus 0.30 sec per fur (GF)

				SP	RR	SF
2724^{7}	**Hawaii Storm (FR) (24)** (DJSffrenchDavis) **9-9-5**(5) RFfrench(1) (hld up & bhd: hdwy 2f out: rdn to ld ins fnl f: r.o wl)	—	**1**	20/1	58?	27
2319^{4}	**Without Friends (IRE) (60)** (JFfitch-Heyes) **3-9-2** BDoyle(4) (hdwy 4f out: led over 1f out tl ins fnl f)	1¼	**2**	$9/2^{2}$	56	17
2228*	**Cape Pigeon (USA) (65)** (LGCottrell) **12-9-10v** DHolland(7) (lw: chsd ldrs: led 3f out: rdn & hdd over 1f out: nt qckn)	¾	**3**	$11/10^{1}$	54	23
2723^{7}	**Jubilee Scholar (IRE) (45)** (GLMoore) **4-9-5** CandyMorris(2) (lw: hdwy 4f out: sn rdn: ev ch over 1f out: one pce)	1	**4**	$5/1^{3}$	47	16
2200^{U}	**Rosalee Royale** (JohnBerry) **5-9-0** TSprake(5) (lw: hld up & bhd: rdn & hdwy 2f out: wknd over 1f out)	2	**5**	33/1	38	7
2171^{9}	**Seamus (36)** (CJHill) **3-8-6**(5) DSweeney(6) (b: a.p: n.m.r on ins over 1f out: wknd ins fnl f)	1½	**6**	33/1	40	1
2577^{9}	**Hatta Sunshine (USA) (34)** (GLMoore) **7-9-10v** MWigham(10) (s.i.s: sn prom: rdn whn n.m.r over 2f out: sn wknd)	5	**7**	14/1	35	4
1383^{16}	**Chopin (IRE) (52)** (RFJohnsonHoughton) **3-8-11** PaulEddery(3) (rdn over 4f out: hdwy 3f out: wknd 2f out)	6	**8**	11/2	18	—
295^{14}	**Embroidered (27)** (SDow) **4-9-0** MRoberts(8) (led: edgd rt & hdd 3f out: wknd 2f out)	6	**9**	40/1	1	—
2407^{9}	**Double-E-I-B-A (50)** (DJSCosgrove) **3-8-11** MRimmer(9) (s.s: a bhd: t.o)	12	**10**	50/1	—	—
				(SP 119.6%)	**10 Rn**	

1m 36.3 (5.00) CSF £96.77 TOTE £16.80: £2.30 £1.50 £1.50 (£20.60) Trio £12.20 OWNER Mr C. C. Capel (UPPER LAMBOURN) BRED Horse France
WEIGHT FOR AGE 3yo-8lb
No bid
319 Hawaii Storm (FR), whose previous win on grass was nearly five years ago, came from behind in typical style on this drop into a seller. (20/1)
2319 Without Friends (IRE) displayed a high head carriage but seemed to get the mile well enough. (9/2)
2228* Cape Pigeon (USA) never really looked like shaking off his rivals but did not go down without a fight. (11/10: evens-6/5)
512 Jubilee Scholar (IRE) was making a quick reappearance on his second outing since changing stables. (5/1: 6/1-4/1)
Rosalee Royale cut little ice in a Wolverhampton selling hurdle forty-eight hours earlier. (33/1)

2749 SOUTH DOWNS H'CAP (0-85) (3-Y.O+) (Class D)

7-50 (7-50) **1m 3f 196y** £3,550.05 (£1,058.40: £504.70: £227.85) Stalls: High GOING minus 0.30 sec per fur (GF)

				SP	RR	SF
2391^{5}	**Wakeel (USA) (74)** (SDow) **5-9-7** MRoberts(7) (hld up & bhd: hdwy 4f out: led 1f out: r.o wl)	—	**1**	16/1	84	66
1934^{5}	**Puce (81)** (LMCumani) **4-9-9**(5) RFfrench(6) (hld up: led over 2f out: hdd 1f out: nt qckn)	nk	**2**	$5/2^{1}$	91	73
1868^{8}	**Davoski (74)** (BWHills) **3-8-9** DHolland(3) (hld up: rdn to ld over 3f out: hdd over 2f out: wknd over 1f out)	10	**3**	20/1	70	40
2218^{8}	**Mr Browning (USA) (66)** (RAkehurst) **6-8-13b** SSanders(1) (led over 8f: wknd 2f out)	11	**4**	11/2	47	29
2574*	**Rising Dough (IRE) (68)** (GLMoore) **5-9-1** 5x MWigham(5) (hld up & bhd: hdwy 4f out: wknd 3f out)	7	**5**	$9/2^{3}$	40	22
2015^{2}	**Canton Venture (76)** (SPCWoods) **5-9-9** WRyan(2) (prom: rdn & wknd 4f out: eased whn no ch over 1f out)	9	**6**	$9/2^{3}$	36	18

2058[14] **Zinzari (FR) (83)** (DRLoder) **3-9-4** DaneO'Neill(4) (chsd ldr 6f: wknd qckly: t.o)....dist 7 100/30 2 — —
(SP 114.0%) **7 Rn**

2m 29.7 (2.10) CSF £50.73 TOTE £12.60: £2.10 £1.90 (£18.40) OWNER Mrs J. M. A. Churston (EPSOM) BRED Gainsborough Farm Inc
WEIGHT FOR AGE 3yo-12lb
STEWARDS' ENQUIRY Wigham susp. 25-26 & 28/7/97 (improper use of whip).
OFFICIAL EXPLANATION Zinzari (FR): no explanation offered.
2391 Wakeel (USA), again at a mile and a half, had a faster surface this time and scored rather cheekily in the end. (16/1)
1934 Puce had the distance in her favour but found the winner waiting to pounce coming to the final furlong. (5/2)
568* Davoski, down 4lb, has yet to prove he really stays this distance. (20/1)
1641* Mr Browning (USA), 5lb higher than when winning over course and distance last month, could never dominate in the way he likes. (11/2: 4/1-6/1)
2015 Canton Venture, 12lb higher than when winning this race last year, was unable to get to his favourite front-running position. (9/2)

2750 TELSCOMBE CLIFFS H'CAP (0-65) (3-Y.O) (Class F)
8-20 (8-21) **1m 1f 209y** £2,277.00 (£627.00: £297.00) Stalls: High GOING minus 0.30 sec per fur (GF)

Form	Horse / details	Dist	Pos	SP	RR	SF
2005[5]	**Who's That Man (57)** (SCWilliams) **3-9-3** DHolland(10) (hld up: hdwy over 3f out: swtchd lft & nt clr run over 1f out: swtchd rt: r.o wl ins fnl f: fin 2nd, s.h: awrdd race)	—	1	9/4 1	66	34
1972[12]	**Interdream (60)** (RHannon) **3-9-6** DaneO'Neill(6) (hld up & bhd: hdwy 5f out: led 2f out: edgd lft over 1f out: all out: fin 1st: disq, plcd 2nd)	s.h	2	4/1 2	69	37
1966[7]	**Keen Waters (36)** (JRArnold) **3-7-10b[1]** NAdams(5) (hld up & bhd: hdwy 3f out: r.o one pce fnl f)	1½	3	12/1	43	11
2132[7]	**Golden Saddle (USA) (59)** (PFICole) **3-9-5** MRoberts(9) (lw: prom: lost pl 5f out: styd on fnl 2f)	¾	4	14/1	64	32
2158[7]	**Il Principe (IRE) (38)** (JohnBerry) **3-7-7(5)** RFfrench(8) (lw: a.p: led 4f out to 3f out: sltly hmpd over 1f out: one pce)	1¼	5	33/1	41	9
2246[4]	**Sound Appeal (61)** (AGFoster) **3-9-7** TSprake(1) (stumbled s: sn prom: hmpd on ins over 1f out: nt rcvr)	1	6	13/2	63	31
2668[10]	**Kingsdown Trix (IRE) (50)** (GLMoore) **3-8-10** RPerham(11) (prom: led 3f out to 2f out: hmpd over 1f out: nt rcvr)	5	7	14/1	44	12
455[4]	**Master Bobby (40)** (RMFlower) **3-7-7(7)** JFowle(2) (lw: bhd fnl 6f)	1¾	8	33/1	31	—
1826[9]	**Hadawah (USA) (60)** (JLDunlop) **3-9-6** BDoyle(4) (trckd ldrs: rdn & wknd over 2f out)	1¾	9	9/2 3	48	16
2522[6]	**Tezaab (50)** (BHanbury) **3-8-10** WRyan(3) (plld hrd: led 6f: sn wknd: t.o)	13	10	9/1	17	—
2183[13]	**Cabcharge Glory (40)** (GGMargarson) **3-8-0** GBardwell(7) (bhd: rdn 7f out: t.o fnl 3f)	12	11	33/1	—	—

(SP 122.1%) **11 Rn**

2m 3.2 (4.90) CSF £10.24 CT £79.60 TOTE £3.30: £1.10 £1.80 £3.00 (£7.40) Trio £18.00 OWNER Mr M Jameson And Mr John T Duffy (NEWMARKET) BRED T. P. Milne and M. Jameson
LONG HANDICAP Keen Waters 7-9
2005 Who's That Man, 3lb higher than when winning at Redcar, had just gone for a run up the inside of Interdream when his ground was taken. Losing far more ground than he was beaten by, he only just failed to get up, which proved vital in the Stewards' room. (9/4: 3/1-2/1)
1633 Interdream, trying a longer trip, just managed to hold on but lost the race for causing Who's That Man to switch. (4/1: 3/1-9/2)
1484 Keen Waters, blinkered for the first time, did not seem inconvenienced by this step up in distance. (12/1: 8/1-14/1)
2132 Golden Saddle (USA) is beginning to look like a horse without a trip. (14/1: 6/1-16/1)
Il Principe (IRE) was 7lb lower than when making his handicap debut. (33/1)
2246 Sound Appeal ran better than her finishing position suggests. (13/2)
906* Kingsdown Trix (IRE) has been dropped 10lb on grass and was unlucky not to have finished closer here. (14/1: 10/1-16/1)
2522 Tezaab (9/1: 6/1-10/1)

2751 LEWES LIMITED STKS (0-60) (3-Y.O+) (Class F)
8-50 (8-53) **5f 59y** £2,277.00 (£627.00: £297.00) Stalls: Low GOING minus 0.30 sec per fur (GF)

Form	Horse / details	Dist	Pos	SP	RR	SF
*2300**	**Pizzicato (60)** (RJRWilliams) **3-8-9(3)** DGriffiths(4) (hld up: hrd rdn to ld over 1f out: all out)	—	1	3/1 3	65	43
2244[6]	**Corniche Quest (IRE) (60)** (MRChannon) **4-8-12(7)** AEddery(3) (hld up & bhd: hdwy over 1f out: rdn & ev ch ins fnl f: r.o)	s.h	2	11/4 2	68	50
1995[5]	**Suite Factors (59)** (KRBurke) **3-8-12** RPerham(5) (led: rdn & hdd 2f out: wknd wl ins fnl f)	4	3	9/2	53	31
1666[6]	**Always Grace (60)** (MissGayKelleway) **5-8-13** DaneO'Neill(2) (stdd s: nvr nr to chal)	2	4	2/1 1	44	26
2536[11]	**Rise 'n Shine (60)** (CACyzer) **3-8-9** WRyan(6) (chsd ldr: led 2f out: sn hdd: wknd ins fnl f)	3½	5	14/1	33	11
	Agwa (58) (JJBridger) **8-8-9(7)** PDoe(1) (bkwd: prom: hrd rdn over 2f out: wknd over 1f out)	1¾	6	20/1	31	13

(SP 114.6%) **6 Rn**

61.6 secs (1.60) CSF £10.96 TOTE £3.60: £2.00 £2.10 (£8.30) OWNER Mr Richard Morris Jr (NEWMARKET) BRED Bolton Grange
WEIGHT FOR AGE 3yo-4lb
2300* Pizzicato seemed to find a bit more when strongly pressed in the closing stages. (3/1: 6/4-7/2)
2244 Corniche Quest (IRE) looked to be coming with a winning run but the winner would not be denied. (11/4)
1995 Suite Factors found himself setting the race up for the first two. (9/2: op 3/1)
1666 Always Grace finds this trip on the sharp side nowadays. (2/1)
1644 Rise 'n Shine ran her best race of the season. (14/1)

T/Plpt: £42.40 (265.98 Tckts). T/Qdpt: £13.60 (54.02 Tckts) KH

2412-CATTERICK (L-H) (Good to Firm)
Wednesday July 16th
WEATHER: fine WIND: fresh half against

2752 SWALE PASTURE MEDIAN AUCTION MAIDEN STKS (2-Y.O) (Class F)
2-15 (2-16) **7f** £2,889.00 (£804.00: £387.00) Stalls: Low GOING minus 0.16 sec per fur (GF)

Form	Horse / details	Dist	Pos	SP	RR	SF
2571*	**Lend A Hand** (MJohnston) **2-9-4** JWeaver(9) (lw: led to 4f out: led 3f out: clr over 1f out: v.easily)	—	1	1/7 1	94+	41
2477[10]	**On The Mat** (JJO'Neill) **2-8-12** JCarroll(8) (w wnr: led 4f out to 3f out: styd on ins fnl f)	11	2	33/1	63	10
1997[7]	**Good On Yer** (SEKettlewell) **2-8-7** JFanning(3) (chsd ldrs: wnt 2nd over 2f out: wknd towards fin)	hd	3	12/1 2	58	5
2394[10]	**Gay Abandon** (KMcAuliffe) **2-8-7** FLynch(2) (outpcd ½-wy: kpt on fnl f: n.d)	5	4	33/1	46	—
	Czar Wars (PTDalton) **2-8-12** LCharnock(12) (neat: bit bkwd: trckd ldrs: outpcd ½-wy: n.d)	½	5	50/1	50	—

				SP	RR	SF
2500^{7}	**Dougs Dream (IRE)** (MrsASwinbank) **2-8-7** RLappin(7) (sn outpcd & drvn along appr fnl f)	1½	**6**	25/1^{3}	42	—
1255^{10}	**Mr Fund Switch** (DNicholls) **2-8-12** AlexGreaves(11) (w ldrs tl rdn & wknd ½-wy)	1¾	**7**	50/1	43	—
2320^{10}	**Silver Joy** (KMcAuliffe) **2-8-7** JQuinn(4) (bit bkwd: chsd ldrs: outpcd 4f out: sn wknd)	d.h	**7**	12/1^{2}	38	—
	Rockette (JWWatts) **2-8-7** NConnorton(6) (cmpt: s.s: a bhd & rn green)	3	**9**	12/1^{2}	31	—
2359^{6}	**Western Lord** (CSmith) **2-8-9**$^{(3)}$ PFessey(10) (chsd ldrs to ½-wy: sn bhd)	3½	**10**	40/1	28	—
	Mecca Princess (RMWhitaker) **2-8-7** ACulhane(5) (cmpt: bit bkwd: s.i.s: a bhd: t.o 3f out)	dist	**11**	50/1	—	—

(SP 128.6%) **11 Rn**

1m 27.6 (4.00) CSF £17.56 TOTE £1.10: £1.10 £3.90 £1.70 (£8.40) Trio £19.90 OWNER Maktoum Al Maktoum (MIDDLEHAM) BRED Gainsborough Stud Management Ltd

2571* Lend A Hand looked in a different league in the paddock and so it proved in the race, but for being eased, he would have had at least fifteen lengths to spare. (1/7)
On The Mat took on the winner. Left for dead turning in, he stuck on to get back up for second near the line. (33/1)
1997 Good On Yer showed a clear second early in the straight but tired and was just pipped for the runner-up spot. (12/1: op 8/1)
Gay Abandon ran her best race so far but that is not saying much. (33/1)
Czar Wars needed this initial outing. (50/1)
Dougs Dream (IRE), who looked very fit, shapes like a stayer. A claimer or seller would be more her mark. (25/1)
Rockette (12/1: op 8/1)

2753 ST. ANNE'S CLAIMING STKS (3-Y.O+) (Class F)

2-45 (2-45) **1m 3f 214y** £2,532.00 (£702.00: £336.00) Stalls: Low GOING minus 0.16 sec per fur (GF)

				SP	RR	SF
2544^{5}	**My Millie (50)** (DWBarker) **4-8-13** TWilliams(4) (lw: sn trckng ldrs: rdn to ld over 1f out: drvn out)	—	**1**	7/2^{2}	52	16
2413^{6}	**Durgams First (IRE) (49)** (MrsMReveley) **5-9-8** ACulhane(6) (hld up: effrt over 2f out: rdn & hung lft over 1f out: styd on wl towards fin)	½	**2**	Evens^{1}	60	24
2200^{B}	**Risky Rose (42)** (RHollinshead) **5-8-12**$^{(3)}$ DGriffiths(3) (chsd ldrs: ev ch over 1f out: kpt on same pce)	1½	**3**	4/1^{3}	51	15
2661^{4}	**Havana Heights (IRE) (40)** (JLEyre) **4-9-1** MGallagher(7) (trckd ldr: led over 5f out tl over 1f out: one pce)	¾	**4**	7/1	50	14
2542^{6}	**Lady Silk (33)** (MissJFCraze) **6-9-1** SWebster(1) (unruly s: sn trckng ldrs: wknd over 2f out)	11	**5**	33/1	36	—
2502^{11}	**Petit Flora (34)** (GHolmes) **5-9-1** TLucas(5) (b.hind: hld up: effrt 3f out: n.d)	1	**6**	14/1	34	—
2034^{9}	**Fox Sparrow (50)** (NTinkler) **7-9-8b** JWeaver(8) (led tl over 5f out: lost pl over 2f out: eased)	7	**7**	14/1	32	—
2479^{4}	**Single Man (IRE)** (FHLee) **4-9-12** RLappin(2) (s.s: a in rr)	1¼	**8**	33/1	34	—

(SP 123.9%) **8 Rn**

2m 41.9 (10.50) CSF £7.36 TOTE £3.50: £1.10 £1.50 £1.70 (£4.30) OWNER Mr D. W. Barker (RICHMOND) BRED P. Asquith
My Millie clmd DCBatey £4,000

2544 My Millie, 10lb best in on official figures, got there with nothing at all to spare. (7/2)
2413 Durgams First (IRE), who has had his fore-legs fired, seemed unhappy on the fast ground and on this sharp, undulating track. After hanging badly, he found his stride inside the last and would have got there in a few more strides. (Evens)
1570 Risky Rose, brought down on her previous outing three weeks ago, had every conceivable chance. (4/1: op 6/1)
2661 Havana Heights (IRE) made the best of her way home but, over this trip, proved woefully one-paced. All she does is stay. (7/1)
1993 Lady Silk would not get this trip in a horse-box. (33/1)
574 Petit Flora (14/1: op 8/1)

2754 LOW GREEN H'CAP (0-75) (3-Y.O+) (Class D)

3-20 (3-21) **5f** £3,691.00 (£1,108.00: £534.00: £247.00) Stalls: Low GOING minus 0.16 sec per fur (GF)

				SP	RR	SF
2536*	**Goretski (IRE) (60)** (NTinkler) **4-9-3** LCharnock(3) (chsd ldrs: rdn ½-wy: styd on wl to ld jst ins fnl f)	—	**1**	4/5^{1}	69	40
2717^{6}	**Johayro (59)** (JSGoldie) **4-9-2v** JQuinn(6) (lw: w ldr: drvn along ½-wy: kpt on same pce)	1½	**2**	10/1	63	34
1759^{13}	**Pleasure Time (63)** (CSmith) **4-9-3b**$^{(3)}$ PFessey(2) (dwlt s: hdwy ½-wy: edgd lft & styd on fnl f)	nk	**3**	9/1	66	37
2203^{11}	**Imp Express (IRE) (40)** (GMMoore) **4-7-11** NCarlisle(4) (outpcd ½-wy: hdwy on ins over 1f out: styd on same pce)	s.h	**4**	50/1	43	14
1671^{5}	**Captain Carat (62)** (DNicholls) **6-9-5b** AlexGreaves(5) (sn outpcd: hdwy over 1f out: nvr nr ldrs)	1	**5**	14/1	62	33
1865^{5}	**Bowcliffe Grange (IRE) (51)** (DWChapman) **5-8-8** ACulhane(1) (led: clr ½-wy: hdd jst ins fnl f: sn wknd)	1¼	**6**	7/1^{3}	47	18
2540^{7}	**Blazing Imp (USA) (51)** (MrsJJordan) **4-8-8** JCarroll(9) (racd wd: hdwy ½-wy: sn chsng ldrs: wknd over 1f out)	1¼	**7**	10/1	43	14
2111^{8}	**Ramsey Hope (62)** (CWFairhurst) **4-9-5v** JWeaver(8) (lw: racd wd: sn outpcd: bhd fr ½-wy)	2½	**8**	20/1	46	17
2563^{13}	**Swan At Whalley (70)** (RAFahey) **5-9-6**$^{(7)}$ RWinston(7) (sn chsng ldrs: wknd 2f out)	¾	**9**	5/1^{2}	52	23

(SP 126.3%) **9 Rn**

60.4 secs (2.70) CSF £10.95 CT £49.45 TOTE £1.90: £1.30 £1.70 £4.30 (£9.40) Trio £86.20 OWNER Mr P. D. Savill (MALTON) BRED Pierre Brichart

2536* Goretski (IRE), raised 11lb for his Bath success, got in here with no penalty. After looking likely to make hard work of it at halfway, in the end he scored in decisive fashion. He is unlikely to rest on his laurels and is likely to be out again on Friday under a single penalty. (4/5)
2717 Johayro put a run of six moderate efforts behind him. (10/1)
1250* Pleasure Time, who missed the break slightly, edged left under pressure causing problems for Captain Carat and the weakening Bowcliffe Grange. (9/1: 13/2-10/1)
223 Imp Express (IRE), who had shown little on his return to turf racing, shaped much better here. (50/1)
1671 Captain Carat had his first outing for forty-two days and, after a moderate effort, will be sharper as a result of it. (14/1)
1865 Bowcliffe Grange (IRE), taken to post early, kicked on, stepped up the pace after a furlong and soon showed three lengths clear. Finding little under pressure, he was weakening when Pleasure Time went across him inside the last. (7/1)
2540 Blazing Imp (USA) (10/1: 12/1-8/1)

2755 COWSTAND BRIDGE (S) STKS (3-Y.O+) (Class G)

3-50 (3-51) **5f 212y** £2,320.00 (£645.00: £310.00) Stalls: High GOING minus 0.16 sec per fur (GF)

				SP	RR	SF
2129^{10}	**Spotted Eagle (64)** (MartynWane) **4-8-11**$^{(3)}$ AWhelan(1) (sn chsng ldr: rdn to ld over 1f out: styd on)	—	**1**	11/4^{1}	52	33
1620^{7}	**Sir Tasker (40)** (JLHarris) **9-9-7** ACulhane(4) (lw: effrt over 2f out: styd on fnl f: nt rch wnr)	1¾	**2**	25/1	54	35
2659^{7}	**Henry the Hawk (45)** (MDods) **6-9-0b** JCarroll(6) (b: swtg: led tl over 1f out: one pce)	s.h	**3**	16/1	47	28
2366^{4}	**Silk Cottage (51)** (RMWhitaker) **5-9-7v** DeanMcKeown(5) (lw: chsd ldrs: outpcd over 2f out: hrd rdn over 1f out: hung lft: one pce)	1¼	**4**	7/1^{3}	51	32
1786^{6}	**Loch Style (50)** (RHollinshead) **4-9-7** FLynch(7) (s.i.s: bhd tl styd on appr fnl f)	2	**5**	10/1	46	27
2540^{8}	**Sense of Priority (57)** (DNicholls) **8-9-7** AlexGreaves(10) (hld up: hdwy ½-wy: sn pushed along: nvr nr ldrs)	½	**6**	11/4^{1}	44	25

2501[6] **Chalice (56)** (MrsASwinbank) **4-8-9** JQuinn(9) (bhd: hdwy on outside 2f out: nvr nr to chal)	1¾	**7**	16/1	27	8
2354[11] **Morning Star (47)** (WMcKeown) **3-7-13**(5) KSked(2) (hld up: effrt over 2f out: n.d)	s.h	**8**	66/1	27	3
1394[7] **Juddy** (JO'Reilly) **3-8-9** JO'Reilly(3) (chsd ldrs tl wknd 2f out)	1	**9**	10/1	30	6
1807[7] **Docklands Carriage (IRE) (63)** (NTinkler) **3-9-2b** KimTinkler(8) (chsd ldrs: sn pushed along: lost pl over 2f out)	2½	**10**	3/1[2]	30	6

(SP 126.1%) **10 Rn**

1m 14.6 (3.70) CSF £72.68 TOTE £3.40: £1.10 £5.20 £2.60 (£33.60) Trio £138.80 OWNER Penny Home Preservation (RICHMOND) BRED Roldvale Ltd
WEIGHT FOR AGE 3yo-5lb
Sold DNicholls 6,800gns

1471 Spotted Eagle, dropped in class, was clear best in on official figures and always looked like doing enough. He was sold at the auction and will be an interesting proposition from David Nicholls' yard. (11/4)
601 Sir Tasker, now bordering on the veteran stage, did amazingly well to finish runner-up, considering he would have been no less than 31lb better off with the winner in a handicap. (25/1)
1816 Henry the Hawk, awash with sweat, was very keen going to post and raced freely, showing his rivals a clean pair of heels for over half a mile. (16/1)
2366 Silk Cottage, who would have been meeting the winner on 20lb better terms in a handicap, had the visor on but, having trouble making the home turn, looked far from keen under strong pressure. (7/1)
687 Loch Style found this trip too short. (10/1)
2540 Sense of Priority was well backed, despite the fact he would have been meeting the winner on a stone better terms in a handicap. He was in trouble soon after halfway. (11/4)
Chalice, who would have been meeting the winner on 3lb better terms in a handicap, was not knocked about at any stage and presumably ran here in the hope of a drop in the official ratings for a handicap. (16/1)
1573* Docklands Carriage (IRE), who had a good chance on official figures, ran one of his poor races, dropping right out at the halfway mark. (3/1: op 5/1)

2756 PALLETT HILL MEDIAN AUCTION MAIDEN STKS (3-Y.O F) (Class F)
4-20 (4-22) **7f** £2,448.00 (£678.00: £324.00) Stalls: Low GOING minus 0.16 sec per fur (GF)

			SP	RR	SF
2234[2] **Mystique Air (IRE) (67)** (EWeymes) **3-8-11** JQuinn(3) (led: shkn up over 2f out: edgd rt & styd on wl fnl f)	—	**1**	13/8[2]	64	26
1858[2] **Moon Fairy** (JGSmyth-Osbourne) **3-8-11** FLynch(6) (lw: hld up: effrt 2f out: sn rdn & hung lft: no imp)	1¾	**2**	11/10[1]	60	22
2040[4] **Daintree (IRE) (50)** (HJCollingridge) **3-8-11** DaleGibson(7) (trckd ldr: drvn along ½-wy: one pce fnl 2f)	2	**3**	3/1[3]	55	17
2523[9] **Joyful Joy (28)** (BPJBaugh) **3-8-11** NCarlisle(2) (trckd ldrs: drvn along ½-wy: wknd over 2f out)	6	**4**	100/1	30 t	4
2234[5] **La Perdoma** (MissMKMilligan) **3-8-11** JCarroll(5) (unruly s: s.s: sme hdwy over 4f out: lost pl over 2f out)	3½	**5**	100/1	22 t	—
1864[9] **Thewrightone (IRE) (35)** (GROldroyd) **3-8-11v** KHodgson(4) (trckd ldrs: rdn & lost pl over 2f out)	3½	**6**	100/1	14 t	—
1690[7] **Pisum Sativum** (JLHarris) **3-8-11** ACulhane(1) (bit bkwd: sn bhd: t.o ½-wy)	dist	**7**	100/1	—	—

(SP 114.7%) **7 Rn**

1m 28.3 (4.70) CSF £3.49 TOTE £2.50: £1.50 £1.10 (£1.70) OWNER Mr T. A. Scothern (MIDDLEHAM) BRED Mrs G. Doyle

2234 Mystique Air (IRE) was given a canny ride. Allowed to dictate her own pace, she quickened off the bend and, despite edging right away from the running rail inside the last, always had it under control. (13/8)
1858 Moon Fairy came with a well-timed effort on the outside two furlongs out but, soon under pressure, she hung left and edged in behind the winner. (11/10: evens-6/4)
2040 Daintree (IRE), hard at work at halfway, proved woefully one-paced. (3/1: op 5/1)
Joyful Joy was flattered in a slowly-run race. (100/1)
2234 La Perdoma, a persistent tail swisher in the paddock, gave problems at the start and tried to give her rivals ten lengths start. (100/1)

2757 BECKSIDE H'CAP (0-70) (3-Y.O) (Class E)
4-50 (4-51) **1m 3f 214y** £3,018.25 (£901.00: £430.50: £195.25) Stalls: Low GOING minus 0.16 sec per fur (GF)

			SP	RR	SF
1804[3] **The Roundsills (54)** (RFJohnsonHoughton) **3-8-8** ACulhane(4) (hdwy & pushed along 6f out: rdn to ld over 1f out: hld on wl)	—	**1**	8/1	62	31
2068[6] **Kingdom Pearl (45)** (MJCamacho) **3-7-13** LCharnock(3) (lw: sn trckng ldrs: rdn to ld over 2f out: hdd over 1f out: kpt on wl)	¾	**2**	8/1	52	21
2189[5] **Hadidi (63)** (DMorley) **3-9-3** DeanMcKeown(2) (lw: trckd ldrs: ev ch & rdn over 2f out: styd on one pce)	4	**3**	11/4[1]	65	34
2189[9] **Fullopep (65)** (MrsMReveley) **3-9-5** FLynch(5) (hld up: hdwy over 2f out: sn rdn: kpt on: nvr nr to chal)	1	**4**	3/1[2]	65	34
2468[4] **Marsh Marigold (67)** (JHetherton) **3-9-0**(7) JennyBenson(8) (hld up: hdwy on outside 2f out: hung lft: nvr rchd ldrs)	½	**5**	9/1	67	36
2387* **Wildmoor (56)** (JDBethell) **3-8-10** TWilliams(7) (hld up: hdwy on ins & n.m.r over 5f out: rdn over 2f out: sn wknd & eased)	11	**6**	4/1[3]	41	10
2170[9] **Zanabay (43)** (WStorey) **3-7-11** NKennedy(6) (swtg: led: hdd & wknd qckly over 2f out)	8	**7**	20/1	17	—
2158[6] **Coral Island (58)** (JGFitzGerald) **3-8-12b**[1] JCarroll(1) (trckd ldrs: rdn 3f out: sn lost pl)	1½	**8**	12/1	30	—
2156[4] **Gymcrak Gorjos (50)** (GHolmes) **3-8-4** TLucas(9) (b.hind: trckd ldrs: effrt over 3f out: sn lost pl)	½	**9**	14/1	22	—
2544[6] **Tribal Mischief (55)** (DMoffatt) **3-8-9** JQuinn(10) (hld up & bhd: effrt 3f out: n.d)	2	**10**	33/1	24	—

(SP 126.0%) **10 Rn**

2m 38.8 (7.40) CSF £69.37 CT £207.38 TOTE £9.00: £3.20 £3.30 £1.90 (£22.90) Trio £21.70 OWNER Lord Leverhulme (DIDCOT) BRED The Rt Hon Viscount Leverhulme

1804 The Roundsills proved well suited by this trip and it took all his rider's skill and strength to keep him off the runner-up inside the last. (8/1)
1863 Kingdom Pearl proved well suited by this extended trip. Kicking on once in line for home, she battled back when headed but the winner always just had the upper hand. (8/1)
2189 Hadidi, who took the eye in the paddock, was almost upsides once in line for home but, soon flat-out, shaped like an out-and-out stayer. (11/4: 2/1-3/1)
1574* Fullopep, given a patient ride, tried to creep closer turning in but, soon flat-out, was never going to get close enough to take a serious hand. (3/1)
2468 Marsh Marigold, held up to get the trip, made ground on the outer once in line for home. Tending to hang left, she stayed on all the way to the line. (9/1)
2387* Wildmoor wore a tongue-strap. Trying to make ground on the inner halfway down the back straight, he ran out of room. Flat-out turning in, his chance went in two strides and he was eased up. (4/1)

T/Plpt: £15.90 (632.03 Tckts). T/Qdpt: £17.10 (24.08 Tckts) WG

2338-DONCASTER (L-H) (Good)

Wednesday July 16th

WEATHER: overcast WIND: slight against

2758 GRESLEY CONDITIONS STKS (2-Y.O) (Class C)

6-30 (6-30) **6f** £4,405.99 (£1,585.62: £758.31: £307.05: £119.03) Stalls: High GOING minus 0.28 sec per fur (GF)

Form	Horse	Dist	Pos	SP	RR	SF
2007*	**Prince Foley** (WGMTurner) **2-9-0**$^{(7)}$ DMcGaffin(3) (lw: trckd ldrs: led on bit 2f out: pushed out fnl f)	—	1	7/1	92	35
2343^{2}	**Alconleigh** (MJohnston) **2-9-1** JWeaver(1) (lw: led 4f: rallied fnl f)	½	2	5/4^{1}	85	28
2140^{2}	**Premium Pursuit** (RAFahey) **2-8-13** ACulhane(2) (chsd ldrs: outpcd over 2f out: no imp after)	5	3	7/2^{2}	69	12
1653^{3}	**Angel Hill** (TDBarron) **2-8-6** LCharnock(5) (chsd ldrs over 3f: sn rdn & btn)	½	4	5/1^{3}	61	4
	Mac's Back (USA) (WAO'Gorman) **2-8-8** EmmaO'Gorman(4) (w'like: bit bkwd: s.s: a outpcd & wl bhd)	19	5	6/1	12	—
				(SP 110.1%)		**5 Rn**

1m 14.31 (3.31) CSF £14.95 TOTE £6.10: £2.70 £1.10 (£5.00) OWNER Foley Steelstock (SHERBORNE) BRED Ian Slocock

2007* Prince Foley, at his first attempt at this trip, travelled extremely well but, once in front, only just found enough to last out. More patient tactics are needed over this longer distance. (7/1)

2343 Alconleigh looked superb and again showed what a game character he is by fighting back when looking well beaten. He should have no problems in staying further. (5/4)

2140 Premium Pursuit was a shade disappointing here, struggling and hanging left some way out and was obviously not on song on this occasion. (7/2)

1653 Angel Hill was very edgy beforehand and never offered a real threat. (5/1: 3/1-11/2)

Mac's Back (USA) needed this both fitness and experience-wise and showed next to nothing, but has the looks of something better. (6/1: op 5/2)

2759 SHADWELL STUD SERIES APPRENTICE H'CAP (0-70) (3-Y.O+) (Class E)

7-00 (7-01) **5f** £3,176.25 (£960.00: £467.50: £221.25) Stalls: High GOING minus 0.28 sec per fur (GF)

Form	Horse	Dist	Pos	SP	RR	SF
2717^{2}	**Cross The Border (54)** (DNicholls) **4-9-1** PRoberts(5) (lw: trckd ldrs: led appr fnl f: rdn & r.o)	—	1	5/2^{1}	66	44
2540^{3}	**Southern Dominion (44)** (MissJFCraze) **5-8-0b**$^{(5)}$ CarolynBales(4) (lw: led tl hdd appr fnl f: kpt on)	1¾	2	12/1	50	28
2480^{3}	**Superbit (67)** (BAMcMahon) **5-9-9**$^{(5)}$ SRighton(6) (lw: chsd ldrs: rdn ½-wy: r.o one pce)	2½	3	9/2^{2}	65	43
1977^{18}	**Antarctic Storm (59)** (RAFahey) **4-9-6** RWinston(3) (hdwy ½-wy: styd on: nrst fin)	s.h	4	12/1	57	35
1865^{3}	**Featherstone Lane (48)** (MissLCSiddall) **6-8-6**$^{(3)}$ TSiddall(9) (hdwy ½-wy: styd on: no imp)	½	5	9/1	45	23
2651^{6}	**Reinhardt (IRE) (47)** (DNicholls) **4-8-1**$^{(7)}$ ANicholls(2) (dwlt: styd on fnl 2f: nvr nrr)	¾	6	16/1	41	19
2675^{13}	**Chemcast (67)** (JLEyre) **4-9-9b**$^{(5)}$ SBuckley(7) (chsd ldrs tl wknd appr fnl f)	2½	7	12/1	53	31
1977^{21}	**The Wad (60)** (DNicholls) **4-9-7** IonaWands(12) (spd 3f: sn btn)	1	8	14/1	43	21
2504^{3}	**Mungo Park (57)** (MrsJRRamsden) **3-9-0v**^{1} TEDurcan(10) (lw: unruly s: nvr wnt pce)	8	9	8/1	14	—
2504^{8}	**Hamilton Gold (40)** (MGMeagher) **4-8-1** GMilligan(11) (sn outpcd)	3	10	33/1	—	—
2480^{6}	**John O'Dreams (40)** (MrsALMKing) **12-8-1** PFessey(8) (b: rel to r: a t.o)	8	11	7/1^{3}	—	—
				(SP 118.9%)		**11 Rn**

60.19 secs (1.79) CSF £31.87 CT £120.21 TOTE £3.30: £1.30 £5.90 £1.90 (£55.80) Trio £36.70 OWNER Mr P. D. Savill (THIRSK) BRED Brook Stud Ltd

WEIGHT FOR AGE 3yo-4lb

2717 Cross The Border, given a good ride, did nothing wrong this time and won it nicely. (5/2)

2540 Southern Dominion is looking particularly well and is obviously in good heart and deserves to find a race. (12/1)

2480 Superbit was surprisingly always finding the pace too strong but this game sort did keep responding to pressure. (9/2)

1468 Antarctic Storm is a real handful and was taken to post early and then in the race just wanted to hang left, but his rider kept him going well. (12/1)

2651 Reinhardt (IRE) missed the kick but did show ability from halfway and is obviously in fair form. (16/1)

2504 Mungo Park was tried in a visor for the first time and almost got down in the stalls a couple of times. This seemed to upset him altogether and he ran no sort of race. (8/1: op 9/2)

2760 BAILEYS ORIGINAL IRISH CREAM H'CAP (0-85) (3-Y.O+) (Class D)

7-30 (7-31) **1m (round)** £3,882.50 (£1,160.00: £555.00: £252.50) Stalls: High GOING minus 0.28 sec per fur (GF)

Form	Horse	Dist	Pos	SP	RR	SF
2006^{10}	**Alfahaal (IRE) (52)** (RFJohnsonHoughton) **4-8-2** GCarter(13) (hld up & bhd: effrt over 2f out: str run to ld nr fin)	—	1	14/1	62	44
2708^{8}	**Sualtach (IRE) (70)** (RHollinshead) **4-9-6** LDettori(2) (lw: hld up: hdwy on ins to ld appr fnl f: r.o u.p: jst ct)	½	2	11/2^{1}	79	61
2290^{12}	**Somerton Boy (IRE) (71)** (PCalver) **7-9-7** NDay(14) (lw: in tch: effrt ½-wy: chal over 2f out: nt qckn fnl f)	1¾	3	10/1	77	59
1775^{11}	**Gulf Shaadi (67)** (EJAlston) **5-9-3** JFEgan(8) (hld up & bhd: effrt over 2f out: styd on towards fin)	½	4	12/1	72	54
2340^{4}	**Mr Teigh (67)** (MrsJRRamsden) **5-9-3** JFortune(7) (trckd ldrs: led over 2f out tl appr fnl f: no ex)	¾	5	7/1^{2}	70	52
2173*	**Liquid Gold (IRE) (74)** (WAO'Gorman) **3-9-2** EmmaO'Gorman(5) (swtg: hld up: hdwy & swtchd over 2f out: rdn & nt qckn fnl f)	s.h	6	8/1^{3}	77	51
2543^{2}	**Kass Alhawa (57)** (DWChapman) **4-8-7** ACulhane(1) (trckd ldrs: nt clr run & hmpd over 2f out: r.o towards fin)	s.h	7	7/1^{2}	60	42
2408^{2}	**Veni Vidi Vici (IRE) (66)** (MJHeaton-Ellis) **4-9-2** SDrowne(11) (hld up: effrt on outside over 2f out: no imp)	¾	8	11/2^{1}	67	49
2465^{8}	**Thatched (IRE) (53)** (REBarr) **7-8-3** DeanMcKeown(3) (lw: bhd: effrt 3f out: n.d)	2½	9	14/1	49	31
2505^{5}	**Attarikh (IRE) (51)** (MrsALMKing) **4-8-1** JQuinn(12) (effrt whn hmpd 2f out: n.d)	2½	10	33/1	42	24
2285^{7}	**Can Can Lady (84)** (MJohnston) **3-9-12** JWeaver(9) (cl up tl wknd 2f out)	1½	11	7/1^{2}	72	46
1972^{11}	**Hopeful Bid (IRE) (53)** (PHowling) **8-8-3** NCarlisle(6) (b.nr hind: chsd ldrs tl wknd & hmpd over 2f out)	5	12	33/1	31	13
2290^{10}	**Mbulwa (54)** (RAFahey) **11-7-11**$^{(7)}$ RWinston(10) (plld hrd: sddle slipped: cl up tl ½-wy: sn lost pl)	19	13	12/1	—	—
1761^{15}	**Look Who's Calling (IRE) (70)** (BAMcMahon) **4-9-6** KDarley(4) (led tl hdd over 2f out: wknd over 1f out)	1	14	14/1	8	—
				(SP 129.7%)		**14 Rn**

1m 40.3 (1.90) CSF £87.43 CT £778.74 TOTE £16.90: £4.20 £1.90 £3.70 (£36.60) Trio £221.70 OWNER Mr C. W. Sumner (DIDCOT) BRED Airlie Stud

WEIGHT FOR AGE 3yo-8lb

OFFICIAL EXPLANATION **Look Who's Calling (IRE): lost his action.**

1385 Alfahaal (IRE) tried different tactics this time and they worked a treat as he produced an incredible turn of foot to win. In this mood, a penalty would not stop him. (14/1)

2201 Sualtach (IRE) looked to have done everything right and, despite his rider trying all he knew, he had to admit he had met one just too good. (11/2)
1560* Somerton Boy (IRE), who looked particularly well, came back to form here but, despite trying hard, he was never quite up to the task. (10/1)
1583 Gulf Shaadi pulled very hard both going to post and early in the race but he did stay on well to show that if he can be settled, the ability is still there. (12/1)
2340 Mr Teigh again had his chances but, over this shorter trip, was tapped for speed. (7/1: 5/1-9/1)
2173* Liquid Gold (IRE) had to do a fair bit of weaving about to find a run but then failed to pick up when asked a serious question, and is probably better with more cut. (8/1)
2543 Kass Alhawa got messed about a good bit and, but for this, would have finished a good deal closer. (7/1)

2761 HALIFAX CAR INSURANCE CONDITIONS STKS (3-Y.O+) (Class C)

8-00 (8-00) **1m (straight)** £4,775.96 (£1,765.64: £845.82: £344.10: £135.05: £51.43) Stalls: Low GOING minus 0.28 sec per fur (GF)

				SP	RR	SF
1257[2]	**Intikhab (USA) (109)** (DMorley) **3-8-10** GCarter(6) (mde most: kpt on wl fnl 2f)	—	1	7/4[1]	105	57
1983*	**Illusion** (MRStoute) **3-9-0** JReid(1) (trckd ldrs: effrt & ch 2f out: kpt on wl fnl f)	¾	2	3/1[2]	108	60
1397[7]	**Hi Nod (96)** (MJCamacho) **7-9-4** LCharnock(2) (hld up: effrt over 2f out: r.o: no imp)	1¾	3	10/1	100	60
2345[4]	**Desert Horizon (100)** (JHMGosden) **3-8-10** LDettori(4) (b: w wnr tl outpcd 2f out: kpt on fnl f)	hd	4	11/2	100	52
2023[6]	**Peartree House (IRE) (100)** (WRMuir) **3-9-2** JWeaver(5) (b.hind: hld up: shkn up over 2f out: nvr able to chal)	1¼	5	5/1[3]	103	55
2023[10]	**Groom's Gordon (FR) (98)** (JLDunlop) **3-8-10b** KDarley(3) (hld up: hdwy ½-wy: rdn & wknd 2f out)	nk	6	8/1	97	49

(SP 113.6%) **6 Rn**

1m 38.52 (1.32) CSF £6.70 TOTE £2.30: £1.40 £2.20 (£2.60) OWNER Mr Hamdan Al Maktoum (NEWMARKET) BRED J. I. Racing Inc. and Marvin Little Jr
WEIGHT FOR AGE 3yo-8lb
1257 Intikhab (USA) looked well in here and, having no reservations about the trip, he dictated things. Once stepping on the gas in the last two furlongs, he was always too strong. (7/4)
1983* Illusion, taking a step up in class, put up a decent effort and, by the way he finished, he should get further. (3/1)
1397 Hi Nod, a seven-furlong specialist, ran well here to show he is coming back to form. (10/1)
2345 Desert Horizon ran reasonably and gave the impression that a bit further might well see improvement. (11/2)
2023 Peartree House (IRE) needed a stronger pace than was set here, and could never get into the final sprint. (5/1)
1544a Groom's Gordon (FR) travels well on the bridle, but once off it there is not any more to come and he appears to keep something for himself. (8/1)

2762 E.B.F. VYNER NOVICE STKS (2-Y.O) (Class D)

8-30 (8-30) **5f** £3,146.50 (£937.00: £446.00: £200.50) Stalls: High GOING minus 0.28 sec per fur (GF)

				SP	RR	SF
	Titanic (IRE) (JHMGosden) **2-8-12** LDettori(1) (cmpt: scope: lw: cl up: led 1½f out: shkn up & qcknd)	—	1	6/4[2]	93+	35
2356[6]	**Perfect Peach** (JBerry) **2-8-7** KDarley(6) (trckd ldrs: effrt over 1f out: r.o: no imp)	3	2	6/1[3]	78	20
2103[6]	**One Singer** (MJohnston) **2-9-2** JWeaver(4) (led tl hdd & hung lft 1½f out: sn btn)	hd	3	11/8[1]	87	29
	Ollie's Chuckle (IRE) (JAGlover) **2-8-12** NDay(5) (cmpt: bhd: hdwy 2f out: styd on wl towards fin)	1	4	20/1	80	22
2467[10]	**Smart Prince** (JJQuinn) **2-8-12** GCarter(3) (swtg: gd spd over 3f: wknd)	5	5	33/1	64?	6
2356[9]	**Barrelbio (IRE)** (JJO'Neill) **2-8-12** ACulhane(7) (stdd s: plld hrd: nvr trbld ldrs)	s.h	6	33/1	64?	6
2324[8]	**Jockweiler (IRE)** (MrsJRRamsden) **2-8-12** JFortune(2) (prom tl wknd fnl 2f)	¾	7	20/1	61?	3

(SP 111.8%) **7 Rn**

60.56 secs (2.16) CSF £8.90 TOTE £2.00: £1.40 £2.00 (£4.50) OWNER Sheikh Mohammed (NEWMARKET) BRED Sheikh Mohammed bin Rashid al Maktoum
Titanic (IRE), a handy sort, did this well and there looks to be something more to come. (6/4: op 4/5)
2356 Perfect Peach took the eye in the paddock, is certainly improving and ran well. (6/1)
2103 One Singer has the speed, but when he came off the bit, he was disappointing. (11/8)
Ollie's Chuckle (IRE) put in a decent first effort here, was not knocked about, and looks likely to improve. (20/1)
Smart Prince, on edge beforehand, showed speed this time but was done with some way out. (33/1)
2140 Barrelbio (IRE) pulls too hard for his own good and needs to learn to settle. (33/1)
Jockweiler (IRE) needs time and probably a trip. (20/1)

2763 ARKSEY TROPHY H'CAP (0-70) (3-Y.O+ F & M) (Class E)

9-00 (9-00) **1m 4f** £3,302.20 (£985.60: £470.80: £213.40) Stalls: Low GOING minus 0.28 sec per fur (GF)

				SP	RR	SF
2380[7]	**Atnab (USA) (56)** (PTWalwyn) **3-8-4**ow1 KDarley(1) (a.p: led wl over 1f out: rdn & r.o)	—	1	15/2	64	32
2564*	**Cashmirie (42)** (JLEyre) **5-8-2** 5x TWilliams(5) (lw: hld up: hdwy 3f out: styd on u.p: nt pce to chal)	1¼	2	100/30[2]	48	29
1623[2]	**Ordained (59)** (EJAlston) **4-9-5** JFEgan(3) (lw: hld up: hdwy 4f out: styd on u.p fnl 2f: nvr able chal)	1¼	3	5/1	64	45
2246*	**Inimitable (64)** (JLDunlop) **3-8-12** LDettori(4) (swtg: led 4f: led over 3f out tl wl over 1f out: sn outpcd)	hd	4	2/1[1]	69	38
2015[12]	**Exactly (IRE) (68)** (JLEyre) **4-10-0** MGallagher(7) (b.hind: cl up: led 8f out tl over 3f out: sn wknd)	15	5	10/1	53	34
2360[2]	**Top (67)** (JRFanshawe) **3-9-1** DHarrison(6) (chsd ldrs: ev ch over 3f out: rdn & fnd nil over 2f out)	¾	6	9/2[3]	51	20

(SP 112.1%) **6 Rn**

2m 35.2 (5.20) CSF £29.32 TOTE £8.30: £3.20 £1.70 (£12.50) OWNER Mr Hamdan Al Maktoum (LAMBOURN) BRED Shadwell Farm Inc
WEIGHT FOR AGE 3yo-12lb
Atnab (USA), trying his longest trip to date, got it well and won nicely. (15/2)
2564* Cashmirie is going up the weights but is still in good form, but despite a gallant effort here, was never quite good enough. (100/30)
1623 Ordained looks very lean and fit and is in good heart, but just lacks that vital turn of foot. (5/1)
2246* Inimitable, who won a moderate race last time, was very stirred up beforehand and, after helping to force the pace, was outbattled in the last two furlongs. (2/1: op 5/4)
Exactly (IRE) helped make the pace but put up little resistance once tackled early in the straight. (10/1)
2360 Top looked none too keen once asked the question halfway up the home straight. (9/2)

T/Plpt: £298.40 (49.19 Tckts). T/Qdpt: £122.70 (6.68 Tckts) AA

2524-SANDOWN (R-H) (Good to firm, Firm ptches Rnd, Good ptches 5f crse)
Wednesday July 16th
WEATHER: humid WIND: almost nil

2764 SINO GROUP DRAGON TROPHY LIMITED STKS (0-90) (3-Y.O+) (Class C)
2-05 (2-05) **1m 3f 91y** £6,710.00 (£2,030.00: £990.00: £470.00) Stalls: High GOING minus 0.33 sec per fur (GF)

				SP	RR	SF
2514[6]	**Rokeby Bowl (90)** (IABalding) **5-9-5** LDettori(1) (lw: a.p: led over 3f out tl over 1f out: led 1f out: rdn out)	—	**1**	7/4[1]	97	65
2026[9]	**Forza Figlio (87)** (MissGayKelleway) **4-9-5** PatEddery(3) (lw: led over 1f: chsd wnr over 2f out: led over 1f out: sn hdd: unable qckn)	¾	**2**	4/1[2]	96	64
1866*	**Khawafi (88)** (EALDunlop) **3-8-4**(3) DO'Donohoe(5) (plld hrd: led 10f out tl over 3f out: one pce)	3	**3**	4/1[2]	91	48
2241[3]	**Smart Play (USA) (90)** (LordHuntingdon) **4-9-5** DHarrison(4) (hld up: rdn 3f out: one pce)	2½	**4**	7/1	88	56
	Technicolour (IRE) (90) (MRStoute) **3-8-6**ow1 JReid(2) (nt grwn: plld hrd: hdwy over 3f out: wknd over 2f out)	8	**5**	9/2[3]	75	31
				(SP 107.0%)	**5 Rn**	

2m 25.04 (1.64) CSF £7.60 TOTE £2.30: £1.30 £2.10 (£4.90) OWNER Mr Paul Mellon (KINGSCLERE) BRED Paul Mellon
WEIGHT FOR AGE 3yo-11lb

2514 Rokeby Bowl, who looked in tremendous shape beforehand, eased his way to the front early in the straight but, headed below the distance, looked booked for second place. However, he managed to get back in front again entering the final furlong and was rousted along to gain his first victory in over two years. (7/4)
1745 Forza Figlio stayed this longer trip and looked likely to prevail as he poked his head in front below the distance. However, he was unable to shake off the winner and, soon collared by that rival, then failed to find another gear. (4/1: 3/1-9/2)
1866* Khawafi took a very keen hold and had soon pulled herself to the front. Collared over three furlongs from home, she was then made to look very one-paced. (4/1)
2241 Smart Play (USA), who went down early, was made to look extremely pedestrian in the straight. (7/1)
Technicolour (IRE) has failed to develop since last year and is still sparely-made. Very free going down to the start and in the early part of the race, she made her move early in the straight but found her earlier exertions taking their toll over a quarter of a mile from home. (9/2: 3/1-5/1)

2765 HSBC TROPHY CONDITIONS STKS (3-Y.O+) (Class C)
2-35 (2-37) **1m 2f 7y** £6,359.00 (£2,381.00: £1,165.50: £502.50: £226.25: £115.75) Stalls: High GOING minus 0.33 sec per fur (GF)

				SP	RR	SF
2338*	**Lord of Men (118)** (JHMGosden) **4-9-8** LDettori(4) (lw: mde all: rdn out)	—	**1**	1/2[1]	113	71
2360*	**Silence Reigns** (MRStoute) **3-8-10** JReid(6) (lw: a.p: chsd wnr over 2f out: ev ch over 1f out: unable qckn)	2½	**2**	14/1	107	55
1769[13]	**Papua (106)** (IABalding) **3-8-6** MRoberts(3) (swtg: plld hrd: chsd wnr over 7f: one pce)	nk	**3**	20/1	103	51
2008*	**Ismaros** (HRACecil) **3-8-10** WRyan(1) (lw: s.i.s: rdn over 2f out: hdwy over 1f out: one pce)	nk	**4**	9/1[3]	106	54
1490[2]	**Helicon (IRE)** (SbinSuroor) **4-9-2** PatEddery(2) (lw: hdwy over 2f out: ev ch 2f out: wknd over 1f out)	3½	**5**	9/2[2]	97	55
	Bahamian Knight (CAN) (DRLoder) **4-9-9** JFortune(5) (bit bkwd: hld up: rdn over 2f out: sn wknd)	7	**6**	16/1	92	50
				(SP 112.2%)	**6 Rn**	

2m 7.78 (1.08) CSF £8.37 TOTE £1.60: £1.20 £2.40 (£6.00) OWNER Sheikh Mohammed (NEWMARKET) BRED Sheikh Mohammed bin Rashid al Maktoum
WEIGHT FOR AGE 3yo-10lb
IN-FOCUS: This looked a hot conditions race.

2338* Lord of Men, fitted with a Monty Roberts blanket for stalls entry, was tackling a mile and a quarter for the first time but had absolutely no problems with it. He was given a super ride by Dettori who reported afterwards that the colt had been distracted by some geese on the inside of the running rail over two furlongs from home. Given three reminders, the colt flashed his tail on each occasion but he lengthened his stride in tremendous style nevertheless, to win with plenty in hand. His trainer was not concerned by the flashing tail, pointing out that the horse was just not used to being shown the whip. Some easier ground would probably help, Gosden later reported, and his action bears that out. He is certainly a very talented individual and a Group race should soon come his way. (1/2)
2360* Silence Reigns, who has a very scratchy action, looked a real threat below the distance before the winner found another gear. He should soon regain the winning thread. (14/1: 8/1-16/1)
1769 Papua, awash with sweat beforehand, took a keen hold and raced in second place. Collared for that position over two furlongs from home, he was once again made to look very pedestrian. (20/1)
2008* Ismaros had far more on his plate this time but, after being out with the washing for much of the trip, moved up nicely below the distance before failing to make any further impression. (9/1: 11/2-10/1)
1490 Helicon (IRE) looked in tremendous shape in the paddock but, after having every chance two furlongs from home, then dropped tamely away. (9/2: 5/2-5/1)
Bahamian Knight (CAN), carrying a 7lb penalty for winning last year's Italian Derby, did not look fully wound up for this reappearance and so it proved as he dropped away approaching the last two furlongs. He could be difficult to place this year. (16/1)

2766 HONG KONG JOCKEY CLUB TROPHY H'CAP (3-Y.O+) (Class B)
3-10 (3-16) **1m 14y** £51,650.00 (£19,250.00: £9,350.00: £3,950.00: £1,700.00: £800.00) Stalls: High GOING minus 0.33 sec per fur (GF)

				SP	RR	SF
2026[14]	**Hawksley Hill (IRE) (98)** (MrsJRRamsden) **4-9-1v[1]** JFortune(14) (rdn over 2f out: hdwy over 1f out: led ins fnl f: drvn out)	—	**1**	10/1	109	77
2334[9]	**Supercal (99)** (DRCElsworth) **3-8-8** DHolland(7) (lw: in rr 5f: gd hdwy over 1f out: str run fnl f: fin wl)	½	**2**	50/1	109	69
2026[19]	**Gold Spats (USA) (95)** (MRStoute) **4-8-12** JReid(8) (a.p: rdn over 2f out: led over 1f out tl ins fnl f: unable qckn)	1¼	**3**	12/1	103	71
2026[25]	**Bold Words (CAN) (108)** (EALDunlop) **3-9-3** MRoberts(1) (lw: a.p: chsd ldr over 2f out: led wl over 1f out: sn hdd: one pce)	s.h	**4**	20/1	115	75
1793*	**Harry Wolton (103)** (HRACecil) **3-8-12** WRyan(13) (hdwy on ins over 1f out: swtchd lft: r.o wl ins fnl f)	1¼	**5**	14/1	108	68
2026[4]	**Dancing Image (89)** (IABalding) **4-8-6** LDettori(3) (stdy hdwy 2f out: rdn over 1f out: r.o one pce)	nk	**6**	9/2[1]	93	61
2137*	**Right Wing (IRE) (95)** (MajorWRHern) **3-8-4** TSprake(17) (hdwy over 2f out: ev ch 1f out: wknd ins fnl f)	1½	**7**	10/1	96	56
2334[2]	**Almushtarak (IRE) (106)** (KMahdi) **4-9-9** PaulEddery(9) (lw: rdn over 2f out: hdwy over 1f out: nvr nrr)	1¼	**8**	14/1	105	73
1737*	**Cosmic Prince (IRE) (96)** (MAJarvis) **3-8-5** GDuffield(16) (swtg: led over 6f)	¾	**9**	11/1	93	53
2026[6]	**Lonely Leader (IRE) (102)** (RHannon) **4-9-5** DaneO'Neill(2) (lw: hld up: rdn over 2f out: wknd fnl f)	1¼	**10**	16/1	97	65
2242[4]	**My Lewicia (IRE) (92)** (PWHarris) **4-8-2**(7) CLowther(15) (a mid div)	hd	**11**	33/1	87	55

Form	Horse	Dist	Pos	SP	RR	SF
2023[3]	**Hornbeam (104)** (JRJenkins) **3-8-13** RCochrane(12) (lw: 9th whn rn wd bnd over 5f out: nt rcvr)	¾	**12**	14/1	97	57
2598[13]	**Concer Un (93)** (SCWilliams) **5-8-10** JFEgan(6) (b: nvr nr to chal)	1	**13**	33/1	84	52
2525*	**Clan Ben (IRE) (95)** (HRACecil) **5-8-12** 4x JLowe(11) (lw: a bhd)	1¾	**14**	16/1	83	51
2338[3]	**Amrak Ajeeb (IRE) (107)** (BHanbury) **5-9-10** MRimmer(5) (a bhd)	1½	**15**	20/1	92	60
2013*	**Fly To The Stars (106)** (MJohnston) **3-9-1** PatEddery(10) (lw: chsd ldr over 5f: wknd over 1f out)	5	**16**	7/1[3]	81	41
2026*	**Red Robbo (CAN) (94)** (RAkehurst) **4-8-11** SSanders(18) (prom over 6f)	s.h	**17**	11/2[2]	69	37
2026[32]	**Saifan (88)** (DMorris) **8-8-5b** NDay(4) (bhd fnl 5f)	18	**18**	40/1	27	—

(SP 131.8%) **18 Rn**

1m 40.83 (-0.37) CSF £434.93 CT £5,609.40 TOTE £14.00: £2.90 £9.90 £3.40 £4.90 (£519.90) Trio £5,269.20 OWNER Mr P. R. C. Morrison (THIRSK) BRED The Wickfield Stud Ltd

WEIGHT FOR AGE 3yo-8lb

OFFICIAL EXPLANATION **Hornbeam: was unable to handle the bend.**

738* Hawksley Hill (IRE), fitted with a visor for the first time, has never travelled so well before according to his jockey afterwards. Picking up ground below the distance, he led inside the final furlong and held on well. He has improved out of all recognition over the last two seasons - his first victory on turf came off just 50 but today he was winning off 98. (10/1)

2023 Supercal, at the tail end of the field for much of the way, really found her feet below the distance but, despite absolutely flying, found the line coming just that little bit too soon. (50/1)

1308* Gold Spats (USA) ran much better here, despite being 9lb higher than when winning at Goodwood back in May, and showed in front below the distance before overhauled inside the final furlong. (12/1)

1456 Bold Words (CAN), who ran a cracking race here in the Whitsun Cup in May, bounced back to form and showed in front a furlong and a half out before being passed soon afterwards. (20/1)

1793* Harry Wolton had no easy task on this handicap debut but acquitted himself well, running on nicely in the last furlong and a half. (14/1)

2026 Dancing Image crept closer a quarter of a mile from home but, although staying on, never looked like finding that vital turn of foot. The Handicapper seems to have his measure at present. (9/2)

2137* Right Wing (IRE) (10/1: 8/1-12/1)

2026* Red Robbo (CAN) laid up with the furious early pace and that took its toll over a furlong from home. (11/2)

2767 SING TAO TROPHY H'CAP (0-90) (3-Y.O+) (Class C)

3-40 (3-46) **1m 6f** £7,100.00 (£2,150.00: £1,050.00: £500.00) Stalls: High GOING minus 0.33 sec per fur (GF)

Form	Horse	Dist	Pos	SP	RR	SF
2194[3]	**Georgia Venture (72)** (SPCWoods) **3-8-2** GDuffield(6) (hdwy over 2f out: hrd rdn over 1f out: led nr fin)	—	**1**	9/1	83	51
2198[2]	**Silently (80)** (JSKing) **5-9-5**(5) RFfrench(9) (a.p: led over 2f out: hrd rdn over 1f out: hdd nr fin)	½	**2**	10/1	90	72
2014[5]	**Shining Dancer (66)** (SDow) **5-8-10** JFEgan(1) (rdn & swtchd rt 2f out: hdwy on ins over 1f out: one pce ins fnl f)	3½	**3**	8/1	72	54
2014[20]	**Midyan Blue (IRE) (67)** (JMPEustace) **7-8-11** RCochrane(2) (rdn over 3f out: hdwy fnl f: nvr nrr)	s.h	**4**	7/1	73	55
2142[2]	**Percy Isle (IRE) (85)** (MRStoute) **3-9-1** JReid(4) (lw: rdn & hdwy over 2f out: one pce)	1	**5**	5/1[2]	90	58
	Bimsey (IRE) (84) (RAkehurst) **7-10-0** SSanders(3) (hdwy 6f out: rdn over 2f out: sn wknd)	1¼	**6**	6/1[3]	88	70
2514[9]	**Mazurek (77)** (MCPipe) **4-9-7** PaulEddery(8) (lw: led 13f out to 10f out: led over 3f out tl over 2f out: wknd over 1f out)	7	**7**	7/1	73	55
1974[2]	**Tudor Island (75)** (CEBrittain) **8-9-5** BDoyle(7) (lw: led 1f: rdn over 3f out: sn wknd)	4	**8**	3/1[1]	66	48
2530[3]	**Bowcliffe Court (IRE) (77)** (RAkehurst) **5-9-0**(7) DDenby(5) (lw: led 10f out tl over 3f out: sn wknd)	12	**9**	10/1	55	37

(SP 120.2%) **9 Rn**

3m 0.59 (1.69) CSF £89.49 CT £692.46 TOTE £14.80: £2.80 £2.30 £2.40 (£62.10) Trio £226.90 OWNER Dr Frank Chao (NEWMARKET) BRED Woodsway Stud

WEIGHT FOR AGE 3yo-14lb

2194 Georgia Venture began to pick up ground over a quarter of a mile from home and, responding to pressure, whittled down the leader near the line. (9/1)

2198 Silently moved to the front over a quarter of a mile from home and appeared to have the race in safe keeping below the distance. However, despite doing nothing wrong, he was overhauled near the line. He has not won for two years. (10/1)

2014 Shining Dancer picked up ground along the inside rail below the distance but, having reached third place early inside the final furlong, could then make no further impression. (8/1)

1162 Midyan Blue (IRE) is not very consistent but did stay on in the final furlong, if finding it all over bar the shouting. He has now won just three times from fifty-four starts. (7/1: 5/1-8/1)

2142 Percy Isle (IRE), pushed along to take closer over two furlongs from home, could then make no further impression. He needs to drop a few pounds in the handicap. (5/1)

Bimsey (IRE), winner of the Aintree Hurdle in April, was having only his third run on the Flat. Taking closer order at the end of the back straight, he had been seen off approaching the final quarter-mile. (6/1: op 3/1)

2768 TIN TIN DAILY NEWS TROPHY MEDIAN AUCTION MAIDEN STKS (2-Y.O) (Class D)

4-10 (4-18) **7f 16y** £3,647.50 (£1,105.00: £540.00: £257.50) Stalls: High GOING minus 0.33 sec per fur (GF)

Form	Horse	Dist	Pos	SP	RR	SF
2286[2]	**Commander Charlie** (IABalding) **2-9-0** PatEddery(4) (lw: stdy hdwy over 2f out: led ins fnl f: r.o wl)	—	**1**	5/2[1]	80	38
2562[4]	**Outsourcing (USA)** (PFICole) **2-9-0** DHolland(6) (chsd ldr: led over 1f out tl ins fnl f: unable qckn)	1½	**2**	11/2[3]	77	35
	Saeedah (JHMGosden) **2-8-9** LDettori(1) (leggy: nt clr run over 2f out: hdwy & n.m.r over 1f out: r.o wl ins fnl f: bttr for r)	1½	**3**	7/1	68+	26
2176[5]	**Middle Temple** (EALDunlop) **2-9-0** WRyan(13) (lw: led over 5f)	3½	**4**	16/1	65	23
2181[10]	**Shannon's Secret (IRE)** (BJMeehan) **2-9-0** RHughes(11) (a.p: rdn over 2f out: one pce)	s.h	**5**	33/1	65	23
2176[6]	**Simlet** (WJarvis) **2-9-0** JReid(12) (lw: n.m.r & sme hdwy over 1f out: wknd fnl f)	3	**6**	16/1	58	16
2482[3]	**Celestial Bay (IRE)** (AGFoster) **2-8-9** TSprake(14) (plld hrd: a.p: rdn 2f out: wknd over 1f out)	½	**7**	16/1	52	10
	King's Hussar (PFICole) **2-9-0** MRimmer(3) (neat: rdn over 3f out: nvr nrr)	s.h	**8**	33/1	57	15
	Lord Warford (GBBalding) **2-9-0** RPrice(2) (str: scope: nvr nr to chal)	1¼	**9**	20/1	54	12
2693[7]	**Daring News** (RHannon) **2-9-0** DaneO'Neill(8) (lw: hdwy on ins 2f out: nt clr run & wknd over 1f out)	1¼	**10**	9/1	52	10
1872[13]	**Fair Game (IRE)** (JLDunlop) **2-9-0** BDoyle(15) (hld up: rdn over 2f out: sn wknd)	nk	**11**	25/1	51	9
2336[5]	**Radar (IRE)** (MAJarvis) **2-9-0** RCochrane(7) (plld hrd: prom 5f)	nk	**12**	3/1[2]	50	8
	Prodigal Son (IRE) (RJRWilliams) **2-9-0** GDuffield(9) (w'like: bit bkwd: s.s: a bhd)	¾	**13**	25/1	48	6
	Zada (GLMoore) **2-9-0** MWigham(5) (str: scope: bkwd: s.s: a bhd)	5	**14**	33/1	37	—

Porthilly Buoy (MJHaynes) **2-9-0** MRoberts(10) (w'like: a bhd) ....4 **15** 66/1 28 —
(SP 131.9%) **15 Rn**

1m 31.64 (3.04) CSF £15.28 TOTE £3.60: £1.70 £1.90 £2.60 (£10.80) Trio £12.00 OWNER Mr David Watson (KINGSCLERE) BRED Britton House Stud

2286 Commander Charlie appreciated the extra furlong and, with experience on his side, came through to lead inside the final furlong. (5/2)
2562 Outsourcing (USA), with his distinctive four white socks, moved to the front below the distance but was passed inside the final furlong. (11/2: op 3/1)
Saeedah, who cost 160,000 guineas, is quite a tall filly but does not have as much substance as one would expect of a Gosden inmate. Nevertheless, she showed a lot of promise, despite not having a clear run, and showed a nice turn of foot inside the final furlong to finish a very pleasing third. A full sister to Bulaxie and a half-sister to Dust Dancer and Zimzalabim, she is sure to come on in leaps and bounds for this and should not be difficult to win with. (7/1: 5/2-8/1)
2176 Middle Temple, tackling an extra furlong, took the field along but, collared over a furlong out, was soon beaten. (16/1)
Shannon's Secret (IRE) ran his best race to date over this longer trip and was close up until tapped for toe in the last two furlongs. (33/1)
2176 Simlet, who did not have a great deal of room in which to manoeuvre below the distance, made a little headway only to tire in the final furlong. (16/1)
2243 Daring News (9/1: 8/1-12/1)
2336 Radar (IRE) (3/1: 4/1-5/2)

2769 CHEVALIER TROPHY H'CAP (0-85) (3-Y.O+) (Class D)
4-40 (4-47) **5f 6y** £3,533.75 (£1,070.00: £522.50: £248.75) Stalls: Low GOING minus 0.33 sec per fur (GF)

	Horse / details	Dist	Pos	SP	RR	SF
2424*	**Faith Alone (77)** (CFWall) **4-9-3**(5) RMullen(5) (b: lw: a.p: rdn over 1f out: led ins fnl f: r.o wl)	—	**1**	100/30 1	83	53
2563 4	**Willow Dale (IRE) (76)** (DRCElsworth) **4-9-7** RCochrane(2) (b.nr hind: rdn over 1f out: gd hdwy fnl f: fin wl)	nk	**2**	11/2 3	81	51
2211 11	**Taoiste (80)** (RWArmstrong) **4-9-11** RPrice(9) (lw: led tl ins fnl f: unable qckn)	nk	**3**	20/1	84	54
2321 3	**Half Tone (54)** (RMFlower) **5-7-13b** JLowe(3) (hdwy over 1f out: hrd rdn: r.o)	½	**4**	9/1	57	27
2590 9	**Dande Flyer (62)** (DWPArbuthnot) **4-8-2**(5) RFfrench(1) (bhd whn nt clr run on ins over 2f out: hdwy fnl f: r.o wl)	¾	**5**	10/1	62	32
2105 30	**Hoh Returns (IRE) (83)** (MBell) **4-10-0** LDettori(8) (lw: hld up: rdn over 1f out: one pce)	2	**6**	12/1	77	47
2321 5	**Master of Passion (66)** (JMPEustace) **8-8-11** JTate(10) (a.p: rdn over 2f out: wknd fnl f)	nk	**7**	20/1	59	29
2590 8	**Kilcullen Lad (IRE) (84)** (PMooney) **3-9-11v** DRMcCabe(4) (lw: outpcd: hdwy 1f out: wknd ins fnl f)	¾	**8**	16/1	74	40
2529 5	**Clan Chief (82)** (JRArnold) **4-9-13** DHarrison(11) (b.off hind: swtg: w ldr over 3f: wknd fnl f)	1¾	**9**	9/2 2	67	37
2289 7	**Lord High Admiral (CAN) (79)** (MJHeaton-Ellis) **9-9-10** MRoberts(7) (lw: spd over 3f)	hd	**10**	10/1	64	34
2529 8	**White Emir (83)** (BJMeehan) **4-10-0b** PatEddery(6) (lw: sme hdwy over 1f out: sn wknd)	¾	**11**	7/1	65	35

(SP 120.4%) **11 Rn**

61.3 secs (1.50) CSF £19.96 CT £292.87 TOTE £4.50: £2.10 £1.80 £5.00 (£10.40) Trio £274.20 OWNER Mrs R. M. S. Neave (NEWMARKET) BRED J. R. Mitchell
WEIGHT FOR AGE 3yo-4lb

2424* Faith Alone, who is currently in foal to Most Welcome, was never far away and managed to get on top inside the final furlong. (100/30)
2563 Willow Dale (IRE) found her stride in no uncertain terms in the final furlong and, absolutely flying, would surely have prevailed with a little further to go. She is a winner without a penalty. (11/2)
1303 Taoiste ran much better here, taking the field along until overhauled inside the final furlong. (20/1)
2321 Half Tone began to pick up ground below the distance but, despite running on, was never going to get there in time. (9/1)
2590 Dande Flyer raced at the back of the field until making up a lot of ground in the final furlong. (10/1)
726 Hoh Returns (IRE) looked in tremendous shape in the paddock and chased the leaders, if tapped for toe from below the distance. (12/1)
2529 Clan Chief disputed the lead until below the distance before tiring. He should not be written off yet. (9/2)
2232* White Emir (7/1: 5/1-8/1)

T/Jkpt: £10,097.00 (0.36 Tckts); £9,101.60 to Leicester 17/7/97. T/Plpt: £426.60 (79.58 Tckts). T/Qdpt: £270.90 (7.85 Tckts) AK

2424- YARMOUTH (L-H) (Good)
Wednesday July 16th
WEATHER: overcast WIND: mod half bhd

2770 UPTON (S) STKS (3-Y.O+) (Class G)
1-50 (1-51) **1m 2f 21y** £2,242.50 (£630.00: £307.50) Stalls: Low GOING minus 0.19 sec per fur (GF)

	Horse / details	Dist	Pos	SP	RR	SF
2577 2	**Bluebell Miss (58)** (MJRyan) **3-8-5** GCarter(1) (chsd ldrs: rdn over 3f out: chal over 2f out: sn led: drvn clr fnl f)	—	**1**	5/2 1	66	38
2428 4	**Soda Pop (IRE) (60)** (CEBrittain) **3-8-10** WJO'Connor(3) (w ldr tl led 4f out: rdn 3f out: hdd 2f out: one pce)	3½	**2**	4/1 3	66	38
2521 11	**Northern Touch (62)** (SCWilliams) **3-7-12**(7) DarrenWilliams(6) (a.p: rdn 4f out: one pce appr fnl f)	½	**3**	11/2	60	32
2332 9	**Blazer's Baby (57)** (JRFanshawe) **3-8-5** NVarley(5) (plld hrd: chsd ldrs: pushed along 4f out: no imp fnl 2f)	1¾	**4**	16/1	57	29
2716*	**Guesstimation (USA) (57)** (JPearce) **8-9-9**(3) CTeague(4) (bhd: effrt over 2f out: sn rdn & no imp)	2	**5**	9/2	65	47
2184 5	**Ajeebah (IRE)** (WJHaggas) **3-8-5** MHills(2) (b.nr fore: lw: led tl rdn & hdd 4f out: sn wknd: t.o)	dist	**6**	3/1 2	—	—

(SP 113.0%) **6 Rn**

2m 8.3 (4.50) CSF £11.81 TOTE £3.00: £1.90 £2.80 (£6.10) OWNER Mr P. E. Axon (NEWMARKET) BRED Denis Bell
WEIGHT FOR AGE 3yo-10lb
No bid

2577 Bluebell Miss, the clear form choice, moved down poorly, but once she came back onto the bridle when moving into a challenging position, it was simply a matter of when and not if. (5/2)
2428 Soda Pop (IRE) certainly appears to have found his trip and he should find a race. (4/1: 9/4-9/2)
1144 Northern Touch stuck on better this time having not elected to force the pace. (11/2)
Blazer's Baby, stepping up in trip, didn't help matters by taking a strong hold. (16/1)
2716* Guesstimation (USA), having his second race in three days, was not weighted to confirm Warwick form with the winner and, brought widest of all, never looked like getting into it. (9/2)
2184 Ajeebah (IRE), dropped sharply in class, failed to see out the trip in very disappointing style. (3/1)

2771 E.B.F. ACLE MAIDEN STKS (2-Y.O) (Class D)

2-25 (2-25) **6f 3y** £3,273.75 (£990.00: £482.50: £228.75) Stalls: High GOING minus 0.19 sec per fur (GF)

				SP	RR	SF
	Headhunter (IRE) (WJHaggas) **2-9-0** MHills(5) (w'like: unf: trckd ldrs: led appr fnl f: rdn out)	—	1	15/2^{3}	80+	44
1932^{8}	**Stone of Destiny** (BJMeehan) **2-9-0** MTebbutt(8) (led wl over 4f: unable qckn fnl f)	1¼	2	16/1	77	41
	Royal Rights (DRLoder) **2-9-0** KDarley(2) (leggy: scope: lw: trckd ldrs: rdn over 1f out: no ex fnl f)	2½	3	8/13^{1}	70	34
	Princess Olivia (MJRyan) **2-8-9** GCarter(6) (neat: unf: bhd: pushed along over 2f out: styd on: nvr nr ldrs)	8	4	12/1	44	8
	Salsette (CEBrittain) **2-8-9** WJO'Connor(7) (str: scope: bit bkwd: w ldr tl wknd over 2f out)	nk	5	11/4^{2}	43	7
	Fritton (IRE) (MHTompkins) **2-9-0** DBiggs(4) (leggy: scope: bit bkwd: nvr nr to chal)	1½	6	33/1	44	8
2363^{6}	**Jus'chillin' (IRE)** (CADwyer) **2-8-9** NVarley(3) (w ldrs over 3f)	¾	7	16/1	37	1
2324^{9}	**Danzino (IRE)** (APJarvis) **2-9-0** SDrowne(1) (prom: rdn & edgd lft 3f out: sn wknd)	1½	8	50/1	38	2
				(SP 124.7%)	**8 Rn**	

1m 13.6 (2.70) CSF £113.23 TOTE £7.50: £1.30 £3.20 £1.30 (£32.60) OWNER Highclere Thoroughbred Racing Ltd (NEWMARKET) BRED Majestic Breeding

Headhunter (IRE), a half-brother to Broadmara who won a Group Three in Ireland as a two-year-old, was taken down steadily, but quickened pleasingly when asked to go and win his race. He has plenty yet to prove but this was a good start and, if he continues to thrive, could yet end up going for the Gimcrack, a race the trainer is keen to win. (15/2: 9/2-8/1)

Stone of Destiny didn't show much from a poor draw on his debut, but tried to make the experience tell by making the running against the stand rail. This brother of Rock Symphony should find a race. (16/1)

Royal Rights, a tall, striking newcomer, moved well to post and looked the part. Travelling smoothly on the heels of the leaders he failed to pick up as well as looked likely. He may need further but a half-brother by Shirley Heights has raced over six furlongs this year. (8/13: 1/2-evens)

Princess Olivia is a good mover but showed little until staying on late in the day. (12/1: 16/1-25/1)

Salsette, well supported in the market, had not come in her coat and looked some way short of peak fitness. This was confirmed by her running but this stocky half-sister to Cool Jazz has a future once fully wound up. (11/4: 9/2-5/2)

Fritton (IRE), a half-brother to the modest Briska and Little Noggins, looked to need this and didn't show a lot. (33/1)

2772 HORSEY H'CAP (0-80) (3-Y.O+ F & M) (Class D)

2-55 (2-56) **1m 3y** £3,452.50 (£1,045.00: £510.00: £242.50) Stalls: High GOING minus 0.19 sec per fur (GF)

				SP	RR	SF
1958^{8}	**Raaha (74)** (RWArmstrong) **3-9-2** AMcGlone(9) (plld hrd: trckd ldrs: led 1f out: rdn out)	—	1	15/2^{3}	81	40
2151^{6}	**Go For Green (58)** (DrJDScargill) **3-8-0** FNorton(10) (lw: a.p: led over 2f out: hdd 1f out: no ex)	1	2	33/1	63	22
2331*	**Prima Verde (78)** (LMCumani) **4-10-0** KDarley(7) (a.p: rdn over 1f out: kpt on one pce)	1¼	3	6/4^{1}	81	48
2346^{6}	**Sue's Return (78)** (APJarvis) **5-10-0** SDrowne(2) (lw: hld up: hdwy 2f out: one pce ins fnl f)	1¼	4	7/1^{2}	78	45
2116^{3}	**Blowing Away (IRE) (72)** (MHTompkins) **3-8-11**(3) MHenry(8) (stdd s: hld up: hdwy over 2f out: no imp appr fnl f)	1	5	7/1^{2}	70	29
2331^{7}	**Our Way (72)** (CEBrittain) **3-9-0** WJO'Connor(5) (prom: rdn & outpcd 4f out: n.d afterwards)	1½	6	8/1	67	26
2645^{11}	**Misty Cay (IRE) (60)** (SDow) **3-8-2** GCarter(1) (swtg: bhd: rdn & hdwy over 2f out: wknd over 1f out: eased)	2½	7	12/1	50	9
2415^{4}	**Literary (72)** (JHMGosden) **3-9-0** GHind(4) (led tl hdd & wknd over 2f out)	½	8	8/1	61	20
2569^{9}	**Badger Bay (IRE) (53)** (CADwyer) **4-8-3** NVarley(6) (in tch: rdn 4f out: sn bhd)	8	9	40/1	26	—
2507^{6}	**Miss Riviera Rose (68)** (GWragg) **3-8-10** MHills(3) (spd 4f)	10	10	14/1	21	—
				(SP 118.7%)	**10 Rn**	

1m 40.2 (4.20) CSF £202.19 CT £493.33 TOTE £9.10: £2.60 £5.70 £1.30 (£148.30) Trio £307.30; £95.23 to Leicester 17/7/97 OWNER Mr Hamdan Al Maktoum (NEWMARKET) BRED Shadwell Estate Company Limited

WEIGHT FOR AGE 3yo-8lb

1958 Raaha may have been held too long in the stalls last time, but for whatever reason failed to run her race. She was well drawn here and made good use of it but didn't entirely impress when going past the runner-up. (15/2)

2151 Go For Green, a wiry, lightly-made filly, looked tuned to the minute and, with the best draw, looked likely to win until the winner pounced. She may be hard pressed to reproduce this. (33/1)

2331* Prima Verde didn't pick up as well on this faster ground and may need further to compensate for her lack of gears. (6/4)

2346 Sue's Return, on the slowest ground towards the centre of the track, ran a fine race to get so close and looks in top form. Strongly-made, giving weight to inferior opponents probably suits her. (7/1)

2116 Blowing Away (IRE), dropped in trip, was reined back at the start and, finally brought to the stands' rail late in the day, did make a little ground. (7/1)

1973 Our Way left behind as the tempo increased, does look to need a truly-run mile as a bare minimum. (8/1)

2059 Miss Riviera Rose (14/1: op 8/1)

2773 EAST COAST MAIDEN STKS (3-Y.O) (Class D)

3-30 (3-31) **7f 3y** £3,420.00 (£1,035.00: £505.00: £240.00) Stalls: High GOING minus 0.19 sec per fur (GF)

				SP	RR	SF
1823^{2}	**Blueygreen (85)** (PWChapple-Hyam) **3-8-9** GHind(6) (lw: mde all: rdn over 1f out: hld on ins fnl f)	—	1	6/4^{1}	81	51
575^{W}	**Kafaf (USA) (82)** (JHMGosden) **3-8-9** AMcGlone(4) (prom: chsd wnr over 2f out: rdn & kpt on fnl f)	½	2	9/4^{2}	80	50
2580^{7}	**Severity** (WJHaggas) **3-9-0** MHills(8) (lw: plld hrd: chsd wnr over 4f: one pce fnl f)	3½	3	11/2^{3}	77	47
164^{5}	**Reeds** (JRFanshawe) **3-9-0** NVarley(2) (bit bkwd: in tch tl lost pl 3f out: n.d afterwards)	8	4	33/1	59	29
2580^{5}	**Select Choice (IRE) (80)** (APJarvis) **3-9-0** SDrowne(3) (chsd ldrs tl rdn & wknd over 1f out)	1¾	5	14/1	55	25
	Il Falco (FR) (SirMarkPrescott) **3-9-0** CNutter(1) (leggy: scope: sn rdn along: nvr nr ldrs)	8	6	20/1	36	6
	Arco Colora (MRStoute) **3-8-9** KDarley(5) (dwlt: a bhd)	16	7	7/1	—	—
	Unforgetable Charm (IRE) (MrsNMacauley) **3-8-9** DBiggs(7) (leggy: unf: b: dwlt: sn bhd)	4	9	33/1	—	—
				(SP 116.0%)	**8 Rn**	

1m 26.4 (2.20) CSF £4.52 TOTE £1.90: £1.10 £1.40 £1.30 (£2.90) OWNER Bloomsbury Stud (MARLBOROUGH) BRED Bloomsbury Stud

1823 Blueygreen, keen going down, broke fast and soon took the advantageous spot on the stands' rail, which may well have made the difference between victory and defeat. (6/4)

Kafaf (USA) went in the stalls this time and ran a decent race although, after looking likely to peg back the winner, failed to do so. (9/4)

Severity, a quite attractive, decent mover, took quite a hold on the winner's quarters. Unable to pick up in the last couple of furlongs, this was a long way in front of his debut a week ago. (11/2)

164 Reeds, off since a couple of runs on the All-Weather in January, looked well in his coat but in need of the run. He didn't shape without promise and his future will depend on what the handicapper does with him now. (33/1)

2580 Select Choice (IRE), racing towards the centre, ran poorly, failing to confirm last week's Folkestone form with Severity. (14/1: op 8/1)

Il Falco (FR), a quite attractive gelding, looked very green going down and was taken off his feet. If he has a future it will be over further. (20/1)

Arco Colora taken down last to post, went down far too freely, running her race before the start, and this ordinary-looking filly will do very well to get a win to put alongside her terrific pedigree before going to stud. (7/1: op 4/1)

2774 TUNSTALL CONDITIONS STKS (3-Y.O F) (Class C)

4-00 (4-02) **7f 3y** £4,532.57 (£1,650.70: £805.35: £344.25: £152.13) Stalls: High GOING minus 0.19 sec per fur (GF)

				SP	RR	SF
2426^{2}	**Imroz (USA) (100)** (HRACecil) **3-8-9** AMcGlone(5) (mde all: rdn & r.o wl fnl f)	—	1	7/4^{2}	105	61
1216^{6}	**Serenity (102)** (JRFanshawe) **3-8-9** MHills(1) (hld up: hdwy to chse wnr over 2f out: one pce fnl f)	3	2	9/2^{3}	98	54
2461a*	**Kenmist** (LMCumani) **3-8-13** KDarley(4) (w'like: hld up: plld out over 1f out: nt pce to chal)	¾	3	8/1	100	56
2023^{19}	**Meshhed (USA) (100)** (BHanbury) **3-9-1** JStack(3) (lw: trckd ldrs: n.m.r wl over 2f out & over 2f out: plld out over 1f out: fnd nil)	¾	4	13/8^{1}	101	57
2506*	**Bint Shihama (USA) (78)** (CEBrittain) **3-8-13** WJO'Connor(2) (lw: chsd wnr tl rdn & wknd over 1f out)	1½	5	16/1	95?	51
				(SP 109.6%)		**5 Rn**

1m 25.6 (1.40) CSF £8.84 TOTE £2.40: £1.10 £2.10 (£5.40) OWNER Mr K. Abdulla (NEWMARKET) BRED Juddmonte Farms

2426 Imroz (USA), whose head again came up, quickened far too well for these in the process and, despite the fact that she does not look to have grown much since last year, she seems to retain most if not all of her ability. (7/4)

1216 Serenity, taken down after the others, accepted restraint on this occasion and ran her race, just finding one too good. (9/2)

2461a* Kenmist, who won over three furlongs further on soft ground on her Italian debut, was given a most negative ride and would need to have been Pegasus to finish significantly closer. She is clearly one to pay close attention to as connections may be angling for a handicap mark. (8/1: 5/1-9/1)

1621* Meshhed (USA), mounted in the saddling boxes as usual, behaved impeccably before the race but clearly hates being crowded and wouldn't go through a narrow gap by the stands rail. Small fields and being allowed to dominate seem to suit her best. (13/8)

2506* Bint Shihama (USA) couldn't cope at all with what was a significant step up in class. (16/1)

2775 FILBY BRIDGE RATED STKS H'CAP (0-100) (3-Y.O+) (Class B)

4-30 (4-31) **7f 3y** £7,274.68 (£2,722.12: £1,331.06: £414.00: £414.00: £129.69) Stalls: High GOING minus 0.19 sec per fur (GF)

				SP	RR	SF
2325^{3}	**Yorkie George (94)** (LMCumani) **3-9-0** KDarley(9) (lw: trckd ldrs: led 2f out: rdn clr fnl f)	—	1	7/2^{2}	103	74
2331^{2}	**Intisab (86)** (RWArmstrong) **4-8-13** GCarter(8) (a.p: rdn & kpt on fnl f)	2½	2	9/1	89	67
2598*	**Tumbleweed Ridge (97)** (BJMeehan) **4-9-10b** 3x MTebbutt(6) (lw: trckd ldrs: rdn & no ex ins fnl f)	nk	3	2/1^{1}	100	78
2105^{19}	**Hello Mister (89)** (TEPowell) **6-8-13**(3) PMcCabe(5) (hld up: hdwy 2f out: r.o fnl f)	s.h	4	25/1	92	70
2105^{17}	**Alamein (USA) (85)** (WJHaggas) **4-8-12b** SDrowne(2) (hld up: hdwy over 1f out: r.o wl ins fnl f)	d.h	4	9/1	88	66
2426^{4}	**Shock Value (IRE) (98)** (MRStoute) **3-9-4** MHills(10) (lw: led: edgd lft & hdd 2f out: sn wknd)	3	6	9/2^{3}	94	65
2326^{9}	**Double Splendour (IRE) (93)** (PSFelgate) **7-9-6** GHind(3) (hld up: hdwy on ins whn nt clr run over 1f out: nt rcvr)	7	7	10/1	73++	51
2478^{7}	**Pleading (86)** (HCandy) **4-8-13** CRutter(1) (trckd ldr centre 4f)	1½	8	11/1	62	40
2026^{24}	**Sky Dome (IRE) (85)** (MHTompkins) **4-8-9**(3) MHenry(7) (lw: w ldrs over 3f)	1¼	9	12/1	58	36
1980^{17}	**Zaretski (83)** (CEBrittain) **3-7-12b1**(5) APolli(4) (spd centre 4f)	3	10	25/1	50	21
				(SP 126.5%)		**10 Rn**

1m 24.9 (0.70) CSF £35.20 CT £74.16 TOTE £3.90: £1.60 £2.70 £1.60 (£11.90) Trio £14.60 OWNER Mr M. J. Dawson (NEWMARKET) BRED Robert Charles Key

WEIGHT FOR AGE 3yo-7lb

2325 Yorkie George, drawn one from the stands rail, took a good hold and tracked the leader along the rail until let through against the fence. With such good fortune, he could hardly help but win, but was still quite impressive. (7/2)

2331 Intisab dropped in trip, ran well but would surely be better over another furlong. (9/1)

2598* Tumbleweed Ridge looked for cover but rather towards the centre of the track, always having at least two horses racing between him and the favoured stands rail. (2/1)

1874 Alamein (USA), with his tongue tied down, worked his way over to the stands rail to beat the draw but had to pull wide to make his final move. This was a good effort and, with the stable back in good form, he should not be long in winning. (9/1)

1596 Hello Mister has never won beyond six furlongs but this run suggests he may be no back number and his last two wins came in the Portland Handicaps of '94 and '95, both off higher marks. (25/1)

2426 Shock Value (IRE), with the best of the draw, made the running until hanging off the stands rail, letting the winner through. Wandering back to the rail, he was already well held. He has not grown much since his two-year-old days and really ought to get this trip, but was most disappointing. (9/2)

738 Sky Dome (IRE) never made a serious bid to get to the stands rail and dominate, running a dismal race. (12/1)

2776 REPPS H'CAP (0-80) (3-Y.O+) (Class D)

5-00 (5-01) **1m 3f 101y** £3,501.25 (£1,060.00: £517.50: £246.25) Stalls: Low GOING minus 0.19 sec per fur (GF)

				SP	RR	SF
2399^{2}	**What A Fuss (58)** (BHanbury) **4-8-8** JStack(8) (lw: trckd ldrs: led 2f out: rdn 1f out: hld on wl nr fin)	—	1	4/1^{2}	67	44
	Burning (USA) (75) (WJHaggas) **5-9-11** MHills(2) (trckd ldrs: outpcd over 2f out: styd on wl appr fnl f: jst failed)	s.h	2	5/1^{3}	84	61
833^{5}	**Leading Note (USA) (74)** (LMCumani) **3-8-13** KDarley(4) (trckd ldrs: rdn over 1f out: kpt on)	¾	3	100/30^{1}	82	48
2374^{4}	**Sarbaron (IRE) (62)** (PWHarris) **3-8-1** FNorton(1) (led over 3f: led 5f out to 2f out: one pce fnl f)	3½	4	9/1	65	31
2483^{2}	**Premier Generation (IRE) (71)** (DWPArbuthnot) **4-9-7** SWhitworth(6) (s.i.s: hdwy over 2f out: no imp appr fnl f)	1½	5	5/1^{3}	72	49
2430^{5}	**Blockade (USA) (60)** (MBell) **8-8-10** MFenton(7) (t: hld up: effrt over 2f out: no imp)	2½	6	6/1	57	34
789^{2}	**Urgent Swift (77)** (APJarvis) **4-9-13** SDrowne(9) (hld up & plld hrd: hdwy whn rdn & edgd lft 3f out: sn btn)	1½	7	7/1	72	49
2550^{7}	**Prospector's Cove (68)** (JPearce) **4-9-4** GHind(5) (dwlt: sn w ldrs: ev ch 3f out: sn wknd)	1	8	10/1	62	39
2512^{6}	**Suivez (52)** (MrsNMacauley) **7-8-2**ow4 DBiggs(3) (b: lw: led 8f out to 5f out: rdn & wknd over 3f out)	15	9	20/1	25	—
				(SP 127.0%)		**9 Rn**

2m 26.4 (4.60) CSF £24.73 CT £70.89 TOTE £4.20: £1.10 £1.10 £2.30 (£22.20) Trio £28.60 OWNER Mr B. Hanbury (NEWMARKET) BRED Gainsborough Stud Management Ltd

WEIGHT FOR AGE 3yo-11lb

2399 What A Fuss, back up in trip, barely saw it out after travelling notably well for much of the race. (4/1)

Burning (USA), having his first run for a new yard, looked very fit and almost snatched the race out of the fire after getting slightly short of room and taking time to respond as the pace quickened. He has run all his best races fresh in the past and this may just have been Cup Final day. (5/1)

833 Leading Note (USA) looked to get this longer trip but is still learning and should prove capable of finding a race off this sort of mark. (100/30)
2374 Sarbaron (IRE), a very poor mover in his slower paces, is not bred to stay this far but seems to last it out, albeit without ever threatening to quicken. (9/1: 5/1-10/1)
2483 Premier Generation (IRE) didn't run badly but found the drying ground against him. (5/1)
2430 Blockade (USA), held up as usual to get this longer trip, failed to do so. (6/1)
2187 Prospector's Cove looks to have gone the wrong way, and his head went ominously high when ridden along halfway up the straight. (10/1)

T/Plpt: £7.80 (1,123.97 Tckts). T/Qdpt: £3.10 (175.29 Tckts) Dk

2531-BATH (L-H) (Good to firm)
Thursday July 17th
WEATHER: unsettled WIND: mod across

2777 WHITE HORSE (S) STKS (4-Y.O+) (Class G)
2-00 (2-02) **1m 3f 144y** £2,234.00 (£624.00: £302.00) Stalls: Low GOING minus 0.46 sec per fur (F)

				SP	RR	SF
*2048**	**Petoskin (51)** (JPearce) **5-9-7** MWigham(2) (mde all: rdn over 2f out: drvn out)	—	1	$4/5^{1}$	58	36
2479^{3}	**Shabanaz (52)** (WRMuir) **12-9-2** JReid(1) (lw: a.p: rdn & nt clr run 2f out: swtchd rt 1f out: r.o)	½	2	$13/8^{2}$	52	30
	Kika (KRBurke) **4-8-11** BDoyle(4) (bit bkwd: a.p: rdn over 3f out: btn whn bmpd 1f out)	3½	3	16/1	43?	21
367^{7}	**Young Frederick (IRE) (40)** (NMBabbage) **4-9-2** TSprake(3) (hdwy 2f out: one pce fnl f)	2	4	$12/1^{3}$	45?	23
	Melos (GThorner) **4-8-11** CRutter(5) (wl bhd fnl 3f: t.o)	dist	5	50/1	—	—
				(SP 109.2%)		**5 Rn**

2m 31.5 (4.80) CSF £2.06 TOTE £1.80: £1.00 £1.90 (£1.50) OWNER Mrs Jean Routledge (NEWMARKET) BRED James Wigan
Bt in 7,300 gns
2048* Petoskin may be better on the sand but this was an uncompetitive race even by selling standards. (4/5: 10/11-evens)
2479 Shabanaz found a soft contest here but could not peg back the winner after not getting the run of the race. (13/8)
Kika will strip fitter for the outing but will struggle to find many affairs as weak as this. (16/1)
280 Young Frederick (IRE) was upped in trip and without headgear on this first run for his new stable. (12/1)

2778 JAMES & COWPER ACCOUNTANTS LIMITED STKS (0-75) (3-Y.O+) (Class D)
2-30 (2-30) **1m 5y** £3,397.00 (£1,021.00: £493.00: £229.00) Stalls: Low GOING minus 0.46 sec per fur (F)

				SP	RR	SF
2695*	**Sword Arm (75)** (RCharlton) **3-9-0v** TSprake(1) (chsd ldr: led over 2f out: r.o wl)	—	1	$7/4^{1}$	85	60
2347^{6}	**Blewbury Hill (IRE) (74)** (RFJohnsonHoughton) **3-8-10** JReid(2) (hld up: chsd wnr fnl 2f: r.o one pce fnl f)	1¼	2	$9/4^{2}$	79	54
2331^{8}	**Scarlet Crescent (72)** (PTWalwyn) **3-8-9** PatEddery(4) (hld up: a bhd)	8	3	$7/2^{3}$	62	37
2201^{12}	**Admirals Flame (IRE) (74)** (CFWall) **6-9-4** GDuffield(3) (b: led tl hdd over 2f out: wknd over 1f out)	3	4	5/1	57	40
				(SP 106.0%)		**4 Rn**

1m 38.2 (Equals best) CSF £5.18 TOTE £2.30: (£2.10) OWNER Mr A. E. Oppenheimer (BECKHAMPTON) BRED Hascombe and Valiant Studs
WEIGHT FOR AGE 3yo-8lb
2695* Sword Arm had the visor refitted because his rider thought he travels better in it as it helps him concentrate. He may now be upped to a mile and a quarter. (7/4)
2347 Blewbury Hill (IRE) was reverting to the right sort of trip. (9/4)
1794* Scarlet Crescent never threatened to take a hand. (7/2)
1782 Admirals Flame (IRE) did not seem suited to front-running tactics. (5/1: op 3/1)

2779 TOTE BOOKMAKERS H'CAP (0-90) (3-Y.O) (Class C)
3-00 (3-00) **5f 11y** £5,791.75 (£1,744.00: £844.50: £394.75) Stalls: High GOING minus 0.46 sec per fur (F)

				SP	RR	SF
180^{3}	**Dominant Air (75)** (SirMarkPrescott) **3-8-10** GDuffield(5) (a.p: led over 1f out: drvn out)	—	1	8/1	78	46
2134^{10}	**Dancethenightaway (86)** (BJMeehan) **3-9-7** PatEddery(7) (hdwy over 2f out: ev ch over 1f out: r.o ins fnl f)	½	2	$6/1^{3}$	87	55
2590^{6}	**Anokato (68)** (KTIvory) **3-8-3b**ow2 BDoyle(6) (rdn over 2f out: hdwy on ins & hmpd over 1f out: r.o ins fnl f)	nk	3	16/1	69	35
2547*	**Cauda Equina (80)** (MRChannon) **3-8-12**(3) 7x PPMurphy(3) (s.i.s: hdwy & squeezed thro over 1f out: nt qckn ins fnl f: fin 4th: ½l: disq: plcd last)		**4d**	$6/1^{3}$	79	47
2134^{14}	**Sabina (84)** (IABalding) **3-9-5** JReid(4) (prom: ev ch 2f out: sn rdn: btn whn bmpd 1f out: fin 5th: 4l: plcd 4th)	4½	4	$2/1^{1}$	70	38
2547^{3}	**Bayford Thrust (76)** (JBerry) **3-8-8**(3) PFessey(1) (b: b.hind: led over 3f: wkng whn hmpd 1f out: fin 6th: 1 ¾l: plcd 5th)	1¾	5	$11/4^{2}$	57	25
2377^{13}	**Mangus (IRE) (72)** (KOCunningham-Brown) **3-8-7** PaulEddery(2) (chsd ldr tl wknd qckly 2f out: fin 7th, 8l: plcd 6th)	8	6	12/1	27	—
				(SP 113.3%)		**7 Rn**

61.1 secs (0.60) CSF £48.33 TOTE £5.60: £2.10 £2.90 (£16.60) OWNER Mr Neil Greig (NEWMARKET) BRED W. N. Greig
STEWARDS' ENQUIRY Murphy susp. 26/7 & 28/7 - 2/8/97 (irresponsible riding).
180 Dominant Air was described by his owner as having come back from semi-retirement. He added that he thought it was a fine training performance. (8/1)
1608 Dancethenightaway was down to only 2lb higher than when winning a nursery on soft ground last season. (6/1)
2590 Anokato, due to go down 3lb, must have gone even closer with a trouble-free run. (16/1)
1018 Sabina seems to need to dominate to show her best. (2/1)
2547 Bayford Thrust was reverting to the minimum trip. (11/4)
2134 Mangus (IRE) (12/1: op 8/1)
2547* Cauda Equina (6/1: 4/1-13/2)

2780 LONGLEAT CLAIMING STKS (3-Y.O+) (Class F)
3-30 (3-32) **5f 11y** £2,617.50 (£730.00: £352.50) Stalls: High GOING minus 0.46 sec per fur (F)

				SP	RR	SF
2567^{9}	**Hard to Figure (75)** (RJHodges) **11-8-9**(3) PPMurphy(5) (lw: gd hdwy over 1f out: str run to ld nr fin)	—	1	13/2	63	33

2575[3]	**Montendre (81)** (RJHodges) **10-8-9** JReid(6) (hdwy over 2f out: r.o wl ins fnl f)	¾	**2**	7/4[1]	58	28
1931[4]	**Mon Bruce (57)** (WRMuir) **3-9-4** PatEddery(7) (a.p: led ins fnl f: hdd nr fin)	hd	**3**	11/2[3]	70	36
2663[4]	**Lucky Dip (68)** (DRCElsworth) **3-8-9b[1]** DHarrison(2) (a.p: rdn over 2f out: ev ch over 1f out: one pce)	1¼	**4**	2/1[2]	57	23
	Rowlandsons Stud (IRE) (KCComerford) **4-8-7**(7) SRighton(1) (lw: led tl ins fnl f)	3	**5**	66/1	49	19
2536[6]	**Delrob (36)** (DHaydnJones) **6-8-7b** AMackay(3) (lw: nvr nrr)	¾	**6**	14/1	40	10
2536[W]	**Chief's Lady (38)** (JMBradley) **5-8-4** TSprake(11) (chsd ldrs: no hdwy fnl 2f)	1	**7**	16/1	33	3
2159[7]	**Moor Hall Princess (34)** (NMBabbage) **3-8-0** JQuinn(4) (chsd ldrs 3f)	3½	**8**	50/1	22	—
	Vaporize (DMHyde) **5-8-6**(3) RHavlin(10) (swtg: a bhd)	8	**9**	66/1	2	—
2311[11]	**Jay-Em-Bee** (JMBradley) **4-8-13**(3) AWhelan(9) (s.s: a bhd)	2	**10**	66/1	3	—
1921[8]	**Nikki Star** (CJHill) **3-8-9** SWhitworth(8) (bit bkwd: swtg: outpcd)	1½	**11**	50/1	—	—
				(SP 119.4%)		**11 Rn**

62.0 secs (1.50) CSF £16.79 TOTE £8.40: £2.30 £1.30 £1.70 (£7.80) Trio £16.00 OWNER Mr J. W. Mursell (SOMERTON) BRED J. W. Mursell
WEIGHT FOR AGE 3yo-4lb
1676 Hard to Figure came with a typical late run to record his first victory over the minimum distance for seven years. (13/2: 4/1-7/1)
2575 Montendre would have been meeting the winner on 12lb worse terms had this been a handicap. (7/4: 5/4-2/1)
1931 Mon Bruce was well supported in the ring despite having a stiff task based on official ratings. (11/2: op 10/1)
2663 Lucky Dip was sharpened up a little by the blinkers. (2/1)
Rowlandsons Stud (IRE) ran a fine race on his comeback despite having a very difficult task at the weights. (66/1)
2536 Delrob is worth a try back at six. (14/1)

2781 AVEBURY MEDIAN AUCTION MAIDEN STKS (2-Y.O) (Class F)

4-00 (4-01) **5f 161y** £2,792.50 (£780.00: £377.50) Stalls: High GOING minus 0.46 sec per fur (F)

				SP	RR	SF
2477[2]	**Lido (IRE)** (BWHills) **2-9-0** MHills(9) (lw: hld up: hdwy over 2f out: led over 1f out: comf)	—	**1**	4/11[1]	85+	41
	Mustique Dream (RCharlton) **2-8-9** TSprake(4) (lengthy: bit bkwd: s.s: hdwy 2f out: r.o ins fnl f: nt trble wnr)	1½	**2**	12/1[3]	76+	32
	Dover Soul (PJMakin) **2-8-9** SSanders(2) (cmpt: hdwy over 2f out: r.o one pce fnl f)	3½	**3**	20/1	66	22
1954[8]	**Regalo** (DMHyde) **2-8-11**(3) RHavlin(10) (led: hdd over 1f out: wknd fnl f)	5	**4**	50/1	57	13
	Tiara (BJMeehan) **2-8-9** GDuffield(7) (w'like: nvr nrr)	2	**5**	14/1	47	3
2509[3]	**Striding King** (MRChannon) **2-9-0** PatEddery(13) (prom: ev ch 2f out: wknd over 1f out)	1	**6**	8/1[2]	49	5
2509[10]	**Tui** (KMcAuliffe) **2-8-9** JReid(6) (chsd ldrs tl wknd 2f out)	¾	**7**	20/1	42	—
1760[11]	**Scene (IRE)** (MartynMeade) **2-8-2**(7) RBrisland(1) (swtg: spd 3f)	2½	**8**	66/1	35	—
2227[5]	**Gaily Mill** (IABalding) **2-8-9** SWhitworth(8) (a bhd)	nk	**9**	16/1	34	—
	Thomas O'Malley (RJO'Sullivan) **2-9-0** AProcter(12) (lengthy: a bhd)	hd	**10**	50/1	39	—
	Tiggy Silvano (MRChannon) **2-8-9** RPainter(3) (lengthy: a bhd)	2½	**11**	50/1	27	—
2509[14]	**Ginnieshope** (SGKnight) **2-8-9** NVarley(5) (a bhd)	1¾	**12**	66/1	22	—
	Sun Dancer (NASmith) **2-9-0** PaulEddery(11) (cmpt: a bhd: t.o)	14	**13**	100/1	—	—
				(SP 124.1%)		**13 Rn**

1m 10.8 (1.30) CSF £5.24 TOTE £1.50: £1.10 £1.60 £4.90 (£5.60) Trio £56.00 OWNER Mr Guy Reed (LAMBOURN) BRED M. Flattery
2477 Lido (IRE) had nothing of the calibre of Little Indian to contend with this time. (4/11: op 4/7)
Mustique Dream is a half-sister to mile and a half winner Oversman and six-furlong juvenile scorer Close Relative. She showed plenty of promise for the future and should appreciate further. (12/1: 3/1-14/1)
Dover Soul, a half-sister to five-furlong juvenile winner Chili Concerto, made a respectable start to her career. (20/1)
Regalo has looked a bit of a short runner over the bare minimum so was not suited by this extended five. (50/1)
Tiara is a 48,000 gns sister to speedy Group Three winner Risky. (14/1: op 7/1)
2509 Striding King travelled strongly on the bridle until finding precious little. (8/1)

2782 WESTONBIRT H'CAP (0-70) (3-Y.O+ F & M) (Class E)

4-30 (4-31) **1m 2f 46y** £3,054.25 (£919.00: £444.50: £207.25) Stalls: Low GOING minus 0.46 sec per fur (F)

				SP	RR	SF
2015[7]	**Saddlers' Hope (70)** (JRFanshawe) **3-9-6** MHills(9) (lw: mde all: clr over 2f out: easily)	—	**1**	10/1	81+	53
1624[3]	**Bathe In Light (USA) (58)** (LordHuntingdon) **3-8-8** DHarrison(2) (lw: a.p: rdn over 3f out: chsd wnr over 2f out: no imp)	4	**2**	4/1[1]	63	35
2550[2]	**Your Most Welcome (56)** (DJSffrenchDavis) **6-8-13**(3) PFessey(8) (hdwy 3f out: one pce fnl 2f)	¾	**3**	4/1[1]	60	42
2552[15]	**Whispering Dawn (63)** (CPEBrooks) **4-9-6**(3) PPMurphy(12) (b: b.hind: a.p: rdn & one pce fnl 2f)	1¼	**4**	20/1	65	47
2487[7]	**Indian Nectar (45)** (RBrotherton) **4-8-5** RPrice(1) (swtg: nvr nr to chal)	1	**5**	33/1	45	27
2550[4]	**Cuban Reef (50)** (WJMusson) **5-8-10** JQuinn(10) (lw: hld up: hdwy 3f out: one pce fnl 2f)	¾	**6**	8/1	49	31
2582[2]	**Mono Lady (IRE) (55)** (DHaydnJones) **4-9-1b** AMackay(11) (s.i.s: hdwy over 3f out: wknd wl over 1f out)	3½	**7**	7/1[3]	48	30
1866[9]	**Off The Rails (64)** (HCandy) **3-9-0** CRutter(7) (plld hrd: a bhd)	nk	**8**	14/1	57	29
1168[13]	**War Shanty (55)** (LadyHerries) **4-9-1** JReid(5) (swtg: a bhd)	nk	**9**	12/1	47	29
1278[5]	**Classic Parisian (IRE) (67)** (RJO'Sullivan) **4-9-13** AProcter(3) (lw: hld up mid div: bhd fnl 2f)	1	**10**	14/1	58	40
2533*	**Hill Farm Blues (64)** (WMBrisbourne) **4-9-10** 6x AGarth(6) (s.s: bhd most of wy)	hd	**11**	5/1[2]	55	37
2374[11]	**Ellway Lady (IRE) (62)** (IABalding) **3-8-12** SWhitworth(4) (lw: chsd ldr: rdn over 3f out: wknd over 2f out: t.o)	9	**12**	16/1	39	11
				(SP 124.0%)		**12 Rn**

2m 8.2 (1.70) CSF £47.41 CT £177.36 TOTE £13.50: £5.30 £1.90 £1.70 (£37.50) Trio £76.90 OWNER Cheveley Park Stud (NEWMARKET)
BRED Cheveley Park Stud Ltd
WEIGHT FOR AGE 3yo-10lb
1301 Saddlers' Hope, down 2lb, made front-running tactics pay off back at this trip with an emphatic victory. (10/1: 8/1-12/1)
1624 Bathe In Light (USA), dropped 2lb, got the best of the separate battle for the runner-up spot. (4/1)
2550 Your Most Welcome was due to go up 2lb in future handicaps. (4/1)
2552 Whispering Dawn was running off the same mark as when scoring at Newmarket last November. (20/1)
Indian Nectar has been given a real chance by the handicapper having dropped 10lb this season. (33/1)
2550 Cuban Reef, due to go down 1lb, was 5lb higher than the highest mark off which she has won. (8/1)
War Shanty (12/1: op 8/1)

T/Plpt: £35.00 (443 Tckts). T/Qdpt: £18.50 (62.59 Tckts) KH

1958-LEICESTER (R-H) (Good, Good to soft patches)
Thursday July 17th
WEATHER: cloudy WIND: slt half bhd

2783 MOUNTSORREL MEDIAN AUCTION MAIDEN STKS (3 & 4-Y.O) (Class F)
2-15 (2-16) **1m 1f 218y** £2,679.00 (£744.00: £357.00) Stalls: High GOING minus 0.08 sec per fur (G)

				SP	RR	SF
2533^{5}	**Go For Salt (USA) (78)** (MRStoute) **3-8-6** KDarley(5) (trckd ldrs: led over 2f out: sn clr: unchal)	—	**1**	$6/5^{1}$	82	31
2059^{2}	**Billy Nomaite** (MrsSJSmith) **3-8-11** OPears(9) (led & sn clr: hdd over 2f out: r.o one pce)	9	**2**	10/1	73	22
2492^{12}	**Minster Star** (JLSpearing) **3-8-6** DaneO'Neill(11) (hld up: hdwy over 2f out: styd on u.p)	¾	**3**	66/1	66	15
1986^{3}	**Shilling (IRE)** (ACStewart) **3-8-6** MRoberts(4) (prom: disp ld 3f out: one pce fnl 2f)	6	**4**	$6/1^{3}$	57	6
2532^{6}	**Woody's Boy (IRE)** (MJHeaton-Ellis) **3-8-11** SDrowne(1) (prom: rdn 3f out: grad wknd)	2	**5**	14/1	59	8
	Lark's Rise (HCandy) **3-8-6** NAdams(10) (leggy: lt-f: bhd: sme hdwy fnl 2f: nvr nrr)	3½	**6**	14/1	48	—
	Announcing (JHMGosden) **3-8-11** GHind(2) (w'like: bit bkwd: s.s: effrt on outside over 2f out: no imp)	¾	**7**	14/1	52	1
2544^{10}	**Dunston Bill** (GBarnett) **3-8-11** NCarlisle(8) (chsd ldrs: pushed along ent st: wknd 3f out)	6	**8**	100/1	42	—
	Pearl Silk (TTBill) **4-9-2** TGMcLaughlin(3) (bkwd: a bhd: t.o fnl 3f)	14	**9**	100/1	15	—
	King Protea (JHMGosden) **3-8-11** LDettori(6) (w'like: scope: bit bkwd: hld up: effrt 4f out: eased whn no imp fnl 3f: t.o)	hd	**10**	$5/2^{2}$	20	—
	Jewel Fighter (CASmith) **3-8-6** VSlattery(7) (w'like: leggy: bkwd: rn green: a bhd: t.o)	22	**11**	100/1	—	—

(SP 121.9%) **11 Rn**

2m 10.3 (6.60) CSF £14.74 TOTE £2.50: £1.10 £1.70 £19.20 (£7.70) Trio £233.20; £167.54 to Newbury 18/7/97 OWNER Mr S. Hanson (NEWMARKET) BRED Brereton C. Jones
WEIGHT FOR AGE 3yo-10lb

2533 Go For Salt (USA) had quite a simple task on this return to maiden company and opened her account in the easiest possible fashion. (6/5)
2059 Billy Nomaite tends to run a bit too free at present, but he continues to perform with credit and his turn will arrive. (10/1: 7/1-12/1)
Minster Star showed much improved form here and if she continues to progress there are races waiting to be picked up. (66/1)
1986 Shilling (IRE) joined issue three furlongs out and looked sure to take a hand in proceedings, but she had no answer when the winner quickened things up and was tenderly handled once her chance had gone. (6/1: 4/1-13/2)
2532 Woody's Boy (IRE) sat much closer to the pace than he had done in his previous races, but he was hard at work from some way out and his chance quickly disappeared. (14/1)
Lark's Rise, a sparsely-made, leggy filly, bred for stamina, was only finding her stride when the race was all but over. (14/1: 8/1-16/1)
Announcing (14/1: 8/1-16/1)
King Protea (5/2: 6/4-11/4)

2784 SUTTON (S) STKS (2-Y.O) (Class G)
2-45 (2-46) **5f 2y** £2,469.00 (£684.00: £327.00) Stalls: High GOING minus 0.08 sec per fur (G)

				SP	RR	SF
2606^{2}	**Daynabee** (NTinkler) **2-8-6** KimTinkler(11) (led after 2f: r.o wl ins fnl f)	—	**1**	$5/1^{3}$	59	7
1274^{4}	**Means Business (IRE)** (BJMeehan) **2-8-11** MTebbutt(8) (hld up: hdwy 2f out: hrd rdn & r.o ins fnl f)	½	**2**	$4/1^{2}$	62	10
2534^{11}	**Corsecan** (SDow) **2-8-11** MRoberts(1) (lw: sn prom: ev ch 1f out: rdn & no ex fnl f)	¾	**3**	14/1	60	8
2664^{3}	**The Imposter (IRE)** (DJGMurraySmith) **2-8-11** KDarley(5) (hdwy wl over 1f out: nrst fin)	3	**4**	11/2	50	—
2412^{4}	**Angry Albert** (CSmith) **2-8-4v(7)** CLowther(2) (chsd ldrs: hrd rdn 2f out: kpt on same pce)	1¼	**5**	16/1	46	—
2233^{3}	**Amington Girl** (PDEvans) **2-8-6** JFEgan(12) (trckd ldrs: shkn up over 1f out: one pce)	1¼	**6**	7/1	37	—
564^{6}	**Suggest** (MartynMeade) **2-8-11b¹** FNorton(10) (bit bkwd: led 2f: prom tl rdn & wknd wl over 1f out)	3	**7**	$11/4^{1}$	33	—
1984^{5}	**Lake Wobegone (IRE)** (JohnBerry) **2-8-11** MFenton(7) (bhd: effrt & rdn 2f out: nt pce to chal)	¾	**8**	20/1	31	—
1789^{9}	**Romantic Secret** (RTJuckes) **2-8-6** VSlattery(6) (chsd ldrs: rdn 2f out: grad wknd)	nk	**9**	50/1	25	—
	Pip's Addition (IRE) (JAGlover) **2-8-6** GCarter(3) (scope: bkwd: s.s: a bhd & outpcd)	nk	**10**	12/1	24	—
2003^{9}	**Lionels Lucky Lady** (JSMoore) **2-8-3(3)** MHenry(4) (prom 3f)	1¾	**11**	33/1	18	—
	Ask Speedy Snaps (JMBradley) **2-8-8(3)** RFfrench(9) (lt-f: unf: bkwd: dwlt: a bhd & outpcd)	4	**12**	33/1	10	—
2066^{7}	**Jen's In The Know** (CMurray) **2-8-1(5)** DSweeney(13) (prom far side over 3f)	¾	**13**	25/1	3	—

(SP 127.9%) **13 Rn**

63.1 secs (4.60) CSF £23.51 TOTE £5.40: £1.90 £3.10 £3.20 (£24.40) Trio £52.70 OWNER Mr T. L. Beecroft (MALTON) BRED G. Middlebrook
No bid

OFFICIAL EXPLANATION **Pip's Addition (IRE): rider was unable to ride out his mount as he had been hit on the knee by a flying horseshoe.**
2606 Daynabee, gaining just reward for some pleasing performances, appreciated this return to the turf and she had the measure of her challengers on the run to the line. (5/1)
1274 Means Business (IRE) is certainly capable of winning at this level but may need a slightly stiffer test of stamina to show his true worth. (4/1)
Corsecan closed up two furlongs out and posed a live threat approaching the final furlong, but when an extra effort was called for he was short of a turn of speed. (14/1: 10/1-16/1)
2664 The Imposter (IRE) found this step down to the minimum trip not in his favour, and he was always at full stretch in an attempt to reach the leaders. (11/2)
2412 Angry Albert, always in the chasing group but never on the bridle, kept plugging away and he may get it right one of these days. (16/1)
2233 Amington Girl could never summon the pace to pose a threat and may well need further. (7/1)
564 Suggest wore blinkers on this first outing for his new stable but he had been out of action for three and a half months and a lack of peak fitness could have been the cause for such a disappointing display (11/4: op 9/2)
Pip's Addition (IRE) (12/1: op 8/1)

2785 BOLLINGER CHAMPAGNE CHALLENGE SERIES GENTLEMEN'S H'CAP (0-70) (3-Y.O+) (Class E)
3-15 (3-18) **7f 9y** £3,499.50 (£1,056.00: £513.00: £241.50) Stalls: Low GOING minus 0.08 sec per fur (G)

				SP	RR	SF
2552^{14}	**Silver Lining (60)** (APJones) **3-11-7** MrJGoldstein(14) (hld up in tch: hdwy to ld over 1f out: jst hld on)	—	**1**	9/1	70	45
2281^{4}	**Lorins Gold (34)** (AndrewTurnell) **7-10-2** MrJRees(17) (lw: hld up: hdwy 2f out: r.o wl fnl f: jst failed)	s.h	**2**	$6/1^{3}$	44	26
2510*	**Welcome Heights (48)** (MJFetherston-Godley) **3-10-9** MrRWakley(15) (hdwy over 2f out: rdn & r.o wl cl home)	¾	**3**	$9/2^{2}$	56	31
2416^{6}	**Dummer Golf Time (58)** (LordHuntingdon) **4-11-12** MrABalding(7) (lw: a.p: ev ch over 1f out: unable qckn)	nk	**4**	9/1	66	48
2463^{5}	**Smart Guest (44)** (DShaw) **5-10-8(4)** MrSDurack(10) (b: chsd ldrs: effrt wl over 1f out: kpt on towards fin)	s.h	**5**	25/1	51	33
2552^{2}	**Delight of Dawn (45)** (EAWheeler) **5-10-9(4)** MrJDewhurst(4) (hdwy 2f out: r.o wl ins fnl f)	1¼	**6**	$4/1^{1}$	50	32

2121[9] **Persephone (25)** (JLHarris) **4-9-3b**(4) MrVLukaniuk(6) (led over 3f out tl hdd & wknd over 1f out)......................5 **7** 40/1 18 —
2760[10] **Attarikh (IRE) (51)** (MrsALMKing) **4-11-1b**(4) MrOMcPhail(5) (lw: chsd ldrs: rdn wl over 1f out: no imp).........s.h **8** 20/1 44 26
1276[12] **Sassy Street (IRE) (48)** (RFJohnsonHoughton) **4-10-12**(4) MrPPhillips(2) (prom: hrd drvn over 2f out: sn btn)1¾ **9** 25/1 37 19
2546[12] **Beano Script (60)** (JHanson) **4-11-10**(4) MrCBHills(13) (lw: prom tl wknd wl over 1f out: eased whn btn) ....hd **10** 12/1 49 31
2577[10] **Euro Superstar (FR) (37)** (SDow) **3-9-8**(4) MrRGuest(3) (a in rr) ....nk **11** 25/1 25 —
2646[9] **Asterix (38)** (JMBradley) **9-10-2b**(4) MrAEvans(9) (b: a in rr) 1¾ **12** 14/1 22 4
2375[10] **Sarum (30)** (JELong) **11-9-8**(4) MrTWaters(8) (b: a bhd) ....¾ **13** 50/1 13 —
2552[17] **Tulsa (IRE) (58)** (BGubby) **3-11-1v**(4) MrJCrowley(18) (prom 4f) ....¾ **14** 20/1 39 14
2302[2] **Failed To Hit (51)** (NPLittmoden) **4-11-1b**(4) MrJTyler-Morris(16) (a in rr) 5 **15** 12/1 20 2
2569[5] **Double Gold (64)** (MBell) **3-11-7**(4) MrCRanson(11) (led to ½-wy: wknd 2f out) ....¾ **16** 9/1 32 7
Rise Up Singing (44) (WJMusson) **9-10-12b** MrTMcCarthy(1) (bkwd: chsd ldrs stands' side 4f)...................2½ **17** 10/1 6 —
(SP 139.1%) **17 Rn**

1m 29.2 (6.60) CSF £59.53 CT £219.13 TOTE £20.60: £3.40 £1.90 £2.50 £1.80 (£36.60) Trio £62.30 OWNER The Lambourn Racing Club (EASTBURY) BRED R. Hutt
LONG HANDICAP Persephone 9-4
WEIGHT FOR AGE 3yo-7lb
OFFICIAL EXPLANATION **Silver Lining: regarding the improvement in form, the trainer stated that on the gelding's previous run at Windsor, he pulled hard and was unsuited by the tight turns of the track. He added that the gelding was pushed wide on the final bend and had benefitted from being run over a furlong less.**
1849* Silver Lining, following up his success in a similar event at Salisbury last month with the same pilot aboard, won the race when kicking clear entering the final furlong for the line arrived only just in time. (9/1)
2281 Lorins Gold, who has been competing over slightly longer trips in his most recent races, was really into his stride inside the last furlong but the post arrived a stride too soon. (6/1)
2510* Welcome Heights came late on the scene and finished in fine style, but the winner had got away and he was never going to make it. He is running consistently well and there is more success to come. (9/2)
2416 Dummer Golf Time had the visor dispensed with on this occasion, but he gave it all he had and only narrowly missed out. (9/1: 8/1-14/1)
2463 Smart Guest, never far away, ran on strongly despite not getting much help from the saddle and he is knocking at the door. (25/1)
2552 Delight of Dawn would have won if she had been given any sort of ride and she could be worth bearing in mind for any near at hand engagements. (4/1)
2239 Beano Script (12/1: 8/1-14/1)
2302 Failed To Hit (12/1: op 8/1)
2569 Double Gold (9/1: 6/1-10/1)

2786 TATTERSALLS AUCTION NURSERY H'CAP (2-Y.O) (Class E)
3-45 (3-46) **5f 218y** £3,535.00 (£1,060.00: £510.00: £235.00) Stalls: High GOING minus 0.08 sec per fur (G)

SP RR SF

2370[4] **Whisky Mack (IRE)** (RHannon) **2-9-6** RHughes(2) (hld up: hdwy & edgd rt to ld over 2f out: sn clr).............— **1** 4/1[2] 85+ 36
2697[5] **Who Nose (IRE)** (BJMeehan) **2-8-8b** MTebbutt(5) (hld up: hdwy 2f out: kpt on ins fnl f: nt rch wnr) 2½ **2** 10/1 66 17
2477[4] **The Groveller** (PDEvans) **2-9-3** WJO'Connor(1) (outpcd: rdn 2f out: styd on wl ins fnl f).................................4 **3** 10/1 65 16
2378* **King Darius (IRE)** (RHannon) **2-9-7** DaneO'Neill(8) (dwlt: hdwy & nt clr run over 2f out: styd on wl appr fnl f) 1¼ **4** 10/1 65 16
2658[2] **Inchalong** (MBrittain) **2-8-4** GCarter(12) (hdwy ½-wy: hung lft over 2f out: sn rdn & btn).................................5 **5** 5/2[1] 35 —
884[10] **O' Higgins (IRE)** (RBoss) **2-8-8** KDarley(9) (prom 4f) ....2 **6** 7/1[3] 34 —
2587[12] **Patricia Olive (IRE)** (MHTompkins) **2-8-1**(3) MHenry(6) (trckd ldrs: hmpd over 2f out: nt rcvr) ....hd **7** 20/1 29 —
2361[4] **Whacker-Do (IRE)** (RHollinshead) **2-8-10** JCarroll(7) (trckd ldrs: rdn & carried rt over 2f out: sn btn)..............1 **8** 16/1 33 —
2578[5] **Muja's Magic (IRE)** (KTIvory) **2-8-4** NAdams(3) (chsd ldrs 4f).....................................¾ **9** 20/1 25 —
2112[3] **Lakeland Pride (IRE)** (PDEvans) **2-9-5** JFEgan(11) (a in rr).....................................2½ **10** 10/1 33 —
2419[2] **Stravsea** (BPJBaugh) **2-7-11** NCarlisle(4) (rdn along ½-wy: a in rr).....................................1 **11** 14/1 8 —
1161[3] **Jackerin (IRE)** (BSRothwell) **2-9-4v**[1] MFenton(10) (bit bkwd: set str pce over 3f: sn rdn & wknd: t.o) ....8 **12** 15/2 8 —
(SP 131.3%) **12 Rn**

1m 14.3 (4.30) CSF £44.96 CT £356.31 TOTE £4.50: £1.80 £2.70 £2.80 (£14.90) Trio £94.40 OWNER The Winning Team (MARLBOROUGH) BRED Springfield House Stud
2370 Whisky Mack (IRE), taken to post early and dismounted, showed his appreciation for this extra furlong and won very much as he pleased. (4/1)
2240 Who Nose (IRE) did not enjoy a clear passage when delivering his challenge between horses and this allowed the winner to get away, but it is doubtful if it cost him the race. (10/1)
2477 The Groveller found the pace much too hot and he was towards the rear until running on strongly under pressure inside the distance. He is bred for stamina on his dam's side and he seems to have inherited it. (10/1)
2378* King Darius (IRE) missed a beat at the start and, encountering trouble when beginning his move, did well in the end to finish so close. (10/1)
2658 Inchalong caused her own trouble by hanging left towards her rivals when galvanised into action approaching the final quarter-mile, and what chance she had had soon gone. (5/2: op 5/1)

2787 APPLEBY CLAIMING STKS (3-Y.O+) (Class F)
4-15 (4-16) **1m 3f 183y** £2,595.00 (£720.00: £345.00) Stalls: High GOING minus 0.08 sec per fur (G)

SP RR SF

2653[7] **Eagle Canyon (IRE) (70)** (BHanbury) **4-9-9** WRyan(6) (lw: hld up: hdwy over 2f out: led ins fnl f: r.o wl)........— **1** 3/1[3] 72 13
2490[4] **Two Socks (54)** (JSKing) **4-9-5** GCarter(8) (hld up in rr: hdwy 2f out: rdn & hung rt: r.o fnl f)...........................¾ **2** 6/1 67 8
2479* **Welsh Mill (IRE) (75)** (MrsMReveley) **8-9-13** KDarley(2) (hld up: hdwy 3f out: led wl over 1f out tl ins fnl f) .....½ **3** 15/8[1] 74 15
2487[8] **Little Miss Rocker (68)** (IABalding) **3-7-13**(3) RFfrench(7) (chsd ldrs: led over 5f out: pushed along over 2f out: hdd wl over 1f out: sn outpcd) ....3½ **4** 5/2[2] 57 —
2365[6] **English Invader (70)** (CADwyer) **6-9-1** RHughes(4) (chsd ldrs: pushed along over 2f out: sn outpcd) ....nk **5** 12/1 57 —
2696[13] **Nikita's Star (IRE) (61)** (DJGMurraySmith) **4-9-9b** DaneO'Neill(9) (hld up in tch: effrt & rdn 3f out: no imp)...3½ **6** 16/1 60 1
2544[13] **Qualitair Beauty** (MissLCSiddall) **4-8-3**(7) TSiddall(5) (led over 6f: rdn & wknd over 2f out: t.o).....................19 **7** 100/1 22 —
Jendali Princess (TTBill) **4-8-8** TGMcLaughlin(1) (bkwd: wnt lft s: a bhd: rdn 3f out: t.o).............................dist **8** 100/1 — —
(SP 118.2%) **8 Rn**

2m 41.8 (13.30) CSF £20.24 TOTE £4.00: £1.90 £1.80 £1.10 (£13.60) Trio £12.00 OWNER Mr Clinton Lane Jnr (NEWMARKET) BRED Mount Coote Stud
WEIGHT FOR AGE 3yo-12lb

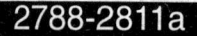

Eagle Canyon (IRE) clmd JPugh £10,000
2297 Eagle Canyon (IRE), adopting more patient tactics for this step down in class, won with a shade to spare and he could be a cheap buy at £10,000. (3/1)
2490 Two Socks took closer order two furlongs out but needed to be straightened after hanging off a true line and his determined late challenge was always being held. (6/1: 4/1-7/1)
2479* Welsh Mill (IRE) was the one to beat after quickening up just inside the quarter-mile pole, but the winner stuck to him and worried him out of it inside the final 200 yards. (15/8)
1986 Little Miss Rocker will put considerable value on herself as a stud prospect when she does eventually win a race, but she is taking time to get it together. (5/2: 7/4-11/4)
753 English Invader did not have the yielding ground that he must have on turf, and off the bridle approaching the final quarter-mile, soon got left behind. (12/1: 7/1-14/1)

2788 BURTON H'CAP (0-70) (3-Y.O+) (Class E)

4-45 (4-46) **5f 218y** £3,327.00 (£996.00: £478.00: £219.00) Stalls: High GOING minus 0.08 sec per fur (G)

				SP	RR	SF
2602^{9}	**Lachesis (42)** (DShaw) **4-8-2** JFanning(14) (hdwy ½-wy: led wl over 1f out: drvn clr)	—	**1**	33/1	51	27
2317^{8}	**Sing With the Band (43)** (BAMcMahon) **6-8-3**ow3 MRoberts(12) (hdwy over 1f out: fin wl)	2	**2**	15/2 [3]	47	20
2179^{13}	**Double Matt (IRE) (59)** (MrsPSly) **5-9-5** NCarlisle(20) (hdwy ½-wy: rdn over 1f out: r.o one pce)	nk	**3**	66/1	62	38
2567^{6}	**Souperficial (52)** (NTinkler) **6-8-12v** KimTinkler(11) (s.i.s: bhd: rdn ½-wy: swtchd lft: gd hdwy appr fnl f: nvr nrr)	½	**4**	10/1	54	30
2372^{3}	**Denbrae (IRE) (67)** (DJGMurraySmith) **5-9-6**(7) CLowther(7) (a.p: ev ch 2f out: kpt on u.p)	s.h	**5**	13/2 [2]	68	44
2665^{6}	**College Night (IRE) (42)** (SCWilliams) **5-7-13**(3) MHenry(17) (hld up: hdwy 2f out: kpt on ins fnl f)	½	**6**	16/1	42	18
2665^{11}	**Silver Purse (60)** (APJones) **3-8-12v¹**(3) JDSmith(5) (chsd ldr stands' side: ev ch 2f out: sn rdn: one pce)	½	**7**	16/1	59	30
2738^{14}	**Napoleon Star (IRE) (50)** (SRBowring) **6-8-10b** DeanMcKeown(10) (hdwy over 1f out: r.o u.p fnl f)	nk	**8**	14/1	48	24
2698*	**Meranti (63)** (JMBradley) **4-9-6**(3) 7x RFfrench(9) (lw: effrt 2f out: sn rdn: nt rch ldrs)	½	**9**	6/1 [1]	60	36
1965^{12}	**Hannah's Usher (53)** (CMurray) **5-8-13** NicolaHowarth(13) (hdwy over 2f out: nt rch ldrs)	s.h	**10**	33/1	49	25
2665^{10}	**May Queen Megan (49)** (MrsALMKing) **4-8-9** DaneO'Neill(2) (mid div: rdn over 2f out: no imp)	2	**11**	33/1	40	16
2416^{7}	**Ohnonotagain (36)** (LRLloyd-James) **5-7-10** NAdams(18) (rdn over 2f out: edgd lft: no rspnse)	1	**12**	40/1	24	—
2422^{5}	**Crissem (IRE) (59)** (RHollinshead) **4-9-5** FLynch(4) (nvr trbld ldrs)	s.h	**13**	14/1	47	23
2651^{W}	**Panther (IRE) (66)** (PDEvans) **7-9-12v** JFEgan(16) (chsd ldrs 4f)	s.h	**14**	14/1	54	30
2308^{4}	**Indian Relative (68)** (RGuest) **4-9-11**(3) DGriffiths(3) (lw: chsd ldrs stands' side: rdn 2f out: sn wknd)	½	**15**	8/1	55	31
2326^{13}	**Bollin Harry (66)** (TDEasterby) **5-9-12** JCarroll(19) (prom: ev ch wl over 1f out: eased whn btn)	½	**16**	6/1 [1]	52	28
2703^{2}	**Beau Venture (USA) (64)** (BPalling) **9-9-5**(5) DSweeney(8) (w ldrs tl wknd 2f out)	1½	**17**	9/1	46	22
	Miss Aragon (36) (MissLCSiddall) **9-7-10** FNorton(15) (lw: a bhd & outpcd)	4	**18**	40/1	7	—
2036^{13}	**Sand Star (55)** (DHaydnJones) **5-9-1v¹** SDrowne(6) (led over 4f: sn rdn & wknd)	¾	**19**	25/1	24	—
1655^{7}	**Sihafi (USA) (50)** (JMCarr) **4-8-10** PBloomfield(1) (racd stands' side: a outpcd)	1½	**20**	8/1	15	—

(SP 145.8%) **20 Rn**

1m 13.7 (3.70) CSF £268.82 CT £14,247.33 TOTE £83.50: £15.50 £1.60 £16.30 £2.10 (£800.50) Trio £857.80; £1,099.44 to Newbury 18/7/97
OWNER Mr J. McManamon (NEWARK) BRED Barouche Stud Ltd
LONG HANDICAP Miss Aragon 7-5 Ohnonotagain 7-7
WEIGHT FOR AGE 3yo-5lb
883 Lachesis caused quite an upset with a comfortably-gained first success and there seemed no fluke about it. (33/1)
2002 Sing With the Band, produced from off the pace, finished with a flourish, but the winner had kicked first and had gone beyond recall. (15/2)
Double Matt (IRE), a lightly-raced five-year-old, showed he is no back number with his best display for two years and if there is any more improvement to come now is the time to strike. (66/1)
2567 Souperficial did his usual and forfeited ground leaving the stalls. In the rear and hard ridden at halfway, he ran on strongly once switched towards the stand rail and only just failed to gain the day. He is a law unto himself but is running well this term. (10/1)
2372 Denbrae (IRE) pushed the pace and battled away right to the finish, but he was being tapped for toe in the dash to the line. (13/2)
2665 College Night (IRE) did not find top gear until late on and the leaders in full flight had taken first run. This was still a promising effort and she is capable of winning another race. (16/1)
1439 Silver Purse, visored for the first time, gave chase to the overall leader on the stands side. With every chance entering the last quarter-mile, she may have done too much too soon, for she was found wanting in the sprint to the line. (16/1)
2497 Napoleon Star (IRE) made up a lot of ground in the closing stages to finish a close-up eighth and he is holding his form. (14/1)
2698* Meranti never really fired and was hard at work to no effect from some way out. (6/1)
2308 Indian Relative (8/1: 6/1-9/1)
2129 Bollin Harry, in the firing line with every chance inside the last quarter-mile, was not persevered with when his chance had gone. It is now thirteen months since he last won a race. (6/1)

T/Jkpt: Not won; £13,965.69 to Newbury 18/7/97. T/Plpt: £275.60 (85.56 Tckts). T/Qdpt: £66.00 (26.88 Tckts) IM

2789a - 2810a (Irish Racing) - See Computer Raceform

2450a-CURRAGH (Newbridge, Ireland) (R-H) (Good to firm)

Sunday July 13th

2811a OMNI RACING ANGLESEY STKS (Gp 3) (2-Y.O)

2-45 (2-46) **6f 63y** IR £19,500.00 (IR £5,700.00: IR £2,700.00: IR £900.00) GOING minus 0.50 sec per fur (F)

				SP	RR	SF
	Lady Alexander (IRE) (CCollins,Ireland) **2-8-7** PShanahan (hld up: 3rd & chal 2f out: led wl over 1f out: jnd early fnl f: r.o u.p)	—	**1**	9/1 [3]	92	42
2451a*	**King Of Kings (IRE)** (APO'Brien,Ireland) **2-8-13** CRoche (hld up in tch: clsd ½-wy: 2nd & effrt over 1f out: ev ch ins last: no ex: r.o: hands & heels)	s.h	**2**	30/100 [1]	98?	48
2466*	**Princely Heir (IRE)** (MJohnston) **2-8-10** DHolland (chsd ldr: led 2f out tl wl over 1f out: no ex: outpcd fnl f)	5	**3**	9/2 [2]	82	32
2439a^{6}	**Retention (IRE)** (KPrendergast,Ireland) **2-8-11**ow1 SCraine (a bhd: n.d)	6	**4**	25/1	68	17

2451a^{4}	**Festival Song (USA)** (APO'Brien,Ireland) **2-8-7b^{1}** JAHeffernan (led: clr after 1½f: hdd 2f out: sn btn & wknd)	3	**5**	25/1	56	6
				(SP 112.8%)		**5 Rn**

1m 15.1 (0.60) OWNER Mrs N. O'Callaghan (THE CURRAGH) BRED Noel O'Callaghan
STEWARDS' ENQUIRY Shanahan susp. 22-24/7/97 (excessive use of whip).
Lady Alexander (IRE) proved that the rather brave decision to supplement her for this race, was indeed the correct one. It was a gutsy performance rather then impressive, and Shanahan got a three-day suspension for using his whip with excessive force and frequency. (9/1)
2451a* King Of Kings (IRE) was not himself, although his demeanour both in the paddock and down at the start gave no indication that he was out of sorts. He appeared to be travelling well although his high head carriage does give some sort of ground for concern. Roche asked him gently for an effort, not using his whip just hand and heels, but there was nothing forthcoming. Subsequently, the trainer confirmed that the horse was off his feed and the Stewards went through the motions of holding an enquiry, but the official vet found nothing wrong. The situation poses some interesting questions as to whether O'Brien will be given the benefit of the doubt concerning the horse's well-being. (30/100)
2466* Princely Heir (IRE) found himself totally outpaced over the last furlong. (9/2)
Retention (IRE) was being pushed along before halfway. (25/1)
2451a Festival Song (USA), in front until one and a half furlongs out, dropped away tamely. (25/1)

2812a - 2813a (Irish Racing) - See Computer Raceform

2814a KILDANGAN STUD IRISH OAKS (Gp 1) (3-Y.O F)

4-20 (4-26) **1m 4f** IR £112,700.00 (IR £38,700.00: IR £18,700.00: IR £6,700.00) GOING minus 0.10 sec per fur (G)

				SP	RR	SF
1738^{6}	**Ebadiyla (IRE)** (JOxx,Ireland) **3-9-0** JPMurtagh (hld up: 9th & hdwy ½-wy: trckd ldrs st: 2nd & chal on ins over 2f out: led 1f out: rdn clr: r.o wl)	—	**1**	9/2^{2}	120	45
2053*	**Yashmak (USA)** (HRACecil) **3-9-0** KFallon (hld up in tch: 4th ½-wy: clsd over 4f out: led st: rdn over 2f out: hdd u.p 1f out: nt qckn w wnr: kpt on)	3	**2**	6/4^{1}	116	41
1916a^{3}	**Brilliance (FR)** (PBary,France) **3-9-0** SGuillot (in tch: 6th ½-wy: wnt 2nd & effrt st: 3rd, rdn & nt rch ldrs 1½f out: kpt on ins last)	hd	**3**	5/1^{3}	116	41
2454a^{8}	**Strawberry Roan (IRE)** (APO'Brien,Ireland) **3-9-0** CRoche (hld up: towards rr: hdwy & 8th st: 5th, rdn & nt trble ldrs 1½f out: styd on fnl f)	5	**4**	6/1	109	34
2267a^{3}	**Family Tradition (IRE)** (APO'Brien,Ireland) **3-9-0b^{1}** WJSupple (towards rr: rdn & styd on in st: nvr nrr)	1½	**5**	33/1	107	32
1738^{5}	**Etoile (FR)** (PWChapple-Hyam) **3-9-0** JReid (mid div: 7th ½-wy: chsd ldrs st: 4th, rdn & nt rch ldrs 1½f out: kpt on same pce)	½	**6**	14/1	107	32
2023^{12}	**Via Verbano (IRE)** (JSBolger,Ireland) **3-9-0** KJManning (mid div: 8th ½-wy: hdwy to chse ldrs st: 5th, rdn & nt trble ldrs 1½f out: one pce)	3	**7**	33/1	103	28
2446a^{3}	**Caiseal Ros (IRE)** (JSBolger,Ireland) **3-9-0** CEverard (led & disp ld early: rn 2nd tl appr st: sn rdn: no imp over 2f out)	4½	**8**	25/1	97	22
2267a^{5}	**Aliya (IRE)** (JOxx,Ireland) **3-9-0** PJSmullen (sn disp ld: led after 2f: hdd & edgd lft st: sn wknd)	hd	**9**	33/1	96	21
1540a^{4}	**Shell Ginger (IRE)** (APO'Brien,Ireland) **3-9-0b^{1}** JAHeffernan (plld hrd: cl up: 5th bef ½-wy: sn wknd: bhd & n.d st)	15	**10**	33/1	76	1
	Absolute Glee (USA) (DKWeld,Ireland) **3-9-0b^{1}** MJKinane (prom early: cl up: 3rd ½-wy: rdn & wknd bef st: n.d)	1	**11**	20/1	75	—
				(SP 116.2%)		**11 Rn**

2m 33.7 (6.70) OWNER H H Aga Khan (CURRABEG)
1738 Ebadiyla (IRE) got a dream run through on the inside as they straightened up off the last bend. Helped in no small measure by her pacemaking stable companion Aliya, she got to the front just over a furlong out and stretched clear. She is improving and the stable has always had a soft spot for the Yorkshire Oaks. She went up 11lb to 121 for this. (9/2)
2053* Yashmak (USA) proved fractious at the start and was reluctant to load. She made her ground smoothly enough on the outside from half a mile out, and set sail for home coming down the hill. Under pressure early in the straight, she looked a sitting duck and was soon outpaced by the winner. She went up 2lb for this to 116. (6/4)
1916a Brilliance (FR) travelled well off the last bend, but lacked the necessary acceleration to get her into a challenging position. It was only in the closing stages that she began to stay on with any effect. (5/1: op 3/1)
2454a Strawberry Roan (IRE) was being ridden along early in the straight and just kept on at the one pace. It doesn't appear that she is that comfortable over this trip. (6/1)
2267a Family Tradition (IRE) kept on at her own pace without ever threatening. (33/1)
1738 Etoile (FR) took a strong tug early on, but held out no hopes with the leaders from the turn in. (14/1: op 8/1)
1533a Via Verbano (IRE) just found herself outclassed. (33/1)
2446a Caiseal Ros (IRE) was prominent until dropping away in the straight. (25/1)
2267a Aliya (IRE) did a good job in the pacemaking role and conveniently moved out to assist the winner turning in. (33/1)
1540a Shell Ginger (IRE) dropped away before the straight. (33/1)
Absolute Glee (USA) ran prominently to the straight. (20/1)

2815a EMIRATES AIRLINE E.B.F. ROCKINGHAM H'CAP (0-110) (Listed) (3-Y.O+)

4-55 (4-56) **5f** IR £36,000.00 (IR £11,400.00: IR £5,400.00: IR £1,800.00) GOING minus 0.50 sec per fur (F)

				SP	RR	SF
	Nakayama Express (IRE) (JGCoogan,Ireland) **4-8-0b$^{(2)}$** EAhern (chsd ldrs: rdn ½-wy: chal over 1f out: led 50y out: r.o.)	—	**1**	9/1	86	29
	Sweet Mazarine (IRE) (CO'Brien,Ireland) **3-7-12^{ow2}** NGMcCullagh (trckd ldrs: chal 1½f out: disp ld ins last: hdd nr fin: r.o.)	nk	**2**	8/1	84	22
1186a^{5}	**Lady Shannon (USA)** (DKWeld,Ireland) **3-7-8$^{(6)}$** DPMcDonogh (prom: led over 1f out: edgd lft: jnd ins last: hdd nr fin: kpt on)	s.h	**3**	11/2^{3}	86	26
1881a^{7}	**Symboli Kildare (IRE)** (JOxx,Ireland) **4-8-7b$^{(10)}$** LisaO'Neill (cl up: ev ch fr 2f out: kpt on ins last)	¾	**4**	14/1	98	41
2056^{23}	**Ailleacht (USA)** (JSBolger,Ireland) **5-9-10** KJManning (prom: rdn & ev ch 2f out: led briefly over 1f out: no ex u.p wl ins last: kpt on)	½	**5**	13/2	103	46
	Another Sky-Lark (IRE) (FBerry,Ireland) **9-8-1$^{(8)ow3}$** FMBerry (chsd ldrs: rdn & kpt on fr over 1f out)	hd	**6**	12/1	88	28
	Royal Affinity (IRE) (APO'Brien,Ireland) **3-8-3$^{(8)}$** CO'Donoghue (towards rr ½-wy: rdn & nt rch ldrs 1½f out: r.o. ins last)	hd	**7**	5/1^{2}	92	32
2105^{9}	**Best Before Dawn (IRE)** (APO'Brien,Ireland) **6-9-9** CRoche (dwlt: sn trckd ldrs: rdn 2f out: nt rch ldrs ins last: kpt on)	nk	**8**	5/2^{1}	100	43

	Sunset Reigns (IRE) (JSBolger,Ireland) **4-9-8b[1]** CEverard (led & disp ld: hdd u.p over 1f out: no ex) 1½	**9**	8/1	95	38
			(SP 120.5%)		**9 Rn**

58.9 secs (0.90) OWNER Patrick McLoughlin (FRIARSTOWN)
Nakayama Express (IRE) got the reward for his consistency. Pulled out just at the right time, he got up in the last few strides. (9/1)
Sweet Mazarine (IRE), from a mark 8lb out of the handicap and carrying 2lb overweight, ran the race of her life but will pay for it in future handicaps. (8/1)
Lady Shannon (USA) showed plenty of foot and got to the front over a furlong out, but edged left under pressure. (11/2)
1532a Symboli Kildare (IRE), with a girl apprentice claiming the full 10lb allowance, seemed to enjoy himself and is coming back to form. (14/1: op 8/1)
1881a Ailleacht (USA) ran fast throughout and had every chance inside the last, but just could not quicken again. (13/2)
Another Sky-Lark (IRE) (12/1: op 8/1)
Best Before Dawn (IRE) again lost ground entering the straight, but was tracking the leaders and holding every chance from two furlongs out. (5/2)

2816a RAGUSA STUD MINSTREL STKS (Gp 3) (3-Y.O+)
5-25 (5-26) **1m** **(New)** IR £19,500.00 (IR £5,700.00: IR £2,700.00: IR £900.00) GOING minus 0.10 sec per fur (G)

			SP	RR	SF
2334*	**Ramooz (USA)** (BHanbury) **4-9-8** KFallon (mod 2nd to st: 3rd on ins & nt clr run fr 2f out: swtchd lft to chal 1f out: sn led: r.o.) ....—	**1**	2/1[2]	115	58
2056[17]	**Burden Of Proof (IRE)** (CO'Brien,Ireland) **5-9-8** JPMurtagh (hld up: towards rr early: clsd to go 2nd st: sn chal: edgd rt 2f out: 3rd, rdn & no ex early ins last: kpt on) 3	**2**	5/4[1]	109	52
2441a[10]	**Eternal Joy** (APO'Brien,Ireland) **3-8-9b** MJKinane (sn led & clr to ½-wy: rdn early st: hdd u.p early fnl f: no ex) ....hd	**3**	16/1	105	39
1060a[3]	**Lil's Boy (USA)** (JSBolger,Ireland) **3-8-9** KJManning (rn 3rd: cld ½-wy: 4th & no ex whn n.m.r 2f out: rdn & nt trble ldrs 1½f out: kpt on) 2½	**4**	3/1[3]	100	34
2447a[5]	**Ministerial Model (IRE)** (APO'Brien,Ireland) **3-8-6** JAHeffernan (towards rr ½-wy: effrt over 2f out: rdn & nt rch ldrs 1½f out: kpt on) ....nk	**5**	20/1	96	30
			(SP 113.4%)		**5 Rn**

1m 38.8 (3.80) OWNER Hilal Salem (NEWMARKET) BRED Gainsborough Stud Management Ltd
2334* Ramooz (USA) found himself with very little room from two furlongs down, but Fallon sat and suffered until a narrow gap came and he went through to lead early inside the last, showing a nice turn of foot to go clear. His next target may be the Beeswing Stakes at Newcastle. (2/1: op 11/10)
1532a* Burden Of Proof (IRE), held up early to get the trip, appeared to be travelling well on the outside keeping Ramooz in, but he was left behind once the winner saw daylight. (5/4)
Eternal Joy made the running and, soon clear, was not headed until just inside the final furlong, but kept on well. This was a big improvement in form and he goes up 8lb to 94. (16/1)
1060a Lil's Boy (USA) was outpaced over the last furlong and a half. (3/1)

2817a (Irish Racing) - See Computer Raceform

2269a-MAISONS-LAFFITTE (France) (Good)
Wednesday July 9th

2818a PRIX MONADE (4-Y.O+)
3-30 (3-33) **1m** £8,979.00

			SP	RR	SF
	Alamo Bay (USA) (AFabre,France) **4-9-2** OPeslier ....—	**1**		114	—
1914a[3]	**Trojan Sea (USA)** (France) **6-9-2** DBoeuf 2½	**2**		109	—
	Folle Tempete (FR) (France) **4-8-13** GMosse 2	**3**		102	—
2393[2]	**Bold Effort (FR)** (KOCunningham-Brown) **5-8-11** FSanchez (btn approx 25l)	**10**		—	—
					10 Rn

1m 38.0 (2.00) P-M 3.00F: 1.20F 1.30F 2.20F (2.70F) OWNER Mr Daniel Wildenstein (CHANTILLY) BRED Allez France Stables Ltd
2393 Bold Effort (FR) tried to repeat last year's one-mile success, but did not get the trip on this occasion. Setting a fast pace early on, he had done too much and, after being headed three furlongs out, soon weakened. An inconsistent sort, he is hard to catch right but a revert to his favourite six furlongs is a must.

2996a-CHANTILLY (France) (R-H) (Good)
Friday July 11th

2819a PRIX LA MOSKOWA (Listed) (4-Y.O+)
3-30 (3-33) **1m 7f** £15,713.00 (£5,387.00: £4,040.00: £2,694.00: £1,347.00)

			SP	RR	SF
2269a*	**Philanthrop (FR)** (J-PGallorini,France) **5-9-0** TGillet ....—	**1**		119	—
2269a[2]	**Yokohama (USA)** (France) **6-8-11** FHead 5	**2**		111	—
1365a[5]	**Fairhonor (FR)** (France) **4-9-0** OPeslier ....nk	**3**		113	—
2055[7]	**Jiyush** (EALDunlop) **4-8-11** RHills (btn approx 6 3/4l)	**5**		109	—
					8 Rn

3m 9.5 (2.50) P-M 2.40F: 1.10F 1.40F 1.50F (3.80F) OWNER J. Menuisier BRED S. Niarchos
1319* Jiyush has been rediscovering his form of late, but put up a slightly disappointing show here.

2639a-DEAUVILLE (France) (R-H) (Good)
Sunday July 13th

2820a PRIX MESSIDOR (Gp 3) (3-Y.O+)
3-00 (3-01) **1m** £24,691.00 (£8,979.00: £4,489.00: £2,694.00)

				SP	RR	SF
	Neuilly (USA) (AFabre,France) **3-8-7** AJunk	—	**1**		118	—
1554a^{3}	**Simon du Desert (FR)** (RCollet,France) **4-9-6** DBoeuf	s.h	**2**		122	—
2453a^{3}	**Polar Prince (IRE)** (MAJarvis) **4-9-6** MRoberts	2	**3**		118	—
2426*	**Snow Kid** (DRLoder) **3-8-7** PatEddery (btn approx 7½l)		**7**		—	—
						7 Rn

1m 37.1 (1.10) P-M 21.10F: 5.00F 1.80F OWNER Mr Paul de Moussac (CHANTILLY) BRED Maylands Stud Company Ltd
2453a Polar Prince (IRE), always close up, kept on well but could do nothing about the shock winner. Busy of late, he will now have a well-earned break and the plan is to return for the Tripleprint Celebration Mile at Goodwood in August.
2426* Snow Kid, supplemented for this, was impressive at Yarmouth last time out and, after leading for a long way here, eventually found things a bit too tough. He prefers soft ground and it was obviously too fast for him here.

0817a-HOPPEGARTEN (Berlin, Germany) (R-H) (Good)
Sunday July 13th

2821a BERLIN BRANDENBERG-TROPHY DER LANDESBANK BERLIN (Gp 2) (3-Y.O+)
4-00 (4-02) **1m** £83,333.00 (£35,985.00: £17,045.00: £9,470.00: £5,682.00)

				SP	RR	SF
2453a^{2}	**Gothenberg (IRE)** (MJohnston) **4-9-6** JWeaver (sn led: clr ½-wy: r.o wl: easily)	—	**1**		122	—
1550a*	**La Blue (GER)** (BSchutz,Germany) **4-9-2** AStarke (mid div: hdwy fr 3f out: nt rch wnr)	2½	**2**		113	—
2097a^{7}	**Eden Rock (GER)** (BSchutz,Germany) **3-8-9** ASuborics (mid div: hdwy 2f out: str run cl home)	nk	**3**		114	—
2272a*	**Kalatos (GER)** (AWohler,Germany) **5-9-6** ABoschert (a.p: rdn & no ex fnl f)	s.h	**4**		116	—
2009^{6}	**Bin Rosie** (DRLoder) **5-9-6b** KDarley (hld up: r.o fr 2f out: nvr nrr)	nk	**6**		116	—
1067a^{3}	**Accento** (RSuerland,Germany) **4-9-6** WRyan (sn chsd ldrs: wknd 1½f out)	1¼	**7**		113	—
	Mill King (GER) (HBlume,Germany) **4-9-6b^{1}** THellier (a in rr)	1¼	**8**		111	—
	Orfijar (FR) (PLautner,Germany) **7-9-6** LPyritz (prom: wknd over 2½f out)	8	**9**		95	—
						9 Rn

1m 37.6 TOTE 37DM: 16DM 12DM 15DM (109DM) OWNER Brian Yeardley Continental Ltd (MIDDLEHAM) BRED Brownstown Stud Farm
2453a Gothenberg (IRE) set a strong pace and, moving five lengths clear with half a mile to run, stayed on strongly. He is a high-class performer when allowed to dominate like this and should continue to thrive in similar mile events on the continent.
2009 Bin Rosie did not have the race run to suit. Held up for his usual late run, he was running on well at the finish and was little more than half a length behind the runner-up.

2644a-SAN SIRO (Milan, Italy) (R-H) (Good)
Sunday July 13th

2822a PREMIO GIUSEPPE DE MONTEL (Listed) (2-Y.O)
4-20 (4-33) **7f 110y** £23,142.00

				SP	RR	SF
2429^{5}	**Timekeeper (USA)** (MBell) **2-8-11** MFenton	—	**1**		82	—
	Special Nash (IRE) (PGuarsegnati,Italy) **2-8-11** ACorniani	½	**2**		81	—
	Diamond Snake (IRE) (GColleo,Italy) **2-8-11** MLatorre	2½	**3**		76	—
						10 Rn

1m 37.2 (12.70) TOTE 42L: 17L 20L 21L (153L) OWNER Mr C. M. Watt (NEWMARKET) BRED Adelphian Ltd
2429 Timekeeper (USA) took the lead inside the final furlong and, holding the renewed effort of the runner-up at bay, kept on in game fashion.

2538-MUSSELBURGH (R-H) (Good to firm)
Friday July 18th
WEATHER: sunny WIND: alm nil

2823 ROBIN COOK AND UNISON STAFF CLAIMING STKS (2-Y.O) (Class D)
2-40 (2-40) **5f** £3,387.50 (£1,025.00: £500.00: £237.50) Stalls: High GOING minus 0.24 sec per fur (GF)

				SP	RR	SF
2412*	**Oriel Girl** (PDEvans) **2-8-2v**^{ow2} JFEgan(3) (lw: led after 2f: drvn out)	—	**1**	7/4^{2}	65	17
2140^{3}	**Always Lucky** (JBerry) **2-8-1**$^{(5)}$ TEDurcan(5) (sn chsng ldrs: rdn ½-wy: kpt on same pce)	1¼	**2**	6/4^{1}	65	19
	Slew Magic (IRE) (WGMTurner) **2-7-9**$^{(7)}$ SCarson(6) (neat: scope: bit bkwd: chsd ldrs: hung lft ½-wy: kpt on u.p)	2	**3**	16/1	55	9
2606^{7}	**Pride of Bryn** (DenysSmith) **2-7-12**^{ow2} TWilliams(2) (led 2f: sn rdn: outpcd fnl 2f)	1¼	**4**	66/1	47	—
2412^{6}	**Dispol Emerald** (SEKettlewell) **2-8-0** LCharnock(4) (racd centre: cl up tl outpcd fnl 2f)	2	**5**	14/1	42	—
2538^{8}	**Ngaere Princess** (WTKemp) **2-7-3**$^{(7)}$ PBradley(1) (lw: racd alone stands' side: s.i.s: sn rcvrd: outpcd fr ½-wy)	2½	**6**	66/1	30	—
2127^{5}	**Junior Muffin (IRE)** (JBerry) **2-8-11** KDarley(7) (outpcd after 2f: sn bhd)	2	**7**	4/1^{3}	39	—
				(SP 111.9%)		**7 Rn**

60.6 secs (2.90) CSF £4.10 TOTE £2.90: £1.20 £1.40 (£2.10) OWNER Mr D. Maloney (WELSHPOOL) BRED Mrs F. A. Veasey
2412* Oriel Girl is getting the winning habit and had the edge from a long way out but it was never easy and she had to be kept up to her work. (7/4)
2140 Always Lucky, easy to back, had her chances but was never doing enough when put under pressure. (6/4)
Slew Magic (IRE) needed this and ran very green and will obviously improve for the experience. (16/1)
Pride of Bryn, who showed nothing on the All-Weather first time, ran better here and there could well be a modest race in her. (66/1)
2412 Dispol Emerald finished closer to the winner this time but there is still plenty more needed. (14/1)

2824 GJW LIMITED STKS (0-55) (3-Y.O+) (Class F)
3-10 (3-10) **1m 4f 31y** £2,931.00 (£888.00: £434.00: £207.00) Stalls: High GOING minus 0.55 sec per fur (F)

				SP	RR	SF
2471^{2}	**Classic Ballet (FR) (52)** (RGuest) **4-8-10**$^{(7)}$ CLowther(8) (lw: trckd ldrs: nt clr run & swtchd over 1f out: chal ins fnl f: r.o to ld nr fin)	—	1	7/1^{3}	60	46
2170*	**Kernof (IRE) (54)** (MDHammond) **4-9-8** JCarroll(7) (a.p: led 2f out: hrd rdn fnl f: r.o: jst ct)	hd	2	8/1	65	51
2503^{5}	**Sherqy (IRE) (54)** (SEKettlewell) **5-9-8** JFortune(5) (a.p: effrt 3f out: sn rdn: one pce appr fnl f)	3	3	10/1	61	47
2564^{7}	**Essayeffsee (55)** (MrsMReveley) **8-9-6** KDarley(1) (lw: hld up & bhd: gd hdwy 3f out: ev ch over 1f out: no ex)	hd	4	7/1^{3}	59	45
2469^{7}	**Lord Advocate (52)** (DANolan) **9-9-5b**$^{(5)}$ KSked(11) (w ldr 4f: cl up: led 3f out to 2f out: grad wknd)	3½	5	14/1	58	44
2652^{4}	**Suga Hawk (IRE) (55)** (EJAlston) **5-9-3**$^{(5)}$ TEDurcan(6) (hld up: effrt & n.m.r 3f out: nvr able to chal)	1¼	6	11/4^{1}	55	41
2479^{2}	**Forzair (50)** (JJO'Neill) **5-9-8** RLappin(10) (lw: mde most tl hdd & wknd 3f out)	¾	7	12/1	54	40
2475^{4}	**Oberons Boy (IRE) (55)** (SDow) **4-9-6** ACulhane(2) (hld up & bhd: hdwy over 3f out: hung rt & wknd over 1f out)	¾	8	4/1^{2}	51	37
2164^{6}	**General Glow (49)** (PDEvans) **4-9-6** JFEgan(4) (chsd ldrs tl wknd over 3f out)	3½	9	14/1	46	32
	Ralitsa (IRE) (55) (RMWhitaker) **5-9-6** DeanMcKeown(3) (effrt over 3f: n.d)	1¾	10	25/1	44	30
2541^{3}	**Get A Life (50)** (JO'Reilly) **4-9-3** VHalliday(9) (b.hind: hld up: effrt 4f out: n.d)	3	11	25/1	37	23

(SP 120.6%) **11 Rn**

2m 35.3 (1.80) CSF £57.95 TOTE £6.80: £2.00 £2.90 £9.30 (£34.30) Trio £233.20 OWNER Mr E. Carter (NEWMARKET) BRED Inversiones Gonfi Inc

2471 Classic Ballet (FR) appreciated this longer trip and was given a fine ride. Now she has broken her duck, further improvement looks likely. (7/1)

2170* Kernof (IRE) is in top form just now and, although she always looked second best here, she never stopped trying and just failed to hang on. (8/1)

2503 Sherqy (IRE) put in a useful effort this time but, under pressure some way out, he was never doing enough and is at his best when things go all his own way. (10/1)

1683 Essayeffsee has never won over his far and, after looking dangerous, he failed to pick up late on. He does look in good form at present. (7/1)

2034 Lord Advocate could never dominate this time and was left struggling in the last couple of furlongs. (14/1)

2652 Suga Hawk (IRE) tried for a run up the inner early in the straight but was short of room and was certainly short of the necessary pace. He has more ability than he sometimes cares to show. (11/4)

2475 Oberons Boy (IRE) has had more hard luck stories than a skint punter but this time it seemed it was his attitude that was the problem. (4/1: op 6/1)

2825 INTERNATIONAL SOLIDARITY H'CAP (0-60) (3-Y.O+) (Class F)
3-40 (3-41) **2m** £2,983.00 (£904.00: £442.00: £211.00) Stalls: High GOING minus 0.55 sec per fur (F)

				SP	RR	SF
2166^{5}	**Thunderheart (46)** (RAllan) **6-9-0** KDarley(7) (lw: hld up: hdwy ½-wy: led 2f out: r.o)	—	1	8/1	58	—
2682^{9}	**Bold Elect (52)** (EJAlston) **9-9-6** JFEgan(12) (hld up & bhd: hdwy 3f out: styd on strly towards fin)	1	2	7/1	63	—
2000^{11}	**Marsayas (IRE) (56)** (MJCamacho) **4-9-10** LCharnock(5) (lw: a.p: effrt appr st: led 3f out to 2f out: one pce)	¾	3	10/1	66	—
2352^{2}	**Charity Crusader (42)** (MrsMReveley) **6-8-10** ACulhane(1) (hld up & bhd: gd hdwy over 3f out: chsng ldrs over 1f out: sn btn)	1½	4	6/1^{2}	51	—
2413^{3}	**Gymcrak Tiger (IRE) (46)** (GHolmes) **7-9-0b** JFortune(15) (b.hind: lw: trckd ldrs: effrt over 3f out: one pce)	½	5	9/1	54	—
2350*	**Vintage Taittinger (IRE) (29)** (JSGoldie) **5-7-4**$^{(7)}$ JMcAuley(8) (lw: hld up & bhd: brought wd & effrt 4f out: edgd rt over 1f out: nvr rchd ldrs)	2	6	11/4^{1}	35	—
2539^{2}	**Valiant Dash (30)** (JSGoldie) **11-7-12**ow2 TWilliams(10) (chsd ldrs: drvn along appr st: outpcd fnl 3f)	2	7	20/1	34	—
2661^{3}	**Cois Na Farraige (IRE) (46)** (MissLAPerratt) **4-8-9**$^{(5)}$ TEDurcan(4) (lw: bhd: effrt on outside 4f out: nvr rchd ldrs)	1½	8	20/1	49	—
2414^{3}	**Wellcome Inn (55)** (JO'Reilly) **3-8-6** JO'Reilly(11) (hld up & bhd: effrt ent st: n.d)	1¾	9	14/1	56	—
2352^{6}	**Breydon (38)** (PMonteith) **4-8-3**$^{(3)}$ KMChin(13) (chsd ldrs tl wknd 4f out)	s.h	10	50/1	39	—
2413^{5}	**Gymcrak Cyrano (IRE) (29)** (NChamberlain) **8-7-11** NKennedy(2) (hld up & bhd: n.d)	5	11	20/1	25	—
2568^{11}	**Meadow Blue (42)** (MissLCSiddall) **4-8-10**ow2 OPears(3) (nvr trbld ldrs)	8	12	50/1	30	—
2114^{2}	**Winnebago (47)** (CWThornton) **4-9-1** DeanMcKeown(9) (led tl hdd 3f out: sn wknd & eased)	5	13	13/2^{3}	30	—
2475^{6}	**Well Armed (IRE) (60)** (JJO'Neill) **6-10-0** JCarroll(14) (chsd ldrs tl wknd over 3f out: eased whn btn)	4	14	25/1	39	—
2662^{7}	**Operatic Dancer (28)** (RMMcKellar) **6-7-3**$^{(7)}$ JennyBenson(6) (cl up tl wknd 7f out)	nk	15	100/1	7	—

(SP 126.7%) **15 Rn**

3m 29.5 CSF £55.76 CT £533.51 TOTE £9.00: £4.20 £2.10 £4.60 (£33.60) Trio £261.20 OWNER Mr Ian Dalgleish (CORNHILL-ON-TWEED) BRED Fittocks Stud Ltd

LONG HANDICAP Valiant Dash 7-0 Operatic Dancer 7-9

WEIGHT FOR AGE 3yo-17lb

OFFICIAL EXPLANATION **Thunderheart: regarding the improved form, the gelding had finished distressed last time and had been treated by a vet straight after the race.**

2166 Thunderheart got the ground he likes here and looked a picture and did the business in good style to show he retains plenty of ability. (8/1)

Bold Elect put in a useful effort here and is obviously coming to hand fast. (7/1)

2000 Marsayas (IRE) is looking particularly well and ran a fine race and is well worth keeping an eye on. (10/1: op 6/1)

2352 Charity Crusader had his chances but when it came down to a struggle he again failed to do enough. (6/1)

2413 Gymcrak Tiger (IRE) both looked and ran well but proved short of toe when put under pressure. (9/1: 12/1-8/1)

2350* Vintage Taittinger (IRE), given a lot to do this time, was always finding the effort beyond him and probably needs riding up with the pace. (11/4: 3/1-2/1)

2826 STUC CENTENARY H'CAP (0-70) (3-Y.O+) (Class E)
4-10 (4-11) **5f** £3,485.00 (£1,055.00: £515.00: £245.00) Stalls: High GOING minus 0.24 sec per fur (GF)

				SP	RR	SF
2657^{9}	**Palacegate Jack (IRE) (65)** (JBerry) **6-9-7b**$^{(5)}$ TEDurcan(2) (lw: mde all stands' side: hld on wl)	—	1	8/1^{3}	73	56
2754*	**Goretski (IRE) (67)** (NTinkler) **4-9-9**$^{(5)}$ 7x PRoberts(1) (chsd wnr stands' side: rdn & ev ch ins fnl f: nt qckn towards fin)	½	2	11/10^{1}	73	56
2755^{4}	**Silk Cottage (51)** (RMWhitaker) **5-8-12** DeanMcKeown(4) (lw: chsd ldrs far side: edgd lft & effrt ½-wy: ev ch ins fnl f: nt qckn)	nk	3	9/1	56	39
2657*	**Pallium (IRE) (52)** (DANolan) **9-8-8b**$^{(5)}$ 7x KSked(6) (racd far side: cl up tl outpcd fnl 2f)	2	4	6/1^{2}	51	34

				SP	RR	SF
2657[5]	**Six for Luck (43)** (DANolan) **5-8-4** JCarroll(5) (disp ld far side 3f: sn outpcd)	1½	**5**	6/1[2]	37	20
2657[4]	**Another Nightmare (IRE) (47)** (RMMcKellar) **5-8-1**(7) JMcAuley(3) (disp ld far side tl outpcd fnl 2f)	2	**6**	10/1	35	18
				(SP 106.4%)	**6 Rn**	

59.6 secs (1.90) CSF £14.21 TOTE £7.10: £2.10 £1.10 (£3.90) OWNER Mr William Burns (COCKERHAM) BRED Brendan and Sheila Powell
2032* Palacegate Jack (IRE) got the favoured stands' rails and showed again that when things go his way he is still quite useful. (8/1: 6/1-10/1)
2754* Goretski (IRE) drifted noticeably in the betting and looked as though he was feeling his hard race of only two days ago but he still put up a useful performance. He is now due to go up another 4lb. (11/10)
2755 Silk Cottage looked in tremendous condition and apparently failed to handle the bend at Catterick last time. He ran much better here and seems to be coming to form. (9/1)
2657* Pallium (IRE) was always racing up the unfavoured far side of the track and was making no impression in the last two furlongs. (6/1: op 4/1)
2657 Six for Luck is running reasonably but it is three years since his previous win. (6/1)
2657 Another Nightmare (IRE) had both the ground and the fact that she raced on the far side against her. (10/1)

2827 DAILY RECORD YES YES (S) STKS (2-Y.O) (Class F)

4-40 (4-43) **7f 30y** £2,814.00 (£852.00: £416.00: £198.00) Stalls: High GOING minus 0.55 sec per fur (F)

				SP	RR	SF
2425[2]	**Captain Bliss** (NTinkler) **2-8-4b**(7) RWinston(1) (disp ld tl led over 3f out: rdn clr fnl f)	—	**1**	3/1[2]	55	—
2383[6]	**Anniemitchellslass** (DMoffatt) **2-8-3**(3) DarrenMoffatt(9) (hld up: effrt over 3f out: styd on wl towards fin)	5	**2**	10/1	39	—
2168[6]	**Cosmic Case** (JSGoldie) **2-8-6** TWilliams(6) (chsd ldrs: hdwy & ev ch over 1f out: wknd)	s.h	**3**	16/1	39	—
2714[7]	**Makahu Don** (WTKemp) **2-9-2** OPears(7) (lw: disp ld tl hdd over 3f out: hung lft & one pce)	3	**4**	13/2[3]	42	—
2493[8]	**Ludere (IRE)** (WWHaigh) **2-8-11** RLappin(8) (effrt ½-wy: n.d)	7	**5**	20/1	21	—
2288[8]	**Wee Christy (IRE)** (WMcKeown) **2-8-11b**[1] NConnorton(12) (sme hdwy fnl 3f: n.d)	hd	**6**	12/1	21	—
2361[9]	**Full Moon** (PDEvans) **2-8-11b**[1] JFEgan(11) (hdwy to jn ldrs after 2f: wknd fnl 2½f)	nk	**7**	16/1	20	—
	Ingle Boy (BMactaggart) **2-8-11** VHalliday(4) (w'like: bit bkwd: a rr div)	1	**8**	33/1	18	—
1626[7]	**Gay da Cheen (IRE)** (JMCarr) **2-8-6** NKennedy(2) (prom 4f: sn wknd)	6	**9**	25/1	—	—
2500[10]	**Petite Tache** (NChamberlain) **2-8-1**(5) KSked(10) (chsd ldrs tl st: sn wknd)	3	**10**	25/1	—	—
948[8]	**La Vaso Verdi** (RMWhitaker) **2-8-3**(3) GParkin(3) (lost tch fr ½-wy)	1¾	**11**	25/1	—	—
2489[W]	***Huxleen*** (WGMTurner) **2-8-6**(5) DSweeney(5) (Withdrawn not under starter's orders: ref to ent stalls)		**W**	7/4[1]	—	—
				(SP 122.5%)	**11 Rn**	

1m 31.2 (5.20) CSF £12.35 TOTE £2.70: £1.10 £1.60 £2.40 (£7.50) Trio £29.80 OWNER Elite Racing Club (MALTON) BRED K. Panos
No bid
2425 Captain Bliss, given a most positive ride, did the business this time and left nothing to chance. (3/1)
2383 Anniemitchellslass does not impress on looks but moves well and certainly responded to pressure. There could be a modest race in her. (10/1)
2168 Cosmic Case showed her first real signs of form here and this is obviously the company she needs but probably over a shorter trip. (16/1)
2714 Makahu Don seems to have lost his way for the time being and all he wanted to do was hang left when asked a question. (13/2)
Ludere (IRE) failed to get into this and is proving disappointing. (20/1)
Wee Christy (IRE) had blinkers on for the first time with little effect. (12/1)

2828 HERALD H'CAP (0-60) (3-Y.O+) (Class F)

5-10 (5-12) **1m 16y** £2,996.00 (£908.00: £444.00: £212.00) Stalls: High GOING minus 0.55 sec per fur (F)

				SP	RR	SF
2109[5]	**Seconds Away (30)** (JSGoldie) **6-7-12** TWilliams(11) (hld up: hdwy to ld wl over 1f out: styd on)	—	**1**	14/1	41	18
2546[8]	**Spanish Verdict (51)** (DenysSmith) **10-9-2**(3) CTeague(6) (cl up: ev ch over 2f out: kpt on wl)	½	**2**	12/1	61	38
2384[8]	**Needle Match (51)** (JJO'Neill) **4-9-5** OPears(10) (hld up & bhd: hdwy 3f out: nt clr run & several positions: styd on towards fin)	½	**3**	16/1	60	37
1683[9]	**Champagne N Dreams (42)** (DNicholls) **5-8-7**(3) GParkin(7) (hld up & bhd: gd hdwy 3f out: swtchd 2f out: sn ev ch: nt qckn fnl f)	½	**4**	12/1	50	27
2416[2]	**Legal Issue (IRE) (55)** (WWHaigh) **5-9-9** RLappin(5) (hld up & bhd: hdwy over 3f out: sn in tch: one pce appr fnl f)	2½	**5**	6/1[3]	58	35
2502*	**Bowcliffe (60)** (EJAlston) **6-10-0** JFEgan(8) (lw: hld up: hdwy on outside 3f out: nvr able to chal)	hd	**6**	7/4[1]	63	40
2316[9]	**Tissue of Lies (USA) (58)** (MJohnston) **4-9-9**(3) KMChin(2) (lw: chsd ldr tl wknd fnl 2f)	1½	**7**	9/1	58	35
2205[10]	**Bulsara (54)** (CWFairhurst) **5-9-3**(5) KSked(14) (chsd ldrs tl wknd over 1f out)	½	**8**	12/1	53	30
2522[7]	**Don't Worry Mike (48)** (FHLee) **3-8-8b**[1] NConnorton(1) (led tl hdd & wknd wl over 1f out)	2½	**9**	20/1	42	11
2546[2]	**Nkapen Rocks (SPA) (49)** (CaptJWilson) **4-8-12**(5) TEDurcan(13) (prom tl wknd 2f out)	5	**10**	7/2[2]	33	10
2564[14]	**Midday Cowboy (USA) (40)** (MDHammond) **4-8-3**(5) DSweeney(12) (cl up tl wknd fnl 2f)	3½	**11**	40/1	17	—
2203[6]	**King of Show (IRE) (42)** (RAllan) **6-8-10v** VHalliday(4) (in tch: rn wd st: sn wknd)	8	**12**	33/1	3	—
1818[9]	**Celia's Rainbow (28)** (RMWhitaker) **4-7-10** NKennedy(9) (a bhd)	2½	**13**	100/1	—	—
	Thorntoun Jewel (IRE) (33) (MissZAGreen) **4-7-8**(7) MMathers(3) (swtg: in tch: rn wd st & racd stands' side: sn btn)	nk	**14**	150/1	—	—
				(SP 130.3%)	**14 Rn**	

1m 41.1 (2.10) CSF £164.16 CT £2,508.23 TOTE £11.80: £2.40 £3.10 £8.80 (£75.70) Trio £263.10; £3.71 to Newbury 19/7/97 OWNER Mr J. S. Goldie (GLASGOW) BRED Mrs E.Campbell
LONG HANDICAP Celia's Rainbow 7-9
WEIGHT FOR AGE 3yo-8lb
2109 Seconds Away won his first race here after thirty-nine attempts and showed some spirit to hold on. (14/1)
1862 Spanish Verdict again showed that despite his years there is a race or two in him. (12/1)
2203 Needle Match would probably have won this had he had any sort of run. (16/1)
Champagne N Dreams, who won her only race on this track, put in her best effort for a while here. (12/1)
2416 Legal Issue (IRE) is running quite well at the moment and is certainly well enough handicapped but was never doing enough when it mattered here. (6/1)
2502* Bowcliffe travelled well but failed to pick up in the last three furlongs. He has shot up the handicap recently which is probably taking its toll. (7/4)

T/Plpt: £622.80 (19.79 Tckts). T/Qdpt: £263.50 (3.3 Tckts) AA

1872-NEWBURY (L-H) (Good to firm)
Friday July 18th
WEATHER: overcast WIND: slt across

2829 E.B.F. ECCHINSWELL NOVICE STKS (2-Y.O) (Class D)
2-30 (2-31) **6f 8y** £3,863.50 (£1,168.00: £569.00: £269.50) Stalls: High GOING minus 0.32 sec per fur (GF)

	Horse	Dist	Pl	SP	RR	SF
	Ariant (USA) (JHMGosden) **2-8-12** LDettori(3) (w'like: scope: stdy hdwy 3f out: led on bit over 2f out: rdn fnl f: r.o wl)	—	1	4/11[1]	85+	32
	Sabhaan (MajorWRHern) **2-8-12** RHills(6) (w'like: scope: bit bkwd: hld up: n.m.r over 1f out: rdn: r.o wl ins fnl f)	nk	2	7/1[2]	84+	31
	Night Owl (RCharlton) **2-8-7** TSprake(7) (neat: n.m.r: swtchd lft & hdwy over 1f out: r.o ins fnl f)	1¼	3	20/1	76+	23
	Tumblweed Prospect (BJMeehan) **2-8-12** MTebbutt(2) (leggy: a.p: ev ch 2f out: unable qckn)	1¼	4	12/1	78	25
	Double Brandy (IABalding) **2-8-12** SWhitworth(10) (unf: lost pl 2f out: nt clr run on ins over 1f out: rallied ins fnl f: r.o)	nk	5	33/1	77	24
	Pips Song (IRE) (IABalding) **2-8-9**(3) MartinDwyer(5) (leggy: unf: rdn & hdwy over 2f out: one pce fnl f)	hd	6	16/1	77	24
2215[3]	**Overture (IRE)** (RHannon) **2-9-4** PatEddery(8) (led over 3f: wknd over 1f out)	¾	7	8/1[3]	81	28
	Storm Fromthe East (RHannon) **2-8-12** DaneO'Neill(4) (str: scope: prom over 4f)	1¾	8	16/1	70	17
	Guaranteed (BWHills) **2-8-12** MHills(1) (str: scope: bkwd: a bhd)	2½	9	12/1	63	10
	Muyassir (IRE) (CJBenstead) **2-8-12** GDuffield(9) (str: scope: bkwd: dwlt: a bhd)	6	10	33/1	47	—

(SP 134.7%) **10 Rn**

1m 14.49 (2.69) CSF £4.49 TOTE £1.60: £1.10 £1.90 £3.50 (£5.80) Trio £31.90 OWNER Sheikh Mohammed (NEWMARKET) BRED Mr and Mrs John C. Mabee

Ariant (USA), a medium-sized colt, looked the part in the paddock and was all the rage in the market. He did not let his supporters down as he cruised through on the bridle over a quarter of a mile from home but needed to be rousted along in the final furlong to hold on. More will be heard of him. (4/11)

Sabhaan, an attractive, good-bodied individual with plenty of scope, was colty in the paddock and looked as though this run was just needed. Nevertheless, he showed plenty of promise and, although not having a great deal of room for a brief time below the distance, ran on in tremendous style to make sure the winner did not have things all his own way. He should have no problem going one better. (7/1: 4/1-8/1)

Night Owl, a plain filly who was certainly a lot smaller than many of her rivals, ran on nicely in the last furlong and a half to finish on the heels of the front two. (20/1)

Tumblweed Prospect, a tall colt who is a half-brother to several winners, had every chance two furlongs from home before tapped for toe. (12/1)

Double Brandy does need time to develop. Outpaced as the race began in earnest a quarter of a mile from home, he did not have the clearest of passages along the inside rail below the distance but, to his credit, stayed on in the closing stages. On this evidence he already needs another furlong. (33/1)

Pips Song (IRE), a tall gelding who has yet to develop, moved up soon after halfway but failed to find another gear in the final furlong. (16/1)

2215 Overture (IRE) (8/1: 5/1-9/1)

Guaranteed (12/1: op 5/1)

2830 WATERMILL CONDITIONS STKS (3-Y.O+) (Class C)
3-00 (3-00) **7f 64y (round)** £4,996.00 (£1,864.00: £907.00: £385.00: £167.50: £80.50) Stalls: Low GOING minus 0.32 sec per fur (GF)

	Horse	Dist	Pl	SP	RR	SF
1776*	**Decorated Hero (117)** (JHMGosden) **5-9-7** LDettori(4) (stdy hdwy over 3f out: led over 1f out: rdn out)	—	1	2/1[1]	123	86
2679[3]	**Restructure (IRE) (110)** (MrsJCecil) **5-9-0** MRoberts(5) (lw: a.p: led over 2f out tl over 1f out: r.o)	nk	2	8/1	115	78
2334[4]	**My Branch (103)** (BWHills) **4-8-9** PatEddery(3) (lw: rdn & hdwy over 1f out: unable qckn)	6	3	9/2[3]	97	60
2009[10]	**Hidden Meadow (115)** (IABalding) **3-8-12** MHills(7) (lw: stdy hdwy over 3f out: rdn over 2f out: one pce)	1	4	9/4[2]	105	61
2476[3]	**Cayman Kai (IRE) (102)** (RHannon) **4-9-0** RHughes(6) (lw: rdn & hdwy over 2f out: one pce)	nk	5	16/1	99	62
2056[9]	**Easy Dollar (106)** (BGubby) **5-9-0b** JWeaver(2) (led 5f)	7	6	8/1	84	47
2172*	**Mithali** (BWHills) **4-9-0** RHills(1) (chsd ldr 4f: wknd over 2f out)	1	7	20/1	82	45
1598[4]	**Raheen (USA) (87)** (WGMTurner) **4-8-7b**(7) DMcGaffin(8) (swvd rt s: bhd fnl 3f)	15	8	100/1	49	12

(SP 116.1%) **8 Rn**

1m 27.5 (-0.60) CSF £17.54 TOTE £2.90: £1.30 £2.80 £1.40 (£16.60) OWNER Exors of the late Mr Herbert Allen (NEWMARKET) BRED Reg Griffin and Jim McGrath

WEIGHT FOR AGE 3yo-7lb

1776* Decorated Hero, who has been working with Benny the Dip and Lord of Men at home, had nothing of that calibre here, leading below the distance and being rousted along to keep the persistent runner-up at bay. He is up to winning a Group Three event. (2/1)

2679 Restructure (IRE) appreciated this slightly easier company and went on over a quarter of a mile from home. Headed below the distance, he kept beavering away at the winner and although unable to get back in front, finished well clear of the remainder. He has been struggling in Group company this season and a Listed race may well be the answer. (8/1: 6/1-9/1)

2334 My Branch made a forward move below the distance but was only fighting for third prize. Three of her four wins to date have come in the Autumn. (9/2)

2009 Hidden Meadow is not proving at all consistent this season and, although, creeping closer at halfway, his jockey did not look entirely happy and he was only fighting for third prize in the final quarter-mile. Both his wins this term have come when he has made the running and a return to those tactics might reap rewards. (9/4)

2476 Cayman Kai (IRE) has failed to recapture the form he showed last year when winning the Free Handicap and finishing fourth in the French Two Thousand Guineas and fifth in the St James's Palace Stakes, and was only scrapping for third prize in the final quarter-mile. (16/1)

1720a Easy Dollar hared off in front but, collared approaching the final quarter-mile, soon had bellows to mend. He has been placed in several Pattern events but his record stands at just two wins from thirty starts. (8/1)

2831 CHATTIS HILL MAIDEN STKS (2-Y.O F) (Class D)
3-30 (3-31) **5f 34y** £3,629.50 (£1,096.00: £533.00: £251.50) Stalls: High GOING minus 0.32 sec per fur (GF)

	Horse	Dist	Pl	SP	RR	SF
	Bayleaf (RFJohnsonHoughton) **2-8-11** JReid(7) (neat: hld up: rdn over 1f out: squeezed thro & bmpd on ins, ins fnl f: led last strides)	—	1	8/1	77	35
880[2]	**Cloudberry** (BJMeehan) **2-8-11** MTebbutt(8) (lw: a.p: led wl over 1f out: edgd rt & bmpd ins fnl f: hdd last strides)	hd	2	20/1	77	35

	Thanksgiving (IRE) (MajorDNChappell) **2-8-11** GCarter(11) (w'like: outpcd: hdwy & edgd lft over 1f out: r.o ins fnl f)	2	**3**	20/1	71	29
2103^{11}	**Quiz Show** (RHannon) **2-8-11** DaneO'Neill(5) (a.p: rdn over 3f out: one pce fnl 2f)	1¾	**4**	$6/1^{3}$	65	23
2534^{3}	**Alpha Whisky (GER)** (IABalding) **2-8-11** LDettori(6) (hld up: rdn 2f out: one pce)	s.h	**5**	15/2	65	23
	Belle de Nuit (IRE) (BJMeehan) **2-8-4**(7) GHannon(1) (leggy: hdwy over 1f out: r.o)	hd	**6**	50/1	65	23
2181^{4}	**First Dance** (RHannon) **2-8-11** RHughes(3) (hdwy & nt clr run over 1f out: nt clr run ins fnl f: nvr nrr)	½	**7**	12/1	63+	21
	Delphic Way (GBBalding) **2-8-11** SDrowne(2) (neat: rdn over 3f out: nvr nr to chal)	2	**8**	$11/2^{2}$	57	15
	Madame Claude (IRE) (JARToller) **2-8-11** SSanders(4) (leggy: prom over 2f)	2	**9**	8/1	51	9
2227^{3}	**Kenkan (IRE)** (PFICole) **2-8-11** CRutter(9) (w ldr: led 2f out tl wl over 1f out: sn wknd)	2	**10**	$4/1^{1}$	44	2
2467^{14}	**First Village (IRE)** (JBerry) **2-8-11b¹** KFallon(10) (b.hind: led 3f)	nk	**11**	$11/2^{2}$	44	2
2227^{6}	**To Love With Love** (WJarvis) **2-8-11** PatEddery(12) (s.s: a bhd)	1½	**12**	14/1	39	—

(SP 124.9%) **12 Rn**

62.21 secs (2.01) CSF £150.74 TOTE £15.80: £3.40 £5.00 £7.20 (£119.40) Trio £539.70 OWNER Lady Rothschild (DIDCOT) BRED Lord Rothschild

Bayleaf is not that big but she showed real guts and determination on this racecourse debut. Throwing down her challenge from below the distance, she had very little room in which to manoeuvre along the inside rail as the runner-up kept on leaning on her but she managed to get up in the last couple of strides. (8/1)

880 Cloudberry, off the course for over eleven weeks, went on early in the final quarter-mile, but she drifted right from below the distance, giving the winner very little room on the inside rail. Responding well to her rider's urgings, she only lost out in the last couple of strides. (20/1)

Thanksgiving (IRE), a medium-sized filly, was unable to go the pace but ran on in good style in the last furlong and a half despite drifting out into the centre of the track. (20/1)

Quiz Show, a leading player throughout, was soon being bustled along and never looked like quickening up in the last two furlongs. (6/1)

2534 Alpha Whisky (GER), with experience on her side, chased the leaders but failed to quicken in the final quarter-mile. She needs further. (15/2)

Belle de Nuit (IRE), whose dame was a half-sister to the high-class Ruby Tiger, is a tall filly who is a half-sister to the useful hurdler Pleasureland. She ran on nicely in the last furlong and a half but never threatened to get there in time. (50/1)

2181 First Dance (12/1: op 5/1)

Delphic Way (11/2: 7/1-4/1)

2227 Kenkan (IRE) (4/1: 2/1-9/2)

2832 WATERFORD FOOD INGREDIENTS H'CAP (0-80) (3-Y.O F) (Class D)

4-00 (4-02) **1m 2f 6y** £3,668.50 (£1,108.00: £539.00: £254.50) Stalls: Low GOING minus 0.32 sec per fur (GF)

				SP	RR	SF
885^{3}	**Enlisted (IRE) (72)** (SirMarkPrescott) **3-8-13** GDuffield(11) (hdwy & n.m.r over 1f out: swtchd lft: str run to ld nr fin)	—	**1**	$6/1^{3}$	81	28
1567*	**Boss Lady (IRE) (75)** (RCharlton) **3-9-2** PatEddery(7) (chsd ldr: rdn over 2f out: led over 1f out: hdd nr fin)	½	**2**	$4/1^{2}$	83	30
2468^{2}	**Inclination (60)** (MBlanshard) **3-8-1** JQuinn(3) (led: rdn over 2f out: hdwy over 1f out: one pce)	1½	**3**	8/1	66	13
2507^{4}	**Lonely Heart (75)** (DRCElsworth) **3-9-2e** RCochrane(2) (lw: s.s: swtchd rt & hdwy over 1f out: r.o)	½	**4**	14/1	80	27
1747^{10}	**Fantastic Flame (IRE) (79)** (PJMakin) **3-9-6** SSanders(5) (rdn over 2f out: hdwy over 1f out: one pce)	nk	**5**	16/1	84	31
2183*	**Sellette (IRE) (80)** (DHaydnJones) **3-9-7** SDrowne(10) (lw: a.p: rdn over 2f out: one pce)	s.h	**6**	8/1	85	32
2062^{14}	**Vanishing Trick (USA) (78)** (HRACecil) **3-9-5v¹** KFallon(6) (hld up: rdn over 3f out: one pce)	2	**7**	10/1	79	26
1823^{11}	**Bellagrana (55)** (MJFetherston-Godley) **3-7-7**(3) RFfrench(4) (bhd fnl 2f)	3½	**8**	16/1	51	—
1777^{2}	**Kaziranga (USA) (76)** (LMCumani) **3-9-3** LDettori(9) (sme hdwy over 2f out: sn wknd)	1¼	**9**	$3/1^{1}$	70	17
886^{12}	**Santa Rosa (IRE) (60)** (JLDunlop) **3-8-1** TSprake(8) (lw: plld hrd: hld up: rdn over 2f out: sn wknd)	4	**10**	12/1	47	—
1845^{9}	**Julietta Mia (USA) (70)** (WRMuir) **3-8-11** JReid(1) (lw: plld hrd: prom over 8f)	1½	**11**	16/1	55	2

(SP 122.6%) **11 Rn**

2m 9.42 (5.42) CSF £28.78 CT £182.29 TOTE £7.70: £2.30 £1.90 £1.80 (£14.20) Trio £34.30 OWNER Mr Neil Greig (NEWMARKET) BRED Mount Coote Stud

LONG HANDICAP Bellagrana 7-8

885 Enlisted (IRE) appreciated this longer trip and, despite an absence of over eleven weeks, made a winning debut in handicap company although she only managed to get up near the line. (6/1: 9/2-7/1)

1567* Boss Lady (IRE) appreciated the step up in trip and eventually got to the front below the distance. Despite doing little wrong, she was worried out of it near the finish. (4/1: op 5/2)

2468 Inclination attempted to make every post a winning one but, collared below the distance, failed to find another gear. She remains a maiden. (8/1)

2507 Lonely Heart, switched off the rails in the final quarter-mile, stayed on without looking likely to get there in time. She remains a maiden. (14/1)

1276 Fantastic Flame (IRE) ran better here, moving up below the distance before tapped for toe. (16/1)

2183* Sellette (IRE), who has been very consistent, found top weight anchoring her and could only go up and down in the same place from below the distance. (8/1)

2833 SHRIVENHAM H'CAP (0-90) (3-Y.O+) (Class C)

4-30 (4-32) **6f 8y** £5,735.00 (£1,730.00: £840.00: £395.00) Stalls: High GOING minus 0.32 sec per fur (GF)

				SP	RR	SF
2563^{3}	**Literary Society (USA) (77)** (JARToller) **4-9-2** SSanders(12) (hld up: rdn over 1f out: led last strides)	—	**1**	$6/1^{2}$	83	54
2347^{4}	**Sir Joey (USA) (83)** (PGMurphy) **8-9-8** SDrowne(8) (hld up: rdn to ld ins fnl f: hdd last strides)	s.h	**2**	$8/1^{3}$	89	60
2347*	**Always Alight (76)** (KRBurke) **3-8-10** JQuinn(4) (lw: hld up: rdn over 1f out: r.o)	½	**3**	$11/2^{1}$	81	47
1975^{7}	**Loving And Giving (80)** (HCandy) **3-9-0** CRutter(7) (hrd rdn & hdwy over 1f out: r.o wl ins fnl f)	½	**4**	16/1	83	49
2665*	**Out Line (68)** (MMadgwick) **5-8-7** 7x NVarley(13) (rdn over 2f out: hdwy over 1f out: r.o)	hd	**5**	$8/1^{3}$	71	42
2598^{11}	**Law Commission (89)** (DRCElsworth) **7-10-0** DHolland(6) (rdn & hdwy over 1f out: r.o wl ins fnl f)	s.h	**6**	16/1	92	63
2779^{D}	**Cauda Equina (80)** (MRChannon) **3-8-7**(7) 7x AEddery(3) (a.p: led over 1f out tl ins fnl f: one pce)	nk	**7**	12/1	82	48
2422*	**Desert Lynx (IRE) (76)** (TRWatson) **4-9-1** RHughes(2) (hrd rdn & hdwy over 1f out: r.o)	hd	**8**	20/1	78	49
1772^{11}	**Lord Olivier (IRE) (77)** (WJarvis) **7-9-2** JReid(11) (lost pl over 4f out: rallied over 1f out: one pce)	1¼	**9**	16/1	75	46
2698^{10}	**Scissor Ridge (61)** (JJBridger) **5-7-7**(7) PDoe(14) (prom 3f)	2	**10**	33/1	54	25
1439^{12}	**La Petite Fusee (79)** (RJO'Sullivan) **6-9-4** KFallon(5) (led over 4f)	s.h	**11**	16/1	72	43
2358^{3}	**Lady Diesis (USA) (84)** (BWHills) **3-9-4** MHills(15) (lw: prom over 4f)	1½	**12**	16/1	73	39
2326^{16}	**Charlie Sillett (89)** (BWHills) **5-9-11**(3) JDSmith(1) (s.s: bhd fnl 2f)	2	**13**	25/1	73	44
2605^{3}	**Tailwind (63)** (WRMuir) **3-7-8**(3) MartinDwyer(9) (prom over 4f)	1½	**14**	20/1	43	9
1772^{10}	**Marl (84)** (RAkehurst) **4-9-9** DHarrison(10) (prom over 4f)	3	**15**	11/1	56	27

2424^{4}	**Never Think Twice (63)** (KTIvory) **4-8-2v**^{ow1} BDoyle(16) (b: a bhd)	9	**16**	12/1	11	—

(SP 121.3%) **16 Rn**

1m 13.19 (1.39) CSF £45.65 CT £269.76 TOTE £5.60: £2.10 £2.30 £1.30 £3.60 (£17.60) Trio £36.10 OWNER Lady Celina Carter (WHITSBURY) BRED William R. and Mrs Buster
WEIGHT FOR AGE 3yo-5lb

2563 Literary Society (USA) chased the leaders and, woken up below the distance, managed to get up in the last few strides to gain his first victory over six furlongs. (6/1)
2347 Sir Joey (USA) may be getting on in age but he travelled supremely well and looked sure to score below the distance. Rousted along, he did not find as much as what was expected but still managed to get to the front inside the final furlong before worried out of it in the last couple of strides. He is a winner without a penalty. (8/1)
2347* Always Alight, 14lb higher than when winning here in May, still ran another sound race, keeping on well inside the final furlong. (11/2)
Loving And Giving found her stride from below the distance but, despite running on strongly, was unable to get there in time. (16/1)
2665* Out Line, 7lb higher for her Lingfield success last Friday over this distance, nearly got caught out by the trip on that occasion and certainly did here for, although running on in the last furlong and a half, she found the line always beating her. A return to seven furlongs is needed. (8/1)
1308 Law Commission, dropping to six furlongs for the first time this this season, ran on in good style in the last furlong and a half if never looking likely to get there in time. He has done all his winning on a fast surface. (16/1)

2834 JULY H'CAP (0-85) (3-Y.O+) (Class D)

5-00 (5-00) **2m** £3,597.00 (£1,086.00: £528.00: £249.00) Stalls: Low GOING minus 0.32 sec per fur (GF)

				SP	RR	SF
728^{4}	**Captain Jack (85)** (MCPipe) **7-10-0** MRoberts(2) (lw: led 12f: led over 1f out: drvn out)	—	**1**	5/1^{2}	96	39
2108^{9}	**Premier Night (81)** (SDow) **4-9-10** JReid(1) (lw: hld up: rdn over 2f out: r.o ins fnl f)	1¼	**2**	13/2	91	34
2327^{10}	**Thaljanah (IRE) (82)** (BSmart) **5-9-11** RCochrane(4) (rdn over 2f out: hdwy over 1f out: r.o ins fnl f)	s.h	**3**	9/1	92	35
2530^{4}	**Nanton Point (USA) (74)** (LadyHerries) **5-9-3** JQuinn(3) (chsd ldrs: led 4f out tl over 1f out: unable qckn)	1¾	**4**	11/2^{3}	82	25
2589^{2}	**Russian Rose (IRE) (70)** (JARToller) **4-8-13** PaulEddery(6) (rdn over 3f out: nvr nr to chal)	2½	**5**	Evens^{1}	75	18
	Chief Mouse (67) (FJordan) **4-8-10** SSanders(5) (prom over 13f)	¾	**6**	20/1	33 t	15

(SP 110.1%) **6 Rn**

3m 33.84 (9.64) CSF £31.26 TOTE £5.50: £1.80 £3.10 (£14.10) OWNER Mr Clive Smith (WELLINGTON) BRED Highclere Stud Ltd
OFFICIAL EXPLANATION **Russian Rose (IRE): ran lifelessly and the race probably came too soon.**

728 Captain Jack, given a three-month break, put up a real battling display for having lost the advantage early in the straight, he managed to get back in front again approaching the final furlong and kept on well. (5/1)
1491* Premier Night appreciated the return to a sounder surface and two miles and ran on for second prize inside the final furlong. (13/2)
1947 Thaljanah (IRE) picked up ground below the distance and, running on, only just failed to take second prize. (9/1: 6/1-10/1)
2530 Nanton Point (USA) went on half a mile from home but, collared below the distance, his lack of acceleration was once again exposed. (11/2)
2589 Russian Rose (IRE), set to rise 6lb in future handicaps, ran a lifeless race and never threatened to get into it. (Evens)
Chief Mouse, winner of three races over hurdles in the spring, was close up until tiring over two furlongs from home. (20/1)

2835 LEVY BOARD H'CAP (0-85) (3-Y.O+) (Class D)

5-30 (5-31) **7f (straight)** £3,759.50 (£1,136.00: £553.00: £261.50) Stalls: High GOING minus 0.32 sec per fur (GF)

				SP	RR	SF
2280^{2}	**Waypoint (82)** (RCharlton) **4-9-11** SSanders(2) (lw: hld up: led over 1f out: hrd rdn: r.o wl)	—	**1**	12/1^{3}	95	77
2420*	**Sheltering Sky (IRE) (81)** (JLDunlop) **3-9-3** PatEddery(5) (b: swtchd rt & hdwy over 2f out: ev ch over 1f out: unable qckn)	1¾	**2**	3/1^{1}	90	65
2576^{7}	**Blue Flyer (IRE) (72)** (RIngram) **4-9-1b** AMcGlone(6) (hld up: rdn over 2f out: one pce fnl f)	3½	**3**	33/1	73	55
2325^{12}	**Iblis (IRE) (80)** (GWragg) **5-9-9** MHills(7) (lw: led over 5f: one pce)	1	**4**	20/1	79	61
2465^{4}	**Duello (68)** (MBlanshard) **6-8-11** MRoberts(12) (lw: rdn over 2f out: hdwy over 1f out: nvr nrr)	nk	**5**	12/1^{3}	66	48
2478^{10}	**Q Factor (80)** (DHaydnJones) **5-9-9** SDrowne(3) (hld up: rdn over 2f out: wknd fnl f)	hd	**6**	20/1	78	60
1680^{2}	**Winsome Wooster (63)** (PGMurphy) **6-8-6** DHarrison(10) (a.p: hrd rdn over 2f out: wknd over 1f out)	2	**7**	14/1	56	38
2573^{2}	**Sea Danzig (57)** (JJBridger) **4-8-0** NAdams(4) (lw: prom over 4f)	½	**8**	16/1	49	31
2546^{10}	**Morocco (IRE) (64)** (MRChannon) **8-8-0**$^{(7)ow4}$ AEddery(11) (hrd rdn & hdwy over 1f out: nvr nrr)	2	**9**	25/1	52	30
2510^{3}	**Giko (60)** (JRPoulton) **3-7-10** NVarley(8) (a mid div)	1	**10**	25/1	45	20
2390^{8}	**Civil Liberty (77)** (GLewis) **4-9-6** PaulEddery(1) (nvr nrr)	¾	**11**	25/1	61	43
2708^{15}	**Zelda Zonk (78)** (BJMeehan) **5-9-7** JWeaver(17) (lw: bmpd s: a mid div)	¾	**12**	20/1	60	42
2695^{2}	**Dulcinea (61)** (IABalding) **3-7-8**$^{(3)ow1}$ MartinDwyer(18) (lw: hdwy over 5f out: wknd wl over 1f out)	5	**13**	4/1^{2}	31	5
2422^{9}	**Frederick James (72)** (MJHeaton-Ellis) **3-8-8** SWhitworth(9) (bhd fnl 3f)	8	**14**	33/1	24	—
2554^{10}	**Davids Revenge (67)** (MajorDNChappell) **3-8-3** GCarter(19) (a bhd)	¾	**15**	20/1	17	—
2390^{4}	**Lynton Lad (69)** (CPEBrooks) **5-8-12** RPerham(13) (bhd fnl 3f)	3½	**16**	20/1	11	—
1691*	**Zugudi (80)** (KMahdi) **3-9-2** JReid(14) (lw: bhd fnl 3f)	2	**17**	14/1	18	—
2346^{12}	**Press On Nicky (67)** (WRMuir) **4-8-10** GDuffield(16) (lw: stumbled & bmpd s: hdwy over 5f out: wknd over 3f out)	8	**18**	25/1	—	—
2337^{4}	**Xenophon of Cunaxa (IRE) (61)** (MJFetherston-Godley) **4-8-4** DaneO'Neill(15) (a bhd)	5	**19**	20/1	—	—

(SP 129.4%) **19 Rn**

1m 24.49 (0.39) CSF £35.98 CT £826.49 TOTE £14.90: £2.60 £1.50 £8.60 £4.40 (£26.50) Trio £1,121.90 OWNER Mr Ray Richards (BECKHAMPTON) BRED Berkshire Equestrian Services Ltd
WEIGHT FOR AGE 3yo-7lb

2280 Waypoint put up a good performance under top weight, leading below the distance and responding to pressure to put the runner-up in his place in the final furlong. (12/1)
2420* Sheltering Sky (IRE), by far and away the least experienced in the field - this was only his third run - came through to have every chance below the distance but, although pulling clear of the remainder, was unable cope with the winner. (3/1)
121* Blue Flyer (IRE) chased the leaders but was unable to contain the front two in the final furlong. (33/1)
1442 Iblis (IRE) ran better here, taking the field along until collared below the distance. (20/1)
2465 Duello stayed on from below the distance without ever threatening to get there. He is not easy to win with. (12/1)
2280* Q Factor, 7lb worse off with the winner for beating him five lengths in the mud at Folkestone last month, chased the leaders until tiring in the final furlong. Although she has won on this ground she seems better suited by some give. (20/1)
1680 Winsome Wooster (14/1: 10/1-16/1)

T/Jkpt: £16,013.20 (0.09 Tckts); £20,524.03 to Newbury 19/7/97. T/Plpt: £729.80 (36.74 Tckts). T/Qdpt: £253.60 (5 Tckts) AK

2596-NEWMARKET (R-H) (Good to Soft)

Friday July 18th

WEATHER: fine WIND: fresh bhd

2836 SPORTING INDEX SPREAD BETTING CLAIMING STKS (3-Y.O) (Class D)

6-30 (6-30) **1m (July)** £3,817.50 (£1,140.00: £545.00: £247.50) Stalls: High GOING minus 0.11 sec per fur (G)

				SP	RR	SF
1807[6]	**Phylida (60)** (PJMakin) **3-7-13** JQuinn(11) (hld up stands' side: hdwy over 2f out: rdn & r.o wl to ld nr fin)	—	1	11/2[2]	60	33
2294[4]	**My Beloved (IRE) (58)** (RHannon) **3-8-2**(3) AWhelan(3) (hld up far side: rdn over 3f out: hdwy to ld ins fnl f: ct nr fin)	½	2	13/2[3]	65	38
1238[15]	**Cold Steel (72)** (WJarvis) **3-8-8** KFallon(4) (chsd ldrs far side: ev ch over 1f out: no ex ins fnl f)	¾	3	9/1	67	40
2583[9]	**Prince de Loir** (DJSCosgrove) **3-9-6** MRimmer(1) (chsd ldr far side: led over 2f out tl ins fnl f: one pce)	½	4	16/1	78	51
2125[5]	**Gresatre (51)** (CADwyer) **3-7-11**(7) JoHunnam(6) (in tch stands' side: no hdwy fnl 3f)	5	5	20/1	52	25
2392[2]	**Don Sebastian (68)** (WJHaggas) **3-9-3**(3) RFfrench(10) (lw: w ldr stands' side: led 5f out: wknd over 1f out)	2½	6	5/2[1]	63	36
2522[3]	**Poker Princess (52)** (MBell) **3-7-12**(5) RMullen(5) (dwlt: hld up far side: nvr nr ldrs)	1	7	11/2[2]	44	17
2733[7]	**Miss Barcelona (IRE) (45)** (MJPolglase) **3-7-11** JLowe(2) (led far side: sn clr: hdd over 2f out: sn wknd)	7	8	25/1	24	—
2724[9]	**Windborn (44)** (CNAllen) **3-7-4**(7) DarrenWilliams(7) (lw: in tch stands' side over 4f)	5	9	33/1	14	—
1690[4]	**Moon Song (60)** (APJarvis) **3-8-4**ow1 DHolland(8) (led stands' side 3f)	10	10	7/1	1	—
				(SP 112.6%)	**10 Rn**	

1m 42.15 (4.15) CSF £35.00 TOTE £7.00: £2.10 £1.80 £2.40 (£14.70) Trio £113.80 OWNER Mrs P. J. Makin (MARLBOROUGH) BRED The Glen Andred Stud and Highfield Stud Ltd

1807 Phylida, warm on her toes beforehand, was keen to post and it was a bit of a shock to see her staying on best on this step up in trip. Racing hard by the stands' rail as her rival scoured the course for the best ground probably helped. (11/2)

2294 My Beloved (IRE) ran much better this time, making hard work of getting to the front towards the far side before being denied by a horse racing wide apart from her. (13/2: 4/1-7/1)

50* Cold Steel, very keen going down, was at the end of his tether on meeting the rising ground over this extra furlong. (9/1)

Prince de Loir, dropped in class, looks to have found his grade and ought to stay a little further. (16/1)

2125 Gresatre, a poor mover these days, never mounted a serious challenge. (20/1)

2392 Don Sebastian looked magnificent, but failed to last home in the conditions with so much use made of him. (5/2)

2837 KINGS GAP CONDITIONS STKS (3-Y.O+) (Class C)

7-00 (7-01) **1m 4f (July)** £4,699.87 (£1,690.50: £807.75: £326.25: £125.63) Stalls: High GOING minus 0.11 sec per fur (G)

				SP	RR	SF
1454[4]	**Corradini (110)** (HRACecil) **5-9-2** KFallon(1) (trckd ldrs: rdn to ld over 1f out: rider lost whip: r.o wl)	—	1	2/1[2]	119	32
2311*	**Pentad (USA)** (RCharlton) **3-8-7** PaulEddery(5) (lw: led: qcknd 5f out: hdd over 1f out: kpt on wl)	1½	2	15/2	120	21
1323[8]	**Captain Horatius (IRE) (105)** (JLDunlop) **8-9-2** PatEddery(2) (lw: hld up: hdwy over 3f out: outpcd appr fnl f)	8	3	4/1[3]	106	19
2514[4]	**Nabhaan (IRE) (105)** (DMorley) **4-9-7** RHills(3) (hld up: rdn over 2f out: no imp)	3½	4	11/8[1]	107	20
2490[2]	**Chabrol (CAN) (60)** (RHarris) **4-9-2** SSanders(4) (trckd ldr: rdn 5f out: sn btn)	13	5	33/1	15 t	—
				(SP 110.1%)	**5 Rn**	

2m 37.81 (8.81) CSF £14.63 TOTE £2.70: £1.70 £2.10 (£6.80) OWNER Mr K. Abdulla (NEWMARKET) BRED Juddmonte Farms

WEIGHT FOR AGE 3yo-12lb

1454 Corradini, dropped back in trip, wisely sat close to the pace and did the job well despite Fallon's whip going flying in the Dip. Keeping his interest in a steadily-run race seemed to help him enormously. (2/1: 6/4-5/2)

2311* Pentad (USA), just out of maiden company, made a bold bid to win this from the front but forfeited any hope of getting an attractive handicap mark in the process. (15/2: 5/1-8/1)

522 Captain Horatius (IRE) tried to use his turn of foot but those in front of him were quickening better from the distance. He is normally kept to ten furlongs these days. (4/1)

2514 Nabhaan (IRE) has shone in fast-run handicaps of late but looked a shadow of that horse in this tactical race. (11/8)

2490 Chabrol (CAN) appeared totally outclassed here once the tempo quickened. (33/1)

2838 HORSE RACING ABROAD MAIDEN STKS (3-Y.O+) (Class D)

7-30 (7-30) **6f (July)** £3,913.25 (£1,166.00: £555.50: £250.25) Stalls: High GOING minus 0.11 sec per fur (G)

				SP	RR	SF
2491[4]	**Bacchus** (ACStewart) **3-9-0** MRoberts(8) (w ldrs: led over 1f out: rdn out)	—	1	4/1[2]	86	63
2427[2]	**Listed Account (USA) (75)** (LMCumani) **3-8-9** LDettori(5) (trckd ldrs: rdn over 1f out: r.o wl ins fnl f)	¾	2	4/1[2]	79	56
1764[2]	**Polish Romance (USA) (77)** (MRStoute) **3-8-9** RHills(7) (stdd s: hdwy 2f out: r.o wl fnl f)	nk	3	6/1	78	55
	Mary Cornwallis (GWragg) **3-8-9** MHills(1) (gd sort: trckd ldrs: ev ch over 1f out: no ex ins fnl f)	s.h	4	5/1[3]	78	55
	Bahamian Beauty (USA) (DRLoder) **3-8-9** PatEddery(4) (lw: tall: w ldrs: ev ch 1f out: wknd ins fnl f)	3	5	11/2	70	47
1237[6]	**Butrinto (76)** (MajorWRHern) **3-9-0b**[1] KFallon(3) (b: swtg: led over 4f: sn wknd)	1¼	6	7/2[1]	72	49
	Tahara (IRE) (LMCumani) **3-8-6**(3) RFfrench(6) (cmpt: scope: bkwd: nvr nr ldrs)	6	7	16/1	51	28
	Noble Story (RAkehurst) **3-8-9** SSanders(9) (lw: sn pushed along: chsd ldrs over 3f)	11	8	12/1	21	—
2420[11]	**Beau Tudor (IRE)** (MissLCSiddall) **3-8-7**(7) TSiddall(2) (sn bhd)	2½	9	66/1	20	—
				(SP 123.6%)	**9 Rn**	

1m 13.85 (1.85) CSF £20.11 TOTE £4.90: £1.80 £1.30 £1.60 (£9.80) Trio £15.10 OWNER Mr M. Hawkes (NEWMARKET) BRED Mrs John Trotter

2491 Bacchus had learnt from his debut and, whilst not entirely impressing with his attitude once in front, proved plenty good enough to hold these. (4/1)

2427 Listed Account (USA), a tall good mover, was again dropped in trip and seemed to find this just too sharp. (4/1)

1764 Polish Romance (USA), trying waiting tactics again, was heavily restrained at the start, almost rearing up. However, she did settle better than usual and finished best of all. (6/1: 4/1-7/1)

Mary Cornwallis has had a few problems which has delayed her racecourse debut but looked pretty straight, although not over-big. A good walker, she showed a good action although slightly green going down and gave the impression she might well have prevailed but for inexperience catching her out on such testing ground. (5/1)

Bahamian Beauty (USA), ex-Irish, was taking a drop in trip but still folded in the last furlong. (11/2: 4/1-6/1)

1237 Butrinto, blinkered for the first time, got warm. He folded rather tamely on meeting the rising ground and may prove tricky to place. (7/2)

Noble Story (12/1: 8/1-14/1)

2839 SPORTING INDEX H'CAP (0-95) (3-Y.O+) (Class C)

8-00 (8-02) **1m 2f (July)** £7,830.00 (£2,340.00: £1,120.00: £510.00) Stalls: High GOING minus 0.11 sec per fur (G)

				SP	RR	SF
2585^{6}	**Manazil (IRE) (81)** (RWArmstrong) **3-8-6** RHills(1) (lw: a.p: rdn to ld over 1f out: r.o)	—	1	7/1	96	49
2118^{8}	**Mutadarra (IRE) (62)** (WJMusson) **4-7-11** JQuinn(7) (lw: hld up & plld hrd: gd hdwy over 1f out: r.o wl: nt rch wnr)	1¼	2	25/1	75	38
2210^{5}	**Roufontaine (77)** (WRMuir) **6-8-12** MRoberts(6) (stdd s: hdwy 6f out: one pce fnl 2f)	2½	3	14/1	86	49
2315*	**Military (USA) (85)** (HRACecil) **3-8-10** KFallon(3) (trckd ldr tl led 3f out: hdd over 1f out: one pce)	¾	4	15/8^{1}	93	46
2296*	**Sky Commander (USA) (89)** (MRStoute) **3-9-0** LDettori(8) (b: hld up: pushed along & hdwy 3f out: nvr rchd ldrs)	1½	5	3/1^{2}	94	47
2710^{21}	**Major Change (93)** (MissGayKelleway) **5-9-11**$^{(3)}$ RFfrench(2) (led 7f: wknd over 1f out)	7	6	14/1	87	50
2585^{6}	**Bold Oriental (IRE) (83)** (NACallaghan) **3-8-8** PatEddery(4) (hld up: effrt 2f out: sn rdn & no hdwy)	1½	7	9/2^{3}	75	28
2574^{6}	**Edan Heights (76)** (SDow) **5-8-11** SSanders(9) (trckd ldrs: rdn over 2f out: eased whn btn ins fnl f)	nk	8	20/1	67	30
680^{18}	**Albaha (USA) (77)** (JEBanks) **4-8-7**$^{(5)}$ RMullen(10) (lw: reard s: pushed along 3f out: a bhd)	9	9	12/1	54	17

(SP 120.1%) **9 Rn**

2m 7.61 (4.01) CSF £150.20 CT £2,172.02 TOTE £8.70: £2.20 £5.60 £2.60 (£89.30) Trio £579.00; £334.40 to 21/7/97 OWNER Mr Hamdan Al Maktoum (NEWMARKET) BRED Shadwell Estate Company Limited
WEIGHT FOR AGE 3yo-10lb

2585 Manazil (IRE), with plenty of use made of her, found her stamina coming into play in these testing conditions. (7/1)
1588 Mutadarra (IRE) took a good hold going down and looked impossible to settle in the race but still finished in great style after threading his way through and is clearly in great heart. (25/1)
1923 Roufontaine ran her race but the handicapper may just have her measure in this grade. (14/1)
2315* Military (USA) did not lead this time but still had plenty of use made of him and looked one-paced. He gives the impression he may still improve over further. (15/8)
2296* Sky Commander (USA) had a hard race to win over course and distance last time and never looked to be finding enough to beat a 3lb hike in the weights. (3/1)
1768 Major Change, dropped a little in class, did not disgrace himself reverting to the front-running tactics which brought him success a couple of years back. (14/1)

2840 SOMERSHAM MAIDEN STKS (2-Y.O F) (Class D)

8-30 (8-31) **7f (July)** £3,817.50 (£1,140.00: £545.00: £247.50) Stalls: High GOING minus 0.34 sec per fur (GF)

				SP	RR	SF
	Glorosia (FR) (LMCumani) **2-8-11** LDettori(9) (str: cmpt: bkwd: led 5f: rallied to ld wl ins fnl f: cleverly)	—	1	9/2^{2}	76+	33
	Particular Friend (EALDunlop) **2-8-11** KFallon(7) (wl grwn: trckd ldrs: led 2f out tl hdd & unable qckn wl ins fnl f)	nk	2	9/2^{2}	75	32
	Alharir (USA) (JLDunlop) **2-8-11** RHills(11) (w'like: scope: trckd ldrs: effrt over 1f out: kpt on ins fnl f)	3	3	13/2^{3}	69+	26
2336^{2}	**Matata (IRE)** (NACallaghan) **2-8-11** PatEddery(10) (lw: a.p: ev ch 2f out: no ex appr fnl f)	½	4	6/4^{1}	67	24
	Little Miss Huff (IRE) (RGuest) **2-8-11** PBloomfield(5) (leggy: sn pushed along: in tch: outpcd over 2f out: styd on fnl f)	1¼	5	33/1	65	22
	Moonstone (IRE) (APJarvis) **2-8-11** DHolland(1) (leggy: scope: sn pushed along: in tch 5f)	4	6	20/1	55	12
	Cantonese (USA) (RCharlton) **2-8-11** PaulEddery(8) (w'like: chsd ldr tl rdn & wknd over 2f out)	s.h	7	8/1	55	12
	Mysterious Ecology (CEBrittain) **2-8-11** MRoberts(6) (w'like: leggy: sn pushed along & bhd: styd on wl fnl f: nrst fin)	hd	8	16/1	55	12
	Doating (IRE) (JWHills) **2-8-11** MHills(3) (w'like: scope: stdd s: hld up: nvr nr ldrs)	2½	9	20/1	49	6
1619^{9}	**Supacalifragilistk** (CEBrittain) **2-8-11** SSanders(2) (chsd ldrs tl wknd 2f out)	2	10	33/1	45	2
	Operatic (MBell) **2-8-11** MFenton(4) (w'like: dwlt: a bhd)	3	11	14/1	38	—

(SP 128.8%) **11 Rn**

1m 27.93 (2.93) CSF £24.16 TOTE £5.30: £1.90 £1.70 £2.40 (£13.50) Trio £23.80 OWNER Mr Robert Smith (NEWMARKET) BRED Alec Head

Glorosia (FR), a well-made newcomer, looked short of peak fitness but belied that impression by rallying for a cheeky win. This fluent mover should go on to better things. (9/2)
Particular Friend, a half-sister to Marl and Davoski, is quite a lengthy individual but shaped with considerable promise and should not be too hard to place. (9/2: 5/2-5/1)
Alharir (USA), a first foal of the stable's Ribblesdale winner Thawakib, who might have done even better but for shoulder problems, moved down very poorly herself but came back in really good style and promises to do even better when stepped up a little in trip. (13/2: 6/4-7/1)
2336 Matata (IRE) did not look entirely happy with life when mounting a challenge and soon faded. The maiden she debuted in has not really worked out so far. (6/4: op 3/1)
Little Miss Huff (IRE), a gangly, rather likeable half-sister to modest hurdler Galaxy High, shaped quite nicely in the closing stages. (33/1)
Moonstone (IRE) did not show very much but has a sprinter's pedigree and time may show that this trip is a little too far. (20/1)
Operatic (14/1: 10/1-16/1)

2841 HARSTON H'CAP (0-80) (3-Y.O+ F & M) (Class D)

9-00 (9-01) **6f (July)** £4,199.25 (£1,254.00: £599.50: £272.25) Stalls: High GOING minus 0.34 sec per fur (GF)

				SP	RR	SF
2491*	**Always On My Mind (75)** (PJMakin) **3-9-5** SSanders(1) (set stdy pce: qcknd 2f out: rdn & hung lft fnl f: r.o wl)	—	1	4/1^{2}	85	56
2244*	**Almasi (IRE) (75)** (CFWall) **5-9-10** GDuffield(3) (trckd ldrs: ev ch whn hmpd ins fnl f: unable qckn nr fin)	¾	2	7/2^{1}	83	59
2496*	**Mary Magdalene (72)** (MBell) **3-9-2** MFenton(6) (w wnr over 4f)	1	3	5/1^{3}	77	48
2192^{3}	**Shalstayholy (IRE) (66)** (GLMoore) **3-8-10** JQuinn(8) (hld up & plld hrd: hdwy over 1f out: r.o wl fnl f)	hd	4	8/1	71	42
2703^{5}	**The Fugative (67)** (PMitchell) **4-8-13**$^{(3)}$ ^{6x} AWhelan(4) (lw: hld up: hdwy over 1f out: nt rch ldrs)	1½	5	6/1	68	44
2529^{9}	**Galine (79)** (WAO'Gorman) **4-10-0** EmmaO'Gorman(5) (trckd ldrs: effrt over 1f out: sn btn)	1	6	6/1	77	53
2505*	**Watch The Fire (66)** (JEBanks) **4-8-10**$^{(5)}$ RMullen(2) (hld up: nvr nr ldrs)	3½	7	11/2	55	31
2216^{13}	**Kind of Light (67)** (RGuest) **4-9-2v^{1}** PBloomfield(7) (lw: trckd ldrs: rdn 2f out: sn wknd)	1¼	8	14/1	53	29

(SP 120.6%) **8 Rn**

1m 13.32 (1.32) CSF £17.84 CT £66.99 TOTE £4.70: £1.50 £1.90 £1.70 (£7.60) OWNER Mascalls Stud (MARLBOROUGH) BRED Mascalls Stud Farm
WEIGHT FOR AGE 3yo-5lb

2491* Always On My Mind was given a canny ride, waiting in front, but gave her pilot a shock when ducking left as pressure was applied. Despite this, she looked the winner on merit and rightly kept the race. (4/1)

2244* Almasi (IRE), in good form at the moment, made a gallant effort to score off a 7lb higher mark than ever before and the winner bumping her and than carrying her across the course can hardly have been in her favour. (7/2)
2496* Mary Magdalene ran straight all the way but could not muster any extra speed in the last furlong and was gradually left behind, although some of the two principals' progress was sideways. (5/1)
2192 Shalstayholy (IRE), keen going down and early in the race, caught the eye in this slowly-run sprint, finishing much the best of all. (8/1)
2703 The Fugative, whose wins to date have come over the minimum trip, was held up and could not make her usual move with the whole field quickening. (6/1)
Galine sat closer to the pace than normal but could not pick up as well as some when the tempo increased. (6/1)
2505* Watch The Fire found the waiting tactics working all against her in a slowly-run race. (11/2)

T/Plpt: £376.10 (48.87 Tckts). T/Qdpt: £28.40 (53.83 Tckts) Dk

2564-PONTEFRACT (L-H) (Good to Firm)
Friday July 18th
WEATHER: fine & sunny WIND: fresh half against

2842 JOSEPH HELER INJURED JOCKEYS HOLIDAY FUND APPEAL MAIDEN AUCTION STKS (2-Y.O) (Class D)
6-45 (6-46) **6f** £3,485.00 (£1,055.00: £515.00: £245.00) Stalls: Low GOING minus 0.59 sec per fur (F)

				SP	RR	SF
	Bergen (IRE) (JHanson) **2-8-7** EJohnson(5) (leggy: lt-f: bit bkwd: dwlt: hdwy on ins ½-wy: swtchd rt 2f out: rdn to ld ins fnl f)	—	**1**	10/1	86+	32
2202[2]	**Panama House** (TDEasterby) **2-8-5** LCharnock(3) (lw: mde most tl rdn & hdd ins fnl f)	1¼	**2**	5/1[2]	81	27
	Good Catch (IRE) (PRWebber) **2-8-6**ow1 JFortune(4) (lt-f: unf: hld up: hdwy 2f out: rdn & r.o ins fnl f)	¾	**3**	25/1	80	25
1933[7]	**Lady Yavanna** (KMcAuliffe) **2-8-4**ow2 FLynch(2) (lw: trckd ldrs: swtchd ins appr fnl f: fin wl)	1¼	**4**	12/1	74	18
2356[5]	**Dancing Rio (IRE)** (PCHaslam) **2-7-12**(5) IonaWands(12) (bit bkwd: chsd ldrs: pushed along & outpcd over 2f out: styd on appr fnl f)	¾	**5**	25/1	71	17
	Golden Fortune (DRLoder) **2-7-13**(3) MHenry(1) (w'like: bit bkwd: disp ld: rdn & one pce appr fnl f)	hd	**6**	9/1	70	16
2359[3]	**Legend of Love** (JAGlover) **2-8-5** NDay(14) (chsd ldrs: rdn over 2f out: r.o one pce)	s.h	**7**	7/1[3]	73	19
	Eastern Purple (IRE) (RAFahey) **2-8-7** ACulhane(13) (cmpt: bkwd: s.s: hdwy after 2f: wknd wl over 1f out)	½	**8**	8/1	74	20
2202[4]	**Elsinore (IRE)** (MrsJRRamsden) **2-8-2** GHind(10) (lw: nvr nrr)	2	**9**	20/1	63	9
695[6]	**Henry The Proud (IRE)** (JBerry) **2-8-10b1** KDarley(18) (trckd ldrs 4f: sn lost tch)	nk	**10**	16/1	71	17
1842[4]	**Balla d'Aire (IRE)** (RBoss) **2-8-7** JCarroll(9) (trckd ldrs: rdn 2f out: sn btn)	hd	**11**	11/4[1]	67	13
	Detroit City (IRE) (JBerry) **2-8-0**(3) PFessey(17) (lt-f: prom 4f)	¾	**12**	12/1	61	7
1577[5]	**Press Ahead** (BAMcMahon) **2-8-3** LNewton(7) (prom tl rdn & wknd wl over 1f out)	5	**13**	33/1	48	—
2545[9]	**Starliner (IRE)** (MBrittain) **2-8-0** GBardwell(15) (outpcd)	5	**14**	33/1	32	—
	Buzz The Agent (MWEasterby) **2-8-4**ow1 TLucas(11) (w'like: leggy: bit bkwd: outpcd: a bhd)	hd	**15**	33/1	35	—
2477[9]	**Lesley's Adventure (IRE)** (CaptJWilson) **2-7-12** DaleGibson(8) (in tch over 3f)	1	**16**	33/1	27	—
2477[5]	**Maggice** (RHollinshead) **2-7-12** DWright(6) (a bhd)	hd	**17**	16/1	26	—
				(SP 137.4%)	**17 Rn**	

1m 15.9 (0.90) CSF £56.38 TOTE £21.60: £4.80 £1.80 £4.10 (£29.30) Trio £190.50; £80.51 to 21/7/97 OWNER Mr J. Hanson (WETHERBY) BRED Norelands Bloodstock

Bergen (IRE), a lightly-made May foal given time to strengthen up, won this readily despite a tardy start and he can only go on from here. (10/1)
2202 Panama House attempted to do it from the front but the outcome was still the same and he is certainly not getting beaten for the want of trying. (5/1)
Good Catch (IRE), a very unfurnished Last Tycoon filly who was reported to have shown promise at home, battled on well in the latter stages and she should be able to earn her share of prizes. (25/1)
1619 Lady Yavanna picked up in fine style after being switched to the inside rail approaching the final furlong and if this had been over the trip she tried at Sandown, she would probably have made it. (12/1: op 6/1)
2356 Dancing Rio (IRE), who made his debut here last month, looked to be in trouble entering the straight but he kept finding extra and is gaining experience all the time. (25/1)
Golden Fortune, a flashy-looking filly with four white socks, could not be described as a good sort as far as fillies go but she did give the impression she would strip fitter for the run and that was definitely the case. (9/1: op 7/2)
Eastern Purple (IRE) (8/1: 4/1-9/1)
1842 Balla d'Aire (IRE), thought by his trainer to need more time, again showed plenty of pace but, when the pressure was on, he quickly beat a retreat. (11/4)

2843 YORKSHIRE-TYNE TEES TELEVISION H'CAP (0-70) (3-Y.O+) (Class E)
7-10 (7-14) **1m 4f 8y** £3,405.00 (£1,020.00: £490.00: £225.00) Stalls: Low GOING minus 0.59 sec per fur (F)

				SP	RR	SF
2199[2]	**Passing Strangers (USA) (57)** (PWHarris) **4-8-8**(7) CLowther(5) (a.p: hrd drvn to ld wl ins fnl f)	—	**1**	6/1[1]	69	39
1683[12]	**Farfields Prince (38)** (DNicholls) **5-7-10** LCharnock(13) (led: hung rt over 1f out: hdd wl ins fnl f)	1½	**2**	33/1	48	18
2316[10]	**Augustan (54)** (SGollings) **6-8-12** FLynch(10) (a.p: rdn wl over 1f out: kpt on same pce)	2½	**3**	14/1	61	31
1481[4]	**Ocean Park (66)** (LadyHerries) **6-9-10** DeanMcKeown(8) (b: hld up: hdwy 4f out: rdn & one pce appr fnl f)	¾	**4**	10/1	72	42
2279[5]	**Admirals Secret (USA) (50)** (CFWall) **8-8-8** SWebster(3) (hld up & bhd: effrt over 2f out: kpt on u.p fnl f)	nk	**5**	10/1	55	25
2702[3]	**May King Mayhem (46)** (MrsALMKing) **4-8-4** JCarroll(1) (hld up: hdwy 3f out: nt rch ldrs)	¾	**6**	6/1[1]	50	20
2164[7]	**Course Fishing (42)** (BAMcMahon) **6-8-0**ow1 LNewton(12) (chsd ldrs: rdn along over 3f out: styd on one pce)	hd	**7**	11/1	46	15
2293[8]	**Road Racer (IRE) (61)** (MrsJRRamsden) **4-9-5** JFortune(2) (lw: hld up: effrt & rdn over 2f out: no imp)	3½	**8**	13/2[2]	61	31
2650[5]	**Meg's Memory (IRE) (55)** (AStreeter) **4-8-13** KDarley(6) (hdwy ½-wy: rdn 3f out: sn wknd)	2½	**9**	10/1	51	21
2071[4]	**Mercury (IRE) (41)** (JAGlover) **4-7-10**(3) PFessey(9) (hld up: hdwy 4f out: rdn & wknd over 2f out: t.o)	7	**10**	14/1	28	—
	Fighting Times (50) (CASmith) **5-8-8** ACulhane(4) (bkwd: trckd ldrs: rdn 4f out: sn wknd: t.o)	4	**11**	25/1	32	2
2696[8]	**Fabulous Mtoto (57)** (MSSaunders) **7-9-1** NCarlisle(14) (in tch: pushed along & n.m.r 3f out: sn wknd: t.o)	½	**12**	16/1	38	8
*2365**	**Our Main Man (41)** (RMWhitaker) **7-7-13** DWright(11) (a in rr: t.o)	1	**13**	13/2[2]	21	—
1574[2]	**Six Clerks (IRE) (58)** (JGFitzGerald) **4-9-2** WRyan(7) (lw: prom: rdn over 2f out: sn wknd: t.o)	9	**14**	8/1[3]	26	—
516[3]	**Mr Speculator (58)** (JEBanks) **4-9-2** GBardwell(15) (a bhd: t.o)	4	**15**	16/1	20	—
				(SP 133.8%)	**15 Rn**	

2m 36.5 (2.20) CSF £203.32 CT £2,490.39 TOTE £7.60: £2.50 £33.90 £5.80 (£757.10) Trio £364.40 OWNER Mrs P. W. Harris (BERKHAMSTED) BRED Gainesway Thoroughbreds Ltd

2199 Passing Strangers (USA) has been promising to find a race and, though he did have to work to wear down the long time leader, he won rather cosily in the end. (6/1)
Farfields Prince has shown little sign of ability before but was allowed to dictate this time and, had he not drifted almost the width of the track inside the distance, may well have held on. (33/1)
2015 Augustan had the ground and trip in his favour and ran well but the leading pair were always going that bit too well for him. (14/1)
1481 Ocean Park, who has enjoyed a seven-week break, moved to post like a crab but he did his best on the return journey only to find the considerable weight concession taking its toll in the closing stages. (10/1: 8/1-12/1)
1636 Admirals Secret (USA) has not won a race for close on two years but he has been showing signs of a return to form in his last couple of outings and there could be another race in him. (10/1)
2702 May King Mayhem won no fans with his action to post and, making hard work of it from the start, was never a factor. (6/1)
2293 Road Racer (IRE), twice a winner here, just could not handle this ever-drying ground and a short-lived effort on the home turn came to nothing. (13/2)

2844 ANTONIA DEUTERS H'CAP (0-80) (3-Y.O+) (Class D)

7-40 (7-46) **5f** £5,572.00 (£1,666.00: £798.00: £364.00) Stalls: Low GOING minus 0.59 sec per fur (F)

				SP	RR	SF
2738^{7}	**Just Dissident (IRE) (57)** (RMWhitaker) **5-8-6** DeanMcKeown(8) (mde all: pushed clr over 2f out: r.o wl)	—	1	20/1	64	46
2738^{6}	**Camionneur (IRE) (47)** (TDEasterby) **4-7-10b** LCharnock(1) (dwlt: hdwy over 1f out: fin wl)	1½	2	16/1	49	31
2567*	**Cim Bom Bom (IRE) (78)** (MBell) **5-9-8v**$^{(5)\ 7x}$ GFaulkner(7) (lw: outpcd wl over 1f out: rdn & r.o wl towards fin)	s.h	3	7/2^{1}	80	62
2717^{4}	**Manolo (FR) (63)** (JBerry) **4-8-5b**$^{(7)}$ CLowther(9) (lw: a chsng ldrs: kpt on u.p ins fnl f)	s.h	4	9/1	65	47
2717^{5}	**Royal Dome (IRE) (67)** (MartynWane) **5-9-2** JCarroll(10) (chsd wnr: hrd drvn over 1f out: wknd ins fnl f)	2	5	10/1	63	45
2717^{3}	**Rich Glow (53)** (NBycroft) **6-8-2** GHind(2) (chsd ldrs: drvn along over 2f out: nt pce to chal)	¾	6	9/2^{2}	46	28
2759^{3}	**Superbit (67)** (BAMcMahon) **5-9-2** LNewton(6) (lw: chsd ldrs: rdn wl over 1f out: sn outpcd)	½	7	10/1	59	41
2220^{4}	**Sharp Pearl (74)** (PRWebber) **4-9-9b** JFortune(14) (drvn along over 2f out: nvr nr to chal)	nk	8	16/1	65	47
2162^{6}	**First Maite (78)** (SRBowring) **4-9-13b** SWebster(13) (bhd: effrt & rdn 2f out: nt pce to chal)	¾	9	16/1	66	48
2675^{9}	**For the Present (79)** (TDBarron) **7-10-0** KDarley(5) (prom: pushed along ½-wy: outpcd fnl 2f)	½	10	16/1	66	48
2738^{5}	**Ned's Bonanza (55)** (MDods) **8-8-4v**^{ow1} FLynch(3) (lw: effrt 2f out: eased whn no ch appr fnl f)	1½	11	8/1	37	18
2567^{2}	**Bowlers Boy (74)** (JJQuinn) **4-9-4**$^{(5)}$ PRoberts(4) (lw: a bhd & outpcd)	s.h	12	7/1^{3}	56	38
2754^{5}	**Captain Carat (62)** (DNicholls) **6-8-11b** AlexGreaves(12) (s.i.s: a bhd & outpcd)	3½	13	16/1	32	14
2497^{9}	**Tutu Sixtysix (47)** (DonEnricoIncisa) **6-7-10b** KimTinkler(11) (s.s: a bhd & outpcd & t.o)	11	14	66/1	—	—

(SP 127.9%) **14 Rn**

61.5 secs (-0.20) CSF £297.67 CT £1,315.42 TOTE £23.20: £4.60 £4.30 £1.90 (£150.40) Trio £274.90 OWNER Mrs C. A. Hodgetts (LEEDS) BRED M. Duffy
LONG HANDICAP Camionneur (IRE) 7-9 Tutu Sixtysix 6-3
1734 Just Dissident (IRE) made all when successful in this event twelve months ago and, showing no signs of stopping, again completed a pillar to post victory. (20/1)
2738 Camionneur (IRE) lost the advantage of his plum draw with a tardy start but he was really into his stride inside the final furlong and another success is beckoning. (16/1)
2567* Cim Bom Bom (IRE), never happy on this lively ground, also found the step back to the minimum trip too much for him and, though he was running on well towards the finish, was never in a position to trouble the winner. (7/2)
2717 Manolo (FR) always looked likely to make a race of it but, when the winner stepped up the pace entering the straight, he was soon flat to the boards and held despite rallying in the closing stages. (9/1)
2717 Royal Dome (IRE) did his level best to keep tabs on the winner but the exertions took their toll and he had shot his bolt once into the final furlong. (10/1)
2717 Rich Glow was always finding the tempo too hot and, though he kept plugging away, was never going to take a hand in proceedings. (9/2)

2845 COUNTRYWIDE FREIGHT H'CAP (0-70) (3-Y.O+) (Class E)

8-10 (8-12) **1m 4y** £3,874.50 (£1,161.00: £558.00: £256.50) Stalls: Low GOING minus 0.59 sec per fur (F)

				SP	RR	SF
2368^{8}	**Pleasure Trick (USA) (41)** (DonEnricoIncisa) **6-8-0** KimTinkler(6) (hdwy over 2f out: str run to ld wl ins fnl f)	—	1	12/1	53	35
2043^{9}	**No Cliches (65)** (DNicholls) **4-9-10** AlexGreaves(11) (a.p: chsd ldr 2f out: str chal ins fnl f: r.o)	s.h	2	12/1	77	59
2660^{3}	**Monte Cavo (47)** (MBrittain) **6-8-6** GBardwell(7) (bhd: effrt & rdn 4f out: gd hdwy appr fnl f: fin wl)	1	3	7/4^{1}	57	39
2408^{9}	**Prime Light (69)** (GWragg) **4-9-9b**$^{1(5)}$ GMilligan(3) (lw: a.p: led over 3f out tl wl ins fnl f)	1¼	4	10/1	76	58
2463^{3}	**Prime Partner (37)** (TDEasterby) **4-7-10** LCharnock(10) (hdwy 3f out: outpcd appr fnl f)	6	5	9/1	32	14
2463^{4}	**Java Red (IRE) (45)** (JGFitzGerald) **5-8-4b** WRyan(9) (hld up: styd on appr fnl f: nvr nrr)	1¼	6	8/1^{3}	38	20
2716^{2}	**Trying Times (IRE) (53)** (JBerry) **4-8-7**$^{(5)}$ PRoberts(13) (nvr nr to chal)	½	7	9/1	45	27
1802^{3}	**Tinklers Folly (57)** (RMWhitaker) **5-9-2** DeanMcKeown(2) (led 3f: rdn & wknd over 2f out)	1	8	12/1	47	29
2339^{9}	**Antonias Melody (64)** (SRBowring) **4-9-9** SWebster(4) (chsd ldrs: rdn over 2f out: sn wknd: t.o)	6	9	14/1	42	24
2471^{3}	**Power Game (54)** (JBerry) **4-8-13b** KDarley(1) (lw: s.s: bhd & rdn 3f out: t.o)	2	10	7/1^{2}	28	10
2502^{9}	**She's Simply Great (IRE) (39)** (JJO'Neill) **4-7-12** DWright(8) (a bhd: rdn 2f out: no imp: t.o)	9	11	20/1	—	—
1615^{8}	**Energy Man (48)** (MDods) **4-8-7v**^{1} JCarroll(12) (chsd ldr: led 5f out tl over 3f out: sn wknd & eased: t.o)	11	12	20/1	—	—

(SP 128.3%) **12 Rn**

1m 42.8 (0.40) CSF £145.67 CT £352.08 TOTE £13.20: £3.20 £4.30 £1.40 (£103.10) Trio £142.20 OWNER Don Enrico Incisa (MIDDLEHAM) BRED W. S. Farish
1800 Pleasure Trick (USA) only just failed to score on his previous visit here last month, so this hard-fought, narrow success was thoroughly deserved. (12/1)
No Cliches delivered a determined last-furlong challenge and might have poked his nose in front for a stride but the winner, in receipt of 24lb, had his head in front when it mattered. This was a much-improved performance and he is ready to strike. (12/1)
2660 Monte Cavo stays this trip extremely well but he took a long time to warm up on ground possibly too lively for him and he always had just too much to do. (7/4)
1837 Prime Light did too much too soon in his first time blinkers and was down to a walk in the final one hundred yards. This effort confirms he has ability and it is just a matter of him getting it together. (10/1)
2463 Prime Partner was not quite so effective on this faster ground and had to admit the principals too smart for him when the dash to the line developed. (9/1)
2463 Java Red (IRE), unable to find top gear until far too late, found the race over by the time he did get going. (8/1)
1802 Tinklers Folly (12/1: op 8/1)
1765 Antonias Melody (14/1: 10/1-16/1)

2471 Power Game never took hold of his bridle after losing ground at the start and ran no race at all. (7/1)

2846 ST JOHN AMBULANCE MAIDEN STKS (3-Y.O) (Class D)

8-40 (8-42) **1m 2f 6y** £3,598.75 (£1,090.00: £532.50: £253.75) Stalls: Low GOING minus 0.59 sec per fur (F)

	Horse / details	Dist	Pos	SP	RR	SF
1625³	**Khayali (IRE) (82)** (DMorley) **3-9-0** JStack(4) (mde all: sn clr: rdn 2f out: swished tail: hld on)	—	1	11/4²	93	53
2126³	**Monitor (88)** (HRACecil) **3-9-0** WRyan(10) (lw: a.p: hdwy to chal wl over 1f out: hrd rdn: unable qckn)	1¼	2	10/11¹	91	51
2315⁷	**Alakdar (CAN)** (ACStewart) **3-9-0** JFortune(1) (a chsng ldrs: rdn & outpcd over 1f out)	12	3	10/1³	72	32
963⁹	**Go Hence** (WJarvis) **3-9-0** NDay(3) (bit bkwd: mid div: styd on appr fnl f: nvr nrr)	1½	4	14/1	70	30
2566⁸	**Stormy Story (USA)** (JHMGosden) **3-9-0** GHind(7) (hld up: hdwy over 3f out: wknd fnl 2f)	3½	5	14/1	64	24
	Rosa Royale (MrsJCecil) **3-8-9** GBardwell(5) (b: lengthy: unf: s.s: drvn along ½-wy: no imp)	9	6	12/1	45	5
2566¹²	**Understudy** (RHollinshead) **3-8-9** FLynch(2) (s.s: a bhd & outpcd)	hd	7	33/1	44	4
2566¹¹	**Sefton Blake** (MGMeagher) **3-9-0** DaleGibson(11) (lw: a in rr)	½	8	50/1	49	9
1646⁷	**Yours In Sport** (JWWatts) **3-9-0** JCarroll(8) (dwlt: a bhd: t.o)	2½	9	33/1	45	5
2045⁹	**Mill Orchid** (JBerry) **3-8-6**(3) PFessey(6) (chsd wnr over 5f: sn pushed along & wknd: t.o)	3	10	33/1	35	—
2492⁹	**Rockie The Jester** (JPLeigh) **3-9-0** DeanMcKeown(9) (lw: a bhd: t.o)	1½	11	100/1	37	—

(SP 120.9%) **11 Rn**

2m 9.5 (-0.10) CSF £5.06 TOTE £4.30: £1.30 £1.30 £1.90 (£1.70) Trio £5.90 OWNER Mr Hamdan Al Maktoum (NEWMARKET) BRED Shadwell Estate Company Limited

1625 Khayali (IRE) opened his account with a readily-gained success on this return to ten furlongs, but he was not at all happy on the prevailing ground and that was more than likely the reason he swished his tail when asked to extend himself. (11/4)

2126 Monitor travelled comfortably and always looked to be going best but with the winner keeping up the gallop, was unable to get the better of him and the position had to be accepted. (10/11)

2315 Alakdar (CAN) had to admit the leading pair much too good for him but he showed more promise than he did on his debut and he is learning the ropes. (10/1)

Go Hence needed the run after a ten week break but he showed a glimpse of promise over this longer trip and should continue to progress. (14/1)

Stormy Story (USA) took closer order before reaching the straight and momentarily did look likely to run into the places. He was only treading ground inside the last quarter-mile and may have needed it more than was apparent. (14/1)

Rosa Royale (12/1: op 8/1)

2847 EUROLEASE LIMITED STKS (0-65) (3-Y.O+) (Class F)

9-10 (9-11) **6f** £2,801.00 (£848.00: £414.00: £197.00) Stalls: Low GOING minus 0.59 sec per fur (F)

	Horse / details	Dist	Pos	SP	RR	SF
2698⁴	**Fairy Prince (IRE) (61)** (MrsALMKing) **4-9-0** JFortune(2) (mde most: rdn & r.o wl)	—	1	100/30¹	73	47
2173⁴	**Shades of Love (62)** (VSoane) **3-8-9** GHind(7) (a w ldrs: str chal fnl f: r.o)	½	2	8/1	72	41
2711¹⁵	**U-No-Harry (IRE) (63)** (RHollinshead) **4-9-0** FLynch(1) (a.p tl rdn & outpcd wl over 1f out)	2½	3	4/1²	65	39
2424²	**Don Pepe (63)** (RBoss) **6-9-3** JCarroll(6) (lw: bhd: hdwy 2f out: r.o wl ins fnl f)	s.h	4	100/30¹	68	42
2703*	**River Tern (63)** (JMBradley) **4-8-13**(7) CLowther(10) (lw: prom tl rdn & outpcd wl over 1f out)	2½	5	5/1³	64	38
2203⁷	**Mr Fortywinks (IRE) (60)** (JLEyre) **3-8-9** MGallagher(3) (a outpcd)	3	6	20/1	50	19
2603¹¹	**Be Warned (54)** (MDods) **6-9-0b** OPears(4) (bhd: rdn over 2f out: no imp)	½	7	20/1	49	23
2543¹⁰	**King Chestnut (30)** (MDods) **6-9-0v¹** LCharnock(8) (trckd ldrs over 4f: sn outpcd)	1½	8	33/1	45	19
2376³	**Farewell My Love (IRE) (60)** (JSWainwright) **3-8-6** RLappin(9) (s.i.s: a in rr)	1¾	9	14/1	37	6
873⁶	**Showgirl (60)** (CaptJWilson) **3-8-6** KDarley(5) (bkwd: prom tl wknd qckly over 2f out: t.o)	17	10	16/1	—	—

(SP 118.9%) **10 Rn**

1m 15.3 (0.30) CSF £27.81 TOTE £4.70: £1.60 £2.40 £1.70 (£23.50) Trio £51.80 OWNER Mr Aiden Murphy (STRATFORD-UPON-AVON) BRED Jim O'Hara and Christian Healy

WEIGHT FOR AGE 3yo-5lb

2698 Fairy Prince (IRE), not winning out of turn, had to dig deep in the closing stages to withstand the persistent runner-up. (100/30)

2173 Shades of Love, returning to sprinting for this first outing out of maiden company, ran a race full of promise and he is improving with every run. (8/1)

1662 U-No-Harry (IRE) failed to take advantage of his number one draw but he was always poised to challenge until the quickening tempo proved beyond him on the approach to the final furlong. (4/1)

2424 Don Pepe can win at this trip but he is much better suited to seven furlongs and his sustained late flourish was never going to get him there. (100/30)

2703* River Tern has been running consistently well this term and he was far from disgraced on this occasion but, with the pace never dropping, had met his match below the distance. (5/1)

Mr Fortywinks (IRE), stepping up from selling company, never got into the race but he was going about his business in workmanlike style towards the finish and he is capable of stepping up on this. (20/1)

T/Plpt: £503.10 (37.53 Tckts). T/Qdpt: £20.70 (67.82 Tckts) IM

2693-SALISBURY (R-H) (Firm, Good to Firm patches)

Friday July 18th

WEATHER: overcast WIND: almost nil

2848 AXMINSTER 100 APPRENTICE H'CAP (0-70) (3-Y.O+) (Class G)

6-20 (6-20) **1m** £2,200.00 (£625.00: £310.00) Stalls: High GOING minus 0.33 sec per fur (GF)

	Horse / details	Dist	Pos	SP	RR	SF
2672⁴	**Eurobox Boy (61)** (APJarvis) **4-9-1**(8) CCarver(7) (a.p: led 1f out: r.o wl)	—	1	7/1	65	48
1878¹⁰	**Absolute Utopia (USA) (53)** (NEBerry) **4-8-10**(5) TField(8) (a.p: led 3f out to 1f out: one pce)	2½	2	12/1	52	35
2004²	**Samara Song (52)** (IPWilliams) **4-8-9**(5) DHayden(14) (hld up: hdwy 2f out: r.o one pce fnl f)	½	3	9/2²	50	33
2696¹⁵	**Royal Acclaim (45)** (KRBurke) **12-7-13v**(8)ow11 EmilyJoyce(4) (bhd tl hdwy on outside fnl 2f: nvr nrr)	¾	4	40/1	42	14
1878¹⁴	**King Parrot (IRE) (55)** (LordHuntingdon) **9-8-9**(8) CCogan(5) (lw: hld up: hdwy 3f out: one pce fnl 2f)	1¾	5	13/2	48	31
1826¹³	**Mary Culi (58)** (HCandy) **3-8-2**(10) BarrySmith(3) (hdwy 3f out: one pce fnl 2f)	s.h	6	16/1	51	26
2375⁷	**Moultazim (USA) (41)** (MrsSDWilliams) **7-7-12**(5)ow7 RSmith(15) (prom tl wknd wl over 1f out)	2½	7	33/1	29	5
	Cointosser (IRE) (63) (MCPipe) **4-9-11** PFredericks(13) (s.s: nvr trbld ldrs)	hd	8	4/1¹	51	34
2395⁷	**River Seine (FR) (43)** (SGKnight) **5-8-0**(5) RCody-Boutcher(1) (hld up & bhd: hdwy over 2f out: nvr trbld ldrs)	½	9	25/1	30	13

2375[3] **Helios (60)** (DJGMurraySmith) **9-9-8** DMcGaffin(12) (led 5f: sn wknd) ....1¼ **10** 6/1[3] 44 27
2723[12] **Ladybower (IRE) (34)** (JRPoulton) **5-7-7**(3) JFowle(6) (prom: ev ch over 2f out: sn wknd) ....2½ **11** 33/1 13 —
2492[7] **Magic Lahr (GER) (58)** (IABalding) **4-8-12**(8) LeanneMasterson(10) (hld up mid div: bhd fnl 2f) ....hd **12** 12/1 37 20
1926[5] **Warren Knight (51)** (CAHorgan) **4-8-8**(5) RBrisland(11) (b: s.s: sn rcvrd: bhd fnl 2f) 2 **13** 12/1 26 9
2310[17] **Amnesty Bay (35)** (MDIUsher) **5-7-6**(5)ow1 KerryBaker(2) (a bhd) ....4 **14** 40/1 2 —
2536[13] **Dancing Jack (38)** (JJBridger) **4-8-0** PDoe(16) (prom over 4f: t.o fnl 2f) ....21 **15** 40/1 — —
(SP 124.3%) **15 Rn**

1m 43.2 (3.20) CSF £77.39 CT £394.26 TOTE £9.40: £2.60 £3.30 £2.50 (£53.10) Trio £132.70 OWNER Mr N. Coverdale (ASTON UPTHORPE) BRED G. Revitt
LONG HANDICAP Royal Acclaim 7-2 Ladybower (IRE) 7-4 Amnesty Bay 6-13
WEIGHT FOR AGE 3yo-8lb
2672 Eurobox Boy, hardly winning out of turn, was only 2lb higher than when second to Dreams End at York. (7/1)
1588 Absolute Utopia (USA) had finished eight lengths behind the winner on 4lb worse terms at Newbury last time. (12/1)
2004 Samara Song, up 2lb, was more patiently ridden over this stiffer mile. (9/2)
360 Royal Acclaim, 8lb out of the handicap, settled better on this occasion on another rare outing on grass. (40/1)
King Parrot (IRE) could have found this testing mile stretching his stamina to the limit. (13/2)
1423 Mary Culi, down 2lb, was again disappointing and it may be she needs a return to seven. (16/1)

2849 NETHERAVON NOVICE STKS (2-Y.O) (Class D)
6-50 (6-51) **6f 212y** £3,671.50 (£1,102.00: £531.00: £245.50) Stalls: High GOING minus 0.33 sec per fur (GF)

SP RR SF
2123[3] **Hujoom (IRE)** (JLDunlop) **2-8-12** BDoyle(3) (chsd ldr: led 2f out: sn hdd: led ins fnl f: rdn out) ....— **1** 4/11[1] 76 25
Bermuda Boy (BJMeehan) **2-8-12** MTebbutt(5) (leggy: bit bkwd: hld up: swtchd lft over 2f out: led wl over 1f out: hdd ins fnl f: r.o) ....nk **2** 14/1[3] 75 24
2336[10] **Fantasy Night (IRE)** (JLDunlop) **2-8-12** WJO'Connor(4) (dwlt: hld up & bhd: rdn 3f out: sn outpcd) 9 **3** 16/1 55 4
1961[5] **Smart Beau (USA)** (RCharlton) **2-8-12** TSprake(6) (hld up & bhd: rdn 3f out: sn outpcd) ....s.h **4** 4/1[2] 55 4
Dragon Boy (IPWilliams) **2-8-12** AClark(2) (neat: bkwd: hld up: rdn 3f out: wknd over 2f out) ....s.h **5** 20/1 54 3
2509[7] **Downclose Duchess** (MBlanshard) **2-8-7** CRutter(1) (led 5f: wknd over 1f out) ....3½ **6** 33/1 41 —
(SP 113.6%) **6 Rn**

1m 29.89 (3.89) CSF £6.87 TOTE £1.50: £1.10 £3.70 (£5.40) OWNER Kuwait Racing Syndicate (ARUNDEL) BRED W. J. Byrne
2123 Hujoom (IRE) displayed a rather high head carriage, but did the business in the end and hopefully it was only greenness. (4/11)
Bermuda Boy, a half-brother to Sawa-id and Sir Talbot, gave those who laid the odds on the hot-pot a real fright. He will not have to improve much to find a race. (14/1: op 8/1)
Fantasy Night (IRE) is a half-brother to several winners including Son of Sharp Shot. (16/1)
1961 Smart Beau (USA), a $110,000 yearling, is the first foal of a mare who scored eleven times at up to nine furlongs in the States. (4/1)
Dragon Boy, is a half-brother to six-furlong juvenile scorer Safety Pin, and a nine-furlong selling winner. (20/1)

2850 ST. JOHN AMBULANCE H'CAP (0-85) (3-Y.O) (Class D)
7-20 (7-20) **1m 4f** £3,730.00 (£1,120.00: £540.00: £250.00) Stalls: Low GOING minus 0.33 sec per fur (GF)

SP RR SF
2537[3] **Irsal (75)** (MCPipe) **3-8-13** RHughes(1) (lw: chsd ldr: rdn to ld over 3f out: all out) ....— **1** 5/4[1] 79 27
2230[5] **Deep Water (USA) (71)** (PFICole) **3-8-9** CRutter(4) (led over 8f: hrd rdn: r.o) ....½ **2** 7/2[3] 74 22
2230[4] **Motet (83)** (GWragg) **3-9-7b**[1] AClark(3) (hld up in rr: rdn 5f out: no rspnse) ....10 **3** 2/1[2] 73 21
2058[19] **Behind The Scenes (72)** (CACyzer) **3-8-10** WJO'Connor(2) (hld up: rdn over 5f out: wknd over 3f out) ....15 **4** 7/1 42 —
(SP 112.5%) **4 Rn**

2m 37.8 (6.80) CSF £5.61 TOTE £2.30 (£2.80) OWNER Richard Green (Fine Paintings) (WELLINGTON) BRED Shadwell Estate Company Limited
2537 Irsal, who has changed stables, was set to go up 4lb the next day. He held on in a dour struggle after committing a long way out for one thought to be a doubtful stayer. (5/4)
2230 Deep Water (USA), down 3lb, was much happier at the head of affairs. He did not go down without a fight but was always just getting the worse of the argument. (7/2)
2230 Motet did not find the blinkers working the oracle. (2/1)
1322* Behind The Scenes (7/1: 5/1-8/1)

2851 NIGHTFALL CONDITIONS STKS (2-Y.O) (Class C)
7-50 (7-50) **5f** £5,025.20 (£1,623.20: £791.60) Stalls: High GOING minus 0.33 sec per fur (GF)

SP RR SF
2314[2] **Desert Lady (IRE)** (RCharlton) **2-8-8** TSprake(2) (lw: hld up & plld hrd: wnt 2nd 3f out: led over 1f out: rdn & hung rt fnl f: r.o wl) ....— **1** 4/11[1] 88 24
1959[3] **Ruzen (IRE)** (BPalling) **2-8-10** DHarrison(3) (led over 3f: hrd rdn: nt qckn ins fnl f) ....1¾ **2** 11/4[2] 84 20
2648[4] **Days of Grace** (MartynMeade) **2-8-5** FNorton(1) (chsd ldr 2f: sn rdn: styd on ins fnl f) ....½ **3** 8/1[3] 78? 14
(SP 111.1%) **3 Rn**

62.49 secs (2.49) CSF £1.66 TOTE £1.30 (£1.20) OWNER The Thoroughbred Corporation (BECKHAMPTON) BRED Theo Waddington (UK) Ltd
2314 Desert Lady (IRE) had to be ridden on one rein to keep her off the runner-up in the last two hundred yards. (4/11)
1959 Ruzen (IRE) seemed to handle the fast ground well enough. (11/4)
2648 Days of Grace did not get home in the soft ground at Ascot when previously tried over six, but is worth another crack at that trip (8/1)

2852 NETTON CLAIMING H'CAP (0-60) (3-Y.O+) (Class F)
8-20 (8-32) **6f** £3,120.00 (£870.00: £420.00) Stalls: High GOING minus 0.33 sec per fur (GF)

SP RR SF
2554* **Distinctive Dream (IRE) (50)** (KTIvory) **3-8-13b** 7x BDoyle(5) (b: hld up: hdwy over 2f out: led over 1f out: edgd rt: r.o wl) ....— **1** 9/2[1] 59 36
2732[3] **Nellie North (45)** (GMMcCourt) **4-8-13** DHarrison(2) (lw: a.p: led over 2f out tl over 1f out: nt qckn) 1½ **2** 8/1 50 32
2723[5] **Abtaal (52)** (RJHodges) **7-9-6** AMackay(8) (s.i.s: hdwy over 2f out: one pce fnl f) 1½ **3** 14/1 53 35
2646[7] **Charlton Imp (USA) (47)** (RJHodges) **4-9-1** TSprake(3) (lw: chsd ldrs: one pce fnl 2f) 1 **4** 12/1 45 27
2393[5] **Justinianus (IRE) (46)** (JJBridger) **5-8-9**(5) ADaly(1) (swtg: a.p: rdn over 2f out: one pce) 1¼ **5** 8/1 41 23
2698[6] **Robellion (56)** (DWPArbuthnot) **6-9-10v** SWhitworth(11) (hdwy 2f out: one pce fnl f) ....½ **6** 11/2[2] 50 32

1931[5] **Lamorna (54)** (MRChannon) **3-9-0**(3) PPMurphy(14) (swtg: s.s: hdwy 3f out: one pce fnl 2f)....hd **7** 6/1[3] 47 24

2278[7] **Secret Strength (49)** (LadyHerries) **3-8-12** AClark(10) (lw: tk keen hold in rr: lost pl 3f out: stdy hdwy fnl f: nvr plcd to chal)....3 **8** 16/1 34 11

1857[5] **Rambold (56)** (NEBerry) **6-9-10** RPerham(9) (w ldr: led 3f out: sn hdd: eased whn btn over 1f out)....6 **9** 7/1 25 7

2698[14] **Mellors (IRE) (55)** (MJHeaton-Ellis) **4-9-9** SDrowne(16) (led: hrd rdn & hdd 3f out: sn wknd)....4 **10** 25/1 14 —

Bella's Legacy (45) (KRBurke) **4-8-13** WJO'Connor(7) (prom 3f)....1¾ **11** 16/1 — —

2665[13] **Beveled Crystal (47)** (CJames) **3-8-10** CRutter(12) (s.i.s: a bhd)....1½ **12** 33/1 — —

2115[6] **Saxon Bay (51)** (KOCunningham-Brown) **5-9-5** AMcGlone(6) (reard stalls: a t.o)....dist **13** 11/1 — —

2177[11] ***Petraco (IRE) (50)*** (NASmith) **9-8-13**(5) AmandaSanders(13) (Withdrawn not under Stater's orders: Completed course after false s).... **W** 12/1 — —

2745[10] ***Divine Miss-P (56)*** (APJarvis) **4-9-3**(7) CCarver(15) (Withdrawn not under Stater's orders: Completed course after false s).... **W** 33/1 — —

(SP 134.5%) **13 Rn**

1m 15.49 (2.49) CSF £36.39 CT £384.22 TOTE £4.90: £2.10 £2.50 £6.00 (£16.60) Trio £117.90 OWNER Mr K. T. Ivory (RADLETT) BRED Peter Kehoe

WEIGHT FOR AGE 3yo-5lb

IN-FOCUS: **All except the runner-up went various distances after a false start.**

2554* Distinctive Dream (IRE), only due to go up 6lb tomorrow, again showed a tendency to go right-handed under pressure. (9/2)

2732 Nellie North had the advantage of not being involved in the false start but, was still unable to hold the runner-up. (8/1)

1965* Abtaal set to drop 2lb tomorrow, appeared to find this drop back to six a bit sharp. (14/1)

1794 Charlton Imp (USA), 2lb lower in future in handicaps, was tried in blinkers last time and rather surprisingly was having another attempt at sprinting. (12/1)

2393 Justinianus (IRE) maybe consistent but has a very poor strike rate. (8/1: 6/1-9/1)

2698 Robellion has a 3lb lower mark from tomorrow. (11/2)

1931 Lamorna (6/1: op 10/1)

Secret Strength, on his handicap debut, was tenderly handled and gave the distinct impression he is capable of better things. (16/1)

2115 Saxon Bay (11/1: 7/1-12/1)

2853 ODSTOCK MAIDEN STKS (3-Y.O+) (Class D)

8-50 (8-54) **1m 6f** £3,743.00 (£1,124.00: £542.00: £251.00) GOING minus 0.33 sec per fur (GF)

SP RR SF

2692[5] **Ultimate Smoothie** (MCPipe) **5-9-7** RHughes(2) (mde all: clr over 2f out: eased fnl f)....— **1** 11/4[2] 74+ 30

1850[2] **Tycooness (IRE)** (MJohnston) **3-8-2** JFanning(3) (hld up: hdwy 6f out: wnt 2nd over 3f out: no ch w wnr)....¾ **2** 4/7[1] 68 10

2692[7] **Ajcombe (IRE)** (LadyHerries) **4-9-7** AClark(5) (hld up: styd on one pce fnl 2f)....¾ **3** 40/1 72 28

Bold Buster (IABalding) **4-9-7** SWhitworth(1) (hld up & bhd: hdwy over 2f out: eased whn btn over 1f out)....5 **4** 10/1[3] 67 23

2182[6] **Baubigny (USA) (63)** (MRChannon) **3-8-4**(3) PPMurphy(4) (hld up: chsd wnr over 4f out tl over 3f out: sn wknd)....12 **5** 12/1 53 —

2323[5] **Ewar Snowflake** (KOCunningham-Brown) **3-8-2** TSprake(6) (chsd wnr over 9f: eased whn no ch fnl 3f)....dist **6** 20/1 — —

(SP 114.3%) **6 Rn**

3m 7.45 (8.75) CSF £4.36 TOTE £3.70: £1.30 £1.10 (£2.20) OWNER Isca Bloodstock (WELLINGTON) BRED Fares Stables Ltd

WEIGHT FOR AGE 3yo-14lb

Ultimate Smoothie, a bumper and hurdle winner, showed why he was so well backed when disappointing recently at Lingfield. He could have won by at least ten lengths. (11/4)

1850 Tycooness (IRE) was extremely flattered by the margin of defeat. (4/7: op 2/9)

Ajcombe (IRE), twenty lengths behind the winner at Lingfield last Saturday, could have been beaten by at least half that distance here. (40/1)

Bold Buster could only manage a token effort. (10/1: 8/1-12/1)

T/Plpt: £12.50 (607.4 Tckts). T/Qdpt: £6.20 (73.91 Tckts) KH

2713-AYR (L-H) (Good to firm)
Saturday July 19th

WEATHER: sunny & warm WIND: nil

2854 HOURSTONS OF AYR AMATEUR H'CAP (0-70) (3-Y.O+) (Class E)

6-55 (6-57) **1m 1f** £2,997.50 (£905.00: £440.00: £207.50) Stalls: Low GOING minus 0.51 sec per fur (F)

SP RR SF

1333* **Epic Stand (68)** (MrsJRRamsden) **3-11-2**(4) MissERamsden(7) (a.p: led wl over 2f out: shkn up appr fnl f: qcknd)....— **1** 2/1[1] 80+ 62

2494[2] **Gold Blade (60)** (JPearce) **8-11-7** MrsLPearce(10) (lw: rr div: hdwy 3f out: chsng wnr appr fnl f: no imp)....2½ **2** 100/30[2] 68 59

2245* **Righty Ho (60)** (PTWalwyn) **3-10-8**(4) MissSSamworth(2) (lw: unruly gng to s: bhd: styd on u.p fnl 3f: nrst fin)....1¾ **3** 5/1[3] 64 46

2237[3] **Marzocco (35)** (TAKCuthbert) **9-9-4**(6)ow10 MissHCuthbert(8) (lw: prom: effrt & ev ch 3f out: one pce fnl 2f)....4 **4** 16/1 32 13

2342[3] **Sagebrush Roller (52)** (JWWatts) **9-10-13** MrCBonner(11) (lw: sn wl bhd: r.o fnl 3f: nrst fin)....¾ **5** 14/1 48 39

2602[4] **Charisse Dancer (38)** (CWThornton) **4-9-7**(6) MrJCrowley(13) (sme hdwy u.p 3f out: nvr rchd ldrs)....4 **6** 12/1 27 18

2564[5] **Maurangi (28)** (BWMurray) **6-8-13b**(4)ow3 MissJWormall(4) (b.hind: in tch: effrt 3f out: sn rdn & one pce)....1¼ **7** 14/1 15 3

1127[11] **Napoleon's Return (37)** (JLEyre) **4-9-12v** MissDianaJones(1) (lw: disp ld tl hdd wl over 2f out: sn btn)....nk **8** 16/1 23 14

2661[5] **School of Science (36)** (DANolan) **7-9-5**(6)ow11 MissDCarter(3) (swtg: prom tl wknd 3f out)....2½ **9** 66/1 18 —

2205[14] **Talented Ting (IRE) (42)** (PCHaslam) **8-9-13v**(4) MrsCWilliams(5) (disp ld tl hdd & wknd over 2f out)....¾ **10** 25/1 22 13

2503[11] **Sabu (60)** (JIACharlton) **5-11-7** MrRHale(14) (prom tl wknd fnl 3f)....10 **11** 66/1 23 14

2660[14] **Hutchies Lady (35)** (RMMcKellar) **5-9-4**(6)ow7 MrCRussell(9) (b.hind: lost tch fnl 4f)....hd **12** 66/1 — —

2659[10] **Aye Ready (25)** (DANolan) **4-8-8b**(6) MrsDWilkinson(12) (s.s: plld hrd & sn chsng ldrs: wknd qckly appr st: t.o)....dist **13** 200/1 — —

(SP 114.7%) **13 Rn**

1m 53.46 (0.10 under best) (2.96) CSF £6.90 CT £26.53 TOTE £2.60: £1.80 £1.10 £1.80 (£3.80) Trio £5.60 OWNER Mr Colin Webster (THIRSK) BRED Cleaboy Farms Co

LONG HANDICAP Maurangi 8-13 School of Science 8-11 Aye Ready 8-5

WEIGHT FOR AGE 3yo-9lb

1333* Epic Stand, returning after two months off, was 8lb higher but won with a great deal of authority, and is obviously still improving. (2/1: op 11/10)
2494 Gold Blade, although well outclassed, does look to be coming back to something like his old form. (100/30: op 6/1)
2245* Righty Ho gave problems aplenty on the way to the post and, finding this surface too fast at this trip, did his running when it was all too late. (5/1)
2237 Marzocco again ran well, but 10lb overweight was bound to make a difference. (16/1)
2342 Sagebrush Roller was not in the mood early on and soon trailed the field, and when he did decide to run it was far too late. (14/1)
2602 Charisse Dancer was staying on in the straight, suggesting that she might need further. (12/1: op 8/1)

2855 BUTE HOUSE NURSING HOME LIMITED STKS (0-80) (3-Y.O) (Class D)
7-25 (7-26) **1m 2f** £3,403.75 (£1,030.00: £502.50: £238.75) Stalls: Low GOING minus 0.51 sec per fur (F)

				SP	RR	SF
1175[5]	**Captain Scott (IRE) (80)** (JAGlover) **3-9-1** JFortune(3) (lw: trckd ldrs: hdwy over 2f out: rdn to ld wl ins fnl f)	—	1	5/2[1]	90	41
	Ferny Hill (IRE) (77) (SirMarkPrescott) **3-8-12** KDarley(7) (lw: trckd ldr: effrt 2f out: sn hrd drvn: led ins fnl f: sn hdd: r.o)	hd	2	5/2[1]	87	38
2059*	**Raivue (80)** (EWeymes) **3-9-1** DeanMcKeown(1) (led: rdn over 2f out: r.o: hdd ins fnl f: rallied)	s.h	3	8/1	90	41
2328[10]	**Contentment (IRE) (78)** (JWHills) **3-8-12**(3) MHenry(4) (hld up: hdwy over 3f out: chsng ldrs 2f out: sn rdn & btn)	6	4	100/30[2]	80	31
2290[5]	**Share Delight (IRE) (79)** (BWHills) **3-8-12**(3) JDSmith(5) (b: swtg: hld up: effrt 3f out: sn rdn & no rspnse)	6	5	7/1[3]	71	22
2113[4]	**Brave Montgomerie (79)** (MissLAPerratt) **3-8-12** NKennedy(2) (s.i.s: nvr wnt pce)	2½	6	14/1	64	15
2224[2]	**Baby Jane (60)** (BMactaggart) **3-8-10**(5) SCopp(6) (chsd ldrs tl wknd 3f out)	6	7	100/1	57	8

(SP 111.5%) **7 Rn**

2m 7.99 (2.19) CSF £7.65 TOTE £3.20: £1.50 £2.90 (£5.30) OWNER The Write State Partnership (WORKSOP) BRED P. D. and Mrs Player
1175 Captain Scott (IRE), returning after over two months on the sidelines, was given a cracking ride and found plenty in a driving finish. He looks a progressive sort. (5/2)
Ferny Hill (IRE), trying his longest trip to date, got it well enough but was always having to struggle and was just tapped for toe. This was still a useful first effort of the season, and there looks to be plenty more to come from this big, imposing colt. (5/2)
2059* Raivue is without doubt on the upgrade, and proved a tough customer, fighting back when looking well beaten. He should certainly appreciate further and looks the type for the National Hunt game. (8/1)
2005* Contentment (IRE) almost got into this two furlongs out, but soon found the effort required too much and was wisely not over-punished. (100/30)
2290 Share Delight (IRE) got a shade warm beforehand and, once asked for an effort early in the straight, he took the easy way out. (7/1)
2113 Brave Montgomerie, who judging from his scratchy action has a problem, was never happy. (14/1: op 8/1)
2224 Baby Jane had no chance in this company. (100/1)

2856 E.B.F. SUNDAY MAIL MAIDEN STKS (2-Y.O) (Class D)
7-55 (7-58) **6f** £3,517.50 (£1,065.00: £520.00: £247.50) Stalls: High GOING minus 0.51 sec per fur (F)

				SP	RR	SF
2473[4]	**Friar Tuck** (MissLAPerratt) **2-9-0** NKennedy(3) (lw: mde all: qcknd over 2f out: hung lft ins fnl f: r.o wl)	—	1	10/1	81	16
2509[2]	**Bold King** (JWHills) **2-8-11**(3) MHenry(2) (trckd ldrs: hdwy over 2f out: styd on: no ch w wnr)	4	2	5/2[2]	70	5
2534[6]	**Defiance** (BWHills) **2-8-11**(3) JDSmith(6) (hld up & bhd: hdwy over 2f out: sn rdn & nvr able to chal)	2½	3	3/1[3]	64	—
2409[2]	**Althib (IRE)** (MRStoute) **2-9-0** KDarley(5) (lw: hld up: effrt over 2f out: rdn & nt qckn)	2½	4	11/8[1]	57	—
	Miss Salsa Dancer (DenysSmith) **2-8-9** JFortune(1) (neat: bit bkwd: prom: drvn along after 2f: outpcd fnl 2f)	1½	5	100/1	48	—
	Si Senorita (BMactaggart) **2-8-9** DeanMcKeown(7) (leggy: effrt ½-wy: no imp)	1¾	6	100/1	43	—
1310[5]	**Solo Song** (DANolan) **2-8-2**(7) RWinston(4) (cl up 3f: sn rdn & wknd)	16	7	50/1	1	—

(SP 108.7%) **7 Rn**

1m 12.6 (2.80) CSF £28.92 TOTE £7.80: £2.60 £1.90 (£13.90) OWNER Cree Lodge Racing Club (AYR) BRED James Thom and Sons
2473 Friar Tuck confirmed his promise of last time in some style, although he was still very green when ridden. (10/1: op 16/1)
2509 Bold King is turning out to be a professional loser, and he could never get in a blow at this useful winner. (5/2)
2534 Defiance tried to come from behind, and met with a little trouble, but was never good enough to make an impression. There does seem to be some improvement in him. (3/1: op 5/1)
2409 Althib (IRE) looked to have everything in his favour, but he was very easy to back and gave the impression that he was not putting his heart into it when the pressure was applied. (11/8: op 1/2)
Miss Salsa Dancer was always struggling with the pace, and either needed the experience or needs further. (100/1)
Si Senorita certainly needed this experience and never got in a blow. (100/1)

2857 ROTHMANS ROYALS NORTH SOUTH CHALLENGE SERIES H'CAP (0-90) (3-Y.O+) (Class C)
8-25 (8-28) **7f** £5,576.00 (£1,688.00: £824.00: £392.00) Stalls: Low GOING minus 0.51 sec per fur (F)

				SP	RR	SF
1397[5]	**Almuhimm (USA) (81)** (TDBarron) **5-9-11** KDarley(7) (hld up & bhd: hdwy on ins over 2f out: rdn to ld cl home)	—	1	8/1	91	46
2708[W]	**Persian Fayre (83)** (JBerry) **5-9-10**(3) MHenry(4) (lw: led: qcknd clr 3f out: hdd & no ex towards fin)	hd	2	6/1[3]	93	48
2326[10]	**For Your Eyes Only (80)** (TDEasterby) **3-9-3** DeanMcKeown(9) (lw: hld up: effrt over 3f out: swtchd ins over 1f out: styd on wl)	2	3	6/1[3]	85	33
2708[4]	**Grey Kingdom (75)** (MBrittain) **6-8-12**(7) DMernagh(2) (chsd ldr: rdn 3f out: r.o one pce)	1¼	4	11/2[2]	77	32
2325[10]	**Royal Ceilidh (IRE) (72)** (DenysSmith) **4-9-2** JLowe(3) (a chsng ldrs: rdn & one pce fnl 3f)	1¾	5	14/1	70	25
1561[6]	**Smokey From Caplaw (74)** (JJO'Neill) **3-8-11** RLappin(1) (effrt ½-wy: nvr able to chal)	nk	6	16/1	72	20
2708*	**Stackattack (IRE) (73)** (MrsJRRamsden) **4-9-3** JFortune(6) (lw: chsd ldrs tl wknd fnl 2½f)	2	7	2/1[1]	66	21
2760[13]	**Mbulwa (54)** (RAFahey) **11-7-5**(7) RWinston(8) (prom 4f: sn outpcd)	½	8	16/1	46	1
2711[10]	**Mister Westsound (52)** (MissLAPerratt) **5-7-10b** NKennedy(10) (dwlt: a bhd)	3½	9	10/1	36	—
2567[3]	**Colway Ritz (75)** (JWWatts) **3-8-12** NConnorton(11) (lw: in tch: rdn ent st: no rspnse)	13	10	10/1	29	—

(SP 125.0%) **10 Rn**

1m 26.14 (1.74) CSF £54.23 CT £290.96 TOTE £11.30: £2.40 £2.30 £2.10 (£32.30) Trio £29.20 OWNER Burke's 5th Family Settlement (THIRSK) BRED Gainsborough Farm Inc.
LONG HANDICAP Mister Westsound 7-9
WEIGHT FOR AGE 3yo-7lb
1397 Almuhimm (USA) was more than a handful in the paddock but he did everything right in the race and, given a smashing ride, led where it mattered. There is plenty more in the tank when things go his way. (8/1)

2325 Persian Fayre tried to pinch this when quickening clear early in the straight and it all but worked. He is obviously in tremendous form but has yet to win off a mark as high as this. (6/1)
2326 For Your Eyes Only is proving difficult to weigh up, but obviously has ability and finished particularly well and, if the key can be found, there is better to come. (6/1)
2708 Grey Kingdom ran his usual brave race, but was tapped for speed early in the straight and his chance had soon gone. (11/2)
1583 Royal Ceilidh (IRE) has not as yet struck form this year, but there were encouraging signs on this occasion. (14/1)
1225* Smokey From Caplaw, after seven weeks off, ran reasonably without offering a threat and is likely to be all the better for it. (16/1)
2708* Stackattack (IRE) was 6lb higher this week but proved very disappointing and it was certainly not the weight that made this much difference. This run is best ignored. (2/1)
2711 Mister Westsound showed no spark at all this time. (10/1)

2858 BAILEYS ORIGINAL IRISH CREAM NURSERY H'CAP (2-Y.O) (Class D)

8-55 (8-56) **6f** £3,468.75 (£1,050.00: £512.50: £243.75) Stalls: High GOING minus 0.51 sec per fur (F)

				SP	RR	SF
2579*	**Regal Revolution** (PTWalwyn) **2-8-6** JLowe(3) (cl up: led 2f out: r.o)	—	**1**	$2/1^{1}$	79	—
2516^{4}	**Sea Magic (IRE)** (BWHills) **2-8-11**(3) JDSmith(2) (lw: hld up: effrt 2f out: sn chsng ldrs: kpt on fnl f)	½	**2**	$5/2^{2}$	86	7
2658*	**Pierpoint (IRE)** (RAFahey) **2-8-6**(7) RWinston(1) (lw: a cl up: hrd rdn 2f out: nt qckn fnl f)	2½	**3**	$2/1^{1}$	78	—
2466^{4}	**Sandside** (JBerry) **2-9-7** KDarley(4) (lw: led 4f: sn rdn & btn)	10	**4**	$6/1^{3}$	59	—
				(SP 109.5%)		**4 Rn**

1m 13.22 (3.42) CSF £6.62 TOTE £2.40 (£4.70) OWNER Mr S. W. E. J. Slack (LAMBOURN) BRED T. R. Lock
2579* Regal Revolution, despite showing a definite tendency to hang left, always had too much courage for these. (2/1)
2516 Sea Magic (IRE) had a big gap to go through but always seemed hesitant about it and she may well be a nervous sort. (5/2)
2658* Pierpoint (IRE), off a 7lb higher mark, was stepping-up in trip and saw plenty of daylight this time but failed to last home. (2/1: op 3/1)
2466 Sandside looked particularly well, but the Handicapper has taken no chances with him and he seems to have lost his form for the time being. (6/1: 4/1-7/1)

2859 DAILY RECORD MAIDEN STKS (3-Y.O+) (Class D)

9-25 (9-25) **1m** £3,371.25 (£1,020.00: £497.50: £236.25) Stalls: Low GOING minus 0.51 sec per fur (F)

				SP	RR	SF
2492^{2}	**Dawam Allail (IRE) (75)** (MAJarvis) **3-8-12** JFortune(2) (lw: mde all: pushed clr appr fnl f)	—	**1**	$1/2^{1}$	85	3
2549^{4}	**Hanajir (IRE)** (CWThornton) **3-8-7** DeanMcKeown(1) (s.s: sn rcvrd: styd on fnl 2f: no ch w wnr)	3½	**2**	$12/1^{3}$	73	—
1682^{3}	**Polenka (IRE)** (JWWatts) **3-8-7** KDarley(4) (b: lw: chsd wnr: rdn over 2f out: sn btn)	3½	**3**	$2/1^{2}$	66	—
2715^{10}	**Chanson d'Amour (IRE) (36)** (MissLAPerratt) **3-8-7** NKennedy(3) (lw: outpcd appr st: n.d after)	3	**4**	50/1	4 t	—
				(SP 109.7%)		**4 Rn**

1m 42.68 (5.28) CSF £6.76 TOTE £1.70 (£4.80) OWNER Sheikh Ahmed Al Maktoum (NEWMARKET) BRED Woodcote Stud Ltd
2492 Dawam Allail (IRE) looked magnificent and, setting a good pace, always had too high a cruising speed for the opposition. He just needed nudging along for a very comfortable win. (1/2)
2549 Hanajir (IRE), wearing a tongue-strap, showed improved form but, despite staying on well, never had a chance with the winner. (12/1: op 6/1)
1682 Polenka (IRE) looked the part, but proved very disappointing when ridden and something may have been amiss. (2/1)
Chanson d'Amour (IRE) had no chance in this company and, in the circumstances, ran quite well. (50/1)

T/Plpt: £205.60 (59.47 Tckts). T/Qdpt: £61.80 (8.11 Tckts) AA

2829-NEWBURY (L-H) (Good to firm)
Saturday July 19th
WEATHER: hot WIND: almost nil

2860 MTOTO DONNINGTON CASTLE CONDITIONS STKS (2-Y.O) (Class B)

1-30 (1-32) **7f (straight)** £8,194.00 (£3,046.00: £1,473.00: £615.00: £257.50: £114.50) Stalls: High GOING minus 0.33 sec per fur (GF)

				SP	RR	SF
1873*	**Trans Island** (IABalding) **2-9-3** KDarley(5) (led to 1f out: hrd rdn: led last strides)	—	**1**	$7/4^{2}$	86	60
722^{4}	**Wrekin Pilot** (RHannon) **2-8-13** DaneO'Neill(2) (hld up: chsd wnr over 1f out: led 1f out tl hdd last strides)	hd	**2**	16/1	82	56
	Dark Moondancer (PWChapple-Hyam) **2-8-7** JReid(4) (leggy: scope: lw: hld up: rdn over 3f out: r.o one pce: rn green)	4	**3**	$11/8^{1}$	67+	41
	Quintus (USA) (PFICole) **2-8-7** PatEddery(1) (leggy: scope: lw: chsd wnr: rdn over 2f out: ev ch wl over 1f out: wknd fnl f)	½	**4**	$7/2^{3}$	66	40
2057^{12}	**Alazan** (DMHyde) **2-8-10** SSanders(6) (lw: prom 3f)	19	**5**	50/1	25	—
	Ida Lupino (IRE) (BWHills) **2-8-2** RHills(3) (str: scope: bkwd: s.s: a bhd)	¾	**6**	14/1	15	—
				(SP 115.2%)		**6 Rn**

1m 25.21 (1.11) CSF £25.68 TOTE £2.50: £1.40 £4.10 (£9.60) OWNER Al Muallim Partnership (KINGSCLERE) BRED Godolphin Management Co Ltd
1873* Trans Island, a strong, plain colt, had to concede weight all round but proved up to the task. Bowling along in front, he was marginally headed a furlong out but, refusing to give way, battled his way back to the front in the last few strides. (7/4: evens-15/8)
722 Wrekin Pilot, who has been gelded since his last run three months ago, appreciated this longer trip and poked a nostril in front entering the final furlong. However, despite doing nothing wrong, he was worried out of it in the last few strides. (16/1)
Dark Moondancer, a tall, attractive colt with plenty of substance and scope, did not know what was required of him on this debut and was being pushed along from halfway. He struggled on and is sure to have learnt a lot from this. He should find a race. (11/8)
Quintus (USA), a tall individual with plenty of scope, raced in second place and had every chance early in the final quarter-mile before tiring in the final furlong. A half-brother to several winners in North America, he should not be long in opening his account. (7/2)
Alazan looked in good shape beforehand but had been seen off by halfway. He needs a real drop in class. (50/1)
Ida Lupino (IRE), a well-built filly who is a half-sister to Chester Vase winner High Baroque, looked far from fit and, after losing ground at the start, was always struggling at the back. (14/1: 5/1-16/1)

2861 RUINART CHAMPAGNE HACKWOOD STKS (Listed) (3-Y.O+) (Class A)

2-00 (2-00) **6f 8y** £12,178.00 (£3,664.00: £1,772.00: £826.00) Stalls: High GOING minus 0.33 sec per fur (GF)

				SP	RR	SF
1855*	**Hattab (IRE) (100)** (PTWalwyn) **3-8-12** PatEddery(5) (lw: hdwy over 2f out: led 1f out: edgd rt: rdn out)	—	**1**	7/1	110	79

2056[13]	**Soviet State (USA) (106)** (PWChapple-Hyam) **3-8-12** JReid(2) (a.p: led over 1f out: sn hdd: unable qckn)	1¼	**2**	10/1	107	76
2775[4]	**Hello Mister (89)** (TEPowell) **6-9-3** MHills(1) (rdn & hdwy over 1f out: one pce ins fnl f)	½	**3**	20/1	105	79
2598[5]	**Cretan Gift (98)** (NPLittmoden) **6-9-3b** JWeaver(11) (hdwy over 1f out: r.o)	hd	**4**	12/1	105	79
2106[4]	**Averti (IRE) (108)** (WRMuir) **6-9-3** DaneO'Neill(4) (stumbled s: nt clr run wl over 1f out: swtchd lft: hdwy fnl f: r.o wl)	½	**5**	4/1[1]	104+	78
2526[7]	**Omaha City (IRE) (99)** (BGubby) **3-8-12** DHarrison(9) (a.p: rdn over 2f out: one pce)	nk	**6**	16/1	103	72
2476*	**Za-Im (105)** (BWHills) **3-8-12** RHills(3) (lw: a.p: led 2f out tl over 1f out: wknd fnl f)	3	**7**	9/2[2]	95	64
2023[17]	**Andreyev (IRE) (107)** (RHannon) **3-9-2** RHughes(10) (lw: hld up: rdn over 2f out: wknd fnl f)	1¾	**8**	12/1	94	63
2476[4]	**Jayannpee (102)** (IABalding) **6-9-7** WRyan(14) (lw: hld up: rdn wl over 1f out: sn wknd)	¾	**9**	10/1	92	66
2526[14]	**Johnny Staccato (93)** (JMPEustace) **3-8-12** JTate(13) (s.s: a bhd)	3	**10**	33/1	80	49
2526[4]	**Proud Native (IRE) (108)** (APJarvis) **3-8-12** KDarley(7) (lw: hld up: rdn over 2f out: wknd over 1f out)	½	**11**	11/2[3]	79	48
	Blue Ridge (VSoane) **3-8-12** BDoyle(8) (led 1f: wkng whn bmpd 2f out)	2½	**12**	50/1	73	42
980[7]	**The Puzzler (IRE) (102)** (BWHills) **6-9-3** ANicholls(6) (b: led 5f out to 2f out: sn wknd)	½	**13**	20/1	71	45
1148[15]	**Sea Dane (96)** (PWHarris) **4-9-7** SSanders(12) (b: a bhd)	1¾	**14**	50/1	71	45

(SP 121.9%) **14 Rn**

1m 11.07 (-0.73) CSF £65.35 TOTE £7.30: £2.50 £2.90 £3.90 (£67.10) Trio £476.70 OWNER Mr Hamdan Al Maktoum (LAMBOURN) BRED Shadwell Estate Company Limited

WEIGHT FOR AGE 3yo-5lb

1855* Hattab (IRE), who flopped in a Listed race at Kempton in May, made no mistake this time, leading a furlong from home and being rousted along to score. (7/1)

745* Soviet State (USA) is well suited by a fast surface and moved into a narrow lead below the distance. Soon collared by the winner, he failed to find another gear. (10/1)

2775 Hello Mister confirmed the promise shown at Yarmouth on Wednesday, moving up below the distance before tapped for toe in the final furlong. He has not won for nearly two years. (20/1)

2598 Cretan Gift ran well on this venture into Pattern company but, although running on from below the distance, never looked like troubling the principals. (12/1)

2106 Averti (IRE) did not have luck on his side and, when he at last got a clear passage in the final furlong, made up a tremendous amount of ground. He has been running well in Pattern company this season and is certainly up to winning a Listed event. (4/1)

1212 Omaha City (IRE) is finding life very hard going in Pattern company this year and never looked like finding another gear in the final quarter-mile. He is proving very difficult to place. (16/1)

2476* Za-Im (9/2: op 3/1)

2862 WEATHERBYS SUPER SPRINT STKS (2-Y.O) (Class B)

2-30 (2-32) **5f 34y** £74,671.60 (£27,864.40: £13,562.20: £5,761.00: £2,510.50: £1,210.30) Stalls: High GOING minus 0.33 sec per fur (GF)

				SP	RR	SF
2103[4]	**Lord Kintyre** (BRMillman) **2-8-7** BDoyle(23) (hld up: rdn over 1f out: led 1f out: edgd lft: r.o wl)	—	**1**	7/1	98	58
2212[3]	**Pure Coincidence** (GLewis) **2-8-8** MHills(24) (a.p: led 2f out to 1f out: hrd rdn: r.o)	¾	**2**	40/1	97	57
2335[6]	**Banningham Blade** (KTIvory) **2-7-12** MartinDwyer(2) (a.p: rdn over 2f out: ev ch over 1f out: unable qckn)	2	**3**	5/1[2]	81	41
2314[4]	**Yorkies Boy** (BAMcMahon) **2-8-7** KDarley(10) (a.p: ev ch over 1f out: one pce)	s.h	**4**	25/1	89	49
2712[2]	**Mysticism** (CEBrittain) **2-8-0** DBiggs(13) (lw: hdwy over 1f out: r.o)	½	**5**	20/1	81	41
2370*	**Ella (IRE)** (LordHuntingdon) **2-8-3** DHarrison(19) (a.p: rdn over 2f out: ev ch over 1f out: one pce)	¾	**6**	13/2[3]	81	41
1954*	**Petarga** (JARToller) **2-8-3** SSanders(5) (rdn over 2f out: hdwy over 1f out: one pce)	1¼	**7**	16/1	78	38
1806[4]	**Be My Wish** (MissGayKelleway) **2-8-5** TSprake(7) (b.hind: rdn over 2f out: hdwy over 1f out: nvr nrr)	½	**8**	50/1	78	38
2147*	**Phone Alex (IRE)** (RHannon) **2-8-1** DaneO'Neill(14) (rdn over 2f out: hdwy over 1f out: r.o one pce)	½	**9**	12/1	72	32
1970*	**Stop Out** (HMorrison) **2-8-5** WRyan(25) (lw: s.s: rdn & hdwy over 1f out: nvr nrr)	hd	**10**	16/1	76	36
1013[4]	**Salamanca** (JBerry) **2-7-13** PFessey(20) (led 3f)	1½	**11**	12/1	66	26
2147[5]	**Relate** (MartynMeade) **2-8-3** FNorton(9) (lw: prom 3f)	¾	**12**	66/1	67	27
2484[2]	**Daunting Lady (IRE)** (RHannon) **2-8-7** PatEddery(21) (lw: a mid div)	½	**13**	11/4[1]	70	30
2306*	**Brandon Frank** (IABalding) **2-8-5** SWhitworth(4) (swtg: a mid div)	½	**14**	20/1	66	26
2578[4]	**Catherines Song** (CADwyer) **2-8-1** JTate(15) (b.off hind: lw: rdn over 2f out: hdwy & hmpd over 1f out: one pce)	¾	**15**	66/1	60	20
2439a[4]	**Occhi Verdi (IRE)** (MJohnston) **2-8-5** JWeaver(6) (prom over 2f)	nk	**16**	16/1	63	23
2538[4]	**Charlies Lad (IRE)** (RGuest) **2-8-5** PBloomfield(17) (a bhd)	2	**17**	100/1	57	17
2545[6]	**Rhinefield Beauty (IRE)** (JSGoldie) **2-7-12** RMullen(11) (lw: a.p: ev ch wl over 1f out: sn wknd)	nk	**18**	100/1	49	9
2684[2]	**Take A Turn** (MRChannon) **2-8-13** PPMurphy(18) (a bhd)	2½	**19**	66/1	56	16
1593[5]	**Persian Sabre** (VSoane) **2-7-13** AWhelan(16) (bhd fnl 2f)	3	**20**	66/1	33	—
2103[14]	**Lady Moll** (RBoss) **2-8-0** RHills(22) (prom over 2f)	1¼	**21**	33/1	30	—
2054[6]	**Rejected** (RHannon) **2-8-13** RHughes(3) (mid div over 4f)	nk	**22**	25/1	42	2
2138[7]	**Dancing Icon (IRE)** (RHannon) **2-8-6** JReid(8) (a bhd)	nk	**23**	16/1	34	—

(SP 140.6%) **23 Rn**

60.52 secs (0.07 under 2y best) (0.32) CSF £265.49 TOTE £9.00: £2.80 £8.60 £2.50 (£139.10) Trio £335.10 OWNER Mr M. Calvert (CULLOMPTON) BRED Rowcliffe Stud

OFFICIAL EXPLANATION **Daunting Lady (IRE): did not act on the firm ground.**

2103 Lord Kintyre came through to lead a furlong out and, despite drifting left, kept on well to fractionally beat the juvenile course record set in this race last year. (7/1)

2212 Pure Coincidence, so impressive on the All-Weather last month, ran his best race on grass. Showing in front a quarter-of-a-mile from home, he was passed by the winner entering the final furlong and, although unable to get back up, kept on well to finish a clear second-best. (40/1)

2335 Banningham Blade is at her best at five furlongs on fast ground and, despite a very tough campaign, ran another fine race off her feather-weight, having every chance over a furlong from home before tapped for toe. She is a real credit to her trainer. (5/1)

2314 Yorkies Boy, at his best on a fast surface, had every chance below the distance before failing to find another gear. (25/1)

2712 Mysticism ran on in the last furlong and a half, but never looked like getting there in time. (20/1)

2370* Ella (IRE) had no problems coping with this faster ground, and had every chance below the distance before failing to find another gear. (13/2)

2484 Daunting Lady (IRE) was a bitter disappointment, and her jockey later reported that she failed to act on the firm ground. (11/4)

2863 ROSE BOWL STKS (Listed) (2-Y.O) (Class A)
3-05 (3-05) **6f 8y** £9,852.00 (£2,976.00: £1,448.00: £684.00) Stalls: High GOING minus 0.33 sec per fur (GF)

				SP	RR	SF
2556^{2}	**Victory Note (USA)** (PWChapple-Hyam) **2-8-11** JReid(5) (b.hind: lw: stdy hdwy over 2f out: led 1f out: pushed out)	—	1	6/5^{1}	103+	66
2648*	**Mugello** (APJarvis) **2-8-6** MHills(2) (led to 1f out: unable qckn)	1½	2	7/2^{2}	94	57
2012^{13}	**Bold Edge** (RHannon) **2-8-11** PatEddery(3) (lw: hld up: rdn 2f out: ev ch 1f out: one pce)	½	3	4/1^{3}	98	61
2584^{7}	**Aix En Provence (USA)** (MJohnston) **2-8-11** JWeaver(7) (lw: stdy hdwy over 2f out: rdn over 1f out: sn wknd)	2½	4	16/1	91	54
2534*	**Hill Magic** (DRCElsworth) **2-8-11** DHarrison(4) (hld up: rdn 2f out: sn wknd)	3½	5	8/1	82	45
2320*	**Batswing** (MartynMeade) **2-8-11b** FNorton(1) (swtg: chsd ldr over 4f)	2	6	20/1	77	40
2588^{4}	**Fiveo'clock Shadow (IRE)** (BJMeehan) **2-8-11** MTebbutt(6) (a bhd)	2	7	33/1	71	34
				(SP 112.4%)	**7 Rn**	

1m 11.91 (0.11) CSF £4.85 TOTE £2.00: £1.40 £2.20 (£2.80) OWNER Mrs J Magnier & Mr R E Sangster (MARLBOROUGH) BRED Walter Swinburn

2556 Victory Note (USA) comes from a stable that has a brilliant record in this event. Creeping closer in the second half of the race, he was shaken-up to lead a furlong out and soon asserted to give Chapple-Hyam his fifth consecutive success in this event. He looks useful. (6/5)

2648* Mugello attempted to make all the running but, collared a furlong from home, was then put in her place. (7/2: 3/1-9/2)

1263* Bold Edge, one of three almost in line a furlong from home, then failed to muster up another gear. (4/1: 5/2-9/2)

2584 Aix En Provence (USA) moved up with the winner soon after halfway, but had shot his bolt approaching the final furlong. (16/1)

2534* Hill Magic chased the leaders, but had been hung out to dry two furlongs out. (8/1)

2320* Batswing found this class and trip his undoing. (20/1)

2864 STEVENTON STKS (Listed) (3-Y.O+) (Class A)
3-35 (3-35) **1m 2f 6y** £12,490.00 (£3,760.00: £1,820.00: £850.00) Stalls: Low GOING minus 0.33 sec per fur (GF)

				SP	RR	SF
1771*	**Arabian Story (108)** (LordHuntingdon) **4-9-3** DHarrison(4) (b: led 1f: rdn 3f out: nt clr run on ins 2f out: swtchd rt: chsd ldr over 1f out: hrd rdn: led last strides)	—	1	2/1^{1}	116	96
1323*	**Germano (111)** (GWragg) **4-9-6** MHills(3) (hld up: chsd ldr over 4f out: led wl over 1f out: hrd rdn: hdd last strides)	nk	2	9/4^{2}	119	99
2274a^{5}	**Royal Amaretto (IRE) (114)** (BJMeehan) **3-8-7** MTebbutt(1) (lw: led 9f out tl wl over 1f out: sn wknd)	5	3	9/4^{2}	108	78
1962*	**Ghataas (103)** (JLDunlop) **3-8-7** RHills(5) (lw: hld up: rdn 3f out: wknd wl over 1f out)	12	4	11/2^{3}	88	58
				(SP 110.3%)	**4 Rn**	

2m 1.42 CSF £6.26 TOTE £3.00 (£3.80) OWNER The Queen (WEST ILSLEY) BRED The Queen
WEIGHT FOR AGE 3yo-10lb

1771* Arabian Story nearly got caught-out by this shorter distance but, freeing himself from a box early in the final quarter mile, whittled down the leader to get on top in the last few strides. A mile and a half is his trip. (2/1)

1323* Germano lost nothing in defeat and made his bid for glory early in the final quarter-mile. Grimly trying to hold on, he was only worn down in the last few strides. He should soon regain the winning thread. (9/4)

2274a Royal Amaretto (IRE) was certainly not going to hang around and set a brisk pace but, collared well over a furlong from home, was soon beaten. (9/4)

1962* Ghataas, held up at the back of the field, was being bustled along in the straight and had shot his bolt well over a furlong out. (11/2)

2865 HANNINGTON H'CAP (0-90) (3-Y.O+) (Class C)
4-05 (4-05) **1m 5f 61y** £5,507.50 (£1,660.00: £805.00: £377.50) Stalls: Low GOING minus 0.33 sec per fur (GF)

				SP	RR	SF
2551*	**Jazz King (80)** (MissGayKelleway) **4-9-10** JReid(7) (lw: chsd ldr 2f: led wl over 1f out: hrd rdn fnl f: r.o wl)	—	1	11/2^{3}	90	66
2512^{3}	**Kinnescash (IRE) (66)** (PBowen) **4-8-10** MHills(2) (chsd ldr over 11f out: led over 2f out tl wl over 1f out: unable qckn)	2	2	4/1^{2}	74	50
2676^{2}	**Remaadi Sun (84)** (MDIUsher) **5-10-0** RStreet(5) (hdwy over 2f out: one pce)	2½	3	8/1	89	65
2514^{2}	**My Learned Friend (80)** (AHide) **6-9-5**(5) RMullen(8) (hrd rdn 3f out: hdwy over 1f out: r.o one pce)	s.h	4	11/4^{1}	85	61
2198^{12}	**Casual Water (IRE) (66)** (AGNewcombe) **6-8-10** SSanders(6) (s.s: stdy hdwy over 3f out: rdn over 2f out: one pce)	nk	5	7/1	70	46
2381^{6}	**Sandy Floss (IRE) (63)** (RHBuckler) **4-8-7** PatEddery(3) (lw: a.p: rdn over 3f out: wknd over 1f out)	1½	6	10/1	65	41
2199^{3}	**Lavender Della (IRE) (58)** (MJFetherston-Godley) **4-8-2** DaneO'Neill(9) (lw: a bhd)	½	7	10/1	60	36
2696^{10}	**Chris's Lad (55)** (BJMeehan) **6-7-10b**(3) MartinDwyer(4) (lw: hld up: rdn 5f out: wknd over 1f out)	¾	8	6/1	56	32
2528^{12}	**Story Line (80)** (DWPArbuthnot) **4-9-10** SWhitworth(1) (lw: led 11f: wknd over 1f out)	s.h	9	25/1	81	57
				(SP 122.0%)	**9 Rn**	

2m 48.99 (2.49) CSF £26.86 CT £165.01 TOTE £5.30: £2.10 £1.90 £3.00 (£10.10) Trio £48.60 OWNER Whitcombe Manor Racing Stables Ltd (WHITCOMBE) BRED Casterbridge Stud and Brook Stud Ltd

2551* Jazz King struck the front early in the final quarter-mile and, given a few reminders inside the distance, kept on well. (11/2)

2512 Kinnescash (IRE) continues to rise in the handicap but this did not stop him running another sound race. Gaining a narrow lead before the quarter-mile pole, he was collared well over a furlong out and then put in his place. (4/1)

2676 Remaadi Sun began a forward move halfway up the straight, but his rider looked extremely weak and the combination made no impression. He is not easy to win with and has now scored just twice from thirty starts. (8/1: op 5/1)

2514 My Learned Friend, under the cosh for the last three furlongs, stayed on from below the distance and only just failed in his bid for third prize. (11/4)

1805 Casual Water (IRE) crept closer over three furlongs from home, but could then make no further impression. (7/1)

1678 Sandy Floss (IRE) was close up until calling it a day below the distance. (10/1: op 16/1)

2199 Lavender Della (IRE) (10/1: 8/1-12/1)

2866 LEVY BOARD SEVENTH RACE H'CAP (0-90) (3-Y.O+) (Class C)
4-35 (4-38) **1m 1f** £5,393.75 (£1,625.00: £787.50: £368.75) Stalls: Low GOING minus 0.33 sec per fur (GF)

				SP	RR	SF
2710^{12}	**Another Time (84)** (SPCWoods) **5-9-11** PatEddery(2) (lw: nt clr run 3f out & over 2f out: swtchd rt: hdwy over 1f out: hrd rdn to ld last stride)	—	1	6/1^{3}	95	75
2528^{13}	**Strazo (IRE) (87)** (LadyHerries) **4-10-0** JReid(5) (hld up: led over 1f out: hrd rdn: hdd last stride)	s.h	2	14/1	98	78
2550^{5}	**Tribal Peace (IRE) (60)** (BGubby) **5-7-12**(3) MartinDwyer(4) (lw: a.p: rdn over 3f out: one pce)	3	3	25/1	66	46

2514^{5}	**Dreams End (83)** (PBowen) **9-9-10** RHills(1) (lw: stdy hdwy & nt clr run on ins over 2f out: n.m.r on ins over 1f out: r.o one pce)	1	**4**	9/2^{1}	87	67
2508*	**Zermatt (IRE) (59)** (MDIUsher) **7-8-0** NAdams(7) (lw: led over 7f)	hd	**5**	14/1	63	43
2026^{16}	**King of Tunes (FR) (83)** (JJSheehan) **5-9-10** DaneO'Neill(3) (nt clr run over 2f out: hdwy over 1f out: nvr nrr)	nk	**6**	10/1	86	66
1739^{4}	**Virtual Reality (78)** (JARToller) **6-9-5** SSanders(11) (nvr nr to chal)	1¾	**7**	5/1^{2}	78	58
2478^{8}	**My Valentina (75)** (BWHills) **3-8-7** TSprake(10) (swtg: nt clr run over 3f out & over 2f out: hdwy fnl f: nvr nrr)	nk	**8**	16/1	74	45
1414^{6}	**Pistol (IRE) (74)** (CAHorgan) **7-9-1** DHarrison(12) (nvr nrr)	1½	**9**	14/1	71	51
2293*	**Mattimeo (IRE) (75)** (APJarvis) **4-9-2** WRyan(8) (bhd fnl 2f)	1½	**10**	8/1	69	49
2666^{5}	**China Red (USA) (85)** (JWHills) **3-9-3** MHills(13) (prom over 7f)	¾	**11**	10/1	78	49
2528^{7}	**Philistar (76)** (KRBurke) **4-9-3** BDoyle(9) (hld up: rdn over 3f out: wknd wl over 1f out)	4	**12**	7/1	62	42
1768^{6}	**Autumn Cover (79)** (PRHedger) **5-9-6** DBiggs(6) (lw: prom over 6f)	1½	**13**	9/1	62	42
				(SP 130.7%)		**13 Rn**

1m 51.06 (0.76) CSF £87.42 CT £1,216.86 TOTE £6.70: £2.20 £6.90 £7.50 (£60.50) Trio £253.90 OWNER Mr D. Sullivan (NEWMARKET) BRED W. G. Barker
WEIGHT FOR AGE 3yo-9lb

2710 Another Time, who had no luck in running in the Magnet Cup last week, did not have the best of runs here, but he found daylight below the distance and ran on strongly to snatch the spoils right on the line. (6/1)
Strazo (IRE), who has failed to shine in two previous runs this season, bounced back to form. Sent to the front below the distance, he did absolutely nothing wrong and was only caught right on the line. He is a winner without a penalty. (14/1)
2550 Tribal Peace (IRE) was never far away, but was made to look very one-paced in the last three furlongs. (25/1)
2514 Dreams End failed to get the best of runs along the inside rail in the straight but, when he did find daylight, stayed on in the final furlong. He has yet to win on ground better than good. (9/2)
2508* Zermatt (IRE) attempted to make all the running but, headed below the distance, had soon shot his bolt. (14/1: op 8/1)
1782* King of Tunes (FR), with nowhere to go behind a wall of horses over a quarter-of-a-mile from home, stayed on from below the distance without ever threatening to get there. (10/1)
1739 Virtual Reality (5/1: op 8/1)
2293* Mattimeo (IRE) (8/1: op 5/1)

T/Jkpt: £25,047.80 (0.4 Tckts); £21,167.22 to Windsor 21/7/97. T/Plpt: £295.30 (112.7 Tckts). T/Qdpt: £37.60 (39.6 Tckts) AK

2836-NEWMARKET (R-H) (Good)
Saturday July 19th

WEATHER: warm & sunny WIND: mod across

2867 FOOD BROKERS-GLOYSTARNE H'CAP (0-85) (4-Y.O+) (Class D)

2-10 (2-11) **1m 6f 175y (July)** £4,347.00 (£1,296.00: £618.00: £279.00) Stalls: High GOING minus 0.28 sec per fur (GF)

				SP	RR	SF
542^{6}	**Beaumont (IRE) (67)** (JEBanks) **7-8-11** RCochrane(3) (swtg: hld up: hdwy 3f out: led 2f out: sn clr: eased nr fin)	—	**1**	14/1	78	54
2592^{4}	**Durham (54)** (GLMoore) **6-7-12b**ow2 CRutter(1) (hld up: rdn & hdwy over 3f out: r.o fnl f: nt trble wnr)	1½	**2**	9/1^{3}	63	37
1325^{6}	**Captain's Guest (IRE) (84)** (MrsAJPerrett) **7-10-0** AClark(7) (b: swtg: hld up & plld hrd: n.m.r over 2f out: hdwy over 1f out: edgd lft & r.o wl fnl f)	2½	**3**	14/1	91	67
2315^{3}	**Colour Code (82)** (MrsASwinbank) **5-9-12** NDay(9) (chsd ldrs: outpcd over 2f out: n.d after)	1¾	**4**	5/2^{1}	87	63
2696^{7}	**Sea Freedom (68)** (GBBalding) **6-8-12v** SDrowne(10) (b: lw: prom: pushed along 6f out: no imp fnl 3f)	5	**5**	7/1^{2}	67	43
1841^{2}	**Pike Creek (USA) (72)** (IABalding) **4-9-2** LDettori(5) (lw: w ldr: rdn & ev ch 4f out: wknd over 1f out)	3	**6**	5/2^{1}	68	44
2776^{8}	**Prospector's Cove (67)** (JPearce) **4-8-11** GHind(8) (chsd ldr tl wknd 3f out)	9	**7**	25/1	53	29
2327^{11}	**Arctic Fancy (USA) (78)** (PWHarris) **4-9-1**(7) CLowther(2) (plld hrd: hdwy 8f out: led on bit over 4f out: rdn over 2f out: sn hdd & wknd)	8	**8**	9/1^{3}	56	32
2498^{4}	**Amiarge (52)** (MBrittain) **7-7-10** GBardwell(6) (led tl over 4f out: sn wknd)	5	**9**	20/1	24	—
2475^{3}	**Classic Find (USA) (70)** (ICampbell) **4-9-0** AMackay(4) (b.hind: hld up: hdwy 6f out: rdn over 3f out: sn wknd)	3	**10**	14/1	39	15
				(SP 118.3%)		**10 Rn**

3m 12.16 (3.66) CSF £123.25 CT £1,645.51 TOTE £12.70: £2.30 £2.00 £3.30 (£61.50) Trio £172.20 OWNER Mr P. Cunningham (NEWMARKET) BRED Mount Coote Stud in Ireland
LONG HANDICAP Amiarge 7-9 Durham 7-8

55 Beaumont (IRE), returning after a break following an unproductive spell mixing hurdling and All-Weather efforts during the winter, moved down well and found the race run to suit his turn of foot. (14/1)
2592 Durham, again on his favoured fast ground, looked to be going nowhere until staying on to great effect. He is hardly his own best friend, but he has slipped to a winning mark if the mood takes him. (9/1)
1325 Captain's Guest (IRE) was again given a waiting ride over a distance short of his best, and was still almost last when the winner went for home. He holds his head awkwardly and must have had his problems but still possesses plenty of ability. (14/1)
2315 Colour Code, stepped-up in trip for his first run in a handicap, is already proven over the distance in bumpers but lacked a turn of foot. (5/2)
2696 Sea Freedom was one of the first in trouble, again finding this trip too sharp. (7/1)
1841 Pike Creek (USA), whose run over the course and distance last month has not really worked out, was left toiling in the Dip. (5/2)
2475 Classic Find (USA) (14/1: 10/1-16/1)

2868 INVESCO H'CAP (0-80) (3-Y.O+) (Class D)

2-40 (2-40) **1m (July)** £4,698.00 (£1,404.00: £672.00: £306.00) Stalls: Low GOING minus 0.28 sec per fur (GF)

				SP	RR	SF
2557^{7}	**Jibereen (56)** (PHowling) **5-8-4** PaulEddery(4) (b: lw: trckd ldrs: plld out 2f out: rdn & r.o to ld wl ins fnl f)	—	**1**	8/1	68	50
2557^{4}	**Toujours Riviera (68)** (JPearce) **7-9-2** LDettori(7) (led tl hdd & unable qckn wl ins fnl f)	nk	**2**	7/2^{1}	79	61
194^{11}	**Priolo Prima (68)** (SirMarkPrescott) **4-9-2** CNutter(10) (lw: dwlt: hdwy 5f out: ev ch ins fnl f: btn whn n.m.r nr fin)	1½	**3**	12/1	76	58
2331^{6}	**Blessed Spirit (78)** (CFWall) **4-9-12** RCochrane(1) (hld up: hdwy over 1f out: r.o wl ins fnl f)	nk	**4**	5/1^{2}	86	68
2346^{7}	**Ca'd'oro (60)** (GBBalding) **4-8-8** SDrowne(6) (hld up: hdwy 2f out: nvr rchd ldrs)	2½	**5**	11/1	63	45
2290^{2}	**Al Masroor (USA) (78)** (JWPayne) **3-9-4** DeanMcKeown(3) (chsd ldrs: rdn & no imp fnl 2f)	1	**6**	8/1	79	53
2408^{7}	**Mr Rough (55)** (DMorris) **6-8-3** NDay(11) (lw: a.p: ev ch 2f out: wknd over 1f out)	2½	**7**	14/1	51	33
1501*	**Safey Ana (USA) (64)** (BHanbury) **6-8-12** JStack(5) (b: swtg: hld up: nvr plcd to chal)	nk	**8**	11/1	59	41

				SP	RR	SF
2645[2]	**Saratoga Red (USA) (61)** (WAO'Gorman) **3-8-1b** EmmaO'Gorman(12) (a bhd)	½	**9**	10/1	55	29
2704[3]	**Awassi (IRE) (69)** (KMahdi) **4-9-3** OPeslier(8) (w ldr 5f: wknd over 1f out)	4	**10**	6/1[3]	55	37
2174[13]	**Saltando (IRE) (52)** (PatMitchell) **6-8-0v**ow2 AMackay(2) (lw: chsd ldrs over 4f)	15	**11**	33/1	8	—
				(SP 118.5%)		**11 Rn**

1m 39.5 (1.50) CSF £33.10 CT £317.40 TOTE £8.10: £2.10 £1.70 £3.30 (£12.50) Trio £253.60 OWNER Mr Liam Sheridan (NEWMARKET) BRED Mrs J. Everitt
WEIGHT FOR AGE 3yo-8lb
2557 Jibereen confirmed the positive impression he has given in recent weeks and is probably not finished yet, as he seemed to deliver his challenge too soon on this occasion. (8/1)
2557 Toujours Riviera has gradually slipped down the handicap since winning on his seasonal debut in 1995, but another hard race merely extends his losing run. He is a big horse and has only once shouldered less than 9st 5lb to victory, so connections may be well served by asking him to concede weight in a more modest race. (7/2)
194 Priolo Prima, back after another six weeks on the sidelines, showed his inexperience at the start but looked fit and ran well, although he was already held when forced to ease in the dying strides. He should not be too hard to place. (12/1: op 7/1)
2331 Blessed Spirit needs to be delivered fast and late, and rather missed the boat on this occasion. (5/1)
2117* Ca'd'oro got going rather too late to take a hand. (11/1: 8/1-12/1)
2290 Al Masroor (USA), off a 4lb higher mark than when runner-up last time, looked harshly treated and could make little impact where it matters. (8/1: op 5/1)

2869 FOOD BROKERS APHRODITE STKS (Listed) (3-Y.O+ F & M) (Class A)
3-15 (3-16) **1m 4f (July)** £11,754.50 (£3,506.00: £1,673.00: £756.50) Stalls: High GOING minus 0.28 sec per fur (GF)

				SP	RR	SF
2333[3]	**Anno Luce** (JHMGosden) **4-9-2v** LDettori(1) (led after 2f: c centre st: clr 2f out: pushed out)	—	**1**	8/1	112	62
2379*	**Kaliana (IRE)** (LMCumani) **3-8-4** DHolland(6) (hld up: hdwy over 2f out: r.o wl fnl f: nt trble wnr)	2	**2**	7/2[2]	109	47
736[12]	**Beauchamp Jade (100)** (HCandy) **5-9-2** CRutter(5) (hld up & plld hrd: c centre st: hdwy over 2f out: r.o fnl f)	¾	**3**	14/1	108	58
2348*	**Dust Dancer (96)** (JLDunlop) **3-8-4** PaulEddery(8) (hld up: hdwy to ld stands' side group 3f out: no imp appr fnl f)	1¼	**4**	6/1[3]	107	45
	Fascinating Rhythm (HRACecil) **3-8-6**ow2 KFallon(3) (lw: hld up: c centre st: rdn over 2f out: sn btn)	12	**5**	3/1[1]	93	29
1722a[3]	**Vagabond Chanteuse (101)** (TJEtherington) **3-8-4** AClark(2) (prom: c centre st: chsd wnr tl wknd over 2f out)	½	**6**	6/1[3]	90	28
2710[16]	**Ball Gown (95)** (DTThom) **7-9-2** DRMcCabe(10) (hld up & plld hrd: btn over 2f out)	1	**7**	12/1	89	39
2513[7]	**Woodren (USA) (90)** (RGuest) **4-9-2** RCochrane(9) (led 2f: led stands' side group st: wknd 3f out)	10	**8**	33/1	75	25
2513[4]	**Star Precision (100)** (GBBalding) **3-8-4** SDrowne(4) (chsd ldrs: c centre st: wknd 3f out)	3½	**9**	8/1	71	9
	Cabaret (IRE) (96) (PWChapple-Hyam) **4-9-2** OPeslier(7) (swtg: prom tl wknd 4f out)	26	**10**	14/1	36	—
				(SP 122.0%)		**10 Rn**

2m 31.25 (2.25) CSF £34.52 TOTE £6.80: £2.30 £2.00 £3.30 (£31.20) Trio £242.80 OWNER Sheikh Mohammed (NEWMARKET) BRED Sheikh Mohammed
WEIGHT FOR AGE 3yo-12lb
2333 Anno Luce, cleverly ridden by Dettori, took half the field down the centre and whilst it is debatable whether the ground was any faster, this denied the other half of the field a decent lead. Set alight going to the quarter-mile pole, she was never in serious danger. (8/1)
2379* Kaliana (IRE) was set a mountainous task by the time she began her move but came home in great style. This was only her second race and she has plenty of progress still in her, as the bare result does not do her justice. (7/2)
Beauchamp Jade, on her toes and slightly keen going down, is having something of a stop-start season, this second outing coming three months after her first. Nevertheless, this run was close to her best of last year. (14/1)
2348* Dust Dancer, forced to commit early by the stands' rail due to the lack of pace in the group, is probably a little better than this. (6/1: op 4/1)
Fascinating Rhythm, not over-big, looked magnificent but was hard at work some way from home and never got going. The maiden she won last year told us little - none of those behind won either of their next two starts - and it remains to be seem if her reputation earlier this year was all hype. (3/1)
1722a Vagabond Chanteuse ran as if not getting the trip at this truer pace. (6/1)
2710 Ball Gown, stepping-up in trip, took a strong hold and, with the field splitting into two in the straight, saw far too much daylight to give herself a chance. (12/1)
934 Woodren (USA) looked and moved well to post although a trifle warm, but ran no race at all. (33/1)
Cabaret (IRE) (14/1: 10/1-16/1)

2870 PRIMULA MAIDEN STKS (2-Y.O) (Class D)
3-45 (3-47) **6f (July)** £4,305.00 (£1,290.00: £620.00: £285.00) Stalls: Low GOING minus 0.28 sec per fur (GF)

				SP	RR	SF
2012[5]	**Hayil (USA)** (DMorley) **2-9-0** KFallon(9) (trckd ldrs: led wl over 1f out: all out)	—	**1**	4/5[1]	81	55
	Iceband (USA) (JHMGosden) **2-9-0** LDettori(1) (gd sort: leggy: a.p: ev ch fnl f: r.o)	s.h	**2**	7/1[3]	81+	55
2295[6]	**Beware** (RWArmstrong) **2-9-0** RPrice(3) (chsd ldrs: ev ch 2f out: one pce)	4	**3**	25/1	70	44
	Prompt Delivery (USA) (MRStoute) **2-9-0** OPeslier(10) (w'like: scope: hld up: hdwy over 1f out: r.o fnl f)	1	**4**	7/2[2]	68	42
	Quiver Tree (DRLoder) **2-8-9** RCochrane(8) (lengthy: scope: bit bkwd: stdd s: hld up: hdwy & nt clr run over 1f out: r.o wl fnl f)	2½	**5**	16/1	56+	30
	Broughtons Mill (WJMusson) **2-9-0** JStack(11) (leggy: bit bkwd: hld up & bhd: hdwy over 1f out: nvr nrr)	1	**6**	66/1	58	32
	Queen Salote (DRLoder) **2-8-2**(7) CLowther(7) (leggy: scope: in tch: no imp fnl 2f)	nk	**7**	20/1	52	26
2176[8]	**Red Pepper (IRE)** (PHowling) **2-9-0** CRutter(4) (led over 4f: sn wknd)	2	**8**	100/1	52	26
	Holy Wine (USA) (DRLoder) **2-8-11**(3) PMcCabe(5) (w'like: scope: trckd ldrs: effrt over 2f out: sn btn)	s.h	**9**	20/1	52	26
	Al Mabrook (IRE) (KMahdi) **2-9-0** PaulEddery(12) (unf: lw: s.i.s: rdn & hdwy 3f out: nvr trbld ldrs)	¾	**10**	33/1	50	24
	Ei Ei (CEBrittain) **2-9-0** DHolland(2) (leggy: unf: lw: in tch 4f)	½	**11**	33/1	49	23
	Delayed Reaction (NACallaghan) **2-9-0** SDrowne(6) (rangy: bit bkwd: plld hrd: prom over 3f)	10	**12**	33/1	22	—
				(SP 120.8%)		**12 Rn**

1m 13.38 (1.38) CSF £5.75 TOTE £1.80: £1.10 £1.80 £3.80 (£4.70) Trio £41.70 OWNER Mr Hamdan Al Maktoum (NEWMARKET) BRED Shadwell Farm Inc
2012 Hayil (USA) made his experience tell, being flat-out to win a very decent maiden. (4/5: evens-8/11)
Iceband (USA), an attractive colt, moved down well and made the winner pull out all the stops. There was plenty to like about this performance and he should not be too hard to place. (7/1: 9/4-15/2)
Beware moved well to post, and was another to frank the form of Linden Heights' maiden here last month. (25/1)

Prompt Delivery (USA) really took the eye going to post and finished in pleasing style, coming from off the pace. This attractive colt is bred to get at least a mile in time. (7/2)
Quiver Tree, a lengthy, rather green-looking newcomer, was too free going down. Steadied from the stalls, she came home well under a tender ride once in the clear, and should come on plenty for this. (16/1)
Broughtons Mill, cheaply bought, gave encouragement by staying in nicely past beaten horses in the closing stages. (66/1)
Delayed Reaction, a tall, quite imposing individual, looks anything but the finished article, and was too free both going down and coming back to really do himself justice. (33/1)

2871 FOOD BROKERS ANIMAL HEALTH TRUST TROPHY RATED STKS H'CAP (0-100) (3-Y.O) (Class B)
4-15 (4-18) **1m (July)** £17,150.00 (£6,350.00: £3,050.00: £1,250.00: £500.00: £200.00) Stalls: Low GOING minus 0.28 sec per fur (GF)

				SP	RR	SF
2585[5]	**Stanton Harcourt (USA) (93)** (JLDunlop) **3-9-4** OPeslier(2) (chsd ldrs: led over 1f out: rdn out)	—	1	5/1[3]	104	63
2492*	**Speculator (IRE) (82)** (WJHaggas) **3-8-7** DHolland(7) (lw: hld up: hdwy 2f out: ev ch wl ins fnl f: unable qckn nr fin)	hd	2	100/30[1]	93	52
2478[2]	**Generous Libra (94)** (DRLoder) **3-9-5** RCochrane(1) (hld up: hdwy 3f out: n.m.r 2f out: kpt on ins fnl f)	1½	3	10/1	102	61
2013[6]	**Nomore Mr Niceguy (91)** (EJAlston) **3-9-2** KFallon(5) (led after 1f: rdn & hdd over 1f out: one pce)	nk	4	16/1	98	57
2309*	**Mara River (85)** (IABalding) **3-8-10** GHind(9) (hld up: hdwy over 1f out: r.o)	1	5	8/1	90	49
2013[21]	**Wasp Ranger (USA) (96)** (PFICole) **3-9-0**[(7)] DavidO'Neill(3) (sn chsng ldr: rdn 3f out: ev ch over 1f out: wknd ins fnl f)	1¾	6	25/1	98	57
737[6]	**Hayes Way (IRE) (96)** (TGMills) **3-9-7** AClark(8) (hld up & plld hrd: rdn over 2f out: styd on fnl f)	½	7	40/1	97	56
2137[2]	**Sugarfoot (90)** (NTinkler) **3-9-1** CRutter(12) (nvr nr to chal)	1¼	8	20/1	88	47
2290[6]	**Tigrello (86)** (GLewis) **3-8-11** PaulEddery(6) (hld up: effrt & nt clr run over 1f out: nvr nr ldrs)	4	9	9/1	76	35
2601*	**Stilett (IRE) (91)** (LMCumani) **3-9-2** LDettori(4) (lw: led 1f: rdn over 2f out: sn btn)	¾	10	7/2[2]	80	39
2549*	**Shawm (88)** (DRLoder) **3-8-6**[(7)] CLowther(11) (lw: chsd ldrs over 5f)	s.h	11	7/1	77	36
2585[8]	**Atlantic Desire (IRE) (90)** (MJohnston) **3-8-12**[(3)] KMChin(10) (lw: prom 4f)	1¾	12	20/1	75	34
				(SP 126.4%)	**12 Rn**	

1m 39.51 (1.51) CSF £20.48 CT £156.72 TOTE £6.50: £2.00 £1.90 £2.70 (£13.90) Trio £48.40 OWNER Mr Cyril Humphris (ARUNDEL) BRED Pamela H. Firman
LONG HANDICAP Speculator (IRE) 8-6
2585 Stanton Harcourt (USA), whose habit of pulling has not aided his cause in the past, seemed well suited by being ridden more prominently over a shorter trip. (5/1)
2492* Speculator (IRE), very keen going down, found a good turn of foot in the Dip, but the winner responded and he could not get up in time. This was a sound first handicap and he should be able to find another race. (100/30)
2478 Generous Libra, a keen sort who follows the family line and races with his head rather high, came home well once in the clear. Blinkers or a visor may well help. (10/1)
2013 Nomore Mr Niceguy, given an enterprising ride, had no answer once the principals began to quicken. He has paid the penalty for the 'crime' of consistency in handicaps, and may well be on a mark from which he cannot win. (16/1)
2309* Mara River seemed in a most unpromising position two furlongs out, but picked up well and may well have been a threat to all with a little more use made of her. (8/1: 6/1-9/1)
1770 Wasp Ranger (USA), who beat another non-stayer when winning a mile maiden, looks a seven-furlong specialist on this evidence. (25/1)
2290 Tigrello, halted briefly when beginning his run, never got into the race. (9/1)
2601* Stilett (IRE) had been held up for both wins, trying to make the pace when a losing favourite in between, so these forcing tactics seemed to make very little sense. (7/2)
2549* Shawm was a real disappointment on a return to a trip that should suit. (7/1)

2872 CHEMIST BROKERS H'CAP (0-100) (3-Y.O+) (Class C)
4-45 (4-46) **5f (July)** £5,531.25 (£1,650.00: £787.50: £356.25) Stalls: Low GOING minus 0.28 sec per fur (GF)

				SP	RR	SF
2675[12]	**Tadeo (92)** (MJohnston) **4-9-11**[(3)] KMChin(11) (chsd ldrs: rdn to ld ins fnl f: r.o)	—	1	20/1	99	81
2711[5]	**Daawe (USA) (81)** (MrsVAAconley) **6-9-3** LDettori(6) (lw: in tch: hdwy over 1f out: rdn & hung lft ins fnl f: unable qckn nr fin)	¾	2	11/2[2]	86	68
2529[12]	**Speed On (91)** (HCandy) **4-9-13** CRutter(8) (lw: in tch: nt clr run 2f out: rdn over 1f out: hdwy whn nt clr run & swtchd ins fnl f: r.o wl nr fin)	¾	3	14/1	93	75
1766[3]	**Anotheranniversary (91)** (GLewis) **4-9-13** PaulEddery(2) (b.hind: led over 4f: unable qckn)	s.h	4	6/1[3]	93	75
2529[3]	**Music Gold (IRE) (92)** (WAO'Gorman) **4-10-0b** EmmaO'Gorman(10) (s.v.s: rdn & hdwy 2f out: no ex fnl f)	1	5	8/1	91	73
2563*	**Gone Savage (83)** (WJMusson) **9-9-5** RCochrane(9) (b: hld up: hdwy & n.m.r over 1f out: nt clr run ins fnl f: eased whn btn)	½	6	100/30[1]	80+	62
1608[5]	**Meliksah (IRE) (92)** (MBell) **3-9-5**[(5)] GFaulkner(5) (swtg: w ldr: ev ch ins fnl f: sn btn)	s.h	7	11/1	89	67
2289[12]	**Swynford Dream (75)** (JFBottomley) **4-8-11** OPeslier(3) (chsd clr ldrs: rdn & hld whn hmpd ins fnl f: nt rcvr)	2	8	9/1	66+	48
2675[8]	**Lago Di Varano (82)** (RMWhitaker) **5-9-4** AClark(7) (lw: nvr nr to chal)	¾	9	9/1	70	52
2590*	**Bowden Rose (83)** (MBlanshard) **5-9-2b**[(3)] PPMurphy(4) (s.i.s: sn rdn along: n.d)	¾	10	6/1[3]	69	51
2560[7]	**Jennelle (88)** (CADwyer) **3-9-6** KRutter(1) (chsd ldrs 3f)	1½	11	25/1	69	47
				(SP 121.8%)	**11 Rn**	

58.87 secs (0.37) CSF £119.13 CT £1,507.29 TOTE £32.50: £6.10 £1.80 £3.90 (£56.40) Trio £487.70 OWNER Mr J. R. Good (MIDDLEHAM) BRED J. R. and Mrs P. Good
WEIGHT FOR AGE 3yo-4lb
STEWARDS' ENQUIRY Dettori susp 28-30/7/97 (careless riding).
1910a Tadeo, well below-par so far this season, bounced back to form, coming with a strong late run having been taken off his feet along with most of the rest of the field. The fact that he had made all the running every time he had scored previously, makes this success all the more of a surprise. (20/1)
2711 Daawe (USA) has hung left before so to see Dettori draw his whip in his right hand was a cause for concern and the combination gave a fair bit of trouble to those behind. Nonetheless, this was a fine effort as his only wins over five furlongs have come on Southwell's notoriously slow surface. (11/2)
1766 Speed On, probably beaten more by the draw the last time, seems in good form and, had the gaps opened for him at the right time, he would have taken some beating. His overall record is a poor reward for his ability, but he should soon put that right. (14/1)
1766 Anotheranniversary, very fast out of the blocks as usual, would be hard to beat over three furlongs and a faster five like Goodwood or Epsom would surely be in his favour. (6/1)

2529 Music Gold (IRE) lost a lot of ground at the start and, in the circumstances, covered himself in glory, for he actually had a chance of sorts entering the final furlong. He is definitely one to keep on the right side of. (8/1)
2563* Gone Savage, keen going down as usual, did not get the breaks this time. (100/30)
1608 Meliksah (IRE) (11/1: 8/1-12/1)
1946 Swynford Dream, on a 4lb lower mark than when winning on the Rowley course last October, had no more than place chances when hampered. (9/1)

2873 CHEMIST BROKERS MAIDEN STKS (3-Y.O) (Class D)
5-20 (5-24) **1m (July)** £3,980.00 (£1,190.00: £570.00: £260.00) Stalls: Low GOING minus 0.28 sec per fur (GF)

				SP	RR	SF
2330³	**Desert Track** (JHMGosden) **3-9-0** LDettori(5) (lw: hld up: hdwy over 1f out: r.o wl to ld nr fin)	—	**1**	7/4¹	71	44
2583¹¹	**Dr Martens (IRE)** (LMCumani) **3-9-0** GHind(7) (bit bkwd: hdwy 3f out: led 1f out tl hdd & unable qckn nr fin)	nk	**2**	10/1	70	43
2591⁵	**Red Guard (80)** (GWragg) **3-9-0** AClark(13) (swtg: chsd ldrs: rdn & hung rt over 1f out: styd on ins fnl f)	3	**3**	11/4²	64	37
	Warning Express (RWArmstrong) **3-8-9** RPrice(2) (leggy: lw: in tch: hdwy over 3f out: led over 2f out to 1f out: wknd ins fnl f)	nk	**4**	20/1	59	32
847⁷	**Tonight's Prize (IRE)** (CFWall) **3-9-0** WLord(1) (in tch: no hdwy fnl 2f)	½	**5**	40/1	63	36
	Grovefair Venture (45) (KMahdi) **3-9-0** MRimmer(4) (led & plld hrd: hdd over 2f out: one pce)	3	**6**	66/1	57	30
2591⁸	**Forestry** (JGSmyth-Osbourne) **3-9-0** GBardwell(6) (swtg: pushed along 3f out: nvr nr ldrs)	2½	**7**	50/1	52	25
1144¹⁴	**Despina** (HCandy) **3-8-9** CRutter(8) (chsd ldrs 4f)	2	**8**	33/1	43	16
	Strength of Vision (CREgerton) **3-9-0** SophieMitchell(9) (wl grwn: bit bkwd: bhd fnl 3f)	3½	**9**	50/1	41	14
2555¹⁰	**Broughtons Lure (IRE)** (WJMusson) **3-8-9** JStack(12) (prom 4f)	nk	**10**	40/1	35	8
	Waterspout (USA) (MrsAJPerrett) **3-9-0** RCochrane(3) (s.i.s: hdwy after 3f: nt clr run over 3f out: sn btn & eased)	1¼	**11**	11/2³	38	11
	Lyphielo (USA) (LMCumani) **3-8-2**(7) DYoung(10) (lengthy: bit bkwd: nvr nr to chal)	1½	**12**	25/1	30	3
	Monacle (DMorris) **3-9-0** NDay(14) (unf: bit bkwd: s.s: effrt 3f out: nvr nr ldrs)	8	**13**	50/1	19	—
	Howaida (IRE) (MRStoute) **3-8-9** KBradshaw(15) (unf: scope: stumbled & uns rdr s)		**U**	10/1	—	—
				(SP 120.4%)		**14 Rn**

1m 41.05 (3.05) CSF £17.12 TOTE £2.40: £1.10 £2.90 £1.60 (£12.30) Trio £14.80 OWNER Sheikh Mohammed (NEWMARKET) BRED Sheikh Mohammed Bin Rashid Al Maktoum
2330 Desert Track, whose only previous outings have been on firm and heavy, may well have been suited by neither and moved well on this surface to win a modest maiden rather cleverly. Now he has got back on track, there should be more to come. (7/4)
2583 Dr Martens (IRE) moved a little better on this slightly easier ground and put in a much improved display, despite there still being plenty to work on. (10/1: 6/1-11/1)
2591 Red Guard seemed to have found the ideal race but showed little heart, and blinkers may be required to get the best out of him. (11/4)
Warning Express, a rather narrow half-sister to Tykeyvor, moves well and made a respectable debut. (20/1)
Tonight's Prize (IRE) is quite a keen sort and, dropped in trip, ran much better than on his debut. (40/1)
Grovefair Venture ran quite well, but pulled too hard in front courtesy of the loose horse. (66/1)
Waterspout (USA) (11/2: 7/2-6/1)

T/Plpt: £2,000.30 (20.38 Tckts). T/Qdpt: £60.90 (43.53 Tckts) Dk

2518-NOTTINGHAM (L-H) (Good to firm)
Saturday July 19th
WEATHER: sunny & very warm WIND: mod bhd

2874 LADIES DAY (S) H'CAP (0-60) (3-Y.O+) (Class G)
2-20 (2-20) **1m 6f 15y** £1,984.50 (£547.00: £259.50) Stalls: High GOING minus 0.63 sec per fur (F)

				SP	RR	SF
2174¹²	**Cohiba (34)** (BJCurley) **4-8-10** GDuffield(13) (hld up in tch: led over 4f out: sn clr: rdn & hld on fnl f)	—	**1**	9/1	48	29
2350³	**Brodessa (52)** (MrsMReveley) **11-10-0** ACulhane(9) (hdwy 6f out: chsd wnr over 3f out: rdn & kpt on wl towards fin)	1½	**2**	2/1¹	64	45
2737⁷	**Ship's Dancer (23)** (DonEnricoIncisa) **4-7-13b** KimTinkler(4) (lw: hdwy 3f out: styd on wl ins fnl f)	¾	**3**	40/1	34	15
2531⁹	**Rose of Glenn (45)** (BPalling) **6-9-2**(5) DSweeney(2) (a chsng ldrs: rdn & outpcd 4f out: styd on fnl f)	nk	**4**	9/1	56	37
1230¹⁴	**Eurolink Windsong (IRE) (41)** (MartynWane) **3-8-0**(3) DO'Donohoe(15) (s.s: hdwy 3f out: styd on u.p appr fnl f)	2½	**5**	33/1	49	16
*2322**	**Bedouin Prince (USA) (39)** (MrsLStubbs) **10-9-1** JFEgan(5) (b: chsd ldrs: rdn over 3f out: r.o one pce)	2	**6**	7/1²	45	26
2511⁷	**China Mail (IRE) (37)** (JABennett) **5-8-13** MFenton(3) (lw: nvr plcd to chal)	2	**7**	33/1	41	22
2662³	**Ballet de Cour (20)** (TJEtherington) **4-7-3**(7) PDoe(8) (lw: nvr nr to chal)	½	**8**	8/1³	23	4
2539³	**Ijab (CAN) (32)** (JParkes) **7-8-8b** WJO'Connor(10) (b: lw: in tch tl rdn & wknd over 3f out)	10	**9**	8/1³	24	5
1095¹⁰	**Marys Path (34)** (SGollings) **3-7-3**(7) JFowle(6) (lw: a in rr)	nk	**10**	66/1	25	—
1288⁴	**Mapengo (36)** (JCullinan) **6-8-12** VSlattery(12) (bit bkwd: chsd ldng pair 4f: sn rdn & lost pl)	nk	**11**	33/1	27	8
1417²	**Side Bar (25)** (KCComerford) **7-7-12v**(3) MBaird(7) (chsd ldr: led 5f out: sn hdd & wknd)	9	**12**	12/1	6	—
2518⁸	**Kindred Greeting (25)** (JO'Reilly) **5-8-1v¹** JO'Reilly(11) (lw: led 9f: wknd 3f out)	2½	**13**	25/1	3	—
2577⁶	**Bold Et Noir (41)** (WJarvis) **3-8-3** MRoberts(1) (hdwy ½-wy: wknd 4f out: t.o)	21	**14**	9/1	—	—
2544¹²	**Dispol Prince (20)** (GROldroyd) **4-7-10** NVarley(14) (a bhd: t.o)	10	**15**	66/1	—	—
				(SP 123.8%)		**15 Rn**

3m 1.3 (2.80) CSF £24.10 CT £661.94 TOTE £9.40: £2.10 £1.50 £6.80 (£20.70) Trio £137.30 OWNER Mrs B. J. Curley (NEWMARKET) BRED Snailwell Stud Co Ltd
LONG HANDICAP Marys Path 7-4
WEIGHT FOR AGE 3yo-14lb
No bid
OFFICIAL EXPLANATION Cohiba: regarding the improvement in form, the trainer's representative reported that the gelding had been dropped in the handicap and in class, and benefited from fourteen furlongs on a faster surface and from being enterprisingly ridden.
Cohiba swept into the lead soon after entering the straight and, driven clear over two furlongs out, had the right man on top to keep him galloping to the end. (9/1: op 6/1)
2350 Brodessa should have been a good thing on this step down to selling company, even with top-weight, but he had allowed the winner to take first run, and that rival had no intention of giving in to someone almost three times his age. (2/1)

1817 Ship's Dancer had shown little sign of ability in the past but, with her stable in form, she produced her best effort yet and there could be a race in her. (40/1)
2175 Rose of Glenn finished much closer to the favourite on these altered terms, but she was inclined to run her race in snatches and never really threatened danger. (9/1: op 6/1)
Eurolink Windsong (IRE), a lightly-raced filly attempting an extended trip for the first time, showed her first glimpse of form and she should be able to win a race at this level. (33/1)
2322* Bedouin Prince (USA) looked ill at ease on this lively ground but, to his credit, he gave it his best shot without ever threatening to trouble the leading pair. (7/1)
2539 Ijab (CAN) (8/1: 6/1-9/1)
1417 Side Bar (12/1: 8/1-14/1)
2577 Bold Et Noir (9/1: 7/1-12/1)

2875 EAST MIDLAND COMMERCIALS MAIDEN STKS (2-Y.O F) (Class D)

2-50 (2-51) **6f 15y** £3,936.25 (£1,180.00: £567.50: £261.25) Stalls: Low GOING minus 0.63 sec per fur (F)

				SP	RR	SF
2312^{2}	**Dazilyn Lady (USA)** (PWHarris) **2-8-11** ACulhane(2) (mde all far side: rdn over 2f out: r.o to ld fnl 100y)	—	**1**	7/1	79	40
1306^{3}	**Taalluf (USA)** (MajorWRHern) **2-8-8**$^{(3)}$ DGriffiths(7) (a.p. stands' side: led over 1f out tl ins fnl f: rallied cl home)	nk	**2**	9/1	78	39
	Alborada (SirMarkPrescott) **2-8-11** GDuffield(19) (lt-f: unf: a.p: hmpd wl over 1f: swtchd lft ent fnl f: r.o)	3	**3**	2/1^{1}	70+	31
	Zambezi (USA) (DRLoder) **2-8-11** MRoberts(17) (lt-f: unf: led: rdn & hung lft over 1f out: sn hdd: no ex fnl f)	1	**4**	6/1^{3}	68	29
	Momentarily (USA) (EALDunlop) **2-8-8**$^{(3)}$ DO'Donohoe(13) (w'like: chsd ldrs: pushed along whn bdly hmpd 1f out: sn btn)	5	**5**	11/2^{2}	55	16
2335^{5}	**Eleonora d'Arborea** (BJMeehan) **2-8-4**$^{(7)}$ GHannon(5) (prom: hmpd & swtchd lft over 1f out: nt rcvr)	nk	**6**	8/1	54	15
2728^{17}	**Sassy (IRE)** (APJarvis) **2-8-4**$^{(7)}$ CCarver(12) (hdwy over 1f out: nrst fin)	nk	**7**	50/1	53	14
2047^{8}	**Great Lyth Lass (IRE)** (PDEvans) **2-8-11** JFEgan(16) (prom tl wknd wl over 1f out)	¾	**8**	16/1	51	12
	Washm (USA) (DMorley) **2-8-11** GCarter(15) (small: lt-f: trckd ldrs stands' side over 4f)	1	**9**	14/1	48	9
2579^{3}	**Roisin Splendour (IRE)** (SDow) **2-8-11** RPerham(11) (trckd ldrs over 4f)	1¼	**10**	14/1	45	6
2367^{4}	**Touchanova** (AHide) **2-8-6**$^{(5)}$ GMilligan(4) (b.nr hind: chsd wnr far side: rdn over 2f out: a outpcd)	3	**11**	33/1	37	—
	Wrought Iron (USA) (MBell) **2-8-11** MFenton(9) (cmpt: bkwd: s.s: a bhd & outpcd: t.o)	8	**12**	14/1	16	—
2571^{5}	**Lilanita** (BPalling) **2-8-6**$^{(5)}$ AimeeCook(10) (outpcd: t.o)	4	**13**	33/1	5	—
2706^{14}	**Wedding Band** (RHannon) **2-8-11** WJO'Connor(6) (bit bkwd: s.s: a bhd: t.o)	½	**14**	20/1	4	—
1425^{13}	**Chiltern Emerald** (KRBurke) **2-8-6**$^{(5)}$ DSweeney(14) (bit bkwd: outpcd: a bhd: t.o)	1¾	**15**	50/1	—	—
	Sporty Spice (IRE) (JLHarris) **2-8-11** FLynch(1) (leggy: lt-f: bkwd: racd far side: a bhd: outpcd: t.o)	nk	**16**	33/1	—	—
	Rita's Rock Ape (RBrotherton) **2-8-11** NVarley(8) (neat: bkwd: outpcd: t.o)	18	**17**	66/1	—	—

(SP 141.5%) **17 Rn**

1m 11.6 (0.10) CSF £69.34 TOTE £6.00: £2.70 £3.40 £1.10 (£40.50) Trio £36.10 OWNER Mr M Parker Mr G Knight & Mrs G Godfrey (BERKHAMSTED) BRED Gainsborough Farm Inc

2312 Dazilyn Lady (USA) decided to remain with a couple of rivals on the far side, and she always had their measure, but she looked in trouble when ridden along soon after halfway, and it came as a surprise to the majority that she was in command inside the last hundred yards. (7/1)
1306 Taalluf (USA) had enjoyed a two-month break since making her debut, and she looked the winner when gaining command on the stands' side approaching the final furlong but, hard as she tried, the verdict went against her. Losses are only lent. (9/1)
Alborada, a lightly-made daughter of a useful race-mare, had got into contention but was being made to work, when she was the meat in a sandwich below the distance. Although she did rally once switched, the damage had been done. She should not be too hard to place. (2/1: 3/1-11/2)
Zambezi (USA), a sharp-looking filly whose dam was twice a winner over sprint distances, forced the pace, but she was beginning to feel the strain when she hung off a true line over a furlong out, and was soon headed and beaten. She will strip fitter for the run. (6/1: 2/1-13/2)
Momentarily (USA) did not catch the eye cantering to post, but she was never far away once the action started, only to be knocked out of her stride below the distance, and that put paid to what chance remained. (11/2)
2335 Eleonora d'Arborea has been very highly-tried in her most recent races and that could have taken the edge off her, for she was being nudged along and looked held when forced to switch violently left in the barging match which took place over a furlong out. (8/1)

2876 EAST MIDLAND COMMERCIALS H'CAP (0-70) (3-Y.O+) (Class E)

3-25 (3-26) **1m 1f 213y** £3,434.25 (£1,029.00: £494.50: £227.25) Stalls: High GOING minus 0.63 sec per fur (F)

				SP	RR	SF
2164^{3}	**African-Pard (IRE) (58)** (DHaydnJones) **5-9-5** MFenton(6) (hld up & bhd: gd hdwy over 2f out: led over 1f out: r.o strly)	—	**1**	14/1	70	29
2430*	**Calendula (63)** (DMorley) **4-9-10** GCarter(1) (hld up: hdwy over 3f out: hmpd & swtchd rt over 2f out: r.o ins fnl f)	2	**2**	9/2^{2}	72	31
2187^{6}	**Bonanza Peak (USA) (61)** (MrsJCecil) **4-9-8** GDuffield(3) (lw: led tl over 3f out: rdn to ld over 2f out: hdd over 1f out: no ex fnl f)	nk	**3**	5/2^{1}	69	28
2523^{8}	**Flotilla (55)** (SMellor) **3-8-6v**^{1} RPerham(8) (prom: led over 3f out tl over 2f out: rdn & one pce fnl f)	1¼	**4**	33/1	61	10
2552^{16}	**Haydn James (USA) (60)** (PWHarris) **3-8-11b** ACulhane(11) (hld up in rr: stdy hdwy 3f out: nvr nrr)	s.h	**5**	16/1	66	15
2668^{5}	**Mazilla (50)** (AStreeter) **5-8-8v**$^{(3)}$ RHavlin(9) (chsd ldrs: rdn over 2f out: r.o one pce)	2	**6**	9/2^{2}	53	12
2660^{5}	**Bedazzle (38)** (MBrittain) **6-7-13** NVarley(2) (trckd ldrs: rdn over 2f out: one pce)	1½	**7**	8/1	39	—
2205^{8}	**Gilling Dancer (IRE) (49)** (PCalver) **4-8-10** FLynch(7) (lw: s.s: a bhd: t.o)	24	**8**	16/1	11	—
2375*	**Clued Up (55)** (PDEvans) **4-9-2v** JFEgan(4) (in tch: drvn along 3f out: sn wknd: t.o)	s.h	**9**	6/1^{3}	17	—
2340^{10}	**Oneoftheoldones (36)** (JNorton) **5-7-8**$^{(3)}$ MBaird(10) (chsd ldr tl ½-wy: wknd 3f out: t.o)	7	**10**	20/1	—	—
1830^{11}	**Desert Cat (IRE) (62)** (MartynWane) **4-9-6**$^{(3)}$ DO'Donohoe(5) (lw: hld up & bhd: effrt over 3f out: no imp: t.o)	23	**11**	14/1	—	—

(SP 123.1%) **11 Rn**

2m 5.4 (2.90) CSF £72.45 CT £198.23 TOTE £17.80: £3.80 £2.10 £1.50 (£34.40) Trio £68.80 OWNER J S Fox and Sons (PONTYPRIDD) BRED Des De Vere Hunt
WEIGHT FOR AGE 3yo-10lb
OFFICIAL EXPLANATION **Gilling Dancer (IRE): lost his action.**

2164 African-Pard (IRE), taken to post very steadily, was restrained in the rear. Pulled into the centre of the track to make progress approaching the last quarter-mile, he surged through to lead over a furlong out and got off the mark with a comfortable success. (14/1: 10/1-16/1)
2430* Calendula was looking short of pace when forced to switch entering the final quarter-mile, and though she stayed on inside the distance it is doubtful if the result was affected. She seems to need further on ground as fast as this. (9/2)
2187 Bonanza Peak (USA) adopted front-running tactics and turned in his best effort yet, and there is no reason why he should not go on improving. (5/2: op 4/1)

Flotilla showed much improved form with a visor and this slightly longer trip, and it would be most surprising if he cannot find a race. (33/1)
Haydn James (USA) has been a big disappointment so far this season, but there was plenty to like about this effort and he could be coming to himself. (16/1)
2668 Mazilla, carrying 5lb less than when successful in this event a year ago, is struggling to find her form this term and it is proving difficult to pinpoint the problem. (9/2)
2375* Clued Up (6/1: 3/1-13/2)

2877 LADIES DAY H'CAP (0-85) (3-Y.O) (Class D)
4-00 (4-01) **1m 54y** £6,388.00 (£1,924.00: £932.00: £436.00) Stalls: High GOING minus 0.63 sec per fur (F)

Form	Horse	Dist	Pl	SP	RR	SF
2374^{10}	**Merciless Cop (67)** (BJMeehan) **3-8-0b**$^{(3)ow4}$ DO'Donohoe(3) (hld up in rr: hdwy on outside to ld over 2f out: rdn out)	—	1	16/1	75	28
2156*	**Muhtafel (85)** (JLDunlop) **3-9-7** GCarter(2) (hld up: hdwy & swtchd ins 2f out: rdn, edgd rt & r.o cl home)	½	2	2/1^{1}	92	49
1234^{2}	**Burning Truth (USA) (80)** (RCharlton) **3-9-2** WJO'Connor(7) (bit bkwd: a.p: drvn to ld over 2f out: sn hdd: one pce fnl f)	2½	3	6/1^{3}	82	39
2495^{4}	**Night Chorus (68)** (BSRothwell) **3-8-4** MFenton(1) (hld up: hdwy over 2f out: rdn & unable qckn ins fnl f)	1	4	16/1	68	25
2214^{4}	**Nominator Lad (75)** (BAMcMahon) **3-8-11** MWigham(4) (bit bkwd: hld up: effrt & drvn along 3f out: no imp)	6	5	8/1	64	21
2495^{2}	**Gharib (USA) (73)** (ACStewart) **3-8-9** MRoberts(5) (b.hind: hld up: hdwy ent st: ev ch over 2f out: drvn along & wknd)	1	6	4/1^{2}	60	17
2331^{5}	**Telemania (IRE) (82)** (WJHaggas) **3-9-4** FLynch(8) (led after 2f tl over 2f out: sn rdn & wknd)	1	7	9/1	67	24
1928^{2}	**Moon Blast (85)** (LadyHerries) **3-9-7** GDuffield(9) (hld up in tch: outpcd over 3f out: sn btn)	s.h	8	6/1^{3}	70	27
2214^{6}	**I Can't Remember (73)** (PDEvans) **3-8-9v**^{1} JFEgan(6) (led 2f: ev ch tl wknd 2f out)	hd	9	20/1	57	14

(SP 119.5%) **9 Rn**

1m 42.2 (0.90) CSF £45.58 CT £208.42 TOTE £14.50: £4.00 £1.50 £1.70 (£27.60) Trio £47.50 OWNER Mr Mario Lanfranchi (UPPER LAMBOURN) BRED G. S. Shropshire
2245 Merciless Cop went to the start like a cat on hot bricks, but there was no faulting the way he came back and, ploughing a lone furrow up the centre of the track, took full advantage of his weight allowance and held on gamely to the finish. (16/1)
2156* Muhtafel had a bit more on his plate conceding weight in this first handicap, but he is still very short on experience and, this will stand him in good stead. (2/1)
1234 Burning Truth (USA) reappearing after a two-month rest, gave the impression cantering to post that he would prefer more cut on the ground. Always close up, he was tapped for speed entering the final furlong but he did stay on, and his luck is due a change. (6/1)
2495 Night Chorus eventually found his stride halfway up the straight, but by then he had got too much to do, and his finishing position was as close as he could get. (16/1)
2495 Gharib (USA) fighting for the lead two furlongs out, was unable to maintain his progress under pressure, and as yet does not appear to be seeing the trip out, or there again does he need a much stiffer test of stamina? (4/1)
1928 Moon Blast, hard at work in an attempt to hold his pitch early in the straight, dropped away tamely and was one of the first beaten. This was not his true running. (6/1)

2878 'BEST DRESSED LADY' CLAIMING STKS (3-Y.O) (Class F)
4-30 (4-31) **1m 54y** £2,785.20 (£772.20: £369.60) Stalls: High GOING minus 0.63 sec per fur (F)

Form	Horse	Dist	Pl	SP	RR	SF
1756^{12}	**Racing Heart (38)** (PJMakin) **3-9-0** GDuffield(10) (hld up: hdwy over 2f out: shkn up to ld ins fnl f: sn clr)	—	1	13/2^{3}	62	31
2669^{7}	**Flood's Hot Stuff (37)** (NPLittmoden) **3-7-12**$^{(5)ow3}$ ADaly(6) (led 1f: led 3f out tl over 1f out: rallied u.p cl home)	2½	2	20/1	46	12
2670^{2}	**Bon Guest (IRE) (53)** (JGMO'Shea) **3-9-2**$^{(3)}$ DGriffiths(3) (lw: hld up: hdwy 3f out: led over 1f out: rdn, edgd lft & hdd ins fnl f)	s.h	3	3/1^{2}	62	31
2733^{8}	**Silent Valley (46)** (MissLCSiddall) **3-8-12v**^{1} MWigham(5) (trckd ldrs: rdn over 2f out: kpt on ins fnl f)	1¾	4	12/1	52	21
2501^{5}	**Italian Symphony (IRE) (44)** (PDEvans) **3-8-9** JFEgan(11) (nvr trbld ldrs)	8	5	9/1	33	2
2392^{3}	**Bobbitt (50)** (WJarvis) **3-8-6** MRoberts(1) (prom: effrt wl over 2f out: sn rdn & wknd)	1	6	7/4^{1}	28	—
1989^{8}	**Geordie Lad (52)** (JABennett) **3-8-9** MFenton(9) (b: led after 1f to 3f out: sn rdn & wknd)	3½	7	20/1	24	—
	April In Paris (CJames) **3-8-6** RPerham(2) (nt grwn: chsd ldrs tl wknd over 2f out)	6	8	20/1	10	—
	Two Bills (58) (AStreeter) **3-9-0**$^{(5)}$ GMilligan(4) (bkwd: s.i.s: a bhd: t.o)	9	9	10/1	5	—

(SP 115.8%) **9 Rn**

1m 42.9 (1.60) CSF £115.33 TOTE £9.70: £2.40 £7.20 £1.50 (£88.80) Trio £143.50 OWNER Avon Industries Ltd (MARLBOROUGH) BRED Avon Industries Bath Ltd
STEWARDS' ENQUIRY Griffiths susp. 28/7-1/8/97 (failure to ensure best possible placing).
1500 Racing Heart much happier on turf, opened her account with a runaway success and, in this class, more success can come her way. (13/2: 4/1-7/1)
Flood's Hot Stuff ran much better with more use made of her and, though she had to admit the winner too good, a repeat could pay dividends. (20/1)
2670 Bon Guest (IRE) gained his only win over course and distance in May, and he looked set to follow up when leading into the final furlong but, once the challenges came, he was unable to respond. (3/1)
1998 Silent Valley shaped a bit better in the visor, but she is short of pace and could not reach a position to cause concern. (12/1)
2392 Bobbitt is very mediocre as yet, and she would have trouble finding a race much weaker than this. (7/4)
Two Bills (10/1: 5/1-11/1)

2879 'LADIES IN HALF PRICE' RATING RELATED MAIDEN STKS (0-65) (3-Y.O) (Class F)
5-00 (5-01) **1m 1f 213y** £2,692.80 (£745.80: £356.40) Stalls: High GOING minus 0.63 sec per fur (F)

Form	Horse	Dist	Pl	SP	RR	SF
	Missfortuna (65) (SirMarkPrescott) **3-8-11** GDuffield(2) (trckd ldrs: led wl over 2f out: clr fnl f: impressive)	—	1	13/8^{1}	74+	23
2420^{6}	**Tarxien (57)** (KRBurke) **3-9-0** JFEgan(8) (lw: hld up: hdwy over 3f out: rdn & one pce appr fnl f)	4	2	8/1^{3}	71	20
2323^{4}	**Walk On By (65)** (RHannon) **3-9-0** RPerham(7) (a.p: rdn wl over 1f out: kpt on one pce)	¾	3	4/1^{2}	69	18
2315^{16}	**Salsee Lad (60)** (JRFanshawe) **3-9-0** WJO'Connor(4) (trckd ldrs: rdn over 2f out: nt clr run & swtchd rt appr fnl f: r.o)	1½	4	12/1	67	16
2389^{8}	**Hope Chest (63)** (DRLoder) **3-8-11** MRoberts(6) (lw: led tl hdd wl over 2f out: sn rdn & outpcd)	½	5	4/1^{2}	63	12
2238^{6}	**Get The Point (65)** (RHollinshead) **3-9-0** FLynch(1) (hld up: effrt 3f out: no hdwy)	2	6	10/1	63	12
2668^{13}	**The Green Grey (47)** (WRMuir) **3-8-11**$^{(3)}$ DO'Donohoe(3) (bhd: rn wd ent st: sn rdn: no imp: t.o fnl 2f)	10	7	25/1	47	—
2430^{10}	**Not Forgotten (USA) (63)** (PAKelleway) **3-9-0b**^{1} MWigham(9) (lw: s.i.s: sn chsng ldrs: wknd 3f out: t.o)	hd	8	16/1	47	—
2487^{14}	**Such Presence (45)** (KSBridgwater) **3-9-0** VSlattery(5) (a bhd: t.o)	hd	9	50/1	24 t	—

				SP	RR	SF
2535[5]	**Showcase (40)** (JWHills) **3-8-11b[1]** MFenton(10) (b.nr hind: chsd ldr tl rdn & wknd 2f out: t.o)	2	**10**	20/1	17 t	—
				(SP 122.4%)	**10 Rn**	

2m 5.1 (2.60) CSF £15.01 TOTE £2.60: £1.10 £2.70 £1.80 (£20.10) Trio £44.90 OWNER Dr St John Collier & Mrs Sherry Collier (NEWMARKET) BRED Dr and Mrs St J. Collier

Missfortuna, a strongly-made, fine-looking filly, did not have to exert herself on this seasonal debut to put paid to this opposition, and she looks a promising prospect. (13/8: 2/1-evens)

Tarxien, returning to a more suitable trip, turned in his best effort yet, and he looks the sort to progress further. (8/1: 7/1-11/1)

2323 Walk On By has been tried at different distances and has not run a bad race yet. His turn will come one of these days. (4/1: tchd 6/1)

1936 Salsee Lad would benefit from more cut in the ground, and it is possible he would have made the frame had he not been forced to check and switch when he was just finding his stride. (12/1: op 7/1)

1372 Hope Chest made the running for almost a mile, but she kept very little in reserve and her measure had been taken below the distance. (4/1: tchd 6/1)

2238 Get The Point ran a very lacklustre race, and if anything he seems to be going backwards. (10/1: 6/1-12/1)

T/Plpt: £48.70 (243.51 Tckts). T/Qdpt: £23.60 (32.52 Tckts) IM

2400-REDCAR (L-H) (Good to firm)
Saturday July 19th

Race 6: No time taken due to poor visibility.
WEATHER: fine WIND: almost nil

2880 FURNITURE FACTORS RACING SCHOOLS APPRENTICE H'CAP (0-60) (3-Y.O+) (Class G)
6-45 (6-45) **1m** £2,398.50 (£671.00: £325.50) Stalls: Low GOING minus 0.56 sec per fur (F)

				SP	RR	SF
2646[6]	**Clytha Hill Lad (31)** (JMBradley) **6-8-1** IonaWands(2) (b: lw: a.p: led over 2f out: hld on wl)	—	**1**	5/1[2]	41	8
2716[9]	**Miletrian City (43)** (MissLAPerratt) **4-8-8b**(5) NPollard(8) (lw: mid div: hdwy to disp ld 2f out: kpt on: jst hld on)	hd	**2**	20/1	53	20
2845[5]	**Prime Partner (37)** (TDEasterby) **4-8-7** DSweeney(6) (lw: pressed ldr: ev ch over 2f out: one pce ins last)	1½	**3**	4/1[1]	44	11
2646[4]	**Zahran (IRE) (32)** (JMBradley) **6-7-11**(5) DarrenWilliams(10) (lw: cl up: outpcd over 2f out: kpt on ins last)	hd	**4**	5/1[2]	39	6
2546[9]	**Forest Robin (57)** (MrsJRRamsden) **4-9-8**(5) ClaireWest(7) (nvr far away: effrt 3f out: kpt on same pce ins last)	½	**5**	11/2[3]	63	30
2651[7]	**General Monty (43)** (TDBarron) **5-8-13** KimberleyHart(5) (prom: pushed along over 2f out: one pce)	2½	**6**	20/1	44	11
1761[6]	**Hotcake (37)** (MissSEHall) **4-8-7** CTeague(4) (hld up: rdn over 2f out: nt pce to chal)	1	**7**	8/1	36	3
1615[3]	**Western Venture (IRE) (30)** (MartynWane) **4-8-0** MBaird(12) (led tl hdd over 2f out: sn btn)	2	**8**	14/1	25	—
1800[11]	**Habeta (USA) (37)** (JWWatts) **11-8-7** RHavlin(11) (hld up: rdn along 3f out: no imp)	3	**9**	13/2	26	—
2531[10]	**Paperwork Pete (IRE) (30)** (WStorey) **5-7-9**(5) JMcAuley(9) (in tch: rdn ½-wy: struggling over 2f out)	1¼	**10**	33/1	16	—
2362[6]	**First Bite (IRE) (53)** (MDHammond) **5-9-6**(3) NHorrocks(3) (bhd: rdn ½-wy: sn btn)	nk	**11**	12/1	39	6
2723[10]	**Paint It Black (54)** (DNicholls) **4-9-3**(7) JoanneDavies(1) (bhd: rdn ½-wy: n.d)	½	**12**	15/2	39	6
				(SP 131.8%)	**12 Rn**	

1m 38.1 (3.10) CSF £102.60 CT £423.60 TOTE £6.90: £3.20 £5.10 £1.90 (£136.50) Trio £134.60; £115.70 to Ayr 21/7/97 OWNER Mrs Marion Morgan (CHEPSTOW) BRED Mrs M. C. Morgan

2646 Clytha Hill Lad finally lost his maiden tag at his eleventh attempt, winning a poor race in determined style under a good ride from Iona Wands. (5/1)

2716 Miletrian City, back over his best trip, turned in an improved effort, just failing to take the honours on the nod. (20/1)

2845 Prime Partner, running for the second time in the space of twenty-four hours, could do more inside the final furlong. (4/1)

2646 Zahran (IRE), a stablemate of the winner and closely matched with him on recent Chepstow form, kept on well in the closing stages but just lacked the foot to make his presence felt. (5/1: tchd 11/)

2152 Forest Robin extended his losing run and is still a maiden after twenty-six attempts. (11/2)

1630 General Monty had had his measure taken approaching the final furlong. (20/1)

2881 E.B.F. BORO REDBOOK MAIDEN STKS (2-Y.O) (Class D)
7-15 (7-17) **7f** £3,619.50 (£1,086.00: £523.00: £241.50) Stalls: Low GOING minus 0.56 sec per fur (F)

				SP	RR	SF
	Abuhail (USA) (DMorley) **2-9-0** JWeaver(11) (w'like: scope: in tch on ins: effrt & swtchd on ins over 2f out: led appr fnl f: r.o wl)	—	**1**	7/2[2]	74+	33
2336[3]	**Eljjanah (USA)** (JLDunlop) **2-9-0** GCarter(9) (in tch gng wl: effrt & ev ch appr fnl f: kpt on)	1¼	**2**	13/8[1]	71	30
2022[2]	**Rioja** (TPTate) **2-9-0** AMackay(4) (lw: led tl hdd appr fnl f: no ex wl ins fnl f)	¾	**3**	6/1	69	28
2022[5]	**Watkins** (FMurphy) **2-9-0** JFanning(2) (unruly bef s: cl up: rdn over 2f out: sn one pce)	3½	**4**	12/1	61	20
2688[7]	**Tarashaan** (SirMarkPrescott) **2-8-11**(3) RHavlin(1) (lw: s.s & wl outpcd: sme late hdwy: n.d)	10	**5**	9/2[3]	39	—
	Wishbone Alley (IRE) (MDods) **2-9-0** AlexGreaves(6) (w'like: bit bkwd: cl up tl wknd over 2f out)	s.h	**6**	16/1	39	—
	Jago (MWEasterby) **2-8-11**(3) GParkin(3) (unf: bit bkwd: s.i.s: sn outpcd & bhd)	1	**7**	33/1	36	—
	Lady Rochelle (TDEasterby) **2-8-9** LCharnock(7) (leggy: unf: scope: bhd: rdn ½-wy: sn struggling)	½	**8**	16/1	30	—
2356[7]	**Eddie Rombo** (NTinkler) **2-9-0** KimTinkler(10) (chsd ldrs tl wknd over 2f out)	2	**9**	25/1	31	—
	Priolette (IRE) (JGFitzGerald) **2-8-9** ACulhane(8) (w'like: bit bkwd: s.i.s: rn green in rr: nvr a factor)	¾	**10**	11/1	24	—
2499[6]	**Prince Nicholas** (KWHogg) **2-9-0** MGallagher(5) (sn outpcd: struggling fr ½-wy)	13	**11**	25/1	—	—
				(SP 131.2%)	**11 Rn**	

1m 24.5 (1.50) CSF £9.69 TOTE £4.30: £2.10 £1.40 £1.60 (£2.70) Trio £6.70 OWNER Mr Hamdan Al Maktoum (NEWMARKET) BRED T. F. Van Meter II

Abuhail (USA), a likeable individual by Silver Hawk and a $170,000 yearling purchase, made a pleasing debut. He was nicely on top in the closing stages and should go on from here. (7/2)

2336 Eljjanah (USA) travelled well throughout the race but, when push came to shove, failed to find the acceleration of the winner and had to admit defeat inside the final furlong. (13/8: evens-7/4)

2022 Rioja fulfilled the promise of his debut effort by running another good race. He should not be a maiden for long. (6/1)

2022 Watkins, never too far away, turned in a respectable effort if just lacking the finishing pace of the first three when the chips were down. (12/1)

Tarashaan, who blotted his copybook on his debut, was very slowly away and was soon rousted along in the rear. Although he made some late headway, he could never get anywhere near the thick of the action. He looks one to treat with some caution. (9/2: op 8/1)

2882 CELLNET RIVERSIDE STADIUM H'CAP (0-75) (3-Y.O+) (Class D)

7-45 (7-45) **2m 4y** £3,769.00 (£1,132.00: £546.00: £253.00) Stalls: Low GOING minus 0.56 sec per fur (F)

				SP	RR	SF
2702^{7}	**Salska (58)** (AStreeter) **6-8-9**$^{(3)}$ RHavlin(5) (a.p: led over 2f out: u.p ins fnl f: hld on gamely)	—	1	12/1	67	19
2000^{2}	**Hullbank (67)** (WWHaigh) **7-9-7** ACulhane(9) (hld up in mid div: smooth hdwy & ev ch over 1f out: nt qckn towards fin)	½	2	5/1^{3}	76	28
2682^{2}	**Here Comes Herbie (62)** (WStorey) **5-8-13**$^{(3)}$ PFessey(1) (lw: hld up & bhd: hdwy 3f out: chsng ldrs over 1f out: no ex ins fnl f)	¾	3	4/1^{1}	70	22
2589^{6}	**Alwarqa (50)** (MartynWane) **4-8-4** AMackay(11) (cl up: led ½-wy tl over 2f out: rallied: no ex ins fnl f)	hd	4	9/1	58	10
2737^{2}	**Highfield Fizz (42)** (CWFairhurst) **5-7-10** LCharnock(7) (hld up: effrt over 2f out: kpt on u.p ins fnl f)	½	5	7/1	49	1
2682^{3}	**Great Oration (IRE) (61)** (FWatson) **8-9-1** JWeaver(10) (hld up: effrt on outside 2f out: kpt on: nrst fin)	hd	6	9/2^{2}	68	20
2589^{14}	**Spa Lane (53)** (MPBielby) **4-8-2**$^{(5)}$ DSweeney(2) (hld up: effrt on outside over 2f out: no imp)	4	7	16/1	56	8
2035^{2}	**Needwood Epic (48)** (BCMorgan) **4-8-2** GCarter(4) (led tl ½-wy: outpcd 2f out: eased)	1½	8	16/1	50	2
2352*	**Forgie (IRE) (70)** (PCalver) **4-9-7**$^{(3)}$ DarrenMoffatt(8) (lw: tk kn hold: chsd ldrs: drvn over 3f out: outpcd 2f out: eased)	3	9	5/1^{3}	69	21
2327^{15}	**Dirab (70)** (TDBarron) **4-9-3**$^{(7)}$ VictoriaAppleby(3) (mid div: lost tch 3f out: sn btn)	1¾	10	8/1	67	19
2000^{13}	**Highflying (65)** (GMMoore) **11-9-0**$^{(5)}$ TEDurcan(6) (prom: losing tch 3f out: sn btn)	1½	11	10/1	60	12

(SP 133.7%) **11 Rn**

3m 32.0 (7.00) CSF £73.61 CT £273.16 TOTE £17.00: £3.30 £3.50 £1.70 (£121.00) Trio £138.20 OWNER Mr P. L. Clinton (UTTOXETER) BRED J. A. Haverhals

LONG HANDICAP Highfield Fizz 7-8

2198 Salska is nothing if not game, and she showed plenty of determination to come out on top in a desperate finish. (12/1)

2000 Hullbank, off a 4lb higher mark than when winning at Beverley, turned in a sound effort but not for the first time found nothing extra off the bridle after making smooth headway to launch his challenge. (5/1)

2682 Here Comes Herbie, held up at the rear in a moderately-run race, was still in last place on the home turn. He made up his ground rapidly to throw down his challenge but could not produce an extra burst to take the spoils. He is in great heart at present. (4/1)

2589 Alwarqa is coming back to form and rallied in splendid style here, after looking likely to be swamped in the closing stages. (9/1)

2737 Highfield Fizz is running well in defeat at present and deserves to find a race before long. She is twice a winner on this course and warrants attention if coming back here in the near future. (7/1)

2682 Great Oration (IRE) produced a sound effort but was not helped by the slightly muddling pace early on. He would have preferred a true end to end gallop. (9/2)

2352* Forgie (IRE) had his bid for a hat-trick scuppered and was put in his place in the final quarter-mile. (5/1)

2883 MIDDLESBROUGH FOOTBALL CLUB (S) H'CAP (0-60) (3-Y.O) (Class G)

8-15 (8-16) **5f** £2,337.50 (£650.00: £312.50) Stalls: Low GOING minus 0.56 sec per fur (F)

				SP	RR	SF
2354^{3}	**College Princess (47)** (SCWilliams) **3-8-5**$^{(7)}$ DarrenWilliams(9) (chsd ldrs: effrt 2f out: led ins fnl f: r.o wl)	—	1	5/1^{2}	52	30
2481^{6}	**Gunners Glory (56)** (BJMeehan) **3-9-2b**$^{(5)}$ TEDurcan(6) (sn rdn: in tch: effrt 2f out: ev ch ins fnl f: hld nr fin)	1	2	6/1^{3}	58	36
2354^{2}	**Hiltons Executive (IRE) (36)** (EJAlston) **3-8-1** LCharnock(11) (chsd ldrs: drvn ½-wy: kpt on fnl f)	hd	3	15/2	38	16
2354^{8}	**Melbourne Princess (43)** (RMWhitaker) **3-8-8** ACulhane(8) (led tl hdd ins fnl f: no ex)	½	4	12/1	43	21
2001^{9}	**Lunar Music (48)** (RonaldThompson) **3-8-13b** JWeaver(3) (lw: prom: nt qckn over 1f out)	2	5	9/2^{1}	42	20
2540^{14}	**Toronto (50)** (JBerry) **3-9-1b** GCarter(7) (chsd ldrs: rdn ½-wy: outpcd fr over 1f out)	3½	6	9/1	32	10
2177^{14}	**Municipal Girl (IRE) (52)** (BPalling) **3-8-12**$^{(5)}$ DSweeney(1) (prom centre: nt qckn fr 2f out)	nk	7	9/1	33	11
1236^{18}	**Emmas Breeze (45)** (GGMargarson) **3-8-10** MFenton(13) (chsd ldrs: rdn ½-wy: sn one pce)	hd	8	20/1	26	4
779^{12}	**Risky Flight (38)** (ASmith) **3-8-0**$^{(3)}$ PFessey(10) (outpcd & bhd tl styd on fnl f)	¾	9	25/1	17	—
1995^{8}	**Northern Sal (52)** (MissLAPerratt) **3-9-0**$^{(3)}$ GParkin(12) (chsd ldrs tl ½-wy: sn btn)	2½	10	6/1^{3}	23	1
2481^{8}	**M T Vessel (42)** (JRJenkins) **3-8-7b** DWright(4) (prom centre tl ½-wy: sn btn)	s.h	11	20/1	12	—
2354^{4}	**Flo's Choice (IRE) (46)** (JO'Reilly) **3-8-11** JO'Reilly(14) (sn outpcd: struggling fr ½-wy)	1½	12	20/1	12	—
2417^{7}	**Donna's Dancer (IRE) (50)** (NTinkler) **3-9-1b** KimTinkler(5) (lw: s.i.s: bdly outpcd: n.d)	nk	13	7/1	15	—
2278^{5}	**Hot News (45)** (JRJenkins) **3-8-10v**^{1} DaleGibson(2) (a outpcd & bhd)	s.h	14	20/1	10	—

(SP 138.3%) **14 Rn**

58.5 secs (1.00) CSF £34.25 CT £221.50 TOTE £6.10: £2.10 £3.20 £2.60 (£21.00) Trio £36.80 OWNER College Farm Thoroughbreds (NEWMARKET) BRED Mrs C. A. Dunnett

No bid

2354 College Princess deserved to win a race and finally found opportunity knocking in this modest event. She was given a good ride by her 7lb claiming apprentice. (5/1)

2481 Gunners Glory had every chance inside the final furlong but could not pull out any extra. (6/1)

2354 Hiltons Executive (IRE), closely matched with the winner on Musselburgh running, ran up to scratch but was unable to quicken when it mattered. (15/2)

2235 Melbourne Princess, dropped 9lb in the handicap, put up a better display. She has yet to win a race after fourteen attempts but should not be written off yet. (12/1)

1730 Lunar Music, with the blinkers back on, had every chance but was put firmly in her place in the final furlong. (9/2: op 7/1)

2235 Toronto is proving a disappointing individual. (9/1)

2032 Donna's Dancer (IRE) missed the break and, completely outpaced early on, had no chance of recovering. (7/1)

2884 RIVERSIDE ROAR LIMITED STKS (0-70) (3-Y.O+) (Class E)

8-45 (8-45) **1m 1f** £2,786.00 (£833.00: £399.00: £182.00) Stalls: Low GOING minus 0.56 sec per fur (F)

				SP	RR	SF
2521^{2}	**Night Mirage (USA) (70)** (MJohnston) **3-8-8** JWeaver(4) (lw: trckd ldrs: rdn to ld 1f out: jst hld on)	—	1	5/2^{2}	74	35
1818^{2}	**Queens Consul (IRE) (69)** (BSRothwell) **7-9-3** MFenton(3) (lw: led tl hdd 1f out: kpt on wl: jst failed)	hd	2	9/4^{1}	74	44
2570^{4}	**Smart Spirit (IRE) (67)** (MrsMReveley) **3-8-8** ACulhane(1) (hld up: improved over 2f out: outpcd over 1f out)	8	3	9/4^{1}	60	21
2785^{10}	**Beano Script (58)** (JHanson) **4-9-6** EJohnson(5) (prom: rdn over 2f out: sn btn)	1¾	4	20/1	60	30
974^{8}	**Tilaal (USA) (67)** (MDHammond) **5-9-6** GCarter(2) (chsd ldrs: rdn appr st: outpcd over 2f out)	2½	5	13/2^{3}	55	25

(SP 108.2%) **5 Rn**

1m 52.0 (1.30) CSF £7.46 TOTE £3.00: £1.50 £1.40 (£3.60) OWNER Mr & Mrs G Middlebrook (MIDDLEHAM) BRED Hartland Farm & James Hayward

WEIGHT FOR AGE 3yo-9lb

2521 Night Mirage (USA) finally and deservedly lost her maiden tag and did so in gutsy fashion, coming out on top after a titanic duel. (5/2)

1818 Queens Consul (IRE), coming back from a six-week break, just failed to return in a blaze of glory after a typically game performance. (9/4)
2570 Smart Spirit (IRE) is proving a disappointment and was put firmly in her place in a matter of strides here when the race developed into a duel in the final quarter-mile. (9/4)
2239 Beano Script, running for the second time in three days, was unable to make his presence felt. (20/1)

2885 STEVE GIBSON H'CAP (0-80) (3-Y.O) (Class D)
9-15 (9-15) **1m 3f** £3,821.00 (£1,148.00: £554.00: £257.00) Stalls: Low GOING minus 0.56 sec per fur (F)

				SP	RR	SF
2421³	**Bally Souza (IRE) (73)** (MJohnston) **3-9-2** JWeaver(4) (lw: mde all: clr over 2f out: unchal)	—	1	5/2¹	89	—
2667⁶	**Mardrew (65)** (RHarris) **3-8-5**(3) RHavlin(3) (chsd ldrs: hdwy to chse wnr over 2f out: no imp)	7	2	8/1	71	—
2410⁵	**Kayfiyah (IRE) (78)** (DMorley) **3-9-7** GCarter(5) (chsd wnr tl over 2f out: sn btn)	10	3	3/1²	69	—
	Rock The Casbah (53) (JHetherton) **3-7-10** DWright(6) (bit bkwd: bhd: wknd 3f out)	10	4	25/1	30	—
2387³	**Quezon City (57)** (MJCamacho) **3-8-0** LCharnock(1) (in tch tl 3f out: sn btn)	1	5	5/2¹	32	—
1747⁹	**Nobel Lad (74)** (JLDunlop) **3-9-3** ACulhane(2) (prom: outpcd 3f out: sn btn)	5	6	5/1³	42	—
				(SP 113.8%)	**6 Rn**	

No Time Taken CSF £20.89 TOTE £3.00: £1.90 £2.50 (£14.20) OWNER Miss Belinda Lee (MIDDLEHAM) BRED Dene Investments N V
LONG HANDICAP Rock The Casbah 7-9
IN-FOCUS: **This race was run in very poor visibility and accordingly no time was taken.**
2421 Bally Souza (IRE) made all the running and ran on strongly in the closing stages to put the issue firmly beyond doubt. (5/2)
2667 Mardrew is running well at present but he had no chance of collaring the decisive winner here. (8/1)
2410 Kayfiyah (IRE) was put firmly in her place in the final two furlongs. (3/1)
Rock The Casbah, making his seasonal reappearance, was under pressure early in the home straight and could never get in a blow. (25/1)
2387 Quezon City was in trouble a long way from home. (5/2: 7/2-9/4)
1271 Nobel Lad was very disappointing. (5/1)

T/Plpt: £10.80 (1,167.14 Tckts). T/Qdpt: £9.50 (62.15 Tckts) O'R

2544-RIPON (R-H) (Good to firm)
Saturday July 19th
WEATHER: sunny & hot WIND: almost nil

2886 E.B.F. LEEDS CHILDRENS HOLIDAY CAMP ASSOCIATION MAIDEN STKS (2-Y.O) (Class D)
2-35 (2-44) **5f** £3,358.60 (£1,016.80: £496.40: £236.20) Stalls: Low GOING minus 0.42 sec per fur (F)

				SP	RR	SF
2545³	**Zizi (IRE)** (KRBurke) **2-8-9** JQuinn(8) (trckd ldrs: rdn to ld over 1f out: r.o wl)	—	1	7/4¹	76	13
1954³	**Quakeress (IRE)** (JohnBerry) **2-8-9** JLowe(11) (led tl over 1f out: kpt on same pce)	3	2	7/1	66	3
2553⁴	**Leofric** (MJPolglase) **2-9-0b¹** TGMcLaughlin(10) (chsd ldrs: kpt on one pce fnl 2f)	1½	3	13/2³	67	4
2361³	**Rich Choice** (JDBethell) **2-8-9** TWilliams(3) (trckd ldrs: effrt ½-wy: sn rdn & hung rt: kpt on one pce)	2	4	13/2³	55	—
	Kings Check (MissJFCraze) **2-9-0** SWebster(6) (cmpt: s.i.s: bhd tl styd on appr fnl f)	2	5	33/1	54	—
2477⁶	**Saint Ann (USA)** (MJohnston) **2-8-6**(3) RFfrench(5) (chsd ldrs: hung rt & outpcd ½-wy: sn wknd)	½	6	7/2²	47	—
2202⁸	**Cherokee Charlie** (RCraggs) **2-8-11**(3) GParkin(7) (s.i.s: a wl outpcd & bhd)	4	7	33/1	39	—
1280⁵	**Turf Moor (IRE)** (JJO'Neill) **2-8-4**(5) TEDurcan(9) (chsd ldrs to ½-wy: sn wknd)	3½	8	16/1	23	—
2684⁴	**Time To Time** (TDEasterby) **2-8-9** LCharnock(1) (unruly s: prom early: outpcd & bhd fr ½-wy)	½	9	13/2³	22	—
2110⁴	***Inshallah*** (MartinTodhunter) **2-8-9** DaleGibson(2) (Withdrawn not under Starter's orders: unruly: ref to ent stalls)		W	10/1	—	—
	Curriculus (IRE) (MartinTodhunter) **2-9-0** JCarroll(4) (Withdrawn not under Starter's orders: unruly: ref to ent stalls)		W	33/1	—	—
				(SP 134.9%)	**9 Rn**	

60.4 secs (2.60) CSF £14.24 TOTE £2.90: £1.20 £1.70 £2.00 (£9.30) Trio £19.50 OWNER Mr Nigel Shields (WANTAGE) BRED Richard Kent
2545 Zizi (IRE) took this modest event in decisive fashion. (7/4: op 3/1)
1954 Quakeress (IRE) has plenty of early speed and is suited by sharp tracks such as this. (7/1)
2553 Leofric, tried in blinkers, does not seem to be progressing. (13/2)
2361 Rich Choice, very keen going down, never settled and hung under pressure. (13/2)
Kings Check, very green going down, has plenty to learn. (33/1)
2477 Saint Ann (USA), dropped back to five, showed a very poor action going to post and hung as if feeling the fast ground. (7/2)
2684 Time To Time was one of just several who gave the starting stall team problems. (13/2)

2887 CENTAUR (S) STKS (3-Y.O+) (Class F)
3-10 (3-11) **1m** £2,600.00 (£725.00: £350.00) Stalls: High GOING minus 0.42 sec per fur (F)

				SP	RR	SF
2463*	**Special-K (47)** (EWeymes) **5-8-9**(7) TSiddall(8) (lw: trckd ldrs: styd on to ld jst ins fnl f: hld on wl)	—	1	5/4¹	56	42
2651W	**My Handsome Prince (30)** (PJBevan) **5-9-2** NCarlisle(7) (chsd ldr: led over 1f out tl jst ins fnl f: nt qckn wl ins fnl f)	nk	2	12/1	55	41
2203¹²	**Shark (IRE) (49)** (KAMorgan) **4-9-2** OPears(10) (plld hrd: led tl over 1f out: grad wknd)	2½	3	33/1	50	36
2488¹⁰	**Katie Komaite (39)** (CaptJWilson) **4-8-6b**(5) PRoberts(3) (racd wd: hld up: hdwy over 2f out: kpt on same pce appr fnl f)	nk	4	6/1	45	31
2701¹⁰	**Grovefair Lad (IRE) (39)** (MartynWane) **3-8-5**(3) RFfrench(1) (lw: bhd: styd on u.p fnl 2f: nvr nr ldrs)	4	5	10/1	42	20
2544³	**Bernard Seven (IRE) (33)** (MDods) **5-9-7b** AlexGreaves(4) (sn trckng ldrs: effrt over 2f out: hung rt & nt run on)	3	6	3/1²	41	27
2671⁸	**Dragonjoy (53)** (NPLittmoden) **4-9-7v** RLappin(9) (prom early: hdwy u.p 5f out: nvr nr to chal)	1	7	7/1	39	25
2602¹³	**Persian Sunset (IRE) (35)** (GWoodward) **5-8-11** JQuinn(2) (hld up: a bhd)	2	8	16/1	25	11
	First Option (28) (RBastiman) **7-9-2**(5) HBastiman(6) (t: s.s: a bhd)	16	9	33/1	3	—
	Lab Test (IRE) (JLEyre) **5-9-7** MGallagher(5) (chsd ldrs: effrt 3f out: sn wknd: p.u over 1f out: b.b.v)		P	11/2³	—	—
				(SP 140.2%)	**10 Rn**	

1m 40.5 (2.30) CSF £22.90 TOTE £2.40: £1.50 £2.60 £7.40 (£13.80) Trio £93.30 OWNER Mr G. Falshaw (MIDDLEHAM) BRED Patrick Diamond
WEIGHT FOR AGE 3yo-8lb
No bid

OFFICIAL EXPLANATION **Lab Test (IRE): was bleeding from the nose.**
2463* Special-K showed that she can handle any sort of ground. It was in mark contrast to Beverley. Well-handled, she was always doing just enough. (5/4)
2488 My Handsome Prince, who would have been meeting the winner on 17lb better terms in a handicap, is still a maiden after twenty-nine attempts but surely there is an opening somewhere for him. (12/1)
Shark (IRE), taken to post early, would not settle in front. Considering how keenly he raced, he did well to last to over a furlong out. (33/1)
2226 Katie Komaite, who raced on the by-pass, ran much better than when gambled on in her previous outing. (6/1)
2226 Grovefair Lad (IRE) shaped better after a dismal effort on his previous start. (10/1)
2544 Bernard Seven (IRE), who would have been meeting the winner on 19lb better terms in a handicap, has no relish for a fight these days. (3/1: op 9/2)
860 Dragonjoy (7/1: op 4/1)

2888 FORTE HOTELS (YORKSHIRE) MEDIAN AUCTION MAIDEN STKS (3-Y.O) (Class E)

3-40 (3-40) **1m 1f** £3,047.50 (£910.00: £435.00: £197.50) Stalls: High GOING minus 0.42 sec per fur (F)

				SP	RR	SF
2583[2]	**Marilaya (IRE)** (LMCumani) **3-8-6**(3) RFfrench(1) (trckd ldrs: plld hrd: sddle slipped: led 3f out: drvn clr fnl f)	—	1	1/8[1]	66	39
2546[3]	**Fancy A Fortune (IRE) (60)** (DNicholls) **3-9-0** AlexGreaves(4) (lw: trckd ldr: led over 3f out: sn hdd: kpt on wl: no ch w wnr)	2½	2	12/1[3]	67	40
	Beach Buoy (IRE) (CaptJWilson) **3-8-9**(5) PRoberts(2) (w'like: bit bkwd: sn chsng ldrs: kpt on same pce fnl 2f: nvr able to chal)	1	3	33/1	65	38
2315[6]	**In The Genes** (JLEyre) **3-9-0** MGallagher(5) (sn outpcd & pushed along: nvr nr ldrs)	8	4	8/1[2]	51	24
1939[7]	**Our Future (IRE) (65)** (RonaldThompson) **3-9-0v**[1] TWilliams(3) (sn drvn along: led tl over 3f out: lost pl over 2f out)	17	5	100/1	20	—

(SP 111.6%) **5 Rn**

1m 53.2 (2.20) CSF £2.70 TOTE £1.20: £1.10 £1.80 (£2.00) OWNER H H Aga Khan (NEWMARKET) BRED His Highness the Aga Khan's Studs S.C.
2583 Marilaya (IRE), backed as if defeat was out of the question, raced keenly and her saddle soon slipped back. Skillfully handled, in the end she scored in workmanlike fashion. (1/8: op 2/7)
2546 Fancy A Fortune (IRE) was asked to do just enough to secure second spot. (12/1: op 7/1)
Beach Buoy (IRE), a good-bodied individual who looked in need of the outing, ran a highly satisfactory first race. (33/1)
2315 In The Genes was soon being taken off his legs over this inadequate trip. (8/1: op 7/2)
Our Future (IRE) has now finished tailed off in three outings this year. (100/1)

2889 TETLEY'S BELL-RINGER H'CAP (0-85) (3-Y.O+) (Class D)

4-10 (4-11) **1m 4f 60y** £6,690.00 (£2,010.00: £970.00: £450.00) Stalls: Low GOING minus 0.42 sec per fur (F)

				SP	RR	SF
2514[8]	**Tessajoe (78)** (MJCamacho) **5-9-8** LCharnock(9) (b.hind: trckd ldr: led over 3f out: drvn out fnl f)	—	1	7/4[1]	86	43
2660[8]	**Gold Desire (52)** (MBrittain) **7-7-10** JLowe(3) (a chsng ldrs: chal over 3f out: kpt on wl fnl f)	¾	2	14/1	59	16
2494[3]	**Leviticus (IRE) (75)** (TPTate) **3-8-7** NConnorton(5) (trckd ldrs: effrt over 3f out: rdn & hung rt over 1f out: kpt on one pce)	1¼	3	10/1	80	25
1832*	**Infatuation (76)** (LadyHerries) **4-9-6** TWilliams(6) (hld up: hdwy & swtchd outside over 2f out: hung rt & kpt on same pce fnl f)	½	4	7/2[2]	81	38
2652[2]	**Slip Jig (IRE) (72)** (KRBurke) **4-9-2** JQuinn(4) (b.nr fore: hld up: hdwy on ins 3f out: n.m.r: nt qckn appr fnl f)	1½	5	5/1[3]	75	32
2763[3]	**Ordained (62)** (EJAlston) **4-8-1**(5)ow3 TEDurcan(2) (trckd ldrs: effrt over 3f out: kpt on fnl 2f: no imp)	hd	6	13/2	65	19
2729[7]	**Break the Rules (84)** (DNicholls) **5-9-9**(5) PRoberts(1) (lw: hld up: nvr nr to chal)	½	7	7/1	86	43
	High Pyrenees (71) (FMurphy) **5-9-1** JFanning(7) (bhd: pushed along ½-wy: n.d)	4	8	33/1	68	25
2548[2]	**Swiftway (64)** (KWHogg) **3-7-5**(5) IonaWands(8) (led tl over 3f out: wknd over 2f out)	1	9	16/1	60	5

(SP 125.7%) **9 Rn**

2m 37.9 (4.40) CSF £30.07 CT £192.80 TOTE £2.80: £1.20 £3.20 £3.10 (£27.10) Trio £94.60 OWNER Riley Partnership (MALTON) BRED A. and Mrs Rhodes
LONG HANDICAP Gold Desire 7-6 Swiftway 7-5
WEIGHT FOR AGE 3yo-12lb
2514 Tessajoe, who seems better than ever, travelled strongly but, in the end, there was next to nothing to spare. (7/4)
2660 Gold Desire, from 4lb out of the handicap, ran right up to his very best. (14/1)
2494 Leviticus (IRE) is proving hard to win with and he hung right and on to the running rail here. (10/1)
1832* Infatuation, from a 5lb higher mark, had to switch to the outside to get a run but, once there, he persisted in hanging back right. He is not a straightforward ride. (7/2: 5/2-4/1)
2652 Slip Jig (IRE), trying for an ambitious run up the inner, probably ran close to his best. (5/1)
2763 Ordained shaped well and gave the impression she will soon regain top form. (13/2)
2528 Break the Rules had a quiet run round and, no doubt, his new connections are hoping the Handicapper shows some mercy. (7/1)
High Pyrenees, who won a maiden at Ayr over two years ago, has had his fore-legs fired. (33/1)

2890 LEEDS HOSPITAL FUND H'CAP (0-80) (3-Y.O+) (Class D)

4-40 (4-42) **1m 2f** £3,850.00 (£1,150.00: £550.00: £250.00) Stalls: High GOING minus 0.42 sec per fur (F)

				SP	RR	SF
2678[6]	**Sandmoor Chambray (77)** (TDEasterby) **6-9-11** LCharnock(12) (mde all: styd on wl fnl f)	—	1	11/2[3]	87	59
1981[13]	**Hazard a Guess (IRE) (80)** (DNicholls) **7-10-0** AlexGreaves(1) (hld up: hdwy over 2f out: styd on strly ins fnl f)	½	2	10/1	89	61
2512*	**Wathbat Nashwan (79)** (LMCumani) **3-9-0**(3) RFfrench(2) (lw: trckd ldrs: rdn & ev ch over 1f out: nt qckn)	nk	3	5/2[1]	88	50
2686[4]	**Gymcrak Premiere (72)** (GHolmes) **9-9-6** TLucas(10) (b.hind: trckd ldrs: effrt over 3f out: n.m.r 2f out: styd on one pce)	1½	4	9/1	78	50
2328[3]	**Ibin St James (69)** (JDBethell) **3-8-7b** TWilliams(9) (chsd ldrs: rdn & hung lft over 2f out: sn outpcd)	5	5	8/1	67	29
2205[9]	**Lay The Blame (73)** (MDHammond) **4-9-7** AMcGlone(6) (hld up: hdwy on outside over 2f out: edgd rt: nvr nr to chal)	nk	6	10/1	71	43
2546*	**Dispol Gem (66)** (PCalver) **4-8-11**(3) DarrenMoffatt(5) (chsd ldrs: effrt over 3f out: sn rdn: no imp)	1¾	7	8/1	61	33
2686*	**Ambidextrous (IRE) (61)** (EJAlston) **5-8-4**(5) TEDurcan(4) (lw: in tch: effrt over 3f out: nvr nr to chal)	s.h	8	4/1[2]	56	28
2546[4]	**Impulsive Air (IRE) (62)** (EWeymes) **5-8-10** JQuinn(8) (in tch: drvn along over 3f out: sn outpcd)	1	9	12/1	55	27

					SP	RR	SF
1979^{16}	**Censor (80)**	(DNicholls) **4-9-9**(5) PRoberts(7) (dwlt s: hld up & plld very hard: nvr nr ldrs)	½	**10**	25/1	73	45
2470*	**White Plains (IRE) (79)**	(KRBurke) **4-9-10**(3) GParkin(11) (hld up: hdwy 4f out: rdn & wknd over 2f out)	¾	**11**	9/1	70	42
2156^{5}	**Quaint Desire (49)**	(MBrittain) **4-7-11** DaleGibson(3) (a in rr)	8	**12**	33/1	28	—

(SP 138.8%) **12 Rn**

2m 5.4 (1.90) CSF £64.36 CT £166.67 TOTE £8.80: £2.20 £4.00 £1.60 (£45.30) Trio £60.80 OWNER Sandmoor Textiles Co Ltd (MALTON) BRED P. and Mrs Venner
WEIGHT FOR AGE 3yo-10lb

2678 Sandmoor Chambray, given a positive ride, certainly seemed to stay the trip alright. (11/2)
1145 Hazard a Guess (IRE), running from a mark 2lb lower than when he last won a handicap at Newcastle eleven months ago, was in no hurry to join issue. Woken up inside the last, he almost caught the winner unawares. (10/1)
2512* Wathbat Nashwan, from a 7lb higher mark, travelled strongly and looked sure to pick off the winner at any time but, under pressure, he could only stay on at the same pace. He is well worth another chance. (5/2: op 6/4)
2686 Gymcrak Premiere, racing towards the inner, was messed about by the winner but would still have only have finished fourth. (9/1)
2328 Ibin St James seemed to appreciate this much faster ground. (8/1)
2686* Ambidextrous (IRE), despite his Chester success, is regarded by connections as being a better horse going right-handed. (4/1)

2891 LEEDS CORN EXCHANGE SHOPS MAIDEN H'CAP (0-70) (3-Y.O+) (Class E)
5-10 (5-13) **6f** £3,210.00 (£960.00: £460.00: £210.00) Stalls: Low GOING minus 0.42 sec per fur (F)

					SP	RR	SF
2177^{2}	**Aquatic Queen (50)**	(CADwyer) **3-8-8**(5) TEDurcan(1) (lw: trckd ldr: led over 1f out: r.o wl)	—	**1**	$9/2^{2}$	61	33
2313^{2}	**Gay Breeze (38)**	(PSFelgate) **4-8-6** DWright(2) (led tl over 1f out: kpt on same pce)	2	**2**	$9/4^{1}$	44	21
2510^{4}	**Presentiment (51)**	(MartynWane) **3-9-0** SWebster(5) (s.i.s: hrd rdn & styd on appr fnl f)	2	**3**	10/1	51	23
1963^{13}	**Madam Zando (29)**	(JBalding) **4-7-11**ow1 NCarlisle(4) (lw: bhd tl styd on appr fnl f)	½	**4**	33/1	28	4
2732^{7}	**Dona Filipa (39)**	(MissLCSiddall) **4-8-4**(3) DarrenMoffatt(9) (bhd tl styd on wl appr fnl f)	nk	**5**	14/1	37	14
2788^{12}	**Ohnonotagain (33)**	(LRLloyd-James) **5-8-1** KimTinkler(8) (a chsng ldrs: rdn over 2f out: one pce)	1	**6**	20/1	29	6
2169^{8}	**Mill End Boy (53)**	(MWEasterby) **3-9-2v**[1] TLucas(11) (bhd: hdwy over 1f out: nvr nr ldrs)	4	**7**	11/1	38	10
2121^{3}	**Gain Line (USA) (54)**	(BobJones) **4-9-8** AMcGlone(15) (mid div: rdn over 2f out: no imp)	nk	**8**	$7/1^{3}$	38	15
2540^{5}	**Maydoro (44)**	(MDods) **4-8-12** MGallagher(6) (swtg: s.i.s: bhd: hdwy & hung rt 2f out: n.d)	4	**9**	14/1	17	—
2313^{21}	**Colonel's Pride (45)**	(RMWhitaker) **3-8-8** VHalliday(17) (swtg: racd far side: n.d)	s.h	**10**	33/1	18	—
2313^{20}	**In Good Nick (60)**	(MWEasterby) **3-9-6b**(3) GParkin(13) (in tch: rdn & outpcd ½-wy: sn lost pl)	1½	**11**	10/1	29	1
2657^{2}	**Belbay Star (31)**	(JLEyre) **4-7-13b** TWilliams(14) (hdwy u.p over 2f out: sn wknd)	6	**12**	$7/1^{3}$	—	—
2354^{6}	**Tom Pladdey (34)**	(RBastiman) **3-7-11b** JQuinn(7) (a bhd)	¾	**13**	20/1	—	—
2235^{3}	**Star of The Road (44)**	(JMCarr) **3-8-7** LCharnock(10) (chsd ldrs tl lost pl over 2f out)	¾	**14**	9/1	—	—
2659^{2}	**Fisiostar (44)**	(MDods) **4-8-12b** DaleGibson(3) (a bhd)	¾	**15**	8/1	—	—
2547^{9}	**Tom Mi Dah (61)**	(MDHammond) **3-9-3**(7) NHorrocks(12) (a bhd)	3½	**16**	25/1	—	—
2704^{11}	**Petsong (40)**	(VSoane) **3-8-3** JFanning(16) (racd far side: bhd fnl 2f)	3½	**17**	33/1	—	—

(SP 157.1%) **17 Rn**

1m 12.5 (2.00) CSF £16.64 CT £104.23 TOTE £5.10: £1.80 £1.60 £4.50 £9.50 (£6.50) Trio £85.80 OWNER Mr J. Johnston (NEWMARKET)
BRED Joseph H. Johnston
LONG HANDICAP Madam Zando 7-8
WEIGHT FOR AGE 3yo-5lb
IN-FOCUS: **A low draw seemed a big advantage. The first two were drawn one and two and only those two horses ever got into contention.**
2177 Aquatic Queen, drawn one, looked really well on her first outing for her new trainer and, after tracking the leader travelling strongly, she took this in comfortable fashion. (9/2)
2313 Gay Breeze broke smartly and made the running but could never shake off the winner. (9/4: op 4/1)
2510 Presentiment, who missed the break, stayed on under an enthusiastic ride. (10/1)
1332 Madam Zando, who showed a glimmer of ability last year, ran easily her best race so far this season. (33/1)
2496 Dona Filipa may be worth a try over six. (14/1)

T/Plpt: £18.60 (755.92 Tckts). T/Qdpt: £7.00 (83.46 Tckts) WG

2700-WARWICK (L-H) (Good to firm)
Saturday July 19th
WEATHER: fine WIND: nil

2892 CLASSIC COTTAGE CARNIVAL APPRENTICE H'CAP (0-70) (3-Y.O+) (Class F)
6-35 (6-36) **7f** £2,406.50 (£684.00: £339.50) Stalls: Low GOING minus 0.34 sec per fur (GF)

					SP	RR	SF
2205^{15}	**King Athelstan (USA) (59)**	(BAMcMahon) **9-8-13**(6) SRighton(3) (a.p: led over 4f out: clr over 1f out: all out)	—	**1**	$7/1^{2}$	61	45
2543^{5}	**The Barnsley Belle (IRE) (46)**	(JLEyre) **4-7-12**(8)ow3 SBuckley(2) (hld up: gd hdwy on ins over 1f out: r.o wl ins fnl f)	hd	**2**	$7/1^{2}$	48	29
2646^{2}	**Dr Woodstock (43)**	(MartynMeade) **3-7-2**(8) RBrisland(4) (hdwy over 4f out: r.o ins fnl f)	s.h	**3**	$4/1^{1}$	45	22
2282^{6}	**Digpast (IRE) (39)**	(JJBridger) **7-7-13** PDoe(1) (bhd tl gd hdwy fnl f: fin wl)	½	**4**	25/1	40	24
2179^{7}	**Press Again (42)**	(PHayward) **5-7-11**(5)ow5 DHayden(8) (hdwy over 1f out: r.o ins fnl f)	¾	**5**	50/1	41	20
2552*	**Whatever's Right (IRE) (66)**	(MDIUsher) **8-9-7**(5) GHannon(13) (swtg: lost pl bnd 3f out: styd on fnl f)	½	**6**	$4/1^{1}$	64	48
2395^{6}	**Havago (61)**	(RHannon) **3-8-6**(8) RSmith(6) (a.p: one pce fnl 2f)	1¼	**7**	$15/2^{3}$	56	33
2220^{7}	**Rock Symphony (68)**	(WJHaggas) **7-10-0** RStudholme(7) (nvr nrr)	hd	**8**	10/1	63	47
2169^{4}	**Hever Golf Mover (60)**	(TJNaughton) **3-8-5**(8) RachaelMoody(12) (nvr nr ldrs)	¾	**9**	10/1	53	30
2418^{9}	**Northern Judge (40)**	(APJames) **4-7-11b**(3) JFowle(10) (a bhd)	3½	**10**	25/1	25	9
2228^{12}	**Fairly Sure (IRE) (36)**	(NEBerry) **4-7-5**(5) PBradley(9) (prom 4f: sddle slipped)	¾	**11**	33/1	19	3
	Leguard Express (IRE) (38)	(OO'Neill) **9-7-12b**ow1 PFredericks(5) (led over 2f: wknd over 1f out)	nk	**12**	14/1	21	4
2174^{16}	**Gulf of Siam (43)**	(EAWheeler) **4-7-11**(6) SCarson(11) (bhd fnl 3f)	3	**13**	33/1	19	3

(SP 117.1%) **13 Rn**

1m 27.1 (2.50) CSF £46.58 CT £175.01 TOTE £8.70: £3.00 £2.00 £1.60 (£21.90) Trio £28.50 OWNER Mr Ian Guise (TAMWORTH) BRED Brushwood Stable
LONG HANDICAP Fairly Sure (IRE) 7-8
WEIGHT FOR AGE 3yo-7lb

OFFICIAL EXPLANATION Fairly Sure (IRE): saddle slipped.
1005* King Athelstan (USA), was 2lb higher than when winning a similar event over seven here in May. (7/1)
2543 The Barnsley Belle (IRE) has slipped to a competitive mark on grass but could not quite pull it off. (7/1)
2646 Dr Woodstock, raised 1lb, is knocking on the door. (4/1)
2282 Digpast (IRE) has plummeted down the ratings on grass this season. He did not seem suited by this shorter distance but seems to be running into form. (25/1)
Press Again appears to be having problems finding her best trip. (50/1)
2552* Whatever's Right (IRE), up 3lb, was 6lb higher than when winning this race last year. (4/1)

2893 TATTERSALLS MAIDEN AUCTION STKS (2-Y.O) (Class E)

7-05 (7-13) **7f** £3,408.25 (£1,021.00: £490.50: £225.25) Stalls: Low GOING minus 0.34 sec per fur (GF)

				SP	RR	SF
2388[2]	**High Sheriff (IRE)** (WJHaggas) **2-8-10** KFallon(2) (mde all: clr 2f out: easily)	—	1	8/13[1]	83+	48
2524[9]	**Primavera** (MJHaynes) **2-8-2**ow1 JFEgan(7) (chsd wnr: no imp fnl 2f)	3	2	33/1	68	32
	Lucky Myst (CEBrittain) **2-8-6** WJO'Connor(5) (w'like: bit bkwd: a.p: one pce fnl 3f)	2½	3	14/1	66	31
2500[6]	**Cool Secret** (ABMulholland) **2-8-7** MRoberts(11) (plld hrd: a.p: btn whn hung lft over 1f out)	s.h	4	12/1[3]	67	32
2509[8]	**Mystagogue** (RHannon) **2-8-9** DaneO'Neill(6) (no hdwy fnl 3f)	2	5	10/1[2]	65	30
2388[9]	**Miss Skye (IRE)** (TJNaughton) **2-8-2** TSprake(15) (nvr nrr)	3½	6	33/1	50	15
2147[4]	**Muftuffenuf** (PRWebber) **2-8-3** DHarrison(12) (hdwy over 3f out: wknd 2f out)	1½	7	10/1[2]	47	12
	Stalwart Legion (IRE) (JWHills) **2-8-3** GDuffield(9) (w'like: bkwd: a bhd)	3	8	25/1	41	6
2562[8]	**Dance To The Beat** (MartynMeade) **2-8-1** FNorton(13) (prom over 3f)	2½	9	12/1[3]	33	—
2534[13]	**Belle de Montfort** (JLSpearing) **2-8-0** NVarley(8) (a bhd)	2	10	50/1	27	—
2693[8]	**Zuryaf (IRE)** (BJMeehan) **2-8-12** MTebbutt(4) (lw: n.d)	1¼	11	10/1[2]	36	1
2500[11]	**Saint Albert** (PTWalwyn) **2-8-6v[1]** DHolland(14) (prom over 3f)	4	12	20/1	21	—
1251[12]	**Espresso** (JWHills) **2-8-6** NAdams(3) (a bhd)	3½	13	25/1	13	—
2509[9]	***Petane (IRE)*** (JRArnold) **2-8-6**(3) AWhelan(1) (Withdrawn not under Starter's orders: ref to ent stalls)		W		—	—
1664[7]	***Make It So*** (JSMoore) **2-7-8**(5) RMullen(10) (Withdrawn not under Starter's orders: unruly s: ref to ent stalls)		W		—	—
				(SP 131.5%)	**13 Rn**	

1m 26.1 (1.50) CSF £40.84 TOTE £1.40: £1.10 £11.10 £3.90 (£34.20) Trio £158.50; £160.79 to Ayr 21/7/97 OWNER Highclere Thoroughbred Racing Ltd (NEWMARKET) BRED M. J. Dargan
2388 High Sheriff (IRE), a half-brother to Hand of Straw, dominated the race throughout over this extra furlong. (8/13)
Primavera, who only cost 3,000 gns, appreciated the combination of faster ground and ease in grade but proved no match for the winner. (33/1)
Lucky Myst is a half-brother to Group One winner Lapierre and useful sprinter Lucky Hunter. He will be sharper for the outing. (14/1: 10/1-16/1)
2500 Cool Secret, trying a longer trip, broke well this time but ran too freely. (12/1)
Mystagogue is a half-brother to dual six furlong scorer Lamorna. (10/1: 6/1-12/1)
Miss Skye (IRE) is a half-sister to Katy-Q. (33/1)

2894 KING OF COTTAGES LIMITED STKS (0-85) (3-Y.O+) (Class D)

7-35 (7-43) **7f** £3,645.60 (£1,087.80: £519.40: £235.20) Stalls: Low GOING minus 0.34 sec per fur (GF)

				SP	RR	SF
2690[5]	**Divina Luna (84)** (JWHills) **4-9-0** MRoberts(6) (lw: a.p: rdn to ld 1f out: r.o wl)	—	1	7/1	94	66
1874[3]	**Volley (IRE) (83)** (MajorDNChappell) **4-9-0** DHarrison(5) (lw: a.p: ev ch 1f out: nt qckn)	¾	2	14/1	92	64
2380[3]	**Apache Star (84)** (GWragg) **3-8-7v[1]** MHills(3) (a.p: led over 2f out to 1f out: one pce)	1¼	3	10/1	89	54
	Consort (85) (MrsAJPerrett) **4-9-3** AClark(1) (bit bkwd: hld up: hdwy on ins over 2f out: swtchd rt over 1f out: r.o)	1	4	16/1	90	62
2561[3]	**Arruhan (IRE) (85)** (PTWalwyn) **3-8-7** RHills(2) (hld up: hdwy 3f out: one pce fnl 2f)	2	5	9/2[2]	83	48
	The In-Laws (IRE) (84) (SirMarkPrescott) **3-8-7** GDuffield(8) (nvr nr to chal)	½	6	6/1[3]	81	46
2143*	**Dundel (IRE) (80)** (BWHills) **3-8-6**(3) RFfrench(10) (lost pl 5f out: rallied over 1f out: one pce)	nk	7	7/1	83	48
2649*	**Dayville (USA) (86)** (JBerry) **3-8-11** DHolland(7) (led over 4f: wknd over 1f out)	½	8	9/1	84	49
2013[24]	**Kaiser Kache (IRE) (83)** (KMcAuliffe) **3-8-12** JFEgan(9) (prom over 4f: t.o)	15	9	16/1	50	15
2775[4]	**Alamein (USA) (85)** (WJHaggas) **4-9-3b** KFallon(4) (hld up: rdn over 3f out: t.o fnl 2f)	18	10	3/1[1]	7	—
				(SP 120.0%)	**10 Rn**	

1m 24.9 (0.30) CSF £93.47 TOTE £7.80: £2.50 £3.60 £2.30 (£52.90) OWNER Mr D. J. Deer (LAMBOURN) BRED Azienda Agricola Colle Cardella
WEIGHT FOR AGE 3yo-7lb
OFFICIAL EXPLANATION Alamein (USA): could not act on the ground.
2690 Divina Luna appreciated this drop in class and repeated last season's win in this event. (7/1)
1874 Volley (IRE), lightly raced, put in another sound effort. (14/1)
2380 Apache Star, tried in a visor, was taking a big drop in distance on faster ground. (10/1)
Consort made a highly respectable seasonal debut and a step up to a mile can pay dividends. (16/1)
2561 Arruhan (IRE) was a bit disappointing. (9/2)
The In-Laws (IRE) should do better in due course but might need further now. (6/1)

2895 DAVID WINTER INTERNATIONAL MOUSE LIMITED STKS (0-70) (3-Y.O+) (Class E)

8-05 (8-10) **5f** £3,018.25 (£901.00: £430.50: £195.25) Stalls: Low GOING minus 0.34 sec per fur (GF)

				SP	RR	SF
2581[2]	**Mousehole (70)** (RGuest) **5-9-2** PBloomfield(2) (hdwy 2f out: led ins fnl f: r.o wl)	—	1	9/4[2]	69	48
2590[2]	**Tuscan Dawn (71)** (JBerry) **7-8-11**(5) PRoberts(1) (chsd ldr: led over 1f out tl ins fnl f)	1	2	2/1[1]	66	45
2703[6]	**Windrush Boy (44)** (MRBosley) **7-8-11**(5) AimeeCook(4) (hld up: hdwy over 1f out: r.o)	¾	3	33/1	63	42
2497[6]	**Tart and a Half (69)** (JLEyre) **5-8-13b** KFallon(9) (a.p: one pce fnl 2f)	1¼	4	7/2[3]	56	35
2422[13]	**Imposing Time (62)** (MissGayKelleway) **6-8-13v**(3) RFfrench(7) (hld up: hdwy over 1f out: one pce ins fnl f)	½	5	14/1	58	37
2581[8]	**Superlao (BEL) (44)** (JJBridger) **5-8-9**(7) PDoe(3) (prom: lost pl over 2f out: rallying on ins whn nt clr run ins fnl f)	1	6	33/1	55	34
2422[12]	**Depreciate (67)** (CJames) **4-9-2v[1]** CRutter(6) (prom 3f)	hd	7	12/1	54	33
2703[7]	**Captain Sinbad (41)** (KSBridgwater) **5-9-2b** VSlattery(8) (led over 3f: wknd ins fnl f)	nk	8	50/1	53	32
2300[6]	**Brin-Lodge (IRE) (28)** (KSBridgwater) **4-8-13b** SDrowne(5) (a bhd)	4	9	100/1	38	17
2197[5]	**Another Batchworth (62)** (EAWheeler) **5-8-8b**(5) ADaly(10) (s.s: sn chsng ldrs: wknd 2f out)	3	10	8/1	28	7
				(SP 120.6%)	**10 Rn**	

59.3 secs (1.30) CSF £6.68 TOTE £3.10: £1.80 £1.60 £2.50 (£3.50) OWNER Mrs Janet Linskey (NEWMARKET) BRED T. H. Rossiter

2581 Mousehole appreciated the fast ground and underlined the fact that he does not need last season's headgear to do the business. (9/4)
2590 Tuscan Dawn ran right up to his form but met one too good. (2/1)
2703 Windrush Boy would have been meeting the first two on much better terms in a handicap but does run well over this course. (33/1)
2497 Tart and a Half had finished a length behind the winner at level weights at Ripon last month. (7/2)
Imposing Time was dropping back from six. (14/1)
2321* Superlao (BEL) had a stiff task at the weights but was unlucky not to finish closer. (33/1)
2162 Depreciate (12/1: op 8/1)

2896 DAVID WINTER FAIRYTALE CHALLENGE (S) H'CAP (0-60) (3-Y.O+) (Class G)
8-35 (8-35) **1m 4f 115y** £1,984.50 (£547.00: £259.50) Stalls: Low GOING minus 0.34 sec per fur (GF)

				SP	RR	SF
2727^{2}	**Le Grand Gousier (USA) (52)** (RJRWilliams) **3-8-10** MHills(6) (mde all: rdn over 3f out: r.o wl)	—	**1**	3/1^{2}	63	32
2701*	**Arzani (USA) (57)** (DJSCosgrove) **6-10-0** MRimmer(2) (b: a.p: chsd wnr fnl f: nt qckn)	1¼	**2**	9/4^{1}	66	48
2531^{3}	**Excelled (IRE) (30)** (CJDrewe) **8-8-1** TSprake(1) (hld up: stdy hdwy on ins 4f out: one pce fnl f)	2	**3**	8/1	37	19
2488^{16}	**Scottish Park (30)** (MCPipe) **8-7-10b**$^{(5)}$ APolli(8) (hdwy 9f out: jnd wnr 6f out: one pce fnl 2f)	¾	**4**	12/1	36	18
2701^{4}	**Whothehellisharry (36)** (PTDalton) **4-8-4**$^{(3)}$ PMcCabe(9) (lw: a.p: no hdwy fnl 3f)	s.h	**5**	7/1	42	24
1926^{14}	**I'm a Nut Man (36)** (CASmith) **6-8-7** CRutter(10) (b: hld up: hdwy 3f out: one pce fnl 2f)	1	**6**	11/1	41	23
2753^{3}	**Risky Rose (42)** (RHollinshead) **5-8-10**$^{(3)}$ DGriffiths(5) (lw: lost pl 5f out: styd on fnl 2f)	¾	**7**	6/1^{3}	46	28
2000^{12}	**Monis (IRE) (35)** (RonaldThompson) **6-8-6** TWilliams(7) (hld up: hdwy over 3f out: wknd over 1f out)	2½	**8**	11/1	35	17
2531^{8}	**Bresil (USA) (25)** (JJBridger) **8-7-3**$^{(7)}$ PDoe(4) (b: plld hrd: bhd fnl 4f)	5	**9**	33/1	19	1
2279^{12}	**Gracious Imp (USA) (28)** (JRJenkins) **4-7-13** JQuinn(3) (prom over 8f: t.o)	26	**10**	33/1	—	—

(SP 123.9%) **10 Rn**

2m 43.1 (5.60) CSF £9.96 CT £45.52 TOTE £3.90: £1.60 £1.60 £1.90 (£4.00) OWNER Entente Cordiale (NEWMARKET) BRED La Haras Inc
LONG HANDICAP Bresil (USA) 7-4
WEIGHT FOR AGE 3yo-13lb
Bt in 7,800 gns
2727 Le Grand Gousier (USA), given a canny ride from the front, went for home leaving the back straight. (3/1)
2701* Arzani (USA), 3lb higher than when winning here a week ago, appeared to stay the longer trip well enough. (9/4)
2531 Excelled (IRE) could not sustain a promising-looking run. (8/1)
Scottish Park, down 10lb, had faster ground this time but has never scored beyond a mile and a quarter. (12/1)
2701 Whothehellisharry was probably not suited by this longer distance. (7/1)
1383 I'm a Nut Man was another trying a longer trip. (11/1)

2897 RICHARD III CLASSIC H'CAP (0-80) (3-Y.O) (Class D)
9-05 (9-06) **1m 2f 169y** £3,613.75 (£1,078.00: £514.50: £232.75) Stalls: Low GOING minus 0.34 sec per fur (GF)

				SP	RR	SF
2645^{6}	**Tangshan (CAN) (68)** (MRStoute) **3-8-10** MHills(5) (mde all: clr 2f out: eased ins fnl f)	—	**1**	7/2^{2}	81	32
2285^{3}	**Dead Aim (IRE) (75)** (IABalding) **3-9-3** BDoyle(6) (hld up in rr: rdn over 3f out: hdwy 2f out: wnt 2nd 1f out: no ch w wnr)	3	**2**	13/8^{1}	84	35
2379^{5}	**Pennys From Heaven (79)** (HCandy) **3-9-7b^{1}** CRutter(1) (chsd wnr: rdn over 3f out: wknd wl over 1f out)	3½	**3**	4/1^{3}	82	33
2522^{2}	**Silvery (54)** (JARToller) **3-7-10** JQuinn(3) (hld up: rdn over 3f out: no hdwy fnl 2f)	1¼	**4**	13/2	56	7
2695^{3}	**Begorrat (IRE) (74)** (BJMeehan) **3-9-2** MTebbutt(4) (hld up: bhd fnl 2f)	15	**5**	9/2	53	4

(SP 111.8%) **5 Rn**

2m 18.7 (4.70) CSF £8.95 TOTE £3.70: £1.70 £1.40 (£2.80) OWNER The Hon Mrs Edgar & Partners (NEWMARKET) BRED Gainsborough Farm Inc and La Ferme du Paturage Inc
LONG HANDICAP Silvery 7-9
2645 Tangshan (CAN), down 2lb, settled much better at the head of affairs over this longer trip. (7/2)
2285 Dead Aim (IRE), again up in distance, was never going to get near the winner. (13/8)
1868 Pennys From Heaven was tried in blinkers after an abysmal run on soft ground last time. (4/1)
2522 Silvery had finished second on soft ground in a poor race last time. (13/2)

T/Plpt: £32.10 (360.29 Tckts). T/Qdpt: £9.10 (76.15 Tckts) KH

2854-AYR (L-H) (Good to firm)
Monday July 21st
WEATHER: sunny WIND: slt against

2898 E.B.F. MAIDEN STKS (2-Y.O) (Class D)
2-15 (2-16) **7f** £3,779.00 (£1,142.00: £556.00: £263.00) Stalls: Low GOING minus 0.16 sec per fur (GF)

				SP	RR	SF
2363^{2}	**Rico Suave (IRE)** (SirMarkPrescott) **2-9-0** SSanders(4) (mde all: rdn appr fnl f: r.o wl)	—	**1**	5/2^{2}	80	29
2524^{3}	**Marran (IRE)** (JLDunlop) **2-9-0** KDarley(3) (hld up: effrt ½-wy: hung lft over 2f out: kpt on: no imp)	4	**2**	4/7^{1}	71	20
2324^{3}	**Tearaway** (JWWatts) **2-9-0** JCarroll(2) (last tl hdwy u.p 3f out: nvr able chal)	4	**3**	12/1^{3}	62	11
	Swaybus (MJohnston) **2-8-9** JWeaver(1) (str: cmpt: bit bkwd: cl up tl wknd wl over 2f out)	8	**4**	16/1	38	—

(SP 105.8%) **4 Rn**

1m 29.18 (4.78) CSF £3.83 TOTE £3.50: (£1.60) OWNER Mr Haydn Kelly (NEWMARKET) BRED Eclipse Bloodstock
2363 Rico Suave (IRE) won this particularly well and is seriously getting his act together, and there looks to be more to come. (5/2)
2524 Marran (IRE), a handy sort, had his chances but also had his limitations exposed, and his tendency to hang under pressure leaves a question mark. (4/7)
2324 Tearaway always seemed to find this ground a bit too quick for his liking and could never get in a blow. (12/1: op 8/1)
Swaybus is built like the proverbial brick outhouse, but needed this and blew up some way from home. (16/1)

2899 JOE PUNTER (S) H'CAP (0-60) (3-Y.O+) (Class F)
2-45 (2-49) **5f** £2,780.00 (£780.00: £380.00) Stalls: Low GOING minus 0.16 sec per fur (GF)

				SP	RR	SF
2780^{6}	**Delrob (35)** (DHaydnJones) **6-8-3b** AMackay(4) (outpcd far side: hdwy 2f out: r.o to ld ins fnl f)	—	**1**	6/1^{2}	45	2
2759^{8}	**The Wad (60)** (DNicholls) **4-9-7**$^{(7)}$ TSiddall(9) (a chsng ldrs centre: rdn 2f out: kpt on wl: nrst fin)	½	**2**	8/1	68	25
2828*	**Seconds Away (36)** (JSGoldie) **6-8-4b** 6x TWilliams(7) (hdwy centre 2f out: styd on wl towards fin)	2	**3**	10/1	38	—

2754[4]	**Imp Express (IRE) (40)** (GMMoore) **4-8-8** JWeaver(2) (lw: chsd ldrs far side: hrd rdn over 1f out: nt qckn) ...	1¾	**4**	8/1	36	—
2540[12]	**Ready Teddy (IRE) (36)** (MissLAPerratt) **4-8-4v[1]** KDarley(3) (led & sn clr far side: hdd & no ex ins fnl f)	½	**5**	14/1	31	—
2738[8]	**Answers-To-Thomas (38)** (JMJefferson) **4-8-6b[1]** WRyan(5) (swtg: chsd ldrs far side: nt qckn fnl 2f)	1¾	**6**	20/1	27	—
2317[10]	**Gormire (30)** (JHetherton) **4-7-12b** DaleGibson(1) (unruly gng to s: rel to r & sn t.o: r.o fnl f)	1	**7**	20/1	16	—
2674[3]	**Marjorie Rose (IRE) (59)** (ABailey) **4-9-13** SSanders(15) (b.hind: racd stands' side: sn outpcd)	1¾	**8**	11/2[1]	39	—
2759[5]	**Featherstone Lane (48)** (MissLCSiddall) **6-9-2** AMcGlone(13) (racd stands' side: sn drvn along: nvr trbld ldrs)	1¼	**9**	8/1	24	—
2659[3]	**Leading Princess (IRE) (49)** (MissLAPerratt) **6-9-3b** JCarroll(10) (spd centre 3f)........	2	**10**	13/2[3]	19	—
1963[12]	**L A Touch (43)** (JJQuinn) **4-8-11** JStack(14) (racd stands' side: rdn ½-wy: no imp)........	1¼	**11**	7/1	9	—
2657[10]	**Lord Cornelious (33)** (DANolan) **4-7-10**(5)ow5 KSked(6) (racd centre: outpcd fr ½-wy)........	s.h	**12**	200/1	—	—
2826[6]	**Another Nightmare (IRE) (46)** (RMMcKellar) **5-8-7**(7) JMcAuley(11) (racd stands' side: rdn ½-wy: no imp after)........	½	**13**	14/1	10	—
2354[9]	**Miss St Kitts (34)** (JSGoldie) **3-7-9v**(3) PFessey(8) (swtg: racd centre: spd to ½-wy)	¾	**14**	100/1	—	—
				(SP 122.3%)		**14 Rn**

61.23 secs (4.23) CSF £48.08 CT £440.33 TOTE £8.10: £3.00 £2.80 £3.10 (£46.30) Trio £439.30 OWNER Mrs E. M. HaydnJones (PONTYPRIDD) BRED J. K. S. Cresswell
LONG HANDICAP Lord Cornelious 7-2
WEIGHT FOR AGE 3yo-4lb
No bid
2780 Delrob is much better on the All-Weather these days but, after getting completely outpaced, she finished strongly to win the day. (6/1)
1662 The Wad ran well and kept responding to pressure and looks in good form just now. (8/1)
2828* Seconds Away just found this trip too sharp, but he certainly finished well and would not have needed much further to get into it. (10/1: 8/1-12/1)
2754 Imp Express (IRE) is a real handful in the preliminaries, but looks well and has ability, although he does not always put it to full use. (8/1)
1311 Ready Teddy (IRE) had a visor on for the first time and showed that she can really shift, but she just failed to see it out. (14/1)
429 Answers-To-Thomas had blinkers on for the first time and had his chances, but he was very edgy and sweaty beforehand and had run himself out approaching the last furlong. (20/1)
Gormire has plenty of ability but refused point-blank to go early on and was soon tailed off, but she finished with a tremendous flourish. If she can be sorted out, races such as this would be easy meat. (20/1)
2674 Marjorie Rose (IRE) prefers easier ground and had no chance from her draw. (11/2)
2826 Another Nightmare (IRE) (14/1: op 8/1)

2900 DAILY RECORD H'CAP (0-90) (3-Y.O+) (Class C)
3-15 (3-18) **6f** £5,407.00 (£1,636.00: £798.00: £379.00) Stalls: Low GOING minus 0.16 sec per fur (GF)

				SP	RR	SF
1259[5]	**Tiler (IRE) (74)** (MJohnston) **5-8-12** JWeaver(8) (lw: a w ldrs: led 2½f out: hld on wl)	—	**1**	7/1	81	39
2857[4]	**Grey Kingdom (75)** (MBrittain) **6-8-6**(7) DMernagh(11) (a w ldrs: disp ld appr fnl f: no ex towards fin)........	nk	**2**	8/1	81	39
2505[6]	**Amron (61)** (JBerry) **10-7-10**(3) PFessey(7) (lw: hdwy 2f out: styd on wl towards fin)	½	**3**	12/1	66	24
2651*	**Myttons Mistake (58)** (ABailey) **4-7-5**(5) IonaWands(13) (prom: outpcd 2f out: kpt on wl fnl f)	1	**4**	10/1	60	18
2721*	**Double Oscar (IRE) (58)** (DNicholls) **4-7-3b**(7) 7x ANicholls(9) (hld up: effrt over 2f out: r.o one pce)	hd	**5**	3/1[1]	60	18
980[8]	**Babsy Babe (89)** (JJQuinn) **4-9-8**(5) TEDurcan(10) (chsd ldrs tl wknd fnl f)........	1¾	**6**	50/1	86	44
2826[4]	**Pallium (IRE) (63)** (DANolan) **9-7-10b**(5)ow5 KSked(6) (sn cl up: led ½-wy: sn hdd: wknd over 1f out)........	2½	**7**	33/1	54	7
2377[8]	**Westcourt Magic (90)** (MWEasterby) **4-10-0** DaleGibson(2) (unruly s: led tl ½-wy: grad wknd)	nk	**8**	13/2[3]	80	38
2711[21]	**Natural Key (69)** (DHaydnJones) **4-8-7** AMackay(14) (outpcd & bhd: sme hdwy 2f out: n.d)........	1½	**9**	8/1	55	13
2711[3]	**Zuhair (90)** (DMcCain) **4-10-0** JCarroll(12) (b: hld up: effrt ½-wy: sn btn)	4	**10**	6/1[2]	65	23
2711[9]	**Mallia (68)** (TDBarron) **4-8-6b** KDarley(4) (effrt ½-wy: no imp)........	1	**11**	12/1	41	—
2517[8]	**Just Visiting (88)** (CaptJWilson) **3-9-0**(7) AngelaHartley(3) (prom 4f: wknd)........	½	**12**	16/1	59	12
2826[5]	**Six for Luck (60)** (DANolan) **5-7-5**(7)ow2 NPollard(1) (dwlt: sn w ldrs: wknd 2f out)	¾	**13**	100/1	29	—
2129[9]	**French Grit (IRE) (78)** (MDods) **5-9-2** WRyan(5) (s.s: a bhd)	7	**14**	12/1	29	—
				(SP 131.3%)		**14 Rn**

1m 12.82 (3.02) CSF £61.60 CT £629.87 TOTE £6.10: £1.70 £2.30 £4.10 (£21.60) Trio £171.60 OWNER Mrs C. Robinson (MIDDLEHAM) BRED J. Mamakos
LONG HANDICAP Myttons Mistake 7-8 Double Oscar (IRE) 7-0 Six for Luck 6-9 Pallium (IRE) 7-0
WEIGHT FOR AGE 3yo-5lb
1259 Tiler (IRE) looked magnificent after over two months off and, off a decent mark, did the business in determined style. (7/1)
2857 Grey Kingdom runs his heart out every time and this was yet another magnificent effort. (8/1)
2505 Amron keeps his condition well and put in a useful effort, but was never quite doing things fast enough. (12/1)
2651* Myttons Mistake probably just found this trip too sharp and, after getting outpaced, was sticking on really well at the end. This was a particularly good effort from his draw. (10/1)
2721* Double Oscar (IRE) is in really good form at the moment but he just found this too competitive for his liking. (3/1)
Babsy Babe, returning after two and a half months off, showed signs of coming back to form. (50/1)
2377 Westcourt Magic, as usual these days was walked to the start, but gave plenty of problems and obviously spent most of his energy. (13/2)
2033 Natural Key is still high enough in the handicap and ran pretty well, particularly from such a high draw. (8/1)

2901 TENNENT CALEDONIAN BREWERIES SCOTTISH CLASSIC STKS (Gp 3) (3-Y.O+) (Class A)
3-45 (3-45) **1m 2f** £21,642.00 (£6,972.00: £3,386.00) Stalls: Low GOING minus 0.16 sec per fur (GF)

				SP	RR	SF
1769[12]	**Crystal Hearted (109)** (HCandy) **3-8-6** AMcGlone(2) (lw: mde all: hld on wl fnl 2f)........	—	**1**	8/1[3]	112	50
1769[6]	**Fahris (IRE) (113)** (BHanbury) **3-8-6** RHills(3) (hld up: hdwy to chal 2f out: hrd rdn: outpcd ins fnl f: kpt on towards fin)	nk	**2**	5/6[1]	112	50
2010[4]	**Even Top (IRE) (119)** (MHTompkins) **4-9-2** WRyan(1) (trckd wnr after 2f: effrt over 2f out: rdn & r.o one pce).	¾	**3**	11/8[2]	110	58
				(SP 107.8%)		**3 Rn**

2m 9.26 (3.46) CSF £13.63 TOTE £7.60: (£3.00) OWNER Mrs C. M. Poland (WANTAGE) BRED Newgate Stud Co
WEIGHT FOR AGE 3yo-10lb
OFFICIAL EXPLANATION **Crystal Hearted: regarding the improved form compared with the Derby, the rider reported that the colt was suited by the drop to ten furlongs and may have been upset by the atmosphere at Epsom.**
1769 Crystal Hearted was without doubt the paddock pick and, given a cracking ride, left his Derby form way behind with a very game

performance. (8/1)
1769 Fahris (IRE) was both edgy and sweaty in the paddock, but looked to be going well for much of the race but, in the end, was comprehensively out-battled. (5/6)
2010 Even Top (IRE) was a shade warm in the preliminaries and, when there was no real early pace, he was sent up to challenge and the tempo immediately increased. However, when the race was seriously on in the last two and a half furlongs, he proved short of toe. Perhaps even more use should be made of him. (11/8)

2902 BURNS COTTAGE MAIDEN STKS (3-Y.O+) (Class D)

4-15 (4-16) **1m 2f** £3,532.00 (£1,066.00: £518.00: £244.00) Stalls: Low GOING minus 0.16 sec per fur (GF)

				SP	RR	SF
1331[3]	**Eshtiaal (USA) (84)** (JLDunlop) **3-8-11b[1]** RHills(4) (lw: sn led: qcknd clr 3f out: unchal)	—	1	1/7[1]	78+	50
2572[4]	**Doubly Sharp (USA)** (MJohnston) **3-8-11** JWeaver(5) (a chsng ldrs: styd on u.p: no ch w wnr)	16	2	7/1[2]	52	24
2420[8]	**Ingleborough** (DMoffatt) **3-8-11** JCarroll(3) (led early: chsd wnr tl wl outpcd fnl 4f)	3½	3	25/1[3]	47	19
2501[8]	**The Vale (IRE)** (RMMcKellar) **5-9-0**(7) JMcAuley(2) (outpcd & lost tch appr st: styd on fnl f: n.d)	1¼	4	100/1	45?	27
2501[7]	**No Problem Jac** (JJO'Neill) **4-8-11**(5) TEDurcan(1) (lw: effrt 4f out: rdn & no imp)	nk	5	40/1	39?	21

(SP 107.3%) **5 Rn**

2m 9.93 (4.13) CSF £1.25 TOTE £1.30: £1.10 £1.60 (£1.50) OWNER Mr Hamdan Al Maktoum (ARUNDEL) BRED Shadwell Farm Inc and Shadwell Estate Co Ltd
WEIGHT FOR AGE 3yo-10lb
1331 Eshtiaal (USA) had blinkers on for the first time and certainly needs them, but found a race that he only had to turn up to win easily. (1/7)
2572 Doubly Sharp (USA) is not very good and really had to struggle to finish second best. (7/1: 5/1-8/1)
Ingleborough looks a likely hurdler and was too slow here. (25/1)
The Vale (IRE) improved a little at this trip but there is a vast amount more needed. (100/1)
No Problem Jac looks well enough but, as yet, has not shown anything positive. (40/1)

2903 GARRY OWEN H'CAP (0-60) (3-Y.O) (Class F)

4-45 (4-45) **7f** £2,883.75 (£870.00: £422.50: £198.75) Stalls: Low GOING minus 0.16 sec per fur (GF)

				SP	RR	SF
2715[2]	**Hi Mujtahid (IRE) (44)** (SEKettlewell) **3-8-6** KDarley(4) (mde most: wandered u.p over 1f out: kpt on wl)	—	1	4/1[2]	56	23
2733*	**High Spirits (IRE) (59)** (TDEasterby) **3-9-2b**(5) TEDurcan(3) (hld up: hdwy 3f out: chal 2f out: wandered u.p: nt qckn towards fin)	¾	2	7/4[1]	69	36
1838[5]	**Murron Wallace (42)** (DHaydnJones) **3-8-4** AMackay(5) (bhd: rdn ½-wy: styd on: no imp)	3	3	6/1	45	12
1756[3]	**Euroquest (40)** (DNicholls) **3-8-2** AMcGlone(8) (lw: sn chsng ldrs: outpcd 3f out: no imp after)	7	4	12/1	27	—
2715[6]	**Naivasha (55)** (JBerry) **3-9-0**(3) PFessey(2) (lw: s.i.s: effrt ½-wy: no imp)	nk	5	11/1	42	9
2715[3]	**Beau Roberto (49)** (JSGoldie) **3-8-11** TWilliams(6) (chsd ldrs tl outpcd fnl 3f)	½	6	5/1[3]	35	2
2659*	**Paldost (46)** (MDHammond) **3-8-8** DaleGibson(7) (swtg: prom tl rdn & wknd over 3f out)	2½	7	10/1	26	—
2715[5]	**Tazibari (48)** (DMoffatt) **3-8-10** JCarroll(1) (in tch: effrt over 3f out: sn btn)	7	8	12/1	12	—

(SP 120.1%) **8 Rn**

1m 29.04 (4.64) CSF £11.01 CT £38.75 TOTE £4.30: £1.60 £1.30 £2.20 (£3.30) OWNER Mr W. B. Imison (MIDDLEHAM) BRED Sheikh Mohammed Obaid Al Maktoum
2715 Hi Mujtahid (IRE) did it well this time, and this would seem to be a much-improved performance. (4/1)
2733* High Spirits (IRE) looked likely to win this from early in the straight, but got slightly unbalanced under pressure and was worried out of it. (7/4)
1838 Murron Wallace ran much better this time and certainly has the ability if she can be persuaded. (6/1)
1756 Euroquest, from a yard in good form, looked particularly well after over six weeks off but may be at his best on the All-Weather. (12/1)
2715 Naivasha looked well enough but did not seem to be co-operating this time. (11/1)
2715 Beau Roberto ran moderately, and it would seem he needs further. (5/1)
2659* Paldost got himself in a state beforehand and did not give his running. (10/1)

T/Plpt: £590.80 (25.79 Tckts). T/Qdpt: £21.90 (46.23 Tckts) AA

2733-BEVERLEY (R-H) (Good to firm)
Monday July 21st

WEATHER: fine & sunny WIND: slt half bhd

2904 SHIPTONTHORPE CLAIMING STKS (2-Y.O) (Class F)

6-35 (6-36) **5f** £2,903.00 (£808.00: £389.00) Stalls: High GOING minus 0.54 sec per fur (F)

				SP	RR	SF
2181[23]	**High Carry** (JEBanks) **2-8-1**(5) CLowther(14) (chsd ldr: led 2f out: drvn out)	—	1	5/1[3]	71	32
2736[4]	**Quiz Master** (EWeymes) **2-8-8v[1]** JQuinn(2) (sn trckng ldrs: ev ch & rdn 1f out: nt qckn)	1¼	2	15/2	67	30
2489[5]	**Figawin** (GLewis) **2-8-4** PaulEddery(12) (b.nr hind: chsd ldrs: kpt on one pce fnl 2f)	5	3	9/2[2]	43	10
1396[13]	**I'm Tef** (TDEasterby) **2-8-9b[1]** LCharnock(10) (chsd ldrs: drvn along ½-wy: hung rt: one pce)	2	4	14/1	42	9
2712[6]	**Penniless (IRE)** (NTinkler) **2-8-4** KimTinkler(15) (led to 2f out: wknd appr fnl f)	hd	5	2/1[1]	36	3
2736[3]	**Miss Eliminator** (MWEasterby) **2-8-2**(3)ow1 GParkin(5) (lw: b.off hind: s.i.s: hdwy & hung rt ½-wy: styd on: nvr nr to chal)	s.h	6	6/1	37	3
2658[4]	**Dispol Lass** (PCalver) **2-7-8**(3) DarrenMoffatt(9) (b.nr hind: bhd tl styd on fnl 2f)	2	7	25/1	23	—
1581[9]	**Gala Miss** (PDEvans) **2-8-2**ow2 JFEgan(13) (outpcd fr ½-wy)	2½	8	20/1	20	—
2739[10]	**Dibola** (JSWainwright) **2-8-11** GDuffield(7) (nvr bttr than mid div)	1	9	33/1	26	—
2553[11]	**Filgrave (IRE)** (CADwyer) **2-8-6v[1]**(3) DO'Donohoe(3) (reminders after s: a bhd)	½	10	14/1	22	—
2304[3]	**Glenstal Lad** (RHollinshead) **2-8-7** ACulhane(1) (hld up: a bhd)	1	11	20/1	17	—
2419[6]	**Sylvan Cloud** (CWFairhurst) **2-7-4v**(7) JennyBenson(6) (sn outpcd: drvn along ½-wy: n.d)	nk	12	33/1	6	—
2022[4]	**The Cannie Rover** (MWEasterby) **2-8-11** TLucas(8) (sn outpcd: nt clr run ½-wy: n.d)	½	13	10/1	18	—
1797[11]	**Mystery Man** (PCHaslam) **2-8-9** JFortune(11) (bit bkwd: unruly in stalls: s.s. sme hdwy ½-wy: sn wknd)	1	14	12/1	13	—
2606[6]	**Pollyteknick** (NPLittmoden) **2-7-13** JLowe(4) (wl bhd fr ½-wy)	6	15	25/1	—	—

(SP 147.4%) **15 Rn**

62.7 secs (0.90) CSF £44.14 TOTE £5.90: £2.00 £2.10 £1.90 (£66.80) Trio £127.70 OWNER Mr Giles Pritchard-Gordon (NEWMARKET) BRED Giles W. Pritchard-Gordon
High Carry clmd Contrac Promotions Limited £12,000

High Carry, all at sea in the mud at Windsor last time, apparently landed some inspired market support. She was claimed and now joins Nigel Tinkler. (5/1)
2736 Quiz Master, in a visor for the first time, was on his toes in the paddock. He ran well from a poor draw and, though not progressing with his racing, he will certainly win a similar event. (15/2)
2489 Figawin, dropped back in distance, was taken to post early. (9/2)
I'm Tef, in blinkers for the first time, was very keen going to post. (14/1)
2712 Penniless (IRE) was hot in the paddock and needed two handlers. She seems to have gone off the boil at present. (2/1)
2736 Miss Eliminator, who has had her shins fired, did not have the run of the race but she contributed to her own trouble. She is not a five-furlong filly. (6/1)
Mystery Man (12/1: op 8/1)

2905 CARIBBEAN NIGHT NOVICE STKS (2-Y.O) (Class D)

7-05 (7-06) **7f 100y** £3,756.00 (£1,128.00: £544.00: £252.00) Stalls: High GOING minus 0.54 sec per fur (F)

			SP	RR	SF
2752*	**Lend A Hand** (MJohnston) **2-9-4** JWeaver(6) (lw: dwlt: sn trckng ldr: led over 1f out: r.o wl towards fin) —	1	6/4[1]	90	55
2584[8]	**Calchas (IRE)** (SirMarkPrescott) **2-9-10** GDuffield(8) (lw: chsd ldrs: effrt over 3f out: styd on fnl f: no imp) 1¼	2	7/2[2]	93	58
2707[4]	**Winsome George** (CWFairhurst) **2-9-4** NKennedy(2) (lw: sn outpcd: hdwy over 3f out: kpt on fnl 2f) 5	3	11/2[3]	77	42
2681[2]	**Out Like Magic** (PDEvans) **2-8-13** JFEgan(5) (chsd ldrs: drvn along 5f out: one pce fnl 2f) 1½	4	11/2[3]	68	33
	Eastern Glory (USA) (MrsJRRamsden) **2-8-12** JFortune(9) (cmpt: unf: s.i.s: shkn up over 2f out: sme hdwy fnl f: nvr nr ldrs) 8	5	10/1	50	15
2680[6]	**Captain McCloy (USA)** (MrsJRRamsden) **2-8-12** OPears(1) (sn bhd: sme hdwy 2f out: n.d) hd	6	20/1	50	15
2467*	**Two Williams** (MWEasterby) **2-9-4** TLucas(3) (plld hrd: led & sn clr: hung rt & hdd over 1f out: wknd & eased) 2	7	15/2	52	17
2499[3]	**Watchman** (TPTate) **2-8-12** NConnorton(4) (sn outpcd & pushed along: nvr nr ldrs) 2½	8	20/1	40	5
			(SP 123.4%)		**8 Rn**

1m 32.3 (0.30) CSF £6.91 TOTE £2.60: £1.30 £1.20 £1.40 (£2.70) Trio £9.20 OWNER Maktoum Al Maktoum (MIDDLEHAM) BRED Gainsborough Stud Management Ltd
2752* Lend A Hand followed up his facile Catterick success, and although he had to work hard, in the end he was right on top. He is a likeable and progressive colt. (6/4)
2215* Calchas (IRE), who is not very big, showed a scratchy action going down but he ran really well under his big weight. (7/2)
2707 Winsome George was struggling to keep up at halfway. Keeping on in his own time, he needs a strongly-run mile. (11/2)
2681 Out Like Magic is nothing to look at but she is certainly tough. (11/2)
Eastern Glory (USA) looked in need of the experience. Showing plenty of knee action going down, he was given an educational run and can only improve for it. (10/1)
2680 Captain McCloy (USA) was having his third outing and now qualifies for a nursery mark. (20/1)
2467* Two Williams, who excelled in a tape start on soft ground over five furlongs here, was very keen going to post. Racing much too freely for his own good and finding trouble handling the bend, he hung right once in line for home as if feeling the fast ground and, dropping right out, was virtually pulled up near the finish. His trainer says he has wind problems but, back over five and on easy ground, there are surely more races to be won with him. (15/2)

2906 JWE MOBILEPHONE GROUP H'CAP (0-70) (3-Y.O+) (Class E)

7-35 (7-37) **7f 100y** £4,440.00 (£1,335.00: £645.00: £300.00) Stalls: High GOING minus 0.54 sec per fur (F)

			SP	RR	SF
2204[6]	**Rymer's Rascal (54)** (EJAlston) **5-8-13** JFEgan(11) (chsd ldrs: led jst ins fnl f: jst hld on) —	1	10/1	66	47
2502[2]	**Euro Sceptic (IRE) (42)** (TDEasterby) **5-7-8b**(7) RWinston(2) (bhd whn hmpd 5f out: hdwy 2f out: styd on wl ins fnl f: jst failed) hd	2	4/1[1]	54	35
2651[10]	**Magic Lake (37)** (EJAlston) **4-7-3v**(7) PBradley(9) (trckd ldrs: led over 1f out tl jst ins fnl f: no ex) ½	3	25/1	48	29
2760[9]	**Thatched (IRE) (53)** (REBarr) **7-8-12** DeanMcKeown(12) (hld up: hdwy over 2f out: n.m.r: styd on fnl f) 1½	4	10/1	61	42
2465[2]	**Night of Glass (58)** (JLEyre) **4-9-3** MGallagher(5) (b: hdwy u.p over 2f out: styd on appr fnl f: nvr nr to chal) ½	5	15/2[3]	64	45
2463[6]	**Oriel Lad (37)** (DonEnricoIncisa) **4-7-10b** KimTinkler(14) (s.i.s: hdwy on ins over 2f out: kpt on same pce fnl f) nk	6	25/1	43	24
2733[3]	**Gipsy Princess (59)** (MWEasterby) **3-8-11** TLucas(8) (chsd ldr tl wknd over 1f out) 1	7	7/1[2]	63	37
2546[7]	**Jedi Knight (68)** (MWEasterby) **3-9-6** LCharnock(3) (s.s: swtchd rt s: hdwy over 2f out: n.m.r over 2f out: nvr nr to chal) hd	8	10/1	71	45
	My Godson (54) (MDods) **7-8-10**(3) CTeague(13) (chsd ldrs: outpcd fnl 2f) ¾	9	33/1	56	37
2672[2]	**Duke Valentino (58)** (RHollinshead) **5-9-0**(3) DGriffiths(10) (bhd whn hmpd 5f out: hdwy 2f out: edgd lft: n.d) ¾	10	10/1	58	39
2733[9]	**Petite Risk (55)** (KWHogg) **3-8-7** JQuinn(15) (led tl over 1f out: sn wknd) ½	11	33/1	54	28
2735*	**Cee-N-K (IRE) (75)** (MJohnston) **3-9-13** 6x BDoyle(6) (lw: bhd & drvn along over 3f out: n.d) 1	12	8/1	72	46
2465[3]	**Superpride (56)** (MrsMReveley) **5-9-1** ACulhane(7) (sn trckng ldrs: hung rt & lost pl over 2f out: eased) 9	13	8/1	34	15
1501[7]	**Gymcrak Flyer (64)** (GHolmes) **6-9-9** JFortune(1) (b.hind: racd wd: bhd & pushed along 3f out: sn wknd & eased) s.h	14	12/1	42	23
2117[7]	**Tassili (IRE) (68)** (LadyHerries) **4-9-13** PaulEddery(4) (chsd ldrs: drvn along 5f out: lost pl over 2f out: eased) nk	15	11/1	45	26
			(SP 132.5%)		**15 Rn**

1m 32.6 (0.60) CSF £47.84 CT £952.23 TOTE £16.00: £3.80 £1.70 £10.20 (£26.50) Trio £472.70; £472.73 to 23/7/97 OWNER Mr Brian Chambers (PRESTON) BRED Mrs Sara Logue and David Lewis
LONG HANDICAP Magic Lake 7-6 Oriel Lad 7-8
WEIGHT FOR AGE 3yo-7lb
1511 Rymer's Rascal made it win number two from thirty-two starts, but he had luck on his side in what was essentially a rough contest. (10/1)
2502 Euro Sceptic (IRE) had it all to do after being hampered when starting the home turn. After having to seek an opening, he really found his stride inside the last and would have won in two more strides. (4/1)
1131 Magic Lake, who has slipped right down the weights, was 4lb out of the handicap. She ran easily her best race this year and can clearly find another opportunity from this sort of mark. (25/1)
2205 Thatched (IRE) won this race last year from a 10lb lower mark. A horse who has to come from the back, like several others he met plenty of trouble. (10/1)
2465 Night of Glass ran with credit on totally different ground. (15/2)
1655 Oriel Lad, from a stable in cracking form, crept up the far rail in the final quarter-mile. (25/1)
2733 Gipsy Princess (7/1: 7/2-8/1)

2546 Jedi Knight, very much on his toes beforehand and very keen to post, ran with credit after a slow break and, like several others, met plenty of trouble. (10/1)

2907 I.J. BLAKEY HAULAGE H'CAP (0-80) (3-Y.O+ F & M) (Class D)

8-05 (8-05) **1m 1f 207y** £4,235.25 (£1,272.00: £613.50: £284.25) Stalls: High GOING minus 0.54 sec per fur (F)

	Horse / details	Dist	Pos	SP	RR	SF
2569*	**Mcgillycuddy Reeks (IRE) (46)** (DonEnricoIncisa) **6-8-2** KimTinkler(1) (sn trckng ldrs: rdn to ld over 2f out: styd on wl fnl f)	—	**1**	8/1	57	23
2043*	**Opalette (72)** (LadyHerries) **4-10-0** JWeaver(2) (lw: led tl over 2f out: nt qckn appr fnl f)	4	**2**	9/4[1]	77	43
2730[6]	**Papita (IRE) (63)** (SDow) **3-8-9** JFEgan(6) (dwlt s: styd on u.p fnl 2f: nvr nr to chal)	1¼	**3**	6/1[3]	66	22
2468*	**Lindrick Lady (IRE) (69)** (BSRothwell) **3-9-1** JFortune(5) (w ldr tl outpcd fnl 2f)	1	**4**	6/1[3]	70	26
2471*	**Lapu-Lapu (54)** (MJCamacho) **4-8-10** LCharnock(7) (trckd ldrs: effrt over 2f out: kpt on same pce fnl 2f)	hd	**5**	3/1[2]	55	21
2502[5]	**Sing And Dance (41)** (EWeymes) **4-7-11** JQuinn(4) (trckd ldrs: rdn & outpcd over 2f out: n.d after)	2½	**6**	7/1	38	4
2757[5]	**Marsh Marigold (67)** (JHetherton) **3-8-6**(7) JennyBenson(3) (hld up: edgd lft & outpcd 3f out: sn bhd)	13	**7**	12/1	43	—

(SP 115.6%) **7 Rn**

2m 5.7 (2.60) CSF £24.60 TOTE £10.10: £3.40 £1.90 (£14.00) OWNER Don Enrico Incisa (MIDDLEHAM) BRED Noel Sweeney
WEIGHT FOR AGE 3yo-10lb

2569* Mcgillycuddy Reeks (IRE), from an 8lb higher mark, took a keen grip and so lay up with the pace in what was a moderately-run race. Vigorously ridden, she came right away in the final furlong. Her stable is in cracking form at present. (8/1)
2043* Opalette, an excitable type, was racing from a 3lb higher mark. Setting just a modest pace, she could not match strides with the winner in the final furlong. (9/4)
2730 Papita (IRE) seemed to appreciate the step-up in distance. (6/1)
2468* Lindrick Lady (IRE), from a 2lb higher mark, was outpaced on this ground in the final quarter-mile in what had been a moderately-run race. (6/1)
2471* Lapu-Lapu, who tends to get a bit excited beforehand, was tapped for foot in the final quarter-mile. This is probably as good as she is. (3/1)
2502 Sing And Dance, still a maiden and lacking any finishing speed, was held up in a moderately-run race. (7/1)

2908 NORWOOD MAIDEN H'CAP (0-65) (3-Y.O) (Class F)

8-35 (8-35) **2m 35y** £2,903.00 (£808.00: £389.00) Stalls: High GOING minus 0.54 sec per fur (F)

	Horse / details	Dist	Pos	SP	RR	SF
2667[4]	**Pen Friend (43)** (WJHaggas) **3-8-1** JLowe(13) (trckd ldrs: led & edgd rt over 1f out: drvn out)	—	**1**	6/1[2]	54	18
1043[2]	**Philosophic (52)** (SirMarkPrescott) **3-8-10** GDuffield(1) (lw: chsd ldrs: pushed along ½-wy: rdn & outpcd 4f out: styd on appr fnl f: no imp towards fin)	1¼	**2**	13/8[1]	62	26
2889[9]	**Swiftway (59)** (KWHogg) **3-9-3** DeanMcKeown(8) (led tl over 1f out: one pce)	3	**3**	20/1	66	30
2132[2]	**Pointe Fine (FR) (56)** (JWHills) **3-9-0** JFortune(3) (trckd ldrs: effrt over 3f out: one pce)	5	**4**	7/1	58	22
2397[8]	**Hippios (43)** (SDow) **3-8-1b**ow5 JFEgan(10) (hdwy 5f out: one pce fnl 3f)	1	**5**	33/1	44	3
1863[6]	**Ziggy's Viola (IRE) (55)** (MrsMReveley) **3-8-8**(5) SCopp(15) (hld up: hdwy & hung rt 2f out: nvr nr to chal)	½	**6**	14/1	55	19
2207[2]	**Arisaig (IRE) (56)** (PCalver) **3-8-11**(3) DarrenMoffatt(11) (lost pl 5f out: t.o 3f out: hdwy over 1f out: swtchd lft & styd on wl towards fin)	hd	**7**	8/1	56	20
2662[4]	**Maremma (38)** (DonEnricoIncisa) **3-7-10** KimTinkler(12) (bhd tl kpt on u.p fnl 2f: n.d)	3	**8**	20/1	35	—
2020[10]	**Avro Avian (40)** (MJCamacho) **3-7-12** LCharnock(14) (lw: w ldrs: drvn along 3f out: lost pl over 1f out)	2½	**9**	8/1	35	—
2357[3]	**Ocean Breeze (38)** (JSWainwright) **3-7-10v[1]** JQuinn(7) (bhd: sme hdwy 5f out: wknd over 1f out)	6	**10**	20/1	27	—
2170[6]	**Ibn Masirah (50)** (MrsMReveley) **3-8-8** ACulhane(4) (a in rr)	9	**11**	11/1	30	—
2757[3]	**Hadidi (63)** (DMorley) **3-9-7** JStack(2) (lw: trckd ldrs: rdn & edgd lft over 2f out: sn wknd)	6	**12**	13/2[3]	37	1
2522[8]	**Miss Alice (38)** (CSmith) **3-7-10** NVarley(6) (bhd & drvn along 5f out)	5	**13**	25/1	7	—
2548[5]	**Noirie (46)** (MBrittain) **3-8-4** GBardwell(9) (bhd & drvn along 7f out: t.o 3f out)	10	**14**	25/1	5	—
1299[10]	**Pertemps Mission (62)** (JPearce) **3-9-6** MWigham(5) (sn pushed along: hdwy to chse ldrs 7f out: wknd qckly 5f out: t.o 3f out)	6	**15**	14/1	15	—

(SP 147.0%) **15 Rn**

3m 36.2 (5.70) CSF £16.46 CT £203.87 TOTE £7.50: £2.30 £1.60 £3.90 (£7.50) Trio £125.00 OWNER Mr B. Haggas (NEWMARKET) BRED Lord Halifax
LONG HANDICAP Ocean Breeze 7-8 Hippios 7-9 Maremma 7-6

2667 Pen Friend proved well suited by the step-up in distance and, battling on in most determined fashion, was always holding the runner-up in the closing stages. He handles fast ground well and may have further improvement in him. (6/1)
1043 Philosophic is an out-and-out stayer. His rider did really well to get him so close, and a more galloping track may suit him better. (13/8: 9/4-6/4)
2548 Swiftway, last of nine at Ripon two days earlier, ran well after being allowed to set his own pace. (20/1)
2132 Pointe Fine (FR) certainly seemed to stay the trip alright. (7/1)
Hippios, who has plummeted down the ratings, shaped a little better. (33/1)
1863 Ziggy's Viola (IRE) seemed to give her rider no help. (14/1)
2207 Arisaig (IRE), an excitable type, seemed to run a temperamental race. Dropping himself right out, he was a long way behind turning in but was putting in some solid work at the line. If he can be persuaded to put his best foot forward throughout the contest, he is certainly capable of winning a stayers' handicap from this sort of mark. (8/1: op 9/2)
2757 Hadidi (13/2: op 4/1)

2909 POCKLINGTON LIMITED STKS (0-65) (3-Y.O+) (Class F)

9-05 (9-05) **1m 1f 207y** £2,804.00 (£842.00: £406.00: £188.00) Stalls: High GOING minus 0.54 sec per fur (F)

	Horse / details	Dist	Pos	SP	RR	SF
2722*	**Regal Reprimand (65)** (GLewis) **3-8-11** PaulEddery(5) (b.hind: lw: hld up: smooth hdwy over 1f out: shkn up & qcknd to ld jst ins fnl f: pushed out)	—	**1**	5/4[1]	74	1
2722[2]	**Marytavy (64)** (SirMarkPrescott) **3-8-6** GDuffield(6) (lw: sn trckng ldrs: effrt over 2f out: ev ch over 1f out: edgd rt u.p: nt pce of wnr)	¾	**2**	7/4[2]	68	—
2415[8]	**Grate Times (62)** (EWeymes) **3-8-9** BDoyle(1) (led: rdn over 2f out: hdd & nt qckn jst ins fnl f)	1¼	**3**	12/1	69	—
1694[8]	**Montecristo (65)** (RGuest) **4-9-0**(5) CLowther(2) (hld up: hdwy over 3f out: hung rt & nt qckn appr fnl f)	nk	**4**	11/2[3]	68	5
	Ile Distinct (IRE) (64) (MrsASwinbank) **3-8-9** JFortune(4) (chsd ldrs: shkn up & outpcd over 2f out: kpt on fnl f)	¾	**5**	16/1	22 t	—

2502[15]	**Nukud (USA) (20)** (GROldroyd) **5-8-12v**[(7)] RFarmer(3) (t: chsd ldr tl lost pl over 2f out)	7	**6**	40/1	11 t	—

(SP 112.2%) **6 Rn**

2m 9.7 (6.60) CSF £3.33 TOTE £2.10: £1.60 £1.10 (£1.50) OWNER The Voice Group Ltd (EPSOM) BRED Godolphin Management Co Ltd
WEIGHT FOR AGE 3yo-10lb

2722* Regal Reprimand, meeting the winner on 2lb worse terms compared with Folkestone, was given a confident ride. Showing a nice turn of foot and coming through between horses, he took this in good style for a horse rated in the mid-sixties. He certainly possesses a good turn of finishing speed. (5/4: evens-11/8)

2722 Marytavy, very keen, rolled off a straight line under pressure and, in the end, the winner beat her comfortably. She will need to settle better. (7/4)

1629 Grate Times, with the blinkers left off and stepping up in distance, was allowed to set his own pace. Showing plenty of knee action, he gave a good account of himself and ran easily his best race so far this year. (12/1: 8/1-14/1)

1694 Montecristo gave his rider no assistance, hanging in behind. (11/2)

Ile Distinct (IRE), an immature type, showed plenty of knee action going down. Tending to hang left on this fast ground, he was not disgraced. (16/1)

1312 Nukud (USA) has been tubed. (40/1)

T/Plpt: £47.30 (394.12 Tckts). T/Qdpt: £8.60 (134.05 Tckts) WG

2602-SOUTHWELL (L-H) (Standard)
Monday July 21st

WEATHER: sunny & hot WIND: slt half against

2910 TURNER H'CAP (0-60) (3-Y.O+) (Class F)
2-30 (2-31) **1m 6f (Fibresand)** £2,277.00 (£627.00: £297.00) Stalls: High GOING minus 0.06 sec per fur (STD)

				SP	RR	SF
2702[*]	**Indigo Dawn (59)** (MJohnston) **3-8-10**[(3)] KMChin(2) (sn pushed along mid div: hdwy 4f out: rdn to ld over 1f out: r.o wl)	—	**1**	5/2[1]	71	25
2607[2]	**Shy Paddy (IRE) (36)** (KOCunningham-Brown) **5-8-4** MRoberts(7) (chsd ldrs: sn pushed along: effrt u.p 2f out: styd on)	1½	**2**	14/1	46	14
2607[*]	**Dashing Invader (USA) (45)** (PWHarris) **4-8-13b** FNorton(10) (led tl hdd over 1f out: sn rdn & btn)	5	**3**	11/4[2]	50	18
2190[5]	**Action Stations (59)** (CACyzer) **3-8-13** GDuffield(6) (lw: trckd ldrs: rdn 5f out: no imp)	14	**4**	12/1	48	2
2518[*]	**Arif (IRE) (37)** (BJCurley) **5-8-5** JFanning(14) (sn chsng ldr: rdn over 2f out: sn wknd)	3½	**5**	6/1[3]	22	—
2668[12]	**Subtle Touch (IRE) (40)** (TTClement) **6-8-3**[(5)ow3] GFaulkner(12) (hld up: hdwy 5f out: nt rch ldrs)	½	**6**	50/1	24	—
	Charlie Bigtime (39) (ICampbell) **7-8-7** RCochrane(11) (bkwd: in rr tl sme late hdwy)	1	**7**	25/1	22	—
2386[8]	**Cittern (56)** (MrsMReveley) **7-9-10** ACulhane(1) (swtg: a in rr: t.o)	6	**8**	33/1	32	—
2660[9]	**One Life To Live (IRE) (50)** (SEKettlewell) **4-9-4** JFortune(8) (a rr div: t.o)	1¼	**9**	25/1	25	—
2474[2]	**Tam O'Shanter (52)** (CWThornton) **3-8-6** DeanMcKeown(4) (chsd ldrs 8f: sn rdn & wknd: t.o)	3½	**10**	9/1	23	—
2541[*]	**Kilnamartyra Girl (44)** (JParkes) **7-8-12** GBardwell(13) (a bhd: t.o)	4	**11**	9/1	10	—
2668[9]	**Sommersby (IRE) (43)** (MrsNMacauley) **6-8-11** SDrowne(3) (b: lw: hdwy 8f out: rdn over 3f out: sn lost tch: t.o)	4	**12**	33/1	4	—
1494[9]	**El Nido (51)** (DWChapman) **9-9-5** LCharnock(9) (bit bkwd: bhd fr ½-wy: t.o)	20	**13**	33/1	—	—
1996[5]	**Finestatetobein (30)** (FWatson) **4-7-12** JQuinn(5) (a in rr: t.o fnl 4f)	6	**14**	20/1	—	—

(SP 127.1%) **14 Rn**

3m 10.2 (12.20) CSF £34.85 CT £100.35 TOTE £3.30: £1.80 £3.20 £1.10 (£34.00) Trio £30.90 OWNER Greenland Park Ltd (MIDDLEHAM) BRED Laharna Ltd
WEIGHT FOR AGE 3yo-14lb

2702* Indigo Dawn, a half-sister to last year's winner Shirley Sue, gave the impression that she had not taken to this surface when driven along in the early stages but, with stamina coming into play, she stayed on relentlessly to gain command approaching the final furlong. She is really on a roll at present. (5/2)

2607 Shy Paddy (IRE) was 14lb better off for a fifteen-length beating with Dashing Invader and, under a firm ride, turned the tables. However, the winner is at the top of her form just now and she was always holding his sustained rally. (14/1)

2607* Dashing Invader (USA) had 15lb more to carry than when annihilating his field on his previous run, and he again attempted to gallop them into the ground but, after looking all over the winner, he was in trouble below the distance as the extra burden took its toll. (11/4)

2518* Arif (IRE) likes to dictate but he was unable to on this occasion and, though he did his best, had shot his bolt soon after turning in. (6/1: 3/1-13/2)

2541* Kilnamartyra Girl (9/1: 6/1-10/1)

2911 KANDINSKY CLAIMING LIMITED STKS (0-55) (3-Y.O+) (Class F)
3-00 (3-00) **1m 3f (Fibresand)** £2,277.00 (£627.00: £297.00) Stalls: Low GOING minus 0.06 sec per fur (STD)

				SP	RR	SF
2541[2]	**Portite Sophie (32)** (MBrittain) **6-8-8**[(5)] CLowther(2) (b: a chsng ldrs: shkn up over 2f out: r.o to ld fnl 100y)	—	**1**	9/2	51	9
2652[7]	**Nicola's Princess (49)** (BAMcMahon) **4-9-5** MRoberts(9) (lw: hld up: hdwy to ld over 2f out: sn rdn: hdd wl ins fnl f)	½	**2**	4/1[3]	56	14
2301[7]	**Tovarich (50)** (RonaldThompson) **6-8-11b**[(5)] DSweeney(4) (led after 1f: rdn & hdd over 2f out: wknd over 1f out)	11	**3**	16/1	37	—
2673[2]	**Esperto (50)** (JPearce) **4-9-4** GBardwell(7) (lw: hld up: hdwy 4f out: rdn over 2f out: no imp)	7	**4**	9/4[1]	29	—
1798[14]	**Dino's Mistral (32)** (FHLee) **4-9-0** DeanMcKeown(3) (trckd ldrs: hrd drvn over 2f out: sn btn)	1¼	**5**	25/1	23	—
2063[8]	**Mowlaie (43)** (DWChapman) **6-8-12** ACulhane(1) (b: hld up & bhd: effrt & hrd rdn 3f out: no imp: t.o)	9	**6**	7/2[2]	8	—
	Modesto (USA) (30) (KOCunningham-Brown) **9-9-2** RCochrane(5) (bit bkwd: led 1f: prom tl rdn & wknd over 4f out: t.o)	5	**7**	16/1	5	—
2701[9]	**Tocco Jewel (20)** (MJRyan) **7-8-9** DRMcCabe(8) (in rr: rdn along over 4f out: no rspnse: t.o)	4	**8**	25/1	—	—
2569[8]	**Cimmerian (50)** (MESowersby) **3-7-9**[(7)] RWinston(6) (trckd ldrs 7f: sn rdn & wknd: t.o)	8	**9**	5/1	—	—

(SP 127.3%) **9 Rn**

2m 31.9 (11.90) CSF £23.24 TOTE £5.90: £2.10 £2.40 £2.00 (£13.60) Trio £122.40 OWNER Ms Maureen Hanlon (WARTHILL) BRED Mr and Mrs R. W. Lycett Green
WEIGHT FOR AGE 3yo-11lb

2541 Portite Sophie, winner of her only previous race on the Fibresand at Wolverhampton, gave notice earlier in the month that she was approaching her peak and, with the help of a considerable weight advantage, ran on strongly to wear down the runner-up halfway through the final furlong. (9/2)
2209 Nicola's Princess travelled strongly and looked well in command when leading early in the straight, but she did not find a lot when challenged, and lack of stamina could be the problem. (4/1: 5/2-9/2)
Tovarich, lightly-raced this term, tied up rather quickly after being headed and it is possible he has not quite come to himself as yet. (16/1)
2673 Esperto moved feelingly to post and was always making hard work of it. There may well be a problem to be sorted out. (9/4)
313 Dino's Mistral, a very lightly-made individual, sat in behind the leaders and was travelling well within himself for the first mile but, once he came of the bridle, there was nothing more to offer. (25/1)
1748* Mowlaie has won both his races on turf on a much sounder surface, and it was quite obvious from some way out that he was not enjoying this at all. (7/2)

2912 UCCELLO LIMITED STKS (0-65) (3-Y.O+) (Class F)

3-30 (3-30) **1m (Fibresand)** £2,277.00 (£627.00: £297.00) Stalls: Low GOING minus 0.06 sec per fur (STD)

				SP	RR	SF
2671[2]	**Mythical (61)** (SirMarkPrescott) **3-8-7** GDuffield(1) (lw: hld up in tch: chal over 1f out: rdn to ld wl ins fnl f)	—	**1**	3/1[2]	71	26
2602[2]	**Kalimat (66)** (WJarvis) **3-8-7** JQuinn(7) (a.p: led over 2f out: sn rdn: hdd & no ex wl ins fnl f)	2	**2**	11/8[1]	67	22
*2602**	**Phoenix Princess (53)** (BAMcMahon) **3-8-10** MRoberts(5) (lw: hld up: hdwy over 3f out: rdn & one pce fnl 2f)	4	**3**	10/1	62	17
2544[7]	**Major Mouse (52)** (WWHaigh) **9-9-4** LCharnock(6) (hld up: effrt & rdn st: kpt on: nt pce to chal)	2½	**4**	20/1	57	20
2542*	**Broctune Gold (65)** (MrsMReveley) **6-9-10** ACulhane(3) (lw: led tl over 2f out: eased whn btn appr fnl f)	6	**5**	8/1	51	14
2744[5]	**Magazine Gap (46)** (PatMitchell) **4-8-13**(5) AmandaSanders(8) (swtg: hld up: pushed along 3f out: no imp)	s.h	**6**	50/1	45	8
2502[8]	**Agent (62)** (JLEyre) **4-9-7** DeanMcKeown(4) (prom: rdn 4f out: wknd over 2f out)	2½	**7**	20/1	43	6
2532[7]	**Dazzling Stone (65)** (LadyHerries) **3-8-10** RCochrane(2) (swtg: chsd ldrs: sn pushed along: outpcd fnl 3f)	2½	**8**	7/2[3]	35	—

(SP 121.0%) **8 Rn**

1m 45.0 (6.00) CSF £7.17 TOTE £2.80: £1.50 £1.10 £2.10 (£3.10) OWNER Lord Fairhaven (NEWMARKET) BRED Barton Stud
WEIGHT FOR AGE 3yo-8lb
2671 Mythical promised to win very easily when joining issue below the distance, but the favourite proved a tough nut to crack, and Duffield had to get serious to make sure late on. (3/1)
2602 Kalimat had no trouble gaining her revenge over Phoenix Princess and she tried hard to pinch the race entering the last quarter-mile, but the winner proved just as strong when the chips were down. (11/8: 2/1-5/4)
2602* Phoenix Princess had less use made of her and she looked a threat turning in but, once the principals took one another on, she was tapped for toe. (10/1: 7/1-12/1)
2128 Major Mouse is finding it difficult to recapture his form of a few seasons ago and, though he did stay on under pressure, was unable to make any significant impression on the leaders. (20/1)
2542* Broctune Gold adopted his usual forceful tactics but could never get away, and he was beaten in a matter of strides once into the straight. (8/1: op 9/2)

2913 DISCOVERY ARGYLL LIMITED EDITION H'CAP (0-70) (3-Y.O+ F & M) (Class E)

4-00 (4-02) **7f (Fibresand)** £3,070.25 (£917.00: £438.50: £199.25) Stalls: Low GOING minus 0.06 sec per fur (STD)

				SP	RR	SF
2427[3]	**Icy Guest (USA) (70)** (PJMakin) **3-9-10** DHolland(1) (lw: mde all: drvn clr 2f out: rdn & r.o wl)	—	**1**	7/1	80	43
2732[8]	**Napier Star (67)** (MrsNMacauley) **4-10-0v** SWebster(11) (b.off hind: trckd ldrs: hdwy to chse wnr over 1f out: sn rdn & no imp)	4	**2**	12/1	68	38
2602[3]	**Arrasas Lady (35)** (JRPoulton) **7-7-3**(7) JFowle(6) (s.s: hdwy 2f out: rdn & r.o wl ins fnl f)	nk	**3**	33/1	35	5
2734[2]	**Bollero (IRE) (56)** (JBerry) **3-8-5**(5) CLowther(9) (lw: prom: rdn over 2f out: r.o one pce)	1	**4**	6/1	54	17
2569[2]	**Al Reet (IRE) (56)** (SRBowring) **6-9-3** DeanMcKeown(4) (lw: trckd ldrs: outpcd ent s: styd on u.p ins fnl f)	nk	**5**	9/2[2]	53	23
2671[10]	**Heathyards Lady (USA) (52)** (RHollinshead) **6-8-13** FLynch(3) (b: nvr nr to chal)	hd	**6**	10/1	49	19
2416[3]	**Kissel (58)** (SEKettlewell) **5-9-5** JFortune(5) (lw: prom: rdn 2f out: sn btn)	2½	**7**	5/1[3]	49	19
2602[7]	**Qualitair Silver (42)** (JFBottomley) **3-7-10b[1]** LCharnock(8) (prom tl rdn & outpcd over 2f out)	6	**8**	20/1	20	—
2463[12]	**Born A Lady (46)** (MrsVAAconley) **4-8-4**(3)ow8 KMChin(10) (b.off hind: hmp after 3f: a in rr: hrd rdn ent st: t.o)	1½	**9**	12/1	20	—
*2672**	**People Direct (57)** (NPLittmoden) **4-9-4** JQuinn(7) (hmpd after 3f: a bhd: t.o)	8	**10**	5/2[1]	13	—
2372[12]	**Strat's Quest (64)** (DWPArbuthnot) **3-8-13**(5) DSweeney(2) (prom over 4f: sn lost tch: t.o)	16	**11**	14/1	—	—

(SP 129.1%) **11 Rn**

1m 31.7 (5.20) CSF £88.07 CT £2,461.25 TOTE £5.90: £2.30 £2.80 £8.50 (£59.80) Trio £331.40 OWNER Dr Carlos Stelling (MARLBOROUGH) BRED Cambremont Limited Partnership
LONG HANDICAP Arrasas Lady 6-9 Qualitair Silver 7-8
WEIGHT FOR AGE 3yo-7lb
2427 Icy Guest (USA) had her full quota of weight for a maiden but, with the inside berth, she made it a true test of stamina and, driven clear on straightening up, finally opened her account. (7/1)
2162 Napier Star, restrained in an attempt to get the trip, was travelling best of all early in the straight but her lack of stamina showed when she was let down, and she could do little more than gallop on the spot. (12/1)
2602 Arrasas Lady, carrying 8lb more than her long handicap weight, did extremely well to finish so close after losing ground at the start and she is certainly capable of finding a race. (33/1)
2734 Bollero (IRE), made to struggle soon after entering the straight, kept plugging away but a turn of finishing speed was badly missing. (6/1)
2569 Al Reet (IRE), off the bridle in an effort to hold her pitch on the approach to the straight, was picking up well again towards the finish, and a return to turf when the ground is suitable could bring its reward. (9/2)
1818 Heathyards Lady (USA), who moved to post poorly, has not yet found her form but she has done most of her winning in the autumn, and she could be coming to herself. (10/1)
2416 Kissel (5/1: op 10/1)
2672* People Direct, the worst sufferer in a barging match at the end of the back straight, was soon out of contention and unable to recover. (5/2)
1141* Strat's Quest (14/1: 10/1-16/1)

2914 MONDRIAN (S) STKS (2-Y.O) (Class G)

4-30 (4-30) **7f (Fibresand)** £1,984.50 (£547.00: £259.50) Stalls: Low GOING minus 0.06 sec per fur (STD)

				SP	RR	SF
2587[6]	**Docklands Dispatch (IRE)** (NTinkler) **2-8-11** KimTinkler(2) (chsd ldr: led 4f out: clr fnl 2f)	—	**1**	6/1	63	11
2681[10]	**Edna's Gift (IRE)** (JBerry) **2-8-6**(5) PRoberts(4) (lw: a chsng ldrs: drvn along ½-wy: kpt on: no ch w wnr)	14	**2**	7/2[2]	31	—

				SP	RR	SF
*2304**	**Rock From The Sun** (WGMTurner) **2-8-6**$^{(5)}$ DSweeney(5) (swtg: led 3f: rdn over 2f out: sn btn)	1¾	**3**	6/5^{1}	27	—
2016^{17}	**Sixth Avenue (IRE)** (RMWhitaker) **2-8-6** DeanMcKeown(1) (trckd ldrs: effrt u.p over 2f out: no imp)	2	**4**	5/1^{3}	17	—
2736^{9}	**Vogue Imperial (IRE)** (PCHaslam) **2-8-4b**$^{1(7)}$ PGoode(7) (dwlt: hung rt thrght: sn wl outpcd)	4	**5**	16/1	13	—
2412^{9}	**E B Treasure** (NBycroft) **2-8-6** ACulhane(6) (b.off hind: a bhd & outpcd: t.o)	15	**6**	40/1	—	—
2412^{10}	**Boccolino** (TDBarron) **2-8-11** LCharnock(3) (bit bkwd: prom tl rdn & outpcd over 2f out: t.o)	4	**7**	8/1	—	—
				(SP 118.1%)	**7 Rn**	

1m 33.5 (7.00) CSF £25.94 TOTE £9.30: £2.80 £2.10 (£7.70) OWNER Mrs Lisa Olley (MALTON) BRED Joseph Crowley
No bid
2587 Docklands Dispatch (IRE), whose husband and wife team are enjoying a purple patch, turned this race into a procession and there would not be much hope for the opposition. (6/1: 7/2-13/2)
2378 Edna's Gift (IRE), driven along turning out of the back straight, could never get in a blow against the winner. (7/2)
2304* Rock From The Sun should have been the one to beat, but she was unable to keep tabs on the winner once in line for home, and proved most disappointing. (6/5: 4/5-5/4)

2915 PICASSO H'CAP (0-60) (3-Y.O+) (Class F)
5-00 (5-01) **6f (Fibresand)** £2,277.00 (£627.00: £297.00) Stalls: Low GOING minus 0.06 sec per fur (STD)

				SP	RR	SF
2567^{14}	**Zain Dancer (42)** (DNicholls) **5-8-10** FLynch(10) (mid div: hdwy 2f out: rdn to ld wl ins fnl f)	—	**1**	100/30^{1}	52	34
*2366**	**Time To Fly (49)** (BWMurray) **4-8-12b**$^{(5)}$ DSweeney(11) (set str pce: sn wl clr: rdn & ct cl home)	¾	**2**	9/1	57	39
*2605**	**Sea Ya Maite (60)** (SRBowring) **3-9-9** SWebster(5) (b: bhd: hdwy wl over 1f out: nrst fin)	2½	**3**	7/1	61	38
2463^{7}	**Legend of Aragon (49)** (JAGlover) **3-8-5**$^{(7)}$ TPengkerego(14) (racd wd: hdwy 2f out: rdn wl over 1f out: fin wl)	½	**4**	20/1	49	26
2603^{7}	**Jilly Beveled (36)** (RonaldThompson) **5-8-4** MGallagher(9) (in tch: effrt 2f out: sn rdn: kpt on)	1	**5**	33/1	33	15
2366^{2}	**Thordis (60)** (PJMakin) **4-10-0v** DHolland(15) (swtg: in tch: hdwy & hrd drvn over 2f out: nvr able chal)	¾	**6**	7/1	55	37
2651^{8}	**Steal 'Em (43)** (ABailey) **4-8-11v** DWright(2) (spd over 4f)	2	**7**	20/1	33	15
2826^{3}	**Silk Cottage (48)** (RMWhitaker) **5-9-2** DeanMcKeown(4) (lw: trckd ldrs: rdn 2f out: no imp)	hd	**8**	5/1^{2}	38	20
2463^{10}	**Bold Street (IRE) (60)** (GMMoore) **7-10-0** JTate(6) (nvr nrr)	s.h	**9**	25/1	50	32
2788*	**Lachesis (34)** (DShaw) **4-8-2**^{7x} JFanning(12) (racd wd: nvr trbld ldrs)	1¼	**10**	13/2^{3}	20	2
1977^{2}	**Afaan (IRE) (59)** (RFMarvin) **4-9-13v** TGMcLaughlin(16) (chsd ldrs: rdn over 2f out: sn btn)	2	**11**	5/1^{2}	40	22
1861^{4}	**La Volta (53)** (MissJFCraze) **4-9-7** NConnorton(1) (lw: a outpcd)	3	**12**	25/1	26	8
2788^{18}	**Miss Aragon (42)** (MissLCSiddall) **9-8-10**^{ow4} OPears(3) (a bhd: t.o)	9	**13**	33/1	—	—
2424^{9}	**Sharp Return (55)** (MJRyan) **3-9-4b** DRMcCabe(13) (outpcd: t.o)	nk	**14**	25/1	3	—
2852^{13}	**Saxon Bay (58)** (KOCunningham-Brown) **5-9-12** MRoberts(7) (outpcd: t.o)	1	**15**	20/1	4	—
2724^{13}	**Sandweld (48)** (CADwyer) **3-8-4b**$^{1(7)}$ JoHunnam(8) (a in rr: t.o)	¾	**16**	20/1	—	—
				(SP 141.2%)	**16 Rn**	

1m 17.6 (4.10) CSF £31.77 CT £199.74 TOTE £4.40: £1.20 £2.60 £1.80 £5.10 (£58.70) Trio £126.60 OWNER Mr S. Aitken (THIRSK) BRED Mrs C. J. Richardson and Mrs A. A. Scott
WEIGHT FOR AGE 3yo-5lb
1754 Zain Dancer landed a right touch for his very shrewd trainer, but he had to work for it before he eventually took the measure of the long-time leader. (100/30: 8/1-3/1)
2366* Time To Fly was soon stretching his pursuers to the limit and he looked set to come home on his own, but these tactics played into the hands of the winner, and he was forced to give best in the final fifty yards. (9/1)
2605* Sea Ya Maite usually races with the pace, but he was taken off his legs this time and only got going when the race was all but over. (7/1)
2206 Legend of Aragon finds this trip a bit short and, forced to race wide from a poor draw, was only into her stride inside the distance. This was not a bad effort and she could pick up a small race in the coming weeks. (20/1)
1786 Jilly Beveled has hardly got the pace to win at this trip, but she shaped with plenty of promise and there could be another race to be won. (33/1)
2366 Thordis began his effort over two furlongs out and stayed on under pressure without being able to summon the speed to get to terms. (7/1)
2826 Silk Cottage (5/1: op 12/1)
2788* Lachesis (13/2: op 4/1)

T/Plpt: £231.40 (68.88 Tckts). T/Qdpt: £57.10 (16.96 Tckts) IM

2727-WINDSOR (Fig. 8) (Good to firm)
Monday July 21st
WEATHER: hot WIND: almost nil

2916 MERCURY ASSET MANAGEMENT (S) H'CAP (0-60) (3-Y.O+) (Class F)
6-20 (6-22) **1m 3f 135y** £2,598.00 (£728.00: £354.00) Stalls: High GOING minus 0.37 sec per fur (F)

				SP	RR	SF
2398^{7}	**Nothing Doing (IRE) (42)** (WJMusson) **8-8-13** KFallon(3) (rdn 3f out: gd hdwy over 1f out: r.o to ld cl home)	—	**1**	6/1^{2}	55	36
2577^{7}	**Sapphire Son (IRE) (42)** (PCClarke) **5-8-10**$^{(3)}$ RFfrench(10) (w ldr: led 3f out tl nr fin)	½	**2**	14/1	54	35
2139^{9}	**Veronica Franco (44)** (RIngram) **4-8-12**$^{(3)}$ AWhelan(7) (hdwy on ins whn hmpd over 1f out: r.o ins fnl f)	3	**3**	8/1	52	33
2199^{13}	**Victor Blum (USA) (35)** (CAHorgan) **4-8-6v**^{1} GCarter(15) (lw: led to 3f out: wknd ins fnl f)	2½	**4**	33/1	40	21
2727^{3}	**Running Free (IRE) (45)** (MJFetherston-Godley) **3-8-4** DaneO'Neill(5) (prom tl wknd over 1f out)	4	**5**	6/1^{2}	44	13
2727^{5}	**Sheilas Dream (45)** (GLMoore) **4-9-2** SWhitworth(12) (prom tl wknd over 1f out)	1¼	**6**	12/1	43	24
2246^{5}	**High Desire (IRE) (48)** (JRArnold) **4-9-5** DHarrison(11) (nvr nr to chal)	1¼	**7**	13/2^{3}	44	25
2518^{7}	**La Spagna (25)** (MDIUsher) **6-7-10** JMarshall(2) (bhd: gd hdwy & rn wd over 2f out: sn btn)	nk	**8**	33/1	20	1
2777^{2}	**Shabanaz (52)** (WRMuir) **12-9-9** PatEddery(9) (bhd tl hdwy 3f out: carried wd over 2f out: sn wknd)	1½	**9**	5/1^{1}	45	26
2896^{2}	**Arzani (USA) (57)** (DJSCosgrove) **6-10-0** MRimmer(6) (b: chsd ldrs tl wknd over 2f out)	3	**10**	13/2^{3}	46	27
2577^{13}	**Proud Brigadier (IRE) (34)** (MRBosley) **9-8-5** CRutter(14) (b: nvr nr ldrs)	nk	**11**	25/1	23	4
46^{4}	**Barnwood Crackers (59)** (MRChannon) **3-9-1**$^{(3)}$ PPMurphy(8) (swtg: a bhd)	s.h	**12**	16/1	48	17
2646^{8}	**Northern Saga (IRE) (37)** (CJDrewe) **4-8-8** AClark(13) (lw: a bhd)	1½	**13**	25/1	24	5
2577^{12}	**Another Fiddle (IRE) (28)** (JELong) **7-7-13** NCarlisle(4) (b.hind: prom 8f)	2	**14**	33/1	12	—

2488[5] **Sweet Seventeen (32)** (HJCollingridge) **4-8-3**ow7 DianaWeeden(1) (gd hdwy 6f out: wknd 3f out) ....7 **15** 25/1 6 —

(SP 123.6%) **15 Rn**

2m 30.6 (4.60) CSF £74.16 CT £619.33 TOTE £5.30: £1.80 £5.50 £2.70 (£41.10) Trio £391.20; £33.06 to 23/7/97 OWNER Broughton Bloodstock (NEWMARKET) BRED Cleaboy Stud

LONG HANDICAP La Spagna 7-7 Sweet Seventeen 7-8

WEIGHT FOR AGE 3yo-12lb

Bt in 5,200gns. Veronica Franco clmd JWhelan £6,000

2279 Nothing Doing (IRE), whose prospects looked remote when under pressure in midfield three furlongs out, suddenly began to run below the distance and snatched the race close home. (6/1)

1636 Sapphire Son (IRE) raced with the leader until taking up the running three furlongs out. Clear at the distance, he could not quite hold the winner's late thrust. (14/1)

1478 Veronica Franco looked very unlucky. She tried for a run on the inside approaching the final furlong when flying but got stopped. She ran on inside the last but it was too late. She was claimed and will now be used as a broodmare. (8/1)

Victor Blum (USA), visored for the first time, made the running until three furlongs out. He stayed on under pressure and should be able to win a seller. (33/1)

2727 Running Free (IRE) was close up until weakening approaching the final furlong. (6/1)

2727 Sheilas Dream (12/1: op 8/1)

2246 High Desire (IRE) (13/2: 9/2-7/1)

2777 Shabanaz, settled at the back of the field, was coming with a run on the outside when carried very wide over two furlongs from home and he soon dropped back. (5/1)

2896 Arzani (USA) (13/2: 4/1-7/1)

2917 E.B.F. CASTLEBROOK PROPERTIES MEDIAN AUCTION MAIDEN STKS (2-Y.O) (Class E)

6-50 (6-59) **5f 10y** £3,095.00 (£935.00: £455.00: £215.00) Stalls: High GOING minus 0.37 sec per fur (F)

	Horse / details	Dist	Pos	SP	RR	SF
2477[8]	**Golden Strategy (IRE)** (RHannon) **2-9-0** RHughes(18) (b.nr hind: lw: mde all: r.o wl)	—	**1**	11/4[1]	78	38
2181[14]	**Bound To Please** (PJMakin) **2-9-0** SSanders(20) (hdwy 2f out: swtchd lft & r.o wl ins fnl f)	s.h	**2**	12/1	78	38
	Tullich Refrain (WRMuir) **2-8-9** KFallon(17) (leggy: lt-f: s.s: gd hdwy 2f out: nrst fin)	1	**3**	12/1	70+	30
	Call To Order (CFWall) **2-9-0** PatEddery(15) (neat: chsd wnr tl wknd fnl f)	4	**4**	4/1[2]	62	22
	Rapid Reliance (DRCElsworth) **2-8-9** RCochrane(7) (neat: stdy hdwy 2f out: r.o wl ins fnl f)	3	**5**	12/1	48+	8
2693[9]	**Magical Dancer (IRE)** (MrsPNDutfield) **2-8-6**(3) RHavlin(13) (spd over 3f)	1¾	**6**	20/1	42	2
2534[14]	**I Cried For You (IRE)** (RHannon) **2-9-0** DaneO'Neill(12) (chsd ldrs: one pce fnl 2f)	1¼	**7**	20/1	43	3
	Bay Prince (IRE) (MRChannon) **2-9-0** RPerham(1) (w'like: bit bkwd: a.p: no hdwy fnl 2f)	nk	**8**	16/1	42	2
	Call Me Vera (EAWheeler) **2-8-4**(5) ADaly(2) (leggy: lt-f: spd 3f)	¾	**9**	50/1	35	—
	Impulsive Decision (IRE) (MartynMeade) **2-8-9** FNorton(14) (leggy: lt-f: nvr plcd to chal)	s.h	**10**	20/1	35	—
2553[12]	**Pippas Pride (IRE)** (MJFetherston-Godley) **2-9-0** CRutter(16) (nvr nr to chal)	nk	**11**	33/1	39	—
2553[8]	**Tom** (LordHuntingdon) **2-9-0** DHarrison(6) (bit bkwd: prom 3f)	2½	**12**	6/1[3]	31	—
	College Rose (SCWilliams) **2-8-9** GCarter(11) (leggy: lt-f: spd 3f)	¾	**13**	50/1	23	—
	Aegean Breeze (MissGayKelleway) **2-8-11**(3) RFfrench(8) (neat: a bhd)	1½	**14**	20/1	24	—
2534[12]	**Second Sun** (JJBridger) **2-8-11**(3) MHenry(4) (outpcd)	hd	**15**	33/1	23	—
2467[8]	**Technician (IRE)** (MAJarvis) **2-9-0** GHind(5) (outpcd)	s.h	**16**	20/1	23	—
2283[4]	**River Frontier (IRE)** (MDIUsher) **2-8-9** RPrice(3) (a bhd)	2	**17**	50/1	12	—
1932[9]	**Vista Alegre** (PJMakin) **2-9-0** AClark(9) (bit bkwd: spd over 2f)	3	**18**	25/1	7	—
2588[8]	**Eastwell Hall** (RCurtis) **2-9-0** SDrowne(10) (a bhd)	1¼	**19**	33/1	3	—
	Mrs Pickles (MDIUsher) **2-8-9** JMarshall(19) (str: bkwd: s.s: a bhd)	3	**20**	20/1	—	—

(SP 137.0%) **20 Rn**

61.4 secs (1.70) CSF £30.61 TOTE £3.60: £1.60 £3.70 £4.60 (£16.50) Trio £134.70 OWNER Mr George Teo (MARLBOROUGH) BRED Frank Barry

2477 Golden Strategy (IRE) made all the running. He looked well in control at the distance but only just lasted home. (11/4)

1959 Bound To Please improved considerably on his two previous outings. He made good headway two furlongs out and, switched left inside the last, almost snatched the race. (12/1)

Tullich Refrain, a leggy filly and rather lightly-made, missed the break and, in the circumstances, did extremely well to reach third place, running on strongly in the closing stages. (12/1: op 4/1)

Call To Order, a useful sort, went with the winner until unable to quicken under pressure in the final furlong. The experience will have done him good. (4/1)

Rapid Reliance, a neatly-made filly, ran on steadily and with great promise in the final quarter-mile. Considerable improvement can be expected. (12/1: 5/1-14/1)

583 Magical Dancer (IRE) was in the firing line until weakening approaching the final furlong. (20/1)

Impulsive Decision (IRE) is not a very attractive filly, but she ran by no means badly for a first appearance, without enjoying the clearest of runs. She is worth keeping an eye on. (20/1)

Tom (6/1: 4/1-7/1)

2918 LADBROKES H'CAP (0-80) (3-Y.O+ F & M) (Class D)

7-20 (7-23) **1m 67y** £3,525.50 (£1,064.00: £517.00: £243.50) Stalls: High GOING minus 0.37 sec per fur (F)

	Horse / details	Dist	Pos	SP	RR	SF
2555*	**Wishing Stone (USA) (72)** (EALDunlop) **3-8-12** KFallon(4) (a.p: led over 2f out: r.o wl)	—	**1**	9/4[1]	82	20
2730[2]	**Fancy Design (IRE) (50)** (PMitchell) **4-7-7**(5)ow2 AimeeCook(2) (b.off hind: lw: hdwy 2f out: r.o wl ins fnl f)	1½	**2**	20/1	57	1
2730*	**Comanche Companion (62)** (TJNaughton) **7-8-10** 5x PatEddery(7) (lw: led tl over 2f out: r.o one pce)	1¾	**3**	11/4[2]	66	12
2119[5]	**Kentucky Fall (FR) (65)** (LadyHerries) **4-8-13** AClark(3) (plld hrd: a.p: ev ch over 1f out: wknd ins fnl f)	nk	**4**	10/1	68	14
1483*	**Sandicliffe (USA) (50)** (JARToller) **4-7-9**(3) RFfrench(9) (plld hrd: chsd ldrs: nt clr run & clipped heels over 1f out: nt rcvr)	¾	**5**	10/1	52+	—
2557[5]	**Fern's Governor (55)** (WJMusson) **5-8-3** GCarter(8) (nvr nr to chal)	3	**6**	4/1[3]	51	—
2645[5]	**What Happened Was (72)** (MartynMeade) **3-8-12** FNorton(10) (b.hind: no hdwy fnl 3f)	s.h	**7**	10/1	68	6
2603[6]	**Palo Blanco (77)** (GLMoore) **6-9-11** SWhitworth(11) (prom tl wknd 2f out)	2	**8**	12/1	69	15
1439[11]	**Bold Tina (IRE) (70)** (RHannon) **3-8-10** DaneO'Neill(6) (plld hrd: prom 3f: sn wknd)	1¼	**9**	16/1	60	—
2691[13]	**Aegean Sound (68)** (KTIvory) **3-8-8** CScally(5) (b.hind: a bhd)	5	**10**	33/1	48	—

(SP 126.0%) **10 Rn**

1m 47.0 (4.80) CSF £50.58 CT £129.16 TOTE £3.10: £1.60 £2.40 £1.60 (£15.80) Trio £12.00 OWNER Maktoum Al Maktoum (NEWMARKET) BRED Gainsborough Farm Inc

LONG HANDICAP Fancy Design (IRE) 6-9
WEIGHT FOR AGE 3yo-8lb
2555* Wishing Stone (USA), upped to handicap company, proved equal to the task. Never far behind the leaders, she went to the front over two furlongs from home and won readily. (9/4)
2730 Fancy Design (IRE) ran a fine race with an unfavourable weight. She improved steadily two furlongs out and ran on well inside the last furlong, without unduly troubling the winner. (20/1)
2730* Comanche Companion tried to make all the running as usual but was headed over two furlongs from home. Though she stayed on at the finish, she never appeared likely to trouble the winner. (11/4)
2119 Kentucky Fall (FR) pulled hard on the heels of the leaders and, after having every chance below the distance, weakened inside the last furlong. (10/1: 8/1-12/1)
1483* Sandicliffe (USA), one of several to take a strong hold, was close up behind the leaders when clipping heels approaching the final furlong. In the circumstances, she did well to reach fifth place and should be followed. (10/1)
2557 Fern's Governor stayed on in the last two furlongs without ever looking likely to reach a challenging position, and may be worth another chance. (4/1)
2645 What Happened Was (10/1: 8/1-12/1)
2603 Palo Blanco (12/1: 8/1-14/1)

2919 SUNLEY CONDITIONS STKS (2-Y.O F) (Class C)
7-50 (7-51) **5f 217y** £4,379.60 (£1,636.40: £798.20: £341.00: £150.50: £74.30) Stalls: High GOING minus 0.37 sec per fur (F)

				SP	RR	SF
2728[3]	**Jay Gee (IRE)** (GGMargarson) **2-8-9** GCarter(3) (lw: led over 3f: led over 1f out: r.o wl)	—	1	16/1	84	23
2597[3]	**Zelanda (IRE)** (JHMGosden) **2-8-9** AGarth(1) (a.p: led over 2f out tl over 1f out)	2	2	8/13[1]	79	18
	Fair Deal (USA) (DRLoder) **2-8-6** DHarrison(5) (leggy: chsd ldrs: outpcd over 1f out: r.o ins fnl f)	nk	3	6/1[3]	75	14
	Pride of My Heart (IABalding) **2-8-3**(3) MartinDwyer(2) (leggy: unf: bit bkwd: s.s: hdwy fnl 2f: nrst fin)	1¼	4	14/1	72	11
2371[2]	**Classy Cleo (IRE)** (RHannon) **2-8-13** PatEddery(6) (w ldrs tl wknd 2f out)	6	5	7/2[2]	63	2
1867[5]	**Lady Ralphina** (JJBridger) **2-8-4**(5) ADaly(4) (spd 3f: t.o)	16	6	100/1	16	—

(SP 112.0%) **6 Rn**

1m 13.3 (2.80) CSF £24.37 TOTE £14.50: £2.70 £1.20 (£8.70) OWNER Mr John Guest (NEWMARKET) BRED Eaton Farms Inc, Red Bull Stable and Joe Hernon
2728 Jay Gee (IRE) made the running until over two furlongs from home. She regained her advantage approaching the final furlong and there was no fluke about her win. (16/1)
2597 Zelanda (IRE) went with the leaders and gained a narrow advantage approaching the two-furlong marker. She was readily outpaced approaching the final furlong. (8/13)
Fair Deal (USA), a leggy filly, raced in fifth place but only two lengths behind the leader. After being tapped for foot approaching the final furlong, she ran on well inside the distance. (6/1: 5/2-7/1)
Pride of My Heart missed the break but was staying on in the last two furlongs. (14/1: 4/1-16/1)
2371 Classy Cleo (IRE) weakened rapidly after going with the leaders for half-a-mile. (7/2)

2920 CADOGAN CHARITY H'CAP (0-80) (3-Y.O+) (Class D)
8-20 (8-21) **1m 2f 7y** £3,467.00 (£1,046.00: £508.00: £239.00) Stalls: High GOING minus 0.37 sec per fur (F)

				SP	RR	SF
2533[2]	**Anak-Ku (75)** (MissGayKelleway) **4-10-0** SSanders(4) (lw: mde all: r.o wl)	—	1	4/1[1]	85	55
1231[0]	**Shahik (USA) (67)** (DHaydnJones) **7-9-6** SDrowne(7) (swtg: jnd wnr 7f out: ev ch tl nt qckn fnl f)	2½	2	33/1	73	43
2570[3]	**Hardy Dancer (67)** (GLMoore) **5-9-6** AClark(3) (hdwy fnl 2f: nvr nrr)	1	3	7/1	71	41
2550[3]	**Princess Danielle (67)** (WRMuir) **5-9-3**(3) MartinDwyer(8) (lw: hdwy on ins whn hmpd twice over 6f out: r.o fr 3 out: nt rch ldrs: fin 4th, s.h: disq: plcd last)	s.h	4d	4/1[1]	71	41
2550*	**Haroldon (IRE) (68)** (BPalling) **8-9-7** DaneO'Neill(1) (bhd tl rdn & hdwy 2f out: nvr nr ldrs: fin 5th, 6l & s.h: plcd 4th)	6	4	11/2[3]	63	33
2660*	**Askern (64)** (DHaydnJones) **6-9-3** AMackay(5) (hdwy 5f out: rdn over 3f out: sn wknd: fin 6th, nk: plcd 5th)	nk	5	4/1[1]	58	28
2380[4]	**Seattle Swing (77)** (MrsAJPerrett) **3-9-6** PatEddery(6) (lw: a bhd: fin 7th, 4l: plcd 6th)	4	6	5/1[2]	65	25
	Woodrising (57) (CREgerton) **5-8-10** MTebbutt(2) (prom early: sn bhd: fin 8th, 6l: plcd 7th)	6	7	20/1	35	5
2687[8]	**Bicton Park (70)** (KCComerford) **3-8-13** WJO'Connor(9) (lw: prom 4f: t.o: fin 9th, dist: plcd 8th)	dist	8	40/1	—	—

(SP 114.7%) **9 Rn**

2m 8.2 (3.30) CSF £125.18 CT £814.51 TOTE £3.70: £1.60 £6.10 £1.90 (£95.00) Trio £166.00 OWNER H R H Sultan Ahmad Shah (WHITCOMBE) BRED John Rose
WEIGHT FOR AGE 3yo-10lb
STEWARDS' ENQUIRY obj to Princess Danielle by Clerk of the Scales sustained. Dwyer susp. 30-31/7/97 (failure to weigh in).
2533 Anak-Ku made all the running and had only the second for company from before the halfway stage. Running on strongly, he was well in command in the final furlong. (4/1)
Shahik (USA) took on the winner after three furlongs and the pair were well clear from half-a-mile out. (33/1)
2570 Hardy Dancer stayed on from the back of the field to snatch third place on the post, but was never on terms with the first two. (7/1)
2550* Haroldon (IRE) never appeared likely to repeat his recent win here. He was at the back of the field until staying on under pressure in the final quarter-mile. (11/2: 4/1-6/1)
2660* Askern (4/1: 3/1-9/2)
2550 Princess Danielle was making headway on the inside when badly checked six furlongs from home. Though she improved to take a remote third place approaching the final furlong, she never threatened to take a hand in the finish. (4/1)

2921 MAXIMS CLUB H'CAP (0-70) (3-Y.O) (Class E)
8-50 (8-56) **5f 217y** £3,160.00 (£955.00: £465.00: £220.00) Stalls: High GOING minus 0.37 sec per fur (F)

				SP	RR	SF
2852*	**Distinctive Dream (IRE) (56)** (KTIvory) **3-8-4b**(3) 7x MartinDwyer(17) (b: a.p: led over 1f out: all out)	—	1	5/1[1]	67	33
1843[6]	**Ella Lamees (55)** (WJMusson) **3-8-6** KFallon(20) (lw: hdwy 2f out: hrd rdn & ev ch fnl f: r.o)	s.h	2	5/1[1]	66	32
1644[6]	**Stock Hill Dancer (53)** (BJMeehan) **3-7-11**(7) GHannon(16) (led over 4f: r.o)	½	3	20/1	63	29
*2669**	**Broadway Melody (63)** (APJarvis) **3-9-0** DHolland(7) (a.p: ev ch 1f out: nt qckn)	3½	4	15/2	63	29
2605[4]	**Big Ben (70)** (RHannon) **3-9-7** DaneO'Neill(19) (lw: hdwy fnl 2f: nvr nrr)	1½	5	7/1[3]	66	32
2665[9]	**Forgotten Times (USA) (61)** (TMJones) **3-8-12** NCarlisle(18) (lw: a.p: no hdwy fnl 2f)	½	6	8/1	56	22
2554[9]	**Heavenly Miss (IRE) (55)** (JJBridger) **3-8-6** SSanders(8) (hdwy over 2f out: hrd rdn over 1f out: nt qckn)	½	7	12/1	49	15
2554[4]	**Nervous Rex (55)** (WRMuir) **3-7-13**(7) JWilkinson(15) (prom 4f)	½	8	13/2[2]	47	13
2732[9]	**Whizz Kid (48)** (JJBridger) **3-7-10**(3)ow1 MHenry(11) (prom 4f)	¾	9	16/1	38	3

				SP	RR	SF
2665[8]	**Midnight Shift (IRE) (67)** (RGuest) **3-9-4** PBloomfield(9) (lw: nvr bttr than mid div)	2	**10**	14/1	52	18
2554[3]	**Will To Win (52)** (PGMurphy) **3-8-3** SDrowne(4) (lw: prom 4f)	s.h	**11**	8/1	37	3
2555[12]	**Imperial Glen (IRE) (48)** (MDIUsher) **3-7-13** JMarshall(10) (lw: a bhd)	2½	**12**	40/1	26	—
2319[9]	**Masterstroke (66)** (BJMeehan) **3-9-3b[1]** MTebbutt(5) (a bhd)	7	**13**	16/1	25	—
1851[7]	**Over The Moon (55)** (MJFetherston-Godley) **3-8-6** FNorton(14) (lw: a wl bhd)	2	**14**	20/1	9	—
2552[13]	**Sun O'Tirol (IRE) (54)** (JRArnold) **3-8-5b** CRutter(2) (prom 3f)	nk	**15**	25/1	7	—
1141[25]	**Class Distinction (IRE) (70)** (RHannon) **3-9-7** RHughes(13) (lw: prom over 3f)	3	**16**	20/1	15	—
885[11]	**Oakbrook Rose (52)** (MPMuggeridge) **3-8-3** SophieMitchell(6) (a wl bhd)	14	**17**	40/1	—	—
2730[13]	***Mighty Flow (52)*** (MrsPNDutfield) **3-8-0**(3) AWhelan(3) (Withdrawn not under Starters's orders: ref to ent stalls)		**W**	33/1	—	—

(SP 145.2%) **17 Rn**

1m 12.4 (1.90) CSF £27.88 CT £355.48 TOTE £5.10: £1.80 £1.90 £6.30 £2.00 (£16.10) Trio £159.60 OWNER Mr K. T. Ivory (RADLETT) BRED Peter Kehoe

2852* Distinctive Dream (IRE) is in terrific form and completed a quick hat-trick but, despite considerable improvement compared with earlier running against several of those behind, he had nothing in reserve at the finish. (5/1)

1843 Ella Lamees was gambled on from 12/1 and, given a great ride nearly pulled it off. This trip may be slightly short for her, and she should soon break her maiden. (5/1: op 10/1)

Stock Hill Dancer made much of the running, and kept going really well. This was her best effort so far, and she can take a similar contest. (20/1)

2669* Broadway Melody probably improved on her Wolverhampton win on her return to turf, and looks to be on the upgrade. (15/2)

2605 Big Ben, who has won twice over seven furlongs this season, seemed to find this trip too short. (7/1)

2554 Forgotten Times (USA) was further behind the winner on more favourable terms compared with their meeting at the beginning of July. His wins have come on the Lingfield All-Weather. (8/1: op 12/1)

1810 Heavenly Miss (IRE) was also better off with the winner on earlier course running. (12/1)

2554 Will To Win (8/1: 6/1-9/1)

T/Jkpt: £19, 085.20 (0.09 Tckts); £24,461.43 to Yarmouth 22/7/97. T/Plpt: £96.50 (237.82 Tckts). T/Qdpt: £11.40 (120.97 Tckts) AK/Hn

2770-**YARMOUTH (L-H) (Good to firm)**

Tuesday July 22nd

WEATHER: overcast WIND: fresh bhd becoming fresh half bhd

2922 SCRATBY H'CAP (0-75) (3-Y.O+) (Class D)

2-15 (2-18) **7f 3y** £3,932.25 (£1,176.00: £563.50: £257.25) Stalls: Low GOING minus 0.52 sec per fur (F)

				SP	RR	SF
2121[7]	**Mezzoramio (48)** (KAMorgan) **5-7-10v**(7)ow1 JoHunnam(11) (b: mde all: rdn fnl f: r.o wl)	—	**1**	4/1[1]	57	39
2557[18]	**Present Generation (72)** (RGuest) **4-9-8**(5) CLowther(1) (bhd: hdwy & drvn along 3f out: chsd wnr appr fnl f: r.o wl)	¾	**2**	25/1	79	62
*2603**	**Alpine Hideaway (IRE) (73)** (BHanbury) **4-9-7**(7) ANicholls(16) (lw: hld up: hdwy ½-wy: styd on wl ins fnl f)	1¼	**3**	10/1	77	60
2563[16]	**Ivory's Grab Hire (65)** (KTIvory) **4-9-3b**(3) MartinDwyer(6) (a.p: rdn over 1f out: unable qckn)	1½	**4**	16/1	66	49
2427*	**Karinska (56)** (MCChapman) **7-8-4**(7) SCarson(9) (lw: chsd ldrs: r.o one pce appr fnl f)	nk	**5**	8/1	56	39
2671[4]	**Wild Palm (67)** (WAO'Gorman) **5-9-8b** EmmaO'Gorman(7) (hld up mid div: effrt & nt clr run wl over 1f out: nt rcvr)	hd	**6**	6/1[2]	67	50
2711[8]	**Prima Silk (69)** (MJRyan) **6-9-10** GCarter(2) (hld up: hdwy 3f out: rdn over 1f out: one pce)	nk	**7**	8/1	68	51
2481[4]	**Hype Energy (56)** (GLewis) **3-8-4** PaulEddery(3) (hld up: hdwy wl over 1f out: nvr nrr)	½	**8**	7/1[3]	54	30
2390[6]	**Pengamon (68)** (HJCollingridge) **5-9-9** JQuinn(5) (trckd ldrs: rdn 2f out: no imp)	¾	**9**	8/1	65	48
2724[5]	**Shermood (41)** (KTIvory) **4-7-3**(7) DarrenWilliams(13) (b: b.hind: hld up: hdwy 3f out: nt rch ldrs)	nk	**10**	50/1	37	20
1631[4]	**Mukhlles (USA) (66)** (BobJones) **4-9-7** NDay(8) (bit bkwd: in tch: effrt & hrd rdn wl over 1f out: sn btn)	nk	**11**	10/1	61	44
2151[8]	**Push A Venture (53)** (SPCWoods) **3-7-12**(3) RFfrench(12) (trckd ldrs: pushed along over 2f out: sn btn)	1¾	**12**	20/1	44	20
2760[12]	**Hopeful Bid (IRE) (53)** (PHowling) **8-8-8** NCarlisle(4) (b: a in rr)	3	**13**	20/1	37	20
	Red Admiral (61) (CMurray) **7-9-2** NicolaHowarth(10) (bkwd: chsd wnr tl rdn & wknd over 2f out)	3½	**14**	20/1	37	20
2747[2]	**Nicker (63)** (WJarvis) **3-8-11** WRyan(14) (a bhd)	3½	**15**	15/2	31	7
	E-Mail (IRE) (72) (JMPEustace) **3-9-6** JTate(15) (nt grwn: bkwd: sn pushed along: a in rr: t.o)	5	**16**	33/1	29	5

(SP 139.0%) **16 Rn**

1m 24.6 (0.40) CSF £114.90 CT £951.63 TOTE £5.30: £1.10 £6.70 £3.50 £4.30 (£453.80) Trio £731.40; £432.67 to Catterick 23/7/97 OWNER Mr T. R. Pryke (MELTON MOWBRAY) BRED Saeed Manana

LONG HANDICAP Shermood 6-8

WEIGHT FOR AGE 3yo-7lb

OFFICIAL EXPLANATION E-Mail (IRE): lost a shoe.

1501 Mezzoramio had the high-numbered stall that is crucial when the ground rides fast and, dominating all the way, was always going to hold on. (4/1: op 6/1)

Present Generation ran well considering he showed such a poor action to post, staying on willingly in the closing stages, and that initial success is well within his reach. (25/1)

2603* Alpine Hideaway (IRE) was far from disgraced in this step-up in class, but did seem to have an almost impossible task at the weights. (10/1)

1509* Ivory's Grab Hire has won at this trip, but he does most of his racing at sprint distances now and he was feeling the strain once into the final furlong. (16/1)

2427* Karinska, not helped by this ever-drying ground, did her best to get into the action but, with the pace not dropping, was unable to land a blow. (8/1: op 5/1)

2671 Wild Palm, once again, had a nightmare run when poised to deliver his challenge and the fact that he did finish so close would suggest he was unlucky. He is continuing to perform with credit and another success cannot be too far away. (6/1)

2923 ELIZABETH SIMPSON (S) STKS (2-Y.O) (Class G)

2-45 (2-46) **7f 3y** £2,406.00 (£666.00: £318.00) Stalls: Low GOING minus 0.52 sec per fur (F)

				SP	RR	SF
2153[3]	**The Honorable Lady** (MRChannon) **2-8-3**(3) PPMurphy(10) (lw: a.p: led 2f out: clr fnl f)	—	**1**	7/1	67	27
2664[2]	**Little Tumbler (IRE)** (SWoodman) **2-8-6** PatEddery(1) (lw: chsd ldrs: rdn 2f out: kpt on ins fnl f: no ch w wnr)	5	**2**	7/4[1]	56	16
2587[5]	**Kite** (MBell) **2-8-6** MFenton(8) (a.p: ev ch 2f out: rdn & one pce fnl f)	nk	**3**	6/1	55	15
2163[3]	**Medina Miss** (WGMTurner) **2-8-1**(5) DSweeney(4) (led tl hdd 2f out: sn rdn: outpcd fnl f)	1½	**4**	11/2[3]	52	12

				SP	RR	SF
2719^{6}	**Bermuda Triangle (IRE)** (MJHaynes) **2-8-3**$^{(3)}$ RFfrench(5) (prom: nt clr run over 2f out: sn rdn & wknd)	5	**5**	7/1	40	—
2786^{9}	**Muja's Magic (IRE)** (KTIvory) **2-8-3**$^{(3)}$ MartinDwyer(9) (a outpcd)	2½	**6**	9/1	34	—
2587^{7}	**Lilian Marks (IRE)** (BJMeehan) **2-8-6** MTebbutt(6) (a in rr)	1¼	**7**	20/1	32	—
2579^{2}	**Shannon (IRE)** (CADwyer) **2-8-3**$^{(3)}$ DO'Donohoe(3) (outpcd: a bhd)	1	**8**	9/2^{2}	29	—
2047^{9}	**Summer River (IRE)** (CMurray) **2-8-11v** PBloomfield(7) (a in rr)	½	**9**	25/1	33	—
	Senor Hurst (MrsPSly) **2-8-11** NCarlisle(2) (unf: scope: bkwd: dwlt: sn chsng ldrs: wknd wl over 2f out: t.o)	26	**10**	25/1	—	—
				(SP 131.7%)	**10 Rn**	

1m 25.9 (1.70) CSF £19.94 TOTE £8.00: £1.80 £1.20 £1.80 (£8.70) Trio £22.10 OWNER Henry Ponsonby & Partners (1) (UPPER LAMBOURN) BRED Stetchworth Park Stud Ltd

Bt in 9,500gns

2153 The Honorable Lady, content to wait on the leaders, took over entering the final quarter-mile and strode clear for a very easy success. She proved costly to retain and her future may well lie in nurseries. (7/1)

2664 Little Tumbler (IRE), always struggling with the pace, came into her own in the latter stages and stamina would seem to be her strong suit. (7/4)

2587 Kite is improving with each run and there is a race waiting to be picked up. (6/1: op 7/2)

2163 Medina Miss, bowling along in the lead from the start, was made to look very slow when the winner quickened things up, and it is doubtful if this longer trip was in her favour. (11/2)

1827 Bermuda Triangle (IRE), engaged in a barging match over two furlongs out, was almost certainly knocked out of her stride, for her chance quickly evaporated. (7/1)

2578 Muja's Magic (IRE) (9/1: 5/1-10/1)

2579 Shannon (IRE) (9/2: op 5/2)

2924 MEDLER MAIDEN STKS (3-Y.O+) (Class D)

3-15 (3-17) **1m 3f 101y** £3,677.45 (£1,097.60: £524.30: £237.65) Stalls: High GOING minus 0.52 sec per fur (F)

				SP	RR	SF
933^{12}	**Invermark (82)** (JRFanshawe) **3-8-12** MHills(7) (hdwy 7f out: led over 3f out tl wl over 1f out: rallied to ld ins fnl f: all out)	—	**1**	8/1^{3}	84	31
2046^{2}	**Awesome Wells (IRE) (85)** (HRACecil) **3-8-12** KFallon(6) (hld up: hdwy 4f out: rdn to ld wl over 1f out: hdd & no ex ins fnl f)	hd	**2**	4/5^{1}	84	31
2532^{4}	**Marsul (USA)** (JHMGosden) **3-8-12** RHills(3) (hld up in tch: rdn wl over 1f out: r.o wl towards fin)	hd	**3**	8/1^{3}	84	31
2389^{4}	**Elbaaha (80)** (MAJarvis) **3-8-7** BDoyle(4) (a chsng ldrs: nt clr run & hung lft fnl 2f: kpt on u.p)	¾	**4**	8/1^{3}	78	25
	Jaseur (USA) (JHMGosden) **4-9-9** GHind(2) (bit bkwd: s.s: hdwy 3f out: sn drvn along & outpcd)	6	**5**	10/1	74	32
2537^{5}	**Devilish Charm (USA)** (MrsAJPerrett) **3-8-12** PatEddery(1) (bit bkwd: led: drvn along & hdd over 3f out: sn btn: t.o)	14	**6**	9/2^{2}	55	2
2687^{5}	**Glittering (USA)** (CEBrittain) **3-8-12** RCochrane(8) (trckd ldrs tl wknd over 3f out: sn t.o)	hd	**7**	40/1	55	2
1130^{8}	**Briggs Turn** (WJarvis) **3-8-12** MTebbutt(5) (prom over 6f: sn lost tch: t.o)	24	**8**	50/1	—	—
				(SP 120.6%)	**8 Rn**	

2m 25.2 (3.40) CSF £14.30 TOTE £7.90: £2.70 £1.10 £1.90 (£6.50) OWNER Sir David Wills (NEWMARKET) BRED Sir David Wills

WEIGHT FOR AGE 3yo-11lb

Invermark found this much easier than the hot handicap he ran in on his previous outing in May, but it was his superior stamina in the latter stages that enabled him to get off the mark. (8/1: op 5/1)

2046 Awesome Wells (IRE) looks to be a hard ride and he is still striving to get winning brackets by his name. Fortune will favour him before long. (4/5: evens-11/10)

2532 Marsul (USA) stayed on really well under strong pressure in the closing stages and he is improving fast. (8/1: op 4/1)

2389 Elbaaha was close enough if good enough throughout the last quarter-mile, but she did not help her cause by hanging to the left towards the rail where there was no room at all. She has the ability and will show her true worth one of these days. (8/1)

Jaseur (USA) is very lightly-raced and did not relish this lively ground, but he ran better than his finishing position might suggest after losing ground at the start, and there must be some reason why he remains in training in such a powerful stable. (10/1: op 6/1)

2537 Devilish Charm (USA) is still not the finished article and he looked ill at ease on the ground, so this performance can safely be put down to a learning process. (9/2: op 7/1)

2925 NORTH WALSHAM H'CAP (0-95) (3-Y.O) (Class C)

3-45 (3-47) **6f 3y** £5,494.90 (£1,640.20: £783.60: £355.30) Stalls: Low GOING minus 0.52 sec per fur (F)

				SP	RR	SF
2560^{2}	**Elnadim (USA) (94)** (JLDunlop) **3-9-7** RHills(5) (lw: a.p: chal over 1f out: hrd rdn to ld cl home)	—	**1**	2/1^{1}	108	65
2590^{5}	**March Crusader (78)** (BHanbury) **3-8-5** JStack(9) (lw: a.p: led over 2f out: hrd rdn & ct nr fin)	hd	**2**	5/1^{2}	92	49
2691^{3}	**Ivory Dawn (75)** (KTIvory) **3-7-13**$^{(3)}$ MartinDwyer(10) (hdwy over 2f out: kpt on ins fnl f)	4	**3**	8/1	78	35
2560^{5}	**Silca Key Silca (85)** (MRChannon) **3-8-5**$^{(7)}$ AEddery(8) (led over 3f: rdn & outpcd appr fnl f)	½	**4**	10/1	87	44
1610^{9}	**Carati (84)** (RBoss) **3-8-11** KFallon(7) (prom tl hrd rdn & wknd 2f out)	3½	**5**	25/1	76	33
2517^{5}	**Blues Queen (78)** (MRChannon) **3-8-2**$^{(3)}$ PPMurphy(2) (in tch: outpcd over 2f out: sn hrd rdn & no imp)	7	**6**	25/1	52	9
694^{2}	**Refuse To Lose (80)** (JMPEustace) **3-8-7** RCochrane(4) (a outpcd)	s.h	**7**	11/2^{3}	54	11
*871**	**Forcing Bid (80)** (SirMarkPrescott) **3-8-7** GDuffield(6) (bit bkwd: bhd: effrt u.p over 2f out: a outpcd)	1¾	**8**	7/1	49	6
	Wait For Rosie (86) (VSoane) **3-8-13** JQuinn(11) (outpcd)	4	**9**	33/1	44	1
1029^{13}	**Moonshiner (USA) (84)** (GWragg) **3-8-11b**^{1} MHills(1) (chsd ldrs over 3f: sn outpcd)	5	**10**	16/1	29	—
2654^{5}	**Hopesay (80)** (JHMGosden) **3-8-7** PatEddery(3) (lw: chsd ldrs: rdn along ½-wy: sn lost tch)	1¼	**11**	8/1	22	—
				(SP 125.7%)	**11 Rn**	

1m 10.6 (-0.30) CSF £11.32 CT £66.50 TOTE £3.30: £1.50 £1.60 £2.20 (£11.00) Trio £22.60 OWNER Mr Hamdan Al Maktoum (ARUNDEL) BRED Shadwell Farm Inc

2560 Elnadim (USA) had to work really hard to win this, but the race was run in a time not far off the record and, with top weight, this will go down as some performance. (2/1)

2590 March Crusader got first run and made the favourite give everything he had to wear him down nearing the line. This was a better than average performance and he can soon make amends. (5/1)

2691 Ivory Dawn appeared to find the early pace more than she could handle, but she began to pick up inside the last quarter-mile and there could be more success to follow. (8/1: 5/1-9/1)

2560 Silca Key Silca needs easier underfoot conditions than she had here, but she forced the pace until past halfway before having to admit the leading pair much too good for her. (10/1)

988 Carati, fresh and well after almost two months out of action, showed up with the pace until finding things much too hot once the battle to the finish really got under way. (25/1)

871* Forcing Bid, twice successful on the All-Weather in the spring, was far from happy on this much faster ground. (7/1: op 4/1)

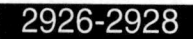

2654 Hopesay (8/1: 6/1-9/1)

2926 E.B.F. SCROBY SANDS MAIDEN STKS (2-Y.O) (Class D)

4-15 (4-16) **5f 43y** £3,351.25 (£1,000.00: £477.50: £216.25) Stalls: Low GOING minus 0.52 sec per fur (F)

				SP	RR	SF
2728^{7}	**Gipsy Moth** (BJMeehan) **2-8-9** PatEddery(6) (lw: mde all: edgd rt fnl 2f: comf)	—	1	10/1	82+	42
2324^{2}	**Clef of Silver** (WJarvis) **2-9-0** MHills(3) (lw: hdwy 2f out: rdn appr fnl f: nt pce of wnr)	2½	2	13/8^{2}	79	39
	Escudo (IRE) (JHMGosden) **2-8-9** GHind(8) (neat: scope: bit bkwd: s.s: hdwy ½-wy: kpt on fnl f: improve)	2	3	6/1^{3}	68+	28
2720^{9}	**Tightrope** (SirMarkPrescott) **2-9-0** GDuffield(4) (outpcd tl sme late hdwy)	3	4	14/1	64	24
1744^{10}	**Naayel (IRE)** (CJBenstead) **2-9-0** RHills(7) (chsd ldrs 3f: sn rdn & outpcd)	1¾	5	20/1	59	19
2597^{6}	**Babanina** (CEBrittain) **2-8-9** BDoyle(1) (chsd wnr tl lost pl fnl 2f)	1½	6	6/4^{1}	49	9
2771^{4}	**Princess Olivia** (MJRyan) **2-8-9** GCarter(5) (bit bkwd: dwlt: a bhd & outpcd)	1¾	7	12/1	44	4
2409^{6}	**Marahill Lad** (PHowling) **2-9-0** PaulEddery(2) (b: rdn ½-wy: sn lost tch: t.o)	8	8	33/1	24	—

(SP 123.5%) **8 Rn**

61.4 secs (0.40) CSF £26.40 TOTE £10.60: £2.20 £1.10 £2.10 (£15.20) OWNER Mrs K. J. Crangle (UPPER LAMBOURN) BRED P. T. Tellwright

1970 Gipsy Moth did it all from the front and, forging clear after edging over to the stands' rail, won very much as she pleased. (10/1)

2324 Clef of Silver had to settle for the runner-up prize once again, but he ran his race out to the finish and his turn will come. (13/8: 6/4-9/4)

Escudo (IRE), a not over-big debutante who failed to impress with her action to post, ran a pleasing race after forfeiting ground at the start, and this half-sister to four winners will not let the family name down. (6/1: 4/1-7/1)

2720 Tightrope could not go the early pace, but he was picking up in the latter stages and is open to further improvement. (14/1: 8/1-16/1)

Naayel (IRE), very keen to post, is hardly giving himself a chance at present and experience should settle him. (20/1)

2597 Babanina was all the rage in the betting ring after such a promising start to her career, but she was in trouble soon after halfway and, as she showed at Newmarket, is better than this. (6/4)

2927 BELTON MAIDEN H'CAP (0-75) (3-Y.O+) (Class D)

4-45 (4-45) **1m 6f 17y** £3,900.40 (£1,166.20: £558.60: £254.80) Stalls: High GOING minus 0.52 sec per fur (F)

				SP	RR	SF
2199^{5}	**Aztec Flyer (USA) (45)** (CEBrittain) **4-8-10b^{1}** BDoyle(1) (chsd ldr: led 6f out: rdn over 2f out: styd on strly)	—	1	15/2	62	22
2592^{11}	**Charming Admiral (IRE) (56)** (CFWall) **4-9-7** GDuffield(5) (chsd ldrs: chal 2f out: sn rdn: r.o one pce)	5	2	9/2	67	27
2230^{9}	**Nordic Crest (IRE) (73)** (PWHarris) **3-9-5**(5) CLowther(4) (lw: hld up: hdwy over 3f out: sn rdn: nt rch ldrs)	10	3	100/30^{2}	73	19
2430^{7}	**Acerbus Dulcis (33)** (MCChapman) **6-7-5**(7)ow2 SCarson(2) (dwlt: effrt 4f out: sn rdn: no imp)	3	4	12/1	30	—
2421^{5}	**Dalwhinnie (57)** (JWharton) **4-9-8b^{1}** KFallon(3) (lw: chsd ldrs: wnt 2nd over 5f out: rdn & wknd wl over 3f out: t.o)	22	5	9/4^{1}	29	—
2692^{4}	**Coble (70)** (BWHills) **3-9-7b^{1}** MHills(6) (led over 8f: wknd qckly: t.o)	hd	6	7/2^{3}	41	—

(SP 113.7%) **6 Rn**

3m 3.7 (5.70) CSF £37.21 TOTE £8.00: £2.70 £2.50 (£15.00) OWNER Mr R. Meredith (NEWMARKET) BRED Raul Martin

LONG HANDICAP Acerbus Dulcis 7-8

WEIGHT FOR AGE 3yo-14lb

2199 Aztec Flyer (USA), much keener in the blinkers, kicked on at the end of the back straight and, keeping up the gallop under a strong ride, proved much too good for these rivals. (15/2: 5/1-8/1)

Charming Admiral (IRE) looked to be travelling just the better when joining issue entering the last quarter-mile, but the winner kept finding extra and worried him out of it. (9/2: 3/1-5/1)

1649 Nordic Crest (IRE) could never get himself in with a shout despite staying on, and he has run his best races at much shorter trips. (100/30: 2/1-7/2)

2421 Dalwhinnie, travelled really well as long as she was on the bridle but, when she was let down, she stopped to nothing. Time will tell it was the lively ground that was the cause for such a below-par performance. (9/4: 2/1-3/1)

T/Jkpt: Not won; £35,831.54 to Catterick 23/7/97. T/Plpt: £79.10 (352.52 Tckts). T/Qdpt: £12.40 (140.21 Tckts) IM

2777-BATH (L-H) (Firm)
Wednesday July 23rd

WEATHER: fine WIND: mod across

2928 ORCHARDLEIGH LIMITED STKS (0-65) (3-Y.O+) (Class F)

2-15 (2-15) **1m 3f 144y** £2,670.00 (£745.00: £360.00) Stalls: Low GOING minus 0.46 sec per fur (F)

				SP	RR	SF
2696^{6}	**Pay Homage (65)** (IABalding) **9-9-1**(3) MartinDwyer(3) (swtg: trckd ldr: rdn over 3f out: r.o to ld last stride)	—	1	7/1^{2}	75	55
2879*	**Missfortuna (65)** (SirMarkPrescott) **3-8-5** 2x GDuffield(6) (a.p: led wl over 2f out: sn hdd: led 1f out: hdd last stride)	hd	2	8/13^{1}	74	42
2421^{2}	**Peppers (IRE) (65)** (KRBurke) **4-9-1** BDoyle(4) (hld up: hdwy over 3f out: led over 2f out to 1f out: nt qckn)	1	3	7/1^{2}	71	51
2373^{10}	**Newport Knight (65)** (RAkehurst) **6-9-4** SSanders(7) (b.hind: hld up & bhd: rdn 3f out: styd on one pce fnl 2f)	5	4	16/1	67	47
2696^{12}	**Statajack (IRE) (60)** (DRCElsworth) **9-9-4b** RCochrane(5) (b: hld up: hdwy 5f out: rdn over 3f out: one pce)	nk	5	10/1^{3}	66	46
2646^{3}	**Java Shrine (USA) (53)** (AJChamberlain) **6-8-11**(7) RCody-Boutcher(8) (hld up: a bhd)	6	6	40/1	58	38
2569^{6}	**Russian Olive (64)** (LMCumani) **3-8-0**(3) RFfrench(1) (sn chsng ldr: led 7f out tl over 3f out: wknd over 2f out)	1¾	7	10/1^{3}	53	21
2694^{6}	**Western Playboy (54)** (RJBaker) **5-9-4** VSlattery(2) (plld hrd: led over 4f: rdn to ld wl over 3f out: hdd wl over 2f out: sn wknd)	5	8	100/1	49	29

(SP 114.4%) **8 Rn**

2m 28.2 (1.50) CSF £10.65 TOTE £10.10: £1.60 £1.10 £1.30 (£5.80) OWNER Miss A. V. Hill (KINGSCLERE) BRED Cheveley Park Stud Ltd

WEIGHT FOR AGE 3yo-12lb

2696 Pay Homage, scoring for the first time beyond nine furlongs, had not won for over two years but does need this sort of trip nowadays. (7/1)

2879* Missfortuna, making a quick reappearance, was again stepping up in trip and got nailed right on the line. (8/13)

2421 Peppers (IRE) again showed she stays beyond a mile and a quarter. (7/1: 5/1-15/2)

Newport Knight has yet to recapture the form that saw him register back to back wins a year ago. (16/1)

2391 Statajack (IRE) had finished five lengths behind the winner when pulling hard at Salisbury last time. (10/1)

2569 Russian Olive (10/1: op 9/2)

2929 BE HOPEFUL MEMORIAL H'CAP (0-80) (3-Y.O+) (Class D)
2-45 (2-45) **1m 5y** £3,556.25 (£1,070.00: £517.50: £241.25) Stalls: Low GOING minus 0.46 sec per fur (F)

				SP	RR	SF
1955[2]	**Blue Imperial (FR) (65)** (JWHills) **3-8-5**(3) MHenry(5) (chsd ldr: rdn over 3f out: led over 2f out: r.o wl)	—	1	5/2[1]	80	46
2848[3]	**Samara Song (53)** (IPWilliams) **4-8-4**ow1 SSanders(1) (hld up: hdwy on ins 3f out: rdn & chsd wnr over 1f out: no imp)	3	2	3/1[2]	62	35
2743*	**Sooty Tern (77)** (JMBradley) **10-9-11**(3) 7x RFfrench(4) (lw: hld up: hdwy 4f out: rdn & one pce fnl 2f)	2½	3	5/1[3]	81	55
2552[8]	**Paddy's Rice (55)** (MBlanshard) **6-8-6** JQuinn(3) (hld up: hdwy 4f out: rdn & one pce fnl 2f)	¾	4	10/1	58	32
2743[6]	**Night Wink (USA) (70)** (GLMoore) **5-9-7v** SWhitworth(7) (plld hrd: led over 5f: sn wknd)	¾	5	11/2	71	45
2315[15]	**Norman Conquest (USA) (69)** (IABalding) **3-8-12** BDoyle(6) (lw: hld up: a bhd)	3½	6	14/1	63	29
	Final Stab (IRE) (73) (PWHarris) **4-9-5**(5) CLowther(2) (hld up: a bhd)	3	7	11/1	61	35
				(SP 109.7%)	**7 Rn**	

1m 39.1 (0.90) CSF £8.43 TOTE £3.60: £1.80 £1.90 (£3.30) OWNER Mr George Tong (LAMBOURN) BRED Haras de Clairfeuille
WEIGHT FOR AGE 3yo-8lb
1955 Blue Imperial (FR), freshened up by a break, had gone up a total of 11lb this season, but continues to improve. He loves fast ground and may go to Glorious Goodwood next week. (5/2)
2848 Samara Song is nothing if not consistent and deserves to break his duck. (3/1)
2743* Sooty Tern found racing off a mark 4lb higher than last week too much. (5/1)
1506* Paddy's Rice had finished eight and a half lengths behind Sooty Tern on 12lb better terms in Brighton in June. (10/1)
2743 Night Wink (USA) ran much too freely in the re-fitted visor. (11/2)
1877 Norman Conquest (USA) (14/1: op 8/1)
Final Stab (IRE) (11/1: 8/1-12/1)

2930 WEST LITTLETON LIMITED STKS (0-80) (3-Y.O+) (Class D)
3-15 (3-15) **1m 2f 46y** £3,419.75 (£1,028.00: £496.50: £230.75) Stalls: Low GOING minus 0.46 sec per fur (F)

				SP	RR	SF
2672[9]	**Farmost (80)** (SirMarkPrescott) **4-9-4** GDuffield(4) (lw: led after 1f: hdd over 2f out: nt clr run & swtchd rt over 1f out: rallied to ld last stride)	—	1	4/1[3]	84	65
1272*	**Space Race (72)** (CACyzer) **3-8-10** KFallon(6) (a.p: wnt 2nd 8f out: led over 2f out: edgd lft over 1f out: ct last stride)	s.h	2	7/2[2]	86	57
2532[3]	**Danzas (80)** (RCharlton) **3-8-8** TSprake(5) (dwlt: hdwy 5f out: one pce fnl 2f)	5	3	7/4[1]	76	47
1092[4]	**Alaflak (IRE) (78)** (MajorWRHern) **6-9-4** PaulEddery(3) (b: b.hind: prom early: rdn over 3f out: sn bhd)	8	4	5/1	64	45
2594[4]	**Polar Champ (78)** (SPCWoods) **4-9-3**(3) RFfrench(2) (hld up: rdn over 3f out: a bhd)	nk	5	5/1	65	46
	Shifting Moon (78) (FJordan) **5-9-4** SSanders(1) (lw: led 1f: reminder over 6f out: wknd 3f out)	½	6	20/1	62	43
				(SP 116.7%)	**6 Rn**	

2m 6.5 (0.10 under best) (equals standard) CSF £17.42 TOTE £5.20: £1.80 £2.10 (£12.40) OWNER Mr W. E. Sturt (NEWMARKET) BRED Hesmonds Stud Ltd
WEIGHT FOR AGE 3yo-10lb
OFFICIAL EXPLANATION **Trainer reported that the gelding had shown nothing this year either at home or on the racecourse, and that this win astonished him.**
1082 Farmost, disappointing in two runs on the sand, has apparently not been working all that well and, although supported in the ring, flabbergasted his trainer. (4/1)
1272* Space Race handled the fast ground and longer trip but may well have lost the race in the Stewards' room had he held on, because he caused the winner to switch. (7/2)
2532 Danzas was again disappointing. (7/4)
1092 Alaflak (IRE) had finished third over hurdles a week ago. (5/1)
2594 Polar Champ (5/1: op 11/4)

2931 E.B.F. MELKSHAM NOVICE STKS (2-Y.O) (Class D)
3-45 (3-45) **5f 11y** £3,568.00 (£998.00: £484.00) Stalls: High GOING minus 0.46 sec per fur (F)

				SP	RR	SF
1990*	**Its All Relative** (JBerry) **2-8-4**(5) CLowther(1) (lw: mde all: edgd rt over 1f out: clr fnl f)	—	1	15/8[2]	89+	6
2370[5]	**Fast Tempo (IRE)** (BPalling) **2-8-13** TSprake(3) (lw: a.p: rdn 2f out: wnt 2nd 1f out: no ch w wnr)	7	2	6/1[3]	71	—
2648[2]	**Tempus Fugit** (BRMillman) **2-8-11** BDoyle(2) (lw: w wnr: rdn over 2f out: btn whn sltly hmpd over 1f out)	2	3	8/13[1]	63	—
				(SP 111.0%)	**3 Rn**	

63.6 secs (3.10) CSF £8.33 TOTE £2.60: (£4.60) OWNER Mr R. Leah (COCKERHAM) BRED R. Leah
OFFICIAL EXPLANATION **Tempus Fugit: the trainer reported that the filly was subsequently found to be jarred up.**
1990* Its All Relative is certainly progressing nicely on this evidence. (15/8)
2370 Fast Tempo (IRE) at least turned around the Windsor form with the favourite on this faster ground. (6/1)
2648 Tempus Fugit possibly found the ground too lively. (8/13)

2932 CHUCKLESTONE H'CAP (0-70) (3-Y.O+) (Class E)
4-15 (4-15) **2m 1f 34y** £2,937.25 (£883.00: £426.50: £198.25) Stalls: High GOING minus 0.46 sec per fur (F)

				SP	RR	SF
1795[7]	**Brighter Byfaah (IRE) (42)** (NAGraham) **4-8-3** TSprake(7) (hld up & bhd: hdwy over 6f out: edgd lft & led over 1f out: jst hld on)	—	1	16/1	56	38
2014[22]	**Shadirwan (IRE) (63)** (RAkehurst) **6-9-10** SSanders(1) (a.p: hrd rdn 3f out: swchd rt over 1f out: styd on wl ins fnl f)	s.h	2	8/1[3]	77	59
2490*	**Manileno (62)** (MCPipe) **3-8-3**(3) MartinDwyer(3) (led: rdn over 2f out: hdd over 1f out: wknd ins fnl f)	5	3	6/5[1]	71	36
2198[7]	**Coh Sho No (54)** (SDow) **4-9-1** RHughes(8) (hld up & bhd: hdwy 10f out: chsd ldr 8f out tl over 3f out: one pce fnl 2f)	2½	4	8/1[3]	61	43
2702[5]	**Royal Circus (45)** (IPWilliams) **8-8-3**(3) PPMurphy(4) (chsd ldr over 9f: rdn over 4f out: wknd over 2f out)	7	5	12/1	45	27
1953[4]	**Coleridge (42)** (JJSheehan) **9-7-12b**(5)ow4 ADaly(6) (wl bhd fnl 5f)	9	6	10/1	34	12
2175[5]	**Longcroft (35)** (CLPopham) **5-7-3**(7) PBradley(2) (swtg: wl bhd fnl 5f)	1½	7	40/1	26	8
762[14]	**Beauchamp Knight (50)** (HCandy) **4-8-11** SWhitworth(9) (hld up: lost tch 5f out: eased fnl 3f)	dist	8	20/1	—	—

				SP	RR	SF
1665*	**Landlord (52)** (PBowen) **5-8-13b** MFenton(5) (prom tl wknd over 6f out: eased fnl 3f)	dist	**9**	6/1[2]	—	—
				(SP 111.8%)	**9 Rn**	

3m 44.6 (3.20) CSF £119.66 CT £244.81 TOTE £22.20: £4.30 £1.40 £1.40 (£36.30) Trio £14.90 OWNER Mr Paul Jacobs (NEWMARKET) BRED Limestone Stud
WEIGHT FOR AGE 3yo-17lb
Brighter Byfaah (IRE), inclined to want to lean on the favourite, was 1lb lower than when winning a Nottingham seller over a mile and three quarters a year ago. (16/1)
831 Shadirwan (IRE) bounced back to form, having tumbled to a mark 7lb lower than when winning at Doncaster's Lincoln meeting last season. (8/1)
2490* Manileno, again up in distance, had been raised a further 5lb. (6/5)
1974 Coh Sho No is back to the same mark as when successful at Folkestone in April. (8/1: op 5/1)
2702 Royal Circus has yet to win beyond a mile and five. (12/1: op 8/1)
1665* Landlord (6/1: op 7/2)

2933 DYRHAM SPRINT H'CAP (0-80) (3-Y.O+) (Class D)
4-45 (4-45) **5f 161y** £3,738.25 (£1,126.00: £545.50: £255.25) Stalls: High GOING minus 0.46 sec per fur (F)

				SP	RR	SF
2780*	**Hard to Figure (80)** (RJHodges) **11-9-13**(3) 7x PPMurphy(3) (lw: bhd tl gd hdwy over 1f out: r.o wl to ld nr fin)	—	**1**	10/1	89	68
2844[8]	**Sharp Pearl (74)** (PRWebber) **4-9-10b** SWhitworth(4) (hdwy 2f out: led ins fnl f: hdd nr fin)	nk	**2**	10/1	82	61
2663[2]	**Ansellman (78)** (JBerry) **7-9-9b**(5) PRoberts(1) (a.p: led 1f out tl ins fnl f)	1¾	**3**	11/2[3]	81	60
2529[13]	**Akalim (61)** (LGCottrell) **4-8-11** MFenton(6) (chsd ldr: led over 1f out: sn hdd: one pce)	¾	**4**	7/1	62	41
2581[6]	**Kildee Lad (66)** (APJones) **7-8-13**(3) JDSmith(2) (rdn & hdwy over 2f out: ev ch over 1f out: one pce)	s.h	**5**	11/4[1]	67	46
2788[17]	**Beau Venture (USA) (66)** (BPalling) **9-9-2** TSprake(8) (led: clr over 2f out: hdd over 1f out: wknd fnl f)	5	**6**	9/1	53	32
2788[9]	**Meranti (61)** (JMBradley) **4-8-11** SophieMitchell(7) (lw: s.i.s: hdwy over 2f out: wknd fnl f)	¾	**7**	7/1	46	25
2743[2]	**Victory Team (IRE) (72)** (GBBalding) **5-9-8** RHughes(5) (a bhd)	3	**8**	5/1[2]	49	28
				(SP 111.9%)	**8 Rn**	

1m 10.0 (0.50) CSF £89.88 CT £547.95 TOTE £6.90: £2.70 £3.00 £1.80 (£45.70) OWNER Mr J. W. Mursell (SOMERTON) BRED J. W. Mursell
2780* Hard to Figure, over the extended five this time, was 21lb lower than his last handicap win which came in the 1993 Ayr Gold Cup. (10/1: 7/1-11/1)
2220 Sharp Pearl had ground conditions in his favour and very nearly pulled it off. (10/1: 8/1-12/1)
2663 Ansellman was possibly just found out by the extended five. (11/2: 4/1-6/1)
Akalim, 15lb lower than when winning a nursery in October 1995, could be finding some form. (7/1)
2581 Kildee Lad, down 3lb, was 10lb lower than when winning this race last season. (11/4)
2703 Beau Venture (USA) has won once over course and distance but the remainder of his victories have come over the bare minimum. (9/1: op 5/1)
2788 Meranti (7/1: op 4/1)

T/Plpt: £123.70 (138.97 Tckts). T/Qdpt: £78.00 (6.87 Tckts) KH

2752-CATTERICK (L-H) (Good to firm, Good patches)
Wednesday July 23rd
WEATHER: overcast & warm with sunny periods WIND: mod across

2934 C.S.S. SDN BHD H'CAP (0-70) (3-Y.O+) (Class E)
2-30 (2-31) **5f** £3,304.25 (£989.00: £474.50: £217.25) Stalls: Low GOING minus 0.12 sec per fur (G)

				SP	RR	SF
2759*	**Cross The Border (54)** (DNicholls) **4-9-0** AlexGreaves(1) (lw: trckd ldrs: smooth hdwy to ld 1f out: pushed out)	—	**1**	11/10[1]	65+	46
2738*	**Young Ben (IRE) (48)** (JSWainwright) **5-8-5b**(3)ow7 7x GParkin(7) (b.hind: in tch centre: hdwy over 1f out: styd on wl towards fin)	1	**2**	12/1	56	30
2899[4]	**Imp Express (IRE) (40)** (GMMoore) **4-8-0** DaleGibson(17) (lw: chsd ldrs stands' side: styd on u.p fnl 2f)	½	**3**	20/1	46	27
1865[7]	**Grand Chapeau (IRE) (50)** (DNicholls) **5-8-10** JWeaver(6) (lw: led 4f: no ex)	¾	**4**	20/1	54	35
	Kabcast (41) (DWChapman) **12-8-1b** TWilliams(16) (led stands' side over 3f: wknd)	2	**5**	100/1	38	19
2754[7]	**Blazing Imp (USA) (50)** (MrsJJordan) **4-8-3**(7) JennyMurphy(3) (racd centre: hdwy over 1f out: no imp)	nk	**6**	20/1	46	27
2738[2]	**Rennyholme (41)** (ABMulholland) **6-8-1** GBardwell(8) (racd centre: sn drvn along & bhd: hdwy over 1f out: nrst fin)	nk	**7**	9/1	37	18
2754[2]	**Johayro (59)** (JSGoldie) **4-9-2**(3) PFessey(15) (w ldr stands' side over 3f: grad wknd)	1¼	**8**	10/1	51	32
2657[8]	**Insider Trader (58)** (MrsJRRamsden) **6-8-13v**(5) DSweeney(2) (cl up: rdn ½-wy: wknd over 1f out)	nk	**9**	7/1[2]	49	30
1865[4]	**Thick as Thieves (39)** (RonaldThompson) **5-7-10**(3) DarrenMoffatt(11) (sn drvn along: racd stands' side after 2f: n.d)	1½	**10**	20/1	25	6
2754[3]	**Pleasure Time (63)** (CSmith) **4-9-9b** JFortune(4) (lw: cl up effrt ½-wy: btn appr fnl f)	s.h	**11**	8/1[3]	49	30
520[15]	**Lennox Lewis (68)** (DNicholls) **5-9-7**(7) ANicholls(13) (racd stands' side: nvr wnt pce)	1¼	**12**	50/1	50	31
2366[5]	**Ticka Ticka Timing (38)** (BWMurray) **4-7-5**(7)ow2 DSalt(14) (racd stands' side: n.d)	1	**13**	100/1	16	—
2540[16]	**Good To Talk (38)** (TDEasterby) **4-7-12b** LCharnock(5) (chsd ldrs 3f: sn wknd)	nk	**14**	25/1	15	—
2540[17]	**Kalar (45)** (DWChapman) **8-8-5b** ACulhane(10) (spd centre 3f: eased whn btn)	¾	**15**	20/1	20	1
1835[14]	**Serious Hurry (41)** (RMMcKellar) **9-7-10b**(5)ow5 KSked(12) (bit bkwd: racd stands' side: sn outpcd)	1¾	**16**	100/1	10	—
				(SP 130.6%)	**16 Rn**	

60.1 secs (2.40) CSF £13.62 CT £193.99 TOTE £1.80: £1.30 £3.30 £2.10 £3.70 (£23.90) Trio £117.40 OWNER Mr P. D. Savill (THIRSK) BRED Brook Stud Ltd
LONG HANDICAP Ticka Ticka Timing 7-4 Serious Hurry 7-7
2759* Cross The Border is in top form and was always going far too well for this bunch. (11/10: 7/4-evens)
2738* Young Ben (IRE) showed his win last time here was no fluke and, despite carrying 7lb overweight, ran a smashing race. (12/1)
2899 Imp Express (IRE) did well here from his draw to show he has the ability when he decides to fully use it. (20/1)
1759 Grand Chapeau (IRE) is off a decent mark after some disappointing efforts. This was his most positive performance for a while. (20/1)
Kabcast, making his seasonal debut, showed all his old speed and, in due course, will no doubt do better. (100/1)
2540 Blazing Imp (USA) keeps running well, though was never doing quite enough to get into this. (20/1)
2738 Rennyholme found this track too sharp but did finish well. (9/1)

2935 HUDDERSFIELD (S) STKS (2-Y.O) (Class G)

3-00 (3-07) **7f** £2,355.00 (£655.00: £315.00) Stalls: Low GOING minus 0.12 sec per fur (G)

				SP	RR	SF
2500[13]	**Semi Circle** (TDEasterby) **2-8-6b[1]** LCharnock(6) (chsd ldrs: styd on u.p to ld wl ins fnl f)	—	**1**	50/1	60	11
2383[2]	**Ribble Assembly** (RAFahey) **2-8-11** JCarroll(9) (lw: sn cl up: rdn to disp ld 1f out: nt qckn)	1¾	**2**	100/30[2]	61	12
2493[W]	**Bint Nadia** (JDBethell) **2-8-6** TWilliams(8) (swtg: led tl hdd & no ex wl ins fnl f)	s.h	**3**	7/2[3]	56	7
1997[5]	**Miss Main Street (IRE)** (JJQuinn) **2-8-6** JFortune(1) (lw: a chsng ldrs: rdn ½-wy: styd on: nvr able chal)	2½	**4**	11/8[1]	50	1
	Jet Set Sarah (USA) (JBerry) **2-8-6** KDarley(3) (lengthy: unf: in tch: reminders ½-wy: no imp)	6	**5**	8/1	37	—
2493[4]	**Last Lap** (TDEasterby) **2-8-6** DeanMcKeown(5) (in tch: sn drvn along: no imp fnl 3f)	hd	**6**	14/1	36	—
2827[5]	**Ludere (IRE)** (WWHaigh) **2-8-11** DHarrison(2) (outpcd tl sme late hdwy 2f out)	2	**7**	25/1	37	—
1829[9]	**Wynbury Flyer** (FMurphy) **2-8-11** JFanning(12) (s.i.s: hdwy u.p ½-wy: sn btn)	1¼	**8**	25/1	34	—
2741[6]	**Jilvarra** (WGMTurner) **2-8-1**(5) DSweeney(11) (w ldrs 5f: wknd qckly)	nk	**9**	10/1	28	—
2493[7]	**Diamond Steve** (NTinkler) **2-9-2v** KimTinkler(7) (swtg: sn outpcd & bhd)	2	**10**	33/1	34	—
2752[4]	**Gay Abandon** (KMcAuliffe) **2-8-6** FLynch(4) (s.i.s: a bhd)	6	**11**	14/1	10	—
1815[9]	**Newgate Noblesse** (BWMurray) **2-8-6** VHalliday(10) (sn bhd: eased fnl 2f: t.o)	dist	**12**	100/1	—	—
				(SP 134.5%)	**12 Rn**	

1m 29.5 (5.90) CSF £211.73 TOTE £82.20: £12.00 £1.30 £1.40 (£104.50) Trio £188.70 OWNER Mr C. H. Stevens (MALTON) BRED Mrs E. C. York

No bid

2018 Semi Circle had blinkers on for the first time and they certainly helped her under a vigorous ride. (50/1)

2383 Ribble Assembly behaved himself this time and was put into the stalls late. He then had his chances but was tapped for toe late on. (100/30: 5/1-3/1)

2288 Bint Nadia was calm on leaving the paddock but, by the time she was put into the stalls, she was in a muck sweat. However, she still ran well, only to be out-pointed late on. (7/2)

1997 Miss Main Street (IRE) looked short of toe here and either needs some cut in the ground or a more galloping track. (11/8: 5/4-evens)

Jet Set Sarah (USA) needed plenty of help from the saddle as she was very green here and, hopefully, this should improve her a little. (8/1)

2493 Last Lap just looks short of pace. (14/1)

Jilvarra (10/1: op 16/1)

2936 LEEDS NURSERY H'CAP (2-Y.O) (Class D)

3-30 (3-30) **7f** £3,847.00 (£1,156.00: £558.00: £259.00) Stalls: Low GOING minus 0.12 sec per fur (G)

				SP	RR	SF
2288[W]	**Tancred Times** (DWBarker) **2-8-3** TWilliams(4) (sn led: qcknd ent st: r.o wl)	—	**1**	9/1	68	11
2060[3]	**Deki (USA)** (DMorley) **2-9-7** JStack(7) (lw: a chsng ldrs: effrt over 2f out: styd on: nvr able chal)	2	**2**	5/2[1]	81	24
2565[D]	**Erro Codigo** (MrsJRRamsden) **2-8-7** JFortune(8) (lw: effrt ½-wy: styd on: nt pce to chal)	2½	**3**	7/2[2]	62	5
2168[4]	**Durham Flyer** (TDEasterby) **2-9-1** DeanMcKeown(5) (led early: chsd wnr: rdn appr st: r.o one pce)	1	**4**	4/1[3]	67	10
2499[7]	**Petara (IRE)** (JSWainwright) **2-8-6**(3) GParkin(2) (bhd: hdwy on outside 2f out: nrst fin)	½	**5**	20/1	60	3
2689[6]	**Oh Never Again (IRE)** (MJohnston) **2-9-4** JWeaver(3) (chsd ldrs: rdn over 2f out: wknd over 1f out)	1	**6**	9/2	67	10
2587[4]	**Three Tenners** (JBerry) **2-8-1**(3) PFessey(1) (in tch tl outpcd fnl 2½f)	1	**7**	10/1	51	—
2396*	**Eastwell Minstrel** (RCurtis) **2-7-10** JLowe(6) (a outpcd & wl bhd)	23	**8**	14/1	—	—
				(SP 119.5%)	**8 Rn**	

1m 29.3 (5.70) CSF £30.38 CT £89.50 TOTE £8.10: £2.70 £1.10 £1.60 (£17.10) OWNER The Ebor Partnership (RICHMOND) BRED W. L. Barker

OFFICIAL EXPLANATION **Eastwell Minstrel: was unsuited by the good to firm going.**

2016* Tancred Times refused to enter the stalls last time but did nothing wrong here and won in useful style to show that, when she behaves herself, she has plenty of ability. (9/1: op 6/1)

2060 Deki (USA) again travelled well enough but, once an effort was needed, he was never coming up with the goods. (5/2: 3/1-2/1)

2565 Erro Codigo tried to come from off the pace and failed to make an impression, but he keeps showing enough to suggest a race can be found. (7/2: op 9/4)

2168 Durham Flyer was a shade disappointing here, looking a bit one-paced, but perhaps he needed this, his first run for over four weeks. (4/1)

2018 Petara (IRE), happier on this faster surface, picked up well in the closing stages. (20/1)

2689 Oh Never Again (IRE) had his chances but did not seem to last the trip out. (9/2)

2937 WILLIE CARSON - PINKER'S POND APPRENTICE H'CAP (0-65) (3-Y.O+) (Class F)

4-00 (4-00) **7f** £2,702.25 (£828.00: £411.50: £203.25) Stalls: Low GOING minus 0.12 sec per fur (G)

				SP	RR	SF
2854[8]	**Napoleon's Return (37)** (JLEyre) **4-8-0v** GWright(1) (prom: nt clr run 2½f out to 1½f out: qcknd to ld ins fnl f)	—	**1**	12/1	44	15
2355[4]	**Miss Pigalle (36)** (MissLAPerratt) **6-7-13b** FionaBrown(5) (hdwy after 3f: swtchd outside appr fnl f: disp ld tl ins fnl f: nt qckn)	½	**2**	14/1	42	13
2573[3]	**Roseate Lodge (35)** (SEKettlewell) **11-7-12** SClarke(13) (hld up: & bhd: stdy hdwy on ins 2f out: n.m.r 1f out: r.o)	1	**3**	7/1[3]	39	10
2317[9]	**Dispol Diamond (49)** (GROldroyd) **4-8-12** RFarmer(15) (a chsng ldrs: ev ch 1f out: kpt on)	½	**4**	10/1	51	22
2205[11]	**Raed (64)** (MrsASwinbank) **4-9-13** DMulhall(2) (led after 1½f tl ins fnl f)	½	**5**	10/1	65	36
2573[10]	**Greatest (55)** (MissGayKelleway) **6-9-4b** ANicholls(3) (lw: led 1½f: chsd ldrs: rdn over 2f out: ev ch tl nt qckn ins fnl f)	s.h	**6**	100/30[1]	56	27
2355[6]	**Chinour (IRE) (50)** (EJAlston) **9-8-13** MelanieWorden(6) (s.i.s: wl bhd tl styd on wl fnl 2f)	s.h	**7**	10/1	51	22
2724[2]	**Lancashire Legend (51)** (SDow) **4-9-0** DSalt(9) (sn trckng ldrs: swtchd wl over 1f out: nt qckn)	1	**8**	6/1[2]	50	21
2063[12]	**Stolen Music (IRE) (33)** (REBarr) **4-7-10** PMQuinn(12) (dwlt: bhd tl sme hdwy fnl 2f)	1	**9**	100/1	30	1
2828[14]	**Thorntoun Jewel (IRE) (33)** (MissZAGreen) **4-7-10** MMathers(14) (swtg: s.i.s: a rr div)	nk	**10**	100/1	29	—
	Saint Amigo (35) (BPJBaugh) **5-7-12**ow2 LisaWatson(4) (chsd ldrs over 4f: wknd)	3	**11**	50/1	24	—
2204[8]	**Welcome Lu (36)** (JLHarris) **4-7-13** PMundy(10) (a bhd)	1¾	**12**	10/1	21	—
2302[4]	**Everset (FR) (44)** (ABailey) **9-8-7** IHudson(7) (b: chsd ldrs tl wknd over 1f out)	nk	**13**	10/1	28	—
2754[8]	**Ramsey Hope (62)** (CWFairhurst) **4-9-11v** SOlley(16) (lw: in tch tl wknd fnl 2f)	3	**14**	25/1	39	10
2544[11]	**Juicy Ting (47)** (PCHaslam) **3-8-3** PGoode(8) (in tch 4f)	1¼	**15**	9/1	22	—
				(SP 127.5%)	**15 Rn**	

1m 28.7 (5.10) CSF £160.49 CT £1,199.63 TOTE £11.80: £2.70 £3.00 £2.70 (£94.40) Trio £420.30 OWNER Mr J. E. Wilson (HAMBLETON) BRED T. K. Knox

LONG HANDICAP Saint Amigo 7-7 Stolen Music (IRE) 7-7
WEIGHT FOR AGE 3yo-7lb
IN-FOCUS: This event was restricted to apprentices who had never ridden a winner.
Napoleon's Return, well handicapped after some moderate efforts, he came right back to form here and did it nicely, despite finding trouble in running. (12/1)
2355 Miss Pigalle looked to have done everything right when switching for a clear run approaching the final furlong but, despite doing her best, she had to admit she met one just too good. (14/1)
2573 Roseate Lodge is still in top form but needs things to go just right and met with trouble here at a vital stage. (7/1)
1655 Dispol Diamond had no excuses here after holding every chance throughout and kept battling on to the line. (10/1)
1833 Raed is gradually slipping down the handicap and ran well here but is yet to win a race. (10/1)
403 Greatest is off his lowest mark for a while and ran reasonably but is certainly better on the All-Weather. (100/30: 5/1-3/1)
2355 Chinour (IRE) is a frustrating customer who runs when in the mood and it was always too late here, but he did make up an incredible amount of ground late on. (10/1)
2724 Lancashire Legend has plenty of ability and is very well just now but he is not the easiest of rides and his only win to date has been on the All-Weather. (6/1: op 4/1)
1998 Juicy Ting (9/1: 6/1-10/1)

2938 LEYBURN CLAIMING STKS (I) (3-Y.O+) (Class F)
4-30 (4-30) **5f 212y** £2,182.00 (£602.00: £286.00) Stalls: High GOING minus 0.12 sec per fur (G)

Form	Horse	Dist	Pos	SP	RR	SF
2899[2]	**The Wad (60)** (DNicholls) **4-8-5**(7) TSiddall(9) (lw: chsd ldrs: led 2f out: styd on wl)	—	1	2/5[1]	64	34
2575[6]	**Seretse's Nephew (41)** (MJPolglase) **3-8-4** DHarrison(4) (led tl hdd 2f out: btn appr fnl f)	4	2	12/1	50	15
1828[13]	**Rotherfield Park (IRE) (30)** (CSmith) **5-8-1**(3) PFessey(2) (bhd: styd on fnl 2½f: nrst fin)	2½	3	11/1[3]	39	9
2177[9]	**Martindale (IRE) (40)** (JHanson) **4-8-11** EJohnson(8) (cl up tl wknd fnl 2f)	2	4	6/1[2]	40	10
2384[7]	**Mu-Arrik (29)** (GROldroyd) **9-8-9v** KHodgson(7) (lw: outpcd ½-wy: n.d after)	1¾	5	20/1	34	4
2734[6]	**Newtons Corner (IRE)** (DNicholls) **3-8-11** JWeaver(3) (s.s: stdy hdwy 2f out: nvr nr to chal)	½	6	16/1	39	4
297[8]	**Peacefull Reply (USA) (24)** (FHLee) **7-8-10b** ACulhane(1) (chsd ldrs: hmpd after 2f: wknd fnl 2f)	s.h	7	33/1	33	3
1861[7]	**Ragazzo (IRE) (29)** (JSWainwright) **7-8-9b** LCharnock(5) (prom to ½-wy)	4	8	33/1	21	—
	February (33) (NPLittmoden) **4-8-4b**[1] GBardwell(6) (t: dwlt: drvn along & hdwy after 2f: wknd over 2f out)	24	9	50/1	—	—

(SP 120.2%) **9 Rn**

1m 14.6 (3.70) CSF £6.19 TOTE £1.50: £1.10 £2.10 £3.40 (£3.50) Trio £14.80 OWNER Mr W. J. Kelly (THIRSK) BRED C. R. and V. M. Withers
WEIGHT FOR AGE 3yo-5lb
2899 The Wad looked to have a simple task here and did it well enough. (2/5)
378 Seretse's Nephew is only a very moderate performer and this was a reasonable effort, but he eventually cried enough approaching the last furlong. (12/1: 6/1-14/1)
Rotherfield Park (IRE) has shown nothing on two previous runs this year so this was a much better effort, but the opposition here was not up to much. (11/1)
795 Martindale (IRE) has not much of an action and seems to have the ability to match. (6/1)
1620 Mu-Arrik last won a race three seasons ago and that was off a 23lb higher mark. (20/1)
2734 Newtons Corner (IRE), having only his second outing, gave definite signs of hope here and was certainly not knocked about. (16/1)

2939 LEYBURN CLAIMING STKS (II) (3-Y.O+) (Class F)
5-00 (5-01) **5f 212y** £2,182.00 (£602.00: £286.00) Stalls: High GOING minus 0.12 sec per fur (G)

Form	Horse	Dist	Pos	SP	RR	SF
1468[9]	**Top of The Form (IRE) (83)** (MJohnston) **3-8-8** JWeaver(7) (mde all: clr ½-wy: rdn out)	—	1	11/4[3]	61	39
2711[19]	**Palacegate Touch (80)** (JBerry) **7-9-4b**(3) PFessey(4) (chsd ldrs: wnt 2nd u.p 1½f out: nt pce to chal)	2	2	9/4[2]	64	47
2891[6]	**Ohnonotagain (33)** (LRLloyd-James) **5-8-4** KimTinkler(5) (outpcd tl styd on fnl 2f: nrst fin)	1¾	3	33/1	42	25
2691[10]	**Paddy Lad (IRE) (83)** (RGuest) **3-9-2** PBloomfield(1) (a chsng ldrs: sn drvn along: one pce fnl 2½f)	hd	4	7/4[1]	59	37
2575[4]	**The Frisky Farmer (45)** (WGMTurner) **4-8-6**(5) DSweeney(2) (chsd wnr over 4f: sn btn)	1½	5	33/1	45	28
2755[6]	**Sense of Priority (53)** (DNicholls) **8-8-12** AlexGreaves(6) (lw: hld up: effrt 2f out: nvr nr to chal)	¾	6	16/1	44	27
	Dauntless Fort (35) (MrsVAAconley) **6-8-4**(3)ow1 RHavlin(3) (s.i.s: a bhd: t.o)	20	7	200/1	—	—
2234[4]	**Running Bear** (MissSEHall) **3-8-11** KDarley(8) (lw: sn chsng ldrs: wknd over 2f out: t.o)	4	8	6/1	—	—

(SP 120.3%) **8 Rn**

1m 14.0 (3.10) CSF £9.05 TOTE £3.90: £1.90 £1.70 £3.30 (£6.50) OWNER Mr R. W. Huggins (MIDDLEHAM) BRED Sean Beston
WEIGHT FOR AGE 3yo-5lb
Top of The Form (IRE) clmd CaptHBarlow £12,000. Ohnonotagain clmd IPrice £3,000
Top of The Form (IRE) showed she retains all her speed from last season and threw off the opposition by halfway, and it was just a question of whether she would see the trip out, which she did well. (11/4)
2472* Palacegate Touch put in a fair performance but was never quite doing enough, and was unluckily in the wrong division of this race. (9/4)
1586 Ohnonotagain is yet to win a race in twenty-six attempts but was keeping on well at the end here. (33/1)
2185 Paddy Lad (IRE), a bit edgy beforehand, had his chances but was disappointing when ridden. (7/4)
2575 The Frisky Farmer had plenty on here and this was not a bad effort. (33/1)
2755 Sense of Priority keeps giving the impression that he is likely to do better. (16/1)

2940 DEWSBURY MAIDEN STKS (3-Y.O+) (Class D)
5-30 (5-32) **1m 5f 175y** £3,717.00 (£1,116.00: £538.00: £249.00) Stalls: Low GOING minus 0.12 sec per fur (G)

Form	Horse	Dist	Pos	SP	RR	SF
1474[4]	**Valagalore (75)** (BWHills) **3-7-13**(3) PFessey(3) (trckd ldrs: effrt 4f out: led 2f out: styd on wl)	—	1	2/1[1]	81	30
2046[7]	**Jazz Track (IRE)** (PWChapple-Hyam) **3-8-4**(3) RHavlin(12) (in tch: hdwy 4f out: led over 2f out: sn hdd: kpt on)	1½	2	11/4[2]	84	33
2131[W]	**Annaletta** (JPearce) **3-8-2** GBardwell(10) (lengthy: unf: chsd ldrs: led over 4f out & sn drvn along: hdd over 2f out: kpt on same pce)	3½	3	16/1[3]	75	24
2749[7]	**Zinzari (FR) (83)** (DRLoder) **3-8-7** KDarley(8) (in tch: effrt 4f out: sn chsng ldrs: one pce fnl 2f)	hd	4	2/1[1]	80	29
2656[6]	**Murchan Tyne (IRE)** (EJAlston) **4-8-9**(7) MelanieWorden(1) (in tch tl outpcd fnl 4f)	11	5	50/1	62	25
2548[3]	**Hoh Explorer (IRE) (60)** (DWBarker) **3-8-7** TWilliams(7) (dwlt: hld up: hdwy 5f out: nvr trbld ldrs)	3½	6	33/1	63	12
	Thahib (JLHarris) **3-8-7** ACulhane(4) (outpcd after 6f: nvr trbld ldrs)	9	7	20/1	53	2
2131[3]	**Stoned Imaculate (IRE)** (FMurphy) **3-8-2** JFanning(9) (cl up tl wknd fnl 4f)	½	8	20/1	47	—
	Highfield Pet (50) (CWFairhurst) **4-9-7** LCharnock(2) (led tl hdd over 4f out: wknd qckly)	15	9	100/1	35	—

				SP	RR	SF
	Powerful Spirit (JGMO'Shea) **5-9-7** JStack(6) (s.s: a bhd)	24	**10**	200/1	7	—
2549^{3}	**Serious Account (USA)** (JLEyre) **4-9-7** MGallagher(11) (outpcd & lost tch 7f out: t.o)	27	**11**	20/1	—	—
				(SP 119.9%)	**11 Rn**	

3m 4.3 (8.30) CSF £6.70 TOTE £3.80: £1.40 £1.10 £4.00 (£4.00) Trio £43.80 OWNER Mrs A. D. Bourne (LAMBOURN) BRED Newgate Stud Co
WEIGHT FOR AGE 3yo-14lb
OFFICIAL EXPLANATION **Serious Account (USA): choked.**
1474 Valagalore did not really look the type for this track but she handled it well and won nicely, and certainly appreciated the trip. (2/1)
2046 Jazz Track (IRE) still looked as though this was needed but put in a useful effort here and further improvement is on the cards. (11/4)
Annaletta, a fair sort, looked particularly fit but needed some strong driving to get her going and was then short of speed late on. She has ability but may also have her share of temperament, as she showed at Redcar last time when refusing to enter the stalls. (16/1)
1647 Zinzari (FR) is proving very difficult to win with and this proved far too competitive in the home straight. (2/1)
Murchan Tyne (IRE), the winner of a bumper, looked pretty slow here and will no doubt do better over hurdles. (50/1)

T/Jkpt: Not won; £52,215.44 to Sandown 24/7/97. T/Plpt: £27.40 (772.94 Tckts). T/Qdpt: £11.40 (88.82 Tckts) AA

2783-**LEICESTER** (R-H) (Good)
Wednesday July 23rd

Visibility poor: Race 6
WEATHER: sunny & v.warm WIND: almost nil

2941 NEXT (S) STKS (3-Y.O) (Class G)
6-30 (6-32) **1m 8y** £2,448.00 (£678.00: £324.00) Stalls: Low GOING minus 0.33 sec per fur (GF)

				SP	RR	SF
2646^{5}	**Circle of Magic (44)** (PJMakin) **3-8-6b** JFortune(3) (hld up: swtchd rt 3f out: chal ent fnl f: rdn to ld wl ins fnl f)	—	**1**	3/1^{1}	58	32
2733^{12}	**Rochea (49)** (MrsNMacauley) **3-8-6** BDoyle(4) (lw: hld up: hdwy over 2f out: led ins fnl f: sn hdd: no ex)	¾	**2**	13/2^{3}	57	31
2750^{10}	**Tezaab (50)** (BHanbury) **3-8-11** WRyan(10) (hdwy 3f out: ev ch over 1f out: hrd rdn: unable qckn)	1¼	**3**	10/1	59	33
2522^{4}	**Sun Fairy (49)** (JAGlover) **3-8-6** GCarter(12) (in tch: hdwy & ev ch ent fnl f: hrd rdn: unable qckn)	2	**4**	4/1^{2}	50	24
	Riverside Girl (IRE) (JSMoore) **3-7-13**(7) PaulCleary(1) (still unf: a.p: led over 2f out tl ins fnl f: one pce)	2	**5**	40/1	46	20
1121^{8}	**Petuntse** (JGSmyth-Osbourne) **3-8-11e** WJO'Connor(13) (bit bkwd: trckd ldrs tl wknd wl over 1f out)	5	**6**	50/1	41	15
2203^{9}	**Terry's Rose (47)** (RHollinshead) **3-8-6** NCarlisle(14) (plld hrd: mde most over 5f: wknd appr fnl f)	3½	**7**	10/1	29	3
	Langara Heights (BJLlewellyn) **3-8-11** JQuinn(8) (leggy: lt-f: s.s: wl bhd tl sme late progress)	10	**8**	50/1	14	—
2770^{6}	**Ajeebah (IRE)** (WJHaggas) **3-8-6** FLynch(11) (rdn & effrt ½-wy: no imp)	1¼	**9**	9/1	7	—
2738^{19}	**Bright Gold (55)** (ASmith) **3-8-11b** DeanMcKeown(2) (prom: stumbled after 3f: wknd over 2f out)	6	**10**	25/1	—	—
2407^{6}	**Fly High (42)** (DMorris) **3-8-6** NDay(9) (bhd fnl 3f)	1¼	**11**	12/1	—	—
	Blue Jay (IRE) (RHannon) **3-8-11** DaneO'Neill(15) (rangy: unf: prom over 5f: eased whn btn)	6	**12**	8/1	—	—
2731^{16}	**Kalmoojid** (CJHill) **3-8-11** GDuffield(6) (nvr nr ldrs: wnt lame 3f out)	1½	**13**	33/1	—	—
	Honiara Bay (MissAStokell) **3-8-6** JLowe(7) (leggy: lt-f: sn bhd & outpcd: t.o)	23	**14**	50/1	—	—
				(SP 120.4%)	**14 Rn**	

1m 37.9 (2.90) CSF £19.31 TOTE £4.50: £1.50 £3.60 £2.30 (£12.60) Trio £114.90 OWNER T W Wellard Partnership (MARLBOROUGH) BRED Tedwood Bloodstock Ltd
Sold MPipe 6,000 gns
OFFICIAL EXPLANATION **Kalmoojid: went lame three furlongs out.**
2646 Circle of Magic, gradually edging over towards the favoured far side from halfway, found all that was needed in the latter stages to get off the mark. (3/1)
2040 Rochea, making significant headway entering the last quarter-mile, led briefly before the winner took over and this could be more her grade. (13/2)
2522 Tezaab has been competing over longer trips of late and he put in a determined challenge approaching the final furlong but lack of a turn of pace caught him out in the battle to the line. He is short on experience and is capable of winning at this level. (10/1)
2522 Sun Fairy, a quick-actioned filly, worked hard to give herself a live chance entering the final furlong but once it developed into a sprint she was found wanting. (4/1)
Riverside Girl (IRE), out of action since the autumn and having only the third race of her life, turned in a very promising display and she should not be too difficult to place. (40/1)
Petuntse, quite a nice sort taken to post early, showed up just behind the leaders until lack of peak condition took its toll below the distance. (50/1)
1998 Fly High (12/1: op 6/1)

2942 WILSON BOWDEN PROPERTIES NURSERY H'CAP (2-Y.O) (Class E)
7-00 (7-01) **5f 2y** £3,093.00 (£924.00: £442.00: £201.00) Stalls: Low GOING minus 0.33 sec per fur (GF)

				SP	RR	SF
2578^{2}	**Mislead (IRE)** (JSMoore) **2-7-12**(3) MHenry(1) (a.p: led wl over 1f out: jst hld on)	—	**1**	8/1^{3}	69	19
2786^{2}	**Who Nose (IRE)** (BJMeehan) **2-8-0b**(7) GHannon(7) (dwlt: bhd: rapid hdwy appr fnl f: fin fast)	s.h	**2**	6/1^{2}	75	25
2697^{7}	**Eleventh Duke (IRE)** (RHannon) **2-9-0** DaneO'Neill(4) (lw: hld up: hdwy u.p 2f out: swtchd rt over 1f out: r.o)	1¼	**3**	9/1	78	28
2578*	**Mishraak (IRE)** (RWArmstrong) **2-9-10** GCarter(5) (led tl wl over 1f out: hrd rdn & one pce ins fnl f)	nk	**4**	6/4^{1}	87	37
1806^{3}	**Really Done It Now (IRE)** (KRBurke) **2-8-7** PaulEddery(2) (lw: a chsng ldrs: rdn over 1f out: r.o)	1½	**5**	8/1^{3}	65	15
2538*	**Mill End Quest** (MWEasterby) **2-8-11** TLucas(3) (w ldrs over 3f)	2	**6**	6/1^{2}	63	13
2578^{6}	**Bliss (IRE)** (MrsPNDutfield) **2-7-6**(5)ow1 AimeeCook(9) (prom tl rdn & outpcd over 1f out)	2	**7**	40/1	42	—
2697^{9}	**Tamerin Bay** (RBoss) **2-8-11** GDuffield(6) (prom: hrd rdn over 1f out: sn wknd: t.o)	12	**8**	14/1	18	—
2520^{3}	**Bandbox (IRE)** (SMellor) **2-8-10** JQuinn(8) (in tch tl outpcd 2f out: t.o)	3½	**9**	11/1	6	—
				(SP 118.2%)	**9 Rn**	

60.8 secs (2.30) CSF £51.51 CT £410.31 TOTE £10.30: £2.50 £1.50 £2.80 (£24.00) Trio £73.40 OWNER Mr P. Henley (HUNGERFORD) BRED Peter Henley Jnr
2578 Mislead (IRE) was able to turn the tables on the favourite on these more advantageous terms but she only hung on by the skin of her teeth. (8/1)
2786 Who Nose (IRE), successful in a couple of sellers over an extra furlong, lost this with a tardy start for his determined late flourish failed by only half a stride. (6/1)
1812 Eleventh Duke (IRE), brought back to the minimum trip, stayed on strongly once switched towards the far side inside the distance and he is certainly ready to strike. (9/1: 6/1-10/1)

2578* Mishraak (IRE) again force the pace but he was conceding plenty of weight all round and he was at the end of his tether inside the last furlong. (6/4)
1806 Really Done It Now (IRE) posed a serious threat on the approach to the final furlong but, when the chips were down, she was tapped for a turn of speed. (8/1)
2538* Mill End Quest showed plenty of pace to share the lead but she was in trouble below the distance and her measure had been taken. (6/1)
1797* Tamerin Bay (14/1: op 8/1)

2943 CLEGG CONSTRUCTION MAIDEN AUCTION STKS (2-Y.O) (Class E)

7-30 (7-31) **7f 9y** £3,327.00 (£996.00: £478.00: £219.00) Stalls: Low GOING minus 0.33 sec per fur (GF)

Form	Horse	Dist	Pos	SP	RR	SF
2700[6]	**Shalad'or** (BRMillman) **2-8-2**[ow3] BDoyle(5) (plld hrd: mde virtually all: hld on wl towards fin)	—	1	11/1	61	23
2699[6]	**Lift The Offer (IRE)** (RHannon) **2-8-11** DaneO'Neill(8) (a.p: rdn over 1f out: kpt on ins fnl f)	1	2	7/2[1]	68	33
2181[19]	**Roborant** (JLDunlop) **2-8-12** GCarter(1) (sn drvn along: hdwy & hung rt 2f out: r.o wl ins fnl f)	hd	3	14/1	69	34
2595[2]	**Danzig Flyer (IRE)** (PWHarris) **2-8-2**(5) CLowther(2) (trckd ldrs: effrt & rdn appr fnl f: unable qckn)	½	4	9/2[3]	62	27
1997[6]	**No Shame** (JGSmyth-Osbourne) **2-8-4** DHarrison(3) (chsd ldrs: rdn wl over 1f out: one pce)	3	5	20/1	53	18
2489[2]	**Petaling (IRE)** (BJMeehan) **2-7-13**(3) MartinDwyer(11) (disp ld early: prom tl rdn & outpcd appr fnl f)	¾	6	14/1	49	14
	Memphis Dancer (JWHills) **2-8-1**(3) MHenry(6) (w'like: scope: bit bkwd: hdwy 3f out: kpt on one pce appr fnl f)	¾	7	25/1	49	14
2306[13]	**Saligo (IRE)** (HMorrison) **2-8-0** CRutter(15) (nvr nr to chal)	1¾	8	50/1	41	6
	After Eight (RWArmstrong) **2-8-12** RPrice(13) (small: bkwd: rdn along ½-wy: a bhd)	¾	9	14/1	52	17
2786[3]	**The Groveller** (PDEvans) **2-8-7** JFortune(14) (mid div: effrt & rdn 2f out: no imp)	2	10	5/1	42	7
2699[5]	**Kate Lane (IRE)** (MrsPNDutfield) **2-7-11**(5) AimeeCook(12) (lw: mid div: rdn along ½-wy: n.d)	½	11	25/1	36	1
	Rude Shock (MHTompkins) **2-8-10** WJO'Connor(9) (neat: bkwd: a bhd & outpcd)	3½	12	20/1	36	1
2519[2]	**Constant Attention** (PFICole) **2-8-7** JQuinn(7) (in tch over 4f: sn wknd)	4	13	4/1[2]	24	—
	Felony (IRE) (DJGMurraySmith) **2-8-9** GDuffield(10) (cmpt: bkwd: rn green: bhd fr ½-wy: t.o)	5	14	33/1	14	—
	Vicky Jazz (JSMoore) **2-8-1** JLowe(16) (lt-f: a bhd)	½	15	50/1	5	—
2519[7]	**Lanara** (MrsNMacauley) **2-8-1**[ow1] DBiggs(4) (sn outpcd: t.o)	dist	16	50/1	—	—

(SP 131.4%) **16 Rn**

1m 25.6 (3.00) CSF £44.47 TOTE £28.70: £6.20 £1.90 £3.60 (£36.00) Trio £104.70 OWNER Mr G. Palmer (CULLOMPTON) BRED Mrs M. Palmer and G. Palmer
2700 Shalad'or decided to attack from the front and, though she showed signs of weakening in the final one hundred yards, had enough in hand to last home. (11/1: 7/1-12/1)
2699 Lift The Offer (IRE) improved on his debut but he showed here that he does need a slightly stiffer test of stamina, and he should not take long in finding a race. (7/2)
Roborant ran his best race yet over this slightly longer trip but he does look to be a difficult ride at present and experience should improve him in time. (14/1)
2595 Danzig Flyer (IRE) was only really beaten for want of a turn of pace inside the final furlong and the longer trip or more testing ground could provide the answer. (9/2)
1997 No Shame is a half-sister to useful sprinter Point of Light and also a thirteen furlong winner and she seems to be more a stayer than a sprinter and even this trip was inadequate. (20/1)
2489 Petaling (IRE) did not stride out freely to post and, though she showed up with the pace, was struggling to hold on in the latter stages. (14/1)
Memphis Dancer was staying on at the finish and she might have what it takes. (25/1)
2519 Constant Attention (4/1: op 5/2)

2944 ALLIANCE & LEICESTER H'CAP (0-90) (3-Y.O+) (Class C)

8-00 (8-00) **1m 3f 183y** £5,715.00 (£1,710.00: £820.00: £375.00) Stalls: Low GOING minus 0.33 sec per fur (GF)

Form	Horse	Dist	Pos	SP	RR	SF
2514[12]	**Wild Rita (79)** (WRMuir) **5-9-10** DaneO'Neill(3) (hld up in tch: hdwy over 2f out: led appr fnl f: r.o wl)	—	1	9/2[2]	89	52
2682*	**Rex Mundi (65)** (PDEvans) **5-8-10** JFortune(7) (led after 1f: shkn up over 2f out: hdd appr fnl f: rallied u.p)	nk	2	13/2	75	38
2391*	**Tappeto (73)** (HCandy) **5-9-4** CRutter(6) (lw: hld up & bhd: hdwy 2f out: rdn & one pce fnl f)	3½	3	9/2[2]	78	41
2380[2]	**Toi Toi (IRE) (75)** (DWPArbuthnot) **3-8-8** SWhitworth(4) (b.hind: lw: hld up: effrt wl over 1f out: styd on u.p: nt pce to chal)	s.h	4	11/2	80	31
2749*	**Wakeel (USA) (79)** (SDow) **5-9-10** 5x GDuffield(1) (lw: swtg: hld up & bhd: hrd rdn 2f out: no imp)	5	5	5/1[3]	77	40
374[3]	**Soldier Mak (59)** (JMackie) **4-8-4** JQuinn(2) (bkwd: prom: jnd ldr 3f out: wknd 2f out: t.o)	10	6	16/1	44	7
2653[2]	**Twilight Sleep (USA) (78)** (MCPipe) **5-9-9** RHughes(5) (led 1f: chsd ldr: ev ch 3f out: sn rdn: wknd wl over 1f out: t.o)	5	7	100/30[1]	56	19

(SP 110.7%) **7 Rn**

2m 32.9 (4.40) CSF £28.19 TOTE £5.10: £1.90 £3.30 (£16.60) OWNER Perspicacious Punters Racing Club (LAMBOURN) BRED Terry Brady
WEIGHT FOR AGE 3yo-12lb
789 Wild Rita has found her form in the second part of the year in the past and this cleverly-gained success shows that she has now come to herself. (9/2)
2682* Rex Mundi is as tough as old boots and he just would not give in after being headed but stamina is his strong suit and the winner proved just too sharp for him in the duel to the line. (13/2)
2391* Tappeto delivered his challenge from off the pace inside the last quarter-mile but, despite staying on, could not muster the speed to prove troublesome. (9/2)
2380 Toi Toi (IRE) continues to improve and an early success will not come out of turn. (11/2)
374 Soldier Mak needed this after an almost five-month break but he performed with credit, and though he had been trying for a long time does look to have the ability to win a race. (16/1)

2945 SAMWORTH BROTHERS H'CAP (0-80) (3-Y.O F) (Class D)

8-30 (8-33) **7f 9y** £3,925.00 (£1,180.00: £570.00: £265.00) Stalls: Low GOING minus 0.33 sec per fur (GF)

Form	Horse	Dist	Pos	SP	RR	SF
2317[6]	**La Dolce Vita (66)** (TDBarron) **3-8-7** JFortune(13) (swtg: trckd ldrs: rdn to ld ins fnl f: veered lft: r.o)	—	1	9/1	75	38
	All Is Fair (80) (SirMarkPrescott) **3-9-7** GDuffield(3) (bit bkwd: hld up: hdwy 2f out: rdn & r.o wl ins fnl f)	1	2	11/4[1]	87	50
2704[8]	**Las Vistas (55)** (HJCollingridge) **3-7-10** NAdams(2) (plld hrd: chsd ldrs: rdn over 1f out: r.o wl)	1	3	33/1	60	23
2369[14]	**Tayovullin (IRE) (64)** (HMorrison) **3-8-5** CRutter(5) (b: lw: chsd ldr: led over 2f out tl ins fnl f)	s.h	4	20/1	68	31
2645[7]	**Tycoon Girl (IRE) (70)** (BJMeehan) **3-8-11** MTebbutt(9) (trckd ldrs: hdwy u.p over 1f out: r.o)	nk	5	20/1	74	37
2705[4]	**Tabasco Jazz (60)** (BJMeehan) **3-7-12**(3) MartinDwyer(12) (led tl over 2f out: rdn & ev ch ent fnl f: one pce)	hd	6	6/1[3]	63	26
2523[6]	**Faym (IRE) (59)** (JWharton) **3-8-0** JQuinn(7) (w ldrs: rdn over 1f out: sn btn)	¾	7	14/1	61	24

				SP	RR	SF
2705[5]	**Halowing (USA) (75)** (JGSmyth-Osbourne) **3-9-2** TSprake(8) (lw: prom: rdn 2f out: grad wknd)	½	**8**	10/1	76	39
2340[8]	**Trading Aces (75)** (MBell) **3-8-11v**(5) RMullen(6) (nvr nr to chal)	nk	**9**	11/1	75	38
675[8]	**Wee Dram (76)** (RHannon) **3-9-3** DaneO'Neill(4) (in tch: effrt & rdn wl over 2f out: sn wknd)	2	**10**	10/1	71	34
2420[10]	**Danehill Princess (IRE) (60)** (RHollinshead) **3-8-1** DaleGibson(10) (a in rr)	3	**11**	25/1	49	12
2133[7]	**Summer Queen (79)** (SPCWoods) **3-9-6** WRyan(1) (lw: hld up: a bhd)	hd	**12**	9/2[2]	67	30
1859[10]	**Pat Said No (IRE) (58)** (DJSCosgrove) **3-7-10b**[1](3) MBaird(11) (lw: sn outpcd: t.o)	dist	**13**	33/1	—	—
				(SP 121.6%)	**13 Rn**	

1m 24.7 (2.10) CSF £29.25 CT £753.77 TOTE £8.30: £1.90 £2.20 £12.60 (£22.90) Trio £401.20; £33.91 to 25/7/97 OWNER Mr Stephen Woodall (THIRSK) BRED D. R. Botterill

LONG HANDICAP Las Vistas 7-7

2317 La Dolce Vita does not win that often but she invariably shows promise and no one will begrudge her this hard-fought success. (9/1)

All Is Fair did not look one hundred per cent for this belated seasonal debut and she took time to really find her stride but there was plenty to like about her commitment and she has trained on. (11/4)

1638 Las Vistas turned in her best performance yet in this first handicap and, from her present mark, looks a ready-made winner. (33/1)

1373 Tayovullin (IRE), in the action all the way, was the one to beat into the final furlong but a turn of finishing speed was missing when it was most needed. She is in fine form and there is another race in her. (20/1)

1679 Tycoon Girl (IRE), taking a step down in distance, did not impress to post but she ran a genuine race and another success is long overdue. (20/1)

2705 Tabasco Jazz, in and out of the lead from the start, only lost out in the sprint to the line. Still to open her account, her forceful tactics could pay off against maidens. (6/1: op 4/1)

2523 Faym (IRE) (14/1: op 8/1)

2946 COX FREEMAN MEDIAN AUCTION MAIDEN STKS (3-Y.O) (Class F)

9-00 (9-01) **5f 2y** £2,469.00 (£684.00: £327.00) Stalls: Low GOING minus 0.33 sec per fur (GF)

				SP	RR	SF
2277[2]	**Goodbye Gatemen (IRE) (68)** (BAPearce) **3-8-11**(3) MartinDwyer(6) (mde all: rdn & edgd lft fnl f: all out)	—	**1**	8/13[1]	52	26
2732[2]	**Dancing Mystery (41)** (EAWheeler) **3-9-0** TSprake(4) (a.p: chal appr fnl f: carried lft: r.o)	nk	**2**	9/4[2]	51	25
2747[10]	**Barbury Ballad (IRE) (40)** (MJHeaton-Ellis) **3-8-9**(5) ADaly(3) (bhd: rdn 2f out: a outpcd)	7	**3**	20/1	29	3
2496[W]	**Harvey's Future** (TTClement) **3-8-9**(5) GFaulkner(7) (b: prom tl rdn & outpcd over 1f out)	nk	**4**	7/1[3]	28	2
2780[11]	**Nikki Star** (CJHill) **3-8-4**(5) DSweeney(2) (swvd lft s: a bhd & outpcd)	19	**5**	16/1	—	—
				(SP 115.8%)	**5 Rn**	

61.1 secs (2.60) CSF £2.25 TOTE £1.60: £1.10 £1.70 (£1.60) OWNER Mrs E. N. Nield (LIMPSFIELD) BRED Miss Ann Quinn

2277 Goodbye Gatemen (IRE) should have found this easy but he continually edged left into the whip when strongly pressed in the latter stages and held on with nothing to spare. (8/13)

2732 Dancing Mystery mounted a serious challenge into the final furlong and was intimidated into drifting left due to the antics of the winner, but his rider never had to stop riding and he was beaten on merit. (9/4)

Harvey's Future showed up with the pace but he was the first one to feel the strain and faded quickly below the distance. (7/1: 7/2-8/1)

T/Plpt: £398.50 (40.93 Tckts). T/Qdpt: £40.40 (26.65 Tckts) IM

2764-SANDOWN (R-H) (Good to firm, Firm patches)
Wednesday July 23rd

Race 5: hand timed

WEATHER: hot WIND: almost nil

2947 HARPERS & QUEEN CLAIMING STKS (3-Y.O+) (Class F)

6-15 (6-16) **1m 14y** £2,905.00 (£880.00: £430.00: £205.00) Stalls: High GOING minus 0.45 sec per fur (F)

				SP	RR	SF
2729[6]	**Yalta (IRE) (81)** (RCharlton) **4-9-11b**[1] PatEddery(11) (lw: mde all: clr over 1f out: rdn out)	—	**1**	3/1[2]	90	63
2441a[4]	**High Premium (84)** (RAFahey) **9-9-0**(7) RWinston(9) (a.p: chsd wnr over 2f out: nt cl run on ins 2f out: swtchd lft: r.o)	1¼	**2**	4/5[1]	84	57
2603[13]	**Golden Ace (IRE) (80)** (RHannon) **4-8-12**(7) RSmith(10) (lw: rdn & hdwy over 2f out: r.o one pce)	9	**3**	16/1	64	37
2724[6]	**Jilly Woo (47)** (DRCElsworth) **3-7-6**(7) JFowle(3) (hld up: rdn over 2f out: one pce)	1¾	**4**	25/1	48	13
2216[9]	**Zurs (IRE) (58)** (MissGayKelleway) **4-9-7**(3) RFfrench(6) (hdwy over 1f out: nvr nrr)	s.h	**5**	10/1[3]	65	38
2748[2]	**Without Friends (IRE) (60)** (JFfitch-Heyes) **3-8-6**(3) AWhelan(14) (swtg: hld up: rdn over 2f out: one pce)	½	**6**	25/1	57	22
2602[5]	**Hadadabble (32)** (PatMitchell) **4-8-10** RCochrane(4) (swtg: nvr nr to chal)	½	**7**	66/1	49	22
	Fengari (53) (MMadgwick) **8-9-0** NVarley(12) (swtg: bit bkwd: rdn & hdwy on ins over 2f out: wknd 1f out)	1¼	**8**	50/1	51	24
2646[17]	**Persian Dawn (30)** (RTPhillips) **4-8-7** JReid(8) (chsd wnr over 5f)	1	**9**	50/1	42	15
2723[2]	**Little Pilgrim (25)** (TMJones) **4-9-0** AMcGlone(13) (swtg: sme hdwy over 1f out: sn wknd)	1¼	**10**	33/1	46	19
236[4]	**Oozlem (IRE) (39)** (LMontagueHall) **8-8-11**(3) DO'Donohoe(7) (bit bkwd: s.i.s: a bhd)	2½	**11**	33/1	41	14
2369[16]	**Cabcharge Blue (53)** (TJNaughton) **5-8-7**(7) RachaelMoody(1) (swtg: hdwy over 5f out: wknd over 3f out)	½	**12**	66/1	40	13
1921[7]	**Moredun (IRE)** (IABalding) **3-8-4** GHind(5) (t: lw: hld up: rdn over 3f out: sn wknd)	½	**13**	50/1	37	2
2281[5]	**Mad Alex (48)** (MJHaynes) **4-9-1** LDettori(2) (b: b.hind: lw: prom over 4f)	9	**14**	33/1	22	—
				(SP 120.9%)	**14 Rn**	

1m 42.16 (0.96) CSF £4.75 TOTE £4.50: £2.10 £1.10 £4.80 (£2.50) Trio £9.00 OWNER Lord Weinstock (BECKHAMPTON) BRED Ballymacoll Stud Farm Ltd

WEIGHT FOR AGE 3yo-8lb

2729 Yalta (IRE) appreciated the drop in class and first-time blinkers and bounced back to form with a pillar-to-post victory, lengthening his stride in good style in the final quarter-mile to keep the runner-up at bay. (3/1)

2441a High Premium was officially best in at the weights after a string of good efforts. Moving into second place over a quarter of a mile from home, he tried to go for a run up the inside but failed and had to be switched left, allowing the winner to get first run. He appeared to find the ground a bit too lively and was not letting himself down properly but, nevertheless, kept on really well to finish well clear of the remainder. On a slightly easier surface, he can regain the winning thread. (4/5: op evens)

1261 Golden Ace (IRE) has been out of form this year and, although staying on, never threatened to trouble the first two. (16/1)

Jilly Woo was made to look extremely slow in the straight. Not surprisingly, she remains a maiden, and is going to have to find an exceptionally bad race if she is to ever win. (25/1)

677 Zurs (IRE), whose only win to date came on the All-Weather, has lost his way this season and not even this drop in class could help. (10/1: 12/1-8/1)

2748 Without Friends (IRE), who ran well in a seller last week, once again had his limitations savagely exposed. (25/1)

2948 JENNIFER'S DIARY E.B.F. MAIDEN STKS (2-Y.O) (Class D)

6-45 (6-47) **7f 16y** £3,517.50 (£1,065.00: £520.00: £247.50) Stalls: High GOING minus 0.45 sec per fur (F)

				SP	RR	SF
2562^{3}	**Trident (USA)** (MRStoute) **2-9-0** JReid(3) (lw: hld up: led 2f out: rdn out)	—	**1**	4/9^{1}	85+	43
	Silvertown (JHMGosden) **2-9-0** PatEddery(1) (w'like: scope: bit bkwd: rdn over 3f out: hdwy 2f out: chsd wnr over 1f out: r.o: bttr for r)	2½	**2**	13/2^{2}	79+	37
2693^{12}	**Cage Aux Folles (IRE)** (JWHills) **2-9-0** MHills(9) (w ldr over 3f: rdn over 2f out: unable qckn)	3½	**3**	50/1	71	29
	Courtly Times (EALDunlop) **2-8-9** KFallon(7) (leggy: s.s: rdn over 3f out: hdwy over 1f out: one pce)	¾	**4**	12/1	65	23
1812^{18}	**Chief Blade** (RAkehurst) **2-9-0** SSanders(11) (led 5f: wknd over 1f out)	3½	**5**	50/1	62	20
	Gallaash (USA) (JHMGosden) **2-9-0** LDettori(6) (w'like: scope: lw: a.p: hung rt on ins over 2f out: wknd over 1f out)	2½	**6**	8/1^{3}	56	14
	Ocean Line (IRE) (APJarvis) **2-9-0** SDrowne(8) (w'like: bit bkwd: a bhd)	1¼	**7**	40/1	53	11
2012^{9}	**Hickory (IRE)** (MJHaynes) **2-9-0** DHolland(4) (prom over 3f)	1	**8**	14/1	51	9
	Opportune (GER) (DRCElsworth) **2-9-0** RCochrane(10) (w'like: scope: bkwd: dwlt: bhd fnl 2f)	1¼	**9**	25/1	48	6

(SP 118.2%) **9 Rn**

1m 30.26 (1.66) CSF £3.54 TOTE £1.60: £1.10 £1.80 £5.80 (£3.40) Trio £63.70 OWNER Highclere Thoroughbred Racing Ltd (NEWMARKET) BRED Albatroz Bloodstock Agency Inc. & Yorkrun Farm Inc

2562 Trident (USA) confirmed the promise shown at Newmarket recently, leading two furlongs from home and being ridden along to keep the runner-up at bay. Reid reported afterwards that he needs every inch of a mile. (4/9)

Silvertown, an attractive, good-sized individual with plenty of strength and scope, looked just in need of this but still ran a very promising race. Fitted with a Monty Roberts blanket for stalls entry, he came through to take second place over a furlong out and, at one stage, looked as if he might trouble the winner. Flashing his tail when hit, he nevertheless kept on, although his jockey eased him down in the last few yards when victory was out of the question. He should have little problems winning. (13/2: 3/1-7/1)

Cage Aux Folles (IRE), racing with his tongue tied down, left his debut run well behind. Disputing the lead to halfway, he failed to find another gear in the straight but did struggle on for third prize. (50/1)

Courtly Times, a tall filly with less substance than many in the field, made a move on the outside below the distance but then failed to find another gear. (12/1: 7/1-14/1)

Chief Blade ran better here, taking the field along until collared two furlongs from home. (50/1)

Gallaash (USA), an attractive, good-bodied colt with plenty of scope, cost $280,000 as a yearling and is out of a mare who is related to Singspiel. Unfortunately, he gave Dettori steering problems and, although against the rails, kept on trying to hang. Dettori slapped him down the side and the combination weakened below the distance. (8/1: 6/1-10/1)

893 Hickory (IRE) (14/1: op 7/1)

2949 SPORTING INDEX H'CAP (0-80) (4-Y.O+) (Class D)

7-15 (7-16) **1m 6f** £3,761.25 (£1,140.00: £557.50: £266.25) Stalls: High GOING minus 0.45 sec per fur (F)

				SP	RR	SF
1763^{4}	**Mawared (IRE) (67)** (JLDunlop) **4-9-1** RHills(7) (b: hdwy over 3f out: rdn over 2f out: led over 1f out: r.o wl)	—	**1**	6/1^{3}	78	46
2767^{2}	**Silently (80)** (JSKing) **5-9-11**(3) RFfrench(9) (lw: hld up: rdn over 3f out: n.m.r over 1f out: hung lft ins fnl f: r.o wl)	2½	**2**	100/30^{1}	88	56
2589^{9}	**Lime Street Blues (IRE) (55)** (TKeddy) **6-8-3**ow1 SSanders(8) (hld up: led over 3f out tl over 1f out: unable qckn)	1¼	**3**	40/1	62	29
2118^{11}	**Nordansk (53)** (MMadgwick) **8-8-1** NVarley(2) (lw: hdwy over 3f out: hrd rdn over 2f out: hung rt over 1f out: one pce)	s.h	**4**	14/1	60	28
2694*	**Tawafek (USA) (70)** (SDow) **4-9-4** JReid(5) (lw: rdn over 5f out: hdwy over 1f out: r.o one pce)	1¼	**5**	6/1^{3}	75	43
2682^{7}	**General Mouktar (48)** (MCPipe) **7-7-10** DWright(6) (lw: rdn over 3f out: hdwy over 1f out: nvr nrr)	hd	**6**	9/1	53	21
2767^{8}	**Tudor Island (75)** (CEBrittain) **8-9-9** LDettori(4) (lw: prom over 12f)	6	**7**	11/2^{2}	73	41
2694^{2}	**Mighty Phantom (USA) (65)** (JWHills) **4-8-13** MHills(3) (chsd ldr: ev ch over 2f out: wknd over 1f out)	1¼	**8**	9/1	62	30
2592^{3}	**Reaganesque (USA) (53)** (PGMurphy) **5-8-1**ow1 SDrowne(1) (led over 10f: wknd wl over 1f out)	3½	**9**	9/1	46	13
2483^{4}	**Rock The Barney (IRE) (51)** (MDIUsher) **8-7-6**(7)ow3 SCarson(10) (lw: bhd fnl 5f)	10	**10**	10/1	32	—

(SP 115.2%) **10 Rn**

3m 2.07 (3.17) CSF £23.63 CT £668.11 TOTE £7.40: £2.60 £1.80 £3.10 (£9.30) Trio £182.70 OWNER Mr Hamdan Al Maktoum (ARUNDEL) BRED Shadwell Estate Company Limited

LONG HANDICAP Rock The Barney (IRE) 7-8

1763 Mawared (IRE) appreciated this longer trip and, rousted along to lead approaching the final furlong, kept on well to the line. (6/1: op 4/1)

2767 Silently, bustled along and going nowhere early in the straight, manoeuvered himself to a clear position entering the final furlong but then drifted out to the centre of the track. Nevertheless, he really found his feet in the last one hundred yards but, despite running on strongly, found the winner was already home and dried. He has now finished second in three of his four runs this season. (100/30)

Lime Street Blues (IRE), 16lb lower than at the beginning of the season, ran his best race as a result. Showing in front early in the straight, he was collared approaching the final furlong and then failed to find another gear. (40/1)

1459 Nordansk appreciated this longer trip but gave his jockey problems in the straight as he tried to hang. Despite Varley's efforts, the gelding could only go up and down in the same place in the final furlong. He is very difficult to win with. (14/1: 8/1-16/1)

2694* Tawafek (USA) stayed on in the last furlong and a half but, by then, it was all over. (6/1)

2381 General Mouktar, racing at the back of the field, never threatened to get into it despite some late headway. (9/1: 5/1-10/1)

2694 Mighty Phantom (USA) (9/1: 6/1-10/1)

2483 Rock The Barney (IRE) (10/1: 8/1-12/1)

2950 EVENING STANDARD H'CAP (0-80) (4-Y.O+) (Class D)

7-45 (7-48) **5f 6y** £4,585.00 (£1,390.00: £680.00: £325.00) Stalls: Low GOING minus 0.45 sec per fur (F)

				SP	RR	SF
2732^{4}	**Mindrace (59)** (KTIvory) **4-8-7** KFallon(5) (led over 3f: led 1f out: all out)	—	**1**	6/1^{3}	67	29
2769^{4}	**Half Tone (55)** (RMFlower) **5-8-3b**ow1 SSanders(8) (lw: a.p: rdn over 1f out: ev ch ins fnl f: r.o wl)	hd	**2**	15/2	63	24
2377^{7}	**Mister Jolson (75)** (RJHodges) **8-9-9** SDrowne(1) (lw: hdwy & swtchd rt over 1f out: r.o)	1¼	**3**	5/1^{2}	79	41
2769^{5}	**Dande Flyer (62)** (DWPArbuthnot) **4-8-7**(3) RFfrench(7) (lw: w ldr: led wl over 1f out to 1f out: unable qckn)	s.h	**4**	8/1	66	28
2649^{4}	**Golden Pound (USA) (77)** (MissGayKelleway) **5-9-11** JReid(4) (b.hind: hld up: rdn over 2f out: one pce)	1¼	**5**	6/1^{3}	77	39
2769^{2}	**Willow Dale (IRE) (77)** (DRCElsworth) **4-9-11** RCochrane(3) (b.nr hind: lw: hld up: rdn over 2f out: wknd fnl f)	2½	**6**	5/2^{1}	69	31
1410^{13}	**Longwick Lad (77)** (WRMuir) **4-9-11** MHills(6) (lw: bhd fnl 2f)	nk	**7**	14/1	68	30

2711[6] **Bayin (USA) (65)** (MDIUsher) **8-8-13** RStreet(2) (a bhd)....1½ **8** 15/2 51 13
(SP 115.1%) **8 Rn**

61.27 secs (1.47) CSF £45.65 CT £221.55 TOTE £6.90: £1.60 £2.00 £1.80 (£28.50) OWNER Mr D. F. Abbott (RADLETT) BRED Mrs P. A. Brown

2732 Mindrace showed real battling qualities for, after setting the pace, he was narrowly headed below the distance. However, he soon fought his way back to the front and, in an all-out struggle, prevailed by the skin of his teeth to gain only the second victory of his career. (6/1: 5/1-15/2)
2769 Half Tone has done all his winning at this trip and was a leading player throughout. Throwing down a very determined challenge in the final furlong, he did little wrong and only just failed to prevail. (15/2)
2377 Mister Jolson, switched as he began to pick up ground below the distance, ran on nicely inside the final furlong to snatch third prize right on the line. (5/1: op 3/1)
2769 Dande Flyer signalled a return to form here last week and again ran well. Disputing the lead, he showed with a narrow advantage early in the final quarter-mile but, headed a furlong out, was tapped for toe in the last one hundred yards. (8/1)
2649 Golden Pound (USA) chased the leaders but failed to quicken in the second half of the race. Both his wins to date have come at six furlongs and a return to that trip is needed. (6/1)
2769 Willow Dale (IRE) has been in fine form this season but she was disappointing on this occasion and was off the bridle before halfway. (5/2)
949* Longwick Lad (14/1: 10/1-16/1)
2711 Bayin (USA) (15/2: 5/1-8/1)

2951 PANMURE GORDON H'CAP (0-85) (3-Y.O) (Class D)

8-15 (8-15) **7f 16y** £4,299.00 (£1,302.00: £636.00: £303.00) Stalls: High GOING minus 0.45 sec per fur (F)

			SP	RR	SF
2704[2]	**Jorrocks (USA) (74)** (IABalding) **3-8-12** LDettori(6) (lw: hld up: shkn up over 1f out: led ins fnl f: r.o wl) ....—	**1**	100/30[2]	83	58
2119[3]	**Song of Skye (80)** (TJNaughton) **3-9-4** DHolland(3) (hdwy over 1f out: r.o wl ins fnl f) ....¾	**2**	7/1	87	62
2528[9]	**Asef Alhind (83)** (BHanbury) **3-9-7** RHills(5) (lw: chsd ldr: led over 2f out: hrd rdn over 1f out: hdd ins fnl f: unable qckn) ....nk	**3**	5/2[1]	90	65
2691[2]	**Impulsif (USA) (72)** (DJSffrenchDavis) **3-8-10** PatEddery(2) (lw: a.p: rdn over 2f out: ev ch wl over 1f out: wknd fnl f) 5	**4**	7/2[3]	67	42
991[9]	**Ijtinab (78)** (RAkehurst) **3-9-2** SSanders(4) (lw: hld up: rdn over 3f out: wknd ins fnl f) 1¼	**5**	9/1	71	46
2313[7]	**Rotor Man (IRE) (60)** (JDBethell) **3-7-9v**[1(3)] RFfrench(1) (lw: led over 4f: wknd over 1f out) 2½	**6**	11/2	47	22

(SP 111.8%) **6 Rn**

1m 28.8 (0.20) CSF £23.20 TOTE £2.70: £1.70 £2.40 (£11.60) OWNER Mr Paul Mellon (KINGSCLERE) BRED Stewart L. Amstrong

2704 Jorrocks (USA) was given a lovely ride by Dettori who patiently waited with the gelding at the back of the field. Still cruising on the bridle entering the final quarter-mile, he woke up the gelding approaching the final furlong and the combination came through to lead in the last one hundred yards. (100/30)
1453 Song of Skye began to pick up ground below the distance but, despite running on strongly, found the winner had got first run. (7/1: 5/1-8/1)
1682* Asef Alhind, who failed to stay a mile and a quarter here at the beginning of the month, made his bid for glory over a quarter of a mile from home but was unable to contain the winner inside the final furlong. A drop of a few pounds in the handicap would help. (5/2)
2691 Impulsif (USA) had every chance early in the final quarter-mile, before tiring in the last two hundred yards. (7/2)
790 Ijtinab, off the course for eleven weeks, was the first off the bridle early in the straight. Nevertheless, he held on grimly until tiring inside the final furlong. He looks on a stiff mark. (9/1: 4/1-10/1)
2313 Rotor Man (IRE) took the field along but he was collared over a quarter of a mile from home and the writing was soon on the wall. (11/2)

2952 CORNERSTONE IMAGING AND HEADWAY TECHNOLOGY MEDIAN AUCTION MAIDEN STKS (3 & 4-Y.O) (Class E)

8-45 (8-46) **1m 2f 7y** £2,739.25 (£829.00: £404.50: £192.25) Stalls: High GOING minus 0.45 sec per fur (F)

			SP	RR	SF
1270[5]	**Agony Aunt (74)** (MrsJCecil) **3-8-6** PatEddery(1) (lw: led over 1f: led over 3f out: drvn out) ....—	**1**	7/2[2]	86	34
2731[3]	**Kamanev (IRE)** (MRStoute) **3-8-11** JReid(4) (lw: hld up: n.m.r over 3f out: chsd wnr wl over 1f out: edgd rt: nt r.o) ....½	**2**	4/5[1]	90	38
2583[7]	**Water Flower** (JRFanshawe) **3-8-6** MHills(8) (b.hind: hld up: rdn & n.m.r over 3f out: wknd over 1f out) 7	**3**	11/2[3]	74	22
2687[2]	**Rumuz (IRE)** (EALDunlop) **3-8-6** RHills(2) (b.nr hind: hld up: chsd wnr over 3f out tl wl over 1f out: sn wknd)..2	**4**	8/1	71	19
1637[9]	**Certain Surprise** (MMadgwick) **3-8-6** NVarley(7) (s.s: a bhd) 3	**5**	66/1	66	14
2731[13]	**Shailendra (IRE)** (JHMGosden) **3-8-6** LDettori(5) (lw: led over 8f out tl over 3f out: sn wknd) 14	**6**	12/1	44	—
2532[9]	**Aegean** (RHannon) **3-8-11** SSanders(6) (a bhd) 23	**7**	33/1	12	—

(SP 116.4%) **7 Rn**

2m 9.39 (2.69) CSF £6.27 TOTE £4.70: £1.90 £1.30 (£3.10) Trio £3.70 OWNER Capt J. Macdonald-Buchanan (NEWMARKET) BRED The Lavington Stud

1270 Agony Aunt put her experience to good use. Sent on over three furlongs from home, she responded to pressure to keep the reluctant runner-up at bay. (7/2)
2731 Kamanev (IRE) stood out in the paddock but unfortunately did not cover himself in glory in the race itself. Moving into second place early in the final quarter-mile, he then ducked in behind the winner and, carrying his head high, simply refused to go past the winner, despite finishing well clear of the remainder. It remains to be seen whether this incident was a one-off. (4/5)
Water Flower, led round by two handlers in the paddock, chased the leaders but she was being bustled along early in the straight and had given her all below the distance. (11/2: 7/1-12/1)
2687 Rumuz (IRE) moved into second place early in the straight but she was collared for that position early in the final quarter-mile and had soon shot her bolt. She is certainly one of the stable's lesser lights. (8/1: op 4/1)

T/Plpt: £28.80 (874.8 Tckts). T/Qdpt: £30.30 (41.26 Tckts) AK

2746-BRIGHTON (L-H) (Firm)
Thursday July 24th

WEATHER: fine but cloudy WIND: moderate against

2953 E.B.F. WOODINGDEAN MEDIAN AUCTION MAIDEN STKS (2-Y.O) (Class E)

2-00 (2-01) **6f 209y** £3,096.25 (£925.00: £442.50: £201.25) Stalls: Low GOING minus 0.42 sec per fur (F)

			SP	RR	SF
2394[2]	**Flow By** (JLDunlop) **2-8-9** GCarter(9) (hld up: hdwy over 2f out: rdn to ld ins fnl f: r.o) ....—	**1**	3/1[2]	73	17
2768[2]	**Outsourcing (USA)** (PFICole) **2-9-0** CRutter(1) (led: hrd rdn & hdd ins fnl f: r.o) ....nk	**2**	2/1[1]	77	21

2509^{13}	**Riley** (RCharlton) **2-9-0** TSprake(8) (lw: a.p: rdn & ev ch 2f out: one pce)	2½	**3**	20/1	72	16
2728^{14}	**Blueberry** (SDow) **2-8-6**(3) DO'Donohoe(6) (stdd s: wl bhd tl hdwy over 3f out: r.o one pce fnl f)	nk	**4**	25/1	66	10
2719^{4}	**Appyabo** (MRChannon) **2-9-0** RHughes(11) (hld up: hdwy over 2f out: one pce fnl f)	½	**5**	33/1	70	14
2320^{9}	**Aldwych Arrow (IRE)** (MBell) **2-9-0** MFenton(4) (prom tl wknd over 1f out)	2	**6**	12/1	65	9
2699^{10}	**Phantom Waters** (RFJohnsonHoughton) **2-8-9** AClark(2) (dwlt: sn rcvrd: nt clr run on ins over 2f out: wknd over 1f out)	s.h	**7**	25/1	60	4
	Colleville (MAJarvis) **2-8-9** MTebbutt(7) (small: bkwd: wl bhd tl hdwy fnl 2f: nvr nrr)	¾	**8**	16/1	58	2
2394^{3}	**Fawning** (MBlanshard) **2-8-9** JQuinn(10) (hld up: hdwy 3f out: wknd 2f out)	2½	**9**	8/1	53	—
2768^{6}	**Simlet** (WJarvis) **2-9-0** WRyan(5) (lw: outpcd: t.o fnl 4f)	4	**10**	16/1	48	—
2746^{2}	**Aegean Dawn** (RHannon) **2-8-9** DaneO'Neill(3) (plld hrd: chsd ldr tl wknd over 2f out)	2	**11**	$7/2^{3}$	39	—
				(SP 126.5%)		**11 Rn**

1m 23.3 (3.30) CSF £8.89 TOTE £3.70: £1.80 £1.20 £5.30 (£2.60) Trio £63.20 OWNER Hesmonds Stud (ARUNDEL) BRED Hesmonds Stud Ltd

2394 Flow By, described by her trainer as having taken time to get the hang of things, handled the fast ground well. She might now go for a nursery if Dunlop considers the Handicapper is not too hard on her. (3/1)

2768 Outsourcing (USA) continues to knock on the door and did not go down without a fight. (2/1)

Riley fared much better than on his debut on this sounder surface and certainly stayed the extra furlong. (20/1)

Blueberry had shown nothing in her two previous runs but came into her own over this longer trip and might be one to keep an eye on. (25/1)

2719 Appyabo is a brother to a ten and eleven furlong winner in Ireland. (33/1)

1842 Aldwych Arrow (IRE), out of a mile and a half winner in Ireland, had surprisingly been dropped back to the minimum trip last time. (12/1)

Colleville, bred to stay, showed some promise for the future. (16/1)

2394 Fawning (8/1: op 7/2)

2954 ROCK GARDENS CLAIMING STKS (3-Y.O+) (Class F)

2-35 (2-36) **6f 209y** £2,277.00 (£627.00: £297.00) Stalls: Low GOING minus 0.42 sec per fur (F)

				SP	RR	SF
2006^{4}	**Kings Harmony (IRE) (71)** (PJMakin) **4-9-8** DHolland(5) (lw: mde all: rdn out)	—	**1**	$7/4^{1}$	69	32
2745^{7}	**Crystal Heights (FR) (63)** (RJO'Sullivan) **9-8-12** SWhitworth(14) (b: s.s: hdwy & edgd lft over 1f out: r.o ins fnl f)	2	**2**	$3/1^{2}$	54	17
2724*	**Rawi (50)** (MissGayKelleway) **4-8-11b**(3) RFfrench(3) (lw: a.p: chsd wnr 3f out: one pce fnl 2f)	s.h	**3**	10/1	56	19
2745^{14}	**Dark Menace (49)** (EAWheeler) **5-8-5b**(7) SCarson(16) (a.p: one pce fnl 2f)	¾	**4**	20/1	53	16
2745^{6}	**Pearl Dawn (IRE) (46)** (PCClarke) **7-8-5** CRutter(17) (hld up: hdwy 2f out: one pce fnl f)	1¾	**5**	14/1	42	5
2724^{4}	**Okay Baby (IRE) (26)** (JMBradley) **5-8-3** TSprake(8) (a.p: rdn over 1f out: wknd fnl f)	¾	**6**	20/1	38	1
2748^{8}	**Chopin (IRE) (52)** (RFJohnsonHoughton) **3-8-5b** AClark(6) (dwlt: nvr nr to chal)	nk	**7**	33/1	46	2
2723^{4}	**Prince of Fortune (47)** (MBlanshard) **3-8-5** JQuinn(9) (no hdwy fnl 3f)	hd	**8**	14/1	46	2
1921^{5}	**Blazing Castle (50)** (WGMTurner) **3-8-4**(7) DMcGaffin(4) (lw: rdn 3f out: no hdwy fnl 2f)	hd	**9**	33/1	52	8
2748^{4}	**Jubilee Scholar (IRE) (45)** (GLMoore) **4-8-12** CandyMorris(7) (dwlt: hmpd & swtchd lft over 2f out: nvr trbld ldrs)	1½	**10**	14/1	42	5
2663^{6}	**Durable George (41)** (JJBridger) **3-7-12**(5) ADaly(15) (lw: bhd whn edgd lft over 2f out)	6	**11**	50/1	26	—
2649^{7}	**Kilvine (77)** (WJHaggas) **4-9-8** SDrowne(12) (lw: prom: eased whn btn over 1f out: sddle slipped)	½	**12**	$7/1^{3}$	37	—
	Captain Picard (DCO'Brien) **3-8-4**ow3 GCarter(2) (s.s: t.o fnl 4f)	16	**13**	50/1	—	—
2542^{7}	**Mirror Four Life (IRE) (65)** (MHTompkins) **3-8-4v**[1] DBiggs(10) (chsd wnr 4f: sn wknd: t.o)	11	**14**	20/1	—	—
				(SP 127.0%)		**14 Rn**

1m 23.0 (3.00) CSF £5.78 TOTE £2.40: £1.10 £1.50 £2.70 (£5.90) Trio £9.90 OWNER Ten of Hearts (MARLBOROUGH) BRED Rathasker Stud

WEIGHT FOR AGE 3yo-7lb

OFFICIAL EXPLANATION **Kilvine: saddle slipped.**

2006 Kings Harmony (IRE), dropped in class, had previously scored twice here on firm ground. (7/4)

879 Crystal Heights (FR), another course specialist down in grade, just got up to snatch second place. (3/1)

2724* Rawi again ran well in what was a more competitive event than at Folkestone last time. (10/1: 7/1-12/1)

1639* Dark Menace does seem to reserve his best for this course and put a disappointing effort here last week behind him. (20/1)

2745 Pearl Dawn (IRE) was back into a claimer this time. (14/1: op 8/1)

2724 Okay Baby (IRE) travelled well for a long way for one who would have been 26lb better off with the winner in a handicap. (20/1)

2723 Prince of Fortune (14/1: op 8/1)

2748 Jubilee Scholar (IRE) (14/1: 7/1-16/1)

2955 KINGSTON (S) H'CAP (0-60) (3-Y.O+) (Class G)

3-10 (3-13) **1m 3f 196y** £1,984.50 (£547.00: £259.50) Stalls: High GOING minus 0.42 sec per fur (F)

				SP	RR	SF
2770^{2}	**Soda Pop (IRE) (60)** (CEBrittain) **3-10-0** WJO'Connor(7) (lw: hld up: rdn & hdwy 3f out: led wl ins fnl f: r.o)	—	**1**	7/1	71	48
2916^{2}	**Sapphire Son (IRE) (42)** (PCClarke) **5-9-5**(3) RFfrench(6) (chsd clr ldr after 3f: led over 2f out tl wl ins fnl f)	¾	**2**	$3/1^{1}$	52	41
2916^{5}	**Running Free (IRE) (45)** (MJFetherston-Godley) **3-8-13** DaneO'Neill(5) (hld up: hdwy 3f out: nt clr run on ins fnl 2f: swtchd rt nr fin: r.o)	1	**3**	12/1	54	31
2150^{6}	**Sovereign Crest (IRE) (45)** (CAHorgan) **4-9-11** DHolland(2) (b: s.s: hld up in rr: hdwy 3f out: nt clr run fnl 2f: r.o)	nk	**4**	$4/1^{3}$	53	42
2577^{8}	**Harlequin Walk (IRE) (34)** (RJO'Sullivan) **6-9-0** JQuinn(9) (dwlt: hld up: hdwy 3f out: hrd rdn & one pce fnl 2f)	1½	**5**	$7/2^{2}$	40	29
2550^{10}	**Tuigamala (32)** (RIngram) **6-8-12** NAdams(4) (lw: hld up & bhd: hdwy 4f out: wknd 2f out)	14	**6**	7/1	19	8
2874^{11}	**Mapengo (36)** (JCullinan) **6-9-2b** VSlattery(3) (led: clr after 3f: rdn over 4f out: hdd over 2f out: sn wknd)	6	**7**	33/1	15	4
2428^{6}	**Tyrolean Dancer (IRE) (50)** (SPCWoods) **3-9-4** DBiggs(8) (hld up: rdn 4f out: sn wl bhd: t.o)	8	**8**	12/1	19	—
2281^{9}	**Kirov Protege (IRE) (36)** (MrsLCJewell) **5-8-9**(7) DarrenWilliams(1) (chsd ldr 3f: rdn & wknd 7f out: t.o fnl 4f)	9	**9**	10/1	—	—
				(SP 119.6%)		**9 Rn**

2m 32.0 (4.40) CSF £26.76 CT £232.53 TOTE £8.50: £2.50 £1.90 £2.70 (£6.40) Trio £17.40 OWNER Mr A. J. Richards (NEWMARKET) BRED Riviere Salee Partnership

WEIGHT FOR AGE 3yo-12lb

Sold CSparrowhawk 7,400gns

2770 Soda Pop (IRE) had not appeared to stay this trip at Sandown three outings ago but this is an easier course and he was able to concede weight to his seniors. (7/1)

2916 Sapphire Son (IRE) was making a quick reappearance off the same mark. (3/1: 2/1-7/2)

2916 Running Free (IRE), nearly ten lengths behind the runner-up at Windsor on Monday night, was due to go down 4lb in future handicaps. He could not get out of a pocket on the rails until it was far too late. (12/1)

2150 Sovereign Crest (IRE), dropping down to selling company, was yet another for Brighton's long list of hard-luck stories. (4/1)
566 Harlequin Walk (IRE) is still 2lb higher than when winning a Folkestone seller a year ago. (7/2)

2956 PEVENSEY H'CAP (0-60) (3-Y.O) (Class F)

3-40 (3-46) **1m 1f 209y** £2,277.00 (£627.00: £297.00) Stalls: High GOING minus 0.42 sec per fur (F)

				SP	RR	SF
2750[2]	**Interdream (60)** (RHannon) **3-9-7** DaneO'Neill(4) (mde all: rdn & qcknd clr over 1f out: eased wl ins fnl f)	—	1	9/4[1]	68+	15
2395[12]	**Indian Blaze (55)** (PWHarris) **3-8-11**(5) CLowther(1) (hld up & plld hrd: hdwy over 1f out: r.o: nt trble wnr)	1½	2	14/1	61	8
2672[5]	**Castles Burning (USA) (54)** (CACyzer) **3-8-12**(3) AWhelan(5) (hld up: hdwy over 1f out: r.o ins fnl f)	2	3	10/1	56	3
2353[2]	**Ceanothus (IRE) (60)** (WJHaggas) **3-9-7** SDrowne(3) (a.p: one pce fnl 2f)	hd	4	7/2[3]	62	9
2750*	**Who's That Man (63)** (SCWilliams) **3-9-10** 6x DHolland(10) (a.p: rdn & ev ch over 2f out: wknd fnl f)	2	5	100/30[2]	62	9
2722[7]	**Be True (57)** (GLMoore) **3-9-4** CandyMorris(7) (hld up & plld hrd: no hdwy fnl 2f)	½	6	33/1	55	2
2750[3]	**Keen Waters (35)** (JRArnold) **3-7-10b** NAdams(2) (s.s: hdwy over 4f out: ev ch over 2f out: wkng whn wandered over 1f out)	¾	7	8/1	32	—
2468[8]	**Lochlass (IRE) (60)** (SPCWoods) **3-9-7** WJO'Connor(8) (chsd wnr over 6f: wkng whn hmpd over 1f out)	2½	8	14/1	53	—
2750[8]	**Master Bobby (40)** (RMFlower) **3-7-8**(7) JFowle(9) (stdd s: wl bhd fnl 4f)	nk	9	33/1	33	—
265[6]	**She's Electric (36)** (JJBridger) **3-7-6**(5)ow1 RMullen(6) (hld up in rr: t.o fnl 5f)	29	10	50/1	—	—
				(SP 117.4%)	**10 Rn**	

2m 5.0 (6.70) CSF £33.12 CT £245.11 TOTE £3.30: £1.70 £2.90 £3.70 (£32.80) Trio £87.90 OWNER Mr Charles Farr & Mr Mark Heaton (MARLBOROUGH) BRED Mrs G. Kindersley
LONG HANDICAP She's Electric 7-5
2750 Interdream, due to go up 2lb following course and distance disqualification, took the initiative when no-one wanted to go on and these unintended tactics worked a treat. (9/4)
Indian Blaze, disappointing when tried in blinkers last time, has been tumbling down the ratings this season and was suited by this step up from seven furlongs. (14/1)
2672 Castles Burning (USA), 20lb lower than on the sand, ran one of his best races on this return to grass. (10/1)
2353 Ceanothus (IRE) had run over a mile as a two-year-old so it came as no surprise to see her stepped up in distance for this handicap debut. (7/2: op 11/2)
2750* Who's That Man could not confirm last week's form with the winner on 6lb worse terms, and had to carry a 6lb penalty when the Handicapper had only raised him 2lb. (100/30)
Be True did not settle even after the slow early pace picked up, but he is due to drop 7lb at the weekend. (33/1)
2750 Keen Waters (8/1: op 4/1)
26 Lochlass (IRE) (14/1: 10/1-16/1)

2957 JOE BLANKS MEMORIAL CHALLENGE CUP H'CAP (0-80) (3-Y.O) (Class D)

4-10 (4-12) **7f 214y** £3,518.20 (£1,048.60: £499.80: £225.40) Stalls: Low GOING minus 0.42 sec per fur (F)

				SP	RR	SF
2695[10]	**Olivo (IRE) (67)** (CAHorgan) **3-9-3** DHolland(3) (chsd clr ldr: led 3f out to 2f out: led 1f out: r.o wl)	—	1	7/1	75	13
2772[7]	**Misty Cay (IRE) (60)** (SDow) **3-8-10** DaneO'Neill(5) (lw: hld up: rdn & lost pl 5f out: hdwy over 3f out: led 2f out to 1f out: nt qckn)	1¼	2	6/1	66	4
2369[10]	**Chain Reaction (IRE) (55)** (MAJarvis) **3-8-5** GCarter(6) (b: hld up: hdwy over 3f out: nt clr run over 2f out: r.o one pce)	1½	3	14/1	58	—
2601[5]	**Signs And Wonders (71)** (CACyzer) **3-9-7** WRyan(4) (lw: dwlt: hdwy 3f out: one pce fnl 2f: sddle slipped)	1½	4	13/8[1]	71	9
2523[11]	**Around Fore Alliss (61)** (TGMills) **3-8-11** AClark(2) (s.s: hdwy 3f out: wknd 2f out)	9	5	9/2[3]	42	—
2408[8]	**Chingachgook (60)** (PWHarris) **3-8-5b**[1](5) CLowther(1) (led: sn clr: hdd 3f out: edgd lft & wknd over 1f out)	½	6	7/2[2]	40	—
				(SP 112.0%)	**6 Rn**	

1m 36.1 (4.80) CSF £42.00 TOTE £5.70: £3.80 £2.00 (£10.80) OWNER Mr J. L. Harrison (PULBOROUGH) BRED Russlson
1870 Olivo (IRE) was down 3lb, and his trainer told the Stewards that he had lost interest after playing up in the stalls last time. (7/1)
2319 Misty Cay (IRE), due to go down 3lb, has gained her wins to date in three claimers on the sand at Lingfield and a juvenile seller here. (6/1)
Chain Reaction (IRE), down 5lb, looked unlucky at first glance but did not quicken up a lot in the closing stages. (14/1: 10/1-16/1)
2601 Signs And Wonders did not look all that unlucky but, obviously, the slipping saddle could not have helped. (13/8)
2523 Around Fore Alliss was down 4lb after disappointing in soft ground last time. (9/2)
1633 Chingachgook took off in the first-time blinkers. (7/2)

2958 PRESTON PARK LIMITED STKS (0-60) (3-Y.O+) (Class F)

4-40 (4-40) **5f 213y** £2,277.00 (£627.00: £297.00) Stalls: Low GOING minus 0.42 sec per fur (F)

				SP	RR	SF
2721[2]	**Resist the Force (USA) (55)** (CACyzer) **7-9-2**(3) RFfrench(3) (lw: hld up: swtchd lft & hdwy over 2f out: led ins fnl f: edgd lft: r.o wl)	—	1	8/1	70	15
2745[5]	**Sharp Imp (59)** (RMFlower) **7-9-2b** SDrowne(2) (lw: hld up & bhd: hdwy on ins over 2f out: squeezed thro over 1f out: hmpd ins fnl f: fin 3rd, ½l: plcd 2nd)	½	2	100/30[2]	62	7
2751[2]	**Corniche Quest (IRE) (60)** (MRChannon) **4-9-5** RHughes(4) (a.p: led over 1f out tl ins fnl f: edgd lft: nt qckn: fin 2nd, 1½l: disq: plcd 3rd)	1½	3	3/1[1]	66	11
2751[4]	**Always Grace (60)** (MissGayKelleway) **5-8-13** AClark(1) (hld up & bhd: hdwy fnl f: r.o)	¾	4	3/1[1]	57	2
2788[7]	**Silver Purse (56)** (APJones) **3-8-5b**[1](3) JDSmith(7) (hdwy 4f out: carried rt 3f out: rdn & one pce fnl 2f)	½	5	15/2	55	—
2557[13]	**Celandine (57)** (AndrewTurnell) **4-8-8**(5) ADaly(9) (led: edgd rt over 1f out: sn hdd: btn whn hmpd ins fnl f)	1½	6	25/1	51	—
2671[11]	**Gwespyr (60)** (RHannon) **4-9-2** DaneO'Neill(6) (b.nr fore: prom: carried rt 3f out: wknd 2f out)	5	7	13/2[3]	41	—
2751[6]	**Agwa (58)** (JJBridger) **8-8-9**(7) PDoe(5) (chsd ldr: edgd rt 3f out: wknd 2f out)	hd	8	16/1	41	—
				(SP 119.0%)	**8 Rn**	

1m 10.7 (3.50) CSF £33.10 TOTE £8.10: £1.70 £2.10 £1.90 (£11.50) Trio £9.20 OWNER Mrs Barbara Hogan (HORSHAM) BRED Ron Con & Barronstown
WEIGHT FOR AGE 3yo-5lb
STEWARDS' ENQUIRY Hughes susp. 2-3/8/97 (careless riding).
2721 Resist the Force (USA) found more patient tactics working the oracle on this continued return to sprinting. (8/1)
2745 Sharp Imp got just the run he wanted up the inside but, unfortunately, the second door was slammed in his face. (100/30)
2751 Corniche Quest (IRE) got her rider in hot water for squeezing up Sharp Imp against the rails. (3/1)
2751 Always Grace got going far too late in the day and might stay seven on this evidence. (3/1)
2788 Silver Purse, in a first-time visor last time, made the switch to blinkers here. (15/2: 5/1-8/1)

Celandine, reverting to sprinting, showed bags of speed from the outside draw and might take some catching at five. (25/1)

T/Plpt: £23.30 (727.3 Tckts). T/Qdpt: £19.50 (65.88 Tckts) KH

2947-SANDOWN (R-H) (Good to firm, Firm patches)
Thursday July 24th
WEATHER: humid WIND: almost nil

2959 TATTERSALLS MAIDEN AUCTION STKS (2-Y.O) (Class E)
2-15 (2-17) **5f 6y** £3,582.50 (£1,085.00: £530.00: £252.50) Stalls: Low GOING minus 0.40 sec per fur (F)

				SP	RR	SF
2831^{2}	**Cloudberry** (BJMeehan) **2-8-5** PatEddery(6) (lw: mde virtually all: drvn out)	—	**1**	8/11^{1}	77	14
2706^{5}	**Statua (IRE)** (PJMakin) **2-8-7** RCochrane(5) (hld up: rdn over 2f out: chsd wnr fnl f: ev ch ins fnl f: r.o wl)	nk	**2**	4/1^{2}	78	15
2553^{6}	**Bala** (HMorrison) **2-8-4** KDarley(7) (lw: a.p: rdn over 2f out: unable qckn)	3½	**3**	14/1	64	1
1821^{11}	**Mercury Falling** (DWPArbuthnot) **2-7-12**(3) MartinDwyer(2) (a.p: rdn over 2f out: wknd fnl f)	1	**4**	33/1	58	—
	Thelonius (IRE) (JGSmyth-Osbourne) **2-8-7** KFallon(3) (neat: outpcd: nvr nr to chal)	2	**5**	20/1	57	—
	Sharp Fellow (IABalding) **2-8-6** LDettori(8) (leggy: hld up: rdn over 2f out: wknd over 1f out)	1¼	**6**	6/1^{3}	52	—
	Natalie's Pet (GLewis) **2-8-3**^{ow2} RPrice(4) (b.hind: w'like: bit bkwd: a bhd)	1¾	**7**	20/1	44	—
2739^{4}	**Life Sentence** (JGSmyth-Osbourne) **2-8-7** DHarrison(1) (lw: jinked & uns rdr s)		**U**	25/1	—	—
				(SP 115.2%)	**8 Rn**	

62.37 secs (2.57) CSF £3.22 TOTE £1.80: £1.10 £1.40 £2.00 (£1.90) OWNER Mrs Douglas Coker (UPPER LAMBOURN) BRED D. A. and Mrs Hicks

2831 Cloudberry put her experience to good use and set only a moderate pace - her jockey knowing only too well that this track can prove too tough for some youngsters. Woken up in the final quarter-mile, she was presented with a very strong challenge from the runner-up in the final furlong but, responding to pressure, just held on. (8/11)

2706 Statua (IRE) was probably not helped by the drop down to five furlongs, even on this stiff track. Moving into second place entering the final furlong, she threw down a very determined challenge and only just failed. A return to six furlongs should see her picking up a similar event. (4/1)

2553 Bala was never far away but failed to find that vital turn of foot in the second half of the race. (14/1)

Mercury Falling does not have much substance, but she broke on level terms this time and ran much better until tiring in the final furlong. (33/1)

Thelonius (IRE) is not that big. Unable to go the pace, he did not help his cause by fly-jumping on several occasions and never threatened to get into it. (20/1)

Sharp Fellow, a tall gelding, chased the leaders but had come to the end of his tether below the distance. (6/1: op 4/1)

2960 SUN BANK MAIDEN STKS (3-Y.O+) (Class D)
2-50 (2-51) **1m 14y** £3,517.50 (£1,065.00: £520.00: £247.50) Stalls: High GOING minus 0.40 sec per fur (F)

				SP	RR	SF
2492^{5}	**Crown of Thorns (USA)** (JHMGosden) **3-8-13** LDettori(10) (lw: a.p: led over 1f out: rdn out)	—	**1**	13/8^{1}	84	44
2566^{5}	**Bright Heritage (IRE) (84)** (DRLoder) **4-9-7** PatEddery(7) (swtg: led over 6f: ev ch ins fnl f: unable qckn)	1	**2**	9/4^{2}	82	50
1611^{8}	**Blot** (MrsJCecil) **3-8-13** PaulEddery(4) (b.hind: hld up: rdn over 1f out: r.o one pce)	1¾	**3**	7/1	79	39
1409^{W}	**Fatal Baraari** (MRStoute) **3-8-13** JReid(5) (a.p: rdn over 2f out: one pce)	3	**4**	4/1^{3}	73	33
	Joust (CEBrittain) **3-8-13** BDoyle(6) (str: scope: bit bkwd: s.s: rdn over 2f out: hdwy over 1f out: one pce)	3½	**5**	20/1	66	26
	Galaxy Flight (MartynMeade) **3-8-8** FNorton(3) (w'like: rdn 4f out: nvr nr to chal)	3½	**6**	66/1	54	14
1297^{10}	**Waasef** (MissGayKelleway) **4-9-7** SSanders(8) (nvr nrr)	s.h	**7**	16/1	59	27
2704^{7}	**Flying Flip** (BCMorgan) **3-8-8** CHodgson(2) (b.hind: bhd fnl 2f)	3½	**8**	25/1	47	7
	Rock River (DCO'Brien) **3-8-8** GBardwell(9) (w'like: bkwd: a bhd)	hd	**9**	100/1	47	7
2555^{11}	**Just Dickens** (RIngram) **3-8-8** AMcGlone(1) (swvd lft s: hdwy 7f out: wknd over 2f out)	1¾	**10**	100/1	43	3
				(SP 119.3%)	**10 Rn**	

1m 43.34 (2.14) CSF £4.90 TOTE £2.90: £1.10 £1.20 £2.00 (£3.90) Trio £9.90 OWNER Sheikh Mohammed (NEWMARKET) BRED Darley Stud Management Co Ltd

WEIGHT FOR AGE 3yo-8lb

2492 Crown of Thorns (USA) looked in very good shape beforehand and, leading over a furlong out, was rousted along to dispose of the runner-up in the last one hundred yards. (13/8)

2566 Bright Heritage (IRE) was better suited by the return to a mile. Bowling along in front, he was collared below the distance but still had every chance inside the final furlong, before the weight allowance to his younger rival proved the stumbling block. (9/4)

1611 Blot, who flopped badly at Newmarket at the end of May, ran better here but, despite staying on for third prize, never looked like finding the vital turn of foot to trouble the front two. (7/1: 5/1-8/1)

Fatal Baraari, who has been gelded since refusing to enter the stalls at Kempton in May, looked very well in the paddock and had no problems entering the stalls this time. Never far away, he was asked for his effort over two furlongs from home but could only go up and down in the same place. (4/1: op 9/4)

Joust, who looked more like a carthorse in the paddock, took closer order below the distance but could then make no further impression. (20/1)

Galaxy Flight, a medium-sized filly who was withdrawn from a seller at Leicester the night before, found this race far too hot and could never get into it. A realistic drop in class is needed. (66/1)

2961 SUN LIFE OF CANADA H'CAP (0-85) (3-Y.O+) (Class D)
3-25 (3-28) **1m 2f 7y** £7,262.50 (£2,200.00: £1,075.00: £512.50) Stalls: High GOING minus 0.40 sec per fur (F)

				SP	RR	SF
2574^{3}	**Traceability (72)** (SCWilliams) **4-9-3** KDarley(15) (chsd ldr: led over 3f out: hrd rdn over 1f out: r.o wl)	—	**1**	10/1	81	53
2653^{3}	**Bardon Hill Boy (IRE) (82)** (BHanbury) **5-9-13** MRimmer(4) (a.p: rdn 3f out: chsd wnr over 1f out: r.o wl)	nk	**2**	16/1	91	63
2722^{3}	**Princess Topaz (65)** (CACyzer) **3-7-11**(3) MartinDwyer(1) (rdn over 2f out: hdwy over 1f out: edgd rt ins fnl f: r.o wl)	¾	**3**	20/1	72	34
2483^{3}	**Typhoon Eight (IRE) (70)** (RWArmstrong) **5-9-1** RPrice(10) (swtg: hld up: rdn 3f out: unable qckn)	1¾	**4**	9/1	75	47
2344*	**Koraloona (IRE) (57)** (GBBalding) **4-8-2** AMcGlone(6) (rdn over 3f out: lost pl over 2f out: rallied fnl f: r.o wl)	s.h	**5**	10/1	62	34
2686^{5}	**Brandon Jack (75)** (IABalding) **3-8-10** LDettori(8) (lw: nt clr run over 3f out: rdn over 2f out: hdwy over 1f out: one pce fnl f)	nk	**6**	12/1	79	41
2118^{9}	**General Haven (70)** (TJNaughton) **4-9-1** JWeaver(7) (lw: hld up: rdn 3f out: btn whn n.m.r ins fnl f)	hd	**7**	20/1	74	46
2485^{5}	**Zidac (69)** (PJMakin) **5-9-0** SSanders(12) (a.p: hrd rdn over 2f out: wknd over 1f out)	1¾	**8**	16/1	70	42
2190^{4}	**Shahboor (USA) (72)** (MRStoute) **3-8-7** JReid(16) (led over 6f: wkng whn nt clr run on ins ins fnl f)	s.h	**9**	6/1^{3}	73	35

	Herr Trigger (72) (DrJDScargill) **6-9-3b** JTate(9) (bit bkwd: nvr nrr) ½	**10**	20/1	72	44
2653[4]	**Sofyaan (USA) (80)** (LadyHerries) **4-9-11** RCochrane(13) (stdy hdwy over 6f out: wknd over 1f out) nk	**11**	12/1	80	52
1934[8]	**Quiet Arch (IRE) (67)** (WRMuir) **4-8-12** KFallon(5) (a bhd) s.h	**12**	20/1	67	39
2537*	**Darapour (IRE) (84)** (LMCumani) **3-9-5** PatEddery(3) (rdn over 3f out: hdwy & n.m.r over 2f out: nt clr run on ins fr over 1f out: nt rcvr) 1½	**13**	4/1[1]	81+	43
2528*	**Trojan Risk (75)** (GLewis) **4-9-6** PaulEddery(2) (lw: a bhd) 3	**14**	11/2[2]	67	39
431[15]	**Superbelle (76)** (MAJarvis) **3-8-11** EmmaO'Gorman(14) (swtg: bhd fnl 2f) 5	**15**	33/1	60	22
2601[12]	**Poker School (IRE) (84)** (NACallaghan) **3-9-5** DHarrison(11) (lw: a bhd) 5	**16**	20/1	61	23

(SP 131.8%) **16 Rn**

2m 8.72 (2.02) CSF £140.56 CT £2,896.32 TOTE £12.60: £2.20 £3.70 £5.10 £2.00 (£62.30) Trio £695.60 OWNER Mr J. W. Lovitt (NEWMARKET) BRED J. S. A. and Mrs Shorthouse

WEIGHT FOR AGE 3yo-10lb

STEWARDS' ENQUIRY Dwyer susp 2-3/8/97 (careless riding).

2574 Traceability, racing with his tongue tied down, has been returning to form of late and opened his account for the season, leading early in the straight and responding well to pressure to hold on. (10/1)

2653 Bardon Hill Boy (IRE) was back at the trip over which he has gained all four of his victories to date. Taking second place approaching the final furlong, he ran on strongly but found the line always beating him. (16/1)

2722 Princess Topaz at last began to pick up ground below the distance but, despite running on strongly inside the final furlong, drifted right in the process. Her jockey was later suspended for two days for careless riding. (20/1)

2483 Typhoon Eight (IRE) was surprisingly dropping back in distance and, bustled along three furlongs from home, never looked like finding that vital turn of foot. He needs to return to a mile and a half. (9/1)

2344* Koraloona (IRE), whose trainer reported that he needs give underfoot after winning last time out, was surprisingly running on this very lively ground. Outpaced over a quarter of a mile from home, he got his second wind in the final furlong but, by then, it was far too late. When the heavens open, he can return to the winner's enclosure. (10/1)

2686 Brandon Jack found this ground much too lively and, although he did weave his way through the pack below the distance, was making no further impression in the final furlong. Some rain is very much required. (12/1)

2537* Darapour (IRE) had a nightmare run. With a wall of horses in front of him in the straight, he did begin to pick up ground but then found himself totally boxed in from below the distance and, from that point, had nowhere to go. This run should most definitely be forgotten and he can soon bounce back into the winner's enclosure, possibly over a bit further. (4/1)

2962 MILCARS STAR STKS (Listed) (2-Y.O F) (Class A)

3-55 (4-02) **7f 16y** £9,048.00 (£2,739.00: £1,337.00: £636.00) Stalls: High GOING minus 0.40 sec per fur (F)

			SP	RR	SF
2516*	**Woodland Melody (USA)** (PWChapple-Hyam) **2-8-12** JReid(1) (hld up: rdn over 2f out: chsd wnr fnl f: led last stride) —	**1**	11/4[2]	94	51
2202*	**Eloquent** (SirMarkPrescott) **2-8-12** SSanders(2) (led 1f: led over 3f out: hrd rdn over 1f out: hdd last stride) s.h	**2**	100/30[3]	94	51
2558[6]	**Forum** (CEBrittain) **2-8-9** BDoyle(3) (led 6f out tl over 3f out: hrd rdn over 1f out: one pce) 2	**3**	15/8[1]	86	43
2597[7]	**Obsessed** (MRStoute) **2-8-9** LDettori(4) (hld up: swtchd lft 3f out: rdn over 2f out: sn wknd) 2½	**4**	5/1	81	38
2394*	**Next Round (IRE)** (MBell) **2-8-12** MFenton(5) (a.p: rdn over 2f out: wknd over 1f out) hd	**5**	14/1	84	41
2697[3]	**Robeena** (CNAllen) **2-8-9** MartinDwyer(6) (lw: a bhd) 2½	**6**	25/1	75	32

(SP 111.7%) **6 Rn**

1m 29.76 (1.16) CSF £11.07 TOTE £3.30: £1.70 £2.40 (£5.70) OWNER Mr R. E. Sangster (MARLBOROUGH) BRED Seahorse Investments

2516* Woodland Melody (USA) took a long time to get going, just like on her debut. Eventually taking second place at the distance, she still had quite a bit of ground to make up on the leader but she eventually whittled that rival down to hit the front right on the line. She looks useful but another furlong would be greatly appreciated. (11/4)

2202* Eloquent was trying to follow the same pattern as stable companion Red Camellia, who won the same Carlisle maiden before putting up a tremendous performance to win this Pattern event. Gaining a slender advantage early in the straight, she responded to pressure and looked to have the race in the bag, only to be caught right on the line. Compensation awaits. (100/30)

2558 Forum had the step up in distance she had been looking for. Soon at the head of affairs, she was narrowly collared early in the straight and failed to quicken in the last furlong and a half. (15/8)

2597 Obsessed, switched to the outside early in the straight, had shot her bolt two furlongs from home. (5/1: 11/4-11/2)

2394* Next Round (IRE) had far more on her plate here but was close up until left for dead from below the distance. (14/1: 10/1-6/1)

2697 Robeena is not going the right way - she was one and three quarter lengths behind the winner on her debut - and was always at the back of the field. (25/1)

2963 PYCRAFT & ARNOLD H'CAP (0-90) (3-Y.O) (Class C)

4-25 (4-30) **1m 6f** £5,135.75 (£1,556.00: £760.50: £362.75) Stalls: High GOING minus 0.40 sec per fur (F)

			SP	RR	SF
2213*	**High Intrigue (IRE) (77)** (HRACecil) **3-8-11** KFallon(8) (mde all: clr over 1f out: hrd rdn: r.o wl) —	**1**	9/1	87	43
2391[2]	**Little Acorn (85)** (SCWilliams) **3-9-5** KDarley(5) (hdwy over 6f out: rdn 4f out: chsd wnr over 2f out: hrd rdn over 1f out: unable qckn) 1¾	**2**	9/1	93	49
2139[4]	**Sudest (IRE) (73)** (IABalding) **3-8-4**(3) MartinDwyer(1) (lw: rdn 5f out: hdwy over 1f out: r.o wl ins fnl f) 1	**3**	7/2[1]	80	36
2676[5]	**Mithak (USA) (87)** (BWHills) **3-9-7b[1]** RHills(10) (rdn & hdwy 2f out: r.o one pce) 1¾	**4**	6/1[3]	92	48
2692*	**Melodica (82)** (MRStoute) **3-9-2** JReid(6) (a.p: hrd rdn over 2f out: one pce) s.h	**5**	7/1	87	43
2230[2]	**Heart of Armor (82)** (PFICole) **3-9-2** PatEddery(3) (lw: rdn & lost pl over 4f out: r.o one pce fnl 2f) ¾	**6**	11/1	86	42
2514[16]	**Assured Gamble (86)** (CEBrittain) **3-9-6** BDoyle(4) (lw: hdwy over 11f out: chsd wnr over 10f out tl over 2f out: wknd 1f out) nk	**7**	14/1	90	46
1649[4]	**Tango King (75)** (JLDunlop) **3-8-9** RCochrane(11) (swtg: nvr nr to chal) hd	**8**	10/1	79	35
2589[5]	**Sun Alert (USA) (75)** (MJPolglase) **3-8-9** MRimmer(2) (lw: prom over 10f) 3½	**9**	20/1	75	31
2850[4]	**Behind The Scenes (72)** (CACyzer) **3-8-6** SSanders(7) (a bhd) 15	**10**	33/1	54	10
2692[2]	**Crystal Hills (IRE) (85)** (JHMGosden) **3-9-5** LDettori(9) (a bhd) 24	**11**	4/1[2]	40	—

(SP 120.8%) **11 Rn**

3m 2.71 (3.81) CSF £81.80 CT £312.99 TOTE £9.20: £3.00 £1.70 £2.10 (£77.40) Trio £85.80 OWNER Mrs E. A. Harris (NEWMARKET) BRED Airlie Stud

OFFICIAL EXPLANATION Crystal Hills (IRE): did not appear to act on the course.

2213* High Intrigue (IRE) put up a game performance from the front. Forging clear below the distance, she was given some strong reminders but was not going to be caught. (9/1: 6/1-10/1)

2391 Little Acorn continues to run consistently, despite a steady rise in the handicap and his tail-flashing antics. Moving into second place over two furlongs from home, he grimly tried to peg back the winner but never looked like finding that vital turn of foot. (9/1)

2139 Sudest (IRE) was well out with the washing turning out of the back straight but his rider was soon bustling him along and, for a long way, there appeared to be no response. At long last, he found his stride from below the distance but, despite finishing with a real flourish, found the winner was already home and dry. (7/2)
2676 Mithak (USA), fitted with blinkers for the first time, was taking a step up in trip to compensate for his lack of acceleration but, although staying on, it was once again blatantly exposed. (6/1)
2692* Melodica once again had her lack of acceleration well exposed as she could only go up and down in the same place in the last three furlongs. (7/1: 5/1-8/1)
2230 Heart of Armor, taking a step up in distance, broke well enough but gradually lost his pitch in the back straight and was quite some way off the leaders once in line for home. He did stay on in the final quarter-mile but never threatened to get back into it. (11/1)

2964 SURREY RACING H'CAP (0-80) (3-Y.O) (Class D)
4-55 (5-03) **5f 6y** £3,485.00 (£1,055.00: £515.00: £245.00) Stalls: Low GOING minus 0.40 sec per fur (F)

				SP	RR	SF
2841^{4}	**Shalstayholy (IRE) (66)** (GLMoore) **3-8-7** KFallon(5) (lw: a.p: led over 2f out: drvn out)	—	**1**	7/1^{3}	76	27
2769^{8}	**Kilcullen Lad (IRE) (80)** (PMooney) **3-9-7v** RCochrane(8) (lw: gd hdwy over 1f out: hrd rdn: r.o wl ins fnl f)	½	**2**	20/1	88	39
2481*	**Sally Green (IRE) (75)** (CFWall) **3-9-2** LDettori(4) (swtg: hld up: rdn over 1f out: r.o wl ins fnl f)	½	**3**	9/2^{1}	82	33
2581^{4}	**Tear White (IRE) (67)** (TGMills) **3-8-8** JReid(11) (hdwy on bit over 1f out: rdn fnl f: unable qckn wl ins fnl f)	½	**4**	20/1	72	23
2655^{4}	**Bramble Bear (70)** (MBlanshard) **3-8-11** JQuinn(10) (hld up: hrd rdn over 1f out: one pce)	1½	**5**	9/1	71	22
2779^{3}	**Anokato (63)** (KTIvory) **3-8-1**(3) MartinDwyer(9) (a.p: hrd rdn over 1f out: wknd fnl f)	nk	**6**	8/1	63	14
2780^{3}	**Mon Bruce (57)** (WRMuir) **3-7-12** JLowe(2) (lw: rdn over 2f out: nvr nr to chal)	nk	**7**	9/2^{1}	56	7
2563^{6}	**Silent Miracle (IRE) (74)** (MBell) **3-9-1** MFenton(7) (lw: prom over 2f)	½	**8**	6/1^{2}	71	22
2580*	**Hever Golf Rocket (73)** (TJNaughton) **3-9-0** PatEddery(6) (a bhd)	½	**9**	8/1	68	19
569^{11}	**Nightingale Song (72)** (MartynMeade) **3-8-13** FNorton(3) (swtg: led over 2f: wknd over 1f out)	1¼	**10**	50/1	63	14
2393^{6}	**Marengo (68)** (JAkehurst) **3-8-9** SSanders(1) (prom 3f)	2	**11**	10/1	53	4
				(SP 115.9%)	**11 Rn**	

61.69 secs (1.89) CSF £125.73 CT £636.71 TOTE £9.80: £2.80 £2.80 £1.90 (£107.90) Trio £173.30 OWNER J B R Leisure Ltd (BRIGHTON) BRED Mrs P. Grubb
2841 Shalstayholy (IRE), who caught the eye last time out, went on at halfway and, responding to stern pressure, just held on to gain her first victory at this trip. (7/1)
2590 Kilcullen Lad (IRE), dropped 4lb by the handicapper, bounced back to form. Slicing his way through the field from below the distance, he ran on really strongly and only just failed. (20/1)
2481* Sally Green (IRE) had more on her plate on this occasion than when winning here at the beginning of the month but, nevertheless, ran on really nicely inside the final furlong. (9/2)
2581 Tear White (IRE) is not the easiest of rides but cruised up on the bridle below the distance. When his rider did ask him for his effort in the final furlong, the response was not as great as first anticipated and the combination failed to quicken. (20/1)
2655 Bramble Bear chased the leaders but failed to find another gear from below the distance. All three of her wins to date have come at this trip. (9/1)
2779 Anokato, set to rise 5lb in future handicaps, was bang in the firing line until tiring in the final furlong. (8/1)
2393 Marengo (10/1: 8/1-12/1)

T/Jkpt: £61,897.40 (0.99 Tckts); £871.79 to Ascot 25/7/97. T/Plpt: £86.00 (388.46 Tckts). T/Qdpt: £49.50 (34.01 Tckts) AK

2965a - 2966a (Irish Racing) - See Computer Raceform

0019a-DOWN ROYAL (Lisburn, Ireland) (R-H) (Good to firm)
Monday July 14th

2967a ULSTER HARP DERBY H'CAP (0-110) (Listed) (3-Y.O+)
3-30 (3-32) **1m 4f 68y** IR £30,000.00 (IR £9,500.00: IR £4,500.00: IR £1,500.00)

				SP	RR	SF
2136^{3}	**Docklands Limo** (BJMcMath) **4-8-5** DHarrison (led early: rn 2nd: led again 4f out: jnd 1½f out: rdn & led ins last: kpt on wl)	—	**1**	7/1	84+	—
	Munif (IRE) (DKWeld,Ireland) **5-9-10** MJKinane (hld up: hdwy & 5th 4f out: 2nd & chal 2f out: disp ld & ev ch wl over 1f out: no ex u.p wl ins last: kpt on)	1½	**2**	5/1^{2}	101	—
	Hill Society (IRE) (NMeade,Ireland) **5-7-12**(6) DPMcDonogh (rn 3rd: 2nd & chal over 3f out: 3rd, rdn & no ex 1½f out: kpt on)	1	**3**	14/1	80	—
809a^{5}	**Rasin (IRE)** (KPrendergast,Ireland) **3-8-4** WJSupple (in tch: 4th ½-wy: chsd ldrs u.p over 2f out: nt rch ldrs over 1f out: kpt on)	nk	**4**	14/1	92	—
2053^{2}	**Akdariya (IRE)** (JOxx,Ireland) **3-8-12** JPMurtagh (hld up towards rr: cld over 3f out: 5th, rdn & nt rch ldrs 1½f out: no ex: kpt on same pce)	nk	**5**	5/4^{1}	100	—
	Afarka (IRE) (SJTreacy,Ireland) **4-8-4** NGMcCullagh (rn 5th: hld up: 7th, rdn & chsd ldrs over 3f out: no imp 1½f out: kpt on)	3½	**6**	12/1	74	—
	Monongahela (IRE) (APO'Brien,Ireland) **3-7-10b** 5x AJNolan (sn led: hdd 4f out: rdn & wknd 2½f out)	3½	**7**	10/1	75	—
	Basanta (IRE) (JSBolger,Ireland) **4-9-2** 7x KJManning (hld up towards rr: 6th & chsd ldrs 4f out: no imp under 3f out: eased: lame)	20	**8**	11/2^{3}	56	—
				(SP 119.1%)	**8 Rn**	

2m 33.8 OWNER Mrs Lisa Olley (NEWMARKET) BRED Majors Racing International Ltd
2136 Docklands Limo became the first English-trained winner of this race since its inception as a handicap nine years ago. In front before the straight, he battled on well under pressure to win gamely. (7/1)
Munif (IRE), successful in this race two years ago, challenged and had every chance over a furlong out. (5/1)
Hill Society (IRE) chased the leader from three furlongs out but just could not quicken. (14/1)
Rasin (IRE) kept on well without quickening over the last furlong. (14/1)
2053 Akdariya (IRE), runner-up to Yashmak in the Ribblesdale, looked nicely treated in this, her first handicap but despite starting favourite, there didn't appear to be a great deal of confidence in her chance and she was last of all with three furlongs to race. Fifth and under pressure a furlong out, she kept on without making any real impression. (5/4)

2968a - 2986a (Irish Racing) - See Computer Raceform

2626a-LEOPARDSTOWN (Dublin, Ireland) (L-H) (Good)
Saturday July 19th

2987a MASTERCHEFS/APRICOTS ROCHESTOWN STKS (Listed) (2-Y.O)
2-30 (2-33) **6f** IR £12,900.00 (IR £3,700.00: IR £1,700.00: IR £500.00) GOING minus 0.18 sec per fur (GF)

	Horse		Pos	SP	RR	SF
1531a6	**Flame Violet (IRE)** (APO'Brien,Ireland) **2-8-7** CRoche (cl up: trckd ldrs: 3rd & chal 2f out: led early fnl f: r.o: hands & heels: hld on)	—	1	2/1 2	88	29
	Abandonment (IRE) (JOxx,Ireland) **2-8-7** PJSmullen (hld up: trckd ldrs: 5th ½-wy: 4th & swtchd rt over 1f out: chal ins last: r.o wl: jst failed)	s.h	2	9/2 3	88	29
	Dane River (IRE) (JSBolger,Ireland) **2-8-10** KJManning (prom: rn 2nd: rdn under 2f out: led over 1f out tl early fnl f: no ex)	1½	3	5/4 1	87	28
2439a9	**Magical Baba (IRE)** (PatrickPrendergast,Ireland) **2-8-10** SCraine (hld up: chsd ldrs: 6th & rdn 1½f out: kpt on ins last: nrst fin)	½	4	10/1	86	27
	Delirious Tantrum (IRE) (GMLyons,Ireland) **2-8-7** NGMcCullagh (6th & in tch ½-wy: effrt over 2f out: 5th & no ex early ins last: kpt on)	2	5	14/1	77	18
	Marilia (IRE) (JSBolger,Ireland) **2-8-7** JoannaMorgan (led tl over 1f out: no ex ins last: wknd)	s.h	6	16/1	77	18
	Musical Myth (USA) (JGBurns,Ireland) **2-8-7** WJSupple (chsd ldrs: 4th ½-wy: 5th & btn 1½f out: wknd)	10	7	12/1	50	—

(SP 125.3%) **7 Rn**

1m 14.1 (3.40) OWNER Mr M. Tabor (PILTOWN)
1531a Flame Violet (IRE) hit the front early inside the last, but didn't deliver all that was expected, just holding on by the minimum. She has a big home reputation and her trainer reckons she is of Group One class, with the Moyglare Stud Stakes as her main target. (2/1)
Abandonment (IRE) found the inside from an outside draw pretty quickly after missing the break. Without the blinkers on this time, she fairly ran threw these at the end and, if her rider had not dropped his whip, there might have been a different result. (9/2: op 3/1)
Dane River (IRE) made the running, but hung left throughout and was readily outpaced inside the last. (5/4)
1531a Magical Baba (IRE), beaten over fourteen lengths behind Tadwiga and Soft Touch at the Curragh last time, probably puts this form into perspective. (10/1)
Musical Myth (USA) (12/1: op 7/1)

2988a - (Irish Racing) - See Computer Raceform

2989a BALLYROAN STKS (Listed) (3-Y.O+)
3-30 (3-30) **1m 4f** IR £12,900.00 (IR £3,700.00: IR £1,700.00: IR £500.00) GOING minus 0.09 sec per fur (G)

	Horse		Pos	SP	RR	SF
2456a4	**Gordi (USA)** (DKWeld,Ireland) **4-9-6** MJKinane (mde all: pushed along over 2f out: reminders 2f out: styd on wl whn chal)	—	1	5/4 2	103+	64
	Carnelly (IRE) (DHanley,Ireland) **3-8-5** EAhern (hld up: rn 3rd: cld over 3f out: rdn 2f out: wnt 2nd ins last: s.o: nt trble wnr)	1	2	10/1 3	99?	48
2446a2	**Chania (IRE)** (JOxx,Ireland) **3-8-5** PJSmullen (rn 2nd: trckd wnr: effrt st: ev ch 2f out: rdn & no ex over 1f out: kpt on same pce)	1½	3	Evens 1	97	46
	On Fair Stage (IRE) (JOxx,Ireland) **4-9-3** JPMurtagh (hld up towards rr: cld fr 4f out: chsd ldrs & effrt 2f out: sn rdn & no imp)	6	4	10/1 3	89	50

(SP 112.6%) **4 Rn**

2m 34.9 (4.90) OWNER Allen Paulson (CURRAGH)
2456a Gordi (USA), with two races on unsuitable ground behind him this season, looked absolutely tremendous and, dominating throughout, was a very comfortable winner. His current rating of 106 precludes any favoured treatment in the Ebor, but the big York handicap is on his agenda and after that it may be Melbourne. (5/4)
Carnelly (IRE) stayed on well inside the last but is greatly flattered by the result and he pays for it by going up 12lb. (10/1)
2446a Chania (IRE) tracked the winner but was floundering early in the straight and just does not stay. (Evens)

2990a - 2995a (Irish Racing) - See Computer Raceform

2457a-CHANTILLY (France) (R-H) (Holding)
Tuesday July 1st

2996a PRIX BERTEUX (Gp 3) (3-Y.O)
3-20 (3-17) **1m 7f** £24,691.00 (£8,979.00: £4,489.00)

	Horse		Pos	SP	RR	SF
1070a7	**New Frontier (IRE)** (AFabre,France) **3-8-12** TJarnet	—	1		107	—
	Ithaca (JEPease,France) **3-8-12** FSanchez	1½	2		105	—
1726a8	**Kashwan (SPA)** (ELellouche,France) **3-8-12** TThulliez	hd	3		105	—

4 Rn

3m 16.5 (9.50) P-M 3.00F: 1.70F 1.80F OWNER Mr M. Tabor (CHANTILLY) BRED Irelandia Holdings Ltd
819a New Frontier (IRE), leading the field from the start, accelerated well in the straight and, pushed out, run clear of his rivals with a length and a half to spare. He is without doubt a promising colt who goes well on the ground and will probably be aimed at the Group Two Hubert du Chaudenay.
Ithaca put in a good performance here. Racing in third place for most of the way, he was ridden in the final two furlongs to quicken and made up a lot of ground in the final one hundred yards. He, like the winner, may also take his chance in the Hubert du Chaudenay.
819a Kashwan (SPA) was having his first outing since his disappointing appearance in the Prix du Jockey-Club. In second place for most of the way, he tried to challenge the leader in the straight but did not quite find enough stamina. Better things may be seen of him.

2457a-CHANTILLY (France) (R-H) (Holding)
Tuesday July 1st

2996b PRIX DE LA CROIX DES VENEURS (2-Y.O) (Class E)
1-20 (1-16) **7f** £10,101.00

Horse	Dist	Pos	SP	RR	SF
Andoya (FR) (MmeMBollack-Badel,France) **2-8-7**(3) SHamel	—	1		—	—
Context (MmeCHead,France) **2-8-13** ODoleuze	s.h	2		—	—
Evening World (FR) (PFICole) **2-8-13** TQuinn	s.nk	3		—	—

8 Rn

1m 34.5 (12.50) P-M 19.30F: 2.40F 1.30F 1.30F (28.30F) OWNER Mme D. Chatelperron (LAMORLAYE) BRED Christian Henty
Evening World (FR) was slowly away but, pulling hard, soon found his way to the front. Taking it up two and a half furlongs out, he still held the advantage but found very little in reserve when headed close home.

0624a-LES LANDES (Jersey) (L-H) (Good to firm)
Friday July 11th

2997a DEUTSCHE MORGAN GRENFELL SPRINT H'CAP (3-Y.O+)
7-30 (7-33) **5f 110y** £900.00

Horse	Dist	Pos	SP	RR	SF
Arkady (IRE) (CMcCready,Jersey) **6-10-12** RMcGhin	—	1		63	—
Misinterrex (MissAVibert,Jersey) **6-9-6** BPowell	1	2		40	—
Newbury Coat (KHarvey,Guernsey) **7-9-12** RPainter	½	3		45	—
Northern Clan (AJChamberlain) **4-10-6** RGreene (btn approx 33½l)		7		—	—

8 Rn

69.0 secs TOTE £10.00: £3.20 £2.20 £7.00 (£4.80) OWNER R A Ltd (JERSEY) BRED Mrs Ian Fox

2998a BARCLAYS PREMIER (3-Y.O+)
8-00 (8-00) **1m 1f** £900.00 (£375.00: £225.00)

Horse	Dist	Pos	SP	RR	SF
Bird Island (CMcCready,Jersey) **6-10-9** RPainter	—	1		55	—
Mans Passion (MissAVibert,Jersey) **5-9-11** BPowell	1	2		41	—
Night Time (AGHobbs) **5-10-12** MissVLucas	3	3		51	—

7 Rn

2m TOTE £9.20: £3.40 £2.40 (£3.20) OWNER Mr Bill Allan (JERSEY) BRED W. Allan and Miss Y. Stead

2999a SBC H'CAP (3-Y.O+)
8-30 (8-30) **1m 7f** £1,200.00 (£500.00)

Horse	Dist	Pos	SP	RR	SF
Brown Fairy (USA) (JSOArthur,Jersey) **9-10-12** VSmith	—	1		60	—
Star Performer (IRE) (AGHobbs) **6-10-12** GShenkin	6	2		54	—
Time Lapse (JSOArthur,Jersey) **8-8-5** RPainter	1	3		18	—

6 Rn

3m 33.3 TOTE £6.60: £3.40 £4.20 (£15.50) OWNER C Barton & C Gruchy & P Warner & P W

2820a-DEAUVILLE (France) (R-H) (Good)
Monday July 14th

3000a PRIX MINERVE (Gp 3) (3-Y.O F)
2-15 (2-15) **1m 4f 110y** £24,691.00 (£8,979.00: £4,489.00)

Form	Horse	Dist	Pos	SP	RR	SF
2275a[3]	**Kassana (IRE)** (AdeRoyerDupre,France) **3-8-9** GMosse	—	1		107	—
	Proud Fillie (FR) (AFabre,France) **3-8-9** OPeslier	hd	2		107	—
	Warbler (PBary,France) **3-8-9** SGuillot	4	3		102	—
1875[3]	**Western Hour (USA)** (PWChapple-Hyam) **3-8-9** JReid (btn approx 16¼l)		7		—	—

8 Rn

2m 38.9 (0.40) P-M 2.80F: 1.20F 1.50F 1.50F (7.60F) OWNER H H Aga Khan (CHANTILLY) BRED H. H. Aga Khan
2275a Kassana (IRE) looked magnificent in the paddock and proved her worth, having been unlucky in her previous race. Brought with a late run having been held up for much of the race, she relished this fast ground and is bound to go on to greater things. She may now take her chance in the Prix de Pomone at Deauville in August.
Proud Fillie (FR) looked as if she was going to have a runaway victory here. Taking the lead two furlongs out, she rallied in the final furlong, only to be headed close home. She, like the winner, may also go for the Prix de Pomone at Deauville.
Warbler was given every possible chance having been prominent for most of the race, but just stayed on in the middle of the track to sneak into third place.
1875 Western Hour (USA) set a good pace and led until the straight. She soon weakened and was never seen with a chance.

3001a PRIX DE RIS-ORANGIS (Gp 3) (3-Y.O+)
3-20 (3-19) **6f** £24,691.00 (£8,979.00: £4,489.00: £2,694.00)

Form	Horse	Dist	Pos	SP	RR	SF
2056[4]	**Monaassib** (EALDunlop) **6-9-4** DO'Donohoe	—	1		119	—
940[5]	**Zamindar (USA)** (AFabre,France) **3-8-13** OPeslier	¾	2		118	—
1719a*	**Nombre Premier** (AdeRoyerDupre,France) **3-8-13** GMosse	hd	3		118	—
2526[10]	**Brave Edge** (RHannon) **6-9-0** DaneO'Neill	s.nk	4		112	—
2273a*	**Occupandiste (IRE)** (MmeCHead,France) **4-9-1** ODoleuze	½	5		112	—
1721a[2]	**Wardara** (FBellenger,France) **5-8-10** MdeSmyter	2½	6		100	—
2106[9]	**Croft Pool** (JAGlover) **6-9-6** GCarter	1	7		108	—

2106[11]	**Deep Finesse** (MAJarvis) **3-8-13** MRoberts	1½ **8**		103	—
2640a[4]	**Hever Golf Rose** (TJNaughton) **6-9-1** PatEddery	s.h **9**		98	—
					9 Rn

1m 9.8 (1.80) P-M 7.10F: 1.50F 1.10F 1.20F (7.60F) OWNER Maktoum Al Maktoum (NEWMARKET) BRED Side Hill Stud in Ireland
2056 Monaassib put up an excellent performance in this Group Three event. Racing in second place, he took the lead one and a half furlongs out to finish strongly and win by three-quarters of a length. He appears to still be improving as a six-year-old and has the ability to quicken off a fast pace. He may well now go for Prix Maurice de Gheest followed by the Haydock Park Sprint Cup.
940 Zamindar (USA), the odds-on favourite, was held up for most of the way to make a late challenge but could not catch the leader inside the final furlong. He may now go for the Sussex Stakes at the end of July, and would seem to have a great chance.
1719a* Nombre Premier tracked the leader on the inside and, switched right to chase the winner over a furlong out, was unlucky not to have taken second place on the line. He may now be rested and brought back for an autumn campaign.
1590 Brave Edge, held up early on, made a brave effort to take fourth from Occupandiste.
1455* Croft Pool, prominent for most of the way, weakened approaching the final furlong.
941* Deep Finesse, ridden in mid-division, weakened in the home straight and the pace may have been to strong for him.
2640a Hever Golf Rose was close up for much of the way but was never a danger in the straight.

2460a-SAINT-CLOUD (France) (L-H) (Good)
Tuesday July 15th

3002a PRIX EUGENE ADAM (Gp 2) (3-Y.O)
2-05 (2-05) **1m 2f** £33,670.00 (£13,468.00: £6,734.00: £3,367.00)

			SP	RR	SF
1725a[3]	**Kirkwall** (AFabre,France) **3-8-11** OPeslier (rn in 3rd tl jst ins fnl f: tk ld bef line: pushed out: impressive)	— **1**		119	—
	Rajpoute (FR) (FDoumen,France) **3-8-11** GMosse (set gd pce: mde all tl hdd ins fnl f)	s.h **2**		119	—
1769[3]	**Romanov (IRE)** (PWChapple-Hyam) **3-8-11** JReid (mid div: styd on fnl stages)	1 **3**		117	—
2274a[6]	**Zenith Rose (FR)** (PLenogue,France) **3-8-11** SGuillot (rn 2nd tl st: wknd 2f fr home: styd on one pce)	4 **4**		111	—
2274a[4]	**Alekos (USA)** (CLaffon-Parias,France) **3-8-11** DBoeuf (rn in 5th: hdwy 2f out: r.o)	1 **5**		109	—
1915a*	**Kaldou Star** (ELellouche,France) **3-8-11** TThulliez (a bhd: n.d)	2 **6**		106	—
					6 Rn

2m 7.9 (4.40) P-M 2.30F: 1.40F 3.70F OWNER Mr K. Abdulla (CHANTILLY) BRED Juddmonte Farms
1725a Kirkwall has only been beaten once in six outings this year when third to Starborough and Mamalik in the Prix Jean Prat. Sat back in third place for most of the race, Peslier timed his run perfectly and Kirkwall had enough in hand to make a late challenge just before the line, to take the lead and win by a short head. Andre Fabre rates this colt very highly and he should be watched with interest. He could now be rested with the Arc de Triomphe in mind.
Rajpoute (FR) set a strong pace and made all until losing his position in the final few strides. This noble-looking son of Double Bed has great prospects for the future and is heading for the Arc in October.
1769 Romanov (IRE) did not live up to expectations after finishing third in the Epsom Derby. Racing in fourth just behind Kirkwall, he ran on impressively under pressure but could not catch the leaders. He may be better suited by ten furlongs.
1205a Zenith Rose (FR) ran in second place for most of the way but weakened considerably in the final stages. He may have found the ground too fast as he acts better when there is more cut in the ground.

3000a-DEAUVILLE (France) (R-H) (Good)
Wednesday July 16th

3003a PRIX CERES (Listed) (3-Y.O F)
2-30 (2-27) **7f** £15,713.00 (£5,387.00: £4,040.00)

			SP	RR	SF
	Heaven's Command (NClement,France) **3-8-11** GMosse	— **1**		108	—
	Clodora (FR) (France) **3-8-11** OPeslier	nk **2**		107	—
	Libria (IRE) (France) **3-8-11** SGuillot	1 **3**		105	—
1621[4]	**Well Warned** (BWHills) **3-8-11** TThulliez (btn over 4½l)	**8**		—	—
					10 Rn

1m 24.6 (0.60) P-M 3.10F: 1.80F 1.40F 1.70F (8.40F) OWNER Ecurie Skymarc Farm (CHANTILLY) BRED Skymarc Farm Inc
1621 Well Warned set a good pace and ran well only to weaken three furlongs out. She never got into contention at the business end and may have found the going too firm.

0920a-FRANKFURT (Germany) (L-H) (Good)
Sunday July 20th

3004a FRANKFURT-POKAL UM DEN PREIS VON LOTTO HESSEN (Gp 3) (3-Y.O+)
3-50 (3-57) **1m 2f** £22,727.00 (£9,091.00: £4,545.00)

			SP	RR	SF
1728a[7]	**Devil River Peek (USA)** (BSchutz,Germany) **5-9-1** AStarke	— **1**		107	—
	Shebar (USA) (DRichardson,Germany) **6-8-13b[1]** StephenDavies	1 **2**		103	—
2459a[7]	**Turbo Drive** (BSchutz,Germany) **3-8-3** NGrant	1½ **3**		101	—
					10 Rn

2m 10.53 TOTE 49DM: 22DM 30DM 40DM OWNER Stall Hoppegarten BRED Fares Farm Inc.
1067a Devil River Peek (USA) waited with at the back of the field, was produced with a strong run on the inside to lead entering the final furlong and was ridden out to the line.
Shebar (USA) tried to make all the running but was headed inside the final furlong.

KREFELD (Germany) (R-H) (Good)
Sunday July 20th

3005a LUDWIG GOEBELS-ERINNERUNGSRENNEN (Listed) (3-Y.O F)
3-35 (3-35) **1m 4f** £22,727.00 (£9,091.00: £4,545.00)

				SP	RR	SF
2458a*	**Anna Thea (IRE)** (HBlume,Germany) **3-9-0** THellier	—	1		96+	—
1875[4]	**Viscoumtess Brave (IRE)** (LordHuntingdon) **3-9-0** KWoodburn	2½	2		93	—
	Open Air (GER) (WHaustein,Germany) **3-9-0** ASchikora	¾	3		92	—
						7 Rn

2m 28.4 TOTE 16DM: 11DM 12DM 18DM OWNER Gestut Rottgen

1875 Viscoumtess Brave (IRE) tracked the leader but had no answer when the very smart winner, who was unpenalised for a recent Group Three success, swept past with over a furlong and a half to run. She did however keep on well for second place.

2818a-MAISONS-LAFFITTE (France) (Good)
Sunday July 20th

3006a PRIX MAURICE DE NIEUIL (Gp 2) (3-Y.O+)
2-40 (2-40) **1m 4f 110y** £33,670.00 (£13,468.00: £6,734.00: £3,367.00)

				SP	RR	SF
1917a[2]	**Surgeon** (JdeRoualle,France) **4-9-4** CAsmussen (hld up: qcknd to chal ins fnl f: r.o to ld cl home)	—	1		121	—
2333*	**Kutta** (RWArmstrong) **5-9-4** RHills (led: set gd pce: qcknd wl over 2f out: ct cl home)	hd	2		121	—
	My Emma (RGuest) **4-9-7** DHolland (hld up: plld 4f out: swtchd lft jst ins fnl f: fin wl)	½	3		123	—
2270a*	**For Valour (USA)** (AFabre,France) **4-9-4** OPeslier (hld up in rr: styd on)	1½	4		118	—
1070a[5]	**Sendoro (IRE)** (AdeRoyerDupre,France) **3-8-6**ow1 GMosse (racd 2nd tl wknd appr fnl f)	¾	5		117	—
						5 Rn

2m 38.6 (4.10) P-M 2.70F: 1.60F 2.70F OWNER Mr K. H. Eng BRED George Strawbridge

1917a Surgeon deserved this success after coming so close in the Grand Prix de Chantilly last time out, although the ground here would not have been as soft as he would have liked it.

2333* Kutta tried to make all here and, trying to slip the field approaching the straight, could never break free from the eventual winner and had to make do with second place.

My Emma, on her first outing since winning last year's Prix Vermeille, put in a decent performance here and, after being slightly bumped and switching a furlong from home, was finishing well close home. She will now go for the Yorkshire Oaks.

3007a PRIX CHLOE (Gp 3) (3-Y.O F)
3-50 (3-49) **1m 1f** £24,691.00 (£8,979.00: £4,489.00)

				SP	RR	SF
1916a[7]	**Golden Arches (FR)** (PDemercastel,France) **3-8-9** TGillet	—	1		113	—
	Sensitivity (USA) (NClement,France) **3-8-9** DBoeuf	½	2		112	—
	Cunning Vixen (IRE) (JEHammond,France) **3-8-9** SGuillot (fin 3rd, 2l: disq: plcd last)	2	**3d**		109	—
1916a[9]	**Queen Maud (IRE)** (JdeRoualle,France) **3-8-13** CAsmussen (fin 4th, 1½l: plcd 3rd)	1½	3		110	—
						10 Rn

1m 53.5 P-M 6.10F: 1.90F 2.50F 1.40F (44.30F) OWNER Ecurie Fabien Ouaki

STEWARDS' ENQUIRY Guillot susp. 4 days (careless riding).

Golden Arches (FR) was driven out after taking the lead inside the final furlong and will now head to Goodwood for the Nassau Stakes.

2822a-SAN SIRO (Milan, Italy) (R-H) (Good)
Sunday July 20th

3008a PREMIO GARIGUANO (2-Y.O F)
3-20 (3-22) **6f** £9,642.00

				SP	RR	SF
	Wren (IRE) (LordHuntingdon) **2-8-9** FJovine	—	1		—	—
	Folling (FR) (LPlanard,France) **2-8-11** MPlanard	2¼	2		—	—
	Soviet Lynk (IRE) (VOriani,Italy) **2-8-11** LPanici	8	3		—	—
						8 Rn

1m 10.9 (2.90) TOTE 37L: 15L 12L 20L (30L) OWNER Anglia Bloodstock Ltd (WEST ILSLEY) BRED Barnane Partnership

Wren (IRE) had been going well on the gallops at home, so this success was no surprise to connections. She started slowly, but gradually made up ground to hit the front two furlongs from home and her jockey never had to resort to the whip.

2133-ASCOT (R-H) (Good, Good to Firm patches)
Friday July 25th
WEATHER: warm WIND: almost nil

3009 TIMEFORM CHARITY DAY MAIDEN STKS (UNRACED 2-Y.O F) (Class D)
2-15 (2-15) **6f** £7,035.00 (£2,130.00: £1,040.00: £495.00) Stalls: Low GOING minus 0.20 sec per fur (GF)

			SP	RR	SF
Shuhrah (USA) (SbinSuroor) **2-8-11** LDettori(1) (str: scope: swvd rt s: mde all: pushed out)	—	1	6/4[2]	90+	38
Ashraakat (USA) (JLDunlop) **2-8-11** RHills(3) (leggy: scope: chsd wnr over 3f: chsd wnr over 1f out: ev ch 1f out: unable qckn)	1½	2	4/6[1]	86+	34
Royal Shyness (GLewis) **2-8-11** PaulEddery(5) (neat: hld up: chsd wnr over 2f out tl over 1f out: ev ch 1f out: one pce)	¾	3	11/1[3]	84 t	32
Glitter Princess (MajorDNChappell) **2-8-11** GCarter(2) (neat: a bhd)	4	4	33/1	73?	21

	Acebo Lyons (IRE) (APJarvis) **2-8-11** DHolland(4) (leggy: bit bkwd: a bhd)	1¼	**5**	50/1	70?	18
				(SP 113.2%)		**5 Rn**

1m 17.02 (3.02) CSF £2.66 TOTE £2.40: £1.30 £1.30 (£1.20) OWNER Godolphin (NEWMARKET) BRED Shadwell Farm Inc

Shuhrah (USA), an attractive, close-coupled filly, with plenty of strength and substance about her, had been working at home for quite some time but a couple of little setbacks kept her off the track. Making the running, she was strongly tackled by the second and third but, shaken up, managed to assert her authority inside the final furlong. (6/4)

Ashraakat (USA), a tall filly who is a half-sister to 1994 Irish One Thousand Guineas winner Mehthaaf, comes from a stable that won this race in 1994 and 1995 with subsequent Classic-placed fillies Aqaarid and Bint Shadayid, and is held in high regard herself. Racing in second place, she did not have a great deal of room in which to manoeuvre below the distance but was one of three in line a furlong out, before the winner found a bit extra. She looks a ready-made winner. (4/6: 1/2-5/6)

Royal Shyness, whose dam who won the Group Two Lowther Stakes, made a highly promising debut. Showing narrowly in second place over a quarter of a mile from home, she was almost in line entering the final furlong, before tapped for toe. Described by her trainer as the best he has got, she should have no problems finding an ordinary maiden. (11/1: 4/1-12/1)

Glitter Princess found this company too hot and was always at the back of the field. (33/1)

Acebo Lyons (IRE), quite a tall filly with little substance, cost a mere Ir1,500gs. Looking just in need of this, she was out-classed from start to finish. (50/1)

3010 FURNITURE VILLAGE BROWN JACK H'CAP (0-80) (3-Y.O+) (Class D)

2-45 (2-45) **2m 45y** £10,698.75 (£3,240.00: £1,582.50: £753.75) Stalls: High GOING minus 0.20 sec per fur (GF)

				SP	RR	SF
2653^{5}	**Rusk (75)** (JPearce) **4-9-10** NDay(7) (hld up: rdn over 2f out: led ins fnl f: r.o wl)	—	**1**	20/1	86	45
2564^{2}	**Benjamins Law (47)** (JAPickering) **6-7-3**(7) JFowle(8) (chsd ldr 15f out: led 1f out tl ins fnl f: r.o)	hd	**2**	25/1	58	17
2483*	**Magic Combination (IRE) (73)** (BJCurley) **4-9-8** LDettori(10) (hld up: rdn over 2f out: squeezed thro ins fnl f: r.o one pce)	1	**3**	11/2 3	83	42
2411^{2}	**Spy Knoll (77)** (MRStoute) **3-8-9** JReid(3) (swtg: led 15f out to 1f out: one pce)	nk	**4**	9/2 2	87	29
2882*	**Salska (61)** (AStreeter) **6-8-10** 3x TSprake(4) (rdn & hdwy over 2f out: r.o one pce)	nk	**5**	12/1	70	29
2139*	**Bolivar (IRE) (72)** (RAkehurst) **5-9-7b** MJKinane(9) (led 1f: rdn over 2f out: btn whn hmpd ins fnl f)	3½	**6**	9/4 1	78	37
2882^{4}	**Alwarqa (51)** (MartynWane) **4-7-11**(3)ow1 AWhelan(1) (rdn over 2f out: nvr nr to chal)	¾	**7**	14/1	56	14
2767^{3}	**Shining Dancer (66)** (SDow) **5-9-1** SSanders(5) (swtg: bhd fnl 7f)	2	**8**	8/1	69	28
2327^{7}	**Burnt Offering (69)** (CEBrittain) **4-9-4** KFallon(6) (hld up: rdn over 2f out: sn wknd)	1½	**9**	8/1	71	30
2702^{6}	**Paradise Navy (64)** (CREgerton) **8-8-13b** RHughes(2) (lw: a bhd)	2	**10**	20/1	64	23
				(SP 114.3%)		**10 Rn**

3m 36.84 (9.64) CSF £379.54 CT £2,821.84 TOTE £39.30: £7.00 £4.60 £1.60 (£138.00) Trio £400.70 OWNER Mrs Jean Connew (NEWMARKET) BRED W. F. Macauley

WEIGHT FOR AGE 3yo-17lb

2653 Rusk appreciated the step up in distance and defied top weight to lose his maiden tag, being rousted along to get on top inside the final furlong. (20/1)

2564 Benjamins Law appreciated this longer trip. Soon racing in second place, he struck the front a furlong out but was unable to cope with the winner in the last one hundred yards. He has yet to win on grass but that should soon be rectified. He will go hurdling next season. (25/1)

2483* Magic Combination (IRE) chased the leaders. Bustled along in the straight, he managed to squeeze through a narrow gap inside the final furlong but, despite struggling on, was unable to get on terms with the front two. (11/2: 4/1-6/1)

2411 Spy Knoll lacks real acceleration and appreciated this longer trip. Bowling along in front, he was eventually overhauled a furlong from home and, once again, was then tapped for toe. (9/2)

2882* Salska had more to do here and, although staying on in the straight, was not going to get there in time. She has done all her winning on a sound surface. (12/1)

2139* Bolivar (IRE) goes particularly well round here - he has yet to win anywhere else in this country - but this was not his day and he was already in trouble when hampered inside the final furlong. (9/4)

3011 IMPERIAL CANCER RESEARCH FUND RATED STKS H'CAP (0-100) (3-Y.O+) (Class B)

3-15 (3-18) **5f** £15,520.49 (£5,809.50: £2,842.25: £1,223.75: £549.38: £279.63) Stalls: Low GOING minus 0.20 sec per fur (GF)

				SP	RR	SF
2717*	**Blessingindisguise (86)** (MWEasterby) **4-8-7b** 3x MJKinane(1) (a.p: led over 1f out: drvn out)	—	**1**	11/2 2	100	53
2289^{3}	**Surprise Mission (89)** (MrsJRRamsden) **5-8-10** JFortune(5) (hld up: swtchd rt over 1f out: ev ch ins fnl f: unable qckn)	1½	**2**	5/1 1	98	51
2289*	**Moon Strike (FR) (90)** (PHowling) **7-8-11** AMunro(7) (b: swtg: hdwy over 1f out: r.o wl ins fnl f)	hd	**3**	11/2 2	99	52
2105^{24}	**Rushcutter Bay (86)** (TTClement) **4-8-7v** DeanMcKeown(4) (lw: a.p: rdn over 2f out: ev ch over 1f out: one pce)	½	**4**	25/1	93	46
2560^{10}	**Prince Dome (IRE) (89)** (MartynWane) **3-8-3**(3)ow3 AWhelan(11) (lw: a.p: rdn over 2f out: one pce)	1	**5**	12/1	93	39
2598^{7}	**World Premier (95)** (CEBrittain) **4-9-2** PatEddery(8) (lw: outpcd: hdwy over 1f out: r.o)	d.h	**5**	10/1	102	55
2675^{3}	**Twice as Sharp (94)** (PWHarris) **5-8-10**(5) CLowther(10) (lw: prom over 3f)	2½	**7**	10/1	90	43
2675^{2}	**Crofters Ceilidh (90)** (BAMcMahon) **5-8-11** JReid(9) (lw: hld up: rdn 2f out: btn whn nt clr run over 1f out)	¾	**8**	9/1 3	84	37
2289^{8}	**Canovas Heart (86)** (BobJones) **8-8-7** NDay(13) (hld up: hrd rdn over 1f out: wknd fnl f)	¾	**9**	20/1	77	30
2289^{11}	**Passion For Life (100)** (GLewis) **4-9-7** PaulEddery(3) (lw: bhd fnl 3f)	2½	**10**	25/1	83	36
2683^{8}	**Blue Iris (100)** (MAJarvis) **4-9-7** LDettori(2) (b.hind: led over 3f)	s.h	**11**	9/1 3	83	36
2861^{10}	**Johnny Staccato (93)** (JMPEustace) **3-8-10** JTate(12) (a bhd)	¾	**12**	33/1	74	23
2377^{6}	**Fond Embrace (91)** (HCandy) **4-8-12** GCarter(6) (bhd fnl 2f)	½	**13**	16/1	70	23
				(SP 114.6%)		**13 Rn**

61.49 secs (1.29) CSF £27.22 CT £148.67 TOTE £6.00: £1.80 £2.10 £2.60 (£10.20) Trio £9.30 OWNER Mr A. G. Black (SHERIFF HUTTON) BRED Mrs A. Meller

LONG HANDICAP Blessingindisguise 7-11 Canovas Heart 8-5 Rushcutter Bay 8-5

WEIGHT FOR AGE 3yo-4lb

2717* Blessingindisguise may have been worse off with both the second and third but he was not going to let that stop him, leading over a furlong out and responding to pressure to register his fifth victory of the season. He has done all his winning at this trip. (11/2)

2289 Surprise Mission, 14lb better off with the winner for being beaten two and a half lengths at Newcastle last week, got closer but was unable to turn the tables. He has done all his winning at five furlongs. (5/1)

2289* Moon Strike (FR), who has changed stables since his last run, was 7lb better off with the winner for beating him a short-head at Newcastle last month but, despite running on strongly in the last furlong and a half, was never going to get there in time. (11/2)

Rushcutter Bay ran his best race so far this season and still had every chance below the distance, before tapped for toe. (25/1)

2560 Prince Dome (IRE), never far away, failed to find that vital turn of foot in the final quarter mile. (12/1)

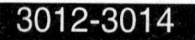

2598 World Premier has not raced at this trip since May 1995 and it was not hard to see why as he got completely outpaced, until running on strongly when it was all over. A return to six or seven furlongs is most definitely required. (10/1)

3012 LEUKAEMIA RESEARCH FUND H'CAP (0-90) (3-Y.O) (Class C)

3-50 (3-51) **1m 2f** £8,988.00 (£2,724.00: £1,332.00: £636.00) Stalls: High GOING minus 0.20 sec per fur (GF)

				SP	RR	SF
2839*	**Manazil (IRE) (86)** (RWArmstrong) **3-9-7** 5x RHills(7) (lw: a.p: hrd rdn over 1f out: led ins fnl f: r.o wl)	—	**1**	8/1	99	44
2601^{7}	**Rudimental (82)** (SirMarkPrescott) **3-9-3** SSanders(3) (hld up: rdn over 2f out: r.o ins fnl f)	1¼	**2**	5/1^{2}	93	38
2645^{3}	**Kewarra (70)** (BRMillman) **3-8-5** TSprake(2) (lw: chsd ldr: led over 2f out tl ins fnl f: unable qckn)	1	**3**	16/1	79	24
2341^{3}	**Pinchincha (FR) (84)** (DMorris) **3-9-5** NDay(9) (rdn over 2f out: hdwy over 1f out: r.o)	¾	**4**	9/1	92	37
2566*	**Song of Freedom (86)** (JHMGosden) **3-9-7** LDettori(8) (lw: bhd whn stumbled 3f out: hdwy over 1f out: r.o one pce)	hd	**5**	9/4^{1}	94	39
2574^{10}	**Another Night (IRE) (84)** (RHannon) **3-9-5** DaneO'Neill(10) (lw: rdn over 2f out: hdwy 5f: nvr nrr)	1	**6**	16/1	90	35
2601^{9}	**Vain Tempest (83)** (PWChapple-Hyam) **3-9-4** JReid(4) (lw: rdn over 2f out: nvr nr to chal)	2	**7**	11/1	86	31
2585^{9}	**Regal Thunder (USA) (73)** (MRStoute) **3-8-8** PatEddery(1) (led over 7f: wknd fnl f)	nk	**8**	13/2^{3}	76	21
2566^{9}	**Russian Ruler (IRE) (82)** (APJarvis) **3-9-3** DHolland(11) (lw: a bhd)	3	**9**	33/1	80	25
1595^{9}	**Sheer Face (85)** (WRMuir) **3-9-6** MHills(6) (lw: hdwy over 4f out: wknd over 1f out)	½	**10**	33/1	82	27
2229^{6}	**Byzantium (85)** (LordHuntingdon) **3-9-6** KFallon(5) (hld up: rdn over 2f out: wknd over 1f out)	3½	**11**	14/1	77	22
				(SP 114.5%)	**11 Rn**	

2m 11.13 (5.63) CSF £42.26 CT £564.50 TOTE £8.70: £2.60 £1.90 £3.70 (£19.10) Trio £61.40 OWNER Mr Hamdan Al Maktoum (NEWMARKET) BRED Shadwell Estate Company Limited

2839* Manazil (IRE), from a stable that has had the virus, followed up last week's success, responding to pressure to get on top inside the final furlong. Armstrong reported afterwards that the whole yard has been coughing since May and, although it has not affected the older horses as much, the two-year-olds are in terrible shape. (8/1: 6/1-9/1)

2601 Rudimental was ridden with more patience this time and returned to form. Hunting up the leaders, he was asked for his effort early in the straight and ran on to take second prize. (5/1)

2645 Kewarra appreciated the step up in distance and gained control early in the straight. Collared inside the final furlong, he was once again tapped for toe. He remains a maiden. (16/1)

2341 Pinchincha (FR) continues in fine heart, despite his rise in the weights but, although running on in the last furlong and a half, was never going to get there in time. (9/1: 6/1-10/1)

2566* Song of Freedom, given top weight on this handicap debut, was at the back of the field when stumbling badly turning for home. This certainly did his cause no good but he never found that vital turn of foot, despite staying on in the last furlong and a half. (9/4: op 7/2)

2137 Another Night (IRE), bustled along and going nowhere at the back of the field early in the straight, struggled on in the final furlong. (16/1)

2045* Vain Tempest (11/1: 8/1-12/1)

2229 Byzantium (14/1: 10/1-20/1)

3013 SUNLEY E.B.F. MAIDEN STKS (2-Y.O) (Class D)

4-25 (4-28) **7f** £7,002.50 (£2,120.00: £1,035.00: £492.50) Stalls: Low GOING minus 0.20 sec per fur (GF)

				SP	RR	SF
2295^{3}	**Setteen** (MAJarvis) **2-9-0** LDettori(5) (lw: hld up: chsd ldr over 2f out: rdn to ld over 1f out: r.o wl)	—	**1**	15/8^{1}	101	56
1418^{6}	**Celtic Pageant** (RAkehurst) **2-9-0** SSanders(8) (lw: led over 5f: unable qckn)	2	**2**	25/1	96	51
	Quiet Assurance (USA) (EALDunlop) **2-9-0** KFallon(1) (b: w'like: scope: lw: hld up: rdn 3f out: one pce)	7	**3**	4/1^{2}	80	35
2556^{4}	**Rainbow High** (BWHills) **2-9-0** MHills(4) (w ldrs over 4f)	2	**4**	7/1	76	31
	Somayda (IRE) (JLDunlop) **2-9-0** RHills(3) (w'like: scope: bhd fnl 3f)	4	**5**	13/2	67	22
2012^{7}	**Speedfit Too (IRE)** (GGMargarson) **2-9-0** GCarter(6) (hld up: rdn 3f out: wknd 2f out)	2	**6**	9/1	62	17
	Angstrom (IRE) (MRStoute) **2-9-0** MJKinane(7) (str: scope: bkwd: bhd fnl 5f: t.o)	30	**7**	16/1	—	—
	Bering Gifts (IRE) (PFICole) **2-9-0** PatEddery(2) (Withdrawn not under Starter's orders: ref to ent stalls)		**W**	5/1^{3}	—	—
				(SP 117.0%)	**7 Rn**	

1m 29.47 (2.27) CSF £34.22 TOTE £2.30: £1.60 £3.80 (£33.00) OWNER Sheikh Ahmed Al Maktoum (NEWMARKET) BRED Godolphin Management Co Ltd

2295 Setteen, an attractive, good-bodied colt, was well suited by the extra furlong. Pulling well clear of the remainder with the runner-up, he got on top below the distance and proved too strong for his rival, to give his trainer his first two-year-old winner of the season. Better things are expected of him. (15/8)

1418 Celtic Pageant ran a tremendous race and, setting a brisk pace, had all bar the winner shaken off in the final quarter-mile. Collared below the distance, he found that rival too good. He should soon be winning. (25/1)

Quiet Assurance (USA), an attractive, medium-sized colt, was made to look very pedestrian in the last three furlongs. (4/1: 5/2-5/1)

2556 Rainbow High disputed the lead until done with approaching the final quarter-mile. (7/1: 5/1-8/1)

Somayda (IRE), a half-brother to champion filly Salsabil, was getting left behind in the last three furlongs. (13/2: 3/1-7/1)

3014 MRS BASIL SAMUEL MAIDEN STKS (3-Y.O) (Class D)

5-00 (5-00) **1m 2f** £6,937.50 (£2,100.00: £1,025.00: £487.50) Stalls: High GOING minus 0.20 sec per fur (GF)

				SP	RR	SF
2731^{2}	**Kayf Tara** (MRStoute) **3-9-0** MJKinane(1) (lw: a.p: chsd ldr 5f out: led 2f out: rdn: r.o wl)	—	**1**	5/2^{2}	97	51
1477^{2}	**Shaya (96)** (MajorWRHern) **3-9-0** RHills(6) (lw: led 8f: unable qckn)	3	**2**	9/4^{1}	92	46
2583^{5}	**Saafeya (IRE)** (JHMGosden) **3-8-9** LDettori(3) (rdn & hdwy over 2f out: r.o one pce)	hd	**3**	11/4^{3}	87	41
2410^{6}	**Bina Gardens** (HRACecil) **3-8-9** KFallon(2) (hld up: rdn over 3f out: wknd 2f out)	7	**4**	5/1	76	30
	Just Alex (IRE) (TGMills) **3-9-0** JReid(4) (w'like: scope: hung lft fnl 2f: nvr nr to chal)	2	**5**	40/1	78	32
2731^{6}	**Kristal Bridge** (PWHarris) **3-8-4**(5) CLowther(8) (lw: bhd fnl 2f)	5	**6**	20/1	65	19
2731^{7}	**Moran** (RFJohnsonHoughton) **3-9-0** PaulEddery(5) (chsd ldrs 5f: wknd 3f out)	19	**7**	16/1	39	—
	Primero (IRE) (ABarrow) **3-8-11**(3) AWhelan(7) (unf: scope: prom 4f: t.o)	dist	**8**	66/1	—	—
				(SP 117.2%)	**8 Rn**	

2m 9.43 (3.93) CSF £7.92 TOTE £2.90: £1.50 £1.10 £1.30 (£3.20) OWNER Sheikh Ahmed Al Maktoum (NEWMARKET) BRED Meon Valley Stud

2731 Kayf Tara, a full-brother to the 1993 King George VI and Queen Elizabeth Diamond Stakes winner Opera House, took the eye in the paddock. Moving into second place at halfway, he grabbed the initiative a quarter of a mile from home and, kept up to his work, ran on strongly. Kinane described him as a big baby afterwards. (5/2)

1477 Shaya is becoming extremely frustrating and, for the fourth time in as many starts, had to settle for being the bridesmaid. He is an out-an-out galloper who has got no turn of foot according to his jockey. He also added that he is above average and needs a mile and a half. Over that trip, he can at last break his duck. (9/4)

2583 Saafeya (IRE) stayed on in the straight but she never looked like finding that vital turn of foot. (11/4)

2410 Bina Gardens chased the leaders, but she was in trouble turning for home and had shot her bolt early in the straight. She is obviously one of the stable's lesser lights. (5/1: op 5/2)
Just Alex (IRE), an attractive, scopey colt, was out of his depth here and, hanging badly in the straight, ended up under the stands rails. (40/1)

T/Jkpt: Not won; £10,878.31 to Ascot 26/7/97. T/Plpt: £57.90 (665.9 Tckts). T/Qdpt: £7.30 (333.26 Tckts) AK

2645-CHEPSTOW (L-H) (Good to firm)
Friday July 25th

Race 6: flip-start
WEATHER: fine WIND: slt behind becoming nil

3015 LYSAGHT AMATEUR H'CAP (0-70) (3-Y.O+) (Class G)
6-30 (6-33) **1m 4f 23y** £2,612.00 (£732.00: £356.00) Stalls: Low GOING minus 0.27 sec per fur (GF)

				SP	RR	SF
843[7]	**Tajar (USA) (31)** (TKeddy) **5-9-7** MrJGoldstein(12) (hld up: hdwy over 3f out: led 2f out: r.o wl)	—	**1**	50/1	41	21
2843[3]	**Augustan (54)** (SGollings) **6-11-2** MrRThornton(6) (hld up: hdwy over 3f out: r.o one pce fnl f)	3	**2**	100/30[1]	60	40
2865[8]	**Chris's Lad (55)** (BJMeehan) **6-11-3b** MissJAllison(8) (hld up & bhd: hdwy over 5f out: styd on wl fnl f)	¾	**3**	7/1[3]	60	40
2843[12]	**Fabulous Mtoto (56)** (MSSaunders) **7-11-4** MrKGoble(4) (lw: plld hrd: a.p: led over 4f out to 2f out: one pce)	1¼	**4**	14/1	59	39
2531[12]	**Perfect Bertie (IRE) (36)** (NMBabbage) **5-9-7**(5) MissJWorkman(3) (prom tl wknd wl over 1f out)	2	**5**	25/1	37	17
2650[2]	**Supermick (38)** (WRMuir) **6-10-0** MrsAPerrett(2) (plld hrd: led 2f: wknd over 1f out)	½	**6**	100/30[1]	38	18
2785[9]	**Sassy Street (IRE) (48)** (RFJohnsonHoughton) **4-10-10** MissEJohnsonHoughton(14) (s.s: nvr nrr)	2½	**7**	50/1	45	25
2696[11]	**Nosey Native (60)** (JPearce) **4-11-8** MrsLPearce(1) (lw: hld up in rr: stdy hdwy fnl 2f: nt rch ldrs)	1½	**8**	9/1	55	35
680[12]	**Reimei (66)** (KCComerford) **8-11-9**(5) DrAKimber(7) (lw: hld up mid div: bhd fnl 3f)	1¾	**9**	40/1	59	39
2682[11]	**Warning Reef (60)** (PEccles) **4-11-3h**(5) MrsNElliott(10) (lw: dwlt: nrst fin)	½	**10**	33/1	52	32
1779[20]	**Contract Bridge (IRE) (49)** (PGMurphy) **4-10-6**(5) MissLGreen(9) (s.s: a bhd)	4	**11**	16/1	36	16
2696[5]	**Courageous Knight (44)** (PHayward) **8-10-6** MrsSBosley(11) (prom 4f)	3	**12**	4/1[2]	27	7
2063[9]	**Phanan (34)** (REPeacock) **11-9-5**(5)ow1 MrsCPeacock(5) (plld hrd: led after 2f tl over 6f out: wknd over 3f out)	2	**13**	66/1	14	—
2144[10]	**Sweet Ciseaux (IRE) (36)** (BJLlewellyn) **4-9-7**(5)ow5 MrSDurack(13) (lw: plld hrd: sn prom: sddle slipped: led over 6f out tl over 4f out: sn wknd)	2½	**14**	50/1	13	—
	Champagne Gold (47) (JCMcConnochie) **10-10-4**(5)ow12 MrMWMancini(15) (a bhd)	6	**15**	50/1	16	—
				(SP 119.8%)	**15 Rn**	

2m 42.1 (9.70) CSF £185.25 CT £1,244.66 TOTE £74.90: £12.80 £1.50 £2.00 (£81.00) Trio £200.10 OWNER The Veg Chef Partnership (HANLEY SWAN) BRED Shadwell Farm Inc
LONG HANDICAP Tajar (USA) 9-6
IN-FOCUS: **Unusually for these events, the pace was muddling to halfway.**
496 Tajar (USA), tried in blinkers in sellers, has tumbled down the handicap, and was coming back after a three-month break. There appeared no fluke about the way he gave his trainer his first Flat winner. (50/1)
2843 Augustan, 3lb higher than when winning this event last year, was due to go up 1lb tomorrow. (100/30)
1779* Chris's Lad, set to go down 2lb in future handicaps, was not suited by the fact there was no pace early on. (7/1)
2533 Fabulous Mtoto would probably have settled better in a stronger-run race. (14/1)
Perfect Bertie (IRE) is well handicapped on some of his old form. (25/1)
2650 Supermick, raised 2lb, is 5lb higher than the highest mark off which he has won. (100/30)

3016 JACK BROWN BOOKMAKER H'CAP (0-70) (3-Y.O+) (Class E)
7-00 (7-02) **5f 16y** £2,956.75 (£889.00: £429.50: £199.75) Stalls: High GOING minus 0.27 sec per fur (GF)

				SP	RR	SF
2732[5]	**Ashkernazy (IRE) (43)** (NEBerry) **6-8-1** NAdams(1) (mde all: all out)	—	**1**	6/1[2]	52	30
2933[6]	**Beau Venture (USA) (66)** (BPalling) **9-9-10** TSprake(7) (swtg: sn chsng wnr: ev ch fnl f: r.o)	nk	**2**	8/1	74	52
2563[10]	**Songsheet (70)** (MSSaunders) **4-9-11**(3) PPMurphy(10) (lw: s.i.s: hdwy over 2f out: ev ch ins fnl f: r.o)	hd	**3**	7/1[3]	78	56
2852[6]	**Robellion (53)** (DWPArbuthnot) **6-8-11v** SWhitworth(5) (lw: hdwy over 1f out: r.o ins fnl f)	½	**4**	6/1[2]	59	37
2703[3]	**Sharp Stock (57)** (RJHodges) **4-9-1** BDoyle(9) (swtg: a.p: one pce fnl f)	hd	**5**	11/2[1]	63	41
2847[5]	**River Tern (69)** (JMBradley) **4-9-10**(3) RFfrench(8) (swtg: hld up: nt clr run 2f out: hdwy over 1f out: swtchd lft ins fnl f: r.o)	¾	**6**	6/1[2]	73	51
2899*	**Delrob (42)** (DHaydnJones) **6-8-0b** 7x AMackay(6) (chsd ldrs: rdn over 3f out: wknd 2f out)	2½	**7**	7/1[3]	38	16
2895[5]	**Imposing Time (62)** (MissGayKelleway) **6-9-6v** NGMcCullagh(2) (lw: tk keen hold: trckd ldrs: wknd over 1f out)	2	**8**	10/1	51	29
2536[5]	**Make Ready (59)** (JNeville) **3-8-13** JLowe(3) (chsd ldrs: wkng whn hmpd 2f out)	nk	**9**	15/2	47	21
2491[12]	**Silent Symphony (38)** (MrsSDWilliams) **5-7-10** FNorton(11) (bhd fnl 2f: t.o)	18	**10**	50/1	—	—
				(SP 117.2%)	**10 Rn**	

58.8 secs (1.80) CSF £48.76 CT £322.06 TOTE £7.00: £2.10 £2.20 £2.90 (£21.10) Trio £116.40 OWNER London Bridge II (UPPER LAMBOURN) BRED G. P. Griffin
LONG HANDICAP Silent Symphony 7-6
WEIGHT FOR AGE 3yo-4lb
2732 Ashkernazy (IRE), down 2lb, was back to the mark she scored off at Windsor last August. (6/1)
2933 Beau Venture (USA), back to the bare minimum, possible found his run two days earlier taking a slight edge off him. (8/1)
2406* Songsheet was no less than 24lb worse off with the winner than when beating her five lengths in a non-handicap at Windsor in June. (7/1)
2852 Robellion was 8lb lower than when successful in this race last season. (6/1)
2703 Sharp Stock ran well without ever quite having every chance. (11/2)
2847 River Tern, 6lb higher than when winning at Warwick, was set to drop 1lb the next day and looked the hard-luck story of the race. (6/1)
2536 Make Ready (15/2: 5/1-8/1)

3017 GOLDEN DAFFODIL STKS (Listed) (3-Y.O+ F & M) (Class A)
7-30 (7-33) **1m 2f 36y** £10,615.20 (£3,976.80: £1,948.40: £842.00: £381.00: £196.60) Stalls: Low GOING minus 0.27 sec per fur (GF)

				SP	RR	SF
	Fiji (HRACecil) **3-8-7**ow2 KFallon(5) (lw: hld up: hdwy 3f out: led wl over 1f out: jst hld on)	—	**1**	3/1[2]	110	45
2180*	**Bint Baladee (98)** (SbinSuroor) **3-8-5** LDettori(2) (lw: hld up & bhd: hdwy over 1f out: r.o ins fnl f: jst failed)	s.h	**2**	5/2[1]	108	45

				SP	RR	SF
1916a[12]	**Dances With Dreams** (PWChapple-Hyam) **3-8-6**[ow1] JReid(8) (b.hind: lw: a.p: led over 2f out tl wl over 1f out: nt qckn ins fnl f)	1¼	**3**	7/2[3]	107	43
2053[9]	**Sarayir (USA) (102)** (MajorWRHern) **3-8-5** RHills(7) (lw: led: rdn & hdd over 2f out: r.o one pce)	½	**4**	6/1	105	42
1875[7]	**The Faraway Tree (84)** (GWragg) **3-8-5** AClark(3) (lw: hld up & bhd: rdn & hdwy over 1f out: nvr nrr)	¾	**5**	14/1	104	41
2219[2]	**Natalia Bay (IRE) (92)** (PFICole) **3-8-5** BDoyle(4) (swtg: plld hrd: a.p: rdn over 2f out: one pce)	1¼	**6**	16/1	102	39
2869[8]	**Woodren (USA) (90)** (RGuest) **4-9-1** RHughes(6) (chsd ldr: rdn over 3f out: wknd over 2f out)	2½	**7**	50/1	98	45
1740[6]	**Gretel (95)** (MRStoute) **3-8-5** TSprake(1) (plld hrd: a in rr)	11	**8**	14/1	81	18

(SP 111.3%) **8 Rn**

2m 8.4 (3.10) CSF £9.36 TOTE £3.20: £1.50 £1.20 £1.60 (£3.20) OWNER H R H Prince Fahd Salman (NEWMARKET) BRED Newgate Stud Co
WEIGHT FOR AGE 3yo-10lb

Fiji, a bit of a madam once on the racecourse, did not come past the stands and eventually consented to go straight to the start. She did nothing wrong in the race, however, and scraped home under 2lb overweight. (3/1)
2180* Bint Baladee, showing the temperament of her two-year-old days, displayed a high head carriage and took an age to pick up. Expertly coaxed along in the closing stages, she had no-one to blame but herself. (5/2)
1916a Dances With Dreams ran a fine race for one who is much more at home with some give in the ground. (7/2: 2/1-4/1)
960 Sarayir (USA), highly tried this season, gave the first indication that she has really trained on. (6/1)
The Faraway Tree shaped as though she will be better suited by a longer trip. (14/1: 10/1-16/1)
2219 Natalia Bay (IRE) stuck on well, considering how hard she had pulled for her head. (16/1)

3018 STEEP HOLM H'CAP (0-70) (3-Y.O+) (Class E)

8-00 (8-00) **7f 16y** £3,132.25 (£943.00: £456.50: £213.25) Stalls: High GOING minus 0.27 sec per fur (GF)

				SP	RR	SF
2880*	**Clytha Hill Lad (36)** (JMBradley) **6-7-7**(3) RFfrench(1) (b: a.p: rdn to ld wl ins fnl f: r.o)	—	**1**	10/1	49	32
2006[18]	**Speedy Classic (USA) (56)** (MJHeaton-Ellis) **8-9-2** AClark(8) (a.p: led 3f out tl wl ins fnl f)	½	**2**	10/1	68	51
2760[2]	**Sualtach (IRE) (68)** (RHollinshead) **4-10-0** LDettori(7) (hld up: hdwy over 2f out: hrd rdn over 1f out: r.o ins fnl f)	½	**3**	11/4[1]	79	62
2651[4]	**Dream Carrier (IRE) (40)** (REPeacock) **9-7-11**(3) PFessey(11) (led 4f: wknd 2f out)	6	**4**	11/1	37	20
2550[9]	**Well Drawn (60)** (HCandy) **4-9-6** NAdams(3) (prom: rdn & wknd over 2f out)	1½	**5**	20/1	54	37
2835[9]	**Morocco (IRE) (60)** (MRChannon) **8-8-13**(7) AEddery(4) (hld up: hdwy over 2f out: nvr nr to chal)	½	**6**	8/1	53	36
2785[6]	**Delight of Dawn (47)** (EAWheeler) **5-8-7** JReid(6) (dwlt: hdwy over 2f out: sn rdn: wknd wl over 1f out)	1¼	**7**	9/2[2]	37	20
2721[8]	**Severn Mill (36)** (JMBradley) **6-7-3**(7) JFowle(13) (s.s: nvr trbld ldrs)	¾	**8**	33/1	24	7
2698[3]	**White Settler (63)** (RJHodges) **4-9-9** TSprake(5) (hld up: hdwy 2f out: wknd over 1f out)	½	**9**	13/2[3]	50	33
2788[19]	**Sand Star (55)** (DHaydnJones) **5-9-1v** SWhitworth(12) (plld hrd: bhd fnl 3f)	1½	**10**	25/1	39	22
2573[5]	**La Chatelaine (44)** (GLewis) **3-7-8**(3) MBaird(2) (bhd fnl 3f)	3½	**11**	13/2[3]	20	—
2510[6]	**Alpine Music (IRE) (46)** (JMBradley) **3-7-10b**(3)ow3 MHenry(10) (chsd ldr over 3f: rdn & wknd over 2f out)	¾	**12**	33/1	20	—

(SP 123.6%) **12 Rn**

1m 21.3 (2.00) CSF £96.21 CT £329.49 TOTE £11.60: £3.10 £2.40 £2.00 (£45.10) Trio £44.80 OWNER Mrs Marion Morgan (CHEPSTOW) BRED Mrs M. C. Morgan
LONG HANDICAP Clytha Hill Lad 7-5 Severn Mill 7-0 Alpine Music (IRE) 7-5
WEIGHT FOR AGE 3yo-7lb

2880* Clytha Hill Lad, not penalised for his recent apprentice race win, was effectively off a mark 3lb higher than his rating from tomorrow because he was out of the handicap. (10/1: 8/1-12/1)
1680 Speedy Classic (USA) was only 2lb higher than when winning over course and distance last September. (10/1)
2760 Sualtach (IRE), down 2lb, was trying to beat the Handicapper, having been set to rise 5lb from the next day. (11/4)
2651 Dream Carrier (IRE), down 2lb, has scored eleven times in all during a long career but never on a straight course. (11/1)
Well Drawn, dropped 8lb after a couple of disappointing runs this season, was coming back in distance. (20/1)
2546 Morocco (IRE) was already set to run off a 1lb lower mark in future handicaps. (8/1)

3019 LUNDY ISLAND MAIDEN AUCTION STKS (2-Y.O) (Class D)

8-30 (8-32) **6f 16y** £3,454.00 (£1,042.00: £506.00: £238.00) Stalls: High GOING minus 0.27 sec per fur (GF)

				SP	RR	SF
	Magical (WRMuir) **2-8-7** JReid(5) (w'like: scope: a gng wl: led & carried lft over 1f out: rdn out)	—	**1**	11/4[2]	76	29
2439a[2]	**Soft Touch (IRE)** (MissGayKelleway) **2-7-12** NGMcCullagh(1) (hld up: swtchd rt & hdwy over 1f out: r.o wl ins fnl f)	nk	**2**	5/4[1]	66	19
2534[4]	**Deva Lady** (MRChannon) **2-8-0** AMackay(8) (led: hdd & edgd lft over 1f out: nt qckn)	1¼	**3**	6/1[3]	65	18
	Short Romance (IRE) (JWHills) **2-7-11**(3) MHenry(3) (cmpt: bkwd: hdwy 3f out: wknd over 1f out)	5	**4**	16/1	52	5
2112[5]	**Clermont City (IRE)** (PWChapple-Hyam) **2-8-0**(7) RCody-Boutcher(4) (prom over 4f)	3	**5**	16/1	51	4
	Bay Watch (IRE) (IABalding) **2-8-10** SWhitworth(2) (str: scope: lw: dwlt: a bhd)	2	**6**	9/1	49	2
	Fair Sonia (KMcAuliffe) **2-7-12** NAdams(6) (w'like: s.i.s: rdn over 3f out: sn bhd)	nk	**7**	25/1	36	—

(SP 111.0%) **7 Rn**

1m 11.9 (2.70) CSF £5.59 TOTE £3.60: £1.80 £1.30 (£3.20) OWNER Mr J. Jannaway (LAMBOURN) BRED James Thom and Sons

Magical, a half-brother to five-furlong juvenile winner Under Pressure, had apparently been working well at home. (11/4)
2439a Soft Touch (IRE) rather overdid the waiting tactics and should get seven if ridden like this. (5/4)
2534 Deva Lady should stay another furlong. (6/1)
Short Romance (IRE) is bred to need further and will strip fitter next time. (16/1)
2112 Clermont City (IRE) was reverting to six. (16/1)
Bay Watch (IRE) looks the type who will need plenty of time. (9/1: 5/1-10/1)

3020 SIR GORDON RICHARDS H'CAP (0-80) (3-Y.O) (Class D)

9-00 (9-00) **2m 49y** £3,533.50 (£1,063.00: £514.00: £239.50) Stalls: Low GOING minus 0.27 sec per fur (GF)

				SP	RR	SF
2535*	**Lady of The Lake (72)** (JLDunlop) **3-9-6** KFallon(4) (swtg: swvd rt s: led over 8f: led 3f out: rdn & edgd rt fnl f: r.o)	—	**1**	4/5[1]	80	35
2410[7]	**Yak Alfaraj (70)** (MRStoute) **3-9-4** JReid(3) (hmpd s: hld up: hdwy 3f out: ev ch 1f out: carried rt: nt qckn)	1	**2**	7/2[3]	77	32
2423[3]	**Ikhtisar (USA) (73)** (PTWalwyn) **3-9-7v**[1] RHughes(2) (swtg: plld hrd early: chsd ldr: led 8f out: rdn over 4f out: hdd 3f out: sn wknd)	15	**3**	3/1[2]	65	20

2397[9] **Nile Valley (IRE) (68)** (PWChapple-Hyam) **3-8-9b**[1](7) RCody-Boutcher(1) (hld up & plld hrd: rdn over 3f out: sn bhd) 9 **4** 6/1 51 6
(SP 117.1%) **4 Rn**

3m 38.1 (10.10) CSF £4.08 TOTE £1.90: (£2.80) OWNER Capt J. Macdonald-Buchanan (ARUNDEL) BRED The Lavington Stud
2535* Lady of The Lake, raised 5lb, drifted away from the far rail in the closing stages, despite Fallon doing everything he could. (4/5)
1434 Yak Alfaraj, the only colt against three fillies, was stepping up considerably in distance for this handicap debut and should not be considered unlucky. (7/2: 5/2-4/1)
2423 Ikhtisar (USA), up 3lb, did not see out the trip in the first-time visor. (3/1)
2397 Nile Valley (IRE) proved difficult to settle in the first-time blinkers. (6/1)

T/Plpt: £33.50 (451.63 Tckts). T/Qdpt: £3.30 (239.11 Tckts) KH

2867-NEWMARKET (R-H) (Good to firm)
Friday July 25th
WEATHER: warm & fine WIND: fresh behind

3021 NGK SPARK PLUGS MAIDEN STKS (3-Y.O) (Class D)
6-20 (6-21) **1m 4f** **(July)** £4,337.50 (£1,300.00: £625.00: £287.50) Stalls: High GOING minus 0.47 sec per fur (F)

					SP	RR	SF
2566[4]	**Zerpour (IRE)** (LMCumani) **3-9-0** DHolland(7) (trckd ldrs: led over 1f out: sn pushed clr)	—	**1**	6/4[1]	93+	45
2311[4]	**Sir Ricky (USA)** (RCharlton) **3-9-0** PatEddery(8) (trckd ldrs: r.o ins fnl f)	3	**2**	7/2[2]	89	41
2583[4]	**Dovedon Star (80)** (PAKelleway) **3-8-4**(5) GMilligan(11) (hld up: hdwy 3f out: rdn over 1f out: one pce)	nk	**3**	8/1	84	36
1258[8]	**Savu Sea (IRE)** (CFWall) **3-8-9** MTebbutt(2) (led 3f: led over 2f out tl over 1f out: sn wknd)	12	**4**	33/1	68	20
1784[5]	**Gallant Heights** (GCBravery) **3-8-9** MRimmer(9) (hld up: hdwy 4f out: nvr able chal)	5	**5**	25/1	61	13
2287[4]	**Chandler's Hall** (MJHeaton-Ellis) **3-9-0** DaneO'Neill(5) (led after 3f tl over 2f out: sn btn)	¾	**6**	33/1	65	17
	Serpentara (HRACecil) **3-8-9** WRyan(3) (leggy: scope: prom: ev ch over 2f out: sn rdn & btn)	½	**7**	7/1[3]	59	11
1866[12]	**Signed And Sealed (USA)** (CACyzer) **3-9-0** WJO'Connor(6) (rdn 3f out: nvr nr to chal)	2	**8**	33/1	62	14
2410[4]	**Aboo Hom (80)** (ACStewart) **3-9-0** JCarroll(4) (lw: sn pushed along: hdwy 6f out: ev ch over 3f out: wknd 2f out)	6	**9**	8/1	54	6
	Snowcap (IRE) (GWragg) **3-8-9** MHills(10) (w'like: unf: a bhd)	5	**10**	14/1	42	—
	Fine Quill (JHMGosden) **3-8-9** AMcGlone(1) (unf: bit bkwd: chsd ldrs tl rdn & wknd 5f out)	14	**11**	16/1	23	—

(SP 122.2%) **11 Rn**

2m 31.2 (2.20) CSF £5.94 TOTE £3.00: £1.70 £1.20 £2.00 (£5.20) Trio £7.10 OWNER H H Aga Khan (NEWMARKET) BRED His Highness the Aga Khan's Studs S.C.
2566 Zerpour (IRE), back up in trip, moved to post poorly on this faster ground but, in the race, was always cruising and looked the winner long before he struck the front. He should continue to progress and, if the handicapper gives him a chance, he should take it. (6/4)
2311 Sir Ricky (USA) took a good hold gong down and, produced by the stands rail, picked up nicely, but not as well as the winner. There should be a race in him. (7/2)
2583 Dovedon Star, accompanied by a late jockey change, was rather keen going down this time. Although she seemed to stay this longer trip, her lack of gears when required was again in evidence. (8/1)
Savu Sea (IRE), a good mover, is gradually getting her act together and her pedigree suggests she will be suited by further. (33/1)
1784 Gallant Heights tried to stay on, switching a couple of times in the process, but could make little impression. (25/1)
2287 Chandler's Hall doesn't look the finished article yet and went rather too freely to post. (33/1)
Serpentara was too keen going down for this debut effort and failed to last home. She comes from a very strong female line, her grandam Sandy Island being closely related to Slip Anchor, and she will surely come on for this. (7/1: 7/2-8/1)
2410 Aboo Hom (8/1: 4/1-9/1)
Snowcap (IRE) (14/1: 10/1-16/1)

3022 SNOWDENS' MARQUEES NOVICE STKS (2-Y.O) (Class D)
6-50 (6-53) **6f** **(July)** £4,142.50 (£1,240.00: £595.00: £272.50) Stalls: High GOING minus 0.47 sec per fur (F)

					SP	RR	SF
2588[3]	**Krispy Knight** (JWHills) **2-8-12** MHills(1) (w ldr: led 1f out: rdn out)	—	**1**	7/4[1]	81	45
2771[2]	**Stone of Destiny** (BJMeehan) **2-8-12** MTebbutt(7) (lw: led 5f: r.o)	1½	**2**	6/1[3]	77	41
1607[9]	**Diamond White** (GCBravery) **2-8-7** AMunro(5) (chsd ldrs: rdn 2f out: one pce appr fnl f)	2½	**3**	12/1	65	29
	Palmetto Bay (IRE) (MRStoute) **2-8-12** KDarley(6) (leggy: scope: chsd ldrs: outpcd 2f out: rdn 1f out: kpt on)	4	**4**	7/1	60	24
2356*	**Suivez La Trace** (RAFahey) **2-9-4** JCarroll(9) (lw: chsd ldrs tl wknd over 1f out)	1¼	**5**	4/1[2]	62	26
	Inn On The Park (SDow) **2-8-12** DaneO'Neill(4) (leggy: unf: s.v.s: a bhd)	7	**6**	25/1	38	2
2588[6]	**Bahamian Melody (USA)** (DRLoder) **2-8-12** PatEddery(8) (lw: bhd fnl 3f)	¾	**7**	6/1[3]	36	—
	Linda (NACallaghan) **2-8-7** WRyan(3) (unf: bit bkwd: swvd lft s: a bhd)	11	**8**	25/1	—	—

(SP 112.8%) **8 Rn**

1m 12.89 (0.89) CSF £11.18 TOTE £2.80: £1.20 £1.70 £2.00 (£5.90) Trio £19.70 OWNER Mr Derek Clee (LAMBOURN) BRED D. D. and Mrs Jean P. Clee
2588 Krispy Knight, given that his pedigree suggests he will improve greatly for a step up in trip, has made a most encouraging start, winning this with some authority. (7/4)
2771 Stone of Destiny ran another sound race but again found one who could quicken up to take him. (6/1)
1607 Diamond White moved particularly well to post but gave a lot of trouble at the start. She stuck to her task in the closing stages but does now need further than six furlongs. (12/1)
Palmetto Bay (IRE), whose dam is a half sister to Aim for the Top, looks the sort to make up into a useful sort but moved to post rather scratchily. Losing his place on the run into the Dip, he rallied on meeting the rising ground and may need a bit more cut to be seen to best advantage. (7/1: op 4/1)
2356* Suivez La Trace moved down well on a surface much faster than that of his debut, but could not handle the step up in class. (4/1)
Inn On The Park is the first foal of a winning mare from a good family, being a half-sister to a number of winners, most notably Ever Genial. He got very stirred up in the stalls as the handlers struggled to get Diamond White into the next stall, almost going down, and almost certainly lost all chance when they opened. A very good mover, she may have some ability. (25/1)
2588 Bahamian Melody (USA) looked in good order, but his long stride seemed to be feeling the ground going down and this probably accounted for another poor display. (6/1)

3023 BAILEYS' IRISH CREAM LIQUEUR CONDITIONS STKS (3-Y.O+) (Class C)
7-20 (7-20) **5f (July)** £5,346.40 (£1,926.40: £923.20: £376.00: £148.00) Stalls: High GOING minus 0.47 sec per fur (F)

	Horse	Dist	Pos	SP	RR	SF
2599[5]	**Coastal Bluff (110)** (TDBarron) **5-8-13** KDarley(3) (b.hind: lw: w ldr: led & rdn over 1f out: eased nr fin: cleverly)	—	1	8/11[1]	114+	59
2599[6]	**Easycall (110)** (BJMeehan) **3-8-9** MTebbutt(1) (swtg: trckd ldrs: ev ch over 1f out: unable qckn ins fnl f)	nk	2	11/4[2]	113	54
3001a[4]	**Brave Edge (106)** (RHannon) **6-8-13** DaneO'Neill(5) (hld up: rdn & r.o fnl f: nt pce to chal)	1½	3	5/1[3]	108	53
1975[6]	**Venture Capitalist (100)** (DNicholls) **8-8-13** AlexGreaves(2) (hld up: rdn 1f out: no imp)	1½	4	12/1	103	48
941[10]	**Midnight Escape (95)** (CFWall) **4-8-13** PatEddery(4) (lw: led over 3f: sn btn)	hd	5	12/1	66 t	48
				(SP 116.6%)		**5 Rn**

58.38 secs CSF £3.03 TOTE £1.80: £1.30 £1.80 (£2.10) OWNER Mrs D. E. Sharp (THIRSK) BRED R. M. West
WEIGHT FOR AGE 3yo-4lb

2599 Coastal Bluff looked to have thrived since his first run and, although the steady pace turned this into a three-furlong sprint, he still held the aces. This was an excellent performance and, whilst the Stewards' Cup may be first on the agenda, a Group success surely awaits. (8/11: 10/11-evens)
2599 Easycall, back over his best trip, bounced back to form and only gave best to the winner in the last fifty yards, having not helped his cause by trying to hang left. (11/4)
3001a Brave Edge at least did not have the draw to blame this time, but found giving the principals a couple of lengths start in the steadily-run early stages too much to overcome, once full throttle was engaged. (5/1: 3/1-11/2)
1975 Venture Capitalist has always needed plenty of cover and a fast pace, and didn't really get enough of either. (12/1)
941 Midnight Escape moved down well and is clearly in good form but, because of the steady pace, may well be flattered by his proximity to those in front. (12/1: tchd 20/1)

3024 TRAVIS PERKINS H'CAP (0-90) (3-Y.O+) (Class C)
7-50 (7-50) **6f (July)** £6,004.00 (£1,792.00: £856.00: £388.00) Stalls: High GOING minus 0.47 sec per fur (F)

	Horse	Dist	Pos	SP	RR	SF
2346[9]	**Geimhriuil (IRE) (81)** (LMCumani) **3-9-1** PatEddery(8) (lw: trckd ldrs: led over 1f out: comf)	—	1	3/1[1]	91+	52
2841[8]	**Kind of Light (67)** (RGuest) **4-8-3**(3) MartinDwyer(4) (trckd ldrs: effrt 3f out: ev ch over 1f out: r.o ins fnl f)	1½	2	20/1	73	39
2900[2]	**Grey Kingdom (75)** (MBrittain) **6-9-0** KDarley(3) (led tl over 1f out: one pce)	s.h	3	7/2[2]	81	47
2567[4]	**The Happy Fox (IRE) (73)** (BAMcMahon) **5-8-12b** JCarroll(7) (lw: w ldr: ev ch over 1f out: no ex wl ins fnl f)	½	4	8/1	78	44
2649[6]	**Shamanic (82)** (SPCWoods) **5-9-7** WRyan(6) (squeezed out s: hld up: n.m.r 2f out: no imp fnl f)	2½	5	8/1	80	46
2833[6]	**Law Commission (86)** (DRCElsworth) **7-9-11** DHolland(9) (hld up: rdn over 1f out: no imp)	½	6	7/2[2]	83	49
	Ursa Major (87) (PAKelleway) **3-9-7** AMunro(2) (bit bkwd: prom tl wknd over 1f out)	3½	7	20/1	74	35
2313*	**Muhandam (IRE) (72)** (PAKelleway) **4-8-6**(5) CLowther(5) (lw: prom: rdn over 2f out: sn wknd)	½	8	7/1[3]	58	24
1972[15]	**Jupiter (IRE) (66)** (GCBravery) **3-8-0** DRMcCabe(1) (lw: stdd s: hdwy over 2f out: rdn & hung lft: sn btn)	hd	9	16/1	52	13
				(SP 119.6%)		**9 Rn**

1m 12.56 (0.56) CSF £60.55 CT £199.97 TOTE £3.60: £1.70 £4.20 £1.40 (£63.70) Trio £50.70 OWNER Mr M. J. Dawson (NEWMARKET) BRED Miss Suzanne O'Neill
WEIGHT FOR AGE 3yo-5lb

1870* Geimhriuil (IRE), clearly well suited by the drop back to sprinting for the first time since his two-year-old days, picked up in tremendous style once let down, and the handicapper may struggle to keep up with him from now on. (3/1)
Kind of Light, who hit form around this time last year, is on a winning mark judged on those displays, but could not match the foot of the winner. She will not always catch such a tartar and a win could be close at hand. (20/1)
2900 Grey Kingdom, having his third run in a row on fast ground, was somewhat scratchy going down, but ran with his usual courage and remains a credit to all concerned. (7/2)
2567 The Happy Fox (IRE), taken to post very quietly after the others, could not get to the front this time but ran well, only tying up in the last fifty yards. To last home over such a stiff six, he probably needs things to go his way. (8/1)
2649 Shamanic did not get the run of the race and is almost certainly capable of better. (8/1)
2833 Law Commission needs every yard of a truly-run six furlongs, and the steady early pace meant that his efforts to follow the winner through came to little. (7/2)

3025 ROY CHAPMAN PROPERTY AGENTS NURSERY H'CAP (2-Y.O) (Class D)
8-20 (8-20) **7f (July)** £4,620.00 (£1,380.00: £660.00: £300.00) Stalls: High GOING minus 0.47 sec per fur (F)

	Horse	Dist	Pos	SP	RR	SF
2681*	**Lord Smith** (MCPipe) **2-9-4**(3) MartinDwyer(5) (mde virtually all: rdn & styd on strly fnl 2f)	—	1	5/2[1]	89	53
2371[6]	**Summer Deal (USA)** (PFICole) **2-8-6**(7) DavidO'Neill(1) (w wnr: ev ch 2f out: one pce)	3½	2	7/1	73	37
2587[2]	**Sick As A Parrot** (CADwyer) **2-8-2**(3) DO'Donohoe(6) (lw: hld up: pushed along & hdwy over 3f out: nt pce to chal)	nk	3	3/1[2]	64	28
2562[6]	**Bobbydazzle** (DrJDScargill) **2-8-10**(3) DGriffiths(4) (rr: hld up: hdwy 4f out: ev ch 2f out: one pce)	¾	4	6/1	71	35
2429[4]	**Kim's Brave** (BJMeehan) **2-9-6** PatEddery(7) (chsd ldrs tl wknd 2f)	7	5	4/1[3]	62	26
2595[5]	**Signatory** (RHannon) **2-8-10** DaneO'Neill(3) (lw: w ldrs over 3f)	3	6	7/1	45	9
2681[6]	**Arm And A Leg (IRE)** (CADwyer) **2-7-13**(5)ow3 CLowther(2) (stdd s: bhd fnl 3f)	5	7	8/1	27	—
				(SP 124.0%)		**7 Rn**

1m 26.09 (1.09) CSF £20.85 TOTE £2.70: £2.30 £4.10 (£15.70) OWNER Mr A. J. Lomas (WELLINGTON) BRED Mrs M. S. Teversham

2681* Lord Smith is a real professional and, not for the first time, made his stamina tell. A mile would hold no terrors. (5/2)
2371 Summer Deal (USA) seemed to cope with this step up in trip, despite going down rather keenly, but was not helped by the 9lb rise in the weights overnight. This neatly-made filly would be interesting with a feather weight. (7/1: 9/2-15/2)
2587 Sick As A Parrot looks the part but again made hard work of getting into contention. His dam, by Niniski, is a half-sister to the ill-fated Arcot, so this trip may prove well short of his best. (3/1: op 6/1)
2562 Bobbydazzle, a half-sister to Tumbleweed Ridge, again looked a none too easy ride. (6/1: 3/1-13/2)
2429 Kim's Brave moved down well but, back on faster ground, proved a big disappointment. (4/1)
2595 Signatory couldn't get to the front this time and didn't run his race. (7/1)

3026 WICKEN FEN H'CAP (0-75) (3-Y.O+) (Class D)
8-50 (8-51) **1m 2f (July)** £4,932.00 (£1,476.00: £708.00: £324.00) Stalls: High GOING minus 0.47 sec per fur (F)

	Horse	Dist	Pos	SP	RR	SF
2839[2]	**Mutadarra (IRE) (62)** (WJMusson) **4-9-4** PatEddery(9) (lw: hld up & bhd: plld out & hdwy over 2f out: led ins fnl f: rdn out)	—	1	2/1[1]	75	51

2845[2]	**No Cliches (65)** (DNicholls) **4-9-7** AlexGreaves(11) (chsd ldrs: led over 1f out tl ins fnl f: rdn & rallied)..........s.h	**2**	8/1	78	54
2782*	**Saddlers' Hope (75)** (JRFanshawe) **3-9-7** 5x MHills(8) (swtg: led tl over 1f out: one pce)..........4	**3**	100/30[2]	82	48
2889[2]	**Gold Desire (48)** (MBrittain) **7-8-4** GBardwell(1) (lw: sn chsng ldrs: outpcd & rdn wl over 1f out: styd on ins fnl f)..........nk	**4**	6/1[3]	54	30
1983[3]	**Sharbadarid (IRE) (73)** (LMCumani) **3-9-5** DHolland(10) (lw: hld up: hdwy 4f out: nvr rchd ldrs)..........6	**5**	13/2	69	35
2744[3]	**Lookingforarainbow (IRE) (60)** (BobJones) **9-9-2** AMcGlone(3) (hld up: hdwy 4f out: no imp appr fnl f).......1½	**6**	9/1	54	30
2430[9]	**Captain Marmalade (41)** (DTThom) **8-7-6**(5) APolli(2) (b: swtg: hld up: hdwy 4f out: wknd over 1f out)..........1½	**7**	33/1	33	9
2399[5]	**Zamalek (USA) (42)** (RMFlower) **5-7-9**(3) MartinDwyer(7) (in tch: rdn 3f out: wknd over 1f out)..........2	**8**	16/1	30	6
2593[4]	**Bubble Wings (FR) (68)** (SPCWoods) **5-9-10** WJO'Connor(12) (hld up: hdwy 4f out: rdn over 2f out: sn btn) nk	**9**	8/1	56	32
2577[14]	**Rehaab (49)** (DMorris) **4-8-5** JCarroll(5) (prom tl wknd over 3f out)..........3	**10**	25/1	32	8
2551[4]	**Rich In Love (IRE) (74)** (CACyzer) **3-9-6b[1]** KDarley(6) (trckd ldrs over 6f)..........½	**11**	14/1	56	22
1665[4]	**Action Jackson (50)** (BJMcMath) **5-8-6** WRyan(4) (swtg: chsd ldrs 5f)..........nk	**12**	16/1	32	8
			(SP 141.5%)		**12 Rn**

2m 5.18 (1.58) CSF £21.79 CT £55.80 TOTE £3.80: £1.70 £4.30 £1.80 (£29.20) Trio £19.70 OWNER Mr B. N. Fulton (NEWMARKET) BRED Mrs T. V. Ryan
WEIGHT FOR AGE 3yo-10lb

2839 Mutadarra (IRE), beaten by a subsequent winner here a week ago, was again held up in the rear and settled rather better for Eddery. Once pulled to the outside and woken up, he found a great turn of foot but it was coming to an end once he hit the front and the post came just in time. (2/1)
2845 No Cliches does not seem to lack courage, far from it, but now has a record of one win and five defeats in photo finishes. (8/1: op 5/1)
2782* Saddlers' Hope, who got warm and was rather free going down, found no more when tackled. This is a tough track to make all the running on and somewhere a little sharper would suit better. (100/30)
2889 Gold Desire loves this place and looked tuned to the minute, but moved down rather poorly and got outpaced at a vital time. Whilst he may be better over a little further these days, he has won the handicap over course and distance at the first August meeting in two of the last three seasons. (6/1)
1983 Sharbadarid (IRE), whose dam is a half-sister to Shahrastani and Shadirwan, was stepping up in trip for this handicap debut, but almost certainly needs further still. (13/2: 7/2-7/1)
2744 Lookingforarainbow (IRE) finds this trip too short these days and is becoming expensive to follow. (9/1)
2593 Bubble Wings (FR) (8/1: 5/1-9/1)

T/Plpt: £9.50 (1,901.79 Tckts). T/Qdpt: £4.70 (216.36 Tckts) Dk

2874-NOTTINGHAM (L-H) (Good to firm)
Friday July 25th
WEATHER: fine and sunny WIND: mod across

3027 PINXTON MINERS' WELFARE (S) STKS (3 & 4-Y.O) (Class G)
6-10 (6-10) **1m 1f 213y** £1,984.50 (£547.00: £259.50) Stalls: Low GOING minus 0.45 sec per fur (F)

			SP	RR	SF
2770[4]	**Blazer's Baby (57)** (JRFanshawe) **3-8-5** DHarrison(2) (swtg: chsd ldrs: drvn along over 4f out: led over 1f out: styd on u.p)..........—	**1**	11/8[1]	55	—
2546[13]	**Scenicris (IRE) (50)** (RHollinshead) **4-9-1** FLynch(6) (lw: hld up: stdy hdwy over 3f out: rdn 1f out: kpt on towards fin)..........1½	**2**	2/1[2]	53	4
2670[6]	**Macari (45)** (BPJBaugh) **3-8-10** GHind(5) (led tl over 1f out: kpt on one pce)..........nk	**3**	7/1[3]	57	—
2568[10]	**Spare My Blushes (39)** (BAMcMahon) **3-8-5** LNewton(8) (trckd ldrs: effrt over 3f out: hung lft: grad wknd)....10	**4**	33/1	36	—
2410[11]	**Stockbrook** (KRBurke) **4-9-6** JQuinn(3) (hld up: drvn along over 4f out: no rspnse)..........1¾	**5**	8/1	38	—
2787[7]	**Qualitair Beauty (35)** (MissLCSiddall) **4-8-8**(7) TSiddall(7) (trckd ldrs: effrt over 4f out: lost pl 3f out)..........2	**6**	40/1	30	—
2911[5]	**Dino's Mistral (30)** (FHLee) **4-9-6** CRutter(4) (trckd ldrs: drvn along over 3f out: sn wknd)..........24	**7**	20/1	—	—
			(SP 109.2%)		**7 Rn**

2m 9.9 (7.40) CSF £3.46 TOTE £2.20: £1.40 £2.10 (£1.70) OWNER Mr K. Brooke (NEWMARKET) BRED B. Brooke
WEIGHT FOR AGE 3yo-10lb
Sold Miss SRudge 3,600gns

2770 Blazer's Baby, who has a high head carriage, settled much better, and took a very modest event even by selling race standards with nothing to spare. She was sold at the auction and is apparently bound to race in Belgium. (11/8: 4/5-6/4)
1660 Scenicris (IRE) has only won once from thirty-nine starts and it is not hard to see why. Making ground on the bridle when put under pressure, she was in two minds whether to go through with it. Consenting to stay on towards the finish, it was too late to trouble the winner. (2/1)
2670 Macari put two poor runs behind him. (7/1)
Spare My Blushes wants to do nothing but hang left. (33/1)
Stockbrook (8/1: 6/1-10/1)

3028 GREASLEY MINERS' WELFARE H'CAP (0-65) (3-Y.O) (Class F)
6-40 (6-40) **2m 9y** £2,277.00 (£627.00: £297.00) Stalls: Low GOING minus 0.45 sec per fur (F)

			SP	RR	SF
2189*	**Ginger Rogers (51)** (DWPArbuthnot) **3-8-9** JQuinn(7) (trckd ldrs: led over 5f out: drvn clr 3f out: pushed out)..........—	**1**	7/2[1]	69	33
2172[10]	**Shelteez (USA) (40)** (MBell) **3-7-7**(5) RMullen(2) (drvn along ½-wy: hdwy over 4f out: wnt 2nd over 2f out: styd on: nt rch wnr)..........1	**2**	20/1	57	21
2725[5]	**Keepsake (IRE) (50)** (MDIUsher) **3-8-8** RStreet(1) (hld up & bhd: hdwy over 4f out: one pce fnl 3f)..........15	**3**	11/1	52	16
2397[2]	**Nick of Time (63)** (JLDunlop) **3-9-7** GCarter(5) (chsd ldrs: wnt 2nd 4f out: wknd over 2f out)..........5	**4**	7/2[1]	60	24
2189[7]	**Jucinda (57)** (JPearce) **3-9-1** DHarrison(8) (hld up: hdwy over 4f out: rdn & wknd 3f out)..........2	**5**	6/1[3]	52	16
2535[4]	**Golden Melody (54)** (MJHeaton-Ellis) **3-8-12** SSanders(3) (b.hind: led: sn drvn along: hdd over 5f out: sn wknd)..........16	**6**	10/1	33	—
2397[3]	**Cadbury Castle (43)** (MBlanshard) **3-8-1** CRutter(9) (sn chsng ldrs: drvn along 5f out: sn wknd)..........2	**7**	8/1	20	—
2650[7]	**Select Star (IRE) (60)** (APJarvis) **3-9-4** SDrowne(6) (b.hind: drvn along & lost pl ½-wy: t.o 4f out)..........21	**8**	12/1	16	—

				SP	RR	SF
2757*	**The Roundsills (58)** (RFJohnsonHoughton) **3-9-2** 4x ACulhane(4) (swtg: chsd ldrs: rdn 7f out: lost pl over 4f out: eased fnl 2f)	hd	**9**	5/1[2]	14	—
				(SP 116.4%)		**9 Rn**

3m 28.0 (5.00) CSF £70.02 CT £639.51 TOTE £2.60: £1.50 £6.10 £4.20 (£185.80) Trio £126.60; £128.41 to 28/7/97 OWNER Mr W. H. Ponsonby (COMPTON) BRED R. Barber

2189* Ginger Rogers, a likeable filly, had this in the bag the minute she stepped up the gallop and took charge going into the home turn. Idling in front, she had to be pushed out towards the finish. She looks to have plenty of further improvement in her. (7/2)

Shelteez (USA), stepping up considerably in trip, went in pursuit of the winner coming to the final quarter-mile. She stayed on but the winning margin slightly flatters her. (20/1)

2182 Keepsake (IRE) proved suited by this step up in distance but she looked woefully one-paced. (11/1: 8/1-12/1)

2397 Nick of Time, from a 3lb higher mark, went in pursuit of the winner once in line for home but had given all with over two furlongs left to run. (7/2)

1853 Jucinda, nibbled at in the market, had been dropped 4lb in the official ratings. Making her move off the bend, she was getting nowhere with three furlongs left to run. (6/1: op 10/1)

2757* The Roundsills, sweating in the paddock, was loaded first. Under pressure at halfway, his rider eventually gave up. (5/1)

3029 RJB MINING H'CAP (0-70) (3-Y.O+) (Class E)

7-10 (7-12) **1m 54y** £3,772.25 (£1,133.00: £546.50: £253.25) Stalls: Low GOING minus 0.45 sec per fur (F)

				SP	RR	SF
2502[3]	**Snowy Mantle (38)** (JDBethell) **4-7-6**(5)ow1 RMullen(8) (trckd ldrs: led over 1f out: sn clr: readily)	—	**1**	9/1	54+	21
2733[4]	**Star Turn (IRE) (60)** (MBell) **3-8-11** MFenton(14) (chsd ldrs: styd on u.p fnl 2f: no ch w wnr)	5	**2**	9/1	66	26
2743[3]	**Chairmans Choice (55)** (APJarvis) **7-9-0** JQuinn(10) (led tl over 1f out: kpt on same pce)	½	**3**	6/1[2]	60	28
2557[14]	**Harmony Hall (67)** (JRFanshawe) **3-9-4** DHarrison(6) (b.hind: chsd ldrs: drvn along over 3f out: one pce)	2	**4**	16/1	68	28
2868[3]	**Priolo Prima (68)** (SirMarkPrescott) **4-9-13** SSanders(9) (trckd ldrs: sddle slipped 4f out: eased appr fnl f)	1¼	**5**	7/2[1]	67	35
2745[12]	**Oxbane (63)** (HCandy) **3-9-0** CRutter(1) (trckd ldrs: effrt over 3f out: one pce)	1½	**6**	16/1	59	19
2239[7]	**Highspeed (IRE) (57)** (SEKettlewell) **5-9-2** JFortune(4) (hld up: hdwy over 3f out: nvr nr to chal)	s.h	**7**	10/1	53	21
2660[2]	**Nobby Barnes (44)** (DonEnricoIncisa) **8-8-3** KimTinkler(15) (s.s: effrt over 3f out: nvr nr ldrs)	s.h	**8**	7/1[3]	40	8
2546[19]	**Darling Clover (64)** (RBastiman) **5-9-4**(5) HBastiman(2) (b.hind: s.i.s: hld up & bhd: kpt on fnl 2f: nvr nr to chal)	1¼	**9**	25/1	58	26
2395[5]	**Prince Zizim (37)** (CADwyer) **4-7-10** DWright(5) (unruly s: chsd ldrs: drvn along 5f out: hrd rdn & wknd 3f out)	1¼	**10**	16/1	28	—
2523[4]	**The Negotiator (61)** (MJHeaton-Ellis) **3-8-12** SDrowne(11) (mid div: drvn along over 3f out: n.d)	2	**11**	10/1	48	8
2546[11]	**Royal South (IRE) (50)** (PSFelgate) **4-8-9** GHind(7) (s.i.s: a bhd: c wd ent st)	5	**12**	16/1	28	—
2828[9]	**Don't Worry Mike (49)** (FHLee) **3-8-0**bow1 LNewton(12) (sddle slipped: c wd & bhd fnl 4f)	8	**13**	20/1	11	—
	The Real McCoy (45) (IPWilliams) **3-7-10** NCarlisle(13) (bolted gng to s: racd wd: plld very hrd: lost pl 5f out: sn wl bhd: t.o)	dist	**14**	14/1	—	—
				(SP 126.0%)		**14 Rn**

1m 43.8 (2.50) CSF £83.64 CT £505.98 TOTE £9.60: £3.20 £4.00 £3.10 (£54.90) Trio £247.80 OWNER Mrs G. Fane (MIDDLEHAM) BRED Mrs G. Fane

LONG HANDICAP Prince Zizim 7-8 The Real McCoy 7-5

WEIGHT FOR AGE 3yo-8lb

2502 Snowy Mantle, who apparently broke a blood-vessel when third at Carlisle last time, came through on the rail and took this in fine style. (9/1)

2733 Star Turn (IRE) ran easily his best race so far this year. (9/1)

2743 Chairmans Choice, who likes to get on with it, might be better over seven. (6/1)

Harmony Hall has more than his fair share of weight and it is hard to know what his best trip will turn out to be. (16/1)

2868 Priolo Prima, whose saddle slipped turning in, lost the weight cloth coming to the final furlong and his rider could do no more than sit still rodeo-style. (7/2)

1265 Oxbane, an excitable type, was stepped up in trip but it brought no improvement. (16/1)

2660 Nobby Barnes, drawn wide, missed the break and was always struggling. (7/1)

Darling Clover hinted that she might do considerably better before much longer. (25/1)

The Real McCoy (14/1: op 33/1)

3030 HARRINGTONS/HARWORTH MINERS' WELFARE MEDIAN AUCTION MAIDEN STKS (3-Y.O) (Class E)

7-40 (7-40) **1m 54y** £3,070.25 (£917.00: £438.50: £199.25) Stalls: Low GOING minus 0.45 sec per fur (F)

				SP	RR	SF
2877[5]	**Nominator Lad (75)** (BAMcMahon) **3-9-0** JFortune(8) (sn trckng ldrs: effrt over 2f out: rdn to ld jst ins fnl f: edgd lft: jst hld on)	—	**1**	9/2[3]	78	28
2602[8]	**Twin Time (60)** (MJHeaton-Ellis) **3-8-9** SDrowne(1) (chsd ldrs: styd on wl fnl f: jst failed)	s.h	**2**	16/1	73	23
2773[3]	**Severity** (WJHaggas) **3-9-0** FLynch(5) (sn led: hdd jst ins fnl f: wknd towards fin)	5	**3**	5/1	68	18
	Encore (JHMGosden) **3-8-9** GHind(6) (lengthy: unf: dwlt s: hdwy over 4f out: kpt on same pce fnl 2f)	1¾	**4**	3/1[2]	60	10
2654[3]	**Sceptre Lady (IRE) (72)** (BWHills) **3-8-9** GCarter(7) (led early: trckd ldrs: rdn & hung lft 2f out: sn wknd)	s.h	**5**	15/8[1]	60	10
	Telloff (MAJarvis) **3-8-9** SSanders(3) (bhd: hdwy over 3f out: kpt on fnl 2f: nvr nr to chal)	2½	**6**	20/1	55	5
	Jonny's Joker (FHLee) **3-9-0** DeanMcKeown(2) (hld up: hdwy over 3f out: sn rdn & hung lft: n.d)	5	**7**	33/1	50	—
2197[14]	**Whisper Low (IRE) (45)** (RHollinshead) **3-8-9** JQuinn(9) (chsd ldrs tl rdn & lost pl over 3f out: sn bhd)	17	**8**	50/1	12	—
2651[12]	**Gablesea (50)** (BPJBaugh) **3-9-0** ACulhane(4) (bhd: sme hdwy over 3f out: sn wknd)	3½	**9**	33/1	10	—
				(SP 113.1%)		**9 Rn**

1m 44.7 (3.40) CSF £58.74 TOTE £7.20: £1.50 £2.80 £1.80 (£59.40) Trio £64.60; £58.27 to 28/7/97 OWNER Mr J. D. Graham (TAMWORTH) BRED J. D. Graham

2214 Nominator Lad, who has apparently taken time to reach full fitness, responded to his rider's urgings but it was desperate near the line. (9/2)

1443 Twin Time, who would have been meeting the winner on 8lb better terms in a handicap, ran easily her best race so far and she proved very willing. (16/1)

2773 Severity, who tended to swish his tail in the paddock, made the running, but seemed to run out of stamina in the closing stages and might be better over seven. (5/1: op 11/4)

Encore, a backward-looking filly, took time to warm to her task after a slow break. Keeping on steadily in her own time, she should improve for the outing and will be suited by further. (3/1: 4/1-9/4)

2654 Sceptre Lady (IRE), a keen-going type, is not progressing and, under pressure, all she wanted to do here was hang left. (15/8: 5/4-2/1)

Telloff, an excitable type, was given a quiet run round on her third ever outing. She is now qualified for a handicap mark but it remains to be seen if she progresses. (20/1)

3031 E.B.F. AND RAINWORTH MINERS' WELFARE MAIDEN STKS (2-Y.O) (Class D)

8-10 (8-11) **5f 13y** £3,588.50 (£1,073.00: £514.00: £234.50) Stalls: High GOING minus 0.45 sec per fur (F)

			SP	RR	SF
2037^{5}	**The Limping Cat (IRE)** (BCMorgan) **2-9-0** DeanMcKeown(8) (led over 3f out: shkn up & r.o strly fnl f).........—	**1**	6/1^{3}	84	31
	Odette (SirMarkPrescott) **2-8-9** SSanders(4) (w'like: lw: w ldrs: rdn over 1f out: nt qckn)..........3	**2**	8/11^{1}	70+	17
2588^{7}	**Above Board** (BWHills) **2-9-0** EJohnson(9) (sn outpcd: shkn up ½-wy: styd on appr fnl f)..........3½	**3**	10/1	63	10
2320^{8}	**Night People** (WJarvis) **2-9-0** EmmaO'Gorman(10) (hld up & bhd: stdy hdwy 2f out: styd on wl towards fin)..½	**4**	20/1	62+	9
2356^{8}	**Shamwari Song** (JAGlover) **2-9-0** GCarter(5) (s.i.s: sn wl bhd: styd on appr fnl f)..........2	**5**	25/1	56+	3
2222^{2}	**Iris May** (JBerry) **2-8-9** JFortune(6) (led over 1f: rdn & wknd over 1f out)..........¾	**6**	7/2^{2}	48	—
2388^{6}	**Balanita (IRE)** (BPalling) **2-9-0** DHarrison(1) (unruly in stalls: sn chsng ldrs: wknd 2f out)..........¾	**7**	16/1	51	—
1941^{11}	**Revenge Is Sweet** (BAMcMahon) **2-9-0** LNewton(2) (chsd ldrs: rdn & outpcd ½-wy: n.d)..........3	**8**	50/1	41	—
	Haunt The Zoo (JLHarris) **2-8-9** ACulhane(3) (lengthy: unf: s.s: a wl bhd)..........nk	**9**	33/1	35	—
2519^{6}	**General Klaire** (BAMcMahon) **2-8-2**(7) SRighton(7) (chsd ldrs 3f: sn lost pl)..........3	**10**	25/1	26	—

(SP 126.7%) **10 Rn**

60.6 secs (1.70) CSF £10.21 TOTE £6.10: £1.10 £1.60 £3.50 (£7.60) Trio £24.80 OWNER Mr G. Whitaker (BURTON-ON-TRENT) BRED Razza Del Pian Del Lago

IN-FOCUS: This was trainer Barry Morgan's first winner since 1994, having temporarily relinquished his licence.

2037 The Limping Cat (IRE), who was carrying plenty of condition, took the favoured stands side and ran on much too strongly for the favourite in the final furlong. He should improve further. (6/1)

Odette, an attractive, sharp daughter of the Queen Mary winner On Tiptoes, was quite keen going to post. After being upsides entering the final furlong with the winner racing on the better ground against the stands'-side rail, she soon proved no match. Heavily supported, she had obviously been showing plenty at home. (8/11: op 11/8)

Above Board, who carries plenty of condition, showed a pronounced knee action going down. Soon being taken off his legs, he stuck on in the final furlong and will do better over further in due course. (10/1: op 6/1)

Night People, an excitable type, proved keen going down. Dropped right out, he picked up ground on the bridle and is now qualified for a handicap mark. Six or even seven will suit him much better. (20/1)

1774 Shamwari Song, soon well off the pace, was staying on in determined fashion under a quiet ride at the line. This was his third outing and it will be interesting to see how he fares in handicaps. (25/1)

2222 Iris May ran another disappointing race, finding little under pressure. (7/2: 5/2-4/1)

3032 CLIPSTONE MINERS' WELFARE LIMITED STKS (0-65) (3-Y.O+) (Class F)

8-40 (8-40) **5f 13y** £2,508.00 (£693.00: £330.00) Stalls: High GOING minus 0.45 sec per fur (F)

			SP	RR	SF
2847*	**Fairy Prince (IRE) (61)** (MrsALMKing) **4-9-5** JFortune(4) (hdwy ½-wy: styd on u.p to ld jst ins fnl f: hld on wl)..........—	**1**	100/30^{2}	71	47
2529^{4}	**Barranak (IRE) (65)** (GMMcCourt) **5-9-8** CRutter(1) (trckd ldrs: ev ch 1f out: nt qckn)..........1¼	**2**	7/2^{3}	70	46
2665^{5}	**Pharaoh's Joy (57)** (JWPayne) **4-8-13** RCochrane(2) (lw: hld up: effrt ½-wy: ev ch 1f out: nt qckn)..........hd	**3**	9/4^{1}	61	37
1294^{8}	**Sylvan Dancer (IRE) (61)** (CFWall) **3-8-9** SSanders(5) (sn outpcd: hdwy over 1f out: kpt on same pce ins fnl f)..........nk	**4**	7/2^{3}	60	32
2895^{10}	**Another Batchworth (62)** (EAWheeler) **5-8-8b**(5) ADaly(3) (led: clr ½-wy: wknd & hdd jst ins fnl f)..........6	**5**	6/1	41	17

(SP 112.6%) **5 Rn**

59.9 secs (1.00) CSF £13.98 TOTE £3.50: £1.40 £2.20 (£5.50) OWNER Mr Aiden Murphy (STRATFORD-UPON-AVON) BRED Jim O'Hara and Christian Healy

WEIGHT FOR AGE 3yo-4lb

2847* Fairy Prince (IRE) found the drop back to five no problem and he proved very willing under pressure. (100/30: 2/1-7/2)

2529 Barranak (IRE), who would have been 6lb better off with the winner in a handicap, was unable to dominate but he almost certainly ran right up to his best here. (7/2: 3/1-6/1)

2665 Pharaoh's Joy, who travelled sweetly off the pace, would have been meeting the winner on 5lb better terms in a handicap. (9/4)

783 Sylvan Dancer (IRE), unable to go the pace, moved up coming to the final furlong, looking as if she would take a serious hand but, under pressure, she looked in two minds about it. (7/2: op 6/1)

2197 Another Batchworth, who has speed to burn, put a poor effort last time behind her. Four or five lengths clear at halfway, she tied up badly entering the final furlong. She has not recovered the sort of form that won her three races last year. (6/1: op 4/1)

T/Plpt: £140.50 (67.89 Tckts). T/Qdpt: £18.70 (32.67 Tckts) WG

2015-THIRSK (L-H) (Good)

Friday July 25th

WEATHER: sunny periods WIND: mod half behind

3033 E.B.F. BBC RADIO YORK JULIA LEWIS MAIDEN STKS (2-Y.O F) (Class D)

2-05 (2-06) **6f** £3,715.50 (£1,119.00: £542.00: £253.50) Stalls: High GOING minus 0.33 sec per fur (GF)

			SP	RR	SF
	Half-Hitch (USA) (DRLoder) **2-8-11** WRyan(6) (leggy: unf: lw: hld up: hdwy ½-wy: led 1f out: r.o wl)..........—	**1**	10/1^{3}	86	30
2516^{2}	**Likely Story (IRE)** (JLDunlop) **2-8-11** KDarley(3) (mde most 5f: r.o)..........2	**2**	1/2^{1}	81	25
1997^{4}	**Delciana (IRE)** (PWHarris) **2-8-11** ACulhane(4) (chsd ldrs: rdn 2f out: sn outpcd)..........9	**3**	10/1^{3}	57	1
2176^{9}	**Chaska** (MJohnston) **2-8-11** JWeaver(5) (dwlt: outpcd & bhd tl sme late hdwy)..........2	**4**	33/1	51	—
1457^{5}	**Ratiyya (IRE)** (BHanbury) **2-8-11** JStack(7) (disp ld over 3f: sn rdn & btn)..........2½	**5**	7/2^{2}	45	—
	Maytong (JBerry) **2-8-6**(5) PRoberts(2) (leggy: unf: scope: sn chsng ldrs: outpcd ½-wy: n.d after)..........nk	**6**	20/1	44	—

(SP 114.8%) **6 Rn**

1m 12.3 (2.60) CSF £14.75 TOTE £6.30: £2.50 £1.20 (£3.10) OWNER Mr E. J. Loder (NEWMARKET) BRED Edmund J. Loder

Half-Hitch (USA) is nothing special to look at but she does use herself well and, given a fine ride here, won authoritatively and is obviously pretty decent. (10/1: op 5/2)

2516 Likely Story (IRE) was brought very late into the paddock and was on her toes but she did little wrong otherwise, only to meet one rival too good. She does deserve a change of luck. (1/2: 4/5-4/9)

1997 Delciana (IRE) again showed speed but these two useful opponents were far too good for her once the pace was really on. (10/1)

Chaska still gives the impression that she needs time to strengthen, and she is gradually improving. (33/1)
1457 Ratiyya (IRE), the pick of the bunch on looks, proved disappointing and may well have needed this after two months off. (7/2)
Maytong showed some ability before lack of experience told in the last two and a half furlongs. (20/1)

3034 TRANSPENNINE EXPRESS H'CAP (0-80) (3-Y.O+) (Class D)

2-35 (2-36) **6f** £3,761.00 (£1,133.00: £549.00: £257.00) Stalls: High GOING minus 0.33 sec per fur (GF)

Form	Horse	Dist	Pos	SP	RR	SF
2711^{2}	**Benzoe (IRE) (73)** (MrsJRRamsden) **7-9-7** DHarrison(15) (lw: hdwy to trck ldrs ½-wy: led stands' side wl over 1f out: r.o u.p to ld overall nr fin)	—	1	$9/4^{1}$	83	53
2934^{4}	**Grand Chapeau (IRE) (50)** (DNicholls) **5-7-12** DaleGibson(2) (racd far side: led & sn clr: eased & ct cl home)	nk	2	12/1	59	29
2844^{2}	**Camionneur (IRE) (48)** (TDEasterby) **4-7-10b** LCharnock(7) (lw: s.i.s: chsng ldrs ½-wy: effrt 2f out: kpt on)	3	3	9/1	49	19
2900*	**Tiler (IRE) (81)** (MJohnston) **5-10-1** 7x JWeaver(1) (s.i.s: chsd ldr far side: rdn ½-wy: nt qckn)	1¼	4	$8/1^{3}$	79	49
2759^{4}	**Antarctic Storm (59)** (RAFahey) **4-8-7** JCarroll(14) (lw: a chsng ldrs: effrt 2f out: nt qckn)	1½	5	$11/2^{2}$	53	23
2567^{8}	**Fame Again (66)** (MrsJRRamsden) **5-9-0** JFanning(12) (hld up: hdwy ½-wy: nt qckn appr fnl f)	1	6	10/1	57	27
2788^{14}	**Panther (IRE) (66)** (PDEvans) **7-8-7b**(7) AMcCarthy(16) (led stands' side over 4f: grad wknd)	2½	7	9/1	51	21
2711^{17}	**Foist (60)** (MWEasterby) **5-8-8** ACulhane(13) (prom over 4f: grad lost pl)	½	8	14/1	43	13
	Knave's Ash (USA) (84) (DNicholls) **6-10-4** AlexGreaves(11) (hdwy 2f out: nvr nr to chal)	½	9	50/1	66	36
1225^{18}	**Middle East (67)** (TDBarron) **4-8-10**(5) KimberleyHart(10) (nvr nr ldrs)	7	10	33/1	30	—
2711^{13}	**Bee Health Boy (66)** (MWEasterby) **4-9-0b** TLucas(9) (lw: in tch over 3f: grad wknd)	nk	11	10/1	28	—
2934^{12}	**Lennox Lewis (68)** (DNicholls) **5-8-9**(7) ANicholls(6) (sn outpcd & wl bhd: sme late hdwy)	1	12	50/1	28	—
2844^{10}	**For the Present (77)** (TDBarron) **7-9-11** KDarley(5) (in tch over 4f: wknd)	2½	13	14/1	30	—
2735^{8}	**Prominent (57)** (MrsVAAconley) **3-8-0**ow4 MDeering(4) (sn outpcd & n.d)	2½	14	33/1	3	—
2472^{4}	**The Lambton Worm (74)** (DenysSmith) **3-8-12**(5) PRoberts(3) (sn outpcd & bhd)	1¼	15	14/1	17	—
2738^{13}	**Dominelle (54)** (TDEasterby) **5-8-2** TWilliams(8) (s.i.s: hdwy ½-wy: sn wknd)	1½	16	25/1	—	—
				(SP 136.8%)	**16 Rn**	

1m 11.3 (1.60) CSF £31.53 CT £219.03 TOTE £3.00: £1.50 £2.50 £1.80 £1.90 (£45.20) Trio £137.20 OWNER Mr Tony Fawcett (THIRSK) BRED Mrs P. Grubb
LONG HANDICAP Prominent 7-9 Camionneur (IRE) 7-8
WEIGHT FOR AGE 3yo-5lb
STEWARDS' ENQUIRY Gibson susp: 3-12/8/97 (failure to ensure best possible placing).
OFFICIAL EXPLANATION Foist: the rider reported that his instructions were to try to dominate, but that he was unable to as the gelding was never moving fluently on the fast ground, and would be better suited by a softer surface.
2711 Benzoe (IRE), given a cracking ride, had to kick a long way from home and kept responding to pressure to beat his only serious rival, who was on the opposite side of the track. (9/4)
2934 Grand Chapeau (IRE) showed here that he is in tremendous form by leaving this field standing but, as he tired late on, his rider dropped his hands some three strides off the line and possibly could have thrown away a winning chance. The Stewards took the appropriate action and banned him for ten days. (12/1)
2844 Camionneur (IRE) is running well at the moment but is not quite doing enough when it matters. (9/1)
2900* Tiler (IRE) was the only one to race with the leader up the far rails and, after a tardy start, he was only struggling to get to grips and never succeeded. (8/1: 6/1-9/1)
2759 Antarctic Storm was well drawn but was again inclined to hang and was never doing enough in the last couple of furlongs. (11/2)
2567 Fame Again, carrying plenty of condition, ran well and will return to form in due course. (10/1)
Panther (IRE) showed his first real signs of form this year and is slipping down the handicap. (9/1: op 14/1)
1259 Foist put up an eye-catching run and the market seems the best guide to his chances. (14/1)
Knave's Ash (USA), having his first run for his new stable, showed enough to suggest that he is worth keeping in mind. (50/1)

3035 BBC RADIO YORK JONATHAN COWAP H'CAP (0-80) (3-Y.O+) (Class D)

3-05 (3-05) **1m 4f** £3,624.50 (£1,091.00: £528.00: £246.50) Stalls: Low GOING minus 0.33 sec per fur (GF)

Form	Horse	Dist	Pos	SP	RR	SF
2885*	**Bally Souza (IRE) (78)** (MJohnston) **3-9-0** 5x JWeaver(4) (lw: cl up: rdn 3f out: led 1f out: styd on strly)	—	1	$10/11^{1}$	87	42
2749^{6}	**Canton Venture (76)** (SPCWoods) **5-9-10** KDarley(3) (led: qcknd ent st: hdd 1f out: kpt on)	2½	2	$3/1^{2}$	82	49
2164^{10}	**In the Money (IRE) (51)** (RHollinshead) **8-7-13** LCharnock(2) (hld up: hdwy over 3f out: rdn & nvr able chal)	5	3	$5/1^{3}$	50	17
2889^{6}	**Ordained (59)** (EJAlston) **4-8-0**(7) PBradley(1) (lw: trckd ldrs: effrt 3f out: sn outpcd)	2	4	6/1	55	22
2763^{5}	**Exactly (IRE) (68)** (JLEyre) **4-9-2** TWilliams(5) (b.hind: cl up tl outpcd ent st: eased whn wl btn fnl 2f)	dist	5	25/1	—	—
				(SP 112.2%)	**5 Rn**	

2m 35.2 (4.50) CSF £3.66 TOTE £1.80: £1.10 £2.10 (£2.40) OWNER Miss Belinda Lee (MIDDLEHAM) BRED Dene Investments N V
WEIGHT FOR AGE 3yo-12lb
2885* Bally Souza (IRE) is really on the upgrade and, by the way she won this, she will stay further. (10/11)
2749 Canton Venture is high enough in the weights but he keeps running well and made the winner fight. (3/1)
2015 In the Money (IRE) can win on turf but he is better on the All-Weather. He likes things to go his way but this was still not a bad effort. (5/1)
2889 Ordained keeps running reasonably without winning, and her limitations were exposed some way from home here. (6/1)
2763 Exactly (IRE) had trouble with a tongue-strap in the preliminaries and that may well have been the reason for her dismal display. She looked distressed in the last two furlongs. (25/1)

3036 BBC RADIO YORK ADAM TOMLINSON CONDITIONS STKS (2-Y.O) (Class C)

3-40 (3-40) **7f** £5,209.50 (£1,677.00: £813.50) Stalls: Low GOING minus 0.33 sec per fur (GF)

Form	Horse	Dist	Pos	SP	RR	SF
2758^{2}	**Alconleigh** (MJohnston) **2-9-2** JWeaver(1) (lw: led: hung bdly rt fr ½-wy: rdn & r.o fnl 3f: bit slipped)	—	1	$11/10^{2}$	90	42
2558^{8}	**Belladera (IRE)** (NTinkler) **2-8-11** KDarley(3) (lw: trckd wnr: effrt ent st: r.o one pce)	2½	2	$5/6^{1}$	79	31
2905^{7}	**Two Williams** (MWEasterby) **2-9-2** TLucas(2) (hld up: hung rt appr st: hdwy 2f out: sn rdn & nt qckn)	1	3	$16/1^{3}$	82?	34
				(SP 108.0%)	**3 Rn**	

1m 27.5 (2.60) CSF £2.19 TOTE £1.80: (£1.10) OWNER Mr David Abell (MIDDLEHAM) BRED Maristow Farms Partnership
2758 Alconleigh would have won this by a street-length had he not persisted in hanging right, and his rider did particularly well. (11/10: 11/10-evens)
1174* Belladera (IRE) looked in tremendous condition but proved disappointing when ridden turning for home, and was never anything like good enough despite the winner's problems. (5/6: evens-4/5)
2905 Two Williams again gave problems by hanging right and he is probably better with more cut in the ground. (16/1)

3037 ARMY BENEVOLENT FUND MAIDEN STKS (3-Y.O) (Class D)

4-10 (4-11) **7f** £3,215.00 (£965.00: £465.00: £215.00) Stalls: Low GOING minus 0.33 sec per fur (GF)

Form	Horse	Btn	Pos	SP	RR	SF
2705^{3}	**Caribbean Star (74)** (MRStoute) **3-8-9v^{1}** WRyan(5) (mde all: qckmd clr over 2f out: jst hld on)	—	**1**	5/2^{1}	77	52
2547^{4}	**Barnburgh Boy (72)** (TDBarron) **3-9-0** KDarley(10) (trckd ldrs: effrt over 2f out: r.o towards fin)	nk	**2**	9/2	81	56
674^{10}	**Beyond Calculation (USA) (78)** (PWHarris) **3-9-0** ACulhane(2) (a chsng ldrs: effrt 3f out: nt pce to chal)	2½	**3**	100/30^{2}	76	51
1777^{3}	**Topton (IRE)** (IABalding) **3-8-11**$^{(3)}$ MartinDwyer(6) (bhd: hdwy over 2f out: r.o u.p: nrst fin)	nk	**4**	5/1	75	50
2654^{2}	**Villarica (IRE)** (PWChapple-Hyam) **3-8-6**$^{(3)}$ RHavlin(1) (lw: chsd ldrs: outpcd 3f out: no imp after)	5	**5**	4/1^{3}	59	34
	Damara (CWFairhurst) **3-8-9** LCharnock(4) (unf: bhd: hdwy on ins 3f out: nvr rchd ldrs)	2	**6**	100/1	54	29
2420^{14}	**General Hastie** (CWThornton) **3-9-0** TWilliams(3) (b.hind: nvr bttr than mid div)	7	**7**	66/1	43	18
2703^{8}	**Night Express (60)** (BHanbury) **3-9-0** JStack(7) (lw: hld up: shkn up 2f out: n.d)	½	**8**	50/1	42	17
2938^{6}	**Newtons Corner (IRE)** (DNicholls) **3-9-0** AlexGreaves(8) (chsd ldrs tl wknd fnl 2½f)	6	**9**	66/1	28	3
2420^{9}	**Perfect Bear** (MrsSJSmith) **3-9-0** OPears(9) (a bhd)	nk	**10**	100/1	27	2
2020^{11}	**Imperial Line (IRE)** (ABMulholland) **3-9-0** TLucas(11) (b: effrt ½-wy: sn btn)	1¾	**11**	100/1	23	—

(SP 114.4%) **11 Rn**

1m 26.1 (1.20) CSF £12.45 TOTE £4.40: £1.50 £1.40 £2.20 (£5.60) Trio £17.50 OWNER Mr W. H. Scott (NEWMARKET) BRED W. Scott and P. Scott

OFFICIAL EXPLANATION **Villarica (IRE): finished distressed.**

2705 Caribbean Star had the visor on for the first time and certainly knew what was required and, intelligently ridden, she stole just enough early in the straight to last home. (5/2)

2547 Barnburgh Boy, taking a step up in trip, got it well and ought to find a race before long. (9/2)

517 Beyond Calculation (USA) has not run for over three months and probably needed this and, in the circumstances, it was not a bad effort. (100/30)

1777 Topton (IRE), dropping back in trip, had a lot of running to do from the home turn and would have needed to be something special to have made it. (5/1)

2654 Villarica (IRE) looked particularly well but proved very disappointing and something may well have been wrong with her. (4/1: op 7/4)

Damara, making her racecourse debut, showed a little ability and some improvement is likely. (100/1)

3038 BBC RADIO YORK ELLY FIORENTINI (S) H'CAP (0-60) (3-Y.O) (Class G)

4-40 (4-42) **1m** £2,442.50 (£680.00: £327.50) Stalls: Low GOING minus 0.33 sec per fur (GF)

Form	Horse	Btn	Pos	SP	RR	SF
2368^{7}	**Polarize (53)** (TDBarron) **3-9-4b** KDarley(5) (lw: trckd ldr: led 3f out: sn clr: styd on)	—	**1**	7/2^{3}	63	30
2245^{4}	**Inkwell (34)** (AHide) **3-7-13** DaleGibson(8) (lw: in tch: hrd rdn over 2f out: styd on: nt pce to chal)	3	**2**	3/1^{2}	38	5
2522^{5}	**Mutahadeth (50)** (DShaw) **3-9-1** JFanning(2) (rr div: hdwy over 3f out: styd on: nvr able to chal)	hd	**3**	6/1	54	21
2715^{11}	**Alisadara (33)** (NBycroft) **3-7-12** LCharnock(6) (a.p: effrt 3f out: r.o one pce)	6	**4**	50/1	25	—
2913^{4}	**Bollero (IRE) (56)** (JBerry) **3-9-2**$^{(5)}$ TEDurcan(11) (lw: led tl hdd 3f out: sn rdn & btn)	1¼	**5**	11/4^{1}	45	12
2503^{10}	**Kalousion (32)** (TJEtherington) **3-7-11b** NCarlisle(7) (sme hdwy 3f out: nvr trbld ldrs)	3	**6**	33/1	15	—
2670^{7}	**Bali-Pet (42)** (JParkes) **3-8-7** TLucas(4) (bhd: hdwy u.p over 2f out: n.d)	½	**7**	20/1	24	—
2208^{7}	**Interaction (31)** (RCraggs) **3-7-3**$^{(7)}$ PBradley(10) (chsd ldrs tl wknd fnl 2½f)	2	**8**	25/1	9	—
2313^{18}	**Onemoretime (40)** (BWMurray) **3-8-5** MDeering(9) (nvr rchd ldrs)	1	**9**	16/1	16	—
2756^{4}	**Joyful Joy (31)** (BPJBaugh) **3-7-5**$^{(5)}$ IonaWands(12) (c wd st & sn rdn: n.d)	1	**10**	14/1	5	—
2603^{14}	**Nordico Melody (IRE) (54)** (MrsSJSmith) **3-9-5** OPears(14) (chsd ldrs 5f: sn lost pl)	6	**11**	20/1	16	—
1730^{12}	**Five-O-Fifty (50)** (JLEyre) **3-8-8**$^{(7)}$ SBuckley(3) (in tch to st)	2½	**12**	33/1	7	—
2745^{11}	**Fan of Vent-Axia (40)** (DJSCosgrove) **3-8-5** TWilliams(13) (s.i.s & drvn along after s: sn in tch: wknd over 3f out)	7	**13**	6/1	—	—

(SP 136.2%) **13 Rn**

1m 40.8 (4.30) CSF £14.14 CT £64.47 TOTE £5.70: £1.70 £1.40 £2.80 (£10.00) Trio £36.50 OWNER Mr J. Baggott (THIRSK) BRED Exors of the late D. Macrae

LONG HANDICAP Joyful Joy 7-7

No bid

STEWARDS' ENQUIRY Deering susp. 3-11/8/97 (excessive & improper use of whip).

2368 Polarize, dropped in class, found this right up his street and had it won a long way out. (7/2)

2245 Inkwell, who looks particularly well, was in the right company and was certainly given an aggressive ride. He kept struggling on but was never quite good enough. (3/1)

2522 Mutahadeth, very much on his toes in the paddock, showed here that he has ability when things go his way. (6/1)

1451 Alisadara ran her best race for a while but looked well short of pace in the last three furlongs. (50/1)

2913 Bollero (IRE) was certainly not at his best here and gave up once passed early in the straight. (11/4: 2/1-3/1)

3039 BBC RADIO YORK APPRENTICE H'CAP (0-70) (3-Y.O+) (Class E)

5-15 (5-16) **1m** £2,796.50 (£857.00: £426.00: £210.50) Stalls: Low GOING minus 0.33 sec per fur (GF)

Form	Horse	Btn	Pos	SP	RR	SF
2937^{3}	**Roseate Lodge (37)** (SEKettlewell) **11-7-7**$^{(3)}$ JennyBenson(4) (lw: hld up & bhd: gd hdwy on ins ent st: led over 1f out: r.o: eased towards fin)	—	**1**	7/1^{2}	46	16
2848*	**Eurobox Boy (66)** (APJarvis) **4-9-8**$^{(3)}$ ^{5x} CCarver(7) (chsd ldrs: outpcd & nt clr run over 2f out: swtchd & r.o: nrst fin)	¾	**2**	11/2^{1}	74	44
2888^{2}	**Fancy A Fortune (IRE) (60)** (DNicholls) **3-8-6**$^{(5)}$ ANicholls(11) (led 6f: kpt on u.p)	nk	**3**	11/2^{1}	67	29
2922^{5}	**Karinska (56)** (MCChapman) **7-9-1** SCarson(1) (hld up: hdwy & prom ent st: sn rdn: styd on: nt pce to chal)	1½	**4**	9/1	60	30
2651^{3}	**Ballard Lady (IRE) (40)** (JSWainwright) **5-7-13** RBrisland(5) (hld up: wnt prom ent st: led 2f out tl over 1f out: wknd)	1½	**5**	10/1	41	11
2937^{7}	**Chinour (IRE) (50)** (EJAlston) **9-8-9** NPollard(8) (s.i.s: c wd & effrt 3f out: nvr nrr)	¾	**6**	8/1^{3}	49	19
1450^{11}	**Gladys Althorpe (IRE) (68)** (JLEyre) **4-9-10**$^{(3)}$ SBuckley(12) (s.i.s: styd on fnl 3f: no imp)	½	**7**	10/1	66	36
2671^{5}	**Naughty Pistol (USA) (49)** (PDEvans) **5-8-5b**$^{(3)}$ AMcCarthy(9) (effrt ent st: c wd & n.d)	½	**8**	14/1	46	16
2880^{3}	**Prime Partner (37)** (TDEasterby) **4-7-10** DarrenWilliams(6) (w ldrs tl wknd fnl 2f)	4	**9**	10/1	26	—
2828^{2}	**Spanish Verdict (48)** (DenysSmith) **10-8-7** PBradley(13) (lw: chsd ldrs tl rdn & wknd fnl 3f)	7	**10**	7/1^{2}	23	—
2368^{9}	**Efipetite (37)** (NBycroft) **4-7-5b**$^{(5)}$ PMQuinn(2) (swtg: prom 4f: sn lost pl)	½	**11**	100/1	11	—

				SP	RR	SF
2884[2]	**Queens Consul (IRE) (69)** (BSRothwell) **7-10-0** JMcAuley(10) (b: s.i.s: sn pushed along & in tch: carried wd st: wknd fnl 2½f)	1½	**12**	11/2[1]	40	10

(SP 127.2%) **12 Rn**

1m 40.2 (3.70) CSF £44.45 CT £219.06 TOTE £11.80: £2.70 £2.90 £2.10 (£35.40) Trio £154.60 OWNER Mr Jon Firth (MIDDLEHAM) BRED Barrettstown Stud Farms Ltd

LONG HANDICAP Roseate Lodge 7-8 Efipetite 6-7

WEIGHT FOR AGE 3yo-8lb

2937 Roseate Lodge had the run of the race. Well ridden, he probably found himself in front too soon but was still always in command. (7/1)

2848* Eurobox Boy, despite his rise in the weights, is still improving and, given an enthusiastic ride, finished strongly after finding trouble in running. (11/2)

2888 Fancy A Fortune (IRE) forced the pace and kept struggling on, suggesting that further might well help. (11/2)

2922 Karinska is in good form at the moment and this was another fair effort. (9/1)

2651 Ballard Lady (IRE) got a dream run up the inner and had her chances, until running out of fuel in the closing stages. (10/1)

2937 Chinour (IRE) runs when in the mood and it was never soon enough here. (8/1)

Gladys Althorpe (IRE) was always struggling to overcome a poor start. (10/1: op 6/1)

2884 Queens Consul (IRE) never fired on this occasion and something was probably wrong. (11/2)

T/Plpt: £22.40 (481.85 Tckts). T/Qdpt: £10.30 (36.91 Tckts) AA

2669-WOLVERHAMPTON (L-H) (Standard)

Friday July 25th

WEATHER: overcast WIND: slt half across

3040 N.M.B. HELLER H'CAP (0-65) (3-Y.O) (Class F)

1-55 (1-55) **5f (Fibresand)** £2,277.00 (£627.00: £297.00) Stalls: Low GOING minus 0.23 sec per fur (FST)

				SP	RR	SF
2510[10]	**Hajat (43)** (JBerry) **3-7-13**(3) PFessey(7) (led after 2f: hrd rdn over 1f out: jst hld on)	—	**1**	3/1[3]	48	16
2605[6]	**Master Foley (59)** (NPLittmoden) **3-8-11**(7) KPierrepont(4) (a.p: hrd rdn over 1f out: sustained chal fnl f: jst failed)	hd	**2**	5/2[1]	64	32
1479[7]	**Midnight Times (46)** (DCO'Brien) **3-8-2**(3) RFfrench(1) (lw: a.p: disp ld over 1f out: rdn & unable qckn fnl f)	1¼	**3**	25/1	47	15
2704[13]	**Badrinath (IRE) (39)** (HJCollingridge) **3-7-7**(5)ow2 RMullen(5) (lw: chsd ldrs: rdn wl over 1f out: kpt on ins fnl f)	hd	**4**	5/1	39	5
2671[7]	**Caspian Morn (48)** (WGMTurner) **3-8-2**(5) DSweeney(6) (slt ld 2f: rdn over 1f out: r.o one pce)	2	**5**	11/4[2]	42	10
2603[10]	**Blue Cheese (37)** (MrsNMacauley) **3-7-10** NAdams(2) (rdn along ½-wy: a outpcd)	¾	**6**	14/1	29	—
2206[5]	**Royal Cascade (IRE) (62)** (BAMcMahon) **3-9-7** LNewton(3) (outpcd: a bhd: t.o)	6	**7**	11/2	34	2

(SP 122.8%) **7 Rn**

62.0 secs (3.10) CSF £11.03 TOTE £3.40: £2.00 £2.40 (£5.10) OWNER Mrs David Brown (COCKERHAM) BRED Shadwell Estate Company Limited

LONG HANDICAP Blue Cheese 7-7 Badrinath (IRE) 7-1

1843 Hajat, having her first run since changing stables, appreciated the step down to the minimum trip. Showing ahead before halfway, she won with nothing to spare but held on determinedly close home. (3/1)

2605 Master Foley could never poke his head in front on this return to five furlongs, but he was doing all his best work late on and was far from disgraced. (5/2)

Midnight Times with the action from the start, remained on the inside and may have led briefly on the approach to the final furlong, but the principals proved just too sharp in the sprint to the line. (25/1)

Badrinath (IRE), taking a big step down in distance, was always struggling with the pace, but he was into his stride in the closing stages and is capable of better. (5/1)

1644 Caspian Morn showed plenty of speed but she was in trouble on straightening up and gradually faded. (11/4)

3041 LOMBARD NATWEST CLAIMING STKS (3-Y.O+) (Class F)

2-25 (2-25) **1m 100y (Fibresand)** £2,277.00 (£627.00: £297.00) Stalls: Low GOING minus 0.23 sec per fur (FST)

				SP	RR	SF
2671[9]	**Colins Choice (57)** (JLSpearing) **3-7-11**(3) PFessey(4) (hld up: hdwy over 2f out: str run to ld nr fin)	—	**1**	16/1	57	30
2785[15]	**Failed To Hit (50)** (NPLittmoden) **4-9-3b** SWhitworth(9) (lw: swtg: mde most: hrd drvn fnl f: ct cl home)	nk	**2**	10/1	65	46
2722[5]	**The Executor (64)** (RJO'Sullivan) **7-8-13** JQuinn(11) (hld up: hdwy ½-wy: styng on whn nt clr run ins fnl f: r.o towards fin)	hd	**3**	7/2[1]	61	42
2569[3]	**Broughton's Pride (IRE) (51)** (JLEyre) **6-8-5**(7) RWinston(7) (lw: trckd ldrs: ev ch whn squeezed for room 200y out: nt rcvr)	2½	**4**	4/1[2]	56	37
*2670**	**Madam Lucy (48)** (PHowling) **3-7-10** FNorton(3) (a chsng ldrs: rdn over 1f out: r.o one pce)	s.h	**5**	4/1[2]	47	20
2646[11]	**Moneghetti (35)** (JLHarris) **6-8-10**(3) RFfrench(8) (wl bhd & outpcd tl sme late hdwy)	6	**6**	14/1	45	26
2603[5]	**Pc's Cruiser (IRE) (38)** (NPLittmoden) **5-8-9v** TGMcLaughlin(6) (hld up: hdwy 5f out: shkn up over 2f out: one pce)	1¼	**7**	6/1[3]	39	20
2603[8]	**Sakharov (46)** (BPalling) **8-8-8**(5) DSweeney(5) (b: prom: rdn & wknd over 2f out)	1¼	**8**	10/1	40	21
2785[13]	**Sarum (27)** (JELong) **11-8-9** LeesaLong(2) (b: w ldr to ½-wy: sn wknd: t.o)	12	**9**	40/1	14	—
	Mrs Pollock (JLHarris) **4-8-8** SDrowne(10) (bkwd: a bhd & outpcd: t.o)	25	**10**	25/1	—	—
	Miss Mighty (JHPeacock) **4-8-4** MFenton(1) (bit bkwd: a bhd: t.o)	8	**11**	66/1	—	—

(SP 115.0%) **11 Rn**

1m 48.8 (3.80) CSF £146.22 TOTE £23.70: £3.10 £3.40 £1.80 (£82.50) Trio £136.90; £11.57 to Ascot 26/7/97 OWNER Mr Colin Ross (ALCESTER) BRED Roldvale Ltd

WEIGHT FOR AGE 3yo-8lb

Madam Lucy clmd JSpearing £3,000

Colins Choice had it all to do turning in, but she delivered a sustained late challenge to gain command nearing the line. (16/1)

2302 Failed To Hit adopted front-running tactics and always appeared to have the situation under control, but the concession of so much weight swayed the scales against him in the dying strides. (10/1: op 5/1)

2722 The Executor took closer order down the back straight and was poised to challenge when short of room just inside the final furlong. Rallying gamely once in the clear, he only just missed out and did look a shade unlucky. (7/2)

2569 Broughton's Pride (IRE) does lack a turn of finishing speed and, though she was tightened up entering the last furlong, may not have been able to mount a challenge even with a clear run. (4/1)

2670* Madam Lucy did not remain in her present yard for long for she was claimed for £1,000 more than she cost when changing hands earlier in the month. (4/1)
2488 Moneghetti, taken off his legs in the early stages, stayed on willingly inside the distance and is capable of better. (14/1)

3042 ROYAL BANK INVOICE FINANCE NURSERY H'CAP (2-Y.O) (Class E)

2-55 (2-56) **6f (Fibresand)** £3,070.25 (£917.00: £438.50: £199.25) Stalls: Low GOING minus 0.23 sec per fur (FST)

				SP	RR	SF
2565^{9}	**Carambo** (JLEyre) **2-9-4** MGallagher(2) (lw: chsd ldrs: drvn along over 2f out: bmpd & led appr fnl f: sn clr)	—	1	7/1	77	27
1872^{8}	**Kennet** (PDCundell) **2-9-7** JQuinn(8) (hld up & bhd: r.o appr fnl f: no ch w wnr)	7	2	10/1	61	11
2571^{3}	**American Cousin** (BJMeehan) **2-9-4** MTebbutt(6) (trckd ldrs: rdn ½-wy: kpt on ins fnl f)	hd	3	$3/1^{2}$	58	8
2222^{3}	**Frisky Lady** (TDEasterby) **2-8-6**(7) RWinston(5) (prom: rdn over 1f out: sn outpcd)	¾	4	9/1	51	1
2658^{5}	**Risky Whisky** (JBerry) **2-8-11b**(3) PFessey(4) (led after 2f: rdn & edgd rt appr fnl f: sn hdd & btn)	¾	5	$4/1^{3}$	50	—
2604^{4}	**Black Jet** (NPLittmoden) **2-8-5**(5) DSweeney(7) (lw: in tch to ½-wy: sn pushed along & outpcd)	1¼	6	12/1	43	—
2681^{8}	**Fast Franc (IRE)** (SCWilliams) **2-9-0** SDrowne(3) (led 2f: hrd drvn 2f out: grad wknd)	1¼	7	$11/4^{1}$	43	—
2786^{8}	**Whacker-Do (IRE)** (RHollinshead) **2-9-4** FLynch(1) (dwlt: hdwy 3f out: rdn 2f out: sn wknd)	1	8	14/1	45	—
				(SP 117.6%)	**8 Rn**	

1m 15.2 (4.00) CSF £68.50 CT £235.14 TOTE £5.20: £1.50 £2.30 £1.60 (£93.80) OWNER C H & D W Stephenson Ltd (HAMBLETON) BRED C. Stephenson
1990 Carambo turned the race into a procession when she took the measure of the leader approaching the final furlong, and she could be coming to herself fast now. (7/1)
836 Kennet was content to bide his time in the rear until being brought wide and staying on strongly to gain the runner-up prize well inside the last furlong. (10/1: op 6/1)
2571 American Cousin, who is a very poor mover, was having his first outing on the All-Weather. Never far away but hard at work at halfway, he did stay on but had to admit the winner in a class of her own. (3/1)
2222 Frisky Lady tried her hardest to keep tabs on the leaders but she was being tapped for toe on straightening up. (9/1: op 6/1)
2658 Risky Whisky helped force the pace, but he was under pressure when edging right into the challenging winner approaching the final furlong, and his measure was soon taken. (4/1)
2383* Fast Franc (IRE), under pressure turning into the straight, was unable to respond, and his first run on Fibresand proved a big disappointment. (11/4)
2361 Whacker-Do (IRE) (14/1: 10/1-16/1)

3043 BUSINESS SEATING AND DESKING MEDIAN AUCTION MAIDEN STKS (3-Y.O) (Class F)

3-25 (3-25) **6f (Fibresand)** £2,277.00 (£627.00: £297.00) Stalls: Low GOING minus 0.23 sec per fur (FST)

				SP	RR	SF
2510^{8}	**Mike's Double (IRE) (60)** (MissGayKelleway) **3-8-11**(3) RFfrench(3) (a.p: rdn over 1f out: led & qcknd fnl 100y)	—	1	$5/4^{2}$	68	33
	Nobalino (MrsNMacauley) **3-9-0** SDrowne(4) (w'like: bit bkwd: a.p: led over 1f out: edgd rt: hdd & no ex ins fnl f)	1¼	2	$8/1^{3}$	65	30
2669^{2}	**Castle Ashby Jack (60)** (PHowling) **3-9-0b** FNorton(6) (b.hind: led tl hdd over 1f out: sn rdn & btn)	2½	3	$4/5^{1}$	58	23
2669^{6}	**Nesbet (41)** (BRCambidge) **3-9-0** NAdams(7) (s.i.s: rdn along over 2f out: nvr nr to chal)	9	4	25/1	34	—
2780^{8}	**Moor Hall Princess (34)** (NMBabbage) **3-8-9** JQuinn(2) (outpcd: drvn along ½-wy: no imp)	3½	5	20/1	20	—
1587^{17}	**Beckenham Insight** (DCO'Brien) **3-8-9v**[1] GBardwell(1) (bit bkwd: s.s: sn rdn along: a outpcd)	2	6	40/1	14	—
	Dyce (JBalding) **3-8-9** JEdmunds(5) (wl grwn: bkwd: s.s: a outpcd & bhd)	2½	7	33/1	8	—
				(SP 125.1%)	**7 Rn**	

1m 14.5 (3.30) CSF £11.19 TOTE £2.60: £1.00 £5.30 (£15.70) OWNER The Money Men (WHITCOMBE) BRED John Kent
2231 Mike's Double (IRE), ridden with plenty of confidence, burst through to lead a hundred yards out and won going away. There could be more success to follow. (5/4)
Nobalino did not look tuned up enough on this racecourse debut, but he ran a promising race in defeat and he does look to have a promising future. (8/1)
2669 Castle Ashby Jack is paying his way in place money and he looked to have found the ideal opportunity to open his account here. However, he was found wanting when the tempo quickened below the distance. (4/5: evens-11/10)

3044 THORPE VERNON AND CO. (ACCOUNTING) H'CAP (0-70) (3-Y.O) (Class E)

4-00 (4-01) **1m 1f 79y (Fibresand)** £3,070.25 (£917.00: £438.50: £199.25) Stalls: Low GOING minus 0.23 sec per fur (FST)

				SP	RR	SF
2671^{6}	**Cherokee Flight (55)** (SMellor) **3-8-6** JQuinn(4) (lw: chsd ldrs: led over 3f out: styd on strly)	—	1	25/1	66	37
1999^{6}	**Sparky (68)** (MWEasterby) **3-9-2b**(3) GParkin(1) (trckd ldrs: effrt ent st: r.o wl towards fin)	1	2	$8/1^{3}$	77	48
2878^{3}	**Bon Guest (IRE) (58)** (JGMO'Shea) **3-8-2**(7) RWinston(9) (lw: hld up: hdwy 4f out: rdn over 1f out: one pce)	2½	3	9/1	63	34
2554^{20}	**Ron's Round (45)** (CADwyer) **3-7-10** NVarley(3) (w ldrs tl rdn & outpcd wl over 1f out)	7	4	20/1	38	9
2246^{15}	**Bold Saint (IRE) (45)** (PWHarris) **3-7-10b** FNorton(5) (mid div: hdwy 5f out: rdn over 2f out: sn btn)	2	5	20/1	35	6
*2912**	**Mythical (66)** (SirMarkPrescott) **3-9-3** 5x CNutter(11) (hld up mid div: effrt 3f out: sn rdn: r.o one pce)	s.h	6	$3/1^{2}$	56	27
2392*	**Impala (60)** (WGMTurner) **3-8-6**(5) DSweeney(8) (mde most tl over 3f out: sn drvn along & wknd)	3½	7	14/1	44	15
2605^{2}	**Zalotto (IRE) (59)** (TJEtherington) **3-8-10b** MGallagher(2) (lw: nvr plcd to chal)	¾	8	14/1	41	12
2733^{5}	**Tipperary Sunset (IRE) (45)** (JJQuinn) **3-7-10** JLowe(12) (a in rr)	1¾	9	25/1	24	—
2052^{7}	**Weet And See (67)** (RHollinshead) **3-9-1**(3) DGriffiths(10) (a in rr: t.o)	14	10	20/1	22	—
2695^{11}	**Triple Term (70)** (JGSmyth-Osbourne) **3-9-7** SWhitworth(7) (chsd ldrs tl rdn & wknd over 3f out: t.o)	2	11	25/1	22	—
2555^{8}	**She's A Cracker (56)** (MrsNMacauley) **3-8-7** SDrowne(6) (a bhd: t.o fnl 4f)	dist	12	9/1	—	—
2671^{3}	**Fife Major (USA) (63)** (BWHills) **3-8-11**(3) RFfrench(13) (lw: stumbled & uns rdr s)		U	$9/4^{1}$	—	—
				(SP 126.0%)	**13 Rn**	

2m 0.1 (4.10) CSF £187.32 CT £1,783.35 TOTE £35.80: £2.60 £3.40 £2.70 (£73.00) Trio £71.80 OWNER Silver Knight Exhibitions Ltd (SWINDON) BRED Highclere Stud Ltd
LONG HANDICAP Bold Saint (IRE) 7-7
2671 Cherokee Flight set sail for home turning out the back straight and gained enough leeway to remain in control to the line. (25/1)
1999 Sparky is consistent and he is not short on stamina, so it is possible more forceful tactics could suit his way of running. (8/1)
2878 Bon Guest (IRE) turned in a pleasing performance and connections should be contented with his continued commitment. (9/1)
Ron's Round did not quite see the trip out but this was one of his better efforts and he would seem to be getting it together. (20/1)
1796 Bold Saint (IRE) could never really get himself into contention, but this was probably not such a bad effort and he should not be written off yet. (20/1)
2912* Mythical obviously did not appreciate running twice in five days and she definitely did not fire this time. (3/1)

2671 Fife Major (USA), well supported in the ring, had the misfortune to lose his footing and unseating his jockey leaving the stalls. (9/4)

3045 HAYS ACCOUNTANCY PERSONNEL (S) STKS (2-Y.O F) (Class G)

4-35 (4-35) **7f (Fibresand)** £1,984.50 (£547.00: £259.50) Stalls: High GOING minus 0.23 sec per fur (FST)

				SP	RR	SF
2840[11]	**Operatic** (MBell) **2-8-8** MFenton(8) (s.s: hdwy 2f out: r.o strly to ld wl ins fnl f)	—	**1**	4/1 2	54	3
2493[5]	**Katie's Cracker** (MRChannon) **2-8-8** RPainter(4) (trckd ldrs: hdwy to ld over 1f out: hdd & no ex wl ins fnl f)	¾	**2**	5/1 3	52	1
2935[6]	**Last Lap** (TDEasterby) **2-8-1b**[1](7) RWinston(6) (hld up in tch: effrt over 2f out: wknd ins fnl f)	3½	**3**	10/1	44	—
2066[8]	**Gorgeous** (NPLittmoden) **2-8-8** TGMcLaughlin(7) (lw: chsd ldr: led over 2f out tl over 1f out: sn outpcd)	5	**4**	6/1	33	—
2664[4]	**Tender Doll (IRE)** (CADwyer) **2-8-8** NVarley(3) (prom tl rdn & wknd over 2f out)	5	**5**	5/1 3	21	—
2304[2]	**Silent Pride (IRE)** (MDIUsher) **2-8-8** JMarshall(1) (swtg: led over 4f: sn rdn & wknd)	1	**6**	10/1	19	—
1432[5]	**Keen Lady** (NPLittmoden) **2-8-8** SWhitworth(2) (bit bkwd: unruly stalls: s.i.s: a bhd: t.o)	7	**7**	14/1	3	—
2823[3]	**Slew Magic (IRE)** (WGMTurner) **2-8-3**(5) DSweeney(5) (bit bkwd: chsd ldrs over 4f: sn lost tch: t.o)	nk	**8**	9/4 1	3	—
				(SP 123.2%)	**8 Rn**	

1m 30.9 (6.20) CSF £24.07 TOTE £4.10: £1.40 £1.70 £2.40 (£21.20) OWNER Cheveley Park Stud (NEWMARKET) BRED Cheveley Park Stud Ltd

Bt in 4,200gns

Operatic again lost ground as the stalls opened, but in this lower grade she had the ability to recover and, in the end, win going away. (4/1: op 5/2)

2493 Katie's Cracker, ridden to forge ahead below the distance, ran her race out to the finish but the winner had the legs of her in the run to the line (5/1)

2935 Last Lap wore blinkers for the first time but they appeared to have little effect and she was never a serious threat. (10/1: 5/1-12/1)

Gorgeous looked to have plenty in hand taking over on the home turn, but she is bred to be a sprinter and lack of stamina was a problem inside the distance. (6/1)

2664 Tender Doll (IRE) has been doing all her best work in the closing stages in her two previous outings over six furlongs, but she sat much closer to the pace this time and had had enough before reaching the straight. (5/1)

2304 Silent Pride (IRE), a very poor mover in her slower paces, weakened rather quickly after leading for over half a mile. (10/1: op 6/1)

2823 Slew Magic (IRE), little bigger than a pony, could have found this race coming far too soon but, then again, perhaps the trip was beyond her at this early stage of her career. (9/4)

3046 CHAROLAIS AMATEUR H'CAP (0-60) (3-Y.O+) (Class G)

5-10 (5-10) **2m 46y (Fibresand)** £1,984.50 (£547.00: £259.50) Stalls: Low GOING minus 0.23 sec per fur (FST)

				SP	RR	SF
	Lake Dominion (38) (KCComerford) **8-9-6**(7)ow1 MrJOwen(7) (bit bkwd: trckd ldrs: led 1f out: hld on wl cl home)	—	**1**	50/1	42	24
2469[3]	**Stalled (IRE) (48)** (PTWalwyn) **7-10-5**(4) MarchionessBlandford(1) (b: chsd ldr: led over 1f out: sn hdd: kpt on u.p nr fin)	½	**2**	9/4 1	52	35
2737*	**Arian Spirit (IRE) (47)** (JLEyre) **6-10-8** 4x MissDianaJones(9) (lw: hld up in tch: hdwy 3f out: rdn over 1f out: one pce)	1¼	**3**	5/1 2	49	32
2737[6]	**Black Ice Boy (IRE) (42)** (RBastiman) **6-9-10b**(7) MissRBastiman(12) (swtg: led & sn clr: wknd & hdd 1f out)	2½	**4**	5/1 2	42	25
2048[2]	**Castle Secret (58)** (DBurchell) **11-10-12**(7) MrGRichards(6) (bhd tl styd on fnl 2f)	½	**5**	7/1 3	57	40
	Mizyan (IRE) (60) (JEBanks) **9-11-0**(7) MrJGTownson(8) (bkwd: hdwy after 5f: rdn & wknd wl over 1f out)	¾	**6**	14/1	59	42
2511[3]	**Spiral Flyer (IRE) (29)** (MDIUsher) **4-9-0**(4) MrsAUsher(3) (hdwy fnl 3f: nvr nrr)	1¼	**7**	8/1	26	9
2696[9]	**Stonecutter (57)** (PJMakin) **4-10-11**(7) MissSDeburiatte(10) (a in rr: t.o)	11	**8**	16/1	44	27
2607[6]	**Swordking (IRE) (31)** (JLHarris) **8-9-2v**(4) MrVLukaniuk(2) (bit bkwd: prom: rdn 5f out: wknd over 2f out: t.o)	¾	**9**	20/1	17	—
	Provence (52) (AWCarroll) **10-10-9v**(4) MrOMcPhail(4) (b: prom to ½-wy: sn wknd: t.o)	15	**10**	25/1	23	6
2350[7]	**Dallai (IRE) (33)** (GPKelly) **6-9-1**(7)ow8 MissSBrotherton(5) (b.nr hind: chsd ldrs 10f: sn wknd: t.o)	12	**11**	66/1	—	—
2146[13]	**Sussex Gorse (34)** (JELong) **6-9-2**(7)ow9 MrTWaters(11) (prom early: sn lost tch: t.o)	dist	**12**	100/1	—	—
				(SP 113.3%)	**12 Rn**	

3m 41.5 (14.50) CSF £137.75 CT £631.06 TOTE £91.00: £14.60 £1.90 £2.00 (£148.50) Trio £216.90; £6.11 to Ascot 26/7/97 OWNER Mrs Betty Bate and Mr Mark Campbell (AYLESBURY) BRED Grange Farm (Barnby Moor) Ltd

LONG HANDICAP Sussex Gorse 8-1

IN-FOCUS: **This race saw the first winner for both rider James Owen and trainer Ken Comerford, an ex-jump jockey.**

Lake Dominion, a winner over hurdles and fences, completed the set with his first success on the Flat. Out of action for six hundred and twenty three days and looking to be carrying condition, he proved the stronger in a spirited duel to the post to supply his rider with his first success on his very first ride. (50/1)

2469 Stalled (IRE) probably better over a slightly shorter trip, worked hard to nose ahead briefly before the winner pounced, and it is to his credit that he was able to fight back nearing the line. (9/4: op 4/1)

2737* Arian Spirit (IRE) did everything right and delivered her challenge entering the final furlong, but she is not quite so effective on this surface and a turn of finishing speed was missing when it was most needed. (5/1: op 3/1)

2737 Black Ice Boy (IRE), at his best when able to dictate, did just that here, but he had set quite a telling gallop and was out on his feet when passed approaching the final furlong. (5/1: op 3/1)

2048 Castle Secret, very much on his toes in the preliminaries, was given far too much to do and was only into his stride when it was all but over. (7/1: 5/1-8/1)

Mizyan (IRE) has not won beyond fourteen furlongs on the Flat, but he ran well here after being of the track since the autumn, and he is no back number yet. (14/1)

T/Plpt: £522.90 (15.33 Tckts). T/Qdpt: £46.40 (12.4 Tckts) IM

3009-ASCOT (R-H) (Soft)

Saturday July 26th

WEATHER: heavy early rain becoming overcast and humid WIND: almost nil

3047 E.B.F. GRANVILLE MAIDEN STKS (UNRACED 2-Y.O C & G) (Class D)

2-00 (2-07) **6f** £6,807.50 (£2,060.00: £1,005.00: £477.50) Stalls: Low GOING: 0.26 sec per fur (G)

			SP	RR	SF
La-Faah (IRE) (BWHills) **2-8-11** RHills(5) (leggy: hld up: led 1f out: rdn out)	—	**1**	10/1	80 t	37
Social Charter (USA) (PWChapple-Hyam) **2-8-11** JReid(6) (scope: a.p: rdn 2f out: ev ch ins fnl f: r.o)	½	**2**	5/2 1	79 t	36
Mutawwaj (IRE) (SbinSuroor) **2-8-11** LDettori(3) (str: scope: led over 4f: ev ch ins fnl f: unable qckn)	1	**3**	7/2 2	76 t	33

Deep Space (IRE) (EALDunlop) **2-8-11** MHills(1) (w'like: scope: hld up: led over 1f out: sn hdd: one pce)	hd	4	15/2	76 t	33
Dower House (WJarvis) **2-8-11** PatEddery(8) (w'like: scope: hld up: jumped path over 3f out: rdn 2f out: wknd over 1f out)	5	5	$4/1^{3}$	62 t	19
Najjar (USA) (PTWalwyn) **2-8-11** MJKinane(4) (leggy: scope: bit bkwd: prom over 3f)	1	6	8/1	60 t	17
Paddy McGoon (USA) (DRCElsworth) **2-8-11** RCochrane(7) (w'like: scope: bit bkwd: bhd fnl 3f)	s.h	7	20/1	60 t	17
Imshishway (IRE) (BJMeehan) **2-8-11** MTebbutt(2) (w'like: scope: bhd fnl 3f)	7	8	25/1	41 t	—

(SP 111.4%) **8 Rn**

1m 19.9 (5.90) CSF £30.46 TOTE £12.20: £2.80 £1.60 £1.30 (£15.80) OWNER Mr Hamdan Al Maktoum (LAMBOURN) BRED Shadwell Estate Company Limited

IN-FOCUS: **With three-quarters of an inch of rain falling in the space of an hour and a half before racing, the ground dramatically changed and officials were so concerned that they had to call an inspection. With the rain still falling heavily, the two-year-olds were very late into the paddock and all rugged-up, making description of the newcomers very difficult indeed.**

La-Faah (IRE), a tall colt, certainly knew what was required of him, being rousted along to lead a furlong from home and keeping on too well for his very persistent rivals. (10/1: 6/1-12/1)

Social Charter (USA), a speedy sort, was the subject of encouraging home reports and was a leading player throughout. Still battling for the advantage inside the final furlong, he gave his all but was just unable to get the better of the winner. On a sounder surface he looks a ready-made winner. (5/2: op 5/4)

Mutawwaj (IRE), an attractive colt with plenty of strength and scope about him, took the field along until collared below the distance. Refusing to lie down, he was still in with every chance inside the final furlong, before tapped for toe. Dettori appeared disappointed afterwards, revealing that the colt did not like the ground and appeared lazy. On a sounder surface, he should have no problems winning. (7/2)

Deep Space (IRE), a medium-sized colt, gained a slender advantage below the distance, but he was soon headed and tapped for toe. (15/2)

Dower House, whose dam is a half-sister to Grand Lodge, who won this race in 1993, chased the leaders until coming to the end of his tether below the distance. (4/1)

Najjar (USA), a tall colt, looked as though the run would do him good and so it proved, as he dropped away approaching the final quarter-mile.(8/1)

3048 SHAH JAHAN DIAMOND LADIES' CONDITIONS STKS (3-Y.O+) (Class C)

2-35 (2-36) **1m (round)** £7,132.50 (£2,160.00: £1,055.00: £502.50) Stalls: High GOING: 0.26 sec per fur (G)

				SP	RR	SF
2868^{4}	**Blessed Spirit (78)** (CFWall) **4-9-5**(3) MissHWebster(5) (dwlt: hdwy 4f out: led over 1f out: r.o wl)	—	1	$10/1^{3}$	75	39
940^{8}	**Cape Cross (IRE) (110)** (JHMGosden) **3-9-5** MrsLPearce(6) (b.hind: w ldr: led over 5f out tl over 3f out: led over 2f out tl over 1f out: ev ch ins fnl f: r.o)	nk	2	$8/15^{1}$	79	35
2654*	**Yabint El Sultan (74)** (BAMcMahon) **3-9-6** MrsSBosley(4) (a.p: rdn over 2f out: unable qckn)	2	3	14/1	76	32
$2642a^{10}$	**Yorkshire (IRE) (102)** (PFICole) **3-9-5** MissSHiggins(9) (led over 2f: led over 3f out tl over 2f out: wknd over 1f out)	2½	4	$3/1^{2}$	70	26
2430^{2}	**Squared Away (47)** (JWPayne) **5-9-13b** MissCLake(3) (lw: dwlt: wl bhd 6f: nvr nrr)	6	5	66/1	58	22
2430^{6}	**Marjaana (IRE) (70)** (PTWalwyn) **4-9-8** MissSSamworth(1) (lw: no hdwy fnl 3f)	s.h	6	14/1	53	17
2492^{11}	**Cold Lazarus (58)** (RTPhillips) **3-9-2**(3) MissElaineMills(7) (swtg: a wl bhd: t.o)	28	7	100/1	2	—
2848^{4}	**Royal Acclaim (26)** (KRBurke) **12-9-13v** MissRJPatman(8) (swtg: a bhd: t.o)	5	8	100/1	—	—
2780^{9}	**Vaporize (38)** (DMHyde) **5-9-13** MrsDMcHale(2) (swtg: prom 4f: t.o)	10	9	100/1	—	—

(SP 117.1%) **9 Rn**

1m 49.63 (8.83) CSF £14.82 TOTE £8.40: £1.40 £1.10 £1.70 (£5.80) Trio £13.70 OWNER Sir William Stuttaford (NEWMARKET) BRED Farmers Hill Stud

WEIGHT FOR AGE 3yo-8lb

2868 Blessed Spirit is no easy ride but she gets on well with her lady jockey, who broke her in as a yearling and rides her out every day at home. Making their first public appearance together, they appeared to have little chance at the weights - Blessed Spirit was rated 25lb behind the hot favourite on official adjusted ratings - but the combination poked a nostril in front below the distance and held on well to give Heather Webster her first-ever winner. (10/1)

692 Cape Cross (IRE), who had only Yorkshire to worry about at the weights, should have won this. Disputing the lead from the outset, he was back in front again early in the straight, but his experienced rider looked absolutely hopeless on him. However, despite little assistance, he struggled on well. (8/15)

2654* Yabint El Sultan had a severe test at the weights as she was 37lb behind Cape Cross on official adjusted ratings but, raced up with the pace, she failed to quicken in the last two furlongs. (14/1)

2642a Yorkshire (IRE), the only danger to the hot-pot on official ratings, was taking a big drop in distance. Disputing the lead from the start, he was collared a quarter-of-a-mile from home, and was left behind from below the distance. Ten furlongs is possibly more his trip. (3/1)

2430 Squared Away, rated a colossal 63lb behind the favourite on official adjusted ratings, was soon miles adrift of the other runners, but struggled on again late in the day. (66/1)

2430 Marjaana (IRE), 35lb behind Cape Cross on official adjusted ratings, was making no impression whatsoever on the principals in the straight. (14/1)

3049 PRINCESS MARGARET STKS (Gp 3) (2-Y.O F) (Class A)

3-05 (3-05) **6f** £23,380.00 (£8,839.00: £4,319.50: £1,961.50) Stalls: Low GOING: 0.26 sec per fur (G)

				SP	RR	SF
2597*	**Embassy** (DRLoder) **2-8-9** PatEddery(6) (stdy hdwy 2f out: led wl over 1f out: rdn out)	—	1	$5/2^{1}$	92	77
2728*	**Miss Zafonic (FR)** (RHannon) **2-8-9** LDettori(5) (plld hrd: hdwy over 1f out: unable qckn)	2	2	$5/2^{1}$	87	72
2024^{15}	**Filey Brigg** (WTKemp) **2-8-9** KFallon(4) (swtg: chsd ldr: rdn over 2f out: ev ch over 1f out: one pce)	hd	3	33/1	86	71
2712*	**Socket Set** (BAMcMahon) **2-8-9** MRoberts(3) (led over 4f)	1½	4	14/1	82	67
1927*	**Filfilah** (PTWalwyn) **2-8-9** RHills(7) (hld up: rdn over 2f out: wknd wl over 1f out)	4	5	$7/1^{3}$	72	57
2558^{3}	**Forest Treasure (IRE)** (JBerry) **2-8-9** GCarter(2) (b.hind: hld up: rdn over 2f out: sn wknd)	hd	6	$7/2^{2}$	72	57
1735^{2}	**Another Fantasy (IRE)** (RHannon) **2-8-9** DaneO'Neill(1) (lw: rdn over 3f out: bhd fnl 2f)	2½	7	8/1	65	50

(SP 112.6%) **7 Rn**

1m 16.8 (2.80) CSF £7.78 TOTE £3.30: £2.10 £2.00 (£3.30) OWNER Sheikh Mohammed (NEWMARKET) BRED Sheikh Mohammed bin Rashid al Maktoum

2597* Embassy, a compact little battleship, put up a sparkling performance in a time over three seconds faster than the two-year-old colts and geldings managed in the opener. This ground did not look ideal for her, judging by her action, but she nevertheless came through to lead approaching the final furlong to gain a decisive victory. She looks very useful and the Lowther Stakes and Cheveley Park are possibles for her. (5/2)

2728* Miss Zafonic (FR), bred by Pat Eddery who was on the winner, comes from a family that prefers firm ground. Taking a keen hold, she moved up below the distance but then got stuck in the ground. It was later revealed she had been bought by Sheikh Mohammed. She should regain the winning thread before long given a fast surface. (5/2)

1653* Filey Brigg, who cost a mere 1,000gs at the Doncaster Yearling Sales, was the most experienced in the line-up. She coped well with the extra furlong and gave a good account of herself, having every chance below the distance before tapped for toe. (33/1)
2712* Socket Set, whose only previous defeat came on soft ground, took the field along but, collared approaching the final furlong, was soon beaten. A return to a sounder surface is needed. (14/1)
1927* Filfilah took the field along until tiring early in the final quarter-mile. (7/1)
2558 Forest Treasure (IRE) disappointed on the ground and had been hung out to dry two furlongs from home. (7/2)

3050 KING GEORGE VI AND THE QUEEN ELIZABETH DIAMOND STKS (Gp 1) (3-Y.O+) (Class A)

3-50 (3-50) **1m 4f** £294,600.00 (£109,600.00: £52,100.00: £22,100.00) Stalls: High GOING: 0.26 sec per fur (G)

				SP	RR	SF
2559[2]	**Swain (IRE)** (SbinSuroor) **5-9-7** JReid(5) (lw: hld up: led over 2f out: edgd rt over 1f out: drvn out)	—	**1**	16/1	135	83
2527*	**Pilsudski (IRE) (128)** (MRStoute) **5-9-7** MJKinane(8) (b.nr hind: lw: hld up: n.m.r & swtchd lft 2f out: hrd rdn over 1f out: chsd wnr fnl f: r.o)	1	**2**	6/1[3]	134	82
2460a*	**Helissio (FR)** (ELellouche,France) **4-9-7** CAsmussen(2) (lw: led 1f: led over 5f out tl over 2f out: 4th whn n.m.r on ins over 1f out: unable qckn)	1¼	**3**	11/10[1]	132	80
1736*	**Singspiel (IRE) (128)** (MRStoute) **5-9-7** LDettori(6) (hld up: rdn over 3f out: chsd wnr over 2f out to 1f out: wknd ins fnl f)	2½	**4**	4/1[2]	129	77
2559*	**Shantou (USA) (123)** (JHMGosden) **4-9-7** GHind(1) (lw: s.s: nt clr run over 6f out: rdn over 3f out: no hdwy fnl 2f)	4	**5**	16/1	123	71
2100a[4]	**Strategic Choice (USA) (122)** (PFICole) **6-9-7** RCochrane(4) (lw: rdn over 3f out: nvr nr to chal)	5	**6**	66/1	117	65
2104*	**Predappio** (SbinSuroor) **4-9-7** GaryStevens(7) (a bhd)	3	**7**	12/1	113	61
2107*	**Kingfisher Mill (USA) (118)** (MrsJCecil) **3-8-9** PatEddery(3) (lw: led 11f out tl over 5f out: wknd over 3f out)	13	**8**	8/1	95	31
				(SP 114.0%)		**8 Rn**

2m 36.45 (6.45) CSF £97.45 TOTE £12.00: £3.90 £2.70 £1.00 (£46.10) OWNER Godolphin (NEWMARKET) BRED Sheikh Mohammed
WEIGHT FOR AGE 3yo-12lb
OFFICIAL EXPLANATION **Kingfisher Mill (USA): was found to have suffered a back injury.**
IN-FOCUS: **The line up for this mile and a half championship of Europe was quite breathtaking with seventeen Group One races won between them - thirty-two Group races in all - with prize-money earned topping nearly £8,500,000 and an average rating of 125.**
2559 Swain (IRE), who did an outstanding piece of work at the weekend, looked absolutely tremendous beforehand and was in his element in the soft ground. Leading early in the straight, he edged over to the rails below the distance, doing Helissio no favours, and, responding to pressure, held on well. A North America campaign has now been scrapped and he will be aimed at the Arc. (16/1)
2527* Pilsudski (IRE), whose connections were delighted when the deluge began in the morning, having been very concerned about the fast ground earlier in the week, ran an absolute cracker. Needing to be switched a quarter of a mile from home, he responded well to pressure and, moving into second place, made sure the winner did not have things all his own way. He will now have a rest before one of the Arc trials. (6/1)
2460a* Helissio (FR), with the heavy early rain being no problem for him, was very disappointing. Not settling very well early on, he went on soon after halfway but he was headed early in the straight and seemed to offer little resistance, giving up very quickly; quite simply, he is not used to horses passing him and did not know what to do. Done no favours by the winner below the distance, it made little difference to his chances but, to his credit, he did struggle on again in the closing stages. There are other days for this brilliant individual. (11/10)
1736* Singspiel (IRE) is an absolute star but the heavy rain which dramatically changed the going was all against him. Nevertheless, he showed his class and, bustled along turning for home, poked his head into second place below the distance. He looked a possible threat but tired in the soft ground in the last one hundred and fifty yards. There will be other days for him. (4/1)
2559* Shantou (USA), who goes well with give underfoot, looked in fine shape beforehand but was making no impression on the principals in the straight. (16/1)
2100a Strategic Choice (USA) had a seriously stiff task, but the deluge beforehand made the task even more daunting and he could never get into it. (66/1)
2104* Predappio had conditions to suit but proved very disappointing on his first venture into Group One company and was always at the back of the field. (12/1: 8/1-14/1)
2107* Kingfisher Mill (USA), the only three-year-old in the line-up, had a very stiff task and, after cutting out the running in the first half of the race, had shot his bolt turning for home. (8/1)

3051 BARNEY BARNATO DIAMOND RATED STKS H'CAP (0-105) (3-Y.O+) (Class B)

4-30 (4-30) **1m 2f** £12,312.00 (£4,608.00: £2,254.00: £970.00: £435.00: £221.00) Stalls: High GOING: 0.26 sec per fur (G)

				SP	RR	SF
2676[7]	**Present Arms (USA) (94)** (PFICole) **4-8-11** GaryStevens(2) (b.hind: lw: nt clr run 2f out: hdwy over 1f out: led ins fnl f: pushed out)	—	**1**	15/2[2]	106	52
2710[3]	**Game Ploy (POL) (94)** (DHaydnJones) **5-8-11** RCochrane(4) (swtg: stdy hdwy & n.m.r 2f out: rdn over 1f out: ev ch ins fnl f: unable qckn)	2½	**2**	5/1[1]	102	48
2690[4]	**Russian Music (99)** (MissGayKelleway) **4-9-2** KFallon(10) (lw: hdwy over 3f out: led over 1f out tl ins fnl: one pce)	1	**3**	20/1	105	51
2710[10]	**Kuala Lipis (USA) (93)** (PFICole) **4-8-10** PatEddery(3) (lost pl over 3f out: r.o one pce fnl 2f)	4	**4**	9/1	93	39
2710[7]	**Wahiba Sands (94)** (JLDunlop) **4-8-11** MJKinane(7) (swtg: hld up: rdn over 2f out: wknd over 1f out)	1	**5**	5/1[1]	92	38
2136[9]	**Wilcuma (103)** (PJMakin) **6-9-6** MRoberts(5) (swtg: rdn over 2f out: hdwy over 1f out: nvr nrr)	¾	**6**	12/1	100	46
2656[3]	**Premier Bay (101)** (PWHarris) **3-8-8b** JReid(8) (led 8f out tl over 1f out: sn wknd)	2½	**7**	14/1	94	30
2766[15]	**Amrak Ajeeb (IRE) (104)** (BHanbury) **5-9-7** MRimmer(6) (nvr nr to chal)	2	**8**	11/1	94	40
2656[2]	**Maralinga (IRE) (100)** (LadyHerries) **5-9-3** PaulEddery(1) (led 2f: rdn over 2f out: wknd over 1f out)	7	**9**	8/1[3]	79	25
2525[3]	**Mukaddar (USA) (96)** (CJBenstead) **3-8-3** RHills(9) (lw: prom 8f)	7	**10**	12/1	64	—
2528[3]	**Night Watch (USA) (94)** (IABalding) **4-8-11** LDettori(11) (b: hld up: rdn over 3f out: sn wknd: t.o)	dist	**11**	5/1[1]	—	—
				(SP 118.0%)		**11 Rn**

2m 13.52 (8.02) CSF £40.97 CT £664.02 TOTE £7.70: £2.90 £2.30 £4.40 (£17.50) Trio £165.30 OWNER H R H Prince Fahd Salman (WHATCOMBE) BRED Tri-Star Stable
WEIGHT FOR AGE 3yo-10lb
OFFICIAL EXPLANATION **Night Watch (USA): was sore on his near-fore.**
2676 Present Arms (USA) appreciated the underfoot conditions. Picking up ground nicely below the distance, he shot into the lead inside the final furlong for a cosy success. (15/2)
2710 Game Ploy (POL) would ideally be suited by faster ground which makes this performance even more commendable. Throwing down his challenge in the final furlong, he may well have got his head in front for a few strides, before the winner asserted. (5/1)
2690 Russian Music coped well with this longer trip and moved to the front below the distance. Headed inside the final furlong, he then failed to find another gear. (20/1)

1016 Kuala Lipis (USA), 7lb higher than he has ever won off, got outpaced turning for home but did struggle on again from below the distance. (9/1)
2710 Wahiba Sands chased the leaders but the writing was on the wall below the distance. (5/1)
1261 Wilcuma, well suited by this ground, struggled on in the last furlong and a half without ever posing a threat. He needs to drop a few pounds in the handicap. (12/1)

3052 CROCKER BULTEEL H'CAP (0-105) (3-Y.O+) (Class B)

5-00 (5-00) **1m (straight)** £13,810.00 (£4,180.00: £2,040.00: £970.00) Stalls: Low GOING: 0.26 sec per fur (G)

				SP	RR	SF
2525^{2}	**Aunty Jane (96)** (JLDunlop) **4-9-8** JReid(7) (lw: a.p: led 2f out: rdn out)	—	**1**	4/1^{1}	109	78
2708^{6}	**Tertium (IRE) (80)** (MartynWane) **5-8-3**$^{(3)}$ AWhelan(10) (rdn 2f out: hdwy over 1f out: chsd wnr fnl f: unable qckn)	2½	**2**	15/2	88	57
987^{15}	**Alhawa (USA) (77)** (RAkehurst) **4-8-3** RHills(2) (lw: rdn over 2f out: hdwy over 1f out: one pce)	1½	**3**	15/2	82	51
2761^{3}	**Hi Nod (96)** (MJCamacho) **7-9-8** LCharnock(5) (a.p: rdn over 2f out: one pce)	1	**4**	8/1	99	68
2525^{5}	**Hal's Pal (97)** (DRLoder) **4-9-9** PatEddery(9) (swtg: stdy hdwy 2f out: rdn over 1f out: one pce)	½	**5**	11/2^{3}	99	68
2525^{8}	**Kayvee (90)** (MrsAJPerrett) **8-9-2** AClark(6) (hld up: ev ch wl over 1f out: wknd fnl f)	1	**6**	9/1	90	59
2708^{3}	**Present Chance (78)** (BAMcMahon) **3-7-10** JQuinn(3) (lw: prom 5f)	2	**7**	12/1	74	35
2508^{3}	**Koathary (USA) (80)** (LGCottrell) **6-8-6** MRoberts(4) (led 6f)	1¾	**8**	11/1	73	42
2766^{10}	**Lonely Leader (IRE) (102)** (RHannon) **4-10-0** LDettori(1) (swtg: bhd fnl 3f)	7	**9**	9/2^{2}	81	50
2766^{18}	**Saifan (85)** (DMorris) **8-8-11b** NDay(8) (lw: hld up: rdn over 2f out: sn wknd)	28	**10**	25/1	8	—
				(SP 118.1%)	**10 Rn**	

1m 44.86 (4.86) CSF £31.55 CT £203.68 TOTE £3.50: £1.40 £2.40 £2.90 (£15.30) Trio £75.80 OWNER Mr Paul Locke (ARUNDEL) BRED P. Locke
WEIGHT FOR AGE 3yo-8lb
2525 Aunty Jane confirmed the promise shown at Sandown at the beginning of the month, leading a quarter of a mile from home and being ridden along to assert her authority. She enjoyed the ground and will now take a step up to Listed company. (4/1)
2708 Tertium (IRE) came through to take second place entering the final furlong, but was unable to get on terms with the winner. (15/2)
832 Alhawa (USA), given an eleven-week break, was certainly fit but, after moving up to take third place entering the final furlong, could then make no further impression. (15/2: 5/1-8/1)
2761 Hi Nod was never far away but never looked like finding another gear in the final quarter-mile. All twelve of his wins to date have come over seven furlongs. (8/1)
2525 Hal's Pal is no easy ride and appeared to be cruising as he crept closer a quarter of a mile from home. However, once let down, he flashed his tail and found disappointingly little. (11/2)
Kayvee showed that he is coming back to form and had every chance early in the final quarter-mile, before tiring in the last two hundred yards. (9/1)

3053 VENETIA DIAMOND H'CAP (0-95) (3-Y.O+) (Class C)

5-35 (5-36) **1m 4f** £7,100.00 (£2,150.00: £1,050.00: £500.00) Stalls: High GOING: 0.26 sec per fur (G)

				SP	RR	SF
2528^{11}	**Tykeyvor (IRE) (86)** (LadyHerries) **7-9-10** GaryStevens(4) (mde all: rdn over 2f out: r.o wl)	—	**1**	6/1	100	56
2653*	**Veridian (79)** (PWHarris) **4-9-3** KFallon(3) (hld up: chsd wnr 3f out: rdn over 2f out: unable qckn)	1½	**2**	9/2^{3}	91	47
2710^{18}	**Sharp Consul (IRE) (82)** (HCandy) **5-9-6** CRutter(6) (stdy hdwy over 2f out: rdn: one pce)	1¼	**3**	11/2	92	48
2726*	**King Kato (88)** (MrsAJPerrett) **4-9-12** JReid(1) (lw: plld hrd: hld up: rdn over 2f out: one pce)	3½	**4**	7/2^{1}	94	50
2865^{3}	**Remaadi Sun (84)** (MDIUsher) **5-9-8b**^{1} RStreet(5) (lw: nvr nr to chal)	s.h	**5**	12/1	90	46
2718^{2}	**Florentino (IRE) (72)** (BWHills) **4-8-10** MHills(10) (b: a.p: chsd wnr over 4f out to 3f out: sn wknd)	3	**6**	11/2	74	30
2729^{4}	**Dance So Suite (87)** (PFICole) **5-9-11** MJKinane(8) (lw: chsd wnr 6f: rdn over 2f out: wknd over 1f out)	4	**7**	4/1^{2}	83	39
267a^{8}	**Ela-Yie-Mou (IRE) (75)** (SDow) **4-8-13** MRoberts(12) (lw: s.s: hdwy on ins over 8f out: chsd wnr 6f out tl over 4f out: sn wknd)	21	**8**	33/1	43	—
2533^{8}	***Filial (IRE) (76)*** (BJMeehan) **4-9-0** MTebbutt(7) (Withdrawn not under Starter's orders: lame)		**W**	20/1	—	—
				(SP 120.9%)	**8 Rn**	

2m 40.9 (10.90) CSF £30.59 CT £143.78 TOTE £7.90: £2.30 £1.60 £1.60 (£15.20) Trio £21.50 OWNER Seymour Bloodstock (UK) Ltd (LITTLEHAMPTON) BRED H. Key
2028 Tykeyvor (IRE) appreciated the return to a mile and a half and, making all the running, was rousted along in the straight to give his American jockey, who had just come over for the day, a double. (6/1: 4/1-13/2)
2653* Veridian poked his head into second place turning for home but, try as he might, was unable to get on terms with the winner. (9/2: op 7/1)
1208 Sharp Consul (IRE) likes this ground and appeared to be cruising as he crept closer in the straight but, once let down, he could only go up and down in the same place. (11/2)
2726* King Kato chased the leaders but could only plod on in his own time in the straight. (7/2)
2865 Remaadi Sun never threatened to get into it. (12/1: op 8/1)
2718 Florentino (IRE) has yet to win over this trip and had been hung out to dry early in the straight. (11/2)

T/Jkpt: Not won; £35,119.28 to 28/7/97. T/Plpt: £14.10 (4,980.52 Tckts). T/Qdpt: £13.90 (179.95 Tckts) AK

2687-LINGFIELD (L-H) (Good to firm, Firm patches, AW Standard)

Saturday July 26th

Race 6 abandoned - course unsafe.
WEATHER: overcast WIND: fresh behind

3054 ARUNDEL APPRENTICE MAIDEN H'CAP (0-70) (3-Y.O+) (Class F)

6-15 (6-21) **1m 2f (Equitrack)** £2,305.00 (£655.00: £325.00) Stalls: High GOING minus 0.50 sec per fur (FST)

				SP	RR	SF
2570^{6}	**Michael Venture (60)** (SPCWoods) **3-9-1** PDoe(2) (mde all: hrd rdn over 1f out: r.o)	—	**1**	10/1	73	38
2668^{8}	**Executive Officer (31)** (RMFlower) **4-7-7b**$^{(3)}$ JFowle(4) (hdwy ½-wy: hrd rdn over 1f out: styd on to go 2nd ins fnl f)	3	**2**	12/1	39	14
2670^{5}	**Bapsford (46)** (GLMoore) **3-7-10**$^{(5)}$ DarrenWilliams(3) (a.p: chsd wnr ½-wy tl ins fnl f: one pce)	2½	**3**	8/1^{3}	50	15
2319^{5}	**Paddy Hurry (41)** (NACallaghan) **3-7-5**$^{(5)}$ RBrisland(10) (hdwy 6f out: sn rdn: kpt on one pce fnl 2f)	5	**4**	10/1	37	2
2199^{7}	**Sam Rockett (36)** (MissGayKelleway) **4-7-12**$^{(3)}$ AMcCarthy(7) (hld up: hrd rdn 4f out: one pce)	s.h	**5**	11/8^{1}	32	7
2246^{10}	**Keen Companion (59)** (TJNaughton) **4-9-2**$^{(8)}$ RachaelMoody(6) (dwlt: bhd tl styd on one pce fnl 2f)	hd	**6**	12/1	55	30

				SP	RR	SF
2896[10]	**Gracious Imp (USA) (33)** (JRJenkins) **4-7-9**(3)ow2 SCarson(5) (mid div whn hmpd & lost pl 5f out: rdn 4f out: no hdwy)	12	**7**	100/1	10	—
2159[6]	**Mogul (60)** (NAGraham) **3-8-8**(7) ANicholls(1) (mid div whn bdly hmpd 5f out: sn lost tch)	2½	**8**	7/1[2]	33	—
2836[9]	**Windborn (46)** (CNAllen) **3-8-1** DMcGaffin(9) (rr: effrt 4f out: sn btn)	4	**9**	11/1	12	—
	Dragon's Back (IRE) (63) (DCO'Brien) **4-9-4**(10) DanielBurchell(8) (chsd wnr to ½-wy: sn wknd)	9	**10**	12/1	15	—

(SP 116.3%) **10 Rn**

2m 6.91 (2.61) CSF £111.71 CT £919.69 TOTE £7.30: £2.30 £4.10 £2.90 (£68.60) Trio £231.20 OWNER Dr Frank Chao (NEWMARKET) BRED Woodsway Stud and Chao Racing and Bloodstock Ltd
LONG HANDICAP Executive Officer 7-7 Paddy Hurry 7-7 Gracious Imp (USA) 7-2
WEIGHT FOR AGE 3yo-10lb

1679 Michael Venture, dropped in class here, was always going best and had the race under control from some way out. (10/1: 7/1-12/1)
Executive Officer kept on well for second up the straight without threatening the winner. (12/1: 14/1-25/1)
2670 Bapsford got the trip alright but looked rather slow. (8/1: 6/1-10/1)
2319 Paddy Hurry kept on in the final two furlongs without looking like taking a hand. (10/1: 6/1-12/1)
1968 Sam Rockett was disappointing and he was under pressure at the top of the hill and making little headway. (11/8)
1297 Keen Companion (12/1: op 8/1)
2724 Windborn (11/1: 6/1-12/1)
Dragon's Back (IRE) (12/1: 10/1-20/1)

3055 DIGICON GEOPHYSICAL (S) STKS (2-Y.O) (Class G)

6-45 (6-51) **5f** £1,984.50 (£547.00: £259.50) Stalls: High GOING minus 0.50 sec per fur (F)

				SP	RR	SF
2784[2]	**Means Business (IRE)** (BJMeehan) **2-8-11b[1]** DaneO'Neill(5) (swtg: mde all: rdn over 1f out: r.o wl ins fnl f)	—	**1**	5/4[1]	62	35
2571[8]	**Ok John (IRE)** (JAkehurst) **2-8-11** AClark(3) (a.p: chsd wnr 2f out: rdn ins fnl f: unable qckn)	2½	**2**	9/4[2]	54	27
2664[5]	**Calliram** (MBlanshard) **2-8-6** JQuinn(4) (chsd ldrs: rdn 2f out: one pce)	3½	**3**	13/2	38	11
2425[5]	**Newhargen (IRE)** (PDEvans) **2-8-11b** MFenton(6) (w wnr tl ½-wy: wknd over 1f out)	2	**4**	4/1[3]	36	9
880[11]	**Polly In Paris (IRE)** (MartynMeade) **2-8-6** FNorton(1) (sn rdn along: bhd fnl 3f)	7	**5**	10/1	9	—
	Waytogomo (MissBSanders) **2-8-3**(3) AWhelan(8) (dwlt: a bhd)	10	**6**	9/1	—	—
	Miss Lady Lydia (JRPoulton) **2-8-6** AMorris(2) (lt-f: s.v.s: a bhd)	4	**7**	25/1	—	—
2396[2]	***Verdant Express*** (WGMTurner) **2-8-1**(5) GMilligan(7) (unf: Withdrawn not under Starter's orders: uns rdr gng to s)		**W**	13/2	—	—

(SP 144.8%) **7 Rn**

57.94 secs (0.94) CSF £4.86 TOTE £2.50: £1.50 £2.10 (£2.40) OWNER Thurloe Thoroughbreds II (UPPER LAMBOURN) BRED T. Connolly
Bt in 9,000gns

2784 Means Business (IRE) had the measure of his rivals from halfway. (5/4)
2571 Ok John (IRE), the subject of a gamble, looked none too keen when pressure was applied. (9/4)
2664 Calliram was well outpaced in the final two furlongs. (13/2)
2425 Newhargen (IRE) showed speed to halfway. (4/1)
Polly In Paris (IRE) (10/1: 8/1-12/1)

3056 BAILEYS ORIGINAL IRISH CREAM H'CAP (0-80) (3-Y.O+) (Class D)

7-15 (7-19) **7f 140y** £3,645.60 (£1,087.80: £519.40: £235.20) Stalls: High GOING minus 0.50 sec per fur (F)

				SP	RR	SF
2868[8]	**Safey Ana (USA) (64)** (BHanbury) **6-9-8** JReid(5) (b: lw: hld up: pushed along ½-wy: hdwy & n.m.r over 1f out: swtchd lft: hrd rdn ins fnl f: led nr fin)	—	**1**	3/1[1]	75	48
2743[7]	**Apollo Red (70)** (GLMoore) **8-10-0** CandyMorris(9) (led: hrd rdn ins fnl f: hdd nr fin)	nk	**2**	8/1	80	53
2833[10]	**Scissor Ridge (58)** (JJBridger) **5-9-2** JQuinn(2) (a.p: chsd ldr over 1f out tl ins fnl f: one pce)	1½	**3**	14/1	65	38
2848[5]	**King Parrot (IRE) (50)** (LordHuntingdon) **9-8-3**(5) AimeeCook(1) (lw: chsd ldrs: rdn over 2f out: one pce)	nk	**4**	7/2[2]	57	30
1745[5]	**Banzhaf (USA) (66)** (GLMoore) **4-9-10** AClark(3) (plld hrd: hld up: hdwy 2f out: hrd rdn ins fnl f: one pce)	1¼	**5**	4/1[3]	70	43
2788[11]	**May Queen Megan (46)** (MrsALMKing) **4-8-4**ow1 MRoberts(7) (chsd ldrs: rdn over 4f out: wknd ins fnl f)	nk	**6**	16/1	49	21
2645[8]	**Jolly Jackson (56)** (RAkehurst) **3-8-6** DHarrison(4) (hld up: rdn 3f out: hdwy over 2f out: wknd 1f out: eased ins fnl f)	3	**7**	11/1	53	18
1002[4]	**Daylight Dreams (75)** (CACyzer) **3-9-11** AMorris(8) (chsd ldr tl over 1f out: sn wknd)	s.h	**8**	20/1	72	37
2743[5]	**Fort Knox (IRE) (49)** (RMFlower) **6-8-7b** DaneO'Neill(6) (hld up in rr: rdn ½-wy: sn btn: eased over 1f out)	3	**9**	8/1	40	13

(SP 115.1%) **9 Rn**

1m 30.35 (1.35) CSF £25.01 CT £265.45 TOTE £4.20: £1.60 £2.80 £3.80 (£16.20) Trio £88.30 OWNER The Optimists Racing Partnership (NEWMARKET) BRED Robert N. Clay
WEIGHT FOR AGE 3yo-8lb

OFFICIAL EXPLANATION **Safey Ana (USA): regarding the apparent improvement in form, the case was referred to Portman Square as the relevant information was unavailable, where connections' explanation was accepted.**

1501* Safey Ana (USA) stepped up on recent form here, and would have won a shade more comfortably had he not found trouble in running. (3/1)
1599 Apollo Red was given a gem of a ride here and only just failed. Racing up the favoured stands side, he attempted to make all and his jockey set a steady pace, then quickened it up at halfway to put all his rivals in trouble. However, he began to tread water in the final furlong and was headed close home. (8/1: 5/1-9/1)
253 Scissor Ridge ran well but gave the impression that this extended seven furlongs is just too far. (14/1: op 8/1)
2848 King Parrot (IRE) raced up the unfavoured centre of the track and ran a bit better than his finishing position suggests. (7/2)
1745 Banzhaf (USA) pulled hard and was another to race up the centre of the track. He is finding his form. (4/1)
2245 Jolly Jackson (11/1: 8/1-12/1)

3057 LADBROKE H'CAP (0-70) (3-Y.O) (Class E)

7-45 (7-46) **2m** £3,096.25 (£925.00: £442.50: £201.25) Stalls: High GOING minus 0.50 sec per fur (F)

				SP	RR	SF
2397[7]	**Sipowitz (47)** (CACyzer) **3-7-12**(3)ow3 AWhelan(1) (lw: a.p: chsd ldr 6f out: led over 3f out: hrd rdn over 1f out: r.o)	—	**1**	14/1	58	—
2725[2]	**Trooper (67)** (RAkehurst) **3-9-7** DHarrison(5) (a.p: chsd wnr over 3f out: hrd rdn 1f out: r.o)	½	**2**	4/1[3]	78	23
2486[3]	**Padauk (64)** (MJHaynes) **3-9-1**(3) RFfrench(6) (hld up: lost footing sltly over 3f out: rdn over 2f out: styd on ins fnl f)	1¾	**3**	13/2	73	18
2397[4]	**Motcombs Club (46)** (NACallaghan) **3-8-0b[1]** JQuinn(3) (led: hdd over 3f out: sn wknd)	17	**4**	9/1	38	—

2667[10] **Frost King (55)** (MissBSanders) **3-8-9** DaneO'Neill(7) (prom tl wknd 6f out)	3½	**5**	20/1	43	—
2397* **Zafarelli (60)** (JRJenkins) **3-9-0** JReid(4) (hld up: hdwy 4f out: wknd over 2f out)	5	**6**	7/4 1	43	—
2189[4] **Aurelian (61)** (MBell) **3-9-1** MFenton(2) (hld up: rapid hdwy 4f out: s.u over 3f out)		**S**	11/4 2	—	—
			(SP 117.8%)	**7 Rn**	

3m 34.0 (10.00) CSF £65.11 TOTE £18.30: £4.70 £2.90 (£59.60) OWNER Mr R. M. Cyzer (HORSHAM) BRED C. A. and R. M. Cyzer
2068 Sipowitz set sail for home early in the straight and saw it out well, despite 3lb overweight. (14/1: 10/1-16/1)
2725 Trooper looked like scoring when challenging strongly in the last two furlongs but gave the impression he was not putting it all in. A pair of blinkers might help. (4/1: 11/4-9/2)
2486 Padauk was a bit unlucky. Held up just behind the leaders and travelling well, he slipped slightly turning for home. Back on an even keel, he stayed on nicely through the final two furlongs and gave the impression he would have gone close, but for his mishap. (13/2)
2397 Motcombs Club raced too freely in first-time blinkers. (9/1: op 6/1)
2397* Zafarelli ran poorly and may have found the ground too lively. (7/4)
2189 Aurelian, whose jockey appeared at least partly to blame for the fall, was asked to make rapid headway running down the hill and was going too fast when he approached the sharp home turn, made slippery by afternoon rain. (11/4)

3058 ASHURST LIMITED STKS (0-65) (3-Y.O+) (Class F)
8-15 (8-17) **7f (Equitrack)** £2,277.00 (£627.00: £297.00) Stalls: High GOING minus 0.50 sec per fur (FST)

			SP	RR	SF
2552[10] **Invocation (63)** (GLMoore) **10-9-8** AClark(5) (lw: hld up in tch: led over 1f out: edgd lft wl ins fnl f: r.o)	—	**1**	5/1	67	40
2957[4] **Signs And Wonders (65)** (CACyzer) **3-8-7**ow1 KFallon(4) (lw: a.p: led ½-wy: hdd over 1f out: btn whn short of room wl ins fnl f)	1½	**2**	6/4 1	56	21
2742* **Radar O'Reilly (62)** (RJRWilliams) **3-8-12** RCochrane(1) (chsd ldr tl ½-wy: ev ch over 1f out: one pce)	3	**3**	11/4 2	54	20
2506[6] **Native Rhythm (IRE) (65)** (PWChapple-Hyam) **3-8-6b1** JReid(2) (led tl ½-wy: sn wknd)	12	**4**	7/2 3	20	—
			(SP 105.6%)	**4 Rn**	

1m 26.45 (2.05) CSF £11.23 TOTE £4.80: (£5.70) OWNER Mr R. Kiernan (BRIGHTON) BRED Juddmonte Farms
WEIGHT FOR AGE 3yo-7lb
490 Invocation was always travelling nicely. He looked like scoring well when leading below the distance but, edging to his left, he had to be kept up to his work. (5/1)
2957 Signs And Wonders took it up at halfway. She was headed below the distance and kept battling on, but was a beaten horse when running out of room late on. (6/4)
2742* Radar O'Reilly was always to the fore but only had the one pace to give in the final furlong. (11/4)
2506 Native Rhythm (IRE) led to halfway and soon said goodnight. (7/2: op 7/4)

3059 SEVENOAKS H'CAP (0-70) (3-Y.O) (Class E)
- Abandoned -Slippery Ground

T/Plpt: £701.70 (18.6 Tckts). T/Qdpt: £57.20 (13.26 Tckts) SM

2324-NEWCASTLE (L-H) (Good)
Saturday July 26th
Races 2 & 5: hand-timed
WEATHER: overcast and rainy WIND: slt behind

3060 TATTERSALLS MAIDEN AUCTION STKS (2-Y.O) (Class E)
2-15 (2-18) **6f** £3,230.00 (£980.00: £480.00: £230.00) Stalls: High GOING minus 0.20 sec per fur (GF)

			SP	RR	SF
Darwell's Folly (USA) (MJohnston) **2-8-6** DHolland(5) (w'like: str: a.p: hdwy to ld appr fnl f: rdn & r.o)	—	**1**	7/2 2	79	25
2842[2] **Panama House** (TDEasterby) **2-8-9** JCarroll(6) (lw: a chsng ldrs: rdn 2f out: kpt on fnl f: nrst fin)	nk	**2**	8/11 1	81	27
2856[5] **Miss Salsa Dancer** (DenysSmith) **2-7-12**(3) PFessey(1) (mde most tl hdd appr fnl f: kpt on wl)	s.h	**3**	16/1	73	19
Kayo (TJEtherington) **2-8-9** ACulhane(4) (w'like: s.i.s: hld up: hdwy 2f out: hung lft: chsng ldrs 1f out: wknd towards fin)	4	**4**	14/1	70	16
Cool Prospect (ABMulholland) **2-8-8** TLucas(8) (leggy: unf: hld up: hdwy 2f out: hung lft: shkn up 1f out: no ex)	1¾	**5**	33/1	65	11
2324[7] **Reach For A Star** (CWThornton) **2-8-12** EJohnson(10) (s.i.s: hung lft most wy: nvr rchd ldrs)	5	**6**	50/1	55	1
2477[14] **Double Appeal (IRE)** (CaptJWilson) **2-8-0** NVarley(2) (w ldr tl wknd wl over 1f out)	3½	**7**	66/1	34	—
One To Go (IRE) (JBerry) **2-8-2**(5) TEDurcan(9) (w'like: leggy: outpcd fr ½-wy)	hd	**8**	15/2 3	41	—
2700[12] **Lavernock Lady** (JJQuinn) **2-8-1** DaleGibson(7) (in tch: shkn up ½-wy: sn lost pl)	8	**9**	66/1	14	—
Carrick View (IRE) (PCalver) **2-8-9** JFortune(3) (leggy: scope: dwlt & wnt lft s: n.d)	2	**10**	16/1	16	—
			(SP 118.2%)	**10 Rn**	

1m 15.04 (3.54) CSF £5.80 TOTE £5.20: £1.60 £1.10 £2.50 (£2.70) Trio £7.60 OWNER S & P Darwell Ltd (MIDDLEHAM) BRED Airlie Stud
OFFICIAL EXPLANATION **Reach For A Star: hung left.**
Darwell's Folly (USA), a really sturdy newcomer, won this nicely despite looking in need of it and there is obviously more to come. (7/2: 5/2-4/1)
2842 Panama House refused to have a tongue-strap fitted and also showed other signs of temperament, but he ran well enough and kept responding to pressure late on. (8/11: evens-8/13)
2856 Miss Salsa Dancer put in a much improved effort, and her debut race at Ayr was probably a hot event. (16/1)
Kayo took the eye in the paddock, but he has a pounding action and was inclined to hang when under pressure. However, he should improve for this experience. (14/1: 10/1-16/1)
Cool Prospect travelled on the bridle but then showed signs of greenness in the closing stages and was not over-punished. There looks to be a race or two in him. (33/1)
Reach For A Star was always giving problems by hanging left and his rider could never get the best out of him. If he can be sorted out, there is obviously better to come. (50/1)
Double Appeal (IRE) showed plenty of speed this time and is obviously learning. (66/1)

3061 ELDON GARDEN SHOPPING H'CAP (0-85) (3-Y.O+) (Class D)
2-50 (2-51) **1m 2f 32y** £3,468.75 (£1,050.00: £512.50: £243.75) Stalls: High GOING minus 0.20 sec per fur (GF)

			SP	RR	SF
2585[13] **Party Romance (USA) (84)** (BHanbury) **3-9-6** WRyan(4) (disp ld to ½-wy: cl up: disp ld wl over 1f out: led ins fnl f: styd on gamely)	—	**1**	5/2 1	95	56

2686[2]	**Keep Battling (50)** (JSGoldie) **7-7-7**(3) PFessey(8) (hld up & bhd: gd hdwy on ins to chal ins fnl f: rdn & no ex)	1	**2**	6/1 3	59	30
2890[6]	**Lay The Blame (71)** (MDHammond) **4-9-3** JCarroll(5) (trckd ldrs: disp ld wl over 1f out: hdd ins fnl f: kpt on same pce)	1¼	**3**	7/1	79	50
2857[5]	**Royal Ceilidh (IRE) (70)** (DenysSmith) **4-9-2** JFortune(2) (hld up: effrt & swtchd over 1f out: styd on: nvr able to chal)	1¼	**4**	10/1	76	47
2760[11]	**Can Can Lady (82)** (MJohnston) **3-9-1**(3) KMChin(7) (lw: hld up: effrt 3f out: r.o one pce)	½	**5**	10/1	87	48
2828[8]	**Bulsara (54)** (CWFairhurst) **5-7-9**(5)ow2 KSked(3) (lw: mde most tl hdd wl over 1f out: grad wknd)	3½	**6**	8/1	53	22
2528[5]	**Flying North (IRE) (80)** (MrsMReveley) **4-9-12** ACulhane(6) (hld up & bhd: effrt 3f out: sn rdn & no imp)	¾	**7**	7/2 2	78	49
2549[6]	**Bold Appeal (IRE) (50)** (WStorey) **5-7-10** NVarley(1) (chsd ldrs tl wknd qckly fnl 2f)	25	**8**	50/1	9	—

(SP 108.8%) **8 Rn**

2m 10.7 (4.00) CSF £14.52 CT £73.15 TOTE £3.30: £1.90 £1.60 £2.80 (£8.70) OWNER Mr Abdullah Ali (NEWMARKET) BRED Mollie E. Boyd & Vinery
LONG HANDICAP Keep Battling 7-8 Bold Appeal (IRE) 7-8
WEIGHT FOR AGE 3yo-10lb
OFFICIAL EXPLANATION **Party Romance (USA): the rider reported that the colt had run too freely last time, but that he had been able to settle him here.**
2585 Party Romance (USA), who seems a difficult customer to weigh-up, came back to form after a poor effort last time and showed too much courage for the runner-up. (5/2)
2686 Keep Battling, despite the steady pace, came through on the bridle to challenge but was then comprehensively outbattled. Nevertheless, he is in really good form and will obviously pick up a race when everything goes his way. (6/1)
2043 Lay The Blame certainly has the ability to win a race but it is now two years since he last found success. (7/1)
2857 Royal Ceilidh (IRE), trying a longer trip, was given every chance to get it but things never went right and he did not have a hard race. (10/1)
2113* Can Can Lady was not really suited by the steady pace here and was out-sprinted in the last couple of furlongs. (10/1: op 6/1)
1862 Bulsara is certainly off a useful mark and had the run of the race, but proved disappointing when tackled. (8/1)

3062 NORTH EAST SLAG CEMENT LTD (S) STKS (2-Y.O) (Class G)
3-25 (3-25) **6f** £2,284.50 (£642.00: £313.50) Stalls: High GOING minus 0.20 sec per fur (GF)

				SP	RR	SF
2784*	**Daynabee** (NTinkler) **2-8-11** KimTinkler(6) (led tl hdd ins fnl f: rallied to ld post)	—	**1**	4/1 2	61	21
2736[5]	**Patsy Culsyth** (MJohnston) **2-8-7** DHolland(5) (hld up: sn trckng ldrs: qcknd to ld ins fnl f: wandered u.p & ct nr fin)	s.h	**2**	4/6 1	57	17
2736[11]	**Snappy Times** (MDods) **2-8-12** DaleGibson(3) (lw: b: in tch: hrd drvn 2f out: styd on wl towards fin)	2	**3**	20/1	57	17
2823[4]	**Pride of Bryn** (DenysSmith) **2-8-4**(3) PFessey(9) (w wnr tl outpcd ins fnl f)	½	**4**	10/1	50	10
2827[4]	**Makahu Don** (WTKemp) **2-9-2** KDarley(1) (chsd ldrs: effrt over 2f out: hung lft: nt qckn fnl f)	½	**5**	8/1 3	58	18
2827[3]	**Cosmic Case** (JSGoldie) **2-8-7** TWilliams(4) (trckd ldrs: effrt over 2f out: btn appr fnl f)	3	**6**	8/1 3	41	1
1137[6]	**Chardania (IRE)** (CaptJWilson) **2-8-7** JCarroll(2) (outpcd & bhd fr ½-wy)	10	**7**	40/1	14	—
2827[11]	**La Vaso Verdi** (RMWhitaker) **2-8-7** DeanMcKeown(7) (sn hrd drvn & bhd: n.d)	1	**8**	50/1	12	—
2545[15]	**Shirleys Girl (IRE)** (WStorey) **2-8-7** JFanning(8) (s.i.s: a outpcd & bhd)	1	**9**	50/1	9	—
2412[8]	**Wilfred Sherman (IRE)** (JBerry) **2-8-11**(5) TEDurcan(10) (outpcd & lost tch fr ½-wy)	3	**10**	20/1	10	—

(SP 127.2%) **10 Rn**

1m 15.7 (4.20) CSF £6.74 TOTE £4.10: £1.30 £1.30 £5.00 (£3.20) Trio £29.00 OWNER Mr T. L. Beecroft (MALTON) BRED G. Middlebrook
No bid. Patsy Culsyth clmd Consult Co. Ltd £6,000
2784* Daynabee, from a yard in form, would not give in here and, after looking beaten, fought back splendidly. (4/1)
2736 Patsy Culsyth, dropped in class, still managed to snatch defeat from the jaws of victory, but there is surely a seller to be picked up with her. (4/6: 4/5-evens)
1797 Snappy Times was given some most determined assistance and kept answering, but the effort was always too late. (20/1)
2823 Pride of Bryn showed enough here to suggest that there is a similar event in her. (10/1: 8/1-12/1)
2827 Makahu Don again spoilt his chances by hanging left. (8/1: op 12/1)
2827 Cosmic Case failed to run up to his form of last time. (8/1: 6/1-9/1)

3063 THOMAS LONSDALE GALLAGHER BEESWING STKS (Gp 3) (3-Y.O+) (Class A)
4-00 (4-03) **7f** £18,729.00 (£7,011.00: £3,430.50: £1,477.50: £663.75: £338.25) Stalls: High GOING minus 0.20 sec per fur (GF)

				SP	RR	SF
2078a*	**Wizard King (116)** (SirMarkPrescott) **6-9-4** DeanMcKeown(1) (mde all: sn clr: shkn up appr fnl f: r.o wl)	—	**1**	7/2 2	127	90
2598[2]	**How Long (105)** (LMCumani) **4-9-0** KDarley(4) (hld up: effrt 3f out: r.o wl fnl f: no ch w wnr)	5	**2**	12/1	112	75
2023[4]	**Captain Collins (IRE) (103)** (PWChapple-Hyam) **3-8-7** DHolland(8) (chsd wnr most of wy: rdn over 2f out: r.o one pce)	1	**3**	12/1	109	65
2816a*	**Ramooz (USA) (107)** (BHanbury) **4-9-4** WRyan(3) (lw: b: hld up: effrt 3f out: styd on: nvr able to chal)	1¼	**4**	9/1 3	110	73
2334[3]	**Wind Cheetah (USA) (105)** (MRStoute) **3-8-7** FLynch(6) (prom: outpcd over 2f out: no imp after)	1¾	**5**	12/1	102	58
2830*	**Decorated Hero (117)** (JHMGosden) **5-9-0** AMcGlone(5) (trckd ldrs: effrt over 2f out: wknd appr fnl f)	nk	**6**	5/6 1	102	65
2679[6]	**Kala Sunrise (88)** (CSmith) **4-9-0** JFortune(2) (swtg: chsd ldrs tl rdn & btn 2f out)	nk	**7**	66/1	101	64
2599[9]	**Lucayan Prince (USA) (116)** (DRLoder) **4-9-4b** JCarroll(7) (hld up & bhd: effrt over 2f out: no rspnse)	7	**8**	16/1	89	52

(SP 117.2%) **8 Rn**

1m 24.16 (-0.34) CSF £41.20 TOTE £4.90: £1.80 £2.40 £1.60 (£24.20) OWNER Sheikh Ahmed bin Saeed Al Maktoum (NEWMARKET) BRED Sheikh Mohammed bin Rashid al Maktoum
WEIGHT FOR AGE 3yo-7lb
2078a* Wizard King, well suited by the rain that fell during the afternoon, he was brilliant here and, allowed to steal a useful advantage early on, found another gear when ridden and was most impressive. (7/2)
2598 How Long seems an unlucky sort who is just too highly rated for handicaps and is not quite good enough for these events, but he is certainly in good form and got the trip particularly well. (12/1)
2023 Captain Collins (IRE) always held a good position, but when asked for an effort he lacked any change of gear. (12/1)
2816a* Ramooz (USA), trying to come from off the pace, had too much on here and was never anything like good enough. (9/1)
2334 Wind Cheetah (USA) had the ground softening in his favour during the afternoon, but he was still struggling for toe a long way out. (12/1)
2830* Decorated Hero did not look at his best and certainly did not give his running here and was obviously not quite right. (5/6: evens-11/10)

3064 CP INSULATIONS H'CAP (0-80) (3-Y.O+) (Class D)

4-35 (4-35) **1m 3y (straight)** £3,550.00 (£1,075.00: £525.00: £250.00) Stalls: High GOING minus 0.20 sec per fur (GF)

			SP	RR	SF
2678^{8}	**Iamus (80)** (TDBarron) **4-9-7**(7) VictoriaAppleby(1) (mde all: hld on wl fnl f) ....——	**1**	8/1	93	76
1761^{9}	**Oriole (48)** (DonEnricoIncisa) **4-7-10** KimTinkler(5) (trckd ldrs: hdwy over 2f out: chal ins fnl f: nt qckn towards fin) ....nk	**2**	20/1	60	43
2828^{4}	**Champagne N Dreams (48)** (DNicholls) **5-7-5**(5) IonaWands(8) (chsd ldrs: outpcd over 2f out: no imp after) ...8	**3**	8/1	44	27
2678^{3}	**Pride of Pendle (71)** (MartynWane) **8-9-5** SSanders(3) (lw: hld up: hdwy over 2f out: rdn & nvr able to chal)...2	**4**	$11/4^{1}$	63	46
2290^{13}	**Gulliver (73)** (MrsJRRamsden) **4-9-7** JFortune(6) (b: hld up: effrt over 2f out: no imp) ....½	**5**	$9/2^{3}$	64	47
2668^{3}	**Sweet Supposin (IRE) (58)** (CADwyer) **6-8-1v**(5)ow3 TEDurcan(7) (cl up: effrt over 2f out: sn btn) 7	**6**	6/1	36	16
2569^{11}	**Whittle Rock (66)** (MrsMReveley) **4-9-0** ACulhane(2) (hld up: rdn over 2f out: n.d) ....nk	**7**	6/1	43	26
2890^{7}	**Dispol Gem (66)** (PCalver) **4-9-0** KDarley(4) (trckd ldrs tl wknd fnl 2½f) 8	**8**	$7/2^{2}$	27	10
			(SP 122.6%)	**8 Rn**	

1m 40.5 (1.90) CSF £141.13 CT £1,223.98 TOTE £11.20: £2.30 £5.10 £1.90 (£92.60) OWNER Burke's 5th Family Settlement (THIRSK) BRED Hesmonds Stud Ltd

LONG HANDICAP Oriole 6-11 Champagne N Dreams 7-4

1782 Iamus tried front-running tactics this time which proved successful last season and, by the looks of things, he will stay further. (8/1)

1128* Oriole put in a tremendous effort from 13lb out of the handicap and may well pick up another race. (20/1)

2828 Champagne N Dreams put in another reasonable effort, but was never doing enough when the pressure was on in the last two and a half furlongs. (8/1)

2678 Pride of Pendle looked well enough but never really fired on this occasion. (11/4)

2290 Gulliver tried to come from well off the pace and did make a little late headway, but was wisely not over-punished when he had no chance. (9/2)

2668 Sweet Supposin (IRE) has won thirteen races, all on the All-Weather. (6/1)

3065 MILLIGAN BAKERY 'FAMOUS FOR OUR FRESHNESS' H'CAP (0-95) (3-Y.O+) (Class C)

5-05 (5-05) **5f** £5,147.00 (£1,556.00: £758.00: £359.00) Stalls: High GOING minus 0.20 sec per fur (GF)

			SP	RR	SF
2872^{9}	**Lago Di Varano (79)** (RMWhitaker) **5-8-12b** DeanMcKeown(3) (lw: mde most: rdn & r.o wl fnl f) ....——	**1**	$8/1^{2}$	86	32
2675^{4}	**Lady Sheriff (77)** (MWEasterby) **6-8-10b** TLucas(8) (lw: a cl up: kpt on wl u.p fnl f) 1	**2**	$9/2^{1}$	81	27
2872*	**Tadeo (96)** (MJohnston) **4-9-12**(3) KMChin(6) (chsd ldrs: effrt 2f out: kpt on wl) ....hd	**3**	$9/2^{1}$	100	46
2683^{9}	**Vax Star (85)** (JLSpearing) **3-9-0b** SSanders(7) (a cl up: ev ch ins fnl f: no ex) ....s.h	**4**	25/1	88	30
2872^{2}	**Daawe (USA) (82)** (MrsVAAconley) **6-9-1** MDeering(5) (a chsng ldrs: hdwy u.p over 1f out: styd on) ....½	**5**	$9/2^{1}$	84	30
2655^{5}	**Darb Alola (USA) (92)** (MRStoute) **3-9-7** WRyan(4) (lw: gd spd 3f: wknd) 3	**6**	$10/1^{3}$	84	26
2560^{4}	**Double Action (94)** (TDEasterby) **3-9-9** KDarley(1) (in tch: effrt 2f out: nt pce to chal) ....hd	**7**	$9/2^{1}$	86	28
2872^{7}	**Meliksah (IRE) (90)** (MBell) **3-9-0**(5) GFaulkner(2) (cl up tl wknd over 1f out) 5	**8**	$9/2^{1}$	66	8
			(SP 115.0%)	**8 Rn**	

61.14 secs (2.74) CSF £40.05 CT £167.83 TOTE £8.30: £2.00 £1.40 £2.10 (£11.20) OWNER The PBT Group (LEEDS) BRED Miss S. E. Hall

WEIGHT FOR AGE 3yo-4lb

2339 Lago Di Varano, who looked particularly well, was suited by the heavy rain during the afternoon and proved most determined under pressure. (8/1)

2675 Lady Sheriff is a real battler and kept plugging away. She is off a mark 9lb higher than she has previously won off. (9/2)

2872* Tadeo, although he still should have beaten the winner on form, did not run badly and kept responding to pressure. (9/2)

Vax Star showed her first real signs of coming back to form here. (25/1)

2872 Daawe (USA) again ran well but probably just found this trip too sharp on turf. (9/2)

2655 Darb Alola (USA) is beginning to slip down the handicap and has the ability when things are right. (10/1)

2560 Double Action was always finding this trip on the sharp side. (9/2)

1608 Meliksah (IRE) (9/2: op 8/1)

T/Plpt: £100.40 (206.42 Tckts). T/Qdpt: £81.30 (9.75 Tckts) AA

2880-REDCAR (L-H) (Good to soft, Soft patches)

Saturday July 26th

WEATHER: raining WIND: almost nil

3066 CLEVELAND AMATEUR LIMITED STKS (0-75) (3-Y.O+) (Class G)

6-35 (6-35) **7f** £2,162.50 (£600.00: £287.50) Stalls: Centre GOING: 0.16 sec per fur (G)

			SP	RR	SF
1824*	**Purple Fling (73)** (DWChapman) **6-11-3** MissRClark(4) (plld hrd: trckd ldrs: rdn to ld jst ins fnl f: hld on wl)...——	**1**	7/1	82	60
2779*	**Dominant Air (79)** (SirMarkPrescott) **3-10-10** MrPScott(2) (lw: trckd ldr: effrt over 2f out: rdn & ev ch over 1f out: nt qckn nr fin) ....nk	**2**	$11/4^{2}$	81	52
2844^{12}	**Bowlers Boy (72)** (JJQuinn) **4-11-3** MrSSwiers(1) (hld up & plld hrd: hdwy over 2f out: ev ch over 1f out: nt qckn towards fin) ....hd	**3**	7/1	81	59
2557^{3}	**Suez Tornado (IRE) (71)** (EJAlston) **4-10-12**(5) MissKimJones(6) (lw: hld up: hdwy ½-wy: sn outpcd: styd on strly fnl f) ....½	**4**	$7/2^{3}$	80	58
1794^{4}	**Solfegietto (74)** (MBell) **3-9-13**(5) MrAEvans(5) (led: hung lft: hdd jst ins fnl f: wknd towards fin: b.b.v) ....¾	**5**	10/1	72	43
2465*	**Opulent (75)** (MrsMReveley) **6-10-12**(5) MrKRO'Ryan(3) (lw: trckd ldrs: drvn along ½-wy: hung bdly lft: lost pl & swvd lft over 1f out) 9	**6**	$2/1^{1}$	58	36
			(SP 116.3%)	**6 Rn**	

1m 29.7 (6.70) CSF £25.14 TOTE £8.10: £2.20 £1.60 (£11.90) OWNER Miss N. F. Thesiger (YORK) BRED Mrs P. Lewis

WEIGHT FOR AGE 3yo-7lb

1824* Purple Fling, having his first outing since being bought for 8,000gns at the Newmarket July Sales, was exceptionally well handled to get home in a tight finish. (7/1)

2779* Dominant Air, who is only a pony, ran really well but, hard as he tried, he could not worry the winner out of it. The trip was no problem. (11/4)

2567 Bowlers Boy, who took a fierce grip, moved up to have every chance and was staying on at the finish. He certainly got the seven. (7/1: tchd 11/1)

2557 Suez Tornado (IRE), who had something to find on official figures, found the trip too short. Badly outpaced soon after halfway, he finished best of all. (7/2)
1794 Solfegietto made the running but hung left throughout. Weakening towards the finish, she broke a blood-vessel. (10/1: 5/1-11/1)
2465* Opulent, who again had his tongue tied down, gave his partner a wretched ride. (2/1)

3067 RYCROFT COMMERCIAL VEHICLE NURSERY H'CAP (2-Y.O) (Class D)
7-05 (7-06) **7f** £3,834.00 (£1,152.00: £556.00: £258.00) Stalls: Centre GOING: 0.16 sec per fur (G)

			SP	RR	SF
1941^{3}	**Bolero Kid** (MWEasterby) **2-9-1** TLucas(6) (lw: hld up: effrt & nt clr run over 1f out: swtchd: r.o wl to ld last 50y) —	**1**	$7/2^{2}$	77+	37
2689^{3}	**Mamora Bay (IRE)** (MHTompkins) **2-8-6**(3) MHenry(7) (hld up: effrt & swtchd outside over 2f out: led over 1f out tl towards fin) 1½	**2**	$4/1^{3}$	68	28
2587^{3}	**Bali Dance** (CBBBooth) **2-7-13b^{1}**(3) PFessey(1) (swvd lft s: sn pushed along: hdwy ½-wy: ev ch over 1f out: swvd lft: styd on same pce) 1	**3**	8/1	58	18
2215^{2}	**Indian Missile** (JLDunlop) **2-9-7** KDarley(8) (lw: trckd ldrs: drvn along ½-wy: nt qckn appr fnl f) 3	**4**	$9/4^{1}$	70	30
2565^{5}	**Heavenly Falls (IRE)** (CADwyer) **2-8-0** NVarley(4) (chsd ldr: led over 2f out tl over 1f out: sn wknd) hd	**5**	9/2	49	9
1626^{6}	**My Bet** (MWEasterby) **2-7-12** NKennedy(2) (led tl over 2f out: grad wknd) 1¾	**6**	50/1	43	3
2714^{4}	**Marske Machine** (NTinkler) **2-7-10** KimTinkler(3) (dwlt s: sn pushed along: hdwy ½-wy: lost pl over 1f out) s.h	**7**	14/1	41	1
2681^{3}	**Lord of Love** (TDEasterby) **2-8-6** TWilliams(5) (chsd ldrs: drvn along ½-wy: lost pl over 2f out) 3½	**8**	9/1	43	3

(SP 120.9%) **8 Rn**

1m 29.3 (6.30) CSF £17.44 CT £98.70 TOTE £6.20: £1.80 £1.20 £1.50 (£14.90) OWNER Mr M. W. Easterby (SHERIFF HUTTON) BRED R. S. A. Urquhart

1941 Bolero Kid, as expected, proved suited by the step up in distance and the soft ground. Full of running with nowhere to go over a furlong out after being switched, he was hit over the head by another rider's whip but still came through to score in good style. He can surely follow up under similar conditions. (7/2)
2689 Mamora Bay (IRE) went to post really well. Coming from off the pace, he took it up on the outside but had no answer when the winner swept by him near the line. (4/1)
2587 Bali Dance, in blinkers for the first time, swerved left leaving the start. She gave her rider plenty of problems, swerving left just inside the last and almost colliding with the runner-up. (8/1: 5/1-9/1)
2215 Indian Missile was coltish in the paddock. Racing on the stands side rail, he was pushed along at halfway and soon had every chance but, under top weight, could find no extra coming to the final furlong. He does not seem as good as connections first hoped he would prove. (9/4)
2565 Heavenly Falls (IRE), well supported in the market, made hard of work of taking it up and was well and truly run out of it in the final furlong. (9/2: 10/1-4/1)
1330 My Bet was doing too much in front. (50/1)
2681 Lord of Love (9/1: 11/2-10/1)

3068 RACING CHANNEL MAIDEN (S) STKS (3-Y.O) (Class G)
7-35 (7-41) **1m 3f** £2,355.00 (£655.00: £315.00) Stalls: Low GOING: 0.36 sec per fur (GS)

			SP	RR	SF
2908^{8}	**Maremma (34)** (DonEnricoIncisa) **3-8-9** KimTinkler(8) (s.s: sn pushed along: hdwy over 3f out: led over 2f out: styd on wl) —	**1**	$5/1^{3}$	52	18
2757^{9}	**Gymcrak Gorjos (46)** (GHolmes) **3-8-9b^{1}** TLucas(7) (trckd ldr: led 4f out tl over 2f out: kpt on: no imp) 3½	**2**	6/1	47	13
1999^{7}	**Kingdom Emperor (47)** (MJCamacho) **3-9-0** JFortune(6) (hld up: hdwy 4f out: sn chsng ldrs: one pce fnl 2f) 4	**3**	$9/2^{2}$	46	12
2487^{15}	**Baaheth (USA) (55)** (SCWilliams) **3-9-0** KDarley(1) (trckd ldr: ev ch tl wknd over 2f out) 2	**4**	$5/1^{3}$	43	9
	Lady Magician (CWFairhurst) **3-8-2**(7) JennyBenson(2) (unf: s.i.s: bhd & pushed along: styd on fnl 2f: nvr nr to chal) 2	**5**	16/1	35	1
2887^{5}	**Grovefair Lad (IRE) (34)** (MartynWane) **3-9-0** SSanders(4) (sn prom: rdn over 3f out: wknd fnl 2f) 17	**6**	$100/30^{1}$	16	—
2602^{12}	**Dance Melody (29)** (GROldroyd) **3-8-9** KHodgson(9) (plld hrd: trckd ldrs: effrt over 3f out: sn wknd) 1¾	**7**	16/1	8	—
2145^{10}	**Emily-Jayne (35)** (MrsMReveley) **3-8-9b^{1}** ACulhane(3) (plld hrd: sn trckng ldrs: drvn along over 5f out: edgd lft & lost pl over 3f out) 2½	**8**	$9/2^{2}$	4	—
2673^{3}	**Ballydinero (IRE) (40)** (CaptJWilson) **3-9-0b** JWeaver(5) (led to 4f out: sn lost pl: virtually p.u) 23	**9**	14/1	—	—

(SP 125.5%) **9 Rn**

2m 31.5 (14.50) CSF £34.93 TOTE £6.30: £2.50 £3.60 £2.40 (£28.80) Trio £41.90 OWNER Don Enrico Incisa (MIDDLEHAM) BRED Godolphin Management Co Ltd
Bt in 7,800gns

2662 Maremma, racing with a tongue-strap, clearly appreciated the rain-softened ground and stayed on far too well for these. This was a very poor event, even by selling race standards. (5/1)
2156 Gymcrak Gorjos, dropped back slightly in distance and fitted with blinkers, set sail for home but it was soon obvious the winner was staying on too well for her. (6/1: op 7/2)
900 Kingdom Emperor looks a nervous sort and had the visor left off. (9/2: 7/2-6/1)
173 Baaheth (USA), who races with his tongue tied down, seems to be going backwards. (5/1: 7/2-11/2)
Lady Magician, backed at long odds, showed a glimmer of ability. (16/1)
2887 Grovefair Lad (IRE), well supported in the market after an improved effort at Ripon last time, was going up and down in the same place early in the straight. (100/30)
Emily-Jayne (9/2: 7/2-11/2)

3069 GREEN HOWARDS TERRITORIAL H'CAP (0-85) (3-Y.O+) (Class D)
8-05 (8-05) **2m 4y** £3,444.00 (£1,032.00: £496.00: £228.00) Stalls: Centre GOING: 0.36 sec per fur (GS)

			SP	RR	SF
2882^{3}	**Here Comes Herbie (62)** (WStorey) **5-9-11** SSanders(1) (trckd ldrs: led on bit 3f out: shkn up & styd on wl fnl f) —	**1**	$11/4^{2}$	74	39
2882^{5}	**Highfield Fizz (41)** (CWFairhurst) **5-8-1**(3) PFessey(4) (b.off hind: hld up: hdwy to chal over 3f out: sn rdn: nt qckn appr fnl f) 2½	**2**	$5/1^{3}$	51	16
2882^{10}	**Dirab (65)** (TDBarron) **4-10-0** KDarley(6) (lw: led to 3f out: one pce) 2½	**3**	$5/2^{1}$	72	37
2682^{5}	**Ramike (IRE) (80)** (MJohnston) **3-9-12** JWeaver(3) (hld up: hdwy 12f out: sn chsng ldrs: outpcd fnl 3f) 4	**4**	$11/4^{2}$	83	31
2737^{5}	**Hasta la Vista (54)** (MWEasterby) **7-9-0b**(3) GParkin(2) (chsd ldrs: rdn over 4f out: lost pl over 2f out) 23	**5**	7/1	34	—
	Alaraby (IRE) (60) (MartynWane) **5-9-9** JCarroll(7) (b: hld up: pushed along 5f out: sn bhd) 5	**6**	100/1	35	—

1162[13]	**Batoutoftheblue (52)** (WWHaigh) **4-9-1** ACulhane(5) (trckd ldrs: pushed along 8f out: wknd over 3f out)	7	**7**	14/1	20	—
				(SP 118.7%)		**7 Rn**

3m 45.1 (20.10) CSF £16.29 TOTE £3.60: £2.00 £2.20 (£6.30) OWNER Mr H. S. Hutchinson (CONSETT) BRED H. Hutchinson
WEIGHT FOR AGE 3yo-17lb
2882 Here Comes Herbie was always travelling well and took this with the minimum of fuss. (11/4)
2882 Highfield Fizz moved upsides just under half a mile from home but, hard as she tried, the winner always had her measure. (5/1)
2142 Dirab set no more than a modest pace. Looking to be cantering turning in, when challenged he could only keep on in his own time. He has slipped down the weights to an attractive mark but needs a flat-out gallop. (5/2)
2682 Ramike (IRE) was left behind in the final three furlongs. (11/4: 7/4-3/1)
2737 Hasta la Vista was in trouble as soon as they straightened up. (7/1: 9/2-8/1)

3070 NORTH YORKSHIRE MEDIAN AUCTION MAIDEN STKS (2-Y.O F) (Class E)

8-35 (8-41) **6f** £3,172.75 (£952.00: £458.50: £211.75) Stalls: Centre GOING: 0.36 sec per fur (GS)

				SP	RR	SF
2875[6]	**Eleonora d'Arborea** (BJMeehan) **2-8-11** KDarley(1) (mde all: drvn out)	—	**1**	11/2[3]	84	45
	Name of Love (IRE) (DRLoder) **2-8-11** WRyan(11) (w'like: leggy: lw: sn chsng wnr: rdn & nt qckn fnl f)	1	**2**	4/5[1]	81	42
2314[3]	**D'Marti** (CBBBooth) **2-8-11** KHodgson(10) (lw: trckd ldrs: effrt 2f out: styd on same pce fnl f)	2	**3**	7/2[2]	76	37
1466[8]	**Bollinger Rose (IRE)** (JJO'Neill) **2-8-11** JCarroll(8) (chsd ldrs: drvn along ½-wy: outpcd fnl 2f)	4	**4**	66/1	65	26
	Nisaba (IRE) (MJohnston) **2-8-11** JWeaver(2) (lengthy: bit bkwd: dwlt s: sn chsng ldrs: outpcd ½-wy: styd on fnl f)	2	**5**	14/1	60+	21
	Nunthorpe (JAGlover) **2-8-11** JFortune(4) (leggy: w ldrs tl over 2f out: grad wknd)	2	**6**	14/1	55+	16
	Joli Fille (JSWainwright) **2-8-11** TWilliams(9) (unf: sn outpcd & bhd: sme hdwy over 1f out: n.d)	¾	**7**	100/1	53	14
1839[9]	**Llanasa** (JBerry) **2-8-8**(3) PFessey(7) (chsd ldrs: drvn along ½-wy: sn outpcd)	d.h	**7**	25/1	53	14
2467[5]	**Kettlesing (IRE)** (MWEasterby) **2-8-11b** TLucas(6) (outpcd fr ½-wy)	3	**9**	16/1	45	6
	Ladyofdistinction (IRE) (JSWainwright) **2-8-11** ACulhane(5) (cmpt: s.i.s: a outpcd)	nk	**10**	100/1	44	5
2520[2]	***Facsimile*** (CaptJWilson) **2-8-11** SSanders(3) (Withdrawn not under Starter's orders: unruly & uns rdr bef s: ref to ent stalls)		**W**	12/1	—	—
				(SP 127.4%)		**10 Rn**

1m 15.9 (5.70) CSF £9.22 TOTE £5.10: £1.40 £1.60 £1.40 (£3.30) Trio £4.40 OWNER Mr Ettore Landi (UPPER LAMBOURN) BRED Filletts Farm Stud
2875 Eleonora d'Arborea, the most experienced runner in the field, revelled in the rain-soaked ground and was right on top at the finish. (11/2: 4/1-6/1)
Name of Love (IRE), who looked very fit, showed a good, fluent action going down. Tracking the winner when she came under pressure, she seemed to flounder slightly in the ground. (4/5: 4/6-5/4)
2314 D'Marti raced keenly. Tapped for foot soon after halfway, she stuck on strongly. It might be well worth a try giving her her head and letting her get on with it. (7/2)
Bollinger Rose (IRE), who showed plenty of knee action going down, stepped up considerably on her first effort. (66/1)
Nisaba (IRE) looked both in need of the outing and the experience. She can do better, especially over further. (14/1: op 6/1)
Nunthorpe, who has plenty of size about her, showed ability on her debut and can do better, especially on a sounder surface. (14/1)

3071 RICHMOND H'CAP (0-80) (3-Y.O) (Class D)

9-05 (9-09) **1m 2f** £3,691.00 (£1,108.00: £534.00: £247.00) Stalls: Low GOING: 0.36 sec per fur (GS)

				SP	RR	SF
2224*	**Fantail (76)** (MHTompkins) **3-9-2**(3) MHenry(5) (trckd ldrs: pushed along 4f out: led 2f out: jinked rt 1f out: jst hld on)	—	**1**	7/2[3]	85	32
2832*	**Enlisted (IRE) (76)** (SirMarkPrescott) **3-9-5** SSanders(1) (lw: sn trckng ldrs: effrt on ins & nt clr run 3f out: swtchd rt over 1f out: ev ch ins fnl f: jst failed)	s.h	**2**	15/8[1]	85	32
2678[11]	**Zorba (67)** (JHetherton) **3-8-10** NKennedy(3) (lw: sn trckng ldr: led over 2f out: sn hdd: one pce appr fnl f)	3	**3**	12/1	71	18
2495[6]	**Lord Discord (60)** (TDEasterby) **3-8-3** JCarroll(4) (hld up: hdwy 4f out: kpt on one pce fnl 2f)	s.h	**4**	16/1	64	11
2551[3]	**Epworth (78)** (JAGlover) **3-9-7** JFortune(2) (led tl over 2f out: sn rdn & wknd: eased)	11	**5**	2/1[2]	64	11
2330[2]	**Northern Flash (69)** (FMurphy) **3-8-12** ACulhane(6) (hld up: drvn along 5f out: sn wl outpcd & eased)	6	**6**	6/1	46	—
				(SP 118.2%)		**6 Rn**

2m 16.1 (12.50) CSF £10.24 TOTE £4.40: £2.30 £1.90 (£2.60) OWNER Pamela, Lady Nelson of Stafford (NEWMARKET) BRED Skyline Racing Limited
2224* Fantail remained cool as a cucumber while he was re-plated. Running over a trip short of his best, he was sent for home two furlongs out, but after jinking away from the rail the post came just in time. (7/2)
2832* Enlisted (IRE) found herself in a bad position on the inside halfway up the straight. Eventually making her way to the outside, she needed one more stride. (15/8)
2128* Zorba, who has slipped down the weights, ran right up to his best. (12/1: op 20/1)
Lord Discord stepped up considerably on his first effort. Sticking on at the finish, he looks a potential juvenile hurdler. (16/1)
2551 Epworth set just a fair pace. Even with the ground in her favour, once the race began in earnest she was soon swept aside and her rider wisely eased her up. (2/1)

T/Plpt: £35.70 (387.18 Tckts). T/Qdpt: £8.90 (82.26 Tckts) WG

2910-SOUTHWELL (L-H) (Standard)

Saturday July 26th

Race 2: poor visibility
WEATHER: showery with some heavy rain WIND: slight across

3072 CHAMPAGNE MEDIAN AUCTION MAIDEN STKS (2-Y.O F) (Class F)

6-25 (6-25) **7f (Fibresand)** £2,277.00 (£627.00: £297.00) Stalls: Low GOING minus 0.21 sec per fur (FST)

				SP	RR	SF
2728[11]	**Sunley Seeker** (MRChannon) **2-8-11** GCarter(2) (bit bkwd: chsd ldrs: led ent st: sn rdn: kpt on gamely)	—	**1**	8/1[2]	81	7
2781[2]	**Mustique Dream** (RCharlton) **2-8-11** TSprake(7) (lw: a.p: ev ch 1f out: sn rdn: unable qckn)	¾	**2**	1/3[1]	79	5
2196[8]	**Catch The Rainbow** (JGSmyth-Osbourne) **2-8-11** GBardwell(5) (lw: outpcd ½-wy: styd on u.p appr fnl f)	17	**3**	16/1	40	—
	Kustom Kit Kate (SRBowring) **2-8-11** SWebster(1) (leggy: lt-f: chsd ldrs: rdn over 2f out: sn outpcd)	hd	**4**	25/1	40	—
1997[11]	**Parlez Moi d'Amour (IRE)** (CWThornton) **2-8-11** EJohnson(6) (trckd ldrs: outpcd over 2f out: sn btn)	½	**5**	16/1	39	—

	Perecapa (IRE) (BPalling) **2-8-6**$^{(5)}$ DSweeney(3) (leggy: lt-f: unf: led 2f: rdn ½-wy: sn lost tch)	8	**6**	10/1^{3}	21	—
2700^{9}	**Ruby Bear** (WMBrisbourne) **2-8-6**$^{(5)}$ RMullen(8) (b.hind: bkwd: a bhd: t.o)	7	**7**	40/1	5	—
2604^{5}	**Miss Bananas** (TTBill) **2-8-11** TGMcLaughlin(4) (bit bkwd: led after 2f tl over 2f out: wknd qckly: t.o)	13	**8**	12/1	—	—

(SP 120.9%) **8 Rn**

1m 32.8 (6.30) CSF £10.68 TOTE £10.00: £1.20 £1.20 £3.10 (£2.60) OWNER Mrs J. M. Jeyes (UPPER LAMBOURN) BRED Sunley Stud

Sunley Seeker, a half-sister to Garnock Valley, showed little on her racecourse debut, but she was much wiser this time and, putting the emphasis on stamina, was always holding the challenge of the favourite. (8/1: 6/1-9/1)

2781 Mustique Dream, very green on her debut, looked to have a simple task here but, though she finished almost a furlong in front of the rest, she found the winner too much of a handful. (1/3)

1251 Catch The Rainbow, a good-looking filly, very much on her toes, won the separate race for the minor prize but was never within striking range of the principals. (16/1)

Perecapa (IRE) (10/1: op 5/1)

3073 G.B. WILLBOND IDEAL STANDARD (S) STKS (3-Y.O+) (Class G)

6-55 (6-55) **1m 4f (Fibresand)** £1,984.50 (£547.00: £259.50) Stalls: Low GOING minus 0.21 sec per fur (FST)

				SP	RR	SF
2531^{2}	**Private Fixture (IRE) (60)** (DMarks) **6-9-9**$^{(5)}$ DSweeney(3) (bhd: hdwy 4f out: rdn to ld over 1f out: r.o wl)	—	**1**	2/1^{1}	78	25
	Royal Square (CAN) (62) (NPLittmoden) **11-9-9** TGMcLaughlin(6) (swtg: bhd: rdn ½-wy: hdwy over 4f out: led over 2f out tl over 1f out: no ex fnl f)	1½	**2**	25/1	71	18
2770*	**Bluebell Miss (60)** (MJRyan) **3-8-11** GCarter(9) (hld up: hdwy over 3f out: rdn & ev ch ent fnl f: one pce)	4	**3**	5/2^{3}	66	1
2342*	**Anyar Reem (67)** (DShaw) **6-10-0b** JFanning(4) (b: swtg: chsd ldrs: drvn along & lost pl over 4f out: sn btn)	14	**4**	9/4^{2}	52	—
1940^{8}	**Red Whirlwind (42)** (RSimpson) **7-9-9** MGallagher(2) (bit bkwd: trckd ldrs: led over 4f out tl over 2f out: sn rdn & wknd)	4	**5**	50/1	42	—
	Red Tel (IRE) (MCPipe) **5-9-6**$^{(3)}$ MartinDwyer(7) (a bhd: t.o fr ½-wy)	9	**6**	12/1	30	—
2911^{3}	**Tovarich (50)** (RonaldThompson) **6-9-4v**$^{(5)}$ CLowther(5) (lw: led over 7f: sn rdn & wknd: t.o)	2½	**7**	20/1	26	—
	Nagobelia (JPearce) **9-9-6**$^{(3)}$ CTeague(8) (bkwd: a bhd: rdn 6f out: sn t.o)	14	**8**	33/1	8	—
2911^{8}	**Tocco Jewel (20)** (MJRyan) **7-9-4** DRMcCabe(1) (swtg: chsd ldrs 6f: sn lost tch: t.o)	25	**9**	50/1	—	—

(SP 115.8%) **9 Rn**

2m 43.8 (10.80) CSF £51.40 TOTE £3.20: £1.80 £4.00 £1.30 (£22.40) Trio £40.40 OWNER Mr John Jackson (UPPER LAMBOURN) BRED Maurice and Jeremiah Sheahan

WEIGHT FOR AGE 3yo-12lb

No bid. Bluebell Miss clmd PDouglas £5,750.

2531 Private Fixture (IRE) landed quite a touch with a smoothly-gained success and he is thriving since being stepped up in distance. (2/1)

Royal Square (CAN), having his first race on the Flat for almost six years, was fit from jumping. Taking a long time to get going, he struck the front soon after straightening up, but the winner wore him down without much difficulty and he had met his match. (25/1)

2770* Bluebell Miss has been pretty consistent on the turf recently and was fancied to make a winning debut on the sand, but after having every chance entering the final furlong seemed to find this extra distance just beyond her. (5/2)

2342* Anyar Reem, narrowly beaten by the winner at this venue last month, was hard at work turning out of the back straight and his measure had been taken. (9/4: 7/4-3/1)

Red Whirlwind, who has been running over longer trips this terms, got to the front on the home turn but he was unable to hold pole position for long, and he was well outpaced once the race really developed. (50/1)

Red Tel (IRE) (12/1: op 8/1)

3074 PARK HOSPITAL H'CAP (0-60) (3-Y.O+ F & M) (Class F)

7-25 (7-41) **1m 4f (Fibresand)** £2,277.00 (£627.00: £297.00) Stalls: Low GOING minus 0.21 sec per fur (FST)

				SP	RR	SF
2824*	**Classic Ballet (FR) (50)** (RGuest) **4-9-5**$^{(5)}$ CLowther(7) (hld up: hdwy 5f out: led over 2f out: sn clr: r.o wl)	—	**1**	5/1^{1}	64	45
2725^{4}	**Perlethorpe (54)** (MBell) **3-8-11**$^{(5)}$ RMullen(2) (lw: sn pushed along: hdwy 4f out: rdn wl over 1f out: kpt on: no ch w wnr)	6	**2**	8/1^{3}	60	29
*2673**	**Mystic Strand (44)** (WGMTurner) **4-8-13**$^{(5)}$ DSweeney(5) (lw: a.p: led 7f out tl over 2f out: rdn & one pce appr fnl f)	½	**3**	9/1	49	30
*2911**	**Portite Sophie (38)** (MBrittain) **6-8-5**$^{(7)}$ 6x DMernagh(10) (b: b.hind: trckd ldrs: effrt & brought wd st: sn rdn: btn over 1f out)	4	**4**	5/1^{1}	38	19
2727^{9}	**Illegally Yours (36)** (LMontagueHall) **4-8-7**$^{(3)}$ DO'Donohoe(9) (s.s: wl bhd tl gd hdwy 4f out: wknd over 2f out)	4	**5**	12/1	31	12
2753^{5}	**Lady Silk (40)** (MissJFCraze) **6-9-0** SWebster(3) (hld up: nvr nr to chal)	5	**6**	33/1	28	9
*2364**	**Mirror Four Sport (60)** (SRBowring) **3-9-1**$^{(7)}$ FBoyle(8) (b: prom over 6f: sn rdn along: grad fdd)	1¾	**7**	8/1^{3}	46	15
245^{7}	**Palacegate Jo (IRE) (23)** (DWChapman) **6-7-11** DWright(4) (bit bkwd: s.s: effrt 5f out: wknd fnl 3f: t.o)	29	**8**	14/1	—	—
2492^{13}	**Charcol (30)** (JEBanks) **4-8-4** GCarter(11) (swtg: hld up: hdwy 6f out: wknd over 3f out: t.o)	¾	**9**	5/1^{1}	—	—
	Comtec's Legend (23) (JPearce) **7-7-11** GBardwell(1) (bkwd: trckd ldrs: rdn & sddle slipped over 4f out: sn t.o)	½	**10**	13/2^{2}	—	—
1840^{7}	**Shirlaty (45)** (CWThornton) **4-9-5** JFanning(6) (led 5f: wknd over 5f out: t.o)	dist	**11**	33/1	—	—

(SP 115.8%) **11 Rn**

2m 40.0 (7.00) CSF £40.17 CT £315.33 TOTE £6.30: £2.80 £2.40 £3.00 (£41.80) Trio £176.20 OWNER Mr E. Carter (NEWMARKET) BRED Inversiones Gonfi Inc

WEIGHT FOR AGE 3yo-12lb

2824* Classic Ballet (FR), at the top of her form at present, quickly put her stamp on proceedings after setting sail for home from the turn into the straight, and she has not finished winning yet. (5/1: 3/1-6/1)

485 Perlethorpe is slowly but surely getting her act together and she has plenty of time on her side. (8/1)

2673* Mystic Strand was unable to cope with this step up in class, but she did not fail for the want of trying and there will be other prizes to be picked up. (9/1: 6/1-10/1)

2911* Portite Sophie, a winner earlier in the week, could have found this race coming too soon for she was never able to land a blow. (5/1)

2322 Illegally Yours walked out of the stalls and was well behind until making smooth progress at the end of the back straight. Flat to the boards turning in, she was soon treading ground and had probably done too much too soon. (12/1: op 8/1)

2364* Mirror Four Sport has changed stables since her last successful run here at the end of last month, but she had more on her plate under a much bigger weight, and was unable to cope with it. (8/1: 5/1-9/1)

3075 STANDEN HOMES (HOLDINGS) H'CAP (0-90) (3-Y.O+) (Class C)

7-55 (8-09) **7f (Fibresand)** £6,016.85 (£1,800.80: £863.90: £395.45) Stalls: Low GOING minus 0.21 sec per fur (FST)

				SP	RR	SF
2598[8]	**Master Boots (90)** (DRLoder) **4-9-9**(5) CLowther(10) (lw: hld up: hdwy over 2f out: r.o to ld wl ins fnl f)	—	**1**	7/1[2]	99	61
2922[7]	**Prima Silk (74)** (MJRyan) **6-8-12** GCarter(2) (in tch: effrt wl over 1f out: str run fnl f: jst failed)	nk	**2**	12/1	82	44
2567[15]	**Desert Invader (IRE) (70)** (DWChapman) **6-8-8** TSprake(4) (mde most tl wl ins fnl f)	1¼	**3**	20/1	76	38
*2663**	**Intiaash (IRE) (69)** (DHaydnJones) **5-8-4**(3) MartinDwyer(9) (hld up: hdwy over 2f out: ev ch ins fnl f: unable qckn)	hd	**4**	10/1	74	36
2547[8]	**Nor-Do-I (75)** (JMPEustace) **3-8-6** JTate(1) (a.p: ev ch ins fnl f: unable qckn)	¾	**5**	25/1	79	34
2603[3]	**Bold Aristocrat (IRE) (69)** (RHollinshead) **6-8-7** FLynch(12) (hld up: hdwy 3f out: rdn wl over 1f out: one pce)	1½	**6**	16/1	69	31
2925[8]	**Forcing Bid (82)** (SirMarkPrescott) **3-8-13** DeanMcKeown(16) (lw: racd wd: trckd ldrs: rdn & hung lft 2f out: no imp)	2½	**7**	10/1	76	31
2672[3]	**Johnnie the Joker (73)** (JPLeigh) **6-8-6b**(5) DSweeney(11) (bhd: hdwy 2f out: nvr nrr)	1	**8**	9/1[3]	65	27
2844[9]	**First Maite (79)** (SRBowring) **4-9-3b** SWebster(8) (chsd ldrs: effrt & rdn over 1f out: sn outpcd)	½	**9**	16/1	70	32
2303[2]	**The Wyandotte Inn (81)** (MrsNMacauley) **3-8-7**(5) AmandaSanders(13) (lw: a in rr)	1¼	**10**	14/1	69	24
2603[4]	**Theatre Magic (68)** (DShaw) **4-8-6** JFanning(14) (b: chsd ldrs over 5f)	1¼	**11**	20/1	53	15
2424[5]	**Oberon's Dart (IRE) (69)** (PJMakin) **4-8-7** DHolland(5) (prom tl wknd fnl 2f)	hd	**12**	12/1	54	16
2732[11]	**Robo Magic (USA) (82)** (LMontagueHall) **5-9-3**(3) DO'Donohoe(7) (b: chsd ldrs: drvn along 2f out: sn outpcd)	2½	**13**	16/1	61	23
2922[3]	**Alpine Hideaway (IRE) (70)** (BHanbury) **4-8-8** JStack(6) (chsd ldrs: hrd rdn 2f out: sn btn)	¾	**14**	3/1[1]	48	10
2567[13]	**Maiteamia (72)** (SRBowring) **4-8-7b**(3) CTeague(3) (b.off hind: prom over 4f)	2½	**15**	20/1	44	6
2708[13]	**Pericles (82)** (MJohnston) **3-8-10**(3) KMChin(15) (lw: s.i.s: sn chsng ldrs: wknd over 2f out: t.o)	18	**16**	9/1[3]	13	—
				(SP 133.5%)	**16 Rn**	

1m 29.4 (2.90) CSF £83.66 CT £1,570.53 TOTE £7.50: £1.90 £2.30 £5.00 £2.00 (£55.50) Trio £452.30; £286.67 to 28/7/97 OWNER Mr Chris Brasher (NEWMARKET) BRED Hesmonds Stud Ltd

WEIGHT FOR AGE 3yo-7lb

2598 Master Boots has taken time to return to form but, brought wide to avoid the kick-back once in line for home, stayed on stoutly to forge ahead inside the last fifty yards. (7/1: 5/1-8/1)

2711 Prima Silk delivered a determined challenge in the final furlong but was unable to make much impression until running on strongly nearing the line. She deserves to find an opening. (12/1)

2305* Desert Invader (IRE) ran one of his best ever races with a brave front-running effort that only came to an end in sight of the post. (20/1)

2663* Intiaash (IRE) produced her customary late challenge and she was fighting for the lead a hundred yards out, before appearing to find the seventh furlong just too much for her. (10/1)

2298 Nor-Do-I, a lightly-raced individual not sure to stay this trip, was only tapped for toe in the sprint to the line and the return to six furlongs could be the ideal move. He is comparatively well handicapped. (25/1)

2603 Bold Aristocrat (IRE) moved his way through from the rear to give himself a sporting chance turning in, but he has yet to win beyond six furlongs and lack of stamina does seem a problem. (16/1)

2925 Forcing Bid (10/1: op 6/1)

2424 Oberon's Dart (IRE) (12/1: op 6/1)

2922 Alpine Hideaway (IRE), from a stable in good form, was well fancied to follow up his success over course and distance earlier in the month, but two races in five days proved a stumbling block and he had shot his bolt early in the straight. (3/1)

3076 CONSTRUCTION EQUIPMENT FINANCE CLAIMING STKS (2-Y.O) (Class F)

8-25 (8-33) **6f (Fibresand)** £2,277.00 (£627.00: £297.00) Stalls: Low GOING minus 0.21 sec per fur (FST)

				SP	RR	SF
2823[2]	**Always Lucky** (JBerry) **2-8-7**(5) PRoberts(5) (led to 2f out: rallied u.p to ld nr fin)	—	**1**	2/1[1]	65	28
2741[3]	**Persian Fortune** (WGMTurner) **2-8-1**(5) RMullen(7) (w wnr: led 2f out: hrd rdn & ct cl home)	hd	**2**	3/1[2]	59	22
2706[10]	**Percy** (JFBottomley) **2-9-3** NCarlisle(4) (chsd ldrs: outpcd over 2f out: styd on ins fnl f)	3	**3**	5/1[3]	62	25
2467[15]	**Catfoot Lane** (WGMTurner) **2-8-3**(5) DSweeney(3) (trckd ldrs: hrd drvn over 2f out: kpt on ins fnl f)	½	**4**	12/1	51	14
2914[5]	**Vogue Imperial (IRE)** (PCHaslam) **2-8-2**(5) CLowther(1) (outpcd)	6	**5**	20/1	34	—
2304[5]	**Talaheart** (CNAllen) **2-7-13b**(3) MartinDwyer(6) (outpcd: t.o)	12	**6**	16/1	—	—
	Lapimi (MrsNMacauley) **2-8-8** SWebster(8) (leggy: lt-f: s.s: a bhd & outpcd: t.o)	4	**7**	33/1	—	—
2276[2]	**Just A Stroll** (JSMoore) **2-8-7** WJO'Connor(2) (chsd ldrs: drvn along 2f out: sn wknd & eased)	¾	**8**	5/1[3]	—	—
				(SP 112.9%)	**8 Rn**	

1m 17.3 (3.80) CSF £7.11 TOTE £2.00: £1.10 £1.10 £1.60 (£3.20) OWNER Miss Lilo Blum (COCKERHAM) BRED Ridgebarn Farm Stud, Mrs L. Jenkins and Mrs T. She

STEWARDS' ENQUIRY Mullen susp. 4-5/7/97 (excessive use of whip).

2823 Always Lucky, having her first crack at six furlongs, rallied gamely to regain the advantage in the last strides. (2/1: op evens)

2741 Persian Fortune, brought back to sprinting, gave as good as she got but just lacked that bit of extra pace in the dying strides. (3/1)

Percy was unable to hold his pitch when the leading pair took one another on, but he did stay on to secure the minor prize nearing the finish. (5/1)

Catfoot Lane, a stable-companion to the runner-up, shaped much better than she did on her debut and she should continue to progress. (12/1)

3077 GIN H'CAP (0-75) (3-Y.O+) (Class D)

8-55 (9-00) **5f (Fibresand)** £3,677.45 (£1,097.60: £524.30: £237.65) Stalls: Centre GOING minus 0.21 sec per fur (FST)

				SP	RR	SF
2921*	**Distinctive Dream (IRE) (63)** (KTIvory) **3-8-9b**(3) 7x MartinDwyer(3) (trckd ldrs: rdn to ld fnl 100y: r.o)	—	**1**	6/1[2]	72	—
2339[6]	**Broadstairs Beauty (IRE) (74)** (DShaw) **7-9-10b**(3) CTeague(7) (b: lw: a.p: rdn & r.o wl towards fin)	1	**2**	6/1[2]	80	—
2826*	**Palacegate Jack (IRE) (66)** (JBerry) **6-9-0b**(5) TEDurcan(1) (led tl wl ins fnl f)	½	**3**	7/2[1]	70	—
2769[7]	**Master of Passion (70)** (JMPEustace) **8-9-9** JTate(8) (a chsng ldrs: kpt on u.p ins fnl f)	hd	**4**	14/1	74	—
2497[7]	**Shadow Jury (62)** (DWChapman) **7-9-1b** LCharnock(9) (a.p: stands' side: rdn & swvd lft appr fnl f: r.o)	½	**5**	10/1[3]	64	—
2913[2]	**Napier Star (67)** (MrsNMacauley) **4-9-6v** SWebster(5) (chsd ldrs: rdn & one pce appr fnl f)	½	**6**	10/1[3]	68	—
2915[3]	**Sea Ya Maite (60)** (SRBowring) **3-8-9** DaleGibson(2) (b: prom tl rdn & no ex ins fnl f)	hd	**7**	6/1[2]	60	—
2738[3]	**Stolen Kiss (IRE) (67)** (MWEasterby) **5-9-6b** DHolland(6) (sn pushed along & outpcd)	1	**8**	6/1[2]	64	—
2844[6]	**Rich Glow (53)** (NBycroft) **6-8-6** SDrowne(10) (effrt wl over 1f out: nt pce to chal)	2	**9**	6/1[2]	44	—
2480[5]	**Perfect Brave (54)** (JBalding) **6-8-7** JEdmunds(11) (swvd bdly lft s: almost uns rdr: nt rcvr)	6	**10**	20/1	26	—
				(SP 123.3%)	**10 Rn**	

56.7 secs CSF £40.49 CT £139.21 TOTE £7.60: £2.90 £2.70 £2.20 (£31.10) Trio £24.50 OWNER Mr K. T. Ivory (RADLETT) BRED Peter Kehoe

WEIGHT FOR AGE 3yo-4lb
IN-FOCUS: **Due to the heavy rain during the evening and water lying on the track, the stalls had to be positioned in the centre of the course, some forty yards short of the five-furlong start, and it did appear to give the advantage to the low-numbered stalls. The time, (which would have generated a speed figure of around 90), whilst giving the true indication of the competitiveness of the race, can not be judged as a course record.**
2921* Distinctive Dream (IRE), striking while the iron is hot, had no trouble in continuing his run in this change to the sand, and he is in unstoppable form at the moment. (6/1: op 3/1)
2339 Broadstairs Beauty (IRE), lightly raced in the past few months, gave notice that he is approaching his peak with a very promising performance under top weight and his turn could be near at hand. (6/1)
2826* Palacegate Jack (IRE) is not the easiest of animals to pass when he is allowed to dictate and it was only very late on that he did finally give best. (7/2)
2321 Master of Passion showed something of a return to form with a most improved performance and he could be on the way back. (14/1)
1759 Shadow Jury racing wide of the principals, showed with the pace all the way but he just drifted off a true line when the pressure was on, otherwise he would surely have made the frame. (10/1: 8/1-12/1)
2913 Napier Star kept tabs on the leaders, but she was always at full stretch and unable to summon the pace to mount a challenge. (10/1)
2915 Sea Ya Maite has been competing over an extra furlong in recent races, and though he pressed the leaders all the way was found wanting in the dash to the post. (6/1: op 4/1)

T/Plpt: £26.90 (400.22 Tckts). T/Qdpt: £17.40 (39.01 Tckts) IM

2953-BRIGHTON (L-H) (Firm, Good to firm last 3f)
Monday July 28th
WEATHER: sunny WIND: almost nil

3078 RAGGETTS (S) STKS (2-Y.O) (Class G)
2-00 (2-00) **6f 209y** £1,984.50 (£547.00: £259.50) Stalls: Low GOING minus 0.37 sec per fur (F)

				SP	RR	SF
2700[8]	**Jato Dancer (IRE)** (MRChannon) **2-8-6** JFEgan(1) (hld up: led over 2f out: rdn out)	—	**1**	7/2[2]	49	—
2875[14]	**Wedding Band** (RHannon) **2-8-6** DaneO'Neill(3) (lw: outpcd: hdwy over 1f out: r.o)	1¾	**2**	4/1[3]	45	—
1812[15]	**Clear View** (BJMeehan) **2-8-11** MTebbutt(7) (hld up: rdn over 3f out: edgd lft wl over 1f out: chsd wnr over 1f out tl wl ins fnl f: unable qckn)	1¼	**3**	5/1	47	—
2893[13]	**Espresso** (JWHills) **2-8-8v[1]**(3) MHenry(5) (outpcd: hdwy fnl f: nvr nrr)	2½	**4**	14/1	41	—
2664[8]	**Sweet Senorita** (MMadgwick) **2-8-6** NVarley(2) (hld up: rdn & ev ch over 2f out: edgd rt 2f out: wknd over 1f out)	1¼	**5**	33/1	34	—
2923[4]	**Medina Miss** (WGMTurner) **2-8-1**(5) DSweeney(6) (b.nr hind: lw: chsd ldr: ev ch over 2f out: wknd over 1f out)	s.h	**6**	5/2[1]	33	—
2240[8]	**Dancing Al** (JSMoore) **2-8-11** NAdams(4) (led over 4f: wknd over 1f out)	1¼	**7**	9/1	36	—
				(SP 107.1%)		**7 Rn**

1m 25.8 (5.80) CSF £14.08 TOTE £5.30: £2.40 £1.90 (£7.60) OWNER Timberhill Racing Partnership (UPPER LAMBOURN) BRED Stephen Stanhope
Bt in 6,300gns
IN-FOCUS: **This race would not have been out of place as the Donkey Derby on Brighton Beach.**
Jato Dancer (IRE) appreciated the drop in class and was rousted along to win a desperate affair. Connections believe she is up to nursery company. (7/2)
2706 Wedding Band appreciated the drop in class and step-up in trip, and showed her first piece of form, staying on from below the distance to take second place in the closing stages. (4/1)
Clear View, taking a step-up in distance and a drop in class, ran better as a result, only losing the runner-up berth in the closing stages. This is his level. (5/1)
Espresso, who had beaten just one horse on his previous two efforts, was completely outpaced until struggling on in the final furlong as the early leaders tired. He is very short on ability. (14/1: 8/1-16/1)
Sweet Senorita, who had beaten only two rivals in her two previous runs, was one of several with every chance before tiring below the distance. (33/1)
2923 Medina Miss again died over seven furlongs. She is extremely exposed and very moderate. (5/2: op 6/4)
Dancing Al (9/1: 8/1-12/1)

3079 CHIPPENDALE MAIDEN STKS (3-Y.O+ F & M) (Class D)
2-30 (2-31) **7f 214y** £3,758.30 (£1,038.80: £494.90) Stalls: Low GOING minus 0.37 sec per fur (F)

				SP	RR	SF
1656[2]	**Alikhlas (79)** (MajorWRHern) **3-8-11** RHills(1) (hld up: led over 1f out: rdn out)	—	**1**	11/10[1]	79	6
2420[3]	**Summerosa (USA) (80)** (PWChapple-Hyam) **3-8-11** JReid(2) (b.nr fore: lw: chsd ldr: ev ch over 1f out: unable qckn)	2	**2**	3/1[3]	75	2
2555[2]	**Slipstream Star (70)** (IABalding) **3-8-8**(3) MartinDwyer(3) (lw: led: rdn over 2f out: hdd over 1f out: wknd fnl f)	3	**3**	15/8[2]	69?	—
				(SP 107.4%)		**3 Rn**

1m 36.7 (5.40) CSF £3.95 TOTE £2.30 (£2.10) OWNER Mr Hamdan Al Maktoum (LAMBOURN) BRED Shadwell Estate Company Limited
1656 Alikhlas, racing with her tongue hanging out, was held up in third place. Asked for her effort, she came through to lead approaching the final furlong and was rousted along to score. (11/10)
2420 Summerosa (USA) may have got her head in front for a few strides, but when the winner went past she was left standing. (3/1: op 7/4)
2555 Slipstream Star set the pace, and grimly held on until collared approaching the final furlong. (15/8)

3080 BRIGHTON SUMMER CHALLENGE CUP H'CAP (0-70) (3-Y.O+) (Class E)
3-00 (3-00) **1m 3f 196y** £3,044.25 (£909.00: £434.50: £197.25) Stalls: High GOING minus 0.37 sec per fur (F)

				SP	RR	SF
2955[4]	**Sovereign Crest (IRE) (45)** (CAHorgan) **4-8-10v[1]** DHolland(6) (s.s: hdwy over 4f out: rdn over 2f out: chsd ldr over 1f out: led wl ins fnl f: r.o wl)	—	**1**	11/2[3]	53	40
2650[4]	**Freedom Chance (IRE) (69)** (JWHills) **3-9-5v[1]**(3) MHenry(4) (lw: a.p: led 5f out: clr over 2f out: hrd rdn over 1f out: hdd wl ins fnl f: unable qckn)	½	**2**	11/2[3]	76	51
2744[2]	**Cheek To Cheek (61)** (CACyzer) **3-8-11**(3) RFfrench(7) (a.p: rdn over 2f out: r.o one pce)	2	**3**	6/1	66	41

1996^{3}	**Afon Alwen (63)** (SCWilliams) **4-10-0** GCarter(9) (hdwy 5f out: chsd ldr 3f out tl over 1f out: one pce)	¾	**4**	9/1	67	54
2318^{3}	**Colour Counsellor (35)** (RMFlower) **4-7-11b**$^{(3)}$ MartinDwyer(5) (lw: led 7f: wknd 3f out)	13	**5**	9/2^{2}	21	8
2182^{9}	**Tasik Chini (USA) (70)** (PFICole) **3-9-2**$^{(7)}$ DavidO'Neill(8) (w ldr 7f)	7	**6**	10/1	47	22
2907^{3}	**Papita (IRE) (55)** (SDow) **3-8-8** JReid(2) (hld up: rdn over 4f out: sn wknd)	5	**7**	11/4^{1}	25	—
1665^{9}	**Chez Catalan (40)** (RAkehurst) **6-8-5b** SSanders(3) (lw: a bhd)	½	**8**	14/1	9	—
2592^{12}	**Prerogative (45)** (GLMoore) **7-8-10b^{1}** CandyMorris(1) (bhd fnl 10f: t.o)	25	**9**	20/1	—	—
				(SP 120.4%)		**9 Rn**

2m 31.2 (3.60) CSF £34.08 CT £174.64 TOTE £6.40: £2.20 £3.60 £2.00 (£34.10) Trio £72.30 OWNER Mrs B. Sumner (PULBOROUGH) BRED Jeremy Hill

WEIGHT FOR AGE 3yo-12lb

OFFICIAL EXPLANATION Papita (IRE): rider reported that the filly became unbalanced and was hanging badly.

2955 Sovereign Crest (IRE) gained compensation for his unlucky run here last Thursday. Appreciating the first-time visor, he went second over a furlong out and gradually reeled in the leader to get on top in the closing stages. (11/2)

2650 Freedom Chance (IRE), fitted with a visor for the first time, went on at the top of the hill and had a very useful advantage over a quarter of a mile from home. However, he began to tie up below the distance and was caught in the closing stages. (11/2)

2744 Cheek To Cheek, a leading light throughout, struggled on in the final quarter-mile if never looking likely to find that vital turn of foot. (6/1)

1996 Afon Alwen, 5lb higher than at the beginning of the season, found that telling. Moving into second place over three furlongs from home, she was collared for the runner-up berth below the distance. (9/1: 11/2-10/1)

2318 Colour Counsellor, whose two wins to date have come in sellers over this course and distance, set the pace. Collared at the top of the hill, he had been hung out to dry three furlongs from home. A drop to plating company is required. (9/2)

1805 Tasik Chini (USA) (10/1: op 6/1)

93 Chez Catalan (14/1: 8/1-16/1)

3081 BEAU BRUMMEL CLAIMING STKS (3-Y.O+) (Class F)

3-30 (3-33) **1m 1f 209y** £2,277.00 (£627.00: £297.00) Stalls: High GOING minus 0.37 sec per fur (F)

				SP	RR	SF
2929^{5}	**Night Wink (USA) (70)** (GLMoore) **5-9-8**$^{(3)}$ MartinDwyer(3) (mde all: shkn up over 1f out: r.o wl)	—	**1**	7/4^{2}	71	44
2956^{7}	**Keen Waters (35)** (JRArnold) **3-8-3**^{ow1} AClark(5) (chsd wnr: rdn over 2f out: unable qckn)	3½	**2**	10/1	53	15
1968^{12}	**Passage Creeping (IRE) (67)** (SDow) **4-9-0** JReid(1) (hld up: rdn over 2f out: one pce)	6	**3**	6/5^{1}	45	18
	Na Huibheachu (IRE) (33) (JSMoore) **6-9-1** RHughes(6) (lw: hld up: rdn over 3f out: one pce)	hd	**4**	12/1	37 t	19
2947^{4}	**Jilly Woo (44)** (DRCElsworth) **3-7-3**$^{(7)}$ JFowle(2) (dwlt: a bhd)	1½	**5**	15/2^{3}	25 t	—
2730^{17}	**Eternally Grateful (25)** (KTIvory) **4-8-3**$^{(7)ow2}$ CCassidy(4) (b: a bhd: t.o fnl 4f)	20	**6**	50/1	6	—
				(SP 112.3%)		**6 Rn**

2m 2.3 (4.00) CSF £17.16 TOTE £2.60: £1.50 £2.70 (£13.20) OWNER Mrs Dyanne Benjamin (BRIGHTON) BRED Gainsborough Farm Inc

WEIGHT FOR AGE 3yo-10lb

Jilly Woo clmd RJGray £2,000

2929 Night Wink (USA) appreciated the drop in class and scooted up under a good ride. Making all the running, he was woken up below the distance and soon put daylight between himself and his rivals for a cosy success. (7/4)

2750 Keen Waters, making a quick reappearance, raced in second place, but was unable to cope with the winner from below the distance. (10/1: 7/1-14/1)

1668 Passage Creeping (IRE), with 8lb or more to spare over her rivals on official adjusted ratings, has shown again and again that she lacks acceleration and that was painfully exposed. She remains a maiden after seventeen attempts. (6/5)

Na Huibheachu (IRE), an ex-Irish gelding, looked very slow on this first run for his new stable. He remains a maiden after eighteen attempts and will need to find a seriously bad race if he is ever to get his head in front. (12/1)

2947 Jilly Woo was always at the back of the field. Amazingly, she was actually claimed after the race. (15/2)

3082 SADDLESCOMBE H'CAP (0-70) (3-Y.O+) (Class E)

4-00 (4-01) **5f 213y** £3,070.25 (£917.00: £438.50: £199.25) Stalls: Low GOING minus 0.37 sec per fur (F)

				SP	RR	SF
2958*	**Resist the Force (USA) (62)** (CACyzer) **7-9-7**$^{(3)}$ ^{7x} RFfrench(5) (hdwy over 1f out: led ins fnl f: rdn out)	—	**1**	5/1^{2}	74	35
2958^{2}	**Sharp Imp (58)** (RMFlower) **7-9-6b** SDrowne(3) (rdn over 3f out: swtchd rt & hdwy over 1f out: unable qckn ins fnl f)	1¼	**2**	3/1^{1}	67	28
2852^{5}	**Justinianus (IRE) (44)** (JJBridger) **5-8-1**$^{(5)}$ ADaly(2) (lw: chsd ldr: rdn over 2f out: led over 1f out tl ins fnl f: one pce)	2	**3**	11/1	47	8
2732^{13}	**Step On Degas (56)** (MJFetherston-Godley) **4-8-13**$^{(5)}$ DSweeney(1) (lw: hdwy & nt clr run over 1f out: swtchd rt: r.o)	nk	**4**	16/1	59	20
2747^{3}	**Ed's Folly (IRE) (55)** (SDow) **4-9-3** SSanders(9) (a.p: rdn over 2f out: one pce)	¾	**5**	12/1	56	17
2698^{12}	**Sizzling (55)** (RHannon) **5-9-3** DaneO'Neill(6) (a.p: rdn over 2f out: wknd 1f out)	2½	**6**	8/1	49	10
2964^{4}	**Tear White (IRE) (67)** (TGMills) **3-9-10** JReid(7) (lw: hld up: rdn over 2f out: nt clr run over 1f out: wknd fnl f)	nk	**7**	8/1	60	16
2922^{4}	**Ivory's Grab Hire (65)** (KTIvory) **4-9-10b**$^{(3)}$ MartinDwyer(10) (led over 4f)	¾	**8**	7/1^{3}	56	17
2933^{5}	**Kildee Lad (66)** (APJones) **7-9-11b^{1}**$^{(3)}$ JDSmith(11) (lw: hld up: rdn over 2f out: wkng whn bmpd over 1f out)	1	**9**	11/1	54	15
2748^{6}	**Seamus (39)** (CJHill) **3-7-5**$^{(5)}$ APolli(8) (t: dwlt: a bhd)	nk	**10**	25/1	27	—
2698^{8}	**Rockcracker (IRE) (53)** (GGMargarson) **5-9-1b** GCarter(4) (lw: a bhd)	s.h	**11**	11/1	40	1
2954^{5}	**Pearl Dawn (IRE) (44)** (PCClarke) **7-8-6** CandyMorris(13) (hdwy over 3f out: wknd over 1f out)	1¾	**12**	14/1	27	—
2852^{10}	**Mellors (IRE) (50)** (MJHeaton-Ellis) **4-8-12** AClark(12) (lw: prom over 3f)	4	**13**	33/1	22	—
				(SP 128.4%)		**13 Rn**

1m 9.9 (2.70) CSF £19.99 CT £139.18 TOTE £5.60: £2.40 £1.30 £2.80 (£6.60) Trio £53.20 OWNER Mrs Barbara Hogan (HORSHAM) BRED Ron Con & Barronstown

LONG HANDICAP Seamus 7-7

WEIGHT FOR AGE 3yo-5lb

2958* Resist the Force (USA) followed up last Thursday's course and distance victory in good style, swooping through to lead inside the final furlong for a cosy success. (5/1)

2958 Sharp Imp, a winner three times around here, was unable to cope with the winner inside the final furlong. For the fifth time in six starts, he had to settle for second best. (3/1: op 5/1)

2852 Justinianus (IRE), very difficult to win with, got his head in front for a few strides below the distance before passed inside the final furlong. (11/1)

325 Step On Degas had no luck in running, for she had a wall of horses in front of her below the distance as she began to pick up ground. Having to be switched as a result, costing her ground she could ill-afford, she ran on, but by then it was all over bar the shouting. (16/1)

2747 Ed's Folly (IRE), a leading player throughout, remains a maiden after seventeen attempts. (12/1: op 7/1)
2179 Sizzling played an active role until coming to the end of his tether over a furlong out. (8/1)
2933 Kildee Lad (11/1: 7/1-12/1)
2954 Pearl Dawn (IRE) (14/1: 10/1-16/1)

3083 FITZHERBERT H'CAP (0-60) (3-Y.O+) (Class F)

4-30 (4-31) **5f 59y** £2,277.00 (£627.00: £297.00) Stalls: Low GOING minus 0.37 sec per fur (F)

Form	Horse	Dist	Pos	SP	RR	SF
2554^{12}	**Chakra (45)** (SDow) **3-9-2** JFEgan(11) (hdwy over 1f out: hrd rdn fnl f: led last stride)	—	**1**	20/1	54	19
2732^{12}	**Bright Paragon (IRE) (39)** (KTIvory) **8-8-11**(3) MartinDwyer(1) (b: a.p: led over 1f out: hrd rdn fnl f: hdd last stride)	s.h	**2**	$9/2^{2}$	48	17
2780^{5}	**Rowlandsons Stud (IRE) (43)** (KCComerford) **4-8-11**(7) SRighton(8) (w ldr: led over 3f out tl over 1f out: ev ch ins fnl f: one pce)	1	**3**	7/1	49	18
2150^{11}	**Moi Canard (42)** (BAPearce) **4-9-3** DHolland(10) (rdn over 2f out: hdwy fnl f: r.o wl)	1¼	**4**	11/1	44	13
2883*	**College Princess (51)** (SCWilliams) **3-9-1**(7) DarrenWilliams(3) (swtg: a.p: edged lft over 1f out: one pce)	hd	**5**	$11/4^{1}$	53	18
2536^{4}	**Moving Up (IRE) (38)** (TEPowell) **4-8-6**(7) RCody-Boutcher(9) (lw: rdn over 3f out: hdwy 1f out: r.o)	1¾	**6**	9/1	34	3
2751^{5}	**Rise 'n Shine (49)** (CACyzer) **3-9-6** JReid(12) (lw: a.p: rdn over 2f out: wknd ins fnl f)	3	**7**	14/1	36	1
2747^{6}	**Sang d'Antibes (FR) (49)** (DJSCosgrove) **3-9-6** JStack(13) (hld up: rdn over 2f out: one pce)	¾	**8**	16/1	34	—
339^{6}	**Allstars Dancer (31)** (TJNaughton) **4-7-13**(7) RachaelMoody(5) (outpcd: hdwy on ins 1f out: hmpd ins fnl f: nvr nrr)	nk	**9**	16/1	15	—
2747^{9}	**Kanawa (41)** (APJones) **3-8-9**(3) JDSmith(4) (hdwy & hung lft over 1f out: wkng whn n.m.r on ins fnl f)	nk	**10**	33/1	24	—
2663^{3}	**Mister Raider (49)** (EAWheeler) **5-9-5b**(5) ADaly(7) (prom over 3f)	nk	**11**	$11/2^{3}$	31	—
2732^{15}	**Double Or Bust (26)** (CJHill) **4-7-8**(7) PDoe(2) (swtg: led over 1f: rdn over 2f out: wknd over 1f out)	1½	**12**	33/1	4	—
2738^{17}	**Singforyoursupper (46)** (GGMargarson) **3-9-0**(3) MHenry(6) (bhd fnl 2f)	1¼	**13**	12/1	20	—

(SP 127.8%) **13 Rn**

63.0 secs (3.00) CSF £103.22 CT £678.90 TOTE £24.00: £5.30 £2.00 £2.20 (£73.30) Trio £270.50 OWNER Eurostrait Ltd (EPSOM) BRED Eurostrait Ltd
WEIGHT FOR AGE 3yo-4lb
Chakra showed his first sign of form. Picking up ground below the distance, he responded to pressure to poke a nostril in front right on the line. (20/1)
2536 Bright Paragon (IRE) got to the front below the distance but, despite doing little wrong, was caught right on the line. He is a winner without a penalty. (9/2)
2780 Rowlandsons Stud (IRE), racing with his tongue tied down, gave a good account of himself. Soon showing in front, he was collared below the distance but, refusing to give way, still had every chance inside the final furlong before tapped for toe. (7/1)
Moi Canard, taking a big drop in distance, was only making an impression in the final furlong, by which time the race was already over. (11/1)
2883* College Princess was never far away, but her rider looked very weak on her and, drifting over to the rails below the distance, she could only plod on at one pace. (11/4)
2536 Moving Up (IRE) ran on in the final furlong, but by then it was far too late. (9/1)
2751 Rise 'n Shine (14/1: 10/1-16/1)
2663 Mister Raider (11/2: op 3/1)
2481 Singforyoursupper (12/1: 6/1-14/1)

T/Plpt: £189.10 (70.12 Tckts). T/Qdpt: £48.80 (28.33 Tckts) AK

3060-NEWCASTLE (L-H) (Good)

Monday July 28th

Races 2 & 6 - hand-timed
WEATHER: overcast WIND: fresh against

3084 ALEX LAWRIE MEDIAN AUCTION MAIDEN STKS (2-Y.O) (Class E)

2-15 (2-15) **7f** £2,869.25 (£869.00: £424.50: £202.25) Stalls: High GOING minus 0.19 sec per fur (GF)

Form	Horse	Dist	Pos	SP	RR	SF
2022^{3}	**Simply Gifted** (TDEasterby) **2-9-0** LCharnock(1) (swvd lft s: hld up: hdwy 3f out: led ins fnl f: pushed out)	—	**1**	$12/1^{3}$	60	20
2693^{11}	**Balaclava (IRE)** (EALDunlop) **2-9-0** KFallon(3) (chsd ldrs: led 2f out tl ins fnl f: no ex)	¾	**2**	$12/1^{3}$	58	18
	Di Matteo (IRE) (BHanbury) **2-9-0** JWeaver(5) (w'like: bit bkwd: cl up: led 3f out to 2f out: one pce)	1¼	**3**	$8/1^{2}$	55	15
	Daybreak (JWWatts) **2-8-9** JCarroll(2) (lt-f: hld up: hdwy over 2f out: sn chsng ldrs: nt qckn fnl f)	2	**4**	20/1	46	6
2881^{8}	**Lady Rochelle** (TDEasterby) **2-8-9** KDarley(4) (prom tl outpcd fnl 3f)	9	**5**	33/1	25	—
884^{9}	**Kantone (IRE)** (JMPEustace) **2-9-0** JTate(7) (bit bkwd: chsd ldrs 4f: sn rdn & wknd)	1	**6**	33/1	28	—
2524^{2}	**Ray's Folly (IRE)** (MAJarvis) **2-9-0** RCochrane(6) (led 4f: sn rdn & wknd)	4	**7**	$1/4^{1}$	19	—

(SP 117.1%) **7 Rn**

1m 29.88 (5.38) CSF £119.95 TOTE £8.60: £3.00 £2.40 (£33.30) OWNER Mr Steve Hammond (MALTON) BRED T. J. Cooper
OFFICIAL EXPLANATION **Ray's Folly (IRE): no explanation offered.**
2022 Simply Gifted is a keen sort, and his rider was in no hurry after a poor start. Improving on the bridle, he settled it well and there would seem to be more in him as he gains experience. (12/1)
Balaclava (IRE) looks likely to benefit from this and put in a much improved effort. (12/1)
Di Matteo (IRE), needing this, showed plenty of ability and should improve. (8/1)
Daybreak would certainly not impress on looks, but showed fair ability and was definitely not over-punished when beaten (20/1)
Lady Rochelle has shown little in two outings so far. (33/1)
Kantone (IRE), still needing this, gave no real signs of encouragement. (33/1)
2524 Ray's Folly (IRE) dropped away very quickly and something would seem to have been amiss. (1/4)

3085 WARD AIR COMMUNICATIONS TROPHY H'CAP (0-80) (3-Y.O+ F & M) (Class D)

2-45 (2-45) **1m 4f 93y** £3,355.00 (£1,015.00: £495.00: £235.00) Stalls: Low GOING minus 0.19 sec per fur (GF)

Form	Horse	Dist	Pos	SP	RR	SF
2421*	**Debutante Days (69)** (ACStewart) **5-9-10** MHills(3) (trckd ldr: led 2½f out: shkn up & qcknd: comf)	—	**1**	$5/4^{1}$	80+	59
*3074**	**Classic Ballet (FR) (61)** (RGuest) **4-8-11**(5) 5x CLowther(2) (lw: led tl hdd 2½f out: kpt on)	1½	**2**	$11/4^{2}$	70	49

			SP	RR	SF
2503[4]	**Daira (58)** (JDBethell) **4-8-13** KFallon(1) (trckd ldrs: effrt 3f out: rdn & no imp) ¾	**3**	3/1[3]	66	45
2753*	**My Millie (43)** (WStorey) **4-7-12** TWilliams(4) (hld up: hdwy 3f out: ch 2f out: sn btn) 3	**4**	7/1	47	26
			(SP 108.6%)		**4 Rn**

2m 42.8 (5.30) CSF £4.49 TOTE £1.90 (£2.50) OWNER Mrs Shirley Brasher (NEWMARKET) BRED Lady McAlpine
2421* Debutante Days is in good form at present and always had more in hand. (5/4)
3074* Classic Ballet (FR) tried her best but was tapped for toe in the last two and a half furlongs and, judging by the way she stayed on, she should get further. (11/4)
2503 Daira seems to have an aversion to winning, but she is generally thereabouts. (3/1)
2753* My Millie managed to scrape home for her first victory last time and has now changed stables. This was a creditable effort in better company. (7/1: 5/1-8/1)

3086 KEITH PATTINSON ESTATE AGENTS MAIDEN STKS (3-Y.O+) (Class D)
3-15 (3-16) **5f** £3,306.25 (£1,000.00: £487.50: £231.25) Stalls: High GOING minus 0.19 sec per fur (GF)

			SP	RR	SF
2838[5]	**Bahamian Beauty (USA)** (DRLoder) **3-8-9** KDarley(5) (lw: a gng wl: led on bit ent fnl f: easily) —	**1**	6/4[1]	66++	18
1858[3]	**Tithcar (66)** (BHanbury) **3-8-9** KFallon(6) (led: rdn over 2f out: hdd ent fnl f: no ch w wnr) 2½	**2**	7/4[2]	58	10
2891[5]	**Dona Filipa (36)** (MissLCSiddall) **4-8-13** OPears(3) (lw: chsd ldrs: effrt 2f out: kpt on: no imp) 1¼	**3**	16/1	54	10
2747[5]	**Blue Lamp (USA) (60)** (MAJarvis) **3-8-9** RCochrane(2) (hld up: effrt ½-wy: sn rdn & prom: one pce appr fnl f) 1½	**4**	5/1[3]	49	1
2738[4]	**Superfrills (34)** (MissLCSiddall) **4-8-13** DeanMcKeown(7) (cl up tl wknd over 1f out) 2½	**5**	12/1	41	—
2838[9]	**Beau Tudor (IRE)** (MissLCSiddall) **3-8-7**(7) TSiddall(1) (effrt ½-wy: sn rdn & btn) 8	**6**	33/1	21	—
2734[4]	**Mischievous Time (41)** (ASmith) **3-9-0** ACulhane(4) (outpcd & bhd fr ½-wy) 1¾	**7**	25/1	15	—
			(SP 113.4%)		**7 Rn**

61.9 secs (3.50) CSF £3.89 TOTE £2.70: £1.50 £1.30 (£1.90) OWNER Lucayan Stud (NEWMARKET) BRED Diane L. Perkins
WEIGHT FOR AGE 3yo-4lb
2838 Bahamian Beauty (USA) made no mistake in this company and, always going supremely well, fairly trotted up. (6/4: evens-13/8)
1858 Tithcar, dropping back in trip, tried to gallop the opposition into the ground, but proved well short of gears, and her rider dropping his whip made absolutely no difference. (7/4)
2891 Dona Filipa seems honest enough, but just stays and was always short of the necessary toe. (16/1)
2747 Blue Lamp (USA) tried to come from off the pace but, when pressure was applied, her limitations were well exposed. (5/1)
2738 Superfrills had little chance in this event and ran as well as could be expected. (12/1: op 20/1)

3087 GEORGE WYNN 65TH BIRTHDAY H'CAP (0-85) (3-Y.O+) (Class D)
3-45 (3-46) **7f** £3,420.00 (£1,035.00: £505.00: £240.00) Stalls: High GOING minus 0.19 sec per fur (GF)

			SP	RR	SF
2422[4]	**Safio (61)** (ABailey) **4-8-9** DWright(5) (hld up: hdwy 3f out: rdn to ld 1f out: styd on wl) —	**1**	11/2[2]	71	27
2922[2]	**Present Generation (72)** (RGuest) **4-9-1**(5) CLowther(1) (lw: cl up: led 4f out: hdd 1f out: nt qckn) 1½	**2**	9/4[1]	79	35
2478[4]	**Weetman's Weigh (IRE) (78)** (RHollinshead) **4-9-12** FLynch(6) (lw: hld up: hdwy 3f out: chsng ldrs & rdn over 1f out: nt pce to chal) nk	**3**	9/4[1]	84	40
2735[7]	**Jay-Owe-Two (IRE) (73)** (RMWhitaker) **3-9-0** DeanMcKeown(7) (a chsng ldrs: rdn 2f out: kpt on one pce) 1¼	**4**	20/1	76	25
2326[12]	**Magic Mill (IRE) (80)** (JLEyre) **4-10-0** KDarley(2) (hld up: effrt 3f out: outpcd fnl 2f) 11	**5**	8/1[3]	58	14
2069[8]	**Keston Pond (IRE) (56)** (MrsVAAconley) **7-8-4** MDeering(3) (hld up: effrt ½-wy: btn 3f out) 3	**6**	10/1	27	—
2900[14]	**French Grit (IRE) (78)** (MDods) **5-9-12** KFallon(4) (led 3f: rdn & btn 3f out) hd	**7**	9/1	49	5
			(SP 111.9%)		**7 Rn**

1m 28.84 (4.34) CSF £15.92 TOTE £6.90: £2.80 £1.70 (£9.00) OWNER Mrs M. A. Clayton (TARPORLEY) BRED Mrs M. A. Clayton
WEIGHT FOR AGE 3yo-7lb
OFFICIAL EXPLANATION **Magic Mill (IRE): choked.**
2422 Safio, given a patient ride, won his first race for two years and there was plenty to like about the way he did it. (11/2)
2922 Present Generation is obviously in good heart at the moment and put in another useful effort, but is still a maiden after several near-misses. (9/4)
2478 Weetman's Weigh (IRE) likes to come from off the pace but was always struggling, and failed to get in a serious blow. (9/4)
2735 Jay-Owe-Two (IRE) ran much better this time and may be coming back to form. (20/1)
1583 Magic Mill (IRE) was disappointing, dropping tamely away once ridden. (8/1)
974 Keston Pond (IRE) does not look quite right yet and this was another poor effort. (10/1)
1799* French Grit (IRE) is a funny customer who needs things to go just right and, after taking too strong a hold and leading early on, he soon decided it was not for him. (9/1)

3088 WARREN BUTTERWORTH CATERING BUTCHERS H'CAP (0-65) (3-Y.O) (Class F)
4-15 (4-15) **7f** £2,536.50 (£714.00: £349.50) Stalls: High GOING minus 0.19 sec per fur (GF)

			SP	RR	SF
2543[7]	**Barresbo (60)** (CWFairhurst) **3-9-4** JWeaver(9) (lw: hld up & bhd: hdwy 3f out: rdn to ld ins fnl f: styd on wl) —	**1**	7/1[3]	73	27
2903*	**Hi Mujtahid (IRE) (51)** (SEKettlewell) **3-8-9** 6x KDarley(3) (lw: racd alone far side: a cl up: rdn over 1f out: no ex ins fnl f) 2½	**2**	4/1[1]	58	12
2756[3]	**Daintree (IRE) (50)** (HJCollingridge) **3-8-8** DaleGibson(10) (trckd ldrs: led over 2f out tl ins fnl f: sn btn) 1¼	**3**	7/1[3]	54	8
2417[5]	**Two On The Bridge (60)** (DenysSmith) **3-9-4** KFallon(8) (a chsng ldrs: effrt over 2f out: btn appr fnl f) 1¾	**4**	5/1[2]	60	14
2891[3]	**Presentiment (50)** (MartynWane) **3-8-8** LCharnock(11) (in tch: hdwy 3f out: chsng ldrs appr fnl f: no ex) nk	**5**	5/1[2]	50	4
2313[6]	**Sparkling Harry (52)** (MissLCSiddall) **3-8-10** DeanMcKeown(1) (lw: in tch: hrd rdn 2f out: r.o one pce) 1	**6**	16/1	50	4
2567[11]	**Martine (63)** (ABailey) **3-9-7** DWright(5) (bhd: hdwy u.p 2f out: nvr rchd ldrs) 2½	**7**	16/1	55	9
2883[9]	**Risky Flight (38)** (ASmith) **3-7-7**(3) PFessey(2) (prom tl wknd fnl 2½f) 6	**8**	33/1	16	—
2891[7]	**Mill End Boy (50)** (MWEasterby) **3-8-5v**(3) GParkin(12) (led tl hdd over 2f out: grad wknd) 2½	**9**	14/1	22	—
2305[8]	**Magic Fizz (58)** (TJEtherington) **3-9-2** ACulhane(7) (prom 4f: wknd) 1½	**10**	20/1	27	—
2847[9]	**Farewell My Love (IRE) (56)** (JSWainwright) **3-9-0** RLappin(13) (s.s: a bhd) 1¼	**11**	14/1	22	—
2032[5]	**My Saltarello (IRE) (45)** (ABMulholland) **3-7-12**(5)ow3 CLowther(6) (cl up over 4f: wknd) 1	**12**	16/1	9	—
2715*	**C-Harry (IRE) (63)** (RHollinshead) **3-9-7** FLynch(4) (cl up tl rdn & wknd 2f out) s.h	**13**	5/1[2]	27	—
			(SP 133.7%)		**13 Rn**

1m 29.56 (5.06) CSF £35.95 CT £205.09 TOTE £9.20: £3.00 £1.80 £2.10 (£19.40) Trio £77.30 OWNER North Cheshire Trading & Storage Ltd (MIDDLEHAM) BRED North Cheshire Trading and Storage Ltd
LONG HANDICAP Risky Flight 7-6
OFFICIAL EXPLANATION **C-Harry (IRE): the trainer reported that the colt saw too much daylight in the race and ran too freely as a result.**

2169 Barresbo, given a really good, patient ride, produced a good run to settle it nicely in the closing stages and gain his first win. He looks likely to go on from here. (7/1)
2903* Hi Mujtahid (IRE) is a real character for he was taken to the far side to race alone, but was just worried out of it. A pair of blinkers may well help. (4/1)
2756 Daintree (IRE) has yet to win a race, but is both looking and running quite well at present. (7/1)
2417 Two On The Bridge had his chances but this stiff track may just have stretched his stamina. (5/1)
2891 Presentiment has ability but is not quite doing enough when it matters and is still a maiden. (5/1)
2313 Sparkling Harry was without the blinkers this time and was not doing enough. (16/1)
2141 Martine is beginning to slip down the handicap and there were some signs of encouragement here. (16/1)
2715* C-Harry (IRE) (5/1: op 3/1)

3089 BOB GORMAN SIGNS MAIDEN STKS (3-Y.O+) (Class D)

4-45 (4-45) **1m 2f 32y** £3,501.25 (£1,060.00: £517.50: £246.25) Stalls: High GOING minus 0.19 sec per fur (GF)

				SP	RR	SF
2566[2]	**Dantesque (IRE) (84)** (GWragg) **4-9-7** MHills(3) (lw: mde all: v.easily)	—	**1**	1/8[1]	73+	40
2846[7]	**Understudy (57)** (RHollinshead) **3-8-6** FLynch(2) (lw: s.i.s: hdwy ent st: styd on u.p: no ch w wnr)	7	**2**	8/1[2]	57	14
	Sabre Dancer (RAllan) **3-8-11** JWeaver(1) (bit bkwd: a.p: hdwy over 2f out: no imp)	3	**3**	10/1[3]	57	14
1755[7]	**Maddie** (WWHaigh) **5-9-2** RLappin(4) (a chsng ldrs: one pce fnl 3f)	1	**4**	100/1	51	18
2902[5]	**No Problem Jac** (JJO'Neill) **4-9-2** JCarroll(6) (chsd wnr tl wknd fnl 2f)	15	**5**	25/1	27	—
	Uncle Errol (GMMoore) **3-8-11** DaleGibson(5) (cmpt: bit bkwd: sn outpcd & bhd: t.o)	18	**6**	50/1	4	—
				(SP 115.9%)		**6 Rn**

2m 13.0 (6.30) CSF £1.97 TOTE £1.10: £1.10 £1.10 (£2.50) OWNER Mollers Racing (NEWMARKET) BRED Islanmore Stud
WEIGHT FOR AGE 3yo-10lb
2566 Dantesque (IRE) found a non-competitive event and, as expected, absolutely trotted up. (1/8)
2360 Understudy had to work really hard to beat some moderate opponents for second place, but he never had a chance with the very easy winner. (8/1)
Sabre Dancer, having his first run in this country, might well be one to watch over hurdles. (10/1)
Maddie improved on her debut but there is still a long way to go. (100/1)

T/Plpt: £166.90 (87.06 Tckts). T/Qdpt: £4.20 (312.44 Tckts) AA

2916-WINDSOR (Fig. 8) (Good to firm)

Monday July 28th

WEATHER: sunny WIND: almost nil

3090 RUMPLESTILTSKIN (S) STKS (2-Y.O) (Class G)

6-15 (6-18) **5f 217y** £2,272.50 (£635.00: £307.50) Stalls: High GOING minus 0.58 sec per fur (F)

				SP	RR	SF
2875[7]	**Sassy (IRE)** (APJarvis) **2-8-6** SDrowne(5) (a.p: hrd rdn & led wl over 1f out: r.o)	—	**1**	7/4[2]	65	5
1812[23]	**Courtney Gym (IRE)** (MRChannon) **2-8-11** RHughes(4) (hdwy over 2f out: ev ch 1f out: nt qckn)	2	**2**	16/1	65	5
2746[3]	**Shanthi** (PJMakin) **2-8-6** SSanders(6) (a.p: ev ch & hrd rdn over 1f out: nt qckn)	hd	**3**	11/8[1]	59	—
2587[9]	**Dot** (RHannon) **2-8-6** DaneO'Neill(7) (lw: nrst fin)	2	**4**	8/1[3]	54	—
1856[5]	**The Hobby Lobby (IRE)** (MissKMGeorge) **2-8-11** MTebbutt(3) (lw: led over 4f)	¾	**5**	10/1	57	—
2741[P]	**Goldenacres** (JNeville) **2-8-11** FNorton(8) (s.i.s: nvr nr to chal)	7	**6**	25/1	38	—
2784[12]	**Ask Speedy Snaps** (JMBradley) **2-8-11** DHarrison(9) (spd 3f)	10	**7**	33/1	12	—
	First Idea (SDow) **2-8-6** GCarter(1) (leggy: unf: s.s: a bhd)	13	**8**	16/1	—	—
2003[12]	**Lamoura** (RBrotherton) **2-8-6** RPrice(2) (w ldr over 3f: wknd qckly)	6	**9**	40/1	—	—
				(SP 119.7%)		**9 Rn**

1m 13.2 (2.70) CSF £27.77 TOTE £3.00: £1.40 £2.10 £1.20 (£20.70) Trio £19.60 OWNER Mr A. L. R. Morton (ASTON UPTHORPE) BRED Lee Valley Farm
No bid
Sassy (IRE), dropped in class, was good enough but it was hard work. Driven to the front below the distance, she stayed on all out. (7/4)
Courtney Gym (IRE), like the winner dropped in class, made ground from halfway but, after having every chance, could not quicken in the final furlong. (16/1)
2746 Shanthi finished third for the fourth time in as many races. There were no excuses, she was always chasing the leaders and failed to quicken. (11/8: 4/5-6/4)
Dot had plenty to do at halfway but was staying on in the closing stages. (8/1: 6/1-9/1)
1370 The Hobby Lobby (IRE) faded after leading for over four furlongs. (10/1: 5/1-11/1)
1758 Goldenacres missed the break and could never reach a challenging position. (25/1)

3091 CANTOR FITZGERALD BONDS AND EQUITIES H'CAP (0-70) (3-Y.O+) (Class E)

6-45 (6-47) **1m 2f 7y** £3,078.75 (£930.00: £452.50: £213.75) Stalls: High GOING minus 0.58 sec per fur (F)

				SP	RR	SF
2668[4]	**Bakers Daughter (57)** (JRArnold) **5-8-12**(3) MartinDwyer(12) (swtg: a.p: led over 1f out: all out)	—	**1**	6/1[2]	69	51
2782[3]	**Your Most Welcome (57)** (DJSffrenchDavis) **6-9-1** GCarter(15) (hdwy 2f out: r.o wl ins fnl f)	s.h	**2**	6/1[2]	69	51
2305[7]	**Ring the Chief (38)** (MDIUsher) **5-7-10** JMarshall(11) (gd hdwy fnl 2f: nvr nrr)	½	**3**	25/1	49	31
2947[5]	**Zurs (IRE) (58)** (MissGayKelleway) **4-9-2** DHolland(1) (lw: a.p: led over 2f out tl over 1f out: nt qckn)	2½	**4**	8/1[3]	65	47
2650[6]	**Westminster (IRE) (63)** (MHTompkins) **5-9-0v**(7) PClarke(9) (lw: hdwy 5f out: rdn 2f out: one pce)	nk	**5**	10/1	70	52
2892[6]	**Whatever's Right (IRE) (66)** (MDIUsher) **8-9-10** JReid(2) (hdwy over 2f out: one pce fnl f)	1½	**6**	10/1	70	52
2880[5]	**Forest Robin (55)** (MrsJRRamsden) **4-8-13** JFortune(13) (prom tl hrd rdn & wknd over 2f out)	¾	**7**	11/2[1]	58	40
2375[9]	**Super Serenade (47)** (GBBalding) **8-8-5** SDrowne(16) (lw: nvr nr to chal)	1¼	**8**	20/1	48	30
2880[4]	**Zahran (IRE) (38)** (JMBradley) **6-7-5**(5) APolli(3) (lw: hdwy 2f out: nt rch ldrs)	hd	**9**	20/1	39	21
	Ember (45) (PHayward) **4-8-0**(3) MHenry(8) (prom tl wknd over 2f out)	hd	**10**	50/1	46	28
2920[4]	**Haroldon (IRE) (68)** (BPalling) **8-9-12** DaneO'Neill(14) (b: swtg: nvr nr to chal)	½	**11**	8/1[3]	68	50
2910[12]	**Sommersby (IRE) (46)** (MrsNMacauley) **6-8-4b** DHarrison(10) (b: lw: hdwy 4f out: wknd 2f out)	7	**12**	33/1	35	17
2576[4]	**Absolutely Fayre (48)** (VSoane) **6-8-6** FNorton(5) (lw: nvr bttr than mid div)	nk	**13**	16/1	36	18
887[7]	**Absolutelystunning (59)** (MrsBarbaraWaring) **4-9-3** NAdams(4) (b: b.hind: nvr on terms)	½	**14**	14/1	47	29
2916[4]	**Victor Blum (USA) (38)** (CAHorgan) **4-7-10v** NCarlisle(6) (w ldr: led 4f out tl wknd over 2f out)	2	**15**	20/1	22	4

2742[2]	**Sifwa (53)** (DCO'Brien) **3-8-1** GBardwell(7) (lw: a bhd)	7	**16**	33/1	26	—
769[9]	**Talk Back (IRE) (60)** (GLewis) **5-8-11**(7) JDennis(17) (bhd fnl 5f)	nk	**17**	25/1	33	15
	Prestige Lass (54) (MissKMGeorge) **4-8-12** SSanders(18) (led to 4f out: sn hrd rdn & wknd qckly: t.o)	dist	**18**	33/1	—	—

(SP 129.7%) **18 Rn**

2m 5.1 (0.20) CSF £34.74 CT £800.87 TOTE £4.90: £1.20 £2.00 £5.10 £1.90 (£8.80) Trio £132.70 OWNER Mrs Sue Baker (UPPER LAMBOURN) BRED C. C. Bromley and Son and A. O. Nerses
LONG HANDICAP Victor Blum (USA) 7-7 Ring the Chief 7-6 Zahran (IRE) 7-3
WEIGHT FOR AGE 3yo-10lb
2668 Bakers Daughter was always close up. She went to the front approaching the final furlong and held on bravely. (6/1)
2782 Your Most Welcome ran another good race. She improved two furlongs out and her strong burst in the final furlong failed by the narrowest margin. (6/1)
2305 Ring the Chief, like the winner, came late, but could not find quite enough. (25/1)
2947 Zurs (IRE) close up throughout, went to the front two furlongs out but could find no extra approaching the final furlong. (8/1)
2650 Westminster (IRE) moved up steadily from halfway, but could not sustain the effort in the last furlong and a half. (10/1)
2892 Whatever's Right (IRE) made good ground two furlongs out, but could not find the pace to trouble the leaders. (10/1)

3092 CANTOR FITZGERALD INTERNATIONAL H'CAP (0-80) (3-Y.O+ F & M) (Class D)

7-15 (7-17) **5f 217y** £3,759.50 (£1,136.00: £553.00: £261.50) Stalls: High GOING minus 0.58 sec per fur (F)

				SP	RR	SF
2921[2]	**Ella Lamees (55)** (WJMusson) **3-8-0** DRMcCabe(4) (lw: swtg: gd hdwy over 1f out: r.o to ld cl home)	—	**1**	5/1[1]	66	27
2705[7]	**Farley Green (66)** (HCandy) **3-8-11** NAdams(5) (a.p: r.o wl ins fnl f)	½	**2**	14/1	76	37
2833[11]	**La Petite Fusee (76)** (RJO'Sullivan) **6-9-9**(3) RHavlin(6) (lw: led tl nr fin)	hd	**3**	8/1[3]	85	51
2590[4]	**Tinker Osmaston (64)** (RJHodges) **6-9-0** TSprake(14) (lw: chsd ldrs: nt clr run & swtchd lft 1f out: r.o)	s.h	**4**	8/1[3]	73	39
2554[17]	**Dayrella (54)** (WRMuir) **3-7-10**(3) MartinDwyer(13) (lw: hdwy 2f out: r.o ins fnl f)	nk	**5**	9/1	63	24
2895[6]	**Superlao (BEL) (46)** (JJBridger) **5-7-3**(7) PDoe(11) (w ldrs tl wknd fnl f)	5	**6**	20/1	41	7
2925[6]	**Blues Queen (78)** (MRChannon) **3-9-9** PaulEddery(2) (lw: hdwy & hrd rdn over 2f out: wknd over 1f out)	1¾	**7**	16/1	68	29
2708[11]	**Mouche (70)** (MrsJRRamsden) **3-9-1** JFortune(8) (lw: prom 4f)	nk	**8**	10/1	60	21
2506[5]	**Grace (65)** (JMBradley) **3-8-10** SDrowne(9) (s.s: nrst fin)	nk	**9**	12/1	54	15
2705[2]	**Secret Combe (IRE) (79)** (PJMakin) **3-9-10** SSanders(12) (in tch tl rdn & wknd over 2f out)	¾	**10**	6/1[2]	66	27
2358[5]	**Husun (USA) (70)** (PTWalwyn) **3-9-1v[1]** RHills(1) (hrd rdn over 2f out: no hdwy whn hmpd over 1f out)	1¼	**11**	12/1	54	15
2852[9]	**Rambold (52)** (NEBerry) **6-8-2** GCarter(7) (w ldrs over 3f: sn wknd)	nk	**12**	14/1	35	1
2852[2]	**Nellie North (47)** (GMMcCourt) **4-7-6v**(5)ow1 RMullen(3) (reard up s: gd hdwy over 2f out: wknd over 1f out)	s.h	**13**	6/1[2]	30	—
2705[12]	**Prospering (51)** (RJHodges) **3-7-10** FNorton(10) (a bhd)	2½	**14**	20/1	27	—

(SP 130.7%) **14 Rn**

1m 11.1 (0.60) CSF £75.69 CT £519.66 TOTE £6.40: £1.70 £5.70 £3.90 (£43.30) Trio £237.80 OWNER Billings & Broughton (NEWMARKET) BRED C. R. and V. M. Withers
LONG HANDICAP Superlao (BEL) 7-8 Prospering 7-7
WEIGHT FOR AGE 3yo-5lb
2921 Ella Lamees, well behind for a long way, came with a strong, late run to snatch the race close home. (5/1)
2705 Farley Green, always hunting up the leaders, put in a good burst in the last furlong but did not find quite enough. (14/1)
1439 La Petite Fusee tried to make all the running and was not collared until the finish. (8/1)
2590 Tinker Osmaston chased the leaders throughout, but did not enjoy the clearest of runs and can be considered unlucky. (8/1)
1810* Dayrella made ground two furlongs out but, though running on inside the last furlong, could not find quite enough. (9/1: 6/1-10/1)
2895 Superlao (BEL) disputed the lead until weakening in the final furlong. (20/1)
2705 Secret Combe (IRE), dropped in trip, was always struggling to go the pace and never held out any hope. (6/1: 4/1-13/2)

3093 CANTOR FITZGERALD GILT EDGED H'CAP (0-70) (3-Y.O+) (Class E)

7-45 (7-46) **1m 3f 135y** £2,948.75 (£890.00: £432.50: £203.75) Stalls: High GOING minus 0.58 sec per fur (F)

				SP	RR	SF
2843[5]	**Admirals Secret (USA) (50)** (CFWall) **8-8-13** JReid(2) (hld up: hdwy on ins over 1f out: led ins fnl f: r.o)	—	**1**	5/1	59	23
2865[6]	**Sandy Floss (IRE) (61)** (RHBuckler) **4-9-10** SDrowne(6) (lw: led tl ins fnl f)	1½	**2**	8/1	68	32
2696[2]	**Fourdaned (IRE) (58)** (SDow) **4-9-7** JFEgan(4) (lw: a.p: ev ch 1f out: nt qckn)	1¼	**3**	3/1[2]	63	27
2928[5]	**Statajack (IRE) (60)** (DRCElsworth) **9-9-9b** DHolland(5) (b: hld up in rr: hdwy over 2f out: nt clr run over 1f out: nt qckn)	1¼	**4**	8/1	64	28
2208[5]	**Yet Again (50)** (MissGayKelleway) **5-8-13** SSanders(1) (a.p: hrd rdn over 2f out: one pce)	s.h	**5**	9/4[1]	53	17
2750[4]	**Golden Saddle (USA) (57)** (PFICole) **3-8-1**(7) DavidO'Neill(3) (in tch tl wknd over 2f out)	7	**6**	9/2[3]	51	3

(SP 112.8%) **6 Rn**

2m 30.2 (4.20) CSF £38.41 TOTE £5.30: £2.70 £3.80 (£16.50) OWNER Mrs C. A. Wall (NEWMARKET) BRED Haras Santa Maria de Araras & Peter M. Brant
WEIGHT FOR AGE 3yo-12lb
2843 Admirals Secret (USA), patiently ridden, found a clear run on the inside to quicken into the lead in the last one hundred and fifty yards. (5/1: op 3/1)
2865 Sandy Floss (IRE) made a game effort to lead throughout. He held off the sustained challenge of Fourdaned, but could not hold the winner inside the final furlong. (8/1: 6/1-10/1)
2696 Fourdaned (IRE) came under pressure over a quarter of a mile from home. He had every chance a furlong out, but was not doing his rider any favours and did not find much. (3/1)
2928 Statajack (IRE), held up in last place, was moving up to challenge when failing to find a clear run approaching the final furlong. It is doubtful he would have troubled the leaders in any case. (8/1: 5/1-10/1)
2208 Yet Again was driven up to try to challenge the two leaders over two furlongs from home, but was struggling from that point and never appeared likely to win. (9/4)
2750 Golden Saddle (USA) dropped back beaten with well over two furlongs left to race. (9/2)

3094 EVENING STANDARD MAIDEN STKS (2-Y.O) (Class D)

8-15 (8-18) **5f 10y** £3,485.00 (£1,055.00: £515.00: £245.00) Stalls: High GOING minus 0.58 sec per fur (F)

				SP	RR	SF
1952[3]	**Monte Lemos (IRE)** (RCharlton) **2-9-0** TSprake(17) (lw: w ldr: led over 2f out: hung bdly lft: drvn out)	—	**1**	100/30[1]	80	34

				SP	RR	SF
2467^{6}	**Nuclear Debate (USA)** (MrsJRRamsden) **2-9-0** JFortune(19) (lw: s.s: gd hdwy fnl f: nt rch wnr)	2	**2**	10/1	74	28
	Raise A King (JWPayne) **2-9-0** GCarter(9) (leggy: gd hdwy over 1f out: bmpd nr fin)	½	**3**	33/1	72	26
2534^{8}	**Allasella (IRE)** (BPalling) **2-8-6**(3) MartinDwyer(18) (chsd ldrs: hung bdly lft over 1f out: veered rt nr fin)	s.h	**4**	33/1	67	21
850^{4}	**Emperor Naheem (IRE)** (BJMeehan) **2-9-0** MTebbutt(8) (led over 2f: ev ch whn edgd lft over 1f out: wknd ins fnl f)	2	**5**	14/1	66	20
2720^{2}	**Dil** (BHanbury) **2-9-0** JStack(6) (lw: a.p: no hdwy fnl 2f)	hd	**6**	$4/1^{2}$	65	19
1954^{5}	**Alpen Wolf (IRE)** (WRMuir) **2-9-0** JReid(15) (gd spd over 3f)	nk	**7**	14/1	64	18
	Noble Demand (USA) (MrsJRRamsden) **2-9-0** JFEgan(10) (w'like: bit bkwd: hdwy 2f out: nt rch ldrs)	2½	**8**	25/1	56	10
2842^{6}	**Golden Fortune** (DRLoder) **2-8-9** WRyan(11) (lw: a abt same pl)	2½	**9**	$13/2^{3}$	43	—
	Have A Break (CREgerton) **2-9-0** RHughes(21) (lengthy: scope: bit bkwd: nvr nr to chal)	1	**10**	25/1	45	—
	Smart Squall (USA) (LordHuntingdon) **2-9-0** DHarrison(13) (small: hmpd s: nt rcvr)	nk	**11**	7/1	44	—
2597^{10}	**Pre Catelan** (MBell) **2-8-9** PaulEddery(4) (prom over 2f)	¾	**12**	12/1	37	—
2771^{8}	**Danzino (IRE)** (APJarvis) **2-9-0** SDrowne(5) (lw: outpcd)	½	**13**	50/1	40	—
	Long Island (RHannon) **2-9-0** DaneO'Neill(20) (small: lengthy: a bhd)	2	**14**	12/1	34	—
2553^{5}	**Sampower Lady** (WJMusson) **2-8-9** DRMcCabe(16) (a bhd)	nk	**15**	20/1	28	—
	Aries Boy (DCO'Brien) **2-9-0** GBardwell(12) (lt-f: wnt rt s: a bhd)	2½	**16**	33/1	25	—
	Taurean (NAGraham) **2-9-0** SSanders(7) (small: cmpt: a bhd)	5	**17**	25/1	9	—
	Oh So Easy (BJMeehan) **2-8-7**(7) GHannon(2) (cmpt: a bhd)	1¼	**18**	25/1	5	—
2919^{6}	**Lady Ralphina** (JJBridger) **2-8-4**(5) ADaly(3) (lw: chsd ldrs: wkng whn clipped heels & uns rdr over 1f out)		**U**	40/1	—	—

(SP 140.1%) **19 Rn**

60.6 secs (0.90) CSF £34.49 TOTE £4.10: £2.10 £5.40 £15.50 (£32.00) Trio £491.90; £436.56 to 30/8/97 OWNER Mr S M De Zoete (BECKHAMPTON) BRED Rathasker Stud

OFFICIAL EXPLANATION **Have A Break: rider reported that the colt hung so badly he was unable to ride him out.**

1952 Monte Lemos (IRE), fast away this time, raced in second place until leading at halfway. Despite hanging badly to the left in the last two furlongs, he never appeared likely to be caught. (100/30)

2467 Nuclear Debate (USA) missed the break but made good late headway to snatch second place near the line without troubling the winner. (10/1: 7/1-12/1)

Raise A King, a leggy individual, was running on strongly in the last furlong until bumped near the finish. He should certainly be able to win a race, possibly over a longer trip. (33/1)

1293 Allasella (IRE), always chasing the leading group, was hanging badly to the left in the last furlong and veered right near the finish as her rider tried to correct her. (33/1)

850 Emperor Naheem (IRE) led to halfway. He was still challenging strongly when edging to the left over a furlong out and losing his chance. (14/1: op 7/1)

2720 Dil, always chasing the leaders, could make no impression in the final quarter-mile. (4/1)

1954 Alpen Wolf (IRE) (14/1: 8/1-16/1)

2842 Golden Fortune (13/2: 7/2-7/1)

Smart Squall (USA), unruly in the stalls, was badly hampered when they opened and, in the circumstances, was far from disgraced in finishing mid-division. (7/1: 9/2-15/2)

Long Island (12/1: op 6/1)

3095 RAPUNZEL MAIDEN STKS (3-Y.O) (Class D)

8-45 (8-47) **1m 67y** £3,662.00 (£1,106.00: £538.00: £254.00) Stalls: High GOING minus 0.58 sec per fur (F)

				SP	RR	SF
2873^{U}	**Howaida (IRE)** (MRStoute) **3-8-9** JReid(10) (a.p: led 2f out: all out)	—	**1**	$5/1^{3}$	71	35
2555^{3}	**Karakia (IRE)** (JHMGosden) **3-8-9** AGarth(9) (lw: a.p: rdn over 3f out: ev ch fnl f: r.o)	nk	**2**	$7/2^{2}$	70	34
	Khazinat El Dar (USA) (MajorWRHern) **3-8-9** RHills(7) (w'like: s.s: sn prom: ev ch over 1f out: nt qckn)	2½	**3**	16/1	66	30
2591^{2}	**Northern Angel (IRE) (81)** (MrsJCecil) **3-9-0** PatEddery(12) (b.hind: chsd ldr: rdn 3f out: one pce fnl 2f)	3	**4**	$5/4^{1}$	65	29
	Rutland Chantry (USA) (LordHuntingdon) **3-9-0** DHarrison(1) (w'like: rdn over 3f out: hdwy fnl 2f: nvr nrr)	nk	**5**	20/1	64	28
2730^{7}	**Perchance To Dream (IRE) (42)** (BRMillman) **3-8-9b¹** TSprake(13) (led tl wknd 2f out)	2½	**6**	50/1	54	18
2591^{7}	**Meilleur (IRE)** (LadyHerries) **3-9-0** PaulEddery(5) (no hdwy fnl 3f)	1	**7**	20/1	58	22
	Evidently (IRE) (IABalding) **3-8-6**(3) MartinDwyer(6) (w'like: s.s: hdwy 5f out: nt rch ldrs)	hd	**8**	25/1	52	16
	Lysandros (IRE) (JHMGosden) **3-9-0** WRyan(4) (cmpt: nvr nr to chal)	2	**9**	33/1	54	18
2873^{10}	**Broughtons Lure (IRE)** (WJMusson) **3-8-9** DRMcCabe(11) (b.hind: dwlt: a bhd)	4	**10**	100/1	41	5
2555^{9}	**Shalverton (IRE)** (WRMuir) **3-8-9** DaneO'Neill(2) (a bhd)	½	**11**	50/1	40	4
2873^{9}	**Strength of Vision** (CREgerton) **3-9-0** RHughes(14) (s.s: a bhd)	1¾	**12**	100/1	41	5
2555^{4}	**Teulada (USA)** (LMCumani) **3-8-9** JFortune(3) (a bhd)	1¾	**13**	8/1	33	—
2492^{16}	**Catherston Lucky** (GBBalding) **3-8-9** SDrowne(8) (in tch tl wknd 4f out: t.o)	25	**14**	100/1	—	—

(SP 123.5%) **14 Rn**

1m 43.4 (1.20) CSF £19.76 TOTE £7.00: £2.10 £1.60 £3.20 (£17.30) Trio £143.80 OWNER Mr Saeed Suhail (NEWMARKET) BRED Mount Coote Stud

Howaida (IRE), who lost her rider at the start on her only previous run, was always close up and travelling well. She went to the front two furlongs out and battled on gamely. (5/1)

2555 Karakia (IRE), as on her previous run, came off the bridle a long way out but kept staying on. She found a clear run near the inside and had every chance in the last furlong. (7/2: 7/4-4/1)

Khazinat El Dar (USA) soon recovered from a slow start and was bang on terms approaching the final furlong. She showed signs of greenness but should be easy to place. (16/1)

2591 Northern Angel (IRE) appeared to be travelling well in second place to halfway, but came under pressure three furlongs out and could not hold his position. He kept staying on and might do better over a longer trip. (5/4: tchd 4/5)

Rutland Chantry (USA), a useful sort, was behind in the early stages but began to pick up ground from halfway. Though never able to reach the leaders, he gave the impression that there is much better to come, and should stay further. (20/1)

Perchance To Dream (IRE), blinkered for the first time, set off at a million miles an hour but soon weakened when headed at the two-furlong marker. (50/1)

2555 Teulada (USA) (8/1: 6/1-10/1)

T/Jkpt: Not won; £48,107.95 to Goodwood 29/7/97. T/Plpt: £289.20 (92.96 Tckts). T/Qdpt: £136.00 (7.6 Tckts) Hn

2922-YARMOUTH (L-H) (Good to firm, Firm bk st)
Monday July 28th
WEATHER: fine WIND: mod half against

3096 J & H BUNN FERTILIZERS H'CAP (0-70) (3-Y.O+) (Class E)
6-00 (6-00) **2m** £2,810.25 (£837.00: £398.50: £179.25) Stalls: High GOING minus 0.36 sec per fur (F)

				SP	RR	SF
2592U	**Children's Choice (IRE) (49)** (WJMusson) **6-9-7** AMcGlone(1) (hld up: hdwy 2f out: led ins fnl f: pushed out)	—	1	3/1 2	57	14
1866 10	**City Hall (IRE) (65)** (MRStoute) **3-9-6** GHind(3) (trckd ldr 9f: swtchd over 3f out: n.m.r fr 2f out: r.o wl towards fin)	½	2	6/1 3	73	13
2908*	**Pen Friend (49)** (WJHaggas) **3-8-4** 6x JLowe(6) (hld up: rdn over 3f out: hdwy to ld over 1f out: hdd & no ex ins fnl f)	¾	3	11/10 1	56	—
1562 6	**John Lee Hooker (56)** (DWPArbuthnot) **5-10-0** SWhitworth(2) (b: b.hind: lw: plld hrd: in tch: rdn over 3f out: n.m.r over 1f out: nvr able to chal)	8	4	10/1	55	12
	Zeliba (40) (PRChamings) **5-8-12** JQuinn(4) (lw: a.p: led 4f out: hdd & wknd over 1f out)	5	5	12/1	34	—
2777*	**Petoskin (55)** (JPearce) **5-9-10**(3) CTeague(5) (set stdy pce: qcknd over 5f out: hdd 4f out: wkng whn hmpd over 1f out)	5	6	13/2	44	1
				(SP 117.0%)		**6 Rn**

3m 36.6 (13.10) CSF £19.90 TOTE £3.80: £2.10 £2.70 (£13.60) OWNER Mrs A. V. Totman (NEWMARKET) BRED M. J. Cassidy
WEIGHT FOR AGE 3yo-17lb

2411 Children's Choice (IRE) had lady luck on her side for a change and, after travelling best, was able to idle a little in front and still last home. (3/1)

City Hall (IRE), leniently handicapped for one who had shown a little promise, clearly does nothing fast and looked in two minds when the gap appeared, but was closing fast at the line. (6/1: 7/2-13/2)

2908* Pen Friend might well have appreciated a more truly-run race. (11/10: 11/8-evens)

1562 John Lee Hooker did not get the greatest of runs on the inside but did not look to be going well enough to win. (10/1: op 6/1)

Zeliba, a recent winner over hurdles, has been racing more freely recently and, made plenty of use of, did not last home as well as she can. (12/1: op 8/1)

2777* Petoskin, back in handicap company, looked a reluctant leader, but did his best to dictate matters until finding the finishing pace too hot. (13/2: 7/2-7/1)

3097 BASTWICK (S) STKS (2-Y.O) (Class G)
6-30 (6-30) **6f 3y** £2,322.00 (£642.00: £306.00) Stalls: High GOING minus 0.21 sec per fur (GF)

				SP	RR	SF
2862 17	**Charlies Lad (IRE)** (RGuest) **2-8-11** PBloomfield(2) (a.p: led over 2f out: edgd lft: rdn out fnl f)	—	1	3/1 3	59	10
2425 6	**Jaybee Silver** (MHTompkins) **2-8-6** DBiggs(1) (dwlt: hdwy over 2f out: ev ch ins fnl f: r.o)	nk	2	12/1	53	4
1370 5	**Dande Times** (DWPArbuthnot) **2-8-11** SWhitworth(4) (b.hind: rdn over 3f out: hdwy over 1f out: nrst fin)	¾	3	7/1	56	7
2827*	**Captain Bliss** (NTinkler) **2-8-9b**(7) RWinston(5) (lw: w ldr: led after 2f: hdd over 2f out: one pce)	2	4	11/4 2	56	7
	Super Geil (CADwyer) **2-8-6** NVarley(3) (unf: sn pushed along: rdn & hdwy 2f out: wknd ins fnl f)	1	5	15/8 1	43	—
1860 9	**Glass River** (PDEvans) **2-8-11** MRoberts(7) (lw: sn rdn along: led 2f: wknd wl over 1f out)	3½	6	11/1	39	—
2606 8	**Bradbury Falls (IRE)** (DJSCosgrove) **2-8-6** JQuinn(6) (in tch over 3f)	3½	7	25/1	25	—
				(SP 118.8%)		**7 Rn**

1m 15.8 (4.90) CSF £35.68 TOTE £3.80: £1.50 £4.20 (£18.40) OWNER M & G Hill Ltd (Environmental Engineers) (NEWMARKET) BRED Mrs Frances M. Duncan
Bt in 4,500 gns. Dande Times clmd DHolgate £6,000.

2538 Charlies Lad (IRE), taking a big drop in class, again showed a tendency to hang left but was always doing just enough. (3/1)

2425 Jaybee Silver, last out as usual, did some useful running in the closing stages, but this looked a modest race even by selling standards. (12/1: 7/1-14/1)

1370 Dande Times, a good mover, is sprint bred but seemed to do better for this step-up in trip. (7/1)

2827* Captain Bliss, dropped in trip, kept trying but looks better over seven. (11/4: 2/1-3/1)

Super Geil, an ordinary-looking newcomer, took a good hold going down and looked a little green early on. A brief effort came to little and this half-sister to the moderate Gresatre has a lot to prove. (15/8)

1860 Glass River shows knee-action and looked unwilling going down and entering the stalls. Ridden along from the break, he downed tools at the first possible opportunity. (11/1)

3098 COTMAN CONDITIONS STKS (2-Y.O) (Class C)
7-00 (7-00) **5f 43y** £4,923.84 (£1,570.44: £750.72) Stalls: High GOING minus 0.21 sec per fur (GF)

				SP	RR	SF
2762*	**Titanic (IRE)** (JHMGosden) **2-9-0** GHind(2) (lw: hld up: hdwy to ld over 1f out: easily)	—	1	4/9 1	90+	22
2758*	**Prince Foley** (WGMTurner) **2-9-0**(7) DMcGaffin(4) (led 1f: rdn 2f out: swtchd lft over 1f out: rdn & r.o fnl f: nt trble wnr)	1¾	2	9/4 2	92	24
2746*	**High Gain** (PHowling) **2-8-6** JQuinn(3) (plld hrd: led after 1f: hdd over 1f out: one pce)	1½	3	9/1 3	72	4
				(SP 110.0%)		**3 Rn**

64.6 secs (3.60) CSF £1.67 TOTE £1.40 (£1.10) OWNER Sheikh Mohammed (NEWMARKET) BRED Sheikh Mohammed bin Rashid al Maktoum

2762* Titanic (IRE), a stockily-built individual, has plenty of speed for one whose half-brother, Puissant, won over a mile. He had another confidence-booster and looks ready to step-up in class. (4/9)

2758* Prince Foley had to switch when denied a clear run against the rails at a vital point, but would not have troubled the winner. (9/4)

2746* High Gain, who took a keen hold going down and early in the race, was far from disgraced. (9/1)

3099 TATTERSALLS MAIDEN AUCTION STKS (2-Y.O F) (Class E)
7-30 (7-30) **7f 3y** £2,914.25 (£869.00: £414.50: £187.25) Stalls: High GOING minus 0.21 sec per fur (GF)

				SP	RR	SF
2597 11	**Optimistic** (MHTompkins) **2-8-7** DBiggs(1) (lw: chsd ldrs: led wl over 1f out: clr fnl f: comf)	—	1	11/4 2	80+	31
2700 10	**Theme Tune** (DrJDScargill) **2-8-3** JQuinn(5) (hld up: hdwy 3f out: no imp fnl f)	4	2	16/1	67	18
2700 7	**Fanti Dancer (IRE)** (BJMeehan) **2-8-3** BDoyle(2) (chsd ldrs: rdn & edgd lft over 2f out: kpt on)	nk	3	9/2 3	66	17
2728 6	**Jungle Story (IRE)** (PTWalwyn) **2-8-6** RCochrane(3) (led over 5f: wknd & eased ins fnl f)	2½	4	4/7 1	64	15

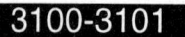

2545^{17} **Woodlands Pride (IRE)** (MCChapman) **2-7-8**(7) SCarson(4) (chsd ldrs 3f: sn rdn & wknd)....11 **5** 50/1 33 —
(SP 116.3%) **5 Rn**

1m 27.8 (3.60) CSF £34.12 TOTE £4.10: £1.60 £3.30 (£18.40) OWNER Mystic Meg Ltd (NEWMARKET) BRED Worksop Manor Stud Farm

Optimistic, a half-sister to the useful Woodbeck, took the eye both in the paddock and on the way to post. Much the best of a modest bunch, she did this in style and looks the sort for nurseries if the Handicapper is kind. (11/4)

Theme Tune, again broke a few lengths behind the others, but this time it looked rather more intentional and she was switched to the stands' rail to make her effort. She does not look anything special although her half-brother, Blue Ridge, did contest Group races last year. (16/1)

Fanti Dancer (IRE) moved to post quite well and gave herself a chance by breaking on terms, but did not find very much once let down. (9/2)

2728 Jungle Story (IRE) went down as if feeling the ground and her return confirmed it, for she was changing her legs and clearly in trouble once asked to stretch. (4/7)

Woodlands Pride (IRE), rather free going down, ran fast in the early stages but, once off the bridle, was soon waving goodbye, (50/1)

3100 ANGLIAN WATER H'CAP (0-75) (3-Y.O+) (Class D)

8-00 (8-05) **7f 3y** £3,709.30 (£1,107.40: £529.20: £240.10) Stalls: High GOING minus 0.21 sec per fur (GF)

				SP	RR	SF
2891^{8}	**Gain Line (USA) (51)** (BobJones) **4-8-7** NDay(10) (a.p: led over 1f out: rdn out)	—	**1**	6/1	62	44
2730^{12}	**On The Green (40)** (AHide) **4-7-7v**(3) MBaird(6) (prom: led 2f out: sn hdd & one pce)	¾	**2**	20/1	49	31
634^{6}	**Sharpo Wassl (68)** (WJHaggas) **3-9-3** RCochrane(11) (lw: hld up: hdwy 2f out: styng on whn n.m.r nr fin)	nk	**3**	13/2	77	52
2847^{4}	**Don Pepe (63)** (RBoss) **6-9-5** BDoyle(4) (hld up: hdwy 2f out: n.m.r & swtchd lft over 1f out: no ex ins fnl f)	1¼	**4**	11/4 1	69	51
2785^{5}	**Smart Guest (46)** (DShaw) **5-8-2**ow2 GHind(12) (b: a.p: ev ch 2f out: one pce fnl f)	s.h	**5**	12/1	52	32
2557^{6}	**Swift (67)** (MJPolglase) **3-9-2** MRimmer(2) (lw: hld up: swtchd rt 3f out: hdwy over 1f out: r.o)	1	**6**	5/1 3	70	45
2663^{8}	**Last Chance (58)** (DJSCosgrove) **3-8-7v¹** SWhitworth(7) (lw: led 4f: kpt on appr fnl f)	2½	**7**	16/1	56	31
2143^{4}	**Ocker (IRE) (69)** (MHTompkins) **3-9-4** DBiggs(3) (stdd s: nvr trbld ldrs)	3	**8**	14/1	60	35
2544^{4}	**Spanish Stripper (USA) (44)** (MCChapman) **6-7-7**(7)ow4 SCarson(9) (lw: dwlt: in tch 4f)	3	**9**	20/1	28	6
2691^{4}	**Eurolink Profile (73)** (LMCumani) **3-9-5**(3) RFfrench(8) (prom: led 3f out tl hdd & wknd 2f out)	1¼	**10**	3/1 2	54	29
2785^{17}	**Rise Up Singing (41)** (WJMusson) **9-7-11b** JQuinn(1) (rdn 4f out: sn bhd)	1¼	**11**	20/1	19	1
	Classic Flyer (IRE) (72) (ICampbell) **4-10-0** AMackay(5) (bkwd: bhd fnl 3f)	1¼	**12**	33/1	47	29

(SP 133.4%) **12 Rn**

1m 26.7 (2.50) CSF £121.52 CT £773.06 **TOTE £8.60**: £2.60 £5.00 £3.20 (£119.00) Trio £424.90 OWNER Legend Racing Club (NEWMARKET) BRED Juddmonte Farms

LONG HANDICAP On The Green 7-7 Spanish Stripper (USA) 7-0

WEIGHT FOR AGE 3yo-7lb

2121 Gain Line (USA) took his usual strong hold but, with plenty of pace on, got a nice lead to the distance. (6/1)

2317 On The Green, moved well to post and ran her best race yet, always being in the firing line. (20/1)

634 Sharpo Wassl, returning after a break of more than three months, looked a bit fresh going down, but came home well and might have prevailed given a totally clear passage. (13/2)

2847 Don Pepe seemed to be going best from some way out, but had to switch at an important stage, costing him momentum and possibly the race. (11/4: op 5/1)

2785 Smart Guest, with most of the field drifting towards the centre of the course, had a clear run against the stands' side fence, running well without ever threatening to quicken enough. (12/1: op 8/1)

2557 Swift again moved down rather poorly, and the cause already looked hopeless when he was brought to the stands' rail to make his run. (5/1)

2143 Ocker (IRE) (14/1: 10/1-16/1)

3101 DAMGATE H'CAP (0-70) (3-Y.O+ F & M) (Class E)

8-30 (8-32) **1m 2f 21y** £2,992.25 (£893.00: £426.50: £193.25) Stalls: Low GOING minus 0.36 sec per fur (F)

				SP	RR	SF
3039^{4}	**Karinska (56)** (MCChapman) **7-9-3**(7) SCarson(5) (plld hrd: wnt prom 5f out: led over 1f out: rdn out)	—	**1**	7/1	61	43
2593^{2}	**Lucky Begonia (IRE) (50)** (WJMusson) **4-9-4** AMcGlone(4) (hld up: hdwy over 1f out: swtchd lft & r.o ins fnl f: nt rch wnr)	1	**2**	7/2 3	53	35
2832^{3}	**Inclination (60)** (MBlanshard) **3-9-4** JQuinn(3) (led: rdn 4f out: hdd over 1f out: one pce)	2½	**3**	2/1 2	60	32
2468^{6}	**Dancing Queen (IRE) (60)** (MBell) **3-9-4** MFenton(1) (a.p: no ex appr fnl f)	1	**4**	12/1	58	30
2487^{4}	**Isis Honda (IRE) (59)** (CEBrittain) **3-9-3** MRoberts(2) (lw: plld hrd: chsd ldr 8f: sn btn)	1¼	**5**	7/4 1	55	27
2730^{8}	**Impetuous Lady (USA) (30)** (WJMusson) **4-7-9**(3) RFfrench(7) (lw: dropped rr 5f out: n.d after)	½	**6**	20/1	25	7
2593^{3}	***Square Mile Miss (IRE) (40)*** (PHowling) **4-8-8** JLowe(6) (Withdrawn not under Starter's orders: uns rdr & bolted bef s)		**W**	12/1	—	—

(SP 124.6%) **6 Rn**

2m 8.2 (4.40) CSF £28.46 TOTE £9.50: £3.40 £1.90 (£12.40) OWNER Mr Geoff Whiting (MARKET RASEN) BRED Sheikh Mohammed bin Rashid al Maktoum

WEIGHT FOR AGE 3yo-10lb

3039 Karinska was scoring over ten furlongs for the first time, but this ninth success saw her show too much ability and resolution for a field of maiden fillies. (7/1)

2593 Lucky Begonia (IRE) got going just too late, and switching inside the winner in the last half furlong did cost her a little ground. She deserves to find a little race. (7/2: 5/2-4/1)

2832 Inclination is hardly an eyecatcher and seems poorly named, as her head carriage suggested she was not enjoying this. A little more cut might help but she does not look one to trust implicitly. (2/1)

1470 Dancing Queen (IRE) travelled best for much of the way but found nothing when the chips were down, as if not getting the trip. This would be very surprising as her dam is a half-sister to last year's mile and three-quarters winner here, Bold Classic. (12/1)

2487 Isis Honda (IRE) raced too freely to save anything for the closing stages and a slight drop in trip might be worth a try. (7/4)

Impetuous Lady (USA), settled to get the trip, did not run as badly as her finishing position suggests, although her effort to close towards the centre of the track entering the final quarter-mile came to nothing. Interestingly, the only times she has shown much promise have been when racing up with the pace over distances short of a mile. (20/1)

T/Plpt: £1,175.60 (10.26 Tckts). T/Qdpt: £188.60 (4.34 Tckts) Dk

2904-BEVERLEY (R-H) (Good, Good to firm patches)
Tuesday July 29th
WEATHER: sunny WIND: strong across

3102 LADYGATE (S) H'CAP (0-60) (3-Y.O) (Class F)
2-00 (2-00) **1m 3f 216y** £2,574.00 (£714.00: £342.00) Stalls: High GOING minus 0.44 sec per fur (F)

				SP	RR	SF
2701²	**Foolish Flutter (IRE) (41)** (RBastiman) **3-8-9b** LCharnock(2) (hld up: hdwy 4f out: rdn to ld appr fnl f: styd on)	—	**1**	11/10¹	51	25
2770³	**Northern Touch (53)** (SCWilliams) **3-9-0**(7) DarrenWilliams(5) (led tl hdd appr fnl f: kpt on same pce)	4	**2**	2/1²	58	32
2068⁸	**Cochiti (37)** (CWThornton) **3-8-5b¹** DeanMcKeown(3) (chsd ldrs: wnt 2nd over 5f out: hrd rdn 2f out: one pce)	1¾	**3**	20/1	39	13
2564¹⁵	**Digital Option (IRE) (40)** (MrsJRRamsden) **3-8-8** MFenton(4) (lw: hld up: effrt appr st: rdn & n.d)	20	**4**	11/2³	16	—
2885⁴	**Rock The Casbah (48)** (JHetherton) **3-9-2** GDuffield(1) (chsd ldr tl rdn & wknd 5f out)	12	**5**	9/1	8	—
				(SP 111.1%)		**5 Rn**

2m 38.3 (5.30) CSF £3.26 TOTE £2.30: £1.30 £1.20 (£2.20) OWNER Mr James Swailes (WETHERBY) BRED Edward Keyes
No bid

2701 Foolish Flutter (IRE), with the blinkers back on and trying her longest trip to date, needed plenty of help from the saddle but saw it out particularly well. (11/10: op 7/4)
2770 Northern Touch, stepping-up in trip, tried to gallop her rivals into the ground, but was all out some way from home and had no answer to the winner. (2/1: 6/4-9/4)
Cochiti had blinkers on for the first time, and ran better given some strong assistance, but was treading water in the last two furlongs. (20/1)
2357 Digital Option (IRE) has been disappointing lately and this was another moderate effort. (11/2: op 3/1)
2885 Rock The Casbah seems to have lost his way and this trip looks well beyond him. (9/1)

3103 E.B.F. MINSTER MOORGATE MAIDEN STKS (2-Y.O) (Class D)
2-30 (2-34) **7f 100y** £3,782.00 (£1,136.00: £548.00: £254.00) Stalls: High GOING minus 0.44 sec per fur (F)

				SP	RR	SF
	Alboostan (DMorley) **2-9-0** MFenton(2) (wl grwn: in tch: hdwy over 2f out: led 1½f: shkn up & r.o)	—	**1**	9/2³	86+	41
2336⁶	**Exit To Somewhere (IRE)** (HRACecil) **2-9-0** WRyan(3) (a chsng ldrs: ev ch 2f out: kpt on)	2	**2**	7/4¹	82	37
2556³	**Indimaaj** (JLDunlop) **2-9-0** BDoyle(5) (in tch: effrt 3f out: styd on appr fnl f: no imp)	2	**3**	2/1²	77	32
2524⁷	**Due South** (EALDunlop) **2-8-9** SWhitworth(8) (dwlt: pushed along & bhd appr st: r.o wl fnl 2f)	1¼	**4**	12/1	70	25
	Hombre (JWWatts) **2-9-0** JCarroll(10) (w'like: bhd: hdwy 2f out: styd on wl)	1½	**5**	33/1	72	27
2688³	**Murmoon** (BHanbury) **2-9-0** JStack(11) (bit bkwd: prom: effrt 3f out: btn appr fnl f)	1¼	**6**	8/1	69	24
2215⁴	**Wathbat Lion** (MAJarvis) **2-9-0** DeanMcKeown(6) (lw: mde most tl hdd & wknd 1½f out)	2½	**7**	16/1	64	19
2752⁹	**Rockette** (JWWatts) **2-8-9** PaulEddery(9) (bhd: hdwy 2f out: nvr nr to chal)	s.h	**8**	50/1	58	13
2768⁵	**Shannon's Secret (IRE)** (BJMeehan) **2-9-0** GDuffield(7) (cl up tl wknd over 2f out)	4	**9**	14/1	55	10
2881⁷	**Jago** (MWEasterby) **2-8-11**(3) GParkin(12) (a outpcd & bhd)	3½	**10**	50/1	47	2
2752¹⁰	**Western Lord** (CSmith) **2-8-11**(3) PFessey(4) (lost tch fr ½-wy)	10	**11**	50/1	26	—
	Premium Quest (RAFahey) **2-9-0** ACulhane(13) (w'like: bit bkwd: dwlt: a outpcd & wl bhd)	9	**12**	25/1	7	—
2917¹⁴	**Aegean Breeze** (MissGayKelleway) **2-8-7**(7) AngelaGallimore(1) (lw: cl up tl wknd qckly fnl 3f)	8	**13**	50/1	—	—
				(SP 133.9%)		**13 Rn**

1m 34.0 (2.00) CSF £12.71 TOTE £6.90: £2.10 £1.10 £1.10 (£7.00) Trio £8.50 OWNER Mr Hamdan Al Maktoum (NEWMARKET) BRED Godolphin Management Co Ltd

Alboostan, a useful type, won this nicely and there looks to be more to come. (9/2: 4/1-6/1)
2336 Exit To Somewhere (IRE) did plenty of squealing in the paddock but he still ran well, only to get tapped for toe in the closing stages. (7/4: 5/2-6/4)
2556 Indimaaj looks the type who needs time to strengthen and, whatever he does this year, another season should see improvement. (2/1: 6/4-9/4)
Due South is going to need longer trips and there is, without doubt, plenty more ability there, but she cannot afford to keep giving the rest so much start. (12/1: op 8/1)
Hombre put in a useful first effort and looks the sort to improve with experience. (33/1)
2688 Murmoon still looked likely to benefit from this and could be one to side with in nurseries. (8/1)
2215 Wathbat Lion was made plenty of use of this time and proved disappointing in the closing stages. (16/1)
Rockette again ran green but was picking up ground nicely in the last two furlongs to show she has ability. (50/1)

3104 TIMEFORM LADIES RACE FOR THE DOROTHY LAIRD TROPHY H'CAP (0-75) (3-Y.O+) (Class E)
3-05 (3-06) **1m 1f 207y** £3,185.75 (£956.00: £460.50: £212.75) Stalls: High GOING minus 0.44 sec per fur (F)

				SP	RR	SF
2907*	**Mcgillycuddy Reeks (IRE) (51)** (DonEnricoIncisa) **6-9-9** 5x KimTinkler(8) (lw: hld up: hdwy on ins over 2f out: led over 1f out: r.o)	—	**1**	3/1¹	65	45
2763²	**Cashmirie (44)** (JLEyre) **5-9-2** MissDianaJones(5) (trckd ldrs: effrt over 2f out: chsng wnr 1f out: kpt on)	1¾	**2**	3/1¹	55	35
2854⁵	**Sagebrush Roller (51)** (JWWatts) **9-9-9** JoHunnam(7) (lw: bhd: hdwy 3f out: nrst fin)	3½	**3**	8/1³	57	37
2843⁸	**Road Racer (IRE) (60)** (MrsJRRamsden) **4-9-13**(5) MissERamsden(2) (lw: bhd: effrt ent st: styd on: nrst fin)	¾	**4**	11/2²	64	44
2824³	**Sherqy (IRE) (55)** (SEKettlewell) **5-9-13** MrsSBosley(1) (led tl hdd over 1f out: sn btn)	1½	**5**	8/1³	57	37
2896⁶	**I'm a Nut Man (35)** (CASmith) **6-8-7** SophieMitchell(4) (b: prom tl outpcd fnl 2f)	2	**6**	12/1	34	14
2469⁵	**High Low (USA) (45)** (MDHammond) **9-8-12**(5) MrsAHammond(6) (chsd ldrs tl wknd fnl 2f)	hd	**7**	12/1	44	24
2164⁴	**Fresh Fruit Daily (70)** (PAKelleway) **5-11-0** AngelaGallimore(9) (hld up: n.m.r appr st: n.d after)	1¼	**8**	10/1	67	47
2494*	**Breezed Well (48)** (KGWingrove) **11-9-1**(5) MrsHNoonan(3) (w ldrs tl wknd fnl 2½f)	½	**9**	14/1	44	24
				(SP 118.7%)		**9 Rn**

2m 6.3 (3.20) CSF £10.71 CT £59.88 TOTE £3.00: £1.40 £1.10 £2.00 (£3.70) Trio £13.30 OWNER Don Enrico Incisa (MIDDLEHAM) BRED Noel Sweeney

2907* Mcgillycuddy Reeks (IRE) looked a good thing after her win the previous week and did the business in style. (3/1)
2763 Cashmirie put in another sound effort off this higher mark but was still always second best. (3/1)
2854 Sagebrush Roller ran well but it is anybody's guess as to what he will do next time. (8/1: op 12/1)
2843 Road Racer (IRE) is off a fair mark and ran a useful race but seems to need much stronger handling. (11/2)
2824 Sherqy (IRE), normally at his best when held up, was made too much use of on this occasion. (8/1)
2896 I'm a Nut Man has ability but is still a maiden and is still an entire, which is probably not in his favour. (12/1)

2164 Fresh Fruit Daily, held up, got messed about turning into the straight and soon decided he wanted none of it. This is best forgotten. (10/1)

3105 SHELPHEN RESOURCE H'CAP (0-80) (3-Y.O+) (Class D)

3-35 (3-35) **1m 100y** £3,998.00 (£1,199.00: £577.00: £266.00) Stalls: High GOING minus 0.44 sec per fur (F)

Form	Horse	Dist	Pos	SP	RR	SF
3039[12]	**Queens Consul (IRE) (69)** (BSRothwell) **7-9-10** MFenton(10) (b: mde all: jst lasted)	—	**1**	9/1	81	54
2678[10]	**Duraid (IRE) (72)** (DenysSmith) **5-9-13** ACulhane(6) (lw: a in tch: effrt over 2f out: r.o u.p towards fin)	hd	**2**	12/1	84	57
2906[5]	**Night of Glass (58)** (JLEyre) **4-8-13v** MGallagher(1) (trckd ldrs: effrt & ev ch 2f out: r.o one pce)	2½	**3**	8/1[3]	65	38
2887*	**Special-K (47)** (EWeymes) **5-8-2** GHind(11) (trckd ldrs: effrt & n.m.r over 2f out: kpt on appr fnl f)	½	**4**	13/2[2]	53	26
2906[4]	**Thatched (IRE) (52)** (REBarr) **7-8-7** DeanMcKeown(7) (lw: hld up: effrt 3f out: n.m.r: styd on: no imp)	2	**5**	8/1[3]	54	27
2845*	**Pleasure Trick (USA) (47)** (DonEnricoIncisa) **6-8-2** KimTinkler(5) (lw: bhd tl swtchd & hdwy 2f out: nrst fin)	½	**6**	10/1	48	21
2906[2]	**Euro Sceptic (IRE) (43)** (TDEasterby) **5-7-5b**(7)ow1 RWinston(3) (lw: trckd ldrs: effrt 2f out: rdn & btn appr fnl f)	s.h	**7**	85/40[1]	44	16
2845[3]	**Monte Cavo (52)** (MBrittain) **6-8-7** GDuffield(12) (chsd wnr tl wknd fnl 2½f)	nk	**8**	8/1[3]	53	26
2071[7]	**In Good Faith (49)** (JJQuinn) **5-8-4v[1]** LCharnock(8) (in tch: effrt 3f out: wknd wl over 1f out)	7	**9**	20/1	37	10
2906[10]	**Duke Valentino (58)** (RHollinshead) **5-8-13** WRyan(4) (swtg: nvr bttr than mid div)	2½	**10**	12/1	41	14
2891[16]	**Tom Mi Dah (56)** (MDHammond) **3-8-3**ow1 JCarroll(9) (a bhd)	4	**11**	25/1	31	—
	Tael of Silver (59) (ABailey) **5-9-0** DWright(2) (sn bhd & pushed along: n.d)	3½	**12**	16/1	28	1

(SP 127.6%) **12 Rn**

1m 45.8 (1.80) CSF £110.14 CT £850.58 TOTE £9.70: £2.10 £3.10 £4.70 (£45.10) Trio £330.80; £139.81 to Goodwood 30/7/97 OWNER Miss Heather Davison (MALTON) BRED Mrs Ann Galvin

WEIGHT FOR AGE 3yo-8lb

3039 Queens Consul (IRE), given a good ride, had her mind made up for him this time and did it in game style. (9/1)
2678 Duraid (IRE) kept responding to pressure and would have won in another two strides. (12/1)
2906 Night of Glass keeps running well and deserves to pick up a race. (8/1)
2887* Special-K is in good form and put up another reasonable effort, but was both short of room and pace at a vital stage. (13/2)
2906 Thatched (IRE) is running well enough to suggest that there is another race in him. (8/1)
2845* Pleasure Trick (USA) is better on the All-Weather but, as he showed last time, can win on turf. This was another reasonable effort, but he was always finishing too late. (10/1)
2906 Euro Sceptic (IRE) has had plenty of chances and probably saw too much daylight on this occasion. (85/40)

3106 FAMILY DAY MAIDEN AUCTION STKS (2-Y.O F) (Class F)

4-10 (4-14) **5f** £2,847.00 (£792.00: £381.00) Stalls: High GOING minus 0.44 sec per fur (F)

Form	Horse	Dist	Pos	SP	RR	SF
2904[6]	**Miss Eliminator** (MWEasterby) **2-8-0b[1]** DaleGibson(11) (b.off hind: trckd ldrs: several positions fr ½-wy: qckned ins fnl f to ld nr fin)	—	**1**	7/1	62	1
1669[5]	**Imperial Honey (IRE)** (MrsASwinbank) **2-8-3** GDuffield(13) (chsd ldrs: led ins fnl f tl ct nr fin)	hd	**2**	16/1	65	4
2473[3]	**Miss Puci** (JBerry) **2-8-3** JFanning(12) (led tl hdd ins fnl f: kpt on)	1	**3**	11/2[2]	62	1
2700[4]	**Sharp Cracker (IRE)** (MJohnston) **2-8-4**(3) KMChin(6) (lw: in tch: effrt ½-wy: kpt on: no imp)	1¼	**4**	7/1	62	1
	Gaelic Quinie (IRE) (GROldroyd) **2-8-0** FNorton(4) (lt-f: unf: s.i.s: hdwy 2f out: sn chsng ldrs: nt qckn ins fnl f)	nk	**5**	25/1	54	—
2538[3]	**Chikapenny** (MrsLStubbs) **2-8-0** DWright(16) (hld up: nt clr run fr ½-wy tl wl ins fnl f)	1	**6**	6/1[3]	50	—
1486[8]	**Russian About (IRE)** (MRChannon) **2-8-3** PaulEddery(10) (unruly s: w ldr tl rdn & btn appr fnl f)	s.h	**7**	11/2[2]	53	—
2784[10]	**Pip's Addition (IRE)** (JAGlover) **2-8-3** JCarroll(7) (dwlt: swtchd lft 2f out: sme late hdwy)	hd	**8**	20/1	53	—
2520[7]	**Tilburg** (MrsNMacauley) **2-7-10**(7)ow3 JoHunnam(14) (sn drvn along: nvr rchd ldrs)	¾	**9**	33/1	50	—
2736[2]	**Gildersleve** (JWWatts) **2-7-11**(3) PFessey(3) (swtg: in tch tl rdn & btn 1f out)	2	**10**	3/1[1]	41	—
2684[5]	**Blarney Park** (CADwyer) **2-8-0** NVarley(5) (chsd ldrs 3f)	½	**11**	20/1	39	—
2545[14]	**Blitz** (MWEasterby) **2-8-0** LCharnock(2) (dwlt: a bhd)	2	**12**	25/1	33	—
2914[6]	**E B Treasure** (NBycroft) **2-8-0** JLowe(15) (sn wl bhd)	½	**13**	33/1	31	—
2412[5]	**Candy Twist** (RonaldThompson) **2-7-11**(3) DarrenMoffatt(1) (a outpcd & bhd)	hd	**14**	33/1	31	—
2736[7]	**Hoyland Common (IRE)** (NTinkler) **2-8-3** KimTinkler(9) (sn bhd)	5	**15**	33/1	18	—
1990[4]	**Crafty Pet (IRE)** (RAFahey) **2-7-7**(7) RWinston(8) (chsd ldrs to ½-wy)	¾	**16**	12/1	13	—

(SP 137.6%) **16 Rn**

64.9 secs (3.10) CSF £105.42 TOTE £9.20: £2.40 £6.80 £2.10 (£51.20) Trio £94.40 OWNER Mr Stephen Curtis (SHERIFF HUTTON) BRED John David Abell

2904 Miss Eliminator had blinkers on which made all the difference, and it was just a question of whether she would find a suitable gap in time. (7/1)
1669 Imperial Honey (IRE), after eight weeks off, took the eye moving well to post and put up a sound effort. (16/1)
2473 Miss Puci made full use of her draw but, despite some determined assistance, she still was not good enough. (11/2)
2700 Sharp Cracker (IRE) ran well from a moderate draw but left the impression that she needs further. (7/1)
Gaelic Quinie (IRE) gave problems before the start but certainly showed ability in the race, and there should be a modest event to be picked up. (25/1)
2538 Chikapenny, without the blinkers on this time, ran a deal better but could never find a gap until far too late. (6/1: 4/1-13/2)
Russian About (IRE) gave problems at the start and that might have made all the difference to the performance. (11/2)
Pip's Addition (IRE) took the eye in the paddock and certainly in the race, and is one to keep in mind. (20/1)

3107 'GO RACING IN YORKSHIRE' LIMITED STKS (0-70) (3-Y.O+) (Class E)

4-45 (4-45) **5f** £2,925.75 (£876.00: £420.50: £192.75) Stalls: High GOING minus 0.44 sec per fur (F)

Form	Horse	Dist	Pos	SP	RR	SF
2844[5]	**Royal Dome (IRE) (66)** (MartynWane) **5-9-5** JCarroll(1) (cl up: led wl over 1f out: styd on wl)	—	**1**	9/2	82	52
2895*	**Mousehole (70)** (RGuest) **5-9-5** PBloomfield(6) (chsd ldrs: outpcd ½-wy: kpt on wl fnl f)	2	**2**	9/4[1]	76	46
3077[2]	**Broadstairs Beauty (IRE) (70)** (DShaw) **7-8-13b**(3) CTeague(2) (b: led over 3f: kpt on one pce fnl f)	1¼	**3**	5/2[2]	69	39
2717[9]	**Just Bob (64)** (SEKettlewell) **8-8-9**(7) JennyBenson(5) (s.i.s: wl bhd tl hdwy 2f out: r.o)	½	**4**	9/1	67	37
2844[4]	**Manolo (FR) (64)** (JBerry) **4-8-9b**(7) PBradley(3) (prom: drvn along ½-wy: no imp after)	1¼	**5**	4/1[3]	63	33
2938[3]	**Rotherfield Park (IRE) (30)** (CSmith) **5-8-10**(3) PFessey(4) (in tch: rdn ½-wy: n.d after)	2	**6**	33/1	42 t	24

(SP 110.5%) **6 Rn**

62.7 secs (0.90) CSF £13.24 TOTE £5.50: £3.30 £1.60 (£8.30) OWNER Mr G. W. Jones (RICHMOND) BRED Michael F. Fogarty

2844 Royal Dome (IRE), well suited by getting a good lead, won with a little in hand. (9/2)
2895* Mousehole, as at Warwick last time, was never on the bridle, but he does respond to pressure, although it was always in vain. (9/4)

3077 Broadstairs Beauty (IRE) keeps trying hard but it is now two seasons since his last win. (5/2)
2504 Just Bob put up an eye-catcher and is likely to do better before long, especially if Jimmy Fortune is back in the saddle. (9/1)
2844 Manolo (FR) had plenty on, and was off the bit by halfway and making no impression thereafter. (4/1)
2938 Rotherfield Park (IRE) ran better than could have been expected. (33/1)

3108 SWINGS AND ROUNDABOUTS H'CAP (0-70) (3-Y.O+) (Class E)

5-15 (5-16) **1m 3f 216y** £3,130.50 (£939.00: £452.00: £208.50) Stalls: High GOING minus 0.44 sec per fur (F)

				SP	RR	SF
2824[2]	**Kernof (IRE) (59)** (MDHammond) **4-9-4** JCarroll(9) (in tch: effrt over 2f out: r.o wl fnl f to ld cl home)	—	**1**	5/1[2]	66	50
2365[2]	**Mister Aspecto (IRE) (56)** (MJohnston) **4-9-1v** BDoyle(6) (led: rdn 2f out: edgd rt: no ex towards fin)	1¼	**2**	11/2[3]	61	45
1853[8]	**High On Life (65)** (ACStewart) **3-8-12** SWhitworth(8) (plld hrd: trckd ldrs: hung rt over 1f out: styd on towards fin)	1	**3**	15/2	69	41
2682[6]	**Dancing Cavalier (65)** (RHollinshead) **4-9-3**(7) PFredericks(10) (b.off hind: bhd: effrt 3f out: styd on wl fnl f: nrst fin)	½	**4**	15/2	68	52
2846[4]	**Go Hence (70)** (WJarvis) **3-9-3** WRyan(5) (bhd: effrt on ins over 2f out: styd on towards fin)	2½	**5**	4/1[1]	70	42
2843[11]	**Fighting Times (45)** (CASmith) **5-8-4** DeanMcKeown(1) (prom tl btn & eased ins fnl f)	4	**6**	25/1	40	24
2682[10]	**Euphoric Illusion (37)** (MrsSJSmith) **6-7-7**(3) PFessey(7) (hld up: effrt 5f out: n.d)	2	**7**	14/1	29	13
2607[3]	**Heighth of Fame (49)** (JHetherton) **6-8-8** GDuffield(3) (prom tl wknd fnl 2½f)	7	**8**	8/1	32	16
	Peep O Day (41) (JLEyre) **6-8-0** TWilliams(4) (chsd ldrs tl wknd over 2f out)	3	**9**	9/1	20	4
1463[14]	**Samim (USA) (53)** (SGollings) **4-8-12b** MFenton(2) (swtg: chsd ldrs tl wknd fnl 2½f)	9	**10**	16/1	20	4
				(SP 113.1%)	**10 Rn**	

2m 35.6 (2.60) CSF £28.74 CT £184.18 TOTE £5.70: £1.70 £1.30 £2.50 (£10.40) Trio £24.20 OWNER Mr J. M. Gahan (MIDDLEHAM) BRED David Wallace

WEIGHT FOR AGE 3yo-12lb

2824 Kernof (IRE) is in the form of his life at the moment and, if reverting to hurdling, he should be followed. (5/1)
2365 Mister Aspecto (IRE) won this race off a 7lb higher mark last year but, despite a determined effort, just failed to last out this time. (11/2)
1282 High On Life was coltish in the paddock and took a strong hold in the race, and he would probably do better if he had a serious visit from the vet. (15/2)
2316 Dancing Cavalier has won off a mark as high as this and put in a reasonable effort, but probably just found this trip too sharp. (15/2)
2846 Go Hence, stepping-up in trip, took an age to get going but there is obviously ability there, once he gets the hang of things. (4/1)
Fighting Times ran much better on this occasion, and was given an easy time once beaten. (25/1)

T/Plpt: £135.40 (106.62 Tckts). T/Qdpt: £65.80 (13.84 Tckts) AA

2344-GOODWOOD (R-H) (Good to firm, Good patches)

Tuesday July 29th

WEATHER: hot WIND: almost nil

3109 WESTMINSTER TAXI INSURANCE GORDON STKS (Gp 3) (3-Y.O) (Class A)

2-15 (2-16) **1m 4f** £22,589.00 (£8,351.00: £4,000.50: £1,627.50: £638.75: £243.25) Stalls: High GOING minus 0.21 sec per fur (GF)

				SP	RR	SF
1399[2]	**Stowaway** (SbinSuroor) **3-8-10** KDarley(5) (lw: a.p: led 3f out: edgd rt over 2f out: hrd rdn over 1f out: r.o wl)	—	**1**	100/30[1]	122+	73
2641a[2]	**Poseidon (107)** (MRChannon) **3-8-10** JFortune(3) (rdn over 4f out: hdwy over 2f out: chsd wnr over 1f out: no imp)	3	**2**	33/1	118	69
2515*	**Ivan Luis (FR) (108)** (MBell) **3-8-10** RCochrane(2) (lw: stdy hdwy on ins over 2f out: swtchd lft over 1f out: hrd rdn: one pce)	½	**3**	15/2[3]	117	68
741[3]	**King Sound (112)** (JHMGosden) **3-8-10** OPeslier(10) (lw: a.p: ev ch 3f out: 2nd & rdn whn n.m.r on ins over 2f out: wknd over 1f out: fin 5th, 4l: plcd 4th)	1½	**4**	9/1	110	61
2107[2]	**Palio Sky (106)** (JLDunlop) **3-8-10** KFallon(1) (lw: hld up: rdn over 4f out: 6th & btn whn nt clr run over 2f out: fin 6th, 3l: plcd 5th)	4	**5**	15/2[3]	106	57
2765[2]	**Silence Reigns (104)** (MRStoute) **3-8-10** JReid(6) (lw: hld up: swtchd lft over 2f out: rdn: one pce: fin 4th, 1½l: disq plcd 6th)	3	**6**	15/2[3]	115	66
2596[2]	**Winter Garden (106)** (LMCumani) **3-8-10** JWeaver(8) (lw: nvr nr to chal)	3	**7**	7/1[2]	102	53
2135*	**Falak (USA) (115)** (MajorWRHern) **3-8-10** RHills(4) (lw: a.p: ev ch 3f out: hrd rdn over 2f out: wknd over 1f out)	3	**8**	100/30[1]	98	49
2107[5]	**Solo Mio (IRE) (98)** (BWHills) **3-8-10** PatEddery(9) (led over 3f: wknd over 3f out)	2½	**9**	20/1	95	46
2135[5]	**Blue River (IRE) (99)** (TGMills) **3-8-10** DHolland(7) (lw: chsd ldrs: led over 8f out to 3f out: sn wknd)	2½	**10**	40/1	91	42
				(SP 114.1%)	**10 Rn**	

2m 33.98 (0.78) CSF £119.34 TOTE £3.10: £1.80 £4.80 £2.50 (£83.00) Trio £289.30 OWNER Godolphin (NEWMARKET) BRED Hesmonds Stud Ltd

STEWARDS' ENQUIRY Reid susp. 7-11/8/97 (irresponsible riding)

1399 Stowaway appreciated the longer trip and, despite an absence of nearly ten weeks, struck the front three furlongs out. With a useful advantage below the distance, he responded to pressure for a decisive victory. (100/30)
2641a Poseidon began a forward move over a quarter of a mile from home but, having taken second place approaching the final furlong, could make no impression. The St Leger is now in the minds of connections. (33/1)
2515* Ivan Luis (FR) continues in good heart but, after being switched left below the distance, failed to find another gear. (15/2)
741 King Sound, without a run in three and a half months, was done no favours as the winner came across him over a quarter of a mile from home, but was already held. (9/1)
2107 Palio Sky chased the leaders but was already sending out distress signals when done no favours by Silence Reigns over two furlongs from home. (15/2)
2765 Silence Reigns was manoeuvred off the rail over a quarter of a mile from home, doing Palio Sky no favours, but made little impression thereafter. Reid was very harshly suspended for five days for irresponsible riding. (15/2: 5/1-8/1)
2135* Falak (USA) was a major disappointment and, after travelling well early in the straight, stopped to nothing below the distance. He is much better than this. (100/30)

3110 GROSVENOR CASINOS CUP H'CAP (0-105) (3-Y.O+) (Class B)

2-45 (2-50) **1m 6f** £35,825.00 (£10,850.00: £5,300.00: £2,525.00) Stalls: High GOING minus 0.21 sec per fur (GF)

Form	Horse	Dist	Pl	SP	RR	SF
2589*	**Media Star (USA) (81)** (JHMGosden) **4-8-7v** OPeslier(1) (lw: mde all: rdn over 3f out: clr over 2f out: r.o wl)	—	**1**	4/1 ^{1}	95	70
2749^{2}	**Puce (84)** (LMCumani) **4-8-10** PatEddery(10) (lw: gd hdwy over 2f out: chsd wnr wl over 1f out: r.o)	2½	**2**	15/2 ^{2}	95	70
2709*	**Benatom (USA) (95)** (HRACecil) **4-9-7** KFallon(3) (rdn over 4f out: hdwy over 3f out: unable qckn)	3½	**3**	4/1 ^{1}	102	77
2865*	**Jazz King (87)** (MissGayKelleway) **4-8-13** JReid(13) (lw: a.p: rdn over 3f out: one pce)	2	**4**	8/1 ^{3}	92	67
2327^{5}	**Top Cees (92)** (MrsJRRamsden) **7-9-4** JFortune(8) (lw: rdn over 4f out: hdwy on ins over 3f out: one pce)	s.h	**5**	9/1	97	72
2348^{3}	**Hoh Express (89)** (IABalding) **5-9-1** KDarley(2) (rdn over 3f out: hdwy & nt clr run 2f out: nvr nrr)	nk	**6**	16/1	94	69
2889^{5}	**Slip Jig (IRE) (70)** (KRBurke) **4-7-10** GBardwell(11) (b.nr fore: rdn over 4f out: no hdwy fnl 3f)	½	**7**	33/1	74	49
2834^{2}	**Premier Night (81)** (SDow) **4-8-7** MRoberts(14) (a.p: rdn over 4f out: chsd wnr over 3f out tl wl over 1f out: sn wknd)	3½	**8**	14/1	81	56
3010^{3}	**Magic Combination (IRE) (73)** (BJCurley) **4-7-13** JQuinn(12) (prom 9f)	1	**9**	12/1	72	47
2327^{9}	**Lallans (IRE) (95)** (MJohnston) **4-9-7** JWeaver(7) (chsd wnr over 10f: wknd over 2f out)	s.h	**10**	20/1	94	69
2776^{2}	**Burning (USA) (78)** (WJHaggas) **5-8-4** FLynch(9) (bhd fnl 3f)	1¼	**11**	15/2 ^{2}	75	50
1974^{4}	**Renzo (IRE) (77)** (MrsAJPerrett) **4-8-3b** AClark(4) (prom over 10f)	10	**12**	33/1	63	38
2596^{5}	**Fletcher (96)** (HMorrison) **3-8-3v ^{1}(5)** CLowther(6) (swtg: bhd fnl 5f)	1¾	**13**	33/1	80	41

(SP 118.5%) **13 Rn**

2m 59.88 (0.88) CSF £28.88 CT £114.11 TOTE £4.40: £1.80 £2.20 £2.00 (£15.40) Trio £18.10 OWNER Mr K. Abdulla (NEWMARKET) BRED Juddmonte Farms

WEIGHT FOR AGE 3yo-14lb

IN-FOCUS: **The inaugural running of this race produced a good, competitive field and a tremendous display from both Media Star and Olivier Peslier.**

2589* Media Star (USA) continues to go from strength to strength and was given a peach of a ride by Peslier, who dictated the whole race from the front. Set alight early in the straight, he soon had all his rivals at it and, clear before the two pole, was never going to be caught. Not surprisingly, he is now favourite for the Tote Ebor and must have a very good chance, even with a 7lb penalty. (4/1)

2749 Puce had no problems with this longer trip but was given an awful lot to do. Still out with the washing when the winner kicked for home, she made up a tremendous amount of ground to go into second place early in the final quarter-mile but was unable to peg him back in time. The Tote Ebor is now being considered. (15/2)

2709* Benatom (USA) likes to hear his feet rattle but, after taking closer order early in the straight, could make no further impression. (4/1: op 6/1)

2865* Jazz King may have had to contend with a 7lb rise in the weights and a step-up in class, but he ran a sound race, disputing second place early in the final quarter-mile, before tapped for toe. (8/1)

2327 Top Cees found this trip too sharp and never looked like finding the necessary turn of foot in the straight. (9/1)

2348 Hoh Express held up to get this longer distance, was never any nearer than at the finish. (16/1)

3111 KING GEORGE STKS (Gp 3) (3-Y.O+) (Class A)

3-20 (3-24) **5f** £27,680.00 (£10,364.00: £4,982.00: £2,174.00) Stalls: Low GOING minus 0.21 sec per fur (GF)

Form	Horse	Dist	Pl	SP	RR	SF
2861^{5}	**Averti (IRE) (108)** (WRMuir) **6-9-0** KFallon(3) (lw: outpcd: hdwy over 1f out: hrd rdn fnl f: led nr fin)	—	**1**	11/1	113	61
2526^{3}	**Cathedral (IRE) (104)** (BJMeehan) **3-8-10** MTebbutt(10) (hld up: rdn over 2f out: led ins fnl f: hdd nr fin)	½	**2**	12/1	111	55
2599^{3}	**Indian Rocket (114)** (JLDunlop) **3-8-10** RHills(9) (a.p: hrd rdn over 1f out: ev ch ins fnl f: r.o)	½	**3**	7/1 ^{3}	110	54
2683^{5}	**Bolshoi (IRE) (105)** (JBerry) **5-9-0b** EmmaO'Gorman(13) (lw: hdwy over 1f out: r.o wl ins fnl f)	s.h	**4**	20/1	110	58
2861^{11}	**Proud Native (IRE) (103)** (APJarvis) **3-8-10** DHolland(15) (hld up: rdn over 2f out: r.o ins fnl f)	¾	**5**	33/1	107	51
3001a ^{8}	**Deep Finesse (110)** (MAJarvis) **3-9-1** MRoberts(1) (w ldr: hrd rdn & ev ch over 1f out: one pce)	s.h	**6**	25/1	112	56
2106*	**Don't Worry Me (IRE)** (GHenrot,France) **5-9-5** OPeslier(14) (hld up: rdn over 2f out: r.o ins fnl f)	nk	**7**	12/1	111	59
2675^{10}	**Crowded Avenue (95)** (PJMakin) **5-9-0** SSanders(5) (a.p: hrd rdn over 1f out: one pce)	s.h	**8**	33/1	106	54
2599^{7}	**Rambling Bear (108)** (MBlanshard) **4-9-5** RCochrane(12) (outpcd: nvr nrr)	1	**9**	16/1	108	56
2526^{8}	**Eveningperformance (116)** (HCandy) **6-9-2** CRutter(2) (led tl ins fnl f: sn wknd)	s.h	**10**	7/1 ^{3}	105	53
2683^{4}	**Ya Malak (116)** (DNicholls) **6-9-0** AlexGreaves(7) (hld up: hrd rdn over 1f out: wknd ins fnl f)	½	**11**	9/2 ^{2}	101	49
2861^{2}	**Soviet State (USA) (103)** (PWChapple-Hyam) **3-8-10** JReid(4) (a bhd)	¾	**12**	14/1	99	43
2677^{3}	**Connemara (IRE) (103)** (CADwyer) **3-8-7** DHarrison(6) (swtg: bhd fnl 2f)	½	**13**	33/1	94	38
3001a ^{7}	**Croft Pool (108)** (JAGlover) **6-9-8** GCarter(11) (bhd fnl 3f)	2	**14**	25/1	99	47
2106^{15}	**Almaty (IRE) (112)** (JHMGosden) **4-9-0** PatEddery(8) (lw: spd over 3f)	2	**15**	11/4 ^{1}	84	32

(SP 127.4%) **15 Rn**

57.75 secs (1.05) CSF £120.02 TOTE £12.30: £3.70 £3.70 £2.10 (£133.10) Trio £242.50 OWNER Mr D. J. Deer (LAMBOURN) BRED D. J. and Mrs Deer

WEIGHT FOR AGE 3yo-4lb

OFFICIAL EXPLANATION **Almaty (IRE): trainer reported the colt was squeezed up leaving the stalls and was never going well thereafter. Ya Malak: the trainer reported that the gelding had a bout of colic on the morning following the race.**

2861 Averti (IRE), unlucky at Newbury last time out, was unable to lay up with the early pace but came with a nice run along the inside rail from below the distance to get up in the last few strides, gaining not only a first Group success for himself, but also a first one for his trainer William Muir. The Group One Nunthorpe Stakes at York is the next obvious target. (11/1)

2526 Cathedral (IRE) ran a tremendous race in this very competitive affair. Eventually getting in front early inside the final quarter-mile, he did nothing wrong and was only worried out of it close home. He is improving and another step-up in class for the Group One Nunthorpe Stakes could be on the cards. (12/1: op 8/1)

2599 Indian Rocket coped well with this drop in distance and had every chance inside the final furlong. A return clash with the first two in the Nunthorpe Stakes looks likely. (7/1)

2683 Bolshoi (IRE) began to find his feet from below the distance but, despite running on strongly, found the line always beating him. (20/1)

2526 Proud Native (IRE) chased the leaders and kept on well in the final furlong. (33/1)

3001a Deep Finesse ran better and had every chance below the distance, before tapped for toe. (25/1)

2683 Ya Malak was found to have a bout of colic the day after the race. (9/2)

2106 Almaty (IRE) was a major disappointment. Racing up with the pace, he did not look to be travelling very well and tamely dropped away below the distance. He is much better than this. (11/4)

3112 WILLIAM HILL CUP H'CAP (4-Y.O+) (Class B)

3-50 (3-54) **1m 2f** £37,125.00 (£11,250.00: £5,500.00: £2,625.00) Stalls: High GOING minus 0.21 sec per fur (GF)

Form	Horse	Dist	Pl	SP	RR	SF
2594*	**Danish Rhapsody (IRE) (90)** (LadyHerries) **4-8-6** JReid(11) (mde all: drvn out)	—	**1**	14/1	101	70

2866* **Another Time (90)** (SPCWoods) **5-8-6** AMunro(15) (stdy hdwy 3f out: nt clr run over 2f out: hrd rdn over 1f out: chsd wnr fnl f: r.o) ....½ **2** 16/1 100 69
1768* **Champagne Prince (95)** (PWHarris) **4-8-6**(5) CLowther(17) (a.p: rdn & ev ch over 2f out: unable qckn) ....1 **3** 7/1[2] 104 73
2514* **Zaralaska (112)** (LMCumani) **6-10-0** PatEddery(5) (lw: hld up: rdn over 1f out: one pce) ....nk **4** 3/1[1] 120 89
2710[9] **Prince of My Heart (103)** (BWHills) **4-9-5** MHills(3) (hdwy over 2f out: hrd rdn over 1f out: r.o) ....nk **5** 25/1 111 80
2710[5] **Secret Aly (CAN) (83)** (CEBrittain) **7-7-13** DBiggs(6) (a.p: nt clr run over 3f out: rdn over 2f out: one pce) ....hd **6** 25/1 91 60
2729[5] **Grief (IRE) (82)** (DRCElsworth) **4-7-5**(7) JFowle(8) (b: nt clr run over 2f out: n.m.r & swtchd lft over 1f out: hdwy fnl f: nvr nrr) ....s.h **7** 20/1 89 58
1768[13] **Hunters of Brora (IRE) (89)** (JDBethell) **7-8-5** DHolland(13) (lw: hdwy over 1f out: r.o) ....hd **8** 16/1 96 65
2710[2] **Najm Mubeen (IRE) (95)** (ACStewart) **4-8-11** MRoberts(12) (nt clr run over 2f out: nvr nrr) ....hd **9** 7/1[2] 102 71
2766* **Hawksley Hill (IRE) (103)** (MrsJRRamsden) **4-9-5v** JFortune(9) (nt clr run over 3f out: hdwy & nt clr run over 2f out: swtchd lft wl over 1f out: one pce) ....½ **10** 8/1[3] 109 78
2710[20] **Fahs (USA) (81)** (RAkehurst) **5-7-11** JQuinn(1) (swtg: a.p: rdn over 3f out: wknd fnl f) 1 **11** 16/1 86 55
2710[4] **Star Manager (USA) (86)** (PFICole) **7-8-2** CRutter(7) (bhd whn hmpd 2f out: nvr nrr) 3 **12** 16/1 86 55
2764[2] **Forza Figlio (88)** (MissGayKelleway) **4-8-1b[1]**(3) RFfrench(16) (lw: prom 8f) 2½ **13** 14/1 84 53
2528[10] **Conspicuous (IRE) (84)** (LGCottrell) **7-7-11**(3) MHenry(18) (lw: hld up: rdn over 3f out: wknd over 1f out) 1¼ **14** 16/1 78 47
2890[2] **Hazard a Guess (IRE) (82)** (DNicholls) **7-7-7**(5) IonaWands(10) (a bhd) 2 **15** 16/1 73 42
2766[14] **Clan Ben (IRE) (96)** (HRACecil) **5-8-12** KFallon(2) (lw: rdn thrght: hdwy 4f out: wkng whn hmpd wl over 1f out) 1 **16** 20/1 85 54
2890[11] **White Plains (IRE) (80)** (KRBurke) **4-7-5**(5) RMullen(4) (swtg: prom over 7f) 8 **17** 40/1 56 25
2866[13] **Autumn Cover (80)** (PRHedger) **5-7-10** GBardwell(14) (prom 7f) ....18 **18** 20/1 28 —
(SP 134.2%) **18 Rn**

2m 7.12 (0.52) CSF £198.84 CT £1,583.94 TOTE £14.40: £2.40 £4.50 £1.90 £1.80 (£204.30) Trio £314.60 OWNER Mr Chris Hardy (LITTLEHAMPTON) BRED Grangemore Stud
LONG HANDICAP White Plains (IRE) 7-8 Autumn Cover 7-7
STEWARDS' ENQUIRY Fortune susp. 7-9/8/97 (careless riding)

2594* Danish Rhapsody (IRE) had more on his plate but put up a fine display from the front and, responding to pressure, was not going to be passed. (14/1: 10/1-16/1)
2866* Another Time likes to hear his feet rattle and, although not having the best of runs, came through to take second place entering the final furlong and kept on really well. This was a fine effort, especially considering he returned with a minor cut on his near-hind leg from which his shoe had also been wrenched. (16/1)
1768* Champagne Prince, who missed the Magnet Cup after failing to sparkle at home, found his winning run coming to an end but had every chance over two furlongs from home, before failing to quicken. The Handicapper appears to have his measure now. (7/1)
2514* Zaralaska ran an absolute cracker, considering the trip was too sharp for him and he has been hiked up 22lb since his first victory two runs ago. When stepped back up in trip, there are more races to be won with him. (3/1)
2710 Prince of My Heart ran on nicely in the straight but was unable to get there in time. (25/1)
2710 Secret Aly (CAN) has never won off a mark as high as this and failed to quicken in the last two furlongs. (25/1)

3113 EVENING STANDARD NURSERY H'CAP (2-Y.O) (Class C)
4-25 (4-27) **6f** £7,570.00 (£2,260.00: £1,080.00: £490.00) Stalls: Low GOING minus 0.21 sec per fur (GF)

SP RR SF

2509* **Halmahera (IRE)** (IABalding) **2-9-7** PatEddery(2) (lw: hld up: nt clr run over 2f out: swtchd rt: hrd rdn to ld ins fnl f: r.o wl) ....— **1** 11/4[1] 89 40
2571[7] **Ron's Pet** (RHannon) **2-8-12** DaneO'Neill(3) (lw: a.p: led over 1f out tl ins fnl f: r.o) ....½ **2** 14/1 79 30
2886* **Zizi (IRE)** (KRBurke) **2-9-1** JQuinn(5) (hld up: nt clr run over 2f out: hrd rdn over 1f out: r.o ins fnl f) ....½ **3** 9/1 80 31
2565[2] **Legs Be Frendly (IRE)** (KMcAuliffe) **2-9-6** JReid(10) (hld up: rdn over 1f out: ev ch ins fnl f: unable qckn) ....¾ **4** 8/1 83 34
2862[19] **Take A Turn** (MRChannon) **2-9-1v[1]** JFortune(6) (rdn over 2f out: hdwy over 1f out: nvr nrr) 1¾ **5** 20/1 74 25
2720[5] **Night Flyer** (JWHills) **2-8-11** MHills(7) (rdn over 2f out: nt clr run over 1f out: swtchd rt: hdwy fnl f: r.o) ....1 **6** 9/2[2] 67 18
1328[8] **Poetto** (BJMeehan) **2-7-13**(3) MartinDwyer(8) (hdwy over 1f out: wknd ins fnl f) 1 **7** 25/1 55 6
2689* **Master Mac (USA)** (RAkehurst) **2-9-5** SSanders(9) (lw: a.p: hrd rdn & ev ch over 1f out: sn wknd) ....s.h **8** 5/1[3] 72 23
2700[2] **Universal Lady** (CJames) **2-8-8** CRutter(4) (spd over 3f) 4 **9** 8/1 51 2
2685[4] **Somosierra (IRE)** (JBerry) **2-9-0** KDarley(1) (led over 4f) ....s.h **10** 12/1 56 7
2741[2] **Private Seal** (GLMoore) **2-8-10** AClark(11) (lw: sme hdwy over 2f out: wkng whn hmpd over 1f out) ....¾ **11** 20/1 50 1
(SP 121.5%) **11 Rn**

1m 13.06 (3.26) CSF £40.58 CT £289.51 TOTE £3.70: £1.80 £3.60 £2.40 (£30.50) Trio £124.70 OWNER Robert & Elizabeth Hitchins (KINGSCLERE) BRED Mrs John McEnery

2509* Halmahera (IRE) was the paddock pick and had no problems with this fast ground, overcoming traffic problems to strike the front inside the final furlong. He would not want much further than six furlongs according to his trainer. (11/4)
1235 Ron's Pet has looked an awkward customer in the past but did not do a great deal wrong here, gaining a slender advantage below the distance, before collared inside the final furlong. (14/1)
2886* Zizi (IRE), with a wall of horses in front of her over a quarter of a mile from home, kept on nicely inside the final furlong for third prize. (9/1)
2565 Legs Be Frendly (IRE) threw down his challenge below the distance and may well have got his head in front for a few strides early inside the final furlong, before tapped for toe. (8/1)
2684 Take A Turn, fitted with a visor for the first time, stayed on from below the distance to be nearest at the line. (20/1)
2720 Night Flyer, who did not get the best of runs, put in some good work in the final furlong but, by then, it was all far too late. (9/2)

3114 GROSVENOR CASINOS SOUTHSEA MAIDEN STKS (2-Y.O F) (Class D)
5-00 (5-01) **6f** £7,067.50 (£2,140.00: £1,045.00: £497.50) Stalls: Low GOING minus 0.21 sec per fur (GF)

SP RR SF

2597[2] **Expect To Shine** (BWHills) **2-8-11** MHills(1) (hld up: led 1f out: rdn out) ....— **1** 6/4[1] 85 40
2349[7] **Jilted (IRE)** (RHannon) **2-8-8**(3) MartinDwyer(3) (led 5f: unable qckn) 2 **2** 14/1 80 35
Yanabi (USA) (PTWalwyn) **2-8-11** DHolland(6) (leggy: unf: s.s: outpcd: hdwy over 1f out: str run fnl f: fin wl: bttr for r) ....¾ **3** 20/1 78+ 33
2597[4] **Elsurur (USA)** (SbinSuroor) **2-8-11** RHills(11) (a.p: rdn over 3f out: one pce) ....¾ **4** 4/1[2] 76 31
2771[5] **Salsette** (CEBrittain) **2-8-11** OPeslier(9) (a.p: ev ch over 1f out: wknd fnl f) ....nk **5** 12/1 75 30
Empirical (USA) (JHMGosden) **2-8-11** KFallon(4) (cmpt: a.p: ev ch over 1f out: wknd fnl f) ....½ **6** 10/1 74 29
1749[2] **Lady From Limerick (IRE)** (JBerry) **2-8-11** KDarley(5) (hld up: rdn over 2f out: sn wknd) 7 **7** 16/1 55 10
Special Treat (DRLoder) **2-8-11** PatEddery(8) (neat: rdn & hdwy over 1f out: sn wknd) ....½ **8** 7/1[3] 54 9

Form	Horse	Dist	Pos	SP	RR	SF
	Star of Grosvenor (IRE) (PWChapple-Hyam) **2-8-11** JReid(12) (neat: hld up: rdn over 2f out: wknd over 1f out)	1	**9**	10/1	51	6
	Uplifting (LGCottrell) **2-8-11** MRoberts(10) (small: bit bkwd: a bhd)	2	**10**	50/1	46	1
2728[12]	**Runaround** (SDow) **2-8-11** SSanders(2) (s.s: bhd fnl 2f)	½	**11**	33/1	44	—
2917[5]	**Rapid Reliance** (DRCElsworth) **2-8-11** RCochrane(7) (a bhd)	3½	**12**	33/1	35	—
				(SP 123.5%)	**12 Rn**	

1m 12.38 (2.58) CSF £23.97 TOTE £2.40: £1.30 £4.10 £5.60 (£21.00) Trio £188.30 OWNER Maktoum Al Maktoum (LAMBOURN) BRED Gainsborough Stud Management Ltd

2597 Expect To Shine is not very big but she certainly knew what was required of her and, leading approaching the final furlong, was rousted along for a decisive victory. (6/4)

2349 Jilted (IRE) attempted to make all the running but, collared a furlong out, was soon put in her place. (14/1)

Yanabi (USA), a leggy filly who needs time to develop, ran a most promising first race for she was totally run off her feet for the majority of the contest. At last realising what was required, she sprouted wings in the final furlong and came flying through for third prize. Over further, she should soon pick up a race. (20/1)

2597 Elsurur (USA), racing with her tongue tied down, was off the bridle before halfway but, to her credit, kept plodding on. (4/1)

2771 Salsette ran much better and was one of four with every chance below the distance, before tiring inside the final furlong. (12/1)

Empirical (USA), a close-coupled individual who is a half-sister to several winners, travelled well for much of the race until tiring in the final furlong. She is sure to step-up on this before long. (10/1: op 5/1)

Special Treat (7/1: 3/1-10/1)

Star of Grosvenor (IRE) (10/1: 3/1-11/1)

3115 LORD GEORGE BENTINCK H'CAP (0-85) (3-Y.O+) (Class D)

5-35 (5-39) **1m** £10,020.00 (£3,000.00: £1,440.00: £660.00) Stalls: High GOING minus 0.21 sec per fur (GF)

Form	Horse	Dist	Pos	SP	RR	SF
2508[2]	**No Extras (IRE) (72)** (GLMoore) **7-9-5** JQuinn(17) (hld up: swtchd lft over 1f out: led 1f out: rdn out)	—	**1**	15/2[2]	84	69
2552[5]	**Clouds Hill (FR) (52)** (RHannon) **4-7-10**(3) RFfrench(13) (lw: hdwy & nt clr run over 2f out: swtchd lft 1f out: r.o wl)	2	**2**	20/1	60	45
2772[4]	**Sue's Return (77)** (APJarvis) **5-9-10** KDarley(15) (lw: a.p: rdn over 3f out: led over 1f out: sn hdd: 2nd & btn whn hmpd ins fnl f)	½	**3**	11/1	84	69
2868[2]	**Toujours Riviera (71)** (JPearce) **7-9-4** OPeslier(19) (lw: a.p: ev ch over 1f out: one pce)	nk	**4**	9/1	77	62
2877[7]	**Telemania (IRE) (81)** (WJHaggas) **3-9-6** FLynch(9) (swtg: hrd rdn & hdwy over 1f out: r.o wl)	hd	**5**	25/1	87	64
2743[4]	**Confronter (57)** (SDow) **8-8-4** MRoberts(10) (swtg: nt clr run over 2f out: hdwy over 1f out: r.o wl)	nk	**6**	25/1	63	48
2760*	**Alfahaal (IRE) (56)** (RFJohnsonHoughton) **4-8-3** GCarter(16) (lw: plld hrd: nt clr run over 2f out: hdwy over 1f out: r.o wl)	¾	**7**	9/1	60	45
2216[6]	**Sovereigns Court (58)** (LGCottrell) **4-8-5** AMunro(11) (plld hrd: nt clr run over 2f out tl over 1f out: hdwy fnl f: r.o wl)	hd	**8**	16/1	62	47
2557*	**Ben Gunn (69)** (PTWalwyn) **5-9-2** RCochrane(6) (swtg: hdwy over 1f out: r.o)	nk	**9**	7/1[1]	72	57
2485[4]	**Baba Au Rhum (IRE) (66)** (IPWilliams) **5-8-13** AClark(18) (led over 5f out tl over 1f out: 4th & btn whn nt clr run on ins, ins fnl f)	s.h	**10**	16/1	69	54
2229[4]	**Hajr (IRE) (82)** (EALDunlop) **3-9-7** KFallon(1) (a.p: rdn over 2f out: wknd fnl f)	2	**11**	15/2[2]	81	58
*238**	**Present Situation (60)** (LordHuntingdon) **6-8-2**(5) AimeeCook(14) (a mid div)	nk	**12**	8/1[3]	59	44
2730[5]	**Queen's Insignia (USA) (57)** (PFICole) **4-8-4** CRutter(12) (hdwy over 2f out: wknd over 1f out)	¾	**13**	20/1	54	39
2877[8]	**Moon Blast (84)** (LadyHerries) **3-9-9v**[1] JReid(20) (s.s: mid div whn hmpd on ins over 2f out)	2	**14**	16/1	77	54
2485[6]	**Fionn de Cool (IRE) (61)** (RAkehurst) **6-8-8** SSanders(7) (prom over 5f)	hd	**15**	16/1	54	39
	Show Faith (IRE) (62) (RHannon) **7-8-9** DaneO'Neill(4) (prom 5f)	½	**16**	50/1	54	39
2508[7]	**Serendipity (FR) (70)** (BRMillman) **4-9-3** TSprake(5) (lw: s.s: a bhd)	3	**17**	14/1	56	41
2660[13]	**Canadian Fantasy (76)** (MJohnston) **3-9-1** JWeaver(2) (led over 2f: wknd over 2f out)	1½	**18**	16/1	59	36
1972[2]	**Desert Time (68)** (CAHorgan) **7-9-1** DHolland(8) (mid div & no ch whn nt clr run over 1f out)	7	**19**	10/1	37	22
				(SP 139.8%)	**19 Rn**	

1m 38.82 (1.62) CSF £153.06 CT £1,558.70 TOTE £9.10: £2.10 £4.70 £3.20 £2.50 (£142.40) Trio £463.00 OWNER Mr K. Higson (BRIGHTON) BRED R. J. Cullen

WEIGHT FOR AGE 3yo-8lb

2508 No Extras (IRE), formerly a useful sprinter, has really bounced back to form and has been running well over this trip. Switched left below the distance, he struck the front entering the final furlong and was rousted along to gain his second victory over a mile. (15/2)

2552 Clouds Hill (FR), who did not get the best of runs, kept on really well in the final furlong, if unable to peg back the winner. He remains a maiden. (20/1)

2772 Sue's Return ran a fine race under top weight and got to the front below the distance, but she was soon headed by the winner and was held when done no favours by that rival soon afterwards. (11/1)

2868 Toujours Riviera, never far away, had every chance below the distance before tapped for toe. He has not won for two years, but this is his ground and trip. (9/1)

2331 Telemania (IRE), racing at the back of the field, ran on from below the distance but found the line was always beating her. (25/1)

2743 Confronter, with a wall of horses in front of him over a quarter of a mile from home, ran on in the last furlong and a half to be nearest at the line. He wins in his turn. (25/1)

T/Jkpt: £39,255.60 (1.3 Tckts). T/Plpt: £118.20 (653 Tckts). T/Qdpt: £37.10 (95.07 Tckts) AK

2758-DONCASTER (L-H) (Good)

Wednesday July 30th

Race 1 - hand timed

WEATHER: overcast WIND: fresh against

3116 DONCASTER RACECOURSE SUNDAY MARKET (S) STKS (3, 4 & 5-Y.O) (Class E)

6-15 (6-15) **1m 4f** £2,966.20 (£883.60: £420.80: £189.40) Stalls: Low GOING minus 0.32 sec per fur (GF)

Form	Horse	Dist	Pos	SP	RR	SF
2777[3]	**Kika** (KRBurke) **4-9-2** JFortune(2) (led tl hdd ins fnl f: rallied to ld last stride)	—	**1**	4/1[3]	48	10
2753[2]	**Durgams First (IRE) (51)** (MrsMReveley) **5-9-11** ACulhane(1) (lw: hld up: hdwy on bit 3f out: shkn up to chal 1½f out: slt ld ins fnl f: hrd rdn & jst ct)	s.h	**2**	10/11[1]	57	19
2916[12]	**Barnwood Crackers (59)** (MRChannon) **3-8-9** JCarroll(7) (chsd ldrs: rdn 3f out: one pce)	4	**3**	100/30[2]	48	—

Form	Horse / details	Dist	Pos	SP	RR	SF
2887[8]	**Persian Sunset (IRE) (23)** (GWoodward) **5-9-2** GCarter(5) (hld up & bhd: sme hdwy 3f out: rdn & nvr able to chal)	½	**4**	40/1	42	4
2937[11]	**Saint Amigo (30)** (BPJBaugh) **5-9-0v**(7) RWinston(6) (hld up: effrt over 3f out: rdn & no imp)	7	**5**	50/1	38	—
	Princess Belfort (GBarnett) **4-9-2** NCarlisle(3) (chsd ldrs: effrt 3f out: sn btn)	5	**6**	50/1	26	—
2824[10]	**Ralitsa (IRE) (50)** (RMWhitaker) **5-9-4**(3) GParkin(4) (rel to r & sn wl t.o)	dist	**7**	10/1	—	—

(SP 110.9%) **7 Rn**

2m 39.9 (9.90) CSF £6.88 TOTE £3.90: £1.70 £1.30 (£2.40) OWNER Mr I. Goldsmith (WANTAGE) BRED Aston House Stud Co
WEIGHT FOR AGE 3yo-12lb
Bt in 6,000gns
2777 Kika, having only her second race, proved to be a real fighter. She met the line on the right stride to have her nose in front. (4/1)
2753 Durgams First (IRE) looked a picture and did little wrong, but just found one too tough in a desperate finish. (10/11: 8/13-evens)
46 Barnwood Crackers needed two attendants in the paddock, but did run better this time. (100/30)
1798 Persian Sunset (IRE), trying to come from off the pace, was never good enough to make an impression. (40/1)
Saint Amigo raced freely and then failed to pick up when asked a question. (50/1)
Ralitsa (IRE) (10/1: 7/1-11/1)

3117 DONCASTER STALLHOLDERS MAIDEN STKS (2-Y.O) (Class D)

6-50 (6-52) **7f** £3,939.50 (£1,181.00: £568.00: £261.50) Stalls: High GOING minus 0.18 sec per fur (GF)

Form	Horse / details	Dist	Pos	SP	RR	SF
2562[2]	**Opera King (USA)** (SbinSuroor) **2-9-0** DHolland(1) (chsd ldrs: rdn to ld ins fnl f: r.o: eased towards fin)	—	**1**	5/6[1]	85	33
2860[4]	**Quintus (USA)** (PFICole) **2-9-0** JQuinn(10) (lw: led tl hdd ins fnl f: kpt on wl)	¾	**2**	4/1[2]	83	31
	Clarity (IRE) (APJarvis) **2-8-9** SDrowne(16) (unf: scope: mid div: shkn up & hdwy over 1f out: r.o wl towards fin)	s.h	**3**	25/1	78	26
	Winsa (USA) (JLDunlop) **2-8-9** GCarter(11) (lengthy: scope: hld up: effrt & nt clr run over 2f out: swtchd appr fnl f: r.o)	1½	**4**	8/1	75+	23
	Blue Dawn (IRE) (EALDunlop) **2-8-9** GHind(17) (lt-f: rr div: hdwy 2f out: styd on wl)	2½	**5**	20/1	69	17
2881[5]	**Tarashaan** (SirMarkPrescott) **2-9-0** GDuffield(8) (in tch: styd on wl fnl f)	s.h	**6**	20/1	74	22
	Former Love (USA) (PRWebber) **2-8-9** JFortune(13) (unf: mid div: hdwy over 1f out: nvr nr to chal)	nk	**7**	50/1	68	16
	Guilsborough (DMorris) **2-9-0** NDay(7) (cmpt: s.i.s: pushed along & hdwy ½-wy: nvr rchd ldrs)	2½	**8**	50/1	68	16
1872[14]	**Sadir** (MajorWRHern) **2-9-0** NCarlisle(15) (prom tl outpcd fnl 2f)	2½	**9**	25/1	62	10
2870[5]	**Quiver Tree** (DRLoder) **2-8-9** WRyan(3) (w ldrs over 5f: grad wknd)	nk	**10**	7/1[3]	56	4
	Torso (JWWatts) **2-9-0** JCarroll(9) (w'like: dwlt: pushed along & bhd: n.d)	hd	**11**	25/1	61	9
2849[4]	**Smart Beau (USA)** (RCharlton) **2-9-0** WJO'Connor(6) (outpcd fr ½-wy)	s.h	**12**	20/1	61	9
	Bay of Delight (EALDunlop) **2-8-9** SWhitworth(14) (unf: scope: s.i.s: hdwy & in tch after 2f: wknd fnl 2f)	1	**13**	14/1	54	2
2037[14]	**Julies Jewel (IRE)** (MCChapman) **2-8-7**(7) SCarson(5) (chsd ldrs over 4f: wknd)	5	**14**	50/1	47	—
	Orleans (IRE) (TPTate) **2-9-0** ACulhane(4) (w'like: bit bkwd: outpcd & bhd fnl 3f)	2	**15**	33/1	43	—
	Count Keni (JMJefferson) **2-9-0** LCharnock(12) (w'like: str: bit bkwd: s.s: a bhd)	hd	**16**	50/1	42	—

(SP 141.4%) **16 Rn**

1m 28.8 (4.30) CSF £3.95 TOTE £1.90: £1.20 £1.90 £17.20 (£4.50) Trio £242.50 OWNER Godolphin (NEWMARKET) BRED W. S. Farish Jr
2562 Opera King (USA) still looked likely to benefit from this, but he did behave himself at the start this time and then had to work to get over to the stands' rails and, in the end, did it really well. There looks to be plenty more to come. (5/6: 8/11-5/4)
2860 Quintus (USA) looked very fit and proved to be a tough sort but, in the end, he had to admit he had met one too good. (4/1)
Clarity (IRE) showed plenty of promise and should have learnt plenty, and will certainly appreciate further. (25/1)
Winsa (USA), one of the best lookers in the race, appeared unlucky and is one to keep on the right side of. (8/1: op 4/1)
Blue Dawn (IRE), although not much to look at, did show plenty of promise, getting the hang of things late on. (20/1)
2881 Tarashaan is beginning to learn to settle and gave plenty of signs of encouragement this time. (20/1)
Former Love (USA) failed to impress on looks but there was enough in her performance to suggest that she can improve. (50/1)
Guilsborough showed signs of ability after a moderate start. (50/1)
2870 Quiver Tree (7/1: op 4/1)
Bay of Delight (14/1: op 8/1)

3118 WARD'S THORNE BEST BITTER CONDITIONS STKS (3-Y.O+) (Class C)

7-25 (7-25) **6f** £5,237.72 (£1,863.32: £894.66: £366.30) Stalls: High GOING minus 0.18 sec per fur (GF)

Form	Horse / details	Dist	Pos	SP	RR	SF
2334[6]	**Abou Zouz (USA) (110)** (DRLoder) **3-9-2** WRyan(1) (lw: cl up: led over 2f out: wandered u.p: kpt on wl towards fin)	—	**1**	5/4[1]	104	24
3023[4]	**Venture Capitalist (100)** (DNicholls) **8-9-7** AlexGreaves(3) (lw: hld up: effrt over 2f out: disp ld 1f out: no ex towards fin)	nk	**2**	5/2[2]	103	28
2526[13]	**Astrac (IRE) (99)** (NTinkler) **6-9-2** KimTinkler(2) (w ldrs tl outpcd appr fnl f)	4	**3**	7/1	88	13
679[10]	**Juwwi (107)** (MajorWRHern) **3-8-11** DHolland(5) (led over 3f: sn rdn & wknd)	13	**4**	3/1[3]	53	—

(SP 110.5%) **4 Rn**

1m 15.36 (4.36) CSF £4.33 TOTE £2.10: (£2.20) OWNER Mr Wafic Said (NEWMARKET) BRED G. Watts Humphrey Jnr
WEIGHT FOR AGE 3yo-5lb
2334 Abou Zouz (USA) looked particularly well and, despite showing a tendency to hang when put under maximum pressure, he did just enough. (5/4)
3023 Venture Capitalist really needs a bigger field to get some cover but still had his chances and, if looks mean anything, he is coming right. (5/2)
980 Astrac (IRE), having his first run for his new stable, was wearing stick-on shoes in front and has obviously had a problem, but he did show something here. (7/1)
Juwwi has yet to show anything positive this season. (3/1)

3119 DONCASTER GOOSEHILL MARKET H'CAP (0-85) (3-Y.O F) (Class D)

7-55 (7-56) **1m (round)** £3,947.50 (£1,180.00: £565.00: £257.50) Stalls: High GOING minus 0.32 sec per fur (GF)

Form	Horse / details	Dist	Pos	SP	RR	SF
2593*	**Right Tune (81)** (BHanbury) **3-9-4** JStack(1) (lw: a cl up: led wl over 1f out: styd on wl fnl f)	—	**1**	8/1	91	59
2672[8]	**Sweet Contralto (81)** (DRLoder) **3-9-4** WRyan(10) (lw: led tl hdd wl over 1f out: one pce)	1¾	**2**	10/1	88	56
2601[4]	**Woodbeck (83)** (JAGlover) **3-9-6** NDay(3) (lw: a chsng ldrs: rdn 2f out: kpt on wl: nt pce to chal)	hd	**3**	11/4[1]	89	57
2894[7]	**Dundel (IRE) (77)** (BWHills) **3-9-0** RHughes(2) (hld up: hdwy over 2f out: chsng ldrs appr fnl f: no ex)	2	**4**	9/1	79	47

				SP	RR	SF
2894[6]	**The In-Laws (IRE) (84)** (SirMarkPrescott) **3-9-7** GDuffield(5) (lw: plld hrd: bhd: hdwy ½-wy: no imp)	5	**5**	13/2	76	44
2495[7]	**Ganga (IRE) (82)** (WJarvis) **3-9-0**(5) CLowther(6) (prom: rdn over 3f out: one pce)	½	**6**	12/1	73	41
2331[3]	**Sleepless (84)** (NAGraham) **3-9-7** DHolland(8) (hld up & bhd: nt clr run 3f out: hdwy 2f out: nvr nr to chal)	¾	**7**	6/1[3]	74	42
2705*	**Midyan Queen (62)** (RHollinshead) **3-7-13** LCharnock(4) (plld hrd: hdwy ½-wy: chsng ldrs 2f out: sn btn)	1¼	**8**	11/1	49	17
2704[5]	**Shoshaloza (USA) (70)** (PRWebber) **3-8-7** JFortune(12) (lw: dwlt: effrt ½-wy: btn & eased fnl f)	1¼	**9**	5/1[2]	55	23
2705[9]	**My Girl Lucy (59)** (PMitchell) **3-7-10** JQuinn(11) (bhd: shkn up ½-wy: n.d)	9	**10**	33/1	26	—
2654[4]	**Chinaberry (72)** (CEBrittain) **3-8-9** WJO'Connor(7) (prom: rdn over 3f out: sn wknd: eased fnl f: sddle slipped)	1½	**11**	12/1	36	4
2062[9]	**Samsung Spirit (74)** (EWeymes) **3-8-11** JCarroll(9) (in tch: rdn ½-wy: sn lost pl)	6	**12**	16/1	26	—
				(SP 133.7%)	**12 Rn**	

1m 40.05 (1.65) CSF £88.17 CT £265.68 TOTE £10.50: £2.90 £4.00 £1.80 (£34.00) Trio £15.50 OWNER Mr Abdullah Ali (NEWMARKET) BRED Gainsborough Stud Management Ltd
LONG HANDICAP My Girl Lucy 7-5
2593* Right Tune is in good form at the moment and got stronger here the further they went. (8/1)
1406* Sweet Contralto, who ran miserably on the All-Weather last time, was back to form here but was outpointed late on and is probably better with more cut in the ground. (10/1)
2601 Woodbeck keeps running well, but leaves the impression that she needs a stronger gallop and probably easy ground. (11/4)
2143* Dundel (IRE) looked the type that needs things to go all her own way, and things proved too tough in the final furlong here. (9/1)
2894 The In-Laws (IRE) looked short of toe here when the pace hotted up from halfway, but does give the impression that, looks-wise, she is coming to hand. (13/2)
2495 Ganga (IRE), who won on very testing ground at Newcastle a couple of runs ago, was always being tapped for speed here. (12/1)
2331 Sleepless, held up, met with trouble in running and this is best ignored. (6/1)

3120 'DAZZLING DONCASTER MARKETS' H'CAP (0-85) (3-Y.O+) (Class D)

8-25 (8-26) **1m 2f 60y** £3,655.00 (£1,090.00: £520.00: £235.00) Stalls: Low GOING minus 0.32 sec per fur (GF)

				SP	RR	SF
2507*	**Capilano Princess (81)** (DHaydnJones) **4-9-12** SDrowne(4) (hld up: hdwy 4f out: led appr fnl f: r.o)	—	**1**	13/2	90	72
2291[3]	**Honourable (81)** (JWWatts) **3-9-2** JCarroll(3) (trckd ldrs: nt clr run & swtchd over 2f out: ev ch 1½f out: kpt on)	1½	**2**	7/4[1]	88	60
2729[8]	**River's Source (USA) (79)** (BWHills) **3-9-0** DHolland(6) (a cl up: slt ld wl over 1f out: hdd appr fnl f & no ex)	2	**3**	12/1	83	55
2574[11]	**Henley (USA) (85)** (DRLoder) **3-9-6** WRyan(5) (led tl hdd wl over 1f out: kpt on one pce)	hd	**4**	7/1	88	60
2574[9]	**Ginzbourg (85)** (JLDunlop) **3-9-6** GCarter(7) (bhd: effrt 4f out: styd on fnl f: nt pce to chal)	s.h	**5**	7/1	88	60
2731[4]	**Mengaab (USA) (82)** (JHMGosden) **3-9-3v** GHind(2) (chsd ldrs: rdn over 3f out: sn outpcd)	4	**6**	11/2[3]	79	51
3026[2]	**No Cliches (70)** (DNicholls) **4-9-1** AlexGreaves(1) (lw: trckd ldrs tl wknd fnl 2f)	½	**7**	7/2[2]	66	48
				(SP 120.0%)	**7 Rn**	

2m 9.3 (1.50) CSF £17.84 TOTE £9.40: £3.40 £1.70 (£10.30) OWNER Mr H. G. Collis (PONTYPRIDD) BRED Mrs O. M. Collis
WEIGHT FOR AGE 3yo-10lb
2507* Capilano Princess, patiently ridden, did this well and always looked as though there was more to come. (13/2)
2291 Honourable, from a yard that is out of form, ran well and there is surely a decent handicap to come his way. (7/4)
690* River's Source (USA) seems to have taken time to get over his hard-fought Newmarket win at the beginning of the season, and this was his first encouragement for a while. (12/1)
1595* Henley (USA), after two moderate runs, ran more encouraging and he is probably better on faster ground. (7/1)
966 Ginzbourg showed enough here to suggest that he should not be written off yet. (7/1)
2731 Mengaab (USA) has a poor action and, once asked to stretch early in the straight, he soon gave up. (11/2)
3026 No Cliches looked well enough but ran poorly and this was not his true running. (7/2)

3121 'COME TO DONCASTER MARKETS' H'CAP (0-70) (3-Y.O) (Class E)

8-55 (9-06) **5f** £3,348.00 (£999.00: £477.00: £216.00) Stalls: High GOING minus 0.18 sec per fur (GF)

				SP	RR	SF
2715[4]	**Storyteller (IRE) (51)** (MrsJRRamsden) **3-8-2v**[ow1] MFenton(10) (lw: hld up & bhd: swtchd 2f out: str run to ld ins fnl f: r.o wl)	—	**1**	9/2[2]	60	21
2964[5]	**Bramble Bear (70)** (MBlanshard) **3-9-7** JQuinn(6) (lw: hld up: nt clr run 2f out tl ins fnl f: r.o wl)	2	**2**	9/1	73	35
2751[3]	**Suite Factors (56)** (KRBurke) **3-8-4**(3) GParkin(11) (led tl hdd appr fnl f: kpt on)	½	**3**	9/1	57	19
2751*	**Pizzicato (64)** (RJRWilliams) **3-9-1** GDuffield(8) (cl up: led appr fnl f: sn hdd & nt qckn)	hd	**4**	4/1[1]	65	27
2738[11]	**Tinker's Surprise (IRE) (48)** (JBalding) **3-7-13** TWilliams(3) (dwlt: hld up: hdwy to chal appr fnl f: no ex)	1	**5**	14/1	46	8
2547[6]	**William's Well (60)** (MWEasterby) **3-8-11b** DaleGibson(12) (a chsng ldrs: sn pushed along: nt qckn fnl 2f)	½	**6**	6/1	56	18
3016[9]	**Make Ready (59)** (JNeville) **3-8-10** SDrowne(7) (chsd ldrs tl rdn & btn 1f out)	1¼	**7**	16/1	51	13
2883[13]	**Donna's Dancer (IRE) (49)** (NTinkler) **3-8-0b** KimTinkler(9) (lw: s.s: outpcd & bhd tl sme late hdwy)	1¼	**8**	20/1	37	—
2891[10]	**Colonel's Pride (48)** (RMWhitaker) **3-7-6**(7)[ow3] RWinston(1) (prom: rdn ½-wy: grad wknd)	1¼	**9**	33/1	32	—
2883[5]	**Lunar Music (46)** (RonaldThompson) **3-7-11** FNorton(5) (spd 3f: sn wknd)	2½	**10**	20/1	22	—
2921[4]	**Broadway Melody (63)** (APJarvis) **3-8-7**(7) CCarver(4) (lw: spd over 3f: sn wknd)	¾	**11**	11/2[3]	37	—
2711[14]	**Van Chino (69)** (BAMcMahon) **3-9-6** JFortune(2) (spd over 3f)	¾	**12**	10/1	40	2
				(SP 122.0%)	**12 Rn**	

61.37 secs (2.97) CSF £40.95 CT £331.30 TOTE £5.60: £2.40 £2.30 £3.20 (£26.70) Trio £38.30 OWNER Mr Paul Green (THIRSK) BRED Paul Green
LONG HANDICAP Colonel's Pride 7-7
2715 Storyteller (IRE), dropped back in trip, looked the part this time and got it right in some style to land a gamble. (9/2: 7/1-4/1)
2964 Bramble Bear appeared very unlucky and would have given the winner something to think about but it is questionable whether she would have beaten him. (9/1)
2751 Suite Factors put up another fair effort and deserves to find a race. (9/1)
2751* Pizzicato had her chances but was short of toe late on. (4/1)
1995 Tinker's Surprise (IRE) has plenty of ability but appears to need things to go just right. (14/1)
2547 William's Well ran reasonably, but was always struggling with the pace and just seems to have lost his edge at the moment. (6/1)
2883 Donna's Dancer (IRE) has plenty more ability if he can be persuaded to put it to full use. (20/1)

T/Plpt: £38.90 (374.42 Tckts). T/Qdpt: £53.60 (19.94 Tckts) AA

3109-GOODWOOD (R-H) (Good to firm)
Wednesday July 30th

Race 1 - flip start
WEATHER: fine WIND: slt against

3122 MARRIOTT HOTELS GOODWOOD H'CAP (0-95) (3-Y.O+) (Class C)

2-15 (2-15) **2m 4f** £14,620.00 (£4,360.00: £2,080.00: £940.00) GOING minus 0.19 sec per fur (GF)

				SP	RR	SF
2589^{3}	**Cloud Inspector (IRE) (75)** (MJohnston) **6-9-4** JWeaver(5) (led over 12f: led wl over 2f out: drvn out)	—	1	$8/1^{3}$	88	64
2932^{2}	**Shadirwan (IRE) (63)** (RAkehurst) **6-8-6** SSanders(10) (swtg: chsd ldr: ev ch 1f out: r.o)	¾	2	$6/1^{1}$	75	51
2014^{2}	**Shirley Sue (70)** (MJohnston) **4-8-10**$^{(3)}$ KMChin(12) (lw: lost pl over 6f out: rallied 1f out: styd on wl)	nk	3	$7/1^{2}$	82	58
2327^{13}	**Go Britannia (85)** (DRLoder) **4-10-0** PatEddery(4) (lw: hld up in rr: hdwy 3f out: swtchd rt over 1f out: r.o)	½	4	12/1	97	73
2327^{18}	**Transom (USA) (83)** (MrsAJPerrett) **6-9-12** JReid(3) (hld up: rdn & hdwy wl over 1f out: r.o)	1½	5	$8/1^{3}$	94	70
2825^{2}	**Bold Elect (55)** (EJAlston) **9-7-12** JQuinn(11) (no hdwy fnl 3f)	2	6	20/1	64	40
3010^{8}	**Shining Dancer (64)** (SDow) **5-8-7** JFEgan(1) (hld up: hdwy over 1f out: nvr nr to chal)	1½	7	11/1	72	48
2327^{3}	**Onefourseven (75)** (JLEyre) **4-9-4** TWilliams(2) (lw: hld up & plld hrd: rdn over 4f out: n.d)	½	8	$6/1^{1}$	82	58
2589^{4}	**Arcady (59)** (JLHarris) **4-7-13**$^{(3)}$ RFfrench(8) (b: lw: a.p: led over 7f out: hdd wl over 2f out: wknd 1f out)	¾	9	$6/1^{1}$	66	42
2867^{5}	**Sea Freedom (66)** (GBBalding) **6-8-9v** SDrowne(7) (b: prom tl wknd 3f out)	s.h	10	$6/1^{1}$	73	49
2963^{9}	**Sun Alert (USA) (77)** (MJPolglase) **3-7-9**$^{(3)ow2}$ MartinDwyer(9) (a bhd)	2½	11	33/1	76 t	34
1027^{8}	**Upper Mount Clair (69)** (CEBrittain) **7-8-12** MRoberts(6) (prom tl wknd over 3f out: t.o)	14	12	25/1	57 t	39
				(SP 119.4%)	**12 Rn**	

4m 20.89 (5.89) CSF £49.65 CT £327.04 TOTE £9.90: £2.90 £2.30 £2.00 (£41.20) Trio £75.80 OWNER Mr Markus Graff (MIDDLEHAM) BRED D. Cordell-Lavarack
WEIGHT FOR AGE 3yo-22lb
STEWARDS' ENQUIRY Chin susp. 8-11/8/97 (excessive use of whip).

2589 Cloud Inspector (IRE) had been raised 9lb without winning this season, and gained due reward for some consistent efforts with a game victory over this marathon trip. (8/1)
2932 Shadirwan (IRE) is certainly back on song, and his trainer said he will now have a rest while they decide where he goes next. (6/1)
2014 Shirley Sue, off the same mark as when second in the Ascot Stakes, again did not adopt her front-running tactics and was fairly flying at the death. Her rider picked a three-day whip ban. (7/1)
1400 Go Britannia, up to a real marathon distance this time, seemed to be coming with a winning run, and it was weight rather than a lack of stamina that prevented him from gaining the day. (12/1)
2327 Transom (USA) was 2lb better off with the winner than when beating him a head over two miles here last month. (8/1)
2825 Bold Elect, raised 3lb, has yet to win over a full two miles but was certainly not disgraced over this extended trip. (20/1)
2767 Shining Dancer (11/1: 8/1-12/1)

3123 LANSON CHAMPAGNE VINTAGE STKS (Gp 3) (2-Y.O) (Class A)

2-45 (2-46) **7f** £23,590.00 (£8,827.00: £4,238.50: £1,844.50) Stalls: High GOING minus 0.19 sec per fur (GF)

				SP	RR	SF
2057*	**Central Park (IRE)** (PFICole) **2-9-0** PatEddery(1) (chsd ldr: rdn over 2f out: led wl over 1f out: r.o wl)	—	1	$5/4^{1}$	111+	53
2699*	**Docksider (USA)** (JWHills) **2-8-11** MHills(5) (lw: hld up & plld hrd: rdn over 1f out: r.o one pce fnl f)	3	2	7/1	101	43
2477*	**Little Indian** (SPCWoods) **2-8-11** WRyan(6) (lw: hld up in rr: outpcd over 2f out: rdn over 1f out: styd on wl ins fnl f)	1¾	3	10/1	97	39
2600^{3}	**Arawak Cay (IRE)** (DRLoder) **2-8-11** MJKinane(4) (lw: led over 5f: wknd ins fnl f)	½	4	$11/2^{3}$	96	38
2600*	**Baltic State (USA)** (HRACecil) **2-9-0** KFallon(3) (lw: hld up: hdwy over 2f out: rdn & ev ch over 1f out: wknd ins fnl f)	hd	5	$11/4^{2}$	99	41
2429^{3}	**Lone Piper** (CEBrittain) **2-8-11** MRoberts(2) (hld up & plld hrd: wknd over 1f out)	1½	6	33/1	92	34
				(SP 111.0%)	**6 Rn**	

1m 27.26 (2.46) CSF £9.54 TOTE £2.10: £1.50 £2.30 (£5.80) OWNER H R H Prince Fahd Salman (WHATCOMBE) BRED Lodge Park Stud

2057* Central Park (IRE) continues to go from strength to strength and, bred to stay a mile and a half, might be more of a Derby than Guineas prospect next year. (5/4)
2699* Docksider (USA), having apparently planned to lead, did not handle the bend all that well under heavy restraint. Highly-regarded by his trainer, there will be other days for him. (7/1)
2477* Little Indian, another who is the apple of his trainer's eye, finished to quite some effect and already appears ready to tackle a mile. (10/1: 8/1-12/1)
2600 Arawak Cay (IRE) did not get home after adopting front-running tactics in a stronger-run race than at Newmarket last time. (11/2)
2600* Baltic State (USA) was friendless in the market, and his rider was rather surprisingly convinced that his mount had failed to stay. They did go a stronger gallop than at Newmarket last time. (11/4: 7/4-3/1)
2429 Lone Piper, out of a sister to Enharmonic, was typically pitched in at the deep-end by his trainer. (33/1)

3124 SUSSEX STKS (Gp 1) (3-Y.O+) (Class A)

3-20 (3-23) **1m** £92,770.00 (£34,791.00: £16,770.50: £7,368.50) Stalls: High GOING minus 0.19 sec per fur (GF)

				SP	RR	SF
2679*	**Ali-Royal (IRE) (120)** (HRACecil) **4-9-7** KFallon(3) (swtg: hld up: hdwy 3f out: led over 1f out: drvn out)	—	1	$13/2^{3}$	129	81
2011*	**Starborough (123)** (DRLoder) **3-8-13** PatEddery(6) (lw: led over 6f: r.o)	¾	2	$9/4^{1}$	128	72
2527^{4}	**Allied Forces (USA) (120)** (SbinSuroor) **4-9-7** JReid(9) (a.p: rdn over 2f out: r.o one pce fnl f)	¾	3	$9/2^{2}$	126	78
2023*	**Among Men (USA) (113)** (MRStoute) **3-8-13** MJKinane(7) (lw: hld up: rdn & hdwy over 2f out: r.o ins fnl f)	1	4	$9/2^{2}$	124	68
2025^{4}	**Classic Park** (APO'Brien,Ireland) **3-8-10** SCraine(8) (hld up: hdwy on ins 3f out: ev ch over 1f out: wknd ins fnl f)	1¾	5	20/1	118	62
2821a*	**Gothenberg (IRE) (119)** (MJohnston) **4-9-7** JWeaver(4) (lw: prom over 5f)	2	6	25/1	117	69
2011^{2}	**Air Express (IRE) (121)** (CEBrittain) **3-8-13** BDoyle(2) (hld up: hdwy 3f out: wknd 2f out)	5	7	7/1	107	51
1460*	**Wolf Mountain (100)** (RHannon) **3-8-13** DaneO'Neill(5) (lw: prom over 5f)	1¾	8	66/1	103	47
2453a*	**Alhaarth (IRE) (121)** (SbinSuroor) **4-9-7** RHills(1) (lw: hld up: bhd fnl 3f)	3½	9	15/2	96	48
				(SP 114.8%)	**9 Rn**	

1m 37.98 (0.78) CSF £19.11 TOTE £8.70: £2.10 £1.60 £1.80 (£13.30) Trio £19.70 OWNER Greenbay Stables Ltd (NEWMARKET) BRED C. H. WACKER III
WEIGHT FOR AGE 3yo-8lb

2679* Ali-Royal (IRE), unable to hold his position early on, put up a very gritty performance and put any doubts to rest that he was not up to this class. Tough and consistent, he does not seem to know how to run a bad race. (13/2)
2011* Starborough certainly kept on bravely when headed and connections, having toyed with stepping up to a mile and a quarter, thought he may have found this course too sharp. (9/4)
2527 Allied Forces (USA), who sweated up badly in the paddock, could not confirm the Queen Anne form with the admittedly unlucky Ali-Royal on 3lb better terms. (9/2)
2023* Among Men (USA), taking on by far his stiffest task to date, really took the eye in the paddock. Not campaigned as a juvenile, his trainer already believes he will make a smashing four-year-old and this evidence suggests he might stay further. (9/2)
2025 Classic Park looked capable of continuing her trainer's fantastic season with a furlong and a half to go, and certainly justified taking on the colts. (20/1)
2821a* Gothenberg (IRE) was unable to dominate with Starborough in the field. (25/1)
2011 Air Express (IRE) was rather disappointing after his good run behind the runner-up at Royal Ascot. (7/1)
1460* Wolf Mountain was taking a big step-up in class on this first attempt at a mile. (66/1)
2453a* Alhaarth (IRE) had to handle quicker ground this time. (15/2)

3125 TOTE GOLD TROPHY H'CAP (0-105) (3-Y.O) (Class B)

3-50 (3-55) **1m 4f** £36,100.00 (£10,900.00: £5,300.00: £2,500.00) Stalls: Low GOING minus 0.19 sec per fur (GF)

				SP	RR	SF
2585[2]	**Maylane (99)** (ACStewart) **3-9-4** MRoberts(15) (hld up in rr: hdwy over 2f out: led ins fnl f: r.o)	—	**1**	13/2	108	64
2585*	**Memorise (USA) (91)** (HRACecil) **3-8-10** KFallon(5) (hld up: rdn & hdwy over 4f out: nt clr run & swtchd rt over 1f out: swtchd lft: r.o wl ins fnl: fin 2nd, ½l: disq: plcd last)	½	**2d**	4/1[1]	99	55
2676*	**Dream of Nurmi (90)** (DRLoder) **3-8-9** MJKinane(4) (lw: a.p: rdn over 3f out: led & edgd rt over 2f out: edgd lft & hdd ins fnl f: fin 3rd, 1¼l: plcd 2nd)	1¼	**2**	9/1	96	52
2548*	**Real Estate (83)** (CFWall) **3-8-2** GDuffield(2) (chsd ldrs: ev ch ins fnl f: nt qckn: fin 4th, nk: plcd 3rd)	nk	**3**	10/1	89	45
2850*	**Irsal (78)** (MCPipe) **3-7-8**(3) MartinDwyer(7) (prom tl wknd over 1f out: fin 5th, plcd 4th)	3	**4**	20/1	80	36
837[9]	**Happy Minstral (USA) (88)** (MJohnston) **3-8-7** JWeaver(11) (hld up & bhd: nt clr run over 1f out: hdwy fnl f: nvr nrr: fin 6th, plcd 5th)	½	**5**	25/1	89	45
2515[4]	**Mandilak (USA) (102)** (LMCumani) **3-9-7** PatEddery(1) (hld up & bhd: hdwy over 4f out: btn whn hmpd over 1f out: fin 7th, plcd 6th)	¾	**6**	10/1	102	58
2764[3]	**Khawafi (85)** (EALDunlop) **3-8-4** RHills(6) (lw: hld up: hdwy over 2f out: nvr trbld ldrs: fin 8th, plcd 7th)	½	**7**	20/1	84	40
2514[10]	**Cyrian (IRE) (87)** (PFICole) **3-8-6** KDarley(10) (lw: led over 9f: bdly hmpd on ins over 1f out: nt rcvr: fin 9th, plcd 8th)	½	**8**	20/1	86	42
2058[5]	**Prairie Falcon (IRE) (89)** (BWHills) **3-8-8** MHills(3) (a bhd: fin 10th, plcd 9th)	½	**9**	11/1	87	43
2963[7]	**Assured Gamble (86)** (CEBrittain) **3-8-5** BDoyle(13) (hld up & plld hrd: bhd fnl 3f: fin 11th, plcd 10th)	1½	**10**	33/1	82	38
2315[2]	**True Glory (IRE) (79)** (JHMGosden) **3-7-12** JQuinn(12) (prom: lost pl over 5f out: n.d after: fin 12th, plcd 11th)	hd	**11**	9/2[2]	75	31
2585[16]	**Cinema Paradiso (94)** (PFICole) **3-8-13** CRutter(8) (lw: plld hrd: prom tl wknd 3f out: fin 13th, plcd 12th)	4	**12**	33/1	85	41
2585[3]	**Mersey Beat (89)** (GLMoore) **3-8-8** AClark(14) (lw: sn bhd: fin 14th, plcd 13th)	1¼	**13**	6/1[3]	78	34
2594[5]	**Happy Go Lucky (84)** (RJO'Sullivan) **3-8-3**[ow3] SSanders(9) (chsd ldr tl rdn & wknd over 3f out: fin 15th, plcd 14th)	7	**14**	40/1	64	17

(SP 128.8%) **15 Rn**

2m 36.64 (3.44) CSF £56.44 CT £549.46 TOTE £6.60: £2.50 £2.80 £2.90 (£34.50) Trio £127.50 OWNER Sheikh Ahmed Al Maktoum (NEWMARKET) BRED Sheikh Ahmed Bin Rashid Al Maktoum
STEWARDS' ENQUIRY Fallon susp. 8-12/8/97 (irresponsible riding).
2585 Maylane, up 4lb, got away on level terms, particularly by his standards and missed all the trouble by coming up the outside. His trainer thinks he will be too highly rated for handicaps now, and is thinking in terms of the Great Voltigeur at York. (13/2)
2676* Dream of Nurmi, raised 6lb, would have been harder to beat had he kept straight but that would have meant that the unlucky Memorise would have got a better run. (9/1)
2548* Real Estate, raised 13lb for winning a couple of Class E handicaps, ran a fine race in this much hotter contest. (10/1)
2850* Irsal, 3lb higher than when winning at Salisbury, had much more on his plate and one cannot help feeling that this trip stretches his stamina to the limit. (20/1)
837 Happy Minstral (USA), coming back after a break, is one to keep an eye on. (25/1)
2515 Mandilak (USA) was making his handicap debut in a very competitive race after some sound efforts in conditions events. (10/1)
2514 Cyrian (IRE), although held, would have finished much closer had Memorise not squeezed him up against the fence. (20/1)
2058 Prairie Falcon (IRE) (11/1: 8/1-12/1)
2585* Memorise (USA) was desperately unlucky in running but, nevertheless, his disqualification was inevitable after he nearly put Cyrian through the inside rail. (4/1)

3126 PEUGEOT 406 COUPE H'CAP (0-80) (4-Y.O+) (Class D)

4-25 (4-28) **5f** £7,570.00 (£2,260.00: £1,080.00: £490.00) Stalls: Low GOING minus 0.19 sec per fur (GF)

				SP	RR	SF
3065[2]	**Lady Sheriff (77)** (MWEasterby) **6-10-0b** MJKinane(13) (mde all: clr over 1f out: r.o wl)	—	**1**	8/1	89	49
2900[5]	**Double Oscar (IRE) (62)** (DNicholls) **4-8-6b**(7) ANicholls(14) (s.s: gd hdwy over 1f out: r.o wl ins fnl f)	1¼	**2**	14/1	70	30
2148[8]	**Sweet Magic (60)** (PHowling) **6-8-11** MRoberts(3) (hdwy over 1f out: r.o)	2½	**3**	20/1	60	20
2950[4]	**Dande Flyer (61)** (DWPArbuthnot) **4-8-9**(3) RFfrench(2) (lw: hdwy 2f out: r.o one pce fnl f)	½	**4**	11/2[1]	59	19
2895[2]	**Tuscan Dawn (70)** (JBerry) **7-9-2**(5) PRoberts(6) (a.p: one pce fnl 2f)	½	**5**	8/1	67	27
2950[2]	**Half Tone (54)** (RMFlower) **5-8-5b** SSanders(11) (hdwy over 2f out: one pce fnl f)	nk	**6**	13/2[2]	50	10
3016[3]	**Songsheet (70)** (MSSaunders) **4-9-7** RCochrane(15) (hdwy over 1f out: nt clr run ins fnl f: nvr nrr)	hd	**7**	16/1	66	26
2950[7]	**Longwick Lad (77)** (WRMuir) **4-10-0** JReid(8) (nvr nr to chal)	hd	**8**	20/1	72	32
2590[3]	**Malibu Man (70)** (EAWheeler) **5-9-2**(5) ADaly(4) (swtg: prom tl hrd rdn & wknd over 1f out)	nk	**9**	7/1[3]	64	24
3016[5]	**Sharp Stock (57)** (RJHodges) **4-8-8** BDoyle(7) (mid div whn n.m.r over 1f out)	1¾	**10**	25/1	46	6
2590[7]	**Runs in the Family (65)** (GMMcCourt) **5-9-2b** DHarrison(10) (lw: chsd wnr: rdn over 1f out: wknd ins fnl f)	nk	**11**	16/1	53	13
2581[5]	**Sally Slade (67)** (CACyzer) **5-9-4** KDarley(9) (outpcd)	½	**12**	12/1	53	13
2950*	**Mindrace (66)** (KTIvory) **4-9-3**[7x] KFallon(16) (lw: bhd fnl 2f)	s.h	**13**	12/1	52	12
2339[12]	**Polly Golightly (66)** (MBlanshard) **4-9-3b** NAdams(12) (chsd ldrs: rdn & wknd over 1f out: eased whn btn ins fnl f)	¾	**14**	16/1	50	10
3032[2]	**Barranak (IRE) (65)** (GMMcCourt) **5-9-2** CRutter(5) (bhd fnl 2f)	3½	**15**	12/1	37	—

2938*	**The Wad (65)** (DNicholls) **4-8-9**(7) 7x TSiddall(1) (reard stalls: uns rdr s)		**U**	16/1	—	—
				(SP 130.1%)		**16 Rn**

59.28 secs (2.58) CSF £109.09 CT £2,082.34 TOTE £6.90: £1.90 £4.10 £6.30 £2.00 (£66.30) Trio £1,026.40 OWNER Mr E. J. Mangan (SHERIFF HUTTON) BRED Jeremy Green and Sons

3065 Lady Sheriff never really looked likely to be caught off a mark 9lb higher than she has ever won off before. (8/1)
2900 Double Oscar (IRE), a stone higher than when winning at Folkestone, is certainly in a purple patch but could not overcome a poor start, especially on this return to five. (14/1)
Sweet Magic showed definite signs of a return to form, having dropped 18lb this season. (20/1)
2950 Dande Flyer has slipped to a mark 6lb lower than when registering two wins in nurseries in October 1995. (11/2)
2895 Tuscan Dawn found this event a bit too competitive. (8/1)
2950 Half Tone was 1lb lower than when a good second a week ago. (13/2)
3016 Songsheet was unlucky not to have finished a bit closer. (16/1)

3127 DONCASTER BLOODSTOCK SALES MAIDEN STKS (2-Y.O C & G) (Class D)

5-00 (5-00) **6f** £7,067.50 (£2,140.00: £1,045.00: £497.50) Stalls: Low GOING minus 0.19 sec per fur (GF)

				SP	RR	SF
2556[5]	**Arkadian Hero (USA)** (LMCumani) **2-8-11** PatEddery(3) (hld up: swtchd lft 2f out: hdwy over 1f out: hrd rdn to ld nr fin)	—	**1**	2/1[1]	102	30
1978[5]	**Bemsha Swing (IRE)** (RHannon) **2-8-11** JReid(7) (a.p: led over 1f out: hrd rdn & hdd nr fin)	nk	**2**	16/1	101	29
2829[2]	**Sabhaan** (MajorWRHern) **2-8-11** RHills(6) (a.p: ev ch over 1f out: sn rdn: wknd fnl f)	6	**3**	11/4[2]	85	13
	Sara Moon Classic (IRE) (KMcAuliffe) **2-8-11** MRoberts(2) (unf: hld up: lost pl over 3f out: sme late hdwy)	5	**4**	50/1	72	—
2771[3]	**Royal Rights** (DRLoder) **2-8-11** MJKinane(5) (lw: led 5f out tl over 1f out: eased whn btn ins fnl f)	¾	**5**	9/1[3]	70	—
	Porto Foricos (USA) (HRACecil) **2-8-11** KFallon(4) (w'like: scope: rn green: rdn over 2f out: sn bhd)	1¼	**6**	2/1[1]	67	—
2571[4]	**Coolin River (IRE)** (KRBurke) **2-8-11** JFEgan(1) (led 1f: rdn & wknd 2f out)	¾	**7**	50/1	65	—
				(SP 113.1%)		**7 Rn**

1m 13.27 (3.47) CSF £31.36 TOTE £3.10: £1.70 £3.10 (£14.90) OWNER Mr M Tabor & Mrs John Magnier (NEWMARKET) BRED Gainesway Thoroughbreds Ltd

2556 Arkadian Hero (USA) is on a learning curve and had to overcome a bit of greenness, but there was no disputing the way he knuckled down. (2/1)
1978 Bemsha Swing (IRE) broke smartly and soon crossed towards the stands' side. He may not have been suited by the give in the ground last time. (16/1)
2829 Sabhaan did not get home after being right up with the pace on this occasion. (11/4)
Sara Moon Classic (IRE), out of a seven-furlong winner in Belgium, ran on after looking a lost cause and will definitely be suited by further. (50/1)
2771 Royal Rights was again disappointing and is not going to live up to entries in the Gimcrack, Middle Park and Dewhurst on this evidence. (9/1: 6/1-10/1)
Porto Foricos (USA), a half-brother to Gay Gallanta and Sportsworld, is also entered up in the top-class two-year-old events. Looking inexperienced, he was not helped by racing on the outside of the others. (2/1)

3128 DRAYTON H'CAP (0-90) (3-Y.O+ F & M) (Class C)

5-35 (5-38) **1m 1f** £7,895.00 (£2,360.00: £1,130.00: £515.00) Stalls: High GOING minus 0.19 sec per fur (GF)

				SP	RR	SF
2894[3]	**Apache Star (82)** (GWragg) **3-9-3v** MHills(8) (hld up & bhd: hrd rdn & hdwy 2f out: r.o to ld last strides)	—	**1**	14/1	92	65
2918*	**Wishing Stone (USA) (77)** (EALDunlop) **3-8-9**(3) 5x DO'Donohoe(1) (hld up: hdwy over 4f out: ev ch fnl f: r.o)	nk	**2**	15/2	87	60
2832[7]	**Vanishing Trick (USA) (75)** (HRACecil) **3-8-10b**[1] KFallon(6) (a.p: led over 2f out: hrd rdn & hdd last strides)	1	**3**	16/1	83	56
2133[4]	**Kalinka (IRE) (86)** (PFICole) **3-9-7** JReid(7) (hld up: hdwy 2f out: r.o one pce fnl f)	1¾	**4**	9/1	91	64
2871[5]	**Mara River (84)** (IABalding) **3-9-2**(3) MartinDwyer(11) (lost pl 6f out: nt clr run 3f out: swtchd lft ins fnl f: r.o wl)	s.h	**5**	6/1[2]	89	62
2907[2]	**Opalette (72)** (LadyHerries) **4-9-2** JWeaver(4) (led over 6f: wknd over 1f out)	3½	**6**	12/1	70	52
2331[4]	**Undercover Agent (IRE) (83)** (JLDunlop) **3-9-4** PatEddery(3) (lw: hdwy 3f out: one pce fnl 2f)	1	**7**	7/1[3]	80	53
2184*	**Alifandango (IRE) (79)** (ACStewart) **3-9-0** MRoberts(10) (hld up & bhd: plld out 3f out: hdwy 2f out: hrd rdn over 1f out: wknd fnl f)	2½	**8**	11/1	71	44
2113[2]	**Stone Flower (USA) (85)** (PWChapple-Hyam) **3-9-6** MDemuro(13) (lw: hld up: squeezed thro on ins over 2f out: wknd wl over 1f out)	2½	**9**	20/1	73	46
2772[6]	**Our Way (70)** (CEBrittain) **3-8-5** DBiggs(2) (s.s: hdwy 6f out: wknd over 2f out)	5	**10**	20/1	49	22
959[9]	**Raindancing (IRE) (89)** (RHannon) **3-9-10** BDoyle(9) (prom 5f)	hd	**11**	33/1	68	41
2888*	**Marilaya (IRE) (85)** (LMCumani) **3-9-6** KDarley(5) (lw: plld hrd: prom tl wknd over 2f out)	5	**12**	11/4[1]	55	28
2380[5]	**Doyella (IRE) (83)** (DRLoder) **3-9-4** MJKinane(12) (prom: wkng whn hmpd over 2f out: eased whn btn)	5	**13**	14/1	44	17
				(SP 122.9%)		**13 Rn**

1m 55.34 (2.34) CSF £105.35 CT £1,618.27 TOTE £16.70: £4.10 £2.40 £4.60 (£82.70) Trio £305.40 OWNER Mr A. E. Oppenheimer (NEWMARKET) BRED Hascombe and Valiant Studs
WEIGHT FOR AGE 3yo-9lb

2894 Apache Star, back to a more suitable trip, was 2lb lower than when making her handicap debut two outings ago. (14/1)
2918* Wishing Stone (USA) continues in fine form but could not quite defy her penalty. (15/2: 5/1-8/1)
1794 Vanishing Trick (USA), down 3lb, was sharpened up by the blinkers, having been tried in a visor last time. (16/1)
2133 Kalinka (IRE) does display a rather high head carriage but seemed to do her best. (9/1)
2871 Mara River is continuing to hold her form and was unlucky not to have finished in the money. (6/1)
2907 Opalette has been raised a total of 9lb for completing a hat-trick this season. (12/1)
2184* Alifandango (IRE) (11/1: 7/1-12/1)
2888* Marilaya (IRE) (11/4: op 9/2)

T/Jkpt: £12,010.80 (0.09 Tckts); £15,394.23 to Goodwood 31/7/97. T/Plpt: £188.30 (385.94 Tckts). T/Qdpt: £42.10 (85.09 Tckts) KH

3027-NOTTINGHAM (L-H) (Good to firm, Good patches)
Wednesday July 30th
WEATHER: overcast WIND: str against

3129 'CHILDRENS DAY' (S) H'CAP (0-60) (3-Y.O) (Class G)
2-30 (2-30) **1m 6f 15y** £1,984.50 (£547.00: £259.50) Stalls: Low GOING minus 0.09 sec per fur (G)

Form	Horse	Dist	Pos	SP	RR	SF
2955^{3}	**Running Free (IRE) (49)** (MJFetherston-Godley) **3-9-2** JFortune(6) (chsd ldrs: disp ld fnl 4f: hrd rdn to ld ins fnl f)	—	1	$2/1^{1}$	61	25
2874^{5}	**Eurolink Windsong (IRE) (37)** (MartynWane) **3-8-4** DeanMcKeown(9) (plld hrd: a.p: led over 4f out tl ins fnl f: hrd rdn: r.o)	hd	2	$11/4^{2}$	49	13
2727^{8}	**Fortune Hopper (49)** (JPearce) **3-9-2** GBardwell(8) (trckd ldrs: hrd rdn ent st: styd on one pce)	10	3	13/2	50	14
2908^{13}	**Miss Alice (39)** (CSmith) **3-8-1**(5)ow1 CLowther(1) (chsd ldrs: led 8f out tl over 4f out: wknd 2f out)	7	4	20/1	32	—
2423^{4}	**Skelton Sovereign (IRE) (54)** (RHollinshead) **3-9-7** FLynch(4) (lw: hld up: effrt over 3f out: sn hrd rdn: no imp)	4	5	$3/1^{3}$	42	6
2874^{10}	**Marys Path (29)** (SGollings) **3-7-3**(7) JFowle(5) (lw: sn chsng ldr: wknd 4f out)	hd	6	50/1	17	—
2750^{11}	**Cabcharge Glory (32)** (GGMargarson) **3-7-10**(3) MHenry(7) (a in rr: t.o)	7	7	50/1	12	—
1951^{12}	**Miss Mezzanine (35)** (EAWheeler) **3-7-9**(7)ow6 SCarson(3) (led to 8f out: sn rdn & wknd: t.o)	1¾	8	50/1	13	—
2190^{8}	**Interregnum (34)** (AGFoster) **3-8-1**ow1 TSprake(2) (bit bkwd: lost pl 10f out: t.o)	8	9	16/1	3	—

(SP 114.9%) **9 Rn**

3m 10.7 (12.20) CSF £6.72 CT £25.04 TOTE £2.10: £1.20 £1.10 £2.10 (£6.00) Trio £11.10 OWNER The BMH Partnership (EAST ILSLEY) BRED Mrs B. M. Browne
LONG HANDICAP Miss Mezzanine 7-8 Marys Path 7-9
Bt in 3,000gns
OFFICIAL EXPLANATION Skelton Sovereign (IRE): the rider reported that the colt did not act on the ground. The Veterinary Officer added that the colt was found to be unlevel behind after the race.
2955 Running Free (IRE) has been promising to win a race, so this hard-fought success was not coming out of turn. The deciding factor was his ability to truly stay the trip. (2/1)
2874 Eurolink Windsong (IRE) had a head-to-head with the winner from the turn into the straight and she did appear to have the edge but, close home, an extra effort proved beyond her. (11/4: 9/4-7/2)
2357 Fortune Hopper was unable to improve on his performance behind the winner over a shorter trip earlier in the month, and was never a factor. (13/2)
2423 Skelton Sovereign (IRE) has won on this ground but his action to post suggested he was ill at ease, and he was never able to get himself into contention. (3/1: op 7/4)

3130 BUSINESS NETWORK H'CAP (0-85) (3-Y.O+) (Class D)
3-05 (3-06) **6f 15y** £3,848.50 (£1,153.00: £554.00: £254.50) Stalls: High GOING minus 0.09 sec per fur (G)

Form	Horse	Dist	Pos	SP	RR	SF
2872^{10}	**Bowden Rose (83)** (MBlanshard) **5-9-9b**(5) DSweeney(14) (mde all: clr fnl f: pushed out)	—	1	$9/1^{3}$	92	71
2339^{10}	**Brecongill Lad (64)** (MissSEHall) **5-8-9** LCharnock(15) (lw: a.p: rdn & edgd lft over 1f out: unable qckn)	1¾	2	14/1	68	47
3034^{13}	**For the Present (76)** (TDBarron) **7-9-7** ACulhane(12) (hdwy u.p 2f out: kpt on wl towards fin)	hd	3	$8/1^{2}$	80	59
2708^{9}	**Delta Soleil (USA) (81)** (PWHarris) **5-9-7**(5) CLowther(3) (hld up: hdwy appr fnl f: nrst fin)	¾	4	$8/1^{2}$	83	62
2649^{3}	**Mr Bergerac (IRE) (80)** (BPalling) **6-9-11** TSprake(7) (lw: effrt & rdn over 2f out: nvr nr to chal)	2	5	$5/1^{1}$	77	56
2844*	**Just Dissident (IRE) (64)** (RMWhitaker) **5-8-9** DeanMcKeown(11) (prom: rdn along wl over 1f out: one pce)	½	6	$8/1^{2}$	60	39
2833^{8}	**Desert Lynx (IRE) (76)** (TRWatson) **4-9-7** RHughes(1) (lw: nvr nr to chal)	½	7	$8/1^{2}$	70	49
2563^{11}	**Pageboy (65)** (PCHaslam) **8-8-10** JFortune(10) (trckd ldrs: kpt on u.p ins fnl f)	½	8	14/1	58	37
2769^{6}	**Hoh Returns (IRE) (81)** (MBell) **4-9-12** MFenton(6) (lw: swtchd rt s: a outpcd)	½	9	$8/1^{2}$	73	52
2833^{12}	**Lady Diesis (USA) (82)** (BWHills) **3-9-5**(3) JDSmith(5) (dwlt: a in rr)	hd	10	16/1	73	47
2497^{5}	**High Domain (IRE) (65)** (JLSpearing) **6-8-10** FLynch(13) (chsd ldrs over 4f: sn rdn & outpcd)	2	11	14/1	51	30
2833^{9}	**Lord Olivier (IRE) (75)** (WJarvis) **7-9-6** MTebbutt(8) (chsd ldrs 4f: sn rdn & outpcd)	¾	12	14/1	59	38
2844^{7}	**Superbit (66)** (BAMcMahon) **5-8-11** LNewton(9) (lw: prom: drvn along ½-wy: grad wknd)	2	13	$8/1^{2}$	45	24
2649^{8}	**Mumkin (79)** (TThomsonJones) **3-9-5** GCarter(4) (racd centre: hrd rdn over 2f out: no imp)	1¼	14	20/1	55	29

(SP 130.6%) **14 Rn**

1m 13.8 (2.30) CSF £127.55 CT £673.43 TOTE £12.60: £4.20 £3.20 £2.70 (£57.10) Trio £95.50 OWNER G H S Bailey & N C D Hall (UPPER LAMBOURN) BRED E. A. Badger
WEIGHT FOR AGE 3yo-5lb
2590* Bowden Rose appreciated this step back to her own company and, in control from the start, won with quite a bit in hand. (9/1: op 6/1)
1977 Brecongill Lad was the only serious threat to the winner inside the distance, but he edged away from the rails when put under pressure, and lacked the speed to mount a challenge. (14/1)
2129 For the Present showed a return to form with a promising staying-on effort, and he could be on the way back. (8/1)
2129 Delta Soleil (USA) found his stride on the approach to the final furlong but, by then, the principals had gone beyond recall. He has been performing well but, over sprint distances, he does seem to need a stiffer test. (8/1)
2649 Mr Bergerac (IRE) could never summon the pace to prove troublesome and this lively ground is not for him. (5/1)
2844* Just Dissident (IRE) likes to blaze a trail but was unable to do so. Although he shared the lead, he could never get to the front and, though he never stopped trying, had met his match below the distance. (8/1)
2422* Desert Lynx (IRE) needs more cut than she had here and, drawn in the slower centre of the track, was never finding the pace to make her presence felt. (8/1)
2497 High Domain (IRE) (14/1: op 8/1)

3131 'PLAYGROUND' NOVICE AUCTION STKS (2-Y.O) (Class F)
3-35 (3-36) **6f 15y** £2,277.00 (£627.00: £297.00) Stalls: High GOING minus 0.09 sec per fur (G)

Form	Horse	Dist	Pos	SP	RR	SF
2519^{3}	**Zena** (WJarvis) **2-8-7** DHolland(12) (hld up in tch: n.m.r over 1f out: qcknd to ld ins fnl f: sn clr)	—	1	$9/2^{2}$	82+	27
2942^{9}	**Bandbox (IRE)** (SMellor) **2-8-12** MWigham(9) (lw: mde most tl ins fnl f)	1¾	2	16/1	82	27
2520*	**Welcome Sunset** (JWharton) **2-8-12** JFortune(5) (lw: hld up: nt clr run over 1f out: swtchd lft: r.o wl towards fin)	hd	3	$9/2^{2}$	82	27
2700^{3}	**Sing For Me (IRE)** (RHollinshead) **2-8-0** NCarlisle(6) (hdwy appr fnl f: fin wl)	¾	4	10/1	68	13
2842^{5}	**Dancing Rio (IRE)** (PCHaslam) **2-8-5**(5) CLowther(3) (lw: a.p: hrd rdn over 1f out: r.o one pce)	hd	5	8/1	78	23

2870[10] **Al Mabrook (IRE)** (KMahdi) **2-8-6**(5) DSweeney(1) (trckd ldrs: drvn along appr fnl f: nvr nrr)..........nk **6** 8/1 78 23
2047[6] **Ra Ra Rasputin** (BAMcMahon) **2-8-10** LNewton(2) (spd over 4f)..........3 **7** 33/1 69 14
2519[4] **Chameli** (MrsLStubbs) **2-8-3** TSprake(8) (in tch on outside: drvn along over 2f out: no imp)..........½ **8** 14/1 61 6
2862[14] **Brandon Frank** (IABalding) **2-9-0** SWhitworth(4) (lw: s.i.s: effrt & rdn over 2f out: nt pce to chal)..........½ **9** 5/2[1] 71 16
2736* **Fashion Victim** (THCaldwell) **2-9-3** ACulhane(7) (prom: hrd rdn 2f out: wknd appr fnl f)..........1¾ **10** 7/1[3] 69 14
Touch of Colour (JWWatts) **2-8-5** JCarroll(10) (unf: scope: bkwd: s.i.s: a bhd & outpcd)..........5 **11** 16/1 44 —
2697[6] ***Blushing Victoria*** (MartynMeade) **2-8-10** FNorton(11) (Withdrawn not under Starter's orders: reard over in stalls).......... **W** 10/1 — —
(SP 139.2%) **11 Rn**

1m 15.6 (4.10) CSF £71.96 TOTE £4.20: £1.80 £4.50 £2.70 (£35.40) Trio £158.70; £6.71 to Goodwood 31/7/97 OWNER Mr N. S. Yong (NEWMARKET) BRED Fares Stables Ltd

2519 Zena was searching for room inside the last quarter-mile and, when a gap did eventually present itself, she was through like a rat up a drainpipe and the contest was over in a matter of strides. (9/2)
2520 Bandbox (IRE), having his first try at six furlongs, ran his best race yet and he is certainly capable of going one better. (16/1)
2520* Welcome Sunset found his path blocked when he was poised to challenge and he had to be switched and, by the time he found top gear, the winner had the prize safely under wraps. (9/2)
2700 Sing For Me (IRE), who showed plenty of knee action, ran on particularly well inside the final furlong and, as her previous race was over seven furlongs, connections obviously realised that she needs further. (10/1)
2842 Dancing Rio (IRE) has hardly run a bad race yet and, though he raced freely to share the lead, he battled on to the finish and will make his mark before long. (8/1)
Al Mabrook (IRE) did at least know he had been in a race this time, and the experience should stand him in good stead. (8/1: op 16/1)
2306* Brandon Frank, slow to find his stride, was made to work approaching the last quarter-mile and, unable to step-up his pace, proved most disappointing. (5/2: 2/1-7/2)

3132 'SCHOOL HOLIDAYS' H'CAP (0-75) (3-Y.O) (Class D)

4-10 (4-10) **1m 54y** £4,046.75 (£1,214.00: £584.50: £269.75) Stalls: Low GOING minus 0.09 sec per fur (G)

SP RR SF

2169[3] **Anetta (51)** (MissSEHall) **3-7-11** LCharnock(6) (b.hind: lw: hld up: hdwy 3f out: led over 2f out: drvn clr fnl f)..........— **1** 8/1 58 19
2184[4] **Love Venture (69)** (SPCWoods) **3-9-1** WJO'Connor(3) (chsd ldr: led 4f out to 3f out: styd on ins fnl f)..........2½ **2** 6/1[3] 71 32
Fearless Cavalier (57) (RHollinshead) **3-8-3** FLynch(4) (wl bhd & outpcd: gd hdwy over 2f out: rdn & one pce fnl f)..........¾ **3** 10/1 58 19
2897[5] **Begorrat (IRE) (72)** (BJMeehan) **3-9-4** MTebbutt(5) (chsd ldrs: led 3f out: sn hdd & rdn: r.o one pce fnl f).....s.h **4** 7/2[2] 73 34
2523* **Saffron Rose (75)** (MBlanshard) **3-9-7** TSprake(7) (hld up: hdwy over 3f out: sn rdn: kpt on towards fin)......s.h **5** 6/4[1] 76 37
2878[2] **Flood's Hot Stuff (50)** (NPLittmoden) **3-7-10** GBardwell(2) (led tl ½-wy: rdn & btn over 2f out)..........2½ **6** 10/1 46 7
2755[10] **Docklands Carriage (IRE) (63)** (NTinkler) **3-8-9** KimTinkler(1) (lw: s.i.s: sn chsng ldrs: rdn along & outpcd over 2f out)..........4 **7** 16/1 51 12
(SP 130.1%) **7 Rn**

1m 47.0 (5.70) CSF £47.00 TOTE £11.20: £2.90 £3.20 (£31.10) OWNER Mr B. McAllister (MIDDLEHAM)
LONG HANDICAP Flood's Hot Stuff 6-11

2169 Anetta came into her own over this longer trip, winning very much as she pleased and, now that she has found her true mark, there could be more success to be had. (8/1)
2184 Love Venture had more than her full quota of weight in this first handicap, but she ran her best race yet and is beginning to get the hang of the game. (6/1: op 5/2)
Fearless Cavalier has filled out a bit since his two-year-old days and looked well tuned up for his first try at this extended trip. Restrained some way behind his rivals, he made smooth progress to give himself every chance approaching the final furlong, but lack of a recent race seemed to take its toll. (10/1: op 13/2)
2695 Begorrat (IRE) gets this trip well, but he does seem to lack a turn of finishing speed and may well need easier underfoot conditions to show his true worth. (7/2)
2523* Saffron Rose, attempting a three-timer over course and distance, just could not cope with this much faster ground and she was unable to get close enough to land a blow. (6/4)

3133 'CHILDREN IN FREE' MEDIAN AUCTION MAIDEN STKS (3-Y.O F) (Class E)

4-45 (4-47) **1m 1f 213y** £2,940.25 (£877.00: £418.50: £189.25) Stalls: Low GOING minus 0.09 sec per fur (G)

SP RR SF

2878[4] **Silent Valley (42)** (MissLCSiddall) **3-8-11v** MWigham(8) (lw: hld up: hdwy 3f out: led appr fnl f: all out)..........— **1** 7/1 62 19
2832[8] **Bellagrana (52)** (MJFetherston-Godley) **3-8-11** DHolland(2) (hld up: hdwy over 2f out: rdn & r.o wl ins fnl f) ..nk **2** 8/1 62 19
2374[7] **Limelight (59)** (JARToller) **3-8-11** DaleGibson(6) (trckd ldrs: rdn 2f out: kpt on one pce fnl f)..........1¼ **3** 7/2[2] 60 17
Little Miss Lucy (MJHeaton-Ellis) **3-8-12**ow1 RHughes(7) (lengthy: unf: bit bkwd: bhd: hdwy 3f out: rdn & rn green ent fnl f: improve)..........2½ **4** 16/1 57 13
2568[9] **Viburnum** (AGFoster) **3-8-11** TSprake(9) (hld up: hdwy u.p wl over 1f out: nt pce to chal)..........nk **5** 5/1[3] 55 12
2956[8] **Lochlass (IRE) (60)** (SPCWoods) **3-8-11** WJO'Connor(5) (chsd ldrs: led 4f out tl over 3f out: rdn & btn appr fnl f)..........1¼ **6** 12/1 53 10
2723[3] **Super Scravels (47)** (KMahdi) **3-8-6**(5) CLowther(1) (s.i.s: hdwy ent st: led over 3f out tl over 1f out: wknd)..........1 **7** 11/4[1] 51 8
2783[3] **Minster Star** (JLSpearing) **3-8-11** FLynch(4) (prom: pushed along 3f out: wknd wl over 1f out)..........4 **8** 11/2 45 2
2731[14] **Fully Booked (47)** (JWHills) **3-8-8**(3) MHenry(3) (swtg: led tl over 4f out: sn rdn & lost tch: t.o)..........dist **9** 12/1 — —
2773[9] **Unforgetable Charm (IRE)** (MrsNMacauley) **3-8-11** SWebster(10) (prom 7f: sn rdn & wknd: t.o)..........8 **10** 25/1 — —
(SP 129.7%) **10 Rn**

2m 11.1 (8.60) CSF £62.90 TOTE £12.20: £2.90 £2.80 £1.20 (£31.40) Trio £72.80 OWNER Mrs S. E. Cooper (TADCASTER) BRED W. R. Jones

2878 Silent Valley, much happier with this step-up to ten furlongs, stayed on to strike the front at the distance and then clung on grimly to the post. (7/1)
Bellagrana taken to post early, was anchored in the pack. Pulled wide to deliver her challenge, she was pegging back the winner all the way to the line but had met a rival who was not in the mood to give best and was still a couple of paces short at the finish. She is improving and consolation awaits. (8/1)
1563 Limelight sat close to the pace and battled on willingly under pressure but she was tapped for toe inside the distance. She is bred to need further and must not be written off just yet. (7/2)
Little Miss Lucy still looks to need time to furnish, but she turned in a pleasing performance on this debut and, with this experience under her belt, will be all the wiser next time. (16/1)

2116 Viburnum could not get herself into a challenging position, despite staying on, but she is gaining experience all the time. (5/1)
26 Lochlass (IRE) did manage to poke her nose in front briefly early in the straight and, though she was unable to sustain the run, should know what is required now. (12/1: op 6/1)
2723 Super Scravels, the subject of some inspired support in the ring, improved quickly to take the lead early in the straight but she had very little left when the winner came on the scene and was soon back-pedalling. (11/4)
2783 Minster Star (11/2: 3/1-6/1)
Fully Booked (12/1: op 8/1)

3134 'SWEETS & ICE CREAM' LIMITED STKS (0-60) (3-Y.O+) (Class F)

5-20 (5-20) **1m 1f 213y** £2,277.00 (£627.00: £297.00) Stalls: Low GOING minus 0.09 sec per fur (G)

				SP	RR	SF
2373[9]	**Monument (60)** (JSKing) **5-9-4** TSprake(2) (a.p: led 3f out: r.o strly ins fnl f)	—	**1**	5/1[3]	71	34
2890[9]	**Impulsive Air (IRE) (59)** (EWeymes) **5-9-4** EmmaO'Gorman(10) (lw: sn chsng ldrs: rn wd & lost pl ent st: rallied 2f out: r.o)	2½	**2**	12/1	67	30
2686[6]	**Tonnerre (59)** (BAMcMahon) **5-9-6** LNewton(4) (lw: a.p: ev ch over 1f out: rdn & edgd lft ins fnl f: unable qckn)	¾	**3**	10/1	68	31
2733[2]	**Sharp Deed (IRE) (55)** (PJMakin) **3-8-3**(5) DSweeney(7) (a.p: kpt on u.p ins fnl f)	hd	**4**	9/2[2]	66	19
3026[12]	**Action Jackson (50)** (BJMcMath) **5-9-1**(3) PMcCabe(1) (led to 3f out: rdn & btn whn hmpd ins fnl f)	¾	**5**	12/1	64	27
2845[8]	**Tinklers Folly (55)** (RMWhitaker) **5-8-13**(5) CLowther(5) (prom: kpt on one pce fnl 2f)	4	**6**	12/1	58	21
2668[7]	**Piquant (60)** (LordHuntingdon) **10-8-13**(5) AimeeCook(11) (a in rr)	7	**7**	15/2	47	10
2843[14]	**Six Clerks (IRE) (55)** (JGFitzGerald) **4-9-4b** MTebbutt(8) (lw: mid div: rdn 3f out: no imp)	¾	**8**	11/1	46	9
2582[3]	**Tart (FR) (56)** (JPearce) **4-9-1** MWigham(3) (hld up: effrt on ins over 2f out: sn rdn: no rspnse)	3½	**9**	5/2[1]	37	—
	Access Adventurer (IRE) (60) (RBoss) **6-9-4** RHughes(12) (bkwd: a bhd: eased whn btn fnl 2f: t.o)	11	**10**	7/1	22	—
2825[12]	**Meadow Blue (35)** (MissLCSiddall) **4-9-1** OPears(6) (bit bkwd: a bhd: t.o fnl 3f)	8	**11**	50/1	6	—
2724[10]	**Mubariz (IRE) (32)** (CSmith) **5-9-4** FLynch(9) (t: a bhd: t.o fnl 3f)	22	**12**	33/1	—	—

(SP 133.1%) **12 Rn**

2m 9.9 (7.40) CSF £65.96 TOTE £6.10: £2.30 £4.80 £3.10 (£35.00) Trio £333.90; £56.44 to Goodwood 31/7/97 OWNER Mr V. Askew (SWINDON) BRED Exors of the late Mrs D. M. de Rothschild
WEIGHT FOR AGE 3yo-10lb
STEWARDS' ENQUIRY Newton susp. 8-10/8/97 (careless riding).
1923 Monument usually finds his form at this time of year, and he hardly had to get serious to shake off this opposition. (5/1)
2546 Impulsive Air (IRE), having another try at this slightly longer trip, may well have made a race of it had he not run so wide entering the straight, for he lost far more ground than he was beaten by. (12/1: op 7/1)
2686 Tonnerre needs to be able to get his toe in but he ran up to his mark, though it must be said that he was fortunate not to be down-graded after he all but put Action Jackson over the rail just inside the final furlong. (10/1)
2733 Sharp Deed (IRE), given every opportunity to get the trip, did not fail for the want of trying and that elusive first success cannot be too far away. (9/2)
1665 Action Jackson forced the pace for almost a mile and then kept staying on under strong pressure, but he was fighting a losing battle when Tonnerre stopped him in his tracks two hundred yards out. (12/1)
1802 Tinklers Folly, a prolific winner over seven furlongs and a mile in the past, just does not get this trip and it would be wise to let him take a step down to his ideal distance. (12/1)
1588 Piquant (15/2: 5/1-8/1)
1574 Six Clerks (IRE) (11/1: 6/1-12/1)
Access Adventurer (IRE) (7/1: op 9/2)

T/Plpt: £724.70 (19.29 Tckts). T/Qdpt: £128.60 (7.22 Tckts) IM

2959-SANDOWN (R-H) (Good to firm)
Wednesday July 30th

WEATHER: warm WIND: almost nil

3135 PACEMAKER & THOROUGHBRED BREEDER RACING SCHOOLS APPRENTICE H'CAP (0-75) (3-Y.O+) (Class E)

6-00 (6-05) **1m 2f 7y** £2,698.75 (£820.00: £402.50: £193.75) Stalls: High GOING minus 0.39 sec per fur (F)

				SP	RR	SF
3026[8]	**Zamalek (USA) (42)** (RMFlower) **5-7-9**(3) JFowle(7) (swtg: led 9f out tl over 7f out: chsd ldr over 2f out: led ins fnl f: r.o wl)	—	**1**	12/1	51	25
2961*	**Traceability (77)** (SCWilliams) **4-10-2**(3) 5x DarrenWilliams(2) (led 1f: led over 3f out tl ins fnl f: r.o)	½	**2**	3/1[1]	85	59
2344[3]	**Dauphin (IRE) (44)** (WJMusson) **4-8-0** PDoe(1) (s.s: hld up: hrd rdn over 2f out: unable qckn)	5	**3**	7/2[2]	44	18
2195*	**Absolute Liberty (USA) (68)** (SPCWoods) **3-9-0** GMilligan(4) (led over 7f out tl over 3f out: one pce)	2	**4**	5/1	65	29
1588[10]	**Dances With Hooves (66)** (DJSffrenchDavis) **5-9-8** DDenby(8) (s.i.s: nvr nr to chal)	1	**5**	20/1	61	35
2772[5]	**Blowing Away (IRE) (70)** (MHTompkins) **3-8-13**(3) PClarke(6) (hld up: rdn over 3f out: sn wknd)	1¾	**6**	9/1	63	27
2375[8]	**Shining Example (70)** (PJMakin) **5-9-12** RHavlin(5) (swtg: sme hdwy on ins wl over 1f out: sn wknd)	2½	**7**	4/1[3]	59	33
2743[8]	**Manaloj (USA) (72)** (RHannon) **4-9-11**(3) RSmith(3) (hld up: rdn over 3f out: sn wknd)	2½	**8**	20/1	57	31

(SP 111.1%) **8 Rn**

2m 10.22 (3.52) CSF £41.26 CT £136.49 TOTE £15.00: £2.00 £1.60 £1.40 (£11.20) OWNER Rare Stakes Partnership (JEVINGTON) BRED Buckram Oak Farm
WEIGHT FOR AGE 3yo-10lb
2399 Zamalek (USA), the early leader, moved into second place early in the straight and eventually managed to wear down the leader inside the final furlong. (12/1: op 8/1)
2961* Traceability, winner over this course and distance last Thursday, valiantly tried to follow up as he moved to the front early in the straight, but his 5lb penalty took its toll and he was overhauled inside the final furlong, the pair finishing well clear of the remainder. (3/1)
2344 Dauphin (IRE) chased the leaders but failed to find that vital turn of foot in the final quarter-mile. Both his wins to date have come over further and a step back up in distance would help. (7/2)
2195* Absolute Liberty (USA) was soon at the head of affairs. Collared early in the straight, he was always being tapped for toe. (5/1)
108* Dances With Hooves, racing at the back of the field, never threatened to get into it. (20/1)
2772 Blowing Away (IRE) had been seen off early in the straight. (9/1)

3136 E.B.F. MEDIAN AUCTION MAIDEN STKS (2-Y.O) (Class D)

6-35 (6-39) **5f 6y** £3,485.00 (£1,055.00: £515.00: £245.00) Stalls: Low GOING minus 0.39 sec per fur (F)

				SP	RR	SF
2370[6]	**Brimstone (IRE)** (DRCElsworth) **2-9-0** AClark(4) (lw: led over 3f out: pushed out)	—	**1**	5/1[2]	78	7
2829[8]	**Storm Fromthe East** (RHannon) **2-9-0** DaneO'Neill(8) (lw: a.p: chsd wnr over 1f out: r.o)	¾	**2**	7/4[1]	76	5
	Hever Golf Machine (TJNaughton) **2-9-0** AMcGlone(5) (str: bit bkwd: outpcd: hdwy over 1f out: unable qckn)	4	**3**	16/1	63	—
1564[11]	**Apple Sauce** (JRArnold) **2-8-9** DHarrison(9) (bit bkwd: a.p: rdn over 2f out: wknd fnl f)	1½	**4**	33/1	53	—
2870[8]	**Red Pepper (IRE)** (PHowling) **2-9-0** CRutter(11) (led over 1f: wknd over 1f out)	2	**5**	16/1	52	—
	Sharp Steel (GLMoore) **2-9-0** CandyMorris(6) (leggy: swtg: hdwy over 2f out: wknd over 1f out)	2	**6**	20/1	45	—
	Saxon Victory (USA) (WJHaggas) **2-9-0** RCochrane(2) (leggy: lw: a bhd)	4	**7**	7/1	33	—
2138[8]	**Surpresa Cara** (GLewis) **2-8-9** PaulEddery(10) (bhd fnl 2f)	1	**8**	6/1[3]	25	—
2781[5]	**Tiara** (BJMeehan) **2-8-9** SSanders(3) (bhd fnl 2f)	hd	**9**	5/1[2]	24	—
	Sabre Girl (RHannon) **2-8-6**(3) AWhelan(1) (neat: stumbled s: a bhd)	7	**10**	14/1	2	—
				(SP 122.6%)	**10 Rn**	

63.39 secs (3.59) CSF £13.58 TOTE £6.60: £2.10 £1.10 £3.80 (£7.70) Trio £34.00 OWNER Seymour Bloodstock (UK) Ltd (WHITCOMBE) BRED Airlie Stud

OFFICIAL EXPLANATION **Sabre Girl: shied away and collided with the rail shortly after the start.**

1842 Brimstone (IRE), with plenty of substance about him, was soon at the head of affairs and needed only to be nudged along to keep the runner-up at bay. (5/1: 4/1-6/1)

Storm Fromthe East, an attractive colt with plenty of substance and scope, came through to take second place below the distance but, despite finishing well clear of the remainder, was unable to overhaul the winner. He should have no problems landing a similar event. (7/4)

Hever Golf Machine, a sturdy colt, was carrying some condition. Picking up ground below the distance, he was making no further impression inside the final furlong. (16/1)

Apple Sauce still looked a bit porky in the paddock, but was close up until tiring in the final furlong. (33/1)

1941 Red Pepper (IRE), the early leader, had shot his bolt below the distance. (16/1)

Sharp Steel, a tall gelding with not much substance, was unruly and worked-up in the paddock. He made an effort at halfway but had nothing left below the distance. (20/1)

Saxon Victory (USA) (7/1: op 3/1)

Surpresa Cara (6/1: 5/2-7/1)

3137 IMBER COURT H'CAP (0-85) (3-Y.O+) (Class D)

7-10 (7-11) **1m 6f** £4,396.50 (£1,332.00: £651.00: £310.50) Stalls: Low GOING minus 0.39 sec per fur (F)

				SP	RR	SF
2949*	**Mawared (IRE) (71)** (JLDunlop) **4-9-0** 4x RHills(7) (b: n.m.r over 3f out: hdwy over 2f out: led over 1f out: rdn out)	—	**1**	7/4[1]	84	45
2694[3]	**Alarico (FR) (62)** (IPWilliams) **4-8-5** AClark(6) (swtg: chsd ldr: led 3f out tl over 1f out: unable qckn)	2½	**2**	10/1	72	33
2949[5]	**Tawafek (USA) (70)** (SDow) **4-8-13** JFEgan(4) (hld up: rdn over 3f out: one pce)	3	**3**	14/1	77	38
2767[6]	**Bimsey (IRE) (82)** (RAkehurst) **7-9-11** SSanders(1) (swtg: hdwy over 4f out: hrd rdn over 2f out: one pce)	hd	**4**	2/1[2]	89	50
2767[4]	**Midyan Blue (IRE) (65)** (JMPEustace) **7-8-8** RCochrane(3) (hld up: hrd rdn over 3f out: sn wknd)	2½	**5**	11/2[3]	69	30
1871[4]	**Castle Courageous (73)** (LadyHerries) **10-8-9**(7) PDoe(5) (b: hld up: hrd rdn over 3f out: wknd over 2f out)	1½	**6**	20/1	75	36
2897[3]	**Pennys From Heaven (75)** (HCandy) **3-8-4** CRutter(8) (lw: led 11f: wknd over 1f out)	6	**7**	10/1	70	17
2764[4]	**Smart Play (USA) (85)** (LordHuntingdon) **4-10-0** DHarrison(2) (lw: a bhd)	21	**8**	14/1	56	17
				(SP 121.4%)	**8 Rn**	

3m 2.91 (4.01) CSF £20.07 CT £180.75 TOTE £2.50: £1.20 £2.70 £3.60 (£19.70) OWNER Mr Hamdan Al Maktoum (ARUNDEL) BRED Shadwell Estate Company Limited

WEIGHT FOR AGE 3yo-14lb

2949* Mawared (IRE) followed up his win here last Wednesday night despite a 4lb penalty and, striking the front approaching the final furlong, was rousted along to score. This is his trip. (7/4)

2694 Alarico (FR) moved to the front early in the straight but, collared approaching the final furlong, failed to cope with the winner. (10/1: 8/1-14/1)

2949 Tawafek (USA), 4lb better off with the winner for a five-length beating here last Wednesday, failed to get any closer. (14/1: 8/1-16/1)

2767 Bimsey (IRE), 2lb lower than when running here two weeks ago, moved up turning for home but was made to look extremely pedestrian in the straight. (2/1)

2767 Midyan Blue (IRE) showed little and had been seen off early in the straight. He is not very consistent and has not won for two years. (11/2)

1871 Castle Courageous has failed to recapture his sparkling form of 1994 and had been seen off over two furlongs from home. (20/1)

3138 PRICE WATERHOUSE H'CAP (0-80) (3-Y.O+) (Class D)

7-40 (7-45) **7f 16y** £4,970.00 (£1,505.00: £735.00: £350.00) Stalls: High GOING minus 0.39 sec per fur (F)

				SP	RR	SF
2835[7]	**Winsome Wooster (63)** (PGMurphy) **6-8-13** JFEgan(10) (a.p: led 2f out: rdn out)	—	**1**	10/1	74	56
2835[5]	**Duello (65)** (MBlanshard) **6-9-1** MRoberts(4) (lw: rdn over 2f out: hdwy over 1f out: str run fnl f: fin wl)	hd	**2**	8/1[3]	76	58
2868[6]	**Al Masroor (USA) (77)** (JWPayne) **3-9-6** DeanMcKeown(12) (a.p: rdn over 2f out: ev ch ins fnl f: unable qckn)	1¼	**3**	12/1	85	60
2785*	**Silver Lining (62)** (APJones) **3-8-5** RCochrane(7) (rdn over 2f out: hdwy over 1f out: r.o wl ins fnl f)	¾	**4**	8/1[3]	68	43
1489[14]	**Perfect Pal (IRE) (72)** (MissGayKelleway) **6-9-5**(3) RFfrench(5) (rdn over 3f out: hdwy over 1f out: r.o wl)	1	**5**	10/1	76	58
2678[12]	**Arterxerxes (78)** (MJHeaton-Ellis) **4-10-0** AClark(13) (lw: led 5f: wknd fnl f)	½	**6**	7/1[2]	81	63
2745[8]	**Coastguards Hero (46)** (MDIUsher) **4-7-3**(7) JFowle(8) (hld up: rdn over 2f out: one pce)	½	**7**	33/1	48	30
2951[2]	**Song of Skye (80)** (TJNaughton) **3-9-9** JWeaver(1) (s.s: hdwy over 1f out: nvr nrr)	¾	**8**	11/2[1]	80	55
2835[8]	**Sea Danzig (58)** (JJBridger) **4-8-8** DHarrison(3) (lw: chsd ldr 4f: wknd over 1f out)	3½	**9**	14/1	50	32
1249[9]	**Masterpiece (72)** (RHannon) **3-9-1** DaneO'Neill(2) (rdn over 2f out: hdwy over 1f out: wknd fnl f)	1	**10**	20/1	62	37
2704[4]	**Kailey Goddess (USA) (65)** (RWArmstrong) **4-9-1** RPrice(6) (lw: a bhd)	s.h	**11**	14/1	55	37
2866[5]	**Zermatt (IRE) (59)** (MDIUsher) **7-8-9** NAdams(14) (lw: hld up: rdn 4f out: wknd wl over 1f out)	3	**12**	10/1	42	24
2576[3]	**Whispered Melody (58)** (RAkehurst) **4-8-8** SSanders(9) (prom over 5f)	5	**13**	11/1	30	12
2835[3]	**Blue Flyer (IRE) (70)** (RIngram) **4-9-6b** AMcGlone(11) (rdn 4f out: bhd fnl 2f)	nk	**14**	7/1[2]	41	23
				(SP 126.9%)	**14 Rn**	

1m 29.44 (0.84) CSF £84.34 CT £930.42 TOTE £12.40: £3.80 £2.50 £3.40 (£25.00) Trio £170.30 OWNER Miss Amanda Rawding (BRISTOL) BRED Mrs J. A. Rawding and G. C. Greenwood

LONG HANDICAP Coastguards Hero 7-2
WEIGHT FOR AGE 3yo-7lb
1680 Winsome Wooster, currently in-foal to Cyrano de Bergerac, struck the front a quarter of a mile from home but found the line only just saving her. This was her last race. (10/1: 8/1-12/1)
2835 Duello only found his stride from below the distance and, absolutely flying, would surely have prevailed in a couple more strides. He is not easy to win with and his record now stands at three victories from fifty-five starts. (8/1)
2868 Al Masroor (USA) ran a fine race. Throwing down his challenge in the final quarter-mile, he was still battling for the advantage inside the final furlong before tapped for toe. (12/1)
2785* Silver Lining began a forward move below the distance but, despite running on strongly, found the line always beating him. Both his wins this season have come over this trip. (8/1)
1237 Perfect Pal (IRE), given a nine-week break, put in some good work in the last furlong and a half without threatening to get there in time. (10/1)
1308 Arterxerxes, looking in fine shape in the paddock, was back over his optimum trip and had been dropped a few pounds by the Handicapper, which makes this performance rather disappointing. (7/1: op 12/1)

3139 PORTSMOUTH ROAD CLAIMING STKS (3-Y.O+) (Class E)
8-10 (8-15) **7f 16y** £2,739.25 (£829.00: £404.50: £192.25) Stalls: High GOING minus 0.39 sec per fur (F)

				SP	RR	SF
3056[5]	**Banzhaf (USA) (66)** (GLMoore) **4-9-8** AClark(7) (lw: chsd ldr: led over 3f out: rdn over 2f out: clr over 1f out: r.o wl)	—	1	11/4[1]	77	51
2575[2]	**Peter Perfect (58)** (GLewis) **3-8-5b** PaulEddery(5) (led over 3f: rdn over 2f out: unable qckn)	1¾	2	7/1	63	30
2954[12]	**Kilvine (77)** (WJHaggas) **4-9-4** RCochrane(1) (lw: rdn over 2f out: hdwy over 1f out: one pce)	s.h	3	13/2[3]	69	43
2921[5]	**Big Ben (70)** (RHannon) **3-9-3** DaneO'Neill(6) (lw: no hdwy fnl 3f)	3	4	11/4[1]	68	35
2748*	**Hawaii Storm (FR) (53)** (DJSffrenchDavis) **9-8-5**(3) RFfrench(4) (rdn over 2f out: nvr nr to chal)	s.h	5	10/1	52	26
2958[4]	**Always Grace (58)** (MissGayKelleway) **5-8-7** SSanders(3) (swtg: a bhd)	4	6	100/30[2]	42	16
2937[8]	**Lancashire Legend (49)** (SDow) **4-8-8** JFEgan(2) (plld hrd: prom 5f)	6	7	12/1	29	3

(SP 119.0%) **7 Rn**
1m 30.67 (2.07) CSF £21.73 TOTE £5.30: £2.60 £2.40 (£16.90) OWNER Mr Bryan Pennick (BRIGHTON) BRED Pope McLean
WEIGHT FOR AGE 3yo-7lb
3056 Banzhaf (USA) appreciated the drop in class and being allowed to race up with the pace. Gaining control early in the straight, he was rousted along to forge clear in the final quarter-mile and gain his first turf success. (11/4)
2575 Peter Perfect, who sped off down to the start, coped with this longer trip and took the field along to halfway. Grimly trying to hold on to the winner, he was put in his place in the final quarter-mile. (7/1)
Kilvine, officially 8lb best-in on adjusted ratings, has been in bad form this season. Moving up to dispute second place below the distance, he was then tapped for toe. (13/2)
2921 Big Ben, who showed a scratchy action going down, was making little impression on the leaders in the straight. (11/4: 21/-3/1)
2748* Hawaii Storm (FR) never threatened to get into it. (10/1)
2958 Always Grace, who pulled hard going down, was always at the back. (100/30)
2937 Lancashire Legend (12/1: 8/1-14/1)

3140 SURREY RACING MAIDEN STKS (3-Y.O) (Class D)
8-40 (8-42) **1m 14y** £3,517.50 (£1,065.00: £520.00: £247.50) Stalls: High GOING minus 0.39 sec per fur (F)

				SP	RR	SF
2242[5]	**Chief Monarch (85)** (BSmart) **3-9-0** RCochrane(7) (lw: hld up: rdn over 2f out: str run to ld wl ins fnl f: r.o wl)	—	1	7/4[1]	81	47
2873[5]	**Tonight's Prize (IRE)** (CFWall) **3-9-0** SSanders(4) (nt clr run over 2f out: hdwy over 1f out: ev ch wl ins fnl f: r.o wl)	hd	2	9/2	81	47
	Kamin (USA) (RWArmstrong) **3-9-0** RHills(2) (a.p: led over 3f out: hrd rdn over 1f out: hdd wl ins fnl f: unable qckn)	1¾	3	100/30[2]	77	43
1625[5]	**Silver Whirl (USA)** (RCharlton) **3-8-9** TSprake(1) (a.p: ev ch over 2f out: hrd rdn over 1f out: one pce)	½	4	4/1[3]	71	37
2492[8]	**Massyar Seventeen** (HJCollingridge) **3-9-0** MRimmer(3) (rdn over 2f out: hdwy over 1f out: one pce)	2½	5	14/1	71	37
1499[7]	**Swan Lane (USA)** (JHMGosden) **3-8-9** AGarth(6) (lw: hld up: rdn over 2f out: sn wknd)	5	6	6/1	57	23
2960[10]	**Just Dickens** (RIngram) **3-8-9** AMcGlone(5) (led over 4f: wknd over 2f out)	17	7	33/1	23	—

(SP 121.5%) **7 Rn**
1m 43.2 (2.00) CSF £10.13 TOTE £2.50: £1.60 £2.80 (£6.30) OWNER Miss N. Jefford (LAMBOURN) BRED James William Mitchell and Simon Edward Mitchell
1741 Chief Monarch, who failed to handle the mud last time out, looked in tremendous shape beforehand, though favourite backers must have been extremely worried a quarter of a mile from home as he appeared to be going nowhere, with the leader beginning to pull away. However, the uphill climb proved to be in his favour and he came with a storming run in the final furlong to snatch the spoils in the last fifty yards. (7/4)
2873 Tonight's Prize (IRE) again showed his liking for this trip. Coming with the winner from below the distance, he had every chance in the closing stages and only just lost out. (9/2: 5/2-5/1)
Kamin (USA), a well-built colt, showed little in two runs last year but is obviously going to be a different proposition this season if this run is anything to go by. Sent on early in the straight, he appeared to have the race won below the distance but, with the winner and second producing a tremendous finish, he was worried out of it in the last fifty yards. He should soon find a race. (100/30: op 5/1)
1625 Silver Whirl (USA), taking a drop in distance, had every chance before tapped for toe. (4/1)
1409 Massyar Seventeen began a forward move below the distance but could then make no further impression. (14/1: op 6/1)
1499 Swan Lane (USA) looked very well but she does not have much substance and is very definitely one of the stable's lesser lights. (6/1: op7/2)

T/Plpt: £89.80 (181.25 Tckts). T/Qdpt: £28.90 (35.24 Tckts) AK

3116-DONCASTER (L-H) (Good, Good to firm patches)
Thursday July 31st
WEATHER: overcast WIND: fresh against

3141 MSF ACCIDENT REPAIR CENTRES "SPIES HECKER" AMATEUR H'CAP (0-80) (3-Y.O+) (Class F)
2-30 (2-30) **2m 110y** £2,553.00 (£708.00: £339.00) Stalls: High GOING minus 0.13 sec per fur (G)

				SP	RR	SF
3010[10]	**Paradise Navy (64)** (CREgerton) **8-10-8b**(5) MissERamsden(4) (lw: trckd ldr: led ½-wy: pushed out cl home)	—	1	15/2	72	37

3046[3] **Arian Spirit (IRE) (37)** (JLEyre) **6-9-0** MissDianaJones(1) (lw: hld up: hdwy 4f out: chsd wnr fnl 2f: styd on strly towards fin) ....nk	**2**	11/8[1]	45	10
2064[2] **Klondike Charger (USA) (74)** (BWHills) **3-10-1**(5) MrCBHills(2) (set slow pce to ½-wy: chsd wnr: effrt ent st: one pce) 10	**3**	5/1[3]	72	20
2696[4] **Sun of Spring (57)** (DWChapman) **7-10-6** MissRClark(3) (lw: hld up: hdwy on ins 4f out: rdn & btn over 2f out) 5	**4**	11/2	50	15
3010[5] **Salska (65)** (AStreeter) **6-10-9**(5)ow5 MrPClinton(6) (lw: racd wd: prom: effrt 4f out: sn btn) 1	**5**	3/1[2]	57	17

(SP 110.9%) **5 Rn**

3m 46.25 (16.25) CSF £16.94 TOTE £6.80: £2.20 £1.60 (£4.30) OWNER Elite Racing Club (CHADDLEWORTH) BRED Stetchworth Park Stud Ltd

LONG HANDICAP Arian Spirit (IRE) 8-13

WEIGHT FOR AGE 3yo-17lb

2702 Paradise Navy, in a messy race, was given a really good ride and the line came just in time. (15/2)

3046 Arian Spirit (IRE) needed a much stronger gallop than was set here and looks in really good form. (11/8)

2064 Klondike Charger (USA), stepping up in trip, was a reluctant leader to halfway and then found it all too much when the pressure was on in the last three furlongs. (5/1)

2696 Sun of Spring should have got this trip the way the race was run, and this was a disappointing effort. (11/2)

3010 Salska had an inexperienced rider on board and this effort is best ignored. (3/1)

3142 VAUX SAMSON CONDITIONS STKS (2-Y.O) (Class C)

3-05 (3-06) **7f** £4,921.00 (£1,701.00: £815.50: £332.50) Stalls: High GOING minus 0.13 sec per fur (G)

		SP	RR	SF
2562* **Haami (USA)** (JLDunlop) **2-9-0** RHills(1) (lw: hld up: smooth hdwy to ld 1½f out: r.o: eased towards fin) ....—	**1**	8/15[1]	95+	56
2707* **Tracking** (HRACecil) **2-9-7** WRyan(2) (lw: trckd ldrs: outpcd over 2f out: hdwy u.p 1f out: r.o wl) ....nk	**2**	9/2[3]	101	62
2905[2] **Calchas (IRE)** (SirMarkPrescott) **2-9-3** SSanders(4) (cl up: led & qcknd over 2f out: hdd 1½f out: sn btn) 2	**3**	7/2[2]	93	54
2863[6] **Batswing** (MartynMeade) **2-9-0** FNorton(3) (led over 4f: sn rdn & btn) 6	**4**	25/1	76	37

(SP 109.5%) **4 Rn**

1m 27.09 (2.59) CSF £3.10 TOTE £1.50 (£1.70) OWNER Mr Hamdan Al Maktoum (ARUNDEL) BRED Shadwell Farm Inc

2562* Haami (USA), ridden with confidence, did it nicely and looks to be going the right way. Much better things look to be in the pipeline. (8/15)

2707* Tracking is certainly a hard ride but he does respond to pressure and, the further he goes, the better he should like it. (9/2)

2905 Calchas (IRE) is a real tough sort who has the scope for improvement. Although slightly outclassed here, this was not a bad effort. (7/2)

2863 Batswing found this company too hot and was put in his place in a few strides approaching the last quarter-mile. (25/1)

3143 FLETCHER MOTORS (LEEDS) PEUGEOT H'CAP (0-70) (3-Y.O+) (Class E)

3-35 (3-37) **7f** £3,703.30 (£1,110.40: £534.20: £246.10) Stalls: High GOING minus 0.13 sec per fur (G)

		SP	RR	SF
2785[3] **Welcome Heights (48)** (MJFetherston-Godley) **3-8-1** FNorton(7) (swtchd rt s: bhd: hdwy & nt clr run over 2f out: swtchd & qcknd to ld ins fnl f) ....—	**1**	8/1	61	33
2785[4] **Dummer Golf Time (58)** (LordHuntingdon) **4-9-4v** DHarrison(18) (in tch: hdwy 2f out: styd on u.p) 1½	**2**	4/1[1]	68	47
3064[2] **Oriole (36)** (DonEnricoIncisa) **4-7-10** KimTinkler(21) (cl up: led over 2f out tl ins fnl f: no ex) ....nk	**3**	6/1[2]	45	24
2708[14] **Bollin Dorothy (52)** (TDEasterby) **4-8-12** TWilliams(15) (hld up & bhd: hdwy 3f out: styd on u.p: no imp) 1¾	**4**	14/1	57	36
3034[11] **Bee Health Boy (66)** (MWEasterby) **4-9-9b**(3) GParkin(5) (lw: swtchd rt s: in tch: effrt 3f out: nt qckn appr fnl f) ....nk	**5**	16/1	70	49
2735[3] **Three For A Pound (68)** (JAGlover) **3-9-7** JFortune(8) (lw: effrt ½-wy: sn prom: nt qckn appr fnl f) ....¾	**6**	10/1	71	43
2937[5] **Raed (64)** (MrsASwinbank) **4-9-10** JSupple(11) (w ldrs: led ½-wy tl over 2f out: wknd) ....½	**7**	20/1	65	44
2788[8] **Napoleon Star (IRE) (47)** (SRBowring) **6-8-7b** DeanMcKeown(19) (lw: bhd tl styd on fnl f) ....nk	**8**	16/1	48	27
2552[9] **Welsh Mountain (38)** (MJHeaton-Ellis) **4-7-12** NVarley(20) (lw: in tch: rdn 3f out: no imp) ....nk	**9**	25/1	38	17
*2915** **Zain Dancer (47)** (DNicholls) **5-8-7** 6x FLynch(17) (dwlt: sn rcvrd: ch over 2f out: wknd over 1f out) 1¼	**10**	15/2	44	23
2567[12] **Lunch Party (45)** (DNicholls) **5-8-0**(5) IonaWands(12) (s.i.s: n.d) ....hd	**11**	25/1	42	21
2892[2] **The Barnsley Belle (IRE) (46)** (JLEyre) **4-7-13**(7) SBuckley(10) (lw: prom tl outpcd fnl 3f) 2	**12**	10/1	38	17
2918[2] **Fancy Design (IRE) (36)** (PMitchell) **4-7-5**(5) AimeeCook(1) (b.off hind: racd far side: hdwy over 2f out: rdn & btn over 1f out) ....½	**13**	7/1[3]	27	6
2674[4] **Marino Street (53)** (PDEvans) **4-8-6v**(7) AMcCarthy(3) (racd far side: chsd ldrs 5f) 2½	**14**	20/1	39	18
3075[11] **Theatre Magic (41)** (DShaw) **4-8-1**ow1 JFanning(13) (b: prom tl wknd fnl 2½f) ....¾	**15**	20/1	25	3
2735[6] **Lady Godiva (57)** (MJPolglase) **3-8-10** TGMcLaughlin(2) (led far side over 5f: wknd) ....½	**16**	20/1	40	12
2368[11] **Awesome Venture (48)** (MCChapman) **7-8-1**(7) SCarson(9) (b.off hind: racd centre: led to ½-wy: sn wknd) 3	**17**	33/1	24	3
2325[11] **Allinson's Mate (IRE) (68)** (TDBarron) **9-9-7b**(7) VictoriaAppleby(6) (racd centre: outpcd & bhd fr ½-wy) 1¼	**18**	14/1	41	20
2569[10] **Catwalk Girl (38)** (RAFahey) **4-7-5**(7)ow2 RWinston(14) (n.d) 1	**19**	33/1	9	—

(SP 145.6%) **19 Rn**

1m 28.07 (3.57) CSF £38.11 CT £210.26 TOTE £10.50: £2.00 £2.10 £1.70 £3.30 (£32.10) Trio £98.00 OWNER The Most Welcome Partnership (EAST ILSLEY) BRED R. E. A. Bott (Wigmore Street) Ltd

LONG HANDICAP Oriole 7-9 Fancy Design (IRE) 7-9 Catwalk Girl 7-8

WEIGHT FOR AGE 3yo-7lb

2785 Welcome Heights produced his customary late run to take this in some style and, using these tactics, he will always be hard to asses by the handicapper. (8/1)

2785 Dummer Golf Time had the visor back on here and kept responding to pressure but was never quite good enough. He deserves a change of luck. (4/1)

3064 Oriole had his chances but was worried out of it and is now due to go up 13lb for his good effort at the weekend. (6/1)

2422 Bollin Dorothy travels well and is slipping back down to a decent handicap mark. (14/1)

2422 Bee Health Boy keeps running reasonably but is never quite doing enough. (16/1)

2735 Three For A Pound ran a fair race and is better on easier ground. (10/1)

2788 Napoleon Star (IRE) has ability but needs luck in running as he is always putting his best work in at the end. (16/1)

2915* Zain Dancer (15/2: 5/1-8/1)

3144 MSF FLEET SERVICES CONDITIONS STKS (3-Y.O+) (Class C)

4-10 (4-11) **1m (round)** £4,775.96 (£1,765.64: £845.82: £344.10: £135.05: £51.43) Stalls: High GOING minus 0.13 sec per fur (G)

		SP	RR	SF
2009[7] **Beauchamp King (110)** (JLDunlop) **4-9-8** GCarter(1) (lw: hld up & bhd: nt clr run over 2f out: hdwy over 1f out: qcknd to ld post) ....—	**1**	4/1[2]	102	70

	Jamrat Jumairah (IRE) (EALDunlop) **4-8-9** RHills(5) (b: hld up: hdwy over 2f out: rdn to ld wl ins fnl f: jst ct) hd	**2**	13/2	89	57
1766[9]	**Kumait (USA) (92)** (DRLoder) **3-8-6** WRyan(7) (led: qcknd over 2f out: r.o: hdd & no ex towards fin) ....hd	**3**	12/1	94	54
2679[2]	**Weet-A-Minute (IRE) (105)** (RHollinshead) **4-9-0** FLynch(4) (a.p: outpcd over 2f out: hmpd over 1f out: swtchd & styd on) 1¼	**4**	9/2 [3]	91	59
	Sunbeam Dance (USA) (SbinSuroor) **3-8-6** JCarroll(3) (cl up: effrt over 2f out: rdn & no rspnse appr fnl f)...2½	**5**	5/2 [1]	86	46
2525[9]	**Warningford (93)** (JRFanshawe) **3-8-10** DHarrison(6) (in tch: hdwy 3f out: rdn & btn appr fnl f).....................hd	**6**	6/1	90	50
	Bin Cyclone (USA) (CEBrittain) **3-8-3** SSanders(2) (w'like: bit bkwd: chsd ldrs tl wknd fnl 2½f) 7	**7**	16/1	69	29

(SP 107.9%) **7 Rn**

1m 40.82 (2.42) CSF £23.86 TOTE £4.40: £2.50 £2.30 (£14.30) OWNER Mr E. Penser (ARUNDEL) BRED E. Penser
WEIGHT FOR AGE 3yo-8lb

830 Beauchamp King looked really well and bounced back to form here, coming from off the pace after finding trouble in running. He obviously needs things to go just right. (4/1)

Jamrat Jumairah (IRE), having her first outing for almost a year, put up a tremendous effort and it would appear that she has fully got over her problems. (13/2)

Kumait (USA), an edgy sort, was given a good ride and almost pinched this but may be slightly flattered by his proximity at the finish. (12/1)

2679 Weet-A-Minute (IRE) needed a stronger pace than was set here and then got messed about, but he did stay on. (9/2)

Sunbeam Dance (USA) had his chances but, when it came down to struggle, he proved very disappointing, and looks to keep something for himself. (5/2)

1976* Warningford, after a poor effort last time, ran better here only to find this company too hot. (6/1)

3145 WARD'S BEST BITTER H'CAP (0-85) (3-Y.O) (Class D)

4-45 (4-46) **6f** £3,655.00 (£1,090.00: £520.00: £235.00) Stalls: High GOING minus 0.13 sec per fur (G)

			SP	RR	SF
2841*	**Always On My Mind (80)** (PJMakin) **3-9-6** SSanders(7) (lw: chsd ldrs: sddle slipped after 1f: rdn to ld wl ins fnl f) ....—	**1**	7/2 [2]	94+	46
2841[3]	**Mary Magdalene (72)** (MBell) **3-8-7**(5) GFaulkner(6) (lw: cl up: led over 2f out: sn hrd rdn: hdd & nt qckn towards fin) ....nk	**2**	5/1 [3]	85	37
2711[11]	**Style Dancer (IRE) (72)** (RMWhitaker) **3-8-12v** DeanMcKeown(2) (led tl hdd over 2f out: one pce) 5	**3**	10/1	72	24
2734*	**Caution (75)** (SGollings) **3-9-1** WRyan(4) (hdwy ½-wy: sn chsng ldrs: nt qckn fnl f)..¾	**4**	12/1	73	25
2517[3]	**Compatibility (IRE) (81)** (JHMGosden) **3-9-7** GHind(5) (lw: chsd ldrs: outpcd ½-wy: no imp after) ....hd	**5**	5/1 [3]	79	31
3100[7]	**Last Chance (58)** (DJSCosgrove) **3-7-9v**(3) MBaird(1) (lw: sn pushed along: nvr trbld ldrs)..............................4	**6**	25/1	45	—
2925[2]	**March Crusader (78)** (BHanbury) **3-9-4** JStack(3) (b: unruly s: s.v.s: nt rcvr)..25	**7**	15/8 [1]	—	—

(SP 111.0%) **7 Rn**

1m 14.29 (3.29) CSF £18.08 TOTE £4.30: £1.90 £3.10 (£13.10) OWNER Mascalls Stud (MARLBOROUGH) BRED Mascalls Stud Farm

2841* Always On My Mind was being hampered by a slipping saddle soon after the start but, given a cracking ride, produced what was needed to settle it. (7/2)

2841 Mary Magdalene was closely handicapped with the winner on the Newbury run and made a real fight of it, but had to admit defeat late on. (5/1)

2547 Style Dancer (IRE) is running quite well and there could well be a modest race to be picked up. (10/1)

2734* Caution looked to have plenty on here but ran a useful race and is obviously still in good heart. (12/1)

2517 Compatibility (IRE) found things happening too quickly here and may well need further. (5/1)

2407 Last Chance could never go the pace. (25/1)

3146 FLETCHER MOTORS (LEEDS) CITROEN LIMITED STKS (0-70) (3-Y.O+) (Class E)

5-20 (5-20) **6f** £3,102.70 (£925.60: £441.80: £199.90) Stalls: High GOING minus 0.13 sec per fur (G)

			SP	RR	SF
3032*	**Fairy Prince (IRE) (68)** (MrsALMKing) **4-9-7** JFortune(3) (lw: w ldr: effrt 2f out: r.o gamely to ld wl ins fnl f)...—	**1**	7/2 [3]	78	53
3107*	**Royal Dome (IRE) (66)** (MartynWane) **5-9-7** 3x JCarroll(2) (mde most tl hdd wl ins fnl f: kpt on wl) ....½	**2**	3/1 [1]	77	52
2496[4]	**Archello (IRE) (65)** (GROldroyd) **3-8-4**(3) GParkin(7) (bhd: hdwy 2f out: styd on wl towards fin).....................1¾	**3**	11/2	63	33
2788[5]	**Denbrae (IRE) (66)** (DJGMurraySmith) **5-9-1** SSanders(6) (hdwy over 2f out: sn chsng ldrs: nt qckn fnl f) ......nk	**4**	100/30 [2]	65	40
2868[10]	**Awassi (IRE) (69)** (KMahdi) **4-9-1** RPrice(4) (chsd ldrs: effrt 2f out: hung lft & sn btn) ....¾	**5**	5/1	63	38
2788[3]	**Double Matt (IRE) (59)** (MrsPSly) **5-9-1** NCarlisle(1) (lw: s.i.s: sn chsng ldrs: wknd fnl 2f)...7	**6**	9/1	45	20
2915[13]	**Miss Aragon (31)** (MissLCSiddall) **9-8-5**(7) TSiddall(5) (lw: a outpcd & bhd) 3	**7**	33/1	34?	9

(SP 115.3%) **7 Rn**

1m 13.88 (2.88) CSF £13.38 TOTE £3.50: £2.10 £2.10 (£4.00) OWNER Mr Aiden Murphy (STRATFORD-UPON-AVON) BRED Jim O'Hara and Christian Healy
WEIGHT FOR AGE 3yo-5lb

3032* Fairy Prince (IRE) is certainly tough and had the right man on board to do the business. (7/2)

3107* Royal Dome (IRE) has yet to win at this trip but he certainly got it well enough. (3/1)

2496 Archello (IRE) without the visor this time, ran much better and got the trip really well, putting in all her best work at the finish. (11/2)

2788 Denbrae (IRE) looked to have a serious chance in these conditions but proved a shade disappointing. (100/30)

2704 Awassi (IRE) has been tried over longer trips recently and was disappointing here once off the bridle. (5/1)

2788 Double Matt (IRE) looked well enough but ran miserably. (9/1)

T/Plpt: £85.50 (207.64 Tckts). T/Qdpt: £21.70 (55.33 Tckts) AA

3122-GOODWOOD (R-H) (Good to firm)

Thursday July 31st

Race 7 - hand timed
WEATHER: damp WIND: almost nil

3147 OAK TREE STKS (Listed) (3-Y.O+ F & M) (Class A)

2-15 (2-15) **7f** £22,710.00 (£6,780.00: £3,240.00: £1,470.00) Stalls: High GOING minus 0.12 sec per fur (G)

			SP	RR	SF
1533a[9]	**Dazzle (112)** (MRStoute) **3-8-7** JReid(7) (hld up: nt clr run over 1f out: swtchd lft ins fnl f: qcknd to ld nr fin)..—	**1**	11/4 [2]	108	48
1836[2]	**Unconditional Love (IRE) (92)** (MJohnston) **4-9-0** JWeaver(4) (dropped rr over 2f out: rallied fnl f: r.o wl)......½	**2**	33/1	107	54
1326[3]	**Miss Riviera (95)** (GWragg) **4-9-0** MHills(3) (lw: hdwy over 2f out: led 1f out: rdn: hdd nr fin) ....nk	**3**	20/1	106	53

2774*	**Imroz (USA) (106)** (HRACecil) **3-8-7** KFallon(2) (swtg: plld hrd: hdwy 4f out: led over 1f out: sn hdd: one pce)	¾	**4**	15/2	105	45
2830[3]	**My Branch (101)** (BWHills) **4-9-0** PatEddery(8) (lw: hld up: rdn over 2f out: nt clr run over 1f out: r.o one pce)	¾	**5**	10/1	103	50
1533a[5]	**Oh Nellie (USA) (114)** (NACallaghan) **3-8-7** OPeslier(1) (led over 5f: wknd fnl f)	3½	**6**	9/4[1]	95	35
2561*	**Noisette (100)** (JHMGosden) **3-8-7** LDettori(6) (rdn & hdwy on ins over 1f out: nt clr run on ins, ins fnl f: nt rcvr)	¾	**7**	3/1[3]	93	33
2773*	**Blueygreen (85)** (PWChapple-Hyam) **3-8-7** DaneO'Neill(5) (lw: chsd ldr over 4f: wkng whn n.m.r over 1f out)	¾	**8**	50/1	56 t	31
				(SP 113.0%)	**8 Rn**	

1m 27.63 (2.83) CSF £78.38 TOTE £3.80: £1.60 £3.10 £3.20 (£45.80) OWNER Cheveley Park Stud (NEWMARKET) BRED Cheveley Park Stud Ltd
WEIGHT FOR AGE 3yo-7lb

1533a Dazzle was ideally suited by the drop down to seven furlongs and certainly lived up to her name. Manoeuvered to get daylight early inside the final furlong, Reid needed to do very little on the filly for her to show a useful turn of foot to surge into the lead in the closing stages. The Haydock Park Sprint Cup over six furlongs is now seriously being considered. (11/4)
1836 Unconditional Love (IRE) is not the easiest of individuals but she ran an absolute cracker and, after dropping back to last place over a quarter of a mile from home, sprouted wings in the final furlong, if just unable to get there. She will be confined to pattern races from now on, with the target of making her into an attractive broodmare, the main priority (33/1)
1326 Miss Riviera, currently in foal to Salse, is not easy to win with and has just one maiden victory to her name. However this looked like being her day as she gained control a furlong out, only to be passed by the winner near the line. She often runs well in these type of events without getting her head in front and she is very frustrating. (20/1)
2774* Imroz (USA) had far more on her plate here. Nevertheless she showed in front below the distance but, soon headed, then failed to find another gear. (15/2)
2830 My Branch, reportedly in foal to Polar Falcon, was locked in with nowhere to go below the distance. When a gap did appear she just stayed on at the one pace. (10/1)
1533a Oh Nellie (USA), very free going to post, was most disappointing, and after cutting out the running, had little more to offer when collared approaching the final furlong. (9/4: 6/4-5/2)
2561* Noisette had absolutely no luck in running and, with nowhere to go inside the final furlong, the situation had to be accepted. (3/1)

3148 SALOMON BROTHERS RICHMOND STKS (Gp 2) (2-Y.O C & G) (Class A)
2-45 (2-45) **6f** £24,466.00 (£9,094.00: £4,397.00: £1,835.00: £767.50: £340.50) Stalls: Low GOING minus 0.12 sec per fur (G)

				SP	RR	SF
2588*	**Daggers Drawn (USA)** (HRACecil) **2-8-11** KFallon(5) (lw: hld up: rdn over 1f out: qcknd to ld ins fnl f: comf)	—	**1**	8/13[1]	114+	44
2862*	**Lord Kintyre** (BRMillman) **2-8-11** BDoyle(4) (hld up: led over 1f out tl ins fnl f: unable qckn)	1½	**2**	10/1	110	40
2484*	**Bodyguard** (PFICole) **2-8-11** LDettori(3) (led over 4f: wkng whn hung rt 1f out)	3½	**3**	9/2[2]	101	31
2584[2]	**Linden Heights** (LMCumani) **2-8-11** PatEddery(2) (lw: a.p: ev ch over 1f out: sn wknd)	1¼	**4**	7/1[3]	97	27
2863[3]	**Bold Edge** (RHannon) **2-8-11** DaneO'Neill(7) (lw: hld up: rdn over 2f out: wknd wl over 1f out)	1½	**5**	33/1	93	23
2639a[2]	**Cortachy Castle (IRE)** (BJMeehan) **2-8-11** MTebbutt(6) (lw: a.p: ev ch 2f out: wknd over 1f out)	4	**6**	15/2	83	13
				(SP 116.4%)	**6 Rn**	

1m 12.62 (2.82) CSF £7.89 TOTE £1.80: £1.40 £3.00 (£7.40) OWNER Cliveden Stud (NEWMARKET) BRED Cliveden Stud

2588* Daggers Drawn (USA) looked in great heart beforehand and put up an extremely impressive performance. Behind a wall of horses over a quarter of a mile from home, luckily a gap presented itself to him below the distance and he sprinted through to lead inside the final furlong and win readily. He looks a high-class individual and is already clear favourite for next year's 2,000 Guineas. It will take something special to lower his colours this season. (8/13)
2862* Lord Kintyre ran another cracking race and made his bid for glory below the distance, but he was unable to cope with the winner inside the final furlong, although still finishing well clear of the remainder. There are more races to be won with him. (10/1)
2484* Bodyguard, who has shown himself to be a very useful two-year-old, was put in his place here when collared over a furlong out. (9/2)
2584 Linden Heights looked really well beforehand but, after having every chance over a furlong out, soon had bellows to mend. (7/1)
2863 Bold Edge was not up to this hot company and had been seen off early in the final quarter-mile. (33/1)
2639a Cortachy Castle (IRE) found the fast ground not to his liking and, after racing alongside the leader, had been burnt off below the distance. (15/2)

3149 CROWSON GOODWOOD CUP STKS (Gp 2) (3-Y.O+) (Class A)
3-20 (3-21) **2m** £38,724.00 (£14,316.00: £6,858.00: £2,790.00: £1,095.00: £417.00) Stalls: High GOING minus 0.12 sec per fur (G)

				SP	RR	SF
2055[8]	**Double Trigger (IRE) (115)** (MJohnston) **6-9-0** MRoberts(1) (lw: mde all: hung lft 1f out: rdn out)	—	**1**	16/1	126	85
2055[2]	**Classic Cliche (IRE) (120)** (SbinSuroor) **5-9-5** LDettori(6) (lw: gd hdwy over 3f out: chsd wnr over 1f out: ev ch 1f out: unable qckn)	1½	**2**	5/4[1]	130	89
2055[6]	**Double Eclipse (IRE) (113)** (MJohnston) **5-9-0** JWeaver(3) (lw: hdwy 3f out: chsd wnr over 2f out tl over 1f out: ev ch 1f out: one pce)	½	**3**	12/1	124	83
2055[3]	**Election Day (IRE) (119)** (MRStoute) **5-9-0v** OPeslier(2) (lw: 3rd whn slipped 9f out: rdn 5f out: lost pl 3f out: r.o one pce fnl 2f)	2½	**4**	7/1[3]	122	81
2055[12]	**Persian Punch (IRE) (113)** (DRCElsworth) **4-9-0** RCochrane(10) (hld up: rdn over 4f out: wknd 2f out)	4	**5**	7/1[3]	118	77
2055[5]	**Samraan (USA) (114)** (JLDunlop) **4-9-0** PatEddery(9) (lw: nvr nr to chal)	hd	**6**	13/2[2]	117	76
2108*	**Canon Can (USA) (102)** (HRACecil) **4-9-0** AMcGlone(8) (lw: a.p: chsd wnr 6f out tl over 2f out: sn wknd)	2½	**7**	25/1	115	74
2055[13]	**Grey Shot (110)** (IABalding) **5-9-3** JReid(4) (chsd wnr 10f: wknd over 2f out)	2½	**8**	20/1	115	74
2596[4]	**State Fair (104)** (BWHills) **3-7-13** TSprake(7) (lw: a bhd)	5	**9**	50/1	109	51
2837*	**Corradini (110)** (HRACecil) **5-9-0** KFallon(5) (lw: a bhd: t.o)	dist	**10**	12/1	—	—
				(SP 114.6%)	**10 Rn**	

3m 24.81 (0.81) CSF £32.04 TOTE £15.90: £2.70 £1.40 £2.70 (£13.00) Trio £19.80 OWNER Mr R. W. Huggins (MIDDLEHAM) BRED Dene Investments N V
WEIGHT FOR AGE 3yo-17lb

OFFICIAL EXPLANATION **Double Trigger (IRE): regarding the improvement in form, the trainer's representative reported that the horse prefers firmer ground than that at Ascot, and that the blinkers he wore there may have contributed to his disappointing run.**
IN-FOCUS: **This race was certainly something to savour and rekindled memories of the 1995 epic between the brothers Double Trigger and Double Eclipse and maybe all those people who believed that these long-distance races do not have an important part to play, should look at the emotional scenes that followed and realise that this is the true spirit of racing.**
891 Double Trigger (IRE) bounced back to his best under a marvellous ride from Roberts and quashed all those doubters who believed he had gone. Making every post a winning one, he looked in serious trouble as the second and third loomed up below the distance, but he dug deep into his reserves and was not going to be denied. The king is certainly back to reclaim his crown and the Doncaster Cup is next on the agenda. (16/1)

2055 Classic Cliche (IRE) was certainly given a lot to do and had a tremendous amount of ground to make up on the winner at the top of the hill. Nevertheless, he cut through the opposition and came through to throw down his challenge below the distance. It looked as if he would master Double Trigger, but he failed to find another turn of foot in the final furlong. Whilst this was a good performance, he has not returned to the same level of form he showed last year. (5/4)
2055 Double Eclipse (IRE) has been plagued with tendon injury which has made training him at home extremely difficult. He made a pleasing reappearance in the Ascot Gold Cup but ran out of his skin here. Coming through to chase his brother over a quarter of a mile from home, he looked a serious threat and had every chance a furlong from home before tapped for toe. If he remains sound, he richly deserves to land a decent staying prize. (12/1: op 8/1)
2055 Election Day (IRE), who likes some cut, got outpaced early in the straight but did stay on again in the final quarter-mile. (7/1)
2055 Persian Punch (IRE) was again disappointing and, rousted along running down the hill, had cooked his goose two furlongs from home. (7/1)
2055 Samraan (USA) never threatened to get into it. (13/2)
2837* Corradini (12/1: op 8/1)

3150 SCHWEPPES GOLDEN MILE H'CAP (3-Y.O+) (Class B)

3-50 (4-10) **1m** £48,250.00 (£14,500.00: £7,000.00: £3,250.00) Stalls: High GOING minus 0.12 sec per fur (G)

				SP	RR	SF
2766[16]	**Fly To The Stars (106)** (MJohnston) **3-9-6** OPeslier(19) (lw: bolted after false s: a.p: rdn over 2f out: led ins fnl f: r.o wl)	—	**1**	14/1	118	71
2598[10]	**Crumpton Hill (IRE) (92)** (NAGraham) **5-9-0** MRoberts(16) (hdwy on ins over 2f out: nt clr run on ins over 1f out: swtchd lft: r.o ins fnl f)	1¼	**2**	12/1	102	63
3064[4]	**Pride of Pendle (74)** (MartynWane) **8-7-5**(5) RMullen(4) (rdn over 2f out: hdwy over 1f out: r.o wl ins fnl f)	nk	**3**	40/1	83	44
2866[2]	**Strazo (IRE) (87)** (LadyHerries) **4-8-9** RCochrane(22) (hld up: rdn over 2f out: r.o ins fnl f)	nk	**4**	8/1 2	95	56
2866[6]	**King of Tunes (FR) (83)** (JJSheehan) **5-8-2**(3) RFfrench(6) (lw: hdwy over 1f out: r.o wl ins fnl f)	s.h	**5**	25/1	91	52
2666*	**Brilliant Red (90)** (PRHedger) **4-8-12** AMcGlone(11) (lw: led: hrd rdn over 1f out: hdd ins fnl f: unable qckn)	½	**6**	16/1	97	58
2666[2]	**Mawingo (IRE) (81)** (GWragg) **4-8-3b1** MHills(17) (lw: bolted after false s: hdwy over 2f out: hrd rdn & hung rt over 1f out: ev ch 1f out: one pce)	nk	**7**	5/1 1	88	49
3052[2]	**Tertium (IRE) (80)** (MartynWane) **5-7-13**(3) AWhelan(12) (nt clr run over 2f out, over 1f out & 1f out: hdwy fnl f)	½	**8**	20/1	86	47
2866[12]	**Philistar (76)** (KRBurke) **4-7-12** JQuinn(7) (nt clr run over 2f out: hdwy over 1f out: r.o ins fnl f)	nk	**9**	40/1	81	42
2708[5]	**Irish Accord (USA) (90)** (MrsJRRamsden) **3-8-4** AMunro(21) (lw: hld up: rdn over 2f out: one pce)	½	**10**	10/1 3	94	47
2871[4]	**Nomore Mr Niceguy (91)** (EJAlston) **3-8-5** JFEgan(15) (bolted in false s: prom 6f)	1¾	**11**	20/1	92	45
2690[3]	**Star Talent (USA) (88)** (IABalding) **6-8-10** LDettori(18) (lw: bolted after false s: a mid div)	6	**12**	8/1 2	77	38
2894*	**Divina Luna (83)** (JWHills) **4-8-2**(3) MHenry(3) (lw: nvr nrr)	hd	**13**	16/1	71	32
3052[9]	**Lonely Leader (IRE) (102)** (RHannon) **4-9-10** RHughes(10) (lw: prom over 6f)	½	**14**	20/1	89	50
2137[8]	**Strathmore Clear (88)** (GLewis) **3-8-2b1** PaulEddery(2) (lw: chsd ldr 5f)	¾	**15**	25/1	74	27
3052[3]	**Alhawa (USA) (77)** (RAkehurst) **4-7-13** LCharnock(13) (lw: s.s: hdwy & n.m.r over 2f out: wkng whn nt clr run 2f out)	½	**16**	14/1	62	23
2871[3]	**Generous Libra (94)** (DRLoder) **3-8-8** PatEddery(9) (plld hrd: hld up: rdn over 2f out: wkng whn hmpd 2f out)	3½	**17**	12/1	72	25
2117[2]	**Artful Dane (IRE) (79)** (MJHeaton-Ellis) **5-8-1v** SDrowne(8) (hld up: rdn over 2f out: sn wknd)	1¼	**18**	33/1	54	15
2871[7]	**Hayes Way (IRE) (96)** (TGMills) **3-8-10** AClark(5) (lw: bhd fnl 3f)	7	**19**	33/1	57	10
2761[5]	**Peartree House (IRE) (100)** (WRMuir) **3-9-0** KFallon(1) (lw: bhd fnl 2f)	2½	**20**	20/1	56	9
2598[16]	***Emerging Market (98)*** (JLDunlop) **5-9-6** KDarley(20) (Withdrawn not under Starter's orders: bolted after false s)		**W**	25/1	—	—
2766[9]	***Cosmic Prince (IRE) (93)*** (MAJarvis) **3-8-7** GDuffield(14) (Withdrawn not under Starter's orders: bolted after false s)		**W**	14/1	—	—
				(SP 136.5%)	**20 Rn**	

1m 39.44 (2.24) CSF £130.44 CT £5,184.96 TOTE £16.10: £3.50 £4.50 £5.80 £2.60 (£104.50) Trio £1,618.00 OWNER Mr P. D. Savill (MIDDLEHAM) BRED Bishop's Down Farm
LONG HANDICAP Pride of Pendle 7-7
WEIGHT FOR AGE 3yo-8lb
IN-FOCUS: **This race was delayed by twenty minutes after six horses bolted following a false start, which had seen some of the stalls open inadvertently before all the horses had been properly loaded.**
2013* Fly To The Stars, who galloped a couple of furlongs in the false start, showed no ill-effects in the race and left his Sandown disappointment well behind. Never far away, he was rousted along in the straight and, gaining the upper-hand inside the final furlong, kept on really well. (14/1)
2026 Crumpton Hill (IRE) ran a blinder. Picking up ground along the inside rail, he did not have the best of runs below the distance and had to be switched left. It did not affect the result but he ran on inside the final furlong for second place. (12/1)
3064 Pride of Pendle, racing at the back of the field, made giant strides below the distance, but despite finishing really well, was never going to get there in time. (40/1)
2866 Strazo (IRE), set to rise 5lb in future handicaps, chased the leaders. Off the bridle over a quarter of a mile from home, he kept on well but was never going to get in a serious blow. (8/1)
2866 King of Tunes (FR), at the back of the field for much of the way, put in some really good work in the last furlong and a half, and only just failed to get into the prize money. (25/1)
2666* Brilliant Red attempted to make every post a winning one but he was eventually overhauled inside the final furlong. (16/1)
2666 Mawingo (IRE), fitted with blinkers for the first time, had a nice exercise gallop beforehand. Picking up ground in the straight, he had every chance entering the final furlong, before quicker rivals had his measure. (5/1)
3052 Tertium (IRE) had absolutely no luck in running and was stopped at least three times in the straight as he tried to pick up ground. He eventually got daylight in the final furlong, but although keeping on really well, the damage had already been done. (20/1)
2690 Star Talent (USA) (8/1: op 12/1)

3151 E.B.F. NEW HAM MAIDEN STKS (2-Y.O F) (Class D)

4-25 (4-42) **7f** £7,165.00 (£2,170.00: £1,060.00: £505.00) Stalls: High GOING minus 0.12 sec per fur (G)

				SP	RR	SF
2597[5]	**Midnight Line (USA)** (HRACecil) **2-8-11** KFallon(9) (chsd ldr: rdn over 3f out: led wl over 1f out tl ins fnl f: led wl ins fnl f: r.o wl)	—	**1**	15/8 1	83+	36
	Doomna (IRE) (EALDunlop) **2-8-11** OPeslier(4) (neat: s.i.s: rdn over 2f out: hdwy over 1f out: led ins fnl f: sn hdd: unable qckn)	½	**2**	6/1 3	82+	35
2875[3]	**Alborada** (SirMarkPrescott) **2-8-11** GDuffield(1) (hld up: rdn over 2f out: r.o one pce fnl f)	1½	**3**	11/4 2	78	31
	Hadayik (PTWalwyn) **2-8-11** RCochrane(2) (w'like: rdn 2f out: hdwy over 1f out: r.o one pce)	nk	**4**	20/1	78	31

				SP	RR	SF
	Vignette (USA) (JHMGosden) **2-8-11** LDettori(3) (leggy: unf: hld up: ev ch over 1f out: wknd fnl f)	2½	**5**	13/2	72	25
2840^{6}	**Moonstone (IRE)** (APJarvis) **2-8-11** KDarley(8) (a.p: rdn over 2f out: wknd fnl f)	2	**6**	33/1	68	21
	Oberon's Mistral (HRACecil) **2-8-11** AMcGlone(6) (small: lenghty: s.s: nvr nr to chal)	½	**7**	25/1	66	19
2227^{7}	**Captivating (IRE)** (RHannon) **2-8-11** DaneO'Neill(5) (prom over 5f)	2½	**8**	33/1	61	14
2870^{7}	**Queen Salote** (DRLoder) **2-8-11** PatEddery(10) (led over 5f)	½	**9**	14/1	60	13
	La Lyonesse (JWHills) **2-8-11** MHills(11) (leggy: bhd fnl 4f)	9	**10**	33/1	39	—
	Anakela Bay (IRE) (BWHills) **2-8-11b^{1}** DHolland(12) (leggy: unf: s.s: a bhd)	17	**11**	33/1	—	—
				(SP 116.1%)	**11 Rn**	

1m 28.99 (4.19) CSF £10.93 TOTE £3.10: £1.30 £2.20 £1.50 (£11.60) Trio £13.00 OWNER H R H Prince Fahd Salman (NEWMARKET) BRED Newgate Stud Farm Inc

2597 Midnight Line (USA) put up a good performance for she was one of the first off the bridle. In front early in the final quarter-mile, she was narrowly passed by the runner-up inside the final furlong but battled her way back to the front and will surely do even better over further. (15/8)

Doomna (IRE), a full sister to Kahal, ran a race full of promise on this debut. Picking up ground nicely below the distance, she poked a whisker in front inside the final furlong but, soon collared by the winner, then failed to cope with that rival. Her trainer reported afterwards that Peslier had said to him that he had ridden a bad race, but that certainly did not look the case from the stands. She looks a ready-made winner. (6/1: 3/1-13/2)

2875 Alborada, bustled along over a quarter of a mile from home, stayed on without ever looking likely to find that vital turn of foot. She is worth a try at a mile. (11/4: 7/4-3/1)

Hadayik, a medium-sized filly, stayed on in the last furlong and a half and only just failed in her bid for third prize. Another furlong would surely be in her favour. (20/1)

Vignette (USA), a tall filly who needs time to develop, was travelling best of all in the straight and had every chance below the distance before lack of a recent run took its toll. She should come on for this and will not be difficult to place. (13/2)

2840 Moonstone (IRE) played an active role until coming to the end of her tether in the final furlong. (33/1)

Queen Salote (14/1: 8/1-16/1)

3152 EQUITY FINANCIAL COLLECTIONS NURSERY H'CAP (2-Y.O) (Class C)

5-00 (5-06) **5f** £7,440.00 (£2,220.00: £1,060.00: £480.00) Stalls: Low GOING minus 0.12 sec per fur (G)

				SP	RR	SF
2942*	**Mislead (IRE)** (JSMoore) **2-8-1**(3) 6x MHenry(4) (lw: a.p: led over 1f out: rdn out)	—	**1**	12/1	76	14
2851*	**Desert Lady (IRE)** (RCharlton) **2-9-4** TSprake(3) (stdy hdwy 2f out: rdn over 1f out: ev ch ins fnl f: r.o)	½	**2**	3/1 1	88	26
2862^{11}	**Salamanca** (JBerry) **2-8-11**(3) PFessey(7) (lw: led: edgd lft over 2f out: hdd over 1f out: unable qckn ins fnl f)	1¼	**3**	12/1	80	18
2473*	**Prix Star** (CWFairhurst) **2-9-2v** LCharnock(6) (lw: lost pl 3f out: rallied 2f out: one pce)	2	**4**	16/1	76	14
2728^{4}	**Sada** (MajorWRHern) **2-8-9** MHills(5) (hdwy over 1f out: one pce)	½	**5**	9/1	67	5
2942^{4}	**Mishraak (IRE)** (RWArmstrong) **2-9-7b^{1}** LDettori(8) (swtg: a.p: hung lft 3f out: rdn over 2f out: wknd over 1f out)	½	**6**	9/2 3	78	16
2942^{2}	**Who Nose (IRE)** (BJMeehan) **2-8-4b** MRoberts(1) (lw: nvr nr to chal)	nk	**7**	7/1	60	—
2553*	**Centre Court** (RHannon) **2-9-3** DaneO'Neill(2) (no hdwy fnl 2f)	1½	**8**	4/1 2	68	6
1635^{4}	**Eastern Lyric** (JBerry) **2-8-13** KDarley(11) (a.p: rdn over 2f out: wknd fnl f)	1¼	**9**	12/1	60	—
2942^{5}	**Really Done It Now (IRE)** (KRBurke) **2-8-4b^{1}** PaulEddery(10) (lw: hdwy over 2f out: wknd over 1f out)	2½	**10**	20/1	43	—
2931^{2}	**Fast Tempo (IRE)** (BPalling) **2-9-0** JReid(9) (spd over 2f)	6	**11**	20/1	34	—
				(SP 124.2%)	**11 Rn**	

60.41 secs (3.71) CSF £46.15 CT £417.19 TOTE £18.00: £3.70 £1.80 £2.80 (£45.70) Trio £186.30 OWNER Mr P. Henley (HUNGERFORD) BRED Peter Henley Jnr

2942* Mislead (IRE), rousted along to lead below the distance, proved just too good for the second and third inside the final furlong. (12/1)

2851* Desert Lady (IRE) to run well and cruised into the action a quarter of a mile from home. One of three battling for the advantage inside the final furlong, she did little wrong if unable to master the winner. Her trainer is now considering stepping her up to Listed company. (3/1)

1013 Salamanca attempted to make all the running, but she was collared below the distance and just failed to find another turn of foot in the last one hundred yards. (12/1)

2473* Prix Star, who looked to be on a stiff mark for this handicap debut, got outpaced before halfway but he got back into it in the final quarter-mile if then tapped for toe. (16/1)

2728 Sada began a forward move below the distance but could then make no further impression. (9/1)

2942 Mishraak (IRE) was close up until tiring below the distance. (9/2: 6/1-4/1)

3153 DRAWING ROOM H'CAP (0-80) (3-Y.O+) (Class D)

5-35 (5-36) **1m 1f** £8,740.00 (£2,620.00: £1,260.00: £580.00) Stalls: High GOING minus 0.12 sec per fur (G)

				SP	RR	SF
2866^{3}	**Tribal Peace (IRE) (60)** (BGubby) **5-8-5**(3) RFfrench(14) (lw: hld up: hung rt & led over 1f out: hrd rdn: r.o wl)	—	**1**	10/1	70	49
2828^{6}	**Bowcliffe (60)** (EJAlston) **6-8-8** JFEgan(12) (gd hdwy over 1f out: r.o wl ins fnl f)	¾	**2**	12/1	69	48
3029^{3}	**Chairmans Choice (55)** (APJarvis) **7-8-3** SDrowne(1) (hdwy over 2f out: ev ch over 1f out: unable qckn)	nk	**3**	20/1	63	42
2478^{9}	**Plan For Profit (IRE) (80)** (MJohnston) **3-9-5** JWeaver(15) (lw: gd hdwy over 1f out: r.o wl ins fnl f)	nk	**4**	14/1	88	58
1745*	**Sharp Shuffle (IRE) (80)** (RHannon) **4-10-0** RHughes(7) (s.s: nt clr run on ins over 2f out: hdwy on ins over 1f out: one pce ins fnl f)	nk	**5**	11/1	87	66
1739^{5}	**Mantles Prince (79)** (GLewis) **3-9-4b** PaulEddery(18) (led over 7f: one pce)	½	**6**	12/1	85	55
1300^{7}	**Smarter Charter (70)** (MrsLStubbs) **4-9-4** KFallon(2) (lw: hdwy over 1f out: nvr nrr)	1¾	**7**	20/1	73	52
3115^{2}	**Clouds Hill (FR) (52)** (RHannon) **4-8-0** JQuinn(13) (n.m.r & lost pl over 2f out: n.m.r over 1f out: one pce)	hd	**8**	13/2 3	55	34
3039^{2}	**Eurobox Boy (65)** (APJarvis) **4-8-6**(7) CCarver(3) (hdwy & n.m.r on ins over 1f out: n.m.r on ins, ins fnl f: nvr nrr)	½	**9**	11/1	67	46
2340^{6}	**Noble Dane (IRE) (71)** (PWHarris) **3-8-5**(5) CLowther(10) (hmpd over 1f out: nvr nrr)	1¼	**10**	33/1	71	41
2150*	**Harvey White (IRE) (56)** (JPearce) **5-8-4** CRutter(4) (lw: a mid div)	1	**11**	12/1	54	33
2118^{5}	**Kedwick (IRE) (60)** (PRHedger) **8-8-8b** AMcGlone(11) (b: nvr nrr)	1½	**12**	11/1	55	34
2672^{7}	**Tallulah Belle (61)** (NPLittmoden) **4-8-9** BDoyle(5) (lw: hld up: rdn 3f out: wkng whn hmpd over 2f out)	nk	**13**	25/1	56	35
2782^{4}	**Whispering Dawn (62)** (CPEBrooks) **4-8-10** RCochrane(8) (b.hind: prom tl wknd & hmpd over 1f out)	½	**14**	25/1	56	35
2929*	**Blue Imperial (FR) (71)** (JWHills) **3-8-7**(3) 6x MHenry(17) (chsd ldr over 7f)	nk	**15**	6/1 2	64	34
2660^{4}	**Best of All (IRE) (74)** (JBerry) **5-9-8b** KDarley(6) (lw: prom over 7f)	nk	**16**	14/1	67	46
2576^{2}	**Renata's Prince (IRE) (60)** (KRBurke) **4-8-8** LDettori(16) (lw: a.p: rdn over 2f out: eased whn btn fnl f)	¾	**17**	5/1 1	52	31
3115^{19}	**Desert Time (68)** (CAHorgan) **7-9-2** DHolland(9) (hmpd over 1f out: a bhd)	14	**18**	20/1	35	14
				(SP 139.7%)	**18 Rn**	

1m 56.8 (3.80) CSF £116.95 CT £2,267.57 TOTE £14.70: £2.70 £5.20 £6.10 £4.00 (£138.50) Trio £1,384.00 OWNER Brian Gubby Ltd (BAGSHOT) BRED Mrs P. H. Burns in Ireland

WEIGHT FOR AGE 3yo-9lb
2866 Tribal Peace (IRE), drifting to his right as he led below the distance, responded to pressure and kept on really well. (10/1)
2828 Bowcliffe, 9lb higher than when successful at Carlisle earlier in the month, made up a tremendous amount of ground in the last furlong and a half and found the line always beating him. (12/1)
3029 Chairmans Choice came to have every chance below the distance but then failed to find another gear. (20/1)
2290 Plan For Profit (IRE) had no problems with this slightly longer trip. Put to sleep at the back of the field, he made up a tremendous amount of ground from below the distance but failed to get there in time. (14/1)
1745* Sharp Shuffle (IRE) has never won beyond a mile and, after moving up along the inside rail below the distance, failed to find another gear inside the final furlong. (11/1)
1739 Mantles Prince attempted to make all the running, but collared below the distance, could only go up and down in the same place. (12/1)

T/Jkpt: Not won; £33,640.28 to Goodwood 1/8/97. T/Plpt: £90.10 (851.35 Tckts). T/Qdpt: £14.80 (320.97 Tckts) AK

3154a - 3171a (Irish Racing) - See Computer Raceform

2810a-CURRAGH (Newbridge, Ireland) (R-H) (St Good to Firm, rnd Good)
Saturday July 26th

3172a MELD STKS (Gp 3) (3-Y.O+)
4-05 (4-05) **1m 2f** IR £19,500.00 (IR £5,700.00: IR £2,700.00: IR £900.00)

				SP	RR	SF
2814a8	**Caiseal Ros (IRE)** (JSBolger,Ireland) **3-8-5**ow1 PJSmullen (sn led: mde all: rdn & styd on whn chal last 2f)	—	1	10/1	106	—
2454a7	**Casey Tibbs (IRE)** (DKWeld,Ireland) **3-8-7** PShanahan (hld up towards rr: clsd in early st: swtchd 1½f out: r.o u.p ins last: nrst fin: fin 3rd: pl 2nd)	nk	2	11/4 2	104	—
2814a4	**Strawberry Roan (IRE)** (APO'Brien,Ireland) **3-8-4** JAHeffernan (hld up in tch: 3rd½-wy: chsd ldrs on ins early st: edgd lft u.p early ins last: kpt on: nt rch wnr: fin 2nd: disq:)	2½	3	5/2 1	105	—
14123	**Green Card (USA)** (SPCWoods) **3-8-7** AMunro (sn chsng ldr: effrt early st: 3rd u.p & no ex ins last: kpt on same pce)	½	4	5/1	103	—
22172	**Amid Albadu (USA)** (JLDunlop) **3-8-7** WJSupple (hld up: 4th & rdn 4f out: effrt u.p early st: btn wl over 1f out)	3½	5	100/30 3	97	—
				(SP 104.1%)		**5 Rn**

2m 6.2 (2.20) OWNER Dermot McAuliffe (COOLCULLEN)
2814a Caiseal Ros (IRE) was able to dominate here and nothing appeared anxious to take her on. She just set her own pace and from early in the straight, it was obvious that the others had made a collective tactical error. She battled on with some determination, but there won't be many Group Three contests that come as easy as this one. (10/1)
2454a Casey Tibbs (IRE) settled at the back door, was still last on the inside with a furlong to run. He switched out and appeared to hang left into the bargain and was slightly hampered by Strawberry Roan's errant ways. His trainer has pencilled in the Secretariat Stakes in Arlington on August 24th, but that would be a couple of steps up the ladder from this. (11/4)
2814a Strawberry Roan (IRE), weak in appearance, hung left when trying to challenge inside the last and disqualified for some minor damage to Casey Tibbs. She looked a bit unfortunate to lose second place and is not the filly that she was thought to be earlier in the year. (5/2: op 5/4)
1412 Green Card (USA) ran in second but looked quite one-paced inside the last furlong. (5/1)
2217 Amid Albadu (USA) was carried left by Casey Tibbs inside the last but was well beaten at that stage. (100/30)

3173a - 3175a (Irish Racing) - See Computer Raceform

MAIA (Merano, Italy) (R-H) (Good)
Saturday July 26th
No Times Taken

3176a PREMIO JAPAN AIRLINES (2-Y.O)
3-00 (3-16) **7f** £15,428.00 (£6,788.00: £3,394.00)

			SP	RR	SF
Krizevac (LCamici,Italy) **2-8-8** MCangiano	—	1		—	—
Gautama (BGrizzetti,Italy) **2-9-1** MTellini	hd	2		—	—
Lionel (FBrogi,Italy) **2-8-8** CFiocchi	1½	3		—	—
Stanott (IRE) (LMCumani) **2-8-8** MDemuro (btn 17½l)		8		—	—
					8 Rn

TOTE 197L: 38L 19L 25L (470L) OWNER C. A. M. M. A BRED Camma S A S
Stanott (IRE) was slowly away and, after making a little progress on the home turn, dropped out quickly in the final three furlongs. This was a very disappointing debut.

3177a PREMIO BANCO AMBROSIANO VENETO (2-Y.O)
3-30 (3-48) **7f 110y** £9,642.00 (£4,243.00: £2,314.00)

			SP	RR	SF
Jar (IRE) (BGrizzetti,Italy) **2-8-11** MTellini	—	1		—	—
Diminsky (IRE) (MCiciarelli,Italy) **2-8-11** MEsposito	½	2		—	—
Elcari (IRE) (VBignami,Italy) **2-8-11** LSorrentino	½	3		—	—
Chief Whip (USA) (LMCumani) **2-8-11** MDemuro (btn 13½l)		10		—	—
					11 Rn

TOTE 72L: 25L 24L 39L (243L) OWNER S. Angilica BRED Az Agr Il Tiglio di Amelia Prevedello
Chief Whip (USA) got upset in the paddock and showed his frustration by unshipping his jockey. Racing in mid division, he was back-pedalling in the final quarter-mile and will surely prove better than this.

3006a-MAISONS-LAFFITTE (France) (Soft)
Saturday July 26th

3178a PRIX ROBERT PAPIN (Gp 2) (2-Y.O C & F)
2-20 (2-21) **5f 110y** £39,282.00 (£15,713.00: £7,856.00: £3,928.00)

				SP	RR	SF
2409*	**Greenlander** (CEBrittain) **2-9-2** SGuillot (bhd most of wy: mid div 2f out: qcknd ins fnl f: pushed out & tk ld: fin strly)	—	1		95	—
2484[3]	**Aurigny** (SDow) **2-8-13** GMosse (hld up bhd: hdwy 2f out: led 1½f out: hdd ins fnl f)	s.nk	2		91	—
2639a*	**Zelding (IRE)** (RCollet,France) **2-8-13** OPeslier (prom: trckd ldrs: rdn over 1f out: styd on u.p fnl f)	nk	3		91	—
	Roi Gironde (IRE) (MmeCHead,France) **2-9-2** FHead (set pce: hdd 1½f out: one pce fnl f)	½	4		92	—
2644a*	**Della Scala (IRE)** (BGrizzetti,Italy) **2-9-2** GForte (rdn mid div: hrd rdn fnl 2f)	½	5		91	—
1669*	**Atlantic Viking (IRE)** (MJohnston) **2-9-2** JWeaver (sn rdn: wknd 2f out: n.d)	8	6		67	—
	Jarnail (FR) (MTurquier,France) **2-9-2** ODoleuze (bhd early: wknd 2f out: t.o)	10	7		38	—

7 Rn

64.9 secs (1.40) P-M 4.80F: 2.80F 6.40F OWNER Sheikh Marwan Al Maktoum (NEWMARKET) BRED Sheikh Marwan al Maktoum

2409* Greenlander was outpaced early on here before coming with a finely-timed late challenge up the stands rail. He ran on really gamely and led in the last few strides. Still a little green, he is sure to improve and he will be rested until the Middle Park Stakes, but his connections might be tempted to have a tilt at the Prix Morny at Deauville.

2484 Aurigny moved up sweetly to challenge at the furlong marker but she could not quite last out to the line. She was probably beaten by the distance. A very fast filly, five furlongs looks to be her best trip and she will now head for a Listed race at Deauville.

Zelding (IRE) looked the likely winner when she hit the front a furlong out, but she did not quite stay the trip. Her forte is speed and a drop back to the minimum distance will be to her advantage. She is probably better than this.

Roi Gironde (IRE) was quickly into his stride and was one of the leaders early on, but was outpaced from a furlong and a half out before running on again in the closing stages.

1669* Atlantic Viking (IRE) was close up until the furlong marker where he dropped out of contention. This was disappointing and is best forgotten, as his jockey thought that the colt did not act well on the soft ground.

3179a PRIX HUBERT DE CHAUDENAY (Gp 2) (3-Y.O)
3-25 (3-26) **1m 7f** £33,670.00 (£13,468.00: £6,734.00: £3,367.00)

				SP	RR	SF
1913a*	**Vertical Speed (FR)** (AFabre,France) **3-9-2** OPeslier (rdn 3rd: led 1½f out: fin strly)	—	1		109+	—
2596[3]	**Book At Bedtime (IRE)** (CACyzer) **3-8-13** FHead (racd 2nd: led 4f out: hdd 1½f out: styd on wl)	4	2		102	—
2996a*	**New Frontier (IRE)** (AFabre,France) **3-9-2** AJunk (led tl hdd 4f out: 2nd st: unable qckn)	¾	3		104	—
	Kaldoun Choice (FR) (RCollet,France) **3-9-2** CHanotel (hld up bhd: hdwy 2f out: styd on one pce)	1½	4		102	—
2996a[2]	**Ithaca** (JEPease,France) **3-9-2** FSanchez (racd in 4th: effrt st: wknd qckly)	6	5		96	—

5 Rn

3m 18.1 (3.60) P-M 1.50F: 1.20F 1.90F OWNER Mr Daniel Wildenstein (CHANTILLY) BRED Allez France Stables

1913a* Vertical Speed (FR) is a top-class horse in the making and he landed his hat-trick in style. Third for much of the race, he slipped into the lead over a furlong out before cantering home unchallenged. A son of Bering, he has both stamina and speed and will go on to much better things. He is expected to be seen out next in the Prix Kergorlay at Deauville and, whatever happens this year, he will turn into a top-class four-year-old.

2596 Book At Bedtime (IRE) ran a thoroughly game race and was given a perfect ride. Second early on, she took the lead four out but could not cope with the finishing speed of the winner, only staying on at the one pace. She will now be given a rest until September, when she will contest either the Park Hill Stakes or the St Leger.

2996a* New Frontier (IRE) led until four out and then stayed on one-paced. He is already the winner of a Group Three race and that appears to be his level.

Kaldoun Choice (FR) was held up for a late run but never really looked dangerous. He is not up to this class.

3180a PRIX DAPHNIS (Gp 3) (3-Y.O)
4-00 (4-04) **1m 1f** £24,691.00 (£8,979.00: £4,489.00: £2,694.00)

				SP	RR	SF
2345*	**Handsome Ridge** (JHMGosden) **3-8-9** SGuillot	—	1		107	—
1915a[3]	**Aneysar (IRE)** (AdeRoyerDupre,France) **3-8-9** GMosse	nk	2		107	—
	Blasket Island (IRE) (AFabre,France) **3-8-9** OPeslier	nk	3		106	—
2457a*	**Night Player (IRE)** (RCollet,France) **3-8-9** TGillet	2	4		102	—
	Stingy (MmeCHead,France) **3-8-9** ODoleuze	½	5		102	—
1361a[3]	**Varxi (FR)** (DSmaga,France) **3-8-12** DBoeuf	15	6		78	—

6 Rn

1m 53.5 P-M 8.40F: 3.10F 1.90F OWNER Platt Promotions Ltd (NEWMARKET) BRED Mrs Willa Harford

2345* Handsome Ridge was always well up and ran on really gamely to beat the long-time leader by a neck. He is certainly an improving sort and may well stay a little further. It would be no surprise to see him back in France for the Prix Guillaume d'Ornano at Deauville, and judging by the way he is going, he could make his presence felt in Group Two company.

1915a Aneysar (IRE) tried to make all and stuck to his guns but he could not repel the winner in the final fifty yards. He looks capable of winning a similar sort of group race in the future.

Blasket Island (IRE) was held up early on and came with a sustained run from one and a half furlongs out. He was given every chance but could not quite get to the leaders. He might be better over a slightly shorter distance.

Night Player (IRE) was a disappointing favourite. He never really settled in the race and put in a half-hearted effort in the straight. He may not have been suited by this track and should be given another chance. His trainer believes that this is best forgotten.

3181a PRIX D'ARCHERES CLAIMING (4-Y.O+)
4-30 (4-34) **1m 1f** £5,612.00

				SP	RR	SF
	Archiduque (SPA) (MRolland,France) **6-9-3** OPeslier	—	1		90	—
	Just Lead (FR) (France) **6-9-6** TGillet	1	2		91	—

					SP	RR	SF
	Nakama (IRE) (France) **7-9-1** MBoutin	s.nk	**3**			86	—
2666[6]	**Henry The Fifth** (CEBrittain) **4-8-13** SGuillot (btn over 5½l)		**9**			76	—

11 Rn

1m 52.9 P-M 5.50F: 2.20F 3.30F 1.80F (37.60F) OWNER Lo Duca BRED Yeguada Torre Duero

1476 Henry The Fifth was well up for much of the race but was a spent force by the furlong marker. He was just staying on at the one pace at the end.

1202a-DUSSELDORF (Germany) (R-H) (Good)
Sunday July 27th

3182a WGZ BANK-DEUTSCHLANDPREIS (Gp 1) (3-Y.O+)
3-40 (3-51) **1m 4f** £68,182.00 (£26,515.00: £13,258.00: £5,682.00)

				SP	RR	SF
2100a[2]	**Luso** (CEBrittain) **5-9-6** LDettori (mde all: clr appr fnl f: r.o strly)	—	**1**		127	—
1724a[2]	**Wurftaube (GER)** (HRemmert,Germany) **4-9-2** KWoodburn (a.p: chal 2f out: no imp)	3	**2**		119	—
2459a[4]	**Protektor (GER)** (ALowe,Germany) **8-9-6** ASuborics (bhd: hdwy 2f out: styd on one pce)	2	**3**		120	—
2104[4]	**Royal Court (IRE)** (PWChapple-Hyam) **4-9-6** JReid (mid div tl outpcd 3f out: sme late prog)	1½	**4**		118	—
2459a[3]	**Mongol Warrior (USA)** (LordHuntingdon) **4-9-6** DHarrison (sn trckd ldr: 3rd fr ½-wy to 1f out: one pce)	nk	**5**		118	—
2459a[5]	**Bad Bertrich Again (IRE)** (ALowe,Germany) **4-9-6** GBocskai (hld up: hdwy st: wknd fnl f: b.b.v)	2	**6**		115	—

6 Rn

2m 27.95 TOTE 25DM: 13DM 11DM (36DM) OWNER Mr Saeed Manana (NEWMARKET) BRED Saeed Manana

2100a Luso had conditions in his favour and, allowed to dominate, won with authority. The runner-up almost got upsides passing the quarter-mile pole, but was fighting a losing battle thereafter. He may return for a couple of German Group One events in the near future, and has the Japan Cup as his long-term goal.

2104 Royal Court (IRE) needs softer ground and a longer trip. Outpaced when the tempo quickened three furlongs from home, he stayed on dourly in the closing stages.

2459a Mongol Warrior (USA) was in the first three until dropping away in the final furlong. The ground had dried out too much for his liking.

3047-ASCOT (R-H) (Good, Good to firm patches)
Friday August 1st
WEATHER: humid WIND: alm nil

3183 BUCKINGHAM PALACE APPRENTICE H'CAP (0-70) (3-Y.O+) (Class E)
6-00 (6-01) **1m 4f** £4,119.00 (£1,257.00: £621.00: £303.00) Stalls: High GOING minus 0.12 sec per fur (G)

				SP	RR	SF
3026[4]	**Gold Desire (54)** (MBrittain) **7-9-0**(3) DMernagh(4) (b.nr hind: lw: hld up: rdn over 1f out: led ins fnl f: r.o wl)	—	**1**	13/2	64	40
2843*	**Passing Strangers (USA) (64)** (PWHarris) **4-9-10**(3) DMcGaffin(6) (chsd ldr: led & hung lft 2f out: hdd ins fnl f)	1¼	**2**	7/2[3]	72	48
2667[13]	**Zorro (55)** (RMFlower) **3-8-7** GMilligan(2) (lw: swtg: hld up & plld hrd: hdwy over 6f out: one pce fnl 2f)	5	**3**	3/1[1]	57	22
2650[3]	**Opera Buff (IRE) (65)** (MissGayKelleway) **6-10-0** JWilkinson(3) (lw: hld up: hdwy over 5f out: lost pl over 4f out: r.o one pce fnl 2f)	1½	**4**	9/2	65	41
2650*	**Glow Forum (58)** (LMontagueHall) **6-9-2**(5) DHayden(5) (b: hld up: rdn over 2f out: sn wknd)	1	**5**	100/30[2]	56	32
2397[11]	**Bint Rosie (44)** (MJFetherston-Godley) **3-7-10** KSked(1) (swtg: led tl hdd & sltly hmpd 2f out: sn wknd)	s.h	**6**	33/1	42	7
2949[10]	**Rock The Barney (IRE) (46)** (MDIUsher) **8-8-4**(5) SCarson(7) (s.s: a bhd)	6	**7**	10/1	36	12

(SP 113.8%) **7 Rn**

2m 37.7 (7.70) CSF £26.49 TOTE £7.30: £2.60 £2.40 (£18.70) OWNER Northgate Lodge Racing Club (WARTHILL) BRED Northgate Lodge Stud Ltd

LONG HANDICAP Bint Rosie 7-8

WEIGHT FOR AGE 3yo-11lb

3026 Gold Desire, reverting to a longer trip, was 6lb higher than at Newmarket a week ago after a good effort from out of the handicap the time before. (13/2)

2843* Passing Strangers (USA), raised a hefty 7lb, might be better suited by going left-handed. (7/2)

1938 Zorro, down 3lb, was only a pound higher than when winning at Yarmouth, but never really looked like making his mark. (3/1: op 5/1)

2650 Opera Buff (IRE) lost his position at a vital stage, and could never get back into it. (9/2)

2650* Glow Forum could not confirm the Chepstow form with Opera Buff, having gone up 2lb in the ratings. (100/30)

Bint Rosie ran her best race to date from 2lb out of the handicap. (33/1)

2483 Rock The Barney (IRE) (10/1: 7/1-12/1)

3184 EVENING STANDARD H'CAP (0-80) (3-Y.O+) (Class D)
6-30 (6-32) **1m 2f** £5,628.00 (£1,704.00: £832.00: £396.00) Stalls: High GOING minus 0.12 sec per fur (G)

				SP	RR	SF
2866[10]	**Mattimeo (IRE) (75)** (APJarvis) **4-10-0** KDarley(1) (lw: hld up: hdwy over 2f out: led ins fnl f: drvn out)	—	**1**	10/1	83	44
2285[2]	**Island Sanctuary (IRE) (80)** (PJMakin) **3-9-10** LDettori(7) (a.p: led wl over 1f out tl ins fnl f)	2½	**2**	9/4[1]	84	36
2187[D]	**North Reef (IRE) (73)** (JPearce) **6-9-12** MWigham(3) (led over 8f: one pce)	¾	**3**	8/1	76	37
2909*	**Regal Reprimand (71)** (GLewis) **3-9-1** 5x PaulEddery(6) (b.hind: hld up: rdn & hdwy 2f out: r.o one pce fnl f)	s.h	**4**	4/1[2]	74	26
2866[9]	**Pistol (IRE) (72)** (CAHorgan) **7-9-11** PatEddery(8) (chsd ldr over 7f: wknd over 1f out)	5	**5**	9/2[3]	67	28
2961[7]	**General Haven (70)** (TJNaughton) **4-9-9** TSprake(4) (lw: hld up: rdn over 2f out: a bhd)	s.h	**6**	7/1	65	26
	Celebrant (68) (AHide) **3-8-12** RCochrane(2) (bkwd: hld up: a bhd)	5	**7**	16/1	55	7
1972[4]	**Soaking (48)** (MDIUsher) **7-7-8**(7) SCarson(5) (hld up: hdwy over 3f out: c wd st: rdn & edgd rt over 2f out: sn wknd)	9	**8**	12/1	20	—

(SP 115.2%) **8 Rn**

2m 12.74 (7.24) CSF £30.19 CT £176.29 TOTE £13.50: £2.90 £1.10 £2.00 (£14.70) OWNER Mrs Monica Keogh (ASTON UPTHORPE) BRED W. J. Byrne

WEIGHT FOR AGE 3yo-9lb

2293* Mattimeo (IRE), 5lb higher than when winning at Newcastle, bounced back after running in a better race last time. (10/1: 7/1-12/1)

2285 Island Sanctuary (IRE), again up another furlong, was 4lb higher than when second last time, and 6lb above the mark off which he scored at Nottingham. (9/4)
2187 North Reef (IRE) was again 4lb higher than when winning at Warwick. (8/1)
2909* Regal Reprimand, because of his penalty, will have been running off a 2lb lower mark from the following day. (4/1)
1414 Pistol (IRE), usually ridden with more restraint, slipped to a mark a pound lower than the last of his four wins last summer. (9/2)

3185 SANATOGEN RATED STKS H'CAP (0-95) (3-Y.O+) (Class C)

7-00 (7-01) **7f** £6,312.60 (£2,363.40: £1,156.70: £498.50: £224.25: £114.55) Stalls: Low GOING minus 0.12 sec per fur (G)

				SP	RR	SF
2649[2]	**Chewit (82)** (GLMoore) **5-8-8** CandyMorris(3) (plld hrd: a.p: led nr fin: pushed out)	—	1	9/1	89	56
3024[6]	**Law Commission (89)** (DRCElsworth) **7-9-1** KFallon(2) (hld up: hdwy over 2f out: hrd rdn to ld ins fnl f: hdd nr fin)	nk	2	15/2	95	62
2691[6]	**Redwing (86)** (JLDunlop) **3-8-6** PatEddery(1) (swtg: led: rdn over 2f out: hdd ins fnl f: r.o)	½	3	11/2[3]	91	52
3138[8]	**Song of Skye (81)** (TJNaughton) **3-8-1** TSprake(5) (lw: hld up: hdwy 2f out: nt clr run over 1f out: swtchd rt: hrd rdn: r.o)	s.h	4	8/1	86	47
2857*	**Almuhimm (USA) (86)** (TDBarron) **5-8-12** KDarley(10) (hld up: hdwy over 1f out: one pce fnl f)	¾	5	5/1[2]	89	56
2447a[8]	**Patsy Grimes (89)** (JSMoore) **7-9-1** LDettori(4) (lw: hld up: rdn over 2f out: nt clr run over 1f out: one pce)	2½	6	14/1	87	54
2390[2]	**Chickawicka (IRE) (95)** (BPalling) **6-9-2**(5) DSweeney(7) (prom tl rdn & wknd 2f out)	5	7	12/1	81	48
3052[6]	**Kayvee (90)** (MrsAJPerrett) **8-9-2** AClark(9) (hdwy over 3f out: wknd over 1f out)	3	8	12/1	69	36
2704*	**Sweet Fortune (USA) (86)** (MRStoute) **3-8-6**ow1 JReid(6) (lw: prom 5f)	¾	9	2/1[1]	64	24
2925[9]	**Wait For Rosie (86)** (VSoane) **3-8-6** JQuinn(8) (w ldr: wkng whn n.m.r over 2f out: eased: t.o)	dist	10	33/1	—	—
				(SP 123.3%)	**10 Rn**	

1m 29.51 (2.31) CSF £72.00 CT £301.63 TOTE £10.20: £2.30 £2.50 £1.90 (£44.10) Trio £103.40 OWNER Ballard (1834) Ltd (BRIGHTON)
BRED B. Minty
LONG HANDICAP Song of Skye 8-0
WEIGHT FOR AGE 3yo-6lb
OFFICIAL EXPLANATION **Sweet Fortune (USA): no explanation offered.**
2649 Chewit, 6lb lower than when fifth over course and distance in the Victoria Cup, ran out a narrow if decisive winner. (9/1)
3024 Law Commission made a valiant attempt to repeat last year's win off a pound higher mark. (15/2)
2691 Redwing did not go down without a fight, having been dropped 4lb by the handicapper. (11/2: 4/1-6/1)
2951 Song of Skye, making a quick reappearance, did not get the best of runs, and was never doing things quickly enough in the closing stages. (8/1)
2857* Almuhimm (USA), dropped 4lb prior to winning at Ayr, was 5lb higher here. (5/1)
2447a Patsy Grimes, down 3lb, was only a pound higher than when she last won nearly a year ago, but unfortunately she did not see much daylight against the stands rails. (14/1)

3186 O'KEEFE CHALLENGE NURSERY H'CAP (2-Y.O) (Class C)

7-30 (7-30) **7f** £5,784.00 (£1,752.00: £856.00: £408.00) Stalls: Low GOING minus 0.12 sec per fur (G)

				SP	RR	SF
2719*	**Country Garden** (RHannon) **2-8-8** KDarley(6) (lw: plld hrd mid div: nt clr run 2f out: swtchd lft over 1f out: squeezed thro to ld wl ins fnl f)	—	1	7/1	77	35
2849*	**Hujoom (IRE)** (JLDunlop) **2-9-6** LDettori(9) (a.p: led on bit wl over 1f out: sn rdn: hdd wl ins fnl f)	1¾	2	11/4[1]	85	43
2181[8]	**Ringleader** (PFICole) **2-8-8** RCochrane(8) (hld up: hdwy over 3f out: ev ch over 1f out: one pce)	1¼	3	9/1	70	28
2858[2]	**Sea Magic (IRE)** (BWHills) **2-9-5** JReid(10) (lw: hld up & bhd: hdwy over 2f out: rdn over 1f out: one pce)	1½	4	10/1	78	36
2509[4]	**Water Force** (GBBalding) **2-8-9** TSprake(7) (hld up & bhd: rdn & hdwy over 2f out: one pce fnl f)	hd	5	20/1	68	26
2768*	**Commander Charlie** (IABalding) **2-9-7** PatEddery(4) (lw: hld up & bhd: nt clr run over 1f out: swtchd rt: hdwy fnl f: nvr nr to chal)	hd	6	100/30[2]	79	37
3067[3]	**Bali Dance** (CBBBooth) **2-7-6**(7) RWinston(1) (hld up: swtchd rt over 1f out: nvr trbld ldrs)	1¼	7	14/1	54	12
2595[3]	**Respond** (GLMoore) **2-8-11** AClark(5) (plld hrd early: rdn over 2f out: wknd 1f out)	½	8	14/1	65	23
2689[8]	**Island Girl (IRE)** (DWPArbuthnot) **2-7-11**(3) RFfrench(2) (led over 5f: btn whn hmpd over 1f out)	2½	9	14/1	49	7
2923*	**The Honorable Lady** (MRChannon) **2-7-11** 5x JQuinn(3) (w ldr: rdn over 2f out: btn whn n.m.r over 1f out: eased)	14	10	6/1[3]	14	—
				(SP 120.4%)	**10 Rn**	

1m 31.36 (4.16) CSF £25.01 CT £164.95 TOTE £6.70: £1.70 £1.60 £2.40 (£9.20) Trio £100.80 OWNER Lord Carnarvon (MARLBOROUGH)
BRED Highclere Stud Ltd
STEWARDS' ENQUIRY Darley susp. 10-11/08/97 (careless riding).
2719* Country Garden, reluctant to go to post, is nothing if not consistent, and got a nice run against the stands rails after weaving his way through. His rider was banned for careless riding after carving up longtime leader Island Girl. (7/1)
2849* Hujoom (IRE) did not find as much as Dettori might have anticipated, and the eight concession proved too great. (11/4: 2/1-3/1)
1842 Ringleader, suited by this extra furlong, would appear to be on a handy mark. (9/1)
2858 Sea Magic (IRE) has given the handicapper far more to work on than the majority of her rivals. (10/1)
2509 Water Force was trying a longer trip. (20/1)
2768* Commander Charlie met trouble in trying to come from last place in the final quarter-mile. (100/30)

3187 GOLDEN GATES MAIDEN STKS (2-Y.O F) (Class D)

8-05 (8-06) **6f** £5,862.00 (£1,776.00: £868.00: £414.00) Stalls: Low GOING minus 0.12 sec per fur (G)

				SP	RR	SF
	Nanoushka (IRE) (RHannon) **2-8-11** PaulEddery(4) (leggy: unf: lw: hld up: hdwy over 1f out: led ins fnl f: r.o wl)	—	1	5/1[3]	89+	45
2728[2]	**Dodo (IRE)** (DRCElsworth) **2-8-11** KFallon(8) (led: rdn over 1f out: hdd ins fnl f)	2	2	2/1[1]	84	40
	Honey Storm (IRE) (MRChannon) **2-8-11** JFEgan(7) (leggy: unf: rdn over 2f out: hdwy whn n.m.r over 1f out: r.o ins fnl f)	3½	3	25/1	74	30
	Oh Hebe (IRE) (PWHarris) **2-8-11** PatEddery(2) (w'like: hld up: swtchd rt over 2f out: hdwy over 1f out: wknd ins fnl f)	nk	4	10/1	74	30
2597[8]	**Cosmic Countess (IRE)** (MAJarvis) **2-8-11** RCochrane(1) (lw: prom tl wknd over 1f out)	1¼	5	4/1[2]	70	26
2829[3]	**Night Owl** (RCharlton) **2-8-11** TSprake(3) (prom tl rdn & wknd over 1f out)	2	6	7/1	65	21
	Wigging (NAGraham) **2-8-11** KDarley(6) (w'like: prom tl wknd over 1f out)	1½	7	8/1	61	17
	Coalminersdaughter (IRE) (JWHills) **2-8-11** AClark(5) (lw: hld up: rdn & hdwy over 2f out: wknd over 1f out)	s.h	8	20/1	61	17

Flush (FR) (JWHills) **2-8-11** LDettori(10) (lengthy: bit bkwd: swvd rt s: a bhd) 1¼	**9**	16/1	57	13
Magic Spring (IRE) (KMcAuliffe) **2-8-11** JReid(9) (lt-f: prom: j.path over 3f out: wknd wl over 2f out) 4	**10**	25/1	47	3
		(SP 121.0%)	**10 Rn**	

1m 16.98 (2.98) CSF £14.22 TOTE £5.80: £1.60 £1.60 £5.10 (£9.80) Trio £121.50 OWNER Thurloe Thoroughbreds II (MARLBOROUGH) BRED Godolphin Management Co Ltd

Nanoushka (IRE), a half-sister to a seven-furlong juvenile winner in Ireland, was the subject of encouraging reports. Well on top in the end, her rider was apparently impressed, and it seems as if an ambitious campaign is being mapped out if things go according to plan. (5/1)
2728 Dodo (IRE) beat the others easily enough, and it sounds as if she came up against a useful sort in the winner. (2/1)
Honey Storm (IRE), a half-sister to five furlong juvenile scorer Hana Marie, is out of a five and six furlong two-year-old winner. She shaped well enough on her debut. (25/1)
Oh Hebe (IRE), a half-sister to Poppy Carew and Calypso Grant, did enough to suggest she can maintain the family name. (10/1: 7/1-11/1)
2597 Cosmic Countess (IRE) is a half-sister to seven-furlong winner Cosmic Prince. (4/1)
2829 Night Owl is a 100,000 guineas half-sister to good stayer Lord Jim and a French miler. (7/1: op 4/1)
Wigging, a half-sister to Bluebook and Myself, has entries in both the Lowther and Cheveley Park. (8/1)

3188 CLASSIC FM MAGAZINE MAIDEN STKS (3-Y.O) (Class D)

8-35 (8-35) **1m 4f** £5,576.00 (£1,688.00: £824.00: £392.00) Stalls: High GOING minus 0.12 sec per fur (G)

			SP	RR	SF
2566[3]	**Ghillies Ball** (RCharlton) **3-9-0** TSprake(4) (lw: hld up & bhd: hdwy 2f out: led 1f out: rdn out) ....—	**1**	4/1	96	47
2568[2]	**Nightlark (IRE) (83)** (DRLoder) **3-8-9** PatEddery(2) (led over 4f: led over 1f out: sn hdd: nt qckn) 2	**2**	5/2 1	88	39
2924[3]	**Marsul (USA)** (JHMGosden) **3-9-0** LDettori(6) (hld up: rdn over 2f out: ev ch 1f out: one pce) 1	**3**	11/4 2	92	43
2513[8]	**Alcalali (USA) (95)** (PAKelleway) **3-8-9** JReid(1) (plld hrd: racd wd: led over 7f out: hdd over 1f out: wknd fnl f) 5	**4**	3/1 3	80	31
2008[13]	**Back Row** (LMCumani) **3-8-9** KDarley(5) (hld up: bhd fnl 2f) 6	**5**	12/1	72	23
2486[5]	**Veuve Clicquot** (RWArmstrong) **3-8-9** MRoberts(3) (bhd fnl 4f: t.o) 25	**6**	14/1	39	—
			(SP 114.6%)	**6 Rn**	

2m 36.25 (6.25) CSF £13.52 TOTE £4.90: £2.00 £1.80 (£7.80) OWNER The Queen (BECKHAMPTON) BRED The Queen
2566 Ghillies Ball did this in the style of a real stayer, and his trainer thinks he might develop into a Gold Cup horse. One cannot help feeling he has the physique to be a more than useful recruit to the Queen Mother's string of jumpers. (4/1: op 5/2)
2568 Nightlark (IRE) again had the role of bridesmaid, and her frustrating run continues. (5/2)
2924 Marsul (USA) was up another furlong, but had more to do this time. (11/4)
2053 Alcalali (USA) went in search of faster ground from the word go, and was joined by the others leaving Swinley Bottom. (3/1)

T/Plpt: £97.40 (189.72 Tckts). T/Qdpt: £15.90 (87.91 Tckts) KH

3147-GOODWOOD (R-H) (Good to Firm)

Friday August 1st

Races 1 & 2 hand timed
WEATHER: humid WIND: almost nil

3189 SEEBOARD H'CAP (0-100) (3-Y.O) (Class C)

2-15 (2-15) **7f** £20,535.00 (£6,180.00: £2,990.00: £1,395.00) Stalls: High GOING minus 0.12 sec per fur (G)

			SP	RR	SF
2951*	**Jorrocks (USA) (80)** (IABalding) **3-7-11**(5) 6x CLowther(8) (hdwy 2f out: led wl ins fnl f: rdn out) ....—	**1**	9/1 3	91	60
1737[9]	**Great Child (84)** (MRStoute) **3-8-6** LDettori(9) (lw: hdwy 2f out: led ins fnl f: sn hdd: unable qckn) ....¾	**2**	6/1 2	93	62
2861[6]	**Omaha City (IRE) (99)** (BGubby) **3-9-7** AClark(12) (swtg: a.p: led 2f out tl ins fnl f: one pce) 2	**3**	16/1	104	73
2871[6]	**Wasp Ranger (USA) (94)** (PFICole) **3-9-2b1** PatEddery(14) (lw: rdn 4f out: hdwy over 1f out: r.o) ....¾	**4**	10/1	97	66
2591[4]	**Silver Kristal (76)** (RAkehurst) **3-7-9**(3) RFfrench(7) (lost pl over 2f out: rallied fnl f: r.o) ....s.h	**5**	9/1 3	79	48
2663[5]	**Just Loui (75)** (KRBurke) **3-7-11** GBardwell(15) (led 5f) 2	**6**	33/1	73	42
2325[6]	**Jeffrey Anotherred (89)** (KMcAuliffe) **3-8-11** JFEgan(4) (hdwy over 1f out: nvr nrr) ....½	**7**	20/1	86	55
2023[15]	**Shaheen (USA) (93)** (HRACecil) **3-9-1v1** KFallon(1) (nvr nrr) 1¼	**8**	10/1	87	56
2517[4]	**Granny's Pet (98)** (PFICole) **3-9-6b** RCochrane(13) (s.s: nvr nr to chal) ....hd	**9**	14/1	92	61
2833[3]	**Always Alight (77)** (KRBurke) **3-7-13** JQuinn(10) (lw: nvr nrr) ....nk	**10**	12/1	70	39
2925[3]	**Ivory Dawn (75)** (KTIvory) **3-7-6**(5) AimeeCook(5) (nvr nrr) ....nk	**11**	33/1	68	37
2426[5]	**Fun Galore (USA) (95)** (BWHills) **3-9-3** MHills(11) (chsd ldr: ev ch 2f out: wknd over 1f out) ....nk	**12**	25/1	87	56
2691[5]	**Gee Bee Dream (79)** (APJarvis) **3-8-1** SDrowne(6) (prom over 4f) ....hd	**13**	20/1	71	40
2013[5]	**Just Nick (84)** (WRMuir) **3-8-6**ow1 JReid(2) (bhd fnl 3f) 11	**14**	11/1	51	19
2591*	**Jawhari (87)** (JLDunlop) **3-8-9** RHills(3) (bhd fnl 3f) 9	**15**	11/4 1	33	2
			(SP 127.0%)	**15 Rn**	

1m 26.2 (1.40) CSF £55.36 CT £797.34 TOTE £12.00: £3.20 £1.90 £6.40 (£34.50) Trio £571.10 OWNER Mr Paul Mellon (KINGSCLERE) BRED Stewart L. Amstrong

OFFICIAL EXPLANATION **Jawhari: the rider reported that the colt ran freely in he early stages, lost his action on the bend and was never really going thereafter. He therefore felt it prudent to ease the colt.**
2951* Jorrocks (USA), produced late as he was last time, responds well to these tactics, and again found a notable turn of foot. He is on the upgrade. (9/1)
1175 Great Child took a while to pick up after being off the bridle early in the straight. This trip is probably a minimum for him, particularly over a track this sharp, and the ground was plenty fast enough too. (6/1)
2861 Omaha City (IRE) has been running well in better company, and confirmed his ability with a bold effort under top weight. (16/1)
2871 Wasp Ranger (USA), blinkered for the first time, was under pressure by halfway, and looked as if he would appreciate a return to a longer trip. (10/1)
2591 Silver Kristal, staying on after being outpaced at a vital stage, may be worth trying over a mile. (9/1: op 6/1)
2663 Just Loui, five times successful on sand, has never won on turf, but put up a creditable effort here. (33/1)
2325 Jeffrey Anotherred finished well after proving unwilling to settle, and is running better at present than his form figures would suggest. (20/1)
2591* Jawhari ran way below his potential, but was reported by his jockey to have been free early on, and was never going well after losing his action on the bend. (11/4)

3190 VOLVO CONTRACTS GLOBETROTTER H'CAP (0-110) (3-Y.O) (Class B)

2-45 (2-47) **1m 2f** £34,800.00 (£10,500.00: £5,100.00: £2,400.00) Stalls: High GOING minus 0.12 sec per fur (G)

				SP	RR	SF
2729[2]	**Future Perfect (88)** (PFICole) **3-8-9** CRutter(1) (mid div whn stumbled 7f out: hdwy over 2f out: led over 1f out: hrd rdn & edgd rt: r.o wl)	—	**1**	25/1	97	71
2058[8]	**Supply And Demand (97)** (GLMoore) **3-9-4** JReid(11) (hdwy 4f out: stumbled over 3f out: rdn 2f out: unable qckn fnl f)	1½	**2**	12/1	104	78
2871[12]	**Atlantic Desire (IRE) (90)** (MJohnston) **3-8-11** JWeaver(10) (lw: plld hrd: hrd rdn & hdwy on ins over 1f out: swtchd lft ins fnl f: r.o)	1½	**3**	20/1	94	68
1875[10]	**Calypso Grant (IRE) (93)** (PWHarris) **3-8-9**(5) CLowther(17) (swtg: a.p: led over 2f out tl over 1f out: one pce)	nk	**4**	33/1	97	71
2601[6]	**Bali Paradise (USA) (92)** (PFICole) **3-8-13** BDoyle(12) (w ldr over 6f: one pce)	½	**5**	25/1	95	69
2761[4]	**Desert Horizon (98)** (JHMGosden) **3-9-5** LDettori(13) (b: a.p: rdn over 2f out: wknd over 1f out)	½	**6**	16/1	100	74
2137[3]	**Lord Eurolink (IRE) (89)** (JLDunlop) **3-8-10** RCochrane(8) (hld up: rdn over 2f out: wknd over 1f out)	¾	**7**	14/1	90	64
2058[10]	**Generous Gift (95)** (EALDunlop) **3-9-2** KFallon(2) (lw: mid div whn hmpd over 4f out: nvr nr to chal)	½	**8**	25/1	95	69
2585[10]	**Priena (IRE) (93)** (DRLoder) **3-9-0** KDarley(14) (lw: led over 7f)	¾	**9**	20/1	92	66
2338[5]	**Barba Papa (IRE) (100)** (LMCumani) **3-9-7** DHolland(9) (plld hrd: hdwy over 1f out: eased whn btn ins fnl f)	2	**10**	25/1	96	70
2528[2]	**Patriot Games (IRE) (85)** (MRStoute) **3-8-6** PaulEddery(5) (hld up: rdn over 2f out: wknd over 1f out)	2	**11**	8/1[3]	78	52
2710[6]	**Southerly Wind (87)** (MrsJRRamsden) **3-8-8** JFortune(7) (lw: bhd fnl 3f)	½	**12**	8/1[3]	79	53
2585[4]	**Amyas (IRE) (97)** (BWHills) **3-9-4** MHills(18) (a bhd)	4	**13**	3/1[1]	82	56
2778*	**Sword Arm (81)** (RCharlton) **3-8-2v** TSprake(16) (prom over 7f)	s.h	**14**	13/2[2]	66	40
1982[6]	**Al Azhar (92)** (IABalding) **3-8-13** PatEddery(3) (hdwy over 1f out: wknd fnl f)	nk	**15**	10/1	77	51
2765[3]	**Papua (99)** (IABalding) **3-9-6** MRoberts(4) (swtg: bhd fnl 5f)	nk	**16**	25/1	83	57
2729*	**Sir Talbot (91)** (RHannon) **3-8-12** DaneO'Neill(6) (prom over 7f)	1¾	**17**	16/1	73	47
2687*	**Labeq (IRE) (85)** (PTWalwyn) **3-8-6** RHills(15) (prom over 7f)	2½	**18**	13/2[2]	63	37
				(SP 140.8%)	**18 Rn**	

2m 8.3 (1.70) CSF £282.20 CT £5,548.93 TOTE £50.00: £7.90 £2.50 £5.10 £8.00 (£370.50) Trio £2,642.50; £1,563.19 to Goodwood 2/8/97
OWNER R O M Racing (WHATCOMBE) BRED Mrs E. C. York

2729 Future Perfect, well suited by this trip nowadays, readily overcame a 3lb rise in his handicap rating. (25/1)
1741 Supply And Demand has been done no favours by the handicapper, but good efforts like this one will encourage no mercy. (12/1)
2292* Atlantic Desire (IRE) needs at least this trip nowadays, and may stay further too. (20/1)
724 Calypso Grant (IRE), a sister to ten-furlong winner Poppy Carew, has never won over this trip herself, but only gave best in the final furlong. (33/1)
2601 Bali Paradise (USA) has not won over a trip as far as this, but lack of acceleration seemed to be the main problem. (25/1)
2761 Desert Horizon, running in his first handicap, may have been installed a pound or two too high in the weights. (16/1)
2585 Amyas (IRE), last of all at halfway, failed to pick up when ridden in the home straight. (3/1)
2778* Sword Arm has looked much better over a shorter trip. (13/2)

3191 SCHRODERS GLORIOUS RATED STKS H'CAP (0-110) (Listed) (4-Y.O+) (Class A)

3-20 (3-20) **1m 4f** £30,405.20 (£11,346.80: £5,523.40: £2,347.00: £1,023.50: £494.10) Stalls: Low GOING minus 0.12 sec per fur (G)

				SP	RR	SF
2108[12]	**Bahamian Sunshine (USA) (95)** (RAkehurst) **6-8-7** JWeaver(7) (swtg: mde all: rdn over 1f out: r.o wl)	—	**1**	20/1	107	69
2656*	**Bright Water (108)** (HRACecil) **4-9-6** KFallon(4) (a.p: rdn 4f out: chsd wnr over 3f out: ev ch over 1f out: unable qckn)	3½	**2**	6/5[1]	115	77
2710[19]	**Humourless (95)** (LMCumani) **4-8-7** LDettori(5) (b.hind: chsd wnr over 8f: hrd rdn over 2f out: one pce)	1	**3**	9/2[2]	101	63
2709[6]	**Better Offer (IRE) (100)** (MrsAJPerrett) **5-8-12** JReid(1) (lw: nvr nr to chal)	7	**4**	10/1	97	59
2869[3]	**Beauchamp Jade (98)** (HCandy) **5-8-10** CRutter(2) (rdn over 4f out: no hdwy fnl 2f)	1¼	**5**	9/2[2]	93	55
2765[6]	**Bahamian Knight (CAN) (108)** (DRLoder) **4-9-6** PatEddery(6) (lw: prom over 8f)	8	**6**	16/1	92	54
1960[5]	**Medaille Militaire (109)** (JLDunlop) **5-9-7** KDarley(3) (s.s: a bhd)	29	**7**	7/1[3]	55	17
				(SP 114.1%)	**7 Rn**	

2m 35.16 (1.96) CSF £40.65 TOTE £18.70: £5.30 £1.50 (£19.80) OWNER Lucayan Stud (EPSOM) BRED Galbreath/Phillips Racing Partnership
LONG HANDICAP Humourless 8-6 Bahamian Sunshine (USA) 8-4
OFFICIAL EXPLANATION Medaille Militaire: finished distressed.

1319 Bahamian Sunshine (USA) failed to stay a marathon trip last time. Given a well judged ride, he responded well to the change of tactics and stretched out willingly when challenged. (20/1)
2656* Bright Water has been running over one-and-a-quarter miles, and is yet to win over a trip as far as this. (6/5)
2710 Humourless put a poor effort in the Magnet Cup behind him with a satisfactory run in this slightly higher grade. (9/2)
2709 Better Offer (IRE) is inconsistent, but the way he stayed on here suggests he is capable of running into form as the season progresses. (10/1)
2869 Beauchamp Jade, who has been troublesome in the stalls at times, was joined by her trainer at the start, but she ran disappointingly and can do better. (9/2: 3/1-5/1)
2765 Bahamian Knight (CAN) won the Italian Derby last season, but has achieved very little since. (16/1)
1960 Medaille Militaire (7/1: 5/1-15/2)

3192 JOCKEY CLUB OF KENYA MOLECOMB STKS (Gp 3) (2-Y.O) (Class A)

3-50 (3-52) **5f** £24,025.00 (£9,040.00: £4,382.50: £1,952.50) Stalls: Low GOING minus 0.12 sec per fur (G)

				SP	RR	SF
2811a*	**Lady Alexander (IRE)** (CCollins,Ireland) **2-8-12** PShanahan(2) (unf: scope: a.p: led wl over 1f out: drvn out)	—	**1**	100/30[1]	101	26
2863[2]	**Mugello** (APJarvis) **2-8-7** MHills(12) (lw: a.p: hrd rdn over 1f out: ev ch fnl f: r.o wl)	½	**2**	11/2[2]	94	19
696[4]	**Chieftain (IRE)** (NACallaghan) **2-8-12** PatEddery(6) (lw: s.s & bmpd s: outpcd: hdwy over 1f out: r.o)	1½	**3**	8/1	95	20
2862[3]	**Banningham Blade** (KTIvory) **2-8-7** BDoyle(5) (hld up: hrd rdn over 1f out: r.o one pce)	hd	**4**	12/1	89	14
2584[5]	**Tippitt Boy** (KMcAuliffe) **2-9-3** JReid(8) (lw: hdwy over 1f out: r.o)	s.h	**5**	16/1	99	24
2862[2]	**Pure Coincidence** (GLewis) **2-8-12** PaulEddery(9) (led over 3f: hrd rdn: one pce)	¾	**6**	13/2[3]	92	17
2931*	**Its All Relative** (JBerry) **2-8-7** KFallon(11) (lw: a.p: hrd rdn over 1f out: one pce)	¾	**7**	12/1	84	9
2862[5]	**Mysticism** (CEBrittain) **2-8-7** LDettori(3) (outpcd: nvr nrr)	2	**8**	14/1	78	3
2639a[4]	**Ouaisne** (RGuest) **2-8-12** DHolland(7) (wnt lft s: bhd fnl 2f)	¾	**9**	10/1	81	6

				SP	RR	SF
2926*	**Gipsy Moth** (BJMeehan) **2-8-7** MTebbutt(13) (bhd fnl 2f)	1½	**10**	33/1	71	—
2314*	**Princess Natalie** (TDBarron) **2-8-7** KDarley(10) (lw: reard s: hdwy 4f out: wknd over 1f out)	2	**11**	9/1	64	—
2024[9]	**Compradore** (MBlanshard) **2-8-7** JQuinn(4) (prom over 3f)	1¼	**12**	33/1	60	—
2740*	**Distinct Vintage (IRE)** (RHannon) **2-8-12** RHughes(1) (lw: bhd fnl 2f)	s.h	**13**	12/1	65	—

(SP 123.5%) **13 Rn**

60.12 secs (3.42) CSF £19.25 TOTE £3.90: £1.80 £2.50 £3.30 (£12.60) Trio £57.00 OWNER Mrs N. O'Callaghan (THE CURRAGH) BRED Noel O'Callaghan

2811a* Lady Alexander (IRE) was coming back to the minimum trip, but she has plenty of speed and her ability to stay further came in handy when joined by the runner-up inside the final furlong. (100/30)

2863 Mugello is a pacey sort, and her natural early speed will keep her out of trouble in her races, and enable her to pick up plenty more prizemoney. (11/2)

696 Chieftain (IRE) missed the break, and was last of all until halfway. He had been off the track for three months, and has definite prospects. (8/1: 6/1-9/1)

2862 Banningham Blade continues to run with admirable consistency. As a 600 guineas purchase, she has been one of the bargains of the season. (12/1)

2584 Tippitt Boy ran well under the harsh burden of a 5lb penalty, imposed as a result of his Royal Ascot victory in which several of his rivals were badly hampered in running. (16/1)

2862 Pure Coincidence has lots of speed, and made a bold attempt to exploit it on this ideal track for speedsters. (13/2)

2639a Ouaisne (10/1: op 6/1)

3193 E.B.F. FOXHALL MAIDEN STKS (2-Y.O C & G) (Class D)

4-25 (4-26) **7f** £7,197.50 (£2,180.00: £1,065.00: £507.50) Stalls: High GOING minus 0.12 sec per fur (G)

				SP	RR	SF
	Chester House (USA) (HRACecil) **2-8-11** KFallon(1) (w'like: scope: rdn 5f out: hdwy over 3f out: wandered over 1f out: edgd rt 1f out: led ins fnl f: r.o wl: rn green)	—	**1**	10/11[1]	81+	47
	Just In Time (TGMills) **2-8-11** JReid(9) (scope: bit bkwd: a.p: nt clr run on ins over 2f out & 1f out: r.o ins fnl f: bttr for r)	½	**2**	25/1	80	46
	Secret Archive (RHannon) **2-8-11** RHughes(3) (w'like: scope: s.s: rdn & hdwy over 3f out: r.o one pce fnl f)	½	**3**	20/1	79	45
2012[14]	**Hadid (USA)** (BWHills) **2-8-11** RHills(10) (led over 5f out: hrd rdn over 1f out: hdd ins fnl f: unable qckn)	s.h	**4**	9/1	79	45
2699[2]	**Night Shot** (IABalding) **2-8-11** LDettori(5) (rdn over 2f out: hdwy over 1f out: one pce)	1¼	**5**	3/1[2]	76	42
	Generosity (PFICole) **2-8-11** PatEddery(2) (unf: lw: rdn over 3f out: nvr nr to chal)	3	**6**	7/1[3]	69	35
2849[2]	**Bermuda Boy** (BJMeehan) **2-8-11** JWeaver(7) (led over 1f: ev ch wl over 1f out: sn wknd)	1¾	**7**	10/1	65	31
2688[4]	**Wildcat (IRE)** (RHannon) **2-8-11** PaulEddery(8) (swtg: s.s: a bhd)	14	**8**	25/1	33	—
2509[6]	**Top Maite** (AGFoster) **2-8-8**(3) AWhelan(6) (prom over 3f)	s.h	**9**	50/1	33	—
2948[7]	**Ocean Line (IRE)** (APJarvis) **2-8-11** KDarley(4) (a bhd)	5	**10**	50/1	21	—

(SP 125.3%) **10 Rn**

1m 28.03 (3.23) CSF £35.32 TOTE £2.10: £1.30 £3.10 £3.60 (£21.30) Trio £95.70 OWNER Mr K. Abdulla (NEWMARKET) BRED Juddmonte Farms

Chester House (USA), whose trainer has played down the Newmarket gossip about him, was unimpressive in victory, but Cecil says he is backward and lazy, and that he should improve with racing. (10/11: 1/2-evens)

Just In Time, a 58,000 guineas yearling, did not get the best of runs, and looks sure to win races. (25/1)

Secret Archive, a 72,000 guineas yearling, made a satisfactory debut, and has scope for improvement. (20/1)

1486 Hadid (USA) would have been third if he had not been eased near the finish when the winner crossed in front of him. He has failed to score in his first three races, but has shown plenty of ability in the process. (9/1: 8/1-12/1)

2699 Night Shot travelled well for a long way, and can be placed to good effect. (3/1: op 12/1)

Generosity, who cost 200,000 francs as a yearling, was going on nicely at the finish after taking an age to get going. He will improve for the experience, and looks sure to appreciate a longer trip in due course. (7/1: 4/1-8/1)

2849 Bermuda Boy was not knocked about when held in the final furlong. (10/1)

3194 CHICHESTER CITY H'CAP (0-90) (3-Y.O) (Class C)

5-00 (5-00) **5f** £7,310.00 (£2,180.00: £1,040.00: £470.00) Stalls: Low GOING minus 0.12 sec per fur (G)

				SP	RR	SF
3082[7]	**Tear White (IRE) (67)** (TGMills) **3-8-1** JQuinn(2) (lw: a.p: led over 1f out: rdn out)	—	**1**	15/2	75	20
2655[6]	**Brutal Fantasy (IRE) (83)** (JLEyre) **3-8-10**(7) RWinston(1) (a.p: hrd rdn over 1f out: r.o ins fnl f)	nk	**2**	12/1	90	35
2779[2]	**Dancethenightaway (87)** (BJMeehan) **3-9-0**(7) GHannon(6) (swtg: s.i.s: outpcd: hdwy & hung rt 1f out: r.o)	½	**3**	7/1	92	37
2964[6]	**Anokato (68)** (KTIvory) **3-8-2b** BDoyle(9) (outpcd: hdwy over 1f out: r.o)	1½	**4**	14/1	69	14
2529[11]	**Rudi's Pet (IRE) (82)** (RHannon) **3-9-2b** PatEddery(7) (lw: lost pl over 1f out: r.o ins fnl f)	½	**5**	4/1[1]	81	26
2833[7]	**Cauda Equina (80)** (MRChannon) **3-9-0** RHughes(3) (swtg: hld up: rdn over 2f out: one pce)	s.h	**6**	13/2[3]	79	24
2779[4]	**Sabina (83)** (IABalding) **3-9-3** LDettori(4) (led over 3f: wknd ins fnl f)	1¼	**7**	5/1[2]	78	23
2044[6]	**Gaelic Storm (78)** (MJohnston) **3-8-12** JWeaver(10) (b.hind: swtg: dwlt: nvr nr to chal)	½	**8**	9/1	71	16
2655[3]	**Swino (80)** (PDEvans) **3-9-0v** JFEgan(8) (lw: hld up: rdn over 2f out: wknd over 1f out)	2½	**9**	12/1	65	10
901[9]	**Antonia's Choice (78)** (JBerry) **3-8-7**(5) CLowther(5) (bhd fnl 2f)	3	**10**	14/1	54	—

(SP 113.0%) **10 Rn**

59.88 secs (3.18) CSF £82.27 CT £608.28 TOTE £10.70: £2.80 £3.40 £2.00 (£69.20) Trio £107.30 OWNER A W Lawson & Co Ltd (EPSOM) BRED A. F. O'Callaghan

2964 Tear White (IRE), a much more amenable character nowadays, was well drawn, and it was to his advantage he was able to claim the rail. He also ran very well when second at this meeting last year. (15/2)

2655 Brutal Fantasy (IRE), dropped 4lb in recent races, showed his appreciation with a return to form, but he was still 5lb above his highest winning mark. (12/1)

2779 Dancethenightaway, hopelessly outpaced and hanging down the hill, ran badly at Epsom earlier in the season, and may be best suited by a flatter track. (7/1)

2964 Anokato was undone by a combination of the draw and his inability to go the early pace. (14/1: 8/1-16/1)

2347 Rudi's Pet (IRE) looked a difficult ride, with his jockey having to stop riding him altogether for much of the last two furlongs, but the ability is there if he can be persuaded to use it. (4/1)

2547* Cauda Equina left the stalls awkwardly, and by halfway was finding this downhill five furlongs a shade too fast. (13/2)

2779 Sabina showed plenty of speed for four furlongs, and was not given a hard time in the final one hundred yards. (5/1)

2655 Swino (12/1: 8/1-14/1)

3195 KINRARA APPRENTICE LIMITED STKS (0-80) (4-Y.O+) (Class D)

5-35 (5-35) **6f** £6,710.00 (£2,030.00: £990.00: £470.00) Stalls: Low GOING minus 0.12 sec per fur (G)

				SP	RR	SF
2377*	**So Intrepid (IRE) (80)** (JMBradley) **7-9-4** RFfrench(2) (lw: chsd ldr: led over 1f out: rdn: r.o wl)	—	1	13/8 1	82	53
2841 2	**Almasi (IRE) (77)** (CFWall) **5-8-12**(3) JoHunnam(5) (lw: hdwy 2f out: chsd wnr fnl f: no imp)	2½	2	7/4 2	72	43
2939 2	**Palacegate Touch (80)** (JBerry) **7-9-4b**(3) CLowther(4) (lw: led over 4f)	2	3	7/2 3	73	44
3092 6	**Superlao (BEL) (44)** (JJBridger) **5-8-12** ADaly(1) (hld up: rdn over 2f out: wknd over 1f out)	1½	4	33/1	60	31
3056 3	**Scissor Ridge (58)** (JJBridger) **5-8-7**(5) PDoe(6) (swtg: hld up: rdn over 2f out: wknd wl over 1f out)	4	5	10/1	49	20
3083 4	**Moi Canard (42)** (BAPearce) **4-8-12** AimeeCook(3) (bhd fnl 4f)	1¾	6	20/1	45	16
				(SP 113.5%)		**6 Rn**

1m 12.5 (2.70) CSF £4.46 TOTE £2.80: £1.70 £1.60 (£2.40) OWNER Mr E. A. Hayward (CHEPSTOW) BRED Crest Stud Ltd
2377* So Intrepid (IRE) won with a bit in hand, and is in prime form at present. (13/8)
2841 Almasi (IRE) was joint top-rated with the winner on official figures, but proved to be no match on the day. (7/4)
2939 Palacegate Touch streaked away in front, apparently going well, but he ended up setting up the race for the winner, and running himself into the ground. (7/2)
3092 Superlao (BEL) had no chance at these weights. (33/1)
3056 Scissor Ridge was up against it on these terms with the leading trio. (10/1)
3083 Moi Canard would have been much better off in a handicap. (20/1)

T/Jkpt: Not won; £58,428.45 to Goodwood 2/8/97. T/Plpt: £961.00 (70.58 Tckts). T/Qdpt: £18.10 (202.02 Tckts) AK

3021-NEWMARKET (R-H) (Good)
Friday August 1st
WEATHER: overcast WIND: slight behind

3196 SIDE HILL (S) STKS (3-Y.O+) (Class E)

6-10 (6-10) **1m (July)** £3,817.50 (£1,140.00: £545.00: £247.50) Stalls: Low GOING minus 0.16 sec per fur (GF)

				SP	RR	SF
2947 3	**Golden Ace (IRE) (80)** (RHannon) **4-9-4** DHarrison(4) (swtg: mde virtually all: rdn & hld on wl fnl f)	—	1	15/8 2	48	30
2549 9	**Windy Treat (USA)** (EALDunlop) **3-8-11** GCarter(3) (plld hrd: rdn & hdwy over 2f out: edgd lft 1f out: no ex ins fnl f)	1¾	2	3/1 3	45	20
2941 6	**Petuntse** (JGSmyth-Osbourne) **3-8-11e** WJO'Connor(5) (b.hind: sn w wnr: ev ch over 1f out: sn rdn & btn)	1¾	3	25/1	41	16
3048 8	**Royal Acclaim (26)** (KRBurke) **12-9-2v**(7) EmilyJoyce(1) (bhd: hdwy over 2f out: nvr rchd ldrs)	4	4	25/1	38	20
2757 8	**Coral Island (54)** (JGFitzGerald) **3-9-2** WRyan(2) (lw: in tch 5f)	2½	5	7/4 1	33	8
2748 5	**Rosalee Royale (32)** (JohnBerry) **5-8-13** MFenton(6) (prom tl rdn & btn 3f out)	¾	6	25/1	22	4
				(SP 107.7%)		**6 Rn**

1m 43.84 (5.84) CSF £6.43 TOTE £2.70: £1.50 £1.50 (£3.70) OWNER Mr George Teo (MARLBOROUGH) BRED Miss Roseanne Millett and Paul McEnery
WEIGHT FOR AGE 3yo-7lb
Sold JPurcell 6,200gns
2947 Golden Ace (IRE), dropped in class, got very warm, but was able to dictate for much of the race and came up the hill in good style. (15/8: 4/5-2/1)
2549 Windy Treat (USA) seemed more amenable on this straight track, if somewhat keen going down. Once the chance was there in the final furlong, he was found wanting. (3/1: 5/1-11/4)
2941 Petuntse, with his tongue tied down, was taken to post very early. He seems to be gradually coming to hand although he again failed to see out an eighth furlong. (25/1)
2848 Royal Acclaim had no chance at the weights, and staying on past beaten horses was as much as could reasonably be expected. (25/1)
2158 Coral Island, back to a mile, moved down well, but again ran below par. (7/4)
2748 Rosalee Royale, taken down steadily, was the first beaten. (25/1)

3197 LUCINDA STOPFORD SACKVILLE LADIES' H'CAP (0-80) (3-Y.O+) (Class E)

6-40 (6-41) **1m 4f (July)** £3,850.00 (£1,150.00: £550.00: £250.00) Stalls: High GOING minus 0.16 sec per fur (GF)

				SP	RR	SF
2961 3	**Princess Topaz (61)** (CACyzer) **3-9-10** MrsSBosley(8) (a.p: led over 1f out: pushed out)	—	1	9/2 3	71	40
2889 4	**Infatuation (75)** (LadyHerries) **4-11-7** MrsMCowdrey(5) (swtg: hld up: hdwy over 4f out: r.o ins fnl f: nt trble wnr)	2½	2	7/1	82	62
3015 3	**Chris's Lad (53)** (BJMeehan) **6-9-13b** MissJAllison(4) (led 3f: led over 5f out: rdn & hdd over 1f out: kpt on)	½	3	4/1 2	59	39
3015 8	**Nosey Native (60)** (JPearce) **4-10-6** MrsLPearce(2) (hld up: hdwy 5f out: one pce fnl 2f)	1¾	4	16/1	64	44
2944 4	**Toi Toi (IRE) (75)** (DWPArbuthnot) **3-10-10** MrsDArbuthnot(1) (lw: b.hind: prom: rdn 2f out: no imp)	hd	5	9/1	79	48
3015 2	**Augustan (55)** (SGollings) **6-10-1** MissDianaJones(3) (chsd ldrs: ev ch wl over 1f out: sn wknd)	3½	6	5/1	54	34
2469 2	**Madison Welcome (IRE) (63)** (MrsJRRamsden) **3-9-7**(5) MissERamsden(9) (bhd fnl 4f)	14	7	7/2 1	43	12
2787 5	**English Invader (54)** (CADwyer) **6-9-9**(5) MrsCWilliams(7) (lw: dwlt: bhd fnl 4f)	12	8	16/1	18	—
2146 6	**Don't Drop Bombs (USA) (41)** (DTThom) **8-9-1v** MissJFeilden(6) (led after 3f tl over 5f out: rdn & edgd lft over 3f out: sn wknd)	8	9	14/1	—	—
				(SP 118.0%)		**9 Rn**

2m 37.17 (8.17) CSF £33.51 CT £125.26 TOTE £5.50: £2.20 £2.40 £1.70 (£31.00) Trio £12.30 OWNER Mr Stephen Crown (HORSHAM) BRED S. Crown
WEIGHT FOR AGE 3yo-11lb
OFFICIAL EXPLANATION **Madison Welcome (IRE): the rider reported that the gelding had been outpaced when the leaders quickened.**
2961 Princess Topaz, tried over this trip for the second time, lasted home well. (9/2)
2889 Infatuation does not look a straightforward ride, but made relentless progress without ever looking like getting there in time. (7/1: op 3/1)
3015 Chris's Lad, making much of his own pace for a change, could not repeat his earlier success, but did not go down without a fight. (4/1)
2469 Nosey Native does appear to be on the way back. (16/1)
2944 Toi Toi (IRE) seemed to struggle to see out the trip in this more truly-run race. (9/1)
3015 Augustan was slightly disappointing, weakening on meeting on meeting the rising ground. (5/1)
2469 Madison Welcome (IRE) never gave his supporters a moment's hope, and looks to need an awful lot of kidding. (7/2)

3198 VARDY CONTINENTAL H'CAP (0-90) (3-Y.O+) (Class C)

7-10 (7-12) **6f (July)** £5,872.50 (£1,755.00: £840.00: £382.50) Stalls: Low GOING minus 0.16 sec per fur (GF)

				SP	RR	SF
2573^{W}	**Rififi (64)** (RIngram) **4-8-3** DRMcCabe(2) (lw: b: in tch: hdwy over 2f out: led 1f out: rdn out)	—	**1**	16/1	77	53
3130^{5}	**Mr Bergerac (IRE) (80)** (BPalling) **6-9-5** DHarrison(12) (in tch: rdn to ld over 1f out: sn hdd & kpt on)	nk	**2**	8/1	92	68
3082*	**Resist the Force (USA) (62)** (CACyzer) **7-8-1** ^{7x} GDuffield(5) (lw: chsd ldrs: ev ch 1f out: unable qckn ins fnl f)	s.h	**3**	7/2 ^{1}	74	50
	Al Muallim (USA) (80) (JWPayne) **3-9-1** AMcGlone(3) (lw: stdd s: hdwy 2f out: styd on wl fnl f)	1¾	**4**	14/1	87	59
3024^{3}	**Grey Kingdom (75)** (MBrittain) **6-9-0** AMunro(1) (w ldrs: one pce appr fnl f)	hd	**5**	11/2 ^{2}	82	58
2766^{13}	**Concer Un (89)** (SCWilliams) **5-10-0** GCarter(4) (b: outpcd tl styd on appr fnl f)	3	**6**	20/1	88	64
2769^{3}	**Taoiste (82)** (RWArmstrong) **4-9-7** RPrice(10) (lw: led over 4f)	1¾	**7**	10/1	77	53
3024^{5}	**Shamanic (82)** (SPCWoods) **5-9-7** WRyan(6) (prom 4f)	5	**8**	10/1	63	39
1772^{12}	**Eastern Prophets (83)** (GLewis) **4-9-5**(3) AWhelan(9) (chsd ldr 4f)	hd	**9**	16/1	64	40
2950^{8}	**Bayin (USA) (65)** (MDIUsher) **8-8-4** RStreet(7) (dwlt: hdwy over 3f out: wknd over 1f out)	s.h	**10**	7/1	46	22
2841^{7}	**Watch The Fire (64)** (JEBanks) **4-7-12**(5) RMullen(11) (dwlt: rdn 2f out: nvr nr to chal)	2½	**11**	12/1	38	14
2833*	**Literary Society (USA) (81)** (JARToller) **4-9-6** SSanders(13) (lw: chsd ldrs over 3f: sn rdn & btn)	2	**12**	6/1 ^{3}	50	26
2872^{11}	**Jennelle (83)** (CADwyer) **3-9-4** KRutter(8) (dwlt: sn rcvrd: rdn over 2f out: sn wknd)	½	**13**	20/1	50	22
				(SP 129.3%)	**13 Rn**	

1m 13.54 (1.54) CSF £136.40 CT £528.94 TOTE £21.90: £4.40 £2.80 £1.40 (£164.40) Trio £153.10 OWNER Brooknight Guarding Ltd (EPSOM) BRED Milton Park Stud Partnership

WEIGHT FOR AGE 3yo-4lb

2006* Rififi looked magnificent and, probably racing on the best ground, was able to swoop late. (16/1)

3130 Mr Bergerac (IRE) can be considered an unlucky loser here, as the field split into two indistinct groups, with those nearer the far side doing much the best, stalls one to five providing the other finishers in the first six. Clear of his group once Taoiste weakened, he looks at his very best just now and should soon be winning. (8/1)

3082* Resist the Force (USA) made a bold hat-trick bid, but his turn of foot was not quite so effective in this higher grade. (7/2)

Al Muallim (USA), who looked big and well, was rather keen going down and Plan A seemed to be to get him settled. Once asked to improve, he kept closing to the line and gave the impression that there was still petrol left in the tank. If he learns to settle, he should get further but, even over this trip, there are races to be won with him on this evidence. (14/1)

3024 Grey Kingdom, having his third run in a fortnight, ran a bit flat, and the handicapper forced his hand as he is due to go up 3lb from Saturday. (11/2: 4/1-6/1)

2161 Concer Un is still paying for the purple patch which saw him win five handicaps in six outings last summer. He has lost ten times since the run ended and this drop in trip smacked a bit of desperation. (20/1)

3024 Shamanic (10/1: 7/1-12/1)

2711 Bayin (USA), with the field dividing into two groups, one towards the centre, the other towards the far side, saw too much daylight and was always doing too much too soon. (7/1)

2841 Watch The Fire (12/1: 7/1-14/1)

2833* Literary Society (USA) (6/1: op 4/1)

3199 ANTEC VIRKON CONDITIONS STKS (3-Y.O+ F & M) (Class C)

7-40 (7-40) **6f (July)** £5,402.25 (£1,723.50: £824.25) Stalls: Low GOING minus 0.16 sec per fur (GF)

				SP	RR	SF
1147^{10}	**Dame Laura (IRE) (102)** (HMorrison) **3-8-8** DHarrison(1) (mde all: rdn over 1f out: hld on wl)	—	**1**	2/1 ^{2}	96	38
2561^{9}	**Conspiracy (95)** (JLDunlop) **3-8-8** GCarter(2) (lw: trckd wnr: chal wl over 1f out: sn rdn & no imp)	1½	**2**	8/11 ^{1}	92	34
3145^{4}	**Caution (75)** (SGollings) **3-9-0** WRyan(3) (hld up: plld out 3f out: sn outpcd: nvr able to chal)	2½	**3**	5/1 ^{3}	55 t	33
				(SP 107.9%)	**3 Rn**	

1m 14.99 (2.99) CSF £3.58 TOTE £2.80 (£1.60) OWNER Mr A. J. Morrison (EAST ILSLEY) BRED Mervyn Stewkesbury

672 Dame Laura (IRE), out of Group company and down in trip for the first time this season, made all in game style. (2/1: 6/4-9/4)

1610 Conspiracy has failed to shine so far this year, and never seriously looked like getting to the winner. (8/11)

3145 Caution, outclassed on paper, ran well without posing a threat. (5/1: 3/1-11/2)

3200 BRITAM INTERNATIONAL H'CAP (0-70) (3-Y.O+) (Class E)

8-10 (8-11) **1m 2f (July)** £4,110.00 (£1,230.00: £590.00: £270.00) Stalls: High GOING minus 0.16 sec per fur (GF)

				SP	RR	SF
3105^{8}	**Monte Cavo (52)** (MBrittain) **6-8-12** GBardwell(9) (in tch: pushed along 6f out: hdwy to ld over 1f out: drvn out)	—	**1**	12/1	64	46
2399*	**Jona Holley (49)** (GLMoore) **4-8-9** MFenton(16) (led 6f: led 2f out: sn hdd: kpt on fnl f)	1¼	**2**	5/1 ^{2}	59	41
3029*	**Snowy Mantle (43)** (JDBethell) **4-7-12**(5) ^{6x} RMullen(1) (plld hrd: w ldrs: led 4f out to 2f out: wknd fnl f)	3	**3**	7/2 ^{1}	48	30
1958^{12}	**Bubbly (70)** (JLDunlop) **3-9-7** GCarter(17) (prom: one pce fnl 2f)	¾	**4**	14/1	74	47
3091^{5}	**Westminster (IRE) (63)** (MHTompkins) **5-9-9v** AMcGlone(7) (hld up: hdwy 2f out: nvr rchd ldrs)	s.h	**5**	10/1	67	49
2782^{6}	**Cuban Reef (48)** (WJMusson) **5-8-8** DHarrison(15) (lw: stdd s: hdwy 5f out: swtchd lft over 2f out: nvr rchd ldrs)	5	**6**	8/1 ^{3}	44	26
3026^{7}	**Captain Marmalade (41)** (DTThom) **8-8-1** GDuffield(5) (b: hdwy 2f out: nrst fin)	¾	**7**	25/1	36	18
2281^{6}	**Golden Touch (USA) (54)** (DJSCosgrove) **5-9-0** JWeaver(6) (chsd ldr 6f)	2½	**8**	12/1	45	27
2843^{10}	**Mercury (IRE) (41)** (JAGlover) **4-8-1** RPrice(8) (chsd ldrs 7f)	2½	**9**	16/1	28	10
2512^{8}	**Alsahib (USA) (64)** (WRMuir) **4-9-10** WJO'Connor(12) (chsd ldrs: rdn over 3f out: sn btn)	2½	**10**	16/1	47	29
2885^{2}	**Mardrew (65)** (RHarris) **3-9-2** SSanders(13) (prom tl wknd over 2f out)	¾	**11**	9/1	47	20
2668^{2}	**Count Tony (65)** (SPCWoods) **3-9-2** WRyan(10) (s.i.s: nvr trbld ldrs)	s.h	**12**	12/1	46	19
2770^{5}	**Guesstimation (USA) (59)** (JPearce) **8-9-2**(3) CTeague(2) (hdwy over 3f out: sn rdn & btn)	nk	**13**	14/1	40	22
2873^{6}	**Grovefair Venture (64)** (KMahdi) **3-9-1** MRimmer(3) (prom: rdn 4f out: sn wknd)	½	**14**	25/1	44	17
2956^{3}	**Castles Burning (USA) (54)** (CACyzer) **3-8-2**(3) AWhelan(4) (lw: a bhd)	1½	**15**	16/1	32	5
	Strictly Hard (58) (GCBravery) **3-8-9** DRMcCabe(14) (a bhd)	8	**16**	20/1	23	—
2836^{3}	**Cold Steel (62)** (WJarvis) **3-8-13b** ^{1} RHills(11) (hdwy 7f out: wknd over 3f out)	hd	**17**	9/1	27	—
				(SP 145.6%)	**17 Rn**	

2m 8.24 (4.64) CSF £74.78 CT £249.84 TOTE £16.50: £3.90 £2.10 £1.70 £3.40 (£107.30) Trio £68.10 OWNER Mr Mel Brittain (WARTHILL) BRED Sheikh Mohammed bin Rashid al Maktoum

WEIGHT FOR AGE 3yo-9lb

2845 Monte Cavo, whose stable-companion Gold Desire has made this race his own, winning it twice in three seasons, made it three out of four for the stable with a strong, late run. Although a failure over a mile and a half already this season, he went close over eleven furlongs on Southwell's slow surface previously, and it is possible the full extent of his stamina is yet to be revealed. (12/1)
2399* Jona Holley confirmed that he gets the trip as he kept plugging away after looking booked for third. (5/1)
3029* Snowy Mantle, stepped back up in trip to try to take advantage of her mark before being re-handicapped, finished weakly after going for home some way out, and looks better over a mile. (7/2)
606* Bubbly lost the plot after his maiden win but, returning big and well after a seven-week break, ran much better over this longer trip. (14/1)
3091 Westminster (IRE), a good mover, got going too late on this occasion as he found himself with plenty to do once the leaders quickened. (10/1)
2782 Cuban Reef, another who comes from behind, found the race not run to suit her. (8/1: 6/1-9/1)

3201 E.B.F. BEACON MAIDEN STKS (2-Y.O) (Class D)

8-40 (8-45) **7f (July)** £4,175.00 (£1,250.00: £600.00: £275.00) Stalls: Low GOING minus 0.16 sec per fur (GF)

				SP	RR	SF
	Elshamms (ACStewart) **2-8-9** RHills(2) (gd sort: lw: w ldrs: led over 2f out: qcknd clr fnl f)	—	**1**	6/5[1]	77+	23
2680[7]	**Rabah** (JLDunlop) **2-9-0** GCarter(15) (lw: w ldrs: outpcd 2f out: kpt on fnl f)	3	**2**	5/1[3]	75	21
	Speaker's Chair (RCharlton) **2-9-0** WJO'Connor(8) (w'like: scope: mde most over 4f: one pce appr fnl f)	nk	**3**	14/1	75	21
	First Consul (USA) (MRStoute) **2-9-0** KBradshaw(4) (gd sort: scope: stdd s: hdwy 2f out: nt pce to chal)	2	**4**	14/1	70	16
	Shaanxi Romance (IRE) (MBell) **2-9-0** MFenton(7) (w'like: scope: s.i.s: hdwy over 1f out: r.o)	2½	**5**	16/1	64	10
	Taverner Society (IRE) (RWArmstrong) **2-9-0** RPrice(1) (cmpt: bkwd: hdwy 3f out: no imp appr fnl f)	¾	**6**	33/1	63	9
2176[7]	**O'Kelly (DEN)** (RGuest) **2-8-9** PBloomfield(3) (trckd ldrs: no hdwy fnl 2f)	1	**7**	40/1	55	1
2768[13]	**Prodigal Son (IRE)** (RJRWilliams) **2-9-0** GDuffield(13) (bmpd 2f out: nvr trbld ldrs)	1¼	**8**	33/1	57	3
	Forty Love (IRE) (JEBanks) **2-8-9**(5) GFaulkner(14) (cmpt: scope: in tch: rdn over 2f out: no imp)	nk	**9**	33/1	57	3
	Eco Friendly (JRFanshawe) **2-9-0** DHarrison(5) (wl grwn: bit bkwd: w ldr over 4f: sn rdn & wknd)	¾	**10**	20/1	55	1
	Hastate (WJarvis) **2-9-0** WRyan(10) (gd sort: bhd fnl 2f)	3½	**11**	10/1	47	—
2556[8]	**River Beat (IRE)** (MHTompkins) **2-9-0** AMcGlone(11) (lw: w ldrs over 4f)	½	**12**	40/1	46	—
	Guenivite (USA) (DRLoder) **2-8-6**(3) PMcCabe(12) (wl grwn: w ldrs tl wknd over 2f out)	s.h	**13**	16/1	41	—
	Five Fairies (NACallaghan) **2-8-9** GBardwell(9) (lt-f: leggy: s.s: rdn & hung lft 3f out: a bhd)	3	**14**	33/1	34	—
	Flight (LMCumani) **2-9-0** JWeaver(6) (neat: scope: stdd s: hld up & plld hrd: plld out 3f out: rdn & hung lft 2f out: sn wknd)	2½	**15**	9/2[2]	33	—
				(SP 135.9%)	**15 Rn**	

1m 29.94 (4.94) CSF £6.95 TOTE £2.40: £1.50 £2.20 £3.40 (£8.20) Trio £15.40 OWNER Mr Hamdan Al Maktoum (NEWMARKET) BRED Shadwell Estate Company Limited
Elshamms, a half-sister to the much vaunted but ultimately disappointing Shaya, has had the dogs barking too, but confirmed the hype, coming clear in devastating fashion. She looks very useful to say the least despite being a bit of a tail flasher in the preliminaries. (6/5: evens-6/4)
2680 Rabah, whose dam is a full-sister to Last Tycoon and a half-sister to Moon Flower and Flowerdrum, looked keen going down but saw the trip out well, coming home in good style after losing his position going into the dip. (5/1)
Speaker's Chair, whose dam is a half-sister to Rainbow Quest, shaped with great promise although looking in need of further already. (14/1: op 7/1)
First Consul (USA), a rather free half-brother to El Volador, took some settling but came home in decent style. (14/1: 6/1-16/1)
Shaanxi Romance (IRE), rather on the leg and a moderate mover, nonetheless caught the eye finishing in fine style and should win a race with normal progress. (16/1)
Taverner Society (IRE), a half-brother to the ill-fated chaser Henley Regatta, showed a good action going down and quite a bit of promise, although probably racing on the best ground. (33/1)
Eco Friendly was unruly when the bell went for the jockeys to mount and gave trouble at the start. Not fully wound up, he should do better as he grows up. (20/1)
Hastate, a really likeable first foal of Lupe winner Gisarne, didn't show an awful lot but will do much better in time. (10/1)
Flight, taken down steadily and missing the beat at the start, was far too free, ruining all chance. (9/2)

T/Plpt: £128.30 (120.79 Tckts). T/Qdpt: £22.70 (45.1 Tckts) Dk

2848-SALISBURY (R-H) (Good to firm)
Friday August 1st

WEATHER: overcast WIND: slight against

3202 NEWNHAM MAIDEN STKS (3-Y.O+) (Class D)

5-50 (5-54) **6f** £3,678.00 (£1,104.00: £532.00: £246.00) Stalls: High GOING minus 0.17 sec per fur (GF)

				SP	RR	SF
2838[6]	**Butrinto (73)** (MajorWRHern) **3-8-12** DHolland(10) (mde all: clr over 2f out: rdn over 1f out: r.o)	—	**1**	5/2[1]	75	34
	First Principle (CFWall) **3-8-12** WLord(2) (unf: scope: bit bkwd: hld up: hdwy fr 2f out: chsd wnr 1f out: r.o)	1¼	**2**	12/1	72	31
2506[8]	**Misty Point (65)** (IABalding) **3-8-7** SWhitworth(7) (hld up: pushed along ½-wy: hdwy over 1f out: styd on ins fnl f)	nk	**3**	15/2	66	25
2580[2]	**Taffs Well** (RAkehurst) **4-9-2** MTebbutt(6) (chsd wnr tl over 2f out: sn hrd rdn: one pce)	3	**4**	3/1[2]	63	26
2704[6]	**Beaucatcher (IRE)** (MJHeaton-Ellis) **3-8-7** SDrowne(1) (chsd ldrs tl wknd over 2f out)	6	**5**	14/1	42	1
2918[9]	**Bold Tina (IRE) (70)** (RHannon) **3-8-7** DaneO'Neill(5) (prom: pushed along ½-wy: wknd 2f out)	s.h	**6**	4/1[3]	42	1
2580[4]	**Turners Way** (SDow) **3-8-12** NCarlisle(4) (chsd wnr over 2f out to 1f out: wknd qckly ins fnl f)	1	**7**	9/1	44	3
	Hawksbill Henry (USA) (MrsAJPerrett) **3-8-5**(7) GayeHarwood(9) (w'like: bit bkwd: dwlt: a bhd)	6	**8**	16/1	28	—
2591[9]	**Borrador** (RCurtis) **3-8-12** JLowe(3) (a bhd)	½	**9**	50/1	27	—
	Jades Shadow (JJBridger) **4-8-13**(3) MHenry(8) (prom tl wknd over 3f out: t.o)	28	**10**	66/1	—	—
				(SP 119.0%)	**10 Rn**	

1m 16.5 (3.50) CSF £32.00 TOTE £3.30: £1.70 £3.10 £1.80 (£21.00) Trio £51.90 OWNER Lady Rothschild (LAMBOURN) BRED Lord Rothschild
WEIGHT FOR AGE 3yo-4lb
OFFICIAL EXPLANATION **Turners Way: bled from the nose.**
2838 Butrinto looked like winning this easily when clear approaching the two pole, but his stride shortened in the final furlong and he looked far from keen near the finish. (5/2)
First Principle ran a promising race here. Held up in the rear, he made steady headway through the final two furlongs without ever being put under severe pressure. He has the scope to improve, and is sure to pick up a similar race. (12/1)

1415 Misty Point was being pushed along to keep in touch at halfway, but to her credit kept staying on. This appears to be her trip. (15/2)
2580 Taffs Well was disappointing, coming under pressure around the halfway mark and gradually dropping away. (3/1)

3203 SPIRE FM H'CAP (0-70) (4-Y.O+) (Class E)
6-20 (6-31) **1m 6f** £3,034.75 (£913.00: £441.50: £205.75) Stalls: High GOING minus 0.17 sec per fur (GF)

				SP	RR	SF
2311[6]	**Height of Heights (IRE) (67)** (LadyHerries) **4-9-11** DHolland(4) (a.p: led over 2f out: hrd rdn over 1f out: r.o)	—	1	9/1	79	61
2867[2]	**Durham (59)** (GLMoore) **6-9-3b** SWhitworth(5) (hld up: rdn 5f out: stdy hdwy fr 3f out: chal strly fnl 2f: unable qckn cl home)	nk	2	5/2 [1]	71	53
3015[12]	**Courageous Knight (44)** (PHayward) **8-7-13**(3) MHenry(1) (rr: rdn 3f out: kpt on one pce fnl 2f)	6	3	9/1	49	31
2702[2]	**Hillswick (40)** (JSKing) **6-7-12** NAdams(3) (led: hdd over 2f out: grad wknd)	1	4	8/1 [3]	44	26
2592[8]	**Serious Trust (50)** (MrsLCJewell) **4-8-8** SophieMitchell(10) (hld up: rdn over 3f out: swtchd lft over 2f out: kpt on one pce ins fnl f)	½	5	20/1	53	35
	Courbaril (58) (MCPipe) **5-9-2b** JLowe(9) (bit bkwd: hld up: hdwy ½-wy: rdn over 3f out: sn btn)	¾	6	5/2 [1]	60	42
	Tommy Cooper (39) (MrsBarbaraWaring) **6-7-11v** FNorton(11) (b: prom tl wknd over 2f out)	s.h	7	33/1	41	23
3015[4]	**Fabulous Mtoto (56)** (MSSaunders) **7-9-0** JFortune(6) (keen hold: hdwy after 4f: ev ch over 2f out: sn rdn & wknd)	nk	8	12/1	58	40
2535[3]	**Oscar Rose (38)** (MJBolton) **4-7-10** NCarlisle(7) (a bhd)	11	9	40/1	27	9
2932[4]	**Coh Sho No (54)** (SDow) **4-8-12** DaneO'Neill(8) (w.r.s & uns rdr)		U	7/1 [2]	—	—
2874[4]	***Rose of Glenn (45)*** (BPalling) **6-8-3** CRutter(2) (Withdrawn not under Starter's orders: sddle slipped & uns rdr gng to s: rn loose)		W	12/1	—	—

(SP 126.3%) **10 Rn**

3m 4.82 (6.12) CSF £27.75 CT £173.09 TOTE £9.10: £2.60 £1.30 £2.60 (£12.20) Trio £94.20 OWNER Mrs Denis Haynes (LITTLEHAMPTON) BRED Wretham Stud
LONG HANDICAP Oscar Rose 6-12
OFFICIAL EXPLANATION Courbaril: no explanation offered.
1106 Height of Heights (IRE) looked far keener than the runner-up in a struggle. (9/1: 6/1-10/1)
2867 Durham appeared to throw this away. He looked sure to win when challenging below the distance, but appeared unwilling to go by. (5/2: 3/1-9/2)
2696 Courageous Knight struggled on in the final two furlongs without ever looking likely to take a hand. (9/1)
2702 Hillswick attempted to make all, but was put in his place in the final two furlongs. (8/1)
Courbaril looked just in need of this on his seasonal debut, and is presumably being readied for a jumps campaign. (5/2: 7/4-3/1)

3204 TRINITY CONDITIONS STKS (2-Y.O) (Class C)
6-50 (6-55) **6f** £4,650.50 (£1,688.00: £819.00: £345.00: £147.50) Stalls: High GOING minus 0.17 sec per fur (GF)

				SP	RR	SF
2295[4]	**Mushraaf** (JLDunlop) **2-8-10** BDoyle(4) (edgd lft s: hld up: swtchd lft over 2f out: hrd rdn over 1f out: str run fnl f: led last stride)	—	1	9/4 [3]	78	28
2860[2]	**Wrekin Pilot** (RHannon) **2-9-0** DaneO'Neill(5) (lw: led: clr over 1f out: hrd rdn ins fnl f: hdd last stride)	s.h	2	6/4 [1]	82	32
2768[7]	**Celestial Bay (IRE)** (AGFoster) **2-8-5** MTebbutt(1) (edgd rt s: chsd ldr: rdn over 1f out: unable qckn)	1½	3	20/1	69	19
2781*	**Lido (IRE)** (BWHills) **2-8-10** DHolland(3) (squeezed stly s: hld up: pushed along after 2f: hrd rdn over 1f out: one pce)	2	4	7/4 [2]	69	19

(SP 111.9%) **4 Rn**

1m 16.84 (3.84) CSF £5.69 TOTE £3.40 (£2.20) OWNER Mr Hamdan Al Maktoum (ARUNDEL) BRED London Thoroughbred Services Ltd and John Gaines
2295 Mushraaf looked anything but the winner at the two pole, but stayed on strongly in the final furlong to grab the spoils. He wants seven already. (9/4: 74/1-5/2)
2860 Wrekin Pilot looked sure to win below the distance, but was foiled by the winner's late run. (6/4)
2482 Celestial Bay (IRE) ran a sound race, chasing up the leaders throughout, but was unable to find the quickening touch. (20/1)
2781* Lido (IRE), squeezed slightly at the start, was being pushed along in the early stages, and never really threatened to take a hand. (7/4)

3205 GUINNESS H'CAP (0-70) (3-Y.O) (Class E)
7-20 (7-21) **1m** £3,207.00 (£966.00: £468.00: £219.00) Stalls: High GOING minus 0.17 sec per fur (GF)

				SP	RR	SF
2731[9]	**Rocky Dance (FR) (64)** (APJarvis) **3-9-1** SDrowne(8) (hld up: hdwy 3f out: led & edgd lft ins fnl f: r.o)	—	1	12/1	76	41
2878*	**Racing Heart (53)** (PJMakin) **3-8-4** DHolland(4) (hld up: n.m.r over 3f out: hdwy 2f out: chal strly whn hmpd & snatched up ins fnl f: swtchd rt: r.o wl: unlucky)	¾	2	4/1 [2]	64	29
2727[4]	**Warrior King (IRE) (45)** (CADwyer) **3-7-3**(7) DarrenWilliams(3) (a.p: led over 2f out: hdd & edgd rt ins fnl f: unable qckn)	nk	3	7/1	55	20
2566[10]	**Bogan (IRE) (65)** (LordHuntingdon) **3-9-2** BDoyle(9) (led: hdd over 2f out: wknd over 1f out)	6	4	14/1	63	28
2705[6]	**Free As A Bird (60)** (MRChannon) **3-8-11** RHughes(2) (prom: ev ch over 2f out: wknd over 1f out)	2	5	5/1 [3]	54	19
2695[9]	**Isca Maiden (45)** (PHayward) **3-7-10** NAdams(1) (chsd ldr tl ½-wy: wknd 3f out: t.o)	17	6	33/1	5	—
2945[5]	**Tycoon Girl (IRE) (70)** (BJMeehan) **3-9-7** MTebbutt(7) (hld up: hdwy over 3f out: wknd over 2f out: t.o)	nk	7	15/2	29	—
2510[12]	**Balladara (IRE) (56)** (RHannon) **3-8-7** DaneO'Neill(5) (a bhd: t.o)	2	8	12/1	11	—
3038*	**Polarize (58)** (TDBarron) **3-8-9b** 5x JFortune(6) (chsd ldrs: cl up whn broke leg & p.u over 3f: dead)		P	3/1 [1]	—	—

(SP 110.9%) **9 Rn**

1m 44.42 (4.42) CSF £51.08 CT £323.29 TOTE £16.50: £3.30 £2.10 £2.20 (£22.60) Trio £23.50 OWNER Mrs Ann Jarvis (ASTON UPTHORPE) BRED Gainsborough Stud Management Ltd
LONG HANDICAP Isca Maiden 7-5
STEWARDS' ENQUIRY Williams susp. 10-13/8/97 (careless riding).
1322 Rocky Dance (FR) was brought through to challenge inside the final furlong, but has to be considered fortunate to hang on for victory. (12/1: 8/1-14/1)
2878* Racing Heart was very unlucky. Held up towards the rear, she was hampered three furlongs out, and then when making good headway to challenge inside the final furlong, Holland had to snatch right up as both the winner and the third squeezed her out. Switched right, she ran on gamely but did not have enough time to make up the leeway. She can be considered a winner without a penalty. (4/1: op 5/2)
2727 Warrior King (IRE) took it up over two furlongs out, and caused most of the damage by hanging to his right inside the final furlong. (7/1)
3038* Polarize was going well just behind the leaders when breaking a leg. (3/1)

3206 DOWNING CLAIMING STKS (3-Y.O) (Class F)

7-50 (7-51) **6f** £2,679.00 (£744.00: £357.00) Stalls: High GOING minus 0.17 sec per fur (GF)

				SP	RR	SF
968^{9}	**Salty Behaviour (IRE) (83)** (RHannon) **3-9-4** DaneO'Neill(4) (a.p: led over 2f out: rdn over 1f out: r.o)	—	**1**	$11/4^{1}$	76	41
2883^{2}	**Gunners Glory (56)** (BJMeehan) **3-8-2b** DBiggs(6) (hld up: hdwy 3f out: ev ch ins fnl f: unable qckn)	1	**2**	$4/1^{2}$	57	22
	Glen Ogil (IABalding) **3-8-6** SWhitworth(7) (w'like: bit bkwd: hld up: hdwy 2f out: rdn over 1f out: styd on ins fnl)	1¼	**3**	16/1	58	23
2724^{8}	**Dorado Beach (34)** (LGCottrell) **3-8-5** NCarlisle(3) (a.p: hmpd over 1f out: styd on one pce ins fnl f)	hd	**4**	33/1	57	22
2734^{5}	**Petite Danseuse (65)** (CADwyer) **3-8-1** NVarley(12) (swtg: a.p: led over 3f out: hdd over 2f out: wknd over 1f out)	3½	**5**	$4/1^{2}$	43	8
2836^{10}	**Moon Song (57)** (APJarvis) **3-8-9** SDrowne(8) (chsd ldrs: rdn over 2f out: wknd over 1f out)	1½	**6**	11/1	47	12
2921^{9}	**Whizz Kid (45)** (JJBridger) **3-7-4**(7) PDoe(9) (chsd ldrs: rdn over 3f out: wknd over 1f out)	hd	**7**	16/1	35	—
2954^{8}	**Prince of Fortune (45)** (MBlanshard) **3-8-4** NAdams(5) (led: hdd over 3f out: wknd over 2f out)	1½	**8**	16/1	38	3
2947^{13}	**Moredun (IRE)** (IABalding) **3-8-2** CRutter(11) (t: a bhd)	8	**9**	14/1	15	—
	Copenhagen (JAkehurst) **3-8-5** MTebbutt(1) (a bhd)	3½	**10**	16/1	9	—
3121^{11}	**Broadway Melody (63)** (APJarvis) **3-8-9** JLowe(10) (prom tl wknd over 2f out)	4	**11**	$6/1^{3}$	2	—

(SP 122.4%) **11 Rn**

1m 16.42 (3.42) CSF £12.78 TOTE £3.40: £1.70 £1.30 £3.30 (£4.70) Trio £36.80 OWNER Mr J. R. Shannon (MARLBOROUGH) BRED Airlie Stud

Glen Ogil clmd W Harrison £6,000

Salty Behaviour (IRE) had not run for eighty-nine days but looked fit enough. He took it up going well over two furlongs out, and saw it out nicely. (11/4)

2883 Gunners Glory challenged strongly in the final two furlongs, but could not quite get his head in front. (4/1)

Glen Ogil made a promising debut, staying on nicely in the final two furlongs. Quite a big gelding, he will no doubt improve. (16/1)

Dorado Beach was slightly unlucky, being hampered below the distance, but he gave the impression that he would only have been third at best. (33/1)

2734 Petite Danseuse took it up over three furlongs out. Headed a furlong later, she did not last much longer. (4/1)

2921 Broadway Melody (6/1: op 7/2)

3207 MAGDALENE H'CAP (0-80) (3-Y.O+ F & M) (Class D)

8-20 (8-22) **6f 212y** £3,886.00 (£1,168.00: £564.00: £262.00) Stalls: High GOING minus 0.17 sec per fur (GF)

				SP	RR	SF
2835^{6}	**Q Factor (78)** (DHaydnJones) **5-10-0** SDrowne(5) (lw: a.p: rdn over 2f out: led 1f out: r.o)	—	**1**	$7/1^{3}$	90	51
2020*	**Karawan (76)** (JHMGosden) **3-9-6** GHind(9) (led: hdd 1f out: unable qckn)	1½	**2**	$11/8^{1}$	85	40
2745^{3}	**Octavia Hill (52)** (PWHarris) **4-7-11**(5) CLowther(4) (chsd ldrs: rdn & outpcd over 2f out: styd on again ins fnl f)	nk	**3**	$5/1^{2}$	60	21
2216^{4}	**Newlands Corner (56)** (JAkehurst) **4-8-6b** MTebbutt(1) (hld up: hdwy over 2f out: sn rdn: one pce)	1½	**4**	9/1	60	21
3092^{7}	**Blues Queen (78)** (MRChannon) **3-9-8** RHughes(8) (hld up: hrd rdn over 2f out: no hdwy)	1½	**5**	12/1	79	34
2945*	**La Dolce Vita (72)** (TDBarron) **3-9-2** 6x JFortune(6) (hld up: hdwy over 2f out: wknd appr fnl f)	½	**6**	$5/1^{2}$	72	27
2730^{3}	**Calamander (IRE) (65)** (WRMuir) **3-8-6**(3) DO'Donohoe(7) (prom: rdn 3f out: sn wknd)	9	**7**	$7/1^{3}$	44	—
1987^{4}	***Good News (IRE) (62)*** (MMadgwick) **3-8-6b** NVarley(3) (Withdrawn not under Starter's orders: jockey injured in stalls)		**W**	12/1	—	—

(SP 125.8%) **7 Rn**

1m 30.04 (4.04) CSF £15.78 CT £44.58 TOTE £7.70: £2.60 £1.70 (£7.70) Trio £17.50 OWNER Mr H. G. Collis (PONTYPRIDD) BRED A. Sofroniou and H. Collis

WEIGHT FOR AGE 3yo-6lb

2835 Q Factor put up a game performance here under top weight, responding well to pressure in the final two furlongs to get on top inside the last. (7/1: op 4/1)

2020* Karawan made a bold bid to make all, but found the winner too strong in the final furlong. (11/8)

2745 Octavia Hill lost a prominent position when getting outpaced approaching the two pole. Although staying on again late, the damage was done. (5/1: op 8/1)

2216 Newlands Corner made a move approaching the two pole, but had only the one pace to give from below the distance. (9/1)

2517 Blues Queen (12/1: 10/1-16/1)

2945* La Dolce Vita was a little bit disappointing here. She made a short-lived effort with two furlongs to run, before weakening inside the last. (5/1: op 3/1)

T/Plpt: £95.30 (97.09 Tckts). T/Qdpt: £14.10 (48.24 Tckts) SM

3033-THIRSK (L-H) (Good)

Friday August 1st

WEATHER: overcast WIND: fresh bhd

3208 GO RACING IN YORKSHIRE H'CAP (0-80) (3-Y.O+) (Class D)

2-25 (2-26) **6f** £3,897.50 (£1,175.00: £570.00: £267.50) Stalls: High GOING minus 0.18 sec per fur (GF)

				SP	RR	SF
3034^{2}	**Grand Chapeau (IRE) (51)** (DNicholls) **5-8-4**ow1 SSanders(15) (lw: mde all: clr 2f out: r.o wl)	—	**1**	$5/2^{1}$	63	32
3034^{3}	**Camionneur (IRE) (48)** (TDEasterby) **4-8-1b** LCharnock(3) (s.s: hdwy ½-wy: styd on: no ch w wnr)	3	**2**	16/1	52	22
3034*	**Benzoe (IRE) (80)** (MrsJRRamsden) **7-10-5** 7x DHarrison(12) (lw: s.i.s: hdwy & nt clr run ½-wy: styd on wl fnl f)	1¾	**3**	$11/4^{2}$	79	48
2934^{8}	**Johayro (59)** (JSGoldie) **4-8-12** ACulhane(14) (cl up: rdn over 2f out: one pce)	1½	**4**	12/1	54	25
3077^{9}	**Rich Glow (53)** (NBycroft) **6-8-6** JCarroll(6) (bhd tl r.o fnl 2f)	hd	**5**	16/1	48	19
2857^{6}	**Smokey From Caplaw (74)** (JJO'Neill) **3-9-9** RLappin(13) (a chsng ldrs: outpcd whn hmpd ent fnl f: nt rcvr)	2	**6**	$8/1^{3}$	64	30
3024^{4}	**The Happy Fox (IRE) (73)** (BAMcMahon) **5-9-12b** LNewton(9) (lw: chsd ldrs tl grad wknd fnl 2f)	2½	**7**	14/1	56	26
2900^{3}	**Amron (61)** (JBerry) **10-8-9**(5) TEDurcan(11) (in tch: effrt ½-wy: no imp)	3½	**8**	10/1	35	7
3066^{3}	**Bowlers Boy (72)** (JJQuinn) **4-9-8**(3) GParkin(5) (lw: in tch 4f)	1¾	**9**	20/1	41	13
2711^{20}	**Thwaab (66)** (FWatson) **5-9-5b** GHind(2) (lw: sn outpcd & bhd)	¾	**10**	16/1	33	5
2788^{4}	**Souperficial (52)** (NTinkler) **6-8-5v** KimTinkler(10) (racd centre fr ½-wy: n.d)	nk	**11**	20/1	18	—

2934[2]	**Young Ben (IRE) (44)** (JSWainwright) **5-7-11b**ow1 TWilliams(4) (b.hind: gd spd over 4f)	hd	**12**	10/1	10	—
2755*	**Spotted Eagle (61)** (DNicholls) **4-9-0** AlexGreaves(7) (lw: in tch 4f)	2½	**13**	25/1	20	—
2933[7]	**Meranti (61)** (JMBradley) **4-9-0** GCarter(8) (in tch to ½-wy)	7	**14**	16/1	2	—
				(SP 135.8%)		**14 Rn**

1m 12.6 (2.90) CSF £45.80 CT £121.92 TOTE £3.00: £1.30 £4.20 £1.60 (£25.00) Trio £29.90 OWNER Mr David Faulkner (THIRSK) BRED Norelands Bloodstock
WEIGHT FOR AGE 3yo-4lb

3034 Grand Chapeau (IRE) had the best draw and as he has shown in the past has speed aplenty. Leaving nothing to chance this week, had this won a long way out. (5/2)
3034 Camionneur (IRE), a real character, did his usual and finished strongly after a slow start. He rarely wins but has the ability and always had to be considered for a place. (16/1)
3034* Benzoe (IRE) found all sorts of trouble this time and but for this would have been a deal closer. (11/4: op 6/1)
2754 Johayro had a good draw and ran well, but was never good enough in the last couple of furlongs. (12/1)
2844 Rich Glow is in good heart should he return to Ayr in the near future. (16/1)
2857 Smokey From Caplaw ran reasonably, but was struggling when almost getting put over the rails entering the final furlong. (8/1)

3209 LEWIS GEIPEL MEMORIAL CHALLENGE CUP NURSERY H'CAP (2-Y.O) (Class D)
2-55 (2-55) **5f** £3,624.50 (£1,091.00: £528.00: £246.50) Stalls: High GOING minus 0.18 sec per fur (GF)

				SP	RR	SF
2712[5]	**Baby Grand (IRE)** (TDBarron) **2-8-5**(5) KimberleyHart(7) (chsd ldrs: led ins fnl f: r.o)	—	**1**	5/1[3]	80	29
2713[4]	**Shalyah (IRE)** (MrsJRRamsden) **2-7-5**(5) RMullen(1) (lw: outpcd ½-wy: styd on wl appr fnl f: nvr able to chal)	1½	**2**	7/1	61	12
*2606**	**Beechwood Quest (IRE)** (BSRothwell) **2-7-10be** LCharnock(5) (led: hung lft thrght: hdd & no ex ins fnl f)	3½	**3**	3/1[2]	50	2
2066[4]	**Bow Peep (IRE)** (MWEasterby) **2-7-10** DaleGibson(6) (lw: in tch: kpt on one pce fnl 2f)	1¾	**4**	14/1	44	—
2823*	**Oriel Girl** (PDEvans) **2-7-8v**(3) PFessey(3) (cl up tl rdn & btn over 1f out)	1½	**5**	11/2	41	—
2739[2]	**Cumbrian Cadet** (TDEasterby) **2-8-4b** JCarroll(4) (lw: chsd ldrs tl wknd appr fnl f)	3	**6**	14/1	38	—
2862[4]	**Yorkies Boy** (BAMcMahon) **2-9-7** LNewton(2) (outpcd & lost tch fr ½-wy)	¾	**7**	5/2[1]	53	4
1614[6]	**Seventh Heaven** (DNicholls) **2-7-5**(5) IonaWands(8) (a outpcd & bhd)	1¼	**8**	33/1	24	—
				(SP 114.4%)		**8 Rn**

60.5 secs (2.90) CSF £35.96 CT £112.06 TOTE £6.00: £1.80 £1.80 £1.50 (£35.90) OWNER Mrs D. E. Sharp (THIRSK) BRED Rathbarry Stud
OFFICIAL EXPLANATION **Yorkies Boy: the rider reported that the going was not firm enough for the colt.**

2712 Baby Grand (IRE) is game and consistent, and had the race set up for her here and won it authoritatively. (5/1)
2713 Shalyah (IRE) found things happening too quickly early on, but finished well suggesting there is much better to come. (7/1)
2606* Beechwood Quest (IRE) spoilt her chances by hanging left, and would seem better suited when she can get a rail on that side to race against. (3/1)
2066 Bow Peep (IRE) showed enough to suggest that there is a race to be picked up. (14/1)
2823* Oriel Girl had no excuses and got run out of it approaching the final furlong. (11/2)
2739 Cumbrian Cadet again had his chances but he looked none too keen when ridden. (14/1)
2862 Yorkies Boy ran miserably and never looked happy at any stage. (5/2)

3210 PETER BELL MEMORIAL H'CAP (0-70) (3-Y.O F) (Class E)
3-30 (3-30) **1m 4f** £3,168.00 (£954.00: £462.00: £216.00) Stalls: High GOING minus 0.18 sec per fur (GF)

				SP	RR	SF
2763[6]	**Top (62)** (JRFanshawe) **3-9-7** SSanders(1) (w ldr: led over 3f out: qcknd: styd on wl)	—	**1**	16/1	71	32
2783[4]	**Shilling (IRE) (60)** (ACStewart) **3-9-5** DHarrison(2) (led tl hdd over 3f out: kpt on one pce)	2	**2**	3/1[2]	66	28
2763*	**Atnab (USA) (60)** (PTWalwyn) **3-9-5** JCarroll(6) (lw: hld up: effrt 5f out: styd on u.p fnl 2f: nt pce to chal)	hd	**3**	15/8[1]	66	28
3074[2]	**Perlethorpe (54)** (MBell) **3-8-8**(5) RMullen(4) (a chsng ldrs: one pce fnl 3f)	3	**4**	9/2[3]	56	19
2757[2]	**Kingdom Pearl (49)** (MJCamacho) **3-8-8** LCharnock(7) (prom tl outpcd fnl 2f)	½	**5**	11/2	51	14
	Chairmans Daughter (62) (JPearce) **3-9-4**(3) CTeague(3) (in tch: effrt to chse ldrs appr st: btn over 3f out)	8	**6**	25/1	53	16
3074[7]	**Mirror Four Sport (45)** (SRBowring) **3-7-11**(7) FBoyle(5) (bhd: outpcd 5f out: n.d)	2½	**7**	25/1	33	—
2399[7]	**Doyenne (43)** (GLewis) **3-7-13**(3) PFessey(8) (lw: bhd: drvn along 4f out: n.d)	3½	**8**	13/2	26	—
				(SP 120.3%)		**8 Rn**

2m 39.7 (9.00) CSF £61.09 CT £124.06 TOTE £17.90: £2.40 £1.60 £1.50 (£19.50) OWNER Lord Halifax (NEWMARKET) BRED Lord Halifax
OFFICIAL EXPLANATION **Top: regarding the improvement in form, the trainer reported that he had no explanation for the filly's poor performance last time, other than that she can be temperamental and was able to dominate here.**

2763 Top was completely transformed here and, always going nicely, put her stamp on the race early in the straight. In this mood she is quite useful. (16/1)
2783 Shilling (IRE) stays well enough but looks short of a turn of foot. (3/1)
2763* Atnab (USA), ridden from just off the pace this time, found this track a bit on the sharp side but was staying on well at the finish. She should have no difficulty in staying further. (15/8)
3074 Perlethorpe stays but is short of any real speed. (9/2)
2757 Kingdom Pearl was always well enough placed if good enough, but when ridden in the straight her limitations were quickly exposed. (11/2: 4/1-6/1)
Chairmans Daughter was having her first run of the season, and over a longer trip, without the blinkers in which she won last year, she blew up someway from home. (25/1)

3211 WEATHERBYS BREEDING SALES MAIDEN STKS (3-Y.O+) (Class D)
4-00 (4-01) **1m** £3,601.75 (£1,084.00: £524.50: £244.75) Stalls: Low GOING minus 0.18 sec per fur (GF)

				SP	RR	SF
2960[3]	**Blot** (MrsJCecil) **3-8-12** JCarroll(10) (lw: b.hind: in tch: hdwy ent st: led 2½f out: r.o wl)	—	**1**	5/2[1]	88	32
3037[2]	**Barnburgh Boy (72)** (TDBarron) **3-8-12** DHarrison(8) (hld up: gd hdwy appr st: effrt over 2f out: kpt on: nt pce to chal)	3½	**2**	5/1[3]	81	26
3052[7]	**Present Chance (78)** (BAMcMahon) **3-8-12** LNewton(4) (chsd ldrs: chal 2½f out: nt qckn)	½	**3**	11/2	80	25
	Talib (USA) (DMorley) **3-8-12** GCarter(2) (s.i.s: stdy hdwy 2f out: nvr plcd to chal)	12	**4**	10/1	56	4
	Royale Rose (FR) (ABailey) **3-8-7** DWright(13) (a chsng ldrs: outpcd fnl 3f)	5	**5**	20/1	41	—
2549[8]	**Es Go** (RBastiman) **4-9-0**(5) HBastiman(3) (dwlt: hld up & bhd: nvr plcd to chal)	3½	**6**	50/1	39	—
2960[4]	**Fatal Baraari** (MRStoute) **3-8-12v**[1] FLynch(1) (lw: led tl hdd 2½f out: sn btn)	2	**7**	7/2[2]	35	—
2888[3]	**Beach Buoy (IRE)** (CaptJWilson) **3-8-7**(5) PRoberts(11) (nvr bttr than mid div)	½	**8**	33/1	34	—
	Flower Miller (JHanson) **4-9-5** EJohnson(6) (chsd ldrs: sn pushed along: wknd fnl 3f)	3	**9**	33/1	28	—

2902[4]	**The Vale (IRE)** (RMMcKellar) **5-8-12**(7) JMcAuley(9) (n.d)	1¼	**10**	250/1	26	—
	Beguine (USA) (WJarvis) **3-8-7** SSanders(7) (lw: sn drvn along: lost tch fnl 3½f)	3	**11**	13/2	15	—
	Jive Boogie (NBycroft) **3-8-12** LCharnock(5) (a rr div)	5	**12**	500/1	10	—
2873[12]	**Lyphielo (USA)** (LMCumani) **3-8-7** GHind(12) (cl up tl wknd fnl 3f)	3½	**13**	16/1	—	—
				(SP 124.4%)		**13 Rn**

1m 41.3 (4.80) CSF £13.96 TOTE £2.30: £1.50 £1.80 £2.10 (£8.70) Trio £18.40 OWNER Bernard Gover Bloodstock Trading Ltd (NEWMARKET) BRED Miss I. G. and Miss E. G. MacGregor

WEIGHT FOR AGE 3yo-7lb

2960 Blot has really got his act together and won well, and ought to stay further. (5/2)

3037 Barnburgh Boy, stepping up in trip yet again, put in another decent effort and deserves a change of luck. (5/1)

2708 Present Chance keeps running well without winning, and probably needs to find an easier race to boost his confidence. (11/2)

Talib (USA) having his first run of the season, showed plenty of promise and, over further, he should improve a good deal. (10/1)

Royale Rose (FR), a French import, ran well in blinkers last time when racing in that country, and this was not too bad an effort without them. (20/1)

2315 Es Go had another dress rehearsal here, and showed plenty without getting anywhere near, and when the market speaks he will be one to watch. (50/1)

2960 Fatal Baraari, in a visor for the first time, ran too freely and gave up once tackled. (7/2)

Beguine (USA) (13/2: 4/1-7/1)

3212 CARPENTER'S ARMS CLAIMING STKS (2-Y.O) (Class F)

4-30 (4-31) **7f** £2,845.00 (£795.00: £385.00) Stalls: Low GOING minus 0.18 sec per fur (GF)

				SP	RR	SF
2784[7]	**Suggest** (WStorey) **2-8-6** SSanders(2) (led tl ½-wy: led appr fnl f: styd on wl)	—	**1**	20/1	70	22
*3045**	**Operatic** (MBell) **2-7-9**(5) RMullen(12) (sn pushed along: rr div tl styd on wl fnl 3f)	2½	**2**	4/1[2]	58	11
2936[5]	**Petara (IRE)** (JSWainwright) **2-8-9v1** RLappin(3) (lw: cl up: led ½-wy tl appr fnl f: sn btn)	3	**3**	11/4[1]	60	13
2936[7]	**Three Tenners** (JBerry) **2-8-3b**(3) PFessey(11) (a chsng ldrs: one pce fnl 3f)	2½	**4**	5/1	52	6
2493[13]	**Disco Tex** (MWEasterby) **2-8-9** TLucas(8) (outpcd & bhd: hdwy 2f out: nrst fin)	hd	**5**	33/1	55	8
1819[9]	**Silver Hope (IRE)** (RHollinshead) **2-8-9** FLynch(6) (outpcd & bhd: styd on wl fnl 3f: nrst fin)	hd	**6**	14/1	54	8
2904[4]	**I'm Tef** (TDEasterby) **2-8-6** LCharnock(1) (chsd ldrs: effrt ent st: wknd over 2f out)	5	**7**	9/2[3]	40	—
2935[2]	**Ribble Assembly** (RAFahey) **2-8-11** JCarroll(10) (hld up & bhd: sme hdwy 2f out: n.d)	4	**8**	5/1	36	—
2493[10]	**Musical Pet (IRE)** (JLEyre) **2-7-13** TWilliams(7) (nvr trbld ldrs)	½	**9**	33/1	23	—
2881[9]	**Eddie Rombo** (NTinkler) **2-8-7** KimTinkler(5) (chsd ldrs tl wknd fnl 3f)	5	**10**	33/1	19	—
2493[9]	**Are Yer There** (MWEasterby) **2-8-4**(3) GParkin(9) (c wd & rdn over 5f out: sn bhd)	3	**11**	33/1	12	—
	Drain Doctor (SEKettlewell) **2-8-5** ACulhane(4) (leggy: bit bkwd: s.i.s: a outpcd & wl bhd)	dist	**12**	33/1	—	21
				(SP 124.3%)		**12 Rn**

1m 29.6 (4.70) CSF £89.04 TOTE £22.00: £4.10 £1.40 £1.90 (£64.50) Trio £184.10; £57.06 to Goodwood 2/8/97 OWNER Bellcoil Ltd (CONSETT) BRED F. M. Kalla

Suggest clmd M F Nolan £6,000

2784 Suggest, having only his fourth run, is now in his third stable. He showed fine courage to win this and looks to be really getting things right. (20/1)

3045* Operatic takes an age to get going, but she certainly stays and that will bring its rewards. (4/1: op 5/2)

2936 Petara (IRE), in a visor for the first time, was made a lot of use of and cried enough approaching the last furlong. (11/4)

2587 Three Tenners had the blinkers back on this time, but they didn't help as things were always happening too quickly for her liking when the pressure was on early in the straight. (5/1)

Disco Tex looks to have some improving to do physically, but showed ability here, staying on well after getting outpaced and running green in the early stages (33/1)

Silver Hope (IRE), who showed nothing on his debut, gave signs of something better here by responding to pressure from halfway. (14/1)

3213 NAG'S HEAD MAIDEN APPRENTICE H'CAP (0-70) (3-Y.O+) (Class F)

5-05 (5-05) **7f** £2,532.50 (£720.00: £357.50) Stalls: Low GOING minus 0.18 sec per fur (GF)

				SP	RR	SF
3039[3]	**Fancy A Fortune (IRE) (60)** (DNicholls) **3-9-4**(5) ANicholls(1) (lw: mde all: kpt on wl fnl f)	—	**1**	11/8[1]	70	46
2878[5]	**Italian Symphony (IRE) (38)** (PDEvans) **3-8-1b** AMcCarthy(2) (a cl up: ev ch over 2f out: nt qckn fnl f)	1	**2**	9/1	46	24
2659[5]	**Carreamia (51)** (JLEyre) **4-9-6** SBuckley(3) (in tch: styd on fnl 2f: nvr able to chal)	5	**3**	5/1[3]	47	31
2937[9]	**Stolen Music (IRE) (30)** (REBarr) **4-7-13** JennyBenson(10) (dwlt: wl bhd tl styd on fnl 3f)	5	**4**	16/1	15	2
2152[7]	**Intrepid Fort (27)** (BWMurray) **8-7-10v** CCogan(4) (chsd ldrs tl outpcd fnl 2½f)	nk	**5**	20/1	11	—
2521[12]	**Petula Boy (33)** (SRBowring) **3-7-10b** FBoyle(7) (nvr able to rch ldrs)	1½	**6**	16/1	14	—
3088[5]	**Presentiment (50)** (MartynWane) **3-8-8**(5) DMulhall(9) (s.i.s: nvr trbld ldrs)	½	**7**	4/1[2]	30	10
3018[8]	**Severn Mill (27)** (JMBradley) **6-7-10** JFowle(6) (in tch tl st: sn rdn & btn)	hd	**8**	10/1	6	—
	Legal Brief (30) (JSWainwright) **5-7-13b** RBrisland(8) (prom tl st: sn wl bhd)	16	**9**	33/1	—	—
	Penygarn Guv'nor (55) (JMBradley) **4-9-10** JMcAuley(5) (cl up tl st: wknd qckly & t.o)	30	**10**	14/1	—	—
				(SP 124.0%)		**10 Rn**

1m 28.8 (3.90) CSF £15.03 CT £49.65 TOTE £2.10: £1.10 £2.40 £1.50 (£6.80) Trio £10.80 OWNER E W & M Tuer (THIRSK) BRED Mellon Stud

LONG HANDICAP Severn Mill 7-9 Intrepid Fort 7-3

WEIGHT FOR AGE 3yo-6lb

IN-FOCUS: This was the first winner for Adrian Nicholls, sixteen-year-old son of trainer David.

3039 Fancy A Fortune (IRE) got it right this week and, very ably handled, did it nicely. (11/8: 4/5-6/4)

2501 Italian Symphony (IRE) showed his first signs of real form for his new stable here, and his attitude might just be changing. (9/1)

2659 Carreamia, wearing a tongue-strap, did her usual and only ran when it was too late, and may need further help. (5/1)

Stolen Music (IRE) had a rider who is a come from behind specialist, but after a very poor start here she always had too much on, but did give some signs of hope. (16/1)

Intrepid Fort, who has never won a race in forty attempts, was put under pressure early in the straight and never looked likely to lose that record. (20/1)

Penygarn Guv'nor (14/1: op 33/1)

T/Plpt: £24.90 (557.42 Tckts). T/Qdpt: £4.10 (213.88 Tckts) AA

3189-GOODWOOD (R-H) (Good to firm, Rnd crse Firm patches)
Saturday August 2nd
WEATHER: hot WIND: almost nil

3214 VODAFONE CONDITIONS STKS (3-Y.O) (Class B)
2-15 (2-16) **1m** £13,256.00 (£4,904.00: £2,352.00: £960.00: £380.00: £148.00) Stalls: High GOING minus 0.23 sec per fur (GF)

				SP	RR	SF
3048^{2}	**Cape Cross (IRE) (110)** (JHMGosden) **3-8-12** LDettori(3) (b.hind: lw: chsd ldr: led 2f out: rdn over 1f out: r.o wl)	—	**1**	3/1^{2}	113	80
2586^{4}	**Dragonada (USA) (102)** (HRACecil) **3-8-11** KFallon(4) (lw: led: rdn 3f out: hdd 2f out: unable qckn)	2½	**2**	7/1^{3}	107	74
2774^{3}	**Kenmist** (LMCumani) **3-8-7** KDarley(5) (a.p: rdn 3f out: r.o one pce fnl f)	nk	**3**	20/1	102	69
2011^{7}	**Running Stag (USA) (107)** (PMitchell) **3-8-12** PatEddery(6) (lw: rdn 3f out: hdwy over 1f out: r.o one pce)	nk	**4**	10/1	107	74
1767^{2}	**Faithful Son (USA) (112)** (MRStoute) **3-9-2** JReid(1) (hld up: rdn over 2f out: one pce)	1¾	**5**	8/11^{1}	107	74
3189^{3}	**Omaha City (IRE) (99)** (BGubby) **3-8-12** AClark(2) (a bhd)	4	**6**	40/1	95	62

(SP 111.7%) **6 Rn**

1m 37.01 (-0.19) CSF £20.99 TOTE £3.50: £1.70 £2.40 (£9.00) OWNER Sheikh Mohammed (NEWMARKET) BRED Sheikh Mohammed Bin Rashid Al Maktoum

OFFICIAL EXPLANATION Faithful Son (USA): no explanation offered.

3048 Cape Cross (IRE), who should have won at Ascot last Saturday, made no mistake on this occasion. Better suited by the return to a fast surface, he gained control a quarter-of-a-mile out, and rousted along, asserted his authority. (3/1)

2586 Dragonada (USA) attempted to make all the running, but she was off the bridle early in the straight, and collared two furlongs from home, failed to find another gear. She gives the impression that a step up in distance would help. (7/1)

2774 Kenmist found this trip on the sharp side, and although never far away, she was being pushed along early in the straight. She did stay on in the closing stages, and only just failed to take second prize. She is now qualified for handicaps, and having won over a mile-and-a-quarter on soft ground, could be an interesting prospect if stepped back up in trip. (20/1)

2011 Running Stag (USA), back in more his own class here, having run in the St James's Palace Stakes at Royal Ascot, struggled on from below the distance, if never seriously threatening. A return to a mile-and-a-quarter would be in his favour. (10/1: 7/1-11/1)

1767 Faithful Son (USA) was very disappointing, for Reid was beginning to get at him early in the straight, and the response was negligible. Maybe the ground was faster than he would have liked, and he is worth another chance on a slightly easier surface. (8/11)

3189 Omaha City (IRE), third here the day before, was out of his depth in this race, and was always at the back. He is proving very difficult to place. (40/1)

3215 VODAFONE NURSERY H'CAP (2-Y.O) (Class C)
2-45 (2-46) **7f** £11,275.00 (£3,400.00: £1,650.00: £775.00) Stalls: High GOING minus 0.23 sec per fur (GF)

				SP	RR	SF
*2706**	**Merlin's Ring (85)** (IABalding) **2-9-5** LDettori(2) (hdwy over 2f out: led over 1f out: all out)	—	**1**	11/4^{1}	95	57
*2595**	**Mantles Star (82)** (GLewis) **2-9-2** PaulEddery(12) (lw: stdy hdwy on ins 3f out: nt clr run wl over 1f out & 1f out: swtchd lft: r.o wl ins fnl f)	hd	**2**	13/2^{3}	92+	54
2786^{4}	**King Darius (IRE) (78)** (RHannon) **2-8-12** DaneO'Neill(4) (rdn over 2f out: hdwy over 1f out: r.o wl ins fnl f)	4	**3**	16/1	79	41
2700*	**Fayrana (IRE) (80)** (JWHills) **2-9-0** KFallon(8) (a.p: rdn over 4f out: ev ch 2f out: unable qckn)	nk	**4**	7/1	80	42
2644a^{6}	**Shawdon (86)** (SirMarkPrescott) **2-9-6** GDuffield(9) (lw: chsd ldr: led over 2f out tl over 1f out: wknd ins fnl f)	¾	**5**	8/1	84	46
2371^{4}	**Gypsy Hill (79)** (DHaydnJones) **2-8-13** SDrowne(3) (rdn over 3f out: hdwy over 1f out: nvr nrr)	5	**6**	20/1	66	28
2714*	**The Rich Man (IRE) (87)** (BWHills) **2-9-7** MHills(6) (prom over 5f)	1¼	**7**	5/1^{2}	71	33
2587*	**Bellow (IRE) (72)** (HMorrison) **2-8-1**(5) CLowther(1) (lw: led: sn clr: hdd over 2f out: sn wknd)	hd	**8**	14/1	56	18
2681^{7}	**Red Maple (USA) (70)** (PFICole) **2-8-4b^{1}** FNorton(7) (bhd fnl 3f)	3	**9**	25/1	47	9
2741^{4}	**Persian Venture (71)** (BJMeehan) **2-8-5** KDarley(5) (a bhd)	2½	**10**	33/1	42	4
2363^{5}	**Mohawk (IRE) (72)** (JLDunlop) **2-8-6** DBiggs(11) (a bhd)	½	**11**	16/1	42	4
2953^{4}	**Blueberry (70)** (SDow) **2-8-4** JFEgan(10) (a bhd)	4	**12**	16/1	31	—

(SP 116.1%) **12 Rn**

1m 27.03 (2.23) CSF £17.32 CT £222.50 TOTE £3.00: £1.50 £2.30 £3.90 (£9.60) Trio £69.60 OWNER Mrs Richard Plummer & Partners (KINGSCLERE) BRED Mrs A. Plummer

2706* Merlin's Ring, moving up in distance, gained control a furlong-and-a-half out, but with the second really flying in the closing stages, he found the line only just saving him. He is liked a lot by his trainer. (11/4)

2595* Mantles Star was very unlucky. Dressed up with nowhere to go in the final quarter-mile, he eventually extricated himself entering the final furlong, but was about a length-and-three quarters down on the winner. Running on really strongly, he would certainly have prevailed in a couple more strides. He is a horse with a big future, according to his trainer. (13/2)

2786 King Darius (IRE) only found his stride below the distance, but ran on really strongly to take third prize, only to find the front two already home and dry. He has shown a liking for cut underfoot. (16/1)

2700* Fayrana (IRE), off the bridle turning for home, had every chance a quarter-of-a-mile out before failing to quicken. (7/1)

2644a Shawdon found seven furlongs in this fast-run race too much for him, for after leading over a quarter-of-mile from home, he was collared below the distance, and had little left in the tank inside the final furlong. (8/1)

2371 Gypsy Hill, racing at the back, stayed on from below the distance to be nearest at the line. (20/1)

2587* Bellow (IRE) (14/1: 10/1-16/1)

3216 VODAFONE NASSAU STKS (Gp 2) (3-Y.O+ F & M) (Class A)
3-20 (3-23) **1m 2f** £48,911.00 (£18,149.00: £8,749.50: £3,622.50: £1,486.25: £631.75) Stalls: High GOING minus 0.23 sec per fur (GF)

				SP	RR	SF
2586*	**Ryafan (USA)** (JHMGosden) **3-8-9** MHills(5) (lw: a.p: led over 2f out: rdn: r.o wl)	—	**1**	9/4^{1}	123	84
1147^{4}	**Entice (FR) (102)** (SbinSuroor) **3-8-6** LDettori(7) (hld up: rdn over 2f out: chsd wnr over 1f out: edgd rt ins fnl f: no imp)	2½	**2**	6/1	116	77
2099a^{2}	**Papering (IRE) (112)** (LMCumani) **4-9-1** PatEddery(1) (swtg: led over 7f: 3rd & btn whn hmpd on ins, ins fnl f)	2	**3**	11/4^{2}	113	83
1200a^{5}	**Grey Way (USA)** (JLDunlop) **4-9-1** KDarley(2) (rdn over 3f out: hdwy over 2f out: wknd over 1f out)	3	**4**	20/1	108	78
922a^{7}	**Last Second (IRE) (118)** (SirMarkPrescott) **4-9-1** GDuffield(6) (hld up: rdn over 3f out: no rspnse)	3½	**5**	7/2^{3}	102	72
2814a^{6}	**Etoile (FR) (112)** (PWChapple-Hyam) **3-8-6** JReid(3) (chsd ldr over 6f: wknd 2f out)	¾	**6**	10/1	101	62
2513^{6}	**Maid of Camelot (99)** (RCharlton) **3-8-6** TSprake(4) (swtg: bhd fnl 3f)	6	**7**	25/1	92	53

(SP 111.6%) **7 Rn**

2m 5.56 (-1.04) CSF £14.05 TOTE £3.10: £1.90 £2.20 (£8.60) OWNER Mr K. Abdulla (NEWMARKET) BRED Juddmonte Farms

WEIGHT FOR AGE 3yo-9lb
OFFICIAL EXPLANATION Last Second (IRE): the trainer's only explanation was that the filly had not trained on.
2586* Ryafan (USA) was sent to the front over a quarter-of-a-mile from home and, ridden along, asserted her authority from below the distance, to win her first race over this trip in thoroughly convincing style. The Group Two Prix de l'Opera on Arc weekend is her big target. (9/4)
1147 Entice (FR), a small, wiry filly, has not been out since disappointing in the Musidora Stakes at York back in May, when the stable was under a cloud. She ran much better here, but having moved into second place approaching the final furlong, had no hope of reeling in the winner. Simon Crisford, the Godolphin Racing Manager, reported afterwards that she would pick up a nice race before the end of the season, although what you saw here was as good as she is. She will now go for the Prix de Psyche over a mile-and-a-quarter at Deauville next Saturday. (6/1)
2099a Papering (IRE) attempted to make all the running, but she was collared over a mile-and-a-quarter from home, and was already held in third place when done no favours by the runner-up inside the final furlong. She has won two listed races to date, but has yet to win a Group race. (11/4)
Grey Way (USA), an ex-Italian filly, who won a Group Two race last year, and has already scored twice this season, was making her debut for John Dunlop. Given no easy task, she made an effort over a quarter-of-a-mile from home, but was left for dead below the distance. (20/1)
922a Last Second (IRE), a delicate filly who needs a lot of time between her races, once again was a major disappointment, and the sad fact seems to be that she simply has not trained on. She has now been retired. (7/2: op 6/4)
2814a Etoile (FR) is finding life tough this season, and had been hung out to dry two furlongs from home. (10/1)

3217 VODAFONE STEWARDS' CUP H'CAP (3-Y.O+) (Class B)

3-50 (3-55) **6f** £48,250.00 (£14,500.00: £7,000.00: £3,250.00) Stalls: Low GOING: 0.04 sec per fur (G)

				SP	RR	SF
2560*	**Danetime (IRE) (100)** (NACallaghan) **3-8-10**[3x] PatEddery(5) (lw: a.p: led 2f out: all out)	—	**1**	5/1[1]	117	82
2529*	**My Best Valentine (95)** (VSoane) **7-8-9** RCochrane(23) (hdwy over 1f out: ev ch ins fnl f: r.o)	nk	**2**	9/1[3]	111	80
2675*	**Dashing Blue (102)** (IABalding) **4-9-2**[3x] LDettori(30) (lw: hdwy over 1f out: ev ch ins fnl f: r.o)	½	**3**	10/1	117	86
2711*	**Faraway Lass (82)** (LordHuntingdon) **4-7-10**[3x] MDemuro(2) (lw: nt clr run over 2f out: swtchd rt: hdwy over 1f out: r.o)	hd	**4**	33/1	97	66
2711[4]	**Oggi (87)** (PJMakin) **6-8-1** AMunro(27) (nt clr run: swtchd left wl over 1f out: hdwy over 1f out: r.o)	¾	**5**	14/1	100	69
2683[6]	**King of Peru (94)** (NPLittmoden) **4-8-8** KFallon(9) (a.p: hrd rdn over 1f out: unable qckn)	s.h	**6**	33/1	107	76
3115*	**No Extras (IRE) (82)** (GLMoore) **7-7-3**(7) [5x] DarrenWilliams(3) (swtg: hdwy over 1f out: r.o)	¾	**7**	33/1	93	62
3065[3]	**Tadeo (95)** (MJohnston) **4-8-6**(3) KMChin(15) (lw: a.p: hrd rdn over 1f out: one pce)	s.h	**8**	25/1	105	74
1980[18]	**Triple Hay (95)** (RHannon) **3-8-2**(3) MHenry(16) (hld up: rdn over 2f out: one pce)	½	**9**	40/1	104	69
2835*	**Waypoint (82)** (RCharlton) **4-7-7v[1]**(3) RFfrench(19) (a.p: hrd rdn over 1f out: wknd ins fnl f)	2	**10**	10/1	86	55
3023*	**Coastal Bluff (110)** (TDBarron) **5-9-10** KDarley(6) (b.hind: a.p: hrd rdn over 1f out: wknd fnl f)	s.h	**11**	6/1[2]	114	83
2717[7]	**Squire Corrie (86)** (DWChapman) **5-7-11**(3) PFessey(17) (lw: led over 2f: wknd over 1f out)	hd	**12**	50/1	89	58
2598[12]	**Double Bounce (88)** (PJMakin) **7-8-2** MRoberts(4) (swtg: nvr nrr)	s.h	**13**	20/1	91	60
2299[3]	**Wildwood Flower (94)** (RHannon) **4-8-8** DaneO'Neill(25) (a mid div)	s.h	**14**	16/1	97	66
2517*	**Nigrasine (99)** (JLEyre) **3-8-9** DeanMcKeown(18) (prom over 4f)	s.h	**15**	25/1	102	67
2833[2]	**Sir Joey (USA) (83)** (PGMurphy) **8-7-11** JLowe(13) (lw: a mid div)	½	**16**	20/1	85	54
2775*	**Yorkie George (97)** (LMCumani) **3-8-7**[3x] JReid(28) (hdwy & bmpd over 1f out: wknd fnl f)	s.h	**17**	16/1	98	63
2861[3]	**Hello Mister (90)** (TEPowell) **6-8-4**[ow1] MHills(1) (nvr nrr)	hd	**18**	16/1	91	59
1980[4]	**Sharp Hat (92)** (RHannon) **3-8-2** JFEgan(11) (spd over 4f)	nk	**19**	40/1	92	57
2526[5]	**To the Roof (IRE) (105)** (PWHarris) **5-9-0**(5) CLowther(29) (lw: hdwy over 3f out: hrd rdn over 1f out: sn wknd)	¾	**20**	20/1	103	72
2655*	**The Gay Fox (86)** (BAMcMahon) **3-7-3**(7) JFowle(7) (bhd fnl 2f)	hd	**21**	50/1	84	49
2950[6]	**Willow Dale (IRE) (82)** (DRCElsworth) **4-7-10** FNorton(24) (hld up: rdn over 2f out: wknd over 1f out)	hd	**22**	50/1	80	49
961[6]	**Loch Patrick (96)** (MMadgwick) **7-8-10b[1]** GDuffield(26) (s.s: a bhd)	s.h	**23**	25/1	94	63
2675[14]	**Sea-Deer (87)** (CADwyer) **8-8-1** SDrowne(10) (bhd fnl 2f)	nk	**24**	33/1	84	53
3075[4]	**Intiaash (IRE) (82)** (DHaydnJones) **5-7-10** NVarley(12) (a bhd)	nk	**25**	50/1	78	47
2769[11]	**White Emir (84)** (BJMeehan) **4-7-12b** DBiggs(14) (outpcd)	2	**26**	50/1	75	44
2526[12]	**Sylva Paradise (IRE) (103)** (CEBrittain) **4-9-3b[1]** BDoyle(22) (a.p: led over 3f out to 2f out: wknd over 1f out)	hd	**27**	50/1	94	63
2211[5]	**Selhurstpark Flyer (IRE) (100)** (JBerry) **6-8-9**(5) PRoberts(20) (b: spd over 3f)	¾	**28**	25/1	89	58
2769[9]	**Clan Chief (83)** (JRArnold) **4-7-11** GBardwell(21) (lw: prom over 3f)	s.h	**29**	25/1	71	40
2964[2]	**Kilcullen Lad (IRE) (86)** (PMooney) **3-7-10v** NAdams(8) (lw: spd over 3f)	7	**30**	50/1	56	21
				(SP 147.3%)	**30 Rn**	

1m 10.95 (1.15) CSF £37.66 CT £424.07 TOTE £7.20: £2.70 £2.80 £2.60 £9.00 (£36.10) Trio £162.10 OWNER Mr M Tabor & Mrs John Magnier (NEWMARKET) BRED Holborn Trust Co
LONG HANDICAP No Extras (IRE) 6-4 Intiaash (IRE) 7-8 Faraway Lass 7-6 The Gay Fox 7-5 Willow Dale (IRE) 7-5 Kilcullen Lad (IRE) 7-8
WEIGHT FOR AGE 3yo-4lb
2560* Danetime (IRE), set to rise 8lb in future handicaps, landed a major gamble - owner Michael Tabor admitting he had won more than £200,000 - recovering all losses sustained in his unlucky defeat in the Wokingham, and more. Gaining a narrow overall lead a quarter-of-a-mile from home, he found the line only just saving him, with strong challenges from the second and third on different parts of the course. It later transpired that the colt had twisted a shoe in the race. Callaghan considers this the highlight of his career, and believes Danetime is up to Group company, although he does need rain - this ground was plenty fast enough for him. (5/1)
2529* My Best Valentine, seventh and sixth in the last two runnings of this race, ran an absolute cracker, and storming through in the centre of the course, looked likely to prevail inside the final furlong, only for the photo finish to reveal he had just lost out. (9/1)
2675* Dashing Blue moved up along the far rail below the distance, and was challenging for the lead inside the final furlong, only just losing out in a very tight finish. (10/1)
2711* Faraway Lass ran a tremendous race, especially considering she encountered traffic problems. When she got a clear run below the distance, she ran on really strongly, but just failed to get there in time. (33/1)
2711 Oggi, who did not have the best of runs, began a forward move below the distance, but despite running on, found the line always beating him. He has done all his winning at this trip. (14/1)
2683 King of Peru, a leading light from the off, was not disgraced, but just failed to find another gear in the last furlong-and-a-half. (33/1)
3115* No Extras (IRE), a winner here over a mile on Tuesday, was 10lb higher on this occasion, and was not suited by the drop in distance. Nevertheless, he was not disgraced, and ran on well from below the distance to be nearest at the line. (33/1)
3023* Coastal Bluff, 19lb higher than when winning this race last year, was far from disgraced, and was close up until his welter burden took its toll in the final furlong. (6/1)

3218 TURF CLUB RATED STKS H'CAP (0-95) (3-Y.O) (Class C)

4-25 (4-26) **1m 6f** £10,098.60 (£3,737.40: £1,793.70: £733.50: £291.75: £115.05) Stalls: High GOING minus 0.23 sec per fur (GF)

				SP	RR	SF
2410[2]	**Liffre (IRE) (78)** (JHMGosden) **3-8-6** LDettori(14) (lw: chsd ldr: led over 2f out: hrd rdn fnl f: r.o wl)	—	**1**	13/2[3]	88	51

2551[2] **Dominant Duchess (78)** (JWHills) **3-8-6** MHills(2) (s.i.s: gd hdwy over 1f out: chsd wnr fnl f: r.o) ....¾ **2** 10/1 87 50
2767* **Georgia Venture (78)** (SPCWoods) **3-8-6** GDuffield(13) (hld up: rdn over 3f out: unable qckn) 2½ **3** 8/1 84 47
2423[2] **Thornby Park (86)** (JLDunlop) **3-9-0** TSprake(7) (hdwy over 3f out: hrd rdn over 2f out: one pce) 1½ **4** 14/1 91 54
2647[3] **Snow Partridge (USA) (82)** (PFICole) **3-8-10** KDarley(10) (a.p: rdn over 3f out: one pce) ....nk **5** 16/1 86 49
2530* **Right Man (82)** (GLewis) **3-8-10** PaulEddery(11) (rdn over 3f out: hdwy & nt clr run on ins over 1f out: r.o one pce) ....s.h **6** 4/1[1] 86 49
2284[2] **Milly of The Vally (88)** (HRACecil) **3-9-2** KFallon(8) (rdn over 3f out: hdwy over 1f out: one pce) 1¼ **7** 10/1 91 54
2423[6] **Brand New Dance (76)** (DWPArbuthnot) **3-8-4** MRoberts(6) (nvr nr to chal) ....nk **8** 33/1 78 41
2291* **Kilma (USA) (90)** (LMCumani) **3-9-4** PatEddery(1) (led over 11f: eased whn btn fnl f) ....1¾ **9** 5/1[2] 90 53
2918[7] **What Happened Was (76)** (MartynMeade) **3-8-4** FNorton(5) (a bhd) 3½ **10** 50/1 72 35
2647[2] **Sausalito Bay (87)** (IABalding) **3-9-1** RCochrane(4) (prom over 10f) ....¾ **11** 8/1 83 46
2327[6] **Flirting Around (USA) (93)** (MRStoute) **3-9-7** JReid(9) (bhd fnl 3f) ....s.h **12** 9/1 89 52
2230[8] **Protocol (IRE) (76)** (JWHills) **3-8-1**(3) MHenry(12) (bhd fnl 3f) 1¾ **13** 25/1 70 33
3069[4] **Ramike (IRE) (76)** (MJohnston) **3-8-4** BDoyle(3) (bhd fnl 3f) ....¾ **14** 16/1 69 32
(SP 127.6%) **14 Rn**

3m 2.81 (3.81) CSF £66.94 CT £497.43 TOTE £6.10: £1.80 £3.10 £4.80 (£53.60) Trio £371.90 OWNER Sheikh Mohammed (NEWMARKET) BRED Sheikh Mohammed Bin Rashid Al Maktoum

LONG HANDICAP What Happened Was 7-12 Brand New Dance 8-3 Ramike (IRE) 8-3

2410 Liffre (IRE) appreciated the longer trip, and made a successful debut in handicap company, leading over a quarter-of-a-mile from home, and holding on well. She is a good staying filly according to her trainer, and the Melrose Stakes at York is a possible. (13/2)

2551 Dominant Duchess ran a fine race over this longer trip. Getting into top gear from below the distance, she ran on really strongly, but just failed to peg back the winner. (10/1)

2767* Georgia Venture, 6lb higher for her recent Sandown win, never really looked like quickening up in the straight. (8/1)

2423 Thornby Park is a real stayer, and despite all her rider's efforts, could only go up and down in the same place in the final quarter-mile. (14/1)

2647 Snow Partridge (USA) was off the bridle as the bugler called, entering the straight, but could only plod on in his own time. (16/1)

2530* Right Man found everything conspiring against him - he was 25lb higher than when winning his first race at Windsor in May, would have been better suited by two miles, and encountered traffic problems at a critical stage. In the circumstances, he did well to finish so close. (4/1)

3219 E.B.F. RICHARD BAERLEIN MAIDEN STKS (UNRACED 2-Y.O) (Class D)

5-00 (5-02) **6f** £7,067.50 (£2,140.00: £1,045.00: £497.50) Stalls: Low GOING: 0.04 sec per fur (G)

SP RR SF

Tamarisk (IRE) (RCharlton) **2-9-0** TSprake(8) (unf: scope: squeezed thro & hdwy over 2f out: led 1f out: pushed out) ....— **1** 11/4[1] 86+ 52
Elhabub (BWHills) **2-9-0** MHills(5) (leggy: scope: bit bkwd: dwlt: nt clr run over 2f out tl over 1f out: swtchd lft 1f out: hdwy fnl f: r.o: bttr for r) ....1 **2** 7/2[2] 83+ 49
Designer (USA) (JHMGosden) **2-9-0** LDettori(7) (w'like: scope: hld up: rdn over 1f out: ev ch ins fnl f: unable qckn) ....1½ **3** 11/4[1] 79 t 45
Surveyor (JLDunlop) **2-9-0** JReid(9) (w'like: scope: stdy hdwy 2f out: rdn over 1f out: ev ch ins fnl f: sn wknd) ....1¼ **4** 9/1 76 t 42
Silca Key Service (MRChannon) **2-8-9** BDoyle(1) (unf: a.p: rdn & swtchd rt wl over 1f out: ev ch over 1f out: one pce) ....s.h **5** 25/1 71 t 37
The Downtown Fox (BAMcMahon) **2-9-0** GDuffield(3) (unf: led to 1f out: sn wknd) ....¾ **6** 16/1 74 t 40
Silversmith (FR) (SDow) **2-9-0** JFEgan(10) (w'like: bit bkwd: nvr nrr) ....2½ **7** 40/1 67 t 33
Golden Reprimand (IRE) (RHannon) **2-9-0** PatEddery(6) (unf: scope: w ldr: rdn over 2f out: wknd over 1f out) ....2½ **8** 6/1[3] 61 t 27
Rubamma (PTWalwyn) **2-9-0** RCochrane(4) (neat: prom over 4f) ....3 **9** 14/1 53 t 19
(SP 118.7%) **9 Rn**

1m 13.22 (3.42) CSF £11.75 TOTE £4.50: £1.50 £2.00 £1.10 (£11.50) Trio £10.20 OWNER Highclere Thoroughbred Racing Ltd (BECKHAMPTON) BRED Mount Coote Stud

Tamarisk (IRE), who cost 78,000 guineas as a yearling at the Newmarket Autumn Sales last year, and was the second-most expensive purchase by Highclere Thoroughbred Racing, has plenty of scope, and will be even better when he strengthens up. Striking the front entering the final furlong, he needed only to be nudged along for a cosy victory. He can win again. (11/4)

Elhabub, a tall colt who stands over a lot of ground, carries some condition. He had absolutely no luck in running, which makes this performance even more commendable. Only finding a clear run in the final furlong, he ate up the ground, but the winner had got first run on him, and he was unable to peg him back in time. He should not be missed next time out. (7/2: op 9/4)

Designer (USA), a decent, rangy sort, who cost $550,000, and has a string of big-race entries, made a very pleasing debut, and was one of several fighting for the lead early inside the final furlong before tapped for toe. He looks a ready-made winner. (11/4: op 6/4)

Surveyor, an attractive individual with scope, was rather colty in the paddock, but concentrated much better on the job in hand in the race itself. One of several with every chance early inside the final furlong, he then tired as lack of a recent run took its toll. He should not be difficult to win with. (9/1)

Silca Key Service needs time to develop, but had every chance below the distance before tapped for toe. (25/1)

The Downtown Fox, a lightly-made colt, took the field along, but collared a furlong out, soon had bellows to mend. (16/1)

Rubamma (14/1: op 8/1)

3220 TRUNDLE LIMITED STKS (0-90) (3-Y.O+) (Class C)

5-35 (5-35) **7f** £6,985.00 (£2,080.00: £990.00: £445.00) Stalls: High GOING minus 0.23 sec per fur (GF)

SP RR SF

2766[6] **Dancing Image (89)** (IABalding) **4-9-2** LDettori(3) (swtg: stdd s: hdwy on bit to ld over 1f out: comf) ....— **1** 13/8[1] 101+ 60
Mashhaer (USA) (90) (MRStoute) **3-8-10** JReid(6) (lw: a.p: ev ch over 1f out: unable qckn) ....2½ **2** 4/1[2] 95 48
3150[13] **Divina Luna (85)** (JWHills) **4-8-12**(3) MHenry(7) (led over 5f: one pce) ....2 **3** 6/1[3] 90 49
2894[2] **Volley (IRE) (83)** (MajorDNChappell) **4-8-13** KDarley(2) (hdwy on ins over 2f out: rdn over 1f out: one pce)...hd **4** 15/2 88 47
2735[2] **Hawait (IRE) (90)** (BWHills) **3-8-12** MHills(1) (hld up: rdn wl over 1f out: sn wknd) 6 **5** 8/1 79 32
2666[4] **Albert The Bear (88)** (JBerry) **4-9-1**(5) CLowther(5) (w ldr over 4f) ....s.h **6** 14/1 81 40
2476[6] **Prends Ca (IRE) (90)** (WRMuir) **4-8-13** DaneO'Neill(4) (prom over 5f) 5 **7** 8/1 62 21
(SP 113.0%) **7 Rn**

1m 26.6 (1.80) CSF £7.25 TOTE £2.20: £1.50 £2.10 (£2.90) OWNER The Queen (KINGSCLERE) BRED The Queen

WEIGHT FOR AGE 3yo-6lb

IN-FOCUS: **A big meeting without some Frankie magic is becoming unthinkable, and the popular Italian celebrated a tremendous 294/1 four-timer with one of his famous flying leaps in the winner's enclosure.**

2766 Dancing Image put up a very polished performance under a super-cool ride from Dettori. Swinging along on the bridle, he cruised into the lead approaching the final furlong, and Dettori only needed to wiggle his arms slightly for the gelding to sprint away for a decisive victory. Although both his previous wins have come over a mile, it was on Frankie's recommendation that he was dropped back to seven furlongs. (13/8)
Mashhaer (USA), trained by Saeed bin Suroor last year to win a Newmarket maiden, was making a belated reappearance, but still showed plenty of promise, having every chance below the distance before left for dead by the winner. This is his level according to his trainer. (4/1: 3/1-9/2)
2894* Divina Luna, never in the hunt here on Thursday, took the field along, but collared approaching the final furlong, could then only struggle on in her own time. Seven furlongs is her absolute minimum according to her trainer. (6/1)
2894 Volley (IRE) picked up ground along the inside rail over a quarter of a mile from home, but could then only struggle on at one pace. (15/2)
2735 Hawait (IRE), held up off the pace, was asked for his effort early in the final quarter-mile, but found little. (8/1: 5/1-9/1)
2666 Albert The Bear had no easy task at the weights, and after disputing the lead, was in trouble over a quarter of a mile from home. (14/1)
2476 Prends Ca (IRE) (8/1: 6/1-9/1)

T/Jkpt: £68,069.00 (0.58 Tckts); £40,266.19 to Chepstow 3/8/97. T/Plpt: £59.90 (1,313.09 Tckts). T/Qdpt: £30.00 (132.49 Tckts) AK

2657-HAMILTON (R-H) (Good)
Saturday August 2nd
WEATHER: fine WIND: almost nil

3221 KITCHEN BATHROOM & TILE COMPANY SERIES (ROUND 5) APPRENTICE H'CAP (0-75) (3-Y.O+) (Class E)
5-55 (5-56) **1m 3f 16y** £3,410.50 (£1,039.00: £512.00: £248.50) GOING minus 0.41 sec per fur (F)

			SP	RR	SF
2469*	**Philmist (41)** (MissLAPerratt) **5-7-11b**(7)ow1 SBuckley(1) (lw: hld up: stdy hdwy 3f out: led ins fnl f: rdn & r.o)—	1	5/2[2]	54	36
1232[3]	**Mentalasanythin (65)** (DHaydnJones) **8-10-0** GFaulkner(8) (lw: chsd clr ldr: led 3f out tl ins fnl f: no ex).......2½	2	8/11[1]	74	57
2660[12]	**Rapid Mover (35)** (DANolan) **10-7-5b**(7)ow2 NPollard(2) (led & sn clr: hdd 3f out: sn outpcd)........7	3	50/1	34	15
2716[3]	**Thisonesforalice (36)** (JSGoldie) **9-7-6**(7) JMcAuley(5) (hld up: hdwy over 3f out: rdn & no imp fnl 2f) ....nk	4	11/2[3]	35	18
2541[4]	**Philgem (33)** (CWFairhurst) **4-7-3v**[1](7) JennyBenson(4) (chsd ldrs: effrt 3f out: no imp) 1¾	5	12/1	29	12
2716[8]	**Knave (35)** (PMonteith) **4-7-12**ow2 ADaly(7) (chsd ldrs: hdwy 4f out: rdn & btn over 2f out)........nk	6	20/1	31	12
2226[11]	**Sweet Note (IRE) (43)** (MissLAPerratt) **3-7-3**(7) ANicholls(3) (bhd: c wd & effrt 5f out: n.d)........8	7	50/1	27	—
			(SP 118.2%)	**7 Rn**	

2m 22.2 (2.80) CSF £4.43 CT £54.24 TOTE £3.10: £1.50 £1.10 (£1.80) OWNER Mr C. D. Barber-Lomax (AYR) BRED Mrs M. Morley
LONG HANDICAP Rapid Mover 6-11 Philgem 7-5 Sweet Note (IRE) 7-0
WEIGHT FOR AGE 3yo-10lb
2469* Philmist had the strong pace she required and, coming from behind, was given a smashing ride and won well. (5/2: 2/1-3/1)
1232 Mentalasanythin put up a brave attempt under topweight, but try as he might he could not match the winner for speed in the final furlong. (8/11)
1615 Rapid Mover was 13lb out of the handicap and hasn't won on the Flat for four years, and this was not a bad effort for him. (50/1)
2716 Thisonesforalice again ran reasonably, but he was never giving it his best shot once an effort was needed. (11/2)
2541 Philgem had the visor on instead of blinkers this time, and failed to come up with the goods when ridden. (12/1)

3222 MOTHERWELL NOVICE AUCTION STKS (2-Y.O) (Class F)
6-25 (6-25) **5f 4y** £2,542.00 (£712.00: £346.00) Stalls: Low GOING minus 0.41 sec per fur (F)

			SP	RR	SF
2739*	**Lets Be Fair** (JHanson) **2-8-13** EJohnson(2) (lw: led after 2f: sn clr: hung rt: easily) ....—	1	8/13[1]	80+	40
2762[3]	**One Singer (91)** (MJohnston) **2-8-11**(5) KSked(1) (outpcd tl styd on u.p fnl 2f: no ch w wnr)........3	2	9/4[2]	73	33
2858[4]	**Sandside (84)** (JBerry) **2-9-1**(3) TEDurcan(4) (lw: led 2f: sn rdn & one pce) 1¾	3	8/1[3]	70	30
2917[10]	**Impulsive Decision (IRE)** (MartynMeade) **2-8-3**(3)ow3 RHavlin(5) (chsd ldrs: sn drvn along & no imp)........1¼	4	33/1	54	11
	French Pride (IRE) (ARDicken) **2-8-2**(5) ADaly(3) (cmpt: scope: bit bkwd: dwlt: a outpcd & bhd)........3	5	16/1	45	5
			(SP 112.6%)	**5 Rn**	

59.6 secs (1.30) CSF £2.12 TOTE £1.60: £1.10 £1.40 (£1.20) OWNER Mr J. Hanson (WETHERBY) BRED Bearstone Stud
2739* Lets Be Fair again won with any amount in hand, but the only worrying thing was her tendency to hang right. (8/13: 4/5-evens)
2762 One Singer was surprisingly left for speed early on, and despite picking up at the end was completely outclassed. (9/4)
2858 Sandside has speed aplenty in the early part of the race, but for some reason at the moment he cannot maintain it. (8/1)
2917 Impulsive Decision (IRE) looked lean and fit, but was always finding things happening too fast here, and may well need a bit further. (33/1)
French Pride (IRE) needed this both fitness and experience-wise and should improve for it. (16/1)

3223 UDDINGSTON (S) STKS (3-Y.O+) (Class G)
6-55 (6-56) **1m 4f 17y** £2,276.00 (£636.00: £308.00) Stalls: High GOING minus 0.41 sec per fur (F)

			SP	RR	SF
2544*	**Sun Mark (IRE) (62)** (MrsASwinbank) **6-9-12** EJohnson(7) (lw: chsd ldrs: led over 2f out: pushed along ent fnl f: eased nr fin)........—	1	7/4[2]	55	47
2386*	**Monaco Gold (IRE) (52)** (MrsMReveley) **5-9-7**(5) SCopp(3) (lw: chsd ldr: led over 3f out tl over 2f out: kpt on u.p fnl f)........hd	2	6/4[1]	55	47
2564[4]	**Craigary (30)** (MrsASwinbank) **6-9-2**(5) ADaly(8) (prom: hdwy 4f out: sn chsng ldrs: rdn 2f out: nvr able to chal)........2½	3	16/1	47	39
2825[10]	**Breydon (33)** (PMonteith) **4-9-7** OPears(1) (a.p: one pce fnl 4f)........8	4	20/1	36	28
2854[9]	**School of Science (22)** (DANolan) **7-9-2**(5) KSked(5) (led tl hdd over 3f out: sn outpcd)........½	5	66/1	35	27
2825[8]	**Cois Na Farraige (IRE) (48)** (MissLAPerratt) **4-9-7b**[1] NKennedy(2) (bhd: effrt 5f out: sn btn: hmpd 2f out).....23	6	6/1[3]	5	—
2859[4]	**Chanson d'Amour (IRE) (30)** (MissLAPerratt) **3-7-12**(7) JMcAuley(4) (lw: outpcd appr st: sn wl bhd: t.o) 24	7	25/1	—	—
2854[10]	**Talented Ting (IRE) (37)** (PCHaslam) **8-9-2**(5) GFaulkner(6) (bhd: hdwy u.p 4f out: no ch whn stumbled & fell 2f out: dead)........	F	16/1	—	—
			(SP 112.5%)	**8 Rn**	

2m 36.6 (4.60) CSF £4.10 TOTE £2.80: £1.30 £1.10 £2.60 (£1.70) OWNER Scotnorth Racing Ltd (RICHMOND) BRED Matt Carr
WEIGHT FOR AGE 3yo-11lb
No bid
OFFICIAL EXPLANATION **Sun Mark (IRE): the rider reported that the gelding finished lame, but was subsequently found to be sound.**
2544* Sun Mark (IRE) always looked to be going best, but in the end despite his rider's confidence there may not have been much to spare. (7/4)
2386* Monaco Gold (IRE) from a yard having a lean spell, kept battling back when looking beaten and probably should have had even more use made of him. (6/4)

2564 Craigary ran better this time and there could well be a modest race to be found. (16/1)
669 Breydon showed little when the pressure was really on in the last half-mile. (20/1)
2661 School of Science is basically not very good, and that was well exposed halfway up the home straight. (66/1)

3224 GLENGOYNE SINGLE HIGHLAND MALT H'CAP (0-85) (3-Y.O+ F & M) (Class D)

7-25 (7-34) **6f 5y** £5,652.25 (£1,708.00: £831.50: £393.25) Stalls: Low GOING minus 0.41 sec per fur (F)

				SP	RR	SF
3039[5]	**Ballard Lady (IRE) (41)** (JSWainwright) **5-7-11**[ow1] TWilliams(7) (prom: drvn along ½-wy: led over 1f out: styd on wl)	—	**1**	6/1[3]	51	21
2717[8]	**Don't Care (IRE) (62)** (MissLAPerratt) **6-9-1b**(3) TEDurcan(5) (a in tch: styd on u.p fnl 2f: nrst fin)	2	**2**	20/1	67	38
2900[9]	**Natural Key (65)** (DHaydnJones) **4-9-7** AMackay(6) (prom: hdwy to chal 2f out: sn hrd rdn & nt qckn)	hd	**3**	5/2[2]	69	40
3024[2]	**Kind of Light (68)** (RGuest) **4-9-10** JWeaver(1) (lw: trckd ldrs: hdwy & ev ch 2f out: rdn & r.o one pce)	½	**4**	7/4[1]	71	42
2657[3]	**Suedoro (45)** (JSGoldie) **7-7-8**(7) JMcAuley(2) (wnt rt s: sn chsng ldrs: led over 2f out tl over 1f out: no ex)	hd	**5**	7/1	48	19
2657[7]	**Sunday Mail Too (IRE) (40)** (MissLAPerratt) **5-7-3**(7) ANicholls(4) (cl up: led after 2f tl over 2f out: sn wknd)	9	**6**	25/1	19	—
2899[10]	**Leading Princess (IRE) (47)** (MissLAPerratt) **6-8-3b** NKennedy(9) (lw: cl up over 3f: hung rt & wknd)	hd	**7**	10/1	26	—
2659[11]	**Ragtime Cowgirl (42)** (DANolan) **4-7-5**(7)ow2 NPollard(3) (dwlt: hung rt most of wy: n.d)	3	**8**	66/1	13	—
2883[10]	**Northern Sal (50)** (MissLAPerratt) **3-8-2** DWright(8) (led 2f: hung rt & wknd fnl 2f)	12	**9**	40/1	—	—
				(SP 113.4%)	**9 Rn**	

1m 11.8 (1.80) CSF £102.19 CT £340.01 TOTE £6.10: £1.80 £2.00 £1.80 (£35.20) Trio £47.40 OWNER Mrs P. Wake (MALTON) BRED Airlie Stud
LONG HANDICAP Ballard Lady (IRE) 7-9 Ragtime Cowgirl 7-5 Sunday Mail Too (IRE) 7-6
WEIGHT FOR AGE 3yo-4lb
STEWARDS' ENQUIRY Williams susp. 11-14/8/97 (improper use of whip).Wainwright fined £230 (failure to inform rdr of horse's hypersensitive skin).
3039 Ballard Lady (IRE) had to work hard at this trip, but she is game, and that won the day. (6/1)
529 Don't Care (IRE) has been very disappointing, but there were signs of hope here. She stayed on well at the end. (20/1)
2900 Natural Key is running reasonably, and is beginning to slip down the handicap. (5/2)
3024 Kind of Light was a shade disappointing here, not quite finding enough when the pressure was on, but she does look well at the moment and should not be written off yet. (7/4)
2657 Suedoro ran reasonably, but had no excuses this time. (7/1)

3225 ROTHMANS ROYALS NORTH SOUTH CHALLENGE SERIES H'CAP (0-80) (3-Y.O) (Class D)

7-55 (7-58) **1m 1f 36y** £5,277.00 (£1,596.00: £778.00: £369.00) Stalls: High GOING minus 0.41 sec per fur (F)

				SP	RR	SF
2884*	**Night Mirage (USA) (70)** (MJohnston) **3-9-2** JWeaver(2) (lw: hld up: hdwy over 3f out: qcknd to ld 1f out: rdn & r.o wl)	—	**1**	11/4[2]	83	45
2877[4]	**Night Chorus (67)** (BSRothwell) **3-8-13** JFortune(4) (in tch: hdwy 3f out: ev ch over 1f out: kpt on)	2½	**2**	5/1[3]	76	38
3071[3]	**Zorba (65)** (JHetherton) **3-8-11** NKennedy(6) (cl up: led 3f out to 1f out: r.o one pce)	1¾	**3**	7/1	71	33
2735[4]	**Ultra Boy (75)** (PCHaslam) **3-9-2**(5) GFaulkner(1) (a.p: hdwy & ev ch 2f out: nt qckn)	3	**4**	6/1	75	37
2903[6]	**Beau Roberto (51)** (JSGoldie) **3-7-11**[ow1] TWilliams(7) (prom tl outpcd & lost pl over 3f out: swtchd outside & styd on: no imp)	1¾	**5**	9/1	48	9
2909[2]	**Marytavy (61)** (SirMarkPrescott) **3-8-7** JCarroll(5) (lw: chsd ldrs: effrt 4f out: hung rt: wknd fnl 2½f)	14	**6**	2/1[1]	34	—
2715[9]	**Biff-Em (IRE) (55)** (MissLAPerratt) **3-8-1** DWright(3) (led tl hdd 3f out: wknd fnl 2f)	3½	**7**	25/1	22	—
				(SP 117.3%)	**7 Rn**	

1m 56.8 (2.50) CSF £16.05 TOTE £3.00: £1.60 £2.90 (£7.60) OWNER Mr & Mrs G Middlebrook (MIDDLEHAM) BRED Hartland Farm & James Hayward
OFFICIAL EXPLANATION Marytavy: was unsuited by the course.
2884* Night Mirage (USA) is really getting the hang of things, and did this particularly well. (11/4)
2877 Night Chorus put up a useful effort, and although well held by the winner, he did keep staying on gamely. (5/1)
3071 Zorba is running well again, and looks likely to need further to come back to his best. (7/1)
2735 Ultra Boy had his chances, but failed to last home at this slightly longer trip. (6/1)
2903 Beau Roberto looks a funny customer, as he did not seem to like it when surrounded by other horses, but once switched outside he then stayed on. (9/1)
2909 Marytavy was nothing like her best here, and just wanted to hang right, and this effort is best forgotten. (2/1)

3226 BAILEYS ORIGINAL IRISH CREAM NURSERY (QUALIFIER) H'CAP (2-Y.O) (Class E)

8-25 (8-25) **6f 5y** £3,241.25 (£980.00: £477.50: £226.25) Stalls: Low GOING minus 0.41 sec per fur (F)

				SP	RR	SF
2714[2]	**Jacmar (IRE) (80)** (MissLAPerratt) **2-9-7** NKennedy(8) (lw: bhd: hdwy ½-wy: led ins fnl f: r.o wl)	—	**1**	7/2[2]	81	33
2565[6]	**Mighty Sure (IRE) (62)** (MWEasterby) **2-8-3** DaleGibson(5) (lw: a.p: led wl over 1f tl ins fnl f: kpt on u.p)	1¼	**2**	6/1	60	12
1038[4]	**Mamma's Boy (74)** (JBerry) **2-8-12**(3) TEDurcan(3) (lw: a chsng ldrs: ev ch & hrd rdn over 1f out: kpt on)	½	**3**	5/1[3]	70	22
3062[6]	**Cosmic Case (56)** (JSGoldie) **2-7-11**[ow1] TWilliams(4) (dwlt: hld up: hdwy over 2f out: rdn & no imp)	1½	**4**	25/1	48	—
2578[3]	**Swanmore Lady (IRE) (56)** (SCWilliams) **2-7-11** DWright(2) (hld up: hdwy on ins 2f out: hrd rdn & no imp fnl f)	½	**5**	11/2	47	—
2851[3]	**Days of Grace (75)** (MartynMeade) **2-8-13**(3) RHavlin(6) (led over 4f: hung rt & wknd)	1¾	**6**	7/1	61	13
2886[6]	**Saint Ann (USA) (70)** (MJohnston) **2-8-11** JWeaver(1) (gd spd over 3f: wknd qckly)	10	**7**	10/1	30	—
2740[2]	**Mystery Guest (IRE) (69)** (SirMarkPrescott) **2-8-10** JCarroll(7) (chsd ldrs over 3f: wknd qckly)	2	**8**	2/1[1]	24	—
				(SP 127.3%)	**8 Rn**	

1m 12.6 (2.60) CSF £25.50 CT £101.64 TOTE £5.20: £1.60 £3.30 £1.80 (£31.60) OWNER Mr John Marett (AYR) BRED Lodge Park Stud
LONG HANDICAP Cosmic Case 7-4
2714 Jacmar (IRE), although not suited by the downhill section early on, does finish strongly, and won this in good style. He is doing well physically. (7/2)
2031 Mighty Sure (IRE) put in a sound effort, and kept battling away, but she had to admit she had met one just too good. Her turn will come. (6/1)
1038 Mamma's Boy, after three months off, and stepping up in trip for the first time, ran well, and looks one to keep in mind. (5/1)
3062 Cosmic Case, dropped out this time, ran better, but was still never doing enough when it mattered late on. (25/1)
2578 Swanmore Lady (IRE) travelled well on the bridle, but was a shade disappointing off it. (11/2)
2851 Days of Grace has the speed, but once off the bit all she wants to do is hang right. (7/1)
2886 Saint Ann (USA) (10/1: op 5/1)

T/Plpt: £9.10 (1,267.16 Tckts). T/Qdpt: £5.90 (109.19 Tckts) AA

3054-LINGFIELD (L-H) (Turf Good to firm, AWT Standard)
Saturday August 2nd
WEATHER: fine WIND: nil

3227 ALEXIR PACKAGING APPRENTICE H'CAP (0-60) (3-Y.O+) (Class G)
6-05 (6-12) **7f 140y** £2,147.50 (£610.00: £302.50) Stalls: High GOING minus 0.42 sec per fur (F)

Last	Horse / details	Dist	Pos	SP	RR	SF
2785[2]	**Lorins Gold (36)** (AndrewTurnell) **7-7-13**(5) DarrenWilliams(6) (a gng wl: swtchd rt & led over 2f out: shkn up over 1f out: sn clr)	—	1	6/1[2]	48	30
3018*	**Clytha Hill Lad (43)** (JMBradley) **6-8-11** TSiddall(12) (b: a.p: rdn over 3f out: r.o ins fnl f)	3	2	6/1[2]	49	31
2646*	**Gold Lance (USA) (53)** (RJO'Sullivan) **4-9-7** PFredericks(7) (lw: hdwy over 3f out: one pce fnl f)	¾	3	7/1[3]	57	39
3018[7]	**Delight of Dawn (47)** (EAWheeler) **5-8-9**(6) SCarson(3) (lw: hdwy over 2f out: one pce fnl f)	½	4	5/1[1]	50	32
2892[11]	**Fairly Sure (IRE) (34)** (NEBerry) **4-7-11**(5) RBrisland(15) (s.i.s: hdwy over 2f out: r.o one pce fnl f)	¾	5	16/1	36	18
1965[10]	**Dancing Lawyer (50)** (KRBurke) **6-8-8**(10) PWright(8) (hdwy over 3f out: one pce fnl 2f)	s.h	6	20/1	51	33
2833[16]	**Never Think Twice (60)** (KTIvory) **4-9-4v**(10) CCassidy(1) (b: swtchd stands' side after 2f: nvr nr to chal)	2½	7	25/1	56	38
3138[9]	**Sea Danzig (58)** (JJBridger) **4-9-12** PDoe(18) (lw: led tl hdd over 2f out: wknd over 1f out)	½	8	8/1	53	35
3083[6]	**Moving Up (IRE) (38)** (TEPowell) **4-8-1**(5) RCody-Boutcher(16) (rdn & hdwy over 3f out: wknd over 1f out)	hd	9	14/1	33	15
1273[14]	**Master Millfield (IRE) (52)** (CJHill) **5-9-6** DMcGaffin(13) (prom tl wknd wl over 1f out)	4	10	14/1	39	21
2848[6]	**Mary Culi (53)** (HCandy) **3-8-4**(10) BarrySmith(14) (nvr nr ldrs)	¾	11	12/1	38	13
2937*	**Napoleon's Return (41)** (JLEyre) **4-8-1v**(8) GWright(9) (n.d)	¾	12	15/2	24	6
2947[10]	**Little Pilgrim (41)** (TMJones) **4-8-2**(7) PMundy(2) (lw: s.s: racd wd over 3f: a bhd)	1¾	13	25/1	21	3
2785[14]	**Tulsa (IRE) (50)** (BGubby) **3-8-6b[1]**(5) RSmith(4) (racd wd over 3f: sn bhd)	hd	14	25/1	30	5
2745[4]	**Multi Franchise (43)** (RMFlower) **4-8-8**(3) JFowle(17) (swtg: w ldr tl wknd over 2f out)	1¼	15	7/1[3]	20	2
2892[5]	**Press Again (37)** (PHayward) **5-8-0**(5) DHayden(5) (racd wd over 3f: a bhd)	hd	16	16/1	14	—
458[3]	**Spencer's Revenge (55)** (PButler) **8-9-4**(5) GHannon(10) (lw: s.s: a bhd)	3	17	12/1	25	7

(SP 149.9%) **17 Rn**

1m 31.05 (2.05) CSF £45.19 CT £256.05 TOTE £7.20: £1.80 £1.70 £2.70 £2.60 (£18.60) Trio £13.70 OWNER Mrs M. R. Taylor (WANTAGE) BRED E. and G. Bosley
WEIGHT FOR AGE 3yo-7lb

2785 Lorins Gold, raised 2lb, was in control from the moment he switched to get right under the stands rails. (6/1: tchd 10/1)
3018* Clytha Hill Lad, up 7lb, could make no impression on the winner, but got the better of a well-contested battle for the runner-up spot. (6/1)
2646* Gold Lance (USA), raised 5lb for winning a Chepstow seller, was the same amount worse off with the runner-up whom he had beaten just over three lengths on that occasion. (7/1)
2785 Delight of Dawn was backed from 14/1 into favouritism, having been better in at the weights with the first two based on her last two outings. (5/1)
Fairly Sure (IRE) recorded her only previous win in this event last year off a 12lb higher mark. (16/1)
1965 Dancing Lawyer, down 5lb, had been tried in blinkers last time on his last outing for Brian Meehan. (20/1)
2848 Mary Culi (12/1: 8/1-14/1)
458 Spencer's Revenge (12/1: 8/1-14/1)

3228 ABACUS RESEARCH (S) STKS (2-Y.O) (Class G)
6-35 (6-42) **6f** £2,337.30 (£647.80: £309.90) Stalls: High GOING minus 0.42 sec per fur (F)

Last	Horse / details	Dist	Pos	SP	RR	SF
2923[5]	**Bermuda Triangle (IRE) (62)** (MJHaynes) **2-8-3**(3) RFfrench(4) (a.p: rdn to ld ins fnl f: r.o)	—	1	7/1	50	17
3097*	**Charlies Lad (IRE) (70)** (RGuest) **2-9-3** PBloomfield(9) (led: edgd lft 2f out: hdd ins fnl f)	¾	2	11/8[1]	59	26
2923[6]	**Muja's Magic (IRE) (59)** (KTIvory) **2-8-6b[1]** NAdams(7) (a.p: ev ch over 1f out: nt qckn)	1½	3	10/1	44	11
2003[5]	**Dixie Crossroads** (SDow) **2-7-13**(7) DSalt(10) (hdwy over 2f out: r.o one pce fnl f)	2½	4	12/1	37	4
3025[7]	**Arm And A Leg (IRE) (63)** (CADwyer) **2-9-0**(3) DO'Donohoe(8) (rdn over 3f out: no hdwy fnl 2f)	1	5	6/1[3]	46	13
2378[4]	**Satis (IRE)** (MRChannon) **2-8-6** PaulEddery(5) (chsd ldr: ev ch over 1f out: wknd fnl f)	nk	6	7/2[2]	34	1
3055[6]	**Waytogomo** (MissBSanders) **2-8-3**(3) AWhelan(6) (no hdwy fnl 2f)	1	7	20/1	31	—
2875[15]	**Chiltern Emerald** (KRBurke) **2-8-6** JQuinn(2) (s.i.s: a bhd)	7	8	16/1	13	—
2781[8]	**Scene (IRE) (53)** (MartynMeade) **2-7-13**(7) RBrisland(1) (a bhd)	5	9	14/1	—	—
3055[7]	**Miss Lady Lydia** (JRPoulton) **2-8-6** AMorris(11) (a bhd: t.o)	13	10	33/1	—	—

(SP 128.1%) **10 Rn**

1m 11.61 (2.61) CSF £17.10 TOTE £8.60: £1.90 £1.10 £3.10 (£6.30) Trio £14.20 OWNER Mr M. J. Haynes (EPSOM) BRED T. Connolly
No bid

2923 Bermuda Triangle (IRE), reverting to six, was never in danger of going missing, and pounced in the final two hundred yards. (7/1)
3097* Charlies Lad (IRE) was attempting a quick follow-up in this grade. (11/8)
2578 Muja's Magic (IRE), tried in blinkers, had finished two-and-a-half lengths behind the winner over seven at Yarmouth last time. (10/1: op 6/1)
2003 Dixie Crossroads, whose rider looked very inexperienced when push came to shove, could never get to grips with the principals. (12/1)
2681 Arm And A Leg (IRE) was dropping back from seven. (6/1)
2378 Satis (IRE) gave the distinct impression she needs to drop back to the minimum distance. (7/2)

3229 BAA LONDON GATWICK H'CAP (0-70) (3-Y.O+) (Class E)
7-05 (7-08) **1m 3f 106y** £3,044.25 (£909.00: £434.50: £197.25) Stalls: High GOING minus 0.42 sec per fur (F)

Last	Horse / details	Dist	Pos	SP	RR	SF
2955[2]	**Sapphire Son (IRE) (46)** (PCClarke) **5-8-7**(3) RFfrench(3) (a.p: led ins fnl f: r.o wl)	—	1	8/1	54	34
3015[6]	**Supermick (38)** (WRMuir) **6-8-2** MRoberts(7) (hld up & bhd: rdn & hdwy on ins over 2f out: styd on ins fnl f)	2	2	6/1[3]	43	23
3080[5]	**Colour Counsellor (35)** (RMFlower) **4-7-13b** JQuinn(1) (hld up: hdwy over 2f out: styd on fnl f)	hd	3	12/1	40	20
2667*	**Krosno (70)** (SCWilliams) **3-9-10** KFallon(4) (lw: led: hrd rdn 2f out: hdd ins fnl f: one pce)	nk	4	10/11[1]	75	45
2592[5]	**Almuhtaram (52)** (GLewis) **5-9-2b** PaulEddery(9) (chsd ldr: rdn over 2f out: eased whn btn wl ins fnl f)	1½	5	11/2[2]	55	35
	Karachi (55) (RJO'Sullivan) **7-9-5** AProcter(8) (bkwd: hld up: hdwy on ins 4f out: wknd over 2f out)	8	6	25/1	46	26
1803[6]	**Printers Quill (40)** (MajorDNChappell) **5-8-4** SophieMitchell(5) (hld up & bhd: sme hdwy over 3f out: wknd over 2f out)	1¾	7	16/1	29	9

				SP	RR	SF
2955^{9}	**Kirov Protege (IRE) (32)** (MrsLCJewell) **5-7-3**(7) DarrenWilliams(6) (a bhd)	5	**8**	20/1	14	—
2955*	**Soda Pop (IRE) (65)** (GLMoore) **3-9-5** CandyMorris(2) (lw: chsd ldrs tl wknd 3f out)	hd	**9**	7/1	47	17

(SP 127.8%) **9 Rn**

2m 28.6 (3.90) CSF £55.84 CT £543.79 TOTE £8.50: £2.00 £1.70 £2.80 (£16.90) Trio £74.90 OWNER Mr D. Cobb (HAILSHAM) BRED Geoffrey Cole
LONG HANDICAP Kirov Protege (IRE) 7-7
WEIGHT FOR AGE 3yo-10lb
2955 Sapphire Son (IRE), up 4lb, had no problem with the step up from selling company in this 0-70. (8/1: op 9/2)
3015 Supermick really needs the full mile-and-a-half as a minimum. (6/1)
3080 Colour Counsellor is another who seems to find this distance the bare minimum. (12/1: op 7/1)
2667* Krosno, raised 7lb, did not have things all his own way on this occasion. (10/11)
2592 Almuhtaram was coming back in distance after a couple of runs at a mile-and-three-quarters. (11/2)

3230 WESTMEAD WINNERS MEDIAN AUCTION MAIDEN STKS (3-Y.O) (Class F)
7-35 (7-38) **7f 140y** £2,669.70 (£739.20: £353.10) Stalls: High GOING minus 0.42 sec per fur (F)

				SP	RR	SF
1973^{8}	**City Gambler (70)** (GCBravery) **3-8-9** MRimmer(9) (a.p: led wl over 1f out: drvn out)	—	**1**	5/4^{1}	63	28
	Miss Kalaglow (CFWall) **3-8-9** MTebbutt(6) (b.hind: hld up & bhd: hdwy fnl 2f: r.o)	nk	**2**	11/1	62	27
2924^{7}	**Glittering (USA)** (CEBrittain) **3-9-0** MRoberts(10) (lw: w ldr: led over 3f out tl over 1f out: nt qckn ins fnl f)	2	**3**	3/1^{2}	63	28
3133^{7}	**Super Scravels (47)** (KMahdi) **3-8-9** PaulEddery(3) (lw: hld up: hdwy over 2f out: wknd over 1f out)	3½	**4**	9/2^{3}	51	16
2960^{6}	**Galaxy Flight** (MartynMeade) **3-8-9** FNorton(1) (lw: prom 5f)	5	**5**	7/1	40	5
2392^{7}	**Moontalk** (MJHaynes) **3-8-2**(7) MCornally(4) (b.nr hind: trckd ldrs: wknd over 2f out)	4	**6**	25/1	32	—
2921^{14}	**Over The Moon (51)** (MJFetherston-Godley) **3-8-9** JQuinn(5) (a bhd)	3	**7**	14/1	26	—
2941^{13}	**Kalmoojid** (CJHill) **3-8-9**(5) APolli(7) (plld hrd: led over 4f: sn wknd: t.o)	12	**8**	33/1	6	—
2580^{8}	**Forward Miss** (CJBenstead) **3-8-9** JLowe(8) (lw: a bhd: t.o)	5	**9**	33/1	—	—
2956^{10}	**She's Electric (28)** (JJBridger) **3-8-2**(7) PDoe(2) (lw: s.s: sn rcvrd: wknd over 2f out: t.o)	1	**10**	33/1	—	—

(SP 127.8%) **10 Rn**

1m 31.66 (2.66) CSF £17.39 TOTE £2.40: £1.10 £4.20 £2.00 (£17.90) Trio £41.70 OWNER Mr J. J. May (NEWMARKET) BRED J. Ward Hill
1784 City Gambler took advantage of a drop in class with a hard-fought win. (5/4: evens-6/4)
Miss Kalaglow, given a fair bit to do, seemed to be coming with a winning run, and is bred to stay further. (11/1: 8/1-12/1)
2360 Glittering (USA), a half-brother to top-class French performer Village Star, was trying a shorter trip. (3/1)
3133 Super Scravels had apparently failed to stay a mile-and-a-quarter at Nottingham three days ago. (9/2)
2960 Galaxy Flight (7/1: 5/1-15/2)
Over The Moon (14/1: 10/1-16/1)

3231 SUN PUNTERS CLUB LIMITED STKS (0-70) (3-Y.O+) (Class E)
8-05 (8-06) **2m (Equitrack)** £2,940.25 (£877.00: £418.50: £189.25) Stalls: Low GOING minus 0.52 sec per fur (FST)

				SP	RR	SF
3108^{2}	**Mister Aspecto (IRE) (69)** (MJohnston) **4-9-8v** BDoyle(4) (lw: chsd ldr: led 6f out: rdn over 1f out: r.o wl)	—	**1**	11/4^{2}	81	45
2963^{10}	**Behind The Scenes (60)** (CACyzer) **3-8-9** AMorris(5) (a.p: rdn over 3f out: ev ch 2f out: one pce)	4	**2**	25/1	79	28
2530^{8}	**Dark Waters (IRE) (66)** (NAGraham) **4-9-3**(5) GMilligan(6) (lw: led 10f: wknd over 4f out)	8	**3**	6/1^{3}	69	33
3110^{7}	**Slip Jig (IRE) (69)** (KRBurke) **4-9-8** KFallon(2) (swtg: hld up: hdwy 10f out: wknd over 4f out)	2	**4**	9/4^{1}	67	31
2014^{23}	**Totem Dancer (69)** (JLEyre) **4-8-12**(7) RWinston(1) (hld up: hdwy 10f out: rdn & wknd over 4f out)	7	**5**	9/4^{1}	57	21
2564^{6}	**Warm Spell (70)** (GLMoore) **7-9-8** MWigham(3) (b: lw: hld up in rr: nvr gng wl: lost tch 8f out: t.o)	12	**6**	13/2	48	12

(SP 119.7%) **6 Rn**

3m 24.81 (3.81) CSF £53.80 TOTE £3.30: £1.60 £4.70 (£25.20) OWNER Aspecto Clothing Co Ltd (MIDDLEHAM) BRED Petra Bloodstock Agency Ltd
WEIGHT FOR AGE 3yo-15lb
3108 Mister Aspecto (IRE), quite content to have a lead from Dark Waters, had twice already scored here on the sand, and ended a frustrating run. (11/4)
1322* Behind The Scenes possibly got outstayed by the winner in the final furlong. (25/1)
1964* Dark Waters (IRE) did nothing more than give the winner a nice lead. (6/1: 4/1-13/2)
1162 Totem Dancer (9/4: 6/4-5/2)
2564 Warm Spell (13/2: 9/2-7/1)

3232 SAXBY H'CAP (0-65) (3-Y.O+ F & M) (Class F)
8-35 (8-35) **1m 2f (Equitrack)** £2,277.00 (£627.00: £297.00) Stalls: Low GOING minus 0.52 sec per fur (FST)

				SP	RR	SF
1999^{9}	**Soden (IRE) (65)** (TGMills) **3-9-7**(3) RFfrench(4) (swtg: chsd ldr: led over 2f out: r.o wl)	—	**1**	7/1	74	47
3058^{2}	**Signs And Wonders (60)** (CACyzer) **3-9-2**(3) AWhelan(2) (hld up & plld hrd: hdwy 2f out: ev ch ins fnl f: nt qckn)	1½	**2**	3/1^{3}	67	40
3085^{2}	**Classic Ballet (FR) (60)** (RGuest) **4-9-9**(5) CLowther(6) (lw: hld up: hdwy over 5f out: one pce fnl 2f)	2	**3**	13/8^{1}	63	45
2955^{5}	**Harlequin Walk (IRE) (44)** (RJO'Sullivan) **6-8-12** JQuinn(1) (hld up & plld hrd: rdn over 3f out: hdwy over 2f out: one pce)	½	**4**	9/4^{2}	47	29
2049^{6}	**Willie Rushton (55)** (GLMoore) **4-9-9** MWigham(5) (b: b.hind: prom: led over 7f out: rdn & hdd over 2f out: wknd 1f out: eased)	7	**5**	14/1	46	28
2920^{7}	**Woodrising (54)** (CREgerton) **5-9-8** MTebbutt(3) (lw: led over 2f: wknd over 5f out: sn t.o)	23	**6**	9/1	9	—

(SP 123.0%) **6 Rn**

2m 6.68 (2.38) CSF £28.25 TOTE £7.70: £2.80 £1.70 (£10.60) OWNER Albert Soden Ltd (EPSOM) BRED Lodge Park Stud
WEIGHT FOR AGE 3yo-9lb
OFFICIAL EXPLANATION Woodrising: the trainer reported that the filly injured herself in the stalls prior to the race.
1416 Soden (IRE), 5lb lower than when third here on grass, was by no means hard-pressed to make a successful debut on the sand. (7/1)
3058 Signs And Wonders, rated 11lb lower than on grass, got a fine run around the inside on the home turn on this step up in distance. (3/1)
3085 Classic Ballet (FR), 10lb higher than her recent win at Southwell, was having her third quick race over a shorter trip. (13/8)
2955 Harlequin Walk (IRE), rated 10lb lower than on grass, was one pound higher than when winning here over a mile-and-a-half in February. (9/4: 7/4-11/4)
Willie Rushton (14/1: 8/1-16/1)

T/Plpt: £47.80 (315.86 Tckts). T/Qdpt: £19.90 (44.05 Tckts) KH

3196-**NEWMARKET (R-H) (Good)**

Saturday August 2nd

WEATHER: overcast WIND: almost nil

3233 HERO CONDITIONS STKS (2-Y.O) (Class C)

2-00 (2-00) **7f (July)** £6,477.00 (£1,773.00) Stalls: Low GOING minus 0.13 sec per fur (G)

				SP	RR	SF
2524*	**Almutawakel** (SbinSuroor) **2-9-1** RHills(2) (lw: mde all: qcknd over 3f out: hld on wl fnl f)	—	1	2/9[1]	101+	36
722*	**Mijana (IRE)** (JHMGosden) **2-9-1** GHind(1) (lw: trckd wnr: plld out & ev ch 1f out: sn rdn & no imp)	2	2	7/2[2]	96	31
				(SP 104.0%)		**2 Rn**

1m 29.45 (4.45) TOTE £1.20 OWNER Godolphin (NEWMARKET) BRED Shadwell Estate Company Limited

2524* Almutawakel, whose dam is a half-sister to White Muzzle, is a good, athletic mover and confirmed the very good impression he left on his debut. (2/9: op 2/5)

722* Mijana (IRE) looked fit despite his layoff and time may tell that to trouble the winner, if only briefly, was an achievement. (7/2: op 7/4)

3234 YE OLDE OAK 'HOT DOG' H'CAP (0-70) (3-Y.O) (Class E)

2-30 (2-32) **1m 4f (July)** £4,207.50 (£1,260.00: £605.00: £277.50) Stalls: High GOING minus 0.13 sec per fur (G)

				SP	RR	SF
2731[12]	**Prince Alex (IRE) (63)** (ACStewart) **3-9-0** SWhitworth(8) (hld up: c centre st: effrt 4f out: hdwy to ld 2f out: hung rt over 1f out: drvn out)	—	1	5/1[2]	74	45
3028[3]	**Keepsake (IRE) (46)** (MDIUsher) **3-7-11** RStreet(10) (hld up: gd hdwy over 1f out: nt rch wnr)	nk	2	14/1	57	28
	Pietro Bembo (IRE) (69) (SirMarkPrescott) **3-9-6** SSanders(11) (dwlt: sn chsng ldrs: ev ch 2f out: kpt on same pce)	1½	3	13/2[3]	78	49
2652[3]	**Arriving (65)** (JWHills) **3-9-2** RHills(7) (hdwy 4f out: hmpd over 1f out: kpt on again ins fnl f)	nk	4	3/1[1]	73	44
2315[14]	**Spick And Span (53)** (CWThornton) **3-8-4** JStack(12) (s.i.s: hdwy 6f out: led over 2f out: sn hdd & btn)	nk	5	33/1	61	32
2064[6]	**Scarrots (70)** (SCWilliams) **3-9-7** DHolland(6) (w ldrs: c centre st: wknd over 2f out)	s.h	6	11/1	78	49
2776[4]	**Sarbaron (IRE) (61)** (PWHarris) **3-8-12** GCarter(2) (prom: rdn over 2f out: sn btn)	4	7	16/1	63	34
1938[10]	**Persian Blue (65)** (RHannon) **3-9-2** WJO'Connor(15) (nvr nr to chal)	2½	8	16/1	64	35
2667[5]	**Rare Talent (64)** (MRChannon) **3-9-1** ACulhane(14) (chsd ldrs over 8f)	3	9	16/1	59	30
2876[4]	**Flotilla (53)** (SMellor) **3-8-4** AMcGlone(9) (plld hrd: prom 7f)	7	10	20/1	39	10
2667[2]	**Bewitching Lady (48)** (DWPArbuthnot) **3-7-8**(5) RMullen(1) (lw: in tch: c centre st: btn over 2f out)	½	11	12/1	33	4
2662[6]	**Frankie (48)** (MHTompkins) **3-7-13** DaleGibson(5) (prom 8f)	2½	12	25/1	30	1
2667[3]	**Swing West (USA) (65)** (PFICole) **3-9-2** MRimmer(3) (lw: trckd ldr tl wknd 3f out)	11	13	14/1	32	3
2591[10]	**Pemberley (IRE) (47)** (WJHaggas) **3-7-12** JQuinn(4) (c centre st: nvr nr ldrs)	7	14	25/1	5	—
2389[5]	**Alpina (USA) (67)** (JHMGosden) **3-9-4** GHind(13) (led tl hdd & wknd over 2f out)	20	15	11/1	—	—
				(SP 125.7%)		**15 Rn**

2m 35.36 (6.36) CSF £66.18 CT £433.03 TOTE £7.70: £2.40 £4.40 £2.70 (£91.90) Trio £383.50 OWNER S Corman Ltd (NEWMARKET) BRED David A. Clarke

2315 Prince Alex (IRE) does himself well as he still carries condition, but got off the mark in his first handicap despite again showing a tendency to hang. His drift into the whip in the dip did cause trouble and under the old rules would have cost him the race as it cost Arriving third place. He looks the sort to progress further and headgear may aid his steering. (5/1: op 8/1)

3028 Keepsake (IRE), dropping half a mile in trip, was hardly made much use of. After having several positions towards the rear in the straight, he finally went for a run towards the stands' side in the dip and would have got up in a few strides. (14/1)

Pietro Bembo (IRE), making a belated seasonal bow, moved down really well and shaped well, although unable to pick up from the dip. On pedigree this trip may just beyond his best. (13/2)

2652 Arriving, back on better ground, would have finished third at least but for meeting interference in the dip. (3/1)

1950 Spick And Span in the lead briefly, was soon left standing once headed and his ability to get this trip is not yet proven. (33/1)

2064 Scarrots couldn't dominate and coming to the centre of the course in the final mile merely served to help others. This can be a daunting place for front-runners. (11/1: 8/1-12/1)

2667 Bewitching Lady (12/1: op 8/1)

2667 Swing West (USA) (14/1: 10/1-16/1)

2389 Alpina (USA) (11/1: 6/1-12/1)

3235 E.B.F. CARTERS SOFT DRINKS MAIDEN STKS (2-Y.O) (Class D)

3-05 (3-06) **6f (July)** £4,110.00 (£1,230.00: £590.00: £270.00) Stalls: Low GOING minus 0.13 sec per fur (G)

				SP	RR	SF
	Teapot Row (IRE) (JARToller) **2-9-0** SSanders(5) (cmpt: mde all: drew clr fnl f: rdn out)	—	1	14/1[3]	93+	63
	Friendly Warning (FR) (JEBanks) **2-8-9** JQuinn(6) (neat: chsd ldrs: rdn 2f out: kpt on: no ch w wnr)	4	2	25/1	77	47
	Hakeem (IRE) (RWArmstrong) **2-9-0** RPrice(3) (w'like: scope: dwlt: hdwy over 2f out: r.o wl fnl f)	1¾	3	14/1[3]	78	48
	Golden Dice (USA) (HRACecil) **2-9-0** WRyan(9) (neat: scope: w wnr: rdn 2f out: sn btn)	1¼	4	7/2[2]	74	44
3131[6]	**Al Mabrook (IRE)** (KMahdi) **2-9-0** DHolland(7) (trckd ldrs: one pce fnl 2f)	2	5	16/1	69	39
	Kheyrah (USA) (EALDunlop) **2-8-9** RHills(10) (w'like: leggy: trckd ldrs: rdn 2f out: sn btn)	2½	6	8/13[1]	57	27
3047[8]	**Imshishway (IRE)** (BJMeehan) **2-9-0** MTebbutt(11) (lw: prom tl rdn & btn 2f out)	2	7	33/1	57	27
	Paarl Rock (DRLoder) **2-8-11**(3) PMcCabe(2) (cmpt: scope: bkwd: rdn 2f out: nvr nr to chal)	1¼	8	14/1[3]	54	24
	Free Option (IRE) (BHanbury) **2-9-0** JStack(4) (w'like: prom 4f)	s.h	9	20/1	54	24
	Confirmation (SirMarkPrescott) **2-9-0** CNutter(1) (wl grwn: bkwd: dwlt: sn pushed along: nvr nr ldrs)	½	10	16/1	52	22
2771[6]	**Fritton (IRE)** (MHTompkins) **2-9-0** DaleGibson(12) (lw: dwlt: a bhd)	3	11	20/1	44	14
	Greeba (RHannon) **2-8-9** WJO'Connor(8) (cmpt: s.v.s: nt rcvr)	4	12	16/1	29	—
	Walpole (DRLoder) **2-9-0** CHodgson(13) (str: cmpt: bkwd: bhd fnl 3f)	4	13	16/1	23	—
				(SP 144.0%)		**13 Rn**

1m 13.74 (1.74) CSF £336.15 TOTE £14.70: £2.20 £4.60 £3.80 (£113.30) Trio £490.30 OWNER Duke of Devonshire (WHITSBURY) BRED Cambremont Ltd Partnership

Teapot Row (IRE), whose dam is a half-sister to last year's maiden winner Green Bopper, is bred to stay well but doesn't take the eye, being compact and rather narrow. Just in front throughout, he had them all in trouble by the two-furlong pole and, the further they went, the better he got. A most promising start. (14/1: op 8/1)

Friendly Warning (FR), a rather small filly, who looked in need of the run, was far too keen going down. To show so well towards the end of the race, given the circumstances, does suggest a degree of promise. (25/1)

Hakeem (IRE), a rather long-backed newcomer, related to a couple of winners, stayed on nicely in the closing stages after looking one of few without a chance just past halfway. (14/1: 8/1-16/1)
Golden Dice (USA) is not very big but moved to post quite pleasingly. Upsides the winner from the off, he was comprehensively outpaced once his rival stepped on the gas. (7/2: 5/2-4/1)
3131 Al Mabrook (IRE), having his second race in three days, was taken down steadily and id gradually getting the hang of things. (16/1)
Kheyrah (USA), backed off the boards, didn't look ready and, despite moving down really well, was caught out by her lack of a race. (8/13)
Imshishway (IRE), who is a very good mover and looks the part, didn't run quite as well as might have been expected but this run could easily have come too soon after his debut. (33/1)
Paarl Rock (14/1: op 8/1)
Free Option (IRE), a tallish newcomer, got a little warm but showed a good action going down and laid up well until the tempo quickened. He will come on for this. (20/1)
Walpole, a very sturdy newcomer, looked well in his coat although just in need of the race and was colty beforehand. A half-brother to a couple of winners, he could go either way. (16/1)

3236 YE OLDE OAK 'ANY TIME SNACKS' H'CAP (0-80) (3-Y.O) (Class D)

3-35 (3-36) **1m (July)** £4,698.00 (£1,404.00: £672.00: £306.00) Stalls: Low GOING minus 0.13 sec per fur (G)

				SP	RR	SF
2408^{3}	**Silk St John (74)** (MJRyan) **3-9-2** GCarter(10) (lw: hld up: hdwy 2f out: str run to ld nr fin)	—	**1**	11/2^{2}	84	56
3100^{6}	**Swift (67)** (MJPolglase) **3-8-9** JTate(2) (trckd ldrs: squeezed thro to ld over 1f out: sn clr: ct nr fin)	½	**2**	14/1	76	48
*3044**	**Cherokee Flight (60)** (SMellor) **3-8-2** JQuinn(9) (hld up: nt clr run fr 2f out: styd on wl fnl f)	1¾	**3**	12/1	66	38
2323^{3}	**Monaco (IRE) (67)** (LMCumani) **3-8-9** DHolland(3) (a.p: led 2f out: sn hdd: wknd ins fnl f)	3	**4**	9/1	67	39
2772*	**Raaha (79)** (RWArmstrong) **3-9-7** RHills(14) (chsd ldrs: rdn & edgd lft over 1f out: no imp)	s.h	**5**	13/2^{3}	78	50
2760^{6}	**Liquid Gold (IRE) (72)** (WAO'Gorman) **3-9-0** EmmaO'Gorman(13) (lw: chsd ldrs: rdn over 2f out: sn btn)	3	**6**	7/1	65	37
2506^{2}	**Quibbling (72)** (HCandy) **3-9-0** AMcGlone(1) (dwlt: bhd tl sme hdwy fnl f)	nk	**7**	7/1	65	37
2585^{12}	**Foot Battalion (IRE) (75)** (RHollinshead) **3-9-0**(3) DGriffiths(6) (chsd ldrs tl rdn & wknd 3f out)	1½	**8**	20/1	65	37
2778^{2}	**Blewbury Hill (IRE) (74)** (RFJohnsonHoughton) **3-9-2** SSanders(5) (w ldr: ev ch 2f out: wknd fnl f)	½	**9**	9/2^{1}	63	35
2877*	**Merciless Cop (73)** (BJMeehan) **3-9-1b** MTebbutt(8) (hld up: hdwy over 2f out: wknd fnl f)	½	**10**	11/1	61	33
1973^{9}	**Maladerie (IRE) (68)** (MRChannon) **3-8-10** ACulhane(7) (led 6f)	4	**11**	33/1	48	20
2772^{2}	**Go For Green (60)** (DrJDScargill) **3-7-13**(3) DO'Donohoe(4) (stdd s: a bhd)	½	**12**	14/1	39	11
2773^{4}	**Reeds (65)** (JRFanshawe) **3-8-7** NDay(11) (rdn 3f out: a bhd)	½	**13**	25/1	43	15
3029^{2}	**Star Turn (IRE) (61)** (MBell) **3-8-3** MFenton(12) (w ldrs: wkng whn hmpd over 1f out)	12	**14**	12/1	15	—
				(SP 130.5%)	**14 Rn**	

1m 41.29 (3.29) CSF £78.06 CT £859.06 TOTE £8.20: £2.70 £5.60 £4.10 (£75.30) Trio £273.70 OWNER C R S Partners (NEWMARKET) BRED L. Audus
2408 Silk St John, a half-brother to Misty Silks, Kingchip Boy and Prima Silk, has probably found his trip and produced an excellent burst of speed to win from an unpromising position. (11/2)
3100 Swift, back on good ground, still moved down poorly but was back to his best. Bursting clear in the dip, he may have done too much, too soon for he was a sitting duck when the winner pounced. (14/1)
3044* Cherokee Flight, couldn't get through when he wanted to but, once in the clear, although staying on well, failed to match the turn of foot of the winner. (12/1)
2323 Monaco (IRE), very free going down, is not giving himself a chance of seeing out the trip he has been trying. (9/1)
2772* Raaha, rather keen going down, didn't have the draw to help him this time and, once off the bit, tended to hang. (13/2)
2760 Liquid Gold (IRE), a half-brother to Exalted, gives the impression that he is worth a try over further. (7/1)
2506 Quibbling, bred to be well suited by middle distances, was very free going down and missed the break, probably to some extent deliberately. She stayed on from an impossible position and will have a future over further if only she settles down. (7/1)
2778 Blewbury Hill (IRE), on the keen side going down, may get this trip with a patient ride but certainly doesn't see it out with so much use made of him. (9/2)
2877* Merciless Cop (11/1: 7/1-12/1)

3237 HERO DRINKS NURSERY H'CAP (2-Y.O) (Class C)

4-10 (4-11) **6f (July)** £17,220.00 (£5,160.00: £2,480.00: £1,140.00) Stalls: Low GOING minus 0.13 sec per fur (G)

				SP	RR	SF
2919*	**Jay Gee (IRE) (82)** (GGMargarson) **2-9-0** GCarter(3) (w ldrs: led over 1f out: rdn out)	—	**1**	13/2^{2}	92	56
2926^{2}	**Clef of Silver (77)** (WJarvis) **2-8-9** RHills(14) (hdwy over 2f out: rdn & hung lft: no ex fnl f)	2	**2**	13/2^{2}	82	46
3022^{3}	**Diamond White (83)** (GCBravery) **2-9-1** DRMcCabe(12) (hdwy over 1f out: r.o wl ins fnl f)	1¼	**3**	16/1	84	48
3042^{2}	**Kennet (73)** (PDCundell) **2-8-5** JQuinn(16) (b.off hind: bhd: gd hdwy fnl f: fin wl)	hd	**4**	20/1	74	38
2545*	**Happy Days Again (IRE) (86)** (JWharton) **2-8-13**(5) RMullen(11) (led tl hdd over 1f out: sn wknd)	2	**5**	8/1^{3}	82	46
2862^{9}	**Phone Alex (IRE) (79)** (RHannon) **2-8-8**(3) AWhelan(5) (chsd ldrs: pushed along over 2f out: edgd lft & sn btn)	2	**6**	9/1	69	33
1475^{6}	**Stately Princess (77)** (MRChannon) **2-8-9** ACulhane(6) (in tch: rdn over 1f out: kpt on fnl f)	s.h	**7**	12/1	67	31
2664*	**Acid Test (65)** (WRMuir) **2-7-8**(3) MBaird(13) (lw: chsd ldrs: ev ch over 2f out: sn btn)	4	**8**	25/1	45	9
2103^{8}	**Minetta (80)** (MBell) **2-8-12** MFenton(10) (nvr nr to chal)	1	**9**	16/1	57	21
1856^{2}	**Lasham (67)** (NACallaghan) **2-7-8**(5) APolli(1) (racd alone: spd over 3f)	2	**10**	25/1	39	3
2886^{3}	**Leofric (75)** (MJPolglase) **2-8-7b** JTate(2) (s.s: sn w ldrs: ev ch over 2f out: rdn & hung lft: sn btn)	2½	**11**	33/1	40	4
2565*	**Composition (84)** (MAJarvis) **2-9-2** WRyan(8) (lw: a bhd)	2	**12**	13/2^{2}	44	8
3067^{2}	**Mamora Bay (IRE) (74)** (MHTompkins) **2-8-6v^{1}** DaleGibson(9) (rdn 2f out: a bhd)	1	**13**	16/1	31	—
2863^{7}	**Fiveo'clock Shadow (IRE) (83)** (BJMeehan) **2-9-1b^{1}** MTebbutt(4) (w ldrs: rdn 2f out: sn btn)	1¼	**14**	20/1	37	1
2786*	**Whisky Mack (IRE) (89)** (RHannon) **2-9-7** WJO'Connor(7) (a bhd)	9	**15**	5/1^{1}	19	—
				(SP 123.3%)	**15 Rn**	

1m 14.22 (2.22) CSF £41.33 CT £619.66 TOTE £6.20: £2.40 £1.90 £3.70 (£16.80) Trio £112.40 OWNER Mr John Guest (NEWMARKET) BRED Eaton Farms Inc, Red Bull Stable and Joe Hernon
OFFICIAL EXPLANATION **Whisky Mack (IRE): no explanation offered.**
2919* Jay Gee (IRE) showed her win was no fluke and, ridden in a similarly aggressive manner, won a trifle readily to give the yard their biggest success. She ought to stay another furlong. (13/2)
2926 Clef of Silver burst through towards the stands' side but, once the chance was there, seemed to want to do little other than hang in behind the winner. The ability is definitely there but he is becoming frustrating. (13/2: 10/1-6/1)
3022 Diamond White, taken down quietly, came home well enough to suggest a nursery over seven could come her way. (16/1)
3042 Kennet only got going when the race was over, finishing best of all, but is not bred to stay much further. (20/1)
2545* Happy Days Again (IRE), stepping up in trip, showed terrific speed until failing to last home. (8/1)

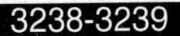

2147* Phone Alex (IRE) has an action which suggests any further ease in the ground would not come amiss. (9/1)
2588 Fiveo'clock Shadow (IRE) was too free in the first-time blinkers. (20/1)

3238 'READY RICE' H'CAP (0-90) (3-Y.O+) (Class C)
4-40 (4-42) **1m 2f (July)** £5,580.00 (£1,665.00: £795.00: £360.00) Stalls: High GOING minus 0.13 sec per fur (G)

				SP	RR	SF
	Mohawk River (IRE) (90) (MRStoute) **4-10-0** SSanders(4) (h.d.w: hld up: rdn over 1f out: str run to ld wl ins fnl f)	—	1	11/1	103	75
2839[4]	**Military (USA) (85)** (HRACecil) **3-9-0** WRyan(9) (trckd ldr: rdn to ld over 1f out: hdd & no ex wl ins fnl f)	¾	2	4/1[1]	97	60
2846*	**Khayali (IRE) (89)** (DMorley) **3-9-4** RHills(1) (lw: led: rdn wl over 1f out: sn hdd & one pce)	2½	3	11/2[3]	97	60
2710[8]	**Bay of Islands (82)** (DMorris) **5-9-6** NDay(7) (prom: rdn 3f out: kpt on same pce)	1¼	4	8/1	88	60
2574[4]	**Vola Via (USA) (83)** (IABalding) **4-9-7** SWhitworth(2) (hld up: hdwy fnl 2f: nt pce to chal)	s.h	5	13/2	89	61
2961[10]	**Herr Trigger (70)** (DrJDScargill) **6-8-8b** JTate(5) (in tch: hdwy over 2f out: sn ev ch: no imp appr fnl f)	s.h	6	12/1	76	48
2961[2]	**Bardon Hill Boy (IRE) (85)** (BHanbury) **5-9-9** MRimmer(6) (chsd ldrs: rdn 3f out: sn btn)	9	7	4/1[1]	76	48
2890[3]	**Wathbat Nashwan (80)** (LMCumani) **3-8-9** DHolland(8) (lw: hld up: hdwy 3f out: wknd wl over 1f out)	hd	8	5/1[2]	71	34
2292[5]	**Cybertechnology (82)** (BWHills) **3-8-11b[1]** GCarter(3) (b: hld up & plld hrd: nvr nr ldrs)	3½	9	16/1	68	31
				(SP 118.4%)	**9 Rn**	

2m 6.73 (3.13) CSF £51.06 CT £250.72 TOTE £13.30: £2.90 £2.10 £1.90 (£33.40) Trio £61.00 OWNER Sheikh Mohammed (NEWMARKET)
BRED Sheikh Mohammed bin Rashid al Maktoum
WEIGHT FOR AGE 3yo-9lb
Mohawk River (IRE), a half-brother to In The Wings and Hawker's News, looks to have done well over the winter but had not quite come in his coat. A slightly scratchy mover, he suddenly found a terrific turn of foot on meeting the rising ground, so much so that his pilot was able to ease down a stride or two before the line, such was his impetus. Older horses from this yard are to be feared and this one is no exception. (11/1)
2839 Military (USA) had to battle to pass Khayali in the dip but, seemed to have the race in safe keeping going a couple of lengths to the good. Whether he took things a little too easy is hard to say but he had no answer when the winner quickened by close home. (4/1)
2846* Khayali (IRE), an eyecatching half-brother to Middle Park winner Balla Cove, does look a bit of a character once ridden, but this looked a hot handicap and there will be other days. (11/2)
2155 Bay of Islands, from some way out, was being niggled along and going not quite well enough to take a hand. To his credit, he stuck to his guns to the line. Every race of his life has been over this trip and it is amazing that he has yet to try a mile and a half. (8/1)
2574 Vola Via (USA) ran respectably but was found wanting for a turn of foot in this company. (13/2)
Herr Trigger, having only his third race in almost two years, ran very well, looking the only one likely to trouble Military and Khayali until the complexion changed completely in the last furlong. (12/1)
2961 Bardon Hill Boy (IRE), up in the handicap and in class, never seriously looked like getting off the mark for the season. (4/1)
2890 Wathbat Nashwan (5/1: 7/2-11/2)

T/Plpt: £16,942.00 (0.7 Tckts); £6,962.47 to Chepstow 3/8/97. T/Qdpt: £1,077.60 (0.29 Tckts); £1,033.99 to Chepstow 3/8/97 Dk

3208-THIRSK (L-H) (Good)
Saturday August 2nd
WEATHER: cloudy

3239 TONY WHITING PUBLIC RELATIONS E.B.F. SUTTON MAIDEN STKS (2-Y.O) (Class D)
2-10 (2-13) **5f** £4,029.00 (£1,212.00: £586.00: £273.00) Stalls: High GOING minus 0.13 sec per fur (G)

				SP	RR	SF
2762[2]	**Perfect Peach** (JBerry) **2-8-6**(3) TEDurcan(12) (lw: mde all: clr over 1f out: comf)	—	1	11/10[1]	78	8
2713[7]	**Happy Days (79)** (DMoffatt) **2-8-11**(3) DarrenMoffatt(1) (a.p: rdn over 1f out: r.o one pce)	2	2	9/1	77	7
	Thistle Park (TDBarron) **2-9-0** JCarroll(6) (leggy: unf: bit bkwd: hld up: hdwy ½-wy: kpt on wl ins fnl f)	1¼	3	16/1	73	3
	Fizzed (MJohnston) **2-8-9** JWeaver(7) (w'like: leggy: unf: bit bkwd: s.s: hdwy 2f out: r.o wl ins fnl f)	hd	4	9/2[2]	67+	—
2762[5]	**Smart Prince** (JJQuinn) **2-8-11**(3) GParkin(9) (a.p: rdn over 1f out: unable qckn)	nk	5	25/1	71	1
1255[5]	**Euro Venture** (DNicholls) **2-9-0** AlexGreaves(3) (bit bkwd: chsd ldrs: rdn & one pce appr fnl f)	½	6	7/1[3]	70	—
2477[13]	**Hey Up Mate (IRE)** (JBerry) **2-9-0** OPears(5) (trckd ldrs: effrt & rdn over 1f out: nt pce to chal)	nk	7	33/1	69	—
	Penny Whistle (TDEasterby) **2-8-9** NKennedy(10) (small: cmpt: bkwd: s.s: nvr nrr)	1	8	25/1	61	—
	Stately Favour (MJCamacho) **2-8-9** LCharnock(4) (w'like: bit bkwd: effrt & rdn wl over 1f out: no imp)	s.h	9	25/1	60	—
	Ray of Sunshine (IRE) (MrsJRRamsden) **2-9-0** JFortune(11) (leggy: scope: bit bkwd: s.s: effrt 2f out: sn rdn: btn whn nt clr run ins fnl f)	s.h	10	14/1	65	—
	Lambs Lane (TDEasterby) **2-9-0** CRutter(8) (w'like: str: bkwd: hld up: hdwy & rdn along 2f out: wknd wl over 1f out)	¾	11	20/1	63	—
	The Fuelologist (MissJFCraze) **2-9-0** SWebster(13) (leggy: lt-f: unf: in tch to ½-wy: sn rdn & wknd)	1¾	12	40/1	57	—
	Far Removed (IRE) (MrsJRRamsden) **2-9-0** MDeering(2) (w'like: leggy: bkwd: outpcd)	½	13	20/1	56	—
				(SP 127.3%)	**13 Rn**	

62.0 secs (4.40) CSF £10.49 TOTE £2.10: £1.10 £1.90 £6.20 (£6.60) Trio £103.70 OWNER Mrs Ann Morris (COCKERHAM) BRED R. J. Vines
2762 Perfect Peach had the perfect draw, and with her added experience to boot, put paid to this opposition in no uncertain terms. (11/10)
1774 Happy Days, in contrast to the winner, was drawn out in the centre of the track, but he had the speed to push the pace until having to admit the favourite much too good for him. (9/1)
Thistle Park, who has been gelded, looked as if he would benefit from this racecourse debut, and he was getting to realise what was needed in the latter stages. (16/1)
Fizzed, a leggy daughter of useful racemare Clicquot, looked ill-at-ease on this lively ground. Hesitant as the stalls opened, she did extremely well to finish so close, and she should not be hard to place. (9/2)
2762 Smart Prince had little chance of reversing his placings with the winner on these identical terms, but he only faded out of the prizemoney inside the distance, and he should be able to find a small race. (25/1)
1255 Euro Venture has enjoyed a ten-week break since his last outing, and remained in close contention until feeling the strain on the approach to the final furlong. (7/1)
Penny Whistle, a not over-big, backward-looking filly bred for speed, was unable to recover from a sluggish start, but she caught the eye running on steadily, and she looks to have what it takes. (25/1)
Ray of Sunshine (IRE) (14/1: op 8/1)

3240 ROCOM LADIES' (S) H'CAP (0-60) (3-Y.O+) (Class E)

2-40 (2-42) **6f** £3,662.00 (£1,106.00: £538.00: £254.00) Stalls: High GOING minus 0.13 sec per fur (G)

Form	Horse	Dist	Pos	SP	RR	SF
2899^{13}	**Another Nightmare (IRE) (44)** (RMMcKellar) **5-10-9**(4) MrsCWilliams(20) (lw: mde all stands' side: clr ins fnl f)	—	**1**	14/1	56	33
2899^{11}	**L A Touch (40)** (JJQuinn) **4-10-9** MissAElsey(1) (trckd ldrs far side: rdn & r.o wl towards fin)	2½	**2**	14/1	45	22
1944^{6}	**Dancing Sioux (47)** (RGuest) **5-10-9**(7) MissZBurkett(19) (b: a.p: stands' side: rdn & one pce fnl f)	½	**3**	14/1	51	28
2657^{6}	**Stephensons Rocket (46)** (RAFahey) **6-10-11**(4) MissSHiggins(4) (trckd ldrs: carried rt over 2f out: r.o wl ins fnl f)	1¾	**4**	10/1	45	22
3039*	**Roseate Lodge (40)** (SEKettlewell) **11-10-2**(7) MissJHarrison(23) (lw: hdwy wl over 1f out: r.o wl cl home)	s.h	**5**	$7/1^{2}$	39	16
2755^{3}	**Henry the Hawk (41)** (MDods) **6-10-6b**(4) MissERamsden(5) (b: lw: led far side 2f out: rdn & one pce ins fnl f)	s.h	**6**	$8/1^{3}$	40	17
2954^{6}	**Okay Baby (IRE) (26)** (JMBradley) **5-9-5b**[1](4) MissHWebster(12) (chsd ldrs stands' side: rdn & outpcd over 1f out)	3½	**7**	12/1	16	—
2759^{6}	**Reinhardt (IRE) (45)** (DNicholls) **4-11-0** MissJAllison(24) (hdwy appr f: fin wl)	hd	**8**	$6/1^{1}$	35	12
2755^{8}	**Morning Star (47)** (WMcKeown) **3-10-12** MissPRobson(3) (chsd ldrs far side: rdn 2f out: sn wknd)	nk	**9**	50/1	36	9
2938^{5}	**Mu-Arrik (29)** (GROldroyd) **9-9-5v**(7) MissAArmitage(21) (nvr nrr)	s.h	**10**	16/1	18	—
2696^{14}	**Burning Cost (25)** (REPeacock) **7-9-4**(4) MrsCPeacock(2) (rdn along far side: nvr rchd ldrs)	hd	**11**	50/1	13	—
2852^{W}	**Petraco (IRE) (50)** (NASmith) **9-10-12**(7) MissAShirley-Priest(10) (prom 4f)	1	**12**	14/1	36	13
2899^{3}	**Seconds Away (34)** (JSGoldie) **6-9-10b**(7) MissDCarter(11) (nvr nr to chal)	1	**13**	12/1	17	—
585^{21}	**Maysimp (IRE) (43)** (BPJBaugh) **4-10-5**(7)ow8 MissSMPotts(13) (a in rr)	½	**14**	50/1	25	—
2934^{15}	**Kalar (41)** (DWChapman) **8-10-10** MissRClark(6) (w ldrs far side 4f: hung bdly rt fr ½-wy)	hd	**15**	14/1	22	—
2887^{9}	**First Option (32)** (RBastiman) **7-9-8**(7)ow9 MissRBastiman(22) (racd stands' side: a bhd & outpcd)	hd	**16**	50/1	13	—
2903^{7}	**Paldost (43)** (MDHammond) **3-10-1**(7) MrsAHammond(8) (outpcd)	nk	**17**	16/1	23	—
3034^{16}	**Dominelle (51)** (TDEasterby) **5-11-2**(4) MissADeniel(9) (nvr gng pce of ldrs)	hd	**18**	14/1	31	8
2780^{7}	**Chief's Lady (35)** (JMBradley) **5-10-0**(4) MissVRoberts(15) (s.s: a bhd)	1	**19**	16/1	12	—
2939^{3}	**Ohnonotagain (38)** (MrsNMacauley) **5-10-7** MissDianaJones(14) (outpcd)	2½	**20**	10/1	9	—
1115^{8}	**Patrita Park (45)** (WWHaigh) **3-10-6**(4) MissEJJones(18) (prom over 3f: sn wknd)	¾	**21**	33/1	14	—
2937^{13}	**Everset (FR) (39)** (ABailey) **9-10-1**(7) MissALHutchinson(16) (b: outpcd)	1	**22**	16/1	5	—
2755^{7}	**Chalice (52)** (MrsASwinbank) **4-11-0**(7) MissLPreston(17) (in tch stands' side over 3f out: sn outpcd)	6	**23**	25/1	2	—
	Vales Ales (25) (RMMcKellar) **4-9-1**(7) MissKWarnett(7) (prom far side 3f: sn lost tch: t.o)	3	**24**	50/1	—	—

(SP 151.6%) **24 Rn**

1m 15.3 (5.60) CSF £204.84 CT £2,634.64 TOTE £22.80: £3.60 £5.40 £3.40 £2.30 (£420.80) Trio £524.90; £295.75 to Chepstow 3/8/97
OWNER GM Engineering (LESMAHAGOW) BRED John J. Ryan
WEIGHT FOR AGE 3yo-4lb
No bid

2826 Another Nightmare (IRE) always had control of her rivals under the stands rails, but she did have to do battle with the far side leaders before proving too smart for them. (14/1)
L A Touch ran her best race for quite some time, but being drawn on the opposite side to the winner certainly did her no favours. (14/1)
1944 Dancing Sioux has performed well at this trip in the past, but he has only ever won at seven furlongs on the All-Weather, so this performance on this step down in class shows he had not lost his ability to win, especially at this level. (14/1)
2657 Stephensons Rocket may well have taken a deal of beating had he not been carried almost the whole width of the track by the hanging Kalar from soon after halfway, and he deserves the chance to put the record straight. (10/1)
3039* Roseate Lodge was not helped by this return to sprinting, but he did finish best of all, and he is retaining his form. (7/1)
2755 Henry the Hawk took control of the far-side group two furlongs out, and soon showed clear, but he failed to sustain the effort, and faded inside the final furlong. (8/1)
2759 Reinhardt (IRE), not the most dependable of animals, took time to find his stride, and by the time he did, the race was all but over. (6/1)

3241 COOPERS & LYBRAND MAIDEN H'CAP (0-70) (3-Y.O+) (Class E)

3-10 (3-11) **6f** £3,874.75 (£1,168.00: £566.50: £265.75) Stalls: High GOING minus 0.13 sec per fur (G)

Form	Horse	Dist	Pos	SP	RR	SF
2674^{5}	**River Ensign (35)** (WMBrisbourne) **4-7-4**(7) AMcCarthy(14) (a.p stands' side: led 2f out: comf)	—	**1**	10/1	47	9
3088^{4}	**Two On The Bridge (60)** (DenysSmith) **3-9-4b**[1] LCharnock(7) (hdwy wl over 1f out: nrst fin)	1¼	**2**	$4/1^{2}$	69	27
3037^{8}	**Night Express (55)** (BHanbury) **3-8-13** JFortune(13) (hdwy ½-wy: rdn & one pce ins fnl f)	hd	**3**	$7/2^{1}$	63	21
2738^{16}	**Skelton Countess (IRE) (41)** (RHollinshead) **4-8-3** FLynch(15) (lw: in tch stands' side: rdn & edgd lft over 1f out: nvr able to chal)	2½	**4**	25/1	43	5
2891^{9}	**Maydoro (41)** (MDods) **4-8-3** TWilliams(11) (chsd ldrs: rdn 2f out: sn outpcd)	4	**5**	10/1	32	—
779^{6}	**Merrily (53)** (MissSEHall) **4-9-1** DHarrison(10) (bkwd: s.i.s: hdwy over 2f out: nt rch ldrs)	1½	**6**	6/1	40	2
2878^{7}	**Geordie Lad (46)** (JABennett) **3-8-4** CRutter(8) (nvr nr to chal)	nk	**7**	20/1	32	—
2602^{11}	**Bent Raiwand (USA) (34)** (DonEnricoIncisa) **4-7-10** KimTinkler(1) (b: effrt & rdn 2f out: nt pce to chal)	¾	**8**	20/1	18	—
2891^{11}	**In Good Nick (56)** (MWEasterby) **3-8-11v**[1](3) GParkin(5) (mid div: effrt 2f: sn rdn & no imp)	¾	**9**	10/1	38	—
3034^{14}	**Prominent (50)** (MrsVAAconley) **3-8-8v**[1] MDeering(12) (spd 4f: sn lost tch)	5	**10**	20/1	19	—
2523^{12}	**Superapparos (42)** (SRBowring) **3-7-7b**[1](7)ow4 FBoyle(3) (led: edgd rt: hdd 2f out: sn btn)	1¼	**11**	20/1	8	—
2891^{4}	**Madam Zando (34)** (JBalding) **4-7-10v**[1] NCarlisle(6) (spd over 3f)	hd	**12**	20/1	—	—
2496^{12}	**Seanchai (IRE) (34)** (PSFelgate) **4-7-5**(5) IonaWands(4) (outpcd)	4	**13**	33/1	—	—
2941^{10}	**Bright Gold (44)** (ASmith) **3-8-2b** RLappin(9) (bhd fr ½-wy: t.o)	10	**14**	33/1	—	—
2506^{9}	**River Tweed (70)** (JHMGosden) **3-10-0** JCarroll(2) (hdwy ½-wy: sddle slipped & virtually p.u fnl 2f)	dist	**15**	$5/1^{3}$	—	—

(SP 134.0%) **15 Rn**

1m 14.1 (4.40) CSF £44.34 CT £166.15 TOTE £18.00: £3.60 £2.10 £1.60 (£38.20) Trio £52.50 OWNER Crispandave Racing Associates (NESSCLIFFE) BRED A. H. Brisbourne
LONG HANDICAP Madam Zando 7-2 Seanchai (IRE) 7-2 Superapparos 7-7
WEIGHT FOR AGE 3yo-4lb

2674 River Ensign, who has been showing promise on the All-Weather, opened her account under a very competent ride, and if not over-faced she could follow up. (10/1)
3088 Two On The Bridge decided to put his best foot forward in the latter stages in his first-time blinkers, and this half-brother to Comanche Companion can make his mark when returning to a longer trip. (4/1)
2510 Night Express gives the impression that he needs a more yielding surface, but he ran up to his mark, and only got tapped for toe inside the final furlong. (7/2)

Skelton Countess (IRE), still struggling to find her correct trip, did not help her cause by hanging left when ridden approaching the final furlong. (25/1)
2540 Maydoro, in the chasing group, was hard at work entering the final quarter-mile, and she lacked the pace to make any impression. (10/1)
469 Merrily was unable to recover from a slow start, but she did look burly after a lengthy break, and she will improve for the run. (6/1)

3242 BARCLAYS BANK H'CAP (0-80) (3-Y.O+) (Class D)
3-40 (3-41) **1m 4f** £4,987.50 (£1,500.00: £725.00: £337.50) Stalls: Low GOING minus 0.13 sec per fur (G)

				SP	RR	SF
	Kilernan (45) (TDBarron) **6-7-11** LCharnock(3) (hld up: hdwy over 2f out: led appr fnl f: r.o wl)	—	**1**	16/1	53	37
1649^{7}	**Rheinbold (75)** (TJEtherington) **3-9-2** CRutter(1) (lw: hld up: hdwy over 2f out: kpt on u.p ins fnl f)	1¼	**2**	16/1	81	54
2839^{9}	**Albaha (USA) (73)** (JEBanks) **4-9-8**(3) DSweeney(5) (led: clr ½-wy: hdd over 1f out: one pce)	1	**3**	7/1^{3}	78	62
655^{7}	**Star Rage (IRE) (75)** (MJohnston) **7-9-13** JWeaver(2) (bit bkwd: hld up in rr: hdwy 3f out: sn drvn: nt rch ldrs)	5	**4**	11/2^{2}	73	57
2907^{4}	**Lindrick Lady (IRE) (68)** (BSRothwell) **3-8-6**(3) GParkin(9) (chsd ldrs: hrd drvn over 2f out: no imp)	5	**5**	9/1	60	33
3035^{2}	**Canton Venture (76)** (SPCWoods) **5-10-0** JFortune(8) (chsd ldr: rdn 3f out: wknd wl over 1f out)	2	**6**	11/4^{1}	65	49
2890^{10}	**Censor (75)** (DNicholls) **4-9-13** AlexGreaves(7) (lw: hld up & bhd: effrt over 2f out: n.d)	½	**7**	14/1	63	47
2327^{8}	**Opaque (69)** (WStorey) **5-9-7** JFanning(4) (s.i.s: drvn along thrght: no imp)	8	**8**	7/1^{3}	47	31
2890^{5}	**Ibin St James (67)** (JDBethell) **3-8-8b** DHarrison(10) (lw: a in rr)	1½	**9**	7/1^{3}	43	16
3061^{3}	**Lay The Blame (70)** (MDHammond) **4-9-8** JCarroll(6) (lw: trckd ldrs: rdn 3f out: sn wknd: t.o)	8	**10**	7/1^{3}	35	19
				(SP 120.5%)	**10 Rn**	

2m 35.9 (5.20) CSF £229.57 CT £1,788.71 TOTE £12.40: £3.10 £5.50 £2.10 (£402.60) Trio £110.60 OWNER Mr J. O. Hall (THIRSK) BRED James Hall
WEIGHT FOR AGE 3yo-11lb
Kilernan won on his only outing of '96, and to produce him fit to win again after a four-hundred-and-eighty-five day absence in this better-grade event, is a credit to his shrewd trainer. (16/1)
1282* Rheinbold, pulled wide to make progress over two furlongs out, took a long time to find top gear, and though he did run on strongly inside the final furlong, the winner had taken first run and was not for catching. (16/1)
389* Albaha (USA) adopted identical tactics to the ones successful on the All-Weather in March, and he looked to have slipped his field entering the straight, but he does struggle a bit on the turf, and with his stride shortening rapidly, had shot his bolt entering the last furlong. (7/1: op 14/1)
133 Star Rage (IRE) can run well when fresh, but he finds this trip inadequate nowadays, and could not muster the pace to deliver his challenge. One to keep in mind when he returns to two miles. (11/2)
3035 Canton Venture had to be content with a lead this time, but he was off the bridle early in the straight, and his bumper weight once again took its toll. (11/4)
3061 Lay The Blame (7/1: 5/1-8/1)

3243 LORDS TAVERNERS H'CAP (0-95) (3-Y.O+) (Class C)
4-15 (4-16) **1m** £7,476.50 (£2,252.00: £1,091.00: £510.50) Stalls: Low GOING minus 0.13 sec per fur (G)

				SP	RR	SF
2601^{10}	**Caviar Royale (IRE) (93)** (TDBarron) **3-9-5** JCarroll(4) (hld up in rr: smooth hdwy on ins to ld appr fnl f: sn clr)	—	**1**	20/1	106	53
2124^{7}	**Mountgate (66)** (MPBielby) **5-7-13** TWilliams(1) (lw: hld up: rdn 3f out: styd on fnl 2f: nrst fin)	2½	**2**	16/1	74	28
3064*	**Iamus (82)** (TDBarron) **4-8-8**(7) VictoriaAppleby(9) (led tl hdd appr fnl f: no ex)	nk	**3**	8/1	89	43
3061^{4}	**Royal Ceilidh (IRE) (68)** (DenysSmith) **4-8-1** JFanning(2) (lw: a.p: jnd ldr 2f out: rdn & one pce fnl f)	½	**4**	5/1^{2}	74	28
2601^{3}	**Attitude (86)** (HCandy) **3-8-12** CRutter(10) (hld up: pushed along ent st: kpt on fnl 2f: nvr able to chal)	3	**5**	9/2^{1}	86	33
2465^{6}	**Bollin Frank (72)** (TDEasterby) **5-8-5** LCharnock(6) (trckd ldrs: rdn 2f out: eased whn btn appr fnl f)	½	**6**	5/1^{2}	71	25
2857^{7}	**Stackattack (IRE) (73)** (MrsJRRamsden) **4-8-6** JFortune(11) (lw: hld up in tch: effrt & drvn along over 2f out: kpt on same pce)	1¼	**7**	11/2^{3}	70	24
1647^{6}	**Our People (82)** (MJohnston) **3-8-8** JWeaver(5) (lw: w ldr tl rdn & wknd 2f out)	2½	**8**	10/1	74	21
1658^{3}	**Van Gurp (85)** (BAMcMahon) **4-9-4** LNewton(8) (swtg: trckd ldrs: rdn along 5f out: sn wknd: t.o)	9	**9**	16/1	59	13
2678^{7}	**Moving Arrow (86)** (MissSEHall) **6-9-5** FLynch(7) (dwlt: bhd & rdn over 4f out: no rspnse: t.o)	¾	**10**	11/1	58	12
1261^{3}	**Almond Rock (95)** (JRFanshawe) **5-10-0** DHarrison(3) (swtg: hld up: effrt & pushed along ent st: sn no imp: eased: t.o)	6	**11**	7/1	55	9
				(SP 124.5%)	**11 Rn**	

1m 40.3 (3.80) CSF £292.03 CT £2,575.63 TOTE £31.70: £8.60 £4.20 £3.50 (£138.00) Trio £445.30; £501.81 to Chepstow 3/8/97 OWNER Burke's 5th Family Settlement (THIRSK) BRED Jerry O'Brien
WEIGHT FOR AGE 3yo-7lb
2601 Caviar Royale (IRE), completing a double for his local stable, enjoyed a charmed run up the inside rail, and came from last to first to win unchallenged. (20/1)
1655 Mountgate again played up when mounted on the track, and he looked to be in serious trouble when ridden soon after turning in, but to his credit he stayed on really well in the closing stages and is on good terms with himself. (16/1)
3064* Iamus, a stable-companion of the winner, tried hard to repeat his all-the-way success at Newcastle eight days ago, and he hung on grimly until forced to give best entering the final furlong. (8/1)
3061 Royal Ceilidh (IRE) joined issue two furlongs out, and did look to have found a winning opportunity, but with the leader giving as good as he got, she was the one who was forced to give best. She left the impression she was not at all happy on this ground. (5/1)
2601 Attitude, as at Newmarket last month, appears to struggle with the pace at this trip, and as he won at seven furlongs in his first season, a stiffer test of stamina looks to be needed. (9/2)
2465 Bollin Frank is finding it hard to make his presence felt this term, and failing to respond to pressure, the position was accepted below the distance. (5/1)
2857 Stackattack (IRE) has yet to prove that he gets the trip, and he could only gallop on the spot when made to work in the latter stages. (11/2)

3244 HALCYON GROUP MAIDEN STKS (3-Y.O F) (Class D)
4-45 (4-47) **7f** £3,795.00 (£1,140.00: £550.00: £255.00) Stalls: Low GOING minus 0.13 sec per fur (G)

				SP	RR	SF
2773^{2}	**Kafaf (USA) (84)** (JHMGosden) **3-8-11** JCarroll(2) (mde all: clr 2f out: very easily)	—	**1**	8/11^{1}	84++	47
2838^{3}	**Polish Romance (USA) (75)** (MRStoute) **3-8-11** FLynch(1) (s.s: hdwy 3f out: chsd wnr fnl 2f: no imp ins fnl f)	2½	**2**	15/8^{2}	78	41
	Amid The Stars (MJohnston) **3-8-11** JWeaver(4) (still unf: chsd wnr 5f: sn rdn & outpcd)	13	**3**	13/2^{3}	49	12

Toss And Tumble (WWHaigh) **3-8-11** RLappin(3) (w'like: scope: bkwd: trckd ldrs: drvn along & outpcd over 2f out) ....6 **4** 33/1 35? —
(SP 109.0%) **4 Rn**

1m 28.1 (3.20) CSF £2.16 TOTE £1.60 (£1.30) OWNER Mr Hamdan Al Maktoum (NEWMARKET) BRED Shadwell Farm Inc

2773 Kafaf (USA), a bit of a handful to load into the stalls, had little more than an afternoon stroll once in action, and this could be the making of her. (8/11)

2838 Polish Romance (USA), taken to post early, and trying a slightly longer trip, stood still as the stalls opened and lost considerable ground. Set alight once in line for home, she went after the winner entering the last quarter-mile, but after threatening danger, could only stay on at one pace throughout the final furlong. (15/8)

Amid The Stars, still very unfurnished, did not impress to post, and after doing her best to keep tabs on the winner, was a spent force from some way out. (13/2)

T/Plpt: £6,412.40 (2.45 Tckts). T/Qdpt: £600.40 (0.4 Tckts); £486.88 to Chepstow 3/8/97 IM

3015-CHEPSTOW (L-H) (Good to firm, becoming Good to Soft)
Sunday August 3rd
WEATHER: raining WIND: nil

3245 DAY OUT H'CAP (0-70) (3-Y.O+) (Class E)
2-10 (2-11) **1m 4f 23y** £2,853.00 (£864.00: £422.00: £201.00) Stalls: Low GOING minus 0.38 sec per fur (F)

	Horse / details	Dist	Pos	SP	RR	SF
3093[5]	**Yet Again (50)** (MissGayKelleway) **5-8-5**(3) RFfrench(7) (hld up: hdwy 6f out: led wl over 1f out: all out)	—	**1**	4/1[1]	60	42
2782[7]	**Mono Lady (IRE) (55)** (DHaydnJones) **4-8-13** AMackay(4) (hld up & bhd: hdwy over 3f out: ev ch fnl f: r.o wl)	s.h	**2**	6/1[3]	65	47
	Bodantree (38) (NMBabbage) **6-7-5**(5) RMullen(3) (lw: hld up & bhd: hdwy over 2f out: one pce fnl f)	3½	**3**	8/1	43	25
2949[9]	**Reaganesque (USA) (51)** (PGMurphy) **5-8-9** SDrowne(5) (led over 10f: wknd fnl f)	1¾	**4**	4/1[1]	54	36
2928*	**Pay Homage (70)** (IABalding) **9-9-7**(7) RFowley(2) (dwlt: plld hrd: hdwy over 3f out: wknd over 1f out)	s.h	**5**	9/2[2]	73	55
2531[4]	**Nornax Lad (USA) (45)** (MartynMeade) **9-8-3b** FNorton(8) (w ldr: rdn 4f out: wknd 2f out)	1½	**6**	12/1	46	28
1677[10]	**Euro Singer (50)** (TKeddy) **5-8-8** SSanders(1) (hld up: wknd 3f out: t.o fnl 2f)	16	**7**	13/2	30	12
2896[3]	**Excelled (IRE) (38)** (CJDrewe) **8-7-10** JLowe(6) (hld up: wknd 4f out: t.o fnl 2f)	10	**8**	14/1	5	—

(SP 111.3%) **8 Rn**

2m 35.5 (3.10) CSF £24.09 CT £159.43 TOTE £3.90: £1.40 £2.00 £2.60 (£12.30) OWNER Mr A. P. Griffin (WHITCOMBE) BRED Aston Park Stud

LONG HANDICAP Bodantree 7-7 Excelled (IRE) 7-2

OFFICIAL EXPLANATION Euro Singer: had breathing problems.

3093 Yet Again defied a mark 10lb higher than his last victory at Brighton in April. (4/1)

2582 Mono Lady (IRE) lost no caste in defeat and only went down after a protracted tussle. (6/1)

Bodantree, who won over nearly two and a half miles over hurdles in June, was by no means disgraced on this first run on the Flat for just over two years. (8/1: op 5/1)

2592 Reaganesque (USA) was dropping back from fourteen furlongs. (4/1)

2928* Pay Homage, raised 4lb, ran too freely for his young rider. (9/2)

2531 Nornax Lad (USA) has come down a total of 6lb after a couple of defeats in sellers over longer trips. (12/1)

Euro Singer (13/2: 7/2-7/1)

3246 DAVID EVANS 50TH BIRTHDAY H'CAP (0-85) (3-Y.O+) (Class D)
2-40 (2-42) **1m 2f 36y** £5,381.00 (£1,628.00: £794.00: £377.00) Stalls: Low GOING minus 0.38 sec per fur (F)

	Horse / details	Dist	Pos	SP	RR	SF
3012[3]	**Kewarra (70)** (BRMillman) **3-8-7** TSprake(9) (tk keen hold: chsd ldr over 4f: rdn over 1f out: edgd rt & led last strides)	—	**1**	13/2[3]	81	44
2920*	**Anak-Ku (80)** (MissGayKelleway) **4-9-9**(3) RFfrench(2) (plld hrd: led: rdn over 1f out: hdd last strides)	nk	**2**	7/2[1]	91	63
2839[3]	**Roufontaine (77)** (WRMuir) **6-9-6**(3) RHavlin(5) (s.s: hdwy on ins 3f out: r.o one pce fnl 2f)	3½	**3**	7/2[1]	82	54
1398[3]	**Voila Premiere (IRE) (66)** (PGMurphy) **5-8-12** SDrowne(3) (hld up: hdwy over 3f out: n.m.r over 2f out: one pce)	s.h	**4**	6/1[2]	71	43
3053[3]	**Sharp Consul (IRE) (82)** (HCandy) **5-9-7**(7) LJames(7) (lw: nvr nr to chal)	1¼	**5**	6/1[2]	85	57
2287[2]	**Tikopia (84)** (IABalding) **3-9-7** SWhitworth(8) (lw: hld up: hdwy over 2f out: wknd over 1f out)	2½	**6**	9/1	83	46
2920[5]	**Askern (64)** (DHaydnJones) **6-8-10** AMackay(6) (s.s: plld hrd: chsd ldr 6f out: wknd over 1f out)	1½	**7**	10/1	61	33
	Hisar (IRE) (80) (CPEBrooks) **4-9-12** CRutter(10) (bit bkwd: a bhd)	3	**8**	14/1	72	44
3091[11]	**Haroldon (IRE) (68)** (BPalling) **8-9-0** NDay(1) (chsd ldrs tl wknd over 3f out)	1¼	**9**	14/1	58	30

(SP 118.8%) **9 Rn**

2m 7.4 (2.10) CSF £27.70 CT £85.94 TOTE £8.40: £2.20 £1.40 £1.60 (£19.80) Trio £17.50 OWNER Mr G. Palmer (CULLOMPTON) BRED Mrs M. Palmer and G. Palmer

WEIGHT FOR AGE 3yo-9lb

3012 Kewarra had less to do off the same mark than when a good third at Ascot last time. (13/2)

2920* Anak-Ku, raised 5lb, was no less than 15lb higher than when winning over course and distance in June. (7/2)

2839 Roufontaine was meeting the runner up on 13lb better terms than when beaten three-quarters length over course and distance in June. (7/2)

1398 Voila Premiere (IRE), down 2lb, failed to pick up after meeting a little trouble in running and was by no means unlucky. (6/1)

3053 Sharp Consul (IRE) did not find the ground easing in time to enhance his chance. (6/1: op 4/1)

2287 Tikopia looked harshly treated on this handicap debut. (9/1)

2660* Askern (10/1: op 6/1)

Hisar (IRE) (14/1: 10/1-16/1)

3247 SUNDAY MEDIAN AUCTION MAIDEN STKS (2-Y.O F) (Class E)
3-10 (3-13) **5f 16y** £2,801.00 (£848.00: £414.00: £197.00) Stalls: High GOING minus 0.38 sec per fur (F)

	Horse / details	Dist	Pos	SP	RR	SF
884[4]	**Santa Faye (IRE)** (BPalling) **2-8-11** TSprake(5) (mde all: rdn over 1f out: r.o wl)	—	**1**	8/1	74	19
2862[12]	**Relate** (MartynMeade) **2-8-8**(3) RHavlin(8) (stumbled s: a.p: hung lft over 1f out: nt qckn fnl f)	2	**2**	4/1[2]	68	13
2781[3]	**Dover Soul** (PJMakin) **2-8-11** SSanders(3) (hmpd s: hdwy over 2f out: r.o one pce fnl f)	nk	**3**	100/30[1]	67	12

3062[2]	**Patsy Culsyth (70)** (MrsLStubbs) **2-8-8v[1]**(3) DO'Donohoe(1) (carried lft s: sn prom: one pce fnl 2f)	1½	**4**	7/1	62	7
2520[5]	**Mountain Magic** (DJSffrenchDavis) **2-8-11** NCarlisle(4) (hld up: one pce fnl 2f)	1	**5**	10/1	59	4
2781[7]	**Tui** (KMcAuliffe) **2-8-8**(3) RFfrench(6) (nvr nr to chal)	1	**6**	25/1	56	1
2917[9]	**Call Me Vera** (EAWheeler) **2-8-6**(5) ADaly(10) (hld up: no hdwy fnl 2f)	½	**7**	25/1	54	—
	Arjan (IRE) (JBerry) **2-8-6**(5) CLowther(9) (cmpt: s.s: a bhd)	s.h	**8**	6/1[3]	54	—
	Silver Sea (USA) (IABalding) **2-8-11** SWhitworth(7) (w'like: a bhd)	3	**9**	6/1[3]	45	—
1444[5]	**Swift Time (60)** (MRBosley) **2-8-11** CRutter(2) (carried lft s: sn prom: wknd 2f out)	2½	**10**	25/1	37	—
				(SP 115.9%)	**10 Rn**	

59.5 secs (2.50) CSF £35.35 TOTE £8.80: £2.30 £2.00 £1.70 (£10.60) Trio £37.20 OWNER Mrs R. M. Williams (COWBRIDGE) BRED Martyn J. McEnery

884 Santa Faye (IRE), a half-sister to a winner in Belgium, responded well when put to the test. (8/1)

2147 Relate was inclined to hang in behind the winner, just as her rival began to assert. (4/1: 3/1-9/2)

2781 Dover Soul may have finished second had she not been crowded at the start, but it is doubtful if she would have beaten the winner. (100/30)

3062 Patsy Culsyth was back to five furlongs for this first run in a visor. (7/1)

2520 Mountain Magic might be worth a try at six furlongs. (10/1)

Tui could be interesting in nurseries when reverting to a longer distance. (25/1)

Arjan (IRE) (6/1: 4/1-13/2)

Silver Sea (USA) (6/1: op 4/1)

3248 MADEMOISELLE LADIES AMATEUR H'CAP (0-70) (3-Y.O+) (Class G)

3-40 (3-44) **1m 14y** £2,347.50 (£660.00: £322.50) Stalls: High GOING minus 0.33 sec per fur (G)

				SP	RR	SF
2730[11]	**Sis Garden (54)** (JCullinan) **4-10-6**(7) MissEmmaGarley(16) (mde virtually all: r.o wl)	—	**1**	20/1	66	48
2285[5]	**Waikiki Beach (USA) (62)** (GLMoore) **6-11-7** MrsJMoore(1) (led far side: ev ch fnl f: nt qckn)	1¼	**2**	16/1	72	54
3104[9]	**Breezed Well (48)** (KGWingrove) **11-10-2**(5) MrsHNoonan(20) (a.p: r.o one pce fnl f)	2½	**3**	16/1	53	35
2868[5]	**Ca'd'oro (59)** (GBBalding) **4-10-13**(5) MissERamsden(14) (hdwy over 1f out: nvr nrr)	hd	**4**	100/30[1]	63	45
2785[12]	**Asterix (35)** (JMBradley) **9-9-3b**(5)ow1 MissVRoberts(10) (b: dwlt: sn chsng ldrs: no hdwy fnl 2f)	1¼	**5**	12/1	37	18
2854[3]	**Righty Ho (60)** (PTWalwyn) **3-10-7v[1]**(5) MissSSamworth(18) (nvr nr to chal)	s.h	**6**	9/1	62	37
2852[4]	**Charlton Imp (USA) (45)** (RJHodges) **4-9-13**(5) MrsCWilliams(7) (hdwy over 2f out: wknd over 1f out)	nk	**7**	14/1	46	28
2651[9]	**Cee-Jay-Ay (42)** (JBerry) **10-10-1** MissRClark(9) (dwlt: hdwy over 3f out: wknd over 1f out)	1½	**8**	12/1	40	22
2507[5]	**Queens Stroller (IRE) (41)** (REPeacock) **6-9-9**(5) MrsCPeacock(4) (racd far side: bhd fnl 2f)	2	**9**	20/1	35	17
3196[4]	**Royal Acclaim (27)** (KRBurke) **12-8-9v**(5) MissRJPatman(13) (n.d)	¾	**10**	25/1	20	2
2564[9]	**Bellas Gate Boy (48)** (JPearce) **5-10-7** MrsLPearce(8) (n.d)	½	**11**	10/1	40	22
2645*	**With A Will (64)** (HCandy) **3-10-9**(7) MrsCDunwoody(17) (prom over 5f)	nk	**12**	13/2[3]	55	30
2913[3]	**Arrasas Lady (45)** (JRPoulton) **7-9-11**(7)ow15 MrsCPoulton(11) (s.s: a bhd)	2½	**13**	33/1	31	—
	Can't Say (IRE) (30) (JMBradley) **5-8-12**(5) MissHWebster(2) (racd far side: a bhd)	½	**14**	50/1	15	—
2065[6]	**Mr Montague (IRE) (56)** (TWDonnelly) **5-10-10**(5) MissJWormall(12) (a bhd)	5	**15**	33/1	31	13
1507[12]	**Efficacious (IRE) (41)** (PEccles) **4-9-7**(7) MrsNElliott(6) (spd over 5f)	nk	**16**	40/1	16	—
3138[12]	**Zermatt (IRE) (59)** (MDIUsher) **7-10-13**(5) MrsAUsher(15) (a bhd)	3½	**17**	6/1[2]	27	9
	The Four Isles (53) (DJWintle) **3-9-12**(7) MissLEvans(19) (a bhd: t.o)	11	**18**	33/1	—	—
				(SP 130.2%)	**18 Rn**	

1m 35.4 (4.20) CSF £276.90 CT £4,870.02 TOTE £38.30: £5.10 £4.20 £11.10 £1.50 (£168.90) Trio £1,409.50 OWNER Alan Spargo Ltd Toolmakers (AYLESBURY) BRED Mrs J. Mackie and Major W. R. Paton Smith

LONG HANDICAP Royal Acclaim 8-13

WEIGHT FOR AGE 3yo-7lb

1640 Sis Garden was coolly ridden from the front, especially when considering it was her rider's first winner. (20/1)

2285 Waikiki Beach (USA) may have got his head in front in the final quarter-mile and ran his best race on turf for a while having slipped a total of 5lb. (16/1)

2494* Breezed Well was 5lb higher than when winning in a bog at Beverley last month. (16/1)

2868 Ca'd'oro not inconvenienced by the change in ground, was 6lb higher than when winning at Goodwood in June. (100/30: 5/1-3/1)

2375 Asterix, a standing dish in these sort of events here, has slipped to a mark 5lb lower than when winning a similar event over a year ago. (12/1)

2854 Righty Ho, tried in a visor, went down early after playing up going to post last time. (9/1)

3249 SUNDAY MARKET (S) STKS (3-Y.O+) (Class G)

4-10 (4-15) **7f 16y** £2,389.50 (£672.00: £328.50) Stalls: High GOING minus 0.23 sec per fur (F)

				SP	RR	SF
2937[6]	**Greatest (55)** (MissGayKelleway) **6-9-4b**(3) RFfrench(14) (a.p: led over 3f out: hung bdly lft over 2f out: r.o wl)	—	**1**	7/1[3]	60	39
2903[3]	**Murron Wallace (42)** (DHaydnJones) **3-8-5** AMackay(9) (hdwy 2f out: carried lft over 1f out: ev ch ins fnl f: nt qckn)	nk	**2**	7/1[3]	49	22
1238[2]	**Golden Fact (USA) (79)** (RHannon) **3-8-3**(7) RSmith(10) (hld up: hdwy 2f out: one pce fnl f)	1¾	**3**	11/4[2]	50	23
2852[3]	**Abtaal (51)** (RJHodges) **7-9-7** SDrowne(8) (s.s: hdwy over 2f out: one pce fnl f)	2½	**4**	10/1	50	29
2883[7]	**Municipal Girl (IRE) (50)** (BPalling) **3-8-10** TSprake(3) (a.p: one pce fnl 2f)	nk	**5**	12/1	44	17
638[8]	**Backhander (IRE) (41)** (RTPhillips) **5-8-11b**(5) CLowther(11) (prom over 4f)	6	**6**	16/1	31	10
2954[4]	**Dark Menace (49)** (EAWheeler) **5-8-9b**(7) SCarson(6) (no hdwy fnl 3f)	nk	**7**	10/1	30	9
2954[2]	**Crystal Heights (FR) (60)** (RJO'Sullivan) **9-9-2** SSanders(12) (s.s: nvr nr ldrs)	5	**8**	5/2[1]	19	—
1429[5]	**Sheraton Girl (43)** (NPLittmoden) **3-8-3**(7) KPierrepont(13) (prom 4f)	1½	**9**	25/1	15	—
2748[7]	**Hatta Sunshine (USA) (31)** (GLMoore) **7-9-4b[1]**(3) AWhelan(1) (s.s: a bhd)	1¼	**10**	33/1	17	—
2192[6]	**Parijazz (IRE) (55)** (MartynMeade) **3-8-5** FNorton(5) (led over 3f: sn wknd)	3	**11**	20/1	1	—
3048[9]	**Vaporize (28)** (DMHyde) **5-9-2** CRutter(7) (a bhd)	7	**12**	50/1	—	—
	Benicia Boy (JCMcConnochie) **5-9-2** MWigham(2) (s.s: a bhd)	nk	**13**	66/1	—	—
	Abduction (RTJuckes) **4-9-2** VSlattery(4) (rdn 4f out: sn bhd)	1½	**14**	66/1	—	—
				(SP 128.5%)	**14 Rn**	

1m 22.9 (3.60) CSF £51.17 TOTE £7.20: £3.10 £1.90 £2.20 (£33.00) Trio £52.50 OWNER Invoshire Ltd (WHITCOMBE) BRED Bloomsbury Stud

WEIGHT FOR AGE 3yo-6lb

No bid

OFFICIAL EXPLANATION **Crystal Heights (FR): was unsuited by the change in going.**

STEWARDS' ENQUIRY Obj. to Greatest by Mackay overruled.

2937 Greatest managed to hold on despite virtually going from one side of the course to the other. (7/1)

2903 Murron Wallace was intimidated into going over to the far rail by the winner, however there was always daylight between them and she certainly could have won if she'd been good enough. (7/1)
1238 Golden Fact (USA) travelled well on this drop in class, but could not take advantage of the winner's antics. (11/4: 7/4-3/1)
2852 Abtaal was back to the right trip on this return to selling company. (10/1)
1661 Municipal Girl (IRE) possibly found this step up to seven furlongs beyond her best. (12/1)

3250 A DAY AT THE RACES MAIDEN STKS (3-Y.O+) (Class D)
4-40 (4-43) **7f 16y** £3,387.50 (£1,025.00: £500.00: £237.50) Stalls: High GOING minus 0.23 sec per fur (F)

			SP	RR	SF
2835[10]	**Giko (55)** (JRPoulton) **3-8-13** SDrowne(3) (mde all: rdn over 1f out: r.o wl) —	**1**	11/2[3]	77	28
3037[4]	**Topton (IRE)** (IABalding) **3-8-13** SWhitworth(4) (hld up: rdn & chsd wnr fnl 2f: no imp) 3	**2**	Evens[1]	70	21
	Feel No Fear (WRMuir) **4-8-11**(3) DO'Donohoe(1) (hld up: rdn over 2f out: wknd over 1f out) 9	**3**	8/1	45	2
2183[4]	**Zabriskie (74)** (GLMoore) **3-8-13b[1]** SSanders(2) (hld up: rdn over 2f out: sn wknd) 12	**4**	2/1[2]	23	—
2941[14]	**Honiara Bay** (MissAStokell) **3-8-5**(3) PPMurphy(5) (rdn 3f out: sn bhd: t.o) 10	**5**	66/1	—	—

(SP 111.3%) **5 Rn**

1m 23.2 (3.90) CSF £10.71 TOTE £6.60: £2.40 £1.10 (£4.40) OWNER V R V Partnership (LEWES) BRED Sheikh Mohammed bin Rashid al Maktoum
WEIGHT FOR AGE 3yo-6lb
2510 Giko took full advantage of the ease in the ground thanks to the incessant rain. (11/2)
3037 Topton (IRE) could not make the best of what had seemed a golden opportunity. (Evens)
Feel No Fear is a half-sister to sprinter Sweet Magic. (8/1)
2183 Zabriskie did not find the blinkers working the oracle on his first run for his new stable. (2/1: op 5/4)

3251 SUNDAY SPECIAL H'CAP (0-75) (3-Y.O+) (Class D)
5-10 (5-11) **6f 16y** £3,631.25 (£1,100.00: £537.50: £256.25) Stalls: High GOING minus 0.23 sec per fur (F)

			SP	RR	SF
2747[4]	**Gold Edge (50)** (MRChannon) **3-7-13** AMackay(8) (mde all: clr over 1f out: r.o wl) —	**1**	9/1	65	40
2780[2]	**Montendre (75)** (MJHeaton-Ellis) **10-10-0** SSanders(3) (lw: hld up: hdwy over 1f out: hrd rdn ins fnl f: no imp) 4	**2**	9/1	80	59
3092[4]	**Tinker Osmaston (64)** (RJHodges) **6-9-3** SDrowne(1) (lw: hld up: hdwy 2f out: rdn over 1f out: one pce) ½	**3**	11/4[1]	67	46
2921[8]	**Nervous Rex (55)** (WRMuir) **3-8-1**(3) DO'Donohoe(7) (hld up: rdn over 2f out: one pce) ¾	**4**	11/1	56	31
3018[2]	**Speedy Classic (USA) (60)** (MJHeaton-Ellis) **8-8-8**(5) ADaly(10) (w wnr 4f: one pce) ½	**5**	5/1[3]	60	39
2698[2]	**Erupt (64)** (GBBalding) **4-9-0**(3) PPMurphy(5) (nvr nr to chal) 2½	**6**	7/2[2]	57	36
1089[8]	**Croeso Cynnes (68)** (BPalling) **4-9-7** TSprake(2) (prom over 4f) ½	**7**	12/1	60	39
1966[5]	**Polgwynne (50)** (BSmart) **3-7-13** CRutter(6) (bhd fnl 2f) 2½	**8**	16/1	35	10
2721[6]	**Priory Gardens (IRE) (47)** (JMBradley) **3-7-7**(3) RFfrench(4) (spd 3f) s.h	**9**	9/1	32	7

(SP 117.5%) **9 Rn**

1m 10.8 (1.60) CSF £80.09 CT £260.20 TOTE £8.90: £2.00 £2.50 £1.50 (£38.20) Trio £52.60 OWNER Mr Frank Chadwick (UPPER LAMBOURN) BRED C. R. and V. M. Withers
LONG HANDICAP Priory Gardens (IRE) 7-6
WEIGHT FOR AGE 3yo-4lb
2747 Gold Edge, dropped 2lb, was well suited by the ease in the ground and finally lost her maiden tag in some style. (9/1)
2780 Montendre had been dropped no less than 18lb since last in a handicap five outings ago. (9/1: 6/1-10/1)
3092 Tinker Osmaston proved just how difficult it is to catch these sprinters right and possibly saw daylight too early on the outside this time. (11/4)
2554 Nervous Rex never gave his supporters much cause for sweaty palms. (11/1: op 7/1)
3018 Speedy Classic (USA), up 4lb, was not suited by the change in the ground. (5/1)
2698 Erupt, back up 3lb, did have some give in the ground this time. (7/2)
2206 Priory Gardens (IRE) (9/1: op 14/1)

T/Jkpt: Not won; £51,673.56 to Windsor 4/8/97. T/Plpt: £58.00 (428.91 Tckts). T/Qdpt: £15.60 (189.92 Tckts) KH

2681-CHESTER (L-H) (Good to firm)
Sunday August 3rd
WEATHER: overcast WIND: slt across

3252 QUEENSFERRY CONDITIONS STKS (3-Y.O+) (Class C)
2-30 (2-31) **7f 2y** £6,491.00 (£2,271.00: £1,110.50: £477.50) Stalls: Low GOING minus 0.33 sec per fur (GF)

			SP	RR	SF
3052[4]	**Hi Nod (96)** (MJCamacho) **7-9-2** LCharnock(1) (lw: trckd ldng pair: hdwy wl over 1f out: rdn to ld wl ins fnl f) —	**1**	9/4[2]	101	41
2211[7]	**My Melody Parkes (94)** (JBerry) **4-8-11** KDarley(2) (led: hrd drvn ent fnl f: hdd & no ex wl ins fnl f) ½	**2**	5/1	95	35
2683[3]	**Ziggy's Dancer (USA) (92)** (EJAlston) **6-9-2** JFEgan(3) (chsd ldr: effrt over 1f out: sn rdn: unable qckn) 2½	**3**	100/30[3]	94	34
2861[4]	**Cretan Gift (98)** (NPLittmoden) **6-8-11b**(5) PRoberts(4) (lw: hld up in rr: effrt & drvn along 2f out: no imp) 1½	**4**	7/4[1]	91	31

(SP 106.9%) **4 Rn**

1m 27.88 (2.68) CSF £10.99 TOTE £3.00 (£7.00) OWNER Mr Brian Nordan (MALTON) BRED B. Nordan
3052 Hi Nod, appreciating this return to his favourite trip, needed to put his best foot forward in the closing stages but he had command in the final 100 yards, making sure he kept up his record of having won in every season since he began. (9/4)
My Melody Parkes, showing her first glimpse of form this season, did not go down without a fight and she could be about to strike. (5/1: 7/2-11/2)
2683 Ziggy's Dancer (USA) has done all his recent running at sprint distances although he has won at this trip in the past, but his determined effort to take the leader's measure below the distance failed to materialise. (100/30)
2861 Cretan Gift has long given the impression that he would be suited by this trip and he adopted his usual patient tactics but a turn of finishing speed was missing and he brought up the rear throughout. (7/4)

3253 E.B.F. SALTNEY MAIDEN STKS (2-Y.O) (Class D)
3-00 (3-01) **7f 2y** £3,615.00 (£1,095.00: £535.00: £255.00) Stalls: Low GOING minus 0.33 sec per fur (GF)

			SP	RR	SF
2286[3]	**Elakik** (JLDunlop) **2-9-0** KDarley(1) (lw: chsd ldr: hrd drvn 2f out: led ent fnl f: all out) —	**1**	13/8[1]	80	28
2829[9]	**Guaranteed** (BWHills) **2-8-11**(3) JDSmith(8) (small: str: bkwd: hld up: hdwy on ins 2f out: str run fnl f: jst failed) hd	**2**	14/1	80	28

				SP	RR	SF
2516[5]	**Rewardia (IRE)** (PDEvans) **2-8-9** JFEgan(2) (chsd ldrs: rdn & outpcd 2f out: rallied ins fnl f: r.o strly)	hd	**3**	20/1	75	23
2699[4]	**After The Rain** (BWHills) **2-9-0** GCarter(5) (hld up: effrt & rdn over 2f out: gd hdwy fnl f: r.o)	s.h	**4**	9/4[2]	79	27
2181[15]	**Khattaff (IRE)** (MajorWRHern) **2-9-0** PaulEddery(3) (bit bkwd: led tl hdd & wknd 1f out)	3	**5**	16/1	73	21
2948[3]	**Cage Aux Folles (IRE)** (JWHills) **2-8-11**(3) MHenry(6) (prom tl rdn & wknd wl over 1f out)	¾	**6**	8/1	71	19
	French Connection (JBerry) **2-8-11**(3) PFessey(7) (trckd ldrs: drvn along 3f out: sn btn)	nk	**7**	14/1	70	18
2477[3]	**Bodfari Pride (IRE)** (ABailey) **2-9-0** KFallon(10) (chsd ldrs: rdn over 2f out: sn outpcd: t.o)	10	**8**	11/2[3]	47	—
2163[6]	**Risknowt Getnowt** (TWall) **2-9-0** DWright(4) (s.s: a bhd & outpcd: t.o)	13	**9**	50/1	18	—

(SP 121.3%) **9 Rn**

1m 28.92 (3.72) CSF £26.12 TOTE £2.40: £1.30 £4.20 £3.50 (£22.00) Trio £319.10 OWNER Mr Hamdan Al Maktoum (ARUNDEL) BRED Shadwell Estate Company Limited

2286 Elakik opening his account on this first attempt at the trip, had to work hard to hold on, but he showed all the right commitment when the pressure was on. (13/8)

Guaranteed a full-brother to My Branch, improved considerably on his racecourse debut and on a slightly stiffer track should soon be able to go one better. (14/1)

Rewardia (IRE), a very fit-looking filly, ran a fine race in defeat and she does appear to have come on in leaps and bounds since her debut last month. (20/1)

2699 After The Rain has taken time to come to himself and he may have found seven furlongs on this track not quite testing enough, but he was pegging back the leaders on the run to the line and his turn is near at hand. (9/4)

Khattaff (IRE) has had a couple of runs but still looks far from the finished article and this much more testing race should have blown away the cobwebs. (16/1)

2948 Cage Aux Folles (IRE) was unable to respond when the tempo lifted on the approach to the straight and on such an easy track looks to need further. (8/1)

3254 MAIL ON SUNDAY MILE (QUALIFIER) H'CAP (0-85) (3-Y.O+) (Class D)

3-30 (3-33) **7f 122y** £8,871.00 (£2,688.00: £1,314.00: £627.00) Stalls: Low GOING minus 0.33 sec per fur (GF)

				SP	RR	SF
2760[5]	**Mr Teigh (66)** (MrsJRRamsden) **5-8-9** KFallon(1) (a chsng ldrs: drvn to ld over 1f out: sn clr)	—	**1**	7/2[1]	77	48
2918[3]	**Comanche Companion (63)** (TJNaughton) **7-8-6** PaulEddery(11) (chsd ldrs: hrd drvn over 1f out: kpt on: nt pce of wnr)	3½	**2**	10/1	67	38
3034[5]	**Antarctic Storm (56)** (RAFahey) **4-7-13** LCharnock(2) (hld up mid div: hdwy u.p wl over 1f out: kpt on ins fnl f)	¾	**3**	14/1	58	29
2900[4]	**Myttons Mistake (57)** (ABailey) **4-8-0** DWright(10) (lw: a.p: led over 2f out tl over 1f out: one pce)	½	**4**	7/1[3]	58	29
3056*	**Safey Ana (USA) (67)** (BHanbury) **6-8-10** JStack(6) (b: bhd: hdwy on ins ent st: wknd & eased ins fnl f)	5	**5**	13/2[2]	57	28
3198[5]	**Grey Kingdom (78)** (MBrittain) **6-9-0**(7) DMernagh(5) (hld up mid div: hdwy 2f out: sn rdn: nvr able to chal)	1¼	**6**	9/1	66	37
2857[3]	**For Your Eyes Only (80)** (TDEasterby) **3-9-2** DeanMcKeown(12) (lw: hld up: effrt 2f out: nt pce to chal)	¾	**7**	13/2[2]	66	30
1920[10]	**Knobbleeneeze (72)** (MRChannon) **7-9-1v** CandyMorris(8) (prom tl outpcd wl over 1f out)	1½	**8**	14/1	55	26
2913[10]	**People Direct (53)** (NPLittmoden) **4-7-7**(3) PFessey(7) (prom tl rdn & wknd qckly over 1f out)	hd	**9**	20/1	36	7
2651[2]	**Silver Harrow (56)** (AGNewcombe) **4-7-6**(7) RWinston(14) (a in rr)	½	**10**	16/1	38	9
2517[7]	**Rock Island Line (IRE) (71)** (JBerry) **3-8-2**(5) PRoberts(9) (hld up: effrt on outside 3f out: rdn & wknd 2f out)	1¾	**11**	12/1	49	13
2346[13]	**Rebel County (IRE) (84)** (ABailey) **4-9-13** DBiggs(13) (lw: bhd: plld wd & effrt over 2f out: sn rdn: no imp)	hd	**12**	33/1	62	33
2760[4]	**Gulf Shaadi (66)** (EJAlston) **5-8-6**(3) DGriffiths(3) (dwlt: nt clr run 3f out & 2f out: a in rr)	½	**13**	8/1	43	14

(SP 126.2%) **13 Rn**

1m 33.7 (1.70) CSF £37.96 CT £429.13 TOTE £4.10: £1.80 £3.80 £3.90 (£29.90) Trio £425.10 OWNER Platinum Racing Ltd (THIRSK) BRED K. G. Bridges

LONG HANDICAP People Direct 7-9

WEIGHT FOR AGE 3yo-7lb

2760 Mr Teigh, continuing his step down in distance, won this competitive event without being asked a serious question and there is plenty more success in this fellow. (7/2: op 6/1)

2918 Comanche Companion, never far away, did her very best to get to terms but over this slightly shorter trip lacked the speed to do so. (10/1)

3034 Antarctic Storm showed much-improved form on this return to a more suitable trip and he can be kept in mind for an early success. (14/1)

2900 Myttons Mistake set sail for home turning in and was always going to be the one to beat, but once the winner was let loose he was soon struggling. (7/1)

3056* Safey Ana (USA) obtained a clear passage on the inside rail entering the straight, but the pace was increasing all the time and the position was accepted once his jockey realised the task was hopeless. (13/2: 4/1-7/1)

3198 Grey Kingdom waited on the leaders on this return to a longer trip, but the exertions of a hard race at Newmarket three days earlier had taken its toll and he was never able to deliver a challenge. (9/1)

2857 For Your Eyes Only never fired at all and it would be hard to look for excuses, and it could also prove costly. (13/2: 4/1-7/1)

3255 ALDFORD RATED STKS H'CAP (0-95) (4-Y.O+) (Class C)

4-00 (4-00) **2m 2f 147y** £14,998.49 (£5,611.50: £2,743.25: £1,178.75: £526.88: £266.13) Stalls: Low GOING minus 0.33 sec per fur (GF)

				SP	RR	SF
2676[3]	**Shaft of Light (84)** (LordHuntingdon) **5-8-3**[ow1] KDarley(3) (a.p: led over 6f out: hrd rdn fnl f: all out)	—	**1**	11/4[1]	92	25
2514[3]	**Raffles Rooster (78)** (AGNewcombe) **5-7-4**(7) RWinston(4) (lw: hld up in rr: stdy hdwy 6f out: ev ch 1f out: kpt on u.p)	½	**2**	7/2	86	20
2709[3]	**Cuff Link (IRE) (95)** (MajorWRHern) **7-9-0** PaulEddery(5) (lw: a.p: rdn to chal ent fnl f: no ex nr fin)	1¼	**3**	100/30[3]	102	36
2882[6]	**Great Oration (IRE) (78)** (FWatson) **8-7-8**(3) PFessey(1) (hld up: effrt & hrd drvn over 4f out: nt rch ldrs)	7	**4**	25/1	79	13
1672*	**Embryonic (IRE) (81)** (MartinTodhunter) **5-8-0**[ow2] GCarter(2) (lw: trckd ldrs: rdn 3f out: wknd & eased over 1f out)	1¾	**5**	3/1[2]	80	12
2327[14]	**Etterby Park (USA) (78)** (MJohnston) **4-7-11** NAdams(6) (led 12f: rdn over 3f out: sn btn)	3	**6**	11/1	74	8
2653[6]	**Rasayel (USA) (78)** (PDEvans) **7-7-4**(7) AMcCarthy(7) (sn chsng ldrs: lost tch 5f out: t.o)	21	**7**	20/1	56	—

(SP 113.9%) **7 Rn**

4m 11.59 (9.09) CSF £11.50 TOTE £3.90: £2.10 £2.30 (£9.30) OWNER The Queen (WEST ILSLEY) BRED The Queen

LONG HANDICAP Great Oration (IRE) 6-7 Etterby Park (USA) 7-8 Rasayel (USA) 7-5

2676 Shaft of Light, winning for only the second time on turf and the first time at such an extended trip, had the inside rail to assist him in an all-out duel to the line. Staying is definitely his game. (11/4)

2514 Raffles Rooster given a very patient ride on this first attempt at the trip, looked to have timed his challenge just right when ranging upsides passing the furlong marker but the winner was in no mood to give best and found just enough to hold him at bay. The Cesarewitch is his Autumn objective. (7/2)
2709 Cuff Link (IRE) was making hard work of it turning for home, but the runner-up egged him on and he stayed on to have every chance entering the final furlong, before the weight began to take its toll. (100/30)
2882 Great Oration (IRE) is usually in his element when given a real test of stamina, but he was never travelling on this occasion and was unable to cause concern. (25/1)
1672* Embryonic (IRE) was onto a hat-trick, but he was unable to get in a blow in the final three furlongs and the position was accepted below the distance. (3/1)
2327 Etterby Park (USA) tried to take advantage of his light weight and set out to make all, but the wheels dropped off once he'd been collared and he faded rather quickly. (11/1)

3256 ECCLESTON H'CAP (0-70) (3-Y.O+ F & M) (Class E)
4-30 (4-30) **1m 4f 66y** £3,485.00 (£1,055.00: £515.00: £245.00) Stalls: Low GOING minus 0.33 sec per fur (GF)

				SP	RR	SF
2744*	**Double Eight (IRE) (65)** (BWHills) **3-9-3**(3) JDSmith(1) (swtg: mde all: shkn up over 1f out: sn clr)	—	**1**	11/8 1	77+	37
2582⁴	**Dizzy Tilly (69)** (TJNaughton) **3-9-10** PaulEddery(2) (chsd wnr thrght: hrd drvn 3f out: wknd appr fnl f)	6	**2**	9/4 2	73	33
2843⁹	**Meg's Memory (IRE) (54)** (AStreeter) **4-8-13**(7) TSiddall(3) (s.i.s: hld up in rr: rdn & lost tch 4f out)	3½	**3**	9/2 3	54	25
3074⁴	**Portite Sophie (43)** (MBrittain) **6-8-9** KDarley(4) (swtg: hld up: effrt over 5f out: outpcd 4f out: sn rdn & btn)	nk	**4**	9/2 3	42	13
				(SP 109.2%)	**4 Rn**	

2m 42.65 (6.45) CSF £4.34 TOTE £1.90 (£1.80) OWNER Mr R. W. Miller (LAMBOURN) BRED Gay O'Callaghan
WEIGHT FOR AGE 3yo-11lb
2744* Double Eight (IRE) has really come into her own since tackling a longer trip and she was always in complete control here. (11/8)
2582 Dizzy Tilly usually does her share of the pace-making, but was denied that role on this occasion and any hope of success had come to an end before reaching the home straight. (9/4)
2650 Meg's Memory (IRE), sluggish leaving the stalls, was hard at work and getting left behind half a mile out, but she did stay on the better to gain third prize in the dying strides. (9/2)
3074 Portite Sophie, very worked up in the preliminaries, looked ill at ease cantering to post and, losing touch with the leading pair four furlongs out, failed to see the trip out. (9/2)

3257 TATTERSALLS AUCTION NURSERY H'CAP (2-Y.O) (Class E)
5-00 (5-00) **6f 18y** £3,436.25 (£1,040.00: £507.50: £241.25) Stalls: Low GOING minus 0.33 sec per fur (GF)

				SP	RR	SF
1760¹⁸	**Sandmoor Tartan (57)** (TDEasterby) **2-7-10** DWright(5) (lw: hld up & bhd: hdwy wl over 1f out: str run to ld nr fin)	—	**1**	12/1	55	25
2685²	**Heavenly Abstone (82)** (PDEvans) **2-9-7v** JFEgan(3) (b: a.p: drvn over 2f out: led ins fnl f tl ct cl home)	hd	**2**	7/2 2	80	50
2516⁹	**Royal Dream (80)** (JBerry) **2-9-2**(3) PFessey(9) (lw: dwlt: bhd: effrt over 2f out: rdn & r.o wl fnl f)	2	**3**	5/1 3	73	43
2412³	**Hayburner (57)** (MWEasterby) **2-7-10b¹** NAdams(6) (led tl hdd ins fnl f)	1	**4**	14/1	47	17
2604³	**Frankie Fair (IRE) (70)** (MAJarvis) **2-8-4**(5) PRoberts(7) (lw: hld up: pushed along ½-wy: nt clr run wl over 1f out: kpt on fnl f)	1½	**5**	13/2	56	26
2024¹⁶	**Bodfaridistinction (IRE) (79)** (ABailey) **2-9-4** KFallon(1) (b.nr hind: prom: rdn 2f out: sn wknd: t.o)	9	**6**	15/8 1	41	11
2886ᵂ	**Inshallah (69)** (MartinTodhunter) **2-8-8** LCharnock(2) (chsd ldrs: rdn 2f out: eased whn btn appr fnl f: t.o)	nk	**7**	6/1	30	—
3055⁴	**Newhargen (IRE) (57)** (PDEvans) **2-7-3**(7) AMcCarthy(8) (chsd ldrs: pushed along wl over 2f out: sn wknd: t.o)	3	**8**	16/1	11	—
				(SP 121.5%)	**8 Rn**	

1m 15.45 (2.15) CSF £52.08 CT £226.51 TOTE £31.70: £5.00 £1.50 £1.60 (£91.70) Trio £47.80 OWNER Sandmoor Textiles Co Ltd (MALTON) BRED Franklin Cunliffe
LONG HANDICAP Sandmoor Tartan 7-9 Hayburner 7-9 Newhargen (IRE) 7-8
948 Sandmoor Tartan completed an across the card double for his connections with a thrilling, last-stride victory, and these waiting tactics obviously suit his style of racing. (12/1)
2685 Heavenly Abstone tries her heart out and she looked set to regain winning form when surging ahead two hundred yards out, but the concession of so much weight swayed the scales against her in the dying strides. (7/2)
2060* Royal Dream has made all in both her wins, but she was a shade slow leaving the start and, forced to race on the outside, did not really get going into it was far too late. (5/1)
2412 Hayburner adapted more forceful tactics on this step up in class, with blinkers fitted for the first time, and he held the call until inside the last furlong. These tactics would pay off with interest in a seller. (14/1)
2604 Frankie Fair (IRE), kept up to her work from halfway, found all sorts of trouble in running entering the straight and she could not get within striking range. (13/2)
1211 Bodfaridistinction (IRE) just cannot handle lively ground and she was one of the first beaten. It would be worth waiting for the Autumn rains to arrive. (15/8)
2110 Inshallah (6/1: 9/2-7/1)

T/Plpt: £158.30 (131.42 Tckts). T/Qdpt: £19.20 (48.28 Tckts) IM

3084-NEWCASTLE (L-H) (Good to Firm)
Sunday August 3rd
Races 2, 5 & 6: hand-timed
WEATHER: sunny WIND: slt bhd

3258 FOX ADVERTISING NURSERY H'CAP (2-Y.O) (Class D)
2-20 (2-20) **6f** £3,631.25 (£1,100.00: £537.50: £256.25) Stalls: High GOING minus 0.46 sec per fur (F)

				SP	RR	SF
1941⁴	**Peter's Imp (IRE) (77)** (JBerry) **2-8-13** GDuffield(5) (chsd ldrs: rdn to ld ins fnl f: r.o)	—	**1**	6/1 3	81	31
2500²	**Aberkeen (80)** (MDods) **2-9-2** JCarroll(8) (chsd ldrs: led 1½f out tl ins fnl f: wandered sltly: kpt on)	¾	**2**	9/1	82	32
2343⁴	**Carbon (85)** (DMorley) **2-9-7** JFortune(2) (lw: hld up: effrt ½-wy: hdwy u.str.p over 1f out: edgd rt: kpt on)	hd	**3**	6/1 3	87	37
2712³	**Grand Estate (69)** (TDEasterby) **2-8-5** TWilliams(4) (a chsng ldrs: nt clr run over 1f out & swtchd twice: kpt on)	nk	**4**	9/2 2	70	20
2893⁴	**Cool Secret (71)** (ABMulholland) **2-8-4**(3) DSweeney(6) (s.i.s: hld up: hdwy 2f out: n.m.r: nvr nr to chal)	½	**5**	10/1	71	21

1860[4] **Dawn Patrol (60)** (KWHogg) **2-7-10** NKennedy(3) (chsd ldrs over 4f: grad wknd) ....6 **6** 20/1 44 —
3106* **Miss Eliminator (67)** (MWEasterby) **2-8-3b** 7x TLucas(10) (b.off hind: plld hrd: led tl hdd over 1f out: sn wknd) ....2½ **7** 4/1[1] 44 —
2842[9] **Elsinore (IRE) (67)** (MrsJRRamsden) **2-8-3** RHills(9) (lw: lost tch ½-wy: n.d after) ....5 **8** 7/1 31 —
3062[5] **Makahu Don (60)** (WTKemp) **2-7-10** JQuinn(7) (prom over 3f: sn lost pl) ....¾ **9** 10/1 22 —
2714[6] **Ellenber (61)** (WMcKeown) **2-7-8b**(3)ow1 DarrenMoffatt(1) (dwlt: rdn ½-wy: nt keen) ....13 **10** 25/1 — —
(SP 116.0%) **10 Rn**

1m 13.48 (1.98) CSF £53.33 CT £315.79 TOTE £5.00: £1.60 £1.80 £2.10 (£15.60) Trio £20.90 OWNER Mr & Mrs Peter Foden (COCKERHAM) BRED Don Kelly
LONG HANDICAP Makahu Don 7-9 Ellenber 7-4
OFFICIAL EXPLANATION **Grand Estate: lost a front plate during the race. Miss Eliminator: was found to be coughing on returning to the yard.**
1941 Peter's Imp (IRE) was returning after seven weeks off. He has been gelded in the meantime and seems to have improved. (6/1)
2500 Aberkeen is in fine form, responded to pressure well and deserves to find another race. (9/1)
2343 Carbon is not the easiest of rides and takes a lot of settling, and he gives the impression that he is not really giving it his best shot in the closing stages. (6/1)
2712 Grand Estate was always a bit short of room here and he does give the impression that there is more to come if he can be persuaded. (9/2)
2893 Cool Secret is a free-running sort and did not have the best of luck here, and there would seem to be a race to be picked up. (10/1)
1860 Dawn Patrol ran better here after seven weeks off. (20/1)
3106* Miss Eliminator spoiled her chances by taking charge early on and leading, and she stopped quickly once tackled. (4/1)

3259 ADIDAS LIMITED STKS (0-80) (3-Y.O+) (Class D)

2-50 (2-50) **1m 4f 93y** £5,509.00 (£1,549.00: £757.00) Stalls: Low GOING minus 0.46 sec per fur (F)

SP RR SF

2855[2] **Ferny Hill (IRE) (77)** (SirMarkPrescott) **3-8-9** GDuffield(3) (lw: hld up: effrt ent st: r.o u.p fnl 2f to ld wl ins fnl f) ....— **1** 9/4[3] 90 40
2944* **Wild Rita (82)** (WRMuir) **5-9-5** JFortune(1) (trckd ldr: chal 2f out: r.o) ....½ **2** 15/8[2] 88 49
3035* **Bally Souza (IRE) (83)** (MJohnston) **3-8-10** JWeaver(2) (lw: led: qcknd ent st: rdn appr fnl f: r.o: hdd & no ex wl ins fnl f) ....½ **3** 11/8[1] 90 40
(SP 107.7%) **3 Rn**

2m 40.2 (2.70) CSF £5.73 TOTE £3.20 (£3.50) OWNER Cheveley Park Stud (NEWMARKET) BRED D. Ryan, M. Moloney and H. King
WEIGHT FOR AGE 3yo-11lb
2855 Ferny Hill (IRE) certainly appreciated this even longer trip and responded in great style to pressure, and seems to be going the right way. (9/4)
2944* Wild Rita is in good hearty still and was always find a race or two and this may well turn out to be useful form. (15/8)
3035* Bally Souza (IRE) still looks in tremendous form but she probably did not set a strong enough pace here and was just out-sprinted late on, despite a gallant effort. (11/8)

3260 E.B.F. CALDERPRINT MAIDEN STKS (2-Y.O) (Class D)

3-20 (3-20) **7f** £3,631.25 (£1,100.00: £537.50: £256.25) Stalls: High GOING minus 0.46 sec per fur (F)

SP RR SF

Fruits of Love (USA) (MJohnston) **2-9-0** JWeaver(5) (w'like: str: bit bkwd: hld up: shkn up & qcknd to ld wl over 1f out: r.o wl) ....— **1** Evens[1] 85+ 38
2870[4] **Prompt Delivery (USA)** (MRStoute) **2-9-0** FLynch(3) (cl up: led 3f out: hdd wl over 1f out: r.o) ....2½ **2** 6/5[2] 79 32
2881[6] **Wishbone Alley (IRE)** (MDods) **2-9-0** AlexGreaves(7) (plld hrd: led 1f: led 4f out to 3f out: outpcd fnl 2f) 8 **3** 33/1 61 14
Vincent (JLHarris) **2-9-0** ACulhane(4) (leggy: dwlt: sn pushed along & prom: wl outpcd fnl 2f) 1¼ **4** 50/1 58 11
Saintes (WMcKeown) **2-9-0** JCarroll(1) (w'like: bit bkwd: dwlt: sn rcvrd: wl outpcd fnl 2f) 1½ **5** 50/1 55 8
2881[4] **Watkins** (FMurphy) **2-9-0** JFanning(2) (hld up: effrt over 2f out: sn btn) ....3½ **6** 14/1[3] 47 —
2875[16] **Sporty Spice (IRE)** (JLHarris) **2-8-9** GDuffield(8) (dwlt: shkn up & hdwy to ld after 1f: hdd 4f out: sn lost pl) .12 **7** 50/1 14 —
(SP 110.9%) **7 Rn**

1m 26.37 (1.87) CSF £2.04 TOTE £2.40: £1.50 £1.20 (£1.30) OWNER Mr M. Doyle (MIDDLEHAM) BRED Mr and Mrs Roy L. Ash
Fruits of Love (USA) is a most imposing individual who came with a massive reputation, vindicated it in emphatic style and looks one to follow. (Evens)
2870 Prompt Delivery (USA) is a typical American-bred on looks and is well put together, but handy rather than well-grown. Inclined to get warm down at the start, his performance was pretty good, but he found this useful winner too strong in the closing stages. (6/5: 4/5-5/4)
Wishbone Alley (IRE) ran pretty well against these two useful rivals and was not over-punished once obviously beaten. (33/1)
Vincent has plenty to learn but this tall individual has the scope for improvement. (50/1)
Saintes needed this, looked very green and was treading water from some way out. (50/1)
2881 Watkins never got in a blow but left the impression that if his sights were lowered, he can do better. (14/1)

3261 BUSINESS FURNITURE CENTRE (S) STKS (3-Y.O+) (Class G)

3-50 (3-51) **6f** £2,211.00 (£621.00: £303.00) Stalls: High GOING minus 0.46 sec per fur (F)

SP RR SF

2734[3] **Skyers Flyer (IRE) (65)** (RonaldThompson) **3-8-11**(3) DSweeney(9) (hld up: smooth hdwy to ld ins fnl f: pushed out) ....— **1** 5/2[1] 54 37
2891[15] **Fisiostar (40)** (MDods) **4-9-4b** JCarroll(2) (dspd ld tl hdd ins fnl f: hrd rdn & styd on towards fin) ....hd **2** 14/1 54 41
2954[3] **Rawi (50)** (MissGayKelleway) **4-9-9b** JFortune(5) (disp ld: hrd rdn appr fnl f: sn hdd & no ex) ....2½ **3** 11/4[2] 52 39
2847[7] **Be Warned (54)** (MDods) **6-9-4b** JWeaver(3) (hld up & bhd: hdwy 2f out: sn rdn & nvr able to chal) ....1 **4** 4/1[3] 44 31
2755[2] **Sir Tasker (48)** (JLHarris) **9-9-9** ACulhane(10) (trckd ldrs: effrt over 2f out: nt qckn) 3½ **5** 8/1 40 27
2828[12] **King of Show (IRE) (38)** (RAllan) **6-9-4b** VHalliday(1) (lw: chsd ldrs: effrt over 2f out: btn over 1f out) 1 **6** 12/1 32 19
2605[7] **Fonzy (64)** (MrsSJSmith) **3-9-0** OPears(7) (chsd ldrs tl wknd fnl 2f) ....s.h **7** 6/1 32 15
1940[P] **Needle Knot (IRE) (50)** (FMurphy) **4-9-4** JFanning(8) (cl up over 3f: wknd qckly) ....13 **8** 25/1 — —
2496[7] **Fancy Clancy (29)** (MissLCSiddall) **4-8-13** TLucas(6) (lw: hld up: effrt over 2f out: sn rdn & btn) ....1¾ **9** 25/1 — —
(SP 122.7%) **9 Rn**

1m 13.14 (1.64) CSF £37.86 TOTE £3.30: £1.30 £3.20 £1.50 (£36.20) Trio £13.20 OWNER Mrs J. Carney (DONCASTER) BRED Denis Brennan
WEIGHT FOR AGE 3yo-4lb
Sold Mrs T Miller 7,800gns
2734 Skyers Flyer (IRE) is a trappy customer to win with but she was given the perfect ride and did just enough. (5/2)
2659 Fisiostar has yet to win a race but, judging by the way he battled back here, he can find an opportunity. (14/1)

2954 Rawi, trying a shorter trip here, tried to compensate by helping force the pace but he had run himself out with a furlong left. (11/4)
863 Be Warned has not won for two years and looks to have his own ideas about the game but he still possesses ability. (4/1: op 6/1)
2755 Sir Tasker ran reasonably but he is certainly better on the All-Weather these days. (8/1)
1311 King of Show (IRE) has been disappointing so far this season but did show a little here, but was always seeing too much daylight. (12/1)

3262 ROTHMANS ROYALS NORTH SOUTH CHALLENGE SERIES H'CAP (0-85) (3-Y.O+) (Class D)

4-20 (4-20) **1m (round)** £7,262.50 (£2,200.00: £1,075.00: £512.50) Stalls: Low GOING minus 0.46 sec per fur (F)

				SP	RR	SF
2903²	**High Spirits (IRE) (63)** (TDEasterby) **3-8-8b** TWilliams(3) (a.p: led over 2f out: sn rdn clr: styd on wl)	—	1	5/1 ²	76	36
3134²	**Impulsive Air (IRE) (59)** (EWeymes) **5-8-11** JQuinn(2) (a chsng ldrs: outpcd over 2f out: hdwy over 1f out: styd on wl)	2½	2	7/2 ¹	67	34
2543*	**Dee Pee Tee Cee (IRE) (75)** (MWEasterby) **3-9-6** TLucas(1) (lw: led tl hdd over 2f out: rdn & r.o one pce)	1¼	3	7/2 ¹	81	41
3029⁸	**Nobby Barnes (44)** (DonEnricoIncisa) **8-7-10** KimTinkler(8) (dwlt: bhd tl r.o fnl 2f)	2	4	14/1	46	13
2906¹²	**Cee-N-K (IRE) (74)** (MJohnston) **3-9-5** JWeaver(5) (a.p: effrt 3f out: one pce)	2	5	7/1 ³	72	32
3064⁵	**Gulliver (72)** (MrsJRRamsden) **4-9-10** JFortune(4) (hld up: effrt 3f out: no imp)	hd	6	9/1	69	36
2547¹¹	**Denton Lad (62)** (WTKemp) **3-8-7** JCarroll(7) (lw: chsd ldrs tl outpcd fnl 3f)	1	7	20/1	57	17
3066⁴	**Suez Tornado (IRE) (71)** (EJAlston) **4-9-9v** ACulhane(6) (lw: hld up: effrt 3f out: n.d)	¾	8	7/2 ¹	65	32
				(SP 117.3%)	**8 Rn**	

1m 40.9 (1.90) CSF £21.40 CT £63.38 TOTE £6.70: £1.70 £1.40 £1.50 (£9.20) OWNER Mrs J. B. Mountifield (MALTON) BRED Sean Twomey
WEIGHT FOR AGE 3yo-7lb
2903 High Spirits (IRE), given a most positive ride, made this race his in a few strides approaching the last two furlongs. (5/1)
3134 Impulsive Air (IRE) always held a good position but runs when in the mood and he only decided to put his best foot forward when the winner was home and dried. (7/2)
2543* Dee Pee Tee Cee (IRE) has had four weeks off and returned looking well, but is now 8lb higher which probably made all the difference. (7/2: op 7/4)
3029 Nobby Barnes, as usual, tried to come from behind and the effort was again far too late. All he needs is a flat-out gallop and everything going his way. (14/1)
2735* Cee-N-K (IRE) was always close enough if good enough but he lacked a change of gear. (7/1)
3064 Gulliver gives the impression that he is coming back to form. (9/1)
3066 Suez Tornado (IRE) needed a stronger pace than was set here and ran no sort of race. (7/2)

3263 LUCKY CHOICE H'CAP (0-95) (3-Y.O+) (Class C)

4-50 (4-51) **1m 2f 32y** £10,747.50 (£3,255.00: £1,590.00: £757.50) Stalls: High GOING minus 0.46 sec per fur (F)

				SP	RR	SF
2890*	**Sandmoor Chambray (80)** (TDEasterby) **6-8-13** JWeaver(7) (lw: mde all: qcknd 3f out: r.o wl)	—	1	5/1 ²	91	57
2766¹¹	**My Lewicia (IRE) (91)** (PWHarris) **4-9-10** ACulhane(1) (trckd ldrs: effrt over 2f out: styd on: nt pce of wnr)	1½	2	11/1	100	66
2839⁶	**Major Change (90)** (MissGayKelleway) **5-9-9** JFortune(3) (a.p: rdn over 2f out: kpt on fnl f: no imp)	3½	3	8/1	93	59
2710¹³	**Wafir (IRE) (84)** (PCalver) **5-9-0**(3) DarrenMoffatt(9) (lw: cl up: rdn 3f out: r.o one pce)	nk	4	6/1	87	53
2574²	**Hachiyah (IRE) (90)** (DMorley) **3-9-0** RHills(2) (hld up: lost pl ½-wy: rdn & hung lft 3f out: nvr rchd ldrs)	4	5	9/4 ¹	86	43
1773*	**Shadoof (79)** (WRMuir) **3-8-3** JQuinn(6) (cl up: effrt 3f out: wknd 2f out)	2½	6	5/1 ²	71	28
2058¹⁸	**Banbury (USA) (94)** (JWWatts) **3-9-4** JCarroll(4) (hld up: rdn 3f out: n.d)	4	7	11/2 ³	80	37
2782¹¹	**Hill Farm Blues (65)** (WMBrisbourne) **4-7-12** AGarth(8) (s.s: hdwy & in tch ½-wy: rdn & wknd over 3f out)	dist	8	10/1	—	—
				(SP 122.3%)	**8 Rn**	

2m 7.1 (0.40) CSF £56.02 CT £404.44 TOTE £4.90: £1.80 £2.70 £1.90 (£41.80) Trio £51.20 OWNER Sandmoor Textiles Co Ltd (MALTON) BRED P. and Mrs Venner
WEIGHT FOR AGE 3yo-9lb
2890* Sandmoor Chambray looked magnificent and, again ridden from the front, revelled in it to score in useful style. (5/1: op 3/1)
2242 My Lewicia (IRE), trying this trip for only the second time, got it well and looks to be coming to hand. (11/1)
2839 Major Change showed up well but it took quite a time for the penny to drop when ridden and, when he did run on, it was all over. He either needs a stronger pace or further. (8/1)
1559* Wafir (IRE) raced up with the pace but this was a far more competitive event than the one he won at Ayr, and he was left struggling in the last couple of furlongs. (6/1)
2574 Hachiyah (IRE) looks the type who is useful when things go her way but she had to struggle here and all she wanted to do was hang. (9/4)
1773* Shadoof has been off the track for two months and seemed to blow up here. (5/1)

T/Plpt: £45.30 (270.55 Tckts). T/Qdpt: £4.80 (160.02 Tckts) AA

2500-CARLISLE (R-H) (Good to firm, Good patches)
Monday August 4th
WEATHER: sunny WIND: mod across

3264 CALDERPRINT CARLISLE CHAMPION APPRENTICE H'CAP (0-70) (3-Y.O+) (Class E)

6-20 (6-21) **7f 214y** £2,854.75 (£868.00: £426.50: £205.75) Stalls: High GOING minus 0.52 sec per fur (F)

				SP	RR	SF
3105⁷	**Euro Sceptic (IRE) (44)** (TDEasterby) **5-8-6b**(3) RWinston(11) (lw: a in tch: swtchd 2f out: led appr fnl f: r.o)	—	1	6/1 ¹	56	22
*3044*²	**Sparky (66)** (MWEasterby) **3-9-10b** GParkin(3) (b: bhd & pushed along ½-wy: hdwy u.p 2f out: styd on wl)	1	2	6/1 ¹	76	35
2109*	**Running Green (62)** (DMoffatt) **6-9-13v** DarrenMoffatt(1) (b: sn bhd: hdwy on ins 3f out: hmpd 2f out: r.o wl fnl f)	2½	3	10/1 ³	67	33
3105⁵	**Thatched (IRE) (51)** (REBarr) **7-9-2** PFessey(2) (lw: s.i.s: hdwy 3f out: styd on: nvr able to chal)	nk	4	6/1 ¹	55	21
3064³	**Champagne N Dreams (42)** (DNicholls) **5-8-4**(3) IonaWands(14) (cl up: led over 3f out tl appr fnl f: grad wknd)	hd	5	10/1 ³	46	12
2906*	**Rymer's Rascal (56)** (EJAlston) **5-9-7** DGriffiths(8) (chsd ldrs: effrt over 2f out: one pce appr fnl f)	1¾	6	7/1 ²	57	23
2880²	**Miletrian City (45)** (MissLAPerratt) **4-8-5b**(5) SBuckley(10) (lw: s.i.s: hdwy whn hmpd 2f out: nvr able to chal)	1½	7	10/1 ³	43	9
3105⁴	**Special-K (47)** (EWeymes) **5-8-7**(5) TSiddall(4) (bhd: c wd & effrt over 2f out: nvr rchd ldrs)	1	8	7/1 ²	43	9
1761¹³	**Pine Ridge Lad (IRE) (60)** (JLEyre) **7-9-11** OPears(9) (led tl hdd over 3f out: grad wknd)	1½	9	16/1	53	19

				SP	RR	SF
2913[7]	**Kissel (58)** (SEKettlewell) **5-9-4**(5) JennyBenson(7) (bhd: effrt on outside 3f out: no imp)	1½	**10**	25/1	48	14
898[10]	**Giftbox (USA) (38)** (NBycroft) **5-8-3** FLynch(13) (chsd ldrs tl wknd fnl 2f)	nk	**11**	50/1	27	—
3039[10]	**Spanish Verdict (53)** (DenysSmith) **10-9-4** CTeague(5) (lw: sn bhd: hdwy on ins whn bdly hmpd 2f out: nt rcvr)	1½	**12**	14/1	39	5
2716[4]	**Mystic Times (34)** (BMactaggart) **4-7-10**(3)ow3 KSked(6) (lw: outpcd fr ½-wy)	½	**13**	33/1	19	—
2686[7]	**Golden Fish (33)** (EJAlston) **5-7-7**(5) PBradley(12) (prom 5f: sn rdn & wknd)	8	**14**	20/1	2	—
				(SP 121.2%)	**14 Rn**	

1m 39.9 (2.90) CSF £35.68 CT £337.81 TOTE £5.00: £2.20 £1.90 £6.10 (£9.80) Trio £87.00 OWNER Mr C. H. Stevens (MALTON) BRED Martyn J. McEnery

LONG HANDICAP Mystic Times 7-7

WEIGHT FOR AGE 3yo-7lb

STEWARDS' ENQUIRY Winston susp. 13-14/8/97 (careless riding).

3105 Euro Sceptic (IRE) at last got things right here but he was lucky to keep the race as he badly hampered three others, one of which might well have beaten him. (6/1)

3044 Sparky did not look to be going that well but he did respond to pressure in the last two furlongs, and has more ability when he decides to fully use it. (6/1: 9/2-7/1)

2109* Running Green appeared unlucky as he got messed about when beginning his run two furlongs out and, although flying at the finish, his chance had then gone. (10/1)

3105 Thatched (IRE) is running pretty well at the moment. (6/1)

3064 Champagne N Dreams is running quite well and certainly has more ability if she can be persuaded. (10/1: 8/1-12/1)

2906* Rymer's Rascal does not win very often and found the struggle too much this time. (7/1)

2880 Miletrian City was just beginning to make ground when he got carved up by the winner two furlongs out. (10/1)

Pine Ridge Lad (IRE) had a good blow out here after two months off. (16/1)

2828 Spanish Verdict normally likes to be up with the pace and, trying to come from behind, got absolutely murdered twice, the first of which was the winner's fault. (14/1: 10/1-16/1)

3265 CUMBRIA LIFE MAIDEN AUCTION STKS (2-Y.O) (Class E)

6-50 (6-50) **5f** £2,892.00 (£876.00: £428.00: £204.00) Stalls: High GOING minus 0.52 sec per fur (F)

				SP	RR	SF
2713[2]	**Selkirk Rose (IRE)** (MissLAPerratt) **2-8-4** KDarley(8) (lw: trckd ldrs: led 1½f out: shkn up & qcknd: eased towards fin)	—	**1**	Evens[1]	75+	34
664[4]	**Three Star Rated (IRE)** (TDBarron) **2-8-4** RLappin(2) (hld up: hdwy 2f out: chsd wnr fnl f: kpt on)	¾	**2**	16/1	73	32
2739[6]	**Rio (IRE)** (JBerry) **2-8-3**(3) TEDurcan(6) (chsd ldrs: effrt ½-wy: styd on wl fnl f)	1¾	**3**	14/1	69	28
3106[6]	**Chikapenny (69)** (MrsLStubbs) **2-7-13** DWright(4) (s.i.s: hdwy u.p 2f out: styd on fnl f)	½	**4**	9/1	60	19
2706[7]	**Heathyards Sheik** (RHollinshead) **2-8-6** FLynch(7) (hmpd after s: hdwy 2f out: nvr rchd ldrs)	1	**5**	9/1	64	23
2904[2]	**Quiz Master (72)** (EWeymes) **2-8-9v** JFortune(9) (disp ld 2f: cl up tl wknd over 1f out)	s.h	**6**	7/1[3]	67	26
3094[5]	**Emperor Naheem (IRE)** (BJMeehan) **2-8-9** MTebbutt(3) (cl up: led after 2f tl 1½f out: sn rdn & btn)	s.h	**7**	11/2[2]	67	26
3070[4]	**Bollinger Rose (IRE)** (JJO'Neill) **2-8-8** JCarroll(1) (outpcd & lost tch fr ½-wy)	8	**8**	12/1	40	—
3062[4]	**Pride of Bryn (53)** (DenysSmith) **2-7-10**(3) PFessey(5) (disp ld 2f: sn bhd)	6	**9**	50/1	12	—
				(SP 120.1%)	**9 Rn**	

60.9 secs (0.70) CSF £19.64 TOTE £1.90: £1.10 £4.80 £2.40 (£25.50) Trio £52.70 OWNER Mr Jim McLaren (AYR) BRED Gay O'Callaghan

2713 Selkirk Rose (IRE), always going best, won nicely but she just gave the impression that if a struggle ensued, she might be found wanting. (Evens)

664 Three Star Rated (IRE) has changed stables and, after nearly four months off, showed plenty this time and looks to be on the upgrade. (16/1)

2739 Rio (IRE) took a long time to get going but certainly finished well and may need a bit further. (14/1)

3106 Chikapenny is beginning to look an iffy sort and certainly has more ability if she can be persuaded. (9/1)

1797 Heathyards Sheik seemed to clip the heels of other runners early on and stumbled badly but, in the end, did quite well and is clearly worth another chance or two. (9/1)

2904 Quiz Master, having his second run in the visor, did not go anything like as well. (7/1)

3094 Emperor Naheem (IRE) (11/2: 4/1-6/1)

3266 PIMMS H'CAP (0-60) (3-Y.O) (Class F)

7-20 (7-21) **5f 207y** £2,724.00 (£764.00: £372.00) Stalls: Centre GOING minus 0.52 sec per fur (F)

				SP	RR	SF
2892[9]	**Hever Golf Mover (58)** (TJNaughton) **3-9-7** JWeaver(9) (lw: trckd ldrs: led wl over 1f out: r.o)	—	**1**	4/1[1]	71	32
2852[7]	**Lamorna (51)** (MRChannon) **3-9-0** ACulhane(11) (s.i.s: effrt ½-wy: styd on fnl 2f: nvr able to chal)	3½	**2**	5/1[2]	55	16
2310[16]	**Ginny Wossername (35)** (MartynMeade) **3-7-12b** FNorton(4) (outpcd & bhd: hdwy over 2f out: styd on wl towards fin)	1	**3**	50/1	36	—
2504[2]	**Bold Brief (51)** (DenysSmith) **3-8-9**(5) CLowther(8) (chsd ldrs: effrt over 2f out: one pce)	¾	**4**	5/1[2]	50	11
2417[3]	**King Uno (50)** (MrsJRRamsden) **3-8-13** JFortune(5) (lw: sn pushed along & bhd: hdwy 2f out: nvr rchd ldrs)	s.h	**5**	4/1[1]	49	10
2903[4]	**Euroquest (35)** (DNicholls) **3-7-12** TWilliams(10) (in tch: outpcd ½-wy: kpt on fnl 2f)	¾	**6**	10/1	32	—
2883[3]	**Hiltons Executive (IRE) (36)** (EJAlston) **3-7-10**(3) PFessey(12) (led over 4f: sn rdn & btn)	3	**7**	8/1[3]	25	—
2941[7]	**Terry's Rose (41)** (RHollinshead) **3-8-4**ow1 KDarley(3) (in tch: outpcd ½-wy: n.d after)	nk	**8**	12/1	29	—
2906[11]	**Petite Risk (47)** (KWHogg) **3-8-10** DeanMcKeown(1) (spd 4f)	1	**9**	20/1	32	—
3038[9]	**Onemoretime (34)** (BWMurray) **3-7-11** DWright(7) (lw: b: s.i.s: a outpcd & bhd)	1½	**10**	33/1	15	—
1566[14]	**Fit For The Job (IRE) (36)** (TWall) **3-7-13** NCarlisle(6) (chsd ldrs 3f: sn wknd)	3½	**11**	50/1	8	—
2715[7]	**Wagga Moon (IRE) (57)** (JJO'Neill) **3-9-6** JCarroll(2) (lw: chsd ldrs: rdn ½-wy: wknd fnl 2f)	¾	**12**	12/1	27	—
				(SP 120.5%)	**12 Rn**	

1m 14.0 (2.20) CSF £21.26 CT £807.62 TOTE £5.80: £2.00 £1.60 £9.40 (£13.30) Trio £261.00; £161.75 to 6/8/97 OWNER Hever Racing Club (EPSOM) BRED Mrs L. Popely

2169 Hever Golf Mover looked a picture and, finding this a pretty uncompetitive event, had it sewn up some way out. (4/1)

1931 Lamorna is dropping down the handicap and showed ability, but seems to also have a problem as she was never striding out with any freedom, and only ran on when it was too late. (5/1)

1921 Ginny Wossername, dropping back in trip here, took a long time to get going but, in the end, she did show some signs of coming back to form. (50/1)

2504 Bold Brief was, as usual, up with the pace but failed to do anything when put under pressure. (5/1)

2417 King Uno did not have the visor on here and that probably made all the difference. (4/1: 3/1-9/2)

2903 Euroquest is certainly more than a bit of a monkey and was never giving it his best here. (10/1)

3267 U.A.P. PROVINCIAL H'CAP (0-80) (3-Y.O+) (Class D)

7-50 (7-50) **1m 4f** £3,420.00 (£1,035.00: £505.00: £240.00) Stalls: High GOING minus 0.52 sec per fur (F)

				SP	RR	SF
2122^{12}	**Al's Alibi (72)** (WRMuir) **4-9-13** KFallon(6) (lw: cl up: led over 2f out: r.o wl)	—	**1**	5/1	82	41
3015*	**Tajar (USA) (41)** (TKeddy) **5-7-10** NCarlisle(5) (hld up & bhd: hdwy gng wl 4f out: chsng wnr appr fnl f: nt qckn)	2½	**2**	5/1	48	7
553*	**Globe Runner (52)** (JJO'Neill) **4-8-7** KDarley(2) (trckd ldrs: hdwy 3f out: rdn & one pce fnl 2f)	2	**3**	5/1	56	15
2889^{3}	**Leviticus (IRE) (75)** (TPTate) **3-9-5** ACulhane(7) (lw: chsd ldrs: outpcd over 3f out: sn lost pl: styd on wl fnl f)	nk	**4**	$9/2^{3}$	79	27
2843^{6}	**May King Mayhem (49)** (MrsALMKing) **4-8-4** TWilliams(3) (lw: rn in snatches: in tch: hdwy u.p 3f out: one pce fnl 2f)	1	**5**	$4/1^{2}$	51	10
2064^{4}	**Stakis Casinos Boy (IRE) (80)** (MJohnston) **3-9-10** JWeaver(4) (lw: led tl hdd over 2f out: sn rdn & wknd)	hd	**6**	$9/4^{1}$	82	30
	Chill Wind (41) (NBycroft) **8-7-7**(3) DarrenMoffatt(1) (bit bkwd: outpcd & wl bhd fnl 5f)	12	**7**	100/1	27	—

(SP 119.9%) **7 Rn**

2m 33.1 (4.10) CSF £28.97 TOTE £5.90: £3.50 £2.20 (£19.30) OWNER The Sussex Stud Ltd (LAMBOURN) BRED The Sussex Stud and Roncon Ltd

LONG HANDICAP Tajar (USA) 7-6 Chill Wind 6-3

WEIGHT FOR AGE 3yo-11lb

1260 Al's Alibi, normally happier on an easier surface, was back down to the mark he won off last year and did it really well again. (5/1)
3015* Tajar (USA), off a 10lb higher mark here, ran a useful race and is obviously in really good heart. (5/1)
553* Globe Runner, having his first run for over four months, showed enough to suggest that he should be all the better for it. (5/1: 7/2-11/2)
2889 Leviticus (IRE) is proving a most frustrating character and, hopefully, he will now come into his own over hurdles as he certainly looks the right type. (9/2)
2843 May King Mayhem has shot up 13lb since winning here last month and ran as well as could be expected. (4/1)
2064 Stakis Casinos Boy (IRE) looked superb but, when the pressure was on, he proved most disappointing. (9/4)

3268 WHINLATTER CLAIMING STKS (3-Y.O) (Class F)

8-20 (8-22) **6f 206y** £2,486.00 (£696.00: £338.00) Stalls: High GOING minus 0.52 sec per fur (F)

				SP	RR	SF
2691^{8}	**Nant Y Gamer (FR) (80)** (JBerry) **3-8-4**(5) CLowther(6) (lw: cl up: rdn to ld 1f out: styd on wl)	—	**1**	$11/10^{1}$	77	29
2665^{3}	**Davis Rock (66)** (WRMuir) **3-8-6**ow1 KFallon(1) (led tl hdd 1f out: no ex u.p)	2	**2**	$11/8^{2}$	69	20
2554^{7}	**Patina (43)** (RHollinshead) **3-8-4** KDarley(4) (a chsng ldrs: one pce fnl 2f)	4	**3**	10/1	58	10
2723^{6}	**Feel A Line (46)** (BJMeehan) **3-8-7b** MTebbutt(3) (lw: prom tl lost pl 3f out: rdn & n.d after)	3½	**4**	$8/1^{3}$	53	5
2756^{5}	**La Perdoma** (MissMKMilligan) **3-7-9**(3) PFessey(5) (bhd: effrt ½-wy: rdn & no imp)	3	**5**	100/1	37	—
1998^{13}	**Greenacres Goddess** (TWall) **3-8-0** NCarlisle(2) (a bhd: lost tch fnl 3f)	26	**6**	100/1	—	—

(SP 111.9%) **6 Rn**

1m 27.6 (1.90) CSF £2.58 TOTE £2.10: £1.40 £1.20 (£1.70) OWNER Lord Mostyn (COCKERHAM) BRED Mrs Carolyn Elwes

2303 Nant Y Gamer (FR) had to fight to get the upper hand but, once in front, he soon had it sewn up. (11/10: 4/5-5/4)
2665 Davis Rock did her utmost to upset the winner but her limitations were exposed late on. (11/8)
2554 Patina had plenty on here and ran fairly well in the circumstances. (10/1)
2407* Feel A Line does not look the easiest of rides and, tending to hang, is probably better suited by a left-handed track. (8/1: op 5/1)
2756 La Perdoma was beaten twelve and a half lengths this time which is the nearest she has finished in three efforts. (100/1)

3269 WRYNOSE LIMITED STKS (0-50) (3-Y.O+) (Class F)

8-50 (8-52) **6f 206y** £2,668.00 (£748.00: £364.00) Stalls: High GOING minus 0.52 sec per fur (F)

				SP	RR	SF
2501^{3}	**Surf City (49)** (WWHaigh) **4-9-2** ACulhane(1) (bhd: hdwy & nt clr run over 2f out: swtchd & rdn to ld ins fnl f: styd on wl)	—	**1**	$11/2^{2}$	56	38
3029^{13}	**Don't Worry Mike (39)** (FHLee) **3-8-10b** KFallon(5) (lw: chsd ldrs: wnt 2nd over 2f out: ev ch ins fnl f: kpt on)	¾	**2**	16/1	54	30
3088^{2}	**Hi Mujtahid (IRE) (50)** (SEKettlewell) **3-8-13b**[1] KDarley(4) (lw: led tl hdd & hung rt ins fnl f: sn btn)	1	**3**	$5/4^{1}$	55	31
3056^{6}	**May Queen Megan (43)** (MrsALMKing) **4-8-13** TWilliams(8) (in tch: rdn over 3f out: styd on: no imp)	1½	**4**	9/1	46	28
3039^{6}	**Chinour (IRE) (48)** (EJAlston) **9-8-9**(7) MelanieWorden(2) (dwlt: bhd tl r.o fnl 2f)	nk	**5**	8/1	48	30
2755^{5}	**Loch Style (48)** (RHollinshead) **4-9-2** FLynch(7) (s.i.s: hdwy u.p ½-wy: sn prom: btn over 1f out)	3	**6**	14/1	41	23
2937^{10}	**Thorntoun Jewel (IRE) (23)** (MissZAGreen) **4-8-13** JFanning(9) (bhd: rdn ½-wy: hdwy 2f out: n.d)	2½	**7**	200/1	32	14
2887^{2}	**My Handsome Prince (30)** (PJBevan) **5-9-2** NCarlisle(10) (chsd ldrs tl wknd over 2f out)	2½	**8**	12/1	29	11
2892^{3}	**Dr Woodstock (43)** (MartynMeade) **3-8-10** FNorton(11) (cl up tl wknd fnl 3f)	¾	**9**	$6/1^{3}$	28	4
2938^{7}	**Peacefull Reply (USA) (24)** (FHLee) **7-9-2v** DeanMcKeown(6) (chsd ldrs tl wknd fnl 2f)	½	**10**	50/1	27	9

(SP 117.9%) **10 Rn**

1m 27.4 (1.70) CSF £81.92 TOTE £5.30: £1.40 £2.80 £1.30 (£36.60) Trio £33.50 OWNER Exors of the late Mr A W Anderson (MALTON) BRED Miss E. Drax

WEIGHT FOR AGE 3yo-6lb

STEWARDS' ENQUIRY Culhane susp. 13-14/8/97 (excessive use of whip).

2501 Surf City won well here, despite getting messed about. (11/2)
855 Don't Worry Mike took the eye in the paddock and ran well and may yet pick up a race. (16/1)
3088 Hi Mujtahid (IRE) had blinkers on for the first time but this caused him to race too freely and he then failed to respond to pressure. (5/4)
May Queen Megan is taking time to find her form this season but was staying on at the end. (9/1)
3039 Chinour (IRE) did his usual and decided to run when it was all too late. (8/1: 6/1-9/1)
2755 Loch Style took a lot of driving to get him going and then failed to make any serious impression. (14/1: op 7/1)
2892 Dr Woodstock (6/1: op 4/1)

T/Plpt: £143.60 (115.4 Tckts). T/Qdpt: £33.60 (31.38 Tckts) AA

2886-RIPON (R-H) (Good to firm)
Monday August 4th
WEATHER: fine WIND: fresh half against

3270 E.B.F. ROUNDABOUT NOVICE STKS (2-Y.O) (Class D)
2-30 (2-32) **6f** £3,327.40 (£1,007.20: £491.60: £233.80) Stalls: Low GOING minus 0.28 sec per fur (GF)

Form	Horse	Dist	Pos	SP	RR	SF
2685[5]	**Marton Moss (SWE) (83)** (TDEasterby) **2-9-4** KFallon(1) (trckd ldrs: effrt 2f out: r.o u.p to ld jst ins fnl f: sn clr)	—	1	3/1[2]	85	43
2658[3]	**Miquelon (93)** (RHollinshead) **2-9-4** KDarley(3) (lw: chsd ldrs: sn pushed along: outpcd ½-wy: styd on ins fnl f: no ch w wnr)	2½	2	5/6[1]	78	36
2500[8]	**Pigeon (59)** (DWBarker) **2-8-7** TWilliams(6) (w ldr: led over 1f out: hdd jst ins fnl f: kpt on same pce)	nk	3	16/1	67?	25
2881[3]	**Rioja** (TPTate) **2-8-12** ACulhane(5) (lw: led: rdn 2f out: sn hdd: one pce)	1	4	7/2[3]	69	27
	Royal Velvet (CWFairhurst) **2-8-7** DeanMcKeown(2) (leggy: unf: unruly s: dwlt: sn wl bhd)	13	5	16/1	29	—
2752[7]	**Mr Fund Switch** (DNicholls) **2-8-12** AlexGreaves(4) (trckd ldrs: outpcd ½-wy: hung rt & sn wl bhd)	8	6	33/1	13	—

(SP 116.5%) **6 Rn**

1m 13.0 (2.50) CSF £5.64 TOTE £5.40: £1.80 £1.40 (£2.60) OWNER Mr T. H. Bennett (MALTON) BRED Mrs M. Campbell Andenaes

2685 Marton Moss (SWE), who apparently found the going too firm at Chester, showed a very scratchy action going down. Tucked away on the stands-side rails, he took a while to get into full stride but, once in front, soon pulled clear. (3/1: tchd 5/1)
2658 Miquelon was soon being driven along. Badly tapped for foot at halfway, he was staying on inside the last but had no chance with the winner. (5/6: evens-4/5)
2500 Pigeon seemed to turn in a much improved effort, but this will not do her nursery handicap mark much good. (16/1)
2881 Rioja set his own pace but was easily swept aside. He probably needs seven furlongs or even a mile. (7/2)
Royal Velvet, who gave plenty of problems at the start, missed the break. (16/1)
Mr Fund Switch, a keen-going type, hung badly right and his rider had no option but to ease him up from halfway. (33/1)

3271 ADAM TOMLINSON AFTERNOON SHOW (S) H'CAP (0-60) (3-Y.O+) (Class F)
3-00 (3-05) **5f** £2,742.40 (£771.40: £377.20) Stalls: Low GOING minus 0.28 sec per fur (GF)

Form	Horse	Dist	Pos	SP	RR	SF
2540[11]	**Bashful Brave (48)** (BPJBaugh) **6-9-6**(5) PRoberts(3) (chsd ldrs: styd on to ld last 75y)	—	1	12/1	57	35
2934[3]	**Imp Express (IRE) (38)** (GMMoore) **4-9-1** JWeaver(8) (lw: w ldr: led over 1f out tl hdd nr fin)	½	2	9/4[1]	45	23
2844[14]	**Tutu Sixtysix (26)** (DonEnricoIncisa) **6-8-3** KimTinkler(6) (bhd: hdwy over 1f out: styd on wl towards fin)	1	3	14/1	30	8
2915[12]	**La Volta (45)** (MissJFCraze) **4-9-8b**[1] SWebster(5) (bhd: styd on wl appr fnl f: nt rch ldrs)	s.h	4	16/1	49	27
2934[14]	**Good To Talk (35)** (TDEasterby) **4-8-5**(7) RWinston(14) (swtchd rt s & racd alone far side: w ldrs: hrd rdn 2f out: kpt on)	½	5	14/1	37	15
3240[6]	**Henry the Hawk (41)** (MDods) **6-9-4b** JCarroll(1) (b: led tl over 1f out: wknd towards fin)	s.h	6	9/2[3]	43	21
2934[5]	**Kabcast (39)** (DWChapman) **12-9-2b** ACulhane(4) (chsd ldrs: sn drvn along: kpt on one pce fnl 2f)	2	7	4/1[2]	35	13
2536[15]	**Mister Sean (IRE) (21)** (JMBradley) **4-7-12** TWilliams(12) (b.hind: hdwy 2f out: kpt on fnl f: nvr nr to chal)	1¾	8	33/1	11	—
	Bee Dee Best (IRE) (36) (JPSmith) **6-8-13** KFallon(10) (s.i.s: bhd tl styd on fnl 2f)	nk	9	14/1	25	3
2788[20]	**Sihafi (USA) (46)** (JMCarr) **4-9-6**(3) GParkin(15) (sn drvn along & outpcd: n.d)	½	10	9/1	34	12
2883[4]	**Melbourne Princess (42)** (RMWhitaker) **3-9-2** DeanMcKeown(9) (w ldrs centre tl wknd 2f out)	3½	11	10/1	19	—
2938[9]	**February (31)** (NPLittmoden) **4-8-8b**ow4 TGMcLaughlin(17) (sn rdn & bhd)	2½	12	33/1	—	—
2899[7]	**Gormire (28)** (JHetherton) **4-8-5b** NKennedy(13) (s.i.s: a in rr)	¾	13	16/1	—	—
2364[5]	**Love Over Gold (30)** (MCChapman) **3-8-4** LNewton(7) (b.hind: unruly in stalls: s.s: a wl bhd)	1¾	14	33/1	—	—
3088[8]	**Risky Flight (34)** (ASmith) **3-8-3**(5) CLowther(11) (in tch: drvn along ½-wy: sn wknd)	¾	15	33/1	—	—
2883[6]	***Toronto (47)*** (JBerry) **3-9-7b** KDarley(2) (Withdrawn not under Starter's orders: v.unruly in stalls)		W	14/1	—	—
3086[5]	***Superfrills (34)*** (MissLCSiddall) **4-8-11** DHarrison(16) (Withdrawn not under Starter's orders: v.unruly & ref to ent stalls)		W	14/1	—	—

(SP 152.6%) **15 Rn**

60.7 secs (2.90) CSF £36.57 CT £293.82 TOTE £16.50: £5.40 £1.70 £2.50 (£26.40) Trio £126.10 OWNER Mr W. P. Burnell (LITTLE HAYWOOD) BRED Mrs G. M. Hay
WEIGHT FOR AGE 3yo-3lb
No bid

1667 Bashful Brave, who apparently injured his back last time, carried top weight here, despite being rated only 48. (12/1: op 8/1)
2934 Imp Express (IRE), dropped 2lb, was heavily backed but, after looking like landing the gamble, the winner showed the greater resolution near the line. (9/4: op 4/1)
2366 Tutu Sixtysix, on a long losing run, carried her proper mark here in what was a very low-class handicap, even by selling race standards. She ran her usual race, putting in her best work at the finish. (14/1)
1861 La Volta, tried in blinkers, got going when it was all over. (16/1)
2167 Good To Talk, taken down quietly and with the blinkers left off, raced in glorious isolation down the far rail. (14/1)
3240 Henry the Hawk, having his second outing in three days, was on edge in the paddock. (9/2: op 3/1)
2934 Kabcast was still carrying plenty of condition. (4/1: op 7/1)

3272 BBC RADIO YORK H'CAP (0-70) (3-Y.O+) (Class E)
3-30 (3-30) **1m 4f 60y** £2,908.25 (£881.00: £430.50: £205.25) Stalls: Low GOING minus 0.28 sec per fur (GF)

Form	Horse	Dist	Pos	SP	RR	SF
2236[2]	**Campaspe (58)** (JGFitzGerald) **5-9-10** KFallon(8) (trckd ldrs: wnt 2nd over 2f out: led over 1f out: sn drvn clr: readily)	—	1	5/2[1]	70	52
2576[5]	**Double Flight (62)** (MJohnston) **3-9-3** JWeaver(6) (led: clr ½-wy: hdd over 1f out: no ch w wnr)	5	2	11/4[2]	68	39
2911[6]	**Mowlaie (53)** (DWChapman) **6-9-5** ACulhane(5) (in tch: pushed along & outpcd ½-wy: styd on fnl 2f)	4	3	10/1	53	35
2843[7]	**Course Fishing (40)** (BAMcMahon) **6-8-6** LNewton(4) (hld up: hdwy over 4f out: sn rdn: kpt on: nvr nr to chal)	1¾	4	4/1[3]	38	20
2843[13]	**Our Main Man (41)** (RMWhitaker) **7-8-4**(3) GParkin(2) (trckd ldrs: drvn along over 5f out: lost pl over 3f out)	3½	5	5/1	34	16
2064[5]	**Monarch's Pursuit (52)** (TDEasterby) **3-8-7** KDarley(3) (trckd ldr tl rdn & wknd over 2f out)	5	6	5/1	39	10
	Dicentra (40) (CWThornton) **4-8-6** DeanMcKeown(7) (outpcd & bhd fr ½-wy)	3½	7	20/1	22	4
	Curtelace (48) (MPBielby) **7-9-0** JCarroll(1) (bit bkwd: hld up & plld hrd: bhd fnl 4f: virtually p.u)	dist	8	16/1	—	—

(SP 128.3%) **8 Rn**

2m 38.6 (5.10) CSF £10.15 CT £58.15 TOTE £2.90: £1.50 £1.10 £4.40 (£3.30) OWNER Mr J. G. FitzGerald (MALTON) BRED J. G. Fitzgerald

WEIGHT FOR AGE 3yo-11lb
2236 Campaspe, well suited by the strong pace, took this weak handicap in decisive fashion. (5/2)
2576 Double Flight set a strong gallop and had all but the winner beaten off halfway up the straight. She might be worth a try over a slightly shorter distance. (11/4)
2911 Mowlaie, tapped for foot turning in, seemed to stay the trip alright. (10/1)
2164 Course Fishing, who won this race a year ago off a 1lb lower mark, was making hard work of it a long way from home. (4/1)
2365* Our Main Man was readily outpaced once the race began in earnest. (5/1)
2064 Monarch's Pursuit, who had the visor left off, looks a potential juvenile hurdler. (5/1)

3273 ARMSTRONG MEMORIAL CHALLENGE CUP RATED STKS H'CAP (0-95) (3-Y.O+) (Class C)

4-00 (4-01) **6f** £6,564.48 (£2,440.32: £1,180.16: £492.80: £206.40: £91.84) Stalls: Low GOING minus 0.28 sec per fur (GF)

				SP	RR	SF
3195*	**So Intrepid (IRE) (80)** (JMBradley) **7-8-11** JFortune(5) (lw: trckd ldrs: led over 1f out: r.o wl u.p)	—	**1**	3/1^{1}	88	47
2326^{5}	**Gadge (81)** (ABailey) **6-8-12** DWright(3) (b: mid div: effrt over 2f out: nt clr run & swtchd over 1f out: styd on wl ins fnl f)	nk	**2**	9/1	88	47
2769*	**Faith Alone (81)** (CFWall) **4-8-12** GDuffield(12) (b: s.i.s: sn trckng ldrs: effrt over 2f out: kpt on same pce appr fnl f)	1½	**3**	11/2^{3}	84	43
2900^{6}	**Babsy Babe (87)** (JJQuinn) **4-9-1**(3) TEDurcan(4) (lw: trckd ldrs: ev ch 2f out: r.o same pce)	hd	**4**	14/1	90	49
3034^{4}	**Tiler (IRE) (79)** (MJohnston) **5-8-10** JWeaver(10) (reard s: led over 4f out tl over 1f out: one pce)	1	**5**	7/1	79	38
3034^{9}	**Knave's Ash (USA) (81)** (DNicholls) **6-8-12** AlexGreaves(1) (trckd ldrs tl grad wknd appr fnl f)	1	**6**	16/1	79	38
3065^{7}	**Double Action (94)** (TDEasterby) **3-9-7** KDarley(7) (lw: trckd ldrs: effrt & n.m.r 2f out: kpt on fnl f)	s.h	**7**	5/1^{2}	92	47
3208^{7}	**The Happy Fox (IRE) (76)** (BAMcMahon) **5-8-7b** LNewton(9) (w ldrs: rdn & hung rt over 2f out: wknd over 1f out)	nk	**8**	16/1	73	32
2900^{8}	**Westcourt Magic (86)** (MWEasterby) **4-9-3** TLucas(2) (led over 1f: chsd ldrs tl wknd 2f out)	1¾	**9**	9/1	78	37
2105^{20}	**Perryston View (85)** (PCalver) **5-9-2** JCarroll(11) (in tch: effrt over 2f out: grad wknd)	1¼	**10**	7/1	74	33
2894^{8}	**Dayville (USA) (86)** (JBerry) **3-8-13** DHolland(14) (racd virtually alone far side: w ldrs tl wknd over 1f out)	¾	**11**	16/1	73	28
2833^{13}	**Charlie Sillett (87)** (BWHills) **5-9-4** MHills(6) (b.hind: s.i.s: bhd: sme hdwy 2f out: sn wknd & eased)	3½	**12**	16/1	64	23
2900^{12}	**Just Visiting (83)** (CaptJWilson) **3-8-5**(5) PRoberts(13) (chsd ldrs: drvn along & outpcd ½-wy: sn wknd)	3½	**13**	33/1	51	6
835^{R}	**Sailormaite (80)** (MissJFCraze) **6-8-11** SWebster(8) (s.i.s: sn drvn along & a outpcd)	2	**14**	33/1	43	2
3065^{4}	**Vax Star (85)** (JLSpearing) **3-8-12b** KFallon(15) (w ldrs far side: hung lft & lost pl ½-wy: eased)	8	**15**	12/1	26	—
				(SP 145.8%)		**15 Rn**

1m 12.2 (1.70) CSF £34.59 CT £149.79 TOTE £4.50: £1.60 £1.80 £2.90 (£28.40) Trio £35.90 OWNER Mr E. A. Hayward (CHEPSTOW) BRED Crest Stud Ltd
LONG HANDICAP The Happy Fox (IRE) 8-4
WEIGHT FOR AGE 3yo-4lb
OFFICIAL EXPLANATION Westcourt Magic: the jockey reported that the gelding hung badly during the race.
3195* So Intrepid (IRE), with no penalty, showed bags of resolution under a hard ride and is a splendid advert for his trainer. (3/1)
2326 Gadge, having his first out for thirty-seven days and incredibly 31lb higher than when his winning run on turf started at Newcastle in March, came from off the pace and made the winner fight hard all the way to the line. He too is a splended advert for his handler. (9/1)
2769* Faith Alone was racing from a mark 13lb higher than when successful at Yarmouth two outings ago. (11/2)
2900 Babsy Babe looked and ran well and is back to her best. (14/1)
3034 Tiler (IRE), 5lb higher than when successful at Ayr and on a mark 1lb higher than he has ever won off, ran well considering for most of the race he was virtually alone up the middle, and also he reared leaving the stalls. (7/1)
3034 Knave's Ash (USA), taken to post quietly, shaped by no means badly. In a shrewd yard, there is no doubt he is on the way back and, no doubt, he will now step up in distance. (16/1)
3065 Double Action, back over his best trip, did not have the best of luck in running and was by no means knocked about. (5/1)
942* Perryston View, having his first outing for forty-five days, was restless in the stalls. Not knocked about at any stage, this was almost certainly the start of his build-up to the Ayr Gold Cup. (7/1)

3274 TOMMY SHEDDEN CHALLENGE TROPHY H'CAP (0-90) (3-Y.O) (Class C)

4-30 (4-30) **1m 1f** £5,481.25 (£1,645.00: £792.50: £366.25) Stalls: High GOING minus 0.28 sec per fur (GF)

				SP	RR	SF
3190^{3}	**Atlantic Desire (IRE) (90)** (MJohnston) **3-9-7** JWeaver(4) (mde all: hld on wl towards fin)	—	**1**	8/11^{1}	98	62
3119^{2}	**Sweet Contralto (81)** (DRLoder) **3-8-12** WRyan(3) (trckd wnr: chal over 2f out: nt qckn ins fnl f)	½	**2**	11/4^{2}	88	52
3012^{10}	**Sheer Face (82)** (WRMuir) **3-8-13** KFallon(2) (lw: hld up: effrt over 2f out: kpt on same pce appr fnl f)	3	**3**	11/2^{3}	84	48
501^{8}	**Largesse (77)** (JohnBerry) **3-8-8** MFenton(5) (trckd ldrs: effrt on ins over 3f out: edgd lft & wknd over 1f out)	6	**4**	20/1	68	32
1834^{6}	**Round Robin (IRE) (71)** (CWThornton) **3-8-2** GDuffield(6) (s.i.s: pushed along over 5f out: hdwy u.p over 3f out: hung bdly rt & wknd 2f out)	½	**5**	12/1	61	25
2537^{7}	**Juggler (74)** (LordHuntingdon) **3-8-5** DHarrison(1) (unruly s: hld up: effrt over 3f out: rdn: edgd rt & lost pl 2f out)	8	**6**	7/1	50	14
				(SP 124.9%)		**6 Rn**

1m 53.2 (2.20) CSF £3.32 TOTE £1.70: £1.10 £2.30 (£2.30) OWNER Atlantic Racing Ltd (MIDDLEHAM) BRED Hamwood Stud
3190 Atlantic Desire (IRE), making a quick reappearance, was taken to post first. Adopting her favoured front-running tactics, she showed real grit and determination to hold off the runner-up's challenge. (8/11)
3119 Sweet Contralto seemed suited by both the step up in distance and the much faster ground. Throwing down a determined challenge, she could not get her head in front. (11/4)
1104 Sheer Face, who looked really well, has been dropped 3lb in the weights but it does not look enough. (11/2: 3/1-6/1)
Largesse, absent for 128 days and stepping up considerably in distance, seemed to run out of stamina after travelling nicely. (20/1)
1834 Round Robin (IRE) showed his true colours here, hanging violently right under pressure. (12/1: op 8/1)
1637 Juggler, who showed plenty of knee action, gave a problem or two at the start. Driven along halfway up the straight, he edged to his right and dropped away beaten two furlongs out. On this evidence, the Handicapper has pitched him in quite a few pounds too high. (7/1: op 4/1)

3275 'GO RACING IN YORKSHIRE' MAIDEN STKS (3-Y.O+) (Class D)

5-00 (5-00) **1m 2f** £3,685.00 (£1,035.00: £505.00) Stalls: High GOING minus 0.28 sec per fur (GF)

				SP	RR	SF
2846^{2}	**Monitor (87)** (HRACecil) **3-8-12** KFallon(2) (lw: mde all: clr 3f out: pushed out)	—	**1**	1/8^{1}	81 t	54
	Nature Dancer (BWHills) **3-8-7** MHills(3) (rangy: dwlt: sn pushed along: wnt 2nd over 3f out: no ch w wnr)	8	**2**	10/1^{3}	63 t	36

Limni (USA) (MrsJCecil) **3-8-12** JCarroll(1) (lengthy: b: chsd wnr: pushed along over 5f out: hung lft & wknd over 3f out)....8 **3** 7/1[2] 55 t 28
(SP 110.5%) **3 Rn**

2m 5.9 (2.40) CSF £2.18 TOTE £1.10 (£1.50) OWNER Buckram Oak Holdings (NEWMARKET) BRED Buckram Thoroughbred Enterprise Inc.
2846 Monitor had a bloodless success. This type of event, with a prohibitive odds-on favourite, is no great advert for "Go Racing in Yorkshire". (1/8: 1/4-1/10)
Nature Dancer, who swished her tail in the paddock, showed a scratchy action going down. (10/1: op 5/1)
Limni (USA), bandaged in front, is a poor walker and a moderate mover. When pushed along, all he wanted to do was hang left. (7/1: 3/1-10/1)

T/Plpt: £7.70 (2,514.82 Tckts). T/Qdpt: £2.50 (329.24 Tckts) WG

3090-WINDSOR (Fig. 8) (Good)
Monday August 4th
WEATHER: warm WIND: almost nil

3276 SORCERERS APPRENTICE (S) H'CAP (0-60) (3-Y.O+) (Class G)
6-05 (6-05) **1m 67y** £2,133.50 (£606.00: £300.50) Stalls: High GOING minus 0.21 sec per fur (GF)

				SP	RR	SF
3091⁸	**Super Serenade (47)** (GBBalding) **8-8-7**(8) FTynan(6) (a.p: led 2f out: r.o wl)	—	**1**	10/1	62	29
2369¹¹	**Rocky Waters (USA) (32)** (MDIUsher) **8-8-0v** ANicholls(1) (b.hind: hdwy over 3f out: chsd wnr over 1f out: no imp)	3½	**2**	20/1	40	7
2947¹¹	**Oozlem (IRE) (33)** (LMontagueHall) **8-8-1b** DHayden(13) (s.s: hdwy over 1f out: r.o)	¾	**3**	8/1[3]	40	7
3041⁷	**Pc's Cruiser (IRE) (38)** (NPLittmoden) **5-7-12**(8)ow5 KPierrepont(18) (mid div whn hmpd on ins 6f out: swtchd lft & hdwy over 1f out: r.o)	1¾	**4**	16/1	41	3
2928⁶	**Java Shrine (USA) (53)** (AJChamberlain) **6-9-7** RCody-Boutcher(9) (lost pl over 3f out: r.o one pce fnl 2f)	1¼	**5**	12/1	54	21
2552¹²	**Noeprob (USA) (52)** (RJHodges) **7-9-6** RBrisland(5) (led 1f: rdn over 2f out: one pce)	½	**6**	6/1[2]	52	19
2941⁵	**Riverside Girl (IRE) (43)** (JSMoore) **3-7-10**(8)ow4 PaulCleary(11) (hdwy over 1f out: nvr nrr)	2	**7**	20/1	39	—
2121¹⁰	**Mediate (IRE) (39)** (AHide) **5-8-7v** JGotobed(7) (nvr nrr)	nk	**8**	25/1	35	2
2777⁴	**Young Frederick (IRE) (40)** (NMBabbage) **4-8-8** SCarson(3) (snatched up & lost pl 5f out: rallied 3f out: wknd over 1f out)	nk	**9**	12/1	35	2
3041⁸	**Sakharov (43)** (BPalling) **8-8-11b¹** GHannon(17) (led over 7f out to 2f out: sn wknd)	¾	**10**	20/1	37	4
2646¹⁴	**Blushing Grenadier (IRE) (31)** (MJFetherston-Godley) **5-7-13** PClarke(4) (hld up: rdn over 2f out: sn wknd)	2	**11**	25/1	21	—
2954¹⁰	**Jubilee Scholar (IRE) (41)** (GLMoore) **4-8-9** DarrenWilliams(10) (a mid div)	¾	**12**	12/1	29	—
2488*	**Queen of Shannon (IRE) (58)** (AWCarroll) **9-9-7**(5) PMundy(15) (a bhd)	nk	**13**	11/2[1]	46	13
1291¹³	**Quinzii Martin (42)** (DHaydnJones) **9-8-2b**(8) JoeleneRichards(14) (a bhd)	3½	**14**	25/1	29	—
3091⁹	**Zahran (IRE) (31)** (JMBradley) **6-7-13** JFowle(2) (b: a bhd)	d.h	**14**	8/1[3]	11	—
2501⁴	**Move With Edes (59)** (WGMTurner) **5-9-13** DavidO'Neill(8) (prom over 6f)	s.h	**16**	9/1	39	6
3248⁵	**Asterix (34)** (JMBradley) **9-8-2b** PFitzsimons(16) (b: dwlt: hdwy 5f out: wknd 2f out)	2½	**17**	10/1	9	—
2997a⁷	**Northern Clan (32)** (AJChamberlain) **4-8-0v** CCogan(12) (bhd fnl 3f)	3	**18**	33/1	1	—

(SP 137.8%) **18 Rn**

1m 47.7 (5.50) CSF £193.36 CT £1,611.61 TOTE £19.90: £3.10 £5.00 £2.60 £2.80 (£266.30) Trio £456.80; £135.13 to 6/8/97 OWNER Mr J. G. Thatcher (ANDOVER) BRED J. Maxwell
WEIGHT FOR AGE 3yo-7lb
No bid
Super Serenade gained control two furlongs out and kept on really well to give his young rider his first ever victory (10/1)
1009 Rocky Waters (USA) struggled into second place over a furlong out but had no hope of reeling in the winner. He is a poor performer these days who has not won since 1994. (20/1)
236 Oozlem (IRE) was putting in all his best work in the last furlong and a half. All five of his wins have come over a mile. (8/1: 6/1-9/1)
2603 Pc's Cruiser (IRE) was done no favours on the long loop three-quarters of a mile from home, and was switched left by his jockey , who looked very ungainly, over a furlong out. The combination continued to drift left, but nevertheless plodded on to be nearest at the line. He is a very poor performer who has done all his winning on the Southwell fibresand. (16/1)
2646 Java Shrine (USA) is a poor performer these days and never threatened here. His only win to date came over three years ago. (12/1)
2552 Noeprob (USA) was made to look very pedestrian in the final quarter-mile. She has done all her winning in selling or claiming company. (6/1)

3277 EVENING STANDARD MAIDEN STKS (3-Y.O+) (Class D)
6-35 (6-35) **1m 2f 7y** £3,642.50 (£1,100.00: £535.00: £252.50) Stalls: High GOING minus 0.21 sec per fur (GF)

				SP	RR	SF
2832⁵	**Fantastic Flame (IRE) (78)** (PJMakin) **3-8-7** SSanders(1) (rdn over 3f out: hdwy 2f out: led over 1f out: r.o wl)	—	**1**	8/1[3]	84	50
2328¹²	**Aerleon Pete (IRE) (75)** (MRStoute) **3-8-12** JReid(13) (a.p: rdn 4f out: ev ch over 1f out: unable qckn)	2	**2**	10/1	86	52
1006⁵	**Sturgeon (IRE) (78)** (PFICole) **3-8-12** CRutter(7) (hdwy over 3f out: ev ch over 1f out: one pce)	2½	**3**	8/1[3]	82	48
1611³	**Easy Song (USA)** (RCharlton) **3-8-12** PatEddery(5) (lw: a.p: led over 3f out tl over 1f out: sn wknd)	5	**4**	11/10[1]	74	40
	Naval Games (SCWilliams) **4-9-7** DaneO'Neill(14) (w'like: bit bkwd: swtchd lft wl over 1f out: hdwy over 1f out: nvr nrr)	s.h	**5**	66/1	74	49
1940⁵	**Sheep Stealer** (REPeacock) **9-9-4**(3) MartinDwyer(15) (led over 6f: wknd over 2f out)	1	**6**	66/1	72	47
2583¹⁰	**Polenista** (JLDunlop) **3-8-7** GCarter(10) (bmpd s: nvr nr to chal)	¾	**7**	14/1	66	32
	Classic Fan (USA) (MRChannon) **3-8-4**(3) PPMurphy(8) (unf: nvr nrr)	hd	**8**	33/1	66	32
2846⁵	**Stormy Story (USA)** (JHMGosden) **3-8-12** GHind(12) (hld up: nt clr run over 2f out: nvr plcd to chal)	2	**9**	16/1	68	34
2853⁴	**Bold Buster** (IABalding) **4-9-7** SWhitworth(4) (reard s: a bhd)	1	**10**	25/1	66	41
2687³	**Versatility** (RFJohnsonHoughton) **4-9-2** PaulEddery(3) (bhd fnl 3f)	5	**11**	12/1	53	28
2924⁵	**Jaseur (USA)** (JHMGosden) **4-9-7** LDettori(6) (hdwy 5f out: wknd over 2f out)	½	**12**	11/2[2]	57	32
2846³	**Alakdar (CAN)** (ACStewart) **3-8-12** RHills(11) (swtg: prom over 6f)	8	**13**	12/1	45	11
	Henbury Princess (RJHodges) **4-9-2** SDrowne(2) (w'like: bit bkwd: a bhd)	22	**14**	33/1	4	—
	Charbertsam (RRowe) **4-9-0**(7) AGarrity(9) (neat: a bhd)	11	**15**	66/1	—	—

(SP 136.5%) **15 Rn**

2m 7.9 (3.00) CSF £84.89 TOTE £7.30: £2.10 £3.80 £2.40 (£220.20) Trio £66.50 OWNER Dr Carlos Stelling (MARLBOROUGH) BRED Cambremont Ltd Partnership

WEIGHT FOR AGE 3yo-9lb

2832 Fantastic Flame (IRE), rousted along early in the straight, came through to lead below the distance and kept on really strongly. (8/1: 5/1-9/1)
1006 Aerleon Pete (IRE), one of several with every chance below the distance, was then unable to contain the winner. This was his best run so far this season. (10/1: op 4/1)
1006 Sturgeon (IRE) ran much better here and threatened to take the lead over a furlong out before tapped for toe. (8/1: 4/1-9/1)
1611 Easy Song (USA) found this longer trip beyond him, for after moving to the front over three furlongs from home, he was collared below the distance and had little left in the tank. (11/10)
Naval Games did not look fully tuned up for this belated racecourse debut but stayed on from below the distance to be nearest at the line. (66/1)
Sheep Stealer took the field along but was collared over three furlongs from home and soon had bellows to mend. (66/1)
1866 Polenista (14/1: op 8/1)
2846 Stormy Story (USA) was certainly looked after in mid-field and never looked like getting into it. He is now qualified for handicaps and looks one to note. (16/1)
2924 Jaseur (USA) (11/2: 3/1-6/1)
2846 Alakdar (CAN) (12/1: op 7/1)

3278 TATTERSALLS MAIDEN AUCTION STKS (2-Y.O) (Class E)

7-05 (7-07) **5f 217y** £3,273.75 (£990.00: £482.50: £228.75) Stalls: High GOING minus 0.21 sec per fur (GF)

				SP	RR	SF
3013^{6}	**Speedfit Too (IRE) (85)** (GGMargarson) **2-8-12** GCarter(23) (a.p: led over 1f out: rdn out)	—	**1**	$9/2^{2}$	94	21
3113^{4}	**Legs Be Frendly (IRE) (85)** (KMcAuliffe) **2-8-10v1** JReid(13) (lw: a.p: chsd wnr over 1f out: unable qckn)	2½	**2**	$7/2^{1}$	85	12
	Canonize (IRE) (JWHills) **2-8-5** RHills(12) (w'like: s.s: swtchd lft over 2f out: hdwy wl over 1f out: one pce fnl f)	nk	**3**	20/1	80	7
2962^{6}	**Robeena (86)** (CNAllen) **2-7-12**(3) MartinDwyer(10) (hdwy over 2f out: rdn over 1f out: one pce)	3	**4**	$9/2^{2}$	68	—
2706^{8}	**Roi de Danse** (JWHills) **2-8-6**(3) MHenry(5) (rdn & hdwy over 1f out: r.o)	1½	**5**	20/1	72	—
	Midnight Sting (MAJarvis) **2-8-2**ow2 MRoberts(11) (b: w'like: scope: bit bkwd: stdy hdwy over 1f out: nvr plcd to chal)	hd	**6**	14/1	64+	—
	Sumbawa (IRE) (DHaydnJones) **2-8-4** SDrowne(18) (leggy: bit bkwd: s.s: hdwy 5f out: rdn over 2f out: one pce)	2½	**7**	33/1	60	—
2893^{W}	**Petane (IRE)** (JRArnold) **2-8-9** GHind(7) (hdwy over 1f out: eased whn btn fnl f)	½	**8**	33/1	63	—
2466^{3}	**Cape Hope** (RBoss) **2-8-3**(3) RFfrench(16) (led over 4f)	¾	**9**	14/1	58	—
	Dawn Treader (USA) (RHannon) **2-8-10** DaneO'Neill(3) (w'like: bit bkwd: s.s: swtchd rt 5f out: nvr nrr)	¾	**10**	16/1	60	—
3033^{3}	**Delciana (IRE)** (PWHarris) **2-8-6** JQuinn(14) (bmpd over 2f out: nvr plcd to chal)	nk	**11**	16/1	55+	—
2191^{7}	**Up The Wall** (RHarris) **2-8-2**(5) ADaly(15) (prom over 4f)	1¼	**12**	50/1	53	—
2553^{7}	**Katyushka (IRE)** (MajorDNChappell) **2-8-4** AClark(17) (s.s: hdwy 5f out: wknd over 1f out)	1	**13**	$7/1^{3}$	47	—
3019^{3}	**Deva Lady (76)** (MRChannon) **2-8-5** PaulEddery(8) (hld up: rdn over 2f out: sn wknd)	2½	**14**	9/1	42	—
2917^{11}	**Pippas Pride (IRE)** (MJFetherston-Godley) **2-8-5**(3) DSweeney(2) (nvr nrr)	3	**15**	33/1	37	—
2306^{8}	**Shecando (IRE)** (CJames) **2-8-3** CRutter(22) (prom over 4f)	nk	**16**	20/1	31	—
	Ivory Charm (KTIvory) **2-8-2** DBiggs(19) (w'like: bit bkwd: a bhd)	2½	**17**	33/1	23	—
2959^{5}	**Thelonius (IRE)** (JGSmyth-Osbourne) **2-8-7** SSanders(24) (prom 3f)	3	**18**	20/1	20	—
2587^{11}	**La Vizelle (IRE)** (RGuest) **2-7-8**(7) DarrenWilliams(4) (a bhd)	1½	**19**	33/1	10	—
	Imperial Court (IRE) (JGMO'Shea) **2-8-7** RPrice(1) (w'like: bit bkwd: a bhd)	8	**20**	33/1	—	—
2579^{9}	**Risque** (MrsAJBowlby) **2-8-7** CandyMorris(9) (bhd fnl 2f)	1¼	**21**	50/1	—	—
	Southdown Cyrano (IRE) (PButler) **2-8-4** JLowe(21) (unf: bit bkwd: s.s: hdwy over 4f out: wknd over 3f out)	18	**22**	50/1	—	—
				(SP 148.8%)	**22 Rn**	

1m 14.6 (4.10) CSF £19.33 TOTE £5.90: £2.10 £1.60 £6.40 (£9.30) Trio £109.60 OWNER Mr John Guest (NEWMARKET) BRED Minch Bloodstock

1812 Speedfit Too (IRE) appreciated this easier assignment and, leading over a furlong out, was rousted along to assert. (9/2: 5/2-5/1)
3113 Legs Be Frendly (IRE) had a battle for second place in the final furlong, and although just succeeding had no hope with the winner. He has now finished second in five of his seven races and deserves a change of luck. (7/2: 5/2-4/1)
Canonize (IRE), whose dam was a multiple winner in the USA, came through to dispute second place in the final furlong and only just lost out. (20/1)
2962 Robeena took closer order over a quarter of a mile from home, but failed to find another gear from below the distance. (9/2)
Roi de Danse, at the back of the field in the early stages, stayed on through the field in the last furlong and a half. (20/1)
Midnight Sting, a scopey individual who looked as though the run would do her good, was given very tender handling, but caught the eye as she stayed on steadily from below the distance. She should soon leave this run behind. (14/1)
3033 Delciana (IRE) was given extremely tender handling in midfield and never looked like troubling the principals. She is now qualified for nurseries and looks one to keep an eye on. (16/1)
2553 Katyushka (IRE) (7/1: 4/1-8/1)

3279 SCOTTISH EQUITABLE/JOCKEYS ASSOCIATION H'CAP (0-75) (3-Y.O+) (Class D)

7-35 (7-36) **1m 3f 135y** £3,603.50 (£1,088.00: £529.00: £249.50) Stalls: High GOING minus 0.21 sec per fur (GF)

				SP	RR	SF
2961^{5}	**Koraloona (IRE) (57)** (GBBalding) **4-8-12** SDrowne(4) (rdn over 3f out: hdwy over 2f out: led wl ins fnl f: r.o wl)	—	**1**	$5/1^{2}$	66	48
2297^{3}	**Isitoff (71)** (SCWilliams) **4-9-12** LDettori(8) (a.p: rdn over 2f out: led ins fnl f: sn hdd: r.o)	nk	**2**	$11/2^{3}$	80	62
2928^{4}	**Newport Knight (60)** (RAkehurst) **6-9-1** AClark(1) (a.p: chsd ldr 5f out: led over 2f out tl ins fnl f: r.o)	nk	**3**	$11/2^{3}$	68	50
2783^{5}	**Woody's Boy (IRE) (61)** (MJHeaton-Ellis) **3-8-5** SSanders(3) (rdn over 3f out: hdwy over 1f out: r.o ins fnl f)	s.h	**4**	14/1	69	40
2949^{8}	**Mighty Phantom (USA) (62)** (JWHills) **4-9-3** RHills(2) (rdn over 2f out: hdwy over 1f out: r.o wl)	¾	**5**	9/1	69	51
2920^{D}	**Princess Danielle (66)** (WRMuir) **5-9-7** JReid(11) (rdn & hdwy over 2f out: swtchd rt wl over 1f out: unable qckn)	1¾	**6**	$4/1^{1}$	71	53
2916*	**Nothing Doing (IRE) (47)** (WJMusson) **8-8-2** JQuinn(6) (nvr nr to chal)	1¼	**7**	8/1	50	32
	Krayyan Dawn (47) (JAkehurst) **7-8-2**ow1 GCarter(5) (b: led 9f)	6	**8**	33/1	42	23
	Silvretta (IRE) (63) (RCSpicer) **4-9-4** MRoberts(9) (plld hrd: hdwy 9f out: wknd over 3f out)	hd	**9**	20/1	58	40
2837^{5}	**Chabrol (CAN) (60)** (RHarris) **4-8-10**(5) ADaly(10) (chsd ldr over 6f: wknd over 3f out)	4	**10**	8/1	49	31

2726[3] **French Mist (72)** (SDow) **3-9-2** JFEgan(7) (lw: hdwy 3f out: wknd over 1f out) ......¾ **11** 12/1 60 31
(SP 121.7%) **11 Rn**

2m 30.6 (4.60) CSF £30.93 CT £146.58 TOTE £7.40: £2.30 £1.90 £1.90 (£18.10) Trio £38.80 OWNER Mr Bernard Keay (ANDOVER) BRED Eaton Farms Inc, Red Bull Stable and Joe Hernon
WEIGHT FOR AGE 3yo-11lb

2961 Koraloona (IRE) launched his challenge from below the distance and eventually managed to get up in the closing stages. (5/1)
2297 Isitoff, a leading light throughout, poked a whisker in front early inside the final furlong, only to be narrowly passed by the winner soon afterwards. (11/2)
2928 Newport Knight has been sliding down the weights after some poor efforts, but ran much better here and gained control over a quarter of a mile from home. Although headed inside the final furlong, he only just lost out in a very tight finish. (11/2)
2783 Woody's Boy (IRE) at last found his feet from below the distance, but despite running on found the line was always coming too soon. (14/1)
2694 Mighty Phantom (USA) found this trip rather on the short side, for although running on in good style in the last furlong and a half, she was never going to get there. (9/1)
2920 Princess Danielle was moving up in distance, but having taken closer order over a quarter of a mile from home, then failed to find the necessary turn of foot. (4/1)
2837 Chabrol (CAN) (8/1: tchd 12/1)

3280 BRIAN BARNES/PROSTATE RESEARCH CAMPAIGN UK H'CAP (0-70) (3-Y.O+) (Class E)
8-05 (8-06) **5f 10y** £2,851.25 (£860.00: £417.50: £196.25) Stalls: High GOING minus 0.21 sec per fur (GF)

				SP	RR	SF
*3077**	**Distinctive Dream (IRE) (63)** (KTIvory) **3-9-1b**(3) MartinDwyer(2) (b: hdwy over 2f out: led over 1f out: hrd rdn & hung rt ins fnl f: r.o wl)	—	**1**	7/2 1	76	52
1667[6]	**Sound the Trumpet (IRE) (50)** (RCSpicer) **5-8-8** MRoberts(1) (hld up: led over 2f out tl over 1f out: unable qckn)	2	**2**	25/1	57	36
3107[2]	**Mousehole (70)** (RGuest) **5-10-0** PBloomfield(8) (hdwy over 2f out: ev ch 1f out: 2nd & btn whn snatched up on ins wl ins fnl f)	hd	**3**	8/1 2	76	55
3016[6]	**River Tern (68)** (JMBradley) **4-9-9**(3) RFfrench(5) (lw: hdwy over 1f out: r.o)	¾	**4**	9/1 3	72	51
2946[2]	**Dancing Mystery (45)** (EAWheeler) **3-7-7**(7) SCarson(13) (lw: a.p: rdn over 1f out: one pce)	nk	**5**	9/1 3	48	24
2698[5]	**Friendly Brave (USA) (64)** (MissGayKelleway) **7-9-8** JReid(3) (lw: hld up: nt clr run over 1f out: r.o one pce)	nk	**6**	10/1	66	45
2841[5]	**The Fugative (66)** (PMitchell) **4-9-10** SSanders(7) (dwlt: hdwy over 1f out: r.o)	hd	**7**	9/1 3	68	47
3016[2]	**Beau Venture (USA) (67)** (BPalling) **9-9-11** TSprake(12) (prom whn nt clr run & lost pl over 3f out: r.o one pce fnl f)	¾	**8**	10/1	66	45
2946[4]	**Harvey's Future (41)** (TTClement) **3-7-10** GBardwell(6) (b: nvr nr to chal)	1¼	**9**	40/1	36	12
2759[11]	**John O'Dreams (38)** (MrsALMKing) **12-7-10** JLowe(9) (b: s.s: a bhd)	1¼	**10**	25/1	29	8
3082[3]	**Justinianus (IRE) (46)** (JJBridger) **5-7-13**(5)ow2 ADaly(14) (lw: bhd fnl 3f)	nk	**11**	16/1	37	14
2732*	**Tommy Tempest (42)** (REPeacock) **8-8-0** JQuinn(4) (a.p: ev ch over 1f out: sn wknd)	½	**12**	12/1	31	10
2946*	**Goodbye Gatemen (IRE) (65)** (BAPearce) **3-9-6** JFEgan(10) (swvd lft s: led over 2f: eased whn btn over 1f out)	2	**13**	9/1 3	48	24
3016*	**Ashkernazy (IRE) (46)** (NEBerry) **6-8-4** NAdams(11) (prom over 2f)	2	**14**	8/1 2	22	1
				(SP 126.3%)	**14 Rn**	

61.6 secs (1.90) CSF £101.77 CT £638.87 TOTE £4.20: £2.30 £5.30 £2.60 (£141.40) Trio £427.80 OWNER Mr K. T. Ivory (RADLETT) BRED Peter Kehoe
LONG HANDICAP Harvey's Future 7-6 John O'Dreams 7-8
WEIGHT FOR AGE 3yo-3lb
OFFICIAL EXPLANATION **Tommy Tempest: the trainer reported that the gelding was struck into behind. Ashkernazy (IRE): no explanation offered.**

3077* Distinctive Dream (IRE) is in the form of his life at present. Leading over a furlong out, he hung badly right inside the final furlong, despite all his rider's efforts, and did the third no favours in the closing stages. However he was certainly the best horse on the day and kept the race after a Stewards' Enquiry to register his fifth consecutive victory. (7/2)
1667 Sound the Trumpet (IRE) moved to the front over a quarter of a mile from home but, headed below the distance, failed to find another gear. He has now won just once from 34 starts. (25/1)
3107 Mousehole continues in fine form and was still challenging for the lead a furlong out. However he appeared held in second place when done no favours by the winner in the closing stages. (8/1)
3016 River Tern stayed on well in the last furlong and a half, but was never going to get there in time. (9/1)
2946 Dancing Mystery was a leading light from the off and, although his jockey did not look very strong, the combination could only go up and down in the same place. He remains a maiden. (9/1)
2698 Friendly Brave (USA) was the meat in the sandwich below the distance, but did struggle on in the closing stages. He is dropping down to an attractive mark in the handicap. (10/1)
3016 Beau Venture (USA) (10/1: 8/1-12/1)
2946* Goodbye Gatemen (IRE) (9/1: 6/1-10/1)

3281 VALKYRIES MAIDEN STKS (3-Y.O) (Class D)
8-35 (8-36) **1m 67y** £3,525.50 (£1,064.00: £517.00: £243.50) Stalls: High GOING minus 0.21 sec per fur (GF)

				SP	RR	SF
930[9]	**Alphabet (84)** (MRStoute) **3-8-9** JReid(6) (lw: a.p: led over 1f out: rdn out)	—	**1**	15/8 1	76	20
3095[3]	**Khazinat El Dar (USA)** (MajorWRHern) **3-8-9** RHills(2) (lw: led 7f: r.o)	½	**2**	2/1 2	75	19
3095[4]	**Northern Angel (IRE) (81)** (MrsJCecil) **3-9-0** PatEddery(7) (b: lw: hld up: rdn 3f out: unable qckn)	8	**3**	3/1 3	65	9
	Swinging The Blues (IRE) (RAkehurst) **3-9-0** AClark(4) (lost pl over 2f out: one pce)	1	**4**	20/1	63	7
	Sycamore Boy (USA) (LordHuntingdon) **3-9-0** MRoberts(1) (a.p: shkn up 3f out: sn wknd)	¾	**5**	7/1	61	5
	Erinrinca (IRE) (JEBanks) **3-8-9** JQuinn(5) (w'like: bit bkwd: dwlt: a bhd)	3	**6**	20/1	51	—
2853[6]	**Ewar Snowflake** (KOCunningham-Brown) **3-8-6v**1(3) MartinDwyer(3) (dwlt: a bhd)	13	**7**	50/1	25	—
				(SP 117.1%)	**7 Rn**	

1m 48.0 (5.80) CSF £5.54 TOTE £3.20: £1.90 £2.00 (£3.60) OWNER Cheveley Park Stud (NEWMARKET) BRED Cheveley Park Stud Ltd and B. A. Cooper

930 Alphabet, given a three-month break, poked a whisker in front approaching the final furlong, and with Reid needing only to use hands and heels, was always just holding the second. (15/8)
3095 Khazinat El Dar (USA) took the field along. Narrowly headed approaching the final furlong, she kept on really well to finish well clear of the remainder, but was always just being held by the winner. She should soon go one better. (2/1)

3095 Northern Angel (IRE) was left for dead by the front two in the last three furlongs. (3/1: 9/4-7/2)
Swinging The Blues (IRE), making a belated seasonal reappearance, got completely outpaced over a quarter of a mile from home and from that point could only plod on in his own time. (20/1)
Sycamore Boy (USA) was never far away, but he showed an awful action, and was a spent force over two furlongs from home. (7/1)

T/Jkpt: £20,665.50 (2.19 Tckts). T/Plpt: £167.00 (150.53 Tckts). T/Qdpt: £9.40 (168.8 Tckts) AK

2934-CATTERICK (L-H) (Good to firm, Good patches)
Tuesday August 5th
WEATHER: overcast WIND: mod across

3282 'PONTEFRACT PARK' MAIDEN STKS (2-Y.O) (Class D)
2-15 (2-17) **7f** £3,411.50 (£1,022.00: £491.00: £225.50) Stalls: Low GOING minus 0.10 sec per fur (G)

				SP	RR	SF
2680²	**Mowbray (USA)** (PFICole) **2-9-0** JReid(6) (chsd ldrs: pushed along appr st: led over 2f out: comf)	—	**1**	4/7 1	77	34
2875⁴	**Zambezi (USA)** (DRLoder) **2-8-9** WRyan(8) (lw: a.p: chsd wnr fnl 2f: no imp)	1¾	**2**	2/1 2	68	25
2898³	**Tearaway** (JWWatts) **2-9-0** JCarroll(5) (sn chsng ldrs: styd on fnl 2f: no imp)	5	**3**	14/1 3	62	19
	Mareeba (MJohnston) **2-8-9** JWeaver(4) (lengthy: unf: s.i.s: bhd tl styd on fnl 2f)	2	**4**	16/1	52	9
*2606*⁴	**Russian Romeo (IRE) (60)** (BAMcMahon) **2-9-0** LNewton(2) (disp ld 3f: rdn & one pce)	1¾	**5**	50/1	53	10
2842¹⁵	**Buzz The Agent** (MWEasterby) **2-8-11**(3) GParkin(3) (effrt ½-wy: nvr trbld ldrs)	1½	**6**	66/1	50	7
1806¹¹	**Isabella** (TKeddy) **2-8-9** NCarlisle(1) (mde most tl hdd & wknd over 2f out)	¾	**7**	50/1	43	—
3103¹⁰	**Jago** (MWEasterby) **2-9-0** TLucas(7) (in tch tl outpcd ½-wy: wknd qckly)	11	**8**	66/1	23	—
				(SP 116.4%)	**8 Rn**	

1m 28.3 (4.70) CSF £1.77 TOTE £1.60: £1.10 £1.10 £1.80 (£1.10) OWNER Sir George Meyrick (WHATCOMBE) BRED Helen C Alexander
OFFICIAL EXPLANATION **Buzz The Agent: the trainer reported that the colt was later found to have sore shins.**
2680 Mowbray (USA) didn't look particularly happy on this track, but he still won well enough and will obviously be better on a more galloping course. (4/7)
2875 Zambezi (USA) hasn't the best of actions, but she has a fair amount of ability and will obviously pick up a run of the mill event. (2/1)
2898 Tearaway stays well, but seems to lack any turn of foot. (14/1)
Mareeba, a green newcomer, gradually improved as the race progressed and there is obviously some improvement there. (16/1)
2606 Russian Romeo (IRE), a free-runner trying his longest trip to date, was left struggling once the pace seriously increased. (50/1)

3283 'REDCAR, RIPON & THIRSK' H'CAP (0-70) (3-Y.O+) (Class E)
2-45 (2-46) **1m 5f 175y** £3,226.25 (£965.00: £462.50: £211.25) Stalls: Low GOING minus 0.10 sec per fur (G)

				SP	RR	SF
3069⁵	**Hasta la Vista (50)** (MWEasterby) **7-8-5b**(3) GParkin(10) (b.nr hind: trckd ldrs: shkn up to ld ins fnl f: r.o)	—	**1**	10/1	61	31
2949³	**Lime Street Blues (IRE) (55)** (TKeddy) **6-8-13** NCarlisle(6) (b.hind: lw: in tch: hdwy to ld over 2f out: hdd ins fnl f: kpt on)	1½	**2**	8/1 3	64	34
3108⁴	**Dancing Cavalier (65)** (RHollinshead) **4-9-2**(7) PFredericks(2) (b.off hind: bhd: hmpd after 5½f: hdwy on outside over 2f out: hung lft: styd on wl towards fin)	nk	**3**	4/1 2	74	44
2236⁹	**Ballpoint (70)** (GMMoore) **4-10-0** JFortune(4) (bhd & hmpd after 5½f: hdwy 6f out: chal 2f out: no ex fnl f)	1	**4**	9/1	78	48
2902²	**Doubly Sharp (USA) (55)** (MJohnston) **3-8-0b**¹ JFanning(11) (sn cl up: led 4f out tl over 2f out: kpt on one pce)	hd	**5**	14/1	63	20
1605⁷	**Clash of Swords (48)** (PCalver) **4-8-6** KDarley(5) (hdwy 5f out: in tch appr st: one pce after)	5	**6**	20/1	50	20
3093*	**Admirals Secret (USA) (54)** (CFWall) **8-8-12** 4x JReid(16) (lw: bhd: effrt 6f out: rdn appr st: nvr rchd ldrs)	3½	**7**	7/2 1	52	22
*3046*⁶	**Mizyan (IRE) (51)** (JEBanks) **9-8-4**(5) CLowther(13) (bhd & pushed along: styd on fnl 3f: n.d)	1½	**8**	10/1	47	17
3085³	**Daira (58)** (JDBethell) **4-8-13**(3) PFessey(3) (lw: chsd ldrs tl outpcd fnl 2½f)	1¾	**9**	8/1 3	52	22
2413⁷	**Karaylar (IRE) (40)** (WStorey) **5-7-12** TWilliams(8) (sn outpcd & bhd: sme hdwy over 2f out: n.d)	s.h	**10**	25/1	34	4
3203ᵂ	**Rose of Glenn (45)** (BPalling) **6-8-3** TSprake(7) (in tch: pushed along over 6f out: wknd over 2f out)	1	**11**	11/1	38	8
*2910*¹¹	**Kilnamartyra Girl (44)** (JParkes) **7-8-2** MFenton(12) (b.hind: a in rr)	2	**12**	20/1	35	5
2932⁵	**Royal Circus (45)** (IPWilliams) **8-8-3** JFEgan(1) (chsd ldrs: outpcd 7f out: sn lost pl)	3½	**13**	14/1	31	1
2825¹³	**Winnebago (46)** (CWThornton) **4-8-4** DeanMcKeown(14) (led tl hdd 4f out: wknd qckly over 2f out)	9	**14**	10/1	22	—
1469¹⁵	**Kissandy (51)** (MrsVAAconley) **3-7-3**(7) JMcAuley(9) (t.o fnl 6f)	30	**15**	200/1	—	—
2880¹¹	**First Bite (IRE) (48)** (MDHammond) **5-8-6** WRyan(15) (prom to ½-wy: t.o)	3	**16**	25/1	—	—
				(SP 141.1%)	**16 Rn**	

3m 5.5 (9.50) CSF £87.94 CT £360.37 TOTE £15.90: £3.60 £1.10 £2.60 £3.10 (£115.90) Trio £201.60 OWNER Mr K. Hodgson (SHERIFF HUTTON) BRED Clanville Lodge Stud
LONG HANDICAP Kissandy 6-3
WEIGHT FOR AGE 3yo-13lb
OFFICIAL EXPLANATION **Hasta La Vista: regarding the improvement in form, the rider reported that the gelding was unable to quicken off a slow pace last time, but the stronger gallop here enabled him to stay on in the closing stages.**
3069 Hasta la Vista, given a chance by the handicapper, was well suited by the strong pace and won it nicely. (10/1: op 6/1)
2949 Lime Street Blues (IRE) hasn't won on the Flat for four seasons - that was on heavy ground - but is obviously in good heart and has certainly slipped down the handicap. (8/1)
3108 Dancing Cavalier got messed about at one stage and always had a lot of running to do and as usual he tended to hang under pressure, but despite a strong finish was always too late. (4/1: op 6/1)
1672 Ballpoint has a dreadful action, but he ran well enough, having every chance after being hampered, only then failing to quicken late on. (9/1: 8/1-12/1)
2902 Doubly Sharp (USA) had blinkers on for the first time and put up a much improved performance. (14/1)
1232 Clash of Swords threw away a winning opportunity on this track last season and was never fully co-operating this time. (20/1)
3093* Admirals Secret (USA) ran moderately and was in trouble some way out, and was not over-punished when beaten. (7/2)
3085 Daira (8/1: 6/1-9/1)

3284 'BEVERLEY WESTWOOD' (S) STKS (3, 4 & 5-Y.O) (Class G)
3-15 (3-16) **1m 7f 177y** £2,162.50 (£600.00: £287.50) Stalls: Low GOING minus 0.10 sec per fur (G)

				SP	RR	SF
2824⁷	**Forzair (50)** (JJO'Neill) **5-9-12** JCarroll(3) (lw: mde all: edgd rt fnl 2f: all out)	—	**1**	9/1 3	57	25

				SP	RR	SF
2825[3]	**Marsayas (IRE) (58)** (MJCamacho) **4-9-8** DeanMcKeown(5) (a chsng ldrs: rdn 4f out: swtchd ins fnl f: kpt on u.str.p)	nk	**2**	10/11 [1]	53	21
2908[10]	**Ocean Breeze (35)** (JSWainwright) **3-8-7v** KDarley(1) (trckd ldrs: chal 7f out: outpcd 4f out: sn btn)	10	**3**	16/1	43	—
2874[3]	**Ship's Dancer (24)** (DonEnricoIncisa) **4-9-3b** KimTinkler(6) (dwlt: effrt ½-wy: nvr able to chal)	1¾	**4**	16/1	36	4
2411[7]	**Swan Hunter (65)** (DJSCosgrove) **4-9-8** MRimmer(2) (swtg: chsd ldrs: chal over 4f out: wknd over 2f out)	10	**5**	11/8 [2]	31	—
1229[11]	**Ihtimaam (FR) (32)** (MrsASwinbank) **5-9-8** EJohnson(4) (s.i.s: lost tch 6f out: sn t.o)	17	**6**	50/1	14	—

(SP 118.2%) **6 Rn**

3m 37.7 (15.70) CSF £17.30 TOTE £11.90: £4.30 £1.20 (£6.80) OWNER Clayton Bigley Partnership Ltd (PENRITH) BRED J. G. Charlton
WEIGHT FOR AGE 3yo-15lb
No bid, Marsayas (IRE) clmd Mrs V. Jordan £5,750
2479 Forzair, trying his longest trip to date, did it the hard way and, despite hanging on under pressure, held on splendidly. (9/1)
2825 Marsayas (IRE) had his chances, but looks slow and perhaps even more use should have been made of him. (10/11: 4/5-evens)
2357 Ocean Breeze looked to have a lot on here, so this was not too bad an effort. (16/1)
2874 Ship's Dancer, despite the fact that her stable is in tremendous form, had no chance at these weights. (16/1)
2175 Swan Hunter, who sweated up and moved very badly to post, proved a big disappointment and dropped away tamely in the home straight. (11/8)

3285 'DONCASTER TOWN MOOR' H'CAP (0-60) (3-Y.O+) (Class F)

3-45 (3-47) **7f** £3,120.00 (£870.00: £420.00) Stalls: Low GOING minus 0.10 sec per fur (G)

				SP	RR	SF
2395[13]	**Mybotye (55)** (RBastiman) **4-9-5**(5) HBastiman(16) (bhd: hdwy on outside 2f out: hrd rdn: hung lft & r.o to ld cl home: fin 1st: disq: plcd last)		**1d**	8/1	66	37
2760[7]	**Kass Alhawa (59)** (DWChapman) **4-10-0** ACulhane(5) (in tch: rdn to ld ins fnl f: ct cl home: fin 2nd, nk: awrdd r)	nk	**1**	8/1	69	40
2788[2]	**Sing With the Band (43)** (BAMcMahon) **6-8-12** JReid(12) (a chsng ldrs: led 1½f out tl ins fnl f: btn whn hmpd nr fin: fin 3rd, 3/4l: plcd 2nd)	¾	**2**	4/1 [1]	52	23
2828[3]	**Needle Match (54)** (JJO'Neill) **4-9-9** JCarroll(1) (s.i.s: bhd: hdwy & nt clr run wl over 1f out: swtchd & r.o strly fnl f: fin 4th, nk: plcd 3rd)	nk	**3**	9/1	62	33
3254[4]	**Myttons Mistake (57)** (ABailey) **4-9-5**(7) IHudson(2) (hdwy ½-wy: sn chsng ldrs: n.m.r fnl f: kpt on: fin 5th, nk: plcd 4th)	nk	**4**	6/1 [2]	64	35
2906[7]	**Gipsy Princess (57)** (MWEasterby) **3-9-6** TLucas(8) (mid div: hdwy over 2f out: sn chsng ldrs: btn whn hmpd wl ins fnl f: fin 6th, 1l: plcd 5th)	1	**5**	7/1 [3]	62	27
2828[5]	**Legal Issue (IRE) (55)** (WWHaigh) **5-9-10** RLappin(10) (lw: mid div: hdwy 2f out: n.m.r & r.o one pce: fin 7th, 1½l: plcd 6th)	1½	**6**	12/1	57	28
1573[7]	**Abstone Queen (50)** (PDEvans) **3-8-13v** JFEgan(11) (hdwy ent st: n.m.r & nvr able to chal: fin 8th, ½l: plcd 7th)	½	**7**	20/1	50	15
2722[8]	**Pardan (50)** (BPalling) **3-8-13** TSprake(3) (led after 1½f tl 1½f out: wknd: fin 9th, 3/4l: plcd 8th)	¾	**8**	25/1	49	14
2567[7]	**Formidable Liz (45)** (MDHammond) **7-9-0** JFortune(14) (nvr trbld ldrs: fin 10th, 3l: plcd 9th)	3	**9**	14/1	37	8
2395[2]	**Sea Spouse (39)** (MBlanshard) **6-8-8** DeanMcKeown(15) (lw: led 1½f: w ldr tl wknd fnl 2f: fin 11th, ½l: plcd 10th)	½	**10**	12/1	30	1
1965[4]	**Super Park (41)** (JPearce) **5-8-10** MWigham(13) (bhd: effrt on outside 2f out: n.d: fin 12th, 2l: plcd 11th)	2	**11**	12/1	27	—
1828[2]	**Pathaze (43)** (NBycroft) **4-8-12** JWeaver(4) (chsd ldrs 5f: wknd: fin 13th, 3½l: plcd 12th)	3½	**12**	16/1	21	—
2937[4]	**Dispol Diamond (49)** (GROldroyd) **4-9-4** KDarley(9) (hdwy u.p 2f out: sn btn: fin 14th, hd: plcd 13th)	hd	**13**	9/1	27	—
2384[5]	**Komlucky (48)** (ABMulholland) **5-8-12v**(5) CLowther(6) (chsd ldrs tl wknd fnl 2f: fin 15th, 3/4l: plcd 14th)	¾	**14**	12/1	24	—
2906[9]	**My Godson (52)** (MDods) **7-9-4**(3) CTeague(17) (effrt 4f out: sn btn: fin 16th, 6l: plcd 15th)	6	**15**	20/1	14	—
793[6]	**Red Embers (56)** (DNicholls) **3-9-5** WRyan(7) (stdd s: a bhd: fin 17th, 2l: plcd 16th)	2	**16**	25/1	14	—

(SP 149.5%) **17 Rn**

1m 28.8 (5.20) CSF £42.53 CT £305.05 TOTE £12.60: £3.60 £1.60 £2.50 £1.50 (£54.80) Trio £217.50 OWNER Mr J. B. Wilcox (YORK) BRED L. H. J. Ward
WEIGHT FOR AGE 3yo-6lb
STEWARDS' ENQUIRY Bastiman susp. 14-23/8/97 (reckless riding) & 25-30/8/97 (excessive & incorrect use of the whip).
OFFICIAL EXPLANATION **Mybotye: regarding the improvement in form, the trainer reported that the gelding's poor run last time had been due to it suffering from the herpes virus. The trainer was fined £200 under instruction H14 for failing to have reported this.**
2760 Kass Alhawa needs to come late and also needs plenty of luck and certainly had more than his fair share of that. (8/1)
2788 Sing With the Band is running well at present and is certainly off a useful mark. (4/1)
2828 Needle Match left the impression that with any luck at all, he might well have won this. (9/1)
3254 Myttons Mistake ran a fair race and had no luck in running, otherwise he would certainly have been in the shake up. (6/1)
2733 Gipsy Princess had her chances and being hampered didn't make that much difference. (7/1)
2828 Legal Issue (IRE) likes the track but is the type that needs things to go just right and they never did here. (12/1)
2567 Formidable Liz (14/1: 10/1-16/1)
571 Mybotye came from way behind and, given some really strong assistance, stayed on to win it, but in doing so carved up half the field and the Stewards had no option but to throw him out. (8/1)

3286 'WETHERBY STEEPLECHASES' CLAIMING STKS (3-Y.O+) (Class F)

4-15 (4-15) **1m 3f 214y** £2,532.00 (£702.00: £336.00) Stalls: Low GOING minus 0.10 sec per fur (G)

				SP	RR	SF
2661*	**Urgent Reply (USA) (56)** (CADwyer) **4-9-2** JCarroll(1) (lw: b: mde virtually all: hrd rdn & kpt on wl appr fnl f)	—	**1**	3/1 [2]	57	27
187[3]	**More Than You Know (IRE) (82)** (KRBurke) **4-9-2** BDoyle(3) (trckd ldrs: hdwy on bit to disp ld over 2f out: rdn appr fnl f: fnd nil)	1½	**2**	2/1 [1]	55	25
2065[5]	**Golden Thunderbolt (FR) (66)** (NTinkler) **4-9-9** JWeaver(5) (bhd: effrt over 5f out: chsng ldrs ent st: one pce appr fnl f)	½	**3**	2/1 [1]	61	31
2911[2]	**Nicola's Princess (49)** (BAMcMahon) **4-8-12** MWigham(4) (b: chsd wnr tl wknd fnl 3f)	17	**4**	4/1 [3]	28	—
2364[6]	**Kirkham** (MrsVAAconley) **3-8-8** NCarlisle(2) (prom tl outpcd over 7f out: t.o fnl 4f)	24	**5**	66/1	3	—

(SP 113.2%) **5 Rn**

2m 41.3 (9.90) CSF £8.85 TOTE £3.50: £1.30 £1.60 (£4.30) OWNER Mr S. Aitken (NEWMARKET) BRED Clovelly Farms
WEIGHT FOR AGE 3yo-11lb
2661* Urgent Reply (USA) again showed what a game sort he is, but in doing so he did have a hard race. He looks the type that should do well over hurdles. (3/1)

187 More Than You Know (IRE) looked to be cantering for much of the trip, but when an effort was required, she just downed tools. (2/1: op 5/4)
2065 Golden Thunderbolt (FR) was struggling with the pace some way out. He managed to get into it turning for home, but then looked slow. (2/1)
2911 Nicola's Princess is probably better on an easier surface and a shade shorter distance. (4/1)

3287 'YORK KNAVESMIRE' H'CAP (0-65) (3-Y.O+) (Class F)

4-45 (4-49) **5f** £2,973.00 (£828.00: £399.00) Stalls: Low GOING minus 0.10 sec per fur (G)

Form	Horse	Dist	Pos	SP	RR	SF
3126^{2}	**Double Oscar (IRE) (62)** (DNicholls) **4-9-11b** AlexGreaves(7) (lw: in tch: hdwy to ld ins fnl f: r.o)	—	**1**	$2/1^{1}$	75	55
	Lady Caroline Lamb (IRE) (60) (RBastiman) **4-9-4**(5) HBastiman(9) (in tch: hdwy over 1f out: nt qckn ins fnl f)	1½	**2**	33/1	68	48
3208^{4}	**Johayro (58)** (JSGoldie) **4-9-7v** KDarley(19) (racd stands' side: a chsng ldrs: kpt on wl)	1	**3**	10/1	63	43
3121^{6}	**William's Well (60)** (MWEasterby) **3-9-3b**(3) GParkin(5) (b.nr fore: in tch: hrd rdn over 1f out: styd on)	1	**4**	20/1	62	39
2703^{4}	**Sotonian (HOL) (44)** (PSFelgate) **4-8-0**(7) RWinston(6) (a chsng ldrs: ev ch ins fnl f: no ex)	1½	**5**	$7/1^{2}$	41	21
3271^{2}	**Imp Express (IRE) (38)** (GMMoore) **4-8-1** NCarlisle(12) (in tch: hdwy ½-wy: nt qckn ins fnl f)	hd	**6**	11/1	35	15
3034^{7}	**Panther (IRE) (62)** (PDEvans) **7-9-11v** JFEgan(8) (lw: styd on fnl 2f: nrst fin)	1	**7**	25/1	56	36
2759^{2}	**Southern Dominion (43)** (MissJFCraze) **5-8-6b** SWebster(2) (prom tl rdn & btn over 1f out)	½	**8**	$7/1^{2}$	35	15
2540*	**Lillibella (56)** (MrsJRRamsden) **4-9-5** JFortune(18) (prom tl lost pl appr fnl f)	s.h	**9**	$8/1^{3}$	48	28
2754^{6}	**Bowcliffe Grange (IRE) (49)** (DWChapman) **5-8-12** ACulhane(10) (led & sn clr: hdd & wknd ins fnl f)	½	**10**	12/1	39	19
2759^{7}	**Chemcast (65)** (JLEyre) **4-9-7b**(7) SBuckley(1) (chsd ldrs over 3f)	½	**11**	12/1	54	34
2934^{6}	**Blazing Imp (USA) (47)** (MrsJJordan) **4-8-10** MFenton(15) (wnt rt s: a bhd)	hd	**12**	20/1	35	15
2759^{10}	**Hamilton Gold (36)** (MGMeagher) **4-7-13** FNorton(11) (chsd ldrs 3f: sn lost pl)	2	**13**	66/1	18	—
2061^{9}	**Time To Tango (57)** (GMMoore) **4-9-6** JWeaver(20) (a bhd)	nk	**14**	20/1	38	18
2895^{3}	**Windrush Boy (52)** (MRBosley) **7-8-10**(5) AimeeCook(3) (in tch 3f: wknd)	hd	**15**	12/1	33	13
2721^{4}	**Tymeera (44)** (BPalling) **4-8-7** TSprake(16) (lw: s.i.s: n.d)	1	**16**	16/1	21	1
3077^{8}	**Stolen Kiss (IRE) (57)** (MWEasterby) **5-9-6b** TLucas(13) (unruly s: a bhd)	1¼	**17**	20/1	30	10
2674^{2}	**Amy Leigh (IRE) (48)** (CaptJWilson) **4-8-4b**(7) AngelaHartley(17) (s.i.s: a bhd)	¾	**18**	40/1	19	—
	Brawling Springs (45) (JJO'Neill) **3-8-5** JCarroll(4) (dwlt: a bhd)	1¾	**19**	66/1	10	—

(SP 147.1%) **19 Rn**

60.3 secs (2.60) CSF £94.52 CT £602.06 TOTE £3.80: £1.40 £7.00 £1.60 £4.30 (£61.70) Trio £632.20 OWNER Trilby Racing (THIRSK) BRED Tasia Limited
WEIGHT FOR AGE 3yo-3lb
OFFICIAL EXPLANATION **Stolen Kiss (IRE): the trainer reported that the ground was too firm for the filly.**
3126 Double Oscar (IRE) is in top form and won this really well. (2/1: op 7/2)
Lady Caroline Lamb (IRE), from a yard that is going well at present, put in a useful effort for her first outing of the season. (33/1)
3208 Johayro is certainly coming back to form, this was a fine effort from his draw. (10/1)
3121 William's Well is running better again and was keeping on determinedly at the end, but does need plenty of driving. (20/1)
2703 Sotonian (HOL) has only ever won on sand, but does have the pace to pick up a race on turf. (7/1)
3271 Imp Express (IRE) has the ability but doesn't always put it in. (11/1)
3034 Panther (IRE) is on his way back to form and over six furlongs he should be kept in mind. (25/1)
2540* Lillibella (8/1: 6/1-9/1)

T/Jkpt: £7,100.00 (0.09 Tckts); £4,195.69 to Newcastle 6/8/97. T/Plpt: £30.50 (807.11 Tckts). T/Qdpt: £9.90 (125.57 Tckts) AA

2719-FOLKESTONE (R-H) (Good to firm, Good patches)

Tuesday August 5th

WEATHER: sunny WIND: slight across

3288 E.B.F. BURWASH NOVICE STKS (2-Y.O) (Class D)

2-00 (2-00) **5f** £3,332.70 (£993.60: £473.80: £213.90) Stalls: Low GOING minus 0.13 sec per fur (G)

Form	Horse	Dist	Pos	SP	RR	SF
2684*	**Huntswood (86)** (RHannon) **2-9-4** RHughes(2) (a.p: led wl over 1f out: rdn: r.o wl)	—	**1**	$4/6^{1}$	86	35
2831^{9}	**Madame Claude (IRE)** (JARToller) **2-8-7** SSanders(4) (hld up: chsd wnr over 1f out: ev ch ins fnl f: unable qckn nr fin)	1	**2**	$5/1^{3}$	72	21
3094^{7}	**Alpen Wolf (IRE)** (WRMuir) **2-8-12v**[1] DaneO'Neill(3) (rdn over 3f out: hdwy over 1f out: one pce wl ins fnl f)	1¾	**3**	8/1	71	20
2942^{8}	**Tamerin Bay (70)** (RBoss) **2-9-0b**[1] GDuffield(1) (led over 3f)	1¾	**4**	12/1	68	17
3055*	**Means Business (IRE) (69)** (BJMeehan) **2-8-12b** MTebbutt(6) (swtg: a.p: rdn over 2f out: wknd over 1f out)	1¼	**5**	$9/2^{2}$	62	11
	Thumbellina (SDow) **2-8-7** MRoberts(5) (neat: a bhd)	5	**6**	20/1	41	—

(SP 118.4%) **6 Rn**

60.8 secs (3.20) CSF £4.57 TOTE £1.50: £1.20 £2.50 (£3.20) OWNER Mrs D. F. Cock (MARLBOROUGH) BRED Patrick Eddery Ltd
2684* Huntswood, the paddock pick of a very moderate bunch, poked his head in front early in the final quarter-mile, but with the second soon challenging it looked as if he had a real fight on his hands. However his jockey had the situation in hand in the closing stages and in the end the combination won with a little bit to spare. (4/6)
Madame Claude (IRE) was facing easier company here and, throwing down her challenge from below the distance, looked a serious threat to the hot favourite. Battling for honours inside the final furlong, the winner found a little bit extra in the closing stages. (5/1)
1954 Alpen Wolf (IRE), fitted with a visor for the first time, began to pick up ground below the distance and looked a possible threat to the front two, only failing to find another gear in the last fifty yards. (8/1: 9/2-9/1)
1797* Tamerin Bay fitted with blinkers for the first time after some poor efforts, took the field along, but collared below the distance was soon a spent force. (12/1: 6/1-14/1)
3055* Means Business (IRE), awash with sweat beforehand, was close up until tiring before the final furlong. (9/2: tchd 7/1)
Thumbellina, a plain, rather spotty filly, did not look fully fit and showed nothing. (20/1)

3289 PAT MARSH SHOW (S) STKS (2-Y.O F) (Class G)

2-30 (2-30) **6f** £1,984.50 (£547.00: £259.50) Stalls: Low GOING minus 0.13 sec per fur (G)

Form	Horse	Dist	Pos	SP	RR	SF
2923^{8}	**Shannon (IRE) (60)** (CADwyer) **2-8-10** KFallon(1) (nt clr run over 2f out: swtchd rt & hdwy over 1f out: led 1f out: all out)	—	**1**	6/1	64	15

				SP	RR	SF
3106[7]	**Russian About (IRE)** (MRChannon) **2-8-7**(3) PPMurphy(4) (lw: a.p: led 2f out to 1f out: hrd rdn: r.o wl)	hd	**2**	5/2[2]	64	15
2786[7]	**Patricia Olive (IRE) (59)** (MHTompkins) **2-8-7**(3) MHenry(5) (lw: hld up: rdn over 2f out: r.o one pce)	2	**3**	9/2[3]	58	9
2923[2]	**Little Tumbler (IRE)** (SWoodman) **2-8-10** PaulEddery(6) (lw: a.p: rdn over 2f out: ev ch 1f out: one pce)	nk	**4**	5/4[1]	58	9
3090[8]	**First Idea** (SDow) **2-8-10** MRoberts(7) (hdwy 3f out: wknd over 1f out)	4	**5**	25/1	47	—
2728[20]	**Secret Tango** (APJones) **2-8-10** GCarter(3) (lw: led 4f: wkng whn hmpd on ins over 1f out)	5	**6**	25/1	34	—
				(SP 113.2%)	**6 Rn**	

1m 15.1 (4.90) CSF £19.72 TOTE £5.50: £1.90 £1.60 (£9.70) OWNER Mr Elias Haloute (NEWMARKET) BRED James Waldron
No bid

2579 Shannon (IRE), a lightly-made filly, was given an inspired ride by Fallon. Switched right to begin her run below the distance, she struck the front entering the final furlong, and although flashing her tail when hit just held on in a desperate finish. (6/1)
3106 Russian About (IRE) appreciated the drop in class and went very close. Sent on a quarter of a mile from home, she looked sure to finish second best when collared entering the final furlong, but she found extra in the closing stages and almost got back up. (5/2)
2587 Patricia Olive (IRE) struggled on in the closing stages but never threatened the front two. (9/2)
2923 Little Tumbler (IRE), who has shown up well in two previous sellers, had every chance entering the final furlong before tapped for toe. (5/4: 11/10-7/4)

3290 ROSS & CO. SOLICITORS H'CAP (0-75) (3-Y.O+) (Class D)
3-00 (3-00) **6f** £3,980.00 (£1,190.00: £570.00: £260.00) Stalls: Low GOING minus 0.13 sec per fur (G)

				SP	RR	SF
2745[2]	**Stand Tall (61)** (LadyHerries) **5-9-0** MRoberts(1) (b.hind: mde all: hrd rdn & edgd rt ins fnl f: r.o wl)	—	**1**	2/1[1]	72	54
3087[2]	**Present Generation (75)** (RGuest) **4-10-0** KFallon(7) (lw: hld up: chsd wnr wl over 1f out: hrd rdn & ev ch ins fnl f: unable qckn)	1	**2**	4/1[2]	83	65
2891*	**Aquatic Queen (58)** (CADwyer) **3-8-4**(3) TEDurcan(8) (lw: a.p: hrd rdn over 1f out: one pce)	2½	**3**	6/1	60	38
2958[3]	**Corniche Quest (IRE) (63)** (MRChannon) **4-8-9**(7) AEddery(2) (a.p: rdn wl over 1f out: sn wknd)	1¼	**4**	6/1	61	43
2369[12]	**Scathebury (55)** (KRBurke) **4-8-8** DHolland(6) (lw: nvr nr to chal)	1¾	**5**	12/1	49	31
3082[11]	**Rockcracker (IRE) (53)** (GGMargarson) **5-8-6b** GBardwell(4) (chsd ldrs: rdn over 3f out: wknd wl over 1f out)	s.h	**6**	9/1	47	29
3016[4]	**Robellion (53)** (DWPArbuthnot) **6-8-6v** SWhitworth(3) (b.hind: hld up: rdn over 2f out: sn wknd)	s.h	**7**	5/1[3]	46	28
2721[7]	**Waders Dream (IRE) (48)** (PatMitchell) **8-7-10v**(5)ow5 AmandaSanders(5) (lw: hld up: rdn 2f out: sn wknd)	s.h	**8**	25/1	41	18
				(SP 120.1%)	**8 Rn**	

1m 12.5 (2.30) CSF £9.76 CT £38.52 TOTE £2.60: £1.10 £1.60 £1.70 (£3.40) OWNER Mr Chris Hardy (LITTLEHAMPTON) BRED Mrs E. Longton
LONG HANDICAP Waders Dream (IRE) 7-6
WEIGHT FOR AGE 3yo-4lb

2745 Stand Tall adopted different tactics on this occasion. Making every post a winning one, he was seriously threatened by the second in the final furlong, but kept up the gallop to dispose of that rival. (2/1: op 3/1)
3087 Present Generation did little wrong and, moving into second place early in the final quarter-mile, looked likely to prevail inside the final furlong. However, the winner found a bit extra and he was tapped for toe. He has now finished second in six of his ten races to date. (4/1)
2891* Aquatic Queen, 8lb higher than when winning a maiden handicap at Ripon last time out, raced in the front rank but was left for dead by the front two from below the distance. (6/1)
2958 Corniche Quest (IRE) was close up until calling it a day over a furlong out. Only one of her five victories to date has come in a handicap. (6/1: 4/1-13/2)
1993 Scathebury found this trip on the sharp side and never threatened to get into it. A return to seven furlongs or a mile is needed. (12/1: 8/1-14/1)
1666* Rockcracker (IRE) continues to disappoint and needs to drop further in the handicap. (9/1)

3291 CHERITON MAIDEN H'CAP (0-70) (3-Y.O+) (Class E)
3-30 (3-30) **1m 4f** £3,261.30 (£974.40: £466.20: £212.10) Stalls: High GOING minus 0.31 sec per fur (GF)

				SP	RR	SF
2916[3]	**Veronica Franco (45)** (PRHedger) **4-8-7** DaneO'Neill(2) (hdwy over 7f out: chsd ldr 3f out: led 2f out: rdn out)	—	**1**	6/1	55	36
2592[2]	**Moon Colony (66)** (LadyHerries) **4-10-0** PaulEddery(4) (led 10f: unable qckn)	3	**2**	5/2[3]	72	53
3091[15]	**Victor Blum (USA) (34)** (CAHorgan) **4-7-7b**[1](3) RFfrench(7) (lw: chsd ldr over 3f: chsd ldr over 7f out tl over 6f out: lost pl over 3f out: one pce)	2	**3**	7/1	37	18
2928[3]	**Peppers (IRE) (65)** (KRBurke) **4-9-13** KFallon(3) (lw: s.s: rdn 3f out: hdwy over 2f out: one pce)	1	**4**	7/4[1]	67	48
	Drift (66) (SirMarkPrescott) **3-9-3** GDuffield(6) (chsd ldrs over 8f out tl over 7f out: chsd ldr over 6f out to 3f out: one pce)	1¼	**5**	2/1[2]	66	36
3101[6]	**Impetuous Lady (USA) (34)** (WJMusson) **4-7-10** JQuinn(5) (nvr nr to chal)	s.h	**6**	33/1	34	15
2667[9]	**Sylvan Jubilacion (54)** (PMitchell) **3-8-5** GCarter(1) (bhd fnl 7f)	28	**7**	33/1	17	—
				(SP 130.9%)	**7 Rn**	

2m 35.8 (4.60) CSF £22.83 TOTE £7.10: £2.70 £1.70 (£15.80) OWNER Mr J. J. Whelan (CHICHESTER) BRED Islanmore Stud
LONG HANDICAP Victor Blum (USA) 7-7 Impetuous Lady (USA) 7-6
WEIGHT FOR AGE 3yo-11lb

2916 Veronica Franco made a winning debut for her new connections, leading a quarter of a mile out and being rousted along to break her duck at the fifteenth attempt in this poor contest. (6/1: op 4/1)
2592 Moon Colony once again attempted to make all, but when the winner got to him two furlongs from home, he was found wanting. (5/2)
2916 Victor Blum (USA) ran his best race to date in this poor event. Losing his pitch over a quarter of a mile from home, he was then made to look very pedestrian. (7/1)
2928 Peppers (IRE) began a forward move turning for home, but was then made to look very one-paced. She lacks acceleration and is proving extremely difficult to win with. (7/4)
Drift, off the track for over a year and taking a big step up in distance, certainly made Duffield work extremely hard, but raced in second place for much of the contest. Collared for that position three furlongs from home, his lack of acceleration was there for all to see. (2/1: 2/1-3/1)

3292 WARREN H'CAP (0-65) (3-Y.O+ F & M) (Class F)
4-00 (4-01) **6f 189y** £2,923.80 (£811.80: £389.40) Stalls: High GOING minus 0.31 sec per fur (GF)

				SP	RR	SF
2665[7]	**Primelta (43)** (RAkehurst) **4-8-6** SSanders(4) (hdwy on ins over 1f out: swtchd lft & hrd rdn: led nr fin)	—	**1**	9/1	54	14
2665[4]	**Tachycardia (36)** (RJO'Sullivan) **5-7-10**(3) RFfrench(3) (led: rdn over 1f out: hdd nr fin)	¾	**2**	6/1	45	5
3088[3]	**Daintree (IRE) (50)** (HJCollingridge) **3-8-7** NAdams(5) (chsd ldr over 5f out tl ins fnl f: one pce)	2	**3**	5/1[2]	55	9

2310^{8} **Rumbustious (50)** (RHannon) **3-8-7** DaneO'Neill(2) (rdn over 2f out: hdwy over 1f out: r.o)....hd	**4**	11/2^{3}	54	8
2723* **Shashi (IRE) (55)** (PatMitchell) **5-9-4** PBloomfield(8) (b.off hind: rdn & no hdwy fnl 2f)....1¼	**5**	8/1	56	16
2788^{15} **Indian Relative (65)** (RGuest) **4-9-11**$^{(3)}$ MartinDwyer(6) (swtg: hld up: rdn over 2f out: one pce)....½	**6**	3/1^{1}	65	25
2957^{3} **Chain Reaction (IRE) (54)** (MAJarvis) **3-8-11** GCarter(9) (b: prom over 5f)....4	**7**	6/1	45	—
2395^{14} **Barbrallen (33)** (MrsLCJewell) **5-7-10** JQuinn(7) (s.s: a bhd)....½	**8**	50/1	23	—
Times of Times (IRE) (65) (GLMoore) **4-10-0** CandyMorris(1) (a bhd)....7	**9**	16/1	38	—

(SP 114.6%) **9 Rn**

1m 25.6 (4.20) CSF £55.91 CT £274.60 TOTE £10.80: £2.70 £2.20 £1.80 (£15.20) Trio £52.20 OWNER Mrs A. Valentine (EPSOM) BRED P. Valentine

LONG HANDICAP Barbrallen 7-0

WEIGHT FOR AGE 3yo-6lb

Primelta left her previous form well behind. Switched off the rail below the distance, she gradually wore the leader down to get on top near the finish. (9/1)

2665 Tachycardia, better known as a sprinter, coped with this longer trip. Indeed she won over a mile at Wolverhampton back in 1994. Adopting her usual front running role, she looked likely to prevail below the distance, but was eventually worn down near the finish. (6/1)

3088 Daintree (IRE), soon in second place, failed to master the leader and was collared for the runner-up berth inside the final furlong. (5/1)

1780* Rumbustious, who has been dropped 10lb in her last two outings, stayed on in the last furlong and a half and only just failed to take third prize. (11/2)

2723* Shashi (IRE) was made to look very one-paced in the straight. (8/1: 6/1-9/1)

2308 Indian Relative never looked like quickening up in the short home straight. (3/1)

3293 KENT MESSENGER GROUP NEWSPAPER MAIDEN H'CAP (0-70) (3-Y.O+) (Class E)

4-30 (4-32) **1m 1f 149y** £3,494.25 (£1,044.00: £499.50: £227.25) Stalls: High GOING minus 0.31 sec per fur (GF)

		SP	RR	SF
2577^{3} **Country Thatch (38)** (CAHorgan) **4-7-7**$^{(3)}$ RFfrench(6) (a.p: led over 1f out: rdn out)....—	**1**	4/1^{3}	46	8
1477^{11} **Bear Hug (70)** (LadyHerries) **4-10-0** PaulEddery(3) (chsd ldrs 8f out: led over 2f out tl over 1f out: r.o)....nk	**2**	11/4^{2}	78	40
2941^{3} **Tezaab (50)** (BHanbury) **3-7-10**$^{(3)}$ MartinDwyer(8) (a.p: rdn over 2f out: unable qckn)....3	**3**	8/1	53	6
2929^{2} **Samara Song (53)** (IPWilliams) **4-8-11** KFallon(4) (lw: rdn & hdwy over 2f out: one pce)....¾	**4**	15/8^{1}	54	16
2772^{8} **Literary (70)** (JHMGosden) **3-9-5** GHind(7) (nvr nr to chal)....2½	**5**	6/1	67	20
3054^{2} **Executive Officer (38)** (RMFlower) **4-7-10b** JQuinn(5) (bhd fnl 2f)....4	**6**	16/1	29	—
3054^{10} **Dragon's Back (IRE) (58)** (DCO'Brien) **4-9-2** GBardwell(2) (lw: led 7f)....7	**7**	20/1	37	—
3196^{6} **Rosalee Royale (38)** (JohnBerry) **5-7-10** JLowe(1) (lw: s.i.s: a bhd)....2	**8**	40/1	14	—

(SP 119.9%) **8 Rn**

2m 3.5 (5.80) CSF £14.86 CT £78.14 TOTE £4.80: £1.20 £1.40 £2.00 (£12.40) OWNER Mrs B. Sumner (PULBOROUGH) BRED Devonia Stud

LONG HANDICAP Executive Officer 6-11 Rosalee Royale 7-4

WEIGHT FOR AGE 3yo-9lb

STEWARDS' ENQUIRY Hind susp. 12-14/8/97 (failure to obtain best possible placing).

2577 Country Thatch confirmed the promise shown here last month, gaining a narrow advantage below the distance and needing to be ridden along to keep the persistent runner-up at bay. (4/1)

1106 Bear Hug ran better here and made his bid for glory over two furlongs from home. Collared below the distance, he refused to lie down and kept on well to the line. (11/4)

2941 Tezaab was never far away, but was decidedly tapped for toe in the straight. (8/1: op 3/1)

2929 Samara Song, reverting to a longer trip, picked up ground turning for home, but was then made to look extremely pedestrian. He remains a maiden after nineteen attempts. (15/8)

2415 Literary, taken to post early, was given a very quiet ride at the back of the field but crept closer in the straight to finish fifth. Hind was later suspended for three days for not obtaining the best possible placing. However not too much should be read into this as the filly is very moderate and perhaps Hind did not see any point in persevering with her in the latter stages. (6/1: op 3/1)

T/Plpt: £145.10 (126.75 Tckts). T/Qdpt: £42.40 (33.17 Tckts) AK

3078-BRIGHTON (L-H) (Good to firm, becoming Good)
Wednesday August 6th

Races 3 & 4 - poor visibility

WEATHER: raining and misty

3294 RINGMER (S) STKS (2-Y.O) (Class G)

2-15 (2-16) **6f 209y** £1,984.50 (£547.00: £259.50) Stalls: High GOING minus 0.17 sec per fur (GF)

		SP	RR	SF
3045^{8} **Slew Magic (IRE)** (WGMTurner) **2-8-3**$^{(3)}$ DSweeney(2) (mde all: rdn ins fnl f: r.o)....—	**1**	11/2^{3}	61	—
3090^{3} **Shanthi (60)** (PJMakin) **2-8-6** SSanders(1) (a.p: chsd wnr 2f out: rdn & edgd rt ins fnl f: unable qckn)....¾	**2**	7/4^{2}	59	—
2699^{13} **Shalabella (IRE)** (MRChannon) **2-8-8**^{ow2} KFallon(5) (chsd wnr to 2f out: sn rdn: n.m.r ins fnl f: one pce)....1¼	**3**	13/2	58	—
3097^{2} **Jaybee Silver** (MHTompkins) **2-8-6** DBiggs(4) (hld up: rdn over 2f out: wknd over 1f out)....11	**4**	13/8^{1}	31	—
3078^{7} **Dancing Al** (JSMoore) **2-8-11** SWhitworth(3) (hld up: rdn over 2f out: sn btn)....5	**5**	14/1	25	—

(SP 109.8%) **5 Rn**

1m 26.5 (6.50) CSF £14.13 TOTE £8.00: £2.40 £1.40 (£5.70) OWNER Mr Basheer Kielany (SHERBORNE) BRED Hans Hintermuller

No bid

3045 Slew Magic (IRE) made all the running and saw it out gamely. (11/2: 3/1-6/1)

3090 Shanthi moved up threateningly below the distance, but didn't look too keen under pressure. (7/4)

Shalabella (IRE) was short of room inside the final furlong, but for which she would have been fighting out second place. (13/2: 3/1-7/1)

Dancing Al (14/1: 8/1-16/1)

3295 MARINA MAIDEN AUCTION STKS (2-Y.O) (Class E)

2-45 (2-46) **6f 209y** £2,992.25 (£893.00: £426.50: £193.25) Stalls: High GOING minus 0.17 sec per fur (GF)

		SP	RR	SF
3113^{2} **Ron's Pet (77)** (RHannon) **2-8-12** DBiggs(2) (lw: led over 5f out: hdd over 1f out: rallied ins fnl f: led nr fin)....—	**1**	7/4^{1}	79	23
2728^{8} **Blue Zola (IRE)** (MBell) **2-8-5** SSanders(1) (chsd ldrs: led over 1f out: rdn ins fnl f: hdd nr fin)....hd	**2**	3/1^{2}	72	16
Jonas Nightengale (CACyzer) **2-8-1**$^{(3)}$ RFfrench(6) (rr: rdn 5f out: kpt on one pce fnl 2f)....8	**3**	25/1	52	—
2689^{4} **Hoh Justice (77)** (IABalding) **2-8-10** SWhitworth(7) (lw: led over 1f: w ldr tl over 2f out: wknd over 1f out)....nk	**4**	7/2^{3}	58	2

2959^{U}	**Life Sentence** (JGSmyth-Osbourne) **2-8-7** DHarrison(8) (prom: ev ch over 2f out: wknd over 1f out)	5	**5**	20/1	43	—
2943^{13}	**Constant Attention** (PFICole) **2-8-7** CRutter(5) (sn rdn along: in tch tl wknd over 2f out)	1¼	**6**	6/1	40	—
2243^{11}	**Lauren's Lad** (GLewis) **2-8-6** PaulEddery(3) (bhd fr ½-wy)	19	**7**	16/1	—	—
3103^{13}	**Aegean Breeze** (MissGayKelleway) **2-8-9** KFallon(4) (a bhd)	2½	**8**	20/1	—	—

(SP 117.1%) **8 Rn**

1m 24.7 (4.70) CSF £6.47 TOTE £2.30: £1.00 £3.10 £3.80 (£3.90) OWNER Mr George Teo (MARLBOROUGH) BRED Daniel James

3113 Ron's Pet saw this seven-furlong trip out well and battled on gamely to regain the lead inside the last, having been headed below the distance. (7/4)

Blue Zola (IRE) stepped up on her debut here. She looked like winning when taking it up below the distance, but just got run out of it close home. She should be able to find a similar event (3/1)

Jonas Nightengale ran here as though a longer trip is required. (25/1)

2689 Hoh Justice dropped away disappointingly in the last two furlongs. (7/2: 5/2-4/1)

2519 Constant Attention (6/1: 4/1-7/1)

3296 TOTE CREDIT SPRINT H'CAP (0-80) (3-Y.O+) (Class D)

3-15 (3-16) **5f 213y** £3,454.50 (£1,029.00: £490.00: £220.50) Stalls: High GOING minus 0.17 sec per fur (GF)

				SP	RR	SF
2950^{5}	**Golden Pound (USA) (75)** (MissGayKelleway) **5-9-12b** KFallon(5) (swtg: hld up: gd hdwy to ld 2f out: rdn ins fnl f: r.o wl)	—	**1**	9/4^{1}	84	42
3082^{8}	**Ivory's Grab Hire (64)** (KTIvory) **4-8-12b**$^{(3)}$ MartinDwyer(3) (rr: hdwy 2f out: sn rdn: styd on to go 2nd ins fnl f)	1¾	**2**	10/1	68	26
2933^{2}	**Sharp Pearl (77)** (PRWebber) **4-10-0b** RHughes(6) (lw: hld up: hdwy 2f out: rdn over 1f out: kpt on one pce ins fnl f)	nk	**3**	6/1	81	39
2954*	**Kings Harmony (IRE) (71)** (PJMakin) **4-9-8** SSanders(4) (lw: chsd ldrs: ev ch 2f out: sn rdn: one pce)	¾	**4**	4/1^{3}	73	31
3056^{2}	**Apollo Red (72)** (GLMoore) **8-9-9** CandyMorris(7) (swtg: led 5f out: hdd 2f out: sn wknd)	5	**5**	11/4^{2}	60	18
2705^{8}	**Song Mist (IRE) (72)** (PFICole) **3-8-12b**$^{1(7)}$ DavidO'Neill(8) (prom tl wknd 2f out)	nk	**6**	10/1	59	13
3083*	**Chakra (52)** (SDow) **3-7-10**$^{(3)}$ ^{7x} RFfrench(1) (led 1f: styd prom: ev ch 2f out: sn rdn & wknd)	2½	**7**	12/1	33	—

(SP 117.6%) **7 Rn**

1m 10.7 (3.50) CSF £24.15 CT £111.11 TOTE £2.70: £1.60 £3.10 (£12.40) Trio £17.90 OWNER Mr A. P. Griffin (WHITCOMBE) BRED Builder's Mart Inc

WEIGHT FOR AGE 3yo-4lb

2950 Golden Pound (USA) was well supported beforehand and, after striking the front two furlongs out, ran on strongly for an emphatic success to give Kieren Fallon his first winner at the course. (9/4)

2922 Ivory's Grab Hire ran a sound race, keeping on for second inside the last, without looking like reaching the winner. (10/1)

2933 Sharp Pearl ran well under his big weight, but found the ten stone beating him in the closing stages. (6/1: 3/1-13/2)

2954* Kings Harmony (IRE) had every chance but was unable to quicken up in the last furlong or so. (4/1)

3056 Apollo Red was the disappointment of the race, but he was sweating quite profusely in the preliminaries and didn't look particularly at ease beforehand. This run is probably best forgotten. (11/4)

2705 Song Mist (IRE) (10/1: op 6/1)

3083* Chakra (12/1: op 6/1)

3297 TOTE BOOKMAKERS H'CAP (0-60) (3-Y.O+) (Class F)

3-45 (3-45) **1m 1f 209y** £2,692.80 (£745.80: £356.40) Stalls: Low GOING minus 0.17 sec per fur (GF)

				SP	RR	SF
3229^{3}	**Colour Counsellor (35)** (RMFlower) **4-8-7b** DaneO'Neill(3) (chsd ldr: led 6f out: clr over 1f out: eased ins fnl f)	—	**1**	9/2^{3}	51+	14
2701^{3}	**Runic Symbol (35)** (MBlanshard) **6-8-7** CRutter(10) (hld up: hdwy 4f out: swtchd lft over 2f out: styd on to go 2nd ins fnl f)	6	**2**	5/1	41	4
3091^{4}	**Zurs (IRE) (53)** (MissGayKelleway) **4-9-11** KFallon(8) (lw: chsd ldrs: rdn 2f out: one pce)	½	**3**	13/8^{1}	59	22
2954^{7}	**Chopin (IRE) (46)** (RFJohnsonHoughton) **3-8-9b** SSanders(11) (rr: rdn 4f out: styd on ins fnl f)	¾	**4**	12/1	50	4
3227^{10}	**Master Millfield (IRE) (52)** (CJHill) **5-9-10** RHughes(2) (lw: led 4f: wknd appr fnl f)	3	**5**	11/1	52	15
3074^{10}	**Comtec's Legend (24)** (JPearce) **7-7-10** GBardwell(4) (bit bkwd: prom: rdn 4f out: wknd over 1f out)	5	**6**	14/1	16	—
2918^{10}	**Aegean Sound (60)** (KTIvory) **3-9-6**$^{(3)}$ MartinDwyer(5) (swtg: bhd fnl 4f)	7	**7**	25/1	40	—
2550^{8}	**Double Rush (IRE) (43)** (TGMills) **5-9-1** JQuinn(7) (b.hind: hld up: hdwy 4f out: rdn over 2f out: sn btn)	5	**8**	7/2^{2}	15	—

(SP 121.7%) **8 Rn**

2m 5.9 (7.60) CSF £26.54 CT £47.85 TOTE £5.30: £1.60 £1.30 £1.40 (£14.40) Trio £5.70 OWNER Mrs G. M. Temmerman (JEVINGTON) BRED M. A. Kirby

LONG HANDICAP Comtec's Legend 7-9

WEIGHT FOR AGE 3yo-9lb

3229 Colour Counsellor ran out a very easy winner here. Leading shortly after halfway, the race was in safe-keeping throughout the final two furlongs. (9/2)

2701 Runic Symbol plugged on for second in the final furlong but was no threat to the winner. (5/1)

3091 Zurs (IRE) ran well under top weight here, but found the impost weighing him down in the final two furlongs. (13/8)

1383 Chopin (IRE) made headway from the rear in the final furlong or so and was never nearer than at the finish. (12/1)

2218 Double Rush (IRE) (7/2: 5/2-4/1)

3298 CLIFTONVILLE MEDIAN AUCTION MAIDEN STKS (3 & 4-Y.O) (Class F)

4-15 (4-17) **1m 3f 196y** £2,277.00 (£627.00: £297.00) Stalls: Low GOING minus 0.17 sec per fur (GF)

				SP	RR	SF
2787^{4}	**Little Miss Rocker (60)** (IABalding) **3-8-5**$^{(3)}$ MartinDwyer(1) (trckd ldng pair: rdn over 3f out: led over 2f out: edgd rt appr fnl f: r.o wl)	—	**1**	3/1^{2}	67	14
2908^{4}	**Pointe Fine (FR) (56)** (JWHills) **3-8-8** KFallon(4) (chsd ldr: hrd rdn 3f out: kpt on one pce fnl 2f)	1¾	**2**	4/1^{3}	65	12
3108^{3}	**High On Life (65)** (ACStewart) **3-8-13** SWhitworth(3) (led: pushed along ½-wy: rdn over 3f out: hdd over 2f out: btn whn n.m.r appr fnl f)	nk	**3**	4/7^{1}	69	16
2782^{2}	***Bathe In Light (USA) (59)*** (LordHuntingdon) **3-8-8** DHarrison(2) (Withdrawn not under Starter's orders)		**W**		—	—

(SP 108.6%) **3 Rn**

2m 37.4 (9.80) CSF £10.19 TOTE £3.60: (£3.30) OWNER Ellway Racing (KINGSCLERE) BRED Mrs A. Plummer

2787 Little Miss Rocker appeared to be travelling best turning for home and, despite edging right nearing the final furlong, won this poor race a shade cosily. (3/1: op 2/1)

2908 Pointe Fine (FR) was under severe pressure for the final two furlongs, but the runner-up prize was the best she could do. (4/1)
3108 High On Life was disappointing, being niggled along some way out and having little resistance in the final two furlongs. (4/7: 1/2-4/5)

3299 EDBURTON MAIDEN H'CAP (0-60) (3-Y.O+) (Class F)
4-45 (4-46) **6f 209y** £2,808.30 (£778.80: £372.90) Stalls: High GOING minus 0.17 sec per fur (GF)

Form	Horse / Details	Dist	Pos	SP	RR	SF
2554^{6}	**Homestead (45)** (RHannon) **3-8-12** DaneO'Neill(4) (a.p: led over 2f out: clr appr fnl f: r.o wl)	—	**1**	100/30^{1}	57	33
3082^{5}	**Ed's Folly (IRE) (55)** (SDow) **4-9-11**$^{(3)}$ RFfrench(12) (a.p: rdn over 2f out: one pce)	3½	**2**	4/1^{2}	59	41
1944^{3}	**Muara Bay (41)** (GLewis) **3-8-1**$^{(7)}$ JDennis(10) (s.v.s: bhd tl hdwy fnl 2f: nrst fin)	1¼	**3**	7/1	42	18
2853^{5}	**Baubigny (USA) (60)** (MRChannon) **3-9-13** RHughes(6) (led: hdd over 2f out: wknd ins fnl f)	3	**4**	10/1	54	30
2945^{3}	**Las Vistas (56)** (HJCollingridge) **3-9-9** NAdams(11) (chsd ldrs: rdn over 2f out: one pce)	½	**5**	7/1	49	25
3083^{9}	**Allstars Dancer (31)** (TJNaughton) **4-7-11**$^{(7)}$ RachaelMoody(3) (nvr nrr)	1½	**6**	12/1	21	3
2353^{3}	**Millpet (46)** (RGuest) **3-8-13** PBloomfield(15) (towards rr: rdn 3f out: kpt on one pce fnl 2f)	1¼	**7**	10/1	33	9
3082^{10}	**Seamus (36)** (CJHill) **3-8-3** CRutter(17) (swtg: nvr bttr than mid div)	6	**8**	25/1	9	—
3030^{6}	**Telloff (55)** (MAJarvis) **3-9-8** SSanders(7) (in tch: wknd 2f out)	1¾	**9**	13/2	24	—
2945^{6}	**Tabasco Jazz (60)** (BJMeehan) **3-9-6**$^{(7)}$ GHannon(9) (prom tl wknd over 2f out)	1¾	**10**	11/2^{3}	25	1
1005^{15}	**Daratown (30)** (CJHill) **4-8-0**$^{(3)}$ MBaird(8) (prom tl wknd over 2f out)	1	**11**	25/1	—	—
3081^{6}	**Eternally Grateful (26)** (KTIvory) **4-7-10b**$^{1(3)ow1}$ MartinDwyer(14) (a bhd)	1¼	**12**	25/1	—	—
2946^{3}	**Barbury Ballad (IRE) (37)** (MJHeaton-Ellis) **3-7-13**$^{(5)}$ ADaly(13) (in tch: rdn 3f out: wknd 2f out)	1¼	**13**	16/1	—	—
				(SP 140.1%)	**13 Rn**	

1m 23.9 (3.90) CSF £17.48 CT £90.42 TOTE £5.10: £2.20 £1.60 £3.50 (£8.30) Trio £73.50 OWNER Mr Geoffrey Greenwood (MARLBOROUGH) BRED Mrs J. A. Rawding and Green Meadow Stud
WEIGHT FOR AGE 3yo-6lb
Homestead was never far away and, after leading early in the straight, soon had the race in safe-keeping. (100/30)
3082 Ed's Folly (IRE) had a prominent position throughout, but only had the one speed to give in the final two furlongs. (4/1)
1944 Muara Bay missed the break and was a long way in arrears for much of the journey. He did stay on to be third, without ever posing a threat to the winner. (7/1: 5/1-8/1)
431 Baubigny (USA) attempted to make all and kept on well enough after being headed early in the straight. (10/1)
2945 Las Vistas had every chance but just had one pace for pressure in the final two furlongs. (7/1: op 4/1)
2353 Millpet (10/1: op 6/1)
2945 Tabasco Jazz (11/2: 4/1-6/1)

T/Plpt: £55.70 (322.33 Tckts). T/Qdpt: £21.50 (47.93 Tckts) SM

2571-EPSOM (L-H) - Wednesday August 6th (Evening)
3300-3305 Abandoned-Waterlogged

3258-NEWCASTLE (L-H) (Good to firm)
Wednesday August 6th
Races 3 & 6 - hand-timed
WEATHER: sunny and warm WIND: slight behind

3306 NEWCASTLE SHOW MEDIAN AUCTION MAIDEN STKS (2-Y.O) (Class F)
2-30 (2-31) **6f** £2,620.50 (£738.00: £361.50) Stalls: Low GOING minus 0.36 sec per fur (F)

Form	Horse / Details	Dist	Pos	SP	RR	SF
2842^{8}	**Eastern Purple (IRE)** (RAFahey) **2-9-0** ACulhane(11) (cl up: led stands' side after 2f: styd on to ld overall wl ins fnl f & hung lft)	—	**1**	2/1^{1}	71+	23
2953^{5}	**Appyabo (74)** (MRChannon) **2-8-11**$^{(3)}$ PPMurphy(10) (chsd ldrs stands' side: kpt on wl fnl f)	½	**2**	11/2^{3}	70	22
3060^{5}	**Cool Prospect** (ABMulholland) **2-9-0** DWright(4) (led far side tl hdd wl ins fnl f)	½	**3**	33/1	68	20
2713^{6}	**Miss Vivien** (MissLAPerratt) **2-8-6**$^{(3)}$ TEDurcan(8) (lw: racd far side: in tch: hdwy 2f out: styd on one pce fnl f)	2	**4**	14/1	58	10
3033^{4}	**Chaska** (MJohnston) **2-8-9** JWeaver(2) (racd far side: outpcd ½-wy: styd on fnl f)	½	**5**	16/1	57	9
1492^{6}	**Prince Ashleigh** (PCHaslam) **2-9-0** MFenton(17) (bhd: hdwy stands' side 2f out: nvr nr to chal)	hd	**6**	14/1	61	13
2936^{4}	**Durham Flyer (74)** (TDEasterby) **2-9-0b**^{1} LCharnock(7) (chsd ldrs far side: outpcd over 2f out: kpt on fnl f)	1½	**7**	9/1	57	9
1760^{5}	**Top Floor (IRE)** (NTinkler) **2-9-0** KimTinkler(5) (b.off hind: racd far side: in tch: rdn over 2f out: no imp)	½	**8**	14/1	56	8
3042^{8}	**Whacker-Do (IRE) (64)** (RHollinshead) **2-9-0** FLynch(14) (chsd ldrs stands' side tl outpcd fnl 2f)	¾	**9**	33/1	54	6
2870^{9}	**Holy Wine (USA)** (DRLoder) **2-9-0** WRyan(6) (chsd ldrs far side over 4f)	nk	**10**	9/2^{2}	53	5
	Missed Domino (MrsASwinbank) **2-8-9** GDuffield(19) (lt-f: dwlt: racd stands' side: n.d)	2	**11**	50/1	43	—
2538^{6}	**Walworth Wizard** (MDods) **2-9-0** JCarroll(9) (bhd far side: sme hdwy 2f out: n.d)	hd	**12**	50/1	48	—
	Asbestaswecan (WJarvis) **2-9-0** KDarley(1) (cmpt: bit bkwd: racd far side: dwlt: sme hdwy fnl 2f: n.d)	nk	**13**	16/1	47	—
3060^{4}	**Kayo** (TJEtherington) **2-9-0** JTate(15) (chsd ldrs stands' side over 3f)	nk	**14**	14/1	46	—
	Jack Ruby (PLGilligan) **2-9-0** DeanMcKeown(18) (unf: b: racd stands' side: a bhd)	2½	**15**	100/1	39	—
	Repose (IRE) (GROldroyd) **2-8-9** KHodgson(12) (neat: unf: dwlt: racd stands' side: a bhd)	hd	**16**	50/1	34	—
2752^{3}	**Good On Yer** (SEKettlewell) **2-8-9** JFanning(3) (racd far side: lost tch fr ½-wy)	1	**17**	33/1	32	—
2324^{10}	**Miss Pugh** (CWFairhurst) **2-8-9** RLappin(16) (racd stands' side: sn bhd)	2½	**18**	50/1	25	—
2604^{7}	**Tamburello (IRE)** (JBerry) **2-8-6**$^{(3)}$ PFessey(13) (led stands' side 2f: hung bdly lft 2f out & wknd qckly)	¾	**19**	33/1	23	—
				(SP 135.9%)	**19 Rn**	

1m 14.76 (3.26) CSF £11.63 TOTE £3.70: £2.00 £2.10 £11.00 (£24.30) Trio £80.90 OWNER Mr T. C. Chiang (MALTON) BRED B. and R. Breeding
OFFICIAL EXPLANATION **Tamburello (IRE): hung badly left from halfway.**
Eastern Purple (IRE), a sturdy individual, knew more about it this time, but was still inclined to hang and there would seem to be more to come. (2/1)
2953 Appyabo was putting in some really good late work, suggesting that longer trips will see improvement. (11/2)
3060 Cool Prospect showed plenty of toe this time but did too much, too soon, but this nevertheless should have done him good. (33/1)
2713 Miss Vivien showed improvement here and is certainly coming to herself lookswise. (14/1)

3033 Chaska is still learning and by the looks of things, distances in excess of this will suit. (16/1)
1492 Prince Ashleigh, having his first run for ten weeks, showed promise, making steady late headway. (14/1)
Asbestaswecan, having an educational, showed something and should improve. (16/1)

3307 C D BRAMALL LDV NURSERY H'CAP (2-Y.O) (Class E)

3-00 (3-02) **7f** £2,986.25 (£905.00: £442.50: £211.25) Stalls: Low GOING minus 0.36 sec per fur (F)

				SP	RR	SF
2935[4]	**Miss Main Street (IRE) (58)** (JJQuinn) **2-8-2** GDuffield(13) (racd centre: hdwy over 2f out: styd on to ld wl ins fnl f)	—	1	10/1	61	29
2057[9]	**Rebalza (IRE) (64)** (JMPEustace) **2-8-8** JTate(2) (in tch: hdwy to ld ins fnl f: hdd & nt qckn towards fin)	¾	2	7/1[2]	65	33
3106[4]	**Sharp Cracker (IRE) (76)** (MJohnston) **2-9-6** JWeaver(11) (lw: racd centre: led tl hdd ins fnl f: kpt on)	nk	3	10/1	77	45
2923[3]	**Kite (55)** (MBell) **2-7-8**(5) RMullen(14) (chsd ldr centre: one pce fnl 2f)	3	4	10/1	49	17
2493[3]	**Dancing Em (52)** (TDEasterby) **2-7-10** DWright(4) (lw: cl up: rdn over 2f out: r.o one pce)	1½	5	20/1	42	10
2681[5]	**Narrogin (USA) (72)** (MRChannon) **2-8-13v**(3) PPMurphy(8) (chsd ldrs: drvn along over 2f out: one pce)	¾	6	12/1	61	29
2499[4]	**Linnetsong (65)** (GROldroyd) **2-8-9v** KHodgson(3) (hld up: effrt 3f out: no imp)	½	7	11/1	53	21
2905[8]	**Watchman (60)** (TPTate) **2-8-4** JFanning(10) (bhd: hdwy 2f out: nvr nr to chal)	1	8	20/1	45	13
2905[6]	**Captain McCloy (USA) (67)** (MrsJRRamsden) **2-8-11v[1]** DeanMcKeown(12) (lw: dwlt: hdwy & prom ½-wy: hrd rdn 2f out: sn wknd)	hd	9	11/2[1]	52	20
2752[2]	**On The Mat (64)** (JJO'Neill) **2-8-5**(3) PFessey(5) (chsd ldrs 5f: rdn & wknd)	3	10	14/1	42	10
2935*	**Semi Circle (59)** (TDEasterby) **2-8-3** LCharnock(15) (racd centre: prom over 4f)	9	11	7/1[2]	17	—
2477[7]	**Fundance (74)** (MDods) **2-9-4** JCarroll(1) (chsd ldrs 5f: wknd)	1	12	12/1	29	—
2786[12]	**Jackerin (IRE) (77)** (BSRothwell) **2-9-7** MFenton(7) (lw: plld hrd: effrt 3f out: sn wknd & eased)	7	13	16/1	16	—
2842[14]	**Starliner (IRE) (62)** (MBrittain) **2-8-6** KDarley(9) (cl up 4f: sn wknd & eased)	3½	14	12/1	—	—
2904[13]	**The Cannie Rover (64)** (MWEasterby) **2-8-5**(3) GParkin(6) (spd to ½-wy: wknd qckly & virtually p.u)	dist	15	15/2[3]	—	—
				(SP 132.9%)	**15 Rn**	

1m 26.89 (2.39) CSF £78.28 CT £690.39 TOTE £12.70: £4.00 £2.20 £2.30 (£36.00) Trio £303.10 OWNER The Main Street Partnership (MALTON) BRED Eamon and Mrs Mary Salmon
LONG HANDICAP Dancing Em 7-8
OFFICIAL EXPLANATION **The Cannie Rover: lost his action. The jockey reported that the colt felt lame and was subsequently sore on returning to the yard.**
2935 Miss Main Street (IRE) showed a tendency to hang here but, well suited by the stiff track, she settled it in good style late on. (10/1)
1692 Rebalza (IRE) put in by far his best effort here and would seem to be off a decent mark. (7/1)
3106 Sharp Cracker (IRE) is really coming to herself physically and put up a fair effort over this longer trip. Her luck will surely turn before long. (10/1)
2923 Kite is running consistently well just now but is short of a finishing kick. (10/1)
2493 Dancing Em looked particularly well and ran a fair race, but was short of toe when put under pressure. (20/1)
2681 Narrogin (USA) was struggling to stay on terms soon after halfway and looked very one-paced. (12/1)
2499 Watchman had shown little previously, but he seems to stay well and gave signs of hope here. (20/1)

3308 NORTH EAST AUTO TRADER APPRENTICE (S) STKS (3-Y.O+) (Class G)

3-30 (3-31) **1m 4f 93y** £2,102.50 (£590.00: £287.50) Stalls: Low GOING minus 0.36 sec per fur (F)

				SP	RR	SF
3104[5]	**Sherqy (IRE) (55)** (SEKettlewell) **5-9-9**(3) PFredericks(3) (hld up: hdwy on bit 3f out: led ins fnl f: rdn & jst hld on)	—	1	5/2[1]	65	47
2824[4]	**Essayeffsee (53)** (MrsMReveley) **8-9-1**(5) ANicholls(2) (hld up: hdwy over 2f out: nt clr run & swtchd 1f out: r.o towards fin)	s.h	2	5/2[1]	59	41
112[4]	**Kulepopsie (IRE)** (ABMulholland) **4-9-1** KSked(6) (cl up: led 1½f out tl ins fnl f: no ex)	3	3	50/1	50	32
3102[3]	**Cochiti (37)** (CWThornton) **3-8-1b**(3) PDoe(5) (led tl hdd 1½f out: one pce)	3½	4	33/1	46	17
2916[9]	**Shabanaz (49)** (WRMuir) **12-9-6** JWilkinson(7) (chsd ldrs: effrt 4f out: no imp after)	nk	5	7/2[3]	50	32
2661[2]	**Latvian (56)** (RAllan) **10-9-12b** RWinston(1) (hld up: hdwy 5f out: rdn & no rspnse over 2f out)	1¾	6	3/1[2]	54	36
	Petrico (PBeaumont) **5-9-3**(3) TSiddall(8) (chsd ldrs tl rdn & wknd over 4f out)	13	7	50/1	31	13
3068[5]	**Lady Magician** (CWFairhurst) **3-7-13**(5) JennyBenson(4) (in tch tl wknd fnl 4f)	5	8	16/1	20	—
				(SP 117.1%)	**8 Rn**	

2m 42.9 (5.40) CSF £8.38 TOTE £4.40: £1.70 £1.10 £8.70 (£7.00) OWNER Miss N. F. Thesiger (MIDDLEHAM) BRED Shadwell Estate Company Limited
WEIGHT FOR AGE 3yo-11lb
Sold K Bjorkling 7,000gns
3104 Sherqy (IRE), given a cracking ride, as he needs tender handling, did just enough. (5/2)
2824 Essayeffsee went really well for his young rider and got the trip well enough this time. (5/2)
112 Kulepopsie (IRE), having her first run on turf, put up by far her best performance. (50/1)
3102 Cochiti has certainly improved with the blinkers, but was done for speed in the last couple of furlongs. (33/1)
2916 Shabanaz was always finding this too competitive for his liking. (7/2)
2661 Latvian was in one of his non-going moods. (3/1)

3309 SANDY BAY HOLIDAY PARK H'CAP (0-70) (3-Y.O+) (Class E)

4-00 (4-00) **2m 19y** £2,843.25 (£861.00: £420.50: £200.25) Stalls: Low GOING minus 0.36 sec per fur (F)

				SP	RR	SF
2737[3]	**Batabanoo (45)** (MrsMReveley) **8-8-12** KDarley(12) (lw: hld up: nt clr run 2f out: swtchd & qcknd to ld ins fnl f: r.o wl)	—	1	9/1	57	36
*2910**	**Indigo Dawn (60)** (MJohnston) **3-8-12** JWeaver(10) (lw: cl up: led 7f out tl ins fnl f: nt qckn)	2	2	9/4[1]	70	34
3069[3]	**Dirab (61)** (TDBarron) **4-9-9**(5) KimberleyHart(11) (in tch: hdwy over 2f out: styd on u.p: nt pce to chal)	nk	3	10/1	71	50
2867[9]	**Amiarge (46)** (MBrittain) **7-8-13b** JCarroll(6) (a in tch: drvn along over 3f out: styd on wl fnl f: nrst fin)	1¾	4	16/1	54	33
1125[3]	**All On (54)** (JHetherton) **6-9-0**(7) TSiddall(13) (a chsng ldrs: one pce fnl 3f)	hd	5	14/1	62	41
2910[8]	**Cittern (56)** (MrsMReveley) **7-9-9** ACulhane(1) (swtg: hld up: nt clr run & snatched up over 2f out: hmpd over 1f out: r.o towards fin)	½	6	50/1	63	42
3057[S]	**Aurelian (61)** (MBell) **3-8-13** MFenton(8) (bhd: hdwy over 1f out: r.o towards fin)	nk	7	8/1	68	32
3069[7]	**Batoutoftheblue (45)** (WWHaigh) **4-8-12** FNorton(7) (bhd: hdwy whn n.m.r 2f out: styd on wl towards fin)	½	8	25/1	52	31
2825*	**Thunderheart (51)** (RAllan) **6-9-1**(3) DGriffiths(3) (lw: a.p: hdwy to chse ldr 3f out: wknd appr fnl f)	3	9	7/1[3]	55	34
2682[4]	**Trilby (56)** (GRichards) **4-9-6v**(3) TEDurcan(9) (in tch: hdwy 3f out: wknd fnl 2f)	1½	10	7/2[2]	58	37

2908[3]	**Swiftway (57)** (KWHogg) **3-8-9** DeanMcKeown(4) (led tl hdd 7f out: wknd 4f out)	5	**11**	12/1	54	18
2535[2]	**Charter (59)** (WStorey) **6-9-12v[1]** JFanning(14) (lw: chsd ldrs: chal 7f out: wknd fnl 3f)	5	**12**	14/1	51	30
2940[9]	**Highfield Pet (50)** (CWFairhurst) **4-9-3v[1]** LCharnock(2) (t.o fnl 7f)	30	**13**	33/1	12	—
				(SP 131.3%)	**13 Rn**	

3m 32.07 (6.57) CSF £29.18 CT £207.08 TOTE £9.20: £3.00 £1.60 £3.00 (£8.90) Trio £41.10 OWNER Mr P. D. Savill (SALTBURN) BRED Clover Stud

WEIGHT FOR AGE 3yo-15lb

OFFICIAL EXPLANATION **Cittern: the Stewards inquired into the running and riding of Cittern. The rider stated that his instructions were to have the gelding handy and finish as close as possible, but on entering the back straight, he felt it prudent not to push the gelding too hard as he had had leg problems and had started to lose position. Entering the straight, the gelding started to pick up from the rear, but suffered problems getting a run.**

2737 Batabanoo was incredible here, showing a blistering turn of foot in the closing stages, and looks in the form of his life. (9/1)

2910* Indigo Dawn looked to have done everything right but she had no answer to the winner's turn of foot. She remains in tremendous heart. (9/4)

3069 Dirab showed he is on his way back to form here. (10/1: 7/1-12/1)

2498 Amiarge is a good, honest stayer who was keeping on really well when having no real chance. (16/1)

1125 All On, after almost three months off, put up a fine effort to show she will be back in due course. (14/1)

Cittern was dripping with sweat beforehand but certainly put in an eye-catching run and found all the trouble going, but for which he might well have chased his stable companion home. (50/1)

3057 Aurelian finished full of running, suggesting that he is not done with yet. (8/1)

Batoutoftheblue showed his first signs of form this season. He is obviously coming right and is really at his best on the All-Weather. (25/1)

2535 Charter (14/1: 10/1-16/1)

3310 NEP H'CAP (0-85) (3-Y.O+) (Class D)

4-30 (4-30) **7f** £3,420.00 (£1,035.00: £505.00: £240.00) Stalls: Low GOING minus 0.36 sec per fur (F)

				SP	RR	SF
2708[10]	**Royal Mark (IRE) (82)** (TDBarron) **4-10-0** JCarroll(6) (lw: trckd ldrs: qcknd to ld ins fnl f: shkn up & r.o)	—	**1**	4/1[2]	92	67
3087[3]	**Weetman's Weigh (IRE) (78)** (RHollinshead) **4-9-7**(3) DGriffiths(5) (trckd ldrs: hdwy over 1f out: r.o: nt pce of wnr)	2½	**2**	100/30[1]	82	57
2567[5]	**Ochos Rios (IRE) (55)** (BSRothwell) **6-7-8**(7) RWinston(2) (led: qcknd 3f out: hdd & no ex ins fnl f)	s.h	**3**	4/1[2]	59	34
2906[8]	**Jedi Knight (67)** (MWEasterby) **3-8-7** LCharnock(4) (b.nr fore: trckd ldrs: outpcd over 2f out: kpt on fnl f)	3	**4**	11/2[3]	64	33
2428[2]	**Trojan Hero (SAF) (70)** (MrsMReveley) **6-9-2** ACulhane(3) (cl up: chal 2f out: wknd ins fnl f)	1½	**5**	7/1	64	39
3034[6]	**Fame Again (64)** (MrsJRRamsden) **5-8-10** MFenton(7) (hld up: lost tch 2f out: n.d after)	1½	**6**	6/1	55	30
3261[4]	**Be Warned (54)** (MDods) **6-8-0b** TWilliams(1) (dwlt: effrt 3f out: sn btn)	2½	**7**	20/1	39	14
				(SP 110.0%)	**7 Rn**	

1m 25.72 (1.22) CSF £14.83 TOTE £4.60: £1.20 £1.80 (£8.10) OWNER Burke's 5th Family Settlement (THIRSK) BRED Barronstown Stud And Ron Con Ltd

WEIGHT FOR AGE 3yo-6lb

2708 Royal Mark (IRE) had this race set up for him and did it well and looks to be in tremendous heart. (4/1)

3087 Weetman's Weigh (IRE) was always well enough placed but the winner had too much pace for him, although he did battle on when all looked lost. (100/30)

2567 Ochos Rios (IRE) helped set the race up but was done for toe in the closing stages. (4/1)

2906 Jedi Knight raced too freely early on but then showed enough to suggest that he is on his way back to form. (11/2)

2428 Trojan Hero (SAF), stepping up in class this time, ran well especially considering that he has had over a month off. (7/1)

3034 Fame Again never got into this but will return to form in due course. (6/1: op 4/1)

3311 BOOTS AT THE METRO CENTRE LIMITED STKS (0-70) (3-Y.O+) (Class E)

5-00 (5-00) **1m 1f 9y** £2,726.25 (£825.00: £402.50: £191.25) Stalls: Low GOING minus 0.36 sec per fur (F)

				SP	RR	SF
3150[3]	**Pride of Pendle (70)** (MartynWane) **8-9-2** JCarroll(4) (hld up: stdy hdwy over 2f out: led 1f out: r.o wl)	—	**1**	5/2[2]	83	53
3225*	**Night Mirage (USA) (70)** (MJohnston) **3-8-10** 2x JWeaver(1) (lw: trckd ldrs: hdwy over 2f out: rdn appr fnl f: kpt on)	1	**2**	7/4[1]	83	45
3105*	**Queens Consul (IRE) (69)** (BSRothwell) **7-9-2** MFenton(3) (led tl hdd 1f out: nt qckn)	¾	**3**	4/1[3]	80	50
2928[2]	**Missfortuna (68)** (SirMarkPrescott) **3-8-8** GDuffield(2) (lw: cl up tl rdn & wknd wl over 1f out)	9	**4**	5/2[2]	64	26
				(SP 113.5%)	**4 Rn**	

1m 54.3 (2.00) CSF £6.93 TOTE £3.10: (£2.30) OWNER Mrs Linda Miller (RICHMOND) BRED James Simpson

WEIGHT FOR AGE 3yo-8lb

3150 Pride of Pendle, having her hundredth race here, was well suited by the strong pace and did the business in style. (5/2)

3225* Night Mirage (USA) put in another sound effort but, despite trying hard, had to admit she had met one just too good. (7/4)

3105* Queens Consul (IRE), the only front-runner in the race, went too fast and just set the race up for the others. (4/1)

2928 Missfortuna looked well enough but ran disappointingly and seems to have lost it for the time being. (5/2)

T/Jkpt: Not won; £8,109.57 to Pontefract 7/8/97. T/Plpt: £270.50 (85.4 Tckts). T/Qdpt: £20.40 (65.21 Tckts) AA

3129-NOTTINGHAM (L-H) (Good to firm)

Wednesday August 6th

WEATHER: sunny and very warm WIND: strong behind

3312 'JAMAICA' (S) STKS (2-Y.O) (Class G)

6-10 (6-10) **6f 15y** £1,984.50 (£547.00: £259.50) Stalls: High GOING minus 0.52 sec per fur (F)

				SP	RR	SF
3067[5]	**Heavenly Falls (IRE) (60)** (CADwyer) **2-8-13**(3) DO'Donohoe(1) (a w ldrs: led over 1f out: rdn & r.o wl)	—	**1**	3/1[1]	64	25
3090[2]	**Courtney Gym (IRE)** (MRChannon) **2-8-11** JFortune(13) (in tch: hdwy wl over 1f out: hrd rdn & hung lft: r.o)	1¼	**2**	3/1[1]	56	17
3106[14]	**Candy Twist** (RonaldThompson) **2-8-3**(3) DarrenMoffatt(9) (a.p: rdn & edgd lft over 2f out: kpt on fnl f)	½	**3**	33/1	49	10
2720[10]	**Chikal** (BPalling) **2-8-11** TSprake(10) (bit bkwd: dwlt: hdwy over 2f out: nrst fin)	1¾	**4**	7/2[2]	50	11
2186[6]	**Eurofen (54)** (PDEvans) **2-8-11b** JFEgan(11) (led after 2f tl hdd over 1f out: sn rdn & btn)	1½	**5**	20/1	46	7
2935[5]	**Jet Set Sarah (USA)** (JBerry) **2-8-1**(5) CLowther(3) (a outpcd)	7	**6**	10/1[3]	22	—

3106[15]	**Hoyland Common (IRE)** (NTinkler) **2-8-6** KimTinkler(6) (trckd ldrs: hrd drvn over 2f out: sn btn)	1¼	**7**	25/1	19	—
2786[11]	**Stravsea (53)** (BPJBaugh) **2-8-2**(5)ow1 PRoberts(8) (urully stalls: w ldrs over 4f: wknd qckly)	1½	**8**	10/1[3]	16	—
3106[13]	**E B Treasure** (NBycroft) **2-8-6** JLowe(12) (outpcd: t.o)	7	**9**	40/1	—	—
3090[7]	**Ask Speedy Snaps** (JMBradley) **2-8-11** AMackay(4) (lw: slt ld 2f: rdn & wknd over 2f out: t.o)	¾	**10**	33/1	—	—
3076[8]	**Just A Stroll** (JSMoore) **2-8-11** WJO'Connor(5) (chsd ldrs over 3f: sn drvn along & wknd: t.o)	2½	**11**	10/1[3]	—	—
2943[16]	**Lanara** (MrsNMacauley) **2-8-6v**[1] BDoyle(7) (s.s: a bhd & outpcd: t.o)	5	**12**	40/1	—	—
				(SP 118.9%)	**12 Rn**	

1m 13.8 (2.30) CSF £9.97 TOTE £3.50: £1.70 £1.50 £6.80 (£4.40) Trio £192.10 OWNER Mr M. E. Hall (NEWMARKET) BRED Mrs Aine O'Farrell Bt in 6,200gns

3067 Heavenly Falls (IRE) proved much the stronger on this return to selling company and was well in control inside the distance. (3/1)

3090 Courtney Gym (IRE) had to switch to deliver his challenge on the approach to the final furlong and, though he did keep on, the winner had too much speed for him. (3/1)

2412 Candy Twist raced prominently but she wandered under pressure soon after halfway, keeping on doggedly in the latter stages. She is capable of winning at this level. (33/1)

Chikal still has a bit left to work on and this improved performance would suggest that he is heading in the right direction. (7/2: op 8/1)

1498 Eurofen held the call on the stands rail for most of the way but he was found wanting once the pressure was on. (20/1)

2935 Jet Set Sarah (USA) (10/1: op 6/1)

3313 'BARBADOS' MEDIAN AUCTION MAIDEN STKS (3-Y.O) (Class F)

6-40 (6-43) **6f 15y** £2,531.10 (£699.60: £333.30) Stalls: High GOING minus 0.52 sec per fur (F)

				SP	RR	SF
2756[2]	**Moon Fairy** (JGSmyth-Osbourne) **3-8-9** TSprake(3) (lw: mde virtually all: qcknd appr fnl f: comf)	—	**1**	4/5[1]	63+	19
2234[6]	**Chief's Spirit** (GMMoore) **3-9-0** JTate(6) (bit bkwd: a.p: hrd rdn over 2f out: chsd wnr appr fnl f: no imp)	2½	**2**	25/1	61	17
2354[5]	**La Doyenne (IRE) (43)** (CBBBooth) **3-8-9** FLynch(4) (hld up: effrt & nt clr run wl over 1f out: swtchd lft: nt pce to chal)	2½	**3**	25/1	50	6
3043[3]	**Castle Ashby Jack (57)** (PHowling) **3-9-0b** BDoyle(7) (b.hind: disp ld: rdn wl over 1f out: wknd ins fnl f)	¾	**4**	3/1[2]	53	9
3030[7]	**Jonny's Joker** (FHLee) **3-9-0** GCarter(1) (lw: trckd ldrs: drvn along over 2f out: sn outpcd: t.o)	12	**5**	20/1	21	—
3133[10]	**Unforgetable Charm (IRE)** (MrsNMacauley) **3-8-9v**[1] SWebster(5) (bhd: rdn over 2f out: no imp: t.o)	7	**6**	33/1	—	—
	Fantasy Flight (MAPeill) **3-8-9** JFortune(2) (Withdrawn not under Starter's orders: ref to ent stalls)		**W**	9/2[3]	—	—
				(SP 95.9%)	**6 Rn**	

1m 13.7 (2.20) CSF £15.67 TOTE £1.40: £1.10 £6.00 (£21.00) OWNER Firm Of M D G Black (TOWCESTER) BRED Mrs P. M. Black

2756 Moon Fairy, taking a step down to six furlongs, was well suited by these more forceful tactics and she had the prize sewn up entering the final furlong. (4/5)

Chief's Spirit, a desperate mover in his slower paces, beat the rest easily enough but he had to admit the winner in a class of his own. (25/1)

2354 La Doyenne (IRE) settled in behind the leaders travelling comfortably but she was tapped for toe when the battle hotted up and, though she needed to be switched to find room, lacked the pace to mount a challenge. (25/1)

3043 Castle Ashby Jack, who does most of his racing on the All-Weather, showed up with the pace, but he was hard at work approaching the final furlong and his measure was soon taken. (3/1)

3314 'TRINIDAD & TOBAGO' CLAIMING STKS (2-Y.O) (Class F)

7-10 (7-10) **5f 13y** £2,277.00 (£627.00: £297.00) Stalls: High GOING minus 0.52 sec per fur (F)

				SP	RR	SF
3062*	**Daynabee (62)** (NTinkler) **2-8-6** KimTinkler(1) (lw: mde all centre: r.o wl ins fnl f)	—	**1**	9/4[1]	64	24
2684[6]	**Just Another Time (69)** (JBerry) **2-8-8**(5) PRoberts(7) (a.p: stands' side: hrd rdn & ev ch appr fnl f: unable qckn)	1¾	**2**	9/2[3]	66	26
3106[11]	**Blarney Park** (CADwyer) **2-8-1**(3) DO'Donohoe(4) (a.p: rdn 2f out: ev ch ent fnl f: nt pce of wnr)	nk	**3**	9/1	56	16
3097[6]	**Glass River (55)** (PDEvans) **2-8-7** JFEgan(6) (chsd ldrs: ev ch appr fnl f: sn rdn: unable qckn)	1¼	**4**	20/1	55	15
	Arbenig (IRE) (BPalling) **2-8-8** TSprake(2) (cmpt: bkwd: s.i.s: trckd ldrs: kpt on one pce fnl f)	1¼	**5**	5/1	52	12
	Justin Hope (CEBrittain) **2-8-13** BDoyle(9) (b: w'like: bkwd: s.s: a bhd & outpcd)	2½	**6**	10/1	49	9
2051[7]	**Sun In The Morning (64)** (BJMeehan) **2-8-8** MTebbutt(8) (chsd ldr stands' side: rdn wl over 1f out: no imp)	nk	**7**	4/1[2]	43	3
2781[4]	**Regalo (67)** (DMHyde) **2-8-10**(3) RHavlin(3) (stumbled sn after s: sn prom: ev ch over 1f out: wknd qckly fnl f)	2½	**8**	14/1	40	—
				(SP 116.1%)	**8 Rn**	

60.2 secs (1.30) CSF £11.61 TOTE £3.00: £1.10 £2.40 £2.10 (£6.10) Trio £16.60 OWNER Mr T. L. Beecroft (MALTON) BRED G. Middlebrook

3062* Daynabee, who is on a roll, had no trouble on this step back to the minimum trip and she galloped her rivals into the ground. (9/4)

2047 Just Another Time always had the lead on the stands side but the winner, racing wide, was always travelling that bit too well for him. (9/2)

Blarney Park looked to be the first in trouble when given reminders two furlongs out, but she battled back to have every chance passing the furlong marker, before the winner found more and left her struggling. (9/1)

3097 Glass River is not quite getting it together yet, for he was close enough if good enough approaching the final furlong, but was soon put in his place when the sprint to the line developed. (20/1)

Arbenig (IRE), a quick-actioned, compact filly very much in need of the run, showed plenty of promise after missing a beat at the start and she should be able to win races. (5/1)

Justin Hope was far from fully wound up for this racecourse debut and a slow start gave him little chance to show what he is made of. (10/1: op 6/1)

3315 ANTIGUA H'CAP (0-70) (3-Y.O+) (Class E)

7-40 (7-42) **1m 1f 213y** £3,434.25 (£1,029.00: £494.50: £227.25) Stalls: Low GOING minus 0.25 sec per fur (GF)

				SP	RR	SF
3104*	**Mcgillycuddy Reeks (IRE) (59)** (DonEnricoIncisa) **6-9-6** 6x KimTinkler(7) (hld up in rr: hdwy over 3f out: rdn to ld wl ins fnl f)	—	**1**	9/2[2]	71	40
2487[3]	**Mowjood (USA) (64)** (MRStoute) **3-9-2v**[1] KDarley(15) (lw: plld hrd: a.p: led over 1f out: hrd rdn: ct nr fin)	hd	**2**	6/1[3]	76	36
2918[6]	**Fern's Governor (53)** (WJMusson) **5-9-0** GCarter(8) (hld up: plld hrd: gd hdwy over 2f out: rdn & one pce fnl f)	2½	**3**	100/30[1]	61	30
2411[8]	**Supreme Sound (63)** (PWHarris) **3-8-10**(5) CLowther(18) (led tl over 1f out: kpt on u.p ins fnl f)	1¾	**4**	16/1	68	28
2896[8]	**Monis (IRE) (36)** (RonaldThompson) **6-7-11**ow1 NCarlisle(1) (hld up: hdwy over 2f out: styd on u.p fnl f)	2½	**5**	25/1	37	5
2876[7]	**Bedazzle (38)** (MBrittain) **6-7-6**(7) DMernagh(14) (lw: hld up: hdwy 5f out: rdn & edgd lft appr fnl f: no ex)	s.h	**6**	16/1	39	8
3153[11]	**Harvey White (IRE) (56)** (JPearce) **5-9-3** NDay(6) (mid div: rdn over 2f out: sn btn)	2	**7**	9/1	54	23
3134[6]	**Tinklers Folly (55)** (RMWhitaker) **5-9-2v**[1] DeanMcKeown(2) (chsd ldrs: rdn 2f out: sn lost tch)	1½	**8**	16/1	50	19
3039[8]	**Naughty Pistol (USA) (46)** (PDEvans) **5-8-7b** JFEgan(9) (lw: trckd ldrs: hrd rdn 2f out: sn outpcd)	½	**9**	11/1	41	10

				SP	RR	SF
2716^{5}	**Diamond Crown (IRE) (42)** (MartynWane) **6-8-0**(3) AWhelan(17) (dwlt: effrt over 2f out: no imp)	4	**10**	16/1	30	—
2876*	**African-Pard (IRE) (62)** (DHaydnJones) **5-9-9** SDrowne(10) (hld up: hdwy on outside 3f out: sn rdn: no imp)	nk	**11**	6/1^{3}	50	19
	Grooms Gold (IRE) (56) (PWHarris) **5-9-3** ACulhane(4) (bkwd: swtg: a in rr)	2	**12**	33/1	40	9
2876^{8}	**Gilling Dancer (IRE) (46)** (PCalver) **4-8-4**(3) DarrenMoffatt(5) (a in rr)	s.h	**13**	33/1	30	—
2776^{9}	**Suivez (46)** (MrsNMacauley) **7-8-7** BDoyle(12) (b: chsd ldrs: rdn & wknd over 2f out)	2½	**14**	33/1	26	—
3134^{3}	**Tonnerre (59)** (BAMcMahon) **5-9-6** LNewton(3) (prom tl rdn & wknd over 2f out)	¾	**15**	12/1	38	7
1001^{15}	**Rival Bid (USA) (63)** (MrsNMacauley) **9-9-10v** SWebster(11) (b: bit bkwd: s.i.s: effrt over 4f out: sn rdn & wknd)	4	**16**	33/1	36	5
538^{13}	**Princely Affair (40)** (JMBradley) **4-8-1** AMackay(13) (bit bkwd: s.i.s: sn chsng ldrs: wknd over 3f out: t.o)	10	**17**	33/1	—	—

(SP 137.9%) **17 Rn**

2m 7.8 (5.30) CSF £30.78 CT £96.47 TOTE £5.90: £1.10 £1.90 £1.60 £3.30 (£12.40) Trio £21.10 OWNER Don Enrico Incisa (MIDDLEHAM) BRED Noel Sweeney

LONG HANDICAP Monis (IRE) 7-5

WEIGHT FOR AGE 3yo-9lb

3104* Mcgillycuddy Reeks (IRE), winning her fourth race within a month, has improved out of all recognition but she has been stepping up the handicap, and she had to work hard in the latter stages to get the better of a willing rival. (9/2)

2487 Mowjood (USA), a strongly-made colt who is a most impressive mover, was visored for the first time. Running very free, he took control below the distance and, despite giving his all, was worn down in the dying strides. He can soon go one better. (6/1)

2918 Fern's Governor, back over a more suitable trip, was given plenty to do. Making rapid progress entering the final quarter-mile, she was unable to sustain the run and was galloping on the spot inside the last one hundred yards. (100/30)

2064 Supreme Sound has run over longer trips in his most recent outings but he was intent on putting the emphasis on stamina by forcing the pace. Taken on and headed below the distance, he did fight back but his measure had been taken on reaching the final furlong. (16/1)

1796 Monis (IRE) still appears to be searching for a correct trip and, though he stayed on to reach his final placings, was never a factor. (25/1)

2660 Bedazzle came with a promising-looking run inside the last quarter-mile but he drifted badly left when pressure was applied, and it could be that this trip is beyond him. (16/1)

3316 ST LUCIA H'CAP (0-70) (3-Y.O+ F & M) (Class E)

8-10 (8-10) **1m 54y** £3,226.25 (£965.00: £462.50: £211.25) Stalls: Low GOING minus 0.25 sec per fur (GF)

				SP	RR	SF
2174^{8}	**Forest Fantasy (50)** (JWharton) **4-9-2** JFortune(6) (a.p: led 2f out: clr ent fnl f: drvn out)	—	**1**	6/1^{3}	62	44
3027^{2}	**Scenicris (IRE) (48)** (RHollinshead) **4-9-0** FLynch(5) (hld up & bhd: hdwy u.p over 2f out: r.o ins fnl f: no ch w wnr)	3	**2**	14/1	54	36
1966^{3}	**Viva Verdi (IRE) (65)** (JLDunlop) **3-9-10** TSprake(9) (hld up & bhd: hdwy 3f out: kpt on u.p ins fnl f)	1½	**3**	13/8^{1}	68	43
3030^{2}	**Twin Time (65)** (MJHeaton-Ellis) **3-9-10** SDrowne(4) (trckd ldrs: effrt & rdn 2f out: kpt on towards fin)	hd	**4**	7/1	68	43
3248*	**Sis Garden (60)** (JCullinan) **4-9-5**(7) 6x RWinston(2) (sn led: rdn & hdd 2f out: wknd ins fnl f)	½	**5**	8/1	62	44
3132*	**Anetta (57)** (MissSEHall) **3-9-2** 6x LCharnock(1) (lw: chsd ldrs: rdn over 2f out: wknd appr fnl f)	4	**6**	5/1^{2}	51	26
2947^{12}	**Cabcharge Blue (46)** (TJNaughton) **5-8-12** GCarter(10) (prom tl rdn & wknd wl over 1f out)	½	**7**	33/1	39	21
244^{4}	**Perpetual Light (52)** (JJQuinn) **4-9-4** AMcGlone(3) (bit bkwd: a in rr)	4	**8**	16/1	38	20
3039^{11}	**Efipetite (30)** (NBycroft) **4-7-10b** JLowe(8) (plld hrd: chsd ldrs tl outpcd fnl 3f)	½	**9**	50/1	15	—
2941^{2}	**Rochea (47)** (MrsNMacauley) **3-8-6** BDoyle(7) (lw: ld early: chsd ldrs: rdn wl over 1f out: sn btn)	½	**10**	10/1	31	6
3027^{4}	**Spare My Blushes (41)** (BAMcMahon) **3-7-7**(7)ow4 SRighton(11) (rel to r: a wl bhd)	s.h	**11**	25/1	25	—

(SP 123.0%) **11 Rn**

1m 44.9 (3.60) CSF £81.00 CT £183.83 TOTE £7.20: £1.40 £3.60 £1.10 (£27.00) Trio £20.30 OWNER Mr G. W. Turner (MELTON MOWBRAY) BRED Mrs Jane Turner

LONG HANDICAP Efipetite 7-0 Spare My Blushes 7-8

WEIGHT FOR AGE 3yo-7lb

1796 Forest Fantasy, winner of her only previous race twelve months ago, was tackling a slightly shorter trip. Set alight to lead two furlongs out, she was soon driven clear and, keeping up the gallop, had gone beyond recall. (6/1)

3027 Scenicris (IRE) took a long time to warm to her task and, though she was into her stride inside the distance, the winner by then was home and dry. (14/1: 10/1-16/1)

1966 Viva Verdi (IRE) always had far too much to do but she did battle on to make the frame late on, and she is capable of better. (13/8: op 5/2)

3030 Twin Time stuck to her task in the closing stages after being tapped for speed when the winner quickened things up, and a maiden event is well within her reach. (7/1)

3248* Sis Garden had a penalty to carry for her success at Chepstow four days earlier, but she was content to blaze the trail and only got run out of the prizes nearing the line. (8/1: 5/1-9/1)

3132* Anetta was unable to follow up her runaway success of last week and it is more than likely she is not up to carrying weight. (5/1: 7/2-11/2)

3317 'CARIBBEAN' H'CAP (0-65) (3-Y.O+) (Class F)

8-40 (8-41) **2m 9y** £2,970.00 (£825.00: £396.00) Stalls: Low GOING minus 0.25 sec per fur (GF)

				SP	RR	SF
2927*	**Aztec Flyer (USA) (50)** (CEBrittain) **4-8-13b** BDoyle(5) (lw: a.p: led 2f out: sn clr: hld on wl cl home)	—	**1**	9/2^{2}	59	40
3096*	**Children's Choice (IRE) (54)** (WJMusson) **6-9-3** 5x AMcGlone(6) (hld up in rr: hdwy on ins over 3f out: str chal fnl f: r.o)	¾	**2**	5/1^{3}	62	43
2867^{7}	**Prospector's Cove (60)** (JPearce) **4-9-9** NDay(1) (chsd ldrs: effrt & rdn over 2f out: styd on fnl f)	3½	**3**	16/1	65	46
2882^{8}	**Needwood Epic (44)** (BCMorgan) **4-8-7v** LCharnock(10) (led to 2f out: sn rdn: styd on one pce)	¾	**4**	7/1	48	29
2908^{7}	**Arisaig (IRE) (56)** (PCalver) **3-8-1**(3) DarrenMoffatt(2) (lw: in tch: pushed along 10f out: hrd rdn over 2f out: styd on)	s.h	**5**	9/1	60	26
1417^{5}	**Mrs Drummond (IRE) (34)** (GMMcCourt) **4-7-11** NCarlisle(9) (trckd ldrs: hdwy 7f out: rdn over 2f out: grad wknd)	2½	**6**	25/1	36	17
3010^{7}	**Alwarqa (50)** (MartynWane) **4-8-10**(3) AWhelan(3) (chsd ldr 13f: rdn 3f out: sn btn)	3½	**7**	6/1	48	29
2539*	**Sushi Bar (IRE) (40)** (MrsMReveley) **6-8-3**ow1 KDarley(11) (hld up in rr: effrt & rdn wl over 2f out: nvr nr to chal)	2	**8**	4/1^{1}	36	16
2592^{6}	**Strat's Legacy (34)** (DWPArbuthnot) **10-7-11** JLowe(8) (sn pushed along: nvr trbld ldrs)	2½	**9**	20/1	28	9
2879^{8}	**Not Forgotten (USA) (58)** (PAKelleway) **3-7-13v**(7) RWinston(12) (lw: hld up: a in rr)	hd	**10**	16/1	51	17
982^{10}	**Blatant Outburst (62)** (MissSJWilton) **7-9-6**(5) CLowther(4) (s.i.s: a bhd: t.o)	23	**11**	33/1	32	13

2940[7]	**Thahib (60)** (JLHarris) **3-8-8** ACulhane(7) (sn pushed along in rr: no imp: t.o)	3	**12**	14/1	28	—
				(SP 121.6%)		**12 Rn**

3m 30.6 (7.60) CSF £24.95 CT £309.35 TOTE £4.20: £1.60 £1.40 £4.80 (£8.30) Trio £105.10 OWNER Mr R. Meredith (NEWMARKET) BRED Raul Martin

WEIGHT FOR AGE 3yo-15lb

2927* Aztec Flyer (USA), pushing the pace from the break, nosed ahead entering the last quarter-mile but needed to put his best foot forward to hold on close home. (9/2)

3096* Children's Choice (IRE), still the back marker turning for home, made relentless progress up the inside rail and delivered a determined challenge in the final hundred yards, but the winner kept finding more and bravely held her at bay. (5/1)

2776 Prospector's Cove travels well throughout a race but he does not always find much at the business end, although it must be admitted that he did not fail for the want of trying this time. (16/1)

2035 Needwood Epic, bowling along in front from the start, stuck on willingly once headed, but her stride was beginning to shorten inside the distance and she had reached the end of her tether. Still to find an opening, she is fresher than many at this late stage of the season. (7/1: op 12/1)

2908 Arisaig (IRE) looks to be a hard ride but he is not short on stamina and, when the ground eases, it might be worth trying a stronger jockey. (9/1: op 11/2)

Mrs Drummond (IRE) has been well beaten in selling company but she did not fare badly here, and is certainly worth persevering with. (25/1)

2539* Sushi Bar (IRE), asked for his effort early in the straight, failed to pick up at all and obviously has two ways of running. (4/1)

T/Plpt: £7.60 (2,249.23 Tckts). T/Qdpt: £4.90 (247.75 Tckts) IM

3096-YARMOUTH (L-H) (Good to firm)
Wednesday August 6th

WEATHER: sunny WIND: fresh across

3318 EAST COAST H'CAP (0-80) (3-Y.O+) (Class D)

5-50 (5-51) **1m 6f 17y** £3,677.45 (£1,097.60: £524.30: £237.65) Stalls: High GOING minus 0.50 sec per fur (F)

				SP	RR	SF
3203[2]	**Durham (59)** (GLMoore) **6-8-11b** MWigham(8) (bhd: pushed along 7f out: hdwy & n.m.r 3f out: rdn to ld wl ins fnl f)	—	**1**	5/2[1]	70	37
2961[9]	**Shahboor (USA) (70)** (MRStoute) **3-8-9** JReid(6) (a.p: led wl over 1f out: sn hdd: led ins fnl f: sn hdd: unable qckn)	hd	**2**	11/2	81	35
2776[7]	**Urgent Swift (75)** (APJarvis) **4-9-13** WRyan(5) (bhd: hdwy 4f out: led over 1f out tl ins fnl f: no ex nr fin)	1	**3**	14/1	85	52
1027[7]	**The Flying Phantom (75)** (MHTompkins) **6-9-13** GHind(4) (led tl hdd & one pce wl over 1f out)	7	**4**	16/1	77	44
3137[3]	**Tawafek (USA) (68)** (SDow) **4-9-6** MRoberts(1) (lw: prom: rdn over 4f out: sn btn)	3	**5**	9/2[3]	66	33
2411[10]	**Chatham Island (65)** (CEBrittain) **9-9-3** RCochrane(7) (b: in tch tl rdn & wknd 3f out)	2½	**6**	12/1	61	28
2952[3]	**Water Flower (72)** (JRFanshawe) **3-8-11** MHills(3) (b.hind: in tch 10f)	6	**7**	9/2[3]	61	15
3137[2]	**Alarico (FR) (62)** (IPWilliams) **4-9-0** AClark(2) (sn chsng ldr: rdn over 3f out: wknd 2f out)	8	**8**	100/30[2]	42	9
				(SP 123.6%)		**8 Rn**

3m 1.3 (3.30) CSF £16.82 CT £153.79 TOTE £3.00: £1.30 £2.80 £2.70 (£10.50) OWNER The Secret Partnership (BRIGHTON) BRED Highclere Stud Ltd

WEIGHT FOR AGE 3yo-13lb

OFFICIAL EXPLANATION Alarico (FR): no explanation offered.

3203 Durham found trouble in the straight but this probably helped, as, when he was switched towards the far rail and found daylight approaching the final furlong, he quickened well enough to gain the day. (5/2)

2190 Shahboor (USA), stepping up half a mile in trip, looked rather keen going down but stuck to his guns and got the trip. A similar race might easily come his way. (11/2)

789 Urgent Swift, a moderate mover, took some time to warm to the task. Getting better as the race went on, he was only just run out of it and stayed the trip. (14/1: op 7/1)

The Flying Phantom has spent much of his life tilting at windmills but is rather onepaced these days, although he would get further. (16/1)

3137 Tawafek (USA) moved down as if feeling the ground and faded early in the straight. (9/2)

1841 Chatham Island, who won this race on his final outing last season, has been well below par since. (12/1)

3319 MANSHIP MAIDEN STKS (3-Y.O+) (Class D)

6-20 (6-21) **1m 3f 101y** £3,557.50 (£1,060.00: £505.00: £227.50) Stalls: Low GOING minus 0.50 sec per fur (F)

				SP	RR	SF
2924[4]	**Elbaaha (76)** (MAJarvis) **3-8-6** RCochrane(5) (led over 2f: led over 3f out: rdn clr appr fnl f: readily)	—	**1**	Evens[1]	79	33
	St Lawrence (CAN) (80) (CEBrittain) **3-8-11** MRoberts(4) (bit bkwd: chsd ldrs: pushed along over 5f out: kpt on appr fnl f: no ch w wnr)	7	**2**	7/2[2]	74	28
2783[7]	**Announcing** (JHMGosden) **3-8-11** GHind(6) (led 9f out tl over 2f out: sn rdn & no ex)	1¼	**3**	7/1	73	27
3012[9]	**Russian Ruler (IRE) (77)** (APJarvis) **3-8-11** MHills(3) (lw: hld up & plld hrd: hdwy 4f out: no imp fnl 3f)	3	**4**	9/2[3]	68	22
	Shirty (DMorley) **3-8-11** AClark(2) (lengthy: unf: bit bkwd: chsd ldrs over 7f)	25	**5**	8/1	33	—
	On Merit (SGollings) **3-8-11** WRyan(1) (w'like: scope: bkwd: s.i.s: a bhd)	22	**6**	33/1	3	—
				(SP 117.0%)		**6 Rn**

2m 24.3 (2.50) CSF £4.69 TOTE £1.80: £1.30 £1.90 (£3.90) OWNER Sheikh Ahmed Al Maktoum (NEWMARKET) BRED Sheikh Ahmed Bin Rashid Al Maktoum

2924 Elbaaha broke her duck in a modest race but really needed to have her mind made up for her going towards the furlong pole. Once she hit her stride, she was allowed to ease off a little. (Evens)

St Lawrence (CAN), taken down very quietly, stayed on from an unpromising position in the straight but did nothing quickly and looks to need further. (7/2)

Announcing, a half-brother to Presenting, was made to look rather pedestrian in the straight but might do better with some ease in the ground. (7/1)

1936 Russian Ruler (IRE), up in trip, took a strong hold and failed to last home. (9/2: 3/1-5/1)

Shirty, a plain gelding making his debut, dropped away quickly once the field straightened for home. (8/1)

On Merit, a sturdy, likeable newcomer, looked well in his coat but badly in need of the run. Steadied at the start, he soon became half a dozen lengths behind and he never got into the race. His future may well be over hurdles. (33/1)

3320 FREETHORPE CLAIMING STKS (3-Y.O) (Class F)

6-50 (6-51) **1m 2f 21y** £2,623.50 (£726.00: £346.50) Stalls: Low GOING minus 0.50 sec per fur (F)

Form	Horse	Dist	Pos	SP	RR	SF
2582[5]	**Laguna Bay (IRE) (56)** (APJarvis) **3-8-8** JReid(7) (a.p: led ins fnl f: rdn out)	—	**1**	4/1[2]	60	19
2468[5]	**River of Fortune (IRE) (55)** (MHTompkins) **3-8-3**(5) RMullen(8) (lw: led tl hdd & no ex ins fnl f)	1½	**2**	7/1	58	17
3044[3]	**Bon Guest (IRE) (53)** (JGMO'Shea) **3-8-13** WRyan(4) (dwlt: hdwy over 3f out: no ex ins fnl f)	¾	**3**	13/2	61	20
2772[10]	**Miss Riviera Rose (62)** (GWragg) **3-8-8** MHills(2) (trckd ldrs: rdn 2f out: edgd lft & fnd nil appr fnl f)	3	**4**	7/2[1]	52	11
2722[6]	**Manikato (USA) (60)** (DJSCosgrove) **3-9-1** MRimmer(5) (lw: trckd ldrs tl btn over 2f out)	3½	**5**	12/1	53	12
2873[13]	**Monacle** (DMorris) **3-8-13** RCochrane(6) (bit bkwd: sn outpcd: nvr nr ldrs)	1½	**6**	10/1	49	8
1998*	**Court House (64)** (MCChapman) **3-8-0**(7) SCarson(1) (plld hrd: chsd ldrs: rdn & wknd over 3f out)	1¾	**7**	5/1[3]	40	—
3027*	**Blazer's Baby (50)** (MrsNMacauley) **3-7-10**(7)ow5 JoHunnam(3) (chsd ldrs tl wknd over 2f out)	1	**8**	5/1[3]	34	—

(SP 118.2%) **8 Rn**

2m 7.9 (4.10) CSF £30.12 TOTE £4.30: £1.80 £1.80 £1.20 (£12.70) OWNER Town and Country Tyre Services Ltd (ASTON UPTHORPE) BRED Mat Farrell

2582 Laguna Bay (IRE), dropping back in trip, went down keenly and got the better of the runner-up after a ding-dong battle. (4/1: op 5/2)
2178 River of Fortune (IRE), made use of for the first time over this trip, didn't do much wrong, but the winner gradually wore her down, seeing her finish second for the seventh time. (7/1)
3044 Bon Guest (IRE), whose stamina is not really proven, looked all over the winner when beginning a move on the outside early in the straight, but, once within a couple of lengths, tended to edge in behind his rivals and found very little. (13/2)
2059 Miss Riviera Rose, dropped in class, suddenly came off the bit with two furlongs left and didn't want to know. (7/2)
1505 Manikato (USA), a frustrating sort who has flattered to deceive in the past, travelled sweetly on the heels of the leaders until his stamina appeared to fail. (12/1: op 8/1)
Monacle looks rather slow but rather more enthusiastic than some of his rivals here. (10/1: 5/1-12/1)
1998* Court House, stepped up in trip, did nothing to remove the view that last time's victory may have been a fluke. (5/1)
3027* Blazer's Baby parted company with her jockey coming out onto the track, but was eventually persuaded to go down very steadily. Going well early in the straight, the writing was quickly on the wall once she came off the bridle. (5/1)

3321 HORSEY (S) H'CAP (0-60) (3 & 4-Y.O) (Class G)

7-20 (7-23) **1m 3y** £2,553.00 (£708.00: £339.00) Stalls: Low GOING minus 0.50 sec per fur (F)

Form	Horse	Dist	Pos	SP	RR	SF
3143[9]	**Welsh Mountain (38)** (MJHeaton-Ellis) **4-9-3** JReid(9) (a.p: led over 1f out: rdn out)	—	**1**	7/1[3]	49	34
3026[10]	**Rehaab (45)** (DMorris) **4-9-10v[1]** RCochrane(10) (hld up: hdwy to ld wl over 1f out: sn hdd: unable qckn wl ins fnl f)	½	**2**	10/1	55	40
2887[3]	**Shark (IRE) (44)** (KAMorgan) **4-9-9** OPears(2) (led: clr after 2f: hdd wl over 1f out: one pce)	4	**3**	12/1	46	31
2916[15]	**Sweet Seventeen (23)** (HJCollingridge) **4-7-11**(5) AimeeCook(11) (hdwy 3f out: nvr rchd ldrs)	4	**4**	16/1	17	2
2836[5]	**Gresatre (51)** (CADwyer) **3-9-2**(7) JoHunnam(4) (chsd ldrs: no imp fnl 2f)	hd	**5**	12/1	45	23
3038[2]	**Inkwell (34)** (AHide) **3-8-6** MHills(3) (lw: hdwy over 3f out: rdn over 1f out: sn btn)	2½	**6**	9/4[1]	23	1
3068[4]	**Baaheth (USA) (45)** (SCWilliams) **3-9-3b[1]** MWigham(13) (in tch tl hmpd & lost pl 3f out: styd on again appr fnl f)	hd	**7**	12/1	34	12
2785[7]	**Persephone (20)** (JLHarris) **4-7-8b**(5) RMullen(5) (lw: bhd: effrt over 2f out: sn hung lft & no imp)	s.h	**8**	20/1	9	—
2947[7]	**Hadadabble (32)** (PatMitchell) **4-8-11** WRyan(12) (lw: n.d)	2½	**9**	20/1	16	1
3038[3]	**Mutahadeth (50)** (DShaw) **3-9-8** GHind(7) (lw: chsd ldrs: rdn over 3f out: sn btn)	4	**10**	11/2[2]	26	4
2922[10]	**Shermood (23)** (KTIvory) **4-7-9**(7) DarrenWilliams(8) (b: b.hind: lw: prom over 5f)	hd	**11**	7/1[3]	—	—
2912[6]	**Magazine Gap (38)** (PatMitchell) **4-8-12**(5) AmandaSanders(6) (swtg: bhd fnl 3f)	7	**12**	20/1	—	—
2071[12]	**Slievenamon (44)** (JEBanks) **4-9-9** MRoberts(1) (chsd ldrs: rdn 4f out: sn wknd)	3	**13**	11/2[2]	—	—
2883[8]	**Emmas Breeze (42)** (GGMargarson) **3-9-0** MRimmer(14) (w ldrs over 4f: sn wknd)	nk	**14**	20/1	—	—

(SP 143.6%) **14 Rn**

1m 38.5 (2.50) CSF £78.16 CT £797.74 TOTE £7.70: £3.30 £2.70 £4.90 (£46.20) Trio £340.60 OWNER Mr F. J. Sainsbury (WROUGHTON) BRED Messinger Stud Ltd
WEIGHT FOR AGE 3yo-7lb
Sold K Morgan 5,250gns

IN-FOCUS: **Although the stalls for the last three races were placed on the far side, none of the competitors raced there, the vast majority heading for the stands rail, with varying degrees of haste. It was surprising that nobody tried to race hard against the far rail, as this appeared an advantage in the earlier round-course races.**
Welsh Mountain, taking a drop in class, was gaining his first placing since his two-year-old days. He came clear with the runner-up in decent style for selling company. (7/1)
1623 Rehaab, dropped in trip and visored for the first time, caught the eye going to post and came through strongly to go clear with the winner. A similar event should be hers for the taking if the visor works as well again. (10/1: 8/1-12/1)
2887 Shark (IRE), taken down early, started the trend of coming stands side with a fast break seeing him bring the whole field over. Hard to pull up after the race, he does have ability but is clearly not the easiest of customers. (12/1: op 8/1)
2488 Sweet Seventeen, dropped back in trip, got going too late to land a blow. (16/1)
2836 Gresatre again finished weakly over this trip. (12/1)
3038 Inkwell, rather keen going to post, may well have been disadvantaged by having to make his move towards the centre of the track. He looked the part and is worth another chance. (9/4)
3068 Baaheth (USA) was the first to get the stands' rail, but paid the penalty when the rest of the field moved across and all but knocked him over. In the circumstances he did quite well. (12/1)
3038 Mutahadeth (11/2: 4/1-6/1)
Slievenamon (11/2: 4/1-6/1)

3322 BANHAM POULTRY CONDITIONS STKS (2-Y.O) (Class D)

7-50 (7-51) **7f 3y** £3,980.00 (£1,190.00: £570.00: £260.00) Stalls: Low GOING minus 0.50 sec per fur (F)

Form	Horse	Dist	Pos	SP	RR	SF
	Mr Cahill (USA) (MRStoute) **2-8-12** JReid(3) (leggy: scope: hld up: n.m.r over 2f out: hdwy to ld ins fnl f: rdn out)	—	**1**	9/2[2]	83+	39
3047[5]	**Dower House** (WJarvis) **2-8-12** WRyan(7) (a.p: led 2f out tl ins fnl f: unable qckn)	1¼	**2**	4/7[1]	80	36
2394[4]	**Campari (IRE)** (MAJarvis) **2-8-7** RCochrane(2) (led 5f: sn outpcd)	6	**3**	8/1[3]	62	18
2524[10]	**Circus** (CEBrittain) **2-8-12** MRoberts(1) (w ldr tl wknd over 1f out)	1¼	**4**	12/1	64	20
	Grecian Prince (JGSmyth-Osbourne) **2-8-12** MHills(4) (unf: scope: s.s: nvr trbld ldrs)	3	**5**	33/1	57	13

				SP	RR	SF
2849[5]	**Dragon Boy** (IPWilliams) **2-8-12** AClark(6) (lw: plld hrd: prom tl rdn & wknd wl over 1f out)	s.h	**6**	16/1	57	13
2394[8]	**Elba Magic (IRE)** (CADwyer) **2-8-7** MRimmer(5) (prom tl rdn & wknd over 2f out)	5	**7**	9/2[2]	40	—

(SP 127.6%) **7 Rn**

1m 25.5 (1.30) CSF £7.78 TOTE £3.40: £4.10 £1.10 (£3.80) OWNER Maktoum Al Maktoum (NEWMARKET) BRED Centaur Farms Inc.
Mr Cahill (USA), a sturdily-made, attractive newcomer, took the eye in the paddock and looked fit, despite rumours that he would need the run. Easy to back, he was always travelling nicely, and getting a run between the favourite and the stands' rail merely made the job a bit easier. He should go on from here. (9/2: 5/2-5/1)
3047 Dower House showed plenty of knee action and there looked to be something left to work on, but he was clearly expected to win. Although eventually worn down by the winner, he looks up to winning an ordinary maiden, probably with some cut in the ground. (4/7)
2394 Campari (IRE) set a steady pace, but couldn't quicken up with the two principals. (8/1)
Circus raced towards the centre of the course and is probably a little better than the bare form suggests. Unusually for a son of Caerleon, his action suggests some cut in the ground would favour him. (12/1: op 8/1)
Grecian Prince, whose dam is a half-sister to Hellenic, looks the sort to improve with time and didn't give himself much of a chance here, losing ground at the start and looking somewhat green. (33/1)
2849 Dragon Boy, bred to get middle-distances, is going to need to settle rather better than this to do so. (16/1)
Elba Magic (IRE) (9/2: op 20/1)

3323 FILBY BRIDGE H'CAP (0-70) (3-Y.O+ F & M) (Class E)

8-20 (8-20) **5f 43y** £3,018.25 (£901.00: £430.50: £195.25) Stalls: Low GOING minus 0.50 sec per fur (F)

				SP	RR	SF
2852[W]	**Divine Miss-P (50)** (APJarvis) **4-8-10** MHills(4) (racd stands' side: mde all: clr over 1f out: unchal)	—	**1**	14/1	63	45
3032[3]	**Pharaoh's Joy (56)** (JWPayne) **4-9-2b[1]** RCochrane(5) (racd stands' side: hld up: hdwy 2f out: kpt on fnl f: nt trble wnr)	2½	**2**	13/8[1]	61	43
3083[5]	**College Princess (51)** (SCWilliams) **3-8-1**(7) DarrenWilliams(6) (b: racd stands' side: chsd wnr: no imp appr fnl f)	2½	**3**	13/2	49	28
3126[14]	**Polly Golightly (66)** (MBlanshard) **4-9-12b** MRoberts(1) (racd centre: gd spd over 3f)	1	**4**	5/1[3]	61	43
3224[4]	**Kind of Light (68)** (RGuest) **4-10-0** JReid(7) (racd stands' side: chsd ldrs: rdn 2f out: edgd lft & sn btn)	3½	**5**	100/30[2]	52	34
3126[12]	**Sally Slade (67)** (CACyzer) **5-9-13** WRyan(2) (racd centre: a bhd)	3	**6**	11/2	42	24
3077[6]	**Napier Star (43)** (MrsNMacauley) **4-8-3v** AClark(3) (lw: racd centre: in tch tl btn & eased appr fnl f)	1	**7**	10/1	14	—

(SP 122.3%) **7 Rn**

61.4 secs (0.40) CSF £36.88 TOTE £14.00: £4.20 £1.50 (£18.80) OWNER Town and Country Tyre Services Ltd (ASTON UPTHORPE) BRED C. C. Bromley and Son and A. O. Nerses
WEIGHT FOR AGE 3yo-3lb
729* Divine Miss-P, dropped in trip, was bounced out of the stalls, made a bee line for the favoured stands' rail and never looked in any danger. (14/1)
3032 Pharaoh's Joy, who had not won in nine races since this contest a year ago, was a touch keen going down in first-time blinkers. Despite doing some good running towards the end, the winner was long gone. (13/8)
3083 College Princess tried to keep tabs on the winner but gave up the unequal struggle from the distance. (13/2: 7/2-7/1)
2148 Polly Golightly showed plenty of foot in the centre of the course, but was almost certainly on the slowest ground and never looked like winning. (5/1)
3224 Kind of Light, dropped back in trip, could never get into this but wasn't helped by drifting out to the centre of the course. (100/30)
2581 Sally Slade may have raced on the slowest ground and may be suited by a little more cut, but still ran an absolute stinker, having got a good deal closer to Ya Malak in a Sandown listed race three outings ago. (11/2)
3077 Napier Star (10/1: op 5/1)

T/Plpt: £139.20 (81 Tckts). T/Qdpt: £71.40 (14.14 Tckts) Dk

2928-BATH (L-H) (Good)
Thursday August 7th

WEATHER: fine & humid WIND: almost nil

3324 FRANCASAL (S) STKS (2-Y.O) (Class G)

2-30 (2-37) **5f 11y** £2,360.00 (£660.00: £320.00) Stalls: High GOING minus 0.35 sec per fur (F)

				SP	RR	SF
2823[7]	**Junior Muffin (IRE)** (JBerry) **2-8-6**(5) CLowther(3) (swtg: rdn 3f out: plld out 2f out: hdwy over 1f out: led ins fnl f: r.o)	—	**1**	8/1	61	21
1954[7]	**Kathies Pet** (RJHodges) **2-8-1**(5) AmandaSanders(1) (lw: a.p: led ins fnl f: sn hdd: r.o)	nk	**2**	10/1	55	15
3106[8]	**Pip's Addition (IRE)** (JAGlover) **2-8-6** GCarter(4) (chsd ldrs: ev ch ins fnl f: r.o)	½	**3**	7/2[1]	54	14
3055[2]	**Ok John (IRE)** (JAkehurst) **2-8-11** AClark(11) (a.p: led over 1f out tl ins fnl f)	hd	**4**	7/2[1]	58	18
	Aviva Lady (IRE) (CADwyer) **2-8-3**(3) DO'Donohoe(9) (leggy: unf: stdd & sltly hmpd s: hdwy over 1f out: nvr nrr)	2	**5**	5/1[2]	47	7
3247[10]	**Swift Time (60)** (MRBosley) **2-8-1**(5) AimeeCook(6) (lw: w ldrs: ev ch 2f out: wknd over 1f out)	3	**6**	9/1	37	—
3090[5]	**The Hobby Lobby (IRE) (55)** (MissKMGeorge) **2-8-11** SWhitworth(2) (led over 2f: wknd over 1f out)	1½	**7**	20/1	38	—
3055[W]	**Verdant Express** (WGMTurner) **2-8-3**(3) DSweeney(10) (uns rdr & unruly bef s: racd wd: prom: led over 2f out tl over 1f out: sn wknd)	1¼	**8**	12/1	29	—
	Celtic Venture (MRChannon) **2-8-11** RHughes(7) (w'like: a bhd)	2½	**9**	6/1[3]	26	—
2917[17]	**River Frontier (IRE)** (MDIUsher) **2-8-6** JMarshall(5) (rdn over 2f out: sn bhd)	nk	**10**	33/1	20	—
	Marion's Pet (RJHodges) **2-8-6** AMackay(8) (neat: s.s: a wl bhd)	s.h	**11**	25/1	20	—
2276[3]	**Wind In The Park** (MSalaman) **2-7-13**(7) SCarson(12) (a bhd)	5	**12**	40/1	4	—

(SP 127.3%) **12 Rn**

63.3 secs (2.80) CSF £80.22 TOTE £11.10: £3.10 £3.10 £1.70 (£56.20) Trio £72.30 OWNER Comerford Brothers Ltd (COCKERHAM) BRED Patrick J. Duffy
No bid
2127 Junior Muffin (IRE) a half-brother to the sprinter Terrhars, was dropped into a seller after some disappointing efforts. Described as not having the best of legs, he was thought to have appreciated the better ground. (8/1: 5/1-9/1)
Kathies Pet who only cost 800 gns., was fitter for her course and distance debut in an auction race, back in June. (10/1)
3106 Pip's Addition (IRE) ran much better having got away on level terms for the first time. (7/2)
3055 Ok John (IRE) seemed to have run his race well enough on this occasion, but simply wasn't good enough. (7/2: op 9/4)

Aviva Lady (IRE) a half-sister to an Irish mile and a half winner, was supported in the ring and will have learned a lot from this. (5/1)
2396 Verdant Express (12/1: op 8/1)

3325 STAYERS H'CAP (0-70) (3-Y.O) (Class E)
3-00 (3-00) **2m 1f 34y** £2,917.75 (£877.00: £423.50: £196.75) Stalls: High GOING minus 0.35 sec per fur (F)

Form	Horse	Dist	Pos	SP	RR	SF
3028*	**Ginger Rogers (58)** (DWPArbuthnot) **3-9-7** JQuinn(1) (chsd ldr: led over 4f out tl over 3f out: led over 2f out: hrd rdn & hdd over 1f out: led last strides)	—	1	2/5^{1}	69	22
2189^{8}	**Sixties Melody (45)** (RBoss) **3-8-5**$^{(3)}$ RFfrench(2) (hld up in rr: stdy hdwy over 6f out: led over 1f out: hrd rdn: hdd last strides)	s.h	2	6/1^{3}	56	9
3057*	**Sipowitz (51)** (CACyzer) **3-8-11**$^{(3)}$ AWhelan(3) (a.p: led over 3f out tl over 2f out: eased whn btn fnl f)	12	3	100/30^{2}	51	4
2537^{8}	**Abbey Theatre (IRE) (42)** (MSalaman) **3-8-5** SWhitworth(4) (led: rdn & hdd over 4f out: eased whn btn 3f out)	dist	4	20/1	—	—

(SP 113.6%) **4 Rn**

3m 54.0 (12.60) CSF £3.41 TOTE £1.20 (£2.80) OWNER Mr W. H. Ponsonby (COMPTON) BRED R. Barber
STEWARDS' ENQUIRY Ffrench susp. 16-17/8/97 (excessive use of whip).
3028* Ginger Rogers completed a hat-trick, despite having gone up a total of 11lb, but it really was hard work. She will now have three or four weeks off and could be aimed at the Cesarewitch. (2/5)
239 Sixties Melody, down 5lb, was 16lb better off with the winner, than when beaten nine lengths at Yarmouth. Pipped virtually on the post, Ffrench received a double whammy when picking up a two-day whip ban. (6/1)
3057* Sipowitz up 4lb, would have finished much closer had the position not been accepted. (100/30: 2/1-7/2)

3326 BBC RADIO BRISTOL SPRINT H'CAP (0-85) (3-Y.O+) (Class D)
3-30 (3-31) **5f 11y** £3,670.00 (£1,105.00: £535.00: £250.00) Stalls: High GOING minus 0.35 sec per fur (F)

Form	Horse	Dist	Pos	SP	RR	SF
3126^{9}	**Malibu Man (70)** (EAWheeler) **5-9-1** BDoyle(5) (swtg: mde all: rdn over 1f out: r.o wl)	—	1	9/1	81	48
2933^{3}	**Ansellman (77)** (JBerry) **7-9-8b** RHughes(3) (chsd wnr: rdn & nt qckn fnl f)	¾	2	7/2^{1}	86	53
2950^{3}	**Mister Jolson (74)** (RJHodges) **8-9-5** AMackay(6) (lw: hdwy wl over 1f out: one pce fnl f)	1½	3	9/2^{2}	78	45
3126^{4}	**Dande Flyer (61)** (DWPArbuthnot) **4-8-6** SWhitworth(2) (lw: hld up: hdwy over 1f out: one pce fnl f)	s.h	4	9/2^{2}	65	32
3126^{7}	**Songsheet (71)** (MSSaunders) **4-9-2** WJO'Connor(4) (chsd ldrs: one pce fnl 2f)	¾	5	7/1^{3}	72	39
3126^{8}	**Longwick Lad (76)** (WRMuir) **4-9-7** MRoberts(9) (nvr nr to chal)	2½	6	10/1	69	36
	Jucea (66) (JLSpearing) **8-8-11** FNorton(8) (nvr trbld ldrs)	1½	7	10/1	55	22
3217^{25}	**Intiaash (IRE) (79)** (DHaydnJones) **5-9-10** RCochrane(7) (s.s: bhd whn rdn over 1f out: eased ins fnl f: fin lame)	hd	8	7/1^{3}	67	34
2655^{7}	**Chili Concerto (82)** (PJMakin) **3-9-10** NDay(10) (lw: chsd ldrs over 2f)	s.h	9	12/1	70	34

(SP 119.5%) **9 Rn**

61.8 secs (1.30) CSF £38.27 CT £150.62 TOTE £13.20: £3.20 £1.30 £1.70 (£23.60) Trio £25.10 OWNER Church Racing Partnership (PANGBOURNE) BRED Mrs M. Chubb
WEIGHT FOR AGE 3yo-3lb
2590 Malibu Man, described as a good horse when hitting the gate running, was said to have been messed about by a riderless horse when fancied at Goodwood last week. (9/1)
2933 Ansellman is running consistently well of late without managing to win. (7/2)
2950 Mister Jolson due to drop another pound at the weekend, may need a return to six, now he is getting older. (9/2)
3126 Dande Flyer, another due to come down a pound in future handicaps, had finished just over a length in front of today's winner at Goodwood last week, when the latter was reportedly unlucky. (9/2)
3126 Songsheet had no excuses here having met trouble late on when finishing just in front of the winner last week. (7/1)
949* Longwick Lad, yet another involved in that Glorious Goodwood race, is due to drop a pound. (10/1)
1294 Chili Concerto (12/1: 8/1-14/1)

3327 SILKWOOD CLAIMING STKS (3-Y.O+) (Class E)
4-00 (4-01) **5f 161y** £3,112.75 (£937.00: £453.50: £211.75) Stalls: High GOING minus 0.35 sec per fur (F)

Form	Horse	Dist	Pos	SP	RR	SF
2933*	**Hard to Figure (84)** (RJHodges) **11-8-11**$^{(3)}$ PPMurphy(12) (hdwy over 2f out: r.o to ld nr fin)	—	1	6/5^{1}	66	50
2354*	**Mystical (62)** (MrsLStubbs) **3-8-6v**$^{(3)}$ RFfrench(7) (lw: a.p: led 3f out: edgd lft & clr over 1f out: ct nr fin)	hd	2	11/2^{3}	65	45
2748^{9}	**Embroidered (22)** (SDow) **4-8-5** MRoberts(2) (lw: sn outpcd: hdwy over 1f out: r.o)	4	3	50/1	46	30
2536^{8}	**Bairn Atholl (36)** (RJHodges) **4-8-1** NAdams(9) (a.p: one pce fnl 2f)	1	4	33/1	39	23
	Spaniards Close (91) (PJMakin) **9-9-10** DHolland(4) (led over 2f: wknd over 1f out)	1½	5	7/2^{2}	58	42
1488^{7}	**Night Harmony (IRE) (56)** (MissSJWilton) **4-8-12** SWhitworth(6) (swtg: hdwy over 2f out: wknd over 1f out)	nk	6	12/1	45	29
3016^{7}	**Delrob (40)** (DHaydnJones) **6-8-1b** AMackay(11) (rdn over 2f out: sn bhd)	3½	7	20/1	24	8
3083^{10}	**Kanawa (41)** (APJones) **3-7-12**$^{(3)}$ MHenry(5) (swtg: bhd fnl 3f)	3½	8	66/1	18	—
2958^{8}	**Agwa (52)** (JJBridger) **8-8-8** JQuinn(8) (chsd ldrs 3f)	2	9	33/1	16	—
2921^{7}	**Heavenly Miss (IRE) (52)** (JJBridger) **3-7-10**$^{(7)}$ PDoe(1) (spd over 3f)	¾	10	20/1	13	—
3207^{5}	**Blues Queen (75)** (MRChannon) **3-8-11v^{1}** RHughes(3) (s.v.s: a bhd)	1½	11	13/2	16	—
2536^{12}	**Forzara (38)** (JLSpearing) **4-8-1** FNorton(10) (hld up & plld hrd: bhd fnl 3f: t.o)	11	12	66/1	—	—

(SP 124.4%) **12 Rn**

1m 10.8 (1.30) CSF £7.39 TOTE £2.10: £1.20 £1.60 £3.90 (£6.40) Trio £144.20 OWNER Mr J. W. Mursell (SOMERTON) BRED J. W. Mursell
WEIGHT FOR AGE 3yo-4lb
2933* Hard to Figure will now be given a break and the way he is going it may be a tilt at the Gold rather than Silver version of next month's big race at Ayr. (6/5: evens-5/4)
2354* Mystical confirmed she remains in good heart. (11/2)
Embroidered, with an apparently impossible task at the weights, could not hold an early position on this big drop in distance. (50/1)
2197 Bairn Atholl is another who would have been better off in a handicap. (33/1)
Spaniards Close would have been 3lb better off with the winner had this been a handicap. (7/2: 3/1-9/2)
1279* Night Harmony (IRE) like most of the field was not well in at the weights. (12/1)

3328 HOLIDAY H'CAP (0-75) (3-Y.O+) (Class D)
4-30 (4-30) **1m 5y** £4,406.00 (£1,328.00: £644.00: £302.00) Stalls: Low GOING minus 0.35 sec per fur (F)

Form	Horse	Dist	Pos	SP	RR	SF
2929^{7}	**Final Stab (IRE) (69)** (PWHarris) **4-9-3**$^{(5)}$ CLowther(3) (chsd ldr: led 3f out: shkn up ins fnl f: comf)	—	1	20/1	80+	47

				SP	RR	SF
2369^{3}	**Vanborough Lad (43)** (MJBolton) **8-7-7**$^{(3)}$ RFfrench(1) (a.p: r.o ins fnl f: nt trble wnr)	2	**2**	6/1^{3}	50	17
3143^{2}	**Dummer Golf Time (58)** (LordHuntingdon) **4-8-11v** DHarrison(10) (hld up: hdwy 2f out: hrd rdn & r.o one pce fnl f)	hd	**3**	4/1^{2}	65	32
2760^{8}	**Veni Vidi Vici (IRE) (65)** (MJHeaton-Ellis) **4-9-4** AClark(4) (lw: hld up: hdwy over 2f out: hrd rdn over 1f out: r.o one pce)	½	**4**	8/1	71	38
3115^{7}	**Alfahaal (IRE) (56)** (RFJohnsonHoughton) **4-8-9** GCarter(5) (lw: tk keen hold: hdwy 4f out: chsd wnr 2f out: one pce fnl f)	½	**5**	2/1^{1}	61	28
3115^{4}	**Toujours Riviera (71)** (JPearce) **7-9-10** NDay(6) (prom: rdn over 3f out: wknd over 1f out)	2	**6**	6/1^{3}	72	39
3091^{6}	**Whatever's Right (IRE) (66)** (MDIUsher) **8-9-5** MRoberts(8) (nvr trbld ldrs)	½	**7**	11/1	66	33
3132^{5}	**Saffron Rose (75)** (MBlanshard) **3-9-7** JQuinn(9) (hld up mid div: bhd fnl 2f)	7	**8**	10/1	61	21
2892^{12}	**Leguard Express (IRE) (43)** (OO'Neill) **9-7-10b** NAdams(2) (led 5f)	3½	**9**	40/1	22	—
444^{22}	**Three Weeks (54)** (WRMuir) **4-8-7** DaneO'Neill(7) (swtg: a bhd)	4	**10**	40/1	25	—

(SP 120.1%) **10 Rn**

1m 41.1 (2.90) CSF £125.10 CT £552.47 TOTE £33.00: £4.40 £1.40 £2.20 (£84.90) Trio £170.10 OWNER Mrs P. W. Harris (BERKHAMSTED) BRED Pendley Farm

LONG HANDICAP Leguard Express (IRE) 7-4 Vanborough Lad 7-7

WEIGHT FOR AGE 3yo-7lb

Final Stab (IRE) down 4lb, has been lightly raced because of a stress fracture, but he certainly seems on the right road now and there is obviously not much mileage on the clock. (20/1)

2369 Vanborough Lad loves it around here, but found himself only playing for the places in the closing stages. (6/1)

3143 Dummer Golf Time, reverting to a mile, was trying to beat the handicapper, having been set to rise 4lb at the weekend. (4/1)

2408 Veni Vidi Vici (IRE) had been dropped back down 1lb, after disappointing last time. (8/1)

2760* Alfahaal (IRE), penalised 4lb for his Doncaster win, has not really settled in his two races since. (2/1)

3115 Toujours Riviera was a bit disappointing after his good effort at Glorious Goodwood. (6/1)

3132 Saffron Rose (10/1: op 6/1)

3329 COLERNE MAIDEN APPRENTICE H'CAP (0-80) (3-Y.O+) (Class E)

5-00 (5-00) **1m 2f 46y** £2,708.50 (£823.00: £404.00: £194.50) Stalls: Low GOING minus 0.35 sec per fur (F)

				SP	RR	SF
2876^{3}	**Bonanza Peak (USA) (61)** (MrsJCecil) **4-9-6** MartinDwyer(6) (lw: hld up: hdwy over 3f out: led over 1f out: rdn out)	—	**1**	7/4^{1}	72	36
3133^{2}	**Bellagrana (52)** (MJFetherston-Godley) **3-8-2** RFfrench(5) (chsd ldr: led over 3f out: edgd rt & hdd over 1f out: rallied ins fnl f)	1	**2**	9/4^{2}	61	16
2246^{3}	**One In The Eye (37)** (JRPoulton) **4-7-10** RMullen(2) (lw: s.s: hdwy 3f out: one pce fnl 2f)	14	**3**	8/1	25	—
2302^{13}	**Haydown (IRE) (37)** (MRBosley) **5-7-3**$^{(7)}$ KelliPhillips(3) (prom over 6f)	4	**4**	33/1	18	—
2521^{6}	**Jean Pierre (48)** (JPearce) **4-8-7** CTeague(4) (lw: led over 6f: wknd over 2f out: t.o)	20	**5**	11/2^{3}	—	—
3071^{5}	**Epworth (75)** (JAGlover) **3-9-4b**$^{1(7)}$ TPengkerego(1) (s.s: plld hrd: hdwy 8f out: wknd over 2f out: t.o)	6	**6**	11/2^{3}	16	—

(SP 112.0%) **6 Rn**

2m 11.6 (5.10) CSF £5.37 TOTE £2.70: £1.40 £1.60 (£2.20) OWNER Gavin Oram and Julie Cecil (NEWMARKET) BRED Eaton Farms Inc. and Red Bull Stable

LONG HANDICAP Haydown (IRE) 7-3 One In The Eye 7-7

WEIGHT FOR AGE 3yo-9lb

2876 Bonanza Peak (USA) had to be kept up to his work to keep the renewed effort of the runner-up at bay in a poor race. (7/4)

3133 Bellagrana is giving the impression she will stay further. (9/4)

2246 One In The Eye apparently needs soft ground to offset his lack of speed. (8/1)

2521 Jean Pierre (11/2: 4/1-6/1)

3071 Epworth (11/2: op 7/2)

T/Plpt: £33.10 (615.1 Tckts). T/Qdpt: £4.30 (364.04 Tckts) KH

2842-PONTEFRACT (L-H) (Good to firm)

Thursday August 7th

WEATHER: hot and sunny WIND: fresh half against

3330 BOLLINGER CHAMPAGNE CHALLENGE SERIES GENTLEMEN'S H'CAP (0-70) (3-Y.O+) (Class F)

2-15 (2-21) **1m 2f 6y** £2,950.00 (£880.00: £420.00: £190.00) Stalls: Low GOING minus 0.55 sec per fur (F)

				SP	RR	SF
3197^{6}	**Augustan (55)** (SGollings) **6-12-0** MrRThornton(3) (trckd ldrs: led over 1f out: styd on wl)	—	**1**	9/2^{3}	66	54
3200^{6}	**Cuban Reef (48)** (WJMusson) **5-11-7** MrTMcCarthy(2) (hld up: hdwy on ins over 3f out: chal 1f out: nt qckn)	2½	**2**	3/1^{2}	55	43
2564^{3}	**Bold Top (44)** (BSRothwell) **5-11-3b** MrJGoldstein(9) (led tl over 1f out: one pce)	3½	**3**	11/4^{1}	45	33
2512^{4}	**Leif the Lucky (USA) (55)** (MissSEHall) **8-11-10**$^{(4)}$ MrGMarkham(5) (hld up: hdwy over 3f out: effrt 2f out: sn wknd)	8	**4**	8/1	44	32
2884^{4}	**Beano Script (55)** (JHanson) **4-11-10**$^{(4)}$ MrCBHills(8) (plld hrd: sn trckng ldrs: chal over 2f out: wknd over 1f out)	7	**5**	25/1	33	21
2876^{9}	**Clued Up (53)** (PDEvans) **4-11-8v**$^{(4)}$ MrAEvans(6) (lw: hld up: effrt over 3f out: rdn 2f out: sn lost pl)	7	**6**	12/1	19	7
3041^{6}	**Moneghetti (37)** (JLHarris) **6-10-6v**$^{1(4)}$ MrJTyler-Morris(4) (lw: plld hrd: racd wd: sn w ldr: lost pl 3f out: sn t.o)	25	**7**	25/1	—	—
2907^{5}	**Lapu-Lapu (53)** (MJCamacho) **4-11-8**$^{(4)}$ MrKRO'Ryan(7) (trckd ldrs: plld hrd: rdn over 2f out: sn lost pl: virtually p.u)	5	**8**	11/2	—	—

(SP 111.7%) **8 Rn**

2m 14.9 (5.30) CSF £15.94 CT £38.28 TOTE £5.90: £1.40 £1.70 £1.10 (£12.40) Trio £11.50 OWNER Mr Robert Jones (LOUTH) BRED Someries Stud

OFFICIAL EXPLANATION **Lapu-Lapu: was found to be in a distressed state after the race.**

3197 Augustan, making a quick reappearance, found the drop back in distance no problem. (9/2)

3200 Cuban Reef, who is in foal, put two disappointing efforts behind her. (3/1)

2564 Bold Top, still a maiden after thirty-one starts, was still made favourite, which underlines what a low-grade handicap this was. (11/4)

2512 Leif the Lucky (USA), on a losing run of twenty-five, is happier with give underfoot. (8/1)

2884 Beano Script gives his riders problems. (25/1)

2375* Clued Up (12/1: 6/1-14/1)
2907 Lapu-Lapu who never settled, finished in a distressed state. (11/2)

3331 CORNMILL HOTEL (HULL) MAIDEN STKS (2-Y.O) (Class D)
2-45 (2-46) **6f** £3,275.50 (£994.00: £487.00: £233.50) Stalls: Low GOING minus 0.55 sec per fur (F)

				SP	RR	SF
	Priceless (WJHaggas) **2-9-0** FLynch(4) (w'like: cmpt: trckd ldrs gng wl: qcknd to ld fnl 50y: readily)	—	**1**	7/1[3]	78+	27
3094[2]	**Nuclear Debate (USA)** (MrsJRRamsden) **2-9-0** KFallon(9) (trckd ldrs: qcknd to ld 2f out: hdd & no ex wl ins fnl f)	1½	**2**	4/5[1]	74	23
2176[10]	**Moothyeb (USA)** (NAGraham) **2-9-0** RHills(6) (trckd ldrs: effrt 2f out: sn rdn: one pce)	4	**3**	9/1	63	12
3094[8]	**Noble Demand (USA)** (MrsJRRamsden) **2-9-0** OPears(8) (sn outpcd: stdy hdwy over 1f out: kpt on: nvr nr to chal)	¾	**4**	33/1	61+	10
2713[3]	**Boulevard Rouge (USA)** (MJohnston) **2-8-9** JWeaver(7) (led to 2f out: wknd appr fnl f)	3½	**5**	5/2[2]	47	—
	Dangerus Precedent (IRE) (CREgerton) **2-9-0** MTebbutt(2) (unf: s.i.s: wl bhd tl hdwy fnl f)	2½	**6**	20/1	45	—
	Shifty Mouse (DMorley) **2-8-9** MFenton(5) (neat: outpcd ½-wy: kpt on fnl f: n.d)	s.h	**7**	14/1	40	—
3070[9]	**Kettlesing (IRE)** (MWEasterby) **2-8-9** ACulhane(1) (w ldr: sn drvn along: rdn over 2f out: lost pl over 1f out)	12	**8**	33/1	8	—
	Sinch (TDBarron) **2-8-9** KDarley(3) (leggy: s.i.s: a wl bhd)	3½	**9**	14/1	—	—

(SP 130.6%) **9 Rn**

1m 17.1 (2.10) CSF £13.31 TOTE £8.80: £2.10 £1.10 £2.00 (£8.20) Trio £34.00 OWNER The Sun Punters Club (NEWMARKET) BRED Jeremy Green and Sons

OFFICIAL EXPLANATION **Kettlesing (IRE): reported that the filly had run with its tongue tied down, made a noise during the race and stopped very quickly.**

Priceless, a likeable sort, was given a very cool ride. He looked happy to settle for second best until suddenly lengthening his stride, and quickening to show ahead near the line. (7/1: 7/2-8/1)
3094 Nuclear Debate (USA), backed as if defeat was out of the question, kicked for home off the bend and was soon four lengths clear. Treading water inside the last, he was readily overhauled near the line. He might be better suited by a flatter track. (4/5)
2176 Moothyeb (USA), who has changed stables, ran much better than on the soft last time, but lacks any scope. (9/1: 6/1-10/1)
Noble Demand (USA) stayed on under a quiet ride, and will be suited by further. Perhaps more significantly, he needs one more run to qualify for a nursery mark. (33/1)
2713 Boulevard Rouge (USA) showed plenty of pace, but found disappointingly little when tackled. (5/2)
Dangerus Precedent (IRE), a plain sort, was very green and should improve in time. (20/1)
Shifty Mouse, a close-coupled type, ran a satisfactory first race. (14/1: 6/1-16/1)

3332 AUGUST CLAIMING STKS (3-Y.O) (Class F)
3-15 (3-16) **5f** £2,574.00 (£714.00: £342.00) Stalls: Low GOING minus 0.55 sec per fur (F)

				SP	RR	SF
2939*	**Top of The Form (IRE) (80)** (RAFahey) **3-8-4**(7) RWinston(7) (lw: led: clr over 2f out: rdn ins fnl f: unchal)	—	**1**	5/4[1]	83	24
2779[5]	**Bayford Thrust (75)** (JBerry) **3-8-10**(3) PFessey(2) (b: b.hind: sltly hmpd s: bhd tl swtchd outside 2f out: styd on fnl f: nt rch wnr)	2	**2**	9/2[3]	79	20
1980[14]	**Treasure Touch (IRE) (88)** (DNicholls) **3-9-2**(5) IonaWands(1) (chsd ldrs: effrt & swtchd outside over 1f out: kpt on same pce)	hd	**3**	11/8[2]	86	27
3030[8]	**Whisper Low (IRE) (49)** (RHollinshead) **3-8-1** LCharnock(4) (sn outpcd: hdwy over 2f out: sn chsng wnr: wknd fnl f)	3	**4**	100/1	19 t	—
2883[12]	**Flo's Choice (IRE) (40)** (JO'Reilly) **3-8-6** JO'Reilly(3) (trckd ldrs tl wknd 2f out)	4	**5**	50/1	11 t	—
2050[10]	**Weet Ees Girl (IRE) (60)** (TWall) **3-8-1** NCarlisle(5) (chsd ldrs tl wknd 2f out)	5	**6**	50/1	—	—

(SP 109.6%) **6 Rn**

63.4 secs (1.70) CSF £6.31 TOTE £2.10: £1.50 £2.00 (£3.40) OWNER Swan at Whalley Premier Partnership (MALTON) BRED Sean Beston
2939* Top of The Form (IRE), put in to be claimed for a realistic £15,000, after being claimed for £3,000 less at Catterick, was best in on official figures. She hit the traps running and soon showed in a clear lead but, though tying up inside the final furlong, she was never going to be overhauled. (5/4: evens-11/8)
2779 Bayford Thrust was messed about at the start and didn't have the clearest of runs but even so would not have beaten the winner. (9/2)
1254* Treasure Touch (IRE), who has shot up the weights after winning four handicaps already this year, was reappearing after an absence of 54 days. He and Bayford Thrust got in each other's way and though they both stayed on, they were never going to overhaul the winner. (11/8)
Whisper Low (IRE) would have met the winner on 21lb better terms in a handicap. (100/1)
2354 Flo's Choice (IRE), beaten in a selling handicap last time, was put in to be claimed for a ridiculous £10,000 and, as a result, met the winner on 35lb worse terms than she would have done in a handicap. (50/1)

3333 ROGERTHORPE MANOR HOTEL H'CAP (0-90) (3-Y.O+) (Class C)
3-45 (3-45) **1m 4f 8y** £7,700.00 (£2,300.00: £1,100.00: £500.00) Stalls: Low GOING minus 0.55 sec per fur (F)

				SP	RR	SF
2514[14]	**Celestial Choir (83)** (JLEyre) **7-9-10** OPears(3) (hld up: stdy hdwy on outside 2f out: led jst ins fnl f: rdn & r.o)	—	**1**	16/1	97	64
2889*	**Tessajoe (83)** (MJCamacho) **5-9-10** LCharnock(11) (b.hind: hld up: hdwy 7f out: led on bit over 2f out: hdd jst ins fnl f: r.o)	2	**2**	9/1	94	61
2767[5]	**Percy Isle (IRE) (82)** (MRStoute) **3-8-12** KFallon(8) (in tch: effrt over 3f out: styd on one pce fnl 2f)	3	**3**	6/1[2]	89	45
2676[12]	**Brandon Magic (80)** (IABalding) **4-9-7** LDettori(4) (hld up: hdwy over 2f out: styd on fnl f)	½	**4**	8/1	87	54
3053[5]	**Remaadi Sun (82)** (MDIUsher) **5-9-9v** RStreet(6) (hld up: hdwy on outside 5f out: rdn over 2f out: one pce)	½	**5**	13/2[3]	88	55
2963[4]	**Mithak (USA) (85)** (BWHills) **3-9-1** RHills(9) (mid div: drvn along 5f out: nvr nr to chal)	2½	**6**	8/1	88	44
2944[2]	**Rex Mundi (67)** (PDEvans) **5-8-8** JFEgan(5) (chsd ldrs: effrt over 2f out: sn rdn: wknd appr fnl f)	1¼	**7**	10/1	68	35
2865[5]	**Casual Water (IRE) (65)** (AGNewcombe) **6-8-6** SDrowne(10) (hld up: effrt over 3f out: n.d)	3	**8**	9/1	62	29
3125[5]	**Happy Minstral (USA) (88)** (MJohnston) **3-9-4** JWeaver(1) (chsd ldr: chal over 2f out: sn rdn & wknd)	nk	**9**	4/1[1]	85	41
2824[11]	**Get A Life (55)** (JO'Reilly) **4-7-10** JO'Reilly(12) (led & sn clr: hdd over 2f out: sn wknd)	3	**10**	100/1	48	15
3183*	**Gold Desire (55)** (MBrittain) **7-7-10** GBardwell(7) (lw: chsd ldrs: ev ch tl wknd over 2f out: eased)	½	**11**	14/1	47	14
2676[4]	**Heart of Gold (IRE) (88)** (MissSEHall) **3-9-4** AMcGlone(2) (swtg: chsd ldrs: sn drvn along: lost pl 3f out)	nk	**12**	10/1	80	36

(SP 121.6%) **12 Rn**

2m 34.3 (0.00) CSF £142.67 CT £891.85 TOTE £17.00: £3.50 £3.60 £2.10 (£74.20) Trio £193.80 OWNER Mrs Carole Sykes (HAMBLETON) BRED J. L. Eyre
LONG HANDICAP Get A Life 7-4 Gold Desire 7-8
WEIGHT FOR AGE 3yo-11lb

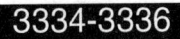

2292 Celestial Choir who won a competitive handicap at York a year ago from a 3lb higher mark, put some disappointing efforts behind her. Nicely handled she was suited by both the serious gallop and the fast ground. She is clearly as good as ever. (16/1)
2889* Tessajoe from a 5lbs higher mark, took it up on the bit turning in, but the back to form winner proved too strong in the closing stages. He has done nothing but improve and is a credit to his yard. (9/1)
2767 Percy Isle (IRE) badly tapped for foot, stuck on at the finish. He seems to have only the one pace and a return to front running tactics looks on the cards. (6/1)
2284 Brandon Magic tailed off on his previous start, has tumbled down the weights. Putting in some good work at the finish, this was a much more encouraging effort. (8/1)
3053 Remaadi Sun did not lie quite as far out of his ground as usual, but his moderate jockey still took the bypass route. (13/2)
2963 Mithak (USA) with the blinkers left off ran another flat race. (8/1)
2865 Casual Water (IRE) who won off a 5lb higher mark at Goodwood a year ago, was never put in the race. The impression was that he will do better soon. (9/1)
3125 Happy Minstral (USA) making a quick reappearance, was awash with sweat in the paddock and soon dropped right out after challenging for the lead turning in. He had disappointed at Leicester a few days after running really well at Catterick two outings ago and he seems to be the type that needs an interval between his races. (4/1)

3334 CHAPLINS CLUB H'CAP (0-70) (3-Y.O+) (Class E)

4-15 (4-17) **5f** £3,980.00 (£1,190.00: £570.00: £260.00) Stalls: Low GOING minus 0.55 sec per fur (F)

				SP	RR	SF
3287*	**Double Oscar (IRE) (69)** (DNicholls) **4-9-10b**(7) [7x] ANicholls(11) (lw: hld up: hdwy on outside over 2f out: edgd lft: styd on wl to ld fnl 50y)	—	**1**	6/1[3]	82	52
3130[2]	**Brecongill Lad (64)** (MissSEHall) **5-9-12** RHills(7) (chsd ldrs: led & edgd lft over 1f out: hdd & no ex towards fin)	1¾	**2**	8/1	71	41
3121*	**Storyteller (IRE) (57)** (MrsJRRamsden) **3-9-2v** [7x] KFallon(4) (lw: chsd ldrs: n.m.r over 1f out: kpt on wl)	1	**3**	9/4[1]	61	28
2895[4]	**Tart and a Half (65)** (JLEyre) **5-9-13v** LDettori(5) (a chsng ldrs: hmpd over 1f out: kpt on wl)	s.h	**4**	9/1	69	39
3208[2]	**Camionneur (IRE) (48)** (TDEasterby) **4-8-10b** PatEddery(9) (s.i.s: hdwy whn nt clr run over 1f out: hmpd: kpt on: nt rch ldrs)	¾	**5**	9/2[2]	50	20
3208[5]	**Rich Glow (53)** (NBycroft) **6-9-1** KDarley(1) (chsd ldrs on ins: sn drvn: nt clr run over 1f out: one pce)	1	**6**	7/1	51	21
3271[3]	**Tutu Sixtysix (34)** (DonEnricoIncisa) **6-7-10** KimTinkler(2) (bhd tl styd on fnl 2f)	nk	**7**	33/1	32	2
2738[15]	**Tropical Beach (60)** (JBerry) **4-9-5b**(3) TEDurcan(10) (sn outpcd: hdwy on outside 2f out: n.m.r & wknd over 1f out)	nk	**8**	20/1	57	27
3130[6]	**Just Dissident (IRE) (64)** (RMWhitaker) **5-9-12** DeanMcKeown(3) (led tl over 1f out: grad wknd)	s.h	**9**	10/1	60	30
3107[4]	**Just Bob (64)** (SEKettlewell) **8-9-5**(7) JennyBenson(14) (s.i.s: bhd tl hdwy on outside 2f out: n.d)	s.h	**10**	25/1	60	30
2738[18]	**Soaked (42)** (DWChapman) **4-8-4b** ACulhane(12) (swtchd lft s: hld up & a in rr)	2	**11**	66/1	32	2
3130[11]	**High Domain (IRE) (65)** (JLSpearing) **6-9-13** JWeaver(8) (chsd ldrs: wkng whn hmpd over 1f out)	s.h	**12**	33/1	55	25
3077[5]	**Shadow Jury (64)** (DWChapman) **7-9-12b** LCharnock(6) (w ldrs: rdn & edgd rt over 1f out: sn lost pl & eased)	3½	**13**	16/1	42	12

(SP 127.8%) **13 Rn**

62.8 secs (1.10) CSF £49.51 CT £136.13 TOTE £9.70: £3.70 £2.30 £1.40 (£59.90) Trio £65.30 OWNER Trilby Racing (THIRSK) BRED Tasia Limited
LONG HANDICAP Tutu Sixtysix 7-2
WEIGHT FOR AGE 3yo-3lb
STEWARDS' ENQUIRY Nicholls susp. 16-17/8/97 (careless riding).
3287* Double Oscar (IRE) having his second outing in three days, overcame a poor draw, sweeping through on the outside, but edging left and tightening up some of those on his inner. Racing with plenty of zest, he won going away and in a matter of strides after the line was six lengths clear. (6/1: 4/1-13/2)
3130 Brecongill Lad who has won off a 1lb higher mark, edged left as he took the lead, contributing to what was an extremely rough race. (8/1)
3121* Storyteller (IRE) under a 7lb penalty, was short of room over a furlong out, but to his credit kept on strongly towards the line. (9/4)
2895 Tart and a Half on a losing run of thirty-five, stuck on after being hampered. (9/1)
3208 Camionneur (IRE) has only won once from forty-two outings now, but he was undoubtedly the unluckiest in what was an particularly rough race. After missing the break, he could not find a run at all, until inside the last. (9/2)
3208 Rich Glow won this event a year ago from a 7lb higher mark. Trapped on the inner, with him it was basically his lack of speed that got him into trouble. (7/1)

3335 MATTY BROWN MEMORIAL MAIDEN STKS (3-Y.O+) (Class D)

4-45 (4-48) **1m 4y** £3,468.75 (£1,050.00: £512.50: £243.75) Stalls: Low GOING minus 0.55 sec per fur (F)

				SP	RR	SF
2960[2]	**Bright Heritage (IRE) (83)** (DRLoder) **4-9-7** PatEddery(3) (mde all: clr 3f out: canter)	—	**1**	1/33[1]	73++	35
3095[12]	**Strength of Vision** (CREgerton) **3-9-0** MTebbutt(2) (hld up: hdwy over 3f out: hung lft & wnt 2nd over 1f out)	18	**2**	33/1[2]	37	—
	Far Atlantic (CADwyer) **4-9-2** KRutter(5) (sn bhd & pushed along: kpt on fnl 2f)	2	**3**	66/1[3]	28	—
2496[9]	**Okra** (JDBethell) **3-8-9** TWilliams(1) (s.i.s: hdwy over 3f out: wnt 2nd over 2f out: one pce)	3½	**4**	66/1[3]	21	—
2783[9]	**Pearl Silk** (TTBill) **4-9-2** TGMcLaughlin(4) (chsd ldrs: wnt 2nd 5f out: lost pl over 2f out)	3	**5**	100/1	15	—
3211[12]	**Jive Boogie** (NBycroft) **3-9-0** JCarroll(6) (chsd wnr 3f: sn drvn along: lost pl over 3f out)	20	**6**	150/1	—	—

(SP 104.6%) **6 Rn**

1m 45.2 (2.80) CSF £1.81 TOTE £1.10: £1.10 £2.00 (£2.10) OWNER Mr John Guest (NEWMARKET) BRED J. Guest
WEIGHT FOR AGE 3yo-7lb
2960 Bright Heritage (IRE) was never out of third gear. (1/33: op 1/20)
Strength of Vision unplaced on his previous two outings, showed a fair bit of knee action. Racing keenly, he still finished second best, but ahead of what? (33/1)
Far Atlantic was tailed off in a claimer last year on her only previous outing. (66/1)
Okra had her only previous run over five furlongs. (66/1)
Pearl Silk was tailed off on her first outing on the Flat proper. (100/1)
Jive Boogie must be a candidate for the worst horse still in training. (150/1)

3336 TALLY HO H'CAP (0-65) (3-Y.O) (Class F)

5-15 (5-18) **1m 4y** £2,805.00 (£780.00: £375.00) Stalls: Low GOING minus 0.55 sec per fur (F)

				SP	RR	SF
3044[9]	**Tipperary Sunset (IRE) (38)** (JJQuinn) **3-7-7**(3) PFessey(12) (s.i.s: hdwy over 2f out: led ins fnl f: styd on)	—	**1**	11/2[3]	50	8
3205[3]	**Warrior King (IRE) (45)** (CADwyer) **3-7-10**(7) AMcCarthy(11) (lw: sn trckng ldrs: led over 1f out tl ins fnl f: kpt on)	nk	**2**	4/1[1]	56	14

3133* **Silent Valley (48)** (MissLCSiddall) **3-8-6v** 6x DeanMcKeown(7) (s.i.s: hld up: hdwy over 2f out: styd on fnl f).1¼ **3** 9/2 2 57 15
2945[11] **Danehill Princess (IRE) (50)** (RHollinshead) **3-8-8** KDarley(6) (hld up: effrt ½-wy: styd on fnl 2f) 3 **4** 14/1 53 11
2757[10] **Tribal Mischief (48)** (DMoffatt) **3-8-3**(3) DarrenMoffatt(2) (s.i.s: hdwy on ins 2f out: n.m.r: kpt on same pce).....2 **5** 25/1 47 5
2669[5] **Falls O'Moness (IRE) (60)** (KRBurke) **3-9-4** JFEgan(1) (hld up: effrt on ins & nt clr run 2f out: rdn & styd on appr fnl f) ....nk **6** 15/2 58 16
2733[6] **Samspet (44)** (RAFahey) **3-7-9**(7) RWinston(5) (chsd ldrs: wknd appr fnl f) ....½ **7** 8/1 41 —
3196[5] **Coral Island (54)** (JGFitzGerald) **3-8-12v**[1] JWeaver(4) (led: edgd lft & hdd over 1f out: sn wknd) 1 **8** 9/1 49 7
3132[7] **Docklands Carriage (IRE) (63)** (NTinkler) **3-9-7** KimTinkler(3) (chsd ldrs: drvn along & lost pl ½-wy)..............1 **9** 16/1 56 14
2315[18] **Bernie's Star (IRE) (46)** (NBycroft) **3-8-4**ow2 JCarroll(9) (chsd ldrs tl lost pl over 2f out) ....3 **10** 33/1 33 —
The Dubious Goose (50) (MrsJRRamsden) **3-8-8** KFallon(13) (trckd ldrs: drvn along over 3f out: lost pl over 1f out) ....6 **11** 13/2 25 —
2182[11] **Sequoia Prince (CAN) (45)** (MBell) **3-8-3v**[1] MFenton(8) (chsd ldrs tl wknd over 2f out) ....2 **12** 14/1 16 —
(SP 125.8%) **12 Rn**

1m 45.6 (3.20) CSF £26.94 CT £102.56 TOTE £9.60: £2.70 £2.20 £2.60 (£25.30) Trio £24.10 OWNER Mrs S. Quinn (MALTON) BRED M. G. Masterson

LONG HANDICAP Tipperary Sunset (IRE) 7-7

2733 Tipperary Sunset (IRE) is only rated 38, but he landed something of a tickle here. (11/2)
3205 Warrior King (IRE) running over his best trip, had to admit defeat near the line. (4/1)
3133* Silent Valley was raised 13lbs after her Nottingham win and will find it even tougher going in future. (9/2)
Danehill Princess (IRE) basically a disappointing filly, had been dropped a whacking 10lbs after her last outing at Leicester. Sticking on at the finish she certainly seemed to stay the trip all right. (14/1)
2544 Tribal Mischief who has been tried at distances up to a mile and a half, has turned in her best two efforts over five furlongs on soft ground at two. (25/1)
2669 Falls O'Moness (IRE) having his eighth outing this year and dropped in the weights and stepped up in distance was punted on. Sticking to the inner, he had a poor run, but would probably have finished no better than fourth anyway. (15/2)
The Dubious Goose gave his rider plenty of problems going to the start. Racing keenly he dropped right out in the straight and might be worth a try in a six furlong selling handicap. (13/2: 4/1-7/1)
Sequoia Prince (CAN) (14/1: 10/1-16/1)

T/Jkpt: Not won; £17,657.11 to Salisbury 8/8/97. T/Plpt: £14.30 (2,107.21 Tckts). T/Qdpt: £7.60 (157.46 Tckts) WG

3337a - 3361a (Irish Racing) - See Computer Raceform

0116a-CORK (Mallow, Ireland) (R-H) (Yielding to Soft becoming Soft)
Sunday August 3rd

3362a DAIRYGOLD PLATINUM STKS (Listed) (3-Y.O+)
4-30 (4-34) **1m 1f** IR £12,900.00 (IR £3,700.00: IR £1,700.00: IR £500.00)

SP RR SF
2446a[5] **Tout A Coup (IRE)** (GACusack,Ireland) **4-9-6** NGMcCullagh (mde all: shaken up under 2f out: r.o.).............— **1** 15/8 1 99+ —
Kilbride Lad (IRE) (MHalford,Ireland) **3-8-10** WJSupple (cl up: 4th½-wy: trckd ldrs st: rdn to chal over 2f out: nt rch wnr u.p ins last: kpt on same pce)....................2½ **2** 10/1 93 —
2989a[4] **On Fair Stage (IRE)** (JOxx,Ireland) **4-9-1** PJSmullen (dwlt: hld up towards rr: hdwy under 4f out: 3rd & effrt 2f out: rdn & no ex ins last: kpt on) ....½ **3** 12/1 89 —
Ridiyara (IRE) (JOxx,Ireland) **3-8-8**ow1 JPMurtagh (in tch: wnt 3rd briefly½-wy: effrt early st: 4th, rdn & no ex over 1f out: kpt on last 100 yds)....................¾ **4** 4/1 2 88 —
Swift Gulliver (IRE) (JSBolger,Ireland) **3-9-1** KJManning (hld up in tch: cl 4th & effrt 3f out: rdn & btn 2f out: eased) ....11 **5** 4/1 2 76 —
1542a[6] **Free To Speak (IRE)** (DKWeld,Ireland) **5-9-4** PShanahan (broke wl: hld up towards rr: rdn & tried to cl early st: no imp fr 2f out) ....1½ **6** 8/1 68 —
No Slouch (IRE) (APO'Brien,Ireland) **3-8-10** CRoche (prom: plld hrd early: 2nd & ev ch st: btn over 2f out: wknd: eased)....................3½ **7** 5/1 3 62 —
(SP 119.3%) **7 Rn**

2m 3.0 OWNER Edmund Loder (NAAS) BRED E. J. Loder
2446a Tout A Coup (IRE) one of the few suited by the desperately heavy ground, made all and won very easily. The Group Three Matron Stakes at the Curragh is her next target. She really enjoyed the ground and was being eased down before the line. (15/8: op 3/1)
Kilbride Lad (IRE) ran his best ever race staying on well from two furlongs out. (10/1: op 6/1)
On Fair Stage (IRE) gained black type by virtue of her ability to act on the ground and she goes up 8lb for this. (12/1: op 8/1)
Ridiyara (IRE) an easy winner of her maiden, was never able to get in a blow. (4/1: op 6/4)
Swift Gulliver (IRE) didn't act on the ground and was eased in the straight. (4/1: op 2/1)
No Slouch (IRE) was another all-at-sea and struggling in the ground from two furlongs out. (5/1: op 2/1)

3363a (Irish Racing) - See Computer Raceform

VICHY (France) (R-H) (Soft)
Wednesday July 30th

3364a GRAND PRIX DE VICHY (Gp 3) (3-Y.O+)
9-25 (9-19) **1m 2f** £24,691.00 (£8,079.00: £4,489.00)

SP RR SF
1554a[4] **Baroud d'Honneur (FR)** (JBernard,France) **4-9-2** FBlondel ....— **1** 120 —
2270a[3] **Bulington (FR)** (H-APantall,France) **5-9-2** OPeslier ....1½ **2** 118 —
2272a[3] **Zero Problemo (IRE)** (BSchutz,Germany) **4-9-2** AStarke ....2 **3** 114 —
5 Rn

2m 5.1 P-M 4.00F: 1.30F 1.10F OWNER Mlle A. Negre BRED Haras d'Etreham
1554a Baroud d'Honneur (FR) was upped in trip and lowered in class. His connections have had this race in mind for some time, and he duly rewarded their patience.

3364a-VICHY (France) (R-H) (Soft)
Thursday July 31st

3365a PRIX LOUIS DESBOUDET (Listed) (4-Y.O+)
9-20 (9-18) **1m 6f** £15,713.00 (£5,387.00: £4,040.00)

				SP	RR	SF
2333⁴	**River North (IRE)** (LadyHerries) **7-8-11** GMilligan	—	1		110	—
	King Cobra (France) **8-8-11** MBoutin	6	2		103	—
2271a³	**Trait De Genie (FR)** (France) **5-8-11** MCesandri	1	3		102	—
						5 Rn

2m 57.9 P-M 8.80F: 2.50F 1.90F OWNER Lady Herries (LITTLEHAMPTON) BRED Lordship and Egerton Studs Ltd
2333 River North (IRE) was found a relatively easy task here and did not fail to make it pay. Held up early, he made progress five furlongs from home to go second behind the clear leader and, ridden along, ran on really well to strike the front inside the final furlong.

3003a-DEAUVILLE (France) (R-H) (Good)
Saturday August 2nd

3366a PRIX DE CABOURG (Gp 3) (2-Y.O)
3-00 (0-30) **6f** £24,691.00 (£8,979.00: £4,489.00)

				SP	RR	SF
	Xaar (AFabre,France) **2-8-11** OPeslier	—	1		105+	—
2639a³	**Charge D'Affaires** (AdeRoyerDupre,France) **2-8-11** GMosse	1½	2		101	—
	Uninhibited (IRE) (SWattel,France) **2-8-8** FHead	2½	3		91	—
2212⁶	**Dernier Croise (FR)** (BJMeehan) **2-8-11b¹** CAsmussen (btn approx 8½l)		5		82	—
						7 Rn

1m 11.7 (3.70) P-M 1.70F: 1.20F 1.40F OWNER Mr K. Abdulla (CHANTILLY) BRED Juddmonte Farms
Xaar looks a top-class horse in the making. A fine-looking individual, he looks tailor-made for the 2,000 Guineas although his connections do not want to talk about the race for the moment following their disappointment with Zamindar. Always close up, he took the lead off the runner-up inside the final furlong and went on to win in style. He appears to have the ability to accelerate on more than one occasion. Connections might miss the Morny and go straight for the Prix Salamandre. This son of Zafonic looks the best two-year-old to be seen out in France so far this year.
Charge D'Affaires was also close up and took control over a furlong out, but could not match the finishing speed of the winner. The colt's trainer was not entirely happy after the race as he thought the lead had been taken too early. He may go for the Prix Morny.
Uninhibited (IRE) made good late progress but never threatened the first two. She finished well clear of the rest and is a filly who is certainly on the upgrade. She will now take her chance in the Prix du Calvados at the end of the month.
2268a Dernier Croise (FR) wore blinkers for the first time but they did not help much. Making all the running, he was a spent force before the furlong marker and does not look up to this standard.

BETTOLE (Varese, Italy) (R-H) (Good)
Sunday August 3rd

3367a CRITERIUM VARESINO MEMORIAL VIRGINIO CURTI (Listed) (2-Y.O)
11-00 (11-00) **7f 110y** £23,142.00

				SP	RR	SF
2822a*	**Timekeeper (USA)** (MBell) **2-9-1** MFenton	—	1		82	—
	Embody (BGrizzetti,Italy) **2-8-11** GForte	1¾	2		74	—
	Sting Umbro (ITY) (GAvvisati,Italy) **2-8-11** SDettori	2½	3		69	—
						9 Rn

0m TOTE 16L: 12L 14L 16L (36L) OWNER Mr C. M. Watt (NEWMARKET) BRED Adelphian Ltd
2822a* Timekeeper (USA) gained his second win in Italy with a very comfortable display. Always prominent behind the leaders, he quickened to lead one and a half furlongs out and ran on well to the line to score impressively.

2097a-COLOGNE (Germany) (R-H) (Soft)
Sunday August 3rd

3368a OPPENHEIM-RENNEN (Listed) (2-Y.O)
3-25 (3-25) **6f** £11,364.00 (£4,545.00: £2,273.00)

				SP	RR	SF
2862⁶	**Ella (IRE)** (LordHuntingdon) **2-8-12** MRoberts	—	1		85	—
	National Academy (GER) (HRemmert,Germany) **2-9-2** KWoodburn	hd	2		89	—
	Blue Marine (GER) (WHaustein,Germany) **2-8-12** AHelfenbein	½	3		83	—
						9 Rn

1m 13.51 (3.71) TOTE 31DM: 16DM 14DM 53DM (86DM) OWNER Coriolan Partnership (WEST ILSLEY) BRED Rocklow Stud
2862 Ella (IRE) made all and just held on in a driving finish from a horse that will almost certainly come on for this.

3369a OSTERMANN-POKAL (Gp 3) (3-Y.O+)
4-45 (4-46) **1m** £22,727.00 (£9,091.00: £4,545.00)

				SP	RR	SF
	Power Flame (GER) (AWohler,Germany) **4-9-2** KWoodburn	—	1		122	—
2821a⁴	**Kalatos (GER)** (AWohler,Germany) **5-9-4** ABoschert	3½	2		117	—
	Sinyar (BSchutz,Germany) **5-9-2** NGrant	¾	3		114	—
2766⁴	**Bold Words (CAN)** (EALDunlop) **3-8-2** MRoberts (btn approx 12 3/4l)		10		—	—
						11 Rn

1m 36.16 (6.16) TOTE 73DM: 22DM 22DM 52DM (317DM) OWNER Rennstall Darboven BRED Gestut Idee
2766 Bold Words (CAN) was in touch until the straight but was soon found out by the strong pace and weakened to finish a very disappointing tenth.

3366a-DEAUVILLE (France) (R-H) (Good)
Sunday August 3rd

3370a PRIX DE POMONE (Gp 2) (3-Y.O+ F & M)
2-30 (2-31) **1m 5f 110y** £33,670.00 (£13,468.00: £6,734.00: £3,367.00) GOING: 0.25 sec per fur (G)

				SP	RR	SF
2104[3]	**Whitewater Affair** (MRStoute) **4-9-4** JReid (broke wl: set gd pce: mde all & r.o wl)	—	**1**		111	54
	Otaiti (IRE) (AFabre,France) **4-9-4** OPeslier (racd in 3rd tl st: rdn 2f out: disp ld 1f out: sn hdd & no ex)	1½	**2**		109	52
2275a[5]	**Legend Maker (IRE)** (AFabre,France) **3-8-6** AJunk (trckd wnr 2f out: hrd rdn & styd on one pce)	nk	**3**		109	40
3000a*	**Kassana (IRE)** (AdeRoyerDupre,France) **3-8-6** GMosse (hld up bhd: wnt wd ent st: hdwy over 2f out: styd on one pce)	3	**4**		105	36
2099a[4]	**Reine Wells (IRE)** (PBary,France) **4-9-4** SGuillot (in rr: fdd st: n.d)	1½	**5**		104	47
1199a[2]	**Maroussie (FR)** (NClement,France) **4-9-4** J-MBreux (racd in 4th: wknd ent st: n.d)	¾	**6**		103	46

6 Rn

3m 3.6 (11.60) P-M 2.30F: 1.50F 1.50F OWNER Mr J. M. Greetham (NEWMARKET) BRED J. M. Greetham

2104 Whitewater Affair looked exceptionally well in the paddock before leading her rivals a merry dance. She made every yard of the running at varying paces and had plenty in hand when tackled in the straight. She was going away from her rivals inside the final furlong like a classy filly and she seems to be on the upgrade. If she recovers well, the Yorkshire Oaks may be on the cards and it will take a decent filly to beat her if she can repeat this sort of performance.

Otaiti (IRE) was warm in the paddock and did not have much gloss in her coat. However, she did nothing wrong in the race and was given every chance. She might now be allowed to take her chance in the Grand Prix de Deauville but looks the perfect type for the Prix de Royallieu in October.

1722a* Legend Maker (IRE) had every chance and raced second until inside the final furlong. She is a good staying filly but rather one paced.

3000a* Kassana (IRE) was held up for a late run but she was much too far out of her ground to ever get in a blow. She did make some late progress but the race was over by the time she arrived on the scene. She might have been feeling the effects of a hard race in the Prix Minerve.

3371a PRIX D'ASTARTE (Gp 2) (3-Y.O+ F & M)
3-00 (3-02) **1m** £33,670.00 (£13,468.00: £6,734.00: £3,367.00) GOING: 0.25 sec per fur (G)

				SP	RR	SF
	Daneskaya (AFabre,France) **4-9-0** AJunk (mid div: rdn ent st: hdwy 2f out: led ins fnl f: pushed out)	—	**1**		111	85
2586[6]	**Rebecca Sharp** (GWragg) **3-9-0** MHills (broke wl: 3rd st: qcknd 2f out: led 1½f out: hdd ins fnl f: r.o wl)	1	**2**		116	83
2766[2]	**Supercal** (DRCElsworth) **3-8-7** JReid (mid div: hdwy st: r.o fnl f)	s.nk	**3**		109	76
3003a*	**Heaven's Command** (NClement,France) **3-8-7** GMosse (prom: hdwy st: r.o fnl f)	¾	**4**		107	74
818a[3]	**Green Lady (IRE)** (AFabre,France) **3-8-7** OPeslier (mid div: u.p 2f out: sltly hmpd: swtchd rt & hrd rdn fnl f)	½	**5**		106	73
2586[2]	**Ocean Ridge (USA)** (SbinSuroor) **3-8-7** LDettori (led tl over 1½f out: sn wknd)	nk	**6**		106	73
1727a[2]	**Basse Besogne (IRE)** (CLaffon-Parias,France) **3-8-7** CAsmussen (a bhd: n.d)	1½	**7**		103	70
2273a[3]	**Whenby (USA)** (MmeCHead,France) **4-9-0** FHead (n.d)	2	**8**		99	73
	Fuenji (FR) (DSmaga,France) **3-8-7** DBoeuf (prom early: r.o wl st: wknd rapidly)	¾	**9**		97	64

9 Rn

1m 39.4 (3.40) P-M 19.80F: 5.80F 3.10F 4.60F (104.60F) OWNER P. Lau (CHANTILLY) BRED Marystead Farm

Daneskaya was brought up the middle of the track with a perfectly-timed challenge. Previous form would suggest that she was not up to this level, but this lightly-raced individual, who is not an easy filly to train, may take her chance in the Jacques Le Marois where the weights will not be so much in her favour.

2586 Rebecca Sharp looked well and ran up to her best. She was raced just behind the leaders and took it up a furlong out before failing to hold the late attack of the winner. This was a good run and her main target is now the Queen Elizabeth II Stakes, and connections will look at both the Jacques Le Marois and the Moulin at Longchamp as a prep. She needs a decent surface to show her best.

2766 Supercal put in a good run and arrived late on the scene having been held up early on. She definitely looks on the upgrade and looks capable of winning a Group Three later on in the season. Her trainer admits that it has taken time to get to know the filly who must be held up to show her best.

Heaven's Command was always close up and stayed on well at the one pace in the final stages. She is genuine and consistent but may not quite stay a mile in decent company.

2586 Ocean Ridge (USA) was a huge disappointment. She was a reluctant leader and, never going well, she was a spent force by the furlong marker. This race may be best forgotten.

3372a PRIX DE CERCLE (Listed) (3-Y.O+)
4-05 (4-07) **5f** £15,713.00 (£5,387.00: £4,040.00: £2,694.00: £1,347.00) GOING: 0.25 sec per fur (G)

				SP	RR	SF
2683[7]	**Struggler** (DRLoder) **5-9-0** LDettori	—	**1**		113	88
	Dyhim Diamond (IRE) (France) **3-8-10** DBoeuf (fin 3rd, s.nk: plcd 2nd)	¾	**2**		110	82
	Linoise (FR) (France) **5-9-1** AJunk (fin 4th, 1½l: plcd 3rd)	1½	**3**		107	81
3023[3]	**Brave Edge** (RHannon) **6-9-0** DaneO'Neill (fin 5th, nk: plcd 4th)	nk	**4**		105	85
2818a[10]	**Bold Effort (FR)** (KOCunningham-Brown) **5-9-0** FSanchez (fin 6th, 1l: plcd 5th)	1	**5**		102	77
1720a[2]	**Roseate Wood (FR)** (UweStoltefuss,Germany) **4-9-1** PHarley (fin 2nd, ½l: disq & plcd 6th)		**6**		112	87

10 Rn

58.4 secs (1.90) P-M 4.00F: 1.90F 2.20F 2.00F (16.80F) OWNER Lord Lloyd-Webber (NEWMARKET) BRED Hesmonds stud Ltd

2526 Struggler led from pillar to post and held on well in the final stages. He is game and very experienced and this was the perfect opportunity for him to open his 1997 account.

3023 Brave Edge never looked like finishing in the frame. Always in mid-division, he ran on at one pace in the final stages.

2818a Bold Effort (FR) was close up but hampered by the runner-up one hundred metres out.

KLAMPENBORG (Copenhagen, Denmark) (R-H) (Good)
Sunday August 3rd

3373a COPENHAGEN GOLDEN MILE (Listed) (3-Y.O+)
2-00 (2-06) **1m** £9,930.00 (£2,979.00: £1,986.00: £1,192.00)

				SP	RR	SF
	Senador (IRE) (LReuterskjold,Sweden) **5-9-4** SusanneBerneklint	—	**1**		94	—
1074a*	**Landsuitor (GER)** (AWohler,Germany) **5-9-4** EDubravka	nk	**2**		93	—

				SP	RR	SF
	Last Dance (DEN) (PiaPallesgaard,Denmark) **6-9-4b¹** JJohansen	s.h	**3**		93	—
2457a⁶	**Hever Golf Glory** (TJNaughton) **3-8-11** PatEddery	3	**4**		87	—
						8 Rn

1m 35.3 TOTE 153Kr: 25Kr 16Kr 20Kr (558Kr) OWNER Mr S. Ekman BRED Dr C. E. Stelling
2457a Hever Golf Glory was never able to get on terms with the leaders. Racing in mid-division, he was fourth into the straight and made his effort over two furlongs out but could only run on at one pace.

3374a SCANDINAVIAN OPEN CHAMPIONSHIP (Listed) (3-Y.O+)
3-05 (3-08) **1m 4f** £59,583.00 (£19,861.00: £9,930.00)

				SP	RR	SF
2333²	**Harbour Dues** (LadyHerries) **4-9-2** PatEddery	—	**1**		117	—
2864*	**Arabian Story** (LordHuntingdon) **4-9-2** DHarrison	nk	**2**		117	—
2559⁴	**Ela-Aristokrati (IRE)** (MHTompkins) **5-9-2** RCochrane	nk	**3**		116	—
						12 Rn

2m 26.2 TOTE 63.20Kr: 20Kr 17Kr 13Kr (89Kr) OWNER Hesmonds Stud (LITTLEHAMPTON) BRED Hesmonds Stud Ltd
2333 Harbour Dues ran an absolute blinder to land this valuable prize very comfortably. Always in touch, this son of Slip Anchor hit the front over a furlong out and soon put a little daylight between himself and his rivals. (/1)
2864* Arabian Story put up a good battling performance. Always close up and tracking the eventual winner, he made his challenge over a furlong out and was hard ridden inside the final furlong, getting up for second in the closing stages.
2559 Ela-Aristokrati (IRE) completed the one-two-three for British trainers here and was quite unlucky not to hang on for second. Held up, he moved into second pace over a furlong out but could find no extra in the closing stages.

1545a-MUNICH (Germany) (L-H) (Soft)
Sunday August 3rd

3375a DALLMAYR COUPE LUKULL (Listed) (3-Y.O+)
2-35 (2-35) **6f 110y** £9,090.00 (£3,636.00: £1,856.00)

				SP	RR	SF
	Nashcash (IRE) (FGang,Germany) **4-8-11** MissSeverineBottani	—	**1**		112	—
2329*	**Tomba** (BJMeehan) **3-8-11** MTebbutt	1	**2**		114	—
	No''ize (GER) (EGroschel,Germany) **6-8-11b** TMundry	2	**3**		105	—
						7 Rn

1m 19.0 TOTE 200DM: 33DM 12DM 24DM (665DM) OWNER Dr M Bottani & H Ochsner BRED Newtonbarry House Stud & Miss S. von Schilcher
2329* Tomba put up a good performance but would have preferred a stronger pace. Always well up with the leaders, he had every chance inside the final furlong but was unable to cope with the speed of the former Con Collins-trained Nashcash.

3376a GROSSER DALLMAYR PREIS-BAYERISCHES ZUCHTRENNEN (Gp 1) (3-Y.O+)
3-50 (3-53) **1m 2f** £82,397.00 (£35,985.00: £17,045.00: £9,470.00: £5,682.00)

				SP	RR	SF
2459a*	**Oxalagu (GER)** (BSchutz,Germany) **5-9-6** AStarke (prom: qcknd to ld over 1f out: drvn out)	—	**1**		122	—
2446a*	**Dance Design (IRE)** (DKWeld,Ireland) **4-9-2** MJKinane (led tl over 1f out: r.o wl u.p: no ex)	½	**2**		117	—
2821a³	**Eden Rock (GER)** (BSchutz,Germany) **3-8-9** TMundry (mid div: kpt on one pce fnl 2f)	3	**3**		114	—
1724a⁴	**Narrabeth (IRE)** (UweStoltefuss,Germany) **4-9-6** DHolland (hld up: some prog fnl 2f: styd on)	1	**4**		115	—
2821a²	**La Blue (GER)** (BSchutz,Germany) **4-9-2** WNewnes (hld up: hdwy 2f out: prog over 1f out: wknd fnl f)	¾	**5**		110	—
2100a⁶	**Needle Gun (IRE)** (CEBrittain) **7-9-6** BDoyle (trckd wnr: wknd 2f out)	¾	**6**		112	—
						6 Rn

2m 4.6 TOTE 39DM: 13DM 11DM OWNER Gestut Rietberg
2446a* Dance Design (IRE) gave a very good account of herself here. She set a good pace and, leading to the distance, ran on well under pressure but could find no extra in the closing stages.
2100a Needle Gun (IRE) was disappointing. He looked to be going well when tracking the winner in the early stages of the race, but when asked the question over two furlongs out, could not quicken and gradually weakened.

2512-HAYDOCK (L-H) (Good to firm)
Friday August 8th
WEATHER: fine and hot WIND: Races 5 & 6 - slight against

3377 WILMSLOW H'CAP (0-85) (3-Y.O) (Class D)
6-10 (6-11) **1m 3f 200y** £3,692.75 (£1,112.00: £538.50: £251.75) Stalls: High GOING minus 0.34 sec per fur (GF)

				SP	RR	SF
	Idrica (82) (JHMGosden) **3-9-6** MJKinane(4) (hld up: dropped rr ½-wy: hdwy u.p 2f out: styd on to ld cl home)	—	**1**	7/2	91	62
2963⁶	**Heart of Armor (80)** (PFICole) **3-9-4** JCarroll(1) (lw: led: hrd rdn appr fnl f: hdd nr fin)	½	**2**	11/4 2	88	59
3259³	**Bally Souza (IRE) (83)** (MJohnston) **3-9-7** JWeaver(5) (hd hld up: hdwy 7f out: jnd ldr 3f out: hrd rdn fnl f: unable qckn)	¾	**3**	5/2 1	90	61
3218¹⁰	**What Happened Was (70)** (MartynMeade) **3-8-8** FNorton(2) (chsd ldr 6f: rdn & wknd over 2f out)	12	**4**	10/1	61	32
1242¹⁰	**Will You Dance (82)** (JLDunlop) **3-9-6** KDarley(3) (bit bkwd: hld up: plld hrd: hdwy 8f out: wknd over 2f out)	3	**5**	3/1 3	69	40
				(SP 111.6%)		**5 Rn**

2m 31.56 (2.16) CSF £12.34 TOTE £4.50: £2.10 £1.90 (£7.20) OWNER Sheikh Mohammed (NEWMARKET) BRED Sheikh Mohammed Bin Rashid Al Maktoum
Idrica, rather surprisingly a drifter in the market seeing that she had won on her racecourse debut last year, did this the hard way and it was due to her undoubted stamina that she was able to gain control nearing the line. (7/2)
2963 Heart of Armor adopted more forceful tactics and they only just failed to succeed. He did prove difficult to wear down but he had been in a battle for the last three furlongs, and that must have taken the finishing punch out of him. (11/4)
3259 Bally Souza (IRE) likes to dictate but she was always losing out on he duel with the runner-up, although it was only late on that she was forced to give best. (5/2)
2645 What Happened Was (10/1: 8/1-12/1)

773* Will You Dance won her maiden well enough but she failed to fire in the mud on her next outing, and she gave the impression this time that this trip could be over-facing her. (3/1)

3378 TARPORLEY CLAIMING STKS (3-Y.O+) (Class F)

6-40 (6-40) **6f** £2,640.00 (£740.00: £360.00) Stalls: High GOING minus 0.34 sec per fur (GF)

Form	Horse	Dist	Pos	SP	RR	SF
3195[3]	**Palacegate Touch (80)** (JBerry) **7-9-10b**[(3)] PFessey(1) (jnd ldr ½-wy: led 2f out: rdn out)	—	**1**	5/2[2]	78	50
3130[12]	**Lord Olivier (IRE) (75)** (WJarvis) **7-9-5** JWeaver(7) (led: rdn & hdd 2f out: rallied nr fin)	1	**2**	7/4[1]	67	39
3287[7]	**Panther (IRE) (62)** (PDEvans) **7-9-1v** JFEgan(2) (hdwy over 2f out: kpt on u.p: nt pce to chal)	1½	**3**	13/2	59	31
2209[5]	**Taragona (54)** (RHollinshead) **4-8-4** FLynch(4) (hung lft 3f out: hrd rdn 2f out: kpt on)	¾	**4**	20/1	46	18
2651[5]	**Best Kept Secret (37)** (LJBarratt) **6-8-2v**[(5)] PRoberts(6) (bhd: effrt & rdn 2f out: nvr able chal)	1¼	**5**	14/1	46	18
2575[5]	**Gopi (63)** (RHannon) **3-8-4**[ow2] DaneO'Neill(3) (prom tl rdn & wknd 2f out)	4	**6**	9/2[3]	36	2
3107[6]	**Rotherfield Park (IRE) (30)** (CSmith) **5-7-7**[(7)] RWinston(5) (lw: a bhd: hrd rdn over 2f out: no imp)	4	**7**	25/1	18	—
3240[14]	**Maysimp (IRE) (35)** (BPJBaugh) **4-8-1**[(3)] DarrenMoffatt(8) (swtg: spd 4f: sn rdn & outpcd)	2½	**8**	50/1	15	—
				(SP 113.7%)	**8 Rn**	

1m 14.01 (2.31) CSF £6.42 TOTE £3.70: £1.70 £1.20 £1.70 (£2.50) OWNER Laurel (Leisure) Ltd (COCKERHAM) BRED The Woodhaven Stud
WEIGHT FOR AGE 3yo-4lb

3195 Palacegate Touch, racing wide of the favourite, joined issue at halfway and, poking his nose in front passing the quarter-mile marker, stayed on willingly under pressure. (5/2: 7/4-11/4)
786* Lord Olivier (IRE), winner of this event twelve months ago, tried to do it from the front again but he was hard at work when headed, and his spirited late rally was to no effect. (7/4: 11/10-2/1)
3287 Panther (IRE), much better when he can get his toe in, ran up to his mark and did not fail for the want of trying. (13/2)
1834 Taragona, returning to sprinting for the first time this season, hung badly left when asked for her effort and, though she did keep running on, lacked the speed to prove troublesome. (20/1)
2651 Best Kept Secret, another returning to sprinting, was always struggling with the pace and was unable to get serious. (14/1)
2575 Gopi ran her usual race and tracked the leaders, but she seemed devoid of speed at the business end of her races and she is still struggling to get it together. (9/2)

3379 COUNTRYWIDE FREIGHT CONDITIONS STKS (2-Y.O) (Class C)

7-10 (7-10) **6f** £4,648.00 (£1,732.00: £841.00: £355.00: £152.50: £71.50) Stalls: High GOING minus 0.34 sec per fur (GF)

Form	Horse	Dist	Pos	SP	RR	SF
	Jazz Club (USA) (PFICole) **2-8-8** FLynch(3) (small: cmpt: bit bkwd: s.s: sn rcvrd: swtchd lft & led over 2f out: pushed out)	—	**1**	8/1[3]	90+	39
2870*	**Hayil (USA) (96)** (DMorley) **2-9-2** JCarroll(6) (hld up: hdwy 2f out: chsd wnr fnl f: no imp)	1¾	**2**	4/5[1]	93	42
2856*	**Friar Tuck** (MissLAPerratt) **2-9-2** KDarley(5) (lw: chsd ldrs: ev ch 2f out: sn rdn: outpcd fnl f)	8	**3**	9/2[2]	72	21
2862[22]	**Rejected (90)** (RHannon) **2-9-2** DaneO'Neill(1) (lw: led: rdn & hdd over 2f out: sn btn)	1½	**4**	9/1	68	17
3226[3]	**Mamma's Boy (74)** (JBerry) **2-8-8**[(3)] TEDurcan(2) (lw: trckd ldrs to ½-wy: sn rdn & lost tch)	5	**5**	20/1	50	—
2648[3]	**Alfiglia (89)** (PJMakin) **2-8-11** MJKinane(4) (swtg: prom over 3f: sn hrd drvn & wknd: t.o)	10	**6**	9/2[2]	23	—
				(SP 117.8%)	**6 Rn**	

1m 13.52 (1.82) CSF £14.51 TOTE £10.70: £3.20 £1.20 (£8.40) OWNER Mr W. S. Farish III (WHATCOMBE) BRED W. S. Farish & Joseph Jamail
OFFICIAL EXPLANATION **Alfiglia: the rider reported that he felt something amiss.**

Jazz Club (USA), a strongly-made colt on short legs, overcame a sluggish start and lack of a previous race to win this in the style of a youngster who looks set to go places. (8/1: 6/1-9/1)
2870* Hayil (USA), ridden with more restraint this time, had let the winner get first run and, though he tried hard, was never able to land a blow. (4/5: tchd evens)
2856* Friar Tuck had his chance two furlongs out but, with the principals increasing the tempo, he quite simply had no answer once the race really developed. (9/2)
2054 Rejected had the speed to lead the way on this step up to six furlongs but he was being ridden along before he was overtaken, and was well outpaced inside the distance. (9/1)
3226 Mamma's Boy was a bit out of his depth here and was fighting a lost cause throughout the final quarter-mile. (20/1)
2648 Alfiglia, thought to need this extra furlong, was in trouble soon after halfway and, according to her jockey, performed as if something was amiss. (9/2: op 3/1)

3380 GATEHOUSE H'CAP (0-85) (3-Y.O+) (Class D)

7-40 (7-40) **1m 2f 120y** £3,601.75 (£1,084.00: £524.50: £244.75) Stalls: High GOING minus 0.34 sec per fur (GF)

Form	Horse	Dist	Pos	SP	RR	SF
2902*	**Eshtiaal (USA) (84)** (JLDunlop) **3-9-12b** KDarley(3) (b.off hind: mde all: qcknd clr 4f out: unchal)	—	**1**	13/8[1]	100	68
3246[7]	**Askern (64)** (DHaydnJones) **6-9-2** AMackay(4) (plld hrd: chsd wnr 7f out: rdn & no imp fnl 2f)	7	**2**	13/2	69	47
2930[5]	**Polar Champ (76)** (SPCWoods) **4-10-0v** MJKinane(5) (chsd ldrs: drvn & outpcd ent st: styd on u.p appr fnl f)	1¼	**3**	11/2[3]	80	58
2890[8]	**Ambidextrous (IRE) (61)** (EJAlston) **5-8-13** JFEgan(6) (lw: hld up in rr: effrt u.p over 2f out: nvr nr to chal)	1¼	**4**	4/1[2]	63	41
3061[2]	**Keep Battling (50)** (JSGoldie) **7-7-13**[(3)] PFessey(2) (swtg: s.s: hdwy on ins over 2f out: wknd appr fnl f)	2½	**5**	4/1[2]	48	26
633[6]	**Obelos (USA) (73)** (MissSJWilton) **6-9-6**[(5)] PRoberts(1) (bit bkwd: chsd ldrs tl wknd over 2f out: t.o)	14	**6**	16/1	50	28
				(SP 112.7%)	**6 Rn**	

2m 13.35 (1.85) CSF £11.76 TOTE £2.50: £1.70 £3.10 (£10.50) OWNER Mr Hamdan Al Maktoum (ARUNDEL) BRED Shadwell Farm Inc and Shadwell Estate Co Ltd
WEIGHT FOR AGE 3yo-10lb

2902* Eshtiaal (USA) has really found his form since forceful tactics were adopted and, in this first handicap, just galloped his rivals into the ground. (13/8)
2660* Askern ran much too free and was soon in pursuit of the winner, but earlier exertions took their toll and it was only the place money he was fighting for in the last couple of furlongs. (13/2: 9/2-7/1)
2594 Polar Champ looked ill at ease cantering to post and he dropped off the pace entering the straight. Driven along, he began to stay on again in the latter stages and does look capable of staying further. (11/2)
2890 Ambidextrous (IRE) performs best when he has plenty of use made of him, but he took a long time to pick up on this occasion and was unable to give his supporters much to shout about. (4/1)
3061 Keep Battling, last to exit from the stalls, made progress up the inside rail in the straight but, with the pace never dropping, had had enough before reaching the final furlong. (4/1)

3381 HAYDOCK PARK PONY CLUB LIMITED STKS (0-70) (3-Y.O+) (Class E)

8-10 (8-10) **1m 2f 120y** £2,762.00 (£836.00: £408.00: £194.00) Stalls: High GOING minus 0.34 sec per fur (GF)

Form	Horse	Dist	Pos	SP	RR	SF
2749[3]	**Davoski (70)** (BWHills) **3-8-11** DHolland(1) (s.i.s: sn drvn along to chse ldr: led 2f out: r.o strly)	—	1	5/1[3]	85	31
3311[2]	**Night Mirage (USA) (70)** (MJohnston) **3-8-10** JWeaver(3) (lw: hld up in rr: hdwy over 2f out: too much to do)	3	2	4/6[1]	79	25
3238[6]	**Herr Trigger (70)** (DrJDScargill) **6-9-5b** JTate(2) (bit bkwd: hld up in rr: hdwy over 2f out: sn rdn: kpt on)	1¼	3	9/2[2]	77	33
2879[6]	**Get The Point (62)** (RHollinshead) **3-8-9** MJKinane(5) (chsd ldrs: hrd drvn 3f out: kpt on same pce)	5	4	8/1	69	15
2832[11]	**Julietta Mia (USA) (66)** (WRMuir) **3-8-3(3)** JDSmith(4) (led: clr over 3f out: rdn & hdd 2f out: sn wknd)	3½	5	14/1	61	7

(SP 112.6%) **5 Rn**

2m 16.4 (4.90) CSF £8.33 TOTE £4.70: £1.70 £1.20 (£2.30) OWNER Mr Robert Ogden (LAMBOURN) BRED Sir Eric Parker

WEIGHT FOR AGE 3yo-10lb

2749 Davoski, stepping back to ten furlongs, was soon being bustled along after missing a beat at the start. Getting the better of the long-time leader two furlongs out, he soon kicked for home and, from then on, there was only going to be one winner. (5/1: op 3/1)

3311 Night Mirage (USA) may have found the ground plenty fast enough but she had all of ten lengths to make up on the leaders turning for home, and the fact that she did get so close was a credit to her. This was her third outing in eight days and it may have been asking too much of a filly. (4/6: 4/5-evens)

3238 Herr Trigger still looks to be coming to himself and, on such a flat track, this trip could be a bit sharp. He can soon recapture his true form. (9/2)

2879 Get The Point, still to get off the mark, looked slow, and he was fighting a losing battle a long way from home. (8/1)

Julietta Mia (USA), very much on her toes in the preliminaries, raced freely and set the pace. She had a useful-looking advantage early in the straight but she had probably done too much too soon, and her stamina gave out entering the last quarter-mile. (14/1)

3382 DEAN DAM H'CAP (0-70) (3-Y.O+) (Class E)

8-40 (8-41) **1m 30y** £3,143.75 (£950.00: £462.50: £218.75) Stalls: Low GOING minus 0.34 sec per fur (GF)

Form	Horse	Dist	Pos	SP	RR	SF
3115[10]	**Baba Au Rhum (IRE) (66)** (IPWilliams) **5-9-11** MJKinane(6) (lw: led after 2f: hrd rdn fnl f: hld on gamely)	—	1	4/1[2]	77	48
2956*	**Interdream (68)** (RHannon) **3-9-6** DaneO'Neill(1) (b.hind: a chsng ldrs: sustained chal fnl f: r.o)	¾	2	100/30[1]	78	42
2845[6]	**Java Red (IRE) (45)** (JGFitzGerald) **5-8-4** KDarley(5) (lw: hld up: hdwy over 2f out: kpt on u.p fnl f)	1¼	3	10/1	52	23
2302[7]	**Wentbridge Lad (IRE) (48)** (ABailey) **7-8-7** DWright(4) (b: b.off hind: hld up: hdwy over 2f out: kpt on u.p ins fnl f)	s.h	4	11/1	55	26
2920[2]	**Shahik (USA) (68)** (DHaydnJones) **7-9-13** AMackay(7) (trckd ldrs: hrd drvn over 2f out: wknd appr fnl f)	3½	5	11/2	68	39
1994[5]	**Riccarton (49)** (PCalver) **4-8-8b[1]** JCarroll(9) (swtg: s.s: sn prom: rdn 2f out: wknd)	4	6	10/1	41	12
3105[6]	**Pleasure Trick (USA) (47)** (DonEnricoIncisa) **6-8-6** KimTinkler(10) (a in rr)	2½	7	9/2[3]	34	5
3264[14]	**Golden Fish (37)** (EJAlston) **5-7-10** FNorton(3) (led 2f: rdn over 2f out: sn btn)	hd	8	25/1	24	—
3213[2]	**Italian Symphony (IRE) (44)** (PDEvans) **3-7-3b(7)** AMcCarthy(8) (hld up: hdwy ½-wy: hrd drvn over 2f out: sn wknd)	s.h	9	16/1	31	—
3105[10]	**Duke Valentino (56)** (RHollinshead) **5-8-12(3)** DGriffiths(2) (lw: bhd fnl 5f: t.o)	8	10	12/1	27	—

(SP 120.6%) **10 Rn**

1m 43.94 (3.34) CSF £16.80 CT £118.92 TOTE £5.10: £2.00 £1.50 £2.30 (£8.00) Trio £26.90 OWNER Mr & Mrs John Poynton (ALVECHURCH) BRED A. Brosnan

LONG HANDICAP Golden Fish 7-6 Italian Symphony (IRE) 7-4

WEIGHT FOR AGE 3yo-7lb

2485 Baba Au Rhum (IRE) got back to winning ways with a very game all-the-way success, but it needed his jockey at his strongest to thwart the persistent runner-up. (4/1)

2956* Interdream had little chance of beating the winner on these terms but he is a progressive sort and, though he is probably better over ten furlongs, gave it his best shot and can soon make amends. (100/30)

2845 Java Red (IRE) never seems to run two races alike but he performed with credit here, and there are more prizes in store when he is in the mood. (10/1)

1575 Wentbridge Lad (IRE), having his first outing for his new stable, ran much better with a professional aboard and, with a bit further to travel, would have gone very close. (11/1: 8/1-12/1)

2920 Shahik (USA) needs a stiffer test of stamina and more yielding ground to produce his best and he was well outpaced when the battle to the line really got underway. (11/2)

1994 Riccarton got very worked up with the application of blinkers and ran far too freely after recovering from a tardy start, and he was a spent force entering the last quarter-mile. (10/1)

T/Plpt: £17.10 (954.66 Tckts). T/Qdpt: £3.30 (380.83 Tckts) IM

3233-NEWMARKET (R-H) (Good to firm)

Friday August 8th

Races 1 & 6 - hand-timed

WEATHER: sunny & hot WIND: almost nil

3383 K & N WAITE CONSTRUCTION H'CAP (0-90) (3-Y.O+) (Class C)

6-00 (6-01) **2m 24y (July)** £5,442.00 (£1,626.00: £778.00: £354.00) Stalls: High GOING minus 0.36 sec per fur (F)

Form	Horse	Dist	Pos	SP	RR	SF
3122[9]	**Arcady (59)** (JLHarris) **4-8-6(5)** RMullen(4) (lw: hld up: plld out & rdn over 2f out: hdwy to ld ins fnl f: r.o)	—	1	6/1	71	37
2850[3]	**Motet (80)** (GWragg) **3-9-3** MHills(5) (hld up: hdwy over 3f out: led over 2f out tl ins fnl f: unable qckn)	½	2	10/1	92	43
3069*	**Here Comes Herbie (66)** (WStorey) **5-9-4** SSanders(6) (hld up: n.m.r over 3f out & 2f out: sn rdn: styd on wl fnl f)	1½	3	7/2[3]	76	42
3122[3]	**Shirley Sue (70)** (MJohnston) **4-9-8** RHills(1) (lw: prom: rdn 4f out: ev ch 2f out: one pce)	s.h	4	11/4[1]	80	46
1100[5]	**Jamaican Flight (USA) (65)** (MrsSLamyman) **4-9-3** PatEddery(3) (led 12f: sn btn)	8	5	6/1	67	33
3010[6]	**Bolivar (IRE) (72)** (RAkehurst) **5-9-10b** LDettori(2) (trckd ldrs: led 4f out: hdd & wknd over 2f out)	4	6	100/30[2]	70	36

(SP 109.6%) **6 Rn**

3m 29.1 (6.10) CSF £51.03 TOTE £8.80: £2.70 £3.50 (£16.50) OWNER Mr J. H. Henderson (MELTON MOWBRAY) BRED A. D. G. Oldrey

WEIGHT FOR AGE 3yo-15lb

OFFICIAL EXPLANATION **Arcady: regarding the improved form, the mare had run too freely last time.**

2589 Arcady did not last home with too much use made of her last time, but was ridden patiently this time and bounced back to her best. (6/1)

2850 Motet had the blinkers dispensed with and this half-mile step up in trip seemed to suit, although the early pace was not over-testing. (10/1)
3069* Here Comes Herbie got into more trouble than he should have done due to the steadily-run race, but was staying on strongly once in the clear. (7/2)
3122 Shirley Sue, dropped half a mile in trip to take advantage of her old mark, found the steady pace against her and was ridden along as soon as the tempo increased. (11/4: 2/1-3/1)
1100 Jamaican Flight (USA) had completed a four-timer over timber since his last run on the Flat, but his usual front-running tactics could not get him clear on this course. (6/1)
3010 Bolivar (IRE) moved down moderately and had to work hard to get to the front, the effort soon petering out. (100/30)

3384 PODINGTON GARDEN CENTRE (S) STKS (2-Y.O) (Class E)

6-25 (6-27) **7f (July)** £3,785.00 (£1,130.00: £540.00: £245.00) Stalls: High GOING minus 0.36 sec per fur (F)

				SP	RR	SF
3212*	**Suggest** (WStorey) **2-9-2** SSanders(1) (lw: mde virtually all: rdn clr fnl f)	—	1	$5/2^{2}$	70	23
2579^{4}	**Won't Forget Me (IRE) (59)** (MHTompkins) **2-8-11** DBiggs(5) (hld up: hdwy over 1f out: r.o fnl f: nt trble wnr)	2½	2	15/2	59	12
2904^{10}	**Filgrave (IRE)** (CADwyer) **2-8-8v**(3) DO'Donohoe(9) (w wnr wl over 5f: one pce)	3	3	25/1	52	5
2394^{6}	**Jazz Singer** (RHannon) **2-8-6** PatEddery(6) (stdd s: hdwy 3f out: outpcd over 1f out: kpt on again nr fin)	3½	4	$13/8^{1}$	39	—
2425^{9}	**Katies Treat (IRE)** (DTThom) **2-8-6v**[1] DRMcCabe(4) (hld up: hdwy over 2f out: wknd ins fnl f)	nk	5	25/1	39	—
1997^{14}	**Dahlidya** (MJPolglase) **2-8-6** JStack(3) (b.hind: swtg: prom: ev ch over 1f out: wknd ins fnl f)	¾	6	25/1	37	—
872^{6}	**Sipping Soda** (KTIvory) **2-8-6** JLowe(2) (dwlt: nvr nr ldrs)	6	7	25/1	23	—
2060^{6}	**Sealed By Fate (IRE)** (JSWainwright) **2-8-11v**[1] MRimmer(8) (plld hrd: prom tl rdn & wknd over 2f out)	1½	8	8/1	25	—
3228^{3}	**Muja's Magic (IRE) (53)** (KTIvory) **2-8-3b**(3) MartinDwyer(7) (b: in tch tl rdn over 2f out: n.m.r & sn btn)	1¾	9	$7/1^{3}$	16	—
				(SP 117.4%)	**9 Rn**	

1m 29.13 (4.13) CSF £18.77 TOTE £3.50: £1.50 £2.00 £4.90 (£13.40) Trio £179.00 OWNER Bellcoil Ltd (CONSETT) BRED F. M. Kalla
Bt in 12,500gns
3212* Suggest seems to have found his feet now, relishing both the trip and the forcing tactics. (5/2)
2579 Won't Forget Me (IRE), with the visor left off this time, got the seventh furlong well and should find a similar race. (15/2)
Filgrave (IRE), a good mover, tried to take the winner on and may have headed him for a few strides around halfway. This step up in trip did seem to suit, although he was leg-weary in the final furlong. (25/1)
2394 Jazz Singer looks to have more stamina than speed on this evidence and, out of a two-mile winner, should stay further in time, despite being by a sprinter. (13/8)
Katies Treat (IRE), visored and stepped up in trip, did rather better than she had in the past without looking to truly stay the distance. (25/1)
Dahlidya, a half-sister to the sprinter Denton Lad, looked to find the seventh furlong beyond her. (25/1)
2060 Sealed By Fate (IRE) (8/1: 6/1-9/1)
3228 Muja's Magic (IRE) (7/1: op 4/1)

3385 BERNARD LLOYD AND PAUL STANBROOK H'CAP (0-85) (3-Y.O+) (Class D)

6-55 (6-55) **6f (July)** £4,659.00 (£1,392.00: £666.00: £303.00) Stalls: High GOING minus 0.36 sec per fur (F)

				SP	RR	SF
3198^{2}	**Mr Bergerac (IRE) (80)** (BPalling) **6-9-13** DHarrison(6) (lw: trckd ldr: pushed along & n.m.r over 2f out: nt clr run over 1f out: qcknd to ld wl ins fnl f)	—	1	$11/4^{1}$	90	47
3280*	**Distinctive Dream (IRE) (69)** (KTIvory) **3-8-9b**(3) 6x MartinDwyer(1) (b: trckd ldrs: led & edgd rt wl over 1f out: rdn & veered lft 1f out: hdd wl ins fnl f)	½	2	$7/2^{2}$	78	31
1029^{6}	**John Emms (IRE) (72)** (MBell) **3-9-1** LDettori(3) (chsd ldrs: rdn & edgd lft whn hmpd 1f out)	1¼	3	8/1	77	30
3130^{3}	**For the Present (72)** (TDBarron) **7-9-5** RCochrane(4) (plld hrd: led over 4f: sn btn)	s.h	4	$11/4^{1}$	77	34
2833^{4}	**Loving And Giving (80)** (HCandy) **3-9-9** CRutter(5) (lw: hld up: plld out wl over 1f out: no imp whn hmpd 1f out)	¾	5	$11/2^{3}$	83	36
2922^{6}	**Wild Palm (67)** (WAO'Gorman) **5-9-0v** EmmaO'Gorman(2) (dwlt: hld up: hdwy over 2f out: btn whn hmpd 1f out)	¾	6	10/1	68	25
				(SP 111.1%)	**6 Rn**	

1m 14.4 (2.40) CSF £11.21 TOTE £3.30: £2.00 £2.20 (£3.90) OWNER Mr P. R. John (COWBRIDGE) BRED Red House Stud
WEIGHT FOR AGE 3yo-4lb
3198 Mr Bergerac (IRE) confirmed the promise of a week ago, but not before giving supporters some heart-stopping moments getting a run. (11/4)
3280* Distinctive Dream (IRE), drawn on the outside, got the run of the race but wandered once in front before suddenly veering across the course when the whip was applied. Given that the winner had found trouble, he might well have held on had he stayed straight. (7/2)
1029 John Emms (IRE) could not quicken up when required and was already drifting when the runner-up went sideways in front of him, causing a concertina effect. This was a tough race for Class D and he deserves a break. (8/1)
3130 For the Present, free going down, set the pace and this probably does not suit. (11/4)
2833 Loving And Giving, a very good mover, was set a very difficult task, being asked to come from the back as the whole field were quickening. (11/2)
2922 Wild Palm again did not get the clearest passage but really needs another furlong. (10/1: 8/1-12/1)

3386 CARWIN MAIDEN STKS (2-Y.O) (Class D)

7-25 (7-26) **7f (July)** £4,045.00 (£1,210.00: £580.00: £265.00) Stalls: High GOING minus 0.36 sec per fur (F)

				SP	RR	SF
	Rabi (IRE) (EALDunlop) **2-9-0** RHills(11) (str: gd sort: bit bkwd: dwlt: hld up: nt clr run 2f out: qcknd to ld over 1f out: sn clr: eased nr fin)	—	1	$2/1^{1}$	91+	27
	The Gene Genie (MJHeaton-Ellis) **2-9-0** SSanders(7) (w'like: hld up: swtchd rt & hdwy over 1f out: r.o: no ch w wnr)	4	2	33/1	82	18
	Rambling Rose (MRStoute) **2-8-9** LDettori(6) (w'like: scope: trckd ldrs: rdn over 1f out: one pce ins fnl f)	1¾	3	$3/1^{2}$	73	9
2562^{7}	**Tensile (IRE)** (LMCumani) **2-8-11**(3) RFfrench(8) (lw: led over 5f: one pce)	1¼	4	$5/1^{3}$	75	11
3201^{15}	**Flight** (LMCumani) **2-9-0** FJovine(5) (w ldr 5f: one pce)	1½	5	25/1	72	8
	Zydeco (IRE) (JLDunlop) **2-9-0** PatEddery(2) (leggy: scope: s.i.s: bhd: rdn 3f out: nvr rchd ldrs)	¾	6	13/2	70	6
	Shape Shifter (IRE) (RHannon) **2-9-0** RHughes(10) (neat: bkwd: chsd ldrs tl rdn & btn over 1f out)	s.h	7	6/1	70	6
1760^{10}	**Festival Flyer** (RBoss) **2-9-0** DHarrison(4) (lw: prom: rdn over 2f out: sn btn)	3½	8	14/1	62	—
	St Enodoc (FR) (JLDunlop) **2-9-0** BDoyle(9) (wl grwn: bkwd: rdn 2f out: a bhd)	1¾	9	25/1	58	—

2509[5] **Santa Court** (RDickin) **2-9-0** CRutter(3) (in tch 5f: sn wknd) ....hd **10** 33/1 58 —
(SP 122.9%) **10 Rn**

1m 28.61 (3.61) CSF £78.38 TOTE £3.10: £1.50 £4.30 £1.30 (£85.70) Trio £84.90 OWNER Mr Hamdan Al Maktoum (NEWMARKET) BRED Neville O'Byrne

Rabi (IRE), a lengthy, attractive newcomer, gave the impression that he was far from fully wound up but did this in great style. He looks one to follow. (2/1: op 5/4)
The Gene Genie, bred to be no great shakes, was taken down steadily after the others and came home really well after a patient ride. (33/1)
Rambling Rose, a half-sister to Mister Pink, is not a great mover but showed enough to suggest she can find a race. (3/1)
2562 Tensile (IRE), allowed to stride along at a sensible pace this time, was gradually left behind from the Dip. (5/1: 7/2-6/1)
3201 Flight, still rather keen to post, was at least under some sort of control this time, and ran much better as a result. (25/1)
Zydeco (IRE), bred to stay well, missed the break and was only really getting going when the race was over. (13/2: 5/2-7/1)
938 Festival Flyer (14/1: tchd 33/1)
St Enodoc (FR), an extremely attractive half-brother to St Mawes, looks to need time to strengthen into his frame and gain full fitness, as he showed precious little in the race. (25/1)

3387 DR. MARTENS NURSERY H'CAP (2-Y.O) (Class D)

7-55 (7-55) **7f (July)** £4,620.00 (£1,380.00: £660.00: £300.00) Stalls: High GOING minus 0.36 sec per fur (F)

				SP	RR	SF
3237[8]	**Acid Test (65)** (WRMuir) **2-8-4**(3) MartinDwyer(2) (lw: a.p: led over 1f out: rdn out)	—	1	16/1	69	22
3025[3]	**Sick As A Parrot (68)** (CADwyer) **2-8-7**(3) DO'Donohoe(6) (lw: w ldr: ev ch over 1f out: edgd lft & unable qckn ins fnl f)	nk	2	6/1 3	71	24
3209[2]	**Shalyah (IRE) (67)** (MrsJRRamsden) **2-8-9** LDettori(4) (dwlt: hld up: n.m.r 2f out & over 1f out: rdn & r.o fnl f: nrst fin)	s.h	3	9/4 1	70+	23
2953*	**Flow By (79)** (JLDunlop) **2-9-7** PatEddery(1) (lw: chsd ldrs: rdn 3f out: one pce appr fnl f)	1½	4	9/4 1	79	32
2516[7]	**Balance The Books (78)** (RHannon) **2-9-6** RHughes(7) (hld up: hdwy over 2f out: nt clr run over 1f out: kpt on ins fnl f)	¾	5	5/1 2	76	29
3025[2]	**Summer Deal (USA) (77)** (PFICole) **2-8-12**(7) DavidO'Neill(3) (led over 5f: sn wknd)	1	6	7/1	73	26
2771[7]	**Jus'chillin' (IRE) (58)** (CADwyer) **2-8-0** NVarley(5) (prom tl rdn & btn 3f out)	16	7	25/1	17	—

(SP 114.7%) **7 Rn**

1m 28.47 (3.47) CSF £97.15 TOTE £25.70: £6.10 £1.90 (£43.90) OWNER Mr A J de V Patrick (LAMBOURN) BRED Cranford Stud
2664* Acid Test went down keenly but got his seventh furlong, although lady luck was on his side. (16/1)
3025 Sick As A Parrot got off on terms this time but, hard as he tried, could never quite get to the winner. (6/1)
3209 Shalyah (IRE), up in trip which certainly ought to suit, did not get the clearest of runs when starting her move and probably should have won. (9/4)
2953* Flow By was making hard work of this some way from home, but kept on trying and should stay further. (9/4)
1149* Balance The Books, given a more patient ride this time, was never given the racing room she needs and the situation was as good as accepted by the time daylight came. She is no forlorn hope off this sort of mark. (5/1: 9/1-4/1)
3025 Summer Deal (USA), able to lead this time, did a little too much in front and failed to last home. (7/1)

3388 RICHARD BOLTON INSURANCE GROUP CONDITIONS STKS (3-Y.O+) (Class C)

8-25 (8-25) **1m 2f (July)** £4,848.40 (£1,795.60: £862.80: £354.00: £142.00: £57.20) Stalls: High GOING minus 0.36 sec per fur (F)

				SP	RR	SF
720a[3]	**Annus Mirabilis (FR)** (SbinSuroor) **5-9-7v** LDettori(2) (lw: trckd ldr: led 2f out: comf)	—	1	8/11 1	113+	52
3017[4]	**Sarayir (USA) (96)** (MajorWRHern) **3-8-2** RHills(4) (lw: plld hrd: trckd ldrs: rdn over 1f out: no imp ins fnl f)	1½	2	13/2 3	101	31
2766[5]	**Harry Wolton (103)** (HRACecil) **3-8-12** WRyan(1) (hld up: hdwy 2f out: r.o fnl f)	1¾	3	7/1	108	38
1836[3]	**Rickenbacker (IRE)** (PWChapple-Hyam) **3-8-10** SWhitworth(5) (chsd ldrs: rdn over 2f out: one pce)	2½	4	20/1	102	32
2345[2]	**Barnum Sands (105)** (JLDunlop) **3-8-7b**[1] PatEddery(6) (led: rdn over 2f out: sn hdd & wknd)	3½	5	5/1 2	93	23
787[3]	**Behaviour (105)** (MrsJCecil) **5-9-2** MHills(3) (hld up: rdn 2f out: no imp)	3½	6	12/1	88	27

(SP 112.8%) **6 Rn**

2m 6.6 (3.00) CSF £5.62 TOTE £1.70: £1.30 £2.40 (£3.30) OWNER Godolphin (NEWMARKET) BRED Darley Stud Management Co Ltd
WEIGHT FOR AGE 3yo-9lb
720a Annus Mirabilis (FR) had run with distinction in Japan and Hong Kong since his last effort on these shores, and was returning after a summer break. This was a good confidence booster which he took well and the plan is to go for the Winter Hill Stakes at Windsor, a race which he won last year before another spell of globetrotting. (8/11)
3017 Sarayir (USA) got pretty warm on a sultry night, but went down well and did enough to suggest that this is now her best trip. A victory this season would improve her stud value but she has clearly trained on, without being out of the top drawer as some had hoped. (13/2)
2766 Harry Wolton ran a cracking race but showed the difficulty 'twilight' horses face, as his trainer could presumably find no alternative to running in a race that he could not win on the book. His good effort could easily see his handicap mark go higher still. (7/1: 5/1-8/1)
1836 Rickenbacker (IRE), a very good mover, acquitted himself well in such company, but may not be easy to place. (20/1)
2345 Barnum Sands, blinkered for the first time, was keen going down and set a strong pace until the effort took its toll. Once his chance was gone, he was not knocked about. (5/1: 3/1-11/2)
787 Behaviour, off since April, didn't move to post well and never looked like improving from the rear once the chips were down. (12/1)

T/Plpt: £777.30 (26.05 Tckts). T/Qdpt: £19.30 (73.85 Tckts) Dk

3202-SALISBURY (R-H) (Good to soft, Good patches)
Friday August 8th

WEATHER: very hot WIND: almost nil

3389 MORRISTON MAIDEN STKS (3-Y.O F) (Class D)

2-00 (2-03) **1m** £3,535.00 (£1,060.00: £510.00: £235.00) Stalls: High GOING minus 0.13 sec per fur (G)

				SP	RR	SF
2537[2]	**Desert Beauty (IRE) (76)** (MRStoute) **3-8-11** PatEddery(10) (chsd ldr: led 2f out: hrd rdn over 1f out: r.o wl)	—	1	10/11 1	68	27
3037[5]	**Villarica (IRE) (70)** (PWChapple-Hyam) **3-8-8**(3) RHavlin(2) (hld up: chsd wnr wl over 1f out: ev ch ins fnl f: r.o)	¾	2	7/1 3	67	26
	Sunny Isle (CFWall) **3-8-11** SSanders(5) (leggy: lt-f: rdn over 2f out: hdwy over 1f out: unable qckn)	2½	3	16/1	62	21
	Hibernica (IRE) (GBBalding) **3-8-11** SDrowne(7) (hld up: rdn over 2f out: one pce)	1	4	25/1	60	19
	Beacon Silver (LordHuntingdon) **3-8-11** MRoberts(4) (str: bit bkwd: a.p: rdn 2f out: wknd over 1f out)	2½	5	10/1	55	14

2846[6]	**Rosa Royale** (MrsJCecil) **3-8-8**(3) MartinDwyer(6) (nvr nr to chal)	1¾	**6**	25/1	51	10
2665[12]	**Curzon Street (67)** (DRCElsworth) **3-8-11** AClark(3) (led 6f)	1½	**7**	14/1	48	7
2506[7]	**Spirit Lady** (JSKing) **3-8-8**(3) RFfrench(8) (a bhd)	7	**8**	33/1	34	—
2832[4]	**Lonely Heart (75)** (DRCElsworth) **3-8-11c** RHughes(1) (s.s: hdwy 7f out: hung bdly rt over 2f out: eased whn btn over 1f out)	1¾	**9**	3/1 2	31	—
1823[W]	**Cherrymentary** (KOCunningham-Brown) **3-8-11** TSprake(9) (leggy: lt-f: a bhd)	22	**10**	25/1	—	—

(SP 126.0%) **10 Rn**

1m 45.85 (5.85) CSF £7.95 TOTE £2.10: £1.10 £1.60 £5.30 (£5.10) Trio £55.50 OWNER Lord Weinstock (NEWMARKET) BRED Ballymacoll Stud Farm Ltd

2537 Desert Beauty (IRE), whose connections were a bit worried the ground would be too soft for her, put up a workmanlike display over a trip that looks rather on the sharp side for her. (10/11: evens-5/4)

3037 Villarica (IRE) threw down her challenge from below the distance but, despite giving her all, just failed to master the winner. She is certainly one of the stable's lesser lights but should be capable of finding a small race. (7/1: op 9/2)

Sunny Isle, a sparely-made filly, moved up below the distance but failed to find another gear in the final furlong. (16/1)

Hibernica (IRE), whose only previous run was over an inadequate six furlongs at Newbury last October where she showed nothing, chased the leaders but could only struggle on at one pace in the final quarter-mile. (25/1)

Beacon Silver, a sturdy filly, did not look fully wound up and so it proved as she dropped away approaching the final furlong, having played a leading role to that point. (10/1: 7/1-11/1)

1988 Curzon Street (14/1: op 8/1)

2832 Lonely Heart (3/1: op 5/1)

3390 H.S. LESTER MEMORIAL CHALLENGE CUP H'CAP (0-70) (3-Y.O) (Class E)

2-30 (2-30) **1m 4f** £3,070.25 (£917.00: £438.50: £199.25) Stalls: High GOING minus 0.13 sec per fur (G)

				SP	RR	SF
3129*	**Running Free (IRE) (50)** (MJFetherston-Godley) **3-8-6** 5x DHolland(1) (mde all: hrd rdn over 1f out: r.o wl)	—	**1**	9/2 2	55	10
1877[5]	**Palaemon (55)** (GBBalding) **3-8-11v** SDrowne(3) (lw: rdn over 5f out: hdwy over 3f out: unable qckn)	1¾	**2**	5/1 3	58	13
2487*	**Come Together (65)** (DWPArbuthnot) **3-9-2**(5) CLowther(7) (hld up: chsd wnr 3f out: hrd rdn over 1f out: one pce)	s.h	**3**	7/4 1	68	23
1866[8]	**Puteri Wentworth (64)** (MissGayKelleway) **3-9-3**(3) RFfrench(6) (b.hind: hld up: rdn 4f out: one pce)	s.h	**4**	13/2	67	22
2004[9]	**Quarterstaff (60)** (CFWall) **3-9-2** SSanders(5) (hdwy over 2f out: wknd over 1f out)	6	**5**	8/1	55	10
2667[7]	**Saltimbanco (45)** (RAkehurst) **3-8-1** NAdams(4) (a.p: rdn over 6f out: chsd wnr 5f out to 3f out: sn wknd)	5	**6**	12/1	33	—
2607[5]	**Bonne Ville (57)** (BPalling) **3-8-13** TSprake(2) (chsd wnr 7f: wknd over 3f out)	4	**7**	10/1	40	—

(SP 112.4%) **7 Rn**

2m 41.9 (10.90) CSF £23.68 TOTE £3.80: £1.60 £2.10 (£10.60) OWNER The BMH Partnership (EAST ILSLEY) BRED Mrs B. M. Browne

3129* Running Free (IRE) followed up his Nottingham selling victory of last week with a pillar-to-post victory. Responding to pressure approaching the final furlong, in the end he won cosily in a very poor event which was no better than a seller. (9/2)

1877 Palaemon, the second off the bridle, moved up over three furlongs from home but was then made to look very one-paced, if just winning the battle for second prize. Not too much should be read into this as he is basically a very moderate performer. (5/1)

2487* Come Together, who showed her first piece of worthwhile form when winning on soft ground at Warwick last time out, again had some cut. Moving into second place three furlongs from home, she failed to find another gear and just lost out in a three-way battle for second place. She does look short on acceleration. (7/4)

Puteri Wentworth, off the bridle half a mile from home, was made to look very one-paced, even in this bad race. (13/2: 4/1-7/1)

Quarterstaff got the longer trip he has been looking for but still did not run much better. He is just a very poor performer. (8/1)

Saltimbanco, off the bridle turning into the long straight, showed in second place for a brief while but had been hung out to dry over two furlongs from home. He has crashed 27lb in the handicap since the beginning of the season but there is still no glimmer of a return to form. (12/1)

3391 CHEVIOT LIMITED STKS (0-90) (3-Y.O+) (Class C)

3-00 (3-01) **1m** £5,085.00 (£1,530.00: £740.00: £345.00) Stalls: High GOING minus 0.13 sec per fur (G)

				SP	RR	SF
3274*	**Atlantic Desire (IRE) (90)** (MJohnston) **3-8-13** 3x DHolland(5) (mde virtually all: all out)	—	**1**	5/2 1	100	36
2601[8]	**Rapier (87)** (RHannon) **3-8-10** RHughes(4) (lw: hdwy over 2f out: hrd drvn over 1f out: ev ch ins fnl f: unable qckn)	1	**2**	6/1	95	31
2133[10]	**Flamboyance (USA) (88)** (JRFanshawe) **3-8-7** PatEddery(3) (a.p: chsd wnr over 2f out: hrd rdn over 1f out: ev ch ins fnl f: one pce)	1¾	**3**	4/1	89	25
3150[6]	**Brilliant Red (90)** (PRHedger) **4-9-6** AMcGlone(2) (w wnr over 5f: swtchd rt & hrd rdn over 1f out: one pce)	½	**4**	7/2 3	94	37
2877[2]	**Muhtafel (90)** (JLDunlop) **3-8-13** RHills(1) (lw: hld up: rdn over 3f out: sn wknd)	18	**5**	11/4 2	58	—

(SP 111.7%) **5 Rn**

1m 45.04 (5.04) CSF £15.67 TOTE £3.00: £1.50 £2.10 (£14.50) OWNER Atlantic Racing Ltd (MIDDLEHAM) BRED Hamwood Stud

WEIGHT FOR AGE 3yo-7lb

OFFICIAL EXPLANATION **Muhtafel: no explanation offered.**

3274* Atlantic Desire (IRE) certainly takes her races extremely well - this was her third outing in a week. Adopting her front-running role, she certainly had another hard race - she was hit thirteen times in the last two furlongs - but managed to keep her rivals at bay. She deserves a break. (5/2)

2013 Rapier will certainly not forget this race in a hurry. Taking closer order over a quarter of a mile from home, his jockey got down to some serious work from below the distance and administered twelve cracks of the whip from that point. Nevertheless, he had every chance inside the final furlong, before tapped for toe. (6/1)

1875 Flamboyance (USA), with 3lb or more to spare on her rivals on official adjusted ratings, was one of three with every chance inside the final furlong, before failing to find another gear. (4/1)

3150 Brilliant Red may well have been feeling the effects of his hard race at Goodwood last week, for he failed to quicken in the last two furlongs. (7/2)

2877 Muhtafel failed to cope with this easier surface and was in trouble over three furlongs from home. (11/4)

3392 KNIGHTS & COMPANY H'CAP (0-80) (3-Y.O+) (Class D)

3-30 (3-31) **1m** £3,678.00 (£1,104.00: £532.00: £246.00) Stalls: High GOING minus 0.13 sec per fur (G)

				SP	RR	SF
2678[13]	**Mihriz (IRE) (60)** (RAkehurst) **5-8-10** AClark(4) (b.nr hind: swtg: hdwy on ins over 3f out: led over 2f out: r.o wl)	—	**1**	8/1 3	79	38
2947*	**Yalta (IRE) (78)** (RCharlton) **4-10-0b** PatEddery(10) (swtg: led 6f out tl over 2f out: rdn over 1f out: unable qckn)	5	**2**	11/2 2	87	46

				SP	RR	SF
3138[3]	**Al Masroor (USA) (77)** (JWPayne) **3-9-6** DeanMcKeown(12) (hld up: rdn over 2f out: one pce)	1¼	**3**	8/1[3]	84	36
3138[2]	**Duello (65)** (MBlanshard) **6-9-1** MRoberts(3) (rdn over 3f out: hdwy over 1f out: eased whn btn fnl f)	2	**4**	7/4[1]	68	27
	Lord Oberon (IRE) (58) (JAkehurst) **9-8-8** GCarter(6) (b: bit bkwd: nvr nr to chal)	6	**5**	20/1	49	8
3014[6]	**Kristal Bridge (73)** (PWHarris) **3-8-11**(5) CLowther(1) (a.p: rdn over 3f out: wknd over 1f out)	nk	**6**	16/1	63	15
3115[8]	**Sovereigns Court (58)** (LGCottrell) **4-8-8** AMunro(5) (hdwy over 2f out: wknd over 1f out)	s.h	**7**	11/2[2]	48	7
2848[13]	**Warren Knight (49)** (CAHorgan) **4-7-10**(3) RFfrench(11) (nvr nrr)	¾	**8**	25/1	37	—
3044[7]	**Impala (67)** (WGMTurner) **3-8-7**(3) RHavlin(9) (lw: prom over 5f)	9	**9**	14/1	37	—
2557[20]	**Broughtons Turmoil (75)** (BRMillman) **8-9-11** TSprake(2) (swtg: led 2f: wknd over 2f out)	8	**10**	14/1	29	—
3053[8]	**Ela-Yie-Mou (IRE) (72)** (SDow) **4-9-8** RHughes(7) (lw: s.s: a bhd)	7	**11**	40/1	12	—
3135[5]	**Dances With Hooves (66)** (DJSffrenchDavis) **5-9-2b[1]** WJO'Connor(8) (bhd fnl 3f)	3½	**12**	25/1	—	—
				(SP 123.5%)	**12 Rn**	

1m 44.61 (4.61) CSF £46.90 CT £345.49 TOTE £11.80: £3.00 £2.60 £1.70 (£41.40) Trio £92.20 OWNER Normandy Developments (London) (EPSOM) BRED Shadwell Estate Company Limited

WEIGHT FOR AGE 3yo-7lb

OFFICIAL EXPLANATION **Mihriz (IRE): regarding the improved form, the trainer reported that the gelding had not liked being bustled along last time.**

1166 Mihriz (IRE) bounced back to form after flopping last time out and, cruising into the lead over a quarter of a mile from home, was bustled along to assert his authority. (8/1)

2947* Yalta (IRE) again found the blinkers helping and was soon at the head of affairs. Collared over a quarter of a mile from home, he proved no match for the winner. (11/2)

3138 Al Masroor (USA) chased the leaders but could only go up and down in the same place in the last two furlongs. (8/1)

3138 Duello, set to rise 3lb in future handicaps, was being pushed along at the back of the field from halfway. He did pick up ground from below the distance but, having got into fourth place, could then make no further impression and his jockey was easy on him in the final furlong. He is probably best at seven furlongs but he is a very frustrating character who is extremely difficult to win with. (7/4)

Lord Oberon (IRE), off the course for two years and now in the OAP category, never threatened to get into it. All eight of his wins to date have come over a mile. (20/1)

2731 Kristal Bridge was taking a drop in distance for this handicap debut and, after racing in close contention, had shot her bolt below the distance. (16/1)

3393 SUTHERLAND H'CAP (0-70) (3-Y.O+ F & M) (Class E)

4-05 (4-06) **6f** £3,226.25 (£965.00: £462.50: £211.25) Stalls: High GOING minus 0.13 sec per fur (G)

				SP	RR	SF
2721[5]	**Supreme Thought (55)** (LGCottrell) **5-9-1** MFenton(8) (mde all: rdn over 1f out: r.o wl)	—	**1**	7/1	64	50
2958[6]	**Celandine (53)** (AndrewTurnell) **4-8-8**(5) ADaly(9) (rdn 2f out: swtchd lft over 1f out: hdwy fnl f: r.o wl)	2	**2**	20/1	57	43
3032[4]	**Sylvan Dancer (IRE) (58)** (CFWall) **3-9-0** SSanders(3) (swtg: hld up: chsd wnr over 1f out: hrd rdn: unable qckn)	s.h	**3**	7/1	62	44
3092[13]	**Nellie North (48)** (GMMcCourt) **4-8-5**(3) MartinDwyer(2) (lw: a.p: rdn over 1f out: one pce)	1	**4**	8/1	49	35
3082[4]	**Step Cn Degas (56)** (MJFetherston-Godley) **4-8-13**(3) RFfrench(1) (hld up: rdn over 2f out: one pce)	2½	**5**	11/4[1]	50	36
2906[3]	**Magic Lake (37)** (EJAlston) **4-7-8v**(3) MBaird(6) (hdwy over 2f out: wknd ins fnl f)	2	**6**	11/2[3]	26	12
1969[7]	**Into Debt (36)** (JRPoulton) **4-7-3b[1]**(7) RBrisland(10) (swtg: s.s: nvr nr to chal)	1	**7**	50/1	22	8
2945[4]	**Tayovullin (IRE) (65)** (HMorrison) **3-9-2**(5) CLowther(4) (b.hind: prom over 4f)	1½	**8**	14/1	47	29
2921[11]	**Will To Win (52)** (PGMurphy) **3-8-8** SDrowne(7) (hld up: rdn 2f out: sn wknd)	3½	**9**	9/1	25	7
2491[3]	**Savona (IRE) (68)** (PJMakin) **3-9-10** PatEddery(5) (lw: a bhd)	4	**10**	9/2[2]	30	12
				(SP 119.7%)	**10 Rn**	

1m 15.8 (2.80) CSF £126.38 CT £956.37 TOTE £7.80: £2.00 £5.20 £2.00 (£57.70) Trio £261.90 OWNER Mr L. G. Cottrell (CULLOMPTON) BRED Derek Simister

LONG HANDICAP Into Debt 7-4

WEIGHT FOR AGE 3yo-4lb

Supreme Thought enjoyed these conditions and, making all the running, was rousted along to belatedly lose her maiden tag. (7/1)

2958 Celandine, down 17lb since the start of the season, was still at the back of the field two furlongs from home. She only began to motor inside the distance and came storming through to snatch second prize right on the line. (20/1)

3032 Sylvan Dancer (IRE), dropped 11lb since the beginning of the season, moved into second place below the distance but she failed to reel in the winner and was caught for second prize right on the line. (7/1)

2852 Nellie North was never far away but lack of acceleration really is the stumbling block with her, and that was again the case here. She is very difficult to win with as one victory from twenty-seven starts testifies. (8/1)

3082 Step On Degas chased the leaders but could only struggle on in her own time in the last two furlongs. She has just one win to her name on turf. (11/4: op 6/1)

2906 Magic Lake, who showed promise last time out, took closer order from halfway but had nothing left in reserve inside the final furlong. One win from twenty-eight starts says it all. (11/2: 4/1-6/1)

3394 AXMINSTER 100 APPRENTICE H'CAP (0-70) (3-Y.O+) (Class G)

4-35 (4-35) **6f 212y** £2,193.00 (£623.00: £309.00) Stalls: High GOING minus 0.13 sec per fur (G)

				SP	RR	SF
3091[3]	**Ring the Chief (35)** (MDIUsher) **5-7-12**(5)ow1 GHannon(6) (swtg: led over 5f out: rdn out)	—	**1**	100/30[2]	48	22
3227[4]	**Delight of Dawn (47)** (EAWheeler) **5-8-12**(3) SCarson(8) (hld up: chsd wnr wl over 1f out: ev ch ins fnl f: r.o)	hd	**2**	5/2[1]	60	35
2848[9]	**River Seine (FR) (40)** (SGKnight) **5-8-3**(5) RCody-Boutcher(2) (swtg: dwlt: hdwy 5f out: hrd rdn over 1f out: unable qckn)	4	**3**	5/1	44	19
2721[12]	**Arnie (IRE) (40)** (JRPoulton) **5-8-3**(5) RBrisland(3) (no hdwy fnl 3f)	7	**4**	8/1	28	3
3016[10]	**Silent Symphony (28)** (MrsSDWilliams) **5-7-7**(3) JFowle(5) (prom over 4f)	4	**5**	50/1	6	—
2721[10]	**Summerville Wood (62)** (PMooney) **3-9-5**(5) PFitzsimons(1) (a bhd)	3½	**6**	9/2[3]	32	1
2958[7]	**Gwespyr (55)** (RHannon) **4-9-4**(5) PDobbs(7) (sme hdwy over 2f out: sn wknd)	6	**7**	8/1	12	—
2777[5]	**Melos (28)** (GThorner) **4-7-5**(5) ANicholls(4) (led over 1f: wknd 4f out: t.o)	dist	**8**	50/1	—	—
				(SP 112.6%)	**8 Rn**	

1m 30.75 (4.75) CSF £10.66 CT £35.53 TOTE £3.70: £1.20 £1.30 £2.20 (£3.50) OWNER Mr G. A. Summers (WANTAGE) BRED Mrs Trisha Dunbar

LONG HANDICAP Melos 7-7

WEIGHT FOR AGE 3yo-6lb

3091 Ring the Chief appreciated the conditions and, soon at the head of affairs, was pushed along to keep the runner-up at bay. (100/30)

3227 Delight of Dawn moved into second place early in the final quarter-mile. She had every chance inside the final furlong and, although her rider looked tidy, he was not that strong and the combination just failed to get on top. Five of her seven wins have come in sellers. (5/2)
349 River Seine (FR) was soon in a handy position but, despite her rider's efforts, failed to quicken in the last furlong and a half. She has yet to win on turf. (5/1)
2115* Arnie (IRE) was made to look very slow in the last three furlongs. (8/1)

T/Jkpt: £20,360.40 (0.1 Tckts); £25,808.99 to Newmarket 9/8/97. T/Plpt: £172.80 (120.68 Tckts). T/Qdpt: £64.90 (16.28 Tckts) AK

3040-WOLVERHAMPTON (L-H) (Standard)
Friday August 8th
WEATHER: sunny WIND: almost nil

3395 DERBYSHIRE NURSERY H'CAP (2-Y.O) (Class E)
2-20 (2-21) **7f (Fibresand)** £3,226.25 (£965.00: £462.50: £211.25) Stalls: Low GOING: 0.43 sec per fur (SLW)

				SP	RR	SF
3019^{5}	**Clermont City (IRE) (64)** (PWChapple-Hyam) **2-8-12** DHarrison(2) (lw: hld up: rdn 4f out: hdwy over 3f out: led over 2f out: drvn out)	—	**1**	14/1	66	19
2681^{9}	**Gralmano (IRE) (62)** (NPLittmoden) **2-8-10** TGMcLaughlin(9) (hdwy 4f out: hung lft ins fnl f: r.o)	1¼	**2**	10/1^{3}	61	14
2500*	**Celtic Comfort (73)** (PCHaslam) **2-9-7** LCharnock(1) (a.p: led 3f out tl over 2f out: r.o one pce)	nk	**3**	5/1^{2}	72	25
2926^{4}	**Tightrope (67)** (SirMarkPrescott) **2-9-1** GDuffield(8) (lw: rdn 4f out: hdwy over 3f out: one pce fnl 2f)	3	**4**	4/6^{1}	59	12
2565^{7}	**Impulse (IRE) (68)** (APJarvis) **2-9-2** DWright(10) (hdwy over 3f out: wknd 2f out)	6	**5**	16/1	46	—
2914^{2}	**Edna's Gift (IRE) (57)** (JBerry) **2-8-2**(3) PFessey(4) (lw: hdwy on ins 3f out: wknd 2f out)	5	**6**	20/1	24	—
3076^{3}	**Percy (68)** (JFBottomley) **2-9-2** NCarlisle(5) (b: bhd fnl 3f)	½	**7**	20/1	33	—
1945^{5}	**Malozza (70)** (PDEvans) **2-9-4b^{1}** JFEgan(6) (b: led after 1f: hdd 3f out: wknd over 2f out)	2½	**8**	20/1	30	—
2914^{4}	**Sixth Avenue (IRE) (49)** (RMWhitaker) **2-7-4**(7)ow1 PDoe(3) (led 1f: wknd over 3f out: t.o)	16	**9**	25/1	—	—
3076^{2}	**Persian Fortune (64)** (WGMTurner) **2-8-9**(3) DSweeney(7) (lw: bhd fnl 3f: t.o)	dist	**10**	14/1	—	—

(SP 123.1%) **10 Rn**

1m 34.3 (9.60) CSF £129.90 CT £755.50 TOTE £26.20: £4.70 £1.90 £2.00 (£91.70) Trio £156.70; £6.62 to Newmarket 9/8/97 OWNER Miss Fiona Feeley (MARLBOROUGH) BRED Mrs C. A. Waters
LONG HANDICAP Sixth Avenue (IRE) 7-9
3019 Clermont City (IRE) found the combination of seven furlongs on sand proving just what the doctor ordered. (14/1)
1577 Gralmano (IRE) does act on this surface and his two best performances by far have come here. (10/1)
2500* Celtic Comfort ran a sound race under top weight. (5/1: 7/2-11/2)
2926 Tightrope, although not beaten far in the end, never appeared set to score. (4/6: op evens)
3076 Persian Fortune (14/1: op 8/1)

3396 STAFFORDSHIRE MAIDEN STKS (3-Y.O) (Class D)
2-50 (2-50) **1m 1f 79y (Fibresand)** £3,709.30 (£1,107.40: £529.20: £240.10) Stalls: Low GOING: 0.43 sec per fur (SLW)

				SP	RR	SF
	All In Leather (75) (WJHaggas) **3-8-9** FLynch(1) (lw: a gng wl: led over 3f out: sn clr: easily)	—	**1**	4/1^{2}	78+	34
3095^{5}	**Rutland Chantry (USA)** (LordHuntingdon) **3-9-0** DHarrison(2) (tk keen hld: rdn & outpcd over 4f out: rallied over 3f out: styd on fnl f: no ch w wnr)	11	**2**	1/2^{1}	64	20
	Cantina (ABailey) **3-8-9** DWright(5) (lt-f: unf: plld hrd: a.p: led 5f out tl over 3f out: no ch w wnr)	3	**3**	16/1	54	10
2960^{8}	**Flying Flip** (BCMorgan) **3-8-9** CHodgson(8) (b.hind: prom over 6f)	8	**4**	33/1	40	—
2420^{7}	**Bustopher Jones** (CREgerton) **3-9-0** MTebbutt(9) (bhd fnl 3f)	7	**5**	20/1	33	—
2360^{7}	**Who Dealt** (RHollinshead) **3-8-9** ACulhane(7) (lw: hld up: sme hdwy over 4f out: wknd over 3f out)	17	**6**	50/1	—	—
2549^{2}	**Weet A Bit (IRE) (45)** (RHollinshead) **3-8-11**(3) DGriffiths(4) (lw: dropped rr over 6f out: t.o)	11	**7**	9/1^{3}	—	—
2300^{8}	**Fortune's Way (IRE)** (JWharton) **3-8-9** JCarroll(3) (swtg: led to 5f out: wknd over 4f out: t.o)	1¼	**8**	33/1	—	—
3119^{10}	**My Girl Lucy (54)** (PMitchell) **3-8-9** JQuinn(6) (bhd fnl 3f: t.o)	hd	**9**	33/1	—	—

(SP 118.1%) **9 Rn**

2m 6.9 (10.90) CSF £5.67 TOTE £4.70: £1.40 £1.10 £2.30 (£1.90) Trio £40.60 OWNER Cheveley Park Stud (NEWMARKET) BRED Cheveley Park Stud Ltd
All In Leather, who like the rest of her stable has been out of sorts, took the eye in the paddock on this belated seasonal reappearance. Taking to the surface like a duck to water, she turned it into a procession and could go on to better things. (4/1: op 6/4)
3095 Rutland Chantry (USA) shaped as though he needs a longer trip but, in any case, the winner was in a different league. (1/2)
Cantina, a half-sister to a bumper winner, did reasonably well on her debut, despite running too freely. (16/1)

3397 LINCOLNSHIRE H'CAP (0-85) (3-Y.O) (Class D)
3-20 (3-20) **1m 100y (Fibresand)** £3,709.30 (£1,107.40: £529.20: £240.10) Stalls: Low GOING: 0.43 sec per fur (SLW)

				SP	RR	SF
3075^{5}	**Nor-Do-I (74)** (JMPEustace) **3-8-12** JTate(7) (mde all: clr over 2f out: rdn wl over 1f out: r.o wl)	—	**1**	6/1^{3}	87	59
3135^{4}	**Absolute Liberty (USA) (75)** (SPCWoods) **3-8-13** GDuffield(3) (lw: sn prom: styd on fnl f: nt trble wnr)	5	**2**	9/2^{2}	79	51
3077^{7}	**Sea Ya Maite (58)** (SRBowring) **3-7-10** DWright(1) (b: chsd wnr: rdn over 3f out: no imp)	½	**3**	8/1	61	33
*3043**	**Mike's Double (IRE) (64)** (MissGayKelleway) **3-8-2** JQuinn(11) (lw: hld up mid div: rdn & hdwy 3f out: one pce fnl 2f)	3	**4**	6/1^{3}	61	33
3320^{3}	**Bon Guest (IRE) (58)** (JGMO'Shea) **3-7-7**(3) PFessey(5) (swtg: hdwy over 3f out: n.d)	9	**5**	8/1	38	10
3075^{10}	**The Wyandotte Inn (80)** (MrsNMacauley) **3-8-13**(5) AmandaSanders(4) (swtg: nvr nr ldrs)	3½	**6**	12/1	53	25
3225^{4}	**Ultra Boy (75)** (PCHaslam) **3-8-13** LCharnock(10) (swtg: prom 5f)	1½	**7**	8/1	45	17
3115^{18}	**Canadian Fantasy (75)** (MJohnston) **3-8-13** JWeaver(6) (prom 4f)	2	**8**	100/30^{1}	42	14
688^{9}	**Mujova (IRE) (83)** (RHollinshead) **3-9-7** MWigham(9) (lw: s.i.s: a bhd)	7	**9**	20/1	36	8
871^{14}	**Komasta (69)** (CaptJWilson) **3-8-2**(5)ow2 PRoberts(8) (bit bkwd: bhd fnl 3f)	½	**10**	25/1	21	—
2836^{6}	**Don Sebastian (76)** (WJHaggas) **3-9-0** FLynch(2) (lw: s.i.s: nvr gng wl: a bhd)	hd	**11**	10/1	28	—

(SP 128.6%) **11 Rn**

1m 52.5 (7.50) CSF £33.26 CT £213.16 TOTE £12.80: £5.80 £3.10 £4.30 (£68.40) Trio £70.30 OWNER The MacDougall Partnership (NEWMARKET) BRED R. E. A. Bott (Wigmore Street) Ltd
3075 Nor-Do-I, hardly bred to stay this sort of distance, was back against his own age-group after being in a stronger race last time. (6/1: op 4/1)
3135 Absolute Liberty (USA) was a hefty 10lb higher than when successful at Lingfield on grass in June. (9/2)

3077 Sea Ya Maite, down 2lb, was still 6lb higher than when winning at Southwell last month and seemed to stay the extended mile well enough. (8/1)
3043* Mike's Double (IRE) was stepping up from six, having finished second over seven at Salisbury three outings ago. (6/1)
2303 The Wyandotte Inn (12/1: op 8/1)

3398 NOTTINGHAMSHIRE H'CAP (0-65) (3-Y.O+) (Class F)

3-50 (3-51) **5f (Fibresand)** £2,277.00 (£627.00: £297.00) Stalls: Low GOING: 0.43 sec per fur (SLW)

Form	Horse / details	Dist	Pos	SP	RR	SF
2581^{9}	**Village Native (FR) (52)** (KOCunningham-Brown) **4-9-5b** DHarrison(2) (s.i.s: sn chsng ldrs: led 2f out: r.o wl)	—	1	20/1	65	48
593^{10}	**Aljaz (50)** (MissGayKelleway) **7-9-3** JQuinn(8) (led over 1f: chsd wnr fnl 2f: no imp)	3	2	$8/1^{2}$	53	36
2915^{2}	**Time To Fly (53)** (BWMurray) **4-9-3b**(3) DSweeney(5) (a.p: one pce fnl 2f)	4	3	$7/4^{1}$	44	27
2177^{17}	**Deerly (53)** (RDickin) **4-9-6** JWeaver(1) (a.p: led over 3f out to 2f out: wknd over 1f out)	1½	4	$10/1^{3}$	39	22
3206^{11}	**Broadway Melody (63)** (APJarvis) **3-9-13** ACulhane(12) (lw: chsd ldrs: no hdwy fnl 2f)	¾	5	$10/1^{3}$	46	26
3287^{18}	**Amy Leigh (IRE) (60)** (CaptJWilson) **4-9-6b**(7) AngelaHartley(6) (lw: nvr nrr)	¾	6	16/1	41	24
2424^{7}	**Shavinsky (60)** (PHowling) **4-9-13** DWright(4) (no hdwy fnl 2f)	1¼	7	25/1	37	20
2915^{8}	**Silk Cottage (45)** (RMWhitaker) **5-8-12** OPears(11) (lw: hld up: sn bhd: nvr plcd to chal)	2	8	$10/1^{3}$	16	—
3083^{3}	**Rowlandsons Stud (IRE) (56)** (KCComerford) **4-9-2**(7) SRighton(9) (lw: chsd ldr over 2f: wknd over 1f out)	1	9	$10/1^{3}$	23	6
3040^{2}	**Master Foley (62)** (NPLittmoden) **3-9-5**(7) KPierrepont(7) (swtg: outpcd)	hd	10	$8/1^{2}$	29	9
*3040**	**Hajat (48)** (JBerry) **3-8-9**(3) PFessey(10) (lw: a bhd)	1½	11	$8/1^{2}$	10	—
2732^{10}	**Littlestone Rocket (56)** (WRMuir) **3-9-1b**(5) PRoberts(13) (lw: a bhd)	2½	12	20/1	10	—
3040^{3}	**Midnight Times (46)** (DCO'Brien) **3-8-10** GBardwell(3) (chsd ldrs tl rdn & wknd over 2f out)	¾	13	16/1	—	—
				(SP 131.2%)	**13 Rn**	

64.3 secs (5.40) CSF £167.61 CT £411.35 TOTE £19.00: £4.40 £1.60 £1.40 (£70.10) Trio £178.80 OWNER Mr A. J. Richards (STOCKBRIDGE) BRED Ewar Stud Farms
WEIGHT FOR AGE 3yo-3lb
2372 Village Native (FR), down 6lb, likes some give in the ground but had not shown a lot on his previous venture on sand on Lingfield's faster surface. (20/1)
391 Aljaz, coming back after a four-month break, was 8lb higher than when winning this race last season. (8/1)
2915 Time To Fly, reverting to the minimum distance, is running consistently well at the moment but had been put up a total of 11lb for his last two performances. (7/4)
1439* Deerly is the type who really needs to dominate from the word go. (10/1)
2921 Broadway Melody is probably more effective at six. (10/1)
2674 Amy Leigh (IRE), 9lb higher than when winning a seller on this course in March, had been raised 3lb for her second here last month. (16/1)
2826 Silk Cottage appeared to be given a quiet run after disappointing when gambled on last time. (10/1)
3083 Rowlandsons Stud (IRE) (10/1: 7/1-12/1)

3399 WEST MIDLANDS (S) STKS (3-Y.O+) (Class G)

4-25 (4-25) **5f (Fibresand)** £1,984.50 (£547.00: £259.50) Stalls: Low GOING: 0.43 sec per fur (SLW)

Form	Horse / details	Dist	Pos	SP	RR	SF
2899^{9}	**Featherstone Lane (58)** (MissLCSiddall) **6-9-2** MWigham(9) (lw: outpcd over 2f out: rallied over 1f out: str run to ld wl ins fnl f)	—	1	$5/1^{2}$	70	32
2899^{8}	**Marjorie Rose (IRE) (63)** (ABailey) **4-8-11** DWright(2) (b.hind: w ldr: led 4f out tl over 2f out: hrd rdn & ev ch ins fnl f: r.o)	1¼	2	$4/6^{1}$	61	23
2934^{13}	**Ticka Ticka Timing (27)** (BWMurray) **4-8-13**(3) DSweeney(1) (lw: a.p: led over 2f out: hrd rdn & hdd wl ins fnl f)	hd	3	40/1	66	28
2602^{16}	**Redspet (25)** (SRBowring) **3-8-5**(3) CTeague(8) (sn outpcd: nvr nr ldrs)	9	4	66/1	32	—
	Malsisio (21) (NPLittmoden) **5-8-11** TGMcLaughlin(7) (outpcd)	3	5	$16/1^{3}$	22	—
2197^{13}	**Breffni (IRE) (48)** (RDickin) **3-8-8** VSlattery(6) (outpcd)	4	6	33/1	10	—
593^{12}	**Efficacy (58)** (APJarvis) **6-8-4**(7) CCarver(4) (lw: led 1f: wknd over 2f out)	¾	7	$5/1^{2}$	7	—
3083^{12}	**Double Or Bust (40)** (CJHill) **4-8-4b**(7) PDoe(5) (swtg: prom over 2f)	3½	8	66/1	—	—
2563^{15}	**General Sir Peter (IRE) (70)** (NACallaghan) **5-9-2b**(5) AmandaSanders(3) (lw: s.i.s: outpcd: 6th whn sddle slipped & uns rdr wl over 2f out)		U	$5/1^{2}$	—	—
				(SP 124.2%)	**9 Rn**	

65.1 secs (6.20) CSF £8.54 TOTE £6.40: £1.60 £1.10 £3.70 (£3.90) Trio £34.80 OWNER Mr D. Parker (TADCASTER) BRED Qualitair Stud Ltd
WEIGHT FOR AGE 3yo-3lb
No bid
1865 Featherstone Lane registered his third win in eighty-eight races, two of which have come over course and distance. (5/1)
2899 Marjorie Rose (IRE) worked hard to get the better of the third but, before she could do that, the winner had swept by. (4/6: op evens)
2366 Ticka Ticka Timing had not shown much since winning a similar event at 33/1 over six furlongs at Southwell just over two years ago. (40/1)
512 Efficacy (5/1: 5/2-11/2)
972 General Sir Peter (IRE) (5/1: op 2/1)

3400 SHROPSHIRE APPRENTICE H'CAP (0-60) (3-Y.O) (Class G)

4-55 (4-55) **1m 6f 166y (Fibresand)** £2,007.50 (£570.00: £282.50) Stalls: High GOING: 0.43 sec per fur (SLW)

Form	Horse / details	Dist	Pos	SP	RR	SF
2398^{10}	**Certain Magic (45)** (WRMuir) **3-8-6** PDoe(4) (hld up: stdy hdwy over 6f out: hrd rdn fnl f: led last stride)	—	1	10/1	55	13
2487^{18}	**Straffan Gold (USA) (50)** (GWragg) **3-8-11** PFredericks(2) (lw: m in snatches: a.p: led 4f out: rdn over 1f out: hdd last stride)	s.h	2	$6/1^{3}$	60	18
3101^{4}	**Dancing Queen (IRE) (60)** (MBell) **3-8-11**(10) DMulhall(5) (hld up: stdy hdwy over 6f out: outpcd 4f out: styd on same pce fnl 3f)	15	3	$3/1^{2}$	54	12
1731^{3}	**Silver Button (42)** (SRBowring) **3-7-9**(8) FBoyle(1) (led: hdd 4f out: wknd 3f out)	14	4	10/1	21	—
3028^{8}	**Select Star (IRE) (55)** (APJarvis) **3-8-10**(6) CCarver(6) (b.hind: w ldr tl hrd rdn & wknd over 4f out: t.o)	26	5	7/1	5	—
2397^{5}	**Alagna (45)** (SCWilliams) **3-8-0**(6) DarrenWilliams(3) (hld up: stdy hdwy over 6f out: rdn 4f out: sn wknd: t.o)	17	6	$5/4^{1}$	—	—
				(SP 114.4%)	**6 Rn**	

3m 28.6 (21.20) CSF £61.08 TOTE £12.30: £4.90 £3.50 (£17.50) OWNER Delamere Partnership (LAMBOURN) BRED D. J. and Mrs Deer
837 Certain Magic has been plummeting down the ratings and was stepping up from a mile and a half on this All-Weather debut. (10/1)

Straffan Gold (USA), taking a big step up in distance on this first outing on sand, was continually on and off the bridle. In fairness, he did little wrong when asked to really put his head down. (6/1)
3101 Dancing Queen (IRE), yet another switching to sand over a longer trip, could do nothing more than plod on. (3/1: op 7/4)
2521 Select Star (IRE) (7/1: 6/1-9/1)
2068 Alagna seems best left alone. (5/4)

T/Plpt: £348.70 (36.05 Tckts). T/Qdpt: £73.30 (11.99 Tckts) KH

2898-AYR (L-H) (Good to firm)
Saturday August 9th
WEATHER: overcast with some light rain WIND: almost nil

3401 MCELROY PRINTERS AMATEUR H'CAP (0-70) (3-Y.O+) (Class F)
2-25 (2-28) **1m 7f** £2,670.00 (£745.00: £360.00) Stalls: Low GOING minus 0.24 sec per fur (GF)

				SP	RR	SF
3141²	**Arian Spirit (IRE) (42)** (JLEyre) **6-10-10v¹** MissDianaJones(6) (a.p: led over 2f out: styd on wl)	—	1	2/1 ¹	50	34
3221⁴	**Thisonesforalice (36)** (JSGoldie) **9-10-0**(4) MrsCWilliams(4) (bhd: gd hdwy to chse wnr over 1f out: kpt on)	1¾	2	33/1	42	26
	Mils Mij (28) (TAKCuthbert) **12-9-3**(7)ow3 MissHCuthbert(10) (outpcd & lost tch ½-wy: styd on wl fnl 2f: nrst fin)	9	3	100/1	25	6
2825⁶	**Vintage Taittinger (IRE) (27)** (JSGoldie) **5-9-9** MissPRobson(2) (lw: chsd ldr: led 3f out: sn hdd & one pce)	nk	4	3/1 ²	23	7
2208³	**Able Player (USA) (41)** (KJDrewry) **10-10-5**(4) MrKDrewry(3) (in tch: outpcd ent st: styd on wl towards fin)	nk	5	33/1	37	21
3197⁴	**Nosey Native (60)** (JPearce) **4-12-0** MrsLPearce(7) (chsd ldrs after 4f tl wknd fnl 2½f)	5	6	10/1	51	35
3046⁴	**Black Ice Boy (IRE) (39)** (RBastiman) **6-10-0b**(7) MissRBastiman(5) (swtg: led & sn clr: hdd 3f out: sn wknd)	2½	7	7/1	27	11
3046²	**Stalled (IRE) (48)** (PTWalwyn) **7-10-12**(4) MarchionessBlandford(1) (lw: in tch: effrt ent st: sn btn)	3½	8	7/2 ³	32	16
2360⁶	**The Orraman (IRE) (47)** (JJO'Neill) **3-9-8**(7) MrJBarcoe(8) (in tch tl wknd appr st)	15	9	100/1	15	—
	Yaakum (28) (SEKettlewell) **8-9-3**(7) MissJHarrison(9) (s.v.s: a t.o)	15	10	40/1	—	—
				(SP 112.4%)	**10 Rn**	

3m 23.71 (13.01) CSF £68.75 CT £4,372.12 TOTE £2.30: £1.10 £3.10 £9.80 (£23.10) Trio £276.90; £132.64 to Epsom Downs 10/8/97
OWNER Mr Martin West (HAMBLETON) BRED M. Ervine in Ireland
LONG HANDICAP Mils Mij 9-2
WEIGHT FOR AGE 3yo-14lb
3141 Arian Spirit (IRE), despite going up 5lb, is still well handicapped and won this nicely. (2/1)
3221 Thisonesforalice seemed to get this trip well enough and ran his best race for a long time. (33/1)
Mils Mij put up a smashing effort and should be kept in mind for a return to chasing. (100/1)
2825 Vintage Taittinger (IRE) ran reasonably and will probably be better suited by easier ground. (3/1)
2208 Able Player (USA) looked in good condition and ran well, suggesting that a return to hurdling might bring success. (33/1)
3197 Nosey Native looked very lean and ran very disappointingly, stopping quickly in the last couple of furlongs. (10/1: op 5/1)

3402 BELLEISLE HOUSE HOTEL MEDIAN AUCTION MAIDEN STKS (2-Y.O) (Class D)
3-00 (3-01) **7f** £3,688.00 (£1,114.00: £542.00: £256.00) Stalls: Low GOING minus 0.24 sec per fur (GF)

				SP	RR	SF
2524⁵	**Nautical Star** (JWHills) **2-8-11**(3) MHenry(1) (lw: chsd ldrs: outpcd over 3f out: swtchd outside & styd on to ld ins fnl f: sn clr)	—	1	8/11 ¹	80+	8
2349⁴	**Lincolnshire (USA) (82)** (PFICole) **2-9-0** MGallagher(3) (swtg: trckd ldr: led wl over 1f out: hdd & no ex ins fnl f)	2½	2	2/1 ²	74	2
2706⁹	**Empire Park** (MJohnston) **2-9-0** JWeaver(4) (lw: led: qckknd ½-wy: hdd wl over 1f out: kpt on one pce)	hd	3	7/2 ³	74	2
	Baylham (JSGoldie) **2-8-11**(3) TEDurcan(2) (leggy: in tch tl outpcd fnl 3f)	8	4	40/1	56	—
				(SP 115.9%)	**4 Rn**	

1m 30.54 (6.14) CSF £2.55 TOTE £1.70: (£1.70) OWNER Mr Michael Wauchope (LAMBOURN) BRED Cheveley Park Stud Ltd
2524 Nautical Star, despite having two extremely edgy rivals, was a real laid-back individual here and his style of racing was similar. He took some getting going but, once he did, he put it beyond doubt in tremendous style in the final furlong. Longer trips will obviously suit. (8/11: op 5/4)
2349 Lincolnshire (USA) is a tall, sweaty and extremely edgy individual but he obviously has ability but, at present, is using most of it in the preliminaries. (2/1: 6/4-9/4)
2706 Empire Park needed two handlers in the paddock and was taken very steadily to post, but he was getting very warm before the race and must learn to settle down. (7/2: 5/2-4/1)
Baylham, a tall newcomer, found this company far too hot. (40/1)

3403 AYR FLOWER SHOW H'CAP (0-90) (3-Y.O+) (Class C)
3-30 (3-31) **1m** £5,377.50 (£1,620.00: £785.00: £367.50) Stalls: Low GOING minus 0.24 sec per fur (GF)

				SP	RR	SF
3254³	**Antarctic Storm (57)** (RAFahey) **4-7-9**(3)ow1 MHenry(2) (mde all: rdn & r.o wl fnl 2f)	—	1	4/1 ²	65	16
2857²	**Persian Fayre (87)** (JBerry) **5-9-11**(3) TEDurcan(6) (lw: trckd ldr: chal over 2f out: nt qckn fnl f)	1¼	2	4/1 ²	93	45
3119⁴	**Dundel (IRE) (77)** (BWHills) **3-8-11** DHolland(1) (a.p: hdwy 2f out: rdn & no ex fnl f)	hd	3	9/2 ³	82	27
2678⁹	**Cashmere Lady (73)** (JLEyre) **5-9-0** MGallagher(7) (a.p: outpcd over 2f out: kpt on towards fin)	1¼	4	6/1	76	28
2906¹³	**Superpride (55)** (MrsMReveley) **5-7-10** DWright(5) (lw: chsd ldrs tl outpcd fnl 2½f)	¾	5	8/1	56	8
3153⁴	**Plan For Profit (IRE) (80)** (MJohnston) **3-9-0** JWeaver(4) (lw: hld up: effrt 3f out: sn rdn & no imp)	1	6	3/1 ¹	79	24
3254¹²	**Rebel County (IRE) (80)** (ABailey) **4-9-4**(3) DGriffiths(3) (hld up & bhd: effrt on ins 3f out: btn 2f out)	8	7	10/1	63	15
				(SP 117.7%)	**7 Rn**	

1m 42.11 (4.71) CSF £19.34 TOTE £5.00: £1.90 £4.20 (£9.70) OWNER Northumbria Leisure Ltd (MALTON) BRED N. and Mrs Bryce-Smith
WEIGHT FOR AGE 3yo-7lb
3254 Antarctic Storm, full of himself as usual, was taken early to post and, despite the fact there were other front-runners, he was given his own way and made full use of it. (4/1: 3/1-9/2)
2857 Persian Fayre was not ridden quite as positively this time and the winner always had first run on him. (4/1)
3119 Dundel (IRE) has plenty of ability but gives the impression that she is saving some for herself. (9/2)
2340 Cashmere Lady left the impression that a bit longer trip would not go amiss. (6/1)
2465 Superpride likes to have his own way and in this race there were too many front-runners, especially at this longer trip. (8/1)
3153 Plan For Profit (IRE) is off a high enough mark and was probably feeling his tremendous Goodwood effort here. (3/1)
Rebel County (IRE) is well handicapped but, as yet, has not shown any signs of encouragement. (10/1: 12/1-20/1)

3404 EVENING TIMES NEWSPAPER OF THE YEAR MAIDEN STKS (3-Y.O+) (Class D)
4-00 (4-02) **1m 2f** £3,759.00 (£1,049.00: £507.00) Stalls: Low GOING minus 0.24 sec per fur (GF)

				SP	RR	SF
2952[2]	**Kamanev (IRE)** (MRStoute) **3-8-11** DHolland(1) (lw: a gng wl: led 1½f out: v.easily)	—	1	2/11[1]	84++	23
3274[5]	**Round Robin (IRE) (71)** (CWThornton) **3-8-11b[1]** JWeaver(3) (lw: led tl hdd 1½f out: no ch w wnr)	6	2	9/2[2]	74	13
2687[7]	**Summer Thyme** (JBerry) **3-8-3**(3) TEDurcan(2) (a last: wl outpcd fnl 4f)	19	3	25/1[3]	39	—
				(SP 106.6%)	**3 Rn**	

2m 12.55 (6.75) CSF £1.22 TOTE £1.10: (£1.10) OWNER Sheikh Mohammed (NEWMARKET) BRED Darley Stud Management Co Ltd
2952 Kamanev (IRE), who looked a real doubtful character last time, had the simplest of tasks here and won with his head in his chest which should have boosted his confidence. (2/11)
3274 Round Robin (IRE) had blinkers on this time and tried hard but was completely out-classed. (9/2)
Summer Thyme does not impress on looks and, performance-wise, she has yet to show anything positive. (25/1)

3405 LADY ISLE (S) H'CAP (0-60) (3-Y.O) (Class F)
4-30 (4-31) **7f** £2,693.00 (£748.00: £359.00) Stalls: Low GOING minus 0.24 sec per fur (GF)

				SP	RR	SF
3268[4]	**Feel A Line (46)** (BJMeehan) **3-9-3b** JWeaver(7) (a cl up: led 3f out: rdn & r.o)	—	1	13/8[1]	56	11
3285[7]	**Abstone Queen (50)** (PDEvans) **3-9-4v**(3) TEDurcan(1) (lw: hld up: hdwy ½-wy: chsd wnr fnl 2f: rdn & nt pce to chal)	1¾	2	9/4[2]	56	11
2891[13]	**Tom Pladdey (32)** (RBastiman) **3-8-3** DWright(8) (led tl hdd 3f out: one pce)	4	3	14/1	29	—
3038[4]	**Alisadara (27)** (NBycroft) **3-7-9**(3)ow2 MHenry(3) (lw: b: trckd ldrs: effrt ½-wy: one pce fnl 2f)	s.h	4	12/1	24	—
3068[6]	**Grovefair Lad (IRE) (31)** (MartynWane) **3-7-9**(7) JennyBenson(5) (s.i.s: sn rcvrd & chsd ldrs: rdn & btn over 2f out)	¾	5	12/1	26	—
3223[7]	**Chanson d'Amour (IRE) (25)** (MissLAPerratt) **3-7-3**(7) JMcAuley(6) (outpcd & bhd ½-wy: n.d after)	1¼	6	25/1	17	—
3121[8]	**Donna's Dancer (IRE) (46)** (NTinkler) **3-9-3b** KimTinkler(2) (s.i.s: drvn along & bhd: n.d)	4	7	9/2[3]	29	—
				(SP 112.9%)	**7 Rn**	

1m 30.44 (6.04) CSF £4.82 CT £30.12 TOTE £1.70: £1.10 £2.80 (£2.40) OWNER Mr J. S. Gutkin (UPPER LAMBOURN) BRED W. R. Jones
LONG HANDICAP Chanson d'Amour (IRE) 7-7 Alisadara 7-9
Bt in 5,500gns
3268 Feel A Line, an edgy sort, was better suited by this left-handed track and, against this moderate opposition, was always too strong. (13/8)
1573 Abstone Queen ran a fair race but just gives the impression that she is not fully putting it in. (9/4)
2354 Tom Pladdey, from a yard in good form, ran better but had no chance in the last two furlongs. (14/1: op 6/1)
3038 Alisadara was always well enough placed but, asked for an effort at halfway, looked very slow. (12/1)
3068 Grovefair Lad (IRE) has more ability but does not often use it. (12/1: op 5/1)
3121 Donna's Dancer (IRE) (9/2: op 5/2)

3406 AILSA CRAIG H'CAP (0-75) (3-Y.O+) (Class D)
5-00 (5-01) **6f** £4,017.75 (£1,212.00: £588.50: £276.75) Stalls: High GOING minus 0.24 sec per fur (GF)

				SP	RR	SF
3087*	**Safio (65)** (ABailey) **4-9-4** DWright(13) (lw: chsd ldrs: effrt 2f out: chal 1f out: rdn to ld cl home)	—	1	3/1[1]	72	44
3287[3]	**Johayro (58)** (JSGoldie) **4-8-8**(3) DGriffiths(9) (lw: cl up: led & qcknd ½-wy: no ex towards fin)	hd	2	4/1[2]	65	37
2964[9]	**Hever Golf Rocket (71)** (TJNaughton) **3-9-6** JWeaver(1) (in tch: hdwy to chal ins fnl f: nt qckn towards fin)	nk	3	6/1[3]	77	45
3208[8]	**Amron (61)** (JBerry) **10-8-11**(3) TEDurcan(6) (in tch: outpcd 2f out: kpt on wl fnl f)	½	4	6/1[3]	66	38
2659[4]	**Shontaine (51)** (MJohnston) **4-8-4** DHolland(2) (effrt ½-wy: styd on wl: nt pce to chal)	1¼	5	14/1	52	24
3224[5]	**Suedoro (44)** (JSGoldie) **7-7-8**(3) DarrenMoffatt(12) (in tch: outpcd ½-wy: kpt on wl towards fin)	¾	6	10/1	43	15
3143[10]	**Zain Dancer (43)** (DNicholls) **5-7-5b**(5) IonaWands(5) (s.s: hdwy ½-wy: kpt on fnl f: nvr able chal)	½	7	7/1	41	13
3334[10]	**Just Bob (64)** (SEKettlewell) **8-8-10**(7) JennyBenson(11) (lw: s.i.s: bhd tl sme late hdwy)	1½	8	10/1	58	30
2422[11]	**Garnock Valley (72)** (JBerry) **7-9-11b** MGallagher(7) (sn pushed along & bhd: sme hdwy fnl f: n.d)	nk	9	14/1	65	37
3285[12]	**Pathaze (45)** (NBycroft) **4-7-9**(3)ow2 MHenry(3) (cl up tl rdn & wknd over 1f out)	2	10	16/1	33	3
3240*	**Another Nightmare (IRE) (51)** (JLEyre) **5-7-11**(7) JMcAuley(10) (led tl ½-wy: grad wknd)	nk	11	8/1	38	10
2659[9]	**Diet (43)** (MissLAPerratt) **11-7-3v**(7) NPollard(4) (lw: outpcd fr ½-wy)	2½	12	200/1	23	—
3224[2]	**Don't Care (IRE) (62)** (MissLAPerratt) **6-9-1b** NKennedy(8) (chsd ldrs tl rdn & wknd fnl 2f)	hd	13	6/1[3]	42	14
				(SP 149.4%)	**13 Rn**	

1m 12.39 (2.59) CSF £17.30 CT £75.96 TOTE £4.00: £1.90 £3.40 £2.80 (£21.20) Trio £95.70 OWNER Mrs M. A. Clayton (TARPORLEY) BRED Mrs M. A. Clayton
LONG HANDICAP Zain Dancer 7-8 Diet 6-7
WEIGHT FOR AGE 3yo-4lb
3087* Safio, who stays further, would have been better suited by a stronger early pace but showed fine battling qualities to make it. (3/1)
3287 Johayro showed he is in tremendous heart and will, no doubt, be back in the winner's enclosure soon, especially over shorter trips or on easier tracks. (4/1)
2580* Hever Golf Rocket ran a useful race off this high mark and his low draw was certainly not in his favour. (6/1)
2900 Amron keeps running reasonably but is not quite firing as he can at the end of his races at the moment. (6/1)
2659 Shontaine is running well and is now back to a handy mark. (14/1: 10/1-16/1)
3224 Suedoro certainly has the ability but is inclined to run in snatches. (10/1)
2915* Zain Dancer has plenty more ability but cannot afford to give so much start to the opposition. (7/1)

T/Plpt: £12.40 (752.09 Tckts). T/Qdpt: £8.50 (59 Tckts) AA

3377-HAYDOCK (L-H) (Good to firm)
Saturday August 9th
WEATHER: sunny and hot WIND: almost nil

3407 TATTERSALLS MAIDEN AUCTION STKS (2-Y.O) (Class E)
2-15 (2-16) **5f** £3,013.75 (£910.00: £442.50: £208.75) Stalls: High GOING minus 0.38 sec per fur (F)

				SP	RR	SF
2862[23]	**Dancing Icon (IRE)** (RHannon) **2-8-7** DaneO'Neill(7) (chsd ldr: rdn to ld ins fnl f: r.o)	—	1	11/2	83	35
2739[8]	**Premium Princess** (JJQuinn) **2-7-10**(3) PFessey(2) (s.i.s: hdwy u.p 2f out: ev ch ent fnl f: unable qckn)	1¼	2	12/1	71	23

			SP	RR	SF
2545[10]	**Italian Rose** (WJMusson) **2-8-0**[ow1] AMackay(5) (bhd: swtchd lft & hdwy ½-wy: led over 1f out tl ins fnl f)......nk	**3**	4/1[2]	71	22
2477[12]	**Cool Mystery** (ABMulholland) **2-8-4** MRoberts(6) (bit bkwd: effrt u.p 2f out: outpcd appr fnl f)..........................4	**4**	20/1	62	14
3247[2]	**Relate** (MartynMeade) **2-8-4**[(3)ow3] RHavlin(1) (lw: prom on outside over 3f)..........................1	**5**	5/1[3]	62	11
3070[3]	**D'Marti (79)** (CBBBooth) **2-8-6** JCarroll(3) (lw: trckd ldrs over 3f: sn outpcd)..........................hd	**6**	5/2[1]	61	13
2545[5]	**Rare Indigo** (JBerry) **2-7-8**[(7)] PBradley(4) (lw: led tl hdd & wknd over 1f out)..........................½	**7**	5/1[3]	54	6

(SP 109.7%) **7 Rn**

60.97 secs (1.47) CSF £54.86 TOTE £5.70: £2.60 £5.20 (£48.30) OWNER Mr J. C. Smith (MARLBOROUGH) BRED Mrs Karen Daley

2138 Dancing Icon (IRE) had shown little on her previous outings but she won this a bit cosily and she has now got the hang of the game. (11/2)

2739 Premium Princess has needed her two previous runs to put an edge on her and she performed well here after a tardy start and, on this evidence, there is a race in her. (12/1: op 8/1)

2545 Italian Rose began to find her stride after being switched towards the centre of the track over two furlongs out. She did forge ahead briefly inside the distance but the winner proved too strong for her in the race to the line. (4/1)

Cool Mystery, a well-grown colt taking a step down to the minimum trip, was always struggling with the pace and was unable to pose a threat. He can still be improved. (20/1)

3247 Relate did her best to hold her pitch down the centre of the track, but she was being made to struggle below the distance and her measure had been taken. (5/1: 4/1-6/1)

3070 D'Marti lacks pace over this trip on such a lively surface, and she was in trouble as soon as the race began in earnest. (5/2)

3408 HARVEY JONES RATED STKS H'CAP (0-90) (3-Y.O+) (Class C)

2-45 (2-46) **1m 30y** £5,158.40 (£1,925.60: £937.80: £399.00: £174.50: £84.70) Stalls: Low GOING minus 0.38 sec per fur (F)

			SP	RR	SF
3311[3]	**Queens Consul (IRE) (74)** (BSRothwell) **7-8-3** DHarrison(1) (b.nr fore: b.hind: mde all: rdn over 2f out: r.o wl)..........................—	**1**	10/1	86	49
3150[8]	**Tertium (IRE) (82)** (MartynWane) **5-8-8**[(3)] AWhelan(4) (hld up: hdwy to chse wnr wl over 1f out: no imp).........2	**2**	5/1[2]	90	53
3153[5]	**Sharp Shuffle (IRE) (81)** (RHannon) **4-8-10**[ow1] RHughes(10) (b: stdd s: hdwy wl over 1f out: styng on whn hmpd & snatched up nr fin)..........................¾	**3**	4/1[1]	88	50
3207*	**Q Factor (82)** (DHaydnJones) **5-8-11** SDrowne(2) (lw: chsd ldr: ev ch 2f out: sn rdn: one pce)..........................1	**4**	7/1	87	50
3063[7]	**Kala Sunrise (88)** (CSmith) **4-9-3** JTate(8) (hld up: hdwy on outside over 2f out: sn rdn: nt pce to chal).........nk	**5**	14/1	92	55
2601[2]	**Zoom Up (IRE) (84)** (MJHeaton-Ellis) **3-8-6** JCarroll(3) (lw: prom: rdn over 1f out: kpt on one pce)..........................2	**6**	11/2[3]	84	40
2585[11]	**Over To You (USA) (82)** (EALDunlop) **3-8-4** RHills(5) (trckd ldrs: shkn up 3f out: grad fdd)..........................nk	**7**	11/2[3]	82	38
2678[4]	**Band on the Run (85)** (BAMcMahon) **10-9-0** MRoberts(9) (lw: trckd ldrs 5f: sn drvn along & outpcd)............3½	**8**	13/2	78	41
2855[5]	**Share Delight (IRE) (77)** (BWHills) **3-7-10**[(3)] PFessey(6) (lw: a in rr)..........................nk	**9**	14/1	69	25

(SP 115.7%) **9 Rn**

1m 41.34 (0.74) CSF £54.07 CT £216.17 TOTE £11.20: £2.10 £2.00 £1.60 (£16.90) Trio £52.70 OWNER Miss Heather Davison (MALTON) BRED Mrs Ann Galvin

WEIGHT FOR AGE 3yo-7lb

STEWARDS' ENQUIRY Whelan susp 18 & 22/8/97 (careless riding).

3311 Queens Consul (IRE), having her second outing in four days, was once again allowed to dictate and, with no challenge coming in once she had shaken off Q Factor, she was able to win with a shade to spare. (10/1)

3150 Tertium (IRE) has not won a race for eighteen months and, though he did his best to reel in the winner inside the distance, lacked the pace to get to terms. (5/1)

3153 Sharp Shuffle (IRE), dropped out at the start, crept through on the inside in the latter stages but he was fighting a lost cause when stopped in his stride and forced to check in sight of the post. Not particularly fluent in his action, an easing of the ground would be in his favour. (4/1)

3207* Q Factor, content to track the winner, delivered her challenge and was a serious threat passing the quarter-mile marker but she was tapped for speed as the tempo was stepped up, and she could do little or nothing about it. (7/1)

2679 Kala Sunrise, back in his own class, had it all to do conceding weight all-round but he gave it his best shot and was far from disgraced. (14/1)

2601 Zoom Up (IRE) found these older rivals a bit too smart for him when the whips were cracking but, for one so lightly raced, he ran up to his mark. (11/2)

3409 PETROS ROSE OF LANCASTER STKS (Gp 3) (3-Y.O+) (Class A)

3-15 (3-15) **1m 2f 120y** £20,920.00 (£7,896.00: £3,848.00: £1,736.00) Stalls: High GOING minus 0.38 sec per fur (F)

			SP	RR	SF
3002a[3]	**Romanov (IRE) (115)** (PWChapple-Hyam) **3-8-7** DHarrison(3) (hld up: pushed along ent st: hdwy 3f out: edgd lft: led over 1f out: rdn & edgd rt: r.o)..........................—	**1**	5/2[1]	115	68
2864[2]	**Germano (111)** (GWragg) **4-9-3** MHills(6) (lw: chsd ldrs: sltly outpcd over 3f out: rallied u.p appr fnl f: r.o wl)..........................½	**2**	4/1[2]	114	77
2901[2]	**Fahris (IRE) (113)** (BHanbury) **3-8-7** RHills(5) (lw: led tl over 1f out: rallied u.p fnl f: no ex nr fin)....................hd	**3**	6/1[3]	114	67
2643a[2]	**Sandstone (IRE) (109)** (JLDunlop) **3-8-7** MJKinane(1) (in tch: effrt 3f out: outpcd fnl 2f)..........................5	**4**	9/1	107	60
2710[15]	**Key to My Heart (IRE) (108)** (MissSEHall) **7-9-3** RHughes(2) (lw: chsd ldrs: rdn wl over 1f out: sn outpcd)......1	**5**	16/1	105	68
1554a[6]	**Tamayaz (CAN)** (SbinSuroor) **5-9-7v** LDettori(4) (lw: hld up: hdwy to chse ldr 5f out: wknd qckly 2f out)......2½	**6**	5/2[1]	105	68
3112[5]	**Prince of My Heart (103)** (BWHills) **4-9-3** MRoberts(7) (hld up: a bhd)..........................2	**7**	20/1	98	61

(SP 112.1%) **7 Rn**

2m 10.52 (-0.98) CSF £11.10 TOTE £3.40: £1.70 £2.20 (£7.60) OWNER Mr R. E. Sangster (MARLBOROUGH) BRED Swettenham Stud

WEIGHT FOR AGE 3yo-10lb

3002a Romanov (IRE) was one of the first off the bridle and he wandered both ways when the pressure was on, but he nosed ahead below the distance and, under a strong ride, held on all-out. (5/2)

2864 Germano had to work hard when the pace increased early in the straight and he looked to have shot his bolt but, with stamina coming into play, he stayed on strongly inside the final furlong. Another try at twelve furlongs could have the desired effect. (4/1)

2901 Fahris (IRE) adopted front-running tactics and turned in his best performance yet, and this lightly-raced colt is really reaching his peak. (6/1)

2643a Sandstone (IRE), narrowly beaten in a Group Three event in Italy last month, was a bit out of his depth here and could never get himself into the action. (9/1)

1960 Key to My Heart (IRE) was feeling the strain over two furlongs out but he is not one to give in easily, and was only shaken off below the distance. (16/1)

1554a Tamayaz (CAN), successful in this race last year, moved through to chased the leader into the straight, but he faded rather quickly entering the final quarter-mile and proved most disappointing. (5/2)

3410 CORAL H'CAP (0-100) (3-Y.O+) (Class C)

3-50 (3-52) **5f** £15,045.00 (£4,560.00: £2,230.00: £1,065.00) Stalls: High GOING minus 0.38 sec per fur (F)

Form	Horse	Dist	Pos	SP	RR	SF
3011[3]	**Moon Strike (FR) (91)** (PHowling) **7-9-5** LDettori(13) (b: hld up: hdwy & swtchd rt over 1f out: r.o strly to ld cl home)	—	1	9/2[1]	101	74
3023[5]	**Midnight Escape (97)** (CFWall) **4-9-11** RHills(9) (lw: w ldr centre: led over 1f out tl wl ins fnl f)	nk	2	16/1	106	79
3011*	**Blessingindisguise (92)** (MWEasterby) **4-9-6b** MJKinane(12) (lw: a.p stands' side: jnd ldrs appr fnl f: unable qckn nr fin)	nk	3	9/2[1]	100	73
3217[8]	**Tadeo (96)** (MJohnston) **4-9-10** MRoberts(6) (lw: a chsng ldrs: rdn over 1f out: kpt on)	1½	4	9/1[2]	99	72
2769[10]	**Lord High Admiral (CAN) (77)** (MJHeaton-Ellis) **9-8-5** SDrowne(18) (led stands' side: rdn appr fnl f: one pce)	1	5	20/1	77	50
3065[5]	**Daawe (USA) (81)** (MrsVAAconley) **6-8-9** FLynch(1) (lw: led far side: ev ch ins fnl f: unable qckn)	nk	6	20/1	80	53
3217[12]	**Squire Corrie (84)** (DWChapman) **5-8-9**(3) PFessey(5) (lw: led centre tl appr fnl f)	hd	7	20/1	83	56
1609[7]	**Young Bigwig (IRE) (92)** (JBerry) **3-8-12**(5) PRoberts(11) (nvr nrr)	¾	8	33/1	88	58
835[2]	**Knotty Hill (76)** (RCraggs) **5-8-4** DHarrison(7) (s.i.s: nvr nrr)	hd	9	20/1	72	45
3146*	**Fairy Prince (IRE) (76)** (MrsALMKing) **4-8-4** DaneO'Neill(8) (nvr trbld ldrs)	s.h	10	12/1	72	45
3011[8]	**Crofters Ceilidh (89)** (BAMcMahon) **5-8-10**(7) SRighton(2) (w ldr far side over 3f)	½	11	16/1	83	56
3111[8]	**Crowded Avenue (100)** (PJMakin) **5-10-0** PaulEddery(15) (outpcd)	1¼	12	14/1	90	63
3065*	**Lago Di Varano (86)** (RMWhitaker) **5-9-0b** DeanMcKeown(3) (racd far side: a outpcd)	nk	13	14/1	75	48
3146[2]	**Royal Dome (IRE) (75)** (MartynWane) **5-8-3** JCarroll(14) (trckd ldrs 3f: sn outpcd)	½	14	10/1[3]	63	36
3194[6]	**Cauda Equina (78)** (MRChannon) **3-8-0**(3) PPMurphy(16) (swtg: outpcd fnl 2f)	nk	15	25/1	65	35
968[6]	**Mile High (93)** (MRChannon) **3-9-4** RHughes(19) (outpcd)	¾	16	25/1	77	47
2675[6]	**That Man Again (86)** (SCWilliams) **5-8-11**(3) AWhelan(10) (chsd ldrs 3f: sn wknd)	1¾	17	16/1	65	38
3011[4]	**Rushcutter Bay (85)** (PLGilligan) **4-8-8v**(5) GFaulkner(4) (lw: dwlt: racd far side: outpcd)	1	18	14/1	61	34
2872[8]	**Swynford Dream (73)** (JFBottomley) **4-8-1** AMackay(17) (swtg: outpcd: a bhd)	½	19	11/1	47	20
				(SP 138.8%)	**19 Rn**	

59.29 secs (-0.21) CSF £74.51 CT £335.57 TOTE £4.60: £1.80 £3.90 £1.90 £2.00 (£90.00) Trio £114.10 OWNER Mr A. Foustok (NEWMARKET) BRED Haras de Manneville in France

WEIGHT FOR AGE 3yo-3lb

3011 Moon Strike (FR), taken to post very steadily, made his way over to the stands side when throwing down his challenge and, finishing strongly, gained control nearing the finish. He is a star performer on his day. (9/2)

3023 Midnight Escape, fighting for supremacy in the centre of the track, took a definite advantage at the distance and gave it all he had but the strong-finishing winner wore him down in the dying strides. This is more like his old self and he deserves to win a decent prize. (16/1)

3011* Blessingindisguise, trying for a four-timer, was the one to beat inside the distance but, hard as he tried, a turn of finishing speed was missing when it was most wanted. (9/2)

3065 Tadeo may have found the ever-drying ground against him, but he stuck to his task and certainly went down fighting. (9/1)

2289 Lord High Admiral (CAN) tried to take full advantage of a plum draw and he battled hard under a strong ride but, in this class, was found wanting in the dash to the line. (20/1)

3065 Daawe (USA), probably better over another furlong now, blazed the trail on the far side but he lacked company in the closing stages, otherwise he would very nearly have won. (20/1)

2717 Squire Corrie showed up in the centre of the track and may well have led briefly but he was unable to maintain the effort, and was held inside the last two hundred yards. (20/1)

3411 E.B.F. EUROLEASE CAR CONTRACTORS MAIDEN STKS (2-Y.O F) (Class D)

4-20 (4-22) **6f** £3,920.25 (£1,182.00: £573.50: £269.25) Stalls: High GOING minus 0.38 sec per fur (F)

Form	Horse	Dist	Pos	SP	RR	SF
2919[2]	**Zelanda (IRE)** (JHMGosden) **2-8-11** LDettori(2) (mde all: brought stands' side: clr over 1f out: unchal)	—	1	2/1[1]	85+	42
2349[6]	**Chocolate (IRE)** (JLDunlop) **2-8-11** MJKinane(10) (a.p: rdn over 1f out: nt pce of wnr)	6	2	7/1[3]	69	26
	Cease Fire (IRE) (MrsJCecil) **2-8-11** JCarroll(9) (b: b.hind: w'like: mid div: hdwy 2f out: kpt on fnl f)	2	3	8/1	64	21
3187[2]	**Dodo (IRE) (89)** (DRCElsworth) **2-8-11** PaulEddery(8) (leggy: lt-f: bit bkwd: a chsng ldrs: rdn & r.o one pce appr fnl f)	1¾	4	3/1[2]	59	16
	Angelina (PHowling) **2-8-11** RHughes(11) (b: unf: scope: bit bkwd: in tch: effrt & swtchd lft appr fnl f: r.o wl)	½	5	33/1	58	15
	Equity Princess (MJohnston) **2-8-11** MRoberts(6) (rn green: sn pushed along: nvr nrr)	s.h	6	9/1	58	15
	Bolshaya (JBerry) **2-8-8**(3) PFessey(4) (rangy: scope: hdwy appr fnl f: nvr nrr)	3	7	14/1	50	7
	Poetry In Motion (IRE) (EJAlston) **2-8-11** SDrowne(1) (unf: scope: prom tl wknd wl over 1f out)	¾	8	16/1	48	5
2409[4]	**Teepee (IRE)** (WJarvis) **2-8-11** RHills(7) (trckd ldrs over 4f)	5	9	11/1	34	—
	Set Trail (IRE) (JHanson) **2-8-11** EJohnson(13) (w'like: scope: chsd wnr over 3f: wknd fnl 2f)	4	10	25/1	24	—
2516[10]	**Caroline's Pet (IRE)** (ABailey) **2-8-11** AMackay(5) (lt-f: sn drvn along: a outpcd)	nk	11	33/1	23	—
2842[17]	**Maggice** (RHollinshead) **2-8-11** FLynch(3) (in tch over 3f)	1	12	33/1	20	—
	Rapture (RHannon) **2-8-11** DaneO'Neill(12) (lt-f: unf: outpcd: hrd rdn ½-wy: t.o)	6	13	10/1	4	—
				(SP 134.6%)	**13 Rn**	

1m 13.21 (1.51) CSF £17.02 TOTE £2.60: £1.30 £2.30 £4.20 (£8.10) Trio £60.50 OWNER Sheikh Mohammed (NEWMARKET) BRED Sheikh Mohammed bin Rashid al Maktoum

2919 Zelanda (IRE) broke smartly from her outside stall and was able to cross to the more favourable stands side. Making all, she proved a class apart and one would wonder how she has been beaten in her previous couple of outings. (2/1)

2349 Chocolate (IRE) kept the winner company for the first half mile but, when that rival lengthened up, she like the rest was left floundering. (7/1)

Cease Fire (IRE), bandaged all-round, was flat-footed as the stalls opened. Asked to improve inside the last quarter-mile, she ran on promisingly and will be all the better for the run. (8/1)

3187 Dodo (IRE) has hardly run a bad race yet but she does lack that bit extra in the closing stages, and that again proved the stumbling block. (3/1)

Angelina will probably come to herself over a longer trip but she shaped well enough on this debut, and the promise is there. (33/1)

Equity Princess is hardly bred for sprinting and, inclined to run green in the early stages, was beginning to realise what was needed in the latter part of the race and the experience will not be lost. (9/1)

Set Trail (IRE), a very late May foal who may well need time, has been pleasing in her homework and, though she dropped away rather quickly in the last couple of furlongs, will be all the wiser for the experience. (25/1)

Rapture (10/1: 8/1-12/1)

3412 NORTH LANCASHIRE H'CAP (0-85) (3-Y.O+) (Class D)

4-50 (4-50) **1m 6f** £3,692.75 (£1,112.00: £538.50: £251.75) Stalls: Centre GOING minus 0.38 sec per fur (F)

				SP	RR	SF
2940*	**Valagalore (78)** (BWHills) **3-8-8**(3) PFessey(8) (dwlt: hdwy over 4f out: led wl ins fnl f: styd on strly)	—	1	11/2	91	52
2676[11]	**Far Ahead (82)** (JLEyre) **5-10-0** RLappin(9) (hld up & bhd: hdwy over 3f out: led 2f out tl wl ins fnl f)	2½	2	11/1	92	66
2718*	**Noufari (FR) (71)** (RHollinshead) **6-9-3** FLynch(1) (a.p: jnd ldr 7f out: hrd rdn 3f out: r.o one pce)	3½	3	9/1	77	51
3035[4]	**Ordained (57)** (EJAlston) **4-8-3** SDrowne(4) (s.i.s: hdwy 3f out: rdn over 1f out: one pce)	2½	4	12/1	60	34
2853*	**Ultimate Smoothie (78)** (MCPipe) **5-9-10** RHughes(2) (led after 3f to 2f out: sn rdn & wknd)	3	5	9/2[2]	78	52
2834[6]	**Chief Mouse (61)** (FJordan) **4-8-7** JCarroll(5) (bhd: rdn 4f out: no imp: t.o)	14	6	20/1	45	19
2589[7]	**Regait (85)** (MAJarvis) **3-9-4** MRoberts(7) (hld up: hdwy & rdn 6f out: wknd over 3f out: t.o)	13	7	5/1[3]	54	15
2963[5]	**Melodica (80)** (MRStoute) **3-8-13** MJKinane(3) (led 3f: hrd rdn 3f out: sn wknd & eased: t.o)	5	8	7/2[1]	43	4
2963[11]	**Crystal Hills (IRE) (82)** (JHMGosden) **3-9-1b**[1] LDettori(6) (trckd ldrs tl wknd over 3f out: t.o)	hd	9	5/1[3]	45	6
				(SP 119.9%)	**9 Rn**	

3m 0.52 (2.32) CSF £60.40 CT £495.18 TOTE £6.60: £2.00 £3.10 £1.90 (£49.60) Trio £108.90 OWNER Mrs A. D. Bourne (LAMBOURN) BRED Newgate Stud Co

WEIGHT FOR AGE 3yo-13lb

OFFICIAL EXPLANATION **Melodica: was making a noise.**

2940* Valagalore has come into her own since tackling an extended trip and stamina played a big part in this comfortable going-away success. (11/2)

1685* Far Ahead moved poorly to the start but he ran well once he was warmed up, and the concession of so much weight must have taken its toll in the closing stages. (11/1: 8/1-12/1)

2718* Noufari (FR) did win on similar ground last month but he does prefer it more yielding, and the leading pair had taken his measure before reaching the final furlong. (9/1)

3035 Ordained has never won beyond eleven furlongs and, ridden to get the trip, did keep plugging away without being able to pose much of a threat. (12/1)

2853* Ultimate Smoothie had more to do in this first handicap, but he did make the majority of the running until fading out of contention inside the distance. (9/2)

2963 Melodica turned in a performance that was too bad to be true and it is almost certain something was amiss. (7/2)

T/Plpt: £284.60 (120.29 Tckts). T/Qdpt: £13.00 (121.62 Tckts) IM

3227-LINGFIELD (L-H) (AW Standard, Turf Good)

Saturday August 9th

WEATHER: very hot WIND: almost nil

3413 LADY EVA (S) H'CAP (0-60) (3-Y.O+) (Class G)

5-50 (5-53) **1m 2f (Equitrack)** £1,984.50 (£547.00: £259.50) Stalls: Low GOING minus 0.56 sec per fur (FST)

				SP	RR	SF
3054[3]	**Bapsford (45)** (GLMoore) **3-8-4** AClark(4) (hld up: led over 2f out: clr over 1f out: r.o wl)	—	1	8/1[3]	55	20
3232[4]	**Harlequin Walk (IRE) (43)** (RJO'Sullivan) **6-8-11** JQuinn(11) (hdwy over 4f out: chsd wnr fnl 2f: no imp)	4	2	4/1[2]	47	21
3044[4]	**Ron's Round (40)** (CADwyer) **3-7-13** NVarley(1) (lw: led 3f: led over 4f out tl over 2f out: one pce)	3	3	12/1	39	4
3276[14]	**Zahran (IRE) (43)** (JMBradley) **6-8-8**(3) DSweeney(5) (b: lw: hdwy over 2f out: one pce)	1	4	12/1	40	14
3200[7]	**Captain Marmalade (35)** (DTThom) **8-8-3** FNorton(9) (b: nvr nr to chal)	4	5	10/1	26	—
2916[6]	**Sheilas Dream (43)** (GLMoore) **4-8-11b**[1] SWhitworth(13) (swtg: a.p: led 7f out tl over 4f out: wknd over 2f out)	7	6	11/1	23	—
2916[10]	**Arzani (USA) (52)** (DJSCosgrove) **6-9-6** MRimmer(2) (b: swtg: prom over 7f)	¾	7	7/2[1]	30	4
2874[14]	**Bold Et Noir (39)** (WJarvis) **3-7-9**(3)ow2 MartinDwyer(8) (hld up: rdn over 3f out: wknd over 2f out)	nk	8	20/1	17	—
2727[7]	**Riscatto (USA) (57)** (WRMuir) **3-8-11b**[1](5) APolli(12) (lw: nvr nrr)	hd	9	14/1	35	—
2848[11]	**Ladybower (IRE) (37)** (JRPoulton) **5-8-0**(5) ADaly(14) (b.hind: a bhd)	1½	10	20/1	12	—
3054[4]	**Paddy Hurry (38)** (NACallaghan) **3-7-11b** GBardwell(10) (prom over 5f)	2½	11	16/1	9	—
2368[14]	**Loxley's Girl (IRE) (37)** (HAkbary) **3-7-10** NAdams(7) (b.hind: bhd fnl 2f)	3½	12	25/1	3	—
2488[12]	**Eastleigh (50)** (RHollinshead) **8-8-11**(7) DHayden(6) (b.off hind: bhd fnl 5f)	4	13	14/1	9	—
2947[8]	**Fengari (60)** (MMadgwick) **8-9-7**(7) PDoe(3) (b: bit bkwd: swtg: bhd fnl 5f)	6	14	10/1	10	—
				(SP 127.8%)	**14 Rn**	

2m 7.27 (2.97) CSF £37.62 CT £367.10 TOTE £11.00: £2.90 £1.80 £3.60 (£16.70) Trio £78.40 OWNER Mr C. J. Pennick (BRIGHTON) BRED Benson Stud

LONG HANDICAP Bold Et Noir 7-8

WEIGHT FOR AGE 3yo-9lb

Bt in 5,000gns

3054 Bapsford moved to the front turning for home and soon forged clear to lose his maiden tag at the thirteenth attempt. (8/1: 5/1-9/1)

3232 Harlequin Walk (IRE) moved into second place turning for home but, try as she might, was unable to peg back the winner. (4/1: 3/1-9/2)

3044 Ron's Round appreciated the drop in class and ran better here. Cutting out most of the running, he was eventually collared turning for home and could only plod on in his own time. (12/1: 8/1-16/1)

2880 Zahran (IRE) moved up over a quarter of a mile from home but could then only struggle on at one pace. This is his level but he is not easy to win with as four victories from sixty-six starts explains. (12/1: 8/1-14/1)

1383 Captain Marmalade is extremely difficult to win with as four victories from ninety-three starts testifies. This is his level. (10/1: 6/1-11/1)

2727 Sheilas Dream, who showed in front briefly, had eventually been disposed of over two furlongs from home. She is a poor performer who remains a maiden. (11/1: 8/1-12/1)

Fengari (10/1: op 20/1)

3414 LOMBARD GOLDEN SPRINT CONDITIONS STKS (2-Y.O) (Class C)

6-20 (6-22) **5f** £4,636.80 (£1,600.80: £765.90: £310.50) Stalls: High GOING minus 0.37 sec per fur (F)

				SP	RR	SF
3152[3]	**Salamanca (82)** (JBerry) **2-8-0**(5) CLowther(3) (mde all: sn clr: unchal)	—	1	7/2[2]	86	49
3192[3]	**Chieftain (IRE)** (NACallaghan) **2-8-7**(3) MartinDwyer(5) (lw: s.s: hdwy to chse wnr over 2f out: no imp)	5	2	2/7[1]	75	38

				SP	RR	SF
3226[6]	**Days of Grace (75)** (MartynMeade) **2-8-0**(7) RBrisland(4) (chsd wnr over 2f: wknd over 1f out)	3½	**3**	20/1 3	61	24
2917[15]	**Second Sun** (JJBridger) **2-8-10** JQuinn(2) (bhd fnl 3f)	15	**4**	33/1	16	—
				(SP 107.7%)		**4 Rn**

57.47 secs (0.47) CSF £4.57 TOTE £3.30: (£1.20) OWNER Mrs Chris Deuters (COCKERHAM) BRED Bearstone Stud

3152 Salamanca burst out of the stalls and, tearing off like a scalded cat, never looked like being caught. This was a very fast time which was a mere 0.22 seconds outside the juvenile course record. (7/2: 5/2-4/1)

3192 Chieftain (IRE) lost ground at the start and, with the winner quickly storming clear, the writing was soon on the wall. He did struggle into second place at halfway, but had no hope of reeling in his rival. A step up to six furlongs would surely help. (2/7)

3226 Days of Grace had no easy task and, in second place to halfway, had then soon been seen off. (20/1)

3415 GUARDWORTH H'CAP (0-70) (3-Y.O+) (Class E)

6-50 (6-51) **2m (Equitrack)** £3,018.25 (£901.00: £430.50: £195.25) Stalls: Low GOING minus 0.56 sec per fur (FST)

				SP	RR	SF
*3231**	**Mister Aspecto (IRE) (69)** (MJohnston) **4-9-13v** BDoyle(9) (chsd ldr: led over 3f out: rdn over 1f out: r.o wl)	—	**1**	9/4 1	81	46
2910[3]	**Dashing Invader (USA) (42)** (PWHarris) **4-8-0b** FNorton(4) (swtg: led over 12f: unable qckn)	2	**2**	9/2 3	52	17
3245[6]	**Nornax Lad (USA) (42)** (MartynMeade) **9-7-7b**(7) RBrisland(7) (rdn & hdwy over 3f out: one pce)	2½	**3**	16/1	50	15
3325[3]	**Sipowitz (53)** (CACyzer) **3-7-10** GBardwell(2) (lw: lost pl over 9f out: rallied 6f out: one pce fnl 4f)	9	**4**	10/1	52	2
3141*	**Paradise Navy (65)** (CREgerton) **8-9-4b**(5) CLowther(3) (lw: dwlt: hdwy over 10f out: rdn over 4f out: no rspnse)	6	**5**	7/2 2	58	23
3232[5]	**Willie Rushton (50)** (GLMoore) **4-8-8** AClark(8) (b: b.hind: lw: hld up: rdn over 4f out: sn wknd)	½	**6**	20/1	42	7
3081[5]	**Jilly Woo (53)** (BAPearce) **3-7-3**(7) DarrenWilliams(6) (swtg: prom over 8f)	26	**7**	33/1	19	—
2874[6]	**Bedouin Prince (USA) (42)** (MrsLStubbs) **10-8-0** JQuinn(1) (b: a bhd: dismntd)	5	**8**	9/1	3	—
2550[R]	**Soojama (IRE) (52)** (RMFlower) **7-8-7b**(3) MartinDwyer(5) (virtually ref to r: a t.o)	dist	**9**	7/1	—	—
				(SP 116.3%)		**9 Rn**

3m 25.08 (4.08) CSF £11.45 CT £117.78 TOTE £3.30: £1.40 £2.10 £9.60 (£9.30) Trio £85.50 OWNER Aspecto Clothing Co Ltd (MIDDLEHAM) BRED Petra Bloodstock Agency Ltd

LONG HANDICAP Jilly Woo 6-3 Sipowitz 7-3

WEIGHT FOR AGE 3yo-15lb

3231* Mister Aspecto (IRE) followed up last Saturday's course and distance victory, leading over three furlongs from home and being rousted along in the straight for a decisive victory. (9/4)

2910 Dashing Invader (USA) again adopted his usual front-running role but, collared over three furlongs from home, proved no match for the winner. (9/2: 3/1-5/1)

3245 Nornax Lad (USA), 23lb lower than when winning here back in February 1994 on his last Equitrack appearance, was bustled along to pick up ground over three furlongs from home but was then made to look very pedestrian. He is very much on the downgrade. (16/1)

3325 Sipowitz was made to look extremely one-paced in the last half-mile and, no doubt, his race at Bath on Thursday was taking its toll. (10/1: 7/1-11/1)

3141* Paradise Navy, winner of this race last year off the same mark, finds little off the bridle and that was very much the case here. (7/2)

3416 E.B.F. LADY MARGARET NOVICE MEDIAN AUCTION STKS (2-Y.O F) (Class F)

7-20 (7-23) **6f** £2,623.50 (£726.00: £346.50) Stalls: High GOING minus 0.37 sec per fur (F)

				SP	RR	SF
3237[6]	**Phone Alex (IRE) (79)** (RHannon) **2-8-9**(5) CLowther(5) (chsd ldrs: rdn over 3f out: led over 1f out: r.o wl)	—	**1**	5/2 2	72	31
1812[9]	**Ambitious** (JRFanshawe) **2-8-8** WRyan(6) (hdwy over 2f out: ev ch fnl f: r.o wl)	nk	**2**	15/8 1	65	24
3265[4]	**Chikapenny (69)** (MrsLStubbs) **2-8-8v1** SSanders(9) (led over 4f: unable qckn)	3	**3**	15/2	57	16
3131[W]	**Blushing Victoria (75)** (MartynMeade) **2-8-13**(3) DSweeney(8) (lw: chsd ldr over 4f: one pce)	1¾	**4**	9/1	61	20
2728[13]	**Pinup** (GLewis) **2-8-8** TSprake(2) (dwlt: nvr nr to chal)	1½	**5**	14/1	49	8
3114[11]	**Runaround** (SDow) **2-8-5**(3) MartinDwyer(7) (no hdwy fnl 3f)	2½	**6**	20/1	42	1
2684[3]	**Farndon Princess** (RHollinshead) **2-8-8** PaulEddery(4) (outpcd)	2½	**7**	5/1 3	35	—
536[13]	**Grosvenor Miss (IRE)** (PWChapple-Hyam) **2-8-5**(3) RHavlin(1) (lw: bhd fnl 3f)	2½	**8**	12/1	29	—
	Little Tolerance (JCullinan) **2-8-8** JQuinn(10) (neat: swtg: bhd fnl 3f)	22	**9**	25/1	—	—
				(SP 124.8%)		**9 Rn**

1m 11.41 (2.41) CSF £7.61 TOTE £2.80: £1.40 £1.60 £1.80 (£5.00) Trio £15.90 OWNER J B R Leisure Ltd (MARLBOROUGH) BRED E. Moloney

3237 Phone Alex (IRE) was given a lovely ride by her young jockey. Already off the bridle by halfway, the filly gained a slender advantage approaching the final furlong and kept on well to keep the very persistent runner-up at bay. (5/2)

Ambitious, reportedly stiff after her Windsor debut, ran much better here. She may well have got her head in front for a few strides as she challenged for the lead from below the distance but, despite doing little wrong, was just unable to get her head in front where it counts. She should soon pick up a race. (15/8)

3265 Chikapenny found the first-time visor helping her for she was smartly out of the stalls but, collared approaching the final furlong, then failed to find another gear. (15/2: 4/1-8/1)

884 Blushing Victoria, racing in second place, failed to quicken in the last furlong and a half. (9/1: 5/1-10/1)

Pinup was not given a hard time at the back of the field but did make some late progress. Further improvement looks likely. (14/1: 8/1-16/1)

2684 Farndon Princess (5/1: op 8/1)

Grosvenor Miss (IRE) (12/1: 7/1-14/1)

3417 MALAYA GATWICK H'CAP (0-70) (3-Y.O+) (Class E)

7-50 (7-53) **6f** £3,252.25 (£973.00: £466.50: £213.25) Stalls: High GOING minus 0.37 sec per fur (F)

				SP	RR	SF
2179[11]	**Walk the Beat (59)** (MartynMeade) **7-9-5** FNorton(12) (hld up: swtchd rt 2f out: led 1f out: hrd rdn: r.o wl)	—	**1**	14/1	69	42
2938[2]	**Seretse's Nephew (41)** (MJPolglase) **3-7-11** JQuinn(9) (chsd ldr: hrd rdn & ev ch 1f out: r.o)	nk	**2**	16/1	50	19
3249[8]	**Crystal Heights (FR) (54)** (RJO'Sullivan) **9-9-0** SSanders(11) (b: s.s: rdn & hdwy over 1f out: r.o)	1	**3**	9/1	61	34
3146[4]	**Denbrae (IRE) (64)** (DJGMurraySmith) **5-9-5**(5) CLowther(4) (hdwy over 1f out: unable qckn ins fnl f)	½	**4**	15/2	69	42
3251*	**Gold Edge (59)** (MRChannon) **3-9-1** BDoyle(6) (led 5f)	1	**5**	7/2 1	62	31
3082[6]	**Sizzling (52)** (RHannon) **5-8-9**(3) MartinDwyer(5) (a.p: rdn over 2f out: one pce)	½	**6**	10/1	53	26
3198[10]	**Bayin (USA) (61)** (MDIUsher) **8-9-7** RStreet(8) (s.s: hdwy over 1f out: nvr nrr)	½	**7**	6/1 3	61	34
3146[6]	**Double Matt (IRE) (57)** (MrsPSly) **5-9-3** DBiggs(10) (s.s: nvr nrr)	½	**8**	16/1	56	29
3077[4]	**Master of Passion (64)** (JMPEustace) **8-9-7**(3) DSweeney(7) (dwlt: hld up: rdn over 2f out: sn wknd)	5	**9**	8/1	49	22
3100[4]	**Don Pepe (63)** (RBoss) **6-9-9** AClark(1) (prom over 3f)	2	**10**	9/2 2	43	16
2244[13]	**Third Party (64)** (SDow) **3-9-6** WRyan(2) (bhd fnl 2f)	1	**11**	14/1	41	10

2848^{15}	**Dancing Jack (36)**	(JJBridger) **4-7-10** GBardwell(3) (prom over 2f)	1¼	**12**	33/1	10	—

(SP 124.7%) **12 Rn**

1m 11.01 (2.01) CSF £209.51 CT £1,265.94 TOTE £22.50: £4.70 £4.20 £2.50 (£128.40) Trio £311.20 OWNER Ladyswood Racing Club (MALMESBURY) BRED R. B. Warren
LONG HANDICAP Dancing Jack 7-1
WEIGHT FOR AGE 3yo-4lb

1743 Walk the Beat left his Windsor disappointment behind and, leading a furlong out, responded to pressure to keep the persistent runner-up at bay. (14/1: 10/1-16/1)
2938 Seretse's Nephew ran a fine race in this better company. With every chance entering the final furlong, he refused to lie down and kept on really well to the bitter end. (16/1)
2954 Crystal Heights (FR) can always be relied on to lose ground at the start and that was again the case here. Nevertheless, he ran on nicely in the last furlong and a half, if never looking likely to get there in time. All six of his turf wins have come at Brighton. (9/1)
3146 Denbrae (IRE) is slipping down the weights but, after moving up on the outside of the field below the distance, was tapped for toe in the last seventy-five yards. (15/2)
3251* Gold Edge, 9lb higher for her win at Chepstow last Sunday, took the field along but, collared a furlong out, then failed to find any extra. (7/2)
3082 Sizzling is sliding down the weights and was a leading light, if failing to quicken in the last two furlongs. He has only one handicap success to his name. (10/1)
1989 Third Party (14/1: 10/1-16/1)

3418 COURIER NEWSPAPERS 125TH ANNIVERSARY LIMITED STKS (0-75) (3-Y.O+) (Class D)

8-20 (8-21) **7f** £3,773.00 (£1,127.00: £539.00: £245.00) Stalls: High GOING minus 0.37 sec per fur (F)

					SP	RR	SF
2420^{2}	**Khafaaq (75)**	(MajorWRHern) **3-8-11b¹** TSprake(10) (lw: nt clr run over 2f out: hdwy to ld over 1f out: rdn: r.o wl)	—	**1**	5/2 ¹	85	49
3189^{11}	**Ivory Dawn (75)**	(KTIvory) **3-8-7**(3) MartinDwyer(6) (hdwy over 3f out: ev ch 1f out: unable qckn)	1¾	**2**	11/2 ³	80	44
3236*	**Silk St John (80)**	(MJRyan) **3-8-13** GCarter(7) (s.s: hdwy over 3f out: ev ch 1f out: one pce)	½	**3**	11/4 ²	82	46
3037*	**Caribbean Star (74)**	(MRStoute) **3-8-10v** WRyan(4) (lw: hld up: rdn over 2f out: one pce)	1½	**4**	11/2 ³	75	39
1238^{7}	**Simple Logic (70)**	(AGFoster) **3-8-8** SWhitworth(1) (b.hind: swtg: led 6f out tl over 1f out: wknd fnl f)	1	**5**	20/1	71	35
3075^{14}	**Alpine Hideaway (IRE) (74)**	(BHanbury) **4-9-5** MRimmer(3) (led 1f: rdn over 2f out: wknd over 1f out)	1	**6**	14/1	74	44
3254^{8}	**Knobbleeneeze (69)**	(MRChannon) **7-9-5v** CandyMorris(9) (hld up: rdn over 2f out: sn wknd)	1¾	**7**	9/1	70	40
871^{7}	**Roffey Spinney (IRE) (75)**	(RHannon) **3-9-1** DBiggs(8) (lw: hld up: rdn 3f out: sn wknd)	9	**8**	20/1	51	15
2161^{4}	**Water Garden (70)**	(GWragg) **3-9-1** AClark(5) (s.s: a bhd)	26	**9**	7/1	—	—
3056^{8}	**Daylight Dreams (70)**	(CACyzer) **3-8-8** AMorris(2) (lw: prom 3f)	nk	**10**	33/1	—	—

(SP 127.6%) **10 Rn**

1m 22.33 (1.13) CSF £16.62 TOTE £3.90: £1.80 £1.80 £1.80 (£12.10) Trio £12.80 OWNER Mr Hamdan Al Maktoum (LAMBOURN) BRED Shadwell Estate Company Limited
WEIGHT FOR AGE 3yo-6lb

2420 Khafaaq found the first-time blinkers helping him to lose his maiden tag and, although not getting the best of runs, led approaching the final furlong and soon asserted. (5/2)
2925 Ivory Dawn, one of several with every chance entering the final furlong, then found the winner had more up his sleeve. (11/2)
3236* Silk St John, with every chance a furlong from home, then failed to find another gear. (11/4)
3037* Caribbean Star chased the leaders but failed to quicken in the last furlong and a half. (11/2)
Simple Logic ran her best race so far this season. Soon at the head of affairs, she was collared approaching the final furlong and tired in the last two hundred yards. (20/1)
3075 Alpine Hideaway (IRE) was close up until tiring approaching the final furlong. (14/1: 10/1-16/1)

T/Plpt: £482.00 (34.5 Tckts). T/Qdpt: £38.70 (33.68 Tckts) AK

3383-NEWMARKET (R-H) (Good to firm)
Saturday August 9th

Races 1, 3 & 6 hand-timed.
WEATHER: sunny & hot WIND: slight across

3419 MONTANA WINES MAIDEN STKS (3-Y.O+) (Class D)

2-00 (2-01) **1m 4f (July)** £3,752.50 (£1,120.00: £535.00: £242.50) Stalls: High GOING minus 0.61 sec per fur (F)

					SP	RR	SF
3188^{3}	**Marsul (USA) (80)**	(JHMGosden) **3-8-10v¹** GHind(4) (lw: mde virtually all: rdn & r.o wl fnl f)	—	**1**	5/1 ²	89	24
3021^{2}	**Sir Ricky (USA) (86)**	(RCharlton) **3-8-10** PatEddery(5) (lw: trckd ldrs: chal 2f out: rdn & hung lft wl ins fnl f: no ex nr fin)	nk	**2**	8/11 ¹	89	24
2940^{2}	**Jazz Track (IRE)**	(PWChapple-Hyam) **3-8-10** SWhitworth(7) (lw: hmpd after 2f: hdwy over 4f out: rdn over 2f out: kpt on)	2	**3**	10/1	86	21
3014^{4}	**Bina Gardens**	(HRACecil) **3-8-5** WRyan(9) (lw: hld up: hdwy 5f out: wknd over 2f out)	4	**4**	7/1 ³	76	11
3014^{5}	**Just Alex (IRE)**	(TGMills) **3-8-10** JQuinn(3) (lw: plld hrd: chsd ldr tl wknd 3f out)	¾	**5**	16/1	80	15
2572^{3}	**Darien**	(RCharlton) **3-8-10** TSprake(2) (lw: dwlt: hdwy 8f out: wknd over 3f out)	¾	**6**	40/1	79	14
3021^{5}	**Gallant Heights**	(GCBravery) **3-8-5** DRMcCabe(1) (chsd wnr 6f)	11	**7**	50/1	59	—
3021^{10}	**Snowcap (IRE)**	(GWragg) **3-8-5** AMcGlone(10) (a bhd)	7	**8**	50/1	50	—
	Panorama	(LMCumani) **3-8-2**(3) RFfrench(6) (unf: bkwd: hdwy 8f out: wknd 5f out)	7	**9**	16/1	40	—
3021^{8}	**Signed And Sealed (USA)**	(CACyzer) **3-8-10** AMorris(8) (hdwy over 6f out: wknd 4f out)	7	**10**	66/1	36	—

(SP 115.8%) **10 Rn**

2m 32.3 (3.30) CSF £8.00 TOTE £6.50: £1.40 £1.30 £1.60 (£3.50) Trio £5.90 OWNER Mr Hamdan Al Maktoum (NEWMARKET) BRED Hidaway Farm

OFFICIAL EXPLANATION Gallant Heights: the trainer reported that the filly was ridden more prominently today and was tiring in the last two furlongs.

IN-FOCUS: This two-day meeting was run on the far side of the July Course. It transpired that during the re-alignment of the course a stake had been put through a cable, which meant that races over a mile and more were not electronically timed on either day. Racereaders' hand-times are substituted.

3188 Marsul (USA), on his toes in the first-time visor, was given a good ride from the front and, although the favourite probably headed him in the Dip, keeping straight won him the day. (5/1: 7/2-11/2)
3021 Sir Ricky (USA), moving keenly and well on the heels of the leader, had to work increasingly hard from the furlong pole. Asked to win the race in the Dip, he soon got upsides but forfeited his chance by veering away from some sharp reminders in the closing stages. It would be unfair to criticise Eddery too much for failing to switch his whip, as he later gave up rides due to dehydration. (8/11: evens-11/10)
2940 Jazz Track (IRE), who was almost found out by his enthusiasm when short of room and clipping heels early on, was outpaced early in the straight. Already proven over further, he stayed on best of all in the last couple of furlongs and should find an opening when back up in trip. (10/1: 8/1-12/1)
3014 Bina Gardens takes a good hold but is only an ordinary mover. Close enough if good enough with three furlongs left, she flashed her tail, as so many by the sire do, when ridden along, and was soon in trouble. A full sister to Bal Harbour, who did most of his winning at ten furlongs, her ability to get this trip is yet to be proven. (7/1: 7/2-8/1)
3014 Just Alex (IRE), free to post, did not give himself a chance of getting this longer trip. (16/1)
2572 Darien, a half brother to Quest For Fame, was racing with his tongue tied down. He briefly flattered but has much to do to live up to his pedigree. (40/1)

3420 EQUITY FINANCIAL COLLECTIONS CLAIMING STKS (3-Y.O+) (Class D)

2-30 (2-33) **7f (July)** £3,785.00 (£1,130.00: £540.00: £245.00) Stalls: Low GOING minus 0.61 sec per fur (F)

				SP	RR	SF
3196[2]	**Windy Treat (USA)** (EALDunlop) **3-8-9** GCarter(1) (dwlt: hld up: hdwy & squeezed thro over 1f out: led ins fnl f: r.o wl)	—	**1**	10/1	75	42
3143[18]	**Allinson's Mate (IRE) (68)** (TDBarron) **9-8-8b**(5) KimberleyHart(3) (hld up: hdwy 3f out: led over 1f out tl ins fnl f: unable qckn)	1¾	**2**	9/2[3]	69	42
3139[4]	**Big Ben (67)** (RHannon) **3-8-11** PatEddery(2) (trckd ldrs: effrt over 1f out: kpt on ins fnl f)	2	**3**	7/2[2]	68	35
2026[31]	**Varnishing Day (IRE) (80)** (PWChapple-Hyam) **5-9-1b**[1] SWhitworth(5) (plld hrd: sn prom: one pce fnl f)	1½	**4**	14/1	63	36
3130[9]	**Hoh Returns (IRE) (78)** (MBell) **4-9-0** MFenton(8) (hld up: hdwy over 2f out: nvr able chal)	2½	**5**	9/4[1]	56	29
2921[16]	**Class Distinction (IRE) (64)** (RHannon) **3-8-11** SSanders(4) (chsd ldrs: rdn & wkng whn nt clr run over 1f out)	½	**6**	16/1	58	25
3100[11]	**Rise Up Singing (41)** (WJMusson) **9-8-9b** RCochrane(10) (led over 5f: n.m.r & sn btn)	4	**7**	16/1	41	14
2071[8]	**Manabar (33)** (MJPolglase) **5-8-8** TGMcLaughlin(6) (a bhd)	¾	**8**	66/1	38	11
	Polar Prospect (70) (BHanbury) **4-9-6** JStack(7) (b: bkwd: bhd fnl 2f)	2½	**9**	14/1	45	18
	Southern Memories (IRE) (WJMusson) **7-8-9** DRMcCabe(11) (bkwd: bhd fnl 3f)	¾	**10**	33/1	32	5
2496[10]	**Just Blink (IRE)** (SCWilliams) **4-8-6** AMcGlone(9) (s.i.s: sn chsng ldrs: wknd over 2f out)	12	**11**	50/1	1	—
				(SP 111.8%)		**11 Rn**

1m 25.08 (0.08) CSF £46.76 TOTE £7.10: £1.80 £2.00 £1.10 (£19.40) Trio £15.90 OWNER Mr Hilal Salem (NEWMARKET) BRED Gainsborough Farm Inc
WEIGHT FOR AGE 3yo-6lb
3196 Windy Treat (USA), again free to post, gave trouble at the stalls but none in the race, finding a good turn of foot to score in good style. He moves like a horse that may have had back trouble, which could account for his Ripon display. (10/1)
2204 Allinson's Mate (IRE) moved poorly to post but ran a sound race without matching the winner's finishing burst. (9/2: op 3/1)
3139 Big Ben, keen going down, was gradually pegging back the runner-up in the final furlong but could not land a blow. This seems his trip. (7/2: op 6/1)
Varnishing Day (IRE), lightly raced, was blinkered for the first time and dropped in class. Taking such a strong hold probably didn't help his cause and a similar race should be within his compass. (14/1)
2769 Hoh Returns (IRE), down in class and up in trip, was set an impossible task by the time he was put to work but his stamina did look stretched. (9/4)
Class Distinction (IRE), back up to seven for the first time this year, already looked in trouble in the Dip when interference ended all hope. (16/1)
Polar Prospect (14/1: op 8/1)

3421 DANDELION LADIES INVITATION AMATEUR H'CAP (0-65) (3-Y.O+) (Class F)

3-05 (3-06) **1m (July)** £4,299.00 (£1,302.00: £636.00: £303.00) Stalls: Low GOING minus 0.61 sec per fur (F)

				SP	RR	SF
2918[5]	**Sandicliffe (USA) (50)** (JARToller) **4-10-11** MissEJohnsonHoughton(5) (trckd ldrs: rdn to ld 1f out: sn pushed clr)	—	**1**	100/30[1]	66	48
2922*	**Mezzoramio (53)** (KAMorgan) **5-11-0v** MrsDArbuthnot(7) (led after 2f: rdn & edgd lft over 1f out: sn hdd: no ex)	5	**2**	4/1[2]	59	41
3321[10]	**Mutahadeth (50)** (DShaw) **3-10-4b**[1] MissASloane(1) (in tch: hdwy over 1f out: r.o wl ins fnl f)	½	**3**	20/1	55	30
3197[9]	**Don't Drop Bombs (USA) (37)** (DTThom) **8-9-12v** MissCNicot(10) (chsd ldrs: ev ch 2f out: one pce fnl f)	½	**4**	16/1	41	23
2892*	**King Athelstan (USA) (60)** (BAMcMahon) **9-11-7** MissERamsden(4) (prom: rdn over 1f out: sn btn)	1¾	**5**	13/2	61	43
2730[9]	**Cats Bottom (45)** (AGNewcombe) **5-10-6** MissLJarven(11) (hld up: hdwy 2f out: no imp fnl f)	1	**6**	11/2[3]	44	26
3056[9]	**Fort Knox (IRE) (47)** (RMFlower) **6-10-8b** MissRClark(12) (s.s: nvr nrr)	½	**7**	10/1	45	27
2146[11]	**Montone (IRE) (55)** (JRJenkins) **7-11-2** MissCGatta(9) (sn pushed along: n.d)	¾	**8**	20/1	51	33
3293[3]	**Tezaab (50)** (BHanbury) **3-10-4** MissJAllison(2) (chsd ldrs over 6f)	hd	**9**	9/1	46	21
2836[8]	**Miss Barcelona (IRE) (42)** (MJPolglase) **3-9-10** MissJFeilden(3) (led 2f: rdn 3f out: sn wknd)	3	**10**	25/1	32	7
2175[9]	**Alisura (30)** (DTThom) **4-9-5b**[1] MissUSchmutzler(6) (prom 5f)	13	**11**	33/1	—	—
2646[15]	**Flagstaff (USA) (31)** (KRBurke) **4-9-6** MrsEVanOrshoven(8) (lw: s.s: a wl bhd)	5	**12**	33/1	—	—
				(SP 116.0%)		**12 Rn**

1m 40.4 (2.40) CSF £13.24 CT £207.04 TOTE £4.10: £1.90 £1.50 £5.80 (£4.30) Trio £78.50 OWNER Ash Partnership (WHITSBURY) BRED Brereton C. Jones
WEIGHT FOR AGE 3yo-7lb
2918 Sandicliffe (USA), rather free going down, showed just how unlucky she had been at Windsor last time, striding clear in great style once in front. (100/30)
2922* Mezzoramio, trying to follow up last year's win in the race, did not find it as easy to dominate but still ran to the line and gave the pilot a good final ride. (4/1)
3038 Mutahadeth, taken down very quietly, settled quite well but finished as if the first-time blinkers had woken him up. (20/1)
2146 Don't Drop Bombs (USA), having his annual crack at the race, was second in 1995, but could not get to the front this time and lacked pace in the last couple of furlongs. (16/1)
2892* King Athelstan (USA), with his tongue tied down, had done his running by the Dip and seemed found out by the stiff mile. (13/2: 7/2-7/1)

2310 Cats Bottom, who has not won on turf since her two-year-old days, never looked like changing that. (11/2)
3293 Tezaab (9/1: op 6/1)

3422 ENZA NEW ZEALAND SWEET SOLERA STKS (Listed) (2-Y.O F) (Class A)

3-35 (3-36) **7f (July)** £9,420.00 (£3,480.00: £1,665.00: £675.00: £262.50: £97.50) Stalls: Low GOING minus 0.61 sec per fur (F)

Form	Horse	Btn	Pl	SP	RR	SF
3237[3]	**Diamond White (83)** (GCBravery) **2-8-8** DRMcCabe(3) (hld up: hdwy 2f out: str run to ld wl ins fnl f)	—	**1**	25/1	95	41
2862[10]	**Stop Out** (HMorrison) **2-8-8** CRutter(5) (lw: hld up: hdwy over 2f out: ev ch wl ins fnl f: unable qckn)	¾	**2**	14/1	93	39
2600[2]	**Silent Tribute (IRE) (100)** (MBell) **2-8-8** MFenton(2) (lw: led 2f: led over 2f out tl ins fnl f: r.o)	s.h	**3**	9/2[3]	93	39
2697*	**Parisian Lady (IRE)** (AGNewcombe) **2-8-8** GHind(7) (plld hrd: led 5f out tl over 2f out: led ins fnl f: sn hdd & one pce)	s.h	**4**	5/2[1]	93	39
2840[2]	**Particular Friend** (EALDunlop) **2-8-8** WRyan(4) (s.i.s: hld up: hdwy over 2f out: one pce appr fnl f)	5	**5**	9/2[3]	82	28
3036[2]	**Belladera (IRE) (85)** (NTinkler) **2-8-8** RCochrane(1) (prom 5f)	¾	**6**	33/1	80	26
2962[2]	**Eloquent** (SirMarkPrescott) **2-8-8** GDuffield(6) (lw: plld hrd: prom tl rdn & btn over 1f out)	2½	**7**	7/2[2]	74	20
3237*	**Jay Gee (IRE) (82)** (GGMargarson) **2-8-11** GCarter(8) (chsd ldrs over 5f)	½	**8**	7/1	76	22

(SP 113.1%) **8 Rn**

1m 25.11 (0.11) CSF £286.69 TOTE £21.30: £3.10 £2.50 £1.40 (£76.60) OWNER Mr Peter Scott (NEWMARKET) BRED Mrs Celia Miller
OFFICIAL EXPLANATION **Eloquent: no explanation offered.**
3237 Diamond White benefited from the step up in trip, although it didn't look that way as she all but bolted to post. In the race she settled well and found a fine turn of foot to pounce late. (25/1)
1970* Stop Out, stepping up from the minimum trip, was the pick on the way down and left her Newbury disappointment behind her. Throwing down a determined challenge from the Dip, she lost little in defeat and looks to have found her distance. (14/1: op 25/1)
2600 Silent Tribute (IRE) ran her race but could not confirm debut placings with the winner. (9/2)
2697* Parisian Lady (IRE), stepping up in trip, took a keen hold and wasn't allowed to dominate by Silent Tribute but still ran a grand race for a bargain basement buy to gain some black type. (5/2)
2840 Particular Friend moved to post notably poorly but didn't perform too badly considering the step up in class, although no match for the principals from the Dip. (9/2)
3036 Belladera (IRE) couldn't make any impression when it mattered and was one of the first beaten. (33/1)
2962 Eloquent, who was restrained this time, refused to settle, failing to run any sort of race. A good mover, she is better than this. (7/2)
3237* Jay Gee (IRE), who beat the winner in a six-furlong nursery here a week ago, moved poorly to post and, having not been able to get in front, failed to see out the extra furlong. (7/1)

3423 JOE JENNINGS BOOKMAKERS H'CAP (0-105) (3-Y.O+) (Class B)

4-10 (4-11) **7f (July)** £19,040.00 (£5,720.00: £2,760.00: £1,280.00) Stalls: Low GOING minus 0.61 sec per fur (F)

Form	Horse	Btn	Pl	SP	RR	SF
2598[18]	**Neuwest (USA) (92)** (RAkehurst) **5-9-11** SSanders(12) (lw: a.p: led over 1f out: sn rdn clr)	—	**1**	9/1[3]	103	70
3150[9]	**Philistar (75)** (KRBurke) **4-8-8** BDoyle(9) (in tch: hdwy over 1f out: fin wl)	2½	**2**	14/1	80	47
3220[4]	**Volley (IRE) (83)** (MajorDNChappell) **4-9-2** GCarter(15) (dwlt: hdwy 3f out: r.o fnl f)	hd	**3**	14/1	88	55
2835[17]	**Zugudi (80)** (KMahdi) **3-8-4**(3) DO'Donohoe(8) (lw: led 1f: led over 3f out tl over 1f out: r.o)	nk	**4**	33/1	84	45
3138[14]	**Blue Flyer (IRE) (70)** (RIngram) **4-8-3** AMcGlone(14) (hdwy & swtchd rt 2f out: r.o ins fnl f)	1¼	**5**	25/1	72	39
3217[13]	**Double Bounce (86)** (PJMakin) **7-9-5** JQuinn(10) (b: hld up: hdwy over 1f out: r.o)	s.h	**6**	16/1	87	54
3185[7]	**Chickawicka (IRE) (95)** (BPalling) **6-10-0** TSprake(13) (led after 1f: hdd over 3f out: one pce fnl f)	½	**7**	25/1	95	62
2211[8]	**Madly Sharp (93)** (JWWatts) **6-9-12** MFenton(7) (hld up: hdwy & swtchd rt 3f out: r.o fnl f)	¾	**8**	10/1	92	59
2598[19]	**Highborn (IRE) (92)** (PSFelgate) **8-9-11** WRyan(3) (hld up: effrt whn nt clr run 2f out: r.o fnl f)	1¼	**9**	20/1	88	55
3150[W]	**Cosmic Prince (IRE) (93)** (MAJarvis) **3-9-6** RCochrane(11) (s.i.s: sn chsng ldrs: rdn over 3f out: btn fnl f)	1¾	**10**	9/2[2]	85	46
2775[8]	**Pleading (82)** (HCandy) **4-9-1** CRutter(17) (s.i.s: hdwy over 2f out: btn over 1f out)	1¼	**11**	16/1	71	38
1309[4]	**Top Banana (91)** (HCandy) **6-9-3**(7) SarahJackson(2) (stdd s: bhd tl hdwy & nt clr run over 1f out)	¾	**12**	25/1	78	45
*3075**	**Master Boots (95)** (DRLoder) **4-9-9**(5) CLowther(16) (w ldr tl wknd over 1f out)	1	**13**	10/1	80	47
3024[7]	**Ursa Major (85)** (PAKelleway) **3-8-12** FJovine(6) (prom: rdn over 3f out: n.m.r 2f out: sn wknd)	nk	**14**	40/1	69	30
3232[2]	**Signs And Wonders (69)** (CACyzer) **3-7-7**(3) RFfrench(1) (prom over 4f: sn wknd)	¾	**15**	20/1	51	12
2961[16]	**Poker School (IRE) (80)** (NACallaghan) **3-8-7** GDuffield(4) (a bhd)	¾	**16**	33/1	61	22
3310*	**Royal Mark (IRE) (87)** (TDBarron) **4-9-6** 5x GHind(5) (dwlt: hdwy & n.m.r over 2f out: nt clr run over 1f out: eased)	1¼	**17**	7/2[1]	65	32

(SP 123.1%) **17 Rn**

1m 24.02 (-0.98) CSF £104.11 CT £1,612.01 TOTE £9.90: £2.40 £3.50 £3.10 £10.50 (£100.10) Trio £284.50 OWNER Mr Paul Green (EPSOM) BRED Robert Bloomer and Sharon L. Bloomer
WEIGHT FOR AGE 3yo-6lb
1874* Neuwest (USA), below his best in the Bunbury Cup, bounced right back and seems much improved since changing stables. (9/1: 6/1-10/1)
1985* Philistar, not beaten far in the Schweppes Golden Mile, finished in great style but the winner had first run on him. (14/1)
3220 Volley (IRE), closely weighted with the winner on their meeting at Newbury in June, took a while to recover from a tardy start and, despite a lot of sterling work in the last couple of furlongs, could never land a blow. She does shape as though she ought to get a mile although soundly beaten on her two efforts at the trip to date. (14/1)
1691* Zugudi, who looked the part and moved well to post, came back to form with a sound effort from the front. (33/1)
2835 Blue Flyer (IRE) has only won once on turf but certainly has the ability to add to that tally. (25/1)
2598 Double Bounce has never won over this trip and was restrained to get it. Staying on well, he could be coming to hand but has not scored in over a year. (16/1)
1737* Cosmic Prince (IRE), given his much publicised problems before the start, was taken down very steadily and it was only when the stalls opened that his chance receded as he missed the break. With plenty of pace on, he was unable to get to the front and was well held in the final furlong. He does give the impression that there is something more to come when everything goes right. (9/2)
3310* Royal Mark (IRE) looked to be cruising when starting his run but had a nightmare run and his jockey gave up in disgust inside the final furlong. He remains in great shape and losses are leant. (7/2)

3424 AUCKLAND H'CAP (0-95) (3-Y.O+) (Class C)

4-40 (4-41) **1m 2f (July)** £5,726.25 (£1,710.00: £817.50: £371.25) Stalls: High GOING minus 0.61 sec per fur (F)

Form	Horse	Btn	Pl	SP	RR	SF
3115[11]	**Hajr (IRE) (82)** (EALDunlop) **3-9-3** WRyan(9) (s.i.s: hld up: hdwy & nt clr run over 2f out: squeezed thro over 1f out: rdn to ld nr fin)	—	**1**	5/1[2]	92+	34

				SP	RR	SF
787[5]	**Silver Groom (IRE) (76)** (RAkehurst) **7-9-6** SSanders(4) (hld up: stdy hdwy to ld ins fnl f: rdn & unable qckn nr fin)	nk	**2**	10/1	86	37
2710[17]	**Orsay (80)** (WRMuir) **5-9-10** TSprake(7) (trckd ldrs: led over 1f out: rdn & hdd ins fnl f: one pce)	1½	**3**	9/1	87	38
2930*	**Farmost (80)** (SirMarkPrescott) **4-9-10** GDuffield(1) (led over 8f: r.o)	nk	**4**	7/1	87	38
2924*	**Invermark (83)** (JRFanshawe) **3-9-4** GCarter(10) (trckd ldrs: pushed along 4f out: btn appr fnl f)	1	**5**	13/2[3]	88	30
2873[3]	**Red Guard (80)** (GWragg) **3-9-1** RCochrane(8) (trckd ldrs: rdn over 2f out: sn btn)	hd	**6**	10/1	85	27
2187*	**American Whisper (75)** (PWHarris) **3-8-5**(5) CLowther(2) (trckd ldrs tl rdn & btn 2f out)	4	**7**	3/1[1]	74	16
2296[7]	**Scoss (84)** (LMCumani) **3-9-5** MDemuro(3) (hld up: hdwy 4f out: no imp fnl 2f)	1¾	**8**	10/1	80	22
2548[4]	**Maradi (IRE) (75)** (MBell) **3-8-10** MFenton(5) (a bhd)	dist	**9**	16/1	—	—

(SP 110.7%) **9 Rn**

2m 5.8 (2.20) CSF £45.69 CT £376.88 TOTE £6.00: £1.60 £2.10 £3.30 (£27.30) Trio £47.20 OWNER Maktoum Al Maktoum (NEWMARKET) BRED Ridgecourt Stud
WEIGHT FOR AGE 3yo-9lb
OFFICIAL EXPLANATION **American Whisper: the trainer reported that the colt could have been dehydrated.**
2229 Hajr (IRE), stepped up in trip, gave the impression that he would have won more decisively had he got daylight sooner. (5/1)
787 Silver Groom (IRE) with trip and ground seemingly ideal, travelled well and ran to his very best, but the 11lb he has gone up since his Flat win fourteen outings ago beat him. (10/1)
2528 Orsay, back to his best in this smaller field, did nothing wrong but he was beaten off a lower mark than this on his first two starts of the year. (9/1)
2930* Farmost ran a fine race and will be right in the shake up in similar conditions on a less testing track. (7/1: 5/1-15/2)
2924* Invermark, surprisingly dropped in trip, found the quickening pace had him in trouble some way out and, despite staying on, could never get back into the shake up. This looked a decent handicap and a step back up in trip should do the trick. (13/2: 9/2-7/1)
2873 Red Guard, back up in trip, again flattered to deceive. He moved down well and travelled strongly before finishing weakly when pressure was applied. (10/1: 7/1-12/1)
2187* American Whisper, up in the handicap as well as in class, challenged rather wide, a move which didn't prove successful during the meeting. (3/1)
1852 Scoss (10/1: 7/1-11/1)

3425 AIR NEW ZEALAND MAIDEN STKS (3-Y.O) (Class D)

5-10 (5-11) **6f (July)** £3,622.50 (£1,080.00: £515.00: £232.50) Stalls: Low GOING minus 0.61 sec per fur (F)

				SP	RR	SF
957[5]	**Midyan Call (92)** (MBell) **3-9-0** MFenton(1) (trckd ldrs: plld out over 1f out: rdn to ld ins fnl f)	—	**1**	6/1[3]	88	61
2838[4]	**Mary Cornwallis** (GWragg) **3-8-9** MHills(4) (led: rdn ins fnl f: sn hdd & no ex)	½	**2**	4/7[1]	82	55
2838[2]	**Listed Account (USA) (75)** (LMCumani) **3-8-9** RCochrane(5) (chsd ldr: ev ch over 2f out: one pce appr fnl f)	3	**3**	9/2[2]	74	47
2045[5]	**Fayik (70)** (AGNewcombe) **3-9-0** GHind(2) (bit bkwd: outpcd: hdwy fnl 2f: fin wl)	3	**4**	25/1	71	44
3241[3]	**Night Express (55)** (BHanbury) **3-9-0** JStack(9) (chsd ldrs: rdn 2f out: no imp)	2	**5**	25/1	65	38
2491[6]	**Hanan (USA) (65)** (PAKelleway) **3-8-6b**[1](3) RFfrench(7) (prom tl rdn & btn 2f out)	1	**6**	16/1	58	31
3202[8]	**Hawksbill Henry (USA)** (MrsAJPerrett) **3-9-0** GayeHarwood(3) (sn pushed along: chsd ldrs tl wknd over 2f out)	½	**7**	50/1	61	34
	Treaty (USA) (KMahdi) **3-9-0** SSanders(8) (w'like: scope: s.i.s: nvr nr ldrs)	7	**8**	16/1	43	16
	Amelia Jane (LMontagueHall) **3-8-6**(3) DO'Donohoe(6) (small: cmpt: bkwd: s.s: sn t.o)	dist	**9**	40/1	—	—

(SP 120.0%) **9 Rn**

1m 10.99 (-1.01) CSF £9.08 TOTE £5.70: £1.90 £1.10 £1.30 (£3.60) Trio £2.50 OWNER Mr Luciano Gaucci (NEWMARKET) BRED C. J. R. Trotter
957 Midyan Call, considered to need cut in the ground, came back to his early-season form behind Captain Collins under a similar patient ride. (6/1: 3/1-13/2)
2838 Mary Cornwallis, on a seemingly more suitable surface, set a tremendous gallop but was tying up and a sitting duck when the winner pulled out of her slipstream in the Dip. (4/7)
2838 Listed Account (USA), who finished in front of the runner-up on softer ground here recently, found this fast surface setting even less of a stamina test. (9/2: 3/1-5/1)
2045 Fayik, sold cheaply since his last run, was surprisingly dropping in trip and totally outpaced as a result, being one of three effectively tailed off at halfway. Finishing in tremendous style, he is one to look out for back up in distance. (25/1)
3241 Night Express stays further than this and could not quicken when the chance was there below the distance. (25/1)
2491 Hanan (USA), blinkered this time, ran a little better but has yet to show she has trained on. (16/1)
Amelia Jane bolted going to post and showed none of that speed coming back. (40/1)

T/Jkpt: Not won; £38,935.61 to Epsom 10/8/97. T/Plpt: £346.60 (113.22 Tckts). T/Qdpt: £288.30 (5.38 Tckts) Dk/CR

3066-REDCAR (L-H) (Good to firm)
Saturday August 9th

WEATHER: fine & sunny WIND: slight half behind

3426 E.B.F. SINNINGTON MAIDEN STKS (2-Y.O F) (Class D)

2-10 (2-10) **7f** £3,671.50 (£1,102.00: £531.00: £245.50) Stalls: High GOING minus 0.54 sec per fur (F)

				SP	RR	SF
2840[3]	**Alharir (USA)** (JLDunlop) **2-8-11** KDarley(2) (trckd ldrs: led on bit over 2f out: pushed wl clr)	—	**1**	1/2[1]	92+	48
	Arctic Air (EWeymes) **2-8-11** OPears(1) (leggy: unf: bit bkwd: swvd lft s: rn green & sn bhd: hdwy over 2f out: kpt on fnl f)	15	**2**	14/1	58	14
	Scent of Success (USA) (MRStoute) **2-8-8**(3) GParkin(7) (tall: sn outpcd & pushed along: hdwy 2f out: styd on towards fin)	1½	**3**	9/2[3]	54	10
3253[3]	**Rewardia (IRE)** (PDEvans) **2-8-4**(7) RWinston(5) (w ldr: led ½-wy tl over 2f out: hung lft & wknd over 1f out)	2½	**4**	4/1[2]	49	5
3070[10]	**Ladyofdistinction (IRE)** (JSWainwright) **2-8-11** TWilliams(4) (s.i.s: hdwy u.p ½-wy: nvr nr ldrs)	2	**5**	40/1	44	—
1819[11]	**Taylor's Pride** (TDBarron) **2-8-11** LCharnock(9) (sn wl outpcd)	1¾	**6**	20/1	40	—
	Tigi (MrsMReveley) **2-8-11** ACulhane(3) (leggy: unf: led tl ½-wy: wkng whn hmpd over 1f out)	1½	**7**	33/1	37	—
2752[6]	**Dougs Dream (IRE)** (MrsASwinbank) **2-8-11** WJO'Connor(6) (sn outpcd)	1¾	**8**	50/1	33	—

1645[11] **Thundering Papoose** (APJames) **2-8-4**(7) JFowle(8) (a wl outpcd) ....2½ **9** 66/1 27 —
(SP 125.1%) **9 Rn**

1m 23.1 (0.10) CSF £9.91 TOTE £1.50: £1.00 £4.70 £1.90 (£7.40) Trio £12.80 OWNER Mr Hamdan Al Maktoum (ARUNDEL) BRED Shadwell Farm Inc

2840 Alharir (USA), who apparently does not show a lot at home, showed a scratchy action going down. In the race itself, she proved totally different class but it was surprising that her rider pushed her out all the way to the line. (1/2)
Arctic Air, a backward-looking type, showed a very poor action going down. Taking time to get the hang of things, she can only improve. (14/1)
Scent of Success (USA), a tall filly, was clueless. After getting messed about, she was putting in some solid work at the line and the outing should have taught her plenty. (9/2)
3253 Rewardia (IRE), unimpressive in the paddock, showed a good action going down but, off the bridle, all she wanted to do was hang left. (4/1: op 6/1)
Ladyofdistinction (IRE), who showed plenty of knee-action going to post, still has plenty to learn. (40/1)

3427 BEDALE (S) STKS (2-Y.O) (Class F)

2-40 (2-41) **6f** £2,574.00 (£714.00: £342.00) Stalls: High GOING minus 0.54 sec per fur (F)

			SP	RR	SF
2606[3]	**Chinaider (IRE)** (JJO'Neill) **2-8-11** KDarley(10) (lw: sn outpcd & pushed along: hdwy ½-wy: led over 1f out: hung lft: drvn out) .... —	**1**	4/1 [2]	69	37
2936[3]	**Erro Codigo (66)** (MrsJRRamsden) **2-8-11** OPears(11) (trckd ldrs: rdn to ld over 2f out: hdd over 1f out: kpt on same pce) 1½	**2**	Evens [1]	65	33
2288[11]	**Circuiteer (IRE)** (JBerry) **2-8-11** JFanning(2) (sn wl outpcd & bhd: hdwy 2f out: styd on towards fin) 3	**3**	16/1	57	25
3062[3]	**Snappy Times (58)** (MDods) **2-8-11** JFEgan(9) (b.nr hind: chsd ldrs: rdn ½-wy: lost pl over 2f out) .... ¾	**4**	11/1 [3]	55	23
	Moonlight Flit (JGFitzGerald) **2-8-6** ACulhane(3) (cmpt: rn green: sn outpcd & bhd: hdwy over 1f out: nvr nr to chal) .... ½	**5**	16/1	49	17
3209[8]	**Seventh Heaven (64)** (DNicholls) **2-8-8**(3) GParkin(6) (led tl over 2f out: wknd over 1f out) 2	**6**	16/1	48	16
3084[5]	**Lady Rochelle** (TDEasterby) **2-8-7**ow1 WJO'Connor(8) (in tch: rdn & outpcd ½-wy: n.d) .... nk	**7**	33/1	44	11
3258[6]	**Dawn Patrol (60)** (KWHogg) **2-7-13**(7) JFowle(7) (w ldr: wknd over 1f out) 4	**8**	11/1 [3]	32	—
	Robert The Bruce (RAFahey) **2-8-4**(7) RWinston(5) (leggy: unf: sn outpcd & bhd: rdn & hung lft ½-wy: n.d) 1¼	**9**	12/1	34	2
3212[7]	**I'm Tef (59)** (TDEasterby) **2-8-11b** LCharnock(1) (chsd ldrs: drvn along ½-wy: wknd 2f out) 2½	**10**	14/1	27	—
3070[7]	**Joli Fille** (JSWainwright) **2-8-6** TWilliams(4) (s.i.s: a outpcd) 2½	**11**	33/1	15	—

(SP 124.6%) **11 Rn**

1m 11.6 (1.40) CSF £8.04 TOTE £4.50: £1.70 £1.20 £4.50 (£3.10) Trio £9.60 OWNER Mr E. A. Brook (PENRITH) BRED James McMullan
Sold T Lomas 12,000gns

2606 Chinaider (IRE) took plenty of stoking up but took it in decisive fashion in the end. Having changed hands at the auction, she apparently now joins Martin Pipe but, with the runner-up rated 66, the Handicapper will be taking no chances with her in nurseries. (4/1)
2936 Erro Codigo, beaten in two nurseries, was on edge in the paddock and was beaten entirely on merit. It is doubtful if he ran up to his nursery mark of 66 here. (Evens)
1819 Circuiteer (IRE), with the blinkers again left off, went keenly to post but, on the way back, was soon struggling, and was out of contention until staying on in good style in the closing stages. (16/1)
3062 Snappy Times carries his head high and has his own ideas. (11/1)
Moonlight Flit, very green going to post, was clueless coming back and can only improve on this initial effort. (16/1)
Robert The Bruce (12/1: op 7/1)

3428 ROTHMANS ROYALS NORTH SOUTH CHALLENGE SERIES H'CAP (0-85) (3-Y.O+) (Class D)

3-10 (3-10) **1m** £4,498.50 (£1,353.00: £654.00: £304.50) Stalls: High GOING minus 0.54 sec per fur (F)

			SP	RR	SF
3052[10]	**Saifan (83)** (DMorris) **8-10-0v** NDay(4) (hld up: effrt ½-wy: led over 1f out tl ins fnl f: rallied to ld post) .... —	**1**	16/1	93	52
2854*	**Epic Stand (76)** (MrsJRRamsden) **3-9-0** ACulhane(5) (hld up: stdy hdwy over 2f out: rdn to ld ins fnl f: jst ct)s.h	**2**	5/2 [1]	86	38
3208[10]	**Thwaab (64)** (FWatson) **5-8-9** JFEgan(6) (trckd ldrs: r.o wl fnl f) .... nk	**3**	12/1	73	32
2890[4]	**Gymcrak Premiere (71)** (GHolmes) **9-9-2** WJO'Connor(2) (b.hind: swvd rt s: sn trckng ldrs: ev ch 2f out: styd on same pce) 2½	**4**	7/1 [3]	75	34
2929[3]	**Sooty Tern (76)** (JMBradley) **10-9-0**(7) RWinston(7) (lw: led tl over 1f out: grad wknd) .... ½	**5**	13/2 [2]	79	38
3153[16]	**Best of All (IRE) (74)** (JBerry) **5-9-5b** LCharnock(1) (trckd ldrs: ev ch 2f out: one pce) .... nk	**6**	7/1 [3]	77	36
2465[5]	**Winston (53)** (JDBethell) **4-7-7**(5) RMullen(10) (sn trckng ldrs: effrt 2f out: sn rdn & no imp) .... ¾	**7**	13/2 [2]	54	13
3064[8]	**Dispol Gem (66)** (PCalver) **4-8-11** KDarley(9) (trckd ldrs: drvn along & ev ch 2f out: sn wknd) .... ¾	**8**	14/1	66	25
3243[2]	**Mountgate (66)** (MPBielby) **5-8-11b**[1] TWilliams(3) (sltly hmpd s: sn drvn along & in tch: hung lft & lost pl over 1f out) 2	**9**	7/1 [3]	62	21
3262[6]	**Gulliver (70)** (MrsJRRamsden) **4-9-1** OPears(8) (trckd ldrs tl lost pl 2f out) 5	**10**	11/1	56	15

(SP 121.3%) **10 Rn**

1m 36.3 (1.30) CSF £53.12 CT £478.54 TOTE £15.30: £3.40 £1.40 £3.90 (£23.90) Trio £257.40; £195.78 to Epsom Downs 10/8/97 OWNER Mrs L. Brook (NEWMARKET) BRED M. M. Nashar
WEIGHT FOR AGE 3yo-7lb
STEWARDS' ENQUIRY Day susp. 18 & 22/8/97 (improper use of whip).

1782 Saifan, who needs a straight track, put three very poor efforts behind him and, answering his rider's every call, regained the advantage right on the line. It was surprising the Stewards did not hold an enquiry into his improved form. (16/1)
2854* Epic Stand, 16lb higher than when reinstated at Newcastle two runs ago, came from off the pace in a race run at a moderate gallop. After going a neck up inside the last, he was just worried out of it. (5/2: op 6/4)
1977 Thwaab, without his usual blinkers and stepping up in distance, finished with quite a flourish. There is no doubt that he is now on a mark from which he can win again. (12/1)
2890 Gymcrak Premiere is happier over an extra quarter-mile. (7/1)
2929 Sooty Tern set just a modest pace. He is not at his best on a straight track and switchback courses suit him ideally. (13/2)
2660 Best of All (IRE) seems high enough in the weights now. (7/1)
1097 Winston, well supported in the market, is better coming from off the pace in a stronger-run race. (13/2: 12/1-6/1)

3429 MARY REVELEY RACING CLUB CLAIMING STKS (3-Y.O+) (Class F)

3-40 (3-41) **1m 6f 19y** £2,511.00 (£696.00: £333.00) Stalls: Centre GOING minus 0.54 sec per fur (F)

			SP	RR	SF
2825[4]	**Charity Crusader (42)** (MrsMReveley) **6-9-1b**(5) SCopp(6) (lw: led: qcknd clr over 3f out: hld on wl towards fin) .... —	**1**	9/4 [2]	47	15

				SP	RR	SF
3116[2]	**Durgams First (IRE) (51)** (MrsMReveley) **5-9-8** ACulhane(4) (lw: hld up: stdy hdwy over 3f out: shkn up & chal over 1f out: nt qckn nr fin)	nk	**2**	4/5[1]	49	17
3089[4]	**Maddie** (WWHaigh) **5-9-7** NDay(1) (trckd ldrs: pushed along over 4f out: kpt on same pce)	3½	**3**	11/1[3]	44	12
2910[14]	**Finestatetobein (30)** (FWatson) **4-9-1** JFEgan(2) (outpcd 8f out: hdwy u.p over 3f out: one pce)	1¼	**4**	20/1	36	4
	Chancancook (JLEyre) **4-8-13** OPears(5) (trckd wnr tl wknd over 2f out)	9	**5**	33/1	24	—
2753[7]	**Fox Sparrow (42)** (NTinkler) **7-9-4b** KDarley(3) (hld up: effrt 3f out: no rspnse)	3	**6**	16/1	26	—
				(SP 108.2%)	**6 Rn**	

3m 7.9 (8.60) CSF £3.66 TOTE £3.90: £1.70 £1.10 (£1.10) OWNER The Mary Reveley Racing Club (SALTBURN) BRED Lavinia Duchess of Norfolk

2825 Charity Crusader, who has no heart for a battle, was allowed to set his own pace. Well handled, when the crunch came he found a fraction more than his equally half-hearted stablemate. (9/4: op 6/4)

3116 Durgams First (IRE), who had 7lb in hand of the winner on official figures, moved up on the bridle to draw almost upsides over a furlong out but, in the dash to the line, he was out-battled by the winner, no hero himself. (4/5)

3089 Maddie, on her toes beforehand, was dropped in class and stepped up in distance. (11/1)

1996 Finestatetobein would have met the winner on a stone better terms in a handicap. (20/1)

Fox Sparrow looked thoroughly out of love with the game. (16/1)

3430 VAUX CIU RED CROSS MAIDEN H'CAP (0-75) (3-Y.O+) (Class D)

4-15 (4-15) **1m 2f** £3,652.00 (£1,096.00: £528.00: £244.00) Stalls: Low GOING minus 0.54 sec per fur (F)

				SP	RR	SF
2907[6]	**Sing And Dance (38)** (EWeymes) **4-7-9**(7) RWinston(2) (lw: hld up: hdwy over 3f out: led & edgd lft over 1f out: styd on u.p)	—	**1**	5/1	50	23
3071[4]	**Lord Discord (58)** (TDEasterby) **3-8-13v[1]** LCharnock(4) (trckd ldrs: led over 3f out: sn rdn: hdd over 1f out: nt qckn)	1¼	**2**	5/2[2]	68	32
1299[13]	**Dulas Bay (47)** (MWEasterby) **3-8-2** JFanning(7) (hld up: hdwy & ev ch over 3f out: hung lft over 2f out: one pce)	2½	**3**	20/1	53	17
2956[4]	**Ceanothus (IRE) (58)** (WJHaggas) **3-8-6**(7) JoHunnam(3) (mde most tl over 3f out: sn wl outpcd)	1½	**4**	9/4[1]	62	26
3225[5]	**Beau Roberto (49)** (JSGoldie) **3-8-4** TWilliams(1) (trckd ldrs: drvn along & ev ch 4f out: edgd rt & lost pl over 2f out)	3½	**5**	8/1	47	11
2783[2]	**Billy Nomaite (70)** (MrsSJSmith) **3-9-11** OPears(6) (w ldr tl wknd qckly over 3f out: sn bhd & eased)	22	**6**	4/1[3]	33	—
				(SP 111.9%)	**6 Rn**	

2m 6.2 (2.60) CSF £16.15 TOTE £5.50: £1.80 £1.50 (£9.20) OWNER Mrs N. Napier (MIDDLEHAM) BRED Mrs N Napier

WEIGHT FOR AGE 3yo-9lb

2907 Sing And Dance looked to have a good chance at the weights, 6lb lower than when third in a better event at Newcastle three outings previously. (5/1)

3071 Lord Discord, in a visor for the first time, looked to have things well under control when taking it up but, off the bridle, he proved woefully one-paced. (5/2)

Dulas Bay, a very tall, narrow sort, probably ran his best race to date. (20/1)

2956 Ceanothus (IRE) appears to have nothing in the way of speed and will be suited by even further. (9/4)

3225 Beau Roberto continues on a downhill slide. (8/1: 6/1-9/1)

2783 Billy Nomaite, on his handicap debut, ran as if something was seriously amiss. (4/1)

3431 GO RACING IN YORKSHIRE H'CAP (0-60) (3-Y.O+) (Class F)

4-45 (4-47) **6f** £2,103.00 (£2,103.00: £444.00) Stalls: High GOING minus 0.54 sec per fur (F)

				SP	RR	SF
3208*	**Grand Chapeau (IRE) (61)** (DNicholls) **5-10-1** AlexGreaves(17) (lw: led: clr over 1f out: jst lasted)	—	**1**	11/4[1]	69	45
3334[5]	**Camionneur (IRE) (48)** (TDEasterby) **4-9-2b** LCharnock(18) (s.i.s: hdwy over 2f out: styd on fnl f)	—	**1**	9/2[2]	56	32
3143[4]	**Bollin Dorothy (52)** (TDEasterby) **4-9-6** TWilliams(23) (trckd ldrs stands' side: kpt on wl fnl f)	1	**3**	10/1	57	33
3240[10]	**Mu-Arrik (29)** (GROldroyd) **9-7-6v**(5)ow1 RMullen(4) (chsd ldrs: edgd rt & styd on same pce appr fnl f)	nk	**4**	50/1	34	9
2711[16]	**Halmanerror (56)** (MrsJRRamsden) **7-9-10** ACulhane(21) (bhd: gd hdwy over 1f out: styd on wl towards fin)	1	**5**	8/1[3]	58	34
3240[4]	**Stephensons Rocket (44)** (RAFahey) **6-8-5**(7) RWinston(6) (chsd ldrs far side: kpt on same pce appr fnl f)	¾	**6**	9/1	44	20
2540[13]	**Mystique Smile (35)** (JSGoldie) **4-8-3** JFanning(12) (w ldr centre: nt qckn appr fnl f)	s.h	**7**	40/1	35	11
3271[10]	**Sihafi (USA) (46)** (JMCarr) **4-9-0** AGarth(19) (a chsng ldrs: rdn over 2f out: one pce)	¾	**8**	20/1	44	20
3240[8]	**Reinhardt (IRE) (43)** (DNicholls) **4-8-11** KDarley(16) (rr div tl styd on fnl 2f)	¾	**9**	14/1	39	15
3241[12]	**Madam Zando (28)** (JBalding) **4-7-3**(7) JFowle(22) (bhd: sme hdwy 2f out: n.d)	nk	**10**	50/1	23	—
3143[8]	**Napoleon Star (IRE) (47)** (SRBowring) **6-8-12**(3) CTeague(10) (hmpd s: bhd & sn drvn along: sme hdwy over 1f out: n.d)	¾	**11**	20/1	40	16
2721[9]	**Kid Ory (39)** (DWChapman) **6-8-2b**(5) KSked(2) (s.i.s: racd far side: sme hdwy ½-wy: wknd over 1f out)	hd	**12**	25/1	32	8
2934[7]	**Rennyholme (46)** (ABMulholland) **6-9-0** WJO'Connor(20) (chsd ldrs over 3f)	hd	**13**	14/1	38	14
3146[7]	**Miss Aragon (31)** (MissLCSiddall) **9-7-6**(7) TSiddall(9) (outpcd fr ½-wy)	nk	**14**	33/1	23	—
3261[2]	**Fisiostar (46)** (MDods) **4-9-0v[1]** JFEgan(15) (in tch: drvn along ½-wy: sn wknd)	2	**15**	11/1	32	8
3034[8]	**Foist (57)** (MWEasterby) **5-9-8**(3) GParkin(3) (in tch: sn drvn along: lost pl over 2f out)	1½	**16**	16/1	39	15
3240[2]	**L A Touch (40)** (JJQuinn) **4-8-8** SophieMitchell(14) (chsd ldrs tl wknd 2f out)	s.h	**17**	10/1	22	—
3266[12]	**Wagga Moon (IRE) (57)** (JJO'Neill) **3-9-7** OPears(1) (swtg: chsd ldrs far side tl wknd 2f out)	½	**18**	50/1	38	10
3241*	**River Ensign (41)** (WMBrisbourne) **4-8-2**(7) AMcCarthy(24) (chsd ldrs: rdn & edgd lft over 2f out: sn wknd)	1½	**19**	10/1	18	—
3037[11]	**Imperial Line (IRE) (34)** (ABMulholland) **3-7-5b[1]**(7) ANicholls(11) (b: swvd lft s: chsd ldrs centre tl lost pl ½-wy)	d.h	**19**	50/1	11	—
3241[6]	**Merrily (49)** (MissSEHall) **4-9-3** NDay(5) (b: b.hind: dwlt s: a bhd)	nk	**21**	16/1	25	1
2203[14]	**Forecast (37)** (KAMorgan) **4-7-12**(7) JoHunnam(13) (sn drvn along: bhd & virtually p.u over 1f out)	dist	**22**	33/1	—	—
				(SP 156.2%)	**22 Rn**	

1m 11.7 (1.50) CSF GC & C £7.38 C & GC £9.06 CT GC, C & BD £59.54 C, GC & BD £63.63 TOTE GC £1.90 C £2.60: GC £1.70 C £1.60 £3.40 £5.60 (£11.80) Trio £20.90 OWNER Mr David Faulkner (THIRSK)/T E F Freight (Scarborough) Ltd (MALTON) BRED Norelands Bloodstock/K. Purfield

LONG HANDICAP Mu-Arrik 7-8 Madam Zando 7-8

WEIGHT FOR AGE 3yo-4lb

OFFICIAL EXPLANATION Foist: finished distressed.

3208* Grand Chapeau (IRE), 10lb higher in the weights, showed three or four lengths clear one and a half furlongs out but, in the end, the post came just in time. He looks in tip-top shape and is a fine advert for his trainer. (11/4)

3334 Camionneur (IRE), having his second outing in three days, deserved a change of luck after his wretched run at Pontefract but, after missing the break slightly and moving up looking sure to win, in the end he had to settle for a share of the spoils. (9/2)
3143 Bollin Dorothy ran right up to her best over her optimum distance. (10/1)
2938 Mu-Arrik, now getting into the veteran stage, has not won for almost three years. Despite his low draw, he ended up racing towards the stands side. (50/1)
1395 Halmanerror, who has won off a 1lb higher mark, was putting in some solid work at the finish and will not be long finding another opening. (8/1)
3240 Stephensons Rocket came out best of those racing towards the far side. (9/1)

T/Plpt: £11.90 (978.84 Tckts). T/Qdpt: £13.90 (26.56 Tckts) WG

3300-EPSOM (L-H) (Good)
Sunday August 10th
WEATHER: very hot WIND: slight half behind

3432 EPSOM AND EWELL BOROUGH COUNCIL DIAMOND JUBILEE LADIES' H'CAP (0-70) (3-Y.O+) (Class E)
2-00 (2-02) **1m 2f 18y** £2,830.25 (£857.00: £418.50: £199.25) Stalls: Low GOING minus 0.25 sec per fur (GF)

				SP	RR	SF
3248^{6}	**Righty Ho (58)** (PTWalwyn) **3-9-11v**(5) MissSSamworth(9) (hdwy over 3f out: led over 1f out: comf)	—	1	11/2^{3}	72	44
3248^{11}	**Bellas Gate Boy (47)** (JPearce) **5-10-0** MrsLPearce(7) (lw: hdwy over 1f out: r.o)	4	2	10/1	55	36
3041^{5}	**Madam Lucy (43)** (JLSpearing) **3-8-10**(5)ow1 MissTSpearing(4) (hdwy over 3f out: unable qckn fnl 2f)	1¼	3	14/1	49	20
3248^{3}	**Breezed Well (46)** (KGWingrove) **11-9-8**(5) MrsHNoonan(5) (a.p: led over 2f out tl over 1f out: wknd ins fnl f)	¾	4	11/1	51	32
	Katie's Kid (35) (DJSffrenchDavis) **7-8-11**(5) MissEFolkes(2) (5th whn hmpd on ins & lost pl over 5f out: rallied & nt clr run over 2f out: one pce)	½	5	40/1	39	20
3048^{5}	**Squared Away (47)** (JWPayne) **5-9-9b**(5) MissCLake(8) (lw: nvr nrr)	¾	6	9/1	50	31
3200^{8}	**Golden Touch (USA) (51)** (DJSCosgrove) **5-10-4** MissERamsden(6) (lw: nvr nrr)	1¾	7	9/2^{2}	51	32
3104^{8}	**Fresh Fruit Daily (68)** (PAKelleway) **5-11-2**(5) MissJWormall(1) (led over 7f)	3½	8	12/1	62	43
1779^{24}	**Lizium (38)** (JCFox) **5-9-0**(5) MissSarah-JaneDurman(3) (lw: a bhd)	nk	9	40/1	32	13
3256^{2}	**Dizzy Tilly (65)** (TJNaughton) **3-10-4**(5) MrsJNaughton(10) (swtg: chsd ldr 7f: wkng whn edgd lft 2f out)	1¼	10	7/2^{1}	57	29
3081^{3}	**Passage Creeping (IRE) (64)** (SDow) **4-11-3** MrsMCowdrey(11) (prom over 7f)	5	11	9/1	48	29

(SP 112.4%) **11 Rn**

2m 10.02 (6.02) CSF £51.59 CT £656.01 TOTE £8.60: £2.30 £1.90 £4.00 (£28.20) Trio £182.50 OWNER Mr Eric Perry (LAMBOURN) BRED B. J. Warren
WEIGHT FOR AGE 3yo-9lb

3248 Righty Ho appreciated the longer trip and, striking the front approaching the final furlong, surged clear to win with plenty in hand. (11/2)
2430 Bellas Gate Boy, racing at the back of the field, at last found his stride from below the distance but, despite running on to take second place in the last fifty yards, found the winner was already home and dry. He is extremely hard to win with and has just one victory to his name from thirty-one starts. (10/1: 8/1-12/1)
3041 Madam Lucy, who has now changed stables twice since winning a claimer last month, took closer order rounding Tattenham Corner but could only go up and down in the same place in the final quarter-mile. (14/1)
3248 Breezed Well certainly has a lot of miles on the clock - this was his 110th race - but he still ran another sound race. (11/1: 6/1-12/1)
Katie's Kid, who has changed stables since his last outing over two years ago, looked reasonably straight considering his lay-off. Losing ground after being hampered along the inside rail just before halfway, he did not have the best of runs over a quarter of a mile out but, when a gap did appear, he could only struggle on at one pace. (40/1)
3048 Squared Away ran a similar race to his one at Ascot two weeks ago, being out with the washing until running on at the death. He has just one victory to his name. (9/1: 5/1-10/1)
3081 Passage Creeping (IRE) (9/1: op 6/1)

3433 WALTER NIGHTINGALL MAIDEN STKS (2-Y.O) (Class D)
2-35 (2-35) **6f** £3,468.75 (£1,050.00: £512.50: £243.75) Stalls: High GOING minus 0.25 sec per fur (GF)

				SP	RR	SF
2571^{2}	**Bernardo Bellotto (IRE) (82)** (MBell) **2-9-0** SSanders(4) (lw: a.p: led over 2f out: drvn out)	—	1	6/4^{1}	78	40
1143^{4}	**The Boy John (USA) (86)** (RHannon) **2-9-0** DHarrison(5) (lw: a.p: chsd wnr over 2f out: hrd rdn & ev ch whn wandered over 1f out: edgd lft ins fnl f: unable qckn)	1	2	5/2^{2}	75	37
2856^{3}	**Defiance** (BWHills) **2-8-11**(3) JDSmith(3) (outpcd: gd hdwy over 1f out: str run fnl f: fin wl)	hd	3	11/2	75+	37
	Naskhi (MJohnston) **2-8-9** MRoberts(1) (b.hind: str: scope: bit bkwd: led over 3f)	3½	4	3/1^{3}	61	23
3084^{6}	**Kantone (IRE)** (JMPEustace) **2-9-0** JTate(2) (spd over 3f)	13	5	33/1	31	—

(SP 111.9%) **5 Rn**

1m 10.46 (2.46) CSF £5.17 TOTE £2.50: £1.40 £1.30 (£2.40) OWNER Richard Green (Fine Paintings) (NEWMARKET) BRED Dr K. A. Roche-Nagle

2571 Bernardo Bellotto (IRE) has been running well this season and richly deserved this success after finishing second in five of his six previous starts. Sent to the front over a quarter of a mile from home, he responded well to pressure to keep the persistent runner-up at bay. (6/4: op 5/2)
1143 The Boy John (USA) looked in good shape for this first run in three months and launched his challenge in the final quarter-mile. Wandering around on the camber, he failed to find another gear inside the final furlong. A race can be found for him. (5/2)
2856 Defiance failed to handle Tattenham Hill and was soon well adrift of the other runners. However, he really found his stride from below the distance and finished in tremendous style. There is a race in him. (11/2: 4/1-6/1)
Naskhi, a plain, well-made filly, was carrying condition but did show with a very slender advantage. She did not handle Tattenham Corner very well and, collared over two furlongs from home, was soon done with. (3/1: op 6/4)

3434 RON SMYTH H'CAP (0-95) (3-Y.O+) (Class C)
3-10 (3-16) **1m 4f 10y** £5,472.00 (£1,656.00: £808.00: £384.00) Stalls: Low GOING minus 0.25 sec per fur (GF)

				SP	RR	SF
3112^{7}	**Grief (IRE) (82)** (DRCElsworth) **4-9-4**(3) RFfrench(9) (b: lw: hld up: led over 1f out: drvn out)	—	1	5/1^{2}	93	71
2944^{5}	**Wakeel (USA) (82)** (SDow) **5-9-7** MRoberts(5) (rdn over 2f out: hdwy over 1f out: r.o wl ins fnl f)	½	2	11/1	92	70
1934^{4}	**Bit on the Side (IRE) (82)** (NEBerry) **8-9-7** SSanders(4) (hdwy over 5f out: hrd rdn over 2f out: unable qckn)	3	3	10/1	88	66
3053^{2}	**Veridian (80)** (PWHarris) **4-9-0**(5) CLowther(7) (hmpd on ins & dropped rr over 5f out: rdn over 3f out: hdwy over 1f out: r.o one pce)	1	4	3/1^{1}	85	63
3112^{12}	**Star Manager (USA) (85)** (PFICole) **7-9-10** CRutter(10) (hdwy over 3f out: hrd rdn over 1f out: one pce)	s.h	5	7/1^{3}	90	68

			Pos	SP	RR	SF
2391[4]	**Artic Courier (82)** (DJSCosgrove) **6-9-7** MRimmer(6) (b: w ldr: led 4f out tl over 1f out: sn wknd)	2	**6**	7/1[3]	84	62
3110[6]	**Hoh Express (89)** (IABalding) **5-9-11**(3) MartinDwyer(3) (lw: hdwy over 3f out: wknd over 2f out)	1¾	**7**	7/1[3]	89	67
2483[5]	**Hawker Hunter (USA) (77)** (RAkehurst) **6-9-2** AClark(2) (led 8f)	16	**8**	7/1[3]	56	34
2180[4]	**Joli's Son (72)** (MJHaynes) **4-8-11** DHarrison(1) (b.hind: prom 6f: t.o)	dist	**9**	33/1	—	—
				(SP 112.0%)	**9 Rn**	

2m 36.76 (2.26) CSF £50.86 CT £475.63 TOTE £5.90: £2.10 £3.30 £1.80 (£23.00) Trio £88.50 OWNER Mr M. Balcomb (WHITCOMBE)

2729 Grief (IRE), who has caught the eye on both his runs this season, struck the front approaching the final furlong and, responding to pressure, held on well. (5/1)

2749* Wakeel (USA), racing at the back of the field, really found his stride from below the distance but, despite finishing really strongly, found the line always just beating him. He is not easy to catch right. (11/1)

1934 Bit on the Side (IRE) at last was stepped up to a more suitable trip but unfortunately did not have the cut in the ground she would have liked, and failed to quicken in the last two furlongs. She can find a race when the ground softens up. (10/1)

3053 Veridian, 7lb higher than when winning at Chester last month, dropped back to last place after being hampered along the inside rail soon after halfway. Picking up ground on the outside of the field below the distance, he did stay on but was never going to get there in time. (3/1)

2710 Star Manager (USA) stayed this longer trip but could only go up and down in the same place in the last two furlongs. He probably needs a break as he seems to run best when fresh. (7/1)

2391 Artic Courier is not easy to win with and, once he had relinquished the lead over a furlong out, was soon done with. (7/1)

2483 Hawker Hunter (USA) (7/1: op 9/2)

3435 MAIL ON SUNDAY MILE (QUALIFIER) H'CAP (0-95) (3-Y.O+) (Class C)

3-40 (3-44) **1m 114y** £7,035.00 (£2,130.00: £1,040.00: £495.00) Stalls: Low GOING minus 0.25 sec per fur (GF)

			Pos	SP	RR	SF
3115[15]	**Fionn de Cool (IRE) (59)** (RAkehurst) **6-7-4**(7) PFitzsimons(2) (lw: led over 7f out: rdn out)	—	**1**	11/1	70	45
2871[2]	**Speculator (IRE) (85)** (WJHaggas) **3-9-1** FLynch(8) (lw: hdwy over 3f out: chsd wnr fnl 2f: unable qckn ins fnl f)	1¾	**2**	6/4[1]	93	60
3185[8]	**Kayvee (86)** (MrsAJPerrett) **8-9-10** AClark(7) (dwlt: in rr whn hmpd 5f out: rdn over 2f out: hdwy fnl f: r.o)	1¾	**3**	16/1	90	65
3115[12]	**Present Situation (60)** (LordHuntingdon) **6-7-7**(5) AimeeCook(6) (lw: lost pl 4f out: rallied over 1f out: r.o one pce)	s.h	**4**	8/1	64	39
3254[2]	**Comanche Companion (64)** (TJNaughton) **7-8-2** PaulEddery(4) (lw: pckd s: led 1f: rdn over 2f out: sn wknd)	1	**5**	13/2	67	42
2951[3]	**Asef Alhind (83)** (BHanbury) **3-8-13** MRimmer(9) (lw: plld hrd: a.p: 2nd whn slipped 5f out: wknd 2f out)	4	**6**	11/2[3]	78	45
3081*	**Night Wink (USA) (68)** (GLMoore) **5-8-3**(3) MartinDwyer(1) (lw: 7th whn b.d 5f out)		**B**	10/1	—	—
2866[7]	**Virtual Reality (77)** (JARToller) **6-9-1** MRoberts(3) (lw: 4th whn stumbled & fell 5f out)		**F**	5/1[2]	—	—
				(SP 119.8%)	**8 Rn**	

1m 43.66 (1.66) CSF £26.78 CT £258.80 TOTE £13.60: £2.50 £1.40 £4.70 (£15.90) Trio £60.60 OWNER Canisbay Bloodstock Ltd (EPSOM)
BRED Ciaran Quigley
WEIGHT FOR AGE 3yo-8lb

2485 Fionn de Cool (IRE) has been extremely difficult to win with but this was to be his day - only his second win from forty-seven starts. Soon at the head of affairs, he was rousted along in the straight to keep the runner-up at bay. He does not like to be slapped according to his trainer. (11/1)

2871 Speculator (IRE) is a progressive colt and moved into second place a quarter of a mile from home. He tended to drift in behind the winner inside the final furlong and this was probably due to the camber. (6/4)

3052 Kayvee is not as good as he was but, nevertheless, ran well considering he was hampered in the melee running down Tattenham Hill. (16/1)

238* Present Situation, who rather lost his place running down Tattenham Hill, stayed on again from below the distance and only just failed in his bid for third prize. (8/1)

3254 Comanche Companion, 7lb higher than when winning earlier in the season, found that telling and had been seen off entering the final quarter-mile. (13/2)

2951 Asef Alhind took a keen hold and had eventually been seen off two furlongs from home. (11/2)

3436 STAFF INGHAM LIMITED STKS (0-90) (3-Y.O+) (Class C)

4-10 (4-14) **6f** £4,908.25 (£1,486.00: £725.50: £345.25) Stalls: High GOING minus 0.25 sec per fur (GF)

			Pos	SP	RR	SF
3130*	**Bowden Rose (88)** (MBlanshard) **5-9-2b**(3) DSweeney(3) (lw: hld up: led over 1f out: r.o wl)	—	**1**	7/2[3]	95	70
3220[7]	**Prends Ca (IRE) (86)** (WRMuir) **4-8-10**(3) JDSmith(5) (rrd s: hdwy over 1f out: hrd rdn ins fnl f: r.o)	¾	**2**	8/1	87	62
3189[7]	**Jeffrey Anotherred (87)** (KMcAuliffe) **3-8-12** JFEgan(2) (swtchd lft & hdwy over 1f out: hrd rdn: r.o)	hd	**3**	5/1	90	61
2677[5]	**China Girl (IRE) (90)** (PWChapple-Hyam) **3-8-6**(3) RHavlin(6) (a.p: led over 2f out tl over 1f out: sn wknd)	5	**4**	11/4[2]	73	44
3280[11]	**Justinianus (IRE) (42)** (JJBridger) **5-9-0**(5) ADaly(1) (lw: prom 2f)	3	**5**	50/1	64 t	46
2872[4]	**Anotheranniversary (90)** (GLewis) **4-8-13** PaulEddery(4) (b.hind: led over 3f: wknd over 1f out)	nk	**6**	2/1[1]	58 t	40
				(SP 112.0%)	**6 Rn**	

1m 8.71 (0.71) CSF £27.01 TOTE £5.40: £2.70 £2.60 (£19.90) OWNER G H S Bailey & N C D Hall (UPPER LAMBOURN) BRED E. A. Badger
WEIGHT FOR AGE 3yo-4lb
STEWARDS' ENQUIRY Obj. to Bowden Rose by Smith overruled.

3130* Bowden Rose continues in great heart and, striking the front approaching the final furlong, kept on well. (7/2)

2476 Prends Ca (IRE) ran better here, running on nicely in the last furlong and a half. Her jockey launched an objection but on what grounds remains a complete and utter mystery, and it was amazing he did not lose his deposit for a most frivolous objection. (8/1: 9/2-9/1)

3189 Jeffrey Anotherred found this six furlongs too sharp and, running on from below the distance, was never going to get there in time. (5/1)

2677 China Girl (IRE) proved disappointing for, after striking the front over two furlongs from home, she was headed below the distance and soon done with. (11/4: op 6/4)

3082 Justinianus (IRE) was a quite ridiculous entry in this race for he was at least 46lb worse off with all his rivals according to official adjusted ratings. (50/1)

2872 Anotheranniversary was unable to cope with the step up to six furlongs and had shot her bolt early in the final quarter-mile. (2/1)

3437 STANLEY WOOTTON MAIDEN STKS (3-Y.O+) (Class D)

4-40 (4-40) **7f** £3,371.25 (£1,020.00: £497.50: £236.25) Stalls: Low GOING minus 0.25 sec per fur (GF)

			Pos	SP	RR	SF
3290[2]	**Present Generation (75)** (RGuest) **4-9-5** SSanders(5) (mde all: clr over 3f out: hrd rdn over 1f out: r.o wl)	—	**1**	9/4[1]	83	47
3244[2]	**Polish Romance (USA) (75)** (MRStoute) **3-8-8** FLynch(1) (a.p: chsd wnr over 2f out: hrd rdn over 1f out: r.o one pce)	¾	**2**	9/4[1]	76	34
3079[2]	**Summerosa (USA) (76)** (PWChapple-Hyam) **3-8-5**(3) RHavlin(7) (b.nr hind: lw: chsd wnr over 4f: one pce)	3	**3**	4/1[3]	69	27

1967[8] **Sandy Saddler** (SDow) **3-8-13** JFEgan(6) (nvr nr to chal) 5	**4**	20/1	63	21
3138[5] **Perfect Pal (IRE) (72)** (MissGayKelleway) **6-9-2**(3) RFfrench(2) (rrd s: no hdwy fnl 3f) ....hd	**5**	100/30[2]	63	27
Raspberry Sauce (CACyzer) **3-8-8** AClark(3) (w'like: bit bkwd: s.s: a bhd) 10	**6**	20/1	35	—
2954[11] **Durable George (35)** (JJBridger) **3-8-8**(5) ADaly(4) (plld hrd: bhd fnl 3f) ....s.h	**7**	50/1	40	—

(SP 116.1%) **7 Rn**

1m 23.05 (2.75) CSF £6.90 TOTE £3.50: £2.50 £1.40 (£3.50) OWNER Mr S. Lury (NEWMARKET) BRED J. M. Ratcliffe
WEIGHT FOR AGE 3yo-6lb

3290 Present Generation gained a richly-deserved first victory. Dictating matters from the front, he forged clear entering the straight and, responding to pressure, was not going to be caught. (9/4)
3244 Polish Romance (USA) is becoming very frustrating to win with. Taking second place over a quarter of a mile from home, she did stay on but never looked like finding that vital turn of foot. There is a maiden to be won with her but it will surely come at one of the smaller tracks. (9/4)
3079 Summerosa (USA) was again shown to be very moderate and was made to look extremely one-paced in the straight. She is certainly one of the stable's lesser lights. (4/1)
Sandy Saddler, racing at the back of the field, passed a few beaten horses to finish a very moderate fourth. (20/1)
3138 Perfect Pal (IRE) is not very consistent and it was all happening far too quickly for him on this very tricky switchback track. (100/30)

T/Jkpt: £47,945.20 (0.1 Tckts); £60,775.63 to Windsor 11/8/97. T/Plpt: £229.00 (91.7 Tckts). T/Qdpt: £52.90 (22.57 Tckts) AK

3426-REDCAR (L-H) (Firm, Good to firm patches)
Sunday August 10th
WEATHER: sunny WIND: fresh across

3438 CAMERA MARTS-PENTAX NURSERY H'CAP (2-Y.O) (Class C)
2-10 (2-10) **6f** £5,249.50 (£1,591.00: £778.00: £371.50) Stalls: High GOING minus 0.49 sec per fur (F)

		SP	RR	SF
3258[5] **Cool Secret (70)** (ABMulholland) **2-8-12** DWright(4) (chsd ldrs: rdn to ld wl over 1f out: styd on wl) ....—	**1**	9/2[2]	80	37
2786[5] **Inchalong (64)** (MBrittain) **2-8-6** GDuffield(8) (lw: unruly s: s.i.s: hdwy u.p ½-wy: nvr able to chal) 4	**2**	7/1	63	20
3314* **Daynabee (69)** (NTinkler) **2-8-11** 7x KimTinkler(3) (led over 4f: kpt on same pce) ....nk	**3**	5/1[3]	68	25
2473[5] **Burnt Yates (IRE) (73)** (MWEasterby) **2-9-1** RCochrane(2) (lw: s.i.s: effrt ½-wy: styd on towards fin) ....hd	**4**	5/1[3]	71	28
3031[5] **Shamwari Song (67)** (JAGlover) **2-8-9** JFortune(9) (sn pushed along: sme hdwy ½-wy: hung lft & sn btn) 3	**5**	11/2	57	14
3257[3] **Royal Dream (79)** (JBerry) **2-9-4**(3) PFessey(5) (cl up tl rdn & btn 2f out) ....hd	**6**	7/2[1]	69	26
3226[4] **Cosmic Case (55)** (JSGoldie) **2-7-11v**[1ow1] TWilliams(1) (s.i.s: rdn ½-wy: n.d) 2½	**7**	16/1	38	—
3067[6] **My Bet (54)** (MWEasterby) **2-7-10** LCharnock(7) (cl up over 3f: wknd) ....½	**8**	16/1	36	—

(SP 113.4%) **8 Rn**

1m 11.4 (1.20) CSF £31.89 CT £148.54 TOTE £5.90: £1.70 £1.60 £1.80 (£18.50) Trio £27.60 OWNER The Gloria Darley Racing Partnership (HAMBLETON) BRED Mrs M. S. Thomas
LONG HANDICAP Cosmic Case 7-9

3258 Cool Secret was a bit on edge and warm beforehand but there was nothing wrong with his performance. (9/2)
2786 Inchalong was playing up in the stalls, causing her to lose ground as they opened and, considering she was off the bit for much of the trip, this was not a bad effort. (7/1)
3314* Daynabee has been running her socks off and, although very warm beforehand, she put up another useful effort here. (5/1)
2473 Burnt Yates (IRE) has been gelded since his last run and gave encouraging signs here that a modest race can be found. (5/1)
3031 Shamwari Song was a big disappointment here and, hanging badly, was obviously not right. (11/2)
3257 Royal Dream showed plenty of toe but failed to see it out and may be better on easier ground. (7/2)

3439 CAMERA MARTS-CANON MAIDEN STKS (3-Y.O+) (Class D)
2-45 (2-45) **1m 1f** £3,650.00 (£1,025.00: £500.00) Stalls: Low GOING minus 0.49 sec per fur (F)

		SP	RR	SF
3095[2] **Karakia (IRE) (75)** (JHMGosden) **3-8-7** JCarroll(1) (mde all: pushed along & r.o wl 2f out: eased towards fin)—	**1**	4/11[1]	79+	21
1322[3] **Good Reputation** (BWHills) **3-8-7** RCochrane(3) (lw: trckd ldr: outpcd over 2f out: kpt on u.p fnl f) 7	**2**	9/4[2]	67	9
Dainty Damsel (RDEWoodhouse) **4-9-1** LCharnock(2) (w'like: bit bkwd: hld up: effrt 4f out: btn over 2f out) .18	**3**	33/1[3]	35?	—

(SP 107.0%) **3 Rn**

1m 54.2 (3.50) CSF £1.33 TOTE £1.40 (£1.10) OWNER Sheikh Mohammed (NEWMARKET) BRED Darley Stud Management Co Ltd
WEIGHT FOR AGE 3yo-8lb

3095 Karakia (IRE) was always far too good for this opposition and showed a useful burst of speed before being eased. This should have done his confidence no end of good. (4/11: op 8/13)
1322 Good Reputation is not the best of movers and was completely outclassed here, but she did look to stay particularly well. (9/4: 6/4-5/2)
Dainty Damsel, a reasonable-looking sort, needed this and showed a little until the pace really hotted up. (33/1)

3440 CAMERA MARTS-VIVITAR H'CAP (0-75) (3-Y.O+) (Class D)
3-20 (3-20) **2m 4y** £3,501.25 (£1,060.00: £517.50: £246.25) Stalls: Centre GOING minus 0.49 sec per fur (F)

		SP	RR	SF
3242[4] **Star Rage (IRE) (75)** (MJohnston) **7-10-0** BDoyle(5) (lw: a.p: led wl over 2f out: styd on) ....—	**1**	7/2[2]	83	50
3141[3] **Klondike Charger (USA) (70)** (BWHills) **3-8-8** GDuffield(7) (cl up: led over 3f out tl wl over 2f out: kpt on u.p)1½	**2**	6/1	77	29
3020[2] **Yak Alfaraj (74)** (MRStoute) **3-8-12** RCochrane(1) (led tl hdd over 3f out: hrd rdn & one pce) 2½	**3**	3/1[1]	78	30
2882[9] **Forgie (IRE) (70)** (PCalver) **4-9-9** JFortune(3) (lw: a chsng ldrs: effrt over 3f out: r.o one pce) 3½	**4**	10/1	71	38
3069[2] **Highfield Fizz (43)** (CWFairhurst) **5-7-10** LCharnock(4) (b.off hind: in tch: pushed along 6f out: outpcd fnl 4f) .8	**5**	9/2[3]	36	3
2718[3] **Sad Mad Bad (USA) (62)** (MrsMReveley) **3-8-0** JQuinn(2) (lw: prom tl lost pl 7f out: n.d after) 9	**6**	16/1	46	—
2291[4] **Ledgendry Line (75)** (MrsMReveley) **4-10-0** ACulhane(6) (lw: hld up & bhd: effrt 4f out: n.d) 11	**7**	9/2[3]	48	15

(SP 112.8%) **7 Rn**

3m 29.7 (4.70) CSF £21.65 TOTE £4.30: £1.80 £2.80 (£16.80) OWNER Mr David Abell (MIDDLEHAM) BRED Killarkin Stud
LONG HANDICAP Highfield Fizz 7-8
WEIGHT FOR AGE 3yo-15lb
OFFICIAL EXPLANATION **Highfield Fizz: gurgled. Sad Mad Bad (USA): lost a front shoe during the race.**

3242 Star Rage (IRE) last won on the Flat two years ago but there was plenty to like about this. Once in front, he was always tending to look about and gave the impression that there was more to come if required. (7/2)
3141 Klondike Charger (USA) keeps running well, is not doing a lot wrong and deserves to pick up a race. (6/1)

3020 Yak Alfaraj made sure there was a pace on this time but, when it came down to a struggle, he flashed his tail and did not look the best of battlers. (3/1)
2882 Forgie (IRE) looked to have plenty on here and ran as well as could be expected. (10/1)
3069 Highfield Fizz was in trouble some way out and this ground may just have been too lively for her. (9/2)
2718 Sad Mad Bad (USA) ran as though he has a problem. (16/1)
2291 Ledgendry Line is a funny customer who needs things to go just right and was obviously not in the mood here. (9/2)

3441 CAMERA MARTS-KODAK H'CAP (0-85) (3-Y.O) (Class D)

3-50 (3-50) **1m 3f** £3,533.75 (£1,070.00: £522.50: £248.75) Stalls: Low GOING minus 0.49 sec per fur (F)

				SP	RR	SF
3125^{11}	**True Glory (IRE) (79)** (JHMGosden) **3-9-5** JCarroll(1) (lw: in tch: sn pushed along: hdwy 4f out: chal 3f out: wl outpcd 2f out: kpt on u.p to ld cl home)	—	**1**	$6/4^{1}$	89	41
2715^{8}	**Pension Fund (69)** (MWEasterby) **3-8-6**(3) GParkin(3) (lw: hld up & bhd: smooth hdwy to ld 3f out: clr 2f out: rdn & fnd nil ins fnl f: ct cl home)	½	**2**	8/1	78	30
3234^{6}	**Scarrots (70)** (SCWilliams) **3-8-10** JFortune(2) (lw: led tl hdd 3f out: sn rdn & btn)	5	**3**	$3/1^{3}$	72	24
1595^{2}	**Regal Patrol (81)** (MRStoute) **3-9-7v¹** RCochrane(4) (trckd ldr: effrt 4f out: rdn & fnd nil)	12	**4**	$2/1^{2}$	66	18
				(SP 109.4%)	**4 Rn**	

2m 20.1 (3.10) CSF £11.01 TOTE £2.30 (£5.20) OWNER Sheikh Mohammed (NEWMARKET) BRED Sheikh Mohammed Bin Rashid Al Maktoum
OFFICIAL EXPLANATION **Regal Patrol: raced too freely wearing the first-time visor and had nothing to give in the latter stages of the race.**
2315 True Glory (IRE) stays particularly well but was always struggling on this fast ground and needed plenty of help from the saddle to make it. She will certainly know she has been in a race here. (6/4)
2715 Pension Fund, taking a big step up in trip and without the blinkers, looked likely to trot up two furlongs out, but the combination of doing too much too soon and stamina limitations just found him out. The ability is certainly there. (8/1)
3234 Scarrots likes to have his own way out in front and, once taken on, he soon gave up. (3/1)
1595 Regal Patrol raced too freely in the visor for the first time and, once asked for an effort, he looked most unco-operative. (2/1)

3442 CAMERA MARTS-RICOH LIMITED STKS (0-60) (3-Y.O+) (Class F)

4-20 (4-20) **1m** £2,696.00 (£756.00: £368.00) Stalls: High GOING minus 0.49 sec per fur (F)

				SP	RR	SF
3262^{2}	**Impulsive Air (IRE) (60)** (EWeymes) **5-9-4** JQuinn(3) (lw: chsd ldr: led over 2f out: rdn & r.o wl)	—	**1**	$7/4^{1}$	69	45
2745^{9}	**Mr Cube (IRE) (56)** (JMBradley) **7-9-7b** JFortune(4) (hld up: stdy hdwy 3f out: effrt 2f out: nt qckn)	4	**2**	5/1	64	40
2716^{6}	**Shamokin (28)** (FWatson) **5-9-1**(3) PFessey(5) (chsd ldrs: ev ch over 2f out: one pce)	4	**3**	33/1	53	29
2876^{11}	**Desert Cat (IRE) (57)** (MartynWane) **4-9-4** JCarroll(6) (chsd ldrs tl rdn & wknd 2f out)	6	**4**	11/1	41	17
*3054**	**Michael Venture (60)** (SPCWoods) **3-8-4**(7) PDoe(7) (led tl hdd over 2f out: sn btn)	5	**5**	$9/4^{2}$	31	—
2909^{6}	**Nukud (USA) (20)** (GROldroyd) **5-8-11v**(7) RFarmer(1) (t: outpcd ½-wy: bhd after)	1¾	**6**	50/1	28	4
3236^{12}	**Go For Green (60)** (DrJDScargill) **3-8-8** RCochrane(2) (lw: sn chsng ldrs: rdn ½-wy: wknd fnl 3f: eased)	13	**7**	$9/2^{3}$	—	—
				(SP 115.2%)	**7 Rn**	

1m 36.5 (1.50) CSF £10.31 TOTE £2.70: £1.20 £2.60 (£5.70) OWNER Mr T. A. Scothern (MIDDLEHAM) BRED Rathasker Stud
WEIGHT FOR AGE 3yo-7lb
3262 Impulsive Air (IRE) won a moderate race here but did it really well. (7/4)
2573* Mr Cube (IRE) travelled particularly well but, when asked for an effort, he was inclined to hang on this fast ground. (5/1)
2716 Shamokin ran one of his better races here but looked very one-paced when ridden. (33/1)
1674 Desert Cat (IRE) has the ability to do better but seems an inconsistent sort. (11/1)
3054* Michael Venture failed to impress on looks and ran moderately. (9/4)
2772 Go For Green looked very lean and fit but ran as though something was wrong and was eased a good deal once beaten. (9/2)

3443 NORTHERN ECHO RACING NORTH H'CAP (0-75) (3-Y.O+) (Class D)

4-50 (4-50) **7f** £2,386.88 (£2,386.87: £542.50: £258.75) Stalls: High GOING minus 0.49 sec per fur (F)

				SP	RR	SF
3143^{3}	**Oriole (48)** (DonEnricoIncisa) **4-8-6** KimTinkler(8) (bhd: hdwy 3f out: chal ins fnl f: r.o)	—	**1**	$7/1^{3}$	58	43
3227^{2}	**Clytha Hill Lad (45)** (JMBradley) **6-8-3** SDrowne(3) (lw: b: a.p: led wl over 1f out: rdn & r.o)	—	**1**	$3/1^{1}$	55	40
2857^{10}	**Colway Ritz (72)** (JWWatts) **3-9-10** JCarroll(7) (lw: hld up & bhd: hdwy 3f out: chsng ldrs over 1f out: no ex)	1¾	**3**	12/1	78	57
3075^{16}	**Pericles (75)** (MJohnston) **3-9-13** BDoyle(1) (lw: chsd ldrs: effrt over 2f out: nt qckn)	2	**4**	8/1	76	55
3207^{6}	**La Dolce Vita (71)** (TDBarron) **3-9-9** JFortune(4) (swtg: hld up & bhd: hdwy 2f out: nvr nr to chal)	½	**5**	$6/1^{2}$	71	50
3064^{7}	**Whittle Rock (62)** (MrsMReveley) **4-9-6** ACulhane(9) (outpcd ½-wy: sme late hdwy: n.d)	1½	**6**	9/1	59	44
3087^{6}	**Keston Pond (IRE) (50)** (MrsVAAconley) **7-8-1**(7) RWinston(11) (chsd ldrs: led wl over 2f out to wl over 1f out: wknd)	s.h	**7**	15/2	47	32
3143^{5}	**Bee Health Boy (66)** (MWEasterby) **4-9-7b**(3) GParkin(6) (led over 4f: sn wknd)	¾	**8**	$7/1^{3}$	61	46
2937^{2}	**Miss Pigalle (38)** (MissLAPerratt) **6-7-10b** NKennedy(10) (chsd ldrs over 4f: wknd)	3½	**9**	$7/1^{3}$	25	10
3431^{12}	**Kid Ory (39)** (DWChapman) **6-7-8b**(3) PFessey(5) (sn cl up: rdn & wknd over 2f out)	5	**10**	12/1	15	—
				(SP 125.0%)	**10 Rn**	

1m 23.5 (0.50) CSF O & CHL £13.88, CHL & O £11.95 CT O, CHL & CR £121.36, CHL, O & CR £107.90 TOTE O £5.00, CHL £1.80: O £3.00, CHL £1.50 £5.20 (£18.40) Trio £112.00 OWNER Don Enrico Incisa (MIDDLEHAM)/Mrs Marion Morgan (CHEPSTOW) BRED Red House Stud/Mrs M. C. Morgan
WEIGHT FOR AGE 3yo-6lb
3143 Oriole, despite going up the weights, showed here that he is in tremendous form and another stride would have seen him with the outright advantage. (7/1: op 9/2)
3227 Clytha Hill Lad keeps his form really well and this was a most gallant effort. (3/1)
2567 Colway Ritz showed something of what he can do here but he does have two ways of running. (12/1)
2303* Pericles, from a stable flying at present, is coming back to form. (8/1: 12/1-7/1)
3207 La Dolce Vita, a sweaty individual, ran well and was not over-punished. (6/1)
2209 Whittle Rock looked none too keen for much of the trip but then ran on when it was all over. (9/1)
3087 Keston Pond (IRE) ran his best race for some time. (15/2)
2937 Miss Pigalle, who ran well last time, failed to impress on looks here and ran poorly. (7/1)

T/Plpt: £50.20 (203.2 Tckts). T/Qdpt: £28.80 (15.97 Tckts) AA

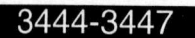

3318-YARMOUTH (L-H) (Good to Firm)
Sunday August 10th
WEATHER: Fine

3444 REEDHAM LIMITED STKS (0-85) (3-Y.O+) (Class D)
2-20 (2-20) **1m 2f 21y** £3,517.50 (£1,065.00: £520.00: £247.50) GOING minus 0.60 sec per fur (F)

			SP	RR	SF
3089*	**Dantesque (IRE) (84)** (GWragg) **4-9-5** MHills(2) (lw: hld up: hdwy & nt clr run over 2f out: rdn to ld fnl 100y) —	**1**	Evens[1]	91	36
2532*	**Meteor Strike (USA) (85)** (MrsAJPerrett) **3-8-10** PatEddery(3) (led 2f: rdn to ld over 1f out: edgd lft: hdd & no ex wl ins fnl f) ½	**2**	100/30[2]	90	26
735[22]	**Diminutive (USA) (77)** (JWHills) **4-9-0**(3) MHenry(1) (hld up & bhd: hdwy 2f out: rdn & one pce fnl f) 3½	**3**	20/1	83	28
3012[4]	**Pinchincha (FR) (84)** (DMorris) **3-9-0** NDay(4) (chsd ldrs: effrt & rdn over 2f out: no imp) 1¼	**4**	5/1	87	23
3112[6]	**Secret Aly (CAN) (83)** (CEBrittain) **7-9-5** DHolland(5) (led 8f out: clr ent st: hdd over 1f out: hmpd appr fnl f: sn btn) 2	**5**	4/1[3]	80	25

(SP 114.5%) **5 Rn**

2m 6.0 (2.20) CSF £4.51 TOTE £1.90: £1.10 £1.70 (£2.20) OWNER Mollers Racing (NEWMARKET) BRED Islanmore Stud
WEIGHT FOR AGE 3yo-9lb

IN-FOCUS: **On another day of continental temperatures, the fresh, welcome breeze off the North Sea made it much more bearable for man and horse alike.**

3089* Dantesque (IRE), short of room when poised to challenge entering the final quarter-mile, did eventually find space but he needed the full treatment to forge ahead well inside the last furlong. (Evens)

2532* Meteor Strike (USA) settled much better once in action than he did on the way to post. Needing to work hard to wear down the long-time leader, he showed his inexperience by drifting badly left under pressure, but at least he battled on and the extra experience should prove beneficial. (100/30)

Diminutive (USA), winner of this event last year, has not seen a racecourse since the spring. Barely hobbling to post, he brought up the rear until staying on inside the last couple of furlongs. (20/1)

3012 Pinchincha (FR) has been on the go since the turn of the year and, running listlessly on this occasion, may well have had enough for the time being. (5/1: 7/2-11/2)

3112 Secret Aly (CAN), a previous winner over course and distance, gained control down the back straight and remained there until below the distance. Ridden along, he looked held when the runner-up took his ground approaching the final furlong and he was forced to accept the situation. (4/1)

3445 HADDISCOE H'CAP (0-80) (3-Y.O F) (Class D)
2-55 (2-55) **1m 2f 21y** £3,517.50 (£1,065.00: £520.00: £247.50) Stalls: Low GOING minus 0.60 sec per fur (F)

			SP	RR	SF
3026[3]	**Saddlers' Hope (77)** (JRFanshawe) **3-9-7** TSprake(3) (chsd ldr: led wl over 2f out: rdn out) —	**1**	5/2[2]	85	42
3153[10]	**Noble Dane (IRE) (68)** (PWHarris) **3-8-12** PatEddery(2) (hld up & bhd: shkn up over 2f out: styd on wl towards fin) 1½	**2**	100/30[3]	74	31
3128[3]	**Vanishing Trick (USA) (77)** (HRACecil) **3-9-7b** WRyan(5) (lw: trckd ldng pair: hrd drvn 2f out: nt pce to chal) ¾	**3**	5/2[2]	81	38
2897*	**Tangshan (CAN) (75)** (MRStoute) **3-9-5** MHills(1) (lw: set str pce: rdn 3f out: sn hdd & wknd: t.o) 15	**4**	9/4[1]	56	13

(SP 111.0%) **4 Rn**

2m 5.5 (1.70) CSF £9.81 TOTE £3.50 (£6.80) OWNER Cheveley Park Stud (NEWMARKET) BRED Cheveley Park Stud Ltd

3026 Saddlers' Hope, prepared to accept the lead, set sail for home soon after passing the three-furlong marker and, though she had two serious rivals to contend with, she always had the situation under control. (5/2)

2340 Noble Dane (IRE) did not pick up immediately when shaken up halfway up the straight but, given no opportunities to shirk the issue, was staying on best of all nearing the finish. (100/30: 3/1-9/2)

3128 Vanishing Trick (USA) is not over-blessed with finishing speed, especially on this lively ground and, though she stuck on under hard driving, never threatened to trouble the winner. (5/2)

2897* Tangshan (CAN) attempted to repeat her all-the-way success at Warwick but she may have run too free for she was legless when collared and dropped away rapidly. (9/4)

3446 WINTERTON NURSERY H'CAP (2-Y.O) (Class D)
3-30 (3-30) **6f 3y** £3,440.00 (£965.00: £470.00) Stalls: High GOING minus 0.60 sec per fur (F)

			SP	RR	SF
2720*	**Moontabeh (85)** (PTWalwyn) **2-9-7** PatEddery(2) (mde virtually all: hrd drvn fnl f: hld on) —	**1**	4/11[1]	85	30
3090*	**Sassy (IRE) (65)** (APJarvis) **2-8-1** NVarley(1) (lw: hld up: hdwy 2f out: rdn to chal ins fnl f: edgd rt: unable qckn) hd	**2**	4/1[2]	65	10
3097[3]	**Dande Times (62)** (KTIvory) **2-7-9b**[1](3) MHenry(3) (swtg: disp ld to ½-wy: sn rdn & outpcd: t.o) 20	**3**	13/2[3]	9	—

(SP 106.7%) **3 Rn**

1m 12.6 (1.70) CSF £1.91 TOTE £1.20 (£1.50) OWNER Mr Hamdan Al Maktoum (LAMBOURN) BRED Gainsborough Stud Management Ltd

2720* Moontabeh has won on this type of ground but he was never happy here and Eddery really earned his fee to enable him to hang on. (4/11)

3090* Sassy (IRE), stepping up considerably from her success in a seller on her previous outing, did veer off a true line under strong pressure nearing the finish but she kept galloping and almost caused a major upset. (4/1)

3097 Dande Times, awash with sweat in his first-time blinkers, ran much too free and had burnt himself out soon after halfway. (13/2: 4/1-7/1)

3447 GREAT YARMOUTH CONDITIONS STKS (3-Y.O+) (Class C)
4-00 (4-01) **6f 3y** £4,518.00 (£1,692.00: £828.50: £357.50: £161.25: £82.75) Stalls: High GOING minus 0.60 sec per fur (F)

			SP	RR	SF
3111[5]	**Proud Native (IRE) (104)** (APJarvis) **3-8-10** DHolland(6) (lw: mde all: qcknd clr appr fnl f: hld on wl nr fin) —	**1**	9/4[1]	107	54
3252[2]	**My Melody Parkes (94)** (JBerry) **4-8-4**(5) PRoberts(7) (lw: chsd ldrs: rdn appr fnl f: fin wl) nk	**2**	10/1	101	52
3124[8]	**Wolf Mountain (100)** (RHannon) **3-9-1** DaneO'Neill(2) (dwlt: hdwy wl over 1f out: rdn appr fnl f: one pce) 2	**3**	100/30[2]	106	53
3217[18]	**Hello Mister (98)** (TEPowell) **6-8-11**(3) PMcCabe(1) (hld up in rr: swtchd lft & gd hdwy appr fnl f: nt pce to chal) 1¼	**4**	11/2	98	49
3111[12]	**Soviet State (USA) (100)** (PWChapple-Hyam) **3-9-1** SWhitworth(4) (trckd ldrs: drvn along 2f out: sn outpcd) nk	**5**	6/1	102	49
2476[2]	**Indian Spark (102)** (WGMTurner) **3-8-10** TSprake(5) (prom: rdn 2f out: sn btn) 2½	**6**	4/1[3]	90	37

(SP 112.6%) **6 Rn**

1m 10.1 (0.30 under best) (-0.80) CSF £22.59 TOTE £2.70: £1.80 £3.10 (£9.90) OWNER Mr L. Fust (ASTON UPTHORPE) BRED Mrs B. A. Headon

WEIGHT FOR AGE 3yo-4lb
3111 Proud Native (IRE), adopting more forceful tactics, showed a return to his useful form of last year and, now that he has got back into the winning mood, should be worth following from now on. (9/4)
3252 My Melody Parkes seems to have lost the habit of winning but she finished in fine style here, and a much-needed change of fortune could be close at hand. (10/1: op 6/1)
3124 Wolf Mountain lost his chance with a tardy start but he shaped promisingly in the circumstances, and this lightly-raced colt can soon bounce back. (100/30)
2861 Hello Mister has not won a race for close on two years and he seems to find this trip on fast ground not quite far enough nowadays. (11/2)
2861 Soviet State (USA), very much on his toes, sat in behind the leaders but he was being made to work two furlongs out and, feeling the strain, was one of the first beaten. (6/1)
2476 Indian Spark was unable to force the pace this time and, flat to the boards two furlongs out, had to admit he had met his match. (4/1)

3448 BROADLAND 102 H'CAP (0-80) (3-Y.O+ F & M) (Class D)

4-30 (4-31) **7f 3y** £5,680.00 (£1,720.00: £840.00: £400.00) Stalls: High GOING minus 0.60 sec per fur (F)

				SP	RR	SF
3026[11]	**Rich In Love (IRE) (69)** (CACyzer) **3-9-7** DHolland(7) (sn pushed along: mde all: drvn clr appr fnl f: unchal)	—	**1**	10/1	81	62
3101*	**Karinska (60)** (MCChapman) **7-8-11**(7) SCarson(6) (lw: a.p: rdn over 1f out: nt pce of wnr)	5	**2**	7/2[2]	61	48
3100[2]	**On The Green (40)** (AHide) **4-7-9v**(3) MBaird(3) (lw: hld up in rr: swtchd rt 3f out: rdn wl over 1f out: one pce)	3½	**3**	4/1[3]	33	20
1589[4]	**Irtifa (72)** (PTWalwyn) **3-9-10** PatEddery(5) (swtg: chsd ldrs: rdn & outpcd wl over 1f out: sn btn)	5	**4**	3/1[1]	53	34
3292[5]	**Shashi (IRE) (55)** (PatMitchell) **5-8-13** DaneO'Neill(4) (chsd ldrs: hrd rdn 2f out: sn wknd)	1¾	**5**	11/1	32	19
2785[16]	**Double Gold (60)** (MBell) **3-8-12** MFenton(2) (lw: trckd ldrs: drvn along 2f out: sn lost tch: t.o)	6	**6**	6/1	24	5
2149[5]	**Tajrebah (USA) (69)** (SPCWoods) **3-9-7** DBiggs(1) (lw: racd centre: effrt & rdn over 2f out: no imp: t.o)	5	**7**	11/2	21	2
				(SP 114.3%)	**7 Rn**	

1m 23.6 (-0.60) CSF £40.68 TOTE £9.90: £4.60 £1.90 (£28.20) OWNER Mr R. M. Cyzer (HORSHAM) BRED Floors Farming
WEIGHT FOR AGE 3yo-6lb
2551 Rich In Love (IRE), taking a big step down in distance, was bustled along to set the pace. Finding an extra gear to draw clear approaching the final furlong, she galloped these rivals into the ground. (10/1: 8/1-12/1)
3101* Karinska performs well at this track but she is better suited to more patient tactics over a longer trip and she was well out-paced when the winner quickened things up. (7/2)
3100 On The Green gradually worked her way over to the favoured stands rail but she lacked the pace to get in a blow against the leading pair. (4/1)
1589 Irtifa, reappearing after a ten week break, pushed the pace until getting left behind inside the last quarter-mile. She probably had more than her full quota of weight. (3/1)
3292 Shashi (IRE) has had quite a busy season and she was in trouble two furlongs out and faded rather tamely. (11/1)

3449 MUNDESLEY MAIDEN H'CAP (0-65) (3-Y.O+) (Class F)

5-00 (5-01) **1m 3f 101y** £2,641.20 (£743.20: £363.60) Stalls: Low GOING minus 0.60 sec per fur (F)

				SP	RR	SF
2927[4]	**Acerbus Dulcis (29)** (MCChapman) **6-7-8**(7) SCarson(1) (hld up: hdwy to ld over 2f out: rdn & r.o strly)	—	**1**	9/2[3]	37	13
3101[2]	**Lucky Begonia (IRE) (52)** (WJMusson) **4-9-10** AMcGlone(2) (lw: swtg: sn chsng ldr: led wl over 2f out: sn hdd: hrd rdn & one pce fnl f)	2½	**2**	Evens[1]	57	33
3044[5]	**Bold Saint (IRE) (42)** (PWHarris) **3-7-13b**(5) CLowther(3) (lw: led: rdn & hdd wl over 2f out: sn btn)	8	**3**	9/4[2]	35	1
2669[4]	**Canton Ron (40)** (HJCollingridge) **3-7-9**(7)ow5 NicolaCole(5) (s.i.s: sn wl outpcd: t.o fr ½-wy)	dist	**4**	13/2	—	—
				(SP 112.3%)	**4 Rn**	

2m 25.4 (3.60) CSF £9.06 TOTE £6.60 (£2.60) OWNER Mr George Hooke (MARKET RASEN) BRED Stetchworth Park Stud Ltd
WEIGHT FOR AGE 3yo-10lb
2430 Acerbus Dulcis got off the mark with a smoothly gained, workmanlike performance and should be able to win over hurdles in the coming season. (9/2)
3101 Lucky Begonia (IRE) looked to have found a moderate race in which to open her account but her action to post would have put many would-be punters off, and she had another hard race for nothing on ground she clearly dislikes. (Evens)
3044 Bold Saint (IRE), one of the stable's lesser lights, again attempted to gallop his rivals into submission but it was he who cracked first, and he was left for dead in the last couple of furlongs. (9/4)

T/Plpt: £826.10 (13.76 Tckts). T/Qdpt: £77.00 (7.2 Tckts)

2941-LEICESTER (R-H) (Good)
Monday August 11th

WEATHER: v.warm WIND: nil

3450 E.B.F. MENPHYS MEDIAN AUCTION MAIDEN STKS (2-Y.O F) (Class E)

5-50 (5-52) **7f 9y** £3,457.00 (£1,036.00: £498.00: £229.00) Stalls: Low GOING minus 0.34 sec per fur (GF)

				SP	RR	SF
2953[8]	**Colleville** (MAJarvis) **2-8-11** RCochrane(11) (a.p: led wl over 1f out: drvn clr)	—	**1**	20/1	86+	38
3072[2]	**Mustique Dream** (RCharlton) **2-8-11** PatEddery(18) (led 4f out tl wl over 1f out: rdn & one pce fnl f)	3	**2**	4/1[2]	79	31
2768[3]	**Saeedah** (JHMGosden) **2-8-11** LDettori(10) (sn chsng ldrs: effrt & ev ch 2f out: sn hrd drvn: one pce)	s.h	**3**	4/5[1]	79	31
2728[10]	**Chlo-Jo** (AGFoster) **2-8-11** GHind(6) (hdwy 2f out: kpt on u.p ins fnl f)	2½	**4**	20/1	73	25
	Bullion (BWHills) **2-8-11** MHills(5) (lt-f: unf: s.s: hdwy over 2f out: one pce fnl f)	2	**5**	14/1	69	21
3009[5]	**Acebo Lyons (IRE)** (APJarvis) **2-8-11** SDrowne(2) (hld up: hdwy over 2f out: styd on wl ins fnl f)	¾	**6**	20/1	67	19
2394[5]	**Latin Nexus (USA)** (PFICole) **2-8-11** CRutter(1) (hdwy over 2f out: rdn & one pce appr fnl f)	hd	**7**	10/1[3]	67	19
	Forgotten Star (IRE) (RFJohnsonHoughton) **2-8-11** SSanders(12) (lengthy: unf: led over 3f: rdn & wknd wl over 1f out)	½	**8**	33/1	66	18
2181[5]	**Hiding Place** (MBell) **2-8-11** MFenton(17) (trckd ldrs: rdn 2f out: sn btn)	nk	**9**	10/1[3]	65	17
2893[8]	**Stalwart Legion (IRE)** (JWHills) **2-8-11** RHills(3) (in tch over 5f)	3	**10**	33/1	58	10
	Trinity Reef (JLDunlop) **2-8-11** BDoyle(16) (leggy: lt-f: prom 5f)	1½	**11**	12/1	55	7
3045[7]	**Keen Lady** (NPLittmoden) **2-8-11** TGMcLaughlin(9) (prom 5f)	3	**12**	66/1	48	—
3136[10]	**Sabre Girl** (RHannon) **2-8-11** WJO'Connor(8) (prom tl wknd over 2f out)	½	**13**	20/1	47	—
	Lady Rockstar (MJRyan) **2-8-11** DRMcCabe(7) (w'like: leggy: bit bkwd: a in rr)	1¾	**14**	33/1	43	—

3072[6]	**Perecapa (IRE)** (BPalling) **2-8-8**(3) DSweeney(19) (a outpcd)	3½	**15**	33/1	35	—
2860[6]	**Ida Lupino (IRE)** (BWHills) **2-8-8**(3) JDSmith(15) (chsd ldrs: rdn & wknd over 2f out)	1¾	**16**	20/1	31	—
2477[11]	**Spice Girl** (PDEvans) **2-8-11** JFEgan(4) (swtg: rdn 3f out: sn lost tch: t.o)	7	**17**	33/1	15	—
	Guest Envoy (IRE) (CNAllen) **2-8-8**(3) MartinDwyer(14) (small: bkwd: a outpcd: t.o)	5	**18**	33/1	4	—
	Freckles (MJRyan) **2-8-8b[1]**(3) MBaird(20) (neat: bit bkwd: s.s: a in rr: t.o)	1¼	**19**	33/1	1	—
	Moonlightandroses (NPLittmoden) **2-8-8**(3) DO'Donohoe(13) (lt-f: s.s: a bhd & outpcd: t.o)	dist	**20**	33/1	—	—

(SP 156.9%) **20 Rn**

1m 24.9 (2.30) CSF £98.06 TOTE £23.90: £9.40 £1.60 £1.10 (£444.90) Trio £39.80 OWNER Mr K. G. Powter (NEWMARKET) BRED K. G. Powter

2953 Colleville, a small filly, had learned a lot from her debut last month and, with stamina the least of her problems, stormed clear for a very comfortable success. (20/1)

3072 Mustique Dream continues to run well but she just seems to lack that bit extra and, once again, had to settle for the runner-up prize. (4/1)

2768 Saeedah was soon chasing up the leaders and had a chance as good as any two furlongs out but she was found wanting when the winner quickened things up and proved a shade disappointing. (4/5)

Chlo-Jo was doing all her best work late on and this would seem more her trip. (20/1)

Bullion, a still-unfurnished filly who looked as though she had done plenty of work, ran extremely well after missing the break and she does look a ready-made winner. (14/1)

3009 Acebo Lyons (IRE) shaped much better over this slightly longer trip and she should not be long in making her mark. (20/1)

2394 Latin Nexus (USA) was unable to maintain her run when the tempo lifted approaching the final furlong but she showed enough to suggest her turn will come. (10/1)

Trinity Reef (12/1: op 7/1)

3451 MERRIMANS (S) NURSERY H'CAP (2-Y.O) (Class G)

6-20 (6-22) **5f 218y** £2,511.00 (£696.00: £333.00) Stalls: Low GOING minus 0.34 sec per fur (GF)

				SP	RR	SF
3067[7]	**Marske Machine (55)** (NTinkler) **2-8-8b[1]** RCochrane(6) (hld up: hdwy wl over 1f out: led wl ins fnl f)	—	**1**	7/1	56	20
3228*	**Bermuda Triangle (IRE) (57)** (MJHaynes) **2-8-5**(5) CLowther(10) (hdwy 2f out: rdn to ld ins fnl f: sn hdd: no ex nr fin)	nk	**2**	7/2[1]	57	21
2545[11]	**Maedaley (52)** (PCHaslam) **2-8-2**(3) MartinDwyer(3) (s.s: hdwy 3f out: rdn & one pce fnl f)	2½	**3**	16/1	46	10
3062[7]	**Chardania (IRE) (44)** (CaptJWilson) **2-7-4**(7)ow1 AngelaHartley(9) (chsd ldrs: led over 1f out to ins fnl f)	1¼	**4**	33/1	34	—
2003[8]	**Fleur-de-Lys (45)** (WJMusson) **2-7-12** FNorton(14) (s.i.s: hdwy to ld 2f out: sn hdd: one pce)	1¾	**5**	12/1	31	—
2914[3]	**Rock From The Sun (55)** (WGMTurner) **2-8-5**(3) DSweeney(11) (led 4f: rdn & outpcd appr fnl f)	3	**6**	12/1	33	—
3395[5]	**Impulse (IRE) (68)** (APJarvis) **2-9-7v[1]** SDrowne(2) (chsd ldrs: rdn over 2f out: ev ch over 1f out: wknd ins fnl f)	s.h	**7**	9/1	45	9
3078[3]	**Clear View (56)** (BJMeehan) **2-8-2**(7) GHannon(5) (nvr trbld dlrs)	1¼	**8**	6/1[3]	30	—
2784[5]	**Angry Albert (53)** (CSmith) **2-8-6v** CRutter(1) (a bhd)	3	**9**	16/1	19	—
2904[7]	**Dispol Lass (43)** (PCalver) **2-7-7**(3) DarrenMoffatt(8) (gd spd 4f)	hd	**10**	20/1	9	—
3045[6]	**Silent Pride (IRE) (50)** (MDIUsher) **2-8-3** JMarshall(12) (w ldrs 4f: drvn along & lost tch)	nk	**11**	12/1	15	—
3045[4]	**Gorgeous (50)** (NPLittmoden) **2-8-3** BDoyle(4) (nvr nr to chal)	s.h	**12**	14/1	15	—
3045[5]	**Tender Doll (IRE) (50)** (CADwyer) **2-8-3** NVarley(7) (trckd ldrs to ½-wy: sn wknd)	2½	**13**	9/1	8	—
2784[6]	**Amington Girl (51)** (PDEvans) **2-8-4v[1]** JFEgan(13) (chsd ldrs: rdn to ld over 2f out: sdn hdd & wknd qckly)	4	**14**	5/1[2]	—	—

(SP 134.9%) **14 Rn**

1m 13.1 (3.10) CSF £32.41 CT £382.46 TOTE £7.90: £2.00 £2.30 £8.30 (£10.00) Trio £207.70; £181.40 to 13/8/97 OWNER Marske Machine Co (MALTON) BRED G. Middlebrook

LONG HANDICAP Chardania (IRE) 7-7

No bid

2714 Marske Machine, from a stable in fine form, responded to the blinkers and surged through to take charge in the last one hundred yards. (7/1)

3228* Bermuda Triangle (IRE) delayed her challenged late on this occasion but she was produced to win inside the last furlong only to be denied in the race to the line. (7/2)

780 Maedaley, flat-footed as the stalls opened, recovered the lost ground but it took its toll in the closing stages on this first attempt beyond the minimum trip. (16/1)

780 Chardania (IRE) looked the likely winner when striking the front below the distance but she was unable to sustain the run and was well outpointed in the sprint to the post. (33/1)

1019 Fleur-de-Lys did not hit the traps but she worked her way into the lead passing the quarter-mile marker before the earlier exertions took their toll and she was made to pay for it. (12/1)

2914 Rock From The Sun attempted to make it a true test of stamina on this step down in trip but she was left standing as the pace lifted approaching the last furlong. (12/1)

1959 Impulse (IRE) had to admit his attempt to concede weight all round too much of a handicap when the final battle developed. (9/1)

3045 Tender Doll (IRE) (9/1: 5/1-10/1)

3452 GRANDSTAND H'CAP (0-70) (3-Y.O) (Class E)

6-50 (6-51) **1m 8y** £3,171.00 (£948.00: £454.00: £207.00) Stalls: Low GOING minus 0.34 sec per fur (GF)

				SP	RR	SF
3230*	**City Gambler (67)** (GCBravery) **3-9-7** MRimmer(4) (hld up in tch: hdwy over 1f out: rdn to ld wl ins fnl f)	—	**1**	12/1	79	55
3205*	**Rocky Dance (FR) (67)** (APJarvis) **3-9-7** SDrowne(3) (hld up & bhd: gd hdwy 2f out: r.o wl fnl f)	1½	**2**	5/1[2]	76	52
3101[3]	**Inclination (60)** (MBlanshard) **3-9-0** RCochrane(1) (led tl wl over 1f out: ev ch ins fnl f: unable qckn)	½	**3**	8/1	68	44
3292[4]	**Rumbustious (50)** (RHannon) **3-8-1**(3) MartinDwyer(5) (chsd ldr: led wl over 1f out tl wl ins fnl f)	½	**4**	9/1	57	33
2945[7]	**Faym (IRE) (57)** (JWharton) **3-8-11** SSanders(11) (stdd s: swtchd lft: hdwy over 1f out: rdn & one pce fnl f)	1½	**5**	14/1	61	37
3205[2]	**Racing Heart (56)** (PJMakin) **3-8-10** GDuffield(2) (hld up: hdwy & swtchd rt over 1f out: hrd rdn: one pce)	1¼	**6**	5/2[1]	58	34
2645[4]	**Silver Secret (67)** (MJHeaton-Ellis) **3-9-7** LDettori(8) (hld up in tch: effrt wl over 1f out: nt pce to chal)	3	**7**	11/2[3]	63	39
2733[13]	**Mendoza (53)** (DJGMurraySmith) **3-8-2**(5) CLowther(7) (prom tl wknd 2f out)	2½	**8**	11/1	44	20
2782[8]	**Off The Rails (61)** (HCandy) **3-9-1** CRutter(10) (chsd ldrs: hrd rdn over 2f out: sn btn)	½	**9**	12/1	51	27
2927[6]	**Coble (65)** (BWHills) **3-9-5** MHills(9) (prom tl rdn & wknd 2f out)	2½	**10**	12/1	50	26
2183[14]	**Aurora Bay (IRE) (48)** (MBell) **3-8-2** MFenton(6) (a bhd: rdn 3f out: t.o)	dist	**11**	25/1	—	—

(SP 123.7%) **11 Rn**

1m 37.0 (2.00) CSF £68.04 CT £371.64 TOTE £10.40: £3.30 £2.60 £1.70 (£24.60) Trio £67.40 OWNER Mr J. J. May (NEWMARKET) BRED J. Ward Hill

3230* City Gambler, winning her second race of the month, found just enough when the battle was on inside the final furlong and she is really thriving now she has the sun on her back. (12/1: op 8/1)

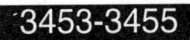

3205* Rocky Dance (FR) produced a determined last-furlong challenge but the winner had taken first run and she was always being held. (5/1)
3101 Inclination once again forced the pace and rallied gamely inside the final furlong. That elusive first victory is well within reach. (8/1)
3292 Rumbustious had far more use made of her this time and she did not give in without a fight but she was tapped for toe in an all-out dash to the line. (9/1)
2523 Faym (IRE), steadied leaving the start and switched in behind, produced a sustained last-furlong challenge but, with the tempo not dropping, could never quite muster the speed of the principals. (14/1: 10/1-16/1)
3205 Racing Heart travelled well for most of the way and she delivered her challenge entering the final furlong but, hard as she tried, she just could not quicken enough to get to terms. (5/2)
642 Mendoza (11/1: 8/1-12/1)

3453 LUMBERS BREITLING H'CAP (0-80) (3-Y.O+) (Class D)

7-20 (7-20) **1m 1f 218y** £3,886.00 (£1,168.00: £564.00: £262.00) Stalls: Low GOING minus 0.34 sec per fur (GF)

				SP	RR	SF
2315^{4}	**Coretta (IRE) (77)** (LMCumani) **3-9-9** LDettori(8) (mde all: hrd drvn 2f out: r.o wl)	—	**1**	$11/4^{2}$	88	45
2660^{6}	**Pekay (64)** (MJohnston) **4-9-5** BDoyle(5) (trckd ldrs: hdwy 2f out: sn ev ch: rdn & one pce fnl f)	2	**2**	$6/1^{3}$	72	38
2832^{2}	**Boss Lady (IRE) (78)** (RCharlton) **3-9-10** PatEddery(4) (a.p: chal 3f out: rdn 2f out: r.o one pce)	4	**3**	$15/8^{1}$	79	36
3140^{5}	**Massyar Seventeen (66)** (HJCollingridge) **3-8-12** MRimmer(6) (swtg: hld up: effrt & pshd along over 3f: styd on appr fnl f)	1¾	**4**	10/1	65	22
3236^{7}	**Quibbling (70)** (HCandy) **3-9-2** CRutter(7) (prom: rdn & outpcd 3f out: n.d afterwards)	1¾	**5**	$6/1^{3}$	66	23
2961^{12}	**Quiet Arch (IRE) (65)** (WRMuir) **4-9-6v^{1}** DaneO'Neill(1) (lw: s.s: effrt 3f out: sn rdn: no imp)	2	**6**	16/1	58	24
2944^{6}	**Soldier Mak (55)** (JMackie) **4-8-10** GCarter(2) (hld up: hdwy 4f out: rdn & wknd 3f out)	nk	**7**	14/1	47	13
2716^{7}	**Majal (IRE) (49)** (JSWainwright) **8-8-4** GDuffield(3) (b: lw: s.s: rdn 3f out: no rspnse o)	3	**8**	25/1	36	2

(SP 115.5%) **8 Rn**

2m 7.9 (4.20) CSF £18.14 CT £34.09 TOTE £4.20: £1.80 £2.10 £1.10 (£14.30) OWNER Mr Gerald Leigh (NEWMARKET) BRED Gerald W. Leigh
WEIGHT FOR AGE 3yo-9lb
2315 Coretta (IRE) got off the mark in her first handicap with a very brave, all the way success and, in winning going away, gave notice that she will be suited by further. (11/4: 2/1-7/2)
2660 Pekay posed a serious threat when mounting a determined challenge below the distance but that was just the spur the winner needed and he was put in his place in the duel to the finish. (6/1: op 4/1)
2832 Boss Lady (IRE) rarely runs a bad race and she tried to make life difficult for the winner early in the straight, but that rival had gears left and she proved much too strong when the chips were down. (15/8)
3140 Massyar Seventeen gave the impression that this trip was more to her liking with a never-nearer, staying-on performance, but he still has more improvement to make to be sure of success. (10/1)
3236 Quibbling got outpaced at a crucial time and from then on could only stay on at the one pace. She is inclined to race freely and she is not yet getting it together. (6/1)
1660 Quiet Arch (IRE) was not at all happy even on this better-than-average going at this time of year, and she was always fighting a losing battle after giving away valuable ground at the start. (16/1)

3454 TRAVELSPHERE CLAIMING STKS (3-Y.O) (Class F)

7-50 (7-51) **7f 9y** £2,847.00 (£792.00: £381.00) Stalls: Low GOING minus 0.34 sec per fur (GF)

				SP	RR	SF
3206^{5}	**Petite Danseuse (60)** (CADwyer) **3-8-7** LDettori(2) (swtg: hld up: hdwy 2f out: led ins fnl f: drvn clr)	—	**1**	$7/2^{2}$	65+	35
3268^{2}	**Davis Rock (66)** (WRMuir) **3-9-2**$^{(3)}$ MartinDwyer(8) (swtg: lw: a.p: ev ch ent fnl f: outpcd towards fin)	3	**2**	$6/1^{3}$	70	40
3029^{6}	**Oxbane (55)** (HCandy) **3-8-1** CRutter(3) (swtg: chsd ldrs: edgd rt 3f out: led 2f tl ins fnl f)	1½	**3**	9/1	49	19
3092^{10}	**Secret Combe (IRE) (79)** (PJMakin) **3-9-5** SSanders(12) (swtchd lft sn after s: hdwy & rdn over 2f out: nt pce to chal)	2½	**4**	$2/1^{1}$	61	31
2921^{13}	**Masterstroke (62)** (BJMeehan) **3-8-6** MTebbutt(6) (swtg: hld up: hdwy ½-wy: wknd 2f out)	8	**5**	16/1	30	—
3206^{6}	**Moon Song (55)** (APJarvis) **3-8-7v^{1}** SDrowne(1) (lw: prom tl wknd u.p 2f out)	3	**6**	16/1	24	—
3145^{6}	**Last Chance (51)** (DJSCosgrove) **3-8-7b^{1}**$^{(5)}$ CLowther(7) (led: edgd rt: sn clr: hdd 2f out & wknd qckly)	½	**7**	16/1	28	—
3316^{10}	**Rochea (47)** (MrsNMacauley) **3-8-7** BDoyle(10) (lw: nvr trbld ldrs)	1¾	**8**	16/1	19	—
3268^{3}	**Patina (43)** (RHollinshead) **3-8-1**$^{(3)}$ RFfrench(13) (hld up in tch: effrt 3f out: rdn & wknd over 1f out)	¾	**9**	8/1	14	—
3088^{11}	**Farewell My Love (IRE) (51)** (JSWainwright) **3-8-7** GDuffield(11) (a bhd: rdn 3f out: t.o)	6	**10**	16/1	4	—
2941^{12}	**Blue Jay (IRE)** (RHannon) **3-8-6** DaneO'Neill(5) (dwlt: a in rr: t.o)	2	**11**	20/1	—	—
3083^{8}	**Sang d'Antibes (FR) (44)** (DJSCosgrove) **3-8-7** GCarter(9) (lw: bhd: effrt over 2f out: no imp: t.o)	1	**12**	20/1	—	—

(SP 129.9%) **12 Rn**

1m 24.9 (2.30) CSF £25.29 TOTE £4.80: £1.90 £2.00 £2.30 (£15.00) Trio £51.10 OWNER Binding Matters Ltd (NEWMARKET) BRED I. D. Livingstone
Oxbane clmd SD Gough £4,000, Farewell My Love (IRE) clmd Mrs S Day £6,000
3206 Petite Danseuse, winning her first race beyond the minimum trip, found the best turn of speed when let down to lead inside the final furlong and won this with ease. (7/2)
3268 Davis Rock, always in the firing line, tried hard to make a race of it but, once the winner found top gear, she was left in her wake. (6/1: 4/1-13/2)
3029 Oxbane gradually worked her way over towards the far side and showed ahead inside the last quarter-mile, but when the dash to the line developed she was found wanting. (9/1)
3092 Secret Combe (IRE), switched in behind the pack soon after the start, did not have a lot of room in which to manoeuvre approaching the last couple of furlongs but it was her own lack of acceleration that was the biggest problem. (2/1)
94* Masterstroke had reached a challenging position over two furlongs out and looked sure to take a hand in the outcome but he found absolutely nothing when set alight and does seem to have a problem. (16/1)

3455 EVANS MERCEDES-BENZ LIMITED STKS (0-65) (3-Y.O) (Class F)

8-20 (8-20) **1m 3f 183y** £2,742.00 (£762.00: £366.00) Stalls: Low GOING minus 0.34 sec per fur (GF)

				SP	RR	SF
2652^{6}	**Lookout (65)** (BWHills) **3-8-8** MHills(7) (hld up in rr: swtchd lft over 3f out: hdwy over 1f out: led wl ins fnl f)	—	**1**	$7/2^{3}$	72	21
3029^{4}	**Harmony Hall (63)** (JRFanshawe) **3-8-11** SSanders(3) (b: b.hind: trckd ldrs: led over 1f out tl ins fnl f: rallied cl home)	½	**2**	9/1	74	23
3234^{4}	**Arriving (65)** (JWHills) **3-8-10** RHills(1) (hld up: hdwy ent st: rdn 2f out: r.o one pce)	3	**3**	$6/4^{1}$	69	18
1465^{4}	**Beauchamp Lion (63)** (JLDunlop) **3-8-11** LDettori(9) (led after 1f: qcknd over 3f out: hdd over 1f out: one pce)	hd	**4**	$3/1^{2}$	70	19

2570^{5}	**Gee Bee Boy (65)** (APJarvis) **3-8-13** SDrowne(4) (lw: hld up: drvn along 3f out: nt rch ldrs)	3½	**5**	16/1	67	16
2182^{5}	**Here's To Howie (USA) (65)** (RHannon) **3-8-13** DaneO'Neill(2) (plld hrd: prom tl n.m.r & wknd wl over 1f out)	¾	**6**	12/1	66	15
2846^{9}	**Yours In Sport (64)** (JWWatts) **3-8-11** PatEddery(6) (swtg: prom: ev ch & rdn 3f out: wknd wl over 1f out)	3	**7**	8/1	60	9
2667^{11}	**Ludo (60)** (RHannon) **3-8-13b^{1}** WJO'Connor(5) (hld up in rr: effrt & rdn 3f out: no rspnse)	3½	**8**	12/1	58	7
3200^{16}	**Strictly Hard (54)** (GCBravery) **3-8-8** DRMcCabe(8) (led 1f: rdn & outpcd 3f out)	2½	**9**	12/1	49	—

(SP 137.3%) **9 Rn**

2m 35.2 (6.70) CSF £38.71 TOTE £4.80: £1.50 £4.30 £1.10 (£21.60) Trio £26.60 OWNER Mr R. D. Hollingsworth (LAMBOURN) BRED R. D. Hollingsworth

2652 Lookout, patiently ridden, landed the gamble readily, but she did need to put her best foot forward to make sure in the dying strides. (7/2: op 8/1)

3029 Harmony Hall has been crying out for this more suitable trip and there is no reason why he cannot find an opening now. (9/1)

3234 Arriving should have had the beating of the winner on the book but she was being tightened up approaching the final furlong, although to make that an excuse could prove costly. (6/4)

1465 Beauchamp Lion, well supported to make it six in a day for Frankie, adopted far more forceful tactics but, after a ten-week break, was feeling the strain when the final battle got under way. (3/1: 9/4-7/2)

2570 Gee Bee Boy could never muster the pace to get himself into the action but he did stay on, although he did have it all to do at the weights. (16/1)

2182 Here's To Howie (USA) refused to settle and, though he was short of room below the distance, he did look to have run his race by then. (12/1)

Strictly Hard (12/1: op 20/1)

T/Plpt: £23.70 (787.72 Tckts). T/Qdpt: £6.90 (202.99 Tckts) IM

3239-THIRSK (L-H) (Good to firm, Firm patches)
Monday August 11th

WEATHER: overcast & v.hot WIND: slt half against

3456 WEST YORKSHIRE (S) H'CAP (0-60) (3-Y.O+) (Class F)

6-05 (6-09) **1m** £3,099.00 (£864.00: £417.00) Stalls: Low GOING minus 0.34 sec per fur (GF)

				SP	RR	SF
3406^{5}	**Shontaine (51)** (MJohnston) **4-9-10** JWeaver(15) (lw: a cl up: led wl over 2f out: styd on wl u.p fnl f)	—	**1**	9/2^{1}	63	45
2857^{8}	**Mbulwa (47)** (RAFahey) **11-9-6** LCharnock(10) (a.p: hdwy to disp ld 2f out: hung rt u.p fnl f: kpt on)	s.h	**2**	7/1^{3}	59	41
3240^{13}	**Seconds Away (34)** (JSGoldie) **6-8-4**(3) PFessey(4) (bhd: hdwy 3f out: styd on: nvr able to chal)	2½	**3**	13/2^{2}	41	23
3315^{8}	**Tinklers Folly (53)** (RMWhitaker) **5-9-12v** DeanMcKeown(16) (swtg: a chsng ldrs: rdn 3f out: one pce)	2½	**4**	14/1	55	37
3143^{17}	**Awesome Venture (38)** (MCChapman) **7-8-4**(7) SCarson(1) (trckd ldrs: effrt 3f out: one pce)	½	**5**	20/1	39	21
3315^{10}	**Diamond Crown (IRE) (42)** (MartynWane) **6-9-1** JCarroll(12) (hld up & bhd: hdwy 3f out: hmpd wl over 1f out: r.o u.p)	2½	**6**	14/1	38	20
2845^{11}	**She's Simply Great (IRE) (32)** (JJO'Neill) **4-8-5** RLappin(5) (unruly s: effrt ½-wy: hmpd wl over 1f out: nvr rchd ldrs)	s.h	**7**	25/1	28	10
2941^{4}	**Sun Fairy (45)** (JAGlover) **3-8-11b^{1}** NDay(17) (in tch tl outpcd fnl 3f)	1¼	**8**	10/1	38	13
2880^{6}	**General Monty (38)** (TDBarron) **5-8-4**(7) VictoriaAppleby(6) (swtg: effrt ½-wy: nvr rchd ldrs)	nk	**9**	9/1	31	13
3382^{8}	**Golden Fish (33)** (EJAlston) **5-8-6** JQuinn(11) (in tch tl outpcd fnl 2½f)	1½	**10**	14/1	23	5
3039^{9}	**Prime Partner (36)** (TDEasterby) **4-8-2**(7) RWinston(13) (in tch to st)	nk	**11**	8/1	25	7
2913^{9}	**Born A Lady (32)** (MrsVAAconley) **4-8-0**(5) APolli(9) (lost tch fr ½-wy)	1¼	**12**	25/1	19	1
2385^{9}	**That Old Feeling (IRE) (45)** (DWChapman) **5-9-4** ACulhane(7) (n.d)	¾	**13**	20/1	30	12
2502^{12}	**Sandblaster (44)** (JLEyre) **4-9-3** OPears(2) (unruly s: led tl hdd wl over 2f out: wknd qckly)	nk	**14**	12/1	29	11
3276^{17}	**Asterix (33)** (JMBradley) **9-8-1b**(5) IonaWands(3) (b: s.s: a bhd)	1	**15**	12/1	16	—
3285^{15}	**My Godson (52)** (MDods) **7-9-8b**(3) CTeague(14) (swtg: bhd & c wd st: n.d)	5	**16**	25/1	25	7
1689^{14}	**Richard House Lad (36)** (RHollinshead) **4-8-9** FLynch(18) (a bhd)	2	**17**	16/1	5	—

(SP 136.5%) **17 Rn**

1m 39.8 (3.30) CSF £32.36 CT £202.02 TOTE £5.90: £1.40 £2.70 £2.80 £3.20 (£13.20) Trio £31.10 OWNER Mr Paul Dean (MIDDLEHAM) BRED Mark Johnston Racing Ltd

WEIGHT FOR AGE 3yo-7lb

Bt in 3,200 gns

3406 Shontaine had not won at this trip previously but he got it particularly well here and showed fine determination, as the runner-up was continually hanging into him. (9/2)

1266 Mbulwa, off his lowest mark for some time, showed his first signs of form this season and, despite his years, looks one to side with. (7/1)

2899 Seconds Away, happier back at this longer trip, ran well without troubling the front pair. (13/2)

3134 Tinklers Folly, excitable and hot beforehand, still ran a fair race. (14/1)

2069 Awesome Venture spends most of his time on the All-Weather at which he is a good deal better, but he did show his well-being here by travelling really well for a long way. (20/1)

2716 Diamond Crown (IRE) tried the impossible attempting to come from last on the home turn, and did well after a bumping match to get so close. (14/1)

1798 She's Simply Great (IRE) has ability but is a real headstrong individual. (25/1)

2941 Sun Fairy (10/1: 7/1-11/1)

2880 General Monty (9/1: 14/1-8/1)

2355* Sandblaster (12/1: op 8/1)

3457 GOLDEN FLEECE HOTEL H'CAP (0-80) (3-Y.O) (Class D)

6-35 (6-35) **1m** £4,272.50 (£1,280.00: £615.00: £282.50) Stalls: Low GOING minus 0.34 sec per fur (GF)

				SP	RR	SF
3310^{4}	**Jedi Knight (67)** (MWEasterby) **3-8-13** LCharnock(6) (a.p: hdwy over 2f out: styd on to ld wl ins fnl f)	—	**1**	11/2^{3}	76	41
3211^{2}	**Barnburgh Boy (73)** (TDBarron) **3-9-5** JCarroll(2) (chsd ldrs: led 2f out: r.o u.p: ct wl ins fnl f)	½	**2**	2/1^{1}	81	46
3213*	**Fancy A Fortune (IRE) (68)** (DNicholls) **3-9-0** AlexGreaves(7) (lw: led 3f: led 3f out to 2f out: sn outpcd)	8	**3**	11/2^{3}	60	25
3088*	**Barresbo (68)** (CWFairhurst) **3-9-0** JWeaver(3) (hld up: effrt 3f out: styd on: n.d)	1¾	**4**	3/1^{2}	57	22
2885^{3}	**Kayfiyah (IRE) (75)** (DMorley) **3-9-7** JStack(1) (s.i.s: sn cl up: led after 3f tl hdd 3f out: sn wknd)	1¾	**5**	10/1	60	25
3236^{8}	**Foot Battalion (IRE) (72)** (RHollinshead) **3-9-4** FLynch(4) (bhd: rdn over 3f out: n.d)	nk	**6**	10/1	56	21

2408[6]	**Unshaken (72)** (EJAlston) **3-8-11**(7) MelanieWorden(5) (outpcd & bhd fnl 3f)	14	**7**	20/1	28	—
				(SP 112.0%)		**7 Rn**

1m 39.2 (2.70) CSF £14.79 TOTE £5.50: £2.70 £1.80 (£6.40) OWNER Mr K. Hodgson (SHERIFF HUTTON) BRED E. J. B. Maude
3310 Jedi Knight still gives the impression that he is a bit of a character, but he won this nicely and there would seem to be more to come. (11/2)
3211 Barnburgh Boy again got run out of it but did not seem to do anything wrong and surely his turn will come. (2/1)
3213* Fancy A Fortune (IRE) went off too fast and was easily picked off in the straight. (11/2)
3088* Barresbo, patiently ridden, found the leaders had got away from him and could never get into it. (3/1)
2885 Kayfiyah (IRE) burst himself by taking the leader on at too fast a pace. (10/1)
1773 Foot Battalion (IRE) is fast dropping down the handicap but did not show any encouragement here. (10/1)

3458 TATTERSALLS MAIDEN AUCTION STKS (2-Y.O) (Class E)
7-05 (7-08) **7f** £3,317.50 (£1,000.00: £485.00: £227.50) Stalls: High GOING minus 0.34 sec per fur (GF)

				SP	RR	SF
3060[2]	**Panama House (79)** (TDEasterby) **2-8-9** LCharnock(2) (lw: mde all: shkn up appr fnl f: r.o)	—	**1**	8/11[1]	70+	37
3239[10]	**Ray of Sunshine (IRE)** (MrsJRRamsden) **2-8-10** JFortune(5) (trckd wnr: effrt over 1f out: nt qckn)	2	**2**	3/1[2]	66	33
3019[4]	**Short Romance (IRE)** (JWHills) **2-8-3** JCarroll(4) (a chsng ldrs: one pce fnl 3f)	3	**3**	9/2[3]	53	20
2752[5]	**Czar Wars** (PTDalton) **2-8-2**(3) PFessey(1) (in tch: rdn ent st: styd on one pce)	1	**4**	25/1	52	19
3212[5]	**Disco Tex** (MWEasterby) **2-8-5**(3) GParkin(3) (b.nr hind: effrt ½-wy: styd on: nvr trbld ldrs)	nk	**5**	25/1	55	22
993[9]	**Desire's Gold** (MBrittain) **2-8-7**ow2 NDay(6) (outpcd & wl bhd fr ½-wy)	14	**6**	50/1	22	—
				(SP 110.7%)		**6 Rn**

1m 27.3 (2.40) CSF £2.74 TOTE £1.60: £1.20 £1.70 (£2.20) OWNER Mr P. England (MALTON) BRED R. B. Warren
3060 Panama House, without the tongue-strap this time, behaved himself well and won in really good style. (8/11)
Ray of Sunshine (IRE) showed signs of temperament but this good-looking sort has plenty of ability when he really decides to use it. (3/1)
3019 Short Romance (IRE) was a very nervy filly in the paddock, almost jumping at her own shadow, and she obviously needs to settle down. (9/2: 5/2-5/1)
2752 Czar Wars looked likely to benefit from this and showed signs of ability. (25/1)
3212 Disco Tex still looks to need time and failed to offer a threat. (25/1)
Desire's Gold did not impress on looks and ran no sort of race. (50/1)

3459 PRESIDIUM - ELMHURST BLOODSTOCK E.B.F. MEDIAN AUCTION MAIDEN STKS (2-Y.O) (Class E)
7-35 (7-36) **5f** £3,382.50 (£1,020.00: £495.00: £232.50) Stalls: High GOING minus 0.34 sec per fur (GF)

				SP	RR	SF
2706[6]	**Naviasky (IRE)** (MrsJRRamsden) **2-9-0** JFortune(8) (lw: hdwy gng wl ½-wy: led appr fnl f: easily)	—	**1**	7/4[2]	79+	11
3239[13]	**Far Removed (IRE)** (MrsJRRamsden) **2-9-0** OPears(9) (trckd ldrs: kpt on wl fnl f)	2	**2**	33/1	73	5
2037[10]	**Double Power** (LRLloyd-James) **2-8-9** KimTinkler(1) (led tl hdd appr fnl f: rdn & no ex)	1½	**3**	20/1	63	—
2706[13]	**Dekelsmary** (JBalding) **2-8-9** JEdmunds(5) (bit bkwd: outpcd & bhd tl r.o wl fnl f)	hd	**4**	40/1	63	—
3239[11]	**Lambs Lane** (TDEasterby) **2-9-0** LCharnock(7) (chsd ldrs: nt qckn fnl 2f)	1½	**5**	14/1	63	—
2762[4]	**Ollie's Chuckle (IRE)** (JAGlover) **2-9-0** NDay(2) (a in tch: drvn along ½-wy: no imp)	1¾	**6**	6/5[1]	57	—
	Time To Hunt (BWMurray) **2-9-0** VHalliday(4) (cmpt: bit bkwd: sn outpcd & bhd)	½	**7**	100/1	56	—
1791[7]	**Stephangeorge** (MBrittain) **2-9-0** JCarroll(10) (swtg: prom 3f: sn wknd)	½	**8**	50/1	54	—
2842[12]	**Detroit City (IRE)** (JBerry) **2-8-11**(3) PFessey(3) (spd over 3f: wknd qckly)	1¼	**9**	8/1[3]	50	—
				(SP 112.7%)		**9 Rn**

61.0 secs (3.40) CSF £56.47 TOTE £3.80: £1.10 £3.30 £4.80 (£21.50) Trio £300.30; £114.23 to 13/8/97 OWNER Mr Nigel Munton (THIRSK) BRED Miss Mary McKeon
OFFICIAL EXPLANATION **Naviasky (IRE): regarding the apparent improvement in form, the trainer reported that the gelding is a quirky, green individual, who has taken time to come to hand and would not have needed to improve on his last run to win here. Ollie's Chuckle (IRE): the jockey reported that the colt had bolted to the start.**
2706 Naviasky (IRE), despite dropping back in class, was different class to these and won like a decent horse. (7/4)
Far Removed (IRE), a stable-companion of the winner, ran with a deal of promise and was certainly not knocked about and, no doubt, the kindness will be repaid. (33/1)
Double Power is a really strong individual who probably still needed this and showed plenty of speed. (20/1)
Dekelsmary, still looking likely to benefit from this, got completely outpaced until showing an amazing burst of speed late on. (40/1)
Lambs Lane is gradually improving but there is plenty more needed. (14/1: 10/1-16/1)
2762 Ollie's Chuckle (IRE) spoiled his chances by bolting on the way to post. (6/5: evens-5/4)

3460 CRAB AND LOBSTER H'CAP (0-80) (3-Y.O) (Class D)
8-05 (8-07) **5f** £4,370.00 (£1,310.00: £630.00: £290.00) Stalls: High GOING minus 0.34 sec per fur (GF)

				SP	RR	SF
3194[8]	**Gaelic Storm (75)** (MJohnston) **3-9-7** JWeaver(6) (lw: s.i.s: hdwy & swtchd 2f out: led ins fnl f: all out)	—	**1**	11/2[3]	84	41
3287[4]	**William's Well (58)** (MWEasterby) **3-8-1b**(3) GParkin(7) (cl up: sn drvn along: led 2f out tl ins fnl f: kpt on wl)	nk	**2**	3/1[2]	66	23
2964[8]	**Silent Miracle (IRE) (73)** (MBell) **3-9-0**(5) GFaulkner(3) (chsd ldrs: ev ch over 1f out: no ex)	3	**3**	8/1	71	28
3121[2]	**Bramble Bear (71)** (MBlanshard) **3-9-3** JQuinn(4) (trckd ldrs: hdwy & ev ch over 1f out: nt qckn)	s.h	**4**	5/2[1]	69	26
3092[8]	**Mouche (66)** (MrsJRRamsden) **3-8-12** JFortune(2) (hld up & bhd: hdwy 2f out: nvr able to chal)	hd	**5**	11/2[3]	64	21
2655[8]	**Nifty Norman (75)** (JBerry) **3-9-4**(3) TEDurcan(5) (cl up 3f: sn rdn & btn)	2½	**6**	8/1	65	22
3121[5]	**Tinker's Surprise (IRE) (50)** (JBalding) **3-7-10b** LCharnock(1) (led 3f: sn wknd)	3	**7**	20/1	30	—
				(SP 111.3%)		**7 Rn**

59.6 secs (2.00) CSF £19.22 TOTE £5.40: £2.80 £2.20 (£10.00) OWNER H C Racing Club (MIDDLEHAM) BRED A. D. G. Oldrey
LONG HANDICAP Tinker's Surprise (IRE) 7-7
2044 Gaelic Storm again lost ground at the start and then had to weave his way through but, given some strong assistance, he was always doing enough and, if his starting problems can be sorted out, there is obviously more to come. (11/2)
3287 William's Well is an honest sort who needs plenty of help from the saddle but keeps responding and really made the winner fight. (3/1: op 11/2)
2563 Silent Miracle (IRE) won her only race on the All-Weather and a return to that surface seems long overdue. (8/1)
3121 Bramble Bear, unlucky last time, this little filly had no excuses here. (5/2)
1021 Mouche is slipping down the handicap and is giving signs o returning to form. (11/2: 3/1-6/1)
2141* Nifty Norman looked uncomfortable in the heat here and found this ground too fast. (8/1)

3461 YORKSHIRE PUDDING H'CAP (0-60) (3-Y.O+) (Class F)

8-35 (8-35) **2m** £3,038.00 (£914.00: £442.00: £206.00) Stalls: Low GOING minus 0.34 sec per fur (GF)

				SP	RR	SF
3096[3]	**Pen Friend (47)** (WJHaggas) **3-8-6** FLynch(1) (lw: mde most: hung rt & hld on wl fnl 3f)	—	**1**	15/8[1]	59	19
3028[2]	**Shelteez (USA) (45)** (MBell) **3-7-13**(5) RMullen(4) (lw: a chsng ldrs: rdn 3f out: kpt on wl towards fin)	nk	**2**	5/2[2]	57	17
3283*	**Hasta la Vista (54)** (MWEasterby) **7-9-11b**(3) 4x GParkin(3) (lw: disp ld tl hdd 9f out: cl up: rdn over 2f out: nt qckn fnl f)	2	**3**	3/1[3]	64	39
3284[4]	**Ship's Dancer (24)** (DonEnricoIncisa) **4-7-12b** KimTinkler(2) (hld up & bhd: hdwy over 3f out: ch over 1f out: sn btn)	½	**4**	33/1	33	8
3317[7]	**Alwarqa (50)** (MartynWane) **4-9-7**(3) AWhelan(6) (hld up: effrt 4f out: sn chsng ldrs: outpcd fnl 2f)	6	**5**	10/1	53	28
2207[3]	**Penny Peppermint (26)** (REBarr) **5-7-7**(7) RWinston(5) (in tch: outpcd 1/2-wy: wknd ent st)	15	**6**	16/1	14	—
2753[4]	**Havana Heights (IRE) (41)** (JLEyre) **4-9-1** MGallagher(7) (prom tl outpcd 5f out: sn bhd)	6	**7**	20/1	23	—
				(SP 111.0%)	**7 Rn**	

3m 32.3 (9.30) CSF £5.76 TOTE £3.00: £1.70 £2.20 (£2.70) OWNER Mr B. Haggas (NEWMARKET) BRED Lord Halifax
WEIGHT FOR AGE 3yo-15lb

3096 Pen Friend, made plenty of use of, proved to be a tough sort but he again hung right under pressure. (15/8)
3028 Shelteez (USA) stays particularly well and, judging by the way she finished, more use should have been made of her. (5/2: op 6/4)
3283* Hasta la Vista might well have won this, had he made it instead of sitting upsides the winner, and continually racing wide. (3/1)
3284 Ship's Dancer showed a useful turn of foot early in the straight but then failed to maintain it. (33/1)
2882 Alwarqa is a moody sort and, after looking dangerous on the home turn, she then came under pressure and found little. (10/1)

T/Plpt: £45.00 (379.13 Tckts). T/Qdpt: £11.20 (92.54 Tckts) AA

3276-WINDSOR (Fig. 8) (Good to firm, Good in St)
Monday August 11th
WEATHER: v.hot WIND: almost nil

3462 STRATFIELD SAYE (S) STKS (3 & 4-Y.O) (Class G)

2-00 (2-00) **1m 3f 135y** £2,146.50 (£599.00: £289.50) Stalls: High GOING minus 0.67 sec per fur (HD)

				SP	RR	SF
2574[5]	**Brighstone (87)** (MCPipe) **4-9-13** AMcGlone(3) (t: lw: mde all: hung lft over 1f out: rdn out)	—	**1**	1/4[1]	66	30
1850[5]	**Foleys Quest (IRE)** (JSMoore) **3-8-1**(7) PaulCleary(2) (b.off fore: swtg: hld up: chsd wnr over 2f out: ev ch over 1f out: r.o)	nk	**2**	12/1	58	11
2535[6]	**Northern Drums (50)** (NMBabbage) **4-9-10v**[1] TSprake(6) (t: swtg: hdwy over 3f out: hung bdly lft 2f out: unable qckn)	1½	**3**	10/1[3]	61	25
2218[7]	**Chief Predator (USA) (51)** (RHannon) **3-8-13b** DaneO'Neill(5) (lw: a.p: chsd wnr 4f out tl over 2f out: one pce)	¾	**4**	6/1[2]	60	13
2301[9]	**Sans Pere** (NMBabbage) **4-9-10** VSlattery(1) (swtg: chsd wnr over 7f: t.o)	dist	**5**	33/1	—	—
				(SP 114.0%)	**5 Rn**	

2m 30.0 (4.00) CSF £4.53 TOTE £1.10: £1.10 £3.20 (£2.70) OWNER Richard Green (Fine Paintings) (WELLINGTON) BRED Michael Poland
WEIGHT FOR AGE 3yo-11lb
Bt in 7,000 gns, Chief Predator (USA) clmd Karen George £5,750

2574 Brighstone, who has been tubed since his last run, appeared to have a simple task but certainly had to work hard. Making every post a winning one, he did not appear to be going as well as the runner-up a quarter of a mile out and then drifted into the centre of the course approaching the final furlong. Rousted along, he just managed to keep his rival at bay. (1/4)
Foleys Quest (IRE) appreciated the drop in class. She appeared to be going better then the winner a quarter of a mile out but, although doing nothing wrong, was unable to get past her rival. (12/1)
888 Northern Drums appreciated the drop in class but he hung badly to his left over a quarter of a mile from home and, from that point, could only plod on at one pace. (10/1: op 5/1)
1971 Chief Predator (USA) is a moderate maiden and, after showing in second place in the straight, could then only go up and down in the same place. He was later claimed to go to Karen George's stable for £5,750. (6/1: op 3/1)

3463 SALAMANCA MAIDEN STKS (3-Y.O+) (Class D)

2-30 (2-31) **1m 67y** £3,642.50 (£1,100.00: £535.00: £252.50) Stalls: High GOING minus 0.67 sec per fur (HD)

				SP	RR	SF
2873[2]	**Dr Martens (IRE)** (LMCumani) **3-9-0** LDettori(14) (a.p: led 2f out: edgd rt ins fnl f: rdn out)	—	**1**	6/4[1]	90	30
3140[2]	**Tonight's Prize (IRE) (78)** (CFWall) **3-9-0** SSanders(18) (swtg: a.p: rdn over 2f out: r.o wl ins fnl f)	hd	**2**	4/1[2]	90	30
3079[3]	**Slipstream Star (70)** (IABalding) **3-8-6**(3) MartinDwyer(4) (swtg: led 6f: 3rd & btn whn shied: hit rail & stmbld ins fnl f)	8	**3**	11/1	69	9
3144[7]	**Bin Cyclone (USA)** (CEBrittain) **3-9-0** WRyan(13) (chsd ldr: led over 2f out: sn hdd: wknd fnl f)	nk	**4**	14/1	74	14
2315[9]	**Hidden Agenda (FR)** (RCharlton) **3-8-9** TSprake(10) (swtg: hld up: rdn 3f out: one pce)	2½	**5**	20/1	64	4
1004[3]	**Flint Knapper** (GWragg) **3-9-0** MHills(7) (lw: no hdwy fnl 3f)	2½	**6**	6/1[3]	64	4
2408[10]	**Doc Ryan's (73)** (MJRyan) **3-9-0** GCarter(6) (hdwy over 3f out: wknd over 2f out)	3	**7**	16/1	58	—
	South China Sea (PFICole) **3-8-9** CRutter(8) (w'like: bit bkwd: s.s: hdwy over 3f out: wknd over 2f out)	2	**8**	14/1	50	—
3211[5]	**Royale Rose (FR)** (ABailey) **3-8-9** DWright(17) (nvr nrr)	2½	**9**	25/1	45	—
	Saramah (USA) (JHMGosden) **3-8-9** RHills(1) (w'like: scope: lw: nvr nrr)	nk	**10**	10/1	44	—
3281[6]	**Erinrinca (IRE)** (JEBanks) **3-8-4**(5) CLowther(9) (nvr nrr)	½	**11**	33/1	43	—
2941[8]	**Langara Heights** (BJLlewellyn) **3-8-7**(7) JWilkinson(15) (a mid div)	hd	**12**	50/1	48	—
	Sheath Kefaah (JRJenkins) **4-9-7** SWhitworth(3) (lw: bhd fnl 4f)	s.h	**13**	66/1	48	—
	Floristan (IRE) (LMCumani) **3-8-11**(3) RFfrench(5) (unf: scope: bit bkwd: a bhd)	½	**14**	25/1	47	—
2687[6]	**Max's Magic (USA)** (GLMoore) **4-9-7** CandyMorris(12) (bit bkwd: prom over 4f)	3	**15**	66/1	41	—
	Got It Wrong Again (KTIvory) **4-9-7** CScally(16) (s.s: a bhd)	1¼	**16**	66/1	39	—
	Nomothetis (IRE) (PFICole) **3-8-9** AClark(11) (cmpt: bit bkwd: s.s: a bhd)	27	**17**	20/1	—	—
				(SP 137.5%)	**17 Rn**	

1m 43.6 (1.40) CSF £6.50 TOTE £2.10: £1.40 £1.40 £3.20 (£4.00) Trio £14.20 OWNER R Griggs Group Ltd (NEWMARKET) BRED Gainsborough Stud Management Ltd
WEIGHT FOR AGE 3yo-7lb

2873 Dr Martens (IRE) struck the front a quarter of a mile out but drifted to his right inside the final furlong and, with Dettori waving his whip, the combination certainly caused the third some problems. Nevertheless, he was certainly the best horse on the day. (6/4)
3140 Tonight's Prize (IRE), never far away, put in some sterling work inside the final furlong, again just losing out in a tight finish. He should soon find a race. (4/1)
3079 Slipstream Star did not have a very happy experience. Setting the pace, she was collared over a quarter of a mile out and was about a length behind Dr Martens inside the final furlong. That rival then edged over towards the rails and, with Dettori waving his whip, the filly shied away, resulting in her hitting the rails and stumbling badly. It did not affect the result but she would certainly have been a great deal closer. (11/1: 8/1-12/1)
Bin Cyclone (USA) struck the front over a quarter of a mile out but he was soon passed and had run out of gas in the final furlong. He is worth a try at seven furlongs. (14/1: 10/1-16/1)
1823 Hidden Agenda (FR) was made to look very pedestrian in the last three furlongs. (20/1)
1004 Flint Knapper never threatened to get anywhere near the principals. (6/1)
Saramah (USA) (10/1: 4/1-12/1)

3464 COPENHAGEN CONDITIONS STKS (2-Y.O) (Class C)

3-00 (3-00) **5f 217y** £4,449.20 (£1,662.80: £811.40: £347.00: £153.50: £76.10) Stalls: High GOING minus 0.44 sec per fur (F)

				SP	RR	SF
3233^{2}	**Mijana (IRE)** (JHMGosden) **2-9-0** LDettori(5) (lw: w ldr: led 3f out: rdn out)	—	**1**	7/4 ^{1}	96	48
3278^{*}	**Speedfit Too (IRE) (89)** (GGMargarson) **2-8-12** GCarter(4) (hld up: chsd wnr wl over 1f out: ev ch ins fnl f: r.o wl)	hd	**2**	13/2	94	46
3113^{*}	**Halmahera (IRE) (93)** (IABalding) **2-8-10** SWhitworth(6) (lw: hld up: rdn 2f out: unable qckn)	2	**3**	11/4 ^{2}	86	38
1293^{*}	**Carrowkeel (IRE)** (BWHills) **2-9-0** MHills(2) (nvr nr to chal)	2	**4**	7/2 ^{3}	85	37
3049^{7}	**Another Fantasy (IRE) (95)** (RHannon) **2-8-9** DaneO'Neill(1) (lw: led 3f: wknd wl over 1f out)	1½	**5**	7/1	76	28
	Spring Fever (BWHills) **2-8-4**$^{(3)}$ JDSmith(3) (w'like: bit bkwd: bhd fnl 3f)	1¼	**6**	25/1	71	23

(SP 114.9%) **6 Rn**

1m 11.4 (0.90) CSF £12.97 TOTE £3.90: £1.50 £3.30 (£15.20) OWNER Mr Nabil Mourad (NEWMARKET) BRED Churchtown House Stud
3233 Mijana (IRE) regained the winning thread. Disputing the lead until showing in front at halfway, he was ridden along to keep the persistent runner-up at bay. (7/4)
3278* Speedfit Too (IRE) lost absolutely nothing in defeat. Throwing down a very determined challenge, he had every chance inside the final furlong and only just lost out. (13/2)
3113* Halmahera (IRE) chased the leaders but failed to find that vital turn of foot when required. (11/4: op 6/4)
1293* Carrowkeel (IRE), held up towards the back of the field, could never summon up the necessary turn of foot to get in a challenge. (7/2)
1735 Another Fantasy (IRE), with a slender advantage to halfway, had shot her bolt early in the final quarter-mile. (7/1: 5/1-15/2)
Spring Fever, quite a powerful colt, was getting left behind from halfway. (25/1)

3465 ROYAL BANK OF SCOTLAND H'CAP (0-70) (3-Y.O+) (Class E)

3-30 (3-32) **1m 67y** £3,268.75 (£985.00: £477.50: £223.75) Stalls: High GOING minus 0.67 sec per fur (HD)

				SP	RR	SF
3227^{3}	**Gold Lance (USA) (53)** (RJO'Sullivan) **4-8-12** LDettori(15) (swtg: hrd rdn over 2f out: hdwy over 1f out: led ins fnl f: r.o wl)	—	**1**	4/1 ^{1}	63	25
3115^{13}	**Queen's Insignia (USA) (56)** (PFICole) **4-9-1** CRutter(5) (hdwy 2f out: led over 1f out tl ins fnl f: unable qckn)	1	**2**	10/1	64	26
3227^{15}	**Multi Franchise (44)** (RMFlower) **4-8-3**^{ow1} DaneO'Neill(16) (swtg: a.p: rdn over 2f out: ev ch ins fnl f: one pce)	hd	**3**	16/1	52	13
3328^{2}	**Vanborough Lad (40)** (MJBolton) **8-7-10**$^{(3)}$ RFfrench(8) (nt clr run over 2f out: hdwy over 1f out: r.o)	1¼	**4**	11/2 ^{2}	46	8
3394^{*}	**Ring the Chief (38)** (MDIUsher) **5-7-11** JMarshall(13) (swtg: hdwy over 1f out: one pce ins fnl f)	½	**5**	8/1	43	5
2748^{3}	**Cape Pigeon (USA) (60)** (LGCottrell) **12-9-5v** DHolland(14) (led 7f out tl over 1f out: one pce)	hd	**6**	10/1	64	26
3115^{16}	**Show Faith (IRE) (59)** (RHannon) **7-8-11**$^{(7)}$ PDobbs(7) (rdn over 2f out: hdwy over 1f out: nvr nrr)	¾	**7**	33/1	62	24
2892^{4}	**Digpast (IRE) (39)** (JJBridger) **7-7-5b**$^{(7)}$ PDoe(17) (s.s: rdn over 2f out: nvr nrr)	½	**8**	20/1	41	3
3230^{3}	**Glittering (USA) (57)** (CEBrittain) **3-8-9** WRyan(4) (a.p: rdn over 2f out: wknd fnl f)	nk	**9**	14/1	58	13
3143^{13}	**Fancy Design (IRE) (50)** (PMitchell) **4-8-4**$^{(5)}$ AimeeCook(1) (b.off hind: hdwy over 1f out: wknd fnl f)	1½	**10**	14/1	48	10
3138^{7}	**Coastguards Hero (38)** (MDIUsher) **4-7-4**$^{(7)}$ JFowle(12) (swtg: a mid div)	3	**11**	16/1	31	—
3139^{*}	**Banzhaf (USA) (69)** (GLMoore) **4-10-0** AClark(9) (swtg: prom over 5f)	¾	**12**	7/1 ^{3}	60	22
	Windswept (IRE) (55) (DJSffrenchDavis) **4-9-0** MTebbutt(2) (swtg: nvr nrr)	s.h	**13**	20/1	46	8
3276^{13}	**Queen of Shannon (IRE) (58)** (AWCarroll) **9-8-10**$^{(7)}$ RStudholme(6) (swtg: dwlt: bhd fnl 2f)	1½	**14**	16/1	46	8
	Protaras Bay (46) (PLGilligan) **3-7-12** EJohnson(10) (bit bkwd: a bhd)	1¼	**15**	40/1	32	—
3105^{12}	**Tael of Silver (57)** (ABailey) **5-9-2v** DWright(11) (led over 1f: ev ch over 2f out: wknd over 1f out)	1¼	**16**	25/1	40	2
1845^{5}	**Deevee (46)** (CJBenstead) **8-8-5** JLowe(3) (lw: a bhd)	2	**17**	14/1	26	—
1499^{8}	**Final Warning (64)** (JEBanks) **3-9-2** MWigham(18) (a bhd)	10	**18**	11/1	24	—

(SP 141.9%) **18 Rn**

1m 44.0 (1.80) CSF £43.59 CT £593.18 TOTE £5.60: £1.90 £1.70 £4.70 £1.60 (£31.80) Trio £493.40 OWNER Mrs Barbara Marchant (WHITCOMBE) BRED Societe Aland
WEIGHT FOR AGE 3yo-7lb
3227 Gold Lance (USA) came through to lead inside the final furlong and ran on strongly to gain his first win outside selling company. (4/1: op 6/1)
2730 Queen's Insignia (USA) came through on the outside of the field to lead below the distance but, headed inside the final furlong, found the winner too good. (10/1)
2745 Multi Franchise, a leading player throughout, still had every chance inside the final furlong, before tapped for toe. He has yet to win a race outside claiming and selling company. (16/1)
3328 Vanborough Lad, making a quick reappearance, did not have the best of runs over a quarter of a mile from home but stayed on from below the distance to be nearest at the line. (11/2)
3394* Ring the Chief, successful at Salisbury on Friday, moved along the inside rail below the distance but failed to find another gear inside the final furlong. (8/1)
2748 Cape Pigeon (USA) was soon at the head of affairs but, collared below the distance, then found younger rivals had the legs of him. Although he has won every year since 1991, he has not won a handicap since 1993. (10/1: 8/1-12/1)

3466 SHADWELL STUD SERIES APPRENTICE H'CAP (0-80) (3-Y.O+) (Class E)

4-00 (4-00) **1m 2f 7y** £2,753.75 (£830.00: £402.50: £188.75) Stalls: High GOING minus 0.67 sec per fur (HD)

				SP	RR	SF
2920^{6}	**Seattle Swing (75)** (MrsAJPerrett) **3-9-11** GMilligan(6) (hld up: rdn over 2f out: led over 1f out: r.o wl)	—	**1**	8/1	85	45

				SP	RR	SF
2843^{4}	**Ocean Park (66)** (LadyHerries) **6-9-11** PDoe(1) (b: lw: a.p: led 3f out tl over 1f out: unable qckn ins fnl f)	1¼	**2**	6/1	74	43
3200*	**Monte Cavo (58)** (MBrittain) **6-9-3** PRoberts(5) (chsd ldr: led over 3f out: sn hdd: hrd rdn over 1f out: one pce)	1¾	**3**	$3/1^{2}$	63	32
3029^{11}	**The Negotiator (60)** (MJHeaton-Ellis) **3-8-10** ADaly(3) (swtg: s.s: rdn over 3f out: hdwy fnl f: nvr nrr)	2	**4**	12/1	62	22
2927^{3}	**Nordic Crest (IRE) (70)** (PWHarris) **3-9-6** CLowther(2) (led over 6f: wknd over 1f out)	nk	**5**	$11/2^{3}$	72	32
3134*	**Monument (62)** (JSKing) **5-9-7** RFfrench(4) (a bhd)	1	**6**	$6/4^{1}$	62	31

(SP 113.5%) **6 Rn**

2m 6.1 (1.20) CSF £48.87 TOTE £11.20: £3.20 £2.40 (£26.00) OWNER The Seattle Swingers (PULBOROUGH) BRED Cheveley Park Stud Ltd
WEIGHT FOR AGE 3yo-9lb

2380 Seattle Swing, sold out of John Gosden's stable for 13,000 guineas after her fourth start, gained her first victory for her new connections, leading below the distance and proving too strong for the runner-up inside the final furlong. (8/1)

2843 Ocean Park went to the front three furlong out and, although headed below the distance, grimly held on until put in his place in the last one hundred yards. (6/1: 4/1-13/2)

3200* Monte Cavo, 23lb higher than when first successful this season, found that telling in the final quarter-mile. (3/1)

2523 The Negotiator was at the back of the field until staying on in the final furlong, by which time it was all far too late. (12/1: 8/1-14/1)

2927 Nordic Crest (IRE), racing with his tongue tied down, was taking a big drop in distance and, after setting the pace, had been seen off below the distance. (11/2: 4/1-6/1)

3134* Monument was very disappointing and was always at the back of the field. He has done all his winning on a fast surface. (6/4)

3467 BOLLINGER CHAMPAGNE CHALLENGE SERIES GENTLEMEN'S H'CAP (0-70) (3-Y.O+) (Class E)

4-30 (4-31) **1m 3f 135y** £2,835.00 (£855.00: £415.00: £195.00) Stalls: High GOING minus 0.67 sec per fur (HD)

				SP	RR	SF
2344^{6}	**Farringdon Hill (65)** (JHMGosden) **6-11-10v^{1}(4)** MrCRanson(2) (b.hind: a.p: led over 4f out: r.o wl)	—	**1**	7/1	74	56
2879^{2}	**Tarxien (62)** (KRBurke) **3-10-10(4)** MrOMcPhail(4) (lost pl over 6f out: rallied over 3f out: ev ch fnl 2f: r.o wl)	s.h	**2**	$5/1^{3}$	71	42
2686^{3}	**Mad Militant (IRE) (63)** (AStreeter) **8-11-12** MrAWintle(5) (lw: hdwy over 2f out: hrd drvn & hung bdly lft over 1f out: unable qckn)	2	**3**	11/2	69	51
3135^{3}	**Dauphin (IRE) (44)** (WJMusson) **4-10-7** MrTMcCarthy(8) (hdwy 3f out: hrd rdn over 1f out: one pce)	1	**4**	$5/2^{1}$	49	31
2824^{9}	**General Glow (45)** (PDEvans) **4-10-4b^{1}(4)** MrAEvans(6) (hdwy 7f out: hrd rdn over 2f out: wknd over 1f out)	nk	**5**	12/1	49	31
3232^{6}	**Woodrising (50)** (CREgerton) **5-10-9(4)** MrPPhillips(12) (led 7f)	11	**6**	14/1	39	21
3276*	**Super Serenade (45)** (GBBalding) **8-10-4(4)** MrJThatcher(3) (lw: prom 7f)	2½	**7**	$3/1^{2}$	31	13
3197^{8}	**English Invader (50)** (RCSpicer) **6-10-13v^{1}** MrJGoldstein(7) (bhd fnl 5f)	1½	**8**	14/1	34	16
	Parish Walk (IRE) (43) (KJDrewry) **6-10-2(4)** MrKDrewry(10) (prom tl hmpd & wknd over 6f out)	14	**9**	25/1	7	—
	Against The Clock (42) (PBowen) **5-10-1(4)ow1** MrGSkone(9) (a bhd: t.o)	dist	**10**	33/1	—	—
3129^{8}	**Miss Mezzanine (53)** (EAWheeler) **3-10-1(4)ow12** MrJDewhurst(11) (swtg: bhd fnl 6f: t.o)	11	**11**	50/1	—	—

(SP 127.9%) **11 Rn**

2m 30.2 (4.20) CSF £41.19 CT £197.57 TOTE £7.50: £2.20 £2.40 £2.00 (£20.30) Trio £18.40 OWNER Mr Christopher Ranson (NEWMARKET) BRED Wick-Dromdiah Investments Ltd
LONG HANDICAP Miss Mezzanine 8-5
WEIGHT FOR AGE 3yo-11lb
STEWARDS' ENQUIRY Wintle susp. 22-23/8/97 (improper use of whip).

2344 Farringdon Hill had the ground to suit and, leading over half a mile from home, just managed to keep the very persistent runner-up at bay. (7/1)

2879 Tarxien ran his best race to date over this longer trip on his handicap debut. Throwing down the gauntlet in the final quarter-mile, he had a tremendous battle with the winner and only just lost out. He is a winner without a penalty. (5/1)

2686 Mad Militant (IRE) began a forward move over a quarter of a mile from home but his jockey then appeared to go berserk on him with the whip from below the distance. Not surprisingly, the gelding hung badly as a result but his rider still did not pull his whip through. Continuing to hit his mount, the combination failed to quicken. His amateur rider can consider himself incredibly lucky that he only received a two-day suspension for not allowing his horse to respond in time. (11/2: 4/1-6/1)

3135 Dauphin (IRE) was racing over a more suitable trip but never looked like finding the vital turn of foot to get into the thick of it in the straight. (5/2)

General Glow, soon in a handy position, had been seen off in the final quarter-mile. (12/1)

3276* Super Serenade (3/1: 2/1-100/30)

3468 WELLINGTON NURSERY H'CAP (2-Y.O F) (Class D)

5-00 (5-01) **5f 217y** £3,306.25 (£1,000.00: £487.50: £231.25) Stalls: High GOING minus 0.44 sec per fur (F)

				SP	RR	SF
2858*	**Regal Revolution (78)** (PTWalwyn) **2-9-0** JLowe(3) (lw: hdwy over 1f out: led ins fnl f: r.o wl)	—	**1**	$4/1^{2}$	82	38
2943*	**Shalad'or (70)** (BRMillman) **2-8-6** TSprake(6) (w ldr: led over 1f out tl ins fnl f: unable qckn)	1½	**2**	$4/1^{2}$	70	26
2893^{7}	**Muftuffenuf (66)** (PRWebber) **2-8-2** AMcGlone(5) (a.p: rdn over 2f out: one pce fnl f)	hd	**3**	14/1	66	22
2176^{2}	**Sandy Shore (78)** (JWharton) **2-8-11(3)** RFfrench(2) (hdwy over 1f out: one pce fnl f)	2	**4**	7/1	72	28
3131*	**Zena (78)** (WJarvis) **2-9-0** DHolland(7) (lw: nvr nr to chal)	nk	**5**	$7/4^{1}$	72	28
3070*	**Eleonora d'Arborea (85)** (BJMeehan) **2-9-7** MTebbutt(9) (lw: led over 4f)	½	**6**	$6/1^{3}$	77	33
2943^{6}	**Petaling (IRE) (64)** (BJMeehan) **2-8-0** DBiggs(4) (prom over 4f)	hd	**7**	14/1	56	12
2138^{3}	**Fire Goddess (74)** (JSMoore) **2-8-7(3)** PPMurphy(1) (prom over 4f)	½	**8**	11/1	65	21

(SP 124.8%) **8 Rn**

1m 12.1 (1.60) CSF £20.52 CT £194.57 TOTE £3.80: £1.60 £1.40 £2.50 (£11.20) Trio £183.30 OWNER Mr S. W. E. J. Slack (LAMBOURN) BRED T. R. Lock

2858* Regal Revolution came through to lead inside the final furlong and soon settled the issue. A step-up in class looks likely. (4/1: op 5/2)

2943* Shalad'or disputed the lead until going on below the distance. Collared inside the final furlong, she proved no match for the winner. (4/1)

2147 Muftuffenuf, not suited by the step up to seven furlongs last time out, ran better here but failed to quicken in the final furlong. (14/1: op 8/1)

2176 Sandy Shore moved up on the outside of the field below the distance but then failed to find another gear in the last two hundred yards. Maybe a step up in trip would help. (7/1)

3131* Zena, unable to go the pace, put in some late work but, by then, it was all far too late. She is a worth a try over further. (7/4)

3070* Eleonora d'Arborea set the pace but, collared over a furlong out, soon had bellows to mend. (6/1)

2138 Fire Goddess (11/1: 8/1-12/1)

T/Jkpt: £14,485.00 (4.88 Tckts). T/Plpt: £111.00 (188.77 Tckts). T/Qdpt: £79.20 (12.57 Tckts) AK

3324-BATH (L-H) (Good)
Tuesday August 12th
WEATHER: fine but cloudy WIND: almost nil

3469 AUGUST (S) STKS (3-Y.O+) (Class G)
2-00 (2-02) **1m 5y** £2,528.00 (£708.00: £344.00) Stalls: Low GOING minus 0.48 sec per fur (F)

			Pos	SP	RR	SF
3041[3]	**The Executor (64)** (RJO'Sullivan) **7-9-3** JReid(9) (lw: hld up: hdwy over 2f out: led ins fnl f: r.o wl)	—	1	5/1[1]	68	46
	Pegasus Bay (MissAEEmbiricos) **6-8-12** RCochrane(4) (b.hind: hld up: stdy hdwy 3f out: ev ch ins fnl f: nt qckn)	1¼	2	7/1	61	39
3276[6]	**Noeprob (USA) (52)** (RJHodges) **7-8-9**(3) PPMurphy(13) (hld up: hdwy 3f out: hrd rdn over 1f out: ev ch ins fnl f: one pce)	1½	3	11/2[2]	58	36
3249*	**Greatest (53)** (MissGayKelleway) **6-9-0b**(3) RFfrench(10) (lw: led tl ins fnl f)	hd	4	6/1[3]	62	40
3082[9]	**Kildee Lad (63)** (APJones) **7-9-3** AClark(7) (hld up & bhd: hdwy over 2f out: hrd rdn over 1f out: one pce)	3	5	10/1	56	34
3297[2]	**Runic Symbol (35)** (MBlanshard) **6-9-3** JQuinn(16) (hdwy over 2f out: wknd over 1f out)	4	6	14/1	48	26
3227[6]	**Dancing Lawyer (47)** (KRBurke) **6-9-3** BDoyle(8) (lw: swtg: prom tl wknd fnl f)	hd	7	12/1	48	26
3269[8]	**My Handsome Prince (30)** (PJBevan) **5-8-12** NCarlisle(6) (lw: nvr trbld ldrs)	2	8	25/1	39	17
3248[7]	**Charlton Imp (USA) (43)** (RJHodges) **4-8-12** SDrowne(14) (hrd rdn & hdwy over 2f out: wknd over 1f out)	½	9	10/1	38	16
	Old Roma (IRE) (60) (JohnBerry) **4-8-7** KDarley(5) (swtg: s.s: nvr nr ldrs)	¾	10	20/1	32	10
3139[5]	**Hawaii Storm (FR) (53)** (DJSffrenchDavis) **9-9-0**(3) MartinDwyer(15) (swtg: s.s: nvr nr ldrs)	nk	11	12/1	41	19
3327[9]	**Agwa (52)** (JJBridger) **8-9-3** GBardwell(2) (plld hrd: prom: rdn 3f out: sn wknd)	½	12	33/1	40	18
3276[10]	**Sakharov (43)** (BPalling) **8-9-3b** TSprake(17) (prom tl wknd qckly over 2f out)	3	13	33/1	34	12
	He Knows The Rules (RHBuckler) **5-8-12** CRutter(3) (bkwd: s.s: a bhd)	½	14	25/1	28	6
243[12]	**Airborne Harris (IRE) (55)** (ABailey) **4-8-12** DWright(11) (plld hrd: chsd ldr: rdn 4f out: wknd over 2f out)	1¾	15	33/1	25	3
1134[9]	**Verro (USA) (15)** (PDPurdy) **10-9-3** SophieMitchell(12) (a bhd: t.o)	16	16	100/1	—	—
3276[18]	**Northern Clan (32)** (AJChamberlain) **4-8-5**(7) SCarson(18) (a bhd: t.o)	3	17	66/1	—	—
				(SP 122.8%)	**17 Rn**	

1m 39.7 (1.50) CSF £32.51 TOTE £6.60: £2.10 £1.90 £2.30 (£35.50) Trio £72.60 OWNER Mr Jack Joseph (WHITCOMBE) BRED Exors of the late Mrs D. M. de Rothschild
No bid
OFFICIAL EXPLANATION Old Roma (IRE): gurgled during the race.
3041 The Executor, a consistent sort, will remain on the Flat because he does not get the trip over hurdles. (5/1)
Pegasus Bay, placed three times in four outings in bumpers, went on to win twice over hurdles but disappointed in two runs over fences this summer. The subject of an old-fashioned gamble on his Flat debut, one can only hope his supporters were on each-way. (7/1: op 25/1)
3276 Noeprob (USA) fared much better than at Windsor last week and would have been 7lb better off with the winner in a handicap. (11/2)
3249* Greatest has won over a mile at Brighton but his other six victories have all been over seven. (6/1)
2933 Kildee Lad, tried in blinkers last time, was dropped in class but had never run beyond six furlongs before. (10/1: op 6/1)
3297 Runic Symbol was dropping back to a mile. (14/1)

3470 MILE MAIDEN H'CAP (0-65) (3-Y.O+) (Class F)
2-30 (2-34) **1m 5y** £2,915.00 (£815.00: £395.00) Stalls: Low GOING minus 0.48 sec per fur (F)

			Pos	SP	RR	SF
2848[2]	**Absolute Utopia (USA) (53)** (NEBerry) **4-9-2** BDoyle(7) (a.p: rdn over 1f out: led & edgd lft ins fnl f: r.o)	—	1	8/1	66	48
3293[4]	**Samara Song (53)** (IPWilliams) **4-9-2** TSprake(18) (a.p: ev ch ins fnl f: r.o)	¾	2	8/1	65	47
2922[11]	**Mukhlles (USA) (65)** (BobJones) **4-10-0** NDay(2) (a.p: led over 2f out: hrd rdn over 1f out: hdd ins fnl f)	¾	3	11/1	75	57
2848[12]	**Magic Lahr (GER) (52)** (IABalding) **4-9-1** LDettori(6) (lw: hld up: hdwy over 2f out: r.o one pce fnl f)	½	4	13/2[3]	61	43
2521[8]	**Prairie Minstrel (USA) (54)** (RDickin) **3-8-10** ACulhane(4) (bit bkwd: hrd rdn & hdwy over 2f out: one pce fnl f)	3	5	20/1	57	32
3207[3]	**Octavia Hill (52)** (PWHarris) **4-8-10b**(5) CLowther(10) (bhd: rdn 4f out: hdwy over 1f out: nvr nrr)	2	6	11/2[2]	51	33
	D J Cat (41) (WRMuir) **4-8-1**(3) MartinDwyer(17) (bkwd: s.i.s: hdw over 1f out: nrst fin)	1¾	7	50/1	37	19
1864[5]	**Rockaroundtheclock (52)** (TRWatson) **3-8-8** DHolland(16) (swtg: nvr nr to chal)	1¼	8	25/1	45	20
2921[12]	**Imperial Glen (IRE) (43)** (MDIUsher) **3-7-13** JMarshall(14) (nvr nrr)	hd	9	50/1	36	11
2573[9]	**Hannalou (FR) (45)** (TGMills) **4-8-5**(3) RFfrench(12) (led over 5f: hrd rdn & wknd over 1f out)	1½	10	14/1	35	17
2892[13]	**Gulf of Siam (40)** (EAWheeler) **4-7-12b**(5)ow1 ADaly(5) (prom over 5f)	hd	11	50/1	30	11
3327[4]	**Bairn Atholl (36)** (RJHodges) **4-7-13** NAdams(11) (nvr trbld ldrs)	2½	12	12/1	21	3
2912[8]	**Dazzling Stone (60)** (LadyHerries) **3-9-2** RCochrane(8) (swtg: a bhd)	nk	13	12/1	44	19
3088[7]	**Martine (57)** (ABailey) **3-8-13** DWright(3) (swtg: plld hrd: prom: rdn over 4f out: wknd over 2f out)	¾	14	25/1	40	15
3230[7]	**Over The Moon (45)** (MJFetherston-Godley) **3-8-1v**[1] FNorton(15) (hrd rdn over 3f out: bhd fnl 2f)	¾	15	50/1	26	1
3134[4]	**Sharp Deed (IRE) (55)** (PJMakin) **3-8-11** JReid(1) (prom over 5f)	½	16	7/2[1]	35	10
2873[8]	**Despina (47)** (HCandy) **3-8-3** CRutter(13) (a bhd)	5	17	20/1	17	—
3056[7]	**Jolly Jackson (54)** (RAkehurst) **3-8-10** SSanders(9) (s.s: a bhd: t.o)	20	18	10/1	—	—
				(SP 137.7%)	**18 Rn**	

1m 39.4 (1.20) CSF £66.46 CT £689.36 TOTE £11.30: £2.40 £1.90 £3.20 £2.00 (£23.60) Trio £191.20 OWNER Mr M. T. Lawrance (UPPER LAMBOURN) BRED Gainsborough Farm Inc
WEIGHT FOR AGE 3yo-7lb
2848 Absolute Utopia (USA), who has had wind problems, will probably have another run on the Flat and then go hurdling. (8/1)
3293 Samara Song, back to his optimum trip, was going strongly early in the home straight but again managed to find one too good. (8/1)
1631 Mukhlles (USA) was 4lb lower than when fourth at Thirsk in June. (11/1)
2492 Magic Lahr (GER), 6lb lower than when making his handicap debut last time, could still be finding this trip on the short side. (13/2)
Prairie Minstrel (USA), down 4lb, was trying a shorter distance. (20/1)
3207 Octavia Hill was stepping up to a mile with the blinkers re-fitted. (11/2)

3471 MENDIP MAIDEN STKS (2-Y.O F) (Class D)
3-00 (3-02) **5f 11y** £3,564.50 (£1,076.00: £523.00: £246.50) Stalls: High GOING minus 0.48 sec per fur (F)

			Pos	SP	RR	SF
2831[11]	**First Village (IRE) (62)** (JBerry) **2-8-11** KDarley(4) (a.p: qcknd to ld ins fnl f: pushed out)	—	1	14/1	80	39

3114^{2}	**Jilted (IRE) (87)** (RHannon) **2-8-8**(3) MartinDwyer(1) (led after 1f tl ins fnl f)	2½	**2**	2/1^{1}	72	31
3187^{4}	**Oh Hebe (IRE)** (PWHarris) **2-8-11** PatEddery(9) (wnt lft s: led 1f: ev ch ins fnl f: nt qckn)	nk	**3**	100/30^{2}	71	30
	Sarah Stokes (IRE) (RGuest) **2-8-11** DHolland(11) (leggy: lt-f: unf: hdwy over 1f out: r.o)	2	**4**	14/1	65	24
	Generous Embrace (DRCElsworth) **2-8-11** JReid(3) (w'like: scope: dwlt: hdwy on ins over 1f out: bttr for r)	4	**5**	16/1	52+	11
2831^{8}	**Delphic Way** (GBBalding) **2-8-11** SDrowne(7) (hmpd s: hdwy 2f out: nt rch ldrs)	s.h	**6**	12/1	52	11
1821^{8}	**Jackies Webb** (BSmart) **2-8-11** SSanders(13) (prom tl hrd rdn & wknd over 1f out)	1¼	**7**	33/1	48	7
	Night Auction (IRE) (BPalling) **2-8-11** TSprake(16) (w'like: scope: s.s: nvr nrr)	1	**8**	33/1	45	4
2959^{4}	**Mercury Falling** (DWPArbuthnot) **2-8-11** SWhitworth(14) (prom over 3f)	hd	**9**	33/1	45	4
	Zamarra (MajorDNChappell) **2-8-11** RHills(10) (w'like: scope: bkwd: s.s: nvr nr ldrs)	¾	**10**	25/1	42	1
2312^{5}	**Robin Lane** (IABalding) **2-8-11** LDettori(12) (rdn & effrt over 2f out: no rspnse)	½	**11**	10/1^{3}	41	—
2831^{6}	**Belle de Nuit (IRE)** (BJMeehan) **2-8-11** MTebbutt(6) (s.i.s: a bhd)	nk	**12**	10/1^{3}	40	—
	Gunzells (USA) (HCandy) **2-8-11** CRutter(2) (lt-f: unf: unruly stalls: s.s: a bhd)	1	**13**	10/1^{3}	36	—
2959^{3}	**Bala** (HMorrison) **2-8-11** DHarrison(17) (chsd ldrs: rdn over 2f out: eased whn btn over 1f out)	1½	**14**	14/1	32	—
3094^{U}	**Lady Ralphina** (JJBridger) **2-8-6**(5) ADaly(8) (lw: hmpd s: prom 3f)	d.h	**14**	66/1	32	—
828^{11}	**Tundra (IRE)** (KMcAuliffe) **2-8-11** JFEgan(15) (a bhd)	4	**16**	50/1	19	—
	Cd Newsround (IRE) (MRChannon) **2-8-11** ACulhane(5) (rangy: bkwd: a bhd)	¾	**17**	33/1	17	—

(SP 136.3%) **17 Rn**

61.5 secs (1.00) CSF £40.58 TOTE £13.00: £3.50 £1.50 £1.60 (£20.50) Trio £16.30 OWNER Dr G. W. W. Tsoi (COCKERHAM) BRED Hugo Merry

2467 First Village (IRE) has had her excuses since making a promising debut. She really got her act together here and can score again. (14/1)
3114 Jilted (IRE), brought back to the minimum trip, yet again had to settle for the role of bridesmaid. (2/1)
3187 Oh Hebe (IRE), dropping back to five, was out-pointed in the final two hundred yards. (100/30: 9/4-7/2)
Sarah Stokes (IRE), a half-sister to smart sprinter Almaty, might not be much to look at but showed promise for the future. (14/1: op 6/1)
Generous Embrace, a half-sister to stayer Embracing and seven-furlong winner Villeggiatura, will come into her own when tackling further. (16/1)
Delphic Way, a half-sister to Ca'd'oro, is another who shaped as though she needs a longer trip. (12/1)
Gunzells (USA) (10/1: op 5/1)

3472 PULTENEY H'CAP (0-75) (3-Y.O+) (Class D)

3-30 (3-30) **2m 1f 34y** £3,533.50 (£1,063.00: £514.00: £239.50) Stalls: High GOING minus 0.48 sec per fur (F)

				SP	RR	SF
3203^{4}	**Hillswick (38)** (JSKing) **6-7-5**(5) APolli(5) (swtg: led over 10f: led over 2f out tl over 1f out: led ins fnl f: all out)	—	**1**	6/1^{2}	51	12
2963^{3}	**Sudest (IRE) (73)** (IABalding) **3-9-2** LDettori(4) (lw: hld up: rdn over 4f out: led over 1f out: edgd lft: hrd rdn & hdd ins fnl f)	1	**2**	1/2^{1}	85	31
3137^{6}	**Castle Courageous (70)** (LadyHerries) **10-10-0** JReid(1) (b: chsd wnr over 10f: rdn & outpcd 3f out: styd on one pce fnl 2f)	5	**3**	8/1^{3}	77	38
3415^{3}	**Nornax Lad (USA) (42)** (MartynMeade) **9-7-7b**(7) RBrisland(3) (hld up: hdwy to ld over 6f out: hdd over 2f out: wknd over 1f out)	1¼	**4**	14/1	48	9
2035^{7}	**Sheriff (50)** (JWHills) **6-8-8** RHills(2) (lw: hld up: rdn 4f out: sn bhd: t.o)	21	**5**	8/1^{3}	37	—

(SP 109.8%) **5 Rn**

3m 48.6 (7.20) CSF £8.74 TOTE £6.00: £1.70 £1.10 (£2.50) OWNER Mr M. G. A. Court (SWINDON) BRED D. T. Byrne
LONG HANDICAP Hillswick 7-9
WEIGHT FOR AGE 3yo-15lb

3203 Hillswick was given a fine ride by the new Italian kid on the block, who managed to knock the whip out of his fellow countryman's hand. (6/1: op 4/1)
2963 Sudest (IRE) worked hard to get in front but the fact that Dettori lost his whip after he was headed made little difference to the outcome. (1/2)
3137 Castle Courageous has been dropped no less than 20lb since making a comeback this season and is certainly on the decline. (8/1)
3415 Nornax Lad (USA) is not the force of old after missing last season. (14/1: op 9/1)

3473 LUCKINGTON LIMITED STKS (0-70) (3-Y.O+) (Class E)

4-00 (4-01) **5f 11y** £2,820.25 (£847.00: £408.50: £189.25) Stalls: High GOING minus 0.48 sec per fur (F)

				SP	RR	SF
3280^{3}	**Mousehole (69)** (RGuest) **5-9-6** PBloomfield(2) (sn rdn along: chsd ldrs: led over 1f out: r.o wl)	—	**1**	2/1^{1}	78	50
3126^{5}	**Tuscan Dawn (69)** (JBerry) **7-8-12**(5) PRoberts(1) (led after 1f tl over 1f out: nt qckn)	2	**2**	5/2^{2}	69	41
2698^{13}	**Pride of Hayling (IRE) (56)** (PRHedger) **6-9-0** SDrowne(5) (rdn over 2f out: hdwy wl over 1f out: r.o ins fnl f)	1	**3**	25/1	63	35
2563^{12}	**Levelled (68)** (MRChannon) **3-9-3**(3) PPMurphy(8) (hld up: rdn & hdwy over 1f out: r.o ins fnl f)	s.h	**4**	14/1	71	40
2964^{11}	**Marengo (65)** (JAkehurst) **3-9-0** SSanders(7) (nvr nr to chal)	¾	**5**	14/1	63	32
3251^{3}	**Tinker Osmaston (66)** (RJHodges) **6-9-3** LDettori(9) (swtchd lft s: hld up & bhd: n.m.r on ins ins fnl f: nvr nrr)	¾	**6**	5/1^{3}	61	33
3280^{8}	**Beau Venture (USA) (67)** (BPalling) **9-9-6** TSprake(3) (led 1f: rdn & wknd over 1f out)	1	**7**	14/1	60	32
3126^{11}	**Runs in the Family (64)** (GMMcCourt) **5-9-6b** DHarrison(6) (w ldrs: rdn over 2f out: wknd over 1f out)	½	**8**	14/1	59	31
2964^{7}	**Mon Bruce (61)** (WRMuir) **3-9-3** JReid(4) (spd over 3f)	2	**9**	16/1	53	22

(SP 115.0%) **9 Rn**

61.3 secs (0.80) CSF £6.36 TOTE £2.90: £1.40 £1.40 £3.50 (£4.20) Trio £103.90 OWNER Mrs Janet Linskey (NEWMARKET) BRED T. H. Rossiter
WEIGHT FOR AGE 3yo-3lb

3280 Mousehole did it the hard way as usual, but was well on top in the end and confirmed the Warwick form with the runner-up, despite being 3lb worse off. (2/1)
3126 Tuscan Dawn was meeting the winner on 3lb better terms than when beaten a length at Warwick. (5/2)
2006 Pride of Hayling (IRE) seems to be coming to hand and a return to six could well pay dividends. (25/1)
2141 Levelled is another finding this minimum trip short of his best. (14/1: 10/1-16/1)
2393 Marengo is usually ridden up with the pace. (14/1)
3251 Tinker Osmaston would have finished a bit closer with a trouble-free run. (5/1)
3016 Beau Venture (USA) (14/1: op 7/1)
2377 Runs in the Family (14/1: op 8/1)

3474 NUNNEY NURSERY H'CAP (2-Y.O) (Class E)
4-30 (4-32) **5f 161y** £2,976.25 (£895.00: £432.50: £201.25) Stalls: High GOING minus 0.48 sec per fur (F)

			SP	RR	SF
2942^{3}	**Eleventh Duke (IRE) (79)** (RHannon) **2-9-1** LDettori(8) (hld up: hdwy over 2f out: led ins fnl f: r.o wl) .... —	**1**	$4/1^{2}$	83	37
3136*	**Brimstone (IRE) (79)** (DRCElsworth) **2-9-1** GDuffield(4) (w ldr: stumbled wl over 2f out: sn led: hdd wl over 1f out: rallied nr fin) .... ¾	**2**	$7/2^{1}$	81	35
3152^{5}	**Sada (77)** (MajorWRHern) **2-8-13** RHills(12) (swtg: a.p: led wl over 1f out tl ins fnl f) .... ½	**3**	$8/1^{3}$	78	32
2558^{12}	**Kawafil (IRE) (85)** (PTWalwyn) **2-9-7** PatEddery(5) (hld up: hdwy whn nt clr run & swtchd rt wl over 1f out: r.o ins fnl f) 1¾	**4**	$7/2^{1}$	81+	35
3113^{5}	**Take A Turn (78)** (MRChannon) **2-8-11v**(3) PPMurphy(9) (lw: chsd ldrs: rdn over 3f out: no hdwy fnl 2f) .... s.h	**5**	16/1	74	28
3113^{7}	**Poetto (63)** (BJMeehan) **2-7-13** DBiggs(10) (swtg: prom: rdn over 3f out: wknd 2f out) 2½	**6**	25/1	52	6
2849^{6}	**Downclose Duchess (60)** (MBlanshard) **2-7-10** JQuinn(3) (swtg: nvr nr to chal) .... ¾	**7**	33/1	46	—
2740^{4}	**Flying Singer (65)** (IABalding) **2-7-12**(3) MartinDwyer(11) (lw: nvr nr to chal) .... hd	**8**	12/1	51	5
2688^{8}	**Ballet Rambert (77)** (MJHeaton-Ellis) **2-8-10**(3) RFfrench(1) (swtg: a bhd) .... s.h	**9**	16/1	63	17
2181^{21}	**Desert Native (62)** (CFWall) **2-7-7**(5) RMullen(6) (s.s: a bhd) 1¼	**10**	14/1	45	—
2689^{9}	**Ben Rinnes (83)** (RFJohnsonHoughton) **2-9-5** JReid(2) (bhd fnl 3f) 5	**11**	12/1	52	6
3113^{10}	**Somosierra (IRE) (76)** (JBerry) **2-8-12** KDarley(7) (led tl over 2f out: sn wknd) 3½	**12**	14/1	35	—
			(SP 122.8%)	**12 Rn**	

1m 11.1 (1.60) CSF £17.42 CT £102.77 TOTE £5.30: £2.10 £1.30 £2.00 (£6.50) Trio £20.90 OWNER Lucayan Stud (MARLBOROUGH) BRED Derek Iceton

LONG HANDICAP Downclose Duchess 7-8

2942 Eleventh Duke (IRE), despite being given three back-handers to assert, appeared to score with a bit in hand. (4/1: 3/1-9/2)
3136* Brimstone (IRE) seemed to appreciate this extended five. (7/2)
3152 Sada is not finding it easy to lose her maiden tag. (8/1)
2227* Kawafil (IRE), covered up this time, was on her best behaviour but did not get the run of the race. (7/2)
3113 Take A Turn was never really in the shake-up. (16/1)
2740 Flying Singer (12/1: 7/1-14/1)
2181* Ben Rinnes (12/1: 8/1-14/1)

3475 ROYAL CRESCENT H'CAP (0-80) (3-Y.O+) (Class D)
5-00 (5-02) **1m 3f 144y** £3,670.00 (£1,105.00: £535.00: £250.00) Stalls: Low GOING minus 0.48 sec per fur (F)

			SP	RR	SF
3137^{7}	**Pennys From Heaven (75)** (HCandy) **3-9-3** CRutter(5) (chsd ldr: led wl over 1f out: pushed out) .... —	**1**	12/1	83	50
2787^{2}	**Two Socks (64)** (JSKing) **4-9-3** DHolland(10) (hld up: stdy hdwy over 3f out: ev ch over 1f out: r.o) .... ½	**2**	12/1	71	49
2696^{3}	**Rising Spray (71)** (CAHorgan) **6-9-10** PaulEddery(9) (lw: hld up & bhd: rdn & hdwy 2f out: r.o ins fnl f) .... ¾	**3**	$7/1^{3}$	77	55
3245^{5}	**Pay Homage (70)** (IABalding) **9-9-6**(3) MartinDwyer(11) (lw: hld up & bhd: hdwy 2f out: r.o one pce fnl f) 1¼	**4**	$7/1^{3}$	75	53
3246^{9}	**Haroldon (IRE) (66)** (BPalling) **8-9-5** DaneO'Neill(4) (b: lost pl 5f out: rdn over 3f out: styd on fnl f) 3½	**5**	20/1	66	44
3203^{3}	**Courageous Knight (46)** (PHayward) **8-7-10**(3)ow3 MHenry(1) (chsd ldrs: rdn over 2f out: no hdwy) 1¼	**6**	16/1	44	19
1169^{10}	**Prospero (73)** (MrsAJPerrett) **4-9-12** AClark(2) (swtg: bit bkwd: hld up: hdwy 7f out: rdn over 2f out: wknd over 1f out) .... ¾	**7**	33/1	70	48
3183^{2}	**Passing Strangers (USA) (64)** (PWHarris) **4-8-12**(5) CLowther(7) (swtg: prom: hrd rdn over 2f out: sn wknd) s.h	**8**	$3/1^{1}$	61	39
2696*	**Credit Squeeze (62)** (RFJohnsonHoughton) **7-9-1** JReid(8) (led: hdd wl over 1f out: sn wknd) 1¼	**9**	$4/1^{2}$	57	35
2731^{8}	**Alarmist (80)** (RCharlton) **3-9-8** TSprake(3) (hld up: hdwy 7f out: hrd rdn over 2f out: sn wknd) .... s.h	**10**	$7/1^{3}$	75	42
1244^{22}	**Danegold (IRE) (68)** (MRChannon) **5-9-0v**(7) AEddery(6) (bit bkwd: a bhd) .... d.h	**10**	20/1	63	41
			(SP 116.2%)	**11 Rn**	

2m 28.5 (1.80) CSF £128.66 CT £992.03 TOTE £11.00: £2.40 £2.10 £2.70 (£36.60) Trio £129.30 OWNER H R H Prince Fahd Salman (WANTAGE) BRED Newgate Stud Co

LONG HANDICAP Courageous Knight 7-8

WEIGHT FOR AGE 3yo-11lb

2897 Pennys From Heaven, who apparently failed to stay Sandown's stiff fourteen furlongs last time, got off the mark here with a narrow but convincing win. (12/1)
2787 Two Socks had been raised 5lb after finishing second in a claimer last time. (12/1)
2696 Rising Spray, raised another 1lb, is just about in the Handicapper's grip. (7/1)
3245 Pay Homage could never get close enough to really make his presence felt. (7/1)
2920 Haroldon (IRE) was 1lb higher than when winning at Windsor last month. (20/1)
3203 Courageous Knight had been tried over a mile and six at Salisbury last time. (16/1)

T/Jkpt: £7,100.00 (0.2 Tckts); £3,419.58 to Salisbury 13/8/97. T/Plpt: £14.60 (1,991.93 Tckts). T/Qdpt: £2.40 (615.84 Tckts) KH

3102-BEVERLEY (R-H) (Good becoming Good to soft)
Wednesday August 13th

Official going changed after 4th race but it had not rained since bef 1st

WEATHER: fine, sunny & hot WIND: almost nil

3476 EAST RIDING YEOMANRY CHALLENGE TROPHY AMATEUR H'CAP (0-80) (3-Y.O+) (Class E)
2-00 (2-00) **7f 100y** £3,137.00 (£941.00: £453.00: £209.00) Stalls: High GOING minus 0.07 sec per fur (G)

			SP	RR	SF
3048^{6}	**Marjaana (IRE) (70)** (PTWalwyn) **4-11-8**(4) MissSSamworth(7) (bmpd s: sn chsng ldrs: styd on wl to ld ins fnl f: drvn out) .... —	**1**	10/1	84	66
3243^{7}	**Stackattack (IRE) (72)** (MrsJRRamsden) **4-12-0** MissERamsden(8) (lw: swvd lft s: led to 4f out: hung bdly lft & led over 1f out: hdd ins fnl f: r.o) 1½	**2**	$7/1^{3}$	83	65
3432^{4}	**Breezed Well (46)** (KGWingrove) **11-9-12**(4) MrsHNoonan(12) (chsd ldrs: sn pushed along: led 4f out tl over 1f out: one pce: fin 3rd, 3l: disq: plcd last) 3	**3d**	10/1	50	32
3248^{8}	**Cee-Jay-Ay (38)** (JBerry) **10-9-1**(7) MissBeverleyKendall(9) (s.i.s: bhd: hdwy on outside 2f out: kpt on fnl f: fin 4th: 2½l: plcd 3rd) 2½	**3**	12/1	37	19
3264*	**Euro Sceptic (IRE) (43)** (TDEasterby) **5-9-9b**(4) MissADeniel(1) (lw: hld up: stdy hdwy 2f out: kpt on: nvr nr to chal: fin 5th: s.h: plcd 4th) .... s.h	**4**	$5/1^{1}$	42	24

3432[6] **Squared Away (47)** (JWPayne) **5-9-13**(4) MissCLake(14) (sn bhd: styd on wl fnl 2f: nt rch ldrs: fin 6th: nk: plcd 5th)....nk **5** 12/1 45 27
2760[14] **Look Who's Calling (IRE) (70)** (BAMcMahon) **4-11-12** MrRThornton(10) (trckd ldrs: hrd rdn over 2f out: grad wknd)....2 **6** 20/1 64 46
3285[11] **Super Park (41)** (JPearce) **5-9-11** MrsLPearce(11) (trckd ldrs: plld hrd: pushed along over 3f out: wknd 2f out)....1¾ **7** 12/1 31 13
3240[5] **Roseate Lodge (40)** (SEKettlewell) **11-9-3**(7) MissJHarrison(13) (bdly hmpd sn after s: bhd tl sme hdwy 2f out: n.d)....nk **8** 5/1[1] 30 12
2708[7] **Takhlid (USA) (68)** (DWChapman) **6-11-10** MissRClark(6) (hld up & plld hrd: nt clr run on ins over 4f out & over 3f out: hrd rdn over 1f out: sn wknd)....nk **9** 14/1 57 39
2577[5] **Chalky Dancer (38)** (HJCollingridge) **5-9-4**(4)ow1 MrsDMcHale(5) (chsd ldrs: c stands' side ent st: wknd over 2f out)....2 **10** 16/1 23 4
2237[12] **Murphy's Gold (IRE) (52)** (RAFahey) **6-10-1**(7) MrCRussell(2) (lw: trckd ldrs: effrt over 2f out: sn lost pl)....½ **11** 12/1 36 18
2708[2] **Anonym (IRE) (62)** (JLEyre) **5-11-4b** MissDianaJones(4) (hld up & plld hrd: effrt over 2f out: sn wknd)....s.h **12** 13/2[2] 45 27
3421[8] **Montone (IRE) (55)** (JRJenkins) **7-10-11v** DrMMannish(3) (sn chsng ldrs: edgd lft over 2f out: sn lost pl)....3 **13** 16/1 32 14

(SP 131.3%) **14 Rn**

1m 37.9 (5.90) CSF £77.95 CT £805.99 TOTE £12.00: £3.60 £3.30 £2.60 (£21.10) Trio £176.50 OWNER Mrs D. C. Samworth (LAMBOURN) BRED Shadwell Estate Company Limited

LONG HANDICAP Chalky Dancer 8-12

STEWARDS' ENQUIRY Noonan susp 22-23 & 25-27/8/97 (irresponsible riding).

OFFICIAL EXPLANATION Murphy's Gold (IRE): injured his near-fore leg during the race.

IN-FOCUS: After five hours' heavy rain in the morning, the going looked soft rather than the official good at the start of the day. It changed to good to soft after the fourth race, but it was certainly dried out by the hot sun and, by the sixth race, it looked to be almost good again.

3048 Marjaana (IRE), back over her best trip and in her right class, was most capably handled. (10/1)

3243 Stackattack (IRE), 5lb higher than when successful at York three outings ago, gave his rider problems by hanging badly left and ending up racing under the stands'-side rail. Had he kept straight, he would have given the winner plenty to do. (7/1)

1677 Cee-Jay-Ay, getting very long in the tooth, last won a handicap over four years ago from a 22lb higher mark. (12/1)

3264* Euro Sceptic (IRE), never reliable at best, ran one of his more tame races. (5/1)

3432 Squared Away as usual stayed on late in the day. (12/1)

3240 Roseate Lodge, drawn on the inside of Breezed Well, was badly hampered after one hundred yards. (5/1)

2205 Murphy's Gold (IRE) was badly struck into. (12/1)

3432 Breezed Well, racing over a trip short of his best, seemed keen to secure the running rail pitch, causing problems for Roseate Lodge. He ran a genuine race but the Stewards took a harsh view of his rider's tactics in the early stages, and handed her a five-day ban. (10/1)

3477 ALLDERS OF HULL CLAIMING STKS (3-Y.O+) (Class E)

2-30 (2-31) **1m 100y** £3,085.00 (£925.00: £445.00: £205.00) Stalls: High GOING minus 0.07 sec per fur (G)

SP RR SF

3266[9] **Petite Risk (47)** (KWHogg) **3-8-4** DeanMcKeown(6) (chsd ldrs: wnt 2nd over 1f out: styd on to ld nr fin)....— **1** 10/1 62 24
2912[5] **Broctune Gold (65)** (MrsMReveley) **6-9-10** KDarley(14) (mde most: clr over 3f out: jst ct)....½ **2** 7/2[2] 74 43
3382[3] **Java Red (IRE) (45)** (JGFitzGerald) **5-9-6v**[1] JFortune(12) (chsd ldrs: wnt 2nd over 3f out: wknd 2f out)....8 **3** 7/1 55 24
3264[8] **Special-K (47)** (EWeymes) **5-8-4**(7) TSiddall(9) (lw: chsd ldrs: outpcd fnl 2f)....2 **4** 5/1[3] 42 11
3221[5] **Philgem (25)** (CWFairhurst) **4-8-3v** NKennedy(13) (chsd ldrs: drvn along over 3f out: wnt 2nd over 2f out: sn wknd)¾ **5** 14/1 33 2
3272[8] **Curtelace (48)** (MPBielby) **7-8-9**(3) GParkin(2) (hld up: effrt over 3f out: sn rdn & wknd)....16 **6** 20/1 11 —
3153[7] **Smarter Charter (68)** (MrsLStubbs) **4-9-10** DHarrison(11) (hdwy on outside over 2f out: sn rdn: no imp)....½ **7** 100/30[1] 23 —
3286[3] **Golden Thunderbolt (FR) (66)** (NTinkler) **4-9-10b**[1] KimTinkler(1) (lw: hdwy on outside 5f out: sn pushed along: lost pl over 3f out)....2 **8** 13/2 19 —
2544[15] **Hatimena** (JGFitzGerald) **3-8-2** FLynch(10) (swtg: a bhd)....2 **9** 16/1 — —
2938[8] **Ragazzo (IRE) (25)** (JSWainwright) **7-8-10b** LCharnock(8) (rr div: effrt on outside over 2f out: n.d)....2 **10** 25/1 — —
3116[5] **Saint Amigo (25)** (BPJBaugh) **5-8-7v**(3) RHavlin(5) (s.i.s: a in rr)....¾ **11** 33/1 — —
2544[8] **Irish Oasis (IRE) (32)** (BSRothwell) **4-9-0** MFenton(3) (sn bhd)....½ **12** 33/1 — —
2828[13] **Celia's Rainbow (20)** (RMWhitaker) **4-8-3** DWright(4) (sn bhd & drvn along)....¾ **13** 33/1 — —
3038[7] **Bali-Pet (36)** (JParkes) **3-8-1b** GBardwell(7) (w ldr 4f: sn lost pl: virtually p.u)....14 **14** 16/1 — —

(SP 132.8%) **14 Rn**

1m 50.2 (6.20) CSF £42.88 TOTE £16.30: £6.40 £1.50 £1.30 (£63.00) Trio £97.90 OWNER Mr K. W. Hogg (ISLE OF MAN) BRED Roldvale Ltd

WEIGHT FOR AGE 3yo-7lb

Broctune Gold clmd IWillder £10,000. Petite Risk clmd PJStephenson £6,000

2495 Petite Risk who is well-named, proved well suited by the morning rain which eased the ground considerably. Proving very willing, she stuck on to get up near the line and, claimed, now joins Jeff Pearce. (10/1: 8/1-12/1)

2912 Broctune Gold, a headstrong sort, was as usual taken to post early. Given a fine ride, he looked to have stolen it when five lengths clear turning in, but was treading water in the final furlong, and was shaded near the line. He too was claimed and now joins Barry Hills. (7/2)

3382 Java Red (IRE), tried in a visor this time, would have met Broctune Gold on 16lb better terms in a handicap. (7/1: op 12/1)

3105 Special-K did not run up to her official handicap mark. (5/1)

3221 Philgem, who had plenty on at the weights, was tried in a visor this time. She is better over further and on soft ground. (14/1)

824 Smarter Charter, who looked to have a good chance in this lower grade, was in real trouble once in line for home. He is not as good as he was. (100/30: 5/2-4/1)

3478 HULL DAILY MAIL H'CAP (0-70) (3-Y.O) (Class E)

3-00 (3-00) **1m 1f 207y** £3,977.00 (£1,196.00: £578.00: £269.00) Stalls: High GOING minus 0.07 sec per fur (G)

SP RR SF

3441[2] **Pension Fund (69)** (MWEasterby) **3-9-7** JFortune(6) (lw: s.s: hld up: hdwy far side over 2f out: led ins fnl f: hld on towards fin)....— **1** 5/2[2] 76 44
3272[2] **Double Flight (62)** (MJohnston) **3-9-0** JWeaver(5) (trckd ldr: led over 3f out tl ins fnl f: rallied nr fin)....½ **2** 7/1[3] 68 36
3315[2] **Mowjood (USA) (64)** (MRStoute) **3-9-2v** KDarley(4) (lw: stdd s: hld up: hdwy over 3f out: sn chsng ldrs: sn rdn & no imp)....7 **3** 7/4[1] 59 27
2593[5] **Misty Rain (62)** (BWHills) **3-8-11**(3) JDSmith(2) (sn outpcd & drvn along: styd far side: kpt on one pce fnl 2f)1¾ **4** 11/1 54 22
3225[3] **Zorba (65)** (JHetherton) **3-9-3** NKennedy(7) (led tl over 3f out: edgd rt & wknd 2f out)....6 **5** 12/1 48 16
3068* **Maremma (49)** (DonEnricoIncisa) **3-8-1** KimTinkler(3) (s.i.s: bhd tl sme hdwy fnl 2f: n.d)....1½ **6** 16/1 29 —
2909[3] **Grate Times (62)** (EWeymes) **3-9-0** DHarrison(10) (chsd ldrs: drvn along over 4f out: wknd 2f out)....7 **7** 11/1 31 —

Form	Horse	Dist	Pos	SP	RR	SF
3211^{4}	**Talib (USA) (67)** (DMorley) **3-9-5** MFenton(8) (trckd ldrs: drvn along over 4f o ut: lost pl over 3f out)	12	**8**	17/2	17	—
2956^{5}	**Who's That Man (59)** (SCWilliams) **3-8-11** DHolland(9) (racd wd: chsd ldrs tl lost pl over 3f out: sn wknd & eased)	25	**9**	12/1	—	—
				(SP 125.9%)	**9 Rn**	

2m 9.9 (6.80) CSF £20.84 CT £36.49 TOTE £4.50: £1.50 £2.00 £1.10 (£13.10) Trio £4.60 OWNER Mr Stephen Curtis (SHERIFF HUTTON) BRED Pitts Farm Stud

3441 Pension Fund had to be ridden differently this time after standing still when the stalls opened. One of two to stick to the far side, he showed the right sort of spirit and should make an interesting juvenile hurdler. (5/2: op 5/1)

3272 Double Flight, down 2lb, made the best of her way home off the bend, bringing the majority of the field with her to the stands side. Proving most willing under pressure, in the end she was just held at bay. (7/1: 5/1-15/2)

3315 Mowjood (USA), a free-going sort, is almost certainly better suited by much faster ground. (7/4)

2178 Misty Rain has slipped 8lb down the handicap after three unpromising efforts. Like the winner, she stayed on the far side. Sticking on at the finish, she might be better suited by further. (11/1)

3225 Zorba (12/1: op 8/1)

2956 Who's That Man (12/1: op 8/1)

3479 E.B.F. JOURNAL MAIDEN STKS (2-Y.O) (Class D)

3-30 (3-36) **7f 100y** £3,912.00 (£1,176.00: £568.00: £264.00) Stalls: High GOING minus 0.07 sec per fur (G)

Form	Horse	Dist	Pos	SP	RR	SF
3103^{4}	**Due South** (EALDunlop) **2-8-9** SWhitworth(1) (prom: sn pushed along: edgd rt & styd on wl to ld towards fin)	—	**1**	5/1 ³	78	21
	Hadith (DMorley) **2-9-0** MFenton(12) (lengthy: unf: chsd ldrs: rdn to ld 1f out: hdd nr fin)	½	**2**	4/1 ²	82	25
2919^{3}	**Fair Deal (USA)** (DRLoder) **2-8-9** KDarley(8) (chsd ldrs: drvn along over 3f out: led over 1f out: sn hdd: keeping on one pce whn hmpd nr fin)	1	**3**	13/8 ¹	75	18
	Mannequin (IRE) (BWHills) **2-8-9** DHolland(6) (neat: s.i.s: bhd: outpcd over 2f out: kpt on wl appr fnl f)	2½	**4**	10/1	69+	12
	Alberich (IRE) (MJohnston) **2-9-0** JWeaver(13) (w'like: str: bit bkwd: dwlt: rn green & sn pushed along: kpt on fnl 2f: nvr nr to chal)	3½	**5**	10/1	67	10
2870^{3}	**Beware** (RWArmstrong) **2-9-0** RPrice(9) (trckd ldrs: effrt over 3f out: wknd fnl f)	¾	**6**	5/1 ³	65	8
2953^{3}	**Riley** (RCharlton) **2-9-0** WJO'Connor(10) (led tl over 1f out: wknd fnl f)	1	**7**	7/1	63	6
3117^{11}	**Torso** (JWWatts) **2-9-0** JFortune(2) (hld up: effrt over 3f out: nvr nr ldrs)	3½	**8**	25/1	56	—
3270^{5}	**Royal Velvet** (CWFairhurst) **2-8-9** DeanMcKeown(7) (a in rr)	nk	**9**	33/1	50	—
3103^{8}	**Rockette** (JWWatts) **2-8-6**(3) PFessey(11) (swtg: hld up: a bhd)	2½	**10**	25/1	45	—
3260^{3}	**Wishbone Alley (IRE)** (MDods) **2-9-0** AlexGreaves(5) (chsd ldrs: ev ch tl wknd 2f out)	1	**11**	25/1	48	—
	Mister Bunch (EWeymes) **2-9-0** DHarrison(4) (str: cmpt: bit bkwd: sn outpcd: rdn & lost pl 4f out)	14	**12**	33/1	17	—
2243^{6}	***Saddlers' Roe (IRE)*** (BWHills) **2-8-11**(3) JDSmith(3) (Withdrawn not under Starter's orders: uns rdr & bolted bef s)		**W**	14/1	—	—
				(SP 146.2%)	**12 Rn**	

1m 38.2 (6.20) CSF £26.22 TOTE £5.90: £2.20 £2.10 £1.10 (£11.50) Trio £7.30 OWNER Maktoum Al Maktoum (NEWMARKET) BRED Gainsborough Stud Management Ltd

3103 Due South is not very big but she is certainly tough. She stuck on under a strong ride to get up near the finish and it will be interesting to see what mark the handicapper pitches her at in mile nurseries. (5/1)

Hadith, green beforehand, was only just denied on his debut. This was probably a fair maiden and he is sure to go one better. (4/1)

2919 Fair Deal (USA), taken to post early, was only sticking on at the same pace when hampered and forced to switch up near the line. This extended seven on easy ground seems to stretch her stamina to the very limit. (13/8)

Mannequin (IRE) may lack size and scope, but she still ran a promising first race, taking time to get her eye in, but keeping on nicely towards the line. (10/1)

Alberich (IRE), a sturdily-made, backward-looking newcomer, ran very green, but there was plenty to like about the way he was picking up ground in the final quarter-mile. (10/1)

2870 Beware seemed to run out of stamina in the final furlong. (5/1: 7/2-11/2)

2953 Riley has no obvious scope for improvement. (7/1)

3480 STEVE AND JOANNE JUST MARRIED NURSERY H'CAP (2-Y.O F) (Class D)

4-00 (4-02) **5f** £3,925.00 (£1,180.00: £570.00: £265.00) Stalls: High GOING minus 0.07 sec per fur (G)

Form	Horse	Dist	Pos	SP	RR	SF
3239*	**Perfect Peach (75)** (JBerry) **2-9-0**(3) TEDurcan(1) (chsd ldrs: led over 1f out: rdn out)	—	**1**	3/1 ¹	78	40
1821^{4}	**Arian Da (74)** (BPalling) **2-9-2** DHarrison(2) (chsd ldrs: kpt on wl fnl 2f: nt qckn ins fnl f)	¾	**2**	11/2 ³	75	37
3438^{2}	**Inchalong (64)** (MBrittain) **2-8-6** GBardwell(5) (sn outpcd & bhd: hdwy over 1f out: styd on wl towards fin)	nk	**3**	8/1	64	26
3226^{2}	**Mighty Sure (IRE) (63)** (MWEasterby) **2-8-5** LCharnock(7) (hmpd & swtchd lft after s: hdwy ½-wy: kpt on same pce appr fnl f)	2	**4**	5/1 ²	56	18
2904*	**High Carry (73)** (NTinkler) **2-9-1** KDarley(6) (racd far side: led tl over 1f out: sn wknd)	5	**5**	11/2 ³	50	12
3106^{16}	**Crafty Pet (IRE) (54)** (RAFahey) **2-7-10v¹** DWright(3) (led stands' side: wknd over 1f out)	1¼	**6**	16/1	27	—
3152*	**Mislead (IRE) (79)** (JSMoore) **2-9-4**(3) MHenry(4) (lw: chsd ldrs tl wknd over 1f out: eased)	14	**7**	3/1 ¹	7	—
				(SP 114.4%)	**7 Rn**	

65.2 secs (3.40) CSF £18.10 TOTE £2.90: £2.30 £3.70 (£15.10) OWNER Mrs Ann Morris (COCKERHAM) BRED R. J. Vines

LONG HANDICAP Crafty Pet (IRE) 7-7

3239* Perfect Peach, who looked to have been put in on a very fair mark, as it turned out had the best of the draw, with all but one of the field choosing to race towards the stands side. She did it tidily. (3/1)

1821 Arian Da, back over her best trip, proved very willing but, hard as she tried, the winner always looked to have her measure. (11/2)

3438 Inchalong was completely taken off her legs in what looked a fast-run race. Well adrift at halfway, she was fast reeling in the first two at the line and is surely better over six. (8/1)

3226 Mighty Sure (IRE) was left short of room on the inside by High Carry soon after the start. Electing to switch to race with the main body of the field towards the stands side, she must have given away a fair amount of ground. Keeping on at the same pace coming to the final furlong, she might be better back over six. (5/1)

2904* High Carry, left alone to race on the far side, seemed to go very fast and looked to be about three lengths clear overall at halfway. It was no surprise to see her tie up badly coming to the final furlong. (11/2)

1990 Crafty Pet (IRE), in a visor for the first time, seemed to set a strong pace on the stands side but she weakened badly over a furlong out. (16/1)

3152* Mislead (IRE), from an 8lb higher mark, tried to match strides with Crafty Pet but it left her without any reserves and, dropping right out, was eased right up. (3/1)

3481 LADIES DAY H'CAP (0-80) (3-Y.O+) (Class D)

4-30 (4-33) **5f** £4,263.00 (£1,284.00: £622.00: £291.00) Stalls: High GOING minus 0.07 sec per fur (G)

			SP	RR	SF
2826^{2}	**Goretski (IRE) (71)** (NTinkler) **4-9-6** DHarrison(11) (swtg: mde all: drvn clr 1f out: styd on wl)...................—	**1**	8/1^{3}	84	61
3240^{18}	**Dominelle (48)** (TDEasterby) **5-7-11** DWright(12) (a chsng ldrs: kpt on wl appr fnl f: no imp)...................3	**2**	14/1	51	28
3334^{2}	**Brecongill Lad (63)** (MissSEHall) **5-8-12** LCharnock(13) (sn trckng ldrs: nt qckn appr fnl f)...................1	**3**	6/1^{2}	63	40
3130^{13}	**Superbit (63)** (BAMcMahon) **5-8-12** LNewton(7) (hdwy ½-wy: kpt on same pce appr fnl f)...................¾	**4**	9/1	61	38
2711^{12}	**Saint Express (79)** (MrsMReveley) **7-10-0** KDarley(3) (chsd ldrs: drvn along & outpcd ½-wy: kpt on appr fnl f)...................½	**5**	9/1	75	52
3208^{9}	**Bowlers Boy (72)** (JJQuinn) **4-9-4**(3) TEDurcan(8) (hdwy ½-wy: n.m.r: kpt on fnl f)...................½	**6**	11/1	67	44
2934^{9}	**Insider Trader (56)** (MrsJRRamsden) **6-8-5v** JFortune(6) (lw: w ldrs tl wknd over 1f out)...................s.h	**7**	10/1	50	27
3334*	**Double Oscar (IRE) (71)** (DNicholls) **4-9-6b** 7x AlexGreaves(9) (lw: hld up & bhd: hdwy & nt clr run 2f out: kpt on: nvr nr ldrs)...................½	**8**	3/1^{1}	64	41
3326^{2}	**Ansellman (77)** (JBerry) **7-9-9b**(3) PFessey(15) (chsd ldrs: wknd over 1f out)...................2½	**9**	8/1^{3}	62	39
3334^{9}	**Just Dissident (IRE) (64)** (RMWhitaker) **5-8-13** DeanMcKeown(5) (bhd: drvn along ½-wy: n.d)...................1	**10**	16/1	46	23
3126^{U}	**The Wad (63)** (DNicholls) **4-8-5**(7) TSiddall(14) (stumbled s: hdwy u.p ½-wy: lost pl over 1f out)...................1¼	**11**	14/1	41	18
2844^{13}	**Captain Carat (59)** (DNicholls) **6-8-8b** WJO'Connor(1) (s.i.s: sme hdwy ½-wy: sn lost pl)...................2½	**12**	16/1	29	6
2847^{3}	**U-No-Harry (IRE) (60)** (RHollinshead) **4-8-9** FLynch(16) (b.nr fore: racd far side: chsd ldrs: edgd lft ½-wy: sn lost pl)...................1	**13**	12/1	26	3
2937^{14}	**Ramsey Hope (60)** (CWFairhurst) **4-8-9v** NKennedy(10) (racd centre: a bhd)...................2½	**14**	33/1	18	—
			(SP 134.7%)	**14 Rn**	

64.1 secs (2.30) CSF £117.63 CT £682.20 TOTE £9.10: £2.60 £3.70 £2.50 (£81.30) Trio £260.50 OWNER Mr P. D. Savill (MALTON) BRED Pierre Brichart

2826 Goretski (IRE) won his sixth handicap this year and from a mark 17lb higher than when he kicked off at Hamilton in May. Pulling clear inside the last, he will now take another hike in the weights. (8/1)

1828 Dominelle put three poor efforts behind her. (14/1)

3334 Brecongill Lad, who won this event here last year from a 2lb higher mark, would have appreciated faster ground. (6/1)

2759 Superbit, who likes to get his toe in, ran much better than on his previous outings. (9/1)

2289 Saint Express seems suited by a stiff five these days. (9/1: op 16/1)

3066 Bowlers Boy, who got into trouble, is probably better over six. (11/1)

3334* Double Oscar (IRE), just 2lb higher in the weights than at Pontefract, seemed to be ridden with a marked lack of urgency. After getting in trouble soon after halfway, his rider seemed quite content to accept defeat. This is best overlooked. (3/1)

3482 GRAPE LANE LIMITED STKS (0-60) (3-Y.O+) (Class F)

5-00 (5-00) **1m 3f 216y** £2,495.00 (£695.00: £335.00) Stalls: High GOING minus 0.07 sec per fur (G)

			SP	RR	SF
2825^{9}	**Wellcome Inn (55)** (JO'Reilly) **3-8-7** JO'Reilly(2) (trckd ldrs: led over 3f out: edgd rt & lft: styd on strly fnl f)...................—	**1**	10/1^{3}	70	—
3286*	**Urgent Reply (USA) (56)** (CADwyer) **4-9-8** DHolland(6) (led: drvn along & hdd over 3f out: swtchd rt & no imp appr fnl f)...................4	**2**	3/1^{2}	69	9
3272*	**Campaspe (58)** (JGFitzGerald) **5-9-5** JFortune(1) (lw: trckd ldr: effrt 3f out: sn rdn: wknd over 1f out)...................1¾	**3**	4/11^{1}	63	3
			(SP 107.4%)	**3 Rn**	

2m 46.7 (13.70) CSF £26.85 TOTE £6.00: (£6.50) OWNER Burntwood Sports Ltd (PONTEFRACT) BRED A. C. Birkle

WEIGHT FOR AGE 3yo-11lb

IN-FOCUS: **This was the first winner as a trainer for Jimmy O'Reilly, as well as his first in the saddle this season.**

2414 Wellcome Inn, well beaten over a much longer trip on his last two outings, made the most of this easy opportunity, a 0-60 limited stakes. No fewer than four of his intended rivals were taken out because of the slight change in the ground. One has to ask just what do their connections want. (10/1)

3286* Urgent Reply (USA) set his own pace. Though forced to switch by the wayward winner, he was beaten entirely on merit. (3/1: op 7/4)

3272* Campaspe, on paper a bitter disappointment, is much happier on faster ground and in bigger fields, ensuring a true pace. (4/11)

T/Plpt: £77.30 (250.54 Tckts). T/Qdpt: £9.20 (153.62 Tckts) WG

3221-HAMILTON (R-H) (Good)

Wednesday August 13th

WEATHER: overcast, raining & v.hot WIND: almost nil

3483 HEATHERY KNOWE (QUALIFIER) CLAIMING STKS (2-Y.O) (Class G)

6-00 (6-00) **5f 4y** £2,192.00 (£612.00: £296.00) Stalls: Low GOING minus 0.21 sec per fur (GF)

			SP	RR	SF
3222^{3}	**Sandside (88)** (JBerry) **2-9-0**(5) PRoberts(3) (lw: trckd ldrs: rdn to ld ins fnl f: styd on wl)...................—	**1**	5/4^{1}	85	32
3209^{5}	**Oriel Girl (66)** (PDEvans) **2-8-8v** JFEgan(5) (cl up: led wl over 1f out tl wl ins fnl f: rallied)...................s.h	**2**	6/4^{2}	74	21
2823^{6}	**Ngaere Princess** (WTKemp) **2-7-5b**(7) JMcAuley(2) (led over 3f: wknd appr fnl f)...................4	**3**	40/1	51	—
1797^{13}	**Scotch Time (58)** (RAFahey) **2-8-9b** JCarroll(4) (lw: dwlt: a outpcd & bhd)...................7	**4**	11/2^{3}	40	—
492^{6}	**Good For You** (SEKettlewell) **2-8-13** JFanning(1) (spd to ½-wy: sn bhd)...................dist	**5**	20/1	—	—
			(SP 107.0%)	**5 Rn**	

61.4 secs (3.10) CSF £2.88 TOTE £3.00: £1.10 £1.30 (£1.10) OWNER Mr J. K. Brown (COCKERHAM) BRED P. Young

3222 Sandside was ridden with patience this time and it did the trick. He was still in front soon enough. (5/4: evens-11/8)

3209 Oriel Girl, back to form here, proved game under pressure and fought back when looking well second best. (6/4)

1990 Ngaere Princess ran her best race to date here. (40/1)

1797 Scotch Time, after over two months off, was ring rusty and never showed after a poor start. (11/2)

492 Good For You has not run for well over four months and, very keen to post, showed little in the race. (20/1)

3484 ARTHUR BALDING H'CAP (0-70) (3-Y.O+) (Class E)

6-30 (6-31) **6f 5y** £3,680.00 (£1,115.00: £545.00: £260.00) Stalls: Low GOING minus 0.21 sec per fur (GF)

			SP	RR	SF
3224^{3}	**Natural Key (65)** (DHaydnJones) **4-10-0** AMackay(13) (in tch: swtchd ½-wy: led wl over 1f out: r.o)...................—	**1**	11/2^{2}	72	55

3334^{7}	**Tutu Sixtysix (33)** (DonEnricoIncisa) **6-7-10** KimTinkler(3) (in tch: hdwy 2f out: kpt on wl)	¾	**2**	20/1	38	21
2857^{9}	**Mister Westsound (51)** (MissLAPerratt) **5-9-0b** GDuffield(9) (dwlt: gd hdwy & swtchd 2f out: nrst fin)	1¾	**3**	8/1	51	34
3221^{3}	**Rapid Mover (34)** (DANolan) **10-7-4b**(7)ow1 NPollard(8) (outpcd tl hdwy over 1f out: r.o wl towards fin)	nk	**4**	66/1	34	16
3271^{6}	**Henry the Hawk (41)** (MDods) **6-8-4b** JCarroll(14) (b: chsd ldrs: rdn ½-wy: ch 2f out: nt qckn)	2	**5**	5/1 1	35	18
3406^{12}	**Diet (33)** (MissLAPerratt) **11-7-3v**(7) JMcAuley(4) (lw: outpcd & bhd tl drifted lft & styd on last 2f)	2½	**6**	66/1	21	4
3334^{8}	**Tropical Beach (60)** (JBerry) **4-9-9** OPears(5) (bhd: hdwy 2f out: styd on towards fin)	hd	**7**	16/1	47	30
3130^{8}	**Pageboy (62)** (PCHaslam) **8-9-6**(5) PRoberts(10) (lw: w ldrs over 4f: grad wknd)	½	**8**	7/1	48	31
3224^{6}	**Sunday Mail Too (IRE) (33)** (MissLAPerratt) **5-7-3**(7) PBradley(6) (lw: cl up 4f: grad wknd)	s.h	**9**	20/1	19	2
3266^{5}	**King Uno (50)** (MrsJRRamsden) **3-8-9v** JFEgan(7) (lw: bhd: drvn along ½-wy: sme late hdwy)	d.h	**9**	13/2 3	36	15
2900^{7}	**Pallium (IRE) (52)** (DANolan) **9-8-10b**(5) KSked(11) (cl up tl wknd wl over 1f out)	¾	**11**	20/1	36	19
3431^{10}	**Madam Zando (34)** (JBalding) **4-7-8**(3)ow1 DarrenMoffatt(2) (racd stands' side: no ch fr ½-wy)	¾	**12**	50/1	16	—
3240^{17}	**Paldost (41)** (MDHammond) **3-8-0b1** DaleGibson(1) (swtg: racd stands' side: outpcd fr ½-wy)	1½	**13**	25/1	19	—
2900^{13}	**Six for Luck (39)** (DANolan) **5-8-2** RLappin(15) (led over 4f: wknd)	hd	**14**	20/1	17	—
3406^{6}	**Suedoro (44)** (JSGoldie) **7-8-7** JFanning(12) (w ldrs 4f: wknd)	hd	**15**	8/1	21	4
3443^{6}	**Whittle Rock (62)** (MrsMReveley) **4-9-6**(5) SCopp(16) (lw: bhd: rdn ½-wy: n.d)	¾	**16**	9/1	37	20
				(SP 123.8%)		**16 Rn**

1m 12.7 (2.70) CSF £107.40 CT £845.95 TOTE £6.10: £1.40 £2.60 £1.90 £8.10 (£61.40) Trio £224.80 OWNER Mr Hugh O'Donnell (PONTYPRIDD) BRED Cheveley Park Stud Ltd

LONG HANDICAP Madam Zando 7-3 Rapid Mover 6-11 Sunday Mail Too (IRE) 7-9 Diet 7-3 Tutu Sixtysix 7-3

WEIGHT FOR AGE 3yo-4lb

3224 Natural Key won her first race of the season here and showed a good turn of foot at the two-furlong marker to pinch it. (11/2)

3271 Tutu Sixtysix is obviously in good form and, although she has never won over further than five furlongs, she stayed well enough here and can end a long losing run before long. (20/1)

2857 Mister Westsound, after a couple of moderate efforts, showed something of his old sparkle here. (8/1)

3221 Rapid Mover was 13lb out of the handicap and apparently at too short a trip but this old character showed he still has the ability when in the mood. (66/1)

3271 Henry the Hawk was always struggling to get on terms and failed to pick up late on. (5/1)

2472 Diet, having his 148th race here, looks really well and gave hope that he might well be in the reckoning again. (66/1)

2504* Tropical Beach, without the blinkers, only got going when it was too late. (16/1)

2563 Pageboy (7/1: 5/1-8/1)

3485 HIGHLANDS H'CAP (0-80) (3-Y.O+) (Class D)

7-00 (7-00) **1m 5f 9y** £3,838.20 (£1,161.60: £566.80: £269.40) Stalls: High GOING minus 0.21 sec per fur (GF)

				SP	RR	SF
3283^{14}	**Winnebago (46)** (CWThornton) **4-8-11** JFanning(5) (mde most: kpt on wl fnl 2f)	—	**1**	10/1	59	40
3221*	**Philmist (45)** (MissLAPerratt) **5-8-3b**(7) SBuckley(8) (in tch: hdwy 3f out: swtchd & qcknd to chal ins fnl f: kpt on one pce)	2½	**2**	9/2 2	55	36
2387^{2}	**Belle Bijou (58)** (MJohnston) **3-8-11** DaleGibson(3) (chsd ldrs tl outpcd & lost pl appr st: styd on fnl 2f: n.d)	4	**3**	5/1 3	63	32
249^{3}	**Chateauherault (IRE) (60)** (PCHaslam) **3-8-8**(5) PRoberts(7) (swtg: chsd ldrs: outpcd 3f out: kpt on fnl f)	1½	**4**	16/1	63	32
3309^{9}	**Thunderheart (51)** (RAllan) **6-9-2** JFEgan(9) (chsd ldrs: effrt 4f out: one pce)	s.h	**5**	6/1	54	35
3108*	**Kernof (IRE) (63)** (MDHammond) **4-10-0** JCarroll(6) (swtg: bhd: effrt 4f out: styd on: n.d)	s.h	**6**	4/1 1	66	47
2824^{5}	**Lord Advocate (52)** (DANolan) **9-8-12b**(5) KSked(1) (b.hind: disp ld tl hdd 6f out: ev ch tl wknd fnl 2f)	1	**7**	7/1	54	35
2757^{6}	**Wildmoor (56)** (JDBethell) **3-8-9** GDuffield(4) (lw: in tch: brought wd st: sn rdn & btn)	11	**8**	7/1	44	13
3223^{6}	**Cois Na Farraige (IRE) (37)** (MissLAPerratt) **4-8-2** AMackay(2) (a bhd)	1	**9**	66/1	24	5
				(SP 110.6%)		**9 Rn**

2m 52.1 (6.40) CSF £46.50 CT £219.78 TOTE £19.60: £3.70 £1.80 £2.20 (£81.60) Trio £132.00 OWNER Mr Guy Reed (MIDDLEHAM) BRED G. Reed

WEIGHT FOR AGE 3yo-12lb

OFFICIAL EXPLANATION **Winnebago: regarding the improvement in form, the trainer reported that the filly had probably gone too fast for her own good at Catterick last time, and appreciated the drop in distance on this occasion.**

2114 Winnebago, who certainly stays well, was at her aggressive best here and galloped her rivals into the ground. She was well on top by the finish. (10/1)

3221* Philmist, stepping up in trip, seemed to get it well enough but just found one too tough. (9/2)

2387 Belle Bijou keeps running as though much longer trips would see her come into her own. (5/1)

2825* Thunderheart ran reasonably but was not helped by the rain-softened ground. He could be interesting if tried over hurdles. (6/1)

3486 LOCHS AND GLENS MAIDEN H'CAP (0-60) (3-Y.O+) (Class F)

7-30 (7-31) **1m 3f 16y** £2,724.00 (£764.00: £372.00) Stalls: High GOING minus 0.21 sec per fur (GF)

				SP	RR	SF
2750^{5}	**Il Principe (IRE) (35)** (JohnBerry) **3-8-7** JFEgan(6) (lw: unruly s: chsd ldrs: reminders 6f out: rdn to ld over 2f out: styd on wl)	—	**1**	9/1	46	24
3223^{3}	**Craigary (35)** (MrsASwinbank) **6-9-3** AMackay(5) (lw: rr div: hdwy 5f out: edgd rt 2f out: kpt on: nt pce to chal)	2	**2**	5/1 3	43	31
2315^{17}	**Classical Dance (IRE) (47)** (MrsMReveley) **3-9-0**(5) SCopp(11) (bhd: hdwy 3f out: styd on u.str.p fnl 2f: nrst f)	1¾	**3**	6/1	53	31
3223^{5}	**School of Science (22)** (DANolan) **7-7-13**(5) KSked(9) (led tl hdd over 2f out: one pce)	nk	**4**	50/1	27	15
2843^{2}	**Farfields Prince (43)** (DNicholls) **5-9-11** GDuffield(12) (lw: a chsng ldrs: one pce fnl 2f)	1¼	**5**	3/1 1	46	34
3108^{6}	**Fighting Times (40)** (CASmith) **5-9-8** JCarroll(8) (b.hind: lw: nvr bttr than mid div)	4	**6**	9/2 2	38	26
3308^{4}	**Cochiti (35)** (CWThornton) **3-8-7b** DaleGibson(10) (prom tl wknd fnl 3f)	¾	**7**	20/1	32	10
2207^{12}	**Bruz (27)** (LLungo) **6-8-9** JFanning(4) (c wd ent st: wknd fnl 2f)	2½	**8**	11/1	20	8
3429^{5}	**Chancancook (25)** (JLEyre) **4-8-7** RLappin(2) (prom tl wknd fnl 3f)	nk	**9**	25/1	17	5
2487^{13}	**Yuppy Girl (IRE) (35)** (CaptJWilson) **4-8-12**(5) PRoberts(7) (lw: mid div tl outpcd fnl 5f)	hd	**10**	14/1	27	15
	Megan Carew (46) (DMoffatt) **3-9-1**(3) DarrenMoffatt(3) (prom to st: sn bhd)	10	**11**	20/1	24	2
1284^{9}	**Burlesque (42)** (JDBethell) **3-9-0**ow2 OPears(1) (bhd fnl 5f)	¾	**12**	10/1	19	—
				(SP 123.6%)		**12 Rn**

2m 26.5 (7.10) CSF £48.66 CT £275.11 TOTE £9.80: £2.60 £1.80 £4.20 (£31.90) Trio £87.30 OWNER The 1997 Partnership (NEWMARKET) BRED J. Costello

WEIGHT FOR AGE 3yo-10lb

2750 Il Principe (IRE) looked a handful both in the paddock and before the start, but he still had too much ability for this bunch and saw it out really well. (9/1)

3223 Craigary looks particularly well and is running consistently. (5/1)
Classical Dance (IRE) has the look of something better but took an age to get going and will probably need further. (6/1)
3223 School of Science, made plenty of use of here, ran his best race for some time. (50/1)
2843 Farfields Prince, after four weeks off, ran pretty well and was certainly not over-punished. (3/1)
2145 Bruz (11/1: 8/1-12/1)
Burlesque (10/1: 8/1-12/1)

3487 THISTLE (S) STKS (3-Y.O+) (Class F)

8-00 (8-00) **1m 1f 36y** £2,514.00 (£704.00: £342.00) Stalls: High GOING minus 0.21 sec per fur (GF)

				SP	RR	SF
2847[6]	**Mr Fortywinks (IRE) (56)** (JLEyre) **3-8-11** MGallagher(10) (mde most: styd on wl fnl 2f)	—	1	9/2[3]	50	21
2906[6]	**Oriel Lad (32)** (DonEnricoIncisa) **4-9-5b** KimTinkler(6) (bhd: effrt & nt clr run 3f out: swtchd 2f out: r.o wl fnl f)	2½	2	10/1	46	25
2887[6]	**Bernard Seven (IRE) (30)** (MDods) **5-9-5b** JCarroll(7) (lw: w wnr tl rdn & btn over 1f out)	1¾	3	14/1	43	22
3264[13]	**Mystic Times (28)** (BMactaggart) **4-8-9**(5) KSked(11) (lw: a chsng ldrs: one pce fnl 3f)	1¾	4	20/1	35	14
	Vintage Red (GRichards) **7-9-5** GDuffield(3) (mid div: c wd & effrt 4f out: hung rt & one pce fnl 2f)	1¾	5	20/1	37	16
2543[9]	**Termon (32)** (MissLAPerratt) **4-9-0** AMackay(2) (bhd: c wd & effrt 5f out: n.d)	s.h	6	20/1	31	10
1470[7]	**Lightning Rebel (65)** (CWThornton) **3-8-11** JFanning(1) (chsd ldrs tl wknd fnl 2f)	½	7	11/4[1]	36	7
2845[7]	**Trying Times (IRE) (44)** (JBerry) **4-9-5**(5) PRoberts(9) (t: chsd ldrs tl wknd fnl 2½f)	2	8	7/2[2]	37	16
3221[6]	**Knave (27)** (PMonteith) **4-9-5** OPears(5) (prom tl wknd over 3f out)	¾	9	50/1	31	10
3264[7]	**Miletrian City (45)** (MissLAPerratt) **4-8-12b**(7) SBuckley(8) (lw: dwlt: hld up: effrt 3f out: hrd rdn & no imp)	½	10	9/1	30	9
3224[8]	**Ragtime Cowgirl (35)** (DANolan) **4-8-7**(7) NPollard(4) (a bhd)	29	11	20/1	—	—
				(SP 113.8%)		**11 Rn**

2m 1.0 (6.70) CSF £38.35 TOTE £6.30: £2.00 £2.90 £3.10 (£57.70) Trio £156.80; £90.59 to 15/8/97 OWNER Miss Nuala Cassidy (HAMBLETON) BRED Miss Fionnuala Cassidy
WEIGHT FOR AGE 3yo-8lb
No bid
2847 Mr Fortywinks (IRE), a warm and edgy individual, appreciated the step up in trip and did it well enough despite sweating profusely during the race. (9/2)
2906 Oriel Lad looked a shade unlucky here as he got stopped at a vital stage and then always had too much on. (10/1)
2887 Bernard Seven (IRE) again had his chance but yet again failed to respond to pressure. (14/1: 10/1-16/1)
2716 Mystic Times had plenty on at these weights and ran pretty well. (20/1)
Vintage Red has ability but was inclined to hang under pressure. This should have put him right for hurdling. (20/1)

3488 FLOWER OF SCOTLAND MAIDEN H'CAP (0-65) (3-Y.O+) (Class F)

8-30 (8-30) **1m 65y** £2,528.00 (£708.00: £344.00) Stalls: High GOING minus 0.21 sec per fur (GF)

				SP	RR	SF
3249[2]	**Murron Wallace (41)** (DHaydnJones) **3-8-5** AMackay(7) (lw: hld up: hdwy on bit 3f out: effrt over 1f out: hrd rdn to ld wl ins fnl f)	—	1	6/4[1]	50	20
2887[4]	**Katie Komaite (39)** (CaptJWilson) **4-8-5v[1]**(5) PRoberts(3) (hld up: qcknd to ld over 2f out: r.o: no ex towards fin)	nk	2	5/1[3]	47	24
3241[8]	**Bent Raiwand (USA) (29)** (DonEnricoIncisa) **4-8-0** KimTinkler(6) (b: trckd ldrs: effrt 2f out: kpt on: nt pce to chal)	3	3	10/1	32	9
3244[3]	**Amid The Stars (62)** (MJohnston) **3-9-12** JFanning(2) (lw: disp ld tl hdd 5f out: ev ch tl outpcd fnl 2f)	6	4	3/1[2]	53	23
3405[6]	**Chanson d'Amour (IRE) (32)** (MissLAPerratt) **3-7-3**(7) JMcAuley(9) (bhd: rdn over 3f out: nvr trbld ldrs)	6	5	33/1	12	—
3105[11]	**Tom Mi Dah (50)** (MDHammond) **3-9-0** JCarroll(8) (bhd: pushed along ½-wy: n.d)	s.h	6	16/1	29	—
3221[7]	**Sweet Note (IRE) (34)** (MissLAPerratt) **3-7-5**(7)ow2 NPollard(4) (dwlt: sn rcvrd: led 5f out tl over 2f out: wknd)	6	7	33/1	2	—
3038[6]	**Kalousion (32)** (TJEtherington) **3-7-3b**(7) PBradley(1) (disp ld tl hdd 5f out: wknd fnl 3f)	1½	8	25/1	—	—
2226[6]	**Northern Maestro (33)** (MrsMReveley) **3-7-11b[1]**ow1 DaleGibson(5) (trckd ldrs tl outpcd over 3f out: sn btn)	3½	9	10/1	—	—
				(SP 115.5%)		**9 Rn**

1m 49.7 (5.60) CSF £8.30 CT £48.20 TOTE £2.30: £1.40 £1.10 £2.70 (£5.20) Trio £20.60 OWNER Dhes-C Partnership (PONTYPRIDD) BRED Mrs B. Skinner and D. F. Powell
LONG HANDICAP Chanson d'Amour (IRE) 7-0 Sweet Note (IRE) 7-3 Kalousion 7-5
WEIGHT FOR AGE 3yo-7lb
STEWARDS' ENQUIRY Mackay susp. 22-23 & 25/8/97 (excessive & improper use of whip).
3249 Murron Wallace at last got it right here but it took a lot of help from the saddle. Perhaps this will have boosted her confidence as she certainly has plenty more ability. (6/4)
2887 Katie Komaite raced in a visor instead of blinkers and took quite a hold and, though responding to pressure, was just worried out of it. She deserves to find a race. (5/1)
Bent Raiwand (USA) has spent much of her career at sprint distances and travelled too keenly here for her own good. (10/1)
3244 Amid The Stars looked very fit indeed but proved disappointing and was off the bit a long way out. (3/1)
2859 Chanson d'Amour (IRE) was 10lb out of the handicap and never gave any signs of hope. (33/1)
2226 Northern Maestro (10/1: 8/1-16/1)

T/Plpt: £63.60 (236.32 Tckts). T/Qdpt: £18.60 (52.39 Tckts) AA

3389-SALISBURY (R-H) (Good to firm)
Wednesday August 13th

WEATHER: unsettled WIND: almost nil

3489 E.B.F. SANDOWN MAIDEN STKS (I) (2-Y.O) (Class D)

1-45 (1-46) **6f** £3,213.50 (£968.00: £469.00: £219.50) Stalls: High GOING minus 0.29 sec per fur (GF)

				SP	RR	SF
3047[2]	**Social Charter (USA)** (PWChapple-Hyam) **2-9-0** JReid(8) (mde all: shkn up over 1f out: pushed out)	—	1	4/7[1]	94+	38
	Majaari (PTWalwyn) **2-9-0** RHills(3) (w'like: hld up: hdwy over 1f out: r.o ins fnl f)	3	2	9/1	86	30
2057[10]	**Exbourne's Wish (USA)** (BWHills) **2-9-0** MHills(4) (swtg: plld hrd: a.p: chsd wnr fnl 2f: sn rdn: no imp)	nk	3	8/1[3]	85	29
2534[5]	**Frolicking** (JLDunlop) **2-8-9** BDoyle(10) (hld up: n.m.r on ins 2f out: r.o one pce fnl f)	3	4	50/1	72	16
	Bless 'im (RHannon) **2-9-0** DaneO'Neill(5) (leggy: lt-f: bhd: rdn over 3f out: nvr nr to chal)	1	5	33/1	75	19

1873^{2}	**Tumbleweed Hero** (BJMeehan) **2-9-0** MTebbutt(9) (bit bkwd: prom: rdn over 2f out: sn wknd)	s.h	**6**	$5/1^{2}$	74	18
	Derryquin (RCharlton) **2-9-0** TSprake(6) (lt-f: unf: bit bkwd: nvr trbld ldrs)	1¾	**7**	33/1	70	14
	Bronzino (GBBalding) **2-9-0** SDrowne(1) (lt-f: swtg: carried lft s: a bhd)	½	**8**	50/1	68	12
1635^{7}	**Sergeant Imp (IRE)** (PMitchell) **2-9-0** AClark(7) (prom 4f)	3½	**9**	100/1	59	3
2926^{5}	**Naayel (IRE)** (CJBenstead) **2-9-0b**[1] RCochrane(2) (swtg: wnt lft s: plld hrd: sn chsng wnr: wknd 2f out)	½	**10**	33/1	58	2
	Mail Shot (IRE) (SDow) **2-9-0** SSanders(11) (lt-f: bkwd: a bhd)	1½	**11**	100/1	54	—
				(SP 116.1%)	**11 Rn**	

1m 15.67 (2.67) CSF £5.59 TOTE £1.50: £1.10 £2.00 £2.40 (£5.10) Trio £10.10 OWNER Mr R. E. Sangster (MARLBOROUGH) BRED Swettenham Stud

3047 Social Charter (USA), beaten by the soft ground on his debut according to his trainer, was quite impressive here. He will now go for the Champion Two-Year-Old Trophy at Ripon prior to a possible tilt at the Mill Reef at Newbury. (4/7)

Majaari, a half-brother to Labeq, stayed on promisingly to snatch second place without causing the winner any anxiety. Normal improvement should see him off the mark and he should not be inconvenienced by an extra furlong. (9/1: op 6/1)

1263 Exbourne's Wish (USA) took a while to settle early on and was probably beaten by a couple of useful recruits. (8/1: op 5/1)

2534 Frolicking, the only filly in the field, had more on her plate here and may do better over seven. (50/1)

Bless 'im will benefit from the experience. (33/1)

1873 Tumbleweed Hero, a half-brother to My Memoirs and Patriach, may just have needed this but this was still disappointing after his promising debut. (5/1)

3490 E.B.F. SANDOWN MAIDEN STKS (II) (2-Y.O) (Class D)

2-15 (2-20) **6f** £3,194.00 (£962.00: £466.00: £218.00) Stalls: High GOING minus 0.29 sec per fur (GF)

				SP	RR	SF
	Harmonic Way (RCharlton) **2-9-0** TSprake(9) (w'like: scope: plld hrd: a.p: led over 1f out: edgd lft & rdn ins fnl f: jst hld on)	—	**1**	$6/4^{1}$	80	4
	Inchtina (HCandy) **2-8-9** CRutter(3) (lt-f: unf: hld up: hdwy 2f out: ev ch wl ins fnl f: jst failed)	s.h	**2**	12/1	75	—
	Asyaad (USA) (BWHills) **2-9-0** MHills(1) (leggy: lt-f: hld up: hdwy over 1f out: r.o ins fnl f)	2½	**3**	$100/30^{2}$	73	—
1749^{5}	**Durar** (JLDunlop) **2-9-0** RHills(4) (lw: a.p: led wl over 1f out: sn hdd: one pce)	1¾	**4**	$5/1^{3}$	69	—
	Orsino (SDow) **2-9-0** SSanders(6) (w'like: scope: led over 4f out tl wl over 1f out: wknd fnl f)	3	**5**	50/1	61	—
	Magical Colours (IRE) (JLDunlop) **2-8-9** BDoyle(10) (lt-f: unf: bkwd: hld up: no hdwy fnl 2f)	3½	**6**	11/1	46	—
	Priors Moor (RWArmstrong) **2-9-0** GCarter(7) (w'like: scope: bkwd: a bhd)	nk	**7**	16/1	50	—
	Lady Felix (SMellor) **2-8-4**(5) ADaly(8) (lt-f: unf: bkwd: uns rdr bef s: led over 1f: rdn & wknd over 2f out)	1¼	**8**	66/1	42	—
	Asinbox (IRE) (BJMeehan) **2-9-0** MTebbutt(5) (w'like: str: bkwd: s.i.s: a bhd)	hd	**9**	20/1	47	—
				(SP 109.9%)	**9 Rn**	

1m 18.34 (5.34) CSF £17.74 TOTE £3.10: £1.30 £1.70 £1.50 (£12.80) Trio £31.20 OWNER Mrs Alexandra Chandris (BECKHAMPTON) BRED Mrs J. Chandris

IN-FOCUS: **This race was slowly-run, being nearly three seconds slower than the first division.**

Harmonic Way, a half-brother to Passiflora, is out of a mile and a half winner who is a half-sister to In The Groove. Proving difficult to settle because of the lack of pace, he showed signs of inexperience in the closing stages but has plenty of scope about him. (6/4)

Inchtina, a half sister to several winners including Polo Kit and Anastina, was only beaten by a whisker and will be even more at home when the emphasis is on stamina. (12/1: 10/1-16/1)

Asyaad (USA), a half-brother to seven-furlong winner Bint Shihama, is out of a sister to Sayyedati and ought to be capable of improving on this. (100/30)

1749 Durar, out of a mile and a quarter winner, is bred to require further. (5/1)

Orsino, already gelded, seems to have more room for physical development than some of his rivals. (50/1)

Magical Colours (IRE) is a half-sister to River Keen and three winners abroad and out of a mare who scored over ten furlongs in Ireland. (11/1)

3491 VIOLET APPLIN CHALLENGE CUP H'CAP (0-70) (3-Y.O+) (Class E)

2-45 (2-50) **1m 1f 209y** £3,346.75 (£1,009.00: £489.50: £229.75) Stalls: High GOING minus 0.29 sec per fur (GF)

				SP	RR	SF
3091^{2}	**Your Most Welcome (58)** (DJSffrenchDavis) **6-9-2** GCarter(4) (hld up: hdwy over 4f out: led wl over 1f out: edgd rt: drvn out)	—	**1**	$5/1^{2}$	69	29
3321^{2}	**Rehaab (45)** (DMorris) **4-8-3v** AClark(14) (plld hrd: lost pl over 6f out: nt clr run over 2f out: swtchd lft & hdwy over 1f out: r.o)	¾	**2**	14/1	55	15
3093^{4}	**Statajack (IRE) (60)** (DRCElsworth) **9-9-4b** KFallon(5) (b: hld up: hdwy over 1f out: r.o ins fnl f)	1	**3**	12/1	68	28
3184^{5}	**Pistol (IRE) (70)** (CAHorgan) **7-10-0** PaulEddery(12) (b.hind: hld up mid div: hdwy over 2f out: one pce fnl f)	1¾	**4**	11/1	75	35
	Alpine Panther (IRE) (64) (MrsMReveley) **4-9-8** LDettori(13) (bit bkwd: led over 5f: sn rdn: wknd fnl f)	nk	**5**	$7/2^{1}$	69	29
3153^{14}	**Whispering Dawn (60)** (CPEBrooks) **4-9-4** RCochrane(10) (s.s: hld up & bhd: hdwy over 1f out: r.o)	nk	**6**	14/1	64	24
3183^{7}	**Rock The Barney (IRE) (42)** (MDIUsher) **8-8-0** DRMcCabe(8) (s.i.s: nvr nrr)	½	**7**	16/1	46	6
3134^{7}	**Piquant (58)** (LordHuntingdon) **10-9-2** JReid(15) (chsd ldr: led over 4f out tl wl over 1f out: sn wknd)	nk	**8**	16/1	61	21
3029^{9}	**Darling Clover (60)** (RBastiman) **5-8-13**(5) HBastiman(6) (b.hind: no hdwy fnl 3f)	¾	**9**	$5/1^{2}$	62	22
3091^{10}	**Ember (42)** (PHayward) **4-8-0** CRutter(16) (tk keen hold: prom tl wknd over 1f out)	2½	**10**	50/1	40	—
2650^{8}	**Bronhallow (38)** (MrsBarbaraWaring) **4-7-10b** JLowe(2) (b.hind: a bhd)	½	**11**	33/1	35	—
2961^{8}	**Zidac (67)** (PJMakin) **5-9-11** SSanders(1) (hld up: hdwy over 5f out: ev ch 2f out: wknd over 1f out)	1½	**12**	12/1	62	22
	Neverold (IRE) (45) (PCRitchens) **7-8-3** NAdams(9) (bkwd: a bhd)	5	**13**	50/1	32	—
1756^{5}	**Shaded (IRE) (55)** (SDow) **3-8-4**ow2 DaneO'Neill(3) (bit bkwd: prom over 7f)	hd	**14**	25/1	42	—
3095^{7}	**Meilleur (IRE) (60)** (LadyHerries) **3-8-9** PatEddery(7) (lw: prom over 7f)	1¾	**15**	$6/1^{3}$	44	—
				(SP 129.4%)	**15 Rn**	

2m 11.43 (6.13) CSF £69.90 CT £752.92 TOTE £5.10: £1.80 £4.80 £2.60 (£26.30) Trio £41.90 OWNER Mrs P. Bedford (UPPER LAMBOURN) BRED Collin Stud

LONG HANDICAP Bronhallow 7-6

WEIGHT FOR AGE 3yo-9lb

3091 Your Most Welcome, raised 1lb for a narrow defeat last time, was hardly winning out of turn and was subsequently described by her trainer as a genuine mare. (5/1)

3321 Rehaab showed her second in a seller when having her first run in a visor a week ago was no flash in the pan. (14/1)

3093 Statajack (IRE), eventually responded to Fallon's urgings and may find this trip on the short side nowadays. (12/1)

3184 Pistol (IRE), down another 2lb, was ridden more patiently this time. (11/1)

Alpine Panther (IRE), having his first run for his new stable, was trying to overcome a long absence. He might well have been strongly backed purely because he had been sent a long way with an eye-catching jockey booking. (7/2: op 6/1)

2782 Whispering Dawn, dropped 2lb, is reported to be in-foal. (14/1)

3492 UPAVON STKS (Listed) (3-Y.O+ F & M) (Class A)

3-15 (3-18) **1m 1f 209y** £10,253.00 (£3,827.00: £1,863.50: £792.50: £346.25: £167.75) Stalls: High GOING minus 0.29 sec per fur (GF)

				SP	RR	SF
2869[4]	**Dust Dancer (96)** (JLDunlop) **3-8-5** BDoyle(2) (hld up: swtchd lft & hdwy over 2f out: qcknd to ld over 1f out: drvn out)	—	1	10/1	114	48
3214[2]	**Dragonada (USA) (104)** (HRACecil) **3-8-7**ow2 KFallon(1) (lw: a.p: led over 3f out tl over 1f out: one pce)	5	2	5/2 [1]	108	40
3017[5]	**The Faraway Tree (94)** (GWragg) **3-8-5** MHills(8) (lw: hld up: hdwy over 5f out: r.o one pce fnl f)	1¼	3	11/1	104	38
3017[2]	**Bint Baladee (98)** (SbinSuroor) **3-8-5** LDettori(10) (lw: hld up: hdwy 2f out: r.o ins fnl f)	½	4	7/2 [2]	103	37
3214[3]	**Kenmist** (LMCumani) **3-8-5** FJovine(4) (a.p: no hdwy fnl 2f)	2½	5	8/1	99	33
3000a[7]	**Western Hour (USA) (95)** (PWChapple-Hyam) **3-8-6**ow1 JReid(6) (lw: prom: rdn over 3f out: wknd over 2f out)	3½	6	10/1	95	28
2028[11]	**Oops Pettie (86)** (MrsJCecil) **4-9-0** PatEddery(9) (hld up: hdwy over 3f out: wknd 2f out)	s.h	7	7/1 [3]	93	36
2869[6]	**Vagabond Chanteuse (100)** (TJEtherington) **3-8-5** AClark(3) (led: rn wd bnd over 6f out: rdn over 4f out: hdd over 3f out: wknd over 2f out)	1¼	8	11/1	91	25
3012*	**Manazil (IRE) (91)** (RWArmstrong) **3-8-5** RHills(7) (rdn over 3f out: a bhd)	11	9	10/1	74	8
	Kinlochewe (97) (JARToller) **4-9-0** SSanders(5) (swtg: a bhd: virtually p.u fnl f)	25	10	25/1	34	—

(SP 122.2%) **10 Rn**

2m 7.64 (2.34) CSF £33.68 TOTE £14.90: £4.00 £1.50 £2.30 (£24.30) Trio £94.70 OWNER Hesmonds Stud (ARUNDEL) BRED Hesmonds Stud Ltd

WEIGHT FOR AGE 3yo-9lb

2869 Dust Dancer was reverting to a mile and a quarter after being thought to have failed to stay at Newmarket. She certainly impressed her trainer here, and he is now thinking of a Group Three at Deauville at the end of the month. (10/1)

3214 Dragonada (USA), trying a longer trip, had most of these in trouble when she went for home, but had no answer when tackled by the winner. (5/2)

3017 The Faraway Tree still seems worth a try at a mile and half. (11/1)

3017 Bint Baladee did not find being coaxed along enough in this company. (7/2)

3214 Kenmist had the longer distance this time but this was quite a hot heat. (8/1)

3000a Western Hour (USA) was reverting to a mile and a quarter. (10/1)

3493 BEMBRIDGE CLAIMING STKS (2-Y.O) (Class F)

3-45 (3-49) **6f 212y** £2,570.00 (£720.00: £350.00) Stalls: High GOING minus 0.29 sec per fur (GF)

				SP	RR	SF
3193[8]	**Wildcat (IRE)** (RHannon) **2-8-11** JReid(9) (led over 2f: swtchd lft over 1f out: rallied to ld nr fin)	—	1	3/1 [1]	72	16
3099[3]	**Fanti Dancer (IRE)** (BJMeehan) **2-8-6** MTebbutt(2) (a.p: jnd ldr 2f out: rdn to ld ins fnl f: hdd nr fin)	½	2	3/1 [1]	66	10
2943[8]	**Saligo (IRE)** (HMorrison) **2-8-6b[1]** CRutter(4) (lw: prom: led over 4f out tl ins fnl f)	2½	3	8/1 [3]	60	4
2227[11]	**Francesca's Folly** (JWHills) **2-8-2** RHills(7) (a.p: r.o one pce fnl 2f)	½	4	25/1	55	—
	Every Penny (APJones) **2-7-12** FNorton(3) (leggy: unf: outpcd: hdwy over 1f out: r.o)	nk	5	33/1	50	—
3078[4]	**Espresso (52)** (JWHills) **2-8-7v** AClark(6) (mid div: sn rdn along: styd on fnl f)	s.h	6	16/1	59	3
	Resurrection (IRE) (RHannon) **2-8-3**(7) RSmith(11) (small: lt-f: hld up & bhd: hdwy over 1f out: nrst fin)	½	7	10/1	61	5
3228[7]	**Waytogomo** (MissBSanders) **2-8-1**(3) AWhelan(8) (prom: rdn 3f out: wknd 2f out)	2	8	20/1	50	—
	Lady Eil (BSmart) **2-8-6** SSanders(5) (lt-f: unf: nvr trbld ldrs)	½	9	20/1	51	—
2579[7]	**Fung Shui (IRE)** (RHannon) **2-9-5** DaneO'Neill(15) (prom over 4f)	6	10	7/1 [2]	51	—
3228[4]	**Dixie Crossroads (48)** (SDow) **2-7-9**(7) DSalt(10) (hld up mid div: bhd fnl 2f)	1	11	10/1	31	—
2693[14]	**Floral Park (49)** (GBBalding) **2-7-10** NVarley(13) (a bhd)	3	12	33/1	18	—
2728[21]	**Princess Deya** (DrJDScargill) **2-8-10** JTate(12) (bkwd: stdd s: outpcd: t.o)	13	13	33/1	2	—
	Sylphide (AJChamberlain) **2-7-10** NAdams(14) (lt-f: bkwd: dwlt: a bhd: t.o)	13	14	50/1	—	—

(SP 121.8%) **14 Rn**

1m 30.87 (4.87) CSF £8.66 TOTE £3.20: £1.70 £1.90 £2.20 (£3.50) Trio £20.10 OWNER Mr George Teo (MARLBOROUGH) BRED M. Grant and W. Hawkings

Wildcat (IRE) clmd Gay Kelleway £8,000

2688 Wildcat (IRE), dropped in class, clawed his way back to strike after looking held. (3/1: op 2/1)

3099 Fanti Dancer (IRE) took a long time to master the third and then found the winner's renewed effort too much. (3/1)

Saligo (IRE), a half-sister to seven-furlong and mile winner Iron Man, showed significant improvement in the blinkers. (8/1)

Francesca's Folly, out of a seven-furlong and mile scorer, benefited from this step up in distance. (25/1)

Every Penny, a half-sister to dual six-furlong juvenile winner Depreciate, was shaping nicely in the closing stages. (33/1)

3078 Espresso was only fourth in a Brighton seller when improving in the visor last time. (16/1)

Resurrection (IRE), given a lot to do, eventually showed signs of life, and this half-sister to amongst others Wildwood Flower and Zaretski seems sure to improve. (10/1)

3494 ISLE OF WIGHT NOVICE STKS (2-Y.O) (Class D)

4-15 (4-16) **6f 212y** £3,701.00 (£1,118.00: £544.00: £257.00) Stalls: High GOING minus 0.29 sec per fur (GF)

				SP	RR	SF
	Soviet Bureau (IRE) (MissGayKelleway) **2-8-12** KFallon(8) (leggy: scope: rdn & hdwy over 3f out: led ins fnl f: drvn out)	—	1	14/1	86+	42
2860[3]	**Dark Moondancer** (PWChapple-Hyam) **2-8-12** JReid(5) (lw: a.p: led over 2f out tl ins fnl f)	1¼	2	2/1 [1]	83	39
3022*	**Krispy Knight** (JWHills) **2-9-4** MHills(3) (lw: trckd ldrs: ev ch over 1f out: one pce)	3½	3	5/2 [2]	81	37
2693[5]	**Close Up (IRE)** (JLDunlop) **2-8-12** FJovine(10) (hld up: r.o one pce fnl 2f)	1¾	4	20/1	71	27
2693[4]	**Santone (IRE)** (RHannon) **2-8-12** PaulEddery(4) (hld up & bhd: stdy hdwy over 1f out: nvr plcd to chal)	½	5	25/1	70	26
	Lear Spear (USA) (DRCElsworth) **2-8-12** AMcGlone(2) (scope: bit bkwd: s.s: nvr nrr)	nk	6	33/1	69	25
2482[2]	**Classic Manoeuvre (USA) (93)** (RHannon) **2-8-12** DaneO'Neill(11) (rdn 3f out: no hdwy)	¾	7	8/1	68	24
3117[2]	**Quintus (USA)** (PFICole) **2-8-12** RCochrane(13) (hld up mid div: bhd fnl 2f)	4	8	5/1 [3]	58	14
	Wintertime (GLewis) **2-8-12** PatEddery(9) (w'like: scope: bkwd: prom over 3f)	hd	9	12/1	58	14
	Sherpa (IRE) (DRCElsworth) **2-8-9**(3) PPMurphy(1) (unf: bit bkwd: a bhd)	hd	10	50/1	58	14
2829[4]	**Tumblweed Prospect** (BJMeehan) **2-8-12** MTebbutt(14) (led over 4f: wknd over 1f out)	½	11	12/1	57	13
1872[6]	**Chief Cashier** (GBBalding) **2-8-12** SDrowne(7) (hld up mid div: wknd over 2f out)	2½	12	33/1	51	7

				SP	RR	SF
2579[5]	**High Jinks** (BSmart) **2-8-12** SSanders(12) (lw: s.s: plld hrd: a bhd)	2	**13**	50/1	46	2
				(SP 130.1%)		**13 Rn**

1m 28.66 (2.66) CSF £39.78 TOTE £21.50: £4.10 £1.50 £1.80 (£54.20) Trio £36.20 OWNER Mr A. P. Griffin (WHITCOMBE) BRED Mrs C. A. Moore

Soviet Bureau (IRE), a half-sister to sprinter Sally Green and winning miler Jackatack, took a while to get the message, but eventually wore the favourite down. Highly regarded at home, he is the first colt his trainer has ever entered for the Derby. (14/1: 10/1-16/1)
2860 Dark Moondancer, a half-brother to Dances With Dreams, is out of an unraced daughter of Soba. He came up against a tartar in the winner if Miss Kelleway is to be believed. (2/1)
3022* Krispy Knight, predictably stepped up in trip, was by no means disgraced under his penalty in what was probably a hot race. (5/2)
2693 Close Up (IRE) seems to be progressing a long the right lines. (20/1)
2693 Santone (IRE) gave the impression that connections have nurseries in mind. (25/1)
Lear Spear (USA), a half-brother to a two-mile winner in Ireland, should be better for the experience. (33/1)
2829 Tumblweed Prospect (12/1: op 8/1)

3495 NEWPORT H'CAP (0-70) (3-Y.O+ F & M) (Class E)
4-45 (4-46) **1m 4f** £3,073.75 (£925.00: £447.50: £208.75) Stalls: High GOING minus 0.29 sec per fur (GF)

				SP	RR	SF
3234[2]	**Keepsake (IRE) (49)** (MDIUsher) **3-8-6** RStreet(7) (hld up in rr: gd hdwy 2f out: r.o to ld last strides)	—	**1**	11/2[2]	60	31
	Siberian Mystic (38) (PGMurphy) **4-8-6** SDrowne(4) (bit bkwd: hld up: stdy hdwy 3f out: led over 1f out: hdd last strides)	hd	**2**	13/2[3]	49	31
3234[8]	**Persian Blue (59)** (RHannon) **3-9-2** DaneO'Neill(8) (hld up & bhd: hdwy 2f out: ev ch ins fnl f: nt qckn)	1	**3**	10/1	69	40
3389[7]	**Curzon Street (67)** (DRCElsworth) **3-9-10** AProcter(9) (hld up in rr: hdwy 2f out: r.o ins fnl f)	¾	**4**	16/1	76	47
3134[9]	**Tart (FR) (54)** (JPearce) **4-9-8** NDay(1) (hld up: stdy hdwy over 3f out: ev ch 2f out: wknd over 1f out)	7	**5**	8/1	53	35
3298[W]	**Bathe In Light (USA) (59)** (LordHuntingdon) **3-9-2** LDettori(2) (lw: plld hrd early: a.p: led on bit wl over 2f out: hdd over 1f out: wknd fnl f)	4	**6**	6/4[1]	53	24
3183[6]	**Bint Rosie (40)** (MJFetherston-Godley) **3-7-11** FNorton(3) (led 1f: led over 3f out: hdd over 2f out: wknd over 1f out)	hd	**7**	33/1	34	5
2532[5]	**Arletty (67)** (HRACecil) **3-9-10** KFallon(10) (lw: prom tl wknd over 2f out)	10	**8**	8/1	47	18
3234[11]	**Bewitching Lady (48)** (DWPArbuthnot) **3-8-5** TSprake(6) (lw: prom tl wknd over 2f out)	s.h	**9**	20/1	28	—
2952[5]	**Certain Surprise (58)** (MMadgwick) **3-9-1** NVarley(11) (rdn 5f out: bhd fnl 3f: t.o)	10	**10**	33/1	25	—
3021[4]	**Savu Sea (IRE) (60)** (CFWall) **3-9-3** MTebbutt(5) (lw: led after 1f: hdd over 3f out: sn wknd: t.o)	16	**11**	12/1	6	—
				(SP 124.3%)		**11 Rn**

2m 36.55 (5.55) CSF £38.97 CT £324.74 TOTE £6.40: £1.70 £1.80 £2.70 (£56.20) Trio £83.20 OWNER Mr Trevor Barker (WANTAGE) BRED Rockville House Stud
WEIGHT FOR AGE 3yo-11lb

3234 Keepsake (IRE), up 3lb, again came from well off the pace but it was timed to perfection on this occasion. (11/2: 4/1-6/1)
Siberian Mystic, 5lb higher than when winning over a mile and quarter a year ago, last ran in May, over hurdles. He looked like landing a gamble until the winner arrived late on the scene. (13/2)
1465 Persian Blue was meeting the winner on 9lb better terms than when beaten just over eight lengths at Newmarket last time. (10/1)
1988 Curzon Street, a sister to In The Groove, proved she stays this sort of trip and could be ridden a bit closer to the pace in the future. (16/1)
2582 Tart (FR), supported in the ring, could not take advantage of a 6lb drop in the ratings. (8/1)
2782 Bathe In Light (USA), a well-backed favourite, did not appear to stay the mile and a half. (6/4: op 3/1)
2532 Arletty (8/1: 6/1-9/1)
3021 Savu Sea (IRE) (12/1: op 7/1)

T/Jkpt: Not won; £6,995.62 to Sandown 14/8/97. T/Plpt: £11.00 (1760 Tckts). T/Qdpt: £7.60 (141.58 Tckts) KH

3135-SANDOWN (R-H) (Rnd crse Good, Good to firm patches, St crse Good) Wednesday August 13th
WEATHER: hot WIND: almost nil

3496 SANDOWN EXHIBITION CENTRE APPRENTICE H'CAP (0-80) (3-Y.O+) (Class E)
5-45 (5-47) **1m 14y** £2,895.25 (£877.00: £428.50: £204.25) Stalls: High GOING minus 0.32 sec per fur (GF)

				SP	RR	SF
3153[9]	**Eurobox Boy (67)** (APJarvis) **4-8-12**(5) CCarver(2) (lw: chsd ldrs over 1f: rdn over 2f out: led ins fnl f: r.o wl)	—	**1**	10/1[3]	78	60
3135*	**Zamalek (USA) (46)** (RMFlower) **5-7-5**(5) JFowle(4) (swtg: a.p: led over 2f out tl ins fnl f: r.o)	hd	**2**	12/1	57	39
3236[3]	**Cherokee Flight (62)** (SMellor) **3-8-5** ADaly(5) (swtg: hld up: rdn over 2f out: r.o)	1	**3**	10/1[3]	80	46
2678[2]	**Therhea (IRE) (76)** (BRMillman) **4-9-12** GMilligan(10) (hdwy over 2f out: rdn over 1f out: r.o)	¾	**4**	7/2[1]	83	65
3248[4]	**Ca'd'oro (58)** (GBBalding) **4-8-5**(3) IonaWands(13) (lw: hdwy over 1f out: r.o)	½	**5**	11/2[2]	64	46
3091*	**Bakers Daughter (59)** (JRArnold) **5-8-9** GFaulkner(1) (swtg: led over 3f: rdn over 3f out: wknd fnl f)	2	**6**	14/1	61	43
3465[10]	**Fancy Design (IRE) (50)** (PMitchell) **4-8-0** AimeeCook(11) (b.hind: hdwy over 1f out: one pce ins fnl f)	1¼	**7**	25/1	50	32
3112[17]	**White Plains (IRE) (76)** (KRBurke) **4-9-12** RMullen(6) (swtg: hdwy over 2f out: wknd fnl f)	nk	**8**	16/1	75	57
3329[3]	**One In The Eye (46)** (JRPoulton) **4-7-5**(5) RBrisland(7) (nvr nrr)	1½	**9**	50/1	42	24
3328*	**Final Stab (IRE) (74)** (PWHarris) **4-9-10** 5x CLowther(3) (lw: chsd ldr over 6f out: led over 4f out tl over 2f out: wknd over 1f out)	nk	**10**	11/2[2]	70	52
3184[8]	**Soaking (48)** (MDIUsher) **7-7-7**(5)ow2 SCarson(14) (a bhd)	6	**11**	12/1	32	12
2492[3]	**Kafil (USA) (76)** (GLMoore) **3-9-0**(5)ow3 MBatchelor(8) (s.i.s: a bhd)	½	**12**	14/1	59	31
3153[8]	**Clouds Hill (FR) (54)** (RHannon) **4-7-13**(5) PDobbs(9) (swtg: mid div over 6f)	3	**13**	12/1	31	13
3227[17]	**Spencer's Revenge (53)** (PButler) **8-7-12**(5)ow1 GHannon(12) (s.i.s: a bhd)	13	**14**	33/1	4	—
				(SP 122.2%)		**14 Rn**

1m 42.73 (1.53) CSF £113.48 CT £756.17 TOTE £17.70: £4.50 £3.80 £2.80 (£108.80) Trio £404.40 OWNER Mr N. Coverdale (ASTON UPTHORPE) BRED G. Revitt
LONG HANDICAP One In The Eye 6-12
WEIGHT FOR AGE 3yo-7lb

3039 Eurobox Boy goes well for his young rider and, always handy, managed to get on top inside the final furlong to give the combination their third win of the year. (10/1)

3135* Zamalek (USA), whose three wins this year have all been over a mile and a quarter, coped with the drop in distance, and moved to the front before the quarter-mile pole. Collared inside the final furlong, he refused to give way and only just lost out. (12/1)
3236 Cherokee Flight chased the leaders, and stayed on up the hill if unable to trouble the front two. (10/1: 8/1-12/1)
2678 Therhea (IRE), a stone higher than when winning at Nottingham in June, has been in good heart since, but the ground was livelier than he would have liked, although he stayed on in the straight to finish on the heels of the principals. (7/2)
3248 Ca'd'oro began to pick up ground on the outside below the distance, but failed to get there in time. (11/2)
3091* Bakers Daughter, in front until the home turn, remained bang in contention until tiring in the final furlong. Her last three victories have all come over a mile and a quarter. (14/1)
3328* Final Stab (IRE) (11/2: 4/1-6/1)

3497 SURREY HERALD NOVICE MEDIAN AUCTION STKS (2-Y.O) (Class E)

6-15 (6-18) **5f 6y** £2,895.25 (£877.00: £428.50: £204.25) Stalls: High GOING: 0.06 sec per fur (G)

				SP	RR	SF
3094[3]	**Raise A King** (JWPayne) **2-8-12** GCarter(9) (hld up: qcknd to ld 1f out: comf)	—	1	7/4[1]	89+	31
3136[2]	**Storm Fromthe East** (RHannon) **2-8-12** PatEddery(8) (lw: led: hung bdly lft & hdd 1f out: unable qckn)	4	2	2/1[2]	76	18
2553[2]	**Loch Laird** (MMadgwick) **2-8-12** JReid(3) (a.p: rdn over 1f out: one pce)	1	3	9/2[3]	73	15
3131[2]	**Bandbox (IRE) (78)** (SMellor) **2-8-12** BDoyle(2) (lw: hld up: rdn over 2f out: one pce)	1¾	4	12/1	68	10
3136[4]	**Apple Sauce** (JRArnold) **2-8-7** CRutter(1) (lw: hdwy over 1f out: wknd fnl f)	4	5	20/1	50	—
3094[18]	**Oh So Easy** (BJMeehan) **2-8-9(3)** MartinDwyer(4) (lw: spd over 3f)	½	6	33/1	53	—
	Prince Oxley (GLMoore) **2-8-12** AClark(6) (str: scope: bit bkwd: a bhd)	3	7	20/1	44	—
3278[22]	**Southdown Cyrano (IRE)** (PButler) **2-8-12** JLowe(7) (bit bkwd: s.i.s: a bhd)	1	8	50/1	41	—
	Legal Lark (IRE) (PHowling) **2-8-12** PaulEddery(5) (w'like: bit bkwd: hld up: rdn over 2f out: sn wknd)	2	9	25/1	34	—
				(SP 113.8%)	**9 Rn**	

64.02 secs (4.22) CSF £4.46 TOTE £3.50: £1.10 £1.30 £1.30 (£2.50) Trio £2.10 OWNER Mr Marwan Tabsh (NEWMARKET) BRED Mrs A. E. Sigsworth

3094 Raise A King, a half-brother to the stable's former star Casteddu, was well backed and did not let his supporters down, showing a useful turn of foot to lead entering the final furlong, and sprinting right away for a decisive victory. (7/4)
3136 Storm Fromthe East was again the paddock pick, but he drifted ominously in the betting, and certainly gave Eddery some steering problems. Setting the pace against the far rails, he drifted towards the centre below the distance, allowing the winner a clear passage up the inner. Collared entering the final furlong, he failed to quicken and ended up in the middle of the track. He can find a race as long as these antics were a one-off. (2/1: evens-9/4)
2553 Loch Laird, a leading light from the off, failed to quicken in the last furlong and a half. (9/2)
3131 Bandbox (IRE), the most exposed in the field, was reverting to five furlongs, but failed to quicken from below the distance. A return to six would surely help. (12/1: 8/1-14/1)
3136 Apple Sauce, out with the washing in the early stages, picked up ground below the distance, but tired in the final furlong. (20/1)
Oh So Easy was in the firing line until tiring over a furlong out. (33/1)

3498 SURREY RACING H'CAP (0-90) (3-Y.O+) (Class C)

6-45 (6-45) **1m 6f** £5,204.00 (£1,577.00: £771.00: £368.00) Stalls: Low GOING minus 0.32 sec per fur (GF)

				SP	RR	SF
2475*	**Turgenev (IRE) (65)** (RBastiman) **8-8-3**ow1 SSanders(7) (chsd ldr 3f: chsd ldr 7f out: led over 2f out: clr 1f out: r.o wl)	—	1	10/1	76	45
2327[4]	**Siege Perilous (IRE) (70)** (SCWilliams) **4-8-5(3)** RFfrench(3) (swtg: hld up: rdn over 3f out: chsd wnr over 1f out: unable qckn)	3	2	7/2[2]	78	48
2944[3]	**Tappeto (73)** (HCandy) **5-8-11** CRutter(2) (hdwy over 1f out: r.o one pce)	¾	3	8/1	80	50
2230[W]	**Badge of Fame (IRE) (85)** (LMCumani) **3-8-10** LDettori(1) (chsd ldr 11f out to 7f out: rdn over 5f out: one pce)	½	4	5/2[1]	91	48
3333[3]	**Percy Isle (IRE) (82)** (MRStoute) **3-8-7** JReid(8) (led over 11f: one pce)	nk	5	6/1[3]	88	45
2865[4]	**My Learned Friend (79)** (AHide) **6-8-12(5)** RMullen(5) (hdwy over 2f out: hrd rdn: one pce)	1½	6	6/1[3]	83	53
3017[7]	**Woodren (USA) (88)** (RGuest) **4-9-12** RCochrane(4) (lw: hld up: rdn over 3f out: wknd over 2f out)	11	7	20/1	80	50
3122[7]	**Shining Dancer (62)** (SDow) **5-7-11(3)** MartinDwyer(6) (bhd fnl 3f)	2½	8	10/1	51	21
				(SP 113.4%)	**8 Rn**	

3m 2.05 (3.15) CSF £40.25 CT £269.67 TOTE £10.40: £2.00 £1.30 £2.00 (£15.70) OWNER Mrs Bridget Tranmer (WETHERBY) BRED Paolo Tomei

WEIGHT FOR AGE 3yo-13lb

2475* Turgenev (IRE) loves Haydock - five of his six previous wins have been there - and some cut in the ground but, despite not having conditions in his favour, still proved up to the task. Leading over a quarter of a mile out, he forged clear inside the last for a decisive victory. (10/1)
2327 Siege Perilous (IRE), only a pound higher than when winning here in June, moved into second place approaching the final furlong, but had no hope of reeling in the winner. (7/2)
2944 Tappeto began to pick up ground on the outside of the field below the distance, but did not look over-enthusiastic about the job in hand, although he struggled on for third. (8/1)
1846* Badge of Fame (IRE) was moving up in distance, but Dettori was already nudging the colt along turning out of the back straight. He was made to look very one-paced in the last three furlongs, and would probably not be inconvenienced by further. (5/2)
3333 Percy Isle (IRE) once again showed that he lacks acceleration for, after setting the pace, he was made to look woefully pedestrian when headed over two furlongs out. (6/1)
2865 My Learned Friend, taking another little step up in distance, moved up over a quarter of a mile out, but failed to find another gear in the closing stages. This trip could well be stretching him to the limit. (6/1)

3499 BERKELEY GROUP CONDITIONS STKS (3-Y.O+) (Class C)

7-15 (7-15) **1m 14y** £5,540.40 (£2,073.60: £1,014.30: £436.50: £195.75: £99.45) Stalls: High GOING minus 0.32 sec per fur (GF)

				SP	RR	SF
	Hirasah (IRE) (RWArmstrong) **3-8-2** RHills(1) (hld up: led over 1f out: rdn out)	—	1	20/1	103+	54
3214*	**Cape Cross (IRE) (110)** (JHMGosden) **3-9-1** LDettori(6) (b.hind: hld up: led 2f out tl over 1f out: ev ch ins fnl f: r.o)	nk	2	8/11[1]	115	66
1159[9]	**Crimson Tide (IRE) (105)** (JWHills) **3-8-7** MHills(4) (hld up: rdn over 1f out: ev ch ins fnl f: unable qckn)	2	3	11/2[3]	103	54
2446a[4]	**Keyboogie (USA) (96)** (RCharlton) **3-8-6** PatEddery(3) (swtg: chsd ldr: led 3f out to 2f out: wknd over 1f out)	5	4	7/2[2]	93	44

931[6] **Royal Crusade (USA)** (WJHaggas) **3-8-7** RCochrane(2) (plld hrd: led 5f: wknd wl over 1f out) 4 **5** 15/2 86 37
(SP 112.0%) **5 Rn**

1m 41.88 (0.68) CSF £33.52 TOTE £12.10: £3.00 £1.20 (£8.70) OWNER Mr Hamdan Al Maktoum (NEWMARKET) BRED Shadwell Estate Company Limited

Hirasah (IRE), off the course since winning a Newmarket maiden over a year ago, has had a lot of problems with her knees and joints, and has done most of her work in the swimming pool. Her trainer has found it difficult to find a race for her, and believes she will be best at six or seven furlongs. Nevertheless, she came through to show with a slender advantage approaching the final furlong, and just kept the very persistent runner-up at bay. Well-regarded at home, she looks up to listed or Group Three company. (20/1)

3214* Cape Cross (IRE), who had everything in his favour, gained control at the quarter-mile pole, but was headed below the distance. He rallied well inside the last, and only just lost out. (8/11: evens-6/5)

1159 Crimson Tide (IRE) made a very encouraging return after a three-month absence, and was one of three almost in line entering the final furlong before tapped for toe. Regarded as a high-class colt by his trainer, he should soon pick up a race, but this is his minimum trip according to his jockey. (11/2: 7/2-6/1)

2446a Keyboogie (USA), dropping back in distance, went for home early in the straight, but she was collared two furlongs out and faded out of contention. (7/2: 5/2-4/1)

931 Royal Crusade (USA), whose rider did very well to get him down to the start, was very anxious to get on with things, but Cochrane did all he could to restrain him. Headed three furlongs from home, he tried grimly to hold on, but a three-month break and his earlier exertions took their toll. Until he learns to settle he looks one to leave alone. (15/2: 5/1-8/1)

3500 HOME-START H'CAP (0-70) (3-Y.O+) (Class E)

7-45 (7-50) **5f 6y** £3,064.25 (£929.00: £454.50: £217.25) Stalls: High GOING: 0.06 sec per fur (G)

			SP	RR	SF
3126[6]	**Half Tone (56)** (RMFlower) **5-9-1b** DaneO'Neill(16) (a.p: led over 1f out: rdn out)	— **1**	3/1[1]	66	48
3327[10]	**Heavenly Miss (IRE) (52)** (JJBridger) **3-8-8b** KFallon(13) (swtg: squeezed out s: outpcd: gd hdwy over 1f out: squeezed thro on ins fnl f: fin wl)	hd **2**	14/1	62	41
3083[2]	**Bright Paragon (IRE) (42)** (KTIvory) **8-7-12**(3) MartinDwyer(7) (b: b.hind: hld up: rdn over 2f out: unable qckn)	2 **3**	12/1	45	27
3121[3]	**Suite Factors (56)** (KRBurke) **3-8-7**(5) CLowther(15) (swtg: led over 2f: edgd lft over 1f out: r.o one pce ins fnl f)	½ **4**	12/1	58	37
3126[15]	**Barranak (IRE) (65)** (GMMcCourt) **5-9-10** CRutter(14) (a.p: led over 2f out tl over 1f out: wknd ins fnl f)	½ **5**	10/1	65	47
3326[4]	**Dande Flyer (60)** (DWPArbuthnot) **4-9-2v**(3) RFfrench(8) (s.s: outpcd: hdwy over 1f out: r.o)	hd **6**	8/1	60	42
3040[4]	**Badrinath (IRE) (42)** (HJCollingridge) **3-7-7**(5)ow2 RMullen(5) (no hdwy fnl 2f)	1¼ **7**	66/1	38	15
3280[5]	**Dancing Mystery (45)** (EAWheeler) **3-7-8**(7) SCarson(17) (prom 3f)	nk **8**	15/2[3]	40	19
2332[11]	**Loganlea (IRE) (50)** (WJMusson) **3-8-6** DRMcCabe(6) (lw: outpcd: hdwy & hmpd over 1f out: nt rcvr)	½ **9**	33/1	43	22
3126[13]	**Mindrace (62)** (KTIvory) **4-9-7** RCochrane(10) (prom 3f)	1½ **10**	9/1	51	33
3287[2]	**Lady Caroline Lamb (IRE) (60)** (RBastiman) **4-9-0**(5) HBastiman(12) (swtg: hld up: rdn over 2f out: wknd over 1f out)	2½ **11**	4/1[2]	41	23
3126[10]	**Sharp Stock (55)** (RJHodges) **4-9-0** BDoyle(9) (swtg: bhd fnl 2f)	¾ **12**	16/1	33	15
3326[7]	**Jucea (66)** (JLSpearing) **8-9-11** SDrowne(2) (lw: a bhd)	2½ **13**	25/1	36	18
45[5]	**Incatime (65)** (AGFoster) **3-9-7** TSprake(4) (swtg: a bhd)	2½ **14**	40/1	27	6
			(SP 125.6%) **14 Rn**		

63.13 secs (3.33) CSF £44.14 CT £435.84 TOTE £4.80: £1.90 £2.60 £3.80 (£38.60) Trio £117.20 OWNER Mrs G. M. Temmerman (JEVINGTON) BRED T. M. Jennings

LONG HANDICAP Badrinath (IRE) 6-12

WEIGHT FOR AGE 3yo-3lb

IN-FOCUS: **Once again the draw had a huge effect, with four of the first five drawn thirteen or higher.**

3126 Half Tone, winner of this race last year off a 6lb lower mark, was blessed with an excellent draw and, striking the front below the distance, soon put daylight between himself and his rivals. This proved very useful, for with the runner-up finishing really fast, he found the line only just coming in time. (3/1: op 5/1)

2921 Heavenly Miss (IRE), unable to go the early pace, made giant strides through the field below the distance and, squeezing through inside the final furlong, may well have prevailed in a couple of strides. (14/1)

3083 Bright Paragon (IRE) chased the leaders but failed to find another gear in the last furlong and a half. (12/1)

3121 Suite Factors, in front to halfway, looked like dropping away below the distance, but stayed on again up the hill. He is not easy to win with, and his record now stands at one win from twenty-eight starts. (12/1)

3032 Barranak (IRE) went on at halfway, but he was collared below the distance, and soon beaten. (10/1: 8/1-12/1)

3326 Dande Flyer, unable to go the early pace, stayed on from below the distance to be nearest at the line. He is on a long losing run, having not won for nearly two years. (8/1)

3501 GO EVENING RACING WITH THE DAILY TELEGRAPH MAIDEN STKS (3-Y.O+) (Class D)

8-15 (8-22) **1m 2f 7y** £3,533.75 (£1,070.00: £522.50: £248.75) Stalls: High GOING minus 0.32 sec per fur (GF)

			SP	RR	SF
3014[2]	**Shaya (92)** (MajorWRHern) **3-8-12** RHills(4) (lw: hld up: led 2f out: hrd rdn over 1f out: r.o wl)	— **1**	11/8[1]	82	26
1103[3]	**Basman (IRE) (102)** (BSmart) **3-8-12** RCochrane(2) (lw: plld hrd: chsd ldr: rdn & ev ch 2f out: r.o one pce ins fnl f)	1½ **2**	11/8[1]	80	24
3021[7]	**Serpentara** (HRACecil) **3-8-7** KFallon(6) (lw: rdn over 2f out: swtchd lft & outpcd 2f out: rallied fnl f: r.o one pce)	hd **3**	7/2[2]	74	18
	Maenad (DJSffrenchDavis) **6-9-2** MTebbutt(3) (led 8f: wknd fnl f)	4 **4**	50/1	68	21
3277[8]	**Classic Fan (USA)** (MRChannon) **3-8-4**(3) PPMurphy(5) (lw: a bhd)	1¾ **5**	25/1[3]	65	9
3277[11]	**Versatility** (RFJohnsonHoughton) **4-9-2** SSanders(1) (a bhd)	1 **6**	33/1	64	17
			(SP 115.2%) **6 Rn**		

2m 12.48 (5.78) CSF £3.24 TOTE £2.70: £1.40 £1.60 (£1.90) OWNER Mr Hamdan Al Maktoum (LAMBOURN) BRED Shadwell Estate Company Limited

WEIGHT FOR AGE 3yo-9lb

3014 Shaya at last had his day after four seconds. Striking the front two furlongs out, he carried his head a little high but, responding to pressure, soon asserted. He maymm prove difficult to place, and a step-up to a mile and a half will surely help. (11/8)

1103 Basman (IRE), off the course since finishing third in the Lingfield Derby Trial in May, took a keen hold racing in second place. One of three in line at the quarter-mile pole, he was then tapped for toe, but stayed on again in the closing stages. This was a slightly disappointing display. (11/8)

3021 Serpentara, outpaced as the real race developed, stayed on up the hill and only just failed to gain second place. (7/2)

Maenad, a tall mare who has shown nothing over hurdles and only moderate form in bumpers, took the field along. Collared a quarter of a mile out, she was only brushed aside in the final furlong. (50/1)

T/Plpt: £83.20 (252.45 Tckts). T/Qdpt: £7.70 (175.98 Tckts) AK

3502a - 3505a (Irish Racing) - See Computer Raceform

0273a-LEOPARDSTOWN (Dublin, Ireland) (L-H) (Yielding)
Monday August 4th

3506a CORK STKS (Listed) (2-Y.O)
2-20 (2-24) **5f** IR £11,287.50 (IR £3,237.50: IR £1,487.50: IR £437.50) GOING minus 0.01 sec per fur (G)

				SP	RR	SF
2054[2]	**Hopping Higgins (IRE)** (APO'Brien,Ireland) **2-8-7** MJKinane (mde all: pushed clr fnl f)	—	**1**	4/6[1]	95+	36
1531a[8]	**Law Library (IRE)** (JSBolger,Ireland) **2-8-10** KJManning (prom: rdn 1½f out: kpt on: nt trble wnr)	3½	**2**	3/1[2]	87	28
	Maduka (IRE) (JSBolger,Ireland) **2-8-7** SCraine (chsd ldrs: no imp over 1f out: styd on ins fnl f)	1	**3**	7/1[3]	81	22
1880a[5]	**Dress Design (IRE)** (JMuldoon,Ireland) **2-8-7** PJSmullen (chsd ldrs: rdn under 2f out: sn btn)	3½	**4**	7/1[3]	69	12
2987a[7]	**Musical Myth (USA)** (JGBurns,Ireland) **2-8-7** WJSupple (a bhd: no imp last 1½f)	2	**5**	20/1	63	6
				(SP 114.8%)		**5 Rn**

60.7 secs (3.20) OWNER Sporting Quest Racing Club (PILTOWN)

2054 Hopping Higgins (IRE), over what is probably her optimum trip, had an easy task and was able to dominate throughout. (4/6)
Law Library (IRE) could make no impression on the winner throughout the last two furlongs, and is not a bad performer in his own class. (3/1: op 2/1)
Maduka (IRE), ridden along in third place over a furlong out, was toiling until finding a surge near the end. (7/1)
Dress Design (IRE) looked quite one-paced from a furlong and a half out and her future probably lies in nurseries. (7/1)

3507a (Irish Racing) - See Computer Raceform

3508a JOE MCGRATH H'CAP (0-105) (3-Y.O+)
3-20 (3-21) **6f** IR £13,500.00 (IR £3,800.00: IR £1,800.00: IR £600.00) GOING minus 0.01 sec per fur (G)

				SP	RR	SF
	Norwegian Blue (IRE) (MBrassil,Ireland) **4-7-12** JoannaMorgan (in tch far side: effrt 1½f out: led early fnl f: kpt on)	—	**1**	10/1	84	28
2900[10]	**Zuhair** (DMcCain) **4-8-10** WJSupple (sn led centre: rdn 2f out: hdd early fnl f: kpt on u.p)	¾	**2**	10/1	94	37
2815a[8]	**Best Before Dawn (IRE)** (APO'Brien,Ireland) **6-9-2**(8) ATKelly (sn cl up towards far side: 2nd ½-wy: led briefly early fnl f: no ex last 150y)	¾	**3**	7/1[2]	106	48
	Maratana (IRE) (EJKearnsJnr,Ireland) **3-7-10**(6)ow6 JPSpencer (bhd: rdn over 2f out: swtchd rt & r.o wl far rail last 1½f: nrst fin)	hd	**4**	14/1	88	28
	Poker-B (IRE) (DGillespie,Ireland) **3-8-10** JPMurtagh (led stands' side: rdn 2f out: no imp on ldrs fr over 1f out)	2½	**5**	6/1[1]	89	29
	Silly Imp (IRE) (JSBolger,Ireland) **3-7-3**(8)ow1 BAHunter (bhd: r.o u.p last 1½f: nvr nrr)	1½	**6**	8/1[3]	72	13
2815a*	**Nakayama Express (IRE)** (JGCoogan,Ireland) **4-8-7b**(2) EAhern (bhd: rdn after 2f: kpt on u.p fr 2f out: n.d)	hd	**7**	7/1[2]	80	24
2815a[9]	**Sunset Reigns (IRE)** (JSBolger,Ireland) **4-9-9** KJManning (prom towards stands' side 4f)	5	**8**	8/1[3]	81	25
	Tinker Amelia (JGMcDonnell,Ireland) **5-7-2**(8) GDPower (cl up centre crse: rdn over 2f out: no imp last 1½f)	s.h	**9**	12/1	53	—
	Diligent Dodger (IRE) (KPrendergast,Ireland) **6-8-7** SCraine (chsd ldrs: lost pl ½-wy: sn n.d)	¾	**10**	6/1[1]	62	8
2815a[4]	**Symboli Kildare (IRE)** (JOxx,Ireland) **4-8-10b**(10) LisaO'Neill (chsd ldrs centre crse: effrt 2f out: sn btn)	½	**11**	8/1[3]	74	19
	Blushing Minstrel (IRE) (JCHarley,Ireland) **3-7-12** RMBurke (chsd ldrs stands' side: rdn ½-wy: bhd & n.d last 2f)	20	**12**	12/1	3	—
				(SP 127.1%)		**12 Rn**

1m 14.6 (3.90) OWNER Ambrose Turnbull (DUNMURRAY) BRED Martyn J. McEnery

Norwegian Blue (IRE), always in the forefront but under a restrained ride, challenged over a furlong out and stayed on well under pressure. (10/1)
2711 Zuhair, up with the pace throughout, was headed a furlong out and looked like dropping away, but he came back with a sustained run near the finish. (10/1)
2815a Best Before Dawn (IRE) is not really the ride for an inexperienced apprentice, but acquitted himself well here after getting to the front a furlong out. (7/1)
Maratana (IRE) finished well after doing a bit of wandering. (14/1)
Poker-B (IRE) is just too high in the handicap. (6/1)
Silly Imp (IRE) kept on under pressure and appears to need further. (8/1)
2815a Symboli Kildare (IRE) (8/1: op 5/1)

3509a (Irish Racing) - See Computer Raceform

3510a BROWNSTOWN STUD STKS (Listed) (3-Y.O+ F & M)
4-20 (4-24) **1m** IR £12,900.00 (IR £3,700.00: IR £1,700.00: IR £500.00) GOING: 0.42 sec per fur (GS)

				SP	RR	SF
2441a[3]	**Inchacooley (IRE)** (MBrassil,Ireland) **5-9-3** EAhern (hld up in tch: 3rd st: swtchd rt & effrt over 1f out: qcknd to ld ins fnl f: r.o wl)	—	**1**	7/1[3]	100+	38
	Khatara (IRE) (JOxx,Ireland) **3-8-10** JPMurtagh (disp ld: w.w: led over 1f out: hdd & no ex ins fnl f)	2½	**2**	9/10[1]	95	27
2814a[7]	**Via Verbano (IRE)** (JSBolger,Ireland) **3-8-10** KJManning (rn 5th: w.w: rdn & no imp 2f out: r.o. fnl f)	1	**3**	5/2[2]	93	26
2816a[5]	**Ministerial Model (IRE)** (APO'Brien,Ireland) **3-8-10** WJSupple (disp ld tl over 1f out: sn btn)	1½	**4**	14/1	90	23
1193a[2]	**Welsh Queen (IRE)** (TStack,Ireland) **3-8-10** PJSmullen (hld up in rr: rdn ent st: kpt on: n.d)	5½	**5**	10/1	79	14
	Society Fair (FR) (MBrassil,Ireland) **4-9-3** SCraine (trckd ldrs: no imp fr over 2f out: wknd over 1f out)	3½	**6**	20/1	72	14
	Desert Ease (IRE) (DKWeld,Ireland) **3-9-2** MJKinane (in tch: rdn & lost pl ent st: sn bhd: eased: t.o)	20	**7**	11/1	38	—
				(SP 122.6%)		**7 Rn**

1m 46.5 (9.50) OWNER P. J. Hyland (DUNMURRAY)

2441a Inchacooley (IRE) successfully made the transition from a handicapper to listed-class performer, with a good effort here. She was been busy in recent weeks, and to win this with such apparent ease suggests she is still improving. (7/1)
Khatara (IRE) has a big home reputation but failed to live up to it here. (9/10)

2814a Via Verbano (IRE) let her consistency carry her into a never-threatening third place. (5/2: op 6/4)
Ministerial Model (IRE) shared the pace with the favourite but weakened quite tamely a furlong out. (14/1)
Desert Ease (IRE) (11/1: op 6/1)

3511a CHALLENGE STKS (Listed) (3-Y.O+)
4-50 (4-52) **1m 6f** IR £12,900.00 (IR £3,700.00: IR £1,700.00: IR £500.00) GOING: 0.42 sec per fur (GS)

				SP	RR	SF
2814a5	**Family Tradition (IRE)** (APO'Brien,Ireland) **3-8-5b** MJKinane (hld up: 4th & clsd st: rdn to chal: styd on u.p to ld nr fin)	—	1	2/1 1	107+	49
2814a9	**Aliya (IRE)** (JOxx,Ireland) **3-8-5** PJSmullen (hld up: 3rd 4f out: chal early st: led over 1f out: hdd u.p nr fin)	nk	2	3/1 3	107	49
2446a6	**Sadlers Home (IRE)** (JSBolger,Ireland) **3-8-5b** JoannaMorgan (rn 2nd: jnd ldr st: hdd u.p over 1f out: no ex: one pce)	5½	3	12/1	100	43
	Mohaajir (USA) (JSBolger,Ireland) **6-9-12** KJManning (led: rdn & jnd st: hdd & no ex over 1f out: wknd)	6	4	11/4 2	102	57
2989a2	**Carnelly (IRE)** (DHanley,Ireland) **3-8-5** WJSmith (hld up: 4th & rdn 4f out: no imp over 2f out)	hd	5	5/1	93	37
				(SP 109.4%)		**5 Rn**

3m 10.1 (13.10) OWNER Mrs John Magnier (PILTOWN)
2814a Family Tradition (IRE), weak in the market, owes this one to Kinane's strength. He practically lifted her up to lead close home. (2/1: op Evens)
2814a Aliya (IRE) looked to have things sewn up over a furlong out, but failed to find anything extra under pressure close home. (3/1)
1698a Sadlers Home (IRE) will have to drop back to handicap company. (12/1)
Mohaajir (USA) badly needed this, his first of the season. (11/4)

3512a - 3533a (Irish Racing) - See Computer Raceform

0378a-LEOPARDSTOWN (Dublin, Ireland) (L-H) (Good to yielding)
Sunday August 10th

3534a HEINZ 57 PHOENIX STKS (Gp 1) (2-Y.O C & F)
3-20 (3-22) **6f** IR £86,000.00 (IR £29,000.00: IR £14,000.00: IR £5,000.00) GOING minus 0.28 sec per fur (GF)

				SP	RR	SF
2811a3	**Princely Heir (IRE)** (MJohnston) **2-9-0** JWeaver (rn 2nd: chsd ldr: rdn to chal fr 2f out: led early fnl f: r.o u.p)	—	1	12/1	104	59
2558*	**Asfurah (USA)** (SbinSuroor) **2-8-11** LDettori (in tch: 4th ½-wy: 3rd & chsd ldrs 1½f out: r.o wl ins last)	hd	2	15/8 1	101	56
2012*	**Harbour Master (FR)** (APO'Brien,Ireland) **2-9-0b** CRoche (chsd ldrs early: 7th ½-wy: 8th u.p & hdwy under 2f out: r.o. ins last)	1½	3	9/4 2	100	55
3506a*	**Hopping Higgins (IRE)** (APO'Brien,Ireland) **2-8-11** WJSupple (led tl early ins last: no ex)	½	4	8/1 3	95	50
	Tarascon (IRE) (TStack,Ireland) **2-8-11** PJSmullen (towards rr early: 6th ½-wy: rdn & nt rch ldrs over 1f out: kpt on ins last)	1½	5	14/1	91	46
25584	**Danyross (IRE)** (APO'Brien,Ireland) **2-8-11b1** KJManning (dwlt & hmpd start: trailing early: hdwy to 5th over 2f out: 4th u.p 1½f out: sn btn)	4	6	12/1	81	36
2987a*	**Flame Violet (IRE)** (APO'Brien,Ireland) **2-8-11** MJKinane (in tch: 5th ½-wy: rdn & nt trble ldrs over 1½f out)	1	7	9/1	78	33
1880a3	**Attractive Crown (USA)** (KPrendergast,Ireland) **2-8-11** SCraine (chsd ldrs: towards rr & rdn ½-wy: no imp fr 2f out)	2½	8	14/1	71	26
25843	**Pool Music** (RHannon) **2-9-0** RHughes (chsd ldrs: 3rd ½-wy: sn rdn: btn & wknd 1½f out)	1½	9	8/1 3	70	25
				(SP 126.5%)		**9 Rn**

1m 11.8 (1.10) OWNER Maktoum Al Maktoum (MIDDLEHAM) BRED Gainsborough Stud Management Ltd
STEWARDS' ENQUIRY Weaver susp. 19-22/8/97 (excessive use of whip).
2811a Princely Heir (IRE), coltish in the preliminaries, was under pressure and chasing the leader hard with two furlongs to race, and did not seem to be enjoying the ground. Leading well inside the last, he showed plenty of determination to just hold on. Weaver hit him fifteen times in all and was handed a four-day ban. He is tough, but definitely needs some give in the ground to help him along. (12/1: op 8/1)
2558* Asfurah (USA) managed to keep in touch but looked in trouble in third place with two furlongs to race. She knuckled down to it inside the last, and ran on well without ever looking likely to get there. (15/8)
2012* Harbour Master (FR) was soon being chased along. He lost his place under pressure after halfway and had only one behind him two furlongs out. The inside was his all the way however, and he ran on strongly inside the last to go third close home. The Prix de la Salamandre may be his next target. (9/4)
3506a* Hopping Higgins (IRE) took them along at a scorching pace but, headed well inside the last, she will be well suited by a return to five furlongs. (8/1)
Tarascon (IRE) appeared to run free early on and, a little one-paced two furlongs out, ran on under pressure to be nearest at the finish. (14/1)
2558 Danyross (IRE) never got into a challenging position. (12/1: op 7/1)
2987a* Flame Violet (IRE) was absolutely no threat from two furlongs out. (9/1: op 6/1)
1880a Attractive Crown (USA) was in last place with two furlongs to race. (14/1)
2584 Pool Music was completely outpaced from halfway. (8/1)

3535a PHOENIX SPRINT STKS (Gp 3) (3-Y.O+)
3-55 (3-56) **6f** IR £19,500.00 (IR £5,700.00: IR £2,700.00: IR £900.00) GOING minus 0.28 sec per fur (GF)

				SP	RR	SF
32524	**Cretan Gift** (NPLittmoden) **6-9-0b** JWeaver (dwlt: sn trailing: rdn & hdwy 2f out: mod 2nd u.p early ins last: kpt on to ld 50y fr fin)	—	1	10/1	108	53
259815	**Azizzi** (CREgerton) **5-9-0** RHughes (sn led: clr 2f out: no ex u.p ins last: hdd 50y fr fin)	2	2	8/1	103	48
2815a5	**Ailleacht (USA)** (JSBolger,Ireland) **5-8-11** KJManning (cl up: 4th u.p over 2f out: no imp over 1f out: kpt on same pce)	3½	3	9/2 3	90	35
1186a*	**Carhue Lass (IRE)** (PO'Leary,Ireland) **3-8-7** NGMcCullagh (prom: sn chsng ldr: rdn & no ex 1½f out)	1½	4	14/1	86	27
3118*	**Abou Zouz (USA)** (DRLoder) **3-9-3** LDettori (cl up early: 5th ½-wy: rdn & no imp 2f out)	s.h	5	7/2 2	96	37
25863	**Theano (IRE)** (APO'Brien,Ireland) **4-8-11** CRoche (sn cl up: 3rd ½-wy: 2nd, rdn & nt trble wnr over 1f out: no ex: lame)	nk	6	5/4 1	85	30
				(SP 111.7%)		**6 Rn**

1m 12.2 (1.50) OWNER T. Clarke (WOLVERHAMPTON) BRED Hesmonds Stud Ltd

3252 Cretan Gift, a 98-rated handicapper, made a nonsense of the Irish pattern. He came out of the stalls slowly and gave them all plenty of start until beginning to make headway with a furlong and a half to race. He ran on with real gusto under pressure to lead fifty yards out. What the BHB Handicapper makes of this will be interesting to see. (10/1: op 6/1)
2329 Azizzi took them along until outpaced by the winner. This appeared another much-improved performance by a handicapper. (8/1)
2815a Ailleacht (USA), in touch on the outside, was being ridden along and finding nothing from two furlongs out. (9/2: op 3/1)
1186a* Carhue Lass (IRE) was always on her head trying to go the pace. (14/1: op 8/1)
3118* Abou Zouz (USA) tracked the leaders but was in trouble from halfway. (7/2)
2586 Theano (IRE) looked a bit unbalanced when she came out, but never got in any sort of a challenge and appeared to be lame afterwards. (5/4)

3536a - 3539a (Irish Racing) - See Computer Raceform

3476-BEVERLEY (R-H) (Good to soft, Soft patches)
Thursday August 14th
WEATHER: sunny WIND: slt half against

3540 TOLL GAVEL (S) H'CAP (0-60) (3-Y.O+) (Class E)
2-00 (2-00) **2m 35y** £2,994.00 (£897.00: £431.00: £198.00) Stalls: High GOING: 0.09 sec per fur (G)

				SP	RR	SF
2539[6]	**Selmeston (IRE) (40)** (SCWilliams) **5-9-0** DHolland(13) (lw: led after 5f: qcknd 4f out: hld on wl)	—	1	8/1	54	20
2874[2]	**Brodessa (54)** (MrsMReveley) **11-9-9**(5) SCopp(5) (lw: hdwy 10f out: sn cl up: effrt 3f out: r.o one pce)	1½	2	4/1 2	67	33
3461[4]	**Ship's Dancer (24)** (DonEnricoIncisa) **4-7-12b** KimTinkler(1) (lw: hld up & bhd: gd hdwy 3f out: sn chsng ldrs: one pce fnl f)	6	3	7/1	31	—
2518[2]	**Liathach (30)** (JRFanshawe) **6-8-4**ow1 DHarrison(8) (prom: hdwy & ev ch 5f out: wknd fnl 2½f)	4	4	9/2 3	33	—
3317[8]	**Sushi Bar (IRE) (39)** (MrsMReveley) **6-8-13** KDarley(12) (lw: a chsng ldrs: outpcd 3f out: no imp after)	3½	5	7/2 1	38	4
2362[2]	**Junior Ben (IRE) (32)** (MESowersby) **5-7-13**(7) NPollard(6) (hdwy ½-wy: sn chsng ldrs: rdn 3f out: sn wknd)	½	6	16/1	31	—
3330[3]	**Bold Top (44)** (BSRothwell) **5-9-4v** MFenton(4) (lw: outpcd & bhd: sme hdwy 3f out: n.d)	4	7	12/1	39	5
2874[13]	**Kindred Greeting (22)** (JO'Reilly) **5-7-10b** JO'Reilly(7) (b.hind: cl up tl wknd 7f out)	15	8	20/1	2	—
2910[13]	**El Nido (40)** (DWChapman) **9-9-0** LCharnock(11) (led 3f: lost tch ½-wy)	1½	9	33/1	18	—
3284*	**Forzair (54)** (JJO'Neill) **5-10-0** 4x JCarroll(3) (led after 3f tl after 5f: cl up tl rdn & wknd over 3f out)	1¾	10	12/1	31	—
3291[6]	**Impetuous Lady (USA) (25)** (WJMusson) **4-7-13** JQuinn(9) (hld up & a bhd)	25	11	14/1	—	—
3308[3]	**Kulepopsie (IRE) (44)** (ABMulholland) **4-9-4** JFortune(10) (prom tl outpcd 6f out: sn lost tch: t.o)	dist	12	14/1	—	—
				(SP 126.3%)	**12 Rn**	

3m 48.6 (18.10) CSF £38.89 CT £224.97 TOTE £10.50: £2.50 £1.60 £2.40 (£28.40) Trio £65.20 OWNER Mr Chris Wright (NEWMARKET) BRED St Simon Foundation
LONG HANDICAP Kindred Greeting 7-8
No bid
2539 Selmeston (IRE), after disappointing last time, has had a rest and was back to his best here. (8/1)
2874 Brodessa, 3lb lower than when winning this last year but, despite another gallant effort, he was never quite good enough and a stronger pace would certainly have suited him better. (4/1: 3/1-9/2)
3461 Ship's Dancer, for the second time in a week, showed an amazing turn of foot early in the straight but it only seems to last for two furlongs and perhaps this trip is just stretching her stamina. (7/1)
2518 Liathach had his chances but he either ran out of stamina or something went wrong as his rider seemed to be looking down approaching the final furlong. (9/2: op 5/2)
3317 Sushi Bar (IRE) has lost the plot for the time being but is probably happier on faster ground. (7/2)
2362 Junior Ben (IRE) has yet to win a race and he proved well short of pace here. (16/1)

3541 E.B.F. WESTWOOD MAIDEN STKS (2-Y.O F) (Class D)
2-30 (2-30) **5f** £3,548.00 (£1,064.00: £512.00: £236.00) Stalls: High GOING: 0.09 sec per fur (G)

				SP	RR	SF
3239[4]	**Fizzed** (MJohnston) **2-8-11** JWeaver(5) (lw: chsd ldrs: hrd rdn to ld ins fnl f: styd on wl)	—	1	2/1 2	84	43
2024[11]	**Folklore (90)** (DRLoder) **2-8-11** KDarley(1) (lw: led tl hdd & no ex ins fnl f)	2	2	4/5 1	78	37
3114[7]	**Lady From Limerick (IRE)** (JBerry) **2-8-8**(3) TEDurcan(4) (swtg: chsd ldrs: rdn ½-wy: no imp after)	4	3	12/1	65	24
3239[9]	**Stately Favour** (MJCamacho) **2-8-11** LCharnock(2) (lw: outpcd tl hdwy 2f out: nt qckn fnl f)	s.h	4	14/1	65	24
2467[2]	**Opopmil (IRE)** (TDEasterby) **2-8-11** WJO'Connor(3) (w ldr tl wknd appr fnl f)	2	5	9/1 3	58	17
2881[10]	**Priolette (IRE)** (JGFitzGerald) **2-8-11** JFortune(6) (sn pushed along & n.d)	1¼	6	33/1	54	13
2728[15]	**Ghorapani (IRE)** (MrsNMacauley) **2-8-11v** DHarrison(7) (nvr wnt pce)	3	7	33/1	45	4
				(SP 119.1%)	**7 Rn**	

65.5 secs (3.70) CSF £3.80 TOTE £3.00: £1.40 £1.20 (£1.90) OWNER Duke of Roxburghe (MIDDLEHAM) BRED D. A. and Mrs Hicks
STEWARDS' ENQUIRY Weaver susp. 23 & 25-27/8/97 (excessive use of whip).
3239 Fizzed knew more about it this time and won well but, in doing so, did have a hard race. (2/1)
1653 Folklore has a poor action which was suited to this softish ground but, after setting the race up, she had nothing in reserve when tackled and this is as good as she is. (4/5: op 6/4)
1749 Lady From Limerick (IRE), a rather warm individual, was taken off her legs at halfway, suggesting that this trip is well short of her best. (12/1: op 8/1)
Stately Favour, a handy sort, was very stuffy in the early stages but did show a little ability without offering a threat. (14/1)
2467 Opopmil (IRE) goes in the ground and has plenty of early pace but, judging by the way she stopped, she may well have needed this after six weeks off. (9/1: 5/1-10/1)

3542 RAPID LAD H'CAP (0-90) (3-Y.O+) (Class C)
3-05 (3-06) **1m 1f 207y** £5,475.00 (£1,650.00: £800.00: £375.00) Stalls: High GOING: 0.09 sec per fur (G)

				SP	RR	SF
3380*	**Eshtiaal (USA) (89)** (JLDunlop) **3-9-5b** 5x KDarley(1) (lw: shkn up to ld after 1f: pushed out)	—	1	Evens 1	100	55
3112[15]	**Hazard a Guess (IRE) (81)** (DNicholls) **7-9-6** AlexGreaves(8) (lw: hld up: hdwy over 2f out: sn chsng ldrs: nt qckn ins fnl f)	1¾	2	9/2 2	89	53
3466[3]	**Monte Cavo (58)** (MBrittain) **6-7-11** GBardwell(2) (led 1f: a chsng ldrs: hdwy 2f out: nt qckn fnl f)	nk	3	10/1	66	30
2292[2]	**Billy Bushwacker (89)** (MrsMReveley) **6-9-9**(5) SCopp(7) (dwlt: effrt & n.m.r over 2f out: one pce appr fnl f)	3½	4	9/2 2	91	55

2328[11] **Sandbaggedagain (77)** (MWEasterby) **3-8-4**(3) GParkin(5) (cl up tl wknd 2f out)..3 **5** 20/1 74 29
3135[2] **Traceability (80)** (SCWilliams) **4-9-5** JCarroll(4) (lw: cl up tl wknd fnl 2f) ....nk **6** 11/2[3] 77 41
(SP 115.6%) **6 Rn**

2m 9.9 (6.80) CSF £5.67 CT £25.63 TOTE £1.90: £1.50 £2.10 (£6.70) OWNER Mr Hamdan Al Maktoum (ARUNDEL) BRED Shadwell Farm Inc and Shadwell Estate Co Ltd
WEIGHT FOR AGE 3yo-9lb
3380* Eshtiaal (USA) has been a revelation since being fitted with the blinkers and, as long as he can dominate, he will take some stopping. (Evens)
2890 Hazard a Guess (IRE) had the race run to suit him but, despite a gallant effort, he was never good enough. This was a much more encouraging run after a poor effort last time. (9/2)
3466 Monte Cavo goes in the ground and had his chances, but his limitations were exposed late on. (10/1: 8/1-12/1)
2292 Billy Bushwacker last one a race over two years ago and is still 7lb higher. (9/2)
2015 Sandbaggedagain, having his first run for almost seven weeks, showed he has the ability if he can be persuaded. (20/1)
3135 Traceability likes to be up with the pace but, off a mark 8lb higher than he has previously won off, he was found out in the closing stages here. He was most likely not helped by the soft ground. (11/2)

3543 CHARLES ELSEY MEMORIAL CHALLENGE TROPHY H'CAP (0-80) (3-Y.O+) (Class D)
3-35 (3-37) **2m 35y** £3,873.00 (£1,164.00: £562.00: £261.00) Stalls: High GOING: 0.09 sec per fur (G)

SP RR SF
3020* **Lady of The Lake (77)** (JLDunlop) **3-9-1** KDarley(9) (trckd ldrs: effrt 3f out: rdn to ld ins fnl f: styd on)...........— **1** 9/2[2] 88 48
3383[5] **Jamaican Flight (USA) (65)** (MrsSLamyman) **4-9-4** JFortune(7) (led tl hdd ins fnl f: kpt on wl) 1 **2** 14/1 75 50
3309[11] **Swiftway (58)** (KWHogg) **3-7-10** LCharnock(8) (cl up: racd far side st: kpt on)...3 **3** 14/1 65 25
3309[3] **Dirab (61)** (TDBarron) **4-8-9**(5) KimberleyHart(3) (hld up & bhd: stdy hdwy 4f out: shkn up 2f out: nt pce to chal) ....1 **4** 100/30[1] 67 42
3309[4] **Amiarge (46)** (MBrittain) **7-7-13b** GBardwell(10) (lw: prom: drvn along 4f out: no imp after) 3 **5** 10/1 49 24
3283[3] **Dancing Cavalier (65)** (RHollinshead) **4-8-11**(7) PFredericks(5) (b.off hind: bhd: hdwy u.p ent st: sn btn).......25 **6** 7/1[3] 43 18
3242[5] **Lindrick Lady (IRE) (67)** (BSRothwell) **3-8-5** MFenton(1) (chsd ldrs tl wknd fnl 3f)..6 **7** 12/1 39 —
3440* **Star Rage (IRE) (80)** (MJohnston) **7-10-5** 5x JWeaver(6) (lw: prom tl outpcd over 2f out: sn wknd)...................8 **8** 100/30[1] 45 20
3309[8] **Batoutoftheblue (45)** (WWHaigh) **4-7-12** JQuinn(2) (lw: hld up & bhd: lost tch & rdn ½-wy: sn btn & eased) dist **9** 7/1[3] — —
(SP 119.5%) **9 Rn**

3m 42.6 (12.10) CSF £61.06 CT £753.36 TOTE £4.90: £2.40 £3.90 £4.30 (£40.20) Trio £302.90 OWNER Capt J. Macdonald-Buchanan (ARUNDEL) BRED The Lavington Stud
LONG HANDICAP Swiftway 7-9
WEIGHT FOR AGE 3yo-15lb
3020* Lady of The Lake stays particularly well and even longer trips should see further improvement. (9/2: 3/1-5/1)
3383 Jamaican Flight (USA) won his only previous race on the Flat over this course and distance and ran his best race for some time here. (14/1)
2908 Swiftway ran well and looks to be coming to form. (14/1)
3309 Dirab is off a useful mark and put in a decent run, and looks one to keep on the right side of. (100/30)
3309 Amiarge is a good, honest stayer but is basically short of pace, and this strongly-run event had him struggling some way out. (10/1)
3283 Dancing Cavalier has done all his winning on left-handed tracks and never seemed happy here. (7/1)
3309 Batoutoftheblue ran a stinker and there was obviously something amiss. (7/1)

3544 HOLDERNESS PONY CLUB CLAIMING STKS (2-Y.O) (Class E)
4-05 (4-06) **5f** £2,925.75 (£876.00: £420.50: £192.75) Stalls: High GOING: 0.09 sec per fur (G)

SP RR SF
3247[4] **Patsy Culsyth (69)** (MrsLStubbs) **2-8-7v** DHarrison(2) (lw: trckd ldr: shkn up to ld 1f out: r.o) ....— **1** 5/2[2] 62 31
*3076** **Always Lucky (68)** (JBerry) **2-8-6**(5) PRoberts(1) (led tl hdd 1f out: sn btn)...4 **2** 8/11[1] 53 22
2886[9] **Time To Time** (TDEasterby) **2-8-7** LCharnock(6) (sn pushed along: hdwy ½-wy: nt pce to chal).......................¾ **3** 5/1[3] 47 16
1829[10] **Miss Beveled (44)** (MBrittain) **2-7-13** GBardwell(4) (a outpcd & bhd)...5 **4** 16/1 23 —
3106[12] **Blitz** (MWEasterby) **2-8-3** DaleGibson(5) (chsd ldrs 3f: sn wknd)..7 **5** 14/1 4 —
(SP 115.7%) **5 Rn**

66.0 secs (4.20) CSF £4.57 TOTE £3.00: £1.10 £1.10 (£1.50) OWNER Contrac Promotions Ltd (COLLINGBOURNE DUCIS) BRED J. Forsyth
3247 Patsy Culsyth had the visor on for the second time and won this uncompetitive event really well. (5/2)
3076* Always Lucky, a very edgy sort, looks her own worst enemy and used up most of her energy before the race began. (8/11: 4/5-evens)
2886 Time To Time does not do anything quickly but does respond to pressure and should stay further. (5/1)
1600 Miss Beveled did not give any signs of encouragement. (16/1)
572 Blitz looked decidedly moderate. (14/1)

3545 PUNCH AND JUDY NURSERY H'CAP (2-Y.O) (Class D)
4-35 (4-36) **7f 100y** £3,593.50 (£1,078.00: £519.00: £239.50) Stalls: High GOING: 0.09 sec per fur (G)

SP RR SF
2936[2] **Deki (USA) (84)** (DMorley) **2-9-6** GCarter(7) (lw: mde most: jst hld on)...— **1** 7/2[2] 87 45
3067* **Bolero Kid (83)** (MWEasterby) **2-9-2**(3) GParkin(5) (lw: b: outpcd & bhd: hdwy u.p 2f out: r.o wl towards fin)..hd **2** 5/2[1] 86 44
2943[4] **Danzig Flyer (IRE) (72)** (PWHarris) **2-8-8** FNorton(1) (a cl up: effrt over 2f out: nt qckn)..................1¾ **3** 7/1[3] 71 29
3307* **Miss Main Street (IRE) (63)** (JJQuinn) **2-7-10**(3) 5x PFessey(11) (sn bhd: hdwy 3f out: chsng ldrs over 1f out: no ex) ....½ **4** 7/1[3] 61 19
2786[6] **O' Higgins (IRE) (60)** (RBoss) **2-7-10** JQuinn(6) (bhd: hdwy over 2f out: nvr able to chal)..................................3 **5** 20/1 52 10
2905[3] **Winsome George (85)** (CWFairhurst) **2-9-7** NKennedy(3) (lw: prom: sn pushed along: no imp fnl 2f)............3½ **6** 8/1 69 27
3468[4] **Sandy Shore (78)** (JWharton) **2-8-9**(5) PRoberts(4) (chsd ldrs tl wknd fnl 2f)..1¼ **7** 8/1 59 17
3131[4] **Sing For Me (IRE) (63)** (RHollinshead) **2-7-13** NCarlisle(2) (hdwy to chse ldrs over 2f out: wknd over 1f out)...4 **8** 11/1 36 —
3258[8] **Elsinore (IRE) (64)** (MrsJRRamsden) **2-8-0** GBardwell(9) (plld hrd: lost tch fnl 3f)...5 **9** 12/1 26 —
3212[3] **Petara (IRE) (65)** (JSWainwright) **2-8-1v** LCharnock(10) (chsd ldrs tl wknd fnl 2f)..1½ **10** 20/1 24 —
(SP 123.6%) **10 Rn**

1m 38.1 (6.10) CSF £12.35 CT £54.61 TOTE £4.30: £1.20 £2.10 £2.90 (£9.90) Trio £21.90 OWNER Mr Hadi Al-Tajir (NEWMARKET) BRED Hadi Al Tajir
STEWARDS' ENQUIRY Parkin susp. 23 & 25-29/8/97 (excessive use of whip).
2936 Deki (USA), at his first attempt on this easy ground, was made plenty of use of and this is obviously the way to ride him. (7/2)

3067* Bolero Kid failed to act on this track until meeting the uphill section and, despite finishing to some purpose, it was always too late. In doing so, he did have a very hard race. (5/2)
2943 Danzig Flyer (IRE) is an excitable sort but, if his energy can be channelled in the right direction, he has the ability. (7/1)
3307* Miss Main Street (IRE) ran a fair race in this much softer ground and remains in good heart. (7/1)
447 O' Higgins (IRE) has been gelded before his run at Leicester last time and, although he showed a little here, there is plenty more needed and perhaps faster ground will help. (20/1)
2905 Winsome George is proving disappointing and was never happy here. (8/1)
2202 Elsinore (IRE) spoiled any chances she had by pulling too hard in the early stages. (12/1: 7/1-14/1)

T/Plpt: £14.60 (1,387.52 Tckts). T/Qdpt: £5.60 (246.69 Tckts) AA

3496-SANDOWN (R-H) (5f Good, Rnd Good to firm, Good patches)
Thursday August 14th
WEATHER: very hot WIND: almost nil

3546 TIMEFORM BLACK BOOK NURSERY H'CAP (2-Y.O) (Class E)
2-15 (2-18) **5f 6y** £2,700.25 (£817.00: £398.50: £189.25) Stalls: High GOING: 0.02 sec per fur (G)

				SP	RR	SF
3094*	**Monte Lemos (IRE) (84)** (RCharlton) **2-9-7** TSprake(2) (a.p: lft in ld over 1f out: edgd rt ins fnl f: rdn out)	—	**1**	4/5[1]	85	27
1386[4]	**Supreme Angel (74)** (MPMuggeridge) **2-8-8**(3) MHenry(3) (a.p: rdn over 1f out: ev ch 1f out: bmpd ins fnl f: r.o)	½	**2**	8/1	73	15
3288[5]	**Means Business (IRE) (69)** (BJMeehan) **2-8-6b** DaneO'Neill(4) (swtg: hld up: rdn over 2f out: 3rd & styng on whn hmpd on ins ins fnl f: nt rcvr)	2	**3**	7/1[3]	62	4
3451[11]	**Silent Pride (IRE) (59)** (MDIUsher) **2-7-3**(7) JFowle(1) (swtg: hld up: rdn over 2f out: one pce)	s.h	**4**	25/1	52	—
2917[2]	**Bound To Please (79)** (PJMakin) **2-9-2** SSanders(6) (led tl fly-jumped, hit rails & uns rdr over 1f out)		**U**	11/4[2]	—	—

(SP 109.7%) **5 Rn**

64.61 secs (4.81) CSF £7.18 TOTE £1.70: £1.10 £2.20 (£5.30) OWNER Mr S M De Zoete (BECKHAMPTON) BRED Rathasker Stud
LONG HANDICAP Silent Pride (IRE) 7-1
3094* Monte Lemos (IRE), who has hung left on both his previous outings, was a rather fortunate winner for he was not going nearly as well as the leader when that rival collided with the rail and unseated his rider below the distance. Left in front, it looked as if he may be in danger as Means Business picked up ground nicely along the inside rail inside the final furlong but that rival got hampered, knocking him out of contention, and Monte Lemos was able to come home in front. (4/5)
1386 Supreme Angel, a leading light from the off, may have been left in front for a few strides when Bound To Please departed over a furlong out. Done no favours inside the final furlong, she nevertheless kept on well to the line. (8/1: op 5/1)
3288 Means Business (IRE), bustled along from halfway, was staying on really nicely along the inside rail when hampered inside the final furlong, from which he could never recover. (7/1: 5/1-8/1)
3045 Silent Pride (IRE), making a quick reappearance and still carrying 2lb more than her long handicap weight despite her rider's claim, is only selling class and needs to return to that level. (25/1)
2917 Bound To Please had a very nasty experience. Setting the pace, he looked to be in command when fly-jumping over a furlong out, causing him to hit the rail and unseat his rider. As long as this episode has not left its mark, he should soon gain compensation. (11/4)

3547 TIMEFORM PERSPECTIVE MAIDEN STKS (2-Y.O F) (Class D)
2-45 (2-48) **7f 16y** £3,582.50 (£1,085.00: £530.00: £252.50) Stalls: High GOING minus 0.36 sec per fur (F)

				SP	RR	SF
	Leggera (IRE) (JLDunlop) **2-8-11** TSprake(4) (leggy: scope: s.s: in rr 5f: gd hdwy over 1f out: str run to ld wl ins fnl f: r.o wl)	—	**1**	25/1	92+	33
	Alignment (IRE) (MRStoute) **2-8-11** JReid(12) (w'like: bit bkwd: plld hrd: hdwy 5f out: ev ch over 1f out: unable qckn ins fnl f)	1¼	**2**	8/1	89+	30
	Bluewain Lady (PWHarris) **2-8-11** GDuffield(11) (str: scope: bit bkwd: a.p: rdn over 3f out: led ins fnl f: sn hdd: one pce)	s.h	**3**	20/1	89	30
2962[3]	**Forum (97)** (CEBrittain) **2-8-11** MRoberts(10) (lw: led tl ins fnl f: one pce)	1¼	**4**	9/4[1]	86	27
2842[3]	**Good Catch (IRE)** (PRWebber) **2-8-11** KFallon(3) (nt clr run 3f out: rdn over 2f out: hdwy over 1f out: r.o)	¾	**5**	8/1	85	26
2919[4]	**Pride of My Heart** (IABalding) **2-8-11** LDettori(13) (a.p: rdn over 3f out: one pce)	½	**6**	9/2[2]	83	24
	Spirit of The Nile (FR) (PFICole) **2-8-11** PatEddery(9) (w'like: bit bkwd: rdn 5f out: lost pl 3f out: r.o one pce fnl f)	½	**7**	6/1	82	23
3117[3]	**Clarity (IRE)** (APJarvis) **2-8-11** SDrowne(5) (rdn over 3f out: hdwy on ins over 2f out: eased whn btn ins fnl f)	s.h	**8**	11/2[3]	82	23
	Sandar (BWHills) **2-8-11** MHills(14) (w'like: bit bkwd: hld up: rdn over 2f out: wknd fnl f)	3	**9**	12/1	75	16
2728[19]	**Safabee** (MJHaynes) **2-8-8**(3) MartinDwyer(2) (bhd fnl 2f)	¾	**10**	33/1	74	15
2713[5]	**Shifting** (CWThornton) **2-8-11** DeanMcKeown(1) (lw: bhd fnl 5f)	nk	**11**	25/1	73	14
	Sweet Dreams (JLDunlop) **2-8-11** WRyan(6) (s.s: a bhd)	1	**12**	25/1	71	12
3019[7]	**Fair Sonia** (KMcAuliffe) **2-8-11** JFEgan(7) (bhd fnl 2f)	3	**13**	33/1	64	5

(SP 130.7%) **13 Rn**

1m 31.62 (3.02) CSF £197.06 TOTE £47.20: £11.20 £3.10 £4.00 (£114.10) Trio £607.80; £770.50 to Newbury 15/8/97 OWNER Mrs H. Focke (ARUNDEL) BRED Mrs Hildegard Focke
Leggera (IRE), a tall, attractive filly with plenty of scope, hardly looked the winner for much of the contest as she hacked round at the back of the field and was last of all entering the straight. However, she made giant strides from below the distance and came storming through to snatch the spoils in the closing stages. This was a very pleasing debut. (25/1)
Alignment (IRE), a plain, medium-sized filly who is a half-sister to Bonny Scot, looked as though the run would do her good and, taking a very keen hold, soon pulled herself into a prominent position. Disputing the lead from below the distance, she was unable to find another gear inside the final furlong but should soon open her account. (8/1: 4/1-9/1)
Bluewain Lady, a well-made filly who is a half-sister to several winners, did not look fully wound up but threw down her challenge below the distance. She managed to poke her head in front inside the final furlong but no sooner had she done so than she was passed by the winner. (20/1)
2962 Forum had a far simpler task on this occasion as she dropped down to maiden company for the first time but she was unable to take advantage of it and, after setting the pace, was overhauled inside the final furlong. (9/4)
2842 Good Catch (IRE) looked as though the step up in trip would help and so it proved. Done no favours early in the straight, she had quite a bit of ground to make up but ran on nicely in the last furlong and a half to be nearest at the line. (8/1)
2919 Pride of My Heart was never far away but was made to look very one-paced in the straight. (9/2)

Spirit of The Nile (FR) (6/1: op 3/1)
3117 Clarity (IRE) (11/2: 8/1-5/1)
Sandar (12/1: op 8/1)

3548 '50 YEARS OF TIMEFORM' H'CAP (0-85) (3-Y.O+) (Class D)
3-20 (3-22) **7f 16y** £4,357.50 (£1,320.00: £645.00: £307.50) Stalls: High GOING minus 0.36 sec per fur (F)

			SP	RR	SF
3254[13] **Gulf Shaadi (66)** (EJAlston) **5-8-12** KFallon(7) (hdwy over 1f out: led ins fnl f: rdn out)	—	1	10/1	77	57
3115[5] **Telemania (IRE) (81)** (WJHaggas) **3-9-7** FLynch(14) (hdwy over 1f out: chsd wnr ins fnl f: unable qckn)	1½	2	11/2 [1]	89	63
3048* **Blessed Spirit (78)** (CFWall) **4-9-10** GDuffield(8) (stdy hdwy on bit 2f out: ev ch 1f out: one pce)	hd	3	8/1	85	65
3115[3] **Sue's Return (78)** (APJarvis) **5-9-10** MHills(10) (lost pl over 4f: rallied over 1f out: r.o wl ins fnl f)	1¾	4	8/1	81	61
3037[3] **Beyond Calculation (USA) (72)** (PWHarris) **3-8-7**(5) CLowther(4) (swtg: s.s: hdwy 2f out: ev ch 1f out: wknd ins fnl f)	1	5	15/2 [3]	73	47
2930[2] **Space Race (79)** (CACyzer) **3-9-5** LDettori(1) (a.p: led over 1f out tl ins fnl f: sn wknd)	1¼	6	11/2 [1]	77	51
1739[15] **Ertlon (70)** (CEBrittain) **7-9-2** MRoberts(2) (hld up: rdn over 2f out: btn whn hmpd ins fnl f)	1	7	14/1	66	46
3115[17] **Serendipity (FR) (66)** (BRMillman) **4-8-12** TSprake(13) (nvr nrr)	¾	8	14/1	60	40
3236[11] **Maladerie (IRE) (63)** (MRChannon) **3-8-0**(3) PPMurphy(6) (a.p: led over 2f out tl over 1f out: sn wknd)	1	9	50/1	55	29
2666[3] **Rakis (IRE) (82)** (MrsLStubbs) **7-10-0** PatEddery(12) (b: lw: hld up: rdn over 2f out: wknd over 1f out)	1¾	10	6/1 [2]	70	50
2691[7] **Topatori (IRE) (73)** (MHTompkins) **3-8-13** DBiggs(11) (lw: prom 5f)	2	11	14/1	57	31
3246[8] **Hisar (IRE) (77)** (CPEBrooks) **4-9-9** CRutter(5) (swtg: led: clr 5f out: hdd over 2f out: wknd wl over 1f out)	3½	12	33/1	53	33
807a[7] **Junikay (IRE) (84)** (RIngram) **3-9-10** AMcGlone(15) (a bhd)	6	13	33/1	46	20
3024[9] **Jupiter (IRE) (64)** (GCBravery) **3-8-4** DRMcCabe(16) (lw: a bhd)	½	14	16/1	25	—
1977[23] **Mansab (USA) (66)** (PGMurphy) **4-8-12** JFEgan(3) (swtg: prom over 4f)	3½	15	20/1	19	—
			(SP 126.6%)	**15 Rn**	

1m 29.51 (0.91) CSF £59.05 CT £446.14 TOTE £11.80: £3.30 £3.10 £2.90 (£72.50) Trio £145.20 OWNER The Bibby Halliday Partnership (PRESTON) BRED Sheikh Mohammed bin Rashid al Maktoum
WEIGHT FOR AGE 3yo-6lb

2760 Gulf Shaadi, a prolific All-Weather winner, had only one Turf victory to his name prior to this. Weaving his way through the pack, he shot into the lead early inside the final furlong and was rousted along to score. He must not be hit according to connections. (10/1)
3115 Telemania (IRE) began to pick up ground below the distance but, having moved into second place inside the final furlong, was unable to peg back the winner. (11/2)
3048* Blessed Spirit showed quite clearly here why she is no easy ride. Absolutely swinging off the bridle as she picked up ground a quarter of a mile out, she had every chance entering the final furlong but, when her rider let her down, she failed to produce the goods. (8/1: 6/1-9/1)
3115 Sue's Return was not helped by the drop down to seven furlongs and lost her pitch turning for home. However, she ran on in good style in the last furlong and a half to finish right on the heels of the principals. She has run some good races this season but has only two wins from thirty-three starts to her name. (8/1)
3037 Beyond Calculation (USA), making his handicap debut, moved up to have every chance a furlong out before tiring in the closing stages. (15/2)
2930 Space Race, pulled out of a hot conditions race here the night before, was taking a drop down in distance but nevertheless got to the front below the distance before swamped for speed inside the final furlong. A return to a longer trip would help. (11/2)
2508 Serendipity (FR) (14/1: 20/1-12/1)
2205 Topatori (IRE) (14/1: 10/1-16/1)

3549 TIMEFORM PHONE SERVICE H'CAP (0-80) (3-Y.O) (Class D)
3-50 (3-51) **1m 6f** £3,598.75 (£1,090.00: £532.50: £253.75) Stalls: Low GOING minus 0.36 sec per fur (F)

			SP	RR	SF
3197* **Princess Topaz (68)** (CACyzer) **3-8-11** MHills(10) (hdwy over 3f out: led over 2f out: clr over 1f out: rdn out)	—	1	7/1 [3]	78	47
3218[8] **Brand New Dance (74)** (DWPArbuthnot) **3-9-3** MRoberts(8) (hdwy over 2f out: chsd wnr over 1f out: unable qckn)	1¼	2	12/1	83	52
3096[2] **City Hall (IRE) (64)** (MRStoute) **3-8-7** JReid(5) (hld up: rdn over 3f out: r.o ins fnl f)	1¾	3	11/4 [1]	71	40
3210[3] **Atnab (USA) (60)** (PTWalwyn) **3-8-3** RHills(2) (hld up: rdn over 3f out: one pce)	1½	4	8/1	65	34
2879[4] **Salsee Lad (60)** (JRFanshawe) **3-8-3** SSanders(4) (rdn over 3f out: nvr nr to chal)	1	5	14/1	64	33
3125[4] **Irsal (78)** (MCPipe) **3-9-7** RHughes(3) (hdwy over 4f out: led 3f out tl over 2f out: wknd over 1f out)	4	6	8/1	77	46
2692[3] **Seattle Art (USA) (75)** (HRACecil) **3-9-4** KFallon(1) (chsd ldr 8f out: led over 3f out: sn hdd: wknd 2f out)	8	7	10/1	65	34
3057[3] **Padauk (65)** (MJHaynes) **3-8-5**(3) MartinDwyer(7) (bhd fnl 5f)	2½	8	20/1	52	21
2592[7] **Wonderboy (IRE) (56)** (RAkehurst) **3-7-10**(3) RFfrench(6) (swtg: chsd ldr 6f: wknd over 3f out)	hd	9	8/1	43	12
2963[8] **Tango King (72)** (JLDunlop) **3-9-1** LDettori(9) (swtg: led over 10f: wknd 2f out)	3½	10	9/2 [2]	55	24
			(SP 118.9%)	**10 Rn**	

3m 2.52 (3.62) CSF £81.15 CT £263.37 TOTE £10.90: £3.10 £4.00 £1.50 (£71.20) Trio £86.40 OWNER Mr Stephen Crown (HORSHAM) BRED S. Crown

3197* Princess Topaz relished the step up in trip and, despite being 7lb higher than when winning at Newmarket last time out, led over a quarter of a mile from home and shot clear below the distance for a decisive victory. (7/1)
1491 Brand New Dance came through to take second place over a furlong out but, despite plodding on, was unable to peg back the winner. (12/1)
3096 City Hall (IRE) was not helped by the drop in distance and, rousted along early in the straight, was going nowhere for a long while. However, he stayed on nicely up the hill for third prize but found the front two already home and dry. A return to two miles is needed. (11/4)
3210 Atnab (USA) was taking a step up in distance but her lack of acceleration was there for all to see in the straight. (8/1)
2879 Salsee Lad was taking a big step up in distance but was still shown to be only moderate. (14/1)
3125 Irsal found this longer trip beyond him. In front early in the straight, he was collared over a quarter of a mile from home and stopped as if shot below the distance. A return to a mile and a half is needed. (8/1: 5/1-9/1)
2692 Seattle Art (USA) (10/1: op 6/1)

3550 COMPUTER TIMEFORM MAIDEN STKS (3-Y.O+ F & M) (Class D)
4-20 (4-24) **7f 16y** £3,338.75 (£1,010.00: £492.50: £233.75) Stalls: High GOING minus 0.36 sec per fur (F)

			SP	RR	SF
Egoli (USA) (GWragg) **3-8-11** MHills(3) (w'like: scope: lw: dwlt: stdy hdwy 3f out: led over 2f out: qckned ins fnl f: easily)	—	1	7/2 [3]	67+	37
2873[4] **Warning Express** (RWArmstrong) **3-8-11** RPrice(1) (hld up: ev ch over 2f out: unable qckn)	3½	2	9/4 [1]	59	29

3250[3]	**Feel No Fear** (WRMuir) **4-9-3** JReid(4) (chsd ldr over 4f: sn wknd)	3½	**3**	16/1	51	27
3095[11]	**Shalverton (IRE)** (WRMuir) **3-8-11** DaneO'Neill(7) (swtg: hld up: rdn 3f out: wknd 2f out)	nk	**4**	33/1	51	21
2838[7]	**Tahara (IRE)** (LMCumani) **3-8-11** LDettori(6) (lw: led over 4f: wknd over 1f out)	1	**5**	7/2 [3]	48	18
	Amarella (IRE) (MJHaynes) **3-8-8**(3) MartinDwyer(2) (sme hdwy over 3f out: sn wknd)	4	**6**	25/1	39	9
2537[6]	***Imperial Scholar (IRE) (84)*** (JMPEustace) **3-8-11** PatEddery(5) (Withdrawn not under Starter's orders: ref to ent stalls)		**W**	3/1 [2]	—	—
				(SP 112.9%)		**6 Rn**

1m 31.24 (2.64) CSF £6.37 TOTE £3.50: £2.70 £1.10 (£2.60) OWNER Mr A. E. Oppenheimer (NEWMARKET) BRED The Hascombe and Valiant Studs

WEIGHT FOR AGE 3yo-6lb

Egoli (USA), an attractive, scopey filly, certainly looked the part in the paddock but drifted very badly in the betting. However, her supporters had absolutely nothing to worry about and, cruising into the lead over a quarter of a mile from home, she quickened right away from her only serious rival to win doing handsprings. She looks a filly with a future and can now go on to better things. (7/2: 5/4-4/1)

2873 Warning Express, an angular filly with not a great deal of substance, was well supported in the market but she was no match for the winner and, after having every chance over a quarter of a mile from home, was put in her place from below the distance. She will not always meet one so good. (9/4)

3250 Feel No Fear raced in second place until over two furlongs from home but was then done with. (16/1)

Shalverton (IRE) chased the leaders but had been hung out to dry two furlongs from home. (33/1)

Tahara (IRE) set the pace but she was collared over a quarter of a mile from home and had shot her bolt below the distance. She looks only moderate. (7/2)

3551 TIMEFORM RACE CARD LIMITED STKS (0-75) (3-Y.O+) (Class D)

4-50 (4-52) **1m 2f 7y** £3,420.00 (£1,035.00: £505.00: £240.00) Stalls: High GOING minus 0.36 sec per fur (F)

				SP	RR	SF
2961[6]	**Brandon Jack (75)** (IABalding) **3-8-11** LDettori(3) (lw: hld up: led over 1f out: rdn out)	—	**1**	2/1 [2]	82	27
2836[4]	**Prince de Loir (73)** (DJSCosgrove) **3-8-9** MRimmer(5) (hld up: rdn 3f out: r.o wl ins fnl f)	¾	**2**	11/1	79	24
2855[4]	**Contentment (IRE) (75)** (JWHills) **3-8-11** RHills(4) (lw: hdwy over 2f out: led 2f out tl over 1f out: unable qckn)	¾	**3**	5/1 [3]	80	25
*3396**	**All In Leather (75)** (WJHaggas) **3-8-8** FLynch(1) (chsd ldr: led 4f out: hrd rdn & hung rt over 2f out: hdd 2f out: sn wknd)	10	**4**	11/8 [1]	61	6
2951[5]	**Ijtinab (75)** (RAkehurst) **3-8-9** SSanders(2) (lw: led 6f: wknd over 2f out)	29	**5**	8/1	15	—
				(SP 111.5%)		**5 Rn**

2m 11.87 (5.17) CSF £19.51 TOTE £3.00: £2.10 £3.70 (£14.10) OWNER Mr R. P. B. Michaelson (KINGSCLERE) BRED Highclere Stud Ltd

2961 Brandon Jack does like to get his toe in and, although unable to do so on this occasion, still proved too good for this moderate bunch, leading over a furlong out and being ridden along to score. (2/1)

2836 Prince de Loir was being bustled along early in the straight and for a long way there was little response. However, he really found his feet in the final furlong and ran on strongly to snatch second prize. (11/1: 8/1-12/1)

2855 Contentment (IRE) came through to show in front two furlongs out but, headed below the distance, failed to find another gear. (5/1: 4/1-6/1)

3396* All In Leather was very disappointing. Sent on turning for home, she hung over to the rails when given a couple of reminders over a quarter of a mile out and, soon headed, was then done with. (11/8)

2951 Ijtinab failed to stay this longer trip and, after setting the pace to the home turn, dropped away over two furlongs out. He has become disappointing. (8/1: 5/1-9/1)

T/Jkpt: Not won; £14,400.88 to Newbury 15/8/97. T/Plpt: £367.70 (76.21 Tckts). T/Qdpt: £26.20 (67.88 Tckts) AK

3370a-DEAUVILLE (France) (R-H) (Soft)
Saturday August 9th

3552a PRIX DE PSYCHE (Gp 3) (3-Y.O F)

3-30 (-) **1m 2f** £24,691.00 (£8,979.00: £4,489.00)

				SP	RR	SF
2275a[2]	**Tenuous** (PBary,France) **3-8-11** SGuillot	—	**1**		108	—
	Majinskaya (FR) (SWattel,France) **3-8-11** FSanchez	¾	**2**		107	—
2458a[2]	**Enigma (GER)** (BSchutz,Germany) **3-8-11** OPeslier	1½	**3**		104	—
						6 Rn

No Time Taken P-M 2.10F: 1.30F 1.40F OWNER Mr K. Abdulla (CHANTILLY) BRED Juddmonte Farms

2275a Tenuous was given an excellent ride and she deserved this Group success. Racing behind the leaders, she was boxed in a little rounding the final turn but her jockey did not panic and the filly was beautifully placed to challenge in the straight. She took the lead one and a half furlongs out and had something in hand when challenged. A daughter of Generous, she is still improving and she may now go for the Prix Vermeille, although the distance of that race is the limit of her range.

Majinskaya (FR) was bought out of a seller in March by her young Deauville trainer and she has improved with every run. Tracking the leader, she looked likely to take the event inside the final furlong but the winner pulled out a little more. She looks capable of taking a Group Three event later on in the season.

2458a Enigma (GER) was unsuited by several changes of pace as she needs an even gallop to show her best. She only got into top gear later on and was running on at the finish.

2821a-HOPPEGARTEN (Berlin, Germany) (R-H) (Good)
Saturday August 9th

3553a ERDGAS TROPHY 97 - GROSSE PREIS VON BERLIN (Gp 3) (3-Y.O+)

3-43 (3-49) **6f 110y** £27,462.00 (£10,985.00: £5,492.00)

				SP	RR	SF
3375a[2]	**Tomba** (BJMeehan) **3-8-12** MTebbutt	—	**1**		117	—
2640a*	**Global Player** (HBlume,Germany) **4-9-6** THellier	½	**2**		120	—
	Aldino (GER) (WKujath,Germany) **3-8-12** StephenDavies	2½	**3**		110	—
						11 Rn

1m 16.3 TOTE 56DM: 30DM 16DM 40DM OWNER Mr J. R. Good (UPPER LAMBOURN) BRED Mrs P. Good

3375a Tomba travelled up from Munich where he was second on his favoured soft ground, to win this more important and valuable prize. With the leaders two furlongs out, he hung left in the closing stages, but had enough in hand to hold the strong late run of the much-improved Global Player. Three-year-olds appeared well in at the weights here and the only ones of that age were first, third and a long-priced last.

3552a-DEAUVILLE (France) (R-H) (Good)
Sunday August 10th

3554a PRIX MAURICE DE GHEEST (Gp 1) (3-Y.O+)
2-35 (2-37) **6f 110y** £56,117.00 (£22,447.00: £11,223.00: £5,612.00)

				SP	RR	SF
3001a5	**Occupandiste (IRE)** (MmeCHead,France) **4-8-12** ODoleuze (mde virtually all: hrd rdn over 1f out: r.o)	—	1		116	—
3001a*	**Monaassib** (EALDunlop) **6-9-2** DO'Donohoe (led early: sn hdd: trckd ldr: swtchd outside st: chal 1f out: styd on)	½	2		119	—
21062	**Titus Livius (FR)** (JEPease,France) **4-9-2** CAsmussen (rdn mid div: hrd rdn 1½f out: swtchd rt ins fnl f: no ex cl home)	¾	3		117	—
26794	**Kahal** (SbinSuroor) **3-8-12** RHills (rdn in 3rd: u.p bef st: chal & ev ch over 1f out: r.o one pce)	1½	4		113	—
	Deadly Dudley (IRE) (RHannon) **3-8-12** OPeslier (rdn in 6th: effrt st: styd on fnl f)	nk	5		113	—
1721a5	**Winning Smile (FR)** (TClout,France) **7-9-2** TGillet (a bhd: wknd st)	5	6		100	—
3001a6	**Wardara** (FBellenger,France) **5-8-13b** MdeSmyter (rdn in rr: u.p 2f out: n.d)	2	7		92	—
3001a3	**Nombre Premier** (AdeRoyerDupre,France) **3-8-12** GMosse (hld up in rr early: wknd fnl 2f)	8	8		76	—
						8 Rn

1m 16.7 (1.70) P-M 9.20F: 1.60F 1.30F 1.10F (15.90F) OWNER Wertheimer Brothers (CHANTILLY) BRED J. Wertheimer & Frere

2273a* Occupandiste (IRE) produced an improved performance on this occasion. She made every yard of the running and pulled out that little extra when challenged in the final furlong. She reversed the form with several of her rivals including the runner-up, and this was due to the testing ground. She is learning about the sprinting game but is bred to stay further. Her target now is the seven-furlong Prix de la Foret in October, a race which looks tailor-made for her.

3001a* Monaassib ran a brave race considering the conditions and would have won if the ground had been firm. He chased the winner virtually throughout but the patchy ground sapped his strength in the final furlong. It was a really decent performance by the gelding, who now goes for the Haydock Sprint. He is a credit to his young trainer who has done so well with him this season.

2106 Titus Livius (FR) took a little time to get into his stride and was putting his best work in at the finish, where he did not exactly have a lot of room. He hit a sticky patch early on and could not go the pace so never really got in a blow. He is now likely to go for the Goldene Peitsche or the Haydock Sprint.

2679 Kahal was always in the leading group and ran on bravely, but was a little one-paced in the final furlong. This was a decent effort by a colt who connections think will mature greatly at four so the 1998 season takes priority.

Deadly Dudley (IRE) appeared outpaced early on but was running on really well at the finish, and this was a good effort as he had not been out for nine months. There is no plan at the moment for him except he will be moving up in trip. He looks one to follow for the remainder of the season.

3553a-HOPPEGARTEN (Berlin, Germany) (R-H) (Good)
Sunday August 10th

3555a BMW EUROPACHAMPIONAT (Gp 2) (3-Y.O)
4-35 (4-42) **1m 4f** £83,334.00 (£35,985.00: £17,045.00: £9,470.00: £5,682.00)

				SP	RR	SF
2642a2	**Baroon** (AWohler,Germany) **3-9-2** ABoschert (mid div: prog 3f out: r.o strly to disp ld ins fnl f: led & edgd lft 100y out: r.o)	—	1		118	—
2642a*	**Borgia (GER)** (BSchutz,Germany) **3-8-12** AStarke (hld up: swtchd 2½f out: hdwy to disp ld ins fnl f: edgd rt & no ex ins fnl 100y)	½	2		113	—
2642a3	**Happy Change (GER)** (AWohler,Germany) **3-9-2** PSchiergen (sn led: qcknd 4f out: kpt on whn hdd ins fnl f)	1¼	3		116	—
1545a*	**Ajano (GER)** (EGroschel,Germany) **3-9-2** ATylicki (prom: chal 4f out: ev ch 1½f out: no ex fnl f)	nk	4		115	—
1553a2	**Ungaro (GER)** (HBlume,Germany) **3-9-2** THellier (prom: rdn & unable qckn 2f out)	2½	5		112	—
	Modigliani (GER) (ALowe,Germany) **3-9-2** KWoodburn (a last: n.d)	9	6		100	—
						6 Rn

2m 33.0 TOTE 25DM: 15DM 19DM OWNER Mr J. Abdullah

Baroon reversed the German Derby form with the runner-up with a narrow success. Making smooth progress with three furlongs left to travel, he came with a strong run to dispute the lead inside the final furlong before running out an impressive winner.

3294-BRIGHTON (L-H) (Good to firm)
Friday August 15th
Races 3 & 4 sea mist
WEATHER: warm & sunny

3556 JIMMY HEAL MEMORIAL TROPHY NURSERY H'CAP (2-Y.O) (Class D)
2-00 (2-01) **5f 59y** £3,234.25 (£964.00: £459.50: £207.25) Stalls: Low GOING minus 0.37 sec per fur (F)

				SP	RR	SF
31526	**Mishraak (IRE) (88)** (RWArmstrong) **2-9-7** RPrice(2) (swtg: broke wl: mde all: clr 2f out: rdn ins fnl f: all out)	—	1	3/1 2	92	26
28297	**Overture (IRE) (82)** (RHannon) **2-9-1** RHughes(1) (swtg: in tch: rdn 3f out: styd on to chse wnr ins fnl f: r.o)	hd	2	15/8 1	86	20
30983	**High Gain (72)** (PHowling) **2-8-5** JQuinn(7) (in tch: chsd wnr 2f out tl ins fnl f: one pce)	2	3	7/2 3	70	4
27406	**Mrs Middle (63)** (NACallaghan) **2-7-7(3)** RFfrench(3) (sn outpcd & bhd: gd hdwy ins fnl f: fin wl)	hd	4	8/1	60	—
311311	**Private Seal (73)** (GLMoore) **2-8-6** AClark(6) (chsd wnr to 2f out: wkng whn n.m.r over 1f out)	3½	5	14/1	60	—
27843	**Corsecan (65)** (SDow) **2-7-12ow2** CRutter(5) (a bhd)	2	6	8/1	46	—
				(SP 110.9%)		**6 Rn**

62.8 secs (2.80) CSF £8.03 TOTE £4.30: £1.70 £1.30 (£3.00) OWNER Mr Hamdan Al Maktoum (NEWMARKET) BRED Scuderia Dello Zodiaco

LONG HANDICAP Mrs Middle 7-9 Corsecan 7-9

3152 Mishraak (IRE) is blessed with very good early pace and handled this sharp downhill course particularly well. (3/1)

2215 Overture (IRE) was always just struggling to go the pace and, though staying on well inside the final furlong, he had too much ground to make up. (15/8)

3098 High Gain had every chance. (7/2)
2740 Mrs Middle was well out the back until staying on strongly in the closing stages. She can pick up a small Nursery especially when returned to six furlongs or even further. (8/1: 6/1-10/1)
2741 Private Seal (14/1: 8/1-16/1)

3557 STANMER CLAIMING STKS (3-Y.O) (Class F)
2-30 (2-32) **7f 214y** £2,277.00 (£627.00: £297.00) Stalls: Low GOING minus 0.37 sec per fur (F)

				SP	RR	SF
3132^{6}	**Flood's Hot Stuff (40)** (NPLittmoden) **3-8-0v^{1}** NAdams(6) (mde all: hrd rdn over 1f out: r.o)	—	**1**	5/1^{3}	46	—
2836^{2}	**My Beloved (IRE) (60)** (RHannon) **3-8-12** RHughes(3) (lw: hld up in tch: chsd wnr fr 3f out: hrd rdn & ev ch wl ins fnl f: r.o)	nk	**2**	8/13^{1}	57	9
3227^{14}	**Tulsa (IRE) (44)** (BGubby) **3-8-6$^{(3)}$** RFfrench(5) (prom: rdn & outpcd 3f out: rallied appr fnl f: keeping on one pce whn n.m.r cl home)	1¼	**3**	4/1^{2}	52	4
3281^{7}	**Ewar Snowflake (26)** (KOCunningham-Brown) **3-7-13b$^{1(3)}$** MHenry(4) (dwlt: sn rcvrd: effrt 3f out: sn btn)	8	**4**	33/1	29	—
2883^{11}	**M T Vessel (38)** (JRJenkins) **3-8-1** CRutter(2) (bhd fnl 3f: t.o)	27	**5**	20/1	—	—
2319^{11}	***Rae Un Soleil*** *(JFfitch-Heyes)* ***3-7-12*** *JQuinn(1) (Withdrawn not under Starter's orders: jockey inj at s)*		***W***	*20/1*	—	—
				(SP 111.0%)		**5 Rn**

1m 36.6 (5.30) CSF £7.31 TOTE £6.10: £2.10 £1.10 (£2.40) OWNER Mr Philip Kirby (WOLVERHAMPTON) BRED R. Powell-Tuck and Partners
2878 Flood's Hot Stuff made all the running and showed plenty of resilience to hang on well. (5/1)
2836 My Beloved (IRE) looked sure to win two furlongs out but either could not or would not go by. (8/13)
1929 Tulsa (IRE) lost a prominent position early in the straight and was keeping on again in the closing stages when running out of room. He would probably only have been third anyway. (4/1)

3558 TARBOT COMPUTER SERVICES H'CAP (0-70) (3-Y.O) (Class E)
3-00 (3-00) **6f 209y** £3,070.25 (£917.00: £438.50: £199.25) Stalls: Low GOING minus 0.37 sec per fur (F)

				SP	RR	SF
3018^{11}	**La Chatelaine (43)** (GLewis) **3-7-10$^{(3)}$** RFfrench(2) (hld up: hdwy over 1f out: sn rdn: styd on to ld wl ins fnl f)	—	**1**	100/30^{2}	54	9
3266*	**Hever Golf Mover (64)** (TJNaughton) **3-9-6** 6x AClark(6) (hld up in tch: led over 1f out: hdd wl ins fnl f: unable qckn)	¾	**2**	9/4^{1}	73	28
3299^{10}	**Tabasco Jazz (60)** (BJMeehan) **3-9-2** DRMcCabe(8) (hld up: rdn over 1f out: styd on ins fnl f)	2½	**3**	9/1	64	19
2892^{7}	**Havago (59)** (RHannon) **3-9-1** RHughes(1) (led: hdd over 1f out: wknd ins fnl f)	2	**4**	7/2^{3}	58	13
2921^{15}	**Sun O'Tirol (IRE) (48)** (JRArnold) **3-8-4** CRutter(7) (chsd ldrs: rdn 3f out: wknd ins fnl f)	1¾	**5**	25/1	43	—
3200^{17}	**Cold Steel (60)** (WJarvis) **3-9-2b** JQuinn(5) (rr: jumped path after 1f: nvr nrr)	1	**6**	9/1	53	8
757^{6}	**Charlton Spring (IRE) (65)** (RJHodges) **3-9-4$^{(3)}$** PPMurphy(4) (hld up in tch: rdn over 2f out: wknd appr fnl f)	1¼	**7**	14/1	55	10
3249^{9}	**Sheraton Girl (40)** (NPLittmoden) **3-7-10** NAdams(3) (chsd ldr: ev ch 2f out: wknd over 1f out)	3½	**8**	10/1	22	—
				(SP 115.7%)		**8 Rn**

1m 23.5 (3.50) CSF £10.40 CT £55.07 TOTE £4.20: £1.40 £1.10 £2.00 (£5.20) OWNER White Bear Ltd (EPSOM) BRED White Bear Ltd
LONG HANDICAP Sheraton Girl 7-9
2573 La Chatelaine, well supported in the market, was brought with a well-timed challenge to lead well inside the final furlong and score with just a little in hand. (100/30: 5/1-3/1)
3266* Hever Golf Mover ran a sound race. She looked like winning when leading below the distance but found the winner too strong late on. (9/4)
2945 Tabasco Jazz stayed on to be a never-nearer third. (9/1: 6/1-10/1)
Havago attempted to make all the running but was put in his place in the last furlong or so. (7/2)
2836 Cold Steel was a bit unlucky not to be closer having jumped a road early on, which left him with an awful lot to do. (9/1: 6/1-10/1)

3559 WEATHERBYS BANKING SERVICE H'CAP (0-80) (4-Y.O+) (Class D)
3-30 (3-32) **1m 3f 196y** £3,613.75 (£1,078.00: £514.50: £232.75) Stalls: High GOING minus 0.37 sec per fur (F)

				SP	RR	SF
3183^{4}	**Opera Buff (IRE) (65)** (MissGayKelleway) **6-8-6$^{(7)}$** JWilkinson(3) (lw: a.p: rdn over 1f out: led ins fnl f: r.o)	—	**1**	11/2	75	34
3229*	**Sapphire Son (IRE) (51)** (PCClarke) **5-7-10$^{(3)}$** RFfrench(6) (led tl ½-wy: led again 2f out: hdd ins fnl f: r.o)	nk	**2**	9/2	61	20
3080*	**Sovereign Crest (IRE) (49)** (CAHorgan) **4-7-11b^{1}** JQuinn(5) (hld up: hdwy 2f out: sn rdn: styd on one pce ins fnl f)	1	**3**	5/2^{1}	57	16
2373^{2}	**Palamon (USA) (72)** (PEccles) **4-9-1$^{(5)}$** GFaulkner(2) (chsd ldr: led ½-wy: hdd 2f out: no ex ins fnl f)	2	**4**	4/1^{3}	78	37
3110^{11}	**Burning (USA) (78)** (WJHaggas) **5-9-12** AClark(4) (chsd ldrs: rdn 2f out: one pce)	½	**5**	7/2^{2}	83	42
2694^{5}	**Prince Danzig (IRE) (60)** (DJGMurraySmith) **6-8-8** CRutter(1) (a bhd)	12	**6**	9/1	49	8
				(SP 114.4%)		**6 Rn**

2m 32.5 (4.90) CSF £27.75 TOTE £5.70: £3.00 £2.40 (£10.10) OWNER Mr D. W. Watson (WHITCOMBE) BRED Juddmonte Farms
3183 Opera Buff (IRE) was given fine ride by his young apprentice. Brought with a smooth challenge from below the two-furlong pole, he got in front inside the final furlong and saw it out well. (11/2)
3229* Sapphire Son (IRE) cut out much of the running and certainly did nothing wrong in defeat. (9/2)
3080* Sovereign Crest (IRE) did not pick up immediately when asked to throw down his challenge from the two-furlong pole. Although staying on inside the final furlong, he never looked like reaching the first two. (5/2)
2373 Palamon (USA) had no more to give in the final furlong. (4/1)
2776 Burning (USA) could do with dropping a few pounds in the weights. (7/2)
1641 Prince Danzig (IRE) (9/1: 6/1-10/1)

3560 ASHFORTH-CARNABY (S) H'CAP (0-60) (3-Y.O+) (Class G)
4-00 (4-02) **1m 3f 196y** £2,219.70 (£614.20: £293.10) Stalls: High GOING minus 0.37 sec per fur (F)

				SP	RR	SF
3081^{2}	**Keen Waters (35)** (JRArnold) **3-8-2** AClark(1) (a.p: led over 2f out: hrd rdn over 1f out: r.o wl)	—	**1**	11/8^{1}	46	22
3329^{4}	**Haydown (IRE) (30)** (MRBosley) **5-8-1$^{(7)}$** KelliPhillips(7) (a.p: chsd wnr over 1f out: unable qckn)	2	**2**	20/1	38	25
3297^{4}	**Chopin (IRE) (46)** (RFJohnsonHoughton) **3-8-13b** JQuinn(6) (hld up: rdn over 2f out: kpt on one pce ins fnl f)	3	**3**	7/2^{2}	50	26
2750^{7}	**Kingsdown Trix (IRE) (47)** (GLMoore) **3-9-0** CRutter(2) (hld up: hdwy over 3f out: ev ch over 2f out: wknd over 1f out)	2½	**4**	9/2^{3}	48	24

				SP	RR	SF
	Telephus (20) (BJMcMath) **8-7-12** EJohnson(4) (in tch: rdn 3f out: wknd wl over 1f out)	3½	**5**	25/1	16	3
3081[4]	**Na Huibheachu (IRE) (33)** (JSMoore) **6-8-11** RHughes(5) (sn led: hdd over 2f out: wknd over 1f out)	8	**6**	7/2[2]	18	5
				(SP 113.3%)	**6 Rn**	

2m 32.9 (5.30) CSF £27.93 TOTE £2.10: £1.10 £6.10 (£18.20) OWNER Mr Richard Young (UPPER LAMBOURN) BRED Mrs B. Skinner
WEIGHT FOR AGE 3yo-11lb
Sold M Oseman 5,500gns
3081 Keen Waters ultimately won this like the price suggested she would but her rider certainly had to get serious to ensure she drew away. (11/8)
Haydown (IRE) ran a sound race under his inexperienced rider but was well held inside the final furlong. (20/1)
3297 Chopin (IRE) stayed on late to go third and appears to have no trip. (7/2)
2750 Kingsdown Trix (IRE) seems unable to reproduce his All-Weather form on the turf. (9/2)

3561 BLACK ROCK LIMITED STKS (0-55) (3-Y.O+) (Class F)

4-30 (4-33) **6f 209y** £2,277.00 (£627.00: £297.00) Stalls: Low GOING minus 0.37 sec per fur (F)

				SP	RR	SF
3393[5]	**Step On Degas (55)** (MJFetherston-Godley) **4-8-11**(3) RFfrench(1) (mde all: hrd rdn ins fnl f: r.o wl)	—	**1**	3/1[2]	60	33
3285[D]	**Mybotye (55)** (RBastiman) **4-9-3** DRMcCabe(6) (chsd ldrs: rdn over 1f out: ev ch ins fnl f: r.o)	hd	**2**	11/4[1]	63	36
3082[12]	**Pearl Dawn (IRE) (40)** (PCClarke) **7-9-0** NAdams(13) (hld up: hdwy 2f out: n.m.r & swtchd rt over 1f out: r.o ins fnl f)	¾	**3**	20/1	58	31
3299[2]	**Ed's Folly (IRE) (53)** (SDow) **4-9-3** RHughes(10) (a.p: ev ch over 1f out: one pce)	1	**4**	11/2	59	32
3417[3]	**Crystal Heights (FR) (54)** (RJO'Sullivan) **9-9-3** AClark(12) (b: s.s: hdwy 3f out: rdn over 2f out: styd on ins fnl f)	½	**5**	4/1[3]	58	31
3143[16]	**Lady Godiva (54)** (MJPolglase) **3-8-8b[1]** JQuinn(11) (nvr nrr)	3½	**6**	12/1	47	14
3276[12]	**Jubilee Scholar (IRE) (41)** (GLMoore) **4-9-3b** JStack(5) (nvr nrr)	nk	**7**	33/1	49	22
3251[8]	**Polgwynne (47)** (BSmart) **3-8-6**(5) GFaulkner(15) (b.hind: chsd ldrs: rdn 2f out: wknd ins fnl f)	nk	**8**	33/1	48	15
2958[5]	**Silver Purse (55)** (APJones) **3-8-8b** RPrice(9) (chsd ldrs tl wknd over 1f out)	2½	**9**	14/1	39	6
2580[6]	**Velvet Jones (39)** (GFHCharles-Jones) **4-9-0**(3) RHavlin(2) (dwlt: a bhd)	1½	**10**	25/1	39	12
3195[6]	**Moi Canard (42)** (BAPearce) **4-8-10**(7) JWilkinson(14) (chsd ldrs: rdn over 2f out: sn wknd)	1	**11**	16/1	37	10
2070[8]	**Soviet Lady (IRE) (40)** (JELong) **3-8-5**(3) MBaird(4) (plld hrd: a bhd)	6	**12**	20/1	20	—
2069[10]	**Newington Butts (IRE) (40)** (KMcAuliffe) **7-9-0** CRutter(7) (chsd ldrs tl wknd 3f out)	18	**13**	33/1	—	—
3421[7]	***Fort Knox (IRE) (47)*** (RMFlower) **6-9-0b**(3) PPMurphy(8) (Withdrawn not under starter's orders: lame at s)		**W**	20/1	—	—
				(SP 134.2%)	**13 Rn**	

1m 22.7 (2.70) CSF £10.62 TOTE £4.00: £1.60 £2.70 £7.00 (£6.50) Trio £95.00 OWNER The Degas Partnership (EAST ILSLEY) BRED A. J. Poulton (Epping) Ltd
WEIGHT FOR AGE 3yo-6lb
3393 Step On Degas made all the running and held on in the gamest fashion. (3/1)
3285 Mybotye got a good run up the inside approaching the final furlong and threw down a strong challenge which only just failed. (11/4: 9/4-7/2)
2954 Pearl Dawn (IRE) was a shade unlucky here. Once clear inside the final furlong, she finished well, but she has let her supporters down before. (20/1)
3299 Ed's Folly (IRE) ran a sound race and had every chance until having to give best inside the final furlong. (11/2)
3417 Crystal Heights (FR) did not help his chances once again with a slow start. (4/1)

T/Plpt: £16.80 (723.2 Tckts). T/Qdpt: £9.50 (52.73 Tckts) SM

3282-CATTERICK (L-H) (Good to firm, Firm patches)

Friday August 15th

WEATHER: sunny WIND: almost nil

3562 TATTERSALLS BOOKMAKERS AMATEUR H'CAP (0-70) (3-Y.O+) (Class G)

5-55 (5-55) **1m 3f 214y** £2,267.50 (£630.00: £302.50) Stalls: Low GOING minus 0.22 sec per fur (GF)

				SP	RR	SF
2652[5]	**Summerhill Special (IRE) (65)** (DWBarker) **6-11-7** MissERamsden(2) (lw: b.nr hind: cl up: led 8f to 4f out: styd on to ld ins fnl f)	—	**1**	7/4[1]	77	52
3297[6]	**Comtec's Legend (30)** (JPearce) **7-9-0** MrsLPearce(1) (trckd ldrs: led 4f out tl wknd & hdd ins fnl f)	2½	**2**	33/1	39	14
608[5]	**Fatehalkhair (IRE) (33)** (BEllison) **5-9-3** MrsCWilliams(5) (bhd tl styd on wl fnl 2f: nrst fin)	4	**3**	11/1	36	11
3141[4]	**Sun of Spring (57)** (DWChapman) **7-10-13** MissRClark(7) (lw: a in tch: hdwy 4f out: sn chsng ldrs & rdn: one pce fnl 2f)	1¼	**4**	5/1[3]	59	34
3540[8]	**Kindred Greeting (31)** (JO'Reilly) **5-8-10b**(5)ow1 MrCWatson(8) (bhd: effrt 4f out: styd on: n.d)	1½	**5**	40/1	31	5
3283[7]	**Admirals Secret (USA) (54)** (CFWall) **8-10-10** MissHWebster(4) (prom tl outpcd 4f out: n.d after)	hd	**6**	100/30[2]	54	29
3432[3]	**Madam Lucy (42)** (JLSpearing) **3-9-1** MissTSpearing(3) (chsd ldrs tl rdn & wknd over 3f out)	20	**7**	7/1	15	—
3421[4]	**Don't Drop Bombs (USA) (37)** (DTThom) **8-9-7v** MissJFeilden(6) (lw: led 4f: chsd ldrs tl wknd over 2f out)	..nk	**8**	6/1	9	—
				(SP 116.6%)	**8 Rn**	

2m 40.8 (9.40) CSF £60.05 CT £464.96 TOTE £2.60: £1.20 £2.70 £2.40 (£9.10) OWNER Alba Racing Syndicate (RICHMOND) BRED Miss Audrey F. Thompson
LONG HANDICAP Comtec's Legend 8-7 Kindred Greeting 8-4
WEIGHT FOR AGE 3yo-11lb
2652 Summerhill Special (IRE), given a good, positive ride, stays well and that proved the decisive factor. (7/4)
Comtec's Legend looked to have this won when sailing past the eventual winner turning for home but she apparently did too much too soon and was comprehensively outstayed. (33/1)
608 Fatehalkhair (IRE) was picking up ground as though longer trips are needed but is obviously well and should be kept in mind for hurdling. (11/1)
3141 Sun of Spring looks well enough but just seems to have lost his spark for the moment. (5/1)
Kindred Greeting found this trip too sharp but he was making reasonable late progress. (40/1)
3283 Admirals Secret (USA) put in another disappointing effort here. (100/30)

3563 IRM LTD (S) STKS (2-Y.O) (Class G)

6-25 (6-26) **7f** £2,267.50 (£630.00: £302.50) Stalls: Low GOING minus 0.22 sec per fur (GF)

				SP	RR	SF
2935[3]	**Bint Nadia (56)** (JDBethell) **2-8-6** TWilliams(6) (a.p: rdn to ld ins fnl f: styd on wl)	—	**1**	9/4[1]	57	6
3427[4]	**Snappy Times (58)** (MDods) **2-8-11** DaleGibson(1) (chsd ldrs: led over 2f out tl 1½f out: kpt on)	2	**2**	6/1[2]	57	6
3045[2]	**Katie's Cracker (50)** (MRChannon) **2-8-6** RPainter(10) (lw: bhd: hdwy 2f out: styd on towards fin)	s.h	**3**	13/2[3]	52	1
2935[8]	**Wynbury Flyer** (FMurphy) **2-8-11** JFanning(9) (prom: rdn ½-wy: kpt on fnl f)	1¼	**4**	33/1	55	4
2383[8]	**Up The Clarets (IRE)** (JJO'Neill) **2-8-11** ACulhane(11) (mid div & drvn along ½-wy: hdwy 2f out: no imp)	½	**5**	25/1	53	2
3395[6]	**Edna's Gift (IRE) (52)** (JBerry) **2-8-6** KDarley(2) (cl up: led 1½f out tl rdn & wknd ent fnl f)	¾	**6**	10/1	47	—
3294*	**Slew Magic (IRE)** (WGMTurner) **2-8-1**(7)ow2 DMcGaffin(8) (rr div: effrt appr str: n.d)	4	**7**	9/4[1]	40	—
3282[5]	**Russian Romeo (IRE) (60)** (BAMcMahon) **2-8-11** LNewton(7) (swtg: prom tl rdn & btn 2f out)	1¾	**8**	7/1	39	—
2827[6]	**Wee Christy (IRE)** (WMcKeown) **2-8-11** OPears(3) (nvr wnt pce)	1	**9**	25/1	36	—
3312[5]	**Eurofen (54)** (PDEvans) **2-8-4**(7) AMcCarthy(4) (bolted gng to s: led tl hdd & wknd over 2f out)	2½	**10**	16/1	31	—
2827[10]	**Petite Tache** (NChamberlain) **2-8-1**(5) KSked(5) (s.s: sn wl t.o)	dist	**11**	50/1	—	—

(SP 129.2%) **11 Rn**

1m 29.3 (5.70) CSF £16.39 TOTE £4.20: £1.30 £2.20 £1.70 (£23.90) Trio £40.50 OWNER Sheikh Amin Dahlawi (MIDDLEHAM) BRED Al Dahlawi Stud Co Ltd

No bid

STEWARDS' ENQUIRY Painter susp. 25-26/8/97 (incorrect use of whip).

OFFICIAL EXPLANATION **Petite Tache: was later found to have pulled muscles in her hindquarters.**

2935 Bint Nadia was again very much on her toes but she did not get into quite the state she did last time and, well handled, won it nicely. (9/4)
3427 Snappy Times had the run of the race by sticking to the inner but just failed to quicken enough. (6/1)
3045 Katie's Cracker, the pick on looks, responded to pressure in the closing stages to show she is coming to form. (13/2)
Wynbury Flyer needs plenty of help from the saddle but, despite staying on, gave the impression that softer ground would probably help. (33/1)
2233 Up The Clarets (IRE) put in his best run to date but he did need plenty of assistance to do so. (25/1)
2914 Edna's Gift (IRE) played a big part in things until running out of stamina in the final furlong. (10/1)
3294* Slew Magic (IRE) wears a pricker on her off-side and, not impressing on looks here, ran poorly. (9/4: op 6/4)
3312 Eurofen lost all chances when bolting on the way to post, using up most of his energy. (16/1)

3564 NORTHERN AGGREGATES NURSERY H'CAP (2-Y.O) (Class E)

6-55 (6-58) **5f 212y** £3,018.25 (£901.00: £430.50: £195.25) Stalls: Low GOING minus 0.22 sec per fur (GF)

				SP	RR	SF
3237[2]	**Clef of Silver (80)** (WJarvis) **2-9-7** JFortune(6) (chsd ldrs: rdn to ld over 1f out: edgd lft: styd on wl)	—	**1**	2/1[1]	85	45
3270[3]	**Pigeon (59)** (DWBarker) **2-8-0** TWilliams(2) (w ldr: led over 2f out tl over 1f out: nt qckn)	1½	**2**	2/1[1]	60	20
3257*	**Sandmoor Tartan (61)** (TDEasterby) **2-8-2** DWright(4) (lw: sn chsng ldrs: outpcd over 2f out: kpt on fnl f)	1¾	**3**	4/1[2]	57	17
3031[6]	**Iris May (75)** (JBerry) **2-9-2** KDarley(7) (lw: led tl hdd over 2f out: ev ch tl wknd fnl f)	1½	**4**	10/1	67	27
2700[5]	**Tremonnow (55)** (JMBradley) **2-7-5**(5) IonaWands(5) (outpcd tl sme late hdwy)	2½	**5**	15/2[3]	41	1
3451[14]	**Amington Girl (55)** (PDEvans) **2-7-3**(7) AMcCarthy(3) (sn outpcd & bhd: n.d)	1½	**6**	66/1	37	—
2233[2]	**Velvet Story (58)** (PDEvans) **2-7-13** DaleGibson(1) (spd 3f: sn wknd)	12	**7**	8/1	7	—

(SP 120.1%) **7 Rn**

1m 13.8 (2.90) CSF £5.91 TOTE £2.30: £1.70 £2.00 (£3.00) OWNER Silver Clef Racing Venture (NEWMARKET) BRED Mrs C. F. Van Straubenzee and Partners

LONG HANDICAP Amington Girl 7-6

3237 Clef of Silver is not the best of movers and is inclined to hang when in front but, given some strong assistance, he was always too good for this bunch. (2/1)
3270 Pigeon again showed signs of temperament at the start but then ran well and, now due to go up 13lb for her run last time, she will probably have made the handicapper think again. (2/1)
3257* Sandmoor Tartan does not look an easy ride but does stay well. (4/1: 3/1-9/2)
3031 Iris May looks well and has the ability but is not coming up with the goods. (10/1)
2700 Tremonnow looked too big and awkward for this track and would seem to need further. (15/2)
2233 Velvet Story raced too freely in the early stages and dropped tamely away from the halfway point. (8/1)

3565 CHARLES CLINKARD FINE FOOTWEAR H'CAP (0-70) (3-Y.O+) (Class E)

7-25 (7-29) **7f** £3,486.25 (£1,045.00: £502.50: £231.25) Stalls: Low GOING minus 0.22 sec per fur (GF)

				SP	RR	SF
3264[6]	**Rymer's Rascal (56)** (EJAlston) **5-9-3** ACulhane(7) (lw: in tch: hdwy to ld ins fnl f: styd on)	—	**1**	8/1	67	49
3285[4]	**Myttons Mistake (57)** (ABailey) **4-9-4** BDoyle(12) (a chsng ldrs: ch ins fnl f: kpt on)	1½	**2**	5/1[2]	65	47
3431[3]	**Bollin Dorothy (52)** (TDEasterby) **4-8-13** TWilliams(17) (mid div: hdwy over 2f out: kpt on fnl f)	s.h	**3**	7/1	60	42
3285[5]	**Gipsy Princess (57)** (MWEasterby) **3-8-12b** OPears(6) (led: clr ½-wy: hdd ins fnl f: no ex)	hd	**4**	7/1	64	40
3443[9]	**Miss Pigalle (38)** (MissLAPerratt) **6-7-13b** NKennedy(3) (mid div: hdwy 2f out: nrst fin)	2½	**5**	20/1	40	22
3476[8]	**Roseate Lodge (40)** (SEKettlewell) **11-7-8**(7) JennyBenson(1) (lw: bhd: effrt ent str: nvr rchd ldrs)	3½	**6**	8/1	34	16
3285[2]	**Sing With the Band (43)** (BAMcMahon) **6-8-4** KDarley(16) (lw: chsd ldrs: effrt over 2f out: wknd fnl f)	½	**7**	9/2[1]	35	17
1800[9]	**Rude Awakening (68)** (CWFairhurst) **3-9-2**(7) TSiddall(2) (lw: chsd ldrs tl grad wknd fnl 2f)	¾	**8**	25/1	59	35
3213[4]	**Stolen Music (IRE) (35)** (REBarr) **4-7-5v**1(5) IonaWands(8) (s.i.s: nvr nrr)	nk	**9**	100/1	25	7
3240[7]	**Okay Baby (IRE) (40)** (JMBradley) **5-7-10v**1(5)ow5 KSked(5) (b.nr fore: mid div: effrt appr str: sn btn)	5	**10**	50/1	19	—
3208[13]	**Spotted Eagle (57)** (DNicholls) **4-9-4** AlexGreaves(11) (cl up over 4f: sn lost pl)	¾	**11**	25/1	34	16
	Kentucky Dreams (35) (MrsAMNaughton) **7-7-3**(7) JMcAuley(10) (in tch: wandered u.p 2f out: sn btn)	nk	**12**	100/1	11	—
3321[8]	**Persephone (36)** (JLHarris) **4-7-11**ow1 DaleGibson(13) (lw: nvr trbld ldrs)	1½	**13**	100/1	9	—
3285[14]	**Komlucky (48)** (ABMulholland) **5-8-6v**(3) PFessey(14) (a bhd)	2	**14**	25/1	16	—
3075[2]	**Prima Silk (66)** (MJRyan) **6-9-13** GBardwell(9) (rdn & bhd fr ½-wy)	6	**15**	6/1[3]	20	2
3208[14]	**Meranti (59)** (JMBradley) **4-9-6** JFortune(4) (cl up tl wknd over 2f out & eased)	7	**16**	10/1	—	—

(SP 126.7%) **16 Rn**

1m 26.4 (2.80) CSF £42.32 CT £288.19 TOTE £11.10: £1.90 £1.30 £1.60 £2.10 (£40.60) Trio £41.50 OWNER Mr Brian Chambers (PRESTON) BRED Mrs Sara Logue and David Lewis

LONG HANDICAP Kentucky Dreams 7-2 Stolen Music (IRE) 6-13 Okay Baby (IRE) 6-13 Persephone 6-9

WEIGHT FOR AGE 3yo-6lb

OFFICIAL EXPLANATION **Meranti: the rider reported that the gelding appeared to be suffering from a back problem.**

3264 Rymer's Rascal looked in tremendous heart and found the hustle and bustle of this big field right up his street and did it well. (8/1)

3285 Myttons Mistake is running consistently well and ought to pick up another race or two in due course. (5/1)
3431 Bollin Dorothy is running well and deserves a change of luck and perhaps easier ground would help. (7/1)
3285 Gipsy Princess appears well enough handicapped and is certainly in good form but, in trying to steal this, she probably did too much too soon and was just caught. (7/1)
3443 Miss Pigalle seems to like this track and finished well, albeit too late. (20/1)
3476 Roseate Lodge ran a fair race but having his second run of the week here probably made all the difference. (8/1: 5/1-10/1)
3285 Sing With the Band had her chances but again failed to take them. (9/2)

3566 HARRISON TAMAR CLAIMING STKS (3-Y.O+) (Class F)
7-55 (7-55) **5f** £2,616.00 (£726.00: £348.00) Stalls: Low GOING minus 0.22 sec per fur (GF)

				SP	RR	SF
3280⁴	**River Tern (68)** (JMBradley) **4-9-0** JFortune(2) (s.i.s: hdwy 2f out: rdn to ld ins fnl f: r.o)	—	**1**	7/1	68	31
3273⁸	**The Happy Fox (IRE) (71)** (BAMcMahon) **5-8-12** LNewton(1) (lw: cl up: led 1½f out tl ins fnl f: kpt on)	¾	**2**	100/30 2	64	27
3481 11	**The Wad (63)** (DNicholls) **4-8-3**(7) TSiddall(7) (lw: chsd ldrs: hdwy over 1f out: kpt on one pce)	2½	**3**	10/1	54	17
3481 12	**Captain Carat (59)** (DNicholls) **6-8-9b** AlexGreaves(4) (lw: trckd ldrs: smooth hdwy to chal 1½f out: sn rdn & no ex)	1	**4**	11/1	49	12
3287⁶	**Imp Express (IRE) (38)** (GMMoore) **4-8-8** DaleGibson(8) (sn drvn along: hdwy 2f out: nvr able to chal)	nk	**5**	25/1	47	10
3378*	**Palacegate Touch (79)** (JBerry) **7-9-2b**(3) PFessey(6) (lw: in tch: drvn along ½-wy: no imp)	s.h	**6**	7/4 1	58	21
3287⁸	**Southern Dominion (43)** (MissJFCraze) **5-8-10b** SWebster(3) (lw: led 3½f: sn rdn & btn)	1½	**7**	33/1	45	8
3326⁸	**Intiaash (IRE) (78)** (DHaydnJones) **5-8-9**(5) KSked(9) (swtg: dwlt: sme hdwy u.p ½-wy: n.d)	1	**8**	9/2 3	45	8
	Redoubtable (USA) (DWChapman) **6-9-5** ACulhane(5) (outpcd & bhd fr ½-wy)	3	**9**	7/1	41	4
				(SP 126.8%)	**9 Rn**	

60.5 secs (2.80) CSF £30.79 TOTE £7.80: £2.00 £1.60 £4.30 (£10.10) Trio £33.70 OWNER Mr M. B. Carver (CHEPSTOW) BRED Bearstone Stud

3280 River Tern is a character but was well suited by his strong rider who handled him to perfection. (7/1)
3024 The Happy Fox (IRE) has the speed and had the draw here but when it came down to a battle he was always second best. (100/30)
2938* The Wad ran well and, with a better draw, would have seriously been in the shake-up. (10/1)
2754 Captain Carat travelled well but failed to do a tap when ridden. (11/1)
3287 Imp Express (IRE) is a frustrating sort who generally has a chance but never quite does enough. (25/1)
3378* Palacegate Touch always found this just too competitive for his liking. (7/4)

3567 DURHAM CHESHIRE HOME MAIDEN H'CAP (0-70) (3-Y.O+) (Class E)
8-25 (8-29) **1m 7f 177y** £3,070.25 (£917.00: £438.50: £199.25) Stalls: Low GOING minus 0.22 sec per fur (GF)

				SP	RR	SF
3283⁶	**Clash of Swords (48)** (PCalver) **4-9-3** KDarley(2) (trckd ldrs: led over 2f out: hld on wl)	—	**1**	7/1 3	56	13
2662W	**Ardarroch Prince (57)** (MrsMReveley) **6-9-12** ACulhane(4) (lw: unruly s: a.p: effrt 4f out: chal over 1f out: hrd rdn & r.o)	hd	**2**	3/1 1	65	22
3429⁴	**Finestatetobein (30)** (FWatson) **4-7-10v¹**(3) PFessey(1) (trckd ldrs: effrt on ins 2f out: n.m.r fnl f: kpt on)	1½	**3**	16/1	36	—
3461⁶	**Penny Peppermint (27)** (REBarr) **5-7-10** NKennedy(7) (bhd: styd on wl fnl 3f: nrst fin)	1¼	**4**	33/1	32	—
2908⁶	**Ziggy's Viola (IRE) (52)** (MrsMReveley) **3-8-6** JFortune(8) (hld up: gd hdwy over 2f out: sn chsng ldrs: nt qckn fnl f)	nk	**5**	7/1 3	57	—
3129²	**Eurolink Windsong (IRE) (46)** (MartynWane) **3-7-9**(5)ow4 KSked(5) (plld hrd: racd wd: effrt 4f out: no imp)	2½	**6**	5/1 2	48	—
3028⁵	**Jucinda (55)** (JPearce) **3-8-9** GBardwell(10) (plld hrd: led after 5f tl over 2f out: wknd)	nk	**7**	9/1	57	—
2387⁵	**Surtsey (65)** (MJohnston) **3-9-5** BDoyle(9) (lw: led 5f: rdn 7f out: wknd appr str)	½	**8**	16/1	67	9
3015 10	**Warning Reef (56)** (PEccles) **4-9-11h** DeanMcKeown(3) (prom tl outpcd 5f out: n.d after)	½	**9**	14/1	57	14
3108⁵	**Go Hence (66)** (WJarvis) **3-9-6** OPears(6) (swtg: rn in snatches: shkn up & hdwy 6f out: wknd appr str & eased)	18	**10**	3/1 1	49	—
				(SP 123.0%)	**10 Rn**	

3m 36.7 (14.70) CSF £27.28 CT £308.78 TOTE £6.70: £2.40 £2.20 £3.80 (£26.30) Trio £120.80 OWNER Mrs Janis MacPherson (RIPON)
BRED Sheikh Mohammed Bin Rashid Al Maktoum
LONG HANDICAP Penny Peppermint 7-9
WEIGHT FOR AGE 3yo-15lb
OFFICIAL EXPLANATION Go Hence: choked.

3283 Clash of Swords threw this race away last year but, given some splendid assistance, did nothing wrong here and showed a good attitude late on. (7/1)
1558 Ardarroch Prince gave problems aplenty before the start and then had his chances but this awkward-looking individual is not entirely suited to this track and this was a decent effort. (3/1)
3429 Finestatetobein ran well with the blinkers on for the first time and had he seen daylight in the closing stages it might have been a close-run thing. (16/1)
2207 Penny Peppermint is slow but sure and was picking up ground when it was all too late. (33/1)
2908 Ziggy's Viola (IRE) gives the impression that she has more ability if she can be persuaded. (7/1)
3129 Eurolink Windsong (IRE) would have preferred a much stronger gallop and spoilt her chances by pulling her rider's arms out. (5/1)
2236 Warning Reef (14/1: 20/1-12/1)
3108 Go Hence, dripping with sweat beforehand, ran no sort of race and would seem to have a problem. (3/1)

T/Plpt: £187.10 (79.11 Tckts). T/Qdpt: £39.50 (27.7 Tckts) AA

3407-HAYDOCK (L-H) (Good to Firm)
Friday August 15th
Race 1 no time taken
WEATHER: fine & warm WIND: nil

3568 SUTTON RACING SCHOOLS APPRENTICE H'CAP (0-80) (3-Y.O+) (Class F)
5-40 (5-40) **1m 3f 200y** £2,416.00 (£676.00: £328.00) Stalls: High GOING minus 0.26 sec per fur (GF)

				SP	RR	SF
3467²	**Tarxien (62)** (KRBurke) **3-8-3** DSweeney(5) (lw: hld up: hdwy to chse ldr 6f out: led over 3f out: shkn up 2f out: r.o)	—	**1**	6/5 1	74	—
3229²	**Supermick (44)** (WRMuir) **6-7-5**(5) PDoe(1) (led tl over 3f out: sn rdn: wknd wl over 1f out)	5	**2**	5/2 2	49	—

2718[4] **Secret Service (IRE) (62)** (CWThornton) **5-8-9b**(5) MNutter(2) (lw: s.s: sn rcvrd to chse ldrs: rdn & outpcd fnl 3f: t.o) ....12 **3** 100/30[3] 51 —
Suvalu (USA) (55) (MGMeagher) **5-8-7** DGriffiths(3) (chsd ldr to ½-wy: rdn & wknd over 4f out: t.o) ....½ **4** 9/1 44 —
(SP 107.1%) **4 Rn**

No Time Taken CSF £3.97 TOTE £1.90 (£1.90) OWNER Mr David Whyte (WANTAGE) BRED Sheikh Mohammed bin Rashid al Maktoum
LONG HANDICAP Supermick 7-5
WEIGHT FOR AGE 3yo-11lb
3467 Tarxien was able to get off the mark in what turned out to be a very moderate affair and he was the only one on the bridle entering the last quarter-mile but he was not doing a lot once in front and not too much should be written into this success. (6/5: op evens)
3229 Supermick did win a couple of races last summer and he has been promising to strike form recently but he was forced to make the running here and, though he did not give in without a fight, had had enough below the distance. (5/2)
2718 Secret Service (IRE) did not do a lot for his inexperienced boy and he was never able to get close enough to cause concern. (100/30)
Suvalu (USA) (9/1: op 5/1)

3569 E.B.F. BELLCHARM RENAULT MAIDEN STKS (2-Y.O) (Class D)
6-10 (6-10) **6f** £3,493.00 (£1,054.00: £512.00: £241.00) Stalls: High GOING minus 0.26 sec per fur (GF)

			SP	RR	SF
3151[5]	**Vignette (USA)** (JHMGosden) **2-8-9** LDettori(9) (mde all: clr wl over 1f out: pushed out fnl f) .... —	**1**	4/6[1]	82+	43
2706[2]	**Requestor** (JGFitzGerald) **2-9-0** KFallon(5) (lw: a.p: chsd wnr fnl 2f: no imp) 4	**2**	9/4[2]	76	37
	Adjutant (BJMeehan) **2-9-0** MTebbutt(2) (w'like: leggy: bit bkwd: s.i.s: sn outpcd: hdwy 2f out: r.o wl) 1¼	**3**	14/1	73	34
2842[7]	**Legend of Love** (JAGlover) **2-9-0** TSprake(3) (lw: mid div: drvn along ½-wy: kpt on appr fnl f) ....hd	**4**	10/1[3]	73	34
3265[5]	**Heathyards Sheik** (RHollinshead) **2-9-0** FLynch(6) (chsd ldrs: rdn over 2f out: sn btn) 2	**5**	33/1	67	28
3127[4]	**Sara Moon Classic (IRE)** (KMcAuliffe) **2-9-0** WJO'Connor(8) (chsd wnr 4f: sn rdn, wknd & eased) 3½	**6**	14/1	58	19
	Laramania (PDEvans) **2-9-0** JFEgan(4) (lt-f: bit bkwd: outpcd: a t.o) 7	**7**	25/1	39	—
3411[11]	**Caroline's Pet (IRE)** (ABailey) **2-8-9** SDrowne(7) (s.s: sn drvn along: a outpcd: t.o) 2	**8**	40/1	29	—
	Bollin Ann (TDEasterby) **2-8-9** JCarroll(1) (lt-f: s.i.s: nvr gng pce of ldrs: t.o) ....nk	**9**	16/1	28	—

(SP 128.3%) **9 Rn**

1m 13.72 (2.02) CSF £2.45 TOTE £2.00: £1.10 £1.20 £2.30 (£1.30) Trio £5.60 OWNER Mr George Strawbridge (NEWMARKET) BRED George Strawbridge Jnr.
3151 Vignette (USA), stepping back a furlong, had little more than a good workout to win this, though her jockey did keep her up to her work in the latter stages just to let her know she had been in a race. (4/6)
2706 Requestor had to admit the winner much too good for him but he ran another promising race and fate will favour him before long. (9/4)
Adjutant, who comes from a good winning family, did look as though he would appreciate easier ground but he picked up well in the closing stages after getting outpaced and should have little trouble winning races. (14/1)
2359 Legend of Love, always struggling with the pace, was finding his stride inside the distance and he should come into his own when tackling a longer trip. (10/1)
3265 Heathyards Sheik is getting the hang of the game now and he should not be brushed aside as yet. (33/1)
3127 Sara Moon Classic (IRE) (14/1: 12/1-20/1)

3570 BAILEYS ORIGINAL IRISH CREAM H'CAP (0-70) (3-Y.O+) (Class E)
6-40 (6-40) **1m 2f 120y** £2,997.50 (£905.00: £440.00: £207.50) Stalls: High GOING minus 0.26 sec per fur (GF)

			SP	RR	SF
3382[4]	**Wentbridge Lad (IRE) (48)** (ABailey) **7-8-10v** JWeaver(1) (b: b.off hind: lw: hld up: swtchd rt & hdwy 2f out: led ins fnl f: comf) .... —	**1**	100/30[2]	61	41
3315*	**Mcgillycuddy Reeks (IRE) (62)** (DonEnricoIncisa) **6-9-10** 5x KimTinkler(2) (lw: hld up: hdwy over 2f out: led over 1f out tl ins fnl f) ....¾	**2**	5/2[1]	74	54
3381*	**Davoski (75)** (BWHills) **3-9-13** 5x DHolland(6) (lw: a.p: led 2f out: rdn & hdd over 1f out: edgd lft & kpt on towards fin) ....nk	**3**	7/2[3]	86	56
3256[4]	**Portite Sophie (39)** (MBrittain) **6-7-8**(7) DMernagh(5) (swtg: a chsng ldrs: effrt & nt clr run over 2f out: swtchd rt & r.o one pce) 1½	**4**	14/1	48	28
3467[5]	**General Glow (45)** (PDEvans) **4-8-7b** JFEgan(8) (chsd ldr: rdn to chal 3f out: one pce fnl 2f) 5	**5**	14/1	47	27
3200[9]	**Mercury (IRE) (38)** (JAGlover) **4-8-0b** TSprake(3) (hld up: a in rr) 2½	**6**	16/1	36	16
	Jimjareer (IRE) (42) (CaptJWilson) **4-8-1**(3)ow1 DSweeney(9) (b.hind: swtg: bkwd: led to 2f out: wknd appr fnl f) ....nk	**7**	20/1	39	18
2570[7]	**Maradata (IRE) (63)** (RHollinshead) **5-9-11** LDettori(7) (s.s: effrt & drvn along over 2f out: no imp) 1¼	**8**	6/1	58	38
3315[17]	**Princely Affair (40)** (JMBradley) **4-8-2b**[1] SDrowne(4) (trckd ldrs over 6f: sn lost tch) 2	**9**	25/1	32	12

(SP 116.0%) **9 Rn**

2m 15.75 (4.25) CSF £11.06 CT £27.59 TOTE £4.10: £1.30 £1.40 £1.60 (£6.00) Trio £5.30 OWNER Mr John Pugh (TARPORLEY) BRED Peter Doyle
WEIGHT FOR AGE 3yo-10lb
3382 Wentbridge Lad (IRE) really appreciated this step up to ten furlongs and, given a very competent ride, readily landed the gamble. He has not been given much time to rest on his laurels as he runs again tomorrow. (100/30)
3315* Mcgillycuddy Reeks (IRE) was unfortunate to meet one too good on this occasion but she ran up to her mark and certainly lost no caste in defeat. (5/2)
3381* Davoski, penalised 5lb for his success over course and distance last week, did edge over to the far rail after being headed but he stuck to the task in hand and there could be more success to be had. (7/2)
3256 Portite Sophie, searching for an opening for the final quarter-mile, had to switch to get any run at all and, by the time she found space, the principals had gone beyond recall. She is running consistently well and compensation awaits. (14/1)
3467 General Glow does his winning at this time of year and he performed with credit here but he was getting no joy in his battle with the long-time leader from the turn for home and that probably took the stuffing out of him. (14/1)
Jimjareer (IRE), having his first outing since December 1996 and trying a slightly longer trip, did a good job of pacemaking until feeling the strain approaching the final furlong. He has only ever won one race and that was over five furlongs but he shaped with promise here and there could be a race in store. (20/1)

3571 RAINHILL NURSERY H'CAP (2-Y.O) (Class E)
7-10 (7-10) **5f** £2,932.50 (£885.00: £430.00: £202.50) Stalls: High GOING minus 0.26 sec per fur (GF)

			SP	RR	SF
3192[10]	**Gipsy Moth (84)** (BJMeehan) **2-9-7** JWeaver(6) (lw: mde all: rdn over 1f out: r.o wl) .... —	**1**	2/1[1]	91	55
3307[13]	**Jackerin (IRE) (77)** (BSRothwell) **2-9-0** MFenton(5) (dwlt: swtchd lft & hdwy wl over 1f out: rdn & edgd rt: r.o)1½	**2**	11/1	79	43

3152^{9}	**Eastern Lyric (79)** (JBerry) **2-8-11**(5) PRoberts(7) (a.p: effrt & squeezed for room ins fnl f: nt rcvr)	2	**3**	5/1^{3}	75	39
3483^{2}	**Oriel Girl (66)** (PDEvans) **2-8-3v** JFEgan(4) (a.p: rdn whn tightened up ins fnl f: one pce)	nk	**4**	5/1^{3}	61	25
3257^{4}	**Hayburner (61)** (MWEasterby) **2-7-5b**(7)ow2 RWinston(3) (prom: ev ch over 1f out: sn rdn: unable qckn)	hd	**5**	6/1	56	18
3239^{2}	**Happy Days (74)** (DMoffatt) **2-8-8**(3) DarrenMoffatt(2) (outpcd: rdn 2f out: no rspnse)	5	**6**	9/2^{2}	53	17
3314^{4}	**Glass River (60)** (PDEvans) **2-7-4**(7)ow1 DMernagh(1) (racd centre: prom: rdn & outpcd fnl 2f)	½	**7**	20/1	37	—

(SP 112.2%) **7 Rn**

61.17 secs (1.67) CSF £22.27 TOTE £2.80: £1.50 £4.00 (£33.40) OWNER Mrs K. J. Crangle (UPPER LAMBOURN) BRED P. T. Tellwright
LONG HANDICAP Hayburner 7-6 Glass River 7-4
2926* Gipsy Moth proved a class apart and always looked well in control. It is doubtful if the trouble behind her had much effect on the final outcome. (2/1)
1161 Jackerin (IRE), returning to the minimum trip, was last to exit the stalls. Pulled off the rails to find room to deliver his challenge, he drifted back under strong pressure and tightened up a couple of rivals and he lacked the pace to reach the winner. (11/1)
1635 Eastern Lyric ran well but she was struggling to hold her pitch when she was impeded two hundred yards out and it may well have cost her the runner-up prize. (5/1)
3483 Oriel Girl was possibly the worst affected in the scrimmaging but she was under strong pressure at the time and her measure had been taken. (5/1)
3257 Hayburner showed plenty of speed to press the winner but he was off the bridle on the approach to the final furlong and had to admit he had met his match. (6/1)

3572 SWAN WITH TWO NECKS (S) STKS (3-Y.O) (Class F)
7-40 (7-40) **1m 30y** £2,528.00 (£708.00: £344.00) Stalls: Low GOING minus 0.26 sec per fur (GF)

				SP	RR	SF
3132^{4}	**Begorrat (IRE) (71)** (BJMeehan) **3-9-0b**^{1} MTebbutt(2) (hld up in tch: jnd ldr 2f out: sn led: rdn clr)	—	**1**	10/11^{1}	74	40
3038^{5}	**Bollero (IRE) (55)** (JBerry) **3-8-11**(3) TEDurcan(4) (lw: led tl wl over 1f out: rallied u.p one pce fnl f)	5	**2**	7/2^{2}	64	30
3313^{3}	**La Doyenne (IRE) (43)** (CBBBooth) **3-8-9** KFallon(3) (lw: chsd ldrs: rdn & outpcd fnl 2f)	6	**3**	14/1	47	13
	Siggiewi (NMBabbage) **3-8-9** TSprake(6) (w'like: scope: bit bkwd: sn bhd & outpcd: styd on fnl 2f: nrst fin)	1¼	**4**	16/1	45	11
3336^{9}	**Docklands Carriage (IRE) (60)** (NTinkler) **3-9-5b** KimTinkler(1) (trckd ldrs: hrd drvn & outpcd over 2f out)	2	**5**	14/1	51	17
3038^{10}	**Joyful Joy (28)** (BPJBaugh) **3-8-9** JFEgan(9) (trckd ldrs: effrt & rdn 2f out: no imp)	1½	**6**	33/1	38	4
3068^{9}	**Ballydinero (IRE) (40)** (CaptJWilson) **3-9-0v**^{1} JCarroll(5) (lw: chsd ldr: rdn over 3f out: sn wknd)	5	**7**	33/1	33	—
3313^{2}	**Chief's Spirit** (GMMoore) **3-9-0** JWeaver(8) (s.s: a bhd t.o)	13	**8**	6/1^{3}	8	—
3250^{5}	**Honiara Bay** (MissAStokell) **3-8-4**(5) PRoberts(10) (in rr: reminders 4f out: no rspnse: t.o)	5	**9**	33/1	—	—

(SP 116.9%) **9 Rn**

1m 44.31 (3.71) CSF £3.75 TOTE £1.90: £1.10 £1.50 £1.70 (£3.30) Trio £15.30 OWNER Mr R. A. Bernard (UPPER LAMBOURN) BRED C. Crowley
Sold M Flynn 8,400gns
3132 Begorrat (IRE), lowered in class and fitted with blinkers for the first time, looked the winner from a long way out and he asserted to prove the point inside the distance. (10/11: evens-4/5)
3038 Bollero (IRE) again tried to make all and she only had the winner to contend with for the final quarter-mile but that rival came there full of running and she quite simply had no answer. (7/2)
3313 La Doyenne (IRE) has done all her racing at sprint distances in the past and her attempt to mount a challenge in the latter stages came to little and she was never a factor. (14/1)
Siggiewi, a Mystiko filly, did not fare badly on this racecourse debut, staying on steadily in the closing stages, and she can only improve with this experience behind her. (16/1)
2755 Docklands Carriage (IRE) is failing to see the trip out and a return to sprinting would seem the obvious solution. (14/1)

3573 KNOTTY ASH H'CAP (0-70) (3-Y.O+) (Class E)
8-10 (8-12) **1m 30y** £3,127.50 (£945.00: £460.00: £217.50) Stalls: Low GOING minus 0.26 sec per fur (GF)

				SP	RR	SF
3443*	**Clytha Hill Lad (51)** (JMBradley) **6-8-13** 6x SDrowne(10) (a chsng ldrs: led ins fnl f: rdn out)	—	**1**	7/1^{2}	62	42
3285^{3}	**Needle Match (54)** (JJO'Neill) **4-9-2** JCarroll(12) (lw: hld up & bhd: hdwy on ins 2f out: swtchd rt: r.o wl towards fin)	1¼	**2**	7/1^{2}	63	43
3264^{12}	**Spanish Verdict (53)** (DenysSmith) **10-9-1** KFallon(13) (lw: hld up: hdwy & rdn 2f out: r.o wl ins fnl f)	1¼	**3**	10/1	59	39
3269^{4}	**May Queen Megan (43)** (MrsALMKing) **4-8-5** MFenton(11) (trckd ldrs: rdn over 2f out: styd on wl fnl f)	hd	**4**	20/1	49	29
3428^{7}	**Winston (53)** (JDBethell) **4-9-1** DHolland(1) (chsd ldrs: effrt on ins 2f out: rdn & edgd lft ins fnl f: unable qckn)	1¼	**5**	10/1	56	36
3143^{6}	**Three For A Pound (66)** (JAGlover) **3-9-7** TSprake(17) (lw: stdd s: hld up: hdwy fnl 2f: nrst fin)	1¼	**6**	12/1	67	40
3456^{11}	**Prime Partner (36)** (TDEasterby) **4-7-5b**(7) RWinston(2) (led: rdn & hdd ins fnl f: btn whn hmpd & snatched up cl home)	nk	**7**	16/1	36	16
3315^{9}	**Naughty Pistol (USA) (46)** (PDEvans) **5-8-8b** JFEgan(5) (prom: rdn wl over 1f out: wknd & eased towards fin)	s.h	**8**	14/1	46	26
3264^{3}	**Running Green (62)** (DMoffatt) **6-9-7v**(3) DarrenMoffatt(7) (hld up: hdwy over 2f out: styng on whn bdly hmpd ins fnl f: nt rcvr)	1½	**9**	10/1	59	39
2828^{7}	**Tissue of Lies (USA) (58)** (MJohnston) **4-9-6** JWeaver(3) (trckd ldrs: rdn over 2f out: grad faded)	1¼	**10**	10/1	53	33
3029^{7}	**Highspeed (IRE) (55)** (SEKettlewell) **5-9-0b**^{1}(3) DSweeney(8) (nvr trbld ldrs)	1	**11**	20/1	48	28
3316*	**Forest Fantasy (56)** (JWharton) **4-8-13**(5) 6x PRoberts(6) (lw: prom: rdn & wknd over 2f out)	1	**12**	5/1^{1}	47	27
2892^{10}	**Northern Judge (37)** (APJames) **4-7-6b**(7) PDoe(4) (in tch: rdn ½-wy: sn wknd)	2	**13**	25/1	24	4
2788^{13}	**Crissem (IRE) (57)** (RHollinshead) **4-9-5** FLynch(16) (lw: s.i.s: a bhd)	5	**14**	20/1	34	14
3310^{3}	**Ochos Rios (IRE) (55)** (BSRothwell) **6-9-0**(3) TEDurcan(9) (a in rr)	s.h	**15**	9/1^{3}	32	12
2868^{7}	**Mr Rough (53)** (DMorris) **6-9-1** NDay(15) (lw: hld up: n.d)	nk	**16**	10/1	30	10

(SP 135.5%) **16 Rn**

1m 43.99 (3.39) CSF £53.26 CT £472.99 TOTE £7.50: £2.00 £1.50 £2.30 £5.00 (£39.90) Trio £87.10 OWNER Mrs Marion Morgan (CHEPSTOW) BRED Mrs M. C. Morgan
WEIGHT FOR AGE 3yo-7lb
3443* Clytha Hill Lad has certainly made hay while the sun shines in the past couple of months and this smoothly-gained success is further evidence that he is still ahead of the handicapper. (7/1)
3285 Needle Match, one of many who found trouble in running in the latter stages, ran on strongly once free but by then the winner had set sail for home. (7/1)
3264 Spanish Verdict, hard at work below the distance, kept staying on and this veteran is still capable of winning another race or two. (10/1)
3269 May Queen Megan, having her first try at a mile, battled on willingly under a forceful ride in the latter stages and she should be able to make her mark at this trip. (20/1)

3428 Winston, never far away, stuck to his work under strong pressure but he was inclined to wander and failed the necessary turn of finishing speed. (10/1)
3143 Three For A Pound, ridden to get the trip, was doing all his best work inside the last couple of furlongs but too late to prove troublesome. (12/1)
2880 Prime Partner set a brisk pace and only gave best inside the final furlong. Held but still battling away, he was forced to take avoiding action when Winston took his ground nearing the finish. (16/1)
3264 Running Green, improving from the rear up the inside rail, was staying on strongly under pressure when he was stopped in his tracks one hundred yards out. It was more than likely that he would have made the frame and he deserves another chance. (10/1)
1878 Mr Rough (10/1: op 16/1)

T/Plpt: £15.10 (1,033.55 Tckts). T/Qdpt: £8.70 (114.03 Tckts) IM

2860-NEWBURY (L-H) (Good to firm)
Friday August 15th
WEATHER: hot WIND: almost nil

3574 GROSVENOR CASINO BRISTOL MAIDEN STKS (2-Y.O F) (Class D)
2-10 (2-12) **6f 8y** £4,276.00 (£1,288.00: £624.00: £292.00) Stalls: Centre GOING minus 0.33 sec per fur (GF)

					SP	RR	SF
	Shmoose (IRE) (SbinSuroor) **2-8-11** LDettori(12) (gd sort: mde all: clr whn hung lft fnl f: comf)	—	1	1/3 1	89+	57
2831 3	**Musical Twist (USA)** (PWChapple-Hyam) **2-8-11** KFallon(4) (w'like: a.p: rdn over 2f out: chsd wnr fnl f: r.o)	1½	2	16/1	85+	53
2831 3	**Thanksgiving (IRE)** (MajorDNChappell) **2-8-11** GCarter(9) (chsd wnr 5f: wknd ins fnl f)	4	3	12/1 3	74	42
	Celtic Cross (LordHuntingdon) **2-8-11** DHarrison(2) (unf: scope: hld up mid div: rdn 3f out: r.o one pce fnl 2f)	hd	4	33/1	74	42
	Sweet Sorrow (IRE) (CFWall) **2-8-11** GDuffield(3) (leggy: hld up mid div: nvr nr to chal)	2½	5	50/1	68	36
2597 12	**Gandoura (USA)** (JHMGosden) **2-8-11** RHills(7) (trckd ldrs: one pce fnl 2f)	½	6	20/1	66	34
	Transylvania (JLDunlop) **2-8-11** PatEddery(11) (unf: prom over 4f)	s.h	7	14/1	66	34
3235 12	**Greeba** (RHannon) **2-8-11** DaneO'Neill(16) (prom 4f)	3	8	33/1	58	26
	Amabel (USA) (IABalding) **2-8-11** SWhitworth(14) (w'like: scope: lost pl after 2f: no hdwy fnl 2f)	1¾	9	50/1	54	22
	Second Chorus (IRE) (PWChapple-Hyam) **2-8-11** JReid(15) (neat: rdn over 3f out: n.d)	s.h	10	7/1 2	53	21
	Maiella (RHannon) **2-8-11** MRoberts(1) (lt-f: a bhd)	½	11	33/1	52	20
	Emmajoun (APJarvis) **2-8-11** JLowe(13) (w'like: s.i.s: sn prom: wknd 2f out: eased whn btn fnl f)	1¼	12	40/1	49	17
	Azulino (IRE) (JWHills) **2-8-11** MHills(6) (leggy: bit bkwd: s.s: a bhd)	2½	13	40/1	42	10
	March Fourteenth (USA) (JHMGosden) **2-8-11** WRyan(5) (a bhd)	1¼	14	33/1	39	7
	Little Cracker (AGNewcombe) **2-8-11** FNorton(10) (leggy: bkwd: a bhd)	5	15	100/1	26	—
	Loubin Lane (AGNewcombe) **2-8-11** JWeaver(8) (w'like: rdn over 4f out: a bhd: t.o)	8	16	66/1	4	—

(SP 135.6%) **16 Rn**

1m 12.55 (0.75) CSF £7.81 TOTE £1.40: £1.10 £3.90 £2.30 (£21.10) Trio £48.30 OWNER Godolphin (NEWMARKET) BRED Sheikh Mohammed bin Rashid al Maktoum
Shmoose (IRE), a half-sister to Kerry Ring out of a 1,000 Guineas runner-up, lived up to her big home reputation and would have won by a wider margin if she had kept straight. More will be heard of this attractive individual who is rather on the small side at the moment. (1/3: op 4/6)
Musical Twist (USA), out of a Fred Darling winner who was unbeaten as a juvenile, was considered the stable's second string here but ran a race full of promise and already seems up to tackling further. (16/1)
2831 Thanksgiving (IRE), a half-sister to Dwingeloo and Suris, paid the penalty for trying to make a race of it with the useful winner. (12/1: 7/1-14/1)
Celtic Cross, bred to need further, looks the type who should do better given time. (33/1)
Sweet Sorrow (IRE), a half-sister to Farewell My Love, made a more than satisfactory start to her career. (50/1)
Gandoura (USA), a half-sister to Intidab and Kafaf, stepped up considerably on her Newmarket debut and may do even better over a longer trip. (20/1)
Transylvania, a half-sister to Sava River, should do better in due course and is bred to eventually require much further. (14/1: 8/1-16/1)
Second Chorus (IRE), a half-sister to Crystal Crossing and Lady Bankes, was disappointing and it will be surprising if she does not turn out to be better than this bare form suggests. (7/1: op 4/1)

3575 BONUSPRINT H'CAP (0-100) (3-Y.O) (Class C)
2-40 (2-41) **1m 2f 6y** £6,027.50 (£1,820.00: £885.00: £417.50) Stalls: Low GOING minus 0.33 sec per fur (GF)

				SP	RR	SF
3012 5	**Song of Freedom (86)** (JHMGosden) **3-8-8** LDettori(12) (hld up: stdy hdwy over 2f out: led ins fnl f: rdn out)	—	1	5/4 1	92+	56
3190 5	**Bali Paradise (USA) (92)** (PFICole) **3-9-0** PatEddery(6) (chsd ldr: led 3f to 1f out: r.o)	nk	2	7/1 2	98	62
1595 8	**Prince of Denial (81)** (DWPArbuthnot) **3-8-3** SWhitworth(1) (lw: hld up: hdwy over 2f out: led 1f out: sn hdd: r.o)	hd	3	12/1	86	50
2561 5	**Marie Dora (FR) (80)** (IABalding) **3-7-13**(3) MartinDwyer(7) (hld up: hdwy over 2f out: n.m.r over 1f out: swtchd lft: r.o)	1¼	4	14/1	83	47
3140*	**Chief Monarch (85)** (BSmart) **3-8-7** JWeaver(11) (lw: s.s: stdy hdwy & nt clr run over 2f out: r.o ins fnl f)	hd	5	10/1	88	52
3263 6	**Shadoof (78)** (WRMuir) **3-7-9**(5) RMullen(3) (lw: hld up: hdwy & n.m.r on ins over 2f out: swtchd rt over 1f out: r.o ins fnl f)	1¼	6	14/1	79	43
3051 7	**Premier Bay (99)** (PWHarris) **3-9-2**(5) CLowther(2) (lw: prom: ev ch over 2f out: sn rdn: wknd 1f out)	3½	7	16/1	95	59
3061*	**Party Romance (USA) (86)** (BHanbury) **3-8-8** WRyan(10) (stdd s: plld hrd: sn chsng ldrs: rdn over 3f out: eased whn btn ins fnl f)	1¼	8	15/2 3	80	44
2729 9	**Gift Token (87)** (MajorDNChappell) **3-8-9** KFallon(4) (mid div: rdn over 4f out: sn bhd)	1¼	9	33/1	79	43
3125 12	**Cinema Paradiso (92)** (PFICole) **3-9-0** JReid(5) (plld hrd: led: sn clr: hdd 3f out: wknd wl over 1f out)	nk	10	33/1	83	47
3128 11	**Raindancing (IRE) (84)** (RHannon) **3-8-6** DaneO'Neill(8) (prom: rdn over 4f out: wknd over 3f out)	3½	11	33/1	70	34
3012 11	**Byzantium (80)** (LordHuntingdon) **3-8-2** MRoberts(9) (lw: bhd fnl 3f)	1½	12	20/1	63	27

(SP 118.3%) **12 Rn**

2m 5.18 (1.18) CSF £8.46 CT £63.52 TOTE £2.20: £1.20 £2.40 £2.90 (£6.30) Trio £54.70 OWNER Sheikh Mohammed (NEWMARKET) BRED Sheikh Mohammed Bin Rashid Al Maktoum
3012 Song of Freedom made no mistake this time off the same mark as when possibly a shade unlucky at Ascot. (5/4)
3190 Bali Paradise (USA) ran a sound race and lost no caste in defeat. (7/1)

1595 Prince of Denial was coming back after injuring a fetlock last time which made this performance all the more creditable. (12/1: op 8/1)
2561 Marie Dora (FR), dropped 6lb, did not get the best of passages at a vital time over this longer distance. (14/1)
3140* Chief Monarch, 2lb lower than when last in a handicap despite winning last time, was reverting to this longer trip and was another who met traffic problems. (10/1)
3263 Shadoof, 3lb higher than when winning at Haydock, was yet another who was a bit of a hard luck story. (14/1)
2656 Premier Bay almost certainly found this ground too quick. (16/1)
3061* Party Romance (USA), raised 2lb, found his old problem of running too freely raising its ugly head. (15/2)

3576 GROSVENOR CASINOS WASHINGTON SINGER STKS (Listed) (2-Y.O) (Class A)
3-10 (3-11) **7f (straight)** £10,008.00 (£3,024.00: £1,472.00: £696.00) Stalls: Centre GOING minus 0.33 sec per fur (GF)

Form	Horse	Dist	Pos	SP	RR	SF
2312*	**Bahr** (BWHills) **2-8-9** MHills(2) (hld up: hdwy to ld 1f out: r.o wl)	—	1	2/1[1]	97+	57
3013[3]	**Quiet Assurance (USA)** (EALDunlop) **2-8-11** KFallon(1) (b: w ldr: led 2f out: rdn & hdd 1f out: nt qckn)	¾	2	8/1[3]	97	57
3260*	**Fruits of Love (USA)** (MJohnston) **2-9-0** JWeaver(3) (led 5f: rdn over 1f out: nt qckn ins fnl f)	1¼	3	11/4[2]	97	57
	City Honours (USA) (PWChapple-Hyam) **2-8-8** JReid(6) (gd sort: dwlt: hld up: rdn over 2f out: styd on ins fnl f)	nk	4	11/4[2]	91+	51
3201[3]	**Speaker's Chair** (RCharlton) **2-8-11** PatEddery(5) (hld up: rdn over 2f out: wknd wl over 1f out)	9	5	14/1	73	33
	Borani (IABalding) **2-8-8** LDettori(4) (str: lengthy: bit bkwd: bhd fnl 2f: t.o)	12	6	20/1	43	3

(SP 109.2%) **6 Rn**

1m 24.81 (0.71) CSF £15.73 TOTE £2.60: £1.90 £3.60 (£15.60) OWNER Sheikh Ahmed Al Maktoum (LAMBOURN) BRED Sheikh Mohammed bin Rashid al Maktoum
2312* Bahr finished up nicely on top against these colts and already seems capable of handling most types of going. (2/1)
3013 Quiet Assurance (USA) could not match the filly in the closing stages but should soon start repaying some of his $180,000 price tag. (8/1: op 5/1)
3260* Fruits of Love (USA) could not defy his penalty but one could not help feeling whatever he achieves this year could be a bonus as he looks a stayer in the making. (11/4)
City Honours (USA), a half-brother to a winner in Spain, is out of a mare who won over ten furlongs and already seems to need a mile. (11/4)
3201 Speaker's Chair had quicker ground to contend with here and could not bring these rivals to order. (14/1: 7/1-16/1)
Borani is out of a half-sister to Dr Massini and Weigh Anchor. (20/1)

3577 GROSVENOR CASINOS HUNGERFORD STKS (Gp 3) (3-Y.O+) (Class A)
3-40 (3-41) **7f 64y (round)** £21,480.00 (£8,049.00: £3,874.50: £1,696.50) Stalls: Low GOING minus 0.33 sec per fur (GF)

Form	Horse	Dist	Pos	SP	RR	SF
3063[6]	**Decorated Hero (117)** (JHMGosden) **5-9-0** LDettori(2) (hld up: stdy hdwy over 2f out: led 1f out: r.o wl)	—	1	11/4[2]	117	77
2821a[6]	**Bin Rosie (111)** (DRLoder) **5-9-3b** PatEddery(1) (a.p: nt clr run over 2f out: swtchd rt 1f out: r.o wl)	1	2	10/1	118	78
3147[2]	**Unconditional Love (IRE) (100)** (MJohnston) **4-8-11** JWeaver(8) (led: hdd 1f out: nt qckn)	¾	3	12/1	110	70
3063[3]	**Captain Collins (IRE) (103)** (PWChapple-Hyam) **3-8-8** DHarrison(4) (sn chsng ldrs: rdn & ev ch over 1f out: one pce)	½	4	12/1	112	66
2766[8]	**Almushtarak (IRE) (106)** (KMahdi) **4-9-0** DO'Donohoe(3) (s.i.s: sn rcvrd: nt clr run on ins over 1f out: rdn & one pce fnl f)	1¾	5	16/1	108	68
3147*	**Dazzle (112)** (MRStoute) **3-8-5** JReid(9) (hld up: stdy hdwy on outside 3f out: sn rdn: one pce)	½	6	7/4[1]	104	58
2690*	**Cadeaux Tryst (106)** (EALDunlop) **5-9-0** RHills(5) (b: hld up: rdn 2f out: no hdwy)	1¼	7	8/1[3]	104	64
2775[3]	**Tumbleweed Ridge (103)** (BJMeehan) **4-9-0b** MTebbutt(6) (hld up & plld hrd: nvr trbld ldrs)	¾	8	16/1	103	63
3147[3]	**Miss Riviera (99)** (GWragg) **4-8-11** MHills(10) (lw: prom 5f)	¾	9	16/1	98	58
3447[4]	**Hello Mister (98)** (TEPowell) **6-9-0** PMcCabe(7) (plld hrd in rr: rdn over 2f out: no rspnse)	3½	10	50/1	93	53

(SP 118.2%) **10 Rn**

1m 27.56 (-0.54) CSF £28.41 TOTE £3.90: £1.80 £2.70 £3.20 (£16.60) Trio £67.00 OWNER Exors of the late Mr Herbert Allen (NEWMARKET) BRED Reg Griffin and Jim McGrath
WEIGHT FOR AGE 3yo-6lb
3063 Decorated Hero, back on song this time, reversed the Beeswing form with Captain Collins. His trainer admitted that it was his fault last time because he ran him too quick and the ground was too loose. (11/4)
2821a Bin Rosie, penalised 3lb for his Group Three win in this race last year, found the winner had obtained first run by the time he got into the clear. (10/1)
3147 Unconditional Love (IRE) would not be inconvenienced by a return to a mile. (12/1)
3063 Captain Collins (IRE) arguably ran his best race to date but could not confirm the Newcastle form with the winner who had excuses that day. (12/1)
2334 Almushtarak (IRE) has certainly been highly tried this season now he is so high in the handicap ratings. (16/1)
3147* Dazzle, not helped by a high draw, saw too much daylight and had a stiffer test of stamina than Goodwood's easy seven. (7/4)

3578 NEWTOWN CONDITIONS STKS (3-Y.O+) (Class C)
4-10 (4-12) **1m 4f 5y** £5,253.00 (£1,698.00: £829.00) Stalls: Low GOING minus 0.33 sec per fur (GF)

Form	Horse	Dist	Pos	SP	RR	SF
2104[10]	**Busy Flight (116)** (BWHills) **4-9-4** MHills(3) (mde all: shkn up over 1f out: r.o wl)	—	1	4/5[1]	113	64
3048[4]	**Yorkshire (IRE) (100)** (PFICole) **3-8-7** JReid(2) (hld up: rdn over 1f out: styd on ins fnl f: nt rch wnr)	1	2	11/2[3]	112	52
3191[2]	**Bright Water (108)** (HRACecil) **4-9-8** KFallon(1) (chsd wnr: rdn over 3f out: no imp fnl 2f)	2	3	6/4[2]	113	64

(SP 110.9%) **3 Rn**

2m 31.64 (1.64) CSF £4.51 TOTE £1.70 (£2.50) OWNER Mr S. WingfieldDigby (LAMBOURN) BRED S. Wingfield Digby
WEIGHT FOR AGE 3yo-11lb
2104 Busy Flight took full advantage of having ground conditions back in his favour. (4/5: 1/2-5/6)
3048 Yorkshire (IRE) will hopefully have found this a useful lesson in being taught to settle. (11/2)
3191 Bright Water was fitted with a tongue-strap for the first time. (6/4)

3579 LEVY BOARD H'CAP (0-85) (3-Y.O+) (Class D)
4-40 (4-40) **2m** £5,267.25 (£1,593.00: £776.50: £368.25) Stalls: High GOING minus 0.33 sec per fur (GF)

Form	Horse	Dist	Pos	SP	RR	SF
3137*	**Mawared (IRE) (77)** (JLDunlop) **4-9-9** RHills(1) (b: lw: a gng wl: led on bit wl over 1f out: easily)	—	1	5/4[1]	93+	63
1950[2]	**Vicki Romara (70)** (MJohnston) **3-8-1** MRoberts(2) (led over 7f: lost pl over 6f out: rallied over 1f out: styd on: no ch w wnr)	3	2	8/1	83	38
3010[2]	**Benjamins Law (53)** (JAPickering) **6-7-6(7)** JFowle(5) (a.p: led over 7f out: hdd wl over 1f out: one pce)	1¾	3	13/2[3]	64	34

				SP	RR	SF
2834[3]	**Thaljanah (IRE) (82)** (BSmart) **5-9-9**(5) ADaly(3) (swtg: chsd ldr: led over 8f out tl over 7f out: wknd over 2f out)	13	**4**	13/2[3]	80	50
3317[2]	**Children's Choice (IRE) (50)** (WJMusson) **6-7-10** JLowe(4) (lw: nvr gng wl: a bhd: t.o fnl 2f)	10	**5**	9/4[2]	38	8

(SP 113.0%) **5 Rn**

3m 27.84 (3.64) CSF £10.93 TOTE £2.00: £1.10 £2.80 (£9.60) OWNER Mr Hamdan Al Maktoum (ARUNDEL) BRED Shadwell Estate Company Limited
LONG HANDICAP Children's Choice (IRE) 7-9
WEIGHT FOR AGE 3yo-15lb
OFFICIAL EXPLANATION **Children's Choice: the trainer reported that the mare was outpaced in the early stages on the fast ground, struggled to take closer order then tired in the final furlong.**
3137* Mawared (IRE), up a further 6lb, completed the hat-trick in effortless style and has really come into his own over these extended trips in typical Dunlop style. (5/4)
1950 Vicki Romara, making her handicap debut, would have preferred a stronger gallop and looks a dour stayer. (8/1)
3010 Benjamins Law, still to win on grass, had been raised 6lb for his narrow defeat at Ascot. (13/2)
2834 Thaljanah (IRE) had plenty to do at these weights. (13/2)
3317 Children's Choice (IRE), set to rise 9lb tomorrow, ran as if something was amiss and was in trouble from the word go. (9/4)

3580 JACK COLLING POLAR JEST APPRENTICE H'CAP (0-90) (3-Y.O+) (Class E)

5-10 (5-10) **6f 8y** £3,139.00 (£952.00: £466.00: £223.00) Stalls: Centre GOING minus 0.33 sec per fur (GF)

				SP	RR	SF
3195[2]	**Almasi (IRE) (77)** (CFWall) **5-9-2**(3) JoHunnam(3) (hld up: led over 1f out: pushed out)	—	**1**	5/1[2]	88	63
3195[5]	**Scissor Ridge (57)** (JJBridger) **5-7-8**(5) RBrisland(10) (chsd ldr: ev ch over 1f out: r.o wl nr fin)	hd	**2**	14/1	68	43
3251[2]	**Montendre (75)** (MJHeaton-Ellis) **10-9-3** ADaly(8) (a.p: hrd rdn & edgd lft over 1f out: r.o ins fnl f)	1¼	**3**	12/1	82	57
3198[3]	**Resist the Force (USA) (68)** (CACyzer) **7-8-7**(3) APolli(2) (lw: hld up: hdwy over 2f out: one pce fnl f)	1¾	**4**	9/2[1]	71	46
3185[6]	**Patsy Grimes (85)** (JSMoore) **7-9-13** AimeeCook(4) (lw: hld up & plld hrd: nt clr run over 2f out & over 1f out: r.o ins fnl f)	nk	**5**	5/1[2]	87	62
3251[6]	**Erupt (63)** (GBBalding) **4-8-0**(5) JFowle(1) (hld up & plld hrd: no hdwy fnl 2f)	s.h	**6**	12/1	65	40
3130[4]	**Delta Soleil (USA) (79)** (PWHarris) **5-9-7** CLowther(5) (rdn over 3f out: no hdwy fnl 2f)	1¾	**7**	9/2[1]	76	51
3280[7]	**The Fugative (66)** (PMitchell) **4-8-3**(5) SCarson(11) (s.s: sn rcvrd: rdn over 2f out: wknd over 1f out)	hd	**8**	12/1	63	38
3251[7]	**Croeso Cynnes (65)** (BPalling) **4-8-2**(5) GHannon(14) (led over 4f: wknd fnl f)	nk	**9**	12/1	61	36
3130[10]	**Lady Diesis (USA) (79)** (BWHills) **3-8-12**(5) ANicholls(6) (lw: bhd: sme hdwy whn nt clr run ins fnl f)	1¼	**10**	8/1[3]	72	43
1148[13]	**Samwar (86)** (MRChannon) **5-9-11**(3) AEddery(7) (s.s: a bhd)	1¼	**11**	16/1	76	51

(SP 124.1%) **11 Rn**

1m 12.65 (0.85) CSF £70.35 CT £757.90 TOTE £5.30: £1.80 £3.70 £2.30 (£60.80) Trio £102.90 OWNER The Equema Partnership (NEWMARKET) BRED Newtownbarry House Stud
WEIGHT FOR AGE 3yo-4lb
STEWARDS' ENQUIRY Daly susp. 25-30/8/97 (incorrect & improper use of whip).
3195 Almasi (IRE), who is holding her form remarkably well, handles all types of ground and was 9lb higher than her latest success. (5/1)
3195 Scissor Ridge has been given a chance by the handicapper following some disappointing efforts in the first half of the season. (14/1)
3251 Montendre is nothing if not genuine and his rider picked up a six-day ban for injuring his mount. (12/1: op 8/1)
3198 Resist the Force (USA) was trying to overcome a 6lb hike in the weights. (9/2: op 3/1)
3185 Patsy Grimes got an even worse run here than at Ascot last time and deserves a change of luck. (5/1)
3251 Erupt ran too freely on the outside of the pack. (12/1: op 8/1)

T/Jkpt: £82.60 (272.19 Tckts). T/Plpt: £17.10 (1,804.39 Tckts). T/Qdpt: £14.40 (73.07 Tckts) KH

3072-SOUTHWELL (L-H) (Standard)

Friday August 15th

WEATHER: sunny & v.hot WIND: almost nil

3581 STARS CLAIMING STKS (I) (3-Y.O+) (Class F)

1-50 (1-52) **7f (Fibresand)** £1,927.00 (£527.00: £247.00) Stalls: Low GOING minus 0.04 sec per fur (STD)

				SP	RR	SF
3075[12]	**Oberon's Dart (IRE) (65)** (PJMakin) **4-9-8** PaulEddery(14) (trckd ldrs: led over 2f out: pushed clr 1f out)	—	**1**	11/2[2]	73	55
3310[7]	**Be Warned (70)** (MDods) **6-8-12v** ACulhane(5) (sn outpcd & bhd: hdwy 2f out: hrd rdn & styd on fnl f)	8	**2**	7/1	45	27
2915[9]	**Bold Street (IRE) (57)** (GMMoore) **7-8-7b** JTate(3) (a chsng ldrs: kpt on same pce fnl 2f)	1¾	**3**	6/1[3]	36	18
3276[14]	**Quinzii Martin (40)** (DHaydnJones) **9-8-8b** SDrowne(7) (swtg: chsd ldrs: one pce fnl 2f)	2½	**4**	11/1	31	13
3240[11]	**Burning Cost (20)** (REPeacock) **7-8-2**(3) DSweeney(8) (bhd & drvn along: kpt on fnl f: nvr rchd ldrs)	4	**5**	33/1	19	1
2041[14]	**Guy's Gamble (33)** (JWharton) **4-8-11b** JFortune(12) (led tl over 2f out: wknd over 1f out)	2	**6**	20/1	20	2
1965[14]	**Bagshot (65)** (GLMoore) **6-8-8b[1]** CandyMorris(11) (b.hind: racd wd: hdwy over 2f out: wknd over 1f out)	2½	**7**	11/4[1]	12	—
3285[8]	**Pardan (50)** (BPalling) **3-8-7**(5) PRoberts(6) (w ldrs: rdn ½-wy: lost pl over 2f out)	hd	**8**	12/1	21	—
2059[12]	**Showstopper** (TJEtherington) **3-8-4** LCharnock(10) (racd wd: t.o ½-wy)	6	**9**	33/1	—	—
3321[11]	**Shermood (23)** (KTIvory) **4-7-13**(3) PFessey(1) (b: b.hind: s.s: hdwy over 4f out: sn rdn: wknd 3f out)	2½	**10**	20/1	—	—
3316[9]	**Efipetite (24)** (NBycroft) **4-8-2b** GBardwell(4) (s.s: racd wd: a bhd)	s.h	**11**	16/1	—	—
3332[6]	**Weet Ees Girl (IRE) (55)** (TWall) **3-8-1** NCarlisle(2) (a in rr)	8	**12**	12/1	—	—

(SP 113.8%) **12 Rn**

1m 30.6 (4.10) CSF £36.04 TOTE £6.70: £2.60 £2.60 £2.70 (£11.50) Trio £36.70 OWNER Mr Peter Wragg (MARLBOROUGH) BRED Ballysheehan Stud
WEIGHT FOR AGE 3yo-6lb
Be Warned clmd JPearce £5,000
OFFICIAL EXPLANATION **Bagshot: the rider reported that the horse was never travelling on the surface.**
2424 Oberon's Dart (IRE), though dropped in class, had plenty to find on official figures but he turned this into a procession. (11/2: 7/2-6/1)
3261 Be Warned, who is on the down-grade, was soon flat out. Sticking on under strong pressure, the winner had flown. (7/1)
2033 Bold Street (IRE) seemed to stay this trip alright. (6/1: 4/1-13/2)
Quinzii Martin ran better than of late. (11/1: 8/1-12/1)
71 Guy's Gamble made the running but soon downed tools when challenged. (20/1)
578 Bagshot, back on his favourite surface and wearing blinkers for the first time, was ridden from off the pace. After improving once in line for home, he was never giving anything like his full shot. (11/4)

Pardan (12/1: 8/1-14/1)

3582 JUPITER H'CAP (0-65) (3-Y.O+) (Class F)

2-20 (2-21) **6f (Fibresand)** £2,277.00 (£627.00: £297.00) Stalls: Low GOING minus 0.04 sec per fur (STD)

Form	Horse	Dist	Pos	SP	RR	SF
3207^{4}	**Newlands Corner (54)** (JAkehurst) **4-9-4b** DBiggs(16) (racd wd: trckd ldrs: led over 1f out: edgd lft: drvn out)	—	**1**	$13/2^{3}$	64	44
3044^{8}	**Zalotto (IRE) (56)** (TJEtherington) **3-9-2b** ACulhane(12) (swtg: chsd ldrs: rdn & hung lft over 1f out: kpt on towards fin)	1½	**2**	7/1	62	38
2788^{10}	**Hannah's Usher (59)** (CMurray) **5-9-9** NicolaHowarth(7) (s.s: hdwy to chse ldrs ½-wy: ev ch over 1f out: nt qckn)	hd	**3**	14/1	65	45
3321^{5}	**Gresatre (64)** (CADwyer) **3-9-10** SDrowne(9) (trckd ldrs: led 2f out: sn hdd: one pce)	2	**4**	16/1	64	40
3040^{7}	**Royal Cascade (IRE) (56)** (BAMcMahon) **3-9-2** JFortune(11) (a chsng ldrs: one pce fnl 2f)	3½	**5**	12/1	47	23
3399^{2}	**Marjorie Rose (IRE) (63)** (ABailey) **4-9-13** DWright(10) (b: b.hind: hdwy ½-wy: rdn & hung lft 2f out: kpt on fnl f)	1¼	**6**	14/1	51	31
2913^{5}	**Al Reet (IRE) (53)** (SRBowring) **6-9-3** DeanMcKeown(5) (chsd ldrs: sn drvn along: outpcd appr fnl f)	½	**7**	$6/1^{2}$	39	19
3287^{17}	**Stolen Kiss (IRE) (64)** (MWEasterby) **5-10-0b** RCochrane(1) (hld up: hdwy & n.m.r over 2f out: nvr nr to chal)	hd	**8**	$11/2^{1}$	50	30
2915^{11}	**Afaan (IRE) (55)** (RFMarvin) **4-9-5** TGMcLaughlin(15) (bhd whn swtchd lft after 1f: swtchd outside over 2f out: kpt on fnl f: nvr nr ldrs)	hd	**9**	$6/1^{2}$	41	21
3227^{7}	**Never Think Twice (59)** (KTIvory) **4-9-9v** CScally(4) (b: s.i.s: nvr nr ldrs)	1¼	**10**	9/1	42	22
2366^{7}	**Komaseph (50)** (RFMarvin) **5-9-0** GBardwell(8) (chsd ldrs: led over 2f out: sn hdd & wknd)	¾	**11**	12/1	31	11
3266^{11}	**Fit For The Job (IRE) (55)** (TWall) **3-9-1** NCarlisle(2) (lw: mde most tl over 2f out: sn lost pl)	10	**12**	20/1	9	—
3398^{7}	**Shavinsky (60)** (PHowling) **4-9-10** PaulEddery(14) (raced wd: chsd ldrs tl lost pl 3f out)	9	**13**	25/1	—	—
1828^{15}	**Oh Whataknight (53)** (RMWhitaker) **4-9-3** OPears(13) (b: racd wd: prom early: bhd fr ½-wy)	½	**14**	25/1	—	—
				(SP 126.8%)	**14 Rn**	

1m 17.5 (4.00) CSF £48.36 CT £588.15 TOTE £7.50: £2.10 £3.70 £6.20 (£24.00) Trio £231.60; £228.34 to Newbury 16/8/97 OWNER The Jolly Skolars (EPSOM) BRED L. A. C. Ashby

WEIGHT FOR AGE 3yo-4lb

3207 Newlands Corner, who completed a hat-trick on turf this time last year, was making her All-Weather debut. Drawn high, she was always travelling nicely and gave her trainer a long overdue change of luck. (13/2)

2605 Zalotto (IRE), even on such a hot day, was awash with sweat beforehand. Dropping down in distance, despite hanging left and looking far from co-operative he kept on inside the last. (7/1: op 9/2)

659 Hannah's Usher, taken to post early as usual, showed a return to form on his favoured surface. (14/1)

3321 Gresatre, 10lb higher than when winning over course and distance in March, ran his best race for quite a while. (16/1)

2206 Royal Cascade (IRE) found five furlongs too sharp last time. (12/1)

2738 Stolen Kiss (IRE), who had won only two of her previous forty-three starts, was an unlikely gamble. After meeting trouble once in line for home, she soon decided that it was too much like hard work. (11/2)

1977 Afaan (IRE) (6/1: op 7/2)

3583 STARS CLAIMING STKS (II) (3-Y.O+) (Class F)

2-50 (2-52) **7f (Fibresand)** £1,927.00 (£527.00: £247.00) Stalls: Low GOING minus 0.04 sec per fur (STD)

Form	Horse	Dist	Pos	SP	RR	SF
2390^{5}	**Deeply Vale (IRE) (60)** (GLMoore) **6-9-0** MWigham(4) (b: lw: trckd ldrs: rdn to ld over 1f out: styd on)	—	**1**	10/1	69	44
2915^{6}	**Thordis (58)** (PJMakin) **4-9-8v** PaulEddery(2) (led tl over 1f out: kpt on one pce)	1¾	**2**	$9/2^{2}$	73	48
2915^{4}	**Legend of Aragon (47)** (JAGlover) **3-8-0**(3) AWhelan(9) (sn pushed along: hdwy 2f out: styd on one pce fnl f)	4	**3**	$5/1^{3}$	51	20
3075^{6}	**Bold Aristocrat (IRE) (69)** (RHollinshead) **6-9-0** FLynch(7) (in tch: effrt over 2f out: hung lft: kpt on fnl f)	s.h	**4**	7/1	56	31
2395^{15}	**Dawalib (USA) (60)** (DHaydnJones) **7-9-2** SDrowne(1) (lw: fly-jumped s: sn chsng ldrs: ev ch tl wknd appr fnl f: eased nr fin)	5	**5**	9/1	46	21
3075^{3}	**Desert Invader (IRE) (70)** (DWChapman) **6-9-2** ACulhane(11) (lw: chsd ldrs: ev ch over 2f out: sn rdn: wknd over 1f out)	8	**6**	$5/2^{1}$	28	3
2915^{5}	**Jilly Beveled (34)** (RonaldThompson) **5-8-0**(3) DarrenMoffatt(8) (sn prom: effrt over 2f out: wknd over 1f out)	s.h	**7**	20/1	15	—
3213^{6}	**Petula Boy (27)** (SRBowring) **3-8-3b**(3) CTeague(13) (racd wd: sn outpcd & drvn along)	2	**8**	33/1	19	—
3320^{4}	**Miss Riviera Rose (62)** (GWragg) **3-8-11** BDoyle(3) (sn pushed along: hdwy to chse ldrs ½-wy: wknd over 1f out: eased)	3	**9**	8/1	18	—
	Lord Naskra (USA) (31) (GWoodward) **8-8-8** RCochrane(5) (b: sn bhd & pushed along)	6	**10**	33/1	—	—
3240^{20}	**Ohnonotagain (30)** (MrsNMacauley) **5-8-7** JFortune(6) (s.i.s: a bhd)	5	**11**	33/1	—	—
				(SP 119.7%)	**11 Rn**	

1m 30.9 (4.40) CSF £48.75 TOTE £9.40: £2.50 £1.50 £2.60 (£27.90) Trio £107.80 OWNER Speedline Telecom (BRIGHTON) BRED Biddestone Stud

WEIGHT FOR AGE 3yo-6lb

2390 Deeply Vale (IRE) recorded his first win since changing stables after winning at Lingfield in November. He was always travelling like a winner here. (10/1)

2915 Thordis, who had plenty to find on official figures, ran a gallant race. (9/2)

2915 Legend of Aragon, without any head-gear, proved suited by the step up in distance and his rider was soon hard at work. (5/1)

3075 Bold Aristocrat (IRE), who was best in on official figures, hung under pressure and never looked happy. (7/1)

1433 Dawalib (USA) stopped quickly in the closing stages. Virtually pulled up near the line, he seems to have some sort of problem. (9/1)

3075 Desert Invader (IRE) was a shade disappointing. (5/2)

3584 A-Z INSURANCE SERVICES H'CAP (0-85) (3-Y.O+) (Class D)

3-20 (3-21) **1m (Fibresand)** £4,776.00 (£1,428.00: £684.00: £312.00) Stalls: Low GOING minus 0.04 sec per fur (STD)

Form	Horse	Dist	Pos	SP	RR	SF
3236^{6}	**Liquid Gold (IRE) (71)** (WAO'Gorman) **3-8-7** EmmaO'Gorman(6) (trckd ldrs: led 2f out: clr ins fnl f: easily)	—	**1**	11/1	88+	53
3264^{2}	**Sparky (72)** (MWEasterby) **3-8-5b**(3) GParkin(8) (b: lw: sn bhd & drvn along: gd hdwy on outside over 2f out: hung lft & kpt on fnl f: no ch w wnr)	6	**2**	$8/1^{2}$	77	42
3075^{8}	**Johnnie the Joker (73)** (JPLeigh) **6-8-13b**(3) CTeague(5) (led 1f: chsd ldrs: one pce fnl 2f)	9	**3**	14/1	60	32
3243^{8}	**Our People (79)** (MJohnston) **3-9-1** BDoyle(12) (chsd ldrs: outpcd ½-wy: kpt on fnl 2f)	½	**4**	14/1	65	30
3030*	**Nominator Lad (70)** (BAMcMahon) **3-8-6** JFortune(15) (racd wd: chsd ldrs: one pce fnl 3f)	s.h	**5**	11/1	56	21

3285[10] **Sea Spouse (60)** (MBlanshard) **6-8-3** DaleGibson(13) (lw: racd wd: chsd ldrs: outpcd ½-wy: n.d)	s.h	**6**	12/1	46	18
3273[14] **Sailormaite (85)** (MissJFCraze) **6-10-0** SWebster(16) (racd wd: chsd ldrs: rdn & hung bdly lft 2f out: no imp)	hd	**7**	33/1	71	43
3476[9] **Takhlid (USA) (70)** (DWChapman) **6-8-13** ACulhane(1) (sn chsng ldrs: led over 2f out: sn hdd & wknd)	4	**8**	16/1	48	20
2369[5] **Bentico (70)** (MrsNMacauley) **8-8-6v**(7) RWinston(3) (b: sn bhd & pushed along n.d)	2	**9**	16/1	44	16
2868* **Jibereen (75)** (PHowling) **5-9-4** PaulEddery(11) (b: lw: racd wd: chsd ldrs tl outpcd over 3f out: sn wknd)	2	**10**	5/1 [1]	45	17
*2913** **Icy Guest (USA) (80)** (PJMakin) **3-9-2** LCharnock(14) (lw: chsd ldrs tl lost pl over 2f out)	6	**11**	9/1 [3]	38	3
426[5] **China Castle (84)** (PCHaslam) **4-9-13** DeanMcKeown(2) (bit bkwd: s.i.s: sme hdwy on outside ½-wy: sn wknd)	3½	**12**	14/1	35	7
2918[8] **Palo Blanco (70)** (GLMoore) **6-8-13** CandyMorris(9) (hld up: nvr plcd to chal)	s.h	**13**	20/1	21	—
2859* **Dawam Allail (IRE) (75)** (MAJarvis) **3-8-11** RCochrane(7) (chsd ldrs: effrt 3f out: sn wknd)	5	**14**	8/1 [2]	16	—
*3397** **Nor-Do-I (79)** (JMPEustace) **3-9-1** 5x JTate(4) (led after 1f tl over 2f out: sn lost pl)	1½	**15**	5/1 [1]	17	—
3024[8] **Muhandam (IRE) (70)** (PAKelleway) **4-8-13** MWigham(10) (chsd ldrs tl lost pl 3f out)	¾	**16**	20/1	6	—

(SP 134.1%) **16 Rn**

1m 42.42 (3.42) CSF £94.19 CT £1,173.97 TOTE £13.60: £3.50 £1.70 £3.50 £5.10 (£94.50) Trio £409.20; £374.69 to Newbury 16/8/97
OWNER Mr N. S. Yong (NEWMARKET) BRED Rowanstown Stud
WEIGHT FOR AGE 3yo-7lb

OFFICIAL EXPLANATION **Palo Blanco: rider reported that her instructions were to drop her mount in, but after two furlongs the mare began to resent the kick-back and was never going thereafter. The rider had also accidently removed both pairs of goggles, impairing her own vision. Nor-Do-I: no explanation offered.**

3236 Liquid Gold (IRE), a fair type, took what looked a competitive handicap in easy fashion as the fourth was beaten over fifteen lengths. He looks to have plenty of improvement in him and could be an interesting prospect on turf at four. (11/1: 7/1-12/1)
3264 Sparky, from a 6lb higher mark, would not go at all. Making ground on the outside turning in, he hung in behind the winner but still finished a long way clear of the third. (8/1: 6/1-9/1)
2672 Johnnie the Joker ran his usual sound race but the handicapper looks to have his measure for the time being. (14/1)
1647 Our People has tumbled down the weights but he did not show a lot of dash here, with the headgear again left off. (14/1)
3030* Nominator Lad found this hard work from the halfway mark from a high draw. (11/1)
2395 Sea Spouse was another not blessed with a favourable starting position. (12/1)
389 China Castle, reappearing after an absence of 151 days and over a distance short of his best, looked burly. (14/1: op 33/1)
2603 Palo Blanco looked to have a quiet run round and was not asked for an effort at any stage. (20/1)
3397* Nor-Do-I, making a quick reappearance, set a strong pace but dropped out in a matter of strides once in line for home. Connections could offer no explanation but there is no doubt that this was a stronger event. (5/1)

3585 ROYAL BANK INVOICE FINANCE H'CAP (0-65) (3-Y.O+ F & M) (Class F)

3-50 (3-50) **1m 4f (Fibresand)** £2,277.00 (£627.00: £297.00) Stalls: Low GOING minus 0.04 sec per fur (STD)

			SP	RR	SF
3232[3] **Classic Ballet (FR) (60)** (RGuest) **4-9-4**(5) PRoberts(6) (lw: trckd ldrs gng wl: led 4f out: shkn up & clr 2f out: eased ins fnl f)	—	**1**	13/8 [1]	70+	21
3102* **Foolish Flutter (IRE) (47)** (RBastiman) **3-7-13b** LCharnock(7) (hld up: wnt 2nd over 4f out: kpt on: no ch w wnr)	6	**2**	7/2 [2]	49	—
3286[4] **Nicola's Princess (48)** (BAMcMahon) **4-8-11** JFortune(2) (sn trckng ldrs: pushed along 5f out: one pce)	7	**3**	10/1	41	—
3390[7] **Bonne Ville (62)** (BPalling) **3-9-0b**[1] RCochrane(3) (led to 4f out: wknd over 2f out)	3	**4**	6/1	51	—
2564[16] **Hobbs Choice (42)** (GMMoore) **4-8-5** JTate(1) (sn drvn along: rdn 9f out: t.o 5f out)	14	**5**	20/1	12	—
3286[2] **More Than You Know (IRE) (64)** (KRBurke) **4-9-10**(3) GParkin(4) (pushed along 9f out: bhd & rdn 6f out: sn t.o)	8	**6**	8/1	23	—
553[11] **Qualitair Pride (34)** (JFBottomley) **5-7-11** NCarlisle(5) (b: w ldrs tl wknd 5f out: sn bhd)	nk	**7**	5/1 [3]	—	—

(SP 116.2%) **7 Rn**

2m 45.8 (12.80) CSF £7.02 TOTE £2.40: £1.30 £3.20 (£5.20) OWNER Mr E. Carter (NEWMARKET) BRED Inversiones Gonfi Inc
WEIGHT FOR AGE 3yo-11lb

3232 Classic Ballet (FR), given a fortnight off after three quick runs, found this simple and recorded a facile success. (13/8)
3102* Foolish Flutter (IRE), 6lb higher and on a different surface, finished clear second best but the winner was much too good. (7/2)
3286 Nicola's Princess, like the others, was hard at work half a mile from home when the winner was still on the bridle. (10/1)
2068 Bonne Ville, who had run poorly on her last two starts, wore blinkers for the first time but, as a result, ran much too freely and set too strong a pace for her own good. (6/1)

3586 VENUS (S) STKS (2-Y.O) (Class G)

4-20 (4-21) **5f (Fibresand)** £1,984.50 (£547.00: £259.50) Stalls: High GOING minus 0.04 sec per fur (STD)

			SP	RR	SF
3209[3] **Beechwood Quest (IRE) (64)** (BSRothwell) **2-8-11be** LCharnock(7) (lw: mde all: styd on u.p fnl f: hld on towards fin)	—	**1**	7/4 [1]	62	24
3324[4] **Ok John (IRE)** (JAkehurst) **2-8-11** PaulEddery(12) (a chsng ldrs: ev ch ins fnl f: nt qckn nr fin)	hd	**2**	5/1 [3]	62	24
3228[2] **Charlies Lad (IRE) (70)** (RGuest) **2-9-2** PBloomfield(1) (a chsng ldrs: ev ch over 1f out: nt qckn)	1¼	**3**	3/1 [2]	63	25
2367[3] **I'm Not Sure (48)** (JBerry) **2-8-3**(3) PFessey(2) (w ldrs: ev ch over 1f out: wknd towards fin)	½	**4**	11/1	51	13
3097[5] **Super Geil** (CADwyer) **2-8-3**(3) AWhelan(13) (chsd ldrs: edgd lft & wknd fnl f)	2	**5**	11/2	45	7
3060[7] **Double Appeal (IRE)** (CaptJWilson) **2-8-6** GBardwell(14) (sn wl outpcd & wl bhd: hrd rdn ½-wy: styd on fnl f)	¾	**6**	25/1	42	4
Thwing (MWEasterby) **2-8-3**(3) GParkin(8) (tall: unf: s.i.s: outpcd & sn drvn along: sme hdwy 2f out: nvr nr ldrs)	nk	**7**	14/1	41	3
3324[10] **River Frontier (IRE)** (MDIUsher) **2-8-6** JMarshall(11) (sn outpcd: sme hdwy over 1f out: n.d)	nk	**8**	33/1	40	2
3312[7] **Hoyland Common (IRE)** (NTinkler) **2-8-6b**[1] RCochrane(5) (chsd ldrs: edgd lft & lost pl over 1f out: eased)	2½	**9**	20/1	32	—
3247[6] **Tui** (KMcAuliffe) **2-8-6** BDoyle(9) (b.hind: prom early: outpcd fr ½-wy)	s.h	**10**	20/1	32	—
2587[8] **Margaret's Dancer (49)** (CSmith) **2-8-8b**(3) TEDurcan(4) (sn outpcd)	2	**11**	33/1	31	—
2935[9] **Jilvarra** (WGMTurner) **2-8-6** DeanMcKeown(10) (s.i.s: hung bdly lft thrght: bhd fr ½-wy)	5	**12**	14/1	10	—
3239[12] **The Fuelologist** (MissJFCraze) **2-8-11** SWebster(3) (sn wl outpcd)	3	**13**	20/1	5	—

(SP 139.1%) **13 Rn**

60.9 secs (3.90) CSF £10.80 TOTE £4.10: £1.10 £2.50 £1.70 (£11.60) Trio £5.60 OWNER Mr B. Valentine (MALTON) BRED W. J. Murphy and T. J. Newman
No bid

3209 Beechwood Quest (IRE) has speed to burn. Answering her rider's every call, there was not an ounce to spare at the line. (7/4)
3324 Ok John (IRE) threw down a strong challenge but, hard as he tried, the winner was always just holding him at bay. (5/1)

3228 Charlies Lad (IRE) found the drop back to five furlongs no problem. (3/1)
2367 I'm Not Sure, who gave a problem or two loading, seems barely to stay the minimum trip. (11/1)
3097 Super Geil ran slightly better than she had done when gambled on on her debut. (11/2: op 3/1)
3060 Double Appeal (IRE) failed completely to go the pace. Given plenty of encouragement from the saddle at the halfway mark, she made up several lengths in the final furlong and is crying out for a longer trip. (25/1)

3587 MARS MAIDEN AMATEUR H'CAP (0-65) (3-Y.O+) (Class G)

4-55 (4-55) **1m 6f (Fibresand)** £1,984.50 (£547.00: £259.50) Stalls: Low GOING minus 0.04 sec per fur (STD)

Form	Horse / details	Dist	Pos	SP	RR	SF
2521^{5}	**Robbo (54)** (CWThornton) **3-10-5b**$^{(5)}$ MrJCrowley(2) (lw: sn trckng ldrs: led over 2f out: rdn & styd on wl fnl f)	—	1	5/1^{3}	67	23
3317^{4}	**Needwood Epic (52)** (BCMorgan) **4-11-7b**^{1} MrRThornton(5) (led tl over 2f out: kpt on: no ch w wnr)	6	2	4/1^{1}	58	27
3317^{6}	**Mrs Drummond (IRE) (30)** (GMMcCourt) **4-9-8**$^{(5)}$ MrsSEddery(6) (hld up: stdy hdwy over 3f out: r.o one pce fnl f)	1¼	3	8/1	35	4
2207^{4}	**Hancock (24)** (JHetherton) **5-9-7** MissPRobson(7) (hdwy 8f out: sn chsng ldrs: effrt over 4f out: wknd fnl f)	¾	4	9/2^{2}	28	—
2910^{6}	**Subtle Touch (IRE) (37)** (PLGilligan) **6-10-6** MrPScott(1) (sn bhd & pushed along: hdwy over 4f out: styd on appr fnl f: n.d)	7	5	12/1	33	2
3317^{10}	**Not Forgotten (USA) (58)** (PAKelleway) **3-11-0b** MrTMcCarthy(4) (lw: trckd ldrs: chal over 4f out: sn rdn & wknd)	12	6	9/1	40	—
2521^{10}	**Slightly Special (IRE) (33)** (DTThom) **5-9-11**$^{(5)}$ MrVLukaniuk(8) (s.i.s: sn pushed along & bhd)	15	7	6/1	—	—
3028^{7}	**Cadbury Castle (40)** (MBlanshard) **3-9-10** MissJAllison(9) (trckd ldrs: pushed along 7f out: lost pl over 5f out)	1	8	6/1	4	—
2846^{11}	**Rockie The Jester (42)** (JPLeigh) **3-9-7**$^{(5)ow4}$ MrSDurack(3) (w ldr: reminders 9f out: hrd rdn & lost pl over 4f out)	26	9	33/1	—	—
				(SP 115.2%)	**9 Rn**	

3m 15.2 (17.20) CSF £22.98 CT £143.16 TOTE £4.70: £1.20 £1.60 £2.10 (£15.00) Trio £20.60 OWNER Mr Guy Reed (MIDDLEHAM) BRED Godolphin Management Co Ltd
WEIGHT FOR AGE 3yo-13lb
2521 Robbo, having his first outing for forty-one days and stepping up in distance, was most capably handled to take this poor event in decisive fashion. (5/1)
3317 Needwood Epic, who has run over a variety of distances, set a strong pace and it was surprising to see her keep going well enough to retain second spot. (4/1: 3/1-9/2)
3317 Mrs Drummond (IRE) was settled off the pace. Making ground on the final turn, she kept on at the same pace in the final furlong. With a more forceful rider in the saddle, she would have secured second place. (8/1)
2207 Hancock, having his first outing for fifty-one days, ran as if needing it, getting very leg-weary in the final furlong. (9/2: 5/2-6/1)
Subtle Touch (IRE) (12/1: op 20/1)
2397 Cadbury Castle (6/1: op 4/1)

T/Plpt: £287.00 (38.93 Tckts). T/Qdpt: £26.10 (28.71 Tckts) WG

3556-BRIGHTON (L-H) (Firm, Good to firm last 6f)

Saturday August 16th

WEATHER: hot WIND: almost nil

3588 ROTTINGDEAN APPRENTICE H'CAP (0-65) (3-Y.O+) (Class F)

5-40 (5-42) **1m 1f 209y** £2,646.60 (£732.60: £349.80) Stalls: High GOING minus 0.38 sec per fur (F)

Form	Horse / details	Dist	Pos	SP	RR	SF
3570*	**Wentbridge Lad (IRE) (53)** (ABailey) **7-9-5v**$^{(5)}$ 6x RStudholme(5) (b: b.off hind: hld up: led 1f out: r.o)	—	1	2/1^{1}	66	48
1632^{12}	**Father Dan (IRE) (53)** (MissGayKelleway) **8-9-7**$^{(3)}$ JWilkinson(2) (b: lw: hld up: led over 2f out to 1f out: r.o)	hd	2	7/1	66	54
3134^{5}	**Action Jackson (50)** (BJMcMath) **5-9-7** APolli(1) (lost pl 7f out: rallied over 1f out: r.o)	2	3	6/1^{3}	60	48
3248^{10}	**Royal Acclaim (30)** (KRBurke) **12-7-10v**$^{(5)}$ EmilyJoyce(3) (hdwy over 1f out: nvr nrr)	3	4	33/1	35	23
2195^{7}	**Roman Reel (USA) (50)** (GLMoore) **6-9-0**$^{(7)}$ CherylBone(7) (lw: led 8f out tl over 4f out: wknd over 3f out)	3½	5	16/1	49	37
3297*	**Colour Counsellor (44)** (RMFlower) **4-9-1b** GFaulkner(4) (led 2f: led over 4f out tl over 2f out: eased whn btn fnl f)	nk	6	7/2^{2}	43	31
3229^{9}	**Soda Pop (IRE) (65)** (GLMoore) **3-9-9**$^{(5)}$ MBatchelor(6) (a.p: ev ch over 2f out: sn wknd)	19	7	10/1	33	13
3101^{W}	**Square Mile Miss (IRE) (40)** (PHowling) **4-8-11** MBaird(8) (b: swtg: rrd s: bhd fnl 3f)	27	8	9/1	—	—
				(SP 110.3%)	**8 Rn**	

2m 1.6 (3.30) CSF £13.89 CT £59.45 TOTE £4.00: £1.80 £1.60 £2.20 (£18.60) OWNER Mr John Pugh (TARPORLEY) BRED Peter Doyle
WEIGHT FOR AGE 3yo-8lb
3570* Wentbridge Lad (IRE) had a 6lb penalty for his Haydock win just twenty-three hours earlier but, despite those exertions and a long journey south, he made it pay. Leading a furlong out, he had the race won when deciding he had done enough in the last few strides, almost being caught by the runner-up. (2/1)
1233 Father Dan (IRE) ran a sound race after an eleven-week break. Showing in front over a quarter of a mile from home, he was headed entering the final furlong and, with the winner stopping in the last few strides, almost got back up. (7/1)
3134 Action Jackson, who lost his pitch after three furlongs, stayed on again from below the distance but was not going to get there in time. Both his wins to date have come in sellers and a drop to that class would help. (6/1: op 3/1)
3196 Royal Acclaim, having his 105th run, is at the OAP stage and has just one win to his name since April 1993. (33/1)
1642* Roman Reel (USA), soon at the head of affairs, was collared at the top of the hill and soon dropped away as he received little assistance from the saddle. (16/1)
3297* Colour Counsellor showed in front again at the top of the hill, but he was collared over a quarter of a mile from home and his jockey was not hard on him in the final furlong when all chance had evaporated. He has done all his winning here. (7/2)
2955* Soda Pop (IRE) (10/1: op 6/1)
2593 Square Mile Miss (IRE) (9/1: op 5/1)

3589 E.B.F. ALFRISTON NOVICE STKS (2-Y.O) (Class D)

6-10 (6-13) **5f 59y** £3,205.00 (£955.00: £455.00: £205.00) Stalls: Low GOING minus 0.38 sec per fur (F)

Form	Horse / details	Dist	Pos	SP	RR	SF
2831^{12}	**To Love With Love** (WJarvis) **2-8-7** JQuinn(7) (hld up: led 2f out: rdn out)	—	1	9/2^{3}	81	22

				SP	RR	SF
3235[5]	**Al Mabrook (IRE)** (KMahdi) **2-8-7**(5) CLowther(6) (hld up: rdn over 2f out: swtchd lft ins fnl f: r.o)	2½	2	11/2	78	19
2862[21]	**Lady Moll (79)** (RBoss) **2-8-13** KFallon(5) (led 1f: led over 2f out: sn hdd: unable qckn)	hd	3	9/4[1]	79	20
2720[11]	**Facile Tigre** (SDow) **2-8-9**(3) DO'Donohoe(1) (s.s & hmpd s: hdwy over 1f out: r.o one pce)	hd	4	12/1	78	19
3136[5]	**Red Pepper (IRE)** (PHowling) **2-8-12** TSprake(3) (a.p: ev ch over 1f out: 3rd & btn whn j.shadow ins fnl f)	1½	5	25/1	73	14
2720[7]	**High Money** (GLewis) **2-8-12b[1]** RPrice(2) (hld up: rdn over 2f out: wknd wl over 1f out)	2	6	11/2	67	8
1735[8]	**Truth Teller (87)** (RHannon) **2-9-2** DaneO'Neill(4) (lw: led 4f out tl over 2f out: wknd over 1f out)	2	7	4/1[2]	65	6
				(SP 111.3%)		**7 Rn**

62.2 secs (2.20) CSF £24.95 TOTE £5.30: £2.40 £2.80 (£20.80) OWNER Mr K. P. Seow (NEWMARKET) BRED Whitsbury Manor Stud
OFFICIAL EXPLANATION **To Love With Love: regarding the improvement in form, the trainer reported that the filly had missed the break last time and never got into the race. Truth Teller: was reportedly unsuited by the track and the fast ground.**

2227 To Love With Love was the subject of a gamble and did not let her supporters down, leading two furlongs out and being rousted along to assert. (9/2: 12/1-4/1)

3235 Al Mabrook (IRE) is going the right way. Switched left as he began a forward move inside the final furlong, he ran on for second prize but found the winner already home and dry. (11/2)

1653 Lady Moll was back in her own class and showed in front before the quarter-mile pole. Soon collared by the winner, she failed to find another gear. (9/4)

Facile Tigre stayed on from below the distance, only just failing to take third prize. (12/1)

3136 Red Pepper (IRE), a leading player throughout, was getting the worst of the argument and was about two lengths down when he jumped the shadow of the half-furlong pole causing his rider to become unbalanced. It made little difference to the result. (25/1)

2018 High Money, fitted with blinkers for the first time, had been seen off early in the final quarter-mile. (11/2)

1504* Truth Teller was the paddock pick but had shot his bolt below the distance. His jockey later reported that the colt was unsuited by the track and the fast ground, which seems rather bizarre as his only win to date came here on fast ground. (4/1: op 2/1)

3590 DOWNS (S) STKS (3-Y.O+) (Class G)

6-40 (6-41) **5f 213y** £1,984.50 (£547.00: £259.50) Stalls: Low GOING minus 0.38 sec per fur (F)

				SP	RR	SF
2939[5]	**The Frisky Farmer (45)** (WGMTurner) **4-8-12**(5) CLowther(7) (mde all: clr over 1f out: hrd rdn: r.o wl)	—	1	20/1	64	35
	Montrestar (60) (ABailey) **4-8-12v**(5) GFaulkner(12) (b.hind: hld up: rdn over 2f out: chsd wnr ins fnl f: r.o wl)	1	2	15/2[3]	61	32
3448[5]	**Shashi (IRE) (53)** (PatMitchell) **5-9-3** PBloomfield(13) (swtg: rdn over 2f out: hdwy over 1f out: r.o wl ins fnl f)	hd	3	14/1	61	32
3280[6]	**Friendly Brave (USA) (62)** (MissGayKelleway) **7-9-3** KFallon(3) (b: b.hind: lw: swtchd lft & nt clr run on ins 2f out: hdwy over 1f out: r.o one pce)	s.h	4	4/5[1]	61	32
3249[7]	**Dark Menace (47)** (EAWheeler) **5-8-10b**(7) SCarson(2) (hdwy on ins over 2f out: chsd wnr over 1f out tl ins fnl f: one pce)	1¼	5	25/1	58	29
3417[11]	**Third Party (64)** (SDow) **3-9-0** DaneO'Neill(4) (rdn over 3f out: hdwy over 1f out: r.o)	1	6	10/1	55	23
3393[4]	**Nellie North (47)** (GMMcCourt) **4-8-12b** PaulEddery(8) (lw: chsd wnr over 4f)	2½	7	10/1	43	14
3040[5]	**Caspian Morn (53)** (WGMTurner) **3-8-2**(7) PDoe(1) (prom over 4f)	½	8	16/1	42	10
2852[11]	**Bella's Legacy (39)** (KRBurke) **4-8-12** TSprake(5) (bhd fnl 2f)	hd	9	33/1	42	13
2922[15]	**Nicker (63)** (WJarvis) **3-9-0** JQuinn(9) (a bhd)	s.h	10	7/1[2]	46	14
3393[7]	**Into Debt (30)** (JRPoulton) **4-8-12b** LeesaLong(6) (swtg: dwlt: a bhd)	hd	11	50/1	41	12
3271[9]	**Bee Dee Best (IRE) (34)** (JPSmith) **6-9-3** RPrice(10) (swtg: prom 4f)	1	12	40/1	44	15
3139[7]	**Lancashire Legend (42)** (SDow) **4-9-0**(3) DO'Donohoe(11) (reluctant to r: a bhd)	1¼	13	20/1	40	11
				(SP 131.3%)		**13 Rn**

1m 9.4 (2.20) CSF £152.43 TOTE £20.50: £2.70 £2.70 £3.10 (£182.70) Trio £186.60 OWNER Mr G. J. Bush (SHERBORNE) BRED Miss Claire Farrow, Dame Elizabeth and Alexander C
WEIGHT FOR AGE 3yo-3lb
No bid

2939 The Frisky Farmer put up a bold display from the front. Forging clear below the distance, he responded to pressure and held on well. He has done all his winning in this grade. (20/1)

Montrestar, who has changed stables since his last run eleven months ago, ran a fine race considering his lay-off and, coming through to take second place inside the final furlong, kept on well. (15/2: 14/1-7/1)

3448 Shashi (IRE) only began to find her feet from below the distance, but ran on really strongly to snatch third prize right on the line. (14/1: 10/1-16/1)

3280 Friendly Brave (USA) was taking a drop in class but did not get the best of rides from Fallon, who showed his inexperience of this tricky course by switching to the inside rail, never a good idea as the horses tend to roll in on the camber. Not surprisingly he failed to get a clear run but, luckily for him, a gap appeared below the distance. Picking up ground, he struggled on but was worried out of the prize money in the closing stages. (4/5: op 5/4)

2954 Dark Menace came through to take second place below the distance but he failed to make any inroads on the winner and was collared for the runner-up berth inside the final furlong. He has gained both his wins here on fast ground. (25/1)

1989 Third Party, taking a drop in class, struggled on in the last furlong and a half from the back of the field without ever looking likely to make her presence felt. (10/1: op 6/1)

3591 SOUTHERN FM CHALLENGE CUP H'CAP (0-70) (3-Y.O) (Class E)

7-10 (7-10) **7f 214y** £2,784.25 (£829.00: £394.50: £177.25) Stalls: Low GOING minus 0.38 sec per fur (F)

				SP	RR	SF
3100[3]	**Sharpo Wassl (69)** (WJHaggas) **3-9-6** KFallon(4) (lw: rdn over 3f out: hdwy over 2f out: led over 1f out: hung lft: all out)	—	1	6/5[1]	78	35
2957*	**Olivo (IRE) (70)** (CAHorgan) **3-9-7** PaulEddery(6) (rdn over 3f out: hdwy over 1f out: r.o wl ins fnl f)	nk	2	9/2[3]	78	35
2005[10]	**Ortelius (67)** (RHannon) **3-9-4** DaneO'Neill(3) (lw: rdn over 3f out: lost pl over 2f out: rallied fnl f: r.o wl)	s.h	3	20/1	75	32
2912[2]	**Kalimat (64)** (WJarvis) **3-9-1b[1]** JQuinn(5) (plld hrd: led over 6f out tl over 1f out: ev ch ins fnl f: r.o)	nk	4	100/30[2]	72	29
2317[13]	**Perfect Poppy (59)** (SDow) **3-8-7**(3) DO'Donohoe(1) (w ldr 6f out: ev ch 2f out: wknd over 1f out)	3	5	12/1	61	18
3200[14]	**Grovefair Venture (58)** (KMahdi) **3-8-4**(5) CLowther(7) (led over 1f: rdn over 3f out: sn wknd)	5	6	14/1	50	7
2309[9]	**Zimiri (68)** (JARToller) **3-9-5** AClark(2) (lw: dwlt: a bhd)	1¼	7	14/1	57	14
				(SP 112.5%)		**7 Rn**

1m 34.6 (3.30) CSF £6.05 TOTE £1.60: £1.80 £2.00 (£3.20) OWNER Mr Ali K Al Jafleh (NEWMARKET) BRED Ali K. Al Jafleh
OFFICIAL EXPLANATION **Zimiri: the trainer reported that he gurgled during the race.**

3100 Sharpo Wassl gave Fallon real problems for, after picking up ground nicely to lead below the distance, he then started to hang on the camber and Fallon had to use his whip in order to try to correct him. The gelding continued to hang throughout the final furlong and, with Fallon beavering away, the combination found the line only just saving them. This was a fine piece of riding. (6/5: 6/4-evens)

2957* Olivo (IRE) began to pick up ground below the distance and, running on strongly inside the final furlong, may well have prevailed with a little further to go. (9/2: op 3/1)
Ortelius, dropped 11lb in the handicap this year after four dismal displays, ran much better and, after getting outpaced, put in some fine work in the final furlong. (20/1)
2912 Kalimat, fitted with blinkers for the first time, took a keen hold and had soon forced her way to the front. Collared below the distance, she refused to lie down and still had every chance inside the final furlong. (100/30)
1219 Perfect Poppy, with every chance a quarter of a mile from home, had shot her bolt approaching the final furlong. (12/1)
1869 Zimiri (14/1: 10/1-16/1)

3592 SOUTH COAST LIMITED STKS (0-50) (3-Y.O) (Class F)
7-40 (7-41) **7f 214y** £2,277.00 (£627.00: £297.00) Stalls: Low GOING minus 0.38 sec per fur (F)

				SP	RR	SF
3299*	**Homestead (50)** (RHannon) **3-9-1** DaneO'Neill(8) (hld up: rdn 2f out: swtchd lft over 1f out: led ins fnl f: r.o wl)	—	**1**	15/8 ^{1}	63	28
3336 ^{2}	**Warrior King (IRE) (47)** (CADwyer) **3-8-12** KFallon(4) (hrd rdn, hdwy & edgd lft over 1f out: hung lft ins fnl f: r.o wl)	½	**2**	7/2 ^{2}	59	24
3421 ^{9}	**Tezaab (49)** (BHanbury) **3-8-12** JStack(6) (chsd ldr: led 2f out: hrd rdn over 1f out: hdd ins fnl f: unable qckn)	1	**3**	8/1	57	22
3230 ^{4}	**Super Scravels (47)** (KMahdi) **3-8-4**(5) CLowther(3) (lw: hdwy & bmpd over 1f out: 4th & btn whn n.m.r & carried lft ins fnl f)	1¾	**4**	8/1	51	16
2852 ^{8}	**Secret Strength (49)** (LadyHerries) **3-8-12** AClark(7) (lw: rdn & hdwy over 2f out: 5th & btn whn carried lft ins fnl f)	2	**5**	9/2 ^{3}	50	15
3133 ^{6}	**Lochlass (IRE) (48)** (SPCWoods) **3-8-6**(3) MHenry(12) (lw: led 6f)	7	**6**	16/1	32	—
2956 ^{6}	**Be True (50)** (GLMoore) **3-8-12v** ^{1} CandyMorris(11) (swtg: prom over 6f)	½	**7**	14/1	34	—
2747 ^{7}	**Royal Emblem (35)** (AGFoster) **3-8-9** TSprake(1) (bhd fnl 3f)	¾	**8**	33/1	30	—
3299 ^{8}	**Seamus (30)** (CJHill) **3-8-7**(5) APolli(5) (swtg: a bhd)	½	**9**	33/1	32	—
1987 ^{6}	**Fable (45)** (JARToller) **3-8-9** PaulEddery(2) (prom over 5f)	4	**10**	20/1	21	—
642 ^{9}	**Talisman (IRE) (45)** (SDow) **3-8-9**(3) DO'Donohoe(9) (lw: s.s: a bhd)	6	**11**	20/1	12	—
				(SP 125.4%)	**11 Rn**	

1m 34.8 (3.50) CSF £7.70 TOTE £2.90: £1.80 £1.40 £2.60 (£3.30) Trio £14.60 OWNER Mr Geoffrey Greenwood (MARLBOROUGH) BRED Mrs J. A. Rawding and Green Meadow Stud
3299* Homestead followed up his win here last week and, rousted along to lead inside the final furlong, kept on strongly. (15/8)
3336 Warrior King (IRE) began to pick up ground below the distance, but Fallon then switched his whip into his right hand and as a result the gelding started to drift left, doing Super Scravels no favours. Fallon failed to bring his whip through and the gelding continued to hang left inside the final furlong. The combination ran on strongly to finish second and the placings were allowed to remain unaltered after a Stewards' Enquiry. (7/2)
3293 Tezaab struck the front two furlongs out but, collared inside the last two-hundred yards, failed to find another gear. (8/1)
3230 Super Scravels, bumped by the drifting second as she picked up ground below the distance, was again done no favours by that rival inside the final furlong, but was beaten at the time. (8/1)
2852 Secret Strength, who caught the eye last time out, had been put in his place when carried left inside the final furlong. (9/2)
3133 Lochlass (IRE) took the field along but, collared two furlongs from home, had nothing in reserve. (16/1)
2956 Be True (14/1: 7/1-16/1)

3593 DUKE OF NORFOLK MEMORIAL H'CAP (0-75) (3-Y.O) (Class D)
8-10 (8-10) **1m 3f 196y** £3,645.60 (£1,087.80: £519.40: £235.20) Stalls: High GOING minus 0.38 sec per fur (F)

				SP	RR	SF
3200 ^{15}	**Castles Burning (USA) (50)** (CACyzer) **3-7-8**(5) APolli(1) (hld up: hrd rdn over 2f out: led over 1f out: r.o wl)	—	**1**	3/1 ^{2}	60	20
3080 ^{2}	**Freedom Chance (IRE) (72)** (JWHills) **3-9-4v**(3) MHenry(4) (hld up: led over 3f out tl over 1f out: unable qckn fnl f)	2½	**2**	13/8 ^{1}	79	39
3495 ^{9}	**Bewitching Lady (48)** (DWPArbuthnot) **3-7-11v** ^{1} JQuinn(3) (led 10f out tl over 3f out: wknd over 1f out)	5	**3**	8/1 ^{3}	48	8
3390*	**Running Free (IRE) (55)** (MJFetherston-Godley) **3-8-4** DaneO'Neill(2) (led 2f: rdn over 3f out: sn wknd)	4	**4**	13/8 ^{1}	50	10
				(SP 112.3%)	**4 Rn**	

2m 32.6 (5.00) CSF £7.79 TOTE £4.00 (£4.30) OWNER Mr R. M. Cyzer (HORSHAM) BRED Robert S. West Jr.
2956 Castles Burning (USA), put to sleep at the back of the field, was given a couple of reminders over a quarter of a mile from home and, leading in the centre of the track approaching the final furlong, kept on strongly under a polished ride from his young apprentice. (3/1)
3080 Freedom Chance (IRE) made his bid for glory over three furlongs from home, but he was collared below the distance and soon put in his place. (13/8)
2667 Bewitching Lady, who has dropped considerably in the handicap this season, was making a quick reappearance and was soon at the head of affairs. Collared early in the straight, she grimly tried to hold on but had been put in her place below the distance. (8/1: 6/1-9/1)
3390* Running Free (IRE), the early leader, had been seen off early in the straight. (13/8)

T/Plpt: £1,658.10 (6.76 Tckts). T/Qdpt: £159.00 (4.13 Tckts) AK

3574-NEWBURY (L-H) (Good to firm)
Saturday August 16th
WEATHER: fine WIND: nil

3594 ANDOVER RATED STKS H'CAP (0-100) (3-Y.O+) (Class B)
2-00 (2-00) **7f 64y (round)** £7,511.04 (£2,799.36: £1,359.68: £574.40: £247.20: £116.32) Stalls: Low GOING minus 0.33 sec per fur (GF)

				SP	RR	SF
1739 ^{6}	**Young Precedent (81)** (PWHarris) **3-7-11**(5) CLowther(8) (chsd ldr: led wl over 2f out: drvn out)	—	**1**	11/1	88	57
3185 ^{2}	**Law Commission (90)** (DRCElsworth) **7-9-2** KFallon(1) (lw: hld up: hdwy over 1f out: hrd rdn & ev ch ins fnl f: nt qckn)	hd	**2**	7/2 ^{2}	97	71
3435 ^{3}	**Kayvee (86)** (MrsAJPerrett) **8-8-12** AClark(3) (hld up: stdy hdwy whn nt clr run over 1f out: swtchd rt: r.o wl ins fnl f)	½	**3**	9/1	92	66
3189 ^{14}	**Just Nick (83)** (WRMuir) **3-8-1**(3) MartinDwyer(4) (a.p: r.o one pce fnl f)	1¼	**4**	10/1	86	55
2229 ^{3}	**Mr Sponge (USA) (86)** (IABalding) **3-8-7** LDettori(10) (a.p: rdn over 2f out: one pce)	nk	**5**	3/1 ^{1}	88	57
3217 ^{19}	**Sharp Hat (91)** (RHannon) **3-8-12** DaneO'Neill(5) (tk keen hold: trckd ldrs: rdn & ev ch over 1f out: wknd ins fnl f)	¾	**6**	10/1	92	61

				SP	RR	SF
2774^{4}	**Meshhed (USA) (100)** (BHanbury) **3-9-7** RHills(7) (led tl wl over 2f out: wknd fnl f)	½	**7**	8/1	100	69
3217^{23}	**Loch Patrick (94)** (MMadgwick) **7-9-6** JReid(6) (hld up: rdn over 4f out: nvr trbld ldrs)	1	**8**	20/1	91	65
1770^{6}	**Tycoon Todd (USA) (95)** (DRLoder) **3-9-2** WRyan(9) (hld up mid div: rdn over 2f out: sn bhd)	2½	**9**	7/1^{3}	87	56
3011^{12}	**Johnny Staccato (89)** (JMPEustace) **3-8-10** JTate(2) (s.s: bhd whn rdn over 2f out: t.o)	16	**10**	33/1	46	15

(SP 115.1%) **10 Rn**

1m 28.26 (0.16) CSF £44.36 CT £340.93 TOTE £11.20: £2.30 £1.70 £2.20 (£22.00) Trio £44.70 OWNER Pendley Knights (BERKHAMSTED) BRED P. V. and Mrs J. P. Jackson

WEIGHT FOR AGE 3yo-5lb

1739 Young Precedent may have benefited from a rest following a cut leg. Dropping back to seven, he seemed a little more resolute than the runner-up at the death. (11/1: 8/1-12/1)

3185 Law Commission came with a well-timed run to win his race, and one cannot help feeling he was outbattled by the winner. (7/2)

3435 Kayvee only got in the clear when it was too late, and does seem at long last to have found some form. (9/1)

2013 Just Nick is holding his form remarkably well and was certainly not disgraced here. (10/1)

2229 Mr Sponge (USA) had no excuses this time, apart of course that he may have been a little over-rated by the Handicapper. (3/1)

1980 Sharp Hat did not get home after failing to settle properly on this step-up to seven. (10/1: 7/1-11/1)

3595 SWETTENHAM STUD ST HUGH'S STKS (Listed) (2-Y.O F) (Class A)

2-30 (2-31) **5f 34y** £9,904.00 (£2,992.00: £1,456.00: £688.00) Stalls: Centre GOING minus 0.33 sec per fur (GF)

				SP	RR	SF
3178a^{2}	**Aurigny (100)** (SDow) **2-8-8** SSanders(11) (s.s: n.m.r 2f out: hdwy over 1f out: led ins fnl f: rdn out)	—	**1**	7/1^{3}	91	39
3192^{4}	**Banningham Blade (97)** (KTIvory) **2-8-11** MartinDwyer(5) (a.p: led over 1f out tl ins fnl f: r.o)	hd	**2**	10/1	94	42
3049^{4}	**Socket Set (97)** (BAMcMahon) **2-8-8** MRoberts(10) (a.p: stands' side: r.o one pce fnl f)	2	**3**	9/2^{2}	85	33
2959*	**Cloudberry (80)** (BJMeehan) **2-8-8** MTebbutt(9) (tk keen hold: hdwy over 1f out: hrd rdn: r.o ins fnl f)	1	**4**	20/1	81	29
2103^{10}	**Contrary Mary (86)** (GLewis) **2-8-8** PatEddery(7) (led stands' side over 3f: one pce)	1	**5**	9/1	78	26
3152^{2}	**Desert Lady (IRE) (91)** (RCharlton) **2-8-11** TSprake(1) (lw: prom far side: ev ch over 1f out: wknd ins fnl f)	½	**6**	7/1^{3}	80	28
3033^{2}	**Likely Story (IRE) (88)** (JLDunlop) **2-8-8** LDettori(3) (lw: outpcd far side: hrd rdn over 1f out: nt clr run ins fnl f: nvr nrr)	½	**7**	8/1	75	23
3192^{2}	**Mugello (100)** (APJarvis) **2-8-8** MHills(4) (lw: w ldrs: led over 2f out tl over 1f out: eased whn btn wl ins fnl f)	nk	**8**	7/2^{1}	74	22
3209*	**Baby Grand (IRE) (88)** (TDBarron) **2-8-8** KimberleyHart(12) (a bhd)	1¼	**9**	20/1	70	18
2713*	**Child Prodigy (IRE) (90)** (JWWatts) **2-8-8** JReid(8) (a.p: led stands' side over 1f out: sn wknd)	nk	**10**	14/1	69	17
3192^{7}	**Its All Relative (94)** (JBerry) **2-8-8** GDuffield(2) (led over 2f: wknd over 1f out)	1¼	**11**	14/1	66	14

(SP 118.5%) **11 Rn**

61.72 secs (1.52) CSF £68.86 TOTE £7.90: £2.10 £3.60 £1.90 (£47.40) Trio £74.40 OWNER J & S Kelly (EPSOM) BRED R. T. Lingwood

3178a Aurigny, described by her trainer as a tough little filly who does not know how to stop trying, had to overcome quite a poor start. Her rider thought he won with a bit up his sleeve. (7/1)

3192 Banningham Blade is another honest sort and remains a credit to all concerned. (10/1: 7/1-11/1)

3049 Socket Set, reverting to the minimum trip, kept on under the stands' rail but could never get to grips with the first two. (9/2: 6/1-4/1)

2959* Cloudberry had a lot more on her plate this time and could be ready to tackle six. (20/1)

1593* Contrary Mary ran on in a style which suggests she might get further. (9/1)

3152 Desert Lady (IRE) saw plenty of daylight from the number one stall. (7/1)

3033 Likely Story (IRE) found this trip too sharp. (8/1)

3192 Mugello (7/2: 5/2-4/1)

2931* Its All Relative (14/1: 10/1-16/1)

3596 TRIPLEPRINT GEOFFREY FREER STKS (Gp 2) (3-Y.O+) (Class A)

3-00 (3-01) **1m 5f 61y** £39,581.00 (£14,787.30: £7,081.15: £3,060.55) Stalls: Low GOING minus 0.33 sec per fur (GF)

				SP	RR	SF
2559^{6}	**Dushyantor (USA) (120)** (HRACecil) **4-9-6** KFallon(5) (tk keen hold: led over 2f out: all out)	—	**1**	9/2^{2}	121	25
2107^{4}	**Panama City (USA) (106)** (PWChapple-Hyam) **3-8-6** DHarrison(4) (lw: led tl over 3f out: rdn over 1f out: r.o)	nk	**2**	9/1^{3}	118	11
3050^{5}	**Shantou (USA) (125)** (JHMGosden) **4-9-9** LDettori(1) (lw: hld up: rdn over 1f out: ev ch ins fnl f: r.o)	hd	**3**	4/7^{1}	124	28
3050^{6}	**Strategic Choice (USA) (120)** (PFICole) **6-9-9** PatEddery(2) (lw: chsd ldr: led over 3f out tl over 2f out: one pce)	3½	**4**	9/2^{2}	119	23

(SP 110.0%) **4 Rn**

2m 55.33 (8.83) CSF £29.34 TOTE £4.20 (£9.30) OWNER Mr K. Abdulla (NEWMARKET) BRED Juddmonte Farms

WEIGHT FOR AGE 3yo-11lb

2559 Dushyantor (USA) wore a tongue-strap for the first time because Cecil believed he had been playing with his tongue. Beaten a neck by Shantou in the St Leger, he was of course meeting his old adversary on 3lb better terms. (9/2)

2107 Panama City (USA) stuck to the far rail like glue while the others came wide, and really battled on against these older horses. It sounds as if connections feel he deserves a crack at the final Classic on this evidence. (9/1)

3050 Shantou (USA), considered by his trainer not to have been suited by a false pace, was trying to confirm his neck defeat in the St Leger of Dushyantor on 3lb worse terms. (4/7)

3050 Strategic Choice (USA) was beaten for finishing speed when the race was really on. (9/2)

3597 LEVY BOARD NURSERY H'CAP (2-Y.O) (Class C)

3-30 (3-31) **7f 64y (round)** £4,991.00 (£1,508.00: £734.00: £347.00) Stalls: Low GOING minus 0.33 sec per fur (GF)

				SP	RR	SF
1945^{4}	**Saffron Lane (IRE) (78)** (RHannon) **2-8-6** LDettori(2) (plld hrd: a.p: nt clr run over 2f out: led ins fnl f: edgd rt: pushed out)	—	**1**	6/1^{2}	85	46
3387*	**Acid Test (69)** (WRMuir) **2-7-8**(3)ow1 MartinDwyer(6) (sn chsng ldr: led wl over 1f out tl ins fnl f)	1¾	**2**	7/1	72	32
3186^{4}	**Sea Magic (IRE) (84)** (BWHills) **2-8-12** JReid(3) (hmpd over 6f out & 5f out: hdwy 2f out: r.o ins fnl f)	½	**3**	9/1	86	47
3022^{2}	**Stone of Destiny (93)** (BJMeehan) **2-9-7** PatEddery(10) (led: hrd rdn & hdd wl over 1f out: one pce)	¾	**4**	5/1^{1}	93	54
3103^{7}	**Wathbat Lion (73)** (MAJarvis) **2-8-1**ow1 MRoberts(8) (a.p: rdn over 1f out: one pce)	½	**5**	8/1	72	32
3278^{11}	**Delciana (IRE) (70)** (PWHarris) **2-7-12** CRutter(5) (hld up & plld hrd: rdn 3f out: no hdwy fnl 2f)	2½	**6**	11/1	64	25
2856^{2}	**Bold King (82)** (JWHills) **2-8-10** MHills(7) (nvr trbld ldrs)	5	**7**	13/2^{3}	65	26
3237^{4}	**Kennet (74)** (PDCundell) **2-8-2** JQuinn(11) (hld up mid div: rdn over 2f out: wknd over 1f out)	nk	**8**	6/1^{2}	56	17
1370^{2}	**Lobuche (IRE) (68)** (RHannon) **2-7-10** NCarlisle(1) (s.i.s: a bhd)	2	**9**	20/1	46	7
3186^{3}	**Ringleader (75)** (PFICole) **2-7-10**(7) DavidO'Neill(4) (plld hrd: stdd & lost pl 5f out: bhd fnl 2f)	1¼	**10**	8/1	50	11

				SP	RR	SF
3142[4]	**Batswing (86)** (MartynMeade) **2-9-0** SSanders(9) (a bhd)	3½	**11**	16/1	53	14
				(SP 122.3%)		**11 Rn**

1m 29.57 (1.47) CSF £45.28 CT £350.89 TOTE £5.00: £2.20 £2.10 £3.40 (£27.10) Trio £82.50 OWNER S L Partnership (MARLBOROUGH) BRED Saffron Breeders Club

LONG HANDICAP Lobuche (IRE) 7-9

1945 Saffron Lane (IRE), coming back after a two-month break, seemed well-suited by this step-up from six. (6/1)

3387* Acid Test could not overcome a 3lb rise in the weights. (7/1)

3186 Sea Magic (IRE) must have gone very close to winning with a trouble-free run. (9/1)

3022 Stone of Destiny, trying a longer distance, was attempting to concede plenty of weight but will not get much respite from the Handicapper on the strength of this effort. (5/1)

3103 Wathbat Lion did not look particularly well handicapped based on what he had achieved previously. (8/1)

3278 Delciana (IRE) looked keen early on on this step-up in distance. (11/1)

3598 E.B.F. YATTENDON MAIDEN STKS (2-Y.O) (Class D)

4-00 (4-03) **7f (straight)** £4,302.00 (£1,296.00: £628.00: £294.00) Stalls: Centre GOING minus 0.33 sec per fur (GF)

				SP	RR	SF
2688[2]	**Mahboob (IRE)** (DMorley) **2-9-0** RHills(7) (chsd ldr: led on bit wl over 1f out: shkn up ins fnl f: r.o)	—	**1**	11/2	85	50
	Prolix (BWHills) **2-9-0** MHills(6) (w'like: scope: hld up: hdwy over 2f out: ev ch ins fnl f: r.o)	1	**2**	14/1	83	48
	Voodoo Saint (USA) (PWChapple-Hyam) **2-9-0** JReid(5) (unf: scope: led over 5f: one pce)	2½	**3**	5/1[3]	77	42
	Kilimanjaro (MRStoute) **2-9-0** PatEddery(17) (cmpt: lw: a.p: rdn over 3f out: one pce fnl 2f)	1½	**4**	5/2[2]	74	39
3013[5]	**Somayda (IRE)** (JLDunlop) **2-9-0** GCarter(14) (rdn & hdwy 2f out: nt rch ldrs)	2	**5**	20/1	69	34
1954[9]	**Praetorian Gold** (RHannon) **2-9-0** WJO'Connor(15) (rdn over 3f out: styd on one pce fnl 2f)	2	**6**	66/1	64	29
	Gurkha (RHannon) **2-9-0** DaneO'Neill(12) (cmpt: prom tl rdn & wknd over 1f out)	1	**7**	33/1	62	27
	Khalas (BWHills) **2-9-0** RStreet(1) (neat: s.s: hld up & bhd: swtchd lft & hdwy over 1f out: nvr plcd to chal)	3½	**8**	50/1	54+	19
	Blueprint (IRE) (LordHuntingdon) **2-9-0** KFallon(19) (leggy: scope: mid div: bhd fnl 2f)	2	**9**	14/1	50	15
	Blue Monk (IRE) (IABalding) **2-9-0** WRyan(10) (w'like: s.s: nvr nr ldrs)	hd	**10**	33/1	49	14
2948[9]	**Opportune (GER)** (DRCElsworth) **2-9-0** AMcGlone(18) (s.s: nvr nr ldrs)	½	**11**	66/1	48	13
	Beauchamp Magic (JLDunlop) **2-9-0** BDoyle(16) (str: scope: bkwd: bhd fnl 2f)	2½	**12**	33/1	43	8
2948[2]	**Silvertown** (JHMGosden) **2-9-0** LDettori(3) (prom: ev ch over 2f out: sn wknd)	s.h	**13**	9/4[1]	42	7
	One Dinar (FR) (JHMGosden) **2-9-0** MRoberts(8) (w'like: swtg: s.s: a bhd)	s.h	**14**	33/1	42	7
	Churlish Charm (RHannon) **2-9-0** DHarrison(13) (wl grwn: rdn 4f out: a bhd)	2	**15**	33/1	38	3
3450[16]	**Ida Lupino (IRE)** (BWHills) **2-8-6**(3) JDSmith(9) (s.s: hld up: a bhd)	nk	**16**	50/1	32	—
	Wave Rock (JLDunlop) **2-9-0** MRimmer(2) (lengthy: s.s: rdn 4f out: a bhd)	5	**17**	50/1	26	—
2482[4]	**Erika's Young Man** (MJHaynes) **2-8-11**(3) AWhelan(11) (bhd fnl 3f)	5	**18**	66/1	14	—
3278[17]	**Ivory Charm** (KTIvory) **2-8-6**(3) MartinDwyer(4) (prom: rdn over 3f out: wknd over 2f out)	hd	**19**	66/1	9	—
				(SP 136.0%)		**19 Rn**

1m 25.79 (1.69) CSF £73.40 TOTE £6.60: £1.80 £3.30 £1.90 (£63.20) Trio £125.20 OWNER Mr Hamdan Al Maktoum (NEWMARKET) BRED Shadwell Estate Company Limited

2688 Mahboob (IRE) scored readily and doubtless dented one or two home reputations. (11/2)

Prolix is a half-brother to mile juvenile winner Ajanta and a useful middle distance performer in Germany. With the winner having the advantage of previous experience, he did nothing wrong and can soon go one better. (14/1)

Voodoo Saint (USA), a well-bred colt, would not have to improve much to find a race. (5/1)

Kilimanjaro, a well-related 500,000 guineas colt, looked well forward in the paddock. Apparently backed for the Derby on the morning of this race, he shaped like a stayer in the making. (5/2: op 6/4)

3013 Somayda (IRE) ran on as though he is going to need a mile to start repaying some of his IR 550,000 guineas purchase price. (20/1)

Praetorian Gold, a half-brother to seven-furlong winner Cunning Plan, improved considerably on his debut over this longer trip. (66/1)

Gurkha, out of a mile and a quarter winner, shaped well for a long way. (33/1)

Khalas is out of a half-sister to At Talaq who won over eleven furlongs in Britain, as well as the Melbourne Cup. Catching the eye of the Stewards, the explanations were accepted but there is no doubt this was a kind introduction. (50/1)

2948 Silvertown (9/4: op 7/2)

3599 TRIUMVIRATE LIMITED STKS (0-90) (3-Y.O+) (Class C)

4-35 (4-35) **1m 4f 5y** £6,127.00 (£2,293.00: £1,121.50: £482.50: £216.25: £109.75) Stalls: Low GOING minus 0.33 sec per fur (GF)

				SP	RR	SF
2764*	**Rokeby Bowl (90)** (IABalding) **5-9-7** LDettori(2) (lw: hld up: hdwy over 2f out: led over 1f out: r.o wl)	—	**1**	9/4[1]	102	55
3053*	**Tykeyvor (IRE) (90)** (LadyHerries) **7-9-7** GDuffield(3) (prom: rdn & outpcd over 3f out: rallied over 1f out: styd on)	1½	**2**	7/2[2]	100	53
1741[7]	**Isle of Man (USA) (88)** (PFICole) **3-8-9** PatEddery(7) (a.p: rdn to ld 2f out: hdd over 1f out: sn wknd)	3	**3**	8/1	94	37
2568*	**Machiavelli (89)** (HRACecil) **3-8-11** KFallon(5) (a.p: ev ch 2f out: wknd 1f out)	½	**4**	9/2[3]	95	38
3053[7]	**Dance So Suite (86)** (PFICole) **5-9-5** JReid(4) (hld up: hdwy to ld over 5f out: hdd 2f out: wknd over 1f out)	nk	**5**	8/1	93	46
3110[13]	**Fletcher (90)** (HMorrison) **3-8-9** DHarrison(1) (hld up in rr: a bhd)	1¼	**6**	14/1	91	34
3110[10]	**Lallans (IRE) (90)** (MJohnston) **4-9-5** MRoberts(6) (led over 5f: wknd over 2f out)	½	**7**	7/1	91	44
				(SP 112.6%)		**7 Rn**

2m 33.44 (3.44) CSF £8.98 TOTE £3.00: £2.00 £2.30 (£4.00) OWNER Mr Paul Mellon (KINGSCLERE) BRED Paul Mellon

WEIGHT FOR AGE 3yo-10lb

2764* Rokeby Bowl had finished about a length behind the winner in the Bessborough on 2lb worse terms. (9/4)

3053* Tykeyvor (IRE) had finished just in front of the winner in the Bessborough on 2lb better terms. (7/2)

1399 Isle of Man (USA) was coming back after a break following a couple of below-par efforts. (8/1: 6/1-9/1)

2568* Machiavelli had more on his plate than when scrambling home at Pontefract. (9/2)

2729 Dance So Suite was only 3lb better off with the runner-up than when beaten thirteen lengths in the soft at Ascot. (8/1: 6/1-9/1)

2596 Fletcher had been tried in a visor at Glorious Goodwood. (14/1)

3600 STRATTON H'CAP (0-95) (3-Y.O+) (Class C)

5-05 (5-06) **5f 34y** £5,381.00 (£1,628.00: £794.00: £377.00) Stalls: Centre GOING minus 0.33 sec per fur (GF)

				SP	RR	SF
3217[22]	**Willow Dale (IRE) (77)** (DRCElsworth) **4-8-12** KFallon(8) (a.p: led over 1f out: r.o wl)	—	**1**	17/2	87	59
3296[3]	**Sharp Pearl (76)** (PRWebber) **4-8-11b** AMcGlone(2) (s.s: sn chsng ldrs: r.o ins fnl f)	1	**2**	14/1	83	55
3011[7]	**Twice as Sharp (93)** (PWHarris) **5-9-9**(5) CLowther(5) (led stands' side over 3f: r.o)	½	**3**	17/2	98	70
3296[2]	**Ivory's Grab Hire (63)** (KTIvory) **4-7-9b**(3) MartinDwyer(6) (a.p: r.o one pce fnl f)	¾	**4**	12/1	66	38

				SP	RR	SF
3273[3]	**Faith Alone (81)** (CFWall) **4-9-2** GDuffield(13) (lw: rdn over 2f out: hdwy fnl f: r.o)	s.h	**5**	4/1 1	84	56
3410[11]	**Crofters Ceilidh (87)** (BAMcMahon) **5-9-8** MRoberts(11) (a.p: one pce fnl 2f)	½	**6**	5/1 2	88	60
3323[4]	**Polly Golightly (63)** (MBlanshard) **4-7-12b** NAdams(3) (racd alone far side: led: sn clr: hdd over 1f out: eased whn btn wl ins fnl f)	1½	**7**	16/1	60	32
3217[29]	**Clan Chief (80)** (JRArnold) **4-9-1** AClark(1) (no hdwy fnl 2f)	1¼	**8**	12/1	73	45
3217[26]	**White Emir (82)** (BJMeehan) **4-9-3b** PatEddery(14) (tk keen hold: nvr nr to chal)	¾	**9**	8/1 3	72	44
3326[6]	**Longwick Lad (73)** (WRMuir) **4-8-8** JReid(9) (prom over 3f)	3½	**10**	16/1	53	25
1957*	**Spender (81)** (PWHarris) **8-8-13**(3) MHenry(15) (lw: a bhd)	2½	**11**	11/1	53	25
2050[6]	**Gi La High (67)** (MartynMeade) **4-8-2** FNorton(4) (a bhd)	1	**12**	20/1	36	8
3410[18]	**Rushcutter Bay (85)** (PLGilligan) **4-9-6v** MTebbutt(12) (outpcd)	2½	**13**	9/1	46	18

(SP 125.7%) **13 Rn**

60.75 secs (0.55) CSF £116.90 CT £969.36 TOTE £9.40: £2.70 £3.50 £3.30 (£78.30) Trio £342.80 OWNER Michael Jackson Bloodstock Ltd (WHITCOMBE) BRED Shunya Seki

2950 Willow Dale (IRE) was back to the minimum trip after running from 5lb out of the handicap in the Stewards' Cup. (17/2)
3296 Sharp Pearl is continuing to knock on the door. (14/1)
2675 Twice as Sharp ran well off a mark 9lb higher than from which he has ever won. (17/2)
3296 Ivory's Grab Hire was dropping back to the minimum distance. (12/1)
3273 Faith Alone has only scored once over five and that was over the testing Sandown track. (4/1)
2675 Crofters Ceilidh, down 2lb, was still 12lb higher than the mark off which she has three times been successful. (5/1)
3323 Polly Golightly, dropped 3lb, showed plenty of dash, but being on her own eventually proved too much of a handicap. (16/1)

T/Jkpt: Not won; £9,544.07 to Pontefract 17/8/97. T/Plpt: £662.10 (81.58 Tckts). T/Qdpt: £92.20 (17.39 Tckts) KH

3270-RIPON (R-H) (Good to firm)
Saturday August 16th
WEATHER: sunny WIND: slt half bhd

3601 HARROGATE (S) H'CAP (0-60) (3-Y.O) (Class F)
2-15 (2-18) **1m 2f** £2,635.30 (£740.80: £361.90) Stalls: High GOING minus 0.47 sec per fur (F)

				SP	RR	SF
3234[9]	**Rare Talent (60)** (MRChannon) **3-9-7** ACulhane(8) (hdwy ½-wy: led over 2f out: hung lft u.p: styd on wl)	—	**1**	11/4 1	71	40
3068[2]	**Gymcrak Gorjos (44)** (GHolmes) **3-8-5b** KDarley(2) (b.nr fore: a.p: hdwy over 3f out: one pce fnl f)	3	**2**	9/2 3	50	19
3321[6]	**Inkwell (36)** (AHide) **3-7-11**ow1 DaleGibson(14) (lw: in tch: drvn along over 4f out: styd on: nvr able to chal)	1½	**3**	7/2 2	40	8
3405[5]	**Grovefair Lad (IRE) (35)** (MartynWane) **3-7-3v**1(7) JennyBenson(3) (s.i.s: styd on u.p fnl 3f)	2	**4**	20/1	36	5
3027[3]	**Macari (50)** (BPJBaugh) **3-8-6**(5) PRoberts(10) (led: sn clr: hdd over 2f out: sn btn)	1½	**5**	10/1	48	17
2357[8]	**Misterton (35)** (JAGlover) **3-7-10b** GBardwell(1) (s.i.s: styd on fnl 3f: n.d)	2½	**6**	8/1	29	—
3405[4]	**Alisadara (35)** (NBycroft) **3-7-10** LCharnock(5) (b.hind: hdwy ½-wy: sn in tch: no imp fnl 2f)	s.h	**7**	25/1	29	—
3477[14]	**Bali-Pet (36)** (JParkes) **3-7-11** TWilliams(4) (sme hdwy 3f out: nvr rchd ldrs)	1	**8**	50/1	29	—
3268[5]	**La Perdoma (35)** (MissMKMilligan) **3-7-7**(3) PFessey(12) (dwlt: hdwy on outside 3f out: n.d)	2½	**9**	25/1	24	—
3271[15]	**Risky Flight (35)** (ASmith) **3-7-10** JLowe(16) (effrt ½-wy: hung rt & no imp)	¾	**10**	50/1	22	—
3038[11]	**Nordico Melody (IRE) (44)** (MrsSJSmith) **3-8-5** JFanning(11) (chsd ldrs tl wknd fnl 2½f)	3	**11**	20/1	27	—
3037[10]	**Perfect Bear (37)** (MrsSJSmith) **3-7-12** DWright(6) (prom tl rdn over 3f out)	3½	**12**	20/1	14	—
2607[8]	**Mister Jay (42)** (KAMorgan) **3-7-10**(7) JoHunnam(9) (nvr bttr than mid div)	½	**13**	33/1	18	—
3285[16]	**Red Embers (50)** (DNicholls) **3-8-11** AlexGreaves(7) (swtg: a rr div)	13	**14**	14/1	5	—
3234[14]	**Pemberley (IRE) (46)** (WJHaggas) **3-8-7**ow5 NDay(15) (chsd ldr over 4f: sn wknd)	8	**15**	14/1	—	—
3196[3]	**Petuntse (45)** (JGSmyth-Osbourne) **3-8-6e**ow5 KHodgson(13) (b.hind: prom tl wknd over 3f out)	3	**16**	8/1	—	—

(SP 140.6%) **16 Rn**

2m 6.8 (3.30) CSF £14.43 CT £46.13 TOTE £4.00: £1.30 £1.40 £1.30 £5.40 (£11.00) Trio £16.10 OWNER Mr A. Merza (UPPER LAMBOURN) BRED Mrs Carol Merza

LONG HANDICAP Risky Flight 7-3 Inkwell 7-9 Grovefair Lad (IRE) 7-2 La Perdoma 7-8 Misterton 7-9 Alisadara 6-13

Bt in 13,000 gns

OFFICIAL EXPLANATION Petuntse: the jockey reported that the saddle slipped.

2667 Rare Talent has dropped down the handicap here, and was taking a big drop in class. He won it well despite showing a tendency to hang when ridden. (11/4: 5/1-5/2)
3068 Gymcrak Gorjos, having her second run in the blinkers, ran well again but the winner was always too classy. (9/2)
3321 Inkwell is slow but sure and, despite staying on under pressure, could never get in a blow. He looks the type that may well to take to hurdling. (7/2: 4/1-6/1)
3405 Grovefair Lad (IRE) had a visor on for the first time and ran better, but only got going when it was all too late. (20/1)
3027 Macari again adopted his attacking policy, but he had risen 5lb in the weights and, once collared by the winner, he soon gave up. (10/1)
2171 Misterton obviously has his own ideas about the game, but he has ability if he can persuaded. (8/1)
793 Red Embers (14/1: op 7/1)
2059 Pemberley (IRE) (14/1: 10/1-16/1)
3196 Petuntse (8/1: op 5/1)

3602 KNARESBOROUGH CONDITIONS STKS (2-Y.O) (Class D)
2-45 (2-48) **6f** £3,308.25 (£1,002.00: £489.50: £233.25) Stalls: Low GOING minus 0.47 sec per fur (F)

				SP	RR	SF
2863[4]	**Aix En Provence (USA) (97)** (MJohnston) **2-9-3** DHolland(3) (mde most: shkn up & r.o wl fnl 2f)	—	**1**	11/10 1	84+	47
2680[4]	**Mihnah (IRE)** (DMorley) **2-8-6** RCochrane(4) (trckd ldrs: smooth hdwy to chal 2f out: sn rdn & no ex)	2½	**2**	6/4 2	66	29
	Moving Princess (MissSEHall) **2-8-6** KDarley(1) (lengthy: bit bkwd: outpcd & lost tch after 2f: styd on wl fnl 2f)	1	**3**	20/1	64+	27
3106[3]	**Miss Puci (68)** (JBerry) **2-8-3**(3) PFessey(2) (w ldrs 4f: grad wknd)	¾	**4**	16/1	62	25
3131[10]	**Fashion Victim (76)** (THCaldwell) **2-9-3** ACulhane(7) (hld up: effrt ½-wy: sn rdn & btn)	5	**5**	20/1	59	22
3152[4]	**Prix Star (83)** (CWFairhurst) **2-9-3v** LCharnock(6) (spd 4f: sn wknd)	½	**6**	9/1 3	58	21
3331[4]	**Noble Demand (USA)** (MrsJRRamsden) **2-8-11** JFortune(8) (lw: prom over 3f: wknd)	¾	**7**	12/1	50	13

	Uniform (MissSEHall) **2-8-6** KHodgson(5) (leggy: scope: s.i.s: a outpcd & bhd) 2	**8**	40/1	40	3
			(SP 123.2%)		**8 Rn**

1m 11.5 (1.00) CSF £2.90 TOTE £2.50: £1.20 £1.10 £2.70 (£1.60) OWNER Featherstone, Bird (MIDDLEHAM) BRED Albatroz, Schumer & Schwartz

2863 Aix En Provence (USA) was back to form and in some style, and looks to be going the right way. (11/10)
2680 Mihnah (IRE), a good mover, travelled well but failed to match the winner for finishing speed. She could well need further and is one to keep an eye on. (6/4)
Moving Princess showed a deal of promise and should have learnt plenty here. She looks one to keep on the right side of, especially when trying longer trips. (20/1)
3106 Miss Puci put in a reasonable effort but found this company too hot in the last furlong and a half. (16/1)
2736* Fashion Victim has lost his way since his win at Beverley. He pulls hard early on and then finds little off the bit. (20/1)
3152 Prix Star likes to dominate and was never good enough here. (9/1)
3331 Noble Demand (USA) (12/1: op 8/1)

3603 BILLY NEVETT MEMORIAL CHALLENGE CUP H'CAP (0-80) (3-Y.O+) (Class D)

3-15 (3-16) **1m 4f 60y** £3,389.00 (£1,022.00: £496.00: £233.00) Stalls: Low GOING minus 0.47 sec per fur (F)

			SP	RR	SF
2824[6]	**Suga Hawk (IRE) (58)** (EJAlston) **5-8-11** JFEgan(2) (lw: trckd ldrs: rdn to ld 1f out: r.o) ....—	**1**	4/1[3]	71	26
3333[11]	**Gold Desire (56)** (MBrittain) **7-8-9** GBardwell(1) (b: lw: mde most tl hdd 1f out: kpt on same pce) 3½	**2**	3/1[2]	64	19
3245*	**Yet Again (55)** (MissGayKelleway) **5-8-8** JCarroll(3) (dwlt: sn cl up: disp ld 3f out tl rdn & btn ent fnl f) 1	**3**	9/4[1]	62	17
	Toshiba Talk (IRE) (43) (BEllison) **5-7-10** LCharnock(4) (hld up: effrt over 3f out: outpcd fnl 2f) 3	**4**	12/1	46	1
3283[4]	**Ballpoint (71)** (GMMoore) **4-9-10** JFortune(5) (prom tl outpcd 3f out: p.u lame 1f out)	**P**	9/4[1]	—	—
			(SP 114.2%)		**5 Rn**

2m 38.5 (5.00) CSF £15.22 TOTE £6.50: £2.20 £1.80 (£16.90) OWNER Mr John Patrick Barry (PRESTON) BRED Countess A. De Laubespin
LONG HANDICAP Toshiba Talk (IRE) 7-9

2824 Suga Hawk (IRE), in a race that turned out to be a six furlong sprint, had the best turn of foot. (4/1)
3183* Gold Desire tried to steal this by quickening on the home turn, but could never get away and, despite trying hard, was clearly second best. He remains in good heart. (3/1)
3245* Yet Again is on a mark 5lb higher than he has previously won off and it just proved too much. (9/4: op 11/8)
Toshiba Talk (IRE) ran well, and this will no doubt have put him straight for hurdling. (12/1: 20/1-10/1)

3604 WILLIAM HILL GREAT ST WILFRID H'CAP (0-105) (3-Y.O+) (Class B)

3-45 (3-48) **6f** £20,470.00 (£6,160.00: £2,980.00: £1,390.00) Stalls: Low GOING minus 0.47 sec per fur (F)

			SP	RR	SF
3410[4]	**Tadeo (95)** (MJohnston) **4-9-8** DeanMcKeown(19) (lw: mde all far side: hrd drvn 2f out: r.o) ....—	**1**	12/1	107	74
3150[W]	**Emerging Market (95)** (JLDunlop) **5-9-8** KDarley(5) (lw: b: s.i.s: hdwy ½-wy: r.o wl u.p fnl f: nrst fin) ....¾	**2**	17/2	105	72
3273[5]	**Tiler (IRE) (78)** (MJohnston) **5-8-5** DHolland(4) (chsd ldr stands' side: ev ch ins fnl f: kpt on) ....hd	**3**	15/2[2]	88	55
3436*	**Bowden Rose (90)** (MBlanshard) **5-9-0b**(3) DSweeney(7) (lw: led stands' side: clr ½-wy: nt qckn ins fnl f) ....s.h	**4**	12/1	100	67
3296*	**Golden Pound (USA) (80)** (MissGayKelleway) **5-8-7b** JCarroll(17) (lw: racd far side: hdwy over 2f out: styd on: nvr able to chal) 1½	**5**	16/1	86	53
3011[9]	**Canovas Heart (83)** (BobJones) **8-8-10** NDay(14) (racd stands' side: chsd ldrs: nt qckn appr fnl f) 2	**6**	33/1	83	50
3254*	**Mr Teigh (74)** (MrsJRRamsden) **5-8-1** JFanning(15) (lw: racd far side: hdwy u.p over 2f out: nvr rchd ldrs) ....nk	**7**	14/1	74	41
3273*	**So Intrepid (IRE) (86)** (JMBradley) **7-8-13** JFortune(20) (lw: chsd ldrs far side tl wknd fnl 1½f) 1	**8**	10/1	83	50
3273[7]	**Double Action (92)** (TDEasterby) **3-9-2** LCharnock(10) (lw: hdwy stands' side 2f out: nvr nr to chal) ....¾	**9**	12/1	87	51
3385[4]	**For the Present (73)** (TDBarron) **7-8-0** DaleGibson(9) (racd stands' side: in tch: rdn ½-wy: no imp after) 1¼	**10**	12/1	65	32
3194[2]	**Brutal Fantasy (IRE) (85)** (JLEyre) **3-8-2**(7) RWinston(18) (b.hind: racd far side: chsd wnr to ½-wy: sn btn) ....nk	**11**	20/1	76	40
3481[8]	**Double Oscar (IRE) (77)** (DNicholls) **4-8-4** FLynch(1) (lw: racd stands' side: swtchd rt ½-wy: n.d) ....½	**12**	8/1[3]	66	33
3273[2]	**Gadge (85)** (ABailey) **6-8-12** DWright(16) (b: racd far side: outpcd & bhd fr ½-wy) 1	**13**	10/1	72	39
3273[4]	**Babsy Babe (86)** (JJQuinn) **4-8-13** ACulhane(21) (swtg: racd far side: rdn ½-wy: sn btn) ....hd	**14**	16/1	72	39
3252[3]	**Ziggy's Dancer (USA) (92)** (EJAlston) **6-9-5** JFEgan(13) (lw: chsd ldrs stands' side tl wknd over 1f out) ....nk	**15**	33/1	78	45
3199[3]	**Caution (75)** (SGollings) **3-7-10**(3) PFessey(2) (racd stands' side: n.d) ....hd	**16**	50/1	60	24
3217[2]	**My Best Valentine (101)** (VSoane) **7-10-0** RCochrane(11) (lw: bhd: drvn along ½-wy: n.d) ....½	**17**	7/2[1]	85	52
3423[14]	**Ursa Major (79)** (PAKelleway) **3-8-3** DBiggs(3) (sn outpcd stands' side) 1	**18**	40/1	60	24
3418[2]	**Ivory Dawn (78)** (KTIvory) **3-8-2** JLowe(6) (outpcd & bhd stands' side fr ½-wy) 2	**19**	33/1	54	18
3118[2]	**Venture Capitalist (100)** (DNicholls) **8-9-13b** AlexGreaves(12) (dwlt: a bhd) 1½	**20**	10/1	72	39
3189[6]	**Just Loui (73)** (KRBurke) **3-7-11** GBardwell(8) (racd stands' side: sn bhd) 6	**21**	25/1	29	—
			(SP 153.9%)		**21 Rn**

1m 9.9 (-0.60) CSF £116.28 CT £808.09 TOTE £15.90: £3.30 £2.00 £2.30 £3.80 (£52.60) Trio £157.70 OWNER Mr J. R. Good (MIDDLEHAM) BRED J. R. and Mrs P. Good
WEIGHT FOR AGE 3yo-3lb

3410 Tadeo had only previously won over the minimum trip, but he used all his speed and, suited by the easy track, did it well. Sticking to the far rails was certainly a help. (12/1)
892 Emerging Market, given a peach of a ride, was produced to win the race on the stands' side, but unluckily for him the winner was on the opposite side of the track. (17/2)
3273 Tiler (IRE), back to his best, tried his heart out and always gives the impression that another furlong would suit. (15/2)
3436* Bowden Rose is in blistering form and has speed to burn and, over the minimum trip, would take some catching. (12/1)
3296* Golden Pound (USA) chased the winner home up the far side but could never summon the speed to get to grips. (16/1)
2289 Canovas Heart loves this track and ran a super race from his draw, but spent most of the race in no man's land. (33/1)
3254* Mr Teigh ran well up the far side but seemed to find this trip too sharp, and only got going when it was too late. (14/1)
3273* So Intrepid (IRE) is on a 6lb higher mark than he had previously won off, and in the circumstances this was not a bad effort. (10/1)
3273 Double Action found the ground too lively and never got going until too late. (12/1)
3118 Venture Capitalist (10/1: op 16/1)

3605 ROTHMANS ROYALS NORTH SOUTH CHALLENGE SERIES H'CAP (0-80) (3-Y.O+) (Class D)

4-15 (4-19) **1m 1f** £5,920.00 (£1,780.00: £860.00: £400.00) Stalls: High GOING minus 0.47 sec per fur (F)

			SP	RR	SF
3262*	**High Spirits (IRE) (69)** (TDEasterby) **3-9-0b** LCharnock(6) (trckd ldrs: rdn to ld ent fnl f: r.o) ....—	**1**	7/2[2]	81	42
3456[2]	**Mbulwa (47)** (RAFahey) **11-7-13** DaleGibson(9) (led tl hdd ent fnl f: r.o) ....½	**2**	11/2	58	26
3153[2]	**Bowcliffe (61)** (EJAlston) **6-8-13** JFortune(5) (lw: trckd ldrs gng wl: hdwy 2f out: nt qckn ins fnl f) 1¼	**3**	5/1[3]	70	38

3105^{2}	**Duraid (IRE) (76)** (DenysSmith) **5-10-0** ACulhane(3) (trckd ldrs: outpcd 2f out: kpt on towards fin) 1	**4**	11/1	83	51
3403^{6}	**Plan For Profit (IRE) (80)** (MJohnston) **3-9-11** DHolland(2) (sn w ldr: effrt over 2f out: one pce appr fnl f) ......nk	**5**	7/1	87	48
3380^{5}	**Keep Battling (49)** (JSGoldie) **7-7-12**(3) PFessey(8) (hld up: effrt over 2f out: styd on: nvr able to chal) 2½	**6**	20/1	51	19
3262^{4}	**Nobby Barnes (44)** (DonEnricoIncisa) **8-7-10** KimTinkler(1) (hld up: effrt over 3f out: nvr rchd ldrs) ....nk	**7**	20/1	46	14
3311*	**Pride of Pendle (76)** (MartynWane) **8-10-0** JCarroll(12) (hld up: effrt 3f out: no imp) 2	**8**	11/4 1	74	42
3091^{7}	**Forest Robin (53)** (MrsJRRamsden) **4-8-5** MDeering(10) (bhd: rn wd st: n.d) 1¾	**9**	20/1	48	16
	Mukhatab (73) (JJQuinn) **5-9-11** JFanning(4) (swtg: hld up & a bhd) 8	**10**	50/1	54	22
3336^{3}	**Silent Valley (55)** (MissLCSiddall) **3-8-0v** GBardwell(7) (dwlt: a bhd) 5	**11**	20/1	27	—
2960^{7}	**Waasef (60)** (MissGayKelleway) **4-8-12** RCochrane(11) (a bhd: virtually p.u fnl 4f) ....dist	**12**	8/1	—	—

(SP 133.9%) **12 Rn**

1m 53.0 (2.00) CSF £22.43 CT £95.75 TOTE £5.50: £2.00 £2.30 £2.00 (£27.40) Trio £37.80 OWNER Mrs J. B. Mountifield (MALTON) BRED Sean Twomey
LONG HANDICAP Nobby Barnes 7-9
WEIGHT FOR AGE 3yo-7lb
OFFICIAL EXPLANATION Waasef: lost his action.
3262* High Spirits (IRE) always held a good position in this messy race and, in top form at present, had the best turn of foot in the closing stages. (7/2)
3456 Mbulwa is running well at the moment and will surely regain winning ways before long. (11/2: 4/1-6/1)
3153 Bowcliffe travelled on the bridle, but would probably have been better suited by a stronger pace and was out-sprinted. (5/1)
3105 Duraid (IRE) ran well in this messy race and remains in good form. (11/1)
3403 Plan For Profit (IRE) always held a good position which was important in this race, but he again showed he has just lost his dash for the moment. (7/1)
3380 Keep Battling needed a stronger pace than was set here. (20/1)
3262 Nobby Barnes had no chance the way this race was run. (20/1)
3311* Pride of Pendle was completely unsuited by the slow pace. (11/4)
Waasef (8/1: 6/1-9/1)

3606 BOROUGHBRIDGE MAIDEN STKS (3-Y.O+) (Class D)
4-50 (4-59) **5f** £3,452.50 (£1,045.00: £510.00: £242.50) Stalls: Low GOING minus 0.47 sec per fur (F)

			SP	RR	SF
3146^{3}	**Archello (IRE) (62)** (GROldroyd) **3-8-9** JFortune(10) (chsd ldrs: led over 1f out: r.o) ....—	**1**	9/4 2	57+	39
2877^{6}	**Gharib (USA) (72)** (ACStewart) **3-9-0** SWhitworth(3) (lw: b.hind: hld up: stdy hdwy 2f out: ev ch ins fnl f: rdn & kpt on) ....½	**2**	2/1 1	60	42
3425^{5}	**Night Express (54)** (BHanbury) **3-8-11**(3) PFessey(1) (lw: trckd ldrs: nt clr run over 1f out: r.o towards fin)......¾	**3**	4/1 3	58	40
3086^{4}	**Blue Lamp (USA) (56)** (MAJarvis) **3-8-9** RCochrane(6) (cl up: chal over 1f out: nt qckn) ....¾	**4**	8/1	51	33
3266^{7}	**Hiltons Executive (IRE) (35)** (EJAlston) **3-8-9** LCharnock(5) (sddle slipped after s: in tch: swtchd over 1f out: r.o towards fin) ....nk	**5**	16/1	50	32
3271^{5}	**Good To Talk (35)** (TDEasterby) **4-8-9**(7) RWinston(4) (led tl hdd appr fnl f: sn btn) 1¾	**6**	16/1	49	33
3086^{3}	**Dona Filipa (39)** (MissLCSiddall) **4-8-11** OPears(12) (effrt ½-wy: sn rdn & nvr able to chal) ....½	**7**	16/1	42	26
2417^{6}	**Prince of Parkes (55)** (JBerry) **3-8-9b**(5) PRoberts(9) (in tch: rdn ½-wy: no imp) 2½	**8**	12/1	39	21
3121^{9}	**Colonel's Pride (42)** (RMWhitaker) **3-9-0v**1 DeanMcKeown(11) (chsd ldrs over 3f: sn rdn & btn) ....nk	**9**	40/1	39	21
	Passionatti (SGollings) **3-8-9** JCarroll(8) (lengthy: unf: bit bkwd: outpcd fr ½-wy) 3	**10**	66/1	24	6
3241^{14}	**Bright Gold (35)** (ASmith) **3-9-0** JLowe(2) (a outpcd & bhd) 2½	**11**	200/1	21	3
3086^{6}	**Beau Tudor (IRE) (38)** (MissLCSiddall) **3-8-7**(7) TSiddall(7) (sn outpcd & bhd) ....¾	**12**	200/1	19	1

(SP 125.5%) **12 Rn**

58.6 secs (0.80) CSF £7.00 TOTE £3.50: £1.20 £2.20 £2.20 (£3.60) Trio £12.90 OWNER Mr E. Gale (YORK) BRED Desmond Mulhall
WEIGHT FOR AGE 3yo-2lb
OFFICIAL EXPLANATION Hiltons Executive (IRE): the rider reported that his saddle slipped.
3146 Archello (IRE) has been consistent all season and got just reward, but may have been a trifle fortunate. (9/4)
2877 Gharib (USA), taking a big drop in distance, went well on the bridle and seemed to respond to pressure this time. Sprinting might be the game for him. (2/1: 6/4-9/4)
3425 Night Express, dropping back in trip, appeared very unlucky as he was denied a clear run at a vital stage. (4/1)
3086 Blue Lamp (USA) had her chances but again failed to take them. (8/1)
2883 Hiltons Executive (IRE) was hampered by a slipping saddle from the start, and by the way she finished she must be counted as very unlucky. (16/1)
3271 Good To Talk has the ability but, as usual, failed to do a tap once off the bridle. (16/1)
2417 Prince of Parkes (12/1: op 8/1)

T/Plpt: £48.10 (547.19 Tckts). T/Qdpt: £20.30 (39.82 Tckts) AA

3395-WOLVERHAMPTON (L-H) (Standard)
Saturday August 16th
WEATHER: sunny & v.warm WIND: nil

3607 E.B.F STARFISH MAIDEN STKS (2-Y.O) (Class D)
7-00 (7-01) **7f (Fibresand)** £4,059.65 (£1,215.20: £583.10: £267.05) Stalls: High GOING minus 0.03 sec per fur (STD)

			SP	RR	SF
2943^{10}	**The Groveller (73)** (PDEvans) **2-9-0** JFEgan(6) (a.p: led ½-wy: hrd rdn fnl f: hld on gamely) ....—	**1**	33/1	81	32
3253^{2}	**Guaranteed** (BWHills) **2-9-0** FLynch(12) (hld up: hdwy 3f out: hrd rdn & r.o wl ins fnl f)..........................½	**2**	7/2 2	80	31
3260^{2}	**Prompt Delivery (USA)** (MRStoute) **2-9-0** KDarley(7) (a.p: ev ch over 1f out: hrd rdn: styd on) ....½	**3**	4/6 1	79	30
3295^{2}	**Blue Zola (IRE)** (MBell) **2-8-4**(5) RMullen(4) (lw: chsd ldrs: effrt ent st: sn rdn: nt pce to chal)....................3½	**4**	13/2 3	66	17
3201^{8}	**Prodigal Son (IRE)** (RJRWilliams) **2-9-0** DRMcCabe(1) (in tch: effrt & rdn wl over 1f out: nvr nr to chal).........5	**5**	33/1	59	10
2768^{8}	**King's Hussar** (PFICole) **2-9-0** MRimmer(9) (bit bkwd: sn bhd & outpcd: sme late hdwy: n.d) ....nk	**6**	14/1	59	10
2295^{8}	**Imbackagain (IRE)** (PCHaslam) **2-9-0** ACulhane(10) (lw: chsd ldrs: hrd drvn over 2f out: sn btn) 4	**7**	50/1	50	1
	Magic Falls (IRE) (MJPolglase) **2-9-0** JTate(3) (w'like: scope: bkwd: sn drvn along: a outpcd)......................1¾	**8**	50/1	46	—
	Zero Three Fifteen (IRE) (MartynMeade) **2-8-11**(3) RHavlin(2) (neat: bit bkwd: trckd ldrs 4f: sn lost tch) ....hd	**9**	33/1	45	—
2768^{11}	**Fair Game (IRE)** (JLDunlop) **2-9-0** BDoyle(11) (outpcd)..hd	**10**	14/1	45	—
3094^{17}	**Taurean** (NAGraham) **2-9-0** SSanders(8) (led over 3f: wknd 2f out: t.o) 6	**11**	50/1	31	—

1026^{6}	**Smart Venture** (RHollinshead) **2-8-11**(3) DGriffiths(5) (outpcd: a bhd)	hd	**12**	33/1	31	—
				(SP 126.5%)		**12 Rn**

1m 30.1 (5.40) CSF £137.30 TOTE £30.40: £5.50 £1.20 £1.10 (£60.90) Trio £24.40 OWNER Mr John Pugh (WELSHPOOL) BRED Mrs M. Tinkler

2786 The Groveller virtually ran away with his jockey to post on this first outing on this surface, and caused quite an upset with a hard-fought, all-out success, but there was certainly no fluke about it. (33/1)
3253 Guaranteed closed up at the end of the back straight and put in a sustained last-furlong challenge, but the winner would not be denied. (7/2)
3260 Prompt Delivery (USA) looked all over the winner turning in, but he was then tapped for toe before rallying under strong pressure nearing the finish. Time may show that his strong suit is stamina. (4/6)
3295 Blue Zola (IRE) tried hard to muster the pace to get at the leaders on straightening up, but her determined efforts were always in vain. (13/2)
Prodigal Son (IRE) raced in touch but, once the tempo lifted, he was short of the necessary acceleration. (33/1)
King's Hussar still has a bit left to work on, and he was only finding his stride when it was all too late. He will come into his own when tackling a mile plus. (14/1)

3608 JUDY'S BIRTHDAY MILE H'CAP (0-65) (3-Y.O+) (Class F)

7-30 (7-34) **1m 100y (Fibresand)** £2,277.00 (£627.00: £297.00) Stalls: Low GOING minus 0.03 sec per fur (STD)

				SP	RR	SF
3285^{6}	**Legal Issue (IRE) (51)** (WWHaigh) **5-9-5** ACulhane(12) (trckd ldrs: led over 2f out: sn drvn clr: jst hld on)	—	**1**	7/1	63	43
2488^{9}	**Sandmoor Denim (39)** (SRBowring) **10-8-7**ow1 SWebster(7) (b: hld up: hdwy 2f out: sn rdn: str chal wl ins fnl f)	nk	**2**	12/1	50	29
3041^{2}	**Failed To Hit (50)** (NPLittmoden) **4-9-4b** SWhitworth(9) (a.p: rdn to chse wnr wl over 1f out: kpt on wl towards fin)	hd	**3**	9/2 2	61	41
*3041**	**Colins Choice (55)** (JLSpearing) **3-9-0**(3) TEDurcan(4) (hld up: hdwy over 4f out: kpt on u.p fnl f)	2	**4**	11/1	63	37
3018^{4}	**Dream Carrier (IRE) (49)** (REPeacock) **9-9-3** SSanders(3) (lw: hld up: hdwy over 2f out: sn rdn: nt rch ldrs)	3	**5**	8/1	51	31
3428^{5}	**Sooty Tern (53)** (JMBradley) **10-9-4**(3) DGriffiths(5) (hld up: hdwy over 2f out: sn rdn: no imp)	nk	**6**	4/1 1	54	34
2912^{3}	**Phoenix Princess (53)** (BAMcMahon) **3-9-1** LNewton(1) (led 7f out tl over 2f out: wknd wl over 1f out)	3½	**7**	6/1	48	22
3249^{6}	**Backhander (IRE) (36)** (RTPhillips) **5-7-13b**(5) RMullen(8) (hld up: hdwy over 3f out: wknd fnl 2f: t.o)	7	**8**	16/1	17	—
3469^{15}	**Airborne Harris (IRE) (55)** (ABailey) **4-9-9** DWright(6) (led over 1f: wknd 3f out: t.o)	2½	**9**	25/1	32	12
3254^{9}	**People Direct (57)** (NPLittmoden) **4-9-11** JFEgan(10) (w ldrs to ½-wy: sn rdn & lost tch: t.o)	s.h	**10**	5/1 3	34	14
3269^{6}	**Loch Style (44)** (RHollinshead) **4-8-12** FLynch(13) (s.s: a bhd: t.o)	10	**11**	14/1	2	—
	Clemency (IRE) (53) (MTate) **5-9-0**(7) VictoriaAppleby(2) (bkwd: reluctant to r: a t.o)	8	**12**	40/1	—	—
3254^{10}	***Silver Harrow (36)*** (AGNewcombe) **4-8-4** AMackay(11) (Withdrawn not under Starter's orders: veterinary advice)		**W**	6/1	—	—
				(SP 141.9%)		**12 Rn**

1m 51.0 (6.00) CSF £86.68 CT £394.47 TOTE £8.00: £2.00 £4.00 £2.50 (£77.30) Trio £149.90 OWNER Mr B. Valentine (MALTON) BRED Naver Enterprises Ltd

WEIGHT FOR AGE 3yo-6lb

3285 Legal Issue (IRE), a choppy mover winning for the first time beyond seven furlongs, slipped his field on the home turn and found just enough to hang on in a thrilling battle to the line. (7/1)
2368 Sandmoor Denim took time to find top gear and his sustained, last-furlong challenge was just a stride too late. (12/1)
3041 Failed To Hit is not enjoying the best of fortune, but he did nothing wrong here and is overdue another success. (9/2)
3041* Colins Choice had it all to do on these altered terms and could not summon the pace to land a blow. (11/1)
3018 Dream Carrier (IRE), held up to get the trip, stayed on in the closing stages without ever threatening to get competitive. (8/1)
3428 Sooty Tern ran a bit flat this time and never held out much hope for his followers. He has run consistently well in most of his races but maybe time is catching up with him. (4/1)

3609 CHEMIQUE ADHESIVES & SEALANTS H'CAP (0-70) (3-Y.O+) (Class E)

8-00 (8-00) **1m 1f 79y (Fibresand)** £3,070.25 (£917.00: £438.50: £199.25) Stalls: Low GOING minus 0.03 sec per fur (STD)

				SP	RR	SF
3496^{3}	**Cherokee Flight (61)** (SMellor) **3-9-1** MWigham(5) (chsd ldrs: chal & nt clr run wl over 1f out: swtchd lft: r.o to ld wl ins fnl f)	—	**1**	9/4 1	70	45
2399^{13}	**Grand Hotel (IRE) (51)** (PWHarris) **3-8-5b^{1}** DHolland(9) (swtg: a.p: ev ch fnl 2f: rdn & edgd rt ins fnl f: r.o)	1¾	**2**	7/1	57	32
2279^{7}	**Wildfire (SWI) (51)** (RAkehurst) **6-8-12** SSanders(6) (b: chsd ldr: led over 5f out: hrd rdn & hdd wl ins fnl f)	nk	**3**	5/1 3	57	39
3153^{13}	**Tallulah Belle (67)** (NPLittmoden) **4-10-0** SWhitworth(10) (hld up: hdwy over 4f out: sn rdn: nt rch ldrs)	12	**4**	7/1	52	34
1116^{10}	**Parsa (USA) (56)** (JLDunlop) **4-9-3** KDarley(8) (trckd ldrs: hrd drvn 3f out: no imp)	7	**5**	9/2 2	29	11
3477^{11}	**Saint Amigo (35)** (BPJBaugh) **5-7-5**(5) IonaWands(1) (a in rr)	1	**6**	40/1	6	—
3396^{9}	**My Girl Lucy (47)** (PMitchell) **3-8-1b**1ow2 JFEgan(4) (led 4f: rdn & outpcd 3f out)	¾	**7**	33/1	17	—
2912^{4}	**Major Mouse (50)** (WWHaigh) **9-8-11** ACulhane(2) (lw: a in rr)	5	**8**	12/1	12	—
3315^{15}	**Tonnerre (57)** (BAMcMahon) **5-9-4** LNewton(7) (lw: lost pl ½-wy: sn wl bhd: t.o)	7	**9**	8/1	7	—
				(SP 114.8%)		**9 Rn**

2m 2.0 (6.00) CSF £16.81 CT £64.73 TOTE £3.30: £1.10 £1.60 £1.60 (£9.20) Trio £20.20 OWNER Silver Knight Exhibitions Ltd (SWINDON) BRED Highclere Stud Ltd

LONG HANDICAP Saint Amigo 7-0

WEIGHT FOR AGE 3yo-7lb

3496 Cherokee Flight is in fine form at present and, though he was the meat in the sandwich when delivering his challenge, it was more than likely he went for a gap that was not there. (9/4)
2159* Grand Hotel (IRE) seems to act well on Fibresand, and he was in the thick of the action from the turn into the straight, only losing out when edging right under pressure in the final one hundred yards. (7/1)
796* Tallulah Belle has not yet recovered her form after a holiday in May and June, but she is gradually finding her way again. (7/1)

3610 WEATHERBYS DASH (DUNSTALL PARK BREEZE UP SALES) CONDITIONS STKS (2-Y.O) (Class B)

8-30 (8-32) **6f (Fibresand)** £18,555.00 (£6,945.00: £3,397.50: £1,462.50: £656.25: £333.75) Stalls: Low GOING minus 0.03 sec per fur (STD)

				SP	RR	SF
3131^{7}	**Ra Ra Rasputin** (BAMcMahon) **2-8-11** SSanders(10) (chsd ldrs: led 2f out: drvn clr fnl f)	—	**1**	50/1	82	37
1045^{2}	**Blue Kite** (NPLittmoden) **2-8-11** TGMcLaughlin(12) (hdwy ½-wy: chsd wnr over 1f out: no imp)	3	**2**	5/1 2	74	29
3257^{2}	**Heavenly Abstone (85)** (PDEvans) **2-8-10v** JFEgan(1) (b: swtg: chsd ldrs: outpcd 2f out: kpt on u.p ins fnl f)	6	**3**	5/1 2	57	12
1684d	**Only For Gold** (JBerry) **2-9-7** KDarley(9) (chsd ldr: led over 2f out: sn hdd: wknd fnl f)	nk	**4**	11/10 1	67	22

				SP	RR	SF
3094^{15}	**Sampower Lady** (WJMusson) **2-8-6** DRMcCabe(11) (hld up: hdwy fnl 2f: nrst fin)	½	**5**	33/1	51	6
2361^{5}	**Tom Dougal (69)** (CSmith) **2-8-11** JTate(6) (outpcd tl kpt on appr fnl f)	s.h	**6**	16/1	56	11
2493*	**Greenbrook (67)** (WGMTurner) **2-8-11** DSweeney(2) (led tl hdd & wknd over 2f out)	nk	**7**	33/1	55	10
3416^{4}	**Blushing Victoria (75)** (MartynMeade) **2-8-10** RHavlin(5) (s.s: a bhd)	2½	**8**	25/1	47	2
3131^{5}	**Dancing Rio (IRE) (73)** (PCHaslam) **2-8-11** JFortune(3) (in tch over 3f)	s.h	**9**	20/1	48	3
3395^{3}	**Celtic Comfort (73)** (PCHaslam) **2-8-11** LCharnock(4) (lw: chsd ldrs over 3f: sn outpcd: t.o)	6	**10**	$12/1^{3}$	32	—
3072^{4}	**Kustom Kit Kate** (SRBowring) **2-8-6** CTeague(8) (lw: outpcd)	¾	**11**	50/1	25	—
3239^{7}	**Hey Up Mate (IRE)** (JBerry) **2-8-11** PFessey(7) (lw: sn drvn along: lost pl ½-wy: t.o)	8	**12**	40/1	9	—
3265^{3}	**Rio (IRE)** (JBerry) **2-8-11** TEDurcan(13) (chsd ldrs tl wknd & eased over 2f out: virtually p.u: t.o)	20	**13**	16/1	—	—

(SP 121.3%) **13 Rn**

1m 15.2 (4.00) CSF £253.78 TOTE £27.10: £4.60 £2.20 £1.60 (£241.00) Trio £89.50 OWNER Mr D. J. Allen (TAMWORTH) BRED D. J. Allen

OFFICIAL EXPLANATION Rio (IRE): lost his action.

Ra Ra Rasputin, a half-brother to Sing with the Band, has shown little sign of ability in the past but he came good in no uncertain terms in this most valuable two-year-old contest, and the ease of his victory had to be seen to be believed. (50/1)

1045 Blue Kite, not the most impressive of movers, ran a fine race on this return to action and, though he failed to match strides with the winner, appeared to be well suited by this step-up to six furlongs. (5/1)

3257 Heavenly Abstone, outpaced on the home turn, renewed her effort once straightened up and ran on strongly to gain third prize right on the line. She is a trier and she seemed to handle this surface. (5/1)

1684* Only For Gold, very keen to post, was unable to adopt his usual front-running tactics, but he probably did too much too soon on this first attempt at six furlongs and was a spent force inside the distance. (11/10)

2553 Sampower Lady, doing all her best work in the latter stages, performed with credit at this first attempt on the sand and over this trip, and she would seem to be coming to herself. (33/1)

2361 Tom Dougal has shown plenty of speed on the turf, but he struggled with the pace and did not begin to pick up until it was far too late. (16/1)

2493* Greenbrook set a brisk pace on this step-up in class but, when the race began in earnest, he was one of the first to crack. (33/1)

3611 SEA HORSE (S) STKS (3, 4 & 5-Y.O) (Class G)

9-00 (9-03) **1m 1f 79y (Fibresand)** £1,984.50 (£547.00: £259.50) Stalls: Low GOING minus 0.03 sec per fur (STD)

				SP	RR	SF
55^{8}	**Red Phantom (IRE) (50)** (SMellor) **5-9-4** MWigham(6) (swtg: dwlt: sn wl bhd: hdwy 3f out: led appr fnl f: comf)	—	**1**	$4/1^{2}$	58	23
3027^{6}	**Qualitair Beauty (30)** (MissLCSiddall) **4-8-13** DeanMcKeown(3) (chsd ldrs: rdn over 2f out: styd on ins fnl f)	2	**2**	25/1	50	15
1965^{16}	**Kayzee (IRE) (43)** (DBurchell) **3-8-1**(5) KSked(7) (led: qcknd over 2f out: hdd appr fnl f: no ex)	hd	**3**	12/1	49	7
2937^{15}	**Juicy Ting (42)** (PCHaslam) **3-8-11** JFortune(9) (a chsng ldrs: rdn & outpcd over 2f out: sn btn)	5	**4**	$5/1^{3}$	46	4
	Zahaalie (USA) (JAPickering) **5-8-11**(7) JFowle(10) (chsd ldrs: rdn & one pce fnl 2f)	nk	**5**	11/1	45	10
3456^{7}	**She's Simply Great (IRE) (32)** (JJO'Neill) **4-8-13** ACulhane(8) (hld up: hdwy 6f out: rdn over 3f out: sn wknd)	7	**6**	$7/2^{1}$	28	—
3335^{5}	**Pearl Silk** (TTBill) **4-8-13** TGMcLaughlin(2) (trckd ldrs: drvn along 3f out: sn wknd)	½	**7**	33/1	28	—
3400^{4}	**Silver Button (42)** (SRBowring) **3-8-8b**¹(3) CTeague(4) (chsd ldr tl wknd over 2f out)	nk	**8**	6/1	32	—
	Pwllglas (SCWilliams) **3-8-11** KDarley(1) (w'like: bkwd: bhd: reminders & swvd lft 5f out: sn t.o)	dist	**9**	$5/1^{3}$	—	—
3268^{6}	**Greenacres Goddess (30)** (TWall) **3-8-6** NCarlisle(5) (a in rr: t.o)	4	**10**	25/1	—	—

(SP 116.5%) **10 Rn**

2m 5.0 (9.00) CSF £92.07 TOTE £5.20: £2.40 £6.00 £3.00 (£70.80) Trio £54.80 OWNER Silver Knight Exhibitions Ltd (SWINDON) BRED K. and Mrs CULLEN

WEIGHT FOR AGE 3yo-7lb

No bid

Red Phantom (IRE), taking a big step down in distance on this first outing since January, completed a rewarding night for connections under a very competent ride, winning rather comfortably in the end. (4/1: op 5/2)

Qualitair Beauty, showing her first real sign of form, was flat to the boards on the home turn but she stayed on well in the latter stages and should be able to pick up a similar race. (25/1)

185 Kayzee (IRE) adopted more forceful tactics over this longer trip and, for most of the way, looked well in control, but she began to tie up on the approach to the final furlong and was down to a walk when collared. (12/1)

3456 She's Simply Great (IRE) (7/2: 6/1-3/1)

1731 Silver Button (6/1: op 10/1)

3612 DOLPHIN MAIDEN APPRENTICE H'CAP (0-65) (3-Y.O+) (Class G)

9-30 (9-30) **1m 4f (Fibresand)** £2,007.50 (£570.00: £282.50) Stalls: Low GOING minus 0.03 sec per fur (STD)

				SP	RR	SF
3449^{3}	**Bold Saint (IRE) (40)** (PWHarris) **3-7-12b**(5) PBradley(3) (led over 8f out tl over 5f out: led 3f out to 2f out: rallied to ld fnl 100y: all out)	—	**1**	11/2	46	16
3430^{4}	**Ceanothus (IRE) (56)** (WJHaggas) **3-9-2**(3) DarrenWilliams(4) (lw: led over 3f: rdn to ld over 5f out: hdd 3f out: led 2f out tl ins fnl f: rallied)	nk	**2**	$7/4^{1}$	62	32
3298^{2}	**Pointe Fine (FR) (60)** (JWHills) **3-9-2**(7) SamDickerson(5) (lw: prom tl lost tch over 4f out: styd on fnl 2f: nrst fin)	2	**3**	$3/1^{2}$	63	33
1164^{15}	**Brynkir (53)** (DJGMurraySmith) **3-9-2** DMcGaffin(1) (bit bkwd: bhd: outpcd 5f out: n.d)	7	**4**	11/2	47	17
3234^{7}	**Sarbaron (IRE) (65)** (PWHarris) **3-10-0** MBatchelor(6) (hld up & bhd: rdn along 7f out: wl bhd fnl 4f: t.o)	11	**5**	$4/1^{3}$	44	14
3134^{11}	**Meadow Blue (35)** (MissLCSiddall) **4-8-8** TSiddall(2) (lw: chsd ldrs: rdn & lost tch 5f out: t.o)	5	**6**	20/1	7	—

(SP 116.9%) **6 Rn**

2m 43.2 (10.70) CSF £14.96 TOTE £4.90: £2.30 £1.30 (£7.90) OWNER Shining Force (BERKHAMSTED) BRED Dr T. J. Molony

WEIGHT FOR AGE 3yo-10lb

3449 Bold Saint (IRE), in a race which developed into a two-horse affair, took full advantage of his significant weight allowance and proved just the stronger in the battle to the line. (11/2)

3430 Ceanothus (IRE), in and out of the lead from the start over this longer trip, gave her all and did not really deserve to have to settle for second best. (7/4: op 3/1)

3298 Pointe Fine (FR) was outpaced at the crucial stage when she last appeared on the All-Weather, and that was the case once again, for she was eating up ground at the finish and would have made it with a little further to travel. (3/1: 5/2-4/1)

T/Plpt: £108.40 (140.51 Tckts). T/Qdpt: £40.50 (14.79 Tckts) IM

3413-LINGFIELD (L-H) (Good to firm)
Sunday August 17th

Race 6 Abandoned - Waterlogging
WEATHER: humid until heavy thunderstorm fr Race 5 WIND: almost nil

3613 HAYS MONTROSE MAIDEN STKS (2-Y.O) (Class D)

2-25 (2-27) **6f** £3,547.45 (£1,075.60: £526.30: £251.65) Stalls: High GOING minus 0.14 sec per fur (G)

				SP	RR	SF
3219[4]	**Surveyor** (JLDunlop) **2-9-0** TSprake(9) (lw: a gng wl: a.p: led over 1f out: qcknd: easily)	—	**1**	11/10[1]	83+	50
3219[7]	**Silversmith (FR)** (SDow) **2-9-0** JFEgan(15) (w ldr: led over 2f out tl over 1f out: unable qckn)	5	**2**	7/1[3]	70	37
2680[5]	**Pay On Red (USA)** (PFICole) **2-9-0** RCochrane(5) (rdn over 3f out: hdwy over 1f out: r.o)	nk	**3**	8/1	69	36
2720[6]	**Jarrayan** (MajorWRHern) **2-8-9** RHills(12) (led over 3f: wknd 1f out)	2	**4**	6/1[2]	59	26
1418[7]	**Campione (IRE)** (MHTompkins) **2-9-0** DBiggs(7) (hld up: rdn over 2f out: one pce)	5	**5**	25/1	50	17
	Twoforten (MMadgwick) **2-9-0** NVarley(10) (w'like: bit bkwd: rdn thrght: nvr nr to chal)	3	**6**	50/1	42	9
	Be My Girl (CFWall) **2-8-9** GDuffield(2) (neat: bit bkwd: dwlt: nvr nrr)	nk	**7**	25/1	36	3
2948[5]	**Chief Blade** (RAkehurst) **2-9-0** SSanders(4) (dwlt: a mid div)	¾	**8**	14/1	39	6
3201[9]	**Forty Love (IRE)** (JEBanks) **2-9-0** AMackay(6) (a mid div)	3	**9**	25/1	31	—
	House On Fire (IRE) (JBerry) **2-8-9**(5) CLowther(8) (lt-f: bhd fnl 2f)	3	**10**	12/1	23	—
3094[13]	**Danzino (IRE)** (APJarvis) **2-9-0** KFallon(1) (a bhd)	hd	**11**	33/1	23	—
3022[6]	**Inn On The Park** (SDow) **2-9-0** DaneO'Neill(16) (a bhd)	nk	**12**	16/1	22	—
	Zillion (IRE) (JWPayne) **2-9-0** AMcGlone(11) (w'like: bkwd: s.s: a bhd)	3	**13**	50/1	14	—
	Pearly Queen (GCBravery) **2-8-9** DRMcCabe(14) (neat: s.s: a wl bhd: t.o)	dist	**14**	50/1	—	—
				(SP 126.1%)	**14 Rn**	

1m 11.45 (2.45) CSF £8.00 TOTE £2.10: £1.10 £1.80 £1.90 (£11.20) Trio £31.20 OWNER The Earl Cadogan (ARUNDEL) BRED Mrs A. Naughton

3219 Surveyor had no problems confirming the promise he had shown on his debut at Goodwood and, always travelling supremely well, cruised into the lead over furlong out and sprinted away to win with a ton in hand. (11/10)

Silversmith (FR) disputed the lead until showing with a slender advantage over a quarter of a mile from home. However, headed below the distance, he was firmly put in his place by the winner. (7/1)

2680 Pay On Red (USA), whose two runs to date have been over seven furlongs, needs further not less and the drop to six furlongs proved all against him. Off the bridle before halfway, he ran on from below the distance and only just failed to take second prize. He is now qualified for nurseries and a step-up to a mile will help. (8/1)

2720 Jarrayan does not have a great deal of substance but nevertheless held a slender advantage until over two furlongs from home. Grimly trying to hold on, she had given best a furlong out. (6/1: op 4/1)

Campione (IRE) looked very fit after a three-month absence, but was made to look very pedestrian in the second half of the race. (25/1)

Twoforten, a stocky colt who looked in need of the run, was being bustled along throughout and never threatened to get near the principals. (50/1)

2948 Chief Blade (14/1: op 8/1)

House On Fire (IRE) (12/1: 8/1-14/1)

3614 JARDINE INSURANCE SERVICES H'CAP (0-85) (3-Y.O) (Class D)

2-55 (2-56) **6f** £3,550.00 (£1,075.00: £525.00: £250.00) Stalls: High GOING minus 0.14 sec per fur (G)

				SP	RR	SF
3198[4]	**Al Muallim (USA) (80)** (JWPayne) **3-9-4** AMcGlone(6) (lw: hld up: led wl over 1f out: drvn out)	—	**1**	11/4[1]	93	66
3473[4]	**Levelled (68)** (MRChannon) **3-8-3**(3) PPMurphy(11) (hld up: swtchd lft 2f out: hrd rdn & ev ch fnl f: r.o wl)	hd	**2**	7/1	81	54
3406[3]	**Hever Golf Rocket (73)** (TJNaughton) **3-8-11** SSanders(12) (w ldr: rdn 3f out: ev ch 2f out: unable qckn)	3½	**3**	11/2[3]	76	49
2951[4]	**Impulsif (USA) (70)** (DJSffrenchDavis) **3-8-8** MTebbutt(4) (swtg: hdwy & n.m.r on ins over 1f out: nvr nrr)	¾	**4**	10/1	71	44
3194[10]	**Antonia's Choice (73)** (JBerry) **3-8-6**(5) CLowther(8) (lw: led over 4f)	5	**5**	25/1	61	34
2838*	**Bacchus (83)** (ACStewart) **3-9-7** KFallon(9) (swtg: hld up: rdn 3f out: wknd over 1f out)	½	**6**	7/2[2]	70	43
3194[4]	**Anokato (66)** (KTIvory) **3-8-1b**(3) MartinDwyer(10) (spd 4f)	¾	**7**	14/1	51	24
3092[5]	**Dayrella (58)** (WRMuir) **3-7-3**(7) PDoe(3) (swtg: dwlt: nvr nr to chal)	5	**8**	14/1	29	2
3145[7]	**March Crusader (83)** (BHanbury) **3-9-7** WRyan(1) (racd alone far side: prom over 4f)	d.h	**8**	8/1	68	41
307[5]	**Countless Times (67)** (WRMuir) **3-8-5** DHarrison(5) (bhd fnl 3f)	10	**10**	25/1	12	—
3250[4]	**Zabriskie (70)** (GLMoore) **3-8-8** AClark(2) (a bhd)	d.h	**10**	40/1	41	14
				(SP 120.4%)	**11 Rn**	

1m 10.61 (1.61) CSF £20.59 CT £94.80 TOTE £3.80: £1.40 £3.90 £1.70 (£19.60) Trio £24.10 OWNER Al Muallim Partnership (NEWMARKET) BRED James T. Gottwald

LONG HANDICAP Dayrella 7-8

3198 Al Muallim (USA) confirmed the promise shown at Newmarket recently, leading early inside the final quarter-mile and responding to pressure to keep the very persistent runner-up at bay. (11/4)

3473 Levelled appreciated the return to six furlongs. Throwing down a very determined challenge from below the distance, he had a tremendous battle royal with the winner and only just lost out. He should soon gain compensation. (7/1)

3406 Hever Golf Rocket disputed the lead, and was still in with every chance two furlongs from home before tapped for toe. (11/2)

2951 Impulsif (USA) found the drop to six furlongs against him. Picking up ground although not having a great deal of room along the inside rail below the distance, he stayed on without ever seriously threatening. A return to a longer trip would help. (10/1: op 6/1)

Antonia's Choice, dropped 7lb after two poor runs this season, needs to drop further for, after showing in front, she was collared below the distance and soon done with. (25/1)

2838* Bacchus chased the leaders but Fallon was already at work at halfway and the combination had nothing more to offer below the distance. (7/2)

3194 Anokato (14/1: op 8/1)

3092 Dayrella (14/1: op 8/1)

2925 March Crusader (8/1: 6/1-9/1)

3615 MAIL ON SUNDAY SERIES (QUALIFIER) H'CAP (0-100) (3-Y.O+) (Class C)

3-25 (3-25) **7f** £7,035.00 (£2,130.00: £1,040.00: £495.00) Stalls: High GOING minus 0.14 sec per fur (G)

				SP	RR	SF
3236[5]	**Raaha (79)** (RWArmstrong) **3-8-12** RHills(7) (a.p: rdn over 2f out: led ins fnl f: r.o wl)	—	**1**	9/1	90	58
3220[6]	**Albert The Bear (86)** (JBerry) **4-9-7**(3) TEDurcan(11) (led: hrd rdn over 1f out: hdd ins fnl f: r.o)	½	**2**	12/1	96	69
3092[3]	**La Petite Fusee (78)** (RJO'Sullivan) **6-9-2** KFallon(10) (rdn over 3f out: hdwy on ins over 1f out: r.o one pce)	1¾	**3**	7/1	84	57

				SP	RR	SF
2894^{4}	**Consort (85)** (MrsAJPerrett) **4-9-9** AClark(8) (lw: hld up: rdn over 3f out: one pce fnl f)	1½	**4**	10/1	87	60
3423^{4}	**Zugudi (80)** (KMahdi) **3-8-10**(3) DO'Donohoe(5) (lw: rdn & lost pl 4f out: eased whn btn ins fnl f)	3	**5**	9/1	76	44
3185*	**Chewit (84)** (GLMoore) **5-9-8** CandyMorris(6) (plld hrd: a.p: ev ch 2f out: hrd rdn over 1f out: wknd qckly)	1¾	**6**	7/2 1	76	49
3185^{4}	**Song of Skye (81)** (TJNaughton) **3-9-0** PaulEddery(3) (rdn over 4f out: nvr nr to chal)	1¾	**7**	13/2 3	69	37
1320*	**Hurtleberry (IRE) (76)** (LordHuntingdon) **4-9-0** DHarrison(9) (hld up: rdn over 3f out: sn wknd)	3	**8**	9/2 2	57	30
2833^{5}	**Out Line (68)** (MMadgwick) **5-8-6** NVarley(2) (bhd fnl 2f)	1½	**9**	9/1	45	18
3423^{5}	**Blue Flyer (IRE) (68)** (RIngram) **4-8-6** AMcGlone(4) (a bhd)	¾	**10**	7/1	44	17

(SP 125.5%) **10 Rn**

1m 23.32 (2.12) CSF £108.91 CT £745.31 TOTE £9.30: £2.60 £2.40 £2.10 (£52.80) Trio £92.20 OWNER Mr Hamdan Al Maktoum (NEWMARKET) BRED Shadwell Estate Company Limited
WEIGHT FOR AGE 3yo-5lb

3236 Raaha, dropping back to seven furlongs, was never far away and, bustled along, got on top inside the final furlong. (9/1)
3220 Albert The Bear, only 2lb higher then when last successful, attempted to make every post a winning one. Eventually overhauled inside the final furlong, he stuck to his guns commendably to the bitter end. (12/1)
3092 La Petite Fusee, who usually front runs, was held up on this occasion and was being pushed along from halfway. She stayed on from below the distance to take third prize but could never get in a serious challenge to the front two. (7/1)
2894 Consort again found this trip a bit sharp and was being pushed along from halfway. Grimly trying to get on terms below the distance, he was tapped for toe in the final furlong. A step-up to a mile would help. (10/1)
3423 Zugudi, who completely lost his pitch half a mile from home, grimly tried to get back into it below the distance, but he failed to do so and his jockey accepted the situation inside the final furlong. (9/1: op 6/1)
3185* Chewit has been in fine form this year but he took too keen a hold early on as he raced up with the pace. He still appeared to be travelling well two furlongs from home but, when asked for his effort below the distance, had nothing in reserve. (7/2)

3616 LUCKY CHOICE H'CAP (0-85) (3-Y.O+) (Class D)

3-55 (3-55) **1m 2f** £10,893.75 (£3,300.00: £1,612.50: £768.75) Stalls: Low GOING minus 0.14 sec per fur (G)

				SP	RR	SF
3315^{4}	**Supreme Sound (61)** (PWHarris) **3-7-12** GBardwell(4) (mde all: hrd rdn 2f out: clr over 1f out: drvn out)	—	**1**	12/1	73	41
*2668**	**La Modiste (66)** (MissGayKelleway) **4-8-11** KFallon(10) (b.hind: hdwy over 3f out: chsd wnr over 1f out: hrd rdn: r.o one pce)	1½	**2**	11/2 2	76	52
2839^{8}	**Edan Heights (73)** (SDow) **5-9-4** JFEgan(1) (lw: hdwy over 8f out: chsd wnr over 2f out tl over 1f out: one pce)	3½	**3**	16/1	77	53
3274^{3}	**Sheer Face (80)** (WRMuir) **3-9-3** DaneO'Neill(9) (swtg: rdn over 2f out: hdwy over 1f out: nvr nrr)	3	**4**	10/1	79	47
3435^{B}	**Night Wink (USA) (68)** (GLMoore) **5-8-8**(5) CLowther(2) (swtg: a.p: chsd wnr over 3f out tl over 2f out: sn wknd)	2½	**5**	10/1	63	39
3112^{11}	**Fahs (USA) (79)** (RAkehurst) **5-9-10** SSanders(3) (lw: chsd wnr 8f out tl over 3f out: wknd 2f out)	½	**6**	3/1 1	73	49
3496*	**Eurobox Boy (67)** (APJarvis) **4-8-5**(7) CCarver(7) (lw: chsd wnr 2f: wknd over 3f out)	4	**7**	11/2 2	55	31
3153*	**Tribal Peace (IRE) (63)** (BGubby) **5-8-5**(3) MartinDwyer(8) (lw: prom 6f)	1½	**8**	13/2 3	49	25
3246*	**Kewarra (74)** (BRMillman) **3-8-11** TSprake(11) (swtg: a bhd)	3	**9**	7/1	55	23
3184^{6}	**General Haven (68)** (TJNaughton) **4-8-13** PaulEddery(5) (swtg: bhd fnl 2f)	2½	**10**	16/1	45	21
2391^{6}	**Rhapsody In White (IRE) (75)** (MAJarvis) **3-8-12** RCochrane(6) (bhd fnl 7f)	5	**11**	12/1	44	12

(SP 126.9%) **11 Rn**

2m 8.45 (3.75) CSF £75.44 CT £999.34 TOTE £14.90: £3.10 £2.10 £5.80 (£33.10) Trio £294.80 OWNER Mrs P. W. Harris (BERKHAMSTED) BRED Pendley Farm
WEIGHT FOR AGE 3yo-8lb

3315 Supreme Sound was given a lovely ride by Gary Bardwell who dictated matters from the front. Vigorously rousting his mount along to go clear well over a furlong out, the combination was never going to be caught. (12/1)
2668* La Modiste began to take closer order turning for home. Moving into second place approaching the final furlong, she stayed on but was unable to get to the winner in time. (11/2: op 3/1)
2574 Edan Heights, dropped 3lb in the handicap, ran his best race for a while. Showing in second place in the straight, he was collared for that position below the distance and failed to find another gear. (16/1)
3274 Sheer Face, held up at the back of the field, stayed on from below the distance without ever posing a threat. (10/1: 8/1-12/1)
3081* Night Wink (USA), who showed in second place early in the straight, had been hung out to dry two furlongs from home. (10/1: 8/1-12/1)
1768 Fahs (USA) was taking a drop in class but, after racing in second place for much of the contest, had shot his bolt two furlongs from home. (3/1)
2391 Rhapsody In White (IRE) (12/1: 8/1-14/1)

3617 SUNDAY (S) STKS (3-Y.O+) (Class F)

4-25 (4-26) **1m 6f** £2,294.00 (£644.00: £314.00) Stalls: High GOING minus 0.14 sec per fur (G)

				SP	RR	SF
1964^{3}	**Hazel (44)** (MissGayKelleway) **5-9-2** KFallon(6) (b: b.hind: hld up: chsd ldr over 2f out: hrd rdn & led over 1f out: eased wl ins fnl f)	—	**1**	6/5 1	35	—
2539^{8}	**Bobby's Dream (25)** (MHTompkins) **5-9-2** DBiggs(2) (led tl over 1f out: unable qckn)	3	**2**	6/1 3	32	—
3390^{6}	**Saltimbanco (45)** (RAkehurst) **3-8-9** AClark(4) (rdn over 3f out: hdwy over 2f out: one pce)	1¾	**3**	2/1 2	35	—
2916^{14}	**Another Fiddle (IRE) (23)** (JELong) **7-9-0**(7) RBrisland(3) (b.hind: chsd ldr 12f out to 7f out: chsd ldr over 3f out tl over 2f out: sn wknd)	5	**4**	16/1	29	—
3073^{8}	**Nagobelia** (JPearce) **9-9-4**(3) CTeague(5) (hld up: chsd ldr 7f out tl over 2f out: sn wknd)	3	**5**	10/1	25	—
1926^{13}	**Challenger (IRE) (30)** (LWells) **4-9-7** PaulEddery(7) (lw: a bhd)	½	**6**	25/1	25	—
3277^{15}	**Charbertsam** (RRowe) **4-9-0**(7) AGarrity(1) (chsd ldr 2f: wknd over 7f out)	15	**7**	25/1	8	—

(SP 115.7%) **7 Rn**

3m 18.39 (20.09) CSF £8.67 TOTE £1.80: £1.30 £2.90 (£4.40) OWNER Mrs Liz Nelson (WHITCOMBE) BRED Roldvale Ltd
WEIGHT FOR AGE 3yo-12lb
No bid

1964 Hazel at last lost her maiden tag in this extremely bad race. Responding to pressure to lead approaching the final furlong, she soon forged clear and was eased down in the closing stages with victory in the bag. The winning distance is not a true reflection of her superiority. (6/5: 11/10-evens)
Bobby's Dream attempted to make all the running but, collared approaching the final furlong, was then left for dead and, with the winner being eased down close home, she is flattered to finish so close. She remains a maiden after twenty-four attempts. (6/1)
3390 Saltimbanco was taking a step-up in distance and a drop in class, but that was still not enough as he could only struggle on at one pace in the final quarter-mile. (2/1)

Another Fiddle (IRE) is just an extremely poor plater as he showed once again. (16/1)
Nagobelia (10/1: 6/1-12/1)

3618 TAUBER APPRENTICE H'CAP (0-75) (3-Y.O+) (Class F)
- Abandoned -Waterlogged

T/Plpt: £80.80 (226.62 Tckts). T/Qdpt: £17.90 (42.15 Tckts) AK

3330-PONTEFRACT (L-H) (Good to firm, Good patches)
Sunday August 17th
WEATHER: hot & humid, thunder storm Race 1 WIND: almost nil

3619 E.B.F. SUNDAY PLATE MAIDEN STKS (2-Y.O) (Class D)
2-15 (2-21) **5f** £3,907.50 (£1,185.00: £580.00: £277.50) Stalls: Low GOING minus 0.11 sec per fur (G)

				SP	RR	SF
2917[8]	**Bay Prince (IRE)** (MRChannon) **2-9-0** JCarroll(5) (mde all: drvn clr over 1f out)	—	**1**	14/1	95	37
	Misty Moor (MJohnston) **2-8-9** DHolland(3) (neat: scope: sn chsng ldrs: rdn & outpcd 2f out: styd on wl fnl f)	6	**2**	5/1	71+	13
	Bawsian (JLEyre) **2-9-0** OPears(8) (cmpt: chsd ldrs: outpcd ½-wy: styd on fnl f)	1¼	**3**	12/1	72	14
3459[2]	**Far Removed (IRE)** (MrsJRRamsden) **2-9-0** JFortune(7) (w ldrs: kpt on same pce appr fnl f)	½	**4**	3/1[1]	70	12
3459[4]	**Dekelsmary** (JBalding) **2-8-9** JEdmunds(10) (plld very hrd: sn trckng ldrs: outpcd ½-wy: kpt on fnl f)	¾	**5**	20/1	63	5
3033[6]	**Maytong** (JBerry) **2-8-4**(5) PRoberts(6) (chsd ldrs tl wknd over 1f out)	hd	**6**	14/1	63	5
3022[7]	**Bahamian Melody (USA)** (DRLoder) **2-9-0** KDarley(2) (lw: sn bhd & drvn along: sme hdwy & n.m.r over 1f out: nvr nr ldrs)	2½	**7**	7/2[2]	60	2
3094[10]	**Have A Break** (CREgerton) **2-9-0** MHills(9) (reard s: sn trckng ldrs: lost pl 2f out: eased)	s.h	**8**	12/1	59	1
3106[9]	**Tilburg** (MrsNMacauley) **2-8-6**(3) PFessey(4) (unruly gng to s: sn bhd)	1½	**9**	33/1	50	—
3136[3]	**Hever Golf Machine** (TJNaughton) **2-9-0** GCarter(1) (sn bhd & drvn along)	1¾	**10**	4/1[3]	49	—
				(SP 120.3%)		**10 Rn**

64.9 secs (3.20) CSF £77.57 TOTE £13.70: £3.90 £2.00 £4.40 (£29.10) Trio £258.50; £76.47 to Hamilton 18/8/97 OWNER Mr D. W. Shepherd (UPPER LAMBOURN) BRED Rathasker Stud

Bay Prince (IRE), mounted on the track and taken down early, did nothing wrong once under way and is clearly a speedy type. (14/1)
Misty Moor, who showed a fair bit of knee action going down, was badly tapped for foot turning in. Sticking on in willing fashion inside the last, she needs six furlongs already. Her stable's juveniles usually improve considerably for their first run. (5/1)
Bawsian, badly left behind at halfway, put in some solid work in the final furlong and will come on for the outing. (12/1: op 8/1)
3459 Far Removed (IRE), stoutly bred on his dam's side, was by no means knocked about and, now qualified for a nursery mark, will no doubt step-up in distance. (3/1)
3459 Dekelsmary again pulled very hard but she is not without some ability. (20/1)
3033 Maytong, on her toes beforehand, continually swished her tail in the paddock. Very keen going down, she showed plenty of speed but proved a very weak finisher. (14/1)
3022 Bahamian Melody (USA) either could not or would not go the pace. After meeting trouble once in line for home, he was by no means knocked about and might be interesting in a nursery over further. (7/2)

3620 MAGIC 828 (S) STKS (3-Y.O+) (Class F)
2-45 (2-48) **1m 4f 8y** £2,598.00 (£728.00: £354.00) Stalls: Low GOING minus 0.11 sec per fur (G)

				SP	RR	SF
3540[7]	**Bold Top (44)** (BSRothwell) **5-9-3be** JFortune(5) (mde all: hrd rdn over 1f out: jst hld on)	—	**1**	5/1[3]	58	27
3308[2]	**Essayeffsee (54)** (MrsMReveley) **8-9-3** KDarley(2) (lw: hld up: stdy hdwy 7f out: effrt 4f out: styd on fnl f)	nk	**2**	5/6[1]	58	27
2607[7]	**Early Peace (IRE) (47)** (MDods) **5-9-3b** DaleGibson(4) (sn bhd & pushed along: hdwy 5f out: styd on same pce appr fnl f)	2½	**3**	12/1	54	23
3380[6]	**Obelos (USA) (73)** (MissSJWilton) **6-9-8** SWhitworth(1) (trckd wnr: chal over 2f out: sn rdn: wknd appr fnl f: eased)	23	**4**	15/8[2]	29	—
	Prince Baltasar (NBycroft) **8-9-3** JCarroll(3) (outpcd 7f out: t.o 4f out)	dist	**5**	50/1	—	—
				(SP 115.6%)		**5 Rn**

2m 44.5 (10.20) CSF £9.38 TOTE £5.30: £1.90 £1.10 (£3.10) OWNER Mrs G. M. Z. Spink (MALTON) BRED Llety Stud
No bid

3330 Bold Top broke his duck at his thirty-fourth attempt, but it took all his brilliant jockey's strength to keep his head in front. (5/1)
3308 Essayeffsee, who would have been meeting the winner on 10lb worse terms in a handicap, began to struggle half a mile from home. Kept right up to his work, he stayed on in the final furlong but was never quite going to get there. (5/6: evens-11/10)
2539 Early Peace (IRE) seemed to appreciate the heavy rain before racing and ran his best race under both codes for a considerable time. (12/1)
633 Obelos (USA) sat on the heels of the winner looking to be going well but, suddenly coming under pressure once in line for home, his stamina gave out completely. It seems a mile and a quarter is as far as he gets. (15/8)
Prince Baltasar, a maiden chaser, was tailed off in the final half-mile. (50/1)

3621 STANLEY LEISURE H'CAP (0-85) (3-Y.O+) (Class D)
3-15 (3-17) **6f** £5,966.00 (£1,808.00: £884.00: £422.00) Stalls: Low GOING minus 0.11 sec per fur (G)

				SP	RR	SF
3310[6]	**Fame Again (64)** (MrsJRRamsden) **5-8-7**(3) DSweeney(8) (swtg: chsd ldrs: effrt 2f out: r.o to ld ins fnl f: hld on wl towards fin)	—	**1**	12/1	75	45
3145[3]	**Style Dancer (IRE) (70)** (RMWhitaker) **3-8-13v** DeanMcKeown(2) (trckd ldrs: n.m.r over 2f out: ev ch ins fnl f: nt qckn)	½	**2**	12/1	80	47
3410[9]	**Knotty Hill (74)** (RCraggs) **5-9-6** DHolland(11) (swtg: w ldrs: led ½-wy: edgd lft over 1f out: hdd ins fnl f: no ex)	3	**3**	9/2[1]	76	46
3208[6]	**Smokey From Caplaw (72)** (JJO'Neill) **3-9-1** JQuinn(10) (lw: racd wd: plld hrd: outpcd ½-wy: styd on wl fnl f)	2½	**4**	10/1	67	34
3410[10]	**Fairy Prince (IRE) (75)** (MrsALMKing) **4-9-7** JFortune(5) (lw: w ldrs: hmpd over 1f out: kpt on one pce)	hd	**5**	13/2[3]	70	40
3431[5]	**Halmanerror (56)** (MrsJRRamsden) **7-8-2** GCarter(3) (sn bhd: hdwy over 1f out: styd on: nt rch ldrs)	s.h	**6**	6/1[2]	51	21
3241[2]	**Two On The Bridge (59)** (DenysSmith) **3-7-13b**(3) PFessey(6) (s.i.s: bhd tl styd on fnl f)	¾	**7**	12/1	52	19
3334[6]	**Rich Glow (51)** (NBycroft) **6-7-11** LCharnock(13) (racd wd: chsd ldrs tl wknd over 1f out)	3	**8**	9/1	36	6

3310[5] **Trojan Hero (SAF) (68)** (MrsMReveley) **6-9-0** ACulhane(7) (hld up: stdy hdwy over 1f out: nvr nr ldrs) 1¼ **9** 14/1 49 19
2788[16] **Bollin Harry (63)** (TDEasterby) **5-8-9** JCarroll(12) (swtg: racd wd: chsd ldrs tl wknd fnl f)................................¾ **10** 8/1 42 12
3420[5] **Hoh Returns (IRE) (75)** (MBell) **4-9-7** MFenton(9) (lw: chsd ldrs: drvn along over 2f out: sn lost pl).................3 **11** 16/1 46 16
2925[5] **Carati (81)** (RBoss) **3-9-10** KDarley(1) (led to ½-wy: wkng whn hmpd over 2f out: eased).............................11 **12** 20/1 23 —
3087[7] **French Grit (IRE) (74)** (MDods) **5-9-6** DaleGibson(4) (hld up: effrt over 2f out: sn wknd: eased).......................2 **13** 14/1 11 —
(SP 123.1%) **13 Rn**

1m 18.0 (3.00) CSF £139.11 CT £711.59 TOTE £21.60: £6.20 £4.30 £2.00 (£77.20) Trio £551.40; £124.26 to Hamilton 18/8/97 OWNER Mr James Ramsden (THIRSK) BRED R. Barbes
WEIGHT FOR AGE 3yo-3lb

3310 Fame Again, back on a more realistic mark, had a lot more use made of her than usual. Really well handled, she was always doing just enough. (12/1)
3145 Style Dancer (IRE) put two moderate efforts behind him. Short of room turning for home, he should not be counted in any way unlucky. (12/1)
835 Knotty Hill presumably needed his outing at Haydock, his first for over three months. He showed plenty of toe here from a poor draw. (9/2)
3208 Smokey From Caplaw is not an easy ride. Keen early on, he dropped everything at halfway but stayed on strongly in the final furlong. There is no doubt he has the ability to win another race when he puts his best foot forward. (10/1: 8/1-12/1)
3146* Fairy Prince (IRE), back over his best trip, was held when Knotty Hill went across him coming to the final furlong. (13/2)
3431 Halmanerror gave a problem or two in the stalls. Shuffled back turning in, he was putting in some solid work at the finish and is back to his best now. (6/1)
3334 Rich Glow, drawn thirteen of thirteen, had much more use made of him than usual. (9/1)
3310 Trojan Hero (SAF) had a quiet run and connections will be hoping the Handicapper will show this ex-South African horse some leniency. (14/1)

3622 ROTHMANS ROYALS NORTH SOUTH CHALLENGE SERIES H'CAP (0-90) (3-Y.O+) (Class C)

3-45 (3-48) **1m 4y** £7,360.00 (£2,230.00: £1,090.00: £520.00) Stalls: Low GOING minus 0.11 sec per fur (G)

SP RR SF

3128* **Apache Star (87)** (GWragg) **3-9-13v** MHills(5) (hld up: hdwy over 2f out: led jst ins fnl f: r.o wl) ....— **1** 7/1[3] 98 61
3403* **Antarctic Storm (60)** (RAFahey) **4-8-6** FNorton(13) (led 1f: racd wd: led over 1f out: hdd jst ins fnl f: styd on same pce)..1½ **2** 10/1 68 37
3457[2] **Barnburgh Boy (73)** (TDBarron) **3-8-13** JCarroll(6) (hld up: stdy hdwy & n.m.r 2f out: kpt on wl ins fnl f).......s.h **3** 10/1 81 44
3190[12] **Southerly Wind (86)** (MrsJRRamsden) **3-9-12** JFortune(4) (hld up: hdwy over 2f out: rdn & styd on strly fnl f)..s.h **4** 6/1[2] 94 57
3243[4] **Royal Ceilidh (IRE) (68)** (DenysSmith) **4-8-7v1**(7) RWinston(2) (trckd ldrs: ev ch over 1f out: wknd towards fin)..1½ **5** 11/1 73 42
3254[7] **For Your Eyes Only (80)** (TDEasterby) **3-9-6** DeanMcKeown(11) (lw: b.nr hind: racd wd: hdwy over 3f out: rdn & outpcd 2f out: styd on ins fnl f)..s.h **6** 10/1 85 48
3408* **Queens Consul (IRE) (79)** (BSRothwell) **7-9-11** MFenton(8) (b.hind: in tch: sn pushed along: styd on same pce fnl 2f)..½ **7** 8/1 83 52
3115[9] **Ben Gunn (69)** (PTWalwyn) **5-9-1** KDarley(7) (swtg: hdwy ½-wy: sn chsng ldrs: rdn over 2f out: nt qckn appr fnl f)..hd **8** 7/2[1] 73 42
2557[8] **Mo-Addab (IRE) (73)** (ACStewart) **7-9-5** SWhitworth(3) (swtg: bhd & drvn along: hdwy over 2f out: rdn & wknd over 1f out)..1¾ **9** 9/1 73 42
3264[9] **Pine Ridge Lad (IRE) (55)** (JLEyre) **7-8-1** RLappin(9) (lw: chsd ldrs: drvn along 3f out: wknd over 1f out)......hd **10** 33/1 55 24
3242[7] **Censor (70)** (DNicholls) **4-9-2** AlexGreaves(12) (lw: plld hrd: led after 1f tl over 1f out: sn wknd & eased)..9 **11** 8/1 52 21
3264[4] **Thatched (IRE) (50)** (REBarr) **7-7-10** JQuinn(10) (lw: s.i.s: bhd: effrt over 3f out: n.d) ....2 **12** 16/1 28 —
(SP 125.7%) **12 Rn**

1m 46.6 (4.20) CSF £72.81 CT £663.47 TOTE £6.50: £2.40 £4.30 £2.60 (£36.50) Trio £113.00 OWNER Mr A. E. Oppenheimer (NEWMARKET) BRED Hascombe and Valiant Studs
WEIGHT FOR AGE 3yo-6lb

3128* Apache Star, from a 5lb higher mark, was restrained well off a furious pace. Getting a dream run through, in the end he took this in decisive fashion. (7/1)
3403* Antarctic Storm, from a 3lb higher mark, raced wide throughout. He ran a gutsy race, but in the end the winner simply proved too good. (10/1)
3457 Barnburgh Boy ran right up to his best and finished in determined fashion. Surely that elusive first win is just around the corner. (10/1)
2710 Southerly Wind, 8lb higher than when winning here first time five outings ago, was suited by the strongly-run mile. Taking time to get into full stride, he was making serious inroads inside the last. A strong-run nine furlongs could prove ideal and he is certainly a likeable type. (6/1)
3243 Royal Ceilidh (IRE) raced keenly in a visor for the first time but, after having every chance, she faded towards the finish. (11/1)
3254 For Your Eyes Only ran much better than Chester. Taking time to get going, he was staying on steadily at the finish and is by no means a forlorn hope. (10/1)
3408* Queens Consul (IRE), from a 1lb higher mark than she has ever won off, was unable to dominate and in the circumstances gave a good account of herself. (8/1)
Censor, who has slipped down the weights and dropped back half-a-mile, carried plenty of market support. Racing much too keenly, when collared he dropped right out and was virtually pulled up. (8/1)

3623 'GO RACING IN YORKSHIRE' H'CAP (0-65) (3-Y.O+) (Class F)

4-15 (4-18) **2m 1f 22y** £3,615.00 (£1,095.00: £535.00: £255.00) Stalls: Centre GOING minus 0.11 sec per fur (G)

SP RR SF

3255[4] **Great Oration (IRE) (60)** (FWatson) **8-9-13** JFortune(6) (hdwy ½-wy: styd on u.p fnl 2f: led nr fin)................— **1** 5/1[3] 72 37
3283[11] **Rose of Glenn (44)** (BPalling) **6-8-6**(5) PRoberts(8) (led & sn clr: kpt on wl fnl f: jst ct)...................................nk **2** 25/1 56 21
3461[2] **Shelteez (USA) (45)** (MBell) **3-7-7**(5) RMullen(11) (lw: hdwy ½-wy: pushed along 5f out: hdwy 2f out: styd on wl towards fin)..nk **3** 2/1[1] 56 7
2825[7] **Valiant Dash (29)** (JSGoldie) **11-7-10** LCharnock(4) (chsd ldrs: pushed along 6f out: one pce fnl 2f).............2½ **4** 50/1 38 3
2702[10] **Romalito (40)** (MBlanshard) **7-8-7** JQuinn(7) (hdwy over 2f out: styd on one pce: nvr nr to chal) 1½ **5** 16/1 48 13
2737[4] **Love Me Do (USA) (61)** (MJohnston) **3-9-0** DHolland(2) (trckd ldrs: effrt over 2f out: one pce appr fnl f)........1¼ **6** 5/1[3] 68 19
3401* **Arian Spirit (IRE) (48)** (JLEyre) **6-9-1v** TWilliams(13) (hld up: stdy hdwy on outside 8f out: rdn over 2f out: wknd over 1f out)..2½ **7** 3/1[2] 52 17

3401^{3} **Mils Mij (29)** (TAKCuthbert) **12-7-3**$^{(7)}$ JMcAuley(3) (b: sn chsng ldrs: pushed along 6f out: sn lost pl: styd on towards fin) ....½ **8** 50/1 33 —
3440^{6} **Sad Mad Bad (USA) (55)** (MrsMReveley) **3-8-8** WJO'Connor(12) (swtg: hld up: nvr plcd to chal) 3 **9** 14/1 56 7
1100^{7} **He's Got Wings (IRE) (52)** (MAPeill) **4-9-5** JCarroll(9) (b.nr hind: hld up: hdwy ½-wy: pushed along 6f out: grad wknd) 2½ **10** 14/1 51 16
3401^{10} **Yaakum (29)** (SEKettlewell) **8-7-3**$^{(7)}$ JennyBenson(5) (hld up & bhd: n.m.r over 3f out: sn wknd & eased)......19 **11** 50/1 10 —
(SP 120.6%) **11 Rn**

3m 53.7 (14.20) CSF £116.10 CT £300.57 TOTE £6.90: £2.10 £3.50 £1.30 (£63.30) Trio £74.80 OWNER M D Hetherington (Packaging) Ltd (SEDGEFIELD) BRED P. F. I. Cole
LONG HANDICAP Mils Mij 7-1 Valiant Dash 7-3 Yaakum 7-9
WEIGHT FOR AGE 3yo-14lb
OFFICIAL EXPLANATION **Sad Mad Bad (USA): was never going, and as a result was hanging and changing his legs.**
3255 Great Oration (IRE), an out and out top-of-the-ground stayer, repeated his success in this event two years ago, but it took all his jockey's strength and determination to force his head in front near the line. (5/1)
2874 Rose of Glenn, who in the past had reserved her best for Catterick, set a good clip and was soon clear. Looking likely to be caught turning in, she pulled three or four lengths clear but was worn down near the line. She deserves full marks for this. (25/1)
3461 Shelteez (USA), an out and out stayer, was again ridden from off the pace. Pushed along over half-a-mile from home, she only made real inroads once in line for home. Despite a tendency to edge left she was reeling in the first two at the line. Surely she needs a lot more use making of her. (2/1)
2539 Valiant Dash, who is by no means consistent, ran one of his better races. (50/1)
1808 Romalito had only won once from fifty starts. (16/1)
2737 Love Me Do (USA), hard at work some way from home, seemed to run out of stamina in the final furlong. (5/1)
3401* Arian Spirit (IRE) (3/1: op 9/2)
3440 Sad Mad Bad (USA), awash with sweat beforehand, from the stands looked to be given a quiet run round, but his jockey explained to the Stewards that the horse was hanging and kept changing his legs. (14/1)

3624 KIDS COME FREE MAIDEN STKS (3-Y.O+) (Class D)
4-45 (4-50) **1m 4y** £3,452.50 (£1,045.00: £510.00: £242.50) Stalls: Low GOING minus 0.11 sec per fur (G)

SP RR SF
3014^{3} **Saafeya (IRE) (84)** (JHMGosden) **3-8-7** GHind(2) (trckd ldrs: led on bit 3f out: sn clr: v.easily) ....— **1** 1/5^{1} 76++ 27
3211^{8} **Beach Buoy (IRE)** (CaptJWilson) **3-8-7**$^{(5)}$ PRoberts(5) (chsd ldrs: drvn along over 3f out: styd on towards fin) ....6 **2** 33/1^{3} 69 20
3211^{7} **Fatal Baraari (73)** (MRStoute) **3-8-12** KDarley(6) (chsd ldrs: pushed along over 3f out: wnt 2nd 1f out: one pce) ....hd **3** 9/2^{2} 69 20
Bodfari Wren (ABailey) **3-8-7** DWright(3) (wl grwn: b: b.hind: led: sn pushed along: hdd 3f out: wknd over 1f out) ....6 **4** 33/1^{3} 52 3
3439^{3} **Dainty Damsel** (RDEWoodhouse) **4-8-13** LCharnock(1) (sn chsng ldrs: wknd qckly over 2f out) ....25 **5** 33/1^{3} 2 —
Hawkers Deal (ARDicken) **4-8-13**$^{(5)}$ ADaly(4) (w'like: bkwd: bolted gng to s: s.s: t.o 5f out) ....dist **6** 100/1 — —
(SP 111.3%) **6 Rn**

1m 48.2 (5.80) CSF £12.53 TOTE £1.30: £1.10 £4.20 (£6.40) OWNER Sheikh Ahmed Al Maktoum (NEWMARKET) BRED Sheikh Ahmed Bin Rashid Al Maktoum
WEIGHT FOR AGE 3yo-6lb
3014 Saafeya (IRE) had been found a soft option and took this without ever engaging second gear. (1/5)
2888 Beach Buoy (IRE), having his third outing, stuck on near the line to take second spot. (33/1)
3211 Fatal Baraari, with the visor left off, looks woefully one-paced. (9/2)
Bodfari Wren, having her first ever outing, was pushed along to make the running. She looked very leg-weary coming to the final furlong. (33/1)
3439 Dainty Damsel dropped out in two strides going into the home turn. (33/1)
Hawkers Deal, whose previous outing was in a National Hunt Flat race, bolted going to the start. (100/1)

3625 FAMILY DAY H'CAP (0-65) (3-Y.O+) (Class F)
5-15 (5-20) **5f** £3,745.00 (£1,135.00: £555.00: £265.00) Stalls: Low GOING minus 0.11 sec per fur (G)

SP RR SF
3290^{4} **Corniche Quest (IRE) (60)** (MRChannon) **4-9-2**$^{(7)}$ AEddery(12) (hdwy on outside 2f out: r.o wl to ld wl ins fnl f) ....— **1** 12/1 72 54
3431* **Camionneur (IRE) (53)** (TDEasterby) **4-9-2b** LCharnock(1) (lw: trckd ldrs: qcknd to ld jst ins fnl f: hdd & no ex towards fin) ....2½ **2** 6/1^{3} 57 39
3334^{11} **Soaked (38)** (DWChapman) **4-8-1b** TWilliams(11) (lw: dwlt: hdwy over 2f out: hung lft & kpt on fnl f)....1¾ **3** 16/1 36 18
*3399** **Featherstone Lane (45)** (MissLCSiddall) **6-8-8** KDarley(8) (chsd ldrs: outpcd 2f out: kpt on wl ins fnl f) ....hd **4** 14/1 43 25
3431* **Grand Chapeau (IRE) (66)** (DNicholls) **5-10-1** AlexGreaves(10) (lw: w ldr: led 2f out tl jst ins fnl f: sn wknd) .1½ **5** 5/1^{2} 59 41
3240^{12} **Petraco (IRE) (46)** (NASmith) **9-8-4**$^{(5)}$ AmandaSanders(2) (a chsng ldrs: one pce fnl 2f) ....½ **6** 20/1 38 20
3481^{10} **Just Dissident (IRE) (62)** (RMWhitaker) **5-9-11** DeanMcKeown(6) (lw: mde most to 2f out: wknd fnl f) ....s.h **7** 10/1 54 36
109^{7} **Plum First (53)** (JLEyre) **7-8-11**$^{(5)}$ KimberleyHart(15) (b: b.hind: sn bhd: hdwy over 2f out: styd on wl ins fnl f) ....s.h **8** 16/1 44 26
3208^{12} **Young Ben (IRE) (47)** (JSWainwright) **5-8-7b**$^{(3)}$ GParkin(14) (b.hind: swtg: chsd ldrs: rdn ½-wy: wknd over 1f out) 2½ **9** 14/1 30 12
3271^{4} **La Volta (45)** (MissJFCraze) **4-8-8b** SWebster(4) (lw: mid div: effrt on ins whn hmpd over 2f out: nt clr run over 1f out: n.d) ....½ **10** 33/1 27 9
3406^{10} **Pathaze (42)** (NBycroft) **4-8-5** ACulhane(13) (swtg: racd wd: nvr nr ldrs) ....s.h **11** 33/1 24 6
3034^{10} **Middle East (63)** (TDBarron) **4-9-5**$^{(7)}$ VictoriaAppleby(16) (s.i.s: a bhd) ....hd **12** 20/1 44 26
3431^{13} **Rennyholme (43)** (ABMulholland) **6-8-6** JCarroll(9) (sn bhd) ....½ **13** 16/1 23 5
3334^{4} **Tart and a Half (65)** (JLEyre) **5-9-7v**$^{(7)}$ RWinston(7) (unruly in stalls: mid div: rdn 2f out: sn btn) ....¾ **14** 4/1^{1} 42 24
2939^{6} **Sense of Priority (48)** (DNicholls) **8-8-11** WJO'Connor(3) (s.i.s: a bhd) ....¾ **15** 14/1 23 5
2844^{11} **Ned's Bonanza (53)** (MDods) **8-9-2** JFortune(5) (sn outpcd & pushed along) 1¼ **16** 7/1 24 6
3417^{2} **Seretse's Nephew (44)** (MJPolglase) **3-8-5** JQuinn(18) (swtg: racd wd: chsd ldrs tl lost pl over 2f out) ....3 **17** 11/1 5 —
(SP 141.6%) **17 Rn**

64.4 secs (2.70) CSF £83.09 CT £1,147.22 TOTE £15.60: £2.50 £2.60 £5.00 £3.00 (£37.80) Trio £498.70 OWNER Mr M. Bishop (UPPER LAMBOURN) BRED K. Molloy
WEIGHT FOR AGE 3yo-2lb

3290 Corniche Quest (IRE), from a stable who has suddenly found form, came from off the pace to shoot clear near the line and take this in good style. (12/1)
3431* Camionneur (IRE), from a 5lb higher mark, tracked the leaders travelling strongly. Possibly hitting the front too soon, in the end the winner ran away from him. He is blooming at present. (6/1)
2305 Soaked, nibbled at in the market, missed the break slightly but, despite giving his rider little help, he was persuaded to stay on in the final furlong. (16/1)
3399* Featherstone Lane has only won three times from eighty-eight starts, two of those on the All-Weather. (14/1)
3431* Grand Chapeau (IRE), 15lb higher compared with when he won at Thirsk two outings ago, sat upsides the leader and the pair seemed to cut each other's throats. It was no surprise to see him fade in the closing stages. (5/1)
3130 Just Dissident (IRE), who likes to dominate, set a very fast pace but had Grand Chapeau upsides him. He had no more to give entering the final furlong. (10/1)
3334 Tart and a Half has only won once from forty-three starts. Giving problems in the stalls, she found nothing at all under pressure. (4/1: 11/2-7/2)

T/Jkpt: Not won; £14,612.44 to Windsor 18/8/97. T/Plpt: £416.40 (45.58 Tckts). T/Qdpt: £23.30 (43.13 Tckts) WG

3483-HAMILTON (R-H) (Good to firm, Good patches)
Monday August 18th
WEATHER: sunny WIND: almost nil

3626 CARFIN H'CAP (0-65) (3-Y.O+) (Class F)
2-15 (2-15) **1m 4f 17y** £2,724.00 (£764.00: £372.00) Stalls: High GOING minus 0.63 sec per fur (F)

				SP	RR	SF
3267[3]	**Globe Runner (52)** (JJO'Neill) **4-9-4** ACulhane(2) (hld up: stdy hdwy to ld ins fnl f: shkn up & qcknd)	—	**1**	4/1[2]	60	39
3486*	**Il Principe (IRE) (41)** (JohnBerry) **3-7-11** 6x DaleGibson(5) (lw: chsd ldr: rdn 5f out: wandered u.p 3f out: kpt on wl)	1¼	**2**	8/1	47	16
2910[7]	**Charlie Bigtime (39)** (ICampbell) **7-8-5** AMackay(7) (outpcd & lost tch 6f out: hdwy 2f out: r.o towards fin)	hd	**3**	33/1	45	24
3485*	**Winnebago (47)** (CWThornton) **4-8-13** 6x DeanMcKeown(8) (lw: led tl hdd ins fnl f: no ex)	1	**4**	100/30[1]	52	31
*3415**	**Mister Aspecto (IRE) (58)** (MJohnston) **4-9-10v** JWeaver(3) (lw: a chsng ldrs: rdn over 3f out: one pce)	1½	**5**	4/1[2]	61	40
3267[7]	**Chill Wind (30)** (NBycroft) **8-7-10** LCharnock(1) (sn outpcd & bhd: hdwy 4f out: nvr able to chal)	2	**6**	100/1	30	9
3485[9]	**Cois Na Farraige (IRE) (37)** (MissLAPerratt) **4-7-12**(5) KSked(6) (lw: prom tl outpcd fnl 3f)	9	**7**	66/1	25	4
3283[9]	**Daira (56)** (JDBethell) **4-9-5b**[1](3) PFessey(4) (in tch: effrt 4f out: fnd nil)	3½	**8**	9/1	40	19
3223[2]	**Monaco Gold (IRE) (45)** (MrsMReveley) **5-8-11** DWright(9) (swtg: chsd ldrs: rdn 5f out: wknd fnl 2½f)	s.h	**9**	9/2[3]	29	8

(SP 107.8%) **9 Rn**

2m 33.9 (1.90) CSF £28.49 CT £717.00 TOTE £5.50: £1.30 £3.30 £3.30 (£33.80) Trio £61.80 OWNER G & P Barker Ltd/Globe Engineering (PENRITH) BRED Badger Hill Stud
LONG HANDICAP Chill Wind 7-0
WEIGHT FOR AGE 3yo-10lb
3267 Globe Runner, well suited by the strong pace here, won this with a fair bit in hand. (4/1)
3486* Il Principe (IRE) is certainly a hard ride but he does stay well and will always need the strongest assistance. (8/1)
Charlie Bigtime failed to win last season but this character showed here that he still has the ability and is certainly on a useful mark. (33/1)
3485* Winnebago put up a brave attempt to repeat the previous week's win but, with quite a few front runners in the race, she was always tending to go that stride or so too fast and was picked off in the closing stages. (100/30)
3415* Mister Aspecto (IRE) can win on turf but is much better on the All-Weather. (4/1: 3/1-9/2)
Chill Wind ran well and is worth keeping in mind for a return to the National Hunt game. (100/1)
3085 Daira had blinkers on this time and they had no effect at all. (9/1)

3627 STONEFIELD (S) H'CAP (0-60) (3-Y.O+) (Class G)
2-45 (2-46) **1m 1f 36y** £2,472.00 (£692.00: £336.00) Stalls: High GOING minus 0.63 sec per fur (F)

				SP	RR	SF
2880[8]	**Western Venture (IRE) (27)** (MartynWane) **4-8-3** LCharnock(9) (swtg: mde most: hld on wl fnl f)	—	**1**	25/1	37	20
3456[3]	**Seconds Away (34)** (JSGoldie) **6-8-10** TWilliams(12) (trckd ldrs: effrt 2f out: styd on towards fin)	½	**2**	7/1[2]	43	26
3487[8]	**Trying Times (IRE) (44)** (JBerry) **4-9-3**(3) TEDurcan(16) (t: a chsng ldrs: kpt on u.p fnl 2f)	nk	**3**	20/1	53	36
3315[5]	**Monis (IRE) (30)** (RonaldThompson) **6-8-3**(3) DarrenMoffatt(17) (mid div: hdwy 3f out: styd on wl towards fin)	½	**4**	10/1	38	21
3486[4]	**School of Science (22)** (DANolan) **7-7-5**(7) NPollard(3) (a chsng ldrs: kpt on u.p fnl 2f)	¾	**5**	33/1	28	11
3487[2]	**Oriel Lad (32)** (DonEnricoIncisa) **4-8-8b** KimTinkler(13) (lw: mid div: hdwy 2f out: kpt on: nvr able to chal)	1	**6**	5/1[1]	37	20
3431[9]	**Reinhardt (IRE) (41)** (DNicholls) **4-9-3** ACulhane(7) (bhd: hdwy u.p 3f out: nvr able to rch ldrs)	1¾	**7**	5/1[1]	43	26
3487[10]	**Miletrian City (45)** (MissLAPerratt) **4-9-7b** JWeaver(14) (hld up & wl bhd: hdwy 2f out: nrst fin)	1¼	**8**	16/1	44	27
2880[7]	**Hotcake (34)** (MissSEHall) **4-8-10** SWebster(15) (b: bhd: sme hdwy u.p fnl 3f: n.d)	2½	**9**	16/1	29	12
3456[4]	**Tinklers Folly (52)** (RMWhitaker) **5-10-0v** DeanMcKeown(1) (chsd ldrs tl wknd fnl 2½f)	1	**10**	14/1	45	28
3104[3]	**Sagebrush Roller (50)** (JWWatts) **9-9-7**(5) PRoberts(4) (lw: bhd tl sme hdwy fnl 2f)	nk	**11**	15/2[3]	43	26
2753[6]	**Petit Flora (30)** (GHolmes) **5-8-6** DaleGibson(11) (b.hind: effrt ½-wy: nvr trbld ldrs)	¾	**12**	25/1	22	5
3442[3]	**Shamokin (33)** (FWatson) **5-8-6**(3) PFessey(2) (chsd ldrs tl wknd fnl 3f)	s.h	**13**	10/1	24	7
3308[7]	**Petrico (35)** (PBeaumont) **5-8-4**(7) TSiddall(18) (in tch 5f)	2	**14**	50/1	23	6
3487[4]	**Mystic Times (28)** (BMactaggart) **4-7-13**(5) KSked(5) (lw: w ldrs tl rdn & wknd fnl 3f)	nk	**15**	16/1	15	—
1845[8]	**Conic Hill (IRE) (37)** (JPearce) **6-8-13v**[1] GBardwell(6) (mid div tl wknd fnl 4f)	1¼	**16**	10/1	22	5
3143[19]	**Catwalk Girl (28)** (RAFahey) **4-7-11v**(7) RWinston(10) (swtg: prom tl wknd fnl 4f)	7	**17**	25/1	1	—
1222[11]	**Stone Cross (IRE) (40)** (MartinTodhunter) **5-9-2** AMackay(8) (b.off hind: lw: a bhd)	8	**18**	33/1	—	—

(SP 133.3%) **18 Rn**

1m 56.3 (2.00) CSF £176.90 CT £3,317.66 TOTE £30.70: £4.60 £1.70 £3.40 £2.50 (£156.90) Trio £771.90; £347.94 to York 19/8/97 OWNER Mr William Graham (RICHMOND) BRED S. Morrin and B. Powell
Bt in 4,700gns
1615 Western Venture (IRE) likes it out in front and proved most determined when tackled. (25/1)
3456 Seconds Away keeps running well and by the way he finished he might well pick up another race. (7/1)
2716 Trying Times (IRE), after two moderate efforts, was back to form here and battled on strongly. (20/1)
3315 Monis (IRE) has not won for four years and keeps trying all sorts of distances but he showed here he still has ability. (10/1)
3486 School of Science has now put in two decent efforts on the trot and it would seem that he is getting it together. (33/1)
3487 Oriel Lad keeps running well but he has not won for some time. (5/1)

3264 Miletrian City, given an impossible task here, ran quite well in the circumstances. (16/1)
1761 Hotcake, given plenty to do, met with trouble in running and had no chance of making up the leeway despite struggling on. (16/1)

3628 CALDERGLEN (QUALIFIER) CLAIMING STKS (2-Y.O) (Class F)

3-15 (3-16) **6f 5y** £2,598.00 (£728.00: £354.00) Stalls: Low GOING minus 0.63 sec per fur (F)

				SP	RR	SF
3306^{5}	**Chaska (64)** (MJohnston) **2-8-10** JWeaver(5) (lw: chsd ldr: led appr fnl f: r.o wl)	—	**1**	Evens ^{1}	68	8
3402^{4}	**Baylham** (JSGoldie) **2-8-8**$^{(3)}$ TEDurcan(2) (trckd ldrs: swtchd & qcknd to chal wl ins fnl f: kpt on)	¾	**2**	33/1	67	7
3257^{7}	**Inshallah (65)** (MartinTodhunter) **2-8-2** AMackay(1) (unruly s: led tl hdd over 1f out: kpt on same pce)	2	**3**	3/1 ^{2}	53	—
3312^{3}	**Candy Twist (51)** (RonaldThompson) **2-7-11**$^{(3)}$ DarrenMoffatt(6) (chsd ldrs tl rdn & nt qckn appr fnl f)	¾	**4**	9/1 ^{3}	49	—
3265^{9}	**Pride of Bryn (48)** (DenysSmith) **2-7-10** LCharnock(7) (cl up: effrt 2f out: wknd fnl f)	hd	**5**	10/1	44	—
2288^{9}	**Castle Friend** (PCHaslam) **2-8-8**$^{(5)}$ PRoberts(8) (prom: effrt 2f out: sn outpcd)	2½	**6**	14/1	55	—
2827^{8}	**Ingle Boy** (BMactaggart) **2-7-11**$^{(5)ow1}$ KSked(9) (sn outpcd & wl bhd: sme late hdwy)	1¾	**7**	50/1	39	—
	Easy Risk (MissLAPerratt) **2-8-0** NKennedy(3) (neat: bit bkwd: s.i.s: sn wl bhd)	19	**8**	25/1	—	—
3070^{7}	**Llanasa (58)** (JBerry) **2-8-3b**$^{1(3)}$ PFessey(4) (rel to r & uns rdr leaving stalls)		**U**	10/1	—	—
				(SP 118.6%)	**9 Rn**	

1m 12.4 (2.40) CSF £45.07 TOTE £1.60: £1.10 £4.10 £2.50 (£17.80) Trio £36.90 OWNER Mr J. R. Good (MIDDLEHAM) BRED J. R. and Mrs P. Good
Chaska clmd B Wilcox £10,000
3306 Chaska is coming to herself looks wise and the further they went the stronger she got. (Evens)
3402 Baylham improved a ton for his initial outing and there is obviously a modest event to be picked up. (33/1)
2110 Inshallah looked a bit of a handful beforehand but she then ran well enough. (3/1)
3312 Candy Twist had her limitations well exposed when the pressure was applied here. (9/1)
3062 Pride of Bryn was disappointing here, dropping tamely away late on. (10/1)
Ingle Boy showed signs of ability. (50/1)
1407 Llanasa (10/1: op 6/1)

3629 PLUMB CENTRE E.B.F. MAIDEN STKS (2-Y.O) (Class D)

3-45 (3-45) **6f 5y** £3,550.00 (£1,075.00: £525.00: £250.00) Stalls: Low GOING minus 0.63 sec per fur (F)

				SP	RR	SF
	Ho Leng (IRE) (MissLAPerratt) **2-9-0** NKennedy(1) (w'like: scope: dwlt: hdwy ½-wy: r.o wl to ld wl ins fnl f)	—	**1**	20/1	88+	26
3278^{2}	**Legs Be Frendly (IRE) (85)** (KMcAuliffe) **2-9-0** JFEgan(6) (lw: cl up: led after 2f: rdn appr fnl f: hdd & no ex towards fin)	1¼	**2**	4/7 ^{1}	85	23
1593^{7}	**Emperor's Gold** (ICampbell) **2-9-0** AMackay(4) (bit bkwd: dwlt: sn pushed along: hdwy ½-wy: no imp)	10	**3**	11/2 ^{2}	58	—
3060^{3}	**Miss Salsa Dancer** (DenysSmith) **2-8-9** LCharnock(5) (chsd ldrs: outpcd whn hmpd over 1f out: n.d after)	hd	**4**	8/1 ^{3}	53	—
2545^{8}	**Mariana** (RMWhitaker) **2-8-9** DeanMcKeown(3) (in tch: hdwy ½-wy: hmpd over 1f out: no imp)	1¾	**5**	16/1	48	—
2886^{5}	**Kings Check** (MissJFCraze) **2-9-0v**^{1} SWebster(2) (chsd ldrs: rdn over 2f out: wknd wl over 1f out)	3½	**6**	33/1	44	—
	Madman's Mirage (FR) (MJohnston) **2-9-0** JWeaver(7) (w'like: scope: bit bkwd: dwlt: sn t.o)	8	**7**	8/1 ^{3}	23	—
2842^{10}	**Henry The Proud (IRE)** (JBerry) **2-8-11**$^{(3)}$ TEDurcan(8) (led 2f: cl up tl wknd fnl 2f)	2½	**8**	12/1	16	—
				(SP 122.5%)	**8 Rn**	

1m 11.3 (1.30) CSF £31.51 TOTE £28.20: £4.10 £1.10 £1.40 (£26.10) OWNER Mr Alan Guthrie (AYR) BRED Brittas House Stud
Ho Leng (IRE), an attractive sort, came from a long way behind to win this really well and there would seem to be plenty more to come. (20/1)
3278 Legs Be Frendly (IRE) looked to have got things right at last but, despite going well clear of the remainder, he yet again found one too good. (4/7)
Emperor's Gold needed this but showed he is learning and there would seem to be some improvement in him. (11/2: op 12/1)
3060 Miss Salsa Dancer looked slow, and being hampered cost her third place. (8/1)
2545 Mariana, an edgy sort, looked very fit but proved disappointing in the race. (16/1)
2886 Kings Check had the visor on for the first time and it did not seem any help at all. (33/1)
Madman's Mirage (FR) (8/1: op 3/1)
695 Henry The Proud (IRE) (12/1: op 8/1)

3630 CAPTAIN J.C. STEWART MEMORIAL H'CAP (0-75) (3-Y.O+) (Class D)

4-15 (4-15) **1m 65y** £3,436.25 (£1,040.00: £507.50: £241.25) Stalls: High GOING minus 0.63 sec per fur (F)

				SP	RR	SF
3328^{6}	**Toujours Riviera (71)** (JPearce) **7-10-0** GBardwell(3) (lw: mde all: qcknd 3f out: r.o wl)	—	**1**	7/2 ^{3}	80	43
3453^{2}	**Pekay (64)** (MJohnston) **4-9-7** JWeaver(4) (trckd ldrs: hdwy to go 2nd appr fnl f: kpt on one pce)	1¼	**2**	9/4 ^{1}	71	34
3100^{12}	**Classic Flyer (IRE) (65)** (ICampbell) **4-9-8** AMackay(5) (chsd wnr: outpcd over 2f out: kpt on)	¾	**3**	14/1	70	33
3285^{*}	**Kass Alhawa (61)** (DWChapman) **4-9-4** ACulhane(1) (trckd ldrs: effrt 2f out: rdn & r.o one pce)	½	**4**	3/1 ^{2}	65	28
3605^{7}	**Nobby Barnes (43)** (DonEnricoIncisa) **8-8-0** KimTinkler(7) (hld up & bhd: effrt over 2f out: nvr able to chal)	½	**5**	10/1	46	9
1837^{9}	**Celebration Cake (IRE) (70)** (MissLAPerratt) **5-9-13** DeanMcKeown(6) (hld up: effrt over 2f out: n.m.r 1f out: no imp)	¾	**6**	8/1	72	35
2880^{9}	**Habeta (USA) (39)** (JWWatts) **11-7-7**$^{(3)}$ PFessey(2) (lw: prom tl outpcd fnl 2½f)	½	**7**	25/1	40	3
				(SP 108.7%)	**7 Rn**	

1m 46.0 (1.90) CSF £9.63 TOTE £4.60: £2.20 £1.40 (£7.10) OWNER Exdreco (NEWMARKET) BRED J. L. C. Pearce
LONG HANDICAP Habeta (USA) 7-5
3328 Toujours Riviera, given a fine ride, got first run on his rivals and thoroughly deserved it. (7/2)
3453 Pekay got outpaced when the tempo increased and that made all the difference. (9/4)
Classic Flyer (IRE) ran pretty well and would seem to be coming to hand. (14/1)
3285* Kass Alhawa was not suited by this messy race and could never get in a serious blow. (3/1)
3605 Nobby Barnes needed a stronger pace than was set here. (10/1: 8/1-12/1)
1837 Celebration Cake (IRE) showed signs of coming back to form and looks well worth keeping an eye on. (8/1)

3631 AULDHOUSE SERIES (ROUND 6) APPRENTICE H'CAP (0-70) (3-Y.O+) (Class F)

4-45 (4-45) **1m 3f 16y** £2,556.00 (£716.00: £348.00) Stalls: High GOING minus 0.63 sec per fur (F)

				SP	RR	SF
2909^{4}	**Montecristo (62)** (RGuest) **4-10-0** PRoberts(6) (lw: trckd ldrs: smooth hdwy to ld over 2f out: rdn & r.o)	—	**1**	5/1 ^{3}	71	43
3485^{7}	**Lord Advocate (52)** (DANolan) **9-9-4b** PFessey(7) (b.hind: rr div: hdwy 4f out: styd on u.p fnl 2f: nvr able to chal)	3½	**2**	10/1	56	28
3264^{11}	**Giftbox (USA) (31)** (NBycroft) **5-7-11** DarrenMoffatt(1) (in tch: hdwy 4f out: chsng ldrs 2f out: r.o one pce)	hd	**3**	25/1	35	7

3484[4]	**Rapid Mover (30)** (DANolan) **10-7-5b**(5) NPollard(2) (chsd clr ldr: sn pushed along: outpcd fnl 3f) 8	**4**	20/1	22	—
3485[2]	**Philmist (45)** (MissLAPerratt) **5-8-6b**(5) SBuckley(4) (chsd ldrs: effrt 4f out: rdn & no imp) 7	**5**	3/1[2]	27	—
3478[2]	**Double Flight (60)** (MJohnston) **3-9-0**(3) KSked(3) (lw: set str pce & sn clr: hdd over 2f out: sn wknd) 10	**6**	Evens[1]	28	—
3211[10]	**The Vale (IRE) (47)** (RMMcKellar) **5-8-8**(5) JMcAuley(5) (a outpcd & wl bhd) ....dist	**7**	33/1	—	—

(SP 112.3%) **7 Rn**

2m 22.0 (2.60) CSF £43.37 TOTE £6.40: £2.60 £1.30 (£24.80) OWNER Mr Rae Guest (NEWMARKET) BRED Lord Matthews
LONG HANDICAP Rapid Mover 7-0
WEIGHT FOR AGE 3yo-9lb
2909 Montecristo, given a confident ride, was well suited by the strong pace and, once striking the front over two furlongs out, there were never any dangers. (5/1)
2824 Lord Advocate seems to be coming back to form and was keeping on really well at the end. (10/1)
Giftbox (USA) has certainly slipped down the handicap and there were definite signs of him coming back to form here. (25/1)
3484 Rapid Mover was always being taken off his legs at the frenetic pace set here but he did stay on. (20/1)
3485 Philmist has put in some useful efforts of late and they looked to have taken their toll here. (3/1)
3478 Double Flight went off at a breakneck pace and was out on her feet when tackled approaching the last quarter-mile. (Evens)

T/Plpt: £380.00 (52.12 Tckts). T/Qdpt: £28.20 (48.48 Tckts) AA

3462-**WINDSOR (Fig. 8) (Good to firm, Good in st)**
Monday August 18th

WEATHER: v.hot WIND: almost nil

3632 BINFIELD MAIDEN STKS (3-Y.O) (Class D)

2-30 (2-33) **1m 2f 7y** £3,662.00 (£1,106.00: £538.00: £254.00) Stalls: High GOING minus 0.56 sec per fur (F)

			SP	RR	SF
3277[2]	**Aerleon Pete (IRE) (78)** (MRStoute) **3-9-0** JReid(8) (chsd ldr: led wl over 1f out: r.o wl) ....—	**1**	4/1	85	35
3218[5]	**Snow Partridge (USA) (82)** (PFICole) **3-9-0** PatEddery(11) (lw: led tl wl over 1f out: r.o) 1¼	**2**	5/2[1]	83	33
	Georgina (IRE) (MajorWRHern) **3-8-9** TSprake(9) (b: b.hind: a.p: ev ch 2f out: one pce) 3½	**3**	11/4[2]	72	22
	Sabadilla (USA) (JHMGosden) **3-9-0** LDettori(7) (unf: scope: bit bkwd: rapid hdwy 7f out: ev ch 2f out: nt qckn) ....nk	**4**	7/2[3]	77	27
	Primeval (PWHarris) **3-8-9**(5) CLowther(10) (str: bit bkwd: hdwy & rdn over 2f out: nrst fin) 6	**5**	25/1	67	17
445[8]	**Ile de Librate** (RJO'Sullivan) **3-9-0** SSanders(5) (nrst fin) ....hd	**6**	50/1	67	17
1851[4]	**Verdi (IRE)** (KMcAuliffe) **3-9-0** KFallon(2) (lw: prom tl wknd over 2f out) 2½	**7**	11/1	63	13
3389[6]	**Rosa Royale** (MrsJCecil) **3-8-6**(3) MartinDwyer(12) (nvr trbld ldrs) 2½	**8**	25/1	54	4
3463[12]	**Langara Heights** (BJLlewellyn) **3-8-7**(7) JWilkinson(6) (swtg: nvr nr to chal) ....½	**9**	50/1	58	8
3095[8]	**Evidently (IRE)** (IABalding) **3-8-9** SWhitworth(1) (prom tl wknd qckly over 2f out) 3	**10**	20/1	49	—
1167[10]	**Mistral Lord (IRE)** (MMadgwick) **3-9-0** NVarley(4) (in tch tl wknd 4f out: t.o) ....dist	**11**	50/1	—	—
	Payaso (RMStronge) **3-9-0** JStack(3) (b: neat: a bhd: t.o) 8	**12**	50/1	—	—

(SP 126.1%) **12 Rn**

2m 7.2 (2.30) CSF £13.26 TOTE £4.30: £1.40 £1.20 £1.60 (£4.20) Trio £11.50 OWNER Mr Paul Locke (NEWMARKET) BRED Mount Coote Stud
3277 Aerleon Pete (IRE) is steadily improving. He raced in second place until driven into the lead below the distance. Staying on bravely, he won decisively. (4/1)
3218 Snow Partridge (USA) made a gallant effort to lead throughout and kept on well for second place when headed approaching the final furlong. (5/2)
Georgina (IRE), bandaged all round and fit for her seasonal debut, only the second race of her career, appeared to be travelling well on the heels of the leaders but, after having every chance two furlongs out, failed to quicken. (11/4)
Sabadilla (USA), a Sadler's Wells colt, needs to furnish. Green in the early stages, he was dashed up to the leader after three furlongs and still had every chance two furlongs out. He could not quicken from that point. (7/2: 2/1-4/1)
Primeval made a satisfactory debut but, though staying on from three furlongs out, was never on terms. (25/1)
Ile de Librate made some late headway but was never in the race with a chance. (50/1)
1851 Verdi (IRE) (11/1: 8/1-12/1)

3633 QUORTINA CHALLENGE CUP H'CAP (0-80) (3-Y.O) (Class D)

3-00 (3-01) **1m 3f 135y** £3,467.00 (£1,046.00: £508.00: £239.00) Stalls: High GOING minus 0.56 sec per fur (F)

			SP	RR	SF
2897[2]	**Dead Aim (IRE) (75)** (IABalding) **3-9-4** LDettori(4) (lw: a.p: led wl over 1f out: r.o wl) ....—	**1**	15/8[1]	84	32
3279[4]	**Woody's Boy (IRE) (61)** (MJHeaton-Ellis) **3-8-4** SSanders(5) (hdwy 2f out: ev ch ins fnl f: r.o) ....¾	**2**	7/2[2]	69	17
2731[5]	**Azores (78)** (PFICole) **3-9-7** PatEddery(1) (led tl over 2f out: ev ch over 1f out: one pce) 1	**3**	7/1	85	33
3200[11]	**Mardrew (65)** (JohnBerry) **3-8-5**(3) RHavlin(3) (hld up: hdwy & ev ch 2f out: one pce) ....¾	**4**	12/1	71	19
3218[13]	**Protocol (IRE) (70)** (JWHills) **3-8-13** RHills(2) (lw: chsd ldr 5f out: led over 2f out tl wknd wl over 1f out) 2	**5**	4/1[3]	73	21
3128[8]	**Alifandango (IRE) (77)** (ACStewart) **3-9-6** MRoberts(6) (chsd ldr tl wknd 5f out) 3½	**6**	6/1	75	23

(SP 111.5%) **6 Rn**

2m 29.7 (3.70) CSF £7.72 TOTE £2.40: £1.40 £1.90 (£3.00) OWNER Al Muallim Partnership (KINGSCLERE) BRED Crichel Farms Ltd and Calogo Bloodstock A. G.
2897 Dead Aim (IRE), well suited by this longer trip, travelled much better than in his previous races. He struck the front below the distance and stayed on strongly. (15/8)
3279 Woody's Boy (IRE), behind for a long way, made ground to challenge approaching the final furlong but could not quite peg back the winner. (7/2)
2731 Azores made the running until over two furlongs out and rallied under some very hard driving without being able to quicken. (7/1: 9/2-15/2)
2885 Mardrew moved up to the leaders smoothly enough approaching the two-furlong marker but, when put to his best, lacked a change of gear. (12/1: 8/1-14/1)
1868 Protocol (IRE), with his tongue tied down, took a narrow lead over two furlongs out but soon weakened when headed approaching the final furlong. (4/1)
2184* Alifandango (IRE) faded quickly after racing in second place to the straight. (6/1: op 4/1)

3634 DUN & BRADSTREET CONDITIONS STKS (3-Y.O+) (Class C)

3-30 (3-30) **1m 2f 7y** £4,510.09 (£1,685.90: £822.95: £352.25: £156.13: £77.68) Stalls: High GOING minus 0.56 sec per fur (F)

				SP	RR	SF
1033[7]	**Salmon Ladder (USA) (113)** (PFICole) **5-9-0** PatEddery(4) (swtg: pushed along: led after 1f: r.o wl)	—	**1**	10/11[1]	112	55
3172a[4]	**Green Card (USA) (107)** (SPCWoods) **3-8-9** JReid(6) (hdwy over 2f out: ev ch over 1f out: no imp)	1½	**2**	3/1[2]	113	48
2642a[12]	**Conon Falls (IRE) (104)** (JHMGosden) **3-8-9** LDettori(1) (hld up: hdwy & ev ch 2f out: r.o one pce)	2	**3**	13/2[3]	109	44
2656[5]	**Acharne (110)** (CEBrittain) **4-9-0** MRoberts(5) (swtg: a.p: rdn & ev ch over 2f out: one pce)	1¾	**4**	10/1	104	47
3388[6]	**Behaviour (103)** (MrsJCecil) **5-9-0** MHills(2) (lw: hld up in rr: effrt & rdn over 2f out: nvr nr to chal)	1½	**5**	12/1	101	44
3051[9]	**Maralinga (IRE) (98)** (LadyHerries) **5-9-5** PaulEddery(3) (led 1f: prom tl wknd over 3f out)	11	**6**	10/1	89	32

(SP 116.6%) **6 Rn**

2m 4.7 (-0.20) CSF £3.74 TOTE £1.80: £1.30 £1.60 (£2.00) OWNER Mr M. Arbib (WHATCOMBE) BRED Robert N. Clay and Michael J. & Mrs Ryan

WEIGHT FOR AGE 3yo-8lb

IN-FOCUS: **This win gave Pat Eddery his twenty-fourth century in the last twenty-five domestic seasons.**

736 Salmon Ladder (USA), over a distance short of his best, had to be driven along to take the lead after a furlong. He looked in trouble approaching the two-furlong marker but was well in control in the final furlong. (10/11: op 6/4)

3172a Green Card (USA), patiently ridden, moved easily enough into second place over a furlong out but could make no impression on the winner. It transpired he had lost his specially fitted shoe in running. (3/1)

2642a Conon Falls (IRE), held up, moved up to challenge two furlongs out but, after having every chance, could find no extra under pressure. (13/2: 9/2-7/1)

2656 Acharne looked a danger momentarily approaching the two-furlong marker but was soon being hard ridden and could find no more. (10/1: 7/1-11/1)

3388 Behaviour, settled at the back of the field, was asked to improve approaching the two-furlong marker but lacked the pace to trouble the leaders. (12/1: 8/1-14/1)

2656 Maralinga (IRE) led for the first furlong but weakened rapidly with more than three furlongs still to race. (10/1: op 6/1)

3635 EARLEY NURSERY H'CAP (2-Y.O) (Class D)

4-00 (4-01) **5f 217y** £3,290.00 (£995.00: £485.00: £230.00) Stalls: High GOING minus 0.56 sec per fur (F)

				SP	RR	SF
2689[7]	**Caversfield (72)** (RHannon) **2-8-13** DaneO'Neill(1) (lw: a.p: led ins fnl f: r.o wl)	—	**1**	11/2[3]	76	17
3237[10]	**Lasham (65)** (NACallaghan) **2-8-6** PatEddery(7) (led: edgd lft 2f out: hrd rdn & edgd rt 1f out: hdd ins fnl f)	1¼	**2**	13/2	66	7
3468[3]	**Muftuffenuf (66)** (PRWebber) **2-8-7** AMcGlone(3) (a.p: ev ch 1f out: one pce)	nk	**3**	6/1	66	7
3446[2]	**Sassy (IRE) (65)** (APJarvis) **2-8-6** DHolland(5) (swtg: hdwy 2f out: hrd rdn 1f out: nt qckn)	1	**4**	9/2[2]	62	3
3215[4]	**Fayrana (IRE) (80)** (JWHills) **2-9-7** MHills(9) (swtg: hld up: hdwy whn bdly hmpd on ins 1f out: nt rcvr)	1¼	**5**	7/2[1]	74	15
3117[12]	**Smart Beau (USA) (68)** (RCharlton) **2-8-9** WJO'Connor(6) (s.s: nrst fin)	1	**6**	12/1	59	—
3289*	**Shannon (IRE) (60)** (CADwyer) **2-8-1** JQuinn(10) (stdd s: effrt & rdn over 1f out: nvr nr to chal)	nk	**7**	10/1	50	—
3289[2]	**Russian About (IRE) (59)** (MRChannon) **2-8-0** CRutter(8) (lw: chsd ldr tl wknd over 2f out)	2½	**8**	7/1	43	—
3152[10]	**Really Done It Now (IRE) (68)** (KRBurke) **2-8-9v[1]** KFallon(2) (b.off hind: nvr trbld ldrs)	hd	**9**	12/1	51	—
3042[3]	**American Cousin (70)** (BJMeehan) **2-8-11b[1]** MTebbutt(4) (lw: prom 3f)	6	**10**	10/1	37	—

(SP 129.5%) **10 Rn**

1m 12.9 (2.40) CSF £41.97 CT £216.78 TOTE £7.30: £1.90 £2.40 £2.20 (£45.70) Trio £104.40 OWNER Mr William Kelly (MARLBOROUGH) BRED Stud-On-The-Chart

STEWARDS' ENQUIRY Eddery susp 27-29/8/97 (careless riding).

1274 Caversfield, more patiently ridden this time, was always on the heels of the leaders and quickened to strike the front inside the final furlong. (11/2: 4/1-6/1)

1856 Lasham tried to make all the running. He edged first to the left and then to the right and could not hold the winner inside the final furlong. (13/2: 5/1-8/1)

3468 Muftuffenuf, always in the first three, had every chance but could find no extra in the last half-furlong. (6/1)

3446 Sassy (IRE) had plenty to do at halfway but, staying on from two furlongs out, was never nearer than at the finish. (9/2)

3215 Fayrana (IRE) was going well on the heels of the leaders on the inside rails when badly hampered going for a gap entering the final furlong. But for this mishap, she would have gone very close. (7/2)

2849 Smart Beau (USA) was slowly away and, though making some headway two furlongs out, could never reach a challenging position. (12/1: 8/1-14/1)

3289* Shannon (IRE) (10/1: 8/1-12/1)

2942 Really Done It Now (IRE) (12/1: 8/1-14/1)

3636 E.B.F. MAIDEN STKS (2-Y.O F) (Class D)

4-30 (4-33) **5f 10y** £3,387.50 (£1,025.00: £500.00: £237.50) Stalls: High GOING minus 0.56 sec per fur (F)

				SP	RR	SF
	Risque Lady (PWHarris) **2-8-11** PatEddery(1) (neat: a.p: led over 1f out: all out)	—	**1**	3/1[2]	83+	43
3009[3]	**Royal Shyness** (GLewis) **2-8-11** PaulEddery(14) (led over 3f: ev ch fnl f: r.o)	s.h	**2**	5/4[1]	83	43
3471[13]	**Gunzells (USA)** (HCandy) **2-8-11** CRutter(13) (swtg: chsd ldrs: r.o ins fnl f)	6	**3**	14/1	64	24
	Zelah (IRE) (BSmart) **2-8-11** MTebbutt(15) (neat: lw: chsd ldrs: styd on ins fnl f)	hd	**4**	14/1	64	24
	Lady Charlotte (DRCElsworth) **2-8-11** JReid(6) (neat: hdwy fnl 2f: nvr nrr)	hd	**5**	33/1	63	23
2862[20]	**Persian Sabre** (VSoane) **2-8-11** RCochrane(9) (hdwy over 1f out: nvr plcd to chal)	1¾	**6**	33/1	58+	18
1970[3]	**Katah** (JHMGosden) **2-8-11** RHills(11) (nvr nr to chal)	½	**7**	6/1[3]	56	16
3324[2]	**Kathies Pet** (RJHodges) **2-8-6(5)** AmandaSanders(3) (nrst fin)	½	**8**	33/1	55	15
3247[7]	**Call Me Vera** (EAWheeler) **2-8-6(5)** ADaly(4) (w ldrs tl wknd qckly over 1f out)	½	**9**	50/1	53	13
	Dancing Wolf (IRE) (MissGayKelleway) **2-8-11** KFallon(12) (b.hind: leggy: unf: hmpd s: a bhd)	1½	**10**	8/1	48	8
3094[9]	**Golden Fortune** (DRLoder) **2-8-11** WRyan(2) (lw: nvr trbld ldrs)	1¼	**11**	20/1	44	4
	Doodle (WJHaggas) **2-8-11** MHills(10) (neat: lw: outpcd)	1	**12**	20/1	41	1
3324[5]	**Aviva Lady (IRE)** (CADwyer) **2-8-11** JQuinn(8) (w ldrs tl wknd 2f out)	1½	**13**	50/1	36	—
	Very Simple (IRE) (JSMoore) **2-8-11** MFenton(7) (small: a wl bhd)	9	**14**	20/1	8	—
	Zeptepi (IRE) (TEPowell) **2-8-6(5)** CLowther(5) (str: bkwd: a wl bhd)	8	**15**	33/1	—	—

(SP 138.1%) **15 Rn**

60.0 secs (0.30) CSF £6.69 TOTE £4.40: £1.70 £1.60 £4.30 (£4.80) Trio £41.00 OWNER Godwin Hollis Lawren Rice (BERKHAMSTED) BRED Pendley Farm

OFFICIAL EXPLANATION **Persian Sabre: Rider reported that his instructions were to settle the filly in behind, cover her up and to come with a long run, but she was denied a clear run in the last two furlongs. The trainer added that he was satisfied with Cochrane's riding and that the filly had been very fractious in the stalls on her previous outing.**
Risque Lady was soon chasing the leaders. She gained a narrow advantage at the distance and gamely held off the favourite's renewed challenge. (3/1)
3009 Royal Shyness tried to make all the running and fought back well when headed approaching the final furlong. (5/4: evens-4/6)
Gunzells (USA) chased the leading group until running on to snatch third place near the finish. (14/1: 10/1-16/1)
Zelah (IRE), backed at long odds, made an encouraging debut. Always hunting up the leaders, she kept on well towards the finish without ever promising to land a blow at the leading pair. Improvement can be expected. (14/1: 33/1-12/1)
Lady Charlotte ran on in the last two furlongs and has scope for improvement. (33/1)
1593 Persian Sabre, having her third run, made steady headway approaching the final furlong without being given a hard race. She should pay to follow. (33/1)
Dancing Wolf (IRE) (8/1: 5/1-10/1)

3637 MARLOW ADDITIONAL APPRENTICE H'CAP (0-70) (3-Y.O+) (Class F)
5-00 (5-04) **5f 10y** £2,371.50 (£674.00: £334.50) Stalls: High GOING minus 0.56 sec per fur (F)

				SP	RR	SF
*2674**	**Opening Range (35)** (NEBerry) **6-7-10** PBradley(2) (hdwy 2f out: led 1f out: r.o wl)	—	**1**	14/1	48	30
3470[12]	**Bairn Atholl (36)** (RJHodges) **4-7-11** JFowle(10) (lw: gd hdwy over 1f out: fin wl)	1½	**2**	25/1	44	26
3206[7]	**Whizz Kid (42)** (JJBridger) **3-8-1** PClarke(3) (hdwy fnl 2f: nvr nrr)	1	**3**	25/1	47	27
3083[11]	**Mister Raider (47)** (EAWheeler) **5-8-0b**(8) BO'Leary(6) (lw: w ldrs: ev ch 1f out: nt qckn)	½	**4**	25/1	51	33
3292[2]	**Tachycardia (36)** (RJO'Sullivan) **5-7-11** DarrenWilliams(7) (a.p: one pce fnl 2f)	¾	**5**	6/1[2]	37	19
2934*	**Cross The Border (62)** (DNicholls) **4-9-9** ANicholls(12) (led tl wknd 1f out)	½	**6**	5/6[1]	62	44
3323*	**Divine Miss-P (58)** (APJarvis) **4-9-2**(3) CCarver(4) (swtg: w ldrs tl wknd fnl f)	hd	**7**	9/1	57	39
3327[2]	**Mystical (62)** (MrsLStubbs) **3-9-4v**(3) GMcDonald(8) (swtg: chsd ldrs: hrd rdn & nt clr run over 1f out: wknd ins fnl f)	1¼	**8**	8/1[3]	57	37
3417[12]	**Dancing Jack (37)** (JJBridger) **4-7-12**ow2 DavidO'Neill(9) (swtg: nvr nr to chal)	2	**9**	50/1	26	6
3249[11]	**Parijazz (IRE) (48)** (MartynMeade) **3-8-4**(3) RBrisland(11) (swtg: outpcd)	2½	**10**	16/1	29	9
3280[12]	**Tommy Tempest (40)** (REPeacock) **8-8-1** PFitzsimons(5) (spd 3f)	½	**11**	10/1	19	1
3600[12]	**Gi La High (67)** (MartynMeade) **4-9-11**(3) ClaireAngell(1) (dwlt: a bhd)	2½	**12**	20/1	39	21
				(SP 129.8%)	**12 Rn**	

59.9 secs (0.20) CSF £308.62 CT £7,745.17 TOTE £17.60: £3.20 £5.50 £3.90 (£298.30) Trio £722.40; £712.31 to York 19/8/97 OWNER In The Purple Racing (UPPER LAMBOURN) BRED Miss E. Drax
LONG HANDICAP Dancing Jack 7-2
WEIGHT FOR AGE 3yo-2lb
2674* Opening Range made good headway to take up the running entering the final furlong. Staying on strongly, she never appeared likely to be caught. (14/1: 10/1-16/1)
3327 Bairn Atholl ran on when it was all too late finishing with a fine flourish. She looks on a handy mark. (25/1)
2321 Whizz Kid, unable to go the early pace, picked up well from two furlongs out but could not quite reach the winner. (25/1)
2663 Mister Raider went with the leaders. He still had every chance entering the final furlong but could then find no more. (25/1)
3292 Tachycardia, always one of the leaders, could find no extra in the last furlong. (6/1)
2934* Cross The Border was too free going to the start and in the race. Held up next time, he will be very hard to beat. (5/6: 5/4-4/5)
2732* Tommy Tempest (10/1: 8/1-12/1)

T/Jkpt: Not won; £27,774.69 to York 19/8/97. T/Plpt: £722.80 (36.87 Tckts). T/Qdpt: £628.30 (2.05 Tckts) AK/Hn

3288-FOLKESTONE (R-H) (Good to firm, Firm patches)
Tuesday August 19th
WEATHER: v.hot WIND: slt half against

3638 JOHN MCCARTHY MAIDEN STKS (2-Y.O F) (Class D)
2-20 (2-25) **6f 189y** £3,643.75 (£1,090.00: £522.50: £238.75) Stalls: Low GOING minus 0.23 sec per fur (GF)

				SP	RR	SF
3114[9]	**Star of Grosvenor (IRE)** (PWChapple-Hyam) **2-8-8**(3) RHavlin(5) (mde all: rdn out)	—	**1**	6/1[3]	77	21
2840[4]	**Matata (IRE)** (NACallaghan) **2-8-11** SDrowne(2) (chsd wnr 6f out: rdn 2f out: ev ch ins fnl f: unable qckn)	½	**2**	11/4[2]	76	20
3033[5]	**Ratiyya (IRE)** (BHanbury) **2-8-11** JStack(8) (a.p: hrd rdn over 1f out: one pce)	1½	**3**	25/1	72	16
3204[3]	**Celestial Bay (IRE) (82)** (AGFoster) **2-8-11** MTebbutt(7) (a.p: hrd rdn over 1f out: one pce)	1½	**4**	14/1	69	13
2840[7]	**Cantonese (USA)** (RCharlton) **2-8-11** TSprake(9) (rdn & hdwy over 1f out: r.o one pce)	½	**5**	8/1	68	12
3151[8]	**Captivating (IRE)** (RHannon) **2-8-11** DaneO'Neill(1) (a.p: hrd rdn over 1f out: one pce)	nk	**6**	25/1	67	11
	Admire (MissGayKelleway) **2-8-8**(3) RFfrench(3) (neat: bit bkwd: hdwy over 1f out: nvr nrr: bttr for r)	2	**7**	10/1	62	6
3187[8]	**Coalminersdaughter (IRE)** (JWHills) **2-8-8**(3) MHenry(13) (nvr nr to chal)	2½	**8**	20/1	57	1
3219[5]	**Silca Key Service** (MRChannon) **2-8-11** ACulhane(12) (lw: s.s: nvr nrr)	½	**9**	15/8[1]	55	—
	Elsaayoura (IRE) (NAGraham) **2-8-11** MRimmer(15) (leggy: lt-f: plld hrd: hld up: rdn over 2f out: sn wknd)	1¼	**10**	33/1	52	—
	Robanna (RAkehurst) **2-8-11** AClark(14) (leggy: lt-f: rdn & hdwy on ins 2f out: wknd over 1f out)	2½	**11**	16/1	47	—
1240[14]	**Miss Chief Maker** (WRMuir) **2-8-8**(3) MartinDwyer(11) (bit bkwd: a bhd)	8	**12**	50/1	28	—
	Tough Nell (IRE) (BobJones) **2-8-11** NDay(6) (unf: bit bkwd: bhd fnl 2f)	10	**13**	25/1	5	—
2959[7]	**Natalie's Pet** (GLewis) **2-8-11** PaulEddery(4) (a bhd)	nk	**14**	50/1	4	—
2728[18]	**Risada (IRE)** (DRLoder) **2-8-11** GCarter(10) (s.s: a bhd)	1¼	**15**	33/1	1	—
				(SP 134.6%)	**15 Rn**	

1m 25.9 (4.50) CSF £21.32 TOTE £20.20: £4.40 £1.20 £7.30 (£16.30) Trio £254.20 OWNER Mr R. E. Sangster (MARLBOROUGH) BRED Swettenham Stud
Star of Grosvenor (IRE) left her debut run well behind and, making all the running, was always just keeping the runner-up at bay. (6/1: 7/2-8/1)
2840 Matata (IRE) was soon racing in second place. Grimly trying to get on terms in the short straight, she found the winner always just holding her. This is her level. (11/4)
3033 Ratiyya (IRE) ran better here and was a leading light throughout, if failing to quicken in the short home straight. (25/1)
3204 Celestial Bay (IRE) was never far away but, despite her rider's efforts, could only go up and down in the same place in the short home straight. (14/1)

Cantonese (USA), pushed along to take closer order in the short straight, could only struggle on at one insufficient pace. (8/1: 6/1-9/1)
Captivating (IRE) was never far away but could only plod on in her own time in the final quarter-mile. (25/1)
Admire may not be that big but she is quite a nice-looking sort. Despite carrying condition and being at the back of the field entering the short straight, she stayed on nicely to be nearest at the line. Improvement can be expected. (10/1)

3639 SMARDEN (S) STKS (2-Y.O) (Class G)

2-50 (2-51) **6f 189y** £1,984.50 (£547.00: £259.50) Stalls: Low GOING minus 0.23 sec per fur (GF)

				SP	RR	SF
3384^{2}	**Won't Forget Me (IRE) (59)** (MHTompkins) **2-8-8**(3) MHenry(5) (hdwy to chse ldr over 1f out: led ins fnl f: rdn out)	—	**1**	5/4^{1}	59	15
2571^{6}	**Pianist (IRE)** (GLewis) **2-8-11** PaulEddery(4) (lw: chsd ldr over 2f: rdn over 3f out: swtchd lft over 1f out: r.o wl ins fnl f)	¾	**2**	3/1^{3}	57	13
3384^{3}	**Filgrave (IRE) (54)** (CADwyer) **2-8-11v** DaneO'Neill(1) (hld up: chsd ldr over 4f out tl over 1f out: hrd rdn: unable qckn fnl f)	hd	**3**	10/1	57	13
3097^{4}	**Captain Bliss (62)** (NTinkler) **2-8-13b**(3) RFfrench(6) (swtg: led tl ins fnl f: sn wknd)	1½	**4**	5/2^{2}	59	15
3384^{7}	**Sipping Soda** (KTIvory) **2-8-6** JLowe(2) (a bhd)	12	**5**	33/1	21	—
2664^{7}	**Global Risk** (CMurray) **2-8-11** NicolaHowarth(3) (bhd fnl 3f)	4	**6**	25/1	16	—
				(SP 113.9%)	**6 Rn**	

1m 26.5 (5.10) CSF £5.00 TOTE £2.10: £1.10 £2.90 (£4.60) OWNER Mrs Jane Bailey (NEWMARKET) BRED Kevin Wallace
No bid
3384 Won't Forget Me (IRE) confirmed the opinion of his Newmarket run and, coming through to take second place below the distance, struck the front inside the final furlong and held on well. (5/4)
2007 Pianist (IRE) appreciated the drop in class and step up in trip but he was still off the bridle at halfway. Appearing to be going nowhere in the straight, he was switched off the rails approaching the final furlong and struck the right key inside the final furlong, running on strongly to snatch second place right on the line. A step up to a mile is needed. (3/1)
3384 Filgrave (IRE) came through to show in second place running down the hill but he was collared for the runner-up berth approaching the final furlong and failed to find another gear. This is his level. (10/1: 7/1-11/1)
3097 Captain Bliss was not going to hang about and raced off in front. Grimly trying to hold on, he had nothing more to offer when collared inside the final furlong. (5/2)

3640 ROCHESTER H'CAP (0-70) (3-Y.O+) (Class E)

3-25 (3-25) **1m 4f** £3,252.25 (£973.00: £466.50: £213.25) Stalls: Low GOING minus 0.23 sec per fur (GF)

				SP	RR	SF
1825*	**Norsong (44)** (JAkehurst) **5-8-2** PaulEddery(3) (mde all: drvn out)	—	**1**	8/1	54	28
3496^{2}	**Zamalek (USA) (46)** (RMFlower) **5-8-4** DaneO'Neill(1) (swtg: rdn & hdwy over 2f out: ev ch ins fnl f: r.o)	½	**2**	9/2^{2}	55	29
3293*	**Country Thatch (43)** (CAHorgan) **4-7-12**(3) RFfrench(10) (a.p: chsd wnr over 1f out tl ins fnl f: unable qckn)	1¼	**3**	4/1^{1}	51	25
647^{16}	**Classic Dame (FR) (63)** (SDow) **4-9-4**(3) MartinDwyer(4) (lw: s.s: rdn & hdwy over 1f out: one pce)	1	**4**	33/1	69	43
	Lear Jet (USA) (70) (BobJones) **4-10-0** NDay(12) (chsd wnr over 10f: one pce)	nk	**5**	9/2^{2}	76	50
3291*	**Veronica Franco (49)** (PRHedger) **4-8-7** SDrowne(9) (rdn & hdwy over 1f out: wknd fnl f)	3	**6**	5/1^{3}	51	25
3203^{5}	**Serious Trust (47)** (MrsLCJewell) **4-8-2**(3) DSweeney(7) (hdwy over 7f out: wknd over 1f out)	¾	**7**	14/1	48	22
	Hoofprints (IRE) (65) (MrsAJPerrett) **4-9-9** AClark(8) (hld up: rdn 3f out: wknd over 1f out)	3	**8**	10/1	62	36
3229^{6}	**Karachi (50)** (RJO'Sullivan) **7-8-8** AProcter(6) (hld up: rdn 3f out: wknd over 1f out)	7	**9**	16/1	38	12
3279^{8}	**Krayyan Dawn (45)** (JAkehurst) **7-8-3** GCarter(2) (b: hdwy over 7f out: wknd 6f out)	20	**10**	25/1	6	—
3449^{4}	**Canton Ron (48)** (HJCollingridge) **3-7-10** NAdams(5) (lw: a bhd)	hd	**11**	50/1	9	—
2116^{4}	**Snow Carnival (55)** (LadyHerries) **4-8-13** TSprake(11) (lw: bhd fnl 6f)	hd	**12**	8/1	16	—
				(SP 125.6%)	**12 Rn**	

2m 37.4 (6.20) CSF £41.89 CT £157.34 TOTE £10.60: £3.10 £2.20 £1.90 (£17.50) Trio £24.40 OWNER The Golfers Partnership (EPSOM)
BRED Deepwood Farm Stud
LONG HANDICAP Canton Ron 6-6
WEIGHT FOR AGE 3yo-10lb
IN-FOCUS: **A serious accident was narrowly averted during this race when the field managed to avoid a car which was partially on the track.**
1825* Norsong, who has changed stables since winning at Salisbury eleven weeks ago, put up another aggressive display from the front and, responding to pressure, just kept the runner-up at bay. (8/1: 6/1-10/1)
3496 Zamalek (USA) had no problems with a step up in distance. Moving up turning into the straight, he threw down his challenge in the final furlong but was just unable to get on top. He is in good heart this year with three wins to his name. (9/2: 3/1-5/1)
3293* Country Thatch ran another sound race off a 5lb higher mark and showed in second place approaching the final furlong, before collared for that position inside the last 150 yards. (4/1: 3/1-9/2)
Classic Dame (FR), who has changed stables since her last run four months ago, moved up below the distance and, although she did not have a great deal of room, her jockey did not stop riding and the filly could only struggle on at one pace. (33/1)
Lear Jet (USA), off the course since pulling up in a novice hurdle at Ascot back in February, was a massive 20lb lower than when last appearing in a handicap and raced in second place until below the distance. (9/2: tchd 7/1)
3291* Veronica Franco moved up below the distance but she had nothing more to offer in the final furlong. She is difficult to win with. (5/1)
1169 Serious Trust (14/1: 16/1-25/1)

3641 GRAFTY GREEN MEDIAN AUCTION MAIDEN STKS (3 & 4-Y.O) (Class F)

4-00 (4-07) **6f** £2,277.00 (£627.00: £297.00) Stalls: Low GOING minus 0.23 sec per fur (GF)

				SP	RR	SF
3452^{7}	**Silver Secret (67)** (MJHeaton-Ellis) **3-9-0** AClark(7) (a.p: rdn over 2f out: led ins fnl f: r.o wl)	—	**1**	Evens^{1}	66	24
3206^{4}	**Dorado Beach (41)** (LGCottrell) **3-8-9** NCarlisle(3) (a.p: led 3f out tl ins fnl f: unable qckn)	2½	**2**	6/1^{2}	54	12
3202^{7}	**Turners Way** (SDow) **3-9-0** DaneO'Neill(6) (hld up: hrd rdn over 1f out: r.o ins fnl f)	s.h	**3**	7/1^{3}	59	17
3299^{13}	**Barbury Ballad (IRE) (32)** (MJHeaton-Ellis) **3-8-9**(5) ADaly(5) (hld up: rdn 3f out: wknd 2f out)	3½	**4**	25/1	50	8
	Able Lass (IRE) (RWArmstrong) **3-8-9** RPrice(4) (leggy: lt-f: s.s: outpcd: nvr nrr)	2½	**5**	9/1	38	—
1292^{17}	**Dozen Roses (38)** (JELong) **3-8-9** TGMcLaughlin(8) (led 3f: wknd wl over 1f out)	3	**6**	33/1	30	—
3313^{4}	**Castle Ashby Jack (49)** (PHowling) **3-9-0b** PaulEddery(2) (b.hind: hld up: rdn over 2f out: wknd wl over 1f out)	½	**7**	6/1^{2}	34	—

			SP	RR	SF
3230^{10} **She's Electric (25)** (JJBridger) **3-8-2**$^{(7)}$ PDoe(1) (lw: s.s: a bhd)	2	**8**	33/1	24	—

(SP 110.8%) **8 Rn**

1m 14.1 (3.90) CSF £6.08 TOTE £1.60: £1.10 £1.60 £1.60 (£4.50) OWNER Mr F. J. Sainsbury (WROUGHTON) BRED Dr Anthony Nicholas Howard

2645 Silver Secret had a much easier task here - he had 18lb or more to spare on official adjusted ratings - and coped with the drop in distance, getting on top inside the final furlong to win this bad race. (Evens)

3206 Dorado Beach ran well in this bad event, showing in front at halfway, before eventually overhauled inside the final furlong. (6/1)

2580 Turners Way, who broke a blood vessel last time out, ran on inside the final furlong and failed by only a whisker to snatch second prize. He is worth a try over seven furlongs. (7/1)

1508 Barbury Ballad (IRE) chased the leaders but had been hung out to dry two furlongs from home. A drop to selling class is his best hope. (25/1)

Able Lass (IRE), a small, lightly-made filly, drifted extremely badly in the betting and never threatened to get into it. (9/1: 9/4-10/1)

3313 Castle Ashby Jack (6/1: 4/1-13/2)

3642 HIGH HALDEN LIMITED STKS (0-60) (3-Y.O+) (Class F)

4-30 (4-33) **6f** £2,277.00 (£627.00: £297.00) Stalls: Low GOING minus 0.23 sec per fur (GF)

			SP	RR	SF
3082^{2} **Sharp Imp (60)** (RMFlower) **7-8-11b**$^{(3)}$ MartinDwyer(2) (gd hdwy on ins over 1f out: str run to ld wl ins fnl f: r.o wl)	—	**1**	5/1^{2}	69	47
3202^{6} **Bold Tina (IRE) (60)** (RHannon) **3-8-8** DaneO'Neill(6) (hld up: led over 1f out tl wl ins fnl f: unable qckn)	1¼	**2**	9/1	63	38
3473^{3} **Pride of Hayling (IRE) (56)** (PRHedger) **6-8-11** SDrowne(3) (lw: hdwy over 2f out: swtchd rt over 1f out: ev ch ins fnl f: one pce)	1¼	**3**	9/2^{1}	59	37
2933^{4} **Akalim (59)** (LGCottrell) **4-8-11**$^{(3)}$ MHenry(5) (a.p: hrd rdn over 1f out: ev ch ins fnl f: sn wknd)	1¼	**4**	13/2	59	37
3582^{10} **Never Think Twice (57)** (KTIvory) **4-8-9v**$^{(5)}$ GFaulkner(7) (b: hdwy over 2f out: hrd rdn over 1f out: one pce ins fnl f)	s.h	**5**	12/1	59	37
3625* **Corniche Quest (IRE) (60)** (MRChannon) **4-8-13**$^{(7)}$ 3x AEddery(8) (rdn & hdwy over 1f out: one pce)	hd	**6**	6/1^{3}	65	43
3500^{6} **Dande Flyer (60)** (DWPArbuthnot) **4-9-0** SWhitworth(9) (hdwy over 1f out: one pce fnl f)	s.h	**7**	6/1^{3}	59	37
3590^{3} **Shashi (IRE) (50)** (PatMitchell) **5-9-0** PBloomfield(4) (rdn over 2f out: mid div whn nt clr run 1f out)	3	**8**	20/1	51	29
3016^{8} **Imposing Time (56)** (MissGayKelleway) **6-8-11**$^{(3)}$ RFfrench(1) (lw: w ldr: led over 2f out tl over 1f out: sn wknd)	¾	**9**	8/1	49	27
3406^{8} **Just Bob (60)** (SEKettlewell) **8-8-7**$^{(7)}$ JennyBenson(10) (lw: a bhd)	3½	**10**	12/1	39	17
3280^{13} **Goodbye Gatemen (IRE) (60)** (BAPearce) **3-9-0** LeesaLong(14) (swtg: led over 3f: wknd wl over 1f out)	4	**11**	20/1	32	7
3195^{4} **Superlao (BEL) (48)** (JJBridger) **5-8-7**$^{(7)}$ PDoe(12) (bhd fnl 2f)	8	**12**	25/1	7	—
3290^{8} **Waders Dream (IRE) (39)** (PatMitchell) **8-8-9v**$^{(5)}$ AmandaSanders(13) (swtg: a bhd)	nk	**13**	33/1	6	—
2922^{14} **Red Admiral (58)** (CMurray) **7-9-0** NicolaHowarth(11) (prom 3f)	3	**14**	25/1	—	—

(SP 133.4%) **14 Rn**

1m 12.4 (2.20) CSF £46.94 TOTE £3.30: £1.60 £3.10 £2.40 (£42.90) Trio £58.80 OWNER Mrs G. M. Temmerman (JEVINGTON) BRED James Wigan

WEIGHT FOR AGE 3yo-3lb

3082 Sharp Imp at last came good after a string of seconds and came with a strong run from below the distance to sweep into the lead in the closing stages. (5/1)

964 Bold Tina (IRE) showed with a narrow advantage against the rails below the distance, but was unable to withstand the late flourish of the winner in the closing stages. (9/1)

3473 Pride of Hayling (IRE) ran another sound race and was one of several with every chance inside the final furlong, before tapped for toe. (9/2: op 3/1)

2933 Akalim again showed promise and may well have got his head in front for a few strides below the distance, before tiring in the closing stages. (13/2)

2424 Never Think Twice, making a quick reappearance, moved up on the outside over a quarter of a mile from home but failed to find another gear in the final furlong. He has just two wins from thirty-five starts to his name. (12/1)

3625* Corniche Quest (IRE) has winning form from five furlongs to a mile and, after taking closer order below the distance, failed to quicken. (6/1: op 7/2)

3643 PAUL COOK APPRENTICE H'CAP (0-70) (3-Y.O) (Class F)

5-00 (5-01) **2m 93y** £2,739.00 (£759.00: £363.00) Stalls: Low GOING minus 0.23 sec per fur (GF)

			SP	RR	SF
3210^{6} **Chairmans Daughter (59)** (JPearce) **3-8-10b** CTeague(3) (swtg: gd hdwy on ins over 2f out: led 1f out: hrd rdn: r.o wl)	—	**1**	7/1	69	36
3210^{4} **Perlethorpe (51)** (MBell) **3-7-13**$^{(3)}$ RMullen(4) (hld up: led over 2f out to 1f out: unable qckn)	2½	**2**	11/4^{2}	59	26
3470^{9} **Imperial Glen (IRE) (45)** (MDIUsher) **3-7-3**$^{(7)}$ JFowle(7) (lw: chsd ldr 13f out tl rn v.wd st: wknd over 1f out)	8	**3**	16/1	45	12
3122^{11} **Sun Alert (USA) (70)** (MJPolglase) **3-9-4**$^{(3)}$ GMilligan(5) (chsd ldr over 3f: rdn over 2f out: wknd over 1f out)	21	**4**	13/8^{1}	49	16
3057^{5} **Frost King (50)** (MissBSanders) **3-8-1v**^{1} AWhelan(1) (led: clr 13f out: hdd over 2f out: sn wknd)	12	**5**	14/1	18	—
2952^{7} **Aegean (45)** (KTIvory) **3-7-10** MartinDwyer(2) (a bhd: t.o fnl 5f)	22	**6**	14/1	—	—
3116^{3} **Barnwood Crackers (45)** (MRChannon) **3-7-10** RFfrench(6) (lw: a bhd: t.o whn p.u ins fnl f: lame)		**P**	3/1^{3}	—	—

(SP 121.5%) **7 Rn**

3m 38.4 (8.40) CSF £26.12 TOTE £9.40: £3.70 £2.60 (£10.40) OWNER Mrs K. J. Crangle (NEWMARKET) BRED Hamilton Bloodstock (UK) Ltd

LONG HANDICAP Imperial Glen (IRE) 7-8 Aegean 7-0 Barnwood Crackers 7-3

3210 Chairmans Daughter was given a tremendous ride. In last place five furlongs from home and some twenty lengths off the leader, she made up a tremendous amount of ground turning for home and was right on terms below the distance. Striking the front entering the final furlong, she was given a few cracks of the whip and ran on strongly. (7/1)

3210 Perlethorpe appreciated the longer trip and showed in front early in the short straight. Collared a furlong out, she was unable to cope with the winner. (11/4: op 6/4)

2287 Imperial Glen (IRE), taking a massive step up in trip, was soon racing in second place but she completely failed to handle the home turn and ran extremely wide. She was left for dead by the front two from below the distance. (16/1)

2589 Sun Alert (USA) was taking a drop in class but still ran poorly and dropped tamely away below the distance. (13/8)

T/Plpt: £28.30 (617.9 Tckts). T/Qdpt: £7.10 (159.28 Tckts) AK

2706-YORK (L-H) (Good)
Tuesday August 19th
WEATHER: hot & humid WIND: slt half bhd

3644 DEPLOY ACOMB CONDITIONS STKS (2-Y.O) (Class B)
2-05 (2-06) **6f 214y** £15,990.00 (£4,370.00: £4,370.00: £1,150.00: £450.00: £170.00) Stalls: High GOING: 0.13 sec per fur (G)

			SP	RR	SF
	Saratoga Springs (CAN) (APO'Brien,Ireland) **2-8-10v1** MJKinane(8) (gd sort: a.p: led 2f out: sn drvn clr)....—	**1**	9/1 3	113	68
3193*	**Chester House (USA)** (HRACecil) **2-9-0** KFallon(4) (s.i.s: sn drvn along: hdwy on ins ½-wy: styd on fnl f: no ch w wnr)....5	**2**	13/8 1	106	61
3047 3	**Mutawwaj (IRE)** (SbinSuroor) **2-8-10** LDettori(6) (lw: w ldr: led over 2f out: sn hdd & outpcd)....d.h	**2**	7/1 2	102	57
3235*	**Teapot Row (IRE)** (JARToller) **2-9-0** SSanders(5) (hld up: hdwy over 2f out: sn rdn: kpt on one pce)....1¾	**4**	7/1 2	102	57
3215*	**Merlin's Ring (94)** (IABalding) **2-8-10** KDarley(1) (trckd ldrs: effrt & rdn over 2f out: sn btn)....1	**5**	7/1 2	95	50
3379*	**Jazz Club (USA)** (PFICole) **2-9-2** PatEddery(2) (b.off fore: led tl hdd & wknd over 2f out)....5	**6**	7/1 2	90	45
3047*	**La-Faah (IRE)** (BWHills) **2-9-0** RHills(7) (hld up in tch: nt clr run 4f out: outpcd fnl 2f)....5	**7**	9/1 3	76	31
3322*	**Mr Cahill (USA)** (MRStoute) **2-9-0** JReid(3) (lw: chsd ldrs tl wknd over 2f out)....1½	**8**	9/1 3	73	28
3123 6	**Lone Piper** (CEBrittain) **2-8-10** MRoberts(9) (bhd: rdn over 3f out: sn t.o)....30	**9**	40/1	—	—

(SP 120.5%) **9 Rn**

1m 26.08 (3.08) CSF SS & CH £11.44, SH & M £33.39 TOTE £14.00: £2.40 CH £1.20 M £2.00 (SS & CH £7.60, SS & M £15.40) Trio £21.20 OWNER Mr M Tabor & Mrs John Magnier (PILTOWN)

Saratoga Springs (CAN), a fine-looking colt already a winner in Ireland over this trip, found much improved form in his first-time visor and quite simply outclassed this opposition. His price for next year's Two Thousand Guineas has been reduced to 20/1. (9/1)
3047 Mutawwaj (IRE) had much faster ground on this occasion and also an extra furlong and, helping force the pace, he gave his best but had to admit the winner a class apart. (7/1)
3193* Chester House (USA) missed the break and was soon bustled along. Sticking to the inside rail, he stayed on well in the closing stages but the winner had taken first run and he was only ever fighting for the places. (13/8)
3235* Teapot Row (IRE) adopted more patient tactics in this higher-class event and despite staying on could not get within striking range of the principals. (7/1)
3215* Merlin's Ring, settled behind the leaders, found this company just a bit too strong for him and he was unable to land a blow. (7/1)
3379* Jazz Club (USA) attempted to make it all but he was taking a step up in class here and he had shot his bolt when collared entering the last quarter-mile. (7/1)

3645 WEATHERBYS INSURANCE LONSDALE STKS (Gp 3) (3-Y.O+) (Class A)
2-35 (2-37) **1m 7f 195y** £24,656.00 (£9,104.00: £4,352.00: £1,760.00: £680.00: £248.00) Stalls: Low GOING: 0.13 sec per fur (G)

			SP	RR	SF
3149 3	**Double Eclipse (IRE) (116)** (MJohnston) **5-9-1** MRoberts(4) (mde all: hrd drvn 2f out: styd on strly)....—	**1**	5/2 2	123	60
3149 6	**Samraan (USA) (114)** (JLDunlop) **4-9-1** LDettori(1) (lw: a.p: jnd wnr over 2f out: hrd rdn: unable to qckn)....2½	**2**	9/1	121	58
2327*	**Windsor Castle (109)** (PFICole) **3-8-4** SSanders(5) (chsd wnr: hrd drvn 5f out: styd on appr fnl f)....1¼	**3**	5/1 3	122	45
2559 5	**Celeric (123)** (DMorley) **5-9-10** PatEddery(3) (lw: hld up & bhd: hdwy 3f out: sn rdn along: no imp)....4	**4**	2/1 1	124	61
3149 4	**Election Day (IRE) (119)** (MRStoute) **5-9-1v** MJKinane(6) (lw: hld up: rdn over 3f out: sn btn)....8	**5**	6/1	107	44
3149 10	**Corradini (110)** (HRACecil) **5-9-1** KFallon(2) (trckd ldrs: effrt over 4f out: rdn & wknd 3f out: t.o)....30	**6**	12/1	77	14

(SP 110.5%) **6 Rn**

3m 29.91 (9.91) CSF £21.07 TOTE £3.00: £1.80 £2.60 (£18.80) OWNER The Middleham Partnership (MIDDLEHAM) BRED Dene Investments N V in Ireland
WEIGHT FOR AGE 3yo-14lb
OFFICIAL EXPLANATION **Corradini: the Vet reported that the horse was lame after the race.**

3149 Double Eclipse (IRE) proved a very popular winner in front of this massive crowd with a very brave all the way success and, in gaining his revenge over the favourite, is a real credit to his stable. (5/2)
3149 Samraan (USA) ran the race of his life and gave backers of the winner a worrying time inside the final quarter-mile before he had to admit the winner just too strong for him. A return to form is imminent. (9/1)
2327* Windsor Castle, the only three-year-old in the race and running without his customary blinkers, was flat to the boards turning in but he is certainly not short where stamina is concerned as he showed at Royal Ascot and he was still galloping on at the finish. (5/1)
2559 Celeric had an almost impossible task trying to concede weight to all his rivals and his effort three furlongs out came to little and he was never a serious factor. (2/1)
3149 Election Day (IRE) should have been thereabouts but he ran very flat and he was treading ground early in the straight. (6/1)
2837* Corradini is a very unimpressive mover at the best of times but he hobbled to post on this occasion and, despite a short-lived effort soon after entering the straight, he eventually finished tailed-off and was reported to have finished lame. (12/1)

3646 JUDDMONTE INTERNATIONAL STKS (Gp 1) (3-Y.O+) (Class A)
3-10 (3-10) **1m 2f 85y** £202,152.00 (£69,312.00: £32,781.00: £12,855.00) Stalls: Low GOING: 0.13 sec per fur (G)

			SP	RR	SF
3050 4	**Singspiel (IRE) (128)** (MRStoute) **5-9-5** LDettori(2) (chsd ldr: led over 3f out: hrd drvn: r.o gamely)....—	**1**	4/1 2	135	90
2454a*	**Desert King (IRE)** (APO'Brien,Ireland) **3-8-11** MJKinane(1) (swtg: plld hrd: hld up: outpcd 3f out: styd on u.p ins fnl f)....1½	**2**	6/1	133	80
2527 2	**Benny The Dip (USA) (126)** (JHMGosden) **3-8-11** WRyan(3) (lw: led tl over 3f out: rdn & one pce appr fnl f)1½	**3**	9/2 3	130	77
2527 3	**Bosra Sham (USA) (133)** (HRACecil) **4-9-2** PatEddery(4) (hld up: effrt over 3f out: sn rdn: no imp)....1¼	**4**	4/5 1	126	81

(SP 108.0%) **4 Rn**

2m 12.1 (3.10) CSF £20.82 TOTE £4.00 (£8.90) OWNER Sheikh Mohammed (NEWMARKET) BRED Sheikh Mohammed bin Rashid al Maktoum
WEIGHT FOR AGE 3yo-8lb
OFFICIAL EXPLANATION **Bosra Sham (USA): lost her near-fore shoe during the race.**

3050 Singspiel (IRE) has had all the superlatives rained on him in the past and this comfortably-gained success was just another to add to his world-wide victories. The fact that Dettori ranks him as the best he as ridden leaves nothing else to be said. (4/1: 9/4-9/2)
2454a* Desert King (IRE), a dual Classic winner in Ireland this year, did himself no favours by taking such a keen tug in the early stages. Tapped for toe when the pace quickened three furlongs out, he was into his stride again inside the distance but, by then, the winner had it all sewn up. (6/1)
2527 Benny The Dip (USA), never afraid to force the pace, kept battling on once headed and he certainly lost no caste in defeat in this company. (9/2)

2527 Bosra Sham (USA) lost her specially-fitted near-fore shoe at halfway and it was sure to have had a bearing on her performance, for she was in trouble passing the three-furlong marker and was unable to deliver a challenge despite staying on. (4/5: op evens)

3647 GREAT VOLTIGEUR STKS (Gp 2) (3-Y.O C & G) (Class A)

3-45 (3-45) **1m 3f 195y** £55,888.00 (£20,113.00: £9,619.00: £3,895.00: £1,510.00) Stalls: Low GOING: 0.13 sec per fur (G)

				SP	RR	SF
3109*	**Stowaway** (SbinSuroor) **3-8-9** LDettori(3) (lw: trckd ldng pair: hdwy 3f out: shkn up 2f out: r.o to ld cl home)	—	**1**	6/5[1]	123	67
2454a[5]	**Silver Patriarch (IRE) (123)** (JLDunlop) **3-8-9** PatEddery(2) (hld up: hdwy 3f out: led 2f out: rdn & edgd lft: ct nr fin)	½	**2**	15/8[2]	122	66
3050[8]	**Kingfisher Mill (USA) (118)** (MrsJCecil) **3-8-12** MJKinane(5) (swtg: chsd clr ldr: led wl over 2f out: sn hdd: nt qckn fnl f)	1¾	**3**	4/1[3]	123	67
1399[3]	**Apprehension (105)** (DRLoder) **3-8-9** RCochrane(1) (lw: hld up: hdwy 3f out: sn ev ch: wknd over 1f out)	4	**4**	16/1	115	59
2515[3]	**Garuda (IRE) (104)** (JLDunlop) **3-8-9** JReid(4) (plld hrd: led & sn wl clr: wknd & hdd wl over 2f out: t.o)	24	**5**	50/1	82	26

(SP 108.1%) **5 Rn**

2m 33.23 (5.43) CSF £3.22 TOTE £2.20: £1.30 £1.20 (£1.80) OWNER Godolphin (NEWMARKET) BRED Hesmonds Stud Ltd

3109* Stowaway had to work hard to take the measure of the runner-up nearing the line but he showed what a progressive colt he really his and will now take his chance in the St Leger over a trip his jockey thinks will be made to measure. (6/5)

2454a Silver Patriarch (IRE) looked sure to win when gaining the advantage two furlongs out but he was inclined to edge left when the pressure was on and forfeited his lead close home. On this occasion he did not appear to be helping his jockey and there was no doubt he should have won this but he will have the chance to gain his revenge over another quarter-mile in the St Leger. (15/8)

3050 Kingfisher Mill (USA), penalised 3lb for winning the King Edward VII Stakes at Royal Ascot, gave a good account of himself at the weights and it was only his lack of finishing speed that was costing him dearly in the battle to the line. (4/1)

1399 Apprehension had little chance of turning the tables on a couple of the principals even over this slightly longer trip but he performed with credit and, for one so short on experience, was far from disgraced. (16/1)

2515 Garuda (IRE) took a fearsome hold to post and took charge once in action, and he only succeeded in running himself into the ground. (50/1)

3648 MELROSE RATED STKS H'CAP (0-100) (3-Y.O) (Class B)

4-15 (4-15) **1m 5f 194y** £16,483.00 (£6,097.00: £2,923.50: £1,192.50: £471.25: £182.75) Stalls: Low GOING: 0.13 sec per fur (G)

				SP	RR	SF
3218[11]	**Sausalito Bay (85)** (IABalding) **3-8-8** KFallon(6) (hld up: hdwy 4f out: led over 2f out: clr fnl f)	—	**1**	10/1	98	68
3333[6]	**Mithak (USA) (85)** (BWHills) **3-8-8v[1]** RHills(3) (bhd: hmpd ent st: gd hdwy 3f out: hung lft appr fnl f: no ch w wnr)	6	**2**	10/1	91	61
3218*	**Liffre (IRE) (85)** (JHMGosden) **3-8-8** LDettori(12) (sn in tch: led over 3f out tl over 2f out: wknd fnl f)	2½	**3**	7/2[3]	88	58
2133[11]	**Marathon Maid (82)** (RAFahey) **3-7-12**(7) RWinston(4) (hdwy 6f out: rdn over 2f out: outpcd)	5	**4**	66/1	79	49
3218[3]	**Georgia Venture (81)** (SPCWoods) **3-8-4** GDuffield(7) (chsd ldrs: led 4f out: sn hdd: wknd appr fnl f)	nk	**5**	10/1	78	48
3125[8]	**Cyrian (IRE) (87)** (PFICole) **3-8-10** KDarley(1) (bhd whn hmpd ent st: styd on fnl 2f)	½	**6**	20/1	84	54
3021*	**Zerpour (IRE) (94)** (LMCumani) **3-9-3** JReid(8) (lw: hld up & bhd: gd hdwy over 4f out: rdn 3f out: sn wknd: t.o)	13	**7**	11/4[1]	76	46
3109[9]	**Solo Mio (IRE) (98)** (BWHills) **3-9-7** PatEddery(5) (trckd ldrs: lost tch over 5f out: t.o)	13	**8**	16/1	65	35
3190[16]	**Papua (95)** (IABalding) **3-9-4** MRoberts(9) (plld hrd: sn prom: wknd over 3f out: t.o)	5	**9**	25/1	56	26
2647[4]	**Ciro's Pearl (IRE) (82)** (MHTompkins) **3-8-5** DBiggs(2) (rdn along 7f out: hmpd appr st: sn t.o)	10	**10**	20/1	31	1
2963*	**High Intrigue (IRE) (81)** (HRACecil) **3-8-4** WRyan(10) (lw: led to 4f out: sn lost pl: t.o)	5	**11**	100/30[2]	25	—
3333[9]	**Happy Minstral (USA) (88)** (MJohnston) **3-8-11** DHolland(11) (swtg: w ldrs: rdn 7f out: hmpd over 3f out: t.o)	s.h	**12**	16/1	31	1

(SP 125.9%) **12 Rn**

2m 59.56 (5.96) CSF £97.90 CT £392.58 TOTE £10.00: £2.20 £3.30 £1.80 (£56.10) Trio £62.40 OWNER Mr J. C. Smith (KINGSCLERE) BRED Littleton Stud

LONG HANDICAP Georgia Venture 8-3

OFFICIAL EXPLANATION **Sausalito Bay: regarding the improvement in form, the colt had been unsuited by the undulating track last time.**

2647 Sausalito Bay had no right to win this on all known form but he knew differently and, leading on the approach to the last quarter-mile, quickly scooted clear to win as he pleased. (10/1)

3333 Mithak (USA), tried in a visor on this occasion, did extremely well to make the frame after finding trouble entering the straight for he was a back-marker at the time, and it is obvious that he has more ability than he cares to show most of the time. (10/1)

3218* Liffre (IRE) was always going to be the one to beat but she was given every chance only for the winner to show her who was boss on this occasion. (7/2)

Marathon Maid is bred to need middle distances but she was jumping into the unknown this time and, from early in the straight, she was struggling to make any impression. At one of the smaller tracks she could well win at this trip. (66/1)

3218 Georgia Venture stays this trip well and she ran up to her mark but, on this more yielding ground, she was very leg-weary approaching the final furlong. (10/1)

3125 Cyrian (IRE), one of the main sufferers entering the straight, did begin to pick up in the latter stages and he is capable of improving on this. (20/1)

3021* Zerpour (IRE), taking on handicappers this time, improved smoothly and put himself in with a winning chance early in the straight but, once off the bridle, he showed his inexperience and gave the impression that he did not see the trip out. (11/4)

3649 EAGLE LANE H'CAP (0-100) (3-Y.O+) (Class C)

4-45 (4-47) **6f** £14,612.50 (£4,375.00: £2,100.00: £962.50) Stalls: High GOING: 0.13 sec per fur (G)

				SP	RR	SF
2561[2]	**Plaisir d'Amour (IRE) (85)** (NACallaghan) **3-8-10** PatEddery(16) (hld up gng wl: hdwy over 2f out: r.o u.p to ld cl home)	—	**1**	8/1[1]	96	70
3604[3]	**Tiler (IRE) (78)** (MJohnston) **5-8-6** DHolland(9) (mde most tl hrd rdn & hdd nr fin)	½	**2**	8/1[1]	88	65
3410[3]	**Blessingindisguise (95)** (MWEasterby) **4-9-9b** MJKinane(21) (racd alone stands' side: gd hdwy & hung lft over 1f out: unable qckn)	hd	**3**	9/1[2]	104	81
3011[5]	**World Premier (94)** (CEBrittain) **4-9-8** MRoberts(17) (chsd ldrs: ev ch fnl f: r.o)	s.h	**4**	10/1[3]	103	80
3208[3]	**Benzoe (IRE) (80)** (MrsJRRamsden) **7-8-8** JFortune(14) (lw: reard s: hdwy fnl 2f: nrst fin)	1¾	**5**	14/1	85	62
3604[7]	**Mr Teigh (74)** (MrsJRRamsden) **5-8-2** FLynch(19) (a chsng ldrs: nt qckn fnl 2f)	2	**6**	12/1	73	50
3385*	**Mr Bergerac (IRE) (86)** (BPalling) **6-9-0** LDettori(3) (lw: hdwy over 2f out: sn rdn: nt rch ldrs)	1½	**7**	11/1	81	58
3273[10]	**Perryston View (83)** (PCalver) **5-8-11** KDarley(2) (lw: w ldrs tl wknd over 1f out)	½	**8**	16/1	77	54
3604[20]	**Venture Capitalist (100)** (DNicholls) **8-10-0** RCochrane(7) (swtchd rt s: hdwy & n.m.r 2f out: nvr nrr)	1	**9**	20/1	91	68
3423[8]	**Madly Sharp (91)** (JWWatts) **6-9-5** JReid(12) (in tch: effrt over 2f out: wknd over 1f out)	½	**10**	16/1	81	58
2925[4]	**Silca Key Silca (83)** (MRChannon) **3-8-5**(3) PPMurphy(8) (trckd ldrs over 4f)	2	**11**	25/1	68	42

				SP	RR	SF
3217[21]	**The Gay Fox (86)** (BAMcMahon) **3-8-11** GDuffield(4) (b: trckd ldrs: rdn over 2f out: sn btn)	nk	**12**	33/1	70	44
3410[8]	**Young Bigwig (IRE) (90)** (JBerry) **3-8-10**(5) PRoberts(10) (in tch tl outpcd fnl 2f)	nk	**13**	25/1	73	47
3437*	**Present Generation (80)** (RGuest) **4-8-8** SSanders(18) (chsd ldrs over 3f)	nk	**14**	20/1	62	39
3508a[2]	**Zuhair (90)** (DMcCain) **4-9-4** JCarroll(15) (b: swtg: prom over 3f)	1	**15**	20/1	70	47
3066*	**Purple Fling (73)** (DWChapman) **6-8-1** JQuinn(11) (n.d)	1	**16**	20/1	50	27
3185[5]	**Almuhimm (USA) (86)** (TDBarron) **5-9-0** KFallon(23) (swtchd lft s: a in rr)	1½	**17**	11/1	59	36
3254[6]	**Grey Kingdom (75)** (MBrittain) **6-8-3** GBardwell(22) (chsd ldrs over 3f)	s.h	**18**	20/1	48	25
3410[6]	**Daawe (USA) (80)** (MrsVAAconley) **6-8-8** MDeering(5) (chsd ldrs far side over 3f)	1	**19**	16/1	50	27
2872[5]	**Music Gold (IRE) (92)** (WAO'Gorman) **4-9-6** EmmaO'Gorman(20) (outpcd)	2½	**20**	12/1	55	32
3410[14]	**Royal Dome (IRE) (73)** (MartynWane) **5-8-1** LCharnock(6) (chsd ldrs far side over 3f)	½	**21**	20/1	35	12
3604[12]	**Double Oscar (IRE) (77)** (DNicholls) **4-7-12b**(7) ANicholls(13) (s.s: a wl bhd)	s.h	**22**	14/1	39	16
3410[13]	**Lago Di Varano (84)** (RMWhitaker) **5-8-12v** DeanMcKeown(1) (b: reard s: a wl bhd)	1	**23**	25/1	43	20
				(SP 147.4%)	**23 Rn**	

1m 12.98 (2.48) CSF £61.79 CT £583.42 TOTE £8.20: £2.30 £2.00 £2.10 £2.90 (£28.30) Trio £62.80 OWNER Mr M Tabor & Mrs John Magnier (NEWMARKET) BRED L. K. and K. McCreery

WEIGHT FOR AGE 3yo-3lb

2561 Plaisir d'Amour (IRE), a very versatile filly, travelled really well behind the leaders. Set alight approaching the final furlong, she had to survive a barging match with Blessingindisguise before asserting her superiority nearing the line. (8/1)

3604 Tiler (IRE), who has been kept busy, set a telling gallop down the centre of the track and, battling on willingly, was only forced to give best in the dying strides. (8/1)

3410 Blessingindisguise, who has done all his winning at the minimum trip, certainly seems to get the six on this evidence. (9/1)

3011 World Premier ran possibly his best race this year, being in the firing line with every chance until finding an extra effort beyond him close home. He is back to something like his best. (10/1)

3208 Benzoe (IRE) gave trouble in the stalls and was on his hind legs as they were released. Content to bide his time, he finished best of all and was without doubt a shade unlucky. (14/1)

3604 Mr Teigh, making a quick reappearance, does not appear to have the speed to win at this trip but he was in with every chance below the distance before being tapped for toe. He is at his peak at present and should be noted when he tackles a more suitable trip. (12/1)

3650 EGLINTON NURSERY H'CAP (2-Y.O) (Class C)

5-15 (5-18) **6f 214y** £12,135.00 (£3,630.00: £1,740.00: £795.00) Stalls: High GOING: 0.13 sec per fur (G)

				SP	RR	SF
3099*	**Optimistic (73)** (MHTompkins) **2-8-2** DBiggs(4) (trckd ldrs: led over 1f out: drvn clr)	—	**1**	11/2[2]	81+	35
3036*	**Alconleigh (92)** (MJohnston) **2-9-7** MRoberts(3) (chsd ldr: led 2f out: sn hdd: outpcd fnl f)	3	**2**	5/1[1]	93	47
2714[3]	**Flower O'Cannie (IRE) (86)** (MWEasterby) **2-9-1** MJKinane(1) (bhd: rdn 3f out: styd on appr fnl f)	¾	**3**	12/1	85	39
3084*	**Simply Gifted (75)** (TDEasterby) **2-8-4** LCharnock(2) (chsd ldrs: styd on u.p fnl 2f)	nk	**4**	8/1	74	28
3258[3]	**Carbon (85)** (DMorley) **2-9-0** KFallon(10) (lw: hdwy u.p ½-wy: styd on towards fin)	nk	**5**	15/2	83	37
3215[3]	**King Darius (IRE) (79)** (RHannon) **2-8-8** PatEddery(9) (outpcd & bhd: hdwy 2f out: nvr nr to chal)	3	**6**	6/1[3]	70	24
3237[11]	**Leofric (70)** (MJPolglase) **2-7-13b** JTate(5) (led: clr ½-wy: wknd & hdd 2f out)	5	**7**	25/1	50	4
3433*	**Bernardo Bellotto (IRE) (84)** (MBell) **2-8-13** LDettori(7) (lw: hld up: hdwy over 2f out: sn rdn & wknd)	2½	**8**	8/1	58	12
2739[3]	**Half A Knicker (67)** (RAFahey) **2-7-10** JQuinn(12) (bhd: rdn ½-wy: no imp)	3½	**9**	12/1	33	—
2786[10]	**Lakeland Pride (IRE) (77)** (PDEvans) **2-8-6** JFEgan(11) (a bhd)	1½	**10**	25/1	40	—
3113[3]	**Zizi (IRE) (83)** (KRBurke) **2-8-7**(5) CLowther(13) (outpcd fr ½-wy)	nk	**11**	11/1	45	—
3387[2]	**Sick As A Parrot (70)** (CADwyer) **2-7-13** GBardwell(8) (outpcd fnl 3f: t.o)	5	**12**	10/1	20	—
*2604**	**Colonel Custer (70)** (CWThornton) **2-7-13** AMackay(14) (unruly s: a bhd: t.o)	10	**13**	16/1	—	—
3438*	**Cool Secret (80)** (ABMulholland) **2-8-9** DWright(6) (sn bhd & rdn along: t.o)	4	**14**	12/1	—	—
				(SP 134.4%)	**14 Rn**	

1m 28.21 (5.21) CSF £33.98 CT £245.75 TOTE £6.40: £2.30 £2.10 £5.30 (£20.60) Trio £144.10 OWNER Mystic Meg Ltd (NEWMARKET) BRED Worksop Manor Stud Farm

3099* Optimistic confirmed the promise shown at Yarmouth with a smoothly-gained success in her first Nursery and she is certainly capable of following up. (11/2)

3036* Alconleigh has been in fine form all season but this attempt to concede 19lb to the improving filly was way beyond him. There was no disgrace in this defeat. (5/1)

2714 Flower O'Cannie (IRE) has only ever won on much more testing ground than she had here and she was only finding top gear when it was all but over. (12/1)

3084* Simply Gifted, still short on experience, stayed on well in the latter stages and there is more improvement to come. (8/1)

3258 Carbon, trying a slightly longer trip, kept staying on under strong pressure without finding the speed to launch a bid. (15/2)

3215 King Darius (IRE), once again, was only finding his stride when the race was as good as over. As he acts in more testing ground, perhaps that is what he needs. (6/1)

T/Jkpt: Not won; £58,598.09 to York 20/8/97. T/Plpt: £108.40 (620.32 Tckts). T/Qdpt: £20.30 (143.88 Tckts) IM

3651a - 3671a : (Irish Racing) - See Computer Raceform

3169a-CURRAGH (Newbridge, Ireland) (R-H) (Good to yielding)
Saturday August 16th

3672a FLAME OF TARA TYROS STKS (Listed) (2-Y.O)

3-00 (3-03) **7f** IR £12,900.00 (IR £3,700.00: IR £1,700.00: IR £500.00) GOING minus 0.06 sec per fur (G)

				SP	RR	SF
2811a[2]	**King Of Kings (IRE)** (APO'Brien,Ireland) **2-9-4** CRoche (hld up: rn 3rd: chal fr 2f out: shkn up to ld over 1f out: led wl over 1f out: drifted rt ins last: r.o.)	—	**1**	2/9[1]	107	60
2680*	**Sharp Play** (MJohnston) **2-9-1** JWeaver (rn 2nd: led over 2f out: hdd wl over 1f out: no ex: kpt on wl: nt trble wnr)	1½	**2**	5/1[2]	101	54
	Photogenic (APO'Brien,Ireland) **2-8-8** JAHeffernan (rn 4th: 3rd & no imp 1½f out: kpt on)	4	**3**	8/1[3]	84	37
	Tittle Tattle (IRE) (GMLyons,Ireland) **2-8-8** KJManning (towards rr: rdn & no imp 2f out)	8	**4**	25/1	66	19
	Pelagius (IRE) (JOxx,Ireland) **2-9-1b** JPMurtagh (led: hdd over 2f out: sn btn & wknd)	3	**5**	8/1[3]	66	19
				(SP 124.6%)	**5 Rn**	

1m 26.1 (3.10) OWNER Mrs John Magnier (PILTOWN)

2811a King Of Kings (IRE) did not impress in this exercise of giving 3lb to a York maiden winner. He quickened to lead but, once in front, looked very indifferent to what he was supposed to be doing. Admittedly, his high head carriage is unattractive, but he edged right in the closing stages and did not appear keen to exert himself. (2/9)
2680* Sharp Play was just done for a turn of foot. His jockey felt he struck into himself two furlongs out. (5/1)

3673a : (Irish Racing) - See Computer Raceform

3674a RIDGEWOOD PEARL DESMOND STKS (Gp 3) (3-Y.O+)
4-00 (4-00) **1m (New)** IR £19,500.00 (IR £5,700.00: IR £2,700.00: IR £900.00) GOING minus 0.06 sec per fur (G)

				SP	RR	SF
3362a5	**Swift Gulliver (IRE)** (JSBolger,Ireland) **3-8-8** KJManning (cl up: 3rd ½-wy: 2nd & chal 2f out: led 1f out: r.o u.p)	—	**1**	10/1	109	48
1062a*	**Dangerous Diva (IRE)** (APO'Brien,Ireland) **3-8-5** JAHeffernan (6th ½-wy: chsd ldrs: 4th u.p 1½f out: kpt on ins last)	¾	**2**	12/1	105	44
3371a3	**Supercal** (DRCElsworth) **3-8-5** SDrowne (hld up towards rr: rdn & hdwy over 2f out: 5th 1f out: kpt on u.p)	nk	**3**	10/1	104	43
2078a2	**Cool Edge (IRE)** (MHTompkins) **6-9-4** RHughes (rn 2nd: led under 3f out: hdd 1f out: no ex u.p: kpt on)	½	**4**	11/2	110	55
	Nobility (IRE) (JOxx,Ireland) **3-8-8** JPMurtagh (hld up in tch: trckd ldrs ½-wy: 3rd & effrt 1½f out: nt rch ldrs ins last: kpt on)	hd	**5**	5/1 3	106	45
2454a6	**Verglas (IRE)** (KPrendergast,Ireland) **3-8-8** WJSupple (hld up in tch: 4th ½-wy: rdn & chsd ldrs 2f out: 6th & no ex 1½f out)	½	**6**	4/1 2	105	44
31246	**Gothenberg (IRE)** (MJohnston) **4-9-7** JWeaver (led: hdd under 3f out: 4th & btn 2f out)	7	**7**	3/1 1	98	43
3144*	**Beauchamp King** (JLDunlop) **4-9-0** MJKinane (towards rr: trailing over 2f out: n.d)	6	**8**	7/1	79	24

(SP 115.4%) **8 Rn**

1m 38.8 (3.80) OWNER Ballylinch Stud (COOLCULLEN)
3362a Swift Gulliver (IRE), not particularly well treated at the weights, bounced back to form with a solid performance. He suffered badly from a muscle problem in the spring, and did not reappear until late July. Eased up when a trailing fifth behind Tout A Coup at Cork last time in heavy ground, he was a revelation here and his trainer, while mindful of the Irish Champion Stakes, says he could well drop back in distance. (10/1)
1062a* Dangerous Diva (IRE), absent since May, is one to keep on the right side of this autumn. (12/1: op 8/1)
3371a Supercal ran best of the English raiders and is another improving three-year-old filly. (10/1)
2078a Cool Edge (IRE) found his younger rivals too strong over the last furlong. (11/2)
Nobility (IRE) had only one pace from a furlong and a half out. (5/1)
2454a Verglas (IRE), presented with his best opportunity of the season, was again a disappointment. (4/1)
3124 Gothenberg (IRE), sent off in front as usual, was never really dominating and weakened two and a half furlongs out. (3/1)
3144* Beauchamp King just did not want to know. (7/1: op 4/1)

3675a ROYAL WHIP STKS (Gp 3) (3-Y.O+)
4-30 (4-33) **1m 2f** IR £19,500.00 (IR £5,700.00: IR £2,700.00: IR £900.00) GOING minus 0.06 sec per fur (G)

				SP	RR	SF
21047	**King Alex** (RCharlton) **4-9-1** MJKinane (hld up: 5th 4f out: 3rd & chal 1½f out: led early ins last: r.o u.p)	—	**1**	7/2 2	118	89
	Rayouni (IRE) (JOxx,Ireland) **3-8-8**ow1 JPMurtagh (rn 3rd: wnt 2nd 3f out: sn chal: disp ld & ev ch 1f out: 2nd, rdn & rallied ins last: r.o.)	s.h	**2**	11/4 1	119+	81
17365	**Oscar Schindler (IRE)** (KPrendergast,Ireland) **5-9-10** SCraine (hld up towards rr: cld 2f out: 4th 1f out: r.o u.p fnl f)	½	**3**	13/2 3	126	97
26564	**Catienus (USA)** (MRStoute) **3-8-7** JWeaver (led tl early ins last: kpt on u.p)	nk	**4**	8/1	117	80
3510a3	**Via Verbano (IRE)** (JSBolger,Ireland) **3-8-4** PJSmullen (hld up: rn 4th: 5th & effrt 2f out: no imp over 1f out)	6	**5**	12/1	104	67
1195a*	**Ashley Park (IRE)** (CO'Brien,Ireland) **3-8-10** CRoche (hld up towards rr: rdn over 2f out: n.d)	11	**6**	13/2 3	92	55
3172a3	**Strawberry Roan (IRE)** (APO'Brien,Ireland) **3-8-4** JAHeffernan (sn chsng ldr tl over 3f out: 3rd u.p 2f out: sn wknd)	¾	**7**	13/2 3	85	48

(SP 107.7%) **7 Rn**

2m 4.8 (0.80) OWNER Mr Wafic Said (BECKHAMPTON) BRED Jon Hanson
2104 King Alex, in a fast-run race, was pushed right out to get his nose in front virtually on the line. He was hampered by the runner-up a furlong and a half out and would have gained the spoils anyway. (7/2)
Rayouni (IRE) edged left a furlong and a half out, hampering the eventual winner, and he got to the front soon after, looking all over a winner until pipped close home. He will improve. (11/4)
1736 Oscar Schindler (IRE), over a distance much too short for him, ran an excellent trial for the Irish St Leger and will bid for a double in that Classic without the benefit of another race. He looks physically better than ever. (13/2)
2656 Catienus (USA), headed inside the last, kept plugging on and this was possibly his best ever performance. (8/1)
3510a Via Verbano (IRE) (12/1: op 8/1)
1195a* Ashley Park (IRE), weak in the market, was very slow to get going and dropped right away in the straight. (13/2)
3172a Strawberry Roan (IRE) seems to have missed the boat now. (13/2)

3676a - 3684a : (Irish Racing) - See Computer Raceform

1587-KEMPTON (R-H) (Good)
Wednesday August 20th
WEATHER: v.hot WIND: almost nil

3685 CARA APPRENTICE H'CAP (0-70) (3-Y.O) (Class E)
5-30 (5-31) **1m 1f (round)** £2,817.25 (£853.00: £416.50: £198.25) Stalls: High GOING minus 0.24 sec per fur (GF)

				SP	RR	SF
33822	**Interdream (70)** (RHannon) **3-9-2**(5) RSmith(3) (b.hind: hdwy 3f out: hung lft & led over 1f out: r.o wl)	—	**1**	3/1 1	80	47
27304	**First Chance (IRE) (68)** (DRCElsworth) **3-9-0**(5) JFowle(2) (hdwy 7f out: led 3f out tl over 1f out: unable qckn)	3½	**2**	4/1 3	72	39
31833	**Zorro (53)** (RMFlower) **3-8-4** JWilkinson(6) (lost pl 4f out: rallied over 1f out: one pce)	3½	**3**	3/1 1	51	18
32994	**Baubigny (USA) (57)** (MRChannon) **3-8-8** AEddery(1) (lw: chsd ldr: led over 4f out to 3f out: wknd over 1f out)	10	**4**	14/1	37	4
33946	**Summerville Wood (62)** (PMooney) **3-8-8**(5) PFitzsimons(4) (bhd fnl 6f)	2	**5**	14/1	38	5
32779	**Stormy Story (USA) (66)** (JHMGosden) **3-9-0**(3) PFredericks(7) (s.s: hdwy over 7f out: wknd over 3f out)	2	**6**	7/2 2	39	6

1256[14]	**Chaluz (47)** (KRBurke) **3-7-12** PDoe(5) (bit bkwd: led over 4f: wknd over 3f out)	24	**7**	12/1	—	—
				(SP 113.2%)		**7 Rn**

1m 54.83 (4.23) CSF £13.63 TOTE £2.80: £2.00 £2.50 (£5.90) OWNER Mr Charles Farr & Mr Mark Heaton (MARLBOROUGH) BRED Mrs G. Kindersley

IN-FOCUS: **This was Richard Smith's first winner in Britain.**

3382 Interdream continues in sparkling form despite being 10lb higher than when last successful. Despite hanging, he led approaching the final furlong and, although ending up on the stands' rails, proved far too good for his rivals. (3/1)

2730 First Chance (IRE) has yet to win on turf but moved to the front entering the straight. Collared below the distance, she was firmly put in her place by the wandering winner. She needs some leniency from the Handicapper. (4/1)

3183 Zorro found the drop in distance a bit too sharp for him for he got outpaced turning for home. Rallying below the distance, to take third place, it looked as if he might trouble the front two but then failed to find another gear. (3/1)

3299 Baubigny (USA) is proving something of a headache for connections who have tried him at various distances between seven furlongs and a mile and three-quarters this season with little success. Not surprisingly, he is tumbling in the handicap, but had been seen off below the distance. (14/1)

772 Summerville Wood never threatened over this longer trip. Both his wins to date have come over six furlongs. (14/1: 8/1-16/1)

3277 Stormy Story (USA) was very disappointing on this handicap debut following an eye-catching run at Windsor last time out and had been hung out to dry turning for home. (7/2)

3686 E.B.F. MEDIAN AUCTION MAIDEN STKS (2-Y.O) (Class E)

6-00 (6-05) **6f** £3,064.25 (£929.00: £454.50: £217.25) Stalls: High GOING minus 0.24 sec per fur (GF)

				SP	RR	SF
3278[5]	**Roi de Danse** (JWHills) **2-9-0** RHills(3) (racd stands' side: hld up: rdn over 2f out: led last strides)	—	**1**	16/1	72	32
504[5]	**Mantles Pride** (GLewis) **2-8-11**(3) AWhelan(5) (b: racd stands' side: a.p: led over 3f out: rdn over 2f out: hdd last strides)	hd	**2**	10/1[3]	72	32
3479[W]	**Saddlers' Roe (IRE)** (BWHills) **2-8-11**(3) JDSmith(6) (racd stands' side: a.p: rdn over 2f out: one pce fnl f)	2	**3**	12/1	66	26
3497[6]	**Oh So Easy** (BJMeehan) **2-9-0** MTebbutt(23) (hdwy over 1f out: one pce fnl f)	5	**4**	33/1	53	13
3306[15]	**Jack Ruby** (PLGilligan) **2-8-9**(5) APolli(16) (a.p: rdn over 1f out: one pce)	1½	**5**	66/1	49	9
2524[6]	**Da Boss** (WRMuir) **2-8-7**(7) JWilkinson(20) (a.p: rdn over 2f out: one pce)	hd	**6**	11/4[1]	49	9
	Tattinger (JRFanshawe) **2-8-9** NVarley(1) (w'like: bit bkwd: racd stands' side: hld up: rdn over 2f out: wknd over 1f out)	½	**7**	14/1	43	3
	Plastered In Paris (IRE) (BJMeehan) **2-9-0** SWhitworth(22) (neat: bit bkwd: hdwy over 1f out: one pce)	1	**8**	16/1	45	5
	Rhapsody In Blue (IRE) (AndrewTurnell) **2-9-0** NAdams(2) (b.off hind: leggy: bit bkwd: racd stands' side: outpcd: nvr nrr)	2½	**9**	66/1	38	—
3084[3]	**Di Matteo (IRE)** (BHanbury) **2-9-0** WRyan(19) (a mid div)	2	**10**	4/1[2]	33	—
2917[12]	**Tom** (LordHuntingdon) **2-9-0** MFenton(18) (dwlt: nvr nrr)	1¼	**11**	20/1	30	—
	Algaleb (HAkbary) **2-9-0** GHind(4) (b: w'like: racd stands' side: led over 2f: wknd over 2f out)	2	**12**	25/1	24	—
	Roberty Bob (IRE) (PTWalwyn) **2-9-0** AMcGlone(24) (str: scope: bkwd: outpcd: nvr nrr)	s.h	**13**	14/1	24	—
3278[8]	**Petane (IRE)** (JRArnold) **2-8-9**(5) GFaulkner(10) (prom over 3f)	nk	**14**	33/1	23	—
2943[9]	**After Eight** (RWArmstrong) **2-9-0** RPrice(14) (spd over 4f)	1	**15**	33/1	21	—
	Komistar (PWHarris) **2-9-0** AClark(12) (neat: dwlt: outpcd)	¾	**16**	20/1	19	—
3136[6]	**Sharp Steel** (GLMoore) **2-9-0** CandyMorris(7) (swtg: prom over 3f)	½	**17**	25/1	17	—
3278[10]	**Dawn Treader (USA)** (RHannon) **2-9-0** DaneO'Neill(17) (dwlt: outpcd)	nk	**18**	16/1	16	—
	Polish Pilot (IRE) (WRMuir) **2-9-0** JStack(15) (w'like: bit bkwd: prom 4f)	¾	**19**	25/1	14	—
1251[9]	**Memorial (IRE)** (RHannon) **2-9-0** CRutter(11) (lw: bhd fnl 2f)	¾	**20**	16/1	12	—
2768[15]	**Porthilly Buoy** (MJHaynes) **2-8-7**(7) MCornally(13) (swtg: a bhd)		**21**	66/1	—	—
3136[9]	**Tiara** (BJMeehan) **2-8-9** NDay(9) (bhd fnl 2f)		**22**	20/1	—	—
	Uther Pendragon (IRE) (JABennett) **2-9-0** SophieMitchell(8) (leggy: bit bkwd: bhd fnl 2f)		**23**	66/1	—	—
				(SP 140.9%)		**23 Rn**

1m 14.48 (3.28) CSF £149.10 TOTE £15.00: £3.10 £3.90 £3.00 (£164.60) Trio £166.40 OWNER Mr A. N. Miller (LAMBOURN) BRED A. N. Miller

OFFICIAL EXPLANATION **Uther Pendragon (IRE): the trainer reported that the colt finished distressed.**

3278 Roi de Danse, the most experienced in the line up, was one of six who elected to race on the stands' side. Throwing down his challenge from below the distance, he had a tremendous duel with the runner-up and managed to poke his head in front in the last couple of strides. (16/1)

504 Mantles Pride, off the course since his debut here back in March, was a different proposition on this occasion now that he has had several months to do develop. Gaining overall control just before halfway, it looked as if he was going to hold on, only to be overhauled in the last couple of strides. He should soon go one better. (10/1: 12/1-8/1)

2243 Saddlers' Roe (IRE) was happier with the return to a sound surface and was always close up on the favoured stands' side. On the heels of the front two below the distance, he then failed to find another gear. (12/1)

3497 Oh So Easy, racing on the far side, came through to show in front on that part of the course inside the final furlong but found the leaders on the stands' side already home and dry. (33/1)

Jack Ruby ran much better here. Moving to the front on the far side over a quarter of a mile from home, he did not have overall control and was collared on that side of the course inside the final furlong. (66/1)

2524 Da Boss, never far away on the far side, could only struggle on in his own time in the final quarter-mile. (11/4)

Tattinger (14/1: 8/1-16/1)

Roberty Bob (IRE) (14/1: 10/1-16/1)

3687 E.B.F. IRISH POST MAIDEN STKS (2-Y.O) (Class D)

6-30 (6-35) **7f (Jubilee)** £3,485.00 (£1,055.00: £515.00: £245.00) Stalls: High GOING minus 0.24 sec per fur (GF)

				SP	RR	SF
3193[3]	**Secret Archive** (RHannon) **2-9-0** PatEddery(8) (mde all: all out)	—	**1**	10/11[1]	79	41
3201[6]	**Taverner Society (IRE)** (RWArmstrong) **2-9-0** RPrice(7) (hdwy 2f out: chsd wnr 1f out: ev ch ins fnl f: r.o)	½	**2**	14/1	78	40
3084[2]	**Balaclava (IRE)** (EALDunlop) **2-9-0** WRyan(1) (a.p: ev ch over 1f out: unable qckn)	2½	**3**	10/1[3]	72	34
	Canadian Puzzler (USA) (PWHarris) **2-9-0** AClark(4) (str: bit bkwd: s.s: rdn & hdwy 2f out: r.o one pce)	2	**4**	16/1	68	30
	Sensory (BWHills) **2-8-11**(3) JDSmith(6) (w'like: scope: rdn over 2f out: hdwy over 1f out: nvr nrr)	¾	**5**	14/1	66	28
	Mister Benjamin (IRE) (SPCWoods) **2-9-0** NDay(11) (leggy: scope: a.p: rdn over 2f out: wknd fnl f)	½	**6**	25/1	65	27
	Royal Ground (IRE) (MRChannon) **2-8-7**(7) AEddery(3) (neat: nvr nrr)	2	**7**	33/1	60	22
2948[6]	**Gallaash (USA)** (JHMGosden) **2-9-0** DaneO'Neill(2) (hld up: rdn 2f out: wknd over 1f out)	1¾	**8**	14/1	56	18
	Mashab (NAGraham) **2-9-0** RHills(17) (w'like: scope: hld up: nt clr run on ins & swtchd lft over 2f out: sn wknd)	1¼	**9**	20/1	53	15
	Miss Dilletante (RFJohnsonHoughton) **2-8-9** AMcGlone(14) (w'like: bit bkwd: a bhd)	1¼	**10**	20/1	45	7

Form	Horse	Dist	Pos	SP	RR	SF
3201[12]	**River Beat (IRE)** (MHTompkins) **2-8-7**(7) PClarke(16) (bdly hmpd on ins 6f out: a bhd)	nk	**11**	50/1	50	12
3151[10]	**La Lyonesse** (JWHills) **2-8-9** NAdams(12) (prom 5f)	1¾	**12**	33/1	41	3
	Caribbean Monarch (IRE) (MRStoute) **2-9-0** JReid(13) (leggy: scope: bit bkwd: plld hrd: hld up: rdn 2f out: wknd over 1f out)	2	**13**	8/1[2]	41	3
	Indy Knight (IRE) (MartynMeade) **2-8-9** FNorton(15) (leggy: s.s: a bhd)	¾	**14**	33/1	35	—
2699[9]	**Green Jacket** (JLDunlop) **2-9-0** GHind(5) (bit bkwd: prom over 4f)	nk	**15**	10/1[3]	39	1
2720[12]	***Zimzie*** (MJHaynes) **2-9-0** SWhitworth(9) (Withdrawn not under Starter's orders: rdr inj at s)		**W**	50/1	—	—
	Noreastern (IRE) (PFICole) **2-9-0** CRutter(10) (Withdrawn not under Starter's orders: ref to ent stalls)		**W**	10/1[3]	—	—

(SP 142.8%) **15 Rn**

1m 27.65 (3.15) CSF £14.06 TOTE £1.80: £1.10 £4.30 £2.00 (£16.20) Trio £21.20 OWNER Mr Mohamed Suhail (MARLBOROUGH) BRED Lord Halifax

3193 Secret Archive confirmed the promise shown at Goodwood on his debut but he will not forget this race in a hurry as it needed Eddery to be at his very strongest to get him home in front. (10/11)

3201 Taverner Society (IRE) ran a fine race here. Coming through to take second place entering the final furlong, he delivered a serious challenge to the winner and, although unable to get on top, made sure his rival had little left in the locker. He should soon go one better. (14/1)

3084 Balaclava (IRE) ran another sound race and threatened to take the lead early in the final quarter-mile. However, he was unable to find another gear in the final furlong. (10/1: 8/1-14/1)

Canadian Puzzler (USA), a half-brother to three winners in North America, looked as though he would benefit from this initial outing. Picking up ground at the same time as the runner-up a quarter of a mile from home, he stayed on if failing to find that vital turn of foot. (16/1)

Sensory, a good-bodied colt with plenty of scope, was being bustled along early in the straight. He stayed on well in the last furlong and a half and will have learnt a lot from this. (14/1: 7/1-16/1)

Mister Benjamin (IRE), quite a tall newcomer with plenty of scope, played an active role until lack of a previous run took its toll in the final furlong. (25/1)

2948 Gallaash (USA) (14/1: 10/1-16/1)

Green Jacket (10/1: 14/1-8/1)

Noreastern (IRE) (10/1: op 6/1)

3688 GUINNESS CONDITIONS STKS (2-Y.O) (Class C)

7-00 (7-01) **7f (Jubilee)** £4,393.29 (£1,644.70: £804.85: £346.75: £155.88: £79.53) Stalls: High GOING minus 0.24 sec per fur (GF)

Form	Horse	Dist	Pos	SP	RR	SF
3282*	**Mowbray (USA)** (PFICole) **2-9-2** JReid(3) (chsd ldr: rdn over 2f out: led nr fin)	—	**1**	5/1[2]	97	36
3103*	**Alboostan** (DMorley) **2-9-2** RHills(5) (led to 1f out: ev ch ins fnl f: r.o)	hd	**2**	5/1[2]	97	36
3215[2]	**Mantles Star (90)** (GLewis) **2-8-11** PatEddery(4) (hld up: led 1f out: hrd rdn: hdd nr fin)	s.h	**3**	13/8[1]	92	31
	Eagle's Cross (USA) (RCharlton) **2-8-8** AClark(6) (unf: bit bkwd: dwlt: rdn over 2f out: hdwy over 1f out: r.o one pce)	2	**4**	14/1	84	23
3331*	**Priceless** (WJHaggas) **2-9-2** WRyan(7) (a.p: rdn over 2f out: wknd fnl f)	nk	**5**	5/1[2]	91	30
2707[3]	**The Glow-Worm (IRE)** (BWHills) **2-8-13**(3) JDSmith(2) (prom over 4f)	1¼	**6**	14/1	89	28
3204[2]	**Wrekin Pilot (95)** (RHannon) **2-9-2** DaneO'Neill(1) (hdwy 2f out: wknd fnl f)	¾	**7**	8/1[3]	87	26

(SP 112.5%) **7 Rn**

1m 28.24 (3.74) CSF £26.26 TOTE £6.30: £2.70 £2.50 (£12.20) OWNER Sir George Meyrick (WHATCOMBE) BRED Helen C Alexander

3282* Mowbray (USA) put up a good display in this hot little race. Racing in second place, he appeared to be in trouble early in the straight but he stuck to his guns really well and eventually got on top near the line. He will be well suited by a step up to a mile. (5/1: 7/2-6/1)

3103* Alboostan ran a fine race in defeat. Taking the field along until collared a furlong out, he refused to lie down without a fight and only just failed in a tremendous three-way photo. He should soon regain the winning thread, possibly over a mile. (5/1)

3215 Mantles Star came through to lead a furlong out but he failed to shake off the front two and was worried out of it near the line. This trip is certainly his limit but he should soon find another race. (13/8)

Eagle's Cross (USA), an unfurnished colt, was certainly pitched in at the deep end on this racecourse debut but, despite looking in need of this and showing a rather high knee action in the straight, stayed on in encouraging style from below the distance to finish fourth. (14/1: op 6/1)

3331* Priceless was taking a step up in class and was running a good race, almost having every chance below the distance, before the extra furlong found him out. (5/1)

2707 The Glow-Worm (IRE) had been seen off early in the straight. (14/1: 10/1-16/1)

3689 EVENING STANDARD H'CAP (0-90) (3-Y.O+) (Class C)

7-30 (7-31) **1m 4f** £5,135.75 (£1,556.00: £760.50: £362.75) Stalls: High GOING minus 0.24 sec per fur (GF)

Form	Horse	Dist	Pos	SP	RR	SF
1922*	**Ridaiyma (IRE) (85)** (LMCumani) **3-9-2** PatEddery(1) (lw: chsd ldr: led 5f out: rdn over 2f out: clr over 1f out: drvn out)	—	**1**	5/2[1]	98	39
2292[4]	**Arctic Owl (82)** (JRFanshawe) **3-8-13** NDay(4) (rdn over 2f out: gd hdwy to chse wnr over 1f out: edgd rt & r.o wl ins fnl f)	nk	**2**	12/1	95	36
3184[2]	**Island Sanctuary (IRE) (81)** (PJMakin) **3-8-12** SSanders(7) (swtg: rdn over 2f out: hdwy over 1f out: r.o one pce)	2½	**3**	9/1	90	31
3026*	**Mutadarra (IRE) (69)** (WJMusson) **4-8-7**(3) JDSmith(3) (swtg: rdn over 2f out: hdwy & nt clr run on ins wl over 1f out: r.o one pce)	1¼	**4**	8/1[3]	77	28
2594[3]	**Myrtlebank (82)** (HRACecil) **3-8-13** WRyan(2) (lw: a.p: chsd wnr 5f out tl over 1f out: sn wknd)	1¾	**5**	13/2[2]	87	28
3434[7]	**Hoh Express (87)** (IABalding) **5-10-0** CRutter(5) (lw: rdn & n.m.r 2f out: hdwy over 1f out: one pce)	¾	**6**	16/1	91	42
2961[4]	**Typhoon Eight (IRE) (70)** (RWArmstrong) **5-8-11** RPrice(11) (swtg: hld up: rdn over 2f out: sn wknd)	3	**7**	9/1	70	21
2949[4]	**Nordansk (55)** (MMadgwick) **8-7-10** NVarley(9) (lw: hdwy over 2f out: wknd over 1f out)	s.h	**8**	16/1	55	6
3053[4]	**King Kato (86)** (MrsAJPerrett) **4-9-13** JReid(10) (led 7f: wknd over 1f out)	1½	**9**	10/1	84	35
3267*	**Al's Alibi (76)** (WRMuir) **4-9-3** DaneO'Neill(12) (swtg: prom over 9f)	3½	**10**	12/1	70	21
3434[6]	**Artic Courier (80)** (DJSCosgrove) **6-9-7** JStack(6) (b: hdwy 4f out: wknd over 2f out)	2	**11**	16/1	71	22
3053[W]	**Filial (IRE) (76)** (BJMeehan) **4-9-3** MTebbutt(8) (lw: hld up: rdn over 2f out: sn wknd)	3½	**12**	33/1	62	13

(SP 118.1%) **12 Rn**

2m 36.33 (6.33) CSF £30.96 CT £217.29 TOTE £3.60: £1.90 £3.80 £2.20 (£18.90) Trio £70.90 OWNER H H Aga Khan (NEWMARKET) BRED His Highness the Aga Khan's Studs S.C.

LONG HANDICAP Nordansk 7-9

WEIGHT FOR AGE 3yo-10lb

1922* Ridaiyma (IRE) may be short on experience but she was up to the task in hand on this handicap debut. Gaining control five furlongs from home, she was bustled clear in the final quarter-mile but, with the second finishing with a real flourish, she found the line coming just in time. (5/2)

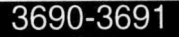

2292 Arctic Owl may not have been suited by the rain-softened ground last time out. Back on a sounder surface, he had no problems with the longer trip and came storming through in the last furlong and a half, if finding the line coming just a few strides too soon. He is learning all the time and should be winning again before long. (12/1: op 8/1)
3184 Island Sanctuary (IRE) saw out this longer trip and stayed on really well in the last furlong and a half to finish third. (9/1)
3026* Mutadarra (IRE), awash with sweat beforehand, has been raised 7lb for his recent victory. Creeping closer along the inside rail, he failed to get a clear run early in the final quarter-mile but, although staying on after a gap appeared, failed to find that vital turn of foot. (8/1: 6/1-9/1)
2594 Myrtlebank moved into second place five furlongs from home but she was collared below the distance and tired as the longer trip found her out. (13/2)
3110 Hoh Express picked up ground below the distance but could then make no further impression. He is not easy to win with and has won just once in the last two years. (16/1)

3690 LONDON IRISH RUGBY FOOTBALL CLUB H'CAP (0-70) (3-Y.O+) (Class E)

8-00 (8-02) **7f (round)** £2,960.25 (£897.00: £438.50: £209.25) Stalls: High GOING minus 0.24 sec per fur (GF)

				SP	RR	SF
3328[3]	**Dummer Golf Time (60)** (LordHuntingdon) **4-9-5v** PatEddery(4) (hdwy over 1f out: led ins fnl f: drvn out)	—	**1**	9/2[1]	70	32
2698[8]	**Mr Speaker (IRE) (58)** (CFWall) **4-9-3** SSanders(6) (hld up: rdn over 2f out: r.o wl ins fnl f)	hd	**2**	25/1	68	30
3139[3]	**Kilvine (67)** (WJHaggas) **4-9-12** FLynch(11) (swtg: rdn over 2f out: hdwy over 1f out: r.o wl ins fnl f)	1¼	**3**	16/1	74	36
3236[14]	**Star Turn (IRE) (61)** (MBell) **3-9-1** MFenton(13) (w ldr: rdn over 2f out: ev ch ins fnl f: unable qckn)	s.h	**4**	25/1	68	25
3202[3]	**Misty Point (65)** (IABalding) **3-9-5** DaneO'Neill(10) (swtg: hdwy over 1f out: styng on whn nt clr run wl ins fnl f)	nk	**5**	14/1	71	28
3092[2]	**Farley Green (68)** (HCandy) **3-9-8** CRutter(9) (a.p: rdn over 2f out: 5th & btn whn hmpd wl ins fnl f)	1	**6**	11/2[2]	72	29
3290*	**Stand Tall (67)** (LadyHerries) **5-9-12** PaulEddery(14) (b.hind: swtg: led: rdn over 1f out: hdd ins fnl f: one pce)	s.h	**7**	6/1[3]	71	33
3420[9]	**Polar Prospect (60)** (BHanbury) **4-9-5** GHind(3) (b: lw: a.p: rdn over 2f out: wknd fnl f)	1½	**8**	25/1	60	22
3392[4]	**Duello (68)** (MBlanshard) **6-9-13** WRyan(5) (lw: hdwy over 1f out: n.m.r 1f out: btn whn nt clr run ins fnl f)	1½	**9**	7/1	65	27
3392[5]	**Lord Oberon (IRE) (58)** (JAkehurst) **9-9-3** MTebbutt(17) (b: nvr nrr)	s.h	**10**	16/1	55	17
3418[7]	**Knobbleeneeze (69)** (MRChannon) **7-10-0v** CandyMorris(12) (hdwy on ins over 1f out: btn whn nt clr run on ins, ins fnl f)	1¼	**11**	16/1	63	25
3251[5]	**Speedy Classic (USA) (58)** (MJHeaton-Ellis) **8-9-3** AClark(16) (hld up: rdn over 2f out: eased whn btn fnl f)	nk	**12**	13/2	51	13
3548[15]	**Mansab (USA) (66)** (PGMurphy) **4-9-11** NDay(15) (swtg: a bhd)	10	**13**	25/1	36	—
3418[5]	**Simple Logic (70)** (AGFoster) **3-9-10** JReid(2) (b.hind: swtg: a.p: rn v.wd bnd over 4f out: wknd over 2f out)	2½	**14**	16/1	35	—

(SP 119.3%) **14 Rn**

1m 28.29 (4.29) CSF £114.63 CT £1,478.45 TOTE £4.20: £2.00 £4.50 £10.20 (£94.10) Trio £569.70 OWNER Coriolan Partnership (WEST ILSLEY) BRED R. M. Whitaker
WEIGHT FOR AGE 3yo-5lb
3328 Dummer Golf Time began to pick up ground below the distance and, striking the front inside the final furlong, responded to pressure to hold on in a tight finish. (9/2)
977 Mr Speaker (IRE) chased the leaders. He was going nowhere for much of the straight but picked up really well inside the final furlong if finding the line just beating him. (25/1)
3139 Kilvine, fitted with a net muzzle, has been in bad form this year and consequently was 18lb lower than when last appearing in a handicap at the end of last season. Racing at the back of the field, he put in some good work in the last furlong and a half but was unable to get there in time. (16/1)
3029 Star Turn (IRE) disputed the lead from the start and was still in with every chance inside the final furlong before tapped for toe. (25/1)
3202 Misty Point, making her handicap debut, was staying on nicely through the field but was not going to get there in time when short of room in the closing stages. (14/1: 10/1-16/1)
3092 Farley Green, never far away, was already getting the worst of the argument when hampered in the closing stages. (11/2)

T/Plpt: £263.70 (51.18 Tckts). T/Qdpt: £21.20 (54.49 Tckts) AK

3450-LEICESTER (R-H) (Good, Good to firm patches)
Wednesday August 20th

WEATHER: overcast, warm & humid WIND: nil

3691 TOM CRIBB LIMITED STKS (0-65) (3-Y.O+) (Class F)

5-40 (5-42) **7f 9y** £2,847.00 (£792.00: £381.00) Stalls: High GOING minus 0.31 sec per fur (GF)

				SP	RR	SF
3417[4]	**Denbrae (IRE) (64)** (DJGMurraySmith) **5-8-11**(5) CLowther(2) (hld up: hdwy 2f out: str run to ld wl ins fnl f)	—	**1**	7/1[2]	74	42
2921[10]	**Midnight Shift (IRE) (64)** (RGuest) **3-8-11** SDrowne(5) (led after 2f: rdn 2f out: ct wl ins fnl f)	½	**2**	9/1	73	36
3452[3]	**Inclination (60)** (MBlanshard) **3-8-5**(3) DSweeney(1) (w ldrs: rdn over 1f out: no ex ins fnl f)	½	**3**	15/2[3]	69	32
3454[2]	**Davis Rock (65)** (WRMuir) **3-8-3**(5) RMullen(8) (chsd ldrs: rdn 2f out: one pce ins fnl f)	3	**4**	100/30[1]	62	25
3100[8]	**Ocker (IRE) (65)** (MHTompkins) **3-8-8**(3) MHenry(4) (in tch: hdwy 2f out: no imp appr fnl f)	nk	**5**	12/1	64	27
2892[8]	**Rock Symphony (64)** (WJHaggas) **7-8-9**(7) JoHunnam(7) (in tch: effrt 2f out: wknd fnl f)	8	**6**	7/1[2]	46	14
3196*	**Golden Ace (IRE) (65)** (RCSpicer) **4-9-2**(3) PPMurphy(6) (nvr trbld ldrs)	5	**7**	10/1	38	6
3121[12]	**Van Chino (65)** (BAMcMahon) **3-8-11** LNewton(9) (prom over 4f)	s.h	**8**	10/1	35	—
1830[13]	**Perilous Plight (43)** (AStreeter) **6-8-13**(3) RHavlin(11) (lw: a bhd)	3½	**9**	14/1	27	—
	Bally Wonder (50) (HJCollingridge) **5-8-13** MRimmer(12) (swtg: sn bhd)	8	**10**	33/1	5	—
3582[11]	**Komaseph (60)** (RFMarvin) **5-9-2** TGMcLaughlin(10) (lw: in tch 3f)	nk	**11**	33/1	8	—
3313*	**Moon Fairy (65)** (JGSmyth-Osbourne) **3-8-11** WJO'Connor(3) (led 2f: wknd 2f out: eased whn btn)	11	**12**	7/1[2]	—	—

(SP 120.8%) **12 Rn**

1m 25.2 (2.60) CSF £63.75 TOTE £6.70: £2.00 £4.00 £2.10 (£37.50) Trio £61.80 OWNER Mr Michael Mellersh (MARKET HARBOROUGH) BRED Mellon Stud
WEIGHT FOR AGE 3yo-5lb
IN-FOCUS: **Despite the stalls being placed on the far rails, the middle of the straight course seemed to provide the fastest ground and the far side was given a wide berth by the majority of the evening's runners.**
3417 Denbrae (IRE), racing beyond six furlongs for the first time in eighteen months, got home with a terrific burst towards the stands' side. (7/1)
2157* Midnight Shift (IRE), stepped up to seven furlongs for the first time since her racecourse debut, seemed to get the trip. (9/1)
3452 Inclination had the best ground for much of the race but failed to pick up over a trip that looks short of her best. (15/2)

3454 Davis Rock moved down moderately and was probably racing on the slowest of the ground, so this was well below her best. (100/30: op 5/1)
2143 Ocker (IRE), taken down early, flattered to deceive for a moment below the distance but was easily held and remains a maiden. (12/1)
Rock Symphony has always looked a sprinter and that, allied with racing on the slowest ground, saw him tying up rapidly in the final furlong. (7/1: op 4/1)
383 Perilous Plight (14/1: op 8/1)

3692 MOLYNEUX (S) STKS (2-Y.O) (Class G)

6-10 (6-11) **5f 218y** £2,595.00 (£720.00: £345.00) Stalls: High GOING minus 0.31 sec per fur (GF)

				SP	RR	SF
3563^{8}	**Russian Romeo (IRE) (60)** (BAMcMahon) **2-8-11v** MRoberts(4) (swtg: wnt lft s: mde all: clr over 1f out: rdn out)	—	1	14/1	74	22
2862^{15}	**Catherines Song (68)** (CADwyer) **2-8-11** DHolland(9) (a.p: rdn & edgd lft over 1f out: kpt on: no imp)	3	2	$6/4^{1}$	66	14
3289^{3}	**Patricia Olive (IRE) (55)** (MHTompkins) **2-8-3**(3) MHenry(2) (lw: hmpd after s: in tch: effrt whn n.m.r wl over 1f out: kpt on on fnl f)	1¼	3	8/1	58	6
3451*	**Marske Machine (55)** (NTinkler) **2-8-11b** KFallon(7) (s.i.s: hdwy 2f out: nrst fin)	½	4	$11/4^{2}$	61	9
3450^{12}	**Keen Lady** (NPLittmoden) **2-8-6** TGMcLaughlin(3) (plld hrd: in tch: rdn 2f out: r.o fnl f)	3	5	33/1	48	—
3446^{3}	**Dande Times (58)** (KTIvory) **2-8-6**(5) CLowther(1) (chsd ldrs over 4f)	nk	6	12/1	53	1
3331^{7}	**Shifty Mouse** (DMorley) **2-8-6** JLowe(10) (spd over 3f)	8	7	$5/1^{3}$	26	—
3055^{3}	**Calliram (50)** (MBlanshard) **2-8-3**(3) PPMurphy(6) (prom: rdn, wandered & wkng whn hmpd over 1f out)	½	8	12/1	25	—
2579^{8}	**Marimbo (IRE)** (CMurray) **2-8-11** NicolaHowarth(5) (bit bkwd: prom: rdn & chsd wnr 2f out: sn wknd)	3	9	40/1	22	—
	Riverlution (JLHarris) **2-8-8**(3) DSweeney(8) (Withdrawn not under Starter's orders)		W	—	—	—

(SP 121.9%) **9 Rn**

1m 13.3 (3.30) CSF £34.11 TOTE £25.80: £3.50 £1.10 £1.70 (£14.00) Trio £48.80 OWNER Mr R. L. Bedding (TAMWORTH) BRED Peadar Devereux
Bt in 5,000gns
3282 Russian Romeo (IRE), dropped a furlong and with the visor back on, was intent on racing down the centre from the start and this proved decisive. (14/1: 10/1-16/1)
2578 Catherines Song looked something of a good thing back in this grade but the draw beat her. (6/4)
3289 Patricia Olive (IRE) had a good draw but lacked the pace to take advantage of it. (8/1)
3451* Marske Machine lost the race at the start but caught the eye making good late progress towards the unfavoured far side. (11/4)
Keen Lady found the trip too short and would be interesting in this grade over further. (33/1)
3446 Dande Times with the blinkers left off, still finished weakly. (12/1: op 8/1)
3331 Shifty Mouse (5/1: op 3/1)
3055 Calliram (12/1: 10/1-16/1)

3693 RADIO LEICESTER H'CAP (0-70) (3-Y.O+) (Class E)

6-40 (6-42) **5f 2y** £3,275.00 (£980.00: £470.00: £215.00) Stalls: High GOING minus 0.31 sec per fur (GF)

				SP	RR	SF
2891^{2}	**Gay Breeze (40)** (PSFelgate) **4-8-0** AMackay(3) (chsd ldr centre tl led over 1f out: jst hld on)	—	1	$5/1^{1}$	48	34
2934^{11}	**Pleasure Time (62)** (CSmith) **4-9-8** JTate(8) (led centre over 3f: chal wl ins fnl f: jst failed)	s.h	2	14/1	70	56
2732^{6}	**Ice Age (56)** (RJRWilliams) **3-9-0** DHolland(5) (s.i.s: hdwy 2f out: ev ch ins fnl f: no ex nr fin)	nk	3	$5/1^{1}$	63	47
3473^{7}	**Beau Venture (USA) (66)** (BPalling) **9-9-9**(3) DSweeney(7) (racd centre: w ldrs: kpt on wl ins fnl f)	½	4	12/1	71	57
3121^{7}	**Make Ready (56)** (JNeville) **3-9-0** SDrowne(1) (racd centre: in tch: rdn 2f out: kpt on fnl f)	1¾	5	14/1	56	40
3326^{5}	**Songsheet (68)** (MSSaunders) **4-9-11**(3) PPMurphy(9) (lw: racd centre: spd over 3f)	1	6	11/1	65	51
3208^{11}	**Souperficial (50)** (NTinkler) **6-8-10v** KimTinkler(4) (s.s: racd centre: nvr nr ldrs)	1½	7	12/1	42	28
2384^{4}	**Flying Harold (47)** (MRChannon) **4-8-7** KFallon(12) (in tch: effrt over 2f out: no imp)	1¼	8	$6/1^{2}$	35	21
2915^{10}	**Lachesis (49)** (DShaw) **4-8-9** JFanning(2) (swtchd rt s: nvr trbld ldrs)	1½	9	10/1	32	18
3280^{2}	**Sound the Trumpet (IRE) (50)** (RCSpicer) **5-8-10** MRoberts(14) (led over 3f: eased whn btn)	1¾	10	$7/1^{3}$	27	13
3280^{10}	**John O'Dreams (36)** (MrsALMKing) **12-7-10** JLowe(6) (lw: s.i.s: a bhd)	3	11	25/1	4	—
3241^{11}	**Superapparos (40)** (SRBowring) **3-7-5b**(7)ow2 FBoyle(11) (lw: prom 3f)	nk	12	25/1	7	—
3481^{4}	**Superbit (63)** (BAMcMahon) **5-9-9** LNewton(13) (w ldr over 3f)	2½	13	8/1	22	8
1942^{9}	**Nampara Bay (43)** (GCBravery) **3-8-1** DRMcCabe(10) (w ldrs tl wknd 2f out)	4	14	16/1	—	—

(SP 130.9%) **14 Rn**

59.9 secs (1.40) CSF £76.09 CT £348.00 TOTE £4.90: £1.20 £7.90 £2.80 (£53.60) Trio £165.80 OWNER Mr P. S. Felgate (MELTON MOWBRAY) BRED Dr W. J. Heffernan
LONG HANDICAP Superapparos 7-7 John O'Dreams 7-8
WEIGHT FOR AGE 3yo-2lb
2891 Gay Breeze couldn't get close to the front early as all the pace was on the far rails, but the situation changed below the distance and he just lasted home, although it certainly didn't look that way to the naked eye. (5/1)
2754 Pleasure Time tried to make all in the centre but looked beaten approaching the final furlong, only to rally and appear to get up on the line. However, the photo showed otherwise. (14/1)
2732 Ice Age was again hindered by a slow break but, after coming with what looked a winning run entering the final furlong, found the effort coming to an end near the finish. (5/1)
3016 Beau Venture (USA) moved poorly to post and couldn't get to the front but stayed on well in the closing stages. (12/1)
2536 Make Ready was again taken off her feet over this trip, but despite hanging somewhat, was staying on well in the final furlong. (14/1)
3326 Songsheet came towards the favoured centre but couldn't land a blow in the closing stages. (11/1)

3694 WEATHERBYS ECLIPSE PEDIGREES H'CAP (0-80) (3-Y.O+ F & M) (Class D)

7-10 (7-11) **1m 3f 183y** £3,704.00 (£1,112.00: £536.00: £248.00) Stalls: High GOING minus 0.31 sec per fur (GF)

				SP	RR	SF
3085*	**Debutante Days (73)** (ACStewart) **5-10-0** KFallon(6) (hld up: dropped rr 4f out: rdn 2f out: rapid hdwy over 1f out: led & edgd rt ins fnl f)	—	1	$7/2^{2}$	84	52
3319*	**Elbaaha (80)** (MAJarvis) **3-9-11** RCochrane(5) (led 1f: led over 3f out tl hdd & unable qckn ins fnl f)	nk	2	$4/1^{3}$	91	49
3445^{2}	**Noble Dane (IRE) (68)** (PWHarris) **3-8-8**(5) CLowther(3) (hld up & plld hrd: hdwy 5f out: rdn & ev ch over 1f out: one pce fnl f)	1¼	3	6/1	77	35
3412^{4}	**Ordained (54)** (EJAlston) **4-8-9** SDrowne(1) (lw: hld up: hdwy over 4f out: chal over 1f out: no ex ins fnl f)	1	4	8/1	62	30
3455*	**Lookout (71)** (BWHills) **3-9-2** 6x DHolland(2) (chsd ldrs: rdn 3f out: no imp appr fnl f)	2½	5	$3/1^{1}$	75	33
3116*	**Kika (43)** (KRBurke) **4-7-12** JQuinn(7) (lw: prom tl wknd 2f out)	4	6	12/1	42	10
2568^{5}	**Rufalda (IRE) (72)** (LMCumani) **3-9-3** DRMcCabe(9) (lw: plld hrd: chsd ldrs 9f: eased whn btn appr fnl f)	2½	7	6/1	67	25

3279^{9}	**Silvretta (IRE) (62)** (RCSpicer) **4-9-3** MRoberts(4) (led after 1f tl over 3f out: rdn & wknd 2f out) 1	**8**	14/1	56	24
	Cliburnel News (IRE) (55) (DShaw) **7-8-5**$^{(5)}$ RMullen(8) (b: nvr trbld ldrs) 1	**9**	33/1	48	16

(SP 124.2%) **9 Rn**

2m 33.6 (5.10) CSF £17.82 CT £77.65 TOTE £4.00: £1.20 £2.20 £1.90 (£11.90) Trio £21.60 OWNER Mrs Shirley Brasher (NEWMARKET) BRED Lady McAlpine

WEIGHT FOR AGE 3yo-10lb

3085* Debutante Days didn't look a contender when dropping back last early in the straight but, pulled towards the stands' side and given a reminder, she picked up in terrific style to steal the spoils in the last half furlong. (7/2)

3319* Elbaaha, set a stiff task in her first handicap, did well but kicking for home down the centre of the track without a rail to help is not easy at the best of times and, when a horse picks up the way the winner did, there is no disgrace in defeat. (4/1)

3445 Noble Dane (IRE), taking another step up in trip, pulled hard early on and that probably decided things, for she just failed to last home after looking a danger. (6/1)

3412 Ordained, back on the mark she won off at Redcar a year ago, didn't impress once the chips were down. (8/1)

3455* Lookout, who shows a bit of knee action, probably had the worst of the ground in the straight and should be forgiven this. (3/1)

3116* Kika couldn't handle the step up in class. (12/1)

3695 SNOW AND ASTILL CENTENARY CLAIMING STKS (3-Y.O) (Class F)

7-40 (7-41) **1m 1f 218y** £2,511.00 (£696.00: £333.00) Stalls: High GOING minus 0.31 sec per fur (GF)

			SP	RR	SF
2836*	**Phylida (58)** (PJMakin) **3-8-10** JQuinn(8) (dwlt: sn chsng ldrs: led over 2f out: rdn & edgd lft ins fnl f: r.o)......—	**1**	3/1^{1}	59	25
2961^{15}	**Superbelle (73)** (MAJarvis) **3-9-2** EmmaO'Gorman(4) (a.p: chal 3f out: sn rdn: kpt on ins fnl f).......................1¾	**2**	4/1^{2}	62	28
3320^{2}	**River of Fortune (IRE) (53)** (MHTompkins) **3-8-9**$^{(5)}$ RMullen(6) (led over 7f: kpt on) ....½	**3**	3/1^{1}	59	25
3133^{4}	**Little Miss Lucy** (MJHeaton-Ellis) **3-9-2** SDrowne(2) (lw: in tch tl outpcd 5f out: n.d afterwards)......................6	**4**	5/1^{3}	52	18
3093^{6}	**Golden Saddle (USA) (54)** (PFICole) **3-9-7** MRoberts(7) (bhd: rdn 5f out: sme hdwy fnl f) ....¾	**5**	7/1	56	22
	Key To (APJarvis) **3-8-12** DHolland(1) (lw: leggy: s.s: sn rdn along: a bhd)...11	**6**	8/1	29	—
3308^{8}	**Lady Magician** (CWFairhurst) **3-8-6** DeanMcKeown(3) (in tch 5f: wknd over 2f out)...................................3½	**7**	25/1	17	—
	Sam's Yer Man (TTClement) **3-9-3** RCochrane(5) (t.o fnl 5f) ....dist	**8**	25/1	—	—

(SP 118.0%) **8 Rn**

2m 9.3 (5.60) CSF £14.36 TOTE £4.00: £1.70 £1.70 £1.50 (£7.20) OWNER Mrs P. J. Makin (MARLBOROUGH) BRED The Glen Andred Stud and Highfield Stud Ltd

2836* Phylida had forged clear by the final furlong but hardly came home strongly, as those outpaced by the three principals on the home turn were closing again at the finish. (3/1)

281 Superbelle looked sure to win when going upsides early in the straight but, soon under pressure, the response was minimal. Coming back for more inside the final furlong, this should hardly be taken as proof of stamina and a mile may suit her better. (4/1)

3320 River of Fortune (IRE) kept plugging away once headed and gave the impression that she saw out the trip better than the two who beat her. (3/1)

3133 Little Miss Lucy, rather keen going down, was left behind on the home turn and, despite staying on, could never get back into it. (5/1)

3093 Golden Saddle (USA) was never going and just stayed on past beaten horses in the closing stages. (7/1)

Key To, a half-brother to a couple of modest middle-distance performers, looked no better, cutting little ice on this debut run. (8/1: op 5/1)

3696 RUTLAND H'CAP (0-70) (3-Y.O) (Class E)

8-10 (8-11) **1m 8y** £3,275.00 (£980.00: £470.00: £215.00) Stalls: High GOING minus 0.31 sec per fur (GF)

			SP	RR	SF
1272^{5}	**Abajany (66)** (MRChannon) **3-9-4** JFortune(11) (bit bkwd: a.p: led over 1f out: drvn out)...............................—	**1**	14/1	78	45
3397^{3}	**Sea Ya Maite (48)** (SRBowring) **3-8-0** NCarlisle(12) (b: lw: chsd ldrs: ev ch over 1f out: no ex ins fnl f)..........1½	**2**	12/1	57	24
2125^{3}	**Time Can Tell (63)** (CMurray) **3-9-1** DeanMcKeown(7) (w ldr: led 5f out tl over 1f out: one pce) ....hd	**3**	16/1	72	39
3452*	**City Gambler (72)** (GCBravery) **3-9-10**^{5x} MRimmer(6) (a.p: one pce fnl f)..1½	**4**	9/2^{3}	78	45
3452^{2}	**Rocky Dance (FR) (67)** (APJarvis) **3-9-5** DHolland(4) (lw: chsd ldrs: no imp appr fnl f) 2	**5**	4/1^{2}	69	36
3336^{6}	**Falls O'Moness (IRE) (54)** (KRBurke) **3-8-6** JQuinn(9) (swtg: hld up: hdwy over 2f out: no imp appr fnl f).......½	**6**	8/1	55	22
3236^{13}	**Reeds (58)** (JRFanshawe) **3-8-10** TSprake(5) (lw: dwlt: rdn 2f out: nvr nr to chal)...2½	**7**	16/1	54	21
2523^{5}	**Welcome Home (53)** (PTDalton) **3-8-5** DRMcCabe(8) (plld hrd: in tch: rdn 2f out: sn btn)................................1½	**8**	16/1	46	13
3470^{5}	**Prairie Minstrel (USA) (54)** (RDickin) **3-8-6b**^{1} MRoberts(3) (hld up & plld hrd: nvr nr ldrs) ....hd	**9**	14/1	47	14
3421^{3}	**Mutahadeth (48)** (DShaw) **3-7-9b**$^{(5)}$ RMullen(1) (in tch tl rdn & wknd 3f out)..10	**10**	8/1	21	—
3236^{4}	**Monaco (IRE) (67)** (LMCumani) **3-9-5** KDarley(2) (lw: in tch: rdn 4f out: btn over 2f out) 2½	**11**	3/1^{1}	35	2
2645^{10}	**Maraud (69)** (JLSpearing) **3-9-7b** SDrowne(10) (led 3f: wknd & eased over 2f out) 11	**12**	33/1	15	—

(SP 127.0%) **12 Rn**

1m 37.9 (2.90) CSF £167.04 CT £2,526.89 TOTE £11.80: £3.30 £2.80 £3.80 (£99.00) Trio £153.00 OWNER John White and Partners (UPPER LAMBOURN) BRED Fares Stables Ltd

IN-FOCUS: **Quickly led across to the centre by Maraud early on, this if anything, seemed to reverse the effect of the draw.**

1272 Abajany, gelded during his spell off, returned looking just in need of the race despite being well in his coat but continued the stable's good run with a hard fought success. (14/1: op 8/1)

3397 Sea Ya Maite transferred his recent All-Weather improvement to turf and should find a similar race on this evidence, as the winner had the best of the ground and was given a notably good ride. (12/1)

2125 Time Can Tell, with the blinkers off, was given an aggressive ride but lacks any finishing kick and his second win is proving rather elusive. (16/1)

3452* City Gambler made a bold hat-trick bid but the 5lb she had been raised for her course win proved the deciding factor. (9/2)

3452 Rocky Dance (FR) moved well to post and raced more keenly than last time but didn't come home as well. (4/1)

3336 Falls O'Moness (IRE) made a brief effort but her maiden status was never in serious danger and her ability to get this trip is far from fully proven. (8/1: op 5/1)

3421 Mutahadeth (8/1: op 14/1)

3236 Monaco (IRE) (3/1: op 5/1)

T/Plpt: £215.80 (65.83 Tckts). T/Qdpt: £47.60 (21.44 Tckts) Dk

2823-MUSSELBURGH (R-H) (Good to firm, Firm patches)
Wednesday August 20th
WEATHER: overcast & warm WIND: slt bhd

3697 ABERLADY RATING RELATED MAIDEN STKS (0-65) (3-Y.O+) (Class F)
2-20 (2-20) **1m 16y** £2,753.75 (£830.00: £402.50: £188.75) Stalls: High GOING minus 0.55 sec per fur (F)

				SP	RR	SF
2909^{5}	**Ile Distinct (IRE) (62)** (MrsASwinbank) **3-8-12** EJohnson(7) (in tch: pushed along ent st: hdwy over 2f out: hung lft: styd on to ld wl ins fnl f: eased towards fin)	—	**1**	Evens^{1}	60	31
3381^{4}	**Get The Point (60)** (RHollinshead) **3-8-9**$^{(3)}$ DGriffiths(5) (mde most tl hdd & no ex wl ins fnl f)	¾	**2**	2/1^{2}	59	30
3627^{5}	**School of Science (22)** (DANolan) **7-8-11**$^{(7)}$ NPollard(2) (disp ld to ½-wy: cl up tl wknd fnl 2f)	8	**3**	100/1	43	20
1958^{W}	**Swan Island (61)** (WMBrisbourne) **3-8-9** JFEgan(1) (b: b.hind: in tch: outpcd over 3f out: no imp)	3	**4**	5/1^{3}	34	5
3241^{10}	**Prominent (45)** (MrsVAAconley) **3-8-12** MDeering(6) (rdn ½-wy: nvr trbld ldrs)	3½	**5**	14/1	30	1
3313^{5}	**Jonny's Joker (44)** (FHLee) **3-8-12** ACulhane(4) (nvr wnt pce)	6	**6**	40/1	18	—
1838^{8}	**Down Hearted (IRE) (39)** (WTKemp) **3-8-12** OPears(3) (chsd ldrs tl st: sn lost pl)	3	**7**	100/1	12	—
				(SP 111.1%)	**7 Rn**	

1m 41.0 (2.00) CSF £2.71 TOTE £2.40: £1.80 £1.10 (£3.00) OWNER Windsor Room Syndicate (RICHMOND) BRED John O'Connor
WEIGHT FOR AGE 3yo-6lb
2909 Ile Distinct (IRE) won this well in the end but it was a struggle to get there and he would seem to need a little further. (Evens)
3381 Get The Point set a scorching pace but, despite trying hard, he just found one too good. (2/1)
3627 School of Science had next to no chance at these weights but did run really well and is obviously in good heart. (100/1)
1048 Swan Island has not run for almost three months and seems happier over shorter distances, and this was also her first run for her new stable. (5/1: op 5/2)
2735 Prominent was in a poor race here and showed little and would seem better over shorter distances. (14/1)

3698 EDMONDS ADVERTISING MAIDEN H'CAP (0-70) (3-Y.O+ F & M) (Class E)
2-55 (2-56) **5f** £2,721.25 (£820.00: £397.50: £186.25) Stalls: High GOING minus 0.30 sec per fur (GF)

				SP	RR	SF
3606^{7}	**Dona Filipa (44)** (MissLCSiddall) **4-8-10**^{ow5} OPears(2) (lw: hld on: smooth hdwy to ld ins fnl f: comf)	—	**1**	15/2	53	27
3086^{2}	**Tithcar (64)** (BHanbury) **3-10-0** EJohnson(5) (lw: chsd ldrs: hdwy & ev ch ins fnl f: no ex)	1¼	**2**	3/1^{2}	69	46
3332^{4}	**Whisper Low (IRE) (49)** (RHollinshead) **3-8-10**$^{(3)}$ DGriffiths(4) (outpcd tl styd on appr fnl f: nvr able chal)	2½	**3**	12/1	46	23
3271^{11}	**Melbourne Princess (42)** (RMWhitaker) **3-8-6**^{ow1} ACulhane(7) (w ldr: led 2f out tl ins fnl f: sn btn)	½	**4**	5/1^{3}	37	13
2921^{3}	**Stock Hill Dancer (56)** (BJMeehan) **3-9-3**$^{(3)}$ TEDurcan(1) (chsd ldrs tl rdn & btn over 1f out)	1½	**5**	15/8^{1}	47	24
3332^{5}	**Flo's Choice (IRE) (40)** (JO'Reilly) **3-8-4** JO'Reilly(3) (hmpd after s: nvr trbld ldrs)	2	**6**	14/1	24	1
2899^{5}	**Ready Teddy (IRE) (32)** (MissLAPerratt) **4-7-12v** NKennedy(6) (t: led 3f: sn rdn & wknd)	1	**7**	5/1^{3}	13	—
				(SP 119.2%)	**7 Rn**	

60.1 secs (2.40) CSF £29.12 TOTE £9.70: £2.10 £1.50 (£8.30) OWNER Mr A. Emmerson (TADCASTER) BRED H. Alexander and R. E. Sangster
WEIGHT FOR AGE 3yo-2lb
3086 Dona Filipa, despite 5lb overweight, proved different class to this lot and, given a most confident ride, won particularly well. (15/2: 7/2-8/1)
3086 Tithcar looked well enough and keeps struggling on under pressure but is woefully short of pace. (3/1)
3332 Whisper Low (IRE) was always finding things happening too quickly but she did stay on when it was all over. (12/1)
2883 Melbourne Princess, this edgy sort, ran fast but found little under pressure. (5/1)
2921 Stock Hill Dancer, after a promising effort last time, was extremely disappointing. (15/8)
3332 Flo's Choice (IRE) got squeezed out after leaving the stalls and was then always struggling to get back into it, which she never achieved. (14/1: op 8/1)

3699 AON/ROYAL & SUNALLIANCE NURSERY H'CAP (2-Y.O) (Class D)
3-30 (3-34) **5f** £3,434.50 (£1,036.00: £503.00: £236.50) Stalls: High GOING minus 0.30 sec per fur (GF)

				SP	RR	SF
3571^{4}	**Oriel Girl (66)** (PDEvans) **2-9-3v** JFEgan(1) (lw: mde most: drvn out)	—	**1**	5/2^{2}	71	32
3571^{5}	**Hayburner (55)** (MWEasterby) **2-8-3b**$^{(3)}$ GParkin(3) (lw: w wnr: hung rt 2f out: kpt on)	1¼	**2**	9/4^{1}	56	17
3438^{7}	**Cosmic Case (51)** (JSGoldie) **2-8-2** DWright(2) (outpcd tl hdwy over 1f out: styd on towards fin)	½	**3**	10/1	50	11
3042^{5}	**Risky Whisky (66)** (JBerry) **2-9-0b**$^{(3)}$ TEDurcan(5) (lw: chsd ldrs over 3f: sn wknd)	7	**4**	6/1	43	4
3106^{2}	**Imperial Honey (IRE) (70)** (MrsASwinbank) **2-9-7** EJohnson(4) (chsd ldrs: sn drvn along: wknd fnl 2f)	2½	**5**	5/1^{3}	39	—
3451^{4}	**Chardania (IRE) (45)** (CaptJWilson) **2-7-3**$^{(7)}$ AngelaHartley(7) (a outpcd & bhd)	1¼	**6**	12/1	10	—
3258^{9}	**Makahu Don (57)** (WTKemp) **2-8-1**$^{(7)}$ JMcAuley(6) (a outpcd & bhd)	5	**7**	7/1	6	—
				(SP 119.6%)	**7 Rn**	

60.2 secs (2.50) CSF £8.38 TOTE £2.60: £1.20 £1.60 (£4.30) OWNER Mr D. Maloney (WELSHPOOL) BRED Mrs F. A. Veasey
LONG HANDICAP Chardania (IRE) 7-5
3571 Oriel Girl, unlucky last time, made no mistake here and she keeps her enthusiasm remarkably well. (5/2)
3571 Hayburner is not the best of movers and, when asked for an effort, he threw his chance away by hanging. (9/4)
3226 Cosmic Case found this trip too sharp but did finish well. (10/1: 6/1-11/1)
3042 Risky Whisky ran poorly here and gave up once ridden soon after halfway, and is probably better with some cut in the ground. (6/1: 4/1-7/1)
3106 Imperial Honey (IRE) was warm and edgy beforehand and ran no sort of race. (5/1)
3451 Chardania (IRE) was not well drawn as it turned out and, very sluggish early on, her chance had soon gone. (12/1: op 7/1)

3700 SCOTTISH BREWERS H'CAP (0-70) (3-Y.O+) (Class E)
4-00 (4-00) **1m 4f 31y** £2,737.50 (£825.00: £400.00: £187.50) Stalls: High GOING minus 0.55 sec per fur (F)

				SP	RR	SF
3626^{2}	**Il Principe (IRE) (41)** (JohnBerry) **3-8-2** ^{6x} JFEgan(2) (trckd ldr: led over 2f out: styd on u.p)	—	**1**	6/4^{1}	54	25
3562^{2}	**Comtec's Legend (25)** (JPearce) **7-7-10** GBardwell(1) (lw: hld up & bhd: hdwy 4f out: chsng wnr 2f out: no ex u.p fnl f)	1¾	**2**	11/4^{2}	36	17
3401^{2}	**Thisonesforalice (40)** (JSGoldie) **9-8-11** OPears(4) (hld up: hdwy over 4f out: sn rdn & no imp)	4	**3**	3/1^{3}	45	26
1763^{11}	**Blenheim Terrace (57)** (CBBBooth) **4-10-0** ACulhane(5) (swtg: hld up: effrt ent st: rdn & no imp)	1¼	**4**	7/1	61	42

3333[10]	**Get A Life (49)** (JO'Reilly) **4-9-6** SWebster(3) (lw: led tl hdd over 2f out: sn btn)	2	**5**	13/2	50	31
				(SP 117.5%)		**5 Rn**

2m 36.3 (2.80) CSF £5.89 TOTE £2.00: £1.10 £1.90 (£3.20) OWNER The 1997 Partnership (NEWMARKET) BRED J. Costello
LONG HANDICAP Comtec's Legend 7-5
WEIGHT FOR AGE 3yo-10lb
3626 Il Principe (IRE) again showed signs of temperament beforehand but he showed, yet again, that he does stay and that was all that was required. (6/4)
3562 Comtec's Legend threw the race away last time and, after looking dangerous again, she ran out of steam late on. (11/4)
3401 Thisonesforalice could never seriously get into this and, judging from his run last time, he needs further. (3/1)
612 Blenheim Terrace gained his only previous win on this track but he was never happy this time, and could well have needed this after two and a half months off. (7/1: op 7/2)
2541 Get A Life raced freely out in front and failed to get home. (13/2)

3701 PINKIE BAR MAIDEN AUCTION STKS (2-Y.O) (Class F)
4-30 (4-30) **7f 30y** £2,753.75 (£830.00: £402.50: £188.75) Stalls: High GOING minus 0.55 sec per fur (F)

				SP	RR	SF
2038[2]	**Demolition Jo (72)** (PDEvans) **2-8-2v** JFEgan(1) (lw: cl up: led 4f out: r.o wl fnl f)	—	**1**	13/8[2]	73	—
3253[7]	**French Connection** (JBerry) **2-8-7**(3) TEDurcan(2) (trckd ldrs: hdwy 3f out: chsng wnr appr fnl f: no imp)	5	**2**	11/4[3]	70	—
3306[2]	**Appyabo (76)** (MRChannon) **2-8-9** ACulhane(8) (cl up: effrt & ev ch ½-wy: one pce fnl 2f)	3	**3**	6/4[1]	62	—
2893[12]	**Saint Albert** (PTWalwyn) **2-8-8** DaleGibson(6) (lw: a chsng ldrs: one pce fnl 3f)	3	**4**	16/1	54	—
3131[11]	**Touch of Colour** (JWWatts) **2-8-4** DWright(3) (led tl hdd 4f out: sn rdn & grad wknd)	hd	**5**	12/1	50	—
	Beau Vienna (ARDicken) **2-8-0** EJohnson(4) (neat: bit bkwd: bhd: effrt ½-wy: nvr trbld ldrs)	nk	**6**	33/1	45	—
	Billy Owl (IRE) (JO'Reilly) **2-8-7** SWebster(7) (unf: bit bkwd: shkn up ½-wy: nvr trbld ldrs)	1¼	**7**	25/1	50	—
2842[16]	**Lesley's Adventure (IRE)** (CaptJWilson) **2-8-2** GBardwell(5) (sn wl bhd)	6	**8**	25/1	31	—
				(SP 129.0%)		**8 Rn**

1m 30.0 (4.00) CSF £6.93 TOTE £2.20: £1.10 £1.40 £1.10 (£4.80) OWNER Mr John Pugh (WELSHPOOL) BRED Bylon Farmers Ltd
2038 Demolition Jo has obviously been crying out for this longer trip and she made no mistake here and, when set alight, got stronger as the race progressed. (13/8)
French Connection looked in good trim and ran a fair race but proved no match for the winner late on. (11/4)
3306 Appyabo had his chances but failed to pick up when ridden and this was disappointing. (6/4: op evens)
Saint Albert is improving but there is plenty more needed. (16/1)
Touch of Colour got into the race this time and should have learnt a little. (12/1)
Beau Vienna needed this and the outing will, no doubt, see some improvement. (33/1)

3702 INVERESK LIMITED STKS (0-60) (3-Y.O+) (Class F)
5-00 (5-01) **7f 30y** £2,802.50 (£845.00: £410.00: £192.50) Stalls: High GOING minus 0.55 sec per fur (F)

				SP	RR	SF
3442*	**Impulsive Air (IRE) (60)** (EWeymes) **5-9-3** DaleGibson(5) (chsd ldrs: rdn to ld wl over 1f out: styd on wl)	—	**1**	5/4[1]	68	11
3269[2]	**Don't Worry Mike (49)** (FHLee) **3-8-9b** ACulhane(1) (lw: led 1f: chsd ldr: rdn over 3f out: one pce)	5	**2**	10/1	54	—
3132[3]	**Fearless Cavalier (57)** (RHollinshead) **3-8-6**(3) DGriffiths(3) (in tch: outpcd ½-wy: sme late hdwy)	3	**3**	7/2[2]	47	—
3378[3]	**Panther (IRE) (59)** (PDEvans) **7-9-0v** JFEgan(6) (lw: led after 1f: sn clr: hdd wl over 1f out: sn btn)	¾	**4**	5/1[3]	45	—
3443[7]	**Keston Pond (IRE) (45)** (MrsVAAconley) **7-9-0** MDeering(2) (outpcd after 2f: n.d after)	hd	**5**	12/1	45	—
2708[12]	**Winter Scout (USA) (60)** (RAFahey) **9-9-1**(5) SCopp(4) (bhd: rdn ½-wy: n.d)	6	**6**	6/1	38	—
				(SP 114.4%)		**6 Rn**

1m 30.0 (4.00) CSF £14.04 TOTE £1.90: £1.10 £3.80 (£4.70) OWNER Mr T. A. Scothern (MIDDLEHAM) BRED Rathasker Stud
WEIGHT FOR AGE 3yo-5lb
3442* Impulsive Air (IRE) is in good form and, after struggling to get on terms, won it really well. (5/4)
3269 Don't Worry Mike looks particularly well and is running consistently but is just short of pace. (10/1)
3132 Fearless Cavalier was never doing enough to make an impression at any stage. (7/2)
3378 Panther (IRE) took charge and went far too fast and this effort is best ignored. (5/1)
3443 Keston Pond (IRE) was disappointing here and probably did not act on this track. (12/1: op 6/1)
2501 Winter Scout (USA), after over five weeks off, ran poorly and obviously needed this. (6/1: op 4/1)

T/Plpt: £8.20 (1,320.74 Tckts). T/Qdpt: £2.80 (200.26 Tckts) AA

3644-YORK (L-H) (Good)
Wednesday August 20th
WEATHER: sunny & warm, becoming cloudy WIND: fresh half bhd

3703 MOTABILITY RATED STKS H'CAP (0-105) (3-Y.O+) (Class B)
2-05 (2-07) **1m 2f 85y** £13,766.40 (£5,097.60: £2,448.80: £1,004.00: £402.00: £161.20) Stalls: Low GOING: 0.00 sec per fur (G)

				SP	RR	SF
3190[13]	**Amyas (IRE) (97)** (BWHills) **3-8-7** MHills(1) (hld up: hdwy on ins over 3f out: rdn to ld wl ins fnl f)	—	**1**	15/2[3]	111	88
3263*	**Sandmoor Chambray (89)** (TDEasterby) **6-8-7** JCarroll(14) (led 1f: led 2f out tl hdd nr fin)	1½	**2**	20/1	101	86
3388[3]	**Harry Wolton (103)** (HRACecil) **3-8-13** KFallon(9) (bhd: sn drvn along: styd on fnl 2f: nvr nrr)	2	**3**	7/1[2]	112	89
3051[2]	**Game Ploy (POL) (96)** (DHaydnJones) **5-9-0** RCochrane(4) (hld up: hdwy over 2f out: hrd rdn & r.o fnl f)	nk	**4**	17/2	104	89
3051[4]	**Kuala Lipis (USA) (91)** (PFICole) **4-8-9b**[1] OPeslier(8) (a chsng ldrs: effrt 3f out: no imp)	2½	**5**	14/1	95	80
3409[7]	**Prince of My Heart (103)** (BWHills) **4-9-7** LDettori(13) (hld up: styd on fnl 3f: nvr nrr)	1¾	**6**	14/1	105	90
3112[3]	**Champagne Prince (96)** (PWHarris) **4-8-9**(5) CLowther(3) (lw: w ldrs: led over 4f out: clr 3f out: rdn & hdd 2f out: sn wknd)	2½	**7**	9/1	94	79
	Freequent (103) (LMCumani) **4-9-7** KDarley(5) (bit bkwd: bhd: drvn along ½-wy: n.d)	7	**8**	33/1	90	75
3112[9]	**Najm Mubeen (IRE) (95)** (ACStewart) **4-8-13v**[1] MRoberts(12) (swtg: stdd s: a in rr)	¾	**9**	9/1	81	66
3051*	**Present Arms (USA) (101)** (PFICole) **4-9-5** PatEddery(7) (b.hind: effrt & rdn 4f out: nt rch ldrs)	1¼	**10**	9/1	85	70
2761[2]	**Illusion (104)** (MRStoute) **3-9-0** JReid(10) (chsd ldrs: rdn along over 3f out: sn wknd)	¾	**11**	13/2[1]	87	64
3112*	**Danish Rhapsody (IRE) (95)** (LadyHerries) **4-8-13** PaulEddery(16) (lw: dwlt: led after 1f tl over 4f out: wknd 3f out)	s.h	**12**	12/1	78	63
3051[6]	**Wilcuma (101)** (PJMakin) **6-9-5b**[1] MJKinane(2) (hld up: a bhd)	1	**13**	20/1	82	67
3190[2]	**Supply And Demand (100)** (GLMoore) **3-8-10** SSanders(6) (prom: effrt over 3f out: sn hrd rdn & wknd)	hd	**14**	12/1	81	58

	Horse		Pos	SP	RR	SF
3190^{8}	**Generous Gift (93)** (EALDunlop) **3-8-3** GCarter(11) (bhd & eased fnl 3f: t.o)	7	**15**	20/1	63	40
3263^{3}	**Major Change (89)** (MissGayKelleway) **5-8-7** JFortune(15) (chsd ldrs 4f: sn lost tch t.o)	2½	**16**	25/1	55	40
				(SP 127.9%)		**16 Rn**

2m 9.59 (0.59) CSF £146.31 CT £1,021.81 TOTE £8.30: £2.00 £5.50 £2.20 £2.50 (£197.20) Trio £348.50 OWNER Mrs J. M. Corbett (LAMBOURN) BRED Mrs Helen Smith

LONG HANDICAP Sandmoor Chambray 8-4

WEIGHT FOR AGE 3yo-8lb

OFFICIAL EXPLANATION **Amyas (IRE): regarding the improvement in form, the trainer reported that the colt was unsuited by the track last time, was better drawn here and preferred the easier ground.**

3190 Amyas (IRE), waiting on the leaders, made relentless progress up the inside rail and stayed on strongly to forge ahead inside the last hundred yards. Very lightly-raced, he could well defy a penalty. (15/2)

3263* Sandmoor Chambray did his level best to complete a hat-trick and made the winner fight hard to take his measure nearing the finish. (20/1)

3388 Harry Wolton does not impress in his slower paces but he certainly has an engine, and he has shown in his most recent races that a longer trip could be more to his advantage. (7/1)

3051 Game Ploy (POL) was probably suited by this fast-run race but does require more cut in the ground and hi staying-on effort would seem to confirm that opinion. (17/2)

3051 Kuala Lipis (USA) sat in behind the leaders travelling comfortably, but he was not able to step up his pace when set alight and it must be said that the blinkers had little effect. (14/1)

3112 Prince of My Heart did a lot of running inside the distance to reach his final placing, but he had left his effort far too late and was never a factor. (14/1)

3112 Champagne Prince had a head to head with the front-running Danish Rhapsody which he eventually won, but it only resulted in him running himself into the ground. This performance can safely be disregarded. (9/1)

2761 Illusion, an improving three-year-old taking on handicappers for the first time, was going well enough in behind the leaders until he came off the bridle early in the straight and then dropped away very quickly. He is better than this. (13/2)

3704 ASTON UPTHORPE YORKSHIRE OAKS STKS (Gp 1) (3-Y.O+ F & M) (Class A)

2-35 (2-50) **1m 3f 195y** £97,345.20 (£35,806.80: £17,003.40: £6,747.00: £2,473.50: £764.10) Stalls: Low GOING: 0.00 sec per fur (G)

	Horse		Pos	SP	RR	SF
3006a^{3}	**My Emma (113)** (RGuest) **4-9-4** DHolland(7) (hld up in rr: hdwy over 2f out: led ins fnl f: comf)	—	**1**	7/1^{2}	122	83
3370a*	**Whitewater Affair (114)** (MRStoute) **4-9-4** JReid(8) (b: led: rdn over 2f out: hdd & no ex ins fnl f)	¾	**2**	7/1^{2}	121	82
2053^{3}	**Crown of Light (113)** (MRStoute) **3-8-8** OPeslier(3) (chsd ldr 9f: styd on wl ins fnl f)	1¾	**3**	12/1	119	70
1738*	**Reams of Verse (USA) (119)** (HRACecil) **3-8-8** KFallon(6) (lw: trckd ldrs: chal 3f out: sn hrd rdn: btn appr fnl f)	2	**4**	4/7^{1}	116	67
3216^{3}	**Papering (IRE) (112)** (LMCumani) **4-9-4** PatEddery(2) (hld up: effrt & rdn 3f out: styd on same pce)	¾	**5**	12/1	115	76
2513*	**Squeak (105)** (JHMGosden) **3-8-8** LDettori(4) (hld up: hdwy over 3f out: wknd over 1f out)	2½	**6**	15/2^{3}	112	63
3188^{4}	**Alcalali (USA) (95)** (PAKelleway) **3-8-8** JFortune(5) (hld up: a in rr)	7	**7**	100/1	81 t	53
2513^{3}	**Attitre (FR) (103)** (CEBrittain) **3-8-8** MRoberts(1) (drvn along to trck ldrs: outpcd wl over 2f out: t.o)	19	**8**	40/1	56 t	28
				(SP 119.2%)		**8 Rn**

2m 30.59 (2.79) CSF £51.91 TOTE £7.60: £1.50 £1.70 £2.50 (£29.00) OWNER Matthews Breeding and Racing (NEWMARKET) BRED Lord Matthews

WEIGHT FOR AGE 3yo-10lb

3006a My Emma has had the Prix de l'Arc de Triomphe as her objective all season, and this comfortably-gained success in such a high-class Group One event would suggest she is well on target. (7/1)

3370a* Whitewater Affair is no slouch herself and her game attempt to make all only came to an end in the closing stages. Possibly better when she can get her toe in, she ran up to her mark here. (7/1)

2053 Crown of Light, very free to post, got rid of her pilot approaching the start and caused a fifteen-minute delay. Tracking the leader for over a mile, she was renewing her challenge in the closing stages and, if she can get more yielding ground, she will always be the one to beat in this type of race. (12/1)

1738* Reams of Verse (USA), very much on edge in the preliminaries, would not have been helped by the delay at the start. Looking to be going every bit like the winner when joining issue three furlongs out, she was unable to get the better of the leader and, finding very little under pressure, was held before reaching the final furlong. (4/7)

3216 Papering (IRE), runner-up in this event last year, was never able to get close enough to mount a challenge and it is possible that she is not quite up to Group One standard. (12/1)

2513* Squeak has been doing extremely well on her step up in class but she had met her match this time, and was unable to get close enough to pose a threat. (15/2)

3705 TOTE EBOR H'CAP (3-Y.O+) (Class B)

3-10 (3-29) **1m 5f 194y** £99,441.25 (£29,905.00: £14,452.50: £6,726.25) Stalls: Low GOING: 0.00 sec per fur (G)

	Horse		Pos	SP	RR	SF
3412^{2}	**Far Ahead (82)** (JLEyre) **5-8-0** TWilliams(10) (trckd ldrs: rdn to ld ins fnl f: hld on gamely)	—	**1**	33/1	98	58
3110*	**Media Star (USA) (88)** (JHMGosden) **4-8-6v** 7x LDettori(15) (led tl over 3f out: led over 1f out tl ins fnl f: kpt on u.p)	nk	**2**	5/1^{1}	104	64
3110^{2}	**Puce (84)** (LMCumani) **4-7-13**(3) RFfrench(17) (b.hind: trckd ldrs: swtchd lft over 2f out: ev ch fnl f: r.o)	hd	**3**	11/2^{2}	100	60
2709^{4}	**Further Flight (100)** (BWHills) **11-9-4** MHills(20) (b.hind: hld up & bhd: hdwy & nt clr over 4f out & over 2f out: styd on wl fnl f)	½	**4**	25/1	115	75
3238*	**Mohawk River (IRE) (94)** (MRStoute) **4-8-12** 4x JReid(18) (lw: trckd ldrs: effrt over 2f out: styd on one pce)	2	**5**	7/1^{3}	107	67
3110^{5}	**Top Cees (92)** (MrsJRRamsden) **7-8-10** JFortune(19) (hld up & bhd: styd on fnl 3f: nvr nrr)	2	**6**	16/1	102	62
2967a*	**Docklands Limo (86)** (BJMcMath) **4-8-4** MRoberts(12) (b.hind: chsd ldr: led over 3f out tl over 1f out: wknd towards fin)	½	**7**	20/1	96	56
3498*	**Turgenev (IRE) (78)** (RBastiman) **8-7-10** 4x FNorton(13) (hld up: hdwy over 2f out: styd on ins fnl f)	nk	**8**	50/1	87	47
3125^{9}	**Prairie Falcon (IRE) (90)** (BWHills) **3-7-7**(3) PFessey(7) (sme hdwy fnl 2f: nvr nr to chal)	4	**9**	33/1	95	43
	Foundry Lane (78) (MrsMReveley) **6-7-10** LCharnock(1) (bhd: sme hdwy 3f out: nvr nrr)	1¾	**10**	33/1	81	41
3255^{2}	**Raffles Rooster (78)** (AGNewcombe) **5-7-3**(7) RWinston(3) (hld up: gd hdwy over 3f out: wknd 2f out)	½	**11**	12/1	80	40
3137^{4}	**Bimsey (IRE) (82)** (RAkehurst) **7-8-0** JQuinn(2) (nvr bttr than mid div)	1¾	**12**	12/1	82	42
3110^{8}	**Premier Night (81)** (SDow) **4-7-10**(3) MartinDwyer(21) (nvr nr to chal)	2	**13**	33/1	79	39
3191^{4}	**Better Offer (IRE) (100)** (MrsAJPerrett) **5-9-4** PatEddery(8) (a in rr)	4	**14**	25/1	93	53
2271a^{2}	**Taufan's Melody (106)** (LadyHerries) **6-9-10** RCochrane(16) (hld up: a bhd)	10	**15**	33/1	88	48
2866^{4}	**Dreams End (83)** (PBowen) **9-8-1** GCarter(22) (b: bhd: effrt 3f out: sn no imp)	3½	**16**	16/1	61	21

2410*	**Purist (95)** (MRStoute) **3-8-1**[ow1] FLynch(4) (lw: chsd ldrs: rdn & wknd over 3f out)	3½	**17**	9/1	69	16
2108[3]	**Daraydan (IRE) (98)** (MCPipe) **5-9-2** KDarley(5) (in tch over 9f)	nk	**18**	33/1	71	31
2709[2]	**Willie Conquer (94)** (RAkehurst) **5-8-12** SSanders(6) (a in rr)	1¾	**19**	10/1	65	25
2989a*	**Gordi (USA) (106)** (DKWeld,Ireland) **4-9-10** MJKinane(11) (chsd ldrs tl wknd over 3f out: t.o)	5	**20**	16/1	72	32
2867[4]	**Colour Code (82)** (MrsASwinbank) **5-8-0**[ow1] GDuffield(14) (lw: uns rdr leaving stalls)		**U**	25/1	—	—
				(SP 132.6%)		**21 Rn**

2m 58.21 (4.61) CSF £166.02 CT £1,000.00 TOTE £64.80: £9.00 £2.00 £1.90 £4.90 (£247.40) Trio £352.60 OWNER Sunpak Potatoes (HAMBLETON) BRED Sir John Astor

LONG HANDICAP Media Star (USA) 7-12 Turgenev (IRE) 6-10 Prairie Falcon (IRE) 7-9 Foundry Lane 7-7

WEIGHT FOR AGE 3yo-12lb

3412 Far Ahead proved a very popular winner for the Yorkshire crowd but his starting price was a true reflection of his chance in such a competitive handicap and, though there was certainly no fluke about this success, he must have had help from above. (33/1)

3110* Media Star (USA) did not deserve to be beaten for he ran his heart out and, with courage like that, this defeat could be just a blip in his progress. (5/1)

3110 Puce, meeting the favourite on 7lb better terms, was entitled to finish ahead of him but her sustained, last-furlong challenge was just not quite enough to enable her to turn the tables. She is continuing to improve with every race and that big prize is well within her reach. (11/2)

2709 Further Flight found all the trouble that was going when attempting to improve from the rear early in the straight, and it is to his credit that he did eventually finish as close as he did. (25/1)

3238* Mohawk River (IRE) ran a first-class race on this step up in distance and class and, though he was unable to land a blow, this was certainly a step in the right direction. (7/1)

3110 Top Cees was unable to improve on his Goodwood run behind a couple of the principals but he does, by right, need a much stiffer test of stamina so this effort was pleasing enough. (16/1)

2967a* Docklands Limo, unproven at the trip, ran possibly his best-ever race here and, though he was out on his legs inside the distance, he never once stopped trying. (20/1)

3706 SCOTTISH EQUITABLE GIMCRACK STKS (Gp 2) (2-Y.O C & G) (Class A)

3-45 (3-54) **6f** £72,307.40 (£26,846.60: £12,955.80: £5,379.00: £2,222.00: £959.20) Stalls: High GOING: 0.00 sec per fur (G)

				SP	RR	SF
3464[4]	**Carrowkeel (IRE)** (BWHills) **2-8-11** PatEddery(1) (led tl ins fnl f: rallied u.p to ld cl home)	—	**1**	16/1	101	54
2584*	**Bold Fact (USA) (100)** (HRACecil) **2-9-0** KFallon(7) (lw: hld up: hdwy over 2f out: led ins fnl f: hdd & no ex nr fin)	¾	**2**	6/4[1]	102	55
2771*	**Headhunter (IRE)** (WJHaggas) **2-8-11** MHills(5) (hld up & bhd: hdwy ½-wy: ev ch over 1f out: wknd ins fnl f)	3	**3**	8/1	91	44
3148[2]	**Lord Kintyre (100)** (BRMillman) **2-8-11** TSprake(2) (plld hrd: trckd ldrs: effrt 2f out: one pce appr fnl f)	1	**4**	11/4[2]	88	41
3306*	**Eastern Purple (IRE)** (RAFahey) **2-8-11** JCarroll(6) (lw: chsd ldrs tl wknd over 1f out)	½	**5**	40/1	87?	40
3489*	**Social Charter (USA)** (PWChapple-Hyam) **2-8-11** JReid(4) (outpcd ½-wy: sn bhd)	1½	**6**	7/2[3]	83	36
2829*	**Ariant (USA)** (JHMGosden) **2-8-11** LDettori(3) (prom 3f: sn lost tch: t.o)	8	**7**	6/1	62	15
				(SP 122.6%)		**7 Rn**

1m 13.39 (2.89) CSF £40.25 TOTE £19.00: £4.40 £1.80 (£28.40) OWNER Sheikh Marwan Al Maktoum (LAMBOURN) BRED D. Houlihan

3464 Carrowkeel (IRE), much sharper after his pipe-opener last week, showed his true battling qualities to win this and his trainer believes he will be even better over seven furlongs. (16/1)

2584* Bold Fact (USA) ran as straight as a dye this time and looked to have control when nosing ahead two hundred yards out, but the winner just would not be denied and proved the stronger nearing the line. (6/4)

2771* Headhunter (IRE) gave connections a good run for their money but he was unable to match strides with the leading pair inside the final furlong and he may well need more time when tackling such hot company. (8/1)

3148 Lord Kintyre refused to settle and hardly gave himself a fair chance, and had shot his bolt entering the final furlong. (11/4)

3306* Eastern Purple (IRE) was far from disgraced on this step up in class and there are plenty of races to be won with this fellow. (40/1)

3707 ROUS (S) STKS (2-Y.O) (Class E)

4-15 (4-20) **6f** £11,527.50 (£3,495.00: £1,710.00: £817.50) Stalls: High GOING: 0.00 sec per fur (G)

				SP	RR	SF
3427*	**Chinaider (IRE) (67)** (MCPipe) **2-8-6** KDarley(15) (lw: a w ldrs: led 2f out: rdn & r.o wl)	—	**1**	6/1[3]	73	43
3209[6]	**Cumbrian Cadet (72)** (TDEasterby) **2-8-11** KFallon(14) (b.hind: a.p: ev ch fnl f: unable qckn)	1¾	**2**	14/1	73	43
3278[14]	**Deva Lady (72)** (MRChannon) **2-8-6** JFortune(9) (a.p: ev ch over 1f out: one pce)	1¼	**3**	10/1	65	35
2858[3]	**Pierpoint (IRE) (80)** (RAFahey) **2-8-11** MJKinane(19) (lw: hld up: hdwy & hung lft fnl 2f: nrst fin)	3½	**4**	11/2[2]	61	31
3306[13]	**Asbestaswecan** (WJarvis) **2-8-11** MHills(17) (lw: s.i.s: hdwy 2f out: nvr nrr)	1½	**5**	10/1	57	27
2942[6]	**Mill End Quest (74)** (MWEasterby) **2-8-6** TLucas(20) (bhd tl styd on fnl 2f)	hd	**6**	10/1	51	21
3483*	**Sandside (88)** (JBerry) **2-8-8**(3) PFessey(8) (led 4f: wknd fnl f)	½	**7**	7/1	55	25
3438[4]	**Burnt Yates (IRE) (72)** (MWEasterby) **2-8-11b**[1] RCochrane(6) (swtg: plld hrd: w ldrs tl wknd over 1f out)	nk	**8**	8/1	54	24
3265[8]	**Bollinger Rose (IRE)** (JJO'Neill) **2-8-6** LDettori(11) (hdwy over 2f out: nt rch ldrs)	½	**9**	16/1	48	18
3610[8]	**Blushing Victoria (72)** (MartynMeade) **2-8-6** TSprake(13) (nvr nr to chal)	¾	**10**	16/1	46	16
2545[7]	**Leather And Scrim (IRE)** (DNicholls) **2-7-13**(7) ANicholls(18) (chsd ldrs over 3f)	½	**11**	20/1	45	15
3295[6]	**Constant Attention (65)** (PFICole) **2-8-6b**[1] OPeslier(1) (mid div: drvn along ½-wy: no imp)	3	**12**	12/1	37	7
1619[10]	**Helenes Hill** (CSmith) **2-8-6** GDuffield(7) (s.i.s: hdwy ½-wy: sn wknd)	nk	**13**	50/1	36	6
	Safari Sam (IRE) (MHTompkins) **2-8-11** DBiggs(3) (w'like: s.s: bhd tl styd on appr fnl f)	2	**14**	16/1	36	6
3306[8]	**Top Floor (IRE)** (NTinkler) **2-8-11** KimTinkler(5) (chsd ldrs over 3f)	1¼	**15**	14/1	32	2
648[9]	**Thecomebackking** (SCWilliams) **2-8-4**(7) DarrenWilliams(10) (outpcd)	1¼	**16**	25/1	29	—
2919[5]	**Classy Cleo (IRE) (83)** (RHannon) **2-8-6** PatEddery(4) (swtg: w ldrs: rdn ½-wy: wknd 2f out)	1¾	**17**	11/4[1]	19	—
2904[9]	**Dibola** (JSWainwright) **2-8-11** DeanMcKeown(2) (swtg: in tch over 3f)	nk	**18**	50/1	23	—
3314[6]	**Justin Hope** (CEBrittain) **2-8-11** JCarroll(16) (outpcd)	5	**19**	16/1	10	—
				(SP 164.3%)		**19 Rn**

1m 13.87 (3.37) CSF £103.79 TOTE £8.10: £2.60 £4.70 £4.40 (£97.70) OWNER Mr A. J. Lomas (WELLINGTON) BRED James McMullan

Bt in 19,500gns. Deva Lady clmd C Allen £10,000.

OFFICIAL EXPLANATION **Mill End Quest: was later found to have a throat infection.**

3427* Chinaider (IRE) was making a quick repayment for the 10,000gs her present owners forked out when she was successful at Redcar earlier in the month. She won this with authority but she also cost a fortune to retain and it is doubtful if she will be seen in this grade again. (6/1)

3209 Cumbrian Cadet did nothing wrong on this step up to six furlongs and another success will come as no surprise. (14/1)

3019 Deva Lady showed plenty of pace all the way and she stuck to her task in the closing stages, but the leading pair were just that bit too good for her. (10/1: 8/1-12/1)

2858 Pierpoint (IRE) could never find the pace to lay up with the leaders and he did not help his jockey when making progress inside the last quarter-mile, for he continually hung left. When he gets his problems sorted out, he will be back to winning ways. (11/2)
3306 Asbestaswecan performed so much better than he did on his debut and the ability is certainly there. (10/1)
2942 Mill End Quest, having her first try at a slightly longer trip, was doing all her best work late on and she is better than the bare form suggests. (10/1: 8/1-12/1)
3483* Sandside held the call in the centre of the track but, as at Ayr on his most recent outing, seems to find this trip beyond him as yet. (7/1)

3708 ROSES STKS (Listed) (2-Y.O C & G) (Class A)
4-45 (4-46) **5f** £12,337.50 (£3,675.00: £1,750.00: £787.50) Stalls: High GOING: 0.00 sec per fur (G)

				SP	RR	SF
3619*	**Bay Prince (IRE)** (MRChannon) **2-8-11** JCarroll(6) (lw: a.p: led over 2f out: styd on wl fnl f)	—	1	16/1	95	50
3209^{7}	**Yorkies Boy (92)** (BAMcMahon) **2-8-11** KDarley(2) (led tl ½-wy: kpt on u.p: no ch w wnr)	1¾	2	20/1	89	44
3031*	**The Limping Cat (IRE)** (BCMorgan) **2-8-11** DeanMcKeown(3) (outpcd 2f out: styd on towards fin)	4	3	20/1	77	32
2685*	**Islamabad (97)** (GLewis) **2-8-11** PaulEddery(1) (b.hind: swtg: w ldrs: rdn ½-wy: outpcd appr fnl f)	1¾	4	$4/1^{2}$	71	26
3446*	**Moontabeh (88)** (PTWalwyn) **2-8-11** RCochrane(4) (lw: sn wl outpcd: effrt u.p 2f out: nvr nrr)	¾	5	12/1	69	24
3098*	**Titanic (IRE)** (JHMGosden) **2-8-11** LDettori(5) (drvn along ½-wy: sn chsng ldrs: wknd wl over 1f out)	nk	6	$8/11^{1}$	68	23
3414^{2}	**Chieftain (IRE) (100)** (NACallaghan) **2-8-11** MJKinane(7) (effrt ½-wy: sn rdn: wknd over 1f out)	2	7	$9/2^{3}$	61	16

(SP 119.2%) **7 Rn**

60.3 secs (2.60) CSF £249.40 TOTE £18.60: £4.20 £4.40 (£65.70) OWNER Mr D. W. Shepherd (UPPER LAMBOURN) BRED Rathasker Stud
3619* Bay Prince (IRE) followed up his very easy success at Pontefract four days earlier with another smoothly-gained win, and he is flying at the moment. (16/1)
3209 Yorkies Boy, the most experienced member of the field, made sure the winner had to assert himself but he was finding the task increasingly difficult inside the distance. (20/1)
3031* The Limping Cat (IRE), sluggish leaving the stalls, could not go the early pace but he did stay on and all is not lost yet. (20/1)
2685* Islamabad helped share the pace-making but he was being stoked up at halfway and was soon finding demands too great. (4/1)
3446* Moontabeh seemed to break well enough but he was soon detached by many lengths. Ridden along, he began to pick up and stayed on steadily but it must be admitted that five furlongs is far too sharp for him. (12/1)
3098* Titanic (IRE) had looked impressive against inferior opposition but he found this a different ball game and he was taken off his legs all the way. (8/11)
3414 Chieftain (IRE) (9/2: 3/1-5/1)

3709 FALMOUTH H'CAP (0-100) (3-Y.O) (Class C)
5-15 (5-16) **5f** £11,355.00 (£3,390.00: £1,620.00: £735.00) Stalls: High GOING: 0.00 sec per fur (G)

				SP	RR	SF
3086*	**Bahamian Beauty (USA) (74)** (DRLoder) **3-8-7** OPeslier(3) (trckd ldrs: led ins fnl f: r.o u.p)	—	1	$4/1^{1}$	82	51
2964*	**Shalstayholy (IRE) (71)** (GLMoore) **3-8-4** JQuinn(2) (a.p: led wl over 1f out tl ins fnl f: rallied u.p)	½	2	12/1	77	46
3011^{5}	**Prince Dome (IRE) (86)** (MartynWane) **3-9-5** LDettori(1) (chsd ldrs: ev ch fnl f: unable qckn)	s.h	3	$5/1^{3}$	92	61
3202*	**Butrinto (75)** (MajorWRHern) **3-8-8** TSprake(7) (swtg: trckd ldrs: rdn wl over 1f out: kpt on)	1¼	4	10/1	77	46
3121^{4}	**Pizzicato (64)** (RJRWilliams) **3-7-8**(3) RFfrench(4) (chsd ldrs: led ½-wy tl over 1f out: sn outpcd)	1¼	5	14/1	62	31
3385^{2}	**Distinctive Dream (IRE) (75)** (KTIvory) **3-8-5**(3) MartinDwyer(8) (swtg: dwlt: hdwy over 1f out: rdn & r.o fnl f)	hd	6	8/1	73	42
3194^{3}	**Dancethenightaway (87)** (BJMeehan) **3-8-13**(7) GHannon(6) (sltly hmpd s: sme hdwy ½-wy: nvr nr to chal)	1	7	12/1	82	51
3145^{2}	**Mary Magdalene (76)** (MBell) **3-8-9** MJKinane(12) (lw: sn outpcd: styd on appr fnl f)	½	8	$9/2^{2}$	69	38
3332*	**Top of The Form (IRE) (80)** (RAFahey) **3-8-6**(7) RWinston(11) (lw: led to ½-wy: wknd over 1f out)	1	9	12/1	70	39
3332^{3}	**Treasure Touch (IRE) (88)** (DNicholls) **3-9-7** RCochrane(10) (chsd ldrs 3f)	2½	10	16/1	70	39
3332^{2}	**Bayford Thrust (75)** (JBerry) **3-8-5b^{1}**(3) PFessey(5) (b: b.hind: s.v.s sn wl bhd: sme late hdwy)	½	11	14/1	55	24
2655^{2}	**Polish Warrior (IRE) (86)** (TDBarron) **3-9-5b** JCarroll(14) (trckd ldrs: shkn up 2f out: sn outpcd)	3	12	10/1	57	26
3273^{15}	**Vax Star (85)** (JLSpearing) **3-9-4b** JFortune(9) (swtg: w ldrs 3f: wknd qckly)	3	13	12/1	46	15

(SP 134.1%) **13 Rn**

60.0 secs (2.30) CSF £54.86 CT £203.41 TOTE £4.60: £2.20 £3.50 £2.50 (£35.80) Trio £86.60 OWNER Lucayan Stud (NEWMARKET) BRED Diane L. Perkins
3086* Bahamian Beauty (USA) has really come to herself now and, though she had a fight on her hands in the closing stages, she was up to it and won cosily in the end. (4/1)
2964* Shalstayholy (IRE), a progressive filly who seems better suited to the minimum trip, gave it her best shot and she ran up to her mark here. (12/1)
3011 Prince Dome (IRE) looked the likely winner inside the last furlong but he was conceding considerable weight and he was tapped for toe close home. This was a better than average contest for three-year-olds. (5/1)
3202* Butrinto, poised to challenge all the way, was unable to quicken sufficiently over this inadequate trip but he kept battling away, and more success is sure to come his way. (10/1)
3121 Pizzicato, still in the process of learning, ran well enough in this class and she is going the right way. (14/1)
3385 Distinctive Dream (IRE) had the blinkers left off this time and missed a beat at the start. Switched towards the stands' rail, he tried hard to mount a challenge in the latter stages but was unable to do so. (8/1)

T/Jkpt: Not won: £107,953.22 to York 21/8/97. T/Plpt: £7,199.20 (11.6 Tckts). T/Qdpt: £388.70 (10.31 Tckts) IM

3489-SALISBURY (R-H) (Good to Firm)
Thursday August 21st
Race 2: no official time taken; Race 5: flip start
WEATHER: showers after Race 4 WIND: slight against

3710 AXMINSTER 100 APPRENTICE H'CAP (0-80) (3-Y.O+) (Class G)
2-15 (2-15) **6f** £2,189.50 (£622.00: £308.50) Stalls: High GOING minus 0.30 sec per fur (GF)

				SP	RR	SF
3385^{3}	**John Emms (IRE) (72)** (MBell) **3-9-4**(3) RMullen(10) (hld up mid div: hdwy to ld over 1f out: r.o wl)	—	1	$4/1^{1}$	83	48
3614^{4}	**Impulsif (USA) (70)** (DJSffrenchDavis) **3-9-5** GMilligan(11) (swtg: a.p: ev ch over 1f out: nt qckn wl ins fnl f)	¾	2	$6/1^{3}$	79	44
3393^{2}	**Celandine (53)** (AndrewTurnell) **4-8-5** ADaly(9) (swtg: hld up & bhd: hdwy over 1f out: r.o ins fnl f)	1¾	3	13/2	57	25
2847^{2}	**Shades of Love (66)** (VSoane) **3-9-1** PRoberts(8) (lw: hld up mid div: hdwy 2f out: one pce fnl f)	2	4	$5/1^{2}$	65	30
2925^{11}	**Hopesay (75)** (JHMGosden) **3-9-10v^{1}** GFaulkner(4) (w ldr: led over 3f out tl over 1f out: wknd fnl f)	1¼	5	12/1	71	36
3241^{7}	**Geordie Lad (47)** (JABennett) **3-7-5**(5) RBrisland(12) (led over 2f: wknd over 1f out)	1¼	6	33/1	39	4

		Dist	Pos	SP	RR	SF
3561^{10}	**Velvet Jones (60)** (GFHCharles-Jones) **4-8-2**$^{(10)ow16}$ CharlotteCox(1) (s.s: nvr trbld ldrs)	nk	**7**	50/1	52	4
3292^{6}	**Indian Relative (62)** (RGuest) **4-8-4**$^{(10)}$ LucyBrown(2) (prom over 3f)	1¼	**8**	8/1	50	18
3327^{11}	**Blues Queen (70)** (MRChannon) **3-8-13**$^{(6)}$ AEddery(5) (s.s: a bhd)	nk	**9**	12/1	57	22
3580^{6}	**Erupt (63)** (GBBalding) **4-8-10**$^{(5)}$ JFowle(3) (s.s: bhd most of wy)	s.h	**10**	9/1	50	18
3018^{9}	**White Settler (63)** (RJHodges) **4-8-12**$^{(3)}$ AmandaSanders(6) (prom 4f)	1¼	**11**	10/1	47	15
3420^{6}	**Class Distinction (IRE) (60)** (RHannon) **3-8-1**$^{(8)}$ PDobbs(7) (prom tl wknd over 1f out: eased whn btn)	5	**12**	16/1	31	—

(SP 120.7%) **12 Rn**

1m 15.33 (2.33) CSF £25.53 CT £125.98 TOTE £6.30: £2.40 £1.90 £2.20 (£27.30) Trio £45.60 OWNER Richard Green (Fine Paintings) (NEWMARKET) BRED Michael and Fiona O'Connor
LONG HANDICAP Velvet Jones 7-5 Geordie Lad 7-5
WEIGHT FOR AGE 3yo-3lb
3385 John Emms (IRE) found this company a little easier and lost his maiden tag. (4/1)
3614 Impulsif (USA) had a stiffer six this time. (6/1)
3393 Celandine remains on a useful mark and might be worth a try at seven. (13/2)
2847 Shades of Love could never get to grips with the leaders on this handicap debut. (5/1)
2654 Hopesay, dropped 5lb, was tried in a visor after some very disappointing efforts this term. (12/1)
Geordie Lad was only running off his true mark because of his rider's allowance. (33/1)

3711 TATTERSALLS MAIDEN AUCTION STKS (2-Y.O) (Class E)

2-45 (2-47) **6f** £3,151.75 (£949.00: £459.50: £214.75) Stalls: High GOING minus 0.30 sec per fur (GF)

		Dist	Pos	SP	RR	SF
3193^{7}	**Bermuda Boy** (BJMeehan) **2-8-12** GDuffield(14) (a.p: led over 3f out: r.o wl)	—	**1**	9/1^{3}	91	54
3411^{3}	**Cease Fire (IRE)** (MrsJCecil) **2-8-0**$^{(3)}$ MartinDwyer(15) (dwlt: plld out & hdwy over 2f out: chsd wnr fnl f: rdn & edgd rt: r.o)	1¼	**2**	4/1^{2}	79	42
3247^{3}	**Dover Soul** (PJMakin) **2-7-12**$^{(3)}$ AWhelan(17) (led over 2f: one pce fnl f)	3½	**3**	10/1	67	30
3192^{8}	**Mysticism (87)** (CEBrittain) **2-7-10**$^{(5)}$ RMullen(11) (chsd ldrs: one pce fnl 2f)	1¼	**4**	4/1^{2}	64	27
3099^{4}	**Jungle Story (IRE)** (PTWalwyn) **2-8-5** RCochrane(16) (chsd ldrs: rdn over 2f out: one pce)	1½	**5**	9/1^{3}	64	27
	Lady Laphroaig (FR) (WRMuir) **2-8-3**^{ow2} GHind(13) (w'like: a.p: no hdwy fnl 2f)	3	**6**	33/1	54	15
3480^{2}	**Arian Da (74)** (BPalling) **2-8-2** SDrowne(8) (w ldrs over 4f)	nk	**7**	14/1	52	15
2181^{16}	**Recognition** (WJarvis) **2-8-8** NDay(10) (lw: chsd ldrs: rdn over 3f out: wknd 2f out)	1¼	**8**	33/1	55	18
	Clouds of Glory (RCharlton) **2-8-6** TSprake(7) (lw: s.s: nvr nrr)	5	**9**	14/1	40	3
	Smiling Voter (IRE) (RHannon) **2-8-6** WJO'Connor(12) (unf: bkwd: dwlt: n.d)	1¾	**10**	25/1	35	—
2893^{5}	**Mystagogue** (RHannon) **2-8-9** PaulEddery(4) (a bhd)	¾	**11**	33/1	36	—
	Ombra di Nube (FR) (CJames) **2-7-13** NAdams(2) (w'like: bkwd: plld hrd early: a bhd)	1¼	**12**	50/1	23	—
	Madame Jones (IRE) (BJMeehan) **2-7-12**$^{(7)ow3}$ GHannon(3) (w'like: a bhd)	¾	**13**	40/1	27	—
3471^{10}	**Zamarra** (MajorDNChappell) **2-8-0** JLowe(5) (prom over 3f)	5	**14**	50/1	8	—
2719^{2}	**Titan** (SDow) **2-8-6** JFEgan(6) (prom over 3f)	3½	**15**	14/1	5	—
3471^{17}	**Cd Newsround (IRE)** (MRChannon) **2-8-1**$^{(3)}$ PPMurphy(1) (a bhd)	½	**16**	33/1	2	—
3278^{3}	**Canonize (IRE)** (JWHills) **2-8-2**$^{(3)}$ MHenry(9) (bolted to s: mid div: rdn over 3f out: sn bhd)	1¼	**17**	5/2^{1}	—	—

(SP 139.6%) **17 Rn**

1m 14.3 (1.30) CSF £43.97 TOTE £10.40: £2.70 £1.70 £4.10 (£32.80) Trio £89.30 OWNER Thurloe Thoroughbreds (UPPER LAMBOURN) BRED Mrs W. H. Gibson Fleming
3193 Bermuda Boy found a drop back to six and this lower grade doing the trick. (9/1)
3411 Cease Fire (IRE), a half-sister to seven-furlong juvenile winner Majestic Heights, had to be switched into the centre of the course and then did not help her cause by drifting over to the far rail. She looks capable of taking a similar event. (4/1)
3247 Dover Soul again had to settle for a place on this step up to six. (10/1)
2862 Mysticism was a little disappointing over this longer trip. (4/1)
3099 Jungle Story (IRE) was reverting to six furlongs. (9/1)
Lady Laphroaig (FR), a 6,000gs yearling, is the first foal of an eleven-furlong winner in France so she is bred to require further. (33/1)
Clouds of Glory (14/1: 10/1-16/1)
3278 Canonize (IRE) was reported by her rider to have run far too freely on the way to post. (5/2)

3712 TOTE BOOKMAKERS H'CAP (0-95) (3-Y.O+) (Class C)

3-20 (3-20) **1m** £5,914.00 (£1,792.00: £876.00: £418.00) Stalls: High GOING minus 0.30 sec per fur (GF)

		Dist	Pos	SP	RR	SF
3112^{14}	**Conspicuous (IRE) (82)** (LGCottrell) **7-8-13**$^{(5)}$ ADaly(1) (hld up in rr: plld out over 2f out: gd hdwy over 1f out: edgd rt & led ins fnl f: rdn out)	—	**1**	10/1	95	49
2117^{8}	**Orange Place (IRE) (75)** (BJLlewellyn) **6-8-4**$^{(7)}$ JWilkinson(2) (led 6f: r.o one pce fnl f)	3	**2**	20/1	82	36
3190^{14}	**Sword Arm (81)** (RCharlton) **3-8-11v** TSprake(10) (a.p: led 2f out: sn rdn: wknd nr fin)	nk	**3**	4/1^{1}	87	35
3254^{5}	**Safey Ana (USA) (67)** (BHanbury) **6-8-3** GHind(6) (hld up: r.o one pce fnl 2f)	1½	**4**	8/1	70	24
3220^{5}	**Hawait (IRE) (88)** (BWHills) **3-9-1**$^{(3)}$ MartinDwyer(5) (lw: hld up: rdn & hdwy whn swtchd lft 2f out: hung lft over 1f out: one pce fnl f)	¾	**5**	12/1	90	38
	Moscow Mist (IRE) (80) (BPalling) **6-8-11**$^{(5)}$ PRoberts(8) (hld up in rr: nvr nr to chal)	½	**6**	33/1	81	35
3150^{4}	**Strazo (IRE) (92)** (LadyHerries) **4-10-0** RCochrane(4) (prom tl rdn & wknd over 2f out)	9	**7**	4/1^{1}	75	29
2835^{11}	**Civil Liberty (70)** (GLewis) **4-8-6** PaulEddery(9) (chsd ldr tl rdn over 3f out: btn whn hmpd over 2f out)	2½	**8**	9/2^{2}	48	2
3153^{15}	**Blue Imperial (FR) (71)** (JWHills) **3-7-12**$^{(3)}$ MHenry(7) (rdn 4f out: a bhd)	5	**9**	7/1^{3}	39	—
3392^{10}	**Broughtons Turmoil (73)** (BRMillman) **8-8-4**$^{(5)}$ GMilligan(3) (plld hrd: prom tl wknd qckly over 3f out: t.o)	14	**10**	12/1	13	—

(SP 114.0%) **10 Rn**

1m 42.9 (2.90) CSF £168.60 CT £865.01 TOTE £13.20: £2.90 £4.10 £1.40 (£106.60) Trio £286.20; £282.21 to Thirsk 22/8/97 OWNER Mrs Jenny Hopkins (CULLOMPTON) BRED Gerry Canavan
WEIGHT FOR AGE 3yo-6lb
2136 Conspicuous (IRE), dropped 2lb, has been highly tried of late and was left with plenty to do when switched for a run on this drop back to an admittedly testing mile. (10/1)
1320 Orange Place (IRE) ran a sound race for his new stable on ground plenty quick enough for him. (20/1)
3190 Sword Arm, reverting to a mile, was 6lb higher than when successful over course and distance in July. (4/1)
3254 Safey Ana (USA) (8/1: 6/1-9/1)
3220 Hawait (IRE) was back to a mark 5lb lower than when winning at Beverley in April. (12/1: op 8/1)
Moscow Mist (IRE) ran respectably on a belated seasonal debut for his new connections. (33/1)

3713 WHITCHURCH CONDITIONS STKS (3-Y.O+) (Class C)

3-55 (3-55) **1m** £4,932.40 (£1,724.40: £842.20: £361.00) Stalls: High GOING minus 0.30 sec per fur (GF)

Form	Horse	Dist	Pos	SP	RR	SF
1412^{7}	**Showboat (98)** (BWHills) **3-8-10** GDuffield(3) (hld up & plld hrd: hdwy over 1f out: hrd rdn to ld wl ins fnl f: r.o)	—	1	$7/2^{2}$	99	27
	Tarski (HRACecil) **3-8-10** JLowe(4) (hld up: swtchd rt & led over 1f out: sn rdn: hdd wl ins fnl f: r.o)	hd	2	$4/1^{3}$	99	27
3220^{2}	**Mashhaer (USA)** (MRStoute) **3-8-10** PaulEddery(1) (led over 5f: rdn to ld wl over 1f out: sn hdd: one pce fnl f)	2	3	$8/11^{1}$	95	23
1160^{14}	**Resounder (USA) (90)** (JHMGosden) **4-9-2** GHind(2) (chsd ldr: led wl over 2f out tl wl over 1f out: sn wknd)	8	4	8/1	79	13
				(SP 111.2%)	**4 Rn**	

1m 44.39 (4.39) CSF £14.90 TOTE £5.30 (£7.20) OWNER Mr R. D. Hollingsworth (LAMBOURN) BRED R. D. Hollingsworth
WEIGHT FOR AGE 3yo-6lb

957 Showboat took a keen hold in a muddling sort of race but certainly delivered the goods under pressure. (7/2)
Tarski lost nothing in defeat but he could be the type who is difficult to place if the Handicapper is none too kind. (4/1: op 5/2)
3220 Mashhaer (USA) was beaten fair and square over this extra furlong. (8/11)
Resounder (USA), coming back after a three-month absence, found little off the bridle. (8/1: 5/1-10/1)

3714 SUMMER OF STELLA H'CAP (0-70) (3-Y.O+) (Class E)

4-25 (4-36) **1m 6f** £3,366.25 (£1,015.00: £492.50: £231.25) GOING minus 0.30 sec per fur (GF)

Form	Horse	Dist	Pos	SP	RR	SF
3640^{7}	**Serious Trust (47)** (MrsLCJewell) **4-8-10** GDuffield(13) (mde all: hrd rdn over 1f out: r.o wl)	—	1	11/1	59	40
3317^{9}	**Strat's Legacy (33)** (DWPArbuthnot) **10-7-10** NAdams(9) (hld up: hdwy 5f out: styd on fnl f)	2	2	20/1	43	24
3455^{2}	**Harmony Hall (63)** (JRFanshawe) **3-9-0** RCochrane(10) (b: b.hind: hld up: stdy hdwy 5f out: chsd wnr over 3f out: ev ch over 1f out: one pce)	s.h	3	$11/2^{1}$	73	42
3559^{3}	**Sovereign Crest (IRE) (49)** (CAHorgan) **4-8-12b** PaulEddery(5) (bhd tl hdwy over 2f out: nt rch ldrs)	5	4	$13/2^{2}$	53	34
2498^{3}	**Classic Line (68)** (JLDunlop) **3-9-5b**^{1} TSprake(12) (rdn over 5f out: sn wl bhd: styd on fnl 2f)	1¼	5	$11/2^{1}$	71	40
3203^{6}	**Courbaril (55)** (MCPipe) **5-9-1v**$^{(3)}$ MartinDwyer(3) (prom tl wknd over 3f out)	2	6	$11/2^{1}$	55	36
3015^{9}	**Reimei (62)** (KCComerford) **8-9-11b**^{1} WJO'Connor(16) (hld up: wknd over 3f out)	2½	7	33/1	59	40
3203^{7}	**Tommy Cooper (35)** (MrsBarbaraWaring) **6-7-12b** JLowe(2) (b: plld hrd: chsd wnr tl rdn over 3f out: sn wknd)	¾	8	16/1	32	13
3475^{6}	**Courageous Knight (41)** (PHayward) **8-8-1**$^{(3)}$ MHenry(11) (hld up: rdn 5f out: bhd fnl 4f)	13	9	10/1	23	4
764^{8}	**The Deejay (IRE) (67)** (MrsMerritaJones) **3-9-1**$^{(3)}$ GParkin(15) (rdn 5f out: bhd fnl 3f)	1¾	10	16/1	47	16
3080^{6}	**Tasik Chini (USA) (65)** (PFICole) **3-9-2b** JFEgan(4) (plld hrd: prom tl rdn & wknd 4f out)	nk	11	14/1	44	13
3015^{11}	**Contract Bridge (IRE) (45)** (PGMurphy) **4-8-8** SDrowne(8) (lw: a bhd)	3	12	33/1	21	2
3046^{7}	**Spiral Flyer (IRE) (33)** (MDIUsher) **4-7-3**$^{(7)}$ JFowle(14) (a wl bhd)	2½	13	20/1	6	—
3277^{13}	**Alakdar (CAN) (66)** (ACStewart) **3-9-3** GHind(7) (swvd lft & uns rdr s)		U	$9/1^{3}$	—	—
2175^{4}	**Ginka (39)** (JWMullins) **6-7-9**$^{(7)ow6}$ SRighton(6) (swvd lft & uns rdr s)		U	25/1	—	—
2511^{6}	***Ronquista d'Or (47)*** (GAHam) **3-7-12** FNorton(1) (Withdrawn not under Starter's orders: lame)		W	33/1	—	—
				(SP 127.5%)	**15 Rn**	

3m 4.17 (5.47) CSF £204.47 CT £1,231.21 TOTE £14.10: £3.40 £9.90 £2.10 (£126.00) Trio £123.70 OWNER Mr Peter Allen (SUTTON VALENCE) BRED W. and R. Barnett Ltd
LONG HANDICAP Spiral Flyer (IRE) 7-6 Ginka 7-5 Strat's Legacy 7-6
WEIGHT FOR AGE 3yo-12lb
OFFICIAL EXPLANATION **Sovereign Crest (IRE): rider reported that the gelding had pulled hard and required settling, and that he met traffic problems as he tried to move out. By the time he found a gap, the leaders had gone, and he felt it prudent not to be over-hard on his mount.**

1169 Serious Trust, nibbled at in the market at Folkestone two days ago, was again supported here and did the business with a game front-running performance. (11/1)
2592 Strat's Legacy battled on from 4lb out of the handicap to secure the runner-up spot right on the line. (20/1)
3559 Sovereign Crest (IRE), trying an extra quarter-mile, caught the eye of the Stewards but the explanations were accepted. (13/2)
2498 Classic Line, 9lb higher than when winning at Redcar, was blinkered for the first time but they could not be described as really having had the desired effect. (11/2)
3203 Courbaril, down 3lb, was switched to a visor from blinkers. (11/2)
2846 Alakdar (CAN) (9/1: 6/1-10/1)

3715 BROAD CHALKE MAIDEN STKS (3-Y.O) (Class D)

4-55 (5-06) **6f 212y** £3,623.00 (£1,094.00: £532.00: £251.00) Stalls: High GOING minus 0.30 sec per fur (GF)

Form	Horse	Dist	Pos	SP	RR	SF
3281^{3}	**Northern Angel (IRE) (75)** (MrsJCecil) **3-8-11**$^{(3)}$ MartinDwyer(6) (mde all: rdn over 1f out: r.o wl)	—	1	$7/1^{3}$	83	35
1823^{3}	**Kawa-Ib (IRE) (81)** (PTWalwyn) **3-8-9** RCochrane(11) (a.p: chal on bit wl over 1f out: sn rdn: nt qckn ins fnl f)	nk	2	$6/5^{1}$	77	29
3463^{4}	**Bin Cyclone (USA)** (CEBrittain) **3-9-0** WJO'Connor(9) (w wnr: rdn over 2f out: wknd over 1f out)	5	3	$7/1^{3}$	71	23
1876^{5}	**Dust** (LordHuntingdon) **3-8-9** TSprake(3) (hld up mid div: no hdwy fnl 2f)	1½	4	$9/2^{2}$	62	14
3437^{4}	**Sandy Saddler** (SDow) **3-9-0** JFEgan(1) (hld up & bhd: shkn up over 2f out: nvr plcd to chal)	1¼	5	20/1	65	17
3389^{4}	**Hibernica (IRE)** (GBBalding) **3-8-9** SDrowne(10) (prom: rdn over 2f out: wknd over 1f out)	s.h	6	10/1	59	11
	Shantarskie (IRE) (CFWall) **3-9-0** GDuffield(2) (lw: hld up & plld hrd: nvr nr ldrs)	hd	7	8/1	64	16
	Hamleys (DMorris) **3-8-9** NDay(12) (neat: dwlt: plld hrd: a bhd)	½	8	25/1	58	10
2229^{5}	**Chili Bouchier (USA) (60)** (DMarks) **3-8-6**$^{(3)}$ AWhelan(4) (a bhd)	1	9	50/1	56	8
1870^{W}	**Swift Sovereign** (JHMGosden) **3-9-0** GHind(5) (a bhd)	2½	10	11/1	55	7
	Trevor Mitchell (JJBridger) **3-8-4**$^{(5)}$ ADaly(8) (bhd fnl 4f)	1	11	66/1	48	—
2591^{13}	**Nobby Beach** (WRMuir) **3-9-0** PaulEddery(7) (bhd fnl 4f: t.o)	13	12	66/1	23	—
				(SP 130.7%)	**12 Rn**	

1m 29.4 (3.40) CSF £15.42 TOTE £6.30: £2.10 £1.40 £2.50 (£6.60) Trio £17.40 OWNER Mr James Stone (NEWMARKET) BRED K. Molloy

3281 Northern Angel (IRE) found this drop back to seven doing the trick. (7/1: op 4/1)
1823 Kawa-Ib (IRE), another down in distance, did not find as much as one anticipated when asked to go and win her race. The first two did pull clear of the third but she does not look the type to take too short a price about. (6/5)
3463 Bin Cyclone (USA), who has not been getting home over a mile, may have to try his luck at sprinting if he continues to be ridden up with the pace. (7/1: op 4/1)
1876 Dust may find a mile off-setting her lack of pace. (9/2)

3437 Sandy Saddler, by no means knocked about, gave the impression he is capable of better things and is now qualified for handicaps. (20/1)
3389 Hibernica (IRE) was having her first run on fast ground. (10/1)
1406 Swift Sovereign (11/1: 7/1-12/1)

T/Plpt: £868.50 (13.52 Tckts). T/Qdpt: £70.50 (8.91 Tckts) KH

3444-YARMOUTH (L-H) (Good to Firm)
Thursday August 21st

WEATHER: fine & humid WIND: fresh half against

3716 BUNGAY H'CAP (0-70) (3-Y.O+ F & M) (Class E)
2-25 (2-35) **6f 3y** £3,278.25 (£981.00: £470.50: £215.25) Stalls: Low GOING minus 0.03 sec per fur (G)

Form	Horse / details	Dist	Pos	SP	RR	SF
2918^{4}	**Kentucky Fall (FR) (64)** (LadyHerries) **4-9-11** AClark(5) (hld up: hdwy to ld wl over 1f out: pushed clr fnl f)	—	1	$9/2^{2}$	74	56
3323^{6}	**Sally Slade (64)** (CACyzer) **5-9-11** MFenton(2) (hdwy 2f out: r.o fnl f)	3	2	10/1	66	48
3266^{2}	**Lamorna (50)** (MRChannon) **3-8-8** MRimmer(1) (s.i.s: hdwy 4f out: ev ch over 1f out: one pce)	2½	3	$4/1^{1}$	45	24
2724^{11}	**Princess Renata (IRE) (39)** (PatMitchell) **4-8-0** JTate(8) (w ldrs: rdn & no ex over 1f out)	1¾	4	50/1	30	12
	Rose Flyer (IRE) (42) (MCChapman) **7-7-10**(7) SCarson(3) (swtg: bkwd: led over 4f)	5	5	50/1	19	1
3241^{15}	**River Tweed (70)** (JHMGosden) **3-10-0** WRyan(4) (w ldrs over 3f)	3	6	9/1	39	18
3290^{3}	**Aquatic Queen (57)** (CADwyer) **3-8-12**(3) TEDurcan(10) (racd alone stands' side: spd over 4f)	½	7	$9/2^{2}$	25	4
3484^{2}	**Tutu Sixtysix (35)** (DonEnricoIncisa) **6-7-10** KimTinkler(6) (n.d)	1¼	8	$8/1^{3}$	—	—
3092^{9}	**Grace (61)** (JMBradley) **3-9-2**(3) RFfrench(9) (lw: a bhd)	1½	9	12/1	22	1
3393^{3}	**Sylvan Dancer (IRE) (58)** (CFWall) **3-9-2** DBiggs(7) (swtg: rdn over 2f out: a bhd)	hd	10	$9/2^{2}$	19	—

(SP 116.4%) **10 Rn**

1m 14.4 (3.50) CSF £44.43 CT £176.22 TOTE £6.70: £2.00 £3.00 £1.80 (£38.00) Trio £46.80 OWNER Mrs Edna Joyce Green (LITTLEHAMPTON) BRED Juddmonte Farms
LONG HANDICAP Tutu Sixtysix 7-2
WEIGHT FOR AGE 3yo-3lb

2918 Kentucky Fall (FR) moved poorly to post but the drop in trip was the key to getting her settled, and she got off the mark in good style. (9/2)
3323 Sally Slade went down very scratchily but, although she has never won above the minimum trip, she did better for a sixth furlong, as she has been outpaced early in her recent starts. (10/1: 6/1-12/1)
3266 Lamorna had to be led to post after flatly refusing to canter to post, delaying the start by several minutes. She soon recovered after failing to break on terms and does seem to have her own ideas about life. (4/1)
Princess Renata (IRE), having only her third run in twenty-five months, ran fast but, when the chips were down, she didn't impress with her head carriage. (50/1)
Rose Flyer (IRE), sweating and on her toes beforehand, was very keen going down for this first run in almost four years. She showed plenty of pace until lack of fitness told and may still have a race in her. All her victories to date have been over seven furlongs on Southwell's Fibresand. (50/1)
2045 River Tweed, again taken down early, gave way tamely soon after halfway. (9/1: op 5/1)

3717 E.B.F. WAXHAM MAIDEN STKS (2-Y.O) (Class D)
2-55 (3-00) **6f 3y** £3,556.00 (£1,063.00: £509.00: £232.00) Stalls: Low GOING minus 0.03 sec per fur (G)

Form	Horse / details	Dist	Pos	SP	RR	SF
3235^{6}	**Kheyrah (USA)** (EALDunlop) **2-8-9** MRimmer(7) (mde all: rdn clr appr fnl f)	—	1	$11/8^{1}$	82+	39
3494^{11}	**Tumblweed Prospect** (BJMeehan) **2-9-0** AClark(8) (plld hrd: chsd ldrs: rdn 3f out: kpt on fnl f)	3½	2	10/1	78	35
3386^{5}	**Flight** (LMCumani) **2-8-11**(3) RFfrench(1) (bit bkwd: trckd ldrs: effrt over 1f out: hung lft & no imp fnl f)	nk	3	$5/1^{3}$	77	34
	Sassy Lady (IRE) (CADwyer) **2-8-6**(3) TEDurcan(2) (unf: bit bkwd: in tch: styd on fnl 2f: nt pce to chal)	3	4	20/1	64	21
	Deep Magic (USA) (HRACecil) **2-8-9** WRyan(6) (neat: scope: lw: w wnr tl wknd 2f out)	7	5	$2/1^{2}$	45	2
3331^{6}	**Dangerus Precedent (IRE)** (CREgerton) **2-9-0** MFenton(3) (nvr nr ldrs)	1½	6	20/1	46	3
3450^{19}	**Freckles** (MJRyan) **2-8-9** GBardwell(4) (bit bkwd: j.path sn after s: sn pushed along & bhd)	3½	7	33/1	32	—
	Polo Venture (SPCWoods) **2-9-0** DBiggs(9) (leggy: bit bkwd: rdn 3f out: sn bhd)	10	8	16/1	10	—
3117^{14}	**Julies Jewel (IRE)** (MCChapman) **2-8-7**(7) SCarson(10) (bhd fnl 3f)	3	9	100/1	2	—

(SP 120.5%) **9 Rn**

1m 14.6 (3.70) CSF £15.29 TOTE £2.00: £1.10 £1.70 £1.60 (£10.90) Trio £10.60 OWNER Mr Hamdan Al Maktoum (NEWMARKET) BRED Shadwell Farm Inc

3235 Kheyrah (USA), again well supported in the ring, looked more the part this time. She is not a typical sprinter on looks, but did this in great style and the fact that her dam is a half-sister to Dunbeath, does give hope of her getting further. (11/8)
2829 Tumblweed Prospect, taken down early after flopping last time, still refused to settle but was made to look rather onepaced by the winner. He will stay further if he learns to settle. (10/1)
3386 Flight looks anything but an easy ride for, after travelling quite well, he did nothing but hang behind when asked to improve. He continues to give the impression that there is plenty more to come if the key can be found. (5/1: op 8/1)
Sassy Lady (IRE), a rather moderate mover, didn't make too bad a debut and should stay further. (20/1)
Deep Magic (USA), a half sister to the dam of Eltish, Fleet River and Yamuna, all of whom won for the yard, looked ready but failed to last home. Not over big, there is surely plenty to come. (2/1: 5/4-5/2)
3331 Dangerus Precedent (IRE) again did not show much, but this half-brother to Hen Harrier will surely stay further in time. (20/1)

3718 WILLIAM YOUNGER EAST ANGLIA H'CAP (0-80) (3-Y.O+) (Class D)
3-30 (3-33) **7f 3y** £3,836.70 (£1,146.60: £548.80: £249.90) Stalls: Low GOING minus 0.03 sec per fur (G)

Form	Horse / details	Dist	Pos	SP	RR	SF
3138^{6}	**Arterxerxes (75)** (MJHeaton-Ellis) **4-9-13** AClark(2) (lw: chsd ldrs tl led over 2f out: drvn out)	—	1	10/1	87	69
3615^{10}	**Blue Flyer (IRE) (68)** (RIngram) **4-9-6** MFenton(1) (lw: hld up: hdwy 2f out: rdn & no imp ins fnl f)	2½	2	16/1	74	56
1658^{13}	**Defined Feature (IRE) (73)** (DrJDScargill) **4-9-11** MRimmer(9) (styd on fnl 2f: nt pce to chal)	1½	3	33/1	76	58
3573^{*}	**Clytha Hill Lad (56)** (JMBradley) **6-8-8** 7x GBardwell(4) (b: lw: hdwy 2f out: nvr rchd ldrs)	nk	4	$5/1^{2}$	58	40
3421^{2}	**Mezzoramio (53)** (KAMorgan) **5-7-12v**(7) JoHunnam(12) (b: led 2f: no imp fnl f)	1¼	5	8/1	52	34
3385^{6}	**Wild Palm (66)** (WAO'Gorman) **5-9-1b**(3) RFfrench(5) (lw: bmpd s: ev ch 2f out: sn rdn & btn)	2½	6	$3/1^{1}$	60	42
3548^{7}	**Ertlon (70)** (CEBrittain) **7-9-1**(7) JGotobed(8) (bhd tl sme hdwy appr fnl f)	3½	7	14/1	56	38

				SP	RR	SF
3448^{3}	**On The Green (44)** (AHide) **4-7-7v**(3) MBaird(11) (racd alone stands' side: led after 2f out tl over 2f out: sn wknd)	5	**8**	14/1	18	—
3477^{2}	**Broctune Gold (65)** (BWHills) **6-9-0**(3) JDSmith(6) (in tch over 4f)	2	**9**	13/2	35	17
2508^{8}	**Flying Pennant (IRE) (55)** (JMBradley) **4-8-7** DBiggs(7) (a bhd)	7	**10**	33/1	9	—
3448*	**Rich In Love (IRE) (80)** (CACyzer) **3-9-13** WRyan(10) (dwlt: sn pushed along: a bhd)	11	**11**	6/1^{3}	9	—

(SP 114.6%) **11 Rn**

1m 27.5 (3.30) CSF £140.64 CT £4,569.66 TOTE £11.60: £2.80 £4.10 £7.20 (£61.20) Trio £375.20; £375.21 to Thirsk 22/8/97 OWNER Mr P G Lowe & Partners (WROUGHTON) BRED S. Tindall and Stowell Hill Ltd

LONG HANDICAP On The Green 7-6

WEIGHT FOR AGE 3yo-5lb

OFFICIAL EXPLANATION Rich In Love (IRE): was in season.

3138 Arterxerxes left his perplexing Sandown effort behind and this certainly is his trip, as he strode clear in the final furlong despite drifting slightly towards the centre of the track. (10/1: 7/1-11/1)

3423 Blue Flyer (IRE) made the best use of his rails draw, sticking to the fence throughout, but could close no more in the final furlong. (16/1)

343 Defined Feature (IRE) ran her best race since changing yards and would be mighty well handicapped if she came back to her very best. (33/1)

3573* Clytha Hill Lad, up in class and down in trip, looked in tremendous shape but with a couple of confirmed front-runners in the race, was unable to go the early pace. (5/1: 7/2-11/2)

3421 Mezzoramio tried to make all but the winner was never far away and took his measure soon after halfway. (8/1: op 5/1)

3385 Wild Palm, sandwiched leaving the stalls then, if anything, saw too much daylight this time and faded disappointingly. The handicapper tends to penalise this type of horse for their consistency. (3/1: op 5/1)

1501 Ertlon (14/1: op 8/1)

3448 On The Green, with the stalls on the far side, was alone in coming to the stands rail but was right up with the leaders until the closing stages. This practice did not look to have the advantage it had held at previous meetings. (14/1: 10/1-16/1)

3448* Rich In Love (IRE) (6/1: op 4/1)

3719 25TH RUNNING OF THE BOTTON BROTHERS LADIES' H'CAP (0-70) (3-Y.O+) (Class G)

4-05 (4-06) **1m 6f 17y** £2,322.00 (£642.00: £306.00) Stalls: High GOING minus 0.36 sec per fur (F)

				SP	RR	SF
3415^{5}	**Paradise Navy (70)** (CREgerton) **8-11-7b** MissERamsden(7) (a.p: led over 4f out: hld on cheekily fnl f)	—	**1**	7/1	80	61
3588^{3}	**Action Jackson (50)** (BJMcMath) **5-10-1** MissSSamworth(3) (a.p: ev ch over 1f out: unable qckn ins fnl f)	½	**2**	6/1	59	40
3279^{5}	**Mighty Phantom (USA) (62)** (JWHills) **4-10-13** MissEJohnsonHoughton(6) (hld up: hdwy 3f out: hung lft & no ex appr fnl f)	2	**3**	4/1^{2}	69	50
3401^{6}	**Nosey Native (60)** (JPearce) **4-10-11** MrsLPearce(2) (hdwy 4f out: one pce appr fnl f)	2	**4**	10/1	65	46
3415^{2}	**Dashing Invader (USA) (35)** (PWHarris) **4-9-0b** MrsCWilliams(8) (lw: led tl hdd over 4f out: rdn & one pce appr fnl f)	¾	**5**	9/2^{3}	39	20
3197^{3}	**Chris's Lad (55)** (BJMeehan) **6-10-6b** MissJAllison(1) (lw: chsd ldrs: rdn over 6f out: no imp fnl 4f)	7	**6**	2/1^{1}	51	32
3421^{11}	**Alisura (35)** (DTThom) **4-9-0v^{1}** MissJFeilden(5) (lw: wl bhd fnl 6f)	15	**7**	66/1	14	—
3449*	**Acerbus Dulcis (35)** (MCChapman) **6-9-0** MrsSBosley(4) (a bhd)	1	**8**	14/1	13	—

(SP 115.6%) **8 Rn**

3m 5.3 (7.30) CSF £44.38 CT £174.45 TOTE £6.80: £1.90 £1.90 £2.10 (£15.10) OWNER Elite Racing Club (CHADDLEWORTH) BRED Stetchworth Park Stud Ltd

LONG HANDICAP Alisura 8-4 Acerbus Dulcis 8-12

3415 Paradise Navy seems to have been called a dog more often than Lassie over the years, but his pilot seems to have found the key - make plenty of use of him but sit motionless in the closing stages. Allowed to do his own thing, he certainly looks genuine enough, although heaven help connections if he gets beaten a short head using such tactics. (7/1)

3588 Action Jackson was taking a dramatic step up in trip from his normal ten furlongs for the second time this year and, again, didn't seem inconvenienced. (6/1)

3279 Mighty Phantom (USA) gave the impression that she should have won this, but ducked in behind when the chance was there. (4/1: 3/1-9/2)

3401 Nosey Native, finishing fourth in the race for the second year running, probably doesn't quite get the trip. (10/1: 7/1-11/1)

3415 Dashing Invader (USA), off the mark she scored off on Fibresand, doesn't seem as good on turf. (9/2)

3197 Chris's Lad is certainly capable of wining off this mark but is running some way below his best at present. (2/1)

Alisura, related to a couple of decent stayers in Elburg and Iota, has lost her way since changing yards and did not take to the visor. (66/1)

3449* Acerbus Dulcis (14/1: op 8/1)

3720 WILLIAM YOUNGER EAST ANGLIA MAIDEN STKS (3-Y.O+) (Class D)

4-35 (4-37) **1m 2f 21y** £3,613.75 (£1,078.00: £514.50: £232.75) Stalls: Low GOING minus 0.36 sec per fur (F)

				SP	RR	SF
2494^{4}	**Grand Splendour (71)** (LadyHerries) **4-9-1** AClark(5) (trckd ldrs: led 3f out: rdn 2f out: lft clr ins fnl f)	—	**1**	9/4^{1}	80	37
3319^{3}	**Announcing** (JHMGosden) **3-8-12** AGarth(1) (dwlt: hdwy over 2f out: lft 2nd ins fnl f)	8	**2**	6/1^{3}	72	21
3132^{2}	**Love Venture (69)** (SPCWoods) **3-8-7** WRyan(8) (led 7f: one pce)	4	**3**	5/1^{2}	61	10
	Double Star (JLHarris) **6-9-3**(3) TEDurcan(2) (lw: chsd ldrs 6f: sn rdn & btn)	½	**4**	20/1	65	22
3419^{9}	**Panorama** (LMCumani) **3-8-4**(3) RFfrench(3) (chsd ldrs: no hdwy fnl 4f)	1¼	**5**	8/1	58	7
2960^{5}	**Joust** (CEBrittain) **3-8-12** MRimmer(7) (bit bkwd: plld hrd: in tch 6f)	1½	**6**	6/1^{3}	61	10
2952^{6}	**Shailendra (IRE)** (JHMGosden) **3-8-7** DaleGibson(9) (hld up & plld hrd: rdn 3f out: nvr nr ldrs)	2½	**7**	16/1	52	1
	Kayesam (JLHarris) **3-8-12** DBiggs(4) (w'like: unf: dwlt: t.o fnl 5f)	dist	**8**	33/1	—	—
992^{4}	**Academy Star** (JRFanshawe) **3-8-7** NVarley(6) (trckd ldrs: reminders 6f out: plld out over 2f out: sn ev ch: hld whn sddle slipped & uns rdr ins fnl f)		**U**	6/1^{3}	—	—

(SP 115.0%) **9 Rn**

2m 7.9 (4.10) CSF £14.42 TOTE £3.00: £1.10 £2.70 £1.40 (£10.40) Trio £6.60 OWNER Mr Andy Holder (LITTLEHAMPTON) BRED GAINSBOROUGH STUD MANAGEMENT LTD

WEIGHT FOR AGE 3yo-8lb

2494 Grand Splendour, with his tongue tied down for the first time, would have won by a length or two but for the incident in the final furlong. She has taken a long time to break her duck and was doing it in a poor race, but this will have done wonders for her. (9/4)

3319 Announcing, dropped in trip, was never going fast enough, but would come into the reckoning if stepped up in trip in a small handicap. (6/1: 4/1-7/1)

3132 Love Venture tried to force the pace and looks short of a change of gear. (5/1)

Double Star, a tall bumper winner, lacked a bit of pace in the straight but looks sure to do better stepped back up in trip. (20/1)

Panorama, a half-sister to Secret Archive, looks to need further than this. (8/1: 5/1-9/1)

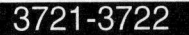

2960 Joust took too strong a hold to see out this longer trip. (6/1: 4/1-13/2)
992 Academy Star would have finished a clear second but for a slipping saddle giving Varley a nasty fall about two hundred yards from home. (6/1: 4/1-13/2)

3721 CROMER LIMITED STKS (0-65) (3-Y.O+) (Class F)

5-05 (5-11) **1m 2f 21y** £2,469.00 (£684.00: £327.00) Stalls: Low GOING minus 0.36 sec per fur (F)

				SP	RR	SF
3200[12]	**Count Tony (62)** (SPCWoods) **3-8-12** WRyan(4) (lw: hld up: hdwy to ld over 1f out: sn clr: rdn out)	—	1	7/1	71	41
3044[U]	**Fife Major (USA) (63)** (BWHills) **3-8-7**(3) JDSmith(2) (lw: plld hrd: trckd ldrs: n.m.r 3f out: plld out 2f out: r.o fnl f: nt trble wnr)	3	2	5/2[1]	64	34
3448[2]	**Karinska (60)** (MCChapman) **7-8-12**(7) SCarson(6) (lw: hld up: hdwy 4f out: one pce appr fnl f)	3	3	100/30[2]	61	39
2487[17]	**Expialiodoocius (63)** (JRFanshawe) **3-8-10** AClark(3) (trckd ldr: ev ch 4f out tl rdn & btn appr fnl f)	3	4	10/1	55	25
*3232**	**Soden (IRE) (65)** (TGMills) **3-8-6**(3) RFfrench(1) (trckd ldr: n.m.r fr 3f out: no ch whn hmpd 1f out)	s.h	5	7/2[3]	54	24
1859[8]	**Cambridge Ball (IRE) (65)** (MJohnston) **3-8-7** JFanning(5) (led tl hdd & wknd over 1f out)	2½	6	6/1	48	18
				(SP 109.7%)		**6 Rn**

2m 7.0 (3.20) CSF £21.54 TOTE £7.60: £2.40 £2.30 (£19.00) OWNER One Dream Partnership (NEWMARKET) BRED Woodsway Stud
WEIGHT FOR AGE 3yo-8lb
2668 Count Tony, taken down early, missed the trouble and produced a good turn of speed on the outside to seal the issue. (7/1)
3044 Fife Major (USA), anchored behind the two leaders to get him to settle over this longer trip, didn't get a clear run in the straight and, by the time he got out, the winner was long gone. (5/2: 2/1-3/1)
3448 Karinska, given a good tactical ride by the pilot who crept up on the outside of his two fellow apprentices on the home turn, holding them in as the leaders tied up. (100/30)
1804 Expialiodoocius, taken down steadily, didn't last home again and might be worth a try over a shorter trip. (10/1)
3232* Soden (IRE) got into all sorts of trouble in the straight and this should be forgotten (7/2: 5/2-4/1)
Cambridge Ball (IRE), having her second run of the season, both over this trip, faded quickly once headed and is not a guaranteed stayer. (6/1: 5/1-8/1)

T/Plpt: £187.30 (80.3 Tckts). T/Qdpt: £117.10 (7.56 Tckts) Dk

3703-**YORK (L-H) (Good)**
Thursday August 21st
WEATHER: humid and raining WIND: mod half bhd

3722 LADBROKE KNAVESMIRE H'CAP (0-95) (3-Y.O+) (Class C)

2-05 (2-07) **1m 3f 195y** £17,220.00 (£5,160.00: £2,480.00: £1,140.00) Stalls: Low GOING: 0.06 sec per fur (G)

				SP	RR	SF
3120[2]	**Honourable (83)** (JWWatts) **3-8-6** LDettori(14) (mde virtually all: styd on wl appr fnl f)	—	1	8/1[3]	98	58
3478*	**Pension Fund (74)** (MWEasterby) **3-7-11** 4x JQuinn(4) (lw: hld up: stdy hdwy & nt clr run over 2f out: styd on fnl f: nt rch wnr)	1¾	2	10/1	87	47
3333[5]	**Remaadi Sun (81)** (MDIUsher) **5-9-0** RStreet(10) (stdd s: hld up & bhd: gd hdwy over 2f out: rdn & edgd lft fnl f: r.o same pce)	2	3	16/1	91	61
3492[7]	**Oops Pettie (86)** (MrsJCecil) **4-9-5** JCarroll(13) (lw: chsd ldrs: chal 3f out: kpt on same pce)	1½	4	9/1	94	64
3444*	**Dantesque (IRE) (86)** (GWragg) **4-9-5** MHills(7) (lw: hld up: hdwy to chse ldrs over 3f out: styd on one pce fnl 2f)	1¾	5	9/2[1]	92	62
2297*	**Shaffishayes (71)** (MrsMReveley) **5-8-4** DeanMcKeown(3) (hld up: hdwy over 2f out: nvr nr ldrs)	5	6	14/1	70	40
3221[2]	**Mentalasanythin (66)** (DHaydnJones) **8-7-13**ow1 AMackay(9) (swtg: w wnr tl wknd 2f out)	nk	7	20/1	64	33
3542[2]	**Hazard a Guess (IRE) (81)** (DNicholls) **7-9-0** AlexGreaves(11) (lw: chsd ldrs tl wknd 2f out)	hd	8	14/1	79	49
3498[6]	**My Learned Friend (79)** (AHide) **6-8-12** AMcGlone(6) (hld up: hdwy over 3f out: rdn over 2f out: no imp)	1	9	12/1	76	46
3263[2]	**My Lewicia (IRE) (94)** (PWHarris) **4-9-8**(5) CLowther(2) (hld up: hdwy on ins over 3f out: sn rdn & no imp)	1	10	20/1	90	60
3333[2]	**Tessajoe (86)** (MJCamacho) **5-9-5** LCharnock(15) (b.hind: hld up: wnt prom 7f out: effrt over 2f out: sn wknd)	1¼	11	14/1	80	50
3333*	**Celestial Choir (89)** (JLEyre) **7-9-8** OPears(1) (lw: chsd ldrs: effrt over 3f out: wknd over 2f out: eased)	4	12	7/1[2]	78	48
1390[5]	**Step N Go (IRE) (73)** (MrsJRRamsden) **3-7-7**(3) PFessey(12) (bit bkwd: plld hrd early: bhd & pushed along 7f out: n.d)	3	13	12/1	58	18
2180[3]	**Darcy (92)** (MRStoute) **3-9-1v**[1] JReid(5) (trckd ldrs: rdn over 3f out: sn lost pl)	2½	14	9/1	73	33
3184*	**Mattimeo (IRE) (80)** (APJarvis) **4-8-13** KDarley(8) (lw: in tch: drvn along 4f out: wknd over 2f out)	3	15	14/1	57	27
				(SP 128.3%)		**15 Rn**

2m 33.3 (5.50) CSF £82.78 CT £1,158.74 TOTE £6.40: £2.50 £2.40 £4.90 (£39.80) Trio £376.50 OWNER Sheikh Mohammed (RICHMOND) BRED Darley Stud Management Co Ltd
LONG HANDICAP Step N Go (IRE) 7-7
WEIGHT FOR AGE 3yo-10lb
3120 Honourable, who raced wide in the early stages, was allowed to set his own pace. Stepping up the gallop halfway up the home straight, in the end he took this in decisive fashion. (8/1)
3478* Pension Fund, ridden to get the trip, rather overdid the waiting tactics. Forced to check halfway up the straight, he put in a good run in the final furlong but the winner was home and dry. He is likely to go up in the ratings as a result of this and connections will no doubt have him out again soon. (10/1)
3333 Remaadi Sun, without any headgear, usually runs well on this track. Given a negative ride as usual, he looked a big danger to the winner coming to the final furlong but, under his veteran jockey, he edged left and ended up on the running rail. (16/1)
Oops Pettie, stepping up in distance, seemed to stay a mile and a half alright. (9/1: 6/1-10/1)
3444* Dantesque (IRE), stepping up in distance, would have been suited by a more strongly-run race. (9/2)
3333 Tessajoe (14/1: op 8/1)
3333* Celestial Choir, who won this a year ago from a 3lb lower mark, was not suited by the slow pace and, once her chance had slipped, she was wisely eased. (7/1)

3723 STAKIS CASINOS LOWTHER STKS (Gp 2) (2-Y.O F) (Class A)

2-35 (2-36) **6f** £45,406.69 (£16,835.30: £8,105.15: £3,343.25: £1,359.13: £565.48) Stalls: High GOING: 0.06 sec per fur (G)

Form	Horse / Details	Dist	Pos	SP	RR	SF
2057[2]	**Cape Verdi (IRE)** (PWChapple-Hyam) **2-8-11** JReid(10) (lw: hld up: hdwy over 2f out: r.o wl fnl f: led post)..	—	**1**	7/4[1]	99	72
3049*	**Embassy** (DRLoder) **2-9-0** PatEddery(6) (lw: sn chsng ldrs: led over 1f out: hrd rdn & edgd lft fnl f: faltered nr fin: jst ct)	s.h	**2**	11/4[2]	102	75
2024*	**Nadwah (USA) (100)** (PTWalwyn) **2-9-0** RHills(1) (lw: sn trckng ldrs: kpt on wl fnl f)	1½	**3**	9/1	98	71
3049[2]	**Miss Zafonic (FR)** (RHannon) **2-8-11** DaneO'Neill(8) (dwlt s: sn trckng ldrs: kpt on same pce fnl 2f)	3	**4**	6/1	87	60
2959[2]	**Statua (IRE)** (PJMakin) **2-8-11** JFortune(2) (hld up: effrt over 2f out: sn outpcd: kpt on wl fnl f)	½	**5**	66/1	86?	59
3411*	**Zelanda (IRE)** (JHMGosden) **2-8-11** OPeslier(4) (led tl hdd & wknd over 1f out)	nk	**6**	10/1	85	58
2875*	**Dazilyn Lady (USA)** (PWHarris) **2-8-11** ACulhane(5) (hld up: effrt over 2f out: sn outpcd: kpt on fnl f)	1	**7**	25/1	82	55
3114*	**Expect To Shine** (BWHills) **2-8-11** MHills(9) (trckd ldrs: effrt over 2f out: wknd over 1f out: eased)	10	**8**	10/1	55	28
3009*	**Shuhrah (USA)** (SbinSuroor) **2-8-11** LDettori(7) (lw: chsd ldrs: pushed along ½-wy: sn outpcd & lost pl: eased)	5	**9**	11/2[3]	42	15
				(SP 126.2%)	**9 Rn**	

1m 12.48 (1.98) CSF £6.77 TOTE £3.00: £1.40 £1.60 £2.30 (£3.70) Trio £13.30 OWNER Mr R. E. Sangster (MARLBOROUGH) BRED Swettenham Stud

2057 Cape Verdi (IRE) was given a confident ride. Racing towards the stands' side, when her jockey realised Embassy was two or three lengths clear towards the far side coming to the final furlong he set her alight and, answering every call, she got up in the very last stride. Stoutly bred, a mile in time will prove no problem but, in truth, this was not a vintage Lowther. (7/4)

3049* Embassy, who has a pronounced round action, really went for home towards the far side coming to the final furlong. Pinching two or three lengths, she edged left and faltered near to the line but, with hindsight, her rider must wish he had ridden her all the way to the wire. Had he done so, she must have hung on. She was giving Cape Verdi 3lb. (11/4)

2024* Nadwah (USA) seemed to be suited by the step up to six and finished clear of the rest. (9/1)

3049 Miss Zafonic (FR) is getting to be too keen for her own good. (6/1: 4/1-13/2)

2959 Statua (IRE), who looked well out of her depth, was far from disgraced. Her proximity to the first two cast doubt as to the overall value of the form. (66/1)

3411* Zelanda (IRE) showed her rivals a clean pair of heels for four furlongs. (10/1)

3009* Shuhrah (USA) (11/2: 4/1-6/1)

3724 NUNTHORPE STKS (Gp 1) (Class A)

3-10 (3-11) **5f** £53,110.00 (£53,110.00: £13,517.75: £5,326.25: £1,913.13: £547.88) Stalls: High GOING: 0.06 sec per fur (G)

Form	Horse / Details	Dist	Pos	SP	RR	SF
3111[11]	**Ya Malak (116)** (DNicholls) **6-9-9** AlexGreaves(4) (lw: hld up: stdy hdwy ½-wy: r.o wl u.p fnl f to jn ldr post)..	—	**1**	11/1	121	79
3217[11]	**Coastal Bluff (110)** (TDBarron) **5-9-9** KDarley(6) (b.hind: bmpd s: bit sn broke: w ldrs: led wl over 1f out: jst lasted)	—	**1**	6/1[2]	121	79
3111*	**Averti (IRE) (108)** (WRMuir) **6-9-9** KFallon(10) (lw: fly-jumped s: hdwy over 1f out: styd on wl towards fin)	hd	**3**	10/1	121	79
2056[18]	**Cyrano's Lad (IRE) (103)** (CADwyer) **8-9-9** JFortune(13) (a chsng ldrs: kpt on wl fnl f)	¾	**4**	50/1	118	76
3111[10]	**Eveningperformance (116)** (HCandy) **6-9-6** CRutter(1) (led to ½-wy: no ex fnl f)	1	**5**	12/1	112	70
3001a[9]	**Hever Golf Rose (107)** (TJNaughton) **6-9-6** JReid(16) (lw: chsd ldrs: rdn & outpcd ½-wy: styd on wl fnl f)	nk	**6**	20/1	111	69
	Mind Games (JBerry) **5-9-9** DHolland(15) (w ldrs: led ½-wy tl over 1f out: grad wknd)	1¼	**7**	9/1[3]	110	68
3111[4]	**Bolshoi (IRE) (105)** (JBerry) **5-9-9b** EmmaO'Gorman(9) (lw: sn outpcd: rdn ½-wy: kpt on wl fnl f)	nk	**8**	20/1	109	67
3111[7]	**Don't Worry Me (IRE)** (GHenrot,France) **5-9-6** OPeslier(5) (lw: in tch: rdn & outpcd ½-wy: styd on appr fnl f)	nk	**9**	10/1	105	63
3111[3]	**Indian Rocket (114)** (JLDunlop) **3-9-7** RHills(14) (lw: mid div: styng on whn nt clr run 1f out)	nk	**10**	9/1[3]	107	63
3111[14]	**Croft Pool (108)** (JAGlover) **6-9-9** GCarter(11) (lw: sn wl outpcd & bhd)	2½	**11**	40/1	99	57
3023[2]	**Easycall (110)** (BJMeehan) **3-9-7** MTebbutt(12) (lw: hld up: sme hdwy ½-wy: hung lft: sn wknd)	¾	**12**	12/1	97	53
3372a*	**Struggler (112)** (DRLoder) **5-9-9** PatEddery(8) (swvd lft s: sn trckng ldrs: hung lft & wknd over 1f out: eased towards fin)	1	**13**	16/1	94	52
2599*	**Compton Place (122)** (JARToller) **3-9-7** SSanders(3) (lw: dwlt s: hdwy u.p ½-wy: wknd 2f out)	8	**14**	9/2[1]	68	24
3111[15]	**Almaty (IRE) (112)** (JHMGosden) **4-9-9** LDettori(2) (chsd ldrs over 3f: sn wknd)	1½	**15**	10/1	63	21
				(SP 123.3%)	**15 Rn**	

59.58 secs (1.88) CSF CB & YM £31.33, YM & CB £33.63 TOTE CB £3.40 YM £6.30: CB £2.80 YM £4.10 £3.40 (£34.10) Trio £109.50
OWNER Contrac Promotions Ltd, Consultco Ltd (THIRSK)/Mrs D. E. Sharp (THIRSK) BRED Mrs R. B. Kennard/R. M. West
WEIGHT FOR AGE 3yo-2lb

IN-FOCUS: **The dead-heat, announced after a twenty-minute delay, meant that Greaves had become the first woman to ride a Group One winner in Britain, and gave Darley just reward for a tremendous ride which ended with him being unseated after the line.**

3111 Ya Malak, who was found to be suffering from colic after Goodwood, came good and is ideally suited by a strong-run race. Ridden to perfection, he battled on to share the prize right on the line. Much improved, he is a credit to his hard-working trainer. (11/1)

3217 Coastal Bluff had a bit which broke soon after the start. Kevin Darley had only the mane to hold on and, with the horse keeping as straight as a dye and running on like a hero, he hung on to share the spoils in a memorable race. (6/1)

3111* Averti (IRE) fly-jumped leaving the stalls and lost more ground than he was eventually beaten by. (10/1)

1596* Cyrano's Lad (IRE), who started life running in two-mile National Hunt Flat races, ran the race of his life and would have been meeting Ya Malak on 12lb better terms in a handicap. (50/1)

Eveningperformance, pipped in this prize a year ago, has speed to burn and ran easily her best race so far this time. (12/1)

3001a Hever Golf Rose proved she is as good as ever. (20/1)

Mind Games, back on the racecourse after a successful time at stud, showed all his old speed but, on this rain-softened ground, he faded in the final furlong. (9/1)

3111 Bolshoi (IRE) ran his usual race, coming from off the pace, and is better suited by tracks with an uphill finish. (20/1)

3111 Indian Rocket was staying on in determined fashion when running completely out of room a furlong out. He is much better suited by six and is one to keep in mind for a nice prize this back-end. (9/1)

2599* Compton Place, dropping back to five, gave away ground at the start. He was never going in the race and this was a shadow of the horse that shone at Newmarket. Whether that was a flash in the pan, only time will tell. (9/2: op 3/1)

3725 BRADFORD & BINGLEY RATED STKS H'CAP (0-105) (3-Y.O+) (Class B)

3-45 (3-47) **7f 202y** £23,563.40 (£8,720.60: £4,185.30: £1,711.50: £680.75: £268.45) Stalls: Low GOING: 0.30 sec per fur (G)

				SP	RR	SF
3198^{6}	**Concer Un (89)** (SCWilliams) **5-8-7** KDarley(1) (b: hdwy over 2f out: styd on wl to ld nr fin)	—	1	9/1	98	70
3112^{10}	**Hawksley Hill (IRE) (103)** (MrsJRRamsden) **4-9-7v** JFortune(12) (hdwy & nt clr run over 2f out: styd on wl to ld ins fnl f: jst ct)	nk	2	8/1	111	83
3051^{3}	**Russian Music (99)** (MissGayKelleway) **4-9-3** KFallon(9) (lw: a chsng ldrs: led over 2f out tl ins fnl f: r.o)	¾	3	16/1	106	78
1982^{5}	**The Prince (93)** (GWragg) **3-8-5** MHills(4) (lw: hld up: gd hdwy over 3f out: ev ch 2f out: wknd fnl f)	3½	4	$6/1^{2}$	93	59
3150^{2}	**Crumpton Hill (IRE) (94)** (NAGraham) **5-8-12** MRoberts(13) (lw: bhd: hdwy 2f out: styd on towards fin)	3	5	9/1	88	60
3190^{4}	**Calypso Grant (IRE) (93)** (PWHarris) **3-8-0**(5) CLowther(6) (bhd: effrt over 3f out: styd on fnl 2f: nvr nr to chal)	2	6	9/1	83	49
2678*	**Jo Mell (93)** (TDEasterby) **4-8-11** JReid(8) (lw: led tl over 2f out: grad wknd)	4	7	$7/2^{1}$	75	47
3189^{4}	**Wasp Ranger (USA) (94)** (PFICole) **3-8-6** PatEddery(10) (lw: w ldrs: wkng whn n.m.r 2f out)	1½	8	12/1	73	39
3189^{2}	**Great Child (89)** (MRStoute) **3-8-1** FLynch(14) (b.off hind: in tch: effrt over 3f out: wknd 2f out)	1½	9	$7/1^{3}$	65	31
3144^{3}	**Kumait (USA) (96)** (DRLoder) **3-8-8** LDettori(3) (lw: hld up: stdy hdwy 3f out: sn pushed along & wknd)	8	10	12/1	55	21
2136^{10}	**Musick House (IRE) (91)** (MissGayKelleway) **4-8-9** SSanders(5) (lw: b.hind: bhd & drvn along 3f out: n.d)	nk	11	25/1	50	22
2766^{17}	**Red Robbo (CAN) (94)** (RAkehurst) **4-8-12** OPeslier(2) (lw: chsd ldrs: ev ch over 2f out: sn wknd)	5	12	$7/1^{3}$	43	15
3252*	**Hi Nod (96)** (MJCamacho) **7-9-0** LCharnock(11) (lw: in tch: drvn along over 4f out: sn wknd & eased)	4	13	12/1	37	9
3243*	**Caviar Royale (IRE) (100)** (TDBarron) **3-8-12** JCarroll(7) (hld up: effrt over 3f out: sn lost pl)	nk	14	16/1	40	6
				(SP 141.3%)		**14 Rn**

1m 39.55 (2.55) CSF £85.01 CT £1,117.92 TOTE £12.40: £3.40 £3.50 £3.90 (£67.10) Trio £244.70 OWNER Miss L. J. Ward (NEWMARKET) BRED Lloyd Bros

LONG HANDICAP Concer Un 8-4

WEIGHT FOR AGE 3yo-6lb

3198 Concer Un, who won this race a year ago from a 1lb lower mark, is as tough as old boots and he ran on with real determination to get up near the line. (9/1)

2766* Hawksley Hill (IRE), well suited by the fast gallop, showed himself to be better than ever. Messed about when starting his run, he had the prize whipped from under his nose near the line. (8/1)

3051 Russian Music ran really well. Up with the pace in a strong-run race, he was only shaded near the line. (16/1)

1982 The Prince, well supported in the market, moved up looking a real danger but, on the rain-softened ground, he tired in the final furlong. Still inexperienced, he will win more races in due course. (6/1)

3150 Crumpton Hill (IRE), from a 2lb higher mark, could not win the way he was ridden. Last of all two furlongs out, it would be interesting to see how he would fare with more use made of him. (9/1)

3190 Calypso Grant (IRE) probably found this trip on the sharp side. (9/1)

2678* Jo Mell was 20lb higher than when his winning run started at Newcastle three outings ago. (7/2)

3726 MOORESTYLE CONVIVIAL MAIDEN STKS (2-Y.O) (Class D)

4-15 (4-21) **6f** £10,672.50 (£3,180.00: £1,515.00: £682.50) Stalls: High GOING: 0.30 sec per fur (G)

				SP	RR	SF
	Bintang (IRE) (PFICole) **2-9-0** PatEddery(4) (w'like: scope: sn trckng ldrs gng wl: led over 2f out: shkn up & qcknd clr over 1f out: eased towards fin)	—	1	5/1	104+	73
3219^{2}	**Elhabub** (BWHills) **2-9-0** RHills(1) (lw: trckd ldr: led after 2f tl over 2f out: no ch w wnr)	8	2	$5/2^{1}$	83	52
3219^{6}	**The Downtown Fox** (BAMcMahon) **2-9-0** SSanders(9) (sn outpcd & pushed along: hung lft thrght: kpt on fnl f)	3	3	14/1	75	44
3127^{6}	**Porto Foricos (USA)** (HRACecil) **2-9-0** KFallon(6) (bit bkwd: led 2f: rdn & wknd 2f out)	7	4	9/1	56	25
	Tornado Prince (IRE) (NACallaghan) **2-9-0** MRoberts(3) (w'like: leggy: s.s: sme hdwy ½-wy: sn wknd & edgd rt: eased)	1	5	10/1	53	22
	Genius (IRE) (PFICole) **2-9-0** KDarley(5) (gd sort: bkwd: sn outpcd & pushed along)	4	6	16/1	43	12
	Naughty Blue (USA) (SbinSuroor) **2-9-0** LDettori(8) (rangy: outpcd ½-wy: sn wl bhd)	10	7	$9/2^{3}$	16	—
3219^{3}	***Designer (USA)*** (JHMGosden) **2-9-0** OPeslier(2) (Withdrawn not under Starter's orders: burst out of stalls)		W	$11/4^{2}$	—	—
				(SP 121.7%)		**7 Rn**

1m 14.1 (3.60) CSF £10.93 TOTE £6.00: £2.70 £1.60 (£5.40) Trio £31.90 OWNER Al Muallim Partnership (WHATCOMBE) BRED J. R. M. and Mrs P. Lewis

Bintang (IRE), a keen type, looked very fit. Very impressive on paper, it remains to be seen how much he progresses. (5/1: 7/2-11/2)

3219 Elhabub proved no match at all for the winner. (5/2)

3219 The Downtown Fox, who had finished behind Elhabub at Goodwood, gave his rider problems. (14/1)

3127 Porto Foricos (USA) banged his head on the stalls' overhead structure when Designer burst out of them, and his effort here is best overlooked. (9/1)

Tornado Prince (IRE), a very immature individual, lost his action completely after moving up at halfway. (10/1)

Genius (IRE) looked badly in need of this initial outing. (16/1)

Naughty Blue (USA) showed nothing at all on his debut. (9/2)

3727 GALTRES STKS (Listed) (3-Y.O+ F & M) (Class A)

4-45 (4-47) **1m 3f 195y** £17,462.50 (£5,200.00: £2,475.00: £1,112.50) Stalls: Low GOING: 0.30 sec per fur (G)

				SP	RR	SF
2869^{2}	**Kaliana (IRE)** (LMCumani) **3-8-8** JReid(4) (hld up: effrt over 3f out: led over 2f out: rdn out)	—	1	$7/4^{1}$	115	77
3492^{3}	**The Faraway Tree (94)** (GWragg) **3-8-8** MRoberts(1) (hld up: hdwy over 3f out: ev ch over 2f out: nt qckn appr fnl f)	3	2	12/1	111	73
$3179a^{2}$	**Book At Bedtime (IRE) (100)** (CACyzer) **3-8-8** DHolland(5) (lw: led tl over 2f out: egd rt & grad wknd)	8	3	15/2	100	62
959^{5}	**Mrs Miniver (USA) (97)** (PAKelleway) **3-8-8** KFallon(7) (trckd ldrs: rdn & wknd over 2f out)	5	4	33/1	94	56
2731*	**Masharik (IRE) (83)** (MajorWRHern) **3-8-8** RHills(2) (trckd ldrs: effrt over 3f out: wknd over 2f out)	nk	5	10/1	93	55
2647*	**Graceful Lass (92)** (DRLoder) **3-8-8** PatEddery(3) (lw: b.nr hind: hld up: pushed along over 5f out: bhd fnl 3f)	7	6	$9/2^{3}$	84	46
3216^{2}	**Entice (FR) (111)** (SbinSuroor) **3-8-8** LDettori(6) (swtg: plld hrd: sn trckng ldr: pshd along over 4f out: no rspnse & sn lost pl: virtually p.u)	dist	7	$9/4^{2}$	—	—
				(SP 116.8%)		**7 Rn**

2m 33.76 (5.96) CSF £22.54 TOTE £2.60: £1.70 £4.00 (£16.50) OWNER H H Aga Khan (NEWMARKET) BRED His Highness the Aga Khan's Studs S.C.

2869 Kaliana (IRE) continued her trainer's domination of this event. Showing a poor action, she proved well suited by the steady rain and, in the end, took this in decisive fashion. A step up to one mile six will be no problem. (7/4)
3492 The Faraway Tree, stepping up in distance, was the only one to make a serious race of it. (12/1)
3179a Book At Bedtime (IRE) set out to make her stamina tell but, when the race began in earnest, she was easily swept aside. All she does is stay and she needs two miles. (15/2)
959 Mrs Miniver (USA) gained some valuable black type. (33/1)
2731* Masharik (IRE) had finished runner-up to the winner on their respective debuts at Chepstow but she was well beaten by her this time. (10/1)
2647* Graceful Lass was unable to manage the step up in class. (9/2: op 7/1)
3216 Entice (FR) would not settle. Finding nothing when pushed along once in line for home, she was virtually pulled up and something was clearly seriously amiss. (9/4: 13/8-5/2)

3728 CITY OF YORK STKS (Listed) (3-Y.O+) (Class A)
5-15 (5-17) **6f 214y** £15,010.00 (£4,480.00: £2,140.00: £970.00) Stalls: High GOING: 0.30 sec per fur (G)

				SP	RR	SF
2830[4]	**Hidden Meadow (115)** (IABalding) **3-9-0** LDettori(6) (trckd ldrs: effrt & hung lft 2f out: r.o to ld wl ins fnl f)	—	**1**	11/2[2]	125	90
2011[5]	**Poteen (USA) (119)** (LMCumani) **3-8-9** PatEddery(3) (lw: sn chsng ldrs: rdn ½-wy: edgd rt & led jst ins fnl f: hdd & nt qckn nr fin)	½	**2**	Evens[1]	119	84
3147[4]	**Imroz (USA) (103)** (HRACecil) **3-8-4** AMcGlone(2) (plld hrd: mde most: wandered & hung bdly rt over 1f out: hdd jst ins fnl f: sn wknd)	4	**3**	10/1	105	70
3144[4]	**Weet-A-Minute (IRE) (100)** (RHollinshead) **4-9-0** FLynch(1) (a chsng ldrs: rdn & outpcd fnl 2f)	1¼	**4**	20/1	107	77
2861*	**Hattab (IRE) (103)** (PTWalwyn) **3-9-0** RHills(8) (lw: hld up: hdwy over 2f out: kpt on same pce)	1	**5**	7/1[3]	110	75
3063[4]	**Ramooz (USA) (107)** (BHanbury) **4-9-8** KFallon(9) (hld up: sme hdwy over 2f out: nv nr to chal)	3	**6**	8/1	106	76
1541a[10]	**Musical Pursuit (116)** (MHTompkins) **3-8-9** JReid(5) (chsd ldrs: outpcd over 2f out: wknd over 1f out)	2	**7**	8/1	93	58
2690[2]	**Tregaron (USA) (103)** (RAkehurst) **6-9-0** OPeslier(7) (sn pushed along: nvr nr ldrs)	½	**8**	9/1	92	62
	Silvering (FR) (MrsJRRamsden) **5-9-0** DHolland(4) (hld up: outpcd ½-wy: eased)	9	**9**	20/1	71	41

(SP 128.7%) **9 Rn**

1m 25.86 (2.86) CSF £11.65 TOTE £6.10: £1.80 £1.30 £2.50 (£5.30) Trio £27.40 OWNER Mr George Strawbridge (KINGSCLERE) BRED I. A. Balding
WEIGHT FOR AGE 3yo-5lb
2830 Hidden Meadow seems to have two ways of running. Given a very quiet ride, despite a tendency to hang he was persuaded to stay on and poke his head in front near the line. On paper this was a good effort giving the runner-up 5lb. (11/2)
2011 Poteen (USA), who looked really fit and well, was worn down near the finish. His suspect stamina gave out on the rain-softened ground. (Evens)
3147 Imroz (USA), who was fitted with a special bridle, gave her rider real problems going down to the start. Refusing to settle, she ducked and dived and is clearly a real madam. (10/1)
3144 Weet-A-Minute (IRE), who looked a little out of his depth, ran with plenty of credit. (20/1)
2861* Hattab (IRE) is probably better from the front over shorter trips. (7/1)
3063 Ramooz (USA) was banging his head against a brick wall under an 8lb penalty. (8/1)
1541a Musical Pursuit, who looked very fit indeed, seemed void of pace and a step up in distance is called for. (8/1: 6/1-9/1)

T/Jkpt: £117,678.90 (0.49 Tckts); £84,529.92 to Goodwood 22/8/97. T/Plpt: £309.10 (284.05 Tckts). T/Qdpt: £48.70 (75.56 Tckts) WG

3554a-DEAUVILLE (France) (R-H) (Good)
Tuesday August 12th

3729a PRIX DE TOURGEVILLE (Listed) (3-Y.O C & G)
1-55 (1-55) **1m** £15,713.00 (£5,387.00: £4,040.00)

				SP	RR	SF
	Marathon (USA) (MmeCHead,France) **3-8-12** FHead	—	**1**		115	—
3150*	**Fly To The Stars** (MJohnston) **3-8-12** OPeslier	1½	**2**		112	—
	Keep Playing (FR) (France) **3-9-2** SGuillot	1½	**3**		113	—

5 Rn

1m 42.4 (6.40) P-M 2.40F: 1.50F 1.50F OWNER Mme A. Head (CHANTILLY) BRED Societe Aland
IN-FOCUS: **This was the final winner in the glittering career of Freddie Head, six-times French champion.**
3150* Fly To The Stars put up a brave effort in this listed event, but he came up against a very useful horse who had been on the sidelines for three months due to a cough. Given every chance, he came to challenge for the lead with the eventual winner but, although running with great credit, he was outclassed inside the final furlong. He will have one more race this season which will either be in Ireland or Turkey.

3729a-DEAUVILLE (France) (R-H) (Good)
Friday August 15th

3730a PRIX GUILLAUME D'ORNANO (Gp 2) (3-Y.O)
3-25 (3-28) **1m 2f** £33,670.00 (£13,468.00: £6,734.00: £3,367.00)

				SP	RR	SF
3002a[2]	**Rajpoute (FR)** (FDoumen,France) **3-8-12** GMosse (trckd ldr tl led ins fnl f: r.o wl)	—	**1**		113	—
2901*	**Crystal Hearted** (HCandy) **3-8-12** AMcGlone (broke wl: set pce: led tl ins fnl f: hdd & no ex cl home)	¾	**2**		112	—
3180a*	**Handsome Ridge** (JHMGosden) **3-8-12** SGuillot (prom: rdn st: wknd fnl f)	nk	**3**		111	—
	Lord Cromby (IRE) (RCollet,France) **3-8-12** DBoeuf (m 4th: r.o wl fnl f)	s.nk	**4**		111	—
3002a*	**Kirkwall** (AFabre,France) **3-9-2** OPeslier (prom: u.p 2f out: one pce cl home)	1	**5**		113	—
2274a[2]	**Ithaki (IRE)** (JEPease,France) **3-8-12** CAsmussen (hld up: n.d)	1½	**6**		107	—

6 Rn

2m 5.5 (0.50) P-M 6.60F: 3.30F 4.80F OWNER Mr J. D. Martin BRED Juddmonte Farms
3002a Rajpoute (FR), in second place most of the way, accelerated well in the final furlong to win with authority. He is certainly on the upgrade and will probably have an American campaign in the autumn as there is little left for him in France. His sire, Double Bed, won his first race in the same event ten years previously.
2901* Crystal Hearted ran his heart out in an attempt to make every yard of the running. Challenged by the winner, he still ran on very gamely, albeit slightly one-paced. He will now be aimed at the Frankfurt Trophy in Germany next month.

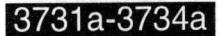

3180a* Handsome Ridge put up another game performance. Always close up, he was outpaced early in the straight before running on again in the final stages. An extremely game performer, he will always take advantage of any weak rivals.
Lord Cromby (IRE), held up, was putting all his best work in at the finish. He looks likely to go on to better things and could take his place in a Group Three in the future.

3730a-DEAUVILLE (France) (R-H) (Good)
Saturday August 16th

3731a PRIX GONTAUT-BIRON (Gp 3) (4-Y.O+)
3-35 (3-43) **1m 2f** £24,691.00 (£8,979.00: £4,489.00)

				SP	RR	SF
2765*	**Lord of Men** (JHMGosden) **4-8-9** SGuillot	—	1		113	—
2270a2	**Si Seductor (USA)** (AFabre,France) **4-8-11** TJarnet	½	2		114	—
1554a5	**Nero Zilzal (USA)** (ELellouche,France) **4-9-0b1** TThulliez	hd	3		117	—
						5 Rn

2m 8.6 (3.60) P-M 1.80F: 1.10F 1.20F OWNER Sheikh Mohammed (NEWMARKET) BRED Sheikh Mohammed bin Rashid al Maktoum
2765* Lord of Men was given a superlative ride to win this. Leading from pillar to post at various speeds, he still had enough in hand in the final furlong to repel his rivals. Staying on well at the finish, it would be no surprise if he turned out for the Prix Foy at Longchamp in September. He is still a fresh horse having missed the whole of his three-year-old career due to a fractured pelvis.
2270a Si Seductor (USA), waited with, challenged the winner throughout the final furlong, and although genuine and consistent, found one too good here.
625a Nero Zilzal (USA), who played up before the start, was not put into the race until halfway up the straight. He may be in for a successful autumn campaign, and another Group race could come his way.

3731a-DEAUVILLE (France) (R-H) (Good)
Sunday August 17th

3732a PRIX DE PONT-L'EVEQUE CLAIMING (3-Y.O)
2-00 (2-00) **1m** £7,856.00

				SP	RR	SF
	Pretty In Pink (USA) (JdeRoualle,France) **3-8-13** CAsmussen	—	1		67	—
	Physicien (FR) (France) **3-9-2** TThulliez	½	2		69	—
	St Petersburg (FR) (France) **3-8-7**(5) AJeuft	nk	3		64	—
34659	**Glittering (USA)** (CEBrittain) **3-8-11** LDettori (btn just over 1¼l)		5		—	—
						13 Rn

1m 43.6 (7.60) P-M 7.30F: 2.50F 2.60F 2.50F (38.00F) OWNER F. A. McNulty
3230 Glittering (USA), running in fifth for most of the way, ran on in the final stages but left his challenge too late.

3733a PRIX DU HARAS DE FRESNAY-LE-BUFFARD-JACQUES LE MAROIS (Gp 1) (3-Y.O+ C & F)
2-35 (2-33) **1m** £112,233.00 (£44,893.00: £22,447.00: £11,223.00)

				SP	RR	SF
12104	**Spinning World (USA)** (JEPease,France) **4-9-4** CAsmussen (rn 4th: u.p wl over 1f out: hdwy & led jst over 1f out: wnt clr wl ins fnl f)	—	1	29/10³	132	—
20113	**Daylami (IRE)** (AdeRoyerDupre,France) **3-8-11** GMosse (hld up early: hdwy 1½f out: trckd ldr: hrd rdn & unable qckn 1f out)	2	2	24/10²	127	—
2820a*	**Neuilly (USA)** (AFabre,France) **3-8-11** TJarnet (in rr: prog over 2f out: u.p 2f out: nvr plcd to chal)	6	3	7/1	115	—
31242	**Starborough** (DRLoder) **3-8-11** LDettori (broke wl: disp ld to 3f out: hdd 2f out: wknd)	3	4	6/5¹	109	—
3001a2	**Zamindar (USA)** (AFabre,France) **3-8-11** OPeslier (rn 3rd: u.p over 2f out: hrd rdn to ld briefly 2f out: hdd & styd on one pce)	½	5	49/10	108	—
	Piperi (IRE) (JEPease,France) **3-8-11** FSanchez (broke wl: disp ld: wknd fnl stages)	dist	6	29/10³	—	—
				(SP 155.6%)		**6 Rn**

1m 34.4 (-1.60) P-M 3.90F: 2.00F 2.00F OWNER Niarchos Family (CHANTILLY)
IN-FOCUS: **For betting purposes, Spinning World (USA) and Piperi (IRE) were cpld.**
1210 Spinning World (USA) was produced in magnificent shape by his trainer, and never looked in the slightest trouble during this mile event which he won last year. His main target is the Breeders' Cup and his next outing will probably come in the Moulin de Longchamp. (29/10)
2011 Daylami (IRE) was given every possible chance, but just could not go with the winner in the final furlong. He too was reappearing after an absence so improvement can be expected next time out in the Moulin. The ground was probably a little bit on the firm side for this colt, who goes well over the round mile at Longchamp. (24/10)
Neuilly (USA), who was stepping up enormously in class, was not at all disgraced. Running on well in the last furlong and a half, he looks as though he may benefit from a longer distance. Relatively inexperienced, he should have benefited from this and a Group race is sure to come his way in the not too distant future. (7/1)
3124 Starborough was taken on by the winner's pacemaker from the start so he never relaxed. He was one of the first under pressure and had no chance from at least two furlongs out. This was certainly not his true form, and he has had quite a tough campaign in top-class company. He still looks a danger to all in the Queen Elizabeth II Stakes at Ascot at the end of September. (6/5)

3734a PRIX DE LESSARD CLAIMING (4-Y.O+)
4-10 (4-11) **1m 4f 110y** £6,734.00

				SP	RR	SF
267a3	**Mon Domino** (RCollet,France) **8-9-2** TJarnet	—	1		93	—
	Katun (FR) (France) **4-9-2** OPeslier	nk	2		93	—
	Paetro (GER) (France) **7-9-2** CAsmussen	2½	3		89	—
30109	**Burnt Offering** (CEBrittain) **4-8-12b** SGuillot (btn approx 7l)		7		—	—
						9 Rn

2m 46.0 (7.50) P-M 7.70F: 1.60F 1.60F 1.20F (23.60F) OWNER M. Clifford (CHANTILLY)
1478 Burnt Offering never looked dangerous during the course of this race.

0918a-DIELSDORF (Zurich, Switzerland) (L-H) (Good)
Sunday August 17th

3735a SATRONIC GRAND PRIX (3-Y.O+)
2-40 (-) **1m** £3,158.00

				SP	RR	SF
2026[21]	**Celestial Key (USA)** (MJohnston) **7-8-12** JWeaver	—	1		95	—
919a[3]	**Roger de Berksted (USA)** (FGang,Germany) **9-9-2** MissSeverineBottani	1¼	2		97	—
271a[3]	**King of Heights (GER)** (MWeber,Germany) **5-9-7** NJeanpierre	1	3		100	—
						8 Rn

1m 43.4 TOTE 3.70SF: 2.80SF 4.40SF OWNER Mr Markus Graff (MIDDLEHAM) BRED Pillar Stud Inc
1074a Celestial Key (USA) gained his first success in Switzerland following four previous outings there this season. Held up towards the rear, he went fourth entering the straight and managed to slip through on the inside to lead well over a furlong out. He will return to England before travelling to Switzerland for his next run.

0719a-GELSENKIRCHEN-HORST (Gelsenkirchen, Germany) (R-H) (Good)
Sunday August 17th

3736a SILBERNE PEITSCHE PREIS DER SPIELBANK HOHENSYBURG (Listed) (3-Y.O+)
2-35 (2-36) **7f** £7,491.00 (£3,030.00: £1,515.00)

				SP	RR	SF
	Barlovento (GER) (UOstmann,Germany) **4-8-9b[1]** GBocskai	—	1		103	—
	Bukett (GER) (FrauEMader,Germany) **4-8-7** ASuborics	1¾	2		97	—
1074a[2]	**Catoki (USA)** (HSteguweit,Germany) **4-8-7** AHelfenbein	1¾	3		93	—
3220[3]	**Divina Luna** (JWHills) **4-8-5** MRoberts (btn approx 4½l)		5		—	—
						9 Rn

1m 26.73 TOTE 26DM: 13DM 23DM 29DM OWNER Mrs U. Ostmann BRED Gestut Rietberg
3220 Divina Luna finished a rather unlucky fifth after her saddle slipped in the closing stages of the race. She disputed the lead until going on at halfway, but, headed over a furlong out, stayed on at one pace.

3737a ARAL-POKAL (Gp 1) (3-Y.O+)
3-45 (3-57) **1m 4f** £79,545.00 (£34,091.00: £18,939.00: £9,470.00: £5,682.00: £3,788.00)

				SP	RR	SF
2642a[4]	**Caitano** (BSchutz,Germany) **3-8-8** AStarke (in tch: chal over 1f out: led ins fnl f: r.o strly)	—	1		124	—
3182a*	**Luso** (CEBrittain) **5-9-6** MRoberts (led tl hdd ins fnl f: one pce)	1¾	2		124	—
1918a*	**Que Belle (USA)** (HRemmert,Germany) **3-8-5** KWoodburn (trckd ldr: rdn to chal 2f out: unable qckn 1f out: styd on wl cl home)	s.h	3		119	—
3182a[3]	**Protektor (GER)** (ALowe,Germany) **8-9-6** ASuborics (hld up in rr: styd on fnl 2f: nvr nr ldrs)	4½	4		118	—
1724a[6]	**Night Petticoat (GER)** (BSchutz,Germany) **4-9-2** TMundry (mid div: one pce st)	1¼	5		112	—
1073a[4]	**Try Again (GER)** (AWohler,Germany) **6-9-6** ABoschert (n.d)	¾	6		115	—
2642a[19]	**Asolo (GER)** (BSchutz,Germany) **3-8-8** WNewnes (prom to 4f out: btn 3f out)	1¾	7		111	—
3182a[6]	**Bad Bertrich Again (IRE)** (ALowe,Germany) **4-9-6** GBocskai (in rr: slt prog 5f out: sn btn)	2	8		110	—
						8 Rn

2m 29.82 TOTE 38DM: 11DM 10DM 10DM OWNER Stall Blauer Reiter
3182a* Luso attempted to make all as he did in this race a year ago. Caitano took the lead inside the final furlong and Luso did well to battle on, but could not catch the winner.

3214-GOODWOOD (R-H) (Good to firm)
Friday August 22nd
WEATHER: Overcast WIND: almost nil

3738 TEMPERATURE'S 50TH ANNIVERSARY MAIDEN STKS (3-Y.O) (Class D)
2-10 (2-10) **1m 2f** £3,460.00 (£1,030.00: £490.00: £220.00) Stalls: Low GOING minus 0.09 sec per fur (G)

				SP	RR	SF
3389[9]	**Lonely Heart (75)** (DRCElsworth) **3-8-9** JReid(5) (mde all: rdn appr fnl f: r.o wl)	—	1	12/1	88	60
2583[3]	**Ricardo** (RCharlton) **3-9-0** PatEddery(3) (lw: hld up: pushed along 5f out: chsd wnr over 3f out: hrd rdn 2f out: one pce)	5	2	8/13[1]	85	57
479[3]	**Majesty (IRE)** (PFICole) **3-9-0** RHills(2) (prom: hrd rdn over 2f out: wknd over 1f out)	3	3	9/2[2]	80	52
683[10]	**Lighten Up** (CEBrittain) **3-8-9** WJO'Connor(1) (chsd wnr 6f out tl over 3f out: wknd over 2f out)	17	4	9/1	48	20
	Shooting Star (IRE) (JHMGosden) **3-9-0** GHind(4) (w'like: a bhd)	5	5	6/1[3]	45	17
				(SP 112.1%)		**5 Rn**

2m 9.94 (3.34) CSF £19.00 TOTE £11.60: £4.10 £1.10 (£4.10) OWNER Mr C. J. Harper (WHITCOMBE) BRED Whitsbury Manor Stud
2832 Lonely Heart made all the running under an enterprising ride, and looked the winner form some way out. (12/1: 7/1-14/1)
2583 Ricardo was a bit disappointing, being niggled some way out, and looking very slow in the closing stages. (8/13)
479 Majesty (IRE) had his chances, but was done with by the two pole. (9/2)
Lighten Up (9/1: 5/1-10/1)
Shooting Star (IRE), not the most pre-possessing of colts, on this showing does not appear to possess much ability. (6/1: 7/2-7/1)

3739 CAFFREY'S IRISH ALE H'CAP (0-85) (3-Y.O+) (Class D)
2-40 (2-40) **1m 4f** £7,440.00 (£2,220.00: £1,060.00: £480.00) Stalls: Low GOING minus 0.09 sec per fur (G)

				SP	RR	SF
3120[6]	**Mengaab (USA) (80)** (JHMGosden) **3-9-4b[1]** GHind(5) (lw: a.p: led 4f out: hdd 1f out: rallied ins fnl f: led last stride)	—	1	9/1	90	62
3318[3]	**Urgent Swift (78)** (APJarvis) **4-9-12** WRyan(7) (hld up: hdwy 3f out: led 1f out: hdd last stride)	s.h	2	9/1	88	70
3381[3]	**Herr Trigger (67)** (DrJDScargill) **6-9-1b** PatEddery(8) (a.p: rdn 2f out: one pce)	3	3	100/30[1]	73	55
3279*	**Koraloona (IRE) (60)** (GBBalding) **4-8-8** SDrowne(6) (chsd ldrs: rdn 3f out: one pce)	1¾	4	4/1[2]	64	46

				SP	RR	SF
3246^{6}	**Tikopia (81)** (IABalding) **3-9-5** JReid(3) (swtg: chsd ldrs: rdn & hung rt over 1f out: one pce)	nk	**5**	8/1	84	56
2749^{4}	**Mr Browning (USA) (65)** (RAkehurst) **6-8-13b** AClark(1) (lw: sn led: hdd 4f out: wknd over 1f out)	3	**6**	13/2^{3}	64	46
*250**	**Steamroller Stanly (78)** (CACyzer) **4-9-12** RHills(2) (hld up: effrt over 3f out: sn btn)	7	**7**	8/1	68	50
3184^{3}	**North Reef (IRE) (72)** (JPearce) **6-9-6** MWigham(4) (swtg: a bhd: lost tch 3f out: t.o)	24	**8**	13/2^{3}	30	12

(SP 112.0%) **8 Rn**

2m 38.15 (4.95) CSF £74.58 CT £294.37 TOTE £16.20: £3.20 £2.90 £1.60 (£70.80) OWNER Sheikh Ahmed Al Maktoum (NEWMARKET) BRED Brereton C. Jones

WEIGHT FOR AGE 3yo-10lb

3120 Mengaab (USA) led early in the straight, but looked cooked when headed at the one pole. To his credit he rallied gamely to get back up right on the post. (9/1)
3318 Urgent Swift was given a patient ride, and he looked sure to score when leading at the one pole, but he was worried out of it late on. (9/1)
3381 Herr Trigger ran well, but gave the impression that this mile and a half stretches his stamina. (100/30)
3279* Koraloona (IRE) was under pressure some way from home, and could probably do with more cut in the ground. (4/1)
3246 Tikopia looked far from keen, hanging in behind his rivals in the final couple of furlongs. (8/1)
2749 Mr Browning (USA) (13/2: 9/2-7/1)

3740 PRESTIGE STKS (Gp 3) (2-Y.O F) (Class A)

3-10 (3-11) **7f** £22,500.00 (£8,440.00: £4,070.00: £1,790.00) Stalls: Low GOING minus 0.09 sec per fur (G)

				SP	RR	SF
3151*	**Midnight Line (USA)** (HRACecil) **2-8-9** WRyan(2) (a.p: pushed along 4f out: hrd rdn ins fnl f: led last stride)	—	**1**	11/2^{3}	88	26
3547^{2}	**Alignment (IRE)** (MRStoute) **2-8-9** JReid(5) (led: hrd rdn ins fnl f: hdd last stride)	s.h	**2**	7/1	88	26
3201*	**Elshamms** (ACStewart) **2-8-9** RHills(3) (lw: tk keen hold: hld up in tch: rdn over 1f out: one pce)	1¼	**3**	5/4^{1}	85	23
3468*	**Regal Revolution (78)** (PTWalwyn) **2-8-9** JLowe(6) (a.p: rdn 2f out: one pce)	1½	**4**	11/1	82	20
3033*	**Half-Hitch (USA)** (DRLoder) **2-8-9** PatEddery(1) (hld up: effrt 3f out: sn btn)	7	**5**	7/2^{2}	66	4
3049^{3}	**Filey Brigg (100)** (WTKemp) **2-8-9** JQuinn(4) (hld up: rdn over 3f out: sn btn)	4	**6**	10/1	57	—

(SP 112.0%) **6 Rn**

1m 29.97 (5.17) CSF £37.44 TOTE £6.50: £2.50 £3.10 (£23.30) OWNER H R H Prince Fahd Salman (NEWMARKET) BRED Newgate Stud Farm Inc

3151* Midnight Line (USA) put up a really game performance here. She was being niggled along to keep in touch early in the straight but, to her credit, she kept finding more. Her jockey's persistence told, and she got up in the shadow of the post. Stamina appears her strong suit. (11/2)
3547 Alignment (IRE), who had shown promise on her debut at Sandown, stepped up on that here, and attempted to make every yard of the running, but was just caught in the final stride. (7/1)
3201* Elshamms moved beautifully to post, but did not help her cause by taking quite a keen hold in the early stages. She still moved up threateningly two furlongs from home, but she had little in the tank late on. She will improve as she learns to settle. (5/4)
3468* Regal Revolution, stepped up in class here, ran a sound race. (11/1: 8/1-12/1)
3033* Half-Hitch (USA) was very disappointing, never really threatening to get in the race. (7/2: op 9/4)
3049 Filey Brigg ran very poorly, and was beaten early in the straight. (10/1)

3741 GEORGE ANTONIADES MEMORIAL H'CAP (0-95) (3-Y.O) (Class C)

3-40 (3-44) **1m 1f** £9,780.00 (£2,940.00: £1,420.00: £660.00) Stalls: Low GOING minus 0.09 sec per fur (G)

				SP	RR	SF
3274^{2}	**Sweet Contralto (83)** (DRLoder) **3-8-9** PatEddery(9) (lw: sn led: hrd rdn ins fnl f: r.o wl)	—	**1**	4/1^{1}	94	61
3190^{15}	**Al Azhar (90)** (IABalding) **3-9-2** AMcGlone(4) (swtg: hld up: hdwy over 2f out: rdn appr fnl f: r.o)	1¼	**2**	12/1	99	66
3403^{3}	**Dundel (IRE) (77)** (BWHills) **3-8-3** GHind(8) (hld up: hdwy over 3f out: chsd wnr over 1f out: rdn ins fnl f: one pce)	s.h	**3**	10/1	86	53
3153^{6}	**Mantles Prince (78)** (GLewis) **3-8-4b** PaulEddery(6) (prom: rdn 2f out: wknd appr fnl f)	5	**4**	6/1^{3}	78	45
3548^{6}	**Space Race (79)** (CACyzer) **3-8-5** AClark(3) (swtg: chsd ldrs: rdn over 2f out: one pce)	3	**5**	11/2^{2}	74	41
3236^{10}	**Merciless Cop (72)** (BJMeehan) **3-7-12b** JQuinn(1) (lw: nvr nrr)	¾	**6**	14/1	65	32
3144^{5}	**Sunbeam Dance (USA) (95)** (SbinSuroor) **3-9-7v^{1}** JReid(7) (prom tl wknd over 2f out)	hd	**7**	8/1	88	55
3591^{2}	**Olivo (IRE) (70)** (CAHorgan) **3-7-10** JLowe(2) (a bhd)	4	**8**	10/1	56	23
3244*	**Kafaf (USA) (86)** (JHMGosden) **3-8-12** RHills(5) (chsd wnr to ½-wy: sn wknd)	1½	**9**	4/1^{1}	69	36

(SP 113.3%) **9 Rn**

1m 55.79 (2.79) CSF £47.32 CT £406.86 TOTE £5.10: £2.00 £3.10 £2.60 (£49.20) Trio £327.20 OWNER Mr S. Frisby (NEWMARKET) BRED Patrick Eddery Ltd

3274 Sweet Contralto was given a really positive ride by Pat Eddery here. She made all the running at a strong pace, and had the race in safe-keeping in the final two furlongs. (4/1)
1982 Al Azhar showed his first sign here of coming back to his two-year-old form, and could be booked for a good autumn. (12/1)
3403 Dundel (IRE) threw down a menacing-looking challenge below the distance, but could not quite muster the pace to get to the winner. (10/1)
3153 Mantles Prince was never that far away, but was a tired horse in the final furlong. (6/1)
3548 Space Race raced in touch, but when put under pressure two furlongs out, only had the one pace to give. (11/2)
3244* Kafaf (USA) ran very disappointingly, being beaten at halfway. Her jockey later reported that she had choked. (4/1)

3742 SURPLICE (S) STKS (2-Y.O) (Class E)

4-15 (4-16) **6f** £3,582.50 (£1,085.00: £530.00: £252.50) Stalls: Low GOING minus 0.09 sec per fur (G)

				SP	RR	SF
2831^{7}	**First Dance (73)** (RHannon) **2-8-6** PatEddery(2) (lw: a.p: led 1f out: hrd rdn ins fnl f: r.o)	—	**1**	4/5^{1}	70	27
3474^{6}	**Poetto (63)** (BJMeehan) **2-8-11** JReid(1) (led: hdd 1f out: hrd rdn ins fnl f: r.o)	s.h	**2**	9/2^{2}	75	32
3314^{3}	**Blarney Park (58)** (CADwyer) **2-8-6** JQuinn(6) (lw: in tch: outpcd over 2f out: rallied 1f out: styd on one pce ins fnl f)	10	**3**	15/2	43	—
3384^{6}	**Dahlidya** (MJPolglase) **2-8-6** JTate(4) (nvr nrr)	½	**4**	25/1	42	—
3451^{2}	**Bermuda Triangle (IRE) (57)** (MJHaynes) **2-8-4**(7) MCornally(8) (lw: nvr nrr)	1¼	**5**	5/1^{3}	44	1
3471^{14}	**Lady Ralphina** (JJBridger) **2-8-6** PaulEddery(3) (chsd ldrs: rdn 2f out: wknd over 1f out)	nk	**6**	40/1	38	—
3324^{6}	**Swift Time (53)** (MRBosley) **2-8-1**(5) AimeeCook(5) (tk keen hold: prom over 3f)	5	**7**	25/1	24	—
1480^{9}	**Far-So-La** (TMJones) **2-8-11** AMcGlone(7) (bit bkwd: bhd fnl 2f)	9	**8**	40/1	5	—

(SP 114.7%) **8 Rn**

1m 13.69 (3.89) CSF £4.08 TOTE £1.60: £1.10 £2.00 £1.70 (£4.10) OWNER Cheveley Park Stud (MARLBOROUGH) BRED Cheveley Park Stud Ltd

Sold Dr J. Scargill 9,000 gns

2181 First Dance looked like winning comfortably when challenging below the distance, but the runner-up ensured that she was driven right out. (4/5)
1255 Poetto made a really bold bid to make all, and battled on most bravely once headed. (9/2)
3314 Blarney Park lost a prominent position when getting outpaced over two furlongs out, and though keeping on again late on, never threatened to get to the two leaders. (15/2)
3384 Dahlidya was never nearer than at the finish. (25/1)

3743 INKPENS MEDIAN AUCTION MAIDEN STKS (2-Y.O) (Class D)
4-45 (4-45) **6f** £3,590.00 (£1,070.00: £510.00: £230.00) Stalls: Low GOING minus 0.09 sec per fur (G)

	Horse / details	Dist	Pos	SP	RR	SF
	Shudder (WJHaggas) **2-9-0** FLynch(3) (w'like: bit bkwd: hld up: gd hdwy over 2f out: led over 1f out: eased nr fin)	—	**1**	13/2	85+	24
3497^{2}	**Storm Fromthe East** (RHannon) **2-9-0** JReid(7) (lw: hld up in tch: gng wl whn nt clr run over 1f out: swtchd rt ent fnl f: r.o wl)	nk	**2**	$6/1^{3}$	84	23
3187^{3}	**Honey Storm (IRE)** (MRChannon) **2-8-9** PaulEddery(6) (a.p: ev ch over 1f out: sn rdn: one pce)	2	**3**	$5/1^{2}$	74	13
$3177a^{10}$	**Chief Whip (USA)** (LMCumani) **2-9-0** WRyan(4) (leggy: scope: a.p: led 2f out: hdd over 1f out: one pce)	¾	**4**	25/1	77	16
3574^{14}	**March Fourteenth (USA)** (JHMGosden) **2-8-9** GHind(2) (chsd ldrs: pushed along 2f out: nt clr run over 1f out tl ins fnl f: one pce)	1¾	**5**	33/1	67	6
	Torrent (PFICole) **2-9-0** PatEddery(1) (w'like: scope: lw: led: hdd 2f out: wknd over 1f out)	nk	**6**	$4/6^{1}$	71	10
	Mismewmew (CJBenstead) **2-8-9** JLowe(5) (unf: bit bkwd: dwlt: a bhd)	4	**7**	50/1	56	—

(SP 113.0%) **7 Rn**

1m 14.46 (4.66) CSF £38.43 TOTE £9.30: £2.70 £2.00 (£33.50) OWNER Mr Ali K Al Jafleh (NEWMARKET) BRED R. J. Reip and Partners
Shudder, quite a compact-looking colt, looked as though the run would do him good, but nonetheless ran out quite an impressive winner. Always going well, he took it up going smoothly below the distance, and his rider was able to ease him down close home. (13/2)
3497 Storm Fromthe East did not get the clearest of runs when moving up ominously below the distance. By the time he got out, the winner had flown. These waiting tactics obviously suit, and compensation awaits. (6/1)
3187 Honey Storm (IRE) had every chance here, but could not quicken up with the principals in the final furlong. (5/1)
3177a Chief Whip (USA), quite a tall, scopey sort, looks as though his best days will come as a three-year-old. Nonetheless, he ran a sound race here, before getting tapped for foot in the closing stages. (25/1)
March Fourteenth (USA) did not get the clearest of runs, but did show some promise for the future. (33/1)
Torrent, a scopey, well-made, sprinting type, showed the way for four furlongs before tiring late on. He will improve. (4/6)

T/Jkpt: £122,018.80 (0.3 Tckts); £120,300.27 to Goodwood 23/8/97. T/Plpt: £244.90 (140.41 Tckts). T/Qdpt: £60.70 (22.45 Tckts) SM

3419-NEWMARKET (R-H) (Good)
Friday August 22nd
WEATHER: Fine and sunny WIND: almost nil

3744 EQUITY FINANCIAL COLLECTIONS MAIDEN STKS (2-Y.O F) (Class D)
2-00 (2-01) **7f (July)** £3,850.00 (£1,150.00: £550.00: £250.00) Stalls: Centre GOING minus 0.45 sec per fur (F)

	Horse / details	Dist	Pos	SP	RR	SF
3009^{2}	**Ashraakat (USA)** (JLDunlop) **2-8-11** MJKinane(2) (mde virtually all: qcknd over 1f out: r.o wl)	—	**1**	$6/5^{1}$	94+	56
	Shimaal (SbinSuroor) **2-8-11** LDettori(1) (leggy: unf: trckd ldrs: effrt & drvn along over 2f out: nt pce to chal)	1¾	**2**	$10/1^{3}$	90	52
	Virtuous (MRStoute) **2-8-11** SSanders(3) (w'like: scope: s.s: hdwy & pushed along 3f out: kpt on wl ins fnl f)	2	**3**	25/1	85+	47
	Jibe (USA) (HRACecil) **2-8-11** KFallon(11) (cmpt: bit bkwd: chsd ldrs: rdn 2f out: kpt on one pce)	nk	**4**	$5/4^{2}$	85	47
$2098a^{5}$	**Frond** (LMCumani) **2-8-8**(3) RFfrench(5) (neat: w wnr tl wknd over 1f out)	4	**5**	50/1	76	38
	Chim Chiminey (BWHills) **2-8-11** MHills(4) (neat: s.i.s: effrt & pushed along 4f out: nvr on terms)	2	**6**	50/1	71	33
3547^{8}	**Clarity (IRE)** (APJarvis) **2-8-11** DHolland(7) (sn chsng ldrs: rdn & outpcd over 1f out)	2½	**7**	25/1	65	27
	Goldtune (MAJarvis) **2-8-11** EmmaO'Gorman(9) (w'like: a in rr)	3	**8**	50/1	59	21
3117^{10}	**Quiver Tree** (DRLoder) **2-8-11** RCochrane(8) (stdd s: a bhd)	1¼	**9**	33/1	56	18
1783^{4}	**Solo Spirit** (JRJenkins) **2-8-11** MRoberts(10) (lw: plld hrd: sn w ldrs: wknd 2f out)	hd	**10**	50/1	55	17
	Dublivia (CADwyer) **2-8-8**(3) DO'Donohoe(6) (scope: lw: trckd ldrs 4f: wknd qckly: t.o: sddle slipped)	14	**11**	50/1	23	—

(SP 119.4%) **11 Rn**

1m 25.15 (0.15) CSF £11.87 TOTE £2.30: £1.10 £1.70 £4.50 (£5.90) Trio £23.40 OWNER Mr Hamdan Al Maktoum (ARUNDEL) BRED Shadwell Farm Inc
3009 Ashraakat (USA) put the emphasis on stamina over this extra furlong, and stepping up the tempo in the Dip, proved far too strong for her challengers. (6/5)
Shimaal, an unfurnished half-sister to high-class Belmez, who is not the best of movers in her slower paces, turned in an encouraging performance on this debut, and with this run to sharpen her up, will soon improve on this. (10/1: 6/1-11/1)
Virtuous,a filly with plenty of scope for improvement, was flat-footed as the stalls opened. Making hard work to recover some of the lost ground, she did extremely well to make the frame, and the experience will not be lost. (25/1)
Jibe (USA), a smallish filly, bred in the purple, looked as though she would benefit from the run. Settling behind the leaders, she was being made to work two furlongs out, and though she battled on, was always finding the task beyond her. (5/4: evens-10/11)
2098a Frond, who made her racecourse debut in Italy just over two months ago, showed up with the pace until feeling the strain running into the Dip. (50/1)
Chim Chiminey has not yet filled to her frame, and could never make her presence felt after a sluggish start. She can only improve on this. (50/1)

3745 GIRTON MAIDEN STKS (2-Y.O C & G) (Class D)
2-35 (2-35) **7f (July)** £4,110.00 (£1,230.00: £590.00: £270.00) Stalls: Centre GOING minus 0.45 sec per fur (F)

	Horse / details	Dist	Pos	SP	RR	SF
	Fantasy Island (IRE) (SbinSuroor) **2-8-11** LDettori(5) (gd sort: mde all: qcknd clr over 1f out: eased nr fin)	—	**1**	$4/9^{1}$	84++	46
	Air Attache (USA) (GLewis) **2-8-11** RCochrane(3) (w'like: a.p: rdn & kpt on fnl f: no ch w wnr)	3½	**2**	50/1	76	38
2409^{3}	**Wuxi Venture** (SPCWoods) **2-8-11** KFallon(1) (lw: chsd ldrs: hrd drvn over 2f out: styd on)	¾	**3**	$10/1^{3}$	74	36
	Gulland (GWragg) **2-8-11** MHills(2) (w'like: scope: bkwd: s.s: hdwy ½-wy: one pce appr fnl f)	1¼	**4**	$7/1^{2}$	71	33
	Florazi (JLDunlop) **2-8-11** MJKinane(6) (w'like: leggy: scope: swvd lft s: hdwy 3f out: wknd wl over 1f out)	6	**5**	14/1	58	20
2943^{12}	**Rude Shock** (MHTompkins) **2-8-11** DBiggs(7) (hld up: nvr plcd to chal)	1¼	**6**	50/1	55	17
1396^{8}	**Dutch Lad** (MHTompkins) **2-8-8**(3) MHenry(4) (hld up in tch: rdn & outpcd 2f out)	½	**7**	50/1	54	16

				SP	RR	SF
	Salford (LMCumani) **2-8-8**(3) RFfrench(8) (gd sort: bkwd: prom: pushed along 4f out: outpcd fnl 2f)	2	**8**	20/1	49	11
	Aspirant Dancer (MBell) **2-8-11** MFenton(9) (cmpt: bkwd: dwlt: sn chsng ldrs: wknd over 2f out: t.o)	10	**9**	50/1	26	—
				(SP 110.1%)	**9 Rn**	

1m 26.02 (1.02) CSF £38.30 TOTE £1.10: £1.10 £4.00 £1.50 (£15.90) Trio £18.20 OWNER Godolphin (NEWMARKET) BRED Gainsborough Stud Management Ltd

Fantasy Island (IRE), a quick-actioned, quality colt, had no trouble making a successful racecourse debut, and though the time was slower than that taken by the fillies, he won easing up, and he is class. (4/9)

Air Attache (USA), an American-bred colt, looking very fit, did his best to give the useful winner a race, but he was always fighting a losing battle, and it is to be hoped he is able to steer clear of him for at least the remainder of this season. (50/1)

2409 Wuxi Venture, one of three with previous racecourse experience, was staying on as well as any up the hill, and he is heading in the right direction. (10/1: 8/1-12/1)

Gulland, a scopey newcomer from a winning family, ran a sound race after losing ground at the start, and with this experience under his belt, improvement can be expected. (7/1: 4/1-8/1)

Florazi, a June foal, very free to post, swerved left as the stalls were released. Taking closer order three furlongs out, he was at the end of his tether below the distance, and was allowed to come home in his own time. (14/1: op 8/1)

3746 NGK SPARK PLUGS APPRENTICE H'CAP (0-80) (3-Y.O+) (Class E)

3-05 (3-05) **6f** **(July)** £3,663.75 (£1,110.00: £542.50: £258.75) Stalls: Centre GOING minus 0.45 sec per fur (F)

				SP	RR	SF
3323^{5}	**Kind of Light (65)** (RGuest) **4-8-13** MartinDwyer(3) (hld up & bhd: hdwy over 1f out: r.o strly to ld nr fin)	—	**1**	3/1^{1}	73	44
3296^{4}	**Kings Harmony (IRE) (69)** (PJMakin) **4-9-3** RHavlin(1) (a.p: rdn over 1f out: slt ld ins fnl f: ct cl home)	½	**2**	7/1^{2}	76	47
1020^{16}	**Princely Sound (63)** (JEBanks) **4-8-11** DSweeney(7) (led: rdn over 1f out: hdd & no ex ins fnl f)	1¼	**3**	8/1^{3}	66	37
2835^{4}	**Iblis (IRE) (76)** (GWragg) **5-9-10** GMilligan(5) (chsd ldrs: rdn to chal ins fnl f: unable qckn)	nk	**4**	3/1^{1}	79	50
2406^{3}	**Shining Cloud (58)** (MBell) **4-8-6** RMullen(2) (hld up: rdn 2f out: styd on wl ins fnl f)	s.h	**5**	7/1^{2}	60	31
3431^{14}	**Miss Aragon (48)** (MissLCSiddall) **9-7-10** PFessey(4) (lw: swtchd lft s: gd hdwy appr fnl f: nt pce to chal)	½	**6**	20/1	49	20
3417^{10}	**Don Pepe (63)** (RBoss) **6-8-11** GFaulkner(8) (lw: hld up: hdwy over 1f out: rdn & one pce ins fnl f)	1	**7**	7/1^{2}	61	32
3398^{4}	**Deerly (51)** (RDickin) **4-7-10**(3) APolli(6) (w ldr tl rdn & outpcd appr fnl f)	3	**8**	20/1	41	12
				(SP 108.1%)	**8 Rn**	

1m 13.14 (1.14) CSF £19.82 CT £119.47 TOTE £3.70: £1.50 £1.80 £2.90 (£8.10) OWNER Mrs B. Mills (NEWMARKET) BRED Theakston Stud

LONG HANDICAP Miss Aragon 6-4

3323 Kind of Light runs well at this track, and given a very confident ride, powered her way through to gain command nearing the line. (3/1)

3296 Kings Harmony (IRE), fighting for the lead from the break, did eventually nose ahead two hundred yards out, but the winner by then was in full flight, and she took his measure close home. (7/1: op 9/2)

323 Princely Sound, off the track for almost four months, has run best when fresh in the past, and he was only worn down inside the final furlong. (8/1)

2835 Iblis (IRE), returning to sprinting for the first time this term, joined issue inside the final furlong, and only just lost out in an all-out dash to the post. This was a very pleasing effort, and he could be approaching his peak. (3/1: op 2/1)

2406 Shining Cloud seems to take a lot of winding up, but she has got more ability than she cares to show at times, and she was really pegging back the leaders at the line. She is not over-raced, and could be worth keeping in mind for a small race. (7/1)

Miss Aragon has won her last two races over course and distance, but that was over two years ago, and her determined late challenge lacked the pace to succeed this time. (20/1)

3747 HOPEFUL STKS (Listed) (3-Y.O+) (Class A)

3-35 (3-36) **6f** **(July)** £11,121.00 (£4,119.00: £1,979.50: £812.50: £326.25: £131.75) Stalls: Centre GOING minus 0.45 sec per fur (F)

				SP	RR	SF
2925*	**Elnadim (USA) (101)** (JLDunlop) **3-8-11** MJKinane(8) (a.p: led & qcknd 2f out: drvn out)	—	**1**	4/1^{2}	121	71
2677^{2}	**Bollin Joanne (107)** (TDEasterby) **4-8-9** KFallon(7) (b: b.off hind: hld up: hdwy 2f out: chsd wnr appr fnl f: no imp)	1¼	**2**	9/4^{1}	113	66
3577^{5}	**Almushtarak (IRE) (106)** (KMahdi) **4-9-0** RCochrane(4) (lw: hld up: hdwy over 1f out: rdn & r.o wl ins fnl f)	1½	**3**	14/1	114	67
3447^{2}	**My Melody Parkes (95)** (JBerry) **4-8-9** GCarter(6) (lw: a.p: led ½-wy to 2f out: rdn & wknd ins fnl f)	2½	**4**	16/1	102	55
2861^{9}	**Jayannpee (100)** (IABalding) **6-9-0** MartinDwyer(3) (b.off hind: chsd ldrs: outpcd over 1f out: rallied u.p fnl f)	½	**5**	16/1	106	59
2683*	**Tedburrow (104)** (EJAlston) **5-9-0** MRoberts(11) (hld up & bhd: effrt & rdn over 1f out: r.o)	¾	**6**	12/1	104	57
3447*	**Proud Native (IRE) (104)** (APJarvis) **3-8-11** DHolland(1) (lw: prom on ins: outpcd over 1f out: styng on whn nt clr run & eased ins fnl f)	1¼	**7**	10/1^{3}	100	50
[illegible]88^{2}	**March Star (IRE) (94)** (JARToller) **3-8-6** SSanders(2) (swtg: trckd ldrs 4f: sn rdn & outpcd)	3½	**8**	33/1	86	36
2599^{8}	**Blue Goblin (USA) (110)** (LMCumani) **3-8-11** LDettori(10) (swtg: hld up: effrt & drvn along 2f out: no imp)	1	**9**	4/1^{2}	88	38
3111^{13}	**Connemara (IRE) (100)** (CADwyer) **3-8-6** DaneO'Neill(9) (hld up: a in rr)	½	**10**	25/1	82	32
3535a^{5}	**Abou Zouz (USA) (106)** (DRLoder) **3-8-11** MHills(5) (led to ½-wy: wknd 2f out)	5	**11**	16/1	74	24
				(SP 118.7%)	**11 Rn**	

1m 11.04 (-0.96) CSF £12.28 TOTE £5.20: £1.60 £1.50 £2.00 (£7.70) Trio £50.00 OWNER Mr Hamdan Al Maktoum (ARUNDEL) BRED Shadwell Farm Inc

WEIGHT FOR AGE 3yo-3lb

2925* Elnadim (USA) won this with more ease than the lower-grade handicap at Yarmouth, and with his stable in such good form, there is no saying how far he can go. (4/1)

2677 Bollin Joanne would have preferred more give in the ground, but she tracked the winner, and tried hard to deliver her challenge inside the last furlong, but her conqueror had taken first run, and he was always well in control. (9/4)

3577 Almushtarak (IRE) had to struggle to hold his place over this shorter trip, but he has got a bit of class about him, and in this kind of form it is only a matter of time before fortune favours him. (14/1)

3447 My Melody Parkes helped force the pace, but she was hard at work in the Dip, and her stamina gave out when faced with the hill. (16/1)

2476 Jayannpee, waiting on the leaders, got outpaced running into the Dip, and though he did rally up the final climb, had to admit the pace too strong. (16/1)

2683* Tedburrow could never get close enough to pose a serious threat, but he stuck on willingly, and he has not stopped winning yet. (12/1: op 8/1)

3447* Proud Native (IRE) was renewing his bid on the far-side rail when forced to take a pull inside the last furlong. It may have cost him some ground, but it is doubtful if he would have troubled the principals. (10/1: 7/1-11/1)

2599 Blue Goblin (USA) again ran no race at all, and his performances in his previous couple of runs could suggest he has gone over the top. (4/1)

3748 BREHENY H'CAP (0-95) (3-Y.O+) (Class C)

4-10 (4-11) **1m 6f 175y (July)** £6,056.00 (£1,808.00: £864.00: £392.00) Stalls: High GOING minus 0.45 sec per fur (F)

Form	Horse / details	Dist	Pos	SP	RR	SF
3579*	**Mawared (IRE) (81)** (JLDunlop) **4-9-10** 4x MJKinane(5) (b: lw: a.p: led ent fnl f: drvn out)	—	1	4/9^{1}	92	39
3543^{8}	**Star Rage (IRE) (78)** (MJohnston) **7-9-7** DHolland(1) (plld hrd: hld up: hdwy wl over 1f out: styd on towards fin)	1¼	2	8/1	88	35
3259^{2}	**Wild Rita (81)** (WRMuir) **5-9-10** DaneO'Neill(3) (lw: chsd ldr: rdn & edgd rt ins fnl f: kpt on)	1¼	3	15/2^{3}	89	36
2949^{7}	**Tudor Island (70)** (CEBrittain) **8-8-13** MRoberts(4) (led: qcknd over 2f out: rdn & hdd ent fnl f: btn whn hmpd & swtchd lft 200y out)	1	4	7/1^{2}	77	24
3318*	**Durham (65)** (GLMoore) **6-8-8b** CRutter(2) (hld up & bhd: rdn & outpcd over 2f out)	10	5	9/1	61	8

(SP 114.6%) **5 Rn**

3m 14.75 (6.25) CSF £4.74 TOTE £1.40: £1.10 £2.40 (£3.50) OWNER Mr Hamdan Al Maktoum (ARUNDEL) BRED Shadwell Estate Company Limited

3579* Mawared (IRE) retained his impressive winning run with another smoothly-gained success, and he has certainly been on a roll in the past couple of months. (4/9)

3440* Star Rage (IRE) travelled well, and looked likely to make a race of it entering the final furlong, but as in the past, he does need all of two miles now, and the winner had his measure when the chips were down. (8/1: 5/1-10/1)

3259 Wild Rita, tackling a slightly longer trip, was prepared to give it all she had, but she was held when edging in front of Tudor Island just inside the final furlong, and was a shade fortunate to hold on to third prize. (15/2)

1974 Tudor Island, bowling along in front, quickened things up soon after passing the three-furlong marker, but he had been collared entering the final furlong, and then had to check when he was stopped in his stride. (7/1)

3749 LONSDALE CLAIMING STKS (3-Y.O) (Class D)

4-40 (4-40) **7f (July)** £3,720.00 (£1,110.00: £530.00: £240.00) Stalls: Centre GOING minus 0.45 sec per fur (F)

Form	Horse / details	Dist	Pos	SP	RR	SF
3443^{5}	**La Dolce Vita (70)** (TDBarron) **3-8-11** KFallon(7) (hld up: swtchd lft ½-wy: led over 1f out: rdn & hld on cl home)	—	1	11/4^{2}	67	47
3454*	**Petite Danseuse (60)** (CADwyer) **3-8-8** LDettori(3) (lw: hld up: hdwy over 1f out: str chal fnl f: no ex nr fin)	nk	2	9/4^{1}	63	43
3206^{2}	**Gunners Glory (56)** (DMarks) **3-8-1**(3) DSweeney(5) (chsd ldrs: outpcd & swtchd rt over 1f out: str run fnl f: r.o)	nk	3	8/1	59	39
3582^{4}	**Gresatre (48)** (CADwyer) **3-8-4v** DHolland(1) (a.p: led 2f out: sn hdd: kpt on u.p fnl f)	½	4	33/1	58	38
3397^{4}	**Mike's Double (IRE) (60)** (MissGayKelleway) **3-9-2**(3) RFfrench(8) (prom: ev ch tl outpcd appr fnl f)	2½	5	10/1	67	47
3268*	**Nant Y Gamer (FR) (78)** (JBerry) **3-9-5**(3) PFessey(2) (lw: mde most 5f: rdn & wknd appr fnl f)	1¾	6	6/1^{3}	66	46
3463^{8}	**South China Sea** (PFICole) **3-9-6** MJKinane(6) (s.i.s: effrt & pushed along 3f out: no imp)	1	7	9/1	62	42
3558^{6}	**Cold Steel (60)** (WJarvis) **3-8-4** SSanders(4) (lw: prom: rdn over 2f out: sn lost pl: t.o)	dist	8	14/1	—	—

(SP 111.5%) **8 Rn**

1m 25.94 (0.94) CSF £8.05 TOTE £3.60: £1.60 £1.40 £2.00 (£4.00) OWNER Mr Stephen Woodall (THIRSK) BRED D. R. Botterill

La Dolce Vita clmd P K Gardner £9,000. Gunners Glory clmd Mrs L Stubbs £5,000

3443 La Dolce Vita poked her head in front running into the Dip, and pulling out all the stops under strong pressure, deservedly held on. (11/4)

3454* Petite Danseuse threw down a strong challenge inside the last furlong, but the winner just would not give best, and was holding her all the way to the line. (9/4)

3206 Gunners Glory, having his first run since changing stables, was without his customary blinkers. Held up to get the seventh furlong, he had trouble finding a clear passage, and though he flew after being switched, the line was always going to arrive too soon. (8/1)

3582 Gresatre ran his best race for quite some time on ground not really ideal, and if conditions do come in his favour in the near future, he should be able to take advantage. (33/1)

3397 Mike's Double (IRE), possibly not quite so effective on this more lively ground, still ran a fine race in defeat, and he is capable of winning another race. (10/1)

3268* Nant Y Gamer (FR) tried to make every post a winning post, but he was being pressed all the way, and had shot his bolt on reaching the last furlong. (6/1: op 4/1)

South China Sea (9/1: op 6/1)

3558 Cold Steel (14/1: 10/1-16/1)

3750 SAXHAM NURSERY H'CAP (2-Y.O) (Class C)

5-10 (5-11) **1m (July)** £5,526.50 (£1,652.00: £791.00: £360.50) Stalls: Centre GOING minus 0.45 sec per fur (F)

Form	Horse / details	Dist	Pos	SP	RR	SF
2953^{2}	**Outsourcing (USA) (82)** (PFICole) **2-9-6** LDettori(4) (mde all: hrd drvn appr fnl f: hld on gamely)	—	1	9/2^{3}	85	30
3295*	**Ron's Pet (83)** (RHannon) **2-9-7** DaneO'Neill(5) (lw: a.p: hrd rdn fnl f: r.o wl)	½	2	10/1	85	30
3307^{6}	**Narrogin (USA) (70)** (MRChannon) **2-8-8** SSanders(8) (a.p: rdn to chal 2f out: kpt on wl ins fnl f)	s.h	3	14/1	72	17
3237^{9}	**Minetta (77)** (MBell) **2-9-1** MFenton(6) (hld up & bhd: hdwy over 1f out: r.o wl towards fin)	s.h	4	16/1	79	24
3025^{5}	**Kim's Brave (78)** (BJMeehan) **2-9-2b1** MTebbutt(2) (trckd ldrs: n.m.r & swtchd rt appr fnl f: r.o)	1	5	16/1	78	23
2943^{3}	**Roborant (77)** (JLDunlop) **2-9-1** MJKinane(1) (prom: pushed along 3f out: nt clr run on ins appr fnl f: nvr able to chal)	s.h	6	5/2^{2}	77	22
3474^{9}	**Ballet Rambert (77)** (MJHeaton-Ellis) **2-9-1** KFallon(3) (hld up in tch: hdwy over 1f out: eased whn btn ins fnl f)	1¾	7	20/1	73	18
3387^{3}	**Shalyah (IRE) (69)** (MrsJRRamsden) **2-8-7** DHolland(10) (hld up & bhd: hdwy on outside 2f out: nt rch ldrs)	1¼	8	9/4^{1}	63	8
2038^{4}	**Cherished (IRE) (64)** (PFICole) **2-8-2** NCarlisle(7) (lw: chsd ldrs tl rdn & wknd wl over 1f out)	1½	9	20/1	55	—
3610^{10}	**Celtic Comfort (73)** (PCHaslam) **2-8-11** MRoberts(9) (trckd ldrs: rdn 3f out: wknd wl over 1f out)	hd	10	9/1	64	9

(SP 124.6%) **10 Rn**

1m 41.73 (3.73) CSF £47.91 CT £539.66 TOTE £3.80: £1.10 £2.30 £3.90 (£7.70) Trio £48.90 OWNER Bernard Gover Bloodstock Trading Ltd (WHATCOMBE) BRED Poole Investments & J. T. L. Jones

2953 Outsourcing (USA) adopted the right tactics over this testing mile, and answering his jockey's every call, held on in an epic duel to the finish. He will not forget this in a hurry. (9/2)

3295* Ron's Pet gave as good as he got, and in the end was a shade unfortunate to meet a rival as courageous as himself. (10/1: 7/1-12/1)

3307 Narrogin (USA), hard at work in an effort to wear down the winner entering the last quarter-mile, never once stopped trying, and success at this trip is well within his reach. (14/1: 7/1-16/1)

1510* Minetta did not find her stride until meeting the rising ground, so stamina has got to be her strong suit. (16/1)

3025 Kim's Brave, denied a clear run inside the distance, ran on well when switched, and it would seem he is better than his bare form suggests. (16/1)

2943 Roborant, drawn on the inside rail, was always with the pace. Nudged along when short of room for the final quarter-mile, he is capable of winning a similar event. (5/2)
3387 Shalyah (IRE), held up off the pace, was unable to quicken when set alight running into the Dip, and she was never a factor. (9/4)

T/Plpt: £7.00 (3020.64 Tckts). T/Qdpt: £4.00 (238.5 Tckts) IM

3456-THIRSK (L-H) (Good, Good to firm patches)
Friday August 22nd
WEATHER: Sunny WIND: mod behind

3751 JOHN CARR (S) STKS (2-Y.O) (Class F)
2-20 (2-23) **7f** £2,792.50 (£780.00: £377.50) Stalls: Low GOING minus 0.34 sec per fur (GF)

				SP	RR	SF
3451[7]	**Impulse (IRE) (64)** (APJarvis) **2-8-11v** KDarley(14) (led after 2f: r.o wl appr fnl f)	—	**1**	6/1[3]	66	27
3563[3]	**Katie's Cracker (50)** (MRChannon) **2-8-6** JCarroll(1) (lw: chsd ldrs: styd on u.p fnl 2f: no ch w wnr)	2½	**2**	9/4[1]	55	16
859[3]	**Pink Ticket (54)** (PDEvans) **2-8-6** JFEgan(16) (chsd ldrs tl lost pl ent st: styd on wl appr fnl f)	1½	**3**	12/1	52	13
3563[2]	**Snappy Times (56)** (MDods) **2-8-11** DaleGibson(12) (b.nr hind: chsd ldrs: effrt & ch 3f out: btn appr fnl f)	¾	**4**	7/1	55	16
3438[8]	**My Bet (50)** (MWEasterby) **2-8-12** TLucas(8) (a chsng ldrs: no hdwy fnl 3f)	2	**5**	20/1	52	13
2886[8]	**Turf Moor (IRE) (57)** (JJO'Neill) **2-8-3**(3) TEDurcan(10) (led 2f: cl up tl wknd wl over 1f out)	2½	**6**	9/1	40	1
3563[4]	**Wynbury Flyer** (FMurphy) **2-8-11** JFanning(3) (sn pushed along: nvr rchd ldrs)	2½	**7**	6/1[3]	39	—
2827[9]	**Gay da Cheen (IRE)** (JMCarr) **2-8-6** LCharnock(2) (nvr trbld ldrs)	4	**8**	50/1	25	—
3544[5]	**Blitz** (MWEasterby) **2-8-3**(3) GParkin(4) (b.off hind: hld up & bhd: nvr nr to chal)	¾	**9**	25/1	23	—
*2914**	**Docklands Dispatch (IRE) (62)** (NTinkler) **2-9-3** KimTinkler(6) (lw: mid div: hrd rdn over 2f out: n.d)	2	**10**	5/1[2]	30	—
3427[9]	**Robert The Bruce** (RAFahey) **2-8-4**(7) RWinston(11) (a outpcd & n.d)	s.h	**11**	12/1	24	—
3563[7]	**Slew Magic (IRE) (59)** (WGMTurner) **2-8-5**(7) DMcGaffin(5) (nvr bttr than mid div)	1	**12**	12/1	22	—
2016[13]	**Eager Hero** (MBrittain) **2-8-11** GBardwell(9) (lw: drvn along thrght: a bhd)	hd	**13**	33/1	21	—
3312[6]	**Jet Set Sarah (USA)** (JBerry) **2-8-1**(5) CLowther(15) (n.d)	1½	**14**	20/1	13	—
3212[12]	**Drain Doctor** (SEKettlewell) **2-8-11** JStack(13) (a bhd)	7	**15**	100/1	2	—
				(SP 140.8%)	**15 Rn**	

1m 28.4 (3.50) CSF £19.93 TOTE £7.90: £2.50 £1.10 £6.30 (£10.90) Trio £62.60 OWNER Mr Terence Lyons II (ASTON UPTHORPE) BRED P. J. Hannon
Sold Mrs JR Ramsden 6,600 gns
3451 Impulse (IRE), very warm beforehand, had his mind made up for him during the race, and did it well. (6/1)
3563 Katie's Cracker does not do anything quickly, but she does stay well, and that should bring its rewards. (9/4)
859 Pink Ticket, stepping up in trip for the first time, got it particularly well, but did not handle the bend on this occasion. (12/1)
3563 Snappy Times had his chances, but when it came down to a struggle he found little. (7/1)
3067 My Bet, very free to post, ran well enough to suggest that there is another race in her. (20/1)
1280 Turf Moor (IRE), an edgy sort, had her chances but proved disappointing when ridden. (9/1)
3563 Wynbury Flyer (6/1: op 12/1)
3544 Blitz ran a shade better, without getting into it, over this trip. (25/1)
Robert The Bruce (12/1: op 50/1)

3752 JAMES HETHERTON LIMITED STKS (0-85) (3-Y.O+) (Class D)
2-50 (2-50) **1m** £3,939.50 (£1,181.00: £568.00: £261.50) Stalls: Low GOING minus 0.34 sec per fur (GF)

				SP	RR	SF
3185[9]	**Sweet Fortune (USA) (83)** (MRStoute) **3-8-13** KDarley(4) (lw: mde all: qcknd over 3f out: r.o strly)	—	**1**	7/4[1]	90	29
3616[4]	**Sheer Face (80)** (WRMuir) **3-8-6**(5) CLowther(3) (chsd wnr: pushed along appr st: kpt on same pce)	2	**2**	13/2	84	23
3079*	**Alikhlas (82)** (MajorWRHern) **3-8-10** TSprake(1) (hld up & bhd: hdwy on bit 2f out: rdn appr fnl f: fnd nil)	2½	**3**	9/4[3]	78	17
3408[2]	**Tertium (IRE) (83)** (MartynWane) **5-9-3** JCarroll(2) (lw: hld up: effrt over 2f out: sn rdn & btn)	6	**4**	2/1[2]	67	12
				(SP 113.8%)	**4 Rn**	

1m 40.4 (3.90) CSF £11.32 TOTE £2.60: (£9.50) OWNER Maktoum Al Maktoum (NEWMARKET) BRED S. D. Brilie
WEIGHT FOR AGE 3yo-6lb
2704* Sweet Fortune (USA) was allowed to dictate things, and was always a gear or two better than these. (7/4)
3616 Sheer Face kept tabs on the winner, but off the bit from halfway, was never good enough despite trying hard. (13/2)
3079* Alikhlas looks a very difficult ride, as she swings off the bit for much of the race, but when it came down to a struggle here, she failed to do a tap. (9/4)
3408 Tertium (IRE) is proving very expensive to follow this year, and was not suited by such a small field. (2/1)

3753 E.B.F. JOHN QUINN MAIDEN STKS (2-Y.O) (Class D)
3-20 (3-25) **6f** £4,157.25 (£1,248.00: £601.50: £278.25) Stalls: High GOING minus 0.34 sec per fur (GF)

				SP	RR	SF
3489[3]	**Exbourne's Wish (USA)** (BWHills) **2-9-0** JCarroll(2) (swtg: unruly s: mde all: r.o wl fnl f)	—	**1**	9/4[2]	85	33
2728[5]	**Robsart (IRE)** (JRFanshawe) **2-8-9** KDarley(9) (chsd ldrs: hdwy to chal 2f out: nt qckn fnl f)	3½	**2**	11/8[1]	71	19
3433[4]	**Naskhi** (MJohnston) **2-8-9** DeanMcKeown(1) (b.hind: cl up: effrt 2f out: nt qckn)	3½	**3**	9/2[3]	61	9
3060[10]	**Carrick View (IRE)** (PCalver) **2-8-11**(3) DarrenMoffatt(6) (drvn along ½-wy: styd on: nvr trbld ldrs)	7	**4**	50/1	48	—
	Walton Grey (IRE) (PDEvans) **2-9-0** JFEgan(11) (cmpt: bit bkwd: styd on fr ½-wy: nvr nr to chal)	1¾	**5**	25/1	43	—
3239[5]	**Smart Prince (69)** (JJQuinn) **2-8-11**(3) GParkin(7) (prom tl outpcd fnl 2f)	hd	**6**	16/1	43	—
	Sea Fig (TDBarron) **2-8-9** ACulhane(5) (cmpt: bit bkwd: sme hdwy over 1f out: n.d)	½	**7**	33/1	36	—
	Esse (EWeymes) **2-8-9** JStack(10) (w'like: scope: nvr bttr than mid div)	1	**8**	20/1	34	—
	Intuitive (JLEyre) **2-8-9** RLappin(12) (lt-f: unf: in tch 4f)	hd	**9**	33/1	34	—
3411[10]	**Set Trail (IRE)** (JHanson) **2-8-9** EJohnson(8) (b.hind: s.i.s: hld up & bhd: nvr nr to chal)	1½	**10**	33/1	30	—
	Mystical Rodge (MDods) **2-9-0** LCharnock(4) (cmpt: unf: chsd ldrs 4f: wknd)	6	**11**	25/1	19	—
	Melodian (MBrittain) **2-9-0** GBardwell(13) (leggy: unf: s.s: a wl bhd)	14	**12**	33/1	—	—
	Nordic Pirjo (MrsJRRamsden) **2-8-9** TSprake(3) (neat: Withdrawn not under Starter's orders: broke out of stalls)		**W**	33/1	—	—
				(SP 126.1%)	**12 Rn**	

1m 12.2 (2.50) CSF £4.85 TOTE £2.70: £1.40 £1.10 £1.70 (£2.50) Trio £2.10 OWNER Mr K. Abdulla (LAMBOURN) BRED Juddmonte Farms

3489 Exbourne's Wish (USA), edgy and sweaty beforehand, gave problems at the start, but did nothing wrong in the race, and won it particularly well. (9/4: op 6/4)
2728 Robsart (IRE), patiently ridden, had her chances, but when it came down to a struggle she found one far too good. (11/8)
3433 Naskhi still looked as though there is something to work on, and time would seem to be the key with her. (9/2)
Carrick View (IRE) showed a fair amount of improvement this time, but there is still plenty more needed. (50/1)
Walton Grey (IRE) needed this, and after looking clueless early on, was learning as the race progressed, and time should see plenty of improvement. (25/1)
3239 Smart Prince found this company too hot, and was wisely not overpunished once beaten. (16/1)
3411 Set Trail (IRE) is certainly not an easy ride, but gave signs of ability here, without getting into the race, and looks one likely to improve. (33/1)

3754 RICHARD FAHEY H'CAP (0-75) (3-Y.O+) (Class D)

3-50 (3-50) **2m** £4,056.50 (£1,217.00: £586.00: £270.50) Stalls: Low GOING minus 0.34 sec per fur (GF)

				SP	RR	SF
3267[4]	**Leviticus (IRE) (73)** (TPTate) **3-9-3** GDuffield(5) (lw: mde all: kpt on wl fnl 2f)	—	**1**	7/1	86	37
3309[12]	**Charter (56)** (WStorey) **6-9-0v** JFanning(2) (hld up: hdwy to chse wnr 4f out: kpt on: nt pce to chal)	1¼	**2**	10/1	68	33
3440[5]	**Highfield Fizz (38)** (CWFairhurst) **5-7-10** LCharnock(7) (b.off hind: hld up & bhd: effrt ent st: styd on: nrst fin)	3½	**3**	8/1	46	11
3309*	**Batabanoo (50)** (MrsMReveley) **8-8-8** KDarley(1) (hld up: shkn up over 2f out: nvr able to chal)	1¾	**4**	2/1[1]	57	22
3440[4]	**Forgie (IRE) (66)** (PCalver) **4-9-7**(3) DarrenMoffatt(4) (chsd wnr after 4f to 4f out: outpcd fnl 2½f)	1¾	**5**	10/1	71	36
3461[3]	**Hasta la Vista (55)** (MWEasterby) **7-8-10b**(3) GParkin(8) (lw: trckd ldrs tl lost pl fnl 2½f)	¾	**6**	11/2[3]	59	24
3419[6]	**Darien (74)** (RCharlton) **3-9-4** TSprake(6) (hld up: effrt appr st: wl outpcd fnl 2½f)	hd	**7**	7/2[2]	78	29
2154[5]	**Anchorena (45)** (DWBarker) **5-8-3** TWilliams(3) (lw: trckd ldrs tl outpcd & lost pl 5f out: n.d after)	6	**8**	16/1	43	8

(SP 118.6%) **8 Rn**

3m 30.5 (7.50) CSF £69.08 CT £526.10 TOTE £9.10: £2.50 £3.10 £1.80 (£67.20) OWNER Mrs S. L. Worthington (TADCASTER) BRED Antonio Boesso

WEIGHT FOR AGE 3yo-14lb

3267 Leviticus (IRE), stepping up in trip, and made plenty of use of, did it well, and staying is obviously the game for him. (7/1)
2535 Charter went after the winner some way out, and kept struggling on, but was never quite doing enough. (10/1)
3440 Highfield Fizz needed a stronger pace than was set here, and despite staying on well, could never get in a blow. (8/1)
3309* Batabanoo did not produce his blistering turn of foot this time, and was not overpunished. (2/1)
3440 Forgie (IRE) is slipping back down the weights, and will return to form in due course. (10/1)
3461 Hasta la Vista was certainly not ridden as positively as normal, and this is best ignored. (11/2)

3755 BRIAN ROTHWELL NURSERY H'CAP (2-Y.O) (Class D)

4-25 (4-27) **6f** £3,782.00 (£1,136.00: £548.00: £254.00) Stalls: High GOING minus 0.34 sec per fur (GF)

				SP	RR	SF
3258[4]	**Grand Estate (69)** (TDEasterby) **2-8-10** KDarley(9) (lw: mde most: kpt on wl fnl f)	—	**1**	2/1[1]	75	28
2712[4]	**Hirst Bridge (IRE) (80)** (MWEasterby) **2-9-0**(7) RWinston(11) (lw: in tch: hdwy u.str.p over 1f out: styd on wl)	1	**2**	10/1	83	36
3480[5]	**High Carry (71)** (NTinkler) **2-8-7**(5) CLowther(7) (a w ldrs: no ex fnl f)	1¼	**3**	14/1	71	24
3239[6]	**Euro Venture (69)** (DNicholls) **2-8-10** AlexGreaves(10) (trckd ldrs: effrt 2f out: nt qckn fnl f)	¾	**4**	4/1[2]	67	20
3307[9]	**Captain McCloy (USA) (65)** (MrsJRRamsden) **2-8-6** TSprake(4) (bhd tl hdwy u.p over 1f out: styd on)	s.h	**5**	25/1	63	16
3480[3]	**Inchalong (64)** (MBrittain) **2-8-5** GBardwell(12) (s.i.s: swtchd lft & hdwy ½-wy: no imp)	2½	**6**	7/1[3]	55	8
3312*	**Heavenly Falls (IRE) (65)** (CADwyer) **2-7-13**(7) AMcCarthy(8) (chsd ldrs: rdn & no imp fnl 2f)	1½	**7**	11/1	52	5
3258*	**Peter's Imp (IRE) (80)** (JBerry) **2-9-7** GDuffield(6) (cl up tl rdn & wknd fnl 2f)	2½	**8**	7/1[3]	61	14
*3042**	**Carambo (76)** (JLEyre) **2-9-3** MGallagher(3) (w ldrs 4f: wknd)	5	**9**	8/1	43	—
2762[6]	**Barrelbio (IRE) (65)** (JJO'Neill) **2-8-6** ACulhane(5) (in tch over 3f)	nk	**10**	10/1	31	—
2361[8]	**King of Dance (70)** (BSRothwell) **2-8-11** LCharnock(2) (a outpcd & wl bhd)	7	**11**	25/1	18	—

(SP 130.3%) **11 Rn**

1m 12.3 (2.60) CSF £24.64 CT £220.25 TOTE £4.10: £2.20 £2.80 £7.00 (£17.60) Trio £96.60 OWNER Mr Ian Armitage (MALTON) BRED C. W. Rogers

3258 Grand Estate made no mistake this time, and won particularly well. (2/1: op 3/1)
2712 Hirst Bridge (IRE), after six weeks off, ran well, but in doing so had quite a hard race. (10/1)
3480 High Carry is a really strong filly, and has plenty of toe. She may be best over the minimum trip at the moment. (14/1: 10/1-16/1)
3239 Euro Venture obviously has ability, but this poor walker seems happiest when on the bridle, and was a shade disappointing off it. (4/1)
2905 Captain McCloy (USA) is certainly coming to himself lookswise, and was picking up well in the closing stages. (25/1)
3480 Inchalong keeps spoiling her chances with her antics at the start, and again missed the break. (7/1)
3042* Carambo (8/1: 6/1-9/1)

3756 MALTON TRAINING ASSOCIATION APPRENTICE H'CAP (0-70) (3-Y.O+) (Class E)

4-55 (5-03) **5f** £3,289.75 (£988.00: £476.50: £220.75) Stalls: High GOING minus 0.34 sec per fur (GF)

				SP	RR	SF
3637[6]	**Cross The Border (62)** (DNicholls) **4-9-8** PRoberts(12) (trckd ldrs: led ent fnl f: r.o)	—	**1**	11/2[2]	76	66
3625[2]	**Camionneur (IRE) (53)** (TDEasterby) **4-8-8**(5) TSiddall(9) (lw: dwlt: hdwy 2f out: r.o towards fin)	2	**2**	11/2[2]	61	51
3287[10]	**Bowcliffe Grange (IRE) (47)** (DWChapman) **5-8-4**(3) KSked(11) (led & sn clr: hdd ent fnl f: no ex)	nk	**3**	5/1[1]	54	44
3566[5]	**Imp Express (IRE) (40)** (GMMoore) **4-8-0** ADaly(14) (in tch: rdn & no ex appr fnl f)	¾	**4**	9/1	44	34
3406[2]	**Johayro (61)** (JSGoldie) **4-9-7v** CLowther(10) (chsd ldrs: rdn ½-wy: no imp after)	2½	**5**	6/1[3]	57	47
3460[2]	**William's Well (59)** (MWEasterby) **3-9-3b** SCopp(4) (b.nr fore: racd centre: chsd ldrs: rdn ½-wy: no imp)	½	**6**	9/1	54	42
3271[7]	**Kabcast (38)** (DWChapman) **12-7-7b**(5) JMcAuley(15) (chsd ldrs 3f)	½	**7**	10/1	31	21
3287[9]	**Lillibella (55)** (MrsJRRamsden) **4-8-12**(3) JoHunnam(17) (lw: s.i.s: hung bdly lft thrght: hdwy after 2f: no imp)	3½	**8**	7/1	37	27
3431[7]	**Mystique Smile (36)** (JSGoldie) **4-7-5**(5) JennyBenson(13) (hung lft ½-wy: nvr trbld ldrs)	½	**9**	9/1	16	6
3143[14]	**Marino Street (48)** (PDEvans) **4-8-3v**(5) AMcCarthy(3) (b.nr fore: racd far side: hld up: n.d)	¾	**10**	25/1	26	16
3454[6]	**Moon Song (55)** (APJarvis) **3-8-8**(5) CCarver(8) (n.d)	nk	**11**	33/1	32	20
3224[9]	**Northern Sal (41)** (MissLAPerratt) **3-7-8**(5) ANicholls(16) (uns rdr & bolted bef s: s.i.s: hdwy after 2f: n.d)	hd	**12**	33/1	18	6
3484[9]	**Sunday Mail Too (IRE) (36)** (MissLAPerratt) **5-7-5**(5) JFowle(2) (a outpcd & bhd)	s.h	**13**	50/1	12	2
2754[9]	**Swan At Whalley (68)** (RAFahey) **5-9-11**(3) RWinston(5) (racd & led far side: outpcd fr ½-wy)	1	**14**	25/1	41	31
3399[3]	**Ticka Ticka Timing (36)** (BWMurray) **4-7-5**(5) PBradley(1) (chsd ldr far side: n.d)	nk	**15**	50/1	8	—
3378[8]	**Maysimp (IRE) (36)** (BPJBaugh) **4-7-7**(3) IonaWands(6) (swtg: outpcd fr ½-wy)	5	**16**	100/1	—	—

				SP	RR	SF
2900[11]	**Mallia (63)** (TDBarron) **4-9-4**(5) VictoriaAppleby(7) (sn outpcd & bhd)	½	**17**	25/1	18	8
				(SP 135.6%)		**17 Rn**

58.2 secs (0.60) CSF £33.92 CT £158.01 TOTE £5.10: £1.90 £2.00 £2.40 £2.10 (£13.50) Trio £61.80 OWNER Mr P. D. Savill (THIRSK) BRED Brook Stud Ltd

LONG HANDICAP Sunday Mail Too (IRE) 7-6 Ticka Ticka Timing 7-4 Maysimp (IRE) 7-4 Mystique Smile 7-7

WEIGHT FOR AGE 3yo-2lb

3637 Cross The Border had this race set up for him, and always going nicely, won it in useful style. (11/2: 7/2-6/1)

3625 Camionneur (IRE) did his usual, gave away many lengths at the start, and then finished like a train, but the effort was again too late. (11/2)

2754 Bowcliffe Grange (IRE) is the fastest horse in the country over three-and-half furlongs, and he seems to be lasting a bit further with every run. (5/1)

3566 Imp Express (IRE) has the ability, but does not quite put it to full use. (9/1)

3406 Johayro likes to dominate, but found these far too fast. (6/1)

3460 William's Well is a hard ride, and always found the pace too strong for his liking here, but was not well drawn. (9/1)

3271 Kabcast just wanted to hang left, and would obviously have been better suited with a left-hand rail to run against. (10/1: 8/1-12/1)

T/Plpt: £187.70 (83.71 Tckts). T/Qdpt: £43.60 (23.28 Tckts) AA

3540-BEVERLEY (R-H) (Good, Good to firm patches)
Saturday August 23rd

WEATHER: overcast WIND: mod half against

3757 E.B.F. ST. JOHN AMBULANCE MAIDEN STKS (2-Y.O F) (Class D)

2-20 (2-22) **7f 100y** £3,600.00 (£1,080.00: £520.00: £240.00) Stalls: High GOING minus 0.63 sec per fur (F)

				SP	RR	SF
2693[2]	**Royal Bounty (IRE)** (MajorWRHern) **2-8-11** TSprake(3) (hld up: hdwy & rdn 2f out: r.o strly to ld cl home)	—	**1**	4/9[1]	84	39
3426[3]	**Scent of Success (USA)** (MRStoute) **2-8-11v[1]** KDarley(4) (led & sn clr: rdn & ct nr fin)	½	**2**	5/1[2]	83?	38
	Elanaaka (DMorley) **2-8-11** JStack(8) (tall: s.i.s: hdwy 2f out: styd on wl ins fnl f)	2½	**3**	16/1	78+	33
	Piccadilly (TJEtherington) **2-8-11** MFenton(2) (w'like: leggy: hld up: hdwy & carried lft ent fnl f: nvr nrr)	4	**4**	33/1	69	24
2953[7]	**Phantom Waters** (RFJohnsonHoughton) **2-8-11** ACulhane(5) (b.hind: chsd clr ldr: rdn over 2f out: sn btn)	1¼	**5**	20/1	66	21
	Moet (IRE) (JLEyre) **2-8-11** OPears(6) (unf: scope: bit bkwd: dwlt: hld up in rr: nvr nr to chal)	3	**6**	20/1	60	15
2875[9]	**Washm (USA)** (DMorley) **2-8-11** JCarroll(7) (chsd ldrs over 4f: sn lost tch)	½	**7**	10/1[3]	59	14
2898[4]	**Swaybus** (MJohnston) **2-8-11** DHolland(1) (swtg: bit bkwd: hld up: effrt over 1f out: rdn & edgd lft: no imp)	3	**8**	20/1	52	7
				(SP 118.1%)		**8 Rn**

1m 32.5 (0.50) CSF £2.61 TOTE £1.30: £1.10 £1.10 £2.40 (£2.20) OWNER Lord Weinstock (LAMBOURN) BRED Ballymacoll Stud Farm Ltd

2693 Royal Bounty (IRE), backed as if defeat was out of the question, had a real battle on her hands entering the final quarter-mile but, with the long-time leader beginning to tie up, she stayed on stoutly to lead in the shadow of the post. (4/9)

3426 Scent of Success (USA) raced freely in her first-time visor, and for most of the way looked to be beyond recall, but she had done too much too soon, and with her stride shortening, was a shade unfortunate to be run out of it nearing the line. (5/1)

Elanaaka must stand all of seventeen hands plus, even at this early stage of her career, but she showed that she does possess ability with a very promising staying-on performance, and given time, she could turn out useful. (16/1)

Piccadilly, an attractive filly, closely related to three winners, was impeded when making a forward move entering the final furlong, but she would not have troubled the principals this time. (33/1)

1927 Phantom Waters, more experienced than any of her rivals, was fighting a losing battle in her attempt to claw back the pace-setter early in the straight, and her exertions took their toll. (20/1)

3758 DRIFFIELD (S) H'CAP (0-60) (3-Y.O+) (Class G)

2-50 (2-50) **1m 3f 216y** £2,616.00 (£726.00: £348.00) Stalls: High GOING minus 0.63 sec per fur (F)

				SP	RR	SF
3540[5]	**Sushi Bar (IRE) (36)** (MrsMReveley) **6-8-10** KDarley(8) (hld up: hdwy 6f out: rdn to ld appr fnl f: r.o wl)	—	**1**	7/1[2]	48	30
3570[4]	**Portite Sophie (39)** (MBrittain) **6-8-6**(7) DMernagh(4) (swtg: a.p: ev ch 1f out: hrd rdn: unable qckn)	1¾	**2**	15/2[3]	49	31
3587[2]	**Needwood Epic (44)** (BCMorgan) **4-9-4b** LCharnock(1) (led tl hdd ent fnl f: one pce)	2	**3**	15/2[3]	51	33
3472[4]	**Nornax Lad (USA) (38)** (MartynMeade) **9-8-9b**(3) RHavlin(15) (swtg: in tch: effrt & rdn 4f out: styd on appr fnl f)	1¾	**4**	15/2[3]	43	25
3491[7]	**Rock The Barney (IRE) (40)** (MDIUsher) **8-8-11**(3) PMcCabe(6) (hld up in rr: styd on fnl 2f: too much to do)	5	**5**	7/1[2]	38	20
3462[2]	**Foleys Quest (IRE) (50)** (JSMoore) **3-9-0** JFEgan(2) (b.off fore: swtg: s.i.s: hld up & bhd: hdwy 5f out: rdn 2f out: one pce)	nk	**6**	11/2[1]	48	20
3461[7]	**Havana Heights (IRE) (36)** (JLEyre) **4-8-3**(7) SBuckley(3) (nvr nr to chal)	¾	**7**	16/1	33	15
3309[13]	**Highfield Pet (40)** (CWFairhurst) **4-8-7**(7) TSiddall(13) (bhd: effrt on outside over 2f out: nt rch ldrs)	¾	**8**	33/1	36	18
3456[6]	**Diamond Crown (IRE) (39)** (MartynWane) **6-8-13** JCarroll(14) (a in rr)	½	**9**	8/1	34	16
2490[5]	**Slapy Dam (44)** (CASmith) **5-9-4** VSlattery(10) (bit bkwd: hld up mid div: effrt & rdn over 3f out: no imp)	1½	**10**	8/1	37	19
2503[6]	**Jubran (USA) (38)** (JLEyre) **11-8-5**(7) RWinston(7) (chsd ldrs: wnt 2nd ent st: sn rdn & wknd)	hd	**11**	12/1	31	13
3456[13]	**That Old Feeling (IRE) (39)** (DWChapman) **5-8-13** OPears(11) (lw: a in rr)	d.h	**12**	25/1	28	10
2503[9]	**Indonesian (IRE) (46)** (PCalver) **5-9-3**(3) DarrenMoffatt(12) (bit bkwd: trckd ldrs: rdn & wknd 4f out)	2½	**12**	16/1	35	17
2170[4]	**Eden Dancer (36)** (MrsMReveley) **5-8-10** ACulhane(9) (bhd: rdn 5f out: no rspnse)	3½	**14**	8/1	21	3
2487[20]	**Banneret (USA) (50)** (JO'Reilly) **4-9-10** AlexGreaves(5) (chsd ldr 9f: sn wknd: t.o)	20	**15**	33/1	8	—
				(SP 138.2%)		**15 Rn**

2m 35.4 (2.40) CSF £60.45 CT £390.90 TOTE £5.20: £1.80 £2.70 £2.60 (£23.90) Trio £51.30 OWNER Mr P. D. Savill (SALTBURN) BRED Scarteen Stud

WEIGHT FOR AGE 3yo-10lb

Bt in 5,200gns

3540 Sushi Bar (IRE) has done all his winning at longer trips, but with the brisk pace, he found everything fitting into place, and once he had struck the front he asserted to pull clear. (7/1)

3570 Portite Sophie came between horses to deliver her challenge entering the last furlong, but hard as she tried, the winner had the legs of her in the race to the line. (15/2)

3587 Needwood Epic, taking a step down in both trip and class, has only one way of running, and once again that bit extra was missing when the final battle developed. (15/2)

3472 Nornax Lad (USA) has been competing over longer trips of late, and though he was hard at work from the turn into the straight, kept staying on, and obviously needs a stiffer test of stamina. (15/2)
2483 Rock The Barney (IRE) should have been in his element in this class, but he was set an almost impossible task, and is capable of improving on this. (7/1)
3462 Foleys Quest (IRE), awash with sweat in the preliminaries, took closer order entering the straight, but she was soon at full stretch, and lacked the speed to reach the leaders. (11/2)

3759 BRIAN MERRINGTON MEMORIAL H'CAP (0-70) (3-Y.O+) (Class E)

3-25 (3-26) **7f 100y** £4,890.00 (£1,470.00: £710.00: £330.00) Stalls: High GOING minus 0.63 sec per fur (F)

Form	Horse	Dist	Pos	SP	RR	SF
3565^{2}	**Myttons Mistake (57)** (ABailey) **4-8-11**(5) PRoberts(13) (hld up in tch: hdwy to ld over 1f out: rdn out)	—	1	9/2^{1}	66	42
3476^{4}	**Euro Sceptic (IRE) (49)** (TDEasterby) **5-8-1b**(7) RWinston(10) (hld up: hdwy & squeezed thro 2f out: fin fast)	¾	2	7/1^{2}	56	32
3573^{2}	**Needle Match (56)** (JJO'Neill) **4-9-1** JCarroll(12) (swtg: hld up & bhd: hdwy over 2f out: rdn & r.o wl fnl f)	hd	3	7/1^{2}	63	39
3627^{7}	**Reinhardt (IRE) (41)** (DNicholls) **4-7-7**(7) ANicholls(2) (sn wl bhd: gd hdwy appr fnl f: nrst fin)	1	4	16/1	46	22
3488^{2}	**Katie Komaite (44)** (CaptJWilson) **4-8-3v**ow1 KDarley(16) (chsd ldrs: led over 1f out: sn hdd: unable qckn)	½	5	12/1	48	23
2913^{6}	**Heathyards Lady (USA) (37)** (RHollinshead) **6-7-10** LCharnock(17) (b: hdwy ent st: sn ev ch: rdn & one pce fnl f)	1	6	25/1	39	15
3622^{12}	**Thatched (IRE) (48)** (REBarr) **7-8-2**(5) KSked(7) (lw: hmpd s: effrt 2f out: rdn appr fnl f: one pce)	hd	7	14/1	50	26
3269*	**Surf City (52)** (WWHaigh) **4-8-11** DaleGibson(15) (lw: hld up mid div: hdwy & nt clr run over 1f out: nt rcvr)	1	8	14/1	51	27
3630^{4}	**Kass Alhawa (61)** (DWChapman) **4-9-6** ACulhane(4) (swtg: trckd ldrs: drvn along 3f: outpcd fnl 2f)	1¼	9	12/1	58	34
3029^{12}	**Royal South (IRE) (43)** (PSFelgate) **4-7-9**(7) JFowle(3) (plld hrd: chsd ldrs 5f)	2½	10	33/1	34	10
3573^{5}	**Winston (50)** (JDBethell) **4-8-9** DHolland(8) (prom: ev ch 2f out: sn rdn & wknd)	s.h	11	9/1^{3}	41	17
3420^{2}	**Allinson's Mate (IRE) (65)** (TDBarron) **9-9-10b** RLappin(9) (hld up: hdwy 3f out: rdn wl over 1f out: sn btn)	nk	12	10/1	56	32
3105^{3}	**Night of Glass (58)** (JLEyre) **4-9-3v** MGallagher(1) (b: wnt rt s: effrt & nt clr run over 2f out: nt rcvr)	½	13	10/1	48	24
3693^{7}	**Souperficial (50)** (NTinkler) **6-8-9v** KimTinkler(6) (hld up: brought wd & hdwy 2f out: wknd fnl f)	hd	14	20/1	39	15
2019^{10}	**Axeman (IRE) (44)** (MartynWane) **5-7-12**(5)ow4 ADaly(14) (led tl hdd & wknd over 1f out)	1¼	15	9/2^{1}	31	3
3582^{7}	**Al Reet (IRE) (54)** (SRBowring) **6-8-13** SWebster(11) (trckd ldrs over 4f)	2	16	14/1	36	12
3421^{5}	**King Athelstan (USA) (60)** (BAMcMahon) **9-8-12**(7) SRighton(5) (swtg: sn chsng ldrs: ev ch ½-wy: sn hrd drvn & wknd: t.o)	11	17	16/1	19	—

(SP 148.2%) **17 Rn**

1m 32.6 (0.60) CSF £37.66 CT £222.58 TOTE £4.80: £1.80 £2.40 £1.90 £4.10 (£15.80) Trio £37.20 OWNER Mr Gordon Mytton (TARPORLEY) BRED R. S. A. Urquhart

IN-FOCUS: **In such a large field, there were the inevitable hard luck stories, for there was very little room to be had inside the last couple of furlongs, and several riders just had to sit and suffer.**

3565 Myttons Mistake has been knocking at the door recently, and he thoroughly deserved to get back to winning ways. Towards the finish he was being made to work, after having the prize sewn up halfway through the final furlong. (9/2)
3476 Euro Sceptic (IRE) carried over a stone more when successful in this race last year, but in what proved to be a rough race in the latter stages, he sustained late rally was never quite going to get him there. (7/1)
3573 Needle Match is running consistently well at present, and he did well to thread his way through a tightly-packed field inside the last quarter-mile, and another win is earmarked. (7/1)
3240 Reinhardt (IRE), beaten in a seller on his most recent outing, has yet to prove he truly stays this trip, but from being some way adrift of his rivals entering the straight, he was putting in some sterling work at the finish, and the ability is there when he cares to use it. (16/1)
3488 Katie Komaite, produced to lead below the distance, was unable to contain the strong-finishing winner, and she was tapped for finishing speed in the run to the line. She is proving hard to win with, but is certainly a trier. (12/1)
2913 Heathyards Lady (USA) usually needs more cut than she had here, but she was fighting for the lead approaching the final furlong, and she could be approaching her peak. (25/1)

3760 RACING CHANNEL MAIDEN STKS (2-Y.O) (Class D)

4-00 (4-01) **1m 100y** £3,385.50 (£1,014.00: £487.00: £223.50) Stalls: High GOING minus 0.63 sec per fur (F)

Form	Horse	Dist	Pos	SP	RR	SF
3479^{5}	**Alberich (IRE)** (MJohnston) **2-9-0** DHolland(3) (bit bkwd: a w ldr: led 2f out: edgd rt fnl f: rdn out)	—	1	6/1^{3}	80+	9
3103^{3}	**Indimaaj** (JLDunlop) **2-9-0** KDarley(4) (chsd ldrs: rdn over 3f out: styd on wl ins fnl f)	1½	2	4/6^{1}	77	6
3047^{6}	**Najjar (USA)** (PTWalwyn) **2-9-0** JLowe(8) (bit bkwd: led to 2f out: sn rdn: no ex)	1¾	3	11/2^{2}	74	3
	Hobart Junction (IRE) (SCWilliams) **2-9-0** PBloomfield(1) (scope: bkwd: swtg: hld up & bhd: styd on appr fnl f: nvr nrr)	2½	4	20/1	69	—
3103^{5}	**Hombre** (JWWatts) **2-9-0** ACulhane(6) (prom: hrd drvn over 2f out: kpt on one pce)	s.h	5	13/2	69	—
	Treasure Chest (IRE) (MajorWRHern) **2-9-0** TSprake(2) (unf: scope: s.i.s: hld up: effrt 3f out: wknd over 1f out)	hd	6	9/1	69	—
3117^{16}	**Count Keni** (JMJefferson) **2-9-0** LCharnock(5) (dwlt: hld up: drvn along over 3f out: sn lost tch: t.o)	12	7	50/1	46	—
	Right Cross Jonny (USA) (PWChapple-Hyam) **2-8-11**(3) RHavlin(7) (w'like: str: bkwd: s.s: a bhd: t.o fnl 3f)	8	8	12/1	31	—

(SP 127.4%) **8 Rn**

1m 48.1 (4.10) CSF £10.64 TOTE £8.20: £1.80 £1.10 £2.10 (£4.40) OWNER Mr David Abell (MIDDLEHAM) BRED Lodge Park Stud

OFFICIAL EXPLANATION **Hombre: choked during the closing stages.**

3479 Alberich (IRE) knew much more this time, and he won with a bit to spare, and as he still looks to be carrying surplus condition, there could be better to come. (6/1)
3103 Indimaaj, a poor mover in his slower paces, was struggling three furlongs out, but with stamina coming into play, he finished best of all, and could find an opening in a mile nursery. (4/6)
3047 Najjar (USA), taken on from the start over this longer trip, ran as if he did not quite see it out on this occasion. He still looks to have something left to work on, and he should continue to progress. (11/2: 7/2-13/2)
Hobart Junction (IRE), a late foal, who is a half-brother to this week's York winner Amyas, will be all the better for this experience, and will win races in time. (20/1)
3103 Hombre, bustled along early in the straight, could do little more than stay on at the one pace, and he just might need a bit more time. (13/2)
Treasure Chest (IRE), whose dam was an out-and-out stayer, was very much in need of this and, flat-footed as the stalls opened, was left trailing when the principals set sail for home. (9/1)
Right Cross Jonny (USA) (12/1: op 8/1)

3761 SNOWY GRAY MEMORIAL H'CAP (0-75) (3-Y.O+) (Class D)

4-30 (4-33) **5f** £3,990.00 (£1,200.00: £580.00: £270.00) Stalls: High GOING minus 0.63 sec per fur (F)

				SP	RR	SF
3756*	**Cross The Border (62)** (DNicholls) **4-9-1** AlexGreaves(16) (mde all: clr appr fnl f: pushed out)	—	1	11/8[1]	74	34
3566[4]	**Captain Carat (56)** (DNicholls) **6-8-9b** JFanning(15) (hdwy over 1f out: fin wl)	1	2	14/1	65	25
3481[3]	**Brecongill Lad (65)** (MissSEHall) **5-9-4** LCharnock(17) (b.nr hind: a.p: hrd drvn appr fnl f: unable qckn)	1¼	3	11/2[2]	70	30
3484[15]	**Suedoro (43)** (JSGoldie) **7-7-10** JLowe(6) (dwlt: hdwy 2f out: r.o wl ins fnl f)	½	4	25/1	46	6
3481[6]	**Bowlers Boy (70)** (JJQuinn) **4-9-9** DaleGibson(13) (chsd ldrs: rdn appr fnl f: r.o one pce)	1¼	5	14/1	69	29
3625[11]	**Pathaze (43)** (NBycroft) **4-7-3**(7) JennyBenson(7) (lw: hdwy over 1f out: nvr nrr)	1½	6	33/1	37	—
3481[13]	**U-No-Harry (IRE) (60)** (RHollinshead) **4-8-13** JFEgan(11) (chsd ldrs: rdn over 1f out: nt pce to chal)	hd	7	20/1	54	14
3625[12]	**Middle East (60)** (TDBarron) **4-8-13** KDarley(9) (trckd ldrs: effrt & rdn over 2f out: no imp)	s.h	8	16/1	54	14
3625[3]	**Soaked (43)** (DWChapman) **4-7-3b**(7) JMcAuley(3) (racd wd: prom tl outpcd appr fnl f)	nk	9	16/1	36	—
3224*	**Ballard Lady (IRE) (48)** (JSWainwright) **5-8-1** TWilliams(18) (hdwy on ins over 1f out: sn rdn: outpcd fnl f)	nk	10	14/1	40	—
3649[21]	**Royal Dome (IRE) (73)** (MartynWane) **5-9-9**(3) RHavlin(8) (lw: gd spd over 3f)	s.h	11	14/1	65	25
3398[3]	**Time To Fly (46)** (BWMurray) **4-7-6b**(7)ow1 RWinston(14) (w ldrs over 3f)	½	12	16/1	36	—
3481[2]	**Dominelle (48)** (TDEasterby) **5-8-1** DWright(2) (lw: nvr gng pce of ldrs)	½	13	10/1[3]	37	—
3075[15]	**Maiteamia (65)** (SRBowring) **4-9-1b**(3) CTeague(10) (b.off hind: w ldrs: rdn 2f out: sn wknd)	1½	14	20/1	49	9
3698*	**Dona Filipa (46)** (MissLCSiddall) **4-7-13** 7x EJohnson(4) (outpcd)	½	15	16/1	28	—
3484[8]	**Pageboy (59)** (PCHaslam) **8-8-7**(5) PRoberts(5) (hld up: effrt over 1f out: sn rdn: wknd ins fnl f)	1¾	16	20/1	36	—
3566[2]	**The Happy Fox (IRE) (68)** (BAMcMahon) **5-9-7b** LNewton(1) (prom: pushed along ½-wy: sn outpcd)	½	17	14/1	43	3
2480[4]	***My Abbey (49)*** (ABailey) **8-8-2** RLappin(12) (Withdrawn not under Starter's orders: veterinary advice)		W	14/1	—	—
				(SP 144.5%)	**17 Rn**	

62.67 secs (0.87) CSF £23.93 CT £98.89 TOTE £2.30: £1.30 £2.60 £1.60 £5.90 (£29.50) Trio £17.70 OWNER Mr P. D. Savill (THIRSK) BRED Brook Stud Ltd

LONG HANDICAP Pathaze 7-6 Suedoro 7-7 Soaked 7-2

3756* Cross The Border, winning his second race within twenty four-hours, set his rivals a merry dance from the start, and he was always going a gear too fast for them. (11/8: 2/1-5/4)

3566 Captain Carat, stable-companion to the winner, only wins in his turn, but he was running on strongly in the latter stages, and all is not lost yet. (14/1)

3481 Brecongill Lad is not being rewarded for some very consistent efforts in the past couple of months, but fate must favour him in this mood. (11/2)

3406 Suedoro did not help her cause on this return to five furlongs by missing the break, but she was really into her stride inside the distance, and is knocking at the door. (25/1)

3481 Bowlers Boy, never far away, kept battling on under pressure in the closing stages, but a turn of finishing speed was missing. (14/1)

1828 Pathaze has not won a race for over two years, but she was running on really well late on, and there could be another small contest to be won. (33/1)

3481 Dominelle could not get in a blow from her outside stall, and this poor effort can safely be disregarded. (10/1)

2480 My Abbey (14/1: 10/1-16/1)

3762 WOODMANSEY MAIDEN APPRENTICE H'CAP (0-60) (3-Y.O+) (Class F)

5-00 (5-06) **1m 1f 207y** £2,434.50 (£692.00: £343.50) Stalls: High GOING minus 0.63 sec per fur (F)

				SP	RR	SF
3382[6]	**Riccarton (46)** (PCalver) **4-8-13**(5) RFarmer(1) (swtg: a.p: led 3f out: sn clr: r.o wl)	—	1	8/1[3]	58	25
3486[5]	**Farfields Prince (43)** (DNicholls) **5-9-1** ANicholls(18) (lw: bhd: hdwy over 2f out: r.o wl ins fnl f)	2½	2	5/2[1]	51	18
3456[8]	**Sun Fairy (44)** (JAGlover) **3-8-3**(5)ow4 TPengkerego(9) (a chsng ldrs: kpt on & drifted rt fnl f: r.o)	s.h	3	8/1[3]	52	7
3442[6]	**Nukud (USA) (24)** (GROldroyd) **5-7-10v** RCody-Boutcher(12) (t: a.p: effrt & rdn over 2f out: one pce)	2½	4	25/1	28	—
3540[6]	**Junior Ben (IRE) (32)** (MESowersby) **5-8-4** NPollard(15) (hdwy 4f out: sn rdn: kpt on same pce)	1¾	5	11/1	33	—
2836[7]	**Poker Princess (52)** (MBell) **3-8-11**(5) DYoung(14) (led after 2f to 5f out: rdn 2f out: sn wknd)	4	6	6/1[2]	47	6
3465[15]	**Protaras Bay (36)** (PLGilligan) **3-8-0** PClarke(13) (bhd tl styd on fnl 2f)	½	7	20/1	30	—
2564[13]	**Silent System (IRE) (24)** (DWChapman) **4-7-10b** JMcAuley(4) (sme late hdwy: nvr nrr)	1	8	25/1	16	—
3431[18]	**Wagga Moon (IRE) (53)** (JJO'Neill) **3-8-12**(5) SOlley(10) (swtg: nvr nr to chal)	s.h	9	12/1	45	4
	Smoke'n'jo (IRE) (56) (MWEasterby) **3-9-6** PBradley(6) (bkwd: trckd ldrs tl rdn & wknd 3f out)	hd	10	14/1	48	7
3321[7]	**Baaheth (USA) (42)** (SCWilliams) **3-8-6b** DarrenWilliams(16) (swtg: nvr trbld ldrs)	½	11	14/1	33	—
3276[7]	**Riverside Girl (IRE) (37)** (JSMoore) **3-7-10**(5) PaulCleary(3) (chsd ldrs 6f: sn pushed along & wknd)	2½	12	10/1	24	—
3213[5]	**Intrepid Fort (24)** (BWMurray) **8-7-10v** CCogan(7) (hld up: hdwy 4f out: wknd over 2f out)	nk	13	25/1	11	—
3608[9]	**Airborne Harris (IRE) (47)** (ABailey) **4-9-0v**1(5) IHudson(5) (led 2f: led 5f out tl 3f out: c wd st: sn wknd)	1¼	14	20/1	32	—
3486[10]	**Yuppy Girl (IRE) (30)** (CaptJWilson) **4-8-2** AngelaHartley(17) (s.s: a bhd & outpcd)	hd	15	14/1	15	—
598[6]	**Whitley Grange Boy (56)** (JLEyre) **4-10-0** SBuckley(11) (swtg: trckd ldrs: drvn along 3f out: sn wknd)	1½	16	9/1	38	5
3583[8]	**Petula Boy (32)** (SRBowring) **3-7-10b** FBoyle(2) (a bhd)	nk	17	25/1	14	—
3601[4]	**Grovefair Lad (IRE) (32)** (MartynWane) **3-7-10v** JennyBenson(8) (lw: ref to r: t.n.p)		R	12/1	—	—
				(SP 152.8%)	**18 Rn**	

2m 6.4 (3.30) CSF £29.29 CT £170.77 TOTE £10.70: £2.10 £1.90 £2.20 £7.60 (£21.10) Trio £39.10 OWNER Mr Kenneth MacPherson (RIPON) BRED Limestone Stud

LONG HANDICAP Silent System (IRE) 7-6 Nukud (USA) 7-6 Intrepid Fort 7-6 Petula Boy 7-5 Grovefair Lad (IRE) 7-8

WEIGHT FOR AGE 3yo-8lb

IN-FOCUS: **This was Irish-born apprentice Richard Farmer's first winner.**

3382 Riccarton has taken an age to win a race, but he was always travelling well with the pace this time and, kicking clear some way out, only has to keep going to open his account. (8/1)

3486 Farfields Prince, restrained in the rear, always had too much to do once the winner went clear, but he did stay on strongly inside the distance, and there is a prize in store. (5/2)

2941 Sun Fairy kept tabs on the leaders, but it was only very late on that she really got down to any serious work. She has been well beaten in sellers, but on this showing success in that grade should be a formality. (8/1)

2909 Nukud (USA), in the action from the start, was only running on at the one pace in the closing stages, but at least this was a step up on what he has achieved so far. (25/1)

3540 Junior Ben (IRE) struggled in his attempt to reach the leaders from the turn for home, and was never a factor. (11/1)

2522 Poker Princess helped share the pace, but she was in trouble as soon as the winner quickened things up in the straight, and she could do little about it. (6/1)

T/Plpt: £9.20 (1,846.06 Tckts). T/Qdpt: £3.40 (200.08 Tckts) IM

3738-GOODWOOD (R-H) (Good to firm)
Saturday August 23rd
WEATHER: hot WIND: slt half against

3763 SPORT ON 5 MARCH STKS (Listed) (3-Y.O) (Class A)
2-15 (2-17) **1m 6f** £13,009.00 (£4,684.00: £2,242.00: £910.00: £355.00) Stalls: High GOING minus 0.19 sec per fur (GF)

Form	Horse	Dist	Pos	SP	RR	SF
2837^{2}	**Pentad (USA) (102)** (RCharlton) **3-8-11** LDettori(1) (swtg: mde virtually all: rdn out)	—	**1**	9/4^{2}	113	39
3109^{6}	**Palio Sky (106)** (JLDunlop) **3-8-11** MJKinane(2) (lw: chsd wnr 13f out: rdn over 2f out: ev ch ins fnl f: unable qckn)	½	**2**	13/8^{1}	112	38
3727^{3}	**Book At Bedtime (IRE) (100)** (CACyzer) **3-8-6** MRoberts(4) (plld hrd: hld up: rdn over 3f out: one pce)	1½	**3**	3/1^{3}	106?	32
3218^{4}	**Thornby Park (86)** (JLDunlop) **3-8-6** GDuffield(5) (hld up: rdn over 3f out: one pce)	2	**4**	14/1	59 t	29
3549*	**Princess Topaz (74)** (CACyzer) **3-8-6** KFallon(3) (hld up: rdn over 3f out: wknd wl over 1f out)	¾	**5**	10/1	59 t	29

(SP 109.6%) **5 Rn**

3m 6.39 (7.39) CSF £5.70 TOTE £2.80: £1.70 £1.60 (£2.80) OWNER Mr K. Abdulla (BECKHAMPTON) BRED George A. Smith and W. E. Johnston

2837 Pentad (USA) was taking a step up in class and distance, and ran a fine race under a lovely ride from Dettori. Making virtually all of the running, he looked in serious trouble as the runner-up loomed upsides in the straight, but ridden along, managed to keep that rival at bay. He is progressing well. (9/4)

3109 Palio Sky, racing in second place, threw down a very determined challenge, and looked a serious threat to the winner. Still in with every chance inside the final furlong, he was unable to get by his rival. The assistant trainer later reported that Kinane had told him he was not sure that the colt went through with his run. Thoughts of the St Leger should now be discarded. (13/8)

3727 Book At Bedtime (IRE), who finished third at York on Thursday, was back over a more suitable trip, but after looking a possible threat over a quarter of a mile from home, could only struggle on at one pace. She has now been placed in six Listed or Group events, but does seem to lack the necessary acceleration to win one. (3/1)

3218 Thornby Park had more on her plate here, and failed to find the necessary turn of foot in the last three furlongs. She is a stayer who does not really quicken sufficiently in this company. (14/1: 10/1-16/1)

3549* Princess Topaz had it all to do at the weights as she stepped up in class, so it was no surprise to see her drop away inside the final quarter-mile. She needs to return to handicap company. (10/1)

3764 CROWSON RATED STKS H'CAP (0-105) (3-Y.O+) (Class B)
2-45 (2-48) **7f** £9,855.00 (£3,645.00: £1,747.50: £712.50: £281.25: £108.75) Stalls: High GOING minus 0.19 sec per fur (GF)

Form	Horse	Dist	Pos	SP	RR	SF
3214^{6}	**Omaha City (IRE) (100)** (BGubby) **3-8-11** RCochrane(8) (s.s: hmpd on ins over 2f out: hdwy over 1f out: sqeezed thro: r.o wl ins fnl f: fin 2nd, nk: awrdd r)	—	**1**	20/1	110	54
2013^{14}	**Swiss Law (103)** (JHMGosden) **3-9-0** LDettori(12) (hdwy over 2f out: squeezed thro to ld ins fnl f: r.o wl: fin 1st: disq & plcd 2nd)	nk	**2**	7/1	114	58
3220*	**Dancing Image (93)** (IABalding) **4-8-9** MJKinane(4) (swtg: stdy hdwy on bit over 2f out: rdn over 1f out: unable qckn)	1½	**3**	7/2^{2}	100	49
2830^{2}	**Restructure (IRE) (105)** (MrsJCecil) **5-9-7** MRoberts(11) (a.p: nt clr run over 2f out: r.o ins fnl f)	1	**4**	11/4^{1}	110	59
2023^{18}	**Cryhavoc (93)** (JRArnold) **3-8-4** JQuinn(13) (led tl ins fnl f: one pce)	nk	**5**	14/1	97	41
3217^{14}	**Wildwood Flower (92)** (RHannon) **4-8-3**(5) CLowther(5) (a.p: rdn over 2f out: ev ch 1f out: one pce)	s.h	**6**	16/1	96	45
3391^{4}	**Brilliant Red (91)** (PRHedger) **4-8-7** GDuffield(6) (prom over 5f)	5	**7**	16/1	83	32
3423^{7}	**Chickawicka (IRE) (93)** (BPalling) **6-8-9** SDrowne(10) (swtg: prom over 3f)	2	**8**	20/1	81	30
3615^{6}	**Chewit (91)** (GLMoore) **5-8-7** CandyMorris(2) (s.s: hdwy over 2f out: rdn over 1f out: eased whn btn fnl f)	s.h	**9**	20/1	79	28
3548^{10}	**Rakis (IRE) (91)** (MrsLStubbs) **7-8-7** DaneO'Neill(9) (lw: bhd fnl 5f)	3	**10**	40/1	72	21
3217^{6}	**King of Peru (94)** (NPLittmoden) **4-8-10** KFallon(3) (mid div over 5f)	s.h	**11**	11/2^{3}	75	24
3423^{12}	**Top Banana (91)** (HCandy) **6-8-0**(7) SarahJackson(7) (rn v.wd st: bhd fnl 4f)	3	**12**	33/1	65	14
3577^{8}	**Tumbleweed Ridge (103)** (BJMeehan) **4-9-5b** MTebbutt(1) (lw: prom 4f)	20	**13**	10/1	31	—

(SP 124.0%) **13 Rn**

1m 26.85 (2.05) CSF £137.30 CT £582.87 TOTE £30.70: £5.30 £2.10 £1.80 (£83.30) Trio £224.00 OWNER Brian Gubby Ltd (BAGSHOT) BRED Brownstown Stud Farm

LONG HANDICAP Chewit 8-0 Brilliant Red 8-6 Top Banana 8-4 Rakis (IRE) 7-11

WEIGHT FOR AGE 3yo-5lb

STEWARDS' ENQUIRY Obj to Swiss Law by Cochrane sustained

3214 Omaha City (IRE) has been very difficult to place this year, but this was to be his day. Hampered by Swiss Law over a quarter of a mile from home, he picked up ground below the distance, and running on really strongly, only just failed to get there. It was no surprise that he was later awarded the race in the Stewards' Room. He will get a mile according to his jockey, which will give connections a few more options with him. (20/1)

1412 Swiss Law, who moved from Saeed bin Suroor's stable six weeks ago, did Omaha City no favours along the inside rail over a quarter of a mile from home. Squeezing through to strike the front inside the final furlong, he just held on, but it was only a matter of time before he lost the race. (7/1)

3220* Dancing Image, who was bought privately by George Strawbridge from the Queen about a week or two ago, came there extremely strongly on the bridle over a quarter of a mile from home, but when asked for his effort below the distance, he failed to find what was expected. (7/2)

2830 Restructure (IRE) was returning to handicap company for the first time this year. Although not having the best of runs over a quarter of a mile from home, he put in some nice work in the closing stages. (11/4)

1551a Cryhavoc ran a fine race back in handicap company, and stayed the seventh furlong, taking the field along until collared inside the last two hundred yards. (14/1)

2299 Wildwood Flower, who showed a very scratchy action on the way to post, was still fighting for the lead entering the final furlong before tapped for toe. Although all four of her wins to date have come over six furlongs, she seemed to cope with the step up to seven. (16/1)

3765 LADBROKE RACING SPRINT H'CAP (0-95) (3-Y.O+) (Class C)
3-15 (3-21) **6f** £15,045.00 (£4,560.00: £2,230.00: £1,065.00) Stalls: Low GOING minus 0.19 sec per fur (GF)

Form	Horse	Dist	Pos	SP	RR	SF
3198*	**Rififi (71)** (RIngram) **4-8-5** DaneO'Neill(12) (b: hdwy 2f out: hrd rdn fnl f: led nr fin)	—	**1**	16/1	86	37
3217^{7}	**No Extras (IRE) (80)** (GLMoore) **7-9-0** JQuinn(15) (swtg: hld up: led over 1f out: hrd rdn: hdd nr fin)	hd	**2**	9/1	95	46
3217^{5}	**Oggi (88)** (PJMakin) **6-9-8** RCochrane(3) (swtg: racd stands' side: hdwy over 2f out: hrd rdn over 1f out: r.o)	1	**3**	13/2^{3}	100	51

3649^{2}	**Tiler (IRE) (80)** (MJohnston) **5-9-0** MRoberts(20) (lw: a.p: ev ch over 1f out: one pce)	1½	**4**	5/1^{2}	88	39
3217^{4}	**Faraway Lass (85)** (LordHuntingdon) **4-9-5** LDettori(1) (lw: racd stands' side: a.p: hrd rdn over 1f out: one pce)	½	**5**	7/2^{1}	92	43
3580^{2}	**Scissor Ridge (62)** (JJBridger) **5-7-3**$^{(7)}$ RBrisland(5) (racd stands' side: gd spd over 3f)	½	**6**	33/1	67	18
3614^{2}	**Levelled (73)** (MRChannon) **3-8-1**$^{(3)}$ PPMurphy(4) (lw: racd stands' side: hdwy over 1f out: nvr nrr)	½	**7**	20/1	77	25
3378^{2}	**Lord Olivier (IRE) (70)** (WJarvis) **7-8-4** EmmaO'Gorman(21) (a.p: hrd rdn over 1f out: wknd fnl f)	1½	**8**	25/1	70	21
3217^{16}	**Sir Joey (USA) (84)** (PGMurphy) **8-9-4** SDrowne(10) (swtg: racd stands' side: nvr nr to chal)	½	**9**	20/1	83	34
3436^{2}	**Prends Ca (IRE) (85)** (WRMuir) **4-9-2**$^{(3)}$ JDSmith(6) (racd stands' side: a mid div)	¾	**10**	25/1	82	33
3604^{21}	**Just Loui (70)** (KRBurke) **3-7-8v**$^{1(7)}$ PDoe(8) (racd stands' side: a.p: hung bdly rt over 2f out: sn wknd)	¾	**11**	40/1	65	13
3604^{4}	**Bowden Rose (92)** (MBlanshard) **5-9-9b**$^{(3)}$ DSweeney(14) (led over 4f)	1	**12**	14/1	84	35
3326^{3}	**Mister Jolson (73)** (RJHodges) **8-8-4**$^{(3)}$ DGriffiths(16) (lw: nvr nrr)	¾	**13**	25/1	63	14
3600*	**Willow Dale (IRE) (82)** (DRCElsworth) **4-9-2** KFallon(9) (b.nr hind: racd stands' side: spd over 4f)	nk	**14**	14/1	71	22
3580^{4}	**Resist the Force (USA) (67)** (CACyzer) **7-7-12**$^{(3)}$ AWhelan(19) (s.s: bhd fnl 2f)	nk	**15**	20/1	56	7
3199^{2}	**Conspiracy (90)** (JLDunlop) **3-9-7** MJKinane(7) (racd stands' side: hdwy over 2f out: wknd over 1f out)	s.h	**16**	25/1	78	26
3423^{6}	**Double Bounce (84)** (PJMakin) **7-9-4b**^{1} MTebbutt(11) (bhd fnl 2f)	nk	**17**	14/1	72	23
3604^{13}	**Gadge (84)** (ABailey) **6-8-13**$^{(5)}$ CLowther(2) (b: racd stands' side: prom 2f)	¾	**18**	20/1	70	21
3604^{8}	**So Intrepid (IRE) (85)** (JMBradley) **7-9-5** GDuffield(17) (b.nr hind: bhd fnl 2f)	2½	**19**	20/1	64	15
3600^{11}	**Spender (79)** (PWHarris) **8-8-13** GBardwell(13) (lw: s.s: a bhd)	15	**20**	33/1	18	—
				(SP 135.6%)	**20 Rn**	

1m 12.31 (2.51) CSF £124.60 CT £990.73 TOTE £16.70: £3.00 £2.20 £2.00 £1.80 (£102.80) Trio £258.80 OWNER Brooknight Guarding Ltd (EPSOM) BRED Milton Park Stud Partnership

LONG HANDICAP Scissor Ridge 7-8

WEIGHT FOR AGE 3yo-3lb

3198* Rififi, a fragile individual who suffers from sore shins according to his trainer, threw down a very determined challenge on the far side from below the distance, and in a tremendous battle-royal with the runner-up, just managed to prevail to give Ingram his biggest success to date. If he comes out of this race alright, he will go for the Portland at Doncaster. (16/1)

3217 No Extras (IRE) goes well on this course, and although unsuited by the drop to six furlongs in the Stewards' Cup, coped much better with it here. Showing in front approaching the final furlong, he had a tremendous ding-dong battle with the winner, and only just lost out. He has certainly returned to form this year, and is still 9lb lower than when winning this race two years ago. (9/1)

3217 Oggi has been in good form this season, and ran another fine race on the unfavoured stands side. Gaining control there a quarter of a mile out, although he did not have overall control, he certainly won the battle on the stands side, but was unable to get on terms with the front two racing on the opposite side of the track. Although 9lb higher than when last successful, there is another race to be won with him this year. (13/2)

3649 Tiler (IRE) may have been having his third run in a week, but he still gave a good account of himself, and was a leading player from the outset until tapped for toe in the final furlong. (5/1)

3217 Faraway Lass ran another fine race under the stands side, and was a leading player on that side of the course until tapped for toe from below the distance. She has done all her winning at this trip. (7/2)

3580 Scissor Ridge took the field along on the stands side, although he did not have overall control, until headed over a quarter of a mile from home. (33/1)

3766 TRIPLEPRINT CELEBRATION MILE STKS (Gp 2) (3-Y.O+) (Class A)

3-50 (3-51) **1m** £37,475.00 (£12,975.00: £6,237.50: £2,562.50) Stalls: High GOING minus 0.19 sec per fur (GF)

				SP	RR	SF
3499^{2}	**Cape Cross (IRE) (110)** (JHMGosden) **3-8-9** LDettori(3) (b.hind: hld up: barged thro to chse wnr 3f out: led wl over 1f out: rdn: r.o wl: fin 1st: disq: plcd 4th)		**1d**	7/2^{3}	126?	66
3124^{4}	**Among Men (USA) (118)** (MRStoute) **3-8-9** MJKinane(2) (lw: led over 6f: unable qckn fnl f: fin 2nd, 2½l: awrdd r)	2½	**1**	8/11^{1}	121	61
2820a^{3}	**Polar Prince (IRE) (113)** (MAJarvis) **4-9-1** RCochrane(4) (hld up: nt clr run 3f out: sn wknd: fin 3rd, btn 2½l & 5l: plcd 2nd)	5	**2**	3/1^{2}	106	52
3150^{20}	**Peartree House (IRE) (100)** (WRMuir) **3-8-9** DaneO'Neill(1) (w wnr tl bmpd & wknd 3f out: fin 4th, btn 11l: plcd 3rd)	11	**3**	33/1	84	24
				(SP 108.1%)	**4 Rn**	

1m 38.34 (1.14) CSF £2.91 TOTE £1.70: (£2.00) OWNER Mr M Tabor & Mrs John Magnier (NEWMARKET) BRED Gail Beitz & Gainsborough Farm

WEIGHT FOR AGE 3yo-6lb

STEWARDS' ENQUIRY Dettori susp. 1-5/9/97 (irresponsible riding).

IN-FOCUS: **This was a day Frankie Dettori will wish to forget, losing two races and picking up a five-day ban which might yet have a bearing on the outcome of the jockeys' championship. Dettori's subsequent appeal against the suspension failed.**

3124 Among Men (USA) was an extremely lucky winner, for after taking the field along, he was collared by Cape Cross early in the final quarter-mile, and was certainly put in his place in the last two hundred yards. There was absolutely no question that he was second-best on merit, but with Cape Cross and Frankie having transgressed the Rules, Among Men was awarded the race. Stoute admitted that he was disappointed with the colt's performance, and believes that he did not handle the course. (8/11)

2820a Polar Prince (IRE) was rather disappointing. Appearing to be travelling well, he got checked three furlongs from home and, soon off the bridle, found little. (3/1)

2761 Peartree House (IRE) was out of his league here, and although given a bump by Cape Cross three furlongs from home, was already beginning to struggle. (33/1)

3499 Cape Cross (IRE) was very unfortunate to lose the race, for he was quite clearly the best horse on the day, but there can be absolutely no denying that Dettori transgressed the Rules. Barging his way through three furlongs from home, giving Peartree House a bump, who in turn checked Polar Prince, he moved to the front early in the final quarter-mile, and asserted his authority in the final furlong for a clear cut success. The Stewards had no option but to hand Dettori a five-day ban for irresponsible riding. As Cape Cross proved here, he is certainly up to winning a Pattern race. (7/2)

3767 CHICHESTER OBSERVER SERIES CLAIMING H'CAP (0-70) (3-Y.O+) (Class E)

4-20 (4-22) **1m 2f** £4,142.50 (£1,240.00: £595.00: £272.50) Stalls: High GOING minus 0.19 sec per fur (GF)

				SP	RR	SF
2533^{10}	**Thatchmaster (IRE) (59)** (CAHorgan) **6-9-5**$^{(3)}$ DO'Donohoe(1) (swtg: mde all: clr over 2f out: r.o wl)	—	**1**	5/1^{3}	73	59
3413^{2}	**Harlequin Walk (IRE) (33)** (RJO'Sullivan) **6-7-10** JQuinn(9) (swtg: hdwy & nt clr run over 2f out: swtchd rt: chsd wnr over 1f out: no imp)	1½	**2**	14/1	45	31
3276^{3}	**Oozlem (IRE) (33)** (LMontagueHall) **8-7-5b**$^{(5)}$ APolli(3) (swtg: rdn over 4f out: gd hdwy fnl f: fin wl)	3½	**3**	14/1	39	25

				SP	RR	SF
3320*	**Laguna Bay (IRE) (56)** (APJarvis) **3-8-11** SDrowne(2) (chsd wnr over 3f: rdn over 3f out: chsd wnr over 2f out tl over 1f out: one pce)	hd	**4**	10/1	62	40
3469*	**The Executor (64)** (RJO'Sullivan) **7-9-13** AProcter(7) (rdn over 3f out: hdwy fnl f: nvr nrr)	2	**5**	8/1	67	53
3491[3]	**Statajack (IRE) (60)** (DRCElsworth) **9-9-9b** KFallon(5) (b.hind: hdwy over 2f out: hung rt over 1f out: one pce)	nk	**6**	7/2[2]	62	48
3617[6]	**Challenger (IRE) (33)** (LWells) **4-7-3**(7) RBrisland(11) (nvr nr to chal)	1	**7**	50/1	34	20
3495[5]	**Tart (FR) (50)** (JPearce) **4-8-13v[1]** GBardwell(6) (a.p: chsd wnr over 6f out tl over 2f out: wknd wl over 1f out)	2	**8**	8/1	47	33
3588*	**Wentbridge Lad (IRE) (57)** (ABailey) **7-9-1v**(5) CLowther(4) (b: b.hind: hdwy over 4f out: wknd over 2f out)	2	**9**	3/1[1]	51	37
3465[3]	**Multi Franchise (45)** (RMFlower) **4-8-5**(3)ow1 JDSmith(12) (swtg: prom over 7f)	¾	**10**	10/1	38	23
2868[11]	**Saltando (IRE) (48)** (PatMitchell) **6-8-11v** DaneO'Neill(10) (a bhd)	12	**11**	25/1	22	8
	Verulam (IRE) (55) (JRJenkins) **4-8-11**(7) JWilkinson(8) (prom 5f)	11	**12**	50/1	11	—

(SP 125.4%) **12 Rn**

2m 10.59 (3.99) CSF £69.68 CT £857.95 TOTE £8.00: £2.60 £2.80 £4.70 (£60.30) Trio £234.60 OWNER Mrs B. Sumner (PULBOROUGH)
BRED Ballysheehan Stud
LONG HANDICAP Challenger (IRE) 7-2 Harlequin Walk (IRE) 7-9
WEIGHT FOR AGE 3yo-8lb
OFFICIAL EXPLANATION **Thatchmaster (IRE): regarding the apparent improvement in form, the trainer described the gelding as much better going right-handed. Tart (FR): gurgled and did not go through with her effort.**

1972 Thatchmaster (IRE), who injured his side when coming out of the stalls at Bath last time out, put up a bold display from the front, and rousted along to forge clear over two furlongs from home, was not going to be caught. (5/1: 7/2-11/2)
3413 Harlequin Walk (IRE), who did not have the clearest of runs early in the straight, moved into second place below the distance, and although pulling clear of the remainder, was unable to throw down a challenge to the winner. She has just one win to her name on turf. (14/1)
3276 Oozlem (IRE), racing at the back of the back of the field, was still only tenth entering the final furlong. He then went into overdrive, and managed to snatch third prize right on the line. (14/1: 10/1-16/1)
3320* Laguna Bay (IRE), who showed in second place for a second time over a quarter of a mile from home, failed to reel in the winner, and was collared for that position below the distance. Her only win to date has come in this class. (10/1)
3469* The Executor stayed on in the final furlong but never threatened. (8/1: 5/1-10/1)
3491 Statajack (IRE) is a tricky customer, who is not easy to win with, and after moving up on the outside over a quarter of a mile from home, could then only plod on in his own time. (7/2)

3768 RICHMOND-BRISSAC TROPHY GENTLEMEN'S H'CAP (0-85) (3-Y.O+) (Class E)

4-50 (4-50) **1m 1f** £3,785.00 (£1,130.00: £540.00: £245.00) Stalls: High GOING minus 0.19 sec per fur (GF)

				SP	RR	SF
3465[7]	**Show Faith (IRE) (54)** (RHannon) **7-10-3** MrCVigors(4) (hld up: led over 2f out: r.o wl)	—	**1**	7/1	65	42
3135[7]	**Shining Example (69)** (PJMakin) **5-11-4** MrLBaker(6) (swtg: a.p: chsd ldr over 5f out tl over 2f out: nt clr run & swtchd rt: chsd wnr over 1f out: ev ch ins fnl f: unable qckn)	3½	**2**	9/2[2]	74	51
3616[8]	**Tribal Peace (IRE) (63)** (BGubby) **5-10-12** MrJRees(1) (lw: hdwy over 1f out: r.o wl ins fnl f)	½	**3**	5/1[3]	67	44
1972[10]	**Superior Force (54)** (MissBSanders) **4-10-3** MrPPailhes(9) (lw: led tl hdd & hung lft over 2f out: sn wknd)	2½	**4**	20/1	53	30
3496[8]	**White Plains (IRE) (75)** (KRBurke) **4-11-10** MrLBarlogh(5) (swtg: hld up: hmpd on ins over 3f out: wknd fnl f)	nk	**5**	12/1	74	51
3115[6]	**Confronter (57)** (SDow) **8-10-6** MrTCuff(2) (hdwy & n.m.r over 2f out: wknd over 1f out)	1½	**6**	9/2[2]	53	30
3466*	**Seattle Swing (78)** (MrsAJPerrett) **3-11-6** MrRThornton(8) (chsd ldr over 3f: wknd over 3f out)	2½	**7**	11/4[1]	70	40
3491[8]	**Piquant (55)** (LordHuntingdon) **10-10-4** MrRWakley(3) (a bhd)	1	**8**	11/1	45	22
3465[8]	**Digpast (IRE) (44)** (JJBridger) **7-9-7b** MrKGoble(7) (s.s: a bhd)	4	**9**	20/1	27	4

(SP 117.7%) **9 Rn**

1m 59.42 (6.42) CSF £35.78 CT £156.41 TOTE £7.40: £2.10 £2.10 £1.70 (£17.80) Trio £68.40 OWNER Mr I. A. N. Wight (MARLBOROUGH)
BRED M. J. Cassidy
LONG HANDICAP Digpast (IRE) 8-13
WEIGHT FOR AGE 3yo-7lb

Show Faith (IRE) has slumped in the weights, and bounced back to form, striking the front over a quarter of a mile from home, and keeping on well to win his first race in over two years. (7/1: 6/1-9/1)
1926* Shining Example regained second place below the distance, and was certainly close enough if good enough early inside the final furlong before tapped for toe. Two of his three wins have come over this trip. (9/2)
3153* Tribal Peace (IRE) stayed on in the last furlong and a half, but found it all over bar the shouting. (5/1)
383 Superior Force took the field along, but collared over two furlongs from home, hung badly left and tamely dropped away. (20/1)
2470* White Plains (IRE), done no favours along the inside rail early in the straight, had been hung out to dry in the final furlong. (12/1: op 8/1)
3115 Confronter found the slightly longer trip beyond him, and had nothing more to offer below the distance. A mile is his trip. (9/2)

3769 E.B.F. SOLENT MAIDEN STKS (2-Y.O F) (Class D)

5-25 (5-26) **7f** £4,269.00 (£1,272.00: £606.00: £273.00) Stalls: High GOING minus 0.19 sec per fur (GF)

				SP	RR	SF
3151[4]	**Hadayik** (PTWalwyn) **2-8-11** JQuinn(3) (mde all: shkn up 2f out: clr over 1f out: r.o wl)	—	**1**	4/5[1]	84	25
3151[7]	**Oberon's Mistral** (HRACecil) **2-8-11** KFallon(2) (lw: hld up: swtchd lft 3f out: chsd wnr fnl 2f: no imp)	2½	**2**	2/1[2]	78	19
	Yanomami (USA) (JHMGosden) **2-8-11** DaneO'Neill(1) (neat: chsd wnr 5f)	3	**3**	9/1	71	12
	Star of The Course (USA) (PFICole) **2-8-8**(3) DO'Donohoe(4) (leggy: lt-f: s.s: a wl bhd)	14	**4**	8/1[3]	39	—

(SP 110.0%) **4 Rn**

1m 29.5 (4.70) CSF £2.48 TOTE £1.80: (£1.60) OWNER Mr Hamdan Al Maktoum (LAMBOURN)

3151 Hadayik, who showed promise on her debut here at the big meeting, had far more scope than her rivals in the paddock, and had little problem opening her account, forging clear from below the distance for a decisive victory. (4/5)
Oberon's Mistral, five lengths behind the winner on her debut at the end of last month, moved into second place two furlongs from home, but had no hope with her rival. (2/1)
Yanomami (USA) is not very big, and after chasing the winner to the two-furlong pole, was easily brushed aside. (9/1: 5/1-10/1)
Star of The Course (USA), a plain filly with little substance and no scope, lost about ten lengths at the start and that was the end of her. (8/1: 5/1-9/1)

T/Jkpt: £149,561.10 (0.3 Tckts); £147,454.69 to Newcastle 25/8/97. T/Plpt: £134.40 (414.89 Tckts). T/Qdpt: £29.10 (46.51 Tckts) AK

3744-NEWMARKET (R-H) (Good to firm)

Saturday August 23rd

WEATHER: fine WIND: mod across

3770 E.B.F. NGK SPARK PLUGS MAIDEN STKS (2-Y.O) (Class D)

2-00 (2-01) **6f (July)** £4,163.50 (£1,243.00: £594.00: £269.50) Stalls: Low GOING minus 0.44 sec per fur (F)

				SP	RR	SF
3127^{2}	**Bemsha Swing (IRE) (90)** (RHannon) **2-9-0** SSanders(4) (lw: mde all: rdn & hld on wl fnl f)	—	**1**	2/1^{1}	101	52
	Ikhteyaar (USA) (RWArmstrong) **2-8-9** RHills(3) (leggy: scope: lw: trckd ldrs: ev ch fnl f: unable qckn nr fin)	nk	**2**	2/1^{1}	95+	46
2962^{4}	**Obsessed** (MRStoute) **2-8-9** JReid(1) (swtg: w wnr: ev ch 2f out: sn rdn: wknd fnl f)	6	**3**	7/2^{2}	79	30
3151^{9}	**Queen Salote** (DRLoder) **2-8-9** AClark(8) (stdd s: hdwy 2f out: nvr able to chal)	4	**4**	20/1	69	20
3717^{8}	**Polo Venture** (SPCWoods) **2-9-0** NDay(2) (lw: prom tl outpcd after 2f)	¾	**5**	25/1	72	23
	Nautical Warning (MHTompkins) **2-9-0** DBiggs(10) (str: cmpt: kpt on fnl 2f: nvr nr ldrs)	1¼	**6**	25/1	68	19
	Holy Smoke (JLEyre) **2-8-9** FLynch(9) (w'like: leggy: nvr nrr)	hd	**7**	25/1	63	14
3235^{8}	**Paarl Rock** (DRLoder) **2-9-0** CHodgson(11) (nvr trbld ldrs)	4	**8**	33/1	57	8
3497^{9}	**Legal Lark (IRE)** (PHowling) **2-9-0** GHind(7) (dwlt: hdwy over 3f out: wknd & eased fnl f)	1¼	**9**	50/1	54	5
	Sconced (USA) (GWragg) **2-9-0** MHills(6) (gd sort: neat: chsd ldrs over 3f)	1½	**10**	10/1^{3}	50	1
	Mantello (MajorDNChappell) **2-9-0** GCarter(5) (wl grwn: bkwd: dwlt: hmpd after 1f: sn wl bhd)	19	**11**	40/1	—	—
				(SP 121.6%)	**11 Rn**	

1m 12.7 (0.70) CSF £5.10 TOTE £2.80: £1.20 £1.40 £1.40 (£3.70) Trio £2.50 OWNER Mr Michael Pescod (MARLBOROUGH) BRED Ben Sangster

3127 Bemsha Swing (IRE), due to run at York during the week, had already flopped once in rain-softened ground and came here instead. Making experience tell, he had to dig deep to resist the challenge of the runner-up. (2/1)

Ikhteyaar (USA), a good-moving half-sister to Mur Taasha, who still has a frame to fill, travelled extremely well and was produced in the Dip. Unable to get past the more experienced winner, she ought to win races. (2/1: 11/10-evens)

2962 Obsessed got rather stirred up beforehand and was keen going down. Failing to impress again when the chips were down, this full sister to Storm Nymph is beginning to look highly strung. (7/2: 5/2-9/2)

Queen Salote, dropped in trip, adopted strangely different tactics, being waited with, and had a hopeless task after the first couple of furlongs. This will at least get her handicapped and she will surely prove better back over further. (20/1)

Polo Venture was somewhat colty beforehand, but probably didn't know what had hit him, this run coming just two days after his debut. A full brother to Polar Champ, there is hope for him. (25/1)

Nautical Warning, a strong, good-bodied newcomer, looks to need a little more time, still being up behind and far from fully fit. A fluent mover, he showed little in the race but will surely leave this run behind. (25/1)

Sconced (USA) (10/1: op 5/1)

3771 CONSTANT SECURITY LADIES' H'CAP (0-85) (3-Y.O+) (Class E)

2-35 (2-36) **5f (July)** £4,012.50 (£1,200.00: £575.00: £262.50) Stalls: Low GOING minus 0.19 sec per fur (GF)

				SP	RR	SF
3600^{2}	**Sharp Pearl (77)** (PRWebber) **4-11-0b** MissERamsden(9) (hld up: hdwy over 1f out: ev ch ins fnl f: led post)	—	**1**	6/1^{2}	85	68
3580^{5}	**Patsy Grimes (84)** (JSMoore) **7-11-2**(5) MrsSMoore(1) (hdwy wl over 1f out: led 1f out: ct post)	s.h	**2**	9/1	92	75
3410^{7}	**Squire Corrie (82)** (DWChapman) **5-11-5** MissRClark(5) (swtg: led over 3f: one pce fnl f)	1¼	**3**	9/1	86	69
3590^{2}	**Montrestar (67)** (ABailey) **4-9-13v**(5)ow10 MissALHutchinson(2) (b.hind: chsd ldrs: one pce fnl f)	½	**4**	14/1	69	42
3460^{3}	**Silent Miracle (IRE) (71)** (MBell) **3-10-6** MrsAPerrett(10) (prom: rdn & one pce fnl f)	½	**5**	9/1	72	53
3406^{11}	**Another Nightmare (IRE) (51)** (RMMcKellar) **5-8-11**(5) MrsCWilliams(11) (lw: racd centre: w ldrs: one pce appr fnl f)	½	**6**	14/1	50	33
3625^{14}	**Tart and a Half (63)** (JLEyre) **5-10-0v** MissDianaJones(6) (a.p: rdn to ld over 1f out: sn hdd & btn)	nk	**7**	7/1^{3}	61	44
3476*	**Marjaana (IRE) (73)** (PTWalwyn) **4-10-5**(5) MissSSamworth(12) (dwlt: nvr nr ldrs)	1½	**8**	10/1	66	49
3582^{9}	**Afaan (IRE) (65)** (RFMarvin) **4-9-11v**(5) MrsMMorris(13) (dwlt: sn chsng ldrs: wknd over 1f out)	s.h	**9**	14/1	58	41
3473*	**Mousehole (73)** (RGuest) **5-10-5**(5) MissZBurkett(3) (s.s: a bhd)	2½	**10**	11/2^{1}	58	41
3198^{9}	**Eastern Prophets (80)** (GLewis) **4-11-3** MrsMCowdrey(7) (nvr nr to chal)	¾	**11**	9/1	63	46
3326*	**Malibu Man (75)** (EAWheeler) **5-10-12** MissJAllison(4) (lw: s.i.s: sn prom: wknd wl over 1f out)	½	**12**	9/1	56	39
3083^{7}	**Rise 'n Shine (51)** (CACyzer) **3-9-0b**^{1} MrsSBosley(8) (bhd fnl 2f)	1¼	**13**	40/1	28	9
				(SP 123.7%)	**13 Rn**	

59.62 secs (1.12) CSF £55.97 CT £465.25 TOTE £6.00: £2.10 £2.50 £3.30 (£22.40) Trio £77.70 OWNER Mr Dennis Yardy (BANBURY) BRED D. MacRae

LONG HANDICAP Rise 'n Shine 8-7

WEIGHT FOR AGE 3yo-2lb

3600 Sharp Pearl, racing with his tongue tied down, didn't break as slowly as he can and was always where his pilot wanted. Challenging throughout the final furlong, he got it on the nod. (6/1)

3580 Patsy Grimes moved to post well and got a clear passage this time, looking sure to win only to be touched off on the line. She is in great heart at present and does deserve to find another race. (9/1)

3410 Squire Corrie, dropped in class, ran his usual sound race in a busy and successful season. (9/1)

3590 Montrestar, basically only a plater, seemed to run out of his skin here but amateur form can be misleading, although he is clearly on good terms with himself. (14/1)

3460 Silent Miracle (IRE) could not pick up when the chance was there and really needs six furlongs on such fast ground. (9/1)

3240* Another Nightmare (IRE) ploughed pretty much a lone furrow down the centre but softer ground or another furlong would have helped. (14/1)

3772 CHRIS BLACKWELL MEMORIAL H'CAP (0-90) (3-Y.O) (Class C)

3-10 (3-10) **7f (July)** £6,116.25 (£1,830.00: £877.50: £401.25) Stalls: Low GOING minus 0.44 sec per fur (F)

				SP	RR	SF
3238^{9}	**Cybertechnology (77)** (BWHills) **3-8-9** MHills(7) (pushed along 4f out: hdwy over 1f out: r.o to ld nr fin)	—	**1**	12/1	86	55
3391^{3}	**Flamboyance (USA) (85)** (JRFanshawe) **3-9-3** JReid(11) (lw: chsd ldrs: led 2f out: rdn fnl f: hdd & unable qckn nr fin)	nk	**2**	10/1	93	62
3614*	**Al Muallim (USA) (87)** (JWPayne) **3-9-5** AMcGlone(8) (lw: plld hrd: trckd ldrs: ev ch fnl f: no ex nr fin)	nk	**3**	11/2	95	64
3140^{3}	**Kamin (USA) (74)** (RWArmstrong) **3-8-6** RHills(3) (swtg: a.p: ev ch 2f out: sn rdn & one pce)	2½	**4**	9/2^{2}	76	45
3189^{15}	**Jawhari (87)** (JLDunlop) **3-9-5** GCarter(12) (hld up: hdwy over 2f out: no imp fnl f)	1¾	**5**	5/1^{3}	85	54

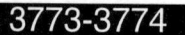

				SP	RR	SF
3189*	**Jorrocks (USA) (89)** (IABalding) **3-9-4**(3) MartinDwyer(6) (hld up: hdwy whn nt clr run wl over 1f out: nvr rchd ldrs)	hd	**6**	4/1 1	87	56
3718[11]	**Rich In Love (IRE) (80)** (CACyzer) **3-8-12** AClark(10) (prom: led over 2f out: sn hdd & btn)	2½	**7**	14/1	72	41
3615[5]	**Zugudi (80)** (KMahdi) **3-8-12** SSanders(13) (led 2f: wkng whn wandered wl over 1f out)	5	**8**	16/1	61	30
3236[2]	**Swift (72)** (MJPolglase) **3-8-4** JTate(5) (nvr nr to chal)	1	**9**	9/1	50	19
840[8]	**Puzzlement (66)** (CEBrittain) **3-7-7**(5) RMullen(9) (swtg: a bhd)	1½	**10**	25/1	41	10
1262[15]	**Mayfair (79)** (PFICole) **3-8-11** MRimmer(2) (in tch tl rdn & wknd over 3f out)	8	**11**	25/1	36	5
3621[12]	**Carati (77)** (RBoss) **3-8-6b**1(3) RFfrench(1) (led after 2f tl over 2f out: sn wknd)	2½	**12**	20/1	28	—

(SP 122.0%) **12 Rn**

1m 25.19 (0.19) CSF £115.48 CT £676.31 TOTE £13.80: £2.90 £3.00 £2.50 (£48.30) Trio £173.00 OWNER Mr W. J. Gredley (LAMBOURN) BRED Stetchworth Park Stud Ltd

2292 Cybertechnology, taking a significant drop in trip after a couple of very poor efforts, hardly looked a total enthusiast but got going fast and late to snatch the race close home. (12/1: op 20/1)

3391 Flamboyance (USA) dropped in trip and, rightly, made plenty of use of, seemed to have battled off her main rivals when the winner pounced. She seems to act well on this ground, is certainly genuine and can win a similar event over a mile. (10/1)

3614* Al Muallim (USA), a very good mover, was still rather keen going down even though he was taken down last. Too free in the early stages, he still looked like winning in the Dip until faltering on the hill. Still finding his feet, there will be other days. (11/2)

3140 Kamin (USA), on his toes beforehand, looked short of pace over this shorter trip. (9/2)

3189 Jawhari moved down well and left his appalling Goodwood effort behind as he was not helped there by the wide draw, and the effort to settle him may have over-compensated. (5/1)

3189* Jorrocks (USA), whose jockey looked to have problems keeping him straight, was further hindered by Zugudi bumping him as he started his move. His action suggests softer ground would suit. (4/1)

3448* Rich In Love (IRE) had coming into season as an excuse for a poor run two days previously, so it was no surprise to see such a quick reappearance. (14/1: 8/1-16/1)

3773 DANEPAK CLASSIC RATED STKS H'CAP (0-95) (3-Y.O+) (Class C)

3-40 (3-47) **1m 2f (July)** £10,318.56 (£3,827.04: £1,843.52: £761.60: £310.80: £130.48) Stalls: High GOING minus 0.44 sec per fur (F)

				SP	RR	SF
3190[18]	**Labeq (IRE) (85)** (PTWalwyn) **3-8-5** GHind(3) (s.i.s: hdwy to ld over 1f out: rdn out)	—	**1**	14/1	95+	49
3424*	**Hajr (IRE) (87)** (EALDunlop) **3-8-7** MHills(2) (lw: s.i.s: hdwy 3f out: ev ch over 1f out: one pce)	2½	**2**	5/1 1	93+	47
2961[13]	**Darapour (IRE) (84)** (LMCumani) **3-8-1**(3) RFfrench(16) (dwlt: hdwy fnl 2f: r.o)	hd	**3**	5/1 1	90+	44
3112[2]	**Another Time (93)** (SPCWoods) **5-9-7** JReid(12) (hld up: hdwy 2f out: r.o wl fnl f)	s.h	**4**	8/1 3	99	61
3575[9]	**Gift Token (83)** (MajorDNChappell) **3-8-3v**1 GCarter(9) (hld up: hdwy 3f out: nvr rchd ldrs)	½	**5**	33/1	88	42
3150[5]	**King of Tunes (FR) (84)** (MJHaynes) **5-8-9**(3) MartinDwyer(11) (lw: hld up: hdwy over 2f out: one pce fnl f)	½	**6**	10/1	88	50
3542[6]	**Traceability (80)** (SCWilliams) **4-8-8** JTate(5) (trckd ldr tl led over 3f out: hdd & wknd over 1f out)	¾	**7**	20/1	83	45
3263[4]	**Wafir (IRE) (83)** (PCalver) **5-8-11** NDay(13) (chsd ldrs tl rdn & btn 5f out)	½	**8**	14/1	85	47
3444[5]	**Secret Aly (CAN) (82)** (CEBrittain) **7-8-10** MRimmer(4) (prom: rdn 4f out: wknd 2f out)	3	**9**	14/1	79	41
1025[3]	**Ihtiyati (USA) (93)** (JLDunlop) **3-8-13** RHills(6) (nvr trbld ldrs)	8	**10**	14/1	78	32
3424[3]	**Orsay (80)** (WRMuir) **5-8-3**(5) RMullen(14) (hld up & plld hrd: hdwy 6f out: wknd wl over 1f out)	½	**11**	12/1	64	26
787[13]	**Time for Action (IRE) (82)** (MHTompkins) **5-8-10** WJO'Connor(8) (lw: led over 6f)	nk	**12**	33/1	65	27
3444[3]	**Diminutive (USA) (79)** (JWHills) **4-8-4**(3) MHenry(10) (nvr trbld ldrs)	2½	**13**	20/1	58	20
2676[9]	**Lomberto (85)** (VSoane) **4-8-13** AMcGlone(15) (prom: rdn 5f out: sn wknd)	1¼	**14**	25/1	62	24
3424[2]	**Silver Groom (IRE) (79)** (RAkehurst) **7-8-7** SSanders(1) (hdwy 4f out: wknd wl over 1f out)	3½	**15**	8/1 3	51	13
3125[13]	***Mersey Beat (89)*** *(GLMoore)* ***3-8-9*** *AClark(7) (swtg: Withdrawn not under Starter's orders: ref to ent stalls)*		**W**	6/1 2	—	—

(SP 118.3%) **15 Rn**

2m 4.14 (0.54) CSF £61.95 CT £281.20 TOTE £15.70: £4.60 £2.30 £2.70 (£42.90) Trio £84.10 OWNER Mr Hamdan Al Maktoum (LAMBOURN) BRED Shadwell Estate Company Limited

LONG HANDICAP Diminutive (USA) 8-5

WEIGHT FOR AGE 3yo-8lb

2687* Labeq (IRE), apparently troubled by a growth on a leg last time, took this in great style despite falling out of the stalls as if not all that keen. In this mood he is a very interesting prospect. (14/1)

3424* Hajr (IRE), almost pulled out at the eleventh hour due to the fast ground, did nothing wrong but couldn't go with the winner from the Dip. (5/1)

2961 Darapour (IRE) dropped back to almost last as the tempo picked up, but came home in fine style and looks to be crying out for further. (5/1)

3112 Another Time, held up as usual, would have preferred an end to end gallop and got going too late. (8/1)

1823* Gift Token, very keen going down in the first-time visor, was restrained in the rear until producing a promising run on the outside entering the Dip. This trip may be stretching her. (33/1)

3150 King of Tunes (FR), stepping back up to this trip for the first time this season, ran well but this is probably a furlong too far. (10/1)

3774 TOTE MULTIBET NURSERY H'CAP (2-Y.O) (Class C)

4-10 (4-15) **6f (July)** £14,265.00 (£4,320.00: £2,110.00: £1,005.00) Stalls: Low GOING minus 0.44 sec per fur (F)

				SP	RR	SF
3464[2]	**Speedfit Too (IRE) (97)** (GGMargarson) **2-9-7** GCarter(4) (in tch: hdwy & squeezed thro over 1f out: sn led: rdn out)	—	**1**	10/1	97	56
3464[3]	**Halmahera (IRE) (93)** (IABalding) **2-9-0**(3) MartinDwyer(9) (hld up: hdwy over 1f out: kpt on fnl f: nt trble wnr)	1½	**2**	12/1	89	48
3331[2]	**Nuclear Debate (USA) (84)** (MrsJRRamsden) **2-8-8** NDay(7) (swtg: hld up & bhd: hdwy 2f out: no ex ins fnl f)	1¼	**3**	15/2	77	36
3706[5]	**Eastern Purple (IRE) (81)** (RAFahey) **2-8-5** GHind(8) (dwlt: hdwy 3f out: ev ch over 1f out: one pce)	¾	**4**	4/1 1	72	31
2917*	**Golden Strategy (IRE) (80)** (RHannon) **2-8-1**(3) MHenry(10) (b.nr hind: a.p: led 2f out: sn hdd & btn)	5	**5**	10/1	57	16
3468[8]	**Fire Goddess (72)** (JSMoore) **2-7-7**(3) MBaird(6) (chsd ldrs: lost pl over 3f out: r.o again appr fnl f)	1¼	**6**	33/1	46	5
3288[3]	**Alpen Wolf (IRE) (73)** (WRMuir) **2-7-6v**(5) RMullen(3) (prom: rdn & wkng whn n.m.r over 1f out)	hd	**7**	25/1	47	6
2862[7]	**Petarga (85)** (JARToller) **2-8-9** SSanders(1) (lw: led 4f: wknd fnl f)	nk	**8**	12/1	58	17
3031[4]	**Night People (72)** (WJarvis) **2-7-7**(3) RFfrench(5) (chsd ldrs: btn whn n.m.r 2f out)	¾	**9**	9/2 2	43	2
2138*	**Ffestiniog (IRE) (88)** (PFICole) **2-8-12** MRimmer(2) (lw: w ldr: wkng whn hmpd over 1f out)	4	**10**	6/1	48	7
3204[4]	**Lido (IRE) (91)** (BWHills) **2-9-1** MHills(11) (a bhd)	½	**11**	11/1	50	9

3186[2]	**Hujoom (IRE) (89)** (JLDunlop) **2-8-13** JReid(12) (a bhd)	1¼	**12**	5/1[3]	45	4
				(SP 129.6%)		**12 Rn**

1m 12.89 (0.89) CSF £123.62 CT £903.33 TOTE £12.80: £2.90 £4.30 £3.00 (£40.00) Trio £416.10 OWNER Mr John Guest (NEWMARKET) BRED Minch Bloodstock

LONG HANDICAP Fire Goddess 7-9 Night People 7-9

3464 Speedfit Too (IRE), who finished in front of both the runner-up here and the subsequent Gimcrack winner last time, had trouble getting through by the far rails but, once in the clear, strode home well despite flashing his tail several times. (10/1: 8/1-12/1)

3464 Halmahera (IRE), on his toes beforehand, came with a storming run in the centre of the course, but the winner had got first run by the far rail. (12/1)

3331 Nuclear Debate (USA) looks a bit of a character and, held onto rather longer this time, probably ran into two very well handicapped horses. (15/2: 5/1-8/1)

3706 Eastern Purple (IRE) appeared to excel in the Gimcrack in the week, making him a good thing off this mark, but he was held by the first two on a line through the winner there, Carrowkeel, and it was this line of form that appeared to be franked. (4/1)

2917* Golden Strategy (IRE), did not break as well as some, but looks all speed at the moment and, after leading into the Dip, did not appear to last home. (10/1)

2138 Fire Goddess, soon taken off her feet, never looked like recovering and is worth a try over further. (33/1)

2138* Ffestiniog (IRE) could not dominate this time but still had place chances when the unwelcome attentions of the winner ended all hope in the Dip. (6/1)

3775 EQUITY FINANCIAL COLLECTIONS MAIDEN STKS (3-Y.O+) (Class D)

4-40 (4-43) **1m (July)** £4,056.25 (£1,210.00: £577.50: £261.25) Stalls: Low GOING minus 0.44 sec per fur (F)

				SP	RR	SF
3463[9]	**Royale Rose (FR)** (ABailey) **3-8-3**(3) RFfrench(3) (lw: led after 1f: edgd rt & hdd 1f out: rallied to ld nr fin)	—	**1**	20/1	74	24
3281[5]	**Sycamore Boy (USA)** (LordHuntingdon) **3-8-11** JReid(10) (dwlt: hdwy 2f out: led 1f out: no ex & ct nr fin)	hd	**2**	13/2	79	29
	Macaribo (JHMGosden) **3-8-11** GHind(6) (w'like: reard s: hdwy 3f out: no ex fnl f)	4	**3**	13/8[1]	71	21
885[8]	**Sharkiyah (IRE) (80)** (RWArmstrong) **3-8-6** GCarter(5) (a.p: rdn over 2f out: one pce)	2½	**4**	4/1[3]	61	11
	Miss Vita (USA) (RJRWilliams) **3-8-3**(3) MartinDwyer(1) (neat: unf: in tch: rdn & outpcd 3f out: no ch afterwards)	¾	**5**	25/1	59	9
	Priluki (CEBrittain) **3-8-6** MRoberts(7) (leggy: scope: led 1f: no imp fnl 3f)	s.h	**6**	7/2[2]	59	9
	Floating Charge (JRFanshawe) **3-8-11** NDay(2) (wl grwn: b.off hind: prom tl rdn & wknd 2f out)	¾	**7**	16/1	63	13
3425[7]	**Hawksbill Henry (USA)** (MrsAJPerrett) **3-8-11** GayeHarwood(4) (w ldrs over 5f)	½	**8**	33/1	62	12
	Cuesta Rey (USA) (JWHills) **3-8-11** MHills(8) (w'like: rdn 2f out: a bhd)	1¼	**9**	12/1	59	9
3463[15]	**Max's Magic (USA)** (GLMoore) **4-9-3** MWigham(9) (dwlt: t.o fnl 3f)	dist	**10**	50/1	—	—
				(SP 120.7%)		**10 Rn**

1m 41.01 (3.01) CSF £131.52 TOTE £17.30: £2.50 £1.80 £1.50 (£51.30) Trio £53.40 OWNER Bodfari Stud Ltd (TARPORLEY) BRED Alec Head

WEIGHT FOR AGE 3yo-6lb

3211 Royale Rose (FR) bounced back to form with a battling success, but would be further improved by the blinkers, as drifting off a true line in the Dip nearly cost her this. (20/1)

3281 Sycamore Boy (USA) looked to be going best in the Dip but wouldn't put his head down and ended up being outbattled by the winner. (13/2)

Macaribo, noisy in the preliminaries, lost ground at the start but moved through easily, only to look a hard ride, holding his head to one side when asked to stretch. His half-brother Mattawan did his winning over a mile and a half and a step up in trip would not go amiss. (13/8: 5/4-9/4)

885 Sharkiyah (IRE), off since April, looked fit enough but found little when coming off the bridle at the two-furlong pole. The way she raced here suggests she may get further, her pedigree does not. (4/1: op 5/2)

Miss Vita (USA), slightly keen going down, shaped respectably for one who will stay further. (25/1)

Priluki, keen going down, was a most reluctant leader early and won't have learnt very much from this debut run. This half-sister to recent Prix Robert Papin winner Greenlander is out of a half sister to Midway Lady, so is certainly bred for the job. (7/2)

Cuesta Rey (USA) (12/1: 8/1-14/1)

T/Plpt: £170.30 (171.43 Tckts). T/Qdpt: £43.80 (25.09 Tckts) Dk

3438-REDCAR (L-H) (Firm, Good to firm patches)

Saturday August 23rd

WEATHER: overcast & raining WIND: almost nil

3776 WESTERDALE NOVICE AUCTION STKS (2-Y.O) (Class E)

5-40 (5-41) **5f** £2,922.50 (£875.00: £420.00: £192.50) Stalls: High GOING minus 0.17 sec per fur (GF)

				SP	RR	SF
3192[6]	**Pure Coincidence (100)** (GLewis) **2-8-13** PaulEddery(1) (w ldrs: led 2f out: comf)	—	**1**	1/8[1]	89+	42
1997[13]	**Torianna (USA)** (DNicholls) **2-8-4** JCarroll(3) (chsd ldrs: shkn up ½-wy: r.o: no ch w wnr)	¾	**2**	20/1	78	31
2886[2]	**Quakeress (IRE)** (JohnBerry) **2-8-5** MFenton(2) (disp ld 3f: sn btn)	4	**3**	11/1[3]	66	19
*3586**	**Beechwood Quest (IRE) (64)** (BSRothwell) **2-8-0be**(3) PFessey(4) (disp ld 3f: sn wknd)	2½	**4**	9/1[2]	56	9
				(SP 112.0%)		**4 Rn**

59.8 secs (2.30) CSF £4.49 TOTE £1.20: (£4.00) OWNER Mrs Andry Muinos (EPSOM) BRED R. and Mrs Parker

3192 Pure Coincidence looked to have a simple task here and was never in danger of defeat but he did need to be asked a question to make sure of it. (1/8)

Torianna (USA) still looked as though she would be all the better for this, but ran well and looks to be improving fast. (20/1)

2886 Quakeress (IRE) was a shade disappointing here and this was certainly not her true form. (11/1: 7/1-12/1)

3586* Beechwood Quest (IRE) found this company far too hot. (9/1)

3777 HERTEL SERVICES H'CAP (0-80) (3-Y.O+) (Class D)

6-05 (6-06) **1m** £3,912.00 (£1,176.00: £568.00: £264.00) Stalls: High GOING minus 0.17 sec per fur (GF)

				SP	RR	SF
3403[4]	**Cashmere Lady (72)** (JLEyre) **5-9-10** OPears(5) (hld up: hdwy 2f out: qcknd to ld wl ins fnl f)	—	**1**	5/1[1]	84	67
3443[4]	**Pericles (73)** (MJohnston) **3-9-5** DHolland(6) (lw: chsd ldrs: led 1½f out: hdd & no ex towards fin)	1½	**2**	7/1[3]	82	59
3443*	**Oriole (52)** (DonEnricoIncisa) **4-8-4** KimTinkler(4) (lw: in tch: effrt over 2f out: styd on u.p. nrst fin)	2½	**3**	11/2[2]	56	39
3262[3]	**Dee Pee Tee Cee (IRE) (75)** (MWEasterby) **3-9-7** TLucas(8) (lw: a chsng ldrs: effrt over 2f out: nt qckn)	¾	**4**	5/1[1]	78	55

1097[6]	**Royal Result (USA) (70)** (TDBarron) **4-9-8** JCarroll(2) (led tl hdd 1½f out: sn wknd)	4	**5**	10/1	65	48
3491[5]	**Alpine Panther (IRE) (64)** (MrsMReveley) **4-9-2** ACulhane(12) (lw: s.i.s: wl bhd tl styd on fnl 2f)	½	**6**	7/1[3]	58	41
3428[10]	**Gulliver (67)** (MrsJRRamsden) **4-9-2**(3) TEDurcan(1) (lw: chsd ldrs tl wknd fnl 2½f)	1¾	**7**	25/1	57	40
3200[3]	**Snowy Mantle (49)** (JDBethell) **4-7-10**(5) IonaWands(3) (chsd ldrs tl rdn & wknd over 2f out)	9	**8**	16/1	21	4
3573[11]	**Highspeed (IRE) (51)** (SEKettlewell) **5-8-0b**(3) PFessey(7) (s.s: hdwy ½-wy: wknd over 2f out)	½	**9**	16/1	22	5
3573[3]	**Spanish Verdict (53)** (DenysSmith) **10-8-5b**[1] PaulEddery(9) (lw: bhd & hrd drvn ½-wy: n.d)	2	**10**	10/1	20	3
3274[4]	**Largesse (73)** (JohnBerry) **3-9-5** MFenton(13) (outpcd & lost tch fr ½-wy)	nk	**11**	7/1[3]	39	16
3621[11]	**Hoh Returns (IRE) (71)** (MBell) **4-9-4**(5) GFaulkner(11) (effrt ½-wy: nvr trbld ldrs)	6	**12**	25/1	25	8
3605[9]	**Forest Robin (50)** (MrsJRRamsden) **4-8-2** MDeering(10) (s.i.s: pushed along & wnt prom after 2f: wknd qckly over 2f out)	29	**13**	20/1	—	—
				(SP 128.6%)	**13 Rn**	

1m 37.5 (2.50) CSF £38.14 CT £188.34 TOTE £7.60: £3.00 £3.10 £2.60 (£34.80) Trio £33.40 OWNER Mrs Sybil Howe (HAMBLETON) BRED J. L. Eyre

WEIGHT FOR AGE 3yo-6lb

3403 Cashmere Lady, confidently ridden, came from way off the pace to win nicely and is obviously in top form. (5/1)
3443 Pericles is running well at the moment but, despite a valiant effort here, he was comprehensively done for speed late on. (7/1)
3443* Oriole was another 4lb higher this time and that seemed to make all the difference. (11/2)
3262 Dee Pee Tee Cee (IRE) is both looking and running well but is off an 8lb higher mark than he has previously won off. (5/1)
1097 Royal Result (USA), after three and a half months off, needed this and ran particularly well and is slipping down to a decent mark. (10/1)
3491 Alpine Panther (IRE), dropped back in trip this time, found things happening too quickly early on but did finish well, suggesting that he is coming right. (7/1: op 9/2)
2239 Highspeed (IRE) has proved disappointing this year but is now on a winning mark and still has the ability if he can be persuaded. (16/1)

3778 RUNSWICK BAY (S) STKS (3-Y.O+) (Class F)

6-35 (6-35) **1m 6f 19y** £2,672.00 (£742.00: £356.00) Stalls: Low GOING minus 0.17 sec per fur (GF)

				SP	RR	SF
1817[2]	**Good Hand (USA) (72)** (SEKettlewell) **11-9-5** KDarley(2) (chsd ldr: pushed along ent st: rdn 3f out: led on bit 2f out: pushed clr fnl f)	—	**1**	4/6[1]	48	16
3429*	**Charity Crusader (48)** (MrsMReveley) **6-9-5b**(5) SCopp(4) (led tl hdd 2f out: no ch w wnr)	5	**2**	7/4[2]	47	15
3562[5]	**Kindred Greeting (16)** (JO'Reilly) **5-9-5b** JO'Reilly(1) (chsd ldrs tl outpcd 4f out: n.d after)	2	**3**	25/1	40	8
3567[3]	**Finestatetobein (30)** (FWatson) **4-8-11v**(3) PFessey(3) (lw: hld up: smooth hdwy & ev ch 4f out: rdn & wknd 2f out)	hd	**4**	5/1[3]	35	3
				(SP 116.9%)	**4 Rn**	

3m 12.7 (13.40) CSF £2.21 TOTE £1.50: (£1.50) OWNER Uncle Jacks Pub (MIDDLEHAM) BRED Tauner Dunlap, Jr. and Brereton C. Jones
No bid

1817 Good Hand (USA) did his usual and was on and off the bit at various stages but, in the end, won really well. (4/6)
3429* Charity Crusader attempted to make all again but found the winner far too strong. (7/4)
3562 Kindred Greeting looked very one-paced once the tempo increased early in the straight. (25/1)
3567 Finestatetobein looked to be going well when challenging half a mile out but, soon asked for a serious effort, she failed to respond. (5/1)

3779 BOLLINGER CHAMPAGNE CHALLENGE SERIES GENTLEMEN'S H'CAP (0-70) (3-Y.O+) (Class F)

7-05 (7-06) **1m 3f** £2,735.00 (£760.00: £365.00) Stalls: Low GOING minus 0.17 sec per fur (GF)

				SP	RR	SF
3467*	**Farringdon Hill (69)** (JHMGosden) **6-11-10v**(4) MrCRanson(1) (s.i.s: sn chsng ldrs: led 4f out: pushed clr: eased towards fin)	—	**1**	7/4[1]	78+	41
3620[2]	**Essayeffsee (54)** (MrsMReveley) **8-10-9**(4) MrTComerford(2) (lw: a chsng ldrs: wnt 2nd 1½f out: no imp)	3	**2**	4/1[3]	59	22
3330*	**Augustan (60)** (SGollings) **6-11-5** MrTMcCarthy(5) (hld up: effrt 4f out: nt pce to chal)	1½	**3**	2/1[2]	63	26
3197[7]	**Madison Welcome (IRE) (63)** (MrsJRRamsden) **3-10-13v**[1] MrSSwiers(4) (lw: hld up: effrt 4f out: rdn & no imp)	s.h	**4**	6/1	65	19
1040[6]	**Brambles Way (54)** (MrsMReveley) **8-10-9**(4) MrNEJones(3) (led tl hdd 4f out: wknd fnl 2f)	1½	**5**	14/1	54	17
				(SP 110.6%)	**5 Rn**	

2m 28.5 (11.50) CSF £8.28 TOTE £3.30: £1.90 £2.30 (£5.40) OWNER Mr Christopher Ranson (NEWMARKET) BRED Wick-Dromdiah Investments Ltd

WEIGHT FOR AGE 3yo-9lb

3467* Farringdon Hill stepped up the tempo once into the straight, and getting first run proved decisive against this bunch. (7/4)
3620 Essayeffsee looked a picture but he is a lazy sort and was never doing enough to get on terms. (4/1)
3330* Augustan had next to no chance as the early pace was slow and did quite well to finish so close. (2/1)
3197 Madison Welcome (IRE) had a visor on for the first time and, although it did wake him up a little, there is still more needed. (6/1)
1040 Brambles Way had a nice pipe-opener after over three months off and this should have put him right for hurdling. (14/1)

3780 WHITBY CONDITIONS STKS (2-Y.O) (Class D)

7-35 (7-38) **7f** £3,437.50 (£1,030.00: £495.00: £227.50) Stalls: High GOING minus 0.17 sec per fur (GF)

				SP	RR	SF
3201[2]	**Rabah** (JLDunlop) **2-8-11** GCarter(3) (lw: cl up: led 3f out: rdn & r.o wl appr fnl f)	—	**1**	4/5[1]	78	46
2741*	**Bettron** (RHannon) **2-8-8**(7) PDobbs(5) (plld hrd: trckd ldrs: hdwy to chal 2f out: r.o)	1	**2**	8/1[3]	80	48
3022[4]	**Palmetto Bay (IRE)** (MRStoute) **2-8-11** KDarley(2) (trckd ldrs: hdwy & ev ch over 2f out: sn rdn & btn)	7	**3**	11/8[2]	60	28
3331[9]	**Sinch** (TDBarron) **2-8-6** LCharnock(1) (hld up: effrt 3f out: no imp)	5	**4**	33/1	43	11
2499[5]	**Crosby Don** (EWeymes) **2-8-11** JCarroll(4) (unruly gng to s: led 4f: sn wknd)	dist	**5**	33/1	—	—
				(SP 114.7%)	**5 Rn**	

1m 25.9 (2.90) CSF £7.85 TOTE £1.40: £1.00 £4.70 (£4.40) OWNER Mr Hamdan Al Maktoum (ARUNDEL) BRED Shadwell Estate Company Limited

3201 Rabah has a good action but is still learning and needed plenty of help from the saddle here but, in the end, did it in great style. (4/5: 4/6-evens)
2741* Bettron, an excitable sort, did not help his cause by pulling hard but, well handled, he did battle on. (8/1)
3022 Palmetto Bay (IRE) is not the best of movers and looks a bit of a handful and, once the tempo increased, he was quickly put in his place. (11/8)
Sinch still needed this and never got into it but time should see a fair bit of improvement. (33/1)
2499 Crosby Don showed temperament problems aplenty beforehand and then ran no sort of race. (33/1)

3781 YORKSHIRE-TYNE TEES TELEVISION H'CAP (0-70) (3-Y.O) (Class E)

8-05 (8-16) **1m 6f 19y** £3,218.25 (£966.00: £465.50: £215.25) Stalls: Centre GOING minus 0.17 sec per fur (GF)

				SP	RR	SF
3623^{6}	**Love Me Do (USA) (60)** (MJohnston) **3-8-12** DHolland(9) (a.p: rdn to ld wl over 1f out: hung lft & r.o)	—	1	11/2^{3}	73	39
3430^{3}	**Dulas Bay (45)** (MWEasterby) **3-7-11** DaleGibson(6) (prom tl lost pl 7f out: hdwy u.p 3f out: sn chsng ldrs: kpt on)	2	2	7/1	56	22
3309^{7}	**Aurelian (58)** (MBell) **3-8-10** MFenton(11) (rr div: hdwy on outside 3f out: styd on: nrst fin)	2½	3	9/2^{2}	66	32
3495*	**Keepsake (IRE) (52)** (MDIUsher) **3-8-4** RStreet(7) (hld up & bhd: hdwy on outside 4f out: chsng ldrs 2f out: no ex fnl f)	hd	4	13/2	60	26
1853^{10}	**Mechilie (44)** (JWPayne) **3-7-7**$^{(3)}$ PFessey(3) (bhd tl styd on fnl 2½f)	1	5	100/1	51	17
3567^{6}	**Eurolink Windsong (IRE) (44)** (MartynWane) **3-7-10** LCharnock(2) (led tl hdd wl over 1f out: no ex)	1½	6	12/1	49	15
3478^{6}	**Maremma (49)** (DonEnricoIncisa) **3-8-1** KimTinkler(4) (sn wl bhd: styd on fnl 2f)	¾	7	14/1	53	19
3455^{4}	**Beauchamp Lion (65)** (JLDunlop) **3-9-3** GCarter(13) (lw: prom tl rdn & btn over 2f out)	1	8	4/1^{1}	68	34
3482*	**Wellcome Inn (62)** (JO'Reilly) **3-9-0** JO'Reilly(8) (dwlt: hdwy to chse ldrs ½-wy: ev ch 4f out: wknd fnl 2f)	s.h	9	10/1	65	31
3441^{3}	**Scarrots (69)** (SCWilliams) **3-9-7** KDarley(10) (lw: chsd ldrs: effrt 4f out: wknd fnl 2f)	½	10	6/1	71	37
3210^{2}	**Shilling (IRE) (61)** (ACStewart) **3-8-13** JCarroll(12) (lw: rr div: hdwy 4f out: rdn & btn over 2f out)	4	11	4/1^{1}	59	25
3485^{4}	**Chateauherault (IRE) (60)** (PCHaslam) **3-8-7**$^{(5)}$ PRoberts(1) (chsd ldrs tl wknd fnl 3f)	nk	12	20/1	57	23
3567^{5}	**Ziggy's Viola (IRE) (52)** (MrsMReveley) **3-8-4**^{ow1} ACulhane(5) (in tch tl rdn & btn 3f out)	2½	13	20/1	47	12
				(SP 147.6%)	**13 Rn**	

3m 7.2 (7.90) CSF £49.40 CT £188.91 TOTE £7.10: £2.70 £6.10 £2.20 (£105.00) Trio Not won; £404.53 to 25/8/97 OWNER Mr M. Doyle (MIDDLEHAM) BRED Robert S. West Jr.

LONG HANDICAP Mechilie 6-10 Eurolink Windsong (IRE) 7-8

3623 Love Me Do (USA), dropped back in trip here, gained his first win on turf and did it well, despite hanging when hitting the front. (11/2)

3430 Dulas Bay, trying his longest trip to date, got it really well and staying seems to be the name of the game with him. (7/1)

3309 Aurelian has slipped back down to a useful mark and is running well. (9/2)

3495* Keepsake (IRE) ran another fine race but is probably at her best over a strongly-run mile and a half. (13/2)

Mechilie, a stone out of the handicap, ran by far her best race to date here and looks likely to need further yet. (100/1)

3567 Eurolink Windsong (IRE) pulled too hard last time, and this time probably went off far too fast and had galloped herself into the ground entering the last two furlongs. (12/1)

3455 Beauchamp Lion (4/1: 11/4-9/2)

3441 Scarrots could never get to the front here and that made all the difference. (6/1)

T/Plpt: £57.00 (151.45 Tckts). T/Qdpt: £30.50 (14.14 Tckts) AA

3632-WINDSOR (Fig. 8) (Good)

Saturday August 23rd

WEATHER: humid WIND: almost nil

3782 GREAT CHARTER (S) STKS (2-Y.O) (Class F)

5-20 (5-22) **5f 217y** £2,738.00 (£768.00: £374.00) Stalls: High GOING minus 0.30 sec per fur (GF)

				SP	RR	SF
2283^{2}	**Rosewood Lady (IRE) (58)** (KRBurke) **2-8-6v^{1}** GDuffield(14) (a.p: led over 1f out: drvn out)	—	1	11/4^{1}	64	30
3546^{4}	**Silent Pride (IRE) (50)** (MDIUsher) **2-8-6** JMarshall(5) (hdwy 2f out: ev ch ins fnl f: r.o)	nk	2	10/1	63	29
3222^{4}	**Impulsive Decision (IRE)** (MartynMeade) **2-8-6** FNorton(9) (s.i.s: hdwy over 1f out: r.o wl ins fnl f)	hd	3	100/30^{2}	63	29
3324^{7}	**The Hobby Lobby (IRE) (53)** (MissKMGeorge) **2-8-11** NAdams(6) (a.p: ev ch over 1f out: r.o ins fnl f)	s.h	4	25/1	68	34
3692^{8}	**Calliram (50)** (MBlanshard) **2-8-3**$^{(3)}$ DSweeney(13) (a.p: ev ch over 1f out: r.o ins fnl f)	nk	5	20/1	62	28
3324^{9}	**Celtic Venture** (MRChannon) **2-8-11** CandyMorris(12) (prom over 4f)	7	6	7/1^{3}	48	14
3586^{12}	**Jilvarra** (WGMTurner) **2-7-13**$^{(7)}$ SCarson(10) (nvr trbld ldrs)	1¼	7	20/1	40	6
2875^{17}	**Rita's Rock Ape** (RBrotherton) **2-8-6** RPrice(3) (led over 4f: eased whn btn ins fnl f)	nk	8	33/1	39	5
3451^{8}	**Clear View (56)** (BJMeehan) **2-8-11b^{1}** MTebbutt(15) (prom over 4f)	1¾	9	9/1	40	6
3294^{4}	**Jaybee Silver (55)** (MHTompkins) **2-8-6** DBiggs(1) (s.s: a bhd)	1¾	10	8/1	30	—
3324^{11}	**Marion's Pet** (RJHodges) **2-8-6** FLynch(4) (bhd fnl 2f)	1½	11	50/1	26	—
3289^{5}	**First Idea** (SDow) **2-8-6** FJovine(8) (a bhd)	½	12	20/1	24	—
3639^{5}	**Sipping Soda** (KTIvory) **2-8-4v^{1}**$^{(7)ow5}$ CCassidy(7) (prom 3f)	5	13	40/1	16	—
1370^{7}	**Primfaheights** (TMJones) **2-8-6** NCarlisle(11) (bhd fnl 3f)	5	14	50/1	—	—
				(SP 119.9%)	**14 Rn**	

1m 13.0 (2.50) CSF £24.78 TOTE £2.90: £1.30 £2.10 £1.70 (£11.30) Trio £13.00 OWNER Mrs Elaine Burke (WANTAGE) BRED St Simon Foundation

No bid

STEWARDS' ENQUIRY Lynch susp. 6, 8-13 & 15-17/9/97 (improper, incorrect & excessive use of whip)

2283 Rosewood Lady (IRE), given a break after a busy June, had the help of the first-time visor. (11/4)

3546 Silent Pride (IRE), back in the selling grade, was suited by this return to six. (10/1)

3222 Impulsive Decision (IRE), a half-sister to May Queen Megan, really appreciated this extra furlong. (100/30)

3090 The Hobby Lobby (IRE) has had plenty of chances but this was certainly one of his better efforts. (25/1)

3055 Calliram, another who has had plenty of shots at goal, ran better than at Leicester three evenings ago. (20/1)

3783 E.B.F. MEDIAN AUCTION MAIDEN STKS (2-Y.O) (Class E)

5-45 (5-51) **5f 217y** £3,143.75 (£950.00: £462.50: £218.75) Stalls: High GOING minus 0.30 sec per fur (GF)

				SP	RR	SF
3471^{12}	**Belle de Nuit (IRE)** (BJMeehan) **2-8-9** MTebbutt(1) (a.p: rdn to ld ins fnl f: r.o)	—	1	15/2^{3}	72	37
	Carinthia (IRE) (CFWall) **2-8-9** GDuffield(6) (lt-f: a.p: led over 3f out tl ins fnl f: r.o)	nk	2	14/1	71	36
3314^{5}	**Arbenig (IRE)** (BPalling) **2-8-6**$^{(3)}$ DSweeney(8) (led over 2f: rdn & n.m.r wl over 1f out: one pce)	1¼	3	12/1	68	33
	Main Street (WJHaggas) **2-9-0** FLynch(3) (unf: a.p: rdn over 1f out: one pce)	2	4	13/8^{1}	68	33
1954^{11}	**Blue Shadow** (RHannon) **2-9-0b^{1}** WJO'Connor(12) (a.p: ev ch over 1f out: wknd ins fnl f)	s.h	5	5/1^{2}	67	32
	The Magistrate (IRE) (MBlanshard) **2-8-11**$^{(3)}$ PPMurphy(9) (cmpt: hdwy fnl 2f: nt rch ldrs)	3	6	16/1	59	24
2699^{8}	**Chayanee's Arena (IRE)** (AGNewcombe) **2-8-9** RPrice(2) (stdd s: hdwy over 2f out: rdn over 1f out: one pce)	¾	7	20/1	52	17

				SP	RR	SF
	Jollyhack (JGMO'Shea) **2-9-0** FJovine(10) (unf: lw: dwlt: nvr nrr)	nk	**8**	33/1	57	22
3306[10]	**Holy Wine (USA)** (DRLoder) **2-9-0** WRyan(4) (hld up mid div: wknd 2f out)	1¼	**9**	5/1[2]	53	18
	Nesala (MartynMeade) **2-8-9** FNorton(14) (w'like: prom 4f)	2½	**10**	25/1	42	7
3687[W]	**Zimzie** (MJHaynes) **2-8-7**(7) MCornally(5) (nvr nr ldrs)	1¼	**11**	33/1	43	8
	Final Settlement (IRE) (JRJenkins) **2-8-11**(3) AWhelan(7) (leggy: unf: prom over 3f)	1¼	**12**	25/1	40	5
	Third Cousin (IRE) (MJHeaton-Ellis) **2-9-0** AClark(15) (lengthy: lw: s.s: bhd fnl 2f)	nk	**13**	12/1	39	4
	Academy (IRE) (AndrewTurnell) **2-9-0** NAdams(11) (w'like: a bhd)	2½	**14**	50/1	32	—
3235[11]	**Fritton (IRE)** (MHTompkins) **2-9-0** DBiggs(16) (swtg: hld up mid div: bhd fnl 2f)	1		14/1	30	—
	Carlasanta (IRE) (AGNewcombe) **2-8-6**(3) DGriffiths(13) (unf: bkwd: s.s: outpcd)	½	**16**	16/1	23	—

(SP 144.0%) **16 Rn**

1m 12.7 (2.20) CSF £109.08 TOTE £12.10: £3.20 £2.50 £5.80 (£27.60) Trio £385.40; £271.42 to 25/8/97 OWNER Mr Richard Withers (UPPER LAMBOURN) BRED Lodge Park Stud

2831 Belle de Nuit (IRE), disappointing last time after a promising debut at Newbury, appreciated this longer trip. (15/2)
Carinthia (IRE), out of a mare placed in sprints, gave every indication that she is up to winning a similar event. (14/1)
3314 Arbenig (IRE), whose dam was a six-furlong juvenile winner in Ireland, looked much more at home over this longer trip. (12/1: op 8/1)
Main Street, a 50,000 guineas yearling, is out of a half-sister to Osario and Only Yours. He should be better for the experience. (13/8)
1486 Blue Shadow, reverting to six furlongs, did not get home in the first-time blinkers. (5/1: op 8/1)
The Magistrate (IRE), a half-brother to seven-furlong, two-year-old winner Magical Belle and a mile winner in Ireland, is out of a half-sister to Topanoora. He seems sure to do better when tackling further. (16/1)
Holy Wine (USA) (5/1: op 3/1)

3784 HAREFIELD CONDITIONS STKS (3-Y.O+) (Class C)

6-15 (6-15) **1m 3f 135y** £4,765.00 (£1,665.00: £812.50: £347.50) Stalls: High GOING minus 0.30 sec per fur (GF)

				SP	RR	SF
3109[5]	**King Sound (108)** (JHMGosden) **3-8-5** LDettori(4) (lw: hld up: rdn to ld over 1f out: r.o)	—	**1**	8/11[1]	110	58
1936*	**Haltarra (USA) (107)** (SbinSuroor) **3-8-8** JReid(1) (led: hdd over 1f out: rdn & r.o)	hd	**2**	9/4[2]	113	61
2180[5]	**Wijara (IRE) (100)** (RHannon) **5-9-1** SSanders(3) (chsd ldr: rdn over 3f out: wknd over 1f out)	5	**3**	12/1	103	61
2837[3]	**Captain Horatius (IRE) (100)** (JLDunlop) **8-9-1** RCochrane(2) (took keen hold: rdn over 3f out: bhd fnl 2f)	8	**4**	11/2[3]	92	50

(SP 111.7%) **4 Rn**

2m 27.1 (1.10) CSF £2.52 TOTE £1.70: (£1.80) OWNER Sheikh Mohammed (NEWMARKET) BRED Newgate Stud Co
WEIGHT FOR AGE 3yo-10lb

3109 King Sound had beaten the runner-up half a length on 3lb worse terms than when lowering the juvenile course record over a mile at Newbury last September. The stable won this race last year with Shantou, prior to winning the St Leger, and it seems as if his trainer might be thinking along the same lines. (8/11)
1936* Haltarra (USA) stepping up from a mile and a quarter, got the trip well but could not quite reverse his narrow defeat by the winner as a two-year-old on 3lb worse terms. (9/4)
2180 Wijara (IRE) probably needs more give in the ground to take on the likes of the first two. (12/1)
2837 Captain Horatius (IRE) is not getting any younger and was again running over the longer trip. (11/2)

3785 WINTER HILL STKS (Gp 3) (3-Y.O+) (Class A)

6-45 (6-45) **1m 2f 7y** £18,840.00 (£7,129.50: £3,489.75: £1,590.75) Stalls: High GOING minus 0.30 sec per fur (GF)

				SP	RR	SF
3388*	**Annus Mirabilis (FR) (116)** (SbinSuroor) **5-9-8v** LDettori(3) (hld up: rdn over 3f out: led wl over 1f out: r.o wl)	—	**1**	11/8[1]	128	91
2901[3]	**Even Top (IRE) (113)** (MHTompkins) **4-9-0** JReid(1) (led over 7f: sn rdn: r.o one pce fnl f)	3½	**2**	100/30[3]	114	77
3409[3]	**Fahris (IRE) (113)** (BHanbury) **3-8-6** RHills(4) (chsd ldr: led over 2f out tl wl over 1f out: one pce fnl f)	nk	**3**	6/4[2]	114	69
2864[4]	**Ghataas (103)** (JLDunlop) **3-8-6** RCochrane(2) (plld hrd in rr: hdwy wl over 1f out: one pce fnl f)	1½	**4**	12/1	93 t	67

(SP 112.9%) **4 Rn**

2m 3.8 (-1.10) CSF £5.92 TOTE £1.90: (£3.20) OWNER Godolphin (NEWMARKET) BRED Darley Stud Management Co Ltd
WEIGHT FOR AGE 3yo-8lb

3388* Annus Mirabilis (FR) duly duplicated last year's victory in this event and will now cross the Atlantic for the Group One Man O' War at Belmont Park. (11/8)
2901 Even Top (IRE) seems ready to tackle a mile and a half. (100/30)
3409 Fahris (IRE) finished three-quarters of a length in front of the runner-up in the Scottish Classic on 2lb worse terms. (6/4: tchd 9/4)
2864 Ghataas would not have minded a little more give in the ground. (12/1: op 8/1)

3786 EGHAM RATED STKS H'CAP (0-90) (3-Y.O+) (Class C)

7-15 (7-17) **1m 67y** £4,760.65 (£1,780.94: £870.47: £373.85: £166.93: £84.16) Stalls: High GOING minus 0.30 sec per fur (GF)

				SP	RR	SF
2678[5]	**Pomona (81)** (PJMakin) **4-9-0** RCochrane(1) (hld up & bhd: rdn over 3f out: rapid hdwy to ld ins fnl f: r.o wl)	—	**1**	10/1	91	71
3128[2]	**Wishing Stone (USA) (81)** (EALDunlop) **3-8-8** WRyan(6) (swtg: hld up: hdwy over 3f out: ev ch over 1f out: nt qckn)	2½	**2**	5/2[1]	86	60
	Glen Parker (IRE) (84) (HRACecil) **4-9-3** KFallon(8) (lw: hld up: hdwy over 3f out: ev ch over 1f out: nt qckn)	1¼	**3**	5/1	87	67
3281*	**Alphabet (84)** (MRStoute) **3-8-11** JReid(7) (hld up: hdwy 4f out: led wl over 1f out tl ins fnl f)	nk	**4**	100/30[2]	86	60
3335*	**Bright Heritage (IRE) (83)** (DRLoder) **4-9-2** LDettori(9) (hld up: hdwy over 3f out: ev ch over 1f out: wknd ins fnl f)	2½	**5**	4/1[3]	80	60
3392[2]	**Yalta (IRE) (79)** (RCharlton) **4-8-12b** SSanders(3) (swtg: led: hdd wl over 1f out: sn wknd)	3½	**6**	8/1	70	50
3112[18]	**Autumn Cover (76)** (PRHedger) **5-8-9** GHind(10) (lw: w ldr tl wknd over 1f out)	7	**7**	14/1	53	33
2211[10]	**West Humble (88)** (MissBSanders) **4-9-7** AClark(2) (hld up: a bhd)	nk	**8**	33/1	65	45
2309[8]	**Sheer Folly (USA) (82)** (PFICole) **3-8-9** AMcGlone(5) (hld up: a bhd)	2	**9**	25/1	55	29
2778[4]	**Admirals Flame (IRE) (74)** (CFWall) **6-8-7** GDuffield(11) (b: swtg: bhd tl sme hdwy over 2f out: wknd wl over 1f out)	2½	**10**	16/1	42	22

(SP 127.9%) **10 Rn**

1m 42.5 (0.30) CSF £35.31 CT £141.56 TOTE £12.40: £2.90 £1.90 £1.80 (£31.20) Trio £139.70 OWNER Skyline Racing Ltd (MARLBOROUGH) BRED R. Kent and Miss R. L. Birchall
LONG HANDICAP Admirals Flame (IRE) 8-5
WEIGHT FOR AGE 3yo-6lb
IN-FOCUS: The two leaders took each other on at a suicidal pace.

2678 Pomona seemed suited by this strongly-run race and went past the leaders as if they were stood still. (10/1)
3128 Wishing Stone (USA) put in another sound effort off a mark 4lb higher than when second at Glorious Goodwood. (5/2)
Glen Parker (IRE), a grand stamp of a horse, took the eye in the paddock but is not particularly well handicapped on what he has achieved. (5/1)
3281* Alphabet was on the same mark as on his handicap debut prior to winning over course and distance last time. (100/30)
3335* Bright Heritage (IRE) found this a good deal more competitive than when causing the management of the Tote a few sleepless nights last time. (4/1)
3392 Yalta (IRE) went off at break-neck speed having been taken on for the lead. (8/1)
1768 Autumn Cover was one of two tearaway leaders who cut each other's throats. (14/1)

3787 BAILEYS ORIGINAL IRISH CREAM H'CAP (0-75) (3-Y.O+ F & M) (Class D)
7-45 (7-46) **1m 67y** £3,681.50 (£1,112.00: £541.00: £255.50) Stalls: High GOING minus 0.30 sec per fur (GF)

				SP	RR	SF
3315^{3}	**Fern's Governor (53)** (WJMusson) **5-8-13** KFallon(11) (hld up: hdwy 3f out: sn rdn: led ins fnl f: r.o wl)	—	1	3/1^{1}	67	49
3316^{5}	**Sis Garden (59)** (JCullinan) **4-9-2**(3) DO'Donohoe(16) (lw: led tl ins fnl f)	3½	2	20/1	66	48
3293^{5}	**Literary (70)** (JHMGosden) **3-9-10** LDettori(6) (lw: hld up & bhd: hdwy over 2f out: r.o ins fnl f)	1¾	3	7/1^{3}	74	50
3465^{2}	**Queen's Insignia (USA) (57)** (PFICole) **4-9-3** JReid(13) (a.p: one pce fnl 2f)	½	4	7/2^{2}	60	42
3465^{13}	**Windswept (IRE) (50)** (DJSffrenchDavis) **4-8-10** MTebbutt(12) (a.p: no hdwy fnl 2f)	1¼	5	16/1	51	33
2285^{6}	**Mimosa (58)** (SDow) **4-9-4** DaneO'Neill(18) (dwlt: hdwy 2f out: nt rch ldrs)	1¼	6	16/1	56	38
3394^{2}	**Delight of Dawn (50)** (EAWheeler) **5-8-3**(7) SCarson(7) (hld up & bhd: hdwy over 1f out: nvr nrr)	1¼	7	8/1	46	28
3469^{3}	**Noeprob (USA) (48)** (RJHodges) **7-8-5**(3) PPMurphy(8) (no hdwy fnl 2f)	¾	8	14/1	42	24
3496^{7}	**Fancy Design (IRE) (44)** (PMitchell) **4-7-13**(5) AimeeCook(2) (prom tl wknd fnl f)	1¼	9	12/1	36	18
3558*	**La Chatelaine (48)** (GLewis) **3-7-13**(3) RFfrench(3) (hdwy on outside over 2f out: wknd over 1f out)	s.h	10	8/1	40	16
3421^{6}	**Cats Bottom (43)** (AGNewcombe) **5-8-3** SDrowne(5) (sme hdwy on outside over 2f out: wknd over 1f out)	3	11	12/1	29	11
3135^{6}	**Blowing Away (IRE) (68)** (MHTompkins) **3-9-8** DBiggs(14) (plld hrd: prom 5f)	d.h	11	20/1	60	36
2778^{3}	**Scarlet Crescent (70)** (PTWalwyn) **3-9-10** RCochrane(10) (a bhd)	5	13	12/1	46	22
3392^{6}	**Kristal Bridge (70)** (PWHarris) **3-9-5**(5) CLowther(9) (prom: rdn over 3f out: wknd over 2 out)	1½	14	20/1	43	19
3550^{6}	**Amarella (IRE) (55)** (MJHaynes) **3-8-9** GHind(15) (chsd ldrs 5f)	10	15	33/1	9	—
3292*	**Primelta (45)** (RAkehurst) **4-8-5** AClark(1) (plld hrd: prom 5f)	3½	16	9/1	—	—

(SP 150.7%) **16 Rn**

1m 44.6 (2.40) CSF £74.76 CT £422.57 TOTE £4.80: £1.40 £4.30 £2.40 £1.60 (£89.50) Trio £315.40 OWNER Fern Components Ltd (NEWMARKET) BRED E. A. Badger
WEIGHT FOR AGE 3yo-6lb
3315 Fern's Governor, whose two previous wins have come over further, was able to sustain her run this time on this return to a mile. (3/1: op 11/2)
3316 Sis Garden put up another brave attempt to make all. (20/1)
3293 Literary did not look suited by this drop back to a mile. (7/1)
3465 Queen's Insignia (USA) likes it around here, but was 4lb higher than when winning over course and distance in June. (7/2)
Windswept (IRE) was 5lb lower than when making her belated seasonal reappearance over course and distance last week. (16/1)
1086 Mimosa, down 2lb, was still 8lb higher than when registering her sole success in June last year. (16/1)
3292* Primelta (9/1: 6/1-10/1)

T/Plpt: £78.00 (155.93 Tckts). T/Qdpt: £7.00 (123.66 Tckts) KH

3245-CHEPSTOW (L-H) (Good to soft)
Monday August 25th
WEATHER: fine but cloudy WIND: almost nil

3788 E.B.F. JULIET MAIDEN STKS (2-Y.O F) (Class D)
2-15 (2-17) **1m 14y** £3,350.00 (£1,010.00: £490.00: £230.00) Stalls: High GOING: 0.24 sec per fur (G)

				SP	RR	SF
3638^{7}	**Admire** (MissGayKelleway) **2-8-8**(3) RFfrench(5) (b.hind: lw: led 2f: led on bit over 2f out: easily)	—	1	100/30^{3}	74+	32
	Casino Ace (IRE) (PWChapple-Hyam) **2-8-11** LDettori(1) (leggy: unf: s.i.s: rdn over 4f out: hdwy over 1f out: r.o ins fnl f: no ch w wnr)	3	2	9/2	68	26
2394^{7}	**Suellajoy** (BSmart) **2-8-11** JStack(7) (a.p: ev ch 2f out: sn rdn: one pce)	nk	3	25/1	68	26
3547^{7}	**Spirit of The Nile (FR)** (PFICole) **2-8-11** WRyan(8) (dwlt: hld up: hmpd over 1f out: hdwy fnl f: r.o)	2½	4	3/1^{2}	63	21
3547^{5}	**Good Catch (IRE)** (PRWebber) **2-8-11** SDrowne(3) (lw: no hdwy fnl 2f)	1¼	5	9/4^{1}	60	18
2222^{5}	**Mary Lou (IRE)** (MRChannon) **2-8-4v**1(7) AEddery(2) (plld hrd: led 6f out tl over 2f out: sn wknd)	5	6	20/1	50	8
3260^{7}	**Sporty Spice (IRE)** (JLHarris) **2-8-11** FJovine(4) (prom over 5f)	4	7	66/1	42	—
	Audeen (SGKnight) **2-8-11** AProcter(6) (neat: bit bkwd: hld up: rn green: rdn over 3f out: sn wl bhd: t.o)	26	8	66/1	—	—

(SP 108.6%) **8 Rn**

1m 38.9 (7.70) CSF £14.84 TOTE £4.20: £1.30 £1.50 £5.00 (£7.60) OWNER Miss Gay Kelleway (WHITCOMBE) BRED Highclere Stud Ltd
3638 Admire had obviously learnt a lot from her debut and justified good market support in effortless style. She can score again. (100/30)
Casino Ace (IRE), a half-sister to Irish St Leger winner Petite Ile, took a real walk in the market and, not surprisingly, shaped like a stayer after appearing rather inexperienced. (9/2: op 6/4)
Suellajoy, a sister to the maiden Threesocks, found the winner galloping all over her. (25/1)
Spirit of The Nile (FR) shaped quite well for one who will eventually need middle distances. (3/1)
3547 Good Catch (IRE) was a bit disappointing on this step up to a mile but the ground was softer this time. (9/4)

3789 E.B.F. ROMEO MAIDEN STKS (2-Y.O C & G) (Class D)
2-45 (2-50) **1m 14y** £3,447.50 (£1,040.00: £505.00: £237.50) Stalls: High GOING: 0.24 sec per fur (G)

				SP	RR	SF
1933^{4}	**Monsajem (USA)** (SbinSuroor) **2-8-11** LDettori(3) (hld up: nt clr run & swtchd rt over 2f out: gd hdwy fnl f: led nr fin)	—	1	11/8^{1}	76	33
3386^{4}	**Tensile (IRE)** (LMCumani) **2-8-8**(3) RFfrench(10) (w ldr: led over 1f out: sn rdn & hung lft: hdd nr fin)	½	2	5/1^{3}	75	32
	Sherganzar (MSalaman) **2-8-11** MWigham(6) (w'like: scope: bkwd: led over 6f: r.o)	½	3	33/1	74	31
	Courteous (PFICole) **2-8-11** WRyan(7) (leggy: scope: bit bkwd: a.p: r.o one pce fnl 2f)	1½	4	7/2^{2}	71	28
3295^{3}	**Jonas Nightengale** (CACyzer) **2-8-11** AMorris(2) (no hdwy fnl 2f)	3	5	14/1	65	22
2768^{9}	**Lord Warford** (GBBalding) **2-8-11** SDrowne(9) (nvr trbld ldrs)	10	6	12/1	45	2

3598[11]	**Opportune (GER)** (DRCElsworth) **2-8-11** AProcter(5) (plld hrd: prom over 5f) 1¼	**7**	33/1	43	—
	Unknown Quest (PFICole) **2-8-11** FJovine(4) (unf: scope: prom over 5f) 2	**8**	16/1	39	—
	Oso Rich (PMRich) **2-8-11** NAdams(8) (w'like: bkwd: s.s: a bhd) 1¼	**9**	66/1	36	—
3219[9]	**Rubamma** (PTWalwyn) **2-8-11** JStack(1) (hld up: rdn over 3f out: wknd over 2f out) 1½	**10**	12/1	33	—
			(SP 116.3%)		**10 Rn**

1m 38.8 (7.60) CSF £7.49 TOTE £2.00: £1.20 £1.20 £3.80 (£3.50) Trio £96.10 OWNER Godolphin (NEWMARKET) BRED D. O'Brien, Ballydoyle Stud, Roncon Ltd, et al

1933 Monsajem (USA), a 290,000 guineas half-brother to mile winner Lothlorien, had a lot to do after running into traffic problems. He is certainly going the right way. (11/8)

3386 Tensile (IRE), suited by this longer trip, did not help his cause by drifting off the stands' rails but the winner would have been an unlucky loser. (5/1: op 3/1)

Sherganzar, a half-brother to several winning sprinters, had no problem with this trip and ran particularly well, considering he appeared to be carrying plenty of condition. (33/1)

Courteous is bred to stay, being a half-brother to a fourteen furlong winner in Ireland and a useful juvenile who won at up to a mile, also in the Emerald Isle. (7/2)

3295 Jonas Nightengale, who only cost 1,000 guineas as a yearling, is a half-brother to Sipowitz. He showed improved form over this longer distance in a much better contest than at Brighton. (14/1)

Lord Warford (12/1: tchd 20/1)

Rubamma (12/1: 8/1-14/1)

3790 FRANKIE DETTORI TON-UP CONDITIONS STKS (3-Y.O+) (Class C)

3-20 (3-20) **7f 16y** £5,034.00 (£1,754.00: £852.00: £360.00) Stalls: High GOING: 0.24 sec per fur (G)

			SP	RR	SF
3577[2]	**Bin Rosie (111)** (DRLoder) **5-9-0b** LDettori(4) (lw: hld up: hdwy over 2f out: led ins fnl f: r.o wl) ....—	**1**	2/7[1]	101	52
672[9]	**Open Credit (101)** (HRACecil) **3-8-4** WRyan(2) (hld up: hdwy over 2f out: led wl over 1f out tl ins fnl f) ....¾	**2**	7/2[2]	94	40
3250*	**Giko (62)** (JRPoulton) **3-8-13** SDrowne(3) (led 2f: led over 2f out tl wl over 1f out: sn wknd) 7	**3**	12/1[3]	57 t	34
	Merci Monsieur (JABOld) **4-8-11**(3) RFfrench(1) (w ldr: led 5f out tl over 2f out: sn wknd) 10	**4**	33/1	30 t	12
			(SP 110.6%)		**4 Rn**

1m 24.6 (5.30) CSF £1.56 TOTE £1.30 (£1.30) OWNER Mr Wafic Said (NEWMARKET) BRED Addison Racing Ltd Inc

WEIGHT FOR AGE 3yo-5lb

3577 Bin Rosie had 5lb in hand of the runner-up based on official ratings. (2/7)

672 Open Credit has obviously had her problems and at least proved she has trained on. (7/2)

3250* Giko is not in the same class as the first two and had an impossible task at the weights. (12/1)

3791 SOUTH WALES ARGUS NURSERY H'CAP (2-Y.O) (Class D)

3-50 (3-50) **5f 16y** £3,194.00 (£962.00: £466.00: £218.00) Stalls: High GOING: 0.24 sec per fur (G)

			SP	RR	SF
3474*	**Eleventh Duke (IRE) (85)** (RHannon) **2-9-7** LDettori(2) (lw: hld up: hdwy 2f out: led ins fnl f: pushed out) ....—	**1**	15/8[1]	89+	44
3497[4]	**Bandbox (IRE) (76)** (SMellor) **2-8-12** MWigham(6) (led: edgd lft over 1f out: hdd & nt qckn ins fnl f) 1¼	**2**	7/1[3]	76	31
1593[2]	**Dim Ots (82)** (BPalling) **2-9-1**(3) RFfrench(1) (w ldr: hung rt & n.m.r over 1f out: rdn & r.o ins fnl f: fin 4th: 1½l: plcd 3rd) ....½	**3**	3/1[2]	81	36
3471*	**First Village (IRE) (85)** (JBerry) **2-9-7** WJO'Connor(5) (lw: a.p: rdn & n.m.r over 2f out: squeezed thro over 1f out: r.o ins fnl f: fin 3rd: ½l: disq: plcd 4th) 1½	**4**	15/8[1]	79	34
3314[7]	**Sun In The Morning (60)** (BJMeehan) **2-7-10** NAdams(3) (swtg: hld up: hrd rdn & wknd over 1f out) 7	**5**	11/1	32	—
3414[4]	**Second Sun (60)** (JJBridger) **2-7-3b**1(7) RBrisland(4) (s.i.s: rdn over 3f out: a bhd) 2½	**6**	33/1	24	—
			(SP 118.3%)		**6 Rn**

61.7 secs (4.70) CSF £15.47 TOTE £2.40: £1.60 £3.00 (£14.70) OWNER Lucayan Stud (MARLBOROUGH) BRED Derek Iceton

LONG HANDICAP Second Sun 6-10

STEWARDS' ENQUIRY O'Connor susp 3-6/9/97 (irresponsible riding)

3474* Eleventh Duke (IRE) did not have too much trouble in defying a 6lb hike in the ratings and again scored without being fully extended. (15/8: 6/4-9/4)

3497 Bandbox (IRE), 5lb better off than when a long way behind the winner at Leicester last month, showed that form to be all wrong. (7/1: 5/1-15/2)

1593 Dim Ots, whose rider had to concentrate on holding her together when she ran out of room, appeared to be third-best on merit. (3/1: op 9/2)

3471* First Village (IRE) found her fair share of problems in running and her rider eventually got himself into hot water. She would not have beaten the winner with a trouble-free run. (15/8)

3792 JOHN & IRIS WATTS CLAIMING STKS (3-Y.O+) (Class F)

4-20 (4-22) **1m 4f 23y** £2,582.50 (£720.00: £347.50) Stalls: High GOING: 0.16 sec per fur (G)

			SP	RR	SF
	Tarry (AStreeter) **4-8-7**(7) PDoe(2) (a.p: rdn over 3f out: led over 2f out: drvn out) ....—	**1**	11/1	56	44
3767[6]	**Statajack (IRE) (60)** (DRCElsworth) **9-9-13b** AProcter(1) (hld up & bhd: hdwy over 2f out: swtchd rt ins fnl f: r.o) 1	**2**	5/2[1]	68	56
	Erlking (IRE) (SMellor) **7-9-3** MWigham(12) (hld up: hdwy over 3f out: ev ch ins fnl f: nt qckn) ....¾	**3**	16/1	57	45
1642[3]	**Araboybill (45)** (JNeville) **6-8-13b** LDettori(3) (led 6f: one pce fnl 2f) 1½	**4**	4/1[2]	51	39
3054[5]	**Sam Rockett (46)** (MissGayKelleway) **4-9-6**(7) JWilkinson(5) (lw: hld up: hdwy over 5f out: one pce 2f) ....½	**5**	7/1	64	52
3308[5]	**Shabanaz (47)** (WRMuir) **12-8-12** WRyan(8) (lw: a.p: hrd rdn over 2f out: wknd fnl f) 2	**6**	6/1[3]	46	34
2955[7]	**Mapengo (29)** (JCullinan) **6-9-1** JStack(7) (lw: w ldr: led 6f out tl over 2f out: wknd over 1f out) 3	**7**	25/1	45	33
3432[9]	**Lizium (32)** (JCFox) **5-8-5**(3) JDSmith(10) (nvr nr ldrs) ....¾	**8**	33/1	37	25
2279[10]	**Zatopek (39)** (JCullinan) **5-9-1** SDrowne(4) (lw: hld up mid div: bhd fnl 3f) 10	**9**	20/1	31	19
3714[12]	**Contract Bridge (IRE) (45)** (PGMurphy) **4-8-9**(3) RFfrench(9) (lw: hld up: stdy hdwy 5f out: wknd 3f out) 2½	**10**	14/1	25	13
3491[13]	**Neverold (IRE) (38)** (PCRitchens) **7-9-0** NAdams(6) (a bhd) 5	**11**	33/1	20	8
3455[8]	**Ludo (58)** (RHannon) **3-9-3b** WJO'Connor(11) (lw: chsd ldrs: rdn 5f out: wknd over 3f out) 6	**12**	7/1	25	3
			(SP 123.2%)		**12 Rn**

2m 42.6 (10.20) CSF £35.19 TOTE £20.90: £4.00 £1.30 £3.60 (£25.70) Trio £209.10 OWNER Mr Alan Baxter (UTTOXETER) BRED Highclere Stud Ltd

WEIGHT FOR AGE 3yo-10lb

Tarry clmd Gay Kelleway £6,000

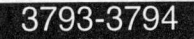

Tarry, successful in a juvenile hurdle at Perth eleven months ago, had not seen a racecourse since breaking a blood-vessel when pulled up at the beginning of March. (11/1: 8/1-12/1)
3767 Statajack (IRE) looked more at home over this extra quarter-mile. (5/2)
Erlking (IRE) seemed to be coming to win his race and might not be the heartiest of battlers. (16/1)
1642 Araboybill had run in a novice seller over hurdles three weeks ago. (4/1: op 6/1)
3054 Sam Rockett landed a seller at Newton Abbot last week. (7/1: op 4/1)
3308 Shabanaz would have preferred a sounder surface and has never won over a full mile and a half. (6/1)

3793 SEVERN BRIDGE H'CAP (0-65) (3-Y.O+) (Class F)

4-50 (4-54) **1m 2f 36y** £2,932.50 (£820.00: £397.50) Stalls: High GOING: 0.16 sec per fur (G)

Form	Horse	Dist	Pos	SP	RR	SF
3315^{11}	**African-Pard (IRE) (62)** (DHaydnJones) **5-10-0** SDrowne(12) (hld up & bhd: gd hdwy & hung lft over 2f out: hung lft & led ins fnl f: r.o wl)	—	**1**	14/1	75	57
1611^{7}	**Dellua (IRE) (65)** (RGuest) **3-9-9** WRyan(9) (hld up: hdwy over 3f out: r.o wl ins fnl f)	2½	**2**	14/1	74	48
3470^{4}	**Magic Lahr (GER) (49)** (IABalding) **4-9-1** LDettori(13) (a.p: led over 2f out tl ins fnl f)	1¼	**3**	$4/1^{1}$	56	38
3470*	**Absolute Utopia (USA) (55)** (NEBerry) **4-9-7** FJovine(8) (hld up mid div: r.o one pce fnl 2f)	1	**4**	7/1	61	43
3588^{2}	**Father Dan (IRE) (56)** (MissGayKelleway) **8-9-5**(3) RFfrench(6) (b: hld up: hdwy over 1f out: r.o)	nk	**5**	$5/1^{2}$	61	43
3227^{8}	**Sea Danzig (55)** (JJBridger) **4-9-0**(7) RStudholme(15) (hdwy over 5f out: one pce fnl 2f)	1¼	**6**	20/1	58	40
2744^{4}	**Blush (56)** (MCPipe) **3-8-7**(7) AEddery(4) (s.s: nvr nrr)	5	**7**	9/1	51	25
870^{9}	**Soldier Cove (USA) (46)** (MartynMeade) **7-8-5**(7) RBrisland(3) (swtg: plld hrd: led: clr over 5f out: hdd over 3f out: sn wknd)	2	**8**	25/1	38	20
3200^{2}	**Jona Holley (53)** (GLMoore) **4-9-5** MWigham(2) (hld up: hdwy on ins to ld over 3f out: hdd over 2f out: eased whn btn ins fnl f)	1¼	**9**	$6/1^{3}$	43	25
3609^{4}	**Tallulah Belle (59)** (NPLittmoden) **4-9-4**(7) KPierrepont(16) (lw: s.s: a bhd)	2½	**10**	25/1	45	27
	Star Entry (60) (MajorDNChappell) **3-9-4** WJO'Connor(10) (swtg: chsd ldrs 6f: sn wknd)	1	**11**	20/1	45	19
3328^{10}	**Three Weeks (48)** (WRMuir) **4-9-0** AProcter(14) (lw: a bhd)	4	**12**	33/1	26	8
3248^{17}	**Zermatt (IRE) (58)** (MDIUsher) **7-9-10** NAdams(7) (sn bhd: hrd rdn over 3f out: no rspnse)	2	**13**	11/1	33	15
2876^{5}	**Haydn James (USA) (58)** (PWHarris) **3-9-2b** JStack(1) (lw: dwlt: a bhd)	hd	**14**	12/1	33	7
3452^{10}	**Coble (60)** (BWHills) **3-9-1v1**(3) JDSmith(5) (swtg: a bhd)	1¾	**15**	12/1	32	6
3605^{12}	**Waasef (60)** (MissGayKelleway) **4-9-5**(7) JWilkinson(11) (prom tl wknd over 3f out: t.o)	25	**16**	20/1	—	—
				(SP 135.4%)		**16 Rn**

2m 13.7 (8.40) CSF £180.18 CT £873.22 TOTE £23.30: £4.40 £1.80 £1.60 £2.20 (£157.00) Trio £69.30 OWNER J S Fox and Sons (PONTYPRIDD) BRED Des De Vere Hunt
WEIGHT FOR AGE 3yo-8lb
2876* African-Pard (IRE), 4lb higher than when winning at Nottingham, proved a difficult ride but was still able to concede weight all round in a decidedly moderate contest. (14/1: op 8/1)
989 Dellua (IRE), coming back after a broken blood-vessel, was a lot less exposed than most of these. Appreciating this longer trip, she could stay even further. (14/1)
3470 Magic Lahr (GER), down another 3lb, had the extra distance this time and it appeared no obvious excuse. (4/1)
3470* Absolute Utopia (USA), raised 2lb, was stepping up from a mile. (7/1)
3588 Father Dan (IRE), up 3lb, seems to find this trip the bare minimum nowadays. (5/1)
2573 Sea Danzig, trying a longer trip, has yet to win beyond seven furlongs. (20/1)
2866 Zermatt (IRE) (11/1: 8/1-12/1)

T/Plpt: £15.70 (704.49 Tckts). T/Qdpt: £7.30 (45.5 Tckts) KH

3432-EPSOM (L-H) (Rnd crse Good to soft, Good ptchs, St crse Good, Good to soft ptchs)
Monday August 25th

WEATHER: overcast & damp WIND: slt half against

3794 CITY INDUSTRIAL SUPPLIES NURSERY H'CAP (2-Y.O) (Class C)

2-05 (2-05) **7f** £8,325.00 (£2,520.00: £1,230.00: £585.00) Stalls: Low GOING: 0.15 sec per fur (G)

Form	Horse	Dist	Pos	SP	RR	SF
3113^{6}	**Night Flyer (75)** (JWHills) **2-8-5**(3) MHenry(5) (swtg: hld up: rdn over 3f out: led ins fnl f: r.o wl)	—	**1**	$4/1^{2}$	74	22
3113^{8}	**Master Mac (USA) (84)** (RAkehurst) **2-9-3** SSanders(3) (lw: led: rdn over 2f out: hdd ins fnl f: unable qckn)	1	**2**	$7/2^{1}$	81	29
2388^{4}	**Iron Mountain (IRE) (69)** (NACallaghan) **2-7-11**(5) APolli(1) (lw: rdn & hdwy over 3f out: ev ch wl over 1f out: one pce)	½	**3**	7/1	65	13
3479^{6}	**Beware (85)** (RWArmstrong) **2-9-4** RPrice(4) (w ldr: rdn over 2f out: ev ch over 1f out: wknd ins fnl f)	1½	**4**	10/1	77	25
3607^{4}	**Blue Zola (IRE) (75)** (MBell) **2-8-8** DHolland(2) (hld up: n.m.r 2f out: one pce)	hd	**5**	$9/2^{3}$	67	15
2693^{6}	**Al's Fella (IRE) (76)** (PFICole) **2-8-9** GCarter(8) (rdn over 3f out: hdwy fnl f: r.o)	nk	**6**	5/1	67	15
3295^{4}	**Hoh Justice (75)** (IABalding) **2-8-8** RCochrane(6) (prom 3f)	4	**7**	8/1	57	5
2689^{10}	**Elleysanta (68)** (AGNewcombe) **2-7-12**(3) AWhelan(9) (bhd fnl 4f)	3½	**8**	25/1	42	—
				(SP 113.6%)		**8 Rn**

1m 27.1 (6.80) CSF £16.53 CT £85.43 TOTE £5.90: £1.90 £1.40 £2.20 (£7.80) Trio £19.60 OWNER The Jampot Partnership (LAMBOURN) BRED Miss K. Rausing
IN-FOCUS: **Following morning rain which changed the going, there was a definite advantage being directly under the stands' rails where the ground was much faster.**
3113 Night Flyer, awash with sweat beforehand, appreciated this slightly longer trip and confirmed Goodwood form with the runner-up. Despite being bustled along early in the straight, he came through to lead inside the last one hundred yards. (4/1)
2689* Master Mac (USA), 1lb worse off with the winner despite being beaten a length by that rival last time out, ran to form, taking the field along until collared by his rival inside the final furlong. (7/2)
2388 Iron Mountain (IRE), who certainly caught the eye here last time out, was given a much more positive ride on this occasion. Bustled along to take closer order in the straight, he came down the centre of the track, the slowest part of the course, but nevertheless had every chance early in the final quarter-mile before tapped for toe. A good-looking, well-built individual, he can pick up a race before long. (7/1: 5/1-15/2)
3479 Beware disputed the lead from the start but, as at Beverley last time out on rain-softened ground, ran out of puff inside the final furlong. He needs a sounder surface to get home over this trip. (10/1: 7/1-11/1)

3607 Blue Zola (IRE) chased the leaders but never looked like quickening up in the straight. (9/2)
2693 Al's Fella (IRE), unable to go the pace, was at the back of the field until making a little late headway. (5/1)
3295 Hoh Justice (8/1: 6/1-9/1)

3795 HEATHORNS BOOKMAKERS H'CAP (0-95) (3-Y.O+) (Class C)
2-35 (2-36) **5f** £10,357.50 (£3,135.00: £1,530.00: £727.50) Stalls: High GOING: 0.05 sec per fur (G)

		Dist	Pos	SP	RR	SF
3460*	**Gaelic Storm (81)** (MJohnston) **3-9-6** DHolland(9) (b.hind: lw: hld up: rdn over 1f out: led wl ins fnl f: r.o wl)	—	1	7/1	89	66
3473^{2}	**Tuscan Dawn (67)** (JBerry) **7-8-3**(5) PRoberts(7) (a.p: rdn over 1f out: led ins fnl f: sn hdd: unable qckn)	½	2	5/1^{3}	73	52
3761*	**Cross The Border (68)** (DNicholls) **4-8-9** 6x SSanders(2) (a.p: led over 1f out tl ins fnl f: one pce)	½	3	6/1	73	52
3126*	**Lady Sheriff (84)** (MWEasterby) **6-9-11b** JReid(10) (w ldr: ev ch over 1f out: one pce)	hd	4	9/4^{1}	89	68
2675^{11}	**Kira (81)** (JLEyre) **7-9-8** OPears(8) (b: b.hind: led over 3f)	2	5	9/2^{2}	79	58
3566*	**River Tern (69)** (JMBradley) **4-8-10** AClark(6) (lw: s.s: outpcd)	2½	6	14/1	59	38
3194^{7}	**Sabina (79)** (IABalding) **3-9-4** RCochrane(4) (s.s: outpcd)	s.h	7	14/1	69	46
2649^{5}	**Youdontsay (80)** (TJNaughton) **5-9-7** DaneO'Neill(3) (bhd fnl 3f)	1½	8	12/1	65	44
3600^{7}	**Polly Golightly (61)** (MBlanshard) **4-7-13b**(3) MHenry(5) (dwlt: outpcd)	2	9	20/1	40	19

(SP 118.2%) **9 Rn**

56.79 secs (2.29) CSF £39.05 CT £206.65 TOTE £7.90: £2.20 £1.70 £1.80 (£16.30) Trio £37.50 OWNER H C Racing Club (MIDDLEHAM) BRED A. D. G. Oldrey
WEIGHT FOR AGE 3yo-2lb

3460* Gaelic Storm put up a good performance especially considering he came with his run in the final furlong down the slowest part of the course, the centre, but managed to get up in the last fifty yards. (7/1)
3473 Tuscan Dawn, 7lb lower than when last successful, ran a fine race and managed to poke a whisker in front inside the final furlong before passed by the winner soon afterwards. He looks ready to strike. (5/1)
3761* Cross The Border is as tough as old boots for this was his fourth race in a week. He still ran a tremendous race and showed in front below the distance before overhauled inside the final furlong. The Handicapper will now have time to re-assess him and he is sure not to look kindly on this recent good run. (6/1: 3/1-7/1)
3126* Lady Sheriff, 7lb higher for her recent Goodwood victory, found that telling and after having every chance below the distance was tapped for toe. All ten of her wins have come over this trip. (9/4)
1772 Kira was probably not helped by the easing in the ground and, after disputing the lead from the start, had nothing more to offer when collared over a furlong out. (9/2)
3194 Sabina (14/1: 8/1-16/1)

3796 MOET & CHANDON SILVER MAGNUM GENTLEMEN'S LIMITED H'CAP (0-90) (3-Y.O+) (Class C)
3-10 (3-11) **1m 4f 10y** £10,406.25 (£3,150.00: £1,537.50: £731.25) Stalls: Low GOING: 0.15 sec per fur (G)

		Dist	Pos	SP	RR	SF
3255*	**Shaft of Light (87)** (LordHuntingdon) **5-11-10v** MrABalding(8) (mde all: clr over 2f out: r.o wl)	—	1	100/30^{1}	103	85
3333^{4}	**Brandon Magic (79)** (IABalding) **4-11-2** MrCBonner(7) (lw: a.p: chsd wnr 4f out: rdn over 3f out: unable qckn)	4	2	13/2	90	72
3599^{5}	**Dance So Suite (86)** (PFICole) **5-11-9** MrFGrasso-Caprioli(6) (hdwy over 4f out: rdn over 2f out: one pce)	hd	3	12/1	97	79
3779^{3}	**Augustan (60)** (SGollings) **6-9-11** MrRWakley(9) (no hdwy fnl 4f)	5	4	11/1	64	46
3643^{4}	**Sun Alert (USA) (70)** (MJPolglase) **3-9-11** MrPJarven(12) (prom over 9f)	5	5	25/1	67	39
3722^{8}	**Hazard a Guess (IRE) (82)** (DNicholls) **7-11-5** MrPPailhes(5) (lw: s.s: nvr nr to chal)	3	6	10/1	75	57
3559*	**Opera Buff (IRE) (68)** (MissGayKelleway) **6-10-5** MrEHennau(4) (nvr nrr)	1	7	7/1	60	42
3585^{6}	**More Than You Know (IRE) (65)** (KRBurke) **4-10-2b^{1}** MrLEBalogh(2) (lw: s.s: hdwy over 9f out: wknd over 4f out)	15	8	33/1	37	19
3333^{8}	**Casual Water (IRE) (63)** (AGNewcombe) **6-10-0** MrRThornton(10) (a bhd)	2½	9	11/2^{2}	32	14
2528^{14}	**Dark Age (IRE) (65)** (RAkehurst) **4-10-2** MrTMcCarthy(1) (lw: bhd fnl 6f)	5	10	12/1	27	9
2344^{4}	**Fairy Knight (64)** (RHannon) **5-10-1** MrCVigors(11) (lw: a bhd)	1½	11	6/1^{3}	24	6
334^{3}	**Squire's Occasion (CAN) (60)** (RCurtis) **4-9-11** MrJGoldstein(3) (prom 5f)	29	12	25/1	—	—

(SP 122.0%) **12 Rn**

2m 43.87 (9.37) CSF £22.61 CT £218.53 TOTE £3.80: £1.80 £3.00 £3.80 (£14.40) Trio £48.60 OWNER The Queen (WEST ILSLEY) BRED The Queen
WEIGHT FOR AGE 3yo-10lb

IN-FOCUS: **This was the only race of the afternoon where the runnners elected to stay on the far side.**
3255* Shaft of Light made every post a winning one and forged clear in the straight to give Lord Huntingdon his third winner in this race in the last four years. (100/30)
3333 Brandon Magic needs cut in the ground and consequently ran a sound race here, if unable to get on terms with the winner in the straight. Although he has not won since his two-year-old days, if the ground remains soft he should at long last return to the winner's enclosure. (13/2)
3599 Dance So Suite took closer order running down Tattenham Hill but could only struggle on at one pace once in line for home. (12/1)
3779 Augustan, who finished third at Redcar on Saturday, was making no impression on the principals in the straight. (11/1: 8/1-12/1)
3643 Sun Alert (USA) was close up until calling it a day over two furlongs from home. (25/1)
3542 Hazard a Guess (IRE) (10/1: op 6/1)

3797 TIFFANY & CO. CONDITIONS STKS (3-Y.O+) (Class C)
3-40 (3-41) **1m 2f 18y** £6,138.00 (£2,238.00: £1,094.00: £470.00: £210.00) Stalls: Low GOING: 0.15 sec per fur (G)

		Dist	Pos	SP	RR	SF
3172a^{5}	**Amid Albadu (USA) (107)** (JLDunlop) **3-8-8b^{1}** GCarter(5) (lw: hld up: led over 2f out: shkn up: r.o wl)	—	1	9/4^{2}	108	21
2136*	**Winter Romance (104)** (EALDunlop) **4-9-2** SSanders(3) (lw: chsd ldr over 1f: rdn over 2f out: chsd wnr ins fnl f: unable qckn)	5	2	13/8^{1}	100	21
2594^{2}	**Zalitzine (USA)** (MRStoute) **3-8-6** JReid(1) (lw: led over 2f: ev ch over 2f out: one pce)	1	3	3/1^{3}	97	10
1456^{17}	**Night City (97)** (KRBurke) **6-9-2** DHolland(4) (led over 7f out tl over 2f out: one pce)	½	4	20/1	37 t	19
3051^{8}	**Amrak Ajeeb (IRE) (102)** (BHanbury) **5-9-2** RCochrane(2) (lw: nvr nr to chal)	s.h	5	7/1	37 t	19

(SP 111.1%) **5 Rn**

2m 14.45 (10.45) CSF £5.83 TOTE £3.20: £1.80 £1.30 (£2.60) OWNER Mr Hamdan Al Maktoum (ARUNDEL) BRED Airlie Stud
WEIGHT FOR AGE 3yo-8lb

3172a Amid Albadu (USA) found the application of blinkers doing the trick and, sent on against the stands' rails over a quarter of a mile from home, was shaken up to forge clear inside the distance. Whilst this was a very good performance, he may well have been slightly flattered as he was certainly racing on the fastest strip of ground directly under the stands' rails. (9/4)

2136* Winter Romance needs some cut in the ground so was well suited by the morning rain. Rousted along over a quarter of a mile from home, he struggled into second place early inside the final furlong but had no hope with the winner. (13/8)
2594 Zalitzine (USA) had every chance over a quarter of a mile from home but could then only keep on at one pace. (3/1)
Night City, who has changed stables since his last run three months ago, soon pulled his way to the front. Collared over a quarter of a mile from home, he could then only keep on in his own time. He has done all his winning in the mud. (20/1)
2338 Amrak Ajeeb (IRE) continues to run poorly and was at the back of the field throughout, if making a little late headway. (7/1)

3798 ROTHMANS ROYALS NORTH SOUTH CHALLENGE SERIES H'CAP (0-90) (3-Y.O+) (Class C)

4-10 (4-14) **1m 114y** £7,165.00 (£2,170.00: £1,060.00: £505.00) Stalls: Low GOING: 0.15 sec per fur (G)

			Pos	SP	RR	SF
3435^{4}	**Present Situation (59)** (LordHuntingdon) **6-7-10**(5) AimeeCook(3) (lw: hld up: led over 1f out: edgd rt: r.o wl)	—	**1**	6/1^{2}	75	48
3616^{2}	**La Modiste (70)** (MissGayKelleway) **4-8-12** RCochrane(8) (hld up: swtchd lft 2f out: chsd wnr fnl f: r.o wl)	1¼	**2**	7/1^{3}	84	57
3616^{6}	**Fahs (USA) (76)** (RAkehurst) **5-9-4** SSanders(10) (a.p: rdn over 3f out: ev ch over 2f out: unable qckn)	5	**3**	7/1^{3}	80	53
3605^{2}	**Mbulwa (54)** (RAFahey) **11-7-5**(5) IonaWands(6) (chsd ldr: led over 2f out tl over 1f out: wknd fnl f)	nk	**4**	16/1	58	31
3145^{5}	**Compatibility (IRE) (78)** (JHMGosden) **3-8-13v**^{1} JReid(9) (swtg: hld up: n.m.r over 2f out: one pce)	1¼	**5**	7/1^{3}	79	45
3772^{9}	**Swift (72)** (MJPolglase) **3-8-7** JTate(13) (lw: nvr nr to chal)	s.h	**6**	14/1	73	39
3594^{3}	**Kayvee (86)** (MrsAJPerrett) **8-10-0** AClark(11) (rdn & hdwy 2f out: one pce)	½	**7**	11/2^{1}	86	59
3712^{8}	**Civil Liberty (70)** (GLewis) **4-8-9b**(3) AWhelan(7) (led 6f)	8	**8**	12/1	55	28
3120^{7}	**No Cliches (70)** (DNicholls) **4-8-5**(7) ANicholls(1) (reluctant to r: nvr nrr)	1½	**9**	10/1	53	26
2303^{7}	**Mr Paradise (IRE) (70)** (TJNaughton) **3-8-5** GCarter(2) (a bhd: sddle slipped 2f out)	2	**10**	10/1	49	15
3548^{13}	**Junikay (IRE) (74)** (RIngram) **3-8-6**(3) MHenry(4) (bhd fnl 3f)	1½	**11**	33/1	50	16
3591^{3}	**Ortelius (69)** (RHannon) **3-8-4**ow1 DaneO'Neill(12) (lw: prom 5f)	5	**12**	11/1	36	1
3608^{6}	**Sooty Tern (75)** (JMBradley) **10-9-3** DHolland(5) (sddle slipped s: a bhd: t.o fnl 4f)	dist	**13**	12/1	—	—

(SP 124.6%) **13 Rn**

1m 47.09 (5.09) CSF £45.43 CT £291.37 TOTE £6.00: £2.10 £2.60 £2.30 (£22.40) Trio £31.20 OWNER Mr Chris van Hoorn (WEST ILSLEY)
BRED The Queen
LONG HANDICAP Mbulwa 7-8
WEIGHT FOR AGE 3yo-7lb

3435 Present Situation comes from a stable that has an excellent 33% strike rate here. Gaining control below the distance, he drifted over to the stands' rails but kept on well to give his trainer a double. (6/1)
3616 La Modiste, switched to the outside a quarter of a mile from home, came through to take second place in the final furlong but, despite forging well clear of the remainder, was unable to overhaul her rival. She has yet to win a handicap on turf. (7/1)
3616 Fahs (USA), who has been running poorly recently, ran better here and had every chance over two furlongs from home before tapped for toe. He would be better suited by a return to further. (7/1)
3605 Mbulwa showed in front over a quarter of a mile from home but he was headed over a furlong out and had little left in the tank. Most of his winning has come on a fast surface. (16/1)
3145 Compatibility (IRE) has certainly looked as if he needs further than six furlongs but, even over this trip, he still looked short on acceleration. (7/1)
3236 Swift, down the field at Newmarket on Saturday and 10lb higher than he has ever won off, never looked like posing a threat. (14/1)
2149* Mr Paradise (IRE) (10/1: 8/1-12/1)
3591 Ortelius (11/1: 8/1-12/1)

3799 LADAS MAIDEN STKS (2-Y.O) (Class D)

4-40 (4-40) **6f** £3,452.50 (£1,045.00: £510.00: £242.50) Stalls: High GOING: 0.15 sec per fur (G)

			Pos	SP	RR	SF
3595^{7}	**Likely Story (IRE) (88)** (JLDunlop) **2-8-9** JReid(5) (lw: hld up: led wl over 1f out: pushed out)	—	**1**	3/1^{2}	84	44
3193^{5}	**Night Shot** (IABalding) **2-9-0** AClark(2) (rdn over 3f out: hdwy over 2f out: ev ch wl over 1f out: eased whn btn wl ins fnl f)	5	**2**	9/4^{1}	76	36
3187^{5}	**Cosmic Countess (IRE)** (MAJarvis) **2-8-9** RCochrane(1) (lw: a.p: rdn over 2f out: wknd wl over 1f out)	2	**3**	7/1	65	25
3433^{2}	**The Boy John (USA) (82)** (RHannon) **2-9-0** DaneO'Neill(6) (lw: a.p: led 3f out tl wl over 1f out: sn wknd)	hd	**4**	7/2^{3}	70	30
1619^{5}	**Indian Silver (79)** (MRChannon) **2-8-9** SSanders(8) (led 3f: wknd over 1f out)	s.h	**5**	10/1	65	25
1440^{11}	**Miss Muffett (IRE)** (PMooney) **2-8-2**(7) PFitzsimons(4) (lw: a bhd)	7	**6**	50/1	46	6
2870^{12}	**Delayed Reaction** (NACallaghan) **2-9-0** GCarter(9) (lw: a bhd)	6	**7**	33/1	35	—
3619^{2}	**Misty Moor** (MJohnston) **2-8-9** DHolland(3) (lw: bhd fnl 3f)	¾	**8**	11/2	28	—
2388^{7}	**Argumentative** (SDow) **2-8-11**(3) DO'Donohoe(7) (a bhd: rein broke)	5	**9**	50/1	20	—

(SP 121.8%) **9 Rn**

1m 12.25 (4.25) CSF £9.81 TOTE £3.50: £1.40 £2.00 £2.40 (£3.80) Trio £9.40 OWNER Mr Michael Page (ARUNDEL) BRED M. L. Page

3595 Likely Story (IRE) appreciated the return to six furlongs and put up a polished display, leading well over a furlong out and needing only to be shaken up to forge clear. (3/1)
3193 Night Shot, bustled along early in the straight, soon picked up ground. Moving into second place well over a furlong out, he failed to contain the winner and when all chance had gone, was eased down in the closing stages. (9/4)
3187 Cosmic Countess (IRE) was never far away but the writing was on the wall early in the final quarter-mile. (7/1)
3433 The Boy John (USA) showed with a slender advantage at halfway but, collared early in the final quarter-mile, was soon done with. A sounder surface would suit. (7/2)
1619 Indian Silver, given a three-month break, found the extra furlong and easy ground too much for her and, after holding a slender lead to halfway, had shot her bolt below the distance. A return to five furlongs is needed. (10/1)

3800 SHERWOOD MAIDEN STKS (3-Y.O) (Class D)

5-10 (5-10) **7f** £3,371.25 (£1,020.00: £497.50: £236.25) Stalls: Low GOING: 0.15 sec per fur (G)

			Pos	SP	RR	SF
3437^{2}	**Polish Romance (USA) (73)** (MRStoute) **3-8-9** DHolland(4) (mde all: pushed out)	—	**1**	5/2^{2}	80	41
3189^{5}	**Silver Kristal (76)** (RAkehurst) **3-8-9** SSanders(8) (chsd wnr: rdn over 2f out: no imp)	1¾	**2**	5/4^{1}	76	37
3437^{3}	**Summerosa (USA) (74)** (PWChapple-Hyam) **3-8-9** JReid(7) (b.nr fore: lw: hdwy 2f out: r.o one pce)	nk	**3**	5/1^{3}	75	36
3250^{2}	**Topton (IRE) (70)** (IABalding) **3-9-0** RCochrane(6) (a.p: rdn over 3f out: one pce)	3½	**4**	6/1	72	33
3048^{7}	**Cold Lazarus (58)** (RTPhillips) **3-9-0** DaneO'Neill(5) (s.s: nvr nrr)	7	**5**	66/1	56	17
2695^{6}	**Mystery Hill (USA) (72)** (JHMGosden) **3-8-9** AGarth(2) (lw: prom over 4f)	1½	**6**	12/1	48	9
3473^{5}	**Marengo (62)** (JAkehurst) **3-9-0** AClark(3) (stdd s: plld hrd: a bhd)	5	**7**	20/1	42	3

				SP	RR	SF
2730^{15}	**Balfour Lady (50)** (JARToller) **3-8-6**(3) AWhelan(1) (bhd fnl 2f)	½	**8**	25/1	35	—

(SP 121.8%) **8 Rn**

1m 25.59 (5.29) CSF £5.79 TOTE £3.20: £1.40 £1.20 £1.70 (£3.10) OWNER Cheveley Park Stud (NEWMARKET) BRED Skara Glen Stables

3437 Polish Romance (USA), who went down very early, at last came good and, making every post a winning one, needed only to be nudged along to keep her rivals at bay. (5/2)

3189 Silver Kristal raced in second place throughout but, despite her rider's efforts, was unable to wear down the winner. She needs further. (5/4)

3437 Summerosa (USA), three lengths behind the winner here earlier in the month, did get closer on this occasion but looked very moderate in the process. She looks one to oppose. (5/1: tchd 8/1)

3250 Topton (IRE) was never far away but was made to look extremely one-paced in the straight. (6/1)

2695 Mystery Hill (USA) (12/1: 6/1-14/1)

T/Plpt: £29.10 (1,220.2 Tckts). T/Qdpt: £7.50 (167.2 Tckts) AK

3306-NEWCASTLE (L-H) (Good)

Monday August 25th

Races 2, 3 & 7: hand timed

WEATHER: overcast, sunny & warm after Race 3 WIND: slt across

3801 UK LAND ESTATES CUP H'CAP (0-90) (3-Y.O+) (Class C)

2-20 (2-21) **7f** £7,230.00 (£2,190.00: £1,070.00: £510.00) Stalls: Low GOING minus 0.20 sec per fur (GF)

				SP	RR	SF
3406*	**Safio (70)** (ABailey) **4-9-0** DWright(5) (swtg: trckd ldrs: rdn to ld appr fnl f: r.o)	—	**1**	13/2^{2}	80	53
3622^{6}	**For Your Eyes Only (79)** (TDEasterby) **3-9-4b**^{1} DeanMcKeown(10) (lw: b.nr hind: chsd ldr: drvn along 3f out: hung rt wl over 1f out: kpt on one pce)	1¼	**2**	11/2^{1}	86	54
3418*	**Khafaaq (83)** (MajorWRHern) **3-9-8b** RHills(2) (lw: effrt 3f out: styd on wl: nt pce to chal)	½	**3**	9/1	89	57
3428^{4}	**Gymcrak Premiere (70)** (GHolmes) **9-9-0v** KFallon(8) (bhd: hdwy 3f out: chsng ldrs appr fnl f: nt qckn)	1½	**4**	14/1	73	46
3273^{6}	**Knave's Ash (USA) (79)** (DNicholls) **6-9-9** AlexGreaves(9) (swtg: in tch: effrt over 2f out: outpcd whn hmpd over 1f out: kpt on)	2	**5**	12/1	77	50
1459^{15}	**Angel Chimes (74)** (JEBanks) **4-9-1**(3) MartinDwyer(12) (swtg: bhd: effrt 3f out: styd on: nvr able to chal)	s.h	**6**	33/1	72	45
3621^{4}	**Smokey From Caplaw (70)** (JJO'Neill) **3-8-9** JQuinn(1) (lw: wl bhd: hdwy over 2f out: nt clr run: styd on wl towards fin)	hd	**7**	12/1	68	36
3185^{3}	**Redwing (85)** (JLDunlop) **3-9-10** KDarley(11) (swtg: led tl hdd appr fnl f: wknd)	hd	**8**	7/1^{3}	82	50
3310^{2}	**Weetman's Weigh (IRE) (78)** (RHollinshead) **4-9-5**(3) DGriffiths(3) (lw: effrt ½-wy: rdn 2f out: nvr trbld ldrs)	¾	**9**	9/1	74	47
1392^{5}	**Blooming Amazing (75)** (JLEyre) **3-9-0** TWilliams(6) (chsd ldrs tl rdn & wknd over 1f out)	1½	**10**	25/1	67	35
3428^{2}	**Epic Stand (78)** (MrsJRRamsden) **3-9-3** JFortune(7) (mid div: effrt & nt clr run over 2f out: sn btn)	1¾	**11**	11/2^{1}	66	34
3428^{3}	**Thwaab (66)** (FWatson) **5-8-7**(3) PFessey(13) (chsd ldrs tl rdn & wknd fnl 2f)	2	**12**	12/1	50	23
3777^{2}	**Pericles (73)** (MJohnston) **3-8-12** MHills(14) (lw: racd alone stands' side: spd to ½-wy: sn wknd)	8	**13**	12/1	38	6
3584^{7}	**Sailormaite (76)** (MissJFCraze) **6-9-6** SWebster(4) (cl up 4f: eased whn btn)	9	**14**	50/1	21	—

(SP 122.8%) **14 Rn**

1m 26.93 (2.43) CSF £38.54 CT £310.00 TOTE £7.30: £2.00 £2.30 £3.00 (£41.30) Trio £157.90 OWNER Mrs M. A. Clayton (TARPORLEY) BRED Mrs M. A. Clayton

WEIGHT FOR AGE 3yo-5lb

3406* Safio, happier at this trip, had slight problems in getting a run but, once he did, the race was always his. (13/2)

3622 For Your Eyes Only had blinkers on for the first time and certainly needs them but, despite running much better, he was still not doing all he can. (11/2: 8/1-5/1)

3418* Khafaaq, having his second run in the blinkers, put up a decent effort but was always having slight traffic problems and could never get to grips. (9/1)

3428 Gymcrak Premiere ran well coming from off the pace, and getting a hefty bump did not help matters. He is also better over slightly further these days. (14/1)

3273 Knave's Ash (USA), from a yard flying at present, ran well but was already struggling when getting almost knocked over entering the last two furlongs. (12/1)

Angel Chimes, after three months off, showed signs of coming back to form. (33/1)

3621 Smokey From Caplaw tried to do the impossible here and come from way behind. He met with all sorts of trouble and is obviously in good heart. (12/1)

3428 Thwaab (12/1: 9/1-14/1)

3802 NEWCASTLE EXHIBITION ALE BLAYDON RACE NURSERY H'CAP (2-Y.O) (Class C)

2-55 (2-57) **1m 3y (straight)** £28,660.00 (£8,680.00: £4,240.00: £2,020.00) Stalls: High GOING minus 0.20 sec per fur (GF)

				SP	RR	SF
3025^{4}	**Bobbydazzle (74)** (DrJDScargill) **2-8-5** JQuinn(9) (lw: hld up centre: effrt over 2f out: r.o to ld wl ins fnl f)	—	**1**	25/1	78	38
3253^{4}	**After The Rain (81)** (BWHills) **2-8-12** MHills(6) (hld up centre: hdwy to ld over 1f out: hdd wl ins fnl f: r.o)	nk	**2**	11/2^{2}	84	44
3479*	**Due South (90)** (EALDunlop) **2-9-7** KFallon(13) (lw: racd stands' side: hdwy over 2f out: chal over 1f out: r.o)	hd	**3**	11/1	93	53
3186*	**Country Garden (81)** (RHannon) **2-8-12** KDarley(14) (lw: chsd ldrs stands' side: hdwy & ev ch 1½f out: nt qckn)	3½	**4**	5/1^{1}	77	37
3613^{3}	**Pay On Red (USA) (76)** (PFICole) **2-8-7** TSprake(11) (trckd ldrs centre: hdwy & ev ch 1½f out: rdn & nt qckn)	½	**5**	11/2^{2}	71	31
3459*	**Naviasky (IRE) (80)** (MrsJRRamsden) **2-8-11** JFortune(2) (lw: hld up & bhd centre: hdwy 2f out: nvr rchd ldrs)	3	**6**	11/2^{2}	69	29
3384*	**Suggest (71)** (WStorey) **2-7-13**(3) MartinDwyer(5) (racd centre: led tl hdd & wknd appr fnl f)	¾	**7**	12/1	59	19
2862^{16}	**Occhi Verdi (IRE) (80)** (MJohnston) **2-8-11** RHills(1) (lw: w ldrs centre tl wknd 1½f out)	½	**8**	16/1	67	27
3282^{3}	**Tearaway (73)** (JWWatts) **2-8-1**(3) PFessey(4) (chsd ldrs centre tl wknd 2f out)	½	**9**	14/1	59	19
3563*	**Bint Nadia (66)** (JDBethell) **2-7-11**ow1 TWilliams(12) (prom stands' side over 5f)	1¾	**10**	33/1	48	7
*3072**	**Sunley Seeker (82)** (MRChannon) **2-8-10**(3) PPMurphy(7) (lw: trckd ldrs centre tl wknd fnl 2½f)	¾	**11**	20/1	63	23
3650^{3}	**Flower O'Cannie (IRE) (86)** (MWEasterby) **2-9-3** TLucas(3) (swtg: w ldrs centre tl wknd over 1f out)	2	**12**	9/1^{3}	63	23
3458*	**Panama House (79)** (TDEasterby) **2-8-10** LCharnock(8) (lw: led stands' side tl wknd over 2f out: chal over 1f out: r.o)	9	**13**	12/1	38	—
3253^{6}	**Cage Aux Folles (IRE) (74)** (JWHills) **2-8-5** JCarroll(16) (chsd ldrs stands' side over 5f: wknd)	5	**14**	20/1	23	—

3395* **Clermont City (IRE) (69)** (PWChapple-Hyam) **2-8-0** DaleGibson(15) (outpcd & bhd stands' side fnl 3f) ....2 **15** 16/1 14 —
(SP 131.3%) **15 Rn**

1m 42.1 (3.50) CSF £148.82 CT £1,546.31 TOTE £41.30: £8.00 £1.80 £2.90 (£80.70) Trio £690.90 OWNER Mrs Bobby Cohen (NEWMARKET) BRED R. A. Dalton

LONG HANDICAP Bint Nadia 7-1

3025 Bobbydazzle looked magnificent and at last confirmed the promise she has been showing, doing this most determinedly. (25/1)

3253 After The Rain was left out in no man's land as the runners failed to cross over to the far rails. He ran well in the circumstances and must be counted as a shade unlucky. (11/2)

3479* Due South needed two attendants in the paddock but did nothing wrong in the race and put up a splendid performance under top weight. (11/1)

3186* Country Garden has improved no end of late but, despite trying hard, her limitations were finally exposed here. (5/1)

3613 Pay On Red (USA) looked to be going particularly well for most of the trip and looked sure to appreciate the extra distance but, when asked a question, proved very one-paced. (11/2)

3459* Naviasky (IRE), taking this step up in trip, was given a lot to do and could never land a blow. (11/2)

3384* Suggest was stepping up in class. This game performer tried his heart out but was well outpointed in the last furlong. (12/1)

2439a Occhi Verdi (IRE) looked and ran well but seemed to run out of stamina. (16/1)

3803 PERTEMPS VIRGINIA RATED STKS H'CAP (0-105) (Listed) (3-Y.O+ F & M) (Class A)

3-25 (3-27) **1m 2f 32y** £12,230.80 (£4,577.20: £2,238.60: £963.00: £431.50: £218.90) Stalls: Low GOING minus 0.20 sec per fur (GF)

				SP	RR	SF
3388[2]	**Sarayir (USA) (96)** (MajorWRHern) **3-9-4** RHills(2) (a.p: rdn to ld ins fnl f: jst hld on)	—	1	4/1[1]	106	62
1146[4]	**Delilah (IRE) (87)** (MRStoute) **3-8-9v[1]** KFallon(4) (hld up: pushed along & hdwy on ins 3f out: swtchd over 1f out: r.o wl towards fin)	s.h	2	8/1	97	53
3453*	**Coretta (IRE) (84)** (LMCumani) **3-8-6** MHills(7) (led tl hdd ins fnl f: kpt on same pce)	1	3	5/1[2]	92	48
3216[7]	**Maid of Camelot (99)** (RCharlton) **3-9-7v[1]** TSprake(3) (lw: hld up & bhd: hdwy over 2f out: chsng ldrs & hrd rdn appr fnl f: kpt on)	1¾	4	14/1	105	61
3445*	**Saddlers' Hope (80)** (JRFanshawe) **3-8-2** JCarroll(1) (cl up: effrt ent st: btn over 1f out)	1½	5	8/1	83	39
3128[4]	**Kalinka (IRE) (85)** (PFICole) **3-8-7** JFortune(8) (in tch: effrt 3f out: outpcd fnl 2f)	1¼	6	8/1	86	42
2676[8]	**Hen Harrier (92)** (JLDunlop) **3-9-0** KDarley(5) (hld up: brought wd st: rdn & nvr able to chal)	1	7	12/1	92	48
3119[3]	**Woodbeck (85)** (JAGlover) **3-8-7** NDay(9) (chsd ldrs: rdn & wknd fnl 2f)	hd	8	7/1[3]	85	41
3575[4]	**Marie Dora (FR) (80)** (IABalding) **3-8-2** MartinDwyer(6) (lw: prom tl outpcd fnl 3f)	1¼	9	7/1[3]	78	34
3277*	**Fantastic Flame (IRE) (78)** (PJMakin) **3-8-0** JQuinn(10) (hld up & bhd: c wd & effrt 3f out: sn wknd)	3	10	9/1	71	27

(SP 119.4%) **10 Rn**

2m 9.7 (3.00) CSF £33.83 CT £151.13 TOTE £4.20: £1.90 £2.40 £2.20 (£12.30) Trio £19.30 OWNER Mr Hamdan Al Maktoum (LAMBOURN) BRED Shadwell Farm Inc. and Shadwell Estate Co. Ltd.

3388 Sarayir (USA) always held a good position, and getting first run on the second made all the difference. (4/1)

1146 Delilah (IRE) had a visor on for the first time but just had trouble in getting a run at a vital stage, otherwise she would have won. She still left the impression that she should stay further. (8/1)

3453* Coretta (IRE) is an honest sort but, despite a valiant effort, she was just picked off. (5/1)

2513 Maid of Camelot had a visor on instead of blinkers this time and travelled particularly well. She was never quite doing enough when asked and has plenty more ability if she can be persuaded. (14/1)

3445* Saddlers' Hope, stepping up in class here, had her limitations exposed approaching the final furlong. (8/1)

3128 Kalinka (IRE), trying her longest trip to date, had her chances but found things too tough in the last couple of furlongs. (8/1)

3804 FCI ROGER VERRALL MEMORIAL CLAIMING STKS (2-Y.O) (Class F)

3-55 (3-56) **5f** £2,671.00 (£808.00: £394.00: £187.00) Stalls: Low GOING minus 0.20 sec per fur (GF)

				SP	RR	SF
3324*	**Junior Muffin (IRE) (64)** (JBerry) **2-8-12**(3) PFessey(3) (trckd ldrs: hdwy to ld 1½f out: all out)	—	1	4/1[3]	73	6
3427[2]	**Erro Codigo (64)** (MrsJRRamsden) **2-8-7** JFortune(2) (disp ld over 3f: hrd rdn & kpt on)	hd	2	11/8[1]	65	—
3544*	**Patsy Culsyth (69)** (NTinkler) **2-8-8v** KimTinkler(5) (chsd ldrs: outpcd 2f out: kpt on wl towards fin)	1	3	15/8[2]	63	—
3331[8]	**Kettlesing (IRE)** (MWEasterby) **2-8-12b** TLucas(1) (disp ld over 3f: rdn & r.o one pce)	nk	4	9/1	66	—
	Lady Emral (MissJFCraze) **2-8-12** SWebster(4) (outpcd ½-wy: sn lost tch)	14	5	25/1	21	—

(SP 110.7%) **5 Rn**

62.95 secs (4.55) CSF £9.17 TOTE £4.00: £1.90 £1.30 (£4.30) OWNER Comerford Brothers Ltd (COCKERHAM) BRED Patrick J. Duffy

3324* Junior Muffin (IRE) is in top form just now and, after travelling best, just found enough when in front. (4/1)

3427 Erro Codigo is proving very difficult to win with and did have a very hard race here. (11/8)

3544* Patsy Culsyth got tapped for foot at a vital stage and, despite finishing well, her chance had gone. (15/8)

2467 Kettlesing (IRE) had the blinkers back on and was dropped in class but was just tapped for foot in the final furlong. (9/1: op 6/1)

3805 STANLEY RACING H'CAP (0-100) (3-Y.O+) (Class C)

4-25 (4-25) **2m 19y** £5,226.75 (£1,584.00: £774.50: £369.75) Stalls: High GOING minus 0.20 sec per fur (GF)

				SP	RR	SF
3383[2]	**Motet (82)** (GWragg) **3-8-6** MHills(3) (lw: hld up: hdwy ½-wy: led 2f out: styd on u.p: swvd rt towards fin)	—	1	11/2[2]	90	32
3218[7]	**Milly of The Vally (86)** (HRACecil) **3-8-10** KFallon(7) (mid div: pushed along appr st: chsng ldrs & n.m.r 2f out: styd on wl towards fin)	nk	2	5/1[1]	94	36
3122[4]	**Go Britannia (89)** (DRLoder) **4-9-13** KDarley(8) (trckd ldrs: stdy hdwy to chal 2f out: sn rdn & r.o: one pce)	hd	3	7/1	97	53
2867*	**Beaumont (IRE) (74)** (JEBanks) **7-8-12** JQuinn(9) (lw: effrt ½-wy: drvn 6f out: chsng ldrs 2f out: kpt on)	½	4	6/1[3]	81	37
3383[4]	**Shirley Sue (75)** (MJohnston) **4-8-13** DeanMcKeown(4) (cl up: led 3f out to 2f out: outpcd whn hmpd 1f out)	hd	5	7/1	82	38
1947*	**Purple Splash (90)** (PJMakin) **7-10-0v** JFortune(6) (bhd: hdwy 3f out: nt clr run over 1f out & ins fnl f: styd on)	s.h	6	9/1	97	53
2475[7]	**Berlin Blue (73)** (JWWatts) **4-8-11** JCarroll(2) (lw: bhd: hdwy 4f out: sn in tch: hrd rdn & no imp fnl 2f)	1¼	7	20/1	79	35
3010*	**Rusk (82)** (JPearce) **4-9-6** NDay(11) (chsd ldrs tl rdn & btn over 2f out)	28	8	9/1	60	16
3412[3]	**Noufari (FR) (68)** (RHollinshead) **6-8-6** FLynch(10) (lw: w ldr: led 9f out to 3f out: wknd qckly)	6	9	16/1	40	—
	Old Red (IRE) (66) (MrsMReveley) **7-8-4** LCharnock(5) (a bhd)	15	10	33/1	23	—
2589[12]	**In Question (85)** (BWHills) **3-8-9** RHills(1) (led 7f: cl up tl wknd qckly 3f out)	12	11	8/1	30	—

(SP 116.0%) **11 Rn**

3m 34.37 (8.87) CSF £29.74 CT £178.12 TOTE £4.80: £1.50 £1.70 £3.00 (£12.60) OWNER Mr A. E. Oppenheimer (NEWMARKET) BRED Hascombe and Valiant Studs

WEIGHT FOR AGE 3yo-14lb

3383 Motet seemed well suited by the very strong pace here and saw it out determinedly, despite ducking at a shadow late on. (11/2)
2284 Milly of The Vally is a real dour stayer and the further she goes the better she will like it. (5/1)
3122 Go Britannia stays well and was well suited by the strong pace but, when it came down to a struggle, he was a shade disappointing. (7/1)
2867* Beaumont (IRE) looked particularly well but had to work hard to get into it and, despite struggling on, could never quite get on terms. (6/1)
3383 Shirley Sue ran well and, after getting squeezed out entering the final furlong, she battled on tenaciously, but the Handicapper is doing her no favours. (7/1)
1947* Purple Splash was trying to come from behind and met with all sorts of trouble. But for this, he would probably have won. (9/1)
1145 Berlin Blue looks to be coming to himself looks-wise and, if he can be persuaded, he still has the ability. (20/1)
2589 In Question helped set a breakneck pace and, in doing so, galloped himself into the ground by the home turn. (8/1)

3806 E.B.F. CHISHOLM BOOKMAKERS MAIDEN STKS (2-Y.O) (Class D)

4-55 (4-59) **7f** £3,696.25 (£1,120.00: £547.50: £261.25) Stalls: Low GOING minus 0.20 sec per fur (GF)

Form	Horse / Trainer / Jockey / Comment	Dist	Pos	SP	RR	SF
3235^{4}	**Golden Dice (USA)** (HRACecil) **2-9-0** KFallon(2) (trckd ldrs: hdwy over 1f out: led ins fnl f: all out)	—	1	$7/4^{1}$	84	36
3598^{8}	**Khalas** (BWHills) **2-9-0** RHills(3) (trckd ldrs: effrt over 2f out: r.o wl towards fin)	s.h	2	$9/2^{2}$	84	36
3411^{6}	**Equity Princess** (MJohnston) **2-8-9** DeanMcKeown(5) (s.i.s: hdwy ½-wy: led 1½f out tl ins fnl f: kpt on)	nk	3	10/1	78+	30
2699^{3}	**Beneventus** (MajorWRHern) **2-8-11**(3) MartinDwyer(8) (lw: sn cl up: led 3f out tl 1½f out: kpt on same pce)	6	4	$13/2^{3}$	70	22
	Saudi (PFICole) **2-9-0** JFortune(15) (leggy: scope: hld up: effrt & rn green over 2f out: styd on: no imp)	2½	5	$13/2^{3}$	64	16
3084^{4}	**Daybreak** (JWWatts) **2-8-9** JCarroll(1) (chsd ldrs: chal over 2f out: wknd over 1f out)	2½	6	16/1	53	5
3619^{3}	**Bawsian** (JLEyre) **2-9-0** TWilliams(12) (bhd: pushed along & hdwy 3f out: nt clr run: n.d)	2	7	12/1	54	6
	Foxie Lady (EALDunlop) **2-8-9** MHills(9) (neat: scope: lw: hld up & bhd: hdwy 2f out: nvr plcd to chal)	¾	8	10/1	47	—
	Desert Sand (MissSEHall) **2-8-9** EJohnson(17) (neat: scope: dwlt: nvr nr to chal)	nk	9	50/1	46	—
	Caraway (RCharlton) **2-8-9** TSprake(14) (w'like: scope: hld up & bhd: hmpd 2½f & 2f out: nt rcvr)	¾	10	16/1	44	—
3602^{8}	**Uniform** (MissSEHall) **2-8-9** KHodgson(16) (bhd tl sme late hdwy)	¾	11	50/1	43	—
1480^{5}	**Saint Malo (USA)** (DRLoder) **2-9-0** KDarley(11) (trckd ldrs: effrt over 2f out: sn btn)	hd	12	11/1	47	—
2110^{U}	**Durgams Delight (IRE)** (BWMurray) **2-8-9** VHalliday(10) (spd 4f)	3½	13	50/1	34	—
1657^{5}	**Allmaites** (DNicholls) **2-9-0** AlexGreaves(6) (chsd ldrs over 4f)	6	14	50/1	26	—
3479^{12}	**Mister Bunch** (EWeymes) **2-9-0** JQuinn(13) (spd over 4f)	hd	15	66/1	26	—
3479^{9}	**Royal Velvet** (CWFairhurst) **2-8-9** LCharnock(7) (led 4f: wknd qckly)	nk	16	66/1	20	—
	Clifton Wood (IRE) (JAGlover) **2-9-0** NDay(4) (w'like: a bhd)	19	17	50/1	—	—

(SP 140.0%) **17 Rn**

1m 28.32 (3.82) CSF £9.35 TOTE £2.50: £1.50 £2.00 £3.10 (£5.70) Trio £24.20 OWNER Mr S. Khaled (NEWMARKET) BRED Palides Investments N. V.

OFFICIAL EXPLANATION **Equity Princess: was unnerved by a horse in a neighbouring stall, and was slowly away as a consequence. Desert Sand: slipped leaving the stalls.**

3235 Golden Dice (USA), a handy sort, travelled well and then responded to some determined driving to gain the day. This should have taught him plenty. (7/4)
3598 Khalas confirmed his promise of last time and showed here he is still learning. There would seem to be plenty more to come. (9/2: op 9/4)
3411 Equity Princess was still very green early on and then showed promise aplenty and should not be long in finding a race. (10/1)
2699 Beneventus went well for a long way, only to find this company too hot when the pressure was really on. (13/2: op 4/1)
Saudi was very green when asked the question and looks likely to improve a good deal for the run. (13/2)
3084 Daybreak again showed promise and a run-of-the-mill maiden can surely be found. (16/1)
3619 Bawsian met with all sorts of trouble and is worth keeping an eye on. (12/1: 8/1-14/1)
Foxie Lady, a handy sort, never got into this but there ought to be plenty of improvement next time. (10/1)
Caraway found more trouble than enough here and is obviously a good deal better than her finishing position suggests. (16/1)
Uniform had an educational and seems to be learning fast. (50/1)
1480 Saint Malo (USA) (11/1: 8/1-12/1)

3807 TELEWEST COMMUNICATIONS MAIDEN STKS (3-Y.O) (Class D)

5-25 (5-29) **1m (round)** £4,162.50 (£1,260.00: £615.00: £292.50) Stalls: Low GOING minus 0.20 sec per fur (GF)

Form	Horse / Trainer / Jockey / Comment	Dist	Pos	SP	RR	SF
	Summer Dance (MRStoute) **3-8-9** KDarley(4) (trckd ldrs: shkn up to ld appr fnl f: r.o: eased towards fin)	—	1	$4/7^{1}$	81+	32
3424^{6}	**Red Guard (79)** (GWragg) **3-9-0** MHills(2) (led tl hdd appr fnl f: no ch w wnr)	2	2	$9/4^{2}$	82	33
3244^{4}	**Toss And Tumble** (WWHaigh) **3-8-9** RLappin(7) (a chsng ldrs: hung lft & outpcd over 2f out: sn btn)	16	3	40/1	45	—
3463^{11}	**Erinrinca (IRE)** (JEBanks) **3-8-9** JQuinn(1) (dwlt: bhd tl sme late hdwy)	1	4	40/1	43	—
1512^{4}	**Kwikpoint** (MartinTodhunter) **3-9-0** DeanMcKeown(5) (cl up tl wknd over 3f out)	9	5	$13/2^{3}$	30	—
	Eat Your Pear (RBastiman) **3-8-9** LCharnock(3) (s.i.s: sn in tch: wl outpcd fnl 4f)	1½	6	25/1	22	—

(SP 116.5%) **6 Rn**

1m 43.5 (4.50) CSF £2.03 TOTE £1.40: £1.20 £1.40 (£1.30) OWNER Cheveley Park Stud (NEWMARKET) BRED Meon Valley Stud

Summer Dance had only one to beat and did that well and was taught her job. (4/7)
3424 Red Guard tried hard to make a race of it but the winner was far too good in the closing stages. (9/4: op 6/4)
Toss And Tumble showed some improvement here but, when ridden, was always inclined to hang. (40/1)
Erinrinca (IRE), having her third run, showed signs of ability, staying on when it was all over. (40/1)
1512 Kwikpoint, after a three-month absence, obviously needed this and no doubt hurdling will be the game for him. (13/2)

T/Jkpt: Not won; £211,081.19 to Ripon 26/8/97. T/Plpt: £91.30 (482.27 Tckts). T/Qdpt: £5.60 (224.14 Tckts) AA

3601-RIPON (R-H) (Good to firm)
Monday August 25th
WEATHER: fine & sunny WIND: slt half bhd

3808 GLASSHOUSES (S) STKS (2-Y.O) (Class F)
2-10 (2-11) **6f** £2,635.30 (£740.80: £361.90) Stalls: Low GOING minus 0.09 sec per fur (G)

				SP	RR	SF
3613⁹	**Forty Love (IRE)** (JEBanks) **2-8-8**(3) DSweeney(5) (chsd ldr: rdn & hung lft over 1f out: styd on wl to ld last stride)	—	**1**	3/1 1	66	26
3782⁶	**Celtic Venture** (MRChannon) **2-8-11** JFanning(2) (chsd ldr: led over 2f out: jst ct)	s.h	**2**	14/1	66	26
3427³	**Circuiteer (IRE) (57)** (JBerry) **2-8-6**(5) CLowther(9) (hung rt thrght: chsd ldr far side: styd on same pce appr fnl f)	3½	**3**	11/2 3	57	17
3586⁶	**Double Appeal (IRE)** (CaptJWilson) **2-8-6** AMcGlone(4) (chsd ldrs: rdn ½-wy: no imp)	5	**4**	14/1	38	—
3427⁵	**Moonlight Flit** (JGFitzGerald) **2-8-6** MRoberts(7) (outpcd & drvn along ½-wy: hung rt: nvr nr to chal)	1¼	**5**	7/2 2	35	—
3106⁵	**Gaelic Quinie (IRE)** (GROldroyd) **2-8-6** FNorton(3) (s.i.s: sn outpcd & bhd: sme hdwy over 1f out: nvr nr to chal)	1	**6**	3/1 1	32	—
2762⁷	**Jockweiler (IRE)** (DWChapman) **2-8-11** ACulhane(10) (s.i.s: sn rdn & wl bhd: sme late hdwy)	3	**7**	16/1	29	—
3072⁸	**Miss Bananas** (TTBill) **2-8-6** JLowe(11) (trckd ldrs far side: wknd 2f out)	1	**8**	33/1	22	—
3692⁵	**Keen Lady** (NPLittmoden) **2-8-6** TGMcLaughlin(6) (sn outpcd & drvn along)	nk	**9**	25/1	21	—
	Makidarti (CWFairhurst) **2-8-6** MFenton(8) (unf: s.i.s: a outpcd)	1½	**10**	20/1	17	—
3451¹⁰	**Dispol Lass (40)** (PCalver) **2-8-6b¹** GHind(1) (led tl over 2f out: wknd)	¾	**11**	33/1	15	—
3427¹⁰	**I'm Tef (49)** (TDEasterby) **2-8-11b** PatEddery(12) (led far side: wknd qckly over 1f out)	1¼	**12**	12/1	16	—
				(SP 129.0%)	**12 Rn**	

1m 14.9 (4.40) CSF £45.40 TOTE £4.70: £1.50 £3.70 £2.10 (£42.50) Trio £41.20 OWNER Mr E. Carter (NEWMARKET) BRED L. and Mrs Hutch
Bt in 8,800gns. Celtic Venture clmd R P Johns £6,000

Forty Love (IRE), dropped appreciably in class, gave his rider problems but finished with quite a flourish to put his head in front right on the line. (3/1)

Celtic Venture was only caught in the very last strides. He was claimed and now joins Linda Stubbs. (14/1)

3427 Circuiteer (IRE) again had the blinkers left off. One of three to race up the middle, he persisted in hanging towards the far rail throughout. (11/2)

3586 Double Appeal (IRE) was stepped up a furlong but did not show any improvement. (14/1: 10/1-16/1)

3427 Moonlight Flit, who had finished just behind Circuiteer on her debut, showed plenty of knee action going down and, on this fast ground, hung right throughout. (7/2)

3106 Gaelic Quinie (IRE) behaved herself down at the stalls but was always up against it after missing the break slightly. (3/1)

2762 Jockweiler (IRE), who has changed stables, is a half-brother to an Ascot Gold Cup winner Ashal. He either could not or would not go the pace but might be an interesting proposition in a mile selling nursery. (16/1)

3809 GRASSINGTON MAIDEN STKS (3-Y.O+) (Class D)
2-40 (2-47) **1m 4f 60y** £3,485.00 (£1,055.00: £515.00: £245.00) Stalls: Low GOING minus 0.09 sec per fur (G)

				SP	RR	SF
2853²	**Tycooness (IRE)** (MJohnston) **3-8-8** JFanning(2) (uns rdr & bolted bef s: s.s: hdwy over 4f out: led over 2f out: shkn up appr fnl f: drvn out)	—	**1**	6/1 3	82	45
	Carisbrooke (HRACecil) **3-8-13** AMcGlone(4) (lengthy: chsd ldr: rdn & outpcd over 2f out: styd on wl towards fin)	1¼	**2**	5/1 2	85	48
3419³	**Jazz Track (IRE) (82)** (PWChapple-Hyam) **3-8-13** PatEddery(5) (lw: led: sn pushed along: hdd over 2f out: nt qckn fnl f: eased nr fin)	hd	**3**	4/5 1	85	48
3396²	**Rutland Chantry (USA)** (LordHuntingdon) **3-8-13** MRoberts(1) (lw: plld hrd: sn trckng ldrs: shkn up over 3f out: no rspnse)	23	**4**	5/1 2	55	18
1434³	**Badenoch (IRE)** (JHMGosden) **3-8-13** GHind(3) (hld up: hdwy 7f out: rdn over 4f out: sn lost pl)	4	**5**	8/1	50	13
3275²	**Nature Dancer** (BWHills) **3-8-3**(5) CLowther(6) (outpcd & pushed along ½-wy: rn wd ent st: sn bhd)	12	**6**	8/1	29	—
				(SP 125.4%)	**6 Rn**	

2m 39.6 (6.10) CSF £35.76 TOTE £6.40: £1.90 £3.00 (£29.80) OWNER Mr J. M. Cullinan (MIDDLEHAM) BRED G. J. Cullinan
STEWARDS' ENQUIRY Eddery susp. 3-6 & 8-9/9/97 (failure to ensure best possible placing)

2853 Tycooness (IRE) unseated her rider leaving the paddock and ran loose but she remained cool and calm throughout. On her two previous outings, both at Salisbury, the races had been started without stalls and she had to be loaded here with the help of a Monty Roberts blanket. She certainly has plenty of temperament but also has an engine and, despite thrashing her tail, she was persuaded to do more than enough. (6/1)

Carisbrooke, badly tapped for toe halfway up the straight, made up four lengths in the final furlong to snatch second place right on the line. He looks a real stayer. (5/1)

3419 Jazz Track (IRE) looks woefully one-paced. Soon being pushed along to maintain the lead, he would definitely have finished second but for being eased near the line and his jockey picked up a five-day ban. (4/5)

3396 Rutland Chantry (USA) is too keen for his own good and, never settling, it was no surprise to see him pull out nothing at all under pressure. (5/1)

1434 Badenoch (IRE) looked very fit, despite an absence of ninety-one days. If this is the best he can do, he is very moderate indeed. (8/1: 6/1-9/1)

3275 Nature Dancer had finished second of three first time. (8/1)

3810 RIPON ROWELS H'CAP (0-100) (3-Y.O+) (Class C)
3-15 (3-15) **1m** £5,803.00 (£1,744.00: £842.00: £391.00) Stalls: High GOING minus 0.09 sec per fur (G)

				SP	RR	SF
3423⁹	**Highborn (IRE) (92)** (PSFelgate) **8-9-11**(3) DSweeney(6) (hld up: hdwy over 4f out: r.o wl to ld ins fnl f)	—	**1**	7/1	100	74
3605⁸	**Pride of Pendle (76)** (MartynWane) **8-8-12** MRoberts(1) (hld up: effrt over 4f out: styd on to ld over 1f out: hdd & nt qckn ins fnl f)	¾	**2**	5/1 3	83	57
3150⁷	**Mawingo (IRE) (83)** (GWragg) **4-9-0**(5) GMilligan(8) (lw: trckd ldrs: nt clr run over 2f out: c outside & kpt on wl fnl f)	nk	**3**	3/1 2	89	63
3605⁴	**Duraid (IRE) (76)** (DenysSmith) **5-8-7**(5) CLowther(3) (lw: hld up: hdwy & nt clr run 2f out: styd on fnl f)	s.h	**4**	6/1	82	56

3243[6]	**Bollin Frank (70)** (TDEasterby) **5-8-6** PatEddery(5) (led tl over 1f out: hung lft: one pce)	½	**5**	11/4[1]	75	49
3584[8]	**Takhlid (USA) (66)** (DWChapman) **6-7-9**(7) RWinston(4) (plld hrd: sn trckng ldr: wknd over 1f out)	2	**6**	16/1	67	41
3428[8]	**Dispol Gem (64)** (PCalver) **4-8-0** JLowe(7) (trckd ldrs: effrt over 2f out: one pce)	¾	**7**	11/1	63	37
3428[9]	**Mountgate (66)** (MPBielby) **5-8-2** DRMcCabe(2) (hld up & bhd: effrt over 3f out: edgd lft: n.d)	3½	**8**	10/1	58	32

(SP 118.4%) **8 Rn**

1m 41.1 (2.90) CSF £39.40 CT £118.60 TOTE £10.50: £2.50 £1.30 £1.50 (£29.40) OWNER Yorkshire Racing Club Owners Group 1990 (MELTON MOWBRAY) BRED Mrs P. F. McQuillan

2124 Highborn (IRE), racing from a mark 3lb higher than he had previously won off, was suited by the slow early pace that did not over-tax his stamina. Well-handled, he ran on with gusto to lead inside the last. (7/1: 5/1-8/1)

3605 Pride of Pendle, from a mark 2lb higher than she has ever won off, is in the form of her life. She would have been better suited by a stronger early pace. (5/1)

3150 Mawingo (IRE), with the blinkers left off, gave his rider no help at all. (3/1)

3605 Duraid (IRE), who met trouble and had to wait for a gap, would have been much better suited by a more strongly-run race. Though 12lb higher in the weights than when he won at Newcastle four outings ago, there is no doubt that when everything goes his way, he is capable of further success. (6/1)

3243 Bollin Frank, allowed to set his own pace, hung badly left entering the last. His three previous victories have come at Haydock and he might be better suited by a left-handed track. (11/4)

2302 Takhlid (USA), well supported at long odds, never settled. Though he won over an extended mile at Epsom almost two years ago, seven furlongs might just suit him better on turf now. (16/1)

3811 RIPON CHAMPION TWO YRS OLD TROPHY, 1997 STKS (Listed) (2-Y.O) (Class A)

3-45 (3-45) **6f** £13,451.00 (£5,009.00: £2,429.50: £1,022.50: £436.25: £201.75) Stalls: Low GOING minus 0.09 sec per fur (G)

				SP	RR	SF
3127*	**Arkadian Hero (USA)** (LMCumani) **2-8-11** PatEddery(1) (lw: mde all: shkn up over 1f out: r.o strly: comf)	—	**1**	6/5[1]	104+	69
2558[9]	**Land of Dreams (100)** (MJohnston) **2-8-6** MRoberts(3) (lw: trckd ldrs: nt clr run 2f out: swtchd outside: r.o u.p: no ch w wnr)	2½	**2**	3/1[3]	92	57
3464*	**Mijana (IRE) (100)** (JHMGosden) **2-9-0** GHind(2) (trckd wnr: rdn over 1f out: styd on same pce)	1½	**3**	9/4[2]	96	61
3270*	**Marton Moss (SWE) (90)** (TDEasterby) **2-8-11** MFenton(4) (lw: stdd s: hld up: hdwy over 2f out: rdn & wknd over 1f out)	5	**4**	20/1	80	45
3019*	**Magical** (WRMuir) **2-8-11** ACulhane(5) (racd wd: chsd ldrs: effrt over 2f out: sn wknd)	1½	**5**	15/2	76	41
3610[2]	**Blue Kite** (NPLittmoden) **2-8-11** TGMcLaughlin(6) (racd wd: chsd ldrs: drvn along 2f out: sn lost pl & eased)	10	**6**	50/1	49	14

(SP 119.7%) **6 Rn**

1m 11.8 (1.30) CSF £5.25 TOTE £1.90: £1.50 £1.80 (£4.30) OWNER Mr M Tabor & Mrs John Magnier (NEWMARKET) BRED Gainesway Thoroughbreds Ltd

3127* Arkadian Hero (USA), a grand type, did it really well and is entitled to take his chance in one of the big two-year-old races this back-end. On this showing, he could be a major player. (6/5)

2558 Land of Dreams, fresh and well after a forty-eight day absence, did not have the run of the race but would not have beaten the winner under any circumstances. (3/1)

3464* Mijana (IRE), whose Windsor win has worked out well, is only small and had his limitations exposed here. (9/4)

3270* Marton Moss (SWE), who again showed a scratchy action going down, was biting off more than he could chew. (20/1)

3019* Magical had his limitations exposed. (15/2)

3812 SUMMER BRIDGE H'CAP (0-80) (3-Y.O) (Class D)

4-15 (4-15) **6f** £3,663.75 (£1,110.00: £542.50: £258.75) Stalls: Low GOING minus 0.09 sec per fur (G)

				SP	RR	SF
3119[12]	**Samsung Spirit (70)** (EWeymes) **3-8-13** JFanning(2) (swtg: mde all: styd on wl fnl f)	—	**1**	12/1	78	47
3269[3]	**Hi Mujtahid (IRE) (53)** (SEKettlewell) **3-7-10b** NKennedy(7) (chsd ldrs: ev ch 1f out: kpt on same pce towards fin)	1	**2**	11/1	58	27
3621[2]	**Style Dancer (IRE) (74)** (RMWhitaker) **3-9-3v** MTebbutt(4) (swtg: trckd ldrs: nt clr run 1f out: kpt on wl towards fin)	hd	**3**	11/2[3]	79	48
3565[4]	**Gipsy Princess (57)** (MWEasterby) **3-8-0b** FNorton(9) (a chsng ldrs: nt qckn fnl f)	½	**4**	8/1	61	30
3460[5]	**Mouche (63)** (MrsJRRamsden) **3-8-3v**[1](3) DSweeney(13) (sltly hmpd s: sn trckng ldrs: ev ch 1f out: wknd towards fin)	hd	**5**	14/1	67	36
3443[3]	**Colway Ritz (72)** (JWWatts) **3-9-1b**[1] GHind(1) (trckd ldrs: shkn up over 2f out: kpt on same pce)	1	**6**	13/2	73	42
3334[3]	**Storyteller (IRE) (59)** (MrsJRRamsden) **3-8-2v** MFenton(3) (lw: bhd: hdwy over 2f out: n.m.r: kpt on: nvr rchd ldrs)	2½	**7**	9/2[1]	53	22
3273[13]	**Just Visiting (77)** (CaptJWilson) **3-8-13**(7) AngelaHartley(11) (a chsng ldrs: rdn 2f out: one pce)	1¾	**8**	50/1	67	36
2326[14]	**Night Flight (74)** (JJO'Neill) **3-8-12**(5) CLowther(12) (chsd ldrs: rdn & outpcd 2f out: n.d)	s.h	**9**	12/1	63	32
3398[10]	**Master Foley (56)** (NPLittmoden) **3-7-13**ow1 DRMcCabe(5) (sn bhd: sme late hdwy)	2½	**10**	14/1	39	7
3410[15]	**Cauda Equina (78)** (MRChannon) **3-9-7** ACulhane(16) (prom rdn over 2f out: wknd over 1f out)	hd	**11**	10/1	60	29
3621[7]	**Two On The Bridge (58)** (DenysSmith) **3-7-8b**(7)ow1 RWinston(15) (racd wd: outpcd fr ½-wy)	½	**12**	16/1	39	7
2847[10]	**Showgirl (54)** (CaptJWilson) **3-7-11**ow1 DWright(8) (sn outpcd & drvn along)	¾	**13**	33/1	33	1
3130[14]	**Mumkin (74)** (MrsLStubbs) **3-8-10**(7) GMcDonald(6) (swvd rt s: swtchd lft & a wl bhd)	1	**14**	33/1	50	19
3710*	**John Emms (IRE) (72)** (MBell) **3-9-1** MRoberts(14) (lw: racd wd: mid div: effrt over 2f out: sn wknd)	1½	**15**	5/1[2]	44	13
2891[14]	**Star of The Road (53)** (JMCarr) **3-7-10** JLowe(10) (in tch: outpcd ½-wy: sn lost pl)	15	**16**	100/1	—	—

(SP 135.5%) **16 Rn**

1m 13.5 (3.00) CSF £137.29 CT £764.10 TOTE £19.60: £3.60 £2.20 £1.80 £2.20 (£176.30) Trio £373.10 OWNER Mr T. A. Scothern (MIDDLEHAM) BRED Red House Stud

LONG HANDICAP Showgirl 7-9 Hi Mujtahid (IRE) 7-9 Star of The Road 7-0

1243 Samsung Spirit, dropped in distance and down the weights, made the most of a favourable draw. (12/1)

3269 Hi Mujtahid (IRE) ran with plenty of credit but is almost certainly better over seven. (11/1)

3621 Style Dancer (IRE) got himself very warm when he had to be re-plated before leaving the paddock. From a 4lb higher mark, he had a poor run and, with better luck, would have troubled the winner. (11/2)

3565 Gipsy Princess ran really well from a moderate draw and seemed to appreciate the drop back to six. (8/1)

3460 Mouche, who has tumbled down the weights, was tried in a visor for the first time. Squeezed out at the start, she ran with plenty of credit considering she was drawn high. (14/1)

3443 Colway Ritz, in blinkers for the first time, went very fast on the way to post. Settled in just behind the leaders, he was not knocked about at any stage. (13/2)
3334 Storyteller (IRE) found it hard to come from behind when the leading group were determined to race as close as possible to the favoured stands' side rail. (9/2)

3813 PATELEY BRIDGE H'CAP (0-70) (3-Y.O) (Class E)

4-45 (4-48) **1m 2f** £3,093.50 (£938.00: £459.00: £219.50) Stalls: High GOING minus 0.09 sec per fur (G)

				SP	RR	SF
3336*	**Tipperary Sunset (IRE) (45)** (JJQuinn) **3-7-3**(7) PBradley(6) (bhd: hdwy over 3f out: led over 1f out: hld on towards fin)	—	**1**	9/1	54	35
3026[5]	**Sharbadarid (IRE) (70)** (LMCumani) **3-9-7** GHind(2) (lw: hld up: hdwy over 3f out: ev ch fnl f: nt qckn towards fin)	nk	**2**	8/1	79	60
3478[4]	**Misty Rain (60)** (BWHills) **3-8-11** PatEddery(12) (in tch: hdwy to ld over 3f out: hdd over 1f out: one pce)	4	**3**	100/30[1]	62	43
3633[4]	**Mardrew (65)** (JohnBerry) **3-9-2** MFenton(10) (bhd: gd hdwy on ins over 3f out: nt clr run 2f out: swtchd lft & styd on fnl f)	1	**4**	12/1	66	47
3430[2]	**Lord Discord (60)** (TDEasterby) **3-8-4**(7) RWinston(1) (chsd ldrs: ev ch tl wknd over 1f out)	1¼	**5**	13/2[3]	59	40
2313[16]	**Tarradale (47)** (CBBBooth) **3-7-12** FNorton(4) (chsd ldrs tl wknd over 1f out)	1¾	**6**	25/1	43	24
3601*	**Rare Talent (66)** (MRChannon) **3-9-3** ACulhane(3) (hld up: hdwy over 3f out: hrd rdn & edgd lft over 2f out: sn lost pl)	13	**7**	11/2[2]	41	22
3230[2]	**Miss Kalaglow (56)** (CFWall) **3-8-7** MTebbutt(5) (b.hind: in tch: effrt & hung lft over 3f out: n.d after)	1¾	**8**	100/30[1]	28	9
3478[5]	**Zorba (64)** (JHetherton) **3-9-1** NKennedy(7) (led: hdd over 3f out: hung lft & sn lost pl)	1¾	**9**	10/1	33	14
3430[6]	**Billy Nomaite (70)** (MrsSJSmith) **3-9-4**(3) DSweeney(9) (w ldr tl wknd over 2f out)	nk	**10**	16/1	39	20
2398[11]	**Top Shelf (60)** (PJBevan) **3-8-6**(5) CLowther(8) (sn outpcd: bhd fnl 4f)	7	**11**	20/1	18	—
155[7]	**Swynford Charmer (45)** (JFBottomley) **3-7-10** JLowe(11) (a bhd)	7	**12**	50/1	—	—
				(SP 129.2%)		**12 Rn**

2m 8.3 (4.80) CSF £77.25 CT £273.59 TOTE £11.90: £3.00 £1.70 £1.90 (£69.30) Trio £192.80 OWNER Mrs S. Quinn (MALTON) BRED M. G. Masterson
LONG HANDICAP Tipperary Sunset (IRE) 7-6 Swynford Charmer 7-4
3336* Tipperary Sunset (IRE), from a 7lb higher mark, came from off the pace and did just enough. He would not want the ground any faster. (9/1)
3026 Sharbadarid (IRE), who has been gelded since his last run, was awkward to load. He did nothing wrong in the race and finished clear second best. Hopefully, now he is settling down and behaving himself, he might improve. (8/1)
3478 Misty Rain made the best of her way home but was readily picked off and needs further. (100/30: 9/2-3/1)
3633 Mardrew, who showed a very poor action going down, had no luck at all in running. (12/1)
3430 Lord Discord had the visor left off this time. (13/2)
1023 Tarradale, who has slipped down the weights, ran his best race for some time. (25/1)
3230 Miss Kalaglow never looked happy and, on this ground and on this undulating track, wanted to do nothing but hang left. (100/30)

T/Plpt: £382.00 (28.83 Tckts). T/Qdpt: £36.90 (13.02 Tckts) WG

2892-WARWICK (L-H) (Soft, Good to soft patches, becoming Good to soft)
Monday August 25th

WEATHER: overcast with sunny periods WIND: almost nil

3814 SSAFA (S) STKS (3-Y.O+) (Class G)

2-30 (2-31) **1m 2f 169y** £1,984.50 (£547.00: £259.50) Stalls: Low GOING minus 0.17 sec per fur (GF)

				SP	RR	SF
3200[13]	**Guesstimation (USA) (57)** (JPearce) **8-9-12** GBardwell(5) (hld up: hdwy ent st: c stands' side: sn rdn: nt clr run & swtchd ins fnl f: r.o: fin 2nd, ½l: awrdd r)	—	**1**	4/1[3]	66	7
3475[5]	**Haroldon (IRE) (61)** (BPalling) **8-9-12** CRutter(2) (b: trckd ldrs: c stands' side: led 1f out: edgd rt: r.o wl: fin 1st: disq: plcd 2nd)	½	**2**	11/4[2]	67	8
3469[2]	**Pegasus Bay** (MissAEEmbiricos) **6-9-7** GDuffield(4) (b: b.hind: a.p: led 4f out: hrd rdn & hdd 1f out: one pce)	1¾	**3**	5/2[1]	59	—
3400[5]	**Select Star (IRE) (55)** (APJarvis) **3-8-12v**[1] JFEgan(8) (b.hind: led 1f: rdn 3f out: r.o one pce)	2	**4**	11/1	56	—
3608[12]	**Clemency (IRE) (45)** (MTate) **5-8-13**(3) TEDurcan(10) (swtg: prom tl rdn & outpcd over 1f out)	nk	**5**	50/1	50	—
3560[2]	**Haydown (IRE) (30)** (MRBosley) **5-9-0**(7) KelliPhillips(3) (s.i.s: led after 1f to 6f out: rdn 2f out: one pce)	1¼	**6**	14/1	12 t	—
3588[4]	**Royal Acclaim (27)** (KRBurke) **12-9-12v** MRimmer(6) (hld up: effrt & rdn over 2f out: no imp)	nk	**7**	25/1	17 t	—
	Irish Groom (AStreeter) **10-9-4**(3) RHavlin(1) (b.off hind: bkwd: chsd ldrs over 6f: sn lost tch)	2½	**8**	50/1	8 t	—
1451[5]	**Supercharmer (60)** (RTJuckes) **3-8-12** PaulEddery(7) (bkwd: prom: racd wd & led 6f out: hdd 4f out: rdn & wknd over 2f out: t.o)	10	**9**	12/1	—	—
				(SP 105.7%)		**9 Rn**

2m 26.1 (12.10) CSF £11.75 TOTE £3.60: £1.70 £2.00 £1.10 (£5.80) Trio £5.10 OWNER The Exclusive Two Partnership (NEWMARKET) BRED Oak Crest Farm
WEIGHT FOR AGE 3yo-9lb
No bid
STEWARDS' ENQUIRY Rutter susp. 3-6/9/97 (careless riding)
2770 Guesstimation (USA) got up on the line to win this event last year and he would probably have succeeded this time with a trouble-free passage, without having to wait for the Stewards to intervene. (4/1)
3475 Haroldon (IRE), dropped in class, led his rivals over to the favoured stands' side once in line for home and he struck the front a furlong out, but his jockey was rather careless in allowing him to drift across the challenging winner and, though he held on, had contravened the Rules and was made to pay for it. (11/4)
3469 Pegasus Bay took command four furlongs out and made his rivals work hard to catch him, but he did the wrong thing in remaining on the far side once in line for home, and he had been picked off entering the final furlong. (5/2)
2521 Select Star (IRE), a bit free in his first-time visor, wore large bandages on both his hind legs. Off the bridle on the home turn, he did battle on but could not muster the pace to get to terms. (11/1)

Clemency (IRE) ran much better than she did on her seasonal debut but she was at full stretch early in the straight, and could only plug on at the one pace. (50/1)
3560 Haydown (IRE), last to leave the stalls, had soon pulled his way into the lead, due to the sedate pace. Although headed, he remained with every chance until the quickening tempo left him struggling inside the last quarter-mile. (14/1)
1451 Supercharmer (12/1: op 8/1)

3815 SEVERN TRENT WATER H'CAP (0-80) (3-Y.O+) (Class D)
3-00 (3-01) **2m 20y** £3,677.45 (£1,097.60: £524.30: £237.65) Stalls: Low GOING minus 0.17 sec per fur (GF)

				SP	RR	SF
3317*	**Aztec Flyer (USA) (56)** (CEBrittain) **4-8-7b** MRimmer(6) (lw: a.p: led 5f out: rdn & styd on strly)	—	**1**	3/1^{2}	62	27
3197^{5}	**Toi Toi (IRE) (75)** (DWPArbuthnot) **3-8-9**$^{(3)}$ RHavlin(2) (lw: chsd ldrs: outpcd over 3f out: rallied appr fnl f: fin wl)	½	**2**	11/2^{3}	81	32
3543^{6}	**Dancing Cavalier (67)** (RHollinshead) **4-8-11**$^{(7)}$ PFredericks(5) (b.off hind: dropped rr 9f out: hdwy 4f out: rdn to chal over 1f out: edgd lft & no ex ins fnl f)	2½	**3**	7/1	70	35
3440^{3}	**Yak Alfaraj (70)** (MRStoute) **3-8-7** GDuffield(4) (lw: led to ½-wy: sn pushed along & lost pl: rallied u.p 2f out: nt pce to chal)	1½	**4**	5/2^{1}	72	23
3392^{11}	**Ela-Yie-Mou (IRE) (69)** (SDow) **4-9-6** JFEgan(1) (lw: trckd ldrs: led 8f out to 5f out: r.o one pce fnl 2f)	2	**5**	25/1	69	34
3498^{3}	**Tappeto (73)** (HCandy) **5-9-10** CRutter(7) (lw: racd wd thrght: lost tch 6f out: t.o)	dist	**6**	3/1^{2}	—	—

(SP 110.3%) **6 Rn**

3m 36.8 (11.30) CSF £16.98 TOTE £4.30: £1.70 £2.70 (£15.50) OWNER Mr R. Meredith (NEWMARKET) BRED Raul Martin
WEIGHT FOR AGE 3yo-14lb
3317* Aztec Flyer (USA) had no trouble handling this softer ground and, though he did have to work in the closing stages, was always firmly in control. He is now being considered for a tilt at the Cesarewitch. (3/1: op 2/1)
3197 Toi Toi (IRE) appreciated this step up in distance and delivered a determined late challenge after getting left behind on the home turn. She was bred to stay and should not take long to get off the mark. (11/2)
3543 Dancing Cavalier took closer order at the end of the back straight and looked a live threat approaching the final furlong but, with the winner showing no signs of stopping, he decided this was not going to be his day. (7/1)
3440 Yak Alfaraj was inclined to run his race in snatches and he had no answer to the relentless gallop the principals kept up in the latter stages. (5/2)
267a Ela-Yie-Mou (IRE), returning to a more suitable trip, was only shaken off inside the last couple of furlongs and was not disgraced with all his weight. (25/1)
3498 Tappeto took the scenic route and probably covered three miles, but he lost touch halfway down the back straight and was soon tailed off. (3/1)

3816 B.B.T. FINANCIAL SERVICES CLAIMING STKS (3-Y.O+) (Class F)
3-30 (3-30) **5f** £2,993.10 (£831.60: £399.30) Stalls: Low GOING minus 0.17 sec per fur (GF)

				SP	RR	SF
3637^{7}	**Divine Miss-P (58)** (APJarvis) **4-8-7** GDuffield(9) (led after 1f: rdn out fnl f)	—	**1**	8/1	65	47
3600^{9}	**White Emir (80)** (BJMeehan) **4-9-3b**$^{(7)}$ GHannon(6) (swtg: hld up: hdwy 2f out: rdn & r.o wl ins fnl f)	1	**2**	11/2^{2}	79	61
3566^{3}	**The Wad (59)** (DNicholls) **4-8-5**$^{(7)}$ TSiddall(4) (lw: a.p: ev ch 1f out: unable qckn)	1	**3**	6/1^{3}	64	46
2922^{8}	**Hype Energy (52)** (GLewis) **3-8-5b**^{1} PaulEddery(1) (hdwy 2f out: r.o wl ins fnl f)	¾	**4**	10/1	56	36
2964^{10}	**Nightingale Song (70)** (MartynMeade) **3-8-4**$^{(3)}$ RHavlin(12) (led 1f: rdn & one pce appr fnl f)	2	**5**	12/1	52	32
3327^{3}	**Embroidered (31)** (SDow) **4-8-5** JFEgan(8) (prom: rdn over 1f out: sn btn)	nk	**6**	16/1	47	29
3378^{6}	**Gopi (60)** (RHannon) **3-8-3** DBiggs(10) (nvr nr to chal)	¾	**7**	14/1	44	24
1275^{4}	**Divide And Rule (69)** (RHollinshead) **3-8-3**$^{(7)}$ DHayden(11) (in tch to ½-wy: sn rdn & outpcd)	3	**8**	11/1	42	22
3077^{3}	**Palacegate Jack (IRE) (69)** (JBerry) **6-9-1b**$^{(3)}$ TEDurcan(13) (lw: w ldrs over 3f: sn rdn & wknd)	½	**9**	5/2^{1}	46	28
3398^{9}	**Rowlandsons Stud (IRE) (43)** (KCComerford) **4-8-1**$^{(7)}$ SRighton(7) (spd to ½-wy: sn lost tch)	1½	**10**	33/1	31	13
3572^{9}	**Honiara Bay (28)** (MissAStokell) **3-7-8v**$^{1(5)}$ RMullen(5) (s.s: a outpcd)	4	**11**	66/1	12	—
2160^{8}	**Blue Havana** (GraemeRoe) **5-8-5** NCarlisle(2) (outpcd: a t.o)	6	**12**	80/1	—	—

(SP 112.7%) **12 Rn**

59.7 secs (1.70) CSF £44.21 TOTE £8.10: £2.40 £2.20 £1.40 (£15.70) Trio £32.10 OWNER Town and Country Tyre Services Ltd (ASTON UPTHORPE) BRED C. C. Bromley and Son and A. O. Nerses
WEIGHT FOR AGE 3yo-2lb
3323* Divine Miss-P is distinctly useful when she can dictate and she was soon calling the tune this time, and won a shade easier than the margin might suggest. She handled the ground really well. (8/1)
2232* White Emir, a heavy-topped individual who should have appreciated the easing of the ground, did not find his stride until too late but he did finish with a flourish and has not stopped winning yet. (11/2)
3566 The Wad, whose form has all been shown on a sounder surface, was in the firing line all the way but the winner proved too strong and he had met his match in the last two hundred yards. (6/1)
2481 Hype Energy, still struggling to find a correct trip, fared so much better in the blinkers and, with another furlong to travel, she would have gone very close. (10/1)
258 Nightingale Song has plenty of pace but she was feeling the strain below the distance, and could do little or nothing about it. (12/1)
3327 Embroidered kept tabs on the leaders but she was unable to raise her pace at the business end, and was easily brushed aside. (16/1)
3077 Palacegate Jack (IRE) had conditions in his favour but he lost out in his battle to set the pace, and he downed tools below the distance. (5/2: 4/1-9/4)

3817 CROSBEE & ATKINS 75TH ANNIVERSARY NURSERY H'CAP (2-Y.O) (Class E)
4-00 (4-01) **6f** £3,122.25 (£933.00: £446.50: £203.25) Stalls: Low GOING minus 0.17 sec per fur (GF)

				SP	RR	SF
3556^{4}	**Mrs Middle (62)** (NACallaghan) **2-7-11** GBardwell(4) (chsd clr ldr: pushed along ½-wy: r.o to ld ins fnl f)	—	**1**	7/2^{2}	66	11
2831^{5}	**Alpha Whisky (GER) (73)** (IABalding) **2-8-8** CRutter(5) (lw: b.hind: a.p: rdn over 1f out: ev ch fnl f: unable qckn)	1½	**2**	11/4^{1}	73	18
3379^{4}	**Rejected (86)** (RHannon) **2-9-7** PaulEddery(3) (lw: chsd ldrs: hrd drvn 2f out: kpt on ins fnl f)	1½	**3**	7/2^{2}	82	27
3571^{3}	**Eastern Lyric (78)** (JBerry) **2-8-13** GDuffield(1) (lw: led & sn clr: wknd & hdd ins fnl f)	1½	**4**	11/4^{1}	70	15
3295^{5}	**Life Sentence (62)** (JGSmyth-Osbourne) **2-7-6v**$^{1(5)ow1}$ RMullen(6) (s.s: a outpcd)	2	**5**	10/1^{3}	49	—

(SP 106.9%) **5 Rn**

1m 16.2 (4.20) CSF £11.41 TOTE £5.30: £2.10 £1.30 (£7.60) OWNER Mr Michael Hill (NEWMARKET) BRED P. T. Tellwright
LONG HANDICAP Life Sentence 7-9

3556 Mrs Middle has been showing signs of improvement in her recent races and, with the softer ground to put more emphasis on stamina, took advantage of her light weight and opened her account going away. (7/2)
2831 Alpha Whisky (GER) looked to have found a suitable opening over this slightly longer trip and she may have poked her nose in front briefly before the winner, but she was found wanting in the dash to the line. (11/4)
3379 Rejected seems to have lost his way but he did stay on under forceful handling, and he did have it all to do at the weights. (7/2)
3571 Eastern Lyric, soon bowling along with a healthy advantage, did look beyond recall but the sixth furlong found her out. (11/4)

3818 ROYAL MERCIAN AND LANCASTRIAN YEOMANRY MAIDEN AUCTION STKS (I) (2-Y.O) (Class F)
4-30 (4-31) **7f** £2,342.80 (£645.80: £306.40) Stalls: Low GOING minus 0.17 sec per fur (GF)

				SP	RR	SF
2840⁵	**Little Miss Huff (IRE)** (RGuest) **2-8-4**ow2 PBloomfield(5) (chsd ldrs: led over 1f out: qcknd clr)	—	1	2/1 1	73+	34
3278¹⁸	**Thelonius (IRE)** (JGSmyth-Osbourne) **2-8-5**(5) RMullen(8) (lw: bhd: drvn along 3f out: hdwy appr fnl f: fin wl)	3½	2	14/1	71	34
3025⁶	**Signatory (68)** (RHannon) **2-8-10** DBiggs(2) (led 1f: led over 2f out tl over 1f out: one pce)	nk	3	11/2 3	70	33
*3607*⁹	**Zero Three Fifteen (IRE)** (MartynMeade) **2-8-4**(3) RHavlin(10) (led after 1f tl over 2f out: rdn & one pce appr fnl f)	hd	4	25/1	67	30
2893⁶	**Miss Skye (IRE)** (TJNaughton) **2-8-5** JFEgan(9) (lw: hdwy over 3f out: kpt on u.p fnl f)	s.h	5	14/1	65	28
3450⁸	**Forgotten Star (IRE)** (RFJohnsonHoughton) **2-7-12** CRutter(12) (hdwy 4f out: rdn 2f out: no imp)	2½	6	4/1 2	52	15
	Misalliance (CFWall) **2-8-2** GDuffield(7) (w'like: scope: bkwd: hdwy ½-wy: wknd wl over 1f out)	1½	7	8/1	53	16
	Yanshan (BobJones) **2-8-4**(3) TEDurcan(6) (w'like: leggy: bit bkwd: s.s: nvr nrr)	2	8	25/1	53	16
3450¹⁰	**Stalwart Legion (IRE)** (JWHills) **2-8-5** PaulEddery(11) (in tch 4f: sn wknd: t.o)	6	9	20/1	38	1
	Mr Miyagi (ABailey) **2-8-7** GBardwell(13) (small: bkwd: s.s: a bhd: t.o)	7	10	16/1	24	—
2719⁵	**Latin Bay** (PWHarris) **2-8-7** MRimmer(3) (chsd ldrs 4f: sn wknd: t.o)	1½	11	20/1	20	—
3278²¹	**Risque** (MrsAJBowlby) **2-8-10** CandyMorris(4) (dwlt: a bhd & outpcd: t.o)	¾	12	66/1	21	—
3253⁹	**Risknowt Getnowt** (TWall) **2-8-7** LNewton(1) (lw: chsd ldrs to ½-wy: sn lost tch: t.o)	5	13	66/1	7	—
				(SP 119.2%)		**13 Rn**

1m 28.1 (3.50) CSF £27.32 TOTE £2.70: £1.30 £7.90 £1.90 (£22.50) Trio £99.30 OWNER Mr M. G. Hill (NEWMARKET) BRED Rose Bank Stud
2840 Little Miss Huff (IRE) followed her promising debut at Newmarket with a clear-cut success and she does look a useful filly in the making. (2/1)
2959 Thelonius (IRE) took time to warm up but he stayed on pleasingly in the closing stages, and this could be more his trip. (14/1)
3025 Signatory, keen to get on with it, does not really give himself the chance to get this sort of trip, although on this occasion, with the winner out of the way he would have taken a great deal of beating. (11/2)
Zero Three Fifteen (IRE), having his first outing on turf, showed a big improvement on his racecourse debut and, if he can maintain the progress, there are races waiting to be won. (25/1)
2893 Miss Skye (IRE) is beginning to get her act together and it is more than possible this easier ground is more to her favour. (14/1)
Forgotten Star (IRE), still not the finished article, did show a bit of promise and there is no reason why she cannot go on improving. (4/1)

3819 ROYAL MERCIAN AND LANCASTRIAN YEOMANRY MAIDEN AUCTION STKS (II) (2-Y.O) (Class F)
5-00 (5-02) **7f** £2,319.70 (£639.20: £303.10) Stalls: Low GOING minus 0.17 sec per fur (GF)

				SP	RR	SF
3458⁴	**Czar Wars** (PTDalton) **2-8-4**(3)ow2 RHavlin(8) (lw: mde all: rdn appr fnl f: r.o wl)	—	1	16/1	83	32
3113⁹	**Universal Lady (72)** (CJames) **2-8-0** CRutter(1) (hdwy 4f out: chsd wnr over 2f out: hrd rdn fnl f: nt qckn)	¾	2	7/4 1	74	25
3493²	**Fanti Dancer (IRE) (62)** (BJMeehan) **2-8-5** GDuffield(10) (lw: chsd ldrs: hrd drvn appr fnl f: kpt on)	2	3	100/30 2	75	26
3545⁸	**Sing For Me (IRE) (61)** (RHollinshead) **2-7-12** NCarlisle(12) (trckd ldrs: rdn & no hdwy fnl 2f)	1½	4	12/1	64	15
3031¹⁰	**General Klaire** (BAMcMahon) **2-8-5** LNewton(5) (hdwy 3f out: styd on ins fnl f)	hd	5	25/1	71	22
3060⁸	**One To Go (IRE)** (JBerry) **2-8-7**(3) TEDurcan(6) (bit bkwd: chsd ldrs: effrt over 1f out: nt pce to chal)	hd	6	16/1	76	27
3458³	**Short Romance (IRE)** (JWHills) **2-8-5** PaulEddery(9) (trckd ldrs: rdn over 2f out: sn btn)	2½	7	6/1 3	65	16
3635⁸	**Russian About (IRE) (59)** (MRChannon) **2-8-2** JFEgan(3) (hdwy ½-wy: rdn wl over 1f out: no imp)	½	8	9/1	61	12
3619⁹	**Tilburg** (MrsNMacauley) **2-7-9**(7)ow4 JoHunnam(11) (nvr nr ldrs)	1½	9	50/1	58	5
	Soap Stone (ABailey) **2-7-12** GBardwell(7) (lt-f: unf: s.s: a bhd: t.o)	5	10	25/1	42	—
2700¹¹	**God Knows (IRE)** (MJFetherston-Godley) **2-8-2** DBiggs(2) (a bhd: t.o)	3	11	50/1	39	—
	Knightcracker (REPeacock) **2-7-5**(7) JFowle(4) (lt-f: unf: bkwd: s.s: a outpcd: t.o)	17	12	50/1	—	—
				(SP 116.8%)		**12 Rn**

1m 28.5 (3.90) CSF £38.33 TOTE £25.40: £4.10 £1.30 £1.50 (£23.80) Trio £19.70 OWNER Mrs Julie Martin (BURTON-ON-TRENT) BRED L. Fuller
3458 Czar Wars decided the best place to be was out in front and, finding extra when strongly pressed in the closing stages, won cosily. He can win again. (16/1)
2700 Universal Lady made her move plenty soon enough and she did look the likely winner when throwing down her challenge into the final furlong, but she was the one to crack as the winner kept his head down and galloped on. Slightly more patient tactics could be the ideal solution. (7/4)
3493 Fanti Dancer (IRE), with the action from the start, did her best to mount a challenge approaching the final furlong but an extra effort proved beyond her. (100/30)
3131 Sing For Me (IRE) seemed to get the trip better than she did at Beverley but she was flat to the boards below the distance and the leaders were not stopping. (12/1: op 8/1)
2519 General Klaire had less use made of her over this trip, and there was plenty to like about the way she was getting down to her work at the finish. (25/1)
One To Go (IRE), still just needing the run, did not fare badly and, tenderly handled when all chance had gone, will repay the kindness. (16/1)
3458 Short Romance (IRE), off the bridle on the entrance to the straight, had nothing more to give and, at this stage of her career, it is possible she is trying to do it all in one go. Experience should settle her. (6/1)

3820 ROYAL NAVY MAIDEN STKS (3-Y.O+) (Class D)
5-30 (5-31) **1m** £3,964.10 (£1,185.80: £568.40: £259.70) Stalls: Low GOING minus 0.17 sec per fur (GF)

				SP	RR	SF
3463⁶	**Flint Knapper** (GWragg) **3-8-12** PaulEddery(3) (lw: hld up: hdwy to ld over 2f out: sn clr: rdn out)	—	1	7/2 2	73	26
3389²	**Villarica (IRE) (74)** (PWChapple-Hyam) **3-8-4**(3) RHavlin(6) (a.p: led 3f out: sn hdd: rdn to chal fnl f: r.o wl)	nk	2	6/4 1	67	20
3389⁵	**Beacon Silver** (LordHuntingdon) **3-8-7** CRutter(9) (bit bkwd: hdwy over 3f out: rdn & wknd wl over 1f out)	11	3	9/2 3	45	—

	Horse	Details	Dist	Pos	SP	RR	SF
	Jovian	(RGuest) **3-8-7** PBloomfield(8) (bkwd: sn drvn along in tch: effrt 2f out: nt rch ldrs)	nk	**4**	20/1	45	—
	Mutabassir (IRE)	(ACStewart) **3-8-12** GDuffield(2) (w'like: str: bkwd: rn green bhd: hdwy over 2f out: nt rch ldrs)	4	**5**	7/2[2]	42	—
3624[4]	**Bodfari Wren**	(ABailey) **3-8-7** GBardwell(7) (b: b.hind: a in rr)	¾	**6**	20/1	35	—
	Burnley Belle	(MRChannon) **5-8-13** CandyMorris(1) (bkwd: a in rr: hrd drvn 2f out: no imp)	4	**7**	20/1	27	—
	Hotstepper	(MrsSDWilliams) **4-8-13** DBiggs(4) (bkwd: led 1f: wknd over 2f out)	½	**8**	66/1	26	—
	Lady of Glendowan	(MrsBarbaraWaring) **4-8-13** EByrne(5) (led after 1f to 3f out: sn rdn & wknd: t.o)	11	**9**	66/1	4	—

(SP 119.9%) **9 Rn**

1m 41.9 (5.50) CSF £8.23 TOTE £5.60: £2.10 £1.50 £1.20 (£3.40) Trio £6.40 OWNER Mr A. E. Oppenheimer (NEWMARKET) BRED Hascombe and Valiant Studs

WEIGHT FOR AGE 3yo-6lb

3463 Flint Knapper, one of only four who were fully wound up, had to put his best foot forward to shake off the very persistent filly. (7/2: op 2/1)

3389 Villarica (IRE), still finding trouble getting off the mark, responded willingly inside the distance and she would have made it in another couple of strides. (6/4)

3389 Beacon Silver moved into a challenging position entering the straight but she was in trouble soon after passing the quarter-mile marker, as lack of peak fitness began to tell. (9/2)

Jovian, off the track since making his debut in the autumn of last year, looks a hard ride and she will strip much fitter with this run under her belt. (20/1)

Mutabassir (IRE), bred to need all of this trip, was too backward to do himself justice on this occasion and, running very green, could come on a ton for the experience. (7/2)

T/Plpt: £34.90 (282.09 Tckts). T/Qdpt: £7.90 (45.74 Tckts) IM

3808-RIPON (R-H) (Good to firm)
Tuesday August 26th

WEATHER: fine & sunny WIND: slt half bhd

3821 RACING CHANNEL MAIDEN AUCTION STKS (2-Y.O) (Class F)

2-30 (2-34) **5f** £2,671.00 (£751.00: £367.00) Stalls: Low GOING minus 0.29 sec per fur (GF)

	Horse	Details	Dist	Pos	SP	RR	SF
3707[2]	**Cumbrian Cadet (72)**	(TDEasterby) **2-8-10** KFallon(11) (b.hind: sn pushed along: hdwy ½-wy: edgd rt & styd on wl to ld nr fin)	—	**1**	5/2[2]	73	35
3306[3]	**Cool Prospect**	(ABMulholland) **2-8-10** TLucas(1) (led: hung bdly rt thrght: hdd nr fin)	½	**2**	9/4[1]	71	33
3610[11]	**Kustom Kit Kate**	(SRBowring) **2-7-12** DaleGibson(10) (swvd rt s: sn rdn along: hdwy ½-wy: styd on fnl f)	½	**3**	100/1	58	20
3459[3]	**Double Power**	(LRLloyd-James) **2-7-12** KimTinkler(3) (lw: w ldrs: hung rt thrght: chal over 1f out: wknd towards fin)	nk	**4**	16/1	57	19
3569[5]	**Heathyards Sheik**	(RHollinshead) **2-8-6** FLynch(4) (lw: sn wl outpcd: hdwy over 1f out: styd on wl towards fin)	nk	**5**	10/1	64	26
2538[7]	**Tangerine Flyer (72)**	(JBerry) **2-8-5**(5) CLowther(6) (a chsng ldrs: kpt on one pce fnl 2f)	¾	**6**	12/1	66	28
3407[2]	**Premium Princess (67)**	(JJQuinn) **2-7-9**(3) PFessey(9) (dwlt: hmpd & swtchd lft after 2f: styd on fnl f)	¾	**7**	7/1	51	13
3278[9]	**Cape Hope (65)**	(RBoss) **2-8-3**(3) RFfrench(12) (lw: hdwy & hung lft 2f out: nvr nr ldrs)	4	**8**	12/1	46	8
	Amber Regent	(PCHaslam) **2-8-10** JFortune(13) (cmpt: scope: outpcd fr ½-wy)	1¾	**9**	33/1	45	7
2706[12]	**Smooth Princess (IRE)**	(JGFitzGerald) **2-8-5** MRoberts(7) (in tch: outpcd ½-wy: sn lost pl)	hd	**10**	20/1	39	1
3282[6]	**Buzz The Agent**	(MWEasterby) **2-8-3** LCharnock(8) (sn wl outpcd)	¾	**11**	33/1	35	—
3426[7]	**Tigi**	(MrsMReveley) **2-7-12** NCarlisle(5) (sn outpcd)	5	**12**	25/1	14	—
3265[2]	**Three Star Rated (IRE)**	(TDBarron) **2-8-5** RLappin(2) (unruly: bolted & uns rdr gng to s: w ldrs to ½-wy: sn wknd)	3	**13**	5/1[3]	11	—

(SP 134.3%) **13 Rn**

59.8 secs (2.00) CSF £8.54 TOTE £4.10: £1.40 £1.30 £17.00 (£6.70) Trio £513.70 OWNER Cumbrian Industrials Ltd (MALTON) BRED Miss Sara Davies and David Lewis

3707 Cumbrian Cadet, dropping back in distance, was given a terrific ride and forced his head in front near the line. This was not a strong event. (5/2: 3/1-9/2)

3306 Cool Prospect, dropping back a furlong, was very keen going to post. Hanging badly right throughout, he must have held on had he kept straight. (9/4: 4/1-2/1)

Kustom Kit Kate, on her first outing on turf, turned in a much improved effort from a poor draw. (100/1)

3459 Double Power, who carries plenty of condition, looked a big danger over a furlong out but contributed to her downfall by hanging badly right. (16/1)

3569 Heathyards Sheik, dropping back in distance, failed completely to go the pace. Putting in some solid work near the line, he will appreciate six or even seven furlongs. (10/1: tchd 16/1)

3407 Premium Princess met all the bad luck going. She seems to lack early speed and needs further. (7/1)

3265 Three Star Rated (IRE), on edge beforehand, bolted going to post. Obviously her temperament is a major stumbling block. (5/1)

3822 DEVERELL CLAIMING STKS (3-Y.O+) (Class F)

3-00 (3-03) **1m** £2,778.10 (£781.60: £382.30) Stalls: High GOING minus 0.47 sec per fur (F)

	Horse	Details	Dist	Pos	SP	RR	SF
3418[6]	**Alpine Hideaway (IRE) (73)**	(BHanbury) **4-8-13** JStack(13) (lw: mde all: hld on wl)	—	**1**	7/1	67	49
3477[4]	**Special-K (46)**	(EWeymes) **5-8-1**(5) CLowther(6) (chsd ldrs: wnt 2nd over 1f out: no imp)	1½	**2**	20/1	57	39
2947[2]	**High Premium (84)**	(RAFahey) **9-8-7**(7) RWinston(3) (sn bhd & pushed along: hdwy over 4f out: hung rt: styd on appr fnl f)	1½	**3**	15/8[1]	62	44
	French Ginger (45)	(LRLloyd-James) **6-8-2** TWilliams(2) (chsd ldrs: chal over 1f out: one pce)	½	**4**	100/1	49	31
3542[4]	**Billy Bushwacker (87)**	(MrsMReveley) **6-9-9** KDarley(14) (lw: dwlt: hdwy over 3f out: kpt on same pce fnl 2f)	½	**5**	100/30[2]	69	51
2760[3]	**Somerton Boy (IRE) (71)**	(PCalver) **7-8-10** NDay(5) (in tch: pushed along 4f out: nvr nr to chal)	1	**6**	6/1	54	36
2894[10]	**Alamein (USA) (85)**	(WJHaggas) **4-9-9b** KFallon(9) (lw: bhd: hdwy u.p 4f out: hung rt: nvr nr ldrs)	2½	**7**	4/1[3]	62	44
3456[5]	**Awesome Venture (33)**	(MCChapman) **7-8-3**(7) SCarson(7) (trckd ldrs: rdn over 2f out: sn wknd)	6	**8**	50/1	37	19
	Spanish Serenade	(MJCamacho) **3-8-7** LCharnock(1) (hld up: hdwy over 3f out: sn chsng ldrs: wknd over 1f out)	2	**9**	20/1	36	12
3627[6]	**Oriel Lad (35)**	(DonEnricoIncisa) **4-8-7b** KimTinkler(11) (lw: sn bhd: hrd rdn over 3f out: n.d)	½	**10**	50/1	29	11

3476[10]	**Chalky Dancer (29)** (HJCollingridge) **5-8-7** JQuinn(12) (chsd wnr tl wknd over 2f out)	7	**11**	100/1	15	—
3378[4]	**Taragona (54)** (RHollinshead) **4-8-4** FLynch(8) (bhd: sme hdwy & edgd lft over 2f out: sn wknd)	3	**12**	20/1	6	—
428[11]	**Lomond Lassie (USA) (32)** (TKersey) **4-8-4** NKennedy(15) (b: sn bhd & pushed along: t.o)	15	**13**	100/1	—	—
3211[9]	**Flower Miller** (JHanson) **4-8-13** EJohnson(4) (s.i.s: a bhd: t.o)	30	**14**	100/1	—	—
3089[6]	**Uncle Errol** (GMMoore) **3-8-7** DaleGibson(10) (sn bhd & drvn along: t.o)	13	**15**	100/1	—	—
				(SP 127.8%)	**15 Rn**	

1m 39.2 (1.00) CSF £130.90 TOTE £12.20: £3.60 £3.50 £1.10 (£70.10) Trio £207.10 OWNER Miss Mary Breslin (NEWMARKET) BRED Roseberry Ltd
WEIGHT FOR AGE 3yo-6lb
Alpine Hideaway (IRE) clmd P Young £10,000
3418 Alpine Hideaway (IRE) made every yard of the running and proved most willing in front. He looked a good buy for only £10,000. (7/1)
3477 Special-K ran out of her skin considering she would have been receiving 20lb from the winner in a handicap. (20/1)
2947 High Premium, best in on official figures, was never going. Hanging under pressure, he was closing the gap on the first two at the line. (15/8)
French Ginger, who ran badly on her final three outings last term, has changed stables. This was easily her best ever effort, she would have been receiving 17lb from the winner in a handicap. (100/1)
3542 Billy Bushwacker has not won on the Flat for over two years and is running a good bit below his official rating of 87. (100/30)
2760 Somerton Boy (IRE) was by no means knocked about. Significantly four of his six wins have come at Ayr. (6/1)
2775 Alamein (USA) showed a very poor action going down and, under pressure, all he wanted to do was hang into the running rail. (4/1)

3823 MARK BIRCH CELEBRATION NURSERY H'CAP (2-Y.O) (Class C)

3-30 (3-32) **5f** £5,004.00 (£1,512.00: £736.00: £348.00) Stalls: Low GOING minus 0.29 sec per fur (GF)

				SP	RR	SF
3541[2]	**Folklore (83)** (DRLoder) **2-9-7** LDettori(16) (mde all far side: r.o wl fnl f)	—	**1**	5/1[2]	93+	54
3619[4]	**Far Removed (IRE) (70)** (MrsJRRamsden) **2-8-8** JFortune(1) (lw: hld up: stdy hdwy over 1f out: r.o strly towards fin)	2½	**2**	8/1[3]	72+	33
2758[4]	**Angel Hill (78)** (TDBarron) **2-9-2** JCarroll(14) (chsd wnr far side: kpt on wl fnl f)	½	**3**	25/1	78	39
3480[4]	**Mighty Sure (IRE) (62)** (MWEasterby) **2-8-0b[1]** DaleGibson(11) (lw: disp ld to ½-wy: edgd rt: kpt on wl fnl f)	¾	**4**	14/1	60	21
3480*	**Perfect Peach (79)** (JBerry) **2-9-0**(3) TEDurcan(9) (w ldrs: led ½-wy: nt qckn appr fnl f)	hd	**5**	9/2[1]	77	38
3438[3]	**Daynabee (68)** (NTinkler) **2-8-6** KimTinkler(3) (w ldrs: kpt on same pce fnl 2f)	s.h	**6**	11/1	66	27
3564[3]	**Sandmoor Tartan (61)** (TDEasterby) **2-7-13** DWright(15) (lw: chsd ldrs far side: styd on same pce appr fnl f)	nk	**7**	12/1	58	19
2736[8]	**Brookhouse Lady (IRE) (62)** (RHollinshead) **2-8-0** NCarlisle(4) (dwlt: bhd tl styd on appr fnl f)	s.h	**8**	20/1	58	19
3650[7]	**Leofric (70)** (MJPolglase) **2-8-8b** DHolland(2) (sn outpcd: styd on appr fnl f)	s.h	**9**	8/1[3]	66	27
3265*	**Selkirk Rose (IRE) (78)** (MissLAPerratt) **2-9-2** KDarley(10) (chsd ldrs: drvn along ½-wy: wknd over 1f out)	s.h	**10**	9/1	74	35
2466[2]	**Branston Berry (IRE) (78)** (JLEyre) **2-9-2** MGallagher(8) (disp ld to ½-wy: wknd over 1f out)	1¼	**11**	25/1	70	31
3258[7]	**Miss Eliminator (69)** (MWEasterby) **2-8-7b** TLucas(13) (swvd rt s: chsd ldrs far side: wknd over 1f out)	nk	**12**	33/1	60	21
3776[4]	**Beechwood Quest (IRE) (64)** (BSRothwell) **2-8-2** LCharnock(6) (w ldrs tl lost pl ½-wy)	4	**13**	20/1	42	3
3571[2]	**Jackerin (IRE) (79)** (BSRothwell) **2-9-3** MFenton(12) (swtchd lft s: outpcd & bhd: sme hdwy & edgd rt over 1f out: n.d)	½	**14**	14/1	56	17
3497[5]	**Apple Sauce (62)** (JRArnold) **2-7-11**(3) RFfrench(5) (sn outpcd & bhd)	½	**15**	12/1	37	—
3589[3]	**Lady Moll (78)** (RBoss) **2-9-2** KFallon(7) (sn outpcd: sme hdwy ½-wy: sn wknd)	1¾	**16**	12/1	48	9
				(SP 132.0%)	**16 Rn**	

59.3 secs (1.50) CSF £41.19 CT £910.96 TOTE £6.00: £1.80 £2.80 £5.30 £3.80 (£29.90) Trio £496.00 OWNER Sheikh Mohammed (NEWMARKET) BRED Sheikh Mohammed bin Rashid al Maktoum
3541 Folklore, one of four who chose to go to the far side, was given her head and turned in a decent effort to defy top weight. (5/1)
3619 Far Removed (IRE) really took the eye in the paddock. Given a negative ride, he suddenly burst through inside the last to win hands down on the stands' side but the winner was over on the other wing. Had his rider shown more sense of urgency, there is no doubt that he could have won this. He will be even better suited by six furlongs and is very much one to keep on the right side of. (8/1: 6/1-9/1)
2758 Angel Hill, fresh and well after a forty-one day absence, went to post keenly. She ran right up to her best. (25/1)
3480 Mighty Sure (IRE), in blinkers for the first time, went from the stands' side to the far side, forfeiting a fair bit of ground. (14/1)
3480* Perfect Peach, racing from a 4lb higher mark, looked to have no excuse. (9/2)
3438 Daynabee acquitted herself well in this much stronger company. (11/1)
3564 Sandmoor Tartan, who raced on the far side, found this trip much too sharp. (12/1)

3824 STEVE NESBITT CHALLENGE TROPHY H'CAP (0-90) (3-Y.O+) (Class C)

4-00 (4-00) **1m 2f** £5,377.50 (£1,620.00: £785.00: £367.50) Stalls: High GOING minus 0.47 sec per fur (F)

				SP	RR	SF
3279[2]	**Isitoff (72)** (SCWilliams) **4-8-13** KDarley(8) (sn chsng ldrs: styd on wl appr fnl f: led post)	—	**1**	13/2	82	33
3703[2]	**Sandmoor Chambray (86)** (TDEasterby) **6-9-13** JCarroll(3) (trckd ldrs: led over 4f out tl last strides)	hd	**2**	5/4[1]	96	47
3279[6]	**Princess Danielle (66)** (WRMuir) **5-8-7** MRoberts(4) (hld up: hdwy over 3f out: sn chsng ldrs: styd on same pce appr fnl f)	2	**3**	11/1	73	24
*3584**	**Liquid Gold (IRE) (71)** (WAO'Gorman) **3-8-4** EmmaO'Gorman(6) (sn trckng ldrs: rdn & ev ch over 1f out: one pce)	nk	**4**	9/2[2]	77	20
2830[7]	**Mithali (85)** (BWHills) **4-9-12** RHills(7) (hld up: nt clr run on ins fr over 3f out: kpt on same pce appr fnl f)	1½	**5**	7/1	89	40
3403[7]	**Rebel County (IRE) (75)** (ABailey) **4-9-2v[1]** DBiggs(5) (plld hrd: effrt 3f out: wknd over 1f out)	4	**6**	10/1	72	23
	Roi du Nord (FR) (65) (NBycroft) **5-8-6** DHolland(1) (w ldr: pushed along over 3f out: wknd over 2f out)	12	**7**	66/1	43	—
2594[6]	**Minersville (USA) (82)** (JHMGosden) **3-9-1** LDettori(2) (lw: led tl over 4f out: lost pl over 2f out: eased)	14	**8**	6/1[3]	38	—
				(SP 121.7%)	**8 Rn**	

2m 6.7 (3.20) CSF £14.67 CT £86.14 TOTE £7.50: £1.70 £1.40 £2.50 (£8.20) OWNER Mr James Brown (NEWMARKET) BRED Mrs Celia Miller
WEIGHT FOR AGE 3yo-8lb
3279 Isitoff answered his brilliant rider's every call to get up right on the line. This trip looks the bare minimum for him nowadays. (13/2)
3703 Sandmoor Chambray, racing from a 3lb lower mark, was put up 6lb after his bold effort at York. Setting sail for home once in the straight and soon stepping up the pace, he did nothing wrong but was caught right on the line. (5/4)
3279 Princess Danielle is running really well at present but the Handicapper looks to have her measure for the time being. (11/1)
3584* Liquid Gold (IRE), above himself in the paddock, was racing from the same mark as at Southwell. On turf he almost certainly needs some give underfoot. (9/2)
2172* Mithali, coltish in the paddock, had little room to work against the far rail but his rider showed no sense of urgency. Possibly nine furlongs will turn out to be his best trip. (7/1)

3403 Rebel County (IRE), in a visor for the first time, raced keenly but pulled out nothing under pressure. (10/1)
2594 Minersville (USA), who has been gelded, did not wear a visor this time. After making the running, he quickly ran up the white flag and is one to have grave reservations about. (6/1)

3825 E.B.F. SAPPER MAIDEN STKS (2-Y.O) (Class D)

4-30 (4-30) **6f** £3,582.50 (£1,085.00: £530.00: £252.50) Stalls: Low GOING minus 0.29 sec per fur (GF)

				SP	RR	SF
3489^{2}	**Majaari** (PTWalwyn) **2-9-0** RHills(2) (lw: mde all: shkn up over 1f out: r.o wl)	—	1	$8/11^{1}$	81+	42
3569^{2}	**Requestor (87)** (JGFitzGerald) **2-9-0** KFallon(1) (lw: trckd ldrs: effrt over 2f out: styd on fnl f: no imp)	2	2	$7/2^{2}$	76	37
3602^{3}	**Moving Princess** (MissSEHall) **2-8-9** KDarley(8) (b.off hind: w ldrs: styd on same pce fnl 2f)	4	3	10/1	60	21
1842^{8}	**Gift of Gold** (ICampbell) **2-9-0** AMackay(6) (dwlt: hld up: effrt over 2f out: kpt on one pce)	2	4	20/1	60	21
	Red Sky Charlie (LordHuntingdon) **2-9-0** MRoberts(3) (w'like: unf: scope: sn outpcd & rn green: hdwy & swtchd rt 2f out: hmpd over 1f out: swtchd lft & styd on wl towards fin)	s.h	5	14/1	60+	21
	Konker (WJHaggas) **2-9-0** FLynch(11) (leggy: scope: swvd rt s: sn chsng ldrs: outpcd fnl 2f)	½	6	20/1	58	19
3459^{5}	**Lambs Lane** (TDEasterby) **2-9-0** JFortune(4) (w ldrs tl wknd over 1f out)	1	7	50/1	56	17
3629^{7}	**Madman's Mirage (FR)** (MJohnston) **2-9-0** DeanMcKeown(9) (bit bkwd: in tch: drvn along ½-wy: sn outpcd)	2	8	20/1	50	11
3464^{6}	**Spring Fever** (BWHills) **2-9-0** MHills(10) (lw: chsd ldrs tl lost pl over 1f out: eased)	hd	9	$6/1^{3}$	50	11
3541^{4}	**Stately Favour** (MJCamacho) **2-8-9** LCharnock(5) (b.hind: plld hrd: outpcd ½-wy: sn lost pl)	5	10	25/1	32	—
				(SP 130.3%)	**10 Rn**	

1m 12.7 (2.20) CSF £3.40 TOTE £1.80: £1.10 £1.20 £1.70 (£2.40) Trio £4.30 OWNER Mr Hamdan Al Maktoum (LAMBOURN) BRED Shadwell Estate Company Limited
3489 Majaari, a laid back individual, took this in fine style and can go on to better things. (8/11: 10/11-evens)
3569 Requestor keeps meeting one just too good but surely his turn is just around the corner. (7/2)
3602 Moving Princess, who showed plenty of promise on her debut, showed a very scratchy action going down. She looked to be beaten nearer eight lengths by the winner than the official six. (10/1)
Gift of Gold kept going surprisingly well considering he raced very keenly. (20/1)
Red Sky Charlie, who showed a poor action going down, met all the bad luck going on his debut. Staying on really strongly at the line, he is capable of a good deal better. (14/1: 10/1-20/1)
Konker looks far from the finished article yet. (20/1)
Madman's Mirage (FR) shaped a lot better than he had on his debut and can only improve further as he gains more experience. (20/1)

3826 WEATHERBYS STALLION BOOK H'CAP (0-70) (3-Y.O+) (Class E)

5-00 (5-00) **2m** £2,989.50 (£906.00: £443.00: £211.50) Stalls: Low GOING minus 0.47 sec per fur (F)

				SP	RR	SF
3543^{5}	**Amiarge (44)** (MBrittain) **7-8-2b** GBardwell(11) (lw: sn bhd & pushed along: hdwy 3f out: styd on wl to ld over 1f out: hld on wl)	—	1	10/1	56	33
3543^{2}	**Jamaican Flight (USA) (68)** (MrsSLamyman) **4-9-12** JFortune(10) (lw: led tl over 1f out: kpt on wl)	1¾	2	$6/1^{3}$	78	55
3543^{4}	**Dirab (61)** (TDBarron) **4-9-5** KDarley(9) (lw: trckd ldrs: rdn & kpt on same pce fnl 2f)	hd	3	$100/30^{1}$	71	48
3461^{*}	**Pen Friend (53)** (WJHaggas) **3-7-11** JLowe(7) (lw: chsd ldrs: rdn over 4f out: one pce)	4	4	$7/2^{2}$	59	22
3203^{U}	**Coh Sho No (50)** (SDow) **4-8-8** JFEgan(4) (mid div: hdwy u.p 4f out: one pce)	½	5	9/1	56	33
3283^{10}	**Karaylar (IRE) (38)** (WStorey) **5-7-10** NKennedy(3) (b: sn outpcd & pushed along: sme hdwy over 3f out: n.d: fin lame)	9	6	16/1	35	12
2702^{8}	**Sarasota Storm (52)** (MBell) **5-8-10** MFenton(6) (dwlt: hdwy on outside over 3f out: grad wknd)	2	7	12/1	47	24
3085^{4}	**My Millie (43)** (WStorey) **4-8-1** JFanning(8) (plld hrd: hdwy over 3f out: sn wknd)	3	8	20/1	35	12
	Alzotic (IRE) (40) (JNorton) **4-7-12** JQuinn(1) (sn trckng ldrs: pushed along over 5f out: lost pl over 2f out)	13	9	33/1	19	—
3754^{8}	**Anchorena (45)** (DWBarker) **5-8-3v** TWilliams(2) (sn trckng ldr: drvn along 4f out: sn lost pl)	s.h	10	20/1	24	1
3440^{2}	**Klondike Charger (USA) (70)** (BWHills) **3-9-0v1** MHills(5) (sn trckng ldrs: hung rt & lost pl over 3f out: eased)	16	11	$7/2^{2}$	33	—
				(SP 126.9%)	**11 Rn**	

3m 28.4 (3.40) CSF £66.20 CT £229.74 TOTE £13.60: £3.50 £2.30 £1.50 (£39.80) Trio £41.80 OWNER Miss Debi Woods (WARTHILL) BRED Follies Partnership
LONG HANDICAP Karaylar (IRE) 7-7
WEIGHT FOR AGE 3yo-14lb
3543 Amiarge, who was not suited by the rain-softened ground at Beverley last time, is an out and out stayer. Suited by the strong gallop, his rider certainly earned his fee. (10/1)
3543 Jamaican Flight (USA), on a 3lb higher mark, made a brave attempt to make all the running. (6/1)
3543 Dirab, undeniably well handicapped and with stronger handling, could not force his head in front. (100/30)
3461* Pen Friend, from a 6lb higher mark, looks one-paced and is a potential hurdler. (7/2: 5/2-4/1)
2932 Coh Sho No is painfully one-paced. (9/1)
2166 Sarasota Storm, after a forty-five day absence, looked and ran as if in need of the outing. (12/1)
3440 Klondike Charger (USA), fitted with a visor, showed no enthusiasm at all and his rider gave up with almost half a mile left to run. (7/2: op 6/1)

T/Jkpt: £268,861.50 (0.87 Tckts); £49,228.18 to Carlisle 27/8/97. T/Plpt: £31.90 (1,743.79 Tckts). T/Qdpt: £8.50 (194.63 Tckts) WG

3827a - 3838a : (Irish Racing) - See Computer Raceform

3532a-LEOPARDSTOWN (Dublin, Ireland) (L-H) (Rnd crse Good to yielding, Good in st)

Saturday August 23rd

3839a DEBUTANTE RACE (Listed) (2-Y.O F)

4-00 (4-05) **7f** IR £12,900.00 (IR £3,700.00: IR £1,700.00: IR £500.00) GOING minus 0.16 sec per fur (GF)

				SP	RR	SF
$3672a^{3}$	**Photogenic** (APO'Brien,Ireland) **2-8-9** JAHeffernan (hld up: hdwy 3f out: 5th & chal fr 2f out: led jst ins last: rdn & edgd lft briefly: r.o.)	—	1	10/1	92	30

Form	Horse / details	Dist	Pl	SP	RR	SF
	Viola Royale (IRE) (CCollins,Ireland) **2-8-9** PShanahan (in tch: chsd ldrs st: 6th & rdn 1½f out: r.o. ins last: 2nd cl home)	¾	2	16/1	90	28
3672a[4]	**Tittle Tattle (IRE)** (GMLyons,Ireland) **2-8-9** NGMcCullagh (towards rr: swtchd to outside & hdwy 2f out: rdn & r.o. ins last: nrst fin)	hd	3	33/1	90	28
	Kitza (IRE) (APO'Brien,Ireland) **2-8-9** CRoche (led & disp ld early: cl up: 3rd ½-wy: chal st: led 2f out: jnd: hdd jst ins fnl f)	hd	4	5/2 [1]	90	28
	Susun Kelapa (USA) (APO'Brien,Ireland) **2-8-9** RMBurke (hld up in tch: 4th ½-wy: chal st: 2nd rdn & ev ch over 1½f out: no ex ins last: kpt on)	nk	5	14/1	89	27
3534a[8]	**Attractive Crown (USA)** (KPrendergast,Ireland) **2-8-9** SCraine (plld hrd: hld up in tch: 5th & chsd ldrs st: 4th & no ex 1f out: kpt on)	½	6	7/1	88	26
	Fairy Flight (IRE) (CO'Brien,Ireland) **2-8-12** WJSupple (hld up: 8th ½-wy: rdn over 2f out: 5th & nt rch ldrs 1½f out: kpt on)	2	7	10/1	86	24
	Badila (IRE) (JOxx,Ireland) **2-8-9** PJSmullen (in tch: 6th ½-wy: rdn & chsd ldrs st: no imp 1½f out: one pce)	3½	8	12/1	75	13
3422[2]	**Stop Out** (HMorrison) **2-8-9** CRutter (cl up: led & disp ld after 2½f tl under 3f out: 3rd, rdn & no ex 2f out: btn & wknd over 1½f out)	5½	9	6/1 [3]	63	1
2987a[2]	**Abandonment (IRE)** (JOxx,Ireland) **2-8-9b** JPMurtagh (s.s: towards rr: 9th ½-wy rdn & no imp 2f out: lame)	3	10	9/2 [2]	56	—
	Jovine (USA) (JSBolger,Ireland) **2-8-9** KJManning (prom: 2nd & disp ld: hdd 2f out: sn no ex & wknd: dropped bhd: eased)	15	11	14/1	22	—

(SP 121.6%) **11 Rn**

1m 34.3 (9.30) OWNER Mrs T. Hyde (PILTOWN)
Photogenic, third behind King of Kings and Sharp Play at the Curragh last time, was still a surprise winner here, battling on well after hitting the front a furlong out. (10/1)
Viola Royale (IRE) finished well and can hardly retain maiden status for much longer. (16/1)
Tittle Tattle (IRE), last into the straight, is another for whom a maiden must appear a formality despite this being her seventh run. (33/1)
Kitza (IRE), the best fancied of the three Aidan O'Brien runners, held every chance all the way up the straight but was outbattled in the closing stages. (5/2)
Susun Kelapa (USA), the outsider of O'Brien's trio, flattered when taking over on the outside turning into the straight, but she could not find any extra inside the last half furlong. (14/1)
Badila (IRE) (12/1: op 8/1)
3422 Stop Out went into the lead after two furlongs but was flying distress signals turning into the straight and faded out quickly. (6/1: op 4/1)

3840a - 3841a : (Irish Racing) - See Computer Raceform

3842a BALLYCULLEN RACE (Listed) (3-Y.O+)

5-30 (5-33) **1m 6f** IR £12,900.00 (IR £3,700.00: IR £1,700.00: IR £500.00) GOING minus 0.16 sec per fur (GF)

Form	Horse / details	Dist	Pl	SP	RR	SF
2454a[2]	**Dr Johnson (USA)** (CO'Brien,Ireland) **3-8-9**ow1 CRoche (hld up: 6th ½-wy: hdwy over 3f out: 2nd & chal 2f out: led 1½f out: clr ins last: r.o: eased nr fin)	—	1	8/13 [1]	106+	6
3511a[2]	**Aliya (IRE)** (JOxx,Ireland) **3-8-5** PJSmullen (led to 1½f out: no ex whn hdd: kpt on same pce: no ch w wnr)	3	2	7/1 [3]	99	—
1698a[6]	**Buddy Marvel (IRE)** (JJMcLoughlin,Ireland) **3-8-12** NGMcCullagh (hld up towards rr: 6th & hdwy over 3f out: 4th st: 3rd 1f out: rdn & styd on: no ch w wnr)	1½	3	10/1	104	5
	Generous Lady (DPKelly,Ireland) **3-8-5** WJSmith (cl up: 3rd ½-wy: rdn 5f out: 2nd & chsd ldr bef st: 3rd & no ex u.p 1½f out: kpt on same pce)	2½	4	33/1	94	—
3511a[4]	**Mohaajir (USA)** (JSBolger,Ireland) **6-9-11** KJManning (rn 2nd: rdn & chsd ldr over 3f out: 5th & btn st: eased)	20	5	7/1 [3]	79	—
	Eldorado (IRE) (MJohnston) **3-8-8** DeanMcKeown (dwlt: hld up: wnt 3rd after ½-wy: 4th & rdn 4f out: 6th & n.d bef st: lame)	1½	6	5/1 [2]	72	—
	Gay's Best Boy (USA) (PatrickJosephGoodwin,Ireland) **10-9-6** JAHeffernan (in tch: wkng 5th ½-wy: rdn & drvn bhd: t.o over 3f out)	dist	7	50/1	—	—

(SP 117.6%) **7 Rn**

3m 10.7 (13.70) OWNER M. V. O'Brien
2454a Dr Johnson (USA) didn't have to run up to anything remotely resembling his Irish Derby form to take this, and was a very easy winner. Ridden to improve his position three furlongs out, he was back on the bridle turning into the straight, and came wide in search of the better ground on a deteriorating track. Roche was patting him down the neck throughout the last half-furlong. This was a nice confidence booster for the colt, who has had a couple of setbacks since that Curragh effort. Whether he will go for the Doncaster St Leger seems to be very much in the air. This was not a stamina test but the twelve-furlong Prix Niel may be a stepping stone en route to the Arc. (8/13)
3511a Aliya (IRE) was made to look very one-paced once headed. (7/1)
1195a Buddy Marvel (IRE) stayed on under pressure without ever getting on challenging terms. (10/1)
Generous Lady ran well above herself here, and has gone up 6lb. (33/1)
3511a Mohaajir (USA) (7/1: op 4/1)
Eldorado (IRE) ruptured the tendons in his near-fore and had to be put down. (5/1)

3843a - 3846a : (Irish Racing) - See Computer Raceform

3588-BRIGHTON (L-H) (Good to firm, Last 6 Furlongs Good)
Wednesday August 27th

WEATHER: overcast & damp WIND: slt half against

3847 E.B.F. MEDIAN AUCTION MAIDEN STKS (2-Y.O F) (Class F)

2-20 (2-21) **5f 213y** £2,484.90 (£686.40: £326.70) Stalls: Low GOING: 0.05 sec per fur (G)

Form	Horse / details	Dist	Pl	SP	RR	SF
	Simply Super (CEBrittain) **2-8-11** MRoberts(3) (str: scope: s.i.s: hdwy 5f out: rdn over 2f out: led 1f out: r.o wl)	—	1	2/1 [1]	63	12
3387[7]	**Jus'chillin' (IRE) (52)** (CADwyer) **2-8-11** KFallon(5) (chsd ldrs: rdn over 4f out: swtchd lft 1f out: r.o ins fnl f)	hd	2	10/1 [3]	63	12

3416[3] **Chikapenny (65)** (MrsLStubbs) **2-8-11v** SSanders(6) (a.p: ev ch over 1f out: unable qckn) ....1 **3** 5/2[2] 60 9
3711[6] **Lady Laphroaig (FR)** (WRMuir) **2-8-11** JReid(1) (led 5f: one pce) ....nk **4** 2/1[1] 59 8
3289[6] **Secret Tango** (APJones) **2-8-11** AClark(4) (lw: dwlt: a bhd) ....24 **5** 50/1 — —
2781[12] **Ginnieshope** (SGKnight) **2-8-8**(3) RFfrench(2) (bhd fnl 3f) ....s.h **6** 33/1 — —
(SP 109.2%) **6 Rn**

1m 13.2 (6.00) CSF £19.03 TOTE £1.90: £1.60 £2.30 (£8.80) OWNER Mr D. Sieff (NEWMARKET) BRED David Sieff

IN-FOCUS: **The Official going remained unchanged despite steady rain during the afternoon, although most of the jockeys thought it was riding soft.**

Simply Super, a well-made filly with plenty of strength and substance, was certainly the paddock pick. Soon recovering from a tardy start, she was bustled along in the straight and managed to get on top a furlong out, winning a shade more comfortably than the winning distance suggests in this appalling race. (2/1: 3/1-6/4)

1854 Jus'chillin' (IRE), who has beaten just two horses in three runs since finishing second on her debut, was soon being pushed along. Switched to the outside below the distance, she ran on inside the final furlong but was unable to overhaul the winner. (10/1: op 5/1)

3416 Chikapenny has certainly been exposed as very moderate and, after having every chance over a furlong out, was then tapped for toe. (5/2)

3711 Lady Laphroaig (FR) took the field along but, collared a furlong from home, could then only keep on in her own time. (2/1: 11/8-9/4)

3848 DITCHLING CLAIMING STKS (3-Y.O+) (Class F)

2-50 (2-50) **1m 1f 209y** £2,277.00 (£627.00: £297.00) Stalls: High GOING: 0.05 sec per fur (G)

SP RR SF

3814* **Guesstimation (USA) (57)** (JPearce) **8-9-8** GBardwell(9) (rdn over 3f out: hdwy over 2f out: led ins fnl f: r.o wl) ....— **1** 13/2 69 49
3616[5] **Night Wink (USA) (64)** (GLMoore) **5-9-7**(3) MartinDwyer(5) (lw: chsd ldr: led over 3f out: rdn over 2f out: hdd ins fnl f: r.o wl) ....s.h **2** 100/30[2] 71 51
3561[3] **Pearl Dawn (IRE) (45)** (PCClarke) **7-8-2**(3) RFfrench(1) (a.p: rdn over 2f out: ev ch ins fnl f: unable qckn) 3 **3** 11/1 47 27
3469[6] **Runic Symbol (35)** (MBlanshard) **6-9-2** JQuinn(2) (lw: hld up: rdn over 2f out: wknd fnl f) 3½ **4** 25/1 53 33
3491[2] **Rehaab (49)** (DMorris) **4-8-9v** RCochrane(10) (hld up: n.m.r over 2f out: nt clr run over 1f out: sn wknd) ....¾ **5** 7/4[1] 44 24
76[8] **Areish (IRE) (35)** (JFfitch-Heyes) **4-8-6**(3) AWhelan(6) (a.p: rdn over 2f out: sn wknd) 5 **6** 50/1 36 16
3477[7] **Smarter Charter (64)** (MrsLStubbs) **4-9-12** KFallon(4) (hld up: rdn over 2f out: wknd over 1f out) ....1¾ **7** 4/1[3] 50 30
3557* **Flood's Hot Stuff (40)** (NPLittmoden) **3-8-3v** NAdams(11) (led over 6f: wknd 2f out) 3 **8** 12/1 31 3
3321[4] **Sweet Seventeen (20)** (HJCollingridge) **4-8-0**(5) AimeeCook(8) (bhd fnl 5f) ....24 **9** 33/1 — —
3469[7] **Dancing Lawyer (44)** (KRBurke) **6-9-4** SSanders(3) (s.s: a bhd) ....4 **10** 25/1 — —
3632[12] **Payaso** (RMStronge) **3-9-4** JStack(7) (dwlt: a bhd) ....21 **11** 50/1 — —
(SP 123.4%) **11 Rn**

2m 5.5 (7.20) CSF £26.13 TOTE £8.00: £2.40 £1.70 £2.00 (£12.40) Trio £45.50 OWNER The Exclusive Two Partnership (NEWMARKET) BRED Oak Crest Farm

WEIGHT FOR AGE 3yo-8lb

Rehaab clmd Miss B Sanders £4,000

3814* Guesstimation (USA) goes well in low-grade events and, after being awarded a race at Warwick on Monday, won this without the Stewards' help, coming through to lead inside the final furlong but, with the second rallying, winning by only a whisker. (13/2: 4/1-7/1)

3616 Night Wink (USA) was back in his ideal class and ran a smashing race. Gaining control early in the straight, he was headed inside the final furlong but, refusing to lie down, failed by only a whisker to get back up. Compensation awaits. (100/30)

3561 Pearl Dawn (IRE), a leading light from the off, challenged for the lead below the distance before failing to quicken in the last one hundred yards. She has yet to win beyond a mile. (11/1: 6/1-12/1)

3469 Runic Symbol had given his all in the final furlong and is not easy to win with, having won just one race from forty-six starts. (25/1)

3491 Rehaab found the visor not working this time for, although meeting traffic problems in the straight, when daylight did appear she soon folded up. (7/4)

3477 Smarter Charter (4/1: 3/1-5/1)

3557* Flood's Hot Stuff (12/1: 8/1-14/1)

3849 QUEENS PARK CENTENARY CHALLENGE CUP H'CAP (0-70) (3-Y.O+) (Class E)

3-20 (3-22) **7f 214y** £3,096.25 (£925.00: £442.50: £201.25) Stalls: Low GOING: 0.05 sec per fur (G)

SP RR SF

3299[3] **Muara Bay (41)** (GLewis) **3-7-7**(3) RFfrench(4) (hdwy over 2f out: nt clr run & swtchd rt over 1f out: str run to ld ins fnl f: r.o wl) ....— **1** 13/2[3] 53 30
3496[13] **Clouds Hill (FR) (54)** (RHannon) **4-9-1v** DaneO'Neill(7) (a.p: led over 4f out: hrd rdn & edgd lft over 1f out: hdd ins fnl f: unable qckn) 2½ **2** 10/1 61 44
3470[2] **Samara Song (53)** (IPWilliams) **4-9-0** KFallon(3) (rdn & hdwy over 2f out: chsd ldr over 1f out tl ins fnl f: one pce) ....s.h **3** 100/30[1] 60 43
3276[2] **Rocky Waters (USA) (35)** (MDIUsher) **8-7-3v**(7) ANicholls(1) (b.hind: rdn over 2f out: hdwy over 1f out: r.o) 4 **4** 10/1 34 17
3561[12] **Soviet Lady (IRE) (41)** (JELong) **3-7-10** GBardwell(8) (a.p: chsd ldr over 3f out tl over 1f out: sn wknd) 1¾ **5** 33/1 36 13
3269[9] **Dr Woodstock (43)** (MartynMeade) **3-7-12** JLowe(9) (a.p: hrd rdn over 2f out: wknd over 1f out) 1¼ **6** 16/1 36 13
3478[3] **Mowjood (USA) (68)** (MRStoute) **3-9-9v** JReid(12) (lw: s.s: nt clr run 2f out: nvr nrr) ....1½ **7** 7/2[2] 58 35
3153[18] **Desert Time (66)** (CAHorgan) **7-9-13** PaulEddery(15) (s.s: nvr nrr) ....½ **8** 11/1 55 38
2915[15] **Saxon Bay (51)** (KOCunningham-Brown) **5-8-9**(3) MartinDwyer(6) (hdwy over 2f out: wkng whn nt clr run over 1f out) 2½ **9** 33/1 35 18
3608[3] **Failed To Hit (44)** (NPLittmoden) **4-8-5b** TGMcLaughlin(5) (led over 3f) 1½ **10** 33/1 25 8
3056[4] **King Parrot (IRE) (49)** (LordHuntingdon) **9-8-5**(5) AimeeCook(14) (bhd fnl 2f) ....7 **11** 7/1 16 —
3469[5] **Kildee Lad (60)** (APJones) **7-9-7** AClark(10) (s.s: hdwy over 2f out: wknd over 1f out) ....nk **12** 33/1 26 9
3207[7] **Calamander (IRE) (64)** (WRMuir) **3-9-5** MRoberts(11) (bhd fnl 3f) ....¾ **13** 16/1 29 6
3690[3] **Kilvine (67)** (WJHaggas) **4-10-0** SDrowne(2) (lw: bhd fnl 3f) 7 **14** 9/1 18 1
1506[15] **Sejaal (IRE) (54)** (RAkehurst) **5-9-1** SSanders(13) (prom over 5f) ....11 **15** 12/1 — —
(SP 138.9%) **15 Rn**

1m 36.4 (5.10) CSF £71.80 CT £241.35 TOTE £7.80: £2.40 £2.90 £1.70 (£38.50) Trio £89.30 OWNER Mr P. A. Idris (EPSOM) BRED J. C. Coombes

LONG HANDICAP Soviet Lady (IRE) 7-5 Rocky Waters (USA) 7-9 Muara Bay 7-7

WEIGHT FOR AGE 3yo-6lb

IN-FOCUS: **This very poor contest was restricted to horses who had not won a Flat race this year.**

3299 Muara Bay at last came good. Encountering traffic problems below the distance, he was switched right and produced a useful run to sweep into the lead inside the final furlong. (13/2)

3115 Clouds Hill (FR) moved to the front at the top of the hill but, despite doing little wrong, was unable to contain the winner inside the final furlong. He remains a maiden. (10/1)
3470 Samara Song is becoming extremely frustrating for, although running a string of sound races, seems incapable of getting his head in front. He remains a maiden after twenty-one attempts. (100/30: op 11/2)
3276 Rocky Waters (USA) has deteriorated into a poor handicapper these days but did stay on in the last furlong and a half to finish a moderate fourth. He has not won since 1994. (10/1)
1115 Soviet Lady (IRE), 5lb out of the handicap, moved into second place early in the straight but she was collared for that position over a furlong out and soon had bellows to mend. She is a poor performer. (33/1)
2892 Dr Woodstock was close up until calling it a day approaching the final furlong. (16/1)
1972 Desert Time (11/1: 8/1-12/1)
3056 King Parrot (IRE) (7/1: 5/1-8/1)
3690 Kilvine (9/1: 6/1-10/1)

3850 GORING MEDIAN AUCTION MAIDEN STKS (3-Y.O) (Class F)
3-50 (3-50) **6f 209y** £2,277.00 (£627.00: £297.00) Stalls: Low GOING: 0.05 sec per fur (G)

Form	Horse	Dist	Pos	SP	RR	SF
3572^{3}	**La Doyenne (IRE) (41)** (CBBBooth) **3-8-9** KFallon(1) (hld up: led over 2f out: clr over 1f out: r.o wl)	—	1	6/1	60	23
2879^{7}	**The Green Grey (47)** (WRMuir) **3-8-11v**$^{1(3)}$ MartinDwyer(5) (dwlt: hld up: chsd wnr 2f out: edgd lft over 1f out: unable qckn)	6	2	33/1	51	14
3500^{14}	**Incatime (61)** (AGFoster) **3-9-0** TSprake(6) (w ldr over 4f: wknd wl over 1f out)	11	3	16/1	26	—
3299^{5}	**Las Vistas (55)** (HJCollingridge) **3-8-9** MRimmer(2) (led over 4f: wknd wl over 1f out)	3	4	$5/2^{3}$	14	—
	Passion (TGMills) **3-8-9** JReid(3) (bhd fnl 4f)	nk	5	$6/4^{1}$	13	—
	Silver Marble (IRE) (RHannon) **3-8-9** DaneO'Neill(4) (unf: scope: s.s: a bhd: virtually p.u fnl 5f: t.o)	dist	6	$9/4^{2}$	—	—
				(SP 122.4%)	**6 Rn**	

1m 26.0 (6.00) CSF £127.21 TOTE £3.90: £1.60 £4.40 (£24.70) OWNER Mrs J. B. Robinson (FLAXTON) BRED Mrs P. Grubb
3572 La Doyenne (IRE) appeared to enjoy the rain-softened ground and, leading over a quarter of a mile from home, was rousted along to forge clear from below the distance to win a desperate race. (6/1: 5/1-8/1)
The Green Grey has shown himself to be a very poor performer on the Flat and in two runs over hurdles but, nevertheless, took second place a quarter of a mile out, if unable to get on terms with the winner. (33/1)
Incatime is a very poor performer and, even in this dire race, he was still beaten out of sight, if picking up third prize. (16/1)
3299 Las Vistas, who looked ill at ease here earlier in the season, took the field along but she was collared over two furlongs from home and was soon hung out to dry. (5/2)
Passion (6/4: op evens)

3851 ARTHUR BORROW KING MEMORIAL H'CAP (0-70) (3-Y.O) (Class E)
4-20 (4-20) **5f 213y** £3,018.25 (£901.00: £430.50: £195.25) Stalls: Low GOING: 0.05 sec per fur (G)

Form	Horse	Dist	Pos	SP	RR	SF
3637^{8}	**Mystical (62)** (MrsLStubbs) **3-9-2v** KFallon(7) (lw: a.p: rdn over 2f out: edgd lft & led ins fnl f: drvn out)	—	1	5/1	70	22
3558^{2}	**Hever Golf Mover (67)** (TJNaughton) **3-9-7** SSanders(3) (hld up: rdn over 2f out: led over 1f out tl ins fnl f: unable qckn)	¾	2	$4/1^{3}$	73	25
3500^{4}	**Suite Factors (55)** (KRBurke) **3-8-6**$^{(3)}$ DSweeney(9) (n.m.r 2f out: hdwy over 1f out: r.o wl ins fnl f)	¾	3	8/1	59	11
3558^{4}	**Havago (56)** (RHannon) **3-8-10** DaneO'Neill(8) (lw: hdwy 3f out: rdn over 1f out: one pce)	1	4	$7/2^{2}$	57	9
3417^{5}	**Gold Edge (57)** (MRChannon) **3-8-11** PaulEddery(5) (lw: a.p: led over 2f out tl over 1f out: wknd ins fnl f)	1¼	5	$3/1^{1}$	55	7
3249^{5}	**Municipal Girl (IRE) (45)** (BPalling) **3-7-10**$^{(3)}$ RFfrench(2) (a.p: hmpd over 1f out: one pce)	s.h	6	10/1	43	—
3614^{7}	**Anokato (63)** (KTIvory) **3-9-0b**$^{(3)}$ MartinDwyer(6) (hld up: rdn over 2f out: wkng whn hmpd over 1f out)	5	7	14/1	47	—
3266^{3}	**Ginny Wossername (42)** (MartynMeade) **3-7-10b** JLowe(4) (a bhd)	9	8	33/1	2	—
3642^{11}	**Goodbye Gatemen (IRE) (60)** (BAPearce) **3-9-0** GBardwell(1) (led: styd far side st: hdd over 2f out: wknd wl over 1f out)	3	9	20/1	12	—
				(SP 118.5%)	**9 Rn**	

1m 12.8 (5.60) CSF £23.72 CT £146.41 TOTE £6.20: £1.90 £1.70 £3.40 (£11.90) Trio £40.90 OWNER Consultco Ltd (COLLINGBOURNE DUCIS) BRED Stud-On-The-Chart
LONG HANDICAP Ginny Wossername 7-1
3327 Mystical, whose only previous victory came on an easy surface, appreciated this rain-softened ground and, under a strong ride from Fallon, managed to get to the front inside the final furlong. (5/1)
3558 Hever Golf Mover, 9lb higher than when last successful, gained a narrow advantage below the distance but was unable to hold off the winner inside the final furlong. (4/1)
3500 Suite Factors knows how to get into the frame but has great trouble getting his head in front and, although running on strongly from below the distance, one win from twenty-nine starts says it all. (8/1: op 5/1)
3558 Havago has dropped 15lb since the beginning of the season after some poor efforts. Although he did not have a great deal of room over a furlong out, it made little difference as he could only plod on at one pace. (7/2)
3417 Gold Edge gained control over a quarter of a mile from home but, headed below the distance, soon had nothing more to offer. (3/1)
3249 Municipal Girl (IRE) was returning to a more suitable trip but she is probably best on a sound surface and this rain-softened ground was not a help. Neither was the interference she encountered over a furlong out, having been travelling well and, from that point, she could only struggle on in her own time. (10/1: 5/1-12/1)
3194 Anokato (14/1: op 7/1)

3852 HANNINGTONS OF BRIGHTON H'CAP (0-80) (3-Y.O+) (Class D)
4-50 (4-51) **5f 59y** £3,581.90 (£1,068.20: £509.60: £230.30) Stalls: Low GOING: 0.05 sec per fur (G)

Form	Horse	Dist	Pos	SP	RR	SF
3600^{4}	**Ivory's Grab Hire (62)** (KTIvory) **4-9-0b**$^{(3)}$ MartinDwyer(10) (lw: hdwy over 2f out: led wl over 1f out: drvn out)	—	1	$4/1^{2}$	76	42
*3398**	**Village Native (FR) (52)** (KOCunningham-Brown) **4-8-4b**$^{(3)}$ RFfrench(2) (a.p: chsd wnr wl over 1f out: ev ch ins fnl f: r.o)	nk	2	$5/1^{3}$	65	31
3642^{7}	**Dande Flyer (59)** (DWPArbuthnot) **4-9-0v** KFallon(1) (s.s: hrd rdn & hdwy over 1f out: unable qckn)	5	3	$3/1^{1}$	57	23
3436^{5}	**Justinianus (IRE) (46)** (JJBridger) **5-8-1** GBardwell(4) (lw: a.p: rdn over 3f out: one pce)	½	4	8/1	42	8
3500^{3}	**Bright Paragon (IRE) (42)** (KTIvory) **8-7-6**$^{(5)ow1}$ RMullen(9) (b: a.p: ev ch wl over 1f out: sn wknd)	¾	5	$4/1^{2}$	36	1
3296^{6}	**Song Mist (IRE) (69)** (PFICole) **3-9-8b** JReid(7) (prom over 3f)	2	6	6/1	57	21
3685^{7}	**Chaluz (47)** (KRBurke) **3-7-7**$^{(7)}$ PDoe(8) (lw: rdn over 2f out: nvr nr to chal)	¾	7	33/1	33	—
3816^{10}	**Rowlandsons Stud (IRE) (43)** (KCComerford) **4-7-5b**$^{1(7)}$ ANicholls(6) (a bhd)	¾	8	16/1	27	—

3292[9] **Times of Times (IRE) (60)** (GLMoore) **4-9-1** CandyMorris(11) (led over 3f).....2½ **9** 16/1 36 2
(SP 121.8%) **9 Rn**

63.8 secs (3.80) CSF £23.56 CT £63.95 TOTE £4.60: £1.60 £2.40 £1.50 (£11.30) Trio £11.80 OWNER Mr Dean Ivory (RADLETT) BRED Japan Bloodstock Ltd

WEIGHT FOR AGE 3yo-2lb

3600 Ivory's Grab Hire is at his best on a fast surface and, although this rain-softened ground was not really ideal for him, he gained control early in the final quarter-mile and responded to pressure to gain his fifth victory of the year. He has done all his winning here and at Lingfield. (4/1: op 5/2)

3398* Village Native (FR), a shock winner last time out, ran another sound race. Delivering his challenge down the centre of the course from below the distance, he kept on, if unable to poke his head in front. (5/1: op 3/1)

3500 Dande Flyer moved up under pressure below the distance but never looked like reeling in the front two in the final furlong. He has not won for nearly two years. (3/1)

3436 Justinianus (IRE) once again demonstrated that he lacks any sort of acceleration and was made to look woefully one-paced in the straight. (8/1)

3500 Bright Paragon (IRE), never far away, had shot his bolt approaching the final furlong. (4/1)

2705 Song Mist (IRE) was returning to five furlongs for the first time since her two-year-old debut but had run out of steam over a furlong out. She is out of form at present. (6/1)

T/Plpt: £157.00 (117 Tckts). T/Qdpt: £11.00 (101.39 Tckts) AK

3264-CARLISLE (R-H) (Firm, Good to firm patches)
Wednesday August 27th

WEATHER: overcast WIND: slt half against

3853 BODDINGTONS, CREAM OF MANCHESTER CLAIMING STKS (3-Y.O+) (Class F)
2-10 (2-11) **1m 4f** £2,430.00 (£680.00: £330.00) Stalls: High GOING minus 0.40 sec per fur (F)

			SP	RR	SF
3429[2]	**Durgams First (IRE) (49)** (MrsMReveley) **5-9-4** ACulhane(7) (lw: trckd ldrs: smooth hdwy over 1f out: shkn up to ld wl ins fnl f).....—	**1**	7/4 1	58	3
3540[10]	**Forzair (53)** (JJO'Neill) **5-9-4** JCarroll(3) (led tl hdd wl ins fnl f: kpt on).....1	**2**	9/4 2	57	2
3477[8]	**Golden Thunderbolt (FR) (65)** (NTinkler) **4-9-7**(5) CLowther(2) (lw: hld up & bhd: hdwy to jn ldr 4f out: sn rdn: one pce appr fnl f).....2½	**3**	9/2 3	61	6
3627[4]	**Monis (IRE) (30)** (RonaldThompson) **6-8-9**(3) DarrenMoffatt(6) (hld up: effrt 3f out: rdn & no imp).....½	**4**	8/1	47	—
	Charlie Chang (IRE) (DWBarker) **4-9-12** JSupple(5) (plld hrd: trckd ldrs: effrt over 1f out: fnd nil).....5	**5**	8/1	54	—
3601[9]	**La Perdoma (26)** (MissMKMilligan) **3-7-12**(3) PFessey(1) (unruly bef s: ref to s & uns rdr in stalls).....	**U**	25/1	—	—

(SP 111.4%) **6 Rn**

2m 39.3 (10.30) CSF £5.30 TOTE £1.90: £1.10 £1.80 (£2.60) OWNER The Mary Reveley Racing Club (SALTBURN) BRED William McGladdery in Ireland

WEIGHT FOR AGE 3yo-10lb

3429 Durgams First (IRE) has now won two races this year, both on this track, and both were slowly-run events. (7/4)

3284* Forzair, whose action suggests that easier ground would help, nevertheless ran well here but did have the run of the race out in front, only to be out-sprinted. (9/4)

3286 Golden Thunderbolt (FR), without the blinkers this time, looked particularly well but this slowly-run event was never going to suit him. (9/2)

3627 Monis (IRE) has yet to show he gets this trip and this muddling event was certainly not conclusive. (8/1)

Charlie Chang (IRE) is an edgy sort who spent most of the trip pulling for his head but, once off the bit, he found absolutely nothing. (8/1: 6/1-10/1)

3854 STELLA ARTOIS H'CAP (0-70) (3-Y.O+ F & M) (Class E)
2-40 (2-42) **7f 214y** £2,918.00 (£884.00: £432.00: £206.00) Stalls: High GOING minus 0.40 sec per fur (F)

			SP	RR	SF
360[8]	**Raindeer Quest (43)** (JLEyre) **5-8-5** RLappin(8) (in tch: hdwy to ld ins fnl f: r.o u.p).....—	**1**	12/1	54	36
3573[4]	**May Queen Megan (43)** (MrsALMKing) **4-8-5** TWilliams(9) (lw: trckd ldrs: led 2½f out tl ins fnl f: no ex).....2½	**2**	9/2 2	49	31
3583[9]	**Miss Riviera Rose (49)** (GWragg) **3-8-5** KDarley(7) (s.i.s: hdwy 2f out: kpt on: nvr able to chal).....1¼	**3**	8/1	53	29
3696[6]	**Falls O'Moness (IRE) (54)** (KRBurke) **3-8-10** JFEgan(3) (swtg: bhd: hmpd after 1f: hdwy 2f out: sn chsng ldrs: no imp fnl f).....1	**4**	12/1	56	32
3487[6]	**Termon (34)** (MissLAPerratt) **4-7-3**(7) JMcAuley(1) (swtg: s.i.s: bhd tl styd on fnl 2f).....1	**5**	12/1	34	16
3572[2]	**Bollero (IRE) (55)** (JBerry) **3-8-8**(3) PFessey(4) (led after 1f tl 2½f out: sn btn).....2	**6**	9/2 2	50	26
3336[4]	**Danehill Princess (IRE) (45)** (RHollinshead) **3-8-1** LCharnock(6) (prom: rdn over 2f out: hung rt over 1f out: wknd).....3	**7**	6/1 3	34	10
3465[16]	**Tael of Silver (47)** (ABailey) **5-8-9v** ACulhane(2) (lw: hld up: hdwy 4f out: rdn & btn over 2f out).....7	**8**	3/1 1	22	4
3488[3]	**Bent Raiwand (USA) (34)** (DonEnricoIncisa) **4-7-10** KimTinkler(5) (b: lw: led 1f: cl up tl rdn & wknd over 2f out).....3½	**9**	14/1	2	—

(SP 116.5%) **9 Rn**

1m 39.0 (2.00) CSF £59.91 CT £338.66 TOTE £13.50: £2.20 £1.70 £1.90 (£30.70) Trio £25.90 OWNER Whitestonecliffe Racing Partnership (HAMBLETON) BRED Stetchworth Park Stud Ltd

LONG HANDICAP Termon 7-6 Bent Raiwand (USA) 7-3

WEIGHT FOR AGE 3yo-6lb

260 Raindeer Quest, having her first run this turf season, was turned out looking fit but did get a shade warm. She really stays further than this and that proved decisive. (12/1)

3573 May Queen Megan again ran well enough at this trip but just lacked a finishing kick. She is, nevertheless, in good form. (9/2)

3320 Miss Riviera Rose has the ability but never got going here until the race was virtually over. (8/1)

3696 Falls O'Moness (IRE) has yet to win a race and, always struggling to improve here, she was never doing enough. (12/1)

2385 Termon has ability but only decided to show any here when it was all too late. (12/1)

3572 Bollero (IRE) has yet to win a handicap. (9/2)

3336 Danehill Princess (IRE) (6/1: 4/1-7/1)

3855 LABATT ICE INVITATION LIMITED STKS (0-65) (3-Y.O+) (Class F)
3-10 (3-14) **6f 206y** £2,570.00 (£720.00: £350.00) Stalls: High GOING minus 0.40 sec per fur (F)

Form	Horse / details	Dist	Pos	SP	RR	SF
3759^{3}	**Needle Match (56)** (JJO'Neill) **4-8-12**$^{(5)}$ CLowther(10) (bhd: hdwy 2f out: r.o wl fnl f to ld nr fin)	—	1	5/1^{3}	72	58
3591^{4}	**Kalimat (64)** (WJarvis) **3-8-6** JFortune(3) (cl up: led 2f out: hrd drvn fnl f: jst ct)	nk	2	7/2^{1}	65	46
3621^{9}	**Trojan Hero (SAF) (65)** (MrsMReveley) **6-9-3** ACulhane(8) (a in tch: hdwy over 2f out: sn chsng ldrs: one pce fnl f)	3½	3	7/1	63	49
3119^{8}	**Midyan Queen (62)** (RHollinshead) **3-8-9** FLynch(1) (bhd: hdwy u.p over 2f out: nvr rchd ldrs)	nk	4	9/1	60	41
2756*	**Mystique Air (IRE) (64)** (EWeymes) **3-8-4**$^{(5)}$ PRoberts(9) (led tl hdd 2f out: grad wknd)	¾	5	9/2^{2}	58	39
3759^{12}	**Allinson's Mate (IRE) (65)** (TDBarron) **9-8-12b**$^{(5)}$ KimberleyHart(6) (lw: mid div: hdwy 3f out: rdn & btn appr fnl f)	1½	6	8/1	57	43
3291^{4}	**Peppers (IRE) (65)** (KRBurke) **4-8-11v^{1}** KDarley(5) (lw: s.i.s: effrt ½-wy: rdn & btn wl over 1f out)	1¾	7	11/2	47	33
3642^{8}	**Shashi (IRE) (50)** (PatMitchell) **5-9-0** PBloomfield(2) (prom tl wknd fnl 2f)	1¾	8	14/1	46	32
3642^{13}	**Waders Dream (IRE) (39)** (PatMitchell) **8-8-9v**$^{(5)}$ AmandaSanders(11) (bhd: hdwy over 3f out: wkng whn hmpd wl over 1f out)	nk	9	100/1	46	32
3612^{6}	**Meadow Blue (30)** (MissLCSiddall) **4-8-4**$^{(7)}$ TSiddall(4) (chsd ldrs tl wknd over 2f out)	11	10	200/1	17	3
	Skyers Tryer (63) (RonaldThompson) **3-8-3**$^{(3)}$ DarrenMoffatt(7) (cl up tl wknd fnl 2f)	1	11	33/1	15	—
				(SP 117.2%)	**11 Rn**	

1m 26.6 (0.90) CSF £20.66 TOTE £4.60: £1.40 £1.80 £3.30 (£9.90) Trio £29.40 OWNER Clayton Bigley Partnership Ltd (PENRITH) BRED Tarworth Bloodstock Investments Ltd
WEIGHT FOR AGE 3yo-5lb
STEWARDS' ENQUIRY Lowther susp. 5/9/97 (careless riding)
3759 Needle Match needs things to go just right and, well-handled, they did exactly that here. (5/1)
3591 Kalimat, without the blinkers this time, looked to have pinched it when kicking on two furlongs out but, despite some serious help from the saddle, she was again caught. (7/2)
3621 Trojan Hero (SAF) ran reasonably and gave the impression that he is slowly and steadily coming back to form. (7/1: 5/1-8/1)
2705* Midyan Queen needs things to go just right and tried to come from behind, but had slight traffic problems and never got in a blow. (9/1)
2756* Mystique Air (IRE), after six weeks off, again tried to make all but was out-battled in the last couple of furlongs. (9/2)
3420 Allinson's Mate (IRE) ran a fair race but his normal finishing kick was never there this time. (8/1: op 5/1)
3291 Peppers (IRE) had a visor on for the first time and looked a picture, but she wanted nothing to do with it when ridden and shied away from the winner at one stage, getting that rival's rider into trouble. (11/2)

3856 MURPHYS IRISH STOUT H'CAP (0-80) (3-Y.O+) (Class D)
3-40 (3-47) **5f** £3,647.50 (£1,105.00: £540.00: £257.50) Stalls: High GOING minus 0.40 sec per fur (F)

Form	Horse / details	Dist	Pos	SP	RR	SF
3649^{22}	**Double Oscar (IRE) (75)** (DNicholls) **4-9-9b** AlexGreaves(16) (s.i.s: bhd tl gd hdwy over 1f out: led ins fnl f: r.o wl)	—	1	7/1^{3}	86	67
3765^{4}	**Tiler (IRE) (80)** (MJohnston) **5-10-0** DHolland(11) (dwlt: gd hdwy 2f out: ev ch ins fnl f: kpt on)	1½	2	2/1^{1}	86	67
3481^{5}	**Saint Express (77)** (MrsMReveley) **7-9-11** ACulhane(12) (sn pushed along: hdwy 2f out: kpt on u.p fnl f: nrst fin)	1½	3	7/1^{3}	78	59
3107^{5}	**Manolo (FR) (63)** (JBerry) **4-8-6b**$^{(5)}$ CLowther(9) (lw: chsd ldr: led ins fnl f: sn hdd & no ex)	¾	4	9/1	62	43
3481^{14}	**Ramsey Hope (60)** (CWFairhurst) **4-8-8v** JFortune(17) (outpcd tl r.o fnl f)	nk	5	20/1	58	39
3625^{7}	**Just Dissident (IRE) (60)** (RMWhitaker) **5-8-8** DeanMcKeown(2) (b: racd wd: led & sn clr: hdd & no ex ins fnl f)	s.h	6	16/1	58	39
3334^{13}	**Shadow Jury (60)** (DWChapman) **7-8-8b** LCharnock(14) (prom: ch over 1f out: nt qckn)	¾	7	20/1	56	37
3761^{13}	**Dominelle (48)** (TDEasterby) **5-7-10** DWright(15) (lw: chsd ldrs: ev ch 1f out: nt qckn)	½	8	13/2^{2}	42	23
3761^{8}	**Middle East (60)** (TDBarron) **4-8-8** KDarley(5) (nvr wnt pce)	hd	9	16/1	54	35
3761^{7}	**U-No-Harry (IRE) (60)** (RHollinshead) **4-8-8** FLynch(3) (b.nr fore: sn pushed along: nvr trbld ldrs)	s.h	10	20/1	53	34
3394^{7}	**Gwespyr (52)** (DonEnricoIncisa) **4-8-0** KimTinkler(7) (s.i.s: nvr trbld ldrs)	s.h	11	66/1	45	26
3761^{4}	**Suedoro (48)** (JSGoldie) **7-7-7**$^{(3)}$ PFessey(6) (lw: chsd ldrs over 3f)	nk	12	25/1	40	21
3484^{11}	**Pallium (IRE) (49)** (DANolan) **9-7-4b**$^{(7)ow1}$ NPollard(1) (in tch tl rdn & btn 2f out)	2	13	20/1	35	15
2934^{10}	**Thick as Thieves (50)** (RonaldThompson) **5-7-9**$^{(3)ow2}$ DarrenMoffatt(4) (sn drvn along: n.d)	1½	14	100/1	31	10
3761^{W}	**My Abbey (51)** (ABailey) **8-7-13**^{ow2} AMackay(18) (chsd ldrs tl wknd qckly over 1f out)	1¾	15	8/1	27	6
3565^{12}	**Kentucky Dreams (48)** (MrsAMNaughton) **7-7-3**$^{(7)}$ PBradley(13) (sn outpcd)	nk	16	300/1	23	4
	Another Episode (IRE) (50) (MissLAPerratt) **8-7-12** NKennedy(8) (spd over 3f: eased whn btn)	6	17	100/1	5	—
3625^{9}	***Young Ben (IRE) (49)*** (JSWainwright) **5-7-11b**^{ow1} TWilliams(10) (b.hind: lw: Withdrawn not under Starter's orders: veterinary advice at s)		W	20/1	—	—
				(SP 136.0%)	**17 Rn**	

60.6 secs (0.40) CSF £18.85 CT £102.83 TOTE £9.50: £2.20 £1.10 £2.10 £2.70 (£10.40) Trio £13.10 OWNER Trilby Racing (THIRSK) BRED Tasia Limited
LONG HANDICAP Thick as Thieves 6-13 Suedoro 7-2 Kentucky Dreams 6-3 Young Ben (IRE) 7-6
3481 Double Oscar (IRE) did what appeared impossible here and came from last to first to win going away. (7/1)
3765 Tiler (IRE), who likes to race up with the pace, was again up to his usual tricks at the start and reared up as the stalls opened. Although he did get into contention, he would no doubt have won had he jumped off on terms. Over longer trips he can get away with this more easily. (2/1: op 7/2)
3481 Saint Express last won a race two seasons ago off a 17lb higher mark and showed here he still has the ability if he can be persuaded. (7/1: 5/1-15/2)
3107 Manolo (FR) is on a reasonable mark and had his chances, but having his first run for a month probably made the difference. (9/1)
1865* Ramsey Hope picked up in good style at the end to show his best form for a while. (20/1)
3625 Just Dissident (IRE) showed blistering speed and, from a better draw, would have taken some catching. (16/1)
3077 Shadow Jury is slipping back down the handicap and ran a fair race. (20/1)
2480 My Abbey (8/1: 5/1-9/1)

3857 E.B.F. 'ROLLING ROCK' MEDIAN AUCTION MAIDEN STKS (2-Y.O) (Class F)
4-10 (4-12) **5f** £2,654.00 (£744.00: £362.00) Stalls: High GOING minus 0.40 sec per fur (F)

Form	Horse / details	Dist	Pos	SP	RR	SF
3602^{4}	**Miss Puci (72)** (JBerry) **2-8-9** KDarley(7) (mde most: all out)	—	1	9/4^{2}	62	26
	Love Again (MBell) **2-8-9** MFenton(4) (neat: s.i.s: nt clr run & swtchd over 1f out: r.o towards fin)	s.h	2	9/2^{3}	62	26

				SP	RR	SF
	Snowballs (MissLAPerratt) **2-9-0** JCarroll(6) (w'like: str: prom tl rn green & lost pl ½-wy: styd on again fnl f)	3½	**3**	8/1	56+	20
	Another Wyn-Bank (JGFitzGerald) **2-8-9** GDuffield(8) (w'like: prom: hdwy u.p over 1f out: sn btn)	1	**4**	25/1	47	11
	Take A Risk (MJohnston) **2-8-9** DHolland(2) (w'like: b.hind: sn w wnr: rdn & btn appr fnl f)	¾	**5**	Evens[1]	45+	9
2739[9]	**Classic Silver (IRE)** (WWHaigh) **2-9-0** ACulhane(1) (prom tl outpcd fnl 2f)	4	**6**	25/1	37	1
3136[7]	**Saxon Victory (USA)** (WJHaggas) **2-8-7**(7) JoHunnam(3) (spd 3f: sn rdn & btn)	¾	**7**	14/1	35	—

(SP 124.4%) **7 Rn**

62.3 secs (2.10) CSF £13.22 TOTE £3.50: £1.60 £5.80 (£7.10) OWNER Mr Jason Puckey (COCKERHAM) BRED Bearstone Stud

3602 Miss Puci made full use of her experience and, responding to some strong driving, just lasted out. (9/4: op 7/2)

Love Again failed to impress with her action but she should have won this but for inexperience and traffic problems. (9/2: 11/4-5/1)

Snowballs, a useful-looking type, probably needed this and was certainly green halfway through the race but did show good signs late on. (8/1)

Another Wyn-Bank ran a fair race and should improve a little for the experience. (25/1)

Take A Risk looked very fit and showed speed aplenty but was found out approaching the final furlong and, like the majority of Risk Mes, may well need easier ground. (Evens)

Saxon Victory (USA) (14/1: op 8/1)

3858 CELLAR SERVICE INVITATION MAIDEN H'CAP (0-60) (3-Y.O+) (Class F)

4-40 (4-40) **2m 1f 52y** £2,612.00 (£732.00: £356.00) Stalls: High GOING minus 0.40 sec per fur (F)

				SP	RR	SF
2940[8]	**Stoned Imaculate (IRE) (49)** (FMurphy) **3-8-4** JFanning(1) (chsd ldrs: led 6f out: drvn clr 3f out: eased towards fin)	—	**1**	7/2[2]	62+	4
3567[4]	**Penny Peppermint (27)** (REBarr) **5-7-7**(3) PFessey(7) (s.s: outpcd & bhd tl hdwy over 2f out: styd on: no ch w wnr)	5	**2**	7/1	35	—
3643[2]	**Perlethorpe (51)** (MBell) **3-8-6** MFenton(4) (lw: chsd ldrs: drvn along appr st: styd on one pce & no imp)	½	**3**	3/1[1]	59	1
2940[5]	**Murchan Tyne (IRE) (55)** (EJAlston) **4-9-10** JFEgan(5) (bhd: hdwy ½-wy: wnt 2nd over 4f out: sn rdn & no imp)	1¼	**4**	5/1[3]	62	18
3400[2]	**Straffan Gold (USA) (50)** (GWragg) **3-8-5** KDarley(3) (chsd ldrs: drvn along 4f out: sn btn)	6	**5**	3/1[1]	51	—
3284[3]	**Ocean Breeze (42)** (JSWainwright) **3-7-11**vow1 TWilliams(9) (chsd ldrs tl wknd over 3f out)	5	**6**	16/1	39	—
3486[11]	**Megan Carew (43)** (DMoffatt) **3-7-9**(3)ow2 DarrenMoffatt(8) (swtg: prom tl lost pl & hmpd ½-wy: n.d after)	1¾	**7**	66/1	38	—
2825[14]	**Well Armed (IRE) (55)** (JJO'Neill) **6-9-10b** JCarroll(2) (b: led tl hdd 6f out: wknd qckly 3f out)	28	**8**	10/1	24	—
3429[3]	**Maddie (43)** (WWHaigh) **5-8-12** ACulhane(6) (a bhd: t.o fnl 4f)	25	**9**	20/1	—	—

(SP 122.6%) **9 Rn**

3m 49.0 (12.00) CSF £27.59 CT £76.89 TOTE £4.90: £2.30 £2.00 £1.60 (£18.50) Trio £18.20 OWNER Mr M. Rowsell (MIDDLEHAM) BRED Mrs Ann Fortune

LONG HANDICAP Megan Carew 7-9 Penny Peppermint 7-9 Ocean Breeze 7-4

WEIGHT FOR AGE 3yo-14lb

2131 Stoned Imaculate (IRE), a winner over hurdles the previous weekend, showed she has got things right by winning this moderate event really well. (7/2)

3567 Penny Peppermint stays but in her own time and needed another circuit to get anywhere near the winner. (7/1)

3643 Perlethorpe has had her chances and again failed to find anything like enough when ridden. (3/1)

2940 Murchan Tyne (IRE) ran her best race to date here but she failed to pull out any extra when ridden in the straight and would probably do better when put over hurdles. (5/1)

3400 Straffan Gold (USA) looked rather moderate here but has the build to make a hurdler. (3/1)

T/Jkpt: £54,662.60 (0.86 Tckts); £10,778.55 to Lingfield 28/8/97. T/Plpt: £18.50 (1,380.27 Tckts). T/Qdpt: £6.00 (163.96 Tckts) AA

3613-LINGFIELD (L-H) (Turf Good to soft, AWT Standard)
Thursday August 28th

WEATHER: unsettled WIND: slt half bhd

3859 LABATT ICE CLAIMING STKS (2-Y.O) (Class F)

2-00 (2-04) **6f** £2,277.00 (£627.00: £297.00) Stalls: High GOING: 0.07 sec per fur (G)

				SP	RR	SF
3471[5]	**Generous Embrace** (DRCElsworth) **2-9-0** JReid(15) (a.p: rdn over 1f out: led ins fnl f: r.o wl)	—	**1**	7/4[1]	74	32
3314[2]	**Just Another Time (68)** (JBerry) **2-8-3**(5) CLowther(7) (b: lw: a.p: rdn over 2f out: led over 1f out tl ins fnl f: r.o)	nk	**2**	4/1[2]	67	25
3468[7]	**Petaling (IRE) (60)** (BJMeehan) **2-8-2b1** GDuffield(1) (racd far side: led over 4f: unable qckn)	4	**3**	8/1	51	9
3589[7]	**Truth Teller (83)** (RHannon) **2-8-7**(7) PDobbs(8) (lw: a.p: rdn over 2f out: one pce)	nk	**4**	16/1	62	20
3692[6]	**Dande Times (58)** (KTIvory) **2-8-2**(3) MartinDwyer(10) (no hdwy fnl 2f)	5	**5**	20/1	39	—
3711[11]	**Mystagogue** (RHannon) **2-8-11** DaneO'Neill(9) (lw: nvr nr to chal)	s.h	**6**	14/1	45	3
3541[7]	**Ghorapani (IRE)** (MrsNMacauley) **2-7-13v**(7) JoHunnam(12) (a mid div)	¾	**7**	40/1	38	—
3411[9]	**Teepee (IRE)** (WJarvis) **2-8-8** LDettori(4) (racd far side: outpcd)	nk	**8**	15/2[3]	40	—
3586[5]	**Super Geil** (CADwyer) **2-7-10**(3) RFfrench(5) (racd far side: bhd fnl 2f)	s.h	**9**	14/1	30	—
3556[6]	**Corsecan (60)** (SDow) **2-8-5** MRoberts(6) (lw: racd far side: prom over 4f)	s.h	**10**	14/1	36	—
3076[4]	**Catfoot Lane** (WGMTurner) **2-8-1**(3) DSweeney(3) (swtg: racd far side: bhd fnl 2f)	1¼	**11**	25/1	32	—
3707[14]	**Safari Sam (IRE)** (MHTompkins) **2-8-11** DBiggs(13) (a bhd)	1¾	**12**	14/1	34	—
	Nuvellino (SGKnight) **2-8-11** SDrowne(11) (leggy: s.s: a bhd)	½	**13**	40/1	33	—
3686[17]	**Sharp Steel** (GLMoore) **2-8-9** CandyMorris(2) (swtg: racd far side: a bhd)	2	**14**	40/1	26	—

(SP 127.7%) **14 Rn**

1m 13.99 (4.99) CSF £7.35 TOTE £2.60: £1.30 £1.10 £2.80 (£4.00) Trio £17.30 OWNER Blandford Thoroughbreds (WHITCOMBE) BRED Glebe Stud and Whitsbury Manor Stud

Generous Embrace clmd MBell £20,000

3471 Generous Embrace confirmed the promise shown on his debut and was suited by the extra furlong, eventually getting on top inside the final furlong. (7/4)

3314 Just Another Time was better served by the return to six furlongs. Showing in front on the stands' side at halfway, he managed to gain overall control below the distance but, although just worried out of it by the winner inside the final furlong, finished well clear of the remainder. The easy surface also seemed to be in his favour and he can win a similar event in this ground. (4/1)

2943 Petaling (IRE) found the first-time blinkers, return to claiming company and the easy ground all helping. Making all the running on the far side, she had overall control until collared below the distance by the stands' side group and, although unable to match the front two, finished well clear of the remainder on her side. (8/1)
3589 Truth Teller ran better on this occasion. Leading the stands' side group to halfway, although he did not have overall control, he was left for dead by the front two in the final furlong. (16/1)
3692 Dande Times again showed that he is extremely moderate and was left for dead in the final quarter-mile. (20/1)
2893 Mystagogue (14/1: 7/1-16/1)
2409 Teepee (IRE) (15/2: 5/1-8/1)
Safari Sam (IRE) (14/1: 8/1-16/1)

3860 MURPHYS IRISH STOUT H'CAP (0-70) (3-Y.O+) (Class E)

2-30 (2-35) **7f (Equitrack)** £3,252.25 (£973.00: £466.50: £213.25) Stalls: Low GOING: 0.07 sec per fur (G)

Form	Horse	Dist	Pos	SP	RR	SF
3205[4]	**Bogan (IRE) (60)** (LordHuntingdon) **3-8-13v[1]** MRoberts(14) (a.p: chsd ldr over 2f out: led ins fnl f: r.o wl)	—	1	14/1	69	39
3583[5]	**Dawalib (USA) (60)** (DHaydnJones) **7-9-4** SDrowne(16) (lw: a.p: rdn over 2f out: r.o ins fnl f)	½	2	16/1	68	43
3690[4]	**Star Turn (IRE) (61)** (MBell) **3-9-0** MFenton(6) (lw: led: rdn over 2f out: hdd ins fnl f: unable qckn)	1	3	10/1	67	37
3423[15]	**Signs And Wonders (62)** (CACyzer) **3-9-1** LDettori(1) (lw: rdn & hdwy over 2f out: r.o ins fnl f)	nk	4	7/1	67	37
3590[13]	**Lancashire Legend (68)** (SDow) **4-9-12** GDuffield(4) (lw: rdn & hdwy 3f out: nt clr run wl over 1f out: one pce)	hd	5	33/1	73	48
3328[7]	**Whatever's Right (IRE) (54)** (MDIUsher) **8-8-12** KFallon(12) (rdn over 3f out: hdwy over 1f out: nvr nrr)	2½	6	4/1[1]	53	28
3420[3]	**Big Ben (67)** (RHannon) **3-9-6** DaneO'Neill(8) (lw: prom over 4f)	½	7	7/1	65	35
*3058**	**Invocation (65)** (GLMoore) **10-9-9** AClark(13) (lw: hdwy 5f out: rdn over 3f out: wknd over 1f out)	1½	8	8/1	59	34
	Le Bam Bam (55) (CNAllen) **5-8-10**(3) MartinDwyer(3) (a mid div)	¾	9	20/1	48	23
3642*	**Sharp Imp (68)** (RMFlower) **7-9-12b** 7x SSanders(7) (a mid div)	4	10	9/2[2]	52	27
3561[4]	**Ed's Folly (IRE) (53)** (SDow) **4-8-8**(3) DO'Donohoe(2) (mid div whn nt clr run on ins over 4f out: bhd fnl 3f)	½	11	7/1	35	10
3261[3]	**Rawi (54)** (MissGayKelleway) **4-8-9b**(3) RFfrench(15) (lw: bhd fnl 3f)	2	12	13/2[3]	32	7
3323[7]	**Napier Star (68)** (MrsNMacauley) **4-9-12v** SWebster(11) (b.nr hind: mid div whn bdly hmpd 5f out: no rcvr)	2	13	20/1	41	16
3642[14]	**Red Admiral (65)** (CMurray) **7-9-9** NicolaHowarth(10) (chsd ldr over 4f)	1¼	14	33/1	35	10
3592[6]	**Lochlass (IRE) (60)** (SPCWoods) **3-8-13** WRyan(5) (lw: bhd fnl 5f)	6	15	25/1	17	—
3561[11]	**Moi Canard (70)** (BAPearce) **4-10-0b[1]** DHolland(9) (a bhd)	1¼	16	20/1	24	—
				(SP 145.8%)	**16 Rn**	

1m 25.8 (1.40) CSF £219.33 CT £2,263.16 TOTE £22.90: £3.50 £4.60 £2.40 £2.30 (£199.70) Trio £611.40; £697.52 to Sandown 29/8/97
OWNER Mr G. Cosmelli (WEST ILSLEY) BRED Clare Dore Ltd
WEIGHT FOR AGE 3yo-5lb
2126 Bogan (IRE) appreciated the drop in distance. Taking second place over a quarter of a mile from home, he managed to wear down the leader inside the final furlong. (14/1: 10/1-16/1)
3583 Dawalib (USA) has done most of his winning at this trip. Never far away, he stuck on well inside the final furlong. (16/1)
3690 Star Turn (IRE) was making his All-Weather debut and coped well with the surface. Bowling along in front, he grimly tried to fend off his rivals and was not overhauled until inside the final furlong. (10/1: 7/1-12/1)
3232 Signs And Wonders began a forward move over a quarter of a mile from home but, despite staying on inside the final furlong, was never going to get there in time. She remains a maiden after sixteen attempts. (7/1)
2937 Lancashire Legend was better behaved this time and, although he did not have a great run turning into the straight, failed to find that vital turn of foot in the closing stages. He is not easy to win with and has just one victory from twenty-seven starts to his name. (33/1)
3091 Whatever's Right (IRE) did not have the run of the race and was out with the washing until staying on when it was all over. (4/1)

3861 BODDINGTONS MANCHESTER GOLD MAIDEN STKS (I) (2-Y.O) (Class D)

3-00 (3-03) **7f 140y** £3,143.25 (£936.00: £445.50: £200.25) Stalls: High GOING: 0.07 sec per fur (G)

Form	Horse	Dist	Pos	SP	RR	SF
	Mutamam (ACStewart) **2-9-0** RHills(9) (w'like: a.p: rdn over 1f out: led ins fnl f: r.o wl)	—	1	Evens[1]	86+	39
	Dancing Phantom (MRStoute) **2-9-0** JReid(6) (w'like: s.s: plld hrd: hdwy 5f out: ev ch over 1f out: r.o)	1¼	2	11/4[2]	83+	36
3638[15]	**Risada (IRE)** (DRLoder) **2-8-9** WRyan(5) (led: hrd rdn over 1f out: hdd ins fnl f: unable qckn)	¾	3	25/1	77	30
1607[8]	**Dashing Chief (IRE)** (MAJarvis) **2-9-0** MRoberts(12) (a.p: rdn 3f out: chsd ldr over 2f out tl over 1f out: eased whn btn fnl f)	7	4	11/2[3]	67	20
	Desert Spa (USA) (PWHarris) **2-9-0** AClark(11) (w'like: scope: s.s: nvr nr to chal)	1¾	5	20/1	64	17
3489[8]	**Bronzino** (GBBalding) **2-9-0** SDrowne(7) (rdn over 4f out: nvr nrr)	1¼	6	20/1	61	14
2520[6]	**Allaton (IRE)** (MrsPSly) **2-9-0** NCarlisle(2) (chsd ldr 5f)	1	7	66/1	59	12
2047[6]	**The Thruster** (MajorWRHern) **2-9-0** TSprake(8) (prom 5f)	2	8	12/1	55	8
	Pairumani Star (IRE) (JLDunlop) **2-9-0** GCarter(10) (w'like: s.s: a bhd)	1¼	9	14/1	52	5
3490[9]	**Asinbox (IRE)** (BJMeehan) **2-9-0** MTebbutt(1) (bhd fnl 4f)	½	10	33/1	51	4
3490[8]	**Lady Felix** (SMellor) **2-8-9** AMcGlone(3) (bit bkwd: a bhd)	4	11	66/1	38	—
				(SP 125.7%)	**11 Rn**	

1m 34.77 (5.77) CSF £3.42 TOTE £2.10: £1.10 £1.40 £6.90 (£2.40) Trio £59.50 OWNER Mr Hamdan Al Maktoum (NEWMARKET) BRED Biddestone Stud
Mutamam, a plain, stocky colt who is the second foal of a half-sister to Mtoto, has entries in all the top staying events. Woken up below the distance, he got on top inside the final furlong and soon asserted his authority. He will be better served by a sounder surface and can go on from here. (Evens)
Dancing Phantom, a medium-sized colt who cost 120,000 guineas, showed a lot of promise, despite taking a very keen hold early on. With every chance over a furlong out, he stuck on well to finish an encouraging second. He should have no problems finding an ordinary maiden. (11/4: 9/4-4/1)
Risada (IRE) left previous form well behind on her first encounter with soft ground and merrily bowled along in front until overhauled inside the final furlong. (25/1)
Dashing Chief (IRE) left his debut run three months ago well behind and showed in second place over a quarter of a mile from home. Collared for that position below the distance, his jockey took things very easy when all chances evaporated in the final furlong and would certainly have finished a lot closer with a bit more effort. (11/2)
Desert Spa (USA), a medium-sized colt who is a half-brother to three winners, lost ground at the start and never threatened to get into it. (20/1)
2047 The Thruster (12/1: op 8/1)
Pairumani Star (IRE) (14/1: 6/1-16/1)

3862 BODDINGTONS MANCHESTER GOLD MAIDEN STKS (II) (2-Y.O) (Class D)

3-30 (3-32) **7f 140y** £3,114.00 (£927.00: £441.00: £198.00) Stalls: High GOING: 0.07 sec per fur (G)

				SP	RR	SF
	Sadian (HRACecil) **2-9-0** KFallon(1) (w'like: scope: a.p: led over 1f out: rdn out)	—	1	3/1[2]	83+	30
3386[6]	**Zydeco (IRE)** (JLDunlop) **2-9-0** LDettori(9) (a.p: rdn over 2f out: ev ch over 1f out: r.o wl)	nk	2	Evens[1]	82	29
	Muhib (USA) (MRStoute) **2-9-0** RHills(11) (leggy: scope: hld up: n.m.r over 2f out: rdn over 1f out: r.o: bttr for r)	1½	3	7/1[3]	79+	26
	Mubrik (IRE) (JHMGosden) **2-9-0** GHind(3) (str: bit bkwd: a.p: ev ch over 1f out: eased whn btn ins fnl f: bttr for r)	3½	4	14/1	72+	19
3450[11]	**Trinity Reef** (JLDunlop) **2-8-9** GCarter(7) (led over 5f)	1½	5	25/1	64	11
3278[7]	**Sumbawa (IRE)** (DHaydnJones) **2-8-9** SDrowne(10) (a.p: led 2f out tl over 1f out: sn wknd)	½	6	25/1	63	10
	Our Molly Malone (DMorley) **2-8-9** MFenton(6) (unf: s.s: nvr nrr)	½	7	25/1	62	9
3598[6]	**Praetorian Gold** (RHannon) **2-9-0** DaneO'Neill(8) (lw: prom over 5f)	1¼	8	8/1	64	11
2893[11]	**Zuryaf (IRE)** (BJMeehan) **2-9-0** MTebbutt(5) (a bhd)	½	9	33/1	63	10
3547[10]	**Safabee** (MJHaynes) **2-8-6**(3) MartinDwyer(4) (prom 4f)	5	10	25/1	48	—
3047[7]	**Paddy McGoon (USA)** (DRCElsworth) **2-9-0** GDuffield(2) (prom over 4f)	6	11	14/1	40	—

(SP 130.3%) **11 Rn**

1m 35.68 (6.68) CSF £6.10 TOTE £5.00: £1.50 £1.20 £2.10 (£3.30) Trio £5.50 OWNER Prince A A Faisal (NEWMARKET) BRED Nawara Stud Co Ltd

Sadian, an attractive colt with plenty of scope, was reported to have been working well at home. Racing down the centre of the course where the ground is often worse after it has rained, he nevertheless struck the front approaching the final furlong and, rousted along, kept the persistent runner-up at bay. From a stable that has an incredible 42% strike rate with its juveniles so far this year, he is sure to come on for the run and is entered in all the top staying races. (3/1: op 2/1)

3386 Zydeco (IRE), much wiser on this occasion, raced in the front rank throughout. He kept on really well inside the final furlong and should have little problem opening his account. (Evens)

Muhib (USA), a tall colt, was given a nice educational introduction. Not having a great deal of room over a quarter of a mile from home, his jockey did push him along below the distance but was not hard on him inside the final furlong, although the colt kept on nicely. Sure to be a lot wiser for this, he should not be difficult to win with. (7/1: 3/1-8/1)

Mubrik (IRE), quite a powerful-looking colt who is a half-brother to the very useful Decorated Hero, did not look fully wound up and so it proved for, after showing plenty of promise to have every chance below the distance, he tired in the final furlong and was not persevered with. Sure to come on a lot for this, he should soon find a race. (14/1: op 6/1)

Trinity Reef took the field along but, collared over two furlongs from home, soon had bellows to mend. (25/1)

Sumbawa (IRE) showed in front a quarter of a mile out but she was collared below the distance and had nothing left in the locker. (25/1)

3863 STELLA ARTOIS CONDITIONS STKS (3-Y.O+) (Class C)

4-00 (4-01) **5f** £4,806.59 (£1,731.22: £829.11: £337.05: £132.03) Stalls: High GOING: 0.07 sec per fur (G)

				SP	RR	SF
3747[4]	**My Melody Parkes (90)** (JBerry) **4-8-9** GCarter(6) (lw: hld up: hrd rdn over 1f out: led ins fnl f: r.o wl)	—	1	9/1[3]	108	70
3111[2]	**Cathedral (IRE) (108)** (BJMeehan) **3-9-1** MTebbutt(7) (chsd ldr: hung lft & led over 1f out: hdd ins fnl f: r.o)	½	2	11/10[1]	114	74
3217[3]	**Dashing Blue (105)** (IABalding) **4-9-0** LDettori(2) (lw: rdn & hdwy over 1f out: unable qckn fnl f)	2	3	13/8[2]	105	67
3425[2]	**Mary Cornwallis** (GWragg) **3-8-7** MHills(3) (b.off hind: lw: led over 3f: wknd fnl f)	2½	4	9/1[3]	92	52
2861[12]	**Blue Ridge (98)** (VSoane) **3-8-12** CRutter(4) (dwlt: a bhd)	1	5	33/1	94?	54

(SP 108.7%) **5 Rn**

58.68 secs (1.68) CSF £17.47 TOTE £9.80: £2.80 £1.40 (£10.80) OWNER Mr Joseph Heler (COCKERHAM) BRED Joseph Heler

WEIGHT FOR AGE 3yo-2lb

3747 My Melody Parkes, who has been running well of late, responded to pressure in the centre of the course and managed to get on top inside the final furlong to gain her first success since her two-year-old debut. (9/1: 6/1-10/1)

3111 Cathedral (IRE) had an easier task here after competing in Pattern company in his last three outings. He did not help his jockey by hanging for much of the contest but, nevertheless, hit the front below the distance. Collared inside the final furlong, he did keep on well, despite his erratic tendencies, but was unable to get back in front. (11/10: op evens)

3217 Dashing Blue, a tremendous third in the Stewards' Cup last time out, picked up ground down the centre of the course below the distance but found the rain-softened ground not to his liking and failed to quicken in the final furlong. (13/8)

3425 Mary Cornwallis had no easy task but showed up well until collared approaching the final furlong. (9/1: 5/1-10/1)

Blue Ridge was always at the back of the field. He has now disappointed in six runs since winning a maiden at Sandown over a year ago, and definitely needs his sights greatly lowered. (33/1)

3864 STELLA DRY CLASSIC H'CAP (0-80) (3-Y.O+) (Class D)

4-30 (4-31) **1m 3f 106y** £3,836.70 (£1,146.60: £548.80: £249.90) Stalls: High GOING: 0.07 sec per fur (G)

				SP	RR	SF
3277[10]	**Bold Buster (64)** (IABalding) **4-9-2** MHills(5) (led 3f: led over 2f out: hrd rdn over 1f out: r.o wl)	—	1	8/1	73	12
3475[7]	**Prospero (70)** (MrsAJPerrett) **4-9-8** JReid(2) (hdwy 3f out: hrd rdn over 1f out: chsd wnr ins fnl f: r.o one pce)	1½	2	16/1	77	16
3390[2]	**Palaemon (58)** (GBBalding) **3-8-1**ow1 RPrice(10) (lw: rdn & hdwy over 2f out: r.o one pce)	1¼	3	10/1	63	—
3279[3]	**Newport Knight (60)** (RAkehurst) **6-8-12** SSanders(9) (b.hind: rdn & hdwy over 2f out: r.o one pce)	s.h	4	7/2[1]	65	4
3277[12]	**Jaseur (USA) (70)** (JHMGosden) **4-9-8v**[1] LDettori(1) (a.p: chsd wnr over 2f out tl ins fnl f: sn wknd)	1½	5	6/1[2]	73	12
3475[2]	**Two Socks (67)** (JSKing) **4-9-5** DHolland(8) (rdn over 3f out: hdwy over 1f out: nvr nrr)	½	6	7/1[3]	69	8
3329[2]	**Bellagrana (54)** (MJFetherston-Godley) **3-7-8**(3) RFfrench(15) (rdn & hdwy over 2f out: nvr nrr)	1	7	7/1[3]	55	—
3475[10]	**Alarmist (75)** (RCharlton) **3-9-4** TSprake(4) (hdwy over 2f out: wknd over 1f out)	1¾	8	12/1	74	4
3382[5]	**Shahik (USA) (68)** (DHaydnJones) **7-9-6** SDrowne(12) (a mid div)	9	9	9/1	54	—
	Elhafid (USA) (68) (MajorWRHern) **3-8-11** RHills(3) (lw: nvr nrr)	¾	10	16/1	53	—
1831[4]	**Bandore (IRE) (75)** (DRLoder) **3-9-4** RCochrane(7) (prom 8f)	6	11	16/1	52	—
3466[5]	**Nordic Crest (IRE) (68)** (PWHarris) **3-8-6**(5) CLowther(16) (lw: a bhd)	5	12	12/1	38	—
3491[14]	**Shaded (IRE) (55)** (SDow) **3-7-9**(3)ow2 MartinDwyer(6) (lw: led over 8f out tl over 2f out: sn wknd)	1¼	13	25/1	23	—
3559[5]	**Burning (USA) (76)** (WJHaggas) **5-10-0** KFallon(11) (prom 8f)	5	14	10/1	37	—
3139[2]	**Peter Perfect (55)** (RCurtis) **3-7-12** JLowe(13) (lw: bhd fnl 3f)	¾	15	20/1	15	—

(SP 142.4%) **15 Rn**

2m 38.42 (13.72) CSF £139.15 CT £1,233.79 TOTE £13.60: £4.50 £5.70 £3.50 (£200.20) Trio Not won; £1,007.43 to Sandown 29/8/97 OWNER Robert & Exors Late Elizabeth Hitchins (KINGSCLERE) BRED Mrs L. Popely

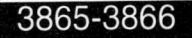

LONG HANDICAP Shaded (IRE) 7-7
WEIGHT FOR AGE 3yo-9lb
2853 Bold Buster, who has been hobdayed, ran by far his best race to date and, showing in front for a second time over a quarter of a mile out, responded to pressure and kept on well. The plan is to send him hurdling. (8/1)
Prospero left two disappointing runs so far this season well behind. Picking up ground in the straight, he came through to take second place inside the final furlong but was unable to get on terms with the winner. (16/1)
3390 Palaemon, rousted along down the centre of the course to pick up ground over a quarter of a mile out, stayed on to snatch third prize on the line. He lacks acceleration. (10/1: 7/1-11/1)
3279 Newport Knight, bustled along as he picked up ground along the inside rail over a quarter of a mile from home, struggled on and failed by only a whisker to take third prize. He has done all his winning at this trip. (7/2)
2924 Jaseur (USA) ran better on this handicap debut and showed in second place over a quarter of a mile from home. Collared for that position inside the final furlong, he had nothing left in the tank. (6/1)
3475 Two Socks, racing at the back of the field, struggled on late in the day but, by then, it was all over bar the shouting. He has just one win to his name. (7/1)

3865 H.P. BULMER H'CAP (0-60) (3-Y.O) (Class F)
5-00 (5-03) **2m (Equitrack)** £2,277.00 (£627.00: £297.00) Stalls: Low GOING minus 0.50 sec per fur (FST)

				SP	RR	SF
3415[4]	**Sipowitz (46)** (CACyzer) **3-8-4**(3) AWhelan(14) (lw: rdn 6f out: hdwy over 2f out: chsd ldr over 1f out: led wl ins fnl f: all out)	—	**1**	13/2	56	22
3700*	**Il Principe (IRE) (44)** (JohnBerry) **3-8-5e** 4x DHolland(13) (a.p: led over 4f out: hrd rdn over 1f out: hdd wl ins fnl f: r.o wl)	hd	**2**	11/2[3]	54	20
2568[8]	**Rear Window (56)** (LordHuntingdon) **3-9-3v**[1] MRoberts(7) (lw: lost pl 12f out: rallied 5f out: chsd ldr over 2f out tl over 1f out: unable qckn)	6	**3**	14/1	60	26
3560*	**Keen Waters (39)** (MrsSDWilliams) **3-7-9**(5) APolli(6) (a.p: rdn over 7f out: chsd ldr over 3f out tl over 2f out: wknd over 1f out)	6	**4**	14/1	37	3
3028[6]	**Golden Melody (51)** (MJHeaton-Ellis) **3-8-12v** SSanders(5) (nvr nr to chal)	3½	**5**	14/1	45	11
2908[5]	**Hippios (37)** (SDow) **3-7-9**(3) RFfrench(1) (nvr nrr)	1¼	**6**	25/1	30	—
3623[9]	**Sad Mad Bad (USA) (55)** (MrsMReveley) **3-9-2** WJO'Connor(10) (a mid div)	2	**7**	12/1	46	12
*3612**	**Bold Saint (IRE) (44)** (PWHarris) **3-8-0b**(5) CLowther(2) (led over 13f out tl over 7f out: led over 5f out tl over 4f out: sn wknd)	nk	**8**	8/1	35	1
3593[3]	**Bewitching Lady (43)** (DWPArbuthnot) **3-8-4** JQuinn(12) (lw: bhd fnl 3f)	8	**9**	14/1	26	—
*3587**	**Robbo (60)** (CWThornton) **3-9-7b** DeanMcKeown(8) (bhd fnl 5f: t.o)	20	**10**	4/1[1]	23	—
2511[9]	**San Glamore Melody (FR) (54)** (RIngram) **3-9-1** AMcGlone(9) (lw: led over 2f: led over 7f out tl over 5f out: sn wknd: t.o)	3	**11**	14/1	14	—
3643[6]	**Aegean (38)** (KTIvory) **3-7-10b**[1](3)ow3 MartinDwyer(4) (bhd fnl 7f: t.o)	17	**12**	40/1	—	—
3567[7]	**Jucinda (51)** (JPearce) **3-8-12** LDettori(3) (bhd fnl 8f: t.o fnl 6f)	dist	**13**	10/1	—	—
3325[2]	**Sixties Melody (49)** (RBoss) **3-8-10** KFallon(11) (mid div whn hmpd 15f out: sn bhd & nvr gng wl: t.o whn p.u 8f out)		**P**	9/2[2]	—	—
				(SP 134.4%)	**14 Rn**	

3m 27.01 (6.01) CSF £43.11 CT £470.15 TOTE £8.60: £2.20 £2.60 £5.80 (£26.60) Trio £119.70 OWNER Mr R. M. Cyzer (HORSHAM) BRED C. A. and R. M. Cyzer
3415 Sipowitz was given a fine ride by Whelan who was already pushing the gelding along at least three-quarters of a mile from home. At last picking up ground over two furlongs out, he came through to lead in the last fifty yards and held on in a tremendous finish. (13/2)
3700* Il Principe (IRE) had no problems with this much longer trip and moved to the front over half a mile from home. Collared in the closing stages, he refused to lie down and was only just beaten. (11/2)
Rear Window coped with the step up in distance on this handicap debut and showed in second place over a quarter of a mile from home. Collared for that position below the distance, he was then left for dead by the front two. (14/1: 10/1-16/1)
3560* Keen Waters, who has changed stables since her last run, was close up until tiring below the distance. This much longer trip seemed a bit too far for her. (14/1)
2535 Golden Melody is a poor performer who was only struggling on past beaten horses. (14/1)
3612* Bold Saint (IRE) (8/1: 6/1-9/1)

T/Jkpt: Not won; £17,910.79 to Sandown 29/8/97. T/Plpt: £127.30 (195.67 Tckts). T/Qdpt: £24.20 (45.44 Tckts) AK

3697-MUSSELBURGH (R-H) (Good)
Thursday August 28th
WEATHER: overcast WIND: almost nil

3866 SALAMANCA (S) STKS (2-Y.O) (Class F)
2-20 (2-21) **5f** £2,626.00 (£736.00: £358.00) Stalls: High GOING minus 0.07 sec per fur (G)

				SP	RR	SF
2746[4]	**Sans Rivale (55)** (BJMeehan) **2-8-6** KDarley(5) (chsd ldrs: led ins fnl f: r.o)	—	**1**	8/1[3]	71	31
3699*	**Oriel Girl (68)** (PDEvans) **2-8-11v** JFEgan(6) (lw: cl up: led after 2f tl ins fnl f: no ex)	1½	**2**	8/15[1]	71	31
3586[4]	**I'm Not Sure (48)** (JBerry) **2-8-3**(3) PFessey(4) (lw: s.i.s: sn chsng ldrs: rdn & no imp fr ½-wy)	6	**3**	10/1	47	7
3636[13]	**Aviva Lady (IRE)** (CADwyer) **2-8-6** JCarroll(2) (s.i.s: sn in tch: rdn ½-wy: r.o one pce)	nk	**4**	6/1[2]	46	6
3483[3]	**Ngaere Princess (50)** (WTKemp) **2-8-1**(5) KSked(3) (lw: led 2f: sn wknd)	1¾	**5**	25/1	40	—
3427[6]	**Seventh Heaven (54)** (DNicholls) **2-8-11b**[1] JFortune(7) (sn drvn along: nvr trbld ldrs)	nk	**6**	11/1	45	5
3062[9]	**Shirleys Girl (IRE)** (WStorey) **2-8-6v**[1] JFanning(1) (s.i.s: sn outpcd & wl bhd)	8	**7**	50/1	14	—
				(SP 113.8%)	**7 Rn**	

60.8 secs (3.10) CSF £11.51 TOTE £8.40: £2.70 £1.10 (£2.40) OWNER Mr David Powell (UPPER LAMBOURN) BRED Catridge Farm Stud Ltd
Sold D Cooper 5,200 gns, Oriel Girl clmd MBarrett £6,000
2746 Sans Rivale won this nicely and could be interesting in nurseries. (8/1: 6/1-9/1)
3699* Oriel Girl did her usual and ran her heart out but just met one too good in this, her fourteenth race of the season. (8/15)
3586 I'm Not Sure has trouble in getting the trip and did not help matters with a tardy start. (10/1: op 6/1)
3324 Aviva Lady (IRE) was always struggling to overcome a moderate start. (6/1)
3483 Ngaere Princess has yet to see the trip out. (25/1)
1614 Seventh Heaven had blinkers on for the first time with no effect. (11/1)

3867 ROYAL SCOTS CUP H'CAP (0-75) (3-Y.O+) (Class D)

2-50 (2-50) **1m 6f** £3,590.50 (£1,084.00: £527.00: £248.50) Stalls: High GOING minus 0.22 sec per fur (GF)

Form	Horse / details	Dist	Pos	SP	RR	SF
3482^{3}	**Campaspe (61)** (JGFitzGerald) **5-9-4** JFortune(1) (a.p: led 3f out: sn pushed clr)	—	1	$4/1^{2}$	73	—
3482^{2}	**Urgent Reply (USA) (60)** (CADwyer) **4-9-3** JCarroll(8) (lw: cl up: led 4f out to 3f out: one pce)	4	2	12/1	67	—
3626^{5}	**Mister Aspecto (IRE) (58)** (MJohnston) **4-9-1v** JWeaver(2) (led tl hdd 4f out: one pce)	2	3	15/2	63	—
*3585**	**Classic Ballet (FR) (61)** (RGuest) **4-8-13**(5) PRoberts(6) (lw: hld up & bhd: gd hdwy over 3f out: sn rdn: btn 2f out)	4	4	$11/4^{1}$	62	—
3631^{2}	**Lord Advocate (47)** (DANolan) **9-7-13b**(5) KSked(4) (lw: b.hind: chsd ldrs: outpcd 4f out: n.d after)	1½	5	10/1	46	—
1452^{9}	**Moonraking (44)** (TJEtherington) **4-8-1** LCharnock(3) (rr div: effrt ent st: no imp)	4	6	25/1	38	—
2486^{2}	**Vrennan (71)** (JRFanshawe) **3-9-2** TWilliams(7) (chsd ldrs: chal 4f out: wknd 3f out)	13	7	$9/2^{3}$	50	—
2787^{3}	**Welsh Mill (IRE) (71)** (MrsMReveley) **8-10-0** KDarley(5) (rr div: outpcd ent st: sn t.o)	24	8	8/1	23	—

(SP 108.4%) **8 Rn**

3m 6.3 CSF £40.57 CT £276.06 TOTE £4.00: £2.40 £3.70 £1.80 (£36.50) OWNER Mr J. G. FitzGerald (MALTON) BRED J. G. Fitzgerald
WEIGHT FOR AGE 3yo-12lb
OFFICIAL EXPLANATION **Vrennan: finished distressed.**

3482 Campaspe, happy on this slightly faster ground, was back to her best and won in really good style. (4/1)
3482 Urgent Reply (USA) finished in front of the winner last time but was firmly put in his place here, and this is as good as he is. (12/1)
3626 Mister Aspecto (IRE) keeps trying hard but he is short of pace on turf. (15/2)
3585* Classic Ballet (FR), trying a longer trip, did not seem to get it. (11/4)
3631 Lord Advocate is beginning to drop back down the handicap and may yet regain his form before the season ends. (10/1)
955 Moonraking had a nice pipe-opener after over three months off and is one to watch if reverting to the All-Weather. (25/1)

3868 PERTEMPS CALEDONIAN RECRUITMENT H'CAP (0-70) (3-Y.O) (Class E)

3-20 (3-20) **7f 30y** £3,241.25 (£980.00: £477.50: £226.25) Stalls: High GOING minus 0.22 sec per fur (GF)

Form	Horse / details	Dist	Pos	SP	RR	SF
3592^{2}	**Warrior King (IRE) (47)** (CADwyer) **3-8-1** JFEgan(9) (bhd: hdwy over 3f out: led 2f out: r.o u.p)	—	1	$11/4^{2}$	59	10
3812^{2}	**Hi Mujtahid (IRE) (52)** (SEKettlewell) **3-8-6b** KDarley(1) (lw: led tl hdd 2f out: one pce)	2	2	$9/4^{1}$	60	11
3292^{3}	**Daintree (IRE) (48)** (HJCollingridge) **3-8-2v¹** DaleGibson(7) (rr div: hdwy over 2f out: n.m.r: styd on towards fin)	¾	3	$5/1^{3}$	54	5
3336^{11}	**The Dubious Goose (43)** (MrsJRRamsden) **3-7-11** LCharnock(2) (bhd: hdwy u.p over 2f out: nvr rchd ldrs)	¾	4	20/1	47	—
3625^{17}	**Seretse's Nephew (45)** (MJPolglase) **3-7-6**(7)ow1 DarrenWilliams(3) (cl up tl wknd wl over 1f out)	nk	5	20/1	49	—
3405*	**Feel A Line (53)** (BJMeehan) **3-8-7b** JCarroll(6) (bhd: effrt over 3f out: rdn & no imp)	2½	6	11/2	51	2
3565^{8}	**Rude Awakening (65)** (CWFairhurst) **3-8-12**(7) TSiddall(8) (lw: chsd ldrs: n.m.r over 2f out: sn btn)	1¼	7	14/1	60	11
2733^{11}	**Freedom of Troy (43)** (JLEyre) **3-7-11** TWilliams(5) (in tch tl wknd fnl 2½f)	5	8	20/1	27	—
	Life On The Street (67) (DNicholls) **3-9-7** AlexGreaves(4) (cl up: wkng whn hmpd wl over 1f out)	6	9	14/1	37	—

(SP 117.1%) **9 Rn**

1m 31.1 (5.10) CSF £8.35 CT £24.80 TOTE £3.70: £1.20 £1.10 £2.50 (£3.60) Trio £7.00 OWNER North End Partnership (NEWMARKET)
STEWARDS' ENQUIRY Darren Williams susp. 8/9/97 (careless riding)

3592 Warrior King (IRE) had to work to improve early in the straight but, once he struck the front, he stayed on particularly strongly. (11/4: op 9/2)
3812 Hi Mujtahid (IRE) did his usual and attempted to make all, but the struggle was always too much for his liking in the last furlong and a half. (9/4)
3292 Daintree (IRE) had a visor on for the first time and needed plenty of encouragement but, to give her her due, she did respond and, in doing so, did meet with some traffic problems. (5/1)
3336 The Dubious Goose, dropping back in trip, showed a little encouragement, staying on when it was all over. (20/1)
3417 Seretse's Nephew showed plenty of speed but looked to have stamina problems. (20/1)
3405* Feel A Line was always struggling and seems better when going left-handed. (11/2)

3869 STEVE WOOD MEMORIAL NURSERY H'CAP (2-Y.O) (Class E)

3-50 (3-51) **7f 30y** £2,576.25 (£765.00: £362.50: £161.25) Stalls: High GOING minus 0.22 sec per fur (GF)

Form	Horse / details	Dist	Pos	SP	RR	SF
3755^{6}	**Inchalong (64)** (MBrittain) **2-8-11** GBardwell(10) (trckd ldrs: led over 1f out: r.o u.p)	—	1	$3/1^{2}$	70	5
3331^{5}	**Boulevard Rouge (USA) (74)** (MJohnston) **2-9-7** JWeaver(3) (lw: bhd: hdwy ½-wy: chsd wnr fnl f: r.o)	1	2	7/1	78	13
3067^{8}	**Lord of Love (67)** (TDEasterby) **2-9-0** LCharnock(5) (a chsng ldrs: kpt on u.p fnl 2f: nt pce to chal)	¾	3	10/1	69	4
3635^{2}	**Lasham (65)** (NACallaghan) **2-8-12** KDarley(2) (led tl hdd & wknd over 1f out)	2½	4	$5/2^{1}$	62	—
2875^{8}	**Great Lyth Lass (IRE) (68)** (PDEvans) **2-9-1v¹** JFEgan(1) (plld hrd: in tch: effrt 3f out: nvr able chal)	2	5	9/1	60	—
2565^{8}	**Blue Anchor (54)** (MrsMReveley) **2-8-1** DaleGibson(7) (hld up & bhd: effrt ½-wy: nvr rchd ldrs)	1½	6	25/1	43	—
3379^{5}	**Mamma's Boy (73)** (JBerry) **2-9-3**(3) TEDurcan(8) (lw: a chsng ldrs: rdn & one pce fnl 3f)	s.h	7	$5/1^{3}$	62	—
3479^{11}	**Wishbone Alley (IRE) (69)** (MDods) **2-9-2** AlexGreaves(4) (hld up & bhd: effrt ½-wy: n.d)	3	8	25/1	51	—
3307^{10}	**On The Mat (61)** (JJO'Neill) **2-8-5b¹**(3) PFessey(6) (cl up 4f: wknd)	½	9	25/1	42	—
3628^{3}	**Inshallah (65)** (MartinTodhunter) **2-8-12** JCarroll(9) (prom tl wknd fnl 3f)	1¼	10	14/1	43	—

(SP 120.0%) **10 Rn**

1m 32.4 (6.40) CSF £22.42 CT £168.77 TOTE £5.90: £1.40 £1.50 £3.60 (£10.00) Trio £40.50 OWNER Northgate Lodge Partnerships (WARTHILL) BRED R. B. Warren

3755 Inchalong behaved in the stalls this time and, jumping out on terms, was always doing enough. (3/1)
3331 Boulevard Rouge (USA), given a chance to get this longer trip, showed a good attitude under pressure and there should be a race to be found. (7/1)
2681 Lord of Love ran a sound race here after a month off and kept responding to pressure in good style. (10/1)
3635 Lasham attempted to make all but found the battle too much late on. (5/2)
1657 Great Lyth Lass (IRE) took too strong a hold in the first-time visor. (9/1)
2165 Blue Anchor obviously needs this longer trip but he also needs to learn to settle. (25/1)
3379 Mamma's Boy looked particularly well but, once ridden, looked woefully short of pace. (5/1)

3870 FORTH A.M. CLAIMING LIMITED STKS (0-70) (3-Y.O) (Class E)

4-20 (4-21) **1m 4f 31y** £2,705.00 (£815.00: £395.00: £185.00) Stalls: High GOING minus 0.22 sec per fur (GF)

Form	Horse / details	Dist	Pos	SP	RR	SF
3272^{6}	**Monarch's Pursuit (50)** (TDEasterby) **3-8-8** JFortune(3) (a cl up: led over 3f out: r.o u.p)	—	1	$6/1^{3}$	59	30
3478^{7}	**Grate Times (60)** (EWeymes) **3-8-12** JCarroll(6) (a chsng ldrs: styd on to chal ins fnl f: no ex)	1¼	2	$6/1^{3}$	61	32

				SP	RR	SF
3695^{3}	**River of Fortune (IRE) (53)** (MHTompkins) **3-8-2**$^{(5)}$ RMullen(5) (led tl hdd over 3f out: grad wknd)	2½	3	11/8^{1}	53	24
3068^{8}	**Emily-Jayne (29)** (MrsMReveley) **3-8-4**^{ow1} KDarley(2) (bhd: effrt ent st: n.d)	11	4	33/1	36	6
2896*	**Le Grand Gousier (USA) (56)** (RJRWilliams) **3-9-3**$^{(3)}$ DGriffiths(4) (chsd ldrs tl rdn & wknd fnl 3f)	11	5	9/4^{2}	37	8
3487^{7}	**Lightning Rebel (52)** (CWThornton) **3-8-10** JFanning(1) (lw: bhd: effrt ent st: sn btn)	5	6	9/1	21	—
				(SP 114.4%)	**6 Rn**	

2m 40.4 (6.90) CSF £37.36 TOTE £5.60: £2.10 £4.20 (£16.60) OWNER Mrs Jean Connew (MALTON) BRED Newgate Stud Co

3272 Monarch's Pursuit probably found a poor race here and was inclined to carry his head high, but his rider certainly made his mind up for him. (6/1)

2909 Grate Times, taking another step up in trip, had his chances but failed to prolong the effort. (6/1: op 3/1)

3695 River of Fortune (IRE) is one-paced and, with his rider undecided about where to race in the home straight, his chance had soon gone. (11/8)

Emily-Jayne has yet to show anything positive. (33/1)

2896* Le Grand Gousier (USA) was inclined to hang in the straight and something would seem to have been wrong with him on this occasion. (9/4)

Lightning Rebel has lost his way at the moment. (9/1)

3871 PERGODA APPRENTICE H'CAP (0-65) (3-Y.O+) (Class F)

4-50 (4-50) **5f** £2,920.00 (£820.00: £400.00) Stalls: High GOING minus 0.07 sec per fur (G)

				SP	RR	SF
3795^{3}	**Cross The Border (69)** (DNicholls) **4-10-7** ^{7x} PRoberts(11) (lw: cl up: led wl over 1f out: r.o)	—	1	5/2^{1}	80	60
3856^{13}	**Pallium (IRE) (48)** (DANolan) **9-8-11b**$^{(3)}$ KSked(7) (hdwy ½-wy: chal ins fnl f: r.o)	½	2	20/1	57	37
3756^{7}	**Kabcast (38)** (DWChapman) **12-8-1b**$^{(3)}$ RWinston(3) (led tl hdd wl over 1f out: kpt on)	2	3	12/1	41	21
3566^{7}	**Southern Dominion (42)** (MissJFCraze) **5-8-3b**$^{(5)}$ CarolynBales(12) (lw: w ldrs far side: edgd lft fr ½-wy: kpt on wl)	s.h	4	20/1	45	25
3271^{W}	**Toronto (47)** (JBerry) **3-8-6b**$^{(5)}$ PBradley(5) (dwlt: hdwy 2f out: nrst fin)	hd	5	25/1	50	28
3271*	**Bashful Brave (53)** (BPJBaugh) **6-9-5** DarrenMoffatt(2) (lw: bhd: effrt ½-wy: styd on: nvr able chal)	½	6	13/2^{3}	54	34
	The Fed (38) (JLEyre) **7-7-13**$^{(5)}$ SBuckley(17) (racd far side: nvr nrr)	1	7	16/1	36	16
3756^{4}	**Imp Express (IRE) (40)** (GMMoore) **4-8-6** TEDurcan(4) (hdwy u.p ½-wy: n.d)	nk	8	7/1	37	17
3709^{5}	**Pizzicato (64)** (RJRWilliams) **3-10-0** DGriffiths(16) (chsd ldrs far side: outpcd fnl 2f)	¾	9	8/1	58	36
3460^{7}	**Tinker's Surprise (IRE) (46)** (JBalding) **3-8-10** RMullen(1) (lw: effrt ½-wy: no imp)	1	10	20/1	37	15
3761^{15}	**Dona Filipa (46)** (MissLCSiddall) **4-8-7**$^{(5)}$ ^{7x} TSiddall(9) (lw: bhd: hdwy ½-wy: n.d)	1¾	11	25/1	32	12
3399^{U}	**General Sir Peter (IRE) (53)** (NACallaghan) **5-9-5** AmandaSanders(13) (s.s: n.d)	½	12	33/1	37	17
3287^{12}	**Blazing Imp (USA) (44)** (MrsJJordan) **4-8-3**$^{(7)}$ JennyMurphy(14) (chsd ldrs far side 3f)	¾	13	33/1	26	6
2540^{6}	**Sunset Harbour (IRE) (44)** (SEKettlewell) **4-8-5**$^{(5)}$ JennyBenson(6) (swtchd & effrt ½-wy: n.d)	¾	14	14/1	23	3
3287^{11}	**Chemcast (62)** (JLEyre) **4-10-0b** OPears(8) (prom tl wknd fnl 2f)	2½	15	14/1	33	13
3756^{3}	**Bowcliffe Grange (IRE) (47)** (DWChapman) **5-8-13b** PFessey(15) (led far side tl wknd fnl 2f)	2½	16	5/1^{2}	10	—
				(SP 137.0%)	**16 Rn**	

60.7 secs (3.00) CSF £60.90 CT £532.30 TOTE £3.00: £1.10 £3.70 £6.60 £4.50 (£50.50) Trio £264.70 OWNER Mr P. D. Savill (THIRSK) BRED Brook Stud Ltd

WEIGHT FOR AGE 3yo-2lb

3795 Cross The Border did well from his draw and remains in tremendous form. (5/2)

2826 Pallium (IRE) ran a cracking race and kept on really well towards the finish. (20/1)

3756 Kabcast had the draw and ran well to show he is likely to pick up a race again this season. (12/1)

2759 Southern Dominion, from a poor draw, again showed he has the ability if he can be persuaded. (20/1)

2883 Toronto is a law unto himself and ran well here after a very poor start. (25/1)

3271* Bashful Brave was always being taken off his legs early on, albeit without offering a threat. (13/2)

The Fed ran well up the unfavoured far side. (16/1)

3756 Bowcliffe Grange (IRE) had the blinkers on for the first time this season and was disappointing, but he was poorly drawn. (5/1)

T/Plpt: £82.90 (216.05 Tckts). T/Qdpt: £27.20 (32.51 Tckts) AA

BORDEAUX (France) (R-H) (Good to firm)
Wednesday August 20th

3872a CRITERIUM DE BEQUET (Listed) (2-Y.O)

6-20 (6-27) **6f** £14,590.00 (£4,938.00: £3,704.00: £2,469.00)

				SP	RR	SF
3008a*	**Wren (IRE)** (LordHuntingdon) **2-8-10** FJovine	—	1		—	—
	River Ball (FR) (France) **2-8-13** J-BEyquem	2½	2		—	—
	Azelna (FR) (France) **2-8-10** PSogorb	1½	3		—	—
3192^{9}	**Ouaisne** (RGuest) **2-8-10** PBloomfield	3¼	4		—	—
						9 Rn

No Time Taken P-M 3.10F: 1.50F 1.50F 2.40F (11.20F) OWNER Anglia Bloodstock Ltd (WEST ILSLEY) BRED Barnane Partnership

3732a-DEAUVILLE (France) (R-H) (Good)
Wednesday August 20th

3873a PRIX DU HARAS DU THENNEY - PRIX DE LA VALLEE D'AUGE (Listed) (2-Y.O)

2-25 (2-25) **5f** £15,713.00 (£5,387.00: £4,040.00: £2,694.00)

				SP	RR	SF
	Sainte Marine (IRE) (RCollet,France) **2-8-8** TJamet	—	1		97+	—
	Petronilla (USA) (France) **2-8-8** FSanchez	2½	2		89	—
	Gold Away (IRE) (France) **2-8-11** ODoleuze	¾	3		90	—
3366a^{5}	**Dernier Croise (FR)** (BJMeehan) **2-8-11** MTebbutt	¾	4		87	—
						5 Rn

58.5 secs (2.00) P-M 4.10F: 1.40F 1.30F (SF 14.00F) OWNER Mr R. C. Strauss (CHANTILLY) BRED Kilfrush Stud Ltd

3366a Dernier Croise (FR) tried to make all, but faded from the furlong marker. The winner looked far superior to the rest, but the second and third are decent performers. As a French-bred he earns extra bonuses in this type of race, and is likely to return for a similar event.

3873a-DEAUVILLE (France) (R-H) (Good)
Saturday August 23rd

3874a CRITERIUM DU FONDS EUROPEEN DE L'ELEVAGE (Listed) (2-Y.O)
2-00 (2-02) **1m** £44,893.00 (£17,957.00: £13,468.00)

				SP	RR	SF
2268a[3]	**Saralea (FR)** (DSmaga,France) **2-8-8** DBoeuf	—	1		82	—
	Milligan (FR) (France) **2-8-11** FSanchez	1½	2		82	—
	Chateau Country (USA) (France) **2-8-11** ODoleuze	s.h	3		82	—
3322[2]	**Dower House** (WJarvis) **2-8-11** OPeslier	¾	4		80	—
3422*	**Diamond White** (GCBravery) **2-8-12** DRMcCabe (btn 11½l)		8		—	—

10 Rn

1m 45.0 (9.00) P-M 8.40F: 1.50F 3.40F 1.20F (65.50F) OWNER Mme M de Chambure (LAMORLAYE)
3322 Dower House put in a decent effort, running on in the closing stages. He was beaten by some pretty fair horses, and a decent maiden should come his way before the end of the season.
3422* Diamond White was well placed early, but was beaten by the furlong marker. She is not quite up to this class.

3875a PRIX DE LIEUREY - PRIX EUROPE 1 (Listed) (3-Y.O+ F & M)
2-35 (2-40) **1m** £44,893.00 (£17,957.00: £13,468.00)

				SP	RR	SF
727*	**Kool Kat Katie (IRE)** (DRLoder) **3-8-8** OPeslier	—	1		110+	—
3371a[7]	**Basse Besogne (IRE)** (France) **3-8-9** TThulliez	¾	2		110	—
3003a[3]	**Libria (IRE)** (France) **3-8-6** SGuillot	nk	3		106	—
3052*	**Aunty Jane** (JLDunlop) **4-8-11** PatEddery (btn approx 3½l)		7		—	—
3144[2]	**Jamrat Jumairah (IRE)** (EALDunlop) **4-8-11** WRyan (btn approx 5½l)		10		—	—
3548[3]	**Blessed Spirit** (CFWall) **4-8-11** DRMcCabe (btn over 5½l)		0		—	—

16 Rn

1m 42.2 (6.20) P-M 10.90F: 4.90F 5.60F 4.20F (147.80F) OWNER Lucayan Stud (NEWMARKET) BRED Lucayan Stud Ltd
727* Kool Kat Katie (IRE), looking superb in the paddock, outclassed her rivals. Always well placed, she took the lead a furlong and a half out and was not hard-pressed to hold her advantage. This was a fine effort on only her second run and her first since April, and her likely targets are the Sun Chariot or the Prix de l'Opera.
3052* Aunty Jane led the field into the straight before fading out of contention.
3144 Jamrat Jumairah (IRE) was never really seen with a chance.
3548 Blessed Spirit was always behind, and never really played a part.

3876a PRIX EUROPE 1 H'CAP (3-Y.O+)
3-05 **5f** £19,080.00

				SP	RR	SF
	Glivana (FR) (DSmaga,France) **3-9-6** DBoeuf	—	1		96	—
	Ebullisante (IRE) (France) **3-8-10** SCoffigny	nk	2		85	—
2096a*	**Arctic Starry (FR)** (France) **5-9-2** AJunk	nk	3		88	—
3372a[5]	**Bold Effort (FR)** (KOCunningham-Brown) **5-10-3** FSanchez (fin 4th btn approx 3/4l: disq & plcd last)		D		—	—

17 Rn

58.5 secs (2.00) P-M 17.20F; 5.80F 2.70F 2.70F (95.40F) OWNER Baron Thierry Van Zuylen (LAMORLAYE) BRED Baron Thierry Van Zuylen
3372a Bold Effort (FR) hampered one of his rivals and was inevitably disqualified.

3877a PRIX DE LA NONETTE (Gp 3) (3-Y.O F)
3-35 (3-41) **1m 2f** £44,893.00 (£16,835.00: £8,418.00)

				SP	RR	SF
3492*	**Dust Dancer** (JLDunlop) **3-9-0** PatEddery	—	1		116	—
1916a*	**Vereva (IRE)** (AdeRoyerDupre,France) **3-9-0** GMosse	hd	2		116	—
1738[2]	**Gazelle Royale (FR)** (JEHammond,France) **3-9-0** CAsmussen	1	3		114	—

6 Rn

2m 13.9 (8.90) P-M 10.70F: 1.10F 1.10F (SF 34.70F) OWNER Hesmonds Stud (ARUNDEL) BRED Hesmonds Stud Ltd
3492* Dust Dancer was given a great ride by Pat Eddery. He was forced to make all after nobody else wanted to lead. After being headed at the furlong marker the filly gamely battled back to beat the Prix de Diane winner and the Oaks runner-up. The Prix Vermeille may now be on the agenda.
1916a* Vereva (IRE) had a harder race than her trainer would have wished. He was very critical of the ground, but the filly probably needed the race, and will strip fitter in the Prix Vermeille.
1738 Gazelle Royale (FR) ran well over a distance short of her best, and was not given a hard time. She will take on the first two in the Vermeille.

3878a COUPE DU FONDS EUROPEEN DE L'ELEVAGE (Listed) (4-Y.O+ F & M)
4-05 (4-11) **1m 2f** £44,893.00 (£17,957.00: £13,468.00)

				SP	RR	SF
	Turning Wheel (USA) (DSepulchre,France) **4-8-11** CAsmussen	—	1		111	—
	L'Annee Folle (FR) (FDoumen,France) **4-8-11** GMosse	2	2		108	—
	Camille (FR) (France) **4-8-11** TGillet	2	3		105	—
2869[10]	**Cabaret (IRE)** (PWChapple-Hyam) **4-8-11** PatEddery (btn approx 11¼l)		9		—	—

9 Rn

2m 7.4 (2.40) P-M 2.30F: 1.20F 1.40F 1.50F (5.10F) OWNER Niarchos Family BRED Flaxman Holdings Ltd
Cabaret (IRE) was totally outclassed, and weakened significantly in the straight.

ARLINGTON PARK (Chicago, USA) (L-H) (Good to soft)
Sunday August 24th

3879a BEVERLY D STKS (Gp 1) (3-Y.O+ F & M)
9-11 (9-14) **1m 1f 110y** £178,571.00 (£59,524.00: £32,738.00)

				SP	RR	SF
	Memories Of Silver (USA) (JToner,USA) **4-8-11** JBailey	—	1		126	—
	Maxzene (USA) (TSkiffington,USA) **4-8-11** MESmith	nk	2		126	—
3376a[2]	**Dance Design (IRE)** (DKWeld,Ireland) **4-8-11** MJKinane	3¼	3		120	—
						6 Rn

1m 54.38 P-M £7.40: PL £3.80 £4.00: SHOW £2.40 £2.60 £2.40 (£11.60) CSF £23.40 OWNER Joan G Phillips & John Phillips
3376a Dance Design (IRE) started favourite for this Grade One event, but may have been unsuited by making the running, and could not hold off the principals in the straight. She will contest the Irish Champion Stakes next.

3880a ARLINGTON MILLION (Gp 1) (3-Y.O+)
10-18 (10-19) **1m 2f** £357,143.00 (£119,048.00: £65,476.00)

				SP	RR	SF
	Marlin (USA) (DWLukas,USA) **4-9-0** GaryStevens	—	1		129	—
628a[3]	**Sandpit (BRA)** (RMandella,USA) **8-9-0** CMcCarron	½	2		128	—
	Percutant (J-PDupuis) **6-9-0b**[1] MJKinane	1¼	3		126	—
3124[3]	**Allied Forces (USA)** (SbinSuroor) **4-9-0** LDettori (btn approx 4¼l)		6		—	—
						8 Rn

2m 2.54 P-M £7.80: PL £4.00 £4.60: SHOW £3.40 £3.60 £8.00 (£14.20) CSF £33.40 OWNER Mr M. Tabor BRED Gilbert G. Campbell
Marlin (USA), whom his trainer believes is the best turf horse in America, justified that view with a comfortable win. He will have one more race before the Breeders' Cup.
3124 Allied Forces (USA) pressed the leader early on, but was left behind when the tempo quickened on the turn for home.

3881a SECRETARIAT STKS (Gp 1) (3-Y.O)
11-25 (11-26) **1m 2f** £142,857.00 (£47,619.00: £26,190.00)

				SP	RR	SF
	Honor Glide (USA) (JDay,Canada) **3-8-11** GGomez	—	1		120	—
3172a[2]	**Casey Tibbs (IRE)** (DKWeld,Ireland) **3-8-6**ow2 MJKinane	1¼	2		113	—
	Glok (USA) (WMott,USA) **3-8-2** JBailey	1¾	3		106	—
						9 Rn

2m 2.74 P-M £7.00: PL £4.20 £12.60 SHOW £2.80 £6.40 £3.80 (£99.40) CSF £112.20 OWNER Mr R. Schaedle BRED Bonnie Heath Farm
Honor Glide (USA) is a very good colt, having previously won the Arlington Classic and the American Derby, and we may well see him contest such as the Rothmans International and the Breeders' Cup later in the year.
3172a Casey Tibbs (IRE) put up a terrific effort, coming through late to hunt up the winner. He will stay in America to contest the Man O' War Stakes, but may possibly be sold to race there.

3874a-DEAUVILLE (France) (R-H) (Good)
Sunday August 24th

3882a PRIX MORNY PIAGET (Gp 1) (2-Y.O C & F)
3-00 (3-06) **6f** £89,783.00 (£35,915.00: £17,957.00: £8,979.00)

				SP	RR	SF
3366a[2]	**Charge D'Affaires** (AdeRoyerDupre,France) **2-8-13** GMosse (hld up: rdn 3f out: hdwy to ld ins fnl f: pushed out)	—	1	10/1	110	—
3366a*	**Xaar** (AFabre,France) **2-8-13** OPeslier (hld up bhd ldr: chal 1f out: led ins fnl f: sn hdd: no ex)	hd	2	3/5[1]	110	—
2024[6]	**Heeremandi (IRE)** (APO'Brien,Ireland) **2-8-10** JReid (trckd ldrs: hrd rdn 1f out: styd on one pce)	1½	3	98/10	103	—
	Khumba Mela (IRE) (AFabre,France) **2-8-10** TJarnet (a.p: outpcd fnl f)	nk	4	53/10[3]	102	—
2012[2]	**Desert Prince (IRE)** (DRLoder) **2-8-13** KFallon (hld up: swtchd lft over 1f out: r.o u.p)	s.h	5	51/10[2]	105	—
3178a[4]	**Roi Gironde (IRE)** (MmeCHead,France) **2-8-13** PatEddery (a bhd: nvr able to chal)	4	6	11/1	94	—
3178a[3]	**Zelding (IRE)** (RCollet,France) **2-8-10** DBoeuf (led tl hdd ins fnl f)	1	7	10/1	89	—
				(SP 130.5%)		**7 Rn**

1m 12.7 (4.70) P-M 11.00F: 1.80F 1.10F (28.30F) OWNER Marquesa de Moratalla (CHANTILLY) BRED Marquesa de Moratalla
3366a Charge D'Affaires was given a perfect ride, with his jockey keeping to the good ground on the rail. He reversed Prix de Cabourg form with the runner-up and, on the upgrade, will probably go for the Prix de la Salamandre. (10/1)
3366a* Xaar can be considered rather unlucky. At halfway his stable companion took his ground, then he had to challenge on the worst going away from the rail. He will go for the Prix de la Salamandre, and looks a good value ante-post bet for the 1998 2,000 Guineas. (3/5)
2024 Heeremandi (IRE) was putting in her best work at the finish. She was not suited by the slow early pace, and will appreciate a longer trip. (98/10)
Khumba Mela (IRE) got worked up in the preliminaries, but ran well despite hampering her stablemate. She is likely to go for the Prix Marcel Boussac. (53/10)
2012 Desert Prince (IRE) was not suited by the way the race was run. He was unable to pick up when the pace quickened, and this performance suggests that further might suit. He should not be written off yet. (51/10)

3883a PRIX KERGORLAY (Gp 2) (3-Y.O+)
3-30 (3-39) **1m 7f** £33,670.00 (£13,468.00: £6,734.00: £3,367.00)

				SP	RR	SF
3149[2]	**Classic Cliche (IRE)** (SbinSuroor) **5-9-4** JReid (a cl up: 4th st: rdn to ld ins fnl f: r.o strly)	—	1		119+	—
2456a*	**Orchestra Stall** (JLDunlop) **5-9-4** PatEddery (a.p: hrd rdn & hung 1f out: r.o ins fnl f)	2	2		117	—
736[8]	**Chief Contender (IRE)** (PWChapple-Hyam) **4-9-4** OPeslier (2nd tl led over 1f out: sn hdd: no ex u.p)	2½	3		114	—
	Eurynome (GER) (PBary,France) **4-9-1** SGuillot (hld up: 5th st: hrd rdn: styd on one pce)	¾	4		110	—
3149[5]	**Persian Punch (IRE)** (DRCElsworth) **4-9-4** KFallon (led tl hdd over 1f out: wknd)	s.nk	5		113	—
	Oliviero (FR) (JYArtu,France) **4-9-4b** AJunk (a bhd)	1½	6		112	—

				SP	RR	SF
1365a*	**Stretarez (FR)** (DSepulchre,France) **4-9-6** FSanchez (mid div: hrd rdn ent st: sn bhd)	20	**7**		92	—

7 Rn

3m 20.9 (12.90) P-M 1.70F: 1.30F 2.20F (SF 6.80F) OWNER Godolphin (NEWMARKET) BRED Lord Victor Matthews in Ireland
3149 Classic Cliche (IRE) outclassed his field in the closing stages despite being a little outpaced turning for home. He has regained his form now and will probably head for the Irish St Leger before a crack at the Melbourne Cup.
2456a* Orchestra Stall put up a decent performance despite hanging in the straight. He was no match for the winner however, and is likely to avoid him in future, his next run being in the Prix Gladiateur.
Chief Contender (IRE) was always close to the pace, but could not cope with the first two in the last furlong. This was an encouraging effort after four months off the track, and he should soon find a suitable opportunity.
Eurynome (GER) was well enough placed in the straight, but did not have the pace to match the principals. A shorter trip might have helped.
3149 Persian Punch (IRE) was always up with the pace, but dropped away tamely in the straight. Connections felt that a stronger pace would have helped, and that the patchy ground was against him. He is likely to meet the winner again in the Irish St Leger.

3735a-DIELSDORF (Zurich, Switzerland) (L-H) (Good)
Sunday August 24th

3884a MERRILL LYNCH SILBERBLAUES BAND VON ZURICH (3-Y.O+)
2-30 (-) **1m 7f** £6,316.00

				SP	RR	SF
3122*	**Cloud Inspector (IRE)** (MJohnston) **6-10-0** JWeaver	—	**1**		95+	—
311a[2]	**Shturm (RUS)** (Switzerland) **4-9-13** RKaderli	7	**2**		87	—
	Grindstone (FR) (Switzerland) **5-9-13** BJollivet	3¾	**3**		83	—

12 Rn

3m 14.2 Tote 1.70SF: 1.20SF 1.30SF 1.80SF (4.50SF) OWNER Mr Markus Graff (MIDDLEHAM) BRED D. Cordell-Lavarack
3122* Cloud Inspector (IRE), who was formerly trained in Switzerland, returned to his old stamping ground and rewarded his connections' enterprise with a comfortable victory. He will return for a race on September 28th, but his ultimate target is the Cesarewitch.

OVREVOLL (Oslo, Norway) (L-H) (Good)
Sunday August 24th

3885a MARIT SVEAAS MINNELOP (Listed) (3-Y.O+)
3-10 **1m 1f** £22,957.00

				SP	RR	SF
	Stato One (RaymondDurant) **5-8-12** LSantos	—	**1**		98	—
	Coneybury (IRE) (WNeuroth,Norway) **7-8-12** FJohansson	1½	**2**		95	—
	Albaran (GER) (Norway) **4-8-12** GNordling	1½	**3**		93	—
3373a[4]	**Hever Golf Glory** (TJNaughton) **3-8-5** SSanders (btn 8l)		**7**		—	—

8 Rn

1m 49.9 Tote 111.40NKr: 16NKr 25NKr 22NKr (1125.80NKr) OWNER Stall R H BRED R. P. Williams
3373a Hever Golf Glory has run all of his last five races overseas, and may be feeling the effects as he produced a moderate effort, and was never in contention.

3252-CHESTER (L-H) (Good to soft)
Friday August 29th
Race 4: hand-timed
WEATHER: fine and warm WIND: fresh across

3886 WIRRAL APPRENTICE H'CAP (0-70) (3-Y.O+) (Class E)
2-10 (2-11) **1m 2f 75y** £2,998.00 (£919.00: £457.00: £226.00) Stalls: High GOING: 0.38 sec per fur (GS)

				SP	RR	SF
3255[7]	**Rasayel (USA) (70)** (PDEvans) **7-9-11**(3) AMcCarthy(8) (dwlt: hld up: hdwy 5f out: led wl over 2f out: pushed out)	—	**1**	12/1	83	44
3767[9]	**Wentbridge Lad (IRE) (57)** (ABailey) **7-8-7v**(8) IHudson(9) (b: b.hind: lw: hld up: hdwy 4f out: styd on wl fnl f)	2½	**2**	9/2 2	66	27
3627[11]	**Sagebrush Roller (50)** (JWWatts) **9-8-8b**1 ANicholls(10) (hld up & bhd: gd hdwy appr fnl f: fin wl)	3	**3**	10/1	55	16
3585[3]	**Nicola's Princess (48)** (BAMcMahon) **4-8-6** FBoyle(4) (lw: chsd ldrs: outpcd over 3f out: styd on ins fnl f)	hd	**4**	12/1	52	13
3758[2]	**Portite Sophie (39)** (MBrittain) **6-7-11** PBradley(2) (led after 2f tl wl over 2f out: wknd appr fnl f)	nk	**5**	7/2 1	43	4
3380[4]	**Ambidextrous (IRE) (60)** (EJAlston) **5-8-10**(8) MelanieWorden(5) (hld up in rr: nvr plcd to chal)	5	**6**	5/1 3	56	17
2876[6]	**Mazilla (48)** (AStreeter) **5-8-6** DHayden(3) (trckd ldrs: drvn along 4f out: sn lost tch: t.o)	12	**7**	10/1	26	—
3570[7]	**Jimjareer (IRE) (38)** (CaptJWilson) **4-7-7**(3) AngelaHartley(6) (lw: led 2f: wknd over 2f out: t.o)	5	**8**	25/1	8	—
3467[3]	**Mad Militant (IRE) (63)** (AStreeter) **8-9-7** RBrisland(1) (lost pl over 6f out: sn t.o)	14	**9**	5/1 3	11	—

(SP 111.2%) **9 Rn**

2m 21.3 (12.60) CSF £56.19 CT £498.51 TOTE £14.20: £2.70 £1.60 £2.40 (£27.10) Trio £32.20 OWNER Pentons Haulage and Cold Storage Ltd (WELSHPOOL) BRED Gainsborough Farm
LONG HANDICAP Jimjareer (IRE) 7-8
2533 Rasayel (USA), taking a big step down in distance, defied top weight with a clear-cut success and also recorded her now familiar August win for the third consecutive year. (12/1)
3588* Wentbridge Lad (IRE) acts well enough with cut in the ground and he did finish best of all, but the winner had got away and he was always fighting a lost cause. (9/2)
3104 Sagebrush Roller, twice a winner here in the past, knows full well where the winning post is but he misjudged his challenge over this longer trip, and only succeeded in gaining third prize right on the line. (10/1: 8/1-12/1)
3585 Nicola's Princess, struggling to stay in touch when the pace lifted out in the country, was staying on in the latter stages and she does seem to need further nowadays. (12/1)
3758 Portite Sophie decided on more forceful tactics on this return to ten furlongs, but the winner took her measure soon after passing the three-furlong marker, and her attempt to hold on to the runner-up prize faded inside the distance. (7/2)
3380 Ambidextrous (IRE) has never won as late as this in the year and he seems to have gone off the boil. (5/1)

3887 E.B.F. GREY FRIARS MAIDEN STKS (2-Y.O) (Class D)

2-45 (2-45) **7f 2y** £3,522.00 (£1,056.00: £508.00: £234.00) Stalls: Low GOING: 0.38 sec per fur (GS)

				SP	RR	SF
3201[7]	**O'Kelly (DEN)** (RGuest) **2-8-9** PBloomfield(6) (a.p: led wl over 2f out: drvn clr ent st: styd on strly)	—	**1**	16/1	79	39
3607[2]	**Guaranteed (84)** (BWHills) **2-9-0** RCochrane(5) (lw: plld hrd: hld up: hdwy over 2f out: kpt on u.p fnl f)	1¾	**2**	9/4[1]	80	40
2943[2]	**Lift The Offer (IRE)** (RHannon) **2-8-11**(3) MartinDwyer(3) (bhd: hdwy wl over 1f out: nvr nrr)	7	**3**	9/2[3]	64	24
3490[4]	**Durar** (JLDunlop) **2-9-0** KDarley(2) (b: lw: prom: hrd drvn over 2f out: wknd fnl f)	¾	**4**	9/2[3]	62	22
3426[4]	**Rewardia (IRE) (72)** (PDEvans) **2-8-9v**[1] JFEgan(4) (led tl hdd wl over 2f out: rdn & wknd ent st)	1½	**5**	14/1	54	14
3687[7]	**Royal Ground (IRE)** (MRChannon) **2-9-0** JFortune(1) (hld up in rr: rdn 2f out: no imp)	9	**6**	7/1	38	—
	Fly By Night (IRE) (MRStoute) **2-9-0** DHolland(8) (cmpt: bkwd: chsd ldrs: effrt 3f out: rdn & wknd 2f out: eased: t.o)	19	**7**	4/1[2]	—	—
3569[7]	**Laramania** (PDEvans) **2-9-0** WJO'Connor(7) (bit bkwd: a in rr: wl bhd fnl 3f: t.o)	7	**8**	40/1	—	—
				(SP 114.6%)	**8 Rn**	

1m 32.49 (7.29) CSF £47.76 TOTE £26.10: £3.80 £1.20 £1.30 (£48.30) OWNER Mr N. Elsass (NEWMARKET) BRED St. Bregnerodgard A/s

O'Kelly (DEN) had been brought along steadily and, gaining command from the long-time leader over two furlongs out, stepped up the gallop and readily out-pointed the hard-ridden runner-up. (16/1)

3607 Guaranteed again showed he needs a stiffer test of stamina, but he never once stopped trying and his turn is near at hand. (9/4)

2943 Lift The Offer (IRE), taken off his legs for most of the way, did begin to pick up once in line for home but he always had far too much to do and was never a serious contender. (9/2)

3490 Durar sat in behind the leader but he was tapped for toe when the winner quickened the tempo, and his run had come to an end on reaching the final furlong. (9/2)

3426 Rewardia (IRE) ran very free in the first-time visor and, hard at work on the home turn, had to admit she had run her race. (14/1)

Fly By Night (IRE), a strongly-made colt on short legs, was too backward to do himself justice on this debut and, showing signs of greenness when shown the whip, was wisely allowed to come home in his own time. (4/1: 5/2-9/2)

3888 EASTGATE RATED STKS H'CAP (0-95) (3-Y.O+) (Class C)

3-15 (3-15) **7f 2y** £6,453.12 (£2,398.08: £1,159.04: £483.20: £201.60: £88.96) Stalls: Low GOING: 0.38 sec per fur (GS)

				SP	RR	SF
3810*	**Highborn (IRE) (95)** (PSFelgate) **8-9-7**(3) 3x DSweeney(13) (lw: hld up: gd hdwy on outside 2f out: str run to ld cl home)	—	**1**	12/1	106	73
3725*	**Concer Un (89)** (SCWilliams) **5-9-4** 3x KDarley(6) (b: dwlt: sn chsng ldrs: rdn to ld ins fnl f: ct nr fin)	hd	**2**	9/4[1]	100	67
3408[4]	**Q Factor (82)** (DHaydnJones) **5-8-11** SDrowne(9) (lw: a.p: led over 2f out tl ins fnl f: unable qckn)	1½	**3**	14/1	89	56
3423[17]	**Royal Mark (IRE) (90)** (TDBarron) **4-9-5** JFortune(5) (hld up: hdwy over 2f out: kpt on u.p ins fnl f)	1¼	**4**	8/1[3]	95	62
3649[7]	**Mr Bergerac (IRE) (86)** (BPalling) **6-9-1** TSprake(2) (lw: hld up: hdwy ent st: swtchd lft & r.o wl fnl f)	1	**5**	11/1	88	55
3397[9]	**Mujova (IRE) (83)** (RHollinshead) **3-8-7** ACulhane(4) (lw: hld up: hdwy 2f out: nt clr run over 1f out: nvr nrr)	1¾	**6**	33/1	81	43
3765[18]	**Gadge (84)** (ABailey) **6-8-8**(5) PRoberts(12) (b: chsd ldrs: effrt over 2f out: wknd over 1f out)	1¾	**7**	14/1	78	45
3615[2]	**Albert The Bear (88)** (JBerry) **4-9-0**(3) TEDurcan(3) (sn led: rdn & hdd 3f out: wknd fnl 2f)	2½	**8**	9/2[2]	77	44
3150[11]	**Nomore Mr Niceguy (90)** (EJAlston) **3-9-0** JFEgan(1) (prom: hrd drvn 2f out: grad wknd)	hd	**9**	8/1[3]	78	40
3604[16]	**Caution (78)** (SGollings) **3-7-13**(3) RFfrench(10) (chsd ldrs: led 3f out: sn hdd & wknd)	nk	**10**	33/1	66	28
3150[12]	**Star Talent (USA) (87)** (IABalding) **6-9-2** RCochrane(8) (trckd ldrs tl outpcd fnl 2f)	1¼	**11**	10/1	72	39
2478[3]	**Double-J (IRE) (80)** (KMcAuliffe) **3-8-4** DHolland(7) (a in rr: t.o)	13	**12**	16/1	35	—
3649[15]	**Zuhair (90)** (DMcCain) **4-9-5** JCarroll(11) (b: chsd ldrs over 4f: sn lost tch: t.o)	½	**13**	25/1	44	11
				(SP 125.2%)	**13 Rn**	

1m 30.81 (5.61) CSF £36.70 CT £382.99 TOTE £16.50: £4.70 £1.50 £5.00 (£15.80) Trio £145.30 OWNER Yorkshire Racing Club Owners Group 1990 (MELTON MOWBRAY) BRED Mrs P. F. McQuillan

LONG HANDICAP Caution 7-10

WEIGHT FOR AGE 3yo-5lb

3810* Highborn (IRE) has shown his liking for this track in the past and, defying a 3lb penalty for a success earlier in the week, again timed his run to perfection and had his head in front where it mattered. (12/1)

3725* Concer Un did his utmost to repeat last year's follow-up from York with another success here, but the well-ridden winner proved just too strong in an all-out battle to the finish. (9/4)

3408 Q Factor looks a picture and continues to perform to the best of her ability but, in this very competitive handicap, the leading pair were just that bit too good for her. (14/1)

3423 Royal Mark (IRE) could have found this rain-softened ground against him but he did battle his way through a tightly-packed field entering the straight and no-one could fault him as far as courage was concerned. (8/1: 6/1-9/1)

3385* Mr Bergerac (IRE), having another try at this longer trip, had to search for an opening when making progress and he did stay on inside the last furlong, but he would have had to fly to reach the leaders. (11/1)

635 Mujova (IRE) did not enjoy a trouble-free passage when attempting to mount a challenge so, in the circumstances, this performance was probably much better than it appears at first sight. (33/1)

3889 COMBERMERE CONDITIONS STKS (2-Y.O F) (Class C)

3-50 (3-51) **6f 18y** £4,677.00 (£1,743.00: £846.50: £357.50: £153.75: £72.25) Stalls: Low GOING: 0.38 sec per fur (GS)

				SP	RR	SF
3595[3]	**Socket Set (96)** (BAMcMahon) **2-8-8** JFortune(6) (a.p: led over 1f out: qcknd clr: drvn out cl home)	—	**1**	10/11[1]	80	46
3610[3]	**Heavenly Abstone (85)** (PDEvans) **2-8-11v** JFEgan(2) (b: hld up: swtchd rt & hdwy over 1f out: rdn & r.o wl fnl f)	1¼	**2**	11/2[3]	80	46
3114[5]	**Salsette** (CEBrittain) **2-8-8** RCochrane(1) (bit bkwd: led tl hdd over 1f out: wknd ins fnl f)	5	**3**	11/2[3]	64	30
3701*	**Demolition Jo (72)** (PDEvans) **2-8-8v** WJO'Connor(5) (chsd ldr: ev ch 2f out: wknd appr fnl f)	3	**4**	9/1	56	22
3416[7]	**Farndon Princess** (RHollinshead) **2-8-8** DHolland(7) (s.i.s: hrd drvn over 2f out: no imp)	hd	**5**	20/1	55	21
3257[6]	**Bodfaridistinction (IRE) (75)** (ABailey) **2-8-11b**[1] DWright(3) (lw: sn pushed along: a bhd)	½	**6**	5/1[2]	57	23
				(SP 114.6%)	**6 Rn**	

1m 19.0 (5.70) CSF £6.10 TOTE £1.90: £1.50 £2.80 (£4.20) OWNER Mr J. C. Fretwell (TAMWORTH) BRED Mrs J. McMahon

3595 Socket Set had a comparatively easy task with her most serious rival failing to show up, and she won just as she should. (10/11)

3610 Heavenly Abstone, switched off the rail to deliver her challenge, ran on strongly in the closing stages but the winner had taken first run and always held a safe cushion. (11/2)

3114 Salsette, a fine-looking filly who still left the impression she is not yet the finished article, had no answer to the winner's pace when taken on approaching the final furlong and her stride shortened inside the last two hundred yards. She should soon be paying her way. (11/2: op 7/2)

3701* Demolition Jo does not know how to run a bad race but she was upped in class here, and found the pressure too much for her from below the distance. (9/1)

3890 BLACKFRIARS H'CAP (0-80) (3-Y.O+) (Class D)

4-20 (4-22) **1m 7f 195y** £3,496.00 (£1,048.00: £504.00: £232.00) Stalls: Low GOING: 0.38 sec per fur (GS)

				SP	RR	SF
3579^{2}	**Vicki Romara (72)** (MJohnston) **3-8-8** DHolland(3) (mde all: clr 7f out: styd on strly)	—	**1**	$4/1^{2}$	86	38
3826^{3}	**Dirab (61)** (TDBarron) **4-8-11** KDarley(7) (lw: hld up: hdwy over 6f out: sn chsng wnr: hrd drvn & swtchd lft appr fnl f: no imp)	3	**2**	$7/2^{1}$	72	38
3603*	**Suga Hawk (IRE) (64)** (EJAlston) **5-9-0** JFortune(4) (lw: hld up: effrt 4f out: rdn & no imp fnl 3f)	10	**3**	10/1	65	31
3309^{10}	**Trilby (53)** (GRichards) **4-8-3v** JCarroll(1) (hld up: hdwy 4f out: sn hrd drvn: no imp)	9	**4**	$7/2^{1}$	45	11
831^{8}	**Unchanged (65)** (CEBrittain) **5-9-1** RCochrane(5) (chsd wnr over 10f: rdn & wknd 4f out: t.o)	13	**5**	9/1	44	10
39^{4}	**Sea Victor (76)** (JLHarris) **5-9-9**(3) RFfrench(2) (bkwd: lost tch 6f out: sn t.o)	5	**6**	10/1	50	16
3579^{3}	**Benjamins Law (53)** (JAPickering) **6-8-0**(3) MartinDwyer(6) (hld up: lost pl 7f out: sn t.o)	dist	**7**	9/1	—	—
3333^{7}	***Rex Mundi (66)*** (PDEvans) **5-9-2** JFEgan(8) (Withdrawn not under Starter's orders: veterinary advice)		**W**	$7/1^{3}$	—	—
				(SP 115.1%)	**7 Rn**	

3m 39.9 (17.00) CSF £13.34 CT £82.42 TOTE £4.50: £2.50 £2.20 (£7.90) OWNER G R Bailey Ltd (Baileys Horse Feeds) (MIDDLEHAM) BRED Sheikh Mohammed Bin Rashid Al Maktoum
WEIGHT FOR AGE 3yo-14lb

3579 Vicki Romara, not winning out of turn, kept up her relentless gallop and proved much too strong for her pursuers. (4/1)
3826 Dirab would have won if he had gone through with his effort at Ripon earlier in the week, and he again looked duck-hearted when asked to go and win his race. He could now need a pair of blinkers to make up his mind. (7/2: 5/2-4/1)
3603* Suga Hawk (IRE), held up to get the trip, was making hard work of it when he tried to take closer order, and he could do little more than gallop on the spot for the final three furlongs. (10/1)
2682 Trilby, driven along for all she was worth entering the last half-mile, failed to make any impression at all and her last couple of runs would suggest she could have gone over the top. (7/2)

3891 RED DEER H'CAP (0-100) (3-Y.O) (Class C)

4-55 (4-57) **1m 2f 75y** £5,540.00 (£1,670.00: £810.00: £380.00) Stalls: High GOING: 0.38 sec per fur (GS)

				SP	RR	SF
3048^{3}	**Yabint El Sultan (74)** (BAMcMahon) **3-7-9**(3) RFfrench(1) (lw: a.p: led 7f out: clr 2f out: unchal)	—	**1**	13/2	93	35
2866^{8}	**My Valentina (72)** (BWHills) **3-7-7**(3) PFessey(10) (hld up & bhd: hdwy over 3f out: hmpd wl over 2f out: styd on wl ins fnl f)	4	**2**	$11/2^{2}$	85	27
3551*	**Brandon Jack (75)** (IABalding) **3-7-10**(3) MartinDwyer(6) (hld up: gd hdwy over 2f out: rdn & one pce appr fnl f)	2	**3**	$6/1^{3}$	85	27
1928*	**Titta Ruffo (84)** (BJMeehan) **3-8-8** KDarley(7) (lw: a.p: chsd wnr over 1f out: wknd fnl f)	5	**4**	9/1	86	28
3594^{9}	**Tycoon Todd (USA) (90)** (DRLoder) **3-9-0** RCochrane(4) (a chsng ldrs: rdn over 2f out: btn whn n.m.r over 1f out)	5	**5**	14/1	84	26
2832^{6}	**Sellette (IRE) (79)** (DHaydnJones) **3-8-3** SDrowne(9) (lw: chsd ldrs tl rdn & wknd over 1f out)	6	**6**	10/1	64	6
3404*	**Kamanev (IRE) (83)** (MRStoute) **3-8-7** DHolland(3) (led over 3f: hrd drvn 3f out: sn btn)	4	**7**	$7/2^{1}$	62	4
3388^{4}	**Rickenbacker (IRE) (97)** (PWChapple-Hyam) **3-9-4**(3) RHavlin(5) (hld up & bhd: outpcd fnl 3f)	s.h	**8**	$11/2^{2}$	76	18
2585^{15}	**Bevier (72)** (CEBrittain) **3-7-10** FNorton(8) (chsd ldrs over 6f: sn pushed along & outpcd: t.o)	18	**9**	20/1	23	—
2930^{3}	**Danzas (77)** (RCharlton) **3-8-1** JFEgan(2) (lw: trckd ldrs: rdn over 3f out: sn lost tch: t.o)	10	**10**	9/1	12	—
				(SP 121.1%)	**10 Rn**	

2m 18.85 (10.15) CSF £39.97 CT £210.65 TOTE £7.60: £1.70 £2.60 £2.00 (£43.40) Trio £54.10 OWNER G S D Imports Ltd (TAMWORTH) BRED J. H. H. Benbow and B. A. McMahon
OFFICIAL EXPLANATION **Kamanev (IRE): no explanation offered.**

3048 Yabint El Sultan took advantage of her lenient handicap mark and, scoring at her first attempt at the trip, sucked her rivals in approaching the straight and sauntered home unchallenged. (13/2)
1264 My Valentina, impeded after finding a smooth run through, lost her momentum at a vital time and, though she finished well, the winner had gone beyond recall. Quite a big filly, she was not at all happy on this tight track. (11/2)
3551* Brandon Jack began to take closer order on the approach to the straight, but the winner by then was in full flight and he was never going to catch her. (6/1: op 4/1)
1928* Titta Ruffo, successful in his first handicap, has since enjoyed a ten-week break. Never far away, he was in hot pursuit of the winner from the turn into the straight before lack of peak fitness took its toll. (9/1)
Tycoon Todd (USA), who changed stables in the summer, races a bit too freely to guarantee he would get this trip and he was already back-peddling when short of room turning in. (14/1)
2832 Sellette (IRE) ran much better than her finishing position would suggest, for she only dropped away from below the distance after chasing the leaders from the start. (10/1)
3404* Kamanev (IRE), given no favours in his first handicap, had a running battle with the winner in the early stages and he had shot his bolt some way from the finish. (7/2)
2930 Danzas (9/1: 6/1-10/1)

T/Plpt: £77.50 (336.84 Tckts). T/Qdpt: £11.00 (145.38 Tckts) IM

3546-SANDOWN (R-H) (Good to soft, Rnd crse Good patches, 5f crse Soft)

Friday August 29th

WEATHER: sunny spells WIND: slt half against

3892 ORLEANS NURSERY H'CAP (2-Y.O) (Class D)

2-00 (2-04) **5f 6y** £3,485.00 (£1,055.00: £515.00: £245.00) Stalls: Low GOING: 0.58 sec per fur (GS)

				SP	RR	SF
3755^{3}	**High Carry (71)** (NTinkler) **2-8-8**(5) CLowther(11) (hld up: rdn over 2f out: led wl over 1f out: r.o wl)	—	**1**	7/1	87	33
3546^{2}	**Supreme Angel (76)** (MPMuggeridge) **2-9-1**(3) MHenry(8) (hld up: rdn over 2f out: unable qckn)	6	**2**	10/1	73	19
3152^{11}	**Fast Tempo (IRE) (79)** (BPalling) **2-9-7** RHills(12) (led over 3f: one pce)	¾	**3**	10/1	74	20
3546^{U}	**Bound To Please (79)** (PJMakin) **2-9-7** SSanders(2) (a.p: hrd rdn over 1f out: one pce)	½	**4**	$5/1^{2}$	72	18
3407^{3}	**Italian Rose (67)** (WJMusson) **2-8-9** LDettori(4) (nt clr run over 2f out: swtchd rt: hdwy over 1f out: r.o one pce)	s.h	**5**	$6/1^{3}$	60	6

Form	Horse (Trainer) Age-Wt Jockey (Comment)	Dist	Pos	SP	RR	SF
3782^{2}	**Silent Pride (IRE) (54)** (MDIUsher) **2-7-3**$^{(7)}$ JFowle(6) (swtg: s.i.s: nvr nr to chal)	3	**6**	20/1	37	—
3228^{6}	**Satis (IRE) (54)** (MRChannon) **2-7-5**$^{(5)}$ APolli(7) (lw: nvr nrr)	6	**7**	20/1	18	—
3589^{4}	**Facile Tigre (77)** (SDow) **2-9-5** MRoberts(9) (rdn over 2f out: hdwy over 1f out: eased whn btn fnl f)	¾	**8**	14/1	39	—
3407*	**Dancing Icon (IRE) (78)** (RHannon) **2-9-6** DaneO'Neill(10) (spd over 2f)	4	**9**	9/2^{1}	27	—
1653^{9}	**Going Places (72)** (KTIvory) **2-9-0** KFallon(5) (spd over 3f)	2½	**10**	8/1	13	—
3546^{3}	**Means Business (IRE) (69)** (BJMeehan) **2-8-11b** MTebbutt(3) (swtg: spd over 2f)	6	**11**	7/1	—	—
				(SP 119.6%)	**11 Rn**	

66.55 secs (6.75) CSF £69.56 CT £635.57 TOTE £8.20: £2.40 £3.00 £5.20 (£36.90) Trio £124.80 OWNER Contrac Promotions Ltd (MALTON) BRED Giles W. Pritchard-Gordon

LONG HANDICAP Satis (IRE) 7-4 Silent Pride (IRE) 7-6

3755 High Carry made the long journey down from Malton pay. Well suited by the return to the minimum trip, she struck the front early in the final quarter-mile and forged clear for a decisive victory. Six furlongs is just too far for her at present. (7/1)

3546 Supreme Angel chased the leaders and, although just winning the scrap for second place, had absolutely no chance with the winner. (10/1)

2931 Fast Tempo (IRE) put her disappointing run at Goodwood last time out behind her but, after setting the pace, was well and truly left behind by the winner when headed early in the final quarter-mile. (10/1)

3546 Bound To Please had the advantage of racing against the stands' rail but failed to quicken in the last furlong and a half. (5/1: 3/1-11/2)

3407 Italian Rose, who did not have a great deal of racing room towards the back of the field at halfway, stayed on from below the distance without ever threatening to get into it. (6/1)

3782 Silent Pride (IRE) could never mount a challenge. She needs to return to six furlongs and selling company. (20/1)

3546 Means Business (IRE) (7/1: 4/1-15/2)

3893 DORKING MAIDEN STKS (3-Y.O F) (Class D)

2-35 (2-36) **1m 2f 7y** £3,485.00 (£1,055.00: £515.00: £245.00) Stalls: High GOING minus 0.03 sec per fur (G)

Form	Horse (Trainer) Age-Wt Jockey (Comment)	Dist	Pos	SP	RR	SF
2583^{6}	**Shaska** (JHMGosden) **3-8-11** LDettori(4) (s.s: hld up: chsd ldr over 2f out: led over 1f out: rdn out)	—	**1**	4/6^{1}	78	11
3495^{4}	**Curzon Street (66)** (DRCElsworth) **3-8-11** AProcter(2) (lw: s.s: stdy hdwy 2f out: rdn over 1f out: ev ch ins fnl f: unable qckn)	1	**2**	7/2^{3}	76	9
3021^{3}	**Dovedon Star (80)** (PAKelleway) **3-8-11** JReid(5) (swtg: chsd ldr: led 3f out tl over 1f out: one pce ins fnl f)	1¼	**3**	5/2^{2}	74	7
3389^{8}	**Spirit Lady** (JSKing) **3-8-11** DBiggs(3) (swtg: led 7f: wknd wl over 1f out)	11	**4**	66/1	57	—
3419^{8}	**Snowcap (IRE)** (GWragg) **3-8-6**$^{(5)}$ GMilligan(1) (hld up: rdn over 2f out: sn wknd)	13	**5**	40/1	36	—
				(SP 114.7%)	**5 Rn**	

2m 17.32 (10.62) CSF £3.41 TOTE £1.50: £1.10 £2.00 (£2.60) OWNER Sheikh Mohammed (NEWMARKET) BRED Cyril Humphris

2583 Shaska bruised her foot after her Newmarket debut last month. Coming through to lead over a furlong out, she tended to carry her head rather high but, given a slap with the whip inside the final furlong, kept on well enough. (4/6: tchd evens)

3495 Curzon Street cruised into the action a quarter of a mile out and appeared to be travelling best of all. With every chance early inside the final furlong, she then found the winner a little bit too strong. (7/2: 9/4-4/1)

3021 Dovedon Star has found lack of acceleration her downfall this season and that was again the problem here for, in the dash to the line in the final furlong, she was tapped for toe. (5/2)

3894 IBC EXECUTIVE TRAVEL H'CAP (0-90) (3-Y.O) (Class C)

3-05 (3-07) **1m 14y** £5,249.50 (£1,591.00: £778.00: £371.50) Stalls: High GOING minus 0.03 sec per fur (G)

Form	Horse (Trainer) Age-Wt Jockey (Comment)	Dist	Pos	SP	RR	SF
2871^{11}	**Shawm (87)** (DRLoder) **3-9-7** KFallon(3) (hdwy 4f out: rn wd st: led over 2f out: edgd rt ins fnl f: drvn out)	—	**1**	9/1^{3}	96	53
3594^{4}	**Just Nick (82)** (WRMuir) **3-9-2** JReid(9) (hdwy over 3f out: chsd wnr 2f out: ev ch ins fnl f: unable qckn)	1	**2**	7/1^{2}	89	46
2332^{5}	**Test The Water (IRE) (78)** (RHannon) **3-8-12** DaneO'Neill(8) (lw: rdn over 2f out: hdwy over 1f out: r.o)	s.h	**3**	25/1	85	42
3418^{3}	**Silk St John (80)** (MJRyan) **3-9-0** GCarter(15) (rdn over 2f out: hdwy over 1f out: r.o one pce)	¾	**4**	7/1^{2}	85	42
3696*	**Abajany (72)** (MRChannon) **3-8-6** 6x PaulEddery(6) (a.p: rdn over 2f out: r.o one pce)	½	**5**	9/1^{3}	76	33
3548^{2}	**Telemania (IRE) (83)** (WJHaggas) **3-9-3** FLynch(1) (hdwy over 2f out: hrd rdn over 1f out: wknd fnl f)	1¼	**6**	9/1^{3}	85	42
3328^{8}	**Saffron Rose (74)** (MBlanshard) **3-8-8** JQuinn(10) (nvr nr to chal)	3½	**7**	16/1	69	26
3243^{5}	**Attitude (85)** (HCandy) **3-9-5** CRutter(4) (lw: prom over 6f)	nk	**8**	16/1	79	36
3408^{6}	**Zoom Up (IRE) (83)** (MJHeaton-Ellis) **3-9-3** SSanders(13) (lw: nvr nrr)	½	**9**	12/1	76	33
3448^{4}	**Irtifa (70)** (PTWalwyn) **3-8-4** RHills(11) (lw: hld up: rdn over 2f out: sn wknd)	5	**10**	16/1	54	11
3392^{3}	**Al Masroor (USA) (77)** (JWPayne) **3-8-11** DeanMcKeown(2) (prom over 5f)	1½	**11**	10/1	58	15
3236^{9}	**Blewbury Hill (IRE) (74)** (RFJohnsonHoughton) **3-8-8** GDuffield(12) (bhd fnl 5f)	hd	**12**	12/1	54	11
2062^{2}	**Green Power (85)** (JRFanshawe) **3-9-5** MJKinane(5) (lw: hdwy over 2f out: wknd over 1f out)	1¼	**13**	5/1^{1}	63	20
3496^{12}	**Kafil (USA) (68)** (GLMoore) **3-8-2**^{ow1} MRoberts(14) (led over 1f: rdn 3f out: wknd wl over 1f out)	2	**14**	16/1	42	—
2695^{7}	**Heart Full of Soul (73)** (PFICole) **3-8-7b** LDettori(7) (lw: led over 6f out tl over 2f out: sn wknd)	3½	**15**	12/1	40	—
				(SP 131.2%)	**15 Rn**	

1m 46.19 (4.99) CSF £69.77 CT £1,463.87 TOTE £11.90: £4.10 £2.30 £4.00 (£78.10) Trio £616.80 OWNER Sheikh Mohammed (NEWMARKET) BRED Sheikh Mohammed Bin Rashid Al Maktoum

2871 Shawm has suffered from breathing problems and swallowed his tongue so, as a result, was fitted with a cross-noseband on this occasion. Racing over his ideal trip, he struck the front over two furlongs form home and, although drifting right under pressure inside the last two hundred yards, kept on well. (9/1)

3594 Just Nick has gained his only victory to date on soft ground. Taking second place a quarter of a mile out, he looked a serious threat to the winner inside the final furlong but just failed to find the necessary turn of foot. (7/1)

2332 Test The Water (IRE), 15lb lower than at the beginning of the season, ran his best race of the campaign, staying on nicely in the last furlong and a half and only just failing to snatch second prize. (25/1)

3418 Silk St John stayed on up the hill in the last furlong and a half and only just lost out in the battle for third prize. (7/1)

3696* Abajany, never far away, struggled on if never looking likely to find the necessary turn of foot. (9/1)

3548 Telemania (IRE) moved up on the outside over two furlongs from home but had run out of gas in the final furlong. (9/1: 6/1-10/1)

3895 SOLARIO STKS (Gp 3) (2-Y.O) (Class A)

3-40 (3-42) **7f 16y** £18,930.00 (£7,164.00: £3,507.00: £1,599.00) Stalls: High GOING minus 0.03 sec per fur (G)

Form	Horse (Trainer) Age-Wt Jockey (Comment)	Dist	Pos	SP	RR	SF
3123^{3}	**Little Indian (100)** (SPCWoods) **2-8-11** JReid(3) (lw: rdn over 3f out: lost pl over 2f out: rallied fnl f: str run to ld nr fin)	—	**1**	12/1	102	61
3142^{2}	**Tracking (100)** (HRACecil) **2-8-11** KFallon(1) (lw: led: rdn over 1f out: hdd nr fin)	½	**2**	5/2^{2}	101	60
3142*	**Haami (USA)** (JLDunlop) **2-8-11** RHills(2) (lw: stdy hdwy over 2f out: chsd ldr over 1f out tl ins fnl f: sn wknd)	2	**3**	15/8^{1}	96	55
3672a^{2}	**Sharp Play** (MJohnston) **2-8-11** JWeaver(5) (chsd ldr over 5f: wknd fnl f)	1¼	**4**	7/2^{3}	94	53

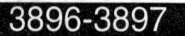

				SP	RR	SF
	Celtic Cavalier (IRE) (APO'Brien,Ireland) **2-8-11v¹** MJKinane(4) (w'like: scope: lw: hld up: rdn over 3f out: wknd over 2f out)	3½	**5**	6/1	86	45
				(SP 107.6%)		**5 Rn**

1m 31.45 (2.85) CSF £36.06 TOTE £15.50: £3.00 £1.80 (£18.90) OWNER Mr G. V. Wright (NEWMARKET) BRED M. S. Anderson

3123 Little Indian found this stiff seven furlongs and the soft ground putting more of an emphasis on stamina - just what the doctor ordered. One of the first off the bridle, he got outpaced over a quarter of a mile from home and looked likely to finish only fourth. However, the Sandown hill can change a finish dramatically and, really finding his feet in the final furlong, he stormed through to snatch the spoils near the line. He is in the Dewhurst and the Racing Post Trophy with connections leaning towards the latter. (12/1)

3142 Tracking, who was trying to chat to his rivals in the paddock, was 7lb better off with Haami for a neck beating last time out. Bowling along in front, he looked to have the measure of his rivals entering the final furlong but was unable to withstand the strong late burst of the winner. He should soon regain the winning thread. (5/2)

3142* Haami (USA), as low as 12/1 for next year's Two Thousand Guineas, looked tremendous in the paddock and cruised closer in the straight, travelling supremely well. Bustled along below the distance, he then failed to find another gear and tired in the closing stages. The soft ground surely played a big part in his downfall as it blunted his acceleration. On a sounder surface, he can bounce back. (15/8: op 5/4)

3672a Sharp Play, second to King of Kings last time out, raced in second place but he was collared for that position approaching the final furlong and tired up the hill. (7/2)

Celtic Cavalier (IRE), an attractive, good-bodied colt who won a maiden at Gowran Park recently, failed to trouble his English opponents and had been seen off approaching the final quarter-mile. (6/1)

3896 IBC EXECUTIVE TRAVEL STAYERS H'CAP (0-70) (3-Y.O+) (Class E)

4-10 (4-14) **2m 78y** £3,696.25 (£1,120.00: £547.50: £261.25) Stalls: High GOING minus 0.03 sec per fur (G)

				SP	RR	SF
3498^{2}	**Siege Perilous (IRE) (70)** (SCWilliams) **4-10-0** LDettori(13) (lw: hdwy over 3f out: led over 2f out tl over 1f out: hrd rdn: led last strides)	—	**1**	$9/2^{2}$	81	52
3714^{6}	**Courbaril (55)** (MCPipe) **5-8-13v** KFallon(12) (lw: hdwy 10f out: rdn over 3f out: led ins fnl f: hdd last strides)	hd	**2**	11/1	66	37
*3073**	**Private Fixture (IRE) (45)** (DMarks) **6-8-3** PaulEddery(3) (swtg: hdwy over 2f out: led over 1f out tl ins fnl f: r.o)	nk	**3**	16/1	56	27
3028^{4}	**Nick of Time (60)** (JLDunlop) **3-8-4** GCarter(8) (stdy hdwy 7f out: hrd rdn over 2f out: ev ch ins fnl f: unable qckn)	½	**4**	10/1	70	27
3472^{3}	**Castle Courageous (67)** (LadyHerries) **10-9-6**(5) GMilligan(5) (b: hdwy over 4f out: hung rt over 1f out: r.o one pce)	½	**5**	16/1	77	48
3472*	**Hillswick (41)** (JSKing) **6-7-8**(5) APolli(16) (a.p: led 8f out tl over 2f out: wknd fnl f)	3	**6**	9/1	48	19
2246^{13}	**Myosotis (52)** (PJMakin) **3-7-10b** GBardwell(15) (nvr gng wl: nvr nrr)	2½	**7**	50/1	56	13
3309^{2}	**Indigo Dawn (61)** (MJohnston) **3-8-5** JWeaver(4) (hld up: rdn 6f out: wknd over 4f out)	21	**8**	$11/4^{1}$	45	2
83^{9}	**Name of Our Father (USA) (65)** (PBowen) **4-9-9** MFenton(1) (swtg: bhd fnl 6f)	17	**9**	20/1	32	3
3587^{5}	**Subtle Touch (IRE) (42)** (PLGilligan) **6-8-0** NAdams(7) (lw: led over 8f: wknd 5f out)	2	**10**	50/1	7	—
3714*	**Serious Trust (51)** (MrsLCJewell) **4-8-9** 4x GDuffield(10) (prom 11f)	½	**11**	10/1	16	—
3057^{6}	**Zafarelli (60)** (JRJenkins) **3-7-13**(5) CLowther(2) (bhd fnl 8f)	nk	**12**	12/1	24	—
3122^{2}	**Shadirwan (IRE) (68)** (RAkehurst) **6-9-12** SSanders(9) (lw: prom 11f)	nk	**13**	$6/1^{3}$	32	3
3587^{6}	**Not Forgotten (USA) (53)** (PAKelleway) **3-7-11b** JLowe(14) (prom over 11f)	1¼	**14**	33/1	16	—
				(SP 126.7%)		**14 Rn**

3m 44.07 (12.07) CSF £50.00 CT £684.49 TOTE £5.50: £2.40 £2.60 £7.30 (£22.70) Trio £310.70 OWNER Mr S. Demanuele (NEWMARKET) BRED Miss Honora Corridan

LONG HANDICAP Myosotis 6-12

WEIGHT FOR AGE 3yo-14lb

3498 Siege Perilous (IRE) has been in good form this season and put up a gritty display. Brought over to the stands' side in search of the better ground, he was one of several fighting for the lead in the straight, but just managed to have his head in front where it mattered to win his first race over this trip. (9/2)

3714 Courbaril bounced back to form after a couple of poor runs this season. Racing down the centre of the track, he got to the front inside the final furlong but was worried out of it in the last few strides. He is a winner without a penalty. (11/1: 7/1-12/1)

3073* Private Fixture (IRE) really enjoyed the step up in trip and managed to get to the front below the distance. Headed inside the final furlong, he only just lost out. He is in great heart at present and, although he has not won on turf since 1993, that should soon be rectified. (16/1)

3028 Nick of Time, who ran well on soft ground at Folkestone earlier in the season, was one of five fighting for the lead inside the final furlong, before just tapped for toe. (10/1)

3472 Castle Courageous is a shadow of his former self these days but, undoubtedly, ran his best race of the season. Despite hanging right below the distance, he was right on the heels of the principals in the final furlong. (16/1)

3472* Hillswick went on at halfway and was probably marginally headed over a quarter of a mile from home. Grimly trying to hold on, he was only shaken off in the final furlong. (9/1)

3714* Serious Trust (10/1: 6/1-11/1)

3122 Shadirwan (IRE) (6/1: op 7/2)

3897 CLAYGATE CLAIMING STKS (3-Y.O) (Class E)

4-45 (4-49) **1m 1f** £2,843.25 (£861.00: £420.50: £200.25) Stalls: High GOING minus 0.03 sec per fur (G)

				SP	RR	SF
3633^{3}	**Azores (78)** (PFICole) **3-9-3** LDettori(4) (hdwy over 2f out: hung rt over 1f out: hrd rdn: led last strides)	—	**1**	$100/30^{2}$	71	54
2601^{15}	**Beryllium (75)** (RHannon) **3-8-9** DaneO'Neill(6) (lw: rdn over 3f out: hdwy over 2f out: hung rt & led ins fnl f: hdd last strides)	½	**2**	14/1	62	45
3741^{6}	**Merciless Cop (72)** (BJMeehan) **3-8-13b** MTebbutt(10) (a.p: rdn over 2f out: led over 1f out tl ins fnl f: one pce)	½	**3**	7/1	65	48
3741^{4}	**Mantles Prince (78)** (GLewis) **3-9-3b** PaulEddery(12) (led 3f: led over 2f out tl over 1f out: one pce)	hd	**4**	$9/4^{1}$	69	52
3557^{3}	**Tulsa (IRE) (44)** (BGubby) **3-8-7** KFallon(1) (rdn over 3f out: hdwy over 1f out: r.o wl ins fnl f)	s.h	**5**	16/1	59	42
1276^{6}	**Bright Fountain (IRE)** (HCandy) **3-8-2** AMcGlone(7) (chsd ldrs: rdn over 3f out: wknd fnl f)	4	**6**	16/1	47	30
3696^{7}	**Reeds (58)** (JRFanshawe) **3-8-5** NDay(3) (rdn over 3f out: hdwy over 1f out: wknd fnl f)	5	**7**	25/1	41	24
2508^{5}	**Orontes (USA) (69)** (RHannon) **3-8-9** JReid(5) (nvr nrr)	3	**8**	12/1	40	23
3601^{3}	**Inkwell (34)** (AHide) **3-7-10b¹**(5) RMullen(9) (s.s: hdwy over 7f out: rdn over 3f out: wknd over 1f out)	2½	**9**	25/1	27	10
	Miskin Heights (IRE) (40) (KRBurke) **3-8-2** JQuinn(2) (swtg: s.s: a bhd)	3	**10**	66/1	23	6
3551^{4}	**All In Leather (70)** (WJHaggas) **3-8-9** FLynch(8) (w ldr: led 6f out tl over 2f out: wknd qckly over 1f out)	5	**11**	$7/2^{3}$	21	4

	Runner	Dist	Pos	SP	RR	SF
2921^{17}	**Oakbrook Rose (46)** (MPMuggeridge) **3-7-11b^{1}**(3) MHenry(11) (a bhd: t.o fnl 2f)	dist	**12**	66/1	—	—
				(SP 125.4%)		**12 Rn**

1m 58.07 (4.97) CSF £46.61 TOTE £3.90: £1.70 £3.90 £2.60 (£51.50) Trio £61.20 OWNER H R H Prince Fahd Salman (WHATCOMBE) BRED Meon Valley Stud
Beryllium clmd CWylie £12,000, Merciless Cop clmd LJones £16,000.

3633 Azores, a half-brother to Oaks winner Lady Carla, appreciated the drop in class and, although wandering about below the distance, responded well to pressure to get up in the last couple of strides. (100/30)
Beryllium appreciated the drop in class and ran his best race of the season. Despite hanging right, he led early inside the final furlong, only to be caught by the winner, racing on the opposite side of the track, in the last couple of strides. (14/1: 10/1-16/1)
2877* Merciless Cop, beaten nearly four lengths by Mantles Prince last week at Goodwood, was 2lb worse off on this occasion but still managed to reverse the form. Showing in front below the distance, he was collared inside the final furlong and tapped for toe. (7/1)
3741 Mantles Prince was not going to hang around and disputed the lead from the start. Eventually overhauled approaching the final furlong, he could only struggle on at one pace. He remains a maiden after thirteen attempts. (9/4: 3/1-100/3)
3557 Tulsa (IRE), off the bridle and well behind entering the straight, stayed on well in the last furlong and a half to be nearest at the line. (16/1)
1276 Bright Fountain (IRE), off the course for three and a half months since her debut, chased the leaders but eventually had to admit defeat in the final furlong. (16/1)
3551 All In Leather (7/2: 5/2-4/1)

3898 GUILDFORD H'CAP (0-80) (3-Y.O+) (Class D)

5-20 (5-23) **5f 6y** £3,810.00 (£1,155.00: £565.00: £270.00) Stalls: Low GOING: 0.58 sec per fur (GS)

	Runner	Dist	Pos	SP	RR	SF
3126^{3}	**Sweet Magic (59)** (PHowling) **6-8-12** MRoberts(11) (racd far side: a.p: led 2f out: rdn out)	—	**1**	11/2^{2}	69	51
3473^{6}	**Tinker Osmaston (64)** (RJHodges) **6-9-3** JQuinn(12) (racd far side: hld up: rdn over 1f out: r.o wl ins fnl f)	½	**2**	5/1^{1}	72	54
2563^{17}	**At Large (IRE) (73)** (JRFanshawe) **3-9-10** NDay(4) (lw: rdn & hdwy over 1f out: r.o wl ins fnl f)	hd	**3**	12/1	81	61
3500^{5}	**Barranak (IRE) (63)** (GMMcCourt) **5-9-2** CRutter(6) (a.p: rdn over 1f out: unable qckn)	1½	**4**	8/1	66	48
3500*	**Half Tone (62)** (RMFlower) **5-9-1b** SSanders(1) (a.p: rdn over 1f out: one pce)	nk	**5**	13/2^{3}	64	46
3642^{6}	**Corniche Quest (IRE) (68)** (MRChannon) **4-9-0**(7) AEddery(3) (lw: hdwy over 1f out: r.o)	hd	**6**	15/2	70	52
3693^{6}	**Songsheet (68)** (MSSaunders) **4-9-4**(3) PPMurphy(10) (lw: a.p: rdn over 2f out: wknd ins fnl f)	1½	**7**	14/1	65	47
3473^{8}	**Runs in the Family (61)** (GMMcCourt) **5-9-0b** KFallon(7) (led 3f: wknd fnl f)	1½	**8**	11/2^{2}	54	36
427^{6}	**Threeplay (IRE) (60)** (JAkehurst) **3-8-11** MTebbutt(5) (bhd fnl 2f)	2	**9**	50/1	46	26
1792^{4}	**Mutasawwar (71)** (MSSaunders) **3-9-8** JReid(2) (lw: a bhd)	1¼	**10**	25/1	53	33
2554^{2}	**Batsman (52)** (WJMusson) **3-8-3** DRMcCabe(8) (a bhd)	5	**11**	8/1	18	—
3500^{13}	**Jucea (61)** (JLSpearing) **8-9-0** JWeaver(9) (lw: prom over 3f)	s.h	**12**	14/1	27	9
				(SP 121.6%)		**12 Rn**

65.4 secs (5.60) CSF £31.02 CT £300.25 TOTE £6.50: £1.90 £1.90 £3.70 (£10.90) Trio £174.40 OWNER Mr C. Hammond (NEWMARKET) BRED Miss K. S. Waddington
WEIGHT FOR AGE 3yo-2lb

3126 Sweet Magic confirmed the promise shown last time out under a very intelligent ride from Roberts who had walked the sprint course before racing and decided that the best ground was on the far side. One of only two to tack over to the far rails - the stalls were on the stands' side - he gained overall control a quarter of a mile out and, rousted along, held on well. (11/2)
3473 Tinker Osmaston, who has won twice on this ground, was the only runner apart from the winner to tack over to the far side. Stalking her rival, she kept on really well inside the final furlong. (5/1)
1119 At Large (IRE) began his effort below the distance but, despite running on strongly to win the stands'-side battle, was just unable to overhaul the front two racing on the opposite side of the track. (12/1: op 8/1)
3500 Barranak (IRE), a leading light from the off, failed to quicken from below the distance. (8/1)
3500* Half Tone, 6lb higher for his recent win here, was never far away but could only plod on at one pace in the final quarter-mile. (13/2)
3642 Corniche Quest (IRE) stayed on from below the distance but never threatened to get there in time. (15/2)

T/Jkpt: Not won; £30,852.00 to Sandown 30/8/97. T/Plpt: £1,234.50 (26.39 Tckts). T/Qdpt: £166.10 (11.41 Tckts) AK

3886-CHESTER (L-H) (Soft, Heavy patches)

Saturday August 30th

Race 1 hand-timed
WEATHER: fine & sunny WIND: mod half against

3899 LINENHALL CONDITIONS STKS (2-Y.O C & G) (Class C)

2-10 (2-10) **6f 18y** £4,764.00 (£1,776.00: £863.00: £365.00: £157.50: £74.50) Stalls: Low GOING: 0.78 sec per fur (S)

	Runner	Dist	Pos	SP	RR	SF
2685^{3}	**Jimmy Too (88)** (BAMcMahon) **2-8-13** JFortune(3) (lw: dwlt: hdwy ½-wy: rdn over 1f out: r.o to ld wl ins fnl f)	—	**1**	9/2^{3}	93	50
3613*	**Surveyor** (JLDunlop) **2-8-13** TSprake(4) (hdwy 3f out: led over 2f out: hrd rdn & hdd wl ins fnl f)	¾	**2**	15/8^{1}	91	48
*3607**	**The Groveller (79)** (PDEvans) **2-8-13** JFEgan(5) (led 1f: rdn & ev ch 2f out: outpcd fnl f)	4	**3**	16/1	81	38
3753*	**Exbourne's Wish (USA) (83)** (BWHills) **2-8-13** MHills(7) (led after 1f tl over 2f out: sn outpcd)	s.h	**4**	3/1^{2}	80	37
3022^{5}	**Suivez La Trace** (RAFahey) **2-8-13** RCochrane(2) (lw: hld up: effrt on outside over 2f out: sn rdn: wknd fnl f)	1½	**5**	8/1	76	33
2856^{4}	**Althib (IRE)** (MRStoute) **2-8-10** SSanders(1) (lw: prom: rdn & wkng whn hmpd over 2f out: eased whn btn: t.o)	17	**6**	9/2^{3}	29	—
				(SP 113.1%)		**6 Rn**

1m 21.5 (8.20) CSF £12.40 TOTE £4.50: £1.80 £1.50 (£4.30) OWNER Mr J. D. Graham (TAMWORTH) BRED J. D. Graham

2685 Jimmy Too has enjoyed a break and, with his stable now in tip-top form, he was able to take advantage of these more testing conditions, battling on to gain command nearing the line. (9/2)
3613* Surveyor set sail for home on the approach to the straight and did look to have control, but the winner relished the conditions better and wore him down late on. (15/8)
3607* The Groveller, in the action all the way, held every chance on sufferance entering the last quarter-mile, but the leading pair proved much too strong in the run to the line. (16/1)
3753* Exbourne's Wish (USA) made the majority of the running until the favourite took over and then lost his pitch. Ridden along, he began to stay on again in the closing stages but had given himself far too much to do. (3/1)

3022 Suivez La Trace, a winner on similar ground on his debut, tried hard to mount a challenge turning in but he had been forced to race on the outside and could not muster the pace to land a blow. (8/1)
2856 Althib (IRE) has not really progressed from his promising debut run and he was already back-pedalling when The Groveller drifted in front of him entering the straight, causing him to be snatched up. (9/2)

3900 ROWTON MOOR H'CAP (0-85) (3-Y.O+) (Class D)

TF

2-45 (2-46) **5f 16y** £6,690.00 (£2,010.00: £970.00: £450.00) Stalls: Low GOING: 0.78 sec per fur (S)

				SP	RR	SF
97 3273[9]	**Westcourt Magic (80)** (MWEasterby) **4-9-11** SSanders(1) (a.p: rdn 2f out: led appr fnl f: edgd rt: r.o wl)	—	**1**	7/2[1]	94	77
9c 3771[3]	**Squire Corrie (82)** (DWChapman) **5-9-13** GDuffield(8) (a.p: rdn & ev ch 1f out: unable qckn fnl 200y)	3	**2**	7/1[2]	87	70
72 3756[14]	**Swan At Whalley (65)** (RAFahey) **5-8-3**(7) RWinston(5) (led tl appr fnl f: sn rdn: no ex)	½	**3**	12/1	68	51
66+ 3795[2]	**Tuscan Dawn (67)** (JBerry) **7-8-7**(5) PRoberts(9) (plld hrd: prom: effrt & rdn wl over 1f out: one pce)	2½	**4**	7/2[1]	62	45
3580[11]	**Samwar (82)** (MRChannon) **5-9-13** JFortune(3) (b.hind: dwlt: sn bhd & outpcd: sme late hdwy: n.d)	1½	**5**	12/1	72	55
3194[9]	**Swino (75)** (PDEvans) **3-9-4b[1]** JFEgan(7) (bhd & outpcd tl r.o u.p fnl f)	s.h	**6**	14/1	65	46
3771[12]	**Malibu Man (75)** (EAWheeler) **5-9-6b[1]** TSprake(11) (s.i.s: hdwy 3f out: sn hrd drvn: wknd over 1f out)	½	**7**	12/1	64	47
3566[6]	**Palacegate Touch (79)** (JBerry) **7-9-7b**(3) TEDurcan(13) (hdwy 3f out: hrd rdn 2f out: sn wknd)	2	**8**	11/1[3]	61	44
	Mazeed (IRE) (76) (PDEvans) **4-9-0**(7) AMcCarthy(4) (bit bkwd: outpcd: a bhd)	2	**9**	25/1	52	35
1243[8]	**Braveheart (IRE) (78)** (MRChannon) **3-9-0**(7) AEddery(2) (bit bkwd: outpcd: a bhd)	¾	**10**	14/1	52	33
3500[11]	**Lady Caroline Lamb (IRE) (64)** (RBastiman) **4-8-9** JQuinn(10) (chsd ldrs to ½-wy: sn rdn & outpcd)	s.h	**11**	12/1	38	21
3457[7]	**Unshaken (67)** (EJAlston) **3-8-10** MHills(12) (outpcd: t.o)	6	**12**	25/1	22	3
				(SP 117.1%)	**12 Rn**	

66.06 secs (5.86) CSF £24.43 CT £240.77 TOTE £4.40: £1.90 £2.60 £2.70 (£11.20) Trio £62.30 OWNER Mr K. Hodgson (SHERIFF HUTTON) BRED C. R. and V. M. Withers
WEIGHT FOR AGE 3yo-2lb

2900 Westcourt Magic has never won on ground as testing as this, but he did win three times in August in his first season, and this is definitely his time of year. (7/2)
3771 Squire Corrie, having his twenty-third outing this season, still retains all his enthusiasm for the game and he more than pays his way. (7/1)
2339* Swan At Whalley has plenty of pace and he led the way until worn down approaching the final furlong, and then found an extra effort more than he could manage. (12/1)
3795 Tuscan Dawn, swinging off the bridle in behind the leaders, was unable to respond when the tempo lifted and was fighting a lost cause from the turn into the straight. (7/2)
Samwar does the majority of his racing over slightly longer trips and a tardy start did him no favours on this track, and he was only finding his stride when the race was as good as over. Suited by some cut in the ground, he could be about to find his form. (12/1: op 7/1)
2655 Swino, taken off his legs, was hard at work from halfway and he did well to get so close at the finish. (14/1)
3326* Malibu Man needs to hit the traps to produce his best but, with the blinkers on, he did miss a beat at the start. Although he recovered to chase the leaders, he had to work to do so and had run himself out before reaching the final furlong. (12/1: op 8/1)
3566 Palacegate Touch (11/1: op 7/1)

3901 ROTHMANS ROYALS NORTH SOUTH CHALLENGE SERIES H'CAP (0-100) (3-Y.O+) (Class C)

3-15 (3-18) **7f 122y** £7,931.50 (£2,392.00: £1,161.00: £545.50) Stalls: Low GOING: 0.78 sec per fur (S)

				SP	RR	SF
3622[7]	**Queens Consul (IRE) (79)** (BSRothwell) **7-8-8** MFenton(9) (chsd ldr: led wl over 3f out: clr appr fnl f: r.o)	—	**1**	10/1	90	69
3548*	**Gulf Shaadi (72)** (EJAlston) **5-8-1** JFEgan(7) (lw: chsd ldrs: rdn to chse wnr over 2f out: no imp)	2	**2**	12/1	79	58
3594[5]	**Mr Sponge (USA) (84)** (IABalding) **3-8-7** SSanders(16) (lw: trckd ldrs: effrt & rdn 2f out: kpt on ins fnl f)	1¼	**3**	10/1	88	61
3112[8]	**Hunters of Brora (IRE) (88)** (JDBethell) **7-9-3** TSprake(1) (lw: hld up: hdwy 2f out: nt clr run & swtchd wl over 1f out: r.o wl towards fin)	nk	**4**	6/1[1]	92	71
3243[11]	**Almond Rock (95)** (JRFanshawe) **5-9-10** RCochrane(18) (swtg: hld up: hdwy on outside over 2f out: rdn & r.o ins fnl f)	s.h	**5**	20/1	98	77
3886[2]	**Wentbridge Lad (IRE) (67)** (ABailey) **7-7-3**(7) DarrenWilliams(11) (b: b.hind: bhd: hdwy u.p 2f out: r.o wl ins fnl f)	1½	**6**	25/1	67	46
3888[8]	**Albert The Bear (88)** (JBerry) **4-9-0**(3) TEDurcan(13) (trckd ldrs: effrt over 2f out: nvr able to chal)	2	**7**	10/1	84	63
3759*	**Myttons Mistake (67)** (ABailey) **4-7-3**(7) PMQuinn(17) (sn chsng ldrs: rdn along 2f out: no imp)	2½	**8**	16/1	58	37
3243[9]	**Van Gurp (84)** (BAMcMahon) **4-8-13** JFortune(6) (hrd drvn over 2f out: nt rch ldrs)	1¼	**9**	25/1	72	51
3801[5]	**Knave's Ash (USA) (79)** (DNicholls) **6-8-8** AlexGreaves(10) (trckd ldrs: rdn & outpcd 2f out)	1¼	**10**	10/1	64	43
3408[8]	**Band on the Run (83)** (BAMcMahon) **10-8-12** AMcGlone(3) (lw: hld up mid div: effrt & rdn 2f out: no imp)	s.h	**11**	16/1	68	47
3457*	**Jedi Knight (73)** (MWEasterby) **3-7-10** JQuinn(5) (in tch tl rdn & wknd over 2f out)	1½	**12**	12/1	55	28
3725[14]	**Caviar Royale (IRE) (98)** (TDBarron) **3-9-7** MHills(2) (lw: a in rr)	¾	**13**	16/1	79	52
2877[9]	**I Can't Remember (73)** (PDEvans) **3-7-3v**(7) AMcCarthy(4) (led 4f: wknd fnl 2f)	hd	**14**	25/1	53	26
3777[4]	**Dee Pee Tee Cee (IRE) (75)** (MWEasterby) **3-7-12** DaleGibson(12) (lw: prom over 4f)	5	**15**	14/1	45	18
3712[6]	**Moscow Mist (IRE) (80)** (BPalling) **6-8-4**(5) PRoberts(15) (b: b.hind: s.i.s: a bhd)	2½	**16**	20/1	44	23
2855*	**Captain Scott (IRE) (81)** (JAGlover) **3-8-4** GCarter(14) (a bhd & outpcd)	1½	**17**	8/1[3]	42	15
3408[3]	**Sharp Shuffle (IRE) (81)** (RHannon) **4-8-10** GDuffield(8) (b: sn drvn along: a bhd: t.o)	8	**18**	7/1[2]	25	4
				(SP 135.0%)	**18 Rn**	

1m 40.83 (8.83) CSF £115.27 CT £1,177.01 TOTE £14.10: £3.40 £5.10 £2.60 £1.60 (£115.50) Trio £248.30 OWNER Miss Heather Davison (MALTON) BRED Mrs Ann Galvin
LONG HANDICAP I Can't Remember 7-5 Jedi Knight 7-6 Myttons Mistake 7-2 Wentbridge Lad (IRE) 7-0
WEIGHT FOR AGE 3yo-6lb

3622 Queens Consul (IRE), enjoying a rewarding season, poked her nose in front soon after halfway and, quickening up to draw clear approaching the final furlong, won very much as she pleased. She is usually at her best with the sun on her back. (10/1)
3548* Gulf Shaadi found all the trouble that was going on his previous visit here last month, but he had the run of the race this time, only for the winner to prove much too smart for him at the weights. (12/1)
3594 Mr Sponge (USA) stuck on well under pressure in the latter stages and, for such an inexperienced individual, he was far from disgraced in this competitive event. (10/1)
934 Hunters of Brora (IRE) had the ideal draw but, for one who has to come from behind, it did not favour her and, though she did weave her way through inside the distance, the line was always going to arrive too soon. (6/1)
1261 Almond Rock enjoys no respite from the Handicapper and he does need a bigger test of stamina, but he showed he is ready to strike form again and should be kept in mind. (20/1)

3886 Wentbridge Lad (IRE), runner-up over ten furlongs here yesterday, ran as well as could be expected on this return to a shorter trip, and his finishing position was as close as he could manage. (25/1)
3615 Albert The Bear (10/1: 8/1-14/1)
2855* Captain Scott (IRE) (8/1: 6/1-10/1)

3902 CHESTER RATED STKS H'CAP (0-110) (Listed) (3-Y.O+) (Class A)

3-50 (3-50) **1m 5f 89y** £15,341.80 (£5,726.20: £2,788.10: £1,185.50: £517.75: £250.65) Stalls: Low GOING: 0.78 sec per fur (S)

				SP	RR	SF
3705[4]	**Further Flight (104)** (BWHills) **11-9-1** MHills(4) (b.hind: hld up: stdy hdwy 5f out: led on bit over 1f out: sn clr: impressive)	—	**1**	9/2[3]	120+	60
3006a[2]	**Kutta (110)** (RWArmstrong) **5-9-7** GCarter(1) (lw: chsd ldrs: led over 3f out tl over 1f out: sn outpcd)	10	**2**	11/4[1]	114	54
3149[8]	**Grey Shot (105)** (IABalding) **5-9-2** JFortune(11) (led tl over 3f out: hrd rdn 2f out: one pce)	5	**3**	15/2	103	43
3705[15]	**Taufan's Melody (105)** (LadyHerries) **6-9-2** RCochrane(5) (lw: hld up: hdwy 5f out: rdn 3f out: styd on one pce)	6	**4**	16/1	96	36
3191[5]	**Beauchamp Jade (97)** (HCandy) **5-8-8** AMcGlone(6) (hld up: effrt over 3f out: styd on: nt rch ldrs)	1	**5**	12/1	87	27
2596[8]	**Rainwatch (102)** (JLDunlop) **3-8-2** TSprake(9) (lw: chsd ldr: rdn & wknd 3f out)	5	**6**	11/1	86	15
3149[9]	**State Fair (104)** (BWHills) **3-8-4** GDuffield(3) (prom tl wknd over 4f out: t.o)	11	**7**	20/1	75	4
3409[5]	**Key to My Heart (IRE) (106)** (MissSEHall) **7-9-3** JFEgan(10) (b: lw: trckd ldrs over 9f: sn wknd: t.o)	9	**8**	12/1	66	6
849[2]	**Star Selection (98)** (JMackie) **6-8-9** JQuinn(8) (prom tl lost pl over 6f out: t.o)	24	**9**	25/1	29	—
3705[5]	**Mohawk River (IRE) (96)** (MRStoute) **4-8-7** SSanders(2) (hld up: wknd over 4f out: t.o)	1½	**10**	4/1[2]	26	—
3492[8]	**Vagabond Chanteuse (99)** (TJEtherington) **3-7-13** DaleGibson(7) (lw: hld up: a in rr: t.o fnl 3f)	dist	**11**	33/1	—	—
				(SP 117.8%)		**11 Rn**

3m 7.09 (17.09) CSF £15.32 CT £83.50 TOTE £4.70: £1.70 £1.70 £2.00 (£6.40) Trio £13.30 OWNER Mr S. WingfieldDigby (LAMBOURN)
BRED S. Wingfield Digby
LONG HANDICAP Mohawk River (IRE) 8-6
WEIGHT FOR AGE 3yo-11lb
OFFICIAL EXPLANATION **Mohawk River (IRE): was unsuited by the testing conditions.**
3705 Further Flight, very unlucky in running in the Ebor, turned this race into a non-event with a very polished performance that was worth going a long way to see. He is a truly marvellous servant to his stable at his advanced age, and it will be a sad day when the likes of him come to the end of their career. (9/2)
3006a Kutta shook the rest off readily enough but the winner was still on the bridle when he cruised past, and he was quite simply outclassed on this occasion. (11/4)
1365a Grey Shot did his best to gallop the opposition into the ground but, forced to give best over three furlongs out, he was soon flat to the boards and his measure had been taken. (15/2)
2271a Taufan's Melody, well behind the winner at York, was meeting him on better terms this time but, as yet, he has still to prove he gets this trip. In this bottomless ground, he was in trouble before reaching the straight and failed to make any impression. (16/1)
3191 Beauchamp Jade did not appear in love with this testing ground and, though she did make some late progress, was never able to get within striking range of the principals. (12/1)
2596 Rainwatch travelled comfortably for quite some way, but he did not find a lot once off the bit and he began to trail inside the final three furlongs. (11/1)
3705 Mohawk River (IRE) should have given the winner something to think about on these slightly beneficial terms, but the soft ground was not for him and he began to tail off out in the country. (4/1: 3/1-9/2)

3903 ROUGE ROSE MAIDEN STKS (3-Y.O+ F & M) (Class D)

4-20 (4-20) **1m 4f 66y** £3,769.00 (£1,132.00: £546.00: £253.00) Stalls: Low GOING: 0.78 sec per fur (S)

				SP	RR	SF
3188[2]	**Nightlark (IRE) (82)** (DRLoder) **3-8-11** RCochrane(5) (mde all: clr 5f out: canter)	—	**1**	10/11[1]	88++	38
3501[5]	**Classic Fan (USA)** (MRChannon) **3-8-11** JFEgan(3) (chsd ldrs: rdn 5f out: sn outpcd: c stands' side st: tk 2nd pl fnl f)	dist	**2**	8/1	—	—
1922[4]	**Dancing Feather** (BWHills) **3-8-11** MHills(2) (bkwd: hld up: chsd wnr 6f out: pushed along & wknd 4f out)	3	**3**	11/4[2]	—	—
3775[5]	**Miss Vita (USA)** (RJRWilliams) **3-8-11** GDuffield(4) (hld up: drvn along over 5f out: sn t.o)	24	**4**	11/2[3]	—	—
	Sostenuto (RHollinshead) **4-9-4**(3) DGriffiths(1) (bkwd: lost tch ½-wy: sn t.o)	27	**5**	16/1	—	—
				(SP 111.4%)		**5 Rn**

2m 54.77 (18.57) CSF £8.26 TOTE £1.90: £1.10 £2.70 (£5.90) OWNER Mr E. J. Loder (NEWMARKET) BRED E. J. Loder
WEIGHT FOR AGE 3yo-10lb
3188 Nightlark (IRE) had nothing more than an exercise workout to win this and, surging clear soon after halfway, she had only to remain on her feet for a facile victory. (10/11: 8/11-evens)
1922 Dancing Feather looked decidedly burly after a ten-week break, and her attempt to gain the runner-up prize came to an end inside the final furlong. (11/4)

3904 EASTGATE CLOCK CENTENARY NURSERY H'CAP (2-Y.O) (Class C)

4-55 (4-56) **7f 2y** £5,605.00 (£1,690.00: £820.00: £385.00) Stalls: Low GOING: 0.78 sec per fur (S)

				SP	RR	SF
3474[5]	**Take A Turn (77)** (MRChannon) **2-8-10v** JFortune(4) (hld up: hdwy 3f out: led appr fnl f: rdn & hung lft: r.o)	—	**1**	10/1	79	29
2176*	**Anita At Dawn (IRE) (80)** (BPalling) **2-8-8**(5) PRoberts(9) (chsd ldr: ev ch appr fnl f: rdn & carried lft nr fin)	¾	**2**	5/1[3]	80	30
3751[6]	**Turf Moor (IRE) (63)** (JJO'Neill) **2-7-3**(7) DarrenWilliams(3) (lw: led tl appr fnl f: rdn & one pce)	3	**3**	33/1	56	6
3650[10]	**Lakeland Pride (IRE) (70)** (PDEvans) **2-7-10b**[1](7) AMcCarthy(11) (hdwy 3f out: c stands' side st: styd on: nt rch ldrs)	1¾	**4**	12/1	59	9
2688[9]	**Opposition Leader (78)** (BWHills) **2-8-11** MHills(8) (bhd tl styd on fnl 2f)	4	**5**	11/2	58	8
2905[4]	**Out Like Magic (84)** (PDEvans) **2-9-3v**[1] JFEgan(10) (prom: rdn over 2f out: sn outpcd)	2½	**6**	7/1	59	9
3545[3]	**Danzig Flyer (IRE) (73)** (PWHarris) **2-8-6** JQuinn(1) (chsd ldrs: rdn & outpcd wl over 1f out)	6	**7**	11/2	34	—
*3610**	**Ra Ra Rasputin (78)** (BAMcMahon) **2-8-11** SSanders(2) (lw: s.i.s: a in rr: rdn over 2f out: no imp: t.o)	8	**8**	7/2[1]	21	—
2962[5]	**Next Round (IRE) (88)** (MBell) **2-9-7** MFenton(5) (chsd ldrs: rdn over 3f out: grad wknd: t.o)	2½	**9**	9/2[2]	25	—
				(SP 120.1%)		**9 Rn**

1m 36.29 (11.09) CSF £56.16 CT £1,480.05 TOTE £12.10: £3.20 £1.80 £6.40 (£25.80) Trio £298.20 OWNER Sheet & Roll Convertors Ltd (UPPER LAMBOURN) BRED B. Burrough
LONG HANDICAP Turf Moor (IRE) 6-11
3474 Take A Turn, well suited by this step up in distance, struck the front approaching the final furlong and looked set to come away, but he continually hung into the whip and had to find extra nearing the finish. (10/1)

2176* Anita At Dawn (IRE) put in a determined challenge entering the last furlong and stayed on really well, but she was slightly impeded and carried left towards the finish and could never quite get to terms. (5/1)
3751 Turf Moor (IRE) found this much tougher than the seller she ran in last time, but she forced the pace and was only shaken off inside the last hundred yards. (33/1)
2112 Lakeland Pride (IRE), blinkered for the first time, was the only one to come wide into the straight, but he ran on well enough, and could well make his mark if lowered in class. (12/1)
2196* Opposition Leader was never going at any stage and was always nearer last than first. (11/2)
2905 Out Like Magic failed to hold her pace when bustled along over two furlongs out, and the visor had little effect on this ground. (7/1)
3610* Ra Ra Rasputin, though so very impressive when successful on the sand earlier in the month, was not the same animal on this return to the turf and he ran no race at all. Horses and women make fools of you. (7/2)

T/Plpt: £71.20 (447.91 Tckts). T/Qdpt: £23.40 (52.76 Tckts) IM

3821-**RIPON** (R-H) (Good)
Saturday August 30th
WEATHER: fine WIND: almost nil

3905 TATTERSALLS MAIDEN AUCTION STKS (2-Y.O) (Class E)
2-30 (2-36) **6f** £3,223.50 (£978.00: £479.00: £229.50) Stalls: Low GOING: 0.05 sec per fur (G)

Form	Horse	Dist	Pos	SP	RR	SF
	Ring Dancer (PJMakin) **2-8-9** DHolland(13) (lengthy: scope: trckd ldrs: led over 1f out: r.o strly)	—	1	9/1[3]	93+	38
3711[2]	**Cease Fire (IRE)** (MrsJCecil) **2-8-3** JCarroll(10) (lw: b: b.hind: dwlt: sn trckng ldrs: led over 2f out tl over 1f out: no ch w wnr)	3	2	10/11[1]	79	24
3239[3]	**Thistle Park** (TDBarron) **2-8-12** KFallon(12) (lw: trckd ldrs: outpcd fnl 2f)	6	3	11/4[2]	72	17
3610[6]	**Tom Dougal (69)** (CSmith) **2-8-7** JTate(19) (chsd ldrs far side: styd on ins fnl f)	½	4	12/1	66	11
	Just Testing (JLEyre) **2-8-2** TWilliams(20) (neat: led far side: wknd ins fnl f)	nk	5	14/1	60	5
3717[9]	**Julies Jewel (IRE)** (MCChapman) **2-8-0**(7) SCarson(1) (mid div: styd on appr fnl f)	½	6	50/1	64	9
	Strictly Rhythm (MrsSABramall,Ireland) **2-8-4**(3) GParkin(17) (racd far side: chsd ldrs tl wknd over 1f out)	1¼	7	50/1	60	5
3106[10]	**Gildersleve** (JWWatts) **2-7-10**(3) PFessey(16) (swtg: racd far side: chsd ldrs tl wknd over 1f out)	nk	8	12/1	51	—
3544[3]	**Time To Time (58)** (TDEasterby) **2-7-13** NKennedy(5) (swvd rt s: led over 3f: grad wknd)	3	9	16/1	43	—
3407[4]	**Cool Mystery** (ABMulholland) **2-8-4** TLucas(4) (lw: trckd ldrs: rdn over 2f out: no imp)	nk	10	20/1	48	—
3753[4]	**Carrick View (IRE)** (PCalver) **2-8-6**(3) DarrenMoffatt(9) (lw: s.i.s: bhd tl sme late hdwy)	1½	11	33/1	49	—
	Celestial Welcome (MrsMReveley) **2-8-0** LCharnock(2) (w'like: scope: bkwd: sn outpcd & drvn along)	¾	12	33/1	38	—
3701[5]	**Touch of Colour** (JWWatts) **2-8-4** NCarlisle(3) (chsd ldrs tl lost pl over 2f out)	½	13	50/1	40	—
2739[5]	**Moy (IRE)** (MBrittain) **2-8-0b[1]** GBardwell(6) (hmpd s: n.d)	1½	14	25/1	32	—
3629[3]	**Emperor's Gold** (ICampbell) **2-8-10** AMackay(21) (lw: swtchd lft s: racd centre: a in rr)	¾	15	16/1	40	—
3458[6]	**Desire's Gold** (MBrittain) **2-7-12**(7) DMernagh(11) (outpcd fr ½-wy)	1½	16	20/1	31	—
3753[8]	**Esse** (EWeymes) **2-8-4** JStack(15) (bit bkwd: racd centre: outpcd fr ½-wy)	1¼	17	20/1	27	—
2739[7]	**Scolding** (KAMorgan) **2-8-0** JLowe(18) (unruly s: racd far side: bhd fnl 2f)	nk	18	50/1	22	—
3707[15]	**Top Floor (IRE)** (NTinkler) **2-8-9** KimTinkler(14) (racd far side: outpcd fr ½-wy)	1¾	19	20/1	27	—
1136[5]	**Benrock (IRE)** (CaptJWilson) **2-8-5** DeanMcKeown(8) (bit bkwd: chsd ldrs to ½-wy: sn lost pl)	1½	20	33/1	19	—
3278[12]	***Up The Wall (60)*** (JohnBerry) **2-8-7** KDarley(7) (Withdrawn not under Starter's orders: burst out of front of stalls)		W	25/1	—	—
				(SP 166.3%)	**20 Rn**	

1m 14.7 (4.20) CSF £18.54 TOTE £14.10: £4.00 £1.20 £1.60 (£8.70) Trio £8.90 OWNER Mitchell Partnership (MARLBOROUGH) BRED Dunchurch Lodge Stud
Ring Dancer, easily the pick of the paddock and a good walker, took this in impressive fashion and is clearly a cut above average. (9/1)
3711 Cease Fire (IRE) was awkward to load and missed the break slightly. After hitting the front, in the end she was outclassed by the winner. (10/11)
3239 Thistle Park, who looked very fit, was by no means knocked about when it was clear the first two were much too good for him. (11/4)
3610 Tom Dougal, taken to post quietly, was putting in his best work at the finish and will be suited by a step up to seven. (12/1)
Just Testing, who is on the small side, showed bags of toe to lead the far-side group. Her stride shortened dramatically inside the last and she could be worth a drop back to five. (14/1)
Julies Jewel (IRE) wore a tongue-strap and will be suited by seven. (50/1)
2736 Gildersleve, awash with sweat in the paddock, took a keen grip going to post and is clearly her own worst enemy. (12/1: op 6/1)

3906 MOORLAND POULTRY H'CAP (0-80) (3-Y.O+ F & M) (Class D)
3-00 (3-02) **1m 2f** £3,615.00 (£1,095.00: £535.00: £255.00) Stalls: High GOING: 0.05 sec per fur (G)

Form	Horse	Dist	Pos	SP	RR	SF
3119[6]	**Ganga (IRE) (78)** (WJarvis) **3-9-9** GHind(3) (hld up: smooth hdwy over 3f out: led over 2f out: styd on wl fnl f)	—	1	10/1	90	64
3570[2]	**Mcgillycuddy Reeks (IRE) (65)** (DonEnricoIncisa) **6-9-4** KimTinkler(6) (lw: hld up: hdwy on outside over 3f out: ev ch over 1f out: nt qckn ins fnl f)	1¼	2	9/2[2]	75	57
3630[3]	**Classic Flyer (IRE) (65)** (ICampbell) **4-9-4** AMackay(9) (lw: led tl over 2f out: r.o one pce)	4	3	9/1	69	51
3430*	**Sing And Dance (43)** (EWeymes) **4-7-7**(3) PFessey(10) (lw: hld up: outpcd over 3f out: n.m.r 2f out: styd on fnl f)	2	4	10/1	43	25
3721[3]	**Karinska (60)** (MCChapman) **7-8-6**(7) SCarson(2) (lw: hld up: hdwy on ins over 3f out: n.m.r: styd on appr fnl f)	1½	5	8/1	58	40
2832[9]	**Kaziranga (USA) (73)** (LMCumani) **3-9-4** KDarley(8) (trckd ldrs: effrt over 3f out: hung rt: one pce fnl 2f)	1¾	6	4/1[1]	68	42
2952*	**Agony Aunt (79)** (MrsJCecil) **3-9-10** JCarroll(4) (trckd ldrs: effrt over 3f out: outpcd fnl 2f)	2	7	11/2[3]	71	45
3696[8]	**Welcome Home (51)** (PTDalton) **3-7-10** LCharnock(1) (chsd ldrs: effrt over 3f out: one pce)	1¼	8	20/1	41	15
3264[10]	**Kissel (53)** (SEKettlewell) **5-8-6** JStack(11) (sn bhd: sme late hdwy)	1½	9	33/1	41	23
3128[13]	**Doyella (IRE) (80)** (DRLoder) **3-9-11** DHolland(5) (w ldr: drvn along 3f out: lost pl over 2f out: eased)	7	10	4/1[1]	56	30
3495[8]	**Arletty (62)** (HRACecil) **3-8-7** KFallon(7) (chsd ldrs: drvn along 4f out: lost pl over 2f out: eased)	5	11	7/1	30	4
				(SP 133.1%)	**11 Rn**	

2m 9.2 (5.70) CSF £56.47 CT £406.93 TOTE £19.10: £5.60 £1.40 £2.30 (£66.90) Trio £283.50 OWNER Cuadra Africa (NEWMARKET) BRED Cambremont Ltd Partnership
LONG HANDICAP Sing And Dance 7-9 Welcome Home 7-6

WEIGHT FOR AGE 3yo-8lb
3119 Ganga (IRE) has disappointed in her two outings since her Newcastle win but as a result has dropped 7lb down in the weights. Appreciating the much easier ground, she was always travelling smoothly and had only to be kept up to her work. (10/1)
3570 Mcgillycuddy Reeks (IRE), 27lb higher than when her winning roll started at Pontefract last month, did well considering she came off the pace in a moderately-run race. In addition connections reckoned she would have appreciated faster ground. (9/2: op 3/1)
3630 Classic Flyer (IRE), running off the same mark, was allowed to just set a modest pace but at the business end the first two quickened away from her. (9/1)
3430* Sing And Dance, from a 5lb higher mark, was held up in a moderately-run race. Tapped for foot and then short of room, she looked third best on merit. (10/1)
3721 Karinska had a very poor run against the far running rail. (8/1)
1777 Kaziranga (USA) wanted to do nothing but hang right under pressure. (4/1)
2380 Doyella (IRE) was allowed to come home in her own time when all chance had gone. (4/1)

3907 CROWTHER HOMES H'CAP (0-80) (3-Y.O+) (Class D)

3-35 (3-35) **1m 4f 60y** £3,840.00 (£1,140.00: £540.00: £240.00) Stalls: Low GOING: 0.05 sec per fur (G)

				SP	RR	SF
3754^{6}	**Hasta la Vista (55)** (MWEasterby) **7-8-4b**(3) GParkin(6) (lw: trckd ldrs: chal over 3f out: led over 1f out: r.o u.p)	—	1	7/1	66	21
3210*	**Top (67)** (JRFanshawe) **3-8-9** KDarley(7) (lw: led tl over 1f out: nt qckn ins fnl f)	½	2	$9/2^{3}$	77	22
3603^{2}	**Gold Desire (56)** (MBrittain) **7-8-8** GBardwell(4) (trckd ldrs: rdn & ev ch over 2f out: r.o on same pce)	1½	3	7/1	64	19
3689^{10}	**Al's Alibi (76)** (WRMuir) **4-10-0** KFallon(3) (trckd ldrs: ev ch over 2f out: kpt on one pce)	nk	4	$4/1^{2}$	84	39
3562*	**Summerhill Special (IRE) (67)** (DWBarker) **6-9-5** TWilliams(8) (lw: b.nr hind: trckd ldrs: ev ch over 2f out: wknd towards fin)	½	5	$9/2^{3}$	74	29
3440^{7}	**Ledgendry Line (71)** (MrsMReveley) **4-9-9** ACulhane(5) (hld up: effrt over 3f out: styd on fnl f: nvr nr to chal)	3	6	$7/2^{1}$	74	29
3267^{2}	**Tajar (USA) (44)** (TKeddy) **5-7-10** NCarlisle(1) (lw: plld hrd: sddle slipped ½-wy: lost pl over 2f out: eased)	12	7	10/1	32	—
2888^{4}	**In The Genes (65)** (JLEyre) **3-8-7** RLappin(2) (plld hrd: effrt over 4f out: wknd 3f out)	1	8	10/1	52	—

(SP 121.8%) **8 Rn**

2m 45.1 (11.60) CSF £37.36 CT £214.81 TOTE £8.40: £2.10 £2.10 £2.20 (£24.10) OWNER Mr K. Hodgson (SHERIFF HUTTON) BRED Clanville Lodge Stud
LONG HANDICAP Tajar (USA) 7-7
WEIGHT FOR AGE 3yo-10lb
3754 Hasta la Vista did really well considering the trip is basically short of his best and the gallop was not a strong one. (7/1)
3210* Top, 5lb higher in the weights, was again allowed to set her own pace. Quickening up once in line for home, despite thrashing her tail she kept on in willing fashion. She seems to be improving with each outing now. (9/2)
3603 Gold Desire, from a stable in cracking form, ran right up to his best. (7/1)
3267* Al's Alibi, 4lb higher than when winning at Carlisle two outings ago, looks to have his measure taken for the time being. (4/1)
3562* Summerhill Special (IRE) raced keenly in a race that was not run at a strong gallop. Possibly seeing too much daylight up the straight, she weakened noticeably towards the finish. (9/2)
3440 Ledgendry Line was held up in a slowly-run race. Over this trip, he needs a good even gallop. (7/2)

3908 RIPON HORN BLOWER CONDITIONS STKS (2-Y.O) (Class B)

4-05 (4-05) **5f** £6,339.00 (£2,361.00: £1,145.50: £482.50: £206.25: £95.75) Stalls: Low GOING: 0.05 sec per fur (G)

				SP	RR	SF
3595^{9}	**Baby Grand (IRE) (88)** (TDBarron) **2-8-7** KimberleyHart(8) (swtchd lft s: hdwy 2f out: r.o wl to ld towards fin)	—	1	14/1	95	37
3178a^{6}	**Atlantic Viking (IRE)** (MJohnston) **2-8-12** DHolland(5) (lw: mde most: edgd lft over 1f out: hdd towards fin)	1	2	$11/10^{1}$	97	39
3595^{2}	**Banningham Blade (100)** (KTIvory) **2-8-11** MartinDwyer(4) (chsd ldrs: rdn ½-wy: styd on fnl f)	½	3	$11/4^{2}$	94	36
3708^{2}	**Yorkies Boy (92)** (BAMcMahon) **2-8-12** KDarley(6) (lw: chsd ldrs: rdn ½-wy: kpt on same pce)	¾	4	$5/1^{3}$	93	35
2168*	**Buzz** (CWThornton) **2-8-10** DeanMcKeown(2) (sn outpcd: hdwy & nt clr run over 1f out: swtchd rt & styd on)	1	5	12/1	88	30
2103^{12}	**Vice Presidential (89)** (TJEtherington) **2-8-10** ACulhane(3) (outpcd ½-wy: kpt on appr fnl f)	1¼	6	20/1	84	26
3036^{3}	**Two Williams (85)** (MWEasterby) **2-8-12** TLucas(7) (lw: chsd ldrs: hung rt & outpcd ½-wy: n.d)	2½	7	20/1	78	20
3414*	**Salamanca (88)** (JBerry) **2-8-9** PFessey(1) (w wnr: rdn & hung rt ½-wy: wkng whn n.m.r over 1f out)	3	8	11/2	65	7

(SP 130.2%) **8 Rn**

61.2 secs (3.40) CSF £31.24 TOTE £16.10: £2.40 £1.20 £1.40 (£19.80) OWNER Mrs D. E. Sharp (THIRSK) BRED Rathbarry Stud
3209* Baby Grand (IRE), the filly no-one wanted when offered for sale as a yearling, had finished well behind Banningham Blade at Newbury. Ridden by a girl apprentice unable to claim her 5lb allowance, she showed real resolution to get up near the line. She has now won five times from nine starts. (14/1)
3178a Atlantic Viking (IRE), having his first outing for thirty-five days, looked to be carrying plenty of condition. Winning the battle for the lead, he rolled on to the stands' side rail over a furlong out and was worn down near the line. Clearly speedy, this will have blown away the cobwebs and he should be spot on next time. (11/10)
3595 Banningham Blade looked to have plenty on with Yorkies Boy on Goodwood running but she improved to come out on top. (11/4)
3708 Yorkies Boy is as tough as teak but he has his limitations. (5/1: 3/1-11/2)
2168* Buzz, having his first outing for sixty-eight days, struggled to go the pace and then met trouble in running. He really needs seven furlongs but this effort will not have done his nursery handicap mark any good. (12/1)
1310 Vice Presidential, absent for seventy-one days, probably needs at least six in this company. (20/1)
3036 Two Williams again tended to hang and almost certainly requires more give underfoot. (20/1)
3414* Salamanca could not get the better of Atlantic Viking up in front and her chance had gone when that rival went across her over a furlong out. (11/2)

3909 BERNADETTE MCWILLIAMS MEMORIAL MAIDEN STKS (3-Y.O+) (Class D)

4-40 (4-41) **1m 2f** £3,680.00 (£1,115.00: £545.00: £260.00) Stalls: High GOING: 0.05 sec per fur (G)

				SP	RR	SF
3419^{4}	**Bina Gardens (72)** (HRACecil) **3-8-7** KFallon(9) (lw: chsd ldrs: led over 3f out: drvn clr appr fnl f)	—	1	$4/6^{1}$	80	39
	Teme Valley (RCharlton) **3-8-12** KDarley(1) (leggy: scope: sn chsng ldrs: drvn along 4f out: styd on appr fnl f: no ch w wnr)	4	2	$7/1^{2}$	79	38
3632^{5}	**Primeval** (PWHarris) **3-8-12** DHolland(5) (lw: sn chsng ldrs: outpcd & edgd lft over 3f out: styd on appr fnl f)	6	3	$7/1^{2}$	69	28
3738^{5}	**Shooting Star (IRE)** (JHMGosden) **3-8-12v**[1] GHind(10) (led tl over 3f out: wknd appr fnl f)	¾	4	12/1	68	27
	Witchfinder (USA) (MrsLStubbs) **5-9-6** TWilliams(2) (bit bkwd: hld up: hdwy over 4f out: sn ev ch: wknd over 1f out)	6	5	50/1	58	25

	Fuwala (DShaw) **3-8-7** JFanning(3) (rangy: scope: bkwd: b: b.hind: sn bhd: sme hdwy over 2f out: n.d)........½	**6**	66/1	52	11
	Notation (IRE) (DWChapman) **3-8-12** ACulhane(6) (bkwd: sn bhd & pushed along: sme hdwy 2f out: n.d) 2	**7**	50/1	54	13
	Quiet Venture (EALDunlop) **3-8-12** JStack(8) (w'like: scope: bit bkwd: hdwy 4f out: sn chsng ldrs: wknd over 2f out)........1½	**8**	15/2 3	52	11
2859 3	**Polenka (IRE)** (JWWatts) **3-8-7** JCarroll(4) (sn w ldr: ev ch tl wknd over 2f out: eased) 2	**9**	9/1	44	3
3463 10	**Saramah (USA)** (JHMGosden) **3-8-7** AGarth(7) (sme hdwy over 4f out: sn lost pl) 10	**10**	16/1	28	—

(SP 125.8%) **10 Rn**

2m 10.5 (7.00) CSF £6.28 TOTE £1.70: £1.10 £1.70 £1.70 (£4.40) Trio £9.60 OWNER Mr K. Abdulla (NEWMARKET) BRED Juddmonte Farms
WEIGHT FOR AGE 3yo-8lb

3419 Bina Gardens, a tall filly, looked the part in the paddock and moved best going to post. Appreciating the drop back in distance, her rider took no chances and kept her right up to her work. (4/6: op 5/4)
Teme Valley, who wore a tongue-strap on his debut, was coltish in the paddock. Showing plenty of knee action going down, he stuck on well and should be able to find a race. (7/1)
3632 Primeval, who moved very short going down, was badly tapped for foot once in line for home. Edging left out to the centre, he kept on and is not without some ability. (7/1)
3738 Shooting Star (IRE), visored for the first time, wore a Monty Roberts-type blanket for stalls entry. Making his own running, this was a better effort but he is clearly very moderate. (12/1)
Witchfinder (USA), having his first outing for two years, has apparently been in Dubai. He moved up travelling comfortably but tired badly over a furlong out. Now qualified for a handicap mark, this outing will not be lost on him. (50/1)
Quiet Venture (15/2: 5/1-8/1)

3910 BARBARA CUNNINGHAM JEWELLERY AND MIDDLEHAM PARK RACING APPRENTICE H'CAP (0-75) (3-Y.O+) (Class F)

5-10 (5-11) **6f** £2,608.00 (£733.00: £358.00) Stalls: Low GOING: 0.05 sec per fur (G)

			SP	RR	SF
3761 5	**Bowlers Boy (67)** (JJQuinn) **4-9-3**(5) RSmith(24) (lw: chsd ldrs far side: led ins fnl f: jst hld on)........—	**1**	10/1	77	59
3756 17	**Mallia (60)** (TDBarron) **4-8-12**(3) VictoriaAppleby(21) (racd far side: chsd ldr: led 1f out: sn hdd: r.o)........s.h	**2**	16/1	70	52
3649 16	**Purple Fling (73)** (DWChapman) **6-9-11**(3) RStudholme(19) (racd far side: hdwy over 2f out: styd on wl ins fnl f)........nk	**3**	14/1	82	64
3637*	**Opening Range (41)** (NEBerry) **6-7-5**(5) PBradley(1) (lw: led stands' side: edgd bdly rt over 1f out: kpt on wl) .1	**4**	15/2 2	47	29
3756 2	**Camionneur (IRE) (53)** (TDEasterby) **4-8-5b**(3) TSiddall(15) (lw: s.i.s: swtchd rt & racd far side: hdwy 2f out: n.m.r: styd on ins fnl f)........nk	**5**	9/2 1	59	41
3812 4	**Gipsy Princess (57)** (MWEasterby) **3-8-4b**(5) SFinnamore(2) (chsd ldrs: kpt on fnl f)........½	**6**	12/1	61	40
3693 9	**Lachesis (47)** (DShaw) **4-7-11**(5) RBrisland(18) (racd far side: trckd ldrs: nt qckn fnl 2f)........1¼	**7**	20/1	48	30
3456*	**Shontaine (56)** (MJohnston) **4-8-4**(7) IGrantham(3) (lw: hdwy over 1f out: styd on towards fin)........½	**8**	10/1	56	38
3625 8	**Plum First (51)** (JLEyre) **7-8-6** KimberleyHart(5) (b: b.hind: mid div: rdn ½-wy: kpt on appr fnl f) 1½	**9**	9/1 3	47	29
3431 6	**Stephensons Rocket (42)** (RAFahey) **6-7-11** RWinston(9) (lw: w ldrs tl wknd over 1f out)........hd	**10**	12/1	37	19
3287 5	**Sotonian (HOL) (41)** (PSFelgate) **4-7-5**(5) JFowle(22) (racd far side: chsd ldrs tl wknd fnl f)........nk	**11**	16/1	36	18
3771 6	**Another Nightmare (IRE) (49)** (RMMcKellar) **5-7-13**(5) JMcAuley(12) (lw: led far side tl hdd & wknd 1f out)...nk	**12**	14/1	43	25
3691 6	**Rock Symphony (60)** (WJHaggas) **7-9-1** JoHunnam(4) (sn outpcd: sme hdwy 2f out: n.d)........½	**13**	10/1	52	34
	Sycamore Lodge (IRE) (70) (MAPeill) **6-9-6**(5) ANicholls(11) (bkwd: nvr bttr than mid div)........½	**14**	25/1	61	43
1227 8	**Naissant (57)** (MartynWane) **4-8-12** KSked(17) (racd far side: chsd ldrs over 3f)........½	**15**	12/1	47	29
3759 15	**Axeman (IRE) (41)** (MartynWane) **5-7-5**(5) JennyBenson(16) (racd centre: nvr nr ldrs) ....nk	**16**	14/1	30	12
3406 4	**Amron (61)** (JBerry) **10-9-2** IonaWands(10) (lw: nvr bttr than mid div)........¾	**17**	10/1	48	30
3580 9	**Croeso Cynnes (62)** (BPalling) **4-8-12**(5) GHannon(23) (racd far side: chsd ldrs tl lost pl 2f out)........1	**18**	11/1	46	28
3582 14	**Oh Whataknight (45)** (RMWhitaker) **4-7-11**(3) DMernagh(6) (b: chsd ldrs over 3f: sn lost pl)........1	**19**	50/1	27	9
3476 6	**Look Who's Calling (IRE) (65)** (BAMcMahon) **4-9-3**(3) SRighton(14) (lw: racd far side: sn outpcd & rdn along)1½	**20**	25/1	43	25
3398 6	**Amy Leigh (IRE) (44)** (CaptJWilson) **4-7-8v**1(5) AngelaHartley(20) (racd far side: outpcd fr ½-wy)........1½	**21**	25/1	18	—
3771 9	**Afaan (IRE) (65)** (RFMarvin) **4-9-1**(5) DHayden(13) (swtchd lft s: sn in tch: hrd rdn ½-wy: sn wknd)........4	**22**	20/1	28	10
3716 5	**Rose Flyer (IRE) (41)** (MCChapman) **7-7-7**(3) SCarson(7) (stumbled s: sn chsng ldrs: lost pl over 2f out) 7	**23**	33/1	—	—
3406 7	**Zain Dancer (41)** (DNicholls) **5-7-10** APolli(8) (reard s: racd centre: a bhd)........1½	**24**	10/1	—	—

(SP 174.5%) **24 Rn**

1m 14.1 (3.60) CSF £185.25 CT £1,288.63 TOTE £17.60: £3.60 £5.60 £5.10 £2.60 (£149.80) Trio £991.40; £153.61 to 1/9/97 OWNER Bowlers Racing (MALTON) BRED Roldvale Ltd
LONG HANDICAP Opening Range 7-9 Axeman (IRE) 7-9 Rose Flyer (IRE) 7-8
WEIGHT FOR AGE 3yo-3lb
STEWARDS' ENQUIRY Polli susp. 8-9/9/97 (incorrect & improper use of whip).

3761 Bowlers Boy, from a winning mark, held on by the skin of his teeth. (10/1)
2711 Mallia, with the blinkers again left off, proved most persistent and, in the end, it was a very close-run thing. (16/1)
3066* Purple Fling is possibly better suited by seven nowadays. (14/1)
3637* Opening Range has speed to burn. Making the running on the stands' side, she edged right across the track and, at the line, was on the quarters of the first three on the far side. She must have given away more ground than she was eventually beaten by. (15/2)
3756 Camionneur (IRE) made it hard work for himself, again missing the break, and his rider seemed unsure from where to deliver his final challenge. (9/2)
3812 Gipsy Princess came out top of those who raced on the stands' side throughout. (12/1)
953 Naissant (12/1: op 20/1)
3406 Zain Dancer (10/1: 8/1-12/1)

T/Plpt: £54.40 (469.86 Tckts). T/Qdpt: £20.30 (52.16 Tckts) WG

3892-SANDOWN (R-H) (Soft)

Saturday August 30th

WEATHER: overcast & damp becoming brighter WIND: almost nil

3911 CHIEF BARKER'S NURSERY (S) H'CAP (2-Y.O) (Class E)

2-00 (2-05) **7f 16y** £2,596.25 (£785.00: £382.50: £181.25) Stalls: High GOING: 0.31 sec per fur (G)

			SP	RR	SF
3692 4	**Marske Machine (59)** (NTinkler) **2-8-13b** LDettori(9) (lw: stdy hdwy over 2f out: hrd rdn fnl f: led nr fin)........—	**1**	11/2 2	61	33

Form	Horse (details)	Dist	Pos	SP	RR	SF
3215^{10}	**Persian Venture (65)** (BJMeehan) **2-9-0**(5) CLowther(10) (lw: hdwy over 5f out: hrd rdn over 2f out: r.o ins fnl f)	hd	2	12/1	67	39
3072^{3}	**Catch The Rainbow (60)** (JGSmyth-Osbourne) **2-9-0** FLynch(8) (chsd ldr: hrd rdn over 2f out: led wl ins fnl f: hdd nr fin)	nk	3	16/1	61	33
3610^{7}	**Greenbrook (67)** (WGMTurner) **2-9-4**(3) DSweeney(3) (led: rdn 1f out: hdd wl ins fnl f: unable qckn)	½	4	4/1^{1}	67	39
3639^{2}	**Pianist (IRE) (57)** (GLewis) **2-8-11** PaulEddery(7) (rdn 4f out: lost pl over 3f out: r.o one pce fnl f)	1¾	5	11/2^{2}	53	25
3228^{5}	**Arm And A Leg (IRE) (57)** (CADwyer) **2-8-8v^{1}**(3) DO'Donohoe(4) (lw: hdwy on ins 4f out: rdn over 2f out: eased whn btn ins fnl f)	½	6	12/1	52	24
3586^{8}	**River Frontier (IRE) (42)** (MDIUsher) **2-7-10** JMarshall(6) (plld hrd: rdn over 3f out: hdwy 2f out: wknd over 1f out)	11	7	50/1	12	—
1498^{5}	**Zig Zag (IRE) (49)** (MHTompkins) **2-8-3** DBiggs(1) (bhd fnl 5f)	3½	8	20/1	11	—
3493^{4}	**Francesca's Folly (52)** (JWHills) **2-8-6** RHills(2) (swtg: a bhd)	3	9	7/1^{3}	7	—
3078*	**Jato Dancer (IRE) (56)** (MRChannon) **2-8-10** PatEddery(5) (prom over 5f)	5	10	11/2^{2}	—	—
				(SP 106.6%)	**10 Rn**	

1m 36.5 (7.90) CSF £54.81 CT £543.47 TOTE £5.40: £1.70 £3.90 £5.10 (£34.90) Trio £87.50 OWNER Marske Machine Co (MALTON) BRED G. Middlebrook

LONG HANDICAP River Frontier (IRE) 7-7

Bt in 13,200 gns. Jato Dancer (IRE) clmd AHill £6,000

3692 Marske Machine made the long journey down from Malton pay. Creeping closer in the straight, she still did not look the likely winner below the distance but, with the leader tying up, she managed to come through and snatch the spoils near the line. (11/2)

2741 Persian Venture appreciated the drop in class. Soon racing in a handy position, he kept on well inside the final furlong to snatch second prize. He would not be inconvenienced by further. (12/1: op 8/1)

3072 Catch The Rainbow enjoyed the drop in class and raced in second place. She eventually managed to get to the front in the closing stages, only to be caught by the winner near the line. (16/1)

3610 Greenbrook was back in his correct grade this time and, bowling along in front, looked the likely winner entering the final furlong. Unfortunately for him, he was worried out of it in the closing stages. (4/1)

3639 Pianist (IRE), as at Folkestone last time out, was off the bridle by halfway and had lost his pitch early in the straight. He did stay on again up the hill but never threatened to get on terms with the principals. He is crying out for a mile. (11/2)

3228 Arm And A Leg (IRE), down 8lb since last appearing in a nursery, was on the heels of the principals below the distance but, when all chance had gone, his jockey was not hard on him inside the final furlong. (12/1: op 8/1)

3493 Francesca's Folly (7/1: 5/1-8/1)

3078* Jato Dancer (IRE) (11/2: 4/1-6/1)

3912 VINTAGE INNS DISTRICT 48 TOP TEN CONDITIONS STKS (2-Y.O) (Class C)

2-35 (2-35) **1m 14y** £4,305.00 (£1,505.00: £735.00: £315.00) Stalls: High GOING: 0.31 sec per fur (G)

Form	Horse (details)	Dist	Pos	SP	RR	SF
3598^{4}	**Kilimanjaro** (MRStoute) **2-8-11** PatEddery(1) (mde all: shkn up over 2f out: qcknd over 1f out: easily)	—	1	2/1^{2}	114+	53
2881*	**Abuhail (USA)** (DMorley) **2-9-0** LDettori(4) (chsd wnr: rdn over 2f out: no imp)	8	2	9/2^{3}	101	40
3450*	**Colleville** (MAJarvis) **2-8-6** WRyan(2) (lw: hld up: rdn over 2f out: sn wknd)	3½	3	8/1	86	25
2693*	**Fakhr (USA)** (JLDunlop) **2-9-0** RHills(3) (hld up: rdn over 2f out: sn wknd)	9	4	11/8^{1}	76	15
				(SP 104.7%)	**4 Rn**	

1m 47.94 (6.74) CSF £8.87 TOTE £2.60: (£4.00) OWNER Mr Tabor Mrs Magnier Lord Lloyd Webber (NEWMARKET) BRED Watership Down Stud

3598 Kilimanjaro appreciated the step up to a mile and, relishing the soft ground, put up an exhilarating display. Making all the running, he showed a fine turn of foot to storm clear of the rest of the field below the distance and win with a ton in hand. He looks to have a very big future. (2/1)

2881* Abuhail (USA) gave chase to the winner but was left for dead by that rival in the final quarter-mile. (9/2)

3450* Colleville had far more on her plate this time and was sending out distress signals approaching the final quarter-mile. (8/1: 10/1-13/2)

2693* Fakhr (USA) was a major disappointment and tamely dropped away a quarter of a mile from home. The soft ground may well have been to blame and he is worth another chance on a sound surface. (11/8)

3913 FORD 21 YEARS CELEBRATION ATALANTA STKS (Listed) (3-Y.O+ F & M) (Class A)

3-05 (3-13) **1m 14y** £11,522.50 (£3,490.00: £1,705.00: £812.50) Stalls: High GOING: 0.31 sec per fur (G)

Form	Horse (details)	Dist	Pos	SP	RR	SF
	One So Wonderful (LMCumani) **3-8-8** PatEddery(8) (gd hdwy over 2f out: led over 1f out: qcknd: easily)	—	1	11/2^{1}	110++	68
3492^{2}	**Dragonada (USA) (102)** (HRACecil) **3-8-8** WRyan(7) (lw: a.p: led over 3f out tl over 1f out: unable qckn)	8	2	11/2^{1}	94	52
3622*	**Apache Star (91)** (GWragg) **3-8-8v** PaulEddery(3) (rdn over 2f out: hdwy over 1f out: r.o)	1¼	3	10/1	92	50
2598^{20}	**Jafn (95)** (BHanbury) **3-8-8** SDrowne(12) (lw: rdn & hdwy over 2f out: one pce)	½	4	25/1	91	49
3716^{2}	**Sally Slade (63)** (CACyzer) **5-9-0** RFfrench(1) (rdn over 3f out: hdwy over 1f out: nvr nrr)	3	5	100/1	85?	49
3499*	**Hirasah (IRE)** (RWArmstrong) **3-8-8** RHills(13) (hld up: ev ch over 2f out: wknd over 1f out)	¾	6	11/2^{1}	83	41
2569^{4}	**Polish Rhythm (IRE) (66)** (GAHubbard) **4-9-0** DO'Donohoe(6) (led over 3f)	3	7	100/1	77	41
2586^{5}	**Khassah (105)** (JHMGosden) **3-8-8** LDettori(4) (lw: rdn over 2f out: hdwy over 1f out: wknd fnl f)	½	8	9/1^{3}	76	34
2561^{8}	**Dancing Drop (100)** (RHannon) **3-8-8** WJO'Connor(5) (prom over 3f)	2	9	16/1	72	30
3017^{3}	**Dances With Dreams** (PWChapple-Hyam) **3-8-8** RHavlin(10) (hld up: ev ch over 2f out: wknd over 1f out)	nk	10	11/2^{1}	72	30
3128^{5}	**Mara River (84)** (IABalding) **3-8-8** CLowther(11) (a.p: ev ch over 2f out: wknd over wl over 1f out)	nk	11	33/1	71	29
3577^{3}	**Unconditional Love (IRE) (101)** (MJohnston) **4-9-0** MRoberts(2) (lw: prom over 3f)	1¼	12	7/1^{2}	69	33
1209^{3}	**Boojum (100)** (BWHills) **3-8-8** JDSmith(9) (bhd fnl 3f)	3½	13	25/1	62	20
3550*	**Egoli (USA)** (GWragg) **3-8-8** AClark(14) (lw: plld hrd: bhd fnl 2f)	2½	14	12/1	57	15
				(SP 119.3%)	**14 Rn**	

1m 46.18 (4.98) CSF £29.93 TOTE £6.50: £2.20 £2.20 £2.30 (£27.90) Trio £91.20 OWNER Helena Springfield Ltd (NEWMARKET) BRED Meon Valley Stud

WEIGHT FOR AGE 3yo-6lb

One So Wonderful, who looked a leading 1,000 Guineas contender after an impressive debut at Kempton last September, wintered very badly and did not come to herself in the spring. As a result, she spent some time at the Meon Valley Stud. Reported to have been working well at home, she put up a breathtaking display and moved up to join the principals from the back of the field in a matter of strides. Striking the front over a furlong out, she showed a tremendous turn of foot to storm clear and win with her head in her chest. She should soon be making up for lost time and a Group race looks a formality, especially if the ground is soft. (11/2)

3492 Dragonada (USA) goes in this ground and moved to the front early in the straight. However, collared by the winner below the distance, she was well and truly put in her place. (11/2: 4/1-6/1)

3622* Apache Star, stepping up in class on the back of two recent handicap victories, gave a good account of herself as she ran on in the last furlong and a half to snatch third prize. (10/1)
1326 Jafn, pushed along to take closer order over a quarter of a mile from home, was then only scrapping for minor honours. (25/1)
3716 Sally Slade, out of her depth here and moving up in distance, was staying on past beaten horses and is surely flattered to finish so close. She has done all her winning at five furlongs. (100/1)
3499* Hirasah (IRE) found a mile in the mud more than she could cope with and, after having every chance over a quarter of a mile from home, had come to the end of her tether below the distance. Dropped to seven furlongs on a sound surface, she is up to winning a similar event. (11/2)
3017 Dances With Dreams (11/2: 4/1-6/1)
3577 Unconditional Love (IRE) flopped in the soft ground, and punters knew their fate turning into the straight. (7/1)

3914 MARSHALL AMPLIFICATION RATED STKS H'CAP (0-100) (3-Y.O+) (Class B)

3-40 (3-43) **5f 6y** £6,697.00 (£2,503.00: £1,221.50: £522.50: £231.25: £114.75) Stalls: High GOING: 0.31 sec per fur (G)

				SP	RR	SF
3194[5]	**Rudi's Pet (IRE) (84)** (RHannon) **3-8-0b**(5) CLowther(7) (mde all: clr 3f out: hrd rdn 1f out: r.o wl)	—	**1**	8/1	94	61
3771[2]	**Patsy Grimes (87)** (JSMoore) **7-8-10** MRoberts(3) (n.m.r 3f out: swtchd rt over 1f out: gd hdwy fnl f: r.o wl)	1¼	**2**	5/1[3]	93+	62
2377[9]	**Repertory (87)** (MSSaunders) **4-8-10** SDrowne(5) (a.p: chsd wnr 3f out: hrd rdn over 1f out: edgd rt ins fnl f: unable qckn)	2	**3**	25/1	87	56
3410*	**Moon Strike (FR) (98)** (PHowling) **7-9-7** LDettori(4) (b: rdn over 2f out: hdwy over 1f out: r.o one pce)	½	**4**	3/1[1]	96	65
3795[8]	**Youdontsay (84)** (TJNaughton) **5-8-4**(3) DO'Donohoe(9) (lw: hld up: rdn over 2f out: r.o one pce fnl f)	s.h	**5**	8/1	82	51
2560[3]	**Soviet Leader (84)** (RGuest) **3-8-2**(3) RFfrench(6) (lw: a.p: rdn over 2f out: one pce)	½	**6**	4/1[2]	80	47
3594[8]	**Loch Patrick (94)** (MMadgwick) **7-9-3** WRyan(8) (lw: rdn over 2f out: hdwy over 1f out: wknd ins fnl f)	1¾	**7**	8/1	85	54
3765[14]	**Willow Dale (IRE) (84)** (DRCElsworth) **4-8-7** PaulEddery(2) (b.nr hind: prom over 3f)	8	**8**	8/1	49	18
3198[7]	**Taoiste (84)** (RWArmstrong) **4-8-7** RPrice(1) (lw: hdwy over 2f out: wknd over 1f out)	3½	**9**	14/1	38	7

(SP 116.6%) **9 Rn**

66.1 secs (6.30) CSF £43.85 CT £883.19 TOTE £9.40: £1.90 £1.40 £7.40 (£15.20) Trio £189.60 OWNER The Broadgate Partnership (MARLBOROUGH) BRED Declan MacPartlin
LONG HANDICAP Youdontsay 8-3 Taoiste 8-3 Willow Dale (IRE) 8-5 Rudi's Pet (IRE) 8-1 Soviet Leader 8-3
WEIGHT FOR AGE 3yo-2lb
3194 Rudi's Pet (IRE) was quick to grab the rails which is always a tremendous advantage when the stalls are placed on the far side and the ground is soft. Making every post a winning one, she had soon forged clear and, responding to pressure, was not going to be caught. (8/1)
3771 Patsy Grimes, switched towards the inside below the distance, ate up the ground in the final furlong but found the line always beating her. She is knocking on the door. (5/1)
877 Repertory is only 1lb lower than when winning in April, despite a string of poor efforts. However, he ran much better here and moved into second place before halfway. Although unable to reel in the winner, he held on to that place until worried out of it in the closing stages. (25/1)
3410* Moon Strike (FR) found another 7lb rise in the weights too much to handle and, although staying on in the last furlong and a half, never seriously threatened. (3/1)
2649 Youdontsay had the best draw of all but was unable to capitalize on it. (8/1: 12/1-7/1)
2560 Soviet Leader was never far away but failed to quicken in the second half of the race. He is better at six furlongs. (4/1: 11/4-9/2)
3600* Willow Dale (IRE) (8/1: 6/1-9/1)
2769 Taoiste (14/1: 8/1-16/1)

3915 SUNLEY H'CAP (0-80) (3-Y.O+) (Class D)

4-10 (4-14) **1m 6f** £3,225.00 (£975.00: £475.00: £225.00) Stalls: Low GOING: 0.31 sec per fur (G)

				SP	RR	SF
	Shooting Light (IRE) (72) (PGMurphy) **4-9-8** SDrowne(7) (a.p: led over 2f out: rdn out)	—	**1**	14/1	83	56
1805*	**Galapino (62)** (MissGayKelleway) **4-8-7**(5) RMullen(18) (hld up: rdn over 2f out: chsd wnr ins fnl f: r.o)	1¼	**2**	14/1	72	45
2867[8]	**Arctic Fancy (USA) (71)** (PWHarris) **4-9-2**(5) CLowther(17) (rdn & hdwy over 2f out: r.o one pce)	1¼	**3**	14/1	79	52
2865[9]	**Story Line (78)** (DWPArbuthnot) **4-9-11**(3) RFfrench(15) (lw: a.p: led 6f out tl over 2f out: one pce)	¾	**4**	33/1	85	58
2652*	**Nichol Fifty (71)** (MHTompkins) **3-8-9** DBiggs(6) (rdn & hdwy over 2f out: r.o one pce)	3	**5**	11/2[3]	75	36
3183[5]	**Glow Forum (58)** (LMontagueHall) **6-8-8** FLynch(5) (b: rdn over 3f out: hdwy over 2f out: one pce)	1½	**6**	14/1	60	33
1649*	**Royal Castle (IRE) (74)** (MajorWRHern) **3-8-12** WRyan(13) (lw: hld up: rdn over 5f out: sn wknd)	6	**7**	9/2[2]	69	30
2725*	**Stahr (73)** (HCandy) **3-8-11b** CRutter(11) (hld up: rdn over 5f out: sn wknd)	¾	**8**	15/2	67	28
3412[5]	**Ultimate Smoothie (75)** (MCPipe) **5-9-11** RHills(1) (led 8f: wknd over 2f out)	hd	**9**	9/1	69	42
3719*	**Paradise Navy (74)** (CREgerton) **8-9-3b**(7) LeanneMasterson(10) (lw: bhd fnl 2f)	5	**10**	20/1	63	36
2589[10]	**Tramline (78)** (MBlanshard) **4-9-11**(3) DSweeney(4) (bhd fnl 7f)	2	**11**	20/1	64	37
2568[7]	**Capsoff (IRE) (73)** (GAHubbard) **4-9-6**(3) DO'Donohoe(9) (hdwy over 6f out: wknd over 3f out: t.o)	dist	**12**	25/1	—	—
2843[15]	**Mr Speculator (56)** (JEBanks) **4-8-6**ow1 RPrice(2) (lw: prom 10f: t.o)	nk	**13**	33/1	—	—
3739*	**Mengaab (USA) (85)** (JHMGosden) **3-9-9b** LDettori(16) (hdwy 6f out: wknd over 3f out: t.o)	2½	**14**	4/1[1]	—	—

(SP 121.3%) **14 Rn**

3m 12.13 (13.23) CSF £167.14 CT £2,536.33 TOTE £23.70: £5.10 £5.70 £2.80 (£251.50) Trio £1,076.40; £1,091.65 to 1/9/97 OWNER Mr J. M. Brown (BRISTOL) BRED The Earl of Harrington
WEIGHT FOR AGE 3yo-12lb
OFFICIAL EXPLANATION **Mengaab (USA) did not act on the ground.**
Shooting Light (IRE), a leading juvenile hurdler last winter who finished third in the Triumph Hurdle, has been off the course since the Cheltenham Festival but was not going to let a near a six-month absence stop him. Striking the front over a quarter of a mile from home, he was pushed along to keep his rivals at bay. Connections must have been absolutely delighted with this as they prepare him for another hurdling campaign. (14/1)
1805* Galapino, without a run in nearly three months, coped with the step up in distance and came through to take second place inside the final furlong. (14/1: 10/1-16/1)
1947 Arctic Fancy (USA), rousted along to take closer order over a quarter of a mile from home, carried his head very awkwardly indeed but nevertheless struggled on to take third prize. (14/1)
Story Line has dropped 16lb in the handicap after four dismal runs this season. However, she ran much better here and moved to the front towards the end of the back straight. Collared over two furlongs out, she could then only struggle on in her own time. (33/1)
2652* Nichol Fifty coped with the step up in trip but, despite staying on in the straight, never threatened to get there in time. (11/2)
3183 Glow Forum has been a model of consistency this year - winning four of her ten races and being placed on five of the other six starts. Taking closer order over a quarter of a mile from home, she then failed to find another gear. (14/1: 10/1-16/1)
1649* Royal Castle (IRE) (9/2: 7/2-11/2)
2725* Stahr (15/2: 5/1-8/1)

3916 WILLIAM HILL H'CAP (0-90) (3-Y.O+) (Class C)

4-45 (4-49) **1m 2f 7y** £4,840.00 (£1,465.00: £715.00: £340.00) Stalls: High GOING: 0.31 sec per fur (G)

				SP	RR	SF
2380*	**Cugina (78)** (GBBalding) **3-8-10** SDrowne(19) (lw: rdn over 4f out: hdwy 3f out: led 2f out: rdn out)	—	**1**	13/2[2]	90	53
3434*	**Grief (IRE) (88)** (DRCElsworth) **4-9-11**(3) RFfrench(6) (b: rdn over 3f out: gd hdwy over 1f out: r.o wl ins fnl f)	hd	**2**	11/1	100	71
3190[11]	**Patriot Games (IRE) (84)** (MRStoute) **3-9-2** WRyan(12) (a.p: rdn over 3f out: r.o ins fnl f)	3½	**3**	8/1[3]	90	53
3689[7]	**Typhoon Eight (IRE) (70)** (RWArmstrong) **5-8-10b** RPrice(3) (hdwy 4f out: hrd rdn over 1f out: unable qckn)	nk	**4**	16/1	76	47
3616[3]	**Edan Heights (72)** (SDow) **5-8-12** MRoberts(18) (hld up: led over 3f out to 2f out: wknd ins fnl f)	1½	**5**	9/1	75	46
3246[4]	**Voila Premiere (IRE) (65)** (PGMurphy) **5-8-0**(5) RMullen(14) (lw: rdn over 3f out: hdwy over 1f out: r.o)	2	**6**	8/1[3]	65	36
3773[14]	**Lomberto (83)** (VSoane) **4-9-9** CRutter(13) (lw: lost pl over 4f out: rallied over 1f out: r.o one pce)	2	**7**	33/1	80	51
3475[10]	**Danegold (IRE) (63)** (MRChannon) **5-8-3v** FNorton(1) (s.i.s: rdn over 3f out: hdwy over 1f out: nvr nrr)	hd	**8**	25/1	60	31
3689[12]	**Filial (IRE) (70)** (BJMeehan) **4-8-10** MTebbutt(15) (hld up: rdn over 3f out: ev ch over 2f out: wknd fnl f)	s.h	**9**	40/1	67	38
3491*	**Your Most Welcome (62)** (DJSffrenchDavis) **6-8-2** DRMcCabe(7) (rdn over 2f out: hdwy over 1f out: one pce fnl f)	nk	**10**	14/1	58	29
3423[16]	**Poker School (IRE) (75)** (NACallaghan) **3-8-2**(5) CLowther(2) (lw: rdn over 3f out: hdwy over 1f out: one pce)	¾	**11**	20/1	70	33
3648[10]	**Ciro's Pearl (IRE) (80)** (MHTompkins) **3-8-12** DBiggs(16) (prom over 5f)	7	**12**	14/1	64	27
3575*	**Song of Freedom (89)** (JHMGosden) **3-9-7** LDettori(9) (lw: bhd fnl 2f)	¾	**13**	3/1[1]	72	35
3281[4]	**Swinging The Blues (IRE) (64)** (RAkehurst) **3-7-3**(7) PFitzsimons(5) (bhd fnl 4f)	1¼	**14**	16/1	45	8
3125[7]	**Khawafi (83)** (EALDunlop) **3-9-1** RHills(4) (led 8f out to 4f out: wknd over 2f out)	hd	**15**	12/1	64	27
3125[14]	**Happy Go Lucky (80)** (RJO'Sullivan) **3-8-9**(3) DO'Donohoe(10) (b.off hind: led 2f: rdn over 3f out: wknd over 2f out)	2½	**16**	40/1	57	20
	Kings Assembly (74) (PWHarris) **5-9-0** AClark(8) (hld up: led 4f out tl over 3f out: wknd over 2f out)	1¾	**17**	20/1	48	19
				(SP 132.9%)	**17 Rn**	

2m 14.99 (8.29) CSF £69.47 CT £550.19 TOTE £7.50: £1.90 £2.90 £2.10 £4.90 (£34.30) Trio £83.60 OWNER Miss B. Swire (ANDOVER) BRED Miss B. Swire

LONG HANDICAP Swinging The Blues (IRE) 7-6

WEIGHT FOR AGE 3yo-8lb

STEWARDS' ENQUIRY Price susp 8-10/9/97 excessive use of whip

2380* Cugina is well suited by this ground and followed up her Chester victory, leading two furlongs out and being ridden along to keep the fast-finishing runner-up at bay. (13/2)

3434* Grief (IRE), rousted along and going nowhere at the back of the field entering the straight, ate up the ground from below the distance but found the line coming just a few strides too soon. A return to a mile and a half would help. (11/1: 8/1-12/1)

2528 Patriot Games (IRE), who disappointed at Goodwood last time out, ran better here and stuck on well inside the final furlong. (8/1: 6/1-9/1)

2961 Typhoon Eight (IRE) was dropped back in distance and, under pressure over a furlong out, failed to find another gear. A return to a mile and half is needed. (16/1)

3616 Edan Heights had the ground in his favour - all three of his wins to date have come with give underfoot. Gaining control early in the straight, he was collared a quarter of a mile out but held on until tiring inside the final furlong. (9/1)

3246 Voila Premiere (IRE) stayed on in the last furlong and a half but never threatened to get there in time. (8/1)

3491* Your Most Welcome (14/1: 10/1-16/1)

2764 Khawafi (12/1: op 8/1)

3917 OASIS LAKELAND VILLAGE MAIDEN STKS (3-Y.O F) (Class D)

5-20 (5-22) **1m 14y** £3,225.00 (£975.00: £475.00: £225.00) Stalls: High GOING: 0.31 sec per fur (G)

				SP	RR	SF
3030[5]	**Sceptre Lady (IRE) (69)** (BWHills) **3-8-11** PatEddery(4) (lw: a.p: rdn over 2f out: led ins fnl f: r.o wl)	—	**1**	10/1	73	38
	Star Gambit (USA) (RAkehurst) **3-8-11** MRoberts(2) (unf: scope: hdwy over 3f out: led over 2f out: wandered 1f out: hdd ins fnl f: r.o)	nk	**2**	14/1	72	37
3281[2]	**Khazinat El Dar (USA)** (MajorWRHern) **3-8-11** RHills(1) (rdn over 4f out: hdwy over 2f out: r.o)	hd	**3**	2/1[1]	72	37
3704[7]	**Alcalali (USA) (84)** (PAKelleway) **3-8-11** MWigham(8) (swtg: led over 6f out tl over 2f out: unable qckn)	2	**4**	10/1	68	33
	La Belle Otero (USA) (HRACecil) **3-8-11** WRyan(11) (leggy: scope: hld up: rdn over 2f out: wknd over 1f out)	6	**5**	9/2[3]	56	21
	Bestemor (HCandy) **3-8-11** CRutter(5) (str: scope: bit bkwd: rdn over 3f out: nvr nr to chal)	3½	**6**	33/1	49	14
2773[7]	**Arco Colora** (DRCElsworth) **3-8-11** AProcter(3) (prom over 5f)	2½	**7**	33/1	44	9
3715[6]	**Hibernica (IRE)** (GBBalding) **3-8-11** SDrowne(6) (b: led over 1f: rdn over 3f out: wknd over 2f out)	3	**8**	33/1	39	4
2952[4]	**Rumuz (IRE)** (EALDunlop) **3-8-8**(3) DO'Donohoe(9) (b.nr hind: hld up: rdn 4f out: sn wknd)	½	**9**	10/1	38	3
	Slieu Whallian (RHannon) **3-8-11** WJO'Connor(10) (unf: scope: a bhd)	7	**10**	25/1	24	—
3030[4]	**Encore** (JHMGosden) **3-8-11** LDettori(7) (a bhd: t.o)	dist	**11**	11/4[2]	—	—
				(SP 124.8%)	**11 Rn**	

1m 49.55 (8.35) CSF £129.58 TOTE £9.60: £2.30 £2.80 £1.20 (£50.20) Trio £92.00 OWNER Sceptre Racing (LAMBOURN) BRED Gay O'Callaghan

3030 Sceptre Lady (IRE) at last came good. Joining issue over a quarter of a mile from home, she gained a narrow advantage early inside the final furlong and held on well. (10/1: 8/1-12/1)

Star Gambit (USA), a lengthy filly who needs time to develop, moved to the front over a quarter of a mile from home. Wandering slightly as the hedge she was running along disappeared a furlong out, leaving her with an expanse of open course all around her, she was collared early inside the final furlong but, to her credit, kept on well to the bitter end. She should soon go one better. (14/1)

3281 Khazinat El Dar (USA) was off the bridle before halfway but she stayed on well up the hill, and can find a similar event before long. (2/1: 5/4-9/4)

3188 Alcalali (USA) finished fourth to Yashmak in the Ribblesdale Stakes but that run was very flattering as she has been beaten in ordinary maidens, including this one. A return to a longer trip looks needed. (10/1: 7/1-11/1)

La Belle Otero (USA), a tall filly with plenty of substance, cost $400,000 and is a half-sister to three Stakes winners in the USA including Grade Three winner Summer Matinee. Chasing the leaders, she only tired from below the distance as lack of a previous run took its toll. She will come on a lot for the outing and should step up on this before long. (9/2: 5/2-5/1)

Bestemor, a well-built filly, was carrying plenty of condition and never threatened to get into it. (33/1)

2952 Rumuz (IRE) (10/1: 6/1-12/1)

T/Jkpt: Not won; £50,726.72 to 1/9/97. T/Plpt: £2,188.30 (26.92 Tckts). T/Qdpt: £337.00 (11.77 Tckts) AK

3626-HAMILTON (R-H) (Good, Good to soft patches becoming Good to soft)
Monday September 1st
WEATHER: overcast WIND: almost nil

3918 HYNDFORD MAIDEN STKS (3-Y.O+) (Class D)
2-15 (2-15) **1m 3f 16y** £3,566.25 (£1,080.00: £527.50: £251.25) Stalls: High GOING minus 0.17 sec per fur (GF)

				SP	RR	SF
1558[3]	**Double Alleged (USA) (88)** (MJohnston) **3-8-13** JWeaver(4) (b: lw: mde all: pushed along 3f out: sn clr: eased ins fnl f)	—	**1**	1/6[1]	78+	39
	Aeolina (FR) (SEKettlewell) **3-8-5**(3) RFfrench(2) (w'like: last tl hdwy over 3f out: styd on: no ch w wnr)	8	**2**	16/1[3]	61	22
3720[4]	**Double Star** (JLHarris) **6-9-7** KFallon(1) (chsd ldrs: rdn 4f out: sn wl outpcd)	14	**3**	5/1[2]	46	15
3488[5]	**Chanson d'Amour (IRE) (20)** (MissLAPerratt) **3-8-1**(7) JMcAuley(3) (chsd wnr tl rdn & btn wl over 2f out)	17	**4**	66/1	17	—

(SP 109.8%) **4 Rn**

2m 25.6 (6.20) CSF £4.03 TOTE £1.10: (£2.50) OWNER Mrs N. J. Huggins (MIDDLEHAM) BRED Gerald W. Leigh
WEIGHT FOR AGE 3yo-8lb

1558 Double Alleged (USA), who just gallops and stays, took no chances even with this moderate opposition and then won as he should have. (1/6)
Aeolina (FR) put in a useful first effort and ought to have learned plenty, despite being out-classed. (16/1)
3720 Double Star looked very slow when the pressure was on in the last half-mile. (5/1)

3919 STONEFIELD (S) H'CAP (0-60) (3-Y.O+) (Class G)
2-45 (2-45) **1m 4f 17y** £2,444.00 (£684.00: £332.00) Stalls: High GOING minus 0.17 sec per fur (GF)

				SP	RR	SF
3486[2]	**Craigary (37)** (MrsASwinbank) **6-9-1** GDuffield(11) (chsd ldrs: led 3f out: rdn clr & styd on wl)	—	**1**	6/1[3]	47	29
3758[7]	**Havana Heights (IRE) (34)** (JLEyre) **4-8-5**(7) SBuckley(16) (a chsng ldrs: kpt on wl fnl 2f)	1½	**2**	25/1	42	24
3758*	**Sushi Bar (IRE) (42)** (MrsMReveley) **6-9-6** KDarley(9) (hld up: hdwy 4f out: styd on wl: nvr able to chal)	½	**3**	11/2[2]	49	31
3488[7]	**Sweet Note (IRE) (27)** (MissLAPerratt) **3-7-3**(7) JMcAuley(4) (s.i.s: hdwy on ins 4f out: swtchd lft 2f out: r.o)	3	**4**	100/1	30	3
3758[9]	**Diamond Crown (IRE) (35)** (MartynWane) **6-8-13** KFallon(12) (hld up & bhd: hdwy 4f out: nrst fin)	1	**5**	8/1	37	19
3626[3]	**Charlie Bigtime (43)** (ICampbell) **7-9-7** AMackay(8) (lw: a in tch: c wd st: one pce fnl 2f)	3	**6**	7/1	41	23
3477[5]	**Philgem (24)** (CWFairhurst) **4-7-11v**(5)ow2 KSked(5) (mid div: hdwy 4f out: rdn & btn appr fnl f)	2	**7**	11/1	19	—
3108[9]	**Peep O Day (38)** (JLEyre) **6-9-2** TWilliams(18) (b.hind: led after 3f to 3f out: wknd)	7	**8**	10/1	24	6
3762[8]	**Silent System (IRE) (20)** (DWChapman) **4-7-12b** JQuinn(2) (trckd ldrs tl wknd over 2f out)	1	**9**	16/1	5	—
3626[7]	**Cois Na Farraige (IRE) (31)** (MissLAPerratt) **4-8-6**(3) TEDurcan(17) (nvr bttr than mid div)	3½	**10**	66/1	11	—
3570[9]	**Princely Affair (25)** (JMBradley) **4-8-0b**(3) RFfrench(6) (n.d)	1	**11**	14/1	4	—
3272[3]	**Mowlaie (50)** (DWChapman) **6-10-0** ACulhane(7) (b: in tch tl wknd fnl 3f)	1½	**12**	14/1	27	9
43[6]	**Mr Bean (40)** (KRBurke) **7-9-4** MFenton(13) (b: led 3f: cl up tl wknd fnl 3f)	½	**13**	20/1	16	—
3792[3]	**Erlking (IRE) (37)** (SMellor) **7-9-1b** MWigham(14) (lw: prom tl wknd fnl 3f)	2½	**14**	5/1[1]	10	—
1686[6]	**Skiddaw Samba (27)** (MrsMReveley) **8-8-5** DWright(1) (hld up & bhd: n.d)	¾	**15**	33/1	—	—
3601[5]	**Macari (47)** (BPJBaugh) **3-9-2** JWeaver(3) (lw: hld up & a bhd)	2	**16**	20/1	16	—
2502[13]	**Bout (27)** (RMMcKellar) **3-7-5v**[1](5) IonaWands(10) (prom to ½-wy)	nk	**17**	100/1	—	—
3401[9]	**The Orraman (IRE) (47)** (JJO'Neill) **3-8-11b**[1](5) CLowther(15) (lw: lost tch fr ½-wy: t.o)	20	**18**	50/1	—	—

(SP 128.3%) **18 Rn**

2m 40.7 (8.70) CSF £147.34 CT £816.22 TOTE £7.30: £1.90 £4.60 £2.00 £24.90 (£163.00) Trio £265.10 OWNER Mr James Cringan (RICHMOND) BRED James A. Cringan
LONG HANDICAP Sweet Note (IRE) 7-3
WEIGHT FOR AGE 3yo-9lb
No bid

3486 Craigary, well-handled, got first run and that proved decisive. (6/1)
2753 Havana Heights (IRE), likely to need further, was made plenty of use of here and did stay on particularly well. (25/1)
3758* Sushi Bar (IRE) was trying to come from off the pace, always had plenty on and never got in a serious blow. (11/2)
2029 Sweet Note (IRE), from 7lb out of the handicap, showed she has plenty of ability if she decides to use it. (100/1)
3456 Diamond Crown (IRE), who likes to come from way behind, always had an impossible task here but he does look on good terms with himself, should things go his way. (8/1)
3626 Charlie Bigtime again ran quite well but he was always having to race wide in the straight, which is never an advantage. (7/1: 5/1-8/1)
Peep O Day (10/1: 12/1-8/1)
3272 Mowlaie (14/1: op 9/1)

3920 E.B.F. MAIDEN STKS (2-Y.O) (Class D)
3-15 (3-16) **1m 65y** £3,517.50 (£1,065.00: £520.00: £247.50) Stalls: High GOING minus 0.17 sec per fur (GF)

				SP	RR	SF
3193[6]	**Generosity** (PFICole) **2-9-0** TQuinn(3) (chsd ldrs: hdwy to disp ld 4f out: led wl over 1f out to 1f out: sn led again: rdn & styd on wl)	—	**1**	4/6[1]	69	25
3825[4]	**Gift of Gold** (ICampbell) **2-9-0** AMackay(1) (a.p: hdwy to ld 1f out: hung lft & sn hdd: kpt on)	nk	**2**	20/1	68	24
3201[5]	**Shaanxi Romance (IRE)** (MBell) **2-9-0** MFenton(6) (disp ld tl led 5½f out: disp ld 4f out tl outpcd appr fnl f)	5	**3**	5/2[2]	59	15
3282[4]	**Mareeba** (MJohnston) **2-8-9** JWeaver(4) (chsd ldrs: effrt & ev ch 4f out: outpcd fnl 2f)	hd	**4**	11/1[3]	54	10
3628[2]	**Baylham** (JSGoldie) **2-8-11**(3) TEDurcan(7) (hld up & bhd: effrt 3f out: nvr nr to chal)	4	**5**	25/1	51	7
3260[4]	**Vincent** (JLHarris) **2-9-0** KFallon(2) (bhd: effrt ½-wy: no imp)	nk	**6**	14/1	50	6
3628[7]	**Ingle Boy** (BMactaggart) **2-8-9**(5) KSked(5) (disp ld 2½f: wknd 4f out)	13	**7**	100/1	25	—

(SP 113.2%) **7 Rn**

1m 50.4 (6.30) CSF £17.06 TOTE £1.60: £1.30 £6.90 (£9.20) OWNER H R H Prince Fahd Salman (WHATCOMBE) BRED Newgate Stud Co

3193 Generosity is certainly a stayer in the making and he needed every yard of this trip. (4/6)
3825 Gift of Gold is improving and there would seem to be a race to be won with him before long. (20/1)
3201 Shaanxi Romance (IRE) was made a lot of use of here and, against a couple of really tough opponents, that probably cost him his chance. (5/2)
3282 Mareeba is improving but this company proved just too hot. (11/1: 8/1-12/1)
3628 Baylham found this company too useful and was wisely not given too hard a time. (25/1)
3260 Vincent never got into this but left the impression that it should have taught him plenty. (14/1)

3921 WILLIAM HILL SCOTTISH TROPHY H'CAP (0-90) (3-Y.O+) (Class C)

3-45 (3-45) **1m 65y** £7,490.00 (£2,270.00: £1,110.00: £530.00) Stalls: High GOING minus 0.17 sec per fur (GF)

			Pos	SP	RR	SF
3622^{2}	**Antarctic Storm (61)** (RAFahey) **4-8-6** FNorton(8) (mde all: r.o wl fnl 2f)	—	1	$6/1^{2}$	72	36
3690^{8}	**Polar Prospect (54)** (BHanbury) **4-7-10**(3) MartinDwyer(11) (b: prom: hdwy & hung lft over 1f out: r.o wl towards fin)	1¼	2	8/1	63	27
3584^{2}	**Sparky (69)** (MWEasterby) **3-8-9b** TLucas(14) (b: lw: trckd ldrs: effrt & ev ch over 1f out: hung rt & nt qckn)	hd	3	10/1	77	36
3722^{7}	**Mentalasanythin (65)** (DHaydnJones) **8-8-10** AMackay(10) (bhd: hdwy on outside 2f out: r.o wl towards fin)	1¼	4	10/1	71	35
3573^{9}	**Running Green (65)** (DMoffatt) **6-8-7v**(3) DarrenMoffatt(13) (b: mid div: n.m.r 3f out: styd on wl fnl 2f)	nk	5	12/1	70	34
3702*	**Impulsive Air (IRE) (62)** (EWeymes) **5-8-7** JQuinn(6) (cl up tl wknd appr fnl f)	1	6	$15/2^{3}$	66	30
3801^{4}	**Gymcrak Premiere (70)** (GHolmes) **9-9-1v** KFallon(12) (lw: hld up & bhd: effrt ½-wy: nt clr run 3f out: no imp)	1¼	7	$9/2^{1}$	71	35
3867^{5}	**Lord Advocate (57)** (DANolan) **9-7-11b**(5)ow6 KSked(4) (b.hind: bhd: brought wd & effrt 4f out: nrst fin)	1¼	8	50/1	56	14
2925^{10}	**Moonshiner (USA) (80)** (GWragg) **3-9-6** KDarley(1) (lw: bhd: effrt & n.m.r 3f out: n.d)	3	9	20/1	73	32
3630^{2}	**Pekay (65)** (MJohnston) **4-8-10** JWeaver(2) (chsd ldrs: effrt 4f out: wknd fnl 2f)	1	10	8/1	56	20
1097^{11}	**Shinerolla (79)** (CParker) **5-9-10** RCochrane(7) (s.i.s: nvr nr to chal)	2½	11	16/1	65	29
3824^{6}	**Rebel County (IRE) (75)** (ABailey) **4-9-1**(5) CLowther(15) (lw: hld up: effrt ½-wy: sn btn)	2½	12	8/1	56	20
3798^{13}	**Sooty Tern (75)** (JMBradley) **10-9-3**(3) RFfrench(5) (chsd ldrs tl wknd fnl 3f)	¾	13	16/1	55	19
	Mister Woodstick (IRE) (56) (CParker) **4-8-1** TWilliams(9) (a rr div)	4	14	33/1	28	—
	Ret Frem (IRE) (67) (CParker) **4-8-12** JCarroll(3) (prom: wkng whn hmpd wl over 2f out)	20	15	25/1	1	—
				(SP 128.7%)	**15 Rn**	

1m 48.4 (4.30) CSF £49.97 CT £457.97 TOTE £6.50: £2.00 £3.50 £2.60 (£54.80) Trio £232.90 OWNER Northumbria Leisure Ltd (MALTON) BRED N. and Mrs Bryce-Smith

LONG HANDICAP Lord Advocate 7-9

WEIGHT FOR AGE 3yo-5lb

3622 Antarctic Storm had things all his own way and, once he had really stepped the pace up approaching the last two furlongs, he was never going to be caught. (6/1)

Polar Prospect is plummeting down the handicap and this was a much better effort, and he can soon find a race. (8/1)

3584 Sparky looks particularly well but is not quite doing all he can and there is certainly more ability there if he would put it in. (10/1)

3221 Mentalasanythin found this trip too sharp and, despite finishing well, the effort was always too late. (10/1)

3573 Running Green seems to find trouble every time he runs which would suggest that he is short of pace at a vital stage and needs a strongly-run event. (12/1)

3702* Impulsive Air (IRE) found this company too competitive and dropped away in the closing stages. (15/2)

3801 Gymcrak Premiere tried to come from way behind and the task was always beyond him. (9/2)

3867 Lord Advocate ran well at a trip too short here. (50/1)

3922 SHOOTING STARS SERIES (FINAL ROUND) APPRENTICE H'CAP (0-70) (3-Y.O+) (Class F)

4-15 (4-20) **5f 4y** £2,892.00 (£812.00: £396.00) Stalls: Low GOING minus 0.17 sec per fur (GF)

			Pos	SP	RR	SF
3856^{12}	**Suedoro (40)** (JSGoldie) **7-7-8**(5) APolli(3) (a chsng ldrs: led appr fnl f: hld on wl)	—	1	20/1	51	25
3910*	**Bowlers Boy (73)** (JJQuinn) **4-9-11**(7) 6x RSmith(1) (lw: prom: qcknd to chal ins fnl f: hung rt: r.o)	s.h	2	14/1	84	58
3756^{6}	**William's Well (60)** (MWEasterby) **3-9-4b** GParkin(9) (chsd ldrs: led wl over 1f out: hdd appr fnl f: kpt on)	1¾	3	$6/1^{3}$	65	38
3398^{11}	**Hajat (46)** (JBerry) **3-8-4** PFessey(4) (bhd: hmpd ½-wy: r.o wl appr fnl f)	nk	4	25/1	50	23
3871^{2}	**Pallium (IRE) (48)** (DANolan) **9-8-0b**(7) NPollard(5) (bhd: hmpd ½-wy: hdwy over 1f out: r.o)	hd	5	12/1	52	26
3771^{4}	**Montrestar (62)** (ABailey) **4-9-4**(3) CLowther(7) (b.hind: chsd ldrs: nt qckn fnl f)	1½	6	$11/2^{2}$	61	35
3406^{13}	**Don't Care (IRE) (62)** (MissLAPerratt) **6-9-7b** TEDurcan(8) (lw: sn drvn along: styd on fnl 2f: n.d)	1¼	7	20/1	57	31
3484^{14}	**Six for Luck (43)** (DANolan) **5-7-11b**(5)ow6 KSked(6) (led 1½f: cl up: edgd lft over 2f out: wknd appr fnl f)	1	8	33/1	35	3
3795^{6}	**River Tern (69)** (JMBradley) **4-10-0** RFfrench(18) (in tch: rdn ½-wy: no imp)	¾	9	13/2	59	33
3761^{6}	**Pathaze (39)** (NBycroft) **4-7-12** DarrenMoffatt(15) (outpcd: sme hdwy over 1f out: n.d)	½	10	12/1	27	1
3856^{5}	**Ramsey Hope (60)** (CWFairhurst) **4-9-0v**(5) TSiddall(17) (nvr wnt pce)	½	11	10/1	46	20
3484*	**Natural Key (68)** (DHaydnJones) **4-9-13** MartinDwyer(13) (chsd ldrs tl wknd over 1f out)	nk	12	$3/1^{1}$	54	28
3756^{13}	**Sunday Mail Too (IRE) (37)** (MissLAPerratt) **5-7-3**(7) PBradley(11) (nvr wnt pce)	nk	13	20/1	22	—
3871^{3}	**Kabcast (38)** (DWChapman) **12-7-6b**(5)ow1 RWinston(10) (led after 1½f tl wl over 1f out: wknd)	s.h	14	16/1	22	—
3484^{6}	**Diet (37)** (MissLAPerratt) **11-7-3v**(7) ANicholls(2) (sn outpcd & bhd)	nk	15	50/1	20	—
3756^{12}	**Northern Sal (41)** (MissLAPerratt) **3-7-8**(5) IonaWands(14) (chsd ldrs over 3f)	3	16	20/1	15	—
3756^{9}	**Mystique Smile (37)** (JSGoldie) **4-7-3**(7) JMcAuley(12) (hld up: effrt ½-wy: n.d)	s.h	17	25/1	11	—
3271^{8}	**Mister Sean (IRE) (37)** (JMBradley) **4-7-3**(7) RThomas(16) (b.hind: sn outpcd & bhd)	1½	18	100/1	6	—
				(SP 137.7%)	**18 Rn**	

60.9 secs (2.60) CSF £253.43 CT £1,802.86 TOTE £15.70: £2.30 £3.60 £2.10 £13.30 (£97.90) Trio £606.70 OWNER Mr Andrew Paterson (GLASGOW) BRED R. Vardy

LONG HANDICAP Six for Luck 7-8 Diet 6-13 Sunday Mail Too (IRE) 7-3 Mystique Smile 7-6 Mister Sean (IRE) 6-6

WEIGHT FOR AGE 3yo-1lb

3761 Suedoro got things right at last here and this is the only track she has won on. (20/1)

3910* Bowlers Boy, poorly drawn, ran a cracker and is obviously in top form. (14/1: op 8/1)

3756 William's Well is running consistently and deserves to find another race. (6/1)

3040* Hajat almost got knocked over at halfway and then finished well to show there is another race or two in her. (25/1)

3871 Pallium (IRE) found trouble at halfway but did run on at the end and remains in good heart. (12/1)

3771 Montrestar is running well but was tapped for speed in the closing stages. (11/2)

3566* River Tern gave problems aplenty leaving the paddock and seemed in an awkward mood on this occasion. (13/2)

3923 TEAM KIER H'CAP (0-80) (3-Y.O) (Class D)

4-45 (4-47) **6f 5y** £3,533.75 (£1,070.00: £522.50: £248.75) Stalls: Low GOING minus 0.17 sec per fur (GF)

			Pos	SP	RR	SF
3614^{8}	**March Crusader (80)** (BHanbury) **3-9-7** KFallon(7) (lw: cl up: led 1½f out: r.o u.p)	—	1	$7/2^{2}$	91	47
3548^{9}	**Maladerie (IRE) (55)** (MRChannon) **3-7-5**(5) APolli(2) (cl up: led ½-wy: hung rt: hdd 1½f out: kpt on)	¾	2	13/2	64	20
3189^{10}	**Always Alight (76)** (KRBurke) **3-9-3** JQuinn(1) (lw: in tch: outpcd ½-wy: hdwy over 1f out: nvr able to chal)	1½	3	$11/4^{1}$	81	37
3716^{9}	**Grace (57)** (JMBradley) **3-7-9**(3) RFfrench(3) (led to ½-wy: n.m.r 2f out: sn wknd)	2½	4	14/1	55	11
2708^{16}	**Osomental (72)** (DHaydnJones) **3-8-13** AMackay(6) (hung bdly rt thrght: sn drvn along: nvr able to chal)	1¼	5	8/1	67	23

3812*	**Samsung Spirit (76)** (EWeymes) **3-9-3** 6x JFanning(4) (chsd ldrs: outpcd ½-wy: n.d after)	6	**6**	7/2 2	55	11
3709 11	**Bayford Thrust (73)** (JBerry) **3-8-11**(3) PFessey(8) (b: b.hind: s.s: hdwy ½-wy: sn wknd)	hd	**7**	6/1 3	52	8
				(SP 116.5%)	**7 Rn**	

1m 13.0 (3.00) CSF £24.58 CT £64.75 TOTE £5.60: £2.30 £2.10 (£7.70) OWNER Maktoum Al Maktoum (NEWMARKET) BRED Gainsborough Stud Management Ltd

2925 March Crusader has proved difficult in the past but he had his mind made up for him here and won it well. (7/2)
Maladerie (IRE) gave definite signs of coming back to form here and is on a useful mark. (13/2)
2833 Always Alight looked tremendously well but found the early pace too strong and, despite finishing well, could never land a blow. (11/4)
2506 Grace has plenty of toe and this was not a bad effort. (14/1)
Osomental just wanted to hang right all the way and his rider did remarkably well to get him so close. (8/1)
3812* Samsung Spirit was disappointing here once the pressure was on. (7/2)
3332 Bayford Thrust cannot afford to keep giving so much ground away at the start. (6/1)

T/Jkpt: £13,078.30 (5.08 Tckts). T/Plpt: £178.10 (162.4 Tckts). T/Qdpt: £97.80 (16.02 Tckts) AA

3638-FOLKESTONE (R-H) (Good, Good to firm patches)
Tuesday September 2nd
WEATHER: warm WIND: slt half bhd

3924 DAVID CAMERON MEMORIAL NURSERY H'CAP (0-75) (2-Y.O) (Class E)
2-30 (2-33) **6f 189y** £3,486.25 (£1,045.00: £502.50: £231.25) Stalls: Low GOING minus 0.20 sec per fur (GF)

				SP	RR	SF
3613 8	**Chief Blade (65)** (RAkehurst) **2-8-11** SSanders(11) (lw: a.p: rdn over 3f out: led ins fnl f: drvn out)	—	**1**	10/1	65	16
2953 10	**Simlet (66)** (WJarvis) **2-8-12** WRyan(14) (lw: hdwy over 1f out: ev ch ins fnl f: r.o wl)	hd	**2**	11/4 1	66	17
3395 10	**Persian Fortune (59)** (WGMTurner) **2-8-2**(3) DSweeney(13) (led: hrd rdn over 1f out: hdd ins fnl f: unable qckn)	1¾	**3**	20/1	55	6
3799 9	**Argumentative (58)** (SDow) **2-8-1**(3) DO'Donohoe(5) (hld up: hrd rdn over 1f out: one pce)	1¼	**4**	33/1	51	2
3215 9	**Red Maple (USA) (65)** (PFICole) **2-8-11** TQuinn(6) (lost pl 5f out: rallied fnl f: r.o one pce)	s.h	**5**	10/1	58	9
3635 4	**Sassy (IRE) (64)** (APJarvis) **2-8-10** SDrowne(7) (rdn 5f out: hdwy over 1f out: r.o one pce)	nk	**6**	13/2 2	56	7
3474 8	**Flying Singer (62)** (IABalding) **2-8-5**(3) MartinDwyer(15) (lw: hld up: nt clr run on ins over 1f out: swtchd lft: one pce)	½	**7**	12/1	53	4
3597 9	**Lobuche (IRE) (64)** (RHannon) **2-8-10** DaneO'Neill(2) (lw: nvr nrr)	1¾	**8**	10/1	51	2
3474 10	**Desert Native (58)** (CFWall) **2-8-4** GDuffield(16) (a.p: rdn over 3f out: wknd fnl f)	nk	**9**	25/1	44	—
3489 9	**Sergeant Imp (IRE) (65)** (PMitchell) **2-8-11** AClark(9) (bhd fnl 4f)	nk	**10**	33/1	50	1
3331 3	**Moothyeb (USA) (75)** (NAGraham) **2-9-7** RHills(3) (bhd fnl 6f)	½	**11**	7/1 3	59	10
3597 6	**Delciana (IRE) (68)** (PWHarris) **2-9-0** JQuinn(10) (lw: w ldr: hrd rdn over 1f out: sn wknd)	½	**12**	11/1	51	2
3817*	**Mrs Middle (68)** (NACallaghan) **2-8-11**(3) 6x RFfrench(12) (dwlt: a bhd)	½	**13**	7/1 3	50	1
3635 6	**Smart Beau (USA) (65)** (RCharlton) **2-8-11** WJO'Connor(8) (sme hdwy on ins over 2f out: wknd over 1f out)	½	**14**	14/1	46	—
3489 4	**Frolicking (75)** (JLDunlop) **2-9-7** JReid(4) (a bhd)	nk	**15**	8/1	55	6
				(SP 140.6%)	**15 Rn**	

1m 26.6 (5.20) CSF £38.38 CT £543.35 TOTE £14.20: £4.10 £1.80 £10.40 (£53.40) Trio £414.00; £425.72 to York 3/9/97 OWNER The Money Men (EPSOM) BRED Mrs John Trotter

STEWARDS' ENQUIRY Obj. to Chief Blade by Ryan overruled

2948 Chief Blade stepped up on his maiden efforts to make a winning debut in handicap company. Pushing along from halfway, Sanders did accidentally strike the runner-up across the head approaching the final furlong but, in a tremendous tussle with that rival, the combination just managed to prevail. (10/1: 7/1-12/1)
2768 Simlet was well supported in the market and ran by far his best race to date. Picking up ground approaching the final furlong, he was accidentally struck on the head but he nevertheless had a tremendous battle-royal with the winner and only just lost out. Compensation awaits. (11/4)
3076 Persian Fortune, who has shown consistent form in claimers, gave a good account of herself here, taking the field along until eventually overhauled inside the final furlong. (20/1)
2388 Argumentative has been competing on soft ground but ran his best race to date on this faster surface, and looked a real danger below the distance before tapped for toe. (33/1)
1961 Red Maple (USA) outpaced after only a couple of furlongs but did stay on again in the last two hundred yards. (10/1: 8/1-12/1)
3635 Sassy (IRE) was off the bridle after only two furlongs, but she was suited by the step up to seven furlongs and was staying on again inside the distance. (13/2)
2740 Flying Singer (12/1: 8/1-14/1)
1370 Lobuche (IRE) (10/1: 6/1-11/1)
3331 Moothyeb (USA) (7/1: op 9/2)
3597 Delciana (IRE) (11/1: 6/1-12/1)
3817* Mrs Middle (7/1: 5/1-8/1)
3635 Smart Beau (USA) (14/1: op 8/1)
3489 Frolicking (8/1: 5/1-9/1)

3925 EPEE CONDITIONS STKS (2-Y.O) (Class C)
3-00 (3-01) **5f** £4,577.89 (£1,696.10: £815.55: £335.25: £135.13: £55.08) Stalls: Low GOING minus 0.20 sec per fur (GF)

				SP	RR	SF
3574 3	**Thanksgiving (IRE)** (MajorDNChappell) **2-8-6** JReid(3) (lw: hld up: led 1f out: pushed out)	—	**1**	4/1 3	89	50
3791*	**Eleventh Duke (IRE) (85)** (RHannon) **2-8-11** DaneO'Neill(1) (lw: lost pl over 2f out: rallied over 1f out: r.o one pce)	1½	**2**	3/1 1	89	50
3556*	**Mishraak (IRE) (93)** (RWArmstrong) **2-8-11** RHills(4) (led 4f: one pce)	¾	**3**	7/2 2	87	48
3595 5	**Contrary Mary (90)** (GLewis) **2-8-6**(3) AWhelan(5) (a.p: rdn over 2f out: one pce fnl f)	¾	**4**	3/1 1	82	43
3873a 4	**Dernier Croise (FR)** (BJMeehan) **2-8-11b** MTebbutt(7) (lw: prom over 3f)	3½	**5**	12/1	73	34
3288 2	**Madame Claude (IRE)** (JARToller) **2-8-6** SSanders(6) (dwlt: bhd fnl 3f)	1½	**6**	12/1	63	24
2926 6	**Babanina** (CEBrittain) **2-8-6** WRyan(2) (a bhd)	4	**7**	12/1	51	12
				(SP 115.3%)	**7 Rn**	

58.9 secs (1.30) CSF £15.21 TOTE £5.40: £3.30 £1.40 (£6.90) OWNER Mrs G. C. Maxwell (PULBOROUGH) BRED J. C. Condon

3574 Thanksgiving (IRE), reverting to the minimum trip, struck the front a furlong out and needed only to be nudged along to win in a fast time which was just under half a second outside the course record set by Pivotal two years ago. (4/1)

3791* Eleventh Duke (IRE), in good form of late, got rather outpaced at halfway but stayed on again from below the distance to take second prize. (3/1)
3556* Mishraak (IRE) once again took the field along but, collared a furlong out, failed to find another turn of foot. (7/2)
3595 Contrary Mary had less to do here and almost had every chance approaching the final furlong before tapped for toe. (3/1)
3873a Dernier Croise (FR), who has been competing in Pattern company abroad, had less on his plate here but had been seen off early in the final quarter-mile. (12/1)
2926 Babanina (12/1: 8/1-14/1)

3926 E.B.F. BROADSWORD MEDIAN AUCTION MAIDEN STKS (I) (2-Y.O) (Class F)
3-30 (3-31) **6f** £2,389.00 (£659.00: £313.00) Stalls: Low GOING minus 0.20 sec per fur (GF)

				SP	RR	SF
3235^{3}	**Hakeem (IRE)** (RWArmstrong) **2-9-0** RPrice(11) (lw: a.p: rdn over 1f out: led ins fnl f: r.o wl)	—	**1**	4/1^{2}	78	44
2917^{4}	**Call To Order** (CFWall) **2-9-0** SSanders(5) (lw: a.p: led over 3f out tl ins fnl f: r.o)	½	**2**	10/1	77	43
3723^{5}	**Statua (IRE) (95)** (PJMakin) **2-8-9** RCochrane(12) (hld up: rdn over 2f out: r.o ins fnl f)	hd	**3**	15/8^{1}	71	37
3416^{2}	**Ambitious** (JRFanshawe) **2-8-9** JReid(10) (hld up: rdn over 1f out: unable qckn)	1	**4**	7/1^{3}	69	35
3574^{12}	**Emmajoun** (APJarvis) **2-8-9** SDrowne(8) (lw: a.p: ev ch over 1f out: wknd ins fnl f)	1	**5**	16/1	66	32
3636^{6}	**Persian Sabre** (VSoane) **2-8-9** CRutter(2) (b.nr fore: led over 2f: wknd 2f out)	2	**6**	16/1	61	27
3597^{10}	**Ringleader (75)** (PFICole) **2-9-0b^{1}** TQuinn(7) (bhd fnl 2f)	2½	**7**	14/1	59	25
2917^{7}	**I Cried For You (IRE)** (RHannon) **2-9-0** DaneO'Neill(9) (lw: prom over 3f)	¾	**8**	25/1	57	23
3278^{6}	**Midnight Sting** (MAJarvis) **2-8-9** WRyan(1) (b: a bhd)	4	**9**	4/1^{2}	41	7
	Critical Air (SirMarkPrescott) **2-9-0** GDuffield(13) (leggy: scope: bit bkwd: prom 3f)	7	**10**	9/1	28	—
	Gone To Press (JWPayne) **2-9-0** MFenton(4) (str: scope: bkwd: s.s: t.o tl p.u over 2f out: lame)		**P**	33/1	—	—
				(SP 131.6%)	**11 Rn**	

1m 12.8 (2.60) CSF £45.37 TOTE £7.90: £2.10 £2.60 £1.20 (£29.90) Trio £21.20 OWNER Mr Ahmed Al Shafar (NEWMARKET) BRED Ahmed Al Shafar
OFFICIAL EXPLANATION Gone To Press: lame on near-fore.
3235 Hakeem (IRE) confirmed the promise of his Newmarket debut and, woken up below the distance, got on top inside the final furlong. (4/1)
2917 Call To Order moved to the front just before halfway and, although collared inside the final furlong, kept on well to the line. He should soon go one better. (10/1: 6/1-12/1)
3723 Statua (IRE), rather flattered in the Group Two Lowther Stakes last time out, was being pushed along soon after halfway but she did run on inside the final furlong, if never looking likely to threaten the winner. (15/8)
3416 Ambitious chased the leaders but failed to find that vital turn of foot from below the distance. A softer surface may help. (7/1)
Emmajoun left her debut run well behind and had every chance below the distance, before tiring in the last one hundred yards. (16/1)
3636 Persian Sabre, who caught the eye last time out, played a far more active role this time but had been seen off two furlongs from home.(16/1)
3186 Ringleader (14/1: op 8/1)
Critical Air (9/1: 3/1-12/1)

3927 E.B.F. BROADSWORD MEDIAN AUCTION MAIDEN STKS (II) (2-Y.O) (Class F)
4-00 (4-01) **6f** £2,389.00 (£659.00: £313.00) Stalls: Low GOING minus 0.20 sec per fur (GF)

				SP	RR	SF
2706^{3}	**Up At The Top (IRE)** (BWHills) **2-8-9** MHills(12) (lw: a.p: led over 1f out: easily)	—	**1**	4/6^{1}	64+	43
3711^{8}	**Recognition** (WJarvis) **2-9-0** JReid(10) (a.p: ev ch over 1f out: unable qckn)	1½	**2**	16/1	65	44
3411^{5}	**Angelina** (PHowling) **2-8-9** PaulEddery(4) (b: s.s: hld up: rdn 3f out: led over 2f out tl over 1f out: one pce)	¾	**3**	13/2^{2}	58	37
3247^{5}	**Mountain Magic** (DJSffrenchDavis) **2-8-9** TQuinn(9) (lw: hld up: rdn over 2f out: wknd over 1f out)	6	**4**	25/1	42	21
938^{7}	**Counsel** (CEBrittain) **2-9-0** WRyan(8) (s.s: nvr nr to chal)	1¼	**5**	10/1	44	23
2953^{9}	**Fawning** (MBlanshard) **2-8-9** JQuinn(1) (led over 3f)	hd	**6**	7/1^{3}	38	17
3686^{8}	**Plastered In Paris (IRE)** (BJMeehan) **2-9-0** MTebbutt(11) (hld up: rdn over 2f out: sn wknd)	1	**7**	12/1	41	20
3707^{16}	**Thecomebackking** (SCWilliams) **2-9-0** MWigham(7) (nvr nrr)	¾	**8**	33/1	39	18
	Carver Doone (MajorDNChappell) **2-9-0** GCarter(2) (w'like: s.s: outpcd: nvr nrr)	s.h	**9**	16/1	39	18
3743^{7}	**Mismewmew** (CJBenstead) **2-8-9** RCochrane(13) (lw: bhd fnl 2f)	nk	**10**	25/1	33	12
3450^{13}	**Sabre Girl** (RHannon) **2-8-9** DaneO'Neill(5) (lw: prom over 3f)	2	**11**	16/1	28	7
3859^{12}	**Safari Sam (IRE)** (MHTompkins) **2-9-0** DBiggs(3) (a bhd)	2	**12**	25/1	27	6
				(SP 134.7%)	**12 Rn**	

1m 12.5 (2.30) CSF £15.60 TOTE £1.40: £1.10 £4.40 £1.60 (£13.80) Trio £36.50 OWNER Mrs E. Roberts (LAMBOURN) BRED H. de Burgh
2706 Up At The Top (IRE) confirmed the promise shown at York on her debut and, striking the front approaching the final furlong, won with plenty more to spare than the official distance would suggest. Hills reported afterwards that she had trouble keeping her balance on these undulations.(4/6)
2181 Recognition left his two previous runs well behind and was fighting for the lead over a furlong out before the winner went by. On this evidence he can find a small race. (16/1)
3411 Angelina gained a slender advantage over a quarter of a mile from home but, headed approaching the final furlong, was then put in her place by the winner. She still finished well clear of the fourth and is up to winning a race such as this before long. (13/2: op 12/1)
3247 Mountain Magic was left for dead by the front three in the final quarter-mile. (25/1)
Counsel, given a four-month break, stayed on to finish a very moderate fifth. He needs further. (10/1: 6/1-12/1)
2394 Fawning took the field along but, collared approaching the last two furlongs, soon had bellows to mend. (7/1: 4/1-8/1)
Plastered In Paris (IRE) (12/1: 6/1-14/1)

3928 CLAYMORE H'CAP (0-65) (3-Y.O+) (Class F)
4-30 (4-32) **2m 93y** £2,277.00 (£627.00: £297.00) Stalls: Low GOING minus 0.20 sec per fur (GF)

				SP	RR	SF
2592^{10}	**Duncombe Hall (35)** (CACyzer) **4-7-12**$^{(3)}$ AWhelan(15) (a.p: reminder over 7f out: rdn over 5f out: chsd ldr wl over 1f out: led ins fnl f: r.o wl)	—	**1**	12/1	49	30
30^{8}	**Red Raja (57)** (PMitchell) **4-9-9** AClark(5) (a.p: led over 5f out: clr over 2f out: hdd ins fnl f: unable qckn)	2	**2**	14/1	69	50
3826^{5}	**Coh Sho No (50)** (SDow) **4-9-2** SSanders(9) (a.p: chsd ldr over 3f out tl wl over 1f out: one pce)	3½	**3**	9/1	59	40
3796^{5}	**Sun Alert (USA) (65)** (MJPolglase) **3-9-4** GCarter(8) (b.hind: lw: hdwy over 2f out: r.o one pce)	7	**4**	16/1	67	35
3549^{4}	**Atnab (USA) (60)** (PTWalwyn) **3-8-13** RHills(16) (hld up: rdn 5f out: sn wknd)	3	**5**	5/1^{1}	59	27
3623^{2}	**Rose of Glenn (50)** (BPalling) **6-8-11**$^{(5)}$ PRoberts(13) (led 11f)	nk	**6**	9/1	49	30
3419^{7}	**Gallant Heights (58)** (GCBravery) **3-8-11** MRimmer(14) (nvr nr to chal)	2½	**7**	16/1	54	22
3462^{4}	**Chief Predator (USA) (51)** (MissKMGeorge) **3-8-1**$^{(3)}$ MartinDwyer(6) (lw: a mid div)	1	**8**	20/1	46	14
3549^{5}	**Salsee Lad (60)** (JRFanshawe) **3-8-13** JReid(10) (lw: nvr nrr)	s.h	**9**	7/1^{2}	55	23

				SP	RR	SF
*660**	**La Menorquina (USA) (32)** (DMarks) **7-7-7**(5) RMullen(11) (bit bkwd: nvr nrr)	1	**10**	7/1[2]	26	7
3694[8]	**Silvretta (IRE) (60)** (RCSpicer) **4-9-12** DaneO'Neill(7) (nvr nrr)	3½	**11**	16/1	51	32
3719[2]	**Action Jackson (53)** (BJMcMath) **5-9-5** TQuinn(3) (a.p: chsd ldr 12f out tl over 5f out: sn wknd)	1½	**12**	8/1[3]	42	23
3714[2]	**Strat's Legacy (40)** (DWPArbuthnot) **10-8-6** NAdams(12) (hdwy 7f out: wknd over 4f out)	hd	**13**	14/1	29	10
3122[12]	**Upper Mount Clair (62)** (CEBrittain) **7-10-0** WRyan(1) (a bhd)	3	**14**	5/1[1]	48	29
3792[4]	**Araboybill (45)** (JNeville) **6-8-11b** SDrowne(2) (bhd fnl 5f)	3	**15**	25/1	28	9
3015[7]	**Sassy Street (IRE) (37)** (RFJohnsonHoughton) **4-7-12**(5)ow2 ADaly(4) (hdwy 7f out: wknd over 4f out)	3½	**16**	14/1	17	—
				(SP 143.4%)	**16 Rn**	

3m 38.4 (8.40) CSF £181.26 CT £1,496.36 TOTE £15.80: £3.10 £5.80 £1.60 £4.30 (£439.40) Trio £344.60 OWNER Mr R. M. Cyzer (HORSHAM) BRED C. A. and R. M. Cyzer
WEIGHT FOR AGE 3yo-13lb

1964 Duncombe Hall certainly had to work hard, but eventually managed to get on top inside the final furlong to lose his maiden tag at the seventeenth attempt. (12/1)
Red Raja, who proved himself a useful juvenile hurdler last winter, ran a cracker after a four and a half month absence. Sent to the front at the top of the hill, he forged clear turning for home and looked likely to prevail, only to be collared inside final furlong. He should soon regain the winning thread. (14/1)
3826 Coh Sho No, 4lb lower than when gaining her only success to date here back in April, moved into second place running down the hill, but she was collared for that position early in the short straight and could only struggle on at one pace. (9/1)
3796 Sun Alert (USA) is slipping down the weights and was staying on past beaten horses when it was all over. (16/1)
3549 Atnab (USA) was taking another step up in distance but had been seen off at the top of the hill. (5/1)

3929 FOIL (S) STKS (3-Y.O+) (Class G)

5-00 (5-01) **1m 4f** £1,984.50 (£547.00: £259.50) Stalls: Low GOING minus 0.20 sec per fur (GF)

				SP	RR	SF
3792[2]	**Statajack (IRE) (60)** (DRCElsworth) **9-9-5b** TQuinn(4) (b: lw: hdwy over 2f out: rdn over 1f out: led wl ins fnl f: r.o wl)	—	**1**	100/30[2]	67	29
3466[2]	**Ocean Park (66)** (LadyHerries) **6-9-0**(5) GMilligan(3) (b: lw: stdy hdwy 4f out: led ins fnl f: sn hdd: r.o wl)	hd	**2**	4/5[1]	67	29
3592[7]	**Be True (47)** (GLMoore) **3-8-10** CandyMorris(10) (dwlt: hdwy over 2f out: rdn over 1f out: unable qckn)	2½	**3**	16/1	64	17
3617[2]	**Bobby's Dream (28)** (MHTompkins) **5-9-0** DBiggs(7) (a.p: led over 1f out tl ins fnl f: sn wknd)	1¼	**4**	20/1	57	19
3814[2]	**Haroldon (IRE) (61)** (BPalling) **8-9-5**(5) PRoberts(8) (lost pl 4f out: rallied over 1f out: r.o one pce)	hd	**5**	6/1[3]	67	29
3588[7]	**Soda Pop (IRE) (62)** (GLMoore) **3-9-1** JReid(5) (led over 10f: wknd ins fnl f)	1½	**6**	8/1	65	18
3617[4]	**Another Fiddle (IRE) (23)** (JELong) **7-8-12**(7) RBrisland(11) (b.hind: bhd fnl 5f)	5	**7**	33/1	53	15
3015[5]	**Perfect Bertie (IRE) (32)** (NMBabbage) **5-9-2**(3) RFfrench(6) (s.s: hdwy over 5f out: wknd over 2f out)	7	**8**	20/1	44	6
3540[4]	**Liathach (29)** (JRFanshawe) **6-9-5** MHills(2) (w ldr 10f out tl over 2f out: sn wknd)	13	**9**	20/1	26	—
	Rocky's Profiles (IRE) (MissKMGeorge) **4-9-5** NAdams(9) (prom 8f)	¾	**10**	14/1	25	—
3695[6]	***Key To*** (APJarvis) **3-8-5** SDrowne(1) (Withdrawn not under Starter's orders: inj bef ent paddock)		**W**	33/1	—	—
				(SP 136.7%)	**10 Rn**	

2m 40.0 (8.80) CSF £6.43 TOTE £3.30: £1.30 £1.50 £13.40 (£3.20) Trio £54.50 OWNER Mrs M. E. Slade (WHITCOMBE) BRED Princess Oettingen-Spielberg
WEIGHT FOR AGE 3yo-9lb
No bid, Ocean Park clmd Mrs E Green £5,750

3792 Statajack (IRE), and his extremely experienced jockey, took full advantage of Milligan's over-confidence and, rousted along in the straight, managed to forge into a narrow lead in the last one hundred yards to win his first race of the season. (100/30)
3466 Ocean Park, taking a drop in class, was best in at the weights and, quite simply, should have won this. Unfortunately, Milligan was brimming with confidence as the gelding inched closer running down the hill, swinging off the bridle in the short straight. Only woken up to lead early inside the final furlong, he was immediately challenged by Statajack and soon passed. Compensation surely awaits. (4/5)
2956 Be True took closer order turning for home but just failed to find the necessary turn of foot in the last furlong and a half. (16/1)
3617 Bobby's Dream gained a slender advantage below the distance, but she was collared early inside the final furlong and soon done with. (20/1)
3814 Haroldon (IRE), who got outpaced running down the hill, stayed on again from below the distance, only to find it all over bar the shouting. (6/1: op 4/1)
2955* Soda Pop (IRE) took the field along, but he was collared over a furlong out and tired inside the last one hundred and fifty yards. (8/1: 5/1-10/1)

3930 SABRE H'CAP (0-80) (3-Y.O+) (Class D)

5-30 (5-31) **6f 189y** £4,027.80 (£1,205.40: £578.20: £264.60) Stalls: Low GOING minus 0.20 sec per fur (GF)

				SP	RR	SF
2933[8]	**Victory Team (IRE) (72)** (GBBalding) **5-9-7** SDrowne(12) (a.p: rdn over 1f out: led ins fnl f: r.o wl)	—	**1**	8/1	82	53
3465[12]	**Banzhaf (USA) (67)** (GLMoore) **4-9-2** AClark(15) (a.p: rdn over 2f out: r.o ins fnl f)	½	**2**	12/1	76	47
2573[6]	**Twin Creeks (63)** (VSoane) **6-8-12** CRutter(7) (lw: hdwy over 3f out: rdn wl over 1f out: r.o ins fnl f)	½	**3**	10/1	71	42
3716*	**Kentucky Fall (FR) (72)** (LadyHerries) **4-9-7** JReid(14) (led tl ins fnl f: unable qckn)	½	**4**	6/1[2]	79	50
3746[2]	**Kings Harmony (IRE) (72)** (PJMakin) **4-9-7** SSanders(2) (a.p: rdn over 1f out: one pce)	¾	**5**	7/1[3]	77	48
3718[7]	**Ertlon (66)** (CEBrittain) **7-9-1** MRimmer(4) (lw: chsd ldr: ev ch over 1f out: wknd fnl f)	1¼	**6**	11/1	68	39
3290[5]	**Scathebury (55)** (KRBurke) **4-8-4** GCarter(3) (lw: rdn & hdwy over 2f out: one pce)	1	**7**	14/1	55	26
3752[3]	**Alikhlas (79)** (MajorWRHern) **3-9-10** RHills(10) (a mid div)	2½	**8**	8/1	73	40
1826[12]	**Oneknight With You (59)** (MJFetherston-Godley) **3-8-1**(3) RFfrench(1) (b: nvr nrr)	hd	**9**	20/1	52	19
3092[11]	**Husun (USA) (67)** (PTWalwyn) **3-8-12** RCochrane(13) (lw: a mid div)	nk	**10**	16/1	60	27
3138[10]	**Masterpiece (67)** (RHannon) **3-8-12** DaneO'Neill(8) (prom over 3f)	nk	**11**	16/1	59	26
2705[10]	**Briska (IRE) (69)** (RAkehurst) **3-9-0** TQuinn(11) (lw: bhd fnl 3f)	½	**12**	10/1	60	27
2415[9]	**Muscatana (64)** (BWHills) **3-8-9** MHills(16) (lw: a bhd)	3½	**13**	16/1	47	14
	Muhandis (74) (GLMoore) **4-9-9** CandyMorris(9) (bit bkwd: a bhd)	½	**14**	25/1	56	27
1958[11]	**Carlton (IRE) (59)** (GLewis) **3-8-4** PaulEddery(5) (a bhd)	5	**15**	14/1	29	—
3442[2]	**Mr Cube (IRE) (56)** (JMBradley) **7-8-5b** GDuffield(6) (lw: a bhd)	2½	**16**	4/1[1]	20	—
				(SP 142.8%)	**16 Rn**	

1m 24.2 (2.80) CSF £107.58 CT £963.31 TOTE £12.50: £2.60 £4.50 £4.00 £1.50 (£91.90) Trio £392.40 OWNER Mr R. J. Lavelle (ANDOVER) BRED Barronstown and Swettenham Studs and Ron Con Ltd
WEIGHT FOR AGE 3yo-4lb

2743 Victory Team (IRE) is well suited by seven furlongs on fast ground and he had his ideal requirements here. Woken up below the distance, he led inside the final furlong and kept on well. (8/1)

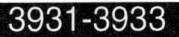

3139* Banzhaf (USA) ran a sound race and, never far away, kept on nicely to take second prize. (12/1)
2573 Twin Creeks took closer order at halfway and kept on in the straight for third prize. (10/1: 8/1-12/1)
3716* Kentucky Fall (FR), 8lb higher for her Yarmouth victory twelve days ago, attempted to make all the running but, collared inside the final furlong, failed to find another gear. (6/1)
3746 Kings Harmony (IRE) was a leading player throughout but failed to find that vital turn of foot in the last furlong and a half. (7/1)
1501 Ertlon, soon racing in second place, had every chance below the distance before tiring. He is not easy to win with - five victories from seventy-one starts says it all - but he is falling in the handicap. (11/1)

T/Jkpt: Not won; £4,358.42 to York 3/9/97. T/Plpt: £91.70 (292.13 Tckts). T/Qdpt: £6.70 (229.89 Tckts) AK

3619-PONTEFRACT (L-H) (Good to soft, Soft patches)
Tuesday September 2nd
WEATHER: sunny periods WIND: slt half bhd

3931 PONTEFRACT SERIES (ROUND 4) APPRENTICE LIMITED STKS (0-65) (3-Y.O+) (Class F)
2-15 (2-17) **1m 4f 8y** £2,378.50 (£676.00: £335.50) Stalls: Low GOING minus 0.16 sec per fur (GF)

				SP	RR	SF
3568*	**Tarxien (65)** (KRBurke) **3-8-10** RWinston(2) (lw: trckd ldrs: brought wd wl over 1f out: sn led: r.o strly)	—	**1**	4/1^{2}	74	20
3080^{4}	**Afon Alwen (62)** (SCWilliams) **4-8-11**$^{(3)}$ DarrenWilliams(8) (chsd ldrs: brought wd st: ev ch over 1f out: r.o)	1½	**2**	5/1^{3}	67	22
3277^{7}	**Polenista (65)** (JLDunlop) **3-8-5** CLowther(1) (hld up: hdwy 4f out: effrt & ch over 1f out: r.o)	5	**3**	2/1^{1}	60	6
3035^{5}	**Exactly (IRE) (61)** (JLEyre) **4-8-11**$^{(3)}$ SBuckley(9) (lw: w ldr: led 5f out tl over 1f out: sn outpcd)	3	**4**	9/1	56	11
3754^{3}	**Highfield Fizz (38)** (CWFairhurst) **5-9-0** TSiddall(6) (b.off hind: hld up: hdwy 4f out: one pce fnl 2f)	5	**5**	12/1	50	5
3272^{4}	**Course Fishing (39)** (BAMcMahon) **6-9-3** SRighton(4) (chsd ldrs tl wknd fnl 2f)	6	**6**	20/1	45	—
1779^{4}	**Non Vintage (IRE) (43)** (MCChapman) **6-9-3** SCarson(3) (swtg: hld up & bhd: effrt over 3f out: n.d)	3½	**7**	16/1	40	—
3463^{5}	**Hidden Agenda (FR) (62)** (RCharlton) **3-7-12**$^{(7)}$ KParsons(5) (bhd: effrt 4f out: n.d)	½	**8**	11/2	36	—
1589^{13}	**Mayflower (60)** (MHTompkins) **3-8-2**$^{(3)}$ PClarke(7) (plld hrd: chsd ldrs tl wknd over 2f out)	8	**9**	16/1	26	—
2911^{9}	**Cimmerian (50)** (MESowersby) **3-8-0**$^{(5)}$ NPollard(10) (led tl hdd 5f out: sn lost pl)	27	**10**	33/1	—	—
				(SP 122.5%)	**10 Rn**	

2m 44.0 (9.70) CSF £23.52 TOTE £4.70: £1.50 £1.60 £1.60 (£8.30) Trio £8.80 OWNER Mr David Whyte (WANTAGE) BRED Sheikh Mohammed bin Rashid al Maktoum
WEIGHT FOR AGE 3yo-9lb
3568* Tarxien, given a intelligent ride and getting the best ground, won in good style. (4/1)
3080 Afon Alwen, well ridden and always picking the best ground round the outside, just met one too good. (5/1)
1866 Polenista won the race up the far side of the track convincingly, but that was much slower ground. (2/1)
3035 Exactly (IRE), racing on the slower ground, ran by far her best race of the season and looks one too keep in mind. (9/1)
3754 Highfield Fizz was always finding this trip a bit on the sharp side and was also racing on the slowest ground, and failed to make a real impression. (12/1)
3272 Course Fishing, a poor mover, has always been a fast-ground specialist and dropped tamely away here. (20/1)

3932 COMPUTER TIMEFORM NURSERY H'CAP (0-85) (2-Y.O) (Class D)
2-45 (2-48) **6f** £3,790.00 (£1,135.00: £545.00: £250.00) Stalls: Low GOING minus 0.16 sec per fur (GF)

				SP	RR	SF
2565^{11}	**Five of Spades (IRE) (68)** (RAFahey) **2-8-1**$^{(7)}$ RWinston(12) (racd wd: a cl up: led wl over 1f out: r.o)	—	**1**	16/1	78	33
3386^{10}	**Santa Court (62)** (RDickin) **2-8-2** GHind(13) (racd wd: s.i.s: sn pushed along: hdwy ½-wy: styd on wl)	2½	**2**	25/1	65	20
2936*	**Tancred Times (70)** (DWBarker) **2-8-10** TWilliams(16) (led & racd wd: hdd wl over 1f out: kpt on)	2	**3**	9/1	68	23
3602^{5}	**Fashion Victim (76)** (THCaldwell) **2-9-2** ACulhane(17) (racd wd: a.p: kpt on fnl f)	½	**4**	20/1	73	28
3468^{6}	**Eleonora d'Arborea (81)** (BJMeehan) **2-9-7** KDarley(14) (racd wd: a chsng ldrs: nt qckn fnl 2f)	3	**5**	15/2^{2}	70	25
3823^{7}	**Sandmoor Tartan (61)** (TDEasterby) **2-8-1** DWright(1) (lw: swtchd rt after s: hdwy ½-wy: swtchd rt again wl over 1f out: nvr able to chal)	½	**6**	9/1	48	3
*1124**	**Summerseat (62)** (CWFairhurst) **2-8-2** LCharnock(6) (racd ins: hdwy ½-wy: eased whn no ch fnl f)	4	**7**	16/1	39	—
3042^{7}	**Fast Franc (IRE) (65)** (SCWilliams) **2-8-5** DHolland(9) (w ldrs ins tl rdn & btn appr fnl f)	hd	**8**	8/1^{3}	41	—
3270^{4}	**Rioja (75)** (TPTate) **2-9-1** TLucas(10) (lw: racd centre: in tch: effrt & hung lft wl over 1f out: no imp)	½	**9**	16/1	50	5
3707^{8}	**Burnt Yates (IRE) (69)** (MWEasterby) **2-8-9** JFortune(8) (racd on ins: sn outpcd: n.d)	½	**10**	14/1	43	—
3899^{3}	**The Groveller (79)** (PDEvans) **2-9-5** JFEgan(5) (lw: chsd ldrs in ins group over 4f)	2	**11**	6/1^{1}	47	2
3247*	**Santa Faye (IRE) (77)** (BPalling) **2-9-3** TSprake(11) (racd ins group: effrt ½-wy: no imp)	s.h	**12**	9/1	45	—
2842^{4}	**Lady Yavanna (76)** (KMcAuliffe) **2-9-2v**^{1} JCarroll(7) (in tch tl outpcd & lost pl fnl 2f)	1¼	**13**	9/1	41	—
3692*	**Russian Romeo (IRE) (65)** (BAMcMahon) **2-7-12v**$^{(7)}$ SRighton(3) (s.i.s: a outpcd & bhd)	1¾	**14**	10/1	25	—
3707^{6}	**Mill End Quest (69)** (MWEasterby) **2-8-9** DaleGibson(4) (chsd ldrs on ins over 3f)	1	**15**	14/1	27	—
1860*	**Wait'n'see (80)** (MWEasterby) **2-9-3**$^{(3)}$ GParkin(2) (led ins group tl rdn & wknd over 2f out)	26	**16**	9/1	—	—
				(SP 135.8%)	**16 Rn**	

1m 18.5 (3.50) CSF £369.17 CT £2,058.09 TOTE £22.90: £3.60 £10.90 £2.90 £9.40 (£373.20) Trio £431.20 OWNER Mr B. L. Cassidy (MALTON) BRED N. and D. Wallace and Co
OFFICIAL EXPLANATION **Wait'n'see: gurgled despite wearing a tongue-strap.**
954 Five of Spades (IRE) obviously revels in the soft and, well-drawn in the circumstances, won in useful fashion. (16/1)
2509 Santa Court was well drawn but did not get the best of breaks. However, he stuck to his task in determined fashion. (25/1)
2936* Tancred Times made full use of his wide draw but, despite a valiant effort, was never quite good enough. (9/1)
3602 Fashion Victim, well drawn, ran much better this time and kept responding to pressure, and obviously likes easy ground. (20/1)
3468 Eleonora d'Arborea was one of the five to race wide throughout and they filled the first five places. (15/2)
3823 Sandmoor Tartan ran a superb race from what was an impossible draw, and his rider did all he could to get to the outside which was virtually impossible. (9/1)
1124* Summerseat ran well from his draw and was not knocked about when obviously beaten. (16/1)

3933 TIMEFORM RACE CARD (S) STKS (3-Y.O+) (Class G)
3-15 (3-20) **1m 2f 6y** £2,721.00 (£756.00: £363.00) Stalls: Low GOING minus 0.16 sec per fur (GF)

				SP	RR	SF
3477^{3}	**Java Red (IRE) (45)** (JGFitzGerald) **5-9-7** KFallon(9) (bhd: effrt 4f out: styd on to ld appr fnl f: sn clr)	—	**1**	7/2^{3}	64	39
3487*	**Mr Fortywinks (IRE) (53)** (JLEyre) **3-8-7** MGallagher(10) (led tl hdd 3f out: kpt on)	4	**2**	100/30^{2}	51	19
3853^{5}	**Charlie Chang (IRE)** (DWBarker) **4-9-0** TWilliams(3) (trckd ldrs: led 3f out tl over 1f out: wknd)	5	**3**	16/1	43	18

3779[2]	**Essayeffsee (54)** (MrsMReveley) **8-9-0** KDarley(14) (mid div: effrt 4f out: sn chsng ldrs & rdn: no imp) 3	**4**	5/2[1]	38	13
	Watch My Lips (MHTompkins) **5-8-11**(3) MHenry(12) (effrt 4f out: styd on: nvr rchd ldrs) 2	**5**	20/1	35	10
3073[9]	**Tocco Jewel (20)** (MJRyan) **7-8-6**(3) PMcCabe(7) (bhd: hdwy over 3f out: nvr able to chal) 1½	**6**	33/1	27	2
3601[11]	**Nordico Melody (IRE) (37)** (MrsSJSmith) **3-8-10**ow3 OPears(1) (chsd ldrs tl rdn & btn 2f out) ....¾	**7**	33/1	34	—
3456[10]	**Golden Fish (27)** (EJAlston) **5-9-0** JFEgan(6) (nvr trbld ldrs) ....½	**8**	20/1	30	5
3620*	**Bold Top (55)** (BSRothwell) **5-9-0be** JFortune(15) (dwlt: jnd ldrs after 2f: wknd over 3f out) 17	**9**	6/1	3	—
	Dig For Gold (MissSEHall) **4-9-0** LCharnock(2) (b.hind: chsd ldrs tl wknd fnl 3f) 1	**10**	14/1	2	—
3413[13]	**Eastleigh (27)** (RHollinshead) **8-9-0**(7) LisaWatson(13) (hld up: lost tch fnl 4f) ....½	**11**	25/1	8	—
3469[10]	**Old Roma (IRE) (55)** (JohnBerry) **4-8-9** DHolland(8) (bhd: effrt over 4f: n.d) ....½	**12**	16/1	—	—
3611[2]	**Qualitair Beauty (30)** (MissLCSiddall) **4-8-9** DeanMcKeown(11) (in tch tl lost pl fnl 4f) 2½	**13**	12/1	—	—
3477[6]	**Curtelace (40)** (MPBielby) **7-8-11**(3) GParkin(4) (chsd ldrs tl wknd over 3f out) 14	**14**	20/1	—	—
3583[10]	**Lord Naskra (USA) (28)** (GWoodward) **8-9-0** ACulhane(5) (b: bhd & rdn ½-wy: wl t.o) ....dist	**15**	50/1	—	—

(SP 140.3%) **15 Rn**

2m 16.5 (6.90) CSF £15.42 TOTE £4.00: £1.80 £2.10 £4.30 (£8.70) Trio £85.80 OWNER Mr Michael Ng (MALTON) BRED Rathasker Stud
WEIGHT FOR AGE 3yo-7lb
No bid

3477 Java Red (IRE) was without either blinkers or a visor this time but he was given some ride and, picking his way through the best ground round the wide outside, won going away. (7/2: op 6/1)
3487* Mr Fortywinks (IRE), a very edgy and excitable sort, again showed he has the ability whilst in the mood. (100/30: 5/2-4/1)
3853 Charlie Chang (IRE) again raced freely but did much better this time, and the ability is there if he can be persuaded. (16/1)
3779 Essayeffsee, not really happy with cut in the ground, ran quite well in the circumstances. (5/2)
Watch My Lips seemed to be having a pipe-opener for hurdling and ran quite well. (20/1)
Tocco Jewel showed signs of ability here which is something she has failed to do on the All-Weather recently. (33/1)

3934 '50 YEARS OF TIMEFORM' FUTURITY CONDITIONS STKS (2-Y.O) (Class B)

3-45 (3-46) **6f** £6,429.00 (£2,249.00: £1,099.50: £472.50) Stalls: Low GOING minus 0.16 sec per fur (GF)

			SP	RR	SF
3723[7]	**Dazilyn Lady (USA) (93)** (PWHarris) **2-8-10** ACulhane(3) (mde most: r.o wl fnl f) ....—	**1**	11/4[2]	96	49
3422[4]	**Parisian Lady (IRE) (98)** (AGNewcombe) **2-8-6** GHind(1) (disp ld: rdn wl over 1f out: nt qckn) 3½	**2**	15/8[1]	83	36
3688[7]	**Wrekin Pilot (92)** (RHannon) **2-9-1** PatEddery(4) (trckd ldrs: effrt over 1f out: sn rdn & btn) 1¾	**3**	100/30	87	40
2024[13]	**Pacifica (97)** (RBoss) **2-8-10** KFallon(2) (chsd ldrs: rdn 2f out: wknd over 1f out) 12	**4**	3/1[3]	50	3

(SP 109.5%) **4 Rn**

1m 17.4 (2.40) CSF £7.55 TOTE £6.60: (£2.90) OWNER Mr M Parker Mr G Knight & Mrs G Godfrey (BERKHAMSTED) BRED Gainsborough Farm Inc

2875* Dazilyn Lady (USA) won this in style and is obviously going the right way. (11/4)
3422 Parisian Lady (IRE) had a hard race last time and showed plenty of courage again here, but she was always second best. (15/8)
3204 Wrekin Pilot sat in behind the leaders waiting to pounce but, when the button was pressed, there was little there. (100/30)
1211 Pacifica has not been out since Royal Ascot and this was disappointing. (3/1)

3935 PHIL BULL TROPHY CONDITIONS STKS (3-Y.O+) (Class C)

4-15 (4-16) **2m 1f 216y** £4,612.90 (£1,680.40: £820.20: £351.00: £155.50) Stalls: Centre GOING minus 0.16 sec per fur (GF)

			SP	RR	SF
2327[17]	**Old Rouvel (USA) (100)** (DJGMurraySmith) **6-9-2** KDarley(2) (trckd ldrs: shkn up over 3f out: led over 1f out: sn clr & eased) ....—	**1**	2/9[1]	66+	19
3826[2]	**Jamaican Flight (USA) (68)** (MrsSLamyman) **4-9-2** JFortune(4) (lw: mde most tl hdd over 1f out: kpt on wl) 1¾	**2**	4/1[2]	64	17
3108[7]	**Euphoric Illusion (32)** (MrsSJSmith) **6-9-2** OPears(1) (w ldr tl wknd fnl 2½f) 13	**3**	33/1[3]	53	6
3858[2]	**Penny Peppermint (26)** (REBarr) **5-8-11** JCarroll(3) (prom tl outpcd fnl 4f: eased whn btn) 15	**4**	66/1	35	—
	Ambuscade (USA) (35) (MrsJJordan) **11-9-2** AlexGreaves(5) (lost tch fnl 7f) ....dist	**5**	33/1[3]	—	—

(SP 109.2%) **5 Rn**

4m 8.2 (16.20) CSF £1.25 TOTE £1.50: £1.10 £1.20 (£1.40) OWNER Mrs R. D. Cowell (MARKET HARBOROUGH) BRED The Bloodstock Agency in USA

2108 Old Rouvel (USA) was so well in here, even he had to win this. (2/9)
3826 Jamaican Flight (USA) is certainly game but the winner was far too good for him. (4/1)
2207 Euphoric Illusion has obviously settled down with hurdling recently and this was a much better effort. (33/1)
3858 Penny Peppermint was out-classed here and ran as well as could be expected. (66/1)

3936 'WWW.TIMEFORM.COM' H'CAP (0-70) (3-Y.O+) (Class E)

4-45 (4-50) **6f** £3,509.00 (£1,052.00: £506.00: £233.00) Stalls: Low GOING minus 0.16 sec per fur (GF)

			SP	RR	SF
3690[7]	**Stand Tall (68)** (LadyHerries) **5-9-12** KDarley(13) (a chsng ldrs: led 1f out: r.o) ....—	**1**	11/2[2]	77	62
3910[9]	**Plum First (51)** (JLEyre) **7-8-4**(5) KimberleyHart(14) (b: b.hind: a chsng ldrs: outpcd 2f out: kpt on wl fnl f)......¾	**2**	12/1	58	43
2895[7]	**Depreciate (61)** (CJames) **4-9-5** TLucas(11) (a chsng ldrs: effrt 2f out: kpt on) ....s.h	**3**	50/1	68	53
3625[5]	**Grand Chapeau (IRE) (66)** (DNicholls) **5-9-10** AlexGreaves(15) (lw: led tl hdd 1f out: no ex) 1½	**4**	8/1[3]	69	54
3621[6]	**Halmanerror (54)** (MrsJRRamsden) **7-8-12** JFortune(9) (in tch: hdwy over 1f out: rdn & nvr rchd ldrs) 3	**5**	9/2[1]	49	34
3565[3]	**Bollin Dorothy (54)** (TDEasterby) **4-8-12** TWilliams(6) (in tch: hdwy 2f out: nvr able to chal) ....hd	**6**	8/1[3]	49	34
3702[4]	**Panther (IRE) (57)** (PDEvans) **7-9-1v** JFEgan(1) (swtchd rt s: in tch: rdn fnl 2f out: nt qckn) 1¾	**7**	14/1	47	32
3573[14]	**Crissem (IRE) (51)** (RHollinshead) **4-8-9** FLynch(17) (s.i.s: styd on wl fnl 2f: nrst fin) 1	**8**	33/1	38	23
3718[6]	**Wild Palm (64)** (WAO'Gorman) **5-9-8b** EmmaO'Gorman(7) (s.s: hdwy 2f out: nvr rchd ldrs) ....¾	**9**	14/1	49	34
3716[7]	**Aquatic Queen (57)** (CADwyer) **3-8-13** KFallon(18) (prom tl rdn & btn over 1f out) ....nk	**10**	11/1	42	25
2711[18]	**Rum Lad (70)** (JJQuinn) **3-9-12** JLowe(16) (bit bkwd: hld up: n.d) ....¾	**11**	14/1	53	36
3484[7]	**Tropical Beach (57)** (JBerry) **4-8-12b**(3) TEDurcan(3) (hld up: effrt ½-wy: wknd over 1f out) ....s.h	**12**	20/1	39	24
3425[4]	**Fayik (70)** (AGNewcombe) **3-9-12** GHind(4) (hld up & bhd: nvr nr to chal) ....nk	**13**	16/1	52	35
1385[15]	**Bataleur (56)** (GWoodward) **4-9-0** DHolland(10) (chsd ldrs 4f) 1¼	**14**	50/1	34	19
1511[12]	**Birchwood Sun (55)** (MDods) **7-8-13b** ACulhane(12) (a outpcd & bhd) ....s.h	**15**	16/1	33	18
3431[16]	**Foist (57)** (MWEasterby) **5-8-12**(3) GParkin(5) (lw: s.i.s: gd hdwy on ins 2f out: wknd over 1f out) 2	**16**	10/1	30	15
3327[6]	**Night Harmony (IRE) (56)** (MissSJWilton) **4-9-0** JCarroll(2) (b: prom 4f: sn bhd) 7	**17**	25/1	10	—

				SP	RR	SF
3261^{7}	**Fonzy (55)** (MrsSJSmith) **3-8-11b** OPears(8) (sn pushed along & bhd)	8	**18**	50/1	—	—
				(SP 130.1%)		**18 Rn**

1m 17.6 (2.60) CSF £63.33 CT £2,770.40 TOTE £7.60: £1.90 £2.20 £7.30 £2.80 (£37.90) Trio £1,033.60; £655.10 to York 3/9/97 OWNER Mr Chris Hardy (LITTLEHAMPTON) BRED Mrs E. Longton
WEIGHT FOR AGE 3yo-2lb
3290* Stand Tall had a good draw, likes the ground and had the speed to get first run. (11/2: op 10/1)
40 Plum First, who goes well in the ground, had the necessary draw, ran a fine race and is obviously in good heart. (12/1)
2162 Depreciate ran his best race for a while and has slipped down the handicap. (50/1)
3625 Grand Chapeau (IRE) had the draw and the speed to make full use of it, but he just failed to last out in these conditions. (8/1)
3621 Halmanerror keeps showing signs of coming to form and this was not a bad effort. (9/2)
3565 Bollin Dorothy ran really well from her draw. (8/1)
3702 Panther (IRE), taken to post early, had an impossible draw and this was a fair effort. (14/1)
2422 Crissem (IRE) has dropped down the handicap dramatically this year and, once she jumps off on terms, there should be more improvement. (33/1)
2417* Rum Lad needed this after a lay-off and had a quiet run. (14/1)
3425 Fayik had a quiet run over what appears too short a trip. (16/1)
3034 Foist (10/1: op 6/1)

3937 TIMEFORM PERSPECTIVE AND RACE RATINGS H'CAP (0-80) (3-Y.O+) (Class D)
5-15 (5-21) **1m 4y** £4,175.00 (£1,250.00: £600.00: £275.00) Stalls: Low GOING minus 0.16 sec per fur (GF)

				SP	RR	SF
2557^{2}	**Kennemara Star (IRE) (80)** (JLDunlop) **3-9-12** PatEddery(16) (lw: mde most after 2f: rdn & r.o wl fnl f)	—	**1**	$15/8^{1}$	96	57
*3608**	**Legal Issue (IRE) (53)** (WWHaigh) **5-8-4** TSprake(17) (lw: a chsng ldrs: chal 1f out: nt qckn towards fin)	1¼	**2**	14/1	67	33
3622^{3}	**Barnburgh Boy (74)** (TDBarron) **3-9-6** JCarroll(13) (a chsng ldrs: kpt on fnl f)	3½	**3**	$7/1^{3}$	81	42
3316^{2}	**Scenicris (IRE) (50)** (RHollinshead) **4-8-1** NCarlisle(4) (hdwy over 2f out: kpt on: nrst fin)	1½	**4**	14/1	54	20
3012^{8}	**Regal Thunder (USA) (71)** (MRStoute) **3-9-3** KDarley(9) (lw: mid div: effrt over 2f out: styd on: n.d)	½	**5**	$6/1^{2}$	74	35
3548^{11}	**Topatori (IRE) (72)** (MHTompkins) **3-9-1**(3) MHenry(18) (a chsng ldrs: effrt over 2f out: one pce)	¾	**6**	16/1	73	34
3777^{13}	**Forest Robin (50)** (MrsJRRamsden) **4-8-1** JFanning(3) (hdwy over 2f out: nvr able to chal)	¾	**7**	25/1	50	16
2906^{14}	**Gymcrak Flyer (64)** (GHolmes) **6-9-1b1** KFallon(5) (chsd ldrs tl wknd fnl 2f)	1½	**8**	12/1	61	27
3605^{10}	**Mukhatab (68)** (JJQuinn) **5-9-5** TLucas(14) (trckd ldrs tl grad wknd fnl 2f)	1¼	**9**	50/1	62	28
3382^{7}	**Pleasure Trick (USA) (47)** (DonEnricoIncisa) **6-7-12** KimTinkler(10) (lw: bhd: sme hdwy fnl 2f: n.d)	nk	**10**	16/1	41	7
	Thaleros (53) (JSWainwright) **7-8-4**ow3 DeanMcKeown(7) (bit bkwd: stdy hdwy 3f out: nvr trbld ldrs)	½	**11**	50/1	46	9
3463^{7}	**Doc Ryan's (67)** (MJRyan) **3-8-13** GBardwell(15) (sme hdwy over 1f out: nvr nr to chal)	1½	**12**	14/1	57	18
3584^{4}	**Our People (79)** (MJohnston) **3-9-11** DHolland(1) (led: racd on ins & hdd after 2f: rdn & btn wl over 1f out)	hd	**13**	16/1	68	29
3777^{6}	**Alpine Panther (IRE) (62)** (MrsMReveley) **4-8-13** ACulhane(12) (bhd: sme hdwy 2f out: n.d)	1	**14**	16/1	49	15
3777^{7}	**Gulliver (64)** (MrsJRRamsden) **4-9-1** JFortune(2) (hld up: effrt 2f out: sn btn)	nk	**15**	20/1	51	17
383^{8}	**Ocean Stream (IRE) (64)** (JLEyre) **4-9-1v1** RLappin(6) (swtg: chsd ldrs tl wknd fnl 3f)	6	**16**	50/1	39	5
1777^{6}	**Zagros (IRE) (58)** (TDEasterby) **3-8-4** LCharnock(8) (bhd & drvn along fr ½-wy)	3	**17**	40/1	27	—
	Xylem (USA) (77) (LMCumani) **6-9-7**(7) DYoung(19) (cl up on ins tl wknd fnl 2½f)	1	**18**	20/1	44	10
3781^{9}	**Wellcome Inn (62)** (JO'Reilly) **3-8-8** JO'Reilly(11) (a bhd)	2½	**19**	25/1	24	—
				(SP 138.3%)		**19 Rn**

1m 46.5 (4.10) CSF £28.60 CT £160.83 TOTE £2.20: £1.10 £2.40 £1.60 £2.60 (£15.20) Trio £29.70 OWNER Windflower Overseas Holdings Inc (ARUNDEL) BRED Windflower Overseas
WEIGHT FOR AGE 3yo-5lb
2557 Kennemara Star (IRE) did this well and is still learning, and there looks to be plenty more to come. (15/8)
3608* Legal Issue (IRE) put in a useful effort but just found the winner too tough. (14/1)
3622 Barnburgh Boy ran another useful race but again found the effort required too much late on. (7/1)
3316 Scenicris (IRE) seems in good heart at the moment and is running consistently well. (14/1)
2585 Regal Thunder (USA) has ability but is not the easiest of rides, and only got going when it was all over. (6/1)
2205 Topatori (IRE), racing on a soft surface for the first time, ran reasonably. (16/1)
2880 Forest Robin is proving difficult to win with but keeps showing signs of promise. (25/1)
Mukhatab showed promise here and was not knocked about and is worth keeping in mind. (50/1)
Thaleros put in a fair first effort of the season and was not given a hard time. (50/1)
3584 Our People raced up the inside of the track, throwing away all chance. (16/1)

T/Plpt: £548.00 (40.56 Tckts). T/Qdpt: £29.00 (44.12 Tckts) AA

3938a - 3960a : (Irish Racing) - See Computer Raceform

3671a-CURRAGH (Newbridge, Ireland) (R-H) (Good to yielding)
Saturday August 30th

3961a TATTERSALLS BREEDERS STKS (2-Y.O)
3-55 (4-04) **6f** IR £73,500.00 (IR £28,500.00: IR £18,500.00: IR £8,500.00) GOING minus 0.08 sec per fur (G)

				SP	RR	SF
3464^{5}	**Another Fantasy (IRE)** (RHannon) **2-8-7** DaneO'Neill (cl up far side group: overall ldr over 1f out: r.o wl)	—	**1**	16/1	102	29
$3506a^{2}$	**Law Library (IRE)** (JSBolger,Ireland) **2-8-10** KJManning (prom: led stands' side group 1½f out: overall 2nd u.p ins last: no ex u.p: r.o)	2½	**2**	$7/1^{3}$	98	25
2862^{13}	**Daunting Lady (IRE)** (RHannon) **2-8-7** MJKinane (cl up far side group: rdn & no ex 1½f out: kpt on ins last)	2½	**3**	$13/2^{2}$	89	16
3226*	**Jacmar (IRE)** (MissLAPerratt) **2-8-10** JWeaver (prom far side group: ev ch fr ½-wy: no ex over 1f out)	s.h	**4**	12/1	92	19
	Balla Sola (IRE) (WPMullins,Ireland) **2-8-10** PJSmullen (sn jnd stands' side group: led stands' side group bef ½-wy: hdd u.p 1½f out: no ex)	¾	**5**	$5/1^{1}$	90	17
2558^{5}	**Conectis (IRE)** (DJSCosgrove) **2-8-7** JReid (cl up: ev ch 2f out: no ex u.p over 1f out: kpt on)	1	**6**	$7/1^{3}$	84	11
	Challenger Two (IRE) (KPrendergast,Ireland) **2-8-10** SCraine (towards rr: rdn & kpt on last 2f: nrst fin)	¾	**7**	20/1	85	12
	Slippery Slope (IRE) (KPrendergast,Ireland) **2-8-7** GMMoylan (trckd ldrs far side group: no ex over 1f out: kpt on)	nk	**8**	14/1	81	8
3743^{3}	**Honey Storm (IRE)** (MRChannon) **2-8-7** PPMurphy (mid div: rdn & chsd ldrs 2f out: no imp over 1½f out: kpt on)	nk	**9**	20/1	80	7

	Horse		Pos	SP	RR	SF
3635[5]	**Fayrana (IRE)** (JWHills) **2-8-7** MHenry (chsd ldrs: rdn ½-wy: nt trble ldrs over 1½f out: kpt on)	s.h	**10**	16/1	80	7
3270[2]	**Miquelon** (RHollinshead) **2-8-10b[1]** PShanahan (prom: ev ch over 2f out: wknd over 1½f out)	s.h	**11**	12/1	83	10
2943[11]	**Kate Lane (IRE)** (MrsPNDutfield) **2-8-7** YOkabe (chsd ldrs far side group: no ex 1½f out: kpt on)	nk	**12**	50/1	79	6
	Deilginis (NMeade,Ireland) **2-8-10** EAhern (mid div: rdn ½-wy: kpt on last 2: nvr nrr)	nk	**13**	20/1	81	8
	Guscott (IRE) (APO'Brien,Ireland) **2-8-10** WJSupple (s.s & wnt lft s: towards rr: kpt on: nvr nrr)	hd	**14**	12/1	81	8
3672a[5]	**Pelagius (IRE)** (JOxx,Ireland) **2-8-10b** JPMurtagh (chsd ldrs far side group: no ex u.p 2f out: kpt on same pce)	nk	**15**	12/1	80	7
	Goldman (IRE) (APO'Brien,Ireland) **2-8-10** RMBurke (chsd ldrs: rdn & no imp 2f out: wknd)	¾	**16**	40/1	78	5
2697[4]	**Oisin (IRE)** (MrsPNDutfield) **2-8-10** DPMcDonogh (mid div: no imp last 2f: kpt on)	1	**17**	33/1	76	3
3151[6]	**Moonstone (IRE)** (APJarvis) **2-8-7** DWright (led & disp ld far side group tl under 2f out: sn no ex)	nk	**18**	33/1	72	—
2987a[5]	**Delirious Tantrum (IRE)** (GMLyons,Ireland) **2-8-7** SWKelly (chsd ldrs: rdn & no imp under 2f out)	nk	**19**	20/1	71	—
	Liffey Ballad (IRE) (GMLyons,Ireland) **2-8-7** JPSpencer (mid div: rdn & no imp over 1½f out)	s.h	**20**	33/1	71	—
	Gold Radiance (APO'Brien,Ireland) **2-8-10** JAHeffernan (chsd ldrs: rdn & no imp under 2f out)	2	**21**	20/1	69	—
3237[7]	**Stately Princess** (MRChannon) **2-8-7** MRimmer (cl up far side group: no ex u.p 1½f out)	1½	**22**	14/1	62	—
2987a[6]	**Marilia (IRE)** (JSBolger,Ireland) **2-8-7** WJSmith (towards rr: cld ½-wy: rdn & btn 1½f out)	1	**23**	20/1	59	—
	Boat Strand (IRE) (APO'Brien,Ireland) **2-8-10b[1]** CRoche (cl up: rdn ½-wy: no imp u.p over 1½f out: wknd)	nk	**24**	12/1	61	—
3306[9]	**Whacker-Do (IRE)** (RHollinshead) **2-8-10** JJBehan (mid div: clsd to chal 2f out: no ex 1½f out: wknd)	¾	**25**	50/1	59	—
	Black Pidgeon (IRE) (MissITOakes,Ireland) **2-8-9**ow2 JMMaguire (dwlt: towards rr: n.d)	½	**26**	100/1	57	—
	Goldbridge (IRE) (APO'Brien,Ireland) **2-8-10** FrancesCrowley (s.i.s: a trailing: n.d)	3½	**27**	40/1	49	—
	Black Rock City (GMLyons,Ireland) **2-8-10** NGMcCullagh (prom: ev ch & rdn ½-wy: wknd over 2f out)	2½	**28**	33/1	42	—
	Carnabrae (IRE) (FBerry,Ireland) **2-8-10** FMBerry (Withdrawn not under Starter's orders)		**W**	10/1	—	—
				(SP 177.8%)	**28 Rn**	

1m 14.5 (4.00) OWNER Mrs P. Jupert (MARLBOROUGH) BRED Jerry O'Brien

IN-FOCUS: **On a different track than usual, further away from the stands, the high-drawn horses suffered no disadvantage here and this was the side where all the pace appeared to lie.**

3464 Another Fantasy (IRE) was always travelling well within herself from halfway. She got to the front over one and a half furlongs out and sprinted clear inside the last. (16/1)

3506a Law Library (IRE) led and disputed the lead on the stands' side but was fighting a losing battle in second place from a furlong out. (7/1)

2862 Daunting Lady (IRE) got herself into a bit of a state beforehand but was always up with the pace on the far side, until unable to find anything extra one and a half furlongs out. She stayed on again to take third place close home. (13/2)

3226* Jacmar (IRE) injected plenty of speed into the far side group but was readily outpaced by the winner from one and a half furlongs out. (12/1: op 8/1)

Balla Sola (IRE), drawn in the centre, made the mistake of coming over towards the stands' side. He led and disputed it until finding no extra from one and a half furlongs out. (5/1)

2558 Conectis (IRE), chasing the leaders on the stands' side, was unable to get in any real sort of a challenge, just keeping on at the one pace. (7/1)

3743 Honey Storm (IRE) showed plenty of pace on the stands' side but was well held over the last one and a half furlongs. (20/1)

3635 Fayrana (IRE), chasing the leaders up the middle, never got on challenging terms from two furlongs out. (16/1)

3270 Miquelon was not able to make any impression over the last one and a half furlongs. (12/1: op 8/1)

2699 Kate Lane (IRE) chased the leaders on the far side but had cried enough with two furlongs to race. (50/1)

Pelagius (IRE) (12/1: op 8/1)

2697 Oisin (IRE), outpaced early, had to switch out to get a run over one furlong out and kept on quite well. (33/1)

3151 Moonstone (IRE) ran fast on the far side to halfway. (33/1)

1475 Stately Princess showed plenty of toe early on but was struggling two furlongs out. (14/1)

2361 Whacker-Do (IRE), prominent to two furlongs out, weakened quickly. (50/1)

3962a FUTURITY STKS (Gp 3) (2-Y.O)

4-25 (4-29) **7f** IR £19,500.00 (IR £5,700.00: IR £2,700.00: IR £900.00) GOING minus 0.08 sec per fur (G)

	Horse		Pos	SP	RR	SF
	Impressionist (IRE) (APO'Brien,Ireland) **2-8-11**ow1 CRoche (sn led & disp ld: clr 3f out: rdn & r.o.)	—	**1**	5/2 [2]	93	46
3576[3]	**Fruits of Love (USA)** (MJohnston) **2-8-10** JWeaver (hld up: chsd ldrs & n.m.r ½-wy: rdn 1½f out: swtchd rt: effrt on ins: r.o. fnl f: nt rch wnr)	1	**2**	7/4 [1]	90	44
	Natalis (IRE) (JOxx,Ireland) **2-8-10** JPMurtagh (hld up: 6th & clsd ½-wy: 3rd & rdn 1½f out: nt trble wnr: kpt on ins last)	¾	**3**	9/2 [3]	88	42
	The King Of Cloyne (USA) (JSBolger,Ireland) **2-8-10** KJManning (cl up: 3rd ½-wy: 2nd u.p & chsd wnr 2f out: no ex over 1f out: kpt on same pce)	¾	**4**	8/1	86	40
3494[3]	**Krispy Knight** (JWHills) **2-8-10** JReid (led early: 2nd & disp ld: 3rd & rdn 3f out: btn 1½f out: kpt on same pce)	2½	**5**	8/1	81	35
	Magical Minty (IRE) (WPMullins,Ireland) **2-8-10** PJSmullen (in tch: 5th 3f out: rdn & nt rch ldrs 1½f out: kpt on)	hd	**6**	12/1	80	34
	Lightning Star (USA) (APO'Brien,Ireland) **2-8-10b[1]** JAHeffernan (chsd ldrs: rdn & no imp fr 2f out)	5½	**7**	20/1	68	22
2057[8]	**Sideman (IRE)** (APO'Brien,Ireland) **2-8-10** MJKinane (hld up in tch: rdn & effrt ½-wy: no imp over 2f out)	¾	**8**	5/1	66	20
				(SP 134.5%)	**8 Rn**	

1m 26.6 (3.60) OWNER Mrs John Magnier (PILTOWN)

Impressionist (IRE), with no pace early on, was forced to make his own running. He went on after two and a half furlongs and was driven clear two furlongs out to effectively seal the matter. He certainly looks useful and this was a big step up (17lb officially) on what he had shown before. (5/2: op 4/1)

3576 Fruits of Love (USA), held up towards the rear, switched to the inside to challenge one and a half furlongs out but there was not much forthcoming. Once he saw a bit more daylight, he ran on well to take second place close home. His jockey would be entitled to feel displeased with his effort. (7/4)

Natalis (IRE), tapped for toe two furlongs out, kept on well over the last furlong and is already in need of a longer trip. (9/2)

The King Of Cloyne (USA), in second place and flying distress signals from three furlongs out, kept on well under pressure from one furlong out. (8/1: op 5/1)

3494 Krispy Knight went with the winner early but was fighting a losing battle from two furlongs out. (8/1)

Magical Minty (IRE) (12/1: op 8/1)

2057 Sideman (IRE), weak in the market, was totally out of contention from two furlongs down. (5/1)

3963a - 3964a : (Irish Racing) - See Computer Raceform

3847-BRIGHTON (L-H) (Good to firm)
Wednesday September 3rd
WEATHER: overcast WIND: slt half against

3965 LADBROKE NURSERY H'CAP (0-85) (2-Y.O) (Class E)
2-20 (2-22) **5f 59y** £2,992.25 (£893.00: £426.50: £193.25) Stalls: Low GOING minus 0.21 sec per fur (GF)

				SP	RR	SF
2942^{7}	**Bliss (IRE) (58)** (MrsPNDutfield) **2-7-10** JQuinn(2) (mde virtually all: rdn out)	—	1	50/1	60	12
3774^{5}	**Golden Strategy (IRE) (78)** (RHannon) **2-9-2** DaneO'Neill(9) (b.hind: lw: rdn over 2f out: hdwy over 1f out: r.o wl ins fnl f)	¾	2	6/1 ^{3}	78	30
3586^{2}	**Ok John (IRE) (62)** (JAkehurst) **2-8-0** DBiggs(7) (b.nr hind: plld hrd: a.p: rdn over 1f out: ev ch ins fnl f: unable qckn)	¾	3	14/1	59	11
3589*	**To Love With Love (78)** (WJarvis) **2-8-13**(3) RFfrench(4) (a.p: rdn over 1f out: one pce)	1¼	4	11/4 ^{2}	72	24
3094^{4}	**Allasella (IRE) (72)** (BPalling) **2-8-10** SSanders(8) (nt clr run 4f out: hdwy over 1f out: nvr nrr)	nk	5	14/1	65	17
2917^{6}	**Magical Dancer (IRE) (58)** (MrsPNDutfield) **2-7-5**(5) APolli(10) (hdwy over 1f out: one pce fnl f)	¾	6	50/1	49	1
3636^{8}	**Kathies Pet (63)** (RJHodges) **2-7-10**(5) AmandaSanders(5) (nvr nr to chal)	1½	7	33/1	49	1
3823*	**Folklore (89)** (DRLoder) **2-9-13** 6x GCarter(11) (lw: a.p: hrd rdn & ev ch over 1f out: eased whn btn ins fnl f)	s.h	8	5/2 ^{1}	75	27
3474^{3}	**Sada (79)** (MajorWRHern) **2-9-3** DHolland(1) (s.s: hdwy over 2f out: rdn over 1f out: wknd ins fnl f)	s.h	9	7/1	65	17
1941^{8}	**Captain Brady (IRE) (61)** (WGMTurner) **2-7-6**(7) AMcCarthy(13) (lw: a bhd)	½	10	50/1	45	—
3817^{4}	**Eastern Lyric (78)** (JBerry) **2-9-2** GDuffield(6) (w wnr 2f: wknd over 2f out)	hd	11	14/1	62	14
3799^{4}	***The Boy John (USA) (80)*** (RHannon) **2-8-11**(7) PDobbs(3) (Withdrawn not under Starter's orders: attempted to break out of stalls.)		W	10/1	—	—
				(SP 119.9%)	**11 Rn**	

63.1 secs (3.10) CSF £266.68 CT £3,514.75 TOTE £70.40: £9.90 £1.90 £3.30 (£229.70) Trio £205.40 OWNER Mr W. A. Harrison-Allan (SEATON) BRED Mrs Margaret Sinanan

LONG HANDICAP Bliss (IRE) 7-8

1293 Bliss (IRE) left previous runs behind and, making every post a winning one, was rousted along to keep his rivals at bay. (50/1)

3774 Golden Strategy (IRE) was still out with the washing a quarter of a mile from home, but he really found his feet from below the distance, only to find the line always coming too soon. (6/1)

3586 Ok John (IRE) took a very keen hold but, nevertheless, was still in with every chance inside the final furlong before failing to find another gear. (14/1)

3589* To Love With Love was never far away but failed to find another turn of foot in the last furlong and a half. (11/4)

3094 Allasella (IRE) stayed on from below the distance without threatening. (14/1)

2917 Magical Dancer (IRE), racing with her tongue tied down, made a forward move in the centre of the course below the distance but could then only keep on in her own time. (50/1)

3823* Folklore (5/2: 7/4-11/4)

3799 The Boy John (USA) (10/1: 8/1-12/1)

3966 BRIGHTON CLAIMING STKS (I) (3-Y.O+) (Class F)
2-50 (2-51) **7f 214y** £1,927.00 (£527.00: £247.00) Stalls: Low GOING minus 0.21 sec per fur (GF)

				SP	RR	SF
2957^{2}	**Misty Cay (IRE) (60)** (SDow) **3-8-4** JFEgan(3) (nvr gng wl: hdwy over 2f out: hrd rdn over 1f out: led ins fnl f: r.o wl)	—	1	2/1 ^{1}	56	16
3849^{15}	**Sejaal (IRE) (54)** (RAkehurst) **5-8-12** DHolland(9) (led tl ins fnl f: unable qckn)	1¼	2	14/1	57	22
3894^{15}	**Heart Full of Soul (73)** (PFICole) **3-9-3b** DaneO'Neill(8) (lw: lost pl 4f out: rallied fnl f: r.o)	3	3	8/1	61	21
3848^{7}	**Smarter Charter (64)** (MrsLStubbs) **4-9-8** SSanders(10) (a.p: hrd rdn over 2f out: one pce)	nk	4	3/1 ^{2}	60	25
	Racing Telegraph (40) (CNAllen) **7-8-10** JQuinn(5) (a.p: styd far side st: rdn over 2f out: one pce)	1	5	33/1	46	11
3206^{3}	**Glen Ogil** (MRChannon) **3-8-10**(3) PPMurphy(6) (b: lw: a.p: rdn over 2f out: sn wknd)	½	6	6/1 ^{3}	53	13
3581^{4}	**Quinzii Martin (34)** (DHaydnJones) **9-8-8b** AMackay(7) (nvr nr to chal)	1¾	7	16/1	39	4
3627^{3}	**Trying Times (IRE) (45)** (JBerry) **4-9-1**(3) TEDurcan(1) (t: lw: hdwy over 4f out: hrd rdn over 2f out: wknd over 1f out)	1¼	8	8/1	47	12
3413^{10}	**Ladybower (IRE) (24)** (JRPoulton) **5-8-3** SDrowne(2) (a bhd)	½	9	25/1	31	—
3229^{8}	**Kirov Protege (IRE) (25)** (GLMoore) **5-8-5**(5) PRoberts(4) (lw: bhd fnl 5f)	nk	10	50/1	37	2
				(SP 116.1%)	**10 Rn**	

1m 36.3 (5.00) CSF £28.94 TOTE £2.70: £1.30 £4.30 £2.30 (£15.40) Trio £60.00 OWNER Mrs A. M. Upsdell (EPSOM) BRED T. Ward

WEIGHT FOR AGE 3yo-5lb

Misty Cay (IRE) clmd Mrs V Ward £6,000

2957 Misty Cay (IRE) was off the bridle from the word go and her jockey did extremely well. The filly at last picked up over a quarter of a mile from home and, under strong riding, got on top inside the final furlong. She has gained all her wins in claiming or selling company. (2/1)

Sejaal (IRE) has been badly out of form for the last two years but ran much better with this drop in class, taking the field along until overhauled inside the final furlong. (14/1: 8/1-16/1)

Heart Full of Soul was taking a drop in class but got outpaced at halfway. He appeared to have no chance below the distance but stayed on in the final furlong to take third prize. (8/1: op 5/1)

3477 Smarter Charter was never far away but failed to quicken in the final quarter-mile. (3/1)

Racing Telegraph, making a belated seasonal bow, was the only runner who elected to stay on the far side in the straight. Bustled along, he failed to find that vital turn of foot. (33/1)

3206 Glen Ogil, tackling a longer trip, was close up until calling it a day two furlongs from home. A drop in distance is required. (6/1)

3967 FRIENDS OF QUEEN PARK (S) STKS (2-Y.O) (Class G)
3-20 (3-21) **6f 209y** £1,984.50 (£547.00: £259.50) Stalls: Low GOING minus 0.21 sec per fur (GF)

				SP	RR	SF
3639*	**Won't Forget Me (IRE) (59)** (MHTompkins) **2-9-2** DBiggs(16) (swtchd rt 2f out: hdwy over 1f out: led ins fnl f: r.o wl)	—	1	7/1 ^{1}	71	24
3586^{3}	**Charlies Lad (IRE) (66)** (RGuest) **2-9-2** PBloomfield(4) (hld up: led over 1f out tl ins fnl f: unable qckn)	1½	2	8/1 ^{3}	68	21
3384^{4}	**Jazz Singer** (RHannon) **2-8-6** DaneO'Neill(12) (a.p: rdn 2f out: one pce)	1¼	3	15/2 ^{2}	55	8

3751^{3}	**Pink Ticket (51)** (PDEvans) **2-8-6** JFEgan(6) (a.p: hrd rdn over 2f out: one pce)	s.h	**4**	8/1^{3}	55	8
3639^{4}	**Captain Bliss (58)** (NTinkler) **2-9-2b** GDuffield(10) (led over 5f)	s.h	**5**	12/1	64	17
3635^{7}	**Shannon (IRE) (59)** (CADwyer) **2-8-8**(3) RFfrench(5) (dwlt: rdn over 2f out: hdwy over 1f out: r.o)	nk	**6**	8/1^{3}	59	12
3751^{14}	**Jet Set Sarah (USA)** (JBerry) **2-8-3v^{1}**(3) TEDurcan(9) (nt clr run over 1f out: hdwy fnl f: nvr nrr)	¾	**7**	25/1	52	5
3788^{6}	**Mary Lou (IRE)** (MRChannon) **2-8-6** GCarter(15) (rdn over 3f out: hdwy fnl f: nvr nrr)	¾	**8**	7/1^{1}	50	3
2493^{12}	**Lady So Bold** (MrsLStubbs) **2-8-6** DHolland(7) (nvr nr to chal)	nk	**9**	25/1	50	3
3782^{4}	**The Hobby Lobby (IRE) (55)** (MissKMGeorge) **2-8-11** NAdams(13) (prom over 5f)	2	**10**	14/1	50	3
2893^{10}	**Belle de Montfort** (JLSpearing) **2-8-6** SDrowne(11) (a bhd)	3	**11**	33/1	38	—
3294^{2}	**Shanthi (55)** (PJMakin) **2-8-6b^{1}** SSanders(14) (hld up: rdn over 2f out: wkng whn hmpd 2f out)	2	**12**	7/1^{1}	34	—
3751^{2}	**Katie's Cracker (53)** (MRChannon) **2-8-6** AMackay(3) (a bhd)	5	**13**	7/1^{1}	22	—
3808^{9}	**Keen Lady** (NPLittmoden) **2-8-6** TGMcLaughlin(1) (a bhd)	2½	**14**	33/1	16	—
3471^{16}	**Tundra (IRE)** (KMcAuliffe) **2-8-6** MTebbutt(8) (b: lw: bhd fnl 3f)	3½	**15**	16/1	8	—
3782^{5}	**Calliram (50)** (MBlanshard) **2-8-6** JQuinn(2) (hld up: rdn over 2f out: sn wknd)	1¼	**16**	14/1	5	—

(SP 135.6%) **16 Rn**

1m 24.7 (4.70) CSF £60.44 TOTE £8.70: £3.20 £3.20 £3.40 (£26.20) Trio £105.90 OWNER Mrs Jane Bailey (NEWMARKET) BRED Kevin Wallace

Bt in 7,200 gns

3639* Won't Forget Me (IRE) followed up his recent Folkestone selling victory. Switched right a quarter of a mile from home, doing a rival no favours, he came with a useful run to strike the front inside the final furlong. (7/1)

3586 Charlies Lad (IRE) coped with this slightly longer trip and showed in front below the distance. Headed inside the final furlong, he was unable to contain the winner. (8/1)

3384 Jazz Singer was always close up but could only struggle on at one pace in the final quarter-mile. (15/2)

3751 Pink Ticket, always well placed, could only keep on in her own time in the last two furlongs. (8/1: 6/1-9/1)

3639 Captain Bliss took the field along but, collared approaching the final furlong, had little left in reserve. (12/1)

3289* Shannon (IRE) stayed on when it was all over. (8/1)

3782 The Hobby Lobby (IRE) (14/1: 10/1-16/1)

3782 Calliram (14/1: 10/1-16/1)

3968 LADBROKE LIMITED STKS (0-60) (3-Y.O) (Class F)

3-50 (3-53) **6f 209y** £2,831.40 (£785.40: £376.20) Stalls: Low GOING minus 0.21 sec per fur (GF)

				SP	RR	SF
3642^{2}	**Bold Tina (IRE) (59)** (RHannon) **3-8-9** DaneO'Neill(2) (hdwy & nt clr run over 1f out: led ins fnl f: r.o wl)	—	**1**	9/2^{2}	65	44
3749^{2}	**Petite Danseuse (60)** (CADwyer) **3-8-9**(3) RFfrench(7) (hld up: rdn over 1f out: ev ch ins fnl f: unable qckn)	1½	**2**	11/4^{1}	65	44
3691^{3}	**Inclination (60)** (MBlanshard) **3-8-9** JQuinn(6) (lw: led: hrd rdn over 1f out: hdd ins fnl f: one pce)	¾	**3**	6/1^{3}	60	39
3592^{4}	**Super Scravels (45)** (KMahdi) **3-8-9** SSanders(9) (lw: rdn over 2f out: hdwy over 1f out: r.o)	3	**4**	20/1	53	32
3697^{2}	**Get The Point (60)** (RHollinshead) **3-8-9**(3) DGriffiths(4) (lw: a.p: hrd rdn & ev ch over 1f out: wknd ins fnl f)	¾	**5**	10/1	54	33
3850*	**La Doyenne (IRE) (41)** (CBBBooth) **3-8-12** FNorton(1) (lw: hld up: rdn over 2f out: wknd fnl f)	5	**6**	7/1	43	22
3558^{7}	**Charlton Spring (IRE) (60)** (RJHodges) **3-8-6**(3) PPMurphy(13) (s.s: rdn over 3f out: nvr nrr)	1	**7**	14/1	37	16
3813^{3}	**Misty Rain (60)** (BWHills) **3-8-9** DHolland(3) (rdn over 2f out: sme hdwy over 1f out: eased whn btn ins fnl f)	hd	**8**	6/1^{3}	37	16
2695^{8}	**Warring (60)** (MSSaunders) **3-8-12** SDrowne(11) (lw: prom over 4f)	1½	**9**	20/1	37	16
3591^{6}	**Grovefair Venture (53)** (KMahdi) **3-8-12** WRyan(10) (lw: prom 4f)	1	**10**	33/1	34	13
2921^{6}	**Forgotten Times (USA) (57)** (TMJones) **3-8-9** NCarlisle(5) (lw: hld up: rdn over 2f out: wknd over 1f out)	3½	**11**	9/1	23	2
3548^{14}	**Jupiter (IRE) (60)** (GCBravery) **3-8-12b^{1}** MRimmer(8) (plld hrd: mid div over 5f)	1¾	**12**	8/1	22	1

(SP 135.3%) **12 Rn**

1m 22.5 (2.50) CSF £17.78 TOTE £5.80: £1.80 £1.90 £2.20 (£10.60) Trio £25.50 OWNER Mrs Chris Harrington (MARLBOROUGH) BRED Mrs Chris Harrington

3642 Bold Tina (IRE), who did not get the best of runs as she picked up ground below the distance, came through to lead inside the final furlong and lose her maiden tag at the twelfth attempt. The change of tactics has been the answer for her. (9/2)

3749 Petite Danseuse chased the leaders. With every chance inside the final furlong, she was then unable to cope with the winner. (11/4)

3691 Inclination again made the frame as she took the field along until overhauled inside the final furlong. She has now finished third in six of her last seven outings. (6/1)

3592 Super Scravels only found her feet from below the distance but, despite running on, never threatened to get near the principals. She remains a maiden. (20/1)

3697 Get The Point was close up until tiring inside the final furlong. He remains a maiden after sixteen attempts. (10/1)

3850* La Doyenne (IRE) had more on her plate this time and had given her best in the final furlong. (7/1)

Charlton Spring (IRE) (14/1: 8/1-16/1)

2921 Forgotten Times (USA) (9/1: 6/1-10/1)

3969 BRIGHTON CLAIMING STKS (II) (3-Y.O+) (Class F)

4-20 (4-21) **7f 214y** £1,927.00 (£527.00: £247.00) Stalls: Low GOING minus 0.21 sec per fur (GF)

				SP	RR	SF
3848^{2}	**Night Wink (USA) (64)** (GLMoore) **5-9-2** WRyan(2) (lw: led 3f: led over 2f out: clr over 1f out: easily)	—	**1**	5/6^{1}	84	38
1874^{8}	**Desert Green (FR) (88)** (RHannon) **8-9-4** DaneO'Neill(7) (lw: hdwy over 1f out: r.o)	9	**2**	9/1	68	22
3469^{11}	**Hawaii Storm (FR) (48)** (DJSffrenchDavis) **9-8-5**(3) RFfrench(9) (lw: a.p: rdn over 2f out: unable qckn)	1¾	**3**	14/1	54	8
3691^{5}	**Ocker (IRE) (63)** (MHTompkins) **3-8-13v^{1}** DBiggs(3) (s.s: plld hrd: hdwy to ld 5f out: hdd over 2f out: wknd fnl f)	1¾	**4**	10/1	61	10
3590^{10}	**Nicker (55)** (WJarvis) **3-8-3** JQuinn(8) (lw: no hdwy fnl 3f)	1¼	**5**	7/1^{3}	48	—
2947^{6}	**Without Friends (IRE) (51)** (JFfitch-Heyes) **3-8-11** GDuffield(4) (nvr nr to chal)	hd	**6**	25/1	56	5
3749^{3}	**Gunners Glory (54)** (MrsLStubbs) **3-8-13** SSanders(1) (lw: prom over 6f)	11	**7**	5/1^{2}	36	—
3469^{12}	**Agwa (40)** (JJBridger) **8-8-5**(5) ADaly(6) (bhd fnl 4f)	½	**8**	40/1	27	—
3816^{12}	**Blue Havana** (GraemeRoe) **5-8-5** NCarlisle(5) (bhd fnl 4f)	12	**9**	50/1	—	—

(SP 117.7%) **9 Rn**

1m 35.3 (4.00) CSF £8.69 TOTE £1.80: £1.10 £2.60 £2.50 (£5.20) Trio £16.50 OWNER Mrs Dyanne Benjamin (BRIGHTON) BRED Gainsborough Farm Inc

WEIGHT FOR AGE 3yo-5lb

Night Wink (USA) clmd Mrs V Ward £7,000

3848 Night Wink (USA) goes well in this class - he demonstrated that again here last week - and, showing in front for his second time over two furlongs out, forged clear to win with a ton in hand. (5/6)

Desert Green (FR), given a three-month break, is not the easiest of rides but stayed on from below the distance to finish a moderate second. (9/1: op 4/1)
3139 Hawaii Storm (FR) is into the veteran stage these days but was close up until tapped for toe in the last two furlongs. (14/1: 10/1-16/1)
3691 Ocker (IRE) pulled his way to the front five furlongs from home. Collared over a quarter of a mile out, he was soon beaten. (10/1: 11/2-11/1)
2747 Nicker (7/1: op 9/2)

3970 GEORGE ROBEY CHALLENGE TROPHY H'CAP (0-70) (3-Y.O+ F & M) (Class E)

4-50 (4-51) **1m 3f 196y** £3,174.25 (£949.00: £454.50: £207.25) Stalls: High GOING minus 0.37 sec per fur (F)

				SP	RR	SF
3245[2]	**Mono Lady (IRE) (60)** (DHaydnJones) **4-9-10b** AMackay(11) (hdwy over 3f out: led over 1f out: pushed out)	—	**1**	12/1	74	61
3495[6]	**Bathe In Light (USA) (58)** (LordHuntingdon) **3-8-13** SSanders(1) (lw: a.p: led over 4f out tl over 1f out: unable qckn)	4	**2**	10/1	67	45
3893[2]	**Curzon Street (66)** (DRCElsworth) **3-9-7** AProcter(12) (lw: hrd rdn & hdwy over 1f out: one pce)	2½	**3**	9/4[1]	71	49
3694[7]	**Rufalda (IRE) (70)** (LMCumani) **3-9-8b**[1](3) RFfrench(2) (lw: hdwy over 3f out: wknd over 1f out)	2½	**4**	8/1[3]	72	50
3793[10]	**Tallulah Belle (59)** (NPLittmoden) **4-9-9** TGMcLaughlin(3) (hdwy over 3f out: wknd over 1f out)	s.h	**5**	25/1	61	48
3767[8]	**Tart (FR) (47)** (JPearce) **4-8-11** GDuffield(6) (a.p: ev ch 2f out: wknd 1f out)	s.h	**6**	12/1	49	36
3495[3]	**Persian Blue (59)** (RHannon) **3-9-0** DaneO'Neill(7) (nvr nr to chal)	3	**7**	11/1	57	35
3495[2]	**Siberian Mystic (40)** (PGMurphy) **4-8-4** SDrowne(8) (hdwy over 4f out: wknd over 2f out)	1½	**8**	5/1[2]	36	23
3415[6]	**Willie Rushton (50)** (GLMoore) **4-9-0** MWigham(9) (a bhd)	3	**9**	33/1	42	29
3695[2]	**Superbelle (59)** (MAJarvis) **3-9-0** EmmaO'Gorman(10) (prom 8f)	19	**10**	16/1	25	3
3640[4]	**Classic Dame (FR) (64)** (SDow) **4-10-0** JFEgan(5) (lw: hld up: rdn over 3f out: sn wknd)	13	**11**	12/1	13	—
3256*	**Double Eight (IRE) (70)** (BWHills) **3-9-11** DHolland(4) (led over 7f)	7	**12**	5/1[2]	9	—
				(SP 128.4%)	**12 Rn**	

2m 30.0 (2.40) CSF £124.74 CT £345.08 TOTE £19.10: £4.10 £4.50 £1.40 (£144.70) Trio £102.30 OWNER Monolithic Refractories Ltd (PONTYPRIDD) BRED Dr. Michael Smurfit
WEIGHT FOR AGE 3yo-9lb
3245 Mono Lady (IRE) struck the front below the distance and needed only to be nudged along for a decisive victory. It later transpired she had lost her off-fore shoe during the race. (12/1: op 8/1)
3495 Bathe In Light (USA) went on at the top of the hill but, collared over a furlong out, was firmly put in her place by the winner. (10/1: 8/1-12/1)
3893 Curzon Street made her effort under pressure below the distance, but could then only go up and down in the same place. (9/4)
2568 Rufalda (IRE), fitted with blinkers for the first time, began a forward move early in the straight but had shot her bolt below the distance. (8/1)
3609 Tallulah Belle took closer order as the runner came into the straight, but had been hung out to dry over a furlong out. (25/1)
3495 Tart (FR) was close up until tiring a furlong from home. (12/1: op 8/1)
3495 Persian Blue (11/1: 5/1-12/1)
3640 Classic Dame (FR) (12/1: 8/1-14/1)

3971 LADBROKE AMATEUR H'CAP (0-70) (3-Y.O+) (Class G)

5-20 (5-24) **1m 1f 209y** £2,592.10 (£720.60: £346.30) Stalls: High GOING minus 0.37 sec per fur (F)

				SP	RR	SF
3588[5]	**Roman Reel (USA) (47)** (GLMoore) **6-10-9** MrsJMoore(8) (hdwy over 2f out: led 1f out: r.o wl)	—	**1**	16/1	58	35
3432*	**Righty Ho (66)** (PTWalwyn) **3-11-7v** MissSSamworth(14) (s.s: hdwy over 2f out: chsd wnr ins fnl f: r.o)	nk	**2**	3/1[1]	77	47
3588[6]	**Colour Counsellor (43)** (RMFlower) **4-10-5b** MrJGoldstein(15) (a.p: rdn over 2f out: ev ch 1f out: unable qckn)	2½	**3**	7/1[3]	50	27
3721[2]	**Fife Major (USA) (63)** (BWHills) **3-10-13**(5) MrCBHills(7) (lw: hdwy 4f out: one pce fnl 3f)	2	**4**	3/1[1]	66	36
3814[7]	**Royal Acclaim (27)** (KRBurke) **12-9-3v** MissRJPatman(13) (hdwy over 1f out: r.o)	s.h	**5**	20/1	30	7
3432[2]	**Bellas Gate Boy (48)** (JPearce) **5-10-10** MrsLPearce(9) (hdwy 4f out: wknd over 1f out)	1	**6**	13/2[2]	50	27
3562[8]	**Don't Drop Bombs (USA) (34)** (DTThom) **8-9-10v** MissJFeilden(11) (lw: led: styd far side st: hdd 1f out: sn wknd)	¾	**7**	7/1[3]	34	11
3496[9]	**One In The Eye (33)** (JRPoulton) **4-9-4**(5) MrIMongan(12) (nvr nrr)	¾	**8**	33/1	32	9
3467[7]	**Super Serenade (57)** (GBBalding) **8-11-5** MrJThatcher(3) (s.s: nvr nrr)	1¾	**9**	16/1	53	30
3581[5]	**Burning Cost (30)** (REPeacock) **7-9-6**ow6 MrsCPeacock(10) (prom 6f)	2	**10**	50/1	23	—
3240[21]	**Patrita Park (37)** (WGMTurner) **3-9-1**(5) MissCStretton(5) (b.hind: bhd fnl 3f)	nk	**11**	33/1	30	—
3041[9]	**Sarum (33)** (JELong) **11-9-4**(5)ow9 MrTWaters(2) (b: prom 6f)	hd	**12**	66/1	26	—
3293[6]	**Executive Officer (25)** (RMFlower) **4-9-1b** MrVLukaniuk(1) (s.s: a bhd)	3½	**13**	20/1	12	—
3792[10]	**Contract Bridge (IRE) (40)** (PGMurphy) **4-9-11**(5) MissLGreen(4) (s.s: a bhd)	12	**14**	33/1	8	—
				(SP 121.9%)	**14 Rn**	

2m 4.8 (6.50) CSF £55.08 CT £351.25 TOTE £12.10: £2.60 £2.70 £2.00 (£34.70) Trio £76.60 OWNER Mr K. Higson (BRIGHTON) BRED Dorothy Price, Jackie W. Ramos & Ken Hickson
LONG HANDICAP Sarum 8-13 Burning Cost 8-12
WEIGHT FOR AGE 3yo-7lb
3588 Roman Reel (USA) came through to lead a furlong out and kept on well to gain his fifth course victory. (16/1)
3432* Righty Ho, 8lb higher for his recent success, began a forward move over a quarter of a mile from home. Coming through to take second place early inside the final furlong, he ran on but was not going to overhaul the winner in time. (3/1)
3588 Colour Counsellor, a leading light throughout, threatened to take the lead below the distance, but was tapped for toe in the final furlong. (7/1)
3721 Fife Major (USA) moved up at the top of the hill but was made to look very pedestrian in the last three furlongs. (3/1)
3588 Royal Acclaim stayed on when it was all over. (20/1)
3432 Bellas Gate Boy took closer order at the top of the hill but had cooked his goose over a furlong out. He has just one win from thirty-two starts to his name. (13/2)

T/Plpt: £160.10 (121.32 Tckts). T/Qdpt: £13.70 (105.11 Tckts) AK

3722-YORK (L-H) (Soft)
Wednesday September 3rd
WEATHER: wet and windy WIND: str half bhd

3972 LEVY BOARD PETRUSHKA VODKA CLAIMING STKS (3-Y.O+) (Class D)
2-10 (2-11) **1m 205y** £5,435.50 (£1,624.00: £777.00: £353.50) Stalls: Low GOING: 0.87 sec per fur (S)

Form	Horse	Btn	Pos	SP	RR	SF
3462*	**Brighstone (81)** (MCPipe) **4-8-11** AMcGlone(8) (t: mde all: clr over 1f out: hung lft: unchal)	—	1	5/1[2]	58+	44
3822[3]	**High Premium (84)** (RAFahey) **9-8-7**(7) RWinston(2) (lw: sn pushed along: hdwy over 5f out: rdn & hung lft over 1f out: kpt on one pce)	5	2	Evens[1]	52	38
3630[5]	**Nobby Barnes (42)** (DonEnricoIncisa) **8-8-10** KimTinkler(1) (dwlt: hdwy 3f out: sn hrd rdn & chsng ldrs: one pce)	hd	3	20/1	48	34
3749[7]	**South China Sea** (PFICole) **3-8-4** TQuinn(4) (trckd wnr: rdn over 2f out: wknd fnl f)	7	4	16/1	35	15
3767[11]	**Saltando (IRE) (43)** (PatMitchell) **6-9-1v** TSprake(6) (lw: chsd ldrs: pushed along 6f out: lost pl 4f out: n.d after)	9	5	33/1	24	10
	Deadline Time (IRE) (MrsMReveley) **4-9-0** KDarley(5) (hld up: effrt over 3f out: sn chsng ldrs: wknd over 2f out)	17	6	6/1[3]	—	—
3768[5]	**White Plains (IRE) (75)** (KRBurke) **4-9-3** KFallon(3) (trckd ldrs: rdn over 3f out: sn lost pl)	17	7	5/1[2]	—	—
3100[9]	**Spanish Stripper (USA) (30)** (MCChapman) **6-8-3**(7) SCarson(7) (swtg: bhd & pushed along 4f out)	3	8	40/1	—	—
				(SP 113.6%)	**8 Rn**	

2m 2.4 (13.40) CSF £9.25 TOTE £5.10: £1.90 £1.10 £2.60 (£3.20) OWNER Richard Green (Fine Paintings) (WELLINGTON) BRED Michael Poland

WEIGHT FOR AGE 3yo-6lb

OFFICIAL EXPLANATION Spanish Stripper (USA): gurgled.

3462* Brighstone, who showed a poor attitude when runner-up over hurdles last time, was allowed to dictate his own pace. Revelling in the ground, he never looked like being challenged. (5/1)

3822 High Premium again made it hard work for his rider. Persisting in hanging left, he was never doing anything like enough to get in a blow with the winner. (Evens)

3630 Nobby Barnes ran really well, considering he would have been in receipt of 38lb from the winner in a handicap. (20/1)

South China Sea, who showed a pronounced knee action going down, seemed to run out of stamina in these testing conditions inside the last. (16/1)

Deadline Time (IRE), who finished lame on his final outing last year, was having his first outing for 357 days and ran as if it was badly needed. (6/1)

3973 BEST BUY PRODUCTS MAIDEN AUCTION STKS (2-Y.O) (Class F)
2-40 (2-42) **7f 202y** £6,524.00 (£1,952.00: £936.00: £428.00) Stalls: Low GOING: 0.87 sec per fur (S)

Form	Horse	Btn	Pos	SP	RR	SF
2996b[3]	**Evening World (FR)** (PFICole) **2-8-4** TQuinn(4) (tall: lw: trckd ldrs: led on bit 3f out: rdn wl clr over 1f out)	—	1	5/4[1]	100+	41
3701[2]	**French Connection** (JBerry) **2-8-10** KDarley(18) (lw: a chsng ldrs: kpt on fnl 2f: no ch w wnr)	14	2	10/1	78	19
3818[6]	**Forgotten Star (IRE)** (RFJohnsonHoughton) **2-7-13** TWilliams(6) (chsd ldrs: rdn over 4f out: sn wl outpcd: styd on appr fnl f)	1½	3	12/1	64	5
	Flight For Freedom (JRFanshawe) **2-8-2** TSprake(5) (unf: scope: hld up: hdwy over 4f out: styd on fnl 2f)	½	4	10/1	66+	7
3818[2]	**Thelonius (IRE)** (JGSmyth-Osbourne) **2-8-5**(5) RMullen(19) (mid div: hdwy to chal 3f out: edgd lft: hrd rdn & wknd over 1f out)	1½	5	11/2[2]	71	12
3869[3]	**Lord of Love (67)** (TDEasterby) **2-8-7** KFallon(7) (lw: mid div: hdwy u.p 3f out: no imp)	s.h	6	9/1	68	9
	Adeste Fideles (MBell) **2-8-5** MFenton(17) (w'like: b.off hind: s.s: bhd tl hdwy 2f out: kpt on: nvr nr ldrs)	nk	7	10/1	65	6
3818[8]	**Yanshan** (BobJones) **2-8-7** NDay(3) (bhd tl styd on fnl 2f)	nk	8	25/1	66	7
3260[6]	**Watkins (66)** (FMurphy) **2-8-7** JFanning(20) (b.hind: chsd ldrs: ev ch over 2f out: wknd over 1f out)	5	9	20/1	56	—
3574[11]	**Maiella** (RHannon) **2-8-2** MRoberts(9) (chsd ldrs: drvn along over 3f out: wknd 2f out)	¾	10	10/1	50	—
	Major Ballaby (IRE) (MrsSABramall,Ireland) **2-8-3**(3)ow2 GParkin(10) (hdwy u.p over 3f out: sn chsng ldrs: wknd 2f out)	1¼	11	33/1	51	—
3103[11]	**Western Lord** (CSmith) **2-8-7** JTate(1) (hld up: sme hdwy over 3f out: sn wknd)	4	12	50/1	44	—
2383[7]	**Just Nobby** (NTinkler) **2-8-4** KimTinkler(12) (sn chsng ldrs: lost pl 3f out)	3½	13	33/1	34	—
3819[5]	**General Klaire** (BAMcMahon) **2-8-5** RCochrane(11) (swtg: chsd ldrs tl wknd over 2f out: eased)	nk	14	8/1[3]	34	—
3760[7]	**Count Keni** (JMJefferson) **2-8-7** LCharnock(2) (hld up: hdwy to chse ldrs over 4f out: wknd 3f out)	1½	15	50/1	33	—
3306[16]	**Repose (IRE)** (GROldroyd) **2-7-13** GBardwell(16) (led to 3f out: sn wknd)	14	16	33/1	—	—
3260[5]	**Saintes** (WMcKeown) **2-8-10** JCarroll(15) (sn bhd & drvn along)	18	17	33/1	—	—
1997[14]	**Townville Cee Cee (60)** (JSWainwright) **2-8-2** RLappin(8) (sn bhd & pushed along)	3	18	33/1	—	—
				(SP 152.2%)	**18 Rn**	

1m 48.46 (11.46) CSF £16.71 TOTE £2.40: £1.40 £1.90 £5.20 (£6.40) Trio £61.80 OWNER Mr T. M. Hely-Hutchinson (WHATCOMBE) BRED Mossborough Stud Company Ltd

2996b Evening World (FR), who looked very fit, was having his first outing since finishing third in a newcomers' race in France sixty-four days earlier. Bought for 50,000gs at the Breeze-up Sale, he took a keen grip but, after hitting the front, his rider left nothing to chance. He is useful at least. (5/4: tchd evens)

3701 French Connection appreciated the testing ground and ran his best race so far. (10/1)

3818 Forgotten Star (IRE) was badly outpaced once in line for home. She was given a very hard ride to snatch third place near the line. (12/1)

Flight For Freedom, who showed plenty of knee action, ran a pleasing first race. (10/1)

3818 Thelonius (IRE) could not confirm Warwick placings with the third, and might be best at seven furlongs for the time being. (11/2)

3869 Lord of Love, under pressure a long way out, looked slow. (9/1)

Adeste Fideles, who showed a very poor action, recovered from a slow start to be staying on at the finish. (10/1: op 6/1)

Yanshan might have further improvement in him. He looks a real stayer. (25/1)

3819 General Klaire (8/1: op 14/1)

3974 BATLEYS CASH & CARRY H'CAP (0-90) (3-Y.O+) (Class C)
3-10 (3-12) **1m 5f 194y** £8,090.00 (£2,420.00: £1,160.00: £530.00) Stalls: Low GOING: 0.87 sec per fur (S)

Form	Horse	Btn	Pos	SP	RR	SF
3754[5]	**Forgie (IRE) (64)** (PCalver) **4-8-13** NDay(10) (hld up: hdwy over 4f out: led over 3f out: edgd rt & clr over 1f out: eased towards fin)	—	1	16/1	76	63

3705^{8} **Turgenev (IRE) (73)** (RBastiman) **8-9-8** DeanMcKeown(11) (trckd ldrs: chal over 3f out: kpt on one pce) 3½ **2**	5/1^{1}	81	68
3242^{8} **Opaque (67)** (WStorey) **5-9-2** JFortune(6) (hdwy 7f out: ev ch over 3f out: one pce fnl 2f)..........1½ **3**	11/1	73	60
3137^{5} **Midyan Blue (IRE) (63)** (JMPEustace) **7-8-12** JTate(13) (chsd ldrs: drvn along & wl outpcd 6f out: styd on wl fnl 2f)..........¾ **4**	12/1	68	55
3705^{10} **Foundry Lane (75)** (MrsMReveley) **6-9-10** ACulhane(14) (hld up: effrt over 4f out: styd on u.p fnl 2f)..........2½ **5**	10/1	78	65
3931* **Tarxien (65)** (KRBurke) **3-8-0**$^{(3)}$ DSweeney(4) (lw: trckd ldrs: effrt over 3f out: outpcd fnl 2f)..........1¾ **6**	8/1	66	42
3498^{4} **Badge of Fame (IRE) (85)** (LMCumani) **3-9-9** JReid(8) (lw: chsd ldrs: outpcd over 3f out: n.d after) 8 **7**	7/1^{3}	76	52
3815^{2} **Toi Toi (IRE) (75)** (DWPArbuthnot) **3-8-13v^{1}** TQuinn(15) (chsd ldrs: rdn 4f out: sn outpcd)..........2½ **8**	12/1	63	39
3319^{2} **St Lawrence (CAN) (77)** (CEBrittain) **3-9-1** MRoberts(9) (led 1f: drvn along 7f out: lost pl over 3f out: eased)..........2½ **9**	16/1	63	39
3377* **Idrica (84)** (JHMGosden) **3-9-8** GHind(7) (led after 1f to 11f out: lost pl over 3f out)..........1½ **10**	15/2	68	44
2596^{7} **One For Baileys (82)** (MJohnston) **3-9-6** JWeaver(5) (chsd ldrs: led 11f out tl over 5f out: wknd over 3f out) 1¾ **11**	10/1	64	40
3010^{4} **Spy Knoll (81)** (MRStoute) **3-9-5v^{1}** KFallon(12) (hdwy 7f out: led over 5f out tl hdd & wknd over 3f out)..........9 **12**	15/2	52	28
3915^{10} **Paradise Navy (74)** (CREgerton) **8-9-4b**$^{(5)}$ AimeeCook(2) (s.i.s: racd far side: sn bhd: t.o 4f out)..........dist **13**	25/1	—	—
3805^{10} **Old Red (IRE) (66)** (MrsMReveley) **7-9-1** LCharnock(1) (racd far side: sn bhd: t.o 6f out)..........4 **14**	33/1	—	—
3648^{2} **Mithak (USA) (85)** (BWHills) **3-9-9v** RHills(3) (racd wd: lost pl over 8f out: t.o 6f out) 1½ **15**	6/1^{2}	—	—
	(SP 138.5%)	**15 Rn**	

3m 11.63 (18.03) CSF £97.65 CT £888.27 TOTE £49.80: £10.80 £2.00 £3.80 (£186.10) Trio £282.10 OWNER Mrs Janis MacPherson (RIPON) BRED Stilvi Compania Financiera And Roncon Ltd.
WEIGHT FOR AGE 3yo-11lb

3754 Forgie (IRE) found the testing conditions no problem and took this in most decisive fashion, much to the surprise of connections. (16/1)
3498* Turgenev (IRE), who had run so well when 10lb wrong at the weights in the Ebor, relished the ground and probably ran close to his best. (5/1)
2327 Opaque had the ground to his liking and put three modest efforts behind him. (11/1)
3137 Midyan Blue (IRE), who's hard to win with, usually runs well here. (12/1)
Foundry Lane had finished third in the Ebor two years ago from a 3lb higher mark. This outing should put him spot on. (10/1)
3931* Tarxien, having his second outing in two days, possibly did not last home in these testing conditions. (8/1)
3498 Badge of Fame (IRE) (7/1: op 9/2)

3975 10TH YEAR OF THE LAWRENCE BATLEY RATED STKS H'CAP (0-105) (3-Y.O+) (Class B)

3-40 (3-43) **6f** £17,527.00 (£6,493.00: £3,121.50: £1,282.50: £516.25: £209.75) Stalls: Low GOING: 0.87 sec per fur (S)

	SP	RR	SF
3604^{9} **Double Action (90)** (TDEasterby) **3-8-6** LCharnock(3) (lw: trckd ldrs: shkn up to ld over 1f out: r.o strly) ....— **1**	6/1^{2}	110	62
2560^{6} **Return of Amin (89)** (JDBethell) **3-8-2**$^{(3)}$ PFessey(7) (s.i.s: hdwy over 2f out: kpt on wl fnl f: no ch w wnr).......8 **2**	10/1	88	40
3709^{3} **Prince Dome (IRE) (89)** (MartynWane) **3-8-2**$^{(3)}$ AWhelan(2) (a chsng ldrs: kpt on same pce fnl 2f)..........nk **3**	12/1	87	39
3649^{12} **The Gay Fox (89)** (BAMcMahon) **3-7-12**$^{(7)}$ SRighton(5) (led: hdd over 1f out: edgd lft: kpt on) ....nk **4**	25/1	86	38
2598^{3} **Elfland (IRE) (89)** (LadyHerries) **6-8-7** RCochrane(10) (swtg: hld up: hdwy over 2f out: styd on same pce appr fnl f) ....nk **5**	4/1^{1}	85	39
3436^{3} **Jeffrey Anotherred (89)** (KMcAuliffe) **3-8-5v^{1}** TSprake(8) (lw: trckd ldrs gng wl: ev ch over 1f out: styd on same pce)..........½ **6**	12/1	84	36
2775^{7} **Double Splendour (IRE) (93)** (PSFelgate) **7-8-8**$^{(3)}$ DSweeney(4) (hld up: effrt over 2f out: nvr nr ldrs)..........¾ **7**	8/1^{3}	86	40
3764^{6} **Wildwood Flower (90)** (RHannon) **4-8-3**$^{(5)}$ CLowther(11) (drvn along & sme hdwy over 2f out: sn wknd).......13 **8**	14/1	48	2
3118^{3} **Astrac (IRE) (95)** (NTinkler) **6-8-13** KFallon(6) (sn outpcd: hdwy over 2f out: sn chsng ldrs: wknd over 1f out: eased) ....hd **9**	9/1	53	7
2861^{13} **The Puzzler (IRE) (100)** (BWHills) **6-9-4** MHills(15) (racd stands' side: swtchd lft over 2f out: sn bhd) ....½ **10**	10/1	57	11
3649^{13} **Young Bigwig (IRE) (89)** (JBerry) **3-8-5** JCarroll(9) (in tch: rdn & edgd lft over 2f out: sn wknd & eased) 12 **11**	25/1	14	—
3217^{9} **Triple Hay (94)** (RHannon) **3-8-10** JReid(14) (racd stands' side: swtchd lft over 2f out: sn bhd) 1 **12**	12/1	16	—
3604* **Tadeo (100)** (MJohnston) **4-9-4** DeanMcKeown(1) (w ldr tl wknd over 2f out) 2 **13**	6/1^{2}	17	—
3747^{5} **Jayannpee (97)** (IABalding) **6-8-12**$^{(3)}$ MartinDwyer(12) (racd stands' side: rdn & lost pl ½-wy: sn bhd)..........8 **14**	10/1	—	—
2861^{7} **Za-Im (105)** (BWHills) **3-9-7** RHills(13) (racd stands' side: bhd fr ½-wy) 1¼ **15**	10/1	—	—
	(SP 143.5%)	**15 Rn**	

1m 17.69 (7.19) CSF £70.76 CT £678.07 TOTE £12.60: £3.60 £3.70 £5.90 (£48.20) Trio £1,340.80; £226.62 to York 4/9/97 OWNER Mr C. H. Stevens (MALTON) BRED Whitsbury Manor Stud
LONG HANDICAP The Gay Fox 7-13 Jeffrey Anotherred 8-1 Young Bigwig (IRE) 8-3 Return of Amin 7-13
WEIGHT FOR AGE 3yo-2lb

3604 Double Action was just 4lb higher than when he won in convincing fashion at Ripon five outings ago. With the ground to suit him, he took this in devastating fashion and, despite the penalty, must have an excellent chance in the Ayr Gold Cup provided the going is on the soft side and he has luck in the draw. His dam won that big prize in 1990. (6/1)
2560 Return of Amin, from 6lb out of the handicap, excelled himself and should have a sound chance in the Silver Cup at Ayr. (10/1)
3709 Prince Dome (IRE) ran really well considering he was 9lb higher in the weights than when he won at Ascot four outings ago. (12/1)
2655* The Gay Fox, from 6lb out of the handicap, showed bags of toe but gave his inexperienced rider problems. (25/1)
2598 Elfland (IRE), in good heart after an absence of fifty-five days, is probably better suited by seven. (4/1)
3436 Jeffrey Anotherred, who has slipped down the weights, traveled strongly in a visor for the first time. Soft ground is not a problem and he too is better over seven. (12/1)
2326 Double Splendour (IRE), on ground possibly too soft for him, gave connections hope. (8/1)
3118 Astrac (IRE) ran by no means badly and is no forlorn hope this back-end. (9/1)
The Puzzler (IRE) was one of four to race on the unfavoured stands' side. (10/1: 9/1-14/1)

3976 BATLEYS PET FOOD CASH & CARRY H'CAP (0-80) (3-Y.O+) (Class D)

4-10 (4-13) **7f 202y** £7,460.00 (£2,240.00: £1,080.00: £500.00) Stalls: Low GOING: 0.87 sec per fur (S)

	SP	RR	SF
3496^{4} **Therhea (IRE) (76)** (BRMillman) **4-9-9**$^{(3)}$ AWhelan(6) (lw: chsd ldrs: led over 2f out: edgd rt: styd on u.p)......— **1**	13/2^{1}	87	58
3759^{13} **Night of Glass (58)** (JLEyre) **4-8-8v** MGallagher(17) (b: hdwy u.p over 3f out: wnt 2nd appr fnl f: kpt on wl) 1 **2**	20/1	67	38
3801^{2} **For Your Eyes Only (79)** (TDEasterby) **3-9-3b**$^{(7)}$ RWinston(22) (lw: a chsng ldrs: ev ch over 2f out: styd on same pce) 1½ **3**	15/2^{2}	85	51
3572* **Begorrat (IRE) (71)** (DMoffatt) **3-8-13b**$^{(3)}$ DarrenMoffatt(20) (a chsng ldrs: one pce fnl 3f) 4 **4**	20/1	69	35
3262^{7} **Denton Lad (60)** (WTKemp) **3-8-5** JCarroll(13) (a chsng ldrs: ev ch over 2f out: one pce)..........nk **5**	33/1	57	23
3403^{5} **Superpride (54)** (MrsMReveley) **5-8-4b** DaleGibson(8) (led: clr over 3f out: edgd rt & hdd over 2f out: grad wknd)..........1½ **6**	25/1	48	19

Form	Horse	Dist	Pos	SP	RR	SF
3542[5]	**Sandbaggedagain (72)** (MWEasterby) **3-9-0**(3) GParkin(11) (sn pushed along: hdwy to chse ldrs over 3f out: no imp)	4	**7**	14/1	58	24
3906[5]	**Karinska (60)** (MCChapman) **7-8-3**(7) SCarson(23) (s.s: bhd: sme hdwy over 2f out: nvr nr ldrs)	6	**8**	16/1	34	5
3901[12]	**Jedi Knight (69)** (MWEasterby) **3-9-0** LCharnock(9) (lw: chsd ldrs tl wknd over 1f out: eased)	hd	**9**	14/1	43	9
3810[2]	**Pride of Pendle (76)** (MartynWane) **8-9-12** MRoberts(18) (hld up: stdy hdwy over 3f out: eased whn no ch fnl 2f)	3	**10**	8/1[3]	44	15
2508[4]	**Phonetic (74)** (GBBalding) **4-9-10** TSprake(19) (lw: s.i.s: bhd: sme hdwy over 2f out: n.d)	½	**11**	12/1	41	12
3548[12]	**Hisar (IRE) (70)** (CPEBrooks) **4-9-6** MHills(2) (bhd: stdy hdwy 2f out: nvr nr to chal)	2	**12**	16/1	33	4
3810[4]	**Duraid (IRE) (76)** (DenysSmith) **5-9-7**(5) CLowther(14) (lw: hld up: effrt over 3f out: edgd lft: sn wknd)	hd	**13**	12/1	39	10
3150[18]	**Artful Dane (IRE) (78)** (MJHeaton-Ellis) **5-10-0v** JReid(12) (chsd ldrs: ev ch & rdn over 2f out: sn wknd)	1¼	**14**	16/1	38	9
2691[9]	**Praeditus (78)** (RHannon) **3-9-9** TQuinn(7) (bhd: sme hdwy over 2f out: sn wknd)	5	**15**	20/1	28	—
3542[3]	**Monte Cavo (58)** (MBrittain) **6-8-8** GBardwell(5) (lw: in tch: effrt over 3f out: sn wknd & eased)	3½	**16**	12/1	1	—
3777*	**Cashmere Lady (77)** (JLEyre) **5-9-13** OPears(16) (lw: sn bhd: eased whn no ch 3f out)	12	**17**	8/1[3]	—	—
2945[9]	**Trading Aces (72)** (MBell) **3-8-12v**(5) RMullen(3) (b.hind: bhd & drvn along 4f out)	nk	**18**	20/1	—	—
3262[8]	**Suez Tornado (IRE) (71)** (EJAlston) **4-9-7v** KFallon(10) (mid div: sme hdwy over 3f out: sn rdn & wknd)	3	**19**	8/1[3]	—	—
3018[3]	**Sualtach (IRE) (73)** (RHollinshead) **4-9-9** KDarley(21) (lw: chsd ldr tl wknd 3f out)	14	**20**	11/1	—	—
3584[10]	**Jibereen (60)** (PHowling) **5-8-10** RCochrane(4) (sn bhd & drvn along: virtually p.u)	18	**21**	12/1	—	—
3855*	**Needle Match (61)** (JJO'Neill) **4-8-11** 5x JFortune(1) (a bhd: virtually p.u)	dist	**22**	12/1	—	—

(SP 162.0%) **22 Rn**

1m 48.85 (11.85) CSF £146.81 CT £997.77 TOTE £6.60: £1.80 £5.10 £2.20 £7.50 (£91.70) Trio £493.60 OWNER Ray Gudge, Colin Lew Calvert (CULLOMPTON) BRED Mrs W. Hanson

WEIGHT FOR AGE 3yo-5lb

3496 Therhea (IRE), a confirmed soft-ground specialist, showed himself to be better than ever. He will be worth keeping on the right side this back-end. (13/2)

3105 Night of Glass did not go down without a struggle. (20/1)

3801 For Your Eyes Only is running better since the blinkers were fitted and he might be worth a try from the front. (15/2)

3572* Begorrat (IRE) acquitted himself well, considering this was an appreciable step up in class. (20/1)

845* Denton Lad, who seems suited by a mile nowadays, ran his best race since changing stables. (33/1)

3403 Superpride showed his rivals a clean pair of heels and kept going surprisingly well. Sweating and taken to post early, he is his own worst enemy. (25/1)

3457* Jedi Knight (14/1: 10/1-16/1)

3810 Pride of Pendle, who does not want the ground as soft as this, was by no means knocked about and is worth bearing in mind, especially at Doncaster and Ayr. (8/1)

Hisar (IRE), a headstrong hurdler, has come down 10lb in the weights after two runs. He was certainly ridden with an eye to the future here. (16/1)

3977 MAYFIELD BITTER & LAGER MAIDEN STKS (3-Y.O) (Class D)

4-40 (4-41) **1m 2f 85y** £6,004.00 (£1,792.00: £856.00: £388.00) Stalls: Low GOING: 0.87 sec per fur (S)

Form	Horse	Dist	Pos	SP	RR	SF
3803[2]	**Delilah (IRE) (87)** (MRStoute) **3-8-9v** JReid(7) (trckd ldrs gng wl: led on bit ins fnl f: v.easily)	—	**1**	5/4[1]	94+	37
2311[3]	**Shadiann (IRE)** (LMCumani) **3-9-0** KDarley(8) (trckd ldrs: rdn to ld over 3f out: hdd ins fnl f: no ch w wnr)	8	**2**	5/1[3]	87	30
	Bel Canto (IRE) (JHMGosden) **3-9-0** AGarth(4) (w'like: bit bkwd: hld up: effrt over 4f out: sn drvn along & outpcd: styd on appr fnl f)	5	**3**	14/1	79	22
2566[6]	**Midnight Watch (USA)** (HRACecil) **3-9-0** KFallon(6) (led tl over 4f out: one pce)	4	**4**	9/2[2]	73	16
3632[4]	**Sabadilla (USA)** (JHMGosden) **3-9-0** GHind(1) (dwlt: hld up: shkn up & hdwy over 4f out: sn outpcd: hdwy to jn ldrs over 2f out: wknd fnl f: eased nr fin)	¾	**5**	9/2[2]	72	15
3738[3]	**Majesty (IRE)** (PFICole) **3-9-0** TQuinn(3) (lw: b.hind: racd far side: sn w ldr: wknd 2f out: eased)	27	**6**	10/1	30	—
3738[4]	**Lighten Up** (CEBrittain) **3-8-9** MRoberts(5) (trckd ldrs: shkn up to ld over 4f out: hung lft & hdd over 3f out: wknd over 2f out: eased)	26	**7**	20/1	—	—
3014[7]	**Moran** (RFJohnsonHoughton) **3-9-0** RCochrane(10) (bolted gng to s: stdd s: sme hdwy over 5f out: sn wknd)	3½	**8**	33/1	—	—
	Taborite (USA) (EJAlston) **3-9-0** ACulhane(9) (wl grwn: unruly in stalls: s.s: sn wl bhd: t.o 4f out)	6	**9**	50/1	—	—
3691[8]	**Van Chino (55)** (BAMcMahon) **3-9-0** JFortune(2) (lw: hld up: effrt over 3f out: sn wknd: eased fnl 2f)	2	**10**	50/1	—	—

(SP 124.9%) **10 Rn**

2m 25.31 (16.31) CSF £7.62 TOTE £2.10: £1.10 £1.70 £3.80 (£5.10) Trio £58.60 OWNER Highclere Thoroughbred Racing Ltd (NEWMARKET) BRED Tullamaine Castle Stud

3803 Delilah (IRE), who shows plenty of knee action, found this testing ground no problem. Never out of third gear, she won this very easily indeed and it can have done her confidence nothing but good. (5/4)

2311 Shadiann (IRE) finished clear second best but, in truth, there was not a second. (5/1: 3/1-11/2)

Bel Canto (IRE), bred in the purple, showed a poor action going down. In need of the outing on his belated debut, after getting outpaced he stayed on in pleasing fashion. (14/1: 10/1-16/1)

2566 Midnight Watch (USA) looks very ordinary and seemed painfully one-paced. (9/2: 3/1-5/1)

3632 Sabadilla (USA), who took a keen grip going down, seemed to improve slightly on his first effort but, if this is the best he can do, he is only moderate. (9/2)

3738 Majesty (IRE) surprisingly opted to race on the slower ground on the inner. (10/1)

3978 KNIGHTSBRIDGE GIN MAIDEN STKS (2-Y.O) (Class D)

5-10 (5-12) **6f 214y** £6,212.00 (£1,856.00: £888.00: £404.00) Stalls: High GOING: 0.87 sec per fur (S)

Form	Horse	Dist	Pos	SP	RR	SF
	Absolutly Sparklin (LMCumani) **2-9-0** KDarley(6) (leggy: scope: lw: led over 5f out: drvn along & r.o strly fnl f)	—	**1**	12/1	92+	32
3806[3]	**Equity Princess** (MJohnston) **2-8-9** JWeaver(4) (hdwy ½-wy: sn chsng ldrs: nt qckn appr fnl f)	4	**2**	11/4[2]	78	18
3013[W]	**Bering Gifts (IRE)** (PFICole) **2-9-0** TQuinn(1) (gd sort: str: lw: led over 1f: rdn over 2f out: wknd over 1f out)	5	**3**	5/4[1]	71	11
	Jayir (IRE) (ACStewart) **2-9-0** RHills(5) (gd sort: cmpt: dwlt: plld hrd: sn w ldrs: n.m.r over 2f out: swtchd & sn wknd)	9	**4**	7/1	51	—
	Highwayman (IRE) (MRStoute) **2-9-0** JReid(2) (w'like: scope: unruly s: trckd ldrs: outpcd ½-wy: wknd over 2f out)	4	**5**	9/2[3]	42	—
	Fear Not (IRE) (MBell) **2-8-9** MFenton(3) (w'like: scope: bit bkwd: sn chsng ldrs: drvn along ½-wy: sn lost pl)	5	**6**	12/1	25	—

(SP 117.2%) **6 Rn**

1m 34.55 (11.55) CSF £42.82 TOTE £10.40: £2.50 £1.60 (£14.30) OWNER Mr M. J. Dawson (NEWMARKET) BRED Worksop Manor Stud Farm

Absolutly Sparklin, who took the eye in the paddock, showed plenty of knee action going down. He took this in really good style and is clearly at least useful. (12/1: op 7/1)
3806 Equity Princess, very edgy in the paddock, struggled slightly to go the pace and, in the end, though clearly second best, she proved no match for the winner. (11/4)
Bering Gifts (IRE), who had to be withdrawn on his intended debut at Ascot, was put into the stalls early and did nothing wrong. Flat out soon after halfway, in this ground he dropped right away coming to the final furlong. He has a big reputation and ought to be able to do much better on a more suitable surface. (5/4: op evens)
Jayir (IRE), noisy in the paddock, would not settle after missing the start. Trapped on the inner, he had to be switched with over two furlongs left to run but soon dropped right away. (7/1)
Highwayman (IRE), who showed a pronounced knee action going down, gave problems at the start. He ran as if badly in need of this initial outing. (9/2: op 3/1)
Fear Not (IRE), who looked in need of the outing, showed a very poor action going down. (12/1: op 7/1)

T/Jkpt: Not won; £10,702.01 to York 4/9/97. T/Plpt: £119.30 (309.2 Tckts). T/Qdpt: £119.70 (12.22 Tckts) WG

3710-SALISBURY (R-H) (Good to soft)
Thursday September 4th
Race 2: hand-timed. Race 4 flip start
WEATHER: fine but cloudy WIND: almost nil

3979 E.B.F. QUIDHAMPTON MAIDEN STKS (I) (2-Y.O F) (Class D)
2-20 (2-22) **6f 212y** £3,213.50 (£968.00: £469.00: £219.50) Stalls: High GOING minus 0.10 sec per fur (G)

				SP	RR	SF
	Flawless (SirMarkPrescott) **2-8-11** GDuffield(11) (w'like: a.p: led over 3f out tl over 1f out: led ins fnl f: r.o wl)	—	**1**	12/1	79+	21
	Millitrix (MRStoute) **2-8-11** DHolland(14) (unf: b.hind: hld up: hdwy over 3f out: led over 1f out tl ins fnl f)	1	**2**	12/1	77+	19
3638[5]	**Cantonese (USA)** (RCharlton) **2-8-11** PaulEddery(12) (lw: plld hrd: a.p: rdn over 1f out: one pce)	4	**3**	16/1	68	10
	Savoury (JLDunlop) **2-8-11** MJKinane(16) (w'like: bkwd: s.s: hdwy fnl f: nvr nrr)	nk	**4**	10/1[3]	67	9
2831[4]	**Quiz Show** (RHannon) **2-8-11** DaneO'Neill(13) (led over 3f: wknd over 1f out)	1¾	**5**	10/1[3]	63	5
3114[3]	**Yanabi (USA)** (PTWalwyn) **2-8-11** RHills(6) (lw: prom stands' side: led over 1f out: no ch w wnr)	nk	**6**	6/5[1]	62	4
3574[9]	**Amabel (USA)** (IABalding) **2-8-11** JQuinn(7) (led stands' side over 5f: one pce)	hd	**7**	16/1	62	4
	Poly Blue (IRE) (MissGayKelleway) **2-8-8**(3) DO'Donohoe(9) (unf: prom stands' side over 4f)	6	**8**	25/1	48	—
	World of Joy (RCharlton) **2-8-11** TSprake(15) (w'like: scope: bit bkwd: prom: rdn over 3f out: wknd over 2f out)	6	**9**	8/1[2]	34	—
3574[16]	**Loubin Lane** (AGNewcombe) **2-8-11** SDrowne(3) (racd stands' side: rdn over 4f out: sn bhd)	hd	**10**	50/1	34	—
	Nocturne (IRE) (JWHills) **2-8-11** AClark(2) (unf: bit bkwd: racd stands' side: a bhd)	½	**11**	20/1	33	—
3613[7]	**Be My Girl** (CFWall) **2-8-11** AMcGlone(1) (racd stands' side: a bhd)	2	**12**	50/1	28	—
	Paradise Soul (USA) (DRLoder) **2-8-11** GCarter(4) (neat: racd stands' side: a bhd)	hd	**13**	14/1	28	—
3769[4]	**Star of The Course (USA)** (PFICole) **2-8-11** OPeslier(10) (prom stands' side over 3f)	6	**14**	14/1	14	—
				(SP 127.8%)	**14 Rn**	

1m 31.8 (5.80) CSF £138.76 TOTE £11.70: £4.30 £3.40 £2.80 (£64.10) Trio £157.00 OWNER Cheveley Park Stud (NEWMARKET) BRED Cheveley Park Stud Ltd
IN-FOCUS: **In the only race where the runners split into two groups, five of the six runners to race on the far side filled the first five places.**
Flawless, a half-sister to Cultured and Seek the Pearl, is out of a mare who won over a mile in France. With the distinct advantage of racing on the far side, she certainly displayed the right sort of attitude. (12/1)
Millitrix, a half-sister to a six-furlong winner in Sweden, is out of a winning miler. She came to win her race, but the winner proved too persistent. (12/1: op 7/1)
3638 Cantonese (USA) is a sister to Easy Listening and a half-sister to Private Song, both of whom won over a mile and a quarter. She gave the impression she would have been suited by further. (16/1)
Savoury, a half-sister to the staying maiden Philosophic, is out of a ten-furlong winner in France, and shaped as though stamina will be her forte. (10/1)
2831 Quiz Show, a half-sister to that good sprinter Mind Games, was stepping up from the minimum distance on slower ground. (10/1)
3114 Yanabi (USA) was the first home on the slower stands' side, and deserves another chance. (6/5)
Amabel (USA), appreciating this longer trip, showed a marked improvement on her debut, and put up a brave effort to finish only just behind the favourite on the unfavoured stands' side. (16/1)
World of Joy (8/1: op 4/1)

3980 WINTERBOURNE H'CAP (0-65) (3-Y.O+) (Class F)
2-50 (2-52) **1m** £2,794.00 (£784.00: £382.00) Stalls: High GOING minus 0.10 sec per fur (G)

				SP	RR	SF
2835[13]	**Dulcinea (65)** (IABalding) **3-9-6**(3) MartinDwyer(11) (a.p: led over 1f out: rdn out)	—	**1**	10/1	74	34
3793[13]	**Zermatt (IRE) (58)** (MDIUsher) **7-9-7** GDuffield(10) (lw: chsd ldr: led wl over 1f out: sn hdd: r.o)	1	**2**	20/1	65	30
3548[8]	**Serendipity (FR) (62)** (BRMillman) **4-9-11** TSprake(2) (hld up & bhd: gd hdwy over 1f out: fin wl)	hd	**3**	20/1	69	34
	Prenonamoss (54) (DWPArbuthnot) **9-9-3** DHolland(6) (hdwy 2f out: r.o ins fnl f)	½	**4**	25/1	60	25
3849[2]	**Clouds Hill (FR) (54)** (RHannon) **4-9-3v** DaneO'Neill(17) (hld up: hdwy over 1f out: r.o one pce fnl f)	¾	**5**	7/1[2]	58	23
3787[2]	**Sis Garden (60)** (JCullinan) **4-9-6**(3) DO'Donohoe(18) (hld up: hdwy 3f out: n.m.r 2f out: one pce)	2½	**6**	10/1	59	24
3496[5]	**Ca'd'oro (58)** (GBBalding) **4-9-7** SDrowne(9) (hld up mid div: rdn over 2f out: no hdwy)	2	**7**	4/1[1]	53	18
2552[3]	**Chasetown Flyer (USA) (61)** (NEBerry) **3-9-5** RHills(12) (lw: trckd ldrs: swtchd lft 2f out: no hdwy)	1¼	**8**	10/1	54	14
34[6]	**Explosive Power (58)** (GCBravery) **6-9-7** MRimmer(13) (led over 6f: sn wknd)	s.h	**9**	25/1	51	16
3018[5]	**Well Drawn (54)** (HCandy) **4-9-3** NAdams(8) (prom: rdn over 3f out: wknd 2f out)	4	**10**	20/1	39	4
3775[8]	**Hawksbill Henry (USA) (60)** (MrsAJPerrett) **3-9-4** GayeHarwood(15) (a bhd)	½	**11**	16/1	44	4
3609[5]	**Parsa (USA) (55)** (JLDunlop) **4-9-4** MJKinane(7) (tk keen hold: sn bhd)	½	**12**	10/1	38	3
3768[6]	**Confronter (57)** (SDow) **8-9-6** OPeslier(5) (hld up mid div: rdn over 2f out: wknd wl over 1f out)	1¼	**13**	9/1[3]	37	2
1484*	**Ivor's Deed (54)** (MissGayKelleway) **4-9-0**(3) AWhelan(16) (plld hrd: prom tl wknd over 1f out)	1	**14**	9/1[3]	32	—
2695[5]	**Sand Cay (USA) (62)** (RHannon) **3-8-13**(7) PDobbs(1) (a bhd)	hd	**15**	20/1	40	—
1680[7]	**Master M-E-N (IRE) (56)** (NMBabbage) **5-9-5v** VSlattery(4) (hld up: rdn over 2f out: sn bhd)	9	**16**	16/1	16	—

768[4] **Hever Golf Magic (IRE) (61)** (TJNaughton) **3-8-12**(7) RachaelMoody(3) (wl bhd fnl 4f: t.o)....10 **17** 16/1 1 —
(SP 133.3%) **17 Rn**

1m 46.5 (6.50) CSF £192.43 CT £3,701.28 TOTE £12.70: £2.70 £4.60 £2.30 £7.10 (£123.50) Trio £466.60; £407.53 to Haydock 5/9/97 OWNER Miss K. Rausing (KINGSCLERE) BRED Miss K. Rausing
WEIGHT FOR AGE 3yo-5lb

2695 Dulcinea, raised 4lb, acts on this sort of going, having suffered from sore shins in the past. (10/1)
2866 Zermatt (IRE), 8lb higher than when winning at Chepstow in July, was due to drop 3lb at the weekend. He is another who likes to get his toe in. (20/1)
2508 Serendipity (FR), who has dropped no less than 20lb this season, came from a long way back and it should be remembered that his only win to date was over ten furlongs. (20/1)
Prenonamoss, off the course for virtually two years, gave every indication that he is no back-number. (25/1)
3849 Clouds Hill (FR) may have preferred a sounder surface. (7/1)
3787 Sis Garden was probably not particularly unlucky, despite having little room at one point. (10/1)
3496 Ca'd'oro was 2lb above the highest mark off which he has won. (4/1)
1484* Ivor's Deed (9/1: op 6/1)

3981 DICK POOLE CONDITIONS STKS (2-Y.O F) (Class B)
3-20 (3-21) **6f** £6,410.00 (£2,260.00: £1,105.00: £475.00) Stalls: High GOING minus 0.10 sec per fur (G)

			SP	RR	SF
3740[4]	**Regal Revolution (95)** (PTWalwyn) **2-8-9** JLowe(5) (mde all: edgd lft 2f out: r.o wl) —	1	3/1 2	82	34
2371*	**Hoh Chi Min (92)** (MBell) **2-9-1** RHills(2) (a.p: nt clr run 2f out tl ins fnl f: r.o) 1¼	2	7/2 3	85	36
3187*	**Nanoushka (IRE)** (RHannon) **2-8-12** PaulEddery(4) (lw: hld up: hdwy over 2f out: ev ch wl over 1f out: sn rdn: one pce) 1¾	3	5/6 1	77	29
3636[10]	**Dancing Wolf (IRE)** (MissGayKelleway) **2-8-9** GDuffield(3) (plld hrd: sn chsng wnr: wknd wl over 1f out) 5	4	10/1	61	15

(SP 110.9%) **4 Rn**

1m 16.79 (3.79) CSF £11.91 TOTE £4.40 (£5.50) OWNER Mr S. W. E. J. Slack (LAMBOURN) BRED T. R. Lock
3740 Regal Revolution, aided by the runner-up getting boxed-in, now heads for the listed Firth of Clyde Stakes at Ayr's Western Meeting. (3/1)
2371* Hoh Chi Min again had give in the ground, but found that the winner was home and dry by the time she got in the clear. (7/2)
3187* Nanoushka (IRE) found disappointingly little when the chips were down, and the form of her Ascot win has not worked out. (5/6)
Dancing Wolf (IRE), a half-sister to Oaks third Mezzogiorno and Rainbow Top, ran much too freely to show her true worth. (10/1)

3982 E.B.F. LOCHSONG H'CAP (0-95) (3-Y.O+ F & M) (Class C)
3-50 (3-51) **6f 212y** £11,137.50 (£3,375.00: £1,650.00: £787.50) Stalls: High GOING minus 0.10 sec per fur (G)

			SP	RR	SF
3798[2]	**La Modiste (70)** (MissGayKelleway) **4-8-5**(3) DO'Donohoe(12) (a.p: led on bit wl over 1f out: sn clr: r.o wl) —	1	7/1 2	86	33
3771[8]	**Marjaana (IRE) (73)** (PTWalwyn) **4-8-11** DHolland(10) (a.p: rdn over 2f out: chsd wnr fnl f: no imp) 3	2	8/1 3	82	29
3423[3]	**Volley (IRE) (84)** (MajorDNChappell) **4-9-8** GCarter(9) (lw: s.s: gd hdwy over 1f out: r.o) 1¼	3	12/1	90	37
3649[11]	**Silca Key Silca (80)** (MRChannon) **3-8-7**(7) AEddery(4) (hld up & bhd: hdwy over 1f out: r.o ins fnl f) nk	4	25/1	86	29
3690[5]	**Misty Point (65)** (IABalding) **3-7-10**(3) MartinDwyer(2) (prom: rdn 3f out: one pce fnl 2f) ¾	5	10/1	69	12
3746*	**Kind of Light (71)** (RGuest) **4-8-6**(3) AWhelan(13) (bhd tl hdwy over 1f out: r.o ins fnl f) ½	6	12/1	74	21
3435[5]	**Comanche Companion (64)** (TJNaughton) **7-8-2**ow1 AMcGlone(14) (led over 5f: wknd fnl f) 1½	7	10/1	63	9
3584[13]	**Palo Blanco (75)** (GLMoore) **6-8-13** GDuffield(17) (plld hrd: no hdwy fnl 2f) nk	8	16/1	74	21
3217[10]	**Waypoint (90)** (RCharlton) **4-10-0** TSprake(7) (lw: plld hrd: a mid div) nk	9	7/1 2	88	35
3119[7]	**Sleepless (84)** (NAGraham) **3-9-4** OPeslier(8) (nvr nrr) 2½	10	8/1 3	76	19
1482[5]	**Ashby Hill (IRE) (67)** (RRowe) **6-8-5** AClark(11) (bit bkwd: plld hrd: prom tl wknd wl over 1f out) hd	11	16/1	59	6
3615[9]	**Out Line (68)** (MMadgwick) **5-8-6** DaneO'Neill(6) (a bhd) 2	12	20/1	55	2
3917[8]	**Hibernica (IRE) (68)** (GBBalding) **3-8-2**ow3 SDrowne(15) (prom: rdn over 3f out: wknd wl over 1f out) 1¾	13	33/1	51	—
2346[4]	**Sweet Wilhelmina (68)** (LordHuntingdon) **4-8-1**(5) AimeeCook(5) (plld hrd: w ldrs over 4f) 2	14	6/1 1	47	—
2390[3]	**Tea Party (USA) (64)** (KOCunningham-Brown) **4-8-2b**ow1 PaulEddery(1) (mid div tl wknd over 2f out) 5	15	14/1	31	—
2774[5]	**Bint Shihama (USA) (90)** (CEBrittain) **3-9-10** MJKinane(3) (a bhd: t.o) 11	16	16/1	32	—

(SP 130.9%) **16 Rn**

1m 29.99 (3.99) CSF £59.46 CT £629.34 TOTE £6.30: £1.70 £2.90 £2.50 £5.20 (£21.00) Trio £298.80 OWNER Mr John Purcell (WHITCOMBE) BRED G. R. Smith (Thriplow) Ltd
WEIGHT FOR AGE 3yo-4lb

3798 La Modiste, already set to go up 5lb in future handicaps, did this in fine style, and is being aimed at the final of the Rothmans series on Cesarewitch day. (7/1)
3476* Marjaana (IRE), 3lbs higher than when winning at Beverley, had raced over an inadequate five furlongs last time. (8/1)
3423 Volley (IRE) again lost ground at the start, but continues to put in some solid efforts. (12/1)
2925 Silca Key Silca, down 3lbs, was still 2lbs higher than when scoring at Lingfield in June. (25/1)
3690 Misty Point, being by Sharpo, should not have minded this easier surface. (10/1)
3746* Kind of Light, trying to defy a 6lb hike in the ratings, has scored off a 2lb higher mark. (12/1)
2346 Sweet Wilhelmina (6/1: 5/1-8/1)

3983 SALISBURY FESTIVAL CONDITIONS STKS (3-Y.O+) (Class C)
4-20 (4-21) **1m 6f** £5,006.80 (£1,750.80: £855.40: £367.00) GOING minus 0.10 sec per fur (G)

			SP	RR	SF
	Clerkenwell (USA) (106) (MRStoute) **4-9-4** MJKinane(3) (h.d.w: hld up: swtchd lft & hdwy over 1f out: led & carried lft ins fnl f: hdd last strides: fin 2nd, s.h: awrdd r) —	1	2/1 2	121+	29
3645[2]	**Samraan (USA) (114)** (JLDunlop) **4-9-4** GCarter(2) (lw: chsd ldr: led over 2f out: sn rdn: hdd & edgd lft ins fnl f: led last strides: fin 1st: disq: plcd 2nd) s.h	2	5/6 1	121	29
3191*	**Bahamian Sunshine (USA) (100)** (RAkehurst) **6-9-4** OPeslier(4) (swtg: led: rdn 3f out: hdd over 2f out: wknd over 1f out) 18	3	4/1 3	100	8
3714U	**Ginka (28)** (JWMullins) **6-8-13v** VSlattery(1) (nvr gng wl: t.o fnl 5f) dist	4	100/1	—	—

(SP 108.9%) **4 Rn**

3m 10.5 (11.80) CSF £3.74 TOTE £2.10 (£1.80) OWNER Sheikh Mohammed (NEWMARKET) BRED Camelot Thoroughbreds and Michael J. Ryan
Clerkenwell (USA), whose rider reported his mount got tired in the last half-furlong, was making a belated seasonal reappearance. He always seemed likely to get the race in the Stewards' room, and is being trained with the Melbourne Cup in mind. (2/1: op 3/1)

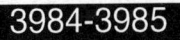

3645 Samraan (USA), who would have been conceding the winner 8lb in a handicap, lost the race after pushing the winner across the course, despite Carter having switched the whip to the correct hand. (5/6: 4/7-10/11)
3191* Bahamian Sunshine (USA) did not have things his own way in this company. (4/1)

3984 BLANDFORD H'CAP (0-80) (3-Y.O+) (Class D)

4-50 (4-53) **5f** £3,824.50 (£1,156.00: £563.00: £266.50) Stalls: High GOING minus 0.10 sec per fur (G)

Form	Horse	Dist	Pos	SP	RR	SF
3410^{5}	**Lord High Admiral (CAN) (75)** (MJHeaton-Ellis) **9-9-9** SDrowne(10) (mde all: clr 2f out: comf)	—	**1**	$6/1^{2}$	91+	73
3898^{7}	**Songsheet (67)** (MSSaunders) **4-8-12**(3) PPMurphy(17) (hld up: hdwy 2f out: chsd wnr fnl f: no imp)	3½	**2**	14/1	72	54
1089^{7}	**Nineacres (71)** (NMBabbage) **6-9-5v** AClark(20) (lw: a.p: rdn 2f out: one pce)	2	**3**	16/1	69	51
3852^{2}	**Village Native (FR) (52)** (KOCunningham-Brown) **4-7-11b**(3) MartinDwyer(15) (a.p: one pce fnl 2f)	¾	**4**	$13/2^{3}$	48	30
3771^{5}	**Silent Miracle (IRE) (69)** (MBell) **3-8-11**(5) GFaulkner(3) (hdwy 3f out: wknd over 1f out)	1¼	**5**	10/1	61	42
3500^{2}	**Heavenly Miss (IRE) (56)** (JJBridger) **3-8-3b** GDuffield(19) (sn rdn along: hdwy over 1f out: r.o one pce fnl f)	nk	**6**	8/1	47	28
3898^{6}	**Corniche Quest (IRE) (68)** (MRChannon) **4-8-9**(7) AEddery(11) (lw: nvr nrr)	1¼	**7**	11/1	55	37
3385^{5}	**Loving And Giving (79)** (HCandy) **3-9-12** GCarter(13) (nvr nr to chal)	s.h	**8**	10/1	66	47
3800^{7}	**Marengo (62)** (JAkehurst) **3-8-9** MTebbutt(2) (lw: nvr nr ldrs)	hd	**9**	25/1	49	30
3771^{11}	**Eastern Prophets (79)** (GLewis) **4-9-13b**^{1} PaulEddery(8) (prom over 3f)	1¾	**10**	20/1	60	42
3693^{13}	**Superbit (60)** (BAMcMahon) **5-8-8** AMcGlone(16) (chsd wnr tl wknd fnl f)	nk	**11**	16/1	40	22
3765^{20}	**Spender (79)** (PWHarris) **8-9-13** MJKinane(12) (lw: dwlt: a bhd)	2	**12**	16/1	53	35
3500^{12}	**Sharp Stock (52)** (RJHodges) **4-8-0v**^{1} AMackay(14) (prom over 3f)	hd	**13**	25/1	25	7
3460^{4}	**Bramble Bear (71)** (MBlanshard) **3-9-4** JQuinn(6) (a bhd)	¾	**14**	9/1	42	23
3334^{12}	**High Domain (IRE) (61)** (JLSpearing) **6-8-2**(7) ANicholls(1) (a bhd)	nk	**15**	11/1	31	13
3393*	**Supreme Thought (61)** (LGCottrell) **5-8-9** NCarlisle(9) (prom 2f)	1¼	**16**	$11/2^{1}$	27	9
	Lough Erne (77) (CFWall) **5-9-11** RHills(7) (hmpd s: a bhd)	5	**17**	16/1	27	9
				(SP 141.6%)	**17 Rn**	

61.5 secs (1.50) CSF £90.57 CT £1,264.24 TOTE £7.20: £2.00 £4.40 £3.60 £1.90 (£122.50) Trio £605.60 OWNER Elite Racing Club (WROUGHTON) BRED Windfields Farm
WEIGHT FOR AGE 3yo-1lb
3410 Lord High Admiral (CAN), who has dropped 15lb this season, likes to dominate and was able do so on this occasion, turning the race into a procession. (6/1)
3693 Songsheet, set to go down 2lbs on Saturday, found the winner calling the tune. (14/1)
1089 Nineacres, raised 7lbs after finishing a close fourth in a conditions event behind Tomba at Haydock, is consequently a stone above the highest mark off which he has won. (16/1)
3852 Village Native (FR) was trying to beat the Handicapper, being due to go up 4lbs at the weekend. (13/2)
3771 Silent Miracle (IRE) could not take advantage of a 2lb drop in the weights. (10/1)
3500 Heavenly Miss (IRE) had been raised 4lb for a narrow defeat last time. (8/1)
2497 High Domain (IRE) (11/1: 8/1-12/1)

3985 E.B.F. QUIDHAMPTON MAIDEN STKS (II) (2-Y.O F) (Class D)

5-20 (5-21) **6f 212y** £3,213.50 (£968.00: £469.00: £219.50) Stalls: High GOING minus 0.10 sec per fur (G)

Form	Horse	Dist	Pos	SP	RR	SF
	Blue Gentian (USA) (RCharlton) **2-8-11** MJKinane(8) (unf: scope: lw: plld hrd early: hdwy over 2f out: led over 1f out: r.o wl)	—	**1**	$2/1^{1}$	80+	31
	Red Rabbit (BWHills) **2-8-11** DHolland(6) (unf: bit bkwd: hld up & bhd: plld out 3f out: gd hdwy over 1f out: nt rch wnr)	2	**2**	9/1	75+	26
	Nebl (MajorWRHern) **2-8-11** RHills(11) (w'like: bit bkwd: a.p: ev ch over 1f out: one pce)	3½	**3**	$4/1^{2}$	67	18
3114^{8}	**Special Treat** (DRLoder) **2-8-11** GCarter(13) (led over 4f out: hung lft 2f out: hdd over 1f out: one pce)	1¾	**4**	14/1	63	14
	Sahara (PFICole) **2-8-11** GDuffield(2) (lt-f: a.p: one pce fnl 2f)	nk	**5**	$8/1^{3}$	63	14
	Akarita (IRE) (BAMcMahon) **2-8-11** AMackay(10) (w'like: bit bkwd: hdwy over 2f out: one pce fnl f)	4	**6**	20/1	54	5
2943^{7}	**Memphis Dancer** (JWHills) **2-8-11** AClark(14) (bit bkwd: nvr nrr)	1¾	**7**	16/1	49	—
3547^{12}	**Sweet Dreams** (JLDunlop) **2-8-11** MRimmer(9) (bhd fnl 2f)	¾	**8**	12/1	48	—
	Tiye (RHannon) **2-8-11** DaneO'Neill(5) (unf: nrst fin)	hd	**9**	12/1	48	—
3788^{4}	**Spirit of The Nile (FR)** (PFICole) **2-8-4**(7) CharlotteCox(15) (a bhd)	6	**10**	12/1	34	—
3806^{10}	**Caraway** (RCharlton) **2-8-11** TSprake(4) (lw: prom over 4f)	1¼	**11**	12/1	31	—
3687^{10}	**Miss Dillettante** (RFJohnsonHoughton) **2-8-11** PaulEddery(1) (led over 2f: wknd over 2f out)	hd	**12**	33/1	31	—
3099^{2}	**Theme Tune** (DrJDScargill) **2-8-11** JQuinn(12) (a bhd)	6	**13**	20/1	17	—
2917^{20}	**Mrs Pickles** (MDIUsher) **2-8-11** JMarshall(3) (bhd fnl 3f)	2	**14**	50/1	12	—
3638^{12}	**Miss Chief Maker** (WRMuir) **2-8-8**(3) MartinDwyer(7) (prom: rdn & wknd qckly over 3f out: t.o)	25	**15**	50/1	—	—
				(SP 134.1%)	**15 Rn**	

1m 30.82 (4.82) CSF £20.24 TOTE £3.80: £2.10 £2.50 £2.30 (£27.20) Trio £40.20 OWNER Mr K. Abdulla (BECKHAMPTON) BRED Juddmonte Farms
Blue Gentian (USA), a half-sister to Sinecure, looks the type to progress. (2/1: op 5/1)
Red Rabbit, a half-sister to Papaha and Lovely Lyca, made a promising start to her career and should appreciate further. (9/1)
Nebl, a half-sister to six-furlong winner Mazeed, should come on for the outing. (4/1: 3/1-5/1)
Special Treat carried her head rather high, and did not help her chances by hanging. (14/1: op 8/1)
Sahara is a full-sister to mile winner Mokuti, and a half-sister to Group One winner Polar Falcon. (8/1: op 4/1)
Akarita (IRE) is a half-sister to Group Two winner Safawan, and Sadapour. (20/1)
Tiye (12/1: op 6/1)
3788 Spirit of The Nile (FR) (12/1: op 6/1)
3806 Caraway (12/1: op 8/1)

T/Plpt: £17,985.40 (0.7 Tckts); £7,391.27 to Haydock 5/9/97. T/Qdpt: £144.80 (9.72 Tckts) KH

3972-YORK (L-H) (Soft, Heavy patches)
Thursday September 4th
Race 3: hand timed
WEATHER: overcast WIND: fresh across

3986 YORKSHIRE-TYNE TEES TELEVISION MAIDEN STKS (2-Y.O) (Class D)
2-10 (2-11) **6f** £6,212.00 (£1,856.00: £888.00: £404.00) Stalls: Low GOING: 0.79 sec per fur (S)

				SP	RR	SF
3598[7]	**Gurkha** (RHannon) **2-9-0** MRoberts(6) (cl up: led ½-wy: pushed along & styd on strly)	—	1	11/2	91	41
2370[7]	**Wolfhunt** (PJMakin) **2-9-0** SSanders(3) (chsd ldrs: effrt & kpt on one pce fnl 2½f)	9	2	9/1	67	17
3743[6]	**Torrent** (PFICole) **2-9-0** TQuinn(4) (lw: plld hrd: trckd ldrs: effrt over 2f out: nt qckn)	2	3	3/1[1]	62	12
3541[6]	**Priolette (IRE)** (JGFitzGerald) **2-8-9** KFallon(7) (s.s: effrt ½-wy: styd on u.p: no imp)	1	4	25/1	54	4
	Persiano (JRFanshawe) **2-9-0** NDay(8) (lengthy: prom: rdn over 2f out: no imp)	5	5	12/1	46	—
3103[6]	**Murmoon** (BHanbury) **2-9-0** WRyan(10) (prom: effrt over 2f out: sn btn)	2½	6	7/2[2]	39	—
3806[14]	**Allmaites** (DNicholls) **2-8-9**(5) IonaWands(1) (led to ½-wy: sn wknd)	2½	7	25/1	32	—
	Alrabyah (IRE) (PTWalwyn) **2-9-0** KDarley(5) (w'like: scope: lw: unruly in stalls & dwlt: sn rcvrd & trckd ldrs: wknd qckly ½-wy: t.o)	23	8	4/1[3]	—	—

(SP 108.0%) **8 Rn**

1m 19.24 (8.74) CSF £43.03 TOTE £6.60: £1.70 £3.10 £1.30 (£19.30) Trio £23.20 OWNER Mr Robert Russell (MARLBOROUGH) BRED Darley Stud Management Co Ltd

3598 Gurkha took the eye in the paddock with a purposeful walk and revelled in these testing conditions, winning in tremendous style. (11/2)
Wolfhunt, returning after over two months off, ran quite well but had no chance at all with the winner. (9/1)
3743 Torrent took a strong hold to post and raced very freely on the way back. He again failed to get home and must learn to settle. (3/1: op 2/1)
Priolette (IRE) fell out of the traps and does not do anything quickly but she does seem to stay. (25/1)
Persiano walks well but his action going to post left something to be desired and he was always struggling in these testing conditions. (12/1: op 8/1)
3103 Murmoon, taken early to post, was all at sea in these conditions once off the bit. (7/2)
Alrabyah (IRE), an attractive sort, looked fit but he showed a poor action. Edgy in the stalls, he missed the kick and then raced too freely and stopped as though something was wrong at halfway. (4/1)

3987 QUINTIN GILBEY SILVER TROPHY H'CAP (0-75) (3-Y.O+) (Class D)
2-40 (2-41) **6f 214y** £9,520.00 (£2,860.00: £1,380.00: £640.00) Stalls: High GOING: 0.79 sec per fur (S)

				SP	RR	SF
3565*	**Rymer's Rascal (60)** (EJAlston) **5-9-1** JFEgan(18) (lw: trckd ldrs: chal over 2f out: carried lft: led ins fnl f: styd on wl)	—	1	14/1	70	49
3690*	**Dummer Golf Time (63)** (LordHuntingdon) **4-9-4v** JReid(7) (hdwy ½-wy: ev ch ins fnl f: kpt on)	nk	2	12/1	72	51
3561[2]	**Mybotye (58)** (RBastiman) **4-8-13** KFallon(20) (prom: hdwy to ld 3f out: hung lft: hdd ins fnl f: no ex)	1	3	9/1[3]	65	44
3649[18]	**Grey Kingdom (73)** (MBrittain) **6-9-7**(7) DMernagh(16) (a cl up: nt qckn fnl 2f)	nk	4	12/1	79	58
3690[11]	**Knobbleeneeze (65)** (MRChannon) **7-9-6v** TQuinn(15) (lw: outpcd ½-wy: styd on u.p appr fnl f: nrst fin)	½	5	6/1[2]	70	49
*3583**	**Deeply Vale (IRE) (64)** (GLMoore) **6-9-5** MWigham(12) (bhd: hdwy 3f out: chsng ldrs over 1f out: no ex)	hd	6	16/1	69	48
3584[5]	**Nominator Lad (70)** (BAMcMahon) **3-9-7** JFortune(24) (bhd: hdwy ½-wy: chsng ldrs 2f out: nt qckn)	1½	7	16/1	72	47
3801[13]	**Pericles (75)** (MJohnston) **3-9-12** JWeaver(1) (chsd ldrs: effrt over 2f out: wknd over 1f out)	hd	8	20/1	76	51
3855[5]	**Mystique Air (IRE) (64)** (EWeymes) **3-8-8**(7) RWinston(8) (in tch: rdn over 2f out: kpt on u.str.p fnl f)	s.h	9	20/1	65	40
3328[4]	**Veni Vidi Vici (IRE) (65)** (MJHeaton-Ellis) **4-9-1**(5) ADaly(6) (bhd: sme hdwy fnl 3f: no imp)	2½	10	14/1	60	39
3901[8]	**Myttons Mistake (59)** (ABailey) **4-8-9**(5) PRoberts(5) (chsd ldrs tl wknd fnl 2f)	1¾	11	12/1	50	29
3690[9]	**Duello (67)** (MBlanshard) **6-9-8** MRoberts(19) (outpcd & bhd: hdwy u.p over 2f out: nvr trbld ldrs)	1½	12	5/1[1]	55	34
3604[19]	**Ivory Dawn (75)** (KTIvory) **3-9-9**(3) DSweeney(21) (mid div: hdwy to chse ldrs over 2f out: sn btn)	4	13	25/1	54	29
3034[15]	**The Lambton Worm (70)** (DenysSmith) **3-9-2**(5) CLowther(2) (sn outpcd & bhd: n.d)	1	14	20/1	47	22
3855[4]	**Midyan Queen (62)** (RHollinshead) **3-8-13** FLynch(9) (hld up: effrt ½-wy: n.d)	½	15	25/1	37	12
3777[5]	**Royal Result (USA) (67)** (TDBarron) **4-9-8** JCarroll(10) (lw: led 4f: sn wknd)	13	16	10/1	13	—
2922[16]	**E-Mail (IRE) (65)** (JMPEustace) **3-9-2** RCochrane(11) (lw: a bhd)	1¼	17	33/1	8	—
3621[3]	**Knotty Hill (73)** (RCraggs) **5-10-0** GHind(22) (bhd: effrt ½-wy: n.d)	1½	18	14/1	12	—
*3581**	**Oberon's Dart (IRE) (65)** (PJMakin) **4-9-6** SSanders(13) (sn pushed along: bhd fr ½-wy)	21	19	9/1[3]	—	—
2678[14]	**Trailblazer (72)** (CWThornton) **3-9-9** DeanMcKeown(17) (sn outpcd & wl bhd)	nk	20	33/1	—	—
3143[7]	**Raed (61)** (MrsASwinbank) **4-9-2** NDay(4) (sn chsng ldrs: wknd 3f out)	1½	21	25/1	—	—
1489[15]	**Barrack Yard (55)** (ACStewart) **4-8-10** WRyan(14) (lw: prom to ½-wy: sn bhd)	½	22	16/1	—	—

(SP 152.5%) **22 Rn**

1m 32.65 (9.65) CSF £170.77 CT £1,536.05 TOTE £19.50: £4.30 £2.70 £2.10 £3.00 (£69.90) Trio £254.40 OWNER Mr Brian Chambers (PRESTON) BRED Mrs Sara Logue and David Lewis
WEIGHT FOR AGE 3yo-4lb

3565* Rymer's Rascal is in the form of his life just now and, with the third all over him like a rash, he needed plenty of courage to gain the day. (14/1)
3690* Dummer Golf Time does not seem to know how to run a bad race and just kept battling away. (12/1: op 8/1)
3561 Mybotye showed what a difficult ride he is here by continually hanging with the strongest assistance, but he certainly has ability. (9/1)
3254 Grey Kingdom is a crackerjack and just keeps running his heart out despite rising 32lb so far this season. (12/1)
1324 Knobbleeneeze is off a useful mark but took time to find his stride here and, although finishing well, could never offer a threat. (6/1)
3583* Deeply Vale (IRE) is a good, consistent sort who spends a lot of his time on the All-Weather these days, but looks pretty useful on turf judging from this. (16/1)
3584 Nominator Lad had plenty to do from his draw and this was not a bad effort. (16/1)
3777 Royal Result (USA) had never raced on such a testing surface before and that found him out in the latter stages. (10/1)

3988 STRENSALL STKS (Listed) (3-Y.O+) (Class A)
3-10 (3-11) **1m 205y** £18,925.00 (£5,650.00: £2,700.00: £1,225.00) Stalls: Low GOING: 0.79 sec per fur (S)

				SP	RR	SF
3797[2]	**Winter Romance (104)** (EALDunlop) **4-9-2** MHills(1) (lw: hld up: effrt over 2f out: led 1f out: drvn out)	—	1	100/30[2]	113	66
3728[4]	**Weet-A-Minute (IRE) (100)** (RHollinshead) **4-9-2** TQuinn(7) (chsd ldrs: led over 2f out to 1f out: hrd rdn & kpt on)	½	2	20/1	112	65
2010[6]	**Balalaika (104)** (LMCumani) **4-9-2** JReid(5) (b.hind: a.p: effrt & ch over 2f out: sn rdn & nt qckn)	5	3	4/1[3]	103	56

3634[4] **Acharne (108)** (CEBrittain) **4-9-2** MRoberts(6) (racd alone on ins: hld up: jnd ldrs ent st: slt ld 3f out: wknd fnl 2f)....3½ **4** 12/1 97 50
3713[2] **Tarski (92)** (HRACecil) **3-8-10** KFallon(4) (hld up: pushed along 6f out: one pce fnl 3f)....2½ **5** 8/1 92 39
3675a[4] **Catienus (USA) (110)** (MRStoute) **3-8-10** KDarley(2) (lw: mde most tl hdd & wknd qckly over 2f out)....17 **6** 6/5[1] 62 9
(SP 112.1%) **6 Rn**

1m 59.8 (10.80) CSF £51.15 TOTE £3.60: £2.00 £3.20 (£22.30) OWNER Maktoum Al Maktoum (NEWMARKET) BRED Gainsborough Stud Management Ltd.
WEIGHT FOR AGE 3yo-6lb
OFFICIAL EXPLANATION **Catienus (USA): no explanation offered.**
3797 Winter Romance likes the ground but did not find as much as looked likely when let down and needed plenty of assistance to keep him going. (100/30: 9/4-7/2)
3728 Weet-A-Minute (IRE) is a tough and consistent sort who kept trying here under the strongest pressure but was always second best. (20/1)
2010 Balalaika was well enough placed if good enough but these testing conditions proved beyond her in the last two and a half furlongs. (4/1)
3634 Acharne likes the soft but his rider took the shortest route throughout and that looked a big mistake. (12/1)
3713 Tarski never seemed happy in this very testing ground. (8/1)
3675a Catienus (USA) has shown in the past he loves testing going which makes this very disappointing effort even more mystifying. (6/5: evens-5/4)

3989 SUN LIFE OF CANADA GARROWBY RATED STKS H'CAP (0-105) (3-Y.O) (Class B)

3-40 (3-41) **1m 3f 195y** £13,302.40 (£4,921.60: £2,360.80: £964.00: £382.00: £149.20) Stalls: Low GOING: 0.79 sec per fur (S)

SP RR SF

3689[2] **Arctic Owl (88)** (JRFanshawe) **3-9-3** NDay(4) (bhd: hdwy 5f out: chal 2f out: disp ld 1f out: hrd rdn & hmpd: kpt on: fin 2nd, s.h: awrdd r)....— **1** 17/2 101 60
3722* **Honourable (90)** (JWWatts) **3-9-5** JCarroll(6) (lw: a cl up: led over 3f out: hung lft u.p: jst hld on: fin 1st: disq: plcd 2nd)....s.h **2** 11/2[3] 103 62
3773[3] **Darapour (IRE) (85)** (LMCumani) **3-9-0** JReid(5) (lw: hld up: hdwy 4f out: outpcd over 2f out: kpt on wl towards fin)....2 **3** 4/1[2] 95 54
3377[3] **Bally Souza (IRE) (82)** (MJohnston) **3-8-11** JWeaver(7) (prom tl outpcd 4f out: kpt on fnl 2f)....11 **4** 12/1 77 36
3071* **Fantail (79)** (MHTompkins) **3-8-5(3)** MHenry(10) (chsd ldrs: pushed along ent st: wknd fnl 3f)....5 **5** 9/1 68 27
3648[4] **Marathon Maid (80)** (RAFahey) **3-8-2(7)** RWinston(2) (chsd ldrs tl lost pl over 4f out)....13 **6** 20/1 51 10
2514[7] **Heritage (92)** (JHMGosden) **3-9-7** GHind(1) (lw: prom: rdn 4f out: wknd over 2f out)....2½ **7** 7/4[1] 60 19
1318[6] **Lycility (IRE) (90)** (CEBrittain) **3-9-5** MRoberts(8) (hld up: hdwy on ins ent st: sn prom: wknd fnl 3f)....9 **8** 25/1 46 5
3599[3] **Isle of Man (USA) (87)** (PFICole) **3-9-2** TQuinn(3) (sn led tl hdd & wknd over 3f out)....5 **9** 14/1 36 —
3722[14] **Darcy (90)** (MRStoute) **3-9-5** KDarley(9) (in tch: hrd rdn ent st: sn lost pl)....5 **10** 10/1 32 —
(SP 124.3%) **10 Rn**

2m 43.24 (15.44) CSF £53.26 CT £203.40 TOTE £10.20: £2.90 £2.10 £1.70 (£27.30) Trio £61.40 OWNER The Owl Society (NEWMARKET) BRED J. M. Greetham
OFFICIAL EXPLANATION **Heritage: was unsuited by sticky and patchy going.**
3689 Arctic Owl certainly stays and acted well in the conditions and, but for the original winner hanging into him, he would probably have won it outright. (17/2)
3722* Honourable travelled well and looked to have the edge from a long way out but when ridden he got completely unbalanced, and with his rider failing to pull his whip through to his left hand the Stewards had no option but to disqualify him. (11/2)
3773 Darapour (IRE) seems that whatever trip or ground he runs over he finishes strongly and there is obviously a lot more ability there when the key is found. (4/1)
3377 Bally Souza (IRE) seems happier on a much faster surface and this was not a bad effort. (12/1)
3071* Fantail, stepping up in class and distance, looked very one-paced. (9/1)
3648 Marathon Maid found the conditions here against her and was left behind once the tempo increased early in the straight. (20/1)
2514 Heritage should have liked the conditions but was again disappointing finding nothing once off the bit. (7/4)

3990 ACMC NURSERY H'CAP (2-Y.O) (Class C)

4-10 (4-12) **7f 202y** £8,480.00 (£2,540.00: £1,220.00: £560.00) Stalls: Low GOING: 0.79 sec per fur (S)

SP RR SF

3602[7] **Noble Demand (USA) (72)** (MrsJRRamsden) **2-7-9(3)** RFfrench(2) (rr div: effrt ½-wy: hdwy & hung lft over 1f out: str run to ld nr fin)....— **1** 7/1[3] 75 26
3474[11] **Ben Rinnes (77)** (RFJohnsonHoughton) **2-7-12(5)** ADaly(1) (chsd ldrs: chal over 3f out: styd on to ld wl ins fnl f: sn hdd & no ex)....2 **2** 12/1 76 27
3650[4] **Simply Gifted (76)** (TDEasterby) **2-8-2** LCharnock(13) (lw: cl up: led over 3f out: hung lft over 2f out: hdd wl over 1f out: nt qckn towards fin)....½ **3** 11/2[2] 74 25
3755[2] **Hirst Bridge (IRE) (82)** (MWEasterby) **2-8-8** KFallon(17) (hdwy ½-wy: sn chsng ldrs: one pce fnl 2f)....6 **4** 8/1 68 19
3904[4] **Lakeland Pride (IRE) (70)** (PDEvans) **2-7-3b(7)** AMcCarthy(10) (a chsng ldrs: effrt over 3f out: one pce)....3 **5** 20/1 50 1
2018* **Carry The Flag (84)** (PFICole) **2-8-10** TQuinn(6) (b.nr hind: cl up: chal 4f out: hmpd over 2f out: sn rdn & btn)....2½ **6** 100/30[1] 59 10
3545[4] **Miss Main Street (IRE) (70)** (JJQuinn) **2-7-3(7)** PBradley(7) (bhd: hdwy ½-wy: rdn & no imp fnl 2½f)....4 **7** 25/1 37 —
3479[10] **Rockette (70)** (JWWatts) **2-7-7b[1](3)** PFessey(12) (s.i.s: effrt appr st: sn rdn & n.d)....5 **8** 20/1 27 —
3638[2] **Matata (IRE) (81)** (NACallaghan) **2-8-2(5)** CLowther(18) (s.i.s: hdwy to chse ldrs after 3f: wknd 4f out)....21 **9** 7/1[3] — —
3628* **Chaska (70)** (ABailey) **2-7-10** DWright(16) (nvr trbld ldrs)....2½ **10** 14/1 — —
1735[5] **Smooth Sailing (95)** (KMcAuliffe) **2-9-7** JFortune(3) (trckd ldrs: hdwy & ev ch over 2f out: nt clr run & swtchd wl over 1f out: sn wknd)....½ **11** 20/1 3 —
2685[6] **Deeceebee (80)** (WStorey) **2-8-6** SSanders(11) (led tl hdd & wknd over 3f out)....8 **12** 11/2[2] — —
3307[15] **The Cannie Rover (74)** (MWEasterby) **2-7-7(7)ow4** RWinston(4) (prom: effrt 4f out: wknd over 2f out)....9 **13** 33/1 — —
3237[13] **Mamora Bay (IRE) (73)** (MHTompkins) **2-7-10(3)** MHenry(9) (bhd fr ½-wy)....9 **14** 20/1 — —
3307[7] **Linnetsong (71)** (GROldroyd) **2-7-11v ow1** FNorton(5) (lost tch fr ½-wy: eased fnl 2f)....26 **15** 33/1 — —
(SP 133.1%) **15 Rn**

1m 48.76 (11.76) CSF £79.90 CT £478.34 TOTE £16.10: £3.40 £3.50 £1.90 (£53.40) Trio £192.50 OWNER Mrs Alison Iles (THIRSK) BRED Brereton C. Jones
LONG HANDICAP Chaska 7-8 Rockette 7-5 The Cannie Rover 7-0 Miss Main Street (IRE) 7-3 Linnetsong 7-2
STEWARDS' ENQUIRY Charnock susp. 13 & 15/9/97 (careless riding).
OFFICIAL EXPLANATION **Linnetsong: was struck into.**

3331 Noble Demand (USA) came from a long way off the pace and was going twice as fast as the rest, and is obviously going to need a stiffish test. (7/1: 5/1-8/1)
2181* Ben Rinnes goes in the ground and is a battler but he had no answer to the winner's amazing late burst . (12/1)
3650 Simply Gifted looked to be going much the best early in the straight, but when in front he hung off a true line and gave the impression that once he strengthens he will do a lot better. (11/2)
3755 Hirst Bridge (IRE) has been running consistently well all year but just found these conditions too much in the last couple of furlongs. (8/1)
3904 Lakeland Pride (IRE) has run some fair races so far without success but the ability is there. (20/1)
2018* Carry The Flag acted well enough in this testing ground, but getting hampered at a vital stage did not help things as he was already feeling the pace. (100/30)
2685 Deeceebee was edgy beforehand and probably went off too fast. (11/2)

3991 PRINCE OF WALES'S OWN REGIMENT OF YORKSHIRE MAIDEN STKS (3-Y.O) (Class D)

4-40 (4-40) **7f 202y** £6,108.00 (£1,824.00: £872.00: £396.00) Stalls: Low GOING: 0.79 sec per fur (S)

				SP	RR	SF
674^{4}	**Solar Storm** (MBell) **3-9-0** MFenton(3) (trckd ldrs: led wl over 2f out: hld on wl)	—	**1**	$4/1^{3}$	88	42
	Brigand (IRE) (DRLoder) **3-9-0** RCochrane(1) (w'like: unf: led tl hdd wl over 2f out: hrd rdn & r.o fnl f)	¾	**2**	5/1	87	41
3463^{14}	**Floristan (IRE)** (LMCumani) **3-8-11**(3) RFfrench(6) (in tch: hdwy over 5f out: effrt 4f out: rdn & r.o one pce)	7	**3**	7/1	72	26
3211^{3}	**Present Chance (78)** (BAMcMahon) **3-9-0** JFortune(4) (chsd ldrs: rdn 4f out: one pce)	11	**4**	$11/4^{1}$	50	4
3775^{3}	**Macaribo** (JHMGosden) **3-9-0** GHind(9) (cl up: effrt 4f out: sn btn)	½	**5**	$3/1^{2}$	49	3
	San Francisco (CWThornton) **3-9-0** DeanMcKeown(8) (wl grwn: bit bkwd: stdd s: effrt over 4f out: sn rdn: n.d)	1¾	**6**	20/1	46	—
	Bob Knows (RFJohnsonHoughton) **3-9-0** JReid(2) (lengthy: bit bkwd: hld up & bhd: shkn up 4f out: n.d)	9	**7**	10/1	27	—
	I See You Sydney (AUS) (MJPolglase) **3-9-0** KDarley(7) (prom tl rdn & wknd over 3f out)	27	**8**	20/1	—	—
				(SP 119.4%)	**8 Rn**	

1m 48.67 (11.67) CSF £23.23 TOTE £5.60: £1.90 £1.90 £2.50 (£16.80) Trio £44.80 OWNER Mr T. F. Harris (NEWMARKET) BRED Cheveley Park Stud Ltd
674 Solar Storm, a continual tail-swisher in the preliminaries, did nothing wrong in the race and showed a fine attitude when tackled. (4/1)
Brigand (IRE) looked green here but then responded to some driving late on only to find the winner too determined. (5/1)
Floristan (IRE) proved to be one-paced once off the bit. (7/1)
3211 Present Chance was disappointing here which can probably be put down to the testing ground. (11/4)
3775 Macaribo found these conditions against him. (3/1)
San Francisco needed the experience and the outing fitness-wise and should improve a little as a result. (20/1)

3992 EQUITY FINANCIAL COLLECTIONS RACING SCHOOLS APPRENTICE H'CAP (0-70) (3-Y.O+) (Class E)

5-10 (5-11) **1m 2f 85y** £4,662.50 (£1,400.00: £675.00: £312.50) Stalls: Low GOING: 0.79 sec per fur (S)

				SP	RR	SF
3907^{3}	**Gold Desire (56)** (MBrittain) **7-9-0** SCopp(15) (lw: b.hind: a chsng ldrs: rdn over 3f out: styd on gamely to ld wl ins fnl f)	—	**1**	$9/1^{3}$	67	54
3609^{9}	**Tonnerre (57)** (BAMcMahon) **5-8-12**(3) FBoyle(22) (led: rdn 3f out: hdd & no ex wl ins fnl f)	1	**2**	12/1	67	54
3691^{7}	**Golden Ace (IRE) (55)** (RCSpicer) **4-8-10**(3) PBradley(18) (in tch: stdy hdwy 4f out: chal 2f out: hung lft & nt qckn ins fnl f)	nk	**3**	20/1	64	51
3793^{9}	**Jona Holley (53)** (GLMoore) **4-8-11** DGriffiths(4) (mid div: hdwy over 3f out: rdn & no imp fnl 2f)	11	**4**	14/1	45	32
3906^{8}	**Welcome Home (47)** (PTDalton) **3-7-9**(3) RBrisland(8) (prom: effrt over 4f out: styd on one pce)	3½	**5**	20/1	34	14
3430^{5}	**Beau Roberto (46)** (JSGoldie) **3-7-8**(3) JMcAuley(14) (chsd ldrs: rdn 4f out: one pce)	½	**6**	20/1	32	12
1039^{4}	**Karisma (IRE) (52)** (DenysSmith) **4-8-10** PFessey(21) (chsd ldrs tl grad wknd fnl 3f)	4	**7**	16/1	32	19
3330^{4}	**Leif the Lucky (USA) (53)** (MissSEHall) **8-8-11** KimberleyHart(19) (chsd ldrs: effrt over 3f out: grad wknd)	hd	**8**	14/1	33	20
3759^{4}	**Reinhardt (IRE) (40)** (DNicholls) **4-7-6**(6) JoanneDavies(1) (s.s: nvr nrr)	4	**9**	14/1	13	—
3694^{9}	**Cliburnel News (IRE) (50)** (DShaw) **7-8-8** DDenby(10) (b: effrt ent st: nvr nr to chal)	2	**10**	25/1	20	7
3691^{10}	**Bally Wonder (40)** (HJCollingridge) **5-7-9**(3) DarrenWilliams(13) (nvr trbld ldrs)	1¾	**11**	25/1	8	—
3916^{6}	**Voila Premiere (IRE) (65)** (PGMurphy) **5-9-9** RMullen(2) (lw: hld up: effrt over 4f out: sn rdn & no imp)	2	**12**	$9/2^{1}$	30	17
3886*	**Rasayel (USA) (75)** (PDEvans) **7-10-5** 5x AMcCarthy(5) (bhd: rdn 5f out: n.d)	3	**13**	$8/1^{2}$	35	22
3608^{2}	**Sandmoor Denim (46)** (SRBowring) **10-8-4** CTeague(17) (b: a bhd)	5	**14**	14/1	—	—
3540^{12}	**Kulepopsie (IRE) (44)** (ABMulholland) **4-8-2** KSked(7) (lost tch fnl 5f)	2	**15**	25/1	—	—
3854*	**Raindeer Quest (48)** (JLEyre) **5-8-6** 5x DSweeney(6) (bhd fnl 4f)	2	**16**	14/1	—	—
3397^{2}	**Absolute Liberty (USA) (67)** (SPCWoods) **3-9-4** MBaird(9) (a bhd)	21	**17**	14/1	—	—
3543^{7}	**Lindrick Lady (IRE) (64)** (BSRothwell) **3-9-1** IonaWands(12) (in tch: hrd rdn over 5f out: sn wknd)	1¼	**18**	14/1	—	—
3813^{2}	**Sharbadarid (IRE) (70)** (LMCumani) **3-9-7** RFfrench(20) (lw: chsd ldrs: rdn ent st: sn wknd)	4	**19**	$9/2^{1}$	—	—
3501^{6}	**Versatility (69)** (RFJohnsonHoughton) **4-9-13** FLynch(3) (s.i.s: a bhd)	3½	**20**	14/1	—	—
3470^{13}	**Dazzling Stone (54)** (LadyHerries) **3-8-5** GMilligan(11) (unruly s: a bhd: t.o)	dist	**21**	14/1	—	—
				(SP 156.9%)	**21 Rn**	

2m 22.86 (13.86) CSF £117.47 CT £2,014.24 TOTE £7.90: £1.70 £5.70 £11.30 £3.30 (£99.20) Trio £1,103.80; £808.43 to Haydock 5/9/97
OWNER Northgate Lodge Racing Club (WARTHILL) BRED Northgate Lodge Stud Ltd
WEIGHT FOR AGE 3yo-7lb
3907 Gold Desire stays further, is tough and, given a most determined ride, his courage won the day. (9/1)
3134 Tonnerre likes the ground and put in a useful effort here but was inclined to wander about when ridden which probably made all the difference. (12/1)
3196* Golden Ace (IRE) looked to be going best for a long way but probably did not quite stay in these conditions. (20/1)
3200 Jona Holley likes the soft and stays well enough but seems high enough in the weights just now. (14/1)
2523 Welcome Home keeps running reasonably but so far without any real success. (20/1)
3430 Beau Roberto showed ability and gives the impression that there is more there if he can be persuaded. (20/1)
3759 Reinhardt (IRE) is a law unto himself but certainly has ability. (14/1)
3916 Voila Premiere (IRE) (9/2: 6/1-4/1)

T/Jkpt: Not won; £17,993.30 to Haydock 5/9/97. T/Plpt: £759.60 (48.78 Tckts). T/Qdpt: £219.50 (9.29 Tckts) AA

0039a-BADEN-BADEN (Germany) (L-H) (Soft)
Friday August 29th

3993a SPRETI-RENNEN (Gp 3) (4-Y.O+)
3-25 (3-50) **1m 2f** £28,409.00 (£11,363.00: £5,681.00: £3,030.00)

				SP	RR	SF
3004a*	**Devil River Peek (USA)** (BSchutz,Germany) **5-9-0** StephenDavies	—	1		121	—
3364a[3]	**Zero Problemo (IRE)** (BSchutz,Germany) **4-8-12** AStarke	1¾	2		116	—
	Sambakonig (GER) (HHorwart,Germany) **4-8-12** WNewnes	1¼	3		114	—
3409[2]	**Germano** (GWragg) **4-8-12** MHills	¾	4		113	—
						12 Rn

2m 4.98 Tote 103DM: 22DM 15DM 37DM (SF 288DM) OWNER Stall Hoppegarten BRED Fares Farm Inc.
3409 Germano was sent off favourite, and chased the leader until going on, travelling strongly, two and a half furlongs out. However, he back-pedalled once challenged a furlong out. The first three came from off the pace, and it may be the leaders went too fast.

CLAIREFONTAINE (Deauville, France) (R-H) (Heavy)
Friday August 29th

3994a PRIX DE COQUAINVILLIER (FRENCH-BRED) (2-Y.O F)
2-00 (2-01) **7f** £7,856.00

				SP	RR	SF
3235[2]	**Friendly Warning (FR)** (JEBanks) **2-9-0** AJunk	—	1		77+	—
	Happy (FR) (France) **2-8-12** SGuillot	1	2		73	—
	Trophy Wife (FR) (France) **2-8-12** DBoeuf	¾	3		71	—
						13 Rn

1m 30.6 P-M 6.00F: 2.50F 2.50F 3.00F (18.20F) OWNER The Allez France Partnership (NEWMARKET) BRED M3 Elevage and Haras d'Etreham
3235 Friendly Warning (FR) was always well placed, and ran out a very comfortable winner of this race, picking up over £12,000 for her owners. She may go for the Rockfel Stakes next, but has the option of returning to France where any prizemoney won is boosted by an 80% owners' bonus.

3882a-DEAUVILLE (France) (R-H) (Very Soft)
Saturday August 30th

3995a PRIX DU HARAS DE LA HUDERIE (Listed) (2-Y.O C & G)
1-55 (1-54) **7f** £15,713.00 (£5,387.00: £4,040.00)

				SP	RR	SF
2860*	**Trans Island** (IABalding) **2-9-2** OPeslier	—	1		91+	—
	Pulsar (FR) (France) **2-9-2** GMosse	4	2		82	—
	My Way (FR) (France) **2-9-2** SGuillot	2½	3		76	—
						6 Rn

1m 30.3 (6.30) P-M 1.70F: 1.40F 2.70F (SF 13.40F) OWNER Al Muallim Partnership (KINGSCLERE) BRED Godolphin Management Co Ltd
2860* Trans Island made virtually all the running and, outclassing his field, won in style. He will not be over-raced this year, and may have just one more outing, in the Horris Hill Stakes. He is a progressive sort who could make a really decent miler next season.

3996a PRIX QUINCEY (Gp 3) (3-Y.O+)
3-30 (3-29) **1m** £24,691.00 (£8,979.00: £4,489.00)

				SP	RR	SF
3729a*	**Marathon (USA)** (MmeCHead,France) **3-8-8** ODoleuze	—	1		113	—
	Parfait Glace (FR) (JEHammond,France) **5-9-0** CAsmussen	1	2		111	—
2818a[2]	**Trojan Sea (USA)** (DSmaga,France) **6-9-2** DBoeuf	1	3		111	—
						8 Rn

1m 43.8 (7.80) P-M 2.30F: 1.50F 2.00F 1.50F (20.00F) OWNER Mr Alec Head (CHANTILLY) BRED Societe Aland
Marathon (USA) has always been held in high regard, but suffered a bad bout of flu when being prepared for the Prix Jean Prat. He has come back in fine style, and had no trouble winning his first Group race. He went to the front a furlong out, and his jockey needed to use only hands and heels from then on. He looks potentially top class, and the Prix de Rond-Point is his next target, possibly followed by the Hollywood Derby. He will remain in training next year, and can become a major force in the top mile events.
Parfait Glace (FR) made most of the running, but had no answer to the winner's challenge. He deserves to win a race at this level.
1914a Trojan Sea (USA) was held up for a late run, but arrived on the scene when the race was over.

3993a-BADEN-BADEN (Germany) (L-H) (Good)
Sunday August 31st

3997a KRONIMUS RENNEN (Listed) (2-Y.O)
1-30 (1-32) **7f 110y** £11,364.00 (£4,545.00: £2,652.00)

				SP	RR	SF
2012[11]	**Chips (IRE)** (DRCElsworth) **2-9-0** DaneO'Neill	—	1		90+	—
3368a[2]	**National Academy (GER)** (Germany) **2-9-0** KWoodburn	½	2		89	—
	Seborga (GER) (DRCElsworth) **2-8-12** ASuborics	2½	3		82	—
						4 Rn

1m 31.84 Tote 32DM: 13DM 12DM (51DM) OWNER Lucayan Stud (WHITCOMBE) BRED Mrs E. M. Gauvain
1411* Chips (IRE) made all to win this listed event comfortably, and was being eased down near the line. He is being aimed at the Racing Post Trophy at Doncaster.

3998a FURSTENBERG-RENNEN (Gp 3) (3-Y.O)
3-25 (3-32) **1m 3f** £28,409.00 (£11,364.00: £5,682.00)

				SP	RR	SF
	March Groom (USA) (AFriebert,Germany) **3-8-12** ASuborics	—	1		105	—
2642a[9]	**Ferrari (GER)** (PLautner,Germany) **3-8-12** WNewnes	1	2		104	—
	Don't Worry (GER) (HBlume,Germany) **3-8-12** THellier	2	3		101	—
3190[17]	**Sir Talbot** (RHannon) **3-8-12** DaneO'Neill (btn approx 8¼l)		8		—	—

13 Rn

2m 16.13 Tote 152DM: 43DM 30DM 32DM (1499DM) OWNER Stall V I P BRED Albert P. Coppola
2729* Sir Talbot was never able to get into a challenging position, and is not in this class.

3998b BLANQUET-RENNEN STKS (3-Y.O+ F & M) (Class E)
4-15 (4-18) **1m 2f** £4,515.00 (£1,818.00: £1,023.00: £569.00)

				SP	RR	SF
	Flamingo Queen (GER) (BSchutz,Germany) **3-8-7** AStarke(0)	—	1		90	—
	Enrica (GER) (HBlume,Germany) **3-9-2** THellier(0)	2½	2		95	—
	Peggy Lane (FR) (DFechner,Germany) **3-9-0** ASuborics(0)	3½	3		87	—
2379[4]	**Polska Princess (GER)** (LordHuntingdon) **3-8-1** StephenDavies(0)	½	4		74	—

16 Rn

2m 5.54 Tote 24DM: 15DM 16DM 31DM (83DM) OWNER Mr H. von Finck
Polska Princess (GER) was in the firing line from the off, but was outpaced by the principals in the closing stages.

3995a-DEAUVILLE (France) (R-H) (Very soft)
Sunday August 31st

3999a PRIX DU CALVADOS (Gp 3) (2-Y.O F)
2-30 (2-35) **7f** £24,691.00 (£8,979.00: £4,489.00)

				SP	RR	SF
2962*	**Woodland Melody (USA)** (PWChapple-Hyam) **2-8-9** OPeslier	—	1		94	—
3873a*	**Sainte Marine (IRE)** (RCollet,France) **2-8-9** TJarnet	5	2		83	—
	Seralia (FR) (PBary,France) **2-8-9** DBoeuf	3	3		76	—

5 Rn

1m 27.3 (3.30) P-M 2.60F: 1.50F 1.80F (SF 6.20F) OWNER Mr R. E. Sangster (MARLBOROUGH) BRED Seahorse Investments
2962* Woodland Melody (USA) made her opponents look rather ordinary and they were not. She lay in second place until one and a half furlongs out, and then drew clear in fine style to win in a canter. A pretty useful filly in the making, she has a lot of scope and will do even better over further. She may now go for the valuable Tattersalls Houghton Sale Race, but is also a possible for the Fillies' Mile and the Prix Marcel Boussac.
Sainte Marine (IRE) tried to make all the running but just stayed on one paced in the final stages. She won a previous race in good style and was rather disappointing on this occasion.
Seralia (FR), who won the Prix Yacowlef, was beaten a total of eight lengths and never really took part in the race. She was thought to have been out of the top drawer.

4000a GRAND PRIX DE DEAUVILLE LANCEL (Gp 2) (3-Y.O+)
3-30 (3-30) **1m 4f 110y** £56,117.00 (£22,447.00: £11,223.00: £5,612.00)

				SP	RR	SF
2559[3]	**Taipan (IRE)** (JLDunlop) **5-9-4** PatEddery (hld up early: wnt 2nd 7f out: cl up ent st: u.p over 2f out: sn led: pushed out)	—	1		120	—
2513[5]	**Camporese (IRE)** (PWChapple-Hyam) **4-9-1** OPeslier (rdn in 2nd: trckd ldr tl st: wnt 3rd: hdwy over 1f out: no ex ins fnl f)	1	2		116	—
3731a*	**Lord of Men** (JHMGosden) **4-9-4** LDettori (set pce: led tl 2f out: hdd, hrd rdn & chal ldr: ev ch over 1f out: styd on one pce)	2½	3		116	—
2271a*	**L'Africain Bleu (FR)** (MmeCHead,France) **4-9-4** ODoleuze (a bhd: wknd st: n.d)	10	4		103	—

4 Rn

2m 58.8 (20.30) P-M 3.40F: 1.90F 1.90F (SF 9.70F) OWNER Lord Swaythling (ARUNDEL) BRED C. H. Wacker III
2559 Taipan (IRE) joined the leader going down the back straight and was brought up the far side of the course with his run in the straight. He revelled on the soft and cut up ground and ran on well in the final stages. He is top-class when conditions are testing and is also beautifully bred. He now heads for the Europa Preis at Cologne and then a campaign in Italy where the ground is nearly always soft in the autumn. He has also been entered in the Prix Foy, and his connections will be keeping a close eye on under foot conditions in Europe over the next few months.
2513 Camporese (IRE) seemed to be in trouble rounding the home turn, but she found a second wind in the straight and ran on well albeit one-paced. She is another who must have soft ground and the Park Hill Stakes could be next, followed by the Prix Royallieu and Prix Royal Oak, which are both ran at Longchamp in October.
3731a* Lord of Men made most of the running. He went rather slowly around the rather dangerous first turn and then accelerated down the back straight. He was joined by the winner rounding the final turn and was brought with a run on the stands side. With his stamina soon drained, he will now be brought back in distance and may well be seen out next in the Prix Dollar.
L'Africain Bleu (FR) was always last and made no show on this occasion.

4001a PRIX DE MEAUTRY (Gp 3) (3-Y.O+)
4-00 (4-02) **6f** £24,691.00 (£8,979.00: £4,489.00)

				SP	RR	SF
960[4]	**Pas De Reponse (USA)** (MmeCHead,France) **3-8-8** ODoleuze	—	1		115	—
3372a[3]	**Linoise (FR)** (AFabre,France) **5-8-11** TJarnet	1	2		112	—
3724[6]	**Hever Golf Rose** (TJNaughton) **6-9-2** JWeaver	1	3		115	—
3372a[4]	**Brave Edge** (RHannon) **6-9-1** PatEddery (btn approx 5¼l)		5		—	—

7 Rn

1m 13.1 (5.10) P-M 1.70F: 1.10F 1.30F (SF 4.10F) OWNER Wertheimer et Frere (CHANTILLY) BRED Wertheimer & Frere
960 Pas De Reponse (USA) looked well and, despite diving right at the furlong marker, accelerated well and dominated the final half-furlong of this sprint. A bad dose of flu had kept her off the course for four months but, now she is back, looks likely to have a successful autumn in a non-vintage year for sprinters. The Prix de l'Abbaye is her main target.

Linoise (FR) is a genuine and consistent mare who ran up to expectations once again. Her next race is likely to be the Prix de Seine-et-Oise at Maisons-Laffitte.
3724 Hever Golf Rose ran her usual honest race, being up with the pace throughout, but running out of steam in the last half-furlong. She will go to Sweden once again before another crack at the Prix de l'Abbaye, where the five furlongs will suit her better.

3794-EPSOM (L-H) (Good)
Friday September 5th
WEATHER: overcast WIND: mod half against

4002 VAILLANT HEATING & HOT WATER H'CAP (0-90) (3-Y.O+) (Class C)
2-05 (2-10) **1m 4f 10y** £7,360.00 (£2,230.00: £1,090.00: £520.00) Stalls: Low GOING minus 0.06 sec per fur (G)

				SP	RR	SF
3796[3]	**Dance So Suite (86)** (PFICole) **5-9-13** TQuinn(6) (a.p: led over 2f out: rdn & r.o wl)	—	**1**	4/1[1]	99	86
2507[2]	**Shalateeno (68)** (BRMillman) **4-8-9** MFenton(3) (a.p: led over 3f out tl over 2f out: unable qckn)	3½	**2**	10/1	76	63
3689[11]	**Artic Courier (78)** (DJSCosgrove) **6-9-5** MRimmer(10) (b: rdn over 3f out: hdwy over 1f out: r.o)	1¼	**3**	14/1	85	72
3115[14]	**Moon Blast (82)** (LadyHerries) **3-9-0** RCochrane(14) (hdwy over 5f out: rdn over 3f out: one pce)	1¼	**4**	20/1	87	65
1934[7]	**Male-Ana-Mou (IRE) (85)** (DRCElsworth) **4-9-12** AProcter(11) (hdwy over 3f out: rdn over 2f out: one pce)	hd	**5**	16/1	90	77
3722[3]	**Remaadi Sun (83)** (MDIUsher) **5-9-10** RStreet(5) (lost pl over 8f out: rallied over 1f out: r.o one pce)	hd	**6**	12/1	88	75
250[5]	**Double Espresso (IRE) (74)** (MJohnston) **3-8-6** MRoberts(7) (bit bkwd: prom over 10f)	2½	**7**	14/1	75	53
2483[7]	**Royal Seaton (70)** (MrsPNDutfield) **8-8-8**(3) RHavlin(8) (nvr nrr)	½	**8**	25/1	71	58
3593[2]	**Freedom Chance (IRE) (72)** (JWHills) **3-8-1v**(3) MHenry(9) (lw: no hdwy fnl 3f)	2½	**9**	12/1	70	48
3694[3]	**Noble Dane (IRE) (70)** (PWHarris) **3-8-2** GCarter(4) (lw: hdwy over 4f out: wknd over 3f out)	nk	**10**	10/1	67	45
3689[5]	**Myrtlebank (80)** (HRACecil) **3-8-12** KFallon(13) (lw: hld up: hrd rdn over 2f out: wknd over 1f out)	¾	**11**	9/1[3]	76	54
3864[2]	**Prospero (72)** (MrsAJPerrett) **4-8-13** AClark(12) (prom over 10f)	5	**12**	10/1	61	48
3897[5]	**Tulsa (IRE) (64)** (BGubby) **3-7-10** JQuinn(2) (bhd fnl 6f)	9	**13**	50/1	42	20
	Hal Hoo Yaroom (82) (RAkehurst) **4-9-9** SSanders(1) (led over 8f: wknd over 2f out)	6	**14**	12/1	52	39
2122[4]	**Life of Riley (85)** (GLewis) **3-9-3** PaulEddery(15) (b: bhd fnl 4f)	6	**15**	8/1[2]	47	25
				(SP 121.2%)	**15 Rn**	

2m 37.55 (3.05) CSF £38.05 CT £475.43 TOTE £4.40: £1.80 £3.10 £3.60 (£24.80) Trio £122.80 OWNER Mr J. S. Gutkin (WHATCOMBE)
BRED Genesis Green Stud and Walter Swinburn Ltd
LONG HANDICAP Tulsa (IRE) 6-6
WEIGHT FOR AGE 3yo-9lb
OFFICIAL EXPLANATION Life of Riley: the rider reported that the colt had lost his off-fore shoe during the race, and also failed to act on the course.
3796 Dance So Suite, on the same mark as when winning over this course and distance last year, hit the front over two furlongs out and soon asserted his authority for a decisive victory. (4/1: op 7/1)
2507 Shalateeno has been a model of consistency this season, and showed in front as the runners entered the straight. Collared over two furlongs out, she was firmly put in her place by the winner. (10/1)
3434 Artic Courier is not easy to win with but did struggle on in the last furlong and a half to take third prize. He has just three victories from forty-one starts to his name. (14/1)
2877 Moon Blast began to inch closer running down Tattenham Hill, but once in line for home could only struggle on at the one pace. Both his wins have come over a mile. (20/1)
1108 Male-Ana-Mou (IRE), without a run in twelve weeks, inched closer early in the straight but was then made to look very pedestrian. (16/1)
3722 Remaadi Sun is on a long losing run but his veteran rider hardly gives him much help, and as usual, he was given far too much to do. (12/1)
250 Double Espresso (IRE) (14/1: 20/1-12/1)
2122 Life of Riley (8/1: 6/1-9/1)

4003 ROOF UNITS FORTUNE STKS (Listed) (3-Y.O+) (Class A)
2-35 (2-39) **1m 114y** £11,054.50 (£3,346.00: £1,633.00: £776.50) Stalls: Low GOING minus 0.06 sec per fur (G)

				SP	RR	SF
2761*	**Intikhab (USA) (109)** (DMorley) **3-8-9** GCarter(1) (a.p: led 1f out: rdn out)	—	**1**	7/2[1]	114	72
3747[3]	**Almushtarak (IRE) (105)** (KMahdi) **4-9-1** PaulEddery(8) (lw: a.p: led over 2f out to 1f out: unable qckn)	1¾	**2**	10/1	111	75
3499[3]	**Crimson Tide (IRE) (104)** (JWHills) **3-8-9** TQuinn(4) (hdwy over 2f out: ev ch 1f out: one pce)	1½	**3**	7/2[1]	108	66
3764[3]	**Dancing Image (93)** (IABalding) **4-9-1** OPeslier(2) (lost pl 4f out: n.m.r over 2f out: swtchd rt: rallied fnl f: r.o)	nk	**4**	14/1	107	71
3766[2]	**Polar Prince (IRE) (113)** (MAJarvis) **4-9-7** RCochrane(7) (hld up: rdn over 2f out: one pce)	1¼	**5**	7/2[1]	111	75
3764*	**Omaha City (IRE) (105)** (BGubby) **3-8-9** KFallon(3) (s.s: a bhd)	8	**6**	9/1[3]	90	48
	Fleet River (USA) (HRACecil) **3-8-4** WRyan(6) (led 6f)	2½	**7**	6/1[2]	80	38
3797[4]	**Night City (97)** (KRBurke) **6-9-1** SSanders(5) (lw: bhd fnl 2f)	9	**8**	33/1	68	32
				(SP 109.7%)	**8 Rn**	

1m 43.67 (1.67) CSF £33.28 TOTE £4.80: £1.60 £2.30 £1.50 (£16.30) OWNER Mr Hamdan Al Maktoum (NEWMARKET) BRED J. I. Racing Inc. and Marvin Little Jr
WEIGHT FOR AGE 3yo-6lb
2761* Intikhab (USA) put up a good display to land his first Listed race, striking the front a furlong out and being rousted along to score. (7/2)
3747 Almushtarak (IRE) has yet to win this season, but put up a bold display and showed in front over a quarter of a mile from home. Headed entering the final furlong, he found the winner too strong. (10/1)
3499 Crimson Tide (IRE), one of three almost in a line a furlong out, was then tapped for toe. He needs further. (7/2)
3764 Dancing Image had more on his plate as he moved up to Listed company, and had real problems coming round Tattenham Corner. He eventually found his feet in the final furlong but by then it was too late. (14/1: 10/1-16/1)
3766 Polar Prince (IRE), with a 6lb penalty for his Group Three victory, was nicely placed entering the straight but when asked for his effort could only go up and down in the same place. (7/2)
3764* Omaha City (IRE) was back in Pattern company, but once again demonstrated that he has been struggling in this league this year. (9/1)
Fleet River (USA) (6/1: op 4/1)

4004 IMI AIR CONDITIONING RATED STKS H'CAP (0-105) (3-Y.O+) (Class B)

3-05 (3-10) **1m 2f 18y** £7,295.56 (£2,730.04: £1,335.02: £574.10: £257.05: £130.23) Stalls: Low GOING minus 0.06 sec per fur (G)

				SP	RR	SF
3824[2]	**Sandmoor Chambray (92)** (TDEasterby) **6-8-10** SSanders(7) (lw: chsd ldr: led over 2f out: clr over 1f out: comf)	—	**1**	11/4[1]	102+	63
3703[12]	**Danish Rhapsody (IRE) (95)** (LadyHerries) **4-8-13** PaulEddery(6) (led over 7f: unable qckn)	2½	**2**	7/1	101	62
	River Usk (97) (HRACecil) **3-8-8** KFallon(1) (swtg: rdn over 4f out: hdwy over 2f out: hung lft over 1f out: r.o one pce)	2½	**3**	6/1[3]	99	53
	Yarob (IRE) (89) (RAkehurst) **4-8-7**[ow2] OPeslier(3) (swtg: hld up: rdn over 2f out: one pce)	3½	**4**	4/1[2]	86	45
3703[8]	**Freequent (103)** (LMCumani) **4-9-7** MRoberts(8) (lw: rdn over 4f out: nvr nr to chal)	2½	**5**	12/1	96	57
3703[10]	**Present Arms (USA) (101)** (PFICole) **4-9-5** TQuinn(4) (lw: prom over 7f)	¾	**6**	6/1[3]	92	53
2136[8]	**Arctiid (USA) (87)** (JHMGosden) **4-8-5** GHind(2) (lw: a bhd)	s.h	**7**	8/1	78	39
3246[2]	**Anak-Ku (86)** (MissGayKelleway) **4-7-13**[(5)] RMullen(5) (b: prom over 6f)	5	**8**	10/1	69	30
				(SP 115.6%)	**8 Rn**	

2m 7.32 (3.32) CSF £20.74 CT £97.20 TOTE £3.50: £1.40 £2.10 £1.90 (£12.30) OWNER Sandmoor Textiles Co Ltd (MALTON) BRED P. and Mrs Venner
LONG HANDICAP Anak-Ku 8-1
WEIGHT FOR AGE 3yo-7lb

3824 Sandmoor Chambray continues in excellent form and, striking the front over two furlongs out, soon forged clear to win with plenty in hand. (11/4)
3112* Danish Rhapsody (IRE) showed his York running to be all wrong, and took the field along until firmly put in his place by the winner over two furlongs out. (7/1)
River Usk, making a belated seasonal debut, was being bustled along rounding Tattenham Corner. He did pick up ground in the straight but he hung left on the camber, although he eventually managed to secure third prize. (6/1: 7/2-13/2)
Yarob (IRE), who spent last winter in the Emirates where he won once, was sold at the Newmarket July Sales for 24,000 guineas. Chasing the leaders, he failed to find another turn of foot in the last two furlongs. (4/1)
Freequent is high in the weights at present, and was running over a trip short of his best, consequently he never looked like getting into it. A return to a mile and a half and a drop in the handicap would make him more interesting. (12/1: 7/1-14/1)
3051* Present Arms (USA) was close up until calling it a day over two furlongs from home. A drop in the weights would be appreciated. (6/1)
Arctiid (USA) (8/1: 6/1-9/1)

4005 SEPTEMBER STKS (Gp 3) (3-Y.O+) (Class A)

3-40 (3-43) **1m 4f 10y** £18,840.00 (£7,129.50: £3,489.75: £1,590.75) Stalls: Low GOING minus 0.06 sec per fur (G)

				SP	RR	SF
3125*	**Maylane (108)** (ACStewart) **3-8-5** MRoberts(2) (faltered s: hdwy 2f out: led 1f out: edgd lft: rdn out)	—	**1**	3/1[2]	118	71
3596*	**Dushyantor (USA) (120)** (HRACecil) **4-9-5** KFallon(6) (rdn 4f out: hdwy 3f out: edgd lft & led over 1f out: sn hdd: unable qckn)	1¾	**2**	10/11[1]	121	83
1476[5]	**Posidonas (118)** (PFICole) **5-9-5** TQuinn(5) (lw: led 1f: led over 5f out tl over 1f out: one pce)	1½	**3**	5/1[3]	119	81
2837[4]	**Nabhaan (IRE) (105)** (DMorley) **4-9-0** RCochrane(1) (hld up: rdn over 2f out: sn wknd)	2½	**4**	12/1	110	72
3501[2]	**Basman (IRE) (97)** (BSmart) **3-8-5** JStack(3) (lw: hld up: hung lft over 2f out: wknd over 1f out)	hd	**5**	33/1	110?	63
3191[6]	**Bahamian Knight (CAN) (105)** (RAkehurst) **4-9-0** OPeslier(4) (led 11f out tl over 5f out: wknd over 2f out: t.o)	dist	**6**	25/1	—	—
				(SP 108.5%)	**6 Rn**	

2m 36.69 (2.19) CSF £5.16 TOTE £3.50: £1.60 £1.30 (£2.20) OWNER Sheikh Ahmed Al Maktoum (NEWMARKET) BRED Sheikh Ahmed Bin Rashid Al Maktoum
WEIGHT FOR AGE 3yo-9lb

3125* Maylane goes extremely well for Michael Roberts, and coped with the step up in class. A temperamental individual, he stopped momentarily a stride after the stalls had opened and lost at least six lengths as a result. Allowed to do his own thing at the back of the field, he started to pick up ground a quarter of a mile out and, striking the front a furlong from home, soon asserted. (3/1)
3596* Dushyantor (USA), again fitted with the tongue-strap, failed to come down Tattenham Hill very well. Bustled along, he eventually got to the front approaching the final furlong, but he was soon headed and failed to find another gear. Lacking that vital turn of foot in top Pattern company is proving his downfall. (10/11)
1476 Posidonas looked in tremendous shape for this first run since the end of May, and inched into a narrow lead running down Tattenham Hill. He looked to be going well early in the straight, but lack of a recent run began to tell and, collared below the distance, he could only keep on at the one pace. Sure to come on for the outing, he is certainly on the way back. (5/1: op 11/4)
2837 Nabhaan (IRE) chased the leaders but had given his all two furlongs from home. (12/1)
3501 Basman (IRE) was certainly given a tough assignment here. Giving his jockey real steering problems in the straight on this tricky camber, he had been seen off early in the final quarter-mile. (33/1)
3191 Bahamian Knight (CAN), who has changed stables since his last outing, continues to run poorly and had given his all over two furlongs from home. (25/1)

4006 UNITED HOUSE NURSERY H'CAP (2-Y.O) (Class D)

4-10 (4-10) **6f** £3,501.25 (£1,060.00: £517.50: £246.25) Stalls: High GOING minus 0.06 sec per fur (G)

				SP	RR	SF
3215[5]	**Shawdon (85)** (SirMarkPrescott) **2-9-3** SSanders(6) (lw: mde all: drvn out)	—	**1**	5/1[2]	90	49
3892*	**High Carry (76)** (NTinkler) **2-8-8**[6x] RCochrane(7) (hld up: rdn over 2f out: chsd wnr over 1f out: r.o)	½	**2**	9/2[1]	80	39
3650[8]	**Bernardo Bellotto (IRE) (81)** (MBell) **2-8-13** KFallon(4) (lw: hld up: rdn over 3f out: unable qckn)	2½	**3**	9/2[1]	78	37
3152[7]	**Who Nose (IRE) (75)** (BJMeehan) **2-8-7b**[ow1] OPeslier(1) (lw: hld up: rdn over 3f out: one pce)	2	**4**	14/1	67	25
1924[2]	**Blakeset (89)** (RHannon) **2-9-7** TQuinn(9) (rdn over 3f out: hdwy fnl f: nvr nrr)	nk	**5**	11/2[3]	80	39
3127[7]	**Coolin River (IRE) (64)** (KRBurke) **2-7-10** JQuinn(8) (lw: chsd wnr over 4f)	1¼	**6**	16/1	52	11
3859[2]	**Just Another Time (66)** (JBerry) **2-7-12** DaleGibson(2) (lw: bhd fnl 2f)	3	**7**	11/2[3]	46	5
3278[4]	**Robeena (76)** (CNAllen) **2-8-5**[(3)] MartinDwyer(3) (s.s: a bhd)	3	**8**	12/1	48	7
3794[3]	**Iron Mountain (IRE) (69)** (NACallaghan) **2-8-1** GCarter(5) (lw: s.s: a bhd)	¾	**9**	8/1	39	—
				(SP 115.2%)	**9 Rn**	

1m 11.16 (3.16) CSF £25.19 CT £98.48 TOTE £6.10: £2.40 £2.00 £1.60 (£7.60) Trio £17.20 OWNER Mr Cyril Humphris (NEWMARKET) BRED C. Humphris

3215 Shawdon appreciated the return to six furlongs and, making every post a winning one, responded well to pressure to keep the runner-up at bay. (5/1: 3/1-11/2)

3892* High Carry, whose trainer only a week earlier had thought six furlongs was beyond her, was surprisingly running over that trip here but at least connections knew it was an easy six furlongs. Coming through to take second place approaching the final furlong, she looked likely to overhaul the winner inside the last two hundred yards but just failed. A return to five furlongs would be in her favour. (9/2: 3/1-5/1)
3433* Bernardo Bellotto (IRE), reverting to six furlongs after flopping over seven furlongs last time out, was bustled along early in the straight but failed to find that vital turn of foot. (9/2)
2942 Who Nose (IRE) failed to come down Tattenham Hill at all well, and could only struggle on at the one pace once in line for home. (14/1: 10/1-16/1)
1924 Blakeset, without a run in twelve weeks, was another who had difficulties running round Tattenham Corner, but did stay on in the final furlong only to find it all over bar the shouting. (11/2)
2571 Coolin River (IRE) gave chase to the winner but was collared for that position approaching the final furlong and had little left to offer. (16/1)

4007 MICHAEL J. LONSDALE MEDIAN AUCTION MAIDEN STKS (2-Y.O) (Class D)

4-40 (4-41) **7f** £3,420.00 (£1,035.00: £505.00: £240.00) Stalls: Low GOING minus 0.06 sec per fur (G)

				SP	RR	SF
3070^{2}	**Name of Love (IRE)** (DRLoder) **2-8-9** KFallon(10) (rdn over 5f out: hdwy over 2f out: chsd ldr over 1f out: led ins fnl f: r.o wl)	—	**1**	9/2^{2}	92	24
	Distinctive Dance (USA) (LordHuntingdon) **2-9-0** WRyan(3) (str: scope: hdwy over 1f out: r.o wl ins fnl f: bttr for r)	1½	**2**	11/1	94	26
3013^{2}	**Celtic Pageant** (RAkehurst) **2-9-0** SSanders(1) (led: clr over 3f out: rdn 2f out: hdd ins fnl f: sn wknd)	¾	**3**	Evens^{1}	92	24
3597^{4}	**Stone of Destiny (94)** (BJMeehan) **2-9-0** OPeslier(15) (swvd rt s: hdwy over 2f out: hrd rdn & edgd lft over 1f out: one pce)	2½	**4**	7/1^{3}	86	18
3117^{7}	**Former Love (USA)** (PRWebber) **2-8-9** AMcGlone(5) (a.p: rdn over 2f out: wknd over 1f out)	5	**5**	25/1	70	2
3743^{5}	**March Fourteenth (USA)** (JHMGosden) **2-8-9** GHind(12) (hld up: rdn over 3f out: sn wknd)	1¼	**6**	25/1	67	—
3070^{5}	**Nisaba (IRE)** (MJohnston) **2-8-9** MRoberts(14) (lw: hld up: rdn over 3f out: wknd over 2f out)	½	**7**	16/1	66	—
3783^{11}	**Zimzie** (MJHaynes) **2-8-11**$^{(3)}$ MartinDwyer(9) (outpcd: nvr nrr)	½	**8**	50/1	70	2
3084^{7}	**Ray's Folly (IRE)** (MAJarvis) **2-9-0** RCochrane(7) (a.p: rdn & wandered 2f out: wknd over 1f out)	1	**9**	10/1	67	—
2524^{8}	**Petruchio (IRE)** (MajorDNChappell) **2-9-0** AClark(4) (bhd fnl 2f)	2	**10**	33/1	63	—
	Mandhar (IRE) (GLewis) **2-9-0** PaulEddery(13) (unf: bit bkwd: a bhd)	1¼	**11**	25/1	60	—
3607^{6}	**King's Hussar** (PFICole) **2-9-0** TQuinn(6) (lw: a bhd)	1¼	**12**	33/1	57	—
3707^{5}	**Asbestaswecan** (WJarvis) **2-9-0** JQuinn(2) (lw: dwlt: a bhd)	s.h	**13**	25/1	57	—
3416^{8}	**Grosvenor Miss (IRE)** (PWChapple-Hyam) **2-8-6b^{1}**$^{(3)}$ RHavlin(11) (lw: prom over 3f)	3	**14**	33/1	45	—
3295^{7}	**Lauren's Lad** (GLewis) **2-9-0** GCarter(8) (dwlt: a wl bhd)	6	**15**	50/1	36	—
				(SP 132.1%)		**15 Rn**

1m 25.49 (5.19) CSF £47.48 TOTE £3.80: £1.40 £3.00 £1.30 (£60.10) Trio £21.40 OWNER Mr William Fox (NEWMARKET) BRED Noel O'Callaghan
3070 Name of Love (IRE) was soon being pushed along, and looked far from the winner. However, she began to find her feet in the straight and came with a nice run to lead inside the final furlong. (9/2)
Distinctive Dance (USA), an attractive, deep-girthed individual with plenty of scope, was not given a hard time but showed bags of promise. Racing well off the pace, Ryan was certainly considerate on him but the combination made up a tremendous amount of ground in the last furlong and a half to snatch second place. He should not be difficult to win with. (11/1: 7/1-14/1)
3013 Celtic Pageant, off the track for six weeks, stormed off in front and was clear entering the straight. He looked sure to succeed but he began to tire from below the distance, and was eventually overhauled inside the final furlong. He should soon be winning. (Evens)
3597 Stone of Destiny the most experienced in the line up, drifted left on the camber below the distance and could only struggle on at the one pace. (7/1)
3117 Former Love (USA) was close up until calling it a day over a furlong out. (25/1)
3743 March Fourteenth (USA) chased the leaders but the writing was on the wall early in the straight. (25/1)
3084 Ray's Folly (IRE) (10/1: 8/1-12/1)

4008 DEAN & WOOD MAIDEN H'CAP (0-70) (3-Y.O+) (Class E)

5-10 (5-14) **7f** £3,025.25 (£917.00: £448.50: £214.25) Stalls: Low GOING minus 0.06 sec per fur (G)

				SP	RR	SF
3470^{6}	**Octavia Hill (52)** (PWHarris) **4-9-0b** KFallon(14) (hdwy 3f out: led 2f out: clr over 1f out: rdn out)	—	**1**	11/2^{1}	63	40
2228^{5}	**Matoaka (60)** (VSoane) **3-9-4** RCochrane(17) (nt clr run over 2f out: swtchd rt & hdwy 1f out: str run fnl f: fin wl)	nk	**2**	12/1	70	43
1273^{13}	**Great Chief (42)** (BobJones) **4-8-4** NDay(6) (lw: dwlt: nt clr run over 2f out: hdwy & n.m.r over 1f out: unable qckn fnl f)	3	**3**	20/1	46	23
3855^{2}	**Kalimat (64)** (WJarvis) **3-9-8** TQuinn(15) (rdn over 3f out: hdwy 2f out: one pce fnl f)	1¼	**4**	13/2^{2}	65	38
3860^{3}	**Star Turn (IRE) (61)** (MBell) **3-9-5** MFenton(4) (lw: a.p: n.m.r over 2f out: one pce)	1½	**5**	11/2^{1}	58	31
3591^{5}	**Perfect Poppy (56)** (SDow) **3-9-0** SSanders(16) (rdn over 3f out: hdwy over 1f out: nvr nrr)	1	**6**	12/1	51	24
3227^{16}	**Press Again (37)** (PHayward) **5-7-10**$^{(3)ow2}$ MHenry(7) (lw: hld up: rdn over 3f out: nt clr run on ins wl over 1f out: sn wknd)	1¼	**7**	20/1	29	4
3710^{7}	**Velvet Jones (44)** (GFHCharles-Jones) **4-7-13**$^{(7)}$ CharlotteCox(11) (nvr nrr)	3½	**8**	20/1	28	5
3868^{3}	**Daintree (IRE) (48)** (HJCollingridge) **3-8-6v** DaleGibson(8) (bmpd s: plld hrd: a.p: led over 2f out: sn hdd: wknd over 1f out)	1	**9**	10/1	30	3
1419^{9}	**Il Doria (IRE) (50)** (AHide) **4-8-12** AMcGlone(2) (led over 4f: wknd over 1f out)	8	**10**	50/1	14	—
3860^{9}	**Le Bam Bam (55)** (CNAllen) **5-9-0**$^{(3)}$ MartinDwyer(3) (prom tl hmpd 4f out)	nk	**11**	25/1	18	—
3800^{5}	**Cold Lazarus (58)** (RTPhillips) **3-9-2v^{1}** GHind(5) (bhd fnl 5f)	1¼	**12**	20/1	18	—
3454^{3}	**Oxbane (53)** (CADwyer) **3-8-11** GCarter(13) (bhd fnl 2f)	½	**13**	11/1	12	—
	Hostile Native (56) (RGuest) **4-9-4** PBloomfield(9) (bmpd s: bhd fnl 3f)	1¾	**14**	9/1^{3}	11	—
3715^{11}	**Trevor Mitchell (45)** (JJBridger) **3-8-3** JQuinn(12) (a bhd)	nk	**15**	40/1	—	—
3715^{3}	**Bin Cyclone (USA) (66)** (CEBrittain) **3-9-10** MRoberts(10) (bmpd s: prom over 4f)	2	**16**	9/1^{3}	16	—
				(SP 124.2%)		**16 Rn**

1m 24.56 (4.26) CSF £59.42 CT £1,189.75 TOTE £5.80: £2.00 £3.40 £5.10 £1.50 (£66.10) Trio £580.70; £736.10 to 8/9/97 OWNER Mrs P. W. Harris (BERKHAMSTED) BRED Pendley Farm
WEIGHT FOR AGE 3yo-4lb
3470 Octavia Hill began her run down the outside in the straight and, striking the front two furlongs out, soon forged clear. However, with the runner-up finishing with a real flourish, she found the line only just coming in time. (11/2: 4/1-6/1)

2228 Matoaka only just failed to lose her maiden tag and make a winning debut for her new stable. Travelling well in the straight, if not having the best of runs, she began to pick up ground in tremendous style inside the distance. Storming through, she would surely have prevailed in a few more strides. (12/1)
Great Chief, off the course for three and a half months, did not have the best of runs but, when he did find daylight, failed to quicken in the final furlong. (20/1)
3855 Kalimat began a forward move two furlongs from home, and after showing briefly in front at the distance, was then tapped for toe. (13/2: 9/2-7/1)
3860 Star Turn (IRE) was never far away but failed to quicken in the last two furlongs. (11/2)
3591 Perfect Poppy stayed on from the back of the field in the last furlong and a half only to find it all over bar the shouting. (12/1)
3454 Oxbane (11/1: 8/1-12/1)
3715 Bin Cyclone (USA) (9/1: op 6/1)

4009 LEVY BOARD MAIDEN STKS (3-Y.O) (Class D)
5-40 (5-43) **1m 114y** £3,371.25 (£1,020.00: £497.50: £236.25) Stalls: Low GOING minus 0.06 sec per fur (G)

				SP	RR	SF
3800^{3}	**Summerosa (USA) (74)** (PWChapple-Hyam) **3-8-6**(3) RHavlin(3) (b.nr fore: lw: hdwy over 2f out: led over 1f out: r.o wl)	—	**1**	4/1 ^{3}	76	46
3277^{4}	**Easy Song (USA) (77)** (RCharlton) **3-9-0** SSanders(9) (lw: a.p: rdn over 3f out: led wl over 1f out: sn hdd: unable qckn)	5	**2**	5/2 ^{1}	72	42
2591^{6}	**Lawz (IRE)** (CJBenstead) **3-9-0** RCochrane(11) (lw: swvd rt s: hdwy over 1f out: edgd lft ins fnl f: one pce)	½	**3**	7/1	71	41
3415^{7}	**Jilly Woo (32)** (PHayward) **3-8-6**(3) MHenry(8) (rdn over 3f out: hdwy over 1f out: nvr nrr)	2½	**4**	50/1	61	31
3775^{9}	**Cuesta Rey (USA)** (JWHills) **3-9-0** KFallon(4) (a.p: led over 2f out tl wl over 1f out: wknd fnl f)	½	**5**	20/1	65	35
2184^{6}	**Sharpwitted** (JHMGosden) **3-8-9** GHind(7) (lw: hld up: rdn over 3f out: wkng whn hung lft 1f out)	1¾	**6**	12/1	57	27
$268a^{9}$	**Palisander (IRE) (70)** (SDow) **3-9-0** MRoberts(2) (chsd ldr: led over 3f out tl over 2f out: sn wknd)	3	**7**	25/1	56	26
3720^{3}	**Love Venture (69)** (SPCWoods) **3-8-9** WRyan(1) (lw: led 5f: wknd over 2f out)	8	**8**	10/1	36	6
3641^{5}	**Able Lass (IRE)** (RWArmstrong) **3-8-9** GCarter(6) (a bhd)	25	**9**	20/1	—	—
3632^{3}	**Georgina (IRE)** (MajorWRHern) **3-8-9** PaulEddery(10) (b: b.hind: nvr gng wl: a wl bhd: t.o whn p.u lame ins fnl f: dead)		**P**	3/1 ^{2}	—	—
3425^{8}	**Treaty (USA)** (KMahdi) **3-8-11**(3) MartinDwyer(5) (lw: ref to r: t.n.p)		**R**	25/1	—	—
				(SP 122.0%)	**11 Rn**	

1m 46.27 (4.27) CSF £12.69 TOTE £5.60: £1.10 £1.60 £2.10 (£7.20) Trio £14.00 OWNER Mr R E Sangster & Mrs J Magnier (MARLBOROUGH) BRED Swettenham Stud and Roncon Ltd
3800 Summerosa (USA) at long last got off the mark and, coming through to lead below the distance, soon forged clear. She still looks one to oppose. (4/1)
3277 Easy Song (USA), racing with his tongue tied down, looked extremely well beforehand and poked a whisker in front early in the final quarter-mile. Soon collared by the winner, he was then left for dead. He should soon find a race. (5/2)
2591 Lawz (IRE) began to pick up ground below the distance, but he drifted left on the camber inside the final furlong and failed to quicken. (7/1)
3081 Jilly Woo, who has changes stables since her last run, is extremely exposed but did stay on to be nearest at the line. She remains a maiden after fifteen attempts. (50/1)
Cuesta Rey (USA) ran much better here and showed in front for a short time early in the straight. (20/1)
2184 Sharpwitted chased the leaders but was already beaten when giving her rider real steering problems a furlong from home. (12/1: op 7/1)
3720 Love Venture (10/1: 7/1-12/1)
3632 Georgina (IRE) (3/1: 2/1-100/30)

T/Plpt: £17.70 (2,128.92 Tckts). T/Qdpt: £2.60 (720.2 Tckts) AK

3568-HAYDOCK (L-H) (Good to soft)
Friday September 5th
WEATHER: fine & sunny WIND: slt half against

4010 BOLLINGER CHAMPAGNE CHALLENGE SERIES GENTLEMEN'S H'CAP (0-70) (3-Y.O) (Class E)
2-15 (2-15) **1m 3f 200y** £2,905.00 (£880.00: £430.00: £205.00) Stalls: High GOING minus 0.01 sec per fur (G)

				SP	RR	SF
*3400**	**Certain Magic (45)** (WRMuir) **3-10-6** MrTMcCarthy(6) (hdwy over 4f out: nt clr run on ins & swtchd over 2f out: styd on wl fnl f: led towards fin)	—	**1**	9/2 ^{2}	55	28
3762^{7}	**Protaras Bay (36)** (PLGilligan) **3-9-7**(4)ow4 MrOMcPhail(3) (hdwy to chse ldrs over 4f out: led over 1f out: hdd nr fin)	nk	**2**	33/1	46	15
3585^{2}	**Foolish Flutter (IRE) (47)** (RBastiman) **3-10-8b** MrRHale(1) (w ldr: led 5f out tl over 1f out: one pce)	2½	**3**	6/1 ^{3}	53	26
3486^{3}	**Classical Dance (IRE) (47)** (MrsMReveley) **3-10-8** MrCBonner(4) (hdwy over 4f out: sn chsng ldrs: one pce fnl 2f)	1¾	**4**	7/2 ^{1}	51	24
3609^{2}	**Grand Hotel (IRE) (42)** (PWHarris) **3-10-3b** MrJGoldstein(9) (in tch: effrt & hung lft 3f out: one pce fnl 2f)	¾	**5**	9/2 ^{2}	45	18
3779^{4}	**Madison Welcome (IRE) (61)** (MrsJRRamsden) **3-11-8v** MrABalding(10) (lw: led to 5f out: lost pl 2f out)	4	**6**	13/2	59	32
3601^{14}	**Red Embers (40)** (DNicholls) **3-9-11**(4) MrVLukaniuk(5) (dwlt: plld hrd: a in rr)	10	**7**	20/1	24	—
3298^{3}	**High On Life (65)** (ACStewart) **3-11-8b1**(4) MrCRanson(2) (lw: s.s: hdwy to chse ldrs 8f out: sddle slipped: virtually p.u over 1f out)	7	**8**	8/1	40	13
3813^{5}	**Lord Discord (60)** (TDEasterby) **3-11-7** MrSSwiers(7) (chsd ldrs tl lost pl over 4f out: sn wl bhd: t.o)	dist	**9**	8/1	—	—
				(SP 116.1%)	**9 Rn**	

2m 42.8 (13.40) CSF £121.09 CT £818.96 TOTE £4.60: £1.90 £6.50 £1.60 (£35.20) Trio £208.40; £211.44 to 8/9/97 OWNER Delamere Partnership (LAMBOURN) BRED D. J. and Mrs Deer
OFFICIAL EXPLANATION **Lord Discord: was found to be distressed after the race. High On Life: saddle slipped.**
3400* Certain Magic met all the trouble going and his rider did well to get him clear and get him up near the line. (9/2)
Protaras Bay, who has tumbled down the weights, lacked nothing in assistance from the saddle. (33/1)
3585 Foolish Flutter (IRE), a keen-going type, probably ran up to the best she is capable of. (6/1)
3486 Classical Dance (IRE) probably ran to the same level of form he showed at Hamilton. (7/2)
3609 Grand Hotel (IRE) gave his rider problems and did not look that enthusiastic. (9/2)
3298 High On Life, tried in blinkers this time, was taken to post early. Losing many lengths at the start, he soon recovered but, with his saddle slipping right round, his rider had no option but to call it a day. (8/1)

4011 HAYDOCK PARK SPRINT CUP STKS (Gp 1) (3-Y.O+) (Class A)

2-50 (2-53) **6f** £75,292.00 (£27,628.00: £13,064.00: £5,120.00: £1,810.00: £486.00) Stalls: High GOING minus 0.01 sec per fur (G)

				SP	RR	SF
2599^{2}	**Royal Applause (118)** (BWHills) **4-9-0** MHills(9) (mde all: qcknd clr over 1f out: r.o wl)	—	1	15/8^{1}	123	59
3553a*	**Tomba (113)** (BJMeehan) **3-8-12** MTebbutt(6) (lw: hmpd after 1f: nt clr run & swtchd lft over 1f out: styd on wl: fin 3rd, ½l: plcd 2nd)	1¼	2	8/1	118	52
3217*	**Danetime (IRE) (109)** (NACallaghan) **3-8-12** MJKinane(3) (lw: plld hrd: swtchd rt after 1f: hdwy & swtchd lft over 1f out: r.o wl: nt rch wnr: fin 2nd, 1¼l: disq: plcd 3rd)	½	3	3/1^{2}	120	54
3724^{3}	**Averti (IRE) (110)** (WRMuir) **6-9-0** JReid(4) (lw: swvd rt & bmpd s: hmpd after 1f: hdwy & hmpd 2f out: hung lft: wknd towards fin)	1¼	4	12/1	115	51
3747^{6}	**Tedburrow (104)** (EJAlston) **5-9-0** ACulhane(2) (hld up: hdwy 2f out: sn chsng ldrs: nt qckn appr fnl f)	2	5	50/1	110	46
940^{10}	**Muchea (115)** (MRChannon) **3-8-12** JFortune(5) (b.nr fore: bmpd s: hmpd after 1f: n.d after)	3½	6	25/1	100	34
3554a^{2}	**Monaassib (114)** (EALDunlop) **6-9-0** DO'Donohoe(7) (chsd ldrs: drvn along ½-wy: wknd 2f out: eased)	6	7	14/1	84	20
3724*	**Coastal Bluff (109)** (TDBarron) **5-9-0** KDarley(1) (b.hind: sn chsng ldrs: rdn 2f out: edgd rt & lost pl over 1f out)	1¼	8	9/2^{3}	81	17
3724^{10}	**Indian Rocket (114)** (JLDunlop) **3-8-12** RHills(8) (lw: plld hrd: chsd ldrs: rdn over 2f out: sn lost pl & eased)	3½	9	8/1	72	6
				(SP 120.4%)	**9 Rn**	

1m 14.46 (2.76) CSF £7.19 TOTE £2.90: £1.20 £2.10 £2.20 (£7.10) Trio £12.10 OWNER Maktoum Al Maktoum (LAMBOURN) BRED Gainsborough Stud Management Ltd

WEIGHT FOR AGE 3yo-2lb

SUBSEQUENT STEWARDS' ENQUIRY Kinane susp. 15-16/9/97 (careless riding). Following an appeal by connections of Tomba, Danetime (IRE) was disqualified and placed third, and Tomba promoted to second.

OFFICIAL EXPLANATION Coastal Bluff: was blowing excessively after the race.

2599 Royal Applause had the plum stands'-side draw, and found the easy ground no problem. Showing all his old speed, he avoided any trouble and took this in decisive fashion, putting his yet to be explained Newmarket flop behind him. He must have sound prospects of emulating Sheikh Albadou who took this prize five years ago before going on to triumph in the Breeders' Cup Sprint. (15/8)

3553a* Tomba, who had the ground to suit, was impeded after a furlong by Danetime. With nowhere to go over a furlong out, he was forced to switch wide and, staying on well, he would certainly have troubled the winner with better luck. Whether he would have beaten him is doubtful. (8/1)

3217* Danetime (IRE) took a keen grip, and after the first furlong his rider pulled him in behind horses to try to get him to settle, causing problems for those on his inside. Forced to switch wide to get a run over a furlong out, he stayed on in good style but too late to trouble the winner. He looks to have further improvement in him and should be a top sprinter next year. (3/1)

3724 Averti (IRE) swerved leaving the stalls, colliding with Muchea, and that was just the start of his problems. Hampered when Danetime was pulled in behind horses after a furlong, he was then pushed wide by that horse over a furlong out, but then compounded his rider's problems by hanging left. (12/1)

3747 Tedburrow, who looked to have plenty to do in this class, again travelled strongly and probably ran his best ever race. (50/1)

737 Muchea collided with Averti at the start and then, like that horse and Tomba, was given problems by Danetime after a furlong. (25/1)

3724* Coastal Bluff, worst drawn, drifted right and dropped right out over a furlong out. He was found to be blowing hard afterwards. Significantly when he took the Stewards' Cup and the Ayr Gold Cup, he had a rail to race against on his right-hand side. (9/2)

3724 Indian Rocket contributed to his own downfall by refusing to settle. (8/1)

4012 E.B.F. BIRKENHEAD MAIDEN STKS (2-Y.O) (Class D)

3-20 (3-25) **5f** £3,777.50 (£1,145.00: £560.00: £267.50) Stalls: High GOING minus 0.01 sec per fur (G)

				SP	RR	SF
2926^{3}	**Escudo (IRE)** (JHMGosden) **2-8-9** JReid(8) (racd far side: trckd ldrs: led over 2f out: r.o wl)	—	1	4/1^{1}	73	34
3471^{4}	**Sarah Stokes (IRE)** (RGuest) **2-8-9** DHolland(12) (hdwy over 2f out: r.o fnl f)	1¼	2	4/1^{1}	69	30
2565^{10}	**Positive Air (61)** (BAMcMahon) **2-8-6**(3) RFfrench(14) (lw: unruly s: w ldrs: led stands' side over 1f out: kpt on)	½	3	20/1	67	28
3094^{6}	**Dil (78)** (BHanbury) **2-9-0** RHills(18) (lw: hld up: hdwy 2f out: styd on wl fnl f)	hd	4	6/1^{2}	72	33
3574^{8}	**Greeba** (RHannon) **2-8-9** MJKinane(16) (chsd ldrs: ev ch over 1f out: kpt on one pce)	2½	5	9/1^{3}	59	20
	Wenda (IRE) (CEBrittain) **2-8-9** KDarley(15) (str: scope: chsd ldrs: rn green: kpt on same pce appr fnl f)	hd	6	12/1	59	20
	Treble Term (PJMakin) **2-8-9** MHills(4) (w'like: lw: racd far side: chsd ldrs: wknd ins fnl f)	s.h	7	12/1	59	20
	Sorridar (JLEyre) **2-8-10**ow1 MGallagher(13) (leggy: unf: lw: dwlt s: hdwy over 1f out: nvr nr to chal)	1¾	8	33/1	54	14
3247^{8}	**Arjan (IRE)** (JBerry) **2-8-6**(3) PFessey(9) (s.i.s: hdwy centre ½-wy: edgd lft & wknd over 1f out)	hd	9	20/1	53	14
2212^{5}	**Super Snip** (ABailey) **2-9-0** DWright(20) (lw: sme hdwy over 1f out: nvr nr ldrs)	hd	10	20/1	57	18
	Surprised (MrsJRRamsden) **2-9-0** JFortune(11) (wl grwn: rn green & sn bhd: hdwy & hung lft 2f out: styd on ins fnl f)	nk	11	12/1	56	17
	Anstand (MrsJRRamsden) **2-9-0** OPears(1) (lt-f: racd far side: sn outpcd: sme hdwy 2f out: n.d)	s.h	12	33/1	56	17
2917^{18}	**Vista Alegre** (PJMakin) **2-9-0** GDuffield(7) (lw: racd far side: chsd ldrs over 2f: sn wknd)	2	13	33/1	50	11
	Game Bird (JLSpearing) **2-8-9** SDrowne(23) (unf: bit bkwd: s.s: a in rr)	1¼	14	33/1	41	2
3686^{5}	**Jack Ruby** (PLGilligan) **2-9-0** DeanMcKeown(6) (led far side: hdd & wknd over 2f out)	nk	15	33/1	45	6
2538^{5}	**Essandess (IRE)** (JLEyre) **2-8-9** TWilliams(2) (bit bkwd: racd far side: w ldrs tl wknd 2f out)	½	16	33/1	38	—
3857^{5}	**Take A Risk** (MJohnston) **2-8-9** JWeaver(22) (b.hind: led stands' side tl hdd & wknd over 1f out)	1½	17	6/1^{2}	34	—
	Lord Lieutenant (MBell) **2-9-0** ACulhane(10) (lengthy: racd far side: sn pushed along: outpcd fr ½-wy)	s.h	18	12/1	38	—
	Carol Singer (USA) (MJohnston) **2-8-9** JFanning(17) (lengthy: unf: w ldrs tl wknd 2f out)	s.h	19	25/1	33	—
	Bollin Ethos (TDEasterby) **2-9-0** LCharnock(3) (w'like: racd far side: sn drvn along & outpcd)	2½	20	33/1	30	—
3239^{8}	**Penny Whistle** (TDEasterby) **2-8-9** NKennedy(5) (s.i.s: racd far side: a bhd)	s.h	21	25/1	25	—
872^{7}	**Lady d'Abo** (RCSpicer) **2-8-9** TSprake(21) (s.s: t.o)	14	22	33/1	—	—
564^{5}	***Sacchetti (IRE)*** (MRChannon) **2-8-11**(3) PPMurphy(19) (Withdrawn not under Starter's orders: reard backwards ent stalls)		W	16/1	—	—
				(SP 160.7%)	**22 Rn**	

62.99 secs (3.49) CSF £17.89 TOTE £4.30: £2.20 £1.80 £5.20 (£7.40) Trio £77.90 OWNER Sheikh Mohammed (NEWMARKET) BRED Miss Rita B. Kennedy

2926 Escudo (IRE) almost certainly raced on the better ground on the far side and took this in convincing fashion. (4/1: op 2/1)

3471 Sarah Stokes (IRE), who showed plenty of knee action going down, was well backed to step up on her promising first effort. She came out best of those on the stands' side but the winner was home and dry on the far side. (4/1)

2312 Positive Air, who gave problems at the start, did nothing wrong once underway. (20/1)

3094 Dil, who showed a good action going down, put in some solid late work and might be interesting in a six or seven-furlong nursery. (6/1)

Greeba, dropped in class, showed a very poor action going to post. (9/1)

Wenda (IRE), whose action left a lot to be desired, showed some ability despite running very green, but she obviously has plenty to learn. (12/1)
Sorridar showed a glimmer of promise after a sluggish start. (33/1)
Surprised, who has plenty of size and scope, is a half-brother to Surprise Mission and Bishops Court. Running green and getting behind and hanging out towards the centre, he did show some ability and there is almost certainly a good deal better to come in time. (12/1)
Lord Lieutenant (12/1: op 7/1)

4013 KING'S REGIMENT CUP LIMITED STKS (0-85) (3-Y.O+) (Class D)

3-50 (3-51) **6f** £3,485.00 (£1,055.00: £515.00: £245.00) Stalls: High GOING minus 0.01 sec per fur (G)

				SP	RR	SF
3580*	**Almasi (IRE) (82)** (CFWall) **5-8-9**(7) JoHunnam(4) (lw: s.i.s: hdwy over 2f out: rdn to ld ins fnl f: r.o wl)	—	**1**	6/1^{3}	94	44
3765^{10}	**Prends Ca (IRE) (82)** (WRMuir) **4-8-10** JReid(3) (lw: hld up: hdwy to ld over 1f out: edgd lft & hdd ins fnl f: no ex)	nk	**2**	15/2	87	37
3709*	**Bahamian Beauty (USA) (81)** (DRLoder) **3-9-0** KDarley(8) (lw: trckd ldrs: ev ch & rdn over 1f out: nt qckn ins fnl f)	½	**3**	11/4^{1}	92	40
3765^{9}	**Sir Joey (USA) (82)** (PGMurphy) **8-8-13** SDrowne(10) (hld up: hdwy over 1f out: styd on wl towards fin)	hd	**4**	4/1^{2}	89	39
514^{3}	**State of Caution (79)** (DShaw) **4-8-13b** JFanning(6) (b: chsd ldrs: rdn 2f out: wknd ins fnl f)	2½	**5**	20/1	82	32
3604^{14}	**Babsy Babe (84)** (JJQuinn) **4-8-10** JFortune(9) (lw: chsd ldrs: effrt over 2f out: one pce)	1½	**6**	4/1^{2}	75	25
3273^{11}	**Dayville (USA) (84)** (JBerry) **3-9-0** DHolland(2) (lw: led tl hdd & wknd over 1f out)	1½	**7**	12/1	77	25
2278*	**Fiametta (85)** (CEBrittain) **3-8-11** MJKinane(1) (dwlt: hdwy over 2f out: rdn & wknd over 1f out)	3	**8**	8/1	66	14
	Scharnhorst (73) (ARDicken) **5-8-8**(5) ADaly(7) (b: bkwd: w ldr tl wknd qckly 2f out: t.o)	21	**9**	20/1	10	—
				(SP 121.0%)	**9 Rn**	

1m 15.67 (3.97) CSF £48.06 TOTE £6.50: £1.40 £1.80 £1.50 (£16.60) Trio £33.90 OWNER The Equema Partnership (NEWMARKET) BRED Newtownbarry House Stud
WEIGHT FOR AGE 3yo-2lb
3580* Almasi (IRE), who has improved about a stone and a half in her last five runs, was well handled after missing the break slightly and, in the end, took this in rather cosy fashion. (6/1)
3436 Prends Ca (IRE), who had a good chance at the weights, is suited by soft ground. Taking a very keen grip, she lacked nothing in assistance from the saddle but close home was definitely second best. (15/2)
3709* Bahamian Beauty (USA) found the reversion to six furlongs no problem. (11/4)
2833 Sir Joey (USA), who is hard to win with, ran his usual race, steaming through at the death. (4/1)
514 State of Caution, having his first outing for one hundred and sixty days, travelled strongly but faded as if in need of the outing. (20/1)
3273 Babsy Babe, best in on official figures never looked like picking up in this ground. (4/1)
2649* Dayville (USA), taken to post early, has speed to burn but, doing too much too soon had nothing at all left in reserve at the business end. (12/1)
2278* Fiametta, an inexperienced filly and a winner of her only previous start, missed the break and with no cover up the middle dropped right out. She possibly needed this and certainly needed the experience. (8/1)

4014 NORWEST HOLST CONSTRUCTION CLAIMING STKS (2-Y.O) (Class F)

4-20 (4-23) **6f** £2,885.00 (£810.00: £395.00) Stalls: High GOING minus 0.01 sec per fur (G)

				SP	RR	SF
3707^{17}	**Classy Cleo (IRE) (74)** (RHannon) **2-8-1**(3) RFfrench(1) (lw: a.p: led over 2f out: r.o wl)	—	**1**	8/1^{3}	68	11
3707*	**Chinaider (IRE) (76)** (MCPipe) **2-8-12** KDarley(7) (a.p: chsd wnr over 1f out: r.o one pce)	1	**2**	7/4^{1}	73	16
3711^{13}	**Madame Jones (IRE)** (BJMeehan) **2-8-7**^{ow1} MTebbutt(5) (lw: hdwy over 1f out: r.o ins fnl f)	1¼	**3**	33/1	65	7
3493^{3}	**Saligo (IRE) (57)** (HMorrison) **2-8-3b**^{ow1} SDrowne(8) (lw: chsd ldrs: r.o one pce fnl f)	½	**4**	25/1	60	2
3707^{7}	**Sandside (76)** (JBerry) **2-8-7** MJKinane(2) (prom tl wknd fnl f)	1¼	**5**	8/1^{3}	60	3
3699^{6}	**Chardania (IRE) (40)** (CaptJWilson) **2-7-10** GBardwell(15) (styd on fnl 2f: nt rch ldrs)	1	**6**	33/1	47	—
3808^{5}	**Moonlight Flit** (JGFitzGerald) **2-7-12** TWilliams(6) (hdyw over 1f out: nt rch ldrs)	1¼	**7**	25/1	45	—
3804^{3}	**Patsy Culsyth (69)** (NTinkler) **2-8-0** KimTinkler(3) (rdn & hdwy over 2f out: one pce appr fnl f)	½	**8**	12/1	46	—
3889^{2}	**Heavenly Abstone (85)** (PDEvans) **2-8-12v** JFEgan(4) (chsd ldrs: rdn over 2f out: wknd over 1f out)	nk	**9**	7/2^{2}	57	—
	City Dance (PJMakin) **2-8-2** GDuffield(10) (leggy: lt-f: unf: s.s: a bhd)	4	**10**	25/1	37	—
3438^{6}	**Royal Dream (79)** (JBerry) **2-7-13**(3) PFessey(9) (lw: w ldrs: hung rt & wknd 2f out)	hd	**11**	8/1^{3}	36	—
3563^{10}	**Eurofen (46)** (PDEvans) **2-8-2b** DWright(16) (sn outpcd)	¾	**12**	25/1	34	—
3789^{9}	**Oso Rich** (PMRich) **2-8-7** NAdams(11) (bit bkwd: s.s: a bhd)	5	**13**	50/1	26	—
3635^{9}	**Really Done It Now (IRE) (64)** (KRBurke) **2-7-9**(7) RWinston(13) (lw: w ldrs over 3f)	nk	**14**	14/1	20	—
3755^{7}	**Heavenly Falls (IRE) (65)** (CADwyer) **2-8-4**(3) DO'Donohoe(14) (chsd ldrs: outpcd fr ½-wy)	5	**15**	20/1	12	—
3908^{7}	**Two Williams (85)** (MWEasterby) **2-9-3** TLucas(12) (led over 3f: sn wknd)	½	**16**	10/1	21	—
				(SP 143.4%)	**16 Rn**	

1m 17.34 (5.64) CSF £22.00 TOTE £10.40: £2.80 £1.40 £10.10 (£13.20) Trio £305.10 OWNER Mrs A. Kane (MARLBOROUGH) BRED Rathasker Stud
Chinaider (IRE) clmd M Leatham £20,000, Classy Cleo (IRE) clmd P D Evans £12,000
OFFICIAL EXPLANATION **Classy Cleo: regarding the current improvement as compared to the filly's previous run at York, the Handicapper explained that on a line with Chinaider, the filly had improved twenty lengths for being 8lb better off on this occasion. The trainer reported that he had no explanation for the poor run at York, but added the filly does suffer slight wind problems.**
2919 Classy Cleo (IRE) does not mind give underfoot, and may not have had the best of the draw when well behind the runner-up at York last time. (8/1: op 5/1)
3707* Chinaider (IRE) could not confirm the York form with the winner on 8lb worse terms, and now goes to be trained by David Nicholls. (7/4)
Madame Jones (IRE) stepped up considerably on her debut, and is going the right way. (33/1)
3493 Saligo (IRE) may have run a bit freely in the first-time blinkers last time, but should be suited to a return to seven on this evidence. (25/1)
3707 Sandside seems at his most effective over the minimum trip. (8/1)
3699 Chardania (IRE) might be worth a try over an extra furlong. (33/1)

4015 NORWEST HOLT CONSTRUCTION H'CAP (0-80) (3-Y.O) (Class D)

4-50 (4-51) **1m 2f 120y** £3,972.50 (£1,205.00: £590.00: £282.50) Stalls: High GOING minus 0.01 sec per fur (G)

				SP	RR	SF
3777^{11}	**Largesse (67)** (JohnBerry) **3-8-8** JFEgan(11) (a.p: led wl over 1f out: clr whn edgd lft ins fnl f: rdn out)	—	**1**	33/1	77	44
3891^{6}	**Sellette (IRE) (79)** (DHaydnJones) **3-9-6** SDrowne(18) (hld up: hdwy 2f out: r.o ins fnl f)	1¼	**2**	25/1	87	54
3633*	**Dead Aim (IRE) (78)** (IABalding) **3-9-5** KDarley(8) (lw: a chsng ldrs: styd on fnl f)	1¾	**3**	9/1^{2}	83	50
3381^{2}	**Night Mirage (USA) (76)** (MJohnston) **3-9-3** JWeaver(9) (a.p: r.o one pce fnl 2f)	nk	**4**	9/1^{2}	81	48

Form	Horse	Dist	Pos	SP	RR	SF
3891*	**Yabint El Sultan (79)** (BAMcMahon) **3-9-3**(3) 5x RFfrench(13) (lw: hld up & bhd: hdwy on outside over 3f out: one pce fnl 2f)	nk	**5**	2/1[1]	84	51
3685*	**Interdream (77)** (RHannon) **3-9-4** MTebbutt(7) (lw: hld up & bhd: hdwy 2f out: rdn & hung lft ins fnl f: nt rch ldrs)	2	**6**	9/1[2]	79	46
3921[3]	**Sparky (69)** (MWEasterby) **3-8-10v**[1] MJKinane(10) (b: hld up & bhd: styd on fnl 2f: nrst fin)	1	**7**	9/1[2]	69	36
2846[8]	**Sefton Blake (60)** (MGMeagher) **3-7-8**(7) RWinston(5) (hdwy over 4f out: nvr trbld ldrs)	1¼	**8**	40/1	58	25
2568[4]	**Legendary Lover (IRE) (80)** (RCharlton) **3-9-7** TSprake(14) (lw: prom: ev ch 2f out: wknd over 1f out)	1¼	**9**	16/1	76	43
2492[4]	**Sahara River (USA) (62)** (RCharlton) **3-8-3** GDuffield(12) (nvr nr ldrs)	nk	**10**	14/1	58	25
3820[2]	**Villarica (IRE) (74)** (PWChapple-Hyam) **3-9-1** JReid(17) (lw: hld up & bhd: hdwy over 2f out: nt clr run & swtchd lft over 1f out: btn whn hmpd ins fnl f)	1½	**11**	9/1[2]	68	35
	Rose Carnival (74) (DRLoder) **3-9-1** MHills(2) (led tl wl over 1f out: sn wknd)	2½	**12**	16/1	64	31
3396[4]	**Flying Flip (55)** (BCMorgan) **3-7-10** LCharnock(16) (b.hind: mid div: effrt over 3f out: sn wknd)	2½	**13**	33/1	41	8
3775*	**Royale Rose (FR) (72)** (ABailey) **3-8-8**(5) GFaulkner(1) (sn chsng ldrs: wknd over 2f out)	hd	**14**	16/1	58	25
3696[3]	**Time Can Tell (63)** (CMurray) **3-8-4** JFanning(3) (prom tl wknd over 2f out)	nk	**15**	25/1	48	15
3071[6]	**Northern Flash (67)** (FMurphy) **3-8-8** DeanMcKeown(4) (prom tl rdn & wknd over 3f out)	3½	**16**	33/1	47	14
3813[7]	**Rare Talent (66)** (MRChannon) **3-8-7** ACulhane(15) (hld up: a bhd)	8	**17**	20/1	34	1
3722[13]	**Step N Go (IRE) (70)** (MrsJRRamsden) **3-8-11** JFortune(6) (hld up: a bhd)	1¾	**18**	10/1[3]	35	2
				(SP 140.5%)	**18 Rn**	

2m 17.75 (6.25) CSF £680.52 CT £7,132.11 TOTE £127.70: £11.90 £7.10 £2.40 £1.90 (£415.40) Trio Not won; £920.67 to Bath 8/9/97
OWNER Mrs Rosemary Moszkowicz (NEWMARKET) BRED Snowdrop Stud Co Ltd

3274 Largesse, dropped a total of 10lb after some disappointing efforts, was stepped up in distance so he could travel on the bridle longer. (33/1)
3891 Sellette (IRE), a bit disappointing at Chester a week ago, was coming back after a break and again had the sort of ground she needs. (25/1)
3633* Dead Aim (IRE), raised 3lb, had won over a bit further at Windsor. (9/1)
3381 Night Mirage (USA), 6lb higher than when scoring at Hamilton last month, has had the benefit of a short rest and is holding her form well. (9/1)
3891* Yabint El Sultan, penalised for her Chester win a week ago, was still 4lb well in on her rating from tomorrow. (2/1)
3685* Interdream, up 7lb, was no less than 17lb higher than when his win after being disqualified at Brighton. (9/1)
3921 Sparky was trying a visor instead of his usual blinkers. (9/1)
2492 Sahara River (USA) (14/1: 12/1-20/1)
3820 Villarica (IRE) would have finished closer with a better run. (9/1)

4016 OUTLAND (S) H'CAP (0-60) (3-Y.O+) (Class G)

5-20 (5-27) **6f** £2,766.00 (£776.00: £378.00) Stalls: High GOING minus 0.01 sec per fur (G)

Form	Horse	Dist	Pos	SP	RR	SF
3484[9]	**King Uno (47)** (MrsJRRamsden) **3-8-13v** GDuffield(17) (s.i.s: rapid hdwy over 1f out: hrd rdn & edgd lft fnl f: led nr fin)	—	**1**	12/1	56	26
3936[5]	**Halmanerror (54)** (MrsJRRamsden) **7-9-8** JFortune(1) (s.s: hdwy over 2f out: led ins fnl f: hdd nr fin)	1½	**2**	9/2[1]	59	31
3856[9]	**Middle East (56)** (TDBarron) **4-9-10** KDarley(8) (racd far side: a.p: led over 1f out tl ins fnl f)	¾	**3**	14/1	59	31
3642[5]	**Never Think Twice (57)** (KTIvory) **4-9-11v** CScally(22) (sn chsng ldrs: led stands' side 1f out: r.o)	1¼	**4**	10/1[3]	57	29
2547[7]	**Fine Times (50)** (CWFairhurst) **3-9-2v** DeanMcKeown(19) (hdwy & edgd lft over 1f out: r.o ins fnl f)	1¼	**5**	16/1	46	16
3936[7]	**Panther (IRE) (57)** (PDEvans) **7-9-11v** JFEgan(5) (chsd ldrs far side: rdn over 2f out: one pce)	nk	**6**	16/1	53	25
3251[4]	**Nervous Rex (54)** (WRMuir) **3-8-13**(7) JWilkinson(3) (racd far side: swtchd rt over 1f out: no hdwy fnl f)	½	**7**	16/1	48	18
3910[8]	**Shontaine (56)** (MJohnston) **4-9-10** JWeaver(14) (nvr nr to chal)	nk	**8**	10/1[3]	49	21
1816[3]	**Densben (47)** (DenysSmith) **13-9-1** ACulhane(11) (s.i.s: hdwy over 1f out: nvr nrr)	¾	**9**	11/1	38	10
3856[8]	**Dominelle (48)** (TDEasterby) **5-9-2** JReid(6) (lw: nvr trbld ldrs)	nk	**10**	10/1[3]	39	11
3910[12]	**Another Nightmare (IRE) (49)** (RMMcKellar) **5-9-3** KimTinkler(12) (led stands' side: wknd over 1f out)	1¾	**11**	20/1	35	7
3698[5]	**Stock Hill Dancer (53)** (BJMeehan) **3-8-12**(7) GHannon(7) (racd far side: led over 4f)	nk	**12**	16/1	38	8
3642[9]	**Imposing Time (51)** (MissGayKelleway) **6-9-2v**(3) RFfrench(23) (b: lw: chsd ldrs 4f)	2½	**13**	14/1	30	2
3756[10]	**Marino Street (45)** (PDEvans) **4-8-6**(7) AMcCarthy(10) (a bhd)	nk	**14**	25/1	23	—
3625[6]	**Petraco (IRE) (44)** (NASmith) **9-8-7**(5) AmandaSanders(16) (chsd ldrs: bmpd over 1f out: wknd fnl f)	½	**15**	14/1	20	—
3816[4]	**Hype Energy (52)** (GLewis) **3-9-1b**(3) AWhelan(24) (prom 3f)	4	**16**	9/1[2]	18	—
3851[5]	**Gold Edge (57)** (MRChannon) **3-9-2**(7) AEddery(9) (reard stalls: a bhd)	s.h	**17**	10/1[3]	23	—
3693[10]	**Sound the Trumpet (IRE) (50)** (RCSpicer) **5-9-4** TSprake(21) (prom over 4f)	1	**18**	20/1	13	—
3470[8]	**Rockaroundtheclock (49)** (TRWatson) **3-9-1b** JFanning(20) (dwlt: a bhd)	s.h	**19**	20/1	12	—
2002[12]	**Beldray Park (IRE) (46)** (MrsALMKing) **4-9-0v**[1] TWilliams(15) (w ldrs tl wknd over 1f out)	½	**20**	33/1	7	—
3871[5]	**Toronto (47)** (JBerry) **3-8-6b**(7) PBradley(18) (prom over 3f)	4	**21**	20/1	—	—
3693[5]	**Make Ready (53)** (JNeville) **3-9-5v**[1] SDrowne(13) (chsd ldrs 3f)	8	**22**	16/1	—	—
				(SP 155.8%)	**22 Rn**	

1m 16.8 (5.10) CSF £66.56 CT £779.08 TOTE £19.80: £4.00 £2.40 £4.00 £2.60 (£70.00) Trio £814.60 OWNER J & M Leisure Ltd (THIRSK)
BRED M. J. Simmonds
WEIGHT FOR AGE 3yo-2lb
Bt in 10,000 gns

3266 King Uno, dropped 3lb, appeared to score something of an own goal here by coming with a storming run to beat his well-backed stable companion. (12/1)
3936 Halmanerror, a well-backed favourite, usually finishes well so it was ironic he should get swept aside by the late rattle of his stablemate. (9/2)
Middle East ran a sound race off a 4lb lower mark. (14/1: op 8/1)
3642 Never Think Twice appreciated this drop in class. (10/1: op 6/1)
2203 Fine Times was 8lb lower than when second in the first-time visor back in May. (16/1)
3936 Panther (IRE) was making a quick reappearance but has won before after only a two-day absence. (16/1)

4017 HAZEL GROVE MEDIAN AUCTION MAIDEN STKS (2-Y.O) (Class E)

5-50 (5-55) **1m 30y** £3,074.00 (£932.00: £456.00: £218.00) Stalls: Low GOING minus 0.01 sec per fur (G)

Form	Horse	Dist	Pos	SP	RR	SF
3450[5]	**Bullion** (BWHills) **2-8-9** MHills(15) (w ldrs: led over 2f out: qcknd clr fnl f)	—	**1**	7/1[3]	76+	30
3201[10]	**Eco Friendly** (JRFanshawe) **2-9-0** JWeaver(13) (lw: led over 4f: r.o fnl f)	3½	**2**	16/1	74	28
3569[3]	**Adjutant** (BJMeehan) **2-9-0** MTebbutt(1) (lw: hld up: hdwy on ins over 5f out: ev ch 2f out: one pce)	¾	**3**	7/2[2]	73	27
3322[3]	**Campari (IRE)** (MAJarvis) **2-8-9** RHills(12) (chsd ldrs: styd on same pce fnl 2f)	nk	**4**	9/1	67	21
3788[2]	**Casino Ace (IRE)** (PWChapple-Hyam) **2-8-9** JReid(3) (lw: hld up: hdwy over 3f out: r.o one pce fnl 2f)	1½	**5**	11/8[1]	64	18

				SP	RR	SF
3818^{10}	**Mr Miyagi** (ABailey) **2-9-0** DWright(2) (chsd ldrs: no hdwy fnl 2f)	1½	**6**	50/1	66	20
	Little Risk (KMcAuliffe) **2-8-9** JFEgan(5) (lengthy: nvr trbld ldrs)	9	**7**	33/1	44	—
3322^{5}	**Grecian Prince** (JGSmyth-Osbourne) **2-9-0** GDuffield(7) (prom: led over 3f out tl over 2f out: wknd fnl f)	s.h	**8**	25/1	48	2
3569^{9}	**Bollin Ann** (TDEasterby) **2-8-9** LCharnock(4) (sme hdwy over 3f out: wknd 2f out)	1½	**9**	33/1	40	—
3686^{13}	**Roberty Bob (IRE)** (PTWalwyn) **2-9-0** JFortune(9) (n.d)	1¼	**10**	16/1	43	—
3312^{4}	**Chikal** (BPalling) **2-9-0** TSprake(17) (hld up & plld hrd: a bhd)	s.h	**11**	33/1	43	—
3489^{5}	**Bless 'im** (RHannon) **2-9-0** MJKinane(18) (lw: a bhd)	1½	**12**	7/1 ^{3}	40	—
3117^{15}	**Orleans (IRE)** (TPTate) **2-9-0** TLucas(11) (a bhd)	¾	**13**	50/1	38	—
3753^{9}	**Intuitive** (JLEyre) **2-8-9** RLappin(16) (prom over 4f)	1½	**14**	50/1	31	—
	Sharp Label (JLHarris) **2-8-9** ACulhane(14) (unf: bit bkwd: a bhd)	2½	**15**	33/1	26	—
	Never Cease (AStreeter) **2-8-7**(7) PDoe(8) (lengthy: bit bkwd: s.s: hdwy 6f out: wknd over 3f out: t.o)	24	**16**	50/1	—	—

(SP 134.5%) **16 Rn**

1m 46.88 (6.28) CSF £105.20 TOTE £10.40: £2.80 £4.20 £1.90 (£68.60) Trio £150.50 OWNER Mr W. J. Gredley (LAMBOURN) BRED Stetchworth Park Stud Ltd

3450 Bullion struck gold with a good performance although the opposition was probably not all that great. (7/1)
3201 Eco Friendly, in the same ownership as the winner, certainly stepped up his Newmarket debut. (16/1)
3569 Adjutant came with a dangerous-looking run but failed to quicken up. (7/2)
3322 Campari (IRE) got the mile well enough. (9/1)
3788 Casino Ace (IRE) never really looked likely to score. (11/8)
Mr Miyagi did enough to suggest he can win a small race. (50/1)

T/Jkpt: Not won; £27,754.79 to Bath 8/9/97. T/Plpt: £55.80 (742.02 Tckts). T/Qdpt: £19.80 (84.66 Tckts) WG/KH

4002-EPSOM (L-H) - Saturday September 6th
4018 Abandoned-funeral of Diana, Princess of Wales

4010-HAYDOCK (L-H) - Saturday September 6th
4023 Abandoned-funeral of Diana, Princess of Wales

3751-THIRSK (L-H) - Saturday September 6th
4029 Abandoned-funeral of Diana, Princess of Wales

3607-WOLVERHAMPTON (L-H) - Saturday September 6th
4036 Abandoned-funeral of Diana, Princess of Wales

3469-BATH (L-H) (Good)
Monday September 8th
WEATHER: fine WIND: slt across

4042 BANES MAIDEN AUCTION STKS (2-Y.O F) (Class E)
2-00 (2-01) **5f 11y** £3,034.75 (£913.00: £441.50: £205.75) Stalls: High GOING minus 0.12 sec per fur (G)

				SP	RR	SF
2558^{10}	**Ajig Dancer (94)** (MRChannon) **2-8-5** TQuinn(10) (chsd ldr: led on bit over 1f out: pushed out)	—	**1**	11/4 ^{1}	82+	32
3711^{7}	**Arian Da (74)** (BPalling) **2-8-3** TSprake(7) (led over 3f: nt qckn)	1¾	**2**	10/1	75	25
	Majalis (RGuest) **2-8-6** PBloomfield(11) (w'like: bit bkwd: a.p: rdn over 2f out: r.o one pce fnl f)	1	**3**	9/1	74	24
3278^{13}	**Katyushka (IRE)** (MajorDNChappell) **2-8-6**ow1 JReid(3) (swtg: chsd ldrs: swtchd rt 2f out: r.o ins fnl f)	s.h	**4**	20/1	74	23
2740^{5}	**Little Fizz** (BJMeehan) **2-8-1** DBiggs(6) (lw: prom tl wknd over 1f out)	1½	**5**	16/1	64	14
3711^{4}	**Mysticism (84)** (CEBrittain) **2-8-2** MRoberts(4) (lw: no hdwy fnl 2f)	hd	**6**	100/30 ^{2}	65	15
2917^{3}	**Tullich Refrain** (WRMuir) **2-8-2** MartinDwyer(15) (lw: s.s: nvr nrr)	nk	**7**	5/1 ^{3}	64	14
3711^{14}	**Zamarra** (MajorDNChappell) **2-7-12**(3) MHenry(2) (no hdwy fnl 2f)	hd	**8**	50/1	63	13
3629^{5}	**Mariana (62)** (RMWhitaker) **2-8-2** NCarlisle(5) (prom tl wknd over 1f out)	2	**9**	50/1	58	8
3711^{16}	**Cd Newsround (IRE)** (MRChannon) **2-8-5** CRutter(12) (hdwy over 2f out: wknd over 1f out)	1	**10**	50/1	57	7
2728^{9}	**Mighty Magic (69)** (MrsPNDutfield) **2-8-4** SSanders(8) (chsd ldrs 3f)	½	**11**	25/1	55	5
	Muji (APJarvis) **2-8-3** SDrowne(1) (unf: s.s: a bhd)	¾	**12**	33/1	51	1
2356^{3}	**Perfect Harmony (IRE)** (BJMeehan) **2-7-13**(7)ow2 GHannon(16) (a bhd)	½	**13**	11/1	53	1
3114^{12}	**Rapid Reliance** (DRCElsworth) **2-8-0** JLowe(9) (a bhd)	1½	**14**	16/1	42	—
1425^{12}	**Heiress of Meath (IRE)** (MDIUsher) **2-8-2** JMarshall(14) (s.s: a bhd)	nk	**15**	66/1	43	—

(SP 124.5%) **15 Rn**

63.4 secs (2.90) CSF £27.67 TOTE £3.30: £1.40 £3.50 £3.30 (£9.50) Trio £113.10 OWNER Timberhill Racing Partnership (UPPER LAMBOURN) BRED Doverlodge Stud

1240 Ajig Dancer, having her first run at the minimum trip, took advantage of a big drop in class with a convincing win. Her trainer admitted she had probably been too highly tried, and she looks capable of scoring again. (11/4: 2/1-3/1)
3480 Arian Da, taken down to the start early, did nothing wrong in the race but simply met one much too sharp. (10/1)
Majalis is a half-sister to sprinter My Abbey and seven furlong winner Peaceful Air. Acquitting herself well on her debut, she looks capable of landing a similar event. (9/1)
2553 Katyushka (IRE), a half-sister to a mile and a quarter winner in France, had handicapped herself by being slowly away on her two previous starts. (20/1)
2740 Little Fizz began to run out of gas coming to the final furlong. (16/1)
3711 Mysticism, back to five, is beginning to look like one who has had more than her fair share of chances. (100/30)
2917 Tullich Refrain, a half-sister to Samsolom and North Song, will do better when she gets her act together leaving the stalls. (5/1)

4043 AUTUMN (S) H'CAP (0-60) (3 & 4-Y.O) (Class G)
2-30 (2-33) **1m 5y** £2,556.00 (£716.00: £348.00) Stalls: Low GOING minus 0.12 sec per fur (G)

				SP	RR	SF
3488*	**Murron Wallace (44)** (DHaydnJones) **3-8-11** AMackay(16) (hdwy over 3f out: rdn over 2f out: led ins fnl f: drvn out)	—	**1**	4/1 ^{1}	56	33

				SP	RR	SF
3608[W]	**Silver Harrow (56)** (AGNewcombe) **4-9-11**(3) DGriffiths(12) (chsd ldr: led 2f out tl ins fnl f)	1	**2**	8/1[3]	66	48
2785[8]	**Attarikh (IRE) (45)** (MrsALMKing) **4-9-3** KFallon(1) (lw: rdn over 3f out: hdwy over 2f out: r.o ins fnl f)	1¼	**3**	10/1	53	35
3470[7]	**D J Cat (36)** (WRMuir) **4-8-8** MartinDwyer(3) (lw: bhd tl hdwy over 2f out: one pce fnl f)	s.h	**4**	12/1	43	25
3413[3]	**Ron's Round (38)** (CADwyer) **3-8-5** JQuinn(15) (lw: prom: lost pl 4f out: styd on fnl f)	hd	**5**	10/1	45	22
3469[9]	**Charlton Imp (USA) (40)** (RJHodges) **4-8-12** RCochrane(11) (lw: a.p: led over 2f out: sn hdd: one pce fnl f)	s.h	**6**	14/1	47	29
3849[6]	**Dr Woodstock (41)** (MartynMeade) **3-8-1**(7) RBrisland(10) (prom tl wknd over 1f out)	2½	**7**	10/1	43	20
644[4]	**Patrick (40)** (DBurchell) **3-8-7** JLowe(13) (bit bkwd: prom early: stdd after 2f: stdy hdwy 2f out: nvr plcd to chal)	1	**8**	16/1	40	17
	Mac Oates (49) (PRHedger) **4-9-7** SSanders(6) (lw: s.s: nvr nrr)	1	**9**	33/1	47	29
3581[8]	**Pardan (39)** (BPalling) **3-8-6b**[1] TSprake(18) (led: clr over 3f out: hdd over 2f out: sn wknd)	hd	**10**	16/1	37	14
3787[5]	**Windswept (IRE) (48)** (DJSffrenchDavis) **4-9-6** MTebbutt(5) (b: prom early: bhd whn nt clr run on ins over 2f out)	2	**11**	5/1[2]	42	24
3848[8]	**Flood's Hot Stuff (40)** (NPLittmoden) **3-8-7v** NAdams(9) (a bhd)	2½	**12**	12/1	29	6
2646[12]	**Finsbury Flyer (IRE) (49)** (RJHodges) **4-9-4**(3) RFfrench(8) (rdn over 3f out: a bhd)	2	**13**	14/1	34	16
3393[6]	**Magic Lake (37)** (EJAlston) **4-8-2**(7) PBradley(14) (lw: a bhd)	1	**14**	14/1	20	2
3454[8]	**Rochea (42)** (MrsNMacauley) **3-8-9v** SDrowne(17) (b.off hind: chsd ldrs over 4f)	nk	**15**	20/1	25	2
3454[5]	**Masterstroke (55)** (BJMeehan) **3-9-1**(7) GHannon(4) (a bhd)	6	**16**	20/1	26	3
2672[6]	**Molly Music (52)** (GGMargarson) **3-9-5** DBiggs(7) (a bhd)	6	**17**	14/1	11	—
1373[14]	**Risking (48)** (RJPrice) **4-9-6** MFenton(2) (lw: chsd ldrs over 4f: t.o)	30	**18**	33/1	—	—
				(SP 144.3%)	**18 Rn**	

1m 43.4 (5.20) CSF £36.41 CT £308.52 TOTE £5.00: £1.70 £2.70 £3.40 £4.10 (£23.70) Trio £103.50 OWNER Dhes-C Partnership (PONTYPRIDD) BRED Mrs B. Skinner and D. F. Powell
WEIGHT FOR AGE 3yo-5lb
Bt in 4,000gns. Windswept (IRE) clmd MSmith £6,000
3488* Murron Wallace, described by her trainer as genuine, certainly needs plenty of driving and won a pretty mediocre event off a 3lb higher mark. (4/1)
2651 Silver Harrow had been poorly drawn when upped in grade last time. (8/1)
2505 Attarikh (IRE), dropped 6lb, could not take advantage of the descent into selling company. (10/1)
D J Cat, down 5lb, seems to find a mile a bit on the short side. (12/1)
3413 Ron's Round is another who appears to need a return to further. (10/1)
2852 Charlton Imp (USA), dropped 5lb, has been rather inconsistent this season and this was one of her better efforts. (14/1)
3849 Dr Woodstock (10/1: 8/1-12/1)
644 Patrick seemed to be given a strange ride, and it will be surprising if he is not capable of better than this. (16/1)

4044 BATHFORD NURSERY H'CAP (2-Y.O) (Class C)
3-00 (3-03) **1m 5y** £5,499.50 (£1,661.00: £808.00: £381.50) Stalls: Low GOING minus 0.12 sec per fur (G)

				SP	RR	SF
3750[5]	**Kim's Brave (80)** (BJMeehan) **2-8-13b** MTebbutt(18) (stdy hdwy 5f out: rdn over 2f out: led & edgd lft over 1f out: hrd rdn & edgd lft ins fnl f: r.o)	—	**1**	16/1	89	38
3468[2]	**Shalad'or (72)** (BRMillman) **2-8-5** MRoberts(14) (plld hrd: led over 2f out tl over 1f out: ev ch whn bmpd ins fnl f: nt qckn)	½	**2**	10/1	80	29
3474[4]	**Kawafil (IRE) (88)** (PTWalwyn) **2-9-7** RCochrane(1) (hld up & bhd: hdwy over 2f out: nt clr run over 1f out: swtchd lft: 3rd & styng on whn nt clr run on ins, ins fnl f: nt rcvr)	½	**3**	11/1	95+	44
3650[6]	**King Darius (IRE) (78)** (RHannon) **2-8-4**(7) PDobbs(8) (lw: dwlt: hdwy fnl 2f: nvr nrr)	3	**4**	10/1	79	28
3597[2]	**Acid Test (72)** (WRMuir) **2-8-5** MartinDwyer(5) (lw: hld up: hdwy over 2f out: wknd over 1f out)	nk	**5**	7/1[3]	72	21
2699[11]	**Naked Oat (73)** (BSmart) **2-8-6** JStack(10) (nvr nr to chal)	1	**6**	33/1	71	20
3794[6]	**Al's Fella (IRE) (74)** (PFICole) **2-8-7** TQuinn(3) (prom tl wknd over 2f out)	1¾	**7**	8/1	69	18
3307[2]	**Rebalza (IRE) (67)** (JMPEustace) **2-8-0** JTate(11) (hdwy 3f out: wknd over 1f out)	½	**8**	12/1	61	10
3961a[17]	**Oisin (IRE) (70)** (MrsPNDutfield) **2-8-0**(3) DSweeney(4) (lw: nvr trbld ldrs)	nk	**9**	33/1	63	12
2898*	**Rico Suave (IRE) (85)** (SirMarkPrescott) **2-9-4** SSanders(6) (led over 6f out: hdd over 2f out: sn wknd)	nk	**10**	9/2[2]	78	27
2953[6]	**Aldwych Arrow (IRE) (75)** (MBell) **2-8-8** MFenton(16) (lw: n.d)	nk	**11**	20/1	67	16
3253*	**Elakik (83)** (JLDunlop) **2-9-2** RHills(12) (lw: prom tl wknd over 2f out)	hd	**12**	4/1[1]	75	24
2943[5]	**No Shame (66)** (JGSmyth-Osbourne) **2-7-10**(3) RFfrench(15) (lw: a bhd)	½	**13**	14/1	57	6
3924[3]	**Persian Fortune (65)** (WGMTurner) **2-7-7**(5)ow2 RMullen(7) (led over 1f: wknd over 2f out)	8	**14**	20/1	40	—
3479[7]	**Riley (78)** (RCharlton) **2-8-11** TSprake(9) (a bhd)	½	**15**	14/1	52	1
2917[19]	**Eastwell Hall (63)** (RCurtis) **2-7-10** JLowe(17) (a bhd: t.o)	9	**16**	50/1	19	—
3859[4]	**Truth Teller (74)** (RHannon) **2-8-7** LDettori(2) (lw: a bhd)	½	**17**	10/1	29	—
				(SP 141.7%)	**17 Rn**	

1m 43.1 (4.90) CSF £167.14 CT £1,777.77 TOTE £22.30: £3.20 £2.00 £2.40 £2.80 (£209.50) Trio £1,118.10 OWNER Mr J. K. Sim (UPPER LAMBOURN) BRED C. R. Mason
LONG HANDICAP Eastwell Hall 7-3 Persian Fortune 7-6
STEWARDS' ENQUIRY Obj. to Kim's Brave by Roberts overruled.
3750 Kim's Brave, raised 2lb, did come off a true line laying grounds for an objection, but proved a tough nut to crack and held on well towards the finish. (16/1)
3468 Shalad'or, also up 2lb, was being held at the death which may have gone against her in the Stewards' room. (10/1)
3474 Kawafil (IRE), up 3lb for her unfortunate run here last time, was even more unlucky on this step-up to a mile. (11/1)
3650 King Darius (IRE) seemed to appreciate the mile but could never get into it after being last to leave the stalls. (10/1: 7/1-12/1)
3597 Acid Test was a further 3lb higher this time. (7/1)
2349 Naked Oat has been gelded since his last run. (33/1)

4045 AVON MAIDEN STKS (3-Y.O+) (Class D)
3-30 (3-35) **1m 3f 144y** £4,011.25 (£1,210.00: £587.50: £276.25) Stalls: Low GOING minus 0.12 sec per fur (G)

				SP	RR	SF
3739[5]	**Tikopia (80)** (IABalding) **3-8-12** MartinDwyer(13) (lw: hld up: rdn & hdwy 3f out: led ins fnl f: rdn out)	—	**1**	6/1[3]	78	53
3419[2]	**Sir Ricky (USA) (86)** (RCharlton) **3-8-12** TSprake(19) (hld up: hdwy 3f out: led wl over 1f out: rdn & hdd ins fnl f)	1¾	**2**	4/5[1]	76	51
3491[15]	**Meilleur (IRE) (56)** (LadyHerries) **3-8-12** RCochrane(3) (lw: hdwy 6f out: led over 2f out tl wl over 1f out: one pce)	6	**3**	25/1	67	42
3793[11]	**Star Entry (55)** (MajorDNChappell) **3-8-7** JReid(1) (prom: led over 5f out tl over 2f out: one pce)	½	**4**	50/1	62	37

Form	Horse / Trainer / Age-Wt / Jockey (comment)	Dist	Pos	SP	RR	SF
2924[6]	**Devilish Charm (USA)** (MrsAJPerrett) **3-8-12** AClark(10) (hld up: hdwy 4f out: wknd 2f out)	5	**5**	8/1	60	35
3439[2]	**Good Reputation (63)** (BWHills) **3-8-7** MHills(9) (hld up mid div: no hdwy fnl 3f)	3½	**6**	8/1	50	25
	Polonaise Prince (USA) (VSoane) **4-9-7** CRutter(18) (bit bkwd: hdwy over 3f out: wknd over 2f out)	2½	**7**	100/1	52	36
	Dubelle (JSKing) **7-9-2** DBiggs(4) (dwlt: plld hrd: hdwy 8f out: wknd over 2f out)	2	**8**	66/1	44	28
3720[2]	**Announcing (75)** (JHMGosden) **3-8-12** LDettori(16) (prom: rdn over 3f out: wknd over 2f out)	7	**9**	9/2[2]	39	14
	Too Logical (PGMurphy) **3-8-12** SDrowne(11) (neat: s.s: a bhd)	1¼	**10**	66/1	38	13
2532[10]	**Negative** (MSalaman) **3-8-7** JQuinn(15) (a bhd: t.o)	16	**11**	100/1	11	—
3277[14]	**Henbury Princess** (RJHodges) **4-8-13**(3) PPMurphy(6) (s.s: a bhd: t.o)	1¼	**12**	100/1	9	—
	Technical Move (IRE) (GAHam) **6-8-9**(7) JFowle(8) (bit bkwd: a bhd: t.o)	16	**13**	100/1	—	—
3572[4]	**Siggiewi** (NMBabbage) **3-8-7** SSanders(5) (a bhd: t.o)	½	**14**	50/1	—	—
	Astrojoy (IRE) (38) (GAHam) **5-9-2** FNorton(12) (swtg: prom tl wknd over 3f out)	2½	**15**	100/1	—	—
98[8]	**Dishy Diamond** (WRMuir) **4-9-2** MRoberts(17) (led: hdd over 5f out: wknd over 3f out)	½	**16**	66/1	—	—
	Cashtal Lace (BJLlewellyn) **4-8-13**(3) PFessey(2) (bit bkwd: a bhd: t.o)	17	**17**	100/1	—	—
3695[4]	**Little Miss Lucy** (MJHeaton-Ellis) **3-8-7** TQuinn(14) (prom tl wknd qckly & p.u lame over 7f out)		**P**	50/1	—	—

(SP 130.4%) **18 Rn**

2m 31.6 (4.90) CSF £10.43 TOTE £8.60: £1.80 £1.10 £4.30 (£4.60) Trio £49.30 OWNER Robert & Exors Late Elizabeth Hitchins (KINGSCLERE) BRED Hesmonds Stud Ltd
WEIGHT FOR AGE 3yo-9lb
3739 Tikopia lost the title of professional loser and is set to go hurdling in the autumn. (6/1)
3419 Sir Ricky (USA) could not cope with an animal who has had plenty of chances. (4/5: tchd evens)
1851 Meilleur (IRE) is certainly staying much further than his pedigree would suggest and should do better in handicaps. (25/1)
Star Entry is another who would have been much better off in a handicap but, of course, being eliminated is the problem this time of year. (50/1)
2924 Devilish Charm (USA) may be finding this trip beyond him at the moment. (8/1)
3439 Good Reputation had no excuses over this longer distance. (8/1)

4046 LETHEBY & CHRISTOPHER MAIDEN H'CAP (0-70) (3-Y.O+) (Class E)

4-00 (4-03) **1m 5f 22y** £3,307.75 (£997.00: £483.50: £226.75) Stalls: High GOING minus 0.12 sec per fur (G)

Form	Horse / Trainer / Age-Wt / Jockey (comment)	Dist	Pos	SP	RR	SF
3864[5]	**Jaseur (USA) (69)** (JHMGosden) **4-10-0v** LDettori(12) (hld up & bhd: hdwy over 2f out: chsd ldr over 1f out: led ins fnl f: r.o wl)	—	**1**	10/1	79	53
3291[2]	**Moon Colony (65)** (LadyHerries) **4-9-10** RCochrane(11) (chsd ldr: led over 5f out: clr 4f out: hdd ins fnl f)	2	**2**	12/1	73	47
3633[2]	**Woody's Boy (IRE) (62)** (MJHeaton-Ellis) **3-8-6**(5) ADaly(6) (bhd tl gd hdwy over 1f out: styd on wl ins fnl f)	s.h	**3**	8/1[3]	70	34
	Brecon (55) (WRMuir) **4-9-0** MartinDwyer(15) (bhd tl hdwy over 2f out: styd on ins fnl f)	hd	**4**	25/1	62	36
3858[4]	**Murchan Tyne (IRE) (52)** (EJAlston) **4-8-11** JQuinn(2) (lw: hld up: hdwy over 1f out: styd on wl ins fnl f)	1	**5**	16/1	58	32
3793[2]	**Dellua (IRE) (67)** (RGuest) **3-9-2** JReid(8) (hld up & plld hrd: hdwy over 3f out: wknd over 1f out)	1½	**6**	9/2[1]	71	35
3754[7]	**Darien (70)** (RCharlton) **3-9-5v[1]** TSprake(13) (hld up: hdwy 6f out: hrd rdn & chsd ldr over 2f out: wknd over 1f out)	nk	**7**	10/1	74	38
3714[3]	**Harmony Hall (68)** (JRFanshawe) **3-9-3** KFallon(3) (b: b.hind: hdwy 8f out: wknd over 2f out)	13	**8**	9/2[1]	56	20
3462[3]	**Northern Drums (52)** (NMBabbage) **4-8-11v** MRoberts(4) (led over 7f: wknd 3f out)	3½	**9**	20/1	36	10
3093[2]	**Sandy Floss (IRE) (63)** (JSKing) **4-9-8** SDrowne(14) (lw: bhd fnl 4f)	4	**10**	14/1	42	16
3903[3]	**Dancing Feather (65)** (BWHills) **3-9-0** MHills(1) (hld up: hmpd over 4f out: rdn over 3f out: sn bhd)	hd	**11**	10/1	44	8
1922[5]	**Jude (63)** (PFICole) **3-8-12** TQuinn(7) (rdn over 4f out: bhd fnl 3f)	4	**12**	14/1	37	1
3057[2]	**Trooper (70)** (RAkehurst) **3-9-5b[1]** SSanders(10) (lw: prom: rdn over 5f out: chsd ldr over 4f out tl wknd over 2f out)	8	**13**	6/1[2]	34	—
1022[11]	**Indiana Princess (56)** (MrsMReveley) **4-9-1** ACulhane(9) (a bhd)	1¼	**14**	16/1	19	—
3632[7]	**Verdi (IRE) (65)** (KMcAuliffe) **3-9-0** AClark(5) (lw: prom over 8f: t.o)	19	**15**	14/1	4	—

(SP 137.1%) **15 Rn**

2m 53.7 (8.00) CSF £128.47 CT £954.15 TOTE £10.50: £3.60 £4.40 £2.70 (£37.20) Trio £287.10 OWNER Sheikh Mohammed (NEWMARKET) BRED Darley Stud Management Co Ltd
WEIGHT FOR AGE 3yo-10lb
3864 Jaseur (USA), appreciating this extended trip, came with a well-timed run without recourse to the whip. (10/1)
3291 Moon Colony stays well and tried to steal this on the home turn. (12/1: op 8/1)
3633 Woody's Boy (IRE) took a long time to get going and stamina was certainly not a problem. (8/1)
Brecon won a novice hurdle at Perth in April and this will have served as a real good pipe-opener for a return to that sphere. (25/1)
3858 Murchan Tyne (IRE), down 3lb, found this distance inadequate. (16/1)
3793 Dellua (IRE), up 2lb, got the stamina test but did not settle as well as her rider would have liked. (9/2)
3419 Darien, down 4lb, was tried in a visor but continued to disappoint. (10/1)

4047 SHERSTON MAIDEN STKS (3-Y.O) (Class D)

4-30 (4-35) **5f 161y** £3,809.75 (£1,148.00: £556.50: £260.75) Stalls: High GOING minus 0.12 sec per fur (G)

Form	Horse / Trainer / Age-Wt / Jockey (comment)	Dist	Pos	SP	RR	SF
3202[2]	**First Principle** (CFWall) **3-9-0** SSanders(3) (hld up: rdn & hdwy over 1f out: led ins fnl f: r.o wl)	—	**1**	3/1[2]	80	51
3698[2]	**Tithcar (62)** (BHanbury) **3-8-9** JStack(6) (lw: w ldr: led over 2f out tl ins fnl f)	1¼	**2**	10/1[3]	72	43
983[6]	**Mr Majica (75)** (BJMeehan) **3-9-0** MTebbutt(12) (bit bkwd: bhd tl gd hdwy fnl f: fin wl)	½	**3**	10/1[3]	75	46
1787[4]	**Persevere** (LordHuntingdon) **3-8-9** MRoberts(9) (hld up: hdwy over 2f out: ev ch ins fnl f: nt qckn)	¾	**4**	12/1	68	39
	Dark Mile (USA) (JHMGosden) **3-8-9** LDettori(7) (hld up: hdwy whn nt clr run over 1f out: one pce fnl f)	hd	**5**	4/5[1]	68	39
3043[2]	**Nobalino** (MrsNMacauley) **3-9-0** SDrowne(10) (s.i.s: hdwy over 1f out: nrst fin)	1¾	**6**	20/1	68	39
3500[8]	**Dancing Mystery (42)** (EAWheeler) **3-8-9**(5) ADaly(1) (no hdwy fnl 2f)	nk	**7**	33/1	67	38
2157[4]	**Marylebone (IRE) (68)** (JBerry) **3-8-11**(3) PFessey(8) (nvr nrr)	nk	**8**	16/1	66	37
2591[11]	**Churchill's Shadow (IRE) (45)** (BAPearce) **3-9-0** JReid(5) (tk keen hold: trckd ldrs: wknd over 1f out)	1¾	**9**	50/1	61	32
3606[5]	**Hiltons Executive (IRE) (35)** (EJAlston) **3-8-9** KFallon(4) (prom tl wknd wl over 1f out)	3	**10**	14/1	48	19
2920[8]	**Bicton Park (64)** (KCComerford) **3-9-0b** MFenton(2) (lw: led: hdd over 2f out: wknd over 1f out)	5	**11**	66/1	39	10
3710[6]	**Geordie Lad (42)** (JABennett) **3-9-0** AClark(11) (bhd fnl 2f)	2	**12**	66/1	33	4
2235[8]	**Heathyards Pearl (USA) (46)** (RHollinshead) **3-8-6v[1]**(3) DGriffiths(13) (prom over 3f)	7	**13**	66/1	9	—

(SP 133.1%) **13 Rn**

1m 12.1 (2.60) CSF £32.87 TOTE £4.40: £1.60 £1.90 £3.40 (£17.40) Trio £43.80 OWNER Sheikh Rashid Bin Ahmed Al Mualla (NEWMARKET) BRED T. Newcombe
3202 First Principle, who did not show much on the sand in Dubai, is a different proposition on grass. (3/1)

3698 Tithcar yet again got run out of it at the business end of the race. (10/1)
983 Mr Majica can certainly get off the mark when reverting to a longer trip. (10/1: op 6/1)
1787 Persevere, rather surprisingly trying her luck at sprinting, was certainly not disgraced. (12/1: op 8/1)
Dark Mile (USA), a half-sister to Fatefully, was backed as if defeat was out of the question on this belated seasonal reappearance. She should not be considered unlucky and possibly needs further. (4/5: tchd 6/4)
3043 Nobalino is another who shaped as though he needed a longer distance. (20/1)

4048 LEVY BOARD SEVENTH RACE H'CAP (0-80) (3-Y.O+) (Class D)
5-00 (5-03) **5f 161y** £4,102.25 (£919.75: £919.75: £283.25) Stalls: High GOING minus 0.12 sec per fur (G)

Form	Horse	Dist	Pos	SP	RR	SF
3580[3]	**Montendre (75)** (MJHeaton-Ellis) **10-9-11** JReid(9) (lw: hld up: gd hdwy fnl f: squeezed thro to ld nr fin)	—	1	14/1	84	64
3922[2]	**Bowlers Boy (70)** (JJQuinn) **4-9-6** SSanders(8) (hdwy over 2f out: led wl ins fnl f: hdd nr fin)	½	2	11/2[2]	78	58
3417[7]	**Bayin (USA) (59)** (MDIUsher) **8-8-9** RStreet(17) (b: s.s: hdwy over 1f out: str run ins fnl f: fin wl)	d.h	2	12/1	67	47
3851[3]	**Suite Factors (55)** (KRBurke) **3-8-0**(3) DSweeney(14) (lw: gd hdwy fnl f: fin wl)	s.h	4	20/1	63	41
3856[3]	**Saint Express (76)** (MrsMReveley) **7-9-12** ACulhane(7) (lw: hdwy over 2f out: ev ch ins fnl f: r.o)	s.h	5	9/1	83	63
3500[10]	**Mindrace (60)** (KTIvory) **4-8-10** JLowe(12) (hdwy over 2f out: r.o fnl f)	1	6	20/1	65	45
3816[5]	**Nightingale Song (60)** (MartynMeade) **3-8-1**(7) RBrisland(13) (chsd ldrs: ev ch ins fnl f: nt qckn)	hd	7	50/1	64	42
2698[7]	**Pointer (55)** (MrsPNDutfield) **5-8-5** CRutter(1) (hdwy on ins over 2f out: led over 1f out tl wl ins fnl f)	s.h	8	11/1	59	39
3566[8]	**Intiaash (IRE) (73)** (DHaydnJones) **5-9-9** SDrowne(19) (hdwy fnl f: r.o)	½	9	20/1	76	56
3852*	**Ivory's Grab Hire (67)** (KTIvory) **4-9-3b** MartinDwyer(2) (lw: prom: ev ch whn bmpd 1f out: one pce)	1¼	10	14/1	66	46
3923[2]	**Maladerie (IRE) (55)** (MRChannon) **3-8-3** AMackay(6) (lw: rdn over 3f out: hdwy on ins whn n.m.r over 1f out: one pce ins fnl f)	¾	11	14/1	52	30
3621[5]	**Fairy Prince (IRE) (73)** (MrsALMKing) **4-9-9** MRoberts(4) (lw: prom: rdn over 2f out: nt clr run over 1f out: eased whn btn fnl f)	½	12	12/1	69	49
3795[7]	**Sabina (76)** (IABalding) **3-9-10** LDettori(5) (dwlt: hdwy & squeezed thro over 1f out: ev ch 1f out: eased whn btn ins fnl f)	nk	13	8/1[3]	71	49
3642[3]	**Pride of Hayling (IRE) (56)** (PRHedger) **6-8-6** TQuinn(15) (lw: prom: led 2f out tl over 1f out: sn wknd)	2	14	8/1[3]	45	25
3898[2]	**Tinker Osmaston (66)** (RJHodges) **6-9-2** JQuinn(18) (n.d)	hd	15	14/1	55	35
3709[4]	**Butrinto (75)** (MajorWRHern) **3-9-9** KFallon(11) (dwlt: a bhd)	s.h	16	7/2[1]	64	42
3910[18]	**Croeso Cynnes (60)** (BPalling) **4-8-10b[1]** TSprake(16) (lw: prom tl wknd over 1f out)	2	17	16/1	43	23
3856[6]	**Just Dissident (IRE) (59)** (RMWhitaker) **5-8-9** AClark(10) (b: lw: led: hdd 2f out: sn wknd)	1¾	18	25/1	37	17
				(SP 146.2%)	**18 Rn**	

1m 11.9 (2.40) CSF M&BO £45.10 M&BA £87.13 CT M,BO&BA £476.49 M,BA&BO £505.83 TOTE £17.40: £2.60 BO £1.40 BA £3.20 S £8.50 (M&BO £22.60 M&BA £61.20) Trio £74.40 OWNER Mr David Mort (WROUGHTON) BRED A. B. Phipps
WEIGHT FOR AGE 3yo-2lb
3580 Montendre came through for a deserved success in the sort of finish the Handicapper dreams about. (14/1)
3198 Bayin (USA) has been slipping down the handicap since his course and distance win in June. (12/1)
3922 Bowlers Boy, down 2lb, was still 3lb higher than when he last won, but very nearly made the long trip south pay off. (11/2)
3851 Suite Factors, again deserting his front-running tactics, finished like a train. (20/1)
3856 Saint Express ran very well in a bunch finish. (9/1)
2950* Mindrace was back to a mark only 1lb higher than when successful at Sandown in July. (20/1)
3816 Nightingale Song was 12lb lower than when last running in a handicap. (50/1)

T/Jkpt: Not won; £36,550.68 to Leicester 9/9/97. T/Plpt: £253.50 (109.64 Tckts). T/Qdpt: £57.80 (33.11 Tckts) KH

3581-SOUTHWELL (L-H) (Standard)
Monday September 8th
WEATHER: fine WIND: mod half bhd

4049 COPENHAGEN CLAIMING STKS (I) (3-Y.O+) (Class F)
1-45 (1-47) **5f (Fibresand)** £1,927.00 (£527.00: £247.00) Stalls: High GOING: 0.00 sec per fur (STD)

Form	Horse	Dist	Pos	SP	RR	SF
3473[9]	**Mon Bruce (75)** (WRMuir) **3-8-10** DaneO'Neill(7) (trckd ldr: led over 1f out: jst hld on)	—	1	6/1[2]	72	54
3327[5]	**Spaniards Close (85)** (PJMakin) **9-9-5** DHolland(2) (trckd ldrs gng wl: chal over 1f out: nt qckn nr fin)	hd	2	9/4[1]	80	63
3398[8]	**Silk Cottage (45)** (RMWhitaker) **5-8-9v** DeanMcKeown(15) (lw: chsd ldrs: hung lft thrght: rdn ½-wy: kpt on wl fnl f)	1¼	3	14/1	66	49
546[3]	**Ma Vielle Pouque (IRE) (54)** (WGMTurner) **3-8-1**(7)ow1 DMcGaffin(10) (in tch: kpt on fnl 2f)	nk	4	14/1	65	46
3484[5]	**Henry the Hawk (39)** (MDods) **6-8-11b** JWeaver(6) (b: lw: led tl over 1f out: sn wknd: eased nr fin)	3½	5	14/1	56	39
3606[3]	**Night Express (77)** (BHanbury) **3-9-0** WRyan(8) (lw: sn outpcd: kpt on appr fnl f: nvr nr ldrs)	2½	6	6/1[2]	52	34
3710[9]	**Blues Queen (66)** (MRChannon) **3-8-13** JFortune(14) (sn outpcd: hdwy ½-wy: hrd rdn & styd on fnl f)	s.h	7	11/1[3]	50	32
2070[14]	**Julia's Relative (50)** (RonaldThompson) **3-7-11b** GBardwell(12) (sn drvn along: hdwy ½-wy: kpt on fnl f)	2½	8	14/1	26	8
3637[11]	**Tommy Tempest (38)** (REPeacock) **8-8-5v** KDarley(9) (chsd ldrs over 3f)	nk	9	20/1	32	15
3565[11]	**Spotted Eagle (50)** (DNicholls) **4-9-1** AlexGreaves(3) (sn outpcd & bhd: sme hdwy over 1f out: nvr nr to chal)	1¼	10	16/1	38	21
3807[3]	**Toss And Tumble** (WWHaigh) **3-8-13** RLappin(4) (sn outpcd)	nk	11	33/1	36	18
	Crees Sqaw (BAMcMahon) **5-9-0** JBramhill(16) (bit bkwd: sn wl bhd)	nk	12	50/1	36	19
3399[4]	**Redspet (25)** (SRBowring) **3-8-4**(3)ow2 CTeague(11) (sn outpcd)	1¾	13	33/1	24	4
	General Equation (42) (JBalding) **4-8-11** JEdmunds(1) (prom far side tl wknd over 1f out)	nk	14	33/1	26	9
3582[12]	**Fit For The Job (IRE) (49)** (TWall) **3-7-9b**(7) PMQuinn(13) (bolted gng to s: sltly hmpd s: a in rr)	2	15	14/1	12	—
	Bankers Order (TDEasterby) **3-8-12** LCharnock(5) (a outpcd & bhd)	5	16	33/1	6	—
				(SP 125.4%)	**16 Rn**	

59.3 secs (2.30) CSF £17.18 TOTE £8.50: £1.90 £1.80 £2.80 (£13.30) Trio £183.80 OWNER Miss Monique Van Bakel (LAMBOURN) BRED E. A. Badger
WEIGHT FOR AGE 3yo-1lb
Mon Bruce clmd ANixon £6,000
2780 Mon Bruce, who has struggled on grass since winning on the Fibresand at Wolverhampton in April, found more under pressure than the runner-up. He was claimed and now joins Michael Dods. (6/1: op 3/1)

3327 Spaniards Close, as usual, travelled strongly but, after looking likely to pick off the winner at any time, in the end he had to just give best. On turf he prefers give underfoot. (9/4: 2/1-3/1)
3398 Silk Cottage has only won once in forty-one starts, but he ran a tremendous race despite showing a marked tendency to hang left. He would have been meeting the winner on two-stone better terms in a handicap. (14/1)
546 Ma Vielle Pouque (IRE), having her first outing for one hundred and sixty days, ran creditably especially considering she would have met the winner on 18lb better terms in a handicap. (14/1)
3484 Henry the Hawk, who had an impossible task at these weights, showed tremendous speed to lead his rivals a merry dance for over three furlongs. (14/1)
2517 Blues Queen (11/1: 7/1-12/1)
293 Fit For The Job (IRE) came in for market support at long odds, but his supporters knew their fate when he bolted going to the start. (14/1: 20/1-12/1)

4050 AMSTERDAM AMATEUR H'CAP (0-70) (3-Y.O+) (Class G)

2-15 (2-17) **1m** **(Fibresand)** £2,070.00 (£570.00: £270.00) Stalls: Low GOING: 0.14 sec per fur (SLW)

				SP	RR	SF
3044[6]	**Mythical (61)** (SirMarkPrescott) **3-10-13**(3) MrPScott(5) (trckd ldrs gng wl: led over 1f out: hung lft: rdn out)	—	1	5/2[1]	73	50
3582[2]	**Zalotto (IRE) (57)** (TJEtherington) **3-10-12b** MrSSwiers(10) (lw: racd wd: in tch: hdwy to chal over 1f out: nt qckn ins fnl f)	¾	2	11/1	68	45
3608[5]	**Dream Carrier (IRE) (47)** (REPeacock) **9-10-2**(5) MrsCPeacock(8) (lw: w ldrs: led 2f out: sn hdd: one pce)	6	3	16/1	46	28
3293[7]	**Dragon's Back (IRE) (51)** (DCO'Brien) **4-10-6**(5) MrVLukaniuk(9) (chsd ldrs: outpcd over 3f out: styd on fnl f)	1½	4	33/1	47	29
3581[2]	**Be Warned (60)** (JPearce) **6-11-6** MrsLPearce(16) (racd wd: lost pl ½-wy: styd on appr fnl f)	1¾	5	9/1[3]	52	34
3793[12]	**Three Weeks (58)** (WRMuir) **4-11-4** MrTMcCarthy(14) (racd wd: sn bhd & pushed along: hdwy over 2f out: nvr rchd ldrs)	s.h	6	25/1	50	32
3822[8]	**Awesome Venture (55)** (MCChapman) **7-10-8**(7) MrNChapman(15) (racd wd: chsd ldrs tl lost pl ½-wy: kpt on fnl f)	2½	7	25/1	42	24
3476[13]	**Montone (IRE) (63)** (JRJenkins) **7-11-6v**(3) DrMMannish(12) (sn bhd: hdwy & edgd lft over 1f out: n.d)	¾	8	25/1	48	30
3696[10]	**Mutahadeth (65)** (DShaw) **3-11-6v[1]** MrCBonner(2) (outpcd ½-wy: hdwy over 2f out: sn rdn & no imp)	hd	9	10/1	50	27
3712[2]	**Orange Place (IRE) (68)** (BJLlewellyn) **6-12-0** MrJLLlewellyn(3) (mde most tl hdd 2f out: sn wknd)	1¼	10	4/1[2]	51	33
870[12]	**Domino Flyer (64)** (MrsASwinbank) **4-11-3**(7) MissLPreston(1) (sn bhd: sme hdwy 2f out: n.d)	2½	11	25/1	42	24
3822[4]	**French Ginger (50)** (LRLloyd-James) **6-10-10** MrJTizzard(13) (racd wd: in tch tl lost pl over 2f out)	1½	12	12/1	25	7
3933[3]	**Charlie Chang (IRE) (60)** (DWBarker) **4-11-6** MrABalding(4) (lw: in tch to st: sn lost pl)	½	13	14/1	34	16
3581[3]	**Bold Street (IRE) (52)** (GMMoore) **7-10-7b**(5) MrsCWilliams(11) (chsd ldrs tl wknd over 2f out)	½	14	14/1	25	7
	Desert Zone (USA) (63) (JohnHarris) **8-11-2**(7) MrsAnnetteHarris(7) (b: unruly & led to post: s.s: reluctant to r)	5	15	25/1	26	8
608[8]	**Live Project (IRE) (58)** (RCraggs) **5-10-11**(7) MissKWarnett(6) (s.v.s: a wl bhd: t.o)	23	16	20/1	—	—

(SP 129.8%) **16 Rn**

1m 47.7 (8.70) CSF £27.29 CT £362.09 TOTE £3.30: £1.20 £3.30 £3.90 £7.30 (£22.60) Trio £106.70 OWNER Lord Fairhaven (NEWMARKET) BRED Barton Stud
WEIGHT FOR AGE 3yo-5lb
3044 Mythical, dropped 5lb and having her first outing for forty-five days, travelled strongly. Skillfully handled, she was persuaded to do just enough. (5/2)
3582 Zalotto (IRE) moved almost upsides over a furlong out but was never going to find quite sufficient to worry the winner out of it. The trip was no problem. (11/1: 8/1-12/1)
3608 Dream Carrier (IRE) seemed to run out of stamina in the final furlong. (16/1)
Dragon's Back (IRE), taken to post early, stuck on again at the finish, giving his new connections some hope. (33/1)
3581 Be Warned, having his first outing since being claimed, dropped right back at the halfway mark, but recovered to be staying on at the finish. His rider is no longer tidy. (9/1)
82 Three Weeks, out of form on turf, seemed to appreciate a reversion to the All-Weather. (25/1)
3421 Mutahadeth (10/1: op 6/1)
3712 Orange Place (IRE) (4/1: 3/1-11/2)
3822 French Ginger (12/1: 8/1-14/1)

4051 COPENHAGEN CLAIMING STKS (II) (3-Y.O+) (Class F)

2-45 (2-46) **5f** **(Fibresand)** £1,927.00 (£527.00: £247.00) Stalls: High GOING: 0.00 sec per fur (STD)

				SP	RR	SF
3816[9]	**Palacegate Jack (IRE) (66)** (JBerry) **6-8-12b**(3) TEDurcan(10) (lw: mde all: clr ½-wy: r.o wl)	—	1	13/8[1]	80	62
3625[4]	**Featherstone Lane (58)** (MissLCSiddall) **6-8-12** MWigham(9) (s.i.s: hdwy 2f out: styd on ins fnl f)	3	2	10/1[3]	67	49
3871[6]	**Bashful Brave (48)** (BPJBaugh) **6-8-4**(5) PRoberts(11) (a chsng ldrs: kpt on one pce fnl 2f)	½	3	10/1[3]	63	45
3583[4]	**Bold Aristocrat (IRE) (67)** (RHollinshead) **6-8-11** KDarley(2) (chsd ldrs: drvn along & outpcd ½-wy: kpt on fnl f)	1¼	4	9/2[2]	61	43
3240[15]	**Kalar (70)** (DWChapman) **8-8-9b** JCarroll(14) (chsd ldrs tl wknd over 1f out)	¾	5	10/1[3]	56	38
3034[12]	**Lennox Lewis (63)** (DNicholls) **5-8-6**(7) ANicholls(1) (trckd ldrs: grad wknd fnl 2f)	2	6	16/1	54	36
102[*]	**Figlia (58)** (JLHarris) **3-8-3b** GDuffield(12) (bhd: hrd rdn & styd on fnl 2f)	nk	7	10/1[3]	44	25
3693[12]	**Superapparos (35)** (SRBowring) **3-8-5**(3) CTeague(3) (s.i.s: hrd rdn & sme hdwy over 1f out: n.d)	s.h	8	33/1	49	30
2738[12]	**Super Rocky (65)** (RBastiman) **8-8-9** DeanMcKeown(7) (lw: in tch: outpcd ½-wy: n.d after)	nk	9	16/1	48	30
3606[10]	**Passionatti** (SGollings) **3-8-13** WRyan(15) (chsd ldrs tl lost pl ½-wy)	nk	10	33/1	52	33
3849[9]	**Saxon Bay (46)** (KOCunningham-Brown) **5-8-5b[1]** LCharnock(4) (s.i.s: a in rr)	1	11	20/1	40	22
3856[W]	**Young Ben (IRE) (29)** (JSWainwright) **5-8-12b**(3) GParkin(6) (b.hind: lw: chsd ldrs: hrd rdn & wknd 2f out)	1¼	12	25/1	46	28
3456[16]	**My Godson (40)** (MDods) **7-8-11b** RLappin(8) (dwlt: a bhd)	1	13	25/1	39	21
2703[9]	**Ioulios (38)** (JEBanks) **3-8-1**(5) CLowther(5) (prom early: outpcd ½-wy: sn bhd)	9	14	33/1	6	—

(SP 125.7%) **14 Rn**

59.1 secs (2.10) CSF £16.36 TOTE £2.80: £1.30 £3.30 £3.70 (£16.50) Trio £48.30 OWNER Mr William Burns (COCKERHAM) BRED Brendan and Sheila Powell
WEIGHT FOR AGE 3yo-1lb
3816 Palacegate Jack (IRE) took this race for the second year running, having had five lengths to spare last time. Showing all his old speed, he had shaken off his rivals by the halfway mark. (13/8)
3625 Featherstone Lane has only won three times from eighty-nine starts. (10/1: 7/1-12/1)
3871 Bashful Brave had plenty on at these weights. (10/1)

3583 Bold Aristocrat (IRE) was run off his feet at halfway and is much better suited by six. (9/2: op 3/1)
2061 Kalar, reverting to his favoured surface, was unable to dominate with Palacegate Jack in the field. (10/1)
Lennox Lewis shaped encouragingly and it will be interesting to see if his trainer can get him back on song. (16/1)

4052 E.B.F. COLOGNE MAIDEN STKS (I) (2-Y.O) (Class D)

3-15 (3-17) **7f (Fibresand)** £3,232.50 (£960.00: £455.00: £202.50) Stalls: Low GOING: 0.14 sec per fur (SLW)

				SP	RR	SF
3687^{6}	**Mister Benjamin (IRE)** (SPCWoods) **2-9-0** NDay(4) (lw: mde all: shkn up & wnt clr ins fnl f: eased towards fin)	—	**1**	11/4^{2}	69+	19
	Flying Bold (IRE) (WRMuir) **2-9-0** JFortune(11) (unf: scope: bit bkwd: racd wd: hdwy over 2f out: edgd lft & styd on fnl f: no ch w wnr)	3	**2**	14/1	62+	12
	Goldfill (WAO'Gorman) **2-8-9** EmmaO'Gorman(9) (cmpt: scope: bit bkwd: shkn up & hdwy ½-wy: styd on ins fnl f)	1¾	**3**	16/1	53+	3
3306^{14}	**Kayo** (TJEtherington) **2-9-0** DHolland(8) (sn bhd & swtchd outside: gd hdwy over 2f out: nt qckn appr fnl f)	½	**4**	20/1	57	7
3629^{6}	**Kings Check** (MissJFCraze) **2-9-0** SWebster(5) (a chsng ldrs: hrd rdn over 2f out: one pce)	1½	**5**	33/1	54	4
	Nuit d'Or (IRE) (MJohnston) **2-9-0** JWeaver(10) (str: bkwd: chsd ldrs: hung lft 2f out: grad wknd)	1¼	**6**	12/1^{3}	51	1
3022^{8}	**Linda** (NACallaghan) **2-8-9** GCarter(6) (chsd ldrs: drvn along over 2f out: sn outpcd)	hd	**7**	25/1	46	—
	King's Mistress (DCO'Brien) **2-8-9** GBardwell(2) (unf: sn pushed along & outpcd: sme late hdwy)	3½	**8**	40/1	38	—
3613^{13}	**Zillion (IRE)** (JWPayne) **2-9-0** AMcGlone(13) (s.i.s: a in rr)	¾	**9**	40/1	41	—
3493^{10}	**Fung Shui (IRE)** (RHannon) **2-9-0** DaneO'Neill(1) (lw: chsd ldrs: hrd rdn & hung lft over 2f out: sn lost pl)	¾	**10**	16/1	39	—
3416^{5}	**Pinup** (GLewis) **2-8-6**$^{(3)}$ AWhelan(3) (chsd ldrs: drvn along ½-wy: wknd 2f out)	hd	**11**	16/1	34	—
3426^{8}	**Dougs Dream (IRE)** (MrsASwinbank) **2-8-9** GDuffield(7) (outpcd & drvn along ½-wy: sn bhd)	8	**12**	40/1	16	—
3607^{3}	***Prompt Delivery (USA)* (83)** (MRStoute) **2-9-0** KDarley(12) (Withdrawn not under Starter's orders: b.b.v at s)		**W**	10/11^{1}	—	—

(SP 129.9%) **12 Rn**

1m 34.4 (7.90) CSF £10.45 TOTE £1.90: £1.10 £2.30 £2.00 (£8.30) Trio £16.30 OWNER Mrs Julie Choy (NEWMARKET) BRED Milltown Stud
3687 Mister Benjamin (IRE) was left with a simple task on paper after the favourite was withdrawn and he made no mistake, taking this in good style and winning easing up. (11/4)
Flying Bold (IRE) looks as though he needs more time yet. Racing wide and travelling strongly, he was by no means knocked about when it was clear the winner knew far too much for him. (14/1)
Goldfill, who looked in need of the outing, ran a pleasing first race. (16/1)
3060 Kayo was pulled wide to avoid the kick-back. Making ground on the wide outside, at one time he looked as though he might take a hand but he could find no more coming to the final furlong. This outing should put him spot on and significantly he is now qualified for a nursery mark. (20/1)
3629 Kings Check did not wear a visor this time. (33/1)
Nuit d'Or (IRE), a strongly-made, burly, backward newcomer, shaped by no means badly. He should come on a good deal for this first outing. (12/1: op 5/1)
3607 Prompt Delivery (USA) (10/11: evens-11/10)

4053 ALFRETON INSURANCE SERVICES MAIDEN H'CAP (0-65) (3-Y.O+) (Class F)

3-45 (3-47) **1m 3f (Fibresand)** £2,277.00 (£627.00: £297.00) Stalls: Low GOING: 0.14 sec per fur (SLW)

				SP	RR	SF
3225^{6}	**Marytavy (61)** (SirMarkPrescott) **3-9-10** GDuffield(9) (lw: cl up: led 5f out: styd on wl)	—	**1**	9/2^{1}	72	27
3486^{6}	**Fighting Times (50)** (CASmith) **5-9-7v^{1}** DaneO'Neill(11) (lw: a chsng ldrs: no ch w wnr fnl 2f)	8	**2**	14/1	49	12
3787^{14}	**Kristal Bridge (65)** (PWHarris) **3-10-0** DHolland(15) (carried wd bnd after 2f: in tch: hdwy 4f out: one pce fnl 2f)	2½	**3**	14/1	61	16
3612^{2}	**Ceanothus (IRE) (59)** (WJHaggas) **3-9-8** KDarley(3) (lw: mid div & pushed along: hdwy 3f out: styd on wl towards fin)	3	**4**	9/2^{1}	50	5
3762^{16}	**Whitley Grange Boy (52)** (JLEyre) **4-9-9** OPears(8) (cl up: led 6f out to 5f out: wknd fnl 3f)	1¾	**5**	16/1	41	4
2878^{6}	**Bobbitt (48)** (WJarvis) **3-8-11** AMcGlone(12) (lw: chsd ldrs: drvn along 4f out: no imp after)	3	**6**	9/1	33	—
3133^{3}	**Limelight (53)** (JARToller) **3-9-2** DaleGibson(7) (lw: sn outpcd & bhd: styd on fnl 4f: n.d)	15	**7**	13/2^{2}	16	—
2859^{2}	**Hanajir (IRE) (49)** (CWThornton) **3-8-12** DeanMcKeown(1) (lw: in tch: rdn 5f out: sn btn)	5	**8**	7/1^{3}	4	—
3632^{9}	**Langara Heights (55)** (BJLlewellyn) **3-8-11**$^{(7)}$ JWilkinson(5) (sn outpcd & t.o: sme late hdwy)	6	**9**	12/1	2	—
3721^{6}	**Cambridge Ball (IRE) (60)** (MJohnston) **3-9-9** JWeaver(13) (sn outpcd & rr div)	6	**10**	10/1	—	—
3762^{10}	**Smoke'n'jo (IRE) (54)** (MWEasterby) **3-9-0**$^{(3)}$ GParkin(4) (prom: sn drvn along: wknd 7f out)	¾	**11**	12/1	—	—
2487^{6}	**So Keen (40)** (ABailey) **4-8-11** DWright(2) (n.d)	¾	**12**	20/1	—	—
3813^{8}	**Miss Kalaglow (53)** (CFWall) **3-9-2** GHind(16) (b.hind: sn pushed along: lost tch fr ½-wy)	1½	**13**	10/1	—	—
995^{19}	**Move The Clouds (55)** (BEllison) **3-9-4** JFortune(6) (led tl hdd & wknd 6f out)	25	**14**	20/1	—	—
3188^{6}	**Veuve Clicquot (56)** (RWArmstrong) **3-9-5** GCarter(14) (carried wd bnd after 2f: sn outpcd & wl bhd)	16	**15**	10/1	—	—

(SP 143.6%) **15 Rn**

2m 32.9 (12.90) CSF £77.10 CT £799.70 TOTE £5.30: £2.70 £9.00 £4.90 (£71.50) Trio £199.10; £201.92 to Leicester 9/9/97 OWNER Lord Roborough (NEWMARKET) BRED Mrs C. S. Knowles
WEIGHT FOR AGE 3yo-8lb
3225 Marytavy really took to this surface and, in a race run at a flat-out gallop, she travelled well and won most emphatically. (9/2: 6/1-4/1)
3108 Fighting Times had a visor on for the first time and it obviously sharpened him up, but he was still no match for the winner. (14/1)
3392 Kristal Bridge had to race wide because of her draw and this probably made a big difference. (14/1)
3612 Ceanothus (IRE) does not do anything quickly but she does stay, and would seem to need further than this. (9/2)
598 Whitley Grange Boy went too fast early on and had burst himself by the home turn. (16/1)
2878 Bobbitt looked pretty fit after almost two months off and, trying her longest trip to date, failed to get home. (9/1)

4054 SUNLINE DIRECT MAIL (S) NURSERY H'CAP (0-65) (2-Y.O) (Class G)

4-15 (4-18) **5f (Fibresand)** £1,984.50 (£547.00: £259.50) Stalls: High GOING: 0.00 sec per fur (STD)

				SP	RR	SF
3859^{9}	**Super Geil (48)** (CADwyer) **2-8-10** DHolland(6) (hdwy ½-wy: led ins fnl f: r.o)	—	**1**	12/1	57	31
3808^{8}	**Miss Bananas (42)** (TTBill) **2-8-4** NKennedy(8) (led tl hdd ins fnl f: no ex)	1½	**2**	33/1	46	20
3751^{4}	**Snappy Times (55)** (MDods) **2-9-3** DaleGibson(2) (a chsng ldrs: kpt on fnl f)	¾	**3**	10/1	57	31
3859^{5}	**Dande Times (52)** (KTIvory) **2-9-0** AMcGlone(17) (lw: spd stands' side: hung lft fr ½-wy: styd on wl fnl f)	1¼	**4**	10/1	50	24
3270^{6}	**Mr Fund Switch (40)** (DNicholls) **2-7-11b^{1}**$^{(5)}$ IonaWands(3) (chsd ldrs: sn drvn along: wknd ins fnl f)	1	**5**	33/1	35	9
3905^{9}	**Time To Time (55)** (TDEasterby) **2-9-3** LCharnock(4) (chsd ldrs: effrt ½-wy: no imp)	hd	**6**	16/1	49	23
3819^{8}	**Russian About (IRE) (55)** (MRChannon) **2-9-3** JFortune(7) (outpcd after 2f: styd on towards fin)	hd	**7**	10/1	49	23
3062^{10}	**Wilfred Sherman (IRE) (59)** (JBerry) **2-9-2**$^{(5)}$ PRoberts(5) (sn outpcd: sme hdwy fnl 2f)	2½	**8**	20/1	45	19

3384[9]	**Muja's Magic (IRE) (50)** (KTIvory) **2-8-12** DeanMcKeown(12) (lw: sn outpcd & bhd: sme late hdwy)	2	**9**	10/1	30	4
3226[5]	**Swanmore Lady (IRE) (53)** (SCWilliams) **2-9-1** KDarley(16) (lw: spd stands' side over 3f)	nk	**10**	13/2[2]	32	6
3808[7]	**Jockweiler (IRE) (47)** (DWChapman) **2-8-9** GDuffield(14) (s.i.s: n.d)	hd	**11**	25/1	25	—
3324[8]	**Verdant Express (47)** (WGMTurner) **2-8-2**(7) DMcGaffin(11) (sn drvn along & bhd)	1	**12**	14/1	22	—
3866[5]	**Ngaere Princess (46)** (WTKemp) **2-8-8** TWilliams(1) (lw: in tch over 3f)	1	**13**	20/1	18	—
3866[3]	**I'm Not Sure (52)** (JBerry) **2-8-9**(5) CLowther(9) (unruly in stalls: s.i.s: nvr rchd ldrs)	s.h	**14**	4/1[1]	24	—
3078[6]	**Medina Miss (52)** (GMMcCourt) **2-9-0** VSlattery(15) (b: b.hind: nvr wnt pce)	2½	**15**	8/1[3]	16	—
3751[9]	**Blitz (45)** (MWEasterby) **2-8-4**(3) GParkin(13) (s.i.s: hung lft: a outpcd & bhd)	1¼	**16**	33/1	5	—
3699[7]	**Makahu Don (53)** (WTKemp) **2-9-1** JCarroll(10) (lw: in tch tl outpcd fr ½-wy)	1¼	**17**	12/1	9	—

(SP 130.9%) **17 Rn**

60.6 secs (3.60) CSF £352.62 CT £3,717.45 TOTE £17.70: £3.90 £7.00 £2.50 £3.40 (£959.70) Trio £256.00; £288.47 to Leicester 9/9/97
OWNER Mr E. R. Kettenacker (NEWMARKET) BRED E. Kettenacker
No bid

3586 Super Geil produced what she had obviously been showing at home before her first run, and this should have done her confidence no harm. (12/1)
2604 Miss Bananas has plenty of toe and this should find her a modest race, either on this surface or on soft ground on turf. (33/1)
3751 Snappy Times, dropping back in trip, ran well but, despite struggling on, was never quite doing enough. (10/1)
3859 Dande Times ran a fair race from what appeared an impossible draw, but his tendency to hang left is quite worrying. (10/1: 8/1-12/1)
3270 Mr Fund Switch had blinkers on for the first time and was given a most aggressive ride, but it all proved in vain. (33/1)
3544 Time To Time ran well at her first attempt on this surface, but looked short of speed at this trip. (16/1)
3808 Jockweiler (IRE) again left the impression that longer trips would see improvement. (25/1)
3866 I'm Not Sure (4/1: op 6/1)
3062 Makahu Don (12/1: op 8/1)

4055 DON NOBLE BOOKMAKER H'CAP (0-65) (3-Y.O+) (Class F)

4-45 (4-45) **1m 6f (Fibresand)** £2,277.00 (£627.00: £297.00) Stalls: Low GOING: 0.14 sec per fur (SLW)

				SP	RR	SF
3865[2]	**Il Principe (IRE) (50)** (JohnBerry) **3-8-2e** JFEgan(5) (lw: a chsng ldrs: rdn to ld 3f out: styd on strly)	—	**1**	7/2[1]	65	21
3928[10]	**La Menorquina (USA) (48)** (DMarks) **7-8-11** JFortune(1) (hdwy u.p 4f out: chsd wnr fnl 2f: hung lft & no imp)	6	**2**	12/1	56	23
3758[3]	**Needwood Epic (52)** (BCMorgan) **4-9-1b** JCarroll(4) (led tl hdd 3f out: sn outpcd)	5	**3**	14/1	54	21
3419[10]	**Signed And Sealed (USA) (50)** (CACyzer) **3-7-13**(3) AWhelan(10) (gd hdwy u.p to chse ldrs 6f out: one pce fnl 3f)	1¼	**4**	20/1	51	7
3919[6]	**Charlie Bigtime (36)** (ICampbell) **7-7-13** GBardwell(8) (sn drvn along & wl bhd: hdwy u.p 6f out: nvr rchd ldrs)	6	**5**	14/1	30	—
3865[10]	**Robbo (60)** (CWThornton) **3-8-12b** DeanMcKeown(12) (in tch: hdwy 6f out: sn rdn & chsng ldrs: wl outpcd fnl 3f)	6	**6**	11/1[3]	47	3
3719[5]	**Dashing Invader (USA) (45)** (PWHarris) **4-8-8b** DHolland(16) (lw: cl up: drvn along 7f out: rdn & wknd 3f out: eased fnl 2f)	¾	**7**	8/1[2]	31	—
68[2]	**Tirmizi (USA) (52)** (MrsASwinbank) **6-9-1** EJohnson(6) (sn outpcd & wl bhd: sme hdwy fnl 4f: n.d)	13	**8**	20/1	24	—
3919[2]	**Havana Heights (IRE) (43)** (JLEyre) **4-7-13**(7)ow6 SBuckley(9) (b.nr hind: prom: drvn along after 4f: lost tch fnl 6f)	9	**9**	8/1[2]	4	—
3291[5]	**Drift (59)** (SirMarkPrescott) **3-8-11** GDuffield(15) (swtg: chsd ldrs: hrd drvn 7f out: wknd fnl 5f)	12	**10**	7/2[1]	7	—
3540[9]	**El Nido (45)** (DWChapman) **9-8-8** LCharnock(17) (n.d)	4	**11**	25/1	—	—
2940[6]	**Hoh Explorer (IRE) (58)** (DWBarker) **3-8-10** TWilliams(13) (sn outpcd & bhd)	10	**12**	20/1	—	—
*3611**	**Red Phantom (IRE) (50)** (SMellor) **5-8-13v** MWigham(11) (effrt ½-wy: sn btn & eased)	6	**13**	8/1[2]	—	—
2882[7]	**Spa Lane (53)** (MPBielby) **4-9-2** AMcGlone(7) (sn outpcd & bhd)	3	**14**	25/1	—	—
3867[6]	**Moonraking (55)** (TJEtherington) **4-9-1**(3) GParkin(2) (sn drvn along & bhd)	27	**15**	16/1	—	—
1964[5]	**Greenwich Fore (60)** (TGMills) **3-8-12** KDarley(14) (b.hind: chsd ldrs tl wknd 4f out)	6	**16**	14/1	—	—

(SP 141.7%) **16 Rn**

3m 11.7 (13.70) CSF £48.43 CT £522.86 TOTE £4.30: £1.70 £2.10 £4.40 £5.00 (£41.70) Trio £140.00 OWNER The 1997 Partnership (NEWMARKET) BRED J. Costello
WEIGHT FOR AGE 3yo-11lb
OFFICIAL EXPLANATION **Dashing Invader: stumbled coming out of the stalls and lost his action in the latter stages of race.**
3865 Il Principe (IRE) has had some hard races recently but seemingly thrives on it, and this was a most emphatic victory. (7/2)
660* La Menorquina (USA) ideally likes further and put up a game effort, but the winner was always far too good. (12/1)
3758 Needwood Epic travelled well out in front but, once asked for an effort, she lacked any further gears. (14/1)
Signed And Sealed (USA), at his first attempt on this surface, showed his first signs of form. (20/1)
3919 Charlie Bigtime found the frenetic early pace way beyond him and could never get into it. (14/1)
3587* Robbo went quite well for a long way, but then proved disappointing once off the bit. (11/1)
3719 Dashing Invader (USA) needs to lead and was never quick enough to do that. (8/1)
3919 Havana Heights (IRE) (8/1: 6/1-9/1)
3291 Drift, very edgy beforehand, ran poorly and was beaten fully six furlongs from home. (7/2: 5/1-3/1)

4056 E.B.F. COLOGNE MAIDEN STKS (II) (2-Y.O) (Class D)

5-15 (5-18) **7f (Fibresand)** £3,200.00 (£950.00: £450.00: £200.00) Stalls: Low GOING: 0.14 sec per fur (SLW)

				SP	RR	SF
3235[10]	**Confirmation** (SirMarkPrescott) **2-9-0** GDuffield(1) (sn trckng ldrs: led 3f out: styd on wl)	—	**1**	11/4[1]	98+	48
3686[10]	**Di Matteo (IRE)** (BHanbury) **2-9-0** WRyan(10) (mid div: sn drvn along: styd on fnl 2f: no ch w wnr)	11	**2**	5/1[2]	73	23
3770[5]	**Polo Venture** (SPCWoods) **2-9-0** NDay(6) (a.p: hdwy over 2f out: no imp)	nk	**3**	10/1	72	22
3686[12]	**Algaleb** (HAkbary) **2-9-0** GHind(5) (b.hind: unruly gng to s: led 4f: grad wknd)	1	**4**	16/1	70	20
2467[13]	**Lunchtime Girl** (JDBethell) **2-8-9** TWilliams(8) (chsd ldrs: rdn 3f out: one pce)	5	**5**	25/1	54	4
3686[18]	**Dawn Treader (USA)** (RHannon) **2-9-0** DaneO'Neill(9) (bhd: drvn along ½-wy: nvr able to chal)	hd	**6**	14/1	58	8
3711[10]	**Smiling Voter (IRE)** (RHannon) **2-8-7**(7) RSmith(11) (sn drvn along & nvr trbld ldrs)	1¾	**7**	20/1	54	4
3806[13]	**Durgams Delight (IRE)** (BWMurray) **2-8-9** VHalliday(4) (unruly gng to s: sn outpcd & bhd: n.d)	5	**8**	50/1	38	—
	Sadeebah (MJohnston) **2-9-0** JWeaver(12) (unf: chsd ldrs tl wknd fnl 2½f)	2½	**9**	13/2	37	—
	Lady Imza (WJHaggas) **2-8-9** JCarroll(7) (cmpt: b.hind: cl up tl wknd fnl 3f)	2	**10**	13/2	28	—
	Goldmaster (WAO'Gorman) **2-9-0** EmmaO'Gorman(3) (unf: scope: unruly in stalls & dwlt: pushed along & n.d)	2	**11**	7/1	28	—

				SP	RR	SF
	Antonio Joli (PFICole) **2-9-0** GCarter(2) (leggy: unf: a outpcd & bhd)	3	**12**	$11/2^{3}$	21	—
				(SP 130.1%)		**12 Rn**

1m 31.8 (5.30) CSF £15.97 TOTE £4.20: £1.40 £1.40 £3.20 (£8.60) Trio £43.40 OWNER Cheveley Park Stud (NEWMARKET) BRED Cheveley Park Stud Ltd

Confirmation has the look of something better and won this nicely. There is obviously more to come. (11/4)
3084 Di Matteo (IRE), unlike his namesake, is short of gears and was always struggling as a result of that. (5/1)
3770 Polo Venture is still learning about the game and time would seem to be the key. (10/1)
Algaleb gave problems aplenty going to the start and finally had to be led all the way, and then ran reasonably. (16/1)
Lunchtime Girl showed a little ability here but looked very one-paced. (25/1)
Dawn Treader (USA) does not do anything quickly and could never get into this. (14/1)

T/Plpt: £280.70 (61.89 Tckts). T/Qdpt: £64.20 (17.24 Tckts) WG/AA

3691-LEICESTER (R-H) (Good to firm)
Tuesday September 9th
WEATHER: fine & sunny WIND: slight bhd

4057 E.B.F. FILBERT MAIDEN STKS (2-Y.O F) (Class D)
2-15 (2-17) **1m 8y** £3,522.00 (£1,056.00: £508.00: £234.00) Stalls: High GOING minus 0.41 sec per fur (F)

				SP	RR	SF
	Bristol Channel (BWHills) **2-8-11** LDettori(4) (b: lt-f: dwlt: hdwy 3f out: led over 1f out: r.o wl)	—	**1**	6/1	84+	37
3386^{3}	**Rambling Rose** (MRStoute) **2-8-11** JReid(7) (a chsng ldrs: led over 2f out tl over 1f out: kpt on u.p)	½	**2**	$3/1^{2}$	83	36
3769^{2}	**Oberon's Mistral** (HRACecil) **2-8-11** WRyan(5) (hld up: hdwy 3f out: jnd ldrs over 2f out: rdn & one pce fnl f)	2½	**3**	$5/1^{3}$	78	31
3547^{3}	**Bluewain Lady** (PWHarris) **2-8-11** PatEddery(9) (led: rdn over 3f out: hdd over 2f out: r.o one pce)	1¼	**4**	$7/4^{1}$	76	29
3744^{6}	**Chim Chiminey** (BWHills) **2-8-11** MHills(6) (hld up: hdwy over 3f out: rdn & ev ch over 2f out: wknd appr fnl f)	5	**5**	11/2	66	19
	Macca Luna (IRE) (MHTompkins) **2-8-8**(3) MHenry(10) (unf: scope: bkwd: s.i.s: hld up in tch: rdn over 2f out: sn btn)	3	**6**	33/1	60	13
2394^{9}	**Siena (GER)** (MRChannon) **2-8-11** JFortune(3) (prom over 5f: sn wknd: t.o)	11	**7**	66/1	38	—
3450^{4}	**Chlo-Jo** (AGFoster) **2-8-11** GBardwell(2) (prom: rdn over 3f out: sn wknd: t.o)	4	**8**	33/1	30	—
3788^{3}	**Suellajoy** (BSmart) **2-8-11** JStack(8) (lw: hld up: lost tch fnl 3f: t.o)	3	**9**	33/1	24	—
3493^{5}	**Every Penny** (APJones) **2-8-11** MRoberts(1) (s.i.s: rdn ½-wy: a bhd: t.o)	9	**10**	33/1	6	—
				(SP 121.0%)		**10 Rn**

1m 37.2 (2.20) CSF £22.27 TOTE £7.30: £1.50 £2.00 £2.30 (£16.10) Trio £16.40 OWNER Mr K. Abdulla (LAMBOURN) BRED Juddmonte Farms

Bristol Channel, a classically-bred, not over-big, sparely-made filly, started her career in the best possible fashion and, with this experience behind her, she could be set to go places. (6/1: op 5/2)
3386 Rambling Rose, still carrying condition despite having had a run, gained a narrow lead entering the final quarter-mile and, proving a tough nut to crack, should have little trouble in making a name for herself. (3/1)
3769 Oberon's Mistral does not really extend herself in her action and she may well benefit from easier ground, but she did run her best race yet, and is getting to know what is required. (5/1)
3547 Bluewain Lady, prepared to force the pace, was given a reminder soon after halfway. Taken on and headed by the runner-up, she stuck to the task in hand but was fighting a losing battle before reaching the final furlong. (7/4: 5/4-15/8)
3744 Chim Chiminey, a stable companion of the winner, put herself in with every chance entering the last couple of furlongs but, once the pace lifted, she had to admit she was a bit out of her class. (11/2)

4058 RANCLIFFE (S) NURSERY H'CAP (0-65) (2-Y.O) (Class G)
2-45 (2-46) **1m 8y** £2,700.00 (£750.00: £360.00) Stalls: High GOING minus 0.41 sec per fur (F)

				SP	RR	SF
3911^{9}	**Francesca's Folly (49)** (JWHills) **2-8-2**(3) MHenry(15) (chsd ldr 5f out: led over 2f out: sn clr: r.o wl)	—	**1**	14/1	55	13
3707^{12}	**Constant Attention (59)** (PFICole) **2-9-1** JReid(12) (dwlt: hdwy 3f out: hrd rdn & chsd wnr over 1f out: nt qckn)	2½	**2**	12/1	60	18
3911^{6}	**Arm And A Leg (IRE) (55)** (CADwyer) **2-8-11v** LDettori(6) (lw: hld up: hdwy over 2f out: r.o ins fnl f)	2	**3**	$7/2^{1}$	52	10
3563^{5}	**Up The Clarets (IRE) (54)** (JJO'Neill) **2-8-10** ACulhane(13) (hdwy 4f out: hrd rdn & r.o one pce fnl f)	½	**4**	25/1	50	8
3692^{3}	**Patricia Olive (IRE) (53)** (MHTompkins) **2-8-4**(5) RMullen(5) (no hdwy fnl 2f)	5	**5**	$10/1^{3}$	39	—
3307^{4}	**Kite (53)** (MBell) **2-8-9** MFenton(10) (prom tl wknd over 1f out: eased whn btn ins fnl f)	nk	**6**	$9/2^{2}$	39	—
3819^{3}	**Fanti Dancer (IRE) (65)** (BJMeehan) **2-9-4b**1(3) TEDurcan(2) (lw: disp ld over 5f)	¾	**7**	$9/2^{2}$	49	7
3750^{9}	**Cherished (IRE) (60)** (PFICole) **2-9-2b**1 TQuinn(11) (lw: hld up: rdn over 2f out: nt run on)	¾	**8**	$9/2^{2}$	43	1
3819^{9}	**Tilburg (55)** (MrsNMacauley) **2-8-11** SSanders(7) (lw: chsd ldrs over 5f: eased whn btn over 1f out)	3	**9**	25/1	32	—
3586^{11}	**Margaret's Dancer (49)** (CSmith) **2-8-2b**(3) PFessey(3) (lw: hld up: hdwy over 3f out: wknd over 2f out)	nk	**10**	40/1	25	—
3751^{10}	**Docklands Dispatch (IRE) (56)** (NTinkler) **2-8-12v**1 KimTinkler(14) (plld hrd: disp ld over 5f: sn hrd rdn & wknd)	1	**11**	12/1	30	—
3967^{8}	**Mary Lou (IRE) (59)** (MRChannon) **2-9-1** JFortune(1) (rdn over 3f out: sn bhd)	3½	**12**	12/1	26	—
3818^{13}	**Risknowt Getnowt (40)** (TWall) **2-7-3**(7) PMQuinn(4) (lw: hld up: hung rt over 4f out: bhd fnl 3f)	1	**13**	50/1	5	—
3819^{11}	**God Knows (IRE) (41)** (MJFetherston-Godley) **2-7-11**ow1 FNorton(9) (prom over 4f)	4	**14**	40/1	—	—
3818^{12}	**Risque (41)** (MrsAJBowlby) **2-7-11**ow1 MartinDwyer(8) (plld hrd: prom tl wknd qckly over 3f out: t.o)	16	**15**	50/1	—	—
				(SP 132.1%)		**15 Rn**

1m 39.1 (4.10) CSF £161.83 CT £685.31 TOTE £15.80: £4.30 £4.60 £1.80 (£90.10) Trio £210.10; £76.95 to Doncaster 10/9/97 OWNER Mr Freddy Bienstock (LAMBOURN) BRED F. Bienstock, John Hills and Mrs S. Wray

LONG HANDICAP Risknowt Getnowt 7-7

Bt in 6,500gns

OFFICIAL EXPLANATION **Francesca's Folly: regarding the improvement in form comparing her previous run at Sandown, the trainer's representative stated that on that occasion she sweated up badly, was reluctant to enter the stalls and never got into the race.**
3493 Francesca's Folly was down 3lb. The Stewards considered her improved form after disappointing on soft ground last time, and were told that the filly had sweated badly and was reluctant to enter the stalls, but today she was much more settled. (14/1)
2519 Constant Attention was a disappointment in blinkers in the valuable six-furlong seller at York's big August meeting. (12/1: 8/1-14/1)
3911 Arm And A Leg (IRE), dropped a further 2lb, was stepping up to a mile. (7/2)
3563 Up The Clarets (IRE) was another trying his luck over a longer trip. (25/1)

3307 Kite (9/2: 3/1-5/1)
3819 Fanti Dancer (IRE) (9/2: op 3/1)
2038 Cherished (IRE), tried in blinkers, seems best left alone. (9/2)

4059 WYMESWOLD H'CAP (0-70) (3-Y.O+) (Class E)

3-15 (3-15) **7f 9y** £3,951.00 (£1,188.00: £574.00: £267.00) Stalls: High GOING minus 0.41 sec per fur (F)

Form	Horse	Dist	Pos	SP	RR	SF
3849^{3}	**Samara Song (53)** (IPWilliams) **4-9-1** MRoberts(10) (lw: hld up: hdwy 2f out: led ins fnl f: comf)	—	**1**	7/1^{2}	60	29
3800^{4}	**Topton (IRE) (68)** (IABalding) **3-9-12v^{1}** LDettori(13) (a.p stands' side: led over 2f out tl ins fnl f)	½	**2**	9/1^{3}	74	39
3328^{5}	**Alfahaal (IRE) (56)** (RFJohnsonHoughton) **4-9-4** JReid(14) (plld hrd: hld up: hdwy 2f out: led ins fnl f: hung rt: sn hdd)	1	**3**	6/1^{1}	60	29
3855^{6}	**Allinson's Mate (IRE) (61)** (TDBarron) **9-9-4**(5) KimberleyHart(5) (hld up: hdwy 2f out: r.o wl ins fnl f)	nk	**4**	16/1	64	33
3937^{8}	**Gymcrak Flyer (64)** (GHolmes) **6-9-12** JFortune(2) (lw: hld up: hdwy over 2f out: one pce appr fnl f)	½	**5**	14/1	66	35
3710^{3}	**Celandine (52)** (AndrewTurnell) **4-8-9**(5) ADaly(4) (nvr nrr)	2½	**6**	12/1	48	17
3691^{2}	**Midnight Shift (IRE) (64)** (RGuest) **3-9-8** PatEddery(19) (led far side: rdn 2f out: hdd & outpcd ins fnl f)	hd	**7**	7/1^{2}	60	25
3759^{8}	**Surf City (51)** (WWHaigh) **4-8-13** ACulhane(8) (trckd ldrs stands' side: no hdwy fnl 2f)	½	**8**	25/1	46	15
3936^{6}	**Bollin Dorothy (54)** (TDEasterby) **4-9-2** TWilliams(17) (prom far side: ev ch over 1f out: sn wknd)	nk	**9**	7/1^{2}	48	17
3868^{2}	**Hi Mujtahid (IRE) (54)** (SEKettlewell) **3-8-12** KDarley(11) (lw: nvr rchd ldrs)	1	**10**	10/1	46	11
3930^{9}	**Oneknight With You (59)** (MJFetherston-Godley) **3-9-3** FNorton(6) (b: nvr nr to chal)	1	**11**	25/1	49	14
3710^{4}	**Shades of Love (63)** (VSoane) **3-9-7** TQuinn(16) (hld up & plld hrd: nvr trbld ldrs)	1¼	**12**	10/1	50	15
3936^{15}	**Birchwood Sun (55)** (MDods) **7-9-3b** JWeaver(15) (swtchd stands' side sn after s: n.d)	1¼	**13**	20/1	39	8
3702^{6}	**Winter Scout (USA) (60)** (RAFahey) **9-9-1**(7) RWinston(20) (lw: prom far side: rdn & ev ch 2f out: wknd over 1f out)	1¼	**14**	16/1	41	10
3641*	**Silver Secret (61)** (MJHeaton-Ellis) **3-9-5** SSanders(18) (lw: chsd ldrs far side over 4f)	1½	**15**	12/1	39	4
3702^{3}	**Fearless Cavalier (56)** (RHollinshead) **3-8-11**(3) DGriffiths(12) (a in rr)	1½	**16**	14/1	30	—
2645^{9}	**Tal-Y-Llyn (IRE) (70)** (BWHills) **3-10-0** MHills(7) (a in rr)	¾	**17**	20/1	43	8
2848^{10}	**Helios (58)** (DJGMurraySmith) **9-9-6** WRyan(3) (led stands' side tl over 2f out: sn wknd)	½	**18**	20/1	29	—
3777^{3}	**Oriole (52)** (DonEnricoIncisa) **4-9-0** KimTinkler(1) (a bhd)	1¾	**19**	20/1	19	—
3614^{10}	**Countless Times (62)** (WRMuir) **3-9-6** MartinDwyer(9) (plld hrd: c stands' side: n.d)	3	**20**	25/1	23	—

(SP 151.0%) **20 Rn**

1m 25.5 (2.90) CSF £69.12 CT £391.25 TOTE £8.30: £1.40 £2.00 £2.30 £4.30 (£27.50) Trio £86.60 OWNER Turton Builders (ALVECHURCH) BRED S. F. Turton
WEIGHT FOR AGE 3yo-4lb

3849 Samara Song appreciated this return to a slightly shorter trip and, given a peach of a ride, at long last had his head in front where it mattered. (7/1)

3800 Topton (IRE), the subject of quite a gamble in a first-time visor, battled for the lead all the way and was only forced to give best nearing the line. He is high in the handicap for a maiden, but should not remain in that grade for long. (9/1)

3328 Alfahaal (IRE), taking a step down in distance and restrained under a fearsome hold, was produced to win his race two hundred yards out, but he drifted over towards the far side rail almost immediately, and forfeited a glorious chance. (6/1: op 4/1)

3855 Allinson's Mate (IRE) rarely runs a bad race and he was doing some sterling work in the closing stages, but the young pretenders were not stopping, and he was unable to land a blow. (16/1)

1501 Gymcrak Flyer wore blinkers for the first time on her previous outing, but they failed to have the desired effect and were discarded this time. Taking closer order over two furlongs out, she looked a serious threat before the weight began to take its toll and she could do no more. (14/1)

3710 Celandine, who has done the majority of her racing over sprint distances, came late on the scene and found it all over bar the shouting. (12/1)

3691 Midnight Shift (IRE) was possibly the overall leader and she really stuck to her guns under strong pressure but, once Alfahaal took her measure, she found the quickening tempo too strong. (7/1)

4060 LEICESTERSHIRE MAIDEN STKS (3-Y.O+) (Class D)

3-45 (3-47) **1m 1f 218y** £4,091.50 (£1,225.00: £588.00: £269.50) Stalls: Low GOING minus 0.41 sec per fur (F)

Form	Horse	Dist	Pos	SP	RR	SF
	Sacho (IRE) (JHMGosden) **4-9-7** LDettori(3) (lw: hld up: hdwy over 3f out: hung rt over 1f out: led ins fnl f: r.o wl)	—	**1**	3/1^{1}	92	59
3463^{2}	**Tonight's Prize (IRE) (83)** (CFWall) **3-9-0** SSanders(8) (plld hrd: a.p: led ins fnl f: sn hdd: nt qckn)	1¼	**2**	3/1^{1}	90	50
3501^{3}	**Serpentara** (HRACecil) **3-8-9** WRyan(12) (chsd ldr tl over 1f out: one pce)	2½	**3**	13/2^{3}	81	41
3909^{8}	**Quiet Venture** (EALDunlop) **3-8-11**(3) DO'Donohoe(17) (lw: led tl ins fnl f)	2	**4**	33/1	83	43
523^{3}	**London Lights** (PFICole) **3-9-0** TQuinn(19) (tk keen hld: a.p: one pce fnl 2f)	s.h	**5**	9/2^{2}	83	43
1499^{5}	**Dukhan (USA)** (RWArmstrong) **3-9-0** KDarley(5) (a.p: hung rt over 1f out: one pce)	nk	**6**	14/1	82	42
3188^{5}	**Back Row** (LMCumani) **3-8-9** PatEddery(15) (hld up: hdwy over 2f out: nt rch ldrs)	6	**7**	12/1	68	28
	Waterwave (USA) (JHMGosden) **4-9-7** MHills(2) (lw: s.s: hdwy fnl 2f: nvr nrr)	hd	**8**	15/2	73	40
3133^{8}	**Minster Star (60)** (JLSpearing) **3-8-9** JFortune(9) (s.i.s: nvr nrr)	nk	**9**	50/1	67	27
518^{7}	**Muhassil (IRE)** (KAMorgan) **4-9-7** OPears(13) (plld hrd: nvr nr ldrs)	s.h	**10**	33/1	72	39
3775^{6}	**Priluki** (CEBrittain) **3-8-9** MRoberts(10) (lw: prom tl wknd over 2f out)	2	**11**	20/1	64	24
	Tyrolean Dream (IRE) (MHTompkins) **3-8-11**(3) MHenry(16) (lw: bhd fnl 3f)	3	**12**	16/1	64	24
3211^{11}	**Beguine (USA)** (WJarvis) **3-8-9** JReid(1) (lw: bmpd 5f out: bhd fnl 3f)	½	**13**	33/1	58	18
	Choice Lady (JLHarris) **3-8-9** DeanMcKeown(7) (w'like: a bhd)	7	**14**	66/1	47	7
	Trienta Mil (PTDalton) **3-9-0** LCharnock(11) (a bhd)	hd	**15**	100/1	52	12
	Thatcham Island (DLWilliams) **4-8-13**(3) DGriffiths(18) (hld up: hdwy on ins 5f out: wknd over 3f out)	5	**16**	100/1	39	6
3909^{6}	**Fuwala** (DShaw) **3-8-9** JFanning(4) (a bhd)	5	**17**	66/1	31	—
3720^{8}	**Kayesam** (JLHarris) **3-9-0** ACulhane(14) (prom tl wknd over 3f out: t.o)	9	**18**	100/1	21	—
3820^{9}	**Lady of Glendowan** (MrsBarbaraWaring) **4-9-2** EByrne(6) (a bhd: t.o)	9	**19**	100/1	2	—

(SP 136.0%) **19 Rn**

2m 5.2 (1.50) CSF £10.69 TOTE £3.90: £1.30 £1.10 £2.50 (£10.60) Trio £19.10 OWNER Sheikh Mohammed (NEWMARKET) BRED Sheikh Mohammed bin Rashid al Maktoum
WEIGHT FOR AGE 3yo-7lb

Sacho (IRE), a one-time leading contender for the 1996 Derby, had not seen a racecourse since last season's Craven meeting because of a very serious hock injury. Despite showing signs of inexperience, he was nicely on top in the end and seems set to make up for lost time. (3/1: 7/4-100/30)

3463 Tonight's Prize (IRE), trying an extra quarter-mile, ran a bit freely but came up against an above-average type in the winner. (3/1)
3501 Serpentara did enough to suggest she is capable of enhancing her paddock value. (13/2)
Quiet Venture fared much better than on his debut and would appear to be going the right way. (33/1)
523 London Lights ran respectably on this comeback after presumably having had some problems. (9/2)
1499 Dukhan (USA) did not look an easy ride. (14/1)
Back Row may do better now she is qualified for handicaps. (12/1)
Waterwave (USA) (15/2: 5/1-8/1)

4061 REMPSTONE MAIDEN STKS (I) (2-Y.O) (Class D)

4-15 (4-17) **7f 9y** £3,587.00 (£1,076.00: £518.00: £239.00) Stalls: High GOING minus 0.41 sec per fur (F)

				SP	RR	SF
	Mudeer (SbinSuroor) **2-9-0** LDettori(13) (gd sort: hld up gng wl: qcknd to ld over 1f out: r.o)	—	**1**	11/4 2	87+	41
3494 4	**Close Up (IRE)** (JLDunlop) **2-9-0** WJO'Connor(17) (hld up: hdwy 3f out: ev ch over 1f out: unable qckn)	1¼	**2**	10/1	84	38
	Last Christmas (BWHills) **2-9-0** MHills(11) (leggy: unf: s.s: hdwy over 2f out: ev ch appr fnl f: unable qckn)	1½	**3**	16/1	81+	35
3687 2	**Taverner Society (IRE)** (RWArmstrong) **2-9-0** MRoberts(16) (a.p: ev ch over 1f out: no ex fnl f)	hd	**4**	5/2 1	81	35
3753 3	**Naskhi** (MJohnston) **2-8-9** JWeaver(18) (mde most tl hdd over 1f out)	1	**5**	12/1	73	27
3745 3	**Wuxi Venture** (SPCWoods) **2-9-0** KDarley(15) (prom: effrt 2f out: r.o one pce)	2	**6**	6/1	74	28
	Diktat (DRLoder) **2-9-0** WRyan(20) (w'like: scope: bkwd: hdwy 3f out: sn ev ch: eased whn btn ins fnl f)	¾	**7**	9/1	72	26
	Allgrit (USA) (EALDunlop) **2-9-0** JFortune(14) (rangy: hld up: effrt 2f out: sn hrd drvn: nt pce to chal)	¾	**8**	14/1	70	24
	Pedro (IRE) (SirMarkPrescott) **2-9-0** SSanders(3) (w'like: str: bkwd: chsd ldrs over 5f)	1¼	**9**	7/1	68	22
3806 5	**Saudi** (PFICole) **2-9-0** TQuinn(19) (prom: ev ch 2f out: wknd over 1f out)	1¾	**10**	12/1	64	18
3494 9	**Wintertime** (GLewis) **2-9-0** PaulEddery(9) (trckd ldrs 4f: sn outpcd)	nk	**11**	20/1	63	17
	Jaazim (USA) (MRStoute) **2-9-0** JReid(6) (w'like: scope: s.s: a in rr)	s.h	**12**	11/2 3	63	17
3117 9	**Sadir** (MajorWRHern) **2-9-0** NCarlisle(10) (hld up: a in rr)	¾	**13**	33/1	61	15
3806 7	**Bawsian** (JLEyre) **2-9-0** OPears(2) (hld up: a in rr)	4	**14**	25/1	52	6
2314 5	**Montano (USA)** (PFICole) **2-9-0** ACulhane(1) (plld hrd: trckd ldrs 5f)	2	**15**	33/1	47	1
3212 6	**Silver Hope (IRE)** (RHollinshead) **2-8-11**(3) DGriffiths(5) (hld up & plld hrd: lost tch wl over 2f out)	4	**16**	50/1	38	—
	Pure Nobility (IRE) (BWHills) **2-9-0** PatEddery(4) (w'like: leggy: bkwd: s.s: a bhd)	nk	**17**	14/1	38	—
2842 13	**Press Ahead** (BAMcMahon) **2-9-0** LNewton(12) (prom: ev ch over 2f out: sn wknd)	½	**18**	50/1	36	—

(SP 169.5%) **18 Rn**

1m 24.4 (1.80) CSF £38.90 TOTE £3.50: £1.50 £4.80 £9.70 (£59.90) Trio £115.20; £146.08 to Doncaster 10/9/97 OWNER Godolphin (NEWMARKET) BRED Meon Valley Stud
Mudeer, a choicely-bred, strongly-made colt who was a late-April foal, knew what was needed and, lengthening up to take control at the distance, won readily. He has entries in the Middle Park and the Royal Lodge Stakes and he looks set to make the grade. (11/4: 6/4-3/1)
3494 Close Up (IRE), improving with each run as he gains experience, was unfortunate to meet one as useful as the winner at this early stage of his career, but he has winner written all over him. (10/1)
Last Christmas still has plenty of filling out to do, but he is a late-May foal, and this very promising racecourse debut stamps him as a colt with a future. (16/1)
3687 Taverner Society (IRE) turned in another encouraging performance and only got tapped for speed inside the distance. Fortune will favour him before long. (5/2)
3753 Naskhi, tackling a slightly longer trip, was in no mood to give best and she did not concede defeat until the winner brushed her aside approaching the final furlong. (12/1)
3745 Wuxi Venture sat in behind the leaders waiting to pounce, but he did not find the expected response when let down and he is not yet getting it together. (6/1: op 12/1)
Diktat, sure to strip much fitter for the run, ran much better than his finishing position would suggest and he is worth bearing in mind for the future. (9/1)
Allgrit (USA), a rangy colt very much on the leg, could not pick up when asked for an effort inside the last quarter-mile, but he did keep galloping and this experience will stand him in good stead. (14/1)

4062 PRESTWOLD CONDITIONS STKS (3-Y.O+) (Class C)

4-45 (4-45) **5f 2y** £5,058.00 (£1,872.00: £898.50: £367.50: £146.25: £57.75) Stalls: High GOING minus 0.41 sec per fur (F)

				SP	RR	SF
3011 11	**Blue Iris (97)** (MAJarvis) **4-8-5** MRoberts(6) (hld up & bhd: hdwy over 1f out: led wl ins fnl f: comf)	—	**1**	7/1	96+	44
3600 6	**Crofters Ceilidh (85)** (BAMcMahon) **5-8-5** SSanders(1) (chsd ldr: led over 2f out tl wl ins fnl f)	¾	**2**	12/1	94	42
3111 9	**Rambling Bear (107)** (MBlanshard) **4-9-2** JReid(4) (lw: hld up & plld hrd: hdwy over 1f out: r.o one pce fnl f)	1¼	**3**	9/4 1	101	49
3011 10	**Passion For Life (96)** (GLewis) **4-9-2** PaulEddery(8) (led over 2f: wknd ins fnl f)	1¼	**4**	20/1	97	45
3747 10	**Connemara (IRE) (97)** (CADwyer) **3-8-4** KDarley(2) (lw: hld up: rdn over 1f out: one pce)	1¼	**5**	13/2 3	82	29
4001a 5	**Brave Edge (106)** (RHannon) **6-8-10** PatEddery(5) (rdn over 2f out: no hdwy)	hd	**6**	5/2 2	86	34
3604 15	**Ziggy's Dancer (USA) (90)** (EJAlston) **6-8-10** ACulhane(7) (lw: plld hrd early: rdn & n.m.r on ins over 2f out: wknd over 1f out)	2	**7**	20/1	80	28
3649 20	**Music Gold (IRE) (90)** (WAO'Gorman) **4-8-10b** JFortune(3) (lw: s.i.s: hld up: a bhd)	1¼	**8**	12/1	76	24

(SP 110.1%) **8 Rn**

59.1 secs (0.60) CSF £71.68 TOTE £6.30: £2.90 £2.00 £1.30 (£40.60) OWNER Mr M. A. Jarvis (NEWMARKET) BRED North Cheshire Trading and Storage Ltd
WEIGHT FOR AGE 3yo-1lb
1766 Blue Iris, wearing a tongue-strap for the first time, adopted totally different tactics and proved something of a revelation. Picking up a 3lb penalty for the Ayr Gold Cup, she is now on 9st and it sounds as if her trainer considers that a real racing weight. (7/1)
3600 Crofters Ceilidh had finished nearly four lengths in front of the winner at level weights at Ascot's King George meeting. (12/1)
2599 Rambling Bear took a strong hold and could not raise his game when the chips were down. (9/4)
1721a Passion For Life showed definite signs of a return to form. (20/1)
2677 Connemara (IRE) is continuing to find life tough as a three-year old and may do better at six furlongs. (13/2)
3372a Brave Edge is another who has been highly tried of late. (5/2)

4063 STAG APPRENTICE H'CAP (0-75) (3-Y.O+) (Class E)

5-15 (5-17) **1m 1f 218y** £3,256.00 (£988.00: £484.00: £232.00) Stalls: High GOING minus 0.41 sec per fur (F)

				SP	RR	SF
3916 5	**Edan Heights (71)** (SDow) **5-9-8**(3) PDoe(16) (a.p: led over 2f out: r.o wl)	—	**1**	10/1	81	60
*3609**	**Cherokee Flight (64)** (SMellor) **3-8-11** ADaly(2) (hld up: hdwy over 2f out: r.o wl ins fnl f)	nk	**2**	7/1 2	74	46

Ref	Horse	Dist	Pos	SP	RR	SF
2722[4]	**Secret Ballot (IRE) (62)** (KMahdi) **3-8-9** DO'Donohoe(4) (hld up mid div: hdwy ½-wy: r.o one pce fnl f)	1¾	**3**	14/1	69	41
3640[2]	**Zamalek (USA) (50)** (RMFlower) **5-8-4** RMullen(19) (a chsng ldrs: ev ch over 1f out: unable qckn)	½	**4**	5/1 [1]	56	35
2782[12]	**Ellway Lady (IRE) (57)** (IABalding) **3-8-4** MartinDwyer(17) (s.i.s: hdwy 4f out: jnd ldrs over 1f out: no ex fnl f)	½	**5**	16/1	62	34
	Scottish Bambi (59) (PRWebber) **9-8-13** MHenry(18) (bit bkwd: hld up: stdy hdwy over 4f out: one pce fnl 2f)	1¼	**6**	14/1	62	41
3620[4]	**Obelos (USA) (65)** (MissSJWilton) **6-9-5** CTeague(7) (hld up in rr: stdy hdwy fnl 2f: nvr nrr)	¾	**7**	16/1	67	46
3616[7]	**Eurobox Boy (72)** (APJarvis) **4-9-7**(5) CCarver(5) (b.nr hind: lw: hld up: hdwy & hung rt over 2f out: one pce)	nk	**8**	10/1	73	52
3694[4]	**Ordained (55)** (EJAlston) **4-8-2**(7) MelanieWorden(10) (chsd ldrs: rdn over 2f out: grad wknd)	hd	**9**	12/1	56	35
3798[4]	**Mbulwa (52)** (RAFahey) **11-8-3**(3) RWinston(14) (led tl hdd & wknd over 2f out)	2½	**10**	9/1	49	28
2483[8]	**Temptress (65)** (JohnHarris) **4-9-0**(5) RStudholme(15) (s.s: effrt on ins 3f out: wknd wl over 1f out)	2½	**11**	16/1	58	37
3824[3]	**Princess Danielle (66)** (WRMuir) **5-9-3**(3) JWilkinson(9) (lw: trckd ldrs 6f: sn lost tch)	½	**12**	7/1 [2]	59	38
3787[3]	**Literary (70)** (JHMGosden) **3-9-3** TEDurcan(6) (hld up: effrt & reminder 3f out: no imp)	hd	**13**	7/1 [2]	62	34
3184[7]	**Celebrant (66)** (AHide) **3-8-10**(3) JoHunnam(11) (b: a in rr)	nk	**14**	20/1	58	30
3315[16]	**Rival Bid (USA) (60)** (MrsNMacauley) **9-8-9v**(5) PFredericks(3) (b: s.s: hdwy over 3f out: wknd over 2f out)	4	**15**	33/1	45	24
3293[2]	**Bear Hug (74)** (LadyHerries) **4-10-0** GMilligan(8) (trckd ldrs tl wknd over 2f out)	hd	**16**	8/1 [3]	59	38
3091[14]	**Absolutelystunning (57)** (MrsBarbaraWaring) **4-8-11** PPMurphy(1) (b: b.hind: a bhd)	½	**17**	16/1	42	21
	Rock Scene (IRE) (55) (AStreeter) **5-8-9** DGriffiths(13) (bkwd: prom over 6f: eased whn btn fnl 2f: t.o)	30	**18**	25/1	—	—

(SP 149.6%) **18 Rn**

2m 5.6 (1.90) CSF £84.64 CT £959.15 TOTE £14.70: £4.00 £3.30 £6.10 £1.80 (£81.30) Trio £340.00; £292.18 to Doncaster 10/9/97 OWNER Mr T. R. Mountain (EPSOM) BRED T. R. Mountain

WEIGHT FOR AGE 3yo-7lb

3916 Edan Heights, at his best at this time of year, handled this lively ground surprisingly well and deservedly hung on nearing the line. (10/1)

3609* Cherokee Flight, given plenty to do, put in a determined last-furlong challenge, but the winner did not falter and was holding him in a spirited duel to the finish. (7/1)

2722 Secret Ballot (IRE) ran well after almost two months out of action and, with more cut in the ground, may well have given the principals more to think about. (14/1)

3640 Zamalek (USA) lacks a turn of finishing speed, but he never stopped trying and he will always pay his way. (5/1)

Ellway Lady (IRE), still to open her account, showed plenty of promise and she could be about to find her way. (16/1)

Scottish Bambi, a winner over fences on his previous outing in the spring, ran extremely well after such a lengthy break, and he will be spot on when he returns to the winter game. (14/1)

3620 Obelos (USA) came from a long way off the pace to reach his final placing and, if he returns to selling company, the hint should be worth taking. (16/1)

3787 Literary (7/1: 5/1-8/1)

3293 Bear Hug (8/1: 5/1-9/1)

4064 REMPSTONE MAIDEN STKS (II) (2-Y.O) (Class D)

5-45 (5-46) **7f 9y** £3,561.00 (£1,068.00: £514.00: £237.00) Stalls: High GOING minus 0.41 sec per fur (F)

Ref	Horse	Dist	Pos	SP	RR	SF
3687[5]	**Sensory** (BWHills) **2-9-0** PaulEddery(15) (hld up & plld hrd: hdwy 2f out: led wl ins fnl f: r.o wl)	—	**1**	7/1 [3]	87+	31
	Shart (IRE) (JHMGosden) **2-9-0** LDettori(9) (gd sort: lw: a.p: led & hung rt 2f out: hrd rdn & hdd wl ins fnl f)	¾	**2**	11/8 [1]	85+	29
3887[7]	**Fly By Night (IRE)** (MRStoute) **2-9-0** JReid(6) (led stands' side: ev ch over 1f out: one pce)	3	**3**	12/1	79	23
3687[4]	**Canadian Puzzler (USA)** (PWHarris) **2-9-0** PatEddery(19) (led centre: one pce fnl 2f)	1½	**4**	3/1 [2]	75	19
	Copernicus (PFICole) **2-9-0** TQuinn(11) (w'like: scope: a.p: no hdwy fnl 2f)	2	**5**	14/1	71	15
	Royal Shock (IRE) (DRLoder) **2-9-0** WRyan(13) (scope: a.p: no hdwy fnl 2f)	¾	**6**	10/1	69	13
	Ridgeway (IRE) (GWragg) **2-9-0** MHills(17) (gd sort: lw: chsd ldr centre tl wknd over 1f out)	¾	**7**	10/1	67	11
3598[17]	**Wave Rock** (JLDunlop) **2-9-0** WJO'Connor(2) (lw: no hdwy fnl 2f)	1¼	**8**	33/1	64	8
	Cherokee Band (USA) (BWHills) **2-9-0** DeanMcKeown(20) (w'like: scope: chsd ldrs centre: wknd 2f out)	¾	**9**	14/1	63	7
	Dilly Lane (USA) (PRWebber) **2-8-9** JFortune(8) (w'like: bit bkwd: nvr nr to chal)	3	**10**	100/1	51	—
3745[7]	**Dutch Lad** (MHTompkins) **2-8-11**(3) MHenry(3) (plld hrd: prom over 4f)	¾	**11**	50/1	54	—
3861[4]	**Dashing Chief (IRE)** (MAJarvis) **2-9-0** MRoberts(4) (lw: nvr nr ldrs)	s.h	**12**	16/1	54	—
3745[9]	**Aspirant Dancer** (MBell) **2-9-0** MFenton(18) (lw: a bhd)	1	**13**	50/1	52	—
3489[11]	**Mail Shot (IRE)** (SDow) **2-9-0** MartinDwyer(10) (s.s: a bhd)	2	**14**	66/1	47	—
	Noble Patriot (RHollinshead) **2-9-0** KDarley(5) (unf: scope: a bhd)	1½	**15**	25/1	44	—
	Cultured King (IRE) (JGSmyth-Osbourne) **2-9-0** GBardwell(7) (lengthy: unf: s.s: a bhd)	½	**16**	33/1	43	—
	Perfect Way (MrsNMacauley) **2-9-0** PBloomfield(12) (lt-f: s.s: a bhd)	6	**17**	66/1	29	—
	Ziggy Stardust (IRE) (MrsAJBowlby) **2-9-0** JStack(1) (unf: hld up mid div: n.m.r 3f out: bhd fnl 2f)	2	**18**	100/1	24	—
	Altitude (IRE) (SirMarkPrescott) **2-9-0** SSanders(14) (gd sort: s.s: a bhd)	4	**19**	16/1	15	—

(SP 149.2%) **19 Rn**

1m 25.3 (2.70) CSF £17.95 TOTE £9.90: £2.10 £1.70 £5.10 (£11.60) Trio £111.50 OWNER Mr K. Abdulla (LAMBOURN) BRED Juddmonte Farms

3687 Sensory, built like a tank, fulfilled the promise of his debut and one cannot help feeling whatever he achieves this year is a bonus. (7/1)

Shart (IRE) looked green when sent about his business and there will be other days for him. (11/8)

3887 Fly By Night (IRE), on faster ground this time, certainly seems capable of winning a race. (12/1)

3687 Canadian Puzzler (USA), who had finished three lengths in front of the winner at Kempton, probably held the overall lead for much of the way. (3/1)

Copernicus, a half-brother to numerous winners, has the scope to go on from here. (14/1)

Royal Shock (IRE), a half-brother to Panata and Shock Value, looks the type to develop into a nice three-year old. (10/1)

Ridgeway (IRE) seemed a nice type of animal in the paddock. (10/1)

T/Jkpt: Not won; £50,746.81 to Doncaster 10/9/97. T/Plpt: £65.00 (450.3 Tckts). T/Qdpt: £14.50 (110.91 Tckts) IM/KH

3859-LINGFIELD (L-H) (Turf Good, Good to firm patches, AWT Standard)
Tuesday September 9th

Race 1: hand-timed
WEATHER: warm & sunny WIND: almost nil

4065 GODSTONE RATING RELATED MAIDEN STKS (0-70) (2-Y.O) (Class E)
2-00 (2-02) **6f** £3,304.25 (£989.00: £474.50: £217.25) Stalls: Low GOING minus 0.30 sec per fur (GF)

				SP	RR	SF
3619^{7}	**Bahamian Melody (USA) (69)** (DRLoder) **2-9-0v^{1}** KFallon(8) (lw: rdn over 3f out: hdwy over 1f out: led 1f out: r.o wl)	—	**1**	5/2^{2}	75	42
3395^{4}	**Tightrope (70)** (SirMarkPrescott) **2-9-0** GDuffield(7) (a.p: rdn over 3f out: ev ch ins fnl f: unable qckn)	1¼	**2**	9/4^{1}	72	39
3823^{9}	**Leofric (67)** (MJPolglase) **2-9-0v^{1}** DHolland(3) (b.off hind: rdn over 2f out: hdwy over 1f out: one pce fnl f)	1¼	**3**	20/1	68	35
3818^{3}	**Signatory (70)** (RHannon) **2-9-0** DaneO'Neill(10) (lw: nt clr run on ins over 2f out: swtchd lft & hdwy over 1f out: one pce fnl f)	hd	**4**	10/1	68	35
3707^{3}	**Deva Lady (70)** (CNAllen) **2-8-6**(5) CLowther(4) (nt clr run & swtchd lft 2f out: hdwy fnl f: r.o)	½	**5**	12/1	64	31
3819^{2}	**Universal Lady (65)** (CJames) **2-8-11** RCochrane(9) (rdn over 2f out: hdwy fnl f: nvr nrr)	1	**6**	7/1	61	28
3774^{7}	**Alpen Wolf (IRE) (70)** (WRMuir) **2-9-0** TSprake(2) (lw: rdn over 2f out: hdwy over 1f out: wknd fnl f)	1¼	**7**	14/1	61	28
3783^{5}	**Blue Shadow (68)** (RHannon) **2-8-11b**(3) RFfrench(5) (a.p: led over 3f out to 1f out: sn wknd)	nk	**8**	20/1	60	27
3635^{3}	**Muftuffenuf (67)** (PRWebber) **2-8-11** AMcGlone(1) (lw: prom over 4f)	1¼	**9**	16/1	54	21
3742^{2}	**Poetto (70)** (BJMeehan) **2-9-0** MTebbutt(12) (led over 2f: wknd over 1f out)	5	**10**	6/1^{3}	43	10
3384^{5}	**Katies Treat (IRE) (45)** (DTThom) **2-8-11v** DRMcCabe(6) (lw: prom over 3f)	6	**11**	66/1	24	—
3742^{6}	**Lady Ralphina (51)** (JJBridger) **2-8-11** JQuinn(11) (spd over 3f)	9	**12**	66/1	—	—
				(SP 128.0%)	**12 Rn**	

1m 11.1 (2.10) CSF £8.24 TOTE £4.70: £1.80 £2.10 £3.00 (£5.20) Trio £76.00 OWNER Lucayan Stud (NEWMARKET) BRED Dr & Mrs R. S. West & Mr & Mrs Mackenzie Miller

3619 Bahamian Melody (USA) needed plenty of driving to get there and the first-time visor was probably a big help. He was better suited by this trip than the five furlongs last time, and runs as if he will stay further. (5/2)
3395 Tightrope, well backed, had every chance and will doubtless be placed to win even if it means a long journey. (9/4)
2886 Leofric ran as well as could be expected, but has had trouble finding an ideal trip. (20/1)
3818 Signatory, ridden with more patience this time, again lacked a turn of foot as the race reached its climax. (10/1: 7/1-12/1)
3707 Deva Lady was going on well at the finish and may be worth a try over an extra furlong. (12/1: 5/1-14/1)
3819 Universal Lady, soon behind on this return to six furlongs, could have done with a longer trip. (7/1: op 7/2)
3288 Alpen Wolf (IRE) (14/1: op 8/1)

4066 E.B.F. NUTFIELD MAIDEN STKS (I) (2-Y.O F) (Class D)
2-30 (2-35) **7f** £3,318.75 (£990.00: £472.50: £213.75) Stalls: Low GOING minus 0.30 sec per fur (GF)

				SP	RR	SF
3744^{4}	**Jibe (USA)** (HRACecil) **2-8-11** KFallon(9) (a.p: led over 2f out: clr over 1f out: easily)	—	**1**	4/9^{1}	92++	33
3117^{4}	**Winsa (USA)** (JLDunlop) **2-8-11** RHills(16) (lw: a.p: rdn over 2f out: unable qckn)	4	**2**	4/1^{2}	83	24
3744^{5}	**Frond** (LMCumani) **2-8-8**(3) RFfrench(7) (lw: a.p: rdn 2f out: one pce)	nk	**3**	20/1	82	23
3574^{5}	**Sweet Sorrow (IRE)** (CFWall) **2-8-11** MTebbutt(17) (rdn over 2f out: hdwy over 1f out: nvr nrr)	2	**4**	7/1^{3}	78	19
	Penrose (IRE) (BWHills) **2-8-11** RStreet(13) (unf: bit bkwd: s.s: swtchd lft 3f out: hdwy over 1f out: one pce: bttr for r)	hd	**5**	25/1	77+	18
3547^{6}	**Pride of My Heart** (IABalding) **2-8-11** AMcGlone(10) (a.p: ev ch over 2f out: wknd over 1f out)	½	**6**	14/1	76	17
	Pixielated (IRE) (DRLoder) **2-8-11** RCochrane(4) (unf: nvr nr to chal)	1½	**7**	20/1	73	14
	Aquarela (MRStoute) **2-8-11** DHolland(6) (w'like: scope: bit bkwd: s.s: hdwy fnl f: nvr nrr: bttr for r)	1¾	**8**	20/1	69+	10
	Ameena (USA) (PFICole) **2-8-11** CRutter(11) (neat: bit bkwd: prom over 4f)	1	**9**	20/1	67	8
	Hevergolf Princess (IRE) (TJNaughton) **2-8-11** AClark(1) (leggy: lw: s.s: nvr nrr: bttr for r)	1	**10**	50/1	64	5
3547^{13}	**Fair Sonia** (KMcAuliffe) **2-8-11** JFEgan(5) (bhd fnl 2f)	s.h	**11**	66/1	64	5
3201^{14}	**Five Fairies** (NACallaghan) **2-8-11** SDrowne(3) (a bhd)	nk	**12**	66/1	63	4
3711^{12}	**Ombra di Nube (FR)** (CJames) **2-8-11** NAdams(15) (led over 4f)	1¾	**13**	100/1	59	—
3493^{7}	**Resurrection (IRE)** (RHannon) **2-8-11** DaneO'Neill(14) (mid div over 5f)	hd	**14**	33/1	59	—
3711^{9}	**Clouds of Glory** (RCharlton) **2-8-11** TSprake(8) (s.s: plld hrd: bhd fnl 2f)	¾	**15**	20/1	58	—
				(SP 144.9%)	**15 Rn**	

1m 24.18 (2.98) CSF £2.60 TOTE £1.50: £1.10 £1.10 £4.30 (£2.20) Trio £8.70 OWNER Mr K. Abdulla (NEWMARKET) BRED Juddmonte Farms

3744 Jibe (USA) won as she liked, and the winning margin could have been doubled if she had been ridden right out. (4/9)
3117 Winsa (USA) had no chance with the winner, but this good-looking sort can pick up a similar race and go on from here. (4/1: 3/1-9/2)
3744 Frond was beaten a similar distance by the winner when they finished down the field last time, but Jibe appears to have made more progress since. (20/1)
3574 Sweet Sorrow (IRE), done for speed in mid-race, ran as if a longer trip would suit. (7/1: 10/1-6/1)
Penrose (IRE), racing from a reasonably high draw, was switched very wide into the centre of the track at halfway but still ran with great promise. Significant improvement is likely. (25/1)
3547 Pride of My Heart has run with credit in her three outings to date and could go well in nurseries. (14/1)
Aquarela shaped well without being knocked about, and this backward sort can do much better in the long run. (20/1)
Hevergolf Princess (IRE), a likeable type, put in some good late work and looks sure to improve. (50/1)

4067 E.B.F. NUTFIELD MAIDEN STKS (II) (2-Y.O F) (Class D)
3-00 (3-06) **7f** £3,318.75 (£990.00: £472.50: £213.75) Stalls: Low GOING minus 0.30 sec per fur (GF)

				SP	RR	SF
	Vocation (IRE) (PRWebber) **2-8-11** DaneO'Neill(5) (lengthy: unf: rdn over 2f out: hdwy over 1f out: led nr fin)	—	**1**	33/1	81	35
3961a^{9}	**Honey Storm (IRE)** (MRChannon) **2-8-11** JCarroll(16) (hdwy over 2f out: hrd rdn over 1f out: ev ch wl ins fnl f: r.o)	nk	**2**	10/1	80	34
	Pride of Place (IRE) (DRLoder) **2-8-11** RCochrane(9) (lt-f: lw: a.p: rdn over 2f out: ev ch wl ins fnl f: r.o)	s.h	**3**	4/1^{3}	80	34
3019^{2}	**Soft Touch (IRE) (85)** (MissGayKelleway) **2-8-11** KFallon(8) (a.p: led 2f out: hrd rdn over 1f out: hdd nr fin)	s.h	**4**	100/30^{2}	80	34
	Muhaba (USA) (SbinSuroor) **2-8-11** RHills(10) (w'like: scope: lw: led 5f: hrd rdn over 1f out: ev ch ins fnl f: unable qckn)	½	**5**	2/1^{1}	79	33
	Balaitini (IRE) (ACStewart) **2-8-11** TSprake(1) (wl grwn: hld up: shkn up over 1f out: one pce: bttr for r)	1½	**6**	16/1	76+	30

				SP	RR	SF
	Queen of Tides (IRE) (MRStoute) **2-8-11** KBradshaw(3) (unf: scope: bit bkwd: shkn up & stdy hdwy over 1f out: nvr plcd to chal)	1½	**7**	16/1	72	26
3187[9]	**Flush (FR)** (JWHills) **2-8-11** AClark(13) (prom over 4f)	½	**8**	25/1	71	25
	Hippocracy (BWHills) **2-8-8**(3) JDSmith(17) (unf: scope: nvr nrr)	2½	**9**	33/1	65	19
	Hever Golf Passion (IRE) (TJNaughton) **2-8-11** AMcGlone(4) (leggy: unf: lw: s.s: nvr nrr)	s.h	**10**	50/1	65	19
3490[6]	**Magical Colours (IRE)** (JLDunlop) **2-8-11** GCarter(7) (hld up: rdn over 2f out: sn wknd)	1½	**11**	25/1	62	16
	Tazkiya (CJBenstead) **2-8-11** GDuffield(14) (leggy: scope: s.s: a bhd)	2½	**12**	25/1	56	10
	Andalish (BWHills) **2-8-11** DHolland(2) (w'like: scope: bit bkwd: racd alone far side: a.p: rdn over 2f out: eased whn btn over 1f out)	4	**13**	10/1	47	1
	Northern Lass (IRE) (MHTompkins) **2-8-11** DBiggs(11) (unf: bit bkwd: a bhd)	2½	**14**	40/1	41	—
2831[10]	**Kenkan (IRE)** (PFICole) **2-8-11** CRutter(15) (prom over 4f)	4	**15**	16/1	32	—
3636[15]	**Zeptepi (IRE)** (TEPowell) **2-8-8**(3) PMcCabe(6) (prom 4f: virtually p.u fnl 2f: t.o)	dist	**16**	100/1	—	—

(SP 135.0%) **16 Rn**

1m 24.01 (2.81) CSF £318.15 TOTE £44.40: £7.90 £3.10 £2.40 (£1,125.00) Trio £347.00; £400.81 to Doncaster 10/9/97 OWNER Elite Racing Club (BANBURY) BRED Jerry O'Brien

Vocation (IRE) won in the style of a horse who will stay further. Still weak at present, she has plenty of room for physical development over the winter. (33/1)
3961a Honey Storm (IRE) has shown enough in her races to date to suggest she can find a winning opportunity. (10/1)
Pride of Place (IRE) is a wiry filly whose best chances may come early in her career, so her connections will be looking hard for an opening in the closing months of the season. (4/1: 7/1-7/2)
3019 Soft Touch (IRE) deserves to win a race and was only run out of it in the last fifty yards. (100/30)
Muhaba (USA) will have disappointed her supporters, but this attractive daughter of Salsabil should find an opening if kept at a realistic level. (2/1: 4/6-11/4)
Balaitini (IRE), a deep-girthed sort, looks sure to step up on this promising debut. (16/1)
Queen of Tides (IRE) was not knocked about and can be expected to improve considerably on this first effort. (16/1)
Tazkiya has plenty to commend her on looks, but she was green and unruly in the paddock and needs to mature mentally. (25/1)
Andalish raced alone on the far side but showed plenty of speed and can be given another chance. (10/1: op 3/1)

4068 C & H (HAULIERS) LTD NURSERY H'CAP (0-75) (2-Y.O) (Class E)

3-30 (3-38) **7f 140y** £3,538.25 (£1,061.00: £510.50: £235.25) Stalls: Low GOING minus 0.30 sec per fur (GF)

				SP	RR	SF
3783[9]	**Holy Wine (USA) (67)** (DRLoder) **2-8-13** RCochrane(16) (lw: hdwy 2f out: led over 1f out: rdn: r.o wl)	—	**1**	4/1[1]	77	35
3924[2]	**Simlet (66)** (WJarvis) **2-8-12** GHind(4) (rdn over 3f out: hdwy over 2f out: ev ch ins fnl f: unable qckn)	3	**2**	6/1[3]	70	28
3819[7]	**Short Romance (IRE) (61)** (JWHills) **2-8-7** RHills(15) (s.s: rdn over 2f out: hdwy over 1f out: r.o one pce)	1	**3**	20/1	63	21
3799[3]	**Cosmic Countess (IRE) (75)** (MAJarvis) **2-9-4**(3) RFfrench(10) (led tl over 1f out: sn wknd)	2	**4**	11/2[2]	72	30
3808*	**Forty Love (IRE) (61)** (JEBanks) **2-8-2**(5) CLowther(14) (a.p: rdn over 2f out: wknd over 1f out)	½	**5**	6/1[3]	57	15
3924[8]	**Lobuche (IRE) (64)** (RHannon) **2-8-10** DaneO'Neill(5) (rdn over 2f out: hdwy over 1f out: nvr nrr)	2	**6**	20/1	56	14
3701[4]	**Saint Albert (59)** (PTWalwyn) **2-8-5** JCarroll(12) (lw: a.p: rdn over 2f out: wknd over 1f out)	¾	**7**	25/1	50	8
2719[8]	**Mari-Ela (IRE) (60)** (JRArnold) **2-8-6** AClark(17) (prom 5f)	1¼	**8**	33/1	48	6
3818[5]	**Miss Skye (IRE) (64)** (TJNaughton) **2-8-10** DHolland(13) (prom 6f)	2½	**9**	16/1	47	5
3967*	**Won't Forget Me (IRE) (64)** (MHTompkins) **2-8-10** 5x DBiggs(6) (nvr nrr)	½	**10**	13/2	46	4
3818[11]	**Latin Bay (58)** (PWHarris) **2-8-4** JQuinn(1) (nvr nrr)	hd	**11**	40/1	40	—
3911[2]	**Persian Venture (67)** (BJMeehan) **2-8-13** MTebbutt(2) (lw: nvr nrr)	1½	**12**	12/1	45	3
3823[15]	**Apple Sauce (60)** (JRArnold) **2-8-6** TSprake(11) (bhd fnl 2f)	½	**13**	33/1	37	—
3924[5]	**Red Maple (USA) (65)** (PFICole) **2-8-11** GCarter(7) (a bhd)	1½	**14**	20/1	39	—
3278[16]	**Shecando (IRE) (64)** (CJames) **2-8-10** CRutter(3) (bhd fnl 2f)	½	**15**	33/1	37	—
3493*	**Wildcat (IRE) (70)** (MissGayKelleway) **2-9-2** KFallon(9) (lw: prom 5f)	3½	**16**	9/1	36	—
3782*	**Rosewood Lady (IRE) (56)** (KRBurke) **2-8-2v** GDuffield(8) (bhd fnl 2f)	2½	**17**	12/1	17	—

(SP 138.0%) **17 Rn**

1m 32.25 (3.25) CSF £25.19 CT £441.61 TOTE £5.60: £2.20 £2.00 £4.00 £1.50 (£33.40) Trio £425.90 OWNER Mr Christopher Ranson (NEWMARKET) BRED Christopher Ranson

Holy Wine (USA) had run over six furlongs on his previous three races but this trip, on his first venture into nursery company, seemed to suit him well. (4/1)
3924 Simlet, not ideally drawn, has run well in his two nurseries to date. (6/1)
3819 Short Romance (IRE) should not be far away in future nurseries off this sort of mark. (20/1)
3799 Cosmic Countess (IRE) has shown plenty of speed in her races and this trip seemed to be stretching her a bit. (11/2)
3808* Forty Love (IRE) was undone by a combination of the step-up in distance and better-quality opposition. (6/1)
1370 Lobuche (IRE) stayed on after being outpaced, but he was never arriving fast enough. (20/1)
3818 Miss Skye (IRE) ran satisfactorily until getting a bit pushed for room and faltering about a furlong and a half from home, after which she was not given a hard time. (16/1)
3911 Persian Venture (12/1: op 8/1)

4069 EDENBRIDGE (S) H'CAP (0-60) (3-Y.O+) (Class G)

4-00 (4-06) **1m 2f (Equitrack)** £2,415.70 (£670.20: £321.10) Stalls: High GOING minus 0.50 sec per fur (FST)

				SP	RR	SF
3767[2]	**Harlequin Walk (IRE) (43)** (RJO'Sullivan) **6-8-11** JQuinn(12) (hld up: hrd rdn over 3f out: led ins fnl f: all out)	—	**1**	11/4[1]	54	21
3321[12]	**Magazine Gap (42)** (PatMitchell) **4-8-5**(5) AmandaSanders(11) (swtg: hld up: rdn over 2f out: ev ch fnl f: r.o wl)	s.h	**2**	20/1	53	20
3971[7]	**Don't Drop Bombs (USA) (40)** (DTThom) **8-8-8v** GDuffield(8) (hld up: chsd ldr over 4f out: led over 2f out tl ins fnl f: unable qckn)	1½	**3**	8/1	49	16
3929[5]	**Haroldon (IRE) (55)** (BPalling) **8-9-9** TSprake(10) (rdn over 5f out: gd hdwy over 1f out: r.o wl ins fnl f)	½	**4**	7/1[2]	63	30
3793[5]	**Father Dan (IRE) (60)** (MissGayKelleway) **8-10-0** KFallon(14) (b: b.hind: rdn over 5f out: nvr nr to chal)	9	**5**	11/4[1]	53	20
3321[13]	**Slievenamon (53)** (JEBanks) **4-9-7v**[1] RCochrane(4) (led over 7f)	3½	**6**	16/1	41	8
3467[8]	**English Invader (58)** (CADwyer) **6-9-12b** DHolland(6) (lw: s.i.s: rdn over 5f out: nvr nrr)	1¼	**7**	14/1	44	11
3762[11]	**Baaheth (USA) (56)** (SCWilliams) **3-9-3v**[1] GCarter(2) (nvr nrr)	2½	**8**	20/1	38	—
3316[7]	**Cabcharge Blue (48)** (TJNaughton) **5-9-2** DaneO'Neill(9) (lw: a mid div)	½	**9**	25/1	29	—
3573[16]	**Mr Rough (50)** (DMorris) **6-9-4** NDay(13) (lw: a bhd)	6	**10**	15/2[3]	21	—
3685[5]	**Summerville Wood (59)** (PMooney) **3-9-6b** DRMcCabe(3) (bhd fnl 5f)	s.h	**11**	16/1	30	—
3691[9]	**Perilous Plight (46)** (AStreeter) **6-8-11v**[1](3) RHavlin(1) (hld up: rdn over 4f out: sn wknd)	5	**12**	12/1	9	—

3762[14]	**Airborne Harris (IRE) (40)** (ABailey) **4-8-8b[1]** DWright(7) (prom over 4f)	1½	**13**	25/1	1	—
3611[3]	**Kayzee (IRE) (41)** (DBurchell) **3-7-11**(5) KSked(5) (prom over 5f: t.o)	29	**14**	14/1	—	—
				(SP 138.7%)		**14 Rn**

2m 8.64 (4.34) CSF £72.74 CT £396.06 TOTE £4.30: £2.00 £10.10 £2.70 (£110.80) Trio £344.60 OWNER Mrs R. J. Doorgachurn (WHITCOMBE) BRED Ronnie Boland in Ireland
WEIGHT FOR AGE 3yo-7lb
Bt in 3,800gns
3767 Harlequin Walk (IRE), on the same mark as when last successful, began to get going running downhill and launched her challenge turning into the straight. Gaining a slender advantage inside the final furlong, she had a tremendous battle with the runner-up and managed to prevail by the skin of her teeth. Four of her five wins have now come on sand. (11/4)
306 Magazine Gap ran by far his best race to date. Throwing down his challenge in the straight, he had a tremendous battle with the winner in the final furlong, but strength from the saddle proved to be the deciding factor and he just failed to get his head in front. (20/1)
3421 Don't Drop Bombs (USA), who is usually amateur-ridden, gained control over a quarter of a mile from home but was unable to hold on inside the final furlong. (8/1)
3929 Haroldon (IRE), pushed along and going nowhere before halfway, was a long way off the front four half a mile from home. Making giant strides in the straight, he finished with a real flourish. (7/1: 5/1-8/1)
3793 Father Dan (IRE) was taking a drop in class but never threatened to get anywhere near the principals. (11/4)
3611 Kayzee (IRE) (14/1: 10/1-16/1)

4070 JARDINES MAIDEN STKS (3-Y.O+) (Class D)
4-30 (4-34) **7f** £4,027.80 (£1,205.40: £578.20: £264.60) Stalls: Low GOING minus 0.30 sec per fur (GF)

				SP	RR	SF
1221[2]	**Darnaway (91)** (HRACecil) **3-9-0** KFallon(12) (lw: a.p: led over 2f out: clr over 1f out: eased ins fnl f)	—	**1**	4/6[1]	90+	49
3775[7]	**Floating Charge** (JRFanshawe) **3-9-0** NDay(14) (b.hind: hld up: rdn over 3f out: chsd wnr fnl f: no imp)	6	**2**	9/1[3]	76	35
1030[10]	**Blushing Desert** (RHannon) **3-8-9** DaneO'Neill(7) (hdwy over 1f out: one pce)	2½	**3**	25/1	66	25
	Injazaat (USA) (75) (MajorWRHern) **3-8-9b** RCochrane(9) (dwlt: hdwy over 2f out: one pce)	1	**4**	14/1	63	22
3715[4]	**Dust** (LordHuntingdon) **3-8-9** RPerham(6) (lw: led over 4f: wknd over 1f out)	3	**5**	16/1	56	15
	Tashkent (RSimpson) **5-9-4** MGallagher(8) (rdn over 3f out: nvr nr to chal)	nk	**6**	50/1	61	24
	Janara (LMCumani) **3-8-6**(3) RFfrench(11) (w'like: prom over 4f)	¾	**7**	14/1	54	13
1409[11]	**Enthrone (USA)** (JHMGosden) **3-8-9** GHind(3) (racd far side: hld up: rdn over 2f out: sn wknd)	1½	**8**	20/1	51	10
	Ikram Boy (USA) (ABailey) **3-9-0** DWright(1) (unf: racd far side: s.s: nvr nrr)	1¼	**9**	40/1	53	12
3775[4]	**Sharkiyah (IRE) (75)** (RWArmstrong) **3-8-9** RHills(4) (racd far side: prom over 4f)	s.h	**10**	14/1	48	7
2773[6]	**Il Falco (FR)** (SirMarkPrescott) **3-9-0** GDuffield(13) (lw: s.s: a bhd)	½	**11**	20/1	52	11
3917[6]	**Bestemor** (HCandy) **3-8-9** CRutter(15) (prom over 4f)	1¾	**12**	20/1	43	2
3550[3]	**Feel No Fear** (WRMuir) **4-8-13** TSprake(2) (racd far side: hld up: rdn over 2f out: sn wknd)	hd	**13**	20/1	42	5
	Croft Sands (RAkehurst) **4-9-4** AClark(5) (racd far side: s.s: a bhd)	12	**14**	25/1	20	—
2580[3]	**Fonteyn (83)** (ACStewart) **3-8-9** DHolland(10) (prom over 4f)	11	**15**	5/1[2]	—	—
				(SP 143.7%)		**15 Rn**

1m 23.05 (1.85) CSF £7.88 TOTE £1.80: £1.20 £2.60 £10.30 (£11.10) Trio £284.30 OWNER Sir David Wills (NEWMARKET) BRED Sir David Wills
WEIGHT FOR AGE 3yo-4lb
1221 Darnaway looked magnificent on this return after a four-month break and had little problem hacking up, leading over a quarter of a mile from home and forging clear to win with a ton in hand (4/6)
Floating Charge, scrubbed along at halfway, struggled into second place a furlong from home but had absolutely no hope with the winner. (9/1: op 14/1)
Blushing Desert, off the course for four months, picked up ground below the distance but could make no further impression in the final furlong. (25/1)
Injazaat (USA), making a belated seasonal debut, was not given a hard time and failed to quicken in the last two furlongs. (14/1: 10/1-16/1)
3715 Dust, in front until past halfway, had shot her bolt over a furlong out. (16/1)
Janara (14/1: 6/1-16/1)
3775 Sharkiyah (IRE) (14/1: 8/1-16/1)

4071 H.B.L.B. BLINDLEY HEATH H'CAP (0-80) (3-Y.O+) (Class D)
5-00 (5-05) **7f** £4,378.15 (£1,313.20: £632.10: £291.55) Stalls: Low GOING minus 0.30 sec per fur (GF)

				SP	RR	SF
3712[4]	**Safey Ana (USA) (66)** (BHanbury) **6-9-0** KFallon(8) (b: swtg: rdn 4f out: hdwy 2f out: led over 1f out: r.o wl)	—	**1**	6/1[2]	77	53
3580[7]	**Delta Soleil (USA) (77)** (PWHarris) **5-9-6**(5) CLowther(11) (rdn over 3f out: hdwy over 1f out: unable qckn)	2	**2**	7/1	83	59
3930*	**Victory Team (IRE) (78)** (GBBalding) **5-9-12** 6x SDrowne(9) (hdwy over 2f out: hrd rdn over 1f out: one pce)	1½	**3**	10/1	81	57
3423[11]	**Pleading (78)** (HCandy) **4-9-12** CRutter(2) (s.s: rdn over 3f out: hdwy over 1f out: one pce)	s.h	**4**	20/1	81	57
3798[8]	**Civil Liberty (63)** (GLewis) **4-8-8**(3) AWhelan(4) (rdn over 3f out: hdwy over 1f out: r.o)	1	**5**	25/1	64	40
2835[12]	**Zelda Zonk (76)** (BJMeehan) **5-9-10** DaneO'Neill(10) (rdn over 3f out: hdwy over 1f out: nvr nrr)	1	**6**	25/1	74	50
3930[4]	**Kentucky Fall (FR) (72)** (LadyHerries) **4-9-6** AClark(1) (lw: a.p: led wl over 1f out: edgd rt: sn hdd: wknd ins fnl f)	1¼	**7**	12/1	68	44
3710[2]	**Impulsif (USA) (74)** (DJSffrenchDavis) **3-9-4** MTebbutt(5) (s.s: swtchd lft over 2f out: nvr nrr)	s.h	**8**	16/1	69	41
2845[4]	**Prime Light (69)** (GWragg) **4-9-3b** RCochrane(7) (nvr nrr)	½	**9**	12/1	63	39
3551[5]	**Ijtinab (70)** (RAkehurst) **3-9-0** NDay(3) (prom 5f)	2	**10**	20/1	60	32
3715*	**Northern Angel (IRE) (75)** (MrsJCecil) **3-9-5** GHind(15) (b.hind: prom 5f)	1	**11**	8/1	62	34
3800*	**Polish Romance (USA) (73)** (MRStoute) **3-9-3** DHolland(14) (lw: led over 5f)	½	**12**	7/2[1]	59	31
2945[8]	**Halowing (USA) (72)** (JGSmyth-Osbourne) **3-9-2** TSprake(16) (nvr nrr)	1	**13**	20/1	56	28
3860[10]	**Sharp Imp (65)** (RMFlower) **7-8-13b** JQuinn(12) (bhd fnl 2f)	nk	**14**	16/1	48	24
3749*	**La Dolce Vita (69)** (NMLampard) **3-8-10**(3) RHavlin(17) (hld up: rdn 3f out: wknd over 2f out)	2	**15**	16/1	48	20
3649[14]	**Present Generation (80)** (RGuest) **4-9-11**(3) RFfrench(18) (lw: prom over 5f)	1½	**16**	13/2[3]	55	31
3075[7]	**Forcing Bid (76)** (SirMarkPrescott) **3-9-6** GDuffield(13) (bhd fnl 2f)	½	**17**	14/1	50	22
3765[11]	**Just Loui (67)** (KRBurke) **3-8-8v**(3) DSweeney(6) (prom over 4f)	½	**18**	33/1	40	12
				(SP 147.2%)		**18 Rn**

1m 22.71 (1.51) CSF £47.68 CT £412.97 TOTE £8.10: £2.30 £2.00 £5.40 £8.40 (£30.60) Trio £124.60 OWNER The Optimists Racing Partnership (NEWMARKET) BRED Robert N. Clay
WEIGHT FOR AGE 3yo-4lb

3254 Safey Ana (USA) is well suited by fast ground but Fallon was already having to push him along before halfway. At last picking up ground a quarter of a mile out, he struck the front approaching the final furlong and ran on strongly to the line. (6/1)
3130 Delta Soleil (USA) began to pick up ground below the distance but failed to find another gear inside the final furlong. He has just one win to his name. (7/1)
3930* Victory Team (IRE) had conditions in his favour, but he was 6lb higher for his Folkestone victory last week and failed to quicken in the last furlong and a half. (10/1)
1397 Pleading picked up ground below the distance but could make no further impression in the final furlong. He goes well with some cut. (20/1)
Civil Liberty has been very disappointing this year and, although running on in the last furlong and a half, never threatened to get there. (25/1)
1935 Zelda Zonk stayed on from the back of the field without posing a threat. (25/1)
3715* Northern Angel (IRE) (8/1: 6/1-9/1)
3800* Polish Romance (USA) (7/2: op 6/1)

4072 JARDINE INSURANCE SERVICES MAIDEN STKS (3-Y.O+) (Class D)
5-30 (5-33) **1m 3f 106y** £3,773.00 (£1,127.00: £539.00: £245.00) Stalls: Low GOING minus 0.30 sec per fur (GF)

				SP	RR	SF
2924²	**Awesome Wells (IRE) (82)** (HRACecil) **3-8-13** KFallon(3) (lw: hld up: chsd ldr over 2f out: led over 1f out: rdn out)	—	1	Evens 1	84	59
3909²	**Teme Valley** (RCharlton) **3-8-13** TSprake(7) (hld up: chsd ldr 6f out: led over 2f out tl over 1f out: unable qckn)	3½	2	5/1 3	79	54
3632²	**Snow Partridge (USA) (82)** (PFICole) **3-8-13** CRutter(4) (lw: led 9f)	14	3	2/1 2	60	35
2008W	**Dunabrattin** (DTThom) **4-9-7** DRMcCabe(10) (lw: nvr nr to chal)	14	4	66/1	40	23
3320⁶	**Monacle** (DMorris) **3-8-13** NDay(6) (nvr nrr)	1¾	5	50/1	38	13
2940⁴	**Zinzari (FR) (76)** (DRLoder) **3-8-13v¹** RCochrane(9) (lw: chsd ldr 10f out to 6f out: sn wknd)	2½	6	10/1	34	9
3720⁶	**Joust** (CEBrittain) **3-8-13** MRimmer(1) (bhd fnl 7f)	½	7	20/1	34	9
	Bursul Lady (26) (MissBSanders) **4-8-13**(3) AWhelan(5) (prom over 4f)	15	8	100/1	8	—
	Dutch (GPEnright) **5-9-7** NAdams(8) (bkwd: a bhd: t.o fnl 6f)	10	9	66/1	—	—
3790⁴	**Merci Monsieur** (JABOld) **4-9-4**(3) RFfrench(11) (a bhd: t.o)	s.h	10	40/1	—	—

(SP 122.2%) **10 Rn**

2m 26.82 (2.12) CSF £6.33 TOTE £2.30: £1.10 £2.10 £1.10 (£6.10) Trio £1.80 OWNER Cliveden Stud (NEWMARKET) BRED Cliveden Stud
WEIGHT FOR AGE 3yo-8lb
2924 Awesome Wells (IRE) at last came good and, striking the front approaching the final furlong, was vigorously ridden along to assert his authority and complete a magnificent five-timer for Fallon. (Evens)
3909 Teme Valley showed in front over a quarter of a mile from home but he was immediately challenged by the winner and, collared by that rival below the distance, failed to find another gear. (5/1: 3/1-11/2)
3632 Snow Partridge (USA) cut out the donkey work but, collared over two furlongs from home, was then left for dead. (2/1)

T/Plpt: £185.10 (118.62 Tckts). T/Qdpt: £35.60 (35.63 Tckts) AK/LMc

4073a - 4089a : (Irish Racing) - See Computer Raceform

3958a-CURRAGH (Newbridge, Ireland) (R-H) (Yielding to soft)
Sunday September 7th

4090a GO AND GO ROUND TOWER STKS (Listed) (2-Y.O)
2-45 (2-45) **6f** IR £12,900.00 (IR £3,700.00: IR £1,700.00: IR £500.00) GOING: 0.23 sec per fur (G)

				SP	RR	SF
3961a²	**Law Library (IRE)** (JSBolger,Ireland) **2-8-10** KJManning (cl up: 3rd ½-wy: 2nd & chal over 2f out: led over 1f out: rdn & kpt on wl)	—	1	6/4 1	97+	48
3839a⁴	**Kitza (IRE)** (APO'Brien,Ireland) **2-8-8**ow1 CRoche (rn 2nd to ½-wy: 3rd & rdn whn n.m.r under 3f out: swtchd: 2nd & kpt on ins last: nt trble wnr)	2	2	6/4 1	90	40
1531a⁴	**Marigot Bay (IRE)** (APO'Brien,Ireland) **2-8-7** JAHeffernan (led tl over 1f out: no ex: wknd ins last)	3	3	7/1 3	81	32
3839a⁷	**Fairy Flight (IRE)** (CO'Brien,Ireland) **2-8-11** JPMurtagh (hld up: mod 4th ½-wy: no imp over 1½f out: kpt on)	½	4	6/1 2	83	34
	Somethingbeautiful (USA) (DGillespie,Ireland) **2-8-7** PShanahan (n.d)	3½	5	33/1	70	21

(SP 109.7%) **5 Rn**

1m 15.2 (4.70) OWNER Mrs J. M. Ryan (COOLCULLEN)
3961a Law Library (IRE) has plenty of experience and his run in the valuable Tattersalls Breeders Stakes here saw him more than good enough to win this. He went to the front well over a furlong out and stretched right away. (6/4: op Evens)
3839a Kitza (IRE) did not have much room between horses two furlongs out, and had to switch out. She was still no match for the winner. (6/4)
1531a Marigot Bay (IRE) made the running but does not really get the sixth furlong. (7/1)
Fairy Flight (IRE) looked pretty one-paced over the last two furlongs. (6/1: op 4/1)

4091a - 4092a : (Irish Racing) - See Computer Raceform

4093a MOYGLARE STUD STKS (Gp 1) (2-Y.O F)
4-15 (4-20) **7f** IR £84,300.00 (IR £28,800.00: IR £13,800.00: IR £4,800.00) GOING: 0.23 sec per fur (G)

				SP	RR	SF
3534a⁵	**Tarascon (IRE)** (TStack,Ireland) **2-8-12**ow1 PJSmullen (cl up: cl 4th ½-wy: rdn to ld early ins last: r.o.)	—	1	7/1	106	50
	Heed My Warning (IRE) (CCollins,Ireland) **2-8-11** WJSupple (prom: led over 2f out: hdd early fnl f: r.o u.p: no ex)	hd	2	10/1	105	50
	Shahtoush (IRE) (APO'Brien,Ireland) **2-8-11** JAHeffernan (towards rr: hdwy 2f out: r.o u.p ins last)	½	3	16/1	104	49
3882a³	**Heeremandi (IRE)** (APO'Brien,Ireland) **2-8-11** CRoche (trckd ldrs: 5th & chal 2f out: ev ch: no ex early fnl f: r.o.)	½	4	3/1 1	103	48
	Mempari (IRE) (APO'Brien,Ireland) **2-8-11** EAhern (hld up: trckd ldrs: chal 1½f out: kpt on u.p fnl f)	s.h	5	16/1	102	47
3534a⁷	**Flame Violet (IRE)** (APO'Brien,Ireland) **2-8-11** SCraine (hld up towards rr: hdwy over 2f out: 7th & nt rch ldrs early fnl f: kpt on)	1	6	14/1	100	45
3192*	**Lady Alexander (IRE)** (CCollins,Ireland) **2-8-11** PShanahan (hld up in tch: effrt over 2f out: rdn & no ex ins last)	½	7	9/2 3	99	44

Remarkable Style (USA) (JSBolger,Ireland) **2-8-11** KJManning (trckd ldrs: 7th & chsd ldrs over 2f out: no ex u.p 1f out) 2½ **8** 12/1 93 38
Karakorum (IRE) (APO'Brien,Ireland) **2-8-11** NGMcCullagh (towards rr early: rdn & chsd ldrs over 2f out: no ex over 1f out) ....s.h **9** 33/1 93 38
Winona (IRE) (JOxx,Ireland) **2-8-11** JPMurtagh (hld up: effrt 2f out: no imp over 1f out) ....s.h **10** 4/1 2 93 38
Cultural Role (DKWeld,Ireland) **2-8-11** MJKinane (prom: 3rd ½-wy: rdn over 2f out: sn wknd: eased) 15 **11** 5/1 59 4
Early Memory (USA) (DKWeld,Ireland) **2-8-11** DPMcDonogh (sn led: hdd over 2f out: sn wknd: dropped bhd: eased) ....4½ **12** 33/1 48 —
(SP 133.4%) **12 Rn**

1m 28.5 (5.50) OWNER Mrs Jane Rowlinson (CASHEL)
3534a Tarascon (IRE), very stoutly bred on her dams side, saw this trip out really well. She had a good battle with the runner-up throughout the last furlong and was always just holding the edge. She went up 5lb from her Phoenix Stakes earned mark to 108. (7/1)
Heed My Warning (IRE), having only here third run, looks a smart staying filly in the making. She was sent to the front two furlongs out, and kept answering everything when challenged throughout the final furlong. (10/1)
Shahtoush (IRE), a maiden having only her second run, put in an eye-catching late run from well off the pace. (16/1)
3882a Heeremandi (IRE), always chasing the leaders, was not going anywhere when inconvenienced by her challenging stable companions on either side of her inside the last. At this stage of her career, this trip might be a bit too far. (3/1)
Mempari (IRE), a beaten favourite on her three previous outings and still a maiden, finished strongly after being switched two furlongs out. She has shot up 20lb for this to 105. (16/1)
3534a Flame Violet (IRE) kept on from behind to be nearest at the finish, and is another to find herself climbing the ratings, going up 10lb to 103. (14/1)
3192* Lady Alexander (IRE) had her chance two furlongs out but weakened inside the last and just did not get the trip. (9/2: op 3/1)
Winona (IRE) dropped away tamely from two furlongs out. (4/1)
Cultural Role stopped dead two and a half furlongs out and was reported to have gurgled. (5/1)

4094a TRUSTED PARTNER MATRON STKS (Gp 3) (3-Y.O+ F & M)
4-45 (4-50) **1m** **(New)** IR £19,500.00 (IR £5,700.00: IR £2,700.00: IR £900.00) GOING: 0.23 sec per fur (G)

SP RR SF

Clerio (H-APantall,France) **3-8-9** MJKinane (hld up: 6th ½-wy: hdwy 3f out: chal to ld over 1f out: rdn & r.o.)— **1** 6/1 3 106 39
3674a3 **Supercal** (DRCElsworth) **3-8-9** SDrowne (hld up towards rr: rdn & hdwy over 2f out: 4th 1f out: r.o u.p: nt rch wnr) 1 **2** 6/1 3 104 37
3674a2 **Dangerous Diva (IRE)** (APO'Brien,Ireland) **3-8-10**ow1 CRoche (hld up in tch: 5th & trckd ldrs 2f out: swtchd lft to chal: 3rd, rdn & no ex early ins last: kpt on) 1½ **3** 9/4 1 102 34
3675a5 **Via Verbano (IRE)** (JSBolger,Ireland) **3-8-9** SCraine (hld up: 7th ½-wy: chsd ldrs early st: 6th & nt rch ldrs 1f out: kpt on ins last) 1 **4** 10/1 99 32
1062a2 **Azra (IRE)** (JSBolger,Ireland) **3-8-9** KJManning (cl up: 4th ½-wy: chal & ev ch 2f out: 2nd & no ex u.p over 1f out: kpt on) ....s.h **5** 8/1 99 32
3362a* **Tout A Coup (IRE)** (GACusack,Ireland) **4-9-0** NGMcCullagh (led early: rn 2nd: rdn & no ex 1½f out: kpt on same pce) ....hd **6** 13/2 99 37
Oriane (JOxx,Ireland) **4-9-0** PJSmullen (towards rr: kpt on last 2f: nvr nrr) 3½ **7** 10/1 92 30
3362a4 **Ridiyara (IRE)** (JOxx,Ireland) **3-8-9** DHogan (led after 1f: clr bef ½-wy: jnd over 1½f out: sn hdd & no ex: wknd) ....hd **8** 14/1 92 25
Velour (JOxx,Ireland) **3-8-9** WJSupple (cl up: 3rd ½-wy: rdn & chsd ldrs st: wknd over 2f out: n.d) 2½ **9** 16/1 87 20
3510a2 **Khatara (IRE)** (JOxx,Ireland) **3-8-9b1** JPMurtagh (hld up towards rr: hdwy on outside early st: rdn & no imp 1½f out) 1 **10** 3/1 2 85 18
(SP 139.5%) **10 Rn**

1m 42.1 (7.10) OWNER Cheik Mohammed Al Maktoum
Clerio, successful in listed company in France at Toulouse and Marseilles, found this step up to Group Three company no problem at all. She came wide up the centre of the track and had things well sewn up from a furlong and a half out. The Prix de l'Opera may be her next target. (6/1: op 7/2)
3674a Supercal came from a long way back and did a fair bit of damage to others on her journey through the field. Her rider was seriously cautioned for careless riding. (6/1: op 4/1)
3674a Dangerous Diva (IRE) ran on over the last furlong and a half without ever getting on challenging terms. (9/4)
3510a Via Verbano (IRE) was entitled to run well but could just find the one pace over the last two furlongs, although she was going on again at the end. (10/1)
1062a Azra (IRE) was staying on when hampered by the second one furlong out. (8/1: op 5/1)
3362a* Tout A Coup (IRE) challenged two furlongs out but was soon found wanting. (13/2)
3510a Khatara (IRE), wearing blinkers for the first time, never got in any sort of challenge. (3/1)

4095a (Irish Racing) - See Computer Raceform

3141-DONCASTER (L-H) (Good to firm)
Wednesday September 10th
WEATHER: fine & sunny WIND: almost nil

4096 QUEEN'S OWN YORKSHIRE DRAGOONS CONDITIONS STKS (2-Y.O) (Class C)
1-30 (1-31) **7f** £4,599.00 (£1,701.00: £815.50: £332.50: £131.25: £50.75) Stalls: High GOING minus 0.40 sec per fur (F)

SP RR SF

36444 **Teapot Row (IRE)** (JARToller) **2-9-1** MRoberts(3) (swvd lft s: plld hrd: led over 1f: nt clr run 2f out: r.o wl u.p to ld cl home) ....— **1** 7/2 2 102 59
37454 **Gulland** (GWragg) **2-8-11** MHills(4) (lw: hld up: hdwy over 2f out: led ins fnl f tl nr fin) ....nk **2** 9/1 97 54
3598* **Mahboob (IRE)** (DMorley) **2-9-1** RHills(2) (lw: trckd ldrs: led 2f out: edgd lft & hdd ins fnl f: nt qckn) ....nk **3** 7/4 1 101 58
3806* **Golden Dice (USA) (85)** (HRACecil) **2-9-1** KFallon(6) (trckd ldrs: ev ch 2f out: hung lft: kpt on same pce) 1¼ **4** 9/1 98 55
3204* **Mushraaf** (JLDunlop) **2-9-3** LDettori(5) (hld up: effrt over 2f out: hung lft & wknd over 1f out) 3 **5** 6/1 93 50
35983 **Voodoo Saint (USA)** (PWChapple-Hyam) **2-8-11** JReid(1) (lw: led over 5f out to 2f out: sn wknd) 1 **6** 9/2 3 85 42
(SP 111.1%) **6 Rn**

1m 25.04 (0.54) CSF £29.08 TOTE £3.30: £1.70 £3.90 (£13.50) OWNER Duke of Devonshire (WHITSBURY) BRED Cambremont Ltd Partnership

3644 Teapot Row (IRE) took plenty of settling. After having to search for an opening, he finished with a real flourish to get up near the line. This event was won by the subsequent Derby winner, Benny The Dip, a year ago, but this year's renewal did not look a vintage contest. (7/2)
3745 Gulland, who has plenty of size and scope, stepped up considerably on his first effort. Only edged out near the line, he should make a very useful stayer at three. (9/1)
3598* Mahboob (IRE), who is not very big, did not help his rider by refusing to settle. (7/4)
3806* Golden Dice (USA), who looked very fit, is an excitable type and, under pressure, all he wanted to do was hang left. (9/1: op 6/1)
3204* Mushraaf, who lacks substance, found this company much tougher. (6/1: 4/1-13/2)
3598 Voodoo Saint (USA) would not settle and soon pulled his way to the front. If he is to progress, he will have to mend his ways. (9/2: op 3/1)

4097 E.B.F. CARRIE RED NURSERY H'CAP (2-Y.O F) (Class C)

2-05 (2-07) **6f 110y** £17,730.00 (£6,570.00: £3,160.00: £1,300.00: £525.00: £215.00) Stalls: High GOING minus 0.40 sec per fur (F)

			SP	RR	SF
3823[11]	**Branston Berry (IRE) (74)** (JLEyre) **2-7-12** AMackay(17) (chsd ldrs: led over 2f out: hld on wl towards fin)...—	**1**	25/1	72	33
2600[4]	**Ascot Cyclone (USA) (94)** (BWHills) **2-9-4** MHills(14) (mid div: hdwy 2f out: ev ch ins fnl f: no ex nr fin)........hd	**2**	9/1[3]	92	53
3650[11]	**Zizi (IRE) (82)** (KRBurke) **2-8-3**(3) DSweeney(12) (lw: hdwy over 2f out: n.m.r over 1f out: ev ch ins fnl f: r.o).hd	**3**	16/1	80	41
3802[8]	**Occhi Verdi (IRE) (80)** (MJohnston) **2-8-4** DHolland(8) (swtg: bhd: hdwy & nt clr run over 2f out: nt clr run over 1f out: r.o wl) 1	**4**	20/1	75+	36
3471[11]	**Robin Lane (73)** (IABalding) **2-7-6**(5)ow1 APolli(1) (racd far side: hdwy: edgd lft & ev ch 1f out: kpt on same pce)........s.h	**5**	33/1	68	28
3471[2]	**Jilted (IRE) (83)** (RHannon) **2-8-7** MartinDwyer(10) (a chsng ldrs: kpt on one pce appr fnl f)........3½	**6**	10/1	69	30
2886[4]	**Rich Choice (73)** (JDBethell) **2-7-6**(5)ow1 RMullen(6) (swvd rt s: led tl over 2f out: edgd rt & grad wknd)........1	**7**	33/1	57	17
3770[4]	**Queen Salote (72)** (DRLoder) **2-7-7**(3) RFfrench(4) (lw: chsd ldrs: effrt over 2f out: one pce) ....½	**8**	7/2[1]	55	16
3783*	**Belle de Nuit (IRE) (72)** (BJMeehan) **2-7-10** JQuinn(9) (mid div: styd on u.p fnl 2f: nvr nr to chal) ....½	**9**	12/1	53	14
3049[5]	**Filfilah (90)** (PTWalwyn) **2-9-0** RHills(16) (lw: bmpd s: sn trckng ldrs: effrt over 2f out: wknd over 1f out) 2½	**10**	8/1[2]	65	26
3541[3]	**Lady From Limerick (IRE) (72)** (JBerry) **2-7-7**(3) PFessey(7) (swtg: reard s: sn drvn along: n.d) ....nk	**11**	20/1	47	8
3750[8]	**Shalyah (IRE) (72)** (MrsJRRamsden) **2-7-10** LCharnock(18) (hld up: effrt over 2f out: n.d) 1	**12**	10/1	44	5
3416*	**Phone Alex (IRE) (78)** (RHannon) **2-7-11**(5) CLowther(15) (swvd rt s: sn drvn along: n.d) ....nk	**13**	8/1[2]	49	10
3638*	**Star of Grosvenor (IRE) (84)** (PWChapple-Hyam) **2-8-8** JReid(19) (chsd ldrs ½-wy: sn lost pl)........1½	**14**	10/1	52	13
3774[6]	**Fire Goddess (72)** (JSMoore) **2-7-7**(3) MBaird(2) (racd far side: chsd ldrs: wkng whn hmpd over 1f out) ....½	**15**	33/1	38	—
3934[4]	**Pacifica (97)** (RBoss) **2-9-7** KFallon(3) (racd far side: sn drvn along: n.d) 5	**16**	20/1	51	12
3422[8]	**Jay Gee (IRE) (94)** (GGMargarson) **2-9-4** GCarter(11) (trckd ldrs: effrt over 2f out: wknd over 1f out)........11	**17**	12/1	21	—
3932[3]	**Tancred Times (73)** (DWBarker) **2-7-11**ow1 TWilliams(5) (sn trckng ldrs: effrt over 2f out: sn wknd) 2	**18**	20/1	—	—
			(SP 134.7%)	**18 Rn**	

1m 19.3 CSF £213.13 CT £3,411.47 TOTE £21.70: £5.10 £2.40 £3.90 £4.90 (£132.00) Trio £1,054.60; £906.12 to Doncaster 11/9/97 OWNER Diamond Racing Ltd (HAMBLETON) BRED J. D. and Mrs Abell
LONG HANDICAP Lady From Limerick (IRE) 7-8 Shalyah (IRE) 7-7 Robin Lane 7-2 Fire Goddess 7-6 Rich Choice 7-4 Queen Salote 7-8 Tancred Times 7-8
STEWARDS' ENQUIRY Polli susp. 19/9/97 (careless riding)
2466 Branston Berry (IRE), much more settled in the paddock on this occasion, proved well suited to the step-up to six, and she certainly showed the right sort of spirit when hotly challenged. (25/1)
2600 Ascot Cyclone (USA), who had plenty on on her two most recent outings, was in the end only just denied. (9/1)
3113 Zizi (IRE), who showed a very scratchy action going down, stuck on strongly after being tightened up over a furlong out. (16/1)
3802 Occhi Verdi (IRE), sweating and on her toes beforehand, was taken to post early. Dropped in at the start, she had no luck at all and must have won with a better run. Whether she will run as well next time, remains to be seen. (20/1)
2312 Robin Lane, 8lb out of the handicap and worst drawn, seemed to turn in a much-improved effort. (33/1)
3471 Jilted (IRE) looked to have been pitched in a pound or two too high on her handicap debut. (10/1)
2886 Rich Choice gave her rider problems going to the start. Out of the weights, she showed her rivals a clean pair of heels but edged right as she tired. By no means a straightforward ride, she might be worth a try over five. (33/1)
3770 Queen Salote was well supported on her handicap debut, but her rider was hard at work some way from home. (7/2: 11/4-9/2)
3750 Shalyah (IRE) (10/1: 8/1-12/1)
3638* Star of Grosvenor (IRE) (10/1: 7/1-11/1)

4098 DONCASTER BLOODSTOCK SALES SCARBROUGH STKS (Listed) (2-Y.O+) (Class A)

2-35 (2-38) **5f** £11,169.00 (£4,131.00: £1,980.50: £807.50: £318.75: £123.25) Stalls: High GOING minus 0.40 sec per fur (F)

			SP	RR	SF
3747[2]	**Bollin Joanne (107)** (TDEasterby) **4-9-2** KFallon(4) (b: trckd ldrs: shkn up to ld over 1f out: r.o strly) ....—	**1**	5/2[1]	115	72
3724[15]	**Almaty (IRE) (108)** (JHMGosden) **4-9-10** LDettori(5) (lw: led to 2f out: styd on ins fnl f)........1¼	**2**	8/1	119	76
	Carmine Lake (IRE) (110) (PWChapple-Hyam) **3-9-1** JReid(6) (lw: unruly s: sn trckng ldrs: effrt & n.m.r over 1f out: kpt on same pce)........hd	**3**	6/1[2]	111	67
2683[2]	**Bishops Court (102)** (MrsJRRamsden) **3-9-6** JFortune(1) (trckd ldrs: effrt over 1f out: edgd lft & kpt on same pce) 1½	**4**	6/1[2]	111	67
3724[12]	**Easycall (108)** (BJMeehan) **3-9-6** MTebbutt(7) (trckd ldrs: led & hung lft 2f out: hdd & wknd over 1f out)........1	**5**	7/1	108	64
4062[6]	**Brave Edge (106)** (RHannon) **6-9-7** DHolland(2) (lw: plld hrd: effrt ½-wy: no imp) ....nk	**6**	20/1	107	64
3724[13]	**Struggler (111)** (DRLoder) **5-9-10** RCochrane(9) (trckd ldrs: drvn along ½-wy: sn outpcd)........1¼	**7**	9/1	106	63
3724[8]	**Bolshoi (IRE) (107)** (JBerry) **5-9-7b** EmmaO'Gorman(10) (lw: sn outpcd: rdn ½-wy: n.d) ....nk	**8**	13/2[3]	102	59
3724[11]	**Croft Pool (108)** (JAGlover) **6-10-0** GCarter(11) (sn outpcd) 3	**9**	16/1	99	56
3649[3]	**Blessingindisguise (97)** (MWEasterby) **4-9-7b** TLucas(3) (lw: uns rdr s)	**U**	11/1	—	—
			(SP 123.1%)	**10 Rn**	

58.05 secs (0.15 under best) (-0.35) CSF £22.57 TOTE £3.70: £1.60 £2.80 £2.00 (£12.10) Trio £48.70 OWNER Lady Westbrook (MALTON) BRED Sir Neil and Lady Westbrook
WEIGHT FOR AGE 3yo-1lb
3747 Bollin Joanne gets better with every outing and she took this in tremendous style, lowering a long-standing track record on ground that looked a good deal firmer than the official version. (5/2)
3111 Almaty (IRE), who wore a tongue-strap for the first time, showed all his old speed but, in the winner, he had met an up and coming filly. (8/1)
Carmine Lake (IRE), who apparently has an arthritic problem, gave trouble at the start on her belated reappearance. She gave a good account of herself and hopefully, if her temperament stands the strain, she will improve on this. (6/1)
2683 Bishops Court, having his first outing for sixty days, looked in tremendous shape beforehand and this outing will have blown away the cobwebs. (6/1)

3023 Easycall hung badly on this very firm ground. (7/1)
4062 Brave Edge was having his second outing in two days. (20/1)
3372a* Struggler travelled strongly but he knows an awful lot about this game and, when the race began in earnest, he was happy to drop himself out. (9/1)
3724 Bolshoi (IRE) is much better suited by tracks with an uphill finish such as Newmarket or Sandown. (13/2)

4099 PARK HILL STKS (Gp 3) (3-Y.O+ F & M) (Class A)

3-10 (3-11) **1m 6f 132y** £20,000.00 (£7,400.00: £3,550.00: £1,450.00: £575.00: £225.00) Stalls: Low GOING minus 0.40 sec per fur (F)

				SP	RR	SF
3763[3]	**Book At Bedtime (IRE) (100)** (CACyzer) **3-8-5** MRoberts(1) (lw: chsd ldrs: pushed along 9f out: led over 2f out: hld on towards fin)	—	**1**	11/1	111	64
3727[2]	**The Faraway Tree (94)** (GWragg) **3-8-5** MHills(4) (hld up: effrt over 3f out: outpcd over 2f out: rallied appr fnl f: nt qckn nr fin)	nk	**2**	7/1	111	64
3705[3]	**Puce (89)** (LMCumani) **4-9-3** KDarley(3) (lw: trckd ldrs: effrt over 4f out: outpcd over 2f out: rallied appr fnl f: nt qckn towards fin)	¾	**3**	13/2 [3]	110	75
2709[5]	**Snow Princess (IRE) (93)** (LordHuntingdon) **5-9-3** JReid(5) (hdwy 7f out: effrt over 4f out: sn rdn & wl outpcd: styd on appr fnl f)	3½	**4**	14/1	106	71
2327[2]	**Sweetness Herself (101)** (MJRyan) **4-9-3** GCarter(2) (sn chsng ldrs: hung lft over 1f out: one pce)	¾	**5**	10/1	105	70
3704[3]	**Crown of Light (113)** (MRStoute) **3-8-5** RCochrane(7) (lw: sn trckng ldr: led over 3f out: hdd over 2f out: wkng whn hmpd over 1f out)	2	**6**	6/4 [1]	103	56
2869*	**Anno Luce** (JHMGosden) **4-9-6v** LDettori(6) (led tl over 3f out: lost pl over 2f out)	8	**7**	3/1 [2]	97	62
				(SP 114.9%)	**7 Rn**	

3m 2.44 (-1.16) CSF £76.37 TOTE £12.90: £3.20 £3.20 (£34.80) OWNER Mr R. M. Cyzer (HORSHAM) BRED Sheikh Mohammed Bin Rashid Al Maktoum
WEIGHT FOR AGE 3yo-12lb
OFFICIAL EXPLANATION Crown of Light: ran too freely and failed to stay.
3763 Book At Bedtime (IRE) has proved a real bargain buy. As tough as old boots, she answered her rider's every call and would not be passed. (11/1)
3727 The Faraway Tree had finished ahead of the winner over a mile and a half at York last time. Tapped for foot halfway up the straight, she rallied gamely coming to the final furlong but, in the end, was just being held. (7/1)
3705 Puce, who had plenty to find on official figures, stuck on strongly after being tapped for foot halfway up the straight. She might be worth a try over two miles. (13/2)
2709 Snow Princess (IRE) stayed on late in the day. She is better over further and on easier ground. (14/1)
2327 Sweetness Herself, very warm beforehand, hung badly on this ground which was too firm for her. (10/1)
3704 Crown of Light raced keenly. After taking it up going well, her stamina seemed to give out and she was well held when hampered. (6/4)
2869* Anno Luce, having her first outing for fifty-three days, possibly needed it and, with all chance gone, was given an easy time. (3/1)

4100 TOTE-PORTLAND H'CAP (0-110) (3-Y.O+) (Class B)

3-40 (3-45) **5f 140y** £18,128.00 (£6,752.00: £3,276.00: £1,380.00: £590.00: £274.00) Stalls: High GOING minus 0.40 sec per fur (F)

				SP	RR	SF
3863[3]	**Dashing Blue (105)** (IABalding) **4-9-12** KDarley(6) (lw: trckd ldrs: led jst ins fnl f: hld on wl)	—	**1**	10/1 [3]	117	81
3594[6]	**Sharp Hat (90)** (RHannon) **3-8-6**(3) RFfrench(22) (lw: hdwy over 2f out: ev ch ins fnl f: no ex nr fin)	½	**2**	14/1	101	63
3604[17]	**My Best Valentine (100)** (VSoane) **7-9-7** RCochrane(19) (lw: s.i.s: gd hdwy over 1f out: nt qckn nr fin)	hd	**3**	13/2 [1]	110	74
3876a[D]	**Bold Effort (FR) (94)** (KOCunningham-Brown) **5-9-1b** JReid(7) (unruly in stalls: hdwy centre over 2f out: kpt on wl fnl f)	¾	**4**	33/1	102	66
3649[23]	**Lago Di Varano (85)** (RMWhitaker) **5-8-6b**ow1 KFallon(21) (lw: in tch: drvn along: nt clr run & wl outpcd ½-wy: kpt on wl fnl f)	nk	**5**	14/1	92	55
3795[4]	**Lady Sheriff (85)** (MWEasterby) **6-7-13b**(7) RWinston(8) (lw: led tl jst ins fnl f)	1	**6**	16/1	90	54
3975[13]	**Tadeo (100)** (MJohnston) **4-9-7** DeanMcKeown(10) (swvd rt s: chsd ldr: hrd rdn & edgd rt over 1f out: kpt on same pce)	s.h	**7**	14/1	104	68
3217[15]	**Nigrasine (102)** (JLEyre) **3-9-7v**1 OPears(15) (chsd ldrs: rdn over 2f out: kpt on one pce)	½	**8**	33/1	105	67
3577[10]	**Hello Mister (96)** (TEPowell) **6-9-0**(3) PMcCabe(1) (racd far side: nvr nr to chal)	s.h	**9**	14/1	99	63
3649[9]	**Venture Capitalist (98)** (DNicholls) **8-9-5** AlexGreaves(5) (lw: hld up: effrt ½-wy: n.m.r: nvr rchd ldrs)	1¼	**10**	16/1	97	61
3914[2]	**Patsy Grimes (90)** (JSMoore) **7-8-8**(3) PPMurphy(20) (hld up: sme hdwy over 1f out: n.d)	hd	**11**	9/1 [2]	89	53
3600[3]	**Twice as Sharp (92)** (PWHarris) **5-8-8**(5) CLowther(14) (in tch: effrt over 2f out: sn wknd)	hd	**12**	12/1	91	55
3900*	**Westcourt Magic (90)** (MWEasterby) **4-8-11** LDettori(9) (nvr nr ldrs)	1¾	**13**	9/1 [2]	84	48
3914[3]	**Repertory (85)** (MSSaunders) **4-8-6** MRoberts(13) (sltly hmpd s: plld hrd: sn in tch: wknd 2f out)	hd	**14**	33/1	78	42
3975[10]	**The Puzzler (IRE) (100)** (BWHills) **6-9-7** MHills(3) (b: racd far side: sme hdwy over 1f out: n.d)	hd	**15**	33/1	93	57
3765[12]	**Bowden Rose (91)** (MBlanshard) **5-8-9b**(3) DSweeney(16) (lw: stdd s: n.d)	hd	**16**	16/1	84	48
3447[6]	**Indian Spark (102)** (WGMTurner) **3-9-0**(7) DMcGaffin(2) (lw: racd far side: n.d)	s.h	**17**	50/1	95	57
3975[3]	**Prince Dome (IRE) (89)** (MartynWane) **3-8-5**(3) AWhelan(18) (chsd ldrs tl hung lft & lost pl 2f out)	hd	**18**	14/1	81	43
3217[27]	**Sylva Paradise (IRE) (98)** (CEBrittain) **4-9-5** JCarroll(4) (swtg: led far side tl wknd over 1f out)	½	**19**	33/1	89	53
3011[2]	**Surprise Mission (90)** (MrsJRRamsden) **5-8-11** JFortune(11) (sltly hmpd s: hmpd after 1f: n.d)	1¾	**20**	9/1 [2]	76	40
3863[5]	**Blue Ridge (93)** (VSoane) **3-8-12** GDuffield(17) (mid div & sn drvn along: bhd fr ½-wy)	1¾	**21**	50/1	74	36
3975[9]	**Astrac (IRE) (95)** (NTinkler) **6-9-2** KimTinkler(12) (lw: n.m.r after 1f: sn bhd)	nk	**22**	50/1	75	39
				(SP 131.7%)	**22 Rn**	

1m 6.67 (-0.33) CSF £127.39 CT £924.94 TOTE £14.50: £4.00 £3.00 £2.10 £5.20 (£162.90) Trio £280.20 OWNER Mrs Duncan Allen (KINGSCLERE) BRED Mrs I. A. Balding
WEIGHT FOR AGE 3yo-2lb
3863 Dashing Blue, ideally suited by fast ground, finds six furlongs testing his stamina to the very limit and this extended five proved ideal. He defied top weight in very game fashion. (10/1)
3594 Sharp Hat, a keen-going sort who likes to get on with it, was in the end only just denied. (14/1)
3217 My Best Valentine put his poor effort at Ripon behind him and was possibly a shade unlucky not to prevail, having slightly missed the break. (13/2)
3876a Bold Effort (FR), who played up in the stalls, had been hoisted in the weights after turning in an apparently improved effort over in France. (33/1)
3065* Lago Di Varano was being tapped for foot when meeting trouble at halfway. Short of room over a furlong out, he was putting in some sterling work at the finish and, though by no means consistent, can surely find a decent sprint when the ground eases this back-end. (14/1)

3795 Lady Sheriff has speed to burn but she barely stays five, and her stamina gave out in the last one hundred and fifty yards. (16/1)
3604* Tadeo ran much better than at York, showing all his old speed. (14/1)
3447 Hello Mister, attempting to win this race for the third time in four years, was one of four to race on the far side and he did best of that group. (14/1)

4101 FARINGDON PLACE MALLARD H'CAP (0-105) (3-Y.O+) (Class B)

4-10 (4-14) **1m 6f 132y** £17,084.00 (£6,356.00: £3,078.00: £1,290.00: £545.00: £247.00) Stalls: Low GOING minus 0.40 sec per fur (F)

				SP	RR	SF
3648*	**Sausalito Bay (92)** (IABalding) **3-9-1** RCochrane(11) (lw: hld up: hdwy over 3f out: led 1f out: hld on wl)	—	**1**	5/1[1]	106	71
3648[5]	**Georgia Venture (80)** (SPCWoods) **3-8-3** GDuffield(4) (trckd ldrs: effrt over 2f out: ev ch ins fnl f: r.o)	hd	**2**	20/1	94	59
3796*	**Shaft of Light (93)** (LordHuntingdon) **5-10-0v** KDarley(7) (trckd ldrs: led over 3f out: hdd 1f out: kpt on same pce)	4	**3**	11/2[2]	103	80
3705[13]	**Premier Night (79)** (SDow) **4-9-0** GCarter(8) (in tch: effrt over 2f out: styd on same pce)	s.h	**4**	33/1	89	66
3890[6]	**Sea Victor (71)** (JLHarris) **5-8-6** DHolland(2) (chsd ldrs: pushed along 6f out: one pce fnl 3f)	2½	**5**	25/1	78	55
3805[7]	**Berlin Blue (71)** (JWWatts) **4-8-6** JCarroll(15) (lw: hld up: hdwy 4f out: n.m.r 2f out: styd on wl)	1¼	**6**	20/1	76	53
1400[2]	**Turnpole (IRE) (74)** (MrsMReveley) **6-8-9** ACulhane(9) (hld up & bhd: styd on fnl 2f: nt rch ldrs)	2	**7**	14/1	77	54
3599[2]	**Tykeyvor (IRE) (92)** (LadyHerries) **7-9-8**(5) CLowther(18) (w ldrs: chal over 3f out: wknd 2f out)	2½	**8**	12/1	92	69
3902[7]	**State Fair (100)** (BWHills) **3-9-6**(3) PFessey(12) (bhd & drvn along 6f out: hdwy & n.m.r 2f out: kpt on)	nk	**9**	33/1	100	65
3599[6]	**Fletcher (90)** (HMorrison) **3-8-10**(3) RFfrench(3) (s.s: bhd: hdwy whn hmpd 2f out: styd on wl towards fin)	s.h	**10**	50/1	90	55
3218[9]	**Kilma (USA) (90)** (LMCumani) **3-8-13** LDettori(13) (lw: bhd: hdwy u.p 3f out: sn wknd)	2½	**11**	8/1[3]	87	52
1592[3]	**Prince Kinsky (78)** (JABOld) **4-8-13** MRoberts(10) (a in rr)	2½	**12**	25/1	73	50
3122[8]	**Onefourseven (75)** (JLEyre) **4-8-10** TWilliams(16) (hdwy u.p 7f out: lost pl & eased 3f out)	½	**13**	16/1	69	46
3419*	**Marsul (USA) (86)** (JHMGosden) **3-8-9v** RHills(5) (chsd ldrs: rdn 4f out: lost pl over 2f out)	hd	**14**	12/1	80	45
3412*	**Valagalore (84)** (BWHills) **3-8-7** MHills(14) (lw: swtchd lft s a in rr)	nk	**15**	5/1[1]	78	43
3110[4]	**Jazz King (87)** (MissGayKelleway) **4-9-8** JReid(6) (led tl over 3f out: sn wknd)	5	**16**	12/1	75	52
3599[4]	**Machiavelli (88)** (HRACecil) **3-8-11** KFallon(1) (lw: chsd ldrs: pushed along 6f out: n.m.r & lost pl 2f out: eased)	17	**17**	14/1	58	23
				(SP 127.2%)		**17 Rn**

3m 2.85 (-0.75) CSF £101.44 CT £537.07 TOTE £6.70: £1.90 £5.10 £1.60 £12.20 (£93.70) Trio £269.60 OWNER Mr J. C. Smith (KINGSCLERE) BRED Littleton Stud
WEIGHT FOR AGE 3yo-12lb

3648* Sausalito Bay is obviously a progressive young stayer. From a 7lb higher mark, he appreciated this flat, galloping track and showed the right sort of spirit in a tight finish. He should make an even better stayer next year. (5/1)
3648 Georgia Venture, who had finished well behind the winner at York, met him on much better terms and gave her all in a tight finish. (20/1)
3796* Shaft of Light, from a 6lb higher mark, took it up travelling easily but was outsprinted in the final furlong. He should go well in the Cesarewitch. (11/2)
2834 Premier Night, a real stayer, put two moderate efforts behind her. (33/1)
39 Sea Victor presumably needed his outing in the mud at Chester last time after a lay-off. He stuck to his guns here and this outing should put him spot on. (25/1)
3805 Berlin Blue ran much better and there is no doubt that he is on a mark from which he can win at present. (20/1)
1400 Turnpole (IRE), having his first outing for one hundred and ninety days, stayed on in promising fashion. He should go close next time. (14/1)
3599 Fletcher, with the headgear again left off, gave the field several lengths' start leaving the stalls. Meeting trouble, he finished with a real flourish and there is no doubt that he has a good deal more ability than his current handicap mark, but when he decides to use it, only he knows. (50/1)
3412* Valagalore, from a 5lb higher mark, ran no race at all. This is best ignored. (5/1)

4102 SITWELL ARMS AT RENISHAW LIMITED STKS (0-85) (3-Y.O+) (Class D)

4-40 (4-48) **1m 2f 60y** £4,698.00 (£1,404.00: £672.00: £306.00) Stalls: Low GOING minus 0.40 sec per fur (F)

				SP	RR	SF
3824[5]	**Mithali (83)** (BWHills) **4-9-6** RHills(10) (lw: mde all: jst hld on)	—	**1**	9/1	97	80
3624*	**Saafeya (IRE) (84)** (JHMGosden) **3-8-10** LDettori(1) (hld up: stdy hdwy & swtchd rt 2f out: ev ch ins fnl f: r.o)	hd	**2**	100/30[2]	94	70
3012[2]	**Rudimental (84)** (SirMarkPrescott) **3-8-13** GDuffield(2) (lw: sn trckng ldrs: effrt on ins 4f out: ev ch over 1f out: nt qckn)	¾	**3**	11/4[1]	96	72
3575[8]	**Party Romance (USA) (85)** (BHanbury) **3-9-1** MHills(6) (trckd ldrs: effrt over 4f out: nt qckn appr fnl f)	1	**4**	11/1	96	72
3128[9]	**Stone Flower (USA) (83)** (PWChapple-Hyam) **3-8-8** JReid(5) (lw: b.nr fore: trckd ldrs: effrt 3f out: styd on same pce)	2½	**5**	16/1	85	61
2855[3]	**Raivue (80)** (EWeymes) **3-8-13** KDarley(4) (trckd ldrs: pushed along over 3f out: one pce)	nk	**6**	10/1	90	66
3822[5]	**Billy Bushwacker (85)** (MrsMReveley) **6-9-4** ACulhane(11) (hld up: hdwy over 2f out: hung lft: nvr rchd ldrs)	1¼	**7**	10/1	86	69
	Palatial Style (76) (PJMakin) **10-9-4** JFortune(7) (bit bkwd: hld up: styd on fnl 2f: nvr nr to chal)	nk	**8**	50/1	85	68
3012[6]	**Another Night (IRE) (82)** (RHannon) **3-8-13** DHolland(8) (b.off hind: bhd: hdwy over 2f out: kpt on: nvr nr to chal)	1	**9**	12/1	86	62
3444[2]	**Meteor Strike (USA) (84)** (MrsAJPerrett) **3-8-13** MRoberts(9) (chsd ldrs: pushed along 4f out: hung lft: wknd over 2f out)	6	**10**	13/2[3]	76	52
3605[11]	**Silent Valley (53)** (MissLCSiddall) **3-8-3v**(7) TSiddall(3) (unruly & led to s: s.s: sme hdwy ½-wy: lost pl 4f out)	11	**11**	66/1	56	32
1949[4]	**Iechyd-Da (IRE) (85)** (MBell) **3-8-11** KFallon(12) (lw: in tch: drvn along over 4f out: wkng whn hmpd 2f out: eased)	1¾	**12**	16/1	55	31
				(SP 122.5%)		**12 Rn**

2m 6.81 (-0.99) CSF £36.72 TOTE £12.50: £3.30 £1.60 £1.60 (£24.30) Trio £31.80 OWNER Mr Hamdan Al Maktoum (LAMBOURN) BRED Shadwell Estate Company Limited
WEIGHT FOR AGE 3yo-7lb

3824 Mithali, who looked outstandingly well, adopted totally different tactics this time and, answering his rider's every call, he would not be collared. (9/1: op 6/1)
3624* Saafeya (IRE) was given a confident ride. Pulled to the outside to start her effort, she was almost upsides inside the last but the winner would not give in. (100/30)
3012 Rudimental, from a stable back on song, stuck to his task and probably ran right up to his very best. (11/4)

3575 Party Romance (USA) seems to settle better when ridden up with the pace. He probably ran right to his best here. (11/1: 8/1-12/1)
2113 Stone Flower (USA) stuck to her guns without threatening to take a serious hand. She might be worth a try over further. (16/1)
2855 Raivue, who was having his first outing for fifty-three days, proved too keen for his own good. The outing will have helped settle him down. (10/1: op 6/1)
3822 Billy Bushwacker looked to have a winning chance on official figures, but he is simply not as good as his current handicap mark and proved it here. (10/1)
Palatial Style, who last won six years ago and was having his first outing for two years, showed that he retains at least some of his former ability. Provided he stands training, it would be no surprise to see him win another race this back-end. (50/1)
3444 Meteor Strike (USA) wanted to do nothing but hang. (13/2: 4/1-7/1)

T/Jkpt: Not won; £67,638.34 to Doncaster 11/9/97. T/Plpt: £2,190.90 (20.67 Tckts). T/Qdpt: £95.70 (38.05 Tckts) WG

3685-KEMPTON (R-H) (Good)
Wednesday September 10th
WEATHER: v.warm WIND: almost nil

4103 E.B.F. MAIDEN STKS (2-Y.O F) (Class D)
1-45 (1-51) **6f** £3,550.00 (£1,075.00: £525.00: £250.00) Stalls: High GOING minus 0.43 sec per fur (F)

				SP	RR	SF
3636[2]	**Royal Shyness** (GLewis) **2-8-11** PaulEddery(12) (a.p: qcknd to ld 1f out: r.o wl)	—	**1**	6/1[2]	96	52
3770[2]	**Ikhteyaar (USA)** (RWArmstrong) **2-8-11** JWeaver(20) (led 5f: hrd rdn: r.o)	½	**2**	2/1[1]	95	51
3686[7]	**Tattinger** (JRFanshawe) **2-8-11** MRimmer(5) (chsd ldrs stands' side: r.o ins fnl f)	4	**3**	25/1	84	40
3744[10]	**Solo Spirit** (JRJenkins) **2-8-11** JFEgan(6) (racd stands' side: gd spd over 4f)	1	**4**	50/1	81	37
3187[6]	**Night Owl** (RCharlton) **2-8-11** TSprake(10) (hdwy 2f out: r.o ins fnl f)	2	**5**	14/1	76	32
	Atuf (USA) (SbinSuroor) **2-8-11** PatEddery(15) (w'like: scope: lw: chsd ldr: ev ch over 1f out: eased whn btn ins fnl f)	1	**6**	2/1[1]	73+	29
1927[4]	**Tajmil (IRE)** (MajorWRHern) **2-8-11** RPerham(4) (racd stands' side: spd over 4f)	½	**7**	25/1	72	28
	Sense of Wonder (BJMeehan) **2-8-11** CRutter(7) (leggy: racd stands' side: styd on fnl 2f)	¾	**8**	33/1	70	26
	Prime Time Girl (IABalding) **2-8-11** AMcGlone(19) (unf: sn t.o: gd late hdwy)	5	**9**	20/1	57	13
	Spree Rose (KOCunningham-Brown) **2-8-11** MFenton(9) (leggy: racd stands' side: nvr trbld ldrs)	s.h	**10**	50/1	57	13
	Qilin (IRE) (MHTompkins) **2-8-11** DBiggs(11) (str: scope: bkwd: nvr bttr than mid div)	½	**11**	33/1	55	11
1970[2]	**Midsummer Night (IRE)** (RHannon) **2-8-11** DaneO'Neill(16) (prom tl wknd 2f out)	1½	**12**	12/1[3]	51	7
	Miss Slender (RHannon) **2-8-11** WJO'Connor(2) (w'like: racd stands' side: outpcd)	½	**13**	20/1	50	6
	Sixpence (GWragg) **2-8-11** AClark(17) (str: bit bkwd: s.s: nvr on terms)	½	**14**	16/1	49	5
3783[3]	**Arbenig (IRE)** (BPalling) **2-8-11** SDrowne(13) (outpcd)	s.h	**15**	20/1	48	4
	Island Race (JRFanshawe) **2-8-11** NDay(3) (w'like: racd stands' side: outpcd)	1	**16**	20/1	46	2
	Mrs Malaprop (MRChannon) **2-8-11** TQuinn(14) (w'like: scope: bit bkwd: prom tl wknd qckly 2f out)	¾	**17**	20/1	44	—
	St Lucia (IRE) (BJMeehan) **2-8-11** FNorton(8) (w'like: scope: racd stands' side: s.s: a bhd)	1	**18**	25/1	41	—
3009[4]	**Glitter Princess** (MajorDNChappell) **2-8-11** WRyan(18) (lw: prom tl wknd qckly 2f out)	1½	**19**	33/1	37	—
	Break For Peace (IRE) (SirMarkPrescott) **2-8-11** SSanders(21) (leggy: unf: a bhd)	hd	**20**	20/1	37	—
	Hebony (JHMGosden) **2-8-11** GHind(22) (Withdrawn not under Starter's orders: unruly in stalls)		**W**	12/1[3]	—	—
				(SP 161.7%)	**20 Rn**	

1m 11.71 (0.51) CSF £16.62 TOTE £6.70: £1.50 £1.30 £8.10 (£6.30) Trio £134.40 OWNER Mr R. D. Hubbard (EPSOM) BRED R. D. Hubbard
3636 Royal Shyness, patiently ridden, moved up smoothly two furlongs out. She quickened to strike the front entering the final furlong and won readily. (6/1: 9/2-7/1)
3770 Ikhteyaar (USA) tried to make all the running. She had shaken off all bar the winner approaching the final furlong and fought back well when headed. (2/1)
Tattinger did best of those racing on the stands' side, running on well inside the final furlong without ever appearing likely to trouble the leading pair. (25/1)
1783 Solo Spirit held a clear lead of the stands'-side group for most of the race, and clearly has enough speed to win a similar event. (50/1)
3187 Night Owl stayed on in the final quarter-mile but was too late to trouble the leaders. (14/1: 8/1-16/1)
Atuf (USA), very fit for her debut, raced in second place. She had every chance below the distance but then came under pressure and was eased when her chance had gone inside the final furlong. (2/1)
Prime Time Girl was badly outpaced and seemed certain to finish in the ruck, but was running on in the closing stages. (20/1)
1970 Midsummer Night (IRE) (12/1: 6/1-14/1)
Hebony (12/1: op 6/1)

4104 SONY CMD-X2000 H'CAP (0-70) (3-Y.O+) (Class E)
2-15 (2-15) **1m 6f 92y** £3,030.00 (£915.00: £445.00: £210.00) Stalls: High GOING minus 0.43 sec per fur (F)

				SP	RR	SF
3694[5]	**Lookout (66)** (BWHills) **3-8-13** PatEddery(8) (a.p: led & qcknd clr over 2f out: hrd rdn over 1f out: r.o)	—	**1**	3/1[1]	78	33
3748[5]	**Durham (65)** (GLMoore) **6-9-9b** CRutter(9) (gd hdwy 2f out: chsd wnr fnl f: hung rt: nt qckn)	1¼	**2**	7/1[2]	76	42
3714[U]	**Alakdar (CAN) (66)** (ACStewart) **3-8-13** TSprake(3) (hdwy 6f out: ev ch over 2f out: r.o one pce)	1¼	**3**	9/1	75	30
2316[8]	**Taufan Boy (65)** (PWHarris) **4-9-9** FNorton(14) (hdwy on ins 4f out: one pce fnl 2f)	1¼	**4**	9/1	73	39
3815[5]	**Ela-Yie-Mou (IRE) (62)** (SDow) **4-9-6** JFEgan(6) (lw: gd hdwy 4f out: one pce fnl 2f)	1¼	**5**	20/1	69	35
3640[5]	**Lear Jet (USA) (70)** (BobJones) **4-10-0** NDay(13) (lw: nvr nr to chal)	1½	**6**	12/1	75	41
3748[4]	**Tudor Island (68)** (CEBrittain) **8-9-12** MRimmer(2) (lw: prom tl lost pl 4f out: no ch after)	1	**7**	7/1[2]	72	38
2853[3]	**Ajcombe (IRE) (67)** (LadyHerries) **4-9-11** AClark(10) (in rr whn hmpd over 4f out: nrst fin)	nk	**8**	10/1	70	36
3867[2]	**Urgent Reply (USA) (60)** (CADwyer) **4-9-4** WRyan(11) (led: hdd over 2f out: wknd over 1f out)	5	**9**	8/1[3]	58	24
3719[6]	**Chris's Lad (55)** (BJMeehan) **6-8-13b** DaneO'Neill(7) (lw: rr div whn stumbled over 4f out: nvr on terms)	3	**10**	8/1[3]	50	16
	Chimborazo (54) (BJMcMath) **6-8-12** JWeaver(12) (bkwd: nvr trbld ldrs)	3½	**11**	33/1	45	11
3283[2]	**Lime Street Blues (IRE) (58)** (TKeddy) **6-9-2** SSanders(4) (nvr on terms)	9	**12**	9/1	39	5
3796[12]	**Squire's Occasion (CAN) (55)** (RCurtis) **4-8-13** JLowe(1) (lw: plld hrd: chsd ldr tl rdn & wknd over 3f out)	5	**13**	20/1	30	—
	My Hero (IRE) (67) (TGMills) **3-9-0** TQuinn(5) (prom tl wknd qckly over 3f out: t.o)	27	**14**	12/1	12	—
				(SP 139.2%)	**14 Rn**	

3m 8.67 (5.67) CSF £24.35 CT £174.36 TOTE £3.00: £1.90 £2.80 £8.40 (£10.50) Trio £100.20 OWNER Mr R. D. Hollingsworth (LAMBOURN)
BRED R. D. Hollingsworth
WEIGHT FOR AGE 3yo-11lb

3694 Lookout travelled well on the heels of the leaders. She went smoothly to the front early in the straight and looked set for an easy win, but she had to be kept up to her work in the last furlong and a half. (3/1)
3318* Durham came from behind to challenge approaching the final furlong but spoiled his chance by hanging right in the closing stages. (7/1)
2846 Alakdar (CAN) moved onto the heels of the winner early in the straight, but failed to quicken and proved one paced in the closing stages. (9/1)
1592 Taufan Boy slipped through on the inside tracking the winner approaching the straight, and stayed on at one pace in the final quarter-mile. (9/1: 6/1-10/1)
3815 Ela-Yie-Mou (IRE), in the ruck in the early stages, moved onto the heels of the leaders on the home turn but could not quicken when it mattered. (20/1)
3640 Lear Jet (USA) ran a very respectable race under a welter burden but could not reach a challenging position. (12/1)

4105 CHERTSEY LOCK CONDITIONS STKS (2-Y.O C & G) (Class C)
2-45 (2-47) **7f (Jubilee)** £4,454.20 (£1,667.80: £816.40: £352.00: £158.50: £81.10) Stalls: High GOING minus 0.43 sec per fur (F)

				SP	RR	SF
3219*	**Tamarisk (IRE)** (RCharlton) **2-9-1** TSprake(11) (lw: mde all: plld hrd: qcknd 2f out: comf)	—	**1**	10/11[1]	103+	55
	Greek Dance (IRE) (MRStoute) **2-8-10** PatEddery(3) (gd sort: a.p: chsd wnr fnl 3f: no imp)	6	**2**	11/4[2]	84	36
3494[6]	**Lear Spear (USA)** (DRCElsworth) **2-8-10** TQuinn(4) (lw: chsd ldrs: r.o one pce fnl 2f)	½	**3**	8/1[3]	83	35
	Close Shave (MRStoute) **2-8-10** KBradshaw(10) (w'like: scope: hdwy 3f out: changed position repeatedly fnl 2f: promising)	1¼	**4**	16/1	80+	32
	Plan-B (JHMGosden) **2-8-10** GHind(7) (w'like: scope: dwlt: sn prom: rdn over 2f out: wknd over 1f out)	1¼	**5**	11/1	77	29
	Cloak of Darkness (IRE) (RHannon) **2-8-10** DaneO'Neill(6) (w'like: nvr nr to chal)	3½	**6**	14/1	69	21
3861[6]	**Bronzino** (GBBalding) **2-8-10** SDrowne(1) (rdn 2f out: no hdwy)	½	**7**	33/1	68	20
	Arctic Star (MRChannon) **2-8-10** RPerham(2) (leggy: s.s: nvr on terms)	3	**8**	14/1	61	13
	Hever Golf Ranger (TJNaughton) **2-8-10** JWeaver(5) (w'like: scope: bit bkwd: in tch tl wknd 3f out)	5	**9**	33/1	50	2
	Anemos (IRE) (MHTompkins) **2-8-10** SSanders(9) (leggy: scope: lw: s.s: a bhd)	hd	**10**	20/1	50	2
	Fiercely Ginger (EAWheeler) **2-8-5**(5) ADaly(8) (w'like: scope: bit bkwd: chsd wnr: sddle slipped 4f out: sn eased & bhd: t.o)	dist	**11**	66/1	—	—

(SP 129.8%) **11 Rn**

1m 25.22 (0.72) CSF £3.41 TOTE £1.70: £1.10 £1.60 £2.10 (£2.00) Trio £8.60 OWNER Highclere Thoroughbred Racing Ltd (BECKHAMPTON) BRED Mount Coote Stud

OFFICIAL EXPLANATION **Close Shave: regarding the apparent tender ride, the rider reported that the colt hung badly left in the straight and could not be ridden out effectively. The colt may also have had a tooth problem.**

3219* Tamarisk (IRE), although refusing to settle, made all the running. He quickened readily when finally given his head at the two-furlong marker, and is clearly a very useful prospect. (10/11)
Greek Dance (IRE), a deep-bodied quality colt, made a satisfactory debut. He took second place before halfway and, though never appearing likely to lose that position, had no chance with the winner from two furlongs out. (11/4: 7/4-3/1)
3494 Lear Spear (USA), always in the leading group, was finding the winner travelling too strongly from halfway but kept on well for third place. (8/1)
Close Shave moved up early in the straight. Though repeatedly changing positions in the last two furlongs, he was running on well. He has scope for improvement and can leave this form far behind. (16/1)
Plan-B soon recovered from a slow start and was on the heels of the leaders early in the straight. He then came under pressure and stayed on at one pace. (11/1: 8/1-12/1)
Cloak of Darkness (IRE), never on terms with the leaders, was nonetheless staying on at the finish. (14/1: op 7/1)
Arctic Star (14/1: 8/1-16/1)

4106 SIRENIA STKS (Listed) (2-Y.O) (Class A)
3-20 (3-20) **6f** £9,706.00 (£2,938.00: £1,434.00: £682.00) Stalls: High GOING minus 0.43 sec per fur (F)

				SP	RR	SF
3811[3]	**Mijana (IRE) (100)** (JHMGosden) **2-8-11** GHind(3) (lw: hld up: qcknd & led over 2f out: r.o wl)	—	**1**	7/2[2]	102	51
2439a*	**Tadwiga** (RHannon) **2-8-6** DaneO'Neill(5) (lw: chsd ldrs: ev ch ins fnl f: r.o)	1¼	**2**	10/1	94	43
3644[5]	**Merlin's Ring (94)** (IABalding) **2-8-11** WRyan(8) (hdwy 2f out: hrd rdn fnl f: nt qckn)	1½	**3**	13/2	95	44
3825*	**Majaari** (PTWalwyn) **2-8-11** TSprake(4) (a.p: ev ch over 1f out: nt qckn)	nk	**4**	4/1[3]	94	43
3799*	**Likely Story (IRE) (89)** (JLDunlop) **2-8-6** SSanders(7) (hld up: ev ch over 1f out: wknd ins fnl f)	1½	**5**	12/1	85	34
2388*	**Toblersong** (RAkehurst) **2-8-11** TQuinn(1) (chsd ldrs: ev ch over 1f out: wknd fnl f)	4	**6**	12/1	79	28
3636*	**Risque Lady** (PWHarris) **2-8-6** PatEddery(2) (hmpd s: hdwy over 3f out: rdn & wknd over 2f out)	2½	**7**	2/1[1]	68	17
2863[5]	**Hill Magic (90)** (DRCElsworth) **2-8-11** SDrowne(6) (lw: a bhd)	2	**8**	20/1	67	16
3925[5]	**Dernier Croise (FR)** (BJMeehan) **2-8-11b** PaulEddery(9) (lw: led over 3f: wknd qckly)	8	**9**	66/1	46	—

(SP 119.6%) **9 Rn**

1m 11.74 (0.54) CSF £36.24 TOTE £4.40: £1.10 £2.90 £1.20 (£34.50) Trio £26.20 OWNER Mr Nabil Mourad (NEWMARKET) BRED Churchtown House Stud

3811 Mijana (IRE), held up just behind the leaders, quickened nicely to strike the front approaching the two-furlong marker. Though strongly pressed all the way to the line, he kept pulling out a bit more. (7/2)
2439a* Tadwiga, buried in mid-field, moved up to challenge entering the final furlong but could make no impression on the winner in the last one hundred yards. (10/1: 7/1-12/1)
3644 Merlin's Ring, dropped in trip and patiently ridden, came with a promising-looking run at the distance but could not quite sustain his effort inside the last furlong. (13/2)
3825* Majaari disputed the lead for much of the way but, despite having every chance, could not quicken in the last furlong. (4/1: 11/4-9/2)
3799* Likely Story (IRE) tracked the leaders on the far rails and found a clear run when it was needed, but lacked the pace to take advantage. (12/1: op 8/1)
2388* Toblersong moved up approaching the two-furlong marker but, despite having every chance, weakened in the final furlong. (12/1: op 8/1)
3636* Risque Lady went to the start too freely and was squeezed out as the stalls opened. She made her effort approaching the two-furlong marker but soon dropped back beaten. (2/1)

4107 SEPTEMBER CONDITIONS STKS (2-Y.O F) (Class C)
3-50 (3-51) **7f** £4,291.80 (£1,606.20: £785.60: £338.00: £151.50: £76.90) Stalls: High GOING minus 0.43 sec per fur (F)

				SP	RR	SF
	Exclusive (MRStoute) **2-8-8** TQuinn(6) (w'like: scope: a.p: led over 2f out: r.o wl)	—	**1**	100/30[2]	99+	31
3574[4]	**Celtic Cross** (LordHuntingdon) **2-8-8** SSanders(8) (led tl over 2f out: styd on)	1¾	**2**	4/1[3]	95	27
3547*	**Leggera (IRE)** (JLDunlop) **2-8-13** PatEddery(4) (lw: chsd ldrs: swtchd lft & rdn over 2f out: r.o one pce)	3½	**3**	Evens[1]	92	24

3744[8]	**Goldtune** (MAJarvis) **2-8-8** MFenton(2) (a.p: r.o one pce fnl 2f)	1	**4**	25/1	85	17
	Storm River (USA) (HRACecil) **2-8-8** WRyan(1) (neat: lw: hld up & bhd: hdwy 2f out: nvr on terms)	hd	**5**	13/2	85	17
3847*	**Simply Super** (CEBrittain) **2-8-8** MRimmer(7) (w ldr tl wknd over 2f out)	1½	**6**	12/1	81	13
	St Clair Shores (USA) (MRStoute) **2-8-8** KBradshaw(3) (unf: scope: nvr nr to chal)	1¾	**7**	20/1	77	9
	Ivory League (GLewis) **2-8-8** PaulEddery(5) (b.nr hind: leggy: scope: a bhd)	3½	**8**	20/1	69	1
				(SP 127.5%)	**8 Rn**	

1m 26.72 (2.22) CSF £17.15 TOTE £4.90: £1.50 £1.10 £1.10 (£15.30) OWNER Cheveley Park Stud (NEWMARKET) BRED Cheveley Park Stud Ltd

Exclusive, an angular half-sister to Entrepreneur with four white socks, looked very fit. Soon pushed along, she nonetheless quickened readily when picked up in earnest approaching the two-furlong marker, and was always in command from that point. (100/30: 9/4-7/2)

3574 Celtic Cross tried to make all the running. She stayed on when headed approaching the two-furlong marker and should have no difficulty in winning a race. (4/1)

3547* Leggera (IRE), in a handy position from the start, was switched left approaching the two-furlong marker and was soon under maximum pressure. She stayed on but lacked a turn of foot. (Evens)

Goldtune, always chasing the leaders, ran on at one pace in the final quarter-mile. (25/1)

Storm River (USA), patiently ridden, tried to come with a run on the wide outside at the two-furlong marker but was never able to get in a blow. She is a neatly-made filly who should be capable of winning a race. (13/2: 3/1-7/1)

3847* Simply Super raced with the leader until weakening approaching the two-furlong marker. (12/1)

4108 TEDDINGTON H'CAP (0-75) (3-Y.O+) (Class D)

4-20 (4-22) **1m 4f** £3,777.50 (£1,145.00: £560.00: £267.50) Stalls: High GOING minus 0.43 sec per fur (F)

				SP	RR	SF
2373[3]	**Alhosaam (73)** (MajorWRHern) **3-9-3** TSprake(8) (lw: hdwy 4f out: led over 2f out: all out)	—	**1**	12/1	84	53
3110[12]	**Renzo (IRE) (75)** (MrsAJPerrett) **4-10-0** AClark(15) (wl bhd tl rapid hdwy over 2f out: ev ch fnl f: nt qckn)	nk	**2**	25/1	86	64
3970[5]	**Tallulah Belle (56)** (NPLittmoden) **4-8-9** JWeaver(7) (s.v.s: gd hdwy 4f out: ev ch over 1f out: nt qckn)	4	**3**	25/1	61	39
3491[4]	**Pistol (IRE) (68)** (CAHorgan) **7-9-7** PaulEddery(19) (stdy hdwy 3f out: ev ch over 2f out: nt qckn)	2	**4**	10/1[3]	71	49
3916[10]	**Your Most Welcome (62)** (DJSffrenchDavis) **6-9-1** DRMcCabe(10) (gd hdwy fnl 2f: nt rch ldrs)	1¼	**5**	12/1	63	41
3815[6]	**Tappeto (72)** (HCandy) **5-9-11b** CRutter(11) (gd hdwy on ins 2f out: one pce fnl f)	1¾	**6**	14/1	71	49
3992*	**Gold Desire (56)** (MBrittain) **7-8-2**(7) DMernagh(9) (b.nr hind: hdwy 4f out: ev ch over 1f out: wknd fnl f)	¾	**7**	7/1[2]	54	32
3318[7]	**Water Flower (70)** (JRFanshawe) **3-9-0** PatEddery(20) (b.hind: no hdwy fnl 4f)	¾	**8**	12/1	67	36
3689[4]	**Mutadarra (IRE) (69)** (WJMusson) **4-9-5**(3) JDSmith(14) (lw: nvr nr to chal)	1¾	**9**	6/1[1]	63	41
3093[3]	**Fourdaned (IRE) (58)** (SDow) **4-8-11** JFEgan(13) (nvr bttr than mid div)	7	**10**	20/1	43	21
2867[6]	**Pike Creek (USA) (72)** (IABalding) **4-9-11** WJO'Connor(18) (lw: prom tl wknd over 2f out)	3	**11**	14/1	53	31
3739[8]	**North Reef (IRE) (72)** (JPearce) **6-9-11** MWigham(6) (nvr on terms)	1	**12**	14/1	52	30
2483[6]	**Dramatic Moment (65)** (JRArnold) **4-9-4** RPerham(16) (prom tl wknd over 2f out)	1¼	**13**	20/1	43	21
3616[11]	**Rhapsody In White (IRE) (70)** (MAJarvis) **3-9-0b[1]** MFenton(12) (prom tl wknd 3f out)	3½	**14**	20/1	43	12
3229[4]	**Krosno (70)** (SCWilliams) **3-9-0** DaneO'Neill(3) (lw: led tl wknd over 2f out)	s.h	**15**	12/1	43	12
3234[3]	**Pietro Bembo (IRE) (70)** (SirMarkPrescott) **3-9-0b[1]** SSanders(2) (prom tl wknd over 2f out)	1¼	**16**	6/1[1]	42	11
789[8]	**Frozen Sea (USA) (63)** (GPEnright) **6-8-9**(7) PDoe(1) (a bhd)	8	**17**	33/1	24	2
3380[3]	**Polar Champ (75)** (SPCWoods) **4-10-0** WRyan(5) (bhd fnl 4f)	3	**18**	16/1	32	10
	Hadabet (59) (RTPhillips) **5-8-12** SDrowne(4) (sn wl bhd)	7	**19**	66/1	7	—
3739[6]	**Mr Browning (USA) (64)** (RAkehurst) **6-9-3b** TQuinn(17) (chsd ldr & rdn along: wknd 3f out: t.o)	dist	**20**	10/1[3]	—	—
				(SP 142.3%)	**20 Rn**	

2m 31.95 (1.95) CSF £283.28 CT £6,630.07 TOTE £17.20: £3.50 £4.70 £3.90 £2.60 (£250.10) Trio Not won; £649.38 to Doncaster 11/9/97
OWNER Sheikh Ahmed Al Maktoum (LAMBOURN) BRED Sheikh Ahmed Bin Rashid Al Maktoum
WEIGHT FOR AGE 3yo-9lb

OFFICIAL EXPLANATION Pietro Bembo (IRE): no explanation offered.

2373 Alhosaam came with a good run on the outside to take the lead approaching the two-furlong marker and held on all-out. (12/1)

1974 Renzo (IRE), held up at the back of the field, came with a storming run on the outside from two furlongs out. He had every chance inside the last furlong but, once again, his high head carriage gave the impression that he could have pulled out a bit more. (25/1)

3970 Tallulah Belle stood still when the stalls opened and lost many lengths. She made good headway to have every chance approaching the final furlong, but the effort of making up so much ground left her with no reserves for the finish. She should win soon. (25/1)

3491 Pistol (IRE) crept into a challenging position below the distance, but then came under strong pressure and could find no more. (10/1)

3491* Your Most Welcome ran on well in the last two furlongs but too late to trouble the leaders. (12/1)

3815 Tappeto came with a good run on the inside two furlongs out, but his head went up when pressure was applied at the distance. (14/1: 10/1-16/1)

3992* Gold Desire moved up to join the leaders at the two-furlong marker, but weakened under pressure in the final furlong. (7/1)

2952 Water Flower (12/1: op 8/1)

3689 Mutadarra (IRE) could never get beyond mid-division and his backers never held much hope. (6/1)

3234 Pietro Bembo (IRE), blinkered for the first time, was on the heels of the leaders until weakening early in the straight. (6/1: op 4/1)

T/Plpt: £89.20 (211.79 Tckts). T/Qdpt: £23.20 (52.74 Tckts) AK

3788-CHEPSTOW (L-H) (Good)

Thursday September 11th

WEATHER: overcast WIND: nil

4109 PASTURE H'CAP (0-80) (3-Y.O+) (Class D)

2-15 (2-18) **1m 2f 36y** £3,946.25 (£1,190.00: £577.50: £271.25) Stalls: Low GOING minus 0.02 sec per fur (G)

				SP	RR	SF
3616[9]	**Kewarra (74)** (BRMillman) **3-9-1** MFenton(9) (lw: a.p: chsd ldr over 2f out: led ins fnl f: jst hld on)	—	**1**	10/1	84	59
3026[9]	**Bubble Wings (FR) (67)** (SPCWoods) **5-9-1** WRyan(5) (swtg: hld up: hdwy 3f out: n.m.r over 1f out: r.o wl ins fnl f)	s.h	**2**	16/1	77	59
3466[6]	**Monument (61)** (JSKing) **5-8-6**(3) RHavlin(10) (led: clr 5f out: hdd ins fnl f)	1¾	**3**	14/1	68	50
3184[4]	**Regal Reprimand (70)** (GLewis) **3-8-11** PaulEddery(1) (hld up: hdwy over 3f out: rdn over 2f out: r.o one pce)	2½	**4**	8/1[3]	73	48
3793[6]	**Sea Danzig (53)** (JJBridger) **4-8-1** NAdams(4) (lw: sn prom: chsd ldr over 3f out tl over 2f out: wknd fnl f)	2½	**5**	25/1	52	34
3916[8]	**Danegold (IRE) (60)** (MRChannon) **5-8-8v** GCarter(8) (s.s: hdwy over 1f out: nvr nrr)	nk	**6**	16/1	59	41

				SP	RR	SF
3246[3]	**Roufontaine (77)** (WRMuir) **6-9-11** DaneO'Neill(12) (hld up: swtchd rt over 3f out: rdn & no hdwy fnl 2f)	¾	**7**	6/1 [1]	75	57
3311[4]	**Missfortuna (68)** (SirMarkPrescott) **3-8-9** SSanders(14) (lw: s.s: hdwy over 6f out: rdn 3f out: sn wknd)	nk	**8**	8/1 [3]	65	40
3916[17]	**Kings Assembly (72)** (PWHarris) **5-9-6** MRimmer(16) (swtg: prom tl wknd over 2f out)	nk	**9**	20/1	69	51
3793*	**African-Pard (IRE) (68)** (DHaydnJones) **5-9-2** SDrowne(2) (n.d)	1¼	**10**	7/1 [2]	63	45
3864[8]	**Alarmist (73)** (RCharlton) **3-9-0v[1]** DHolland(3) (lw: hld up: rdn & wknd over 2f out)	nk	**11**	14/1	67	42
3475[4]	**Pay Homage (70)** (IABalding) **9-9-4** MartinDwyer(15) (lw: s.s: nvr nr ldrs)	½	**12**	9/1	64	46
3768[7]	**Seattle Swing (78)** (MrsAJPerrett) **3-9-0(5)** GMilligan(11) (lw: hld up: hdwy over 3f out: wknd over 2f out)	½	**13**	12/1	71	46
2824[8]	**Oberons Boy (IRE) (53)** (SDow) **4-7-8(7)** PDoe(6) (b: bkwd: a bhd)	2½	**14**	20/1	42	24
	Indrapura (IRE) (54) (JELong) **5-8-2** GBardwell(13) (w ldr tl wknd over 3f out: t.o)	14	**15**	50/1	21	3
	Hillzah (USA) (78) (RBastiman) **9-9-7(5)** HBastiman(7) (bkwd: a bhd: t.o fnl 3f)	3	**16**	33/1	40	22

(SP 119.2%) **16 Rn**

2m 10.1 (4.80) CSF £132.87 CT £2,039.02 TOTE £15.80: £3.10 £3.20 £6.80 £1.90 (£239.60) Trio £440.50; £105.49 to Doncaster 12/9/97
OWNER Mr G. Palmer (CULLOMPTON) BRED Mrs M. Palmer and G. Palmer
WEIGHT FOR AGE 3yo-7lb

3246* Kewarra, disappointing when poorly drawn at Lingfield last time, was again 4lb higher than when scoring over course and distances and is the sort who needs to be coaxed along. (10/1)
2593 Bubble Wings (FR) ran her best race of the season. She only just failed to peg back the winner and might stay further. (16/1)
3466 Monument looked much happier forcing the pace than when held up last time. (14/1)
3184 Regal Reprimand had been pulled up on soft ground over hurdles last week. (8/1)
3793 Sea Danzig, dropped 2lb, was again trying a mile and a quarter and will need to be more patiently ridden to last home. (25/1)
482 Danegold (IRE) had slipped to a mark 18lb lower than when he last won two years ago. (16/1)
3246 Roufontaine is 9lb above the highest mark off which she has scored. (6/1)
3311 Missfortuna (8/1: 6/1-9/1)
2287 Alarmist (14/1: 10/1-16/1)

4110 LESTER PIGGOTT CONDITIONS STKS (3-Y.O F) (Class C)

2-45 (2-46) **1m 2f 36y** £4,500.80 (£1,635.80: £795.40: £337.00: £146.00) Stalls: Low GOING minus 0.02 sec per fur (G)

				SP	RR	SF
3909*	**Bina Gardens (75)** (HRACecil) **3-8-13** WRyan(5) (lw: hld up: hdwy to ld over 2f out: rdn out)	—	**1**	6/1	103	54
3916*	**Cugina (84)** (GBBalding) **3-8-10** SDrowne(2) (hld up: rdn over 3f out: hdwy & hung lft over 2f out: chsd wnr over 1f out: no imp)	2	**2**	7/2 [3]	97	48
3797[3]	**Zalitzine (USA) (92)** (MRStoute) **3-8-13** DHolland(3) (lw: chsd ldr: rdn 3f out: one pce fnl 2f)	3½	**3**	5/2 [2]	94	45
3190[9]	**Priena (IRE) (90)** (DRLoder) **3-8-10** GCarter(1) (lw: led: sn clr: hdd over 2f out: one pce)	½	**4**	2/1 [1]	91	42
	Folgore (USA) (JLDunlop) **3-8-10** PaulEddery(4) (bit bkwd: hld up in rr: rdn 5f out: t.o fnl 3f)	21	**5**	8/1	58	9

(SP 109.5%) **5 Rn**

2m 10.5 (5.20) CSF £23.67 TOTE £5.00: £1.70 £1.90 (£6.70) OWNER Mr K. Abdulla (NEWMARKET) BRED Juddmonte Farms
3909* Bina Gardens, said to have taken time to come to hand this season, followed up her Ripon success despite some tail-swishing. (6/1)
3916* Cugina was inclined to duck in behind and gave the impression she really needs some give in the ground. (7/2)
3797 Zalitzine (USA) is proving a bit disappointing. (5/2)
1875 Priena (IRE) had been finding things tough in competitive handicaps after finishing second in a couple of Listed races. (2/1)
Folgore (USA) (8/1: 6/1-9/1)

4111 PAT EDDERY MAIDEN STKS (I) (2-Y.O) (Class D)

3-20 (3-29) **7f 16y** £3,129.00 (£942.00: £456.00: £213.00) Stalls: High GOING: 0.06 sec per fur (G)

				SP	RR	SF
	Casino King (IRE) (PWChapple-Hyam) **2-8-11(3)** RHavlin(10) (leggy: unf: s.i.s: sn trckng ldrs: rdn over 2f out: rn green & led ins fnl f: rdn out)	—	**1**	8/1 [3]	85+	30
3806[2]	**Khalas** (BWHills) **2-9-0** GCarter(7) (a.p: led over 1f out tl ins fnl f: r.o)	nk	**2**	4/5 [1]	84	29
3687[15]	**Green Jacket** (JLDunlop) **2-9-0** WJO'Connor(3) (a.p: rdn over 1f out: one pce)	3	**3**	50/1	78	23
3745[2]	**Air Attache (USA)** (GLewis) **2-9-0** PaulEddery(13) (led: rdn over 2f out: hdd over 1f out: wknd ins fnl f)	½	**4**	9/2 [2]	76	21
	Mutafarij (USA) (EALDunlop) **2-9-0** MRimmer(11) (w'like: str: bkwd: s.s: swtchd lft & hdwy over 1f out: nrst fin)	hd	**5**	14/1	76+	21
3686[6]	**Da Boss (79)** (WRMuir) **2-9-0** WRyan(2) (lw: no hdwy fnl 2f)	nk	**6**	14/1	76	21
3598[10]	**Blue Monk (IRE)** (IABalding) **2-9-0** MartinDwyer(6) (bit bkwd: nvr nrr)	nk	**7**	16/1	75	20
3973[9]	**Watkins (66)** (FMurphy) **2-9-0** JFanning(9) (chsd ldr: rdn over 3f out: wknd wl over 1f out)	2	**8**	50/1	70	15
3726[6]	**Genius (IRE)** (PFICole) **2-9-0** CRutter(4) (bkwd: bhd fnl 2f)	2	**9**	16/1	66	11
3861[11]	**Lady Felix** (SMellor) **2-8-9** RPerham(8) (bit bkwd: plld hrd early: bhd fnl 2f)	5	**10**	66/1	50	—
	Arcane Star (IRE) (APJarvis) **2-9-0** SDrowne(1) (w'like: scope: bkwd: s.s: a bhd)	5	**11**	33/1	43	—
	Lycian (IRE) (SirMarkPrescott) **2-9-0** SSanders(12) (gd sort: bit bkwd: dwlt: rdn over 3f out: sn bhd)	¾	**12**	12/1	42	—
1872[17]	***Gunboat Diplomacy*** (MJFetherston-Godley) **2-9-0** DHolland(14) (Withdrawn not under Starter's orders: burst out under front of stalls: uns rdr & bolted)		**W**	50/1	—	—

(SP 128.0%) **12 Rn**

1m 25.2 (5.90) CSF £14.09 TOTE £8.90: £1.60 £1.10 £9.60 (£10.10) Trio £139.60 OWNER Mr R. E. Sangster (MARLBOROUGH) BRED Swettenham Stud
Casino King (IRE), a half-brother to mile and a half winner Tintara, was described as a lazy worker who had been showing ability at home. Despite displaying definite signs of inexperience, he proved too good for the hot-pot. (8/1: 6/1-10/1)
3806 Khalas could not make his previous racecourse experience tell against a rival who ran green. (4/5: op 2/1)
Green Jacket, a half-brother to several winner including Private Tender, showed his outing last time at Kempton to be all wrong. (50/1)
3745 Air Attache (USA) had plenty of use made of him here. (9/2: 9/4-5/1)
Mutafarij (USA), a half-brother to amongst others French 1,000 Guineas winner Ta Rib and Tabdea, was getting the hang of things late on and is one to note. (14/1: 7/1-16/1)
3686 Da Boss did not appear to be given too hard a race and might be the sort for a nursery. (14/1: 8/1-16/1)
Blue Monk (IRE), a half-brother to useful sprinter Blue Siren and a ten-furlong winner in Norway, is being brought along quietly and seems to have ability. (16/1)
Lycian (IRE) (12/1: 6/1-14/1)

4112 MEADOW H'CAP (0-60) (3-Y.O+) (Class F)

3-50 (4-03) **7f 16y** £3,037.50 (£850.00: £412.50) Stalls: High GOING: 0.06 sec per fur (G)

Form	Horse / details	Dist	Pos	SP	RR	SF
3987[3]	**Mybotye (58)** (RBastiman) **4-9-12** WRyan(8) (a.p: led ins fnl f: all out)	—	1	8/1[2]	70	53
4059*	**Samara Song (59)** (IPWilliams) **4-9-8**(5) 6x PRoberts(1) (lw: hld up: hdwy wl over 1f out: ev ch ins fnl f: r.o)	nk	2	9/1[3]	70	53
3642[4]	**Akalim (57)** (LGCottrell) **4-9-11** DHolland(18) (a.p: ev ch ins fnl f: r.o)	s.h	3	16/1	68	51
3143*	**Welcome Heights (55)** (MJFetherston-Godley) **3-9-5** FNorton(14) (lw: bhd tl hdwy 2f out: hrd rdn & r.o wl ins fnl f)	s.h	4	7/1[1]	66	45
3465[14]	**Queen of Shannon (IRE) (53)** (AWCarroll) **9-9-0**(7) RStudholme(11) (s.s: hdwy over 1f out: r.o ins fnl f)	1½	5	20/1	61	44
4048[11]	**Maladerie (IRE) (55)** (MRChannon) **3-9-5** GCarter(16) (bhd: rdn over 3f out: hdwy over 1f out: r.o)	1¼	6	20/1	60	39
3690[2]	**Mr Speaker (IRE) (60)** (CFWall) **4-10-0** SSanders(13) (hld up: no hdwy fnl 2f)	2½	7	14/1	59	42
3690[12]	**Speedy Classic (USA) (57)** (MJHeaton-Ellis) **8-9-11** AClark(20) (lw: led: rdn over 2f out: hdd & wknd ins fnl f)	1	8	8/1[2]	54	37
3058[4]	**Native Rhythm (IRE) (60)** (PWChapple-Hyam) **3-9-7**(3) RHavlin(19) (lw: chsd ldrs: rdn over 2f out: wknd over 1f out)	2	9	16/1	52	31
2533[7]	**Mislemani (IRE) (51)** (AGNewcombe) **7-9-2**(3) DGriffiths(7) (bit bkwd: prom 5f)	½	10	14/1	42	25
3718[4]	**Clytha Hill Lad (56)** (JMBradley) **6-9-10** GHind(5) (b: hld up: eased whn btn over 1f out)	½	11	9/1[3]	46	29
3249[4]	**Abtaal (51)** (RJHodges) **7-9-2**(3) PPMurphy(15) (a abt same pl)	s.h	12	20/1	41	24
	Spicetress (55) (JLSpearing) **3-9-5** DaneO'Neill(4) (nvr nr ldrs)	¾	13	40/1	43	22
3930[7]	**Scathebury (55)** (KRBurke) **4-9-9** JFEgan(2) (lw: plld hrd: prom over 5f)	nk	14	25/1	43	26
2698[11]	**Caudillo (IRE) (60)** (MrsPNDutfield) **4-9-9**(5) AimeeCook(3) (lw: dwlt a bhd)	½	15	16/1	47	30
2422[6]	**Macgillycuddy (IRE) (56)** (MrsPNDutfield) **8-9-10** CRutter(6) (bhd: rdn over 3f out: hmpd 2f out)	hd	16	33/1	42	25
120[5]	**Double March (60)** (KTIvory) **4-10-0** MartinDwyer(17) (dwlt: a bhd)	½	17	33/1	45	28
3860[2]	**Dawalib (USA) (50)** (DHaydnJones) **7-9-4b1** SDrowne(9) (chsd ldr: rdn over 2f out: sn wknd)	1¾	18	12/1	31	14
3980[2]	**Zermatt (IRE) (55)** (MDIUsher) **7-9-9** RPerham(10) (prom over 4f)	¾	19	12/1	35	18
3697[4]	**Swan Island (57)** (WMBrisbourne) **3-9-7b** AGarth(12) (b.hind: s.s: a bhd: eased whn no ch fnl 2f)	20	20	20/1	—	—
				(SP 132.3%)	**20 Rn**	

1m 24.2 (4.90) CSF £66.56 CT £1,086.30 TOTE £6.90: £2.10 £2.00 £3.50 £3.00 (£13.70) Trio £172.40 OWNER Mr Anthony Moroney (WETHERBY) BRED R. S. A. Urquhart

WEIGHT FOR AGE 3yo-4lb

STEWARDS' ENQUIRY Studholme susp. 20-21/9/97 (careless riding).

3987 Mybotye found the combination of a different type of bit and a pricker on his left side doing the trick. (8/1)

4059* Samara Song could not quite defy a penalty for his Leicester success two days ago. (9/1)

3642 Akalim, dropped 4lb, was by no means inconvenienced by this extra furlong. (16/1)

3143* Welcome Heights, raised 7lb for his Doncaster win, was 15lb higher than his win over six here earlier in July. (7/1)

2488* Queen of Shannon (IRE), down 5lb, was 4lb higher than when winning a seller at Warwick over a mile and does seem to require that trip. (20/1)

3923 Maladerie (IRE) was making a quick reappearance, being set to go up 3lb at the weekend. (20/1)

3251 Speedy Classic (USA) (8/1: op 12/1)

4113 PAT EDDERY MAIDEN STKS (II) (2-Y.O) (Class D)

4-20 (4-34) **7f 16y** £3,129.00 (£942.00: £456.00: £213.00) Stalls: High GOING: 0.06 sec per fur (G)

Form	Horse / details	Dist	Pos	SP	RR	SF
3094[11]	**Smart Squall (USA)** (LordHuntingdon) **2-9-0** WRyan(11) (s.s: hdwy over 2f out: hrd rdn over 1f out: r.o to ld wl ins fnl f)	—	1	8/1[3]	81	24
3489[6]	**Tumbleweed Hero** (BJMeehan) **2-9-0** MTebbutt(5) (lw: a.p: led over 2f out tl wl ins fnl f)	¾	2	Evens[1]	79	22
3494[12]	**Chief Cashier** (GBBalding) **2-9-0** SDrowne(9) (hld up: hdwy over 2f out: ev ch fnl f: nt qckn)	1¾	3	16/1	75	18
3253[5]	**Khattaff (IRE)** (MajorWRHern) **2-9-0** DHolland(12) (chsd ldr: led over 3f out tl over 2f out: btn whn hung lft ins fnl f)	1¼	4	8/1[3]	73	16
3783[6]	**The Magistrate (IRE)** (MBlanshard) **2-8-11**(3) PPMurphy(6) (hld up: hdwy over 2f out: hung lft over 1f out: one pce fnl f)	1¼	5	12/1	70	13
3783[8]	**Jollyhack** (JGMO'Shea) **2-9-0** DaneO'Neill(7) (hdwy whn hung lft 2f out: no imp)	4	6	33/1	61	4
3687[W]	**Noreastern (IRE)** (PFICole) **2-9-0** CRutter(8) (leggy: unf: sn rdn along: chsd ldrs over 4f)	5	7	6/1[2]	49	—
3193[10]	**Ocean Line (IRE)** (APJarvis) **2-9-0** AMcGlone(13) (lw: bhd fnl 2f)	nk	8	50/1	49	—
	Rhein Hill (IRE) (PWHarris) **2-9-0** AClark(4) (w'like: scope: bit bkwd: s.s: a bhd)	½	9	14/1	48	—
1744[11]	**Goodwood Cavalier** (JLDunlop) **2-9-0** WJO'Connor(2) (bkwd: rdn over 3f out: a bhd)	2	10	16/1	43	—
3783[16]	**Carlasanta (IRE)** (AGNewcombe) **2-8-9** FNorton(1) (bhd fnl 2f)	1½	11	50/1	35	—
	Desert Valentine (LGCottrell) **2-9-0** MFenton(3) (leggy: bkwd: tk keen hold: led over 3f: wknd over 2f out)	6	12	50/1	26	—
	Son of Good Times (PGMurphy) **2-9-0** SSanders(10) (w'like: bkwd: prom over 4f)	2½	13	50/1	20	—
3426[9]	**Thundering Papoose** (APJames) **2-8-2**(7) JFowle(14) (dwlt: rdn over 3f out: a bhd: t.o)	9	14	66/1	—	—
				(SP 124.9%)	**14 Rn**	

1m 25.7 (6.40) CSF £15.01 TOTE £9.40: £2.00 £1.50 £2.50 (£5.40) Trio £18.10 OWNER Mr George Ward (WEST ILSLEY) BRED Centaur Farms Inc.

3094 Smart Squall (USA), who has had remedial stalls training, really appreciated this longer trip and the further they went the better he got. (8/1: 4/1-9/1)

3489 Tumbleweed Hero, stepping up to seven, could not hold the winner but is knocking firmly at the door. (Evens)

1872 Chief Cashier possibly found the ground a bit lively at Salisbury last time. (16/1)

3253 Khattaff (IRE) is well related, being a half-brother to amongst others Middle Park winner Balla Cove. (8/1)

3783 The Magistrate (IRE) had the longer distance but showed signs of a little inexperience. (12/1)

Noreastern (IRE) (6/1: 3/1-7/1)

Rhein Hill (IRE) (14/1: 5/1-16/1)

4114 COPSE (S) STKS (3-Y.O+) (Class G)

4-50 (5-10) **1m 14y** £2,496.50 (£699.00: £339.50) Stalls: High GOING: 0.06 sec per fur (G)

Form	Horse / details	Dist	Pos	SP	RR	SF
2390[R]	**Rock Falcon (IRE) (85)** (LadyHerries) **4-9-8b1** MTebbutt(18) (mde all: clr over 3f out: v.easily)	—	1	8/1	73+	48

				SP	RR	SF
3767[5]	**The Executor (62)** (RJO'Sullivan) **7-9-8** WRyan(6) (hld up: rdn over 3f out: hdwy over 1f out: r.o ins fnl f: no ch w wnr)	4	**2**	9/2[1]	65	40
3848[10]	**Dancing Lawyer (44)** (KRBurke) **6-9-3** DaneO'Neill(15) (lw: hld up: hdwy over 2f out: chsd wnr 1f out: no imp)	1	**3**	20/1	58	33
3897[6]	**Bright Fountain (IRE)** (HCandy) **3-8-7** AMcGlone(5) (hdwy over 2f out: r.o ins fnl f)	½	**4**	11/1	52	22
3814[3]	**Pegasus Bay** (MissAEEmbiricos) **6-9-3** GCarter(19) (b: b.hind: chsd wnr tl wknd fnl f)	hd	**5**	13/2	57	32
3848[4]	**Runic Symbol (35)** (MBlanshard) **6-9-3** CRutter(17) (rdn over 3f out: hdwy over 2f out: one pce fnl f)	2	**6**	20/1	53	28
3787[6]	**Mimosa (56)** (SDow) **4-8-12** JFEgan(10) (nvr nr to chal)	3	**7**	6/1[3]	42	17
	Gemolly (IRE) (MartynMeade) **4-8-5**(7) RBrisland(14) (bkwd: chsd ldrs: btn whn edgd rt over 1f out)	1¼	**8**	66/1	40	15
3787[8]	**Noeprob (USA) (45)** (RJHodges) **7-8-9**(3) PPMurphy(1) (lw: hld up: hdwy 3f out: wknd 2f out)	1½	**9**	12/1	37	12
3254[11]	**Rock Island Line (IRE) (70)** (JBerry) **3-8-12**(5) PRoberts(2) (dwlt: nvr nr ldrs)	2	**10**	5/1[2]	43	13
2723[9]	**Move Smartly (IRE) (42)** (MrsLStubbs) **7-9-3v** DHolland(11) (prom tl hrd rdn & wknd over 2f out)	1¾	**11**	25/1	34	9
2783[11]	**Jewel Fighter** (CASmith) **3-8-7** MFenton(12) (swtg: a bhd)	5	**12**	66/1	19	—
	Accommodate You (JMBradley) **4-8-12** SDrowne(20) (bkwd: s.s: a bhd)	8	**13**	66/1	3	—
	Grovefair Dancer (IRE) (60) (FJYardley) **3-8-7** NAdams(3) (bit bkwd: bhd fnl 3f)	hd	**14**	50/1	3	—
3230[9]	**Forward Miss (25)** (CJBenstead) **3-8-7** TWilliams(7) (swtg: a bhd)	1¾	**15**	66/1	—	—
3972[5]	**Saltando (IRE) (43)** (PatMitchell) **6-9-3v** PBloomfield(8) (rdn over 3f out: a bhd)	2½	**16**	33/1	—	—
3249[13]	**Benicia Boy** (JCMcConnochie) **5-9-3** MWigham(4) (bit bkwd: bhd fnl 3f: t.o)	dist	**17**	66/1	—	—
2228[7]	**Baba Sadhu** (PJMakin) **3-8-12** SSanders(13) (bkwd: a bhd: t.o)	1¼	**18**	14/1	—	—
	Dear John (IRE) (MissAStokell) **4-9-3** AClark(9) (bkwd: s.s: a wl bhd: t.o)	21	**19**	25/1	—	—
1426[7]	**Pow Wow (45)** (PEccles) **3-8-7**(5) GFaulkner(16) (bkwd: prom: rdn over 4f out: sn wknd: t.o)	6	**20**	66/1	—	—
				(SP 127.3%)	**20 Rn**	

1m 36.9 (5.70) CSF £36.32 TOTE £10.60: £3.00 £2.20 £14.80 (£58.50) Trio £126.20 OWNER Mr E. Reitel (LITTLEHAMPTON) BRED Juddmonte Farms
WEIGHT FOR AGE 3yo-5lb
Bt in 8,500gns

1087* Rock Falcon (IRE), switching to blinkers this time, has been treated by a horse psychologist, having refused to race in his two previous runs. Looking a reformed character, he justified market support with ridiculous ease. (8/1)
3767 The Executor, back to a mile, came through to win the separate race for the runner-up spot. (9/2: 3/1-5/1)
3227 Dancing Lawyer, like the rest of the field, found the winner proving a revelation. (20/1)
3897 Bright Fountain (IRE) was taking a drop in both class and distance. (11/1: 8/1-12/1)
3814 Pegasus Bay, reverting to a mile, may have cut his own throat in vain pursuit of the winner. (13/2)
3848 Runic Symbol is having difficulty settling on the right trip but his sole win did come over the extra quarter-mile. (20/1)
3787 Mimosa (6/1: 9/2-7/1)
Baba Sadhu (14/1: 10/1-16/1)

4115 SPINNEY H'CAP (0-65) (3-Y.O+) (Class F)

5-20 (5-41) **5f 16y** £2,827.50 (£790.00: £382.50) Stalls: High GOING: 0.06 sec per fur (G)

				SP	RR	SF
3871[12]	**General Sir Peter (IRE) (46)** (NACallaghan) **5-8-4b**(5) AmandaSanders(2) (hdwy over 1f out: sustained chal fnl f: led last stride)	—	**1**	33/1	57	39
3984[2]	**Songsheet (65)** (MSSaunders) **4-9-11**(3) RHavlin(11) (hdwy over 2f out: led ins fnl f: hdd last stride)	s.h	**2**	6/1[2]	76	58
4048[8]	**Pointer (55)** (MrsPNDutfield) **5-9-4** CRutter(4) (lw: hdwy far side over 1f out: ev ch ins fnl f: r.o)	s.h	**3**	10/1[3]	66	48
3393[9]	**Will To Win (50)** (PGMurphy) **3-8-12** MFenton(6) (b.hind: a.p: led over 2f out tl ins fnl f)	1¾	**4**	16/1	55	36
3693[8]	**Flying Harold (46)** (MRChannon) **4-8-6**(3) PPMurphy(17) (hdwy over 1f out: r.o)	s.h	**5**	10/1[3]	51	33
3761[2]	**Captain Carat (58)** (DNicholls) **6-9-7b** JFanning(7) (s.s & swtchd rt: hdwy fnl f: nrst fin)	1½	**6**	11/2[1]	58	40
3898[8]	**Runs in the Family (60)** (GMMcCourt) **5-9-2v**(7) RStudholme(19) (led stands' side: one pce fnl 2f)	½	**7**	10/1[3]	59	41
3290[7]	**Robellion (49)** (DWPArbuthnot) **6-8-12v** WRyan(8) (lw: hdwy far side over 2f out: wknd over 1f out)	nk	**8**	14/1	47	29
3851*	**Mystical (65)** (MrsLStubbs) **3-9-13v** TWilliams(9) (nvr nr to chal)	1½	**9**	10/1[3]	58	39
3287[15]	**Windrush Boy (49)** (MRBosley) **7-8-7**(5) AimeeCook(12) (lw: prom stands' side over 3f)	1	**10**	16/1	39	21
3606[4]	**Blue Lamp (USA) (53)** (MAJarvis) **3-8-10**(5) PRoberts(13) (n.d)	½	**11**	14/1	41	22
3398[12]	**Littlestone Rocket (56)** (WRMuir) **3-9-4b** DaneO'Neill(1) (n.d)	¾	**12**	20/1	42	23
3296[7]	**Chakra (49)** (SDow) **3-8-11** JFEgan(18) (lw: chsd ldrs stands' side over 2f)	1¼	**13**	20/1	31	12
3984[15]	**High Domain (IRE) (61)** (JLSpearing) **6-9-10b** PaulEddery(16) (chsd ldr stands' side 3f)	½	**14**	20/1	41	23
3898[9]	**Threeplay (IRE) (55)** (JAkehurst) **3-9-3** MTebbutt(20) (outpcd)	¾	**15**	33/1	33	14
4016[12]	**Stock Hill Dancer (53)** (BJMeehan) **3-8-8b**(7) GHannon(3) (swtg: led over 2f: wknd over 1f out)	2½	**16**	20/1	23	4
1966[11]	**Hever Golf Lover (IRE) (50)** (TJNaughton) **3-8-12** AClark(10) (a bhd)	¾	**17**	20/1	18	—
3868[9]	**Life On The Street (63)** (DNicholls) **3-9-11** SSanders(14) (lw: s.s: a bhd)	3½	**18**	16/1	20	1
3850[3]	**Incatime (55)** (AGFoster) **3-9-3b** DHolland(5) (swtg: spd far side 3f)	¾	**19**	33/1	9	—
				(SP 129.6%)	**19 Rn**	

60.4 secs (3.40) CSF £190.20 CT £2,029.01 TOTE £34.50: £4.90 £1.50 £2.80 £4.60 (£186.00) Trio £368.80 OWNER Mrs Anna Sanders (NEWMARKET) BRED Hamilton Bloodstock (UK) Ltd
WEIGHT FOR AGE 3yo-1lb

972 General Sir Peter (IRE) sprang a surprise off a mark 26lb lower than when winning the second of two nurseries at Doncaster as a juvenile. (33/1)
3984 Songsheet, 2lb lower than when second at Salisbury, was just pipped under a welter burden. (6/1)
2232 Pointer had run well after a break at Bath on Monday. (10/1)
2554 Will To Win, down 2lb, had been given a month off following a couple of below-par efforts. (16/1)
2384 Flying Harold, 4lb higher than when scoring here over six in June, does seem better suited by the additional furlong. (10/1)
3761 Captain Carat, raised 2lb, was apparently the first runner at the course for his stable. (11/2: 4/1-6/1)

T/Plpt: £153.70 (115.43 Tckts). T/Qdpt: £6.90 (181.85 Tckts) KH

4096-DONCASTER (L-H) (Good to firm, Firm patches in st)
Thursday September 11th
WEATHER: overcast WIND: almost nil

4116 RALPH RAPER MEMORIAL PRINCE OF WALES CUP NURSERY H'CAP (2-Y.O) (Class C)
2-05 (2-06) **1m (straight)** £20,050.00 (£7,450.00: £3,600.00: £1,500.00: £625.00: £275.00) Stalls: High GOING minus 0.50 sec per fur (F)

				SP	RR	SF
2905*	**Lend A Hand (94)** (MJohnston) **2-9-5** JWeaver(4) (lw: racd far side: mde all: shkn up over 1f out: r.o wl)	—	**1**	8/1 2	103+	58
3780*	**Rabah (88)** (JLDunlop) **2-8-13** RHills(10) (lw: racd far side: hdwy to chse wnr appr fnl f: r.o: nt pce to chal)	1½	**2**	12/1	94	49
3688 6	**The Glow-Worm (IRE) (88)** (BWHills) **2-8-13** PatEddery(3) (racd far side: hdwy 2f out: styd on: nrst fin)	2½	**3**	14/1	89	44
4044*	**Kim's Brave (88)** (BJMeehan) **2-8-13b** 8x KDarley(5) (chsd ldrs far side: one pce fnl 2½f)	1½	**4**	16/1	86	41
3789*	**Monsajem (USA) (83)** (SbinSuroor) **2-8-8** LDettori(19) (in tch stands' side: hdwy 3f out: styd on: nvr able to chal)	1½	**5**	11/2 1	78	33
4014 2	**Chinaider (IRE) (76)** (DNicholls) **2-7-8**(7) RWinston(6) (chsd ldrs far side tl outpcd fnl 2½f)	1¼	**6**	14/1	69	24
3794*	**Night Flyer (79)** (JWHills) **2-8-1**(3) MHenry(2) (prom far side 5f: wknd)	1½	**7**	25/1	69	24
3802 6	**Naviasky (IRE) (80)** (MrsJRRamsden) **2-8-2**(3) DSweeney(12) (lw: bhd stands' side: nt clr run over 2f out & over 1f out: r.o towards fin)	hd	**8**	16/1	69	24
3802*	**Bobbydazzle (79)** (DrJDScargill) **2-8-4** JQuinn(7) (swtchd rt s: hdwy stands' side ½-wy: rdn & no imp fnl 3f)	nk	**9**	14/1	68	23
3757*	**Royal Bounty (IRE) (80)** (MajorWRHern) **2-8-5** TSprake(14) (w ldrs stands' side: rdn 3f out: no imp)	1½	**10**	9/1 3	66	21
3932 13	**Lady Yavanna (74)** (KMcAuliffe) **2-7-8**(5) APolli(16) (disp ld stands' side 5f: wknd)	¾	**11**	50/1	58	13
3686 3	**Saddlers' Roe (IRE) (75)** (BWHills) **2-7-11**(3) PFessey(18) (swtg: chsd ldrs stands' side tl outpcd fnl 2½f)	½	**12**	14/1	58	13
3387 5	**Balance The Books (76)** (RHannon) **2-8-1** DBiggs(24) (trckd ldrs stands' side: rdn 3f out: sn btn)	nk	**13**	20/1	59	14
3862 8	**Praetorian Gold (72)** (RHannon) **2-7-11** DWright(23) (cl up stands' side over 5f)	d.h	**13**	33/1	55	10
3789 2	**Tensile (IRE) (81)** (LMCumani) **2-8-3**(3) RFfrench(17) (racd stands' side: effrt ½-wy: n.d)	½	**15**	14/1	63	18
3802 13	**Panama House (77)** (TDEasterby) **2-8-2** LCharnock(13) (chsd ldrs stands' side over 5f)	½	**16**	25/1	58	13
3802 2	**After The Rain (85)** (BWHills) **2-8-10** MHills(11) (racd stands' side: hdwy ½-wy: rdn & no imp)	½	**17**	8/1 2	65	20
3908 5	**Buzz (91)** (CWThornton) **2-9-2** DeanMcKeown(15) (trckd ldrs stands' side 5f: wknd)	1½	**18**	20/1	68	23
3117 6	**Tarashaan (76)** (SirMarkPrescott) **2-8-1** GDuffield(21) (led stands' side: rdn 3f out: sn btn)	hd	**19**	12/1	52	7
3687 3	**Balaclava (IRE) (80)** (EALDunlop) **2-8-5** MRoberts(9) (racd far side: wl outpcd fr ½-wy)	1¼	**20**	16/1	54	9
3750 3	**Narrogin (USA) (72)** (MRChannon) **2-7-11v** AMackay(20) (w ldrs stands' side 5f: sn rdn & btn)	10	**21**	33/1	26	—
				(SP 139.0%)	**21 Rn**	

1m 37.52 (1.56 under 2y best) (0.32) CSF £93.65 CT £1,260.69 TOTE £6.30: £1.60 £3.50 £3.40 £10.30 (£48.20) Trio £324.30 OWNER Maktoum Al Maktoum (MIDDLEHAM) BRED Gainsborough Stud Management Ltd

2905* Lend A Hand continued his improvement here and, looking magnificent beforehand, won in tremendous style. (8/1)
3780* Rabah ran his heart out but, despite a valiant effort, he had to admit he had met one far too good. (12/1)
3688 The Glow-Worm (IRE) gave the impression that he needs either easier ground or a stiffer test of stamina. (14/1)
4044* Kim's Brave is obviously in good heart and ran well again here but his limitations were exposed late on. (16/1)
3789* Monsajem (USA) has the look of a bit of a character about him, but he certainly has ability and, as it turned out here, he was drawn on the wrong side, so not so much should be made of this. (11/2)
4014 Chinaider (IRE) ran quite well but just failed to see the trip out. (14/1)
3802 Naviasky (IRE) finished second on the stands side but met with a fair amount of trouble and still gives the impression that there is a lot more to come. (16/1)
3802* Bobbydazzle made the mistake of switching to join the stands'-side group just after the start, and ran a useful race in the circumstances. (14/1)

4117 BRITAIN'S FASTEST RAILWAY PARK STKS (Gp 3) (3-Y.O+) (Class A)
2-35 (2-35) **1m (round)** £21,450.00 (£7,950.00: £3,825.00: £1,575.00: £637.50: £262.50) Stalls: High GOING minus 0.50 sec per fur (F)

				SP	RR	SF
4003 2	**Almushtarak (IRE) (106)** (KMahdi) **4-9-0** RCochrane(4) (trckd ldrs: shkn up to ld wl over 1f out: hld on wl)	—	**1**	25/1	120	82
3577*	**Decorated Hero (117)** (JHMGosden) **5-9-4** LDettori(5) (lw: hld up & bhd: effrt over 2f out: chal ins fnl f: nt qckn towards fin)	nk	**2**	9/4 1	123	85
1740*	**Samara (IRE) (105)** (JLDunlop) **4-8-11** PatEddery(9) (a cl up: rdn to chal 2f out: kpt on u.p)	hd	**3**	11/1	116	78
3728 2	**Poteen (USA) (119)** (LMCumani) **3-8-9b1** KFallon(7) (lw: hld up: effrt 3f out: sn hrd drvn: edgd lft & kpt on fnl f: no imp)	¾	**4**	9/4 1	118	75
2009 4	**Nwaamis (USA) (110)** (JLDunlop) **5-9-0** RHills(2) (lw: led: qcknd over 3f out: hdd wl over 1f out: kpt on same pce)	2½	**5**	7/1 2	113	75
3725 2	**Hawksley Hill (IRE) (103)** (MrsJRRamsden) **4-9-0v** JFortune(1) (hld up: effrt over 3f out: rdn & no imp)	¾	**6**	9/1 3	111	73
2011 6	**In Command (IRE) (112)** (BWHills) **3-8-9** MHills(3) (prom tl outpcd fnl 2 ½f)	hd	**7**	7/1 2	111	68
3577 4	**Captain Collins (IRE) (103)** (PWChapple-Hyam) **3-8-9** JReid(6) (plld hrd: bhd: effrt 3f out: sn btn)	2½	**8**	14/1	106	63
				(SP 115.4%)	**8 Rn**	

1m 36.02 (-2.38) CSF £74.77 TOTE £28.50: £4.10 £1.30 £2.70 (£27.50) Trio £99.70 OWNER Mr H. Al-Mutawa (NEWMARKET) BRED Stonethorn Stud Farms Ltd
WEIGHT FOR AGE 3yo-5lb

4003 Almushtarak (IRE), given a good ride, always held a prominent position, and once in front he answered his rider's calls in game style. (25/1)
3577* Decorated Hero, given plenty to do, showed a splendid turn of foot but the effort of getting there just sapped his strength at the end. Ridden closer to the pace, he might have won. (9/4)
1740* Samara (IRE), after a three-month layoff, had everything going her way here and battled on well under pressure, but was never quite good enough. (11/1)
3728 Poteen (USA) had the blinkers on for the first time, but was still not sharp enough despite keeping on. It would seem he is keeping plenty for himself. (9/4)
2009 Nwaamis (USA) off the track for three months, tried to pinch this by quickening from halfway but his limitations were exposed in the last furlong and a half. (7/1)
3725 Hawksley Hill (IRE), trying Group company for the first time, was not disgraced but was never quite good enough. (9/1)
2011 In Command (IRE), having his first run since mid-June, did not impress in the paddock and ran moderately. (7/1)

3577 Captain Collins (IRE) ran far too freely for his own good. (14/1)

4118 GREAT NORTH EASTERN RAILWAY DONCASTER CUP STKS (Gp 3) (3-Y.O+) (Class A)

3-10 (3-12) **2m 2f** £19,156.50 (£6,894.00: £3,297.00: £1,335.00: £517.50) Stalls: Low GOING minus 0.50 sec per fur (F)

				SP	RR	SF
3149[7]	**Canon Can (USA) (102)** (HRACecil) **4-9-0** KFallon(3) (lw: trckd ldrs: led over 3f out: rdn & r.o fnl 2f)	—	**1**	6/1[3]	120	58
3883a[5]	**Persian Punch (IRE) (113)** (DRCElsworth) **4-9-3** TQuinn(1) (trckd ldrs: ev ch over 2f out: kpt on same pce)	1¼	**2**	13/2	122	60
3902*	**Further Flight (100)** (BWHills) **11-9-0** MHills(5) (b.hind: hld up & bhd: hdwy over 3f out: chsng ldrs over 1f out: nt qckn)	nk	**3**	9/2[2]	119	57
3149*	**Double Trigger (IRE) (119)** (MJohnston) **6-9-5** MRoberts(2) (lw: led: pushed along ½-wy: hdd over 3f out: sn btn)	6	**4**	8/13[1]	118	56
3935*	**Old Rouvel (USA) (100)** (DJGMurraySmith) **6-9-0** KDarley(4) (bhd: pushed along ½-wy: wl outpcd fnl 4f)	14	**5**	33/1	101	39

(SP 110.6%) **5 Rn**

3m 52.17 (0.83 under best) (0.17) CSF £36.67 TOTE £5.60: £1.80 £2.30 (£13.00) OWNER Canon (Anglia) O A Ltd (NEWMARKET) BRED Elkay Stables

OFFICIAL EXPLANATION **Double Trigger (IRE): was found to have an unusually low heart-rate.**

2108* Canon Can (USA) took the eye in the paddock and showed here he is really on the upgrade with a super performance, and the stiffer the task, the better he likes it. (6/1: 10/1-11/2)

3883a Persian Punch (IRE) came back to form here and ran his socks off but was never quite up to the task. Despite his hard race, he should now find opportunities this back-end. (13/2)

3902* Further Flight ran another super race but this ground was a shade too lively for him, and he now goes to try and gain his sixth victory in the Jockey Club Cup. (9/2: 9/4-5/1)

3149* Double Trigger (IRE) never looked happy on this occasion but these days he is inclined to run that way. When things go right, he is as good as ever and is never one to be crossed off entirely. (8/13)

3935* Old Rouvel (USA) always found the effort needed here too much for his liking. (33/1)

4119 MAY HILL STKS (Gp 3) (2-Y.O F) (Class A)

3-40 (3-41) **1m (round)** £15,768.00 (£5,832.00: £2,796.00: £1,140.00: £450.00: £174.00) Stalls: High GOING minus 0.50 sec per fur (F)

				SP	RR	SF
3740*	**Midnight Line (USA) (100)** (HRACecil) **2-9-0** KFallon(9) (lw: hung rt appr st & bhd: pushed along & hdwy ½-wy: chal over 1f out: styd on u.p to ld cl home)	—	**1**	3/1[1]	105	67
3979*	**Flawless** (SirMarkPrescott) **2-8-9** GDuffield(6) (shkn up after s: sn chsng ldr: led 2f out: qcknd over 1f out: hdd & no ex towards fin)	½	**2**	12/1	99	61
2840*	**Glorosia (FR)** (LMCumani) **2-8-9** LDettori(5) (trckd ldrs: effrt over 2f out: r.o one pce)	3	**3**	100/30[2]	93	55
3744[3]	**Virtuous** (MRStoute) **2-8-9** MJKinane(2) (lw: in tch: effrt 3f out: kpt on fnl f: no imp)	2	**4**	7/2[3]	89	51
3426*	**Alharir (USA)** (JLDunlop) **2-8-9** RHills(3) (hld up & bhd: effrt & n.m.r over 2f out: swtchd & no imp)	1¼	**5**	5/1	87	49
3769*	**Hadayik** (PTWalwyn) **2-8-9** JCarroll(1) (led tl hdd 2f out: sn btn)	s.h	**6**	12/1	86	48
3650*	**Optimistic (82)** (MHTompkins) **2-8-9** DBiggs(8) (pushed along ½-wy: nvr rchd ldrs)	2½	**7**	20/1	81	43
3422[6]	**Belladera (IRE) (85)** (NTinkler) **2-8-9** RCochrane(7) (chsd ldrs over 5f: wknd)	15	**8**	33/1	51	13
3788*	**Admire** (MissGayKelleway) **2-8-9** PatEddery(4) (trckd ldrs tl wknd qckly fnl 3½f)	30	**9**	14/1	—	—

(SP 116.7%) **9 Rn**

1m 37.49 (0.83 under 2y best) (-0.91) CSF £36.77 TOTE £3.30: £1.50 £2.70 £1.60 (£22.60) Trio £33.70 OWNER H R H Prince Fahd Salman (NEWMARKET) BRED Newgate Stud Farm Inc

3740* Midnight Line (USA) had problems with the turn and looked in trouble but she is game and stays particularly well and, with the right man on board, did it in good style in the end. (3/1: 2/1-100/30)

3979* Flawless, who won on easy ground last time, handled these very fast conditions well and almost stole this, getting first run on the winner, but she just failed to last out. (12/1)

2840* Glorosia (FR) ran well but, after almost two months off, again gave the impression she can be made fitter. Time should see improvement. (100/30)

3744 Virtuous looked the part but proved short of toe halfway through the race and needs something to sharpen her up. (7/2)

3426* Alharir (USA), excitable in the paddock, ran into trouble when the pace was quickening and all chance of a place had soon gone. (5/1)

3769* Hadayik, edgy in the paddock, had run herself into the ground entering the last couple of furlongs. (12/1)

3650* Optimistic, stepping up in class, was edgy in the paddock and was never good enough to make an impression in the race. (20/1)

4120 KYOTO SCEPTRE STKS (Listed) (3-Y.O+ F & M) (Class A)

4-10 (4-11) **7f** £11,662.00 (£4,318.00: £2,074.00: £850.00: £340.00: £136.00) Stalls: High GOING minus 0.50 sec per fur (F)

				SP	RR	SF
3875a[7]	**Aunty Jane (103)** (JLDunlop) **4-8-10** PatEddery(8) (lw: cl up: led over 2f out: hld on wl)	—	**1**	8/1	100	51
3577[6]	**Dazzle (112)** (MRStoute) **3-8-9** JReid(9) (lw: hld up & bhd: hdwy on bit over 1f out: nt clr run ins fnl f: swtchd & r.o: jst failed)	hd	**2**	100/30[2]	103+	50
3577[9]	**Miss Riviera (99)** (GWragg) **4-8-10** MHills(1) (trckd ldrs: chal 2f out: kpt on u.p)	hd	**3**	12/1	100	51
3772[2]	**Flamboyance (USA) (86)** (JRFanshawe) **3-8-6** TQuinn(12) (lw: chsd ldrs: effrt 2f out: r.o one pce)	½	**4**	25/1	98	45
2945[2]	**All Is Fair (83)** (SirMarkPrescott) **3-8-6** GDuffield(3) (dwlt: hld up & bhd: hdwy 2f out: styd on wl towards fin)	1¼	**5**	20/1	96	43
3003a[8]	**Well Warned (106)** (BWHills) **3-8-6** KDarley(4) (in tch: effrt over 2f out: no imp)	¾	**6**	14/1	94	41
3147[7]	**Noisette (100)** (JHMGosden) **3-8-6** LDettori(2) (stumbled s: hdwy ½-wy: rdn & nt qckn fnl 2f)	2	**7**	11/4[1]	89	36
3790[2]	**Open Credit (100)** (HRACecil) **3-8-6** KFallon(6) (cl up: chal over 2f out: sn rdn: wknd over 1f out)	½	**8**	15/2[3]	88	35
3913[6]	**Hirasah (IRE) (98)** (RWArmstrong) **3-8-6** RHills(10) (chsd ldrs: rdn 2f out: wknd over 1f out)	½	**9**	9/1	87	34
3913[12]	**Unconditional Love (IRE) (101)** (MJohnston) **4-8-10** JWeaver(11) (led tl hdd over 2f out: sn wknd)	2½	**10**	8/1	81	32

(SP 116.7%) **10 Rn**

1m 24.66 (0.16) CSF £31.74 TOTE £7.10: £1.70 £1.80 £2.80 (£10.30) Trio £47.40 OWNER Mr Paul Locke (ARUNDEL) BRED P. Locke

WEIGHT FOR AGE 3yo-4lb

OFFICIAL EXPLANATION **Noisette: stumbled and lost a shoe shortly after leaving the stalls.**

3875a Aunty Jane, normally better with cut in the ground, showed fine courage to win this. (8/1: 6/1-9/1)

3577 Dazzle needs holding up but also needs things to go just right and they never did here, but for which she would have won. (100/30: 9/4-7/2)

3147 Miss Riviera is difficult to win with these days but there was nothing wrong with her attitude here. (12/1)

3772 Flamboyance (USA) is a tough sort who stays slightly further than this but is just short of that vital turn of foot to make her quite useful.(25/1)

2945 All Is Fair, last away, only got going when it was all too late and she seems to have plenty more ability when things go her way. (20/1)

3003a Well Warned has ability but was never quite doing enough here when put under maximum pressure. (14/1)
3147 Noisette stumbled badly leaving the stalls and almost had her rider on the floor, and not surprisingly ran no sort of race. (11/4)
3790 Open Credit disappointed here, stopping quickly when serious pressure was applied. (15/2)

4121 DONCASTER FREE PRESS LADIES DAY H'CAP (0-90) (3-Y.O+) (Class C)
4-40 (4-43) **7f** £7,042.50 (£2,115.00: £1,020.00: £472.50) Stalls: High GOING minus 0.50 sec per fur (F)

Form	Horse / Trainer / Wgt / Jockey / Comment	Dist	Pos	SP	RR	SF
3801*	**Safio (75)** (ABailey) **4-8-13** DWright(22) (hld up stands' side: hdwy over 2f out: r.o wl to ld cl home)	—	**1**	6/1[1]	84	45
3772[3]	**Al Muallim (USA) (88)** (JWPayne) **3-9-8** PatEddery(4) (hld up far side: hdwy to ld ins fnl f: r.o: jst ct)	½	**2**	9/1[2]	96	53
3649[6]	**Mr Teigh (73)** (MrsJRRamsden) **5-8-11** JFortune(20) (lw: chsd ldrs stands' side: led 2f out tl ins fnl f: kpt on wl)	hd	**3**	10/1[3]	81	42
3772*	**Cybertechnology (81)** (BWHills) **3-9-1** MHills(12) (lw: hld up stands' side: hdwy 3f out: ev ch over 1f out: kpt on wl)	s.h	**4**	11/1	89	46
3982[3]	**Volley (IRE) (84)** (MajorDNChappell) **4-9-8** KDarley(11) (hld up stands' side: hdwy over 2f out: chsng ldrs & hrd rdn over 1f out: kpt on)	nk	**5**	16/1	91	52
3801[3]	**Khafaaq (83)** (MajorWRHern) **3-9-3b** GDuffield(21) (lw: hld up stands' side: hdwy 3f out: chsng ldrs over 1f out: kpt on u.p)	nk	**6**	12/1	89	46
3975[5]	**Elfland (IRE) (89)** (LadyHerries) **6-9-13** RCochrane(10) (hld up far side: hdwy over 2f out: chal 1f out: wknd towards fin)	nk	**7**	9/1[2]	95	56
3764[12]	**Top Banana (85)** (HCandy) **6-9-2**(7) LJames(2) (led far side tl hdd ins fnl f: no ex)	nk	**8**	33/1	90	51
3752[4]	**Tertium (IRE) (82)** (MartynWane) **5-9-6** MRoberts(13) (hld up stands' side: hdwy 2f out: nt qckn fnl f)	hd	**9**	16/1	87	48
2561[6]	**Blane Water (USA) (86)** (JRFanshawe) **3-9-6** TQuinn(8) (chsd ldrs far side tl outpcd fnl 2f)	2	**10**	20/1	86	43
3649[17]	**Almuhimm (USA) (84)** (MWEasterby) **5-9-8** TLucas(7) (b.off hind: hld up far side: effrt 3f out: no imp)	1	**11**	16/1	82	43
3888[3]	**Q Factor (82)** (DHaydnJones) **5-9-6** AMackay(17) (hld up stands' side: hdwy 3f out: wknd over 1f out)	½	**12**	20/1	79	40
3772[8]	**Zugudi (78)** (KMahdi) **3-8-12** JQuinn(9) (racd far side: effrt 3f out: n.d)	¾	**13**	33/1	73	30
3888[5]	**Mr Bergerac (IRE) (85)** (BPalling) **6-9-9** JWeaver(14) (chsd ldrs stands' side tl wknd fnl 2f)	½	**14**	20/1	79	40
3888[9]	**Nomore Mr Niceguy (88)** (EJAlston) **3-9-8** MJKinane(18) (chsd ldrs stands' side tl wknd fnl 2½f)	nk	**15**	16/1	81	38
3496[10]	**Final Stab (IRE) (76)** (PWHarris) **4-8-9**(5) CLowther(5) (cl up far side tl wknd over 2f out)	nk	**16**	25/1	68	29
3786[4]	**Alphabet (83)** (MRStoute) **3-9-3** JReid(15) (chsd ldrs stands' side over 5f)	½	**17**	11/1	74	31
3615*	**Raaha (82)** (RWArmstrong) **3-9-2** RHills(1) (chsd ldrs far side over 5f)	hd	**18**	10/1[3]	73	30
1935[9]	**Mullitover (83)** (MJHeaton-Ellis) **7-9-7** JCarroll(16) (cl up stands' side 6f)	nk	**19**	33/1	73	34
3725[11]	**Musick House (IRE) (88)** (MissGayKelleway) **4-9-12** KFallon(3) (racd far side: outpcd & lost tch fnl 3f)	nk	**20**	33/1	78	39
3772[7]	**Rich In Love (IRE) (78)** (CACyzer) **3-8-9**(3) AWhelan(19) (led stands' side 6f: wknd)	3	**21**	33/1	61	18
				(SP 133.2%)	**21 Rn**	

1m 25.43 (0.93) CSF £47.28 CT £501.18 TOTE £5.70: £1.80 £2.00 £2.20 £2.50 (£19.60) Trio £72.00 OWNER Mrs M. A. Clayton (TARPORLEY) BRED Mrs M. A. Clayton
WEIGHT FOR AGE 3yo-4lb
3801* Safio was always going pretty well and, getting the required run just in time, pounced to take it late on and show that he is still improving. (6/1)
3772 Al Muallim (USA) looked to have done everything right but had no answer to the winner's late burst. (9/1)
3649 Mr Teigh was back to something like his best here but, because the leaders were on the opposite side of the track, he had to kick from a long way out which probably made some difference. (10/1)
3772* Cybertechnology is in good form, but this proved just beyond him in a driving finish. (11/1)
3982 Volley (IRE) likes to come from behind and kept responding to pressure, giving the impression that she should stay a little further. (16/1)
3801 Khafaaq ran well again in the blinkers and may well pick up another race before the season ends. (12/1)
3975 Elfland (IRE) ran well up the far side but his weight just anchored him late on. Nevertheless, he is coming right. (9/1)
2561 Blane Water (USA), after over two months off, proved short of toe on this very fast ground. (20/1)

T/Jkpt: Not won; £105,516.30 to Doncaster 12/9/97. T/Plpt: £461.70 (127.94 Tckts). T/Qdpt: £60.60 (48.07 Tckts) AA

3997a-BADEN-BADEN (Germany) (L-H) (Good)
Tuesday September 2nd

4122a OETTINGEN RENNEN (Gp 3) (3-Y.O+)
4-10 (4-21) **1m** £28,409.00 (£11,364.00: £5,682.00)

Form	Horse / Trainer / Wgt / Jockey	Dist	Pos	SP	RR	SF
811a[2]	**Waky Nao** (BSchutz,Germany) **4-9-2** THellier	—	**1**		121	—
3376a[3]	**Eden Rock (GER)** (BSchutz,Germany) **3-8-9** AStarke	1½	**2**		116	—
3674a[7]	**Gothenberg (IRE)** (MJohnston) **4-9-4** JWeaver	½	**3**		119	—
						6 Rn

1m 37.33 TOTE 118DM: 35DM 18DM OWNER Mr H. von Finck BRED H. von Finck
3674a Gothenberg (IRE) put up another decent display. Always in contention, he briefly hit the front over a furlong out but was unable to sustain his advantage. He found no extra in the closing stages and ran on at one pace.

4122a-BADEN-BADEN (Germany) (L-H) (Good)
Wednesday September 3rd

4123a BADENER STEHER CUP (Listed) (4-Y.O+)
3-00 (3-00) **2m** £18,939.00 (£7,576.00: £4,356.00: £2,462.00)

Form	Horse / Trainer / Wgt / Jockey	Dist	Pos	SP	RR	SF
	Pasolini (WKujath,Germany) **6-9-1** StephenDavies	—	**1**		114	—
2055[10]	**Camp David (GER)** (AWohler,Germany) **7-9-7** ABoschert	nk	**2**		120	—
3255[3]	**Cuff Link (IRE)** (MajorWRHern) **7-9-1** PaulEddery	3	**3**		111	—
3365a*	**River North (IRE)** (LadyHerries) **7-9-7** GMilligan	½	**4**		116	—
						6 Rn

3m 29.62 TOTE 169DM: 30DM 15DM OWNER Stall Marowi BRED Frau E & A Steigenberger

3255 Cuff Link (IRE), close up for most of the way, found himself outpaced three furlongs out and was never able to get back on terms. Finishing well inside the final furlong, he was not beaten all that far in the end.
3365a* River North (IRE) made his move three furlongs from home but, with every chance over a furlong out, could find no extra in the closing stages.

4124a JACOBS GOLDENE PEITSCHE (Gp 2) (3-Y.O+)
4-10 (4-16) **6f** £47,348.00 (£18,939.00: £9,470.00: £6,061.00)

				SP	RR	SF
3724[9]	**Don't Worry Me (IRE)** (GHenrot,France) **5-8-12** GMosse (hld up in rr: hdwy 2f out: led ins fnl f: r.o wl)	—	1		116	—
3372a[2]	**Dyhim Diamond (IRE)** (CLaffon-Parias,France) **3-8-13** GGuignard (led 2f: led again 2f out tl ins fnl f: kpt on)	1½	2		115	—
3553a[2]	**Global Player** (HBlume,Germany) **4-9-2** THellier (in rr early: nt clr run 2f out: r.o fnl f)	1½	3		112	—
1910a[2]	**Hakiki (IRE)** (WNeuroth,Norway) **5-9-2** FDiaz (a.p: kpt on fnl f)	1	4		109	—
3554a[3]	**Titus Livius (FR)** (JEPease,France) **4-9-2** CAsmussen (mid div: rdn ½-wy: styd on same pce)	½	5		108	—
3372a[6]	**Roseate Wood (FR)** (UweStoltefuss,Germany) **4-8-12** AStarke (a.p: ev ch 1½f out: wknd)	2	6		99	—
1910a[3]	**Troon** (RHaugen,Norway) **7-9-2** YvonneDurant (mid div: unable qckn 1½f out)	½	7		101	—
2640a[2]	**Fifire (GER)** (PPietsch,Germany) **5-9-2** WJakovlev (spd 3f)	nse	8		101	—
816a[2]	**Munaaji (USA)** (AWohler,Germany) **6-9-2b** ABoschert (prom: led after 2f tl 2f out: wknd)	½	9		100	—
	Lagarto (GER) (HJentzsch,Germany) **5-9-2** PSchiergen (a bhd)	2	10		95	—
2640a[3]	**Nautiker (GER)** (PRemmert,Germany) **6-9-2** ASuborics (a outpcd)	7	11		76	—
						11 Rn

1m 9.65 TOTE 68DM: 23DM 27DM 29DM OWNER Mr J. F. Gribomont BRED Irish National Stud Co Ltd
2106* Don't Worry Me (IRE), who won the King's Stand over five furlongs on soft ground, gets this trip well when the going is good. She has had a good summer campaign and, if placed well, can add to her successes again this season.
Dyhim Diamond (IRE), stepped up in class here, was no match for this winner.

3002a-SAINT-CLOUD (France) (L-H) (Good to soft)
Wednesday September 3rd

4125a PRIX RIDGWAY (Listed) (3-Y.O C & G)
2-50 (2-48) **1m** £15,713.00 (£5,387.00: £4,040.00: £2,694.00)

				SP	RR	SF
	Such Charisma (CAN) (MmeCHead,France) **3-9-2** TJarnet	—	1		110	—
3180a[5]	**Stingy** (France) **3-9-2** ODoleuze	3	2		104	—
	Blue Sky (IRE) (France) **3-9-2** OPeslier	½	3		103	—
3214[4]	**Running Stag (USA)** (PMitchell) **3-9-2** AClark	½	4		102	—
						7 Rn

1m 40.7 (2.20) P-M 1.70F: 1.70F 1.70F OWNER R. Romanet (CHANTILLY) BRED Ferme Du Bois Vert & Gainsborough Stud
3214 Running Stag (USA) held third position for most of the way, but after being given every chance, found little acceleration in the final furlong and a half. He could be suited by a longer trip.

4123a-BADEN-BADEN (Germany) (L-H) (Good)
Friday September 5th

4126a RAAB KARCHER BAUSTOFFE-CUP (124 ZUKUNFTS RENNEN) (Gp 2) (2-Y.O)
3-25 (3-33) **6f** £37,879.00 (£15,152.00: £7,576.00: £3,788.00: £2,273.00)

				SP	RR	SF
1723a*	**El Maimoun** (MHofer,Germany) **2-9-2** ASuborics (s.s: hdwy ½-wy: qcknd to ld 1f out: r.o strongly)	—	1		101	—
	Sharp Domino (RSuerland,Germany) **2-9-2** ATylicki (a.p: disp ld ½-wy: led 2f out to 1f out: one pce)	1¾	2		96	—
	Evening Set (GER) (BSchutz,Germany) **2-8-12** AStarke (cl up: r.o fnl 2f)	s.h	3		92	—
3708*	**Bay Prince (IRE)** (MRChannon) **2-9-2** JCarroll (disp ld to 2f out: wknd fnl 100y)	½	4		95	—
3192[13]	**Distinct Vintage (IRE)** (RHannon) **2-9-2** DaneO'Neill (spd 3f)	7	5		76	—
	Royal Star (GER) (WBaltromei,Germany) **2-8-12** DavidEddery (a outpcd)	15	6		32	—
						6 Rn

1m 10.34 TOTE 59DM: 22DM 39DM (437DM) OWNER Stall Mabrouk BRED Belgravia Bloodstock Ltd
3708* Bay Prince (IRE) was a disappointing odds-on favourite. Showing good speed, he disputed the lead until two furlongs out but, once asked the question, found very little in the tank. He is capable of better.
2740* Distinct Vintage (IRE) showed good early speed but he looked out of his depth in this class.

4126a-BADEN-BADEN (Germany) (L-H) (Good)
Sunday September 7th

4127a MERCEDES BENZ - GROSSER PREIS VON BADEN (Gp 1) (3-Y.O+)
3-45 (3-49) **1m 4f** £123,106.00 (£49,242.00: £24,621.00: £11,363.00)

				SP	RR	SF
3555a[2]	**Borgia (GER)** (BSchutz,Germany) **3-8-5** KFallon (hld up: hdwy 4f out: led 1f out: sn hung lft & rt: drvn out)..	—	1		122	—
3737a[2]	**Luso** (CEBrittain) **5-9-6** RCochrane (hld up in tch: mid div st: ev ch over 1f out: kpt on u.p fnl f)	1½	2		126	—
3050[7]	**Predappio** (SbinSuroor) **4-9-6** LDettori (disp ld after 2f: 2nd st: led wl over 1f out to 1f out: no ex)	½	3		125	—
3376a[4]	**Narrabeth (IRE)** (UweStoltefuss,Germany) **4-9-6** KWoodburn (s.s: wl bhd after 2f: hdwy st: styd on fnl 2f: nrst fin)	3½	4		121	—
3737a*	**Caitano** (BSchutz,Germany) **3-8-9** AStarke (a.p: 3rd st: ev ch wl over 1f out: wknd appr fnl f)	2	5		116	—
3555a[5]	**Ungaro (GER)** (HBlume,Germany) **3-8-9** TMundry (mid div & rdn along 4f out: nvr able to chal)	s.h	6		116	—
3737a[5]	**Night Petticoat (GER)** (BSchutz,Germany) **4-9-2** NGrant (led tl wl over 1f out)	4	7		109	—
	Szarlatan (POL) (FrauDKaluba,Poland) **5-9-6** ATylicki (prom 7f: t.o)	20	8		86	—

				SP	RR	SF
	Druzus (POL) (FrauDKaluba,Poland) **4-9-6** EmilZahariev (pushed along fr s: t.o fr 4f out)	30	**9**		46	—
						9 Rn

2m 28.56 TOTE 49DM: 15DM 19DM 14DM OWNER Gestut Ammerland BRED Gestut Ammerland
2642a* Borgia (GER) ran possibly the best race of her career to add another Group One race to her growing list of successes. Held up towards the rear, she made some progress four furlongs out and was brought wide into the straight. She hit the front a furlong out and, despite hanging right and left, she won quite comfortably. She is a very useful filly.
3737a Luso yet again did not disappoint his connections and ran another gallant race. Rather than make the running as is generally the norm, he was held up in touch until making progress down the straight and kept on steadily under pressure inside the final furlong.
3050 Predappio pleased connections with this performance. Disputing the lead after two furlongs, he was then restrained in second and tracked the leader turning into the straight. Taking the lead well over a furlong out, he was soon headed by the winner with a furlong to go and was unable to quicken in the closing stages. He may now go to Woodbine, Toronto for his next race.

CASCINE (Florence, Italy) (L-H) (Good)
Sunday September 7th

4128a PREMIO TOSCANA (Listed) (2-Y.O)
4-00 (4-11) **7f 110y** £23,142.00 (£10,183.00: £5,554.00)

				SP	RR	SF
2822a[2]	**Special Nash (IRE)** (PGuarsegnati,Italy) **2-8-12** ACorniani	—	**1**		81	—
3367a*	**Timekeeper (USA)** (MBell) **2-9-2** MFenton	1½	**2**		82	—
	Sighisoara (ITY) (MGuarnieri,Italy) **2-8-8** CColombi	1	**3**		72	—
						7 Rn

1m 34.0 TOTE 28L: 15L 12L (18L) OWNER Luisa Samataro
3367a* Timekeeper (USA) put up a decent display seeing as he had to give weight away to all his rivals. Always prominent, he was asked to quicken two furlongs out, but did not quite have the pace of the winner.

2273a-LONGCHAMP (Paris, France) (R-H) (Good)
Sunday September 7th

4129a EMIRATES PRIX DU MOULIN DE LONGCHAMP (Gp 1) (3-Y.O+ C & F)
2-30 (2-29) **1m** £101,010.00 (£40,404.00: £20,202.00: £10,101.00)

				SP	RR	SF
3733a*	**Spinning World (USA)** (JEPease,France) **4-9-2** CAsmussen (rdn 4th: hdwy to ld 1½f out: wnt clr: r.o strly)	—	**1**	6/4[2]	130	—
3050[3]	**Helissio (FR)** (ELellouche,France) **4-9-2** OPeslier (rn in 3rd: rdn to ld briefly fr 2f out: styd on one pce)	3	**2**	Evens[1]	124	—
3733a[2]	**Daylami (IRE)** (AdeRoyerDupre,France) **3-8-11** GMosse (rn in mid div: 6th st: r.o strly)	½	**3**	36/10[3]	123	—
3371a*	**Daneskaya** (AFabre,France) **4-8-13** AJunk (hld up bhd early: rdn ent st: prog 2f out: styd on)	s.nk	**4**	306/10	120	—
3124[5]	**Classic Park** (APO'Brien,Ireland) **3-8-8** JReid (in rr: u.p st: styd on one pce: nvr nr to chal)	hd	**5**	539/10	119	—
3733a[3]	**Neuilly (USA)** (AFabre,France) **3-8-11** TJarnet (rn 5th: hrd rdn ent st: prog 2f out: sn btn)	1	**6**	19/1	120	—
3371a[2]	**Rebecca Sharp** (GWragg) **3-8-8** MHills (a bhd: n.d)	2½	**7**	318/10	112	—
628a[B]	**Bijou d'Inde** (MJohnston) **4-9-2** JWeaver (prom: trckd ldr to 2f out: ev ch & wknd qckly)	8	**8**	44/1	99	—
3733a[6]	**Piperi (IRE)** (JEPease,France) **3-8-11** FSanchez (led 6f: sn wknd & lost tch)	15	**9**	6/4[2]	69	—
				(SP 167.0%)		**9 Rn**

1m 37.1 (2.10) P-M 2.50F: 1.10F 1.10F 1.10 (3.00F) OWNER Niarchos Family (CHANTILLY)
IN-FOCUS: **For betting purposes Spinning World (USA) and Piperi (IRE) were cpld.**
3733a* Spinning World (USA) could not have impressed more. Smartly out of the stalls, he was always travelling easily and, allowed to go on a furlong and a half out, his acceleration made his top-class opponents look rather ordinary. Great credit must be given to his trainer who once again produced his colt fresh and at a peak. This was his fourth Group One success, and he will not run again until the Breeders' Cup at Hollywood Park in November. As there are two turns in the mile, this may be rejected in favour of the Classic on sand. He has never ceased to improve and it will take a very good horse to beat him in the autumn. (6/4)
3050 Helissio (FR) settled well but was slightly interfered with running down to the straight. Holding the lead two out, he had no answer to the winner's acceleration. He ran on gamely but his head did hang a little to the left under pressure. He now goes for the Arc de Triomphe where he will probably be reunited with Dominique Boeuf. It was a sporting gesture to let him take his chance in this mile contest, and it must be hoped that he has not been sharpened up too much for the big race. (Evens)
3733a Daylami (IRE) raced in mid division and took a little time to get into top gear. He was putting in his best work at the end, taking third place close home. He would have preferred more cut in the ground and it looked as if a longer trip would be to his advantage. He may now be allowed to take his chance in the Champion Stakes and, if the ground is soft, he should give a good account of himself. (36/10)
3371a* Daneskaya, held up, was brought wide on the outside in the straight and ran an excellent race considering the class of the field. She may yet be suited by further. (306/10)
3124 Classic Park was held up before running on one-paced in the straight. She only lost fourth place by a head and is a brave little filly. (539/10)
3371a Rebecca Sharp was never seen with much of a chance. Waited with, no response was forthcoming when asked for an effort in the straight. She should however, not be written off. (318/10)
628a Bijou d'Inde, prominent for most of the way, was struck into by Helissio before the straight and lost a hind shoe. Running well up to that point, he was soon a spent force and dropped back very quickly. This was his first outing since being brought down in the Dubai World Cup, and although his trainer was discouraged, he may well line up for the Queen Elizabeth II Stakes. (44/1)

4130a PRIX GLADIATEUR (Gp 3) (3-Y.O+)
3-30 (3-29) **1m 7f 110y** £24,691.00 (£8,979.00: £4,489.00)

				SP	RR	SF
3883a[2]	**Orchestra Stall** (JLDunlop) **5-9-6** PatEddery	—	**1**		122+	—
3645*	**Double Eclipse (IRE)** (MJohnston) **5-9-6** JWeaver	5	**2**		117	—
3883a[3]	**Chief Contender (IRE)** (PWChapple-Hyam) **4-9-4** OPeslier	s.h	**3**		115	—
						7 Rn

3m 18.3 (2.30) TOTE 4.00F: 1.80F 1.40F OWNER Mr D. Sieff (ARUNDEL) BRED Alan Gibson
3883a Orchestra Stall gained one of the easiest wins seen in France this year. He slipped into the lead a furlong out and the gelding's jockey spent his time looking over his shoulder for a non-existent challenger. He literally cantered the final furlong and was being eased at the post. When there is cut in the ground, he is a very useful performer, and he will be kept at distances of around two miles with the Prix Royal-Oak at the end of October his next target.

3645* Double Eclipse (IRE), attempting to make all the running, was given a reminder down the back straight and started to battle early in the straight. He ran on bravely but had no answer when the winner came to challenge and his trainer believes he did not run up to scratch on this occasion. He will probably travel to France for the Prix de Cadran and the Royal-Oak, but an alternative would be to run in the Melbourne Cup.
3883a Chief Contender (IRE) was always close up and was the first to attack the leader in the straight. They both ran on one-paced and he just failed in his effort to take second place.

3008a-SAN SIRO (Milan, Italy) (R-H) (Good)
Sunday September 7th

4131a PREMIO FEDERICO TESIO (Gp 3) (4-Y.O+)
4-15 (4-25) **1m 3f** £32,461.00 (£14,780.00: £8,208.00)

				SP	RR	SF
3704^{5}	**Papering (IRE)** (LMCumani) **4-8-8** FJovine	—	**1**		121+	—
3634*	**Salmon Ladder (USA)** (PFICole) **5-8-11** TQuinn	3	**2**		120	—
$1549a^{4}$	**Pay Me Back (IRE)** (GVerricelli,Italy) **7-8-11** SDettori	4½	**3**		113	—

6 Rn

2m 12.5 (4.50) TOTE 18L: 12L 13L (17L) OWNER Sheikh Mohammed (NEWMARKET) BRED Sheikh Mohammed bin Rashid al Maktoum
3704 Papering (IRE) proved to be very much the class horse of the race. In front from the word go, he was always going well and never looked in any danger.
3634* Salmon Ladder (USA) was unable to match the pace of the winner but was always travelling well in second place. He tried to get on terms down the straight but the winner was able to keep him at bay. He is certainly capable of winning another pattern race.

4116-DONCASTER (L-H) (Good to firm)
Friday September 12th
WEATHER: fine & windy WIND: fresh half against

4132 AMCO CORPORATION MAIDEN STKS (2-Y.O) (Class D)
1-30 (1-30) **1m (straight)** £3,200.00 (£950.00: £450.00: £200.00) Stalls: High GOING: 0.07 sec per fur (G)

				SP	RR	SF
3576^{4}	**City Honours (USA)** (PWChapple-Hyam) **2-9-0** JReid(7) (lw: dwlt s: sn pushed along: hdwy ½-wy: wl outpcd over 1f out: str run to ld post)	—	**1**	$11/10^{1}$	103+	44
3598^{2}	**Prolix** (BWHills) **2-9-0** MHills(3) (lw: hld up: hdwy over 2f out: led over 1f out tl post)	s.h	**2**	$3/1^{2}$	103	44
3644^{2}	**Mutawwaj (IRE)** (SbinSuroor) **2-9-0** RHills(1) (trckd ldrs: hung lft thrght: led over 2f out tl over 1f out: styd on u.p)	½	**3**	$7/2^{3}$	102	43
	Kahtan (JLDunlop) **2-9-0** PatEddery(4) (w'like: s.i.s: sn drvn along & bhd: gd hdwy over 2f out: sn chsng ldrs: wknd fnl f: eased nr fin)	4	**4**	10/1	94+	35
	Double Blade (MJohnston) **2-9-0** MRoberts(6) (w'like: str: mde most tl over 2f out: wknd over 1f out)	6	**5**	16/1	82	23
3789^{5}	**Jonas Nightengale** (CACyzer) **2-9-0** KFallon(8) (chsd ldrs: drvn along 3f out: lost pl over 2f out)	4	**6**	50/1	74	15
	Shantung (IRE) (KMcAuliffe) **2-8-9** SSanders(2) (neat: unf: chsd ldrs: outpcd fnl 2f)	2½	**7**	66/1	64	5
3770^{7}	**Holy Smoke** (JLEyre) **2-8-10**^{ow1} OPears(5) (b.hind: w ldr tl wknd 2f out)	4	**8**	50/1	57	—

(SP 115.2%) **8 Rn**

1m 43.0 (5.80) CSF £4.19 TOTE £2.30: £1.20 £1.60 £1.20 (£2.40) OWNER Mr R. E. Sangster (MARLBOROUGH) BRED Swettenham Stud
3576 City Honours (USA) walked around the paddock like and old sheep. Falling out of the stalls and soon being pushed along, he suddenly warmed to his work at halfway. Left well behind in what was only a two furlong sprint coming to the final furlong, he finished with a rare rattle to lead right on the line. He still has plenty to learn and will be suited by a more true test of stamina. (11/10)
3598 Prolix, who showed plenty of knee action going down, quickened to go a length up coming to the final furlong but was picked off right on the line. (3/1)
3644 Mutawwaj (IRE), who showed a sharp action, gave his rider problems by hanging left throughout. He does not seem the type who will progress. (7/2: op 2/1)
Kahtan, who has plenty of size and scope, showed a pronounced knee action going down. Very green, he came from way off the pace to get on to the heels of the leaders but, tiring in the final furlong, was sensibly eased. He will improve a good deal for the outing. (10/1)
Double Blade, a sturdily-made newcomer, was very green going to post. Making the running on sufference, he was easily swept aside when the sprint for the line began. He should improve a good deal for the experience but this relative of the Gold Cup winner Celeric will not be seen at anything like his best until next year. (16/1)

4133 RJB MINING CONDITIONS STKS (3, 4 & 5-Y.O) (Class B)
2-05 (2-05) **1m 2f 60y** £7,320.00 (£2,520.00: £1,200.00: £480.00) Stalls: Low GOING minus 0.17 sec per fur (GF)

				SP	RR	SF
3214^{5}	**Faithful Son (USA) (112)** (MRStoute) **3-9-1** JReid(2) (lw: hld up: hdwy to ld jst ins fnl f: drvn out)	—	**1**	$11/8^{1}$	115	58
2013^{20}	**Alezal (96)** (WJarvis) **3-8-9** SSanders(1) (led: shkn up & qcknd over 2f out: hdd jst ins fnl f: no ex)	1¼	**2**	$7/1^{2}$	107	50
1769^{8}	**Musalsal (IRE) (113)** (BWHills) **3-8-13** MHills(5) (trckd ldrs: rdn over 1f out: kpt on same pce)	hd	**3**	$11/8^{1}$	111	54
$2462a^{3}$	**Yavlensky (IRE) (100)** (JLDunlop) **3-8-9** JWeaver(4) (trckd ldr: racd keenly: lost pl over 4f out: sn bhd & eased)	19	**4**	$8/1^{3}$	77	20

(SP 107.8%) **4 Rn**

2m 11.24 (3.44) CSF £9.58 TOTE £2.10: (£4.70) OWNER Maktoum Al Maktoum (NEWMARKET) BRED Gainsborough Farm Inc
3214 Faithful Son (USA), given forty-one days off, put his disappointing effort last time behind him where apparently the ground was too firm for him. Fitted with special shoes, he was confidently ridden, and quickened through to lead, needing only to be kept up to his work. Now he has regained the winning thread, he should progress further. (11/8: op evens)
1404* Alezal was given a good ride from the front. Setting sail for home halfway up the straight, he stuck on when headed. (7/1)
1769 Musalsal (IRE), absent since the Derby, was tapped for foot when the final sprint began. Keeping on towards the finish, he is better suited by a mile and a half. (11/8)
2462a Yavlensky (IRE), who made no appeal in the paddock, never settled and his rider gave up some way from home. (8/1)

4134 O & K TROY STKS (Listed) (3-Y.O+) (Class A)

2-35 (2-35) **1m 4f** £10,936.75 (£3,943.00: £1,891.50: £772.50: £306.25) Stalls: Low GOING minus 0.17 sec per fur (GF)

				SP	RR	SF
3578*	**Busy Flight (116)** (BWHills) **4-9-1** MHills(1) (lw: trckd ldr: smooth hdwy to ld over 2f out: sn pushed clr: readily)	—	**1**	11/8[1]	121+	81
3125[D]	**Memorise (USA) (99)** (HRACecil) **3-8-6** KFallon(3) (lw: sn pushed along: hdwy over 4f out: chsd wnr over 2f out: no imp)	3	**2**	2/1[2]	117	68
4005[6]	**Bahamian Knight (CAN) (105)** (RAkehurst) **4-9-1b[1]** PatEddery(5) (led tl over 2f out: hung lft & fnd nil)	8	**3**	20/1	106	66
852[2]	**Multicoloured (IRE) (108)** (MRStoute) **4-9-1** JReid(4) (lw: hld up: effrt 3f out: sn drvn along & wknd)	1½	**4**	7/2[3]	104	64
3902[8]	**Key to My Heart (IRE) (103)** (MissSEHall) **7-9-1** JWeaver(2) (lw: b: hld up: effrt over 4f out: no imp: eased ins fnl f)	14	**5**	11/1	86	46
				(SP 110.8%)		**5 Rn**

2m 30.69 (0.69) CSF £4.04 TOTE £2.30: £1.30 £1.50 (£2.30) OWNER Mr S. WingfieldDigby (LAMBOURN) BRED S. Wingfield Digby
WEIGHT FOR AGE 3yo-9lb

3578* Busy Flight repeated his victory in this event last year, taking it in tremendous style, and he is clearly right back to his very best. (11/8: evens-6/4)

3125 Memorise (USA) had 17lb to find on official figures if he was to beat the winner. A very lazy sort, he took a deal of driving, but to his credit kept up to his work in vain pursuit all the way to the line. (2/1)

4005 Bahamian Knight (CAN), in blinkers, set a strong gallop, but when tackled by the winner found absolutely nothing. (20/1)

852 Multicoloured (IRE), absent since Sandown in April, must surely have needed the outing. He has clearly had his problems but there is still sufficient of the season left for him to make up for lost time. (7/2)

3409 Key to My Heart (IRE), who is not running up to his best at present, found this company much too tough. (11/1)

4135 LAURENT-PERRIER ROSE CHAMPAGNE STKS (Gp 2) (2-Y.O C & G) (Class A)

3-05 (3-05) **7f** £54,912.25 (£19,831.00: £9,540.50: £3,927.50: £1,588.75) Stalls: High GOING: 0.07 sec per fur (G)

				SP	RR	SF
3148*	**Daggers Drawn (USA)** (HRACecil) **2-9-0** KFallon(4) (lw: trckd ldrs: nt clr run over 2f out: squeezed thro to ld ins fnl f: drvn out)	—	**1**	4/6[1]	113	75
3123[2]	**Docksider (USA) (100)** (JWHills) **2-8-10** MHills(1) (w ldr: led over 2f out tl ins fnl f: r.o)	½	**2**	9/1[3]	108	70
3644*	**Saratoga Springs (CAN)** (APO'Brien,Ireland) **2-8-10v** MJKinane(2) (lw: trckd ldrs: ev ch & rdn over 1f out: nt qckn)	1¾	**3**	5/2[2]	104	66
3706*	**Carrowkeel (IRE) (100)** (BWHills) **2-9-0** PatEddery(5) (trckd ldrs: effrt over 2f out: swtchd lft: no imp)	3	**4**	9/1[3]	101	63
4007[4]	**Stone of Destiny (94)** (BJMeehan) **2-8-10b[1]** KDarley(3) (lw: led tl over 2f out: sn lost pl)	11	**5**	50/1	72	34
				(SP 110.5%)		**5 Rn**

1m 26.92 (2.42) CSF £7.03 TOTE £1.60: £1.10 £3.30 (£5.80) OWNER Cliveden Stud (NEWMARKET) BRED Cliveden Stud

3148* Daggers Drawn (USA), who shows the white of his eye, showed a very poor action going down. Trapped in behind the second and the third, his rider chanced his arm, squeezing through between horses. Once in front he never looked like pulling clear and had to be driven right out to the line. If this is the best he can do, he is no champion. (4/6)

3123 Docksider (USA) made the winner battle all the way to the line, paying a big compliment to Central Park who defeated him three lengths at Goodwood. (9/1)

3644* Saratoga Springs (CAN) looked better beforehand than he did at York. His rider seemed in great pains to keep the favourite trapped in. Pushed slightly sideways when the winner looked for room, he was beaten entirely on merit. (5/2)

3706* Carrowkeel (IRE), stepping up to seven, had to switch wide to get a clear run, but once he saw daylight he made no impression whatsoever. (9/1)

4007 Stone of Destiny, tried in blinkers, led on sufferance before dropping right away. (50/1)

4136 JOY U.K. H'CAP (0-100) (3-Y.O+) (Class C)

3-35 (3-38) **1m 4f** £4,800.00 (£1,425.00: £675.00: £300.00) Stalls: Low GOING minus 0.17 sec per fur (GF)

				SP	RR	SF
3722[5]	**Dantesque (IRE) (85)** (GWragg) **4-8-12(5)** GMilligan(12) (lw: trckd ldrs: qcknd to ld over 1f out: hung lft: pushed out towards fin)	—	**1**	15/2[3]	97	79
3694[2]	**Elbaaha (84)** (MAJarvis) **3-8-7** RCochrane(13) (in tch: drvn along 3f out: styd on appr fnl f: no imp)	1¼	**2**	10/1	94	67
3259*	**Ferny Hill (IRE) (84)** (SirMarkPrescott) **3-8-7** SSanders(14) (lw: chsd ldrs: drvn along 4f out: styd on same pce fnl 2f)	2	**3**	8/1	92	65
3739[7]	**Steamroller Stanly (75)** (CACyzer) **4-8-7** MFenton(9) (chsd ldr: led over 3f out tl over 1f out: kpt on one pce)	nk	**4**	20/1	82	64
3722[12]	**Celestial Choir (88)** (JLEyre) **7-9-6** OPears(11) (lw: hld up: stdy hdwy over 2f out: nvr rchd ldrs)	2	**5**	12/1	93	75
4002[6]	**Remaadi Sun (83)** (MDIUsher) **5-9-1** RStreet(7) (hld up: hdwy over 2f out: kpt on: nt rch ldrs)	hd	**6**	12/1	88	70
2596[6]	**Catchable (84)** (HRACecil) **3-8-7** KFallon(15) (sn outpcd & bhd: hdwy over 2f out: styd on: nt rch ldrs)	nk	**7**	7/1[2]	88	61
3648[8]	**Solo Mio (IRE) (95)** (BWHills) **3-9-4** PatEddery(4) (lw: hdwy u.p 6f out: hrd rdn & kpt on fnl 3f: nvr nr ldrs)	nk	**8**	14/1	99	72
3051[5]	**Wahiba Sands (92)** (JLDunlop) **4-9-10** MJKinane(10) (hld up: effrt over 2f out: nvr nr to chal)	1¾	**9**	8/1	93	75
3722[9]	**My Learned Friend (75)** (AHide) **6-8-2(5)** RMullen(5) (lw: trckd ldrs: effrt over 3f out: wknd 2f out)	2	**10**	11/1	74	56
3444[4]	**Pinchincha (FR) (83)** (DMorris) **3-8-6** NDay(16) (hld up: sme hdwy over 2f out: nvr nr to chal)	s.h	**11**	16/1	82	55
3773[12]	**Time for Action (IRE) (78)** (MHTompkins) **5-8-10** JWeaver(3) (lw: led tl hdd over 3f out: sn lost pl)	7	**12**	33/1	67	49
	Golden Hello (72) (TDEasterby) **6-8-4** LCharnock(1) (bhd: drvn along 4f out: sn lost tch)	6	**13**	50/1	53	35
3705[7]	**Docklands Limo (84)** (BJMcMath) **4-9-2** MRoberts(8) (lw: trckd ldrs: pushed along 5f out: lost pl over 3f out: eased)	15	**14**	9/2[1]	45	27
1698a[4]	**Kris Green (IRE) (94)** (RHannon) **3-9-3** KDarley(2) (bhd: drvn along 5f out: sn t.o)	8	**15**	33/1	45	18
3110[9]	**Magic Combination (IRE) (75)** (BJCurley) **4-8-7** JQuinn(6) (lw: chsd ldrs: pushed along 7f out: lost pl over 3f out)	4	**16**	12/1	20	2
				(SP 130.3%)		**16 Rn**

2m 31.31 (1.31) CSF £75.97 CT £583.31 TOTE £8.40: £1.80 £2.10 £2.20 £2.90 (£35.50) Trio £61.40 OWNER Mollers Racing (NEWMARKET)
BRED Islanmore Stud
WEIGHT FOR AGE 3yo-9lb
OFFICIAL EXPLANATION Docklands Limo: was found to have a viral infection.

3722 Dantesque (IRE) was much better suited by this more truly-run race and, after taking it up travelling strongly, he won with something in hand. (15/2) GOING !!

3694 Elbaaha, from a 4lb higher mark, is an improving type. The winner got first run on her and she lacked the pace to reel him in. (10/1)
3259* Ferny Hill (IRE) has the action of a real stayer. Driven along turning in, he put in some solid work in the final quarter-mile. (8/1: 6/1-9/1)
250* Steamroller Stanly, who made the bast of his way home, is about 10lb better on an All-Weather surface. (20/1)
3722 Celestial Choir, 5lb higher than when successful at Pontefract two outings ago, was by no means knocked about. (12/1)
4002 Remaadi Sun was given his usual negative ride by his veteran jockey. (12/1)
2596 Catchable, on this fast ground, took an age to get going. Putting in some solid work at the line, some mud underfoot should see him in a much more favourable light. (7/1)
3705 Docklands Limo, from a stable completely out of form, dropped right out and was virtually pulled up. (9/2)

4137 FENNER CONVEYOR BELTING H'CAP (0-80) (3-Y.O+) (Class D)

4-10 (4-15) **5f** £3,200.00 (£950.00: £450.00: £200.00) Stalls: High GOING: 0.07 sec per fur (G)

				SP	RR	SF
3642[10]	**Just Bob (57)** (SEKettlewell) **8-8-5** DeanMcKeown(5) (dwlt s: swtchd rt: hdwy 2f out: styd on wl u.p to ld towards fin)	—	**1**	25/1	68	43
3709[2]	**Shalstayholy (IRE) (74)** (GLMoore) **3-9-7** KFallon(10) (lw: mid div & sn drvn along: hdwy ½-wy: ev ch ins fnl f: r.o)	½	**2**	8/1[3]	83	57
3871*	**Cross The Border (76)** (DNicholls) **4-9-10** AlexGreaves(4) (mde most tl wl ins fnl f: no ex)	nk	**3**	6/1[2]	84	59
3761[17]	**The Happy Fox (IRE) (65)** (BAMcMahon) **5-8-13b** MRoberts(19) (mid div: hdwy over 1f out: styd on towards fin)	1	**4**	16/1	70	45
3900[7]	**Malibu Man (75)** (EAWheeler) **5-9-2**(7) SCarson(18) (lw: s.i.s: sn chsng ldrs: kpt on ins fnl f)	2	**5**	20/1	74	49
3621[10]	**Bollin Harry (60)** (TDEasterby) **5-8-8** JCarroll(9) (lw: in tch: rdn ½-wy: kpt on same pce)	1¼	**6**	16/1	55	30
3856[7]	**Shadow Jury (59)** (DWChapman) **7-8-7b** LCharnock(13) (in tch: styd on wl towards fin)	nk	**7**	25/1	53	28
3649[19]	**Daawe (USA) (78)** (JAGlover) **6-9-12v** JReid(2) (led far side: kpt on wl appr fnl f)	hd	**8**	12/1	72	47
3194*	**Tear White (IRE) (71)** (TGMills) **3-9-4** JQuinn(8) (w ldrs tl wknd over 1f out)	½	**9**	16/1	63	37
3606*	**Archello (IRE) (62)** (GROldroyd) **3-8-9** KDarley(7) (mid div: sn drvn along: n.d)	nk	**10**	20/1	53	27
3910[3]	**Purple Fling (75)** (DWChapman) **6-9-9** ACulhane(21) (bhd: stdy hdwy ½-wy: n.m.r 1f out: nvr nr to chal)	½	**11**	14/1	64	39
3816[3]	**The Wad (58)** (DNicholls) **4-8-6** RCochrane(11) (chsd ldrs over 3f: sn wknd)	nk	**12**	20/1	46	21
3812[7]	**Storyteller (IRE) (57)** (MrsJRRamsden) **3-8-4v** MFenton(20) (bhd: hdwy & swtchd lft over 1f out: nvr nr ldrs)	½	**13**	10/1	44	18
3900[4]	**Tuscan Dawn (69)** (JBerry) **7-8-12**(5) PRoberts(14) (lw: w ldr 3f: sn wknd)	¾	**14**	14/1	53	28
3898[4]	**Barranak (IRE) (62)** (GMMcCourt) **5-8-10** JWeaver(17) (chsd ldrs 3f: btn whn hmpd 1f out)	1¼	**15**	14/1	42	17
3900[3]	**Swan At Whalley (65)** (RAFahey) **5-8-6**(7) RWinston(12) (w ldrs 3f: sn wknd)	hd	**16**	16/1	45	20
3795[9]	**Polly Golightly (58)** (MBlanshard) **4-8-6b** NAdams(3) (w ldr far side 3f: sn wknd)	1	**17**	33/1	35	10
3984*	**Lord High Admiral (CAN) (82)** (MJHeaton-Ellis) **9-10-2** 7x SDrowne(15) (w ldrs tl wknd 2f out)	1	**18**	5/1[1]	56	31
3746[3]	**Princely Sound (63)** (JEBanks) **4-8-6**(5) CLowther(6) (lw: racd far side: sn wl outpcd)	1	**19**	20/1	34	9
3816[2]	**White Emir (77)** (BJMeehan) **4-9-11b** PatEddery(1) (lw: racd far side: sn bhd & drvn along)	1½	**20**	14/1	43	18
3460[6]	**Nifty Norman (73)** (JBerry) **3-9-3**(3) TEDurcan(22) (unruly in stalls: a wl bhd)	¾	**21**	25/1	36	10
3693[2]	**Pleasure Time (63)** (CSmith) **4-8-11** JTate(16) (hld up: hdwy on ins & bdly hmpd over 1f out: nt rcvr)	5	**22**	16/1	10	—

(SP 148.5%) **22 Rn**

61.47 secs (3.07) CSF £205.60 CT £1,294.60 TOTE £27.80: £5.40 £1.50 £2.20 £2.70 (£218.00) Trio £557.90 OWNER Mr J. Fotherby (MIDDLEHAM) BRED Mrs D. Whittingham
WEIGHT FOR AGE 3yo-1lb

3107 Just Bob, who has tumbled down the weights, did not forfeit as much ground at the start as usual. Switched to join the stands'-side group, he ran on gamely to get up near the line. (25/1)
3709 Shalstayholy (IRE), from a 3lb higher mark, was struggling at halfway. Upsides inside the last, she was just shaded. Clearly effective over the minimum trip, she is well worth a try over six on turf. (8/1)
3871* Cross The Border, 22lb higher in the weights than when winning for the first time this season in July, showed bags of toe to overcome a poor draw and was only worn down near the line. (6/1: 5/1-15/2)
3566 The Happy Fox (IRE), last of seventeen behind Cross The Border at Beverley on his previous outing, ran well, finishing with quite a flourish, but he is a good deal better on the All-Weather. (16/1)
3900 Malibu Man, who for once missed the start, seemed to pose his rider problems inside the last, but even so, was keeping on grimly at the line. (20/1)
2788 Bollin Harry won from an 18lb higher mark last year and he ran one of his better races here. (16/1)
3856 Shadow Jury showed that he is back on song. (25/1)
3410 Daawe (USA), having his first outing since changing stables, showed all his old speed to show in a clear lead on the far side over a furlong out, but he had no chance with the first six on the stands side. (12/1)
3910 Purple Fling ran an encouraging race and is almost certainly better suited by six. (14/1)
3984* Lord High Admiral (CAN), under a 7lb penalty, was unable to dominate and called it a day soon after halfway. (5/1: 6/1-4/1)

4138 SUN PRINCESS INJURED JOCKEYS FUND CHALLENGE TROPHY CONDITIONS STKS (3-Y.O) (Class C)

4-40 (4-41) **1m (round)** £4,950.00 (£1,575.00: £750.00) Stalls: High GOING minus 0.17 sec per fur (GF)

				SP	RR	SF
1541a[6]	**Revoque (IRE) (123)** (PWChapple-Hyam) **3-8-11** JReid(3) (lw: trckd ldr: led on bit 3f out: pushed out: readily)	—	**1**	6/5[2]	126+	59
	Bahhare (USA) (121) (JLDunlop) **3-8-11** RHills(1) (hld up: effrt over 2f out: kpt on wl fnl f)	1¼	**2**	10/11[1]	124	57
3725[10]	**Kumait (USA) (92)** (DRLoder) **3-8-11** KFallon(2) (lw: led tl 3f out: sn wknd & eased)	23	**3**	9/1[3]	78	11

(SP 107.8%) **3 Rn**

1m 40.63 (2.23) CSF £2.44 TOTE £2.00: (£1.20) OWNER Mr R. E. Sangster (MARLBOROUGH) BRED Minch Bloodstock
1541a Revoque (IRE), who definitely achieved more at two than Bahhare, was having his first outing since the Irish 2,000 Guineas. He took this in really good style and a step up to a mile and a quarter will be no problem. (6/5: evens-5/4)
Bahhare (USA) was making a belated reappearance after apparently fracturing his pelvis amongst his other problems. Travelling strongly, he was by no means knocked about and the outing would have blown away the cobwebs. He will soon be making up for lost time. (10/11: 4/5-evens)
3144 Kumait (USA), who led on sufferance, seems to be going the wrong way temperamentally. (9/1: 8/1-14/1)

T/Jkpt: £19,292.60 (7.96 Tckts). T/Plpt: £13.00 (3,483.57 Tckts). T/Qdpt: £7.40 (261.73 Tckts) WG

3763-**GOODWOOD** (R-H) (Good, Good to soft St after race 1)

Friday September 12th

WEATHER: early showers becoming sunny

4139 EYDON HALL FARM MACMILLAN NURSES H'CAP (0-70) (3-Y.O+) (Class E)

2-10 (2-11) **1m** £4,565.00 (£1,370.00: £660.00: £305.00) Stalls: High GOING: 0.09 sec per fur (G)

				SP	RR	SF
3465*	**Gold Lance (USA) (56)** (RJO'Sullivan) **4-9-1** LDettori(19) (a.p: rdn over 4f out: led last stride)	—	**1**	6/1^{1}	66	48
3561*	**Step On Degas (52)** (MJFetherston-Godley) **4-8-8**(3) RFfrench(22) (led over 4f: led wl over 1f out: rdn: hdd last stride)	nk	**2**	11/1	61	43
3980^{7}	**Ca'd'oro (58)** (GBBalding) **4-9-0**(3) PPMurphy(15) (lw: rdn over 3f out: hdwy over 1f out: r.o wl ins fnl f)	¾	**3**	14/1	66	48
3392^{7}	**Sovereigns Court (56)** (LGCottrell) **4-9-1v^{1}** DHolland(10) (lw: rdn over 3f out: hdwy on ins over 1f out: unable qckn wl ins fnl f)	hd	**4**	12/1	64	46
3987^{5}	**Knobbleeneeze (65)** (MRChannon) **7-9-10v** JFortune(6) (rdn over 3f out: hdwy over 1f out: one pce ins fnl f)	1	**5**	8/1^{2}	71	53
3297^{3}	**Zurs (IRE) (54)** (JRPoulton) **4-8-13** MartinDwyer(2) (rdn over 3f out: hdwy over 1f out: one pce ins fnl f)	1¼	**6**	20/1	57	39
3916^{14}	**Swinging The Blues (IRE) (60)** (RAkehurst) **3-9-0** AClark(21) (rdn over 3f out: hdwy over 1f out: n.m.r ins fnl f: one pce)	hd	**7**	20/1	63	40
3435*	**Fionn de Cool (IRE) (64)** (RAkehurst) **6-9-9** TQuinn(1) (lw: rdn over 3f out: hdwy over 1f out: r.o one pce)	1½	**8**	10/1^{3}	64	46
3980^{8}	**Chasetown Flyer (USA) (61)** (NEBerry) **3-9-1** GHind(14) (nvr nrr)	nk	**9**	14/1	60	37
1217^{4}	**Penlop (59)** (ACStewart) **3-8-13** GDuffield(3) (rdn over 3f out: mid div whn nt clr run over 2f out)	2	**10**	20/1	54	31
3557^{2}	**My Beloved (IRE) (59)** (RHannon) **3-8-13** DaneO'Neill(11) (lw: nvr nrr)	3	**11**	20/1	48	25
3470^{3}	**Mukhlles (USA) (63)** (BobJones) **4-9-8** GCarter(17) (lw: prom over 6f)	1¾	**12**	10/1^{3}	49	31
3153^{3}	**Chairmans Choice (55)** (APJarvis) **7-9-0** WRyan(18) (w ldr: led over 3f out tl wl over 1f out: sn wknd)	2	**13**	10/1^{3}	37	19
3768^{8}	**Piquant (53)** (LordHuntingdon) **10-8-7**(5) AimeeCook(13) (bhd fnl 3f)	nk	**14**	25/1	34	16
3969^{3}	**Hawaii Storm (FR) (48)** (DJSffrenchDavis) **9-8-4**(3) PMcCabe(20) (dwlt: a bhd)	s.h	**15**	25/1	29	11
3453^{5}	**Quibbling (65)** (HCandy) **3-9-5** CRutter(9) (lw: nvr nrr)	3½	**16**	14/1	39	16
3916^{9}	**Filial (IRE) (67)** (BJMeehan) **4-9-12b^{1}** MTebbutt(8) (a bhd)	2½	**17**	33/1	36	18
3849^{8}	**Desert Time (64)** (CAHorgan) **7-9-9** PaulEddery(16) (mid div over 6f)	½	**18**	16/1	32	14
3909^{5}	**Witchfinder (USA) (59)** (MrsLStubbs) **5-9-4** TWilliams(12) (lw: prom over 6f: eased whn btn fnl f)	1½	**19**	14/1	24	6
3860^{6}	**Whatever's Right (IRE) (65)** (MDIUsher) **8-9-10** RPerham(7) (a bhd)	1¾	**20**	20/1	27	9
3768^{4}	**Superior Force (52)** (MissBSanders) **4-8-8v^{1}**(3) AWhelan(4) (prom over 5f)	1	**21**	20/1	12	—
3591^{7}	**Zimiri (64)** (JARToller) **3-9-4** NCarlisle(5) (a bhd: t.o)	dist	**22**	50/1	—	—

(SP 142.4%) **22 Rn**

1m 42.84 (5.64) CSF £61.32 CT £874.10 TOTE £5.60: £1.60 £2.50 £4.50 £4.80 (£15.60) Trio £122.30 OWNER Mrs Barbara Marchant (WHITCOMBE) BRED Societe Aland

WEIGHT FOR AGE 3yo-5lb

OFFICIAL EXPLANATION Zimiri: gurgled during the race.

3465* Gold Lance (USA) continues to progress and, although being pushed along before halfway, he kept on finding what was required and got up in the last few strides. He is lazy according to Dettori. (6/1)

3561* Step On Degas coped with the extra furlong and disputed the lead from the outset. Asserting from below the distance, it looked as if she might hold on, only to be caught in the last few strides. (11/1: 8/1-12/1)

3980 Ca'd'oro had the ground and trip in his favour but, despite running on really strongly in the last furlong and a half, found the line always going to beat him. (14/1)

2216 Sovereigns Court has been steadily falling in the handicap this year after a number of poor efforts, and this was definitely his best run so far this season. (12/1)

3987 Knobbleeneeze is not very consistent and is not easy to win with these days. He looked a real possibility as he picked up ground below the distance but his effort petered out inside the final furlong. (8/1)

3297 Zurs (IRE), who has changed stables since his last run, has only an All-Weather Lingfield maiden win to his name. Making headway below the distance, he was making no further impression inside the final furlong. (20/1)

3435* Fionn de Cool (IRE) (10/1: 8/1-12/1)

4140 BELLWAY HOMES STARDOM STKS (Listed) (2-Y.O) (Class A)

2-40 (2-42) **1m** £13,247.50 (£3,955.00: £1,890.00: £857.50) Stalls: High GOING: 0.09 sec per fur (G)

				SP	RR	SF
3688^{2}	**Alboostan** (DMorley) **2-8-11** GCarter(2) (mde all: rdn out)	—	**1**	11/2^{3}	101	56
3233*	**Almutawakel** (SbinSuroor) **2-8-11** LDettori(1) (lw: chsd wnr over 5f out: rdn over 2f out: r.o one pce)	1	**2**	8/13^{1}	98	54
3802^{3}	**Due South (94)** (EALDunlop) **2-8-6** TQuinn(5) (chsd wnr over 2f: rdn over 2f out: r.o one pce)	½	**3**	9/2^{2}	92	48
3688^{5}	**Priceless** (WJHaggas) **2-8-11** JFortune(3) (bhd fnl 3f)	11	**4**	12/1	75	31
	Pichon Baron (USA) (BJMeehan) **2-8-11** MTebbutt(4) (leggy: unf: a bhd)	7	**5**	33/1	61	17

(SP 106.1%) **5 Rn**

1m 41.74 (4.54) CSF £8.00 TOTE £5.70: £3.60 £1.10 (£2.40) OWNER Mr Hamdan Al Maktoum (NEWMARKET) BRED Godolphin Management Co Ltd

3688 Alboostan appreciated the step up to a mile and put up a very good display. Not inconvenienced by the slightly easier ground, he made every post a winning one and, given a couple of cracks of the whip, was not going to be overhauled. (11/2)

3233* Almutawakel, soon racing in second place, was asked for his effort over a quarter of a mile from home but he could not quicken up on this easier ground, although he did stay on. Back on a sounder surface he can regain the winning thread. (8/13)

3802 Due South had more on her plate here and, bustled along over two furlongs from home, failed to find that vital turn of foot, if staying on. (9/2)

3688 Priceless was getting left behind in the last three furlongs. A drop in class and distance is needed. (12/1: 7/1-14/1)

Pichon Baron (USA), an ex-French colt who won two claimers over there last month, is a lightly-made individual who was completely outclassed in both the paddock and the race. A serious drop in class is required. (33/1)

4141 SCHRODER INVESTMENT MANAGEMENT H'CAP (0-100) (3-Y.O+) (Class C)

3-10 (3-12) **1m 1f** £15,067.50 (£4,515.00: £2,170.00: £997.50) Stalls: High GOING: 0.09 sec per fur (G)

				SP	RR	SF
4004^{2}	**Danish Rhapsody (IRE) (95)** (LadyHerries) **4-10-0** WRyan(8) (mde all: clr wl over 1f out: r.o wl)	—	**1**	10/1^{3}	106	72
3773^{6}	**King of Tunes (FR) (83)** (MJHaynes) **5-9-2** JFortune(10) (rdn over 2f out: hdwy over 1f out: r.o wl ins fnl f)	1¼	**2**	10/1^{3}	92	58
3119^{5}	**The In-Laws (IRE) (81)** (SirMarkPrescott) **3-8-8** GDuffield(7) (nt clr run on ins over 2f out: swtchd lft: hdwy over 1f out: r.o wl ins fnl f)	1½	**3**	20/1	87	47

				SP	RR	SF
3768^{3}	**Tribal Peace (IRE) (63)** (BGubby) **5-7-7**(3) RFfrench(1) (lw: hdwy over 3f out: rdn over 2f out: unable qckn)....¾	**4**		20/1	68	34
3190^{10}	**Barba Papa (IRE) (97)** (LMCumani) **3-9-10** LDettori(12) (nt clr run 3f out: swtchd lft: hdwy over 1f out: nvr nrr)....2	**5**		12/1	98	58
3798*	**Present Situation (66)** (LordHuntingdon) **6-7-8**(5) AimeeCook(14) (a.p: rdn over 2f out: wknd ins fnl f)....1¾	**6**		9/1^{2}	64	30
3713^{3}	**Mashhaer (USA) (88)** (MRStoute) **3-9-1** TQuinn(16) (prom over 7f)....s.h	**7**		9/1^{2}	86	46
3894^{8}	**Attitude (84)** (HCandy) **3-8-11** CRutter(15) (lw: nvr nr to chal)....1	**8**		33/1	80	40
3725^{6}	**Calypso Grant (IRE) (93)** (PWHarris) **3-9-6** GBardwell(19) (lost pl over 4f out: nt clr run on ins over 1f out: one pce)....nk	**9**		14/1	89	49
3894^{9}	**Zoom Up (IRE) (82)** (MJHeaton-Ellis) **3-8-9** GCarter(17) (lw: nvr nrr)....nk	**10**		33/1	77	37
3052^{8}	**Koathary (USA) (78)** (LGCottrell) **6-8-11** DHolland(4) (b.nr fore: lw: nvr nrr)....¾	**11**		20/1	72	38
3891^{3}	**Brandon Jack (75)** (IABalding) **3-8-2** JFEgan(3) (lw: nvr nrr)....s.h	**12**		12/1	69	29
431*	**Miracle Kid (USA) (86)** (JHMGosden) **3-8-13** GHind(18) (bit bkwd: prom over 7f)....nk	**13**		10/1^{3}	79	39
3150^{15}	**Strathmore Clear (85)** (GLewis) **3-8-12** PaulEddery(20) (prom over 6f)....½	**14**		25/1	77	37
3392*	**Mihriz (IRE) (70)** (RAkehurst) **5-8-3** AClark(11) (lw: a bhd)....2½	**15**		5/1^{1}	58	24
3773^{11}	**Orsay (80)** (WRMuir) **5-8-13** JStack(6) (hdwy over 2f out: wknd over 1f out)....¾	**16**		16/1	67	33
3712*	**Conspicuous (IRE) (88)** (LGCottrell) **7-9-2**(5) ADaly(5) (lw: a bhd)....½	**17**		14/1	74	40
3551^{3}	**Contentment (IRE) (73)** (JWHills) **3-7-11**(3) MHenry(2) (lw: bhd fnl 2f)....7	**18**		20/1	46	6

(SP 127.3%) **18 Rn**

1m 58.25 (5.25) CSF £89.70 CT £1,811.50 TOTE £12.20: £2.70 £2.30 £4.30 £4.80 (£90.90) Trio £319.60 OWNER Mr Chris Hardy (LITTLEHAMPTON) BRED Grangemore Stud

WEIGHT FOR AGE 3yo-6lb

4004 Danish Rhapsody (IRE) continues in tremendous form and put up a very useful front-running display under his welter burden, forging clear in the final quarter-mile to win in fine style. He was bought by connections for a mere 1,300 gns at the beginning of the season but has already amassed nearly £66,000 in prize money for them. A step up to listed company looks on the cards. (10/1)

3773 King of Tunes (FR) began to find his feet below the distance but, despite running on really strongly inside the final furlong, found the line always beating him. (10/1)

3119 The In-Laws (IRE), who failed to get a clear run along the inside rail in the straight, managed to pick up ground below the distance but, despite running on strongly, was never going to get there in time. Another furlong would not go amiss. (20/1)

3768 Tribal Peace (IRE) goes well here and moved up as the Bugler called entering the straight. Bustled along over a quarter of a mile from home, he failed to find that vital turn of foot. (20/1)

2338 Barba Papa (IRE) stayed on in the last furlong and a half without seriously threatening. The Handicapper has done him no favours on his British form. (12/1)

3798* Present Situation, 7lb higher for his recent success, was always in the firing line but tired inside the final furlong. (9/1)

431* Miracle Kid (USA) (10/1: 6/1-12/1)

4142 THEO FENNELL CONDITIONS STKS (3-Y.O) (Class C)

3-40 (3-41) **7f** £7,154.00 (£2,474.00: £1,187.00: £485.00) Stalls: High GOING: 0.09 sec per fur (G)

			SP	RR	SF
3554a^{4}	**Kahal (109)** (SbinSuroor) **3-8-12** LDettori(3) (lw: hld up: led over 1f out: qcknd & edgd rt: easily)....—	**1**	13/8^{2}	107++	52
829^{5}	**Latalomne (USA)** (EALDunlop) **3-9-1** TQuinn(1) (led 5f: btn whn wandered fnl f)....3½	**2**	8/1^{3}	102	47
2011^{8}	**Mamalik (USA)** (JHMGosden) **3-9-1** GHind(2) (chsd ldr: led 2f out tl over 1f out: btn whn bmpd nr fin)....s.h	**3**	10/11^{1}	102	47
3913^{14}	**Egoli (USA)** (GWragg) **3-8-10** DHolland(4) (a in rr)....5	**4**	12/1	86	31

(SP 109.3%) **4 Rn**

1m 29.2 (4.40) CSF £11.41 TOTE £2.00: (£4.00) OWNER Godolphin (NEWMARKET) BRED Shadwell Estate Company Limited

3554a Kahal may have drifted in the betting but he still put up an impressive display, leading below the distance and quickening right away to win doing handsprings. A return visit for the Supreme Stakes later in the month is next on the agenda. (13/8: evens-7/4)

829 Latalomne (USA), who returned lame after flopping at Sandown at the end of April, was having his first run since. Bowling along in front, he was narrowly collared a quarter of a mile from home and certainly put in his place by the winner from below the distance. (8/1: 5/1-9/1)

2011 Mamalik (USA), without a run since flopping at Royal Ascot, poked a nostril in front a quarter of a mile from home, but when the winner was let loose below the distance, there was little he could do. (10/11)

3550* Egoli (USA) again had the ground against her and was in last place from start to finish. (12/1)

4143 TATTERSALLS AUCTION NURSERY H'CAP (2-Y.O) (Class D)

4-15 (4-17) **7f** £4,110.00 (£1,230.00: £590.00: £270.00) Stalls: High GOING: 0.09 sec per fur (G)

			SP	RR	SF
3711^{15}	**Titan (74)** (SDow) **2-8-6** JFEgan(3) (nt clr run over 3f out: swtchd lft over 2f out: hdwy over 1f out: hrd rdn: led nr fin)....—	**1**	8/1^{3}	76	14
3711^{5}	**Jungle Story (IRE) (69)** (PTWalwyn) **2-8-1** JLowe(6) (lw: nt clr run on ins over 3f out tl over 2f out: swtchd lft: hdwy over 1f out: str run fnl f: fin wl)....hd	**2**	9/2^{2}	71	9
4006^{4}	**Who Nose (IRE) (74)** (BJMeehan) **2-8-6b** MTebbutt(1) (lw: rn wd bnd over 5f out: stdy hdwy over 2f out: led over 1f out: edgd rt: hrd rdn fnl f: hdd nr fin)....nk	**3**	10/1	75	13
3908^{6}	**Vice Presidential (89)** (TJEtherington) **2-9-7** LDettori(5) (led over 5f: one pce)....2½	**4**	4/1^{1}	84	22
3289^{4}	**Little Tumbler (IRE) (64)** (SWoodman) **2-7-5**(5) APolli(8) (hdwy over 2f out: r.o one pce)....hd	**5**	25/1	59	—
3186^{5}	**Water Force (74)** (GBBalding) **2-8-3**(3) PPMurphy(9) (lw: prom over 4f)....2½	**6**	9/1	63	1
3686*	**Roi de Danse (82)** (JWHills) **2-8-11**(3) MHenry(2) (lw: rn wd bnd over 5f out: hdwy 4f out: rdn over 2f out: wknd over 1f out)....2½	**7**	9/2^{2}	66	4
3924^{10}	**Sergeant Imp (IRE) (65)** (PMitchell) **2-7-8**(3) RFfrench(7) (lw: a.p: bmpd 3f out: rdn over 2f out: wknd wl over 1f out)....2½	**8**	20/1	43	—
2681^{4}	**Flame Tower (IRE) (64)** (RHannon) **2-7-10** MartinDwyer(4) (lw: prom tl wknd & bmpd 3f out)....8	**9**	10/1	24	—
3379^{6}	**Alfiglia (88)** (PJMakin) **2-9-6b^{1}** JFortune(10) (prom over 4f)....5	**10**	9/1	36	—

(SP 114.3%) **10 Rn**

1m 31.99 (7.19) CSF £39.12 CT £341.59 TOTE £17.90: £3.90 £2.20 £2.40 (£42.10) Trio £112.00 OWNER J & S Kelly (EPSOM) BRED Matthews Breeding and Racing Ltd

LONG HANDICAP Flame Tower (IRE) 7-8 Little Tumbler (IRE) 7-0

OFFICIAL EXPLANATION **Titan: regarding the improved performance, the trainer reported that the colt appreciated today's easier surface and more patient tactics.**

2719 Titan left his disappointing Salisbury run well behind and, beginning his effort below the distance, got up near the line. (8/1: 6/1-9/1)

3711 Jungle Story (IRE) can be considered very unlucky. With nowhere to go along the inside rail in the straight, she was switched left a quarter of a mile out and did not really begin to pick up until approaching the final furlong. Absolutely flying in the last two hundred yards, she would surely have won in a few more strides. She is a winner without a penalty. (9/2)
4006 Who Nose (IRE), who had problems coming around the first bend, was pulling double in the straight and cruised into the lead approaching the final furlong. Drifting right, he came under pressure inside the last one hundred and fifty yards and was worried out of it near the line. (10/1)
3908 Vice Presidential was taking a step up in distance but cut out the donkey work until collared approaching the final furlong. Maybe six furlongs would be the answer for him. (4/1)
3289 Little Tumbler (IRE), still carrying 5lb more than his long handicap, despite her rider's allowance, edged closer over a quarter of a mile from home, but then failed to find the necessary turn of foot. (25/1)
3186 Water Force was in trouble over a quarter of a mile from home. (9/1)
3379 Alfiglia (9/1: op 6/1)

4144 TILNEY PORTFOLIO LIMITED STKS (0-80) (3-Y.O+) (Class D)

4-50 (4-50) **1m 4f** £3,720.00 (£1,110.00: £530.00: £240.00) Stalls: Low GOING: 0.09 sec per fur (G)

				SP	RR	SF
3632*	**Aerleon Pete (IRE) (80)** (MRStoute) **3-8-12** DHolland(2) (hld up: led over 2f out: rdn: r.o wl)	—	1	7/2[2]	94	49
3475*	**Pennys From Heaven (79)** (HCandy) **3-8-12** CRutter(1) (carried stands' side st: swtchd rt & rdn over 3f out: hdwy over 1f out: r.o one pce)	6	2	7/1	86	41
3906[7]	**Agony Aunt (77)** (MrsJCecil) **3-8-9** GHind(5) (lw: led 2f: led 4f out tl over 2f out: one pce)	nk	3	14/1	83	38
2776[3]	**Leading Note (USA) (75)** (LMCumani) **3-8-7** LDettori(7) (lw: hld up: c stands' side st: rdn over 3f out: wknd over 2f out)	4	4	7/2[2]	75	30
3897*	**Azores (78)** (PFICole) **3-8-12** TQuinn(4) (lw: a.p: rdn over 2f out: sn wknd)	1¼	5	6/1[3]	79	34
3424[4]	**Farmost (80)** (SirMarkPrescott) **4-9-7** GDuffield(6) (lw: led 10f out to 4f out: wknd 3f out)	8	6	100/30[1]	68	32
3720*	**Grand Splendour (75)** (LadyHerries) **4-9-4** AClark(3) (s.s: a bhd)	1¼	7	8/1	63	27
				(SP 112.1%)		**7 Rn**

2m 41.42 (8.22) CSF £24.14 TOTE £3.50: £2.00 £1.90 (£12.80) OWNER Mr Paul Locke (NEWMARKET) BRED Mount Coote Stud
WEIGHT FOR AGE 3yo-9lb
STEWARDS' ENQUIRY Dettori susp. 21-26/9/97 (irresponsible riding).
3632* Aerleon Pete (IRE) struck the front down the centre of the course over a quarter of a mile from home and, rousted along, strode clear for a thoroughly decisive victory. (7/2: 5/2-4/1)
3475* Pennys From Heaven, who was forced to come over to the stands side by Leading Note, was switched round that rival early in the straight. He did stay on in the last furlong and a half to just snatch second prize, but found the winner was already home and dried. (7/1)
2952* Agony Aunt showed in front for a second time half a mile from home but collared over a quarter of a mile out, had no answer to the winner. (14/1)
2776 Leading Note (USA) elected to come over to the stands side in the straight in search of the better ground but, in doing so, brought Pennys From Heaven with her. Soon bustled along, she was a spent force over two furlongs from home. (7/2)
3897* Azores, a leading light from the outset, had shot his bolt two furlongs from home. (6/1)
3424 Farmost, taking a step up in trip, was soon in front but, headed half a mile out, soon had bellows to mend. (100/30)

4145 E.B.F. CUCUMBER MAIDEN STKS (2-Y.O) (Class D)

5-20 (5-21) **6f** £5,300.75 (£1,586.00: £760.50: £347.75) Stalls: Low GOING: 0.32 sec per fur (G)

				SP	RR	SF
2870[2]	**Iceband (USA)** (JHMGosden) **2-9-0** LDettori(7) (lw: a.p: led over 1f out: comf)	—	1	4/5[1]	98	44
	Title Bid (USA) (MRStoute) **2-9-0** TQuinn(3) (w'like: hld up: nt clr run over 2f out: rdn over 1f out: r.o one pce)	3	2	9/1	90+	36
3127[3]	**Sabhaan** (MajorWRHern) **2-9-0** DHolland(6) (lw: led over 4f: one pce)	1¾	3	11/2[2]	85	31
3743[4]	**Chief Whip (USA)** (LMCumani) **2-8-11**(3) RFfrench(13) (hdwy over 1f out: one pce fnl f)	1¼	4	14/1	82	28
3490[5]	**Orsino** (SDow) **2-9-0** JFEgan(2) (rdn 3f out: hdwy fnl f: nvr nrr)	½	5	25/1	81	27
	Dilkusha (IRE) (BJMeehan) **2-9-0** MTebbutt(10) (leggy: a.p: rdn over 2f out: wknd over 1f out)	1¾	6	33/1	76	22
	Masha-Il (IRE) (JHMGosden) **2-9-0** GHind(14) (w'like: hld up: nt clr run over 2f out: wknd over 1f out)	2	7	14/1	71	17
3686[2]	**Mantles Pride** (GLewis) **2-9-0** PaulEddery(1) (b: hld up: rdn 3f out: wknd over 1f out)	1¼	8	7/1[3]	67	13
4012[W]	**Sacchetti (IRE)** (MRChannon) **2-9-0** JFortune(8) (prom over 4f)	s.h	9	20/1	67	13
	Seven (BSmart) **2-9-0** JStack(9) (w'like: a bhd)	hd	10	33/1	67	13
2781[10]	**Thomas O'Malley** (RJO'Sullivan) **2-9-0** AProcter(11) (prom 4f)	4	11	66/1	56	2
3791[6]	**Second Sun (46)** (JJBridger) **2-9-0** MWigham(4) (lw: a bhd)	7	12	66/1	38	—
				(SP 124.2%)		**12 Rn**

1m 15.52 (5.72) CSF £8.02 TOTE £1.70: £1.10 £1.90 £1.80 (£7.30) Trio £10.50 OWNER Sheikh Mohammed (NEWMARKET) BRED William Floyd
2870 Iceband (USA) confirmed the promise shown on his debut and, striking the front approaching the final furlong, was shaken up for a decisive victory. (4/5)
Title Bid (USA), a medium-sized colt, was blocked in behind a wall of horses over a quarter of a mile from home. Bustled along below the distance, he stayed on to take second place inside the final furlong, but had no hope with the winner. (9/1: op 9/2)
3127 Sabhaan took the field along but, collared approaching the final furlong, could only go up and down in the same place. He should soon find an ordinary maiden. (11/2)
3743 Chief Whip (USA) began a promising-looking effort on the outside of the field below the distance, but failed to make any real impression in the final furlong. (14/1)
3490 Orsino, racing at the back of the field, put in some late work without ever threatening. (25/1)
Dilkusha (IRE), a tall gelding, was close up until calling it a day approaching the final furlong. (33/1)
Masha-Il (IRE) (14/1: 10/1-16/1)
3686 Mantles Pride (7/1: op 9/2)

T/Plpt: £234.80 (124.67 Tckts). T/Qdpt: £87.60 (13.84 Tckts) AK

4132-DONCASTER (L-H) (Good to firm)
Saturday September 13th
WEATHER: sunny periods & showers WIND: fresh half against

4146 GREAT NORTH EASTERN RAILWAY CONDITIONS STKS (2-Y.O) (Class C)
2-00 (2-01) **6f** £4,639.60 (£1,716.40: £823.20: £336.00: £133.00: £51.80) Stalls: High GOING: 0.05 sec per fur (G)

	Horse	Dist	Pos	SP	RR	SF
3726*	**Bintang (IRE)** (PFICole) **2-9-1** TQuinn(4) (hld up: effrt 2f out: led ins fnl f: rdn & r.o)	—	**1**	8/11^{1}	109	57
	Sky Rocket (MRStoute) **2-8-8** JReid(2) (w'like: leggy: scope: a.p: effrt 2f out: ev ch 1f out: kpt on wl)	1¼	**2**	8/1	99+	47
3379^{2}	**Hayil (USA) (100)** (DMorley) **2-9-1** RHills(6) (lw: led: qcknd over 2f out: hdd & no ex ins fnl f)	1¼	**3**	4/1^{2}	102	50
3490*	**Harmonic Way** (RCharlton) **2-9-1** KFallon(1) (lw: hld up: effrt & prom 2f out: r.o one pce)	4	**4**	9/1	92	40
1735^{3}	**Flaming Ember (IRE) (95)** (BJMeehan) **2-8-13** PatEddery(5) (lw: spd 4f: sn outpcd)	½	**5**	7/1^{3}	88	36
3569^{6}	**Sara Moon Classic (IRE)** (KMcAuliffe) **2-8-11** JFEgan(3) (cl up over 3f: wknd)	14	**6**	50/1	49	—

(SP 113.5%) **6 Rn**

1m 14.28 (3.28) CSF £7.01 TOTE £1.70: £1.40 £2.40 (£3.90) OWNER Al Muallim Partnership (WHATCOMBE) BRED J. R. M. and Mrs P. Lewis

3726* Bintang (IRE) is a hard puller who was taken extremely cautiously to post, and then anchored out the back in the race. He did what he had to do but was not that impressive, and obviously needs to channel all of his energy into racing. (8/11)
Sky Rocket, a useful newcomer, showed plenty of promise and should not be hard to place to advantage and will appreciate a little further. (8/1)
3379 Hayil (USA) tried to steal this when quickening soon after halfway, but he was never good enough despite a valiant effort. (4/1)
3490* Harmonic Way, taking a step-up in class here, ran well but lacked the pace to really get into it, and should appreciate further. (9/1)
1735 Flaming Ember (IRE), returning here after over three months off, proved ring-rusty. (7/1)
3127 Sara Moon Classic (IRE) was completely outclassed here. (50/1)

4147 ROTHMANS ROYALS NORTH SOUTH CHALLENGE SERIES SEMI-FINAL H'CAP (0-100) (3-Y.O+) (Class C)
2-30 (2-36) **1m (round)** £19,820.00 (£5,960.00: £2,880.00: £1,340.00) Stalls: Low GOING minus 0.32 sec per fur (GF)

	Horse	Dist	Pos	SP	RR	SF
3801^{11}	**Epic Stand (78)** (MrsJRRamsden) **3-8-13** JFortune(5) (in tch: hdwy over 1f out: r.o wl to ld wl ins fnl f)	—	**1**	10/1^{2}	90	51
3901*	**Queens Consul (IRE) (85)** (BSRothwell) **7-9-11** MFenton(18) (bhd: gd hdwy on outside over 2f out: chal ins fnl f: kpt on wl)	½	**2**	14/1	96	62
3408^{5}	**Kala Sunrise (88)** (CSmith) **4-10-0** JTate(2) (lw: bhd: nt clr run over 3f out: hdwy 2f out: r.o wl towards fin)	½	**3**	25/1	98	64
3976^{13}	**Duraid (IRE) (76)** (DenysSmith) **5-8-11**(5) CLowther(9) (lw: s.i.s: hdwy & nt clr run 3f out: nt clr run appr fnl f: swtchd & fin fast)	1¼	**4**	16/1	84	50
3243^{10}	**Moving Arrow (82)** (MissSEHall) **6-9-8** DHolland(12) (in tch: hdwy to chal over 1f out: slt ld ins fnl f: sn hdd & no ex)	hd	**5**	33/1	89	55
3605^{3}	**Bowcliffe (63)** (EJAlston) **6-8-3** JFEgan(15) (lw: hld up: stdy hdwy over 2f out: kpt on: nt pce to chal)	hd	**6**	20/1	70	36
3605*	**High Spirits (IRE) (75)** (TDEasterby) **3-8-10b** LCharnock(14) (a.p: rdn to ld 1½f out: hdd ins fnl f: sn btn)	¾	**7**	10/1^{2}	81	42
3921^{11}	**Shinerolla (77)** (CParker) **5-9-3b^{1}** PatEddery(17) (bhd: gd hdwy 3f out: chsng ldrs appr fnl f: nt qckn)	1½	**8**	16/1	80	46
3810^{8}	**Mountgate (66)** (MPBielby) **5-8-6**ow2 ACulhane(10) (bhd: hdwy ½-wy: sn in tch: kpt on u.p fnl f)	¾	**9**	33/1	67	31
3901^{11}	**Band on the Run (81)** (BAMcMahon) **10-9-7** TQuinn(22) (bhd: nt clr run 3f out: hdwy 2f out: no imp)	½	**10**	25/1	81	47
3810^{5}	**Bollin Frank (69)** (TDEasterby) **5-8-9** OPeslier(19) (in tch tl wknd fnl 1½f)	½	**11**	20/1	68	34
3901^{2}	**Gulf Shaadi (74)** (EJAlston) **5-9-0** KFallon(1) (chsd ldrs: effrt over 2f out: sn rdn & btn)	nk	**12**	10/1^{2}	73	39
3901^{4}	**Hunters of Brora (IRE) (88)** (JDBethell) **7-10-0** JReid(25) (dwlt: hld up & bhd: nt clr run 3f out: nt rcvr)	s.h	**13**	12/1^{3}	86	52
3937^{3}	**Barnburgh Boy (74)** (TDEasterby) **3-8-9** JCarroll(20) (bhd: gd hdwy 2f out: wknd over 1f out)	nk	**14**	25/1	72	33
3976^{19}	**Suez Tornado (IRE) (70)** (EJAlston) **4-8-10** DWright(7) (w ldrs tl wknd appr fnl f)	1	**15**	16/1	66	32
3976^{3}	**For Your Eyes Only (80)** (TDEasterby) **3-9-1b** LDettori(6) (mde most tl hdd & wknd 1½f out)	nk	**16**	4/1^{1}	75	36
3976^{10}	**Pride of Pendle (77)** (MartynWane) **8-9-3** MRoberts(23) (hld up & bhd: effrt & plld wd 3f out: n.d)	s.h	**17**	14/1	72	38
3987^{4}	**Grey Kingdom (74)** (MBrittain) **6-8-7**(7) DMernagh(16) (chsd ldrs: effrt 2f out: sn wknd)	nk	**18**	20/1	69	35
3976^{17}	**Cashmere Lady (77)** (JLEyre) **5-9-3** OPears(3) (outpcd & bhd fnl 3f)	1¼	**19**	16/1	69	35
3901^{7}	**Albert The Bear (86)** (JBerry) **4-9-9**(3) TEDurcan(13) (chsd ldrs: rdn over 2f out: grad wknd)	s.h	**20**	33/1	78	44
4015^{4}	**Night Mirage (USA) (76)** (MJohnston) **3-8-11** JWeaver(11) (chsd ldrs 6f: wknd)	3	**21**	16/1	62	23
3901^{10}	**Knave's Ash (USA) (75)** (DNicholls) **6-9-1** AlexGreaves(8) (in tch tl wknd over 3f out)	5	**22**	12/1^{3}	51	17
3039^{7}	**Gladys Althorpe (IRE) (65)** (JLEyre) **4-8-5** TWilliams(24) (prom tl ½-wy: sn btn)	s.h	**23**	20/1	41	7
3798^{9}	**No Cliches (70)** (DNicholls) **4-8-10** SSanders(4) (lw: in tch: drvn along ½-wy: sn lost pl)	1¼	**24**	25/1	43	9
3921*	**Antarctic Storm (66)** (RAFahey) **4-8-6** FNorton(21) (lw: bolted riderless bef s: cl up tl ½-wy: sn wknd & eased)	25	**25**	20/1	—	—

(SP 153.4%) **25 Rn**

1m 40.39 (1.99) CSF £130.20 CT £3,225.15 TOTE £11.40: £2.90 £4.10 £12.80 £5.90 (£119.20) Trio £694.70 OWNER Mr Colin Webster (THIRSK) BRED Cleaboy Farms Co
WEIGHT FOR AGE 3yo-5lb

3428 Epic Stand, like many in this race, had traffic problems, but when he saw daylight, he had the required turn of foot to make full use of it. (10/1)
3901* Queens Consul (IRE), poorly drawn, had to come from off the pace this time and ran a cracker in the circumstances. (14/1)
3408 Kala Sunrise likes to come from off the pace and had no luck at all in running, but for which he would probably have won this. (25/1)
3810 Duraid (IRE) found all the trouble going and did well to finish so close and he obviously remains in good form. (16/1)
2341 Moving Arrow ran his best race for some time and is certainly off a useful mark if remaining in this mood. (33/1)
3605 Bowcliffe does not seem to know how to run a bad race these days despite shooting up the handicap. (20/1)
3605* High Spirits (IRE) put in his usual gallant effort, but his rise in the weights looked to have anchored him. (10/1)
444 Shinerolla, in blinkers for the first time, ran well and seems to be coming to hand. (16/1)
3901 Hunters of Brora (IRE), trying the impossible, to come from behind in such a competitive and large field, never saw daylight. (12/1)
3976 For Your Eyes Only was a ridiculous price. He has never looked a battler and was probably made too much use of here. (4/1)

4148 PORCELANOSA RATED STKS H'CAP (0-105) (3-Y.O+) (Class B)
3-05 (3-07) **1m (straight)** £13,534.40 (£5,009.60: £2,404.80: £984.00: £392.00: £155.20) Stalls: High GOING: 0.05 sec per fur (G)

	Horse	Dist	Pos	SP	RR	SF
3725^{3}	**Russian Music (100)** (MissGayKelleway) **4-9-2** KFallon(8) (lw: hld up: effrt over 2f out: r.o u.p to ld wl ins fnl f)	—	**1**	8/1	111	82
3712^{5}	**Hawait (IRE) (91)** (BWHills) **3-7-13b^{1}**(3) PFessey(10) (bhd: gd hdwy over 2f out: led appr fnl f: hdd & nt qckn towards fin)	½	**2**	25/1	101	67

3741[2] **Al Azhar (91)** (IABalding) **3-8-2** CRutter(3) (lw: hld up: hdwy 2f out: kpt on: nt pce to chal)..........nk **3** 8/1 100 66
3217[17] **Yorkie George (99)** (LMCumani) **3-8-10** LDettori(4) (hld up: hdwy 2f out: nt clr run ins fnl f: styd on towards fin)..........2½ **4** 6/1[3] 103 69
3786* **Pomona (91)** (PJMakin) **4-8-7** JFortune(9) (bhd: hdwy 3f out: sn chsng ldrs & edgd lft: one pce fnl f)..........s.h **5** 8/1 95 66
3725[7] **Jo Mell (93)** (TDEasterby) **4-8-9** LCharnock(5) (trckd ldrs: hdwy to disp ld over 2f out tl hdd appr fnl f: nt qckn)..........1½ **6** 15/2 94 65
3764[4] **Restructure (IRE) (105)** (MrsJCecil) **5-9-7** MRoberts(6) (lw: trckd ldrs: hdwy to disp ld over 2f out: hdd over 1f out: one pce)..........s.h **7** 11/4[1] 106 77
3575[7] **Premier Bay (97)** (PWHarris) **3-8-8b** JReid(7) (trckd ldrs: effrt over 2f out: sn btn)..........6 **8** 20/1 86 52
3051[10] **Mukaddar (USA) (95)** (CJBenstead) **3-8-6** RHills(1) (chsd ldrs tl rdn & wknd wl over 1f out)..........2 **9** 20/1 80 46
2871* **Stanton Harcourt (USA) (97)** (JLDunlop) **3-8-8** PatEddery(11) (swtchd lft after 1f: hdwy ½-wy: rdn & btn over 2f out)..........8 **10** 4/1[2] 66 32
892[25] **Yeast (105)** (WJHaggas) **5-9-7** TQuinn(2) (led tl hdd & wknd over 2f out)..........9 **11** 12/1 56 27
(SP 127.1%) **11 Rn**

1m 39.43 (2.23) CSF £186.48 CT £1,557.03 TOTE £10.00: £2.10 £11.70 £2.60 (£158.00) Trio £416.20 OWNER The Seventh Heaven Partnership (WHITCOMBE) BRED Mrs N. F. M. Sampson
LONG HANDICAP Pomona 8-3 Hawait (IRE) 7-11 Al Azhar 8-1
WEIGHT FOR AGE 3yo-5lb
STEWARDS' ENQUIRY Fortune susp. 22-23/9/97 (careless riding)
3725 Russian Music was ridden with restraint this time, and it worked the oracle as he responded to pressure to snatch it late on. (8/1)
3712 Hawait (IRE) had blinkers on for the first time and was 5lb out of the handicap but, as it turned out, he may have hit the front too soon. He seems to have more ability if things go his way. (25/1)
3741 Al Azhar, dropping back in trip, kept staying on under pressure and left the impression that further is needed. (8/1)
2775* Yorkie George had no luck in running, and although it is unlikely that he would have won he would have finished a deal closer. (6/1)
3786* Pomona is a difficult ride and just wants to hang left, and there is certainly more ability there if it can be coaxed out. (8/1)
3725 Jo Mell ran a useful race off his present high mark. (15/2)
3764 Restructure (IRE) had his chances but was never really firing and being slightly hampered made no difference. (11/4)
2871* Stanton Harcourt (USA) was left on his own on the stands side after the start, and his rider then switched him right over to join the others after that. He certainly did not give his running. (4/1)

4149 PERTEMPS ST LEGER STKS (Gp 1) (3-Y.O C & F) (Class A)

3-40 (3-45) **1m 6f 132y** £183,776.00 (£67,784.00: £32,342.00: £13,010.00: £4,955.00: £1,733.00) Stalls: Low GOING minus 0.32 sec per fur (GF)

SP RR SF

3647[2] **Silver Patriarch (IRE) (123)** (JLDunlop) **3-9-0** PatEddery(9) (a in tch: rdn along 3f out: led wl over 1f out: styd on strly u.p)..........— **1** 5/4[1] 127 54
3179a* **Vertical Speed (FR)** (AFabre,France) **3-9-0** OPeslier(8) (w'like: lw: trckd ldrs: qcknd to ld over 2f out: sn hdd: ev ch tl wknd ins fnl f)..........3 **2** 7/2[2] 124 51
2454a[9] **The Fly (107)** (BWHills) **3-9-0** MHills(3) (hld up & bhd: hdwy 3f out: chsng ldrs over 1f out: kpt on)..........nk **3** 10/1[3] 123 50
4099* **Book At Bedtime (IRE) (100)** (CACyzer) **3-8-11** MRoberts(2) (led 2f: chsd ldrs: hrd drvn over 3f out: kpt on wl: nt pce to chal)..........1½ **4** 14/1 119 46
3645[3] **Windsor Castle (115)** (PFICole) **3-9-0b** TQuinn(7) (b.nr fore: a chsng ldrs: chal 5f out: one pce fnl 2f)..........s.h **5** 10/1[3] 122 49
3596[2] **Panama City (USA) (116)** (PWChapple-Hyam) **3-9-0** JReid(6) (lw: rr div: effrt ent st: styd on: nvr able chal).3½ **6** 12/1 118 45
3501* **Shaya (97)** (MajorWRHern) **3-9-0** RHills(10) (hld up & bhd: effrt 4f out: rdn & nvr able to chal)..........2½ **7** 33/1 115 42
3109[2] **Poseidon (109)** (MRChannon) **3-9-0** JFortune(5) (hld up & bhd: hdwy 4f out: hrd drvn & in tch 2f out: sn wknd)..........2 **8** 25/1 113 40
3784[2] **Haltarra (USA) (109)** (SbinSuroor) **3-9-0** LDettori(11) (racd wd first 4f: led after 2f tl over 2f out: sn wknd).....10 **9** 16/1 102 29
851[6] **Besiege (111)** (HRACecil) **3-9-0** KFallon(4) (trckd ldrs: hdwy 6f out: rdn & wknd fnl 3f)..........1 **10** 10/1[3] 101 28
(SP 121.0%) **10 Rn**

3m 6.92 (3.32) CSF £5.14 TOTE £2.20: £1.40 £2.40 £2.20 (£4.40) Trio £16.80 OWNER Mr Peter Winfield (ARUNDEL) BRED Peter Winfield
IN-FOCUS: **Pat Eddery's fourteenth Classic success was also his 4,000th winner in Britain, a tally exceeded only by Sir Gordon Richards and Lester Piggott.**
3647 Silver Patriarch (IRE) appreciated the trip, and the further they went the stronger he got. In the end it was a most emphatic victory. (5/4)
3179a* Vertical Speed (FR) has done all of his winning on soft ground and in the circumstances this was a tremendous effort, but these conditions found him out in the closing stages. (7/2: 5/2-4/1)
2454a The Fly was given a terrible tactical ride last time, but was ridden much more sensibly here and ran a storming race. Although he was never going to trouble the winner in the last furlong and a half, he kept on well and would have been second with a little further to go. (10/1)
4099* Book At Bedtime (IRE) stays particularly well but got outpaced at a vital stage, and when this game filly began to make progress it was all too late. (14/1)
3645 Windsor Castle, who is basically a soft-ground stayer, ran well in conditions that were far too quick. (10/1)
3596 Panama City (USA) seems to go on any ground and stays well, but lacked the pace to ever seriously get into this. (12/1)
3501* Shaya had plenty on here and this angular colt was never good enough to get in a blow. (33/1)
3109 Poseidon, stepping up in trip, ran reasonably but did not appear to get home. (25/1)
3784 Haltarra (USA) set a useful pace until his stamina gave out in the last two furlongs. (16/1)
851 Besiege looked very fit and keen beforehand and had run himself out early in the straight. (10/1)

4150 POLYPIPE PLC FLYING CHILDERS STKS (Gp 2) (2-Y.O) (Class A)

4-15 (4-16) **5f** £25,670.00 (£9,470.00: £4,520.00: £1,820.00: £695.00: £245.00) Stalls: High GOING: 0.05 sec per fur (G)

SP RR SF

3811[2] **Land of Dreams (100)** (MJohnston) **2-8-7** DHolland(5) (lw: hld up: stdy hdwy to ld ins fnl f: qcknd: impressive)..........— **1** 15/8[1] 98+ 52
3192[5] **Tippitt Boy (100)** (KMcAuliffe) **2-9-3** JFEgan(1) (trckd ldrs: rdn to ld appr fnl f: hdd & no ch w wnr ins fnl f)...2½ **2** 12/1 100 54
3708[6] **Titanic (IRE) (95)** (JHMGosden) **2-8-12** LDettori(6) (trckd ldrs: n.m.r & outpcd 1½f out: styd on wl towards fin)..........nk **3** 7/2[2] 94 48
2831* **Bayleaf** (RFJohnsonHoughton) **2-8-7** JReid(4) (lw: cl up: disp ld wl over 1f out: no ex ins fnl f)..........¾ **4** 7/1 87 41
3908[3] **Banningham Blade (100)** (KTIvory) **2-8-7** KFallon(3) (cl up: wkng whn hmpd over 1f out)..........nk **5** 6/1 86 40
3595[8] **Mugello (100)** (APJarvis) **2-8-7** MHills(2) (led tl hdd appr fnl f: sn btn)..........¾ **6** 13/2 83 37

3595* **Aurigny (100)** (SDow) **2-8-7** SSanders(7) (hld up: effrt 2f out: nvr able chal) 1½ **7** 9/2 3 79 33
(SP 123.0%) **7 Rn**

60.94 secs (2.54) CSF £26.23 TOTE £3.00: £1.60 £5.30 (£18.70) OWNER Maktoum Al Maktoum (MIDDLEHAM) BRED Gainsborough Stud Management Ltd

3811 Land of Dreams, trying the minimum trip for the first time, was given a most patient ride and did the business in some style. She is going to be one to be reckoned with in top-class sprints next year. (15/8)
3192 Tippitt Boy ran his heart out but was completely outclassed by the winner in the closing stages. (12/1)
3708 Titanic (IRE) was short of pace and room at a vital stage and then ran on, but was never good enough and looks to need further. (7/2)
2831* Bayleaf, the winner of a hot maiden last time, was tapped for toe late on. (7/1)
3908 Banningham Blade ran a fair race, but was already feeling the pace and was going nowhere when she was hampered approaching the final furlong. (6/1)
3192 Mugello attempted to make all but had her limitations exposed in the closing stages. (13/2)
3595* Aurigny travelled well, but disappointing failed to pick up when ridden. (9/2)

4151 LADBROKE H'CAP (0-95) (3-Y.O+) (Class C)

4-45 (4-47) **1m 2f 60y** £14,996.00 (£5,564.00: £2,682.00: £1,110.00: £455.00: £193.00) Stalls: Low GOING minus 0.32 sec per fur (GF)

				SP	RR	SF
3197 2	**Infatuation (77)** (LadyHerries) **4-8-11** JWeaver(11) (hld up & bhd: hdwy 4f out: str run appr fnl f to ld wl ins fnl f)	—	**1**	16/1	88	71
3773 10	**Ihtiyati (USA) (93)** (JLDunlop) **3-9-6** RHills(18) (hld up: effrt over 2f out: rdn to ld ins fnl f: hdd & nt qckn towards fin)	½	**2**	20/1	103	79
3773 8	**Wafir (IRE) (81)** (PCalver) **5-9-1** JFortune(8) (hdwy 4f out: chsng ldrs 2f out: kpt on u.p)	1½	**3**	16/1	89	72
3575 6	**Shadoof (77)** (WRMuir) **3-8-4** MRoberts(9) (hdwy 4f out: chsng ldrs over 1f out: kpt on ins fnl f)	nk	**4**	14/1	84	60
3916 13	**Song of Freedom (89)** (JHMGosden) **3-9-2** LDettori(6) (hdwy over 4f out: chsng ldrs whn n.m.r over 2f out: styd on fnl f)	nk	**5**	7/2 1	96	72
3798 3	**Fahs (USA) (76)** (RAkehurst) **5-8-10** DHolland(1) (led 2f: w ldrs: led wl over 2f out tl ins fnl f: no ex)	nk	**6**	9/1	83	66
3722 15	**Mattimeo (IRE) (80)** (APJarvis) **4-8-9**(5) CLowther(17) (lw: hld up: hdwy on outside 3f out: styd on: nvr able to chal)	s.h	**7**	25/1	86	69
4063*	**Edan Heights (71)** (SDow) **5-7-12**(7) PDoe(5) (chsd ldrs tl wknd fnl f)	1½	**8**	14/1	75	58
3752 2	**Sheer Face (79)** (WRMuir) **3-8-6**ow1 JReid(4) (prom: pushed along over 3f out: ev ch over 1f out: wknd ins fnl f)	½	**9**	20/1	82	57
3906 2	**Mcgillycuddy Reeks (IRE) (69)** (DonEnricoIncisa) **6-8-3** KimTinkler(10) (bhd: hdwy on outside 3f out: nvr rchd ldrs)	2	**10**	20/1	69	52
3703 5	**Kuala Lipis (USA) (89)** (PFICole) **4-9-9b** TQuinn(14) (lw: in tch: effrt 4f out: wknd fnl 2f)	1	**11**	10/1	88	71
3575 5	**Chief Monarch (85)** (BSmart) **3-8-12** JStack(7) (chsd ldrs tl wknd fnl 2½f out)	3	**12**	13/2 2	79	55
3722 10	**My Lewicia (IRE) (94)** (PWHarris) **4-10-0** PatEddery(3) (chsd ldr tl wknd fnl 2½f)	4	**13**	20/1	82	65
2889 7	**Break the Rules (81)** (DNicholls) **5-9-1** AlexGreaves(16) (bhd & rdn 4f out: n.d)	2½	**14**	25/1	65	48
3921 12	**Rebel County (IRE) (70)** (ABailey) **4-8-4** DBiggs(2) (effrt 4f out: n.d)	5	**15**	25/1	46	29
3722 4	**Oops Pettie (86)** (MrsJCecil) **4-9-6** JCarroll(19) (lw: in tch: rdn over 3f out: wknd fnl 2f)	2½	**16**	8/1 3	58	41
3238 3	**Khayali (IRE) (89)** (DMorley) **3-9-2** KFallon(13) (led after 2f tl wl over 2f out: wknd)	4	**17**	11/1	55	31
3061 7	**Flying North (IRE) (79)** (MrsMReveley) **4-8-13** ACulhane(15) (hmpd after s: bhd tl hdwy 4f out: sn rdn & btn)	2½	**18**	20/1	41	24
3499 5	**Royal Crusade (USA) (90)** (WJHaggas) **3-9-3** SSanders(12) (plld hrd: bhd: effrt over 3f out: n.d)	hd	**19**	25/1	52	28
3705 16	**Dreams End (83)** (PBowen) **9-9-3** MFenton(20) (b: bhd: effrt 4f out: n.d)	6	**20**	9/1	36	19

(SP 148.4%) **20 Rn**

2m 7.68 (-0.12) CSF £300.92 CT £4,722.11 TOTE £20.40: £3.80 £8.60 £8.40 £4.00 (£535.30) Trio £2,253.00 OWNER Lady Katharine Phillips (LITTLEHAMPTON) BRED Cheveley Park Stud Ltd
WEIGHT FOR AGE 3yo-7lb

3197 Infatuation has to be held up and races with his head very high, but he has bags of ability and possesses an amazing turn of foot, which won the day. (16/1)
1025 Ihtiyati (USA) travelled well and looked to have done everything right, only to get caught late on. He looks in really good form at the moment. (20/1)
3263 Wafir (IRE) is coming back to form and kept struggling on here but was just short of a turn of foot and needs a bit further. (16/1)
3575 Shadoof ran well and kept staying on. He seems on a useful mark. (14/1)
3575* Song of Freedom ran well despite being short of room and would obviously have been a lot closer with any luck. (7/2: op 11/2)
3798 Fahs (USA) ran a useful race but it just proved too competitive for his liking in the closing stages. (9/1)
3184* Mattimeo (IRE) is 5lb higher than he has previously won off but, running well, was staying on when it was all over. (25/1)

4152 H. L. BROWN DIAMOND NURSERY H'CAP (0-85) (2-Y.O) (Class D)

5-15 (5-18) **6f** £5,166.00 (£1,548.00: £744.00: £342.00) Stalls: High GOING: 0.05 sec per fur (G)

				SP	RR	SF
3823 2	**Far Removed (IRE) (72)** (MrsJRRamsden) **2-8-8** JFortune(11) (lw: in tch: effrt 2f out: led appr fnl f: all out)	—	**1**	5/2 1	79	47
3811 6	**Blue Kite (75)** (NPLittmoden) **2-8-11** JWeaver(6) (bhd: hdwy over 1f out: ev ch ins fnl f: kpt on)	½	**2**	12/1	81	49
3799 2	**Night Shot (85)** (IABalding) **2-9-7** LDettori(8) (lw: bhd: hdwy over 2f out: chsng ldrs appr fnl f: kpt on)	1½	**3**	100/30 2	87	55
3869*	**Inchalong (69)** (MBrittain) **2-8-5** GBardwell(3) (hdwy u.p ½-wy: led wl over 1f out: sn hdd: kpt on)	nk	**4**	12/1	70	38
3823 3	**Angel Hill (79)** (TDBarron) **2-9-1** KFallon(10) (bhd: hdwy over 2f out: hrd rdn & edgd rt: styd on wl fnl f)	1½	**5**	9/1 3	76	44
3892 5	**Italian Rose (65)** (WJMusson) **2-8-1** JFEgan(9) (prom: effrt & ev ch over 1f out: wknd ins fnl f)	½	**6**	16/1	61	29
3823 8	**Brookhouse Lady (IRE) (60)** (RHollinshead) **2-7-10** NCarlisle(5) (outpcd tl styd on wl fnl f)	s.h	**7**	16/1	55	23
3904 8	**Ra Ra Rasputin (72)** (BAMcMahon) **2-8-8** MRoberts(4) (a chsng ldrs: rdn wl over 1f out: wknd ins fnl f)	1¼	**8**	14/1	64	32
3212 4	**Three Tenners (60)** (JBerry) **2-7-7b**(3) PFessey(1) (swvd lft s: swtchd rt & bhd: hdwy & hmpd over 1f out: styd on wl)	s.h	**9**	14/1	52	20
3905 10	**Cool Mystery (60)** (ABMulholland) **2-7-10** DWright(7) (mid div: pushed along ½-wy: no imp)	¾	**10**	20/1	50	18
3686 20	**Memorial (IRE) (62)** (RHannon) **2-7-12**ow2 CRutter(14) (hdwy u.p ½-wy: nvr trbld ldrs)	s.h	**11**	16/1	52	18
2758 3	**Premium Pursuit (83)** (RAFahey) **2-8-12b1**(7) RWinston(13) (led & sn clr: hdd wl over 1f out: sn wknd)	1¼	**12**	10/1	70	38
3932 15	**Mill End Quest (66)** (MWEasterby) **2-8-2** DaleGibson(2) (in tch tl hung lft & wknd fr ½-wy)	2½	**13**	25/1	46	14
3817 5	**Life Sentence (61)** (JGSmyth-Osbourne) **2-7-11b1**ow1 FNorton(12) (chsd ldrs tl wknd & hmpd over 1f out)	6	**14**	25/1	25	—
3103 9	**Shannon's Secret (IRE) (71)** (BJMeehan) **2-8-7** PatEddery(15) (chsd ldrs to ½-wy: wl btn whn bdly hmpd over 1f out)	2½	**15**	14/1	28	—

3825[7]	**Lambs Lane (69)** (TDEasterby) **2-8-5b**[1] LCharnock(16) (chsd ldrs 4f) ...3½	**16**	20/1	17	—	
			(SP 141.0%)			**16 Rn**

1m 14.53 (3.53) CSF £34.97 CT £104.44 TOTE £3.30: £1.50 £3.20 £1.40 £2.10 (£33.80) Trio £36.00 OWNER Mrs J. R. Ramsden (THIRSK) BRED R. J. McAlpine and D. O. Pickering

LONG HANDICAP Memorial (IRE) 7-9 Three Tenners 7-8

3823 Far Removed (IRE) did the business at last here but it needed a lot of help from the saddle. This will probably have taught him plenty. (5/2)
3610 Blue Kite had a lot of running to do from halfway and responded to pressure in gallant style, only to find one just too determined. (12/1)
3799 Night Shot put in a useful effort under top weight and ought to appreciate longer trips. (100/30)
3869* Inchalong was up to her old tricks in the stalls here, but still ran a fair race. (12/1: 8/1-14/1)
3823 Angel Hill took a lot of persuading to get going but she did finish particularly well. (9/1)
3892 Italian Rose had her chances but seemed to run out of stamina. (16/1)
861 Brookhouse Lady (IRE) ran as though a little further might help. (16/1)
3212 Three Tenners gave away a lot of ground at the start and then found trouble in running, and but for this would have finished a lot closer. (14/1)
2758 Premium Pursuit had blinkers on for the first time and went far too freely. (10/1)

T/Jkpt: Not won; £10,762.15 to 15/9/97. T/Plpt: £1,778.00 (37.11 Tckts). T/Qdpt: £214.00 (12.79 Tckts) AA/WG

4139-GOODWOOD (R-H) (St crse Good to soft, Rnd crse Good)
Saturday September 13th

WEATHER: sunny WIND: mod half against

4153 MGM ASSURANCE RATED STKS H'CAP (0-105) (3-Y.O+) (Class B)
2-15 (2-16) **7f** £9,529.80 (£3,568.20: £1,746.60: £753.00: £339.00: £173.40) Stalls: Low GOING minus 0.01 sec per fur (G)

			SP	RR	SF
3594[2]	**Law Commission (91)** (DRCElsworth) **7-8-9** SDrowne(7) (rdn over 1f out: hdwy 1f out: led ins fnl f: r.o wl)...—	**1**	4/1[1]	99	52
3913[9]	**Dancing Drop (98)** (RHannon) **3-8-12** DaneO'Neill(11) (a.p: rdn over 2f out: ev ch ins fnl f: unable qckn) 1	**2**	7/1	104	53
1737[15]	**Bachelors Pad (93)** (WJarvis) **3-8-7** WRyan(4) (a.p: rdn over 2f out: r.o ins fnl f) ...1¼	**3**	20/1	96	45
3764[13]	**Tumbleweed Ridge (103)** (BJMeehan) **4-9-7b** MTebbutt(5) (lw: chsd ldr: led 2f out tl ins fnl f: one pce).........hd	**4**	7/1	106	59
1170[4]	**Speedball (IRE) (96)** (IABalding) **3-8-10** MartinDwyer(6) (rdn over 3f out: hdwy fnl f: nvr nrr) ...¾	**5**	7/1	97	46
3713*	**Showboat (95)** (BWHills) **3-8-9** GDuffield(1) (rdn over 2f out: hdwy fnl f: nvr nrr) ...nk	**6**	9/2[2]	95	44
3604[18]	**Ursa Major (90)** (PAKelleway) **3-8-4**ow1 GHind(10) (led 5f: wknd ins fnl f) ...nk	**7**	50/1	90	38
2273a[8]	**Craigievar (99)** (JRFanshawe) **3-8-13** NDay(2) (hdwy over 2f out: wknd over 1f out) ...1¾	**8**	4/1[1]	95	44
4100[9]	**Hello Mister (96)** (TEPowell) **6-8-11**(3) PMcCabe(12) (a bhd) ...¾	**9**	7/1	90	43
3423[10]	***Cosmic Prince (IRE) (93)*** (MAJarvis) **3-8-7** RCochrane(9) (Withdrawn not under Starter's orders: bolted bef s) ...	**W**	5/1[3]	—	—
			(SP 131.6%)		**9 Rn**

1m 28.26 (3.46) CSF £29.20 CT £454.97 TOTE £4.10: £1.30 £2.20 £4.50 (£15.50) Trio £123.20 OWNER Mr Raymond Tooth (WHITCOMBE) BRED Airlie Stud

LONG HANDICAP Ursa Major 7-2

WEIGHT FOR AGE 3yo-4lb

3594 Law Commission has done all his previous winning on fast ground but, under a lovely ride, he came with a useful run to sweep into the lead in the last seventy-five yards. (4/1)
2133 Dancing Drop left her last two disappointing runs behind. Always close up, she had every chance inside the final furlong before the winner swept by. (7/1: 6/1-10/1)
1462 Bachelors Pad, a previous course winner but without a run in three months, was never far away, and kept on well inside the final furlong. (20/1)
2775 Tumbleweed Ridge may have disappointed on his last two outings, but he is still 9lb higher than when successful in the Bunbury Cup in July. Nevertheless, he gave a good account of himself, showing in front a quarter of a mile out before overhauled inside the final furlong. (7/1)
1170 Speedball (IRE), without a run in four months, only got going in the final furlong. Another furlong may well help him. (7/1)
3713* Showboat was not helped by the drop back to seven furlongs and, when he did pick up ground, it was all far too late. A return to a mile is needed. (9/2)
4100 Hello Mister (7/1: 6/1-9/1)

4154 WESTMINSTER TAXI INSURANCE SELECT STKS (Gp 3) (3-Y.O+) (Class A)
2-45 (2-45) **1m 2f** £22,960.00 (£8,585.50: £4,117.75: £1,786.75) Stalls: Low GOING minus 0.01 sec per fur (G)

			SP	RR	SF
3785[3]	**Fahris (IRE) (113)** (BHanbury) **3-8-7** RCochrane(2) (lw: mde all: rdn over 2f out: clr over 1f out: r.o wl) ....—	**1**	100/30[2]	119	61
1159[2]	**Desert Story (IRE) (115)** (MRStoute) **3-8-10** WRyan(5) (hld up: rdn over 2f out: chsd wnr over 1f out: no imp) 6	**2**	5/4[1]	112	54
3634[2]	**Green Card (USA) (107)** (SPCWoods) **3-8-7** NDay(1) (hld up: rdn over 2f out: one pce) ...½	**3**	5/1[3]	109	51
3797*	**Amid Albadu (USA) (107)** (JLDunlop) **3-8-7b** GCarter(4) (lw: rdn over 3f out: hdwy 2f out: one pce).............hd	**4**	100/30[2]	108	50
3988[4]	**Acharne (108)** (CEBrittain) **4-9-0** GDuffield(3) (lw: hld up: rdn over 2f out: sn wknd) ...2½	**5**	25/1	104	53
			(SP 111.1%)		**5 Rn**

2m 10.38 (3.78) CSF £7.34 TOTE £3.30: £1.50 £1.30 (£2.70) OWNER Mr Hamdan Al Maktoum (NEWMARKET) BRED Shadwell Estate Company Limited

WEIGHT FOR AGE 3yo-7lb

3785 Fahris (IRE), unsuited by the Windsor track last time, put up a thoroughly impressive display. Perfectly at home on this slightly easier surface, he made every post a winning one and, quickening up in the straight, forged clear below the distance for a decisive victory. The Champion Stakes or possibly the St Simon Stakes are his targets. (100/30: 9/4-7/2)
1159 Desert Story (IRE), rather sore and stressed after finishing second in the Dante in May, was having his first run since. Moving into second place approaching the final furlong, he was well and truly put in his place by the winner. He is due to meet the winner again in the Champion Stakes, but on this evidence will have to come on a lot for the run. (5/4)
3634 Green Card (USA) has been given some tough assignments since winning a Ripon maiden back in April and, bustled along over two furlongs out, failed to make any further progress. (5/1)
3797* Amid Albadu (USA), the first one to be pushed along, made ground a quarter of a mile out, but was then only battling for minor honours. (100/30)
3988 Acharne is not up to winning at this level, although he has run some decent races. He has got just one win to his name. (25/1)

4155 WILLIAM HILL SPRINT CUP H'CAP (0-95) (3-Y.O+) (Class C)

3-20 (3-22) **6f** £15,565.00 (£4,720.00: £2,310.00: £1,105.00) Stalls: High GOING: 0.22 sec per fur (G)

				SP	RR	SF
3975^{8}	**Wildwood Flower (90)** (RHannon) **4-9-12** DaneO'Neill(16) (hdwy over 1f out: str run fnl f: led nr fin)	—	1	20/1	100	76
3765^{2}	**No Extras (IRE) (85)** (GLMoore) **7-9-7** JQuinn(20) (nt clr run over 1f out: gd hdwy fnl f: r.o wl)	s.h	2	$11/2^{1}$	95	71
3936^{4}	**Grand Chapeau (IRE) (66)** (DNicholls) **5-8-2** GDuffield(19) (led: rdn over 1f out: hdd nr fin)	½	3	20/1	75	51
1101^{3}	**Lochangel (93)** (IABalding) **3-9-13** RCochrane(29) (lw: a.p: rdn over 1f out: one pce ins fnl f)	½	4	$14/1^{3}$	100	74
3923*	**March Crusader (86)** (BHanbury) **3-9-6** WRyan(9) (lw: a.p: rdn over 1f out: one pce)	nk	5	20/1	92	66
3856*	**Double Oscar (IRE) (81)** (DNicholls) **4-8-10b**(7) ANicholls(21) (hdwy over 1f out: r.o wl ins fnl f)	hd	6	$12/1^{2}$	87	63
3765^{6}	**Scissor Ridge (60)** (JJBridger) **5-7-3**(7) RBrisland(27) (a.p: rdn over 2f out: one pce ins fnl f)	hd	7	16/1	66	42
3982^{6}	**Kind of Light (70)** (RGuest) **4-8-6** SDrowne(24) (hdwy over 1f out: r.o)	nk	8	25/1	75	51
3580^{10}	**Lady Diesis (USA) (73)** (BWHills) **3-8-4**(3) JDSmith(13) (lw: hdwy over 1f out: r.o wl ins fnl f)	¾	9	40/1	76	50
3975^{6}	**Jeffrey Anotherred (85)** (KMcAuliffe) **3-9-5** GHind(17) (lw: a.p: rdn over 2f out: one pce)	nk	10	20/1	87	61
3765*	**Rififi (78)** (RIngram) **4-9-0** DRMcCabe(10) (b: lw: racd stands's side: nvr nrr)	s.h	11	$12/1^{2}$	80	56
3615^{3}	**La Petite Fusee (77)** (RJO'Sullivan) **6-8-10**(3) RHavlin(1) (racd stands' side: prom 3f)	½	12	20/1	78	54
3914^{6}	**Soviet Leader (82)** (RGuest) **3-8-13**(3) RFfrench(15) (lw: prom over 4f)	hd	13	$14/1^{3}$	83	57
3604^{5}	**Golden Pound (USA) (80)** (MissGayKelleway) **5-8-11b**(5) RMullen(3) (racd stands' side: prom over 4f)	½	14	20/1	79	55
3709^{6}	**Distinctive Dream (IRE) (74)** (KTIvory) **3-8-8b** MartinDwyer(7) (racd stands' side: a mid div)	hd	15	20/1	73	47
3145*	**Always On My Mind (86)** (PJMakin) **3-9-6** PaulEddery(5) (lw: racd stands' side: prom over 4f)	hd	16	$12/1^{2}$	85	59
3914^{7}	**Loch Patrick (90)** (MMadgwick) **7-9-5**(7) AEddery(28) (lw:.nvr nrr)	1¼	17	33/1	85	61
4048^{2}	**Bayin (USA) (60)** (MDIUsher) **8-7-10** RStreet(18) (b: nvr nrr)	hd	18	16/1	55	31
3910^{2}	**Mallia (63)** (TDBarron) **4-7-13** AMackay(14) (a mid div)	s.h	19	$12/1^{2}$	58	34
4013^{5}	**State of Caution (78)** (DShaw) **4-9-0b** JFanning(25) (b: s.s: outpcd)	nk	20	33/1	72	48
3771*	**Sharp Pearl (84)** (PRWebber) **4-9-3b**(3) DSweeney(12) (lw: racd stands' side: a bhd)	nk	21	25/1	77	53
4016^{17}	**Gold Edge (62)** (MRChannon) **3-7-5**(5) APolli(26) (prom 5f)	hd	22	66/1	55	29
3764^{5}	**Cryhavoc (91)** (JRArnold) **3-9-11** AClark(22) (prom 3f)	nk	23	20/1	83	57
3987^{13}	**Ivory Dawn (72)** (KTIvory) **3-8-6v**^{1} JLowe(2) (lw: racd stands' side: a bhd)	nk	24	40/1	64	38
3982^{15}	**Tea Party (USA) (63)** (KOCunningham-Brown) **4-7-10b**(3) MHenry(23) (lw: prom over 3f)	s.h	25	40/1	54	30
4048^{12}	**Fairy Prince (IRE) (73)** (MrsALMKing) **4-8-9** MTebbutt(6) (racd stands' side: prom 4f)	nk	26	33/1	64	40
3900^{5}	**Samwar (80)** (MRChannon) **5-9-2** GCarter(11) (b.hind: s.s: a bhd)	1	27	16/1	68	44
3984^{6}	**Heavenly Miss (IRE) (62)** (JJBridger) **3-7-10** NAdams(4) (racd stands' side: a bhd)	2	28	50/1	45	19
3914^{5}	**Youdontsay (81)** (TJNaughton) **5-9-0**(3) DO'Donohoe(8) (lw: racd stands' side: bhd fnl 2f)	½	29	33/1	62	38
				(SP 145.5%)	**29 Rn**	

1m 13.48 (3.68) CSF £101.49 CT £2,142.80 TOTE £21.60: £4.90 £2.30 £8.10 £4.10 (£76.20) Trio £216.30 OWNER Mr G. Howard-Spink (MARLBOROUGH) BRED Sir Stephen Hastings and G. Howard-Spink

LONG HANDICAP Bayin (USA) 7-9 Heavenly Miss (IRE) 7-3 Gold Edge 7-3

WEIGHT FOR AGE 3yo-2lb

3764 Wildwood Flower bounced back to form, and came with a tremendous rattle to snatch the verdict near the line. She has done all her winning at six furlongs. (20/1)

3765 No Extras (IRE) loves this course and, although 5lb higher for his recent head second here, was still only on a mark of 85, compared with 102 at the end of 1995. Messed about as he tried to pick up ground, he came with a real flourish in the final furlong, and failed by only a whisker. He is in sparkling form, and can land another decent handicap before the season is over. (11/2)

3936 Grand Chapeau (IRE) adopted his usual front-running role, and held on grimly until caught near the line. This was a fine effort, but a return to five furlongs should see him back in the winner's enclosure. (20/1)

1101 Lochangel, off the course since her seasonal debut four months ago, was back over a more suitable trip, but was given an extremely tough task by the Handicapper. Nevertheless, she ran a tremendous race, and was in the front rank throughout, if just tapped for toe inside the final furlong. (14/1)

3923* March Crusader was never far away, but failed to find that vital turn of foot in the last furlong. (20/1)

3856* Double Oscar (IRE) has been in sparkling form this season, but has shot up in the weights - his first handicap victory came off 48, and he was rated 81 here. Nevertheless, he ran on nicely from below the distance to finish right on the heels of the principals. (12/1)

2358 Lady Diesis (USA) has been running poorly this year and, as a result, has dropped from 92 to 73. However, she caught the eye, running on nicely in the final furlong to be nearest at the line. (40/1)

4156 HIGHLAND SPRING/ROA H'CAP (0-90) (3-Y.O+) (Class C)

3-55 (3-55) **2m** £7,440.00 (£2,220.00: £1,060.00: £480.00) Stalls: Low GOING minus 0.01 sec per fur (G)

				SP	RR	SF
3648^{11}	**High Intrigue (IRE) (81)** (HRACecil) **3-8-6** WRyan(2) (lw: chsd ldr over 4f: led over 2f out: drvn out)	—	1	$7/2^{2}$	92	39
3543*	**Lady of The Lake (86)** (JLDunlop) **3-8-11** GCarter(7) (hld up: rdn over 3f out: chsd wnr over 1f out: hrd rdn: r.o wl ins fnl f)	hd	2	$3/1^{1}$	97	44
3748^{2}	**Star Rage (IRE) (79)** (MJohnston) **7-9-3** GDuffield(9) (rdn over 2f out: hdwy over 1f out: r.o)	1½	3	6/1	88	48
2834^{4}	**Nanton Point (USA) (72)** (LadyHerries) **5-8-10v**^{1} RCochrane(4) (rdn & hdwy over 2f out: unable qckn ins fnl f)	2	4	8/1	79	39
4002^{5}	**Male-Ana-Mou (IRE) (83)** (DRCElsworth) **4-9-7** DaneO'Neill(8) (led over 5f: led 3f out tl over 2f out: wknd ins fnl f)	½	5	$11/2^{3}$	90	50
3805^{6}	**Purple Splash (90)** (PJMakin) **7-10-0v** AClark(1) (nvr nr to chal)	1	6	6/1	96	56
	Great Tern (59) (NMBabbage) **5-7-6**(5)ow1 RMullen(3) (plld hrd: hdwy over 12f out: chsd ldr over 11f out: led over 10f out: clr over 9f out: hdd over 3f out: sn wknd)	2	7	14/1	63	22
3475^{3}	**Rising Spray (72)** (CAHorgan) **6-8-10** PaulEddery(5) (s.s: a bhd)	6	8	12/1	70	30
				(SP 116.6%)	**8 Rn**	

3m 34.3 (10.30) CSF £13.47 CT £55.23 TOTE £4.00: £1.60 £1.30 £1.80 (£5.30) Trio £10.80 OWNER Mrs E. A. Harris (NEWMARKET) BRED Airlie Stud

LONG HANDICAP Great Tern 6-13

WEIGHT FOR AGE 3yo-13lb

OFFICIAL EXPLANATION **High Intrigue (IRE): regarding the apparent improvement from last time out at York, the jockey stated that he may have set too strong a pace in the early stages on that occasion.**

2963* High Intrigue (IRE) showed his York run to be all wrong, and bounced back to form, leading early in the straight and responding well to pressure to keep the persistent runner-up at bay. (7/2)

3543* Lady of The Lake, hiked up 9lb after completing a hat-trick at Beverley, gave her all in her bid to make it four. Taking second place approaching the final furlong, she made sure the winner did not have things all his own way, and only just failed to get up. (3/1)
3748 Star Rage (IRE) has been a grand servant to connections, but this easier surface was not really in his favour. Nevertheless, he ran on to some effect late on to take third prize. (6/1)
2834 Nanton Point (USA) pushed along as he edged closer early in the straight, once again found lack of acceleration his downfall. (8/1)
4002 Male-Ana-Mou (IRE) almost saw out this longer trip, and regained the advantage early in the straight. Collared over a quarter of a mile from home, he refused to give way and was only shaken off inside the final furlong. A mile and three-quarters may be the answer. (11/2)
3805 Purple Splash likes some cut in the ground but could never get into it. He is currently 2lb higher than his highest winning mark. (6/1: 11/1-7/1)
3475 Rising Spray (12/1: op 8/1)

4157 E.B.F. ROYAL NAVY MAIDEN STKS (2-Y.O) (Class D)

4-30 (4-31) **1m** £4,207.50 (£1,260.00: £605.00: £277.50) Stalls: Low GOING minus 0.01 sec per fur (G)

				SP	RR	SF
2057[3]	**Wales** (PFICole) **2-9-0** RCochrane(12) (lw: a.p: rdn over 2f out: led ins fnl f: r.o wl)	—	**1**	4/9[1]	82	61
2680[3]	**Success And Glory (IRE)** (HRACecil) **2-9-0** WRyan(8) (chsd ldr: led over 1f out tl ins fnl f: unable qckn)	1½	**2**	5/1[2]	79	58
3576[6]	**Borani** (IABalding) **2-9-0** MartinDwyer(11) (led over 6f: ev ch ins fnl f: one pce)	2	**3**	33/1	75	54
2898[2]	**Marran (IRE)** (JLDunlop) **2-9-0** GCarter(6) (rdn & hdwy over 2f out: wknd over 1f out)	5	**4**	10/1[3]	65	44
3760[6]	**Treasure Chest (IRE)** (MajorWRHern) **2-9-0** PaulEddery(13) (s.s: hld up: rdn 3f out: wknd over 1f out)	hd	**5**	16/1	65	44
3887[6]	**Royal Ground (IRE)** (MRChannon) **2-9-0** GHind(10) (nt clr run over 3f out: rdn over 2f out: nvr nr to chal)	hd	**6**	33/1	65	44
3490[7]	**Priors Moor** (RWArmstrong) **2-9-0** AClark(7) (nt clr run over 3f out: rdn over 2f out: nvr nrr)	5	**7**	33/1	55	34
3783[12]	**Final Settlement (IRE)** (JRJenkins) **2-8-11**(3) AWhelan(9) (lw: prom over 5f)	3½	**8**	66/1	48	27
3887[3]	**Lift The Offer (IRE) (79)** (RHannon) **2-9-0** DaneO'Neill(2) (lw: bhd fnl 4f)	1¼	**9**	14/1	45	24
3789[7]	**Opportune (GER) (59)** (DRCElsworth) **2-9-0** SDrowne(5) (a bhd)	5	**10**	66/1	35	14
3613[12]	**Inn On The Park** (SDow) **2-9-0** RPerham(1) (a bhd)	1	**11**	66/1	33	12
4007[8]	**Zimzie** (MJHaynes) **2-9-0** GDuffield(4) (prom over 4f)	3	**12**	100/1	27	6
3598[14]	**One Dinar (FR)** (JHMGosden) **2-9-0** JLowe(3) (lw: bhd fnl 3f)	4	**13**	33/1	19	—
				(SP 124.8%)	**13 Rn**	

1m 40.75 (3.55) CSF £2.66 TOTE £1.60: £1.10 £1.50 £5.90 (£3.00) Trio £37.80 OWNER H R H Prince Fahd Salman (WHATCOMBE) BRED Newgate Stud Co
2057 Wales needed every yard of this mile. Pushed along behind the front two over a quarter of a mile from home, he looked in a little bit of trouble, but he eventually got on top inside the final furlong, and lengthened his stride in good style. (4/9: op 4/5)
2680 Success And Glory (IRE) appreciated the extra furlong, and managed to get to the front below the distance. Collared inside the final furlong, he was unable to contain the winner. He should soon pick up a race. (5/1)
3576 Borani, who was given a baptism of fire on his debut, was dropped to more suitable company. Bowling along in front, he was collared below the distance, but still had every chance inside the final furlong, before tapped for toe. He finished well clear of the remainder, and should find an ordinary maiden. (33/1)
2898 Marran (IRE), driven along to take closer order halfway up the straight, was left for dead below the distance. (10/1)
3760 Treasure Chest (IRE), sluggish leaving the stalls, was being hustled along early in the straight, and had given his all below the distance.(16/1)

4158 CITY OF PORTSMOUTH MAIDEN STKS (3-Y.O) (Class D)

5-00 (5-02) **1m 2f** £3,850.00 (£1,150.00: £550.00: £250.00) Stalls: Low GOING minus 0.01 sec per fur (G)

				SP	RR	SF
2897[4]	**Silvery (52)** (JARToller) **3-8-6**(3) RFfrench(8) (hld up: rdn over 2f out: led ins fnl f: r.o wl)	—	**1**	16/1	75	50
	Tough Act (82) (MrsAJPerrett) **3-9-0** AClark(3) (a.p: chsd ldr 6f out: led wl over 1f out tl ins fnl f: nt run on)	nk	**2**	4/1[2]	80	55
1587[12]	**Dick Turpin (USA)** (LordHuntingdon) **3-9-0** WRyan(4) (shkn up over 2f out: hdwy over 1f out: r.o wl ins fnl f)	½	**3**	7/2[1]	79	54
3917[7]	**Arco Colora (60)** (DRCElsworth) **3-8-9** SDrowne(6) (led over 8f: ev ch ins fnl f: sn wknd)	2½	**4**	25/1	70	45
3720[U]	**Academy Star** (JRFanshawe) **3-8-9** NDay(7) (hld up: rdn 3f out: one pce)	¾	**5**	7/2[1]	69	44
2929[6]	**Norman Conquest (USA) (62)** (IABalding) **3-9-0** RCochrane(10) (lw: prom 4f)	6	**6**	12/1	64	39
	Tidewater (RCharlton) **3-8-9** GCarter(9) (w'like: s.s: a bhd)	3	**7**	6/1[3]	54	29
	Catchment (MrsAJPerrett) **3-9-0** GayeHarwood(5) (w'like: scope: a bhd)	s.h	**8**	25/1	59	34
3909[4]	**Shooting Star (IRE)** (JHMGosden) **3-9-0v** GHind(11) (lw: prom over 6f)	hd	**9**	15/2	59	34
3632[6]	**Ile de Librate** (RJO'Sullivan) **3-9-0** GDuffield(2) (a bhd)	2	**10**	16/1	56	31
				(SP 117.6%)	**10 Rn**	

2m 12.02 (5.42) CSF £72.64 TOTE £14.70: £2.80 £2.40 £1.80 (£46.10) Trio £98.30 OWNER Mr Philip Wroughton (WHITSBURY) BRED Highfield Stud Ltd and the Glen Andred Stud
OFFICIAL EXPLANATION Dick Turpin(USA): lost his near-fore shoe in the race.
IN-FOCUS: This looked a very moderate maiden.
2897 Silvery, quite a sparely-made individual, chased the leaders. She eventually managed to get on top inside the final furlong, and just held off the very reluctant runner-up. (16/1)
Tough Act hardly covered himself in glory on his return after an eleven-month absence. Striking the front early in the final quarter-mile, he held his head extremely high, and looked thoroughly unco-operative. Doing his utmost to throw in the towel, he was eventually collared inside the final furlong. (4/1)
Dick Turpin (USA), who reportedly coughed when running poorly on his seasonal debut back in May, was given a very considerate ride, but made eyecatching headway from below the distance to finish right on the heels of the front pair. He is now qualified for handicaps, and looks one to note. (7/2)
2773 Arco Colora, moving up in trip, attempted to make all the running. Collared early in the final quarter-mile, she refused to give up, and still had every chance inside the final furlong before tiring. (25/1)
3720 Academy Star, a tall, unfurnished filly, was bustled along three furlongs from home, but could make no real impression (7/2)
1877 Norman Conquest (USA) looked in very good shape in the paddock, but the writing was on the wall at the top of the hill. (12/1)
Tidewater (6/1: 4/1-7/1)

T/Plpt: £40.00 (972.88 Tckts). T/Qdpt: £7.10 (233 Tckts) AK

3866-MUSSELBURGH (R-H) (Good to firm)
Monday September 15th
WEATHER: sunny periods WIND: fresh half against

4159 E.B.F. MEDIAN AUCTION MAIDEN STKS (2-Y.O F) (Class E)
2-10 (2-15) **5f** £2,937.25 (£883.00: £426.50: £198.25) Stalls: High GOING minus 0.19 sec per fur (GF)

Form	Horse	Dist	Pos	SP	RR	SF
4012[17]	**Take A Risk** (MJohnston) **2-8-11** DHolland(10) (b.hind: hld up: hdwy 2f out: r.o to ld post)	—	1	10/1	61	11
3857[2]	**Love Again** (MBell) **2-8-11** MFenton(11) (prom: hdwy 2f out: led wl ins fnl f: jst ct)	s.h	2	6/4[1]	61	11
3847[3]	**Chikapenny (63)** (MrsLStubbs) **2-8-11v** JFEgan(1) (prom: hdwy to disp ld over 1f out: nt qckn towards fin)	nk	3	8/1[3]	60	10
3407[7]	**Rare Indigo** (JBerry) **2-8-11** KDarley(7) (mde most tl hdd & no ex wl ins fnl f)	nk	4	10/1	59	9
4012[8]	**Sorridar** (JLEyre) **2-8-11** MGallagher(3) (s.i.s: hdwy 2f out: nrst fin)	1¾	5	4/1[2]	53	3
3821[4]	**Double Power (61)** (LRLloyd-James) **2-8-11** KimTinkler(9) (lw: cl up: hung rt most of wy: wknd over 1f out)	1¾	6	12/1	48	—
3857[4]	**Another Wyn-Bank** (JGFitzGerald) **2-8-11** JFortune(8) (chsd ldrs tl rdn & btn appr fnl f)	3½	7	12/1	37	—
	Clanblue Chick (JBerry) **2-8-6**(5) PRoberts(4) (leggy: lt-f: unf: w ldrs over 3f: sn btn)	1½	8	33/1	32	—
3821[12]	**Tigi** (MrsMReveley) **2-8-11** ACulhane(2) (sn outpcd & bhd)	1¾	9	50/1	26	—
	Crystal Waters (IRE) (GROldroyd) **2-8-4**(7) RFarmer(6) (cmpt: sn outpcd & bhd)	1	10	100/1	23	—
	Pabella Bluebird (IRE) (GROldroyd) **2-8-11** KHodgson(12) (lt-f: bit bkwd: s.i.s: a bhd)	8	11	50/1	—	—
	Sun Dancing (IRE) (PMonteith) **2-8-11** OPears(5) (Withdrawn not under Starter's orders: ref to ent stalls)		W	33/1	—	—

(SP 115.5%) **11 Rn**

61.7 secs (4.00) CSF £21.79 TOTE £9.70: £2.70 £1.10 £1.50 (£8.20) Trio £19.00 OWNER Mr P. McMahon (MIDDLEHAM) BRED Mark Johnston Racing Ltd

3857 Take A Risk was ridden with restraint for the first time, and it just worked. (10/1)
3857 Love Again, like the winner, was not well drawn, but she looked to have done everything right only to get worried out of it near the line. (6/4)
3847 Chikapenny had the best draw and certainly had her chances but the struggle proved just too much late on. (8/1)
2545 Rare Indigo has plenty of speed and this was her best effort to date. (10/1)
4012 Sorridar has trouble in jumping off on terms and on such a sharp track as this it left her with an impossible task. She has more ability and should find a race. (4/1)
3821 Double Power looks the type who will be ideally suited once she can find a right-handed rail to run against. (12/1: op 8/1)
3857 Another Wyn-Bank found things happening too quickly on this sharp track. (12/1)

4160 BLACK CASTLE H'CAP (0-70) (3-Y.O+) (Class E)
2-40 (2-43) **2m** £3,112.75 (£937.00: £453.50: £211.75) Stalls: High GOING minus 0.34 sec per fur (GF)

Form	Horse	Dist	Pos	SP	RR	SF
*4055**	**Il Principe (IRE) (55)** (JohnBerry) **3-8-3**ow4 5x JFEgan(13) (trckd ldrs: led 4f out: hld on wl)	—	1	7/2[1]	67	—
3931[5]	**Highfield Fizz (38)** (CWFairhurst) **5-7-10**(3) PFessey(8) (b.off hind: hld up: hdwy ent st: ev ch over 1f out: nt qckn towards fin)	½	2	12/1	50	—
3919[3]	**Sushi Bar (IRE) (43)** (MrsMReveley) **6-8-4** KDarley(2) (bhd: hdwy 3f out: styd on wl: nrst fin)	2½	3	8/1[3]	52	—
3309[6]	**Cittern (56)** (MrsMReveley) **7-9-3** ACulhane(15) (swtg: in tch: hdwy 4f out: sn chsng ldrs & rdn: one pce appr fnl f)	1¾	4	8/1[3]	63	—
	Trump (35) (CParker) **8-7-10** NKennedy(6) (rr div: hdwy 4f out: styd on: nvr able to chal)	hd	5	50/1	42	—
3890[4]	**Trilby (50)** (GRichards) **4-8-11** JCarroll(9) (lw: in tch: effrt ½-wy: effrt & hdwy 4f out: wknd fnl 2f)	s.h	6	9/1	57	—
3826[7]	**Sarasota Storm (49)** (MBell) **5-8-10** MFenton(3) (lw: hld up & bhd: brought wd & effrt ent st: no imp)	8	7	8/1[3]	48	—
3485[5]	**Thunderheart (49)** (RAllan) **6-8-10** DHolland(12) (chsd ldrs: effrt 4f out: wknd 2f out)	1¾	8	10/1	46	—
4104[9]	**Urgent Reply (USA) (60)** (CADwyer) **4-9-2**(5) PRoberts(11) (led after 2f to 4f out: grad wknd)	8	9	16/1	49	—
3781[7]	**Maremma (48)** (DonEnricoIncisa) **3-7-10** KimTinkler(10) (a in rr)	½	10	25/1	37	—
2564[11]	**Teejay'n'aitch (IRE) (36)** (JSGoldie) **5-7-11**ow1 TWilliams(1) (led 2f: chsd ldrs: rdn 6f out: wknd over 3f out)	2	11	33/1	23	—
3890[2]	**Dirab (64)** (TDBarron) **4-9-11b**[1] JFortune(14) (lw: trckd ldrs tl wknd fnl 3f)	10	12	5/1[2]	41	—
3694[6]	**Kika (43)** (KRBurke) **4-8-4** GBardwell(7) (trckd ldrs tl wknd fnl 4f)	5	13	16/1	15	—
3116[7]	**Ralitsa (IRE) (36)** (RMWhitaker) **5-7-8b**[1](3)ow1 DarrenMoffatt(5) (bhd: rel to r after 6f & sn wl t.o: virtually p.u)	dist	14	100/1	—	—

(SP 120.5%) **14 Rn**

3m 30.3 CSF £41.77 CT £293.39 TOTE £4.20: £1.60 £2.30 £1.90 (£25.60) Trio £62.70 OWNER The 1997 Partnership (NEWMARKET) BRED J. Costello

LONG HANDICAP Teejay'n'aitch (IRE) 7-5 Maremma 7-8
WEIGHT FOR AGE 3yo-13lb
OFFICIAL EXPLANATION Cittern: finished lame

4055* Il Principe (IRE) showed yet again just how tough he is and refused to be passed. (7/2)
3931 Highfield Fizz is proving difficult to win with this season and has slipped down the handicap but, despite a useful effort here, she had to admit she had met one just too determined. (12/1)
3919 Sushi Bar (IRE) has won over shorter trips but she does look a real stayer. (8/1)
3309 Cittern, again sweated profusely, and this time had his chances but failed to respond to pressure. He was reportedly lame. (8/1)
Trump, having his first run on the Flat for almost three years, put up a fair effort and looks in good trim for the National Hunt game. (50/1)
3890 Trilby is the type who needs things to go just right and they never really did here. (9/1: op 6/1)
3826 Sarasota Storm, a winner four times on this track, tried his usual tactics but they never looked likely to pay off. (8/1)
3485 Thunderheart (10/1: 12/1-8/1)
3890 Dirab had blinkers on for the first time and raced far too freely. (5/1)

4161 FORT H'CAP (0-70) (3-Y.O+) (Class E)
3-10 (3-12) **1m 4f 31y** £3,132.25 (£943.00: £456.50: £213.25) Stalls: High GOING minus 0.34 sec per fur (GF)

Form	Horse	Dist	Pos	SP	RR	SF
3700[4]	**Blenheim Terrace (52)** (CBBBooth) **4-9-1** FNorton(1) (bhd: hdwy appr st: led appr fnl f: styd on)	—	1	10/1	62	43
3867[4]	**Classic Ballet (FR) (60)** (RGuest) **4-9-9** KDarley(15) (a chsng ldrs: ev ch over 2f out: kpt on)	¾	2	3/1[1]	69	50
3906[3]	**Classic Flyer (IRE) (65)** (ICampbell) **4-10-0** AMackay(6) (cl up: disp ld 5f out: led 4f out tl appr fnl f: kpt on)	nk	3	6/1[2]	74	55
3906[4]	**Sing And Dance (42)** (EWeymes) **4-8-5** DaleGibson(16) (lw: outpcd & bhd after 4f: hdwy 3f out: styd on wl towards fin)	½	4	10/1	50	31

3886[6] **Ambidextrous (IRE) (60)** (EJAlston) **5-9-9** JFEgan(12) (lw: hld up & bhd: hdwy over 3f out: nvr able to chal)	3½	**5**	10/1	63	44
3853* **Durgams First (IRE) (53)** (MrsMReveley) **5-9-2** ACulhane(13) (lw: bhd: hdwy 4f out: chsng ldrs 2f out: no imp)	hd	**6**	9/1	56	37
4015[7] **Sparky (71)** (MWEasterby) **3-9-8b**(3) GParkin(3) (b: hdwy & in tch 8f out: ev ch & rdn over 1f out: hung lft & sn btn)	nk	**7**	12/1	74	46
3992[7] **Karisma (IRE) (50)** (DenysSmith) **4-8-13** JFortune(2) (lw: mid div: swtchd 2f out: no imp)	3	**8**	8/1[3]	49	30
3624[2] **Beach Buoy (IRE) (60)** (CaptJWilson) **3-8-9**(5) PRoberts(14) (b.off hind: in tch tl wknd fnl 3f: fin lame)	hd	**9**	12/1	59	31
Pickens (USA) (56) (DonEnricoIncisa) **5-9-5** KimTinkler(11) (b: sn t.o: r.o fnl 2f: nrst fin)	2½	**10**	50/1	51	32
3919[12] **Mowlaie (45)** (DWChapman) **6-8-8** JCarroll(4) (b: in tch tl wknd fnl 3f)	3½	**11**	20/1	36	17
3298* **Little Miss Rocker (60)** (ARDicken) **3-9-0** OPears(10) (b.off hind: chsd ldrs tl wknd fnl 3f)	1¼	**12**	14/1	49	21
Raased (40) (FWatson) **5-8-0**(3) PFessey(8) (mde most tl hdd & wknd 4f out)	2	**13**	100/1	27	8
3937[11] **Thaleros (50)** (JSWainwright) **7-8-13** DeanMcKeown(9) (cl up tl wknd ent st)	3	**14**	20/1	33	14
3400[3] **Dancing Queen (IRE) (58)** (MBell) **3-8-12** MFenton(5) (mid div tl lost tch fnl 4f)	18	**15**	16/1	17	—

(SP 128.1%) **15 Rn**

2m 37.9 (4.40) CSF £37.24 CT £190.92 TOTE £9.70: £2.70 £1.90 £2.60 (£25.30) Trio £50.50 OWNER Exors of the late Mr A Lyons (FLAXTON) BRED A. Lyons

WEIGHT FOR AGE 3yo-9lb

OFFICIAL EXPLANATION Beach Buoy (IRE): had been struck into.

3700 Blenheim Terrace travelled well and this time went through with the effort but he still thought about it. (10/1)

3867 Classic Ballet (FR), back to her optimum distance, ran well but was always second best. (3/1)

3906 Classic Flyer (IRE), trying her longest trip for a while, put up a fair effort and was keeping on at the end. (6/1)

3906 Sing And Dance was left way behind and then finished strongly, but needed another half-furlong to make it. (10/1)

3886 Ambidextrous (IRE) is still running well off a mark a couple of pounds higher than he has ever won off. (10/1)

3853* Durgams First (IRE) ran a fair race but the struggle was always proving beyond him in the closing stages. (9/1)

4015 Sparky had his chances, but he looked a doubtful character under pressure and this trip was probably stretching his stamina. He seems happier on the All-Weather. (12/1: op 8/1)

3624 Beach Buoy (IRE) (12/1: op 8/1)

4162 PINKIE NURSERY H'CAP (0-75) (2-Y.O) (Class E)

3-40 (3-41) **5f** £3,015.25 (£907.00: £438.50: £204.25) Stalls: High GOING minus 0.34 sec per fur (GF)

			SP	RR	SF
3821[13] **Three Star Rated (IRE) (70)** (TDBarron) **2-9-5** JCarroll(6) (hld up: hdwy to ld 1f out: r.o strly)	—	**1**	12/1	90+	45
2165* **Ellenbrook (IRE) (67)** (JBerry) **2-8-13b**(3) PFessey(5) (led tl hdd 1f out: kpt on same pce)	4	**2**	3/1[1]	74	29
3986[7] **Allmaites (65)** (DNicholls) **2-8-9**(5) IonaWands(7) (lw: in tch: hdwy 2f out: ch over 1f out: nt qckn)	s.h	**3**	16/1	72	27
3699[2] **Hayburner (55)** (MWEasterby) **2-8-4b** TLucas(3) (lw: chsd ldrs tl rdn & btn 1½f out)	1¾	**4**	5/1[2]	56	11
3791[5] **Sun In The Morning (56)** (BJMeehan) **2-8-5** DeanMcKeown(11) (w ldrs tl wknd appr fnl f)	hd	**5**	12/1	57	12
3866* **Sans Rivale (65)** (JLEyre) **2-9-0** RLappin(12) (prom: effrt ½-wy: r.o one pce)	1¼	**6**	6/1[3]	62	17
3823[6] **Daynabee (67)** (NTinkler) **2-9-2** KimTinkler(4) (prom tl outpcd fr ½-wy)	s.h	**7**	6/1[3]	64	19
2862[18] **Rhinefield Beauty (IRE) (63)** (JSGoldie) **2-8-12** ACulhane(9) (s.i.s: outpcd & bhd tl sme late hdwy)	¾	**8**	12/1	58	13
3545[9] **Elsinore (IRE) (61)** (MrsJRRamsden) **2-8-10** JFortune(10) (lw: nvr wnt pce)	¾	**9**	12/1	53	8
3544[4] **Miss Beveled (47)** (MBrittain) **2-7-3b**[1](7) DMernagh(8) (drvn along & a bhd)	1¼	**10**	50/1	35	—
3742[3] **Blarney Park (55)** (CADwyer) **2-8-4** JFEgan(2) (outpcd & bhd after 2f)	hd	**11**	8/1	43	—
3474[12] **Somosierra (IRE) (72)** (JBerry) **2-9-7** KDarley(1) (hdwy after 2f: sn lost pl)	2½	**12**	14/1	52	7

(SP 126.6%) **12 Rn**

60.1 secs (2.40) CSF £46.62 CT £558.99 TOTE £14.10: £4.70 £3.10 £15.70 (£16.80) Trio £320.50; £320.59 to Sandown 16/9/97 OWNER Miss J. Salt (THIRSK) BRED Edmond and Richard Kent

LONG HANDICAP Miss Beveled 7-1

STEWARDS' ENQUIRY Meehan fined £80 under Rule 145 (horse arrived at the post without surcingle).

3821 Three Star Rated (IRE), kept under control before hand and saving all her energies for the race, won in some style and will no doubt be made to pay for it by the handicapper. (12/1: 8/1-14/1)

2165* Ellenbrook (IRE), returning after almost three moths off, failed to impress on the way to post with a moderate action, but she still ran pretty well only to get trounced late on. (3/1)

1657 Allmaites put up a decent effort here and is obviously coming to hand. (16/1)

3699 Hayburner again had his chances but yet again he failed to come up with the goods. (5/1)

2051 Sun In The Morning had plenty to do from her draw and was always fighting a lost cause when the pressure was on after halfway. (12/1)

3866* Sans Rivale moved moderately to post and, poorly drawn, was always struggling. (6/1)

2545 Rhinefield Beauty (IRE) (12/1: 16/1-10/1)

3545 Elsinore (IRE) (12/1: op 8/1)

4163 CARBERRY TOWER CLAIMING STKS (2-Y.O) (Class F)

4-10 (4-11) **1m 16y** £2,682.00 (£752.00: £366.00) Stalls: High GOING minus 0.34 sec per fur (GF)

			SP	RR	SF
4052[4] **Kayo** (TJEtherington) **2-8-13** DHolland(2) (stdd s & sn wl bhd: hdwy over 2f out: r.o fnl f to ld post)	—	**1**	7/1	66	27
3911[4] **Greenbrook (67)** (WGMTurner) **2-8-11**(7) DMcGaffin(7) (lw: led: rdn 2f out: r.o: jst ct)	s.h	**2**	11/10[1]	71	32
4058[8] **Cherished (IRE) (60)** (NTinkler) **2-7-11v**[1](7) RWinston(5) (hld up: effrt over 2f out: swtchd ins: hrd rdn & r.o towards fin)	½	**3**	15/2	56	17
4058[11] **Docklands Dispatch (IRE) (56)** (NTinkler) **2-8-8** KimTinkler(8) (chsd ldrs: effrt over 2f out: kpt on)	2	**4**	20/1	56	17
3905[15] **Emperor's Gold (66)** (ICampbell) **2-8-8v**[1] AMackay(1) (dwlt: sn rcvrd & prom: hung rt over 1f out: nt qckn)	1¾	**5**	6/1[2]	53	14
2827[2] **Anniemitchellslass** (DMoffatt) **2-8-0**(3) DarrenMoffatt(6) (effrt ent st: nvr rchd ldrs)	2½	**6**	13/2[3]	43	4
3967[7] **Jet Set Sarah (USA) (50)** (JBerry) **2-8-4b**[1] KDarley(3) (chsd ldrs tl wknd fnl 3f)	11	**7**	12/1	22	—
4054[13] **Ngaere Princess (46)** (WTKemp) **2-7-11** TWilliams(9) (a wl bhd)	s.h	**8**	50/1	15	—
4014[6] **Chardania (IRE) (52)** (CaptJWilson) **2-8-1** GBardwell(4) (chsd ldrs 5f: sn wknd)	1½	**9**	14/1	16	—

(SP 120.6%) **9 Rn**

1m 43.3 (4.30) CSF £14.37 TOTE £6.90: £2.70 £1.30 £1.20 (£10.00) Trio £15.30 OWNER Mr David Abell (MALTON) BRED Bridge End Bloodstock

4052 Kayo, again given a lot to do, produced a useful turn of foot to make it and leaves the impression that easier ground would help further. (7/1)

3911 Greenbrook seems to go on any ground but, despite a useful effort here, was just worried out of it. (11/10)

4058 Cherished (IRE), in a visor for the first time, did not have the best of runs and would have made it with a little further to go. (15/2)

2914* Docklands Dispatch (IRE), after two poor efforts, ran well here, but does seem better suited by the All-Weather surface. (20/1)

3629 Emperor's Gold, in a visor for the first time, is a funny customer but he has the ability if it can be coaxed out of him. (6/1: op 4/1)
2827 Anniemitchellslass needed this after two months off. (13/2)

4164 HONEST TOUN MAIDEN H'CAP (0-60) (3-Y.O+) (Class F)
4-40 (4-42) **7f 30y** £2,752.00 (£772.00: £376.00) Stalls: High GOING minus 0.34 sec per fur (GF)

Form	Horse	Dist	Pos	SP	RR	SF
4050[12]	**French Ginger (45)** (LRLloyd-James) **6-9-6** TWilliams(9) (lw: mde all: clr over 2f out: styd on u.p)	—	**1**	25/1	60	22
3812[12]	**Two On The Bridge (55)** (DenysSmith) **3-9-12** GBardwell(13) (lw: in tch: effrt over 3f out: styd on u.p towards fin)	1	**2**	14/1	68	26
3854[4]	**Falls O'Moness (IRE) (49)** (KRBurke) **3-9-6** JFEgan(2) (a.p: hdwy u.p over 2f out: sn chsng wnr: one pce fnl f)	1½	**3**	10/1	58	16
3759[5]	**Katie Komaite (41)** (CaptJWilson) **4-9-2v** KDarley(3) (effrt ½-wy: styd on: nvr able to chal)	2½	**4**	9/1[3]	45	7
3813[6]	**Tarradale (43)** (CBBBooth) **3-9-0** FNorton(14) (lw: effrt ½-wy: styd on: nvr nr to chal)	1½	**5**	20/1	43	1
3592[5]	**Secret Strength (44)** (LadyHerries) **3-8-8**(7) PDoe(12) (bhd: styd on u.p fnl 2½f: nrst fin)	hd	**6**	9/2[2]	44	2
3431[15]	**Fisiostar (42)** (MDods) **4-9-3v** JCarroll(8) (lw: bhd: effrt on outside 3f out: nvr rchd ldrs)	nk	**7**	16/1	42	4
3470[14]	**Martine (50)** (ABailey) **3-9-2**(5) PRoberts(4) (effrt on outside ½-wy: n.d)	1¼	**8**	14/1	47	5
2951[6]	**Rotor Man (IRE) (57)** (JDBethell) **3-10-0** DHolland(1) (chsd ldrs tl wknd fnl 3f)	2½	**9**	10/1	48	6
3702[2]	**Don't Worry Mike (49)** (FHLee) **3-9-6b** OPears(5) (cl up tl wknd fnl 2½f)	1¼	**10**	10/1	37	—
3868[4]	**The Dubious Goose (41)** (MrsJRRamsden) **3-8-12** JFortune(7) (drvn along ½-wy: n.d)	2	**11**	12/1	25	—
2940[11]	**Serious Account (USA) (40)** (JLEyre) **4-9-1** MGallagher(6) (sn drvn along & a rr div)	1¾	**12**	7/2[1]	20	—
4008[14]	**Hostile Native (53)** (RGuest) **4-10-0b**[1] MFenton(11) (cl up tl wknd fnl 3f)	12	**13**	14/1	6	—
4050[2]	**Zalotto (IRE) (52)** (TJEtherington) **3-9-9b** ACulhane(10) (sn drvn along & t.o)	15	**14**	9/2[2]	—	—

(SP 138.0%) **14 Rn**

1m 30.7 (4.70) CSF £351.21 CT £3,505.46 TOTE £46.80: £6.60 £5.00 £3.70 (£443.70) Trio £393.20; £249.26 to Sandown 16/9/97 OWNER Mr David Dyer (MALTON) BRED Derek R. Price
WEIGHT FOR AGE 3yo-4lb

3822 French Ginger, given a most positive ride, left nothing to chance here and had it won halfway up the straight, but she still needed keeping up to her work. (25/1)
3241 Two On The Bridge was keeping on particularly well at the end and really deserves to find a race. (14/1: op 8/1)
3854 Falls O'Moness (IRE) is slipping down the handicap and had her chances here but she failed to respond to pressure. (10/1)
3759 Katie Komaite keeps running reasonably but never quite comes up with the goods. (9/1)
3813 Tarradale is now on a realistic mark but he seems his own worst enemy. (20/1)
3592 Secret Strength obviously has ability but getting him to use it seems to be the problem. (9/2)
3868 The Dubious Goose (12/1: op 8/1)
2549 Serious Account (USA) was well supported here but never gave punters the slightest hope. (7/2: 5/1-3/1)
Hostile Native (14/1: op 8/1)

T/Plpt: £174.90 (119.11 Tckts). T/Qdpt: £39.90 (23.09 Tckts) AA

3312-NOTTINGHAM (L-H) (Good to firm)
Monday September 15th
WEATHER: cloudy & windy WIND: str against

4165 E.B.F. NOTTINGHAM MAIDEN STKS (2-Y.O) (Class D)
2-00 (2-00) **1m 54y** £4,115.00 (£1,235.00: £595.00: £275.00) Stalls: Low GOING minus 0.22 sec per fur (GF)

Form	Horse	Dist	Pos	SP	RR	SF
	Asakir (SbinSuroor) **2-9-0** LDettori(11) (lengthy: a.p: led over 2f out: rn green & edgd lft over 1f out: r.o wl)	—	**1**	4/1[3]	84+	31
3479[2]	**Hadith** (DMorley) **2-9-0** RHills(6) (lw: a.p: nt clr run on ins & swtchd rt over 1f out: r.o wl ins fnl f)	1	**2**	5/2[2]	82	29
	Wadi (HRACecil) **2-9-0** KFallon(7) (w'like: leggy: bit bkwd: hld up: rdn & hdwy over 3f out: ev ch 2f out: one pce fnl f)	½	**3**	11/8[1]	81+	28
4056[7]	**Smiling Voter (IRE)** (RHannon) **2-9-0** DaneO'Neill(4) (lw: hld up: rdn & hdwy over 2f out: styd on fnl f)	3½	**4**	25/1	74	21
2870[11]	**Ei Ei** (BWHills) **2-9-0** PaulEddery(12) (hld up & plld hrd: hdwy 3f out: one pce fnl 2f)	1½	**5**	16/1	71	18
3861[9]	**Pairumani Star (IRE)** (JLDunlop) **2-9-0** GCarter(8) (bit bkwd: bhd tl hdwy over 1f out: nvr nrr)	1¾	**6**	20/1	68	15
1872[9]	**Free** (PFICole) **2-9-0** PatEddery(9) (led over 3f: wknd 3f out)	8	**7**	12/1	53	—
4056[12]	**Antonio Joli** (PFICole) **2-9-0** JWeaver(3) (bit bkwd: nvr trbld ldrs)	1¾	**8**	20/1	49	—
3799[7]	**Delayed Reaction** (NACallaghan) **2-9-0** SDrowne(17) (nvr nr ldrs)	1½	**9**	33/1	46	—
3760[3]	**Najjar (USA)** (PTWalwyn) **2-9-0** WRyan(15) (prom: rn wd bnd over 4f out: wknd over 1f out)	1	**10**	10/1	44	—
3806[15]	**Mister Bunch** (EWeymes) **2-9-0** SSanders(1) (a bhd)	¾	**11**	50/1	43	—
3745[6]	**Rude Shock** (MHTompkins) **2-9-0** DBiggs(5) (a bhd)	hd	**12**	20/1	43	—
	Common View (IRE) (NTinkler) **2-9-0** CRutter(14) (str: bkwd: s.i.s: hld up: a bhd)	s.h	**13**	33/1	43	—
3927[5]	**Counsel** (CEBrittain) **2-9-0** GDuffield(10) (w ldr: led over 4f out tl over 2f out: wknd wl over 1f out)	1¼	**14**	20/1	40	—
	Blanche The Almond (CASmith) **2-8-9** VSlattery(2) (lt-f: unf: bkwd: s.s: a bhd)	1¼	**15**	50/1	33	—
	Dockland Executive (BSmart) **2-9-0** JStack(13) (unf: bkwd: a bhd)	4	**16**	33/1	30	—
1827[9]	**Fleet Lady (IRE) (54)** (MrsPNDutfield) **2-8-9** JQuinn(16) (sn chsng ldrs: rn wd bnd over 4f out: sn wknd)	5	**17**	50/1	15	—

(SP 150.9%) **17 Rn**

1m 46.3 (5.00) CSF £14.65 TOTE £5.50: £2.40 £1.10 £1.10 (£11.20) Trio £3.00 OWNER Godolphin (NEWMARKET) BRED Shadwell Estate Company Limited

Asakir, a half-brother to Tahdid, Estimraar and Anam, is entered in the Derby. Described as being a bit lazy at home, he will have one more run before being wintered in Dubai and should come on for the experience. (4/1: op 2/1)
3479 Hadith, a half-brother to Yarob and Ihtriraz, would have given the winner more to think about given a trouble free run and his turn is merely delayed. (5/2)
Wadi, a half-brother to this season's five-furlong winner Furnish, is out of a half-sister to Quest For Fame. He looks the type who could develop into a nice sort for next season. (11/8: 4/5-13/8)
Smiling Voter (IRE) appears to be getting the hang of things and could be the type for a nursery. (25/1)
Ei Ei is a brother to Call to Arms and half-brother to Superluminal and War Beat. Stepping up on his debut, he will do even better when learning to settle. (16/1)
Pairumani Star (IRE) is a half-brother to amongst others Kennemara Star, Dawning Street and Special Dawn. He appears to be going the right way. (20/1)

4166 NOTTINGHAMSHIRE COUNTY CRICKET CLUB NURSERY H'CAP (0-75) (2-Y.O F) (Class E)

2-30 (2-32) **6f 15y** £3,642.25 (£1,093.00: £526.50: £243.25) Stalls: High GOING minus 0.04 sec per fur (G)

				SP	RR	SF
3636[11]	**Golden Fortune (63)** (DRLoder) **2-8-10** KFallon(19) (trckd ldrs stands' side: led 2f out: rdn & r.o wl)	—	**1**	9/4[1]	68	26
4012[3]	**Positive Air (74)** (BAMcMahon) **2-9-7** MRoberts(6) (hdwy far side over 1f out: fin wl)	½	**2**	12/1	78	36
3619[5]	**Dekelsmary (63)** (JBalding) **2-8-10** JEdmunds(4) (hdwy far side 2f out: r.o wl fnl f)	hd	**3**	20/1	66	24
3979[5]	**Quiz Show (74)** (RHannon) **2-9-7** DaneO'Neill(2) (b.nr hind: chsd ldr far side: led 2f out tl ins fnl f)	½	**4**	10/1[3]	76	34
4014[4]	**Saligo (IRE) (65)** (HMorrison) **2-8-12** CRutter(1) (prom far side: one pce ins fnl f)	½	**5**	14/1	66	24
3821[7]	**Premium Princess (64)** (JJQuinn) **2-8-11** SSanders(10) (prom stands' side: ev ch over 1f out: one pce)	½	**6**	10/1[3]	64	22
3817[2]	**Alpha Whisky (GER) (74)** (IABalding) **2-9-7** LDettori(16) (b.hind: led stands' side 4f: one pce appr fnl f)	1½	**7**	4/1[2]	70	28
3927[4]	**Mountain Magic (64)** (DJSffrenchDavis) **2-8-11** JWeaver(9) (lw: nvr nrr)	nk	**8**	20/1	59	17
3821[3]	**Kustom Kit Kate (62)** (SRBowring) **2-8-6**(3) CTeague(12) (nvr nr to chal)	hd	**9**	20/1	57	15
4012[5]	**Greeba (69)** (RHannon) **2-9-2** PatEddery(5) (s.s: racd far side: a bhd)	½	**10**	10/1[3]	62	20
3973[18]	**Townville Cee Cee (54)** (JSWainwright) **2-8-1** JBramhill(11) (prom over 4f)	nk	**11**	25/1	46	4
3307[14]	**Starliner (IRE) (56)** (MBrittain) **2-8-3** GCarter(14) (outpcd)	1	**12**	33/1	46	4
3545[7]	**Sandy Shore (74)** (JWharton) **2-9-4**(3) RFfrench(18) (nvr nr ldrs)	¾	**13**	12/1	62	20
3857*	**Miss Puci (72)** (JBerry) **2-9-0**(5) CLowther(15) (outpcd)	¾	**14**	10/1[3]	58	16
3924[9]	**Desert Native (55)** (CFWall) **2-8-2** GDuffield(20) (a in rr)	1	**15**	25/1	38	—
3967[6]	**Shannon (IRE) (56)** (CADwyer) **2-8-3** SDrowne(13) (a in rr)	½	**16**	16/1	38	—
3965[6]	**Magical Dancer (IRE) (55)** (MrsPNDutfield) **2-8-2** MartinDwyer(17) (in tch 4f: sn wknd)	5	**17**	25/1	24	—
3474[7]	**Downclose Duchess (56)** (MBlanshard) **2-8-3** JQuinn(7) (a in rr)	s.h	**18**	25/1	25	—
3904[3]	**Turf Moor (IRE) (61)** (JJO'Neill) **2-8-5**(3) TEDurcan(8) (lw: s.i.s: a bhd: t.o)	9	**19**	25/1	6	—
3965[5]	**Allasella (IRE) (70)** (BPalling) **2-9-3** TSprake(3) (led far side: sn clr: hdd & wknd 2f out: t.o)	1¼	**20**	12/1	12	—
				(SP 159.2%)	**20 Rn**	

1m 16.2 (4.70) CSF £33.01 CT £499.34 TOTE £2.40: £1.60 £3.20 £4.30 £3.70 (£45.80) Trio Not won; £399.74 to Sandown 16/9/97 OWNER Lucayan Stud (NEWMARKET) BRED P. D. and Mrs Player

2842 Golden Fortune, well supported in this first handicap, had to put her best foot forward to hold on nearing the finish but she had the man of the moment on top and he made sure she stuck her neck out. (9/4)

4012 Positive Air began to stay on strongly below the distance and, finishing really well, only just failed to gain the day. There is a race to be won with her. (12/1)

3619 Dekelsmary had her tongue tied this time and, coming out of the pack inside the distance, finished well. (20/1)

3979 Quiz Show, stepping down from seven furlongs, was always in the firing line on the far side but she was unable to hang on to her advantage inside the last one hundred yards. (10/1)

4014 Saligo (IRE) had the blinkers left off on this occasion and ran as well as ever but a turn of finishing speed was missing inside the last furlong. (14/1)

3821 Premium Princess, having her first try beyond the minimum trip, did not impress to post but she was in the action all the way under the stands' side rail until tapped for toe inside the final furlong. (10/1)

3817 Alpha Whisky (GER) had more use made of her but she had kept nothing in reserve and was brushed aside inside the distance. (4/1)

4167 E.B.F. SEPTEMBER MAIDEN STKS (2-Y.O) (Class D)

3-00 (3-01) **6f 15y** £4,466.00 (£1,343.00: £649.00: £302.00) Stalls: High GOING minus 0.04 sec per fur (G)

				SP	RR	SF
2588[2]	**Deterrent (94)** (JHMGosden) **2-9-0** LDettori(5) (hld up: hdwy far side over 2f out: led over 1f out: easily)	—	**1**	7/4[1]	81+	28
	Captain Tim (DRLoder) **2-9-0** PatEddery(1) (gd sort: chsd ldrs far side: r.o ins fnl f: nt trble wnr)	2	**2**	7/2[3]	76	23
	Jila (IRE) (RWArmstrong) **2-9-0** GCarter(16) (str: scope: chsd ldrs: led stands' side 1f out: no ch w wnr)	2½	**3**	9/2	69+	16
3031[9]	**Haunt The Zoo** (JLHarris) **2-8-9** SSanders(9) (bit bkwd: a.p: led stands' side over 3f out to 1f out: r.o one pce)	½	**4**	50/1	63	10
	Eminent (LordHuntingdon) **2-9-0** WRyan(11) (rangy: dwlt: hdwy over 1f out: nvr nrr)	½	**5**	14/1	67	14
	Young Josh (JHMGosden) **2-9-0** GHind(8) (cmpt: bkwd: chsd ldr far side: led 2f out: sn hdd: wknd fnl f)	1	**6**	14/1	64	11
	Redswan (SCWilliams) **2-9-0** PBloomfield(17) (leggy: s.s: nrst fin)	½	**7**	50/1	63	10
	Serengetti (JBerry) **2-8-4**(5) CLowther(14) (lw: s.s: nvr nr ldrs)	¾	**8**	20/1	56	3
3471[8]	**Night Auction (IRE)** (BPalling) **2-8-9** TSprake(2) (racd far side: bhd fnl 2f)	nk	**9**	33/1	55	2
3986[5]	**Persiano** (JRFanshawe) **2-9-0** NDay(12) (lw: nvr trbld ldrs)	1	**10**	20/1	57	4
3193[4]	**Hadid (USA) (88)** (BWHills) **2-9-0** RHills(7) (led far side 4f: eased whn btn ins fnl f)	¾	**11**	3/1[2]	55	2
	The Artful Dodger (RJRWilliams) **2-9-0** GDuffield(10) (w'like: bkwd: a bhd)	¾	**12**	33/1	53	—
	Krisamba (BJMeehan) **2-9-0** MTebbutt(6) (w'like: scope: dwlt: a bhd)	3	**13**	20/1	45	—
	Dudley Allen (TTClement) **2-9-0** JQuinn(3) (unf: scope: a bhd)	2½	**14**	33/1	39	—
3322[6]	**Dragon Boy** (IPWilliams) **2-9-0** KFallon(4) (racd far side: bhd fnl 3f)	2	**15**	33/1	33	—
3607[11]	**Taurean** (NAGraham) **2-9-0** AMcGlone(13) (prom over 3f)	3½	**16**	100/1	24	—
3782[11]	**Marion's Pet** (RJHodges) **2-8-9** NAdams(15) (led stands' side over 2f: sn wknd: sddle slipped)	6	**17**	100/1	3	—
				(SP 147.1%)	**17 Rn**	

1m 16.3 (4.80) CSF £8.17 TOTE £3.00: £1.80 £3.00 £1.20 (£4.70) Trio £11.40 OWNER Sheikh Mohammed (NEWMARKET) BRED Aylesfield Farms Stud

2588 Deterrent had no Daggers Drawn to contend with this time and duly obliged in what was probably an above-average event. (7/4)

Captain Tim, a half-brother to Musetta and Fiametta is entered in the Middle Park and looks sure to win races. (7/2)

Jila (IRE), out of a half-sister to Gabr, won the race on the stands side and should find a suitable opening before long. (9/2)

Haunt The Zoo only cost 3,000gns and must have delighted connections with this effort. (50/1)

Eminent, a half-brother to Bangles and Faraway Lass, took a while to grasp what was required and seems sure to improve. (14/1)

Young Josh, the first foal of a Group Three King George Stakes winner, ran very well until lack of condition took its toll and will last longer next time. (14/1)

Redswan, a brother to six-furlong juvenile winner Moody, should have learnt a lot from this. (50/1)

4168 BRANSTON ABBY H'CAP (0-70) (I) (3-Y.O+ F & M) (Class E)

3-30 (3-31) **6f 15y** £3,171.00 (£948.00: £454.00: £207.00) Stalls: High GOING minus 0.04 sec per fur (G)

				SP	RR	SF
3812[5]	**Mouche (63)** (MrsJRRamsden) **3-9-9v** KFallon(20) (hld up stands' side: hdwy 2f out: led over 1f out: r.o wl)	—	**1**	3/1[1]	70	38
3922[10]	**Pathaze (37)** (NBycroft) **4-7-13** MartinDwyer(4) (trckd ldrs far side: nt clr run & swtchd rt fnl f: fin wl)	½	**2**	20/1	43	13
3922*	**Suedoro (46)** (JSGoldie) **7-8-5**(3) RFfrench(6) (hdwy far side over 1f out: r.o wl towards fin)	nk	**3**	8/1[3]	51	21

				SP	RR	SF
3590^{6}	**Third Party (53)** (SDow) **3-8-13** SSanders(16) (hld up: hdwy wl over 1f out: fin wl)	1	**4**	16/1	55	23
*3582**	**Newlands Corner (57)** (JAkehurst) **4-9-5b** DBiggs(7) (chsd ldrs far side: led 1f out tl hdd & no ex nr fin)	nk	**5**	8/1^{3}	59	29
3968*	**Bold Tina (IRE) (62)** (RHannon) **3-9-8** DaneO'Neill(19) (hdwy over 1f out: r.o wl fnl f)	1	**6**	11/2^{2}	61	29
3614^{5}	**Antonia's Choice (66)** (JBerry) **3-9-7**(5) CLowther(3) (prom far side: led over 1f out: sn hdd & wknd)	3½	**7**	20/1	56	24
3561^{8}	**Polgwynne (45)** (BSmart) **3-8-5** JStack(17) (lw: nvr nr to chal)	hd	**8**	20/1	34	2
3418^{10}	**Daylight Dreams (65)** (CACyzer) **3-9-11** AMorris(1) (led far side over 4f)	¾	**9**	14/1	52	20
2723^{8}	**Smiling Bess (34)** (JSKing) **4-7-5**(5) APolli(14) (swtg: prom over 4f)	½	**10**	33/1	20	—
3923^{4}	**Grace (54)** (JMBradley) **3-9-0** SDrowne(10) (nvr nrr)	s.h	**11**	10/1	40	8
3266^{8}	**Terry's Rose (38)** (RHollinshead) **3-7-12** NCarlisle(18) (led stands' side tl hdd & wknd over 1f out)	½	**12**	20/1	23	—
3323^{3}	**College Princess (49)** (SCWilliams) **3-8-2**(7) DarrenWilliams(11) (b: effrt over 2f out: rdn & hung lft: no imp)	½	**13**	16/1	32	—
3693^{14}	**Nampara Bay (39)** (GCBravery) **3-7-13b**^{1}ow1 DRMcCabe(13) (a in rr)	½	**14**	16/1	21	—
3074^{6}	**Lady Silk (34)** (MissJFCraze) **6-7-10** JLowe(5) (lw: dwlt: a in rr)	nk	**15**	25/1	15	—
3860^{13}	**Napier Star (39)** (MrsNMacauley) **4-8-1v** JQuinn(9) (lw: b.off hind: spd far side over 3f: wknd qckly)	7	**16**	20/1	2	—
3590^{7}	**Nellie North (45)** (GMMcCourt) **4-8-7b** CRutter(12) (w ldrs stands' side over 3f)	1	**17**	16/1	5	—
3716^{4}	**Princess Renata (IRE) (38)** (PatMitchell) **4-8-0**ow1 JTate(15) (w ldrs stands' side to ½-wy)	¾	**18**	25/1	—	—
3852^{9}	**Times of Times (IRE) (55)** (GLMoore) **4-9-3v**^{1} GDuffield(2) (prom far side over 4f: wknd qckly)	¾	**19**	20/1	11	—
3968^{7}	**Charlton Spring (IRE) (53)** (RJHodges) **3-8-10**(3) PPMurphy(8) (outpcd)	2	**20**	20/1	4	—

(SP 145.9%) **20 Rn**

1m 16.2 (4.70) CSF £70.14 CT £460.16 TOTE £4.00: £1.90 £3.60 £2.50 £5.70 (£99.30) Trio £882.80 OWNER Mr M. J. Simmonds (THIRSK) BRED M. J. Simmonds

LONG HANDICAP Smiling Bess 7-8 Lady Silk 7-6

WEIGHT FOR AGE 3yo-2lb

OFFICIAL EXPLANATION **Charlton Spring (IRE): saddle slipped approaching final furlong.**

3812 Mouche, successful here in the Spring, had to work hard to wear down the far-side leaders inside the final one hundred yards. (3/1)

3761 Pathaze has almost forgotten what winning is all about but, with a clear passage, she may well have put the record straight here. (20/1)

3922* Suedoro does not stride out on this lively ground but she is in fine form at present and will win again when conditions come in her favour. (8/1)

3590 Third Party stayed on strongly inside the final furlong and showed that she is capable of winning more races when caught in the mood.(16/1)

3582* Newlands Corner took command on the far side entering the final furlong and looked set to come away but her stride shortened when pressure was applied and the principals had the legs of her where it mattered. (8/1)

3968* Bold Tina (IRE), a winner over an extra furlong earlier in the month, did not find top gear until the race was as good as over. (11/2)

3614 Antonia's Choice had plenty on her plate at the weights but she ran up to her mark and this lightly-raced filly would seem to be coming right. (20/1)

4169 BRANSTON ABBY H'CAP (0-70) (II) (3-Y.O+ F & M) (Class E)

4-00 (4-03) **6f 15y** £3,145.00 (£940.00: £450.00: £205.00) Stalls: High GOING minus 0.04 sec per fur (G)

				SP	RR	SF
3625^{10}	**La Volta (42)** (MissJFCraze) **4-8-4b** MRoberts(2) (prom far side: led ins fnl f: r.o)	—	**1**	20/1	54	41
4043^{14}	**Magic Lake (37)** (EJAlston) **4-7-10v**(3) MHenry(17) (lw: s.s: hdwy over 2f out: led stands' side over 1f out: edgd lft: r.o)	¾	**2**	16/1	47	34
3198^{11}	**Watch The Fire (64)** (JEBanks) **4-9-7**(5) CLowther(4) (hdwy far side 2f out: r.o ins fnl f)	1½	**3**	12/1	70	57
3637^{12}	**Gi La High (62)** (MartynMeade) **4-9-10** JReid(6) (chsd ldr far side: led 1f out tl ins fnl f)	nk	**4**	20/1	67	54
3910^{15}	**Naissant (53)** (MartynWane) **4-8-12**(3) AWhelan(13) (hdwy over 1f out: r.o)	½	**5**	14/1	57	44
3565^{10}	**Okay Baby (IRE) (34)** (JMBradley) **5-7-3**(7) RThomas(20) (prom stands' side: r.o one pce fnl f)	½	**6**	50/1	37	24
3716^{3}	**Lamorna (48)** (MRChannon) **3-8-5**(3) PPMurphy(3) (nvr nrr)	1	**7**	8/1^{2}	48	33
3637^{2}	**Bairn Atholl (35)** (RJHodges) **4-7-11** NAdams(1) (prom far side: ev ch 1f out: wknd)	s.h	**8**	8/1^{2}	35	22
3565^{7}	**Sing With the Band (43)** (BAMcMahon) **6-8-5** LNewton(11) (lw: prom stands' side over 4f: r.o)	hd	**9**	8/1^{2}	43	30
3922^{17}	**Mystique Smile (34)** (JSGoldie) **4-7-7**(3) RFfrench(12) (swtg: prom stands' side over 4f)	½	**10**	16/1	32	19
3816^{6}	**Embroidered (36)** (SDow) **4-7-12** MartinDwyer(5) (lw: n.d)	1¼	**11**	14/1	31	18
3756^{8}	**Lillibella (55)** (MrsJRRamsden) **4-9-0**(3) DSweeney(10) (led far side: hdd 1f out: wknd)	1¾	**12**	10/1	45	32
3968^{3}	**Inclination (59)** (MBlanshard) **3-9-5** JQuinn(9) (lw: n.d)	nk	**13**	9/1^{3}	49	34
3871^{11}	**Dona Filipa (46)** (MissLCSiddall) **4-8-8** KFallon(16) (lw: a bhd)	hd	**14**	9/1^{3}	35	22
3854^{7}	**Danehill Princess (IRE) (43)** (RHollinshead) **3-8-3** NCarlisle(14) (a bhd)	1¼	**15**	20/1	29	14
3851^{2}	**Hever Golf Mover (68)** (TJNaughton) **3-10-0** JWeaver(8) (a bhd)	nk	**16**	8/1^{2}	53	38
4048^{17}	**Croeso Cynnes (60)** (BPalling) **4-9-8** TSprake(18) (led stands' side: hdd & wknd over 1f out)	1¾	**17**	20/1	41	28
3761^{10}	**Ballard Lady (IRE) (48)** (JSWainwright) **5-8-10** LDettori(19) (a bhd)	nk	**18**	4/1^{1}	28	15
3746^{8}	**Deerly (48)** (RDickin) **4-8-10v**^{1} GHind(15) (spd stands' side 3f)	6	**19**	16/1	12	—
3590^{9}	**Bella's Legacy (39)** (KRBurke) **4-8-1** DBiggs(7) (outpcd)	1¼	**20**	25/1	—	—

(SP 157.1%) **20 Rn**

1m 14.6 (3.10) CSF £323.01 CT £3,772.61 TOTE £22.90: £3.60 £6.50 £3.80 £7.60 (£417.80) Trio Not won; £636.14 to Sandown 16/9/97

OWNER Mr J. Lynam (YORK) BRED K. G. Bridges

LONG HANDICAP Okay Baby (IRE) 7-0 Mystique Smile 7-8

WEIGHT FOR AGE 3yo-2lb

OFFICIAL EXPLANATION **Ballard Lady (IRE): finished distressed.**

3271 La Volta, bought out of Jimmy FitzGerald's stable for 4,400gns in June, took advantage of being given a chance by the handicapper having been disappointing this season. (20/1)

3393 Magic Lake, 3lb lower than when winning over seven at Ayr in July last year, is another who has been basically out of form this season.(16/1)

2841 Watch The Fire has been beaten in a couple of competitive handicaps at Newmarket since his back-to-back victories. (12/1)

1957 Gi La High, down to a 1lb lower mark, than when runner-up at Bath in June, is still awaiting that elusive first win on grass. (20/1)

953 Naissant has dropped to a useful mark but needs a return to seven on ground as fast as this. (14/1)

2954 Okay Baby (IRE) was by no means disgraced over an inadequate trip from out of the handicap. (50/1)

3698* Dona Filipa (9/1: op 6/1)

4170 CARLTON H'CAP (0-65) (I) (3-Y.O+) (Class F)

4-30 (4-31) **2m 9y** £1,927.00 (£527.00: £247.00) Stalls: Low GOING minus 0.22 sec per fur (GF)

				SP	RR	SF
3858*	**Stoned Imaculate (IRE) (56)** (FMurphy) **3-9-3** KFallon(10) (lw: hld up in tch: led over 2f out: drvn out)	—	**1**	9/4^{1}	70	27
3928^{3}	**Coh Sho No (46)** (SDow) **4-9-6** SSanders(11) (lw: trckd ldrs: lost pl 9f out: rallied u.p over 2f out: styd on)	1¼	**2**	15/2	59	29

3781^{5} **Mechilie (42)** (JWPayne) **3-8-3**ow2 GCarter(7) (hld up: hdwy over 3f out: styd on wl ins fnl f)....1½ **3** 10/1 53 8
3865^{4} **Keen Waters (39)** (MrsSDWilliams) **3-8-0** MartinDwyer(13) (hld up & bhd: hdwy & hung lft 4f out: styd on u.p)....2½ **4** 14/1 48 5
3896^{6} **Hillswick (40)** (JSKing) **6-8-9**(5) APolli(1) (mde most tl hdd over 2f out: one pce)....s.h **5** 9/2^{2} 49 19
3896^{14} **Not Forgotten (USA) (48)** (PAKelleway) **3-8-9** GHind(16) (lw: prom: lost pl 10f out: rallied over 2f out: r.o)...1½ **6** 25/1 55 12
4055^{14} **Spa Lane (48)** (MPBielby) **4-9-8** AMcGlone(12) (nvr nrr)....2½ **7** 14/1 53 23
2937^{12} **Welcome Lu (31)** (JLHarris) **4-8-0**(5) RMullen(14) (hld up: hdwy ent st: rdn & wknd fnl 2f)....3 **8** 25/1 33 3
*3046** **Lake Dominion (37)** (KCComerford) **8-8-11** WJO'Connor(5) (b: hmpd after s: nvr nr to chal)....1¼ **9** 14/1 38 8
3758^{4} **Nornax Lad (USA) (36)** (MartynMeade) **9-8-3b**(7) RBrisland(8) (lw: plld hrd: prom: sddle slipped early: bhd fnl 3f)....½ **10** 14/1 36 6
3928* **Duncombe Hall (39)** (CACyzer) **4-8-10**(3) AWhelan(9) (lw: prom: ev ch over 2f out: wknd appr fnl f)....½ **11** 5/1^{3} 39 9
3928^{6} **Rose of Glenn (50)** (BPalling) **6-9-10** DaneO'Neill(4) (hmpd after s: hld up: hdwy ½-wy: rdn 3f out: sn btn) ...hd **12** 12/1 49 19
3931^{6} **Course Fishing (39)** (BAMcMahon) **6-8-13** GDuffield(6) (lw: chsd ldrs tl rdn & wknd wl over 1f out)....½ **13** 11/1 38 8
4053^{9} **Langara Heights (55)** (BJLlewellyn) **3-8-9**(7) JWilkinson(17) (plld hrd: nvr nr ldrs)....½ **14** 20/1 53 10
2498^{5} **Kinoko (45)** (KWHogg) **9-9-5** JBramhill(15) (bit bkwd: chsd ldrs: rdn over 4f out: grad wknd)....2 **15** 11/1 41 11
3626^{6} **Chill Wind (22)** (NBycroft) **8-7-10** DWright(3) (hmpd after s: a bhd)....1¼ **16** 16/1 17 —
2365^{3} **Big Bang (55)** (MBlanshard) **3-9-2** JQuinn(2) (bhd fnl 3f)....nk **17** 12/1 50 7
(SP 163.5%) **17 Rn**

3m 34.7 (11.70) CSF £24.18 CT £163.62 TOTE £3.40: £1.20 £1.60 £4.90 £6.70 (£11.30) Trio £305.20 OWNER Mr M. Rowsell (MIDDLEHAM) BRED Mrs Ann Fortune
LONG HANDICAP Chill Wind 7-8
WEIGHT FOR AGE 3yo-13lb
OFFICIAL EXPLANATION Nornax Lad (USA): saddle slipped shortly after start.
3858* Stoned Imaculate (IRE), none the worse for her fall at the first over hurdles three days earlier, is in fine fettle at present and she could be called the winner from some way out. (9/4)
3928 Coh Sho No ran in snatches but she stayed on really well in the latter stages and was far from disgraced in defeat. (15/2)
3781 Mechilie seemed well suited by this step up in distance and stamina would seem to be her strong suit. (10/1)
3865 Keen Waters looked ill at ease cantering to post and she continually hung left when making progress but she did stay on and is holding her form. (14/1)
3896 Hillswick tried to make this a true test of stamina but he was given no peace in the lead and the quickening tempo proved too much for him in the latter stages. (9/2)
1218 Not Forgotten (USA), running without the blinds, dropped himself out down the back straight and his attempt to get back into it was always beyond him. (25/1)
3758 Nornax Lad (USA), taking a fierce hold which caused his saddle to slip forward, pressed the leaders on sufferance until fading once in line for home. This effort can be disregarded. (14/1)
2498 Kinoko (11/1: op 7/1)

4171 CARLTON H'CAP (0-65) (II) (3-Y.O+) (Class F)
5-00 (5-00) **2m 9y** £1,927.00 (£527.00: £247.00) Stalls: Low GOING minus 0.22 sec per fur (GF)

SP RR SF

3992^{10} **Cliburnel News (IRE) (47)** (DShaw) **7-8-13**(5) RMullen(7) (b: hld up & bhd: stdy hdwy 4f out: led on bit wl over 1f out: rdn & r.o wl)....— **1** 14/1 58 40
3754^{4} **Batabanoo (50)** (MrsMReveley) **8-9-7** JReid(10) (lw: hld up: stdy hdwy 8f out: chsd ldr over 3f out tl over 1f out: styd on)....3 **2** 7/2^{2} 58 40
3325* **Ginger Rogers (63)** (DWPArbuthnot) **3-9-7** JQuinn(12) (b: swtg: a.p: led over 4f out tl wl over 1f out: one pce)....2½ **3** 11/4^{1} 69 38
3928^{7} **Gallant Heights (55)** (GCBravery) **3-8-13** DRMcCabe(13) (s.s: hdwy 3f out: hrd rdn over 1f out: one pce)......½ **4** 8/1 60 29
*3865** **Sipowitz (48)** (CACyzer) **3-8-3**(3) AWhelan(4) (hld up: stdy hdwy 8f out: one pce fnl 2f)....4 **5** 6/1^{3} 49 18
Moving Out (53) (MissHCKnight) **9-9-5**(5) CLowther(5) (bkwd: prom: lost pl 6f out: n.d after)....½ **6** 20/1 54 36
3865^{P} **Sixties Melody (49)** (RBoss) **3-8-4**(3) RFfrench(16) (hld up: lost pl 8f out: n.d after)....5 **7** 9/1 45 14
3865^{6} **Hippios (38)** (SDow) **3-7-5**(5) APolli(6) (hdwy 10f out: wknd over 2f out)....nk **8** 25/1 33 2
Sea Buck (41) (HCandy) **11-8-5b**1(7) BarrySmith(14) (bkwd: nvr trbld ldrs)....1½ **9** 25/1 35 17
3781^{6} **Eurolink Windsong (IRE) (40)** (MartynWane) **3-7-12** MartinDwyer(1) (plld hrd: prom tl wknd over 2f out)......nk **10** 12/1 33 2
122^{3} **Toulston Lady (IRE) (46)** (JWharton) **5-9-3** KFallon(11) (bkwd: bhd tl hdwy 4f out: wknd over 2f out)....4 **11** 10/1 36 18
Irish Stamp (IRE) (40) (FMurphy) **8-8-11** JFanning(2) (bit bkwd: a bhd)....4 **12** 25/1 26 8
865^{16} **Sudden Spin (38)** (JNorton) **7-8-9** JWeaver(8) (bhd fnl 8f)....5 **13** 12/1 19 1
1953^{5} **Suitor (34)** (SDow) **4-8-5** SSanders(9) (a bhd)....nk **14** 14/1 14 —
2498^{2} **Memorable (30)** (KWHogg) **6-8-1** JBramhill(15) (prom 8f)....¾ **15** 12/1 9 —
2607^{9} **Sophie Lockett (35)** (KWHogg) **4-8-1**(5) ADaly(3) (led over 11f: wknd 3f out: t.o)....dist **16** 25/1 — —
(SP 149.9%) **16 Rn**

3m 32.1 (9.10) CSF £65.84 CT £173.34 TOTE £20.70: £2.60 £1.80 £1.10 £2.60 (£34.80) Trio £62.70 OWNER Mr K. Nicholls (NEWARK) BRED St Simon Foundation
LONG HANDICAP Hippios 7-9
WEIGHT FOR AGE 3yo-13lb
Cliburnel News (IRE), 8lb lower than the second of her wins in the spring of 1995, bounced back to form over this longer distance in no uncertain manner. (14/1)
3754 Batabanoo, again 5lb higher than when scoring at Newcastle, found the winner galloping all over him entering the final quarter-mile.(7/2)
3325* Ginger Rogers, up a further 5lb, had no answer to the winner. (11/4)
3021 Gallant Heights, down 3lb, appeared to get the two miles well enough. (8/1)
3865* Sipowitz had finished twelve lengths behind the third on 8lb worse terms at Bath. (6/1)
Moving Out was having a much needed pipe-opener for a return to hurdles. (20/1)

4172 TRENT LIMITED STKS (0-65) (3-Y.O+) (Class F)
5-30 (5-30) **1m 1f 213y** £2,277.00 (£627.00: £297.00) Stalls: Low GOING minus 0.22 sec per fur (GF)

SP RR SF

3697* **Ile Distinct (IRE) (62)** (MrsASwinbank) **3-8-13** GDuffield(13) (lw: hld up: hdwy over 4f out: led wl over 1f out: rdn out)....— **1** 10/1 75 50
3455^{3} **Arriving (65)** (JWHills) **3-8-10** RHills(4) (hld up: stdy hdwy over 3f out: jnd wnr over 1f out: hrd rdn: r.o).........hd **2** 6/1^{1} 72 47
3491^{12} **Zidac (65)** (PJMakin) **5-9-4** SSanders(8) (hld up: hdwy over 2f out: kpt on u.p fnl f)....4 **3** 10/1 66 48

				SP	RR	SF
3767*	**Thatchmaster (IRE) (65)** (CAHorgan) **6-9-3**(3) DO'Donohoe(3) (led tl over 3f out: rdn appr fnl f: r.o one pce)	1½	**4**	6/1[1]	66	48
3631[6]	**Double Flight (65)** (MJohnston) **3-8-8** MRoberts(2) (trckd ldrs: effrt & rdn 2f out: kpt on one pce)	½	**5**	7/1[3]	60	35
3772[10]	**Puzzlement (64)** (CEBrittain) **3-8-11** WRyan(12) (prom: led over 3f out tl wl over 1f out: rdn & wknd ins fnl f)	1¾	**6**	20/1	60	35
3971[4]	**Fife Major (USA) (63)** (BWHills) **3-8-11** PatEddery(10) (lw: hld up: effrt over 4f out: sn drvn along: no imp)	½	**7**	13/2[2]	60	35
4063[3]	**Secret Ballot (IRE) (62)** (KMahdi) **3-8-13** JReid(1) (lw: prom: hmpd on ins 7f out: rdn & wknd fnl 2f)	s.h	**8**	8/1	62	37
3721[5]	**Soden (IRE) (60)** (TGMills) **3-8-7**(3) RFfrench(6) (nvr nrr)	2	**9**	16/1	55	30
3824[7]	**Roi du Nord (FR) (63)** (NBycroft) **5-9-4** GCarter(11) (a in rr)	1½	**10**	33/1	54	36
3455[6]	**Here's To Howie (USA) (64)** (RHannon) **3-8-13** DaneO'Neill(7) (chsd ldrs: rdn along 3f out: sn btn)	nk	**11**	20/1	55	30
3496[6]	**Bakers Daughter (59)** (JRArnold) **5-9-3** MartinDwyer(15) (swtg: hld up: hdwy 5f out: rdn & wknd over 2f out)	3	**12**	12/1	48	30
3968[5]	**Get The Point (59)** (RHollinshead) **3-8-8**(3) DGriffiths(9) (chsd ldrs: hrd drvn over 2f out: sn outpcd)	1½	**13**	20/1	46	21
1117[9]	**Onefortheditch (USA) (65)** (JRFanshawe) **4-9-1** KFallon(18) (bit bkwd: hld up: hdwy over 5f out: rdn over 2f out: grad wknd)	¾	**14**	7/1[3]	42	24
3992[2]	**Tonnerre (58)** (BAMcMahon) **5-9-6** LNewton(14) (lw: a bhd: t.o)	5	**15**	10/1	39	21
4063[7]	**Obelos (USA) (65)** (MissSJWilton) **6-9-6** SWhitworth(17) (a in rr: t.o)	1½	**16**	20/1	37	19
4063[15]	**Rival Bid (USA) (60)** (MrsNMacauley) **9-8-13v**(5) AmandaSanders(16) (b: s.v.s: a bhd: t.o)	3	**17**	33/1	30	12
3720[7]	**Shailendra (IRE) (63)** (JHMGosden) **3-8-8** LDettori(5) (s.s: a bhd: t.o)	18	**18**	12/1	—	—
				(SP 151.5%)	**18 Rn**	

2m 6.1 (3.60) CSF £70.92 TOTE £15.70: £3.10 £2.40 £3.30 (£153.50) Trio £672.90; £94.78 to Sandown 16/9/97 OWNER Windsor Room Syndicate (RICHMOND) BRED John O'Connor

WEIGHT FOR AGE 3yo-7lb

3697* Ile Distinct (IRE) needed to show his true battling qualities inside the last quarter-mile but he has really come to himself now and there could be more success in store. (10/1)

3455 Arriving looked all over the winner when she ranged upsides below the distance but the winner just would not give best and her valiant attempt was to prove in vain. (6/1)

2485 Zidac found the ground firmer than he really cares for and, though he did stay on under pressure, was never in the race with a chance. (10/1)

3767* Thatchmaster (IRE) did his utmost to gallop his rivals into submission but he had plenty of chances early in the straight and he was fighting a losing battle below the distance. (6/1)

3631 Double Flight is finding it hard to win in handicap company but she did not fail for the want of trying and her turn will come. (7/1)

509 Puzzlement nosed ahead early in the straight and battled away after being headed and, given easier ground, he is ready to win another race. (20/1)

3971 Fife Major (USA) could never muster the pace to reach the leaders but he did stay on and may benefit from a longer trip. (13/2)

3992 Tonnerre (10/1: 7/1-11/1)

T/Jkpt: £11,066.90 (0.2 Tckts); £12,469.81 to Sandown 16/9/97. T/Plpt: £745.30 (32.38 Tckts). T/Qdpt: £70.10 (16.51 Tckts) KH/IM

3911-SANDOWN (R-H) (Rnd Good to firm, St Good, Good to firm patches)
Tuesday September 16th

WEATHER: warm WIND: almost nil

4173 'INNINGS OPENING' NURSERY H'CAP (2-Y.O) (Class D)
2-15 (2-16) **5f 6y** £3,533.75 (£1,070.00: £522.50: £248.75) Stalls: High GOING: 0.08 sec per fur (G)

				SP	RR	SF
3965*	**Bliss (IRE) (64)** (MrsPNDutfield) **2-7-10** JQuinn(8) (a.p: led over 1f out: drvn out)	—	**1**	10/1	70	23
4006[2]	**High Carry (82)** (NTinkler) **2-8-9**(5) CLowther(6) (swtg: hld up: chsd wnr over 1f out: ev ch ins fnl f: r.o)	½	**2**	7/2[3]	86	39
3965[2]	**Golden Strategy (IRE) (81)** (RHannon) **2-8-13** DaneO'Neill(2) (b.nr hind: lw: hdwy on ins over 2f out: hrd rdn over 1f out: unable qckn)	2½	**3**	3/1[2]	78	31
2689[2]	**Ivory's Joy (70)** (KTIvory) **2-7-13**(3) RFfrench(5) (b: lw: led over 3f out tl over 1f out: wknd ins fnl f)	¾	**4**	10/1	64	17
3899[6]	**Althib (IRE) (72)** (MRStoute) **2-8-4v**[1] GCarter(1) (swtg: plld hrd: rdn over 2f out: hdwy fnl f: nvr nrr)	1¾	**5**	15/2	61	14
3571*	**Gipsy Moth (88)** (BJMeehan) **2-9-6** PatEddery(7) (lw: led over 1f: rdn over 2f out: wknd over 1f out)	3	**6**	11/4[1]	67	20
3222[2]	**One Singer (89)** (MJohnston) **2-9-7** JWeaver(3) (lw: prom over 2f)	¾	**7**	8/1	66	19
				(SP 114.9%)	**7 Rn**	

63.71 secs (3.91) CSF £41.13 CT £120.68 TOTE £11.40: £3.40 £2.40 (£13.00) OWNER Mr W. A. Harrison-Allan (SEATON) BRED Mrs Margaret Sinanan

LONG HANDICAP Bliss (IRE) 7-9

3965* Bliss (IRE) may have won at 50/1 last time out, but she showed that run to be no fluke, sweeping into the lead over a furlong out and responding to pressure to keep the persistent runner-up at bay. (10/1: 6/1-11/1)

4006 High Carry was back over her ideal trip. Passed by the winner over a furlong out, she nevertheless kept on well to the line if always just being held by that rival. (7/2)

3965 Golden Strategy (IRE) took closer order along the inside rail at halfway, but although struggling into third place, never looked like finding that vital turn of foot. (3/1)

2689 Ivory's Joy gave a good account of herself after a near ten-week absence and only faded inside the final furlong. Although both her wins have come in sellers, she has proved she is up to this better class but might prefer the ground not quite so fast. (10/1)

3899 Althib (IRE) took a keen hold at the back of the field. Tending to wander about a bit over a furlong out, he did stay on when it was all over. He showed a very high knee action and, although he has flopped on a soft surface, maybe this ground was too fast. (15/2: 5/1-8/1)

3571* Gipsy Moth, 4lb higher for his latest success, was bang in the firing line until tiring approaching the final furlong. (11/4)

4174 E.B.F. 'GRASS WIDOWS' MAIDEN STKS (2-Y.O) (Class D)
2-45 (2-46) **7f 16y** £3,533.75 (£1,070.00: £522.50: £248.75) Stalls: High GOING minus 0.37 sec per fur (F)

				SP	RR	SF
	Abreeze (USA) (SbinSuroor) **2-9-0** LDettori(10) (gd sort: bit bkwd: a.p: led over 1f out: qcknd: comf)	—	**1**	7/2[2]	94++	53
3494[2]	**Dark Moondancer** (PWChapple-Hyam) **2-9-0** JReid(11) (chsd ldr: led 2f out tl over 1f out: unable qckn)	5	**2**	5/4[1]	83	42
	Peak Path (IRE) (MRStoute) **2-9-0** PatEddery(7) (w'like: scope: bit bkwd: s.i.s: rdn over 3f out: hdwy over 1f out: r.o)	2	**3**	9/1[3]	78+	37
3806[4]	**Beneventus** (MajorWRHern) **2-9-0** TSprake(9) (lw: stdy hdwy over 2f out: ev ch wl over 1f out: one pce)	½	**4**	9/1[3]	77	36
4105[6]	**Cloak of Darkness (IRE)** (RHannon) **2-9-0** DaneO'Neill(1) (lost pl over 2f out: r.o one pce fnl f)	2	**5**	16/1	73	32

3745[5] **Florazi** (JLDunlop) **2-9-0** TQuinn(13) (plld hrd: hdwy on ins over 5f out: rdn over 2f out: ev ch over 1f out: sn wknd) .... ½ **6** 16/1 71 30
Bombastic (BWHills) **2-9-0** PaulEddery(6) (str: scope: lw: s.s: rdn over 3f out: hdwy & nt clr run over 1f out: nvr nr) 2 **7** 14/1 67 26
Mark of Prophet (IRE) (JEBanks) **2-9-0** JQuinn(4) (leggy: bit bkwd: hld up: rdn over 2f out: wknd over 1f out) 1½ **8** 20/1 64 23
Fayez (KMcAuliffe) **2-9-0** JFEgan(8) (leggy: unf: bit bkwd: a bhd) 4 **9** 50/1 54 13
3861[10] **Asinbox (IRE)** (BJMeehan) **2-9-0** MTebbutt(5) (lw: bhd fnl 2f) 3½ **10** 66/1 47 6
651[7] **Zielana Gora** (JGSmyth-Osbourne) **2-8-9** MRoberts(12) (bit bkwd: led 5f) .... ½ **11** 50/1 40 —
4007[10] **Petruchio (IRE)** (MajorDNChappell) **2-9-0** GDuffield(2) (prom over 4f) .... s.h **12** 50/1 45 4
3497[8] **Southdown Cyrano (IRE)** (PButler) **2-9-0** SDrowne(3) (bhd fnl 3f) .... 9 **13** 100/1 25 —
(SP 118.2%) **13 Rn**

1m 29.98 (1.38) CSF £7.05 TOTE £4.20: £1.80 £1.10 £2.40 (£3.70) Trio £6.40 OWNER Godolphin (NEWMARKET) BRED Darley Stud Management Inc

Abreeze (USA), a quality, deep-girthed colt with plenty of strength and substance, appeared to be carrying quite a lot of condition and drifted extremely badly in the betting. However he silenced his doubters in no uncertain terms as he swept into the lead over a furlong out, and quickened away for a very decisive victory. He is described as one of the better Godolphin juveniles and looks to have a big future. (7/2: evens-9/2)
3494 Dark Moondancer was not entirely convincing with his commitment as Reid was niggling him along entering the straight. He managed to struggle to the front a quarter of a mile out, but when passed by the winner, was firmly put in his place. He looks one to have reservations about, although he certainly has the ability to win a maiden. (5/4)
Peak Path (IRE), a plain, well-made individual, was rather colty leaving the paddock. Looking as though the run would do him good, he was very slow to find his stride and was going nowhere at the back of the field entering the straight. However he grasped what was required of him in the last furlong and a half and stayed on in encouraging style to take third prize. He is sure to come on a lot for this and should be able to pick up a race before long, maybe over an extra furlong. (9/1: 7/2-10/1)
3806 Beneventus cruised into the action in the straight and certainly had every chance early in the final quarter-mile before tapped for toe. He may do better in nurseries. (9/1)
4105 Cloak of Darkness (IRE) got outpaced early in the straight but did struggle on again from below the distance. Another furlong would not go amiss. (16/1)
3745 Florazi took a keen hold and was soon up with the leaders. With every chance below the distance, he then tired as his earlier antics took their toll. (16/1)
Bombastic (14/1: 7/1-16/1)

4175 'LEG BEFORE' LIMITED STKS (0-80) (3-Y.O+) (Class D)
3-20 (3-22) **7f 16y** £3,631.25 (£1,100.00: £537.50: £256.25) Stalls: High GOING minus 0.37 sec per fur (F)

SP RR SF

3888[6] **Mujova (IRE) (80)** (RHollinshead) **3-8-11** ACulhane(5) (nt clr run over 2f out: swtchd rt: hdwy over 1f out: squeezed thro 1f out: led ins fnl f: r.o wl) .... — **1** 16/1 85 54
2925[7] **Refuse To Lose (77)** (JMPEustace) **3-8-11** JTate(13) (lw: led over 4f: ev ch ins fnl f: unable qckn) 1 **2** 10/1 83 52
3095* **Howaida (IRE) (80)** (MRStoute) **3-8-11** JReid(11) (a.p: n.m.r over 1f out: r.o) .... nk **3** 11/4[1] 82 51
4071[6] **Zelda Zonk (76)** (BJMeehan) **5-8-11** MTebbutt(1) (rdn over 2f out: hdwy over 1f out: r.o one pce) .... ¾ **4** 14/1 77 49
3066[2] **Dominant Air (79)** (SirMarkPrescott) **3-9-0** GDuffield(6) (lw: a.p: led over 1f out tl ins fnl f: one pce) .... ¾ **5** 7/1 82 51
3930[8] **Alikhlas (76)** (MajorWRHern) **3-8-11** TSprake(3) (stdd s: nt clr run over 2f out: hdwy & nt clr run over 1f out: r.o) .... nk **6** 20/1 78+ 47
4121[13] **Zugudi (78)** (KMahdi) **3-9-0b[1]** MRimmer(4) (lw: plld hrd: nt clr run over 3f out: rdn over 2f out: hdwy fnl f: nvr nrr) 1 **7** 20/1 79 48
3798[5] **Compatibility (IRE) (78)** (JHMGosden) **3-9-0b[1]** LDettori(7) (hld up: rdn over 2f out: one pce) 2½ **8** 9/1 73 42
403[6] **Nordinex (IRE) (74)** (DRCElsworth) **5-8-11**(3) RFfrench(8) (b: lw: a.p: led over 2f out tl over 1f out: sn wknd) 1½ **9** 25/1 67 39
3715[2] **Kawa-Ib (IRE) (77)** (PTWalwyn) **3-8-8** TQuinn(10) (hld up: rdn over 2f out: 4th whn hmpd on ins 1f out: nt rcvr) .... ¾ **10** 13/2[3] 62+ 31
2945[12] **Summer Queen (77)** (SPCWoods) **3-8-11** JFortune(9) (hld up: rdn over 2f out: wknd over 1f out) .... ½ **11** 20/1 64 33
3764[10] **Rakis (IRE) (80)** (MrsLStubbs) **7-9-0** PatEddery(2) (hld up: rdn over 2f out: wknd over 1f out) .... nk **12** 6/1[2] 63 35
505[5] **Galibis (FR) (80)** (RHannon) **3-8-11** DaneO'Neill(12) (bkwd: a bhd) 3½ **13** 20/1 55 24
(SP 121.3%) **13 Rn**

1m 29.66 (1.06) CSF £140.71 TOTE £17.80: £3.50 £2.80 £1.80 (£84.80) Trio £131.10 OWNER Mr J. D. Graham (UPPER LONGDON) BRED Peter Kelly
WEIGHT FOR AGE 3yo-3lb

3888 Mujova (IRE), who failed to get a trouble-free run last time out, again did not have the clearest of runs. Manoeuvered over to the rails a furlong out, doing Kawa-Ib no favours, he was rousted along to lead in the last one hundred yards. (16/1)
694 Refuse To Lose appreciated the extra furlong. Bowling along in front, he was marginally collared over a quarter of a mile from home, but actually managed to get his head back in front for a few strides inside the final furlong before the winner went by. (10/1: 7/1-11/1)
3095* Howaida (IRE), never far away, did not have a great deal of room below the distance, but she ran on inside the final furlong if flashing her tail when hit. (11/4)
4071 Zelda Zonk has been in the Handicapper's grip this year. Making a promising effort down the centre of the course below the distance, she stayed on but was unable to get there in time. Both her wins to date have come over this trip on fast ground. (14/1: 10/1-16/1)
3066 Dominant Air, who saw out seven furlongs last time out, moved to the front below the distance but, collared inside the final furlong, failed to find another gear. (7/1: 5/1-15/2)
3752 Alikhlas has not looked the easiest of rides but she certainly had no luck in running on this occasion. Drifting badly in the betting, she got stopped a number of times in the straight, but when she did find daylight, stayed on well in the final furlong. (20/1)
3715 Kawa-Ib (IRE) chased the leaders and was struggling on in fourth place when hampered by the winner entering the final furlong. But for this incident, she would certainly have finished a lot closer. (13/2)

4176 MARTIN BICKNELL BENEFIT H'CAP (0-80) (3-Y.O) (Class D)
3-50 (3-54) **1m 14y** £4,533.00 (£1,374.00: £672.00: £321.00) Stalls: High GOING minus 0.37 sec per fur (F)

SP RR SF

3894[5] **Abajany (71)** (MRChannon) **3-9-0** JFortune(13) (a.p: led over 1f out: rdn: r.o wl) .... — **1** 7/1[2] 83 60
3798[10] **Mr Paradise (IRE) (70)** (TJNaughton) **3-8-13** JWeaver(15) (lw: nt clr run over 2f out: hdwy over 1f out: r.o ins fnl f) 2 **2** 14/1 78 55
4151[9] **Sheer Face (78)** (WRMuir) **3-9-2**(5) CLowther(1) (s.i.s: rdn over 2f out: hdwy over 1f out: r.o wl ins fnl f) .... ½ **3** 14/1 85 62
3897[4] **Mantles Prince (74)** (GLewis) **3-9-3b** PaulEddery(11) (chsd ldr: led over 2f out tl over 1f out: unable qckn) .... ½ **4** 8/1 80 57

3772[4]	**Kamin (USA) (72)** (RWArmstrong) **3-9-1** GCarter(7) (lost pl 2f out: rallied fnl f: r.o)	¾	**5**	15/2[3]	77	54
3685[2]	**First Chance (IRE) (68)** (DRCElsworth) **3-8-8**(3) RFfrench(17) (hdwy & n.m.r on ins over 2f out: rdn wl over 1f out: one pce fnl f)	1½	**6**	13/2[1]	70	47
3987[7]	**Nominator Lad (68)** (BAMcMahon) **3-8-11** GDuffield(10) (lw: a.p: hrd rdn over 1f out: wknd ins fnl f)	hd	**7**	12/1	69	46
3200[4]	**Bubbly (69)** (JLDunlop) **3-8-12** PatEddery(14) (led over 5f: ev ch over 1f out: wknd ins fnl f)	2½	**8**	7/1[2]	65	42
3457[6]	**Foot Battalion (IRE) (67)** (RHollinshead) **3-8-10** ACulhane(16) (lw: rdn over 2f out: hdwy over 1f out: one pce ins fnl f)	hd	**9**	33/1	63	40
2309[6]	**Faringdon Future (77)** (BWHills) **3-9-6** TQuinn(12) (swtg: hdwy over 2f out: hrd rdn over 1f out: sn wknd)	1½	**10**	20/1	70	47
3980[11]	**Hawksbill Henry (USA) (54)** (MrsAJPerrett) **3-7-11** GayeHarwood(3) (lw: nvr nrr)	hd	**11**	50/1	47	24
3798[11]	**Junikay (IRE) (67)** (RIngram) **3-8-10** AMcGlone(6) (nt clr run over 2f out: sme hdwy over 1f out: sn wknd)	1¼	**12**	33/1	58	35
3894[11]	**Al Masroor (USA) (76)** (JWPayne) **3-9-5** DeanMcKeown(5) (swtg: prom over 6f)	nk	**13**	14/1	66	43
3478[9]	**Who's That Man (59)** (SCWilliams) **3-8-2** JQuinn(4) (rdn over 2f out: hdwy over 1f out: wknd fnl f)	3	**14**	20/1	43	20
4015[11]	**Villarica (IRE) (73)** (PWChapple-Hyam) **3-9-2** JReid(8) (lw: bhd fnl 2f)	¾	**15**	10/1	56	33
3976[15]	**Praeditus (75)** (RHannon) **3-9-4b[1]** DaneO'Neill(9) (prom over 4f)	¾	**16**	20/1	56	33
3741[8]	**Olivo (IRE) (70)** (CAHorgan) **3-8-10**(3) DO'Donohoe(18) (sme hdwy on ins over 1f out: sn wknd)	2½	**17**	16/1	46	23
3463[3]	**Slipstream Star (72)** (IABalding) **3-9-1** LDettori(2) (bhd fnl 2f)	6	**18**	9/1	36	13

(SP 136.0%) **18 Rn**

1m 42.06 (0.86) CSF £93.71 CT £1,301.44 TOTE £10.90: £2.30 £3.00 £3.50 £1.80 (£117.80) Trio £469.40 OWNER John White and Partners (UPPER LAMBOURN) BRED Fares Stables Ltd

3894 Abajany returned to winning ways on this sounder surface and, striking the front over a furlong out, soon shot clear. He is a different horse since he has been gelded according to his trainer. (7/1)

2149* Mr Paradise (IRE) began to pick up ground below the distance but, despite running inside the final furlong for second prize, found the winner was already home and dry. (14/1)

3752 Sheer Face making a quick reappearance, is gradually coming down the handicap. At the back of the field and appearing to have no chance early in the straight, he sprouted wings from below the distance but found the line always coming too soon. (14/1)

3897 Mantles Prince got to the front over a quarter of a mile from home but, headed below the distance, could only go up and down in the same place. He remains a maiden. (8/1)

3772 Kamin (USA) got outpaced a quarter of a mile from home but did stay on again at the death. (15/2)

3685 First Chance (IRE) edged closer along the inside rail in the straight, but failed to quicken inside the distance. She needs to drop a few pounds. (13/2)

4015 Villarica (IRE) (10/1: 8/1-12/1)

4177 KENNINGTON OVAL MAIDEN STKS (3-Y.O) (Class D)

4-25 (4-26) **1m 2f 7y** £3,452.50 (£1,045.00: £510.00: £242.50) Stalls: High GOING minus 0.37 sec per fur (F)

				SP	RR	SF
1168[10]	**Flagship (72)** (MajorWRHern) **3-8-9** TSprake(12) (hdwy over 1f out: led ins fnl f: rdn out)	—	**1**	14/1	87	49
4060[2]	**Tonight's Prize (IRE) (83)** (CFWall) **3-9-0** GDuffield(5) (hld up: rdn over 2f out: led 1f out tl ins fnl f: unable qckn)	2	**2**	6/4[1]	89	51
	Messina (IRE) (RCharlton) **3-8-9** PatEddery(1) (w'like: scope: rdn over 3f out: hdwy over 1f out: r.o wl ins fnl f)	1½	**3**	9/1	81	43
3820[3]	**Beacon Silver** (LordHuntingdon) **3-8-9** MRoberts(7) (lw: a.p: led over 2f out to 1f out: eased whn btn ins fnl f)	2	**4**	20/1	78	40
3095[9]	**Lysandros (IRE)** (JHMGosden) **3-9-0** JCarroll(2) (lw: rdn 3f out: nvr nr to chal)	3	**5**	25/1	78	40
3727[4]	**Mrs Miniver (USA) (89)** (PAKelleway) **3-8-9** JReid(8) (a.p: led over 3f out tl over 2f out: wknd 1f out)	2½	**6**	9/2[3]	70	32
3977[3]	**Bel Canto (IRE)** (JHMGosden) **3-9-0** LDettori(9) (lw: hld up: rdn 4f out: eased whn btn ins fnl f)	nk	**7**	11/4[2]	74	36
2583[8]	**Pradesh** (JHMGosden) **3-8-9** GHind(10) (bit bkwd: led over 6f: wknd over 2f out)	1¼	**8**	20/1	67	29
3903[4]	**Miss Vita (USA)** (RJRWilliams) **3-8-9** JQuinn(6) (bhd fnl 8f)	1¼	**9**	33/1	65	27
4060[6]	**Dukhan (USA)** (RWArmstrong) **3-9-0** GCarter(11) (prom over 8f)	3	**10**	12/1	65	27
1567[6]	**After Hours (50)** (DJSffrenchDavis) **3-8-9** JWeaver(4) (bit bkwd: a bhd)	7	**11**	50/1	49	11

(SP 127.5%) **11 Rn**

2m 8.62 (1.92) CSF £33.27 TOTE £26.30: £4.50 £1.10 £1.90 (£41.70) Trio £56.00 OWNER Mr R. D. Hollingsworth (LAMBOURN) BRED R. D. Hollingsworth

Flagship left her only previous run four months ago well behind and, coming with a good run from below the distance, struck the front inside the final furlong. (14/1)

4060 Tonight's Prize (IRE) again did nothing wrong and managed to get to the front a furlong out but, for the fourth consecutive time, had to settle for second best as the winner went by. He deserves a change of luck. (6/4)

Messina (IRE), a medium-sized, likeable filly, was going nowhere at the back of the field early in the straight. She at last grasped what was required of her from below the distance and ran on in encouraging style to take third prize. (9/1: 5/1-10/1)

3820 Beacon Silver was moving up in distance and showed in front over a quarter of a mile from home. Headed a furlong out, her jockey was not hard on her when all chance had evaporated. (20/1)

Lysandros (IRE) never looked like posing a serious threat. (25/1)

3727 Mrs Miniver (USA) may have been taking a drop in class, but that did not help her and, after showing in front early in the straight, she had shot her bolt a furlong from home. (9/2: 11/4-5/1)

3977 Bel Canto (IRE) was not helped by the slow pace and Dettori was pushing him along turning into the straight. Failing to find the necessary turn of foot, he was allowed to come home in his own time inside the final furlong, when all chance had gone. A step up to a mile and a half would help. (11/4)

4060 Dukhan (USA) (12/1: 8/1-14/1)

4178 'DISMISSAL' CLAIMING STKS (2-Y.O) (Class E)

4-55 (4-55) **5f 6y** £2,882.25 (£873.00: £426.50: £203.25) Stalls: High GOING: 0.08 sec per fur (G)

				SP	RR	SF
4042[14]	**Rapid Reliance** (DRCElsworth) **2-7-9**(3) RFfrench(9) (hld up: rdn over 1f out: led ins fnl f: r.o wl)	—	**1**	25/1	72	32
3707[4]	**Pierpoint (IRE) (75)** (RAFahey) **2-8-1v[1]**(7) RWinston(15) (lw: a.p: hrd rdn over 1f out: unable qckn)	1¼	**2**	7/2[2]	78	38
3804*	**Junior Muffin (IRE) (73)** (JBerry) **2-8-4**(5) CLowther(14) (rdn over 2f out: swtchd lft & hdwy over 1f out: r.o wl ins fnl f)	½	**3**	5/1[3]	77	37
3782[8]	**Rita's Rock Ape** (RBrotherton) **2-8-4** SDrowne(3) (a.p: led 1f out tl ins fnl f: sn wknd)	1¼	**4**	50/1	69	29
3770[9]	**Legal Lark (IRE)** (PHowling) **2-8-7** MRoberts(1) (s.i.s: rdn over 2f out: hmpd over 1f out: hdwy fnl f: nvr nrr)	1	**5**	50/1	68	28
3237[5]	**Happy Days Again (IRE) (86)** (JWharton) **2-8-10** JCarroll(12) (lw: led 4f)	1¾	**6**	11/10[1]	66	26
3862[10]	**Safabee (60)** (MJHaynes) **2-7-10** NCarlisle(7) (outpcd: nvr nrr)	hd	**7**	50/1	51	11

3911[7] **River Frontier (IRE) (39)** (MDIUsher) **2-7-10** JMarshall(13) (lw: outpcd: nvr nr to chal) ....½	**8**	33/1	50	10
3927[11] **Sabre Girl (52)** (RHannon) **2-8-4** DaneO'Neill(10) (outpcd) 1	**9**	25/1	55	15
3866[2] **Oriel Girl (69)** (BJMeehan) **2-8-2** GDuffield(8) (spd over 3f) ....hd	**10**	7/1	52	12
3859[10] **Corsecan (53)** (SDow) **2-7-11**(7) PDoe(4) (lw: prom over 2f) 1½	**11**	25/1	50	10
Hot Topic (IRE) (PAKelleway) **2-8-8** JReid(5) (neat: bit bkwd: s.i.s: a bhd) 8	**12**	20/1	28	—
4066[14] **Resurrection (IRE)** (RHannon) **2-7-11**(3) MHenry(6) (s.i.s: a bhd) ....½	**13**	25/1	19	—

(SP 128.0%) **13 Rn**

63.23 secs (3.43) CSF £100.09 TOTE £36.90: £3.70 £1.80 £1.70 (£92.70) Trio £138.60 OWNER Mr A. J. Allright (WHITCOMBE) BRED A. B. Barraclough
Rapid Reliance clmd R Ingram £6,000
OFFICIAL EXPLANATION **Rapid Reliance: regarding the improvement in form compared with her previous run at Bath, the trainer reported that the filly had traffic problems at Bath and is also temperamental.**
2917 Rapid Reliance caught the eye on her Windsor debut, but then showed absolutely nothing on her next two outings. Nevertheless, on this occasion she came through to lead in the final furlong and ran on strongly. (25/1)
3707 Pierpoint (IRE) had the plum draw and stuck to the favoured far rails. In a handy position throughout, he managed to get up for second prize but failed to find that necessary turn of foot. (7/2)
3804* Junior Muffin (IRE) had more on his plate here but still gave a good account of himself, running on really strongly inside the last furlong and a half, only just failing to take second prize. (5/1)
Rita's Rock Ape left previous form well behind and got to the front a furlong from home before passed by the winner soon afterwards. (50/1)
Legal Lark (IRE), taking a drop in class after showing nothing in two runs to date, soon made up lost ground to race in midfield. Hampered below the distance, he did stay on in the closing stages. (50/1)
3237 Happy Days Again (IRE) was dropped back to five furlongs after failing to last home over six furlongs last time out. However, this is a very stiff track which takes a lot of getting and, after blazing the trail, he had nothing in reserve when collared a furlong out. (11/10: evens-6/5)

4179 END OF SEASON APPRENTICE H'CAP (0-70) (3-Y.O+) (Class E)
5-25 (5-29) **1m 2f 7y** £2,738.00 (£839.00: £417.00: £206.00) Stalls: High GOING minus 0.37 sec per fur (F)

		SP	RR	SF
3758[5] **Rock The Barney (IRE) (40)** (MDIUsher) **8-7-12b**[1](5) ANicholls(15) (gd hdwy & swtchd rt 2f out: led 1f out: r.o wl) ....—	**1**	8/1[2]	55	37
2668[6] **Law Dancer (IRE) (48)** (TGMills) **4-8-1**(10) LisaHackett(2) (hdwy over 3f out: led over 2f out to 1f out: unable qckn) 2	**2**	20/1	60	42
3907[7] **Tajar (USA) (41)** (TKeddy) **5-8-4** TSiddall(19) (swtg: rdn over 3f out: hdwy over 1f out: r.o) 1	**3**	16/1	51	33
3465[5] **Ring the Chief (37)** (MDIUsher) **5-7-11**(3) DarrenWilliams(1) (swtg: rdn over 2f out: hdwy over 1f out: one pce fnl f) ....½	**4**	8/1[2]	46	28
3413[7] **Arzani (USA) (60)** (DJSCosgrove) **6-9-1**(8) SGaillard(18) (b: rdn over 2f out: hdwy over 1f out: nvr nrr) 3	**5**	16/1	65	47
2373[5] **Herbshan Dancer (56)** (BRMillman) **3-8-13** RStudholme(5) (lw: hdwy 4f out: wknd over 1f out) 5	**6**	16/1	53	29
3796[10] **Dark Age (IRE) (60)** (RAkehurst) **4-9-1**(8) PFitzsimons(4) (lw: a.p: ev ch over 2f out: wknd fnl f) ....½	**7**	14/1	56	38
3714[7] **Reimei (58)** (KCComerford) **8-9-0b**(7) JBosley(14) (rdn & no hdwy fnl 3f) ....s.h	**8**	25/1	54	36
3227[11] **Mary Culi (48)** (HCandy) **3-7-9**(10) BarrySmith(7) (lw: nvr nr to chal) ....½	**9**	14/1	43	19
4063[4] **Zamalek (USA) (50)** (RMFlower) **5-8-10v**(3) JFowle(11) (swtg: plld hrd: led 3f: rdn over 2f out: wknd over 1f out) ....¾	**10**	4/1[1]	44	26
3690[10] **Lord Oberon (IRE) (51)** (JAkehurst) **9-9-0** JDennis(12) (b: hdwy on ins over 1f out: sn wknd) 1	**11**	12/1	43	25
3793[7] **Blush (53)** (MCPipe) **3-8-7b**[1](3) PBradley(17) (nvr nrr) 2½	**12**	12/1	41	17
3848[5] **Rehaab (49)** (MissBSanders) **4-8-9v**(3) GHannon(6) (prom over 7f) 2½	**13**	8/1[2]	33	15
4063[17] **Absolutelystunning (57)** (MrsBarbaraWaring) **4-9-6** VictoriaAppleby(20) (b: b.hind: a bhd) 8	**14**	25/1	29	11
3448[6] **Double Gold (57)** (MBell) **3-8-4**(10) SRussell(3) (plld hrd: hdwy 8f out: led 7f out tl over 2f out: sn wknd) ....nk	**15**	16/1	28	4
3798[12] **Ortelius (67)** (RHannon) **3-9-4**(6) RSmith(13) (lw: bhd fnl 3f) 3½	**16**	16/1	32	8
3315[7] **Harvey White (IRE) (55)** (JPearce) **5-9-1**(3) PClarke(9) (lw: bhd fnl 2f) 2	**17**	9/1[3]	17	—
3886[4] **Nicola's Princess (46)** (BAMcMahon) **4-8-9** SRighton(10) (lw: prom 7f) 2	**18**	12/1	5	—
2873[7] **Forestry (54)** (JGSmyth-Osbourne) **3-8-6**(5) DHayden(16) (bit bkwd: bhd fnl 2f) 13	**19**	20/1	—	—

(SP 146.4%) **19 Rn**

2m 9.44 (2.74) CSF £165.86 CT £2,358.16 TOTE £8.90: £2.20 £6.00 £4.10 £2.10 (£117.30) Trio £765.00 OWNER Mrs Satu Marks (WANTAGE) BRED Mrs Mary Travers
WEIGHT FOR AGE 3yo-6lb
3758 Rock The Barney (IRE), who was given far too much to do last time out, made amends here. Weaving his way through the pack, he struck the front a furlong from home and kept on well to gain his first victory in over two years. (8/1)
2668 Law Dancer (IRE) seems better suited by the All-Weather where he has gained both his successes to date, but he still gave a good account of himself after a near ten-week absence and moved to the front down the centre of the course over a quarter of a mile from home. Headed a furlong out, he then found the winner too good. (20/1)
3267 Tajar (USA), 10lb higher than when winning at the end of July, ran on in the last furlong and a half for third prize. (16/1)
3465 Ring the Chief picked up ground below the distance but was making no further impression in the final furlong. All three of his wins to date have come over seven furlongs. (8/1)
2896 Arzani (USA), 6lb higher than he has ever won off, has gained both his wins this year in selling company, but did stay on from below the distance to be nearest at the line. (16/1)
2373 Herbshan Dancer took closer order entering the straight but had shot his bolt below the distance. He remains a maiden. (16/1)

T/Jkpt: Not won; £19,927.66 to Sandown 17/9/97. T/Plpt: £111.10 (269.8 Tckts). T/Qdpt: £40.60 (36.49 Tckts) AK

3716-YARMOUTH (L-H) (Good to firm, Firm bk st)
Tuesday September 16th
WEATHER: fine WIND: str across

4180 BROOKE CLAIMING STKS (3-Y.O) (Class E)
2-05 (2-06) **1m 3f 101y** £3,201.75 (£954.00: £454.50: £204.75) Stalls: Low GOING minus 0.45 sec per fur (F)

		SP	RR	SF
3865[9] **Bewitching Lady (43)** (DWPArbuthnot) **3-8-4** MartinDwyer(2) (lw: trckd ldrs: led over 1f out: r.o wl) ....—	**1**	25/1	57	32
3767[4] **Laguna Bay (IRE) (56)** (APJarvis) **3-8-12** KDarley(7) (lw: hld up: hdwy on ins & nt clr run over 2f out & over 1f out: swtchd rt: r.o fnl f) ....¾	**2**	11/4[2]	64	39

3567^{10} **Go Hence (63)** (WJarvis) **3-8-11** WRyan(4) (lw: hld up in rr: hdwy 3f out: hrd rdn over 1f out: nt pce to chal)....	2	**3**	5/2 ^{1}	60	35
3870^{5} **Le Grand Gousier (USA) (53)** (RJRWilliams) **3-9-3b^{1}** RCochrane(5) (lw: a.p: led over 2f out tl over 1f out: rdn whn hmpd ent fnl f: nt rcvr)	4	**4**	9/1	61	36
3970^{10} **Superbelle (55)** (MAJarvis) **3-8-12b^{1}** EmmaO'Gorman(3) (sn led: hdd over 2f out: wknd wl over 1f out)	½	**5**	6/1	55	30
3966^{3} **Heart Full of Soul (60)** (PFICole) **3-9-7b** SSanders(1) (chsd ldrs: hrd rdn 4f out: sn lost tch: t.o)....	9	**6**	5/1 ^{3}	51	26
4043^{8} **Patrick (40)** (DBurchell) **3-8-9** KFallon(6) (hld up & bhd: drvn along over 3f out: sn lost tch: t.o)....	15	**7**	12/1	18	—

(SP 107.7%) **7 Rn**

2m 24.7 (2.90) CSF £75.15 TOTE £25.50: £7.70 £1.60 (£54.20) OWNER Mr Noel Cronin (COMPTON) BRED Miss E. Drax

3593 Bewitching Lady took a step down in trip to open her account and, once in front, was in no mood to give best. (25/1)

3767 Laguna Bay (IRE) should have won this, but was continually stopped in her tracks, and when she did eventually find space the winner had set sail for home. Consolation awaits. (11/4)

3567 Go Hence had his tongue tied down, and was fully expected to outclass these rivals, but his action to post suggested he was not at all happy on this lively ground, and he just could not summon the pace to mount a challenge. (5/2)

3870 Le Grand Gousier (USA), always in the firing line, was flat to the boards when he was denied much room up the inside rail entering the final furlong, and the position had to be expected. (9/1: op 6/1)

3695 Superbelle had more use made of her in her first-time blinkers, but she could never get away from her pursuers, and she was struggling to hold on from below the distance. (6/1: 4/1-13/2)

3966 Heart Full of Soul, having his first run at beyond a mile, was in trouble early in the straight, and it would seem lack of stamina could have been the main reason. (5/1: 3/1-11/2)

4043 Patrick (12/1: 8/1-14/1)

4181 JOHN MUSKER STKS (Listed) (3-Y.O+ F & M) (Class A)

2-35 (2-37) **1m 2f 21y** £11,874.70 (£3,541.60: £1,689.80: £763.90) Stalls: Low GOING minus 0.45 sec per fur (F)

			SP	RR	SF
3727^{7} **Entice (FR) (111)** (SbinSuroor) **3-8-7** DHolland(6) (a chsng ldrs: chal appr fnl f: r.o to ld towards fin).....	—	**1**	15/8 ^{1}	109+	38
3594^{7} **Meshhed (USA) (100)** (BHanbury) **3-8-7** RHills(1) (a.p: led over 2f out: hrd drvn & hdd wl ins fnl f)....	½	**2**	8/1	108	37
2126* **Bombazine (IRE) (85)** (LMCumani) **3-8-7** RCochrane(2) (hld up in tch: effrt over 2f out: sn hrd drvn: nvr able to chal)....	2½	**3**	6/1 ^{3}	104	33
1738^{12} **Ukraine Venture (92)** (SPCWoods) **3-8-7** WRyan(3) (bit bkwd: hld up: hdwy over 3f out: nt clr run over 2f out: nt rcvr)....	1¾	**4**	13/2	102	31
3803^{4} **Maid of Camelot (97)** (RCharlton) **3-8-11v** MHills(7) (led after 1f tl over 2f out: rdn & outpcd fnl f)....	¾	**5**	6/1 ^{3}	104	33
3803^{7} **Hen Harrier (91)** (JLDunlop) **3-8-7** KDarley(8) (dwlt: rdn along over 3f out: no imp)....	7	**6**	12/1	89	18
2869^{5} **Fascinating Rhythm** (HRACecil) **3-8-7** KFallon(5) (bit bkwd: led 1f: ev ch over 2f out: sn wknd & eased)....	4	**7**	9/2 ^{2}	83	12
3976^{8} **Karinska (59)** (MCChapman) **7-8-13** SCarson(4) (lw: dwlt: effrt & rdn over 3f out: no rspnse: t.o)....	28	**8**	66/1	39	—

(SP 115.2%) **8 Rn**

2m 5.9 (2.10) CSF £16.49 TOTE £3.60: £1.10 £2.40 £2.40 (£10.90) OWNER Godolphin (NEWMARKET) BRED Darley Stud Management Co. Ltd.

WEIGHT FOR AGE 3yo-6lb

OFFICIAL EXPLANATION **Entice (FR): regarding the improvement in form compared with her previous run at York, the trainer reported that she was unsuited by the yielding ground and did not stay the mile and a half.**

3727 Entice (FR) left her poor York run behind her with a very comfortably-gained success. Although she is beginning to get her winter coat, she is lightly-raced and clearly useful on her day. (15/8)

2774 Meshhed (USA) ran possibly her best race yet. Forced to admit defeat nearing the line, she never once stopped trying, and is worth following from now on. (8/1)

2126* Bombazine (IRE) won her maiden on her previous run three months ago and came here fresh and well but, on this much faster ground, in a higher-graded event, she just could not find the speed to deliver a challenge. She is going the right way. (6/1)

1738 Ukraine Venture, out of action since finishing last in the Oaks over three months ago, does run well when fresh, but she looked in need of this pipe-opener. In the circumstances, she was not disgraced. (13/2)

3803 Maid of Camelot has been highly tried in recent races, and although she adopted more forceful tactics on this occasion she was fighting a lost cause inside the final furlong. (6/1)

2869 Fascinating Rhythm may not have fully recovered from a reported lung infection earlier in the year, for she found absolutely nothing when put to the test, and was once again tenderly handled when all chance had gone. (9/2)

4182 THOMAS PRIOR MAIDEN STKS (3-Y.O+) (Class D)

3-10 (3-10) **6f 3y** £3,785.00 (£1,130.00: £540.00: £245.00) Stalls: High GOING minus 0.45 sec per fur (F)

			SP	RR	SF
4047^{3} **Mr Majica (75)** (BJMeehan) **3-8-12** KDarley(2) (chsd ldng pair: hrd drvn over 2f out: r.o u.p to ld cl home)	—	**1**	100/30 ^{2}	86	28
681^{6} **Gingersnap** (HRACecil) **3-8-7** KFallon(1) (bit bkwd: chsd ldr: led over 2f out: rdn & edgd lft: hdd nr fin)	½	**2**	7/1 ^{3}	80	22
3863^{4} **Mary Cornwallis (85)** (GWragg) **3-8-7** MHills(3) (led over 3f: sn hrd rdn: swtchd lft appr fnl f: no imp)	2½	**3**	4/9 ^{1}	73	15
675^{20} **Shalaal (USA) (82)** (MCChapman) **3-8-5(7)** SCarson(4) (bkwd: trckd ldrs: outpcd fnl 2f)....	7	**4**	40/1	59	1
4070^{11} **Il Falco (FR)** (SirMarkPrescott) **3-8-12** SSanders(5) (outpcd: a bhd)	3½	**5**	50/1	50	—

(SP 109.2%) **5 Rn**

1m 13.1 (2.20) CSF £21.79 TOTE £4.30: £1.50 £1.70 (£7.30) OWNER Mr C. J. Metcalfe (UPPER LAMBOURN) BRED M. Reditt and Son Ltd

4047 Mr Majica was one of the first off the bridle, but his jockey cajoled him into maintaining his run, and it eventually paid off close home. (100/30)

681 Gingersnap still looked to have a bit left to work on on her first outing since the spring. She looked to have the prize in safe-keeping when shaking off the favourite, but she drifted left, into the whip, and was run out of it nearing the line. (7/1: op 9/4)

3863 Mary Cornwallis looked to have a simple task to get off the mark, but she was in trouble soon after losing the lead, and this strongly-made filly may well need to get her toe in to produce her best. (4/9: 8/13-2/5)

4183 BRIAN TAYLOR H'CAP (0-90) (3-Y.O+) (Class C)

3-40 (3-41) **5f 43y** £5,677.50 (£1,695.00: £810.00: £367.50) Stalls: High GOING minus 0.45 sec per fur (F)

			SP	RR	SF
3984^{12} **Spender (77)** (PWHarris) **8-9-5** DHolland(12) (lw: a.p: rdn to ld ins fnl f: hld on gamely)	—	**1**	14/1	88	59
3198^{12} **Literary Society (USA) (80)** (JARToller) **4-9-8** SSanders(10) (lw: hdwy 2f out: chal ins fnl f: unable qckn nr fin)	nk	**2**	12/1	90	61
3410^{17} **That Man Again (83)** (SCWilliams) **5-9-11b** KDarley(9) (led tl ins fnl f)....	1	**3**	10/1	90	61
3217^{30} **Kilcullen Lad (IRE) (82)** (PMooney) **3-9-9v** RCochrane(8) (lw: s.i.s: hdwy & nt clr run 2f out: r.o wl ins fnl f) .	1¼	**4**	16/1	85	55
3765^{7} **Levelled (72)** (MRChannon) **3-8-13** MHills(4) (s.i.s: hdwy 2f out: sn rdn: nt pce to chal)	1¾	**5**	9/1 ^{3}	70	40
4137^{3} **Cross The Border (76)** (DNicholls) **4-9-4** AlexGreaves(5) (lw: w ldrs tl wknd & eased ent fnl f)....	nk	**6**	3/1 ^{2}	73	44

				SP	RR	SF
4048[10]	**Ivory's Grab Hire (67)** (KTIvory) **4-8-9b** MartinDwyer(2) (hdwy over 1f out: nvr nrr)	nk	**7**	16/1	63	34
3761[11]	**Royal Dome (IRE) (70)** (MartynWane) **5-8-9**(3) AWhelan(6) (trckd ldrs over 3f)	nk	**8**	16/1	65	36
4048[18]	**Just Dissident (IRE) (59)** (RMWhitaker) **5-8-1** FNorton(1) (prom tl rdn & wknd over 1f out)	¾	**9**	25/1	52	23
4013[3]	**Bahamian Beauty (USA) (85)** (DRLoder) **3-9-12** KFallon(13) (sn pushed along: a bhd & outpcd)	1¾	**10**	9/4[1]	72	42
3851[7]	**Anokato (63)** (KTIvory) **3-8-4b** GBardwell(11) (outpcd: a bhd)	½	**11**	33/1	49	19
3065[8]	**Meliksah (IRE) (87)** (MBell) **3-9-9**(5) GFaulkner(3) (chsd ldrs 3f: sn lost tch)	2	**12**	14/1	67	37
3600[13]	**Rushcutter Bay (81)** (PLGilligan) **4-9-9** WRyan(7) (a bhd & outpcd)	¾	**13**	33/1	58	29
				(SP 123.3%)		**13 Rn**

61.3 secs (0.30) CSF £158.57 CT £1,044.98 TOTE £16.10: £3.50 £3.50 £3.30 (£52.60) Trio £219.30 OWNER The Entrepreneurs (BERKHAMSTED) BRED The Mount Coote Partnership

WEIGHT FOR AGE 3yo-1lb

1957* Spender acts on all types of ground and wins in all seasons, and this return to form showed he has lost none of his speed. (14/1)

2833* Literary Society (USA) went to post like a crab, but he ran his race out to the finish on this return to the minimum trip, and he made sure the winner had to pull out all the stops to hold him at bay. (12/1: op 8/1)

2675 That Man Again has not won for some time, but he showed an instant return to form here and his turn could be close at hand. (10/1)

2964 Kilcullen Lad (IRE) looked to be a most unlucky loser after missing a beat at the start, for he was denied any sort of run until approaching the final furlong, and the fact that he was able to finish so close is a credit to him. (16/1)

3614 Levelled likes to come from off the pace, but he was being made to work after a tardy start and was never able to get within striking range of the principals. (9/1)

4137 Cross The Border went with the pace, but was feeling the strain inside the distance and was eased once his measure had been taken. (3/1)

4013 Bahamian Beauty (USA), off the bridle from the start, failed to pick up at any stage, and this was certainly not her true running. (9/4)

4184 CAISTER (S) STKS (3-Y.O+) (Class G)

4-15 (4-17) **7f 3y** £2,763.00 (£768.00: £369.00) Stalls: High GOING minus 0.45 sec per fur (F)

				SP	RR	SF
3921[7]	**Gymcrak Premiere (68)** (GHolmes) **9-9-5v** KFallon(16) (hld up: hdwy to ld wl over 1f out: rdn out)	—	**1**	13/8[1]	75	43
4016[8]	**Shontaine (56)** (MJohnston) **4-9-5** DHolland(19) (hdwy 2f out: str chal fnl f: r.o)	nk	**2**	10/1[3]	74	42
3855[8]	**Shashi (IRE) (47)** (PatMitchell) **5-9-0** PBloomfield(20) (in tch stands' side: r.o appr fnl f: nvr nrr)	5	**3**	14/1	58	26
3968[2]	**Petite Danseuse (60)** (CADwyer) **3-8-11** SSanders(11) (a chsng ldrs: rdn & one pce ins fnl f)	s.h	**4**	11/4[2]	58	23
3969[7]	**Gunners Glory (51)** (MrsLStubbs) **3-8-11v[1]** RCochrane(13) (hdwy fnl 2f: nrst fin)	nk	**5**	12/1	57	22
3855[9]	**Waders Dream (IRE) (36)** (PatMitchell) **8-8-9v**(5) AmandaSanders(9) (trckd ldrs stands' side: rdn 2f out: sn btn)	2½	**6**	40/1	51	19
3297[7]	**Aegean Sound (53)** (KTIvory) **3-8-6** MartinDwyer(14) (led stands' side over 5f: sn rdn & wknd)	1½	**7**	33/1	43	8
3261[5]	**Sir Tasker (46)** (JLHarris) **9-9-5** AlexGreaves(17) (chsd ldrs over 5f)	1½	**8**	33/1	50	18
4059[13]	**Birchwood Sun (53)** (MDods) **7-9-5b** AClark(10) (chsd ldrs: rdn 2f out: grad wknd)	¾	**9**	33/1	48	16
3910[16]	**Axeman (IRE) (36)** (MartynWane) **5-8-11**(3) AWhelan(6) (racd far side: rdn & drifted rt over 1f out: eased whn btn)	¾	**10**	40/1	41	9
3966[6]	**Glen Ogil** (MRChannon) **3-8-11** RPerham(8) (b: nvr trbld ldrs)	¾	**11**	16/1	39	4
2922[13]	**Hopeful Bid (IRE) (44)** (PHowling) **8-9-0b** KDarley(18) (b.hind: s.s: a in rr)	¾	**12**	33/1	38	6
3749[4]	**Gresatre (48)** (CADwyer) **3-9-2** WRyan(1) (racd far side: bhd fnl 3f)	½	**13**	14/1	42	7
3565[13]	**Persephone (17)** (JLHarris) **4-8-4b**(5) RMullen(4) (prom far side over 4f)	nk	**14**	50/1	31	—
4114[11]	**Move Smartly (IRE) (42)** (MrsLStubbs) **7-8-7b**(7) GMcDonald(3) (led far side over 4f: sn outpcd)	5	**15**	40/1	25	—
3933[12]	**Old Roma (IRE) (45)** (JohnBerry) **4-8-9b[1]** MFenton(12) (prom stands' side 4f: t.o)	7	**16**	40/1	4	—
1991[4]	**Time of Night (USA) (55)** (JLEyre) **4-8-9** MGallagher(5) (racd far side: rdn along ½-wy: a bhd: t.o)	3½	**17**	12/1	—	—
424[14]	**Wahab (25)** (RFMarvin) **4-9-0v[1]** TGMcLaughlin(2) (b.hind: bit bkwd: racd far side: a bhd: t.o)	5	**18**	40/1	—	—
3321[14]	**Emmas Breeze (36)** (GGMargarson) **3-8-6** GBardwell(15) (prom to ½-wy: wknd qckly: t.o)	13	**19**	50/1	—	—
				(SP 136.3%)		**19 Rn**

1m 26.1 (1.90) CSF £17.90 TOTE £2.60: £1.90 £3.30 £5.60 (£12.40) Trio £45.90 OWNER The Gymcrak Thoroughbred Racing Club (PICKERING) BRED Cheveley Park Stud Ltd

WEIGHT FOR AGE 3yo-3lb

No bid

3921 Gymcrak Premiere found no trouble in running despite the size of the field and, cruising through to take charge just inside the quarter-mile marker, answered his rider's every call. (13/8)

3456* Shontaine promised to wear down the favourite when putting in a sustained last-furlong challenge but, hard as he tried, the winner matched him stride for stride. (10/1)

3590 Shashi (IRE) battled on willingly inside the distance, but the leading pair had got away and she was unable to land a blow. (14/1)

3968 Petite Danseuse is running consistently well at present, but the leading pair proved much too good for her and she was left for dead inside the last furlong. (11/4)

3749 Gunners Glory, really into his stride inside the distance, had left his effort far too late and was never a factor. (12/1)

Waders Dream (IRE) again failed to see out the trip, and a return to sprinting could prove beneficial, especially if he finds his form at this time of year. (40/1)

4185 JACK LEADER CHALLENGE TROPHY NURSERY H'CAP (0-85) (2-Y.O F) (Class D)

4-45 (4-55) **7f 3y** £3,947.50 (£1,180.00: £565.00: £257.50) Stalls: High GOING minus 0.45 sec per fur (F)

				SP	RR	SF
4097[9]	**Belle de Nuit (IRE) (72)** (BJMeehan) **2-8-9** KFallon(9) (a.p: led over 2f out: hrd rdn: hld on wl)	—	**1**	14/1	73	36
3411[2]	**Chocolate (IRE) (81)** (JLDunlop) **2-9-4** KDarley(11) (trckd ldrs: hdwy over 1f out: rdn to chal ins fnl f: unable qckn)	nk	**2**	9/2[2]	81	44
3387[6]	**Summer Deal (USA) (77)** (PFICole) **2-9-0** SSanders(12) (led over 4f out tl over 2f out: rdn & unable qckn fnl f)	1	**3**	14/1	75	38
3638[3]	**Ratiyya (IRE) (78)** (BHanbury) **2-9-1** RHills(10) (hdwy 3f out: ev ch over 1f out: sn rdn: no ex)	1¾	**4**	9/1	72	35
3924[6]	**Sassy (IRE) (63)** (APJarvis) **2-8-0** NVarley(4) (hdwy 4f out: rdn & wknd 2f out)	5	**5**	16/1	46	9
3799[6]	**Miss Muffett (IRE) (59)** (PMooney) **2-7-10** JLowe(2) (dwlt: swtchd rt sn after s: rdn 3f out: n.d)	3	**6**	50/1	35	—
3911[10]	**Jato Dancer (IRE) (59)** (JRArnold) **2-7-10** MartinDwyer(13) (led 3f: rdn & wknd over 2f out)	5	**7**	33/1	23	—
3861[3]	**Risada (IRE) (73)** (DRLoder) **2-8-10** RCochrane(8) (led 4f out tl over 2f out: sn rdn & wknd)	2	**8**	5/1[3]	33	—
3927*	**Up At The Top (IRE) (84)** (BWHills) **2-9-7** MHills(7) (a bhd: rdn over 2f out: no imp)	1½	**9**	13/8[1]	40	3

					SP	RR	SF
3924^{13}	**Mrs Middle (67)** (NACallaghan) **2-8-4** GBardwell(1) (trckd ldrs on outside 4f)	3	**10**	33/1	17	—
4065^{5}	**Deva Lady (70)** (CNAllen) **2-8-4**(3) JDSmith(3) (hld up: in tch whn clipped rival's heels & uns rdr after 2f)		**U**	14/1	—	—

(SP 116.7%) **11 Rn**

1m 25.9 (1.70) CSF £67.85 CT £832.38 TOTE £15.30: £2.60 £1.30 £3.50 (£22.90) Trio £46.50 OWNER Mr Richard Withers (UPPER LAMBOURN) BRED Lodge Park Stud

LONG HANDICAP Jato Dancer (IRE) 7-7 Miss Muffett (IRE) 7-5

OFFICIAL EXPLANATION Up At The Top (IRE): unsuited by the fast ground.

3783* Belle de Nuit (IRE) appreciated having plenty of use made of her and, kicking on some way out, found all that was needed to win readily. (14/1: op 8/1)

3411 Chocolate (IRE) tries hard enough, but she does seem to lack a turn of finishing speed, and although she put in a sustained last-furlong challenge, that bit extra that was needed was not forthcoming. (9/2)

3387 Summer Deal (USA) deserves to win a race and she gave this her best shot, but she was found wanting when the battle to the line really hotted up. (14/1: op 8/1)

3638 Ratiyya (IRE) ran as if she did not really last the trip, after having a chance as good as any approaching the final furlong. (9/1)

3861 Risada (IRE) (5/1: 5/2-11/2)

3927* Up At The Top (IRE), at full stretch three furlongs out, could never make the slightest impression, and she was reported not to have handled the fast ground. (13/8)

4065 Deva Lady (14/1: 10/1-16/1)

T/Plpt: £374.50 (51.83 Tckts). T/Qdpt: £121.80 (8.92 Tckts)

4186a - 4190a (Irish Racing) - See Computer Raceform

0664a-GALWAY (Ireland) (R-H) (Yielding to soft)
Tuesday September 9th

4191a ARDILAUN HOUSE HOTEL OYSTER STKS (Listed) (3-Y.O+)
3-35 (3-36) **1m 4f** IR £9,675.00 (IR £2,775.00: IR £1,275.00: IR £375.00)

				SP	RR	SF
3842a^{2}	**Aliya (IRE)** (JOxx,Ireland) **3-8-7** PJSmullen (sn led: mde all: rdn & styd on last 2f)	—	**1**	7/2^{2}	107	—
2441a*	**Vivo (IRE)** (JOxx,Ireland) **4-9-5** JPMurtagh (hld up: mid div: hdwy over 4f out: 3rd & nt trble ldrs st: rdn & styd on fnl f)	¾	**2**	8/1	109	—
3842a^{5}	**Mohaajir (USA)** (JSBolger,Ireland) **6-9-12** CEverard (chsd ldr tl ½-wy: rdn 3f out: nt trble wnr u.p ins last: kpt on same pce)	1½	**3**	9/1	114	—
	Theatreworld (IRE) (APO'Brien,Ireland) **5-9-9**ow1 CRoche (dwlt: early reminders: towards rr: rdn & hdwy 5f out: 7th bef st: styd on fnl f: nrst fin)	3½	**4**	5/2^{1}	106	—
3842a^{3}	**Buddy Marvel (IRE)** (JJMcLoughlin,Ireland) **3-8-13** NGMcCullagh (hld up: hdwy ½-wy: rdn & chsd ldrs over 4f out: no imp fr 2f out: kpt on same pce)	4½	**5**	7/1	99	—
2267a^{6}	**Rossmore Girl (IRE)** (PJFlynn,Ireland) **4-9-2** SCraine (cl up: wnt 2nd ½-wy tl under 3f out: 4th & no imp st: one pce)	2	**6**	13/2^{3}	91	—
2267a^{8}	**Red Affair (IRE)** (JOxx,Ireland) **3-8-10** PShanahan (mid div: 6th & chsd ldrs appr st: no imp: kpt on)	3½	**7**	16/1	89	—
	Last Dream (IRE) (MJGrassick,Ireland) **3-8-7** EAhern (towards rr: 9th 4f out: no imp fr 4f out)	1½	**8**	33/1	84	—
	Curiously (JOxx,Ireland) **3-8-7** WJSupple (towards rr: n.d: kpt on)	1½	**9**	20/1	82	—
2967a^{7}	**Monongahela (IRE)** (APO'Brien,Ireland) **3-8-13** JAHeffernan (in tch: rdn 5f out: no imp appr st)	11	**10**	25/1	73	—
	Western Chief (IRE) (DKWeld,Ireland) **3-8-10b** MJKinane (towards rr: n.d)	9	**11**	10/1	58	—
3511a^{5}	**Carnelly (IRE)** (DHanley,Ireland) **3-8-7** JJBehan (mid div: rdn ½-wy: no imp fr 4f out: dropped bhd st: p.u nr fin: (bit wnt thro mouth))		**P**	10/1	—	—

(SP 133.4%) **12 Rn**

2m 42.3 OWNER H H Aga Khan (CURRABEG)

3842a Aliya (IRE), whose trainer took this race with Russian Snows and Predappio, is a full sister to disqualified Oaks winner Aliysa and she has the Prix de Lutece at Longchamp next month pencilled in. She made all the running and would appreciate even further than this as well as softer ground. A tough filly, she will be a better four-year-old. Up 3lb for this, she is now rated 101. (7/2)

2441a* Vivo (IRE) finished well from way off the pace and, although he appeared to get the trip, he would definitely be more comfortable over shorter distances. (8/1)

3511a Mohaajir (USA), out of form so far this season, showed positive signs of a comeback with this effort. (9/1)

Theatreworld (IRE), with plenty on his plate in this company, stayed on well without ever getting on terms. He needs an extra half-mile. (5/2)

3842a Buddy Marvel (IRE) ran nowhere near the form he displayed at Leopardstown, when only a length and a half behind the winner when finishing second and third respectively behind Dr Johnson. (7/1)

4192a - 4202a (Irish Racing) - See Computer Raceform

3836a-LEOPARDSTOWN (Dublin, Ireland) (L-H) (Good)
Saturday September 13th

4203a THE FLYING FIVE STKS (Gp 3)
3-30 (3-33) **5f** IR £19,500.00 (IR £5,700.00: IR £2,700.00: IR £900.00) GOING minus 0.16 sec per fur (GF)

				SP	RR	SF
3410^{2}	**Midnight Escape** (CFWall) **4-9-9** KDarley (prom: disp ld ½-wy: 2nd 2f out: led ins fnl f: rdn & r.o.)	—	**1**	6/1^{3}	105+	51
3534a^{4}	**Hopping Higgins (IRE)** (APO'Brien,Ireland) **2-7-11** WJSupple (cl up: hdwy ½-wy: led over 2f out: hdd & rdn ins fnl f: kpt on: no ex)	¾	**2**	13/8^{1}	99	23
3837a^{4}	**Ailleacht (USA)** (JSBolger,Ireland) **5-9-6** KJManning (chsd ldrs: mod 5th ½-wy: nt trble ldrs over 1f out: kpt on)	3	**3**	6/1^{3}	90	36
3837a*	**Poker-B (IRE)** (DGillespie,Ireland) **3-9-8** JPMurtagh (towards rr: no imp 2f out: kpt on ins last: nt trble ldrs)	s.h	**4**	6/1^{3}	92	38
	Lady Assassin (IRE) (CCollins,Ireland) **3-9-5** PShanahan (towards rr early: rdn & no imp 2f out: kpt on ins last)	1½	**5**	20/1	84	30
3837a^{2}	**Best Before Dawn (IRE)** (APO'Brien,Ireland) **6-9-9b1** CRoche (prom: disp ld ½-wy: rdn 2f out: btn wl over 1f out)	1	**6**	3/1^{2}	85	31

3837a5 **Carhue Lass (IRE)** (PO'Leary,Ireland) **3-9-5** NGMcCullagh (led & disp ld: rdn ½-wy: 4th & btn 1½f out: wknd)7 **7** 12/1 58 4
(SP 118.4%) **7 Rn**

59.9 secs (2.40) OWNER Mervyn Ayers (NEWMARKET) BRED M. L. Ayers
3410 Midnight Escape was yet another British raider to underline the paucity of talent amongst Irish sprinters. Fast away and disputing on the rail early, he gained the advantage just over one furlong out and was good value for the official margin. (6/1)
3534a Hopping Higgins (IRE), in front on the outer from halfway, never quite got the opportunity to demonstrate her undoubted speed. The first pair had sorted themselves out with two furlongs to race but the juvenile was always playing second fiddle. (13/8: op Evens)
3837a Ailleacht (USA) was struggling from two furlongs out and there are still no signs that she is anywhere near as good as she was last season. (6/1)
3837a* Poker-B (IRE) needs the extra furlong now. (6/1)

4204a ESAT DIGIFONE IRISH CHAMPION STKS (Gp 1) (3-Y.O+ C & F)
4-00 (4-04) **1m 2f** IR £88,800.00 (IR £28,800.00: IR £13,800.00: IR £4,800.00) GOING minus 0.16 sec per fur (GF)

					SP	RR	SF
3050²	**Pilsudski (IRE)** (MRStoute) **5-9-4** MJKinane (hld up: hdwy gng wl appr st: chal st: led 2f out: qcknd clr 1½f out: r.o. strly: easily)	—	1		5/4 1	140	84
3646²	**Desert King (IRE)** (APO'Brien,Ireland) **3-8-11** CRoche (hld up: rdn 4f out: hdwy appr st: 2nd & effrt 2f out: nt qckn w wnr: kpt on)	4½	2		11/8 2	133	70
3124⁹	**Alhaarth (IRE)** (SbinSuroor) **4-9-4** KDarley (cl up: rdn & chsd ldrs 3f out: 4th & nt qckn under 2f out: no imp)	14	3		9/1 3	110	54
3675a²	**Rayouni (IRE)** (JOxx,Ireland) **3-8-11** JPMurtagh (hld up in rr: rdn 4f out: 6th 2f out: kpt on: n.d)	2	4		10/1	107	44
4094a³	**Dangerous Diva (IRE)** (APO'Brien,Ireland) **3-8-8** JAHeffernan (a.p: led bef st: hdd 2f out: sn wknd & no imp)	3	5		33/1	99	36
3362a⁷	**No Slouch (IRE)** (APO'Brien,Ireland) **3-8-11** WJSupple (sn led: hdd bef st: wknd qckly 2f out)	10	6		100/1	86	23
3674a*	**Swift Gulliver (IRE)** (JSBolger,Ireland) **3-8-11** KJManning (hld up in rr: rdn 4f out: n.d)	8	7		14/1	74	11

(SP 116.2%) **7 Rn**

2m 4.7 (0.70) OWNER Lord Weinstock (NEWMARKET) BRED Ballymacoll Stud Co
3050 Pilsudski (IRE), with the pace and ground to suit, was tremendously impressive. He arrived on the outer just before the turn-in literally cruising, and had taken over as soon as they straightened up and, going three lengths clear at the furlong marker, Kinane was able to look round and ease his mount up close home. The ground, faster than the official 'Good', might have been a contributory factor to a very fast pace but this was an awesome performance which, on his new mark of 135, puts him above Singspiel. (5/4)
3646 Desert King (IRE), a dual classic winner, was truly humbled here. Roche looked uncomfortable in fifth place at halfway and wasn't travelling anything like as well as the winner when throwing down his challenge early in the straight. Pursuit was unavailing over the last furlong and the step back to a mile and a half looks essential if he is to regain status. Only soft ground in Paris would make him a serious Arc contender. (11/8)
3124 Alhaarth (IRE), running in third place throughout, was totally outpaced by two class performers. (9/1: op 6/1)
3675a Rayouni (IRE), with his tongue tied down, never got in any sort of a blow. (10/1)
4094a Dangerous Diva (IRE) backed up No Slouch in a pace-making role, but the pair of them stopped as though hitting a wall turning into the straight. (33/1)

4205a - 4207a (Irish Racing) - See Computer Raceform

3757-BEVERLEY (R-H) (Good to firm)
Wednesday September 17th
WEATHER: sunny WIND: almost nil

4208 HUMBER ESTUARY (S) NURSERY H'CAP (0-65) (2-Y.O) (Class G)
2-25 (2-26) **7f 100y** £2,635.00 (£735.00: £355.00) Stalls: High GOING minus 0.62 sec per fur (F)

				SP	RR	SF
4014⁷	**Moonlight Flit (54)** (JGFitzGerald) **2-8-12b¹** JFortune(1) (rr div: gd hdwy 2f out: r.o to ld wl ins fnl f)	—	1	11/1	63	34
3451³	**Maedaley (51)** (PCHaslam) **2-8-6**(3) PFessey(11) (lw: led tl hdd & no ex wl ins fnl f)	2½	2	8/1 3	55	26
3686¹¹	**Tom (54)** (LordHuntingdon) **2-8-12v¹** JWeaver(5) (mid div: hdwy u.p 2f out: one pce fnl f)	1½	3	9/2 1	54	25
3802¹⁰	**Bint Nadia (56)** (JDBethell) **2-9-0** TWilliams(2) (a.p: hdwy over 2f out: kpt on one pce fnl f)	¾	4	6/1 2	55	26
3751⁵	**My Bet (50)** (MWEasterby) **2-8-5**(3) GParkin(13) (a chsng ldrs: effrt 3f out: wknd ins fnl f)	¾	5	14/1	47	18
3927⁸	**Thecomebackking (61)** (SCWilliams) **2-9-5** KDarley(17) (b.hind: a chsng ldrs: effrt 3f out: no imp)	4	6	11/1	50	21
3628⁴	**Candy Twist (50)** (RonaldThompson) **2-8-5**(3) DarrenMoffatt(6) (mid div: hrd drvn over 2f out: no imp)	½	7	16/1	38	9
4058⁹	**Tilburg (55)** (MrsNMacauley) **2-8-13** SWebster(12) (bhd tl styd on fnl 2f)	2	8	33/1	38	9
3973¹²	**Western Lord (53)** (CSmith) **2-8-11b¹** MFenton(16) (in tch: effrt 3f out: btn over 1f out)	½	9	33/1	35	6
3639³	**Filgrave (IRE) (56)** (CADwyer) **2-9-0v** JFEgan(10) (chsd ldrs: chal ent st: wknd 2f out)	hd	10	8/1 3	38	9
3427⁷	**Lady Rochelle (50)** (TDEasterby) **2-8-8** LCharnock(14) (cl up tl wknd over 2f out)	s.h	11	14/1	32	3
3905¹³	**Touch of Colour (53)** (JWWatts) **2-8-11** GDuffield(4) (sn prom: wknd fnl 3f)	1¾	12	16/1	31	2
3307⁸	**Watchman (55)** (TPTate) **2-8-13** TLucas(15) (swtg: a outpcd & bhd)	1¼	13	10/1	30	1
3990⁸	**Rockette (63)** (JWWatts) **2-9-7** JCarroll(7) (swtg: s.i.s: a bhd)	4	14	12/1	30	1
2383⁵	**Moss Side Monkey (50)** (JBerry) **2-8-5**(3) TEDurcan(8) (bhd fr ½-wy)	2½	15	14/1	12	—
*2604*⁶	**Hope Value (55)** (TDEasterby) **2-8-13b** DeanMcKeown(3) (s.i.s: a bhd)	1½	16	8/1 3	13	—
3866⁶	**Seventh Heaven (51)** (DNicholls) **2-8-9** ACulhane(9) (sn bhd)	5	17	20/1	—	—

(SP 141.7%) **17 Rn**

1m 33.1 (1.10) CSF £99.37 CT £448.58 TOTE £25.80: £4.40 £2.40 £1.20 £1.90 (£185.00) Trio £280.40 OWNER Mr N. H. T. Wrigley (MALTON) BRED Exors of the Late M. H. Wrigley
Bt in 12,400gns, Tom clmd C Fairhurst £6,000.
3808 Moonlight Flit had been crying out for this trip and, in the first time blinkers, made up a tremendous amount of ground in the straight. (11/1)
3451 Maedaley, stepping up in trip, had no fears about it and kept battling on but had no answer to the winner's late surge. (8/1)
Tom, a useful-looking type, had blinkers on for the first time and ran better but failed to pick up late on. He gives the impression that he has more to come if he can be persuaded. (9/2)
3563* Bint Nadia behaved pretty well beforehand this time and had her chances, only to find the effort too much. (6/1)
3751 My Bet had plenty of chances but it all proved beyond her in the closing stages. (14/1)
Thecomebackking showed up behind the leaders but proved short of pace and room early in the straight and all chances had soon gone. (11/1)

4209 TATTERSALLS MAIDEN AUCTION STKS (2-Y.O) (Class E)

2-55 (2-58) **7f 100y** £3,897.50 (£1,175.00: £570.00: £267.50) Stalls: High GOING minus 0.62 sec per fur (F)

Form	Horse	Dist	Pos	SP	RR	SF
	Central Committee (IRE) (PWChapple-Hyam) **2-8-6**(3) RHavlin(16) (w'like: unf: scope: a.p: led 1½f out: r.o wl)	—	**1**	4/5[1]	88+	41
	Long Bond (IRE) (MJohnston) **2-8-8** JWeaver(4) (wl grwn: bit bkwd: s.i.s: outpcd & wl bhd tl hdwy 2f out: hung rt & r.o wl)	3	**2**	9/1[3]	81+	34
3794[5]	**Blue Zola (IRE) (75)** (MBell) **2-8-5** MFenton(12) (chsd ldrs: chal over 2f out: one pce appr fnl f)	2½	**3**	7/1[2]	72	25
3818[7]	**Misalliance** (CFWall) **2-8-1** GDuffield(2) (hld up: stdy hdwy 2f out: nvr plcd to chal)	s.h	**4**	14/1	68	21
3760[4]	**Hobart Junction (IRE)** (SCWilliams) **2-8-8** KDarley(1) (chsd ldrs: effrt 3f out: r.o one pce)	1¼	**5**	7/1[2]	72	25
3757[4]	**Piccadilly** (TJEtherington) **2-8-5** DaleGibson(6) (drvn along thrght: nvr bttr than mid div)	2½	**6**	12/1	64	17
3821[10]	**Smooth Princess (IRE)** (JGFitzGerald) **2-8-2** FNorton(5) (plld hrd: w ldrs tl wknd fnl 2½f)	¾	**7**	33/1	59	12
3760[5]	**Hombre** (JWWatts) **2-8-6** JCarroll(11) (a chsng ldrs: rdn & grad wknd fnl 2½f)	s.h	**8**	9/1[3]	63	16
3819[6]	**One To Go (IRE)** (JBerry) **2-8-4**(3) PFessey(15) (led tl hdd 1½f out: sn btn)	½	**9**	20/1	63	16
4064[16]	**Cultured King (IRE)** (JGSmyth-Osbourne) **2-8-10** SWhitworth(8) (mid div: effrt & nt clr run over 1f out: n.d)	s.h	**10**	33/1	66	19
3306[11]	**Missed Domino** (MrsASwinbank) **2-8-0** EJohnson(10) (mid div: nt clr run appr fnl f: nvr nr to chal)	1¼	**11**	25/1	54	7
3753[W]	**Nordic Pirjo** (MrsJRRamsden) **2-8-1**ow1 JFEgan(13) (leggy: unf: bit bkwd: hld up: hdwy whn nt clr run over 1f out: eased)	3	**12**	20/1	48	—
3427[11]	**Joli Fille** (JSWainwright) **2-7-13** TWilliams(3) (dwlt: a bhd)	1	**13**	40/1	44	—
3973[11]	**Major Ballaby (IRE)** (MrsSABramall) **2-8-4**(3)ow3 GParkin(7) (cl up: chal 3f out: sn wknd)	2	**14**	40/1	48	—
3103[12]	**Premium Quest** (RAFahey) **2-8-8** ACulhane(17) (a bhd)	4	**15**	25/1	40	—
2467[12]	**Itsnotyetnamed** (ASmith) **2-8-4** JLowe(9) (dwlt: a bhd)	½	**16**	25/1	35	—

(SP 146.7%) **16 Rn**

1m 32.2 (0.20) CSF £9.39 TOTE £1.90: £1.70 £3.20 £1.80 (£11.80) Trio £26.40 OWNER Mr R. E. Sangster (MARLBOROUGH) BRED Swettenham Stud

Central Committee (IRE) came with a big reputation. He did the business in convincing style and should have learnt plenty. (4/5: op 5/4)
Long Bond (IRE) proved clueless early on and, despite running on splendidly in the straight, was still very green, and there would seem to be a lot of improvement once he realises what the game is all about. (9/1)
3794 Blue Zola (IRE) again had her chances but she lacks any change of gear. (7/1)
Misalliance, poorly drawn, showed a great deal of promise under a tender ride and looks one to side with. (14/1)
3760 Hobart Junction (IRE) ran a fair race from the worst draw and ought to pick up a modest race. (7/1)
3757 Piccadilly looks well short of toe and was never on the bridle at any stage but she did struggle on. (12/1)
3760 Hombre (9/1: op 6/1)
Missed Domino never got into this but never had much luck in running and gave the impression that there is plenty more to come. (25/1)

4210 JOHN MANGLES MEMORIAL H'CAP (0-65) (3-Y.O+) (Class F)

3-30 (3-31) **1m 100y** £3,215.00 (£965.00: £465.00: £215.00) Stalls: High GOING minus 0.62 sec per fur (F)

Form	Horse	Dist	Pos	SP	RR	SF
3759[2]	**Euro Sceptic (IRE) (51)** (TDEasterby) **5-9-0b** KDarley(11) (lw: mid div: hdwy over 2f out: led wl ins fnl f: all out)	—	**1**	9/2[1]	63	38
4063[10]	**Mbulwa (52)** (RAFahey) **11-9-1** LCharnock(12) (trckd ldrs: led 1½f tl wl ins fnl f: rallied)	s.h	**2**	14/1	64	39
3933*	**Java Red (IRE) (53)** (JGFitzGerald) **5-9-2** ACulhane(13) (mid div: hdwy 2f out: ch ins fnl f: nt qckn)	1¾	**3**	10/1	62	37
3921[2]	**Polar Prospect (56)** (BHanbury) **4-9-5** GHind(19) (b: led 2f: chsd ldrs: nt clr run over 2f out: styd on fnl f)	1¾	**4**	11/2[2]	61	36
3573[6]	**Three For A Pound (65)** (JAGlover) **3-9-10** JFortune(3) (bhd: hdwy over 2f out: swtchd & styd on wl)	½	**5**	11/1	69	40
4147[6]	**Bowcliffe (63)** (EJAlston) **6-9-12** JFEgan(14) (lw: mid div: hdwy over 3f out: one pce appr fnl f)	hd	**6**	6/1[3]	67	42
3584[3]	**Johnnie the Joker (53)** (JPLeigh) **6-8-13b**(3) CTeague(8) (led after 2f to 1½f out: grad wknd)	1½	**7**	14/1	54	29
3777[10]	**Spanish Verdict (51)** (DenysSmith) **10-9-0** GDuffield(18) (mid div: nt clr run over 1f out: nt rcvr)	1¼	**8**	14/1	50	25
3976[16]	**Monte Cavo (57)** (MBrittain) **6-8-13**(7) DMernagh(1) (cl up tl wknd over 1f out)	s.h	**9**	14/1	56	31
3573[15]	**Ochos Rios (IRE) (55)** (BSRothwell) **6-8-11**(7) RWinston(17) (bhd: effrt on ins 3f out: nt clr run: gd hdwy appr fnl f: n.d)	½	**10**	12/1	53	28
3977[10]	**Van Chino (55)** (BAMcMahon) **3-9-0** JCarroll(16) (in tch tl wknd over 1f out)	1¾	**11**	25/1	50	21
3937[15]	**Gulliver (61)** (MrsJRRamsden) **4-9-7**(3) TEDurcan(7) (lw: nvr bttr than mid div)	½	**12**	16/1	55	30
3491[9]	**Darling Clover (56)** (RBastiman) **5-9-0**(5) HBastiman(5) (in tch: racd wd: rdn & btn over 2f out)	1¼	**13**	13/2	47	22
3640[12]	**Snow Carnival (50)** (LadyHerries) **4-8-13** DHolland(6) (lw: s.i.s a bhd)	s.h	**14**	16/1	41	16
3868[7]	**Rude Awakening (60)** (CWFairhurst) **3-9-5** SWhitworth(9) (a bhd)	hd	**15**	25/1	51	22
4015[15]	**Time Can Tell (63)** (CMurray) **3-9-8** DeanMcKeown(4) (a bhd)	s.h	**16**	20/1	54	25
3921[10]	**Pekay (65)** (MJohnston) **4-10-0** JWeaver(2) (cl up tl wknd fnl 2f)	nk	**17**	12/1	55	30
3248[12]	**With A Will (64)** (HCandy) **3-9-2**(7) LJames(15) (prom tl wknd fnl 2½f)	¾	**18**	14/1	53	24
3864[15]	**Peter Perfect (53)** (RCurtis) **3-8-12** JLowe(10) (a rr div)	nk	**19**	16/1	41	12

(SP 157.4%) **19 Rn**

1m 45.0 (1.00) CSF £78.58 CT £607.83 TOTE £5.20: £1.50 £4.90 £2.00 £2.30 (£77.50) Trio £317.80 OWNER Mr C. H. Stevens (MALTON) BRED Martyn J. McEnery
WEIGHT FOR AGE 3yo-4lb

3759 Euro Sceptic (IRE) is a track specialist and, given plenty of assistance from the saddle, did just enough. (9/2)
3798 Mbulwa ran well and is obviously in really good form and deserved to find a race. (14/1)
3933* Java Red (IRE) looks tremendously well and ran a useful race and is obviously in tremendous heart. (10/1)
3921 Polar Prospect was short of room at a vital stage here and his chance had soon gone. (11/2)
3573 Three For A Pound always seems happier on easier ground which makes this a useful effort. (11/1)
4147 Bowcliffe ran quite well yet again but that final dash was never forthcoming. (6/1)
3573 Spanish Verdict is proving difficult to win with this year but he had no luck at all in running here. (14/1)
3029 Darling Clover (13/2: 10/1-6/1)

4211 ARAGON MAIDEN STKS (2-Y.O) (Class D)

4-00 (4-02) **5f** £4,034.00 (£1,217.00: £591.00: £278.00) Stalls: High GOING minus 0.62 sec per fur (F)

Form	Horse	Dist	Pos	SP	RR	SF
4012[18]	**Lord Lieutenant** (MBell) **2-9-0** ACulhane(18) (mde all: qcknd clr 2f out: unchal)	—	**1**	12/1	79	38
4012[2]	**Sarah Stokes (IRE)** (RGuest) **2-8-9** DHolland(11) (lw: a chsng ldrs: rdn 2f out: kpt on: no ch w wnr)	1½	**2**	9/4[2]	69	28
3031[2]	**Odette** (SirMarkPrescott) **2-8-9** GDuffield(9) (lw: a chsng ldrs: rdn ½-wy: kpt on: nt pce to chal)	¾	**3**	6/4[1]	67	26

				SP	RR	SF
4012^{11}	**Surprised** (MrsJRRamsden) **2-9-0** JFortune(3) (styd on fnl 2f: nvr nr to chal)	2	**4**	$6/1^{3}$	65+	24
3825^{3}	**Moving Princess** (MissSEHall) **2-8-9** JWeaver(8) (in tch: kpt on wl fnl f)	1¼	**5**	9/1	56	15
	Lake Taal (MJCamacho) **2-8-9** LCharnock(12) (leggy: unf: bit bkwd: s.s: stdy hdwy fnl 2f)	¾	**6**	25/1	54+	13
3459^{9}	**Detroit City (IRE)** (JBerry) **2-9-0** KDarley(15) (chsd wnr tl rdn & btn wl over 1f out)	s.h	**7**	25/1	59	18
3821^{9}	**Amber Regent** (PCHaslam) **2-9-0** DaleGibson(10) (s.i.s: stdy hdwy fr ½-wy: n.d)	hd	**8**	25/1	59+	18
	Mary Jane (JBerry) **2-8-6**$^{(3)}$ TEDurcan(14) (w'like: bit bkwd: spd over 3f)	½	**9**	20/1	52	11
3265^{6}	**Quiz Master (70)** (EWeymes) **2-9-0** GHind(1) (racd wd: prom: grad wknd appr fnl f)	1½	**10**	14/1	52	11
	Westcourt Ruby (MWEasterby) **2-8-6**$^{(3)}$ GParkin(17) (unf: scope: bit bkwd: hdwy ½-wy: nvr nr to chal)	1½	**11**	20/1	42	1
3636^{12}	**Doodle** (WJHaggas) **2-8-9** JCarroll(16) (s.i.s: hld up & a bhd)	4	**12**	14/1	30	—
	Anditz (IRE) (JLEyre) **2-8-10**^{ow1} OPears(2) (unf: a bhd)	5	**13**	25/1	15	—
3753^{12}	**Melodian** (MBrittain) **2-9-0** MWigham(7) (sn outpcd & bhd)	1¾	**14**	33/1	13	—
3586^{13}	**The Fuelologist** (MissJFCraze) **2-9-0v**^{1} SWebster(13) (chsd ldrs to ½-wy: wknd qckly)	2½	**15**	40/1	5	—
3094^{12}	**Pre Catelan** (MBell) **2-8-9** MFenton(4) (sn bhd)	nk	**16**	16/1	—	—
4012^{12}	***Anstand*** (MrsJRRamsden) **2-9-0** MDeering(5) (Withdrawn not under Starter's orders: veterinary advice at s)		**W**	14/1	—	—
				(SP 158.9%)	**16 Rn**	

62.4 secs (0.60) CSF £38.84 TOTE £32.80: £5.40 £1.20 £1.50 (£34.40) Trio £32.10 OWNER Highclere Thoroughbred Racing Ltd (NEWMARKET) BRED Fulling Mill Farm and Stud

Lord Lieutenant had the best draw and, making full use of it, won in tremendous style and is obviously improving fast. (12/1)

4012 Sarah Stokes (IRE) had her chances but was short of toe halfway through the race and may need a little further or easier ground. (9/4)

3031 Odette, after over two months off, was obviously a bit ring rusty here and was short of toe in the last couple of furlongs. She should be all the better for this. (6/4)

4012 Surprised showed plenty of promise from a poor draw and was wisely not over punished and seems to be learning fast. (6/1)

3825 Moving Princess ran well and, over further, should improve a fair deal. (9/1)

Lake Taal, needing this, showed plenty of hope for the future after a poor start. (25/1)

Amber Regent was slow to realise what was required but was picking up in the closing stages to show some promise for the future. (25/1)

4212 E.B.F. GARROWBY MAIDEN STKS (I) (2-Y.O F) (Class D)

4-35 (4-35) **7f 100y** £3,124.00 (£937.00: £451.00: £208.00) Stalls: High GOING minus 0.62 sec per fur (F)

				SP	RR	SF
3151^{3}	**Alborada** (SirMarkPrescott) **2-8-11** GDuffield(9) (lw: mde all: drvn clr over 1f out: unchal)	—	**1**	$2/5^{1}$	77+	44
	Niki (IRE) (JHMGosden) **2-8-11** GHind(8) (w'ike: trckd ldr: effrt over 3f out: kpt on: no ch w wnr)	6	**2**	$7/1^{3}$	64	31
3547^{9}	**Sandar** (BWHills) **2-8-11** JWeaver(4) (trckd ldrs: styd on same pce fnl 2f)	1¾	**3**	9/1	60	27
3985^{6}	**Akarita (IRE)** (BAMcMahon) **2-8-11** JFEgan(3) (hld up: hdwy over 2f out: sn rdn: styd on one pce)	1½	**4**	11/1	57	24
	Chimes of Peace (JLEyre) **2-8-11** OPears(6) (leggy: unf: bit bkwd: trckd ldrs: effrt over 3f out: wknd over 1f out)	½	**5**	50/1	56	23
	Slipper (LMCumani) **2-8-11** DHolland(2) (neat: unf: in tch: effrt on outside over 2f out: hung rt & no imp)	d.h	**5**	$11/2^{2}$	56	23
	Stone Beck (JMJefferson) **2-8-11** JCarroll(5) (w'like: leggy: dwlt: hdwy over 2f out: kpt on: nvr nr ldrs)	1½	**7**	66/1	53	20
3426^{6}	**Taylor's Pride** (TDBarron) **2-8-11** LCharnock(1) (sn bhd)	9	**8**	66/1	34	1
	Skyers A Kite (RonaldThompson) **2-8-8**$^{(3)}$ DarrenMoffatt(7) (unf: in tch tl wknd qckly 3f out: sn bhd)	½	**9**	100/1	33	—
				(SP 123.6%)	**9 Rn**	

1m 32.1 (0.10) CSF £4.27 TOTE £1.40: £1.10 £2.20 £1.40 (£4.00) Trio £6.90 OWNER Miss K. Rausing (NEWMARKET) BRED Miss K. Rausing

3151 Alborada looked a cut above her rivals in the paddock but her rider left nothing to chance. She was tending to hang into the fence. (2/5)

Niki (IRE), a moderate mover, kept on to finish second best but the winner was in a different league. (7/1: 5/1-8/1)

Sandar was very keen and took some settling. She should have a little more improvement in her. (9/1)

3985 Akarita (IRE) showed a very moderate action going down. (11/1)

Slipper, who showed a sharp action going down, tended to hang in behind her rivals but to her credit kept going all the way to the line. Easier ground might suit her. (11/2)

Chimes of Peace, a poor mover, was by no means knocked about on her debut. (50/1)

Stone Beck, a backward newcomer, showed a glimmer of promise after a slow break. (66/1)

4213 PORT OF HULL H'CAP (0-75) (3-Y.O+) (Class D)

5-05 (5-07) **1m 3f 216y** £4,125.00 (£1,245.00: £605.00: £285.00) Stalls: High GOING minus 0.62 sec per fur (F)

				SP	RR	SF
3867*	**Campaspe (67)** (JGFitzGerald) **5-9-7** JFortune(4) (lw: sn prom: styd on to ld over 1f out: drvn out)	—	**1**	$9/4^{1}$	80	48
3781^{10}	**Scarrots (65)** (SCWilliams) **3-8-11** KDarley(8) (lw: chsd ldrs: led over 3f out tl over 1f out: kpt on wl)	1¼	**2**	$11/2^{2}$	76	36
3796^{4}	**Augustan (60)** (SGollings) **6-9-0** DHolland(9) (hmpd & lost pl after 2f: hdwy 3f out: styd on same pce appr fnl f)	3	**3**	$11/2^{2}$	67	35
3781^{11}	**Shilling (IRE) (61)** (ACStewart) **3-8-7** SWhitworth(10) (bhd: hdwy u.p 4f out: styd on one pce)	1¾	**4**	$13/2^{3}$	66	26
3461^{5}	**Alwarqa (45)** (MartynWane) **4-7-13** FNorton(2) (lw: sn bhd: styd on u.p fnl 3f: nvr nr to chal)	3	**5**	16/1	46	14
3992^{5}	**Welcome Home (50)** (PTDalton) **3-7-7**$^{(3)}$ PFessey(14) (lw: chsd ldrs: one pce fnl 3f)	1	**6**	25/1	50	10
3937^{19}	**Wellcome Inn (60)** (JO'Reilly) **3-8-6** JO'Reilly(15) (lw: s.i.s: hdwy on outside over 2f out: hung rt: nvr nr to chal)	1½	**7**	14/1	58	18
3886^{5}	**Portite Sophie (43)** (MBrittain) **6-7-4**$^{(7)ow1}$ DMernagh(7) (sltly hmpd after 2f: hdwy to chse ldrs 7f out: wknd 2f out)	1¾	**8**	12/1	38	5
2787^{6}	**Nikita's Star (IRE) (57)** (DJGMurraySmith) **4-8-11b** JCarroll(6) (hld up: effrt 3f out: n.d)	4	**9**	20/1	47	15
3992^{18}	**Lindrick Lady (IRE) (64)** (BSRothwell) **3-8-10** MFenton(5) (led tl over 3f out: wknd 2f out)	2½	**10**	14/1	51	11
2487^{9}	**Hever Golf Charmer (56)** (BSRothwell) **3-8-2** LCharnock(13) (chsd ldrs tl lost pl over 3f out: eased)	20	**11**	25/1	16	—
3485^{8}	**Wildmoor (56)** (JDBethell) **3-8-2** TWilliams(1) (chsd ldrs: rdn 4f out: sn lost pl & eased)	nk	**12**	16/1	16	—
3822*	**Alpine Hideaway (IRE) (70)** (MWEasterby) **4-9-10** TLucas(3) (plld hrd: sn trckng ldrs: lost pl over 3f out: eased)	4	**13**	10/1	24	—
				(SP 129.2%)	**13 Rn**	

2m 34.2 (1.20) CSF £13.39 CT £59.56 TOTE £2.80: £1.70 £1.40 £2.30 (£7.10) Trio £9.70 OWNER Mr J. G. FitzGerald (MALTON) BRED J. G. Fitzgerald

LONG HANDICAP Portite Sophie 7-7 Welcome Home 7-5

WEIGHT FOR AGE 3yo-8lb

3867* Campaspe repeated her victory in this race last year, but this time from a 21lb higher mark. After taking until four to break her duck, on the whole she has never stopped improving since. (9/4)

3781 Scarrots, who likes to dominate, set sail for home early in the straight but, in the end, the winner proved too strong. When he has everything his own way, he will be adding to his record. (11/2)

3796 Augustan did well to recover after being badly hampered on the turn into the back straight after the first quarter-mile. (11/2)
3210 Shilling (IRE), dropped back two furlongs in distance, seems to have nothing in the way of finishing speed. Her rider was hard at work half a mile out to no avail. (13/2)
3461 Alwarqa stayed on late in the day and seems to need extreme distances. (16/1)

4214 END OF SEASON MAIDEN STKS (3-Y.O+) (Class D)

5-35 (5-40) **5f** £3,696.00 (£1,113.00: £539.00: £252.00) Stalls: High GOING minus 0.62 sec per fur (F)

Form	Horse	Dist	Pos	SP	RR	SF
3606^{2}	**Gharib (USA) (70)** (ACStewart) **3-8-13** SWhitworth(14) (b.hind: hdwy ½-wy: styd on u.p fnl 2f: led ins fnl f: hung rt: kpt on)	—	**1**	$7/2^{2}$	77	48
3898^{3}	**At Large (IRE) (75)** (JRFanshawe) **3-8-13** KDarley(4) (a chsng ldrs: ev ch ins fnl f: no ex)	1¼	**2**	$7/2^{2}$	73	44
4047^{5}	**Dark Mile (USA)** (JHMGosden) **3-8-8** GHind(19) (lw: prom: effrt & swtchd lft 2f out: rdn & hung rt: styd on towards fin)	hd	**3**	$7/4^{1}$	68	39
4047^{6}	**Nobalino** (MrsNMacauley) **3-8-13** JWeaver(2) (prom: hdwy to ld over 1f out: hung rt & hdd ins fnl f: wknd towards fin)	½	**4**	16/1	71	42
3715^{7}	**Shantarskie (IRE)** (CFWall) **3-8-13** GDuffield(18) (in tch: effrt 2f out: one pce whn hmpd nr fin)	½	**5**	$9/2^{3}$	70	41
4051^{10}	**Passionatti** (SGollings) **3-8-8** JCarroll(5) (unruly s: w ldrs: led ½-wy tl over 1f out: sn wknd)	3½	**6**	66/1	53	24
3241^{4}	**Skelton Countess (IRE) (38)** (RHollinshead) **4-8-9** JFortune(15) (w ldrs tl wknd over 1f out)	4	**7**	40/1	41	13
4049^{12}	**Crees Sqaw** (BAMcMahon) **5-8-9** JBramhill(13) (dwlt: hdwy ½-wy: styd on appr fnl f)	1¼	**8**	66/1	37	9
3261^{9}	**Fancy Clancy (29)** (MissLCSiddall) **4-8-10**ow1 OPears(8) (lw: in tch: rdn & hung rt ½-wy: no imp)	½	**9**	66/1	36	7
	Distant King (GPKelly) **4-8-7**(7) RWinston(10) (bit bkwd: sn outpcd: rdn ½-wy: n.d)	hd	**10**	100/1	40	12
3601^{7}	**Alisadara (24)** (NBycroft) **3-8-8** DHolland(12) (b.hind: outpcd ½-wy: sme late hdwy)	s.h	**11**	66/1	34	5
3606^{12}	**Beau Tudor (IRE) (36)** (MissLCSiddall) **3-8-13** MWigham(7) (lw: sn outpcd)	2½	**12**	66/1	31	2
4049^{16}	**Bankers Order** (TDEasterby) **3-8-13** DeanMcKeown(11) (led to ½-wy: sn wknd)	nk	**13**	66/1	30	1
3280^{9}	**Harvey's Future (37)** (PLGilligan) **3-8-13** EJohnson(3) (b: unruly s: s.i.s: a bhd)	hd	**14**	66/1	30	1
	Teddy's Bow (IRE) (MWEasterby) **3-8-8** TLucas(16) (sn outpcd & drvn along)	nk	**15**	40/1	24	—
	Violette Sabo (TJEtherington) **3-8-8** LCharnock(17) (w'like: str: s.s: a wl bhd)	3	**16**	66/1	15	—
3812^{16}	**Star of The Road (43)** (JMCarr) **3-8-13** ACulhane(1) (racd wd: sn bhd)	4	**17**	50/1	7	—
1582^{9}	**Locksill (40)** (ASmith) **3-8-13** JLowe(9) (unruly s: sn wl bhd)	4	**18**	66/1	—	—
3854^{9}	***Bent Raiwand (USA) (24)*** (DonEnricoIncisa) **4-8-9** KimTinkler(6) (Withdrawn not under Starter's orders: lame at s)		**W**	50/1	—	—

(SP 128.1%) **18 Rn**

61.7 secs (-0.10) CSF £14.48 TOTE £4.50: £1.70 £2.00 £1.20 (£7.00) Trio £3.80 OWNER Sheikh Ahmed Al Maktoum (NEWMARKET) BRED Gainesway Thoroughbreds Ltd
WEIGHT FOR AGE 3yo-1lb

3606 Gharib (USA) came from off the pace and took all his rider's strength to get him home. He apparently now goes to Dubai. (7/2)
3898 At Large (IRE), from a poor draw, had to give best in the last one hundred yards. He is knocking at the door but is finding it hard to get his head in front. (7/2: 2/1-4/1)
4047 Dark Mile (USA) gave her rider problems. Pulled to the outside to make an effort, she persisted in hanging in behind her rivals but was staying on in good style towards the finish. She has plenty of ability but her jockey told the Stewards that he felt she was not giving her all. (7/4: op 11/10)
4047 Nobalino faded badly towards the finish. He is now qualified for a handicap mark and might do better on easier ground. (16/1)
Shantarskie (IRE), who showed ability in Dubai earlier this year, was well supported in the market but was held when hampered near the line. (9/2: op 8/1)
Passionatti, who obviously has plenty of temperament, also possesses a fair amount of speed but she tied up badly towards the finish. (66/1)
Crees Sqaw showed a glimmer of ability. A five-year-old, this was only her third ever outing and she might do better in handicap company. (66/1)

4215 E.B.F. GARROWBY MAIDEN STKS (II) (2-Y.O F) (Class D)

6-05 (6-05) **7f 100y** £3,124.00 (£937.00: £451.00: £208.00) Stalls: High GOING minus 0.62 sec per fur (F)

Form	Horse	Dist	Pos	SP	RR	SF
3757^{2}	**Scent of Success (USA)** (MRStoute) **2-8-11** KDarley(6) (trckd ldr: rdn to ld over 1f out: styd on)	—	**1**	$7/4^{1}$	81	36
3757^{3}	**Elanaaka** (DMorley) **2-8-11** JStack(7) (lw: led tl over 1f out: kpt on same pce)	1¼	**2**	$7/4^{1}$	78	33
	Kingdom Queen (IRE) (MJCamacho) **2-8-11** LCharnock(5) (leggy: unf: bit bkwd: trckd ldrs: drvn along & outpcd ½-wy: styd on appr fnl f)	8	**3**	33/1	61+	16
3986^{4}	**Priolette (IRE) (69)** (JGFitzGerald) **2-8-11** ACulhane(1) (chsd ldrs: rdn 3f out: outpcd over 1f out)	hd	**4**	14/1	61	16
	Tugela (USA) (BWHills) **2-8-11** JWeaver(4) (cmpt: unf: dwlt: sme hdwy over 2f out: nvr nr to chal)	2	**5**	$6/1^{3}$	57	12
4017^{9}	**Bollin Ann** (TDEasterby) **2-8-11** DeanMcKeown(2) (hld up: hdwy over 2f out: grad wknd)	nk	**6**	20/1	56+	11
3806^{11}	**Uniform** (MissSEHall) **2-8-11** KHodgson(3) (sn pushed along: outpcd 3f out: n.d)	nk	**7**	33/1	55	10
	Imelda (USA) (DRLoder) **2-8-11** JFortune(8) (leggy: unf: chsd ldrs: drvn along & outpcd over 3f out: sn wknd)	6	**8**	$7/2^{2}$	43	—
3426^{5}	**Ladyofdistinction (IRE)** (JSWainwright) **2-8-11** TWilliams(9) (hld up: effrt & edgd lft over 2f out: sn wknd)	10	**9**	33/1	21	—

(SP 129.5%) **9 Rn**

1m 32.8 (0.80) CSF £4.91 TOTE £2.70: £1.30 £1.10 £8.70 (£2.30) Trio £73.40 OWNER Mr Saeed Suhail (NEWMARKET) BRED Gainsborough Farm Inc

OFFICIAL EXPLANATION **Bollin Ann: failed to stay, lost her action and was unsuited by the ground.**

3757 Scent of Success (USA) had the visor left off this time. With more patient tactics adopted, she stayed on just the better to confirm the form showed with the runner-up here last time. (7/4)
3757 Elanaaka, dwarfed her rivals in the paddock but had to give best in the final furlong. (7/4)
Kingdom Queen (IRE) looked as if the outing would do her a power of good. Running green at the halfway mark, she gave encouragement for the future, staying on at the line. (33/1)
3986 Priolette (IRE) possibly ran out of stamina in the final furlong and is worth dropping back to six. (14/1)
Tugela (USA), a narrow type, showed a very poor action going down and she needs more time yet. (6/1)
Bollin Ann, having her third outing, was held up off the pace. Making a brief forward move halfway up the straight, she was not persevered with. She is significantly now qualified for a handicap mark and looks capable of better. (20/1)
Imelda (USA) (7/2: op 9/4)

T/Plpt: £4.80 (3,840.95 Tckts). T/Qdpt: £1.80 (583.41 Tckts) AA/WG

4173-SANDOWN (R-H) (Good to firm, Rnd crse Firm ptchs, 5f Crse Good ptchs) Wednesday September 17th

WEATHER: warm WIND: almost nil

4216 SURBITON MAIDEN AUCTION STKS (2-Y.O) (Class E)

2-15 (2-17) **5f 6y** £2,882.25 (£873.00: £426.50: £203.25) Stalls: High GOING minus 0.18 sec per fur (GF)

				SP	RR	SF
4042²	**Arian Da (74)** (BPalling) **2-8-1** TSprake(14) (mde all: hrd rdn over 1f out: r.o wl)	—	1	4/1¹	75	45
3791²	**Bandbox (IRE) (78)** (SMellor) **2-8-6** JReid(2) (swtg: a.p: rdn over 2f out: chsd wnr fnl f: r.o wl)	¾	2	14/1	78	48
3926²	**Call To Order** (CFWall) **2-8-13** PatEddery(7) (lw: a.p: chsd wnr over 3f out to 1f out: unable qckn)	1¾	3	4/1¹	79	49
3686⁴	**Oh So Easy (66)** (BJMeehan) **2-8-6** MTebbutt(11) (lw: hdwy over 1f out: r.o)	1¼	4	7/1	68	38
3794⁷	**Hoh Justice (73)** (IABalding) **2-8-9v¹** TQuinn(16) (lw: a.p: rdn over 3f out: one pce)	1¼	5	5/1²	67	37
4042³	**Majalis** (RGuest) **2-8-4** PBloomfield(8) (a.p: rdn over 2f out: wknd over 1f out)	2½	6	6/1³	54	24
	Sabo's Joy (CNAllen) **2-7-12** MartinDwyer(9) (lengthy: bit bkwd: dwlt: no hdwy fnl 2f)	1½	7	25/1	43	13
4042⁷	**Tullich Refrain** (WRMuir) **2-7-10**(5) RMullen(1) (dwlt: outpcd: nvr nrr)	¾	8	14/1	44	14
*4056*⁹	**Sadeebah** (MJohnston) **2-8-6** RHills(5) (lw: prom 3f)	1¾	9	16/1	43	13
1593⁹	**The Druidess (IRE)** (GCBravery) **2-7-13**ow1 DRMcCabe(6) (bit bkwd: mid div over 3f)	2	10	33/1	30	—
	Magic Powers (GBBalding) **2-8-6** SDrowne(3) (leggy: mid div over 3f)	1¼	11	33/1	33	3
	Algebra (RHannon) **2-8-6** WJO'Connor(15) (b.hind: str: scope: bit bkwd: a bhd)	4	12	16/1	20	—
	Merch Rhyd-Y-Grug (DLWilliams) **2-8-0**(7)ow9 PaulCleary(10) (leggy: unf: dwlt: a bhd)	nk	13	33/1	20	—
3598¹⁹	**Ivory Charm** (KTIvory) **2-8-1** NAdams(12) (a bhd)	1¾	14	33/1	9	—

(SP 124.2%) **14 Rn**

61.32 secs (1.52) CSF £55.65 TOTE £5.00: £1.60 £2.30 £1.70 (£27.50) Trio £11.10 OWNER Mr J. Hamilton-Jones (COWBRIDGE) BRED S. C. Palmer

OFFICIAL EXPLANATION **Majalis: gurgled during the race.**

4042 Arian Da, led round by two handlers in the paddock, at last came good under a fine ride from Sprake. Making all the running, Sprake wisely did not allow her to go storming off in front on this tough uphill course. Responding to pressure below the distance, she held on well. (4/1)

3791 Bandbox (IRE) did well from his bad draw and was always close up down the centre of the course. Moving into second place entering the final furlong, he kept on well but never looked like overhauling the winner in time. (14/1: 10/1-16/1)

3926 Call To Order looked in fine shape in the paddock and was soon racing in second place. Collared for that position a furlong out, he then failed to find another gear. (4/1)

3686 Oh So Easy, racing in midfield, stayed on in the last furlong and a half to finish on the heels of the principals. (7/1)

3295 Hoh Justice had the plum draw but he was soon being pushed along and never looked like finding the necessary turn of foot. (5/1)

4042 Majalis was close up until calling it a day approaching the final furlong. (6/1: op 3/1)

4217 E.B.F. MAIDEN STKS (2-Y.O F) (Class D)

2-45 (2-46) **1m 14y** £3,225.00 (£975.00: £475.00: £225.00) Stalls: High GOING minus 0.53 sec per fur (F)

				SP	RR	SF
3985³	**Nebl** (MajorWRHern) **2-8-11** RHills(4) (lw: led 2f: led 3f out: rdn over 1f out: r.o wl)	—	1	11/2²	91	29
3985⁵	**Sahara** (PFICole) **2-8-11** TQuinn(1) (chsd wnr over 1f: rdn over 3f out: chsd wnr over 1f out: r.o one pce)	2½	2	6/1³	86	24
3788⁵	**Good Catch (IRE) (79)** (PRWebber) **2-8-11** DaneO'Neill(5) (lw: rdn 3f out: hdwy & nt clr rn on ins over 1f out: swtchd lft: one pce)	3	3	13/2	80	18
3450⁶	**Acebo Lyons (IRE)** (APJarvis) **2-8-11** SDrowne(2) (lw: rdn 3f out: nvr nr to chal)	¾	4	20/1	79	17
3985²	**Red Rabbit** (BWHills) **2-8-11** PatEddery(3) (lw: plld hrd: led 6f out to 3f out: wknd over 1f out)	1	5	8/15¹	77	15

(SP 113.0%) **5 Rn**

1m 43.66 (2.46) CSF £32.59 TOTE £6.80: £2.10 £2.60 (£16.00) OWNER Mr Hamdan Al Maktoum (LAMBOURN) BRED Shadwell Estate Company Limited

OFFICIAL EXPLANATION **Red Rabbit: no explanation offered.**

3985 Nebl, beaten three and a half lengths by the hot favourite on her debut, decisively reversed the form. Regaining the advantage early in the straight, she was woken up below the distance and soon forged clear for a decisive victory. (11/2: op 7/2)

3985 Sahara was soon racing in third place. Pushed along early in the straight, she struggled into second place approaching the final furlong, but had no hope with the winner. (6/1: 4/1-13/2)

3788 Good Catch (IRE), racing at the back of the field, did not have the best of runs below the distance but it made little difference to her chances. (13/2)

3450 Acebo Lyons (IRE) found this company far too hot to handle and never threatened to get into it. (20/1)

3985 Red Rabbit pulled far too hard for her own good and had soon forced her way to the front. Marginally collared early in the straight, she had, not surprisingly, run out of steam approaching the final furlong. (8/15)

4218 SANDOWN FUTURITY CONDITIONS STKS (2-Y.O) (Class C)

3-20 (3-23) **1m 14y** £4,460.00 (£1,560.00: £762.50: £327.50) Stalls: High GOING minus 0.53 sec per fur (F)

				SP	RR	SF
3013*	**Setteen** (MAJarvis) **2-9-1** LDettori(4) (lw: mde all: easily)	—	1	2/9¹	96+	41
3597*	**Saffron Lane (IRE) (86)** (RHannon) **2-8-10** DaneO'Neill(2) (chsd wnr: rdn over 2f out: no imp)	3	2	5/1²	85	30
3990¹¹	**Smooth Sailing (91)** (KMcAuliffe) **2-9-1** PatEddery(1) (hld up: rdn 3f out: swtchd lft wl over 1f out: one pce)	5	3	12/1³	80	25
4140⁵	**Pichon Baron (USA)** (BJMeehan) **2-9-7** MTebbutt(3) (plld hrd: a in rr)	13	4	33/1	60	5

(SP 109.1%) **4 Rn**

1m 42.76 (1.56) CSF £1.63 TOTE £1.20 (£1.30) OWNER Sheikh Ahmed Al Maktoum (NEWMARKET) BRED Godolphin Management Co Ltd

3013* Setteen looked in tremendous shape in the paddock and had little more than an exercise gallop as he disposed of his three rivals without turning a hair. He looks a very useful prospect and a step up to Listed company is now on the cards as his trainer adopts a softly softly approach. (2/9: op 2/5)

3597* Saffron Lane (IRE) gave chase to the winner but had no hope with that rival in the final quarter-mile. (5/1: 5/2-11/2)

1735 Smooth Sailing is not up to this class and was only treading water in the last furlong and a half. A return to shorter trips will probably be in his favour. (12/1: op 6/1)

4140 Pichon Baron (USA) was once again totally outclassed and a drop in class is essential, both his wins in France came in claimers. (33/1)

4219 WEATHERBYS SPONSORSHIP IN RACING H'CAP (0-80) (3-Y.O+) (Class D)

3-50 (3-53) **7f 16y** £3,810.00 (£1,155.00: £565.00: £270.00) Stalls: High GOING minus 0.53 sec per fur (F)

Form	Horse / details	Dist	Pos	SP	RR	SF
3987[11]	**Myttons Mistake (59)** (ABailey) **4-8-4**(5) PRoberts(1) (swtg: a.p: rdn over 1f out: led wl ins fnl f: r.o wl)	—	**1**	12/1	70	52
3202[4]	**Taffs Well (69)** (RAkehurst) **4-9-5** TQuinn(7) (chsd ldr: led over 2f out tl wl ins fnl f: unable qckn)	½	**2**	8/1[3]	79	61
4050[10]	**Orange Place (IRE) (75)** (BJLlewellyn) **6-9-4**(7) JWilkinson(11) (lw: a.p: rdn 2f out: one pce)	1¼	**3**	25/1	82	64
3418[4]	**Caribbean Star (74)** (MRStoute) **3-9-7v** JReid(13) (a.p: rdn over 2f out: n.m.r over 1f out: one pce)	hd	**4**	11/1	81	60
3930[3]	**Twin Creeks (63)** (VSoane) **6-8-13** CRutter(12) (hld up: rdn over 2f out: r.o ins fnl f)	¾	**5**	12/1	68	50
3987[10]	**Veni Vidi Vici (IRE) (63)** (MJHeaton-Ellis) **4-8-13** SDrowne(15) (lw: hdwy over 2f out: hrd rdn over 1f out: one pce)	1¾	**6**	12/1	64	46
3987[2]	**Dummer Golf Time (66)** (LordHuntingdon) **4-9-2v** PatEddery(8) (swtg: nt clr run over 2f out: hdwy over 1f out: nvr nrr)	1	**7**	5/1[1]	65	47
3982[11]	**Ashby Hill (IRE) (64)** (RRowe) **6-9-0** AClark(6) (dwlt: rdn & hdwy on ins over 2f out: wknd ins fnl f)	1¼	**8**	12/1	60	42
3198[8]	**Shamanic (76)** (SPCWoods) **5-9-12** TSprake(10) (swtg: plld hrd: nt clr run over 2f out: swtchd lft: nvr nr to chal)	½	**9**	25/1	71	53
2392[5]	**Effervescence (68)** (RHannon) **3-9-1** DaneO'Neill(5) (lw: a bhd)	2½	**10**	20/1	57	36
3987[12]	**Duello (65)** (MBlanshard) **6-9-1** LDettori(2) (a bhd)	s.h	**11**	10/1	54	36
3936[13]	**Fayik (69)** (AGNewcombe) **3-9-2** PaulEddery(3) (mid div over 5f)	s.h	**12**	11/2[2]	58	37
3392[12]	**Dances With Hooves (60)** (DJSffrenchDavis) **5-8-10** MTebbutt(16) (a bhd)	nk	**13**	33/1	48	30
4016[20]	**Beldray Park (IRE) (46)** (MrsALMKing) **4-7-3**(7) RBrisland(9) (bhd fnl 2f)	hd	**14**	50/1	34	16
4059[3]	**Alfahaal (IRE) (56)** (RFJohnsonHoughton) **4-8-6** RHills(4) (nt clr run on ins over 2f out: a bhd)	¾	**15**	11/2[2]	43	25
4109[15]	**Indrapura (IRE) (54)** (JELong) **5-8-4** NCarlisle(14) (b: lw: led over 4f)	1¾	**16**	33/1	37	19
				(SP 127.0%)	**16 Rn**	

1m 28.49 (-0.11) CSF £92.12 CT £2,271.73 TOTE £22.20: £4.40 £2.50 £4.10 £2.70 (£174.40) Trio £1,094.40; £1,387.37 to Newbury 18/9/97
OWNER Mr Gordon Mytton (TARPORLEY) BRED R. S. A. Urquhart
LONG HANDICAP Beldray Park (IRE) 7-7
WEIGHT FOR AGE 3yo-3lb
OFFICIAL EXPLANATION **Myttons Mistake: the changed ground accounted for the improvement in form.**

3759* Myttons Mistake appreciated the return to a fast surface and, in the front rank throughout, managed to get on top in the closing stages. (12/1)

3202 Taffs Well gave a very good account of himself on this handicap debut and eased his way to the front over a quarter of a mile from home. Grimly trying to hold on, he was worried out of it in the last fifty yards. (8/1)

3712 Orange Place (IRE), always close up, failed to find the necessary turn of foot in the last two furlongs. He has done all his winning at this trip but has scored just once since 1994. (25/1)

3418 Caribbean Star, never far away, did not have a great deal of room in which to manoeuvre below the distance but, when a gap did appear, she could only plod on at one pace. (11/1: 8/1-12/1)

3930 Twin Creeks chased the leaders and kept on well up the hill. (12/1)

3328 Veni Vidi Vici (IRE) took closer order over a quarter of a mile from home, but failed to find another gear from below the distance. Both his wins to date have come over a mile. (12/1)

1482 Ashby Hill (IRE) (12/1: 8/1-14/1)

3936 Fayik was heavily supported in the offices in the morning but punters knew their fate halfway up the straight. (11/2: 4/1-6/1)

4220 LADBROKE H'CAP (0-85) (3-Y.O F) (Class D)

4-25 (4-28) **1m 14y** £4,201.50 (£1,272.00: £621.00: £295.50) Stalls: High GOING minus 0.53 sec per fur (F)

Form	Horse / details	Dist	Pos	SP	RR	SF
2137[9]	**Irish Light (USA) (83)** (MRStoute) **3-9-7** LDettori(9) (lw: rdn & hdwy 2f out: led ins fnl f: r.o wl)	—	**1**	11/4[1]	92	48
4015[14]	**Royale Rose (FR) (70)** (ABailey) **3-8-3v[1]**(5) GFaulkner(8) (lw: hld up: rdn over 2f out: r.o ins fnl f)	1¼	**2**	13/2	77	33
3894[10]	**Irtifa (68)** (PTWalwyn) **3-8-6v[1]** RHills(4) (lw: led over 6f out: hrd rdn over 1f out: hdd ins fnl f: unable qckn)	¾	**3**	10/1	73	29
2380[8]	**Calypso Lady (IRE) (70)** (RHannon) **3-8-8** DaneO'Neill(2) (a.p: rdn over 2f out: one pce)	¾	**4**	20/1	74	30
3930[13]	**Muscatana (59)** (BWHills) **3-7-6**(5) RMullen(3) (swtg: hdwy 2f out: rdn over 1f out: one pce)	½	**5**	12/1	62	18
3119[9]	**Shoshaloza (USA) (67)** (PRWebber) **3-8-5** TSprake(1) (nvr nr to chal)	7	**6**	12/1	56	12
4009*	**Summerosa (USA) (75)** (PWChapple-Hyam) **3-8-13** JReid(5) (b.nr fore: lw: hld up: rdn 4f out: wknd 3f out)	3	**7**	4/1[2]	58	14
2491[10]	**Eliza (67)** (LordHuntingdon) **3-8-5** RPerham(6) (led over 1f: rdn over 2f out: wknd over 1f out)	1¼	**8**	14/1	47	3
3189[13]	**Gee Bee Dream (77)** (APJarvis) **3-9-1** SDrowne(7) (hld up: rdn over 2f out: wknd over 1f out)	½	**9**	5/1[3]	56	12
				(SP 112.6%)	**9 Rn**	

1m 42.65 (1.45) CSF £18.37 CT £139.24 TOTE £3.30: £1.80 £1.60 £2.70 (£16.00) Trio £131.10 OWNER Cheveley Park Stud (NEWMARKET)
BRED Newgate Stud Farm Inc.
OFFICIAL EXPLANATION **Summerosa (USA): swallowed her tongue.**

1110* Irish Light (USA), given a three-month break since flopping at Ascot, appreciated the sounder surface and, set alight in the final quarter-mile, came through to lead inside the final furlong. (11/4)

3775* Royale Rose (FR) chased the leaders. She kept on up the hill to take second place but was not going to trouble the winner. (13/2)

3448 Irtifa, fitted with a visor for the first time, was soon at the head of affairs. Grimly trying to fend off her rivals, she was only overhauled inside the final furlong. (10/1)

1813 Calypso Lady (IRE), 15lb lower than at the beginning of the season after several dismal efforts, ran her best race of the campaign, if failing to quicken in the last two furlongs. (20/1)

2214 Muscatana began a forward move a quarter of a mile from home but then could only plod on at one pace. (12/1: 8/1-14/1)

2704 Shoshaloza (USA) (12/1: 7/1-14/1)

1851 Eliza (14/1: 8/1-16/1)

4221 WILLOW CLAIMING STKS (3-Y.O+) (Class E)

4-55 (5-00) **5f 6y** £3,090.25 (£937.00: £458.50: £219.25) Stalls: High GOING minus 0.53 sec per fur (F)

Form	Horse / details	Dist	Pos	SP	RR	SF
3982[8]	**Palo Blanco (74)** (GLMoore) **6-8-3** CandyMorris(17) (mde virtually all: r.o wl)	—	**1**	9/2[3]	64	42
4016[16]	**Hype Energy (50)** (GLewis) **3-7-11b** DWright(19) (b: a.p: chsd wnr over 1f out: no imp)	1½	**2**	12/1	54	31
4051[2]	**Featherstone Lane (42)** (MissLCSiddall) **6-8-6** DRMcCabe(11) (lw: rdn & hdwy on ins over 1f out: r.o ins fnl f)	1	**3**	33/1	59	37
4100[10]	**Venture Capitalist (98)** (DNicholls) **8-9-5** AlexGreaves(9) (rdn & hdwy over 1f out: r.o one pce)	s.h	**4**	6/4[1]	72	50

				SP	RR	SF
4115[8]	**Robellion (49)** (DWPArbuthnot) **6-8-7** TSprake(10) (b: lw: hld up: n.m.r over 1f out: r.o ins fnl f)	nk	**5**	33/1	59	37
4048[9]	**Intiaash (IRE) (73)** (DHaydnJones) **5-8-6** SDrowne(1) (racd stands' side: hrd rdn & hdwy over 1f out: r.o wl ins fnl f)	nk	**6**	16/1	57	35
4115[10]	**Windrush Boy (49)** (MRBosley) **7-7-12**(5) AimeeCook(15) (swtg: a.p: rdn over 1f out: one pce)	1	**7**	33/1	51	29
3900[8]	**Palacegate Touch (77)** (JBerry) **7-8-9b**(5) PRoberts(13) (prom over 3f)	¾	**8**	4/1[2]	59	37
4016[4]	**Never Think Twice (55)** (KTIvory) **4-8-5v** NAdams(7) (b: lw: outpcd: nvr nrr)	nk	**9**	25/1	50	28
4016[13]	**Imposing Time (48)** (MissGayKelleway) **6-8-5v** DaneO'Neill(8) (a mid div)	1¼	**10**	50/1	46	24
4115[12]	**Littlestone Rocket (56)** (WRMuir) **3-8-4b** MartinDwyer(16) (a.p: chsd wnr over 2f out tl over 1f out: sn wknd)	¾	**11**	33/1	43	20
3693[3]	**Ice Age (57)** (RJRWilliams) **3-8-8b[1]** TQuinn(2) (lw: racd stands' side: plld hrd: hdwy over 1f out: wknd fnl f)	nk	**12**	16/1	46	23
3693[11]	**John O'Dreams (32)** (MrsALMKing) **12-8-3** AClark(12) (outpcd)	2	**13**	50/1	34	12
3425[9]	**Amelia Jane** (LMontagueHall) **3-7-7**(5) APolli(18) (w wnr over 2f)	3	**14**	50/1	20	—
4049[4]	**Ma Vielle Pouque (IRE) (56)** (WGMTurner) **3-7-9**(5) RMullen(6) (lw: racd stands' side: bhd fnl 2f)	¾	**15**	50/1	20	—
3852[4]	**Justinianus (IRE) (45)** (JJBridger) **5-8-6** PaulEddery(3) (lw: racd stands' side: bhd fnl 2f)	nk	**16**	66/1	24	2
4070[6]	**Tashkent** (RSimpson) **5-9-5** MGallagher(14) (a bhd)	1¼	**17**	66/1	33	11
3641[6]	**Dozen Roses (35)** (JELong) **3-8-1** CRutter(5) (swtg: racd stands' side: a bhd)	2½	**18**	66/1	8	—
3206[10]	**Copenhagen** (JAkehurst) **3-7-13** NCarlisle(20) (lw: a bhd)	hd	**19**	50/1	6	—
304[8]	**Logie Pert Lad (23)** (JJBridger) **5-7-10**(7) RBrisland(4) (swtg: racd stands' side: a bhd)	3	**20**	66/1	—	—
				(SP 129.0%)	**20 Rn**	

61.60 secs (1.80) CSF £49.06 TOTE £5.40: £2.20 £3.50 £4.40 (£20.30) Trio £184.50 OWNER Mr A. S. Reid (BRIGHTON) BRED P. and D. H. Cockcroft

WEIGHT FOR AGE 3yo-1lb

3584 Palo Blanco made virtually all the running and kept up the gallop in good style. (9/2: 5/1-11/1)

3816 Hype Energy, never far away, took second place approaching the final furlong but was unable to get on terms with the winner. (12/1)

4051 Featherstone Lane began a forward move along the inside rail below the distance and, running on, snatched third place right on the line. He is not easy to win with and has won just three races from ninety-one starts. (33/1)

3118 Venture Capitalist was 9lb or more ahead of his rivals on official adjusted ratings but, although moving up below the distance, failed to find that vital turn of foot to successfully get on terms with the winner. (6/4)

3016 Robellion, who did not have a great deal of room below the distance, stayed on up the hill and only just failed to take fourth prize. He is on a long losing run at present. (33/1)

3075 Intiaash (IRE) did extremely well considering she was racing on the unfavoured stands' side, running on nicely in the last furlong a half. (16/1)

3566 Palacegate Touch (4/1: 3/1-9/2)

4222 LEVY BOARD H'CAP (0-70) (3-Y.O+) (Class E)

5-25 (5-28) **1m 6f** £3,207.25 (£973.00: £476.50: £228.25) Stalls: Low GOING minus 0.53 sec per fur (F)

				SP	RR	SF
3640[6]	**Veronica Franco (49)** (PRHedger) **4-8-9** DaneO'Neill(1) (hdwy 7f out: rdn over 1f out: led ins fnl f: r.o wl)	—	**1**	14/1	58	19
3915[2]	**Galapino (67)** (MissGayKelleway) **4-9-8**(5) RMullen(13) (swtg: nt clr run 3f out: rdn over 2f out: hdwy over 1f out: r.o wl ins fnl f)	nk	**2**	6/1[2]	76	37
4104*	**Lookout (70)** (BWHills) **3-9-6** 4x PatEddery(11) (swtg: led: hrd rdn over 1f out: hdd ins fnl f: unable qckn)	1	**3**	2/1[1]	78	29
3781[4]	**Keepsake (IRE) (52)** (MDIUsher) **3-8-2** RStreet(5) (hdwy on ins over 1f out: r.o)	½	**4**	10/1	59	10
3796[9]	**Casual Water (IRE) (61)** (AGNewcombe) **6-9-7** SDrowne(12) (hdwy over 2f out: rdn over 1f out: r.o ins fnl f)	hd	**5**	6/1[2]	68	29
4045[4]	**Star Entry (55)** (MajorDNChappell) **3-8-5** CRutter(9) (chsd ldr over 12f: one pce)	s.h	**6**	16/1	62	13
4104[12]	**Lime Street Blues (IRE) (58)** (TKeddy) **6-9-4** JReid(7) (a.p: rdn over 2f out: wknd ins fnl f)	1½	**7**	16/1	63	24
3767[7]	**Challenger (IRE) (36)** (LWells) **4-7-3**(7) RBrisland(14) (lw: lost pl over 2f out: rallied fnl f: r.o one pce)	1	**8**	50/1	40	1
1434[11]	**Copper Shell (70)** (APJones) **3-9-6** TSprake(6) (lw: hld up: rdn over 2f out: btn whn nt clr run over 1f out)	3	**9**	33/1	71	22
3714[4]	**Sovereign Crest (IRE) (49)** (CAHorgan) **4-8-9v** PaulEddery(4) (s.s: nt clr run over 2f out: hdwy 2f out: wknd over 1f out)	2½	**10**	12/1	47	8
3593*	**Castles Burning (USA) (55)** (CACyzer) **3-8-5** RHills(8) (lw: bhd fnl 3f)	3	**11**	14/1	49	—
3792*	**Tarry (49)** (MissGayKelleway) **4-8-6**(3) DO'Donohoe(3) (swtg: nt clr run on ins over 2f out: a bhd)	4	**12**	10/1	39	—
3491[11]	**Bronhallow (36)** (MrsBarbaraWaring) **4-7-10b** NCarlisle(10) (plld hrd: hld up: rdn over 2f out: sn wknd)	2	**13**	33/1	23	—
3781[8]	**Beauchamp Lion (63)** (JLDunlop) **3-8-13** LDettori(15) (lw: prom over 11f)	8	**14**	13/2[3]	41	—
				(SP 134.1%)	**14 Rn**	

3m 4.88 (5.98) CSF £96.15 CT £229.59 TOTE £34.00: £5.00 £2.40 £1.40 (£43.90) Trio £58.20 OWNER Mr J. J. Whelan (CHICHESTER) BRED Islanmore Stud

LONG HANDICAP Bronhallow 7-8 Challenger (IRE) 6-13

WEIGHT FOR AGE 3yo-10lb

3640 Veronica Franco, who edged closer in the back straight, was set alight below the distance and managed to get on top inside the final furlong. (14/1)

3915 Galapino, trapped in behind a wall of horses at the back of the field early in the straight, only found his feet below the distance but ran on really strongly and may well have prevailed with a little further to go. (6/1)

4104* Lookout took the field along and still appeared to be travelling well in the straight. Given reminders approaching the final furlong, she was eventually overhauled inside the last one hundred and fifty yards. (2/1)

3781 Keepsake (IRE), put to sleep at the back of the field, ran on in the last furlong and a half but by then it was all too late. (10/1)

3333 Casual Water (IRE) edged closer in the straight and kept on well up the hill. (6/1)

4045 Star Entry raced in second place until approaching the final furlong from which point she could only struggle on at one pace. (16/1)

T/Jkpt: £26,535.30 (0.39 Tckts); £22,797.94 to Newbury 18/9/97. T/Plpt: £754.60 (32.25 Tckts). T/Qdpt: £65.60 (19.38 Tckts) AK

4180-YARMOUTH (L-H) (Firm)
Wednesday September 17th

WEATHER: fine & sunny WIND: mod across

4223 GOLDEN JUBILEE CHALLENGE TROPHY H'CAP (0-90) (3-Y.O+) (Class C)

2-05 (2-06) **1m 2f 21y** £5,872.50 (£1,755.00: £840.00: £382.50) Stalls: Low GOING minus 0.62 sec per fur (F)

				SP	RR	SF
3616*	**Supreme Sound (68)** (PWHarris) **3-8-7** GBardwell(1) (lw: racd keenly: mde all: r.o wl)	—	**1**	4/1[2]	79	43

3820*	**Flint Knapper (79)** (GWragg) **3-9-4** MHills(5) (lw: hld up: hdwy u.p over 2f out: chsd wnr appr fnl f: unable qckn)	1¼	**2**	7/2^{1}	88	52
4009^{2}	**Easy Song (USA) (73)** (RCharlton) **3-8-12** SSanders(6) (lw: trckd ldrs: rdn over 2f out: styd on fnl f)	½	**3**	7/2^{1}	81	45
3773^{9}	**Secret Aly (CAN) (79)** (CEBrittain) **7-9-10** WRyan(9) (hld up & bhd: hdwy over 2f out: nt rch ldrs)	1¾	**4**	11/2^{3}	85	55
4015*	**Largesse (73)** (JohnBerry) **3-8-12** KFallon(4) (in tch: effrt & rdn over 3f out: one pce fnl 2f)	2	**5**	11/2^{3}	75	39
3061^{5}	**Can Can Lady (80)** (MJohnston) **3-9-5** JFanning(2) (lw: trckd ldrs tl rdn & wknd over 1f out)	nk	**6**	11/1	82	46
3773^{13}	**Diminutive (USA) (75)** (JWHills) **4-9-3**(3) RFfrench(8) (hld up: effrt 3f out: rdn & edgd rt 2f out: no imp)	5	**7**	14/1	69	39
3424^{9}	**Maradi (IRE) (71)** (MBell) **3-8-10** RCochrane(7) (lw: sn chsng wnr: rdn & wknd 3f out: t.o)	18	**8**	25/1	36	—
				(SP 114.1%)	**8 Rn**	

2m 3.5 (0.70 under best) (-0.30) CSF £16.67 CT £47.85 TOTE £4.60: £1.60 £1.30 £1.40 (£9.50) Trio £10.90 OWNER Mrs P. W. Harris (BERKHAMSTED) BRED Pendley Farm

WEIGHT FOR AGE 3yo-6lb

3616* Supreme Sound, very much on his toes, repeated his all the way success at Lingfield and, with his stable in such good form, he may well defy a penalty. (4/1: 5/2-9/2)

3820* Flint Knapper, working hard in an attempt to reel in the winner inside the last quarter-mile, was not quite so effective on this much faster ground, and he was always fighting a losing battle. (7/2)

4009 Easy Song (USA), a good-looking colt who ran with his tongue tied down, was taking on handicappers for the first time. Made to work entering the final quarter-mile, he kept staying on, and he seems to be finding his way. (7/2)

3444 Secret Aly (CAN) won this event twelve months ago, but he did look ill at ease on this ever-firming ground, and he failed to summon up the pace to make his presence felt. (11/2)

4015* Largesse had the ground he needs when successful on his previous outing, but this was a different ball game and he was in trouble from some way out. (11/2: op 7/2)

3061 Can Can Lady won over a mile in her first season, so she should have no trouble staying this trip, but with so much use made of her, she gradually dropped away inside the distance. (11/1)

4224 NEWTON (S) STKS (3-Y.O+) (Class G)

2-35 (2-36) **1m 2f 21y** £2,742.00 (£762.00: £366.00) Stalls: Low GOING minus 0.62 sec per fur (F)

				SP	RR	SF
4114^{5}	**Pegasus Bay** (MissAEEmbiricos) **6-9-3** RCochrane(7) (b: hld up: hdwy over 2f out: squeezed thro ins fnl f: rdn to ld nr fin)	—	**1**	9/2^{2}	62+	35
3848*	**Guesstimation (USA) (60)** (JPearce) **8-9-8** GBardwell(6) (hld up: hdwy over 2f out: rdn to ld ins fnl f: sn hdd: r.o)	s.h	**2**	15/8^{1}	67	40
3390^{5}	**Quarterstaff (54)** (CFWall) **3-8-11** SSanders(2) (hld up: hdwy 3f out: led ins fnl f: sn hdd: rdn & edgd lft: no ex)	1½	**3**	6/1^{3}	60	27
4053^{6}	**Bobbitt (48)** (WJarvis) **3-8-6b^{1}** WRyan(13) (hld up: hdwy over 2f out: rdn & r.o wl ins fnl f)	3½	**4**	10/1	49	16
3897^{7}	**Reeds (49)** (JRFanshawe) **3-8-11v^{1}** KFallon(3) (a.p: led 2f out tl ins fnl f: hrd rdn whn hmpd & snatched up: nt rcvr)	1¾	**5**	8/1	51	18
4069^{10}	**Mr Rough (53)** (DMorris) **6-9-8v^{1}** NDay(4) (sn led: clr ½-wy: hdd 2f out: btn whn hmpd ins fnl f)	½	**6**	8/1	55	28
4114^{6}	**Runic Symbol (35)** (MBlanshard) **6-9-3** JQuinn(10) (hdwy over 2f out: nt rch ldrs)	2½	**7**	20/1	47	20
3972^{8}	**Spanish Stripper (USA) (30)** (MCChapman) **6-8-10**(7) SCarson(12) (s.s: effrt 3f out: rdn & one pce fnl 2f)	¾	**8**	33/1	45	18
4114^{16}	**Saltando (IRE) (43)** (PatMitchell) **6-8-12**(5) AmandaSanders(8) (prom: rdn & wknd wl over 1f out)	1¾	**9**	40/1	43	16
3321^{9}	**Hadadabble (26)** (PatMitchell) **4-8-9**(3) RFfrench(15) (mid div tl rdn & wknd 3f out)	3½	**10**	33/1	32	5
1800^{13}	**Generous Present (46)** (JWPayne) **4-9-3b^{1}** GCarter(5) (prom: rdn & wknd over 2f out)	2	**11**	20/1	34	7
4114^{13}	**Accommodate You** (JMBradley) **4-8-9**(3) PPMurphy(11) (bkwd: a bhd: t.o)	10	**12**	50/1	13	—
528^{P}	**Bright Desert** (MartynWane) **4-9-0**(3) AWhelan(9) (s.i.s: a bhd: t.o)	nk	**13**	50/1	18	—
3560^{5}	**Telephus (17)** (BJMcMath) **8-9-0**(3) DSweeney(14) (bit bkwd: hld up: a in rr: t.o)	nk	**14**	50/1	17	—
	Bob's Saintly Aim (BJMcMath) **3-8-6** DBiggs(1) (unf: scope: bkwd: s.s: a t.o)	dist	**15**	40/1	—	—
				(SP 124.7%)	**15 Rn**	

2m 5.8 (2.00) CSF £11.26 TOTE £5.40: £1.90 £1.20 £2.10 (£4.70) Trio £12.20 OWNER Mr Don Cantillon (NEWMARKET) BRED R. P. Dineen

WEIGHT FOR AGE 3yo-6lb

Bt in 7,000gns, Quarterstaff clmd RW Carson £6,000.

4114 Pegasus Bay, given a very patient ride, gained his revenge over the runner-up, and he would undoubtedly have won more easily had the gaps opened sooner. (9/2)

3848* Guesstimation (USA) just failed to complete his hat-trick, but he gave his all once again and was only beaten on the nod. (15/8)

3390 Quarterstaff will not remain a maiden for much longer if he continues to race in this grade. This would seem to be his correct trip. (6/1)

4053 Bobbitt could have been fancied to run much better in the blinkers, but she does not seem to do anything fast, and never really got into serious contention. (10/1)

2773 Reeds, tackling the trip for the first time, had plenty of use made of him and he did appear to have shot his bolt when knocked out of his stride just inside the final furlong. With more restraint, he does look a ready made winner if he remains in this grade. (8/1)

1878 Mr Rough has yet to prove he really stays this trip, and his attempt to make all was already doomed when he was short of room two-hundred yards out. (8/1: 6/1-9/1)

4225 DANNY WRIGHT H'CAP (0-80) (3-Y.O+) (Class D)

3-10 (3-14) **1m 3y** £5,127.00 (£1,536.00: £738.00: £339.00) Stalls: High GOING minus 0.62 sec per fur (F)

				SP	RR	SF
4059^{5}	**Gymcrak Flyer (62)** (GHolmes) **6-8-10** KFallon(3) (hld up: hdwy 2f out: led ins fnl f: sn clr: wknd nr fin)	—	**1**	11/2^{1}	74	39
3930^{6}	**Ertlon (63)** (CEBrittain) **7-8-11** JQuinn(14) (lw: hld up: hdwy over 3f out: led over 2f out tl ins fnl f: rallied u.p cl home)	nk	**2**	8/1	74	39
3630*	**Toujours Riviera (74)** (JPearce) **7-9-8** GBardwell(13) (a.p: led 3f out tl over 2f out: rdn & one pce fnl f)	3	**3**	10/1	79	44
3100*	**Gain Line (USA) (56)** (BobJones) **4-8-4**ow3 NDay(12) (lw: a.p: led over 3f out: sn hdd: kpt on fnl f)	1¼	**4**	8/1	59	21
4071*	**Safey Ana (USA) (71)** (BHanbury) **6-9-5** 5x WRyan(11) (lw: hdwy 2f out: styd on: nvr able to chal)	hd	**5**	11/2^{1}	74	39
4071^{2}	**Delta Soleil (USA) (77)** (PWHarris) **5-9-6**(5) CLowther(5) (hdwy over 1f out: nrst fin)	¾	**6**	15/2^{3}	78	43
3937^{18}	**Xylem (USA) (72)** (LMCumani) **6-8-13**(7) DYoung(7) (prom: ev ch 3f out: outpcd fnl 2f)	3	**7**	33/1	67	32
3718^{3}	**Defined Feature (IRE) (70)** (DrJDScargill) **4-9-4** MRimmer(9) (nvr bttr than mid div)	s.h	**8**	10/1	65	30
2505^{2}	**Court Express (67)** (TJEtherington) **3-8-11** RCochrane(1) (lw: swtchd rt s: nvr nr ldrs)	½	**9**	16/1	61	22
4112^{11}	**Clytha Hill Lad (56)** (JMBradley) **6-8-1**(3) RFfrench(6) (b: nvr nr to chal)	¾	**10**	14/1	49	14
3718^{2}	**Blue Flyer (IRE) (67)** (RIngram) **4-9-1b** AMcGlone(15) (swtg: a in rr)	1¼	**11**	6/1^{2}	57	22
3435^{F}	**Virtual Reality (77)** (JARToller) **6-9-11** SSanders(4) (led tl over 3f out: eased whn btn appr fnl f)	¾	**12**	14/1	66	31
832^{11}	**Night Dance (76)** (KAMorgan) **5-9-7**(3) AWhelan(10) (bkwd: effrt over 3f out: sn rdn: no imp)	½	**13**	25/1	64	29

3921[13] **Sooty Tern (73)** (JMBradley) **10-9-0**(7) RThomas(2) (racd centre: prom over 5f)....3½	**14**	20/1	54	19
		(SP 128.0%) **14 Rn**		

1m 36.3 (0.30) CSF £46.40 CT £416.28 TOTE £6.10: £2.10 £2.90 £3.10 (£27.60) Trio £107.70 OWNER The Gymcrak Thoroughbred Racing Club (PICKERING) BRED D. G. Mason
WEIGHT FOR AGE 3yo-4lb

4059 Gymcrak Flyer came back to form with what should have been a very comfortable success, but she idled after going clear, and in the end only just held on. (11/2)
3930 Ertlon has not won at this trip for several years, but this is his time of year, and this promising effort would suggest he is ready to add to his score. (8/1)
3630* Toujours Riviera, pushing the pace from the break, found the task beyond him inside the final furlong as the weight concession took its toll. (10/1)
3100* Gain Line (USA) opened his account oven seven furlongs at this venue on his previous run, and he gave a good account of himself here but the eighth furlong did seem that bit too far. (8/1)
4071* Safey Ana (USA) has been in good form and has won at the trip, but the progress was slow on this occasion, and he was too late to deliver his challenge. (11/2)
4071 Delta Soleil (USA), very short cantering to post, did make some late progress but never threatened to take a hand in proceedings. (15/2)
Xylem (USA), a winner on the soft in the Autumn of '93, has been very lightly raced since but he ran much better than his finishing position might suggest this time and he could be on the way back. (33/1)

4226 NORTH SEA CONDITIONS STKS (3-Y.O+) (Class C)
3-40 (3-43) **6f 3y** £4,768.25 (£1,763.34: £845.17: £344.35: £135.68: £52.21) Stalls: High GOING minus 0.62 sec per fur (F)

		SP	RR	SF
3747[8] **March Star (IRE) (94)** (JARToller) **3-8-6** SSanders(5) (lw: a.p: led 2f out: hrd rdn: r.o wl)....—	**1**	14/1	93	45
3728[3] **Imroz (USA) (103)** (HRACecil) **3-8-11** KFallon(2) (lw: a.p: drvn along ½-wy: ev ch 1f out: hrd rdn: nt qckn).....½	**2**	11/8[1]	97	49
3975[7] **Double Splendour (IRE) (91)** (PSFelgate) **7-8-10**(3) DSweeney(1) (lw: hld up: hdwy 2f out: rdn & one pce fnl f)....1¼	**3**	10/1	93	47
Palisade (USA) (HRACecil) **3-8-6** WRyan(3) (still unf: hld up: hdwy over 1f out: nt pce to chal)....1½	**4**	8/1	84	36
2025[6] **Moonlight Paradise (USA) (108)** (SbinSuroor) **3-8-13** MHills(6) (bit bkwd: a chsng ldrs: effrt 2f out: edgd rt: no imp)....1¾	**5**	9/4[2]	87	39
4062[5] **Connemara (IRE) (97)** (CADwyer) **3-8-6** RCochrane(4) (led to 2f out: wknd appr fnl f)....1½	**6**	13/2[3]	76	28
		(SP 113.1%) **6 Rn**		

1m 10.4 (-0.50) CSF £31.44 TOTE £15.90: £5.10 £1.40 (£20.60) OWNER Mr G. M. Cobey (WHITSBURY) BRED Noel O'Callaghan
WEIGHT FOR AGE 3yo-2lb

988 March Star (IRE) came back to form with a bang to overturn the hotpot, and there was certainly no fluke about this. (14/1)
3728 Imroz (USA) did not find this step back to sprinting as straightforward as seemed likely, and her attempt to put her stamp on proceedings failed to materialise. (11/8)
3975 Double Splendour (IRE) was unable to maintain his promising-looking run on this lively ground, but he lost no caste in defeat against these younger rivals and, when conditions come in his favour, he can soon get back to winning ways. (10/1)
Palisade (USA), making a belated seasonal debut, has not furnished in the interim and though she is a daisy cutter, she held her head high as if not enjoying the thought of giving it her best on this ground, and was never nearer than at the finish. She was successful over an extra furlong on her racecourse debut and this trip could be inadequate. (8/1: 6/1-10/1)
2025 Moonlight Paradise (USA) looked just in need of the run after three months out of action and this step back to sprinting did not seem to be in her favour. (9/4)
4062 Connemara (IRE) made sure this was a telling test of speed but she has only ever proved herself at the minimum trip, and she had run her race approaching the final furlong. (13/2)

4227 E.B.F. HALVERGATE MAIDEN STKS (2-Y.O F) (Class D)
4-15 (4-16) **6f 3y** £3,882.50 (£1,160.00: £555.00: £252.50) Stalls: High GOING minus 0.62 sec per fur (F)

		SP	RR	SF
3925[6] **Madame Claude (IRE) (74)** (JARToller) **2-8-11** SSanders(7) (led over 1f: led over 2f out tl over 1f out: rallied u.p to ld cl home)....—	**1**	11/1	78	14
Opening Meet (DRLoder) **2-8-11** KFallon(6) (w'like: scope: bit bkwd: a.p: led appr fnl f: hrd rdn & ct nr fin)...hd	**2**	1/3[1]	78	14
Marie Loup (FR) (LMCumani) **2-8-8**(3) RFfrench(4) (scope: bkwd: outpcd: gd hdwy over 1f out: fin fast).......hd	**3**	9/1[3]	78+	14
1961[6] **Face-Off (63)** (CFWall) **2-8-11** AMcGlone(2) (hdwy ½-wy: ev ch over 1f out: rdn & wknd fnl f)....1½	**4**	50/1	74	10
3744[11] **Dublivia** (CADwyer) **2-8-11** RCochrane(1) (hld up: effrt wl over 1f out: sn rdn: nt pce to chal)....¾	**5**	40/1	72	8
3979[12] **Be My Girl** (CFWall) **2-8-11** WRyan(5) (led over 4f out tl over 2f out: sn rdn: outpcd)....6	**6**	66/1	56	—
Water's Edge (GWragg) **2-8-11** MHills(3) (lt-f: unf: bkwd: s.s: a bhd & outpcd)....1¼	**7**	13/2[2]	52	—
Jolly Harbour (WJHaggas) **2-8-11** NDay(8) (leggy: lt-f: unf: s.s: a bhd & outpcd)....1½	**8**	20/1	48	—
		(SP 117.3%) **8 Rn**		

1m 13.0 (2.10) CSF £14.17 TOTE £7.80: £1.40 £1.00 £2.20 (£4.50) OWNER Mr P. C. J. Dalby (WHITSBURY) BRED Newtownbarry House Stud and Miss S. von Schilcher

3288 Madame Claude (IRE) put her previous experience to good use and, finding the extra furlong made to measure, worried the favourite out of it right on the line. (11/1)
Opening Meet, a late foal who was all the rage, did look as though she would strip fitter for the run, and in the end it was that which beat her. She will be the one to beat next time. (1/3)
Marie Loup (FR), outpaced for most of the way, began to pick up below the distance and her sustained late flourish only just failed. She ought to benefit from the easing of the ground and looks a promising prospect. (9/1)
1961 Face-Off was another who tried to put her previous experience to good use, and in running her best race yet, is definitely going in the right direction. (50/1)
Dublivia had the slipping saddle to contend with on her racecourse debut. With no such problem this time, she ran a great deal better and the longer trip looks a must. (40/1)

4228 SHADWELL STUD SERIES APPRENTICE H'CAP (0-70) (3-Y.O+) (Class E)
4-45 (4-46) **7f 3y** £3,191.00 (£968.00: £474.00: £227.00) Stalls: High GOING minus 0.62 sec per fur (F)

		SP	RR	SF
3143[11] **Lunch Party (38)** (DNicholls) **5-8-0** IonaWands(17) (led after 3f: clr 2f out: jst hld on)....—	**1**	3/1[1]	48	30
4184[10] **Axeman (IRE) (38)** (MartynWane) **5-8-0**ow2 PPMurphy(20) (trckd ldrs: rdn 2f out: str chal fnl f: jst failed).........hd	**2**	20/1	48	28
3718[5] **Mezzoramio (51)** (KAMorgan) **5-8-13v** JoHunnam(15) (b: lw: led 3f: rdn appr fnl f: r.o wl)....nk	**3**	7/1[2]	60	42
3421* **Sandicliffe (USA) (57)** (JARToller) **4-9-5** RFfrench(2) (a chsng ldrs: outpcd 2f out: str run fnl f: fin fast) ....s.h	**4**	3/1[1]	66	48

3718[10] **Flying Pennant (IRE) (49)** (JMBradley) **4-8-6b**[1](5) DarrenWilliams(18) (hdwy over 1f out: sn rdn: unable qckn fnl f)	1	**5**	33/1	56	38
3854[2] **May Queen Megan (43)** (MrsALMKing) **4-8-5** GMilligan(13) (s.s: hdwy 2f out: fin wl)	1½	**6**	12/1	46	28
3966[5] **Racing Telegraph (40)** (CNAllen) **7-8-2** CLowther(11) (hdwy over 2f out: kpt on ins fnl f)	1½	**7**	20/1	40	22
3936[2] **Plum First (53)** (JLEyre) **7-8-10**(5) SBuckley(3) (hdwy over 1f out: nvr nrr)	¾	**8**	14/1	51	33
4184[6] **Waders Dream (IRE) (36)** (PatMitchell) **8-7-12v** AmandaSanders(9) (nvr nrr)	hd	**9**	33/1	34	16
3868* **Warrior King (IRE) (53)** (CADwyer) **3-8-9**(3) AMcCarthy(14) (nvr bttr than mid div)	s.h	**10**	8/1 3	51	30
4059[4] **Allinson's Mate (IRE) (61)** (TDBarron) **9-9-9b** KimberleyHart(12) (nvr trbld ldrs)	¾	**11**	10/1	57	39
3787[7] **Delight of Dawn (49)** (EAWheeler) **5-8-11** ADaly(10) (nvr nr to chal)	nk	**12**	12/1	44	26
3852[7] **Chaluz (42)** (KRBurke) **3-8-1** DSweeney(8) (a in rr)	s.h	**13**	25/1	37	16
3746[7] **Don Pepe (61)** (RBoss) **6-9-6**(3) NHorrocks(19) (nvr plcd to chal)	hd	**14**	9/1	56	38
3787[11] **Blowing Away (IRE) (65)** (MHTompkins) **3-9-3**(7) JSavage(6) (lw: mid div: effrt over 2f out: wknd wl over 1f out)	½	**15**	25/1	59	38
4181[8] **Karinska (59)** (MCChapman) **7-9-4**(3) SCarson(4) (trckd ldrs 5f: sn rdn & outpcd)	2	**16**	20/1	48	30
3718[8] **On The Green (38)** (AHide) **4-8-0v** PDoe(1) (racd alone far side: bhd fnl 3f)	½	**17**	16/1	26	8
4043[2] **Silver Harrow (56)** (AGNewcombe) **4-9-4** DGriffiths(7) (a in rr)	2½	**18**	14/1	39	21
3565[16] **Meranti (59)** (JMBradley) **4-9-2**(5) JFowle(5) (lw: prom centre 5f)	1	**19**	25/1	39	21
			(SP 159.0%)	**19 Rn**	

1m 24.5 (0.30) CSF £81.80 CT £336.60 TOTE £8.50: £2.50 £3.60 £2.40 £1.90 (£87.70) Trio £239.70 OWNER Mr S. Aitken (THIRSK) BRED Aston Park Stud

WEIGHT FOR AGE 3yo-3lb

610 Lunch Party landed something of a gamble, but his supporters must have had their hearts in their mouths inside the last one hundred yards. He was given a very competent ride. (3/1: 7/2-6/1)
Axeman (IRE) had a much more favourable draw than he had yesterday and his determined last-furlong challenge only just failed. This was a decent effort and he could find a small race in the coming weeks. (20/1)
3718 Mezzoramio ran up to his best and it was not for the want of trying that he failed to follow up his success here in July. (7/1)
3421* Sandicliffe (USA) was beaten by the draw for she was in front two yards past the post and she must be considered a most unfortunate loser. (3/1: tchd 9/2)
1920 Flying Pennant (IRE), blinkered for the first time, produced a promising-looking run entering the final furlong but, once there, failed to sustain the run. If lowered in class, there are races to be won with him. (33/1)
3854 May Queen Megan did extremely well to finish so close after losing ground at the start, and she was without doubt an unlucky loser. (12/1)
3966 Racing Telegraph has not won for quite some time and he did not impress to post, but he was doing all his best work late on and it is likely he is capable of stepping up on this. (20/1)
4059 Allinson's Mate (IRE) (10/1: 8/1-12/1)

4229 E.B.F. FLEGGBOROUGH MAIDEN STKS (2-Y.O) (Class D)

5-15 (5-16) **7f 3y** £3,915.00 (£1,170.00: £560.00: £255.00) Stalls: High GOING minus 0.62 sec per fur (F)

			SP	RR	SF
3726[7] **Naughty Blue (USA)** (SbinSuroor) **2-9-0** RCochrane(5) (hld up: hdwy 2f out: qcknd to ld appr fnl f: sn clr)	—	**1**	9/1 3	85+	50
Brimming (HRACecil) **2-9-0** KFallon(4) (neat: a.p: drvn along over 2f out: led over 1f out: sn hdd: outpcd fnl f)	5	**2**	4/6 1	74	39
3978[5] **Highwayman (IRE)** (MRStoute) **2-9-0** SSanders(7) (bit bkwd: a.p: hrd drvn & ev ch over 1f out: sn outpcd)	1½	**3**	5/2 2	70	35
3770[10] **Sconced (USA)** (GWragg) **2-9-0** MHills(2) (bhd: effrt 2f out: nt rch ldrs)	6	**4**	9/1 3	57	22
4056[11] **Goldmaster** (WAO'Gorman) **2-9-0** EmmaO'Gorman(8) (trckd ldrs tl outpcd over 1f out)	3	**5**	33/1	50	15
3201[11] **Hastate** (WJarvis) **2-9-0** WRyan(9) (bit bkwd: led tl hdd & wknd over 1f out)	1	**6**	25/1	47	12
4111[12] **Lycian (IRE)** (SirMarkPrescott) **2-9-0** CNutter(1) (bit bkwd: sn pushed along: a in rr)	3	**7**	25/1	41	6
2926[8] **Marahill Lad** (PHowling) **2-9-0** JQuinn(3) (prom over 4f)	5	**8**	50/1	29	—
Rock Sounds (NACallaghan) **2-9-0** GCarter(6) (lt-f: unf: a t.o)	14	**9**	25/1	—	—
			(SP 125.0%)	**9 Rn**	

1m 23.9 (-0.30) CSF £14.86 TOTE £8.10: £1.40 £1.10 £1.10 (£6.10) Trio £6.00 OWNER Godolphin (NEWMARKET) BRED Darley Stud Management Inc

3726 Naughty Blue (USA), much wiser after the experience gained at York, won this in the style of a useful colt and it would be surprising if he can not continue the progress. (9/1: 6/1-10/1)
Brimming, by a Derby winner, out of a Lancashire Oaks winner, is bred to need a much stiffer test of stamina and it was not surprising he was not unable to compete with the winner in the dash to the line. This is probably a better performance than it appears at first sight. (4/6)
3978 Highwayman (IRE) ran much better than he did on his debut and, given easier ground, will soon improve on this. (5/2)
Sconced (USA) is not yet the finished article and he was never able to trouble the principals. (9/1)
Goldmaster, ill-at-ease on this ground, tracked the leaders until getting left behind when the sprint to the post developed. (33/1)
3201 Hastate got the best of the start and made the running for over five furlongs before calling enough. (25/1)

T/Plpt: £18.90 (1,040.95 Tckts). T/Qdpt: £13.00 (63.87 Tckts). IM

3401-AYR (L-H) (Good to soft, Soft patches)
Thursday September 18th

WEATHER: sunny WIND: almost nil

4230 EAGLE TAVERNS (S) STKS (2-Y.O) (Class E)

2-00 (2-01) **5f** £3,610.00 (£1,090.00: £530.00: £250.00) Stalls: High GOING: 0.18 sec per fur (G)

			SP	RR	SF
3804[4] **Kettlesing (IRE) (65)** (MWEasterby) **2-8-6b** DHolland(6) (b.off fore: squeezed out s: hdwy after 2f: chal & hung lft 1f out: styd on to ld wl ins fnl f)	—	**1**	15/2	66	39
4014[8] **Patsy Culsyth (63)** (NTinkler) **2-8-11v** KimTinkler(8) (lw: mde most tl ct wl ins fnl f: kpt on)	½	**2**	14/1	69	42
4012[19] **Carol Singer (USA)** (MJohnston) **2-8-6** JWeaver(3) (s.i.s: hdwy ½-wy: disp ld ins fnl f: nt qckn towards fin)	nk	**3**	8/1	63	36
3932[10] **Burnt Yates (IRE) (67)** (MWEasterby) **2-8-11** TLucas(5) (lw: cl up tl rdn & btn appr fnl f)	2	**4**	9/2 1	62	35
4014[5] **Sandside (74)** (JBerry) **2-8-13**(3) PFessey(1) (a chsng ldrs: nt qckn appr fnl f)	¾	**5**	9/2 1	65	38
3905[8] **Gildersleve (61)** (JWWatts) **2-8-6** JCarroll(11) (prom: outpcd 2f out: kpt on fnl f)	1	**6**	12/1	51	24
3869[5] **Great Lyth Lass (IRE) (65)** (PDEvans) **2-8-6b**[1] JFEgan(4) (in tch: sn drvn along: no hdwy fnl 2f)	1¼	**7**	13/2 3	47	20

				SP	RR	SF
3628[5]	**Pride of Bryn (46)** (DenysSmith) **2-8-1**(5) CLowther(9) (sn outpcd & bhd)	hd	**8**	25/1	47	20
4042[10]	**Cd Newsround (IRE)** (MRChannon) **2-8-6** KDarley(7) (prom tl rdn & btn 1½f out)	1¼	**9**	6/1[2]	43	16
4012[21]	**Penny Whistle** (TDEasterby) **2-8-6** LCharnock(2) (outpcd & lost tch fr ½-wy)	8	**10**	16/1	18	—
3055[5]	**Polly In Paris (IRE)** (MartynMeade) **2-7-13**(7) RBrisland(12) (dwlt: a outpcd & wl bhd)	6	**11**	50/1	—	—
2016[16]	**Sunshine Pet (IRE) (41)** (JJO'Neill) **2-8-6** ACulhane(10) (s.i.s: a outpcd & wl bhd)	6	**12**	50/1	—	—

(SP 114.9%) **12 Rn**

60.85 secs (3.85) CSF £93.40 TOTE £9.90: £3.70 £1.80 £2.50 (£34.30) Trio £92.00 OWNER Mr I. Bray (SHERIFF HUTTON) BRED Liam Phelan

No bid

3804 Kettlesing (IRE) has always had the ability and this poor race proved just up her street, but she did not look one to rely on. (15/2: 5/1-8/1)

3804 Patsy Culsyth looks particularly well at the moment and has always to be considered in such events. (14/1: 8/1-16/1)

Carol Singer (USA) does not impress on looks but, in this class, has the right engine and this should have taught her plenty. (8/1)

3438 Burnt Yates (IRE) has proved disappointing and failed to pull out anything under pressure here. (9/2)

4014 Sandside was always seeing too much daylight on the outside of the field. (9/2: op 3/1)

3905 Gildersleve did not have the best of luck in running here and gave the impression that there could be a modest event in her. (12/1: 8/1-14/1)

4231 HOLIDAY IN AYRSHIRE & ARRAN E.B.F. MAIDEN STKS (2-Y.O) (Class D)

2-30 (2-32) **7f** £4,536.00 (£1,368.00: £664.00: £312.00) Stalls: High GOING: 0.18 sec per fur (G)

				SP	RR	SF
3426[2]	**Arctic Air** (EWeymes) **2-8-9** KDarley(8) (lw: chsd ldr: rdn to ld 1f out: styd on strly)	—	**1**	6/1[3]	76	26
3753[10]	**Set Trail (IRE)** (JHanson) **2-8-9** EJohnson(9) (b.hind: led tl hdd 1f out: kpt on same pce)	1¼	**2**	33/1	73	23
3825[2]	**Requestor (88)** (JGFitzGerald) **2-9-0** ACulhane(6) (hmpd after s: hdwy ½-wy: rdn & no imp fnl 2f)	5	**3**	13/8[1]	67	17
3306[4]	**Miss Vivien** (MissLAPerratt) **2-8-6**(3) TEDurcan(2) (mid div: hdwy 3f out: sn prom: one pce fnl 2f)	1½	**4**	16/1	58	8
	Gypsy Passion (IRE) (MJohnston) **2-9-0** DHolland(4) (wl grwn: bit bkwd: in tch: pushed along appr st: styd on: no imp)	2	**5**	7/1	59+	9
	Fearless Brave (CWThornton) **2-9-0** DeanMcKeown(5) (w'like: lengthy: bhd: styd on fnl 2f: nrst fin)	1	**6**	50/1	56+	6
3973[17]	**Saintes** (WMcKeown) **2-8-9**(5) CLowther(3) (in tch tl outpcd fnl 3f)	5	**7**	100/1	45	—
	Arctic Star (MRChannon) **2-9-0** AMackay(7) (hld up & bhd: effrt ½-wy: n.d)	1	**8**	20/1	43	—
3770[6]	**Nautical Warning** (MHTompkins) **2-9-0** JWeaver(14) (lw: in tch: effrt 3f out: wknd over 1f out)	1¼	**9**	4/1[2]	40	—
3806[6]	**Daybreak** (JWWatts) **2-8-9** JCarroll(12) (hld up: effrt ½-wy: n.d)	1¼	**10**	20/1	32	—
	Repton (MrsASwinbank) **2-9-0** JLowe(10) (leggy: unf: s.s: n.d)	nk	**11**	66/1	36	—
3753[5]	**Walton Grey (IRE)** (PDEvans) **2-9-0** JFEgan(1) (hld up & bhd: n.d)	2½	**12**	50/1	31	—
3687[14]	**Indy Knight (IRE)** (MartynMeade) **2-8-6**(3) RHavlin(13) (sn chsng ldrs: wknd 3f out)	s.h	**13**	50/1	26	—
	Ryefield Star (JBerry) **2-9-0** AMcGlone(11) (w'like: str: bit bkwd: chsd ldrs to ½-wy: wknd)	3½	**14**	20/1	23	—

(SP 116.4%) **14 Rn**

1m 31.43 (7.03) CSF £174.62 TOTE £5.70: £1.70 £6.30 £1.20 (£623.60) Trio £111.40 OWNER Mr T. A. Scothern (MIDDLEHAM) BRED The Overbury Stud

3426 Arctic Air looked really well after almost six weeks off and proved to be a most determined sort, getting stronger as the race progressed. (6/1: 4/1-7/1)

3753 Set Trail (IRE), stepped up in trip and ridden positively, improved a great deal and a race will surely be found. (33/1)

3825 Requestor never had the run of the race and this effort is best forgotten. (13/8)

3306 Miss Vivien ran well after six weeks off and should be all the better for it. (16/1)

Gypsy Passion (IRE), a big, backward sort, does not do anything quickly but this should have taught him something. (7/1: op 9/2)

Fearless Brave was learning as the race progressed and, given stiffer tests, better will be seen. (50/1)

Arctic Star looks a headstrong individual but there is ability there. (20/1)

4232 TIMEFORM HARRY ROSEBERY TROPHY STKS (Listed) (2-Y.O) (Class A)

3-00 (3-02) **5f** £9,992.00 (£3,728.00: £1,814.00: £770.00: £335.00: £161.00) Stalls: High GOING: 0.18 sec per fur (G)

				SP	RR	SF
3774[2]	**Halmahera (IRE) (97)** (IABalding) **2-8-11** MartinDwyer(2) (lw: hdwy ½-wy: led wl ins fnl f: edgd rt)	—	**1**	9/4[1]	96	58
3595[11]	**Its All Relative (94)** (JBerry) **2-8-6** DHolland(6) (led: rdn 2f out: hdd wl ins fnl f: kpt on)	¾	**2**	10/1	89	51
3379[3]	**Friar Tuck (89)** (MissLAPerratt) **2-8-11** JFEgan(4) (lw: cl up: chal 2f out: sn rdn: btn whn hmpd towards fin)	1	**3**	10/1	90	52
3774[4]	**Eastern Purple (IRE) (92)** (RAFahey) **2-8-11b1** JCarroll(8) (s.i.s: hdwy ½-wy: ch 1f out: kpt on)	nk	**4**	6/1[3]	89	51
3908*	**Baby Grand (IRE) (99)** (TDBarron) **2-8-11** KimberleyHart(3) (unruly: bhd & drvn along: hdwy 2f out: nrst fin)	1¾	**5**	7/1	84	46
4152[2]	**Blue Kite (75)** (NPLittmoden) **2-8-11** JWeaver(1) (lw: outpcd & bhd: hdwy 2f out: nvr rchd ldrs)	¾	**6**	14/1	81	43
3925[2]	**Eleventh Duke (IRE) (94)** (RHannon) **2-8-11** KDarley(7) (chsd ldrs: rdn over 2f out: wknd over 1f out)	s.h	**7**	7/2[2]	81	43
3597[11]	**Batswing (82)** (MartynMeade) **2-8-11b** RHavlin(5) (chsd ldrs: sn rdn: wknd fnl 2f)	nk	**8**	25/1	80	42
3926[5]	**Emmajoun** (APJarvis) **2-8-6** CLowther(9) (spd 3f: sn wknd)	7	**9**	20/1	53	15

(SP 113.2%) **9 Rn**

60.0 secs (3.00) CSF £23.11 TOTE £2.50: £1.30 £3.10 £2.30 (£20.40) Trio £61.30 OWNER Robert & Exors Late Elizabeth Hitchins (KINGSCLERE) BRED Mrs John McEnery

3774 Halmahera (IRE), despite this trip being on the sharp side for him, did it well but his inclination to hang when in front is quite worrying. (9/4)

2931* Its All Relative is a game sort who will always find her share of races and should stay a little further. (10/1)

3379 Friar Tuck gave problems at the start last time and was again a bit edgy beforehand but he did give his running here and, if he would settle down, there is better to come. (10/1: 8/1-12/1)

3774 Eastern Purple (IRE) had blinkers on for the first time and ran well but just failed to pick up late on. He looks the sort to do better as he strengthens to his frame. (6/1)

3908* Baby Grand (IRE) gave problems before the start and never got into the race and, by the way she finished, she might well be worth a crack at six furlongs. (7/1: 5/1-8/1)

4152 Blue Kite was always finding this trip too sharp. (14/1)

3925 Eleventh Duke (IRE) ran a bit flat here and was beaten some way out. (7/2)

4233 ISLE OF ARRAN H'CAP (0-85) (3-Y.O+) (Class D)

3-30 (3-35) **5f** £6,482.50 (£1,960.00: £955.00: £452.50) Stalls: High GOING: 0.18 sec per fur (G)

				SP	RR	SF
4137*	**Just Bob (64)** (SEKettlewell) **8-8-7** 7x DeanMcKeown(6) (lw: racd far side: bhd tl hdwy 2f out: r.o wl to ld wl ins fnl f)	—	**1**	7/1[2]	73	55

3910[5] **Camionneur (IRE) (53)** (TDEasterby) **4-7-10b** LCharnock(8) (hld up & bhd far side: hdwy 2f out: r.o)	1½	**2**	14/1	57	39
3410[19] **Swynford Dream (70)** (JHetherton) **4-8-13** JLowe(3) (cl up far side: led over 1f out tl wl ins fnl f)	½	**3**	14/1	73	55
4155[22] **Gold Edge (55)** (MRChannon) **3-7-11** AMackay(24) (sn drvn along stands' side: hdwy 2f out: r.o wl towards fin)	nk	**4**	16/1	57	38
3856[17] **Another Episode (IRE) (53)** (MissLAPerratt) **8-7-3**(7) JMcAuley(4) (w ldrs far side: nt qckn ins fnl f)	nk	**5**	200/1	54	36
3816* **Divine Miss-P (58)** (APJarvis) **4-7-12**(3) PFessey(22) (led stands' side: hung lft fnl f: kpt on)	s.h	**6**	14/1	59	41
4100[6] **Lady Sheriff (85)** (MWEasterby) **6-9-7b**(7) SFinnamore(2) (lw: racd far side: a chsng ldrs: sn drvn along: no imp fnl 2f)	1½	**7**	20/1	81	63
3481* **Goretski (IRE) (80)** (NTinkler) **4-9-9** DHolland(17) (lw: chsd ldrs stands' side: nt qckn fnl 2f)	½	**8**	5/1[1]	74	56
3756[5] **Johayro (60)** (JSGoldie) **4-8-3** TWilliams(5) (racd far side: led tl hdd over 1f out: sn btn)	hd	**9**	16/1	54	36
3621[8] **Rich Glow (53)** (NBycroft) **6-7-10** DWright(19) (racd stands' side: effrt ½-wy: swtchd lft & styd on: nvr rchd ldrs)	nk	**10**	10/1[3]	46	28
3922[3] **William's Well (60)** (MWEasterby) **3-8-2b** DaleGibson(12) (racd stands' side: drvn along thrght: in tch: no imp fnl 2f)	½	**11**	14/1	51	32
3856[4] **Manolo (FR) (62)** (JBerry) **4-8-0b**(5) CLowther(7) (unruly in stalls: s.i.s: racd far side: nvr able to chal)	hd	**12**	25/1	53	35
3900[6] **Swino (73)** (PDEvans) **3-9-1** JFEgan(23) (dwlt: racd stands' side: nrst fin)	s.h	**13**	33/1	64	45
3761[3] **Brecongill Lad (64)** (MissSEHall) **5-8-7** JWeaver(9) (racd far side: in tch: hung rt fr ½-wy: no imp)	nk	**14**	12/1	54	36
3910[17] **Amron (61)** (JBerry) **10-8-4** KDarley(16) (racd stands' side: nvr wnt pce)	¾	**15**	16/1	48	30
3922[5] **Pallium (IRE) (60)** (DANolan) **9-7-12b**(5)ow7 KSked(11) (chsd ldrs centre over 3f)	s.h	**16**	33/1	47	22
4137[12] **The Wad (58)** (DNicholls) **4-7-10**(5) IonaWands(14) (prom stands' side over 3f)	nk	**17**	50/1	44	26
3922[8] **Six for Luck (57)** (DANolan) **5-7-7**(7)ow4 NPollard(20) (racd stands' side: in tch tl wknd fnl 2f)	nk	**18**	200/1	42	20
4115[5] **Flying Harold (53)** (MRChannon) **4-7-5**(5) APolli(15) (chsd ldrs stands' side over 3f)	1½	**19**	33/1	34	16
4016[11] **Another Nightmare (IRE) (53)** (RMMcKellar) **5-7-10** KimTinkler(10) (racd far side: spd 3f: hung rt & wknd)	1¾	**20**	50/1	28	10
4051[6] **Lennox Lewis (63)** (DNicholls) **5-7-13**(7) ANicholls(26) (racd stands' side: bhd & hmpd over 1f out: n.d)	hd	**21**	33/1	38	20
3224[7] **Leading Princess (IRE) (53)** (MissLAPerratt) **6-7-3b**(7) PBradley(13) (unruly bef s: n.d)	nk	**22**	100/1	27	9
3900[2] **Squire Corrie (83)** (DWChapman) **5-9-12** ACulhane(18) (lw: cl up stands' side over 3f: wknd)	¾	**23**	14/1	54	36
1946[11] **Pride of Brixton (80)** (CWThornton) **4-9-9** JCarroll(1) (racd far side: prom to ½-wy: sn wknd)	s.h	**24**	50/1	51	33
4048[7] **Nightingale Song (60)** (MartynMeade) **3-7-9**(7) RBrisland(21) (racd stands' side: n.d)	hd	**25**	20/1	31	12
			(SP 129.9%)	**25 Rn**	

59.94 secs (2.94) CSF £83.50 CT £1,251.70 TOTE £6.60: £1.70 £2.60 £4.60 £7.20 (£59.50) Trio £648.70 OWNER Mr J. Fotherby (MIDDLEHAM) BRED Mrs D. Whittingham

LONG HANDICAP Pallium (IRE) 7-9 Flying Harold 7-3 Another Nightmare (IRE) 7-3 Another Episode (IRE) 7-0 Leading Princess (IRE) 7-0 Rich Glow 7-6 Six for Luck 6-6

WEIGHT FOR AGE 3yo-1lb

4137* Just Bob is a typical sprinter-in-form and won this really well. He looks likely to continue in this vein. (7/1)

3910 Camionneur (IRE) is still in tremendous form but his run was always too late to trouble the winner this time. (14/1)

2872 Swynford Dream is dropping down the handicap fast and this was a useful effort. (14/1)

3851 Gold Edge won the race up the stands' side and finished like the proverbial train to show she is coming back to form. (16/1)

Another Episode (IRE) has speed to burn and will surely pick up a race before the season ends. (200/1)

3816* Divine Miss-P did all the donkey work up the stands' side and this may well turn out to be a decent effort. (14/1: 10/1-16/1)

4100 Lady Sheriff, with an inexperienced rider on board, could never summon the speed to make her presence felt. (20/1)

3621 Rich Glow, back at his favourite track, never had any luck in running and should be forgiven this. (10/1)

4234 MIKE FLYNN 50TH YEAR (AWRIGHTLA) (BOGSIDE CUP) H'CAP (0-95) (3-Y.O) (Class C)

4-00 (4-00) **1m 7f** £7,158.00 (£2,154.00: £1,042.00: £486.00) Stalls: High GOING: 0.18 sec per fur (G)

			SP	RR	SF
3333[12] **Heart of Gold (IRE) (87)** (MissSEHall) **3-9-7** AMcGlone(9) (h.d.w: in tch: effrt 3f out: led appr fnl f: styd on wl)	—	**1**	10/1	97	59
2568[3] **Royal Crown (IRE) (84)** (PWChapple-Hyam) **3-9-1**(3) RHavlin(3) (hld up: hdwy 6f out: led over 3f out tl appr fnl f: kpt on)	1¼	**2**	7/1	93	55
3974[6] **Tarxien (70)** (KRBurke) **3-8-4** JFEgan(8) (lw: hld up: smooth hdwy to disp ld over 2f out: btn appr fnl f)	2½	**3**	9/1	76	38
3915[5] **Nichol Fifty (70)** (MHTompkins) **3-8-4** DBiggs(2) (a chsng ldrs: one pce fnl 3f)	½	**4**	11/2[3]	76	38
4015[3] **Dead Aim (IRE) (78)** (IABalding) **3-8-12** MartinDwyer(4) (lw: pushed along & hdwy 7f out: chal ent st: outpcd fnl 2½f)	4	**5**	13/2	79	41
3989[6] **Marathon Maid (75)** (RAFahey) **3-8-2**(7) RWinston(10) (bhd tl styd on u.p fnl 3f: n.d)	2½	**6**	20/1	74	36
2963[2] **Little Acorn (86)** (SCWilliams) **3-9-6** KDarley(11) (chsd ldrs: effrt 3f out: sn wknd)	18	**7**	5/1[2]	65	27
3648[3] **Liffre (IRE) (85)** (JHMGosden) **3-9-5b**[1] JCarroll(5) (led tl hdd over 3f out: sn wknd)	1¼	**8**	11/4[1]	63	25
3974[8] **Toi Toi (IRE) (77)** (DWPArbuthnot) **3-8-11** SWhitworth(6) (b.hind: prom tl rdn & lost pl ½-wy: sn bhd)	13	**9**	12/1	41	3
3455[7] **Yours In Sport (62)** (JWWatts) **3-7-10** LCharnock(7) (cl up tl wknd qckly ent st: sn bhd)	5	**10**	33/1	21	—
			(SP 119.0%)	**10 Rn**	

3m 22.11 (11.41) CSF £72.67 CT £603.73 TOTE £11.00: £2.40 £2.30 £2.40 (£47.40) Trio £205.80 OWNER Mr C. Platts (MIDDLEHAM) BRED Miss Fiona Meehan

LONG HANDICAP Yours In Sport 7-8

OFFICIAL EXPLANATION **Heart of Gold (IRE): the longer trip and easier ground may have benefited the colt.**

2676 Heart of Gold (IRE) has always looked a stayer and this, his longest trip to date, suited him well. He won it in style and still seems to be improving. (10/1)

2568 Royal Crown (IRE), stepping up in trip, is obviously a stayer and will get further yet. (7/1)

3974 Tarxien travelled well but this trip was probably just beyond him. (9/1)

3915 Nichol Fifty seems to stay well enough but he is just short of a real turn of foot. (11/2)

4015 Dead Aim (IRE) is certainly a hard ride and appears to stay but is short of pace. (13/2)

3648 Liffre (IRE) had blinkers on for the first time but seemed to resent them and ran no sort of race. (11/4)

4235 KILKERRAN AMATEUR H'CAP (0-70) (3-Y.O+) (Class F)

4-30 (4-30) **1m 2f 192y** £3,095.00 (£935.00: £455.00: £215.00) Stalls: High GOING: 0.18 sec per fur (G)

			SP	RR	SF
3631[5] **Philmist (45)** (MissLAPerratt) **5-10-3b** MissAElsey(15) (hdwy & prom 7f out: led over 2f out: r.o wl)	—	**1**	14/1	56	49
3933[2] **Mr Fortywinks (IRE) (44)** (JLEyre) **3-9-9** MissDianaJones(7) (a chsng ldrs: hdwy over 2f out: styd on wl)	1¼	**2**	16/1	53	39
3762[2] **Farfields Prince (43)** (DNicholls) **5-10-1** MrCBonner(3) (hdwy 4f out: styd on u.p fnl 2f: nrst fin)	3	**3**	7/1[3]	48	41
3864* **Bold Buster (69)** (IABalding) **4-11-13** MrABalding(11) (lw: a.p: effrt 3f out: r.o one pce)	¾	**4**	4/1[1]	73	66

3907[5]	**Summerhill Special (IRE) (67)** (DWBarker) **6-11-8**(3) MissERamsden(2) (hld up: effrt ent st: sn chsng ldrs & rdn: nt qckn fnl 2f)	1¼	**5**	7/1[3]	69	62
3890[W]	**Rex Mundi (66)** (PDEvans) **5-11-5**(5) MrAEvans(12) (led tl hdd over 2f out: one pce)	¾	**6**	10/1	67	60
3937[14]	**Alpine Panther (IRE) (59)** (MrsMReveley) **4-11-3** MrSSwiers(5) (lw: hld up: hdwy 4f out: sn in tch & rdn: no imp fnl 2f)	¾	**7**	11/2[2]	59	52
3234[5]	**Spick And Span (53)** (CWThornton) **3-9-13**(5) MrJCrowley(20) (outpcd tl styd on fnl 3f: nrst fin)	nk	**8**	14/1	52	38
3992[6]	**Beau Roberto (44)** (JSGoldie) **3-9-4**(5) MrsCWilliams(4) (hld up & bhd: effrt on ins over 2f out: nvr rchd ldrs)	1¼	**9**	50/1	41	27
3886[3]	**Sagebrush Roller (48)** (JWWatts) **9-9-13b**(7) MrTJBarry(13) (bhd: sme late hdwy: n.d)	1½	**10**	20/1	43	36
3921[8]	**Lord Advocate (50)** (DANolan) **9-10-1b**(7) MrsDWilkinson(14) (in tch tl outpcd ent st: n.d after)	3½	**11**	25/1	40	33
4168[3]	**Suedoro (54)** (JSGoldie) **7-10-5**(7)ow8 MrCDunbar(10) (sn t.o: sme late hdwy)	3	**12**	50/1	40	25
3971[2]	**Righty Ho (70)** (PTWalwyn) **3-11-2v**(5) MissSSamworth(1) (hld up: effrt ent st: no imp)	½	**13**	10/1	55	41
4161[11]	**Mowlaie (45)** (DWChapman) **6-10-3** MissRClark(8) (b: in tch: stumbled 7f out: wknd 4f out)	10	**14**	25/1	15	8
3921[4]	**Mentalasanythin (65)** (DHaydnJones) **8-11-2**(7) MrJDelahunt(6) (bhd: hdwy & prom ½-wy: c wd st: sn wknd)	½	**15**	8/1	34	27
3853[2]	**Forzair (51)** (JJO'Neill) **5-10-9** MrRHale(9) (cl up: sn pushed along: wknd over 3f out)	2	**16**	25/1	17	10
3316[8]	**Perpetual Light (48)** (JJQuinn) **4-10-1**(5) MrVLukaniuk(17) (lost tch fnl 4f)	9	**17**	25/1	1	—
4050[11]	**Domino Flyer (70)** (MrsASwinbank) **4-11-7**(7) MissLPreston(18) (prom to st)	1¼	**18**	33/1	21	14
3779[5]	**Brambles Way (56)** (MrsMReveley) **8-10-7**(7)ow6 MrNEJones(19) (prom to ½-wy: sn bhd)	4	**19**	33/1	1	—
3200[5]	**Westminster (IRE) (62)** (MHTompkins) **5-11-1v**(5) MrMJenkins(16) (bhd: effrt appr st: sn wknd)	22	**20**	12/1	—	—

(SP 146.5%) **20 Rn**

2m 26.65 (10.75) CSF £213.96 CT £1,600.10 TOTE £20.50: £3.20 £2.40 £2.00 £1.60 (£99.40) Trio £110.50 OWNER Mr C. D. Barber-Lomax (AYR) BRED Mrs M. Morley

WEIGHT FOR AGE 3yo-7lb

OFFICIAL EXPLANATION **Philmist: the trainer reported that the mare's last run had come too soon.**

3631 Philmist loves these strongly-run events and won this particularly well. (14/1)

3933 Mr Fortywinks (IRE) was calm and cool on this occasion and ran a game race, sticking on well at the end, suggesting that this longer trip suited particularly well. (16/1)

3762 Farfields Prince took some galvanizing into action but he did pick up well late on to show he has the ability. (7/1: op 12/1)

3864* Bold Buster had his chances but lacked any turn of foot to take them. (4/1)

3907 Summerhill Special (IRE) goes well in these strongly-run events but this time she had her limitations exposed in the last two furlongs. (7/1)

2944 Rex Mundi ran well but this trip was on the sharp side for him. (10/1)

3777 Alpine Panther (IRE) was always struggling for both room and pace and never landed a real blow. He is probably better when more use is made of him. (11/2)

3234 Spick And Span ran as though longer trips are needed. (14/1: 10/1-16/1)

4236 TATTERSALLS MAIDEN AUCTION STKS (2-Y.O) (Class D)

5-00 (5-01) **6f** £3,727.00 (£1,126.00: £548.00: £259.00) Stalls: High GOING: 0.18 sec per fur (G)

				SP	RR	SF
3806[9]	**Desert Sand** (MissSEHall) **2-8-0** EJohnson(13) (bhd: hdwy ½-wy: rdn to ld ins fnl f: m green: r.o)	—	**1**	10/1[2]	76	28
	Ryefield (MissLAPerratt) **2-8-12** JWeaver(7) (rangy: led tl hdd ins fnl f: no ex)	3	**2**	12/1[3]	80+	32
3869[7]	**Mamma's Boy (70)** (JBerry) **2-8-5**(3) TEDurcan(1) (w'like: sn chsng ldrs: ev ch appr fnl f: nt qckn)	1¼	**3**	14/1	73	25
3407[5]	**Relate (70)** (MartynMeade) **2-7-11**(7) RBrisland(6) (cl up: ev ch over 1f out: no ex)	hd	**4**	14/1	68	20
4111[11]	**Arcane Star (IRE)** (APJarvis) **2-8-7** JFEgan(8) (cl up: effrt 2f out: nt qckn fnl f)	s.h	**5**	33/1	71	23
4042[12]	**Muji** (APJarvis) **2-7-13**(3) PFessey(3) (in tch: effrt over 2f out: kpt on same pce)	1¼	**6**	33/1	63	15
	Arab Gold (MissSEHall) **2-8-7** AMcGlone(14) (leggy: unf: hld up & bhd: effrt ½-wy: rdn & no imp)	1½	**7**	33/1	64	16
3905[3]	**Thistle Park** (TDBarron) **2-8-12** KDarley(4) (cl up tl rdn appr fnl f)	nk	**8**	3/1[1]	68	20
	Pas de Memoires (IRE) (MHTompkins) **2-8-8** DBiggs(10) (effrt ½-wy: nvr trbld ldrs)	hd	**9**	14/1	64	16
3610[13]	**Rio (IRE) (70)** (JBerry) **2-8-0**(5) CLowther(11) (lw: in tch: rdn ½-wy: wknd fnl 2f)	1	**10**	12/1[3]	58	10
	Ginner Morris (CBBBooth) **2-8-9** ACulhane(9) (lengthy: unf: in tch tl outpcd fnl 2f)	s.h	**11**	12/1[3]	62	14
3857[3]	**Snowballs** (MissLAPerratt) **2-8-9** JCarroll(12) (bit bkwd: sn drvn along: nvr trbld ldrs)	1	**12**	12/1[3]	59	11
4017[6]	**Mr Miyagi** (ABailey) **2-8-6** DWright(2) (in tch: drvn along ½-wy: sn btn)	4	**13**	3/1[1]	46	—
	Always Trying (MJohnston) **2-8-7** DHolland(5) (leggy: unf: spd to ½-wy: sn bhd)	nk	**14**	12/1[3]	46	—

(SP 126.4%) **14 Rn**

1m 14.85 (5.05) CSF £117.43 TOTE £27.30: £4.90 £4.70 £3.40 (£140.00) Trio £231.20; £263.81 to Newbury 19/9/97 OWNER Mr J. Hanson (MIDDLEHAM) BRED Bylon Farmers Ltd

Desert Sand, given plenty of help from the saddle, won well despite showing definite signs of greenness when seeing the front. (10/1)

Ryefield, a useful sort, looked likely to benefit from this and showed plenty. (12/1)

3869 Mamma's Boy keeps running well but never quite seems to come up with the goods. (14/1: 10/1-16/1)

3407 Relate, after almost six weeks off, ran well and ought to be all the better for it. (14/1)

Arcane Star (IRE) showed a fair amount of improvement on his run last week and is obviously learning. (33/1)

Muji is learning with experience but more time is needed. (33/1)

Arab Gold showed some ability, improving at halfway, only then to blow up. (33/1)

3905 Thistle Park is proving disappointing at the moment and found nothing once off the bit. (3/1)

3857 Snowballs (12/1: 8/1-14/1)

4017 Mr Miyagi (3/1: op 6/1)

Always Trying (12/1: 8/1-14/1)

T/Plpt: £310.30 (69.43 Tckts). T/Qdpt: £80.80 (13.94 Tckts) AA

3594-NEWBURY (L-H) (Good to firm)

Thursday September 18th

WEATHER: fine WIND: nil

4237 AMERADA MAIDEN STKS (2-Y.O) (Class D)

2-10 (2-11) **7f (straight)** £11,283.75 (£3,420.00: £1,672.50: £798.75) Stalls: High GOING minus 0.09 sec per fur (G)

				SP	RR	SF
	Dr Fong (USA) (HRACecil) **2-9-0** KFallon(5) (leggy: scope: lw: hld up: rdn over 3f out: hdwy wl over 1f out: led ins fnl f: r.o wl)	—	**1**	8/1	82+	46

				SP	RR	SF
	Distant Mirage (IRE) (PWChapple-Hyam) **2-9-0** JReid(1) (scope: a.p: rdn over 2f out: ev ch ins fnl f: r.o)	½	**2**	5/4 1	81+	45
3862 4	**Mubrik (IRE)** (JHMGosden) **2-9-0** RHills(13) (w'like: scope: led tl ins fnl f)	½	**3**	13/2 3	80	44
	Misbah (USA) (BHanbury) **2-9-0** SDrowne(8) (b.hind: w'like: scope: hld up: hdwy 2f out: one pce fnl f)	3½	**4**	33/1	72	36
	Grand Slam (IRE) (RHannon) **2-9-0** DaneO'Neill(2) (str: s.s: hdwy fnl 2f: r.o: bttr for r)	hd	**5**	33/1	72+	36
	Pelagos (FR) (RCharlton) **2-9-0** TSprake(6) (w'like: bit bkwd: no hdwy fnl 2f)	nk	**6**	16/1	71	35
3825 5	**Red Sky Charlie** (LordHuntingdon) **2-9-0** RCochrane(4) (nvr nr to chal)	¾	**7**	14/1	69	33
	Shanillo (MRChannon) **2-9-0** JFortune(15) (wl grwn: prom over 5f)	1	**8**	33/1	67	31
	Superchief (MissBSanders) **2-9-0** CRutter(12) (w'like: scope: hld up & bhd: nt clr run 2f out: stdy hdwy over 1f out: bttr for r)	¾	**9**	33/1	65+	29
	Guildhall (BJMeehan) **2-9-0** MTebbutt(11) (w'like: scope: bit bkwd: a mid div)	1½	**10**	33/1	62	26
	First Master (MissGayKelleway) **2-9-0** SSanders(10) (b: w'like: prom 5f)	2½	**11**	33/1	56	20
	Incepta (BWHills) **2-9-0** WJO'Connor(14) (w'like: scope: s.s: sn rcvd: wknd over 1f out)	2½	**12**	33/1	50	14
	Pantar (IRE) (IABalding) **2-9-0** LDettori(16) (prom over 5f)	s.h	**13**	4/1 2	50	14
	Rainmaker (MAJarvis) **2-9-0** PaulEddery(7) (str: scope: a bhd)	1¼	**14**	33/1	47	11
	Frankie Ferrari (IRE) (DRLoder) **2-8-11**(3) MHenry(17) (str: scope: bhd fnl 2f)	hd	**15**	10/1	47	11
	Chrysolite (IRE) (BWHills) **2-9-0** TQuinn(3) (w'like: a bhd)	½	**16**	33/1	46	10
3598 12	**Beauchamp Magic** (JLDunlop) **2-9-0** MRimmer(9) (lw: a bhd)	1½	**17**	33/1	43	7

(SP 139.9%) **17 Rn**

1m 27.87 (3.77) CSF £17.56 TOTE £3.50: £1.10 £1.50 £2.80 (£7.20) Trio £9.00 OWNER The Thoroughbred Corporation (NEWMARKET) BRED Prestonwood Farm Inc

Dr Fong (USA), a $425,000 colt, is out of a winning sprinter in the States. Described by Fallon as a lovely horse with a good attitiude, there was plenty to like about the way he picked up the leaders. He would appear to have a bright future. (8/1: 4/1-10/1)

Distant Mirage (IRE), a 210,000 guineas half-brother to mile winner Roses In The Snow, was well touted beforehand, and showed more than enough to win a race. (5/4)

3862 Mubrik (IRE) had the advantage of previous racecourse experience, but seems to be going the right way. (13/2: 4/1-8/1)

Misbah (USA), a $175,000 first foal of a mare who won at up to seven furlongs in the USA, made a promising enough start to his career. (33/1)

Grand Slam (IRE), a half-brother to a winner in Ireland, is out of a mile juvenile winner, also from the Emerald Isle, who comes from the family of Ardross. He will know more next time. (33/1)

Pelagos (FR), a half-brother to mile winner Twosixtythreewest, should come on for the outing. (16/1)

Superchief, the first foal of an unraced mare, has already been gelded, but showed enough to suggest he is one to keep an eye on. (33/1)

Pantar (IRE) (4/1: 3/1-9/2)

Frankie Ferrari (IRE) (10/1: 5/1-12/1)

4238 DOUBLEPRINT ARC TRIAL STKS (Listed) (3-Y.O+) (Class A)

2-40 (2-40) **1m 3f 5y** £31,433.75 (£11,465.00: £5,607.50: £2,412.50: £1,081.25) Stalls: Low GOING minus 0.09 sec per fur (G)

				SP	RR	SF
4005 3	**Posidonas (118)** (PFICole) **5-9-2** TQuinn(5) (lw: hld up: hdwy over 4f out: rdn over 2f out: led ins fnl f: all out)	—	**1**	8/1 3	119	80
3374a 2	**Arabian Story (109)** (LordHuntingdon) **4-9-2** KFallon(3) (b: hld up: chsd ldr 7f out: rdn over 3f out: rallied over 1f out: ev ch ins fnl f: r.o)	s.h	**2**	11/2 2	119	80
3050*	**Swain (IRE) (131)** (SbinSuroor) **5-9-9** LDettori(1) (hld up in rr: hdwy over 3f out: led over 1f out tl ins fnl f: r.o)	s.h	**3**	1/2 1	126	87
3741 7	**Sunbeam Dance (USA) (92)** (SbinSuroor) **3-8-9** RHills(4) (led: clr 7f out: hdd over 1f out: one pce)	3½	**4**	100/1	114?	68
3983*	**Clerkenwell (USA) (114)** (MRStoute) **4-9-2** JReid(2) (lw: chsd ldr 4f: wknd over 3f out)	6	**5**	9/1	105	66

(SP 104.2%) **5 Rn**

2m 18.97 (1.77) CSF £38.59 TOTE £7.30: £2.50 £1.90 (£19.20) OWNER Mr Athos Christodoulou (WHATCOMBE) BRED A. Christodoulou

WEIGHT FOR AGE 3yo-7lb

4005 Posidonas fulfilled the promise of his comeback race, having wrenched muscles in the spring, and was then held up by fast ground during the summer. Connections are keen to go for the Arc, and there is no doubting he will go to Longchamp a fresh horse. (8/1: op 5/1)

3374a Arabian Story, still to be confirmed a definite runner in the Melbourne Cup, must have gone a long way to booking his passage with this first-class performance. (11/2)

3050* Swain (IRE), on ground plenty fast enough for him, was said by Dettori to have taken a blow just after striking the front. Although pushed out to 10/1 by the bookmakers, he still remains on target for the Arc, a race in which he has been placed for the last two seasons. (1/2)

3144 Sunbeam Dance (USA), a pacemaker for Swain, ran so well that his rider was looking to see where the others were coming to the quarter-mile pole. Tried in a visor last time, he should not be hard to place on this evidence. (100/1)

3983* Clerkenwell (USA), vulnerable over this shorter trip, apparently had a corn two days ago, and may now go for next weekend's Cumberland Lodge at Ascot. (9/1: op 5/1)

4239 DUBAI AIRPORT WORLD TROPHY STKS (Listed) (3-Y.O+) (Class A)

3-10 (3-12) **5f 34y** £31,795.00 (£11,905.00: £5,827.50: £2,512.50: £1,131.25: £578.75) Stalls: High GOING minus 0.09 sec per fur (G)

				SP	RR	SF
3724 5	**Eveningperformance (107)** (HCandy) **6-8-8** CRutter(5) (swtg: mde all: rdn over 1f out: r.o wl)	—	**1**	9/1 3	116	77
4100*	**Dashing Blue (105)** (IABalding) **4-8-13** TQuinn(6) (a.p: chsd wnr fnl 2f: r.o)	1	**2**	7/1 2	118	79
4098*	**Bollin Joanne (107)** (TDEasterby) **4-8-8** KFallon(14) (b: b.off hind: a.p stands' side: hrd rdn & hung lft over 1f out: r.o)	1¼	**3**	2/1 1	109	70
4098 9	**Croft Pool (108)** (JAGlover) **6-9-4** TSprake(16) (hld up: rdn over 2f out: hdwy over 1f out: r.o)	1	**4**	40/1	116	77
4062 3	**Rambling Bear (107)** (MBlanshard) **4-8-13** JReid(15) (lw: hld up & bhd: hdwy over 1f out: r.o)	nk	**5**	14/1	110	71
4098 5	**Easycall (108)** (BJMeehan) **3-8-12b1** MTebbutt(2) (prom tl wknd fnl f)	hd	**6**	20/1	110	70
	Tipsy Creek (USA) (BHanbury) **3-8-12** RHills(3) (b.hind: lw: no hdwy fnl 2f)	¾	**7**	12/1	107	67
3914 4	**Moon Strike (FR) (98)** (PHowling) **7-8-13** RCochrane(11) (b: dwlt: nrst fin)	¾	**8**	25/1	105	66
4203a*	**Midnight Escape (102)** (CFWall) **4-9-2** 3x SSanders(12) (swtg: prom stands' side over 3f)	s.h	**9**	16/1	108	69
4100 19	**Sylva Paradise (IRE) (98)** (CEBrittain) **4-8-13** MRimmer(7) (swtg: bhd fnl 2f)	1¼	**10**	66/1	101	62
4098 6	**Brave Edge (106)** (RHannon) **6-8-13** DaneO'Neill(8) (nvr nrr)	1	**11**	40/1	98	59
4100 11	**Patsy Grimes (90)** (JSMoore) **7-8-8** WJO'Connor(4) (rdn over 2f out: sn bhd)	¾	**12**	66/1	91	52
3724 4	**Cyrano's Lad (IRE) (113)** (CADwyer) **8-8-13** JFortune(1) (prom: rdn over 2f out: wknd over 1f out)	2½	**13**	10/1	88	49
4098 2	**Almaty (IRE) (108)** (JHMGosden) **4-8-13v** LDettori(9) (lw: prom over 3f)	¾	**14**	9/1 3	86	47

				SP	RR	SF
4001a[3]	**Hever Golf Rose (107)** (TJNaughton) **6-8-11** PaulEddery(13) (prom over 2f)	1	**15**	16/1	80	41
3111[6]	**Deep Finesse (110)** (MAJarvis) **3-9-1** SDrowne(10) (swtg: s.i.s: sn rcvrd: rdn 3f out: sn wknd)	¾	**16**	20/1	83	43

(SP 122.3%) **16 Rn**

60.66 secs (0.46) CSF £60.18 TOTE £10.70: £2.90 £2.70 £1.40 (£34.10) Trio £51.40 OWNER Mrs David Blackburn (WANTAGE) BRED Mrs R. D. Peacock
WEIGHT FOR AGE 3yo-1lb

3724 Eveningperformance has taken time to come to hand this season, but impressed her trainer so much that impending retirement to the paddocks could be put on hold, and she may now go for the Prix de L'Abbaye. (9/1: 6/1-10/1)
4100* Dashing Blue ran yet another fine race, and was up against a very useful performer. (7/1: 5/1-8/1)
4098* Bollin Joanne continues in top form, and knuckled down well despite giving her rider problems in the later stages. (2/1)
3001a Croft Pool put up by far his best performance since winning the Temple Stakes on his seasonal reappearance, having finished nine lengths behind the third on 2lb worse terms at Doncaster last week. (40/1)
4062 Rambling Bear settled much better in this strongly-run event, but is the type who is hard to catch right. (14/1)
4098 Easycall, 2lb better off than when finishing four lengths behind Bollin Joanne last week, did not get home in the first-time blinkers. (20/1)
Tipsy Creek (USA) was making a belated reappearance, having suffered a hock injury in the spring. (12/1)

4240 DUBAI DUTY FREE CUP STKS (Listed) (3-Y.O+) (Class A)

3-40 (3-41) **7f (straight)** £32,955.00 (£12,345.00: £6,047.50: £2,612.50: £1,181.25: £608.75) Stalls: High GOING minus 0.09 sec per fur (G)

				SP	RR	SF
1596[3]	**Russian Revival (USA) (110)** (JHMGosden) **4-9-0** LDettori(6) (led over 5f out: shkn up ins fnl f: comf)	—	**1**	8/1	123	78
3728*	**Hidden Meadow (115)** (IABalding) **3-8-11** TSprake(4) (lw: led over 1f: rdn & ev ch over 1f out: nt qckn)	¾	**2**	11/2	121	73
2009[2]	**Centre Stalls (IRE) (116)** (RFJohnsonHoughton) **4-9-0** TQuinn(9) (swtg: hld up: rdn & hdwy over 2f out: one pce fnl f)	2½	**3**	9/2[3]	116	71
2677*	**Bint Albaadiya (USA) (108)** (MRStoute) **3-8-6** JReid(1) (hld up: rdn over 2f out: one pce)	nk	**4**	7/2[1]	110	62
3447[5]	**Soviet State (USA) (99)** (PWChapple-Hyam) **3-8-11** PaulEddery(10) (swtg: hld up & bhd: hdwy over 1f out: nvr nrr)	1¼	**5**	33/1	112	64
3423*	**Neuwest (USA) (102)** (RAkehurst) **5-9-0** SSanders(11) (lw: prom: rdn over 2f out: wknd over 1f out)	nk	**6**	16/1	111	66
3728[5]	**Hattab (IRE) (103)** (PTWalwyn) **3-8-11** RHills(2) (lw: hld up: lost pl 4f out: n.d after)	3½	**7**	16/1	103	55
4011[6]	**Muchea (115)** (MRChannon) **3-8-11** JFortune(3) (lw: a bhd)	1¾	**8**	12/1	99	51
3649[4]	**World Premier (96)** (CEBrittain) **4-9-0** DaneO'Neill(8) (lw: prom 5f)	¾	**9**	33/1	98	53
4003[6]	**Omaha City (IRE) (105)** (BGubby) **3-8-11** RCochrane(7) (s.s: a bhd)	5	**10**	33/1	86	38
1541a[4]	**Yalaietanee (120)** (MRStoute) **3-9-0** KFallon(5) (lw: sn prom: rdn over 4f out: wknd over 2f out)	6	**11**	4/1[2]	76	28

(SP 115.2%) **11 Rn**

1m 25.18 (1.08) CSF £45.20 TOTE £7.80: £2.20 £1.70 £1.70 (£29.10) Trio £32.40 OWNER Maktoum Al Maktoum (NEWMARKET) BRED Swettenham Stud
WEIGHT FOR AGE 3yo-3lb

1596 Russian Revival (USA), transferred out of the Godolphin operation to make way for some new two-year olds, produced an impressive display. He hardly came off the bridle and will now go for next week's Diadem at Ascot providing there is some cut in the ground. (8/1)
3728* Hidden Meadow did nothing wrong but simply met one too smart on the day. (11/2: 7/2-6/1)
2009 Centre Stalls (IRE) really needs a mile on ground as fast as this. (9/2)
2677* Bint Albaadiya (USA), stepping up from six, is bred to stay a mile and could easily have found this ground a bit lively. (7/2)
3447 Soviet State (USA), ridden to get this extra furlong, would have been 11lb better off with the winner had this been a handicap. (33/1)
3423* Neuwest (USA) had a tough task here and would have been receiving 8lb off the winner in a handicap. (16/1)

4241 TRIPLEPRINT H'CAP (0-105) (3-Y.O+) (Class B)

4-10 (4-10) **2m** £14,070.00 (£4,260.00: £2,080.00: £990.00) Stalls: High GOING minus 0.09 sec per fur (G)

				SP	RR	SF
2819a[5]	**Jiyush (102)** (EALDunlop) **4-9-11** RHills(4) (swtg: hld up: led on bit over 2f out: r.o wl)	—	**1**	9/1	115	74
3902[3]	**Grey Shot (105)** (IABalding) **5-10-0** LDettori(10) (a.p: chsd wnr fnl 2f: no imp)	2½	**2**	6/1[2]	116	75
3805[3]	**Go Britannia (90)** (DRLoder) **4-8-13** RCochrane(5) (hld up: hdwy 2f out: styd on fnl f)	1¾	**3**	9/1	99	58
4123a[3]	**Cuff Link (IRE) (95)** (MajorWRHern) **7-9-4** PaulEddery(7) (lw: chsd ldr 9f: rdn over 3f out: one pce)	2½	**4**	9/1	101	60
4101[3]	**Shaft of Light (93)** (LordHuntingdon) **5-9-2v** TQuinn(3) (lw: led: hdd over 2f out: sn hrd rdn: wknd ins fnl f)	1	**5**	3/1[1]	98	57
4101[4]	**Premier Night (81)** (SDow) **4-8-4ow2** SSanders(1) (no hdwy fnl 3f)	2½	**6**	8/1	84	41
4101[9]	**State Fair (100)** (BWHills) **3-8-11** JReid(9) (a bhd)	3	**7**	16/1	100	47
3705[11]	**Raffles Rooster (80)** (AGNewcombe) **5-8-3** SDrowne(6) (hld up: hdwy on ins over 2f out: wknd wl over 1f out)	½	**8**	13/2[3]	79	38
4101[10]	**Fletcher (90)** (HMorrison) **3-7-12(3)** RFfrench(2) (lw: a bhd)	7	**9**	20/1	82	29
4156[3]	**Star Rage (IRE) (79)** (MJohnston) **7-8-2** NAdams(8) (s.i.s: hdwy 7f out: rdn 5f out: wknd 3f out)	¾	**10**	8/1	71	30

(SP 115.5%) **10 Rn**

3m 29.87 (5.67) CSF £55.98 CT £458.54 TOTE £7.70: £2.90 £2.00 £2.40 (£14.30) Trio £40.00 OWNER Mr Hamdan Al Maktoum (NEWMARKET) BRED Shadwell Estate Company Limited
WEIGHT FOR AGE 3yo-12lb

2819a Jiyush, given a break after disappointing in France last time, bounced back to form with a bang and does seem at his best at this time year. (9/1)
3902 Grey Shot found the winner travelling far too strongly and had to content with playing second fiddle. (6/1)
3805 Go Britannia does seem to find two miles the bare minimum these days. (9/1)
4123a Cuff Link (IRE) definitely prefers a stiffer test of stamina than he encountered here. (9/1)
4101 Shaft of Light, again 6lb higher than when scoring at Epsom, is set to go up a further 1lb and did not prove he really stays two miles. (3/1)
4101 Premier Night, a short head behind Shaft of Light on the same terms at Doncaster last week, had previously proved he stays two miles. (8/1)
4156 Star Rage (IRE) (8/1: 6/1-9/1)

4242 BONUSPRINT H'CAP (0-85) (3-Y.O F) (Class D)

4-40 (4-45) **1m 2f 6y** £14,915.00 (£4,520.00: £2,210.00: £1,055.00) Stalls: Low GOING minus 0.09 sec per fur (G)

				SP	RR	SF
4172[2]	**Arriving (65)** (JWHills) **3-7-12(3)** MHenry(17) (hld up & bhd: gd hdwy over 1f out: str run to ld nr fin)	—	**1**	16/1	77	53
3893*	**Shaska (79)** (JHMGosden) **3-9-1** LDettori(2) (swtg: hld up: n.m.r over 2f out: hdwy over 1f out: led wl ins fnl f: hdd nr fin)	nk	**2**	7/1[2]	91	67

				SP	RR	SF
4015^{5}	**Yabint El Sultan (83)** (BAMcMahon) **3-9-5** JFortune(15) (lw: a.p: led 3f out: clr over 1f out: hdd wl ins fnl f)	2	**3**	14/1	91	67
3140^{4}	**Silver Whirl (USA) (67)** (RCharlton) **3-8-3** TSprake(11) (a.p: rdn over 2f out: one pce)	1¼	**4**	20/1	73	49
3773^{5}	**Gift Token (82)** (MajorDNChappell) **3-9-1v**(3) RFfrench(14) (lw: hld up & bhd: nt clr run over 3f out, over 2f out & wl over 1f out: swtchd rt: gd hdwy fnl f: fin wl)	s.h	**5**	25/1	88+	64
3891^{2}	**My Valentina (74)** (BWHills) **3-8-10** PaulEddery(16) (swtg: hld up: nt clr run over 3f out & over 2f out: hdwy whn hmpd over 1f out: one pce)	1½	**6**	12/1	78	54
3786^{2}	**Wishing Stone (USA) (82)** (EALDunlop) **3-9-4** KFallon(10) (swtg: rdn over 3f out: hdwy over 1f out: nvr nrr)	d.h	**6**	7/1 ^{2}	88	64
4002^{10}	**Noble Dane (IRE) (68)** (PWHarris) **3-8-4** CRutter(9) (hld up & plld hrd: nvr nr to chal)	nk	**8**	25/1	71	47
3803^{6}	**Kalinka (IRE) (83)** (PFICole) **3-9-5** TQuinn(6) (lw: hld up: hdwy & nt clr run over 1f out: eased whn btn ins fnl f)	½	**9**	14/1	86	62
3807*	**Summer Dance (85)** (MRStoute) **3-9-7** JReid(7) (hld up & plld hrd: rdn over 3f out: hdwy over 2f out: wknd fnl f)	nk	**10**	7/4 ^{1}	87	63
3916^{16}	**Happy Go Lucky (77)** (RJO'Sullivan) **3-8-13** DaneO'Neill(8) (swtg: prom: rdn over 3f out: eased whn btn fnl f)	nk	**11**	50/1	79	55
3390^{3}	**Come Together (68)** (DWPArbuthnot) **3-8-4**ow1 SSanders(5) (mid div whn hmpd over 1f out: nt rcvr)	4	**12**	33/1	63	38
3903*	**Nightlark (IRE) (82)** (DRLoder) **3-9-4** RCochrane(12) (prom tl wknd 2f out)	nk	**13**	9/1 ^{3}	77	53
3803^{9}	**Marie Dora (FR) (80)** (IABalding) **3-9-2v**^{1} MTebbutt(3) (led 7f: wknd 2f out)	9	**14**	25/1	60	36
3928^{4}	**Sun Alert (USA) (60)** (MJPolglase) **3-7-10v** NAdams(4) (b.off hind: swtg: chsd ldr over 2f: wknd 3f out)	hd	**15**	50/1	40	16
4015^{2}	**Sellette (IRE) (82)** (DHaydnJones) **3-9-4** SDrowne(13) (rdn over 3f out: bhd fnl 2f)	1½	**16**	20/1	60	36
3917^{3}	**Khazinat El Dar (USA) (74)** (MajorWRHern) **3-8-10** RHills(1) (bhd fnl 2f)	3½	**17**	12/1	46	22

(SP 133.9%) **17 Rn**

2m 7.09 (3.09) CSF £112.23 CT £1,512.93 TOTE £18.50: £2.30 £2.50 £3.90 £3.80 (£62.00) Trio £549.80 OWNER Wyck Hall Stud (LAMBOURN) BRED L. H. J. Ward

4172 Arriving managed to come from behind in a race which had more than its fair share of trouble. (16/1)
3893* Shaska did nothing wrong here and perhaps her earlier idiosyncrasies were purely down to greenness. (7/1)
4015 Yabint El Sultan seemed to have stolen this but could not hold on off a mark 9lb higher than her handicap win at Chester. (14/1)
3140 Silver Whirl (USA) may do better when reverting to a mile and a half. (20/1)
3773 Gift Token encountered more problems than the Chancellor on Black Wednesday and has to be considered unlucky. (25/1)
3891 My Valentina, up 2lb, was still 7lb better off with the third than when beaten four lengths at Chester and met even more trouble in running this time. (12/1: 8/1-14/1)
3786 Wishing Stone (USA), raised another 1lb, did not seem inconvenienced by this longer trip and it may be the handicapper has her measure. (7/1)
3807* Summer Dance is bred to stay but ran too freely over this extra quarter-mile. (7/4)

T/Jkpt: Not won; £37,411.73 to Newbury 19/9/97. T/Plpt: £384.60 (99.76 Tckts). T/Qdpt: £39.90 (67.04 Tckts) KH

4223-YARMOUTH (L-H) (Firm)
Thursday September 18th
WEATHER: fine & sunny WIND: slt across

4243 GROSVENOR CASINO GREAT YARMOUTH MAIDEN H'CAP (0-60) (3-Y.O+) (Class F)
2-20 (2-24) **1m 3y** £3,886.00 (£1,168.00: £564.00: £262.00) Stalls: High GOING minus 0.51 sec per fur (F)

				SP	RR	SF
3321^{3}	**Shark (IRE) (42)** (KAMorgan) **4-8-10** OPears(2) (lw: led after 1f: hrd drvn over 1f out: r.o wl)	—	**1**	16/1	55	26
3980^{5}	**Clouds Hill (FR) (53)** (RHannon) **4-9-7v** RPerham(20) (lw: led 1f: rdn over 1f out: unable qckn fnl f)	1½	**2**	4/1 ^{1}	63	34
3937^{7}	**Forest Robin (47)** (MrsJRRamsden) **4-9-1** MWigham(4) (dwlt: swtchd rt sn after s: hdwy over 1f out: r.o strly fnl f)	¾	**3**	10/1	56	27
3558^{3}	**Tabasco Jazz (58)** (BJMeehan) **3-9-1**(7) GHannon(19) (bhd: hdwy over 2f out: r.o wl ins fnl f)	nk	**4**	14/1	66	33
2019^{14}	**Godmersham Park (55)** (PSFelgate) **5-9-9** GDuffield(12) (bit bkwd: prom: rdn wl over 1f out: kpt on)	nk	**5**	10/1	62	33
3860^{15}	**Lochlass (IRE) (43)** (SPCWoods) **3-8-7b**^{1} GBardwell(18) (bhd: hdwy fnl 2f: nrst fin)	nk	**6**	25/1	50	17
4008^{3}	**Great Chief (42)** (BobJones) **4-8-10** NDay(14) (hld up: hdwy 2f out: r.o u.p ins fnl f)	s.h	**7**	7/1 ^{3}	49	20
3592^{3}	**Tezaab (46)** (BHanbury) **3-8-10** JStack(16) (trckd ldrs: hrd drvn 2f out: r.o one pce)	nk	**8**	10/1	52	19
3478^{8}	**Talib (USA) (60)** (DMorley) **3-9-10** GCarter(13) (hld up in tch: effrt 2f out: sn rdn: no imp)	¾	**9**	9/1	65	32
3854^{3}	**Miss Riviera Rose (46)** (GWragg) **3-8-10** MHills(10) (hld up: hdwy over 2f out: wknd wl over 1f out)	nk	**10**	5/1 ^{2}	50	17
3685^{4}	**Baubigny (USA) (53)** (MRChannon) **3-9-0**(3) PPMurphy(7) (hld up: rdn & hdwy 2f out: nt clr run wl over 1f out: nt rcvr)	3	**11**	14/1	51	18
3721^{4}	**Expialiodoocius (58)** (JRFanshawe) **3-9-8** WRyan(1) (a bhd)	½	**12**	14/1	55	22
3205^{8}	**Balladara (IRE) (50)** (RHannon) **3-9-0b**^{1} GHind(17) (a bhd: rdn 3f out: no imp)	3½	**13**	25/1	40	7
4043^{3}	**Attarikh (IRE) (45)** (MrsALMKing) **4-8-13** JQuinn(3) (a in rr)	2	**14**	16/1	31	2
1238^{9}	**Joli's Prince (46)** (CMurray) **3-8-10** NicolaHowarth(9) (a in rr)	1¾	**15**	20/1	29	—
3762^{6}	**Poker Princess (50)** (MBell) **3-9-0** MFenton(8) (chsd ldrs over 5f: sn lost tch)	7	**16**	16/1	19	—
3864^{13}	**Shaded (IRE) (49)** (SDow) **3-8-10**(3) DO'Donohoe(6) (lw: hld up: hdwy ½-wy: rdn over 2f out: no imp)	3	**17**	20/1	12	—
225^{7}	**Verinder's Gift (55)** (DrJDScargill) **3-9-2**(3) DGriffiths(5) (a in rr)	s.h	**18**	33/1	17	—
4112^{17}	**Double March (60)** (KTIvory) **4-9-9**(5) GFaulkner(11) (prom over 5f: sn wknd: t.o)	5	**19**	25/1	12	—

(SP 148.1%) **19 Rn**

1m 38.5 (2.50) CSF £78.73 CT £685.49 TOTE £31.00: £6.40 £1.50 £3.00 £4.20 (£195.80) Trio £388.90; £498.56 to Newbury 19/9/97 OWNER Mr M. J. Harmer (MELTON MOWBRAY) BRED James Mulcahy
WEIGHT FOR AGE 3yo-4lb

3321 Shark (IRE) has been unable to win a seller recently but he succeeded in making all on this occasion to open his account. (16/1)
3980 Clouds Hill (FR) had far more use made of him and he was a live factor entering the final furlong, but the winner kept finding more and he had to admit he had met his match. (4/1)
3937 Forest Robin, switched towards the stands' side soon after the start, weaved his way through in the closing stages and finished best of all. He does seem to be getting it together. (10/1: 7/1-12/1)
3558 Tabasco Jazz, buried in the pack, was putting her best foot forward in the closing stages and there is certainly a race to be won with her. (14/1)
1501 Godmersham Park ran much better over this slightly longer trip and he is sure to strip fitter with this first outing in three months under his belt. (10/1)

3592 Lochlass (IRE), restrained in her first-time blinkers, burst through inside the last furlong and it would seem she is capable of finding a race or two. (25/1)
4008 Great Chief, much more effective when ridden from off the pace, was running on well in the closing stages and his action to post would suggest he will benefit from more yielding ground. (7/1)
3592 Tezaab (10/1: 7/1-12/1)

4244 E.B.F. FREETHORPE MAIDEN STKS (2-Y.O) (Class D)

2-50 (2-50) **1m 3y** £3,512.10 (£1,048.80: £501.40: £227.70) Stalls: High GOING minus 0.51 sec per fur (F)

Form	Horse	Dist	Pos	SP	RR	SF
3874a[4]	**Dower House** (WJarvis) **2-9-0** WRyan(1) (lw: chsd ldr: led wl over 1f out: pushed out)	—	1	5/4[1]	84+	37
4105[5]	**Plan-B** (JHMGosden) **2-9-0** GHind(2) (led tl wl over 1f out: kpt on: no ch w wnr)	1¼	2	7/4[2]	82	35
4052[3]	**Goldfill** (WAO'Gorman) **2-8-9** EmmaO'Gorman(6) (hdwy 3f out: styd on ins fnl f)	4	3	14/1	69	22
3861[5]	**Desert Spa (USA)** (PWHarris) **2-9-0** MHills(7) (lw: trckd ldrs: wknd 2f out)	5	4	8/1[3]	64	17
3973[8]	**Yanshan** (BobJones) **2-9-0** NDay(8) (nvr gng pce of ldrs)	7	5	33/1	50	3
4064[19]	**Altitude (IRE)** (SirMarkPrescott) **2-9-0** GDuffield(3) (chsd ldrs: rdn after 3f: wknd over 2f out)	½	6	33/1	49	2
	Ardleigh Charmer (CADwyer) **2-8-11**(3) DO'Donohoe(4) (w'like: leggy: s.s: a bhd: t.o)	12	7	33/1	25	—
	Shohra Wa Jaah (MAJarvis) **2-9-0** GCarter(5) (lt-f: unf: chsd ldrs: rdn 3f out: sn wknd: t.o)	nk	8	9/1	24	—
				(SP 117.4%)	**8 Rn**	

1m 37.8 (1.80) CSF £3.34 TOTE £2.30: £1.10 £1.30 £1.60 (£1.50) OWNER Lord Howard de Walden (NEWMARKET) BRED Lord Howard de Walden
3874a Dower House has been highly tried but he won this cosily enough and it could be the first of many. (5/4: evens-11/8)
4105 Plan-B, a nice, easy mover, got off on terms this time and set the pace. Doing his best to respond when the winner threw down his challenge, he was not knocked about when held and he should soon be able to go one better. (7/4)
4052 Goldfill always looked to be struggling to keep tabs on the leaders but she stayed on pleasingly inside the distance and will not always have to contend with such useful rivals. (14/1)
3861 Desert Spa (USA), intent on keeping within striking range of the leading pair, probably took too much out of himself and he had shot his bolt below the distance. (8/1)

4245 LOTTIE AND ALBERT BOTTON MEMORIAL NURSERY H'CAP (0-85) (2-Y.O) (Class E)

3-20 (3-20) **1m 3y** £3,356.25 (£1,005.00: £482.50: £221.25) Stalls: High GOING minus 0.51 sec per fur (F)

Form	Horse	Dist	Pos	SP	RR	SF
3650[12]	**Sick As A Parrot (70)** (CADwyer) **2-8-6v**[1] MHills(3) (mde all: shkn up over 1f out: r.o wl)	—	1	3/1[1]	72	18
4044[8]	**Rebalza (IRE) (67)** (JMPEustace) **2-8-3** JTate(9) (a chsng ldrs: effrt u.p over 1f out: kpt on wl fnl f)	¾	2	7/1[3]	68	14
3912[3]	**Colleville (85)** (MAJarvis) **2-9-7** WRyan(5) (hld up: hdwy over 2f out: hrd rdn & one pce fnl f)	1¾	3	3/1[1]	82	28
3386[8]	**Festival Flyer (67)** (RBoss) **2-8-3** NDay(10) (hld up & bhd: hdwy over 2f out: hrd rdn & no ex fnl f)	1¼	4	14/1	62	8
3755[5]	**Captain McCloy (USA) (63)** (MrsJRRamsden) **2-7-13** JQuinn(8) (hld up: swtchd lft 3f out: hdwy fnl 2f: nt pce to chal)	d.h	4	9/2[2]	58	4
3757[5]	**Phantom Waters (68)** (RFJohnsonHoughton) **2-8-4** GCarter(1) (b.hind: prom: rdn over 2f out: grad fdd)	nk	6	16/1	62	8
4044[13]	**No Shame (66)** (JGSmyth-Osbourne) **2-8-2** GBardwell(7) (lw: sn drvn along: a bhd)	2½	7	20/1	55	1
3990[14]	**Mamora Bay (IRE) (70)** (MHTompkins) **2-8-1**(5) RMullen(2) (lw: in tch: rdn over 3f out: sn wknd: t.o)	6	8	12/1	47	—
3607[5]	**Prodigal Son (IRE) (70)** (RJRWilliams) **2-8-6** GDuffield(6) (prom: rdn 3f out: sn wknd: t.o)	1½	9	14/1	44	—
				(SP 112.4%)	**9 Rn**	

1m 39.0 (3.00) CSF £21.49 CT £60.68 TOTE £3.50: £1.30 £1.80 £1.80 (£10.00) Trio £20.20 OWNER Mrs Shelley Dwyer (NEWMARKET) BRED Helshaw Grange Farms Ltd, Miss Powner & A. Hampton
OFFICIAL EXPLANATION **Sick As A Parrot: regarding the improvement in form compared with his previous run at York, the trainer explained that the colt became very unbalanced early on and was unable to hold his position last time out.**
3387 Sick As A Parrot decided on more forceful tactics over this slightly longer trip and, quickening up to hold a healthy advantage into the final furlong, was always proving too strong for his pursuers. (3/1)
3307 Rebalza (IRE) ran a sound race in defeat and, as he was pegging back the winner towards the finish, there is no reason why he will not stay further. (7/1)
3912 Colleville, forced to concede weight all round, turned in a very game performance and, when she is given a chance by the handicapper, she should be able to return to winning ways. (3/1)
3755 Captain McCloy (USA) had finished behind the runner-up before but he did close the gap on these better terms and all is not lost yet. (9/2)
938 Festival Flyer is a half-brother to a mile winner and, in running his best race yet, showed that stamina could be his strong suit. (14/1)
3757 Phantom Waters, ridden along to hold her pitch over two furlongs out, found the task beyond her, though to her credit she did not drop away until approaching the final furlong. (16/1)
3607 Prodigal Son (IRE) (14/1: 10/1-16/1)

4246 GROSVENOR CASINOS STAYERS H'CAP (0-95) (3-Y.O+) (Class C)

3-50 (3-50) **2m 2f 51y** £5,361.30 (£1,598.40: £762.20: £344.10) Stalls: Low GOING minus 0.51 sec per fur (F)

Form	Horse	Dist	Pos	SP	RR	SF
3805*	**Motet (85)** (GWragg) **3-9-10** MHills(4) (lw: hld up & bhd: hdwy on ins to ld over 1f out: r.o wl)	—	1	7/2[2]	96	57
3255[6]	**Etterby Park (USA) (70)** (MJohnston) **4-9-8** JFanning(1) (a.p: led over 2f out tl appr fnl f: sn rdn: no ex)	1½	2	13/2[3]	80	54
3549[3]	**City Hall (IRE) (70)** (MRStoute) **3-8-9v**[1] WRyan(3) (hld up: hdwy over 3f out: sn drvn along: styd on wl fnl f)	hd	3	7/2[2]	80	41
3890[5]	**Unchanged (60)** (CEBrittain) **5-8-12** JQuinn(2) (lw: hld up: gd hdwy 2f out: rdn & one pce fnl f)	2	4	7/1	68	42
4101[5]	**Sea Victor (71)** (JLHarris) **5-9-9** GDuffield(5) (chsd ldr over 12f: rdn over 3f out: sn btn)	3½	5	9/4[1]	76	50
3935[2]	**Jamaican Flight (USA) (72)** (MrsSLamyman) **4-9-10** MWigham(6) (lw: led tl over 2f out: sn rdn & wknd)	3½	6	15/2	74	48
				(SP 112.8%)	**6 Rn**	

3m 57.2 (9.80 under best) (2.60) CSF £23.40 TOTE £4.00: £2.10 £3.00 (£18.40) OWNER Mr A. E. Oppenheimer (NEWMARKET) BRED Hascombe and Valiant Studs
WEIGHT FOR AGE 3yo-13lb
3805* Motet, a much improved performer since he has tackled extended trips, won this readily and, with only 7st 10lb to carry in the Cesarewitch, he could be more than a lively outsider. (7/2)
3255 Etterby Park (USA) tried to slip his field entering the last quarter-mile but he failed to get away on ground plenty fast enough for him and was tapped for toe when the final battle did develop. (13/2)
3549 City Hall (IRE) wore a visor for the first time and did look a serious threat when making stealthy progress but it was not until well inside the final furlong that he really found top gear. (7/2)

Unchanged stays this trip well and she can act on the ground, but she hardly had sufficient use made of her here and was unable to get to terms despite staying on. (7/1)
4101 Sea Victor played a prominent role until the pace lifted early in the straight and, once off the bridle, he found disappointingly little. (9/4)
3935 Jamaican Flight (USA) is a confirmed front-runner and he held the call for most of the way but, once the race began to take shape, he quite simply found himself out of his depth. (15/2)

4247 GROSVENOR CASINO GREAT YARMOUTH CONDITIONS STKS (2-Y.O) (Class C)

4-20 (4-20) **6f 3y** £4,807.60 (£1,685.60: £807.80: £329.00) Stalls: High GOING minus 0.51 sec per fur (F)

				SP	RR	SF
3497*	**Raise A King** (JWPayne) **2-8-13** GCarter(4) (hld up in rr: swtchd lft & hdwy wl over 1f out: rdn to ld wl ins fnl f)	—	**1**	11/4[2]	89+	40
4006*	**Shawdon (92)** (SirMarkPrescott) **2-9-3** GDuffield(1) (led: rdn over 1f out: hdd wl ins fnl f)	1¼	**2**	9/2[3]	90	41
3726[W]	**Designer (USA)** (JHMGosden) **2-8-11** GHind(5) (chsd ldr: ev ch appr fnl f: sn rdn: unable qckn)	½	**3**	4/5[1]	82	33
3934[3]	**Wrekin Pilot (92)** (RHannon) **2-9-1** RPerham(3) (hld up: effrt over 2f out: sn rdn & outpcd: t.o)	11	**4**	15/2	57	8
				(SP 112.2%)	**4 Rn**	

1m 11.9 (1.00) CSF £12.96 TOTE £3.60 (£5.50) OWNER Mr Marwan Tabsh (NEWMARKET) BRED Mrs A. E. Sigsworth
3497* Raise A King, stepping up in class, found all that was needed when he was asked to quicken and he does look a progressive sort. (11/4)
4006* Shawdon adopted the forceful tactics that were successful at Epsom but the winner prove much too good for him when the chips were down. (9/2: op 3/1)
3219 Designer (USA) was fancied to outclass his rivals but he lacked a change of gear inside the final furlong and it may be that he was still in need of racecourse experience. (4/5)
3934 Wrekin Pilot (15/2: 5/1-8/1)

4248 GROSVENOR CASINO MEMBERS H'CAP (0-60) (I) (3-Y.O+) (Class F)

4-50 (4-52) **6f 3y** £3,249.00 (£972.00: £466.00: £213.00) Stalls: High GOING minus 0.51 sec per fur (F)

				SP	RR	SF
3693*	**Gay Breeze (43)** (PSFelgate) **4-8-4**(7) JFowle(20) (mde all: rdn & hld on gamely cl home)	—	**1**	5/1[1]	54	37
4008[13]	**Oxbane (49)** (CADwyer) **3-8-12**(3) DO'Donohoe(15) (hld up: hdwy 2f out: rdn & hung lft appr fnl f: r.o wl cl home)	¾	**2**	14/1	58	39
4112[6]	**Maladerie (IRE) (58)** (MRChannon) **3-9-10** MHills(18) (chsd ldrs: effrt appr fnl f: r.o)	¾	**3**	6/1[3]	65	46
3910[4]	**Opening Range (41)** (NEBerry) **6-8-9** WRyan(12) (trckd ldrs: hdwy & ev ch over 1f out: unable qckn)	hd	**4**	5/1[1]	48	31
3852[5]	**Bright Paragon (IRE) (41)** (KTIvory) **8-8-4**(5) GFaulkner(8) (b: a.p: ev ch over 1f out: rdn & one pce fnl f)	¾	**5**	12/1	46	29
4155[18]	**Bayin (USA) (59)** (MDIUsher) **8-9-13** RStreet(19) (b: hld up: hdwy 2f out: rdn & nt qckn fnl f)	½	**6**	11/2[2]	62	45
4168[18]	**Princess Renata (IRE) (37)** (PatMitchell) **4-8-5** JTate(13) (hdwy over 2f out: sn rdn: nt pce to chal)	s.h	**7**	33/1	40	23
3771[13]	**Rise 'n Shine (44)** (CACyzer) **3-8-7**(3) AWhelan(17) (lw: trckd ldrs stands' side 4f)	5	**8**	33/1	34	15
3323[2]	**Pharaoh's Joy (56)** (AGNewcombe) **4-9-7**(3) DGriffiths(1) (trckd ldrs: effrt & rdn wl over 1f out: no imp)	¾	**9**	12/1	44	27
3082[13]	**Mellors (IRE) (46)** (MJHeaton-Ellis) **4-9-0** GDuffield(9) (hmpd s: nvr nrr)	nk	**10**	25/1	33	16
3290[6]	**Rockcracker (IRE) (49)** (GGMargarson) **5-9-3v** GBardwell(14) (lw: a in rr)	s.h	**11**	9/1	36	19
3637[5]	**Tachycardia (36)** (RJO'Sullivan) **5-8-4** NVarley(11) (chsd ldrs over 4f)	¾	**12**	14/1	21	4
3937[16]	**Ocean Stream (IRE) (58)** (JLEyre) **4-9-12v** OPears(6) (a bhd)	2	**13**	33/1	38	21
3417[6]	**Sizzling (50)** (RHannon) **5-9-4** RPerham(3) (prom to ½-wy: sn rdn & wknd)	4	**14**	14/1	19	2
	Last Ambition (IRE) (33) (RChampion) **5-8-1** JQuinn(7) (bit bkwd: prom: rdn & wknd over 2f out)	1½	**15**	10/1	—	—
4115[6]	**Captain Carat (58)** (DNicholls) **6-9-12b** JFanning(2) (dwlt: in rr whn hmpd over 3f out: nt rcvr)	2	**16**	10/1	18	1
3088[10]	**Magic Fizz (54)** (TJEtherington) **3-9-6b[1]** JStack(5) (in tch on outside over 4f: sn wknd: t.o)	10	**17**	33/1	—	—
3852[8]	**Rowlandsons Stud (IRE) (41)** (KCComerford) **4-8-2**(7) JBosley(10) (in rr whn sddle slipped & uns rdr over 3f out)		**U**	33/1	—	—
				(SP 145.1%)	**18 Rn**	

1m 12.0 (1.10) CSF £77.15 CT £315.00 TOTE £8.40: £1.80 £5.70 £2.40 £1.60 (£173.80) Trio £122.90 OWNER Mr P. S. Felgate (MELTON MOWBRAY) BRED Dr W. J. Heffernan
WEIGHT FOR AGE 3yo-2lb
STEWARDS' ENQUIRY Faulkner susp. 27-30/9/97 (irresponsible riding).
3693* Gay Breeze has really come to himself now and, taking advantage of his high draw, always had too much pace for his valiant pursuers. (5/1: 4/1-6/1)
3454 Oxbane, returning to sprinting, ran possibly her best race yet and had she not hung when ridden inside the final furlong, would have given the winner more to think about. (14/1)
4112 Maladerie (IRE) is continuing to run well but he does seem short of a turn of finishing speed and he may need more cut in the ground than he had here. (6/1)
3910 Opening Range delivered a determined challenge entering the final furlong but she was unable to sustain it and it would seem the minimum trip is as far as she really needs. (5/1: 3/1-11/2)
3852 Bright Paragon (IRE), most impressive cantering to post, was in the firing line all the way. Hard at work, he held every chance until feeling the strain inside the last two hundred yards. (12/1)
4048 Bayin (USA) would have picked this field up from where he was entering the final furlong but age is catching up with him and he now lacks that final flourish. (11/2)
3290 Rockcracker (IRE) (9/1: 6/1-10/1)

4249 GROSVENOR CASINO MEMBERS H'CAP (0-60) (II) (3-Y.O+) (Class F)

5-20 (5-29) **6f 3y** £3,223.00 (£964.00: £462.00: £211.00) Stalls: High GOING minus 0.51 sec per fur (F)

				SP	RR	SF
4050[5]	**Be Warned (44)** (JPearce) **6-8-12v** MWigham(15) (hld up: hdwy over 1f out: str run to ld wl ins fnl f)	—	**1**	7/1[3]	55	32
4228[3]	**Mezzoramio (51)** (KAMorgan) **5-9-0v**(5) JoHunnam(13) (mde most tl hdd wl ins fnl f)	1¼	**2**	7/1[3]	59	36
4048[4]	**Suite Factors (55)** (KRBurke) **3-9-4**(3) DSweeney(2) (lw: a.p far side: ev ch fnl f: r.o)	½	**3**	12/1	61	36
3871[4]	**Southern Dominion (41)** (MissJFCraze) **5-8-9v** SWebster(18) (chsd ldrs stands' side: gd hdwy fnl f: fin wl)	nk	**4**	5/1[1]	47	24
4016[3]	**Middle East (56)** (TDBarron) **4-9-10** GCarter(6) (lw: chsd ldrs far side: rdn over 2f out: r.o)	1½	**5**	8/1	58	35
3637[4]	**Mister Raider (45)** (EAWheeler) **5-8-8b**(5) ADaly(4) (racd far side: prom: rdn & one pce fnl f)	nk	**6**	20/1	46	23
4184[8]	**Sir Tasker (46)** (JLHarris) **9-9-0** NDay(19) (hdwy over 1f out: nvr nrr)	½	**7**	11/1	45	22
3761[16]	**Pageboy (56)** (PCHaslam) **8-9-10** WRyan(14) (lw: prom stands' side: rdn over 1f out: one pce)	hd	**8**	13/2[2]	55	32
3969[4]	**Ocker (IRE) (58)** (MHTompkins) **3-9-5v**(5) RMullen(20) (a chsng ldrs stands' side: no hdwy appr fnl f)	¾	**9**	9/1	55	30
3582[3]	**Hannah's Usher (50)** (CMurray) **5-9-4** NicolaHowarth(16) (hdwy over 2f out: ev ch appr fnl f: sn outpcd)	hd	**10**	16/1	47	24
4048[6]	**Mindrace (60)** (KTIvory) **4-9-9**(5) GFaulkner(10) (w ldrs stands' side: rdn over 1f out: sn wknd)	nk	**11**	14/1	56	33

				SP	RR	SF
3871[7]	**The Fed (36)** (JLEyre) **7-8-4** RLappin(11) (chsd ldrs over 4f)	s.h	**12**	10/1	32	9
3710[8]	**Indian Relative (58)** (RGuest) **4-9-9**(3) AWhelan(3) (racd far side: chsd ldrs over 4f: eased whn btn)	1¾	**13**	12/1	49	26
3251[9]	**Priory Gardens (IRE) (43)** (JMBradley) **3-8-9** GBardwell(8) (outpcd)	½	**14**	20/1	33	8
4115[17]	**Hever Golf Lover (IRE) (50)** (TJNaughton) **3-9-2** RPerham(12) (b.hind: nvr trbld ldrs)	1¼	**15**	20/1	37	12
3910[23]	**Rose Flyer (IRE) (34)** (MCChapman) **7-7-9**(7) SCarson(1) (unruly: led far side 4f: wknd qckly)	2½	**16**	33/1	14	—
3641[4]	**Barbury Ballad (IRE) (40)** (MJHeaton-Ellis) **3-8-6** GDuffield(7) (outpcd)	9	**17**	20/1	—	—
3868[5]	**Seretse's Nephew (44)** (MJPolglase) **3-8-10** JQuinn(9) (b: b.hind: trckd ldrs: rdn & outpcd fr ½-wy)	7	**18**	20/1	—	—
				(SP 148.2%)	**18 Rn**	

1m 12.4 (1.50) CSF £55.19 CT £587.51 TOTE £7.70: £1.90 £1.80 £3.10 £1.90 (£23.80) Trio £60.80 OWNER Mr A. J. Thompson (NEWMARKET) BRED Patrick Eddery Ltd
WEIGHT FOR AGE 3yo-2lb
4050 Be Warned has never won on ground as lively as this but, benefiting from a very cool ride, quickened up appreciably to steal the prize in the last fifty yards. (7/1)
4228 Mezzoramio usually races over longer trips but he coped with this step down admirably and held the call until run out of it nearing the finish. He had a hardish race yesterday, so this goes to prove what a tough individual he really is. (7/1)
4048 Suite Factors won the race on the far side but the draw once again proved decisive and he was the unlucky one. (12/1)
3871 Southern Dominion has won at six furlongs but he does the majority of his racing at the minimum trip. Never far away under the stands' rail, he finished with quite a burst but the photo showed that he had just missed out in the duel for third prize. (5/1)
4016 Middle East, one of eight to race on the far side, was being stoked up soon after halfway but he responded and is certainly knocking at the door. (8/1)
3637 Mister Raider, always pushing the pace on the far side, could have found the ground faster than he cares for, for he was unable to mount a challenge despite running on. (20/1)
3261 Sir Tasker (11/1: 8/1-12/1)
3292 Indian Relative (12/1: 8/1-14/1)

T/Plpt: £72.60 (229.27 Tckts). T/Qdpt: £30.50 (24.08 Tckts) IM

2819a-CHANTILLY (France) (R-H) (Soft)
Wednesday September 10th

4250a PRIX D'AUMALE (Gp 3) (2-Y.O F)
2-20 (2-17) **1m** £24,691.00 (£8,979.00: £4,489.00)

				SP	RR	SF
	Anna Palariva (IRE) (AFabre,France) **2-8-9** OPeslier	—	**1**		—	—
	Fairly Grey (FR) (AFabre,France) **2-8-9** TJarnet	nk	**2**		—	—
	Cortona (IRE) (MmeCHead,France) **2-8-9** ODoleuze	2	**3**		—	—
						9 Rn

1m 38.1 (1.60) P-M 2.10F: 1.20F 1.70F 1.80F (7.10F) OWNER Sheikh Mohammed (CHANTILLY) BRED Sheikh Mohammed
Anna Palariva (IRE) is a high-class filly in the making. She made virtually every yard of the running and held on well to beat one of her stable companions. Unbeaten in her only two races so far, she looks like a filly for the Oaks next year. She still has scope for improvement and will now head for the Prix Marcel Boussac.
Fairly Grey (FR), well placed throughout, came with a well timed challenge halfway up the straight, but did not have the necessary needed to catch the winner. She looks up to Group standard and something like the Prix des Reservoirs could be well within her capabilities.
Cortona (IRE), waited with, made her challenge halfway up the straight. Finishing well, she never threatened the first two.

4251a PRIX MICHEL HOUYVET (Listed) (3-Y.O)
3-20 (3-20) **1m 7f** £15,713.00 (£5,387.00: £4,040.00)

				SP	RR	SF
3763[2]	**Palio Sky** (JLDunlop) **3-8-12** SGuillot	—	**1**		119+	—
	Niederhoff (FR) (France) **3-8-12** TThulliez	3	**2**		116	—
3006a[5]	**Sendoro (IRE)** (France) **3-8-12** GMosse	2½	**3**		113	—
						4 Rn

3m 13.6 (6.60) P-M 2.40F: 1.40F 1.40F OWNER Mr J. E. Nash (ARUNDEL) BRED Montealto Stud Establishment
3763 Palio Sky, whose plans for the St Leger were abandoned after his previous effort at Goodwood, gained some compensation here.

VELIEFENDI (Istanbul, Turkey) (R-H) (Good to firm)
Saturday September 13th

4252a TOPKAPI TROPHY (Gp 2) (3-Y.O+ C & G)
2-00 (2-02) **1m** £47,619.00 (£19,048.00: £9,524.00)

				SP	RR	SF
3409[4]	**Sandstone (IRE)** (JLDunlop) **3-8-11** TSprake	—	**1**		111	—
3728[6]	**Ramooz (USA)** (BHanbury) **4-9-6** AMcGlone	nk	**2**		114	—
3729a[2]	**Fly To The Stars** (MJohnston) **3-8-11** WJO'Connor	1½	**3**		107	—
						11 Rn

1m 34.56 TOTE 2.25L: 1.40L 2.00L 2.10L (8.25L) OWNER Mr Peter Winfield (ARUNDEL) BRED Barouche Stud Ltd
3409 Sandstone (IRE) ran a first-class race and just managed to hold off the fast-finishing Ramooz. Racing in mid-division, he made his effort two and a half furlongs out and hit the front with a furlong to go. He ran on well all the way to the line and had just enough left in the tank.
3728 Ramooz (USA) only just failed by a neck to land the spoils. Racing in mid-division, he left his challenge until inside the final furlong. He was flying on the outside at the finish but could not quite catch the winner.
3729a Fly To The Stars, although putting up a brave performance, did not quite have the finishing pace of the first two. Making good headway in third to go to the front two and a half furlongs out, he was headed at the furlong marker and could find no extra in the closing stages.

1552a-CAPANNELLE (Rome, Italy) (R-H) (Heavy)
Sunday September 14th

4253a PREMIO DIVINO AMORE (Listed) (2-Y.O)
4-00 (4-12) **5f** £23,142.00

				SP	RR	SF
2098a3	**Blu Carillon (IRE)** (OPessi,Italy) **2-8-8** MMonteriso	—	**1**		106+	—
	Teishebaini (IRE) (AColchetti,Italy) **2-8-8** OFancera	3	**2**		96?	—
3176a3	**Lionel** (FBrogi,Italy) **2-8-8** CFiocchi	½	**3**		95?	—
4126a4	**Bay Prince (IRE)** (MRChannon) **2-8-13** JCarroll (btn 8½l)		**7**		84?	—
						10 Rn

59.7 secs TOTE 82L: 24L 18L 22L (269L) OWNER O. Pessi
4126a Bay Prince (IRE) followed up his disappointing run in Germany with another lacklustre display. Once again he showed good speed for three furlongs, but could find no more when asked.

HANOVER (Germany) (L-H) (Good)
Sunday September 14th

4254a PREIS DER STADTSPARKASSE HANNOVER UND DER VGH - DEUTSCHER STUTENPRIES (Gp 3) (3-Y.O+ F & M)
3-40 (3-45) **1m 4f**

				SP	RR	SF
	Lomita (GER) (BSchutz,Germany) **3-8-9** ABoschert	—	**1**		114	—
3998b*	**Flamingo Queen (GER)** (BSchutz,Germany) **3-8-9** AStarke	nk	**2**		114	—
3005a*	**Anna Thea (IRE)** (HBlume,Germany) **3-8-9** TMundry	2½	**3**		110	—
						9 Rn

2m 35.1 TOTE 174DM: 18DM 12DM 11DM (491DM) OWNER Gestut Wittekindshof BRED Gestut Wittekindshof
Lomita (GER), the outsider of the field, sprang quite a surprise.

4129a-LONGCHAMP (Paris, France) (R-H) (Good)
Sunday September 14th

4255a PRIX DES CHENES (Gp 3) (2-Y.O C & G)
2-35 (2-42) **1m** £24,691.00 (£8,979.00: £4,489.00) GOING minus 0.32 sec per fur (GF)

				SP	RR	SF
	Second Empire (IRE) (APO'Brien,Ireland) **2-9-2** MJKinane	—	**1**		110+	69
2482*	**Muhtathir** (JHMGosden) **2-9-2** RHills	2½	**2**		105	64
	Tenbyssimo (IRE) (RFeligioni,Italy) **2-9-2** CAsmussen	5	**3**		95	54
						10 Rn

1m 35.4 (0.40) P-M 2.50F 1.50F 2.30F 1.80F (6.90F) OWNER Mr M. Tabor (PILTOWN)
Second Empire (IRE) put up a significant winning performance in this race and he very much looks like Classic material in the making. On only his second outing, she was ridden in mid-division before making a forward move early in the straight. Taking control of the race one and a half furlongs out, his rider never had to resort to the whip. This was an exceptionally fast time and he has scope for improvement. He may return to France for the Grand Criterium.
2482* Muhtathir was given every possible chance, but simply could not go with the winner in the final stages. Always close up, he held the lead two out before staying on at the one pace. Highly-rated, the ground may have been a little firm and one of the targets for him may be the Racing Post Trophy at Doncaster.
Tenbyssimo (IRE) was given every chance but could only stay on at the one pace in the final furlong and a half. All things considered, this was not a bad effort.

4256a PRIX VERMEILLE (Gp 1) (3-Y.O F)
3-10 (3-11) **1m 4f** £89,787.00 (£35,915.00: £17,957.00: £8,979.00) GOING minus 0.32 sec per fur (GF)

				SP	RR	SF
3007a3	**Queen Maud (IRE)** (JdeRoualle,France) **3-9-0** OPeslier (prom: u.p over 2f out: hdwy to ld 1f out: r.o wl)	—	**1**		117	57
3877a3	**Gazelle Royale (FR)** (JEHammond,France) **3-9-0** CAsmussen (hld up bhd early: in rr st: rdn over 1f out: ev ch cl home: no ex)	1	**2**		116	56
2814a3	**Brilliance (FR)** (PBary,France) **3-9-0** SGuillot (hld up bhd early: u.p ent st: hdwy 2f out & r.o strly: no ex cl home)	nse	**3**		116	56
1916a2	**Mousse Glacee (FR)** (JLesbordes,France) **3-9-0** GMosse (rdn prom: mid div ent st: hdwy 2f out: styd on wl)	nse	**4**		116	56
3727*	**Kaliana (IRE)** (LMCumani) **3-9-0** JReid (rdn mid div: styd on one pce)	2	**5**		113	53
3689*	**Ridaiyma (IRE)** (LMCumani) **3-9-0** PCoppin (led tl hdd 2f out: wknd)	5	**6**		106	46
3877a*	**Dust Dancer** (JLDunlop) **3-9-0** PatEddery (rn 2nd to st: wknd over 1f out)	hd	**7**		106	46
3370a3	**Legend Maker (IRE)** (AFabre,France) **3-9-0** TJarnet (n.d)	21	**8**		78	18
2275a*	**Silver Fun (FR)** (MmeCHead,France) **3-9-0** ODoleuze (prom: no ex fnl stages)	nk	**9**		78	18
						9 Rn

2m 28.2 (2.20) P-M 18.40F: 4.00F 2.20F 2.10F (69.40F) OWNER Mr Gary Tanaka BRED Barronstown Stud & Ron Con Ltd
921a* Queen Maud (IRE), given a fine ride, raced on the rail and took the lead a furlong out. Her breeding would suggest that she would not stay the distance, but she did, and really well. Showing good previous form this season, she may now either go for the Arc de Triomphe or the Flower Bowl at Belmont Park. She is honest, gutsy and a credit to her trainer.
3877a Gazelle Royale (FR) arrived on the scene halfway up the straight and ran on well inside the final furlong, but just lacked the speed to catch the winner. She, like the winner, may either go for the Arc de Triomphe or the Flower Bowl.
2814a Brilliance (FR), held up for a late run, came up the centre of the track in the final furlong. She does not quite appear to stay a mile and a half in top-class company, but she always puts in a good effort. A run in the Arc is a possibility, but she may be destined for a campaign in America.

1916a Mousse Glacee (FR) ran on well in the closing stages but may not quite get twelve furlongs. She has been thereabouts in top company all season and deserves a win. She may go for the Flower Bowl or the EP Taylor Stakes.
3727* Kaliana (IRE) was a long way off the pace for most of the trip, and one of the last into the straight. She made some late progress but never looked like taking a hand in the finish. Her outside draw did not help and she lacked any early pace to settle into a handy position. She is a one-paced but improving filly, who will go rather well in the Prix de Royallieu.
3689* Ridaiyma (IRE) was soon cutting out the pace which she did until early in the straight.
3877a* Dust Dancer ran well until one and a half furlongs out, before dropping back through lack of stamina. In second place, her stride began to shorten in the straight and a return to shorter distances might be worth a try.

4257a PRIX NIEL (Gp 2) (3-Y.O C & F)
3-40 (3-41) **1m 4f** £44,893.00 (£17,957.00: £8,979.00: £4,489.00) GOING minus 0.32 sec per fur (GF)

				SP	RR	SF
3730a*	**Rajpoute (FR)** (FDoumen,France) **3-9-2** GMosse (prom: rdn over 2f out: sn led: pushed out)	—	**1**		119	41
2274a*	**Peintre Celebre (USA)** (AFabre,France) **3-9-2** OPeslier (hld up: nt clr run on ins st: hdwy over 1f out: qcknd v.impressively: fin strly)	nk	**2**		119	41
3109³	**Ivan Luis (FR)** (MBell) **3-9-2** JReid (hld up: rdn 2f out: qcknd wl: no ex ins fnl f)	1	**3**		117	39
3179a³	**New Frontier (IRE)** (AFabre,France) **3-9-2** TJarnet (led tl st: one pcd)	4	**4**		112	34
3730a⁶	**Ithaki (IRE)** (JEPease,France) **3-9-2** CAsmussen (rn 3rd: rdn 2f out: styd on one pce)	¾	**5**		111	33
						5 Rn

2m 30.9 (4.90) P-M 6.70F OWNER Mr J. D. Martin BRED Juddmonte Farms
IN-FOCUS: **After this controversial race, Peslier accused Asmussen of having deliberately prevented him from winning, while Fabre announced he would no longer train for the Niarchos family, Ithaki's owners.**
3730a* Rajpoute (FR) landed a gallant victory. An honest and solid sort, he runs with his head low and, with a trouble-free run, took the advantage halfway up the straight before staying on bravely to the line. He has been well handled and will go for either the Turf Classic or the Rothman's International.
2274a* Peintre Celebre (USA) had a rotten and controversial run. Boxed in for much of the race, his jockey decided not to go for a narrow gap early in the straight. He was eventually extracted from the rail and put in a tremendous burst of acceleration during the final furlong and a half. He only failed by a neck and would have won in a few more strides. This was not exactly an ideal trial, but he did have a lovely blow in the straight. He has come out of the race in good condition and will be difficult to beat in the Arc if luck goes his way.
3109 Ivan Luis (FR), held up last, looked to have second place in the bag until Peintre Celebre came bursting though in the final furlong. This was a good, honest run and although he acted on the ground, connections believe he will be more effective on a softer surface. He has an outside chance in the Arc.

4258a PRIX FOY (Gp 3) (4-Y.O+ C & F)
4-15 (4-15) **1m 4f** £24,691.00 (£8,979.00: £4,489.00) GOING minus 0.32 sec per fur (GF)

				SP	RR	SF
2819a²	**Yokohama (USA)** (MmeCHead,France) **6-9-2** ODoleuze	—	**1**		122	35
	Nothin' Leica Dane (AUS) (JEHammond,France) **5-9-2** GMosse	1	**2**		121	34
1736³	**Le Destin (FR)** (PDemercastel,France) **4-9-2** TGillet	½	**3**		120	33
2270a⁵	**Tamure (IRE)** (JHMGosden) **5-9-2** LDettori (btn approx 2l)		**5**		119	—
						8 Rn

2m 31.8 (5.80) P-M 21.40F: 4.20F 2.90F 2.00F (106.60F) OWNER Madeleine Paulson (CHANTILLY)
Yokohama (USA) ran a gallant race. Leading from pillar to post at a moderate pace, he stayed on gamely to the line. He does not have much pace, but is a resolute galloper and he thoroughly deserved his first Group win. He was sent to France to be trained for the Arc which will be his next target, but as game as he is, it is difficult to see him taking a hand in the finish.
Nothin' Leica Dane (AUS) put in a decent performance. A really tough individual, he stuck to his guns until the end, and with hindsight, his connections may have preferred to let him make the running. He needs a softer surface and a stronger pace to show his best and, benefiting greatly from this outing, he may have a little each-way squeak in the Arc.
1736 Le Destin (FR), held up as usual, came rattling along at the end at the end of the race. He needs a really fast gallop in a race and this was not the case here. He has not won for some time, but he is honest and will take his place in the Arc.
2270a Tamure (IRE), close up for most of the way, was only one-paced in the closing stages. He needs cut and may have been slightly inconvenienced by this drying ground.

4131a-SAN SIRO (Milan, Italy) (R-H) (Good to firm)
Sunday September 14th

4259a PREMIO NOVELLA (Listed) (2-Y.O F)
4-15 (4-16) **1m** £23,142.00 (£10,183.00: £5,554.00)

				SP	RR	SF
3422³	**Silent Tribute (IRE)** (MBell) **2-8-8** MFenton	—	**1**		92+	—
	Andoya (ARenzoni,Italy) **2-8-8** FJovine	1¼	**2**		90	—
	Sopran Dandy (IRE) (Italy) **2-8-10** SDettori	3½	**3**		85	—
						7 Rn

1m 33.2 (3.20) TOTE 15L: 13L 19L (37L) OWNER Mrs E. A. Harris (NEWMARKET) BRED Rathbarry Stud
3422 Silent Tribute (IRE) had the measure of all of her rivals. A daughter of Lion Cavern, she made all and quickened clear in the closing stages to score comfortably.

1909a-TABY (Stockholm, Sweden) (L-H) (Good to soft)
Sunday September 14th

4260a TABY OPEN SPRINT CHAMPIONSHIP (Listed) (3-Y.O+)
2-05 (2-09) **6f** £30,743.00 (£8,540.00: £6,832.00: £6,832.00: £1,708.00)

				SP	RR	SF
	Options Open (AHyldmo,Norway) **5-9-4b¹** YvonneDurant	—	**1**		105	—
4124a⁷	**Troon** (RHaugen,Norway) **7-9-4** MSantos	½	**2**		104	—
4124a⁴	**Hakiki (IRE)** (WNeuroth,Norway) **5-9-4** FDiaz	½	**3**		102	—
	Masterkind (IRE) (WNeuroth,Norway) **3-9-2** FJohansson	d.h	**3**		102	—

					SP	RR	SF
4001a3	**Hever Golf Rose** (TJNaughton) **6-9-0** JWeaver	1	**5**			96	—

13 Rn

1m 13.0 TOTE 31.04: 3.50 2.60 H1.68 M1.57 (274.81) OWNER Pegasus (UK) Ltd BRED D. H. Jones
4001a Hever Golf Rose made the early running but was steadied up into fourth place. Racing in fifth as the field turned into the straight, she made no further headway approaching the line.

4261a LAND ROVER STOCKHOLM CUP INTERNATIONAL (Gp 3) (3-Y.O+)
2-35 (2-40) **1m 4f** £51,238.00 (£17,079.00: £8,540.00)

				SP	RR	SF
3374a*	**Harbour Dues** (LadyHerries) **4-9-6** RCochrane	—	**1**		105	—
	Duty Time (AHyldmo,Norway) **6-9-6** YvonneDurant	½	**2**		104	—
	Kutbeya (USA) (ALund,Norway) **6-9-2** MLarsen	nk	**3**		100	—
36474	**Apprehension** (DRLoder) **3-8-11** KFallon (btn approx 13l)		**10**		88	—

11 Rn

2m 35.4 TOTE 3.60: 1.64 2.80 4.15 (36.05) OWNER Hesmonds Stud (LITTLEHAMPTON) BRED Hesmonds Stud Ltd
3374a* Harbour Dues raced in second place until taking the lead two and half furlongs out. He was pushed out to the line and will now go into quarantine in preparation for the Melbourne Cup at Flemington in November.
3647 Apprehension raced in mid-division and was in sixth place from halfway. Weakening in the final four furlongs, he finished very disappointingly. The trainer reported that he had bled during the race.

4262a BBA (3-Y.O+ F & M)
3-05 (3-10) **1m 1f 165y** £15,371.00 (£4,270.00: £3,416.00)

				SP	RR	SF
	In Waiting (IRE) (MKahn,Sweden) **5-9-4** KAndersen	—	**1**		71	—
	Next Going (IRE) (MKahn,Sweden) **5-9-4** WRyan	2	**2**		68	—
39827	**Comanche Companion** (TJNaughton) **7-9-4** JWeaver	nk	**3**		67	—

9 Rn

2m 6.0 TOTE 2.29: 1.61 1.35 3.46 (14.70) OWNER Stall Falk & Stall Lambada BRED Ballymacoll Stud Farm Ltd
3435 Comanche Companion was close up in fifth place before making good headway in the closing stages, and taking third on the line.

4252a-VELIEFENDI (Istanbul, Turkey) (R-H) (Firm)
Sunday September 14th

4263a BOSPHOROUS TROPHY (3-Y.O+ C & F)
2-00 (2-02) **1m 4f** £47,619.00 (£19,048.00: £9,534.00)

				SP	RR	SF
35964	**Strategic Choice (USA)** (PFICole) **6-9-7b** TQuinn	—	**1**		119+	—
	Aristid (GER) (HBlume,Germany) **4-9-6** THellier	3	**2**		114	—
	Bold Pilot (TUR) (YKara,Turkey) **4-9-6** HKaratas	1½	**3**		112	—

10 Rn

2m 27.26 TOTE 1.25: 1.05 1.05 1.05 (3.15) OWNER Mr M. Arbib (WHATCOMBE) BRED M. Arbib
3596 Strategic Choice (USA) gained his first win of the season with considerable ease. Always close up, he took up the running on the bit well over two furlongs out. He was soon well clear and Quinn eased him right down approaching the finishing line.

4230-AYR (L-H) (Good to soft)
Friday September 19th
WEATHER: sunny WIND: mod bhd

4264 VLADIVAR CLASSIC CLAIMING STKS (3-Y.O+) (Class D)
2-00 (2-02) **1m 1f** £3,766.00 (£1,138.00: £554.00: £262.00) Stalls: High GOING: 0.06 sec per fur (G)

				SP	RR	SF
41643	**Falls O'Moness (IRE) (49)** (KRBurke) **3-8-2** JFEgan(5) (lw: hld up & bhd: hdwy ent st: led 1f out: rdn & r.o)	—	**1**	33/1	71	43
415114	**Break the Rules (81)** (DNicholls) **5-9-6** AlexGreaves(2) (lw: a.p: effrt over 2f out: led over 1f out: sn hdd: r.o)	nk	**2**	6/1 3	84	61
38139	**Zorba (62)** (JHetherton) **3-8-6** NKennedy(12) (chsd ldrs: led over 2f out tl over 1f out: sn wknd)	5	**3**	20/1	66	38
40038	**Night City (94)** (KRBurke) **6-9-10** DHolland(11) (cl up: rn wd st: sn outpcd: kpt on fnl f)	1¾	**4**	11/2 2	76	53
24702	**Scaraben (73)** (SEKettlewell) **9-8-9** JFortune(4) (in tch: swtchd over 2f out: styd on one pce)	5	**5**	6/1 3	52	29
39726	**Deadline Time (IRE) (78)** (MrsMReveley) **4-8-11** KDarley(1) (trckd ldrs: effrt 3f out: wknd over 1f out)	1½	**6**	12/1	51	28
34135	**Captain Marmalade (37)** (DTThom) **8-8-7v** AmandaSanders(10) (b.nr fore: sn wl bhd: sme late hdwy)	2½	**7**	50/1	43	20
3972*	**Brighstone (81)** (MCPipe) **4-8-9** AMcGlone(8) (t: led tl hdd over 2f out: sn wknd)	3½	**8**	11/8 1	38	15
39668	**Trying Times (IRE) (45)** (JBerry) **4-8-5(3)** TEDurcan(6) (t: bhd: effrt over 3f out: n.d)	½	**9**	33/1	36	13
39184	**Chanson d'Amour (IRE) (20)** (MissLAPerratt) **3-7-7(7)** JMcAuley(3) (bhd fnl 4f)	6	**10**	100/1	23	—
382214	**Flower Miller (25)** (JHanson) **4-8-7** EJohnson(7) (prom tl rdn & wknd appr st)	24	**11**	33/1	—	—

(SP 110.3%) **11 Rn**

1m 55.81 (5.31) CSF £180.66 TOTE £31.30: £4.10 £2.40 £3.00 (£187.00) Trio £470.10; £470.15 to Ayr 20/9/97 OWNER Piquet Opera House Partnership (WANTAGE) BRED Ballinacurra Stud
WEIGHT FOR AGE 3yo-5lb
OFFICIAL EXPLANATION **Brighstone: no explanation offered.**
4164 Falls O'Moness (IRE) sprang a surprise here to win her first ever race but there was certainly no fluke about it. (33/1)
2889 Break the Rules was back to form here after his pipe-opener last week and, no doubt, he will go one better before long. (6/1: 4/1-7/1)
3225 Zorba, after two poor efforts, showed something of his old form here and looks worth keeping an eye on. (20/1)
3797 Night City helped set the race up by taking the favourite on but he was always struggling after running slightly wide into the straight. (11/2)
2470 Scaraben, having his first run for almost two months, gave the impression that he will be all the better for it. (6/1)
3972 Deadline Time (IRE) ran better than at York last time and is obviously coming right. (12/1)
3972* Brighstone was never allowed to have things his own way and, once put under pressure, he soon curled up. (11/8)

4265 AON CONSULTING 'DEBRA' NURSERY H'CAP (2-Y.O) (Class C)

2-30 (2-31) **1m** £7,886.00 (£2,378.00: £1,154.00: £542.00) Stalls: High GOING: 0.06 sec per fur (G)

Form	Horse	Btn	Pos	SP	RR	SF
3932[4]	**Fashion Victim (74)** (THCaldwell) **2-8-8** ACulhane(1) (hld up: hdwy over 3f out: led ins fnl f: r.o)	—	1	25/1	79	19
3802[9]	**Tearaway (70)** (JWWatts) **2-8-4** GDuffield(2) (s.i.s: shkn up & sn in tch: led over 2f out tl ins fnl f: kpt on)	¾	2	25/1	74	14
3802[12]	**Flower O'Cannie (IRE) (87)** (MWEasterby) **2-9-4**[(3)] GParkin(13) (a chsng ldrs: led over 3f out tl over 2f out: kpt on same pce)	3	3	20/1	85	25
3450[9]	**Hiding Place (66)** (MBell) **2-7-9**[(5)] RMullen(12) (chsd ldrs: outpcd 3f out: kpt on u.p fnl 2f)	¾	4	14/1	62	2
3387[4]	**Flow By (78)** (JLDunlop) **2-8-12** KDarley(7) (in tch: rdn over 3f out: styd on one pce)	½	5	9/2[2]	73	13
3629[4]	**Miss Salsa Dancer (68)** (DenysSmith) **2-7-13**[(3)] PFessey(11) (chsd ldrs: ev ch 3f out: wknd fnl 2f)	1	6	33/1	61	1
3744[7]	**Clarity (IRE) (79)** (APJarvis) **2-8-8**[(5)] CLowther(3) (bhd & pushed along: hdwy 3f out: nvr rchd ldrs)	¾	7	12/1[3]	71	11
4068*	**Holy Wine (USA) (72)** (DRLoder) **2-8-6** [5x] RCochrane(4) (lw: hld up & bhd: effrt over 3f out: styd on: nt pce to chal)	2½	8	11/4[1]	59	—
3990[10]	**Chaska (67)** (ABailey) **2-8-1v[1]** DWright(10) (led tl hdd over 3f out: sn wknd)	5	9	25/1	44	—
3904*	**Take A Turn (82)** (MRChannon) **2-9-2** JCarroll(16) (lw: in tch: effrt over 3f out: sn btn)	3	10	14/1	53	—
3060[6]	**Reach For A Star (62)** (CWThornton) **2-7-10** EJohnson(5) (swtg: chsd ldrs to st: sn wknd)	¾	11	33/1	31	—
3042[6]	**Black Jet (62)** (NPLittmoden) **2-7-7**[(3)] RFfrench(6) (sn outpcd & wl bhd: n.d)	nk	12	50/1	30	—
3306[7]	**Durham Flyer (70)** (TDEasterby) **2-8-4** LCharnock(9) (mid div: drvn along ½-wy: n.d)	s.h	13	16/1	38	—
3458[5]	**Disco Tex (63)** (MWEasterby) **2-7-11**[ow1] DaleGibson(8) (sn outpcd & wl bhd: n.d)	½	14	25/1	30	—
4116[8]	**Naviasky (IRE) (80)** (MrsJRRamsden) **2-9-0** JFortune(15) (lw: hld up: hdwy appr st: c wd: sn btn & eased)	7	15	9/2[2]	33	—
				(SP 117.9%)		**15 Rn**

1m 45.12 (7.72) CSF £463.99 CT £11,161.48 TOTE £35.60: £4.60 £3.50 £4.40 (£292.20) Trio Not won; £612.12 to Ayr 20/9/97 OWNER Mr R. S. G. Jones (WARRINGTON) BRED Theakston Stud

LONG HANDICAP Reach For A Star 7-5 Black Jet 7-6

3932 Fashion Victim did this in good style to show he is back in top form. (25/1)

3282 Tearaway has the ability but is not an easy ride, as he is inclined to hang, but he should still find a race in due course. (25/1)

3650 Flower O'Cannie (IRE) ran a sound race under top weight here and keeps her enthusiasm particularly well. (20/1)

2181 Hiding Place certainly does not do anything quickly but she does stay well and may need more testing ground. (14/1)

3387 Flow By stayed well enough but was short of pace halfway through the race. (9/2)

3629 Miss Salsa Dancer again had her chances but lacked the pace to ever take them. (33/1)

3117 Clarity (IRE) looks likely to need further and the Handicapper has taken no chances with her. (12/1)

4068* Holy Wine (USA), given plenty to do, could never get into it when set alight and looks worth another chance. (11/4)

4266 ROYAL CALEDONIAN HUNT CONDITIONS STKS (2-Y.O) (Class C)

3-00 (3-02) **7f** £5,112.00 (£1,908.00: £929.00: £395.00: £172.50: £83.50) Stalls: High GOING: 0.06 sec per fur (G)

Form	Horse	Btn	Pos	SP	RR	SF
*4056**	**Confirmation** (SirMarkPrescott) **2-9-5** GDuffield(1) (lw: led tl hdd 2½f out: rallied to ld ins fnl f: styd on wl)	—	1	7/4[1]	104	39
3629*	**Ho Leng (IRE)** (MissLAPerratt) **2-9-5** NKennedy(4) (lw: trckd ldrs: smooth hdwy to ld 2½f out: hdd & no ex ins fnl f)	1¼	2	8/1	101	36
	King of The River (USA) (PWChapple-Hyam) **2-8-12** KDarley(3) (w'like: a chsng ldrs: rdn 3f out: kpt on: nt pce to chal)	3	3	6/1[3]	87	22
4116[18]	**Buzz (91)** (CWThornton) **2-9-3** DeanMcKeown(5) (trckd ldrs: effrt ½-wy: r.o one pce)	1¾	4	12/1	88	23
2842*	**Bergen (IRE)** (JHanson) **2-9-5** EJohnson(2) (b.hind: cl up: chal ½-wy: wknd wl over 1f out)	3	5	2/1[2]	83	18
4236[13]	**Mr Miyagi** (ABailey) **2-8-12** DWright(6) (a outpcd & bhd)	28	6	33/1	12	—
				(SP 105.7%)		**6 Rn**

1m 30.24 (5.84) CSF £12.71 TOTE £2.80: £1.80 £2.30 (£9.20) OWNER Cheveley Park Stud (NEWMARKET) BRED Cheveley Park Stud Ltd

4056* Confirmation was by far the best looker in a useful field and he showed he is progressing here, but needed plenty of help from the saddle and is obviously going to stay further. (7/4)

3629* Ho Leng (IRE) was cruising early in the straight but, as it turned out, his rider probably went for home too soon and gave the gutsy winner plenty of time to fight back. There will be other opportunities for him. (8/1)

King of The River (USA), a decent-looking newcomer, just needed this and it was lack of experience that cost him his chance. He should know much more about it next time. (6/1: op 7/2)

3908 Buzz is a useful sort who seems to have more than his fair share of weight in nurseries and was never quite good enough in this company. (12/1)

2842* Bergen (IRE) ran too freely and dropped disappointingly away in the last two furlongs. He was said to have travelled badly to the meeting. (2/1)

4267 SHADWELL STUD FIRTH OF CLYDE STKS (Listed) (2-Y.O F) (Class A)

3-30 (3-31) **6f** £18,592.00 (£6,928.00: £3,364.00: £1,420.00: £610.00: £286.00) Stalls: High GOING: 0.06 sec per fur (G)

Form	Horse	Btn	Pos	SP	RR	SF
3981*	**Regal Revolution (98)** (PTWalwyn) **2-8-13** JLowe(10) (mde most: hld on gamely fnl f)	—	1	16/1	97	75
2335[4]	**Sapphire Ring (95)** (RCharlton) **2-8-8** KDarley(6) (lw: trckd ldrs: chal over 1f out: hrd rdn & edgd lft: nt qckn towards fin)	nk	2	5/2[1]	91	69
3925*	**Thanksgiving (IRE) (95)** (MajorDNChappell) **2-8-11** GCarter(14) (lw: chsd ldrs: hdwy 2f out: nt qckn ins fnl f)	2	3	12/1[3]	89	67
3981[2]	**Hoh Chi Min (100)** (MBell) **2-8-11** RCochrane(11) (bhd: hdwy ½-wy: styd on: nvr able to chal)	3	4	7/1[2]	81	59
4106[5]	**Likely Story (IRE) (89)** (JLDunlop) **2-8-8** JWeaver(8) (hld up & bhd: hdwy 2f out: nrst fin)	s.h	5	12/1[3]	78	56
4097[2]	**Ascot Cyclone (USA) (94)** (BWHills) **2-8-8** PaulEddery(9) (bhd: hdwy u.p over 2f out: nvr able rch ldrs)	2½	6	7/1[2]	71	49
3541*	**Fizzed** (MJohnston) **2-8-8** DHolland(12) (lw: sn outpcd & bhd: hmpd over 2f out: styd on towards fin)	nk	7	12/1[3]	70	48
3595[4]	**Cloudberry (92)** (BJMeehan) **2-8-8** GDuffield(13) (bhd & hmpd wl over 2f out: sme late hdwy)	s.h	8	20/1	70	48
4106[2]	**Tadwiga** (RHannon) **2-8-13** DaneO'Neill(4) (lw: drvn along thrght: nvr nr ldrs)	hd	9	7/1[2]	75	53
3961a[6]	**Conectis (IRE) (100)** (DJSCosgrove) **2-8-8** JCarroll(7) (chsd ldrs 4f)	2	10	16/1	65	43
3823[10]	**Selkirk Rose (IRE) (78)** (MissLAPerratt) **2-8-8** AMcGlone(5) (gd spd 4f: wknd)	s.h	11	50/1	64	42
3740[6]	**Filey Brigg (100)** (WTKemp) **2-8-13** SDrowne(1) (racd wd: spd 4f)	3	12	20/1	61	39
3411[8]	**Poetry In Motion (IRE)** (EJAlston) **2-8-8** JFEgan(3) (chsd ldrs over 4f)	7	13	100/1	38	16
4042*	**Ajig Dancer (94)** (MRChannon) **2-8-8** JFortune(2) (disp ld 3f: sn wknd: lame)	2½	14	12/1[3]	31	9
				(SP 121.1%)		**14 Rn**

1m 11.73 (1.93) CSF £49.49 TOTE £16.70: £4.20 £1.80 £4.60 (£32.80) Trio £196.70 OWNER Mr S. W. E. J. Slack (LAMBOURN) BRED T. R. Lock

OFFICIAL EXPLANATION Ajig Dancer: was found to be lame.
3981* Regal Revolution has never run a bad race all season and this game filly had far too much courage for the runner-up here. (16/1)
2335 Sapphire Ring always looked likely to win this but, when it came down to a struggle, she proved disappointing and was never giving it her best shot. (5/2)
3925* Thanksgiving (IRE) travelled pretty well on the leaders' heels but then failed to pick up in the closing stages and may be better at the minimum trip for the time being. (12/1)
3981 Hoh Chi Min takes time to find her stride and only got going when it was too late. She seems to need a bit further. (7/1)
4106 Likely Story (IRE), dropped right out, was then always finding the task set beyond her but she did stay on well. (12/1)
4097 Ascot Cyclone (USA) responds to pressure but was always finding this trip too sharp. (7/1)
3541* Fizzed, after five weeks off, seemed ring-rusty and also met with trouble and should be forgiven this. (12/1)
3595 Cloudberry found trouble in running and would have obviously have finished a little closer. (20/1)
4106 Tadwiga was most disappointing here, never travelling at any stage, and obviously something was wrong. (7/1)

4268 FAUCETS FOR MEYNELL SAFEMIX THERMOSTATIC VALVES AND SHOWERS H'CAP (0-90) (3-Y.O+ F & M) (Class C)

4-00 (4-01) **1m 2f** £5,800.00 (£1,750.00: £850.00: £400.00) Stalls: High GOING: 0.06 sec per fur (G)

Form	Horse / running	Dist	Pos	SP	RR	SF
3120*	**Capilano Princess (86)** (DHaydnJones) **4-10-0** SDrowne(4) (hld up: stdy hdwy 3f out: led over 1f out: rdn & r.o)	—	1	3/1[1]	95	69
4151[15]	**Rebel County (IRE) (70)** (ABailey) **4-8-9**(3) RFfrench(11) (hld up & bhd: hdwy 3f out: ch over 1f out: styd on wl)	½	2	14/1	78	52
3937[6]	**Topatori (IRE) (70)** (MHTompkins) **3-8-6** DBiggs(8) (prom: hdwy to ld over 2f out: hdd over 1f out: kpt on)	½	3	14/1	77	45
3803[10]	**Fantastic Flame (IRE) (78)** (PJMakin) **3-9-0** JFortune(12) (lw: hld up: hdwy over 3f out: chsng ldrs over 1f out: rdn & one pce)	2	4	10/1	82	50
3855[7]	**Peppers (IRE) (63)** (KRBurke) **4-8-5**ow1 DHolland(1) (hld up & bhd: gd hdwy 2f out: sn rdn: hung lft & nt run on)	2½	5	10/1	63	36
4015[18]	**Step N Go (IRE) (68)** (MrsJRRamsden) **3-8-4** JFEgan(10) (bhd: drvn along ent st: sme hdwy 2f out: n.d)	10	6	10/1	52	20
3741*	**Sweet Contralto (87)** (DRLoder) **3-9-9** RCochrane(6) (cl up: led over 3f out tl over 2f out: grad wknd)	1¼	7	9/2[2]	69	37
3428[6]	**Best of All (IRE) (73)** (JBerry) **5-9-1b** KDarley(2) (chsd ldrs: effrt over 3f out: wknd over 2f out)	3	8	16/1	50	24
3377[4]	**What Happened Was (67)** (MartynMeade) **3-7-10**(7) RBrisland(3) (led tl hdd & wknd over 3f out)	6	9	20/1	35	3
1435[5]	**Ajayib (USA) (79)** (JLDunlop) **3-9-1** GCarter(5) (swtg: bhd & rdn ent st: n.d)	8	10	13/2[3]	34	2
4102[5]	**Stone Flower (USA) (83)** (PWChapple-Hyam) **3-9-2**(3) RHavlin(9) (b.nr fore: chsd ldrs tl wknd fnl 3f)	1	11	16/1	36	4

(SP 113.6%) **11 Rn**

2m 11.66 (5.86) CSF £41.24 CT £459.96 TOTE £3.70: £1.70 £2.60 £5.30 (£23.20) Trio £141.30 OWNER Mr H. G. Collis (PONTYPRIDD) BRED Mrs O. M. Collis
WEIGHT FOR AGE 3yo-6lb
3120* Capilano Princess, despite going up the weights, keeps her form really well, but she had to pull out all the stops this time. (3/1)
3824 Rebel County (IRE) at last produced something like her old form here and this was her second outing wearing a tongue-strap, which seems to have made the difference. (14/1)
3937 Topatori (IRE), taking a step up in trip, seemed to get it well enough but was just tapped for toe late on. (14/1: op 8/1)
3277* Fantastic Flame (IRE) went well enough for a long way but, when put under pressure, she failed to pick up. She seems held by the Handicapper. (10/1: 8/1-12/1)
3855 Peppers (IRE) has so much ability but as yet has not given it anything like she can. (10/1)
1390 Step N Go (IRE) was tried in a tongue-strap here for the first time and it never made the slightest difference. (10/1)

4269 ROBERT WYPER MOTORS (EGLINTON & WINTON CHALLENGE CUP) H'CAP (0-80) (3-Y.O+) (Class D)

4-30 (4-31) **2m 1f 105y** £5,265.50 (£1,589.00: £772.00: £363.50) Stalls: High GOING: 0.06 sec per fur (G)

Form	Horse / running	Dist	Pos	SP	RR	SF
3540*	**Selmeston (IRE) (47)** (SCWilliams) **5-7-7**(3) RFfrench(9) (trckd ldrs: led over 3f out: rdn over 2f out: hld on wl)	—	1	8/1[3]	55	31
3974[3]	**Opaque (66)** (WStorey) **5-9-1** JFortune(6) (lw: bhd: hdwy over 3f out: hrd drvn 2f out: styd on to disp ld wl ins fnl f: nt qckn cl home)	hd	2	9/2[1]	74	50
3623[7]	**Arian Spirit (IRE) (48)** (JLEyre) **6-7-11v** TWilliams(7) (hld up: smooth hdwy to trck ldrs 3f out: rdn over 2f out: edgd lft & one pce)	3	3	10/1	53	29
3714[5]	**Classic Line (66)** (JLDunlop) **3-8-3b** GCarter(8) (prom tl outpcd & lost pl appr st: styd on u.p fnl 3f)	nk	4	9/1	71	35
3815*	**Aztec Flyer (USA) (59)** (CEBrittain) **4-8-8b** RCochrane(4) (lw: chsd ldrs: ev ch 3f out: wknd over 1f out)	¾	5	11/2[2]	63	39
3805[5]	**Shirley Sue (75)** (MJohnston) **4-9-10** JWeaver(2) (lw: rr div: effrt ½-wy: styd on u.p fnl 3f: nvr able to chal)	1½	6	11/2[2]	78	54
3907*	**Hasta la Vista (58)** (MWEasterby) **7-8-4b**(3) GParkin(10) (lw: trckd ldrs: effrt ent st: sn hrd drvn & grad wknd)	15	7	10/1	47	23
	Great Easeby (IRE) (63) (WStorey) **7-8-12** JFanning(3) (bit bkwd: mid div: rdn appr st: sn btn)	4	8	16/1	48	24
2530[6]	**Grand Cru (65)** (JCullinan) **6-9-0** KDarley(12) (bhd: hdwy ½-wy: outpcd fnl 3f)	3½	9	14/1	47	23
4055[12]	**Hoh Explorer (IRE) (59)** (DWBarker) **3-7-7**(3) DarrenMoffatt(11) (chsd ldrs: pushed along 7f out: sn wknd)	7	10	33/1	35	—
3935[5]	**Ambuscade (USA) (47)** (MrsJJordan) **11-7-3**(7) ANicholls(13) (a bhd)	hd	11	100/1	23	—
4160[8]	**Thunderheart (49)** (RAllan) **6-7-12b**1 DWright(5) (led tl hdd over 3f out: sn wknd)	3½	12	20/1	22	—
3485[3]	**Belle Bijou (59)** (MJohnston) **3-7-10** JLowe(1) (cl up tl wknd rapidly over 7f out: sn t.o)	dist	13	16/1	—	—

(SP 115.4%) **13 Rn**

3m 54.77 (12.27) CSF £37.81 CT £333.61 TOTE £10.30: £2.90 £1.40 £2.00 (£34.00) Trio £128.10 OWNER Mr Chris Wright (NEWMARKET) BRED St Simon Foundation
LONG HANDICAP Hoh Explorer (IRE) 7-9 Ambuscade (USA) 6-12 Belle Bijou 7-9
WEIGHT FOR AGE 3yo-12lb
STEWARDS' ENQUIRY Fortune susp 28/9-1/10/97 (excessive use of whip).
3540* Selmeston (IRE) is at his best after a rest and gives the impression that he will always pull out that bit extra when challenged. (8/1)
3974 Opaque needed some very strong driving to get him going and then had to admit he had met one just too tough. (9/2)
3401* Arian Spirit (IRE) spends much of the race on the bridle but, when it comes down to a struggle, she does not find as much as looks likely. (10/1)
3714 Classic Line looks slow but sure and was keeping on at the end after looking well beaten turning in. (9/1)
3815* Aztec Flyer (USA) went well for a long way but, once a struggle was really on, it all proved beyond him. (11/2)
3805 Shirley Sue was not ridden at all positively and only got going when it was too late. She gives the impression that she can do better. (11/2)

4270 WHYTE & MACKAY SPECIAL RESERVE H'CAP (0-90) (3-Y.O+) (Class C)
5-00 (5-02) **7f** £6,612.50 (£2,000.00: £975.00: £462.50) Stalls: High GOING: 0.06 sec per fur (G)

				SP	RR	SF
4139[5]	**Knobbleeneeze (65)** (MRChannon) **7-8-6** JFortune(9) (lw: chsd ldrs: drvn along over 2f out: hdwy 1f out: styd on wl to ld post)	—	**1**	7/1[2]	75	35
3801[9]	**Weetman's Weigh (IRE) (78)** (RHollinshead) **4-9-2**(3) DGriffiths(12) (in tch: hdwy 2f out: led 1f out: r.o: jst ct)	s.h	**2**	16/1	88	48
3987[8]	**Pericles (73)** (MJohnston) **3-8-11** DHolland(11) (a chsng ldrs: ev ch 1f out: kpt on wl)	nk	**3**	16/1	82	39
3987[16]	**Royal Result (USA) (65)** (MWEasterby) **4-8-6** TLucas(14) (swtg: hld up: racd wd: hdwy over 2f out: styd on wl fnl f: nrst fin)	s.h	**4**	16/1	74	34
2835[2]	**Sheltering Sky (IRE) (85)** (JLDunlop) **3-9-9** KDarley(3) (b: a chsng ldrs: effrt 2f out: one pce appr fnl f)	1	**5**	2/1[1]	92	49
3987*	**Rymer's Rascal (65)** (EJAlston) **5-8-6** JFEgan(6) (lw: plld hrd: cl up: led 2f out to 1f out: no ex)	¾	**6**	17/2[3]	70	30
3262[5]	**Cee-N-K (IRE) (72)** (MJohnston) **3-8-10** JWeaver(10) (chsd ldrs: rdn 3f out: wknd fnl 2f)	3	**7**	20/1	70	27
4219*	**Myttons Mistake (67)** (ABailey) **4-8-3**(5)ow2 6x PRoberts(16) (racd wd: hld up: hdwy over 2f out: nvr rchd ldrs)	2½	**8**	11/1	60	18
3937[5]	**Regal Thunder (USA) (69)** (MRStoute) **3-8-7v[1]** PaulEddery(5) (chsd ldrs: rdn 3f out: wknd 2f out)	hd	**9**	10/1	61	18
3406[9]	**Garnock Valley (70)** (JBerry) **7-8-11b** GCarter(7) (bhd: effrt ½-wy: no imp)	2	**10**	20/1	58	18
3630[6]	**Celebration Cake (IRE) (69)** (MissLAPerratt) **5-8-10** DeanMcKeown(13) (lw: in tch: rdn 3f out: sn btn)	1¼	**11**	16/1	54	14
3709[10]	**Treasure Touch (IRE) (86)** (DNicholls) **3-9-10** AlexGreaves(4) (led tl hdd & wknd 2f out)	1¼	**12**	25/1	68	25
3691*	**Denbrae (IRE) (65)** (DJGMurraySmith) **5-8-1**(5) CLowther(2) (dwlt: hdwy 3f out: n.d)	nk	**13**	12/1	46	6
3812[9]	**Night Flight (72)** (JJO'Neill) **3-8-7**(3) RFfrench(17) (sn wl bhd: n.d)	s.h	**14**	25/1	53	10
3987[14]	**The Lambton Worm (67)** (DenysSmith) **3-8-2**(3) PFessey(1) (sn drvn along: a bhd)	1¾	**15**	33/1	44	1
3921[6]	**Impulsive Air (IRE) (62)** (EWeymes) **5-8-3** DaleGibson(8) (drvn along after s: n.d)	nk	**16**	20/1	39	—
3812[6]	**Colway Ritz (72)** (JWWatts) **3-8-10b** JCarroll(18) (dwlt: a bhd)	½	**17**	25/1	47	4
3566[9]	**Redoubtable (USA) (65)** (DWChapman) **6-8-6** ACulhane(15) (plld hrd: cl up: led 2f out to 1f out: no ex)	dist	**18**	100/1	—	—
				(SP 134.8%)	**18 Rn**	

1m 29.5 (5.10) CSF £101.67 CT £1,632.06 TOTE £7.90: £2.00 £3.30 £6.50 £3.50 (£45.20) Trio £368.40 OWNER Mr Anthony Andrews (UPPER LAMBOURN) BRED A. and Mrs Andrews
WEIGHT FOR AGE 3yo-3lb
OFFICIAL EXPLANATION **Redoubtable (USA): the trainer reported that the horse returned home with a back problem.**
4139 Knobbleeneeze is a grand sort who takes some riding but he was kidded along in tremendous style here and did just enough. (7/1)
3310 Weetman's Weigh (IRE) ran up to his best but, despite a gallant effort, was just touched off. (16/1)
3777 Pericles keeps promising to win a race and kept plugging away here and is certainly off a useful mark. (16/1)
3987 Royal Result (USA) ran well for his new stable here and was keeping on most determinedly at the end. (16/1)
2835 Sheltering Sky (IRE), backed as though defeat was out of the question, was a shade disappointing once off the bit. (2/1)
3987* Rymer's Rascal ran too freely for his own good and in the circumstances this was not a bad effort. (17/2)
4219* Myttons Mistake, poorly drawn, was always having to race wide and can be forgiven this effort. (11/1)
3630 Celebration Cake (IRE) had his chances but showed very little sparkle when ridden. (16/1)
3332 Treasure Touch (IRE) had a nice blow out here and, dropped back in distance, would be well worth keeping an eye on. (25/1)
3691* Denbrae (IRE) (12/1: 8/1-14/1)

T/Plpt: £3,643.20 (7.37 Tckts). T/Qdpt: £31.10 (59.85 Tckts) AA

4237-NEWBURY (L-H) (Good becoming Good to soft becoming Soft)
Friday September 19th
WEATHER: raining WIND: almost nil

4271 HMV STORES NURSERY H'CAP (2-Y.O) (Class C)
2-10 (2-11) **7f 64y (round)** £5,865.00 (£1,770.00: £860.00: £405.00) Stalls: Low GOING: 0.04 sec per fur (G)

				SP	RR	SF
3802[11]	**Sunley Seeker (75)** (MRChannon) **2-8-11** LDettori(1) (lw: led over 2f: rdn over 1f out: led ins fnl f: r.o wl)	—	**1**	14/1	81	39
4044[5]	**Acid Test (71)** (WRMuir) **2-8-7** MartinDwyer(16) (lw: a.p: led 5f out tl ins fnl f: unable qckn)	2½	**2**	12/1	72	30
4017*	**Bullion (84)** (BWHills) **2-9-6** MHills(6) (a.p: hrd rdn over 1f out: one pce)	1¼	**3**	4/1[1]	82	40
3924[15]	**Frolicking (72)** (JLDunlop) **2-8-8** TSprake(17) (s.i.s: rdn over 3f out: hdwy 2f out: one pce fnl f)	3	**4**	16/1	63	21
4116[4]	**Kim's Brave (86)** (BJMeehan) **2-9-8b** 6x MTebbutt(8) (rdn over 2f out: hdwy over 1f out: nvr nrr)	nk	**5**	6/1[2]	77	35
4143[6]	**Water Force (74)** (GBBalding) **2-8-7**(3) PPMurphy(11) (lw: rdn over 3f out: hdwy over 1f out: nvr nrr)	1	**6**	20/1	62	20
3859*	**Generous Embrace (76)** (MBell) **2-8-12** JReid(5) (hld up: rdn over 2f out: wknd over 1f out)	5	**7**	6/1[2]	53	11
3750[7]	**Ballet Rambert (74)** (MJHeaton-Ellis) **2-8-10** KFallon(2) (rdn over 3f out: hdwy & nt clr run over 1f out: eased whn btn fnl f)	5	**8**	12/1	40	—
4042[11]	**Mighty Magic (69)** (MrsPNDutfield) **2-8-5** AClark(4) (lw: prom 6f)	½	**9**	25/1	34	—
2768[10]	**Daring News (72)** (RHannon) **2-8-8** TQuinn(7) (swtg: nvr nrr)	3	**10**	10/1[3]	31	—
4065[6]	**Universal Lady (65)** (CJames) **2-7-12**(3) MHenry(15) (a bhd)	nk	**11**	16/1	23	—
3794[2]	**Master Mac (USA) (85)** (RAkehurst) **2-9-0**(7) PFitzsimons(9) (bhd fnl 3f)	1½	**12**	14/1	40	—
3927[6]	**Fawning (63)** (MBlanshard) **2-7-13** JQuinn(12) (bhd fnl 2f)	1	**13**	33/1	16	—
3186[9]	**Island Girl (IRE) (62)** (DWPArbuthnot) **2-7-12** NAdams(13) (b: b.hind: swtg: a bhd)	s.h	**14**	33/1	15	—
3924[4]	**Argumentative (60)** (SDow) **2-7-3**(7) PDoe(3) (hld up: hrd rdn 3f out: wknd over 2f out)	nk	**15**	33/1	12	—
3932[2]	**Santa Court (65)** (RDickin) **2-8-1** CRutter(10) (s.s: a bhd)	s.h	**16**	16/1	17	—
3131[3]	**Welcome Sunset (77)** (JWharton) **2-8-13** SSanders(14) (swtg: rdn & hdwy over 3f out: wknd over 2f out)	¾	**17**	20/1	27	—
				(SP 126.2%)	**17 Rn**	

1m 33.32 (5.22) CSF £147.75 CT £759.40 TOTE £15.20: £3.60 £2.00 £1.80 £5.60 (£139.40) Trio £149.80 OWNER Mrs J. M. Jeyes (UPPER LAMBOURN) BRED Sunley Stud
LONG HANDICAP Argumentative 7-7
3072* Sunley Seeker appreciated the return to seven furlongs and bounced back to form. The early leader, she travelled well throughout the race and, woken up below the distance, struck the front inside the final furlong. (14/1)
4044 Acid Test, still 6lb higher than when successful at Newmarket last month, nevertheless gave a good account of himself. Soon at the head of affairs, he grimly tried to hold on but was eventually overhauled inside the final furlong. (12/1)
4017* Bullion was never far away but, despite all her rider's efforts, failed to quicken. A return to a mile is needed. (4/1)

3489 Frolicking began an effort on the outside of the field a quarter of a mile from home but could make no further impression in the final furlong. (16/1)
4116 Kim's Brave was not helped by the slight drop in distance and, although staying on from below the distance, never threatened to get near the leaders. (6/1)
4143 Water Force struggled on from the back of the field in the last furlong and a half. (20/1)

4272 TONY STRATTON SMITH MEMORIAL CONDITIONS STKS (3-Y.O+) (Class B)

2-40 (2-41) **1m 2f 6y** £7,631.20 (£2,771.20: £1,345.60: £568.00: £244.00) Stalls: Low GOING: 0.04 sec per fur (G)

				SP	RR	SF
3112^{16}	**Clan Ben (IRE) (95)** (HRACecil) **5-9-0** KFallon(2) (lw: chsd ldr over 4f: chsd ldr over 4f out: led over 2f out tl over 1f out: led ins fnl f: rdn out)	—	**1**	7/1	111	28
4003^{3}	**Crimson Tide (IRE) (102)** (JWHills) **3-8-8** MHills(5) (chsd ldr over 7f out tl over 4f out: w ldr over 2f out: led over 1f out tl ins fnl f: unable qckn)	¾	**2**	$9/4^{1}$	110	21
3634^{3}	**Conon Falls (IRE) (104)** (JHMGosden) **3-8-10** LDettori(3) (lw: plld hrd: led: sn clr: hdd over 2f out: one pce)	3½	**3**	$9/4^{1}$	106	17
1323^{6}	**Proper Blue (USA) (105)** (TGMills) **4-9-0** TQuinn(1) (hdwy over 3f out: rdn over 2f out: sn wknd)	3	**4**	$9/2^{2}$	99	16
3797^{5}	**Amrak Ajeeb (IRE) (100)** (BHanbury) **5-9-0** JReid(4) (lw: a in rr)	6	**5**	$11/2^{3}$	90	7

(SP 107.6%) **5 Rn**

2m 13.12 (9.12) CSF £19.93 TOTE £7.50: £2.10 £1.60 (£10.40) OWNER Angus Dundee Plc (NEWMARKET) BRED T. Hillman
WEIGHT FOR AGE 3yo-6lb
2525* Clan Ben (IRE) had a stiff task at the weights - he would have been at least 5lb better off in a handicap with all his rivals - but he does like this ground and put up a fine battling display to win his first race beyond a mile. (7/1)
4003 Crimson Tide (IRE) had the longer trip he needed and appeared to be hacking over the winner. Poking a head in front below the distance, he found disappointingly little in a fight and, collared inside the final furlong, was unable to cope with the winner. He certainly has bags of ability but looks one to have reservations about. (9/4)
3634 Conon Falls (IRE) likes this ground but he raced far too freely and stormed off in front. Quickly coming back to his field and headed over a quarter of a mile from home, he looked certain to drop right away but, to his credit, plodded on to the bitter end. (9/4)
1323 Proper Blue (USA) took closer order over three furlongs from home but the combination of a four-month absence and soft ground found him out and he had run out of gas a quarter of a mile from home. (9/2)
3797 Amrak Ajeeb (IRE) has completely lost his way and was in last place from start to finish. (11/2)

4273 POLYGRAM MONSTER SALE CONDITIONS STKS (2-Y.O F) (Class B)

3-10 (3-12) **7f (straight)** £6,354.10 (£2,311.60: £1,125.80: £479.00: £209.50) Stalls: High GOING: 0.22 sec per fur (G)

				SP	RR	SF
3979^{7}	**Amabel (USA)** (IABalding) **2-8-8** MHills(5) (mde all: rdn out)	—	**1**	14/1	88	48
	Hollow Haze (USA) (PWChapple-Hyam) **2-8-8** JReid(3) (leggy: scope: hld up: chsd wnr over 1f out: r.o ins fnl f)	1½	**2**	$13/8^{1}$	85+	45
3985*	**Blue Gentian (USA)** (RCharlton) **2-8-13** LDettori(4) (lw: chsd wnr over 5f: unable qckn)	2½	**3**	$13/8^{1}$	84	44
3979^{2}	**Millitrix** (MRStoute) **2-8-8** TQuinn(1) (rdn & hdwy 2f out: one pce fnl f)	¾	**4**	$3/1^{2}$	77	37
3985^{9}	**Tiye** (RHannon) **2-8-8** KFallon(2) (hld up: rdn over 3f out: wknd over 1f out)	4	**5**	$12/1^{3}$	68	28

(SP 115.5%) **5 Rn**

1m 29.39 (5.29) CSF £35.60 TOTE £17.10: £2.90 £1.70 (£46.60) OWNER Mr George Strawbridge (KINGSCLERE) BRED George Strawbridge Jr
OFFICIAL EXPLANATION **Amabel (USA): regarding the improvement in form compared with his previous run at Salisbury, the trainer stated that on that occasion the filly ran up the unfavoured stands side.**
3979 Amabel (USA) left her two previous runs well behind. Making all the running, she violently flashed her tail when hit below the distance but, rousted along, was not going to be denied. (14/1: 12/1-20/1)
Hollow Haze (USA), quite a tall filly with substance and scope, moved into second place approaching the final furlong but, despite pulling away from her rivals, was unable to get to the winner. She will have learnt from this and should soon go one better. (13/8: evens-7/4)
3985* Blue Gentian (USA) looked in tremendous shape in the paddock but this soft ground did not look to be in her favour and, after racing in second place until approaching the final furlong, she could then only struggle on in her own time. (13/8)
3979 Millitrix took closer order a quarter of a mile from home but was left for dead in the final furlong. (3/1: 2/1-100/30)
Tiye, off the bridle by halfway, had shot her bolt below the distance. (12/1: op 7/1)

4274 HAYNES, HANSON AND CLARK CONDITIONS STKS (2-Y.O C & G) (Class B)

3-40 (3-42) **1m (straight)** £9,416.20 (£3,431.20: £1,675.60: £718.00: £319.00) Stalls: High GOING: 0.22 sec per fur (G)

				SP	RR	SF
	Duck Row (USA) (JARToller) **2-8-10** SSanders(4) (w'like: scope: dwlt: hld up: chsd ldr 3f out: led 1f out: rdn out)	—	**1**	$7/2^{3}$	100	53
3576^{2}	**Quiet Assurance (USA)** (EALDunlop) **2-8-10** KFallon(2) (b: lw: chsd ldr: led over 5f out to 1f out: unable qckn)	1½	**2**	$13/8^{1}$	97	50
3973*	**Evening World (FR)** (PFICole) **2-8-10** TQuinn(5) (lw: racd alone stands' side: a.p: rdn over 2f out: wknd over 1f out)	3½	**3**	$2/1^{2}$	90	43
	Glory of Grosvenor (IRE) (PWChapple-Hyam) **2-8-10** JReid(3) (w'like: scope: lw: hld up: chsd ldr over 4f out to 3f out: wknd over 1f out)	1	**4**	11/2	88	41
3598^{9}	**Blueprint (IRE)** (LordHuntingdon) **2-8-10** LDettori(1) (lw: led over 2f: wknd 3f out)	4	**5**	9/1	80	33

(SP 119.0%) **5 Rn**

1m 43.81 (5.81) CSF £9.61 TOTE £5.30: £1.90 £1.80 (£6.00) OWNER Duke of Devonshire (WHITSBURY) BRED Cambremont Limited Partnership
Duck Row (USA), a likeable medium sized colt, made a very pleasing start to his racing career in this useful race and, coming through to lead a furlong from home, was rousted along to assert. (7/2: 9/4-4/1)
3576 Quiet Assurance (USA) looked in very good shape beforehand and was soon at the head of affairs. Although unable to cope with the winner when collared by that rival a furlong out, he still finished well clear of the remainder. He should soon go one better. (13/8)
3973* Evening World (FR), who won on the soft last time out, had more on his plate on this occasion. Ploughing a lone furrow down the stands' rail, he was bang in contention until feeling the pinch below the distance. (2/1)
Glory of Grosvenor (IRE), an attractive, medium-sized individual, was never far away but had nothing more to offer approaching the final furlong. (11/2: 5/4-6/1)

4275 WILLIAM HILL SILVER CLEF LADIES' H'CAP (0-70) (3-Y.O+) (Class E)

4-10 (4-12) **1m 4f 5y** £4,708.50 (£1,428.00: £699.00: £334.50) Stalls: Low GOING: 0.22 sec per fur (G)

Form	Horse	Dist	Pos	SP	RR	SF
3631*	**Montecristo (66)** (RGuest) **4-10-12**(5) MissRFlynn(16) (hdwy over 1f out: led ins fnl f: r.o wl)	—	**1**	10/1	76	46
3864[6]	**Two Socks (66)** (JSKing) **4-11-3** MissSSamworth(4) (lw: hdwy over 1f out: r.o one pce)	3	**2**	10/1	72	42
	Saint Ciel (USA) (40) (FJordan) **9-9-5** MissEJJones(6) (a.p: led over 3f out: hung rt over 1f out: hdd ins fnl f: one pce)	nk	**3**	20/1	46	16
3028[9]	**The Roundsills (59)** (RFJohnsonHoughton) **3-10-2** MissEJohnsonHoughton(10) (hdwy over 2f out: one pce)	4	**4**	16/1	59	21
4002[12]	**Prospero (70)** (MrsAJPerrett) **4-11-7** MrsAPerrett(5) (hld up: hrd rdn over 2f out: wknd over 1f out)	1¾	**5**	13/2[1]	68	38
3796[7]	**Opera Buff (IRE) (68)** (MissGayKelleway) **6-11-0**(5) MissLVollaro(19) (hdwy over 1f out: nvr nrr)	3	**6**	14/1	62	32
895[21]	**Punkah (USA) (70)** (GMMcCourt) **4-11-2**(5) MissMO'Sullivan(22) (s.i.s: hdwy over 3f out: wknd 1f out)	1½	**7**	20/1	62	32
3401[8]	**Stalled (IRE) (48)** (PTWalwyn) **7-9-13** MarchionessBlandford(7) (lw: hdwy over 1f out: nvr nrr)	nk	**8**	10/1	40	10
3476[D]	**Breezed Well (45)** (KGWingrove) **11-9-10** MrsHNoonan(2) (hdwy over 4f out: wknd wl over 1f out)	½	**9**	20/1	36	6
3970[8]	**Siberian Mystic (40)** (PGMurphy) **4-9-0**(5) MissLGreen(11) (hdwy over 3f out: wknd over 2f out)	¾	**10**	9/1[3]	30	—
3714[11]	**Tasik Chini (USA) (60)** (PFICole) **3-10-3** MissSHiggins(18) (racd wd bk st: led over 8f)	2	**11**	25/1	47	9
4108[17]	**Frozen Sea (USA) (63)** (GPEnright) **6-10-9**(5) MrsMEnright(14) (lw: nvr nrr)	3	**12**	33/1	46	16
	Haya Ya Kefaah (66) (NMBabbage) **5-11-3** MissDianaJones(3) (bit bkwd: hdwy over 3f out: wknd 2f out)	2	**13**	12/1	47	17
4179[13]	**Rehaab (49)** (MissBSanders) **4-10-0v** MissLSheen(17) (hdwy over 4f out: wknd over 2f out)	1¾	**14**	20/1	27	—
3758[6]	**Foleys Quest (IRE) (50)** (JSMoore) **3-9-7** MrsSMoore(9) (b: prom 9f)	s.h	**15**	20/1	28	—
3928[13]	**Strat's Legacy (37)** (DWPArbuthnot) **10-9-2** MrsJMoore(1) (b: prom over 6f)	1	**16**	20/1	14	—
3568[2]	**Supermick (40)** (WRMuir) **6-9-5** MrsMCowdrey(13) (hld up: rdn over 3f out: sn wknd)	1	**17**	10/1	16	—
3277[6]	**Sheep Stealer (65)** (REPeacock) **9-11-2** MrsCPeacock(21) (s.s: hdwy over 10f out: wknd over 2f out)	5	**18**	33/1	34	4
2854[2]	**Gold Blade (60)** (JPearce) **8-10-11** MrsLPearce(15) (lw: hld up: shkn up over 4f out: sn wknd)	3½	**19**	7/1[2]	24	—
3640[10]	**Krayyan Dawn (44)** (JAkehurst) **7-9-4**(5)ow4 MrsKHills(12) (prom 8f)	24	**20**	33/1	—	—
3640*	**Norsong (49)** (JAkehurst) **5-10-0** MissJAllison(8) (bhd fnl 5f)	1½	**21**	10/1	—	—
				(SP 142.8%)	**21 Rn**	

2m 44.85 (14.85) CSF £95.20 CT £1,850.33 TOTE £14.20: £4.20 £2.80 £5.30 £7.10 (£75.20) Trio £2,148.10; £2,148.15 to Ayr 20/9/97
OWNER Mr Rae Guest (NEWMARKET) BRED Lord Matthews
WEIGHT FOR AGE 3yo-8lb

3631* Montecristo followed up his recent success and came with a useful run in the final quarter-mile to sweep into the lead inside the final furlong. Jockey Rachel Flynn, wife of the winning trainer, was having her first ride. (10/1)

3864 Two Socks began to pick up ground below the distance but, despite staying on, was unable to get to the winner. (10/1)

Saint Ciel (USA) is better known as a hurdler and has not been seen on the Flat since September 1995. Without a run in four and a half months, he nevertheless got to the front towards the stands' side over three furlongs from home but he hung right below the distance and, collared inside the final furlong, could only keep on at one pace. (20/1)

3028 The Roundsills was back over a more suitable trip but, after moving up over two furlongs from home, could then only go up and down in the same place. (16/1)

3864 Prospero had the big advantage of one of the most experienced and proficient riders in the field but, after looking dangerous on the far rails in the straight, had nothing more to offer from below the distance. (13/2)

3559* Opera Buff (IRE) stayed on from the back of the field in the final quarter-mile without posing a threat. (14/1)

4276 COOPERS & LYBRAND H'CAP (0-95) (3-Y.O+) (Class C)

4-40 (4-43) **7f 64y (round)** £6,287.50 (£1,900.00: £925.00: £437.50) Stalls: Low GOING: 0.22 sec per fur (G)

Form	Horse	Dist	Pos	SP	RR	SF
3772[6]	**Jorrocks (USA) (87)** (IABalding) **3-9-8** LDettori(7) (lw: rdn & hdwy over 1f out: led ins fnl f: r.o wl)	—	**1**	4/1[2]	100	52
3982[2]	**Marjaana (IRE) (75)** (PTWalwyn) **4-8-13** RHills(6) (a.p: rdn over 2f out: ev ch ins fnl f: unable qckn)	2	**2**	7/1[3]	84	39
3894[12]	**Blewbury Hill (IRE) (72)** (RFJohnsonHoughton) **3-8-7** JReid(12) (a.p: led over 1f out tl ins fnl f: one pce)	1¾	**3**	12/1	77	29
4120[5]	**All Is Fair (83)** (SirMarkPrescott) **3-9-4** SSanders(10) (lw: s.s & swvd rt s: rdn 2f out: hdwy over 1f out: r.o wl ins fnl f)	½	**4**	11/4[1]	87	39
	Primo Lara (85) (PWHarris) **5-9-9** MHills(4) (led over 5f: wknd ins fnl f)	2½	**5**	16/1	83	38
2913[11]	**Strat's Quest (64)** (DWPArbuthnot) **3-7-13** MartinDwyer(11) (a.p: rdn over 2f out: wknd over 1f out)	s.h	**6**	20/1	62	14
3801[6]	**Angel Chimes (70)** (JEBanks) **4-8-8** JStack(5) (s.s: nvr nr to chal)	nk	**7**	10/1	67	22
3888[11]	**Star Talent (USA) (85)** (IABalding) **6-9-9** SWhitworth(2) (lw: s.s: a bhd)	11	**8**	12/1	58	13
3712[3]	**Sword Arm (81)** (RCharlton) **3-9-2v** TSprake(1) (bhd fnl 2f)	2½	**9**	10/1	49	1
4155[14]	**Golden Pound (USA) (80)** (MissGayKelleway) **5-9-4** KFallon(3) (lw: bhd fnl 2f)	2½	**10**	9/1	42	—
				(SP 113.4%)	**10 Rn**	

1m 34.41 (6.31) CSF £28.40 CT £277.70 TOTE £2.80: £1.50 £2.10 £2.70 (£13.50) Trio £37.20 OWNER Mr Paul Mellon (KINGSCLERE) BRED Stewart L. Amstrong
WEIGHT FOR AGE 3yo-3lb

3772 Jorrocks (USA) is no easy ride and needs exaggerated tactics. Only picking up ground below the distance, he hung his head extremely awkwardly to one side but, despite this, got on top inside the final furlong and in the end won a shade comfortably. (4/1)

3982 Marjaana (IRE), 13lb higher than when first successful this season, was always close up and had every chance inside the final furlong before the winner asserted. (7/1)

3236 Blewbury Hill (IRE) got to the front below the distance but, collared inside the final furlong, failed to find another gear. He remains a maiden. (12/1)

4120 All Is Fair once again demonstrated she needs further. Still out with the washing two furlong from home, she finished with a real flourish from below the distance but was never going to get there in time. (11/4: 2/1-3/1)

Primo Lara, making a belated seasonal reappearance, was 20lb higher than when first successful. Bowling along in front, he was collared approaching the final furlong and soon tired. He has done all his winning on a fast surface. (16/1)

1141* Strat's Quest found this too far and, after racing up with the pace, had shot her bolt below the distance. Both her wins have come over six furlongs. (20/1)

4277 AMERADA MAIDEN STKS (3-Y.O) (Class D)

5-10 (5-11) **1m (straight)** £3,746.50 (£1,132.00: £551.00: £260.50) Stalls: High GOING: 0.22 sec per fur (G)

Form	Horse	Dist	Pos	SP	RR	SF
	Ghalib (IRE) (MajorWRHern) **3-9-0** RHills(9) (b.off hind: w'like: scope: lw: a.p: chsd ldr over 2f out: led ins fnl f: r.o wl)	—	**1**	7/2[2]	89	67
3991[2]	**Brigand (IRE)** (DRLoder) **3-9-0** KFallon(2) (lw: led: rdn over 2f out: hdd ins fnl f: unable qckn)	1	**2**	3/1[1]	87	65

	Horse	Dist	Pos	SP	RR	SF
1409[2]	**Mount Holly (USA)** (JHMGosden) **3-9-0** LDettori(3) (lw: hld up: swtchd rt over 2f out: one pce)	5	**3**	3/1[1]	77	55
3275[3]	**Limni (USA)** (MrsJCecil) **3-9-0** GHind(10) (b: lw: s.s: rdn over 2f out: hdwy over 1f out: nvr nrr)	3½	**4**	20/1	70	48
3917[2]	**Star Gambit (USA)** (RAkehurst) **3-8-9** TQuinn(8) (lw: a.p: rdn over 2f out: wknd over 1f out)	2½	**5**	7/2[2]	60	38
	Eider Hill (DMorris) **3-8-9** NDay(6) (unf: scope: s.s: nvr nr to chal)	3½	**6**	33/1	53	31
4009[3]	**Lawz (IRE) (72)** (CJBenstead) **3-9-0** SSanders(7) (hld up: rdn over 2f out: sn wknd)	nk	**7**	8/1[3]	57	35
3632[10]	**Evidently (IRE)** (IABalding) **3-8-9** MartinDwyer(1) (s.s: nvr nrr)	hd	**8**	33/1	52	30
4070[12]	**Bestemor** (HCandy) **3-8-9** CRutter(5) (a bhd)	1½	**9**	50/1	49	27
3991[7]	**Bob Knows** (RFJohnsonHoughton) **3-9-0** JReid(11) (prom over 5f)	5	**10**	33/1	44	22
	Pride of Narvik (MRChannon) **3-9-0** MHills(4) (w'like: bhd fnl 2f)	10	**11**	20/1	24	2
3470[17]	**Despina (40)** (HCandy) **3-8-9b1** NAdams(12) (lw: a bhd)	nk	**12**	50/1	19	—

(SP 127.8%) **12 Rn**

1m 42.8 (4.80) CSF £13.35 TOTE £4.70: £2.30 £1.40 £1.70 (£9.00) Trio £9.20 OWNER Mr Hamdan Al Maktoum (LAMBOURN) BRED Shadwell Estate Company Limited

Ghalib (IRE), an attractive, good-bodied colt with plenty of scope, looked in tip top shape and put up a sparkling performance. Always handy, he was rousted along to lead inside the final furlong and kept on really well. He could be useful but we will need to see how he handles a sound surface. (7/2: 2/1-4/1)

3991 Brigand (IRE) looked in tremendous shape beforehand and merrily bowled along in front. Eventually collared inside the final furlong, he finished well clear of the remainder. He is knocking on the door. (3/1: op 7/4)

1409 Mount Holly (USA) has certainly matured since his only previous run this season back in May but, although keeping on for third prize, had no hope with the front two. There is a race to be found with him. (3/1)

3275 Limni (USA) stayed on from the back of the field in the last furlong and a half without ever posing a threat. (20/1)

3917 Star Gambit (USA) was close up until tiring approaching the final furlong. A sounder surface may well help her find a race. (7/2)

Eider Hill, who still needs time to fully develop, never threatened to get into it. (33/1)

4009 Lawz (IRE) (8/1: 12/1-20/1)

T/Jkpt: Not won; £58,130.83 to Newbury 20/9/97. T/Plpt: £594.50 (64.25 Tckts). T/Qdpt: £79.40 (25.47 Tckts) AK

4264-AYR (L-H) (Good, Good to soft patches bk st)
Saturday September 20th

WEATHER: sunny periods WIND: almost nil

4278 E.B.F. TULIP COMPUTERS MAIDEN STKS (2-Y.O) (Class D)

1-55 (1-56) **1m** £4,380.00 (£1,320.00: £640.00: £300.00) Stalls: High GOING: 0.05 sec per fur (G)

	Horse	Dist	Pos	SP	RR	SF
3978[2]	**Equity Princess (80)** (MJohnston) **2-8-9** DHolland(8) (hld up: effrt 3f out: r.o v.wl to ld wl ins fnl f: eased towards fin)	—	**1**	Evens[1]	81	42
	Corniche (IRE) (PFICole) **2-9-0** RCochrane(9) (w'like: scope: led after 1½f: qcknd clr ½-wy: r.o wl: hdd & no ex towards fin)	½	**2**	11/4[2]	85+	46
	Lady Rachel (IRE) (JLEyre) **2-8-9** MGallagher(4) (neat: b.hind: s.i.s: sn in tch: outpcd 3f out: kpt on towards fin)	11	**3**	33/1	58	19
3978[6]	**Fear Not (IRE)** (MBell) **2-8-9** MFenton(6) (chsd ldrs: one pce fnl 3f)	1½	**4**	14/1	55	16
	Glory of Love (JHetherton) **2-9-0** DeanMcKeown(10) (w'like: bit bkwd: dwlt: hdwy on ins 3f out: nrst fin)	s.h	**5**	50/1	60	21
2713[8]	**Pleasant Dreams** (DenysSmith) **2-8-9** JCarroll(5) (chsd ldrs tl outpcd fnl 3f)	2	**6**	100/1	51	12
3479[8]	**Torso** (JWWatts) **2-9-0** JFortune(1) (effrt ½-wy: nvr trbld ldrs)	2½	**7**	25/1	51	12
3825[8]	**Madman's Mirage (FR)** (MJohnston) **2-9-0** JWeaver(12) (bhd: effrt ½-wy: n.d)	3	**8**	33/1	45	6
4236[5]	**Arcane Star (IRE)** (APJarvis) **2-8-9(5)** CLowther(7) (lw: led 1½f: chsd ldr tl wknd fnl 3f)	10	**9**	25/1	25	—
3726[5]	**Tornado Prince (IRE)** (NACallaghan) **2-9-0** PaulEddery(3) (hld up & bhd: nvr nr to chal)	1½	**10**	7/1[3]	22	—
2473[8]	**Nebuchadnezzar** (JJO'Neill) **2-9-0** KDarley(2) (prom tl bdly hmpd after 2f: sn bhd)	5	**11**	50/1	12	—
1797[14]	**Pitchmark (IRE)** (EWeymes) **2-8-9** JQuinn(11) (in tch 5f: wknd)	2	**12**	66/1	3	—

(SP 115.8%) **12 Rn**

1m 42.79 (5.39) CSF £2.89 TOTE £2.00: £1.30 £1.60 £3.60 (£2.20) Trio £33.40 OWNER Maktoum Al Maktoum (MIDDLEHAM) BRED Gainsborough Stud Management Ltd

OFFICIAL EXPLANATION **Tornado Prince (IRE): hung right throughout and lost his action.**

3978 Equity Princess took time to settle and the leader had stolen a march by then but she showed just how useful she is and made up some eight lengths in three furlongs to score a shade cheekily. (Evens)

Corniche (IRE), from a stable whose charges are normally lit up, was a most laid back individual. He was given a tremendous ride and almost pinched it but in the end the lack of a run probably just made the difference. (11/4: 7/4-3/1)

Lady Rachel (IRE) ran reasonably and was keeping on well, suggesting that stiffer tests will suit in time. (33/1)

3978 Fear Not (IRE) is learning but there is plenty more needed. (14/1)

Glory of Love, a lengthy sort, needed this and showed signs of greenness but was staying on, suggesting that time and longer trips will see improvement. (50/1)

4279 JOHNNIE WALKER WHISKY H'CAP (0-90) (3-Y.O+) (Class C)

2-25 (2-25) **1m 5f 13y** £5,832.50 (£1,760.00: £855.00: £402.50) Stalls: High GOING: 0.05 sec per fur (G)

	Horse	Dist	Pos	SP	RR	SF
3705[6]	**Top Cees (90)** (MrsJRRamsden) **7-10-0** JFortune(3) (trckd ldrs: hdwy to ld appr fnl f: shkn up & r.o wl)	—	**1**	9/2[1]	103	63
4108[7]	**Gold Desire (59)** (MBrittain) **7-7-4(7)** DMernagh(4) (chsd ldrs: led over 2f out tl appr fnl f: kpt on)	2½	**2**	16/1	69	29
3626*	**Globe Runner (60)** (JJO'Neill) **4-7-12** JQuinn(11) (lw: hld up & bhd: gd hdwy over 2f out: ch appr fnl f: no ex)	½	**3**	9/2[1]	69	29
3907[6]	**Ledgendry Line (70)** (MrsMReveley) **4-8-8** ACulhane(10) (hld up & bhd: styd on fnl 3f: nvr nrr)	1¼	**4**	9/1[3]	78	38
3722[6]	**Shaffishayes (70)** (MrsMReveley) **5-8-8** DeanMcKeown(7) (hld up & bhd: effrt over 3f out: nrst fin)	1¼	**5**	14/1	76	36
3809[3]	**Jazz Track (IRE) (80)** (PWChapple-Hyam) **3-8-6(3)** RHavlin(5) (lw: chsd ldrs: rdn over 3f out: wknd fnl 2f)	6	**6**	9/1[3]	79	30
3907[4]	**Al's Alibi (76)** (WRMuir) **4-9-0** DaneO'Neill(2) (led tl hdd over 2f out: grad wknd)	nk	**7**	10/1	75	35
4235[11]	**Lord Advocate (58)** (DANolan) **9-7-7b(3)** PFessey(6) (cl up tl wknd fnl 3f)	1½	**8**	50/1	55	15
1992[6]	**The Butterwick Kid (61)** (RAFahey) **4-7-6(7)ow1** RWinston(12) (hld up: effrt over 3f out: n.d)	3	**9**	16/1	54	13
3805[9]	**Noufari (FR) (68)** (RHollinshead) **6-8-6** KDarley(15) (in tch: pushed along 7f out: wknd 4f out)	s.h	**10**	12/1	61	21
4235[15]	**Mentalasanythin (65)** (DHaydnJones) **8-8-3** AMackay(14) (hld up & bhd: effrt ent st: n.d)	3	**11**	14/1	54	14
3267[6]	**Stakis Casinos Boy (IRE) (77)** (MJohnston) **3-8-6** DHolland(9) (chsd ldrs tl wknd over 3f out)	13	**12**	10/1	50	1

				SP	RR	SF
3739^{2}	**Urgent Swift (81)** (APJarvis) **4-9-0**(5) CLowther(1) (hld up & bhd: hdwy 7f out: rdn 4f out: sn wknd)	5	**13**	15/2^{2}	48	8
2676^{10}	***Manful (74)*** (MissLAPerratt) **5-8-12b** NKennedy(8) (Withdrawn not under Starter's orders: veterinary advice in paddock)		**W**	20/1	—	—

(SP 125.8%) **13 Rn**

2m 53.38 (8.58) CSF £75.21 CT £318.20 TOTE £4.40: £2.60 £6.00 £2.00 (£35.90) Trio £122.70 OWNER Mr R. E. Sangster (THIRSK) BRED Pendley Farm

LONG HANDICAP Lord Advocate 7-2

WEIGHT FOR AGE 3yo-9lb

3705 Top Cees was back to his best here, running on strongly and, by the looks of things, he should be given serious consideration for the Cesarewitch. (9/2)

4108 Gold Desire did his usual and ran his heart out but he was never a match for the winner. (16/1)

3626* Globe Runner is still in tremendous form but this trip proved just beyond him. (9/2)

3907 Ledgendry Line looks in great heart at the moment and ran a fair race here. Should things continue to go his way, better is likely. (9/1)

2297* Shaffishayes, trying a longer trip, seemed to get it well enough but needed a stronger gallop to give him a chance of making up the ground in the straight. (14/1)

3809 Jazz Track (IRE) had his chances but proved disappointing when put under pressure. (9/1)

1992 The Butterwick Kid, having his first run for three months, will obviously be all the better for it. (16/1)

4280 LADBROKE (AYR) SILVER CUP H'CAP (3-Y.O+) (Class B)

3-05 (3-05) **6f** £12,427.50 (£3,720.00: £1,785.00: £817.50) Stalls: High GOING: 0.05 sec per fur (G)

				SP	RR	SF
3649^{8}	**Perryston View (81)** (PCalver) **5-9-6v** KDarley(28) (mde all stands' side: clr over 2f out: r.o wl)	—	**1**	11/1	98	81
4013*	**Almasi (IRE) (82)** (CFWall) **5-9-2**(5) JoHunnam(22) (racd stands' side: hdwy 2f out: r.o wl towards fin)	1¼	**2**	10/1^{3}	96	79
3327*	**Hard to Figure (84)** (RJHodges) **11-9-9** JQuinn(3) (racd far side: hdwy 2f out: r.o wl: nrst fin)	1½	**3**	25/1	94	77
3795^{5}	**Kira (81)** (JLEyre) **7-9-6** RLappin(4) (b: led & clr far side: no ex towards fin)	nk	**4**	25/1	90	73
4121^{14}	**Mr Bergerac (IRE) (85)** (BPalling) **6-9-10** RHills(24) (outpcd & bhd stands' side tl r.o wl fnl 2f)	½	**5**	25/1	93	76
3923^{3}	**Always Alight (76)** (KRBurke) **3-8-10**(3) DSweeney(8) (racd far side: in tch: hdwy 2f out: styd on)	nk	**6**	33/1	83	64
3856^{2}	**Tiler (IRE) (80)** (MJohnston) **5-9-5** JWeaver(12) (racd far side: s.i.s: hdwy ½-wy: hrd rdn & kpt on: nt pce to chal)	½	**7**	5/1^{1}	85	68
4155^{6}	**Double Oscar (IRE) (75)** (DNicholls) **4-9-0b** AlexGreaves(26) (lw: hdwy stands' side 2f out: styd on: no imp)	½	**8**	15/2^{2}	79	62
3914*	**Rudi's Pet (IRE) (85)** (RHannon) **3-9-3b**(5) CLowther(9) (lw: racd far side: chsd ldrs tl rdn & btn appr fnl f)	nk	**9**	20/1	88	69
4155^{13}	**Soviet Leader (82)** (RGuest) **3-9-5** DHolland(1) (chsd ldrs far side: effrt over 2f out: btn appr fnl f)	½	**10**	20/1	84	65
3765^{19}	**So Intrepid (IRE) (85)** (JMBradley) **7-9-10** WRyan(15) (racd far side: in tch: effrt ½-wy: no imp: collapsed after r: dead)	½	**11**	33/1	86	69
4137^{8}	**Daawe (USA) (78)** (JAGlover) **6-9-3v** DaneO'Neill(16) (prom stands' side: rdn over 2f out: nt qckn)	s.h	**12**	20/1	79	62
4147^{18}	**Grey Kingdom (73)** (MBrittain) **6-8-5**(7) DMernagh(13) (chsd ldrs far side: rdn ½-wy: nt qckn)	d.h	**13**	50/1	73	56
4137^{11}	**Purple Fling (73)** (DWChapman) **6-8-12** ACulhane(7) (lw: racd far side: hdwy u.p over 1f out: n.d)	nk	**13**	25/1	73	56
3975^{4}	**The Gay Fox (83)** (BAMcMahon) **3-9-6** JFEgan(2) (b: chsd ldrs far side tl rdn & btn wl over 1f out)	½	**15**	20/1	81	62
3765^{13}	**Mister Jolson (72)** (RJHodges) **8-8-11** RCochrane(6) (hdwy far side 2f out: n.m.r & n.d)	1¼	**16**	25/1	67	50
3604^{6}	**Canovas Heart (82)** (BobJones) **8-9-7** MWigham(20) (racd stands' side: spd 4f)	nk	**17**	25/1	76	59
4121^{3}	**Mr Teigh (73)** (MrsJRRamsden) **5-8-12** MFenton(14) (effrt stands' side ½-wy: n.d)	s.h	**18**	16/1	67	50
3649^{5}	**Benzoe (IRE) (80)** (MrsJRRamsden) **7-9-5** JFortune(5) (hld up & bhd far side: effrt over 2f out: n.m.r & n.d)	nk	**19**	14/1	73	56
3888^{7}	**Gadge (82)** (ABailey) **6-9-7** DWright(11) (b: chsd ldrs far side 4f)	½	**20**	25/1	74	57
3975^{2}	**Return of Amin (83)** (JDBethell) **3-9-3**(3) PFessey(18) (racd stands' side: n.d)	1¼	**21**	14/1	72	53
3982^{4}	**Silca Key Silca (80)** (MRChannon) **3-9-3** AMackay(21) (lw: in tch stands' side 4f)	2½	**22**	33/1	62	43
4100^{13}	**Westcourt Magic (85)** (MWEasterby) **4-9-10** TLucas(27) (racd stands' side: outpcd & bhd after 2f)	nk	**23**	14/1	66	49
3987^{18}	**Knotty Hill (73)** (RCraggs) **5-8-12** LCharnock(10) (prom far side 4f: sn wknd)	1¾	**24**	33/1	50	33
3746^{4}	**Iblis (IRE) (76)** (GWragg) **5-9-1** PaulEddery(25) (a outpcd & bhd stands' side)	2½	**25**	25/1	46	29
4270^{14}	**Night Flight (74)** (JJO'Neill) **3-8-4**(7) RWinston(29) (a bhd stands' side)	nk	**26**	50/1	43	24
4155^{27}	**Samwar (82)** (MRChannon) **5-9-7** JCarroll(17) (b.hind: racd stands' side: n.d)	2	**27**	33/1	46	29
4013^{9}	**Scharnhorst (73)** (ARDicken) **5-8-12** EJohnson(23) (prom stands' side 4f: wknd qckly)	14	**28**	66/1	—	—

(SP 141.7%) **28 Rn**

1m 11.73 (1.93) CSF £86.05 CT £2,550.83 TOTE £10.00: £2.50 £2.90 £4.00 £7.40 (£37.00) Trio £500.00 OWNER Mrs Janis MacPherson (RIPON) BRED Mrs V. E. Hughes

WEIGHT FOR AGE 3yo-2lb

3273 Perryston View, given a most positive ride, had the whole field stretched by halfway and, sticking to the stands' rails like glue, he was never going to be pegged back. (11/1)

4013* Almasi (IRE) has been running out of her skin this season and, stepping up in class here, showed just what a genuine sort she is. Despite finishing strongly, the effort was always too late. (10/1)

3327* Hard to Figure has really come back to something like his old self of late and this was a splendid effort, staying on strongly to win the race up the far side of the track but always too late to catch the stands' side runners. (25/1)

3795 Kira is basically a five furlong horse but can win over an easy six and put up a tremendous effort here, leading the far side group by a clear margin only to run out of steam late on. (25/1)

3888 Mr Bergerac (IRE) is still in good form and, by the way he finished, with a little further to go, he would seriously have been in the shake up. (25/1)

3923 Always Alight seems to take time to find his stride but he did stick to his task particularly well and was putting in all his best work at the finish. (33/1)

3856 Tiler (IRE) did his usual these days and just missed the break and, in these very competitive events, that makes all the difference. (5/1: op 12/1)

4155 Double Oscar (IRE) looked the part but, after improving just after halfway, he soon found the effort required here too much for his liking. (15/2)

4137 Daawe (USA) had an in-between draw and, in the circumstances, ran pretty well. (20/1)

4281 FAUCETS FOR PEMBREY IN WALES DOONSIDE CUP STKS (Listed) (3-Y.O+) (Class A)

3-35 (3-37) **1m 2f 192y** £11,224.80 (£4,183.20: £2,031.60: £858.00: £369.00: £173.40) Stalls: High GOING: 0.05 sec per fur (G)

				SP	RR	SF
3785^{4}	**Ghataas (103)** (JLDunlop) **3-8-4** RHills(7) (cl up: led 7f out: qcknd clr ent st: r.o strly)	—	**1**	6/1	113	70
4004*	**Sandmoor Chambray (100)** (TDEasterby) **6-8-11** JWeaver(1) (lw: a.p: hdwy 3f out: styd on wl: no ch w wnr)	3½	**2**	7/2^{2}	108	72
3988*	**Winter Romance (105)** (EALDunlop) **4-9-1** JFortune(6) (lw: in tch: effrt 3f out: n.m.r: styd on: nvr able to chal)	1	**3**	6/1	110	74

3988[2]	**Weet-A-Minute (IRE) (104)** (RHollinshead) **4-8-11** KDarley(3) (chsd ldrs: effrt & edgd lft over 2f out: r.o one pce)	2	**4**	11/2[3]	103	67
3902[9]	**Star Selection (95)** (JMackie) **6-8-11** JQuinn(2) (led 4f: outpcd whn hmpd over 2f out: n.d after)	1¾	**5**	33/1	101	65
4060*	**Sacho (IRE)** (JHMGosden) **4-8-11** GHind(8) (lw: in tch: effrt ent st: hrd drvn over 2f out: sn btn)	½	**6**	5/2[1]	100	64
4004[3]	**River Usk (97)** (HRACecil) **3-8-4** WRyan(4) (bhd: drvn along 4f out: n.d)	1½	**7**	6/1	98	55
4264[4]	**Night City (94)** (KRBurke) **6-8-11** DHolland(5) (s.s: effrt ent st: n.d)	½	**8**	50/1	79 t	61

(SP 113.9%) **8 Rn**

2m 19.0 (3.10) CSF £24.64 TOTE £6.70: £1.80 £1.60 £2.00 (£15.00) OWNER Mr Hamdan Al Maktoum (ARUNDEL) BRED Shadwell Estate Company Limited

WEIGHT FOR AGE 3yo-7lb

3785 Ghataas, a hard puller, was allowed to have his head this time and, well ridden, stole a clear advantage turning for home and there were never any dangers. (6/1)

4004* Sandmoor Chambray ran a cracking race, sticking on determinedly and the Cambridgeshire should suit him ideally. (7/2)

3988* Winter Romance was always struggling to improve and was never good enough to get in a serious blow and the ground might have just dried out too much liking. (6/1: op 4/1)

3988 Weet-A-Minute (IRE) had a hard race last time and seemed to be feeling that here. (11/2)

849 Star Selection stuck on well after getting completely outpaced and chopped for room early in the straight and is obviously coming back to form and is one to keep on the right side of for jumping. (33/1)

4060* Sacho (IRE) proved disappointing once asked to really stretch early in the straight. (5/2)

4004 River Usk never gave any signs of hope and this was a pretty moderate effort. (6/1)

4282 LADBROKE (AYR) GOLD CUP H'CAP (3-Y.O+) (Class B)

4-15 (4-16) **6f** £49,972.50 (£15,030.00: £7,265.00: £3,382.50) Stalls: High GOING: 0.05 sec per fur (G)

				SP	RR	SF
4155*	**Wildwood Flower (97)** (RHannon) **4-9-3** 7x DaneO'Neill(24) (bhd stands' side: hdwy 2f out: r.o wl to ld ins fnl f)	—	**1**	14/1	108	79
3975*	**Double Action (97)** (TDEasterby) **3-9-1** 7x LCharnock(9) (lw: cl up far side: rdn to ld ins fnl f: r.o: hdd & no ex towards fin)	¾	**2**	10/1	106	75
941[8]	**Superior Premium (100)** (RAFahey) **3-9-4** JCarroll(1) (lw: a chsng ldrs far side: kpt on strly fnl f)	½	**3**	33/1	108	77
3535a[2]	**Azizzi (98)** (CREgerton) **5-9-4** JQuinn(7) (lw: led far side tl ins fnl f: kpt on wl)	1¼	**4**	33/1	102	73
4147[20]	**Albert The Bear (88)** (JBerry) **4-8-5b[1]**(3) PFessey(22) (chsd ldrs stands' side: outpcd 2f out: kpt on wl fnl f)	nk	**5**	66/1	92	63
3795*	**Gaelic Storm (88)** (MJohnston) **3-8-6** 7x DHolland(5) (b: swtg: hld up & bhd far side: hdwy 2f out: styd on wl fnl f)	d.h	**5**	14/1	92	61
4062[7]	**Ziggy's Dancer (USA) (90)** (EJAlston) **6-8-10** JFEgan(3) (cl up far side: effrt 2f out: kpt on)	nk	**7**	50/1	93	64
4098[U]	**Blessingindisguise (97)** (MWEasterby) **4-9-3b** TLucas(21) (led stands' side tl ins fnl f: no ex)	1½	**8**	14/1	96	67
3765[3]	**Oggi (91)** (PJMakin) **6-8-11** RCochrane(28) (hdwy stands' side 2f out: hrd rdn & nvr able to chal)	hd	**9**	6/1[1]	90	61
3764[8]	**Chickawicka (IRE) (91)** (BPalling) **6-8-8**(3) DSweeney(6) (b.hind: in tch far side: kpt on one pce fnl f)	hd	**10**	66/1	89	60
3649[10]	**Madly Sharp (88)** (JWWatts) **6-8-8b[1]** JFortune(18) (drvn along stands' side ½-wy: styd on: nvr able to chal)	hd	**11**	25/1	86	57
4100[2]	**Sharp Hat (90)** (RHannon) **3-8-8** GHind(13) (prom far side tl wknd appr fnl f)	nk	**12**	16/1	87	56
4011[5]	**Tedburrow (104)** (EJAlston) **5-9-10** ACulhane(20) (hdwy stands' side over 2f out: chsng ldrs 1f out: wknd)	¾	**13**	20/1	99	70
3604[2]	**Emerging Market (98)** (JLDunlop) **5-9-4** KDarley(8) (b: racd far side: drvn along ½-wy: n.d)	¾	**14**	16/1	91	62
4100[8]	**Nigrasine (102)** (JLEyre) **3-9-6v** DeanMcKeown(10) (chsd ldrs far side 4f)	nk	**15**	50/1	94	63
3863*	**My Melody Parkes (93)** (JBerry) **4-8-13** 3x RHills(29) (lw: gd spd stands' side tl wknd 1f out)	s.h	**16**	7/1[2]	85	56
3747[7]	**Proud Native (IRE) (104)** (APJarvis) **3-9-3**(5) CLowther(16) (in tch stands' side 4f)	nk	**17**	20/1	95	64
3403[2]	**Persian Fayre (87)** (JBerry) **5-8-4**(3) TEDurcan(23) (w ldrs stands' side over 4f)	1	**18**	33/1	76	47
4100[22]	**Astrac (IRE) (95)** (NTinkler) **6-9-1** KimTinkler(25) (outpcd stands' side ½-wy: hmpd over 1f out: n.d)	hd	**19**	66/1	84	55
3535a*	**Cretan Gift (103)** (NPLittmoden) **6-9-9b** JWeaver(12) (lw: racd far side: a bhd)	s.h	**20**	20/1	91	62
3217[28]	**Selhurstpark Flyer (IRE) (97)** (JBerry) **6-8-12**(5) PRoberts(19) (b: outpcd & bhd stands' side)	¾	**21**	33/1	83	54
3649*	**Plaisir d'Amour (IRE) (91)** (NACallaghan) **3-8-9** WRyan(26) (bhd stands' side: hmpd over 1f out: n.d)	1¼	**22**	9/1[3]	74	43
4062[4]	**Passion For Life (96)** (GLewis) **4-9-2** PaulEddery(11) (cl up far side 4f)	s.h	**23**	16/1	79	50
4100[7]	**Tadeo (100)** (MJohnston) **4-9-6** AlexGreaves(17) (lw: spd stands' side 4f)	hd	**24**	33/1	83	54
4121[7]	**Elfland (IRE) (89)** (LadyHerries) **6-8-4**(5) GMilligan(2) (a bhd far side)	¾	**25**	14/1	70	41
3888[13]	**Zuhair (88)** (DMcCain) **4-8-3b[1]**(5) RMullen(4) (a bhd far side)	2	**26**	50/1	63	34
4100[4]	**Bold Effort (FR) (94)** (KOCunningham-Brown) **5-8-11b**(3) RHavlin(27) (w ldrs stands' side over 4f)	hd	**27**	25/1	69	40
3764[11]	**King of Peru (94)** (NPLittmoden) **4-9-0b[1]** TGMcLaughlin(14) (racd far side: in tch: hung rt & wknd fr ½-wy)	2	**28**	25/1	64	35
3425*	**Midyan Call (92)** (MBell) **3-8-10** MFenton(15) (racd far side: prom to ½-wy: sn wknd)	5	**29**	33/1	48	17

(SP 144.0%) **29 Rn**

1m 11.64 (1.84) CSF £121.51 CT £4,221.38 TOTE £13.10: £3.30 £3.10 £15.40 £9.20 (£111.30) Trio £8,702.00; £8,579.50 to Haydock 21/9/97 OWNER Mr G. Howard-Spink (MARLBOROUGH) BRED Sir Stephen Hastings and G. Howard-Spink

WEIGHT FOR AGE 3yo-2lb

4155* Wildwood Flower has found her form of late and her rider is particularly good coming from off the pace. These tactics suit her ideally. (14/1)

3975* Double Action ran his socks off to win the race up the far side, but the ground had dried out too much for him to win it overall. (10/1)

501* Superior Premium ran a storming race after almost five months off, and looks likely to find plenty of other opportunities this backend. (33/1)

3535a Azizzi had the speed to get the far rails, and made full use of that, but was just outstayed. (33/1)

3795* Gaelic Storm did not help matters by sweating profusely before being loaded into the stalls, and was then dropped out, which set him a stiffish task. He did finish to some purpose, certainly stayed the extra furlong, and is not done with yet. (14/1)

3615 Albert The Bear stays further, and had blinkers on for the first time to sharpen him up. With another furlong, he would certainly have been in the shake-up. (66/1)

3252 Ziggy's Dancer (USA) was back to something like his old self, but was just tapped for toe late on. (50/1)

3649 Blessingindisguise behaved himself at the start this time, and put up a useful effort, but this six furlongs just found him out. (14/1)

3765 Oggi was always struggling for both pace and room, and although finishing well, could never get into it. (6/1)

Madly Sharp had blinkers on for the first time, and was given plenty of help from the saddle, but his draw was a disadvantage that he could not overcome. (25/1)

3649* Plaisir d'Amour (IRE), in trying to come from behind, never got a run at any stage, and this is best ignored. (9/1)

4283 LADBROKES AYRSHIRE H'CAP (0-90) (3-Y.O+) (Class C)

4-45 (4-49) **1m** £20,470.00 (£6,160.00: £2,980.00: £1,390.00) Stalls: High GOING: 0.05 sec per fur (G)

				SP	RR	SF
3991*	**Solar Storm (85)** (MBell) **3-9-9** MFenton(1) (trckd ldrs: led wl over 1f out: hrd rdn & r.o)	—	**1**	11/1	95	68
3822[6]	**Somerton Boy (IRE) (69)** (PCalver) **7-8-11** JCarroll(6) (lw: hld up & bhd: hdwy over 2f out: n.m.r: r.o strly fnl f)	1	**2**	16/1	77	54
4121*	**Safio (77)** (ABailey) **4-9-5** DWright(8) (lw: trckd ldrs: hdwy 2f out: chsng ldr whn 1f out: nt qckn)	nk	**3**	11/2[2]	84	61
4268[2]	**Rebel County (IRE) (66)** (ABailey) **4-8-8v** JFortune(16) (hld up & bhd: hdwy on ins whn n.m.r 2f out: styd on wl towards fin)	¾	**4**	12/1	72	49
3423[2]	**Philistar (76)** (KRBurke) **4-9-1**(3) DSweeney(19) (hld up & bhd: nt clr run over 2f out & over 1f out: r.o wl towards fin)	½	**5**	12/1	81	58
4270[11]	**Celebration Cake (IRE) (69)** (MissLAPerratt) **5-8-11** DeanMcKeown(17) (in tch: outpcd 3f out: kpt on wl u.p fnl f)	1¼	**6**	33/1	71	48
3548[4]	**Sue's Return (77)** (APJarvis) **5-9-0**(5) CLowther(9) (in tch: effrt 3f out: styd on one pce)	s.h	**7**	10/1	79	56
3976[4]	**Begorrat (IRE) (70)** (DMoffatt) **3-8-5b**(3) DarrenMoffatt(7) (rr div: hdwy 3f out: sn rdn: styd on one pce appr fnl f)	½	**8**	25/1	71	44
4268[8]	**Best of All (IRE) (73)** (JBerry) **5-9-1b** RCochrane(13) (bhd: hdwy ½-wy: rdn & no imp appr fnl f)	¾	**9**	33/1	73	50
3937*	**Kennemara Star (IRE) (87)** (JLDunlop) **3-9-11** KDarley(14) (lw: trckd ldrs: stdy hdwy to chal 3f out: rdn & wknd appr fnl f)	s.h	**10**	4/1[1]	87	60
3921[5]	**Running Green (67)** (DMoffatt) **6-8-2v**(7)ow2 TSiddall(5) (rr div: effrt 3f out: n.d)	¾	**11**	25/1	65	40
4147[17]	**Pride of Pendle (76)** (MartynWane) **8-9-4** JWeaver(12) (hld up & bhd: effrt 3f out: n.d)	1¾	**12**	16/1	71	48
4270[9]	**Regal Thunder (USA) (69)** (MRStoute) **3-8-7v** JQuinn(2) (led tl hdd & wknd wl over 1f out)	2½	**13**	20/1	59	32
3894[3]	**Test The Water (IRE) (79)** (RHannon) **3-9-3** DaneO'Neill(3) (effrt on ins 3f out: hrd rdn & n.d)	nk	**14**	13/2[3]	68	41
4147[5]	**Moving Arrow (82)** (MissSEHall) **6-9-10** DHolland(11) (chsd ldrs tl wknd fnl 2½f)	3½	**15**	8/1	64	41
4147[11]	**Bollin Frank (68)** (TDEasterby) **5-8-10** LCharnock(10) (chsd ldrs tl rdn & wknd 2f out)	2½	**16**	16/1	45	22
4121[9]	**Tertium (IRE) (81)** (MartynWane) **5-9-4**(5) RMullen(15) (a bhd)	¾	**17**	20/1	57	34
3622[5]	**Royal Ceilidh (IRE) (66)** (DenysSmith) **4-8-5v**(3) PFessey(18) (chsd ldrs tl wknd over 2f out)	6	**18**	25/1	30	7
3901[16]	**Moscow Mist (IRE) (77)** (BPalling) **6-9-0**(5) PRoberts(20) (in tch tl wknd 3f out)	13	**19**	33/1	15	—
				(SP 140.2%)	**19 Rn**	

1m 41.59 (4.19) CSF £163.07 CT £1,006.11 TOTE £24.40: £4.10 £3.90 £2.10 £3.30 (£270.50) Trio £643.10 OWNER Mr T. F. Harris (NEWMARKET) BRED Cheveley Park Stud Ltd

WEIGHT FOR AGE 3yo-4lb

3991* Solar Storm, at his first attempt in handicap company, did it well getting first run and then responding to pressure in game style. (11/1: 8/1-12/1)

3822 Somerton Boy (IRE) likes this track and loves to come from off the pace but he was always finding traffic problems and his effort was then always to late. (16/1)

4121* Safio ran his usual game race but this extra distance just proved beyond him. (11/2)

4268 Rebel County (IRE) has now run consistently well in consecutive days and is obviously knocking at the door. (12/1)

3423 Philistar never saw daylight until too late and is obviously on top form after six weeks off. (12/1)

4270 Celebration Cake (IRE) ran better this time but was still lacking a real turn of speed. (33/1)

4147 Moving Arrow (8/1: 20/1-7/1)

4284 FORD SCOTTISH DEALER NURSERY H'CAP (2-Y.O) (Class D)

5-15 (5-17) **6f** £4,666.00 (£1,408.00: £684.00: £322.00) Stalls: High GOING: 0.05 sec per fur (G)

				SP	RR	SF
3774[12]	**Hujoom (IRE) (87)** (JLDunlop) **2-9-7** KDarley(11) (bhd: hdwy 2f out: styd on to ld wl ins fnl f)	—	**1**	10/1	91	52
4152[12]	**Premium Pursuit (81)** (RAFahey) **2-9-1** RCochrane(9) (cl up: led wl over 1f out: hdd & no ex towards fin)	½	**2**	14/1	84	45
3699[3]	**Cosmic Case (63)** (JSGoldie) **2-7-6**(5)ow1 APolli(12) (bhd: hdwy over 2f out: chsng ldrs over 1f out: kpt on)	1¼	**3**	33/1	62	22
4152[5]	**Angel Hill (79)** (TDBarron) **2-8-13** JCarroll(4) (a.p: effrt 2f out: r.o one pce)	2	**4**	15/2	73	34
4143[4]	**Vice Presidential (86)** (TJEtherington) **2-9-6** ACulhane(10) (chsd ldrs: chal over 1f out: nt qckn)	½	**5**	12/1	79	40
3821*	**Cumbrian Cadet (76)** (TDEasterby) **2-8-10** JFortune(6) (lw: chsd ldrs tl rdn & btn appr fnl f)	1¼	**6**	6/1[3]	65	26
3932*	**Five of Spades (IRE) (77)** (RAFahey) **2-8-4**(7) RWinston(2) (lw: in tch: effrt 2f out: btn appr fnl f)	1½	**7**	9/1	62	23
3869[4]	**Lasham (66)** (NACallaghan) **2-7-11**(3) DarrenMoffatt(3) (rr div: effrt ½-wy: n.d)	1¼	**8**	12/1	48	9
3904[2]	**Anita At Dawn (IRE) (83)** (BPalling) **2-9-3** DHolland(13) (mde most over 4f: wkng whn hmpd appr fnl f)	s.h	**9**	5/1[2]	65	26
3920[5]	**Baylham (66)** (JSGoldie) **2-8-0** JQuinn(7) (bhd: effrt ½-wy: n.d)	1	**10**	25/1	45	6
3288*	**Huntswood (85)** (RHannon) **2-9-5** DaneO'Neill(5) (lw: bhd: rdn ½-wy: n.d)	5	**11**	9/4[1]	51	12
3899[5]	**Suivez La Trace (86)** (JJO'Neill) **2-9-1b**[1](5) CLowther(1) (outpcd & bhd fr ½-wy)	2½	**12**	20/1	45	6
2314[6]	**Katy Thomas (66)** (JBerry) **2-7-11**(3) PFessey(8) (disp ld to ½-wy: wknd qckly)	8	**13**	16/1	4	—
				(SP 132.1%)	**13 Rn**	

1m 13.79 (3.99) CSF £139.97 CT £2,462.35 TOTE £9.50: £2.70 £2.80 £6.00 (£37.60) Trio £281.70 OWNER Kuwait Racing Syndicate (ARUNDEL) BRED W. J. Byrne

LONG HANDICAP Cosmic Case 6-13

OFFICIAL EXPLANATION **Hujoom (IRE): the colt had been drawn on the wrong side last time and had seen too much daylight.**

3186 Hujoom (IRE), after four weeks off and a poor run last time, he returned to form in fine style and looks likely to stay a bit further. (10/1)

4152 Premium Pursuit, without the blinkers this time, was back to his best and ought to pick up another race in due course. (14/1)

3699 Cosmic Case ran well from 11lb out of the handicap and is in really good form just now. (33/1)

4152 Angel Hill had his chances this time but, despite some determined assistance, was never doing enough. (15/2)

4143 Vice Presidential races with every chance until getting out-battled late on. (12/1)

3821* Cumbrian Cadet showed up behind the leaders but was always too short of room and pace to do anything about him. (6/1)

T/Plpt: £167.00 (316.43 Tckts). T/Qdpt: £108.40 (22.72 Tckts) AA

3562-CATTERICK (L-H) (Good to firm, Firm patches)
Saturday September 20th
WEATHER: fine WIND: mod half bhd

4285 LEVY BOARD NURSERY H'CAP (0-75) (2-Y.O) (Class E)
2-20 (2-22) **7f** £3,564.25 (£1,069.00: £514.50: £237.25) Stalls: Low GOING minus 0.32 sec per fur (GF)

Form	Horse / details	Dist	Pos	SP	RR	SF
3545^{10}	**Petara (IRE) (60)** (JSWainwright) **2-8-11v** FLynch(6) (mid div: styd on to ld ins fnl f: drvn out)	—	**1**	14/1	65	29
2840^{10}	**Supacalifragilistk (58)** (BWHills) **2-8-6**(3) DO'Donohoe(13) (sn bhd: gd hdwy on outside 2f out: styd on strly towards fin)	1¼	**2**	$9/1^{3}$	60	24
4152^{4}	**Inchalong (70)** (MBrittain) **2-9-7** GBardwell(16) (lw: s.i.s: hdwy ½-wy: hrd rdn over 2f out: styd on wl appr fnl f)	1	**3**	$11/2^{2}$	70	34
3751*	**Impulse (IRE) (63)** (MrsJRRamsden) **2-9-0** DBiggs(9) (lw: s.i.s: hdwy on outside 2f out: edgd lft: styd on wl towards fin)	hd	**4**	$11/2^{2}$	63	27
3438^{5}	**Shamwari Song (64)** (JAGlover) **2-9-1** VHalliday(14) (bhd: hdwy u.p 2f out: edgd lft & styd on ins fnl f)	1	**5**	14/1	61	25
4152^{9}	**Three Tenners (57)** (JBerry) **2-8-8b** JFanning(3) (s.i.s: bhd: hdwy on outside over 2f out: styng on whn n.m.r ins fnl f)	nk	**6**	14/1	54	18
4061^{14}	**Bawsian (65)** (JLEyre) **2-9-2** OPears(8) (sn outpcd: nt clr run & swtchd outside over 1f out: styd on towards fin)	½	**7**	$7/2^{1}$	61	25
4097^{18}	**Tancred Times (69)** (DWBarker) **2-9-6** TWilliams(7) (led tl hdd & wknd jst ins fnl f)	½	**8**	14/1	63	27
3186^{10}	**The Honorable Lady (63)** (MRChannon) **2-8-11**(3) JBramhill(1) (chsd ldrs tl wknd over 1f out)	1	**9**	12/1	55	19
3905^{4}	**Tom Dougal (69)** (CSmith) **2-9-6** JTate(17) (lw: racd wd: sn chsng ldrs: wknd over 1f out)	hd	**10**	16/1	61	25
3628^{6}	**Castle Friend (58)** (PCHaslam) **2-8-9** DaleGibson(5) (plld hrd: sn trckng ldrs: drvn along ½-wy: lost pl over 2f out)	1¾	**11**	16/1	46	10
3924^{7}	**Flying Singer (61)** (IABalding) **2-8-12** SWhitworth(11) (mid div: sn drvn along: outpcd fr ½-wy)	1¼	**12**	12/1	46	10
3307^{11}	**Semi Circle (58)** (TDEasterby) **2-8-9b** LNewton(2) (s.i.s: a in rr)	1¾	**13**	12/1	39	3
3821^{11}	**Buzz The Agent (58)** (MWEasterby) **2-8-2**(7) SFinnamore(15) (b.nr fore: racd wd: chsd ldrs tl lost pl 2f out)	s.h	**14**	33/1	39	3
3905^{11}	**Carrick View (IRE) (60)** (PCalver) **2-8-11** JStack(4) (lw: chsd ldrs tl wknd over 2f out)	hd	**15**	16/1	41	5
3990^{13}	**The Cannie Rover (60)** (MWEasterby) **2-8-8**(3) GParkin(10) (hld up: nt clr run 2f out: hmpd 1f out: nt rcvr)	1½	**16**	33/1	37	1
4014^{15}	**Heavenly Falls (IRE) (60)** (CADwyer) **2-8-11** FNorton(12) (chsd ldrs: drvn along ½-wy: lost pl over 2f out)	nk	**17**	12/1	37	1
				(SP 144.0%)	**17 Rn**	

1m 26.9 (3.30) CSF £143.01 CT £765.62 TOTE £27.20: £3.80 £3.60 £1.90 £1.50 (£256.40) Trio £159.50; £159.59 to Haydock 21/9/97
OWNER Mr J. H. Pickard (MALTON) BRED Lt-Col and Mrs J. A. Dene

3212 Petara (IRE), who finished last of ten on much easier ground at Beverley on his previous start, proved well suited by this sharper track. (14/1)
1321 Supacalifragilistk, having her first outing for sixty-four days during which time she has changed stables, stuck on strongly and would have troubled the winner with a bit further to go. (9/1)
4152 Inchalong is as tough as old boots and ran really well from a poor draw, especially considering she missed the break. (11/2)
3751* Impulse (IRE), who has been gelded since Thirsk, was edgy beforehand and was taken to post early. Awkward exiting the stalls, making his effort on the wide outside, he tended to edge in. He is certainly on a winning mark and a mile will suit him better. (11/2)
3438 Shamwari Song, having his first outing for forty-one days, gave his rider problems but was staying on at the line. A mile might suit him better. (14/1)
4152 Three Tenners again had no luck in running. (14/1)
3806 Bawsian, who struggled to go the pace, met trouble in running and would be better suited by a mile. (7/2)

4286 E.B.F. MAIDEN STKS (2-Y.O) (Class D)
2-50 (2-51) **5f 212y** £3,541.50 (£1,062.00: £511.00: £235.50) Stalls: High GOING minus 0.32 sec per fur (GF)

Form	Horse / details	Dist	Pos	SP	RR	SF
4145^{2}	**Title Bid (USA)** (MRStoute) **2-9-0** FLynch(1) (lw: hld up: hdwy after 2f: wnt 2nd 2f out: r.o u.p to ld ins fnl f)	—	**1**	$8/11^{1}$	82+	43
3794^{4}	**Beware (83)** (RWArmstrong) **2-9-0** FNorton(7) (sn trckng ldrs: effrt 2f out: styd on fnl f: nt rch wnr)	1¾	**2**	$5/1^{3}$	77	38
3564^{4}	**Iris May (72)** (JBerry) **2-8-9b¹** JFanning(9) (led: sn clr: hdd ins fnl f: kpt on same pce)	1¼	**3**	11/1	69	30
3490^{3}	**Asyaad (USA)** (BWHills) **2-8-11**(3) DO'Donohoe(8) (lw: hld up & sn bhd: stdy hdwy on outside 2f out: edgd lft & styd on wl: nt rch ldrs: eased ins fnl f)	2	**4**	$7/2^{2}$	69+	30
3905^{7}	**Strictly Rhythm** (MrsSABramall) **2-8-11**(3) GParkin(4) (chsd ldrs: one pce fnl 2f)	1½	**5**	33/1	65	26
3411^{7}	**Bolshaya** (JBerry) **2-8-9** DaleGibson(6) (racd wd: chsd ldrs: drvn along ½-wy: outpcd fnl 2f)	4	**6**	25/1	49	10
4211^{5}	**Moving Princess** (MissSEHall) **2-8-9** KHodgson(10) (sn outpcd & bhd: sme hdwy 2f out: n.d)	4	**7**	12/1	38	—
3459^{7}	**Time To Hunt** (BWMurray) **2-9-0** VHalliday(2) (mid div: pushed along ½-wy: sn wl outpcd)	¾	**8**	33/1	41	2
3857^{7}	**Saxon Victory (USA)** (WJHaggas) **2-9-0** SWhitworth(5) (a in rr)	¾	**9**	25/1	39	—
				(SP 126.4%)	**9 Rn**	

1m 12.9 (2.00) CSF £4.92 TOTE £1.80: £1.20 £1.20 £2.10 (£4.10) Trio £11.60 OWNER Sheikh Mohammed (NEWMARKET) BRED Darley Stud Management

4145 Title Bid (USA), who showed a fair bit of knee action going down, knuckled down willingly and, in the end, scored in ready fashion. Seven will prove no problem. (8/11: 10/11-evens)
3794 Beware took a while to get into full stride. Putting in his best work inside the last, seven and a more galloping track will suit him a lot better. (5/1)
3564 Iris May, blinkered for the first time, soon showed in a clear lead but she did not get home. (11/1)
3490 Asyaad (USA), a keen going type, seemed to be given a poor ride. Giving the leaders plenty of rope, he made his ground on the outside once in line for home. Tending to edge left towards the far rail, his rider seemed in no hurry whatsoever and decided to take things easily inside the last. Presumably, he was ridden with a view to a nursery with one more outing under his belt. (7/2)
Strictly Rhythm showed a poor action going down. (33/1)
4211 Moving Princess moved very short to post and seems to have lost her way after a promising first run. (12/1)

4287 SKYRAM H'CAP (0-65) (3-Y.O+) (Class F)
3-20 (3-23) **1m 7f 177y** £3,141.00 (£876.00: £423.00) Stalls: Low GOING minus 0.32 sec per fur (GF)

Form	Horse / details	Dist	Pos	SP	RR	SF
4160*	**Il Principe (IRE) (59)** (JohnBerry) **3-8-11** 5x GBardwell(7) (lw: chsd ldrs: drvn along 7f out: led jst ins fnl f: styd on)	—	**1**	$7/2^{1}$	71	41
	Ranger Sloane (33) (GFierro) **5-7-11**ow1 NCarlisle(17) (b: bit bkwd: sn trckng ldrs: effrt over 2f out: led over 1f out: hdd jst ins fnl f: nt qckn nr fin)	½	**2**	33/1	45	26

				SP	RR	SF
3931[4]	**Exactly (IRE) (55)** (JLEyre) **4-9-5** TWilliams(4) (trckd ldrs: led over 5f out tl over 1f out: kpt on one pce)	3	**3**	13/2[3]	64	46
4045[6]	**Good Reputation (58)** (BWHills) **3-8-7**(3) DO'Donohoe(11) (lw: a.p: drvn along 5f out: one pce fnl 2f)	2	**4**	7/1	64	34
3778[4]	**Finestatetobein (36)** (FWatson) **4-7-9**(5)ow4 KimberleyHart(14) (plld hrd: stdy hdwy 10f out: effrt 4f out: kpt on: nvr nr to chal)	3½	**5**	16/1	39	17
3754[2]	**Charter (60)** (WStorey) **6-9-10v** JFanning(15) (lw: hld up: hdwy 10f out: chsd ldrs over 4f out: sn rdn & no imp)	2	**6**	5/1[2]	61	43
4213[5]	**Alwarqa (45)** (MartynWane) **4-8-6**(3) PPMurphy(6) (sn trckng ldrs: rdn & outpcd over 3f out: n.d after)	1½	**7**	9/1	44	26
	Uncle Doug (60) (MrsMReveley) **6-9-5**(5) SCopp(9) (bit bkwd: bhd: sme hdwy 3f out: nvr nr ldrs)	6	**8**	16/1	53	35
3486[8]	**Bruz (32)** (LLungo) **6-7-3**(7) PBradley(10) (s.s: plld hrd & bhd: sme hdwy over 4f out: n.d)	7	**9**	33/1	18	—
4170[15]	**Kinoko (45)** (KWHogg) **9-8-9** JBramhill(12) (mid div: effrt & drvn along 5f out: sn wl outpcd)	½	**10**	20/1	31	13
3781[2]	**Dulas Bay (48)** (MWEasterby) **3-8-0** DaleGibson(5) (lw: trckd ldrs: drvn along ½-wy: lost pl 4f out)	1¾	**11**	8/1	32	2
3933[9]	**Bold Top (52)** (BSRothwell) **5-9-2be** JStack(3) (s.i.s: sn chsng ldrs: drvn along 6f out: lost pl 4f out)	7	**12**	20/1	29	11
461[11]	**Taniyar (FR) (45)** (RHollinshead) **5-8-9** FLynch(8) (sn bhd)	hd	**13**	20/1	22	4
3858[5]	**Straffan Gold (USA) (47)** (MrsMReveley) **3-7-13** FNorton(13) (hld up: a in rr)	3½	**14**	10/1	20	—
3992[15]	**Kulepopsie (IRE) (39)** (ABMulholland) **4-8-3b**[1] DBiggs(1) (led tl over 5f out: sn wknd: virtually p.u)	14	**15**	33/1	—	—
				(SP 129.8%)	**15 Rn**	

3m 27.9 (5.90) CSF £133.21 CT £680.76 TOTE £3.30: £1.60 £47.90 £2.20 (£220.30) Trio Not won; £249.93 to Haydock 21/9/97 OWNER The 1997 Partnership (NEWMARKET) BRED J. Costello

LONG HANDICAP Bruz 7-0 Ranger Sloane 7-0 Finestatetobein 7-9

WEIGHT FOR AGE 3yo-12lb

4160* Il Principe (IRE) is certainly not resting on his laurels. Making it five wins from seven starts, from a 4lb higher mark than Musselburgh, he would not be denied. (7/2)

Ranger Sloane, a winner over hurdles in February, was racing from 10lb out of the handicap but connections went for quite a touch and, in the end, they were only just denied. (33/1)

3931 Exactly (IRE), racing over an extended trip, surprisingly made the best of her way home but, in the end, the first two proved too strong. A mile six might prove ideal. (13/2)

4045 Good Reputation seemed to stay alright but has nothing in the way of finishing speed. (7/1)

3778 Finestatetobein, who is not one to rely on, ran a much better race. (16/1)

3754 Charter was flat out and getting nowhere turning in. (5/1)

Uncle Doug, making a belated reappearance, was certainly not knocked about. (16/1)

4288 CONSTANT SECURITY SERVICES H'CAP (0-85) (3-Y.O+) (Class D)

3-50 (3-50) **1m 3f 214y** £3,850.00 (£1,150.00: £550.00: £250.00) Stalls: Low GOING minus 0.32 sec per fur (GF)

				SP	RR	SF
3722[11]	**Tessajoe (85)** (MJCamacho) **5-9-9**(5) SCopp(4) (b.hind: trckd ldrs: gng wl: shkn up to ld over 1f out: drvn along: hld on wl)	—	**1**	5/2[1]	94	65
3970[12]	**Double Eight (IRE) (70)** (BWHills) **3-8-2**(3) DO'Donohoe(5) (plld hrd: sn trckng ldr: led over 2f out: nt qckn ins fnl f)	1	**2**	11/2	78	41
3886[9]	**Mad Militant (IRE) (63)** (AStreeter) **8-8-6** NCarlisle(6) (hld up: hdwy over 3f out: styd on same pce fnl 2f)	2½	**3**	13/2	67	38
3809*	**Tycooness (IRE) (78)** (MJohnston) **3-8-13** JFanning(2) (lw: pushed along & outpcd over 7f out: hdwy over 2f out: kpt on: nvr able to chal)	nk	**4**	3/1[2]	82	45
2014[25]	**Nigel's Lad (IRE) (80)** (PCHaslam) **5-9-9** DaleGibson(3) (bit bkwd: chsd ldrs: outpcd & drvn along over 7f out: kpt on fnl 2f: n.d)	4	**5**	7/1	79	50
3242[6]	**Canton Venture (75)** (SPCWoods) **5-9-4** FLynch(7) (chsd ldrs: ev ch over 2f out: wknd over 1f out: eased towards fin)	2	**6**	5/1[3]	71	42
4136[13]	**Golden Hello (69)** (TDEasterby) **6-8-12** TWilliams(1) (led tl over 2f out: sn wknd & eased)	4	**7**	33/1	60	31
				(SP 114.4%)	**7 Rn**	

2m 34.5 (0.30 under best) (3.10) CSF £15.20 TOTE £3.90: £1.90 £2.00 (£11.00) OWNER Riley Partnership (MALTON) BRED A. and Mrs Rhodes

WEIGHT FOR AGE 3yo-8lb

OFFICIAL EXPLANATION **Tessajoe: regarding the improvement in form compared with the gelding's previous run at York, the trainer stated thet the gelding was unsuited by the slow early pace on that occasion. He added that he shows better form on sharp tracks.**

3333 Tessajoe, who was unsuited by the easy ground and false run race at York, repeated his win in this event a year ago, from a stone higher mark. Very willing, he is ideally suited by sharp tracks and fast ground. (5/2)

3256* Double Eight (IRE) put a poor effort behind her last time and made the winner fight all the way to the line. (11/2)

3467 Mad Militant (IRE) usually runs well on sharp tracks like this. (13/2)

3809* Tycooness (IRE) looked to have plenty on at the weights on her handicap debut. Taken to post early, she did nothing wrong at the start but, seeming to drop herself out before staying on at the finish, she is clearly something of a madam. (3/1)

1648* Nigel's Lad (IRE) was having his first outing since Royal Ascot ninety-five days previously. Rallying after losing his place, he will be an interesting proposition in a handicap hurdle. (7/1)

3242 Canton Venture seemed not to appreciate being able to dominate. (5/1)

Golden Hello ran much better than on his reappearance and will no doubt be seen in action under National Hunt Rules before too much longer. (33/1)

4289 CATTERICK 'OPEN MORNING' NEXT SATURDAY (S) STKS (3-Y.O) (Class G)

4-25 (4-25) **1m 5f 175y** £2,197.50 (£610.00: £292.50) Stalls: Low GOING minus 0.32 sec per fur (GF)

				SP	RR	SF
3781[13]	**Ziggy's Viola (IRE) (50)** (MrsMReveley) **3-8-2**(3) DO'Donohoe(7) (trckd ldrs: led 3f out: sn drvn clr: unchal)	—	**1**	7/4[1]	58	2
3714[W]	**Ronquista d'Or (47)** (GAHam) **3-8-10** FNorton(5) (prom: drvn along 6f out: styd on fnl f: no ch w wnr)	4	**2**	9/2[3]	58	2
1733[6]	**Hever Golf Angel (IRE) (50)** (PCHaslam) **3-8-5** DaleGibson(1) (hld up: effrt over 3f out: kpt on one pce fnl 2f)	1¼	**3**	12/1	52	—
3129[5]	**Skelton Sovereign (IRE) (54)** (RHollinshead) **3-9-0** FLynch(3) (lw: hld up: jnd ldrs after 5f: effrt over 4f out: sn rdn: wknd over 1f out)	3	**4**	2/1[2]	57	1
4114[14]	**Grovefair Dancer (IRE) (60)** (FJYardley) **3-8-5** JFanning(2) (hld up: hdwy 7f out: sn chsng ldrs: wknd 2f out)	6	**5**	14/1	42	—
3486[7]	**Cochiti (30)** (CWThornton) **3-8-5b** TWilliams(6) (lw: led to 3f out: edgd rt & sn wknd: eased)	8	**6**	6/1	32	—
3816[11]	**Honiara Bay (28)** (MissAStokell) **3-8-2**(3) PPMurphy(4) (trckd ldrs: stumbled 7f out: sn lost pl: t.o 3f out)	dist	**7**	20/1	—	—
				(SP 121.3%)	**7 Rn**	

3m 7.4 (11.40) CSF £10.18 TOTE £2.60: £2.00 £4.90 (£11.40) OWNER Mrs C. T. Woodley (SALTBURN) BRED Stonethorn Stud Farms Ltd

No bid

3567 Ziggy's Viola (IRE), taken to post early, proved much too good for this lot. Her rider left nothing at all to chance. She does not lack ability, but is not always inclined to show it. (7/4)

2301 Ronquista d'Or proved very one-paced, the winner was much too good. (9/2)
Hever Golf Angel (IRE) seemed to stay the trip alright, especially considering her first outing this season was over five furlongs. (12/1: 16/1-10/1)
3129 Skelton Sovereign (IRE) ran a very tame race. (2/1)

4290 RACING CHANNEL MAIDEN STKS (3-Y.O) (Class D)

4-55 (4-59) **7f** £3,821.00 (£1,148.00: £554.00: £257.00) Stalls: Low GOING minus 0.32 sec per fur (GF)

				SP	RR	SF
3396[3]	**Cantina** (ABailey) **3-8-4**(5) GFaulkner(10) (mde virtually all: styd on wl appr fnl f)	—	**1**	14/1	68	38
4059[2]	**Topton (IRE) (68)** (IABalding) **3-9-0v** SWhitworth(8) (lw: sn chsng ldrs: effrt & hung lft over 1f out: kpt on: no imp)	2	**2**	5/2[3]	68	38
3991[4]	**Present Chance (75)** (BAMcMahon) **3-9-0** LNewton(7) (b.hind: lw: sn chsng ldrs: effrt 2f out: edgd lft & kpt on same pce)	3	**3**	7/4[1]	62	32
3550[2]	**Warning Express** (RWArmstrong) **3-8-9** FNorton(3) (plld hrd: trckd ldrs: rdn over 2f out: wknd over 1f out)	5	**4**	9/4[2]	45	15
3807[5]	**Kwikpoint** (MartinTodhunter) **3-9-0** JStack(15) (hld up: shkn up & stdy hdwy 2f out: styd on wl towards fin: nvr plcd to chal)	¾	**5**	20/1	48	18
4047[8]	**Marylebone (IRE) (63)** (JBerry) **3-9-0** OPears(2) (chsd ldrs: drvn along ½-wy: wknd over 1f out)	1¼	**6**	12/1	46	16
3431[19]	**Imperial Line (IRE) (34)** (ABMulholland) **3-9-0b** NCarlisle(14) (b: plld hrd: hdwy ½-wy: kpt on fnl 2f: nvr nr to chal)	1	**7**	50/1	43	13
945[8]	**Nite Owler** (JO'Reilly) **3-9-0** JFanning(4) (chsd ldrs: drvn along ½-wy: no imp)	nk	**8**	33/1	43	13
3313[W]	**Fantasy Flight** (MAPeill) **3-8-6**(3) DO'Donohoe(9) (mid div: sn pushed along: nvr nr to chal)	1	**9**	33/1	35	5
3068[7]	**Dance Melody (29)** (GROldroyd) **3-8-9** KHodgson(6) (prom: rdn ½-wy: sn lost pl)	½	**10**	50/1	34	4
3396[6]	**Who Dealt** (RHollinshead) **3-8-9** FLynch(13) (hld up: nvr nr ldrs)	2	**11**	33/1	30	—
	The Munro's (JSGoldie) **3-8-11**(3) PPMurphy(11) (unf: bkwd: dwlt: a bhd: t.o ½-wy)	½	**12**	40/1	34	4
	Six Shooter (EWeymes) **3-8-9** DaleGibson(1) (bkwd: sn outpcd & bhd)	½	**13**	33/1	27	—
3037[6]	**Damara** (CWFairhurst) **3-8-9** JTate(12) (bit bkwd: s.i.s: a bhd)	½	**14**	20/1	26	—
2143[8]	**Ballantrae Boy** (JSGoldie) **3-9-0** TWilliams(5) (bit bkwd: s.i.s: a bhd)	¾	**15**	50/1	30	—
				(SP 139.7%)	**15 Rn**	

1m 26.0 (2.40) CSF £48.04 TOTE £18.40: £2.60 £1.30 £1.70 (£17.00) Trio £21.60 OWNER B K Racing (TARPORLEY) BRED K. Benson and R. Kinsey

STEWARDS' ENQUIRY Pears susp. 29/9 & 1/10/97 (incorrect use of whip). SUSEQUENT STEWARDS' ENQUIRY Todhunter fined £1,500 & Stack susp. 14-22/10/97 under rule 151(ii) (schooling in public). Kwikpoint susp. 10/10-/8/11/97.

3396 Cantina settled well in front, and certainly stepped up on her first effort. Further improvement is likely. (14/1)
4059 Topton (IRE), with the visor again fitted, tended to hang in behind the winner, and was never doing enough to seriously trouble her. (5/2)
3991 Present Chance is finding it very hard indeed to get his head in front. (7/4)
3550 Warning Express raced far too keenly. (9/4: op 6/4)
3807 Kwikpoint, having his third outing, was given a negative ride. Running on in fine style at the finish, the impression was that he would have finished on the heels of the third with more forceful tactics. (20/1)
2157 Marylebone (IRE), stepping up in distance, found nothing under pressure. His rider was suspended for using his whip over shoulder height. Perhaps the Stewards should have asked Stack on the fifth why he was not as energetic. (12/1: op 8/1)

4291 'RACING AGAIN NEXT SATURDAY' H'CAP (0-60) (3-Y.O+ F & M) (Class F)

5-30 (5-30) **7f** £3,015.00 (£840.00: £405.00) Stalls: Low GOING minus 0.32 sec per fur (GF)

				SP	RR	SF
4169[7]	**Lamorna (48)** (MRChannon) **3-9-0**(3) PPMurphy(1) (chsd ldrs: led over 1f out: hld on towards fin)	—	**1**	8/1	59	43
4228[12]	**Delight of Dawn (49)** (EAWheeler) **5-9-0b**(7) SCarson(10) (trckd ldrs: edgd lft & styd on fnl f)	½	**2**	14/1	59	46
4059[6]	**Celandine (50)** (AndrewTurnell) **4-9-8** DaleGibson(4) (sn pushed along: hdwy over 2f out: styd on fnl f)	¾	**3**	6/1[3]	58	45
3936[8]	**Crissem (IRE) (49)** (RHollinshead) **4-9-7** FLynch(7) (bhd: hdwy on outside 2f out: wnt lft: styd on wl towards fin)	nk	**4**	20/1	57	44
3854[8]	**Tael of Silver (43)** (ABailey) **5-9-1** FNorton(11) (chsd ldrs: rdn & outpcd over 2f out: kpt on appr fnl f)	1	**5**	12/1	48	35
3909[9]	**Polenka (IRE) (50)** (JWWatts) **3-9-5** JFanning(2) (b: sn outpcd & bhd: hdwy on ins 2f out: styd on ins fnl f)	hd	**6**	10/1	55	39
3565[14]	**Komlucky (42)** (ABMulholland) **5-8-9v**(5) GFaulkner(3) (led over 1f: w ldrs tl wknd appr fnl f)	1	**7**	12/1	45	32
3285[13]	**Dispol Diamond (48)** (GROldroyd) **4-9-6** KHodgson(17) (mid div: hdwy on outside 2f out: carried lft: kpt on: nvr nr to chal)	1	**8**	16/1	48	35
4169*	**La Volta (48)** (MissJFCraze) **4-9-6b** 6x SWebster(9) (lw: plld hrd: trckd ldrs tl wknd over 1f out)	s.h	**9**	9/2[2]	48	35
3910[6]	**Gipsy Princess (57)** (MWEasterby) **3-9-5b**(7) SFinnamore(13) (lw: sn bhd & pushed along: sme hdwy 2f out: n.d)	¾	**10**	10/1	56	40
	Grey Again (48) (DShaw) **5-9-3**(3) CTeague(6) (dwlt: bhd tl sme hdwy 2f out: nvr nrr)	hd	**11**	25/1	46	33
4169[5]	**Naissant (53)** (MartynWane) **4-9-8**(3) DO'Donohoe(12) (led over 5f out tl hdd & wknd over 1f out)	hd	**12**	9/1	51	38
3854[6]	**Bollero (IRE) (55)** (JBerry) **3-9-10** OPears(14) (chsd ldrs tl wknd 2f out)	2	**13**	14/1	49	33
3316[6]	**Anetta (56)** (MissSEHall) **3-9-6**(5) SCopp(8) (chsd ldrs tl wknd 2f out)	½	**14**	12/1	48	32
4059[9]	**Bollin Dorothy (52)** (TDEasterby) **4-9-10** TWilliams(5) (in tch: effrt over 2f out: sn wknd & eased)	2	**15**	4/1[1]	40	27
3241[9]	**In Good Nick (51)** (MWEasterby) **3-9-3b**(3) GParkin(15) (s.i.s: bhd tl styd on fnl 2f: nt rch ldrs)	1¾	**16**	16/1	35	19
3812[13]	**Showgirl (47)** (CaptJWilson) **3-9-2** JTate(16) (hld up: sme hdwy ½-wy: sn wknd & eased)	13	**17**	25/1	1	—
				(SP 152.4%)	**17 Rn**	

1m 26.2 (2.60) CSF £127.97 CT £716.71 TOTE £10.60: £2.20 £3.80 £1.50 £5.10 (£65.20) Trio £84.00 OWNER Mr W. H. Ponsonby (UPPER LAMBOURN) BRED E. M. Thornton

WEIGHT FOR AGE 3yo-3lb

OFFICIAL EXPLANATION Showgirl: bled from the nose.

3716 Lamorna, taken to post early, proved well suited by the return to seven furlongs. She showed the right sort of spirit in a tight finish, in a race that was a selling handicap in all but name, the top weight being rated just 57. (8/1)
3394 Delight of Dawn is on a losing run of twenty-five, but she appeared to give her all. (14/1)
4059 Celandine is running right up to her best at present. (6/1)
3936 Crissem (IRE) ran her best race for a long time. (20/1)
Tael of Silver ran easily her best race this year, and there should be better to come this backend. (12/1)
2859 Polenka (IRE), taken to post early, found this seven on a sharp track too short on her debut in handicap company. (10/1)
3936 Bollin Dorothy had gone in her coat, and she turned in a poor effort. (4/1)

T/Plpt: £42.40 (324.4 Tckts). T/Qdpt: £10.70 (52.69 Tckts) WG

4271-NEWBURY (L-H) (Good to soft)
Saturday September 20th
WEATHER: unsettled WIND: mod bhd

4292 AMERADA CONDITIONS STKS (3-Y.O+) (Class C)
2-00 (2-00) **1m 7y (round)** £4,650.50 (£1,688.00: £819.00: £345.00: £147.50) Stalls: Low GOING: 0.09 sec per fur (G)

				SP	RR	SF
3790*	**Bin Rosie (111)** (DRLoder) **5-9-4b** KFallon(5) (lw: hld up: led 2f out: rdn out)	—	1	4/5^{1}	124	81
1740^{4}	**Fatefully (USA) (104)** (EALDunlop) **4-8-9** MHills(3) (a.p: led 3f to 2f out: one pce)	4	2	5/2^{2}	107	64
3728^{7}	**Musical Pursuit (110)** (MHTompkins) **3-8-10** TQuinn(4) (hld up: rdn wl over 1f out: one pce)	1½	3	6/1^{3}	109	62
3766^{3}	**Peartree House (IRE) (100)** (WRMuir) **3-9-0** MartinDwyer(2) (b.hind: w ldr: led over 4f out: hdd 3f out: rdn over 2f out: wknd over 1f out)	5	4	10/1	103	56
4072^{10}	**Merci Monsieur** (JABOld) **4-8-11**$^{(3)}$ RFfrench(1) (lw: plld hrd: led over 3f: wknd over 2f out: t.o)	25	5	100/1	49	6

(SP 108.5%) **5 Rn**

1m 38.73 (2.73) CSF £2.65 TOTE £1.70: £1.30 £1.50 (£1.50) OWNER Mr Wafic Said (NEWMARKET) BRED Addison Racing Ltd Inc
WEIGHT FOR AGE 3yo-4lb

3790* Bin Rosie, whose trainer described his high head-carriage as a family trait, seems set to be campaigned in the States in the near future. (4/5: tchd evens)

1740 Fatefully (USA), who has left the Godolphin operation, was at her best about this time of year last season, and has presumably been trained for an autumn campaign. (5/2)

3728 Musical Pursuit, found to have had a virus when disappointing in the Irish 2,000 Guineas, at least ran better than on his comeback over seven at York last month. (6/1)

3766 Peartree House (IRE) has been highly-tried this season, and would have been getting another 11lb off the winner in a handicap. (10/1)

4293 BONUSPRINT MILL REEF STKS (Gp 2) (2-Y.O) (Class A)
2-30 (2-30) **6f 8y** £33,144.99 (£12,434.25: £5,997.13: £2,638.63) Stalls: High GOING: 0.09 sec per fur (G)

				SP	RR	SF
3811*	**Arkadian Hero (USA) (100)** (LMCumani) **2-8-12** KFallon(5) (dlwt: plld hrd: hdwy to ld over 3f out: all out)	—	1	4/9^{1}	99	58
3899*	**Jimmy Too (91)** (BAMcMahon) **2-8-12** AClark(8) (racd stands side: hdwy 2f out: hung lft over 1f out: r.o)	nk	2	16/1	98?	57
3534a^{9}	**Pool Music (100)** (RHannon) **2-8-12** MHills(3) (lw: led over 2f: rdn over 2f out: swtchd lft ins fnl f: nt qckn)	1	3	12/1^{3}	96	55
4106*	**Mijana (IRE) (100)** (JHMGosden) **2-8-12** AMcGlone(1) (lw: hld up: hrd rdn over 1f out: one pce)	1	4	6/1^{2}	93	52
3148^{5}	**Bold Edge (100)** (RHannon) **2-8-12** WJO'Connor(7) (lw: racd stands side: a.p: hung lft over 2f out: one pce)	1½	5	12/1^{3}	89	48
4150^{5}	**Banningham Blade (100)** (KTIvory) **2-8-7** MartinDwyer(2) (w ldr over 2f: wknd fnl f)	nk	6	16/1	83	42
4146^{5}	**Flaming Ember (IRE) (95)** (BJMeehan) **2-8-12** TQuinn(4) (hrd rdn over 2f out: sn bhd)	3½	7	66/1	79	38

(SP 112.2%) **7 Rn**

1m 15.05 (3.25) CSF £8.36 TOTE £1.60: £1.40 £2.80 (£7.20) OWNER Mr M Tabor & Mrs John Magnier (NEWMARKET) BRED Gainesway Thoroughbreds Ltd

3811* Arkadian Hero (USA), backed as if defeat was out of the question, was intended to make all the running. He got tired in the softish ground, but showed the same determination he had done at Goodwood. His trainer wants to keep him to six furlongs this season, and thinks the Middle Park may come too soon, while his owner was talking in terms of the Dewhurst, but that is over seven, so it will be interesting to see where he goes. (4/9)

3899* Jimmy Too again showed his liking for give in the ground, and found the winner just too strong after being inclined to duck in behind his rival. (16/1)

3534a Pool Music bounced back to form after a disappointing effort in Ireland. (12/1)

4106* Mijana (IRE) was 3lb better off than when beaten three lengths by the winner on faster ground at Ripon. (6/1: op 4/1)

3148 Bold Edge has not really lived up to his trainer's expectations, but it should be remembered that his only win came over course and distance on even softer ground than this. (12/1: op 8/1)

4150 Banningham Blade was having her sixteenth outing of the season, but only her second beyond the minimum trip. (16/1)

4294 COURAGE H'CAP (0-105) (3-Y.O+) (Class B)
3-00 (3-00) **1m 2f 6y** £16,187.49 (£6,062.50: £2,968.75: £1,281.25: £578.13: £296.88) Stalls: Low GOING: 0.09 sec per fur (G)

				SP	RR	SF
3246^{5}	**Sharp Consul (IRE) (80)** (HCandy) **5-8-7** CRutter(5) (hld up: stdy hdwy 4f out: led over 1f out: pushed out)	—	1	9/1^{3}	93	67
3916^{7}	**Lomberto (81)** (VSoane) **4-8-8** RPerham(10) (lw: chsd ldr: rdn to ld over 4f out: hdd over 1f out: one pce)	2	2	33/1	91	65
3824*	**Isitoff (76)** (SCWilliams) **4-8-3** AMcGlone(3) (a.p: ev ch over 1f out: one pce)	¾	3	14/1	85	59
3434^{5}	**Star Manager (USA) (84)** (PFICole) **7-8-11** TQuinn(2) (lw: a.p: rdn over 3f out: one pce fnl 2f)	½	4	10/1	92	66
3575^{2}	**Bali Paradise (USA) (94)** (PFICole) **3-9-1** MTebbutt(6) (led over 5f: swtchd rt 2f out: one pce)	nk	5	14/1	101	69
3891^{4}	**Titta Ruffo (82)** (BJMeehan) **3-8-3** MartinDwyer(7) (hdwy fnl 2f: nvr nrr)	2½	6	25/1	85	53
4102^{8}	**Palatial Style (77)** (PJMakin) **10-8-4** TSprake(8) (hdwy over 3f out: sltly hmpd 2f out: one pce)	½	7	33/1	80	54
3703^{4}	**Game Ploy (POL) (96)** (DHaydnJones) **5-9-9** KFallon(11) (hld up & bhd: hdwy 3f out: wknd wl over 1f out)	8	8	9/2^{1}	86	60
	Migwar (98) (LMCumani) **4-9-11** WJO'Connor(13) (lw: hdwy over 3f out: wknd 2f out)	9	9	14/1	73	47
4151^{8}	**Edan Heights (75)** (SDow) **5-7-9**$^{(7)}$ PDoe(14) (lw: prom: hrd rdn over 3f out: wknd 2f out)	½	10	16/1	50	24
3703^{7}	**Champagne Prince (96)** (PWHarris) **4-9-9** AClark(16) (hld up mid div: bhd fnl 3f)	hd	11	14/1	71	45
3773^{2}	**Hajr (IRE) (87)** (EALDunlop) **3-8-8** MHills(15) (bhd fnl 3f)	s.h	12	6/1^{2}	61	29
3916^{2}	**Grief (IRE) (93)** (DRCElsworth) **4-9-3**$^{(3)}$ RFfrench(12) (b: a bhd)	1¼	13	9/2^{1}	65	39
2869^{7}	**Ball Gown (91)** (DTThom) **7-9-4** JLowe(1) (s.s: a bhd)	2	14	16/1	60	34
3773^{15}	**Silver Groom (IRE) (79)** (RAkehurst) **7-8-6** SSanders(9) (lw: prom over 5f: t.o)	dist	15	16/1	—	—

(SP 123.8%) **15 Rn**

2m 7.95 (3.95) CSF £262.71 CT £3,722.36 TOTE £10.20: £2.70 £11.20 £4.70 (£162.40) Trio £1,412.00; £1,412.03 to Haydock 21/9/97
OWNER Mrs David Blackburn (WANTAGE) BRED B. Barnwell
WEIGHT FOR AGE 3yo-6lb

3246 Sharp Consul (IRE), relishing the give underfoot, had been dropped 2lb, and his trainer thinks he is best when fresh. (9/1)

2296 Lomberto, 2lb lower than when second to Sky Commander at Newmarket following his Salisbury win, found the winner far too much of a handful on the day. (33/1)

3824* Isitoff, raised 4lb, was kept to ten furlongs, but the ground did put the emphasis on stamina. (14/1)

3434 Star Manager (USA), 2lb lower than when fourth in the Magnet Cup, was dropping back to what is probably his best trip, although he is yet to win beyond a mile. (10/1)

3575 Bali Paradise (USA) scored as a juvenile on this type of ground, but had been raised 2lb for his good second here last month. (14/1)

3891 Titta Ruffo, only 2lb higher than when successful at Goodwood in June, seems to be running into form. (25/1)
4102 Palatial Style took another step along the comeback trail, and it should be remembered he started 9/2 favourite for the 1991 Cambridgeshire. (33/1)
3703 Game Ploy (POL) (9/2: 6/1-4/1)
Migwar (14/1: 10/1-16/1)

4295 TOTE BOOKMAKERS AUTUMN CUP H'CAP (0-100) (3-Y.O+) (Class C)

3-30 (3-30) **1m 5f 61y** £14,265.00 (£4,320.00: £2,110.00: £1,005.00) Stalls: Low GOING: 0.09 sec per fur (G)

				SP	RR	SF
3989[3]	**Darapour (IRE) (87)** (LMCumani) **3-8-11** KFallon(9) (s.i.s: rdn over 4f out: hdwy 3f out: led 1f out: r.o wl)	—	**1**	9/4[1]	98	54
3902[5]	**Beauchamp Jade (95)** (HCandy) **5-10-0** CRutter(8) (hld up & bhd: hdwy over 2f out: styd on fnl f)	1¼	**2**	14/1	105	70
4002[2]	**Shalateeno (70)** (BRMillman) **4-8-3** TSprake(5) (chsd ldr: led wl over 1f out: hdd 1f out: nt qckn)	nk	**3**	10/1	79	44
3974[5]	**Foundry Lane (72)** (MrsMReveley) **6-8-5** NDay(6) (lw: hdwy over 2f out: r.o one pce fnl f)	1¾	**4**	6/1[3]	79	44
3902[6]	**Rainwatch (100)** (JLDunlop) **3-9-10** WJO'Connor(3) (lw: led tl wl over 1f out: one pce)	hd	**5**	14/1	107	63
2834[5]	**Russian Rose (IRE) (75)** (JARToller) **4-8-8** MartinDwyer(12) (hld up & bhd: hdwy fnl 2f: nvr nrr)	nk	**6**	14/1	82	47
3694*	**Debutante Days (78)** (ACStewart) **5-8-11** SSanders(10) (s.i.s: hdwy 3f out: wknd wl over 1f out: eased whn btn fnl f)	24	**7**	5/1[2]	56	21
	Danesman (IRE) (90) (WRMuir) **4-9-9** MRichards(7) (hld up mid div: eased whn btn over 1f out)	nk	**8**	33/1	67	32
4101[16]	**Jazz King (85)** (MissGayKelleway) **4-9-1**(3) RFfrench(13) (hld up: wknd 3f out)	2	**9**	11/1	60	25
	Easy Listening (USA) (85) (NJHawke) **5-9-4** MRimmer(4) (plld hrd: prom tl hrd rdn & wknd 3f out)	4	**10**	50/1	55	20
3434[2]	**Wakeel (USA) (86)** (SDow) **5-9-5** TQuinn(14) (racd wd bk st: prom tl wknd over 3f out: t.o)	19	**11**	11/1	33	—
1122[4]	**Random Kindness (70)** (RIngram) **4-8-3** AMcGlone(11) (bhd fnl 4f: sn t.o)	1½	**12**	33/1	15	—
4002[15]	**Life of Riley (83)** (GLewis) **3-8-7** AClark(1) (prom 7f: t.o fnl 4f)	16	**13**	12/1	9	—

(SP 123.0%) **13 Rn**

2m 54.6 (8.10) CSF £34.69 CT £254.30 TOTE £2.90: £1.70 £3.90 £2.60 (£32.10) Trio £150.50 OWNER H H Aga Khan (NEWMARKET) BRED His Highness the Aga Khan's Studs S.C.
WEIGHT FOR AGE 3yo-9lb

3989 Darapour (IRE) is inclined to lose ground at the start, and is described by his trainer as 'quirky' at the stalls. Appreciating the cut in the ground, he will be gradually upped in distance, although the Cesarewitch is apparently not on the agenda. (9/4)
3902 Beauchamp Jade, dropped 2lb, did not have to contend with ground as deep as last time, and ran yet another fine race in a competitive handicap. (14/1: 10/1-16/1)
4002 Shalateeno, 6lb higher than when winning at Salisbury, did not seem to mind this extended trip. (10/1)
3974 Foundry Lane has slipped to a useful mark, but is shaping as though he may need two miles. (6/1)
3902 Rainwatch was 10lb higher than on the second of his two victories. (14/1: 10/1-16/1)
2834 Russian Rose (IRE), coming back after a break, found this trip inadequate and, despite being 10lb higher than when winning at Bath, looks set for a profitable autumn campaign. (14/1)
3434 Wakeel (USA) (11/1: 8/1-12/1)
2122 Life of Riley (12/1: 8/1-14/1)

4296 SOUTH CROYDON CONSERVATIVE CLUB NURSERY H'CAP (2-Y.O) (Class C)

4-00 (4-02) **5f 34y** £4,900.00 (£1,480.00: £720.00: £340.00) Stalls: High GOING: 0.09 sec per fur (G)

				SP	RR	SF
4173[4]	**Ivory's Joy (70)** (KTIvory) **2-7-10** MartinDwyer(4) (b: lw: hmpd s: swtchd rt: hdwy over 1f out: led wl ins fnl f: r.o)	—	**1**	6/1[2]	73	40
3265[7]	**Emperor Naheem (IRE) (73)** (BJMeehan) **2-7-13** DRMcCabe(11) (plld hrd: a.p: led 2f out tl wl ins fnl f)	nk	**2**	12/1	75	42
3546*	**Monte Lemos (IRE) (88)** (RCharlton) **2-9-0** TSprake(10) (a.p: led over 2f out: sn hdd: ev ch ins fnl f: r.o)	nk	**3**	5/1[1]	89	56
3965[11]	**Eastern Lyric (74)** (JBerry) **2-8-0** NAdams(9) (hdwy over 2f out: ev ch ins fnl f: r.o)	s.h	**4**	12/1	75	42
3908[4]	**Yorkies Boy (97)** (BAMcMahon) **2-9-9** SSanders(8) (chsd ldrs: rdn over 2f out: one pce fnl f)	1¼	**5**	7/1[3]	94	61
3892[2]	**Supreme Angel (76)** (MPMuggeridge) **2-7-13**(3) MHenry(2) (hld up: hdwy over 3f out: rdn over 2f out: one pce fnl f)	nk	**6**	6/1[2]	72	39
3965[W]	**The Boy John (USA) (80)** (RHannon) **2-8-3**(3) RFfrench(5) (lw: nvr nr to chal)	1¼	**7**	6/1[2]	72	39
3892[8]	**Facile Tigre (74)** (SDow) **2-7-7**(7) PDoe(6) (lw: no hdwy fnl 2f)	nk	**8**	20/1	65	32
3892[3]	**Fast Tempo (IRE) (77)** (BPalling) **2-8-3** CRutter(1) (led over 2f: btn whn hmpd ins fnl f)	5	**9**	14/1	53	20
3899[4]	**Exbourne's Wish (USA) (87)** (BWHills) **2-8-13** MHills(7) (prom over 2f: no ch whn hmpd ins fnl f)	¾	**10**	5/1[1]	61	28
3152[8]	**Centre Court (83)** (RHannon) **2-8-2**(7) PDobbs(3) (lw: hld up: rdn over 2f out: sn wknd)	2½	**11**	12/1	49	16

(SP 123.2%) **11 Rn**

63.12 secs (2.92) CSF £72.50 CT £366.34 TOTE £6.50: £2.00 £4.10 £2.40 (£131.40) Trio £251.90 OWNER Mr K. T. Ivory (RADLETT) BRED David S. Leggate

4173 Ivory's Joy, making a quick reappearance, was squeezed out at the start, but that may have proved a blessing in disguise, given the way she came through late on. (6/1)
3094 Emperor Naheem (IRE) seemed to enjoy this easier ground, and might have prevailed had he not run quite so freely. (12/1)
3546* Monte Lemos (IRE) put up a sound effort off a mark 4lb higher than when fortunate to score last time. (5/1)
3817 Eastern Lyric again showed she can handle this easier surface. (12/1)
3908 Yorkies Boy, 6lb higher than on his previous nursery appearance, was paying the penalty for his second in listed company at the York Ebor meeting. (7/1)
3892 Supreme Angel looked unlucky when beaten half-a-length by Monte Lemos at Sandown, but could not reverse the form on 2lb better terms. (6/1)
3892 Fast Tempo (IRE) (14/1: 10/1-16/1)

4297 ROTHMANS ROYALS NORTH SOUTH CHALLENGE SERIES SEMI-FINAL H'CAP (0-100) (3-Y.O+) (Class C)

4-30 (4-32) **1m 7y (round)** £18,075.00 (£5,475.00: £2,675.00: £1,275.00) Stalls: Low GOING: 0.09 sec per fur (G)

				SP	RR	SF
3575[3]	**Prince of Denial (83)** (DWPArbuthnot) **3-8-12** TQuinn(8) (s.i.s: gd hdwy over 1f out: str run to ld nr fin)	—	**1**	14/1	95	74
3982[14]	**Sweet Wilhelmina (68)** (LordHuntingdon) **4-7-12**(3) RFfrench(3) (chsd ldr: led over 3f out: edgd rt over 1f out: hdd nr fin)	nk	**2**	9/1[3]	79	62
3982*	**La Modiste (80)** (MissGayKelleway) **4-8-13** KFallon(7) (rdn & hdwy over 2f out: chsd ldr over 1f out: nt qckn)	1¼	**3**	9/2[1]	89	72
3428*	**Saifan (86)** (DMorris) **8-9-5v** NDay(2) (lw: a.p: r.o one pce fnl 2f)	1¾	**4**	16/1	91	74
3712[10]	**Broughtons Turmoil (71)** (BRMillman) **8-8-4** TSprake(4) (hld up: hdwy over 2f out: n.m.r ins fnl f: one pce)	hd	**5**	33/1	76	59

4176[2]	**Mr Paradise (IRE) (70)** (TJNaughton) **3-7-13** CRutter(5) (lw: hld up & bhd: hdwy over 1f out: nvr nrr)	s.h	**6**	16/1	75	54
3976*	**Therhea (IRE) (81)** (BRMillman) **4-8-11**(3) AWhelan(18) (lw: prom tl wknd fnl f)	½	**7**	8/1[2]	85	68
3622[8]	**Ben Gunn (69)** (PTWalwyn) **5-8-2** JLowe(6) (hld up & bhd: hdwy over 2f out: nt rch ldrs)	hd	**8**	12/1	73	56
3901[3]	**Mr Sponge (USA) (84)** (IABalding) **3-8-13** SSanders(10) (lw: hdwy 2f out: eased whn btn ins fnl f)	2½	**9**	10/1	83	62
3901[18]	**Sharp Shuffle (IRE) (80)** (RHannon) **4-8-10**(3) MHenry(1) (nvr nr ldrs)	4	**10**	20/1	71	54
4141[11]	**Koathary (USA) (75)** (LGCottrell) **6-8-5**(3) DGriffiths(12) (lw: prom tl wknd over 1f out: eased whn btn ins fnl f)	¾	**11**	20/1	65	48
2557[12]	**Family Man (80)** (JRFanshawe) **4-8-13** AClark(14) (plld hrd: hdwy 4f out: wknd over 2f out)	hd	**12**	14/1	69	52
3913[3]	**Apache Star (96)** (GWragg) **3-9-11v** MHills(9) (a bhd: eased fnl f)	2½	**13**	9/1[3]	80	59
3976[14]	**Artful Dane (IRE) (76)** (MJHeaton-Ellis) **5-8-4v**(5) ADaly(16) (rdn over 2f out: no rspnse)	¾	**14**	20/1	59	42
3980[3]	**Serendipity (FR) (63)** (BRMillman) **4-7-10** MartinDwyer(11) (dwlt: a bhd)	hd	**15**	14/1	46	29
3622[9]	**Mo-Addab (IRE) (70)** (ACStewart) **7-8-3** AMcGlone(19) (a bhd)	½	**16**	16/1	52	35
3696[4]	**City Gambler (71)** (GCBravery) **3-8-0** DRMcCabe(17) (b.hind: prom tl rdn & wknd 3f out)	hd	**17**	20/1	52	31
4112[19]	**Zermatt (IRE) (63)** (MDIUsher) **7-7-10** NAdams(13) (lw: led over 4f: wknd over 2f out)	s.h	**18**	50/1	44	27
3901[5]	**Almond Rock (95)** (JRFanshawe) **5-10-0** NVarley(15) (prom: rdn over 3f out: sn wknd)	hd	**19**	16/1	76	59
4141[6]	**Present Situation (66)** (LordHuntingdon) **6-7-8**(5) AimeeCook(20) (lw: a bhd: t.o)	14	**20**	12/1	19	2

(SP 141.2%) **20 Rn**

1m 38.91 (2.91) CSF £126.67 CT £628.59 TOTE £18.50: £3.60 £2.10 £1.90 £11.00 (£66.20) Trio £568.50 OWNER Mr J. S. Gutkin (COMPTON) BRED R. E. Crutchley
LONG HANDICAP Zermatt (IRE) 7-5 Serendipity (FR) 7-9
WEIGHT FOR AGE 3yo-4lb
3575 Prince of Denial, raised 2lb for his promising comeback over ten furlongs here last month, found a mile on yielding going just the ticket. (14/1)
2346 Sweet Wilhelmina ran too freely at Salisbury after her summer break, but was back to her best this time. (9/1)
3982* La Modiste continues to hold her form, but a 10lb hike in the ratings proved too much. (9/2: op 8/1)
3428* Saifan had to contend with a round mile, but ran here so he would be eligible for the final of this series. (16/1)
2161 Broughtons Turmoil, only 1lb higher than winning at Ascot in the spring, settled much better this time, and showed definite signs of a return to form. (33/1)
4176 Mr Paradise (IRE), making a quick reappearance, gives the impression he would not mind a shade f...ther. (16/1)
3976* Therhea (IRE) had been raised 5lb for his win at York. (8/1: 6/1-9/1)

4298 E.B.F. HARWELL MAIDEN STKS (2-Y.O) (Class D)

5-00 (5-04) **6f 8y** £3,902.50 (£1,180.00: £575.00: £272.50) Stalls: High GOING: 0.09 sec per fur (G)

				SP	RR	SF
3979[8]	**Poly Blue (IRE)** (MissGayKelleway) **2-8-6**(3) RFfrench(13) (lw: hld up: hdwy over 1f out: led wl ins fnl f: r.o wl)	—	**1**	16/1	80	53
3717[2]	**Tumblweed Prospect (78)** (BJMeehan) **2-9-0** MTebbutt(17) (a.p: led wl over 1f out tl wl ins fnl f)	¾	**2**	8/1[2]	83	56
	Astrologer (WRMuir) **2-9-0** WJO'Connor(8) (w'like: scope: trckd ldrs: swtchd rt over 1f out: r.o wl ins fnl f: bttr for r)	3	**3**	10/1	75+	48
	Atlanta (JLDunlop) **2-8-9** MRimmer(1) (unf: scope: a.p: ev ch over 1f out: one pce)	nk	**4**	20/1	69	42
4103[18]	**St Lucia (IRE)** (BJMeehan) **2-8-2**(7) GHannon(7) (a.p: one pce fnl 2f)	1¾	**5**	50/1	65	38
	Aganon (MRChannon) **2-9-0** RPerham(20) (w'like: scope: bit bkwd: rdn over 2f out: hdwy over 1f out: nvr nrr)	3	**6**	33/1	62	35
	Waff's Folly (GFHCharles-Jones) **2-8-9** CRutter(10) (unf: s.s: swtchd rt 2f out: hdwy fnl f: nrst fin)	nk	**7**	50/1	56	29
	Epsom Cyclone (USA) (BWHills) **2-9-0** MHills(3) (b.hind: str: scope: bit bkwd: a.p: ev ch over 1f out: eased whn btn ins fnl f: bttr for r)	nk	**8**	8/1[2]	60+	33
	Browning (LordHuntingdon) **2-8-9**(5) AimeeCook(16) (unf: scope: nvr nrr)	¾	**9**	33/1	58	31
	Lucayan Indian (IRE) (DRLoder) **2-9-0** AClark(2) (w'like: scope: bit bkwd: nvr nr ldrs)	½	**10**	10/1	57	30
3770[11]	**Mantello** (MajorDNChappell) **2-9-0** NAdams(6) (prom over 3f)	nk	**11**	33/1	56	29
3047[4]	**Deep Space (IRE)** (EALDunlop) **2-9-0** KFallon(14) (prom: led over 2f out tl wl over 1f out: sn wknd)	1½	**12**	5/4[1]	52	25
	La Galleria (JSMoore) **2-8-6**(3) MHenry(18) (leggy: scope: bhd fnl 2f)	nk	**13**	50/1	46	19
	Robin Goodfellow (PTWalwyn) **2-9-0** TSprake(5) (str: scope: bit bkwd: s.s: a bhd)	½	**14**	9/1[3]	50	23
3985[12]	**Miss Dilletante** (RFJohnsonHoughton) **2-8-9** MartinDwyer(12) (prom 4f)	hd	**15**	33/1	45	18
3927[9]	**Carver Doone** (MajorDNChappell) **2-9-0** AMcGlone(19) (a bhd)	4	**16**	33/1	39	12
	Baby Spice (MRChannon) **2-8-9** CandyMorris(4) (leggy: unf: s.s: a bhd)	s.h	**17**	20/1	34	7
2829[10]	**Muyassir (IRE)** (CJBenstead) **2-8-11**(3) AWhelan(15) (bit bkwd: prom 3f)	¾	**18**	33/1	37	10
2181[9]	**Zeppo (IRE)** (MJHeaton-Ellis) **2-9-0** JLowe(11) (led over 4f)	1½	**19**	20/1	33	6

(SP 138.5%) **19 Rn**

1m 15.25 (3.45) CSF £123.99 TOTE £29.50: £4.90 £2.60 £3.30 (£78.30) Trio £326.10 OWNER Sheet & Roll Convertors Ltd (WHITCOMBE) BRED Dr Michael Dargan
OFFICIAL EXPLANATION **Deep Space (IRE): no explanation offered.**
Poly Blue (IRE), is out a half-sister to dual Ascot Gold Cup winner Sadeem. She had raced on the 'wrong' side, like yesterday's winner Amabel, when making her debut over an extra furlong in similar conditions at Salisbury. (16/1)
3717 Tumblweed Prospect settled better, and handled the ground well enough. (8/1)
Astrologer, a half-brother to the useful sprinter Averti, had to check around the weakening favourite, and it does not need Mystic Meg to see him winning races. (10/1: 8/1-12/1)
Atlanta, who only cost 1,000 guineas, is the first foal of a mare related to Electric. She is looking more than a useful buy. (20/1)
St Lucia (IRE), a half-sister to Shimmering Scarlet, showed tremendous improvement on her debut run at Kempton. (50/1)
Aganon, a brother to seven-furlong winner Serious Fact, and a half-brother to Plain Fact, should do better when trying further. (33/1)
Waff's Folly, the second foal of a mile and a half winner, is another who should improve over a longer trip. (50/1)
Epsom Cyclone (USA), the first foal of a daughter of 1,000 Guineas runner-up Dabaweyaa, was not knocked about when his chance had gone, and seems sure to come on for the run. (8/1: 5/1-9/1)
Lucayan Indian (IRE) (10/1: op 5/1)
3047 Deep Space (IRE) (5/4: op 4/5)

T/Jkpt: £42,596.50 (1.5 Tckts). T/Plpt: £200.80 (236.15 Tckts). T/Qdpt: £337.70 (4.6 Tckts) KH

4036-WOLVERHAMPTON (L-H) (Standard)

Saturday September 20th

WEATHER: overcast WIND: almost nil

4299 E.B.F. MALI MAIDEN STKS (2-Y.O) (Class D)

7-00 (7-00) **1m 100y (Fibresand)** £3,518.20 (£1,048.60: £499.80: £225.40) Stalls: Low GOING minus 0.13 sec per fur (FST)

				SP	RR	SF
4061^{9}	**Pedro (IRE)** (SirMarkPrescott) **2-9-0** SSanders(4) (lw: plld hrd: led 2f: led 3f out: rdn out)	—	**1**	$11/4^{1}$	76+	27
4064^{5}	**Copernicus** (PFICole) **2-9-0** TQuinn(8) (sn rdn along: hdwy over 3f out: wandered & r.o fnl f)	nk	**2**	$5/1^{3}$	75	26
4061^{6}	**Wuxi Venture** (SPCWoods) **2-9-0** NDay(5) (a.p: n.m.r over 1f out: kpt on fnl f)	1	**3**	$4/1^{2}$	74	25
4017^{5}	**Casino Ace (IRE)** (PWChapple-Hyam) **2-8-2**(7) JFowle(3) (lw: led over 6f out to 3f out: ev ch over 1f out: no ex ins fnl f)	hd	**4**	6/1	68	19
3920^{2}	**Gift of Gold (78)** (ICampbell) **2-9-0** DRMcCabe(2) (chsd ldrs tl wknd over 3f out)	5	**5**	11/2	64	15
4064^{6}	**Royal Shock (IRE)** (DRLoder) **2-9-0v¹** KFallon(7) (sn pushed along: rn wd after 1f: hdwy over 3f out: wknd 2f out)	½	**6**	11/2	63	14
4052^{2}	**Flying Bold (IRE)** (WRMuir) **2-9-0** MartinDwyer(6) (prom tl wknd over 3f out)	20	**7**	16/1	25	—
	Lascensa (USA) (PAKelleway) **2-8-9** GBardwell(1) (unf: a bhd)	2½	**8**	33/1	15	—

(SP 117.2%) **8 Rn**

1m 51.5 (6.50) CSF £15.75 TOTE £5.80: £1.50 £1.50 £1.90 (£11.90) OWNER Mr G. D. Waters (NEWMARKET) BRED G. D. Waters

Pedro (IRE), an attractive, keen sort, was much fitter than for his debut, and proved willing in the final struggle. (11/4: 2/1-3/1)

4064 Copernicus looks sure to progress, but is very green and, had his pilot not stopped riding for a few strides before the finish, he may well have caused serious interference, for he continually hung away from the whip, no matter how often it was switched. (5/1)

4061 Wuxi Venture moved down rather better on this surface, but did not really pick up until the race was over. (4/1)

4017 Casino Ace (IRE) seemed to be going as well as any for much of the race, but stuck to the inside, rarely a good tactic here, and found little for her late replacement pilot when the chips were down. (6/1: op 4/1)

3920 Gift of Gold could not transfer his recent improvement to this surface, and did not seem to stay. (11/2)

4064 Royal Shock (IRE) had finished on the heels of the runner-up in a Leicester maiden earlier in the month but, visored this time, did not look a total enthusiast when put under pressure. (11/2: 4/1-6/1)

4300 L.A. METALS 10TH ANNIVERSARY MAIDEN H'CAP (0-70) (3-Y.O+) (Class E)

7-30 (7-31) **1m 100y (Fibresand)** £3,154.00 (£874.00: £418.00) Stalls: Low GOING minus 0.13 sec per fur (FST)

				SP	RR	SF
3030^{9}	**Gablesea (44)** (BPJBaugh) **3-8-7** JFEgan(10) (in tch: hdwy 5f out: led & edgd rt over 1f out: drvn out)	—	**1**	25/1	53	14
3248^{13}	**Arrasas Lady (35)** (JRPoulton) **7-7-9**(7) JFowle(13) (bhd: gd hdwy to ld over 2f out: hdd over 1f out: unable qckn)	1¾	**2**	13/2	41	6
3470^{18}	**Jolly Jackson (65)** (RAkehurst) **3-10-0** TQuinn(11) (hdwy over 2f out: edgd lft & no imp appr fnl f)	9	**3**	$11/2^{3}$	54	15
	Prince Jordan (43) (ICampbell) **3-8-6** AMackay(12) (bhd: rn wd after 1f: stdy hdwy fnl 2f: nvr plcd to chal)	2	**4**	25/1	28	—
2492^{10}	**Kosevo (IRE) (40)** (MGMeagher) **3-8-0**(3) AWhelan(5) (prom: led 4f out to 3f out: sn btn)	1	**5**	20/1	23	—
4060^{16}	**Thatcham Island (43)** (DLWilliams) **4-8-3**(7) PaulCleary(9) (lw: plld hrd: hld up: kpt on fnl 2f: nvr rchd ldrs)	hd	**6**	25/1	26	—
1012^{10}	**With The Tempo (IRE) (35)** (DrJDScargill) **4-8-2** GBardwell(6) (nvr nr to chal)	hd	**7**	20/1	18	—
3715^{9}	**Chili Bouchier (USA) (53)** (DMarks) **3-8-13**(3) RHavlin(1) (prom tl wknd over 3f out)	1½	**8**	12/1	33	—
4055^{10}	**Drift (55)** (SirMarkPrescott) **3-9-4** SSanders(8) (in tch: effrt 4f out: rdn over 2f out: sn wknd)	6	**9**	$4/1^{2}$	23	—
3606^{9}	**Colonel's Pride (42)** (RMWhitaker) **3-8-5** DRMcCabe(3) (w ldrs over 4f)	½	**10**	20/1	10	—
4043^{4}	**D J Cat (36)** (WRMuir) **4-8-3** MartinDwyer(2) (prom over 5f)	3½	**11**	$3/1^{1}$	—	—
3822^{12}	**Taragona (47)** (RHollinshead) **4-9-0** KFallon(7) (prom: led 3f out: sn hdd & wknd)	5	**12**	6/1	—	—
3814^{9}	**Supercharmer (65)** (RTJuckes) **3-10-0v¹** SophieMitchell(4) (led over 4f: sn wknd)	4	**13**	25/1	9	—

(SP 125.4%) **13 Rn**

1m 52.2 (7.20) CSF £157.88 CT £694.09 TOTE £23.40: £5.20 £2.50 £1.90 (£297.40) Trio £73.70; £63.40 to 22/9/97 OWNER Messrs Chrimes, Winn & Wilson (LITTLE HAYWOOD) BRED M. V. S. and Mrs Aram

WEIGHT FOR AGE 3yo-4lb

STEWARDS' ENQUIRY Mackay susp. 29/9-2/10/97 (schooling in public) & Campbell fined £500.00 under Rule 151(ii) (schooling in public).Prince Jordan susp.30 days

2020 Gablesea, a late withdrawal from two races earlier on the week, found the right opening here, scoring in good style. (25/1)

2913 Arrasas Lady, at her best on All-Weather surfaces, is still her maiden, but her day may come in a similar race. (13/2: 4/1-7/1)

2245 Jolly Jackson, back on the All-Weather where he finished runner-up twice last winter, did not run badly, but the Handicapper has hardly been lenient. (11/2: 4/1-6/1)

Prince Jordan, making a belated seasonal debut, stayed on past beaten horses without being asked for an effort, and the displeasure of the Stewards seemed entirely understandable. However, whether the horse has much ability is still open to question, as this was a notably poor race and he was beaten a fair way. (25/1)

Kosevo (IRE) has weakened towards the end of all his races, and the only hope seems to be different tactics or a shorter trip. (20/1)

Thatcham Island, a tail-swishing sister to Chatham Island, again hinted at some ability, but looks highly-strung. (25/1)

4055 Drift (4/1: 3/1-9/2)

4301 KENYA H'CAP (0-70) (3-Y.O+) (Class E)

8-00 (8-03) **6f (Fibresand)** £3,262.00 (£976.00: £468.00: £214.00) Stalls: Low GOING minus 0.13 sec per fur (FST)

				SP	RR	SF
3810^{6}	**Takhlid (USA) (68)** (DWChapman) **6-9-12** ACulhane(10) (a.p: led 1f out: rdn out)	—	**1**	16/1	79	39
3548^{5}	**Beyond Calculation (USA) (69)** (PWHarris) **3-9-6**(5) CLowther(8) (w ldr: led 4f out to 1f out: r.o ins fnl f)	2½	**2**	$11/2^{2}$	73	31
4168^{16}	**Napier Star (68)** (MrsNMacauley) **4-9-12v** TQuinn(11) (lw: prom: ev ch 1f out: sn rdn & btn)	nk	**3**	12/1	72	32
4249^{10}	**Hannah's Usher (60)** (CMurray) **5-9-4** NicolaHowarth(3) (b.hind: in tch: effrt over 2f out: no imp appr fnl f)	3	**4**	11/1	56	16
3987^{22}	**Barrack Yard (68)** (ACStewart) **4-9-12** SWhitworth(12) (dwlt: outpcd: hdwy 3f out: rdn 2f out: no imp)	¾	**5**	$3/1^{1}$	62	22
3583^{6}	**Desert Invader (IRE) (70)** (DWChapman) **6-9-11**(3) DSweeney(2) (prom: outpcd over 3f out: n.d after)	4	**6**	12/1	53	13
3710^{10}	**Erupt (60)** (GBBalding) **4-9-4** SDrowne(7) (dwlt: sn pushed along: nvr nr to chal)	2½	**7**	12/1	36	—
3777^{12}	**Hoh Returns (IRE) (64)** (BPreece) **4-9-8** SSanders(6) (sn outpcd)	1	**8**	16/1	38	—
3860^{16}	**Moi Canard (60)** (BAPearce) **4-9-4** KFallon(9) (lw: prom over 4f: eased whn btn)	nk	**9**	$10/1^{3}$	33	—
907^{2}	**Little Ibnr (59)** (PDCundell) **6-9-3** NDay(4) (led 2f: wknd 2f out)	2½	**10**	$10/1^{3}$	25	—
4137^{7}	**Shadow Jury (61)** (DWChapman) **7-9-5b** JFortune(1) (dwlt: a bhd)	hd	**11**	11/1	27	—
1089^{9}	**Leigh Crofter (59)** (PDCundell) **8-9-3** RPerham(13) (sn outpcd)	½	**12**	20/1	24	—

				SP	RR	SF
4169^{3}	**Watch The Fire (64)** (JEBanks) **4-9-8** AMackay(5) (s.i.s: a bhd)	1	**13**	11/2^{2}	26	—
				(SP 130.2%)		**13 Rn**

1m 15.5 (4.30) CSF £100.79 CT £1,038.29 TOTE £16.90: £4.80 £1.80 £4.20 (£41.90) Trio £92.60; £65.23 to 22/9/97 OWNER Miss N. F. Thesiger (YORK) BRED Cheveley Park Stud Ltd

WEIGHT FOR AGE 3yo-2lb

3810 Takhlid (USA) was back to sprinting for the first time since March, and this seems to be his forte. (16/1)

3548 Beyond Calculation (USA), back to sprinting for the first time since finishing fourth to Revoque on his debut, took to the surface and made good use of a fast break, being in the firing line throughout. He came back to snatch second place in the last furlong. (11/2: 4/1-6/1)

3077 Napier Star, racing closer to the pace than she usually does, bounced back to form but, after looking the likely winner early in the straight, could do no more. (12/1: op 20/1)

3582 Hannah's Usher planted himself when mounted to be taken down early but, once the stalls opened, ran his usual race. (11/1)

1020 Barrack Yard, tasting defeat on the All-Weather for the first time, finds this trip a bare minimum and could not afford a tardy start. (3/1)

3583 Desert Invader (IRE), drawn on the inside, was taken off his feet as he had to steady into the bend. (12/1)

907 Little Ibnr (10/1: 8/1-12/1)

4137 Shadow Jury (11/1: 8/1-12/1)

4169 Watch The Fire (11/2: 4/1-6/1)

4302 MOZAMBIQUE LIMITED STKS (0-60) (3-Y.O+) (Class F)

8-30 (8-31) **1m 6f 166y (Fibresand)** £2,070.00 (£570.00: £270.00) Stalls: High GOING minus 0.13 sec per fur (FST)

				SP	RR	SF
4055^{6}	**Robbo (57)** (CWThornton) **3-8-9b** DeanMcKeown(12) (hdwy 5f out: led over 2f out: sn clr: easily)	—	**1**	10/1	81+	8
4055^{2}	**La Menorquina (USA) (48)** (DMarks) **7-9-3** JFortune(1) (bhd: hdwy 4f out: chsd wnr fnl 2f: no imp)	7	**2**	4/1^{2}	70	8
3928^{9}	**Salsee Lad (58)** (JRFanshawe) **3-8-7** SSanders(2) (hdwy 7f out: ev ch over 2f out: sn outpcd: eased ins fnl f)	3½	**3**	13/2^{3}	68	—
3432^{8}	**Fresh Fruit Daily (50)** (PAKelleway) **5-9-0**(5) CLowther(8) (lw: prom: rdn & no imp fnl 3f)	3	**4**	16/1	65	3
4170^{9}	**Lake Dominion (44)** (KCComerford) **8-8-13**(7) JFowle(4) (b: prom tl lost pl 8f out: rallied 3f out: r.o)	2	**5**	16/1	64	2
3974^{13}	**Paradise Navy (60)** (CREgerton) **8-9-7b**(3) RFfrench(11) (prom: led 6f out tl over 2f out: sn rdn & wknd)	nk	**6**	13/2^{3}	68	6
4053^{4}	**Ceanothus (IRE) (59)** (WJHaggas) **3-8-4** SDrowne(7) (lw: in tch: rdn & no imp fnl 4f)	¾	**7**	13/2^{3}	58	—
4055^{4}	**Signed And Sealed (USA) (49)** (CACyzer) **3-8-4**(3) AWhelan(10) (effrt 5f out: nvr nr ldrs)	1¾	**8**	16/1	59	—
3612^{3}	**Pointe Fine (FR) (60)** (JWHills) **3-8-7**ow3 KFallon(5) (chsd ldrs tl wknd 5f out)	dist	**9**	11/4^{1}	—	—
351^{6}	**Broughtons Formula (58)** (WJMusson) **7-9-4** DRMcCabe(6) (prom tl wknd 6f out)	hd	**10**	10/1	—	—
3896^{10}	**Subtle Touch (IRE) (32)** (PLGilligan) **6-9-4v**1 JStack(3) (led over 8f: sn wknd)	3	**11**	33/1	—	—
3046^{9}	**Swordking (IRE) (26)** (JLHarris) **8-9-4b** ACulhane(9) (Withdrawn not under Starter's orders: lame at s)		**W**	33/1	—	—
				(SP 128.4%)		**11 Rn**

3m 21.9 (14.50) CSF £48.46 TOTE £13.90: £3.30 £1.50 £3.40 (£59.90) Trio Not won; £89.95 to 22/9/97 OWNER Mr Guy Reed (MIDDLEHAM) BRED Godolphin Management Co Ltd

WEIGHT FOR AGE 3yo-11lb

OFFICIAL EXPLANATION Pointe Fine (FR): no explanation offered.

4055 Robbo, trying an extended trip for the first time at this track, cruised through on the outside to lead, and fairly bolted up. (10/1)

4055 La Menorquina (USA) ignored the early pace, and found her stamina coming into play in the last half-mile. Further still suits her. (4/1)

3549 Salsee Lad, making his debut on the surface and with his tongue tied down, was comprehensively done for toe rounding the home turn. (13/2: op 4/1)

3104 Fresh Fruit Daily, trying a longer trip, ran well below her best but the stable is having a poor run at present. (16/1)

3046* Lake Dominion, who caused an upset over further here in the summer, was in trouble from halfway but kept on trying. (16/1)

3719* Paradise Navy, ridden in the manner that has brought success recently, could never shake off his pursuers and found as little as ever once off the bit. (13/2)

4053 Ceanothus (IRE) (13/2: op 4/1)

351 Broughtons Formula (10/1: 8/1-12/1)

4303 DUNSTALL PARK 2-Y-O (S) STKS (2-Y.O) (Class G)

9-00 (9-03) **7f (Fibresand)** £1,725.00 (£475.00: £225.00) Stalls: High GOING minus 0.13 sec per fur (FST)

				SP	RR	SF
4068^{16}	**Wildcat (IRE) (70)** (MissGayKelleway) **2-9-2** KFallon(10) (lw: chsd ldrs: led over 2f out: sn clr: easily)	—	**1**	6/4^{1}	73+	11
3967^{4}	**Pink Ticket (51)** (PDEvans) **2-8-6** JFEgan(12) (prom: rdn 2f out: no ch w wnr)	4	**2**	9/2^{2}	54	—
4163^{5}	**Emperor's Gold (66)** (ICampbell) **2-8-11** AMackay(4) (dlwt: rdn & hdwy over 3f out: r.o fnl f)	1½	**3**	11/1	55	—
	Sharp Monkey (MrsNMacauley) **2-8-11** SSanders(7) (leggy: unf: lw: hdwy over 3f out: nvr rchd ldrs)	1¼	**4**	25/1	53	—
3451^{6}	**Rock From The Sun (53)** (WGMTurner) **2-8-8b**1(3) DSweeney(6) (led over 4f: wknd ins fnl f)	½	**5**	6/1^{3}	51	—
3967^{5}	**Captain Bliss (60)** (NTinkler) **2-9-2b** KimTinkler(8) (lw: prom tl wknd over 2f out)	5	**6**	8/1	45	—
4052^{7}	**Linda** (NACallaghan) **2-8-6** SDrowne(2) (lw: chsd ldrs over 3f)	5	**7**	6/1^{3}	24	—
3493^{9}	**Lady Eil** (BSmart) **2-8-6** JStack(1) (sn pushed along: nvr nr to chal)	1¾	**8**	12/1	20	—
3574^{15}	**Little Cracker** (AGNewcombe) **2-8-6** FNorton(5) (bhd fnl 3f)	3½	**9**	20/1	12	—
3686^{23}	**Uther Pendragon (IRE)** (JABennett) **2-8-11** GBardwell(11) (prom over 3f: sn bhd)	2	**10**	33/1	12	—
	Ivory Girl (IRE) (KGWingrove) **2-8-6** NDay(9) (w'like: s.s: a bhd)	s.h	**11**	33/1	7	—
				(SP 128.4%)		**11 Rn**

1m 31.5 (6.80) CSF £7.95 TOTE £2.40: £1.30 £1.70 £2.20 (£4.90) Trio £24.70 OWNER Miss Gay Kelleway (WHITCOMBE) BRED M. Grant and W. Hawkings

Wildcat (IRE) sold Claes Bjorling 9,000 gns

3493* Wildcat (IRE) looked a real handful, being last into the parade ring and dropping the pilot coming out on to the course. Despite the facile win, connections may not be too despondent about losing him as he seems temperamental. (6/4)

3967 Pink Ticket, proven over the trip and on the surface, was not in the same league as the winner. (9/2)

4163 Emperor's Gold, a bit free going down, again missed the kick but kept finding a little when ridden from halfway. (11/1: 5/1-12/1)

Sharp Monkey, making his debut, was unruly entering the stalls and green in the race but showed a little promise. (25/1)

3451 Rock From The Sun, despite having won over course and distance when slipping her field, looked a doubtful stayer on this occasion. (6/1: 5/1-8/1)

3967 Captain Bliss, making his debut on the surface, did not excel. (8/1: op 9/2)

Lady Eil (12/1: 8/1-14/1)

4304 ZAMBIA H'CAP (0-60) (3-Y.O+) (Class F)

9-30 (9-31) **1m 4f (Fibresand)** £1,932.00 (£532.00: £252.00) Stalls: Low GOING minus 0.13 sec per fur (FST)

Form	Horse and details	Dist	Pos	SP	RR	SF
4069^{7}	**English Invader (55)** (CADwyer) **6-9-10** JFortune(5) (lw: hdwy over 4f out: chal & edgd lft over 1f out: rdn to ld post)	—	**1**	16/1	67	22
2052^{3}	**Royal Roulette (57)** (SPCWoods) **3-9-4v** NDay(8) (hdwy 6f out: led & bmpd over 1f out: ct post)	s.h	**2**	10/1	69	16
3915^{13}	**Mr Speculator (52)** (JEBanks) **4-9-7v** GBardwell(11) (w ldrs: led wl over 1f out: sn hdd & one pce)	3½	**3**	11/1	59	14
3609^{3}	**Wildfire (SWI) (51)** (RAkehurst) **6-9-6** SSanders(3) (led over 5f out: rdn 3f out: hdd over 1f out: sn btn)	4	**4**	$7/1^{3}$	53	8
3901^{6}	**Wentbridge Lad (IRE) (53)** (ABailey) **7-9-5v(3)** RFfrench(4) (b: b.hind: lw: hld up: hdwy 2f out: nvr rchd ldrs)	hd	**5**	$4/1^{1}$	55	10
4046^{4}	**Brecon (56)** (WRMuir) **4-9-11** MartinDwyer(1) (led 1f: rdn 7f out: wknd over 3f out)	1½	**6**	$5/1^{2}$	56	11
4069^{5}	**Father Dan (IRE) (58)** (MissGayKelleway) **8-9-13** KFallon(12) (b: b.hind: in tch: effrt 3f out: rdn & btn 2f out)	1½	**7**	$4/1^{1}$	56	11
3272^{5}	**Our Main Man (57)** (RMWhitaker) **7-9-12** OPears(2) (in tch tl rdn & btn 3f out)	6	**8**	8/1	47	2
4055^{13}	**Red Phantom (IRE) (50)** (SMellor) **5-9-5v** MWigham(10) (lw: dwlt: a bhd)	1½	**9**	12/1	38	—
4045^{7}	**Polonaise Prince (USA) (50)** (VSoane) **4-9-5** CRutter(9) (plld hrd: hdwy over 7f out: rdn 4f out: wknd over 2f out)	hd	**10**	14/1	38	—
1312*	**Good Day (55)** (CWThornton) **3-9-2b** DeanMcKeown(7) (led after 1f tl hdd over 5f out: sn wknd)	25	**11**	12/1	9	—
	Young Butt (57) (BAPearce) **4-9-7(5)** CLowther(6) (b: bkwd: dwlt: t.o fnl 6f)	dist	**12**	33/1	—	—

(SP 128.6%) **12 Rn**

2m 44.3 (11.80) CSF £164.56 CT £1,704.72 TOTE £22.10: £4.70 £3.50 £4.60 (£93.80) Trio £96.90; £122.85 to 22/9/97 OWNER Mrs Shelley Dwyer (NEWMARKET) BRED Bloodstock Management Int Pty Ltd

WEIGHT FOR AGE 3yo-8lb

2787 English Invader, who won a 0-55 Limited Stakes over course and distance earlier in the year, came back to that form but was lucky to keep the race, having appeared to give a slight bump to the runner-up as the first three got tight entering the final furlong. Sticking on strongly near the line, the photo showed he had just got up, to the surprise of many, but the narrowness of the margin made the decision that accidental interference had not affected the placings a little hard to swallow. The head-on must have looked rather different. (16/1)

2052 Royal Roulette looked to have battled her way home but the photo showed otherwise. Both in the picture and in the Stewards' Room, she was unlucky not to get this. (10/1)

516 Mr Speculator disputed the lead virtually all the way back on his favoured surface, may have drifted towards the first two on his outside as battle commenced but did not look the sole cause of the problem from side on. (11/1: 8/1-12/1)

2279 Wildfire (SWI) seems exposed over this trip, which is probably just beyond his best. (7/1)

3901 Wentbridge Lad (IRE) was a useful horse her at his best, winning off 74 in his time, and this latest yard seemed to have found a new lease of life for him by stepping him up in trip. He caught the eye in what was probably an experiment to see if he stayed the trip and he could prove very well handicapped if returning. (4/1)

4046 Brecon did not get the run of the race by sticking to the inner and is worth keeping in mind. (5/1)

4069 Father Dan (IRE) (4/1: 9/2-3/1)

T/Plpt: £639.40 (22.7 Tckts). T/Qdpt: £410.00 (0.6 Tckts); £221.66 Dk

4023-HAYDOCK (L-H) (Good)

Sunday September 21st

WEATHER: sunny WIND: slt half bhd

4305 BIRD IN HAND CONDITIONS STKS (2-Y.O) (Class C)

2-20 (2-20) **5f** £4,803.30 (£1,750.80: £855.40: £367.00: £163.50) Stalls: High GOING minus 0.30 sec per fur (GF)

Form	Horse and details	Dist	Pos	SP	RR	SF
4106^{7}	**Risque Lady** (PWHarris) **2-8-9** KFallon(3) (dwlt: hdwy 2f out: jnd ldr 1f out: rdn to ld cl home)	—	**1**	$11/4^{2}$	96	65
3776*	**Pure Coincidence (100)** (GLewis) **2-8-11** PaulEddery(1) (lw: led: rdn 1f out: hdd nr fin)	nk	**2**	$15/8^{1}$	97	66
1091*	**Star** (MAJarvis) **2-8-6** RCochrane(5) (s.i.s: drvn along 2f out: kpt on: nt pce to chal)	2	**3**	$4/1^{3}$	86	55
1486^{3}	**Shalford's Honour (IRE)** (WJarvis) **2-8-11** JFortune(4) (bkwd: prom: ev ch whn n.m.r over 1f out: swtchd lft: wknd ins fnl f)	½	**4**	9/2	89	58
3791^{4}	**First Village (IRE) (86)** (JBerry) **2-8-9** KDarley(2) (chsd ldrs: rdn wl over 1f out: sn btn)	5	**5**	9/1	71	40

(SP 109.6%) **5 Rn**

59.7 secs (0.20) CSF £7.51 TOTE £2.80: £1.20 £1.40 (£2.30) OWNER Godwin Hollis Lawren Rice (BERKHAMSTED) BRED Pendley Farm

4106 Risque Lady, not so highly tried on the return to the minimum trip, had to work hard to get the better of the colt but she did it willingly and won in a decent time. (11/4)

3776* Pure Coincidence may well have won had he put his head down in the dying strides, but he is inclined to stick it in the air, though it must be said he does look to give of his best. (15/8)

1091* Star won well on her debut over four months ago and she is being brought along steadily but, in this better class event, she could not summon the pace to make her presence felt. (4/1)

1486 Shalford's Honour (IRE) has enjoyed a lengthy break since making his debut in May and he did look burly, but he did show plenty of promise and should be able to go on from here. (9/2)

4306 BAY HORSE LIMITED STKS (0-90) (3-Y.O+) (Class C)

2-55 (2-55) **1m 2f 120y** £5,199.00 (£1,572.00: £766.00: £363.00) Stalls: High GOING minus 0.30 sec per fur (GF)

Form	Horse and details	Dist	Pos	SP	RR	SF
3128^{12}	**Marilaya (IRE) (84)** (LMCumani) **3-8-9** KDarley(3) (dwlt: sn prom: led 7f out: clr ent st: drvn out)	—	**1**	$7/2^{1}$	94	28
	Triple Leap (87) (JHMGosden) **4-9-3** JCarroll(4) (bit bkwd: chsd ldrs: effrt & drvn along 2f out: kpt on same pce)	1¼	**2**	6/1	93	34
3703^{15}	**Generous Gift (90)** (EALDunlop) **3-8-12** KFallon(6) (hld up & bhd: hdwy over 3f out: kpt on u.p fnl f)	hd	**3**	$4/1^{2}$	95	29
2839^{5}	**Sky Commander (USA) (89)** (MRStoute) **3-9-0** RCochrane(1) (hld up: hdwy & swtchd rt over 2f out: sn rdn: no imp)	3½	**4**	$7/2^{1}$	92	26
4151^{11}	**Kuala Lipis (USA) (87)** (PFICole) **4-9-5** DaneO'Neill(5) (lw: led over 3f: hrd drvn over 2f out: sn btn)	1¾	**5**	$9/2^{3}$	87	28
3913^{13}	**Boojum (90)** (BWHills) **3-8-7** PaulEddery(2) (chsd ldrs tl rdn & wknd over 2f out)	2	**6**	8/1	79	13
344^{8}	**Bend Wavy (IRE) (84)** (THCaldwell) **5-9-3** ACulhane(7) (bkwd: plld hrd: hld up in rr: outpcd over 2f out: t.o)	16	**7**	50/1	58	—

(SP 110.0%) **7 Rn**

2m 17.03 (5.53) CSF £20.65 TOTE £4.00: £2.60 £2.70 (£14.80) OWNER H H Aga Khan (NEWMARKET) BRED His Highness the Aga Khan's Studs S.C.

WEIGHT FOR AGE 3yo-7lb
OFFICIAL EXPLANATION Marilaya (IRE): regarding the improvement in form compared with her run at Goodwood, her jockey reported that on that occasion she ran too freely, but here she seemed to settle once she got to the front.
2888* Marilaya (IRE) raced much too freely on her previous outing two months ago and she had pulled her way into the lead at the end of the back straight here, but she did seem to relax once out on her own and was never in much danger of being caught. (7/2)
Triple Leap looked far from fully wound up for this belated return to action but he ran a fine race in defeat and will be worth keeping in mind from now on. (6/1)
1742* Generous Gift does appear to need a stiffer test of stamina, for he was at full stretch from someway out and lacked a turn of speed to deliver a challenge. (4/1)
2839 Sky Commander (USA), fresh and well and very much on his toes, probably found the ground faster than he really cares for, for he was never able to muster the pace to mount a challenge. (7/2)
3703 Kuala Lipis (USA) has only ever won at a mile and he does seem to find this trip just that bit too far, being hard at work and in trouble passing the quarter-mile marker. (9/2)
1209 Boojum should be well suited by this trip, seeing that she won over an extended seven furlongs in her first season but, as yet she has failed to last home and it is proving difficult to find a valid excuse. (8/1)

4307 TOMMY WALLIS H'CAP (0-90) (3-Y.O+) (Class C)

3-25 (3-28) **6f** £5,745.00 (£1,740.00: £850.00: £405.00) Stalls: High GOING minus 0.30 sec per fur (GF)

				SP	RR	SF
4013^{2}	**Prends Ca (IRE) (81)** (WRMuir) **4-9-6**(5) PRoberts(8) (hld up: smooth hdwy over 2f out: led ent fnl f: sn clr)	—	1	15/2^{2}	94	77
3936*	**Stand Tall (74)** (LadyHerries) **5-9-4** KDarley(5) (lw: a.p: hrd drvn wl over 1f out: r.o one pce)	2½	2	5/1^{1}	80	63
4048^{5}	**Saint Express (78)** (MrsMReveley) **7-9-8** ACulhane(2) (lw: a chsng ldrs: led over 1f out: sn hdd: one pce fnl f)	¾	3	10/1	82	65
4121^{15}	**Nomore Mr Niceguy (85)** (EJAlston) **3-9-13** JFEgan(7) (lw: hdwy over 2f out: hrd rdn & r.o wl ins fnl f)	¾	4	20/1	87	68
3604^{10}	**For the Present (70)** (TDBarron) **7-9-0** JFortune(12) (in tch: effrt wl over 1f out: kpt on ins fnl f)	1¼	5	9/1	69	52
4155^{3}	**Grand Chapeau (IRE) (69)** (DNicholls) **5-8-13** AlexGreaves(11) (led tl hdd over 1f out: sn rdn & btn)	s.h	6	5/1^{1}	68	51
3709^{8}	**Mary Magdalene (76)** (MBell) **3-9-4** MFenton(14) (mid div: rdn over 2f out: nvr nr to chal)	½	7	8/1^{3}	74	55
3975^{11}	**Young Bigwig (IRE) (85)** (JBerry) **3-9-13b^{1}** RCochrane(15) (lw: nvr nr to chal)	s.h	8	16/1	82	63
4137^{6}	**Bollin Harry (57)** (TDEasterby) **5-8-1** LCharnock(3) (prom tl wknd appr fnl f)	¾	9	11/1	52	35
4155^{20}	**State of Caution (77)** (DShaw) **4-9-2b**(5) RMullen(13) (b: outpcd)	s.h	10	16/1	72	55
3614^{6}	**Bacchus (80)** (ACStewart) **3-9-8** SWhitworth(6) (bhd: effrt u.p 2f out: no imp)	½	11	12/1	74	55
964*	**Smart Kid (IRE) (85)** (PFICole) **3-9-13** KFallon(10) (bkwd: a bhd & outpcd: eased whn btn fnl 2f)	8	12	9/1	58	39
	Dovebrace (82) (TDBarron) **4-9-12** JCarroll(9) (bit bkwd: dwlt: a bhd)	3	13	33/1	47	30
				(SP 120.8%)	**13 Rn**	

1m 12.16 (0.46) CSF £41.22 CT £351.77 TOTE £8.70: £2.40 £2.20 £3.60 (£19.10) Trio £179.00 OWNER Mr B. Bull (LAMBOURN) BRED Sheikh Mohammed Bin Rashid Al Maktoum
WEIGHT FOR AGE 3yo-2lb
4013 Prends Ca (IRE) gave notice at the previous meeting that she was finding her form and, though she had to contend with this rapidly drying ground, she won very much as she pleased and should be able to defy her penalty. (15/2)
3936* Stand Tall has enjoyed a rewarding season and he rarely runs a bad race, but he had to admit the winner much too good for him on this occasion. (5/1)
4048 Saint Express, still to win beyond the minimum trip, ran a race full of promise and, on this evidence, he is certainly knocking at the door. (10/1)
2871 Nomore Mr Niceguy, making a return to sprinting, was taken off his legs in the early exchanges but he battled on under pressure inside the distance and, if stepping up a furlong, he is performing well enough to find another race. (20/1)
3385 For the Present, always chasing the leaders, could never muster the speed to throw down his challenge and he is finding it hard to get back to winning ways. (9/1)
4155 Grand Chapeau (IRE) gives of his best every time he runs, but forceful tactics are sure to take their toll in time and that appears to be the case with this fellow. (5/1)

4308 CLAUDE HARRISON MEMORIAL CHALLENGE TROPHY H'CAP (0-90) (3-Y.O) (Class C)

3-55 (3-58) **1m 30y** £5,797.00 (£1,756.00: £858.00: £409.00) Stalls: Low GOING minus 0.30 sec per fur (GF)

				SP	RR	SF
3894*	**Shawm (90)** (DRLoder) **3-9-7** KFallon(1) (lw: hld up in tch: hdwy over 2f out: led wl over 1f out: sn clr: readily)	—	1	3/1^{1}	102+	67
3389*	**Desert Beauty (IRE) (76)** (MRStoute) **3-8-7** KDarley(12) (hld up: hdwy & rdn 2f out: r.o wl towards fin)	¾	2	11/2^{3}	87	52
3894^{13}	**Green Power (83)** (JRFanshawe) **3-9-0** JCarroll(7) (hld up in tch: effrt 2f out: styd on one pce fnl f)	6	3	10/1	82	47
3775^{2}	**Sycamore Boy (USA) (74)** (LordHuntingdon) **3-8-5** DaneO'Neill(8) (bhd: hrd drvn over 3f out: styd on ins fnl f)	2½	4	9/1	68	33
4176*	**Abajany (77)** (MRChannon) **3-8-8** 6x JFortune(5) (a.p: chsng wnr whn wnt lame & eased ins fnl f)	3½	5	5/1^{2}	64	29
3225^{2}	**Night Chorus (68)** (BSRothwell) **3-7-13v^{1}** LCharnock(9) (lw: prom: rdn along 2f out: r.o one pce appr fnl f)	1¼	6	16/1	53	18
2013^{16}	**Sharp Temper (83)** (BWHills) **3-9-0** PaulEddery(3) (hld up: hdwy 4f out: wknd wl over 1f out)	¾	7	20/1	66	31
4220^{2}	**Royale Rose (FR) (70)** (ABailey) **3-8-1v** AMackay(6) (led over 5f out tl wl over 1f out: sn outpcd)	nk	8	7/1	52	17
3457^{3}	**Fancy A Fortune (IRE) (65)** (DNicholls) **3-7-3**(7) ANicholls(13) (a in rr)	¾	9	16/1	46	11
3575^{10}	**Cinema Paradiso (90)** (PFICole) **3-9-7** RCochrane(4) (led over 2f: wknd over 2f out)	1¼	10	25/1	69	34
3408^{7}	**Over To You (USA) (80)** (EALDunlop) **3-8-11v^{1}** SWhitworth(10) (lw: bhd: effrt & rdn over 2f out: no rspnse)	2½	11	14/1	54	19
4210^{5}	**Three For A Pound (65)** (JAGlover) **3-7-10** JBramhill(11) (lw: a in rr)	3	12	20/1	33	—
3801^{7}	**Smokey From Caplaw (68)** (JJO'Neill) **3-7-13** MartinDwyer(2) (lw: sddle slipped & c wd ent st: sn t.o: p.u appr fnl f)		P	16/1	—	—
				(SP 126.3%)	**13 Rn**	

1m 41.91 (1.31) CSF £17.54 CT £146.32 TOTE £3.60: £1.60 £2.70 £3.40 (£6.10) Trio £55.60 OWNER Sheikh Mohammed (NEWMARKET) BRED Sheikh Mohammed Bin Rashid Al Maktoum
LONG HANDICAP Fancy A Fortune (IRE) 7-8
3894* Shawm, in the form of his life at present, stole this race by quickening clear below the distance and, though he was being reeled in towards the finish, was never in any danger of being caught. (3/1)
3389* Desert Beauty (IRE), having her first run in handicap company, came from a long way back to reach her final placing and, given the easier ground that she prefers, we will soon be hearing more of her. (11/2)

2062 Green Power, someway adrift of the winner at Sandown, was only 3lb better off in the weights but he turned in a much improved effort and he is capable of finding another opening. (10/1)
3775 Sycamore Boy (USA), taking on handicappers for the first time, did not get going until far too late but there is plenty to like about this effort and it is possible he may well get further. (9/1)
4176* Abajany would not have gained his revenge on the winner but he was in hot pursuit when his jockey thought he had gone lame and eased him right up inside the last two hundred yards. (5/1)
3225 Night Chorus took a keen hold in his first-time visor and only succeeded in running himself into the ground. If he will settle, there could be more prizes to be won. (16/1)

4309 BULLS HEAD MAIDEN STKS (2-Y.O) (Class D)

4-30 (4-33) **7f 30y** £5,129.25 (£1,554.00: £759.50: £362.25) Stalls: Low GOING minus 0.30 sec per fur (GF)

				SP	RR	SF
	Fleetwood (IRE) (HRACecil) **2-9-0** KFallon(6) (gd sort: str: mde all: qcknd clr over 1f out: impressive)	—	**1**	4/6[1]	95++	53
	Mawsoof (MRStoute) **2-9-0** KDarley(4) (cmpt: a.p: drvn along over 2f out: kpt on: no ch w wnr)	8	**2**	11/1	77	35
4064[2]	**Shart (IRE)** (JHMGosden) **2-9-0** JCarroll(9) (chsd wnr: ev ch 2f out: sn drvn along & outpcd)	½	**3**	3/1[2]	76	34
4007[5]	**Former Love (USA)** (PRWebber) **2-8-9** DaneO'Neill(7) (chsd ldrs: rdn along 2f out: kpt on one pce)	6	**4**	50/1	58	16
	National Wish (USA) (EALDunlop) **2-9-0** JFortune(1) (w'like: scope: bkwd: bhd & outpcd: plld wd 2f out: styd on fnl f)	2½	**5**	14/1	57	15
	The Blues Academy (IRE) (MJohnston) **2-9-0v[1]** DeanMcKeown(3) (w'like: leggy: mid div: rdn over 2f out: no imp)	¾	**6**	25/1	55	13
4064[10]	**Dilly Lane (USA)** (PRWebber) **2-8-9** JFEgan(10) (trckd ldrs tl rdn & wknd wl over 1f out)	hd	**7**	66/1	50	8
	Ambiguous (DRLoder) **2-9-0** RCochrane(5) (gd sort: lw: s.s: a bhd & outpcd)	nk	**8**	10/1[3]	54	12
4017[13]	**Orleans (IRE)** (TPTate) **2-9-0** TLucas(2) (s.i.s: a bhd)	5	**9**	66/1	43	1
	Manila Moon (USA) (JJO'Neill) **2-9-0** ACulhane(8) (Withdrawn not under starter's orders: ref to ent stalls)		**W**	50/1	—	—
				(SP 119.8%)	**9 Rn**	

1m 29.8 (1.80) CSF £9.06 TOTE £1.70: £1.10 £2.20 £1.10 (£6.30) Trio £6.10 OWNER H R H Prince Fahd Salman (NEWMARKET) BRED Newgate Stud Co

Fleetwood (IRE) may not stand above fifteen hands, but he is a powerful, classy colt and the way he spread-eagled this field on this racecourse debut would suggest he has a good future ahead of him. The Group Three Horris Hill Stakes at Newbury next month is one of several big race entries he holds in the autumn. (4/6)
Mawsoof, a strongly-made compact colt, made a very pleasing start to his racing career and, though he was made to look second-rate when the winner quickened, he will not always come up against one so smart. (11/1)
4064 Shart (IRE), with a race under his belt, tried hard to make a race of it with the winner but, once that rival stepped up a gear, he was left in his wake. (3/1: 2/1-7/2)
4007 Former Love (USA) had to admit this company much too strong for her, but she did stay on and stamina would seem to be her strong suit. (50/1)
National Wish (USA), with plenty left to work on, was struggling with the pace for much of the way but he did begin to pick up in the latter stages and he will be all the wiser next time. (14/1: op 8/1)
The Blues Academy (IRE) wore a visor on this racecourse debut and was colty in the paddock. Settled off the pace, he did make an effort early in the straight but could do little more than gallop on the spot. (25/1)

4310 GOLDEN PHEASANT H'CAP (0-85) (3-Y.O) (Class D)

5-00 (5-01) **1m 3f 200y** £3,598.75 (£1,090.00: £532.50: £253.75) Stalls: Low GOING minus 0.30 sec per fur (GF)

				SP	RR	SF
4223[5]	**Largesse (73)** (JohnBerry) **3-8-11** JFEgan(3) (a.p: led over 1f out: rdn clr)	—	**1**	11/1	83	53
3424[5]	**Invermark (82)** (JRFanshawe) **3-9-6** RCochrane(4) (disp ld 8f: led over 3f out tl over 1f out: nt pce of wnr)	3½	**2**	13/2	87	57
4045*	**Tikopia (80)** (IABalding) **3-9-4** MartinDwyer(7) (lw: a.p: rdn over 1f out: r.o one pce)	2	**3**	15/2	83	53
3012[7]	**Vain Tempest (81)** (PWChapple-Hyam) **3-9-2**(3) RHavlin(2) (lw: trckd ldrs: rdn & nt clr run 3f out: styd on fnl f)	2	**4**	14/1	81	51
3813[4]	**Mardrew (65)** (JohnBerry) **3-7-12b[1]**(5)ow1 ADaly(6) (hld up & bhd: hdwy over 2f out: nvr nrr)	nk	**5**	14/1	65	34
3689[3]	**Island Sanctuary (IRE) (83)** (PJMakin) **3-9-7** JFortune(1) (hld up in rr: sme late hdwy: nvr nrr)	2½	**6**	6/1[3]	79	49
2328[5]	**Sioux (77)** (CWThornton) **3-9-1** DeanMcKeown(8) (mid div: rdn & outpcd over 3f out)	3	**7**	14/1	69	39
4151[4]	**Shadoof (77)** (WRMuir) **3-9-1** KFallon(5) (hld up & bhd: effrt over 3f out: sn rdn: no imp)	2½	**8**	2/1[1]	66	36
4102[9]	**Another Night (IRE) (80)** (RHannon) **3-9-4** DaneO'Neill(10) (b.hind: in tch: effrt u.p 4f out: no imp)	¾	**9**	12/1	68	38
3377[2]	**Heart of Armor (80)** (PFICole) **3-9-4** KDarley(9) (w ldr: led 4f out: sn rdn & hdd: wknd 2f out)	1½	**10**	11/2[2]	66	36
				(SP 124.1%)	**10 Rn**	

2m 32.12 (2.72) CSF £78.23 CT £534.63 TOTE £17.30: £4.40 £2.30 £2.30 (£86.40) Trio £90.40 OWNER Mrs Rosemary Moszkowicz (NEWMARKET) BRED Snowdrop Stud Co Ltd

4223 Largesse obviously thrives on hard work for this was his second outing in five days. Trying a longer trip, he won going away and, though he is a son of Cadeaux Genereux, he is not lacking in stamina. (11/1)
3424 Invermark had plenty of use made of him and he may have settled better without company, but he did nothing wrong and he could win again before the close. (13/2)
4045* Tikopia kept tabs on the leaders and kept battling away under pressure but the principals proved too strong for him when the whips were cracking. (15/2)
2045* Vain Tempest, searching for room and out-paced early in the straight, did well to eventually finish so close but, in truth, he only stayed on past beaten rivals. (14/1)
3813 Mardrew moved scratchily to post and was in the rear until staying on late in the day. (14/1)
3689 Island Sanctuary (IRE) began to stay on inside the distance, but the leaders had got away and he was never able to pose a threat. (6/1)
4151 Shadoof, held up to get the trip, gave the impression that he found it all too much and he never really fired. (2/1)

T/Plpt: £51.90 (407.99 Tckts). T/Qdpt: £14.20 (85.08 Tckts) IM

4103-KEMPTON (R-H) (Good)

Sunday September 21st

Race 1: hand timed
WEATHER: hot WIND: almost nil

4311 SUNBURY MAIDEN STKS (2-Y.O) (Class D)

2-10 (2-15) **5f** £3,712.50 (£1,125.00: £550.00: £262.50) Stalls: Low GOING minus 0.38 sec per fur (F)

			SP	RR	SF
1961⁷	**Refined (IRE)** (LMCumani) **2-8-6**(3) RFfrench(8) (led over 3f out: qcknd over 1f out: pushed out)—	**1**	5/1 2	76+	32
4103¹⁷	**Mrs Malaprop** (MRChannon) **2-8-9** GCarter(1) (bit bkwd: led over 1f: rdn over 1f out: r.o ins fnl f) 1¼	**2**	8/1	72	28
3981⁴	**Dancing Wolf (IRE)** (MissGayKelleway) **2-8-9** JReid(2) (lw: s.s: hld up: rdn over 1f out: r.o ins fnl f) hd	**3**	5/1 2	72	28
2103¹³	**Wandering Wolf** (RHannon) **2-9-0** OPeslier(10) (lw: a.p: rdn over 2f out: unable qckn) 2½	**4**	4/1 1	69	25
4012¹⁴	**Game Bird** (JLSpearing) **2-8-9** SDrowne(5) (a.p: rdn over 2f out: wknd over 1f out) 1¼	**5**	20/1	60	16
	Pinochet (USA) (JHMGosden) **2-8-9** WRyan(4) (neat: nvr nr to chal) 1	**6**	6/1 3	57+	13
3636⁵	**Lady Charlotte** (DRCElsworth) **2-8-4**(5) CLowther(13) (hdwy over 1f out: wknd fnl f) 1½	**7**	6/1 3	52	8
3589⁵	**Red Pepper (IRE)** (PHowling) **2-9-0** TSprake(3) (prom over 2f) 1¼	**8**	20/1	53	9
4012¹³	**Vista Alegre (65)** (PJMakin) **2-9-0** MHills(7) (a bhd) ¾	**9**	25/1	50	6
4065¹²	**Lady Ralphina (51)** (JJBridger) **2-8-6**(3) AWhelan(6) (a bhd) ½	**10**	100/1	44	—
3686¹⁹	**Polish Pilot (IRE)** (WRMuir) **2-9-0** JWeaver(9) (bit bkwd: prom over 2f) hd	**11**	20/1	48	4
	Royal Blue (MDIUsher) **2-9-0** JMarshall(12) (leggy: a bhd) 3	**12**	25/1	39	—
4012²²	**Lady d'Abo** (RCSpicer) **2-8-6**(3) DO'Donohoe(11) (ref to r: t.n.p)	**R**	100/1	—	—

(SP 117.0%) **13 Rn**

59.9 secs (1.70) CSF £36.02 TOTE £4.60: £1.30 £2.90 £1.50 (£50.30) Trio £87.10 OWNER Sheikh Mohammed (NEWMARKET) BRED W. Maxwell Ervine

1961 Refined (IRE), who found the ground a bit soft and was not suited by the ups and downs of the track when a well beaten favourite on her debut at Leicester three months ago, was a different kettle of fish this time and soon at the head of affairs, forged clear from below the distance for a very decisive victory. (5/1)

Mrs Malaprop still did not look fully wound up despite a recent run but nevertheless was in the firing line throughout. Unable to keep tabs on the winner when that rival forged ahead below the distance, she was staying on again at the death. (8/1)

3981 Dancing Wolf (IRE), a tall filly, looked in good order and ran her best race to date, running on nicely inside the final furlong and only just losing out in the battle for second prize. (5/1)

Wandering Wolf, who rather ambitiously made his debut at Royal Ascot, was having his first run since and was dropped to more suitable company. Looking really well beforehand, he was certainly the paddock pick but failed to quicken in the last two furlongs. (4/1: op 5/2)

Game Bird was in the thick of the action until calling it a day approaching the final furlong. (20/1)

Pinochet (USA) lacks substance and is certainly a lot smaller than the robust types you tend to associate with the Gosden stable. Not given a particularly hard time, she did catch the eye, staying on in the closing stages. She should come on for this. (6/1: 5/2-7/1)

3636 Lady Charlotte (6/1: op 4/1)

4312 KIDS RACE FREE CONDITIONS STKS (3-Y.O+) (Class C)

2-45 (2-46) **1m 2f (Jubilee)** £4,635.75 (£1,692.00: £828.50: £357.50: £161.25) Stalls: High GOING minus 0.38 sec per fur (F)

			SP	RR	SF
3388⁵	**Barnum Sands (105)** (JLDunlop) **3-8-8** TSprake(1) (lw: mde all: clr over 2f out: drvn out)—	**1**	9/4 2	109	69
4149⁹	**Haltarra (USA) (109)** (SbinSuroor) **3-8-12** JReid(3) (lw: hld up: chsd wnr over 6f out to 2f out: chsd wnr ins fnl f: hrd rdn: r.o) nk	**2**	Evens 1	113	73
3703¹³	**Wilcuma (100)** (PJMakin) **6-9-0b** RHills(5) (hld up: chsd wnr 2f out tl ins fnl f: unable qckn) 1¾	**3**	7/1 3	106	72
1261⁹	**Royal Philosopher (100)** (JWHills) **5-9-0** MHills(2) (hld up: rdn 3f out: wknd over 2f out) 16	**4**	8/1	80	46
4072⁴	**Dunabrattin** (DTThom) **4-9-0** DRMcCabe(4) (lw: chsd wnr over 3f: wknd 5f out: t.o) dist	**5**	40/1	—	—

(SP 106.8%) **5 Rn**

2m 2.62 (-0.88) CSF £4.15 TOTE £3.40: £1.40 £1.10 (£1.60) OWNER Aylesfield Farms Stud Ltd (ARUNDEL) BRED Aylesfield Farms Stud
WEIGHT FOR AGE 3yo-6lb

3388 Barnum Sands, who ran too freely in blinkers last time out, had them dispensed with here and, making all the running, forged clear early in the straight. However, with the second sticking on well, his jockey needed to get serious although the combination never looked liked being overhauled. (9/4)

4149 Haltarra (USA) was back over a more suitable distance having failed to stay the St Leger trip last time out. He likes to make the running and being held up may have been partially to blame for this rather disappointing display for Reid was already pushing him along entering the straight. The colt did run on under pressure inside the final furlong but never looked like overhauling the winner. (Evens)

3051 Wilcuma is well suited by some give but still ran a sound race here and moved into second place a quarter of a mile from home. Collared for that spot early inside the final furlong, he then failed to find another gear. (7/1)

Royal Philosopher, without a run in four months, had shot his bolt early in the straight. He has done all his winning at a mile. (8/1: 6/1-9/1)

Dunabrattin was completely out of his depth here but still picked up some prize-money for finishing tailed off. (40/1)

4313 GEOFFREY HAMLYN H'CAP (0-85) (3-Y.O+) (Class D)

3-15 (3-16) **1m 6f 92y** £3,631.25 (£1,100.00: £537.50: £256.25) Stalls: High GOING minus 0.38 sec per fur (F)

			SP	RR	SF
4108²	**Renzo (IRE) (79)** (MrsAJPerrett) **4-9-8** AClark(3) (stdy hdwy over 2f out: led over 1f out: r.o wl)—	**1**	12/1	92	56
4246⁵	**Sea Victor (69)** (JLHarris) **5-8-12** OPeslier(8) (a.p: led over 2f out tl over 1f out: unable qckn) 1¾	**2**	4/1 1	80	44
4104⁵	**Ela-Yie-Mou (IRE) (56)** (SDow) **4-7-6**(7) PDoe(1) (lw: hdwy 6f out: rdn over 2f out: wknd over 1f out) 5	**3**	7/1 3	62	26
4156⁸	**Rising Spray (72)** (CAHorgan) **6-8-12**(3) RFfrench(10) (lw: s.s: hdwy 3f out: wknd wl over 1f out) 2½	**4**	7/1 3	75	39
4002³	**Artic Courier (78)** (DJSCosgrove) **6-9-7** MRimmer(9) (b: hdwy over 2f out: wknd wl over 1f out) 12	**5**	9/1	67	31
3579⁵	**Children's Choice (IRE) (55)** (WJMusson) **6-7-12** JQuinn(5) (sme hdwy over 2f out: sn wknd) 1¼	**6**	12/1	43	7
4002¹⁴	**Hal Hoo Yaroom (82)** (RAkehurst) **4-9-11** JWeaver(6) (led over 3f: wknd over 2f out) 5	**7**	12/1	65	29
3318²	**Shahboor (USA) (75)** (MRStoute) **3-8-8** JReid(2) (led over 10f out tl over 2f out: sn wknd) ¾	**8**	5/1 2	57	11
2189³	**Tommy Tortoise (73)** (MissGayKelleway) **3-8-6** GCarter(7) (lw: bhd fnl 9f) 3	**9**	11/1	51	5
3915³	**Arctic Fancy (USA) (74)** (PWHarris) **4-8-12**(5) CLowther(4) (s.s: hdwy over 12f out: wknd over 2f out) 3	**10**	8/1	49	13

(SP 114.2%) **10 Rn**

3m 6.59 (2.67 under best) (3.59) CSF £53.10 CT £333.84 TOTE £12.80: £2.50 £1.80 £2.20 (£14.00) Trio £74.80 OWNER Mr K. J. Buchanan (PULBOROUGH) BRED K. J. and Mrs Buchanan
WEIGHT FOR AGE 3yo-10lb

4108 Renzo (IRE) is certainly not one to rely on but things went his way on this occasion and this was to be his day. Gradually creeping closer in the last half-mile, he cruised into the lead below the distance and although his rider only shook him up, he nevertheless still carried his head ominously high and looked far from enthusiastic. He still looks one to steer well clear of. (12/1: op 7/1)
4246 Sea Victor, making a quick reappearance, has dropped a handy few pounds this season. Pushed along in the back straight, he then came back on the bridle turning for home and cruised into the lead early in the straight. Collared below the distance, he then found the winner too strong but still finished well clear of the remainder. (4/1)
4104 Ela-Yie-Mou (IRE), who has slumped in the handicap this year, took closer order three-quarters of a mile from home but was left for dead from below the distance. He has just one win to his name. (7/1)
3475 Rising Spray again showed that this distance is beyond him - his only victory at this trip was in a farcically slow-run race - and he had run out of gas early in the final quarter-mile. (7/1)
4002 Artic Courier is not easy to win with but this trip is beyond him and he had shot his bolt early in the final quarter-mile. All three of his victories have come over a mile and a half. (9/1)
3579 Children's Choice (IRE) (12/1: op 8/1)
Hal Hoo Yaroom (12/1: op 7/1)
3318 Shahboor (USA) (5/1: 7/2-11/2)

4314 SUNDAY RACING RATED STKS H'CAP (0-95) (3-Y.O+) (Class C)

3-45 (3-46) **1m (Jubilee)** £6,405.40 (£2,398.60: £1,174.30: £506.50: £228.25: £116.95) Stalls: High GOING minus 0.38 sec per fur (F)

				SP	RR	SF
3786^{6}	**Yalta (IRE) (80)** (RCharlton) **4-8-7b** TSprake(2) (lw: mde all: clr over 2f out: drvn out)	—	1	12/1	88	70
3894^{4}	**Silk St John (80)** (MJRyan) **3-8-3** GCarter(10) (rdn over 2f out: hdwy to chse wnr over 1f out: r.o wl ins fnl f)	nk	2	8/1	87	65
	Secret Spring (FR) (80) (PRHedger) **5-8-7** SDrowne(6) (s.s: hdwy over 1f out: r.o)	3½	3	25/1	80	62
3888^{2}	**Concer Un (93)** (SCWilliams) **5-9-3**(3) RFfrench(9) (b: lw: a.p: rdn over 2f out: wknd 1f out)	2	4	$3/1^{1}$	89	71
3786^{3}	**Glen Parker (IRE) (84)** (HRACecil) **4-8-11** WRyan(3) (lw: prom tl wknd & squeezed out over 2f out: fin 6th, hd: plcd 5th)	½	5	$7/2^{2}$	79	61
3725^{4}	**The Prince (93)** (GWragg) **3-9-2** MHills(8) (lw: s.s: hdwy 3f out: edgd rt & chsd wnr over 2f out to over 1f out: sn wknd: fin 5th, ½l: disq: plcd 6th)	hd	6	$11/2^{3}$	88	66
3752*	**Sweet Fortune (USA) (88)** (MRStoute) **3-8-11** JReid(1) (chsd wnr over 5f)	7	7	$11/2^{3}$	69	47
3725^{12}	**Red Robbo (CAN) (94)** (RAkehurst) **4-9-7b^{1}** OPeslier(5) (hld up: rdn over 4f out: sn wknd)	27	8	7/1	21	3
				(SP 113.1%)		**8 Rn**

1m 36.76 (-0.94) CSF £91.40 CT £2,139.08 TOTE £17.50: £3.10 £1.80 £4.00 (£65.30) Trio £160.00 OWNER Lord Weinstock (BECKHAMPTON) BRED Ballymacoll Stud Farm Ltd
LONG HANDICAP Yalta (IRE) 8-5
WEIGHT FOR AGE 3yo-4lb

3786 Yalta (IRE) likes to front run and, making all the running, forged clear over a quarter of a mile from home. However, with the second finishing with a real flourish, he found the line only just saving him. (12/1)
3894 Silk St John has been running well this season and ran another good race. Moving into second place over a furlong out, he ran on really strongly but found the line just beating him. (8/1)
Secret Spring (FR), who showed himself to be a useful novice hurdler last winter, made an encouraging return to action after a five month absence and was putting in some eye-catching work in the last furlong and a half. This run should have blown away the cobwebs and he should be ready to strike before long. (25/1)
3888 Concer Un, a leading player from the outset, had run out of steam a furlong from home. (3/1)
3786 Glen Parker (IRE) was up with the pace but was feeling the pinch and beginning to back-pedal when squeezed out by The Prince early in the straight. He was later promoted a place. (7/2)
3725 The Prince took closer order turning into the straight but, in the process of moving into second place over a quarter of a mile out, edged right doing Glen Parker no favours. Collared for the runner-up berth below the distance, he soon had bellows to mend. He was later demoted a place at the Stewards' enquiry. (11/2)

4315 CHILDREN'S CHOICE NURSERY H'CAP (2-Y.O) (Class D)

4-20 (4-20) **6f** £3,663.75 (£1,110.00: £542.50: £258.75) Stalls: Low GOING minus 0.38 sec per fur (F)

				SP	RR	SF
3899^{2}	**Surveyor (90)** (JLDunlop) **2-9-7** TSprake(1) (lw: hld up: squeezed thro to ld over 1f out: r.o wl)	—	1	$5/4^{1}$	93	66
3597^{8}	**Kennet (74)** (PDCundell) **2-8-5** RPerham(4) (a.p: led 3f out tl over 1f out: unable qckn)	1¼	2	10/1	74	47
4216^{4}	**Oh So Easy (66)** (BJMeehan) **2-7-11** CRutter(6) (lw: hld up: ev ch wl over 1f out: one pce)	2½	3	$6/1^{2}$	59	32
3743^{2}	**Storm Fromthe East (85)** (RHannon) **2-9-2** JReid(5) (lw: hld up: rdn over 2f out: one pce)	3	4	$6/1^{2}$	70	43
3973^{5}	**Thelonius (IRE) (71)** (JGSmyth-Osbourne) **2-8-2** GBardwell(8) (a.p: rdn over 2f out: wknd over 1f out)	2	5	20/1	51	24
3610^{5}	**Sampower Lady (65)** (WJMusson) **2-7-10** JQuinn(2) (lw: s.s: a bhd)	4	6	12/1	34	7
4106^{8}	**Hill Magic (87)** (DRCElsworth) **2-9-1**(3) RFfrench(7) (prom over 3f)	½	7	12/1	55	28
3708^{5}	**Moontabeh (86)** (PTWalwyn) **2-9-3** RHills(3) (led 3f: wknd over 1f out)	2	8	$7/1^{3}$	48	21
				(SP 114.8%)		**8 Rn**

1m 11.67 (0.47) CSF £13.78 CT £51.89 TOTE £2.20: £1.40 £2.30 £1.70 (£11.40) OWNER The Earl Cadogan (ARUNDEL) BRED Mrs A. Naughton

3899 Surveyor appreciated the return to a sounder surface and put up a very convincing display, squeezing through to lead approaching the final furlong and scooting clear for an emphatic victory. Connections are now contemplating the Group Three Cornwallis Stakes at Ascot next month. (5/4)
3237 Kennet, who did not stay an extended seven furlongs last time out, gained a slender advantage at halfway but, collared by the winner approaching the final furlong, was well and truly put in his place. (10/1)
4216 Oh So Easy, making a quick reappearance, had every chance early in the final quarter-mile before tapped for toe. (6/1)
3743 Storm Fromthe East again adopted waiting tactics but failed to quicken in the last two furlongs. He looks harshly handicapped. (6/1: op 7/2)
3973 Thelonius (IRE) was close up until left for dead from below the distance. He needs to return to further. (20/1)
2863 Hill Magic (12/1: 8/1-14/1)
3708 Moontabeh (7/1: op 4/1)

4316 SEPTEMBER MAIDEN STKS (3-Y.O) (Class D)

4-50 (4-52) **7f** £3,550.00 (£1,075.00: £525.00: £250.00) Stalls: High GOING minus 0.38 sec per fur (F)

				SP	RR	SF
1087^{8}	**Musharak (86)** (JLDunlop) **3-9-0** RHills(10) (plld hrd: swtchd lft over 2f out: gd hdwy to ld 1f out: comf)	—	1	$3/1^{1}$	92	57
3800^{2}	**Silver Kristal (75)** (RAkehurst) **3-8-9** OPeslier(1) (led 6f: unable qckn)	6	2	$100/30^{2}$	73	38

				SP	RR	SF
	Mozambique (IRE) (MrsJCecil) **3-8-11**(3) RFfrench(7) (w'like: scope: s.s: rdn & hdwy over 2f out: one pce fnl f)	nk	**3**	20/1	78	43
	Finarts Bay (MrsJCecil) **3-8-9** JWeaver(9) (rdn & hdwy over 2f out: r.o one pce)	2½	**4**	14/1	67	32
1304[3]	**Star Invader** (MRStoute) **3-9-0** JReid(3) (lw: hmpd s: rdn & hdwy over 2f out: r.o one pce)	½	**5**	4/1[3]	71	36
	Madame Maxi (PRHedger) **3-8-9** SDrowne(2) (leggy: nvr nr to chal)	1¾	**6**	50/1	62	27
4009[5]	**Cuesta Rey (USA)** (JWHills) **3-9-0** MHills(8) (lw: prom 3f)	nk	**7**	12/1	66	31
1629[2]	**Spanish Knot (USA) (73)** (LordHuntingdon) **3-8-9** RPerham(12) (w ldr: ev ch over 1f out: wknd fnl f)	¾	**8**	8/1	59	24
4070[4]	**Injazaat (USA) (75)** (MajorWRHern) **3-8-9b** AClark(5) (hdwy over 3f out: wknd over 1f out)	1	**9**	8/1	57	22
3917[11]	**Encore** (JHMGosden) **3-8-9** WRyan(6) (prom over 5f)	5	**10**	14/1	46	11
3787[15]	**Amarella (IRE) (45)** (MJHaynes) **3-8-9** GCarter(4) (bhd fnl 5f)	1¼	**11**	50/1	43	8
3715[8]	**Hamleys** (DMorris) **3-8-9** NDay(11) (prom over 3f)	2	**12**	33/1	38	3
	My Brother (SEarle) **3-9-0** TSprake(13) (leggy: unf: s.s: a bhd)	1	**13**	50/1	41	6

(SP 124.9%) **13 Rn**

1m 25.3 (0.80) CSF £11.86 TOTE £3.50: £1.60 £1.50 £4.90 (£8.30) Trio £87.70 OWNER Mr Hamdan Al Maktoum (ARUNDEL) BRED Shadwell Estate Company Limited

503 Musharak, who had troubled hocks when flopping at Lingfield back in May, bounced back here. Taking a keen hold at the back of the field, he was switched left early in the straight and, although he had an awful lot of ground to make up, did so in a very short space of time. Storming through to lead striking the furlong pole, he sprinted clear for a very emphatic victory. His trainer describes him as quite a nice horse if he stays alright. (3/1)

3800 Silver Kristal took the field along but, collared a furlong from home, was well and truly left for dead by the winner. She should soon find a race. (100/30)

Mozambique (IRE), a likeable good-bodied colt, began a forward move early in the straight but he had no hope with the winner in the final furlong and was only fighting for the runner-up spot. (20/1)

Finarts Bay, making a belated seasonal reappearance, stayed on in the straight to finish fourth. (14/1)

1304 Star Invader, who finished lame on his debut at Goodwood back in May, looked in good shape for the first run since and struggled on in the straight. (4/1: 3/1-9/2)

4009 Cuesta Rey (USA) (12/1: op 25/1)

1629 Spanish Knot (USA) (8/1: 5/1-9/1)

3030 Encore (14/1: 10/1-16/1)

T/Jkpt: £7,100.00 (0.1 Tckts); £2,675.39 to Kempton 22/9/97. T/Plpt: £454.20 (45.55 Tckts). T/Qdpt: £205.00 (4.19 Tckts) AK

4311-KEMPTON (R-H) (Good to firm)
Monday September 22nd

WEATHER: warm WIND: almost nil

4317 E.B.F. MAIDEN STKS (2-Y.O F) (Class D)

2-00 (2-01) **7f (Jubilee)** £3,322.50 (£1,005.00: £490.00: £232.50) Stalls: High GOING minus 0.46 sec per fur (F)

				SP	RR	SF
3114[4]	**Elsurur (USA)** (SbinSuroor) **2-8-11** JReid(14) (mde all: shkn up over 2f out: r.o wl)	—	**1**	3/1[2]	84+	37
3490[2]	**Inchtina** (HCandy) **2-8-11** CRutter(3) (rdn & hdwy 2f out: chsd wnr fnl f: r.o)	1¾	**2**	7/1	80	33
3979[6]	**Yanabi (USA)** (PTWalwyn) **2-8-11** DHolland(11) (lw: chsd wnr over 5f: r.o one pce)	¾	**3**	2/1[1]	78	31
	Bint Kaldoun (IRE) (DRLoder) **2-8-11** RCochrane(12) (leggy: a.p: rdn over 2f out: chsd wnr over 1f out to 1f out: one pce)	2	**4**	16/1	74	27
	Red Leggings (JWHills) **2-8-8**(3) MHenry(9) (neat: bit bkwd: a.p: rdn over 2f out: wknd over 1f out)	1	**5**	33/1	71	24
4057[4]	**Bluewain Lady** (PWHarris) **2-8-11** KFallon(6) (lw: a.p: rdn over 2f out: wknd over 1f out)	1¼	**6**	8/1	69	22
3117[5]	**Blue Dawn (IRE)** (EALDunlop) **2-8-11** GHind(8) (b.hind: lw: a.p: rdn over 2f out: sn wknd)	s.h	**7**	14/1	69	22
	Caledonian Express (JLDunlop) **2-8-11** TSprake(4) (str: scope: bkwd: shkn up over 2f out: hdwy fnl f: nvr nrr: bttr for r)	½	**8**	33/1	67	20
3638[11]	**Robanna** (RAkehurst) **2-8-11** SSanders(1) (a mid div)	1¾	**9**	33/1	63	16
	Act of Folly (LadyHerries) **2-8-11** AClark(15) (w'like: scope: s.s: a bhd)	1¾	**10**	33/1	59	12
	Lamsaat (IRE) (MAJarvis) **2-8-11** PaulEddery(2) (unf: bkwd: plld hrd: nvr plcd to chal)	nk	**11**	33/1	59	12
3979[4]	**Savoury** (JLDunlop) **2-8-11** TQuinn(5) (bhd fnl 2f)	¾	**12**	6/1[3]	57	10
4103[19]	**Glitter Princess** (MajorDNChappell) **2-8-11** GCarter(7) (s.s: a bhd)	3½	**13**	33/1	49	2
	Stylish Storm (USA) (BWHills) **2-8-11** MHills(10) (leggy: unf: scope: bit bkwd: s.s: a bhd)	½	**14**	25/1	48	1

(SP 130.3%) **14 Rn**

1m 26.24 (1.74) CSF £22.79 TOTE £4.50: £2.20 £1.70 £1.50 (£13.30) Trio £14.50 OWNER Godolphin (NEWMARKET) BRED Shadwell Farm Inc

3114 Elsurur (USA) may have been gleaming in the paddock, but her coat looked as if it was about to go and she had sweated up by the time she had reached the start. Nevertheless, she convincingly reversed Goodwood form with Yanabi, who had beaten her three-quarters of a length. Putting up a stylish front-running display, she had all her rivals at it early in the straight and never looked like being caught. (3/1)

3490 Inchtina appreciated the extra furlong but, despite moving into second place entering the final furlong and keeping on, was unable to peg back the winner. She should soon pick up a race. (7/1)

3979 Yanabi (USA), rather edgy in the paddock, was a little disappointing as she was unable to confirm superiority over the winner. In second place until early in the straight, she stayed on but never threatened to find the necessary turn of foot. (2/1)

Bint Kaldoun (IRE), a tall, plain filly who cost FF1,400,000, showed in front briefly over a furlong out before tapped for toe. (16/1)

Red Leggings is not very big and certainly did not impress in her coat. Looking as though the run would do her good, she was close up until tiring approaching the final furlong. (33/1)

4057 Bluewain Lady, reverting to seven furlongs, was close up until calling it a day over a furlong out. (8/1)

Lamsaat (IRE), a plain filly who needs time, was carrying plenty of condition and was given a very tender ride towards the back of the field. Improvement can be expected. (33/1)

4318 E.B.F. BEDFONT MAIDEN STKS (2-Y.O) (Class D)

2-30 (2-33) **1m (Jubilee)** £3,387.50 (£1,025.00: £500.00: £237.50) Stalls: High GOING minus 0.46 sec per fur (F)

				SP	RR	SF
4061[4]	**Taverner Society (IRE) (85)** (RWArmstrong) **2-9-0** GCarter(1) (a.p: led 2f out: rdn out)	—	**1**	9/2[3]	81	49
	Mantusis (IRE) (PWHarris) **2-9-0** AClark(9) (unf: scope: s.s: hdwy over 2f out: chsd wnr fnl f: r.o one pce)	2	**2**	10/1	77+	45
	Golden Hawk (USA) (PFICole) **2-9-0** TQuinn(3) (leggy: lw: chsd ldr: ev ch 2f out: one pce)	2	**3**	10/1	73	41

				SP	RR	SF
2840^{8}	**Mysterious Ecology** (BWHills) **2-8-9** MHills(7) (s.i.s: plld hrd: hdwy over 3f out: one pce fnl 2f)	2	**4**	20/1	64	32
4061^{12}	**Jaazim (USA)** (MRStoute) **2-9-0** KFallon(6) (hld up: rdn 4f out: one pce fnl 2f)	1¼	**5**	9/4^{1}	67	35
2388^{8}	**Lucky Double** (RHannon) **2-9-0** DaneO'Neill(4) (led 6f: wknd over 1f out)	1¼	**6**	14/1	64	32
3905^{W}	**Up The Wall (60)** (JohnBerry) **2-9-0** JQuinn(10) (rdn & hdwy over 2f out: nvr nrr)	1½	**7**	33/1	61	29
	Methmoon (IRE) (SbinSuroor) **2-9-0** DHolland(14) (w'like: scope: s.s: shkn up 6f out: sme hdwy on ins over 1f out: eased whn btn fnl f: rn green)	3	**8**	7/2^{2}	55+	23
	Tales of Bounty (IRE) (DRCElsworth) **2-9-0** SDrowne(11) (w'like: scope: nvr nrr)	1¾	**9**	20/1	52	20
3745^{8}	**Salford** (LMCumani) **2-9-0** JWeaver(8) (a mid div)	s.h	**10**	20/1	51	19
	Almazhar (IRE) (EALDunlop) **2-8-11**(3) DO'Donohoe(15) (b.off fore: str: scope: bit bkwd: s.s: nvr nrr)	3½	**11**	12/1	44	12
2768^{12}	**Radar (IRE)** (MAJarvis) **2-9-0** RCochrane(12) (nvr nrr)	¾	**12**	20/1	43	11
	Roy (HMorrison) **2-9-0** CRutter(16) (str: scope: bit bkwd: a bhd)	3	**13**	33/1	37	5
4007^{11}	**Mandhar (IRE)** (GLewis) **2-9-0** PaulEddery(17) (prom 4f)	1¾	**14**	25/1	33	1
	Red Brook Lad (SDow) **2-9-0** SSanders(5) (w'like: lw: s.s: a bhd)	½	**15**	33/1	32	—
	General Monck (DMorley) **2-9-0** MFenton(2) (str: scope: s.s: bhd fnl 4f)	3½	**16**	33/1	25	—
3927^{7}	**Plastered In Paris (IRE)** (BJMeehan) **2-9-0** MTebbutt(13) (prom 4f)	nk	**17**	33/1	25	—
				(SP 141.3%)	**17 Rn**	

1m 38.78 (3.72 under 2y best) (1.08) CSF £45.65 TOTE £6.20: £1.80 £3.70 £2.70 (£29.60) Trio £103.10 OWNER Pink & Blue Ribbon Racing Syndicate (NEWMARKET) BRED Theo Waddington (UK) Ltd

4061 Taverner Society (IRE) deserved to win a race and he made no mistake this time, leading a quarter of a mile out and being rousted along to assert his authority. (9/2)

Mantusis (IRE), a lengthy colt who is a half-brother to several winners, came through to take second place a furlong out but, despite staying on, never threatened to get near the winner. (10/1: 14/1-8/1)

Golden Hawk (USA), a tall, attractive colt, was gleaming in his coat. One of three almost in line a quarter of a mile from home, he was then tapped for toe. (10/1)

Mysterious Ecology, who took a keen hold early on, took closer order turning for home but could only struggle on at one insufficient pace in the last two furlongs. (20/1)

Jaazim (USA), bustled along from halfway, was made to look very pedestrian in the straight. He needs further. (9/4: 5/4-3/1)

Lucky Double set the pace but, collared two furlongs from home, lack of a recent run then took its toll and he soon tired. (14/1: 10/1-16/1)

Methmoon (IRE) (7/2: 6/4-4/1)

Almazhar (IRE) (12/1: 4/1-14/1)

4319 SPELTHORNE H'CAP (0-75) (3-Y.O+) (Class D)

3-00 (3-02) **1m (round)** £3,826.25 (£1,160.00: £567.50: £271.25) Stalls: High GOING minus 0.46 sec per fur (F)

				SP	RR	SF
735^{11}	**Myrtle Quest (74)** (RCharlton) **5-9-13** TSprake(6) (lw: rdn over 2f out: hdwy over 1f out: led nr fin)	—	**1**	14/1	86	66
3913^{7}	**Polish Rhythm (IRE) (66)** (GAHubbard) **4-9-5** JReid(3) (lw: a.p: led over 2f out: hrd rdn over 1f out: hdd nr fin)	½	**2**	12/1^{3}	77	57
4219^{6}	**Veni Vidi Vici (IRE) (63)** (MJHeaton-Ellis) **4-9-2** SDrowne(9) (hdwy over 2f out: chsd wnr over 1f out tl ins fnl f: one pce)	¾	**3**	7/1^{1}	73	53
3980^{6}	**Sis Garden (59)** (JCullinan) **4-8-9**(3) DO'Donohoe(1) (a.p: rdn over 2f out: one pce)	1½	**4**	16/1	66	46
3793^{4}	**Absolute Utopia (USA) (55)** (NEBerry) **4-8-8** RPerham(13) (hdwy over 2f out: hrd rdn over 1f out: one pce)	3	**5**	8/1^{2}	56	36
4008^{2}	**Matoaka (65)** (VSoane) **3-9-0** RCochrane(15) (hdwy & nt clr run over 1f out: swtchd rt: nvr nrr)	1	**6**	7/1^{1}	64	40
4112^{3}	**Akalim (57)** (LGCottrell) **4-8-10** DHolland(5) (lw: prom over 5f)	1¾	**7**	8/1^{2}	52	32
4139^{9}	**Chasetown Flyer (USA) (60)** (NEBerry) **3-8-9** KFallon(14) (rdn over 3f out: nvr nrr)	½	**8**	8/1^{2}	54	30
3992^{3}	**Golden Ace (IRE) (56)** (RCSpicer) **4-8-9** DeanMcKeown(17) (rdn over 2f out: nvr nrr)	½	**9**	12/1^{3}	49	29
3980^{4}	**Prenonamoss (54)** (DWPArbuthnot) **9-8-7** MTebbutt(7) (rdn over 2f out: nvr nrr)	¾	**10**	12/1^{3}	46	26
3930^{12}	**Briska (IRE) (64)** (RAkehurst) **3-8-13** TQuinn(2) (a mid div)	1	**11**	14/1	54	30
4219^{11}	**Duello (65)** (MBlanshard) **6-9-4** JQuinn(18) (a bhd)	1¼	**12**	12/1^{3}	52	32
	The Stager (IRE) (70) (JRJenkins) **5-9-9** NDay(11) (led over 5f)	¾	**13**	33/1	56	36
	Lucky Archer (75) (JMBradley) **4-9-11**(3) PPMurphy(12) (lw: a bhd)	2½	**14**	33/1	56	36
4008^{16}	**Bin Cyclone (USA) (64)** (CEBrittain) **3-8-13b^{1}** SSanders(10) (lw: prom over 6f)	1	**15**	20/1	43	19
4139^{16}	**Quibbling (60)** (HCandy) **3-8-9b^{1}** CRutter(8) (w ldr over 4f)	6	**16**	16/1	27	3
3977^{8}	**Moran (67)** (RFJohnsonHoughton) **3-9-2** MRimmer(16) (swtg: prom 4f)	5	**17**	16/1	24	—
				(SP 130.7%)	**17 Rn**	

1m 37.81 (0.61) CSF £163.85 CT £1,186.49 TOTE £16.10: £4.10 £3.90 £1.90 £4.00 (£151.90) Trio £298.80 OWNER Miss M. Sheriffe (BECKHAMPTON) BRED Miss M. Sheriffe and A. J. Tree

WEIGHT FOR AGE 3yo-4lb

499 Myrtle Quest, absent since April when he ran two poor races, gained his only previous win over this trip, and came with a real rattle from below the distance to strike the front near the line. (14/1)

2569 Polish Rhythm (IRE) appreciated the return to handicap company and ran a sound race, showing in front early in the straight before worried out of it near the finish. (12/1)

4219 Veni Vidi Vici (IRE) took closer order early in the straight. In second place below the distance, he was collared for that position inside the final furlong. Both his wins to date have come over this trip. (7/1)

3980 Sis Garden was never far away, but could only go up and down in the same place in the final quarter-mile. She is currently 5lb higher than she has ever won off. (16/1)

3793 Absolute Utopia (USA) began to thread his way through the pack early in the straight, but was only treading water from below the distance. (8/1)

4008 Matoaka again encountered traffic problems and could never get near the principals. (7/1)

4320 STAINES LIMITED STKS (0-85) (3-Y.O+) (Class D)

3-30 (3-33) **1m 4f** £3,468.75 (£1,050.00: £512.50: £243.75) Stalls: High GOING minus 0.46 sec per fur (F)

				SP	RR	SF
4136^{3}	**Ferny Hill (IRE) (84)** (SirMarkPrescott) **3-8-13** SSanders(1) (lw: led over 2f: led over 2f out: drvn out)	—	**1**	5/2^{2}	96	52
4002^{4}	**Moon Blast (81)** (LadyHerries) **3-9-1** RCochrane(2) (rdn over 2f out: hdwy over 1f out: r.o wl ins fnl f)	¾	**2**	10/1	97	53
3989^{9}	**Isle of Man (USA) (85)** (PFICole) **3-8-11** TQuinn(3) (hld up: rdn over 2f out: ev ch wl over 1f out: unable qckn fnl f)	hd	**3**	6/1	93	49
3916^{3}	**Patriot Games (IRE) (84)** (MRStoute) **3-8-13** JReid(5) (hld up: n.m.r over 2f out: rdn: one pce fnl f)	2½	**4**	9/2^{3}	92	48
4072*	**Awesome Wells (IRE) (82)** (HRACecil) **3-8-13** KFallon(4) (lw: chsd ldr: led over 9f out tl over 2f out: wknd over 1f out)	19	**5**	7/4^{1}	66	22

	Fasil (IRE) (83) (JGMO'Shea) **4-9-5** MFenton(6) (a bhd)	28	**6**	20/1	27	—
				(SP 111.3%)		**6 Rn**

2m 31.23 (1.23) CSF £23.19 TOTE £3.40: £1.50 £3.00 (£14.30) OWNER Cheveley Park Stud (NEWMARKET) BRED D. Ryan, M. Moloney and H. King
WEIGHT FOR AGE 3yo-8lb
OFFICIAL EXPLANATION Awesome Wells (IRE): no explanation offered.
4136 Ferny Hill (IRE), the early leader, regained the advantage over a quarter of a mile from home and, responding to pressure, just managed to hold off the runner-up. He would not be inconvenienced by further. (5/2)
4002 Moon Blast may have gained both his victories at a mile, but he went into overdrive in the last furlong and a half and finished really well. (10/1: 7/1-12/1)
3599 Isle of Man (USA) appreciated the return to a fast surface, and had every chance early in the final quarter-mile before tapped for toe. (6/1: 4/1-13/2)
3916 Patriot Games (IRE), taking a step up in distance, was right on the heels of the principals a furlong from home, before failing to find another gear. (9/2)
4072* Awesome Wells (IRE), a big, heavy-topped individual who does nothing fast, moved to the front turning into the back straight but, collared over a quarter of a mile from home, tamely dropped away. (7/4)

4321 SHEPPERTON H'CAP (0-85) (3-Y.O+) (Class D)

4-00 (4-03) **6f** £3,533.75 (£1,070.00: £522.50: £248.75) Stalls: Low GOING minus 0.46 sec per fur (F)

				SP	RR	SF
4155[15]	**Distinctive Dream (IRE) (73)** (KTIvory) **3-9-2b** RCochrane(9) (s.s: nt clr run over 2f out: hdwy over 1f out: led wl ins fnl f: drvn out)	—	**1**	11/1	85	65
4175[5]	**Dominant Air (79)** (SirMarkPrescott) **3-9-8** SSanders(1) (a.p: led over 1f out tl wl ins fnl f: r.o)	nk	**2**	7/1[2]	90	70
4183[5]	**Levelled (72)** (MRChannon) **3-9-1** TQuinn(2) (lw: hld up: rdn over 1f out: eased whn btn ins fnl f)	2	**3**	6/1[1]	78	58
4071[7]	**Kentucky Fall (FR) (71)** (LadyHerries) **4-9-2** AClark(6) (a.p: led 2f out tl over 1f out: wknd fnl f)	1½	**4**	9/1	73	55
3984[5]	**Silent Miracle (IRE) (68)** (MBell) **3-8-6**(5) GFaulkner(7) (lw: a.p: rdn over 2f out: one pce)	hd	**5**	16/1	70	50
4248[6]	**Bayin (USA) (61)** (MDIUsher) **8-8-6** RStreet(4) (b: dwlt & bmpd s: hdwy over 1f out: nvr nrr)	¾	**6**	15/2[3]	61	43
3984[14]	**Bramble Bear (69)** (MBlanshard) **3-8-12** JQuinn(5) (s.s & hmpd s: nvr nr to chal)	1½	**7**	20/1	65	45
4048*	**Montendre (80)** (MJHeaton-Ellis) **10-9-11** JReid(15) (lw: hdwy over 2f out: wknd over 1f out)	2½	**8**	15/2[3]	69	51
3417*	**Walk the Beat (64)** (MartynMeade) **7-8-9** FNorton(8) (hld up: rdn over 2f out: wknd over 1f out)	1	**9**	16/1	50	32
2747*	**Senorita Matilda (USA) (74)** (RHannon) **3-9-3** DaneO'Neill(12) (a bhd)	1	**10**	12/1	58	38
3984[10]	**Eastern Prophets (76)** (GLewis) **4-9-7** PaulEddery(10) (prom 4f)	1½	**11**	20/1	56	38
4137[20]	**White Emir (75)** (BJMeehan) **4-9-6b** MTebbutt(13) (led 4f)	½	**12**	20/1	53	35
4155[12]	**La Petite Fusee (77)** (RJO'Sullivan) **6-9-5**(3) RHavlin(3) (bhd fnl 2f)	6	**13**	8/1	39	21
4048[15]	**Tinker Osmaston (65)** (RJHodges) **6-8-10** KFallon(11) (bhd fnl 2f)	d.h	**13**	12/1	27	9
3984[8]	**Loving And Giving (76)** (HCandy) **3-9-5** CRutter(14) (a bhd)	8	**15**	12/1	17	—
				(SP 128.9%)		**15 Rn**

1m 10.91 (-0.29) CSF £80.88 CT £477.16 TOTE £16.50: £4.20 £3.90 £1.90 (£83.90) Trio £102.10 OWNER Mr K. T. Ivory (RADLETT) BRED Peter Kehoe
WEIGHT FOR AGE 3yo-2lb
3709 Distinctive Dream (IRE) may be 10lb higher than when last successful, but that was not going to stop him and he came through to snatch the spoils in the closing stages. The Handicapper will not look kindly on this. (11/1)
4175 Dominant Air seemed better suited by the return to six furlongs, and moved to the front below the distance only to be worried out of it in the closing stages. (7/1)
4183 Levelled inched closer to the front two below the distance but, when it was apparent he was going to be no better than third, his jockey eased him down in the closing stages. (6/1)
3930 Kentucky Fall (FR), reverting to six furlongs, showed in front a quarter of a mile from home but, headed below the distance, she had little more to offer. (9/1: op 6/1)
3984 Silent Miracle (IRE) has been dropped a few pounds by the Handicapper recently, but failed to find the necessary turn of foot in the last two furlongs. (16/1)
4248 Bayin (USA), making a quick reappearance, stayed on from below the distance but found it all over bar the shouting. (15/2)

4322 SEASON'S END MAIDEN STKS (3-Y.O) (Class D)

4-30 (4-31) **1m 4f** £3,485.00 (£1,055.00: £515.00: £245.00) Stalls: High GOING minus 0.46 sec per fur (F)

				SP	RR	SF
3809[2]	**Carisbrooke** (HRACecil) **3-9-0** KFallon(3) (a.p: hrd rdn over 2f out: led over 1f out: r.o wl)	—	**1**	11/10[1]	86	41
3977[5]	**Sabadilla (USA)** (JHMGosden) **3-9-0** GHind(10) (lw: a.p: led over 2f out tl over 1f out: unable qckn)	5	**2**	5/1[3]	79	34
4072[2]	**Teme Valley** (RCharlton) **3-9-0** TSprake(2) (chsd ldr 11f out: led over 3f out tl over 2f out: wknd over 1f out)	2½	**3**	7/4[2]	76	31
1168[11]	**Eternity** (JRFanshawe) **3-8-9** NDay(5) (lost pl 4f out: no hdwy fnl 3f)	9	**4**	20/1	59	14
2783[6]	**Lark's Rise** (HCandy) **3-8-9** CRutter(8) (hld up: rdn over 3f out: sn wknd)	3½	**5**	16/1	54	9
4158[8]	**Catchment** (MrsAJPerrett) **3-9-0** GayeHarwood(7) (lw: nvr nrr)	2	**6**	33/1	57	12
	Joli Flyers (MJHaynes) **3-9-0** DaneO'Neill(9) (unf: scope: bit bkwd: a bhd)	3	**7**	33/1	53	8
3991[8]	**I See You Sydney (AUS)** (MJPolglase) **3-9-0** TGMcLaughlin(4) (bhd fnl 3f)	hd	**8**	66/1	53	8
1239[15]	**Pleasure Boat** (NAGraham) **3-9-0** DHolland(1) (a bhd)	nk	**9**	33/1	52	7
2731[10]	**My Roland (IRE)** (JFfitch-Heyes) **3-9-0** SSanders(6) (led over 8f)	8	**10**	66/1	42	—
				(SP 123.1%)		**10 Rn**

2m 33.06 (3.06) CSF £6.75 TOTE £2.00: £1.10 £1.60 £1.10 (£4.40) Trio £1.20 OWNER Mr Michael Poland (NEWMARKET) BRED Newgate Stud Co
3809 Carisbrooke, the type of horse who always looks to be carrying condition, was off the bridle early in the straight with Fallon scrubbing the ears off him. However, he came through to lead approaching the final furlong, and the further he went, the further he pulled away. This is certainly his minimum trip. (11/10: evens-4/5)
3977 Sabadilla (USA) inched into a narrow lead over a quarter of a mile from home but, headed below the distance, was well and truly put in his place by the winner. A small maiden should be found for this moderate Gosden inmate. (5/1)
4072 Teme Valley showed in front turning for home, but he was collared early in the straight and had nothing more to offer below the distance. (7/4)
Eternity, without a run since May, looks very slow. (20/1)

4323 LEVY BOARD H'CAP (0-70) (3-Y.O+ F & M) (Class E)

5-00 (5-03) **1m 3f 30y** £2,986.25 (£905.00: £442.50: £211.25) Stalls: High GOING minus 0.46 sec per fur (F)

Form	Horse	Dist	Pos	SP	RR	SF
4108^{3}	**Tallulah Belle (56)** (NPLittmoden) **4-9-0** JWeaver(8) (hdwy to ld over 2f out: clr over 1f out: r.o wl)	—	**1**	8/1^{2}	71	49
3906^{11}	**Arletty (57)** (HRACecil) **3-8-8** KFallon(17) (hdwy over 2f out: chsd wnr over 1f out: no imp)	6	**2**	10/1	63	34
4109^{8}	**Missfortuna (66)** (SirMarkPrescott) **3-9-3** SSanders(11) (rdn 4f out: hdwy over 1f out: r.o)	½	**3**	12/1	72	43
3931^{8}	**Hidden Agenda (FR) (55)** (RCharlton) **3-8-6** TSprake(12) (hdwy on ins over 2f out: one pce)	3	**4**	14/1	56	27
4180^{2}	**Laguna Bay (IRE) (56)** (APJarvis) **3-8-7** DaneO'Neill(13) (lw: rdn over 2f out: hdwy over 1f out: nvr nrr)	2	**5**	8/1^{2}	55	26
3080^{3}	**Cheek To Cheek (59)** (CACyzer) **3-8-10** MFenton(18) (a.p: chsd ldr 4f out tl over 1f out: sn wknd)	5	**6**	16/1	50	21
1301^{6}	**Fantasy Girl (IRE) (62)** (JLDunlop) **3-8-13** TQuinn(10) (lw: hdwy over 3f out: wknd over 1f out)	1¾	**7**	9/1^{3}	51	22
3915^{6}	**Glow Forum (56)** (LMontagueHall) **6-8-9**(5) APolli(6) (s.s: hdwy & swtchd rt 2f out: mid div whn stumbled bdly on ins over 1f out: nvr nr to chal)	2½	**8**	8/1^{2}	41	19
3915^{12}	**Capsoff (IRE) (68)** (GAHubbard) **4-9-9**(3) DO'Donohoe(9) (a mid div)	1	**9**	33/1	52	30
3977^{7}	**Lighten Up (58)** (CEBrittain) **3-8-9** MRimmer(4) (hdwy 9f out: wknd 2f out)	7	**10**	16/1	32	3
4242^{15}	**Sun Alert (USA) (60)** (MJPolglase) **3-8-11v** TGMcLaughlin(1) (b.off hind: a mid div)	1¼	**11**	25/1	32	3
4222^{4}	**Keepsake (IRE) (52)** (MDIUsher) **3-8-3** RStreet(19) (prom over 8f)	½	**12**	13/2^{1}	23	—
2704^{9}	**Made Bold (70)** (HCandy) **3-9-7** CRutter(7) (nvr nrr)	3½	**13**	12/1	36	7
4063^{14}	**Celebrant (61)** (AHide) **3-8-12** RCochrane(15) (b: prom 8f)	4	**14**	20/1	21	—
4108^{13}	**Dramatic Moment (62)** (JRArnold) **4-9-6** RPerham(3) (s.s: hdwy 9f out: wknd 6f out)	hd	**15**	14/1	22	—
4060^{13}	**Beguine (USA) (64)** (WJarvis) **3-9-1** JReid(16) (mid div & wkng whn hmpd 4f out)	7	**16**	14/1	14	—
4046^{11}	**Dancing Feather (62)** (BWHills) **3-8-13** GHind(2) (a.p: led 5f out: clr over 3f out: wandered & hdd over 2f out: eased whn btn wl over 1f out)	1¼	**17**	16/1	10	—
4179^{14}	**Absolutelystunning (53)** (MrsBarbaraWaring) **4-8-11v^{1}** EByrne(14) (b: b.hind: bhd fnl 3f)	½	**18**	33/1	1	—
3893^{4}	**Spirit Lady (51)** (JSKing) **3-8-2**ow1 SDrowne(5) (a bhd)	17	**19**	33/1	—	—
4053^{3}	**Kristal Bridge (60)** (PWHarris) **3-8-11b^{1}** DHolland(20) (lw: led 6f)	7	**20**	20/1	—	—

(SP 141.0%) **20 Rn**

2m 20.42 (1.62) CSF £81.31 CT £909.23 TOTE £8.60: £1.90 £3.30 £3.30 £4.40 (£87.80) Trio £287.70 OWNER Trojan Racing (WOLVERHAMPTON) BRED Bowler (Presswork) Services Ltd

WEIGHT FOR AGE 3yo-7lb

IN-FOCUS: **This belated first victory at Kempton means that Jason Weaver has now ridden a winner at every Flat track in Britain.**

4108 Tallulah Belle confirmed the promise shown at the last meeting and, sweeping through to lead early in the straight, forged clear below the distance to win in decisive style. (8/1)

2532 Arletty, who has been dropped in the handicap after two poor runs, came through to take second place approaching the final furlong, but found the winner already home and dry. (10/1: 8/1-12/1)

3311 Missfortuna, off the bridle turning for home, ran on in the last furlong and a half to snatch third prize. (12/1: op 8/1)

3463 Hidden Agenda (FR) ran her best race to date, moving up along the inside rail early in the straight, before tapped for toe. (14/1)

4180 Laguna Bay (IRE) stayed on in the last furlong and a half to be nearest at the line. (8/1)

3080 Cheek To Cheek, in second place half a mile from home, was collared for that position approaching the final furlong and had nothing more to offer. (16/1)

1301 Fantasy Girl (IRE) (9/1: 6/1-10/1)

3915 Glow Forum was picking up ground in mid-field when almost falling along the inside rail below the distance. This run is best forgotten and a return to a mile and a half would help. (8/1)

T/Jkpt: Not won; £6,529.91 to Nottingham 23/9/97. T/Plpt: £84.60 (277.43 Tckts). T/Qdpt: £24.80 (61.99 Tckts) AK

4057-LEICESTER (R-H) (Good to firm, Good patches)

Monday September 22nd

Visibility: hazy

WEATHER: fine & sunny WIND: almost nil

4324 HIGHFIELDS LIMITED STKS (0-60) (3-Y.O+) (Class F)

2-20 (2-21) **1m 8y** £3,225.00 (£900.00: £435.00) Stalls: Centre GOING minus 0.36 sec per fur (F)

Form	Horse	Dist	Pos	SP	RR	SF
4139^{6}	**Zurs (IRE) (52)** (JRPoulton) **4-8-9**(5) RMullen(12) (lw: hdwy 5f out: led over 2f out: rdn out)	—	**1**	7/1^{3}	64	46
3966^{4}	**Smarter Charter (60)** (MrsLStubbs) **4-9-0** SWhitworth(8) (hld up: hdwy wl over 1f out: r.o wl ins fnl f)	1½	**2**	10/1	61	43
4112^{2}	**Samara Song (59)** (IPWilliams) **4-8-12**(5) PRoberts(14) (lw: hld up: hdwy over 2f out: rdn & one pce fnl f)	nk	**3**	4/1^{1}	63	45
3573^{12}	**Forest Fantasy (58)** (JWharton) **4-9-0** KDarley(11) (hld up: hdwy 2f out: rdn over 1f out: r.o one pce)	1½	**4**	6/1^{2}	57	39
4224^{9}	**Saltando (IRE) (36)** (PatMitchell) **6-9-0** PBloomfield(13) (lw: hld up: hdwy over 2f out: no ex wl ins fnl f)	s.h	**5**	33/1	57	39
3632^{8}	**Rosa Royale (56)** (MrsJCecil) **3-8-7** MartinDwyer(17) (chsd ldrs: rdn & one pce fnl 2f)	1	**6**	8/1	52	30
3269^{5}	**Chinour (IRE) (45)** (EJAlston) **9-9-0** JFEgan(19) (nvr nr to chal)	2	**7**	14/1	51	33
4164*	**French Ginger (45)** (LRLloyd-James) **6-9-0** TWilliams(18) (chsd ldrs: rdn over 2f out: sn btn)	2½	**8**	12/1	46	28
4069^{2}	**Magazine Gap (32)** (PatMitchell) **4-9-0** AmandaSanders(7) (swtg: lw: dwlt: hdwy 2f out: nvr nr ldrs)	s.h	**9**	25/1	46	28
3849^{13}	**Calamander (IRE) (60)** (WRMuir) **3-8-2**(5) CLowther(16) (prom: reminders ½-wy: outpcd fnl 2f)	s.h	**10**	10/1	43	21
3931^{9}	**Mayflower (55)** (MHTompkins) **3-8-7v^{1}** DBiggs(2) (in tch: rdn 2f out: sn btn)	1¼	**11**	20/1	41	19
4059^{16}	**Fearless Cavalier (53)** (RHollinshead) **3-8-10** FLynch(5) (effrt 3f out: sn rdn: no imp)	1	**12**	16/1	42	20
4109^{5}	**Sea Danzig (51)** (JJBridger) **4-9-0** NAdams(4) (led over 5f: sn wknd)	1½	**13**	16/1	39	21
2750^{6}	**Sound Appeal (60)** (AGFoster) **3-8-7v^{1}** DaleGibson(6) (a in rr)	hd	**14**	10/1	36	14
3320^{7}	**Court House (57)** (MCChapman) **3-8-6**(7) SCarson(10) (w ldr 5f: sn lost tch)	6	**15**	20/1	30	8
2733^{10}	**Rambo Tango (46)** (BRCambidge) **3-8-10** JLowe(20) (bit bkwd: a bhd)	2	**16**	50/1	23	1
	Young Benson (60) (TWall) **5-9-0** LNewton(15) (bkwd: a bhd)	hd	**17**	25/1	22	4
3850^{4}	**Las Vistas (53)** (HJCollingridge) **3-8-7** NCarlisle(3) (unruly: chsd ldrs to ½-wy: sn lost tch)	1	**18**	20/1	17	—
3758^{15}	**Banneret (USA) (45)** (JO'Reilly) **4-9-0b^{1}** JO'Reilly(9) (prom over 3f: sn rdn & lost tch)	3	**19**	50/1	14	—
3611^{5}	**Zahaalie (USA) (38)** (JAPickering) **5-8-7**(7) JFowle(1) (lw: a in rr)	1½	**20**	25/1	11	—

(SP 144.0%) **20 Rn**

1m 37.0 (2.00) CSF £70.45 TOTE £11.50: £3.60 £2.90 £1.50 (£36.30) Trio £59.30 OWNER Glendale Partnership Ltd (LEWES) BRED Mrs A. Whitehead

WEIGHT FOR AGE 3yo-4lb

4139 Zurs (IRE) moved into a prominent position before halfway and, nosing ahead entering the final quarter-mile, was driven out firmly to the line. (7/1)
3966 Smarter Charter did not impress with his action to post, but he ran on strongly inside the distance, and it is easy to understand why he has been tried at ten furlongs. (10/1)
4112 Samara Song, given another try at a mile, stuck on willingly under pressure but never promised to find the speed to trouble the winner. (4/1)
3316* Forest Fantasy made significant progress from off the pace in the latter stages but failed to quicken sufficiently to pose a serious threat. She has been lightly-raced and there could be another race to be won. (6/1)
1219 Saltando (IRE) has run without the visor in his most recent races and, though he delivered his challenge up the centre of the track inside the last quarter-mile, he was never quite doing enough to give his supporters much hope. (33/1)
Rosa Royale, short on experience and still searching for her correct trip, was being made to struggle inside the distance and she may well need a slightly longer trip. (8/1: 6/1-9/1)

4325 KEGWORTH CONDITIONS STKS (2-Y.O) (Class C)
2-50 (2-50) **7f 9y** £5,511.10 (£1,762.60: £846.30) Stalls: High GOING minus 0.36 sec per fur (F)

				SP	RR	SF
3386*	**Rabi (IRE)** (EALDunlop) **2-9-2** RHills(2) (bit bkwd: chsd ldr: shkn up to ld over 1f out: sn clr)	—	**1**	1/6[1]	96+	66
3889[4]	**Demolition Jo (76)** (PDEvans) **2-8-6v** JFEgan(1) (led tl rdn & hdd over 1f out)	5	**2**	10/1[3]	75	45
4067*	**Vocation (IRE)** (PRWebber) **2-8-11** WRyan(3) (lw: s.i.s: a bhd & outpcd)	21	**3**	13/2[2]	32	2
				(SP 108.1%)	**3 Rn**	

1m 22.9 (0.30 under 2y best) (0.30) CSF £2.34 TOTE £1.10 (£2.20) OWNER Mr Hamdan Al Maktoum (NEWMARKET) BRED Neville O'Byrne
3386* Rabi (IRE), still looking burly, did not have much to beat, but he was always running away on the heels of the leader. Needing to be sent about his work to strike the front, he sauntered clear at will and the only surprising factor was that he actually broke the two-year-old track record at this trip. (1/6)
3889 Demolition Jo was well rewarded for making this a fair test, but she was out of her depth against the well-regarded winner. (10/1)
4067* Vocation (IRE) made a winning debut earlier in the month but, the way she performed here, one would be right to ask if it is the same filly. (13/2)

4326 GOLDEN HAND (S) STKS (3-Y.O) (Class G)
3-20 (3-22) **1m 1f 218y** £2,490.00 (£690.00: £330.00) Stalls: Centre GOING minus 0.36 sec per fur (F)

				SP	RR	SF
4015[17]	**Rare Talent (63)** (MRChannon) **3-8-11** AMackay(16) (a chsng ldrs: led appr fnl f: all out)	—	**1**	3/1[2]	66	39
4043[5]	**Ron's Round (38)** (CADwyer) **3-8-11** JFEgan(15) (a.p: str chal fnl f: hrd rdn: unable qckn)	hd	**2**	8/1	66	39
4114[4]	**Bright Fountain (IRE) (52)** (HCandy) **3-8-6** AMcGlone(14) (chsd ldrs: outpcd 3f out: sn rdn: styd on appr fnl f)	3	**3**	11/4[1]	56	29
4180[6]	**Heart Full of Soul (60)** (PFICole) **3-9-4b** KDarley(1) (led: qcknd over 3f out: hdd appr fnl f: sn btn)	1¼	**4**	7/1[3]	66	39
	Chilli Boom (40) (RSimpson) **3-8-6b[1]** MGallagher(8) (chsd ldrs: rdn over 3f out: no imp)	8	**5**	40/1	41	14
3396[7]	**Weet A Bit (IRE) (54)** (RHollinshead) **3-8-8**(3) DGriffiths(7) (lw: hld up: hdwy 3f out: no imp appr fnl f)	1½	**6**	10/1	44	17
3897[9]	**Inkwell (34)** (AHide) **3-8-11v[1]** DaleGibson(11) (trckd ldrs: effrt 4f out: rdn & wknd over 2f out)	1½	**7**	33/1	41	14
3909[7]	**Notation (IRE)** (DWChapman) **3-8-11** ACulhane(9) (wl bhd tl sme late hdwy)	1¼	**8**	10/1	39	12
4184[5]	**Gunners Glory (51)** (MrsLStubbs) **3-9-2v** SWhitworth(3) (lw: hld up: effrt ½-wy: wknd 2f out)	nk	**9**	10/1	44	17
3601[10]	**Risky Flight (28)** (ASmith) **3-8-11b** JLowe(5) (lw: plld hrd: in tch over 6f)	1¼	**10**	50/1	37	10
1620[8]	**Swiss Coast (IRE) (47)** (RTJuckes) **3-8-6**(5) CLowther(12) (lw: a bhd)	3	**11**	20/1	32	5
4008[12]	**Cold Lazarus (50)** (RTPhillips) **3-8-11** WRyan(10) (a in rr: t.o)	9	**12**	16/1	18	—
4114[15]	**Forward Miss (20)** (CJBenstead) **3-8-6** TWilliams(13) (swtg: plld hrd: prom: wkng whn stumbled wl over 1f out: t.o)	½	**13**	50/1	12	—
3271[14]	**Love Over Gold (25)** (MCChapman) **3-7-13**(7) SCarson(2) (a bhd: t.o: p.u over 2f out)		**P**	50/1	—	—
3230[8]	***Kalmoojid (32)*** (CJHill) **3-8-11** FLynch(4) (Withdrawn not under Starter's orders: ref to ent stalls)		**W**	33/1	—	—
				(SP 127.4%)	**14 Rn**	

2m 7.1 (3.40) CSF £24.44 TOTE £3.00: £1.40 £3.00 £1.60 (£18.10) Trio £20.50 OWNER Mr A. Merza (UPPER LAMBOURN) BRED Mrs Carol Merza
Sold S Gollings 9,500gns
OFFICIAL EXPLANATION **Love Over Gold: returned lame.**
3601* Rare Talent, from in an in-form yard and back in his own class, needed to put his best foot forward in the closing stages to hold off a very willing rival. He proved costly to retain when winning at Ripon, and connections were forced to let him go this time. (3/1: 2/1-100/30)
4043 Ron's Round looked sure to win when ranging upsides inside the last furlong, but the winner had kept a bit up his sleeve and just held him at bay. He should be able to pick up a race of this description. (8/1: op 12/1)
4114 Bright Fountain (IRE), tapped for toe early in the straight, renewed her effort but she hung off a true line and lacked the pace to mount a challenge. It is possible she needs more cut than she had here. (11/4)
4180 Heart Full of Soul, lowered in class, did his best to run his rivals off their feet, but his stride shortened below the distance and he was very leg-weary in the last two hundred yards. (7/1)
Notation (IRE) (10/1: op 20/1)

4327 LEICESTER SOUND NURSERY H'CAP (0-75) (2-Y.O F) (Class E)
3-50 (3-50) **5f 218y** £3,561.00 (£1,068.00: £514.00: £237.00) Stalls: Centre GOING minus 0.36 sec per fur (F)

				SP	RR	SF
4054[10]	**Swanmore Lady (IRE) (53)** (SCWilliams) **2-7-11**(3) RFfrench(8) (a.p: led over 2f out: jst hld on)	—	**1**	12/1	58	22
4166[3]	**Dekelsmary (63)** (JBalding) **2-8-10** JEdmunds(9) (lw: dwlt: hdwy & wnt lft 2f out: r.o wl towards fin)	hd	**2**	6/1[2]	68	32
3924[12]	**Delciana (IRE) (65)** (PWHarris) **2-8-12** ACulhane(7) (a.p: ev ch fnl 2f: unable qckn fnl f)	1¼	**3**	10/1	66	30
4058[6]	**Kite (51)** (MBell) **2-7-7**(5) RMullen(1) (a chsng ldrs stands' side: kpt on u.p fnl f)	¾	**4**	9/1	50	14
4152[6]	**Italian Rose (63)** (WJMusson) **2-8-10** JFEgan(12) (in tch: rdn over 2f out: kpt on ins fnl f)	¾	**5**	13/2[3]	60	24
4097[11]	**Lady From Limerick (IRE) (68)** (JBerry) **2-9-1** KDarley(10) (chsd ldrs: rdn over 2f out: wknd over 1f out)	2½	**6**	8/1	59	23
3564[5]	**Tremonnow (52)** (JMBradley) **2-7-13** LCharnock(15) (prom: rdn 2f out: wknd appr fnl f)	s.h	**7**	14/1	43	7
3892[6]	**Silent Pride (IRE) (51)** (MDIUsher) **2-7-5**(7) JFowle(2) (swtg: hmpd after 1f: n.d)	nk	**8**	20/1	41	5
3782[10]	**Jaybee Silver (50)** (MHTompkins) **2-7-11**ow1 DaleGibson(11) (trckd ldrs 4f)	3	**9**	20/1	32	—
4162[7]	**Daynabee (67)** (NTinkler) **2-9-0** KimTinkler(13) (lw: led over 3f)	¾	**10**	9/1	47	11
4166[4]	**Quiz Show (74)** (RHannon) **2-9-2**(5) CLowther(4) (lw: sn drvn along: a bhd)	s.h	**11**	9/2[1]	54	18
4054[7]	**Russian About (IRE) (55)** (MRChannon) **2-8-2** AMackay(6) (mid div tl wknd 2f out)	1¼	**12**	12/1	31	—
4042[9]	**Mariana (62)** (RMWhitaker) **2-8-9** NCarlisle(3) (chsd ldrs over 3f)	4	**13**	14/1	28	—

				SP	RR	SF
4162^{11}	**Blarney Park (55)** (CADwyer) **2-8-2** TWilliams(5) (chsd ldrs: rdn whn bdly hmpd 2f out: virtually p.u: t.o)	dist	**14**	12/1	—	—

(SP 131.9%) **14 Rn**

1m 12.3 (2.30) CSF £82.18 CT £705.28 TOTE £21.60: £5.00 £2.90 £3.20 (£58.60) Trio £178.70; £88.13 to Nottingham 23/9/97 OWNER Mr A. G. Axton (NEWMARKET) BRED A. O'Brien

STEWARDS' ENQUIRY Edmunds susp. 1-2/10/97 (careless riding).

OFFICIAL EXPLANATION Quiz Show: was unbalanced coming down the hill and appeared to be in season after the race.

3226 Swanmore Lady (IRE) threw down the gauntlet over two furlongs out, but had to find more when strongly pressed throughout the final furlong. She was very well handled. (12/1)

4166 Dekelsmary once again showed that she is crying out for a seventh furlong and, the sooner she does step-up in trip, the sooner she will break her duck. (6/1: 4/1-13/2)

3597 Delciana (IRE), with a chance as good as any throughout the last quarter-mile, had to admit that extra surge of pace was beyond her in the last hundred yards. She is performing with credit and deserves to win a race. (10/1)

3307 Kite, brought back to sprinting, was never far away under the stands' rail, and she battled on well in the closing stages without ever looking likely to find the necessary turn of foot. (9/1)

4152 Italian Rose, tracking the leaders, came off the bridle two furlongs out and looked set to drop away, but she began to stay on under pressure and, this half-sister to a couple of winners, should not let the family name down. (13/2)

3541 Lady From Limerick (IRE) comes from a winning family, but she is having trouble getting her act together, and was finding demands too great for her on the run to the final furlong. (8/1)

4166 Quiz Show may have found this race coming far too soon, for she ran her worst race yet and was always off the bridle and struggling in the rear. (9/2)

4328 CHARNWOOD CLAIMING STKS (3 & 4-Y.O) (Class F)

4-20 (4-23) **5f 218y** £3,015.00 (£840.00: £405.00) Stalls: Centre GOING minus 0.36 sec per fur (F)

				SP	RR	SF
4184^{4}	**Petite Danseuse (60)** (CADwyer) **3-8-4** FLynch(17) (hld up: hdwy 2f out: led ins fnl f: r.o wl)	—	**1**	4/1 1	67	45
4115^{9}	**Mystical (65)** (MrsLStubbs) **3-8-12v** JFEgan(15) (a.p: led over 1f out tl ins fnl f)	2	**2**	7/1	70	48
4016^{7}	**Nervous Rex (50)** (WRMuir) **3-8-9** SophieMitchell(16) (mid div: hdwy 2f out: r.o wl fnl f)	2	**3**	20/1	61	39
4221^{9}	**Never Think Twice (55)** (KTIvory) **4-8-3v** NAdams(22) (b: bhd: rdn & hdwy 2f out: one pce ins fnl f)	1	**4**	10/1	51	31
4168^{8}	**Polgwynne (45)** (BSmart) **3-7-12**(5)ow3 ADaly(21) (lw: mid div: effrt & rdn 2f out: r.o)	3	**5**	25/1	45	20
3590*	**The Frisky Farmer (54)** (WGMTurner) **4-8-10**(5) CLowther(13) (lw: led 4f: rdn & one pce appr fnl f)	nk	**6**	16/1	54	34
3431^{19}	**River Ensign (41)** (WMBrisbourne) **4-7-5**(7) AMcCarthy(6) (prom: rdn 2f out: grad wknd)	1½	**7**	33/1	33	13
3691^{4}	**Davis Rock (65)** (WRMuir) **3-9-1**(5) PRoberts(9) (chsd ldrs: no hdwy fnl 2f)	½	**8**	12/1	56	34
3851^{6}	**Municipal Girl (IRE) (42)** (BPalling) **3-8-1**(3) DSweeney(10) (trckd ldrs: rdn 2f out: sn btn)	¾	**9**	33/1	38	16
4016^{21}	**Toronto (44)** (JBerry) **3-7-8b**(7) PBradley(19) (prom: led 2f out: sn hdd & wknd)	hd	**10**	33/1	34	12
3930^{5}	**Kings Harmony (IRE) (72)** (PJMakin) **4-9-5** WRyan(7) (chsd ldrs: hrd rdn 2f out: sn btn)	¾	**11**	5/1 2	48	28
3590^{11}	**Into Debt (30)** (JRPoulton) **4-7-7b**(5) RMullen(11) (swtg: outpcd)	½	**12**	33/1	26	6
2835^{19}	**Xenophon of Cunaxa (IRE) (58)** (MJFetherston-Godley) **4-8-7** ACulhane(18) (s.s: a bhd)	¾	**13**	25/1	33	13
3637^{3}	**Whizz Kid (40)** (JJBridger) **3-8-0** GBardwell(5) (dwlt: a in rr)	nk	**14**	20/1	27	5
4155^{24}	**Ivory Dawn (70)** (KTIvory) **3-8-12** MartinDwyer(1) (lw: trckd ldrs stands' side over 3f)	1½	**15**	6/1 3	35	13
3816^{8}	**Divide And Rule (62)** (RHollinshead) **3-8-6**(3) DGriffiths(14) (nvr nr to chal)	½	**16**	20/1	31	9
3710^{12}	**Class Distinction (IRE) (55)** (RHannon) **3-8-13** DBiggs(12) (lw: chsd ldrs over 3f: sn wknd: t.o)	6	**17**	16/1	19	—
4016^{22}	**Make Ready (50)** (JNeville) **3-8-0** JLowe(4) (spd over 3f: t.o)	3½	**18**	16/1	—	—
3923^{7}	**Bayford Thrust (73)** (JBerry) **3-8-13** KDarley(8) (b: b.hind: s.v.s: nt rcvr: t.o)	3	**19**	9/1	1	—
4049^{15}	**Fit For The Job (IRE) (32)** (TWall) **3-8-1b** LNewton(3) (prom 3f: sn lost tch: t.o)	3½	**20**	33/1	—	—
421^{13}	**Niteowl Raider (IRE) (38)** (JO'Reilly) **4-8-7** JO'Reilly(20) (spd 3f: eased whn btn: t.o)	s.h	**21**	50/1	—	—

(SP 146.5%) **21 Rn**

1m 10.9 (0.90) CSF £29.17 TOTE £4.00: £2.40 £2.80 £9.10 (£17.20) Trio £309.60; £218.06 to Nottingham 23/9/97 OWNER Binding Matters Ltd (NEWMARKET) BRED I. D. Livingstone

WEIGHT FOR AGE 3yo-2lb

4184 Petite Danseuse, successful over an extra furlong here in August, produced a telling burst of speed to lead halfway through the final furlong and win going away. She is certainly paying her way. (4/1)

3851* Mystical rarely races on ground as lively as this, but she kicked for home below the distance only to be swamped for speed when the winner appeared on the scene. (7/1)

3251 Nervous Rex looks to need a slightly stiffer test of stamina when the ground rides so fast, and this spirited late effort was never going to get him there. (20/1)

4016 Never Think Twice, driven along to improve two furlongs out, failed to sustain his run once inside the final furlong. He looked ill at ease on the ground. (10/1)

361* Polgwynne won her only race on the All-Weather and, though she tried hard, she just could not muster the pace to reach the leaders. (25/1)

3590* The Frisky Farmer is not the easiest of individuals to catch but, once he loses the lead, his hopes then fade rather quickly. (16/1)

4329 LIGHTNING H'CAP (0-80) (3-Y.O+) (Class D)

4-50 (4-51) **5f 2y** £3,691.00 (£1,108.00: £534.00: £247.00) Stalls: Centre GOING minus 0.36 sec per fur (F)

				SP	RR	SF
3481^{9}	**Ansellman (78)** (JBerry) **7-9-9b**(5) CLowther(13) (a chsng ldr: hrd drvn over 1f out: r.o to ld post)	—	**1**	13/2 2	86	63
3032^{5}	**Another Batchworth (58)** (EAWheeler) **5-8-3b**(5) ADaly(12) (lw: led: sn clr: wknd & ct fnl strides)	hd	**2**	14/1	66	43
4051^{12}	**Young Ben (IRE) (46)** (JSWainwright) **5-7-7b**(3) RFfrench(11) (a chsng ldrs: effrt & rdn over 1f out: r.o)	½	**3**	25/1	52	29
2738^{9}	**Here Comes a Star (46)** (JMCarr) **9-7-10** DWright(9) (hdwy over 2f out: r.o wl ins fnl f)	1	**4**	20/1	49	26
4137^{22}	**Pleasure Time (63)** (CSmith) **4-8-13** JTate(8) (chsd ldrs: rdn & r.o ins fnl f)	nk	**5**	7/1 3	65	42
3693^{4}	**Beau Venture (USA) (65)** (BPalling) **9-8-12**(3) DSweeney(5) (in tch: kpt on fnl 2f: nvr nrr)	¾	**6**	8/1	65	42
3922^{9}	**River Tern (68)** (JMBradley) **4-9-4** ACulhane(6) (lw: dwlt: effrt wl over 1f out: nvr nrr)	1¼	**7**	8/1	64	41
4137^{15}	**Barranak (IRE) (60)** (GMMcCourt) **5-8-10** JFEgan(10) (chsd ldrs tl wknd over 1f out)	nk	**8**	8/1	55	32
4249^{11}	**Mindrace (60)** (KTIvory) **4-8-10v** MartinDwyer(2) (trckd ldrs stands' side 3f)	¾	**9**	14/1	52	29
4221^{12}	**Ice Age (57)** (RJRWilliams) **3-8-6b** WRyan(7) (dwlt: swtchd lft over 2f out: sn rdn: no imp)	nk	**10**	7/1 3	48	24
3910^{11}	**Sotonian (HOL) (46)** (PSFelgate) **4-7-3**(7) JFowle(14) (outpcd)	½	**11**	20/1	36	13
4233^{10}	**Rich Glow (49)** (NBycroft) **6-7-13b** LCharnock(1) (lw: a bhd: rdn 2f out: no rspnse)	¾	**12**	5/1 1	36	13
3856^{11}	**Gwespyr (47)** (DonEnricoIncisa) **4-7-11** KimTinkler(4) (outpcd)	nk	**13**	20/1	33	10
3871^{16}	**Bowcliffe Grange (IRE) (47)** (DWChapman) **5-7-11** TWilliams(15) (s.s: effrt wl over 1f out: nt rch ldrs)	1¾	**14**	7/1 3	28	5

2001^{6}	**Alamode (63)** (JGSmyth-Osborne) **3-8-12** KDarley(3) (in tch: hrd rdn wl over 2f out: sn wknd)	12	**15**	14/1	5	—
				(SP 139.0%)		**15 Rn**

59.5 secs (1.00) CSF £94.00 CT £1,298.34 TOTE £9.00: £2.60 £6.50 £3.90 (£101.20) Trio £375.40 OWNER Ansells of Watford (COCKERHAM) BRED W. L. Caley
LONG HANDICAP Here Comes a Star 7-6 Young Ben (IRE) 7-8 Sotonian (HOL) 7-2
WEIGHT FOR AGE 3yo-1lb
3326 Ansellman always appeared to be fighting a lost cause in pursuit of the clear leader, but he kept persevering and eventually got up right on the line. (13/2)
3032 Another Batchworth has only ever won in October, but she set such a scorching pace she looked home and dry inside the final furlong. However, she was at the end of her tether close home and was just touched off. If there were races over four furlongs, she would no doubt be a star. (14/1)
2934 Young Ben (IRE) only has a single win to his name but he ran up to his best and, if he remains in his own class, it will be surprising if he cannot add to his score in the near future. (25/1)
2203 Here Comes a Star is falling out of the bottom of the handicap and he has not won a race for over two years, but he still retains his ability, though he does seem to need a sixth furlong nowadays. (20/1)
3693 Pleasure Time, narrowly beaten over course and distance in August, was coming back for more nearing the finish but the line was always going to arrive too soon. (7/1)
3693 Beau Venture (USA) usually helps force the pace, but he was unable to do so on this occasion and was never a threat. (8/1)
3922 River Tern forfeited his chance with a sluggish start, but he was running on really well in the latter stages and another success is within his reach. (8/1)
4233 Rich Glow showed what he thinks of having to race twice in five days, and he sauntered home in his own time. (5/1)

T/Plpt: £152.20 (100.22 Tckts). T/Qdpt: £101.50 (9.7 Tckts) IM

4165-**NOTTINGHAM (L-H) (Good to firm, Good patches)**
Tuesday September 23rd
WEATHER: sunny periods WIND: moderate behind

4330 E.B.F. RNIB MAIDEN STKS (2-Y.O F) (Class D)
2-15 (2-17) **1m 54y** £3,773.75 (£1,130.00: £542.50: £248.75) Stalls: Low GOING minus 0.17 sec per fur (GF)

				SP	RR	SF
4057^{2}	**Rambling Rose** (MRStoute) **2-8-11** JReid(3) (sn chsng ldrs: styd on u.p to ld fnl 200y)	—	**1**	$9/2^{3}$	83	53
	Tuning (HRACecil) **2-8-11** KFallon(13) (w'like: leggy: scope: hld up: hdwy over 3f out: led over 2f out: hdd & no ex ins fnl f)	¾	**2**	$3/1^{2}$	82+	52
	Night Rule (BHanbury) **2-8-11** WRyan(1) (w'like: leggy: scope: dwlt: hdwy on ins over 3f out: one pce fnl 2f)	6	**3**	11/1	70	40
3744^{2}	**Shimaal** (SbinSuroor) **2-8-11** JCarroll(8) (trckd ldrs: effrt over 2f out: sn drvn along: no imp)	4	**4**	$6/4^{1}$	62	32
3985^{8}	**Sweet Dreams** (JLDunlop) **2-8-11** TSprake(7) (w ldrs tl wknd wl over 1f out)	1¾	**5**	25/1	59	29
	Dixie d'Oats (EALDunlop) **2-8-11** DBatteate(5) (leggy: unf: b.hind: s.i.s: hdwy over 2f out: nvr nrr)	¾	**6**	16/1	57	27
4007^{7}	**Nisaba (IRE)** (MJohnston) **2-8-11** DHolland(4) (led tl hdd & wknd over 2f out)	3	**7**	25/1	52	22
3862^{5}	**Trinity Reef** (JLDunlop) **2-8-11** GCarter(10) (hld up: nvr nr to chal)	5	**8**	25/1	42	12
4066^{10}	**Hevergolf Princess (IRE)** (TJNaughton) **2-8-11** JWeaver(6) (chsd ldrs tl rdn & wknd 3f out)	hd	**9**	50/1	42	12
	Feel Free (IRE) (LordHuntingdon) **2-8-11** MRoberts(11) (w'like: bit bkwd: hdwy over 4f out: sn pushed along: wknd fnl 2f)	hd	**10**	14/1	41	11
	On Call (SirMarkPrescott) **2-8-11** SSanders(12) (w'like: unf: scope: in tch over 4f)	¾	**11**	7/1	40	10
	Agami (USA) (DRLoder) **2-8-11** PaulEddery(14) (w'like: w ldrs tl lost pl over 3f out)	s.h	**12**	16/1	40	10
3979^{10}	**Loubin Lane** (AGNewcombe) **2-8-8**(3) PPMurphy(9) (a bhd)	½	**13**	100/1	39	9
	Kierans Bridge (IRE) (APJarvis) **2-8-11** SDrowne(2) (cmpt: bkwd: b.nr hind: s.s: a bhd)	4	**14**	50/1	31	1
				(SP 138.9%)		**14 Rn**

1m 44.2 (2.90) CSF £18.75 TOTE £5.60: £1.30 £1.70 £6.00 (£8.60) Trio £76.90 OWNER Sir Evelyn De Rothschild (NEWMARKET) BRED Southcourt Stud
4057 Rambling Rose, delaying her challenge as late as possible, responded well when asked to quicken and her previous experience paid off on this occasion. (9/2: op 3/1)
Tuning, a newcomer with room for improvement, struck the front entering the last quarter-mile and battled on willingly when pressed, but the race-fit winner had her measure in the final hundred yards. She will have no trouble winning races. (3/1)
Night Rule, a sparely-made half-sister to three winners, showed plenty of promise after a sluggish start and she should have little trouble in improving on this. (11/1)
3744 Shimaal, very weak in the ring, was always in close contention, but she did not find a lot when sent about her work and was easily brushed aside. (6/4: op 10/11)
Sweet Dreams, running her best race yet, was in the thick of the action until finding demands too great inside the distance. If she can continue the improvement, she could well strike before the season ends. (25/1)
Dixie d'Oats, an unfurnished debutante who is an April foal, did extremely well to finish as close as she did after being one of the last to exit from the stalls and, with this experience under her belt, she should go on from here. (16/1)

4331 DHL MAIDEN STKS (3-Y.O+) (Class D)
2-45 (2-47) **1m 54y** £4,154.00 (£1,247.00: £601.00: £278.00) Stalls: Low GOING minus 0.17 sec per fur (GF)

				SP	RR	SF
	Northern Blessing (PWHarris) **3-8-9** JReid(9) (leggy: scope: sn trckng ldrs: led over 1f out: drvn clr)	—	**1**	9/1	85	52
2877^{3}	**Burning Truth (USA) (80)** (RCharlton) **3-9-0** TSprake(6) (lw: led tl over 1f out: sn rdn: unable qckn)	5	**2**	$4/9^{1}$	80	47
4060^{8}	**Waterwave (USA)** (JHMGosden) **4-9-4** GHind(2) (bit bkwd: b.hind: sn w ldrs: rdn over 2f out: one pce)	2½	**3**	$7/2^{2}$	75	46
1443^{4}	**Occam (IRE) (57)** (GWragg) **3-9-0** PaulEddery(4) (bit bkwd: racd keenly: trckd ldrs: outpcd fnl 3f)	3	**4**	$8/1^{3}$	70	37
1106^{12}	**Moonshift** (HJCollingridge) **3-9-0** JWeaver(10) (a in rr)	14	**5**	66/1	43	10
4214^{12}	**Beau Tudor (IRE) (36)** (MissLCSiddall) **3-9-0** KFallon(7) (a in rr: t.o)	8	**6**	100/1	27	—
4290^{8}	**Nite Owler** (JO'Reilly) **3-9-0** JFanning(3) (chsd ldrs: rdn along 4f out: sn lost tch: t.o)	5	**7**	50/1	17	—
3820^{7}	**Burnley Belle** (MRChannon) **5-8-13** SSanders(5) (bit bkwd: a bhd & outpcd: t.o)	16	**8**	40/1	—	—
3319^{6}	***On Merit*** (SGollings) **3-9-0** JCarroll(8) (Withdrawn not under Starter's orders: unruly in stalls)		**W**	100/1	—	—
				(SP 120.4%)		**8 Rn**

1m 44.1 (2.80) CSF £13.03 TOTE £9.60: £1.50 £1.10 £1.10 (£4.00) Trio £5.20 OWNER The Twelve Apostles (BERKHAMSTED) BRED Pendley Farm

WEIGHT FOR AGE 3yo-4lb

Northern Blessing, appropriately owned by the Twelve Apostles, made a winning debut with a runaway success, and this half-sister to a couple of winners could turn out useful when she strengthens up. (9/1)

2877 Burning Truth (USA) promises so much but he still remains a maiden after seven runs, and this attractive colt is proving difficult to win with. (4/9)

Waterwave (USA), stepping down from ten furlongs, broke on terms this time and pushed the pace until fading under pressure inside the final quarter-mile. He still looks burly and there is more improvement to follow. (7/2: op 2/1)

1443 Occam (IRE) took quite a bit of settling and, when the tempo was stepped up early in the straight, was caught flat-footed and his chance soon disappeared. (8/1)

4332 MSAS CARGO INTERNATIONAL MAIDEN STKS (2-Y.O F) (Class D)

3-15 (3-18) **6f 15y** £4,027.25 (£1,208.00: £581.50: £268.25) Stalls: High GOING minus 0.43 sec per fur (F)

				SP	RR	SF
4103[2]	**Ikhteyaar (USA)** (RWArmstrong) **2-8-11** RHills(11) (mde all: clr 2f out: comf)	—	**1**	8/13[1]	89+	46
	Final Tango (JHMGosden) **2-8-11** GHind(18) (w'like: scope: hld up: hdwy over 2f out: r.o fnl f: no ch w wnr)	3½	**2**	10/1[3]	80+	37
3187[7]	**Wigging** (NAGraham) **2-8-11** NDay(12) (chsd wnr: r.o one pce fnl 2f)	1¾	**3**	16/1	75	32
	Mahab (USA) (SbinSuroor) **2-8-11** JReid(10) (w'like: dwlt: hdwy over 2f out: styd on ins fnl f)	2½	**4**	9/2[2]	69	26
4167[9]	**Night Auction (IRE)** (BPalling) **2-8-11** SSanders(1) (mde all far side: rdn & kpt on fnl f)	nk	**5**	50/1	68	25
2473[6]	**Oare Kite** (PTWalwyn) **2-8-11** JCarroll(8) (prom stands side over 4f)	¾	**6**	20/1	66	23
3961a[18]	**Moonstone (IRE)** (APJarvis) **2-8-6(5)** CLowther(13) (sn chsng ldrs: outpcd fnl 2f)	hd	**7**	16/1	66	23
	Implicitly (WJarvis) **2-8-11** WRyan(14) (unf: scope: s.s: hdwy 2f out: styd on ins fnl f)	hd	**8**	20/1	65	22
	Only In Dreams (BJMeehan) **2-8-11** MTebbutt(15) (neat: nvr trbld ldrs)	nk	**9**	20/1	65	22
	Silken Dalliance (LordHuntingdon) **2-8-11** MRoberts(4) (w'like: lengthy: nvr gng pce of ldrs)	1¼	**10**	20/1	61	18
3979[9]	**World of Joy** (RCharlton) **2-8-11** TSprake(17) (nvr bttr than mid div)	1½	**11**	14/1	57	14
3862[6]	**Sumbawa (IRE)** (DHaydnJones) **2-8-11** SDrowne(9) (a bhd)	6	**12**	33/1	41	—
884[8]	**Fey Rouge (IRE)** (RHollinshead) **2-8-8(3)** DGriffiths(7) (unruly s: a in rr)	1¼	**13**	66/1	38	—
4216[13]	**Merch Rhyd-Y-Grug** (DLWilliams) **2-8-4(7)** PaulCleary(6) (outpcd)	s.h	**14**	66/1	38	—
	Shotley Marie (IRE) (NBycroft) **2-8-11** LCharnock(5) (lt-f: bkwd: a bhd)	1½	**15**	50/1	34	—
3862[7]	**Our Molly Malone** (DMorley) **2-8-11** MFenton(2) (swtchd rt s: n.d)	5	**16**	50/1	21	—
	Perfect Lady (JMPEustace) **2-8-11** JTate(16) (lengthy: unf: bit bkwd: a bhd & outpcd)	2½	**17**	33/1	14	—
3450[20]	**Moonlightandroses** (NPLittmoden) **2-8-11** TGMcLaughlin(3) (racd far side: a outpcd)	3½	**18**	100/1	5	—
				(SP 142.4%)	**18 Rn**	

1m 12.4 (0.90) CSF £7.76 TOTE £1.40: £1.10 £3.40 £4.70 (£18.40) Trio £92.60 OWNER Mr Hamdan Al Maktoum (NEWMARKET) BRED Shadwell Farm Inc

4103 Ikhteyaar (USA) was able to make it third time lucky with a very straightforward success and, when she is allowed to put the emphasis on stamina, she will always take some beating. (8/13: 11/10-4/7)

Final Tango, whose dam was a winner in France at around nine furlongs, turned in a pleasing performance on this racecourse debut and, if she can steer clear of such as the winner, she will soon lose her maiden tag. (10/1: 8/1-12/1)

3187 Wigging looked far from happy cantering to post, but she gave it her best shot on the return journey and does look the sort to go on improving, especially when the ground eases. (16/1)

Mahab (USA), flat-footed as the stalls were released, stayed on under tender handling in the latter stages and she will be all the sharper next time. (9/2: 3/1-5/1)

Night Auction (IRE) was always winning the race with a lone rival on the far side and, ridden along, stayed on really well to show she is no forlorn hope. (50/1)

2473 Oare Kite, keen to post, raced freely once in action, and she only got shaken off below the distance. (20/1)

Implicitly, a late-April foal from a winning family, lost her chance with a slow start, but she was noted running on pleasingly in the closing stages, and the experience will not be lost. (20/1)

4333 ASHTON CORRUGATED MIDLANDS LIMITED STKS (0-60) (3-Y.O+) (Class F)

3-45 (3-48) **6f 15y** £3,131.70 (£871.20: £419.10) Stalls: High GOING minus 0.43 sec per fur (F)

				SP	RR	SF
4249[5]	**Middle East (56)** (TDBarron) **4-8-13b[1]** JCarroll(1) (a.p far side: led over 2f out: rdn & r.o wl)	—	**1**	9/1[3]	66	48
4248[3]	**Maladerie (IRE) (56)** (MRChannon) **3-8-11** TQuinn(12) (chsd ldrs stands side: kpt on wl ins fnl f)	1	**2**	9/2[1]	63	43
3984[11]	**Superbit (59)** (BAMcMahon) **5-9-2** LNewton(10) (chsd ldrs stands side: styd on ins fnl f)	1½	**3**	12/1	62	44
4168[4]	**Third Party (53)** (SDow) **3-8-11** SSanders(3) (racd far side: styd on wl fnl 2f)	1	**4**	25/1	57	37
3746[5]	**Shining Cloud (58)** (MBell) **4-8-10** MFenton(14) (w ldrs stands side: led over 2f tl over 1f out: one pce fnl f)	½	**5**	8/1[2]	53	35
4184[3]	**Shashi (IRE) (47)** (PatMitchell) **5-8-13** PBloomfield(6) (swtchd lft & racd far side: kpt on fnl 2f)	1½	**6**	25/1	52	34
4137[10]	**Archello (IRE) (60)** (GROldroyd) **3-8-8(3)** GParkin(13) (a chsng ldrs: one pce fnl 2f)	¾	**7**	11/1	50	30
4059[15]	**Silver Secret (60)** (MJHeaton-Ellis) **3-9-0v[1]** AClark(2) (racd far side: bhd tl some hdwy fnl 2f)	1½	**8**	16/1	49	29
3710[11]	**White Settler (60)** (RJHodges) **4-8-13b[1]** SDrowne(17) (nvr nrr)	½	**9**	14/1	44	26
2496[2]	**Hype Superior (IRE) (58)** (ABailey) **3-8-11** DWright(20) (nvr bttr than mid div)	nk	**10**	12/1	44	24
3759[14]	**Souperficial (48)** (NTinkler) **6-9-2v** KimTinkler(15) (dwlt: hdwy ½-wy: edgd lft: nvr nr to chal)	nk	**11**	25/1	46	28
4184[7]	**Aegean Sound (53)** (KTIvory) **3-8-8** MartinDwyer(9) (n.d)	nk	**12**	33/1	39	19
3614[8]	**Dayrella (55)** (WRMuir) **3-9-0** JReid(18) (lw: a in rr)	nk	**13**	16/1	44	24
4059[12]	**Shades of Love (60)** (VSoane) **3-8-11** CRutter(7) (outpcd)	¾	**14**	12/1	39	19
4115[3]	**Pointer (58)** (MrsPNDutfield) **5-8-10(3)** RFfrench(8) (lw: a outpcd)	hd	**15**	10/1	39	21
3984[9]	**Marengo (59)** (JAkehurst) **3-8-11v** MTebbutt(11) (a outpcd)	1½	**16**	16/1	35	15
4115[18]	**Life On The Street (60)** (DNicholls) **3-8-3(5)** PRoberts(19) (chsd ldrs stands side over 3f)	1¾	**17**	9/1[3]	27	7
4210[15]	**Rude Awakening (60)** (CWFairhurst) **3-8-11b** KFallon(5) (led far side over 3f: sn rdn & wknd)	3	**18**	12/1	22	2
4070[5]	**Dust (58)** (LordHuntingdon) **3-8-8** MRoberts(16) (led stands side tl hdd & wknd 2f out: t.o)	10	**19**	8/1[2]	—	—
				(SP 147.4%)	**19 Rn**	

1m 12.4 (0.90) CSF £51.16 TOTE £13.90: £3.70 £2.80 £4.80 (£30.60) Trio £580.80 OWNER Mrs J. Hazell (THIRSK) BRED Miss M. Grantmyre

WEIGHT FOR AGE 3yo-2lb

4249 Middle East, winning his first race for fourteen months, was helped in no small way by the application of blinkers and, forging clear on the far side, won cosily. (9/1)

4248 Maladerie (IRE) ran another good race and he finished ahead of the stands' side group, but the winner, racing the course width apart, was just that bit too good for him on the day. (9/2)

3481 Superbit runs well on this track and he was fighting for the lead all the way but, on ground more lively than he cares for, was unable to match strides late on. (12/1)
4168 Third Party remained on the far side and did not really pick up until it was too late, so it could be worth giving her a try over an extra furlong. (25/1)
3746 Shining Cloud showed ahead on the stands' side briefly but, once the favourite took her measure, she was unable to do anything about it. Her turn will come and she must not be written off yet. (8/1: op 5/1)
4184 Shashi (IRE) decided it was best to make her way over to the far side rail, but she took time to really find her stride and, when she did, the race was all but over. (25/1)
3606* Archello (IRE) (11/1: 8/1-12/1)

4334 HAMBLIN GRAND CASINO NURSERY H'CAP (0-75) (2-Y.O) (Class E)

4-15 (4-17) **1m 1f 213y** £3,538.25 (£1,061.00: £510.50: £235.25) Stalls: Low GOING minus 0.17 sec per fur (GF)

Form	Horse	Dist	Pos	SP	RR	SF
4116[19]	**Tarashaan (71)** (SirMarkPrescott) **2-9-5** SSanders(7) (s.i.s: sn chsng ldrs: led 3f out: hrd rdn & r.o wl)	—	1	7/2[1]	74	34
4006[9]	**Iron Mountain (IRE) (68)** (NACallaghan) **2-9-2** KFallon(13) (sn pushed along: hdwy over 3f out: chsd wnr fnl 2f: hrd rdn: r.o)	½	2	13/2[3]	70	30
4116[21]	**Narrogin (USA) (72)** (MRChannon) **2-9-6** JCarroll(17) (hld up: hdwy on outside over 2f out: rdn & edgd lft: styd on)	1½	3	12/1	72	32
4068[14]	**Red Maple (USA) (62)** (PFICole) **2-8-10b** TQuinn(11) (a in tch: rdn over 2f out: edgd lft & styd on)	hd	4	16/1	62	22
3911[5]	**Pianist (IRE) (57)** (GLewis) **2-8-5** PaulEddery(6) (bhd: hdwy u.p over 2f out: kpt on: nvr nrr)	3½	5	12/1	51	11
4132[6]	**Jonas Nightengale (73)** (CACyzer) **2-9-7** JFEgan(15) (in tch: effrt over 2f out: styd on one pce)	3½	6	14/1	61	21
3395[2]	**Gralmano (IRE) (55)** (NPLittmoden) **2-8-3** MFenton(12) (a chsng ldrs: rdn over 2f out: no imp)	4	7	13/2[3]	37	—
3973[3]	**Forgotten Star (IRE) (64)** (RFJohnsonHoughton) **2-8-12** TWilliams(2) (chsd ldrs tl wknd fnl 2f)	½	8	9/1	45	5
2697[8]	**After Dawn (IRE) (54)** (MrsPNDutfield) **2-7-13**(3) RFfrench(3) (hld up: some hdwy over 2f out: nvr plcd to chal)	1¾	9	40/1	32	—
4044[6]	**Naked Oat (70)** (BSmart) **2-9-4** JStack(16) (hdwy on outside ent st: nvr nr to chal)	1½	10	5/1[2]	46	6
3973[6]	**Lord of Love (68)** (TDEasterby) **2-9-2** LCharnock(5) (lw: trckd ldrs: ev ch 3f out: sn drvn along: grad wknd)	nk	11	10/1	44	4
4044[11]	**Aldwych Arrow (IRE) (72)** (MBell) **2-9-1**(5) GFaulkner(18) (lw: chsd ldrs 6f)	3	12	16/1	43	3
4058[12]	**Mary Lou (IRE) (54)** (MRChannon) **2-8-2** AMackay(1) (a in rr)	1¼	13	16/1	23	—
3607[10]	**Fair Game (IRE) (65)** (JLDunlop) **2-8-13** GCarter(8) (a bhd & outpcd)	2	14	14/1	30	—
4044[16]	**Eastwell Hall (56)** (RCurtis) **2-8-4** MRoberts(10) (mde most tl hdd & wknd 3f out)	1¾	15	33/1	19	—
3911[3]	**Catch The Rainbow (61)** (JGSmyth-Osbourne) **2-8-9** FLynch(9) (a bhd)	¾	16	12/1	22	—
3904[7]	**Danzig Flyer (IRE) (73)** (PWHarris) **2-9-2**(5) CLowther(4) (swtg: trckd ldrs: effrt 3f out: sn rdn & wknd)	¾	17	10/1	33	—
4017[11]	**Chikal (57)** (BPalling) **2-8-5** TSprake(14) (lw: w ldrs over 6f: sn wknd)	hd	18	16/1	17	—
				(SP 159.1%)	**18 Rn**	

2m 9.3 (6.80) CSF £30.54 CT £266.25 TOTE £4.60: £1.50 £2.30 £6.10 £4.20 (£15.10) Trio £159.80 OWNER Mr E. B. Rimmer (NEWMARKET) BRED Deerfield Farm

3117 Tarashaan came into his own over this extended trip and landed a fair touch in the process and, in this class, he can win again. (7/2)
3794 Iron Mountain (IRE) seemed well-suited by the step-up in distance and, though he came out second best this time, it would seem only a matter of time before he does strike it rich. (13/2: op 10/1)
3750 Narrogin (USA), a heavy-topped colt probably not ideally suited by such fast ground, is an out-and-out stayer, and the way he was plugging on towards the finish would suggest that initial success is just around the corner. (12/1)
3924 Red Maple (USA) needs this sort of trip and, though he stuck on gamely under a strong ride, could never find enough to land a blow. He has come to himself now and is worth following. (16/1)
3911 Pianist (IRE), staying on when it was all over, is just the type to win a seller at this trip. (12/1: op 8/1)
3789 Jonas Nightengale had it all to do under top weight in this first handicap and, despite never being far away, could only stay on at the one pace. (14/1)
3395 Gralmano (IRE) (13/2: op 10/1)

4335 BOLLINGER CHAMPAGNE CHALLENGE SERIES GENTLEMEN'S H'CAP (0-70) (3-Y.O+) (Class F)

4-45 (4-47) **1m 1f 213y** £2,923.80 (£811.80: £389.40) Stalls: Low GOING minus 0.17 sec per fur (GF)

Form	Horse	Dist	Pos	SP	RR	SF
4071[5]	**Civil Liberty (60)** (GLewis) **4-11-6** MrABalding(5) (a.p: led over 2f out: hld on wl towards fin)	—	1	11/1	70	49
3762*	**Riccarton (50)** (PCalver) **4-10-10** MrCBonner(2) (hld up: gd hdwy on ins 3f out: ev ch ins fnl f: rdn & unable qckn)	½	2	9/1	59	38
4213[3]	**Augustan (60)** (SGollings) **6-11-6** MrRWakley(11) (lw: mid div: hdwy 3f out: styd on u.p fnl f)	2	3	6/1	66	45
4179[3]	**Tajar (USA) (41)** (TKeddy) **5-10-1** MrJGoldstein(18) (a chsng ldrs: ev ch over 1f out: one pce)	½	4	9/1	46	25
3933[4]	**Essayeffsee (51)** (MrsMReveley) **8-10-7**(4) MrTComerford(15) (lw: a chsng ldrs: one pce fnl 2f)	4	5	12/1	50	29
4235[19]	**Brambles Way (50)** (MrsMReveley) **8-10-6**(4) MrNEJones(1) (hld up & bhd: styd on appr fnl f: nvr nrr)	1¾	6	20/1	46	25
3787*	**Fern's Governor (60)** (WJMusson) **5-11-6** MrTMcCarthy(10) (hld up: effrt on outside over 3f out: nt rch ldrs)	½	7	3/1[1]	55	34
3330[6]	**Clued Up (53)** (PDEvans) **4-10-9v**(4) MrAEvans(9) (hld up & bhd: some late hdwy: n.d)	¾	8	16/1	47	26
	Disallowed (IRE) (63) (DNicholson) **4-11-9** MrOMcPhail(3) (hld up: some hdwy over 2f out: nvr nrr)	1	9	20/1	55	34
4069[11]	**Summerville Wood (59)** (PMooney) **3-10-9**(4) DrAKimber(16) (racd wd: in tch tl outpcd fnl 3f)	1	10	50/1	50	23
4002[13]	**Tulsa (IRE) (46)** (BGubby) **3-10-0** MrJRees(12) (chsd ldrs over 6f)	nk	11	25/1	36	9
4050[8]	**Montone (IRE) (47)** (JRJenkins) **7-10-7b** DrMMannish(6) (sn led: rdn & hdd over 2f out: wknd qckly)	hd	12	25/1	37	16
414[2]	**Aspecto Lad (IRE) (55)** (DLWilliams) **3-10-5**(4) MrSDurack(8) (a in rr)	4	13	25/1	39	12
30[5]	**Tremendisto (46)** (DMcCain) **7-10-2**(4) MrGLake(4) (s.i.s: effrt on ins 3f out: nvr rchd ldrs)	1½	14	33/1	27	6
3779*	**Farringdon Hill (68)** (JHMGosden) **6-11-10v**(4) MrCRanson(13) (b.hind: trckd ldrs: effrt 3f out: sn rdn & wknd)	½	15	7/2[2]	49	28
3335[2]	**Strength of Vision (47)** (CREgerton) **3-9-11**(4)ow2 MrPPhillips(14) (plld hrd: w ldrs tl wknd 3f out)	3	16	20/1	23	—
2171*	**Flashtalkin' Flood (66)** (CADwyer) **3-11-6** MrPScott(17) (trckd ldrs: rdn 4f out: sn wknd)	2½	17	11/2[3]	38	11
1493[5]	**Fortune Hunter (IRE) (54)** (JNorton) **3-10-4v1**(4) MrRayBarrett(7) (in tch: rdn over 3f: sn lost pl: t.o)	12	18	50/1	6	—
				(SP 151.5%)	**18 Rn**	

2m 10.8 (8.30) CSF £107.28 CT £630.73 TOTE £13.60: £2.60 £1.70 £2.30 £3.20 (£44.60) Trio £66.00 OWNER Midcourts (EPSOM) BRED Patrick Eddery Ltd

WEIGHT FOR AGE 3yo-6lb

4071 Civil Liberty, given a very confident ride and always travelling smoothly, had to work to hold on towards the finish, but he gave the impression he always had the situation under control. (11/1)

3762* Riccarton delivered his challenge on the inside of the winner and looked to give it his all, but he was up against a rival who just would not give best. (9/1)
4213 Augustan continues to run well, but he seems to need a slightly stiffer test of stamina these days, and his determined last furlong effort was never going to get him there. (6/1)
4179 Tajar (USA) looked a live threat when joining issue below the distance, but he was unable to sustain the run under strong pressure, and was fighting a lost cause inside the final furlong. (9/1)
3933 Essayeffsee sat closer to the pace than he usually does and was always poised to challenge, but was unable to respond when the tempo picked up and was easily brushed aside. (12/1)
3779 Brambles Way, settled off the pace, began to stay on late in the day but he had allowed the principals too much start. (20/1)
3787* Fern's Governor always had far too much to do and, though she did make a brief forward move, the position was hopeless. (3/1)
3779* Farringdon Hill (7/2: op 2/1)

4336 STAYBRITE WINDOWS LEVY BOARD H'CAP (0-70) (3-Y.O) (Class E)

5-15 (5-16) **2m 9y** £3,951.00 (£1,188.00: £574.00: £267.00) Stalls: Low GOING minus 0.17 sec per fur (GF)

				SP	RR	SF
4170*	**Stoned Imaculate (IRE) (61)** (FMurphy) **3-8-12** ^{5x} KFallon(5) (mid div: hdwy & pushed along 4f out: led over 1f out: styd on strly)	—	**1**	6/4^{1}	75	38
4171^{5}	**Sipowitz (48)** (CACyzer) **3-7-13** TWilliams(3) (lw: a.p: led over 3f tl over 1f out: r.o one pce)	1¼	**2**	12/1	61	24
3317^{5}	**Arisaig (IRE) (56)** (PCalver) **3-8-7b^{1}** NDay(7) (chsd ldrs: rdn & drifted lft fnl 2f: one pce)	6	**3**	12/1	63	26
3400^{6}	**Alagna (49)** (SCWilliams) **3-8-0b**^{1ow4} AMackay(14) (hld up: hdwy over 3f out: ev ch wl over 1f out: one pce)	2½	**4**	16/1	53	12
3896^{8}	**Indigo Dawn (60)** (MJohnston) **3-8-11** DHolland(10) (a chsng ldrs: sn drvn along: wknd wl over 1f out)	3½	**5**	9/1	61	24
4275^{11}	**Tasik Chini (USA) (60)** (PFICole) **3-8-11** TQuinn(15) (hld up: hdwy 6f out: styd on appr fnl f)	2	**6**	25/1	59	22
4010^{6}	**Madison Welcome (IRE) (58)** (MrsJRRamsden) **3-8-6**$^{(3)}$ RFfrench(9) (lw: in tch: drvn along 5f out: wknd 2f out)	nk	**7**	16/1	57	20
4046^{13}	**Trooper (70)** (RAkehurst) **3-9-7** JWeaver(11) (mde most 9f: rdn & wknd 2f out)	4	**8**	16/1	65	28
4160^{10}	**Maremma (46)** (DonEnricoIncisa) **3-7-11** KimTinkler(2) (bhd: some hdwy fnl 2f: nvr nrr)	1¼	**9**	33/1	39	2
3864^{11}	**Bandore (IRE) (70)** (DRLoder) **3-9-7** MRoberts(4) (trckd ldrs tl rdn & wknd over 2f out)	½	**10**	14/1	63	26
3781^{3}	**Aurelian (58)** (MBell) **3-8-9** MFenton(16) (hld up: effrt 3f out: nvr nr ldrs)	3½	**11**	7/1^{3}	47	10
4046^{3}	**Woody's Boy (IRE) (63)** (MJHeaton-Ellis) **3-9-0** SSanders(13) (in tch: rdn & wknd over 3f out)	nk	**12**	6/1^{2}	52	15
4171^{8}	**Hippios (45)** (SDow) **3-7-3**$^{(7)}$ PDoe(6) (trckd ldrs 10f: sn lost tch)	2	**13**	33/1	32	—
3903^{2}	**Classic Fan (USA) (62)** (MRChannon) **3-8-13** JCarroll(17) (hld up: effrt over 3f out: sn no imp)	6	**14**	25/1	43	6
3336^{10}	**Bernie's Star (IRE) (45)** (NBycroft) **3-7-10** LCharnock(1) (bhd & drvn along ½-wy: t.o)	8	**15**	100/1	18	—
1312^{2}	**Guard A Dream (IRE) (45)** (MrsMReveley) **3-7-10** JLowe(8) (plld hrd: a bhd: t.o)	nk	**16**	20/1	18	—
4104^{3}	**Alakdar (CAN) (64)** (ACStewart) **3-9-1** RHills(12) (trckd ldrs: led 7f tl over 3f out: wknd 2f out: t.o)	1¼	**17**	7/1^{3}	36	—
373^{9}	**Melodic Squaw (45)** (MPBielby) **3-7-10** DWright(18) (drvn along fr ½-wy: bhd fnl 5f: t.o)	nk	**18**	100/1	16	—
				(SP 149.3%)	**18 Rn**	

3m 32.1 (9.10) CSF £23.91 CT £190.30 TOTE £2.20: £1.10 £5.30 £2.60 £5.80 (£14.90) Trio £150.40 OWNER Mr M. Rowsell (MIDDLEHAM) BRED Mrs Ann Fortune

LONG HANDICAP Hippios 7-2 Bernie's Star (IRE) 7-1 Guard A Dream (IRE) 7-5 Melodic Squaw 7-9

4170* Stoned Imaculate (IRE) was the only one anyone wanted to be on and she defied the penalty to complete her hat-trick to show that stamina is really her strong suit. She has been well placed. (6/4)
4171 Sipowitz has shown in the past that he needs to get his toe in, so to race him on such lively ground is asking for trouble but, that said, he lost no cast in defeat here and, if he does return to the All-Weather, could prove a ready-made winner. (12/1)
3317 Arisaig (IRE), much sharper in the blinkers, was inclined to drift off a true line when pressure was applied, but he did stay on and there is a race in him. (12/1)
3400 Alagna made relentless progress once in line for home and posed a serious threat just inside the last quarter-mile but, with the pace continuing to lift, he was soon left struggling. (16/1)
3309 Indigo Dawn is a hard ride and she was soon being nudged along, but she remained in the chasing group until fading below the distance. (9/1)
1805 Tasik Chini (USA), tackling his longest trip yet, did keep staying on without having the speed to get involved. (25/1)
3057 Trooper set the pace but attempted to run back into the paddock soon after passing the stands, and it was a good job that his pilot was alert. Maintaining the lead for five furlongs, he did not drop away until approaching the last quarter-mile. (16/1)

T/Jkpt: Not won; £12,649.70 to Goodwood 24/9/97. T/Plpt: £143.50 (206.03 Tckts). T/Qdpt: £55.00 (31.74 Tckts) IM

4337a - 4343a (Irish Racing) - See Computer Raceform

4089a-CURRAGH (Newbridge, Ireland) (R-H) (Yielding to soft)

Saturday September 20th

4344a AON MACDONAGH BOLAND STKS (Gp 3) (3-Y.O+)

2-45 (2-46) **7f** IR £19,500.00 (IR £5,700.00: IR £2,700.00: IR £900.00) GOING: 0.56 sec per fur (GS)

				SP	RR	SF
3063*	**Wizard King** (SirMarkPrescott) **6-9-7** PShanahan (trckd ldrs: rn 3rd: n.m.r over 2f out: chal 1½f out: led early ins last: rdn clr: r.o.)	—	**1**	7/4^{1}	127	67
2820a^{7}	**Snow Kid** (DRLoder) **3-8-12**^{ow1} LDettori (2nd & disp ldt: led 2f out: hdd early ins last: no ex)	2½	**2**	6/1^{3}	115	51
3554a^{5}	**Deadly Dudley (IRE)** (RHannon) **3-8-11** MJKinane (hld up in tch: 4th ½-wy: 3rd, rdn & no ex 1f out: kpt on same pce)	1	**3**	5/1^{2}	112	49
3535a^{6}	**Theano (IRE)** (APO'Brien,Ireland) **4-8-11** CRoche (hld up: 7th ½-wy: effrt 1½f out: kpt on u.p ins last)	s.h	**4**	7/1	109	49
4094a^{5}	**Azra (IRE)** (JSBolger,Ireland) **3-8-8** KJManning (hld up: 5th ½-wy: rdn & no ex over 1f out: kpt on)	s.h	**5**	12/1	109	46
3674a^{4}	**Cool Edge (IRE)** (MHTompkins) **6-9-4** PJSmullen (led & disp ld: hdd 2f out: wkng whn sltly hmpd 1f out: no ex)	1	**6**	8/1	114	54
4117*	**Almushtarak (IRE)** (KMahdi) **4-9-4** JReid (hld up in tch: 4th & effrt 2f out: no ex 1f out: kpt on)	s.h	**7**	10/1	113	53
3674a^{5}	**Nobility (IRE)** (JOxx,Ireland) **3-8-11b^{1}** JPMurtagh (towards rr: rdn after ½-wy: n.d & trailing 2f out)	15	**8**	10/1	75	12
				(SP 116.8%)	**8 Rn**	

1m 30.1 (7.10) OWNER Sh Ahmed Bin Saeed Al Maktoum (NEWMARKET) BRED Sheikh Mohammed bin Rashid al Maktoum

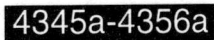

3063* Wizard King again underlined his amazing consistency when gaining his seventeenth win. He came through between horses to lead inside the last, and won with plenty in hand. He is likely to return to Tipperary next month for the Group Three Concorde Stakes, an event he won last season. (7/4)
2820a Snow Kid took up the running with less than two furlongs to race, but was totally outpaced once headed by the winner. (6/1: op 4/1)
3554a Deadly Dudley (IRE) kept on without seriously troubling the first two but will certainly get his turn before the end of the season. (5/1: op 3/1)
3535a Theano (IRE) ran on well late after being switched to the outside. (7/1: op 4/1)
4094a Azra (IRE) kept on over the last furlong and a half without quickening. (12/1)
3674a Cool Edge (IRE) took them along at a very steady pace, but was headed and weakening when slightly hampered by the winner one furlong out. (8/1: op 5/1)
4117* Almushtarak (IRE) looked very onepaced over the last furlong with none of his Doncaster dash on display. (10/1)

4345a (Irish Racing) - See Computer Raceform

4346a JEFFERSON SMURFIT MEMORIAL IRISH ST LEGER (Gp 1) (3-Y.O+)

3-50 (3-51) **1m 6f** IR £88,800.00 (IR £28,800.00: IR £13,800.00: IR £4,800.00) GOING: 0.56 sec per fur (GS)

				SP	RR	SF
3675a[3]	**Oscar Schindler (IRE)** (KPrendergast,Ireland) **5-9-8** SCraine (hld up: hdwy 5f out: 3rd & clsd to trck ldrs bef st: chal between horses over 2f out: led under 2f out: rdn clr fnl f)	—	**1**	2/1[1]	130+	74
4118[2]	**Persian Punch (IRE)** (DRCElsworth) **4-9-8** JPMurtagh (sn chsng ldr: disp ld & rdn bef st: ev ch u.p over 2f out: no ex over 1f out: kpt on same pce)	2	**2**	12/1	128	72
3704[2]	**Whitewater Affair** (MRStoute) **4-9-5** JReid (led & disp ld: hdd under 2f out: rdn & no ex fr 1½f out: kpt on same pce)	2½	**3**	4/1[2]	122	66
3511a*	**Family Tradition (IRE)** (APO'Brien,Ireland) **3-8-9b** CRoche (towards rr: 6th u.p & no imp under 2f out: kpt on same pce)	6	**4**	20/1	115	49
	Stage Affair (USA) (DKWeld,Ireland) **3-8-12** MJKinane (hld up towards rr: mod 5th st: mod 4th & no imp under 2f out: kpt on same pce)	1	**5**	11/1[3]	117	51
3983[2]	**Samraan (USA)** (JLDunlop) **4-9-8** PJSmullen (in tch: 4th ½-wy: rdn 4f out: no imp over 2f out: one pce)	1½	**6**	12/1	115	59
3883a*	**Classic Cliche (IRE)** (SbinSuroor) **5-9-8** LDettori (hld up in tch: 3rd & pushed along ½-wy: rdn & wknd over 5f out: dropped bhd)	dist	**7**	2/1[1]	—	—
				(SP 115.1%)	**7 Rn**	

3m 6.4 (13.40) OWNER Oliver Lehane (FRIARSTOWN) BRED Oliver Lehane
3675a Oscar Schindler (IRE) repeated last year's success and possibly had less to do at the end than twelve months ago. The ground proved no problem and he had matters well sewn up when leading between horses a furlong and a half out. The Arc is the next step and one could envisage some Australian interest in the possibility of a change of ownership before the Melbourne Cup. (2/1)
4118 Persian Punch (IRE), running in second and off the bridle from halfway, stayed on under pressure without quickening. (12/1: op 8/1)
3704 Whitewater Affair set off in front but when headed a furlong and a half out, didn't find anything in reserve. (4/1)
3511a* Family Tradition (IRE) stayed on past beaten horses to go a never threatening fourth over a furlong out. (20/1)
Stage Affair (USA), possibly unsuited by the ground, moved into fourth place early in the straight, but never got on terms. (11/1)
3983 Samraan (USA), tracking the leaders to the straight, found absolutely nothing. (12/1: op 8/1)
3883a* Classic Cliche (IRE), niggled along after halfway, dropped away from the four furlong marker and finished completely tailed off. Nothing untoward was disclosed at the subsequent veterinary inspection, and the five-year-old has now been retired. (2/1)

4347a - 4355a (Irish Racing) - See Computer Raceform

4343a-CURRAGH (Newbridge, Ireland) (R-H) (Yielding to soft)
Sunday September 21st

4356a SOLONAWAY STKS (Listed) (3-Y.O+)

3-40 (3-40) **1m 1f** IR £12,900.00 (IR £3,700.00: IR £1,700.00: IR £500.00) GOING: 0.29 sec per fur (G)

				SP	RR	SF
2441a[5]	**Quws** (KPrendergast,Ireland) **3-8-10** SCraine (hld up: 5th ½-wy: trckd ldrs: 4th & chal fr 2f out: led 150y out: rdn clr: r.o.)	—	**1**	9/4[1]	109+	68
1198a[4]	**Mr Lightfoot (IRE)** (CCollins,Ireland) **3-8-10** PShanahan (rn 2nd: chal to led over 2f out: hdd 150 y out: no ex)	2½	**2**	6/1	105	64
4094a[4]	**Via Verbano (IRE)** (JSBolger,Ireland) **3-8-7** KJManning (hld up in tch: 3rd ½-wy: chal & ev ch fr over 2f out: no ex whn hmpd early ins last: kpt on same pce)	¾	**3**	9/2[3]	100	59
2989a[3]	**Chania (IRE)** (JOxx,Ireland) **3-8-7** PJSmullen (hld up towards rr: 6th ½-wy: rdn bef st: chsd ldrs u.p over 2f out: kpt on ins last: nt rch ldrs)	1	**4**	11/4[2]	98	57
	Handaza (IRE) (JOxx,Ireland) **3-8-7** TQuinn (hld up in tch: 4th ½-wy: chsd ldrs st: 5th & no ex 1½f out: one pce)	5	**5**	8/1	90	49
4204a[6]	**No Slouch (IRE)** (APO'Brien,Ireland) **3-8-10** CRoche (led: hdd over 2f out: no ex 1½f out: wknd: eased)	1	**6**	8/1	91	50
	Carlisle Bay (IRE) (JOxx,Ireland) **3-8-10** JPMurtagh (dwlt: towards rr: rdn & no imp 2f out)	7	**7**	10/1	78	37
				(SP 121.2%)	**7 Rn**	

1m 55.0 (4.50) OWNER Mr Hamdan Al Maktoum (FRIARSTOWN)
Quws, an easy winner of the Irish Cambridgeshire last time, started a well backed favourite here, and justified confidence in no uncertain style. He will step back in distance now when taking on Wizard King in a Group Three in Tipperary next month. (9/4)
Mr Lightfoot (IRE) hung left inside the last and certainly inconvenienced the third. He might have been fortunate to hold on to his placing. (6/1: op 3/1)
4094a Via Verbano (IRE) was not making much impression when carried left by the runner-up inside the last. She has had three hard races in the same number of weeks and has to be termed unlucky. (9/2: op 3/1)
2989a Chania (IRE) was disappointing, finding only one pace after being given reminders two furlongs out. (11/4)
Handaza (IRE) (8/1: op 9/2)
3362a No Slouch (IRE) again adopted front running tactics but did not go off at anything like the same pace employed in the Champion Stakes at Leopardstown. Headed two furlongs out, he was then eased up. (8/1: op 5/1)
Carlisle Bay (IRE) (10/1: op 5/1)

4357a AGA KHAN STUDS NATIONAL STKS (Gp 1) (2-Y.O C & F)
4-15 (4-16) **1m (New)** IR £112,600.00 (IR £38,600.00: IR £18,600.00: IR £6,600.00) GOING: 0.29 sec per fur (G)

				SP	RR	SF
3672a*	**King Of Kings (IRE)** (APO'Brien,Ireland) **2-9-0** CRoche (hld up: trckd ldrs: n.m.r 2f out: opening & chal between horses 1f out: qcknd to ld 100y fr fin: rdn & r.o nr fin)	—	**1**	4/9[1]	107	36
3895[5]	**Celtic Cavalier (IRE)** (APO'Brien,Ireland) **2-9-0** MJKinane (hld up in tch: 5th ½-wy: chal on outside fr over 2f out: 3rd & no ex u.p ins last: kpt on)	¾	**2**	20/1	106	35
2243*	**Mountain Song** (SirMarkPrescott) **2-9-0** SSanders (sn led: hdd u.p 100y fr fin: no ex: kpt on)	s.h	**3**	7/1[2]	105	34
3688*	**Mowbray (USA)** (PFICole) **2-9-0** TQuinn (disp ld early: cl up: cl 3rd, chal & ev ch fr over 2f out: no ex u.p ins last: kpt on)	¾	**4**	7/1[2]	104	33
3962a[6]	**Magical Minty (IRE)** (WPMullins,Ireland) **2-9-0** KJManning (hld up: 6th & chsd ldrs early st: nt rch ldrs 1f out: kpt on wl)	¾	**5**	25/1	102	31
	Takarian (IRE) (JOxx,Ireland) **2-9-0** PJSmullen (hld up: 6th ½-wy: effrt 2f out: 7th, rdn & nt rch ldrs 1f out: kpt on)	½	**6**	16/1	101	30
3962a[3]	**Natalis (IRE)** (JOxx,Ireland) **2-9-0** JPMurtagh (disp ld early: rn 2nd: chal & ev ch early st: no ex ins last)	½	**7**	10/1[3]	100	29
3962a[8]	**Sideman (IRE)** (APO'Brien,Ireland) **2-9-0** JAHeffernan (hld up: 8th & rdn over 2f out: no imp)	6	**8**	20/1	88	17
	Galahad (IRE) (TStack,Ireland) **2-9-0** PShanahan (dwlt: a towards rr: n.d)	3	**9**	25/1	82	11

(SP 126.4%) **9 Rn**

1m 43.3 (8.30) OWNER Mrs John Magnier (PILTOWN)

3672a* King Of Kings (IRE) had to demonstrate some determination to get through a gap inside the last, and with whips flashing in front of his face as a manoeuvre was contemplated, he had plenty of time to shirk the issue. But he did everything willingly enough, and the winning margin does not reflect his superiority over his stable companion in the runner-up spot. His trainer is not keen to take him to England this season, and he is now finished for the year. (4/9)

3895 Celtic Cavalier (IRE) was an eye-catching second under what appeared to be a caring ride from Kinane. He is possibly flattered by this run, but certainly displayed a useful turn of foot in the closing stages. (20/1)

2243* Mountain Song made the running. He was being driven along from two furlongs out and kept on producing that bit extra until headed when weakening well inside the last. (7/1)

3688* Mowbray (USA) was bang in contention with his sustained challenge from two furlongs out, and the winner had to battle to beat him early inside the last. There was not much forthcoming close home. (7/1)

Magical Minty (IRE) should have been totally outclassed in this company, but kept on well on the inside over the final two furlongs, to be nearest at the finish. (25/1)

3962a Natalis (IRE) found little inside the last, but still ran up to his previous best. (10/1: op 6/1)

3962a Sideman (IRE) was no threat turning into the straight. (20/1)

Galahad (IRE) never got into contention. (25/1)

4358a - 4359a (Irish Racing) - See Computer Raceform

3899-CHESTER (L-H) (Good)
Wednesday September 24th
WEATHER: sunny periods WIND: almost nil

4360 CARDEN MAIDEN STKS (3-Y.O+) (Class D)
2-20 (2-23) **1m 5f 89y** £3,798.50 (£1,148.00: £559.00: £264.50) Stalls: Low GOING: 0.12 sec per fur (G)

				SP	RR	SF
3974[12]	**Spy Knoll (79)** (MRStoute) **3-8-12** DHolland(8) (mde all: clr 3f out: rdn out)	—	**1**	3/1[2]	89	50
	Spartan Heartbeat (102) (CEBrittain) **4-9-7** WJO'Connor(2) (swtg: b: bkwd: a.p: wnt 2nd over 3f out: r.o wl towards fin)	1¼	**2**	5/1	88	58
3021[9]	**Aboo Hom (76)** (ACStewart) **3-8-12** MRoberts(5) (bit bkwd: dwlt: pushed along 8f out: hdwy over 3f out: nt rch ldrs)	8	**3**	4/1[3]	78	39
3918[2]	**Aeolina (FR)** (SEKettlewell) **3-8-7** JFortune(7) (a chsng ldrs: rdn over 3f out: no imp)	12	**4**	25/1	59	20
4287[13]	**Taniyar (FR) (45)** (RHollinshead) **5-9-7** RCochrane(3) (hld up: a bhd)	14	**5**	50/1	47	17
3977[4]	**Midnight Watch (USA) (78)** (HRACecil) **3-8-12** KFallon(6) (hld up: hdwy 6f out: rdn & wknd over 3f out: t.o)	2½	**6**	13/8[1]	44	5
3903[5]	**Sostenuto** (RHollinshead) **4-8-13(3)** DGriffiths(1) (a in rr: t.o fnl 5f)	27	**7**	66/1	7	—
2753[8]	**Single Man (IRE)** (BPJBaugh) **4-9-7** ACulhane(4) (chsd wnr to ½-wy: rdn & lost tch 5f out: t.o)	16	**8**	100/1	—	—

(SP 108.1%) **8 Rn**

2m 59.43 (9.43) CSF £14.42 TOTE £4.70: £1.10 £1.60 £1.50 (£8.80) OWNER Mr J. H. Richmond-Watson (NEWMARKET) BRED Lawn Stud
WEIGHT FOR AGE 3yo-9lb

OFFICIAL EXPLANATION **Spy Knoll: refused to face the visor last time, and had been unable to act on the soft ground. Midnight Watch (USA): hung right throughout.**

3010 Spy Knoll has been very disappointing on the whole but today was to be his day, and he succeeded in making all in a race where there were questions to be asked about several of his rivals. (3/1)

Spartan Heartbeat, far from disgraced in group races when he was last in action almost fourteen months ago, showed he had lost none of his ability and, with a recent run under his best, would have had little trouble winning this. Given a polished ride by a much under-used competent jockey, he should soon go one better. (5/1: op 9/4)

2410 Aboo Hom gave the impression that run would do him good after a couple of months on the sidelines. (4/1)

3977 Midnight Watch (USA) is failing to progress at all and, in serious trouble out in the country, weakened quickly as his stamina gave out. (13/8)

4361 MARFORD MAIDEN STKS (2-Y.O) (Class D)
2-50 (2-51) **7f 2y** £3,436.25 (£1,040.00: £507.50: £241.25) Stalls: Low GOING: 0.12 sec per fur (G)

				SP	RR	SF
4061[17]	**Pure Nobility (IRE)** (BWHills) **2-9-0** DHolland(7) (dwlt: sn chsng ldrs: led wl over 1f out: pushed out)	—	**1**	14/1	85	37
	Freedom Quest (IRE) (SirMarkPrescott) **2-9-0** SSanders(8) (leggy: lt-f: unf: hdwy 4f out: hrd drvn & outpcd ent st: r.o wl ins fnl f)	1¾	**2**	7/4[1]	81+	33
3887[5]	**Rewardia (IRE) (70)** (PDEvans) **2-8-9** JFEgan(9) (hld up: hdwy 2f out: rdn & r.o wl fnl f)	½	**3**	16/1	75	27
3306[6]	**Prince Ashleigh** (PCHaslam) **2-9-0** JFortune(6) (a.p: rdn appr fnl f: one pce)	nk	**4**	10/1	79	31
4113[5]	**The Magistrate (IRE)** (MBlanshard) **2-9-0** RCochrane(2) (bhd: hdwy 2f out: nrst fin)	1	**5**	10/1	77	29
3322[7]	**Elba Magic (IRE)** (CADwyer) **2-8-9** KFallon(3) (chsd ldrs tl rdn & outpcd over 2f out)	4	**6**	12/1	63	15

4064[9] **Cherokee Band (USA)** (BWHills) **2-9-0** RHills(4) (hld up: effrt & rdn over 2f out: no imp)	½	**7**	4/1[2]	67	19
4111[9] **Genius (IRE)** (PFICole) **2-9-0** MTebbutt(1) (a bhd & outpcd)	hd	**8**	12/1	66	18
4111[6] **Da Boss (78)** (WRMuir) **2-9-0** MRoberts(5) (lw: led tl hdd & wknd wl over 1f out)	1¾	**9**	5/1[3]	62	14
			(SP 119.1%) **9 Rn**		

1m 31.26 (6.06) CSF £36.58 TOTE £20.50: £5.10 £1.70 £2.30 (£34.70) Trio £141.50 OWNER Mr Bassam Freiha (LAMBOURN) BRED Sheikh Mohammed bin Rashid al Maktoum

Pure Nobility (IRE) ran no race at all on his debut but he was certainly much wiser this time and won very much as he pleased. A May foal, he could still be the one open to most improvement. (14/1: 10/1-16/1)

Freedom Quest (IRE), a sparely-made half-brother to a winner, ran green and got out-paced at a crucial time but he picked up in fine style in the closing stages and should have learned much from this. (7/4: 11/10-2/1)

3887 Rewardia (IRE), the only one with previous experience of the track, adopted more patient tactics and stayed on willingly inside the distance and she will get it right one of these days. (16/1)

3306 Prince Ashleigh, who shows plenty of knee action, was continuing his step up in distance. Never far away, he battled on well nearing the finish and is gradually getting it together. (10/1)

4113 The Magistrate (IRE) has shown a glimpse of promise in all his races so far and his turn will come. (10/1)

Elba Magic (IRE) (12/1: op 8/1)

4362 DEVA NURSERY H'CAP (2-Y.O) (Class D)

3-20 (3-22) **7f 2y** £4,396.50 (£1,332.00: £651.00: £310.50) Stalls: Low GOING: 0.12 sec per fur (G)

			SP	RR	SF
4230[4] **Burnt Yates (IRE) (67)** (MWEasterby) **2-8-11** SSanders(3) (hld up in tch: hdwy to ld over 1f out: rdn clr)	—	**1**	10/1	72	49
4061[15] **Montano (USA) (66)** (PFICole) **2-8-10** JFortune(2) (a.p: ev ch over 1f out: no ch w wnr)	2½	**2**	11/1	65	42
4285[3] **Inchalong (70)** (MBrittain) **2-9-0** NDay(6) (chsd ldr: led over 3f out tl over 1f out: sn rdn: one pce)	2	**3**	8/1[3]	65	42
4325[2] **Demolition Jo (76)** (PDEvans) **2-9-6v** JFEgan(10) (trckd ldrs: hdwy over 2f out: hrd rdn & one pce fnl f)	¾	**4**	7/1[2]	69	46
3819[4] **Sing For Me (IRE) (56)** (RHollinshead) **2-8-0** NCarlisle(7) (hld up: hdwy 3f out: rdn over 1f out: nt rch ldrs)	6	**5**	20/1	35	12
4116[20] **Balaclava (IRE) (77)** (EALDunlop) **2-9-7** KFallon(12) (pushed along ½-wy: hdwy 2f out: nt rch ldrs)	1¼	**6**	10/1	54	31
4006[8] **Robeena (71)** (CNAllen) **2-9-1** RCochrane(13) (bhd: effrt & drvn over 2f out: nvr nrr)	2	**7**	20/1	43	20
4166[2] **Positive Air (74)** (BAMcMahon) **2-9-4** MRoberts(4) (sn pushed along: a in rr)	¾	**8**	4/1[1]	44	21
3866[4] **Aviva Lady (IRE) (53)** (CADwyer) **2-7-4**(7)ow1 JFowle(14) (a in rr)	3¼	**9**	20/1	16	—
4152[15] **Shannon's Secret (IRE) (68)** (BJMeehan) **2-8-12b[1]** MTebbutt(1) (led over 3f: wknd fnl 2f)	2½	**10**	25/1	25	2
4178[3] **Junior Muffin (IRE) (73)** (JBerry) **2-8-12**(5) CLowther(5) (chsd ldrs tl outpcd fnl 2f)	3	**11**	10/1	23	—
4113[4] **Khattaff (IRE) (76)** (MajorWRHern) **2-9-6** RHills(8) (a in rr: t.o)	5	**12**	10/1	15	—
3869[2] **Boulevard Rouge (USA) (77)** (MJohnston) **2-9-7** DHolland(9) (lw: hld up in tch: drvn along ½-wy: sn wknd: t.o)	2½	**13**	10/1	10	—
1577[8] **Thanks Keith (66)** (JJO'Neill) **2-8-10b[1]** TWilliams(11) (bkwd: lost tch 3f out: sn t.o)	3	**14**	20/1	—	—
			(SP 120.3%) **14 Rn**		

1m 29.99 (4.79) CSF £95.23 CT £850.95 TOTE £12.80: £3.00 £3.50 £2.30 (£49.70) Trio £148.30 OWNER Mr I. Bray (SHERIFF HUTTON) BRED John Bernard O'Connor

LONG HANDICAP Aviva Lady (IRE) 7-9

OFFICIAL EXPLANATION **Positive Air: rider reported that the filly was never going.**

4230 Burnt Yates (IRE) has been beaten in sellers over sprint distances but he was always swinging along on the bridle at this first attempt at this more suitable trip, and he won this going away. (10/1)

2314 Montano (USA), pressing the leaders from the break, had his chance below the distance but, once the winner quickened the tempo, he had to admit he had met his match. (11/1)

4285 Inchalong took command soon after halfway and did her best to get away, but there were several rivals waiting to pounce and she was well out-paced in the dash to the post. (8/1)

4325 Demolition Jo, content to drop in behind the leaders on this second outing of the week, tried hard to mount a challenge turning in, but the pace was maintained and she was unable to deliver a challenge. (7/1)

3819 Sing For Me (IRE) came from off the pace but she was hard at work on the approach to the straight and failed to get competitive. (20/1)

3687 Balaclava (IRE), nudged along at halfway, did begin to stay on entering the last couple of furlongs but, with the pace not dropping, was unable to make his presence felt. (10/1)

4166 Positive Air usually stalks the leaders, but she was off the bit all the way round this very sharp track and was always nearer last than first. (4/1)

4363 WEATHERBYS INFORMATION TECHNOLOGY H'CAP (0-80) (3-Y.O+) (Class D)

3-50 (3-51) **1m 7f 195y** £4,123.50 (£1,248.00: £609.00: £289.50) Stalls: Low GOING: 0.12 sec per fur (G)

			SP	RR	SF
3974* **Forgie (IRE) (70)** (PCalver) **4-9-9** NDay(3) (lw: hld up: hdwy 6f out: led wl over 3f out: styd on strly)	—	**1**	17/2	81	63
4101[7] **Turnpole (IRE) (74)** (MrsMReveley) **6-9-13** ACulhane(2) (a chsng ldrs: hrd drvn 3f out: styd on ins fnl f)	1¼	**2**	5/1[2]	84	66
4246[2] **Etterby Park (USA) (70)** (MJohnston) **4-9-9** DHolland(6) (a.p: rdn 2f out: r.o one pce fnl f)	s.h	**3**	8/1	80	62
4108* **Alhosaam (78)** (MajorWRHern) **3-9-5** RHills(5) (hld up: hdwy & pushed along 6f out: hrd rdn 2f out: fin tired)	3½	**4**	9/2[1]	84	54
3805[4] **Beaumont (IRE) (74)** (JEBanks) **7-9-13** RCochrane(4) (hld up in rr: effrt over 5f out: nvr nr ldrs)	12	**5**	7/1[3]	68	50
New Inn (48) (SGollings) **6-8-1** TWilliams(1) (bkwd: led tl wl over 3f out: wknd 2f out)	2	**6**	33/1	40	22
Drama King (43) (BJLlewellyn) **5-7-10** JBramhill(9) (bkwd: chsd ldrs: rdn ½-wy: wknd 4f out)	1¼	**7**	100/1	34	16
4213* **Campaspe (72)** (JGFitzGerald) **5-9-11** 5x KFallon(11) (lw: hld up: hdwy 5f out: eased whn btn fnl 2f)	5	**8**	9/2[1]	58	40
4235[6] **Rex Mundi (66)** (PDEvans) **5-9-5** JFEgan(7) (chsd ldrs: hrd drvn over 2f out: sn btn)	3	**9**	12/1	49	31
3907[2] **Top (69)** (JRFanshawe) **3-8-10** MRoberts(10) (prom 10f: sn wknd: t.o)	dist	**10**	10/1	—	—
3623* **Great Oration (IRE) (67)** (FWatson) **8-9-6** JFortune(8) (a bhd: virtually p.u fnl f: t.o)	23	**11**	11/1	—	—
			(SP 116.2%) **11 Rn**		

3m 33.6 (10.70) CSF £45.55 CT £324.76 TOTE £11.30: £3.20 £2.10 £2.20 (£44.60) Trio £61.50 OWNER Mrs Janis MacPherson (RIPON) BRED Stilvi Compania Financiera And Roncon Ltd.

LONG HANDICAP Drama King 7-2

WEIGHT FOR AGE 3yo-12lb

3974* Forgie (IRE) is enjoying a very rewarding season and he had this prize sewn up from someway out. He has won on slightly faster ground but he does like to get his toe in and conditions still favoured him here. (17/2)

4101 Turnpole (IRE), travelling well behind the leaders, got tapped for toe when the winner kicked for home and, though he stayed on strongly inside the final furlong, was never going to reach him. Still to succeed beyond fourteen furlongs, he certainly has no stamina doubts. (5/1)

4246 Etterby Park (USA) did his best to keep tabs on the winner once that rival had struck the front, but he was soon at full stretch and his measure had been taken. (8/1)
4108* Alhosaam, taking on experienced stayers at this first attempt at the trip, failed to see it out and finished very leg-weary. (9/2)
New Inn, having his first outing since the spring, did look as though the run was needed but, setting a reasonable pace, he did not drop away after being headed and only called enough inside the final quarter-mile. He has not won on the Flat since 1995 but he did win over hurdles last season and that could be where his future lies. (33/1)
4213* Campaspe may well have found this ground softer than she really needs because she was beaten too far out for the excuse to be lack of stamina. (9/2)

4364 HESWALL CONDITIONS STKS (2-Y.O) (Class C)

4-20 (4-21) **7f 122y** £5,120.30 (£1,794.30: £879.65: £380.75) Stalls: Low GOING: 0.12 sec per fur (G)

				SP	RR	SF
3861*	**Mutamam** (ACStewart) **2-9-0** RHills(3) (hld up: hdwy on outside to ld 100y out: sn clr: impressive)	—	1	2/1 2	102++	26
4096 4	**Golden Dice (USA) (98)** (HRACecil) **2-9-0** KFallon(1) (lw: chsd ldr: led over 1f out tl hdd & one pce fnl f)	1¾	2	6/4 1	98	22
4266*	**Confirmation** (SirMarkPrescott) **2-9-5** SSanders(2) (lw: led tl over 1f out: sn hrd drvn: outpcd)	3	3	4/1 3	97	21
4044 3	**Kawafil (IRE) (92)** (PTWalwyn) **2-8-9** RCochrane(4) (hld up & bhd: hdwy 2f out: hrd drvn over 1f out: sn outpcd)	nk	4	5/1	86	10

(SP 110.0%) **4 Rn**

1m 39.62 (7.62) CSF £5.00 TOTE £3.20: (£2.50) OWNER Mr Hamdan Al Maktoum (NEWMARKET) BRED Biddestone Stud
3861* Mutamam was even more impressive than he was on his debut in this higher grade event and, at this stage, he does look a star in the making. (2/1)
4096 Golden Dice (USA) must have thought the prize was his after forging ahead below the distance, but the winner powered past him as if he was standing still. (6/4)
4266* Confirmation could have been attempting the impossible in trying to concede weight to the winner and only time will tell. (4/1)
4044 Kawafil (IRE), the only filly in the race, crept through on the inside to deliver her challenge entering the straight but, when the pace lifted again, she lacked the speed to hold her pitch. (5/1)

4365 TARPORLEY H'CAP (0-85) (3-Y.O+) (Class D)

4-55 (4-56) **5f 16y** £3,452.50 (£1,045.00: £510.00: £242.50) Stalls: Low GOING: 0.12 sec per fur (G)

				SP	RR	SF
4137 16	**Swan At Whalley (63)** (RAFahey) **5-8-6** RCochrane(3) (trckd ldrs: hdwy wl over 1f out: led ins fnl f: jst hld on)	—	1	13/2 2	70	47
3888 10	**Caution (70)** (SGollings) **3-8-12** KFallon(1) (sn pushed along & outpcd: rapid hdwy appr fnl f: fin fast)	hd	2	8/1 3	77	53
4233 7	**Lady Sheriff (85)** (MWEasterby) **6-10-0b** SSanders(9) (chsd ldrs: rdn over 1f out: r.o wl fnl f)	1	3	8/1 3	89	66
4155 21	**Sharp Pearl (84)** (PRWebber) **4-9-13b** JFortune(10) (lw: s.i.s: hdwy 2f out: r.o fnl f)	nk	4	9/1	87	64
4137 17	**Polly Golightly (55)** (MBlanshard) **4-7-12b** DaleGibson(8) (a.p: rdn to ld ins fnl f: sn hdd & unable qckn)	nk	5	20/1	57	34
4233 13	**Swino (73)** (PDEvans) **3-9-1** JFEgan(12) (bhd: hrd rdn 2f out: r.o wl towards fin)	nk	6	20/1	74	50
3856 10	**U-No-Harry (IRE) (56)** (RHollinshead) **4-7-13** NCarlisle(7) (b.nr fore: in tch: effrt & rdn over 1f out: one pce fnl f)	¾	7	16/1	54	31
4233 23	**Squire Corrie (83)** (DWChapman) **5-9-12** ACulhane(11) (lw: sn drvn along: prom: rdn & ev ch whn edgd lft jst ins fnl f)	nk	8	12/1	80	57
3709 9	**Top of The Form (IRE) (80)** (RAFahey) **3-9-1**(7) RWinston(6) (chsd ldrs: rdn whn squeezed out 200y out)	1½	9	12/1	73	49
4169 4	**Gi La High (62)** (MartynMeade) **4-8-5** FNorton(2) (outpcd)	hd	10	8/1 3	54	31
4183 3	**That Man Again (83)** (SCWilliams) **5-9-12v1** DHolland(4) (lw: outpcd: a bhd)	s.h	11	4/1 1	75	52
4137 19	**Princely Sound (61)** (JEBanks) **4-8-1**(3) DSweeney(13) (prom over 3f)	2½	12	16/1	45	22
*4051**	**Palacegate Jack (IRE) (68)** (JBerry) **6-8-8b**(3) TEDurcan(5) (lw: led tl hdd & wknd ins fnl f)	5	13	8/1 3	37	14

(SP 124.5%) **13 Rn**

63.43 secs (3.23) CSF £54.95 CT £400.97 TOTE £7.20: £2.30 £2.20 £3.70 (£19.00) Trio £80.20 OWNER Mrs C. M. Barlow (MALTON) BRED R. L. Cox
WEIGHT FOR AGE 3yo-1lb
STEWARDS' ENQUIRY Culhane susp. 6-7/10/97 (improper use of whip).
3900 Swan At Whalley, a winner over course and distance over three years ago, responded to these more patient tactics and, bursting through to take it up halfway through the final furlong, held on by the skin of his teeth. (13/2)
3199 Caution has never won at this trip and was unable to take advantage of her plum draw. The tail-ender turning in, she did have the gaps to make progress and, flying in the latter stages, only just failed to get up. (8/1: 16/1-7/1)
4233 Lady Sheriff had to work from her poor draw to stay within striking range of the leaders and, though she battled on gamely throughout the final furlong, was never quite going to make it. (8/1)
3771* Sharp Pearl would have been the unlucky one for he missed a beat at the start and had to come on the wide outside to finish on top of the principals. He should be given another chance. (9/1)
3600 Polly Golightly, much more effective on a livelier surface, worked hard to poke her nose in front two hundred yards out but the winner pounced and took her measure. (20/1)
3900 Swino needs a stiffer test on such a tight track but he is a trier and, responding to a forceful ride, ran on to be nearest at the finish. (20/1)
4183 That Man Again failed to hit the traps which is a must for him and, failing to take hold of his bit, ran very flat indeed. (4/1)

T/Plpt: £528.00 (47.77 Tckts). T/Qdpt: £149.70 (10.17 Tckts). IM

4153-GOODWOOD (R-H) (St crse Good, Rnd crse Good to firm)
Wednesday September 24th

WEATHER: fine WIND: mod half behind

4366 'GO HURDLING' (S) STKS (2-Y.O) (Class E)

2-00 (2-00) **1m 1f** £3,385.50 (£1,014.00: £487.00: £223.50) Stalls: High GOING minus 0.46 sec per fur (F)

				SP	RR	SF
4057 7	**Siena (GER) (53)** (MRChannon) **2-8-6** CandyMorris(13) (hdwy over 1f out: squeezed thro ins fnl f: led nr fin)	—	1	33/1	61	—
4058 2	**Constant Attention (63)** (PFICole) **2-8-6** TQuinn(3) (a.p: rdn over 3f out: r.o wl ins fnl f)	½	2	100/30 2	60	—
4157 6	**Royal Ground (IRE) (76)** (MRChannon) **2-8-11** GHind(4) (lw: a.p: rdn & hung lft 2f out: led over 1f out: wandered fnl f: hdd nr fin)	s.h	3	5/2 1	65	2

4058[3]	**Arm And A Leg (IRE) (56)** (CADwyer) **2-8-11** JReid(2) (lw: led over 5f: ev ch ins fnl f: one pce)	1¼	**4**	8/1	63	—
4157[10]	**Opportune (GER) (59)** (DRCElsworth) **2-8-8**(3) RFfrench(11) (nt clr run on ins over 3f out: hdwy over 2f out: nt clr run ins fnl f: nt rcvr)	s.h	**5**	12/1	63	—
4058*	**Francesca's Folly (57)** (JWHills) **2-8-3**(3) MHenry(7) (a.p: rdn over 3f out: ev ch over 1f out: one pce)	½	**6**	7/1[3]	57	—
4066[12]	**Five Fairies** (NACallaghan) **2-8-6** SDrowne(1) (lw: chsd ldr: led over 3f out tl over 1f out: one pce ins fnl f)	½	**7**	7/1[3]	56	—
4054[9]	**Muja's Magic (IRE) (50)** (KTIvory) **2-8-6** NAdams(12) (bhd fnl 2f)	4	**8**	16/1	49	—
3294[3]	**Shalabella (IRE) (53)** (MRChannon) **2-8-6** JCarroll(6) (bhd fnl 3f)	18	**9**	12/1	17	—
3598[18]	**Erika's Young Man (40)** (MJHaynes) **2-8-4**(7) MCornally(10) (lw: a bhd)	5	**10**	33/1	13	—
3742[8]	**Far-So-La (40)** (TMJones) **2-8-11b**[1] RPerham(8) (b.nr hind: plld hrd: bhd fnl 3f)	8	**11**	50/1	—	—
	Pride of Fashion (SGKnight) **2-8-11** VSlattery(5) (str: bkwd: dwlt: a bhd: t.o fnl 5f)	dist	**12**	50/1	—	—
				(SP 118.8%)	**12 Rn**	

1m 59.72 (6.72) CSF £126.69 TOTE £65.50: £10.90 £1.30 £1.50 (£131.50) Trio £152.40 OWNER Mr M. Channon (UPPER LAMBOURN) BRED H. Leisten

No bid. Opportune (GER) clmd R Reynolds £6,000, Constant Attention clmd A Stafford £6,000

Siena (GER) appreciated the drop in class and left previous form behind under a cool ride, coming with a nice run from below the distance and squeezing through to get up near the line. (33/1)

4058 Constant Attention again showed she needs a trip for, after going nowhere early in the straight, she was running on in good style inside the final furlong. (100/30)

Royal Ground (IRE) was taking a drop in class but certainly gave his rider steering problems in the straight. Nevertheless, he got to the front approaching the final furlong, only to be worried out of it in the closing stages. (5/2: 6/4-11/4)

4058 Arm And A Leg (IRE) took the field along and, although collared early in the straight, refused to give way and still had every chance inside the final furlong, before tapped for toe. This is his level. (8/1)

Opportune (GER), taking a big drop in class, had no luck in running but still ran his best race to date. Again denied a clear passage inside the final furlong, he could never really recover but was staying on nicely at the death. (12/1)

4058* Francesca's Folly had every chance below the distance before tapped for toe. (7/1)

4367 ST. IVEL 'GOLD CUP' MAIDEN STKS (2-Y.O) (Class D)

2-30 (2-31) **1m** £3,720.00 (£1,110.00: £530.00: £240.00) Stalls: High GOING minus 0.46 sec per fur (F)

				SP	RR	SF
4132[3]	**Mutawwaj (IRE) (100)** (SbinSuroor) **2-9-0** JReid(2) (a.p: led over 1f out: edgd rt ins fnl f: rdn out)	—	**1**	10/11[1]	91	42
2720[3]	**Achilles** (RAkehurst) **2-9-0** JWeaver(7) (led 3f: led over 3f out tl over 1f out: r.o)	¾	**2**	10/1[3]	90	41
4105[3]	**Lear Spear (USA)** (DRCElsworth) **2-9-0** SDrowne(6) (lw: a.p: rdn over 2f out: unable qckn)	3½	**3**	10/1[3]	83	34
	High Tension (USA) (PFICole) **2-9-0** TQuinn(8) (leggy: scope: lw: a.p: led 5f out tl over 3f out: wknd over 1f out)	4	**4**	9/4[2]	75	26
4061[8]	**Allgrit (USA)** (EALDunlop) **2-9-0** MRimmer(3) (lw: rdn & no hdwy fnl 3f)	hd	**5**	14/1	74	25
3386[9]	**St Enodoc (FR)** (JLDunlop) **2-9-0** TSprake(4) (lw: a bhd)	5	**6**	20/1	64	15
	Santarene (IRE) (PHowling) **2-8-9** PaulEddery(1) (b.nr hind: leggy: a bhd)	5	**7**	66/1	49	—
3760[8]	**Right Cross Jonny (USA)** (PWChapple-Hyam) **2-8-11**(3) RHavlin(5) (lw: s.s: nvr gng wl: a bhd)	24	**8**	33/1	6	—
				(SP 117.2%)	**8 Rn**	

1m 38.94 (0.50 under 2y best) (1.74) CSF £10.83 TOTE £2.00: £1.10 £2.20 £2.20 (£5.00) OWNER Godolphin (NEWMARKET) BRED Shadwell Estate Company Limited

4132 Mutawwaj (IRE) at last came good and, gaining a slender advantage approaching the final furlong, was ridden along to score. (10/11: 4/6-evens)

2720 Achilles appreciated the longer trip and ran a first-class race after a ten week break. Regaining the advantage early in the straight, he was collared approaching the final furlong but refused to go down without a fight and finished well clear of the remainder. He should soon go one better. (10/1)

4105 Lear Spear (USA) was never far away but failed to find that vital turn of foot in the final quarter-mile. (10/1: op 6/1)

High Tension (USA), who cost $625,000 as a yearling, is quite a tall individual. He showed plenty of promise on his debut and only tired below the distance. Entered for some decent races, he should soon find a suitable event. (9/4)

4061 Allgrit (USA) was making little impression on the principals in the straight. (14/1)

4368 SCOTTISH EQUITABLE AUCTION STKS (2-Y.O) (Class C)

3-00 (3-00) **7f** £4,802.00 (£1,778.00: £854.00: £350.00: £140.00: £56.00) Stalls: High GOING minus 0.46 sec per fur (F)

				SP	RR	SF
3235[7]	**Imshishway (IRE)** (BJMeehan) **2-8-10** KDarley(8) (nt clr run over 3f out: swtchd lft & hdwy over 1f out: led wl ins fnl f: r.o wl)	—	**1**	14/1	83	25
4143*	**Titan (76)** (SDow) **2-8-4** TQuinn(7) (lw: s.s: hdwy 2f out: led over 1f out tl wl ins fnl f: unable qckn)	½	**2**	9/1	76	18
4014[3]	**Madame Jones (IRE)** (BJMeehan) **2-7-13** JQuinn(2) (hld up: hrd rdn & edgd rt 1f out: ev ch ins fnl f: one pce)	1¼	**3**	16/1	68	10
4209*	**Central Committee (IRE)** (PWChapple-Hyam) **2-8-9** JReid(1) (a.p: ev ch & n.m.r over 1f out: bmpd ins fnl f: one pce)	s.h	**4**	11/8[1]	78	20
4007[15]	**Lauren's Lad (45)** (GLewis) **2-8-4b**[1] PaulEddery(3) (led over 4f: ev ch whn bmpd ins fnl f: one pce)	1¾	**5**	50/1	69	11
4140[4]	**Priceless (90)** (WJHaggas) **2-8-8** FLynch(6) (hld up: nt clr run & swtchd rt over 1f out: n.m.r & hmpd on ins ins fnl f)	¾	**6**	5/1[3]	71+	13
3819*	**Czar Wars (72)** (PTDalton) **2-8-1** LCharnock(5) (lw: chsd ldr over 3f: wknd over 1f out)	2	**7**	10/1	50	2
3780[2]	**Bettron** (RHannon) **2-7-12**(3) RFfrench(4) (a.p: led over 2f out tl over 1f out: btn whn hmpd 1f out)	hd	**8**	9/2[2]	49	1
				(SP 110.6%)	**8 Rn**	

1m 27.55 (2.75) CSF £111.56 TOTE £26.50: £4.40 £1.80 £2.50 (£60.10) OWNER Mr A. S. Helaissi (UPPER LAMBOURN) BRED Hugo Merry

3235 Imshishway (IRE) left his two previous runs well behind, coming with a good rattle on the outside of the field to snatch the spoils in the closing stages. (14/1)

4143* Titan, successful over this course and distance last time out, moved up to lead below the distance but was unable to contain the winner in the closing stages. (9/1: op 6/1)

4014 Madame Jones (IRE) continues to progress and was happy by the step up to seven furlongs. Drifting right under pressure from below the distance, resulting in a concertina effect which caused interference inside the final furlong, she was tapped for toe in the last one hundred yards. (16/1)

4209* Central Committee (IRE) may not have had a great deal of room to manoeuvre in the final quarter-mile but lack of acceleration prevented him from getting out of trouble. He definitely needs further. (11/8)

Lauren's Lad took the field along and, although collared over a quarter of a mile from home, was still battling hard for the advantage when given a bump inside the final furlong as several runners tightened up. (50/1)

4140 Priceless was better suited by the return to seven furlongs and drop in class but had a nightmare run. Switched over to the rails below the distance in an attempt to get a clear passage, he tried to go for a narrow gap along the inside rail inside the final furlong, resulting in him getting badly hampered. But for this, he would certainly have finished a lot closer. (5/1: 7/2-11/2)

4369 R.O.A. FOUNDATION STKS (Listed) (3-Y.O+) (Class A)

3-30 (3-31) **1m 2f** £17,300.00 (£5,150.00: £2,450.00: £1,100.00) Stalls: High GOING minus 0.46 sec per fur (F)

				SP	RR	SF
4141*	**Danish Rhapsody (IRE) (100)** (LadyHerries) **4-9-0** PaulEddery(1) (lw: mde all: rdn out)	—	**1**	$3/1^{2}$	111	39
4272^{4}	**Proper Blue (USA) (105)** (TGMills) **4-9-0** TQuinn(4) (nt clr run over 3f out: swtchd lft over 1f out: hdwy fnl f: r.o wl)	½	**2**	$4/1^{3}$	110	38
4252a*	**Sandstone (IRE) (108)** (JLDunlop) **3-8-8** TSprake(3) (hld up: rdn over 2f out: r.o ins fnl f)	s.h	**3**	$11/8^{1}$	110	32
$4125a^{4}$	**Running Stag (USA) (107)** (PMitchell) **3-8-8** AClark(5) (lw: hld up: nt clr run over 2f out: chsd wnr over 1f out tl wl ins fnl f: unable qckn)	¾	**4**	9/2	109	31
3738*	**Lonely Heart (77)** (DRCElsworth) **3-8-3** SDrowne(2) (lw: chsd wnr over 8f)	2½	**5**	20/1	100	22

(SP 110.0%) **5 Rn**

2m 9.43 (2.83) CSF £13.53 TOTE £2.70: £1.80 £1.90 (£6.50) OWNER Mr Chris Hardy (LITTLEHAMPTON) BRED Grangemore Stud

WEIGHT FOR AGE 3yo-6lb

4141* Danish Rhapsody (IRE) continues to go from strength to strength and landed his fifth race of the season under a masterly ride from Eddery. Setting a brisk pace for the first couple of furlongs as he established himself in front, Eddery then slowed the tempo right down going to the top of the hill and the runners were almost at a crawl. Quickening things up again over a quarter of a mile from home, he soon had his rivals at full stretch and was not going to be denied as he landed his first Pattern race. He is a real credit to his trainer. (3/1)

4272 Proper Blue (USA) appreciated the return to a fast surface and was held up at the back of the field. Pulled out below the distance, he found his feet in the final furlong but the line was always coming too soon. Over this trip and on this ground, he can find a race before the season is out. (4/1)

4252a* Sandstone (IRE) was nicely placed early in the straight but, when the winner quickened the tempo over a quarter of a mile from home, he was unable to respond immediately. He did run on inside the final furlong and only just failed in his bid for second prize. (11/8)

4389a Running Stag (USA) was not really helped by the slow pace and, although he moved into second position below the distance, he was tapped for toe and worried out of it in the closing stages. (9/2)

3738* Lonely Heart was out of her depth here but held onto second place until below the distance. (20/1)

4370 FRIALATOR INTERNATIONAL H'CAP (0-70) (3-Y.O+) (Class E)

4-00 (4-04) **5f** £4,175.00 (£1,250.00: £600.00: £275.00) Stalls: Low GOING minus 0.31 sec per fur (GF)

				SP	RR	SF
4329^{6}	**Beau Venture (USA) (65)** (BPalling) **9-9-11** TSprake(20) (lw: a.p: led over 1f out: rdn out)	—	**1**	$9/1^{3}$	75	58
4233^{19}	**Flying Harold (45)** (MRChannon) **4-8-5** JCarroll(8) (s.s: hdwy on ins over 1f out: r.o wl ins fnl f)	½	**2**	20/1	53	36
	Lucy In The Sky (IRE) (39) (BJMeehan) **3-7-12**^{ow2} CRutter(1) (hdwy over 1f out: r.o wl ins fnl f)	nk	**3**	50/1	46	26
4115^{2}	**Songsheet (68)** (MSSaunders) **4-9-11**$^{(3)}$ PPMurphy(4) (lw: hdwy over 1f out: r.o ins fnl f)	¾	**4**	$9/1^{3}$	73	56
3898^{5}	**Half Tone (61)** (RMFlower) **5-9-7b** TQuinn(7) (hld up: rdn over 2f out: r.o ins fnl f)	s.h	**5**	12/1	66	49
3898*	**Sweet Magic (63)** (PHowling) **6-9-9** KDarley(3) (a.p: rdn over 1f out: unable qckn ins fnl f)	s.h	**6**	$8/1^{2}$	68	51
4183^{11}	**Anokato (63)** (KTIvory) **3-9-1b**$^{(7)}$ CCassidy(19) (hdwy over 1f out: one pce ins fnl f)	s.h	**7**	33/1	68	50
4047^{7}	**Dancing Mystery (45)** (EAWheeler) **3-7-13b**$^{(5)}$ ADaly(17) (hld up: rdn over 1f out: one pce)	nk	**8**	25/1	49	31
4047^{9}	**Churchill's Shadow (IRE) (45)** (BAPearce) **3-8-4** DRMcCabe(9) (hdwy 1f out: r.o ins fnl f)	hd	**9**	25/1	48	30
3590^{4}	**Friendly Brave (USA) (60)** (MissGayKelleway) **7-9-3**$^{(3)}$ RFfrench(15) (lw: rdn over 2f out: hdwy over 1f out: one pce ins fnl f)	¾	**10**	$7/1^{1}$	61	44
3771^{7}	**Tart and a Half (61)** (MPitman) **5-9-4**$^{(3)}$ MHenry(18) (lw: a.p: ev ch ins fnl f: sn wknd)	¾	**11**	16/1	60	43
4137^{9}	**Tear White (IRE) (69)** (TGMills) **3-10-0** JQuinn(2) (lw: led over 3f)	s.h	**12**	11/1	67	49
4248^{5}	**Bright Paragon (IRE) (41)** (KTIvory) **8-8-1** MartinDwyer(12) (b: a.p: hrd rdn over 1f out: wknd fnl f)	½	**13**	14/1	38	21
4155^{7}	**Scissor Ridge (60)** (JJBridger) **5-8-13**$^{(7)}$ RBrisland(11) (hld up: rdn over 2f out: wknd over 1f out)	¾	**14**	$8/1^{2}$	54	37
3580^{8}	**The Fugative (64)** (PMitchell) **4-9-10** JReid(14) (lw: rdn over 2f out: hdwy over 1f out: wknd ins fnl f)	nk	**15**	14/1	57	40
4221^{7}	**Windrush Boy (46)** (MRBosley) **7-8-1**$^{(5)}$ AimeeCook(21) (hdwy 1f out: wknd ins fnl f)	1¼	**16**	25/1	35	18
4168^{10}	**Smiling Bess (36)** (JSKing) **4-7-5**$^{(5)}$ APolli(23) (swtg: a bhd)	3	**17**	50/1	16	—
4051^{5}	**Kalar (38)** (DWChapman) **8-7-12b** LCharnock(5) (bhd fnl 3f)	½	**18**	25/1	16	—
3922^{14}	**Kabcast (36)** (DWChapman) **12-7-10b** DWright(13) (prom over 3f)	½	**19**	20/1	13	—
4008^{10}	**Il Doria (IRE) (43)** (AHide) **4-8-3** AMcGlone(6) (prom 3f)	3	**20**	50/1	10	—
3280^{14}	**Ashkernazy (IRE) (46)** (NEBerry) **6-8-6** NAdams(16) (prom 2f)	¾	**21**	20/1	11	—
	Wychwood Sandy (43) (HJCollingridge) **6-8-3** MFenton(22) (b: bit bkwd: prom 3f)	¾	**22**	50/1	5	—
4048^{14}	**Pride of Hayling (IRE) (55)** (PRHedger) **6-9-1b**^{1} SDrowne(10) (lw: bhd tl broke leg & fell over 2f out: dead)		**F**	12/1	—	—

(SP 138.1%) **23 Rn**

58.0 secs (1.30) CSF £173.90 CT £7,711.50 TOTE £10.50: £2.60 £4.20 £10.50 £3.60 (£106.50) Trio Not won; £2,048.70 to Pontefract 25/9/97 OWNER Mrs A. L. Stacey (COWBRIDGE) BRED Mrs C. Oliver Iselin III

LONG HANDICAP Smiling Bess 7-6 Lucy In The Sky (IRE) 7-1

WEIGHT FOR AGE 3yo-1lb

4329 Beau Venture (USA) showed no ill effects of his race at Leicester just two days ago and, striking the front in the centre of the course approaching the final furlong, was ridden along to keep his rivals at bay. (9/1)

4115 Flying Harold, who lost ground at the start, really found his feet from below the distance but, despite absolutely flying, found the line just beating him. He has just one win to his name. (20/1)

Lucy In The Sky (IRE), an ex-Irish filly, showed her first sign of ability, despite carrying 11lb more than her long handicap weight. Taking a drastic drop in distance, having competed over one mile five furlongs last time out, she ran on in good style in the last furlong and a half to finish an encouraging third. Sprint distances are obviously the answer to her. (50/1)

4115 Songsheet found her feet from below the distance but, despite running on, was not going to get there in time. She has done all her winning at this trip. (9/1)

3898 Half Tone was going nowhere over a quarter of a mile from home, but did stay on inside the final furlong. (12/1)

3898* Sweet Magic, given an enterprising ride to win at Sandown last time out, was always to the fore but failed to quicken inside the final furlong. (8/1)

4371 WATSON AND PHILIP CLAIMING H'CAP (0-60) (I) (3-Y.O+) (Class E)

4-35 (4-38) **1m** £3,947.50 (£1,180.00: £565.00: £257.50) Stalls: High GOING minus 0.46 sec per fur (F)

				SP	RR	SF
*4069**	**Harlequin Walk (IRE) (34)** (RJO'Sullivan) **6-8-4** JQuinn(10) (a.p: rdn over 2f out: led over 1f out: drvn out)	—	**1**	8/1^{3}	50	22
4114^{3}	**Dancing Lawyer (44)** (KRBurke) **6-9-0** DaneO'Neill(21) (hdwy over 2f out: rdn wl over 1f out: chsd wnr ins fnl f: unable qckn)	1¼	**2**	10/1	58	30
4069^{9}	**Cabcharge Blue (36)** (TJNaughton) **5-8-6** TSprake(11) (hld up: nt clr run over 2f out: r.o ins fnl f)	½	**3**	33/1	49	21
4179^{11}	**Lord Oberon (IRE) (51)** (JAkehurst) **9-9-7** GCarter(18) (rdn over 2f out: hdwy over 1f out: r.o ins fnl f)	2	**4**	7/1^{2}	60	32
4210^{2}	**Mbulwa (51)** (RAFahey) **11-9-7** LCharnock(19) (chsd ldr 6f out: led over 2f out tl over 1f out: wknd ins fnl f)	nk	**5**	11/4^{1}	59	31
3969^{6}	**Without Friends (IRE) (46)** (JFfitch-Heyes) **3-8-12** JWeaver(14) (swtg: rdn over 2f out: hdwy over 1f out: r.o ins fnl f)	hd	**6**	16/1	54	22
3767^{10}	**Multi Franchise (44)** (RMFlower) **4-9-0b** MartinDwyer(12) (swtg: a.p: rdn over 2f out: one pce)	¾	**7**	16/1	50	22
4224^{6}	**Mr Rough (53)** (DMorris) **6-9-9v** SWhitworth(9) (lw: rdn over 3f out: hdwy on ins over 2f out: nt clr run on ins over 1f out: swtchd lft: one pce)	¾	**8**	16/1	58	30
4248^{2}	**Oxbane (49)** (CADwyer) **3-8-12**(3) RFfrench(1) (lw: a mid div)	4	**9**	10/1	46	14
3860^{8}	**Invocation (45)** (GLMoore) **10-9-1** AClark(5) (lw: a mid div)	s.h	**10**	20/1	42	14
3972^{4}	**South China Sea (54)** (PFICole) **3-9-6** TQuinn(6) (prom over 5f)	¾	**11**	16/1	49	17
3640^{3}	**Country Thatch (45)** (CAHorgan) **4-9-1** PaulEddery(8) (a mid div)	½	**12**	11/1	39	11
3227^{13}	**Little Pilgrim (35)** (TMJones) **4-8-5** AMcGlone(3) (lw: nvr nrr)	hd	**13**	20/1	29	1
76^{9}	**Memory's Music (38)** (MMadgwick) **5-8-8** NVarley(2) (a mid div)	nk	**14**	33/1	31	3
4050^{6}	**Three Weeks (40)** (WRMuir) **4-8-10** SophieMitchell(17) (lw: a bhd)	¾	**15**	33/1	32	4
4158^{6}	**Norman Conquest (USA) (58)** (IABalding) **3-9-10v^{1}** KDarley(22) (lw: led 6f out tl over 2f out: wknd over 1f out)	1¼	**16**	14/1	47	15
3496^{11}	**Soaking (43)** (MDIUsher) **7-8-13** DRMcCabe(13) (a bhd)	4	**17**	12/1	24	—
	Great Bear (40) (DWChapman) **5-8-10** DWright(16) (led 2f: wknd over 3f out)	12	**18**	33/1	—	—
124^{15}	**Nattie (45)** (CJHill) **3-8-6b^{1}**(5) APolli(20) (s.s: a bhd)	1¼	**19**	25/1	—	—
2670^{8}	**Forget To Remindme (48)** (JSMoore) **3-8-11**(3) PPMurphy(4) (a bhd)	10	**20**	20/1	—	—

(SP 144.6%) **20 Rn**

1m 40.08 (2.88) CSF £81.88 CT £2,399.04 TOTE £7.80: £1.70 £2.10 £9.80 £2.50 (£45.10) Trio £1,048.00; £590.46 to Pontefract 25/9/97 OWNER Mrs R. J. Doorgachurn (WHITCOMBE) BRED Ronnie Boland in Ireland

WEIGHT FOR AGE 3yo-4lb

4069* Harlequin Walk (IRE) coped with the drop in distance and, leading approaching the final furlong, responded to pressure and kept on well. (8/1: op 5/1)

4114 Dancing Lawyer has been badly out of form until running much better last time out. He showed that effort to be no flash in the pan and moved into second place inside the final furlong, if unable to reel in the winner. (10/1)

Cabcharge Blue ran her best race for a very long time, running on nicely inside the final furlong. She has not won on turf for nearly three years. (33/1)

3392 Lord Oberon (IRE) picked up ground below the distance and ran on inside the final furlong to take fourth prize. All eight of his wins have come over this distance on ground no worse than good. (7/1)

4210 Mbulwa moved to the front over a quarter of a mile from home but, collared below the distance, was soon hung out to dry. (11/4)

2947 Without Friends (IRE) has been exposed as extremely moderate and, although running on from below the distance, not too much should be read into this. (16/1)

4248 Oxbane (10/1: 6/1-11/1)

3640 Country Thatch (11/1: 6/1-12/1)

4372 MERBURY CATERING CONSULTANTS H'CAP (0-80) (3-Y.O) (Class D)

5-05 (5-05) **1m 4f** £3,817.50 (£1,140.00: £545.00: £247.50) Stalls: Low GOING minus 0.46 sec per fur (F)

				SP	RR	SF
1405^{3}	**Zibeth (54)** (SDow) **3-7-3**(7) PDoe(5) (lw: hld up: led 7f out: hrd rdn & hung bdly lft 2f out: r.o wl)	—	**1**	25/1	65	8
4109^{13}	**Seattle Swing (76)** (MrsAJPerrett) **3-9-4** JReid(8) (lw: a.p: ev ch fnl 2f: r.o)	¾	**2**	10/1^{3}	86	29
3234*	**Prince Alex (IRE) (67)** (ACStewart) **3-8-9** SWhitworth(1) (lw: rdn over 3f out: hdwy 2f out: edgd lft 1f out: r.o)	nk	**3**	4/1^{2}	77	20
3915^{7}	**Royal Castle (IRE) (74)** (MajorWRHern) **3-9-2** TSprake(2) (lw: a.p: rdn over 3f out: r.o wl ins fnl f)	s.h	**4**	3/1^{1}	84	27
4179^{6}	**Herbshan Dancer (56)** (BRMillman) **3-7-9**(3) RFfrench(3) (lw: rdn over 3f out: hung bdly lft 2f out: nvr nr to chal)	7	**5**	12/1	56	—
4144^{2}	**Pennys From Heaven (79)** (HCandy) **3-9-7** TQuinn(4) (a bhd)	5	**6**	3/1^{1}	73	16
4072^{3}	**Snow Partridge (USA) (78)** (PFICole) **3-9-6b^{1}** KDarley(6) (lw: hld up: rdn over 3f out: wknd over 1f out)	1½	**7**	11/1	70	13
4176^{17}	**Olivo (IRE) (70)** (CAHorgan) **3-8-12** PaulEddery(7) (led 5f: wknd over 3f out)	10	**8**	14/1	48	—
2910^{4}	**Action Stations (59)** (CACyzer) **3-8-1v^{1}** MartinDwyer(9) (lw: a bhd)	1¾	**9**	25/1	35	—

(SP 109.5%) **9 Rn**

2m 38.99 (5.79) CSF £211.80 CT £1,029.43 TOTE £21.40: £3.20 £2.90 £1.80 (£58.10) Trio £203.90 OWNER Mr J. E. Mills (EPSOM) BRED Sheikh Mohammed Bin Rashid Al Maktoum

1405 Zibeth, who has changed stables since her last run four months ago, moved to the front fully seven furlongs from home. Hanging badly left in the straight, resulting in her ending up on the stands' rail, she managed to keep the persistent runner-up at bay. (25/1)

3466* Seattle Swing saw out this longer trip and threw down a determined challenge in the centre of the course. She may well have got her head in front for a few strides but unfortunately did not have it in front where it really mattered. (10/1)

3234* Prince Alex (IRE) began to pick up ground a quarter of a mile from home, but he too ended up on the stands' rails and only just failed to take second prize. (4/1: op 5/2)

1649* Royal Castle (IRE) appreciated the return to a sound surface but he was off the bridle and going nowhere early in the straight. However, he got his second wind inside the final furlong and, running on, only just failed to take third prize. (3/1)

4179 Herbshan Dancer, another who hung badly left ending up on the stands' rails, never threatened to get into it. He remains a maiden and would probably be helped by a bit of rain. (12/1)

4373 WATSON AND PHILIP CLAIMING H'CAP (0-60) (II) (3-Y.O+) (Class E)

5-35 (5-37) **1m** £3,915.00 (£1,170.00: £560.00: £255.00) Stalls: High GOING minus 0.46 sec per fur (F)

				SP	RR	SF
4043^{9}	**Mac Oates (44)** (PRHedger) **4-8-9**(5) ADaly(10) (lw: n.m.r over 3f out: hdwy over 2f out: led over 1f out: rdn out)	—	**1**	16/1	57	32

			SP	RR	SF
3860[12] **Rawi (45)** (MissGayKelleway) **4-9-1b** JCarroll(3) (lw: a.p: led 2f out tl over 1f out: unable qckn)	1¼	**2**	14/1 3	56	31
4114[7] **Mimosa (51)** (SDow) **4-9-7** TQuinn(22) (hdwy over 1f out: str run fnl f: fin wl)	1½	**3**	10/1 2	59	34
4179[4] **Ring the Chief (37)** (MDIUsher) **5-8-0**(7) GHannon(18) (a.p: rdn over 2f out: one pce)	nk	**4**	4/1 1	44	19
4184[13] **Gresatre (48)** (CADwyer) **3-9-0v** KDarley(20) (hdwy over 2f out: hrd rdn over 1f out: one pce)	½	**5**	16/1	54	25
3787[9] **Fancy Design (IRE) (42)** (PMitchell) **4-8-7**(5) AimeeCook(14) (b.hind: lw: hdwy 2f out: hrd rdn over 1f out: r.o one pce)	s.h	**6**	20/1	48	23
4139[2] **Step On Degas (54)** (MJFetherston-Godley) **4-9-7**(3) RFfrench(11) (led 6f: wknd fnl f)	½	**7**	4/1 1	59	34
4112[14] **Scathebury (50)** (KRBurke) **4-9-6** DaneO'Neill(6) (lw: rdn over 2f out: hdwy over 1f out: nvr nrr)	4	**8**	10/1 2	47	22
3573[7] **Prime Partner (35)** (TDEasterby) **4-8-5** LCharnock(2) (nvr nr to chal)	hd	**9**	14/1 3	32	7
4008[8] **Velvet Jones (40)** (GFHCharles-Jones) **4-8-10** SWhitworth(4) (rdn over 3f out: nvr nrr)	nk	**10**	20/1	36	11
4228[7] **Racing Telegraph (40)** (CNAllen) **7-8-10b1** MartinDwyer(21) (lw: prom 6f)	nk	**11**	16/1	35	10
3561[7] **Jubilee Scholar (IRE) (38)** (GLMoore) **4-8-8** JQuinn(17) (nvr nrr)	2½	**12**	16/1	28	3
3849[11] **King Parrot (IRE) (47)** (LordHuntingdon) **9-8-10**(7) CCogan(15) (lw: prom over 5f)	1¼	**13**	10/1 2	35	10
3465[17] **Deevee (42)** (CJBenstead) **8-8-12** JReid(5) (lw: s.s: nvr nrr)	2½	**14**	20/1	25	—
2006[23] **Belzao (53)** (RSimpson) **4-9-9** MGallagher(13) (hld up: rdn over 3f out: wknd over 2f out)	2½	**15**	33/1	31	6
3420[10] **Southern Memories (IRE) (40)** (WJMusson) **7-8-10** DRMcCabe(19) (prom 6f)	hd	**16**	20/1	18	—
3787[10] **La Chatelaine (47)** (GLewis) **3-8-13** PaulEddery(12) (a bhd)	1¼	**17**	14/1 3	22	—
4008[15] **Trevor Mitchell (37)** (JJBridger) **3-7-10**(7) PDoe(9) (bhd fnl 2f)	hd	**18**	50/1	12	—
3029[10] **Prince Zizim (32)** (RCSpicer) **4-7-11**(5) RMullen(8) (swtg: bhd fnl 2f)	1¼	**19**	33/1	5	—
4047[12] **Geordie Lad (38)** (JABennett) **3-8-4** TSprake(1) (bhd fnl 3f)	hd	**20**	33/1	10	—
3276[8] **Mediate (IRE) (36)** (AHide) **5-8-6v** AMcGlone(7) (lw: s.i.s: a bhd)	1½	**21**	33/1	5	—
3640[9] **Karachi (45)** (RJO'Sullivan) **7-9-1** AClark(16) (bhd fnl 3f)	13	**22**	20/1	—	—
			(SP 148.3%)	**22 Rn**	

1m 39.96 (2.76) CSF £212.67 CT £2,237.54 TOTE £31.60: £4.80 £3.60 £4.40 £1.50 (£171.30) Trio Not won; £1,445.05 to Pontefract 25/9/97
OWNER Mr D. N. Larke (CHICHESTER) BRED D. N. Larke
WEIGHT FOR AGE 3yo-4lb
Mimosa clmd M Pitman £8,000

Mac Oates has fallen in the handicap and, striking the front approaching the final furlong was ridden along to lose his maiden tag. (16/1)
3261 Rawi cruised into the lead a quarter of a mile from home but, collared by the winner approaching the final furlong, failed to find another gear. All three of his wins to date have come over seven furlongs. (14/1)
3787 Mimosa began a forward move below the distance and going into overdrive in the final furlong, finished in tremendous style. She is not easy to win with and has just one victory from thirty-four starts. (10/1: tchd 16/1)
4179 Ring the Chief was always close up but failed to find the necessary turn of foot in the last furlong and a half. All three of his wins to date have come over seven furlongs. (4/1)
3749 Gresatre took closer order over a quarter of a mile from home but could then only go up and down in the same place. He has just one win from twenty-six starts to his name. (16/1)
2918 Fancy Design (IRE) took closer order a quarter of a mile from home and struggled on without finding that vital turn of foot. She remains a maiden after twenty-six attempts. (20/1)
4139 Step On Degas (4/1: 3/1-9/2)
3573 Prime Partner (14/1: 10/1-16/1)
3558* La Chatelaine (14/1: 8/1-16/1)

T/Jkpt: Not won; £20,253.23 to Goodwood 25/9/97. T/Plpt: £617.80 (45.18 Tckts). T/Qdpt: £487.30 (2.58 Tckts) AK

4366-GOODWOOD (R-H) (Rnd Good to firm, St Good)
Thursday September 25th

WEATHER: fine WIND: almost nil

4374 UCELLO II AND UBU III TROPHY (NATIONAL HUNT JOCKEYS) H'CAP (0-70) (3-Y.O+) (Class E)

2-00 (2-01) **2m** £3,663.75 (£1,110.00: £542.50: £258.75) Stalls: Low GOING minus 0.46 sec per fur (F)

			SP	RR	SF
Father Sky (63) (OSherwood) **6-11-8b** JAMcCarthy(5) (b: hld up: hdwy over 3f out: chsd ldr over 2f out: led over 1f out: r.o)	—	**1**	12/1	77	65
Wilkins (48) (RJO'Sullivan) **8-10-7** AMcCabe(11) (a.p: led ½-wy: hdd over 1f out: one pce)	2	**2**	12/1	60	48
3864[3] **Palaemon (57)** (GBBalding) **3-10-4** BFenton(8) (chsd ldrs: rdn 3f out: styd on one pce fnl 2f)	3½	**3**	6/1 3	66	42
4170[5] **Hillswick (41)** (JSKing) **6-10-0** TJMurphy(7) (led 1f: styd prom: rdn 3f out: one pce)	hd	**4**	6/1 3	49	37
4046[10] **Sandy Floss (IRE) (63)** (JSKing) **4-11-8** BPowell(2) (a.p: chsd ldr over 5f out tl over 2f out: grad wknd)	s.h	**5**	25/1	71	59
3928[2] **Red Raja (58)** (PMitchell) **4-11-3** MRichards(6) (hld up: rdn 4f out: kpt on one pce fnl 2f)	1½	**6**	7/2 1	65	53
4104[2] **Durham (65)** (GLMoore) **6-11-10b** DGallagher(9) (hld up: hdwy over 3f out: wknd 2f out)	1¼	**7**	4/1 2	71	59
Chief's Song (42) (SDow) **7-10-1** JRKavanagh(3) (hld up: rdn 3f out: no hdwy)	3½	**8**	10/1	44	32
3689[8] **Nordansk (54)** (MMadgwick) **8-10-13** MAFitzgerald(13) (nvr nrr)	s.h	**9**	12/1	56	44
3983[4] **Ginka (41)** (JWMullins) **6-10-0** SCurran(12) (led after 1f: hdd ½-wy: wknd over 3f out)	4	**10**	50/1	39	27
4104[8] **Ajcombe (IRE) (65)** (LadyHerries) **4-11-10** CLlewellyn(10) (swtg: a bhd)	2	**11**	14/1	61	49
Via Del Quatro (IRE) (50) (JWMullins) **5-10-9** VSlattery(4) (bit bkwd: bhd fnl 4f)	5	**12**	50/1	41	29
4179[10] **Zamalek (USA) (50)** (RMFlower) **5-10-9** CMaude(14) (swtg: a bhd)	½	**13**	16/1	41	29
4222[8] **Challenger (IRE) (41)** (LWells) **4-10-0** LHarvey(1) (chsd ldrs tl wknd over 4f out)	14	**14**	33/1	18	6
607[8] **Classy Chief (65)** (JELong) **4-11-10** LeesaLong(15) (b: dwlt: a bhd: t.o whn p.u & dismntd 3f out)		**P**	25/1	—	—
			(SP 130.1%)	**15 Rn**	

3m 30.17 (6.17) CSF £138.94 CT £886.10 TOTE £9.30: £2.80 £4.00 £2.50 (£49.00) Trio £99.40 OWNER Mr Kenneth Kornfeld (UPPER LAMBOURN) BRED Sheikh Mohammed
LONG HANDICAP Hillswick 9-13 Ginka 9-1 Challenger (IRE) 8-12
WEIGHT FOR AGE 3yo-12lb

Father Sky, who won two races on the Flat in Ireland in 1994, scored his first success on the level in this country here in good style. He will appear again on Saturday week in the Mercedes-Benz Chase at Chepstow. (12/1: op 7/1)
Wilkins made a brave bid to steal the race early in the straight, but was just worn down by the winner. (12/1: 8/1-14/1)
3864 Palaemon got this two miles pretty well, but is woefully short of pace. (6/1)
3928 Red Raja, unusually, did not make the running, and these tactics appeared to backfire as he only had the one pace all the way up the straight. (7/2)

Chief's Song (10/1: 8/1-12/1)
2949 Nordansk (12/1: op 8/1)

4375 SCATS H'CAP (0-85) (3-Y.O) (Class D)

2-30 (2-31) **7f** £3,980.00 (£1,190.00: £570.00: £260.00) Stalls: Low GOING minus 0.46 sec per fur (F)

	Horse	Dist	Pos	SP	RR	SF
4121[6]	**Khafaaq (82)** (MajorWRHern) **3-9-6b** RHills(11) (lw: hld up & bhd: hdwy to ld over 1f out: r.o wl)	—	**1**	11/4[1]	91	48
1238[4]	**Dandy Regent (65)** (CACyzer) **3-8-0**(3) RFfrench(4) (a.p: rdn 2f out: kpt on ins fnl f)	1¾	**2**	25/1	70	27
3894[6]	**Telemania (IRE) (83)** (WJHaggas) **3-9-7** KFallon(9) (s.i.s: hld up: hdwy 3f out: rdn 2f out: styd on ins fnl f)	hd	**3**	7/1[3]	88	45
4220[3]	**Irtifa (68)** (PTWalwyn) **3-8-6v** WRyan(6) (hld up: hdwy over 2f out: rdn over 1f out: kpt on one pce ins fnl f)	hd	**4**	12/1	73	30
3900[10]	**Braveheart (IRE) (70)** (MRChannon) **3-8-8** SSanders(10) (led: hdd over 1f out: one pce)	hd	**5**	20/1	74	31
4175[2]	**Refuse To Lose (77)** (JMPEustace) **3-9-1** RCochrane(8) (chsd ldr: chal strly fr 3f out: ev ch over 1f out: wknd ins fnl f)	1¼	**6**	4/1[2]	79	36
4276[9]	**Sword Arm (81)** (RCharlton) **3-9-5v** TSprake(5) (chsd ldrs: rdn over 2f out: in tch whn rdr lost iron over 1f out: nt rcvr)	1¾	**7**	9/1	79	36
	Salty Jack (IRE) (82) (VSoane) **3-9-6** CRutter(1) (a bhd)	4	**8**	20/1	70	27
4059[7]	**Midnight Shift (IRE) (63)** (RGuest) **3-8-1** MartinDwyer(2) (a bhd)	hd	**9**	11/1	51	8
4220[9]	**Gee Bee Dream (77)** (APJarvis) **3-9-1** JReid(7) (hld up: brief effrt 3f out: sn btn)	nk	**10**	16/1	64	21
4071[10]	**Ijtinab (65)** (RAkehurst) **3-8-3** MRoberts(3) (chsd ldrs tl wknd over 2f out)	4	**11**	8/1	43	—

(SP 115.6%) **11 Rn**

1m 26.26 (1.46) CSF £73.08 CT £407.51 TOTE £3.80: £1.70 £7.10 £1.60 (£63.40) Trio £64.00 OWNER Mr Hamdan Al Maktoum (LAMBOURN) BRED Shadwell Estate Company Limited
OFFICIAL EXPLANATION **Sword Arm: the jockey reported that his foot slipped out of his near side iron in the closing stages of the race, and consequently, was unable to ride out to the line.**
4121 Khafaaq has been running consistently well of late and fully deserved his success. (11/4)
1238 Dandy Regent ran probably his best race to date and could well pick up a similar event before the season finishes. (25/1)
3894 Telemania (IRE) ran well under her big weight, keeping on all the way to the line. (7/1)
4220 Irtifa ran on nicely in the final furlong and is finding her form. (12/1: op 8/1)
Braveheart (IRE) finds even this seven furlongs stretches his stamina, and has an action that suggests softer ground would suit. (20/1)
3712 Sword Arm (9/1: op 6/1)

4376 N.F.U. RATED STKS H'CAP (0-100) (3-Y.O+) (Class B)

3-00 (3-00) **2m** £7,870.56 (£2,715.36: £1,297.68: £524.40) Stalls: Low GOING minus 0.46 sec per fur (F)

	Horse	Dist	Pos	SP	RR	SF
4101[2]	**Georgia Venture (86)** (SPCWoods) **3-8-0**(3) RFfrench(1) (hld up in tch: hdwy to ld 2f out: r.o wl)	—	**1**	5/2[2]	98	43
3705[2]	**Media Star (USA) (93)** (JHMGosden) **4-9-8v** OPeslier(3) (lw: a.p: chal & ev ch 2f out: rdn over 1f out: one pce)	1	**2**	Evens[1]	104+	61
4156[5]	**Male-Ana-Mou (IRE) (82)** (DRCElsworth) **4-8-11** DaneO'Neill(4) (led: hdd 2f out: grad wknd)	7	**3**	9/1	86	43
4156[2]	**Lady of The Lake (91)** (JLDunlop) **3-8-8** GCarter(2) (chsd ldr: pushed along & lost pl over 6f out: rcvrd to chse ldr over 4f out: ev ch 2f out: sn wknd)	3	**4**	9/2[3]	92	37

(SP 106.8%) **4 Rn**

3m 25.76 (1.76) CSF £4.86 TOTE £3.70 (£2.10) OWNER Dr Frank Chao (NEWMARKET) BRED Woodsway Stud
WEIGHT FOR AGE 3yo-12lb
4101 Georgia Venture, who ran so well at Doncaster, proved well suited by the step-up to two miles. (5/2)
3705 Media Star (USA) did not make the running as he usually does, but still lost no caste in defeat. Staying on strongly all the way to the line, he looks sure to run well in the Cesarewitch. (Evens)
4156 Male-Ana-Mou (IRE) set the pace but was put in his place in the final two furlongs. (9/1)
4156 Lady of The Lake ran very much in snatches. (9/2: 5/2-5/1)

4377 CHARLTON HUNT SUPREME STKS (Gp 3) (3-Y.O+) (Class A)

3-30 (3-31) **7f** £22,638.00 (£8,474.40: £4,072.20: £1,775.40) Stalls: Low GOING minus 0.46 sec per fur (F)

	Horse	Dist	Pos	SP	RR	SF
4117[2]	**Decorated Hero (113)** (JHMGosden) **5-9-2** OPeslier(6) (hld up: pushed along to improve over 2f out: led 2f out: r.o)	—	**1**	6/4[1]	118	64
4148[7]	**Restructure (IRE) (105)** (MrsJCecil) **5-9-2** MRoberts(4) (chsd ldrs: rdn 3f out: chsd wnr fnl 2f: r.o)	1¼	**2**	16/1	115	61
4117[5]	**Nwaamis (USA) (110)** (JLDunlop) **5-8-12** RHills(5) (lw: dwlt: hld up: hdwy 2f out: rdn over 1f out: one pce: fin lame)	1½	**3**	5/1[3]	108	54
1203a[3]	**Red Camellia (111)** (SirMarkPrescott) **3-8-6** SSanders(1) (lw: chsd ldr: ev ch 2f out: wknd over 1f out)	3½	**4**	2/1[2]	97	40
3147[6]	**Oh Nellie (USA) (114)** (NACallaghan) **3-8-6** WRyan(2) (led: set str pce: hdd 2f out: sn wknd)	1¼	**5**	6/1	94	37
3147[8]	**Blueygreen (89)** (PWChapple-Hyam) **3-8-6** DaneO'Neill(3) (in tch tl wknd qckly 3f out: t.o)	16	**6**	66/1	57	—

(SP 111.7%) **6 Rn**

1m 24.64 (-0.16) CSF £22.79 TOTE £2.30: £1.50 £3.00 (£9.40) OWNER Exors of the late Mr Herbert Allen (NEWMARKET) BRED Reg Griffin and Jim McGrath
WEIGHT FOR AGE 3yo-3lb
OFFICIAL EXPLANATION **Nwaamis (USA): lame.**
4117 Decorated Hero is a really consistent gelding, and gained another thoroughly deserved success. Pushed along to improve early in the straight, the issue was never in doubt in the final two furlongs. (6/4)
4148 Restructure (IRE), who ran poorly in a handicap at Doncaster, bounced back to form and ran as well as he has done all season. (16/1)
4117 Nwaamis (USA) made a promising move over two furlongs out but, when put under pressure, had nothing extra to offer. It later transpired that he had finished lame. (5/1)
1203a Red Camellia, along with Oh Nellie, very much cut their own throats, and had no more to offer when challenged in the final two furlongs. (2/1)
3147 Oh Nellie (USA) set too strong a pace and was a tired horse in the final two furlongs. (6/1)

4378 EQUITY FINANCIAL COLLECTIONS MAIDEN STKS (3-Y.O) (Class D)

4-00 (4-00) **1m 2f** £3,785.00 (£1,130.00: £540.00: £245.00) Stalls: Low GOING minus 0.46 sec per fur (F)

	Horse	Dist	Pos	SP	RR	SF
4177[7]	**Bel Canto (IRE)** (JHMGosden) **3-9-0** OPeslier(1) (lw: hld up in tch: rdn & lost pl over 4f out: rallied over 2f out: led ins fnl f: r.o)	—	**1**	10/1	83	28

				SP	RR	SF
4158^{2}	**Tough Act (75)** (MrsAJPerrett) **3-9-0** AClark(3) (chsd ldrs: rdn 2f out: ev ch ins fnl f: unable qckn)	¾	**2**	11/2	82	27
4060^{4}	**Quiet Venture** (EALDunlop) **3-9-0** KFallon(10) (a.p: led over 2f out: hrd rdn over 1f out: hdd ins fnl f: unable qckn)	nk	**3**	$7/2^{2}$	81	26
4158^{3}	**Dick Turpin (USA) (71)** (LordHuntingdon) **3-9-0** WRyan(4) (hld up: hdwy over 2f out: ev ch ins fnl f: one pce)	hd	**4**	$3/1^{1}$	81	26
4177^{8}	**Pradesh** (JHMGosden) **3-8-9** AGarth(2) (hld up: hdwy over 2f out: rdn over 1f out: one pce)	2	**5**	20/1	73	18
3800^{8}	**Balfour Lady (43)** (JARToller) **3-8-9** MRoberts(8) (hld up in rr: rdn over 2f out: styd on one pce ins fnl f)	1¼	**6**	33/1	71	16
3970^{3}	**Curzon Street (74)** (DRCElsworth) **3-8-9** JReid(6) (hld up: plld hrd: chsd ldr 6f out to 3f out: n.m.r over 2f out tl over 1f out: wknd appr fnl f)	2½	**7**	$4/1^{3}$	67	12
4053^{7}	**Limelight (53)** (JARToller) **3-8-9b¹** SSanders(5) (led: hdd over 2f out: grad wknd)	4	**8**	33/1	61	6
837^{8}	**Mutabari (USA) (73)** (KMahdi) **3-9-0** RCochrane(7) (prom: rdn over 2f out: wknd over 1f out)	½	**9**	14/1	65	10
3720^{5}	**Panorama** (LMCumani) **3-8-6**(3) RFfrench(9) (chsd ldrs tl wknd over 3f out)	2½	**10**	25/1	56	1

(SP 112.9%) **10 Rn**

2m 10.89 (4.29) CSF £53.69 TOTE £10.10: £2.50 £1.80 £1.20 (£38.70) Trio £37.20 OWNER Sheikh Mohammed (NEWMARKET) BRED Airlie Stud

4177 Bel Canto (IRE) won this despite getting outpaced early in the straight, and would be very well suited by a step-up to a mile and a half. (10/1: 6/1-11/1)

4158 Tough Act was second again, but appeared to do little wrong in the final furlong. (11/2: op 7/2)

4060 Quiet Venture, quite a scopey sort, made a brave bid for home over two furlongs out and battled all the way to the line when challenged. (7/2: 9/2-3/1)

4158 Dick Turpin (USA) moved up menacingly two furlongs out and looked like he might succeed, but he did not quite find that quickening burst. (3/1: 2/1-100/30)

Pradesh ran a promising race, staying on steadily in the final two furlongs, and she will improve. (20/1)

4379 E.B.F. MAIDEN STKS (2-Y.O) (Class D)

4-35 (4-36) **6f** £4,199.25 (£1,254.00: £599.50: £272.25) Stalls: Low GOING minus 0.31 sec per fur (GF)

				SP	RR	SF
4167^{6}	**Young Josh** (JHMGosden) **2-9-0** OPeslier(10) (hld up: hdwy ½-wy: led ent fnl f: r.o)	—	**1**	$5/4^{1}$	83	39
4145^{4}	**Chief Whip (USA)** (LMCumani) **2-8-11**(3) RFfrench(3) (lw: a.p: rdn & outpcd 1f out: styd on strly cl home)	nk	**2**	$4/1^{2}$	82	38
3114^{10}	**Uplifting** (LGCottrell) **2-8-9** MRoberts(4) (led: hdd ent fnl f: hrd rdn: r.o)	d.h	**2**	33/1	77	33
3986^{3}	**Torrent** (PFICole) **2-9-0** CRutter(1) (hld up in tch: rdn over 1f out: styd on ins fnl f)	1¼	**4**	13/2	79	35
4145^{5}	**Orsino** (SDow) **2-9-0** WRyan(9) (chsd ldrs: rdn over 1f out: one pce)	4	**5**	$5/1^{3}$	68	24
3613^{6}	**Twoforten** (MMadgwick) **2-9-0** NVarley(2) (prom: hrd rdn 3f out: wknd over 1f out)	1¾	**6**	33/1	64	20
4231^{8}	**Arctic Star** (MRChannon) **2-9-0** SSanders(7) (chsd ldrs: rdn over 2f out: sn btn)	1½	**7**	10/1	60	16
4145^{11}	**Thomas O'Malley** (RJO'Sullivan) **2-9-0** AProcter(6) (hld up: hrd rdn over 2f out: sn btn)	1¼	**8**	66/1	56	12
	My Tyson (IRE) (KMahdi) **2-9-0** MartinDwyer(8) (w'like: scope: bit bkwd: s.i.s: a bhd)	6	**9**	25/1	40	—
4064^{14}	**Mail Shot (IRE)** (SDow) **2-8-7**(7) PDoe(5) (in tch to ½-wy)	5	**10**	50/1	27	—

(SP 116.7%) **10 Rn**

1m 12.09 (2.29) CSF YJ & CW £2.72, YJ & U £27.20 TOTE £2.50: £1.40 CW £1.40 U £4.10 (YJ & CW £3.10, YJ & U £14.10) Trio £26.70 OWNER Mr D. H. Armitage (NEWMARKET) BRED B. Burrough

4167 Young Josh moved up smoothly at halfway and looked sure to win comfortably when taking it up entering the final furlong but, in the end, was all out to score. Even this sharp six furlongs stretches his stamina at the moment. (5/4)

4145 Chief Whip (USA) was outpaced entering the final furlong, before staying on very strongly in the final hundred yards. He is crying out for seven. (4/1)

Uplifting, bidding to make all, battled on very gamely when headed. (33/1)

3986 Torrent was held up further back on this occasion and, although staying on nicely in the final furlong, never really threatened to take a hand. (13/2: op 9/4)

4380 ST JOHN AMBULANCE BRIGADE NURSERY H'CAP (0-85) (2-Y.O) (Class D)

5-05 (5-07) **1m** £3,200.00 (£950.00: £450.00: £200.00) Stalls: Low GOING minus 0.46 sec per fur (F)

				SP	RR	SF
4044^{10}	**Rico Suave (IRE) (85)** (SirMarkPrescott) **2-9-7** SSanders(6) (chsd ldr: hrd rdn over 2f out: styd on to ld wl ins fnl f)	—	**1**	$5/1^{1}$	88	37
3861^{8}	**The Thruster (60)** (MajorWRHern) **2-7-10b¹** MartinDwyer(7) (plld hrd: sn led: clr over 2f out: hdd wl ins fnl f: no ex)	¾	**2**	8/1	62	11
4044^{12}	**Elakik (83)** (JLDunlop) **2-9-5b¹** RHills(1) (lw: hld up: hdwy over 2f out: rdn over 1f out: r.o)	¾	**3**	$11/2^{2}$	83	32
4068^{3}	**Short Romance (IRE) (63)** (JWHills) **2-7-10**(3)ow1 MHenry(10) (lw: hld up: rdn over 3f out: kpt on one pce fnl 2f)	hd	**4**	$5/1^{1}$	63	11
3926^{7}	**Ringleader (72)** (PFICole) **2-8-8b** CRutter(5) (chsd ldrs: hrd rdn over 2f out: one pce)	2	**5**	14/1	68	17
4271^{8}	**Ballet Rambert (74)** (MJHeaton-Ellis) **2-8-10** KFallon(8) (hld up: effrt 3f out: n.m.r over 2f out: sn rdn: one pce)	2	**6**	$13/2^{3}$	66	15
4105^{7}	**Bronzino (72)** (GBBalding) **2-8-5**(3) PPMurphy(2) (hld up in rr: hdwy over 2f out: wknd ins fnl f)	s.h	**7**	10/1	64	13
4056^{3}	**Polo Venture (71)** (SPCWoods) **2-8-7**ow1 JReid(3) (sn pushed along: bhd fnl 3f)	3½	**8**	$13/2^{3}$	56	4
4143^{5}	**Little Tumbler (IRE) (61)** (SWoodman) **2-7-6**(5)ow1 APolli(4) (prom: rdn 4f out: sn wknd)	5	**9**	14/1	36	—
4056^{6}	**Dawn Treader (USA) (61)** (RHannon) **2-7-8**(3) RFfrench(11) (prom tl wknd 4f out)	7	**10**	14/1	22	—

(SP 115.6%) **10 Rn**

1m 40.08 (2.88) CSF £40.41 CT £212.23 TOTE £6.90: £2.40 £2.50 £2.00 (£28.20) Trio £56.80 OWNER Mr Haydn Kelly (NEWMARKET) BRED Eclipse Bloodstock

LONG HANDICAP The Thruster 7-5

2898* Rico Suave (IRE) had to work hard all the way up the straight to reel in the clear leader, and did so in the last one hundred yards. (5/1)

2047 The Thruster pulled hard but soon set up a commanding advantage. Halfway up the straight it looked like he might hold on, but he was grabbed when inside the final furlong. (8/1)

3253* Elakik made headway halfway up the straight, and stayed on all the way to the line. (11/2: op 7/2)

4068 Short Romance (IRE) came under pressure well over three furlongs out and, although plugging on, never really looked like reaching the principals. (5/1)

3186 Ringleader was never that far away, but only had the one pace for pressure in the final three furlongs. (14/1: 10/1-16/1)

Bronzino (10/1: op 6/1)

4056 Polo Venture (13/2: 4/1-7/1)

T/Jkpt: £27,189.90 (0.58 Tckts); £16,084.22 to Folkestone 26/9/97. T/Plpt: £236.10 (119.91 Tckts). T/Qdpt: £33.90 (38.12 Tckts) SM

3931-PONTEFRACT (L-H) (Good to firm)
Thursday September 25th
WEATHER: overcast WIND: slight half against

4381 E.B.F. POPPIN LANE MAIDEN STKS (2-Y.O) (Class D)
2-40 (2-41) **6f** £4,169.00 (£1,262.00: £616.00: £293.00) Stalls: Low GOING minus 0.42 sec per fur (F)

Form	Horse and running	Dist	Pos	SP	RR	SF
4052^{W}	**Prompt Delivery (USA) (84)** (MRStoute) **2-9-0** KDarley(16) (trckd ldrs: led ½-wy: drvn clr over 1f out: hld on towards fin)	—	**1**	$3/1^{2}$	82	44
3070^{6}	**Nunthorpe** (JAGlover) **2-8-9** NDay(10) (bit bkwd: trckd ldrs: hdwy & ev ch ins fnl f: r.o)	nk	**2**	14/1	76	38
4065^{3}	**Leofric (67)** (MJPolglase) **2-9-0v** JWeaver(1) (b.hind: mid div: sn drvn along: hdwy over 1f out: styd on same pce)	5	**3**	8/1	68	30
4159^{5}	**Sorridar** (JLEyre) **2-8-9** MGallagher(13) (a chsng ldrs: rdn & hung lft over 1f out: styd on)	1	**4**	14/1	60	22
4286^{5}	**Strictly Rhythm** (MrsSABramall,Ireland) **2-8-11**(3) GParkin(11) (led to ½-wy: one pce fnl 2f)	s.h	**5**	33/1	65	27
3711^{17}	**Canonize (IRE)** (JWHills) **2-8-9** MHills(9) (a chsng ldrs: rdn 2f out: no imp)	2	**6**	$9/4^{1}$	55	17
1839^{6}	**My Lost Love** (MJohnston) **2-9-0** DHolland(2) (bit bkwd: hdwy over 2f out: kpt on: nvr nr ldrs)	½	**7**	10/1	58	20
	Captain Logan (IRE) (DRLoder) **2-9-0** JCarroll(7) (w'like: scope: s.i.s: hld up & bhd: styd on fnl 2f: nvr nr to chal)	hd	**8**	$11/2^{3}$	58+	20
4012^{16}	**Essandess (IRE)** (JLEyre) **2-8-9** TWilliams(6) (in tch: drvn along ½-wy: n.d)	hd	**9**	25/1	53	15
	Brave Maple (JMPEustace) **2-9-0** JTate(5) (str: cmpt: bkwd: s.i.s: bhd: sme hdwy over 1f out: n.d)	1¾	**10**	16/1	53	15
	Happy Wanderer (PCHaslam) **2-9-0** JFortune(15) (cmpt: scope: bit bkwd: s.i.s: bhd: sme hdwy over 1f out: n.d)	¾	**11**	33/1	51	13
4229^{5}	**Goldmaster** (WAO'Gorman) **2-9-0** EmmaO'Gorman(4) (sn bhd: rdn ½-wy: n.d)	2½	**12**	25/1	45	7
4165^{8}	**Antonio Joli** (PFICole) **2-9-0** TQuinn(8) (s.i.s: a outpcd & sn drvn along)	7	**13**	16/1	26	—
	Total Tropix (WJHaggas) **2-8-9** FLynch(3) (lt-f: unf: sn wl bhd)	1¼	**14**	14/1	18	—
3610^{12}	**Hey Up Mate (IRE)** (JBerry) **2-8-9**(5) CLowther(14) (w ldrs: rdn ½-wy: wknd 2f out)	2	**15**	33/1	17	—
4064^{13}	**Aspirant Dancer** (MBell) **2-9-0** MFenton(12) (lw: s.i.s: racd wd: a in rr)	4	**16**	25/1	7	—
				(SP 143.5%)	**16 Rn**	

1m 16.5 (1.50) CSF £46.15 TOTE £3.20: £1.10 £4.90 £1.90 (£31.40) Trio £79.20 OWNER Maktoum Al Maktoum (NEWMARKET) BRED Gainsborough Farm Inc

3607 Prompt Delivery (USA), happily none the worse for his unfortunate experience at Southwell, was again taken to post early and this time remained cool and calm at the start. Overcoming a poor draw, he never had to be brought under maximum pressure and always looked to just have the edge. (3/1)

3070 Nunthorpe, absent for sixty-one days, looked on the burly side. Showing a round action going down, she ran really well to push the winner all the way to the line. She should improve quite a bit in time. (14/1)

4065 Leofric, with the visor on again, was taken to post quietly. He looks as though he will appreciate a step up to seven. (8/1)

4159 Sorridar, who has run up light, appreciated the extra furlong. (14/1)

4286 Strictly Rhythm was having his third run here and now qualifies for a handicap mark, but unfortunately they will be taking no liberties with him. (33/1)

3711 Canonize (IRE), who bolted going to the start this time, was warm in the paddock and very keen going to post. She seem to be her own worst enemy. (9/4)

1839 My Lost Love, warm beforehand and taking a keen grip on the way to post, will hopefully settle down with racing. (10/1)

Captain Logan (IRE), who has plenty of size and scope, is a lazy walker and looks half asleep in the paddock. After missing the break, he was given an educational first outing and should improve a good deal in time and as he gains experience. (11/2)

Happy Wanderer looked in need of the outing but showed a glimmer of ability on his debut. (33/1)

4382 PORTERS LODGE NURSERY H'CAP (0-85) (2-Y.O F) (Class D)
3-10 (3-11) **1m 4y** £3,702.25 (£1,108.00: £531.50: £243.25) Stalls: Low GOING minus 0.42 sec per fur (F)

Form	Horse and running	Dist	Pos	SP	RR	SF
4061^{5}	**Naskhi (77)** (MJohnston) **2-9-3** DHolland(3) (lw: b.hind: hld up: stdy hdwy over 3f out: shkn up to ld jst ins fnl f: styd on wl)	—	**1**	$4/1^{2}$	79+	42
4185^{3}	**Summer Deal (USA) (77)** (PFICole) **2-9-3** KDarley(11) (sn chsng ldrs: led over 2f out: r.o)	¾	**2**	9/1	78	41
4017^{4}	**Campari (IRE) (74)** (MAJarvis) **2-9-0** JWeaver(4) (swtg: trckd ldrs: plld v.hrd: rdn & hung bdly lft over 1f out: kpt on)	4	**3**	10/1	67	30
4152^{7}	**Brookhouse Lady (IRE) (58)** (RHollinshead) **2-7-12** NCarlisle(10) (pushed along & hdwy over 3f out: rdn 2f out: wknd towards fin)	nk	**4**	11/1	50	13
4208*	**Moonlight Flit (60)** (JGFitzGerald) **2-8-0b** 6x JQuinn(7) (lw: trckd ldrs: effrt & n.m.r over 2f out: sn wknd)	6	**5**	$11/2^{3}$	40	3
4217^{3}	**Good Catch (IRE) (79)** (PRWebber) **2-9-5** JFortune(2) (lw: sn bhd & pushed along: sme hdwy 3f out: hung lft & no imp)	9	**6**	11/1	41	4
3307^{5}	**Dancing Em (56)** (TDEasterby) **2-7-10** LCharnock(8) (mde most tl over 2f out: sn wknd)	2½	**7**	33/1	13	—
3598^{16}	**Ida Lupino (IRE) (56)** (BWHills) **2-7-7**(3) PFessey(6) (hmpd s: plld v.hrd: sn trckng ldrs: wknd over 2f out)	3	**8**	14/1	7	—
4185^{2}	**Chocolate (IRE) (81)** (JLDunlop) **2-9-7b**[1] TQuinn(1) (sn pushed along: sme hdwy whn sltly hmpd over 2f out: sn wknd)	3	**9**	$5/2^{1}$	26	—
3990^{7}	**Miss Main Street (IRE) (63)** (JJQuinn) **2-8-3** JCarroll(9) (lw: sn bhd)	12	**10**	14/1	—	—
4245^{7}	**No Shame (62)** (JGSmyth-Osbourne) **2-8-2v**[1] GBardwell(5) (w ldrs: hung bdly rt & lost pl ½-wy: t.o 2f out: virtually p.u)	dist	**11**	25/1	—	—
				(SP 119.8%)	**11 Rn**	

1m 45.1 (2.70) CSF £37.25 CT £316.93 TOTE £4.70: £2.20 £2.70 £2.30 (£23.60) Trio £48.20 OWNER Mr Saeed Manana (MIDDLEHAM) BRED Saeed Manana

LONG HANDICAP Dancing Em 7-2 Ida Lupino (IRE) 7-4

4061 Naskhi, stepping up in distance, was given a much more patient ride and, after taking time to get on top, did it in good style in the end. She will improve again. (4/1)

4185 Summer Deal (USA) made the best of her way home but, in the end, was comprehensively beaten. (9/1)

4017 Campari (IRE) is a headstrong filly who is a very difficult ride. She will do anything but run in a straight line. (10/1)

4152 Brookhouse Lady (IRE), picking up ground soon after halfway, seemed to run out of stamina in the closing stages. Seven furlongs might prove her ideal trip. (11/1)

4208* Moonlight Flit, who came from behind in lesser company at Beverley, had much more use made of her and she did not reproduce that effort. (11/2)
4217 Good Catch (IRE) was almost certainly flattered by her effort in a slowly-run race at Sandown last time. (11/1)
2860 Ida Lupino (IRE) is her own worst enemy, as she simply would not settle. (14/1)
4185 Chocolate (IRE), tried in blinkers, ran a very tame race and was already starting to struggle when she was hampered going into the final turn. Her rider soon called it a day. (5/2)

4383 DALBY SCREW-DRIVER RATED STKS H'CAP (0-95) (3-Y.O+) (Class C)

3-40 (3-41) **1m 2f 6y** £6,581.60 (£2,434.40: £1,167.20: £476.00: £188.00: £72.80) Stalls: Low GOING minus 0.42 sec per fur (F)

				SP	RR	SF
3542*	**Eshtiaal (USA) (94)** (JLDunlop) **3-9-6b** KDarley(9) (mde all: hld on towards fin)	—	**1**	5/1[3]	105	71
4136[11]	**Pinchincha (FR) (81)** (DMorris) **3-8-7** NDay(1) (a chsng wnr: hrd rdn & ev ch 1f out: r.o)	¾	**2**	14/1	91	57
4151*	**Infatuation (83)** (LadyHerries) **4-9-1** JWeaver(5) (lw: hld up & bhd: hdwy over 2f out: styd on fnl f: nt rch ldrs)	2½	**3**	5/2[1]	89	61
4148[8]	**Premier Bay (95)** (PWHarris) **3-9-7b** DHolland(10) (trckd ldrs: drvn along over 2f out: kpt on one pce)	¾	**4**	16/1	100	66
4151[3]	**Wafir (IRE) (82)** (PCalver) **5-9-0** JFortune(2) (lw: sn bhd: hdwy on outside over 2f out: hung lft: nvr nr to chal)	1¾	**5**	11/2	84	56
3725[8]	**Wasp Ranger (USA) (93)** (PFICole) **3-9-5** TQuinn(7) (bhd: hdwy & n.m.r 2f out: swtchd ins: nvr nr to chal)	½	**6**	14/1	94	60
3989[8]	**Lycility (IRE) (87)** (CEBrittain) **3-8-13** MRimmer(4) (lw: trckd ldrs: wkng whn n.m.r over 1f out)	5	**7**	33/1	80	46
3570[3]	**Davoski (76)** (BWHills) **3-7-13**(3) PFessey(6) (in tch: pushed along 4f out: lost pl over 2f out)	5	**8**	6/1	61	27
1982[4]	**Jack The Lad (IRE) (80)** (JHetherton) **3-8-6** MTebbutt(3) (a in rr)	nk	**9**	20/1	65	31
4141[3]	**The In-Laws (IRE) (81)** (SirMarkPrescott) **3-8-7** DeanMcKeown(8) (lw: chsd ldrs: pushed along 4f out: wknd over 2f out: eased)	7	**10**	9/2[2]	54	20

(SP 120.0%) **10 Rn**

2m 9.6 (0.00) CSF £67.95 CT £198.70 TOTE £4.50: £1.60 £3.10 £1.70 (£39.90) Trio £30.40 OWNER Mr Hamdan Al Maktoum (ARUNDEL) BRED Shadwell Farm Inc and Shadwell Estate Co Ltd
WEIGHT FOR AGE 3yo-6lb
OFFICIAL EXPLANATION **The In-Laws (IRE): the jockey reported that when he asked the question three furlongs out, his mount failed to pick up and felt wrong. He therefore felt it prudent not to persevere and finished last.**
3542* Eshtiaal (USA) was 10lb higher in the weights than when he won his first handicap at Haydock two outings ago. Transformed by blinkers, he does just enough in front. (5/1)
3444 Pinchincha (FR), 6lb higher than when winning here in June, never gave up trying but the winner was always going to contain his challenge. (14/1)
4151* Infatuation, 6lb higher than at Doncaster, needs to come very late and everything has to go just right. With the winner stretching the field, he was never going to reach a challenging position on this occasion. (5/2)
3575 Premier Bay ran one of his better races and will appreciate some ease in the ground. (16/1)
4151 Wafir (IRE), closely-matched with the third on their Doncaster running, gave his rider real problems. (11/2)
3189 Wasp Ranger (USA), stepping up in distance, did not have the best of runs but basically what he needs is some mercy from the Handicapper. (14/1)
4141 The In-Laws (IRE) was in trouble a long way out. Her rider gave up before the home turn, feeling that she did not feel right. (9/2)

4384 FRIER WOOD MAIDEN STKS (2-Y.O) (Class D)

4-10 (4-11) **1m 4y** £3,387.50 (£1,025.00: £500.00: £237.50) Stalls: Low GOING minus 0.42 sec per fur (F)

				SP	RR	SF
4061[2]	**Close Up (IRE) (88)** (JLDunlop) **2-9-0** KDarley(6) (lw: trckd ldr: led jst ins fnl f: drvn out)	—	**1**	6/5[1]	85	31
3235[9]	**Free Option (IRE)** (BHanbury) **2-9-0** JStack(9) (bit bkwd: trckd ldrs: hung lft over 1f out: styd on wl towards fin)	2½	**2**	12/1	80	26
4064[3]	**Fly By Night (IRE)** (MRStoute) **2-9-0** TQuinn(12) (lw: led tl jst ins fnl f: no ex)	½	**3**	5/1[3]	79	25
4116[17]	**After The Rain (85)** (BWHills) **2-9-0** MHills(11) (lw: hdwy ½-wy: sn chsng ldrs: kpt on same pce fnl 2f)	s.h	**4**	7/2[2]	79	25
4209[14]	**Major Ballaby (IRE)** (MrsSABramall,Ireland) **2-8-11**(3) GParkin(1) (hld up: effrt & outpcd 3f out: hdwy over 1f out: nvr nr ldrs)	2	**5**	66/1	75	21
2196[12]	**Dentardia (IRE)** (JMPEustace) **2-9-0** JTate(8) (bit bkwd: sn chsng ldrs: one pce fnl 2f)	1	**6**	50/1	73	19
3825[6]	**Konker** (WJHaggas) **2-9-0** FLynch(2) (sn trckng ldrs: effrt & n.m.r over 2f out: styd on fnl f)	s.h	**7**	20/1	73	19
	Asset Manager (MJohnston) **2-9-0** DHolland(10) (lengthy: scope: bkwd: outpcd & pushed along ½-wy: hdwy over 2f out: rn green: kpt on)	hd	**8**	5/1[3]	73+	19
	Southern-Be-George (WGMTurner) **2-8-11**(3) DSweeney(3) (wl grwn: str: bkwd: sn prom: drvn along over 2f out: sn wknd)	13	**9**	50/1	47	—
4165[13]	**Common View (IRE)** (NTinkler) **2-9-0** LCharnock(13) (bit bkwd: sn bhd)	2	**10**	50/1	43	—
4231[12]	**Walton Grey (IRE)** (PDEvans) **2-9-0** JFEgan(5) (chsd ldrs tl lost pl over 2f out)	s.h	**11**	50/1	43	—
	Sledmere (IRE) (NTinkler) **2-9-0** KimTinkler(7) (unf: scope: bkwd: s.i.s: a bhd)	3	**12**	50/1	37	—
4061[16]	**Silver Hope (IRE) (60)** (RHollinshead) **2-9-0** ACulhane(4) (sn bhd & drvn along)	1¼	**13**	50/1	34	—

(SP 126.7%) **13 Rn**

1m 45.9 (3.50) CSF £17.86 TOTE £2.40: £1.40 £3.40 £1.60 (£18.30) Trio £36.50 OWNER Mr Ian Cameron (ARUNDEL) BRED Lowquest Ltd
4061 Close Up (IRE), who looked very fit, was very keen going to post. Taking time to get into top gear, in the end he did it nicely. He seems to be improving with every outing. (6/5)
3235 Free Option (IRE), edgy in the paddock, has an awkward head carriage. Clearly suited by the mile, he should have further improvement in him. (12/1)
4064 Fly By Night (IRE), a fluent mover, might be suited by a drop back to seven. (5/1)
3802 After The Rain clearly has his limitations. (7/2)
Major Ballaby (IRE) was having his third run in this country and now qualifies for a handicap mark. He is certainly not without ability. (66/1)
Dentardia (IRE), who showed a very poor action going down, showed a glimmer of ability on the way back. (50/1)
3825 Konker, who was not knocked about, did not have the best of runs. Still immature, he looks the type who might do alright in handicap company at three. (20/1)
Asset Manager, who looked on the burly side, showed a poor action going down but showed plenty of promise in the race itself, despite being very inexperienced. The outing will have taught him plenty. (5/1)

4385 NEVISON H'CAP (0-70) (3-Y.O+) (Class E)

4-45 (4-47) **5f** £3,327.00 (£996.00: £478.00: £219.00) Stalls: Low GOING minus 0.42 sec per fur (F)

				SP	RR	SF
*4049**	**Mon Bruce (57)** (MDods) **3-9-0** JCarroll(15) (w ldrs: led over 1f out: hld on towards fin)	—	**1**	14/1	66	35

3898[12] **Jucea (55)** (JLSpearing) **8-8-13** JWeaver(4) (a chsng ldrs: kpt on wl ins fnl f) ....nk **2** 16/1 63 33
4233[14] **Brecongill Lad (64)** (MissSEHall) **5-9-8** AMcGlone(17) (trckd ldrs: ev ch ins fnl f: nt qckn nr fin) ....hd **3** 12/1 72 42
4115* **General Sir Peter (IRE) (51)** (NACallaghan) **5-8-9** AmandaSanders(12) (racd wd: hmpd after 1½f: hdwy on outside over 1f out: styd on strly towards fin) ....s.h **4** 12/1 59 29
4169[12] **Lillibella (55)** (MrsJRRamsden) **4-8-13** OPears(3) (unruly: hdwy 2f out: hung lft: styd on towards fin) ....nk **5** 16/1 62 32
4051[3] **Bashful Brave (53)** (BPJBaugh) **6-8-8**(3) PRoberts(10) (chsd ldrs: kpt on appr fnl f) ....½ **6** 16/1 58 28
3936[14] **Bataleur (53)** (GWoodward) **4-8-11b**[1] DHolland(8) (dwlt: sn chsng ldrs: nt qckn appr fnl f) ....½ **7** 33/1 56 26
2759[9] **Mungo Park (55)** (MrsJRRamsden) **3-8-12** JFortune(11) (lw: unruly in stalls: dwlt s: hmpd after 1½f: hdwy on outside over 1f out: styd on nr fin) ....nk **8** 12/1 57 26
3984[7] **Corniche Quest (IRE) (65)** (MRChannon) **4-9-2**(7) AEddery(7) (hld up & bhd: swtchd rt after 1½f: hdwy 2f out: styd on ins fnl f) ....hd **9** 7/1[2] 67 37
4183[9] **Just Dissident (IRE) (57)** (RMWhitaker) **5-9-1v** DeanMcKeown(6) (lw: led tl over 1f out: grad wknd) ....½ **10** 10/1[3] 58 28
4183[8] **Royal Dome (IRE) (70)** (MartynWane) **5-10-0** SWhitworth(9) (in tch: effrt over 1f out: nvr rchd ldrs) ....½ **11** 16/1 69 39
3936[12] **Tropical Beach (55)** (JBerry) **4-8-10b**(3) TEDurcan(2) (mid div: sn pushed along: hmpd ½-wy: n.d) ....hd **12** 16/1 54 24
3625[16] **Ned's Bonanza (49)** (MDods) **8-8-7** ACulhane(18) (sme hdwy over 1f out: n.d) ....nk **13** 16/1 47 17
4016[6] **Panther (IRE) (54)** (PDEvans) **7-8-12v** JFEgan(14) (hld up & bhd: sme hdwy over 1f out: n.d) ....nk **14** 16/1 51 21
4329[12] **Rich Glow (49)** (NBycroft) **6-8-7** KDarley(16) (sn outpcd & drvn along: n.d) ....¾ **15** 12/1 43 13
4233[2] **Camionneur (IRE) (53)** (TDEasterby) **4-8-11b** LCharnock(1) (lw: s.i.s: sme hdwy on ins whn sltly hmpd ½-wy: wknd & eased over 1f out) ....5 **16** 5/2[1] 31 1
4049[6] **Night Express (54)** (BHanbury) **3-8-11** JStack(5) (lw: chsd ldrs 3f: sn lost pl) ....3½ **17** 16/1 21 —
(SP 137.6%) **17 Rn**

63.5 secs (1.80) CSF £224.80 CT £2,639.55 TOTE £29.10: £4.80 £3.40 £2.90 £3.80 (£165.40) Trio £1,332.50 OWNER Mr N. A. Riddell (DARLINGTON) BRED E. A. Badger
WEIGHT FOR AGE 3yo-1lb
STEWARDS' ENQUIRY Eddery susp 4-5/10/97 (careless riding).
IN-FOCUS: There was plenty of trouble in this tightly-packed field and, no doubt, there will have been several hard-luck stories afterwards.
4049* Mon Bruce opened his account on turf on his first outing for his new yard after being claimed. (14/1)
Jucea, who has tumbled down the weights, ran easily her best race so far this year. (16/1)
3761 Brecongill Lad, produced with a perfectly-timed challenge, certainly seemed to be saving something for himself in a tight finish. (12/1)
4115* General Sir Peter (IRE) showed his Chepstow win was no fluke and, but for racing wide and being hampered, he might well have got there. (12/1: op 8/1)
2540* Lillibella is a real madam but she certainly possesses ability and, despite hanging off a true line, she was persuaded to stay on towards the line. Whether this was sufficient for connections to delay her retirement to stud, remains to be seen. (16/1)
4051 Bashful Brave stuck on and will appreciate six. (16/1)
2759 Mungo Park, fresh and well on his first outing for seventy-one days and with the visor left off, gave trouble in the stalls. Hampered in the early stages, he was making relentless ground at the finish. (12/1)
3898 Corniche Quest (IRE) interfered with Mungo Park who in turn interfered with General Sir Peter when pulled wide to get some daylight after a furlong and a half. (7/1)
4233 Camionneur (IRE), who has to come from behind, was drawn one. After missing the break, it was always going to be hard work for him and, after meeting some interference going into the final turn, he found nothing at all and was allowed to come home in his own time. Sent off a ludicrously short-priced favourite in such a big and competitive field, it is no wonder the bookies make millions. (5/2: 7/2-9/4)

4386 NEW HALL LIMITED STKS (0-70) (3-Y.O+) (Class E)
5-15 (5-19) **1m 2f 6y** £2,970.00 (£900.00: £440.00: £210.00) Stalls: Low GOING minus 0.42 sec per fur (F)

SP RR SF

4109[2] **Bubble Wings (FR) (70)** (SPCWoods) **5-8-13** NDay(11) (s.i.s: sn drvn along: hdwy over 3f out: rdn to ld over 1f out: hung lft & sn clr: eased nr fin) ....— **1** 100/30[1] 77 51
3976[12] **Hisar (IRE) (67)** (CPEBrooks) **4-9-2** TQuinn(3) (hld up gng wl: hdwy & nt clr run over 2f out & over 1f out: swtchd ins: kpt on wl: no ch w wnr) 1½ **2** 6/1 78 52
4172* **Ile Distinct (IRE) (62)** (MrsASwinbank) **3-9-0** EJohnson(8) (lw: puhsed along 6f out: sn lost pl: hdwy on outside 2f out: hung lft & styd on same pce) ....1 **3** 9/2[2] 80 48
3053[6] **Florentino (IRE) (70)** (BWHills) **4-9-4** MHills(10) (lw: b: unruly s: hld up: stdy hdwy on outside over 2f out: kpt on same pce appr fnl f) ....1¼ **4** 11/2[3] 76 50
4060[10] **Muhassil (IRE) (67)** (KAMorgan) **4-9-2** OPears(5) (b: trckd ldrs: drvn along 4f out: wknd over 1f out) 4 **5** 20/1 68 42
4172[16] **Obelos (USA) (64)** (MissSJWilton) **6-9-4** SWhitworth(7) (sn drvn along: chsd ldrs: led 2f out: sn hdd & wknd) 5 **6** 33/1 62 36
4151[10] **Mcgillycuddy Reeks (IRE) (69)** (DonEnricoIncisa) **6-9-7** KimTinkler(13) (in tch: effrt over 2f out: n.m.r: sn rdn & no imp) 1½ **7** 12/1 62 36
4141[18] **Contentment (IRE) (70)** (JWHills) **3-8-12** JCarroll(4) (lw: hld up: effrt on ins & nt clr run over 2f out: nvr nr ldrs) 1¼ **8** 12/1 57 25
3134[10] **Access Adventurer (IRE) (58)** (RBoss) **6-9-2** JFortune(9) (swtg: unruly in stalls: led after 1f: hdd & n.m.r 2f out: sn wknd) 1 **9** 33/1 54 28
3029[5] **Priolo Prima (69)** (SirMarkPrescott) **4-9-2** KDarley(1) (bit bkwd: hld up: nt clr run & lost pl over 2f out: eased) ....1½ **10** 11/2[3] 51 25
4108[14] **Rhapsody In White (IRE) (66)** (MAJarvis) **3-8-12b** DHolland(12) (sn chsng ldrs: rdn & wknd over 2f out) 3 **11** 20/1 49 17
House of Dreams (55) (GMMoore) **5-9-2** JTate(6) (bit bkwd: led 1f: chsd ldrs tl lost pl over 2f out) 4 **12** 33/1 40 14
4102[11] **Silent Valley (53)** (MissLCSiddall) **3-8-9v** GHind(2) (s.v.s: a bhd: virtually p.u fnl f) ....25 **13** 50/1 — —
(SP 122.0%) **13 Rn**

2m 11.3 (1.70) CSF £19.85 TOTE £3.60: £1.40 £2.70 £1.90 (£14.60) Trio £36.20 OWNER Dr Frank Chao (NEWMARKET) BRED H. S. Verrerie, Gue Foulon and Florent Couturier
WEIGHT FOR AGE 3yo-6lb
4109 Bubble Wings (FR), best in on official figures, showed that she is right back to her best, winning this easing up despite giving her rider a problem or two on the way. (100/30)
3976 Hisar (IRE), who was never put in the race at York on his previous outing, came in for quite a bit of market support. Running away, he met all the trouble going but would not have beaten the winner anyway. Some would say connections got what they deserved. (6/1)
4172* Ile Distinct (IRE), very warm beforehand, ran a peculiar race, seeming to drop himself out and then staying on despite hanging. (9/2)
3053 Florentino (IRE) gave problems when being loaded into the stalls. (11/2)
Muhassil (IRE) ran creditably and will be an interesting proposition over hurdles in the near future. (20/1)
3906 Mcgillycuddy Reeks (IRE) (12/1: op 8/1)

3029 Priolo Prima, a luckless sort, looked burly on his first outing for sixty-two days and, after meeting trouble on the bend, his rider wisely called it a day. (11/2: 7/2-6/1)

T/Plpt: £104.80 (247.84 Tckts). T/Qdpt: £15.50 (120.87 Tckts) WG

4250a-CHANTILLY (France) (R-H) (Good)
Monday September 15th

4387a PRIX D'ARENBERG (Gp 3) (2-Y.O)
2-25 (2-21) **5f 110y** £24,691.00 (£8,979.00: £4,489.00: £2,694.00)

				SP	RR	SF
	Starkey (BHellier,Germany) **2-8-11** KWoodburn	—	**1**		97	—
3743*	**Shudder** (WJHaggas) **2-8-11** MHills	nse	**2**		97	—
	River Flare (USA) (MmeCHead,France) **2-8-8** ODoleuze	1½	**3**		90	—
	Meatball (FR) (PBary,France) **2-8-11** SGuillot	¾	**4**		90	—
3368a*	**Ella (IRE)** (LordHuntingdon) **2-8-8** OPeslier	¾	**5**		85	—

5 Rn

65.9 secs (3.40) P-M 1.90F: 1.50F 2.40F OWNER S Karlheinz & J Wilde BRED Roldvale Ltd
IN-FOCUS: This was Cologne-based trainer Bruce Hellier's 600th winner.
3743* Shudder failed by the narrowest of margins in an all out battle to the line. Tracking the eventual winner, he made his move to take the lead two furlongs out, but could not shrug off that persistent rival and was headed inside the final furlong. He was second to a useful individual here who is unbeaten in four outings.
3368a* Ella (IRE) led early on but, after being ridden along, could only keep on at the one pace.

4125a-SAINT-CLOUD (France) (L-H) (Good)
Tuesday September 16th

4388a PRIX DE LA COCHERE (Listed) (3-Y.O F)
2-55 (2-58) **1m** £15,713.00 (£5,387.00: £4,040.00)

				SP	RR	SF
	Souris Grise (USA) (ELellouche,France) **3-8-12** TGillet	—	**1**		109	—
	Kart Star (IRE) (France) **3-8-12** DBoeuf	nk	**2**		108	—
3913²	**Dragonada (USA)** (HRACecil) **3-8-12** CAsmussen	¾	**3**		107	—

10 Rn

1m 38.5 (0.00) P-M 27.90F: 4.00F 3.90F 1.60F (220.20F) OWNER F. Krief BRED W. C. Kaufman
3913 Dragonada (USA) given every possible chance, took command of the race rounding the final turn and was then outpaced in the final furlong. She only went under by a length and would have been suited by more cut in the ground. She stays in France and has been sent to Pascal Bary's stable at Chantilly.

4255a-LONGCHAMP (Paris, France) (R-H) (Good)
Thursday September 18th

4389a PRIX DU LION D'ANGERS (Listed) (3-Y.O C & G)
3-05 (3-05) **1m 3f** £15,713.00 (£5,387.00: £4,040.00)

				SP	RR	SF
	Majorien (MmeCHead,France) **3-9-2** ODoleuze	—	**1**		115	—
4125a⁴	**Running Stag (USA)** (PMitchell) **3-9-2** AClark	5	**2**		108	—
	Kaizen (FR) (France) **3-9-2** FSanchez	s.h	**3**		108	—

7 Rn

2m 15.4 (1.40) P-M 2.40F: 1.80F 8.60F OWNER Maktoum Al Maktoum (CHANTILLY) BRED Francois Geffroy
4125a Running Stag (USA), held up early on, he made his effort from two furlongs out and then battled on most gamely to hold on to second place. He was much better over this longer trip and his connections are now hoping he will be able to run in the Hong Kong International Vase in December.

4387a-CHANTILLY (France) (R-H) (Good)
Friday September 19th

4390a PRIX DE SEINE-ET-OISE (Gp 3) (3-Y.O+)
3-20 (3-17) **6f** £24,691.00 (£8,979.00: £4,489.00)

				SP	RR	SF
4124a²	**Dyhim Diamond (IRE)** (CLaffon-Parias,France) **3-8-12** GGuignard	—	**1**		118	—
4001a²	**Linoise (FR)** (AFabre,France) **5-8-10** TJarnet	nk	**2**		113	—
	Kistena (FR) (MmeCHead,France) **4-9-3** ODoleuze	5	**3**		107	—

5 Rn

1m 11.8 (2.80) TOTE 4.50F: 1.80F 1.50F OWNER Mr Salem Suhail (CHANTILLY) BRED Knocklong House Stud
4124a Dyhim Diamond (IRE) thoroughly deserved this victory. He has been racing against older horses for much of the season and always with distinction. He took up the running two furlongs out and held on gamely to the bitter end. His trainer will now resist the temptation to run the colt in the L'Abbaye de Longchamp, and he may be put away for the season. He should turn into a top European sprinter in 1998.
4001a Linoise (FR) was always close up and slipped into top-gear at the furlong marker. She was cutting down the winner in the final stages but the post came a little too early. She may be even better over five furlongs.
Kistena (FR), on her first outing of the season, was slowly away and outpaced early on. She found her stride one and a half furlongs out and was putting in her best work at the finish. The winner of last year's l'Abbaye de Longchamp, she has had a back problem since being operated on for a chip on the knee. She looks likely to miss the l'Abbaye and will probably finish her career in the Petit Couvert.

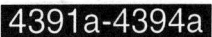

4389a-LONGCHAMP (Paris, France) (R-H) (Good)
Saturday September 20th

4391a PRIX DE LA SALAMANDRE (Gp 1) (2-Y.O C & F)
2-45 (2-48) **7f** £44,893.00 (£17,957.00: £8,979.00: £4,489.00)

				SP	RR	SF
3882a2	**Xaar** (AFabre,France) **2-9-0** OPeslier (mid div: hdwy 2f out: led over 1f out: pushed out: r.o strly)	—	1	6/5 1	115+	—
3882a*	**Charge D'Affaires** (AdeRoyerDupre,France) **2-9-0** GMosse (hld up mid div: hdwy 2f out: no ex cl home)	3	2	27/10 2	108	—
3774*	**Speedfit Too (IRE)** (GGMargarson) **2-9-0** GCarter (rdn in 6th: swtchd rt st: hdwy over 2f out: led briefly over 1f out: outpcd)	5	3	17/1	97?	—
3178a*	**Greenlander** (CEBrittain) **2-9-0** SGuillot (mid div: styd on fnl stages)	1½	4	37/10 3	93	—
3534a3	**Harbour Master (FR)** (APO'Brien,Ireland) **2-9-0b** CAsmussen (hld up early: rdn st: n.d)	1½	5	52/10	90	—
3999a2	**Sainte Marine (IRE)** (RCollet,France) **2-8-11** TJarnet (prom: u.p over 2f out: prog over 1f out: wknd qckly)	2	6	12/1	82	—
3997a*	**Chips (IRE)** (DRCElsworth) **2-9-0** SDrowne (set gd pce: led tl over 1f out: wknd cl home)	6	7	24/1	72	—
4090a3	**Marigot Bay (IRE)** (APO'Brien,Ireland) **2-8-11** JAHeffernan (trckd ldrs: 2nd st: one pcd)	5	8	52/10	57	—
				(SP 143.3%)	**8 Rn**	

1m 21.6 (2.60) P-M 2.20F: 1.10F 1.10F 1.60F (2.90F) OWNER Mr K. Abdullah (CHANTILLY) BRED Juddmonte Farms
OFFICIAL EXPLANATION **For betting purposes, Harbour Master (FR) and Marigot Bay (IRE) were cpld.**
3882a Xaar could not have won this race in better style. Like several of his opponents, he was outpaced early on and, finding his balance halfway up the straight, began to make his challenge. Taking the lead one and a half furlongs out, he drew clear of the runner-up in the final furlong, and the further he went, the better he looked. He has now confirmed his superiority and can be confidently described as classic material. All being well, this son of Zafonic goes for the Dewhurst and next year, the 2,000 Guineas. (6/5)
3882a* Charge D'Affaires was waited with and had to be slightly extracted to challenge with Xaar in the final furlong and a half. He did not have the acceleration to go with the winner and may lack a little stamina. He may take on Xaar again in the Dewhurst Stakes or he could be diverted to the Grand Criterium which is run over a mile, but on a very different part of the Longchamp track. A son of Kendor, he is genuine and consistent and another decent race will come his way. (27/10)
3774* Speedfit Too (IRE) ran an excellent race in representing his small stable. He was brought with a run up the rail after being raced behind the leaders and, running on well, he was never a threat to the winner or runner-up. He will now have a rest and be trained for next year's 2,000 Guineas by way of the Craven Stakes. (17/1)
3178a* Greenlander was always in mid division and rather one-paced in the straight. He would probably be better suited to a longer distance and maybe a drop into Group Three company. (37/10)
3534a Harbour Master (FR), outpaced and under pressure early in the straight, just stayed on in the final stages on ground which looked a little too firm for him. (52/10)
3997a* Chips (IRE) started like a rocket and led until the two-furlong marker where he dropped out quickly. He probably cut his own throat and this race is best forgotten. (24/1)
4090a Marigot Bay (IRE) tried to share the lead with Chips but faded at the same time as him, only a lot quicker. (52/10)

4392a PRIX DU PRINCE D'ORANGE (Gp 3) (3-Y.O)
3-15 (3-14) **1m 2f** £24,691.00 (£8,979.00: £4,489.00)

				SP	RR	SF
2454a3	**Loup Sauvage (USA)** (AFabre,France) **3-8-12** OPeslier	—	1		117	—
1726a9	**Bonapartiste (FR)** (PDemercastel,France) **3-8-12** GMosse	1½	2		115	—
3730a3	**Handsome Ridge** (JHMGosden) **3-9-0** SGuillot	½	3		116	—
						5 Rn

2m 14.0 (14.00) P-M 1.60F: 1.10F 1.10F OWNER Mr Daniel Wildenstein (CHANTILLY) BRED Allez France Stables Ltd
2454a Loup Sauvage (USA) had a perfect trial for the Champion Stakes which will be his next race. He was held up behind the leaders and moved up smoothly to take the lead halfway up the straight. Stretching out to the line, he was never put under the slightest pressure and the best is still to come from him. He will be a tough nut to crack in the Champion Stakes, particularly if there is cut in the ground.
Bonapartiste (FR), waited with, was brought with a late run, but he never had a chance of catching the winner and he is not up to this standard.
3730a Handsome Ridge tried to make every yard of the running. Sticking gamely to his task in the straight, he held on courageously until going into third place. Not suited by this ground, he was giving a kilo to his opponents so this was a brave performance. His next run will be determined by under-foot conditions but he is entered in the Prix Dollar.

4393a PRIX DU PIN (Listed) (3-Y.O+)
3-45 (3-45) **7f** £15,713.00 (£5,387.00: £4,040.00: £2,694.00)

				SP	RR	SF
	Vert Val (USA) (MmeCHead,France) **3-8-6** ODoleuze (fin 2nd, 1l: plcd 1st)	—	1		112	—
2818a*	**Alamo Bay (USA)** (AFabre,France) **4-8-12** OPeslier (fin 3rd, hd: plcd 2nd)	hd	2		114	—
	Keos (USA) (JEHammond,France) **3-8-9** CAsmussen (fin 1st: disq & plcd 3rd)	1	3		117	—
41203	**Miss Riviera** (GWragg) **4-8-8** SGuillot	1	4		108	—
						7 Rn

1m 22.8 (3.80) P-M 4.70F: 2.30F 1.80F OWNER Wertheimer Brothers (CHANTILLY) BRED Wertheimer & Frere
4120 Miss Riviera ran freely early on while being held up for a late run. Putting in her best work inside the final furlong, she was running on best of all at the finish and it looks as if a mile might be to her advantage.

WOODBINE (Toronto, Canada) (L-H) (Good)
Saturday September 20th

4394a WOODBINE MILE (3-Y.O+)
8-40 **1m (Turf)** £129,870.00 (£43,290.00: £23,809.00)

				SP	RR	SF
	Geri (USA) (WMott,USA) **5-8-5** CAntley	—	1		130	—
	Helmsman (USA) (WDollase,USA) **5-8-5** CNakatani	1½	2		127	—
	Crown Attorney (USA) (JMacKenzie,Canada) **4-8-5** TKabel	hd	3		127	—
37852	**Even Top (IRE)** (MHTompkins) **4-8-5** JSantos (btn 12½l)		11		—	—
						12 Rn

1m 36.2 (-1.60) P-M 18.90: (1-2) 8.90 11.20 (1-2-3) 7.40 8.60 15.10 OWNER A. E. Paulson BRED A. E. Paulson

3785 Even Top (IRE) disappointed on his last run for trainer Mark Tompkins. Held up behind, he was unable to quicken when asked the question, and weakened over two furlongs out.

1912a-BELMONT PARK (New York, USA) (L-H) (Fast)
Sunday September 21st

4395a MAN O'WAR STKS (Gp 1) (3-Y.O+)
9-45 **1m 3f** **(Turf)** £142,857.00 (£47,619.00: £26,190.00)

				SP	RR	SF
	Influent (CAN) (MTesher,USA) **6-9-0** JBailey	—	1		131	—
	Val's Prince (USA) (JPicou,USA) **5-9-0** MSmith	2	2		128	—
	Awad (USA) (DDonk,USA) **7-9-0** PDay	¾	3		127	—
3785*	**Annus Mirabilis (FR)** (SbinSuroor) **5-9-0v** GaryStevens (btn jst over 3l)		5		—	—

10 Rn

2m 11.69 P-M 5.80: (1-2) 3.90 7.70 (1-2-3) 2.80 5.00 3.80 OWNER ANKM Stable & Turfnpaddock Farm BRED Austin Taylor
3785* Annus Mirabilis (FR) was not beaten all that far, but did not quite have the pace of the leaders from over one furlong out.

3004a-FRANKFURT (Germany) (L-H) (Good)
Sunday September 21st

4396a FLUGHAFEN FRANKFURT TROPHY (Gp 2) (3-Y.O+)
3-55 (4-00) **1m 2f** £27,462.00 (£10,985.00: £5,492.00: £3,409.00)

				SP	RR	SF
3730a[2]	**Crystal Hearted** (HCandy) **3-8-8** AMcGlone (mde all: rdn out)	—	1		112	—
2642a[6]	**Baleno (GER)** (BSchutz,Germany) **3-8-6** NGrant (mid div: styd on wl fr over 1f out: nt rch ldr)	¾	2		109	—
2643a[3]	**Hondero (GER)** (BOlsson,Germany) **7-9-0b[1]** PPiatkowski (cl up: nt clr run 1½f out: r.o fnl f)	1	3		109	—
2642a[11]	**Icemoon (GER)** (HBlume,Germany) **3-8-6** ABest (hld up in rr: str run fr 1½f out: no ex cl home)	hd	4		107	—
3004a[2]	**Shebar (USA)** (DRichardson,Germany) **6-9-0b** LHammer-Hansen (chsed ldr to st: one pce fnl f)	nse	5		109	—
3993a[3]	**Sambakonig (GER)** (HHorwart,Germany) **4-9-0** PHarley (rr tl st: kpt on wl fnl 2f: nrst fin)	nk	6		109	—
	Allandro (GER) (FrauEMader,Germany) **3-8-6** LMader (mid div: rdn & btn 2f out)	2	7		103	—
4133[3]	**Musalsal (IRE)** (BWHills) **3-8-6** DHolland (racd in 4th: rdn & unable to qckn 2f out)	1¾	8		101	—
3369a[2]	**Kalatos (GER)** (AWohler,Germany) **5-9-2** ABoschert (a bhd)	2	9		101	—

9 Rn

2m 7.02 TOTE 30DM: 14DM 20DM 32DM (229DM) OWNER Mrs C. M. Poland (WANTAGE) BRED Newgate Stud Co
3730a Crystal Hearted put up a great display to make all and hold off the strong challenge of the runner-up. He remains in training next season.
4133 Musalsal (IRE) was never going well according to his pilot and found the ground just a bit too quick. Racing in mid-division, he was unable to quicken when asked two furlongs out.

4259a-SAN SIRO (Milan, Italy) (R-H) (Good to firm)
Sunday September 21st

4397a PREMIO SIGNORINETTA (2-Y.O F)
1-35 (1-35) **7f 110y** £23,142.00 (£10,183.00: £5,554.00)

				SP	RR	SF
	Sopran Londa (IRE) (LCamici,Italy) **2-8-9** MPasquale	—	1		—	—
	Bardonecchia (ITY) (LCamici,Italy) **2-8-9** MCangiano	1	2		—	—
	Lea Grande (LMCumani) **2-8-9** FJovine	3¾	3		—	—

8 Rn

1m 32.9 (8.40) TOTE 23L: 13L 17L 19L (92L) OWNER Az Agr Uberto BRED Azienda Agricola Uberto in Cerrecchie srl
Lea Grande put up a fair performance for this debut and will almost certainly come on for it. Held up in rear, she stayed on well in the final two furlongs and took third place close home.

4398a GRAN PREMIO SAN SIRO (3-Y.O)
3-35 (3-50) **1m 4f** £96,427.00 (£42,428.00: £23,142.00)

				SP	RR	SF
	War Declaration (IRE) (BGrizzetti,Italy) **3-9-2** MTellini	—	1		106	—
2462a[2]	**Honey Colour (IRE)** (ACalchetti,Italy) **3-9-2** OFancera	¾	2		105	—
2462a*	**Jaunty Jack** (LMCumani) **3-9-2** FJovine	½	3		104	—
4133[4]	**Yavlensky (IRE)** (JLDunlop) **3-9-2b[1]** MLatorre (btn 36¼l)		12		—	—

13 Rn

2m 27.6 (7.60) TOTE 119L: 23L 18L 13L (348L) OWNER Scuderia Il Poggio
2462a* Jaunty Jack may have found the ground a bit lively, but nevertheless, put up a brave performance. Racing in third, he switched to the outside soon after entering the straight and went to the front two and a half furlongs from home. Drifting into the rails, he was headed a furlong out and found little when asked inside the final furlong, only running on at the one pace.
4133 Yavlensky (IRE) was held up in rear, he made his effort on the outside three furlongs out, but was soon beaten and was eased.

4399a GRAN PREMIO DEI PROPRIETARI (4-Y.O+)
4-35 (4-54) **1m 2f** £57,856.00 (£23,142.00: £13,885.00)

				SP	RR	SF
4004[5]	**Freequent** (LMCumani) **4-8-12** FJovine	—	1		116	—
2100a[5]	**Toto le Moko (IRE)** (AVerdesi,Italy) **4-8-12** MMonteriso	1	2		114	—
	Concepcion (GER) (HJentzsch,Germany) **7-9-0** SEccles	2½	3		112	—

10 Rn

2m 1.5 (7.50) TOTE 49L: 21L 20L 36L (146L) OWNER Fittocks Stud (NEWMARKET) BRED Fittocks Stud
4004 Freequent returned to his best form and really appreciated this firm ground. Racing in mid-division, he made good headway to track the leaders with two furlongs left to run. He was ridden to hit the front half a furlong from home, and ran on well all the way to the line.

3924-FOLKESTONE (R-H) (Firm)
Friday September 26th
WEATHER: warm WIND: mod half against

4400 EUROTUNNEL DEVELOPMENTS LTD. MAIDEN STKS (3-Y.O+ F & M) (Class D)
2-10 (2-10) **1m 1f 149y** £4,123.35 (£1,234.80: £592.90: £271.95) Stalls: High GOING minus 0.20 sec per fur (GF)

				SP	RR	SF
4046[6]	**Dellua (IRE) (67)** (RGuest) **3-8-10** DaneO'Neill(5) (mde all: clr over 1f out: comf)	—	**1**	11/10[1]	68+	14
4060[11]	**Priluki** (CEBrittain) **3-8-10** MRoberts(2) (hld up: rdn 3f out: swtchd rt 1f out: r.o)	1½	**2**	3/1[2]	66	12
4177[9]	**Miss Vita (USA)** (RJRWilliams) **3-8-10** GCarter(6) (swtg: a.p: chsd wnr 3f out: hrd rdn over 1f out: r.o)	nk	**3**	9/1	65	11
	Rhein Lady (RRowe) **3-8-10** AClark(7) (w'like: bkwd: s.i.s: rdn over 2f out: nvr nr to chal)	11	**4**	6/1[3]	47	—
3211[13]	**Lyphielo (USA)** (LMCumani) **3-8-7**(3) RFfrench(3) (b.off fore: lw: hld up: rdn over 2f out: sn wknd)	¾	**5**	6/1[3]	46	—
	Nancys Gem (DCO'Brien) **3-8-10** GBardwell(4) (str: bkwd: plld hrd: chsd wnr over 6f)	18	**6**	20/1	16	—
4060[19]	**Lady of Glendowan** (MrsBarbaraWaring) **4-9-3**ow1 EByrne(1) (a bhd)	9	**7**	66/1	2	—
				(SP 117.4%)	**7 Rn**	

2m 5.4 (7.70) CSF £4.40 TOTE £1.80: £1.30 £2.20 (£2.80) OWNER Mr Khalid Affara (NEWMARKET) BRED Holborn Trust Co
WEIGHT FOR AGE 3yo-6lb

4046 Dellua (IRE) was the clear form choice and had little problem making all the running to win this very bad race. She is a slow-maturing filly according to her trainer and will be better with a bit of cut. (11/10: 4/5-11/8)

3775 Priluki ran better in this very poor race. Pushed along towards the bottom of the hill, she was switched right entering the final furlong and, running on, just managed to snatch second prize. (3/1)

3775 Miss Vita (USA), a lightly-made filly with no scope, moved into second place three furlongs from home, but she had no chance with the winner despite staying on and was caught for the runner-up spot in the last couple of strides. (9/1)

Rhein Lady looked very tubby in the paddock and, after struggling into fourth place entering the short straight, could make little impression. (6/1)

Lyphielo (USA) lacks ability and was left for dead over two furlongs from home. (6/1: 3/1-7/1)

Nancys Gem looked as fat as a pig in the paddock, and it was absolutely astonishing that she managed to hold on to second place until over three furlongs from home. (20/1)

4401 KENT DEVELOPERS GROUP CLAIMING STKS (2-Y.O) (Class F)
2-40 (2-45) **6f** £2,854.50 (£792.00: £379.50) Stalls: Low GOING minus 0.20 sec per fur (GF)

				SP	RR	SF
4178[5]	**Legal Lark (IRE)** (PHowling) **2-9-0** MRoberts(6) (a.p: w ldr over 1f out: led ins fnl f: rdn out)	—	**1**	3/1[2]	68	41
4006[7]	**Just Another Time (69)** (JBerry) **2-8-9**(3) PRoberts(1) (b.off fore: lw: chsd ldr: led over 1f out: wandered: hdd ins fnl f: r.o)	hd	**2**	9/4[1]	66	39
2003[6]	**Lady Almitra** (CJHill) **2-8-0**(5) RMullen(5) (bit bkwd: hld up: rdn over 2f out: r.o)	1½	**3**	10/1	55	28
4166[16]	**Shannon (IRE) (56)** (CADwyer) **2-8-5** AClark(9) (rdn 4f out: hdwy over 1f out: unable qckn fnl f)	3	**4**	7/1[3]	47	20
4052[11]	**Pinup (60)** (GLewis) **2-7-10**(3) RFfrench(11) (rdn over 2f out: hdwy over 1f out: one pce fnl f)	½	**5**	7/1[3]	39	12
4068[15]	**Shecando (IRE) (57)** (CJames) **2-8-9v**[1] DRMcCabe(8) (bhd whn stumbled over 4f out: hung rt 1f out: nvr nrr)	2	**6**	14/1	44	17
4157[12]	**Zimzie (60)** (MJHaynes) **2-8-4** TSprake(7) (outpcd: nvr nrr)	½	**7**	14/1	38	11
4327[9]	**Jaybee Silver (49)** (MHTompkins) **2-8-3v**[1] DBiggs(4) (hld up: rdn over 2f out: wknd wl over 1f out)	2½	**8**	16/1	30	3
4054[15]	**Medina Miss (52)** (GMMcCourt) **2-7-13v**[1] NVarley(2) (led over 4f)	2½	**9**	10/1	19	—
3094[16]	**Aries Boy** (DCO'Brien) **2-8-6** GBardwell(3) (b: lw: a bhd)	2½	**10**	33/1	20	—
	Moonclaret (CJames) **2-8-7** MTebbutt(10) (leggy: lt-f: bhd fnl 3f)	9	**11**	25/1	—	—
				(SP 125.0%)	**11 Rn**	

1m 13.0 (2.80) CSF £9.94 TOTE £4.30: £1.80 £1.30 £3.50 (£5.10) Trio £44.50 OWNER Six Furlong Racing Club (NEWMARKET) BRED Thomas Downey

4178 Legal Lark (IRE) appreciated the return to six furlongs and, throwing down his challenge below the distance, managed to force his head in front inside the final furlong. Described as a "screwball" by his trainer, he has already put one person in hospital. (3/1: 5/1-11/4)

3859 Just Another Time gained control over a furlong out, but he then wandered badly in front. Passed by the winner inside the final furlong, he nevertheless kept on well to the line. A small claimer can be found for him before long. (9/4: 7/4-11/4)

2003 Lady Almitra looked in need of this first run in four months but nevertheless kept on well inside the final furlong. (10/1: op 6/1)

3967 Shannon (IRE), a sparely-made filly, was soon being bustled along. She did pick up ground below the distance, but was making no further impression in the final furlong. (7/1)

3416 Pinup has shown herself to be a poor performer and, although taking closer order below the distance, was then only treading water. (7/1)

Shecando (IRE) (14/1: 10/1-16/1)

4402 E.B.F. CHERITON PARK MEDIAN AUCTION MAIDEN STKS (2-Y.O) (Class F)
3-10 (3-14) **5f** £2,808.30 (£778.80: £372.90) Stalls: Low GOING minus 0.20 sec per fur (GF)

				SP	RR	SF
4216[3]	**Call To Order** (CFWall) **2-8-9**(5) RMullen(6) (lw: hld up: led over 1f out: shkn up: comf)	—	**1**	4/5[1]	78+	36
	Missed The Cut (IRE) (RHannon) **2-8-9** DaneO'Neill(2) (leggy: lt-f: rdn & hdwy over 1f out: unable qckn wl ins fnl f)	nk	**2**	13/2[2]	72	30
4311[8]	**Red Pepper (IRE)** (PHowling) **2-9-0** GHind(5) (a.p: ev ch over 1f out: one pce)	1¼	**3**	20/1	73	31
4143[8]	**Sergeant Imp (IRE) (58)** (PMitchell) **2-9-0b**[1] AClark(3) (swtg: a.p: led over 2f out tl over 1f out: one pce)	1	**4**	20/1	70	28
	Ballasilla (BPalling) **2-8-9** TSprake(7) (w'like: bit bkwd: s.s: hld up: rdn over 2f out: one pce)	1¾	**5**	10/1	59	17
4159[3]	**Chikapenny (63)** (MrsLStubbs) **2-8-9v** SWhitworth(4) (nvr nr to chal)	2½	**6**	15/2[3]	51	9
3821[8]	**Cape Hope (61)** (RBoss) **2-9-0** NDay(10) (lw: led over 2f: wknd over 1f out)	hd	**7**	12/1	56	14
3926[10]	**Critical Air** (SirMarkPrescott) **2-9-0** CNutter(9) (spd over 3f)	2½	**8**	20/1	48	6
3636[9]	**Call Me Vera** (EAWheeler) **2-8-4**(5) ADaly(8) (swtg: s.s: bhd fnl 2f)	1¾	**9**	25/1	37	—
2304[6]	**Remember Frimley** (CJHill) **2-8-6**(3) PRoberts(1) (a bhd)	1½	**10**	33/1	33	—
				(SP 118.5%)	**10 Rn**	

60.2 secs (2.60) CSF £5.08 TOTE £1.60: £1.10 £2.20 £4.40 (£4.20) Trio £28.60 OWNER Induna Racing Partners (NEWMARKET) BRED David Sinden, Mervyn Ayers and Richard Brunger

4216 Call To Order has run well this season, and had no problem mopping-up this race under a cool ride from Mullen. Moving to the front approaching the final furlong, he was shaken up and, although the runner-up looked a possible danger inside the final furlong, his jockey was confident enough to stop riding nearing the line. This is his ground. (4/5: 5/4-8/11)

Missed The Cut (IRE), a tall filly with no substance, made an encouraging debut. Picking up ground nicely below the distance, she looked a possible threat to the winner inside the final furlong, but that rival was toying with her in the closing stages and she is flattered to finish quite so close. (13/2: 3/1-7/1)
3589 Red Pepper (IRE), in the firing-line throughout, had every chance approaching the final furlong before tapped for toe. (20/1)
985 Sergeant Imp (IRE) appreciated the drop in distance and ran his best race to date, showing in front from halfway before put in his place when collared below the distance. (20/1)
Ballasilla, quite a tall, plain filly, looked in need of this and was only struggling on at the one insufficient pace in the final quarter-mile. (10/1: 4/1-12/1)
4159 Chikapenny may have been placed five times this season, but she is thoroughly exposed and never threatened to get into it. (15/2: 5/1-8/1)
2466 Cape Hope (12/1: op 6/1)

4403 ORBITAL PARK LTD. NURSERY H'CAP (0-85) (2-Y.O) (Class D)

3-40 (3-41) **5f** £3,322.00 (£991.00: £473.00: £214.00) Stalls: Low GOING minus 0.20 sec per fur (GF)

			SP	RR	SF
4145^{8} **Mantles Pride (78)** (GLewis) **2-9-3**(3) RFfrench(1) (b: rdn over 2f out: hdwy to chse ldr over 1f out: led ins fnl f: r.o wl)	—	**1**	8/1	83	55
4216* **Arian Da (80)** (BPalling) **2-9-8** 6x TSprake(3) (lw: led tl ins fnl f: unable qckn)	¾	**2**	8/1	83	55
3965^{3} **Ok John (IRE) (63)** (JAkehurst) **2-8-0**(5) ADaly(2) (chsd ldr over 3f: one pce)	2	**3**	7/1	59	31
4012* **Escudo (IRE) (79)** (JHMGosden) **2-9-7** GHind(7) (s.s: stdy hdwy over 2f out: rdn over 1f out: one pce)	½	**4**	2/1 1	74	46
3544^{2} **Always Lucky (65)** (JBerry) **2-8-4**(3) PRoberts(5) (b.nr hind: a.p: rdn over 1f out: one pce)	½	**5**	6/1 3	58	30
4178* **Rapid Reliance (61)** (RIngram) **2-8-3** 6x DRMcCabe(8) (bhd fnl 2f)	3½	**6**	100/30 2	43	15
4042^{4} **Katyushka (IRE) (74)** (MajorDNChappell) **2-9-2** GCarter(6) (swtg: a bhd)	½	**7**	8/1	54	26
4065^{8} **Blue Shadow (66)** (RHannon) **2-8-8b** DaneO'Neill(4) (a bhd)	½	**8**	10/1	45	17

(SP 125.6%) **8 Rn**

59.4 secs (1.80) CSF £69.30 CT £345.49 TOTE £10.40: £2.20 £2.30 £2.00 (£29.90) OWNER Mr David Barker (EPSOM) BRED R. B. Stokes
3686 Mantles Pride showed his recent Goodwood run to be all wrong and, taking second place below the distance, got up inside the final furlong. (8/1: 4/1-9/1)
4216* Arian Da attempted to make all the running as she had done at Sandown last week, but was eventually overhauled inside the final furlong. (8/1)
3965 Ok John (IRE), in second place until below the distance, then failed to raise his work-rate. (7/1)
4012* Escudo (IRE), well supported in the market, gradually eased her way into the action at halfway but, in the battle to the line from below the distance, she was tapped for toe. She needs further than this minimum trip. (2/1)
3544 Always Lucky, given a six-week break after being beaten at odds-on last time out, was in the firing line until tapped for toe from below the distance. (6/1: 4/1-13/2)
4042 Katyushka (IRE) (8/1: op 5/1)
3783 Blue Shadow (10/1: op 6/1)

4404 LEVY BOARD APPRENTICE H'CAP (0-70) (3-Y.O+) (Class E)

4-10 (4-13) **6f 189y** £2,401.62 (£2,401.62: £534.50: £247.25) Stalls: High GOING minus 0.20 sec per fur (GF)

			SP	RR	SF
4324* **Zurs (IRE) (58)** (JRPoulton) **4-9-2** 6x RMullen(13) (a.p: rdn over 1f out: led ins fnl f: r.o wl)	—	**1**	9/2 3	71	37
3297^{5} **Master Millfield (IRE) (47)** (CJHill) **5-8-2**(3) JWilkinson(7) (lw: hdwy on ins over 1f out: nt clr run on ins ins fnl f: r.o wl)	—	**1**	14/1	60	26
4139^{12} **Mukhlles (USA) (62)** (BobJones) **4-8-13**(7) GemmaJones(11) (lw: hdwy over 1f out: r.o wl ins fnl f)	nk	**3**	14/1	74	40
3930^{2} **Banzhaf (USA) (68)** (GLMoore) **4-9-7**(5) MBatchelor(16) (lw: a.p: rdn over 1f out: r.o one pce)	1	**4**	4/1 2	78	44
4112^{8} **Speedy Classic (USA) (55)** (MJHeaton-Ellis) **8-8-13** ADaly(6) (led tl ins fnl f: one pce)	hd	**5**	12/1	65	31
3590^{5} **Dark Menace (47)** (EAWheeler) **5-8-0b**(5) SCarson(5) (hdwy over 1f out: r.o ins fnl f)	s.h	**6**	16/1	57	23
4228* **Lunch Party (44)** (DNicholls) **5-8-2** 6x PRoberts(3) (w ldr: ev ch ins fnl f: sn wknd)	1	**7**	2/1 1	51	17
4228^{14} **Don Pepe (61)** (RBoss) **6-9-5** GFaulkner(4) (a.p: rdn over 1f out: n.m.r ins fnl f: one pce)	½	**8**	20/1	67	33
3980^{14} **Ivor's Deed (54)** (MissGayKelleway) **4-8-12** RFfrench(10) (lw: hld up: rdn over 1f out: nt clr run ins fnl f: one pce)	nk	**9**	8/1	59	25
4249^{3} **Suite Factors (57)** (KRBurke) **3-8-12** JDSmith(1) (nvr nr to chal)	½	**10**	10/1	61	24
4008^{6} **Perfect Poppy (53)** (SDow) **3-8-5**(3) PDoe(12) (prom over 5f)	½	**11**	14/1	56	19
4373^{19} **Prince Zizim (40)** (RCSpicer) **4-7-12**ow2 AWhelan(14) (lw: a bhd)	½	**12**	40/1	42	6
3787^{16} **Primelta (45)** (RAkehurst) **4-8-0**(3) DDenby(9) (lw: a bhd)	1¾	**13**	12/1	43	9
3608^{8} **Backhander (IRE) (38)** (RTPhillips) **5-7-5b**(5) DarrenWilliams(8) (lw: a bhd)	1¾	**14**	33/1	32	—

(SP 143.1%) **14 Rn**

1m 25.2 (3.80) CSF Z & MM £35.96; MM & Z £40.46 CT Z, MM & M £411.86; MM, Z & M £449.61 TOTE Z £3.20; MM £7.90: Z £2.20 MM £4.90 M £5.30 (£118.60) Trio £357.10 OWNER Glendale Partnership Ltd (LEWES)/Mr John Hill (BARNSTAPLE) BRED Mrs A. Whitehead/A. M. F. Persse
LONG HANDICAP Prince Zizim 7-4 Backhander (IRE) 7-8
WEIGHT FOR AGE 3yo-3lb
4324* Zurs (IRE) followed up his Leicester win on Monday, but was undoubtedly lucky to share the spoils as the runner-up failed to get a clear run inside the final furlong. He did not handle this track according to his trainer. (9/2)
Master Millfield (IRE) has slumped in the handicap after a string of poor efforts - he was 18lb lower than when last successful - but bounced back, and was desperately unlucky not to have won this outright. Trapped in with nowhere to go along the inside rail inside the final furlong, a gap did appear in the last thirty yards and he shot through to share the spoils. (14/1: op 8/1)
3470 Mukhlles (USA), whose apprentice was having her first ever ride, looked extremely well beforehand and was certainly the paddock pick. Beginning a forward move below the distance, she ran on really nicely inside the final furlong and only just failed. (14/1: 12/1-20/1)
3930 Banzhaf (USA), who ran an encouraging race here last time out, again showed plenty of promise and, not given a hard time, was staying on nicely in the closing stages. (4/1)
3251 Speedy Classic (USA) is a real All-Weather specialist, having notched up eight of his eleven victories on the sand. Nevertheless, he did a good job of pacemaking and was not overhauled until inside the final furlong. (12/1)
3590 Dark Menace, racing in midfield, stayed on in the last furlong and a half to be nearest at the line. (16/1)
1484* Ivor's Deed (8/1: 5/1-10/1)
4249 Suite Factors (10/1: op 6/1)
4008 Perfect Poppy (14/1: 10/1-16/1)
3292* Primelta (12/1: 8/1-14/1)

4405 KENT H'CAP (0-70) (3-Y.O+) (Class E)

4-40 (4-40) **1m 7f 92y** £3,278.25 (£981.00: £470.50: £215.25) Stalls: High GOING minus 0.20 sec per fur (GF)

				SP	RR	SF
4246[4]	**Unchanged (60)** (CEBrittain) **5-9-5** MRoberts(2) (mde virtually all: sddle slipped over 2f out: hrd rdn over 1f out: r.o wl)	—	1	5/1[3]	73	55
3549[8]	**Padauk (60)** (MJHaynes) **3-8-8** TSprake(1) (lw: hdwy over 3f out: chsd wnr fnl 2f: r.o)	1½	2	16/1	71	42
4170[2]	**Coh Sho No (46)** (SDow) **4-8-5** DaneO'Neill(10) (hdwy over 3f out: rdn over 2f out: unable qckn)	2½	3	2/1[2]	55	37
4170[11]	**Duncombe Hall (42)** (CACyzer) **4-7-12**(3)ow3 AWhelan(4) (hld up: rdn 5f out: chsd wnr over 3f out to 2f out: one pce)	nk	4	10/1	51	30
3291[3]	**Victor Blum (USA) (37)** (CAHorgan) **4-7-7v**(3) RFfrench(11) (lw: nvr nr to chal)	2	5	33/1	44	26
4161[3]	**Classic Flyer (IRE) (65)** (ICampbell) **4-9-10** GCarter(9) (lw: chsd wnr 12f)	3	6	11/1	68	50
3080[8]	**Chez Catalan (37)** (RAkehurst) **6-7-10b** NAdams(5) (bhd fnl 5f)	5	7	20/1	35	17
2474[3]	**Heubach Boy (48)** (JPearce) **3-7-5**(5) RMullen(3) (a bhd)	½	8	25/1	46	17
4287*	**Il Principe (IRE) (59)** (JohnBerry) **3-8-7** 5x GBardwell(7) (lw: prom over 11f)	5	9	7/4[1]	52	23
				(SP 121.2%)	**9 Rn**	

3m 24.4 (6.40) CSF £73.21 CT £195.36 TOTE £6.20: £1.40 £4.50 £1.40 (£49.20) Trio £37.50 OWNER Mr M. J. Simmonds (NEWMARKET) BRED M. J. Simmonds
LONG HANDICAP Victor Blum (USA) 7-3 Chez Catalan 7-8 Heubach Boy 7-6
WEIGHT FOR AGE 3yo-11lb
OFFICIAL EXPLANATION **Il Principe (IRE): the trainer reported that the gelding was over the top.**

4246 Unchanged, 2lb lower than when winning this race two years ago, had plenty of use made of her under a lovely ride from Roberts, who had to contend with a slipping saddle in the straight. Nevertheless, she responded to pressure and was not going to be caught. (5/1)
3057 Padauk is an exposed maiden. Moving into second place two furlongs from home, he ran on but never seriously looked like overhauling the winner. (16/1)
4170 Coh Sho No, whose only victory to date came over this course and distance in April off an 8lb higher mark, took closer order running down the hill but could make no impression in the straight. (2/1)
3928* Duncombe Hall once again demonstrated that he is very hard work, and was being shunted along at the top of the hill fully five furlongs from home. He did show in second place for a while but was tapped for toe in the straight. (10/1)
3291 Victor Blum (USA) never threatened to get into it and remains a maiden. (33/1)
4161 Classic Flyer (IRE) found this step-up in distance too much and, after racing in second place until over three furlongs from home, had little more to offer. She has just one win to her name. (11/1)

4406 ORBITAL TWO LIMITED STKS (0-70) (3-Y.O+) (Class E)

5-10 (5-10) **1m 4f** £3,200.25 (£957.00: £458.50: £209.25) Stalls: High GOING minus 0.20 sec per fur (GF)

				SP	RR	SF
4275[6]	**Opera Buff (IRE) (68)** (MissGayKelleway) **6-9-0**(7) JWilkinson(6) (lw: hdwy over 2f out: led over 1f out: rdn out)	—	1	9/2[2]	78	58
4108[4]	**Pistol (IRE) (67)** (CAHorgan) **7-9-0**(3) RFfrench(10) (b: b.nr hind: hdwy over 1f out: r.o wl ins fnl f)	hd	2	2/1[1]	74	54
2885[6]	**Nobel Lad (70)** (MCPipe) **3-8-9** TSprake(5) (hld up: chsd ldr over 5f out: led 4f out tl over 1f out: wknd ins fnl f)	5	3	12/1	67	39
4108[12]	**North Reef (IRE) (70)** (JPearce) **6-9-5** MWigham(4) (chsd ldr: led 6f out to 4f out: wknd over 1f out)	1	4	9/1	68	48
3452[9]	**Off The Rails (57)** (HCandy) **3-8-6** NAdams(1) (lw: hdwy over 5f out: chsd ldr over 2f out tl over 1f out: sn wknd)	1½	5	14/1	61	33
4275[12]	**Frozen Sea (USA) (60)** (GPEnright) **6-8-10**(7) PDoe(2) (lw: a bhd)	18	6	10/1	40	20
4002[9]	**Freedom Chance (IRE) (70)** (JWHills) **3-8-11v** MRoberts(9) (lw: prom 6f)	1¾	7	6/1[3]	40	12
4108[16]	**Pietro Bembo (IRE) (70)** (SirMarkPrescott) **3-8-9** CNutter(3) (prom over 6f)	s.h	8	7/1	38	10
4108[15]	**Krosno (70)** (SCWilliams) **3-8-13** GCarter(7) (lw: led 6f)	8	9	7/1	31	3
				(SP 124.3%)	**9 Rn**	

2m 35.9 (4.70) CSF £13.75 TOTE £5.80: £2.40 £2.00 £2.00 (£5.70) Trio £31.80 OWNER Mr D. W. Watson (WHITCOMBE) BRED Juddmonte Farms
WEIGHT FOR AGE 3yo-8lb

4275 Opera Buff (IRE) has gained five of his eight previous victories over this trip and, striking the front approaching the final furlong, was ridden along to hold off the runner-up. (9/2)
4108 Pistol (IRE) shot through with all guns blazing below the distance and, looking a serious threat to the winner inside the final furlong, only just failed to get up in a tight finish. (2/1)
2885 Nobel Lad, who has changed stables since his last run ten weeks ago, moved to the front running down the hill, but that was probably too early in this fast-run race and, collared below the distance, he was soon in trouble. He can find a race. (12/1: 8/1-14/1)
3184 North Reef (IRE), moved to the front in the back straight, but he was collared half a mile from home and was out on his feet below the distance. This trip seems to be beyond him. (9/1)
1420 Off The Rails, who was dropped in distance to a mile last time out, was tried over much further this time as connections desperately tried to find a trip that will bring about improvement. She showed in second place for a brief time early in the straight but, collared for that position below the distance, had little left in reserve. (14/1)
3229 Krosno (7/1: op 4/1)

T/Jkpt: £7,890.10 (2.6 Tckts). T/Plpt: £87.90 (250.1 Tckts). T/Qdpt: £49.40 (23.05 Tckts) AK

4305-HAYDOCK (L-H) (Good)

Friday September 26th

WEATHER: cloudy WIND: slight bhd

4407 STANLEY 49'S MAIDEN STKS (3-Y.O) (Class D)

2-30 (2-31) **1m 2f 120y** £3,582.50 (£1,085.00: £530.00: £252.50) Stalls: Low GOING minus 0.20 sec per fur (GF)

				SP	RR	SF
3389[3]	**Sunny Isle** (CFWall) **3-8-9** JReid(1) (chsd ldr: led over 1f out: r.o wl)	—	1	7/4[1]	69	18
4177[4]	**Beacon Silver** (LordHuntingdon) **3-8-9** WRyan(2) (lw: led: rdn & hdd appr fnl f: r.o one pce)	1¼	2	2/1[2]	67	16
740[9]	**Mowelga** (LadyHerries) **3-9-0** PaulEddery(4) (bit bkwd: s.s: hld up: hdwy on ins over 2f out: rdn & one pce fnl f)	¾	3	7/1	71	20

Form	Horse	Dist	Pos	SP	RR	SF
4277^{4}	**Limni (USA)** (MrsJCecil) **3-9-0** JCarroll(6) (b: hld up: hdwy over 3f out: hrd rdn & one pce fnl f)	½	**4**	4/1^{3}	70	19
	All Girls Forget (JDBethell) **3-8-4**(5) CLowther(7) (cmpt: bkwd: chsd ldrs tl wknd over 2f out: t.o)	22	**5**	20/1	32	—
3977^{9}	**Taborite (USA)** (EJAlston) **3-9-0** JFEgan(3) (bkwd: prom tl wknd 3f out: sn t.o)	d.h	**5**	33/1	70	19
				(SP 109.9%)	**6 Rn**	

2m 19.4 (7.90) CSF £4.79 TOTE £2.30: £1.80 £1.70 (£2.20) OWNER Mr S. Fustok (NEWMARKET) BRED Deerfield Farm

3389 Sunny Isle, whose dam was a useful racemare in the States, took the leader's measure entering the final furlong and, galloping on strongly, won with a shade to spare. She had no trouble seeing out the extra quarter-mile, but she did not have a lot to beat. (7/4)

4177 Beacon Silver, behind the winner on her debut in August, has had the benefit of a couple of runs since then but, despite more forceful tactics, her run had come to an end approaching the last furlong. (2/1)

Mowelga, a fine-looking colt returning after a five-month absence, looked in need of this but, with the company being somewhat moderate, he performed with credit, and if he had a turn of finishing pace he could well have nicked it. (7/1)

4277 Limni (USA), still carrying plenty of condition, took closer order in the straight and was close enough if good enough inside the distance, but he found very little when put to the test and has not really come to himself yet. (4/1)

4408 STANLEY LEISURE MAIDEN STKS (3-Y.O) (Class D)

3-00 (3-00) **7f 30y** £3,566.25 (£1,080.00: £527.50: £251.25) Stalls: High GOING minus 0.20 sec per fur (GF)

Form	Horse	Dist	Pos	SP	RR	SF
3921^{9}	**Moonshiner (USA) (75)** (GWragg) **3-9-0v^{1}** PaulEddery(6) (lw: mde all: drew wl clr over 1f out: unchal)	—	**1**	13/2	87	58
4175^{10}	**Kawa-Ib (IRE) (77)** (PTWalwyn) **3-8-9** RHills(1) (hld up & bhd: hdwy 2f out: kpt on fnl f: no ch w wnr)	6	**2**	2/1^{2}	69	40
	Maypole (IRE) (DRLoder) **3-9-0** RCochrane(2) (nt grwn: bkwd: chsd wnr: rdn over 2f out: sn btn)	¾	**3**	7/4^{1}	72	43
4290^{3}	**Present Chance (75)** (BAMcMahon) **3-9-0** LNewton(3) (b.hind: chsd ldrs: rdn over 2f out: sn wknd)	4	**4**	9/2^{3}	63	34
3335^{4}	**Okra** (JDBethell) **3-8-9** JReid(4) (hld up & bhd: rdn 3f out: no imp)	1¼	**5**	33/1	55	26
	Celestial Ridge (IRE) (JMCarr) **3-8-9** JFEgan(5) (unf: scope: bkwd: b: a in rr: t.o fnl 3f)	dist	**6**	33/1	—	—
				(SP 107.1%)	**6 Rn**	

1m 30.12 (2.12) CSF £16.48 TOTE £7.20: £2.90 £1.50 (£9.50) OWNER Baron G Von Ullmann (NEWMARKET) BRED Edmund J. Loder

674 Moonshiner (USA), returning to maiden company after several attempts in handicaps, changed his tactics and galloped the opposition into the ground. With the favourite short of peak fitness he probably did not have a great deal to beat. (13/2)

4175 Kawa-Ib (IRE) gave the impression cantering to post that she might benefit form easier ground. Settled off the pace, she began to stay on in the latter stages but the winner had got away and she was never a threat. (2/1)

Maypole (IRE), an attractive sort who has not grown since last year, was too backward to win on this seasonal debut and his attempt to hang on to the winner had come to an end soon after passing the two-furlong marker. (7/4)

4290 Present Chance continues to disappoint, and if he could not at least offer threat in this company he is not going to be easy to win with. (9/2: op 3/1)

4409 STANLEY RACING H'CAP (0-90) (3-Y.O+) (Class C)

3-30 (3-32) **1m 3f 200y** £5,667.00 (£1,716.00: £838.00: £399.00) Stalls: Low GOING minus 0.20 sec per fur (GF)

Form	Horse	Dist	Pos	SP	RR	SF
4101^{14}	**Marsul (USA) (83)** (JHMGosden) **3-9-0v** RHills(5) (mde all: clr ent fnl f: hld on cl home)	—	**1**	8/1	95	50
4102^{7}	**Billy Bushwacker (80)** (MrsMReveley) **6-9-5** RCochrane(2) (lw: s.s: hld up in rr: gd hdwy u.p appr fnl f: fin wl)	½	**2**	6/1^{2}	91	54
4144*	**Aerleon Pete (IRE) (87)** (MRStoute) **3-9-4** JReid(3) (s.i.s: hdwy over 2f out: rdn & styd on wl nr fin)	½	**3**	15/8^{1}	98	53
4161*	**Blenheim Terrace (58)** (CBBBooth) **4-7-11** 6x FNorton(1) (s.s: hdwy on ins over 3f out: hrd rdn appr fnl f: r.o)	1	**4**	11/1	67	30
3475^{8}	**Passing Strangers (USA) (64)** (PWHarris) **4-7-12**(5) CLowther(9) (lw: hld up in tch: effrt wl over 2f out: unable qckn ins fnl f)	s.h	**5**	14/1	73	36
3915^{8}	**Stahr (73)** (HCandy) **3-8-4b** CRutter(4) (prom: drvn along over 2f out: sn btn)	4	**6**	14/1	77	32
4136^{10}	**My Learned Friend (73)** (AHide) **6-8-12b^{1}** AMcGlone(6) (lw: plld hrd: chsd ldrs: rdn 2f out: grad wknd)	½	**7**	15/2^{3}	76	39
4136^{5}	**Celestial Choir (87)** (JLEyre) **7-9-5**(7) SBuckley(7) (trckd ldrs: brought wd & rdn 3f out: sn lost tch)	2	**8**	6/1^{2}	88	51
4102^{10}	**Meteor Strike (USA) (83)** (MrsAJPerrett) **3-9-0** PaulEddery(8) (lw: chsd wnr 9f: sn rdn: wknd fnl 2f)	5	**9**	11/1	77	32
				(SP 116.2%)	**9 Rn**	

2m 34.18 (4.78) CSF £50.60 CT £116.45 TOTE £9.10: £2.20 £2.00 £1.60 (£24.30) Trio £32.30 OWNER Mr Hamdan Al Maktoum (NEWMARKET) BRED Hidaway Farm

WEIGHT FOR AGE 3yo-8lb

3419* Marsul (USA) won his maiden at this trip last month and then failed to see out the extra couple of furlongs at Doncaster, but he was not afraid to force the pace and, keeping up the gallop, proved too strong for a host of challengers nearing the finish. (8/1)

4102 Billy Bushwacker has not won since the spring of 1995, but he showed something of a return to form on this first attempt at this longer trip, and it should only be a matter of time before he finally gets back to winning ways. (6/1)

4144* Aerleon Pete (IRE), failed in his bid to complete a hat-trick in a slightly higher grade, and he looked to be galloping on the spot when ridden below the distance but, with the strong-finishing runner-up to egg him on, he too was reeling in the winner towards the finish. (15/8)

4161* Blenheim Terrace was stepping up in class here, and was well suited by the strong pace, but he could never quite muster the speed to deliver a challenge. There was no disgrace in this defeat and he is at his peak at present. (11/1)

3183 Passing Strangers (USA) made steady progress and was in pursuit of the winner approaching the final furlong but, hard as he tried, he just could not raise his pace when it was most needed. (14/1)

2725* Stahr is not up to this class and, though he sat in behind for quite some way, he failed to respond when pressure was applied and dropped away tamely. (14/1)

4410 STANLEY LEISURE DREAM MILE H'CAP (0-85) (3-Y.O+) (Class D)

4-00 (4-02) **1m 30y** £3,891.25 (£1,180.00: £577.50: £276.25) Stalls: Low GOING minus 0.20 sec per fur (GF)

Form	Horse	Dist	Pos	SP	RR	SF
4147^{4}	**Duraid (IRE) (76)** (DenysSmith) **5-9-0**(5) CLowther(4) (chsd ldrs: led wl over 1f out: r.o wl)	—	**1**	11/2^{1}	88	57
3976^{9}	**Jedi Knight (69)** (MWEasterby) **3-8-8** FNorton(8) (hld up: effrt over 1f out: r.o wl fnl f)	2	**2**	11/1	77	42
3976^{2}	**Night of Glass (61)** (JLEyre) **4-8-4v** MGallagher(2) (a.p: led 2f out: rdn & edgd lft: sn hdd: no ex fnl f)	½	**3**	7/1^{3}	68	37
3976^{20}	**Sualtach (IRE) (71)** (RHollinshead) **4-9-0** WRyan(6) (lw: hld up: hdwy over 2f out: kpt on u.p fnl f)	1¼	**4**	14/1	76	45
4176^{3}	**Sheer Face (77)** (WRMuir) **3-9-2** JReid(18) (lw: hld up: effrt & rdn 2f out: styng on whn nt clr run wl ins fnl f)	1	**5**	13/2^{2}	80	45
4147^{15}	**Suez Tornado (IRE) (68)** (EJAlston) **4-8-8**(3) MHenry(7) (hld up: hdwy 3f out: nt rch ldrs)	1¼	**6**	16/1	68	37
4147^{10}	**Band on the Run (79)** (BAMcMahon) **10-9-8** PaulEddery(17) (lw: chsd ldrs: rdn 2f out: sn btn)	4	**7**	10/1	71	40
4213^{13}	**Alpine Hideaway (IRE) (70)** (MWEasterby) **4-8-13** TLucas(11) (nvr nr to chal)	hd	**8**	14/1	62	31
2136^{7}	**Master Beveled (73)** (PDEvans) **7-9-2** JFEgan(15) (bit bkwd: nvr nrr)	2	**9**	16/1	61	30
3910^{14}	**Sycamore Lodge (IRE) (65)** (MAPeill) **6-8-8** JCarroll(3) (s.s: hdwy on ins 3f out: nt clr run wl over 1f out: nt rcvr)	nk	**10**	33/1	53	22
3812^{8}	**Just Visiting (73)** (CaptJWilson) **3-8-12** CRutter(1) (mde most to 2f out: sn wknd)	nk	**11**	33/1	60	25

2866^{11} **China Red (USA) (82)** (JWHills) **3-9-7** RHills(13) (a in rr)	nk	**12**	14/1	68	33
4283^{6} **Celebration Cake (IRE) (69)** (MissLAPerratt) **5-8-12** DeanMcKeown(9) (trckd ldrs tl rdn & wknd 2f out)	½	**13**	10/1	55	24
1775^{13} **Grand Musica (84)** (IABalding) **4-9-13** RCochrane(14) (bit bkwd: s.s: a in rr)	nk	**14**	20/1	69	38
4308^{P} **Smokey From Caplaw (68)** (JJO'Neill) **3-8-7** AMcGlone(16) (lw: a in rr)	s.h	**15**	16/1	53	18
4147^{9} **Mountgate (64)** (MPBielby) **5-8-7** DWright(12) (a bhd: t.o)	7	**16**	25/1	35	4
4219^{3} **Orange Place (IRE) (75)** (BJLlewellyn) **6-8-11**(7) SBuckley(10) (w ldr tl wknd 3f out: t.o)	2	**17**	12/1	42	11

(SP 127.6%) **17 Rn**

1m 43.56 (2.96) CSF £58.69 CT £402.22 TOTE £5.80: £2.00 £3.20 £1.70 £2.90 (£51.70) Trio £219.80 OWNER Mr A. Suddes (BISHOP AUCK-LAND) BRED Hussein Hurami

WEIGHT FOR AGE 3yo-4lb

4147 Duraid (IRE) enjoyed a much better run than he endured at Doncaster and, showing ahead below the distance, soon forged clear to land the gamble readily. (11/2)

3457* Jedi Knight, waiting on the leaders, mounted a determined challenge at the same time as the winner, but that rival beat him to the punch and always had his measure. (11/1)

3976 Night of Glass finished ahead of the principals on his most recent race at York, and he did kick for home two furlongs out, but he drifted off a true line when given a crack with the whip and, losing his advantage, was not given a second chance. (7/1)

3018 Sualtach (IRE), still to succeed at this trip, delivered his challenge from off the pace but, despite staying on, was comfortably held in the closing stages. (14/1)

4176 Sheer Face, working his way through on the inside rail, was staying on but at full stretch when he was tightened up inside the final furlong, and what small chance he had quickly came to an end. (13/2)

3262 Suez Tornado (IRE) took closer order in the straight but was unable to make enough progress to land a blow. (16/1)

Sycamore Lodge (IRE), having another try at this longer trip, was creeping up on the inside rail when finding his path blocked below the distance and, forced to snatch up, had no chance of getting going again. (33/1)

4411 STANLEY CASINOS NURSERY H'CAP (0-85) (2-Y.O) (Class D)

4-30 (4-33) **6f** £3,355.00 (£1,015.00: £495.00: £235.00) Stalls: High GOING minus 0.35 sec per fur (F)

			SP	RR	SF
3717* **Kheyrah (USA) (83)** (EALDunlop) **2-9-6** RHills(3) (lw: a w ldrs: chal 1f out: rdn to ld fnl 50y)	—	1	$6/4^{1}$	83	66
4097* **Branston Berry (IRE) (78)** (JLEyre) **2-8-8**(7) SBuckley(11) (b.hind: a.p: led over 2f out tl wl ins fnl f)	nk	2	9/1	77	60
3755^{8} **Peter's Imp (IRE) (80)** (JBerry) **2-9-3** JCarroll(2) (a.p: rdn & ev ch 1f out: one pce fnl f)	3	3	16/1	71	54
3650^{14} **Cool Secret (78)** (ABMulholland) **2-9-1** DWright(7) (s.i.s: swtchd lft & hdwy 2f out: r.o wl towards fin)	¾	4	20/1	67	50
4014* **Classy Cleo (IRE) (74)** (PDEvans) **2-8-11** JFEgan(5) (mde most over 3f: rdn & one pce fnl f)	nk	5	$15/2^{3}$	62	45
1821^{9} **Miss Dangerous (59)** (MRChannon) **2-7-10** JQuinn(1) (prom on outside tl rdn & wknd appr fnl f)	1¾	6	25/1	43	26
4211^{10} **Quiz Master (70)** (EWeymes) **2-8-2v**(5) CLowther(6) (hdwy u.p & drifted lft 2f out: nvr nrr)	1½	7	25/1	50	33
3821^{5} **Heathyards Sheik (71)** (RHollinshead) **2-8-8** RCochrane(8) (spd over 3f: sn wknd)	3½	8	16/1	41	24
4271^{2} **Acid Test (71)** (WRMuir) **2-8-8** MartinDwyer(10) (swtg: sn drvn along: a outpcd)	1¼	9	$4/1^{2}$	38	21
4068^{5} **Forty Love (IRE) (61)** (JEBanks) **2-7-12b**[1] CRutter(9) (a bhd)	¾	10	14/1	26	9
3192^{11} **Princess Natalie (84)** (MWEasterby) **2-9-7** TLucas(4) (drvn along over 3f out: a bhd)	1	11	9/1	46	29

(SP 122.7%) **11 Rn**

1m 12.32 (0.62) CSF £15.00 CT £150.48 TOTE £2.30: £1.50 £2.50 £3.60 (£10.70) Trio £100.50 OWNER Mr Hamdan Al Maktoum (NEWMAR-KET) BRED Shadwell Farm Inc

3717* Kheyrah (USA) had to work much harder to win this, and it was more strength from the saddle that could have swayed the issue. (6/4)

4097* Branston Berry (IRE) has got plenty of speed and, with the stands' rail for company, made the winner pull out all the stops to get the better of her nearing the finish. The boy did nothing wrong, and the combination could make their mark before the season closes. (9/1)

3258* Peter's Imp (IRE) pressed the leaders and had every chance until finding demands too great inside the last two-hundred yards. (16/1)

3438* Cool Secret did not get the best of the start and was buried in the pack until switched towards the centre of the track to make progress inside the distance. Running on really well in the closing stages, it is possible he will get further ridden this way. (20/1)

1616 Miss Dangerous, returning after a break of over three months, showed up with the pace in the centre of the track until lack of peak condition began to tell on the approach to the final furlong. With her stable back to form she is worth keeping an eye on from now on. (25/1)

4271 Acid Test (4/1: op 7/1)

2314* Princess Natalie (9/1: op 6/1)

4412 STANLEY LEISURE CHILDREN IN NEED CONDITIONS STKS (3-Y.O+) (Class C)

5-00 (5-00) **1m 6f** £5,413.80 (£1,750.80: £855.40) Stalls: Centre GOING minus 0.20 sec per fur (GF)

			SP	RR	SF
4099^{2} **The Faraway Tree (104)** (GWragg) **3-8-1**ow1 PaulEddery(3) (lw: chsd ldr: chal 2f out: led appr fnl f: jst hld on)	—	1	$8/11^{1}$	108	25
2709^{W} **Poltarf (USA) (100)** (JHMGosden) **6-9-1** JCarroll(1) (set str pce: sn clr: hdd appr fnl f: rallied u.p cl home)	s.h	2	$3/1^{2}$	112	40
4005^{4} **Nabhaan (IRE) (105)** (DMorley) **4-9-5** RHills(2) (hld up & bhd: effrt 2f out: hrd drvn: nt pce to chal)	4	3	$3/1^{2}$	111	39

(SP 107.9%) **3 Rn**

3m 6.31 (8.11) CSF £2.85 TOTE £1.60 (£1.70) OWNER Mr A. E. Oppenheimer (NEWMARKET) BRED Hascombe and Valiant Studs

WEIGHT FOR AGE 3yo-10lb

4099 The Faraway Tree was made to work really hard to win this, and the 13lb she was receiving from the runner-up obviously tipped the scales her way. She will not forget this in a hurry. (8/11: evens-4/6)

2269a Poltarf (USA), withdrawn from his intended outing at York in July on veterinary advice, had been without a race in over three months. Carrying plenty of condition as usual, he ran a very honest race in defeat, and was certainly the winner on merit. (3/1)

4005 Nabhaan (IRE) does not find much once off the bridle, and his attempt to let the leaders cut their own throats was never going to materialize. (3/1)

T/Plpt: £13.60 (1,817.46 Tckts). T/Qdpt: £6.90 (154.99 Tckts) IM

3776-REDCAR (L-H) (Firm, Good to Firm patches)

Friday September 26th

WEATHER: overcast WIND: almost nil

4413 E.B.F. MAIDEN STKS (2-Y.O) (Class D)

2-20 (2-21) **1m 1f** £3,333.50 (£998.00: £479.00: £219.50) Stalls: High GOING minus 0.55 sec per fur (F)

			SP	RR	SF
Sinon (IRE) (MJohnston) **2-9-0** DHolland(10) (w'like: leggy: scope: cl up: led wl over 2f out: r.o)	—	1	20/1	85+	21

4132[5] **Double Blade** (MJohnston) **2-9-0** JWeaver(6) (trckd ldrs: ev ch over 2f out: put head in air & hung lft: nt run on)....2½ **2** 2/1[1] 81 17
3979[13] **Paradise Soul (USA)** (DRLoder) **2-8-9** KFallon(2) (lw: bhd: effrt ent st: sn prom: rdn over 2f out: nt pce to chal)....nk **3** 12/1[3] 75 11
4244[3] **Goldfill** (WAO'Gorman) **2-8-9** EmmaO'Gorman(7) (swtg: in tch: effrt 4f out: styd on one pce)....3½ **4** 9/2[2] 69 5
Little Brave (JMPEustace) **2-9-0** JTate(5) (w'like: bit bkwd: bhd tl styd on fnl 3f: nt pce to chal)....½ **5** 16/1 73 9
4165[6] **Pairumani Star (IRE)** (JLDunlop) **2-9-0** KDarley(8) (prom tl lost pl appr st: sn rdn & no imp after)....5 **6** 2/1[1] 64 —
4215[3] **Kingdom Queen (IRE)** (MJCamacho) **2-8-9** LCharnock(4) (cl up: led 4f out tl wl over 2f out: grad wknd)....1¾ **7** 14/1 56 —
4244[6] **Altitude (IRE)** (SirMarkPrescott) **2-9-0** SSanders(1) (lw: prom tl outpcd fnl 3½f)....hd **8** 20/1 61 —
4056[8] **Durgams Delight (IRE)** (BWMurray) **2-8-9** VHalliday(9) (led tl hdd & wknd 4f out)....¾ **9** 50/1 54 —
3395[9] **Sixth Avenue (IRE) (42)** (RMWhitaker) **2-8-9** DaleGibson(3) (sn wl bhd: t.o)....dist **10** 100/1 — —
(SP 117.6%) **10 Rn**

1m 54.4 (3.70) CSF £53.99 TOTE £19.70: £3.80 £1.10 £3.50 (£14.40) Trio £36.00 OWNER Ridings Racing (MIDDLEHAM) BRED C. Crowley

Sinon (IRE) is a big, strong individual, and won this well. There looks to be a fair bit more to come, and he now goes for Newmarket's Zetland Stakes. (20/1)
4132 Double Blade did not impress in the paddock this time, and in the race his attitude was the problem. Until he changes that he is one to be wary of. (2/1)
Paradise Soul (USA) is not much to look at, but she does seem to stay well and had quite a hard race here. (12/1)
4244 Goldfill got rather warm beforehand and just looks a stayer, and lacked any turn of foot to make a real impression. (9/2)
Little Brave took a while to realise what was required, but this real stayer was noted keeping on at the end. (16/1)
4165 Pairumani Star (IRE) failed to handle this awkward turn into the straight, and looked very one-paced thereafter. (2/1)
4215 Kingdom Queen (IRE) (14/1: 10/1-16/1)

4414 MICHAELMAS APPRENTICE H'CAP (0-80) (3-Y.O+) (Class E)

2-50 (2-53) **6f** £3,288.25 (£991.00: £480.50: £225.25) Stalls: High GOING minus 0.55 sec per fur (F)

SP RR SF

4233[9] **Johayro (60)** (JSGoldie) **4-8-10** DGriffiths(3) (mde most: hld on wl)....— **1** 12/1 69 42
4307[3] **Saint Express (78)** (MrsMReveley) **7-9-11**(3) SCopp(12) (a w ldrs: kpt on u.p fnl 2f)....hd **2** 6/1[3] 87 60
3801[12] **Thwaab (65)** (FWatson) **5-8-8v**(7) PBradley(1) (bhd: hdwy 2f out: styd on wl towards fin)....nk **3** 12/1 73 46
3621[13] **French Grit (IRE) (70)** (MDods) **5-9-6** FLynch(5) (trckd ldrs: n.m.r over 1f out: styd on wl towards fin)....nk **4** 16/1 77 50
3910[10] **Stephensons Rocket (49)** (RAFahey) **6-7-8v**[1](5)ow3 RWinston(13) (chsd ldrs: chal ½-wy: no ex ins fnl f)....½ **5** 14/1 55 25
4137[13] **Storyteller (IRE) (55)** (MrsJRRamsden) **3-8-3v** TEDurcan(7) (lw: hld up: hdwy ½-wy: styd on: nvr able to chal)....s.h **6** 11/2[2] 61 32
4221[8] **Palacegate Touch (77)** (JBerry) **7-9-13b** PFessey(11) (chsd ldrs: effrt 2f out: nt qckn)....1½ **7** 20/1 79 52
4301[11] **Shadow Jury (56)** (DWChapman) **7-8-6b** GParkin(2) (prom: effrt 2f out: r.o one pce)....hd **8** 20/1 57 30
4235[12] **Suedoro (46)** (JSGoldie) **7-7-7**(3) APolli(9) (w ldrs tl wknd ins fnl f)....½ **9** 12/1 46 19
4228[8] **Plum First (53)** (MAPeill) **7-7-10**(7) ANicholls(14) (b.hind: bhd: rdn ½-wy: nvr rchd ldrs)....½ **10** 9/1 52 25
4155[19] **Mallia (62)** (TDBarron) **4-8-7**(5) VictoriaAppleby(15) (lw: effrt ½-wy: no imp)....hd **11** 6/1[3] 61 34
4233* **Just Bob (70)** (SEKettlewell) **8-8-13**(7) 7x JennyBenson(6) (lw: s.i.s: nvr nr to chal)....nk **12** 9/2[1] 68 41
4291[10] **Gipsy Princess (57)** (MWEasterby) **3-7-12b**(7) SFinnamore(10) (s.i.s: sn drvn along: n.d)....½ **13** 20/1 53 24
3710[5] **Hopesay (72)** (JHMGosden) **3-9-6v** RHavlin(4) (unruly in paddock: in tch tl wknd fnl 2f)....1 **14** 12/1 66 37
3855[3] **Trojan Hero (SAF) (63)** (MrsMReveley) **6-8-8**(5) KimberleyHart(8) (lw: hld up: effrt 2f out: n.d)....nk **15** 25/1 56 29
4233[21] **Lennox Lewis (60)** (DNicholls) **5-8-3**(7) JoanneDavies(16) (spd to ½-wy: grad lost pl)....½ **16** 20/1 52 25
1993[5] **Antithesis (IRE) (47)** (JSHaldane) **4-7-4**(7)ow1 JMcAuley(17) (s.i.s: a outpcd & bhd)....½ **17** 50/1 37 9
(SP 140.3%) **17 Rn**

1m 10.6 (0.40) CSF £78.27 CT £878.09 TOTE £13.40: £3.30 £1.70 £2.40 £5.50 (£48.50) Trio £266.10 OWNER Mr Frank Brady (GLASGOW) BRED R. M. Whitaker
LONG HANDICAP Stephensons Rocket 7-2 Antithesis (IRE) 7-4
WEIGHT FOR AGE 3yo-2lb

3756 Johayro found this sharp six furlongs right up his street, and showed a really good attitude to hold on. (12/1)
4307 Saint Express keeps running well without getting his head in front but a return to winning form is not beyond the realms of possibility. (6/1)
3428 Thwaab ran well and is certainly off a useful mark just now, and if someone of the likes of Kieren Fallon gets back on board he could be very interesting. (12/1)
3087 French Grit (IRE), after a lay-off, is obviously in good heart and never had much luck in running here. (16/1)
3431 Stephensons Rocket ran one of his better races from 8lb out of the handicap, and there is plenty more ability if he can be persuaded. (14/1)
3812 Storyteller (IRE) ran well and was short of room late on and is obviously coming to form. (11/2)
4137 Shadow Jury showed signs of returning to form. (20/1)

4415 TEESSIDE (S) H'CAP (0-60) (3, 4 & 5-Y.O) (Class G)

3-20 (3-22) **1m 2f** £2,670.00 (£745.00: £360.00) Stalls: High GOING minus 0.55 sec per fur (F)

SP RR SF

3970[6] **Tart (FR) (42)** (JPearce) **4-8-10** KFallon(11) (mid div: hdwy 4f out: led ins fnl f: edgd lft: r.o)....— **1** 9/2[1] 52 34
4139[17] **Filial (IRE) (60)** (BJMeehan) **4-9-7**(7) GHannon(1) (a chsng ldrs: effrt 3f out: kpt on: nt pce of wnr)....½ **2** 8/1[3] 69 51
4243[6] **Lochlass (IRE) (43)** (SPCWoods) **3-8-5b** SSanders(2) (in tch: led over 2f out tl ins fnl f: btn whn n.m.r towards fin)....½ **3** 8/1[3] 51 27
3992[16] **Raindeer Quest (49)** (JLEyre) **5-9-3** RLappin(13) (swtg: hld up & bhd: nt clr run over 3f out: swtchd: styd on wl fnl 2f: nrst fin)....s.h **4** 5/1[2] 57 39
4161[10] **Pickens (USA) (56)** (DonEnricoIncisa) **5-9-10** KimTinkler(17) (b: bhd: styd on fnl 3f: nrst fin)....6 **5** 20/1 55 37
3933[8] **Golden Fish (28)** (EJAlston) **5-7-10** JBramhill(9) (bhd tl styd on fnl 2½f)....1½ **6** 33/1 24 6
3870[2] **Grate Times (60)** (EWeymes) **3-9-8** KDarley(4) (cl up: led over 3f out tl over 2f out: wknd)....6 **7** 9/2[1] 47 23
4326[6] **Weet A Bit (IRE) (54)** (RHollinshead) **3-8-13**(3) DGriffiths(7) (nvr bttr than mid div)....s.h **8** 33/1 41 17
1754[15] **Bison Belting (40)** (JAGlover) **3-8-2** TWilliams(10) (hdwy over 4f out: sn prom: wknd over 1f out)....hd **9** 16/1 27 3
4171[10] **Eurolink Windsong (IRE) (40)** (MartynWane) **3-8-2** NCarlisle(8) (in tch tl outpcd fnl 4f)....1¼ **10** 14/1 25 1
4371[18] **Great Bear (40)** (DWChapman) **5-8-1**(7) RWinston(6) (bhd: sme hdwy 4f out: n.d)....nk **11** 100/1 24 6
4161[13] **Raased (40)** (FWatson) **5-8-8** JFortune(5) (led tl hdd & wknd over 3f out)....nk **12** 12/1 24 6
3758[8] **Highfield Pet (36)** (CWFairhurst) **4-8-4** LCharnock(15) (a bhd)....s.h **13** 20/1 19 1
3758[12] **That Old Feeling (IRE) (35)** (DWChapman) **5-8-0**(3) PFessey(16) (a bhd)....5 **14** 25/1 10 —

4243[8]	**Tezaab (46)** (BHanbury) **3-8-8** JStack(3) (chsd ldrs tl wknd fnl 3f)	2	**15**	9/1	18	—
3919[16]	**Macari (46)** (BPJBaugh) **3-8-5**(3)ow2 GParkin(12) (cl up tl wknd fnl 4f)	4	**16**	16/1	12	—
2701[7]	**Acquittal (IRE) (39)** (AStreeter) **5-8-4v**(3)ow1 RHavlin(14) (prom tl wknd 4f out)	13	**17**	10/1	—	—
				(SP 140.7%)	**17 Rn**	

2m 5.6 (2.00) CSF £39.70 CT £279.10 TOTE £4.00: £1.10 £2.00 £2.60 £2.10 (£14.80) Trio £46.90 OWNER Wroughton House Partnership (NEWMARKET) BRED Lord Samuel Vestey
LONG HANDICAP Golden Fish 7-7
WEIGHT FOR AGE 3yo-6lb
Sold D Nicholls for 6,600 gns
3970 Tart (FR), well supported, was given plenty of assistance from the saddle, and despite showing a tendency to hang left was always doing enough. (9/2)
Filial (IRE) had his chances throughout and kept staying on, but never quite looked likely to make it and may need a bit further. (8/1)
4243 Lochlass (IRE), from a yard in good form, ran well, but being slightly hampered late on may well have cost her second place. (8/1: 6/1-9/1)
3854* Raindeer Quest needs things to go just right and they never quite did here, and her effort was always too late. (5/1)
Pickens (USA) was staying on as though further might well help. (20/1)
Golden Fish has not much to recommend him, but he was picking up well in the closing stages. (33/1)
874 Bison Belting showed a good turn of foot early in the straight and then either blew up or found this trip too far, but he certainly has plenty of ability (16/1)

4416 CONSTANT SECURITY RATED STKS H'CAP (0-95) (3-Y.O+) (Class C)

3-50 (3-51) **1m 6f 19y** £4,528.52 (£1,642.90: £796.45: £334.75: £142.38) Stalls: Centre GOING minus 0.55 sec per fur (F)

				SP	RR	SF
4320*	**Ferny Hill (IRE) (87)** (SirMarkPrescott) **3-8-10** 3x SSanders(5) (led 3f: trckd ldrs: n.m.r over 3f out: hdwy over 1f out: str run to ld post)	—	**1**	7/4[1]	95	31
4136[9]	**Wahiba Sands (90)** (JLDunlop) **4-9-9** KDarley(3) (lw: b.hind: hld up: hdwy on bit over 2f out: slt ld appr fnl f: sn rdn: no ex towards fin)	hd	**2**	13/2	98	44
4136[4]	**Steamroller Stanly (75)** (CACyzer) **4-8-8** DHolland(2) (led: qcknd over 3f out: hdd over 1f out: kpt on wl)	½	**3**	5/2[2]	82	28
4136[7]	**Catchable (84)** (HRACecil) **3-8-7**ow2 KFallon(1) (cl up tl outpcd fnl 2f)	5	**4**	3/1[3]	86	20
3778*	**Good Hand (USA) (73)** (SEKettlewell) **11-8-6** JFortune(4) (chsd ldrs: effrt 4f out: sn outpcd)	7	**5**	20/1	67	13
				(SP 108.0%)	**5 Rn**	

3m 2.9 (3.60) CSF £11.49 TOTE £2.50: £1.80 £2.10 (£6.80) OWNER Cheveley Park Stud (NEWMARKET) BRED D. Ryan, M. Moloney and H. King
LONG HANDICAP Good Hand (USA) 8-5
WEIGHT FOR AGE 3yo-10lb
4320* Ferny Hill (IRE) takes time to find his stride as he has shown on every occasion, and although his rider managed to get him shut in here the extra distance helped in the end. He is a real progressive sort. (7/4)
3051 Wahiba Sands, trying his longest trip to date, looked likely to trot up, but when ridden he never found anything like as much as looked likely, and was just run out of it. There is certainly plenty of ability there. (13/2)
4136 Steamroller Stanly stays well and is honest, but was just tapped for toe at the business end. Nevertheless, his courage will always find him success. (5/2)
4136 Catchable has now disappointed twice at this trip, but on both occasions the ground was against him. (3/1)
3778* Good Hand (USA) found this company too hot and is worth keeping in mind for a return to hurdling. (20/1)

4417 AUTUMN MAIDEN STKS (3-Y.O+) (Class D)

4-20 (4-21) **7f** £3,691.00 (£1,108.00: £534.00: £247.00) Stalls: High GOING minus 0.55 sec per fur (F)

				SP	RR	SF
	Ricky Ticky Tavie (USA) (DRLoder) **3-9-0** KFallon(7) (lw: trckd ldrs: led over 2f out: rdn & r.o)	—	**1**	2/5[1]	80	55
4147[14]	**Barnburgh Boy (73)** (TDEasterby) **3-9-0** SSanders(3) (lw: a.p: chsd wnr fnl 2f: edgd lft 1f out: kpt on)	1¼	**2**	4/1[2]	77	52
4270[17]	**Colway Ritz (72)** (JWWatts) **3-9-0** LCharnock(9) (in tch: effrt over 2f out: nt pce to chal)	2½	**3**	16/1	71	46
1656[4]	**Speedboat (USA) (67)** (JLEyre) **3-9-0** OPears(5) (led tl hdd over 2f out: one pce)	4	**4**	14/1[3]	62	37
4172[13]	**Get The Point (59)** (RHollinshead) **3-9-0** FLynch(6) (a.p: effrt 3f out: r.o one pce)	1¼	**5**	33/1	59	34
3583[11]	**Ohnonotagain (30)** (NTinkler) **5-8-12** KimTinkler(1) (in tch: no hdwy fnl 3f)	5	**6**	100/1	43	21
3910[20]	**Look Who's Calling (IRE) (60)** (BAMcMahon) **4-9-3** KDarley(4) (cl up tl wknd fnl 2½f)	nk	**7**	14/1[3]	47	25
3484[12]	**Madam Zando (25)** (JBalding) **4-8-12** JEdmunds(10) (effrt ½-wy: nvr trbld ldrs)	2½	**8**	100/1	37	15
	Northern Accord (MrsJRRamsden) **3-9-0** JFortune(2) (lengthy: unf: bit bkwd: nvr wnt pce)	½	**9**	14/1[3]	41	16
4214[10]	**Distant King** (GPKelly) **4-8-10**(7) SFinnamore(12) (b: outpcd fr ½-wy)	½	**10**	100/1	39	17
4326[8]	**Notation (IRE)** (DWChapman) **3-8-11b**[1](3) GParkin(8) (s.i.s: pushed along thrght: a bhd)	hd	**11**	100/1	39	14
3822[15]	**Uncle Errol** (GMMoore) **3-9-0** DaleGibson(11) (lost tch fr ½-wy: t.o)	dist	**12**	100/1	—	—
				(SP 125.2%)	**12 Rn**	

1m 22.7 (-0.30) CSF £2.31 TOTE £1.50: £1.10 £1.10 £2.80 (£2.20) Trio £7.50 OWNER Maktoum Al Maktoum (NEWMARKET) BRED Geret Farm Corporation
WEIGHT FOR AGE 3yo-3lb
Ricky Ticky Tavie (USA) is not very big but is quite gutsy, and although the betting suggests this should have been easy he needed to work hard. (2/5)
3937 Barnburgh Boy ran his usual sound race, but was just inclined to edge left under maximum pressure and was never quite doing enough. (4/1)
3812 Colway Ritz has plenty of ability but has his own ideas about how and when to use it. (16/1)
1656 Speedboat (USA) behaved quite well on this occasion, and there is ability there if he can ever be trusted. (14/1)
3968 Get The Point ran reasonably without really getting into it, and never quite seems to come up with the goods. (33/1)
Northern Accord (14/1: op 8/1)

4418 RED CROSS MAIDEN STKS (2-Y.O F) (Class D)

4-50 (4-50) **6f** £3,489.50 (£1,046.00: £503.00: £231.50) Stalls: High GOING minus 0.55 sec per fur (F)

				SP	RR	SF
3985[4]	**Special Treat** (DRLoder) **2-8-11b**[1] KFallon(4) (disp ld: rdn to ld over 2f out: r.o strly)	—	**1**	7/4[1]	82	37
3769[3]	**Yanomami (USA)** (JHMGosden) **2-8-11** KDarley(1) (lw: disp ld after 1f tl over 2f out: nt qckn)	4	**2**	7/4[1]	71	26
	Lindesberg (MJohnston) **2-8-11** DHolland(3) (leggy: scope: bit bkwd: rn green early: hdwy ½-wy: nt qckn fnl 2f)	hd	**3**	2/1[2]	71+	26

3306[19]	**Tamburello (IRE)** (JBerry) **2-8-11** JFortune(2) (bit bkwd: disp ld to ½-wy: sn wknd)	10	**4**	33/1[3]	44	—
				(SP 109.0%)		**4 Rn**

1m 11.0 (0.80) CSF £4.73 TOTE £2.50 (£2.00) OWNER Cheveley Park Stud (NEWMARKET) BRED David John Brown
3985 Special Treat had blinkers on for the first time and that, coupled with some strong assistance, made all the difference. (7/4)
3769 Yanomami (USA) doesn't look anything special and that turned out to be the case when the pressure was applied. (7/4)
Lindesberg, a stoutly-made filly, was clueless early on but gave signs of something better as the race progressed. (2/1)
Tamburello (IRE) needed this after a lay-off, and dropped away once the pressure was applied. (33/1)

4419 SEPTEMBER NURSERY H'CAP (0-75) (2-Y.O) (Class E)

5-20 (5-21) **5f** £3,081.75 (£924.00: £444.50: £204.75) Stalls: High GOING minus 0.55 sec per fur (F)

				SP	RR	SF
3823[4]	**Mighty Sure (IRE) (61)** (MWEasterby) **2-8-12**(3) GParkin(4) (lw: a w ldrs: hrd rdn to ld cl home)	—	**1**	3/1[2]	60	39
4327*	**Swanmore Lady (IRE) (59)** (SCWilliams) **2-8-13** 6x KDarley(8) (lw: a cl up: led 2f out: r.o u.p: jst ct)	s.h	**2**	3/1[2]	58	37
4162[2]	**Ellenbrook (IRE) (67)** (JBerry) **2-9-4b**(3) PFessey(6) (led 3f: rdn & no ex)	4	**3**	9/4[1]	53	32
4162[8]	**Rhinefield Beauty (IRE) (63)** (JSGoldie) **2-9-3** TWilliams(3) (dwlt: sn chsng ldrs: effrt 2f out: nt qckn)	hd	**4**	12/1	49	28
4152[13]	**Mill End Quest (62)** (MWEasterby) **2-8-9**(7) SFinnamore(5) (chsd ldrs: effrt 2f out: nt qckn)	¾	**5**	14/1	45	24
4054[5]	**Mr Fund Switch (42)** (DNicholls) **2-7-5b**(5) IonaWands(7) (prom to ½-wy: sn outpcd)	3½	**6**	12/1	14	—
4152[10]	**Cool Mystery (57)** (ABMulholland) **2-8-11** NCarlisle(2) (spd 3f)	½	**7**	7/1[3]	28	7
1510[13]	**Asprilla (IRE) (50)** (BEllison) **2-8-4** NKennedy(1) (sn outpcd & bhd)	10	**8**	33/1	—	—
				(SP 118.3%)		**8 Rn**

58.2 secs (0.70) CSF £11.83 CT £21.71 TOTE £5.00: £1.30 £1.50 £1.30 (£6.20) OWNER Mr C. J. Rusbridge (SHERIFF HUTTON) BRED St Simon Foundation
LONG HANDICAP Mr Fund Switch 7-6
3823 Mighty Sure (IRE) needed to battle to win this, and was certainly given plenty of assistance from the saddle. (3/1)
4327* Swanmore Lady (IRE) is in good form and ran a sound race here. She responded in game style when ridden, and had the advantage of the rails to race against but was still not quite good enough. (3/1)
4162 Ellenbrook (IRE) is running consistently but lacks any kick at the business end of the race at the moment. (9/4)
2545 Rhinefield Beauty (IRE) gives the impression that she has more ability, and just needs things to go her way. (12/1)
3707 Mill End Quest ran reasonably but over this shorter trip was tapped for toe late on. (14/1)
4054 Mr Fund Switch (12/1: op 7/1)

T/Plpt: £62.30 (300.97 Tckts). T/Qdpt: £8.10 (130.49 Tckts) AA

3183-ASCOT (R-H) (St crse Gd to frm, Gd ptchs, Rnd crse Gd, Gd to frm ptchs)
Saturday September 27th

WEATHER: fair WIND: almost nil

4420 CUMBERLAND LODGE STKS (Gp 3) (3-Y.O+) (Class A)

2-00 (2-00) **1m 4f** £32,150.00 (£12,170.00: £5,960.00: £2,720.00) Stalls: High GOING minus 0.04 sec per fur (G)

				SP	RR	SF
3647[3]	**Kingfisher Mill (USA) (118)** (MrsJCecil) **3-8-11** MJKinane(2) (lw: hld up: led over 1f out: all out)	—	**1**	7/2[2]	125	81
3409*	**Romanov (IRE) (115)** (PWChapple-Hyam) **3-8-9** JReid(8) (rdn over 2f out: hdwy over 1f out: r.o wl ins fnl f)	hd	**2**	100/30[1]	123	79
3784*	**King Sound (108)** (JHMGosden) **3-8-6** LDettori(7) (rdn & hdwy over 1f out: r.o)	1½	**3**	10/1	118	74
4154*	**Fahris (IRE) (117)** (BHanbury) **3-8-9** RHills(6) (chsd ldr: led 4f out tl over 1f out: wknd ins fnl f)	3	**4**	9/2[3]	117	73
4149[8]	**Poseidon (109)** (MRChannon) **3-8-6** SSanders(4) (rdn over 3f out: nvr nr to chal)	4	**5**	25/1	109	65
3182a[5]	**Mongol Warrior (USA) (111)** (LordHuntingdon) **4-9-3** JWeaver(1) (prom over 9f)	28	**6**	40/1	74	38
4131a[2]	**Salmon Ladder (USA) (111)** (PFICole) **5-9-3** TQuinn(5) (swtg: led 8f: wknd over 2f out)	2½	**7**	9/1	71	35
4005*	**Maylane (112)** (ACStewart) **3-8-9** MRoberts(3) (swtg: swvd lft & uns rdr s)		**U**	7/2[2]	—	—
				(SP 111.1%)		**8 Rn**

2m 31.71 (1.71) CSF £13.33 TOTE £4.20: £1.50 £1.40 £1.90 (£6.50) OWNER Lord Howard de Walden (NEWMARKET) BRED Lord Howard de Walden
WEIGHT FOR AGE 3yo-8lb
3647 Kingfisher Mill (USA) again demonstrated that he is one of the leading one and-a-half-mile three-year-olds. Striking the front over a furlong out, he responded well to pressure but, with the second finishing really well, he found the line only just saving him. He will not run again this season but will stay in training next year. (7/2)
3409* Romanov (IRE) again showed that he is a high-class individual. Bustled along early in the straight, he really found his stride from below the distance and, running on really strongly, would surely have prevailed in a few more strides. Connections are thinking about the Canadian International in four weeks and he will remain in training next year. (100/30)
3784* King Sound was certainly not disgraced in finishing third. Travelling nicely in behind a wall of horses early in the straight, he picked up ground below the distance but, although running on to finish clear of the remainder, was always just being held by the front two. (10/1)
4154* Fahris (IRE) does not stay this distance. Gaining a slender advantage half a mile from home, he was collared below the distance and, although grimly trying to hold on, had nothing left in the tank inside the final furlong. He has shown himself to be a very useful individual but a mile and a quarter is his trip. (9/2)
4149 Poseidon, who failed to stay the St Leger trip last time out, never threatened to get into it. (25/1)
3182a Mongol Warrior (USA) was campaigned solely abroad last year and managed to pick up four races. This season he has found it tough going and the three occasions he has been placed have all been abroad. Racing close up, he had given his all early in the straight. This ground was too fast for him. (40/1)
4131a Salmon Ladder (USA), second in this race last year, proved disappointing and, after cutting out the pace for the first mile, had shot his bolt early in the straight. He has not lived up to the sparkling form he showed last year and it may well be that all those hard races he had have taken their toll. (9/1)

4421 RACAL DIADEM STKS (Gp 2) (3-Y.O+) (Class A)

2-35 (2-37) **6f** £59,430.00 (£22,319.00: £10,784.50: £4,766.50) Stalls: Low GOING minus 0.16 sec per fur (GF)

				SP	RR	SF
3747*	**Elnadim (USA) (108)** (JLDunlop) **3-8-12** RHills(11) (lw: mde all: hrd rdn over 1f out: r.o wl)	—	**1**	4/1[2]	128++	105
4011[7]	**Monaassib (114)** (EALDunlop) **6-9-0** DO'Donohoe(12) (lw: a.p: ev ch over 1f out: edgd lft ins fnl f: unable qckn)	3	**2**	9/1	120	99
4011[4]	**Averti (IRE) (115)** (WRMuir) **6-9-0** KFallon(2) (rdn over 2f out: hdwy over 1f out: r.o ins fnl f)	s.h	**3**	6/1	120	99

				SP	RR	SF
4240*	**Russian Revival (USA) (110)** (JHMGosden) **4-9-0** LDettori(3) (lost pl 2f out: rallied 1f out: 4th & btn whn nt clr run on ins ins fnl f)	½	**4**	3/1[1]	119	98
4120[2]	**Dazzle (112)** (MRStoute) **3-8-9** JReid(15) (hld up: rdn 2f out: one pce)	¾	**5**	5/1[3]	114	91
4240[8]	**Muchea (115)** (MRChannon) **3-8-12** TQuinn(8) (hld up: rdn over 2f out: r.o one pce fnl f)	nk	**6**	40/1	116	93
4239[5]	**Rambling Bear (107)** (MBlanshard) **4-9-0** MRoberts(14) (rdn over 2f out: hdwy over 1f out: one pce)	1	**7**	20/1	113	92
4204a[7]	**Swift Gulliver (IRE)** (JSBolger,Ireland) **3-8-12b[1]** KJManning(1) (lw: rdn over 2f out: hdwy fnl f: nvr nrr)	nk	**8**	40/1	112	89
4155[4]	**Lochangel (93)** (IABalding) **3-8-9** RCochrane(13) (a.p: rdn over 2f out: wknd over 1f out)	½	**9**	12/1	108	85
4282[20]	**Cretan Gift (103)** (NPLittmoden) **6-9-0b** JWeaver(16) (rdn over 2f out: nvr nrr)	hd	**10**	40/1	111	90
3199*	**Dame Laura (IRE) (99)** (HMorrison) **3-8-9** KDarley(9) (mid div 5f)	1¾	**11**	50/1	103	80
4100[3]	**My Best Valentine (100)** (VSoane) **7-9-0** CRutter(5) (bhd fnl 2f)	hd	**12**	16/1	106	85
4239[13]	**Cyrano's Lad (IRE) (113)** (CADwyer) **8-9-0** MJKinane(10) (lw: spd 4f)	10	**13**	20/1	79	58
961[7]	**Daring Destiny (110)** (KRBurke) **6-9-1b** TSprake(7) (a bhd)	hd	**14**	50/1	80	59
				(SP 120.3%)		**14 Rn**

1m 12.56 (-1.44) CSF £33.68 TOTE £4.90: £2.20 £2.10 £2.10 (£23.70) Trio £64.80 OWNER Mr Hamdan Al Maktoum (ARUNDEL) BRED Shadwell Farm Inc

WEIGHT FOR AGE 3yo-2lb

3747* Elnadim (USA) is a very progressive colt who has come a long way since winning a maiden at Pontefract on his reappearance in June. This really was a tremendous front-running display, winning in emphatic style in a time that was a mere 0.03 seconds outside the course record set over five years ago. He looks a really exciting six-furlong prospect for next year. (4/1: 3/1-9/2)

3554a Monaassib, who found the ground easier than he would have liked when running his only poor race of the season last time out, bounced back on this fast surface and had every chance approaching the final furlong before the winner asserted. Winner of five races this season including a Listed event and two Group Three races, he is a real credit to his trainer. (9/1)

4011 Averti (IRE), who had no luck in running last time out, picked up ground below the distance but, despite running on, had no hope of getting near the winner. (6/1)

4240* Russian Revival (USA) may not have won on ground worse than good but his trainer believes he needs some cut and this surface did look a bit lively for him. Outpaced a quarter of a mile from home, he was grimly trying to get back into it, although having no hope of getting near the winner when chopped for room by Monaassib inside the final furlong. On a slightly easier surface, he can find another Pattern race. (3/1)

4120 Dazzle needs to be covered up and being produced late and the outside draw was not in her favour. Pushed along a quarter of a mile from home, she failed to find the necessary turn of foot. Seven furlongs suits her better. (5/1)

4011 Muchea has found life a great deal tougher this year and, although failing to find the necessary turn of foot, was staying on again at the death. (40/1)

4422 QUEEN ELIZABETH II STKS (Gp 1) (3-Y.O+) (Class A)

3-20 (3-23) **1m (round)** £187,839.99 (£70,078.25: £33,476.63: £14,380.13) Stalls: High GOING minus 0.04 sec per fur (G)

				SP	RR	SF
3124[7]	**Air Express (IRE) (120)** (CEBrittain) **3-8-11** OPeslier(7) (hdwy over 2f out: led over 1f out: all out)	—	**1**	9/1	128	92
4129a[7]	**Rebecca Sharp (113)** (GWragg) **3-8-8** MHills(9) (stdy hdwy on ins 3f out: nt clr run on ins over 2f out tl over 1f out: swtchd lft: str run fnl f: fin wl)	s.h	**2**	16/1	125	89
4133*	**Faithful Son (USA) (112)** (MRStoute) **3-8-11** KFallon(8) (a.p: rdn over 2f out: ev ch over 1f out: unable qckn)	2	**3**	16/1	124	88
4138[2]	**Bahhare (USA) (121)** (JLDunlop) **3-8-11** RHills(4) (swtg: rdn over 2f out: hdwy over 1f out: r.o wl ins fnl f)	s.h	**4**	15/2[3]	124	88
4129a[8]	**Bijou d'Inde** (MJohnston) **4-9-1** JWeaver(5) (chsd ldr: led over 3f out tl over 1f out: one pce)	nk	**5**	20/1	123	91
3880a[6]	**Allied Forces (USA) (120)** (SbinSuroor) **4-9-1** LDettori(6) (swtg: led over 4f: ev ch over 1f out: one pce)	½	**6**	9/2[2]	122	90
1769[4]	**Entrepreneur (124)** (MRStoute) **3-8-11** MJKinane(2) (lw: lost pl over 2f out: r.o one pce fnl f)	1	**7**	9/2[2]	120	84
4138*	**Revoque (IRE) (123)** (PWChapple-Hyam) **3-8-11** JReid(3) (lw: plld hrd: hld up: rdn over 2f out: no rspnse)	3½	**8**	9/4[1]	113	77
4240[3]	**Centre Stalls (IRE) (116)** (RFJohnsonHoughton) **4-9-1** TQuinn(1) (lw: bhd fnl 3f)	nk	**9**	14/1	113	81
				(SP 112.1%)		**9 Rn**

1m 40.9 (0.10) CSF £122.70 TOTE £12.50: £2.40 £2.90 £2.30 (£66.60) Trio £153.90 OWNER Mr Mohamed Obaida (NEWMARKET) BRED Gainsborough Stud Management Ltd

WEIGHT FOR AGE 3yo-4lb

OFFICIAL EXPLANATION **Revoque (IRE): no explanation offered. Air Express (IRE): regarding the improvement in form, the trainer stated that the colt did not appear to handle the camber at Goodwood last time out.**

IN-FOCUS: With the official electronic timing system not working properly for the day's showpiece, the judge gave an official hand-time of 1m 39.81. Whilst the judge was adamant this was correct, it was seriously wrong as four independent clockers all agreed with AK's time of 1m 40.9, including fellow Raceform racereader Lee McKenzie who went down to the Racetech van and obtained electronic times of both the start and finish to verify the Raceform time.

3124 Air Express (IRE), who was not suited by the Goodwood camber last time out, came through to strike the front below the distance, which was earlier than his jockey had wanted. With the second finishing with a tremendous rattle, he found the line coming not a stride too soon. Whilst this was a fine performance, he would have undoubtedly been beaten by the runner-up had that rival had a clear run. (9/1)

4129a Rebecca Sharp has not been very consistent this season but she was certainly on form here and was incredibly unlucky not to have won. Boxed in with nowhere to go along the inside rail in the straight, she was eventually extricated a furlong from home but, by then, the winner had already stolen a good few lengths. Eating up the ground, she would certainly have prevailed in another stride. She will look for compensation in the Group Two Challenge Stakes at Newmarket next month. (16/1)

4133* Faithful Son (USA) was certainly up against it here but ran a first-class race, especially considering the ground was faster than he would have liked, having every chance over a furlong out before tapped for toe. (16/1)

4138 Bahhare (USA), awash with sweat in the paddock, was hardly given a good ride by Hills who held him up in last place in a slowly-run race. Hardly a sensible thing to do for, when the dash to the line began entering the straight, he found himself with a lot of ground to make up. Nevertheless, he did so in fine style and failed by only a whisker to take third prize. Whilst this was an encouraging performance which pleased connections, he could have finished closer under a better ride. (15/2)

4129a Bijou d'Inde did not take to the sand in Dubai in the spring and, after a long lay-off following a serious tendon injury, was well below his best in the Prix Moulin at Longchamp three weeks ago. He ran a great deal better here and showed in front over three furlongs from home before collared below the distance. (20/1)

3880a Allied Forces (USA) was sweating buckets by the time the runners left the paddock but, back over his ideal trip, gave a good account of himself. Setting only a very sedate pace, he was narrowly collared over three furlongs from home but still had every chance below the distance before tapped for toe. (9/2)

1769 Entrepreneur, who sustained a hamstring injury when disappointing in the Derby, had a public workout here last week but was having his first race since the Blue Riband event. Looking in good shape beforehand, he got outpaced early in the straight but was staying on again inside the final furlong. Kinane reported afterwards that the colt was still rusty and a step up to a mile and a quarter looks on the cards. (9/2: 3/1-5/1)

4138* Revoque (IRE) looked an absolute picture in the paddock but was a bitter disappointment for, after pulling hard in the early stages, when Reid asked him for an effort early in the straight he found absolutely nothing. (9/4)
4240 Centre Stalls (IRE) found this company too hot and was getting left behind in the straight. (14/1)

4423 TOTE FESTIVAL H'CAP (3-Y.O+) (Class B)

3-55 (3-58) **7f** £50,005.00 (£15,040.00: £7,270.00: £3,385.00) Stalls: Low GOING minus 0.16 sec per fur (GF)

				SP	RR	SF
4148[6]	**Jo Mell (93)** (TDEasterby) **4-9-0** OPeslier(2) (chsd ldr: led over 2f out: comf)	—	**1**	14/1	109	92
3798[7]	**Kayvee (86)** (MrsAJPerrett) **8-8-7** AClark(7) (hdwy over 1f out: r.o ins fnl f)	2½	**2**	14/1	96	79
3725[5]	**Crumpton Hill (IRE) (94)** (NAGraham) **5-9-1** MRoberts(4) (lw: a.p: rdn over 2f out: unable qckn)	nk	**3**	12/1	104	87
4148*	**Russian Music (105)** (MissGayKelleway) **4-9-12** 5x KFallon(10) (lw: rdn over 2f out: hdwy over 1f out: r.o one pce)	3½	**4**	14/1	107	90
3728[8]	**Tregaron (USA) (103)** (RAkehurst) **6-9-10** TQuinn(3) (a.p: rdn over 2f out: one pce)	1½	**5**	20/1	101	84
4120[4]	**Flamboyance (USA) (86)** (JRFanshawe) **3-8-4** MHills(9) (hdwy over 1f out: nvr nrr)	nk	**6**	14/1	84	64
4280[21]	**Return of Amin (83)** (JDBethell) **3-8-1** CRutter(21) (racd far side: hdwy over 1f out: one pce fnl f)	hd	**7**	33/1	80	60
4153[5]	**Speedball (IRE) (96)** (IABalding) **3-9-0v**[1] JReid(20) (lw: racd far side: hdwy 3f out: one pce fnl 2f)	hd	**8**	33/1	93	73
3894[2]	**Just Nick (83)** (WRMuir) **3-8-1** MartinDwyer(1) (led over 4f)	¾	**9**	25/1	78	58
3765[5]	**Faraway Lass (86)** (LordHuntingdon) **4-8-7**ow1 JWeaver(5) (rdn over 2f out: hdwy fnl f: nvr nrr)	hd	**10**	10/1 3	81	63
4283[5]	**Philistar (76)** (KRBurke) **4-7-6**(5) RMullen(23) (lw: racd far side: nvr nrr)	1¼	**11**	16/1	68	51
3982[9]	**Waypoint (90)** (RCharlton) **4-8-11** TSprake(18) (lw: racd far side: a mid div)	hd	**12**	20/1	82	65
4282[14]	**Emerging Market (98)** (JLDunlop) **5-9-5** KDarley(12) (lw: nvr nrr)	s.h	**13**	20/1	90	73
4240[10]	**Omaha City (IRE) (105)** (BGubby) **3-9-6**(3) RFfrench(8) (prom over 5f)	s.h	**14**	33/1	97	77
4155[2]	**No Extras (IRE) (85)** (GLMoore) **7-8-6** JQuinn(22) (swtg: racd far side: rdn over 2f out: hdwy over 1f out: one pce)	¾	**15**	13/2 1	75	58
4003[4]	**Dancing Image (93)** (IABalding) **4-9-0** MJKinane(19) (racd far side: hdwy over 1f out: wknd ins fnl f)	¾	**16**	7/1 2	81	64
3594*	**Young Precedent (83)** (PWHarris) **3-8-1** GBardwell(24) (racd far side: prom over 5f)	1½	**17**	14/1	68	48
4121[5]	**Volley (IRE) (84)** (MajorDNChappell) **4-8-5** RHills(25) (racd far side: hdwy 3f out: wknd fnl f)	hd	**18**	33/1	69	52
4071[16]	**Present Generation (80)** (RGuest) **4-7-12**(3) AWhelan(6) (mid div over 5f)	½	**19**	50/1	64	47
4283[3]	**Safio (80)** (ABailey) **4-8-1** 5x DWright(13) (lw: bhd fnl 2f)	nk	**20**	12/1	63	46
4153[W]	**Cosmic Prince (IRE) (93)** (MAJarvis) **3-8-11** RCochrane(11) (prom 4f)	4	**21**	20/1	67	47
4153[7]	**Ursa Major (78)** (PAKelleway) **3-7-5**(5) APolli(14) (racd far side: prom over 5f)	5	**22**	50/1	40	20
4282[10]	**Chickawicka (IRE) (91)** (BPalling) **6-8-12** DaneO'Neill(17) (racd far side: prom over 3f)	1	**23**	50/1	51	34
4240[6]	**Neuwest (USA) (102)** (RAkehurst) **5-9-9** SSanders(15) (lw: bhd fnl 3f)	½	**24**	16/1	61	44
4153[4]	**Tumbleweed Ridge (103)** (BJMeehan) **4-9-10b** LDettori(16) (racd far side: prom 5f: eased whn btn over 1f out: t.o)	dist	**25**	12/1	—	—

(SP 143.6%) **25 Rn**

1m 26.74 (-0.46) CSF £173.74 CT £2,259.07 TOTE £22.10: £4.50 £2.80 £4.20 £3.30 (£153.40) Trio £985.40 OWNER C H Newton Jnr Ltd (MALTON) BRED D.B. Lamplough
LONG HANDICAP Safio 7-5 Ursa Major 7-6
WEIGHT FOR AGE 3yo-3lb

IN-FOCUS: The draw played a big part with those racing on the far side having no chance in the final quarter-mile.
4148 Jo Mell, described as a difficult horse to ride by his trainer, turned this very competitive handicap into a one-horse race for, after striking the front over a quarter of a mile from home, he forged clear from below the distance to win with plenty in hand. (14/1)
3594 Kayvee, third in this race in 1993 and 1994 and second in it last year, put up his best performance of the season, running on nicely in the last furlong and a half to take second place. (14/1)
3725 Crumpton Hill (IRE) goes well in this type of event and had more use made of him, although unable to find the necessary turn of foot in the final quarter-mile. (12/1)
4148* Russian Music, third in this race last year, is probably better at further these days and, although running on from below the distance, was never going to get there in time. (14/1)
2690 Tregaron (USA), 9lb higher than when last successful, likes to hear his feet rattle and was always close up, if tapped for toe in the last two furlongs. (20/1)
4120 Flamboyance (USA), set to rise 7lb in future handicaps, stayed on from below the distance but never looked like getting there in time. A return to a mile is needed. (14/1)
3975 Return of Amin did best of those on the far side but the principals racing on the stands' were already home and dry. He would prefer some cut in the ground. (33/1)

4424 ROSEMARY RATED STKS H'CAP (0-105) (Listed) (3-Y.O+ F & M) (Class A)

4-30 (4-36) **1m (straight)** £18,763.80 (£7,024.20: £3,437.10: £1,480.50: £665.25: £339.15) Stalls: Low GOING minus 0.16 sec per fur (GF)

				SP	RR	SF
3492[5]	**Kenmist (97)** (LMCumani) **3-9-0** KDarley(3) (rdn over 2f out: hdwy over 1f out: led 1f out: drvn out)	—	**1**	10/1	110	77
4110[4]	**Priena (IRE) (88)** (DRLoder) **3-8-5b**[1]ow1 RCochrane(2) (a.p: led over 1f out: sn hdd: r.o)	nk	**2**	10/1	100	66
4120[7]	**Noisette (100)** (JHMGosden) **3-9-3** LDettori(11) (lw: rdn & hdwy over 1f out: unable qckn ins fnl f)	¾	**3**	9/2 2	111	78
4148[5]	**Pomona (87)** (PJMakin) **4-8-8** MJKinane(1) (hld up: rdn over 2f out: n.m.r ins fnl f: one pce)	1¼	**4**	6/1 3	95	66
3736a[5]	**Divina Luna (86)** (JWHills) **4-8-7** MHills(4) (w ldr: led over 2f out tl over 1f out: one pce fnl f)	½	**5**	14/1	93	64
3913[11]	**Mara River (86)** (IABalding) **3-8-3** MartinDwyer(6) (hdwy over 2f out: hrd rdn & ev ch over 1f out: wknd ins fnl f)	1¾	**6**	16/1	90	57
4220*	**Irish Light (USA) (87)** (MRStoute) **3-8-4** TQuinn(12) (stdy hdwy over 2f out: rdn over 1f out: wknd fnl f)	2½	**7**	7/2 1	86	53
4147[2]	**Queens Consul (IRE) (88)** (BSRothwell) **7-8-9** MFenton(7) (led over 5f)	nk	**8**	6/1 3	86	57
4120[10]	**Unconditional Love (IRE) (100)** (MJohnston) **4-9-7** JWeaver(13) (prom over 5f)	3	**9**	16/1	92	63
4121[10]	**Blane Water (USA) (86)** (JRFanshawe) **3-8-3** TSprake(10) (hdwy over 4f out: rdn over 2f out: wknd over 1f out)	1¾	**10**	25/1	75	42
2690[8]	**Tsarnista (90)** (JLDunlop) **4-8-11** MRoberts(8) (bhd fnl 2f)	1½	**11**	20/1	76	47

(SP 114.2%) **11 Rn**

1m 40.84 (0.84) CSF £93.59 CT £475.38 TOTE £14.10: £3.10 £2.80 £1.80 (£46.70) Trio £121.80 OWNER Dr Saini Fasanotti (NEWMARKET)
BRED Azienda Agricola Il Tiglio di Amelia Prevedello
LONG HANDICAP Divina Luna 8-6 Blane Water (USA) 8-0 Mara River 8-1
WEIGHT FOR AGE 3yo-4lb

3492 Kenmist put up a fine display and, coming through to strike the front a furlong out, responded to pressure to hold off her persistent rivals. (10/1)
4110 Priena (IRE) appreciated the drop in distance and poked a whisker in front below the distance. Although soon collared, she refused to lie down and made sure the winner fought hard to the bitter end. (10/1: 8/1-12/1)
4120 Noisette, who had valid excuses for her last two runs, encountered no problems here and ran much better. Picking up ground nicely on the outside below the distance, she got to the heels of the front two but was then unable to get on level terms. (9/2: op 3/1)
4148 Pomona chased the leaders. Although she momentarily did not have a great deal of room inside the final furlong, it made little difference to her chances as she was already tapped for toe at the time. (6/1)
3736a Divina Luna disputed the lead until going on over a quarter of a mile from home. Headed below the distance, she then failed to find another gear. This is her ground. (14/1)
3128 Mara River was not disgraced and was close enough if good enough below the distance, before weakening inside the final furlong.(16/1)

4425 BLUE SEAL CONDITIONS STKS (2-Y.O F) (Class B)

5-00 (5-06) **6f** £11,964.00 (£4,476.00: £2,188.00: £940.00: £420.00: £212.00) Stalls: Low GOING minus 0.16 sec per fur (GF)

				SP	RR	SF
4012^{6}	**Wenda (IRE)** (CEBrittain) **2-8-8** OPeslier(7) (stdy hdwy over 2f out: led ins fnl f: drvn out)	—	**1**	14/1	86	65
4103^{6}	**Atuf (USA)** (SbinSuroor) **2-8-8** LDettori(4) (lw: led: rdn over 1f out: hdd ins fnl f: r.o)	hd	**2**	$4/1^{2}$	86	65
	Shfoug (USA) (BWHills) **2-8-8** MHills(3) (unf: scope: s.s: rdn over 2f out: hdwy over 1f out: r.o ins fnl f: bttr for r)	1¼	**3**	12/1	82+	61
4227^{3}	**Marie Loup (FR)** (LMCumani) **2-8-8** KFallon(5) (lw: hld up: rdn over 2f out: unable qckn)	1¾	**4**	$15/8^{1}$	78	57
	Astrapi (MRStoute) **2-8-8** JReid(8) (unf: scope: a.p: rdn 2f out: ev ch over 1f out: wknd fnl f)	hd	**5**	7/1	78	57
4212^{2}	**Niki (IRE)** (JHMGosden) **2-8-8** RHills(6) (lw: chsd ldr: ev ch over 1f out: wknd fnl f)	nk	**6**	10/1	77	56
	Tabasco (IRE) (MRChannon) **2-8-8** MJKinane(2) (wl grwn: a bhd)	2½	**7**	12/1	70	49
4298^{*}	**Poly Blue (IRE)** (MissGayKelleway) **2-8-11** TQuinn(1) (lw: prom over 3f)	3½	**8**	$5/1^{3}$	64	43
				(SP 115.1%)	**8 Rn**	

1m 15.07 (1.07) CSF £63.36 TOTE £12.70: £2.40 £1.50 £2.80 (£23.80) OWNER Mr B. H. Voak (NEWMARKET) BRED Sean Collins
IN-FOCUS: **A memorable afternoon for Peslier, who completed a brilliant 2,249/1 treble.**
4012 Wenda (IRE) appreciated the extra furlong. Throwing down her challenge below the distance, she got on top inside the final furlong and held on well. (14/1)
4103 Atuf (USA) stepped up on her initial run at Kempton earlier in the month. Attempting to make all the running, she was only passed inside the final furlong and kept on well to the line. She should soon go one better. (4/1: op 9/4)
Shfoug (USA), who needs time to develop, made a very pleasing debut. Although losing ground at the start, she moved up promisingly below the distance and kept on nicely inside the final furlong. She should not be hard to win with. (12/1: 8/1-14/1)
4227 Marie Loup (FR) chased the leaders but Fallon was already working hard on her over a quarter of a mile from home and she could only go up and down in the same place. She is crying out for an extra furlong. (15/8)
Astrapi, a lean, good-quartered filly who is a full-sister to the useful Polydamas, was never far away and had every chance below the distance before tiring. She should soon find a race. (7/1: 4/1-8/1)
4212 Niki (IRE) found the drop in trip not in her favour for, after having every chance approaching the final furlong, was then left standing. A return to seven furlongs is required. (10/1: 6/1-12/1)
Tabasco (IRE) (12/1: 8/1-14/1)

4426 'MAGNIFICENT SEVEN' GORDON CARTER H'CAP (0-95) (3-Y.O+) (Class C)

5-35 (5-35) **2m 45y** £14,590.00 (£4,420.00: £2,160.00: £1,030.00) Stalls: High GOING minus 0.04 sec per fur (G)

				SP	RR	SF
4046^{*}	**Jaseur (USA) (74)** (JHMGosden) **4-8-12v** LDettori(12) (lw: hdwy over 2f out: led over 1f out: r.o wl)	—	**1**	$9/2^{2}$	88+	70
3763^{5}	**Princess Topaz (77)** (CACyzer) **3-8-0**(3) RFfrench(4) (rdn over 2f out: hdwy over 1f out: chsd wnr ins fnl f: unable qckn)	3½	**2**	8/1	88	58
4313^{*}	**Renzo (IRE) (86)** (MrsAJPerrett) **4-9-10** AClark(1) (hdwy over 2f out: chsd wnr over 1f out tl ins fnl f: one pce)	1¾	**3**	9/1	95	77
4241^{10}	**Star Rage (IRE) (82)** (MJohnston) **7-9-6** JWeaver(3) (lw: nt clr run over 2f out: hdwy over 1f out: r.o)	1¼	**4**	14/1	90	72
3498^{8}	**Shining Dancer (60)** (SDow) **5-7-12** JQuinn(10) (nt clr run over 2f out: hdwy over 1f out: r.o)	¾	**5**	16/1	67	49
4313^{2}	**Sea Victor (74)** (JLHarris) **5-8-12** OPeslier(9) (a.p: rdn over 2f out: one pce)	½	**6**	$9/4^{1}$	80	62
4108^{11}	**Pike Creek (USA) (70)** (IABalding) **4-8-8** MartinDwyer(14) (a.p: rdn over 2f out: wknd fnl f)	½	**7**	20/1	76	58
3318^{5}	**Tawafek (USA) (68)** (SDow) **4-8-6** RPerham(6) (rdn over 2f out: hdwy & nt clr run over 1f out: nt rcvr)	1	**8**	20/1	73	55
3763^{4}	**Thornby Park (86)** (JLDunlop) **3-8-12** TSprake(11) (lw: prom over 14f)	s.h	**9**	$7/1^{3}$	91	61
3915^{4}	**Story Line (80)** (DWPArbuthnot) **4-9-4** TQuinn(13) (lw: led tl over 1f out: sn wknd)	nk	**10**	16/1	85	67
2514^{11}	**Whitechapel (USA) (82)** (LordHuntingdon) **9-9-6** KFallon(2) (rdn over 2f out: hdwy over 1f out: wknd fnl f)	s.h	**11**	10/1	87	69
4222^{2}	**Galapino (69)** (MissGayKelleway) **4-8-2**(5) RMullen(5) (hdwy & nt clr run on ins over 1f out: nt rcvr)	nk	**12**	$7/1^{3}$	73	55
3469^{14}	**He Knows The Rules (58)** (RHBuckler) **5-7-3**(7) PDoe(8) (prom over 13f)	18	**13**	50/1	44	26
	Shahrur (USA) (75) (GLMoore) **4-8-13** MJKinane(7) (a bhd: t.o fnl 5f)	dist	**14**	25/1	—	—
				(SP 137.9%)	**14 Rn**	

3m 32.07 (4.87) CSF £41.15 CT £307.49 TOTE £4.80: £1.90 £3.00 £2.80 (£48.80) Trio £87.20 OWNER Sheikh Mohammed (NEWMARKET)
BRED Darley Stud Management Co Ltd
LONG HANDICAP He Knows The Rules 7-5
WEIGHT FOR AGE 3yo-12lb
IN-FOCUS: **Dettori used a special golden saddle, given to him by a Japanese jockey, for this race.**
4046* Jaseur (USA) appreciated the longer trip. Coming through to lead below the distance, he soon forged clear, much to the delight of Dettori who waved and saluted to a cheering crowd. (9/2: 5/2-5/1)
3763 Princess Topaz, out of her depth in Listed company last time out, saw out this longer trip and came through to take second place inside the final furlong, if having no hope of reeling in the winner. (8/1)
4313* Renzo (IRE) began his effort early in the straight and came through to take second place approaching the final furlong, but he carried his head very high as usual and was overhauled for the runner-up berth inside the last two hundred yards. (9/1)
4156 Star Rage (IRE) had the ground in his favour but failed to get a clear run at the back of the field early in the straight. He weaved his way through the pack from below the distance and, in the circumstances, did well to finish fourth. (14/1)
2767 Shining Dancer, who failed to get a clear run early in the straight, stayed on through the pack in the last furlong and a half to be nearest at the line. (16/1)
4313 Sea Victor failed to reverse Kempton form with Renzo on 2lb better terms and, after racing in a prominent position, could only plod on at one pace in the last two furlongs. (9/4)

T/Jkpt: Not won; £18,843.28 to Ascot 28/9/97. T/Plpt: £2,411.60 (40.66 Tckts). T/Qdpt: £643.80 (5.86 Tckts) AK

4285-CATTERICK (L-H) (Good, Good to firm patches)
Saturday September 27th

WEATHER: overcast WIND: slight across

4427 'OPEN-MORNING' NURSERY H'CAP (0-85) (2-Y.O F) (Class E)

2-10 (2-12) **7f** £3,226.25 (£965.00: £462.50: £211.25) Stalls: Low GOING: 0.07 sec per fur (G)

Form	Horse	Dist	Pos	SP	RR	SF
4143^{2}	**Jungle Story (IRE) (70)** (PTWalwyn) **2-9-1** AMcGlone(4) (in tch: rdn along ½-wy: hdwy over 1f out: r.o wl to ld wl ins fnl f)	—	**1**	$2/1^{1}$	74	31
3636^{7}	**Katah (71)** (JHMGosden) **2-9-2** JCarroll(7) (chsd ldrs: rdn to ld ins fnl f: nt qckn towards fin)	1½	**2**	$7/2^{2}$	72	29
4285^{9}	**The Honorable Lady (60)** (MRChannon) **2-8-5** CandyMorris(3) (lw: chsd ldrs: hdwy on ins 2f out: n.m.r ent fnl f: kpt on one pce)	2	**3**	8/1	56	13
3911*	**Marske Machine (62)** (NTinkler) **2-8-7b** KimTinkler(1) (outpcd & bhd tl styd on wl fnl f)	hd	**4**	8/1	58	15
4285^{8}	**Tancred Times (68)** (DWBarker) **2-8-13** TWilliams(5) (led ½f: cl up: led over 2f out tl ins fnl f: wknd)	1½	**5**	$7/1^{3}$	60	17
3468^{5}	**Zena (76)** (WJarvis) **2-9-7** JFortune(2) (prom tl outpcd appr st: n.d after)	½	**6**	$7/1^{3}$	67	24
4208^{2}	**Maedaley (53)** (PCHaslam) **2-7-9**$^{(3)}$ PFessey(8) (led after 1½f tl over 2f out: sn wknd)	1½	**7**	8/1	41	—
4209^{7}	**Smooth Princess (IRE) (60)** (JGFitzGerald) **2-8-5** LCharnock(6) (hld up: effrt ½-wy: sn btn)	5	**8**	14/1	36	—

(SP 120.6%) **8 Rn**

1m 29.8 (6.20) CSF £8.77 CT £43.54 TOTE £2.70: £1.60 £1.90 £2.20 (£4.10) OWNER Major & Mrs Kennard and Partners (LAMBOURN) BRED Barronstown Stud

4143 Jungle Story (IRE), a leggy filly, needed every yard of this trip on this sharp and undulating track. (2/1)
1970 Katah, stepping up in trip, put up an improved performance but she left the impression that she is keeping something for herself. (7/2)
2923* The Honorable Lady took the eye in the paddock but she hesitated at a gap entering the final furlong and any chance had soon gone. (8/1)
3911* Marske Machine, brought into the paddock last and taken to post first as she is a real handful, found this track on this fast ground too sharp, and only ran on when it was too late. (8/1: 6/1-9/1)
3932 Tancred Times is slipping down the handicap and is running quite well. (7/1)
3468 Zena has been off the track for almost seven weeks and she never looked happy here. (7/1)

4428 DUTTON-FORSHAW, STOCKTON, LAND ROVER MAIDEN STKS (2-Y.O) (Class D)

2-40 (2-43) **5f** £3,567.50 (£1,070.00: £515.00: £237.50) Stalls: Low GOING: 0.07 sec per fur (G)

Form	Horse	Dist	Pos	SP	RR	SF
4311^{2}	**Mrs Malaprop** (MRChannon) **2-8-9** JCarroll(13) (lw: chsd ldrs: led 1½f out: r.o strly)	—	**1**	$3/1^{2}$	82+	47
4211^{4}	**Surprised** (MrsJRRamsden) **2-9-0** JFortune(8) (trckd ldrs: hdwy over 1f out: styd on: no ch w wnr)	5	**2**	$9/4^{1}$	71	36
4230^{3}	**Carol Singer (USA)** (MJohnston) **2-8-9** JFanning(11) (mde most tl hdd 1½f out: one pce)	1	**3**	10/1	63	28
2706^{4}	**Howies Choice (IRE)** (KMcAuliffe) **2-9-0** DaleGibson(9) (a chsng ldrs: nt qckn appr fnl f)	1	**4**	$9/2^{3}$	65	30
4211^{13}	**Anditz (IRE)** (JLEyre) **2-8-10**^{ow1} OPears(14) (stdy hdwy ½-wy: nvr nr to chal)	3	**5**	50/1	51	15
1854^{4}	**Great Melody (IRE)** (JMPEustace) **2-8-11**$^{(3)}$ PFessey(7) (a chsng ldrs: nt qckn fnl 2f)	1¼	**6**	8/1	51	16
3619^{6}	**Maytong** (JBerry) **2-8-6**$^{(3)}$ TEDurcan(2) (outpcd tl sme late hdwy)	¾	**7**	14/1	44	9
4159^{11}	**Pabella Bluebird (IRE)** (GROldroyd) **2-8-9** KHodgson(12) (outpcd & bhd tl sme late hdwy)	½	**8**	100/1	42	7
4211^{11}	**Westcourt Ruby** (MWEasterby) **2-8-6**$^{(3)}$ GParkin(6) (sn drvn along & bhd: n.d)	2½	**9**	20/1	34	—
	Crystal Lough (IRE) (GROldroyd) **2-8-4**$^{(7)ow2}$ RFarmer(4) (neat: scope: prom over 3f)	s.h	**10**	100/1	36	—
4211^{8}	**Amber Regent** (PCHaslam) **2-9-0** LCharnock(3) (cl up 3f: wknd)	½	**11**	16/1	37	2
2604^{8}	**Lawful Contract (IRE)** (RHollinshead) **2-8-11**$^{(3)}$ DGriffiths(1) (lw: sn drvn along & n.d)	1½	**12**	100/1	32	—
3804^{5}	**Lady Emral** (MissJFCraze) **2-8-9** SWebster(10) (s.i.s: a outpcd & bhd)	4	**13**	100/1	15	—
4012^{9}	**Arjan (IRE)** (JBerry) **2-8-6**$^{(3)}$ PRoberts(5) (b.nr fore: reard in stalls: ref to s)		**R**	7/1	—	—

(SP 129.9%) **14 Rn**

61.0 secs (3.30) CSF £9.93 TOTE £2.70: £1.60 £1.50 £2.00 (£5.00) Trio £11.40 OWNER Mr Michael Foy (UPPER LAMBOURN) BRED Olympic Bloodstock Ltd and Partners

4311 Mrs Malaprop looked useful here, winning in style from a poor draw, and there would seem to be more to come from this attractive sort. (3/1)
4211 Surprised ran well and was certainly not over-punished. He does not look the ideal type for this track and there is better to come. (9/4)
4230 Carol Singer (USA) ran well again and there should be a modest event to be found for this very sharp sort. (10/1)
2706 Howies Choice (IRE) had not run for over two months and this was not a bad effort in the circumstances. (9/2)
Anditz (IRE) had the worst draw but gave definite signs of ability, gradually picking up ground from halfway. (50/1)
1854 Great Melody (IRE) had his only previous run three and a half months ago and gave problems here by continually hanging left. (8/1)

4429 JOHN MORGAN - YORKSHIRE EVENING POST H'CAP (0-70) (3-Y.O) (Class E)

3-10 (3-10) **1m 3f 214y** £3,148.25 (£941.00: £450.50: £205.25) Stalls: Low GOING: 0.07 sec per fur (G)

Form	Horse	Dist	Pos	SP	RR	SF
3210^{5}	**Kingdom Pearl (47)** (MJCamacho) **3-8-2** LCharnock(2) (lw: trckd ldrs: smooth hdwy to ld over 2f out: sn qcknd clr: eased ins fnl f)	—	**1**	9/1	58+	21
4060^{7}	**Back Row (64)** (LMCumani) **3-9-5** JCarroll(3) (chsd ldr: ev ch over 2f out: rdn & nt qckn)	3	**2**	$9/4^{2}$	71	34
4242^{4}	**Silver Whirl (USA) (66)** (RCharlton) **3-9-7** JFortune(4) (led tl hdd over 2f out: sn wknd)	14	**3**	$8/11^{1}$	54	17
3807^{4}	**Erinrinca (IRE) (48)** (JEBanks) **3-8-0**$^{(3)}$ PFessey(6) (lw: prom tl outpcd & lost tch 5f out: n.d after)	9	**4**	$11/2^{3}$	24	—
3581^{9}	**Showstopper (42)** (TJEtherington) **3-7-4**$^{(7)ow1}$ PBradley(1) (a outpcd & bhd)	1½	**5**	100/1	16	—
1820^{11}	**Al Ava Consonant (42)** (JDBethell) **3-7-11**^{ow1} TWilliams(5) (hld up: shkn up & hdwy 7f out: wknd appr st)	nk	**6**	33/1	16	—

(SP 118.0%) **6 Rn**

2m 42.3 (10.90) CSF £28.53 TOTE £6.30: £1.90 £1.60 (£11.90) OWNER G B Turnbull Ltd (MALTON) BRED Mrs N. F. M. Sampson

LONG HANDICAP Showstopper 6-11 Al Ava Consonant 7-9

OFFICIAL EXPLANATION **Silver Whirl (USA): no explanation offered.**

3210 Kingdom Pearl seems to have had a problem last time as she has now had two months off but, obviously all the better for that, won this in some style. (9/1)
4060 Back Row had her chances but was made to look very one-paced by the winner. (9/4)
4242 Silver Whirl (USA) had some reasonable-looking form but ran badly and something must have been amiss. (8/11: 4/5-evens)
3807 Erinrinca (IRE), taking a big step up in trip, never looked happy and this was a most disappointing effort. (11/2)
Showstopper has yet to show anything positive. (100/1)
Al Ava Consonant keeps stepping up in trip but her performances are certainly not improving. (33/1)

4430 THEAKSTON APPRENTICE LIMITED STKS (0-85) (3-Y.O+) (Class G)

3-45 (3-45) **5f 212y** £2,238.00 (£618.00: £294.00) Stalls: Low GOING: 0.07 sec per fur (G)

				SP	RR	SF
4282[5]	**Gaelic Storm (87)** (MJohnston) **3-8-10**(7) IGrantham(2) (lw: b.hind: disp ld tl led over 2f out: edgd lft & r.o: comf)	—	1	Evens[1]	82+	50
4282[5]	**Albert The Bear (87)** (JBerry) **4-8-12b**(7) PBradley(3) (cl up: chsd wnr fnl 1½f: no imp)	2½	2	6/4[2]	75	45
3594[10]	**Johnny Staccato (85)** (JMPEustace) **3-9-0** PFessey(5) (s.s: styd on fnl 3f: nrst fin)	5	3	5/1[3]	59	27
4417[6]	**Ohnonotagain (30)** (NTinkler) **5-8-5**(5) IonaWands(1) (disp ld tl hdd over 2f out: sn outpcd)	2½	4	100/1	46	16
3746[6]	**Miss Aragon (38)** (MissLCSiddall) **9-8-5**(5) TSiddall(4) (trckd ldrs tl outpcd fnl 2½f)	2	5	25/1	41	11
				(SP 111.5%)		**5 Rn**

1m 14.9 (4.00) CSF £2.57 TOTE £1.90: £1.10 £1.30 (£1.30) OWNER H C Racing Club (MIDDLEHAM) BRED A. D. G. Oldrey
WEIGHT FOR AGE 3yo-2lb
IN-FOCUS: **This was Ian Grantham's first winner.**
4282 Gaelic Storm was well handled by his young rider, won with something to spare and gives the impression that there is still a useful race or two to be picked up this season. (Evens)
4282 Albert The Bear ran a fair race but, at this trip, he was always second best for speed. (6/4)
1975* Johnny Staccato has problems at the start and, until that is sorted out, he is best avoided. (5/1)
2939 Ohnonotagain, having her second run in consecutive days, ran as well as could be expected in this company. (100/1)
3746 Miss Aragon had next to no chance at these weights. (25/1)

4431 BEDALE MEDIAN AUCTION MAIDEN STKS (3-Y.O) (Class F)

4-20 (4-21) **5f 212y** £2,532.00 (£702.00: £336.00) Stalls: Low GOING: 0.07 sec per fur (G)

				SP	RR	SF
4214[6]	**Passionatti (53)** (SGollings) **3-8-9** TWilliams(8) (swtg: plld hrd: w ldr: led over 2f out: drvn out)	—	1	8/1[3]	53	33
3982[5]	**Misty Point (64)** (IABalding) **3-8-9** SWhitworth(1) (lw: chsd ldrs: drvn along ½-wy: r.o fnl f: nrst fin)	¾	2	2/5[1]	51	31
4043[10]	**Pardan (34)** (BPalling) **3-8-11**(3) PRoberts(3) (lw: led tl hdd over 2f out: kpt on same pce)	¾	3	10/1	54	34
4008[9]	**Daintree (IRE) (47)** (HJCollingridge) **3-8-9v** DaleGibson(4) (lw: trckd ldrs: effrt over 2f out: r.o one pce)	nk	4	6/1[2]	48	28
4214[16]	**Violette Sabo** (TJEtherington) **3-8-9** LCharnock(2) (dwlt: nvr trbld ldrs)	6	5	50/1	32	12
4168[12]	**Terry's Rose (33)** (RHollinshead) **3-8-9** NCarlisle(7) (chsd ldrs over 3f: sn rdn & btn)	1	6	20/1	29	9
4300[10]	**Colonel's Pride (42)** (RMWhitaker) **3-9-0** OPears(6) (s.i.s: a bhd)	4	7	33/1	24	4
	Woodetto (IRE) (EWeymes) **3-9-0** JFanning(5) (bit bkwd: outpcd fr ½-wy)	½	8	14/1	22	2
				(SP 122.2%)		**8 Rn**

1m 15.6 (4.70) CSF £11.26 TOTE £7.80: £1.80 £1.10 £3.70 (£3.90) OWNER Mr A. E. Moss (LOUTH) BRED Mrs J. M. Gollings
4214 Passionatti needed two handlers in the paddock and looked a real handful before the start but, positively ridden, she did all that was necessary in the race. (8/1)
3982 Misty Point is nothing special to look at and was very much on her toes beforehand. In this poor race, she took an age to get going, which proved her undoing. (2/5)
Pardan, dropping back in trip here, certainly has the speed but was never quite good enough. (10/1: 8/1-12/1)
3868 Daintree (IRE) always seems to have a chance but is yet to come up with the goods. (6/1)
Violette Sabo improved on her debut but there is plenty more needed. (50/1)
Woodetto (IRE) (14/1: 10/1-16/1)

4432 HIPSWELL H'CAP (0-70) (3-Y.O+) (Class E)

4-50 (4-51) **1m 7f 177y** £3,096.25 (£925.00: £442.50: £201.25) Stalls: Low GOING: 0.07 sec per fur (G)

				SP	RR	SF
4287[2]	**Ranger Sloane (38)** (GFierro) **5-8-10** NCarlisle(10) (b: hld up: hdwy gng wl 6f out: led 2f out: r.o)	—	1	6/1[3]	49	20
4269[7]	**Hasta la Vista (55)** (MWEasterby) **7-9-10b**(3) GParkin(3) (lw: trckd ldrs: hdwy to chal over 1f out: hrd rdn & nt qckn)	2½	2	5/1[2]	64	35
4170[8]	**Welcome Lu (26)** (JLHarris) **4-7-12** FNorton(6) (hld up: hdwy to chse ldrs ent st: kpt on: nt pce to chal)	½	3	12/1	34	5
2757[4]	**Fullopep (62)** (MrsMReveley) **3-9-8** JFortune(8) (lw: hld up: hdwy & prom 4f out: shkn up over 1f out: r.o one pce)	½	4	13/2	70	29
4170[13]	**Course Fishing (34)** (BAMcMahon) **6-8-6** LNewton(4) (lw: trckd ldrs: effrt ent st: r.o one pce)	¾	5	14/1	41	12
3826[8]	**My Millie (38)** (WStorey) **4-8-10** JFanning(1) (hld up & bhd: sme hdwy 3f out: nvr nr to chal)	9	6	16/1	36	7
4269[3]	**Arian Spirit (IRE) (49)** (JLEyre) **6-9-7v** TWilliams(9) (hld up: hdwy ½-wy: led over 2f out: sn hdd & no ex)	nk	7	9/4[1]	46	17
4287[5]	**Finestatetobein (31)** (FWatson) **4-8-0**(3) PFessey(2) (in tch tl outpcd fnl 4f)	2	8	14/1	26	—
	Home Counties (IRE) (55) (DMoffatt) **8-9-10**(3) DarrenMoffatt(7) (hld up & a bhd)	10	9	20/1	40	11
4235[16]	**Forzair (51)** (JJO'Neill) **5-9-9** AMcGlone(5) (lw: mde most tl hdd & wknd over 2f out)	1½	10	20/1	35	6
4170[12]	**Rose of Glenn (45)** (BPalling) **6-9-0**(3) PRoberts(11) (disp ld tl wknd 6f out)	9	11	6/1[3]	20	—
				(SP 125.8%)		**11 Rn**

3m 38.3 (16.30) CSF £35.34 CT £325.64 TOTE £10.20: £2.80 £1.80 £4.50 (£29.90) Trio £339.90; £95.76 to Ascot 28/9/97 OWNER Mr G. Fierro (HEDNESFORD) BRED T. Barratt
WEIGHT FOR AGE 3yo-12lb
4287 Ranger Sloane is in tremendous form and won this nicely. (6/1)
3907* Hasta la Vista loves this track and ran his heart out yet again, but had to admit that he had met one too useful. (5/1)
Welcome Lu ran her best race of the season here and would appear to be coming to hand. (12/1)
2757 Fullopep, after over two months off, ran well and will be worth noting when put over hurdles. (13/2)
3931 Course Fishing has slipped down to a useful mark but this scratchy mover seems to lack a change of gear these days. (14/1)
3085 My Millie is slipping down the handicap and probably needed this, her first run for a month. (16/1)
3623 Rose of Glenn (6/1: op 4/1)

T/Plpt: £25.20 (503.79 Tckts). T/Qdpt: £11.30 (29.85 Tckts) AA

4407-HAYDOCK (L-H) (Good)
Saturday September 27th
WEATHER: cloudy WIND: mod half bhd

4433 E.B.F. KNUTSFORD MAIDEN STKS (2-Y.O) (Class D)
2-30 (2-31) **7f 30y** £3,582.50 (£1,085.00: £530.00: £252.50) Stalls: Low GOING minus 0.15 sec per fur (GF)

			SP	RR	SF
4061[3]	**Last Christmas** (BWHills) **2-9-0** PaulEddery(6) (led 2f: shkn up to ld appr fnl f: r.o wl) ....—	**1**	4/5[1]	83	49
3386[2]	**The Gene Genie** (MJHeaton-Ellis) **2-9-0** SDrowne(9) (lw: chsd ldrs: effrt over 1f out: r.o wl towards fin).........½	**2**	9/2[2]	82	48
	Doraid (IRE) (JHMGosden) **2-9-0** GHind(8) (w'like: bit bkwd: a.p: led over 1f out: sn hdd: one pce fnl f).......1½	**3**	11/2[3]	79	45
	Alcayde (JLDunlop) **2-9-0** WRyan(2) (neat: bkwd: hld up & bhd: hdwy fnl 2f: nvr nrr).......3	**4**	12/1	72	38
3789[6]	**Lord Warford** (GBBalding) **2-8-11**(3) PPMurphy(1) (trckd ldrs: effrt 2f out: r.o one pce).......1½	**5**	50/1	68	34
	Wosaita (JLDunlop) **2-8-9** GCarter(7) (unf: scope: bkwd: hld up in rr: styd on appr fnl f: nrst fin).......s.h	**6**	10/1	63	29
4052[6]	**Nuit d'Or (IRE)** (MJohnston) **2-9-0** DHolland(12) (bit bkwd: led after 2f tl hdd & wknd over 1f out).......1¼	**7**	16/1	66	32
4309[6]	**The Blues Academy (IRE)** (MJohnston) **2-9-0v** DeanMcKeown(11) (chsd ldrs 5f: sn rdn & wknd).......1¼	**8**	20/1	63	29
3887[8]	**Laramania** (PDEvans) **2-9-0** JFEgan(5) (a bhd).......nk	**9**	40/1	62	28
3569[8]	**Caroline's Pet (IRE)** (ABailey) **2-8-2**(7) JBosley(3) (prom to ½-wy: sn rdn & lsot pl).......5	**10**	50/1	46	12
3411[12]	**Maggice** (RHollinshead) **2-8-9** FLynch(4) (s.s: a bhd).......hd	**11**	66/1	46	12
	College Mount (MPBielby) **2-9-0** ACulhane(10) (gd sort: bkwd: s.s: a bhd & outpcd: t.o).......29	**12**	66/1	—	—
			(SP 125.9%)		**12 Rn**

1m 31.22 (3.22) CSF £4.31 TOTE £1.90: £1.10 £1.40 £1.60 (£2.90) Trio £4.30 OWNER Mr A. D. Shead (LAMBOURN) BRED W. F. Macauley

4061 Last Christmas ran in a race that is turning out plenty of winners on his debut and, though he was still green here, he did all that was required to open his account. (4/5)

3386 The Gene Genie, led around by two handlers in the paddock and once again taken to post steadily, took time to find top gear, but he was really into his stride inside the last furlong and gave supporters of the favourite a worrying time late on. (9/2)

Doraid (IRE), sure to strip fitter for the run, showed lots of promise on this debut and he will be all the wiser for this experience. (11/2)

Alcayde, a neatly-turned colt with something left to work on, did all his best work in the closing stages and should be able to win races. (12/1)

Lord Warford had shown little in two previous runs and is bred to stay, so this performance is a sign that he is getting to know what the game is all about. (50/1)

Wosaita, closely related to several winners, was not fully wound up for this debut and did not impress to post, but she did begin to stay on in the latter stages and the experience should prove beneficial. (10/1)

4434 AKZO NOBEL HOLDINGS H'CAP (0-90) (3-Y.O+) (Class C)
3-00 (3-00) **5f** £5,732.00 (£1,736.00: £848.00: £404.00) Stalls: High GOING minus 0.30 sec per fur (GF)

			SP	RR	SF
4239[12]	**Patsy Grimes (87)** (JSMoore) **7-9-8**(3) PPMurphy(5) (lw: bhd & outpcd: rdn 2f out: str run fnl f to ld last stride).......—	**1**	5/1[3]	94	77
4329*	**Ansellman (84)** (JBerry) **7-9-3b**(5) 6x CLowther(6) (lw: hld up: hdwy wl over 1f out: rdn & r.o wl cl home)........hd	**2**	13/2	91	74
4365[8]	**Squire Corrie (81)** (DWChapman) **5-9-5** ACulhane(7) (lw: led tl ct cl home).......s.h	**3**	8/1	88	71
4280[4]	**Kira (81)** (JLEyre) **7-9-5** RLappin(3) (b: chsd ldrs: effrt u.p over 1f out: r.o wl towards fin).......nk	**4**	7/2[1]	87	70
4233[4]	**Gold Edge (61)** (MRChannon) **3-7-12**ow2 AMackay(1) (chsd ldrs: hrd rdn over 1f out: r.o).......1¼	**5**	10/1	63	43
4137[18]	**Lord High Admiral (CAN) (84)** (MJHeaton-Ellis) **9-9-8** SDrowne(2) (w ldrs over 3f: sn rdn & outpcd).......3½	**6**	4/1[2]	74	57
4233[3]	**Swynford Dream (70)** (JHetherton) **4-8-8** JLowe(4) (lw: spd 3f: sn rdn & wknd).......1¾	**7**	7/2[1]	55	38
			(SP 114.6%)		**7 Rn**

59.9 secs (0.40) CSF £33.54 TOTE £6.20: £2.10 £2.40 (£11.10) OWNER Mr J. K. Grimes (HUNGERFORD) BRED J. C. Fox
LONG HANDICAP Gold Edge 7-6
WEIGHT FOR AGE 3yo-1lb

3914 Patsy Grimes has not won at this trip for three years but, ridden to perfection here, swooped to conquer right on the line. (5/1)

4329* Ansellman is running well, and he did look the likely winner in the final fifty yards until the strong-finishing winner beat him to the punch. (13/2)

3900 Squire Corrie is a truly marvellous servant and, in running right up to his best, was a shade unfortunate to be pipped on the post. (8/1: 6/1-9/1)

4280 Kira struggles at this trip in such company and, though she was in the thick of the action nearing the finish, she just lacked that bit extra. (7/2)

4233 Gold Edge probably needs all of six furlongs but she is a trier and was far from disgraced here. (10/1)

4137 Lord High Admiral (CAN), much more effective when he can get his toe in, was in trouble soon after halfway and he had to admit his measure taken. (4/1)

4233 Swynford Dream comes good at this time of year when he has the cut that he needs, but he found this surface just too lively. (7/2)

4435 E.B.F. 'REPROCOLOR' H'CAP (0-90) (3-Y.O+ F & M) (Class C)
3-35 (3-36) **1m 2f 120y** £11,186.25 (£3,390.00: £1,657.50: £791.25) Stalls: High GOING minus 0.15 sec per fur (GF)

			SP	RR	SF
4102[2]	**Saafeya (IRE) (84)** (JHMGosden) **3-9-10** GHind(1) (lw: chsd ldr: led over 2f out: rdn clr: hld on cl home).......—	**1**	7/2[1]	97	44
4268[10]	**Ajayib (USA) (76)** (JLDunlop) **3-9-2b**[1] WRyan(5) (hld up mid div: drvn along 3f out: gd hdwy appr fnl f: fin wl)½	**2**	10/1	88	35
4144[3]	**Agony Aunt (76)** (MrsJCecil) **3-9-2** GCarter(7) (lw: led tl hdd over 2f out: sn hrd drvn: one pce fnl f).......1¾	**3**	14/1	86	33
4063[9]	**Ordained (53)** (EJAlston) **4-8-0** AMackay(4) (hld up & bhd: hdwy wl over 1f out: styd on fnl f).......nk	**4**	20/1	62	16
4242[3]	**Yabint El Sultan (84)** (BAMcMahon) **3-9-3**(7) SRighton(9) (lw: a chsng ldrs: rdn over 1f out: no ex fnl f)........1¼	**5**	8/1	91	38
4242*	**Arriving (70)** (JWHills) **3-8-7**(3) MHenry(2) (hld up: effrt & rdn 3f out: no imp).......1¾	**6**	9/2[3]	75	22
4242[6]	**My Valentina (74)** (BWHills) **3-9-0** PaulEddery(6) (trckd ldrs: rdn 2f out: sn btn).......2½	**7**	4/1[2]	75	22
4144[7]	**Grand Splendour (72)** (LadyHerries) **4-9-5** SDrowne(10) (lw: chsd ldrs tl rdn & wknd over 2f out).......3½	**8**	11/1	68	22
3906*	**Ganga (IRE) (84)** (WJarvis) **3-9-10** DHolland(3) (hld up & bhd: plld wd & effrt over 2f out: no imp).......s.h	**9**	8/1	79	26
3992[13]	**Rasayel (USA) (74)** (PDEvans) **7-9-7** JFEgan(8) (hld up: a in rr).......5	**10**	16/1	62	16
			(SP 117.4%)		**10 Rn**

2m 18.28 (6.78) CSF £35.92 CT £400.89 TOTE £3.50: £1.70 £2.80 £3.10 (£13.30) Trio £63.80 OWNER Sheikh Ahmed Al Maktoum (NEWMARKET) BRED Sheikh Ahmed Bin Rashid Al Maktoum
WEIGHT FOR AGE 3yo-7lb

4102 Saafeya (IRE) gained compensation for her narrow defeat at Doncaster and won a shade easier than the official margin suggests. She does appear to be a very progressive filly. (7/2)

1435 Ajayib (USA), running by far her best race this term, does seem to take time to pick up but she really found her stride in the final hundred yards and the blinkers have obviously woken her up. Her turn is close at hand. (10/1)
4144 Agony Aunt performs best when she can dictate and she did just that here until the winner proved much too strong inside the distance. (14/1)
3694 Ordained ran as if she does need a stiffer test of stamina and, as she has been tried over fourteen furlongs, connections are obviously of the same opinion. (20/1)
4242 Yabint El Sultan had 7lb taken off her back and she gave a good account of herself, but she is better when she can get her toe in and is performing well enough to pick up another race. (8/1)
4242* Arriving always comes from behind, but she was hard at work early in the straight and never promised to get herself concerned in the outcome. (9/2)
3720* Grand Splendour (11/1: 8/1-12/1)

4436 AKZO NOBEL PREMIER H'CAP (0-80) (3-Y.O) (Class D)

4-10 (4-13) **7f 30y** £3,858.75 (£1,170.00: £423.13: £423.13) Stalls: Low GOING minus 0.15 sec per fur (GF)

				SP	RR	SF
4176[7]	**Nominator Lad (67)** (BAMcMahon) **3-8-8** AMackay(2) (hld up & bhd: hdwy centre over 2f out: rdn to ld wl ins fnl f)	—	**1**	11/1	77	49
4176[13]	**Al Masroor (USA) (74)** (JWPayne) **3-9-1** DeanMcKeown(16) (lw: chsd ldrs: rdn to ld ins fnl f: sn hdd: unable qckn)	1	**2**	12/1	82	54
3812[3]	**Style Dancer (IRE) (75)** (RMWhitaker) **3-9-2v** FLynch(5) (lw: hld up & bhd: hdwy & swtchd lft over 2f out: nt clr run & swtchd rt fnl f: fin wl)	1	**3**	14/1	81	53
3584[15]	**Nor-Do-I (70)** (JMPEustace) **3-8-11** JTate(7) (a.p: led over 2f out tl ins fnl f)	d.h	**3**	16/1	76	48
3801[10]	**Blooming Amazing (71)** (JLEyre) **3-8-12** WRyan(12) (lw: trckd ldrs: rdn over 1f out: one pce fnl f)	hd	**5**	14/1	76	48
4175*	**Mujova (IRE) (82)** (RHollinshead) **3-9-9** ACulhane(8) (bhd: hdwy 2f out: nt clr run & swtchd rt ins fnl f: one pce)	1	**6**	14/1	85	57
4219[4]	**Caribbean Star (74)** (MRStoute) **3-9-1v** DHolland(6) (hld up in tch: hdwy & nt clr run 2f out & 1f out: nt rcvr)	hd	**7**	7/2[1]	77	49
4270[7]	**Cee-N-K (IRE) (71)** (MJohnston) **3-8-12** GCarter(9) (lw: trckd ldrs: kpt on u.p ins fnl f)	½	**8**	12/1	73	45
3591*	**Sharpo Wassl (70)** (WJHaggas) **3-8-6**(5) JoHunnam(4) (lw: hld up: hdwy on ins & nt clr run wl over 1f out: nt rcvr & eased)	9	**9**	15/2[3]	52	24
3987[9]	**Mystique Air (IRE) (62)** (EWeymes) **3-7-10**(7) RWinston(15) (bhd: hdwy on outside 3f out: sn rdn: no imp)	1¾	**10**	20/1	40	12
3937[13]	**Our People (76)** (MJohnston) **3-9-0**(3) MHenry(13) (lw: bhd: effrt & rdn over 2f out: no imp)	¾	**11**	25/1	52	24
4290*	**Cantina (70)** (ABailey) **3-8-6**(5) CLowther(11) (led tl over 2f out: sn rdn & wknd)	1	**12**	6/1[2]	44	16
4175[6]	**Alikhlas (76)** (MajorWRHern) **3-9-3** GHind(10) (s.s: hdwy & swtchd ins over 2f out: nt clr run & eased)	1¾	**13**	9/1	46	18
3457[4]	**Barresbo (65)** (CWFairhurst) **3-8-6** PaulEddery(3) (a bhd)	2	**14**	14/1	30	2
3900[12]	**Unshaken (61)** (EJAlston) **3-8-2v**[ow1] SDrowne(14) (lw: chsd ldrs tl wknd qckly over 2f out)	2½	**15**	33/1	21	—
				(SP 126.1%)	**15 Rn**	

1m 30.77 (2.77) CSF £126.62 CT NL, AM & SD £877.18; NL, AM & NDI £992.76 TOTE £13.90: £2.80 £4.50 SD £1.40 NDI £3.20 (£120.60) Trio £366.00; £309.36 to Ascot 28/9/97 OWNER Mr J. D. Graham (TAMWORTH) BRED J. D. Graham
IN-FOCUS: **Due to the fact that there were so many in contention throughout the last three furlongs, this turned out to be a very rough contest and there were many hard-luck stories.**
3987 Nominator Lad, bringing up the rear turning for home, missed all the trouble by pulling wide and, staying on strongly under pressure, ran on to lead well inside the final furlong. (11/1)
3392 Al Masroor (USA) showed a return to form with a much-improved effort and another success is possible before the season closes. (12/1)
3812 Style Dancer (IRE), one of the main sufferers in the general bunching inside the last quarter-mile, was without doubt an unlucky loser and, as he won in the autumn last year, maybe this is his time of year. (14/1)
3584 Nor-Do-I, running his best race yet on this livelier ground, was only worn down inside the final furlong and he does seem to be thriving. (16/1)
1392 Blooming Amazing has given the impression that he does need further and it was only a lack of finishing speed that was missing inside the distance. (14/1)
4175* Mujova (IRE), staying on when forced to switch inside the last furlong, could never really get going again but, with top weight, this was a better than average performance. (14/1)
4219 Caribbean Star had a nightmare run when poised to deliver her challenge and it did seem that she was probably the worst sufferer. (7/2)
3591* Sharpo Wassl (15/2: 5/1-8/1)

4437 E.B.F. SALE MAIDEN STKS (2-Y.O F) (Class D)

4-40 (4-40) **1m 30y** £3,517.50 (£1,065.00: £520.00: £247.50) Stalls: High GOING minus 0.15 sec per fur (GF)

				SP	RR	SF
4067[5]	**Muhaba (USA)** (SbinSuroor) **2-8-11** GHind(2) (mde all: qcknd over 3f out: sn clr: unchal)	—	**1**	4/1[3]	99+	49
4107[5]	**Storm River (USA)** (HRACecil) **2-8-11** WRyan(1) (chsd ldrs: wnt 2nd over 3f out: sn rdn: no imp)	6	**2**	7/2[2]	87	37
4066[2]	**Winsa (USA)** (JLDunlop) **2-8-11** GCarter(7) (dwlt: hdwy 4f out: rdn over 2f out: one pce)	2½	**3**	6/4[1]	82	32
4067[2]	**Honey Storm (IRE) (81)** (MRChannon) **2-8-11** AMackay(6) (chsd ldrs: rdn over 2f out: sn outpcd)	1¼	**4**	8/1	80	30
2840[9]	**Doating (IRE)** (JWHills) **2-8-8**(3) MHenry(4) (bit bkwd: hld up: effrt & outpcd 3f out: n.d)	½	**5**	25/1	79	29
4067[7]	**Queen of Tides (IRE)** (MRStoute) **2-8-11** DHolland(8) (b.hind: chsd wnr over 4f: outpcd 3f out: sn bhd)	9	**6**	7/1	61	11
3905[17]	**Esse** (EWeymes) **2-8-11** ACulhane(3) (a outpcd & bhd: t.o)	dist	**7**	50/1	—	—
				(SP 111.6%)	**7 Rn**	

1m 44.03 (3.43) CSF £15.87 TOTE £4.40: £2.10 £1.90 (£6.20) OWNER Godolphin (NEWMARKET) BRED Shadwell Farm Inc
4067 Muhaba (USA), much sharper for the run at Lingfield earlier in the month, adopted identical tactics over this longer trip and, quickening the tempo to draw clear early in the straight, came home unchallenged. (4/1)
4107 Storm River (USA) had more use made of her on this occasion and she never once stopped trying, but the winner proved to be in a class of her own. (7/2)
4066 Winsa (USA), sluggish as the stalls opened, tried to mount a challenge entering the last quarter-mile but, by then, the winner had set sail for home and she was unable to do anything about it. (6/4)
4067 Honey Storm (IRE) was unable to confirm her form with the winner, though she did remain in the action until finding demands too great halfway up the home straight. (8/1)
Doating (IRE) ran better than she did on her debut, but she is still far from the finished article and she should improve in time. (25/1)
4067 Queen of Tides (IRE), three lengths behind the winner at Lingfield, could have been expected to improve, but her attempt to stay within striking range disappeared early in the straight and she was one of the first beaten. (7/1)

4438 SEPTEMBER MAIDEN H'CAP (0-70) (3-Y.O+) (Class E)

5-15 (5-16) **1m 6f** £3,338.75 (£1,010.00: £492.50: £233.75) Stalls: Low GOING minus 0.15 sec per fur (GF)

Form	Horse	Dist	Pos	SP	RR	SF
4045[5]	**Devilish Charm (USA) (65)** (MrsAJPerrett) **3-9-8** GCarter(13) (hld up: hdwy 6f out: led wl over 1f out: rdn out)	—	**1**	8/1	78	38
4235[7]	**Alpine Panther (IRE) (57)** (MrsMReveley) **4-9-10** ACulhane(6) (lw: trckd ldrs: hrd rdn & ev ch over 1f out: one pce)	1¼	**2**	9/1	69	39
3970[4]	**Rufalda (IRE) (65)** (LMCumani) **3-9-8** DHolland(7) (lw: hld up in rr: hdwy over 2f out: styd on wl fnl f)	nk	**3**	9/2[2]	76	36
3826[9]	**Alzotic (IRE) (35)** (JNorton) **4-8-2** NKennedy(14) (bit bkwd: hld up: hdwy over 4f out: led over 2f out: sn rdn & hdd: one pce)	4	**4**	40/1	42	12
4170[3]	**Mechilie (42)** (JWPayne) **3-7-13** AMackay(11) (hld up & bhd: hdwy & hrd drvn 3f out: styd on)	nk	**5**	3/1[1]	48	8
4161[8]	**Karisma (IRE) (44)** (DenysSmith) **4-8-6**(5) CLowther(9) (s.s: hdwy 5f out: rdn 2f out: one pce)	nk	**6**	11/2[3]	50	20
4161[9]	**Beach Buoy (IRE) (54)** (CaptJWilson) **3-8-11** JFEgan(12) (b.off hind: chsd ldrs: rdn over 2f out: sn btn)	2½	**7**	7/1	57	17
4053[5]	**Whitley Grange Boy (52)** (JLEyre) **4-9-5** RLappin(3) (a.p: led over 3f out tl over 2f out: wknd appr fnl f)	s.h	**8**	16/1	55	25
4302[9]	**Pointe Fine (FR) (61)** (JWHills) **3-9-1**(3) MHenry(10) (hdwy 6f out: rdn & edgd lft over 2f out: sn wknd)	1¼	**9**	10/1	63	23
4046[14]	**Indiana Princess (51)** (MrsMReveley) **4-8-11**(7) RWinston(1) (led tl rn wd & hdd after 2f: wknd 3f out: t.o)	13	**10**	20/1	38	8
4222[13]	**Bronhallow (30)** (MrsBarbaraWaring) **4-7-11** DeclanO'Shea(8) (chsd ldrs over 10f: sn wknd: t.o)	1¾	**11**	25/1	15	—
4104[11]	**Chimborazo (50)** (BJMcMath) **6-9-0**(3) PMcCabe(15) (a bhd: t.o)	hd	**12**	25/1	35	5
5[5]	**What Jim Wants (IRE) (37)** (JJO'Neill) **4-8-4** GHind(4) (bkwd: led after 2f to 9f out: wknd ent st: t.o)	nk	**13**	20/1	21	—
	Most Wanted (IRE) (36) (WMcKeown) **4-8-3** JLowe(5) (swtg: bkwd: led 9f out tl over 3f out: sn wknd: t.o)	8	**14**	40/1	11	—
				(SP 129.2%)	**14 Rn**	

3m 8.25 (10.05) CSF £70.01 CT £342.00 TOTE £10.50: £2.90 £3.30 £2.20 (£39.50) Trio £24.00 OWNER Mr K. Abdulla (PULBOROUGH) BRED Juddmonte Farms

WEIGHT FOR AGE 3yo-10lb

4045 Devilish Charm (USA) came into his own over this extended trip and, now that he has found his true mark, there should be more success to follow. (8/1)

4235 Alpine Panther (IRE) showed he is not short of stamina with a very gutsy battling performance, and he should have little trouble in finding a staying event. (9/1: 6/1-10/1)

3970 Rufalda (IRE) had a lot of running to do inside the last half-mile but she put her head down and battled on gamely and, in finishing best of all, gave notice that this could be her trip. (9/2)

Alzotic (IRE) could, at long last, be coming to himself if this much improved effort is anything to go by, for he only dropped away inside the last two hundred yards. (40/1)

4170 Mechilie stayed on under strong driving in the closing stages but she had been hard at work for quite some time and the progress was slow. (3/1: 2/1-7/2)

1039 Karisma (IRE) stays extremely well but he gave away significant ground with a slow start, so this performance could be better than it seems at first glance. (11/2: op 10/1)

T/Plpt: £368.10 (71.95 Tckts). T/Qdpt: £79.00 (12.06 Tckts) IM

4420-ASCOT (R-H) (Good to firm)
Sunday September 28th

WEATHER: fine WIND: almost nil

4439 SUNDAY CONDITIONS STKS (2-Y.O) (Class B)

2-00 (2-00) **7f** £12,022.00 (£4,498.00: £2,199.00: £945.00: £422.50: £213.50) Stalls: Low GOING minus 0.19 sec per fur (GF)

Form	Horse	Dist	Pos	SP	RR	SF
4061*	**Mudeer** (SbinSuroor) **2-9-0** LDettori(7) (lw: hld up: led 2f out: edgd lft over 1f out: pushed out)	—	**1**	8/13[1]	98	67
	Pegnitz (USA) (CEBrittain) **2-8-11** MRoberts(6) (leggy: scope: lw: s.s: stdy hdwy over 2f out: ev ch over 1f out: unable qckn ins fnl f: bttr for r)	2	**2**	12/1[3]	90+	59
4111*	**Casino King (IRE)** (PWChapple-Hyam) **2-9-0** JReid(1) (lw: w ldr: led 4f out tl 2f out: one pce)	3½	**3**	5/1[2]	85	54
	Ghali (USA) (JLDunlop) **2-8-11** TQuinn(2) (w'like: scope: lw: shkn up & hdwy over 1f out: sn wknd)	2½	**4**	20/1	77	46
3978*	**Absolutly Sparklin** (LMCumani) **2-9-0** KDarley(3) (lw: hld up: rdn over 3f out: wknd over 2f out)	3½	**5**	5/1[2]	72	41
3789[3]	**Sherganzar** (MSalaman) **2-8-11** MJKinane(4) (led 3f: ev ch over 2f out: wknd over 1f out)	3½	**6**	20/1	61	30
	Mizog (JELong) **2-8-6** TGMcLaughlin(5) (leggy: scope: s.s: hld up: rdn over 2f out: sn wknd)	17	**7**	100/1	17	—
				(SP 113.4%)	**7 Rn**	

1m 28.56 (1.36) CSF £8.40 TOTE £1.60: £1.30 £3.30 (£7.50) OWNER Godolphin (NEWMARKET) BRED Meon Valley Stud

4061* Mudeer certainly took the eye in the paddock and put up a useful display. Sent on a quarter of a mile from home, he drifted over to the rails and flashed his tail when hit, but nevertheless, needed only to be nudged along in the final furlong to put the runner-up in his place. A very laid-back individual at home, there is plenty of stamina on his dam's side and he really needs a mile. (8/13: op evens)

Pegnitz (USA), a tall, attractive colt with plenty of scope, has reportedly been working well at home and made a very pleasing debut. Cruising into the action over a quarter of a mile from home, he looked a serious threat to the winner below the distance but his rider was not hard on him and the combination failed to quicken inside the final furlong. Sure to have learnt a lot from this, he should not be difficult to win with. (12/1)

4111* Casino King (IRE) looked well in the paddock but was just beginning to go in his coat. Leading half a mile from home, he was collared two furlongs out and could then only struggle on at one pace. (5/1: 7/2-11/2)

Ghali (USA), an attractive, deep-girthed individual, was given no easy introduction and an effort on the outside of the field below the distance proved to be short-lived. (20/1)

3978* Absolutly Sparklin was never happy on this fast surface and had been hung out to dry over two furlongs from home. His win at York came in the mud and some rain is definitely needed. (5/1: op 3/1)

3789 Sherganzar, led round by two handlers in the paddock, had far more on his plate here but still had every chance approaching the final quarter-mile, before tiring below the distance. (20/1)

4440 GTECH ROYAL LODGE STKS (Gp 2) (2-Y.O C & G) (Class A)

2-35 (2-36) **1m (round)** £74,028.00 (£27,914.90: £13,582.45: £6,104.65) Stalls: High GOING minus 0.19 sec per fur (GF)

Form	Horse	Dist	Pos	SP	RR	SF
4096*	**Teapot Row (IRE)** (JARToller) **2-8-11** SSanders(4) (hld up: hrd rdn & led 1f out: edgd lft: drvn out)	—	**1**	9/1	107	71
4132[2]	**Prolix** (BWHills) **2-8-11** MHills(3) (dwlt: hdwy & n.m.r over 1f out: r.o)	¾	**2**	11/1	106	70
4132*	**City Honours (USA)** (PWChapple-Hyam) **2-8-11** JReid(1) (lw: rdn over 2f out: hdwy fnl f: r.o)	hd	**3**	7/1	105	69

3912*	**Kilimanjaro** (MRStoute) **2-8-11** MJKinane(2) (rdn & lost pl over 5f out: rallied 1f out: r.o)	nk	**4**	9/4[1]	105+	69
4140[2]	**Almutawakel** (SbinSuroor) **2-8-11** LDettori(8) (lw: a.p: rdn over 2f out: unable qckn ins fnl f)	hd	**5**	8/1	105	69
2556*	**Craigsteel** (HRACecil) **2-8-11** KFallon(6) (chsd ldr: led over 1f out: sn hdd: one pce ins fnl f)	nk	**6**	6/1[3]	104	68
3895[4]	**Sharp Play** (MJohnston) **2-8-11** DHolland(5) (a.p: rdn over 2f out: one pce)	1¼	**7**	25/1	101	65
4255a[2]	**Muhtathir (100)** (JHMGosden) **2-8-11** RHills(7) (lw: led over 6f)	4	**8**	3/1[2]	93	57
				(SP 115.8%)		**8 Rn**

1m 41.74 (0.94) CSF £92.78 TOTE £10.60: £1.70 £2.10 £1.90 (£39.50) OWNER Duke of Devonshire (WHITSBURY) BRED Cambremont Ltd Partnership

IN-FOCUS: **With a blanket covering the first six, a big question-mark must loom over the validity of this form.**

4096* Teapot Row (IRE) lacked the substance of many of his rivals in the paddock but put up a gutsy display. Travelling well early in the straight, he was under pressure to lead a furlong out but, despite drifting left, held on in a very tight finish. (9/1)

4132 Prolix, a short-head behind City Honours last time out, was put to sleep at the back of the field. Picking up ground below the distance, he ran on but, for the third consecutive time, had to settle for second best. He has been running really well and richly deserves to get his head in front. (11/1)

4132* City Honours (USA), pushed along early in the straight, only really found his stride in the final furlong and ran on in very pleasing style. Connections are excited about his prospects over a mile and a half next year and believe he has a terrific chance in the Derby. Chapple-Hyam believes he is the best he has had since Dr Devious. (7/1)

3912* Kilimanjaro was in his element in the mud at Sandown last time out where his stamina came into play, but this ground proved too quick for him over this trip and he had soon lost his pitch. He did run on in the final furlong but found the line always beating him. Staying will be his game next year. (9/4: 7/4-11/4)

4140 Almutawakel was happier with the return to a fast surface and was a leading player throughout, only being tapped for toe inside the final furlong. This was a sound performance. (8/1)

2556* Craigsteel, who has had some trouble with sandcracks in his heels since his last run twelve weeks ago, looked dull in his coat for this return. Nevertheless, he got to the front below the distance but, soon headed, then failed to quicken. A lazy worker at home, connections think he prefers soft ground. (6/1)

4255a Muhtathir looked in tremendous shape in the paddock but took a very keen hold in front. Collared below the distance, he tamely folded up. This was a very disappointing performance and he is certainly a lot better than this. Some cut in the ground would be helpful. (3/1)

4441 MAIL ON SUNDAY MILE FINAL H'CAP (3-Y.O+) (Class B)

3-10 (3-12) **1m (straight)** £29,570.00 (£8,960.00: £4,380.00: £2,090.00) Stalls: Low GOING minus 0.19 sec per fur (GF)

				SP	RR	SF
4147[12]	**Gulf Shaadi (74)** (EJAlston) **5-8-6** SSanders(10) (hdwy 2f out: rdn to ld over 1f out: r.o wl)	—	**1**	20/1	87	69
3615[4]	**Consort (82)** (MrsAJPerrett) **4-9-0** MJKinane(11) (lw: hdwy over 3f out: rdn over 2f out: unable qckn)	3	**2**	8/1[2]	89	71
4297[2]	**Sweet Wilhelmina (72)** (LordHuntingdon) **4-8-4** MRoberts(3) (rdn over 2f out: hdwy over 1f out: r.o wl ins fnl f)	hd	**3**	6/1[1]	79	61
4297[7]	**Therhea (IRE) (81)** (BRMillman) **4-8-10**(3) AWhelan(9) (lw: rdn over 2f out: hdwy over 1f out: r.o one pce)	1	**4**	16/1	86	68
4147[25]	**Antarctic Storm (69)** (RAFahey) **4-7-8**(7)ow3 RWinston(14) (led over 6f)	nk	**5**	25/1	73	52
3764[7]	**Brilliant Red (89)** (PRHedger) **4-9-7** KDarley(6) (a.p: rdn over 2f out: one pce)	hd	**6**	25/1	93	75
4297[5]	**Broughtons Turmoil (71)** (BRMillman) **8-8-3** MFenton(12) (s.s & swtchd lft s: nt clr run over 2f out: hdwy on ins over 1f out: r.o)	nk	**7**	12/1	74	56
4297[16]	**Mo-Addab (IRE) (67)** (ACStewart) **7-7-10**(3) PFessey(4) (swtg: nt clr run over 2f out: hdwy over 1f out: r.o)	3	**8**	11/1	64	46
4147[16]	**For Your Eyes Only (79)** (TDEasterby) **3-8-7** LDettori(2) (rdn over 2f out: hdwy fnl f: nvr nrr)	1	**9**	9/1[3]	74	52
4297[20]	**Present Situation (66)** (LordHuntingdon) **6-7-7**(5) AimeeCook(8) (rdn & hdwy over 2f out: eased whn btn ins fnl f)	nk	**10**	20/1	61	43
4283[4]	**Rebel County (IRE) (72)** (ABailey) **4-8-1v**(3) RFfrench(17) (lw: hdwy over 2f out: wknd over 1f out)	¾	**11**	12/1	65	47
4147[19]	**Cashmere Lady (75)** (JLEyre) **5-8-7** RLappin(23) (prom over 6f)	½	**12**	16/1	67	49
4151[6]	**Fahs (USA) (76)** (RAkehurst) **5-8-8** DHolland(22) (lw: prom over 5f)	3	**13**	16/1	62	44
4283[12]	**Pride of Pendle (74)** (MartynWane) **8-8-6** MartinDwyer(18) (hdwy over 2f out: wknd over 1f out)	1¼	**14**	20/1	58	40
4262a[3]	**Comanche Companion (65)** (TJNaughton) **7-7-11** JLowe(15) (lw: prom over 4f)	hd	**15**	25/1	49	31
4153*	**Law Commission (96)** (DRCElsworth) **7-10-0** TQuinn(13) (mid div over 6f)	1	**16**	16/1	78	60
4175[7]	**Zugudi (76)** (KMahdi) **3-7-13b**(5)ow2 CLowther(7) (lw: prom over 5f)	s.h	**17**	20/1	58	34
2835[18]	**Press On Nicky (64)** (WRMuir) **4-7-5**(5) IonaWands(19) (swtg: s.s: bhd fnl 2f)	nk	**18**	66/1	45	27
3476[12]	**Anonym (IRE) (65)** (JLEyre) **5-7-11b**ow1 TWilliams(20) (a bhd)	1½	**19**	40/1	43	24
4219[13]	**Dances With Hooves (64)** (DJSffrenchDavis) **5-7-10** NCarlisle(5) (a bhd)	s.h	**20**	100/1	42	24
3435[2]	**Speculator (IRE) (86)** (WJHaggas) **3-9-0b**[1] MHills(16) (lw: prom over 5f)	1	**21**	8/1[2]	62	40
4225[11]	**Blue Flyer (IRE) (67)** (RIngram) **4-7-13b** AMackay(1) (a bhd)	6	**22**	33/1	31	13
				(SP 132.2%)		**22 Rn**

1m 40.59 (0.59) CSF £146.37 CT £1,029.83 TOTE £43.10: £8.20 £2.10 £1.70 £5.80 (£186.90) Trio £315.60 OWNER The Bibby Halliday Partnership (PRESTON) BRED Sheikh Mohammed bin Rashid al Maktoum

LONG HANDICAP Dances With Hooves 7-0 Press On Nicky 7-8 Anonym (IRE) 7-8

WEIGHT FOR AGE 3yo-4lb

3901 Gulf Shaadi gained by far and away his biggest success to date and, rousted along to lead below the distance, soon shot clear for a decisive victory. He may well take his chance in the Cambridgeshire next Saturday. (20/1)

3615 Consort appreciated the return to a mile and a drop of 3lb in the handicap. Taking closer order soon after halfway, he was bustled along in the final quarter-mile but, although winning the battle for second prize, had no hope with the winner. (8/1)

4297 Sweet Wilhelmina at last found her stride below the distance and, running on really strongly inside the final furlong, only just failed to take second prize. (6/1)

4297 Therhea (IRE) is at his best on a soft surface but he still gave a good account of himself on this much faster ground, staying on in the last furlong and a half. (16/1)

3921* Antarctic Storm took the field along but, collared over a furlong out, had little more in reserve. (25/1)

3391 Brilliant Red, never far away, could only go up and down in the same place in the final quarter-mile. Both his wins have come on fast ground. (25/1)

4442 FILLIES' MILE STKS (Gp 1) (2-Y.O F) (Class A)

3-50 (3-50) **1m (round)** £92,950.00 (£34,860.00: £16,805.00: £7,385.00) Stalls: High GOING minus 0.19 sec per fur (GF)

				SP	RR	SF
4119[3]	**Glorosia (FR)** (LMCumani) **2-8-10** LDettori(4) (stdy hdwy to ld 2f out: rdn over 1f out: r.o wl)	—	**1**	10/1	100	64
4066*	**Jibe (USA)** (HRACecil) **2-8-10** KFallon(7) (hld up: rdn & n.m.r over 2f out: chsd wnr fnl f: r.o wl)	¾	**2**	2/1[1]	99	63

4107* **Exclusive** (MRStoute) **2-8-10** MJKinane(6) (b.off hind: lw: dwlt: swtchd lft over 2f out: hdwy 2f out: chsd wnr over 1f out tl 1f out: unable qckn) 2 **3** 5/1 3 95 59
3723 8 **Expect To Shine (90)** (BWHills) **2-8-10** MHills(1) (s.s: hdwy over 1f out: wknd ins fnl f)....5 **4** 16/1 85 49
4119* **Midnight Line (USA) (100)** (HRACecil) **2-8-10** WRyan(8) (lw: hld up: nt clr run over 2f out: hmpd over 1f out: nt rcvr)....2½ **5** 11/4 2 80+ 44
4273 2 **Hollow Haze (USA)** (PWChapple-Hyam) **2-8-10** JReid(2) (hld up: ev ch whn hung rt 2f out: wknd over 1f out)7 **6** 10/1 66 30
3740 2 **Alignment (IRE)** (MRStoute) **2-8-10** TQuinn(5) (plld hrd: led 6f: wkng whn n.m.r on ins over 1f out)....9 **7** 10/1 48 12
4267 12 **Filey Brigg (100)** (WTKemp) **2-8-10** KDarley(3) (w ldr tl wknd & hmpd over 2f out)....1¾ **8** 66/1 44 8
(SP 111.3%) **8 Rn**

1m 42.31 (1.51) CSF £26.22 TOTE £11.00: £2.30 £1.40 £1.70 (£16.20) OWNER Mr Robert Smith (NEWMARKET) BRED Alec Head

4119 Glorosia (FR), all the better for her recent run, picked up ground to lead a quarter of a mile out. Getting first run on Jibe, she kept on well and was not going to be caught. Her trainer believes she should develop into an Oaks filly. (10/1)
4066* Jibe (USA), well regarded at home, did not have the best of runs early in the straight and, when she did get into full flight, the winner had got first run and was not for catching in time. She looks an exciting prospect for next year. (2/1)
4107* Exclusive was stepping up markedly in class but ran a fine race and showed in second place briefly below the distance, before tapped for toe. (5/1)
3114* Expect To Shine found this longer trip against her for, after cruising early in the straight and picking up ground nicely below the distance, she was then left for dead in the final furlong. A drop in distance is needed. (16/1)
4119* Midnight Line (USA), a real stayer in the making, had a diabolical run in the straight and could never recover. This run should be categorically ignored. (11/4)
4273 Hollow Haze (USA) gave her jockey real steering problems in the straight, causing problems to some of her rivals, and had been hung out to dry below the distance. (10/1)

4443 TOTE SUNDAY SPECIAL H'CAP (3-Y.O+) (Class B)

4-25 (4-25) **1m 4f** £47,551.25 (£14,285.00: £6,892.50: £3,196.25) Stalls: High GOING minus 0.19 sec per fur (GF) SP RR SF

4256a 6 **Ridaiyma (IRE) (92)** (LMCumani) **3-8-4** KDarley(12) (lw: 4th whn squeezed out & lost pl 3f out: rallied over 1f out: r.o wl ins fnl f: fin 2nd, ¾l, awrdd r)....— **1** 9/2 1 103 64
3902 4 **Taufan's Melody (104)** (LadyHerries) **6-9-10** JReid(9) (a.p: led over 2f out: hrd rdn 1f out: r.o wl: fin 1st: disq: plcd 2nd)....¾ **2** 20/1 116 85
3989* **Arctic Owl (92)** (JRFanshawe) **3-8-4** 4x NDay(3) (rdn over 2f out: hdwy over 1f out: str run fnl f: fin wl)....½ **3** 10/1 102 63
3705 14 **Better Offer (IRE) (95)** (MrsAJPerrett) **5-9-1** MJKinane(5) (lw: rdn over 2f out: hdwy over 1f out: r.o)....1¼ **4** 7/1 2 104 73
3705 19 **Willie Conquer (94)** (RAkehurst) **5-9-0** TQuinn(11) (mid div whn hmpd 3f out: rallied over 1f out: r.o)....¾ **5** 14/1 102 71
4151 5 **Song of Freedom (89)** (JHMGosden) **3-8-1** TWilliams(6) (lw: hdwy & swtchd rt over 2f out: ev ch over 1f out: wknd ins fnl f)....2 **6** 8/1 3 94 55
2572* **Taunt (91)** (DMorley) **3-8-3** DHolland(14) (rdn over 2f out: hdwy over 1f out: one pce)....¾ **7** 8/1 3 95 56
3599* **Rokeby Bowl (94)** (IABalding) **5-9-0** LDettori(2) (lw: hdwy over 2f out: wknd fnl f)....¾ **8** 7/1 2 97 66
4136 2 **Elbaaha (84)** (MAJarvis) **3-7-7**(3) PFessey(13) (prom over 9f)....8 **9** 8/1 3 76 37
3989 2 **Honourable (90)** (JWWatts) **3-7-13**(3) RFfrench(8) (led over 7f: wknd over 2f out)....2½ **10** 7/1 2 79 40
4136 6 **Remaadi Sun (83)** (MDIUsher) **5-8-3** RStreet(7) (sme hdwy on ins 2f out: n.m.r & wknd wl over 1f out)....nk **11** 25/1 72 41
4279 7 **Al's Alibi (76)** (WRMuir) **4-7-10** MartinDwyer(4) (swtg: bhd fnl 3f)....1¾ **12** 33/1 62 31
4101 8 **Tykeyvor (IRE) (92)** (LadyHerries) **7-8-12v** FLynch(10) (a.p: led over 4f out tl over 2f out: sn wknd)....nk **13** 14/1 78 47
Arctic Thunder (USA) (92) (BPalling) **6-8-12** SSanders(1) (bit bkwd: bhd fnl 3f)....30 **14** 66/1 38 7
(SP 124.5%) **14 Rn**

2m 31.19 (1.19) CSF £94.74 CT £802.03 TOTE £5.20: £2.40 £5.00 £3.00 (£76.30) Trio £431.50 OWNER H H Aga Khan (NEWMARKET) BRED His Highness the Aga Khan's Studs S.C.
WEIGHT FOR AGE 3yo-8lb
STEWARDS' ENQUIRY Obj. to Taufan's Melody by Darley sustained.

4256a Ridaiyma (IRE), who acted as pacemaker in the Prix Vermeille last time out, was only about half a length down on the winner when squeezed out by that rival on the home turn. It cost her several lengths and she looked in serious trouble early in the straight but she dug deep into her reserves and, running on really strongly, was cutting back the leeway all the way to the line. The incident certainly cost her the race and she was later awarded the contest in the Stewards' room. (9/2)
3902 Taufan's Melody, winner of this race in 1995, was happier with the return to a mile and a half. Striking the front over a quarter of a mile from home, he responded to pressure and held on well. Unfortunately, he had caused some interference to Ridaiyma on the home turn and was demoted to second place. (20/1)
3989* Arctic Owl, still at the back of the field entering the straight, found his stride in no uncertain terms from below the distance and was absolutely flying in the final furlong. He is worth a try at further. (10/1)
3191 Better Offer (IRE), winner of this race last year, ran his best race so far this season, running on nicely in the last furlong and a half. (7/1)
2709 Willie Conquer had no luck in running and was hampered by Ridaiyma, who in turn had been squeezed out by Taufan's Melody. He did run on from below the distance but the damage had already been done. All three of his wins to date have come over this trip. (14/1)
4151 Song of Freedom, taking a step up in distance, had every chance below the distance before tiring in the closing stages. (8/1: 6/1-9/1)

4444 CLIVEDEN RUINART CHAMPAGNE RATED STKS H'CAP (0-105) (3-Y.O+) (Class B)

5-00 (5-02) **5f** £15,680.00 (£5,870.00: £2,872.50: £1,237.50: £556.25: £283.75) Stalls: Low GOING minus 0.19 sec per fur (GF) SP RR SF

4282 13 **Tedburrow (105)** (EJAlston) **5-9-7** KFallon(8) (lw: a.p: led 1f out: rdn out)....— **1** 7/1 118 87
3410 12 **Crowded Avenue (95)** (PJMakin) **5-8-11** SSanders(1) (hdwy & nt clr run over 1f out: r.o ins fnl f)....2 **2** 8/1 102 71
4282 8 **Blessingindisguise (96)** (MWEasterby) **4-8-12b** MJKinane(5) (led over 2f: ev ch 1f out: unable qckn)....¾ **3** 4/1 1 100 69
4100 16 **Bowden Rose (91)** (MBlanshard) **5-8-4b**(3) DSweeney(4) (lw: bmpd s: w ldr: led over 2f out to 1f out: one pce)....nk **4** 20/1 94 63
4153 9 **Hello Mister (94)** (TEPowell) **6-8-7**(3) PMcCabe(7) (s.s: rdn over 1f out: hdwy 1f out: nvr nrr)....1 **5** 14/1 94 63
4282 3 **Superior Premium (103)** (RAFahey) **3-9-4** JCarroll(9) (lw: a.p: ev ch over 1f out: one pce)....s.h **6** 6/1 3 103 71
4282 12 **Sharp Hat (93)** (RHannon) **3-8-5**(3) RFfrench(12) (swtg: hdwy 2f out: rdn over 1f out: wknd ins fnl f)....nk **7** 10/1 92 60
4100 12 **Twice as Sharp (91)** (PWHarris) **5-8-2**(5) CLowther(3) (bmpd s: no hdwy fnl 2f)....¾ **8** 10/1 88 57
4239 10 **Sylva Paradise (IRE) (95)** (CEBrittain) **4-8-11** MRoberts(10) (hld up: rdn 2f out: wknd over 1f out)....2 **9** 16/1 85 54
4239 8 **Moon Strike (FR) (98)** (PHowling) **7-9-0** LDettori(6) (b: hld up: rdn over 2f out: wknd over 1f out: lame)....1¼ **10** 9/2 2 84 53

3975[14] **Jayannpee (97)** (IABalding) **6-8-13** MartinDwyer(11) (stdy hdwy over 2f out: wknd over 1f out) 1 **11** 14/1 80 49
(SP 118.2%) **11 Rn**

60.34 secs (0.14) CSF £56.76 CT £238.54 TOTE £10.60: £3.40 £2.30 £1.70 (£47.50) Trio £92.60 OWNER Mr Philip Davies (PRESTON) BRED Lady Matthews
LONG HANDICAP Bowden Rose 8-5
WEIGHT FOR AGE 3yo-1lb
OFFICIAL EXPLANATION Moon Strike (FR): returned lame.
IN-FOCUS: Eric Alston enjoyed the biggest pay-day of his training career as he completed a 167/1 double.
4011 Tedburrow has been in good heart this year. Striking the front a furlong from home, he was rousted along to assert his authority. (7/1)
2675 Crowded Avenue, stuck in behind a wall of horses a quarter of a mile out, came through to take second place inside the final furlong but was unable to peg back the winner. He has done all his winning over five furlongs on fast ground. (8/1)
4282 Blessingindisguise ran another sound race. In front to halfway, he still had every chance entering the final furlong, before tapped for toe. (4/1)
3604 Bowden Rose disputed the lead until showing marginally in front at halfway. Collared a furlong out, she could then only struggle on at one pace. (20/1)
4100 Hello Mister, racing at the back of the field, stayed on in the final furlong but it was all too late. He has not won for two years and needs further than this five furlongs. (14/1)
4282 Superior Premium, never far away, had every chance below the distance before tapped for toe. He has done all his winning on a soft surface. (6/1)
4100 Sharp Hat (10/1: 7/1-11/1)

4445 HARVEST STKS (Listed) (3-Y.O+ F & M) (Class A)
5-35 (5-35) **1m 4f** £24,167.50 (£7,315.00: £3,570.00: £1,697.50) Stalls: High GOING minus 0.19 sec per fur (GF)

				SP	RR	SF
4099[3]	**Puce (103)** (LMCumani) **4-9-0** LDettori(1) (rdn 3f out: hdwy over 1f out: led ins fnl f: r.o wl)	—	1	11/8[1]	103	56
3727[6]	**Graceful Lass (92)** (DRLoder) **3-8-6** TQuinn(3) (hdwy over 2f out: squeezed thro to ld over 1f out: hdd ins fnl f: r.o)	nk	2	10/1	103	48
3803[3]	**Coretta (IRE) (85)** (LMCumani) **3-8-6** MHills(2) (a.p: rdn over 2f out: r.o)	hd	3	10/1	103	48
3977*	**Delilah (IRE) (92)** (MRStoute) **3-8-6v** JReid(5) (swtg: hld up: rdn over 2f out: bmpd over 1f out: unable qckn ins fnl f)	½	4	7/2[2]	102	47
2053[6]	**Tempting Prospect (100)** (LordHuntingdon) **3-8-6** KDarley(6) (lw: a.p: led over 2f out tl over 1f out: one pce ins fnl f)	hd	5	6/1	102	47
3704[8]	**Attitre (FR) (103)** (CEBrittain) **3-8-6v[1]** MRoberts(4) (swtg: led over 9f)	14	6	11/2[3]	83	28

(SP 112.2%) **6 Rn**

2m 33.93 (3.93) CSF £14.65 TOTE £2.30: £1.40 £2.60 (£13.00) OWNER Fittocks Stud (NEWMARKET) BRED Fittocks Stud
WEIGHT FOR AGE 3yo-8lb
4099 Puce just coped with the drop in distance. The first off the bridle turning for home, she found her feet from below the distance and came through to lead in a tight finish inside the final furlong to complete a hat-trick for both Cumani and Dettori. (11/8)
3727 Graceful Lass ran much better here and squeezed through to lead below the distance. Collared by the winner inside the final furlong, she nevertheless kept on well to the line. (10/1)
3803 Coretta (IRE) appreciated this step up in distance and, never far away, ran on nicely inside the final furlong. (10/1)
3977* Delilah (IRE), given a bump by Graceful Lass over a furlong out, was close enough if good enough inside the final furlong, but she did not look to be thoroughly enjoying herself and failed to quicken. (7/2)
2053 Tempting Prospect, without a run in three months, went on early in the straight. Collared below the distance, she was tapped for toe inside the final furlong. (6/1)
2513 Attitre (FR) took the field along but, collared over two furlongs from home, was soon in trouble. (11/2: 3/1-6/1)

T/Jkpt: Not won; £31,331.48 to Hamilton 29/9/97. T/Plpt: £464.60 (120.38 Tckts). T/Qdpt: £21.10 (159.58 Tckts) AK

3965-BRIGHTON (L-H) (Firm)
Sunday September 28th
WEATHER: fine WIND: almost nil

4446 REID MINTY MAIDEN STKS (2-Y.O) (Class D)
2-30 (2-31) **5f 213y** £4,970.00 (£1,505.00: £735.00: £350.00) Stalls: Low GOING minus 0.45 sec per fur (F)

				SP	RR	SF
4068[4]	**Cosmic Countess (IRE) (74)** (MAJarvis) **2-8-9** TSprake(4) (lw: mde all: rdn over 1f out: r.o)	—	1	11/4[2]	72	30
4296[7]	**The Boy John (USA) (80)** (RHannon) **2-9-0** DaneO'Neill(7) (hld up: hdwy 4f out: chsd wnr ins fnl f: unable qckn)	1¼	2	5/2[1]	74	32
	Territory (IRE) (GLewis) **2-9-0** AClark(8) (w'like: lw: a.p: ev ch over 1f out: sn rdn: one pce)	nk	3	6/1	73	31
	Mansa Musa (IRE) (MRChannon) **2-9-0** RPerham(2) (unf: bit bkwd: mid div: rdn over 2f out: kpt on one pce ins fnl f)	1¼	4	12/1	70	28
3978[4]	**Jayir (IRE)** (ACStewart) **2-9-0** SWhitworth(6) (lw: towards rr: sme hdwy over 2f out: sn rdn: one pce)	1	5	4/1[3]	67	25
	Hopeful Star (IRE) (MissGayKelleway) **2-9-0** JQuinn(5) (w'like: bit bkwd: dwlt: effrt over 2f out: sn btn)	4	6	15/2	56	14
4105[11]	**Fiercely Ginger** (EAWheeler) **2-8-11(3)** ADaly(3) (a bhd)	16	7	10/1	13	—
3985[15]	**Miss Chief Maker (40)** (WRMuir) **2-8-9** JFEgan(1) (sn rdn along: bhd fr ½-wy)	6	8	50/1	—	—

(SP 120.0%) **8 Rn**

1m 8.8 (1.60) CSF £9.75 TOTE £4.10: £1.10 £1.50 £1.70 (£5.60) OWNER Cosmic Greyhound Racing Partnership II (NEWMARKET) BRED R. V. Young
4068 Cosmic Countess (IRE) put her previous racecourse experience to good use here. Breaking smartly, she made all the running and saw it out well. (11/4)
3799 The Boy John (USA) moved up threateningly entering the final furlong and appeared to run his race, but never really looked like reeling in the winner. (5/2)
Territory (IRE) is quite an attractive colt and ran a sound race here. He looked very dangerous below the distance but just could not quicken up. A similar race should be found. (6/1: 3/1-13/2)
Mansa Musa (IRE) looked just in need of the race beforehand but ran well enough on his debut, just plugging on at the one speed in the final furlong. (12/1)
3978 Jayir (IRE) was all at sea coming round the bend and might be suited by a more straightforward track. (4/1: 5/2-9/2)

Hopeful Star (IRE) (15/2: 8/1-12/1)

4447 KVAENER NURSERY H'CAP (0-85) (2-Y.O) (Class C)

3-05 (3-05) **6f 209y** £5,628.00 (£1,704.00: £832.00: £396.00) Stalls: Low GOING minus 0.45 sec per fur (F)

				SP	RR	SF
4157[4]	**Marran (IRE) (79)** (JLDunlop) **2-9-7** JQuinn(5) (a.p: chsd ldr 4f out: led over 2f out: hrd rdn ins fnl f: all out)	—	**1**	5/2[1]	79	47
4116[7]	**Night Flyer (78)** (JWHills) **2-9-3**(3) MHenry(6) (lw: hld up: hdwy 3f out: rdn & edgd lft 1f out: str run fnl f: r.o wl)	nk	**2**	3/1[2]	77	45
4381[3]	**Leofric (67)** (MJPolglase) **2-8-9** DaneO'Neill(4) (hld up: hdwy over 2f out: sn rdn: one pce)	3	**3**	4/1[3]	59	27
4044[15]	**Riley (75)** (RCharlton) **2-9-3b[1]** TSprake(1) (led: hdd over 2f out: wknd 1f out)	1¾	**4**	6/1	63	31
2578[8]	**Lisa's Pride (IRE) (70)** (MissGayKelleway) **2-8-12** JFEgan(3) (bhd fnl 3f)	1¾	**5**	13/2	54	22
4068[6]	**Lobuche (IRE) (60)** (RHannon) **2-7-13**(3) ADaly(2) (swtg: chsd ldr 3f: sn wknd)	2½	**6**	7/1	39	7

(SP 113.7%) **6 Rn**

1m 21.5 (1.50) CSF £9.54 TOTE £2.40: £2.00 £2.00 (£4.30) OWNER Prince A A Faisal (ARUNDEL) BRED Nawara Stud Co Ltd

4157 Marran (IRE) put up a fair performance here under top weight. He was always going well and took it up over two furlongs out but, in the end, was all out to hold on. (5/2: 3/1-2/1)

3794* Night Flyer was a slightly unlucky loser. Like many horses, he hung under pressure down the camber around the one pole. His rider soon straightened him out and he finished well, but the damage had been done. (3/1)

4381 Leofric is in reasonable form at the moment and appeared to run up to his mark here. (4/1: 3/1-9/2)

3479 Riley cut out much of the running but was put in his place in the final two furlongs. (6/1)

4068 Lobuche (IRE) (7/1: op 9/2)

4448 SCOTTISH EQUITABLE H'CAP (0-75) (3-Y.O+) (Class D)

3-40 (3-42) **7f 214y** £4,947.25 (£1,498.00: £731.50: £348.25) Stalls: Low GOING minus 0.45 sec per fur (F)

				SP	RR	SF
4225[3]	**Toujours Riviera (74)** (JPearce) **7-10-0** GBardwell(2) (a.p: n.m.r on ins 2f out: swtchd rt over 1f out: str run ins fnl f: led on line)	—	**1**	15/2[3]	87	52
4291[5]	**Tael of Silver (42)** (ABailey) **5-7-10** DWright(8) (a.p: led 2f out: rdn ins fnl f: hdd on line)	nk	**2**	16/1	54	19
3592*	**Homestead (51)** (RHannon) **3-8-1** JQuinn(4) (mid div: rdn over 2f out: kpt on one pce fnl f)	2	**3**	3/1[2]	59	20
4371[7]	**Multi Franchise (44)** (RMFlower) **4-7-7**(5) RMullen(6) (mid div: rdn over 2f out: styd on one pce ins fnl f)	1	**4**	12/1	50	15
3296[5]	**Apollo Red (72)** (GLMoore) **8-9-12** CandyMorris(7) (led: hdd 2f out: wknd ins fnl f)	nk	**5**	12/1	78	43
3930[16]	**Mr Cube (IRE) (54)** (JMBradley) **7-8-1b**(7) RThomas(1) (nvr nrr)	¾	**6**	10/1	58	23
4225[2]	**Ertlon (67)** (CEBrittain) **7-9-7** TSprake(5) (prom: ev ch 2f out: wknd over 1f out)	2½	**7**	5/2[1]	66	31
4112[10]	**Mislemani (IRE) (49)** (AGNewcombe) **7-8-0**(3) PPMurphy(9) (nvr nrr)	¾	**8**	11/1	47	12
4139[15]	**Hawaii Storm (FR) (45)** (DJSffrenchDavis) **9-7-6**(7)ow2 KerryBaker(11) (a bhd)	s.h	**9**	20/1	43	6
4228[5]	**Flying Pennant (IRE) (49)** (JMBradley) **4-7-10b**(7) DarrenWilliams(12) (hld up: effrt on outside over 3f out: wknd 2f out)	1¼	**10**	16/1	44	9
1464[8]	**Pastiche (55)** (TGMills) **3-8-5** JFEgan(10) (in tch tl wknd over 2f out)	6	**11**	33/1	38	—
3138[13]	**Whispered Melody (56)** (RAkehurst) **4-8-10** AClark(3) (a bhd)	10	**12**	15/2[3]	19	—

(SP 129.4%) **12 Rn**

1m 33.1 (1.80) CSF £120.57 CT £417.69 TOTE £9.80: £3.10 £4.10 £2.50 (£58.40) Trio £102.40 OWNER Exdreco (NEWMARKET) BRED J. L. C. Pearce

LONG HANDICAP Tael of Silver 7-9

WEIGHT FOR AGE 3yo-4lb

4225 Toujours Riviera put up a good performance under top weight and would have won more emphatically with a clear run. (15/2)

4291 Tael of Silver made a bold bid for home and bolted for glory two furlongs out but was just grabbed in the shadow of the post. (16/1)

3592* Homestead came under pressure early in the straight and, to his credit, kept on trying, but could never muster the pace to put in a serious challenge. (3/1)

3465 Multi Franchise kept on in the last two furlongs without ever looking likely to pose a serious threat. (12/1)

3296 Apollo Red cut out the pace as normal. (12/1: 8/1-14/1)

4225 Ertlon ran prominently as usual but dropped away tamely from below the distance. He did not look as well as usual in the paddock. (5/2: op 4/1)

4449 MIRROR H'CAP (0-90) (3-Y.O+) (Class C)

4-15 (4-16) **1m 1f 209y** £9,940.00 (£3,010.00: £1,470.00: £700.00) Stalls: High GOING minus 0.45 sec per fur (F)

				SP	RR	SF
4144[6]	**Farmost (80)** (SirMarkPrescott) **4-9-11** CNutter(5) (sn led: clr over 2f out: r.o)	—	**1**	10/1	91	64
4323*	**Tallulah Belle (61)** (NPLittmoden) **4-8-6** 5x JQuinn(3) (hld up in rr: gd hdwy on ins over 2f out: chsd wnr ins fnl f: r.o)	1	**2**	2/1[1]	70	43
4223*	**Supreme Sound (72)** (PWHarris) **3-8-11** GBardwell(1) (a.p: rdn over 3f out: kpt on one pce fnl 2f)	1¼	**3**	9/2[2]	79	46
3971*	**Roman Reel (USA) (54)** (GLMoore) **6-7-10**(3)ow2 MHenry(6) (a.p: rdn 2f out: one pce)	hd	**4**	11/1	61	32
4297[17]	**City Gambler (70)** (GCBravery) **3-8-9** RPerham(10) (chsd ldrs: rdn over 2f out: one pce)	1½	**5**	16/1	75	42
4176[5]	**Kamin (USA) (71)** (RWArmstrong) **3-8-10** FNorton(7) (hld up in rr: pushed along 3f out: hdwy & n.m.r 2f out & over 1f out: swtchd lft: kpt on one pce fnl f)	½	**6**	5/1[3]	75	42
4235[13]	**Righty Ho (70)** (PTWalwyn) **3-8-9v** TSprake(11) (a mid div)	2	**7**	12/1	71	38
4304[5]	**Wentbridge Lad (IRE) (62)** (ABailey) **7-8-7v** DWright(8) (b: b.hind: a bhd)	1¼	**8**	12/1	61	34
4141[4]	**Tribal Peace (IRE) (63)** (BGubby) **5-8-8** AClark(4) (bhd fnl 3f)	2½	**9**	12/1	58	31
4139[18]	**Desert Time (60)** (CAHorgan) **7-8-2**(3) ADaly(2) (a bhd)	1½	**10**	25/1	52	25
3128[6]	**Opalette (72)** (LadyHerries) **4-9-3** JFEgan(9) (chsd ldrs: rdn 3f out: wkng whn n.m.r 2f out)	4	**11**	7/1	58	31

(SP 130.9%) **11 Rn**

1m 59.1 (0.80) CSF £30.78 CT £103.85 TOTE £11.90: £2.30 £1.50 £2.40 (£30.60) Trio £17.40 OWNER Mr W. E. Sturt (NEWMARKET) BRED Hesmonds Stud Ltd

WEIGHT FOR AGE 3yo-6lb

OFFICIAL EXPLANATION **Farmost: regarding the improvement in form compared with his previous run at Goodwood, the trainer's representative stated that the gelding was better suited by the faster ground here.**

4144 Farmost was given a really positive ride here by Nutter, partnering his first winner of the season. Despite coming back to the runner-up in the final furlong, he looked to have this race in safe keeping for most of the straight. (10/1)

4323* Tallulah Belle was held up and given a lot to do but, to be fair, he looked like picking up the winner with a furlong to run but only gradually closed. (2/1)

4223* Supreme Sound could not get to the front as he likes but, nonetheless, ran a thoroughly game race. (9/2)
3971* Roman Reel (USA) was never far away but just found the quickening gear beyond him. (11/1)
3696 City Gambler hunted up the leading pack but, when put under pressure halfway up the straight, just had the one pace to give. (16/1)
4176 Kamin (USA) was the unlucky horse in the race. He was making headway when running out of room a couple of times in the straight and his rider accepted it in the final furlong. He gave the impression he would have been concerned in the battle for third. (5/1)
3128 Opalette (7/1: 8/1-9/2)

4450 POST OFFICE FREEDOM CLAIMING STKS (3-Y.O+) (Class D)

4-50 (4-52) **1m 3f 196y** £4,162.50 (£1,260.00: £615.00: £292.50) Stalls: High GOING minus 0.45 sec per fur (F)

Form	Horse	Dist	Pos	SP	RR	SF
4304⁷	**Father Dan (IRE) (56)** (MissGayKelleway) **8-8-11**(7) JWilkinson(4) (b: b.hind: chsd ldrs: hrd rdn 2f out: styd on strly ins fnl f to ld last stride)	—	1	15/8²	62	43
4180*	**Bewitching Lady (48)** (DWPArbuthnot) **3-8-5** TSprake(7) (lw: led: hrd rdn ins fnl f: hdd last stride)	hd	2	7/4¹	57	30
3966¹⁰	**Kirov Protege (IRE) (25)** (GLMoore) **5-9-0v** JQuinn(3) (chsd ldr: ev ch over 1f out: wknd ins fnl f)	3½	3	25/1	53	34
2218ᵂ	**At Liberty (IRE) (65)** (RHannon) **5-9-12** DaneO'Neill(6) (lw: hld up: hdwy 4f out: rdn 3f out: wknd 2f out)	6	4	2/1³	57	38
3929⁷	**Another Fiddle (IRE) (23)** (JELong) **7-8-3**(7) RBrisland(2) (b: b.hind: hld up: rdn over 3f out: sn btn)	6	5	50/1	33	14
	Most Welcome News (GLMoore) **5-9-0** CandyMorris(5) (chsd ldrs tl wknd 4f out)	19	6	50/1	11	—
4322⁸	**I See You Sydney (AUS)** (MJPolglase) **3-8-13**(5) GMilligan(1) (s.v.s: bhd: brief effrt over 3f out: sn btn)	4	7	40/1	18	—

(SP 114.7%) **7 Rn**

2m 30.9 (3.30) CSF £5.04 TOTE £2.70: £1.80 £2.00 (£3.20) OWNER Miss Gay Kelleway (WHITCOMBE) BRED John Michael
WEIGHT FOR AGE 3yo-8lb
STEWARDS' ENQUIRY Wilkinson susp. 7-8/10/97 (excessive use of whip). Kelleway fined £230 (failure to inform rdr of horse's hyper-sensitive skin).
4069 Father Dan (IRE) did not look like winning when coming under pressure halfway up the straight but, staying on strongly in the final furlong, he got up in the shadow of the post. (15/8)
4180* Bewitching Lady looked to have won this when shaking off Kirov Protege below the distance, but had no answer to the winner's late burst. (7/4)
2195 Kirov Protege (IRE) moved up smoothly at the two-furlong pole to challenge but, once let off the bridle, found very little. (25/1)
1809 At Liberty (IRE) was disappointing, being beaten halfway up the straight. (2/1)

4451 TOTE LADIES IN RED LIMITED STKS (0-70) (3-Y.O+) (Class E)

5-20 (5-21) **6f 209y** £4,299.00 (£1,302.00: £636.00: £303.00) Stalls: Low GOING minus 0.45 sec per fur (F)

Form	Horse	Dist	Pos	SP	RR	SF
3765⁸	**Lord Olivier (IRE) (68)** (WJarvis) **7-9-6** JQuinn(4) (a.p: led 1f out: r.o)	—	1	6/1	77	65
4176⁸	**Bubbly (67)** (JLDunlop) **3-9-3** TSprake(7) (chsd ldr: ev ch 1f out: unable qckn)	1½	2	7/2²	74	59
4404⁴	**Banzhaf (USA) (68)** (GLMoore) **4-9-6** AClark(2) (chsd ldrs: pushed along 4f out: kpt on u.p fnl 2f)	¾	3	4/1³	72	60
4063¹³	**Literary (69)** (JHMGosden) **3-8-11** AGarth(1) (lw: hld up: hdwy on ins over 2f out: sn rdn: kpt on one pce ins fnl f)	½	4	9/1	65	50
3852⁶	**Song Mist (IRE) (66)** (PFICole) **3-8-11** RPerham(8) (led: hdd 1f out: no ex)	hd	5	11/1	64	49
2745*	**Barbason (66)** (GLMoore) **5-9-12** CandyMorris(12) (dwlt: pushed along & sme hdwy 3f out: sn rdn: one pce)	1¼	6	7/1	74	62
4221¹⁶	**Justinianus (IRE) (41)** (JJBridger) **5-9-0**(3) ADaly(9) (hld up: rdn over 2f out: grad wknd)	3	7	50/1	58	46
3227⁵	**Fairly Sure (IRE) (31)** (NEBerry) **4-8-7**(7) DDenby(10) (a bhd)	2½	8	50/1	49	37
4071⁸	**Impulsif (USA) (70)** (DJSffrenchDavis) **3-8-9**(5) GMilligan(5) (mid div: rdn over 2f out: sn wknd)	1¼	9	11/4¹	49	34
3900⁹	**Mazeed (IRE) (70)** (PDEvans) **4-9-3** JFEgan(3) (lw: bhd fnl 3f)	hd	**10**	14/1	49	37
4228⁹	**Waders Dream (IRE) (34)** (PatMitchell) **8-9-3v** AmandaSanders(6) (dwlt: a bhd)	3½	**11**	25/1	41	29
3849⁵	**Soviet Lady (IRE) (33)** (JELong) **3-8-11** GBardwell(13) (chsd ldrs: rdn 5f out: wknd over 3f out)	9	**12**	33/1	17	2

(SP 131.4%) **12 Rn**

1m 20.0 (0.00) CSF £27.16 TOTE £8.00: £3.30 £2.60 £2.90 (£26.20) Trio £30.40 OWNER Miss V. R. Jarvis (NEWMARKET) BRED Michael Staunton in Ireland
WEIGHT FOR AGE 3yo-3lb
3378 Lord Olivier (IRE), better known as a sprinter, had no trouble with the trip here. He was always going well just behind the two leaders and, after taking it up at the furlong marker, the issue was not in doubt. (6/1)
3200 Bubbly ran much better here than last time and seven furlongs is his best trip. (7/2)
4404 Banzhaf (USA) ran a sound race. He was pushed along to keep tabs on the leaders before the home turn and, to his credit, kept staying on under pressure. (4/1)
3787 Literary moved up early in the straight but, once put under pressure, only had the one pace to offer. (9/1)
3852 Song Mist (IRE) cut out the running but had no more to give when headed at the furlong pole. (11/1: 7/1-12/1)
2745* Barbason, returning from a short break, ran a sound enough race here, just keeping on in the final two furlongs. He looked fit enough in the paddock, but no doubt the race will bring him on. (7/1: 5/1-8/1)
Mazeed (IRE) (14/1: 10/1-16/1)

4452 HBLB H'CAP (0-80) (3-Y.O+) (Class D)

5-50 (5-50) **5f 59y** £4,123.50 (£1,248.00: £609.00: £289.50) Stalls: Low GOING minus 0.45 sec per fur (F)

Form	Horse	Dist	Pos	SP	RR	SF
4321³	**Levelled (70)** (MRChannon) **3-9-3** DaneO'Neill(4) (chsd ldrs: led ent fnl f: r.o)	—	1	7/4¹	81	50
3425³	**Listed Account (USA) (74)** (LMCumani) **3-9-7** TSprake(5) (chsd ldrs: rdn over 2f out: styd on ins fnl f)	1	2	4/1²	82	51
4248⁹	**Pharaoh's Joy (56)** (AGNewcombe) **4-8-1b**(3) PPMurphy(2) (a.p: rdn over 1f out: one pce)	nk	3	16/1	63	33
4329²	**Another Batchworth (58)** (EAWheeler) **5-8-3b**(3) ADaly(7) (led: hdd ent fnl f: no ex)	1	4	9/2³	62	32
4183⁷	**Ivory's Grab Hire (65)** (KTIvory) **4-8-13b** DBiggs(1) (rr: rdn over 3f out: nvr nrr)	½	5	10/1	68	38
4370¹²	**Tear White (IRE) (69)** (TGMills) **3-9-2** JQuinn(8) (prom: rdn 2f out: wknd ins fnl f)	½	6	7/1	70	39
4370¹⁵	**The Fugative (64)** (PMitchell) **4-8-9**(3) AWhelan(6) (a bhd)	2½	7	12/1	57	27
4183*	**Spender (82)** (PWHarris) **8-9-11**(5) GMilligan(3) (dwlt: a bhd)	12	8	9/2³	39	9

(SP 127.9%) **8 Rn**

60.7 secs (0.70) CSF £9.43 CT £85.12 TOTE £2.80: £1.10 £2.00 £3.20 (£6.50) OWNER Maygain Ltd (UPPER LAMBOURN) BRED J. F. Watson
WEIGHT FOR AGE 3yo-1lb
4321 Levelled always appeared to be going best and, after taking it up entering the final furlong, was not hard pushed to score. (7/4)
3425 Listed Account (USA) was being ridden halfway up the straight and it was only late on that she really began to stay on. She wants six furlongs at least. (4/1)
3323 Pharaoh's Joy raced prominently throughout and kept on gamely for pressure. (16/1)
4329 Another Batchworth showed her usual blistering early pace but had no more to give once headed. (9/2)

3852* Ivory's Grab Hire was out the back-door before staying on late, without ever threatening to take a hand. (10/1)
3194* Tear White (IRE) travelled well until the two-furlong marker but then had little more to give. (7/1)
2841 The Fugative (12/1: 8/1-14/1)

T/Plpt: £29.80 (434.36 Tckts). T/Qdpt: £9.90 (65.32 Tckts) SM

4330-NOTTINGHAM (L-H) (Good)
Sunday September 28th
WEATHER: cloudy WIND: almost nil

4453 SUNDAY FUNDAY (S) H'CAP (0-60) (3-Y.O+) (Class G)
3-00 (3-03) **1m 1f 213y** £2,536.80 (£714.80: £350.40) Stalls: Low GOING: 0.03 sec per fur (G)

Form	Horse	Dist	Pos	SP	RR	SF
4053^{2}	**Fighting Times (39)** (CASmith) **5-8-7v** DeanMcKeown(2) (b: a.p: led 3f out: sn clr: comf)	—	1	8/1	52+	21
4224*	**Pegasus Bay (56)** (MissAEEmbiricos) **6-9-10** GHind(6) (b: b.hind: in tch: chsd wnr over 2f out: sn rdn & no imp)	4	2	2/1 ^{1}	63	32
4264^{7}	**Captain Marmalade (37)** (DTThom) **8-8-5** DeclanO'Shea(12) (b: hld up: hdwy 3f out: styd on u.p fnl f)	hd	3	20/1	43	12
3980^{9}	**Explosive Power (55)** (GCBravery) **6-9-9** DRMcCabe(18) (hld up: hdwy over 3f out: rdn & one pce appr fnl f)	1¾	4	7/1 ^{3}	59	28
1441^{8}	**Dannistar (47)** (WMBrisbourne) **5-8-8**$^{(7)}$ AMcCarthy(17) (sn chsng ldr: rdn 2f out: sn wknd)	3	5	6/1 ^{2}	46	15
4055^{9}	**Havana Heights (IRE) (39)** (JLEyre) **4-8-0**$^{(7)ow3}$ SBuckley(16) (b.nr hind: chsd ldrs: sn drvn along: one pce fnl 2f)	hd	6	16/1	38	4
4335^{10}	**Summerville Wood (59)** (PMooney) **3-9-7b** WJO'Connor(3) (trckd ldrs: outpcd ent st: n.d afterwards)	1¾	7	20/1	55	18
4179*	**Rock The Barney (IRE) (45)** (MDIUsher) **8-8-6b**$^{(7)}$ ANicholls(1) (b: reluctant to r: wl bhd tl sme late hdwy)	5	8	6/1 ^{2}	33	2
418^{2}	**Honestly (54)** (BSmart) **4-9-8** JStack(8) (plld hrd: hld up & racd wd: n.d)	2	9	14/1	39	8
	Oakbury (IRE) (36) (MissLCSiddall) **5-8-4**^{ow1} AMcGlone(5) (lw: chsd ldrs 6f: sn wknd)	1½	10	40/1	18	—
4219^{14}	**Beldray Park (IRE) (40)** (MrsALMKing) **4-8-8** NAdams(11) (sn drvn along: a outpcd)	2	11	40/1	19	—
3320^{8}	**Blazer's Baby (50)** (MrsNMacauley) **3-8-12** SDrowne(10) (b: swtg: chsd ldrs to ½-wy: sn lost pl)	1	12	20/1	27	—
2411^{9}	**African Sun (IRE) (40)** (MCChapman) **4-8-8** LNewton(4) (prom tl wknd 3f out)	nk	13	20/1	17	—
4235^{14}	**Mowlaie (37)** (DWChapman) **6-8-5** ACulhane(14) (b: swtg: led tl 3f out: wknd qckly: t.o)	20	14	10/1	—	—
280^{6}	**Callaloo (53)** (KGWingrove) **4-9-7** KRutter(9) (Withdrawn not under Starter's orders: bolted bef s)		W	50/1	—	—

(SP 133.0%) **14 Rn**

2m 11.5 (9.00) CSF £22.00 CT £308.12 TOTE £11.20: £3.90 £1.60 £3.40 (£14.50) Trio £135.50 OWNER Julian Graves Ltd (HANLEY SWAN) BRED C. Hitchings
WEIGHT FOR AGE 3yo-6lb
Bt in 6,200gns
STEWARDS' ENQUIRY Obj. to Captain Marmalade by McCabe overruled. Newton susp. 7/10/97 (improper use of whip).
4053 Fighting Times appreciated having more use made of him and, stretching clear entering the last quarter-mile, was soon beyond recall. Now that he has opened his account, there is no reason why he should not follow up. (8/1)
4224* Pegasus Bay showed at Yarmouth that he is a much better animal if ridden from off the pace but he was never far away this time although, unable to quicken with the winner, he was fighting a lost cause throughout the last couple of furlongs. (2/1: op 3/1)
3413 Captain Marmalade is still capable of winning at this level but he is inclined to run in snatches and, on this occasion, was never nearer than at the finish. (20/1)
Explosive Power, very lightly raced, has only ever won on the All-Weather and, though he performed with credit, lacked the speed on this much faster ground to pose a serious threat. (7/1)
1001 Dannistar has changed stables since he last ran four months ago and, though she did look well forward in condition, was feeling the strain below the distance and her chance had soon gone. (6/1)
4179* Rock The Barney (IRE) (6/1: 4/1-13/2)
3272 Mowlaie (10/1: 12/1-20/1)

4454 LETHEBY & CHRISTOPHER MAIDEN STKS (2-Y.O) (Class D)
3-35 (3-36) **1m 54y** £4,952.00 (£1,496.00: £728.00: £344.00) Stalls: Low GOING: 0.03 sec per fur (G)

Form	Horse	Dist	Pos	SP	RR	SF
	Giveaway (HRACecil) **2-9-0** AMcGlone(16) (w'like: leggy: scope: a.p: chal over 1f out: hrd drvn to ld last stride)	—	1	6/4 ^{1}	80+	41
4309^{2}	**Mawsoof** (MRStoute) **2-9-0** GHind(5) (chsd ldr: led wl over 2f out: rdn & hdd post)	s.h	2	2/1 ^{2}	80	41
4064^{4}	**Canadian Puzzler (USA)** (PWHarris) **2-9-0** SDrowne(6) (sn trckng ldrs: styd on one pce fnl 2f)	4	3	7/1 ^{3}	72	33
4064^{8}	**Wave Rock** (JLDunlop) **2-9-0** MRimmer(11) (hld up: hdwy 3f out: kpt on ins fnl f)	1	4	25/1	70	31
	Double Classic (USA) (MRStoute) **2-9-0** KBradshaw(7) (w'like: a in tch: one pce fnl 3f)	1¼	5	14/1	68+	29
4174^{5}	**Cloak of Darkness (IRE)** (RHannon) **2-9-0** PaulEddery(3) (chsd ldrs tl outpcd fnl 2f)	2½	6	8/1	63	24
3770^{8}	**Paarl Rock** (DRLoder) **2-9-0** GCarter(2) (s.i.s: nvr nr to chal)	2	7	25/1	59+	20
2849^{3}	**Fantasy Night (IRE)** (JLDunlop) **2-9-0** JStack(8) (dwlt: bhd tl sme late hdwy)	2	8	14/1	55+	16
4017^{10}	**Roberty Bob (IRE)** (PTWalwyn) **2-9-0** DaleGibson(13) (sn bhd & drvn along: nvr on terms)	2	9	25/1	51	12
4017^{15}	**Sharp Label** (JLHarris) **2-8-9** LCharnock(15) (unruly s: mid div tl wknd 3f out: t.o)	9	10	66/1	29	—
	Citrus Express (SWE) (PMooney) **2-9-0** WJO'Connor(4) (lengthy: bit bkwd: sn bhd & pushed along: t.o)	12	11	33/1	11	—
	Out On The Street (USA) (TDBarron) **2-9-0** ACulhane(10) (cmpt: bit bkwd: stdd s: a in rr: t.o)	s.h	12	10/1	10	—
4303^{11}	**Ivory Girl (IRE)** (KGWingrove) **2-8-10**^{ow1} KRutter(14) (led & sn wl clr: wknd & hdd wl over 2f out: t.o)	4	13	66/1	—	—
	Windspeed (BPJBaugh) **2-8-11**$^{(3)}$ PRoberts(9) (leggy: bit bkwd: a bhd: t.o)	13	14	50/1	—	—

(SP 138.8%) **14 Rn**

1m 47.3 (6.00) CSF £4.67 TOTE £2.40: £1.50 £1.10 £2.20 (£2.20) Trio £8.50 OWNER Mr K. Abdulla (NEWMARKET) BRED Juddmonte Farms
Giveaway, with plenty of stamina in his breeding, did look as though he would benefit from easier ground. Always in the action, he ranged upsides before reaching the final furlong but had to really stretch out to force his head in front in the dying strides. He is a good-looking colt who should get better with experience. (6/4)
4309 Mawsoof could have found this race coming plenty soon enough but he kicked on some way out and made the winner fight all the way to the line. (2/1)
4064 Canadian Puzzler (USA) has not run a bad race yet but he does appear to lack a turn of finishing speed and more forceful tactics would seem the obvious solution now that he has gained experience. (7/1)
Wave Rock ran his best race yet over this slightly longer trip and he is slowly but surely getting it together. (25/1)

Double Classic (USA) travelled comfortably in behind the leaders but began to struggle three furlongs out . Driven along, he kept responding and, with stamina not a problem, will be all the wiser next time he appears. (14/1)
Out On The Street (USA) (10/1: op 16/1)

4455 PLAYQUEST H'CAP (0-70) (3-Y.O+ F & M) (Class E)

4-10 (4-10) **1m 54y** £3,754.50 (£1,131.00: £548.00: £256.50) Stalls: Low GOING: 0.03 sec per fur (G)

				SP	RR	SF
4228[16]	**Karinska (57)** (MCChapman) **7-8-11**(7) SCarson(7) (hld up & bhd: hdwy over 2f out: r.o to ld cl home)	—	**1**	16/1	69	35
4169[20]	**Bella's Legacy (35)** (KRBurke) **4-7-10** NVarley(6) (hld up: hdwy over 2f out: led ins fnl f: ct post)	s.h	**2**	40/1	47	13
4228[6]	**May Queen Megan (41)** (MrsALMKing) **4-8-2** NAdams(8) (chsd ldrs: hdwy to ld over 2f out: hdd & no ex ins fnl f)	2	**3**	5/1[2]	49	15
2281*	**Bold Faith (47)** (WJMusson) **4-8-8** DRMcCabe(10) (hld up: hdwy 2f out: fin wl)	1	**4**	10/1	53	19
4008[4]	**Kalimat (62)** (WJarvis) **3-9-0**(5) JoHunnam(2) (led tl over 3f out: rallied & ev ch over 1f out: one pce)	nk	**5**	6/1[3]	68	30
4225*	**Gymcrak Flyer (67)** (GHolmes) **6-10-0** DeanMcKeown(3) (trckd ldrs: drvn along 3f out: no imp)	2	**6**	7/2[1]	69	35
3442[7]	**Go For Green (58)** (DrJDScargill) **3-9-1** MRimmer(12) (chsd ldrs tl wknd over 2f out)	½	**7**	16/1	59	21
4070[3]	**Blushing Desert (65)** (RHannon) **3-9-8** PaulEddery(1) (trckd ldrs: rdn & outpcd over 2f out)	6	**8**	6/1[3]	54	16
3810[7]	**Dispol Gem (62)** (PCalver) **4-9-9** GCarter(9) (chsd ldr: led over 3f out tl over 2f out: sn rdn & wknd)	s.h	**9**	8/1	51	17
4291[11]	**Grey Again (48)** (DShaw) **5-8-6**(3) CTeague(5) (b: unruly s: sn wl bhd: t.o)	4	**10**	16/1	29	—
1985[5]	**Princess of Hearts (61)** (MCPipe) **3-9-4b** MWigham(14) (s.i.s: a bhd: t.o)	2½	**11**	10/1	37	—
3266[10]	**Onemoretime (40)** (BWMurray) **3-7-11**[ow1] DeclanO'Shea(4) (b.hind: a bhd: t.o)	2½	**12**	50/1	11	—
				(SP 118.8%)	**12 Rn**	

1m 48.4 (7.10) CSF £477.81 CT £3,306.49 TOTE £24.00: £3.40 £14.20 £1.70 (£343.20) Trio £281.30 OWNER Mr Geoff Whiting (MARKET RASEN) BRED Sheikh Mohammed bin Rashid al Maktoum
LONG HANDICAP Bella's Legacy 7-9 Onemoretime 7-1
WEIGHT FOR AGE 3yo-4lb
OFFICIAL EXPLANATION **Bold Faith: rider reported that his instructions were to drop the filly out, get her relaxed and ask her a question from the two-furlong marker, but only use hands and heels. He added that the filly was keen and became unbalanced early on.**
3906 Karinska may well have ended her career on a high as she is only allowed to race for another week before her time is up as a pregnant mare. In recording her tenth success, she certainly deserves to retire on a winning note. (16/1)
Bella's Legacy, unlike the winner, is still a maiden, but this was her best effort yet on her first appearance at this trip and it will come as a surprise if she cannot pick up a small race in the coming weeks. (40/1)
4228 May Queen Megan seems to need all at this trip nowadays. Though she was forced to give best inside the final furlong, she is continuing to knock at the door. (5/1)
2281* Bold Faith has enjoyed a three-month break since opening her account on the soft at Folkestone and she did give the impression that this was needed, so this fast-finishing performance would suggest that there is more success to follow. (10/1: 8/1-12/1)
4008 Kalimat is high in the handicap for a maiden, which is preventing her from striking it rich, but she rarely runs a bad race. (6/1)

4456 TOTE NOTTINGHAM STEWARDS CUP H'CAP (0-85) (3-Y.O+) (Class D)

4-40 (4-42) **6f 15y** £9,686.50 (£2,932.00: £1,431.00: £680.50) Stalls: High GOING: 0.03 sec per fur (G)

				SP	RR	SF
4307[2]	**Stand Tall (74)** (LadyHerries) **5-9-4** PaulEddery(14) (s.i.s: gd hdwy 2f out: hrd rdn to ld post)	—	**1**	8/1[2]	84	61
4414[11]	**Mallia (62)** (TDBarron) **4-8-6** LCharnock(18) (lw: a.p: led over 1f out: hrd rdn & ct last stride)	s.h	**2**	25/1	72	49
3765[17]	**Double Bounce (82)** (PJMakin) **7-9-12** GCarter(11) (b: hdwy over 2f out: hrd rdn & r.o wl cl home)	s.h	**3**	20/1	92	69
4183[13]	**Rushcutter Bay (75)** (PLGilligan) **4-9-5** NAdams(6) (racd centre: a.p: led over 2f out tl over 1f out: rallied u.p)	nk	**4**	14/1	84	61
4155[11]	**Rififi (78)** (RIngram) **4-9-8** DRMcCabe(13) (b: hld up: hdwy & n.m.r over 2f out: styd on fnl f)	1½	**5**	8/1[2]	83	60
4385[9]	**Corniche Quest (IRE) (65)** (MRChannon) **4-8-2**(7) AEddery(3) (lw: s.i.s: sn chsng ldrs: r.o one pce fnl f)	nk	**6**	20/1	69	46
4071[4]	**Pleading (75)** (HCandy) **4-9-5** CRutter(20) (drvn along ½-wy: kpt on wl fnl f)	s.h	**7**	10/1[3]	79	56
4048[2]	**Bowlers Boy (75)** (JJQuinn) **4-8-12**(7) RSmith(19) (chsd ldrs: rdn & unable qckn appr fnl f)	1	**8**	14/1	76	53
4280[7]	**Tiler (IRE) (80)** (MJohnston) **5-9-10** DeanMcKeown(16) (lw: unruly stalls: chsd ldrs tl over 1f out)	nk	**9**	100/30[1]	81	58
4168*	**Mouche (68)** (MrsJRRamsden) **3-8-10v** MRimmer(2) (racd centre: outpcd ½-wy: kpt on appr fnl f)	nk	**10**	10/1[3]	68	43
4280[19]	**Benzoe (IRE) (78)** (MrsJRRamsden) **7-9-8** JFanning(15) (lw: dwlt: hdwy whn nt clr run over 1f out: n.d)	½	**11**	14/1	77	54
4121[8]	**Top Banana (83)** (HCandy) **6-9-6**(7) LJames(8) (lw: racd centre: nvr nr ldrs)	1¾	**12**	10/1[3]	77	54
4414[3]	**Thwaab (65)** (FWatson) **5-8-9** GHind(4) (racd centre: w ldrs over 3f)	nk	**13**	16/1	58	35
4221*	**Palo Blanco (70)** (GLMoore) **6-9-0** MWigham(12) (w ldrs tl wknd over 1f out)	hd	**14**	14/1	63	40
4221[6]	**Intiaash (IRE) (70)** (DHaydnJones) **5-9-0** SDrowne(1) (hdwy over 1f out: hrd rdn: nt pce to chal)	½	**15**	11/1	62	39
4137[4]	**The Happy Fox (IRE) (65)** (BAMcMahon) **5-8-9b** LNewton(17) (led tl over 2f out)	1½	**16**	12/1	53	30
4307[13]	**Dovebrace (78)** (TDBarron) **4-9-8** JStack(5) (s.i.s: racd centre: effrt 2f out: wknd appr fnl f)	nk	**17**	40/1	65	42
4183[4]	**Kilcullen Lad (IRE) (80)** (PMooney) **3-9-8v** WJO'Connor(9) (chsd ldrs over 4f)	hd	**18**	14/1	67	42
				(SP 143.6%)	**18 Rn**	

1m 14.6 (3.10) CSF £201.54 CT £3,695.84 TOTE £7.50: £2.70 £5.00 £2.90 £4.30 (£67.60) Trio £674.50; £228.02 to Hamilton 29/9/97 OWNER Mr Chris Hardy (LITTLEHAMPTON) BRED Mrs E. Longton
WEIGHT FOR AGE 3yo-2lb
4307 Stand Tall gained a last gasp success that looked almost non-existent entering the final furlong. (8/1)
3910 Mallia has hardly been sighted in his last couple of races since getting touched off on the line at Ripon but this was more like his old self and, when he gets the easier ground that suits him, he should be able to make it pay from his present mark. (25/1)
3423 Double Bounce ran a fine race in defeat here and he may well have poked his head in front briefly before reaching the line. It will be unfortunate if he cannot retain his record of having won every season since 1993. (20/1)
3011 Rushcutter Bay, still to win beyond the minimum trip, was only tapped for toe in the dying strides and there is still plenty of time for him to add to his score. (14/1)
3765* Rififi has had several punishing races this season and has been on the go since February, and his last couple of outings would suggest that is could be time for a break. (8/1: op 5/1)

4457 SUNDAY CONDITIONS STKS (3-Y.O+) (Class C)

5-10 (5-10) **5f 13y** £5,186.00 (£1,886.00: £918.00: £390.00: £170.00) Stalls: High GOING: 0.03 sec per fur (G)

				SP	RR	SF
4282[24]	**Tadeo (100)** (MJohnston) **4-9-0** DeanMcKeown(2) (mde all: hrd rdn & hld on wl nr fin)	—	**1**	5/2[1]	101	67
4062[2]	**Crofters Ceilidh (94)** (BAMcMahon) **5-8-9** LNewton(4) (hld up: n.m.r over 1f out: r.o u.p wl ins fnl f)	nk	**2**	5/1[3]	95	61
2872[3]	**Speed On (90)** (HCandy) **4-9-0** CRutter(5) (hdwy ½-wy: ev ch 1f out: unable qckn cl home)	nk	**3**	100/30[2]	99	65

					SP	RR	SF
4282[16]	**My Melody Parkes (95)** (JBerry) **4-9-1** GCarter(3) (trckd ldrs: effrt & rdn over 1f out: nvr able to chal)	2	**4**	5/2[1]	94	60
4282[23]	**Passion For Life (97)** (GLewis) **4-9-0b** PaulEddery(1) (w wnr: rdn ½-wy: wknd over 1f out)	2½	**5**	13/2	85	51
				(SP 110.2%)		**5 Rn**

60.9 secs (2.00) CSF £13.56 TOTE £4.10: £1.60 £2.10 (£8.50) OWNER Mr J. R. Good (MIDDLEHAM) BRED J. R. and Mrs P. Good

4100 Tadeo got the best of the start and led these speedsters a merry dance and, showing the right attitude to strong driving, refused to give in. (5/2)

4062 Crofters Ceilidh, tightened up against the stands' rail, always seemed to be searching for an opening but, when one did present itself, she was unable to take it immediately and her strong, late flourish was always going to be too late. (5/1)

2872 Speed On has had a very light season but he showed definite signs of a return to form here and, with his stable out of the doldrums, is one to stay on the right side of from now on. (100/30)

3863* My Melody Parkes was always being taken along faster than she cared for and her attempt to mount a challenge approaching the final furlong came to little. (5/2)

4062 Passion For Life had the blinkers back on again but they had no effect at all and he seems to have lost his zest for racing. (13/2)

4458 BBC RADIO NOTTINGHAM MAIDEN AUCTION STKS (I) (2-Y.O) (Class E)

5-40 (5-41) **6f 15y** £3,156.50 (£947.00: £456.00: £210.50) Stalls: High GOING: 0.03 sec per fur (G)

				SP	RR	SF
	Swing Sister (PRWebber) **2-8-3** SDrowne(8) (cmpt: dwlt: hdwy ½-wy: rdn to ld nr fin)	—	**1**	25/1	66+	30
4166[6]	**Premium Princess (64)** (JJQuinn) **2-7-13** DaleGibson(10) (a chsng ldrs: rdn 2f out: str run fnl f: jst failed)	s.h	**2**	6/1	62	26
3307[12]	**Fundance (70)** (MDods) **2-8-10** ACulhane(12) (led: rdn & drifted lft ins fnl f: hdd nr fin)	½	**3**	16/1	72	36
3927[2]	**Recognition (81)** (WJarvis) **2-8-8** AMcGlone(6) (prom: rdn & hung lft over 1f out: sn outpcd)	5	**4**	9/4[1]	56	20
3726[3]	**The Downtown Fox** (BAMcMahon) **2-8-12** LNewton(4) (chsd ldrs over 4f)	1¾	**5**	3/1[2]	56	20
4167[4]	**Haunt The Zoo** (JLHarris) **2-8-0** LCharnock(2) (trckd ldrs: rdn 2f out: sn wknd)	nk	**6**	5/1[3]	43	7
4065[11]	**Katies Treat (IRE) (45)** (DTThom) **2-8-0v** DRMcCabe(5) (outpcd)	3½	**7**	50/1	34	—
4167[12]	**The Artful Dodger** (RJRWilliams) **2-8-8** GCarter(1) (outpcd)	2	**8**	33/1	37	1
4216[9]	**Sadeebah** (MJohnston) **2-8-7** DeanMcKeown(3) (chsd ldrs: drvn along ½-wy: wknd wl over 1f out)	s.h	**9**	20/1	35	—
4056[4]	**Algaleb** (HAkbary) **2-8-11** JStack(7) (w ldr: rdn ½-wy: wknd 2f out)	2	**10**	14/1	34	—
4103[13]	**Miss Slender** (RHannon) **2-8-5** PaulEddery(11) (outpcd)	2½	**11**	16/1	22	—
	Czech Maite (MrsJRRamsden) **2-8-1** DeclanO'Shea(9) (w'like: unf: scope: s.s: a bhd & outpcd)	6	**12**	25/1	2	—
				(SP 122.5%)		**12 Rn**

1m 15.8 (4.30) CSF £151.26 TOTE £25.60: £6.00 £2.00 £5.90 (£60.00) Trio Not won; £219.53 to Hamilton 29/9/97 OWNER Lady Bamford (BANBURY) BRED Compagnia Generale S R L

Swing Sister, a not over-big debutante who looked well tuned up, recovered from a sluggish start and put her head down at the right time to get up close home. (25/1)

4166 Premium Princess produced a sustained run up the stands' side inside the last furlong and only just failed to gain the day. She was one of the most experienced in the field and should be able to win a race of this description. (6/1)

2110 Fundance tried hard to make it all and, had he not drifted off a true line under pressure in the last two hundred yards, may well have succeeded. (16/1)

3927 Recognition showed up with the pace but he hung left when the pressure was on approaching the final furlong and his chance had gone. (9/4)

3726 The Downtown Fox, taking a step down in class this time, pushed the pace and had every chance until fading below the distance. (3/1)

4459 BBC RADIO NOTTINGHAM MAIDEN AUCTION STKS (II) (2-Y.O) (Class E)

6-05 (6-06) **6f 15y** £3,156.50 (£947.00: £456.00: £210.50) Stalls: High GOING: 0.03 sec per fur (G)

				SP	RR	SF
4116[13]	**Praetorian Gold (69)** (RHannon) **2-8-8** WJO'Connor(4) (a.p: rdn 2f out: r.o to ld nr fin)	—	**1**	11/8[1]	66	36
3905[6]	**Julies Jewel (IRE) (62)** (MCChapman) **2-8-0**(7) SCarson(8) (led: clr ½-wy: rdn & hdd cl home)	nk	**2**	16/1	64	34
	Grace Browning (HCandy) **2-8-0** CRutter(3) (cmpt: a.p: rdn 2f out: edgd rt & one pce fnl f)	1¾	**3**	5/1[2]	53	23
4309[7]	**Dilly Lane (USA)** (PRWebber) **2-8-4** SDrowne(6) (swvd lft s: sn chsng ldrs: one pce fnl 2f)	4	**4**	15/2	46	16
4381[15]	**Hey Up Mate (IRE)** (JBerry) **2-8-5**(3) PRoberts(10) (chsd ldrs over 3f)	6	**5**	14/1	34	4
	Dare (CJames) **2-8-8** TLucas(7) (leggy: unf: hld up: effrt 2f out: nvr nr to chal)	nk	**6**	16/1	33	3
4216[10]	**The Druidess (IRE)** (GCBravery) **2-7-13** DRMcCabe(2) (chsd ldrs 4f: sn rdn & wknd)	1¼	**7**	25/1	21	—
4209[12]	**Nordic Pirjo** (MrsJRRamsden) **2-8-0** LCharnock(9) (outpcd)	¾	**8**	13/2[3]	20	—
	Eiffel Tiger (IRE) (BobJones) **2-8-8** GCarter(11) (neat: bkwd: s.i.s: a outpcd)	1½	**9**	10/1	24	—
4058[13]	**Risknowt Getnowt (33)** (TWall) **2-8-6** LNewton(5) (prom over 3f: sn rdn & outpcd)	s.h	**10**	50/1	22	—
4165[15]	**Blanche The Almond** (CASmith) **2-8-2** DaleGibson(1) (outpcd)	2	**11**	33/1	13	—
				(SP 120.1%)		**11 Rn**

1m 15.7 (4.20) CSF £25.24 TOTE £2.40: £1.10 £3.80 £1.80 (£21.70) Trio £69.20 OWNER The Gold Buster Syndicate (2) (MARLBOROUGH) BRED Witney Stud Farm

3598 Praetorian Gold won this courtesy of his superior stamina and a very determined ride from the man on top. He was at full stretch all the way over this inadequate trip and made up all of three lengths inside the final furlong to get up a stride from the line. (11/8)

3905 Julies Jewel (IRE) adopted more forceful tactics and bowled along in a commanding lead, and there was only the winner who was able to get anywhere near him. These tactics will pay dividends. (16/1)

Grace Browning, a small late-April foal who has a bit left to work on, showed plenty of promise, and if brought along steadily should be able to win races. (5/1)

Dilly Lane (USA) looked unwilling to let herself down and was easily shaken off when the battle to the finish got under way. (15/2: 4/1-8/1)

Hey Up Mate (IRE) (14/1: 10/1-16/1)

T/Plpt: £585.30 (24.34 Tckts). T/Qdpt: £548.30 (0.29 Tckts); £526.15 to Hamilton 29/9/97 IM

4042-BATH (L-H) (Good to firm)

Monday September 29th

WEATHER: fine WIND: almost nil

4460 E.B.F. DODINGTON MAIDEN STKS (2-Y.O) (Class D)

2-00 (2-03) **1m 2f 46y** £3,291.50 (£992.00: £481.00: £225.50) Stalls: Low GOING minus 0.41 sec per fur (F)

				SP	RR	SF
	St Helensfield (MJohnston) **2-9-0** JWeaver(1) (leggy: hld up: rdn over 3f out: qckn to ld over 2f out: r.o wl)	—	**1**	9/2[2]	86+	34

4278[2] **Corniche (IRE)** (PFICole) **2-9-0** TQuinn(3) (lw: mde most tl hdd over 4f out: led over 2f out: sn hdd: outpcd over 1f out: rallied ins fnl f)	½	**2**	1/3[1]	85	33
4157[5] **Treasure Chest (IRE)** (MajorWRHern) **2-9-0** TSprake(2) (disp ld tl led over 4f out: hdd over 2f out: btn on ins whn n.m.r ins fnl f)	1½	**3**	13/2[3]	83	31
3545[5] **O' Higgins (IRE) (56)** (RBoss) **2-9-0** LDettori(4) (hld up: hrd rdn & wknd over 1f out)	6	**4**	25/1	74	22
			(SP 110.4%)	**4 Rn**	

2m 10.4 (3.90) CSF £6.19 TOTE £6.10: (£1.90) OWNER Mr Paul Dean (MIDDLEHAM) BRED Hesmonds Stud Ltd
St Helensfield, a half-brother to Group Two winner Stowaway, hails from a stable who seem to specialise in these back-end long-distance juvenile events. (9/2: op 2/1)
4278 Corniche (IRE), a half-brother to a winner in France, seemed to be taken by surprise when the winner went for home and could never peg his rival back. (1/3)
4157 Treasure Chest (IRE), out of a French Gold Cup winner, is not surprisingly blessed with stamina rather than speed. (13/2: op 4/1)
3545 O' Higgins (IRE) was up in both class and distance. (25/1)

4461 WEATHERBYS DATA SERVICES H'CAP (0-80) (3-Y.O+) (Class D)
2-30 (2-30) **2m 1f 34y** £3,533.50 (£1,063.00: £514.00: £239.50) Stalls: High GOING minus 0.41 sec per fur (F)

			SP	RR	SF
4246[3] **City Hall (IRE) (70)** (MRStoute) **3-8-12** TQuinn(3) (mde all: rdn 4f out: r.o wl)	—	**1**	2/1[1]	85	51
4275[5] **Prospero (66)** (MrsAJPerrett) **4-9-6** AClark(7) (hld up: hdwy 6f out: chsd wnr over 3f out: rdn & ev ch over 1f out: nt r.o)	1¼	**2**	9/2[3]	80	58
Torch Vert (IRE) (70) (MCPipe) **5-9-10b** RHills(5) (lw: hld up: rdn & wknd over 3f out)	10	**3**	12/1	75	53
3218[14] **Ramike (IRE) (72)** (MJohnston) **3-9-0** JWeaver(2) (rdn 7f out: a bhd)	¾	**4**	5/1	76	42
3915[9] **Ultimate Smoothie (72)** (MCPipe) **5-9-12** MHills(1) (sn chsng wnr: wknd over 2f out)	8	**5**	10/1	68	46
3203* **Height of Heights (IRE) (74)** (LadyHerries) **4-10-0** LDettori(6) (lw: prom: rdn & wknd over 5f out: eased whn no ch over 2f out)	dist	**6**	11/4[2]	—	—
			(SP 111.6%)	**6 Rn**	

3m 44.3 (2.90) CSF £10.20 TOTE £2.50: £1.30 £2.10 (£7.40) OWNER Lord Weinstock (NEWMARKET) BRED Ballymacoll Stud Farm Ltd
WEIGHT FOR AGE 3yo-12lb
OFFICIAL EXPLANATION **Height of Heights (IRE): gurgled.**
4246 City Hall (IRE), without the visor this time, was pushed along leaving the stalls to get the lead and these completely different tactics did the trick. (2/1)
4275 Prospero, dropped 4lb, did not seem to relish the battle over this longer trip. (9/2)
Torch Vert (IRE) was blinkered for the first time, having fallen when tried in them over hurdles earlier in the month. (12/1: 7/1-14/1)
3069 Ramike (IRE) has been gelding since his last start. (5/1)

4462 E.B.F. SHEILAH HERN MAIDEN STKS (2-Y.O) (Class D)
3-00 (3-00) **5f 161y** £3,428.00 (£1,034.00: £502.00: £236.00) Stalls: High GOING minus 0.41 sec per fur (F)

			SP	RR	SF
4311[7] **Lady Charlotte** (DRCElsworth) **2-8-9** TQuinn(4) (lw: hld up: rdn over 2f out: hdwy over 1f out: led ins fnl f: drvn out)	—	**1**	14/1[3]	82	32
2875[2] **Taalluf (USA)** (MajorWRHern) **2-8-9** RHills(3) (lw: w ldr: led on bit 2f out: hrd rdn & hdd ins fnl f)	1½	**2**	1/4[1]	78	28
4166[7] **Alpha Whisky (GER) (73)** (IABalding) **2-8-9** LDettori(1) (b.hind: led: rdn & hdd 2f out: wknd ins fnl f)	2	**3**	4/1[2]	72	22
4113[13] **Son of Good Times** (PGMurphy) **2-9-0** MFenton(2) (hld up: rdn 3f out: sn bhd)	16	**4**	66/1	33	—
			(SP 108.2%)	**4 Rn**	

1m 11.4 (1.90) CSF £17.44 TOTE £8.40: (£2.80) OWNER Lucayan Stud (WHITCOMBE) BRED Mount Coote Stud
3636 Lady Charlotte was described by her rider as still rather green and he also thought she would be better over further. (14/1: 8/1-16/1)
2875 Taalluf (USA) went to the front smoothly enough but in the end she was beaten fair and square. (1/4)
4166 Alpha Whisky (GER) is bred to need further than she has tackled so far. (4/1)

4463 MORRIS DANCER CONDITIONS STKS (3-Y.O+) (Class C)
3-30 (3-30) **1m 5y** £4,817.00 (£1,677.00: £813.50: £342.50) Stalls: Low GOING minus 0.41 sec per fur (F)

			SP	RR	SF
4272[2] **Crimson Tide (IRE) (102)** (JWHills) **3-8-10** MHills(2) (lw: chsd clr ldr: rdn to ld 1f out: comf)	—	**1**	2/1[1]	106	61
4142[2] **Latalomne (USA) (95)** (EALDunlop) **3-8-12** TQuinn(3) (lw: led: sn clr: rdn & hdd 1f out: one pce)	3½	**2**	5/2[2]	101	56
2766[7] **Right Wing (IRE) (95)** (MajorWRHern) **3-9-0** TSprake(4) (hld up: rdn over 1f out: r.o one pce fnl f)	½	**3**	5/1[3]	102	57
4276* **Jorrocks (USA) (93)** (IABalding) **3-8-10** LDettori(1) (lw: hld up: rdn over 1f out: one pce)	nk	**4**	2/1[1]	97	52
			(SP 111.9%)	**4 Rn**	

1m 38.2 (Equals best) (0.00) CSF £6.79 TOTE £2.80: (£4.20) OWNER Mr Christopher Wright (LAMBOURN) BRED Barronstown Stud and Roncon Ltd
4272 Crimson Tide (IRE) had the race run to suit him in that the pacemaker had nothing left after running himself into the ground. His trainer certainly retains his faith in the colt, and is already thinking in terms of his campaign for next year. (2/1)
4142 Latalomne (USA), soon given his head, paid the penalty for going off like a scalded cat. (5/2)
2137* Right Wing (IRE) is at his most effective on soft ground. (5/1)
4276* Jorrocks (USA) had more on his plate in this race sponsored by his owner. (2/1)

4464 DICK HERN MAIDEN STKS (3-Y.O+) (Class D)
4-00 (4-01) **1m 5y** £3,488.00 (£1,049.00: £507.00: £236.00) Stalls: Low GOING minus 0.41 sec per fur (F)

			SP	RR	SF
4277[2] **Brigand (IRE)** (DRLoder) **3-9-0** LDettori(3) (lw: led over 1f: led 2f out: pushed out)	—	**1**	1/2[1]	80	45
4176[10] **Faringdon Future (73)** (BWHills) **3-9-0** MHills(2) (lw: led over 6f out: hdd 2f out: one pce)	2	**2**	6/1[3]	76	41
4316[4] **Finarts Bay** (MrsJCecil) **3-8-9** JWeaver(4) (hld up: rdn 3f out: sn wknd)	13	**3**	11/4[2]	45	10
Oh Dearie Me (JGMO'Shea) **5-8-13** MFenton(1) (bkwd: bhd fnl 4f: t.o)	12	**4**	25/1	21	—
			(SP 111.5%)	**4 Rn**	

1m 40.1 (1.90) CSF £3.90 TOTE £1.30: (£2.20) OWNER Sheikh Mohammed (NEWMARKET) BRED Newtownbarry House Stud
WEIGHT FOR AGE 3yo-4lb
4277 Brigand (IRE), a half-brother to Italian Oaks winner Lady Bentley, had a lot less to do following two seconds on soft ground. (1/2: 2/7-8/15)
2309 Faringdon Future was having his second outing since being gelded. (6/1)
4316 Finarts Bay was most disappointing on this step up to a mile. (11/4)

4465 ALDIE MAIDEN APPRENTICE H'CAP (0-60) (3-Y.O+) (Class F)

4-30 (4-36) **1m 5y** £2,708.00 (£763.00: £374.00) Stalls: Low GOING minus 0.41 sec per fur (F)

Form	Horse	Dist	Pos	SP	RR	SF
3850[2]	**The Green Grey (42)** (WRMuir) **3-8-12** JoHunnam(5) (hld up: hdwy over 4f out: chsd ldr over 2f out: led 1f out: r.o wl)	—	1	10/1	57	38
4326[2]	**Ron's Round (39)** (CADwyer) **3-8-4**(5)ow1 JGotobed(8) (prom: lost pl over 4f out: rallied over 1f out: styd on ins fnl f)	2½	2	11/4 [1]	49	29
3971[8]	**One In The Eye (31)** (JRPoulton) **4-8-2**(3) JFowle(3) (hld up & bhd: swtchd rt & gd hdwy over 1f out: fin wl)	1¾	3	12/1	38	23
3470[10]	**Hannalou (FR) (40)** (TGMills) **4-8-7v[1]**(7) LisaHackett(18) (led: clr over 5f out: hdd 1f out: wknd)	1¼	4	16/1	44	29
4243[14]	**Attarikh (IRE) (43)** (MrsALMKing) **4-9-3** AEddery(7) (lw: a.p: one pce fnl 2f)	nk	5	7/1 [3]	46	31
4112[20]	**Swan Island (53)** (WMBrisbourne) **3-9-6**(3) AMcCarthy(9) (hld up & bhd: hdwy over 2f out: one pce fnl f)	s.h	6	20/1	56	37
4373[18]	**Trevor Mitchell (37)** (JJBridger) **3-8-2**(5) RBrisland(6) (no hdwy fnl 2f)	1¼	7	50/1	38	19
4373[12]	**Jubilee Scholar (IRE) (38)** (GLMoore) **4-8-7b**(5) DarrenWilliams(12) (hld up: hdwy over 2f out: nt clr run & swtchd rt ins fnl f: n.d)	s.h	8	20/1	39	24
4300[11]	**D J Cat (36)** (WRMuir) **4-8-10** JWilkinson(14) (lw: n.d)	2½	9	10/1	32	17
3470[16]	**Sharp Deed (IRE) (55)** (PJMakin) **3-9-6v[1]**(5) GHannon(10) (nvr nr ldrs)	hd	10	8/1	51	32
4051[11]	**Saxon Bay (42)** (KOCunningham-Brown) **5-9-2b** DDenby(1) (chsd ldrs: rdn over 2f out: sn wknd)	¾	11	33/1	36	21
2300[7]	**Blue Calvine (37)** (CJHill) **3-8-2**(5) RCody-Boutcher(4) (bhd tl hdwy over 2f out: wknd over 1f out)	nk	12	20/1	31	12
4404[14]	**Backhander (IRE) (36)** (RTPhillips) **5-8-5b**(5) ANicholls(11) (chsd ldr over 5f: sn wknd)	¾	13	16/1	28	13
755[12]	**Ilandra (IRE) (34)** (GLMoore) **5-8-8** PDoe(17) (bkwd: sn bhd)	7	14	20/1	12	—
3820[8]	**Hotstepper (36)** (MrsSDWilliams) **4-8-5**(5) CCarver(16) (lw: a bhd)	2½	15	33/1	9	—
4016[19]	**Rockaroundtheclock (47)** (TRWatson) **3-9-0**(3) RStudholme(2) (bhd fnl 2f)	nk	16	33/1	19	—
2487[12]	**Misellina (FR) (45)** (RAkehurst) **3-8-10**(5) PFitzsimons(15) (lw: reard in stalls: ref to r: t.n.p)		R	6/1 [2]	—	—
2488[F]	***Spirit of Sport (30)*** (AGNewcombe) **4-8-1**(3) DMcGaffin(13) (Withdrawn not under Starter's orders: reard up & uns rdr s: dead)		W	50/1	—	—

(SP 134.0%) **17 Rn**

1m 40.6 (2.40) CSF £32.93 CT £330.80 TOTE £8.40: £1.80 £1.20 £3.00 £3.40 (£10.40) Trio £69.20 OWNER Mrs Barbara Jean Martin (LAMBOURN) BRED Green Meadow Stud and P. Crane

WEIGHT FOR AGE 3yo-4lb

3850 The Green Grey, without the visor this time, was a stone lower than when last in a handicap on turf and seemed suited by this return to a mile. (10/1)

4326 Ron's Round was not suited by this drop back to a mile. (11/4)

3329 One In The Eye is another who is better suited by further. (12/1)

1506 Hannalou (FR), who has dropped 20lb in the ratings, was more keen than ever with the fitting of the headgear. (16/1)

4043 Attarikh (IRE) had finished just in front of the runner-up on 3lb better terms over course and distance three weeks ago. (7/1)

3697 Swan Island has come down a total of 11lb following some disappointing performances. (20/1)

3134 Sharp Deed (IRE) (8/1: 6/1-9/1)

Misellina (FR) (6/1: 4/1-13/2)

T/Plpt: £1,186.40 (11.32 Tckts). T/Qdpt: £116.20 (5.24 Tckts) KH

3918-HAMILTON (R-H) (Good, Good to soft patches)
Monday September 29th

WEATHER: overcast WIND: almost nil

4466 BILL MCHARG MEMORIAL H'CAP (0-85) (3-Y.O+) (Class D)

2-20 (2-20) **1m 4f 17y** £4,838.50 (£1,468.00: £719.00: £344.50) Stalls: High GOING minus 0.20 sec per fur (GF)

Form	Horse	Dist	Pos	SP	RR	SF
3231[5]	**Totem Dancer (69)** (JLEyre) **4-9-2** KFallon(10) (lw: rr div: hdwy & swtchd 3f out: qcknd to ld ins fnl f: r.o)	—	1	7/1 [2]	82	59
4279[8]	**Lord Advocate (49)** (DANolan) **9-7-7b**(3) PFessey(6) (led: qcknd 3f out: hdd ins fnl f: kpt on wl)	1¾	2	25/1	60	37
4161[2]	**Classic Ballet (FR) (63)** (RGuest) **4-8-5**(5) CLowther(8) (lw: a chsng ldrs: outpcd 3f out: kpt on appr fnl f)	4	3	13/2 [1]	68	45
3916[12]	**Ciro's Pearl (IRE) (78)** (MHTompkins) **3-9-0**(3) TEDurcan(15) (mid div: effrt 4f out: styd on fnl 2f: nvr able chal)	½	4	9/1	83	52
4235[5]	**Summerhill Special (IRE) (65)** (DWBarker) **6-8-12** KDarley(9) (b.nr hind: a.p: hdwy & ev ch 4f out: outpcd fnl 2f)	s.h	5	7/1 [2]	70	47
4287[3]	**Exactly (IRE) (55)** (JLEyre) **4-8-2** TWilliams(2) (chsd ldrs tl grad wknd fnl 2f)	2½	6	7/1 [2]	56	33
4279[11]	**Mentalasanythin (60)** (DHaydnJones) **8-8-7** SDrowne(12) (in tch: outpcd 3f out: no imp after)	4	7	8/1 [3]	56	33
2421[4]	**Kathryn's Pet (64)** (MrsMReveley) **4-8-11** ACulhane(13) (bhd: gd hdwy on ins 5f out: sn in tch: one pce fnl 2f)	hd	8	12/1	60	37
3919*	**Craigary (50)** (MrsASwinbank) **6-7-8**(3)ow1 RFfrench(7) (lw: bhd: effrt 4f out: n.d)	½	9	12/1	45	21
4310[7]	**Sioux (75)** (CWThornton) **3-9-0** DeanMcKeown(3) (lw: hld up & bhd: effrt 5f out: hung rt & n.d)	1¾	10	10/1	68	37
746[7]	**Slasher Jack (IRE) (65)** (RAFahey) **6-8-5**(7) RWinston(5) (bhd: effrt & nt clr run 3½f out: n.d)	2½	11	25/1	55	32
3648[12]	**Happy Minstral (USA) (85)** (MJohnston) **3-9-10** DHolland(1) (lw: bhd: effrt 8f out: outpcd ent st: n.d)	3½	12	10/1	70	39
4279[W]	**Manful (74)** (MissLAPerratt) **5-9-7b** NKennedy(4) (chsd ldrs tl wknd fnl 3f)	3½	13	20/1	54	31
4160[9]	**Urgent Reply (USA) (55)** (CADwyer) **4-7-11**(5) IonaWands(17) (chsd ldrs: sn pushed along: wknd fnl 4f)	hd	14	14/1	35	12
	Canny Chronicle (49) (PMonteith) **9-7-10** JBramhill(16) (a bhd: t.o)	27	15	100/1	—	—
	Prophits Pride (IRE) (49) (PMonteith) **5-7-10** LCharnock(11) (lw: a bhd: t.o)	6	16	100/1	—	—
	Grog (IRE) (55) (BMactaggart) **8-8-2** JFanning(14) (bit bkwd: dwlt: a bhd: t.o)	s.h	17	100/1	—	—

(SP 127.6%) **17 Rn**

2m 35.8 (3.80) CSF £171.31 CT £1,105.52 TOTE £7.80: £1.40 £5.60 £1.50 £2.70 (£186.80) Trio £650.90; £247.54 to Newmarket 30/8/97 OWNER Diamond Racing Ltd (HAMBLETON) BRED Sheikh Mohammed Bin Rashid Al Maktoum

LONG HANDICAP Lord Advocate 7-6 Canny Chronicle 7-8 Prophits Pride (IRE) 7-1 Craigary 7-3

WEIGHT FOR AGE 3yo-8lb

1162 Totem Dancer, who certainly stays further than this, came from off the pace here to win in most determined style and there looks to be more to come. (7/1)

3921 Lord Advocate, although 4lb out of the handicap, was off a decent mark and, on a track he loves here, ran his heart out. There is only one meeting left at Musselburgh, the other track that he wins at these days, and unless he goes to the All-Weather, opportunities are few and far between. (25/1)

4161 Classic Ballet (FR) is a game and consistent sort but she seems held by the Handicapper on turf at the moment. (13/2)
2647 Ciro's Pearl (IRE), after two moderate efforts, showed something of her old form here but she was always struggling for speed. (9/1)
4235 Summerhill Special (IRE) keeps running consistently well and can pick up another race before the season ends. (7/1)
4287 Exactly (IRE), a stable-companion of the winner here, is running well just now. (7/1)
2421 Kathryn's Pet, a soft-ground specialist, ran a useful race after almost three months off. (12/1)

4467 GERBER LANDA & GEE CONDITIONS STKS (3-Y.O+) (Class C)

2-50 (2-50) **6f 5y** £5,017.60 (£1,878.40: £919.20: £396.00: £178.00: £90.80) Stalls: Low GOING minus 0.01 sec per fur (G)

				SP	RR	SF
4239[11]	**Brave Edge (103)** (RHannon) **6-9-0** DaneO'Neill(1) (lw: trckd ldrs: led appr fnl f: drvn out)	—	1	100/30[3]	96	58
4120[8]	**Open Credit (95)** (HRACecil) **3-8-7** KFallon(7) (lw: a.p: effrt & ev ch 2f out: nt qckn ins fnl f)	1¼	2	2/1[1]	88	48
4221[4]	**Venture Capitalist (92)** (DNicholls) **8-9-7** AlexGreaves(3) (hld up: effrt 2f out: kpt on ins fnl f: nvr able chal)	1½	3	14/1	96	58
4282[7]	**Ziggy's Dancer (USA) (89)** (EJAlston) **6-9-0** JFEgan(6) (lw: a chsng ldrs: rdn over 2f out: r.o one pce)	1¾	4	3/1[2]	84	46
4100[17]	**Indian Spark (100)** (WGMTurner) **3-8-9(3)** DSweeney(2) (led: edgd rt fnl 2f: hdd appr fnl f: no ex)	s.h	5	5/1	84	44
3922[12]	**Natural Key (68)** (DHaydnJones) **4-8-9** SDrowne(4) (cl up tl wknd over 1f out)	s.h	6	25/1	79	41
4280[28]	**Scharnhorst (65)** (ARDicken) **5-8-11(3)** ADaly(5) (b: cl up to ½-wy: sn rdn & btn)	7	7	200/1	65	27

(SP 109.1%) **7 Rn**

1m 12.7 (2.70) CSF £8.56 TOTE £3.90: £2.00 £1.80 (£4.70) OWNER Horris Vale Racing Partnership (MARLBOROUGH) BRED Mrs G. A. Whent
WEIGHT FOR AGE 3yo-2lb

4098 Brave Edge, who has been disappointing this season, was well handled here and found this drop in class right up his street and this will surely have boosted his confidence. (100/30)
4120 Open Credit, dropped back in trip for the first time this season, ran better but there was still little to come when pressure was seriously applied. (2/1)
4221 Venture Capitalist has the ability but does need things to go just right and, this season, they never really have. (14/1: op 7/1)
4282 Ziggy's Dancer (USA) is a difficult customer to weight up but, basically, he has plenty of ability when it suits him and it never did here. (3/1)
3447 Indian Spark has plenty of speed but was inclined to hang when the pressure was applied and ran out of fuel with a furlong to go. (5/1)
3484* Natural Key likes this track but had an impossible task in this company. (25/1)

4468 HAMILTON PARK (LORD HAMILTON OF DALZIEL) SERIES FINAL NURSERY H'CAP (2-Y.O) (Class C)

3-20 (3-21) **6f 5y** £8,335.00 (£2,530.00: £1,240.00: £595.00) Stalls: Low GOING minus 0.01 sec per fur (G)

				SP	RR	SF
3961a[4]	**Jacmar (IRE) (90)** (MissLAPerratt) **2-9-2** KFallon(10) (lw: bhd far side tl hdwy over 3f out: led appr fnl f: hung lft & r.o wl)	—	1	3/1[1]	93+	60
4362[4]	**Demolition Jo (76)** (PDEvans) **2-8-2v** JFEgan(6) (racd stands' side: in tch: hdwy ½-wy: hung rt appr fnl f: r.o)	1½	2	11/2[3]	75	42
4178[2]	**Pierpoint (IRE) (75)** (RAFahey) **2-7-8(7)ow2** RWinston(7) (lw: w ldrs far side: rdn over 2f out: kpt on)	hd	3	11/2[3]	74	39
4232[3]	**Friar Tuck (95)** (MissLAPerratt) **2-9-7** KDarley(12) (lw: sn chsng ldrs far side: led wl over 1f out tl appr fnl f: no ex)	1¼	4	5/1[2]	90	57
4173[7]	**One Singer (85)** (MJohnston) **2-8-11** DHolland(4) (sn outpcd & bhd stands' side: swtchd far side over 2f out & hdwy: wknd fnl f)	6	5	14/1	65	32
4401[2]	**Just Another Time (70)** (JBerry) **2-7-7(3)** RFfrench(2) (b: w ldrs stands' side: rdn ½-wy: no imp after)	4	6	25/1	39	6
3307[3]	**Sharp Cracker (IRE) (77)** (MJohnston) **2-8-3** JFanning(1) (racd stands' side: outpcd fr ½-wy)	½	7	14/1	45	12
4419[3]	**Ellenbrook (IRE) (70)** (JBerry) **2-7-7b(3)** PFessey(11) (led far side over 4f: wknd)	1½	8	14/1	34	1
4284[10]	**Baylham (72)** (JSGoldie) **2-7-12ow2** TWilliams(8) (chsd ldrs far side 4f: wknd)	3	9	50/1	28	—
4284[3]	**Cosmic Case (70)** (JSGoldie) **2-7-5(5)** APolli(3) (b: racd stands' side: nvr trbld ldrs)	1¾	10	25/1	21	—
4284[5]	**Vice Presidential (84)** (TJEtherington) **2-8-10** ACulhane(9) (cl up far side 4f: sn wknd)	nk	11	15/2	34	1
4054[17]	**Makahu Don (70)** (WTKemp) **2-7-3b(7)** PBradley(5) (led stands' side 4f: wknd qckly)	7	12	150/1	2	—

(SP 114.5%) **12 Rn**

1m 12.7 (2.70) CSF £16.12 CT £77.80 TOTE £3.70: £1.50 £2.50 £1.70 (£11.00) Trio £40.50 OWNER Mr John Marett (AYR) BRED Lodge Park Stud
LONG HANDICAP Just Another Time 7-7 Baylham 7-4 Cosmic Case 7-5 Ellenbrook (IRE) 7-8 Makahu Don 6-6

3961a Jacmar (IRE) goes particularly well on this track and had a good draw here and, given some determined assistance, the race was his once he found his stride from halfway. (3/1)
4362 Demolition Jo was 10lb better in with the winner for a head beating earlier in the season but she was not well drawn and having to race up the stands' side made a big difference. (11/2)
4178 Pierpoint (IRE) had a decent draw and ran a sound race but was never quite up to the task. (11/2)
4232 Friar Tuck was again edgy in the stalls but did run well and is perhaps better suited by a stiff five furlongs at the moment. (5/1)
3222 One Singer raced up the wrong side of the track until switching just after halfway and, after improving quickly, he had soon shot his bolt. This is best ignored. (14/1)
4401 Just Another Time raced up the unfavoured stands' side and had no chance from halfway. (25/1)
3307 Sharp Cracker (IRE) (14/1: op 8/1)

4469 ABERCROMBY MAIDEN STKS (3-Y.O) (Class D)

3-50 (3-51) **1m 1f 36y** £3,468.75 (£1,050.00: £512.50: £243.75) Stalls: High GOING minus 0.20 sec per fur (GF)

				SP	RR	SF
4060[12]	**Tyrolean Dream (IRE) (77)** (MHTompkins) **3-9-0** KFallon(6) (a.p: effrt ½-wy: styd on u.p to ld nr fin)	—	1	5/4[1]	57	35
4176[18]	**Slipstream Star (70)** (IABalding) **3-8-9** KDarley(1) (chsd ldr: led 3½f out: styd on u.p: edgd lft ins fnl f: jst ct)	s.h	2	5/4[1]	52	30
	Its My Pleasure (WSCunningham) **3-8-9** SSanders(10) (tall: unf: dwlt: nt clr run 3f out & 2f out: styd on wl towards fin)	9	3	100/1	36	14
3919[4]	**Sweet Note (IRE) (23)** (MissLAPerratt) **3-8-2(7)** JMcAuley(2) (bhd: gd hdwy 4f out: chsng ldrs 2f out: sn wknd)	nk	4	33/1	36	14
4290[9]	**Fantasy Flight** (MAPeill) **3-8-9** JCarroll(7) (rr div: effrt over 4f out: nvr rchd ldrs)	1	5	66/1	34	12
3991[6]	**San Francisco** (CWThornton) **3-9-0** DeanMcKeown(9) (bhd: effrt ½-wy: n.d)	4	6	6/1[2]	32	10
4290[12]	**The Munro's** (JSGoldie) **3-8-9(5)** APolli(3) (prom: ran wd st: sn wknd)	3½	7	66/1	26	4
2846[10]	**Mill Orchid** (JBerry) **3-8-6(3)** PFessey(5) (in tch 4f: sn wknd)	5	8	25/1[3]	12	—
4429[6]	**Al Ava Consonant (40)** (JDBethell) **3-8-9v[1]** DHolland(8) (led tl hdd 3½f out: wknd over 2f out)	9	9	33/1	—	—

4290[15] **Ballantrae Boy** (JSGoldie) **3-9-0** TWilliams(4) (chsd ldrs tl wknd over 4f out)....13 **10** 100/1 — —
(SP 117.9%) **10 Rn**

1m 59.7 (5.40) CSF £2.54 TOTE £2.40: £1.50 £1.10 £3.00 (£1.80) Trio £22.50 OWNER Mr P. Heath (NEWMARKET) BRED Miss Honora Corridan

Tyrolean Dream (IRE), who disappointed on his only previous run this season, needed plenty of help from the saddle and, staying particularly well, just made it. (5/4)

3463 Slipstream Star, trying her longest trip for a while, looked to have pinched it but, when serious pressure was applied, she just wanted to hang and was worried out of it. (5/4: evens-11/8)

Its My Pleasure, looking in need of this, met with a fair amount of trouble in running and, but for this, would have finished a good deal closer. (100/1)

3919 Sweet Note (IRE) has ability but is yet to put it to full use. (33/1)

Fantasy Flight is learning and may need further yet. (66/1)

3991 San Francisco looked pretty slow. (6/1)

4470 J. WATSON SCOTT & CO E.B.F. MEDIAN AUCTION MAIDEN STKS (2-Y.O) (Class F)

4-20 (4-20) **1m 65y** £2,780.00 (£780.00: £380.00) Stalls: High GOING minus 0.20 sec per fur (GF)

SP RR SF

4057[6] **Macca Luna (IRE)** (MHTompkins) **2-8-9** KFallon(6) (lw: chsd ldrs: led over 3f out: styd on wl: sn clr)....— **1** 4/9[1] 62+ 18
4236[14] **Always Trying** (MJohnston) **2-9-0** DHolland(7) (bhd & outpcd over 5f out: swtchd outside & styd on fnl 3½f: no ch w wnr)....11 **2** 5/1[2] 46 2
4163[8] **Ngaere Princess (40)** (WTKemp) **2-8-9** TWilliams(4) (a.p: effrt over 3f out: no imp)....½ **3** 66/1 40 —
3973[13] **Just Nobby (47)** (NTinkler) **2-9-0** KimTinkler(8) (led tl hdd over 3f out: sn outpcd)....3 **4** 33/1 39 —
4208[9] **Western Lord (46)** (CSmith) **2-9-0b** KDarley(1) (bhd tl styd on wl fnl 2f)....½ **5** 16/1[3] 38 —
1557[7] **Anka Lady (53)** (DMoffatt) **2-8-6**(3) DarrenMoffatt(5) (bit bkwd: trckd ldrs: effrt over 3f out: wknd fnl 2½f)....1½ **6** 16/1[3] 30 —
4278[11] **Nebuchadnezzar** (JJO'Neill) **2-8-11**(3) TEDurcan(9) (effrt after 3f: sn rdn & n.d)....1¾ **7** 16/1[3] 32 —
3060[9] **Lavernock Lady** (JJQuinn) **2-8-9** SDrowne(2) (a rr div)....hd **8** 33/1 27 —
3563[11] **Petite Tache** (NChamberlain) **2-8-9** DeanMcKeown(10) (stdd s: a bhd)....11 **9** 100/1 5 —
432[14] **The Other Risk** (DANolan) **2-9-0** JCarroll(3) (a bhd: wl t.o)....dist **10** 25/1 — —
(SP 115.8%) **10 Rn**

1m 50.4 (6.30) CSF £2.41 TOTE £1.60: £1.10 £1.60 £5.20 (£2.80) Trio £30.90 OWNER Mr B. McAllister (NEWMARKET) BRED Ash Hill Stud

Macca Luna (IRE) found this uncompetitive event just what she needed and, although there was nothing really impressive about her performance, she did gallop on splendidly to win as she pleased and her confidence should have been boosted no end. (4/9)

Always Trying is just an out-and-out galloper, who needs time and space to manoeuvre and is still learning. (5/1)

3866 Ngaere Princess, who has previously looked a short runner, did much better over this extended trip. (66/1)

Just Nobby had shown little previously and, apart from the winner and probably the runner-up, this was a pretty poor event. (33/1)

611 Anka Lady, having her first run since the end of May, obviously needed it and, taking a step up in trip, blew up in the last two and a half furlongs. (16/1)

4471 BRYCELAND ENTERTAINMENT H'CAP (0-60) (I) (3-Y.O+) (Class F)

4-50 (4-51) **1m 65y** £2,416.00 (£676.00: £328.00) Stalls: High GOING minus 0.20 sec per fur (GF)

SP RR SF

4184[2] **Shontaine (55)** (MJohnston) **4-9-11** DHolland(10) (lw: a cl up: led appr fnl f: r.o wl)....— **1** 13/2[3] 65 46
4164[4] **Katie Komaite (39)** (CaptJWilson) **4-8-9v** KDarley(15) (hld up: nt clr run over 3f tl over 1f out: styd on wl towards fin)....½ **2** 9/1 48 29
3759[11] **Winston (48)** (JDBethell) **4-9-4** KFallon(2) (mid div: hdwy 2f out: disp ld appr fnl f: no ex towards fin)....s.h **3** 6/1[2] 57 38
4415[4] **Raindeer Quest (47)** (JLEyre) **5-9-3** RLappin(4) (hld up & bhd: hdwy on ins & prom over 4f out: sn rdn: styd on towards fin)....1½ **4** 6/1[2] 53 34
1560[4] **Stormless (58)** (JSGoldie) **6-10-0** TWilliams(12) (trckd ldrs: led over 3f tl appr fnl f: grad wknd)....1¾ **5** 14/1 61 42
2660[11] **Principal Boy (IRE) (48)** (TJEtherington) **4-9-4** DaleGibson(13) (trckd ldrs: effrt over 2f out: btn over 1f out) 2½ **6** 16/1 46 27
3630[7] **Habeta (USA) (34)** (JWWatts) **11-8-1**(3) RFfrench(8) (mid div: effrt over 3f out: nvr rchd ldrs)....½ **7** 16/1 31 12
4161[4] **Sing And Dance (43)** (EWeymes) **4-8-8**(5) CLowther(1) (lw: bhd: sme hdwy over 2f out: n.d)....1¼ **8** 12/1 38 19
3565[5] **Miss Pigalle (36)** (MissLAPerratt) **6-8-6b** JCarroll(11) (chsd ldrs tl rdn & btn over 2f out)....½ **9** 14/1 30 11
3476[3] **Cee-Jay-Ay (36)** (JBerry) **10-8-3**(3) PRoberts(9) (s.i.s: sme hdwy 3f out: n.d)....¾ **10** 14/1 28 9
4415[11] **Great Bear (40)** (DWChapman) **5-8-10** LCharnock(7) (in tch tl wknd over 3f out)....½ **11** 100/1 31 12
3972[3] **Nobby Barnes (42)** (DonEnricoIncisa) **8-8-12** KimTinkler(5) (s.i.s: n.d)....2 **12** 12/1 29 10
3937[4] **Scenicris (IRE) (49)** (RHollinshead) **4-9-5** FLynch(14) (effrt 4f out: sn wknd)....6 **13** 6/1[2] 25 6
4043* **Murron Wallace (49)** (DHaydnJones) **3-9-1** SDrowne(3) (effrt on outside 4f out: n.d)....½ **14** 5/1[1] 24 1
4233[20] **Another Nightmare (IRE) (46)** (RMMcKellar) **5-9-2** SSanders(16) (led tl hdd over 3f out: sn wknd)....10 **15** 33/1 1 —
Jamaica Bridge (40) (MrsAMNaughton) **7-8-10** ACulhane(6) (chsd ldrs tl wknd qckly 4f out: t.o)....24 **16** 100/1 — —
(SP 134.9%) **16 Rn**

1m 48.9 (4.80) CSF £64.57 CT £366.82 TOTE £5.60: £2.30 £2.40 £2.70 £2.30 (£32.60) Trio £111.40 OWNER Mr Paul Dean (MIDDLEHAM) BRED Mark Johnston Racing Ltd

WEIGHT FOR AGE 3yo-4lb

4184 Shontaine is a game sort who is very versatile, regarding both trip and ground, and is now in top form. (13/2)

4164 Katie Komaite is yet to win a race and, although she was unlucky here, the question is, can she be relied upon to do it next time? (9/1)

3573 Winston had an impossible draw and was always being forced wide, probably losing more ground than he was beaten by. (6/1)

4415 Raindeer Quest is running consistently well and surely a modest race can be found, even though she is not one to fully rely on. (6/1)

1560 Stormless ran a cracking race after four months off and is obviously in good heart. (14/1)

2385 Principal Boy (IRE), a winner twice already on this track this season, put in a decent effort here after almost three months off. (16/1)

4161 Sing And Dance (12/1: 8/1-14/1)

4472 BRYCELAND ENTERTAINMENT H'CAP (0-60) (II) (3-Y.O+) (Class F)

5-20 (5-22) **1m 65y** £2,402.00 (£672.00: £326.00) Stalls: High GOING minus 0.20 sec per fur (GF)

SP RR SF

3622[10] **Pine Ridge Lad (IRE) (50)** (JLEyre) **7-9-6** RLappin(12) (mde all: clr ½-wy: styd on)....— **1** 14/1 60 36
3627[2] **Seconds Away (35)** (JSGoldie) **6-8-5** TWilliams(6) (a in tch: hdwy 3f out: styd on: nt pce to chal)....2 **2** 10/1 41 17
4210[8] **Spanish Verdict (49)** (DenysSmith) **10-9-5** KFallon(16) (lw: a chsng ldrs: effrt 3f out: rdn & r.o one pce: nvr able chal)....s.h **3** 9/2[1] 55 31
3976[5] **Denton Lad (59)** (WTKemp) **3-9-11b**[1] JCarroll(1) (hld up: effrt over 2f out: styd on: nvr able chal)....1½ **4** 14/1 62 34

4164[5]	**Tarradale (40)** (CBBBooth) **3-8-6** LCharnock(10) (prom: hdwy to chse wnr over 2f out: wknd over 1f out)	½	**5**	20/1	42	14
4182[5]	**Il Falco (FR) (52)** (SirMarkPrescott) **3-9-4** SSanders(4) (lw: in tch: outpcd over 2f out: btn whn hmpd appr fnl f)	2½	**6**	6/1[3]	49	21
3813*	**Tipperary Sunset (IRE) (50)** (JJQuinn) **3-8-9(7)** PBradley(3) (lw: effrt ½-wy: styd on: nvr rchd ldrs)	s.h	**7**	11/2[2]	47	19
3465[4]	**Vanborough Lad (44)** (MJBolton) **8-8-11(3)** RFfrench(7) (lw: chsd ldrs: outpcd 3f out: no imp after)	¾	**8**	9/2[1]	40	16
4228[10]	**Warrior King (IRE) (52)** (CADwyer) **3-9-4** JFEgan(9) (rr div: effrt over 4f out: nvr rchd ldrs)	hd	**9**	9/1	48	20
3627[8]	**Miletrian City (43)** (MissLAPerratt) **4-8-6b(7)** JMcAuley(14) (s.s: hdwy on outside 2f out: hung rt: n.d)	1¼	**10**	16/1	36	12
4228[2]	**Axeman (IRE) (40)** (MartynWane) **5-8-7(3)** AWhelan(2) (bhd: hdwy on ins ½-wy: sn in tch: wknd fnl 2f)	1	**11**	6/1[3]	31	7
3886[8]	**Jimjareer (IRE) (35)** (CaptJWilson) **4-8-5ow2** KDarley(8) (n.d)	2	**12**	25/1	22	—
3336[7]	**Samspet (44)** (RAFahey) **3-8-3(7)** RWinston(15) (chsd ldrs tl wknd 3f out)	2½	**13**	16/1	27	—
3336[5]	**Tribal Mischief (42)** (DMoffatt) **3-8-5(3)** DarrenMoffatt(11) (a bhd)	5	**14**	16/1	15	—
4304[11]	**Good Day (57)** (CWThornton) **3-9-9b** DeanMcKeown(5) (chsd ldrs to ½-wy: sn wknd)	2½	**15**	66/1	25	—
1043[13]	**Broctune Line (45)** (MrsMReveley) **3-8-11** ACulhane(13) (a bhd)	3½	**16**	20/1	6	—
				(SP 145.3%)		**16 Rn**

1m 49.5 (5.40) CSF £153.51 CT £723.50 TOTE £12.90: £2.80 £1.70 £2.70 £3.70 (£164.90) Trio £365.40 OWNER Whitestonecliffe Racing Partnership (HAMBLETON) BRED Whitechurch Stud in Ireland

WEIGHT FOR AGE 3yo-4lb

3264 Pine Ridge Lad (IRE), on a track suited to front-runners, had his own way throughout and, once he poached a clear lead approaching halfway, was never going to be caught. (14/1)

3627 Seconds Away is difficult to win with but he did stay on here, suggesting that further might well help. (10/1)

4210 Spanish Verdict had no excuses this time, other than the ground might just have been slightly slower than he ideally prefers. (9/2)

3976 Denton Lad, poorly drawn, ran pretty well and is obviously on good terms with himself. (14/1: op 8/1)

4164 Tarradale has ability but, as yet, has not come up with the goods. (20/1)

2773 Il Falco (FR) left the impression that longer trips might well suit. (6/1)

T/Jkpt: £2,241.50 (17.19 Tckts). T/Plpt: £7.60 (4,026.99 Tckts). T/Qdpt: £4.00 (543.73 Tckts) AA

3770-**NEWMARKET** (R-H) (Good to firm, St Good)

Tuesday September 30th

WEATHER: overcast WIND: slt across

4473 E.B.F. JERSEY LILY NURSERY H'CAP (2-Y.O F) (Class C)

12-50 (12-53) **7f (Rowley)** £18,260.00 (£5,480.00: £2,640.00: £1,220.00) Stalls: Low GOING minus 0.28 sec per fur (GF)

				SP	RR	SF
4166*	**Golden Fortune (68)** (DRLoder) **2-7-10(3)** MHenry(9) (a.p: rdn over 1f out: led ins fnl f: r.o)	—	**1**	5/1[1]	78	43
4185*	**Belle de Nuit (IRE) (77)** (BJMeehan) **2-8-8** KFallon(15) (led tl ins fnl f: r.o)	1	**2**	11/1	85	50
4362[3]	**Inchalong (71)** (MBrittain) **2-7-9(7)** DMernagh(5) (trckd ldrs: outpcd 2f out: kpt on appr fnl f)	4	**3**	20/1	70	35
4366[2]	**Constant Attention (65)** (PMitchell) **2-7-7(3)** RFfrench(7) (hdwy over 1f out: nrst fin)	3	**4**	33/1	57	22
4097[4]	**Occhi Verdi (IRE) (81)** (MJohnston) **2-8-12** DHolland(14) (swtg: hld up: rdn 2f out: styd on fnl f)	nk	**5**	6/1[2]	72	37
3961a[10]	**Fayrana (IRE) (80)** (JWHills) **2-8-11** MHills(11) (chsd ldrs 5f)	hd	**6**	10/1	71	36
4097[16]	**Pacifica (88)** (RBoss) **2-9-5** TQuinn(6) (lw: prom: pushed along over 3f out: no imp)	hd	**7**	33/1	79	44
4116[6]	**Chinaider (IRE) (76)** (DNicholls) **2-8-7** KDarley(3) (nvr nr to chal)	hd	**8**	10/1	66	31
4097[14]	**Star of Grosvenor (IRE) (82)** (PWChapple-Hyam) **2-8-13** JReid(13) (lw: in tch: rdn over 2f out: sn btn)	nk	**9**	20/1	72	37
4216[8]	**Tullich Refrain (65)** (WRMuir) **2-7-10** MartinDwyer(10) (lw: dwlt: hld up & plld hrd: no ch fnl 2f)	3½	**10**	10/1	47	12
3889[3]	**Salsette (80)** (CEBrittain) **2-8-11** MRoberts(1) (dwlt: bhd: plld out over 1f out: no imp)	1¾	**11**	12/1	58	23
3904[9]	**Next Round (IRE) (85)** (MBell) **2-9-2** MFenton(2) (swtg: hld up: a bhd)	nk	**12**	20/1	62	27
4097[13]	**Phone Alex (IRE) (76)** (RHannon) **2-8-7** DaneO'Neill(4) (dwlt: rdn 3f out: a bhd)	nk	**13**	20/1	52	17
4227*	**Madame Claude (IRE) (74)** (JARToller) **2-8-5** SSanders(12) (prom over 4f)	14	**14**	8/1[3]	18	—
4218[2]	**Saffron Lane (IRE) (90)** (RHannon) **2-9-7** LDettori(8) (in tch: rdn over 3f out: sn wl bhd)	½	**15**	6/1[2]	33	—
				(SP 124.6%)		**15 Rn**

1m 26.01 (1.51) CSF £50.01 CT £958.69 TOTE £8.60: £2.50 £2.90 £4.00 (£61.40) Trio £254.50 OWNER Lucayan Stud (NEWMARKET) BRED P. D. and Mrs Player

LONG HANDICAP Constant Attention 7-8

4166* Golden Fortune has been a revelation since her statutory three runs for a handicap mark and won in good style eventually, having rather hung fire when challenging in the Dip. (5/1)

4185* Belle de Nuit (IRE) tried to force the pace for the first time and did not go down without quite a scrap, the first two pulling nicely clear. (11/1: 8/1-12/1)

4362 Inchalong is no oil painting but tries hard and, despite being outpaced, kept plugging away for her placing. (20/1)

4366 Constant Attention, having her first run for a new yard, was not suited by the drop in distance and was doing all her best work when the race was over. (33/1)

4097 Occhi Verdi (IRE), who got warm by the time the horses left the paddock, was ridden to get the trip but was never doing enough. (6/1)

3961a Fayrana (IRE) looked to find this trip a touch too far, given the uphill finish. (10/1)

3638* Star of Grosvenor (IRE) seemed harshly handicapped and more patient tactics did not change things. (20/1)

4042 Tullich Refrain (10/1: 7/1-11/1)

4474 TATTERSALLS HOUGHTON SALES CONDITIONS STKS (2-Y.O) (Class B)

1-30 (1-31) **7f (Rowley)** £18,634.80 (£6,913.20: £3,331.60: £1,378.00: £564.00: £238.40) Stalls: Low GOING minus 0.28 sec per fur (GF)

				SP	RR	SF
4105*	**Tamarisk (IRE)** (RCharlton) **2-9-0** TSprake(14) (lw: mde all: qcknd clr over 1f out: pushed out)	—	**1**	5/4[1]	106+	69
4267[2]	**Sapphire Ring (95)** (RCharlton) **2-8-9** KDarley(13) (lw: a.p: chsd wnr wl over 1f out: no imp)	3½	**2**	7/1[3]	93	56
	Putuna (IABalding) **2-8-9** MartinDwyer(6) (wl grwn: lw: hld up: hdwy over 1f out: r.o)	5	**3**	33/1	82	45
3706[3]	**Headhunter (IRE)** (WJHaggas) **2-9-0** MHills(12) (chsd ldrs: styd on same pce fnl 2f)	1¾	**4**	9/2[2]	83	46
	Magic of Aloha (IRE) (BWHills) **2-8-9** DHolland(9) (w'like: scope: plld hrd: w wnr over 4f: btn whn edgd lft 1f out)	nk	**5**	25/1	77	40
3839a*	**Photogenic** (APO'Brien,Ireland) **2-8-9** RHills(4) (gd sort: lw: hld up & bhd: hdwy whn n.m.r 1f out: swtchd & r.o nr fin)	¾	**6**	8/1	75	38
4237[13]	**Pantar (IRE)** (IABalding) **2-9-0** TQuinn(2) (lw: in tch: pushed along 3f out: btn whn n.m.r ins fnl f)	nk	**7**	12/1	80	43

Razor (SCWilliams) **2-9-0** DaneO'Neill(1) (cmpt: b.hind: dwlt: bhd: plld out over 1f out: nvr nr ldrs) ....nk **8** 33/1 79 42
1531a[10] **Apache Red (IRE)** (JSBolger,Ireland) **2-9-0** JReid(3) (neat: lw: plld hrd: in tch: btn whn hmpd ins fnl f) ....¾ **9** 33/1 77 40
3322[4] **Circus** (CEBrittain) **2-9-0** MRoberts(5) (plld hrd: prom: rdn 3f out: wkng whn hmpd ins fnl f)..........................1½ **10** 33/1 74 37
4064[7] **Ridgeway (IRE)** (GWragg) **2-9-0** PaulEddery(11) (lw: carried rt s: rdn & hdwy over 3f out: wknd 2f out).......1¼ **11** 14/1 71 34
4103[5] **Night Owl** (RCharlton) **2-8-9** KFallon(10) (lw: carried rt s: hld up: a bhd)...2 **12** 33/1 61 24
Xwife (IRE) (WNeuroth,Norway) **2-8-9** LDettori(7) (w'like: chsd ldrs: rdn & wknd over 3f out) ....17 **13** 25/1 22 —
(SP 123.0%) **13 Rn**

1m 25.02 (0.52) CSF £8.81 TOTE £2.30: £1.50 £2.30 £7.80 (£5.50) Trio £74.90 OWNER Highclere Thoroughbred Racing Ltd (BECKHAMPTON) BRED Mount Coote Stud

IN-FOCUS: **In addition to the basic prizemoney, Tamarisk won his owners a bonus of £100,000, while Sapphire Ring earned £50,000 for finishing second plus £30,000 for being the first filly home.**

4105* Tamarisk (IRE), who has a marvellous action, was stepped up in class but confirmed the impression he left at Kempton, quickening in great style from the front. On pedigree, he has a great chance of getting a mile and, whether he is supplemented for the Dewhurst or not, he looks a serious Guineas prospect for next year. (5/4)

4267 Sapphire Ring, taken to post steadily after the others, did not seem hindered by the step up in trip and came home well but her stable-companion had first run and she was not going well enough to do anything about it. (7/1: 5/1-8/1)

Putuna, a tall if slightly narrow newcomer, is a half-sister to Tykeyvor and, after showing a good action going down, she finished strongly when switched to the outside entering the Dip. (33/1)

3706 Headhunter (IRE), in the same ownership as the winner, stuck to his task well but was unable to quicken up to any noticeable degree. (9/2)

Magic of Aloha (IRE), still on the leg but with scope to develop, ran surprisingly well given that she seemed far too keen both going down and in the first half-mile coming back. Clearly tired in the Dip, she rolled into the whip, causing quite a bit of mayhem behind. (25/1)

3839a* Photogenic, the chosen runner for the powerful O'Brien team, was never travelling terribly well but was making significant strides when stopped in his tracks. He could well have made the first four but for the interference. (8/1: op 5/1)

Apache Red (IRE), another who took a strong hold early on, was beginning to fade when Reid was forced to stand up in the irons inside the final furlong. He should have finished a little closer. (33/1)

4064 Ridgeway (IRE) (14/1: 10/1-16/1)

4475 SHADWELL STUD CHEVELEY PARK STKS (Gp 1) (2-Y.O F) (Class A)

2-00 (2-00) **6f (Rowley)** £69,700.49 (£25,879.50: £12,489.75: £5,186.25: £2,143.13: £925.88) Stalls: Low GOING minus 0.28 sec per fur (GF)

SP RR SF

3723[2] **Embassy (100)** (DRLoder) **2-8-11** KFallon(3) (hld up: pushed along 4f out: hdwy to ld 1f out: rdn & qcknd clr) ....— **1** 5/2[2] 106 65
2558[2] **Crazee Mental (100)** (DHaydnJones) **2-8-11** DHolland(2) (lw: bhd: nt clr run 2f out: plld out over 1f out: str run fnl f: edgd lft nr fin) 2½ **2** 16/1 99 58
4103* **Royal Shyness** (GLewis) **2-8-11** PaulEddery(4) (hld up: hdwy 2f out: r.o fnl f)................................1¼ **3** 16/1 96 55
3723* **Cape Verdi (IRE) (100)** (PWChapple-Hyam) **2-8-11** JReid(6) (hld up: rdn 3f out: styd on appr fnl f)...............1¼ **4** 11/8[1] 93 52
4093a[4] **Heeremandi (IRE)** (APO'Brien,Ireland) **2-8-11v[1]** MJKinane(8) (w'like: prom: led over 1f out: wandered & sn hdd: one pce) ....nk **5** 20/1 92 51
3723[3] **Nadwah (USA) (100)** (PTWalwyn) **2-8-11** RHills(5) (lw: prom: rdn over 2f out: wknd fnl f) 1½ **6** 10/1 88 47
3574* **Shmoose (IRE)** (SbinSuroor) **2-8-11** LDettori(1) (led wl over 4f: sn wknd)...2½ **7** 11/2[3] 81 40
3723[4] **Miss Zafonic (FR) (100)** (RHannon) **2-8-11** DaneO'Neill(7) (lw: stdd s: plld hrd: sn w ldrs: wknd wl over 1f out) ....nk **8** 16/1 80 39
(SP 117.6%) **8 Rn**

1m 12.26 (0.46) CSF £38.59 TOTE £3.60: £1.10 £2.40 £3.90 (£22.40) OWNER Sheikh Mohammed (NEWMARKET) BRED Sheikh Mohammed bin Rashid al Maktoum

3723 Embassy seemed to handle this faster ground well although it did not always look that way as she appeared to be being bustled along in typical Fallon style after just a couple of furlongs. Sticking to the stands' side, she looked uncertain to get a run until Miss Zafonic weakened. Once in the gap, she quickened in superb style to put her seal on the race in a matter of strides. Not over-big, she ought to just about get a mile on pedigree but has so much speed that this cannot be a certainty. (5/2)

2558 Crazee Mental, second best at least on merit, could be regarded as a touch unfortunate, as the winner got the run that might have come her way, necessitating her being switched wide. Finding a tremendous burst, her tendency to hang was much less pronounced than in the past, only showing when in the clear towards the centre of the track near the finish. It looks likely that six furlongs is her trip. (16/1)

4103* Royal Shyness did not show the blinding speed of the first two but still came home in fine style. She shapes as if sure to get further. (16/1)

3723* Cape Verdi (IRE) found six furlongs too sharp, particularly with no great pace on through the first quarter-mile. Off the bit once the tempo increased, she just kept staying on. She has had no luck with the ground since her debut as early drizzle took any sting out of the ground. Now joining the Godolphin team, she would merit enormous respect in a fast-ground 1,000 Guineas or Oaks, as her pedigree offers great hope of stamina, making the decision to come here rather than the Fillies' Mile at Ascot a trifle hard to fathom. (11/8)

4093a Heeremandi (IRE), dropped back in trip, wore a first-time visor but still wandered around when briefly hitting the front. Outpaced rather than outstayed, her recent efforts in Ireland and France would suggest that this was an excellent renewal. (20/1)

3723 Nadwah (USA), speedily-bred, failed to confirm Ascot placings with Crazee Mental and, the way this was run, did not seem to see out the sixth furlong as she had appeared to do at York. (10/1: 8/1-12/1)

3574* Shmoose (IRE), very weak in the market, has an awkward head carriage and did not seem to be helping her pilot once battle commenced. Her dam was slightly wayward on occasions and it is to be hoped that she is not going the same way. (11/2: 5/2-6/1)

4476 NGK SPARK PLUGS RATED STKS H'CAP (0-100) (3-Y.O+) (Class B)

2-40 (2-41) **1m 4f (Rowley)** £8,064.96 (£2,984.64: £1,432.32: £585.60: £232.80: £91.68) Stalls: High GOING minus 0.28 sec per fur (GF)

SP RR SF

4136[8] **Solo Mio (IRE) (92)** (BWHills) **3-8-12** MHills(1) (chsd ldr: led over 2f out: clr over 1f out: styd on wl) ....— **1** 9/1 104 65
4101[11] **Kilma (USA) (87)** (LMCumani) **3-8-7** LDettori(9) (in tch: hdwy over 1f out: r.o fnl f) ....2½ **2** 7/2[1] 96 57
4002* **Dance So Suite (93)** (PFICole) **5-9-7** TQuinn(4) (b: trckd ldrs: rdn over 2f out: one pce appr fnl f) ....¾ **3** 7/2[1] 101 70
3112[13] **Forza Figlio (87)** (RAkehurst) **4-9-1** SSanders(7) (b.nr hind: hdwy over 2f out: sn rdn: no imp fnl f) ....1½ **4** 6/1[3] 93 62
3125[10] **Assured Gamble (83)** (CEBrittain) **3-8-3** MRoberts(2) (swtg: led tl hdd over 2f out: wknd fnl f) 3 **5** 10/1 85 46
3648[9] **Papua (90)** (IABalding) **3-8-10** KDarley(3) (swtg: hld up: hdwy over 4f out: rdn 3f out: sn btn) 1¼ **6** 14/1 90 51
2108[6] **Inchcailloch (IRE) (82)** (JSKing) **8-8-7**(3) RFfrench(6) (in tch: outpcd over 4f out: styd on wl fnl f)..................2 **7** 25/1 79 48
4294[12] **Hajr (IRE) (87)** (EALDunlop) **3-8-7** KFallon(5) (lw: dwlt: hld up: rdn over 4f out: nvr nr ldrs) ....1¾ **8** 5/1[2] 82 43
4294[5] **Bali Paradise (USA) (93)** (PFICole) **3-8-13** MJKinane(8) (swtg: chsd ldrs tl wknd over 2f out) ....½ **9** 8/1 87 48

			Pos	SP	RR	SF
2589[8]	**Mister Pink (82)** (RFJohnsonHoughton) **3-8-2** MartinDwyer(10) (rdn over 4f out: a bhd)	4	**10**	20/1	71	32
				(SP 120.9%)		**10 Rn**

2m 31.75 (1.25) CSF £38.35 CT £123.91 TOTE £9.40: £2.20 £1.90 £2.00 (£16.20) Trio £23.80 OWNER Mr Wafic Said (LAMBOURN) BRED London Thoroughbred Services Ltd and Roncon Ltd

WEIGHT FOR AGE 3yo-8lb

2107 Solo Mio (IRE) has not prospered the way that looked possible earlier in the year but, with more forcing tactics again employed, could be called the winner some way from home. (9/1)

2291* Kilma (USA), dropped back to her winning trip, did little but stay on once in the clear. (7/2)

4002* Dance So Suite, raised in class and up steeply in the handicap after his Epsom win, did not do too badly in the circumstances. (7/2)

2764 Forza Figlio lacks gears and is going to need things to go his own way to win off this sort of mark unless a further step up in distance can improve him. (6/1)

1218* Assured Gamble, back in his front-running role, was broken by the winner passing the Bushes but showed enough to suggest he is back in form. (10/1)

2765 Papua, the winner of the sales race on this day last year, has done precious little since and looked none too enthusiastic. (14/1)

2108 Inchcailloch (IRE), over a trip well short of his best, was just beginning to get going as the race ended and this should be ideal preparation for his defence of the Cesarewitch. (25/1)

3773 Hajr (IRE) was stepping up in trip but that alone cannot account for such a moderate display. (5/1)

4294 Bali Paradise (USA) (8/1: 6/1-9/1)

4477 SHADWELL STUD SERIES FINAL APPRENTICE H'CAP (0-85) (3-Y.O+) (Class E)

3-10 (3-11) **1m 2f (Rowley)** £7,165.00 (£2,170.00: £1,060.00: £505.00) Stalls: Low GOING minus 0.28 sec per fur (GF)

			Pos	SP	RR	SF
4223[2]	**Flint Knapper (80)** (GWragg) **3-9-6** GMilligan(8) (lw: hld up: hdwy over 3f out: sn rdn: styd on to ld post)	—	**1**	3/1[1]	89	72
41517	**Mattimeo (IRE) (80)** (APJarvis) **4-9-12** PRoberts(5) (hld up: hdwy 2f out: led ins fnl f: hung rt: ct post)	s.h	**2**	7/1[3]	89	78
4210[4]	**Polar Prospect (56)** (BHanbury) **4-8-2** JWilkinson(6) (b: w ldr: led over 1f out tl ins fnl f: r.o)	nk	**3**	9/2[2]	64	53
4141[10]	**Zoom Up (IRE) (80)** (MJHeaton-Ellis) **3-9-6b[1]** ADaly(3) (chsd ldrs: n.m.r 1f out: kpt on same pce)	1¼	**4**	20/1	86	69
4310[5]	**Mardrew (63)** (JohnBerry) **3-8-3** JoHunnam(7) (lw: hld up: hdwy over 2f out: lost pl over 1f out: r.o nr fin)	2	**5**	14/1	66	49
4136[12]	**Time for Action (IRE) (75)** (MHTompkins) **5-9-7** TEDurcan(4) (led tl over 1f out: sn btn)	s.h	**6**	11/1	78	67
4108[9]	**Mutadarra (IRE) (68)** (WJMusson) **4-9-0** DSweeney(10) (swtg: hld up: hdwy whn n.m.r over 1f out: hmpd ins fnl f: nt rcvr)	¾	**7**	9/1	70	59
4308[9]	**Fancy A Fortune (IRE) (62)** (DNicholls) **3-7-11**(5) ANicholls(2) (chsd ldrs tl rdn & wknd over 3f out)	7	**8**	16/1	53	36
4224[2]	**Guesstimation (USA) (60)** (JPearce) **8-8-6** RMullen(13) (b.hind: hld up & plld hrd: rdn 2f out: nvr nr ldrs)	2	**9**	10/1	48	37
4063[16]	**Bear Hug (72)** (LadyHerries) **4-9-4** PDoe(9) (prom: ev ch over 2f out: sn rdn & btn)	4	**10**	11/1	53	42
4319[9]	**Golden Ace (IRE) (56)** (RCSpicer) **4-8-2** RWinston(1) (rdn 3f out: a bhd)	3	**11**	12/1	32	21
3992[17]	**Absolute Liberty (USA) (67)** (SPCWoods) **3-8-7** RFfrench(12) (chsd ldrs 7f)	3	**12**	12/1	39	22
933[15]	**Blurred (IRE) (80)** (MHTompkins) **4-9-5**(7) JSavage(14) (hdwy 5f out: wknd qckly over 3f out)	17	**13**	20/1	24	13
	Classic Defence (IRE) (70) (JWHills) **4-9-2** PPMurphy(11) (b: bhd fnl 4f)	9	**14**	33/1	—	—
				(SP 131.8%)		**14 Rn**

2m 5.83 (1.13) CSF £23.27 CT £92.84 TOTE £3.30: £1.90 £2.90 £2.60 (£16.10) Trio £26.70 OWNER Mr A. E. Oppenheimer (NEWMARKET) BRED Hascombe and Valiant Studs

WEIGHT FOR AGE 3yo-6lb

4223 Flint Knapper does not do anything quickly and needed every yard of the trip to get his head in front. A lightly-raced half-brother to Don Michelotto, he has a fine action and should make further progress, possibly over further. (3/1)

4151 Mattimeo (IRE) should have won. Produced on the outside, he had nothing to race with and came off a true line, surrendering the advantage by the narrowest of margins. (7/1)

4210 Polar Prospect, upped in trip, was given a positive ride after taking a good hold early and saw out the trip. (9/2)

3408 Zoom Up (IRE), stepped up in trip, did not have much room when switching in the Dip but could not have got much closer. (20/1)

4310 Mardrew moved down poorly as usual and a promising move ended abruptly going into the Dip, only for him to run on again late on meeting rising ground. (14/1)

626a Time for Action (IRE) made the running as usual but lasted longer than he has been doing of late and may be returning to form. (11/1)

4108 Mutadarra (IRE), who needs to be held up, ran two good races on the July course in the summer and would have run another here but for a nightmare passage. (9/1: 6/1-10/1)

4478 E.B.F. GEI INTERNATIONAL MAIDEN STKS (2-Y.O C & G) (Class D)

3-45 (3-45) **1m (Rowley)** £5,435.50 (£1,624.00: £777.00: £353.50) Stalls: Low GOING minus 0.28 sec per fur (GF)

			Pos	SP	RR	SF
4157[2]	**Success And Glory (IRE) (89)** (HRACecil) **2-8-11** KFallon(7) (trckd ldrs: rdn to ld wl over 1f out: styd on wl)	—	**1**	11/10[1]	93	40
1607[3]	**Way Out Yonder** (BWHills) **2-8-11** MHills(3) (led: hdd wl over 1f out: sn rdn & one pce)	5	**2**	3/1[2]	83	30
	Jamorin Dancer (MAJarvis) **2-8-11** RCochrane(4) (w'like: chsd ldr: rdn over 2f out: sn outpcd)	4	**3**	16/1	75	22
	Free As The Wind (IRE) (PWChapple-Hyam) **2-8-11** JReid(6) (w'like: bkwd: hld up: effrt over 2f out: no imp)	1	**4**	10/1	73	20
	Almandab (IRE) (JHMGosden) **2-8-11** LDettori(5) (wl grwn: bit bkwd: dwlt: hld up: rdn 2f out: no imp)	s.h	**5**	5/1[3]	73	20
	Banker Dwerry (FR) (SPCWoods) **2-8-11** NDay(1) (wl grwn: bkwd: chsd ldrs: rdn over 4f out: sn btn)	5	**6**	33/1	63	10
	Freddie Mac (IRE) (GCBravery) **2-8-11** DRMcCabe(2) (w'like: leggy: s.s: plld hrd: wl bhd fnl 3f)	12	**7**	40/1	39	—
	Pinsharp (IRE) (PHowling) **2-8-11** PaulEddery(8) (w'like: scope: bit bkwd: wl bhd fnl 3f)	17	**8**	50/1	5	—
				(SP 111.6%)		**8 Rn**

1m 40.44 (3.14) CSF £3.78 TOTE £2.10: £1.10 £1.10 £4.00 (£2.20) OWNER The Thoroughbred Corporation (NEWMARKET) BRED Premier Bloodstock

4157 Success And Glory (IRE), probably beaten by a good horse at Goodwood, stays the mile really well and did the job in good style. (11/10: evens-7/4)

1607 Way Out Yonder, off since May and stepped up two furlongs in trip, was outpointed by the winner in the Dip but still looked the sort who should find a maiden. (3/1: op 2/1)

Jamorin Dancer, a cheaply-bought and rather ordinary-looking newcomer, ran quite well although readily left behind in the last couple of furlongs. (16/1)

Free As The Wind (IRE), a half-brother to the dam of Even Top, is quite sturdily made and should improve with racing. (10/1: 3/1-11/1)

Almandab (IRE), a big, staying type, has the pedigree to match but badly needed this and was left behind from halfway. Out of a dam who won over two miles, he could easily improve as the trips become more suitable next year. (5/1)

T/Jkpt: £7,100.00 (0.7 Tckts); £1,839.82 to Newcastle 1/10/97. T/Plpt: £60.50 (632.44 Tckts). T/Qdpt: £6.90 (383.4 Tckts) Dk

4299-WOLVERHAMPTON (L-H) (Standard)
Tuesday September 30th
WEATHER: overcast then rain WIND: nil

4479 CHEF'S LARDER MAIDEN AUCTION STKS (2-Y.O) (Class F)
2-25 (2-27) **5f (Fibresand)** £2,277.00 (£627.00: £297.00) Stalls: Low GOING: 0.26 sec per fur (SLW)

				SP	RR	SF
4232^{6}	**Blue Kite (87)** (NPLittmoden) **2-8-6** TGMcLaughlin(3) (chsd ldrs: rdn to ld 200y out: hung lft: r.o)	—	**1**	Evens ^{1}	72	45
4159^{2}	**Love Again** (MBell) **2-8-2**(3) AWhelan(9) (lw: a.p: led 2f out tl ins fnl f: r.o)	1½	**2**	6/1 ^{2}	66	39
4211^{9}	**Mary Jane** (JBerry) **2-7-12**(3) PFessey(10) (bit bkwd: w ldrs tl rdn & one pce fnl f)	2½	**3**	16/1	54	27
3905^{5}	**Just Testing** (JLEyre) **2-8-5** TWilliams(8) (outpcd tl sme late hdwy)	6	**4**	6/1 ^{2}	39	12
4042^{5}	**Little Fizz (67)** (BJMeehan) **2-7-12** CRutter(12) (prom over 3f)	hd	**5**	9/1 ^{3}	32	5
3794^{8}	**Elleysanta (64)** (AGNewcombe) **2-7-12** JQuinn(2) (sn pushed along: nvr on terms)	1½	**6**	20/1	27	—
3821^{6}	**Tangerine Flyer (72)** (JBerry) **2-8-5**(5) CLowther(4) (mde most 3f: sn rdn & wknd)	hd	**7**	9/1 ^{3}	39	12
	Abstone Pet Girl (PDEvans) **2-7-5**(7) AMcCarthy(7) (small: unf: dwlt: outpcd)	nk	**8**	50/1	26	—
954^{7}	**Dorton Grange** (KCComerford) **2-7-5**(7) JBosley(11) (chsd ldrs over 3f)	2	**9**	50/1	19	—
	Itch (RBastiman) **2-8-6** DeanMcKeown(5) (scope: s.s: a outpcd)	1	**10**	16/1	24	—
3707^{13}	**Helenes Hill** (JLHarris) **2-8-1** LCharnock(6) (outpcd)	nk	**11**	50/1	18	—
4332^{14}	**Merch Rhyd-Y-Grug** (DLWilliams) **2-7-12** JLowe(1) (outpcd: t.o)	8	**12**	50/1	—	—
	Precisely (IRE) (JWharton) **2-8-6** JCarroll(13) (cmpt: bkwd: s.s: a t.o)	5	**13**	25/1	—	—

(SP 126.8%) **13 Rn**

62.9 secs (4.00) CSF £6.60 TOTE £1.50: £1.10 £1.60 £4.50 (£2.30) Trio £28.20 OWNER Mr T. Clarke (WOLVERHAMPTON) BRED B. Minty

4232 Blue Kite, taking a big step down in class with the sole purpose of collecting an extra £1,000 for being purchased at the Dunstall Park Breeze-Up Sale, ran out a ready winner despite hanging left into the whip throughout the final furlong. Suited by a stiffer test of stamina, he could now be stepped up to seven furlongs. (Evens)

4159 Love Again, having her first outing on the All-Weather, was unable to improve on her efforts on the turf, but she gave of her best and will lose her bridesmaid tag before long. (6/1: op 4/1)

Mary Jane could have still needed the run but she pressed the leaders until feeling the strain once into the last furlong. (16/1)

3905 Just Testing, surprisingly for a Sharpo filly, did not stride out fluently on this easier surface, and she was always struggling with the pace once the contest got under way. (6/1)

4042 Little Fizz raced freely and did not last much further than the three-furlong marker before beating a retreat. (9/1: 6/1-10/1)

2306 Elleysanta, returning to the minimum trip, was off the bridle all the way and unable to go the pace. (20/1)

4480 HAPPY SHOPPER APPRENTICE CLAIMING LIMITED STKS (0-55) (I) (3-Y.O+) (Class G)
3-00 (3-00) **1m 100y (Fibresand)** £1,657.50 (£470.00: £232.50) Stalls: Low GOING: 0.26 sec per fur (SLW)

				SP	RR	SF
3608^{4}	**Colins Choice (51)** (JLSpearing) **3-8-4**(4) PBradley(8) (prom: outpcd 2f out: rallied to ld ins fnl f: sn clr)	—	**1**	7/2 ^{1}	55	30
4210^{11}	**Van Chino (47)** (BAMcMahon) **3-8-13** SRighton(7) (lw: set str pce: pushed along over 2f out: hdd & one pce fnl f)	3½	**2**	10/1	53	28
4168^{15}	**Lady Silk (40)** (MissJFCraze) **6-8-4**(4) CarolynBales(9) (chsd ldrs: lost pl 5f out: rallied ins fnl f)	¾	**3**	20/1	43	22
4228^{13}	**Chaluz (51)** (KRBurke) **3-8-13** RStudholme(12) (w ldr: rdn over 2f out: wknd ins fnl f)	s.h	**4**	16/1	52	27
3608^{11}	**Loch Style (40)** (RHollinshead) **4-8-8**(7) SClarke(1) (s.s: bhd tl hdwy 3f out: kpt on ins fnl f)	1	**5**	25/1	48	27
1939^{5}	**Avanti Blue (45)** (KMcAuliffe) **3-8-11** AMcCarthy(10) (bit bkwd: chsd ldrs: effrt & rdn 2f out: r.o one pce)	1	**6**	14/1	46	21
4371^{15}	**Three Weeks (53)** (WRMuir) **4-8-9**(4) GHannon(11) (lw: hld up: hdwy 4f out: nvr nrr)	1	**7**	5/1 ^{3}	42	21
4300^{2}	**Arrasas Lady (40)** (JRPoulton) **7-8-12** JFowle(3) (trckd ldrs: rdn over 2f out: no imp)	¾	**8**	12/1	40	19
4455^{10}	**Grey Again (48)** (DShaw) **5-8-4v1**(4) RBrisland(6) (swtg: a in rr)	¾	**9**	20/1	34	13
4069^{6}	**Slievenamon (51)** (JEBanks) **4-8-7v**(4) DarrenWilliams(13) (chsd ldrs: drvn along over 2f out: wknd appr fnl f)	4	**10**	7/1	30	9
4300^{12}	**Taragona (40)** (RHollinshead) **4-8-2**(4) DHayden(4) (chsd ldrs over 5f: sn lost pl)	1½	**11**	25/1	22	1
4448^{2}	**Tael of Silver (38)** (ABailey) **5-8-1**(7) JBosley(2) (prom 5f: sn rdn & wknd)	5	**12**	9/2 ^{2}	15	—
4243^{13}	**Balladara (IRE) (45)** (RHannon) **3-8-9**(4) RSmith(5) (a in rr: t.o fnl 3f)	20	**13**	16/1	—	—

(SP 122.0%) **13 Rn**

1m 53.8 (8.80) CSF £34.36 TOTE £4.50: £1.60 £2.30 £9.10 (£24.80) Trio £233.80; £263.46 to Newcastle 1/10/97 OWNER Mr Colin Ross (ALCESTER) BRED Roldvale Ltd

WEIGHT FOR AGE 3yo-4lb

3608 Colins Choice, a previous course and distance winner, looked to be in trouble when losing her pitch on the home turn, but she picked up well once in line for the judge and won very easily in the end. (7/2: 9/4-4/1)

1777 Van Chino went off at a rate of knots on this debut on the sand, and he stuck on surprisingly well when the pressure was on, but the winner proved much too strong for him inside the distance. (10/1: 7/1-12/1)

2753 Lady Silk is a sprinter through and through and it is surprising that she is asked to tackle trips beyond her. To her credit, she did stay on after getting her second wind on the home turn, and maybe success at a mile in these lower-grade events is within her reach. (20/1)

600 Chaluz performs well on this surface, but he did too much too soon in his head to head with the runner-up and in the end it took its toll. (16/1)

3269 Loch Style stood still as the stalls were released, and with the brisk early pace was always being taken off his legs. He began to stay on in the latter stages and there could be another race to be won if he could master the art of trapping. (25/1)

1939 Avanti Blue, without the shades on this return after a mid-summer break, showed up well until lack of peak condition began to tell from the turn from home. (14/1: op 8/1)

4050 Three Weeks (5/1: op 8/1)

4300 Arrasas Lady (12/1: 7/1-14/1)

4448 Tael of Silver (9/2: 3/1-5/1)

4481 MALTHOUSE VINTNER H'CAP (0-70) (3-Y.O+) (Class E)
3-30 (3-30) **1m 6f 166y (Fibresand)** £3,070.25 (£917.00: £438.50: £199.25) Stalls: High GOING: 0.26 sec per fur (SLW)

				SP	RR	SF
4101^{13}	**Onefourseven (57)** (JLEyre) **4-9-4** TWilliams(4) (led after 1f: clr 2f out: styd on strly)	—	**1**	11/4 ^{1}	70	35

				SP	RR	SF
3543[9]	**Batoutoftheblue (64)** (WWHaigh) **4-9-11** ACulhane(12) (hld up: hdwy over 4f out: hrd rdn 2f out: kpt on: no ch w wnr)	4	**2**	11/2[2]	73	38
3867[7]	**Vrennan (65)** (JRFanshawe) **3-9-1** GCarter(8) (swtg: a chsng ldrs: rdn & one pce fnl 2f)	1½	**3**	12/1	72	26
4222[11]	**Castles Burning (USA) (70)** (CACyzer) **3-9-6** AClark(7) (in tch: hdwy 5f out: rdn & outpcd over 2f out)	6	**4**	14/1	71	25
3046[5]	**Castle Secret (56)** (DBurchell) **11-8-10**(7) RBrisland(10) (hld up in tch: lost pl over 5f out: styd on again fnl 2f)	5	**5**	12/1	51	16
4288[5]	**Nigel's Lad (IRE) (64)** (PCHaslam) **5-9-6**(5) CLowther(2) (chsd ldrs to ½-wy: sn rdn along: grad fdd)	3½	**6**	9/1	55	20
4275[8]	**Stalled (IRE) (53)** (PTWalwyn) **7-9-0** JLowe(11) (b: a in rr)	4	**7**	10/1	40	5
3020[4]	**Nile Valley (IRE) (65)** (PWChapple-Hyam) **3-8-12**(3) RHavlin(1) (chsd ldrs to 7f out: sn pushed along & wknd)	2½	**8**	12/1	49	3
*4304**	**English Invader (59)** (CADwyer) **6-9-6** JCarroll(3) (chsd ldrs: pushed along 5f out: sn wknd)	1¼	**9**	6/1[3]	42	7
660[10]	**Shakiyr (FR) (62)** (RHollinshead) **6-9-9** FLynch(5) (bkwd: trckd ldrs tl lost pl 5f out: sn t.o)	25	**10**	16/1	18	—
4302[10]	**Broughtons Formula (55)** (WJMusson) **7-9-2** MWigham(9) (a wl bhd)	s.h	**11**	16/1	11	—
	Armston (55) (JWharton) **5-9-2** JQuinn(6) (bkwd: chsd ldrs tl lost pl 6f out: t.o)	1	**12**	33/1	10	—
				(SP 119.9%)	**12 Rn**	

3m 23.9 (16.50) CSF £15.46 CT £145.48 TOTE £2.50: £1.60 £1.50 £3.90 (£12.30) Trio £48.00 OWNER Mr J. Roundtree (HAMBLETON) BRED Peter Storey

WEIGHT FOR AGE 3yo-11lb

2327 Onefourseven has only a featherweight to carry in the Cesarewitch and this comfortably-gained, clear-cut success could have put him in the right frame of mind. (11/4)

3543 Batoutoftheblue, the gamble of the race, came good at this time last year and, showing signs of a return to form, can safely be followed from now on. (11/2: op 10/1)

2486 Vrennan, still struggling to get off the mark, was making her All-Weather debut. Never far away, she did keep staying on without ever looking likely to mount a challenge. (12/1: op 7/1)

3593* Castles Burning (USA) has yet to prove he stays this trip, for his effort to get himself into the action had come to an end before reaching the home straight. (14/1)

3046 Castle Secret stays extremely well, but he only does as much as he wants and in this instance he did not start to pick up until the race was as good as over. (12/1)

4288 Nigel's Lad (IRE), having his first run on the All-Weather in over eleven months, seems to have gone off the boil after a successful spring campaign and it could be the handicapper has his measure. (9/1)

4304* English Invader (6/1: op 7/2)

4482 GORDON CROWE CLASSIC H'CAP (0-85) (3-Y.O+) (Class D)

4-05 (4-06) **6f (Fibresand)** £3,836.70 (£1,146.60: £548.80: £249.90) Stalls: Low GOING: 0.26 sec per fur (SLW)

				SP	RR	SF
4307[10]	**State of Caution (82)** (DShaw) **4-9-6v**[1](5) CLowther(7) (b: a.p: led over 1f out: rdn out)	—	**1**	14/1	90	61
4137[5]	**Malibu Man (77)** (EAWheeler) **5-9-6** JQuinn(11) (led after 1f tl over 2f out: r.o u.p ins fnl f)	½	**2**	5/1[1]	84	55
4071[17]	**Forcing Bid (80)** (SirMarkPrescott) **3-9-7** GDuffield(5) (lw: a.p: led over 2f out tl over 1f out: rdn & no ex fnl f)	1½	**3**	6/1[2]	83	52
4219[5]	**Twin Creeks (75)** (VSoane) **6-9-4** CRutter(12) (lw: in tch: hdwy wl over 1f out: nrst fin)	1¼	**4**	8/1[3]	74	45
4270[3]	**Pericles (81)** (MJohnston) **3-9-8** JFanning(13) (lw: led 1f: prom tl rdn & outpcd over 1f out)	1¼	**5**	6/1[2]	77	46
3075[9]	**First Maite (75)** (SRBowring) **4-9-1b**(3) CTeague(2) (plld hrd: chsd ldrs: one pce fnl 2f)	1	**6**	14/1	68	39
4233[24]	**Pride of Brixton (75)** (CWThornton) **4-9-4** DeanMcKeown(9) (prom: rdn 2f out: wknd appr fnl f)	nk	**7**	25/1	68	39
4270[10]	**Garnock Valley (70)** (JBerry) **7-8-13b** GCarter(8) (outpcd)	2	**8**	20/1	57	28
3922[11]	**Ramsey Hope (76)** (CWFairhurst) **4-9-5v** NKennedy(10) (lw: chsd ldrs over 3f)	½	**9**	16/1	62	33
3075[13]	**Robo Magic (USA) (80)** (LMontagueHall) **5-9-9** FLynch(4) (b: lw: outpcd: t.o)	9	**10**	20/1	42	13
4249[8]	**Pageboy (73)** (PCHaslam) **8-9-2** SDrowne(3) (lw: sn pushed along: a outpcd: t.o)	3	**11**	14/1	27	—
*4301**	**Takhlid (USA) (74)** (DWChapman) **6-9-3** ACulhane(1) (prom whn bdly hmpd over 3f out: nt rcvr: t.o)	1¼	**12**	6/1[2]	25	—
4049[2]	**Spaniards Close (77)** (PJMakin) **9-9-6** JCarroll(6) (outpcd: a bhd: t.o)	¾	**13**	8/1[3]	26	—
				(SP 121.0%)	**13 Rn**	

1m 16.1 (4.90) CSF £74.05 CT £449.40 TOTE £9.20: £2.60 £2.20 £3.00 (£34.30) Trio £165.40 OWNER Mr J. C. Fretwell (NEWARK) BRED C. Wiggins

WEIGHT FOR AGE 3yo-2lb

STEWARDS' ENQUIRY Duffield susp. 9-11/10/97 (careless riding).

4013 State of Caution seems to reserve his best for the sand and, forging ahead below the distance, was being reeled in close home, but always appeared to have the measure of the strong-finishing favourite. (14/1: 10/1-16/1)

4137 Malibu Man, successful over the minimum trip on his previous outing here in June, gave supporters of the winner a worrying time when he renewed his challenge nearing the finish, but try as he might, the task was always beyond him. (5/1)

2925 Forcing Bid, back over what could prove his ideal trip, took a lot of wearing down, but he did seem to lack a turn of finishing speed and is probably high enough in the handicap for a three-year-old. (6/1)

4219 Twin Creeks has yet to win a race short of seven furlongs and his determined effort to reach the leaders was always doomed to failure. (8/1)

4270 Pericles finds he has hardly got the speed to win at sprint distances nowadays, but he ran well with all of his weight, and he only got shaken off when the dash to the line developed. (6/1: op 3/1)

2162 First Maite took a very strong hold on the heels of the leaders, but only succeeded in beating himself for he had nothing left when a final effort was called for. (14/1)

2563 Pageboy (14/1: op 8/1)

4301* Takhlid (USA) was lucky not to be forced through the inside rail when a rival took his ground turning out of the back straight. Brought to a standstill, his rider wisely let him complete in his own time. This performance can safely be disregarded. (6/1)

4483 BOOKER CASH & CARRY (S) STKS (2-Y.O F) (Class G)

4-40 (4-40) **6f (Fibresand)** £1,984.50 (£547.00: £259.50) Stalls: Low GOING: 0.26 sec per fur (SLW)

				SP	RR	SF
3395[8]	**Malozza (62)** (PDEvans) **2-9-0** JFEgan(11) (a.p: led over 2f out: drvn out)	—	**1**	13/2[3]	59	28
3892[7]	**Satis (IRE) (48)** (MRChannon) **2-8-9** ACulhane(6) (trckd ldrs: effrt 2f out: kpt on wl ins fnl f)	2	**2**	8/1	49	18
4327[4]	**Kite (51)** (MBell) **2-8-9** MFenton(4) (led over 3f: rdn & outpcd appr fnl f)	6	**3**	7/2[1]	33	2
4068[17]	**Rosewood Lady (IRE) (54)** (KRBurke) **2-9-0v** AClark(12) (lw: hdwy ½-wy: rdn & one pce appr fnl f)	¾	**4**	6/1[2]	36	5
4427[7]	**Maedaley (53)** (PCHaslam) **2-8-6**(3) PFessey(2) (prom tl rdn & wknd wl over 1f out)	nk	**5**	8/1	30	—
3967[12]	**Shanthi (53)** (PJMakin) **2-8-9b** JCarroll(3) (bhd & outpcd tl some late hdwy)	1½	**6**	13/2[3]	26	—
4303[7]	**Linda (52)** (NACallaghan) **2-8-9b**[1] SDrowne(13) (lw: hdwy u.p 2f out: nt rch ldrs)	3	**7**	16/1	18	—
3859[11]	**Catfoot Lane (53)** (WGMTurner) **2-8-2**(7) DMcGaffin(1) (swtg: a bhd & outpcd)	1¾	**8**	20/1	13	—
3808[6]	**Gaelic Quinie (IRE)** (GROldroyd) **2-8-9v**[1] FNorton(7) (dwlt: a bhd)	4	**9**	10/1	3	—
4166[18]	**Downclose Duchess (53)** (MBlanshard) **2-8-9** JQuinn(5) (trckd ldrs over 3f)	1	**10**	14/1	—	—

				SP	RR	SF
3563^{6}	**Edna's Gift (IRE) (55)** (JBerry) **2-8-9**$^{(5)}$ CLowther(10) (prom: rdn & wknd 2f out: t.o)	6	**11**	12/1	—	—
4162^{10}	**Miss Beveled (38)** (MBrittain) **2-8-2**$^{(7)}$ DMernagh(9) (sn drvn along: a outpcd: t.o)	nk	**12**	25/1	—	—
4166^{19}	**Turf Moor (IRE) (56)** (JJO'Neill) **2-8-9** TWilliams(8) (in tch 3f: wknd qckly: t.o)	19	**13**	15/2	—	—
				(SP 135.1%)	**13 Rn**	

1m 17.8 (6.60) CSF £59.96 TOTE £12.10: £5.90 £2.20 £2.00 (£51.90) Trio £36.00 OWNER Mr D. Maloney (WELSHPOOL) BRED W. R. Jones
No bid

1945 Malozza got back to winning ways in this first-time seller with a very smooth success and connections were able to retain her without a bid. She is beginning to get her winter coat and that could be a sure sign that she is ready for a break. (13/2: 4/1-7/1)

3228 Satis (IRE) ran a bit too free when she last ran in a seller and she was restrained here. Asked for an effort entering the straight, she stayed on relentlessly, but the winner had got away and was certainly not stopping. (8/1)

4327 Kite tried her best to run her rivals into the ground, but she was forced to give best soon after halfway and finally called enough on the approach to the final furlong. (7/2)

3782* Rosewood Lady (IRE) could never summon the pace to get involved despite staying on. (6/1)

4208 Maedaley, returning to a slightly shorter trip, went with the pace and had every chance until calling enough soon after entering the straight. (8/1)

3294 Shanthi did not appear to take to this surface for she was always at full stretch and being taken off her legs. (13/2: 3/1-7/1)

4484 HAPPY SHOPPER APPRENTICE CLAIMING LIMITED STKS (0-55) (II) (3-Y.O+) (Class G)

5-10 (5-10) **1m 100y (Fibresand)** £1,657.50 (£470.00: £232.50) Stalls: Low GOING: 0.26 sec per fur (SLW)

				SP	RR	SF
*3413**	**Bapsford (53)** (GLMoore) **3-8-13** MBatchelor(12) (hdwy 4f out: led over 2f out: sn clr: hld on)	—	**1**	4/1 1	66	35
4213^{8}	**Portite Sophie (43)** (MBrittain) **6-8-8** DMernagh(7) (hld up: hdwy 4f out: chsd wnr over 1f out: styd on)	1¾	**2**	8/1	54	27
3933^{11}	**Eastleigh (46)** (RHollinshead) **8-8-4**$^{(7)}$ LisaWatson(8) (b.nr hind: in rr tl r.o fnl 2f: nvr nrr)	3½	**3**	25/1	50	23
4373^{9}	**Prime Partner (49)** (TDEasterby) **4-8-9** DMcGaffin(6) (hdwy 4f out: rdn 2f out: nt rch ldrs)	1½	**4**	10/1	45	18
3562^{7}	**Madam Lucy (48)** (JLSpearing) **3-8-8** SRighton(13) (hld up: hdwy over 3f out: styng whn nt clr run ins fnl f)	1¾	**5**	8/1	45	14
1943^{5}	**Medland (IRE) (36)** (BJMcMath) **7-8-9** RStudholme(2) (bkwd: prom: led over 4f out tl over 2f out: wknd over 1f out)	2	**6**	33/1	38	11
3787^{11}	**Cats Bottom (53)** (AGNewcombe) **5-8-8** SCarson(9) (nvr nr to chal)	1¼	**7**	11/2 3	35	8
4043^{11}	**Windswept (IRE) (46)** (MCPipe) **4-8-8** JFowle(10) (swtg: mid div tl wknd wl over 2f out)	1	**8**	9/2 2	33	6
4415^{14}	**That Old Feeling (IRE) (35)** (DWChapman) **5-8-7b** TSiddall(11) (lw: chsd ldrs over 5f: sn lost tch: t.o)	10	**9**	33/1	13	—
4291^{13}	**Bollero (IRE) (54)** (JBerry) **3-8-6**$^{(4)}$ PBradley(5) (chsd ldrs 5f: sn wknd: t.o)	3	**10**	6/1	14	—
4184^{17}	**Time of Night (USA) (50)** (JLEyre) **4-8-4**$^{(4)}$ SBuckley(3) (s.s: a bhd: t.o)	1¾	**11**	10/1	5	—
2573^{11}	**Cheval Roc (55)** (RHannon) **3-8-9**$^{(4)}$ RSmith(1) (swtg: bit bkwd: led to ½-wy: sn lost tch: t.o)	20	**12**	14/1	—	—
4069^{14}	**Kayzee (IRE) (39)** (DBurchell) **3-7-10**$^{(4)}$ RBrisland(4) (swtg: prom: drvn along & wknd over 3f out: t.o)	9	**13**	16/1	—	—
				(SP 130.5%)	**13 Rn**	

1m 53.7 (8.70) CSF £35.82 TOTE £4.30: £2.60 £1.60 £5.90 (£29.60) Trio £86.80 OWNER Mr C. J. Pennick (BRIGHTON) BRED Benson Stud
WEIGHT FOR AGE 3yo-4lb
Bapsford clmd CSBraga £8,000

3413* Bapsford made the long journey from Brighton pay off with another readily-gained success over this slightly shorter trip and he is really flying at present. (4/1)

3886 Portite Sophie edged closer in the last half-mile and went in hot pursuit of the winner approaching the final furlong but that rival had kicked clear and she was always fighting a lost cause. (8/1)

2070 Eastleigh has only ever won on the sand and he was getting down to some serious work in the latter stages here, but he had mis-timed his effort and the line was always going to arrive too soon. (25/1)

3573 Prime Partner has proved something of a disappointment and it is almost twelve months since he last ran on this surface. Though he did stay on, it was very much in his own time and he was never a factor. (10/1)

3432 Madam Lucy, probably better over another furlong, was beginning to stay on when she was denied a clear run inside the last furlong, otherwise she may have finished third. (8/1)

1134 Medland (IRE) ran well after over three months on the sidelines, and though he has not won since January '95, the ability is there when he cares to put it to good use. (33/1)

3787 Windswept (IRE) (9/2: 3/1-5/1)

3854 Bollero (IRE) (6/1: 7/2-13/2)

4485 RED BAND H'CAP (0-70) (3-Y.O+) (Class E)

5-40 (5-43) **1m 1f 79y (Fibresand)** £3,174.25 (£949.00: £454.50: £207.25) Stalls: Low GOING: 0.26 sec per fur (SLW)

				SP	RR	SF
4449*	**Farmost (76)** (SirMarkPrescott) **4-10-6** 6x GDuffield(5) (lw: mde all: drvn clr 2f out: r.o wl)	—	**1**	6/4 1	90	72
3809^{4}	**Rutland Chantry (USA) (60)** (LordHuntingdon) **3-8-13** GCarter(10) (chsd ldrs: effrt 3f out: wnt 2nd wl over 1f out: no imp)	3½	**2**	7/1 2	68	45
4172^{9}	**Soden (IRE) (70)** (TGMills) **3-9-9** TWilliams(11) (lw: in tch: hdwy 4f out: styd on wl ins fnl f)	6	**3**	15/2 3	68	45
3584^{6}	**Sea Spouse (59)** (MBlanshard) **6-9-3** NAdams(8) (a.p: r.o one pce fnl 2f)	nk	**4**	10/1	56	38
3584^{9}	**Bentico (67)** (MrsNMacauley) **8-9-11v** SWebster(2) (b: a chsng ldrs: rdn over 2f out: no imp)	1¼	**5**	14/1	62	44
4264^{3}	**Zorba (65)** (JHetherton) **3-9-4** NKennedy(3) (w wnr: rdn over 2f out: sn wknd)	1½	**6**	12/1	58	35
3108^{8}	**Heighth of Fame (65)** (JHetherton) **6-9-9** LCharnock(12) (bit bkwd: nvr nr ldrs)	3	**7**	14/1	52	34
4139^{10}	**Penlop (67)** (ACStewart) **3-9-6** SWhitworth(6) (nvr bttr than mid div)	5	**8**	8/1	46	23
4371^{10}	**Invocation (63)** (GLMoore) **10-9-7** AClark(9) (a in rr)	2½	**9**	14/1	38	20
4050^{15}	**Desert Zone (USA) (63)** (JohnHarris) **8-9-2**$^{(5)}$ CLowther(4) (b: dwlt: sn chsng ldrs: wknd 3f out)	3	**10**	25/1	33	15
1993^{7}	**Genuine John (IRE) (70)** (JParkes) **4-10-0** ACulhane(7) (bit bkwd: a wl bhd: t.o)	14	**11**	20/1	16	—
4335^{13}	**Aspecto Lad (IRE) (61)** (DLWilliams) **3-8-11v**$^{1(3)}$ DGriffiths(13) (a in rr: eased over 3f out: t.o)	3	**12**	16/1	1	—
1023^{14}	**Eastern Eagle (IRE) (62)** (JMPEustace) **3-9-1** JTate(1) (bkwd: in tch over 5f: sn wknd: virtually p.u fnl f: t.o)	26	**13**	16/1	—	—
				(SP 132.5%)	**13 Rn**	

2m 3.6 (7.60) CSF £12.38 CT £65.21 TOTE £2.00: £1.10 £2.50 £5.10 (£9.60) Trio £52.20 OWNER Mr W. E. Sturt (NEWMARKET) BRED Hesmonds Stud Ltd
WEIGHT FOR AGE 3yo-5lb

4449* Farmost had a welter-weight to carry due to the penalty for winning at Brighton three days previous, but he has the build of a three-mile chaser, and he shook off the extra weight without any trouble at all and still won unchallenged. (6/4)

3809 Rutland Chantry (USA), a lightly-made maiden who was runner-up on his previous visit here, showed that he is progressing in the right direction and that first success could be just round the corner. (7/1)

3721 Soden (IRE) stayed on to gain third prize nearing the finish, but the winner was always going much too well for her and she did not seem up to carrying so much weight in this sort of class. (15/2)
3584 Sea Spouse, always on the heels of the leaders, began to struggle when the winner injected more pace into the race on the home turn, and from then on it was just a case of could he hold on to the minor prize. (10/1)
2369 Bentico appeared to be waiting on the leaders, but he was being made to work to hold his place over two furlongs out and was always short of the necessary acceleration. (14/1)
4264 Zorba likes to dictate but the winner is also a front-runner and he lost out on the battle this time. (12/1)

T/Plpt: £58.10 (321.57 Tckts). T/Qdpt: £19.70 (44.84 Tckts) IM

4486a - 4499a (Irish Racing) - See Computer Raceform

4446-BRIGHTON (L-H) (Firm)
Wednesday October 1st
WEATHER: sunny WIND: mod half against

4500 SEAGULL (S) STKS (2-Y.O) (Class G)
2-20 (2-20) **5f 59y** £1,984.50 (£547.00: £259.50) Stalls: Low GOING minus 0.39 sec per fur (F)

				SP	RR	SF
3556^{5}	**Private Seal (70)** (GLMoore) **2-8-11** AClark(4) (hld up: rdn over 2f out: hung lft & led over 1f out: r.o wl)	—	1	$7/4^{1}$	69	22
3589^{6}	**High Money (67)** (GLewis) **2-8-8**(3) RFfrench(6) (outpcd: hdwy over 1f out: r.o wl ins fnl f)	¾	2	$11/4^{2}$	67	20
3571^{7}	**Glass River (55)** (PDEvans) **2-8-11** JFEgan(2) (lw: a.p: rdn over 2f out: unable qckn)	3½	3	10/1	56	9
4162^{5}	**Sun In The Morning (54)** (BJMeehan) **2-8-11** MTebbutt(1) (led over 3f: wknd ins fnl f)	nk	4	10/1	55	8
4054^{12}	**Verdant Express (47)** (WGMTurner) **2-8-3**(3) DSweeney(5) (bhd fnl 2f)	6	5	16/1	32	—
4178^{10}	**Oriel Girl (66)** (BJMeehan) **2-8-11b**[1] CandyMorris(3) (prom over 3f)	½	6	$7/2^{3}$	35	—
2784^{11}	**Lionels Lucky Lady** (JSMoore) **2-7-13**(7) PaulCleary(7) (a bhd)	13	7	33/1	—	—
				(SP 112.3%)		**7 Rn**

62.4 secs (2.40) CSF £5.86 TOTE £1.80: £2.00 £2.00 (£2.80) OWNER Mr K. Higson (BRIGHTON) BRED K. Higson
No bid
2741 Private Seal appreciated the drop in class. With valuable experience on this very tricky course, he gained control approaching the final furlong, despite hanging left and, having got first run on the runner-up, was not going to be caught. (7/4)
3589 High Money was taking a drop in class but he was unable to go the early pace which proved his downfall for, although running on strongly in the last furlong and a half, was unable to get to the winner in time. He can find a similar event. (11/4)
3314 Glass River was always to the fore but failed to quicken in the final quarter-mile. (10/1)
4162 Sun In The Morning was dropping back into a seller but, after setting the pace until below the distance, had little left to offer in the final furlong. (10/1: 7/1-12/1)
2396 Verdant Express, who went down very early, was getting left behind in the final quarter-mile. Her only piece of form has come on soft ground. (16/1)
3866 Oriel Girl ran poorly with the visor left off last time out but had the blinkers on here. Nevertheless, she had come to the end of her tether below the distance. (7/2)

4501 NEWHAVEN NURSERY H'CAP (0-85) (2-Y.O) (Class E)
2-50 (2-50) **5f 213y** £2,810.25 (£837.00: £398.50: £179.25) Stalls: Low GOING minus 0.39 sec per fur (F)

				SP	RR	SF
4044^{17}	**Truth Teller (66)** (RHannon) **2-8-1**(3) RFfrench(5) (lw: hld up: rdn 2f out: led & edgd lft 1f out: r.o wl)	—	1	5/1	66	—
4165^{14}	**Counsel (65)** (CEBrittain) **2-8-3**ow2 MRoberts(4) (lost pl over 2f out: rallied ins fnl f: r.o wl)	2	2	$9/2^{3}$	60	—
4286^{2}	**Beware (83)** (RWArmstrong) **2-9-7** SSanders(1) (led: sheepskin noseband slipped 3f out: hdd 1f out: unable qckn)	nk	3	$4/5^{1}$	77	8
4296^{8}	**Facile Tigre (70)** (SDow) **2-8-1**(7) PDoe(3) (a.p: hrd rdn & ev ch over 1f out: wknd fnl f)	1¾	4	$4/1^{2}$	59	—
				(SP 110.4%)		**4 Rn**

1m 11.3 (4.10) CSF £22.04 TOTE £5.70: (£17.90) OWNER Mr J. C. Smith (MARLBOROUGH) BRED Elsdon Farms
3859 Truth Teller gained his only previous win here on fast ground but, on another occasion, his jockey reported that he was unsuited by the track and fast ground. He certainly looked ill at ease negotiating the downhill turn over three furlongs from home but, despite this, he came through to lead entering the final furlong and kept on well. (5/1: 3/1-11/2)
3927 Counsel, who ran out of puff over a mile last time out, was reverting back to six but found it too sharp on this track for, after getting outpaced over a quarter of a mile from home, was staying on in really good style in the last one hundred yards. Seven furlongs on a galloping course may prove best for him. (9/2: 4/1-6/1)
4286 Beware took the field along but could not have been helped by his sheepskin noseband riding upwards and to the side from halfway. Whether it impaired his vision is debatable but it must have been a hindrance to him at least and, collared a furlong from home, he failed to find another gear. (4/5)
3589 Facile Tigre, who went down very early, had every chance below the distance before tiring inside the last two hundred yards. (4/1: op 2/1)

4502 E.B.F. SOMPTING MAIDEN STKS (2-Y.O) (Class D)
3-25 (3-25) **6f 209y** £3,380.50 (£1,009.00: £482.00: £218.50) Stalls: Low GOING minus 0.39 sec per fur (F)

				SP	RR	SF
3547^{4}	**Forum (91)** (CEBrittain) **2-8-9** MRoberts(3) (hld up: shkn up over 3f out: led over 1f out: rdn out)	—	1	$3/1^{2}$	84	30
4361^{2}	**Freedom Quest (IRE)** (SirMarkPrescott) **2-9-0** SSanders(2) (hdwy over 5f out: nt clr run on ins over 1f out: r.o wl ins fnl f)	2	2	$13/8^{1}$	84	30
3780^{3}	**Palmetto Bay (IRE)** (MRStoute) **2-9-0** WRyan(1) (lw: w ldr: led over 4f out tl over 1f out: wknd ins fnl f)	2½	3	13/2	79	25
3789^{10}	**Rubamma** (PTWalwyn) **2-8-11**(3) RFfrench(8) (lw: a.p: nt clr run wl over 1f out: one pce)	nk	4	20/1	78	24
4067^{8}	**Flush (FR)** (JWHills) **2-8-9** MHills(4) (s.s: rdn over 2f out: hdwy fnl f: nvr nrr)	1¼	5	14/1	70+	16
4067^{3}	**Pride of Place (IRE)** (DRLoder) **2-8-9** RCochrane(6) (lw: led over 2f: rdn over 2f out: ev ch over 1f out: eased whn btn ins fnl f)	½	6	$7/2^{3}$	69	15
4157^{7}	**Priors Moor** (RWArmstrong) **2-9-0** AClark(7) (lw: bhd fnl 5f)	6	7	50/1	60	6
4381^{14}	**Total Tropix** (WJHaggas) **2-8-9** AMcGlone(5) (a bhd)	nk	8	50/1	54	—
				(SP 114.0%)		**8 Rn**

1m 22.4 (2.40) CSF £7.39 TOTE £3.30: £1.30 £1.10 £2.10 (£2.70) OWNER Wyck Hall Stud (NEWMARKET) BRED Wyck Hall Stud Ltd

OFFICIAL EXPLANATION Flush (FR): rider reported that the filly became unbalanced, stumbled at halfway and was unsuited by the firm ground. She stayed on through tired horses in the latter stages.

3547 Forum had by far and away her easiest task to date but her big frame was probably not ideal for this track. Shaken up from halfway, she led approaching the final furlong but she carried her head rather high and had to be ridden along to secure victory. She has demonstrated this season that she does have plenty of ability but looks one to have reservations about. (3/1)

4361 Freedom Quest (IRE) found himself boxed in entering the final quarter-mile and, when he did find daylight, the winner had got first run on him and was not for catching. He should soon be winning. (13/8: 6/4-9/4)

3780 Palmetto Bay (IRE) disputed the lead until going on at the top of the hill. Collared below the distance, he had little left in reserve. (13/2)

Rubamma, who failed to stay a mile last time out, was dropped back to seven. Not getting a clear run entering the final quarter-mile, he could only struggle on at one pace when daylight appeared. (20/1)

Flush (FR), racing at the back of the field, was given a couple of cosmetic reminders below the distance and caught the eye as she stayed on in the final furlong. It will be interesting to see how she gets on in nurseries. (14/1: 8/1-16/1)

4067 Pride of Place (IRE) is all legs and no substance and, after having every chance below the distance, was eased when all hope had evaporated inside the final furlong. If she is to find a race it will be a very small affair. (7/2: 5/2-4/1)

4503 LEVY BOARD MAIDEN H'CAP (0-70) (3-Y.O+) (Class E)

3-55 (3-56) **1m 3f 196y** £3,044.25 (£909.00: £434.50: £197.25) Stalls: High GOING minus 0.39 sec per fur (F)

				SP	RR	SF
3929[3]	**Be True (35)** (GLMoore) **3-7-4**(7) PDoe(8) (s.s: hdwy 4f out: led over 2f out: clr whn hrd rdn, edgd lft & hit rail wl over 1f out: easily)	—	**1**	4/1[2]	61+	37
4300[9]	**Drift (59)** (SirMarkPrescott) **3-9-7** SSanders(10) (lw: w ldr: led 4f out tl over 2f out: unable qckn)	14	**2**	16/1	66	42
4063[5]	**Ellway Lady (IRE) (56)** (IABalding) **3-9-4** MartinDwyer(2) (lw: rdn over 3f out: hdwy over 2f out: one pce)	2	**3**	6/1	61	37
3211[6]	**Es Go (49)** (RBastiman) **4-8-13**(5)ow2 HBastiman(11) (hld up: rdn over 3f out: one pce)	1	**4**	3/1[1]	52	33
3864[7]	**Bellagrana (53)** (MJFetherston-Godley) **3-8-12**(3) RFfrench(5) (lost pl over 4f out: one pce fnl 2f)	½	**5**	7/1	56	32
4336[4]	**Alagna (45)** (SCWilliams) **3-8-7v[1]** JFEgan(7) (lw: a.p: rdn over 3f out: wkng whn n.m.r over 2f out & nt clr run wl over 1f out)	nk	**6**	11/1	47	23
4172[7]	**Fife Major (USA) (62)** (BWHills) **3-9-10** MHills(6) (lw: hld up: rdn over 3f out: wknd over 2f out)	hd	**7**	9/2[3]	64	40
4179[9]	**Mary Culi (44)** (HCandy) **3-8-6** AMcGlone(1) (hld up: rdn over 4f out: sn wknd)	3½	**8**	14/1	41	17
3848[6]	**Areish (IRE) (30)** (JFfitch-Heyes) **4-7-13** GBardwell(9) (a bhd)	1½	**9**	33/1	25	8
4372[9]	**Action Stations (59)** (CACyzer) **3-9-7** MRoberts(4) (led 8f: wknd over 2f out)	9	**10**	16/1	42	18
3814[6]	**Haydown (IRE) (30)** (MRBosley) **5-7-6**(7) KelliPhillips(3) (prom over 7f)	21	**11**	20/1	—	—
				(SP 124.4%)	**11 Rn**	

2m 29.6 (2.00) CSF £64.35 CT £359.31 TOTE £5.30: £1.20 £4.60 £2.90 (£59.70) Trio £75.40 OWNER Mr F. L. Hill (BRIGHTON) BRED J. A. E. Hobby

WEIGHT FOR AGE 3yo-7lb

3929 Be True turned this race into a procession. Unfortunately, having struck the front over a quarter of a mile out, his young rider was going to take no chances and enthusiastically drove him along, resulting in the gelding drifting left and hitting the rails. Keeping his mount right up to his work until the closing stages, despite needing a pair of binoculars to see his toiling rivals, Doe was obviously not thinking about the Handicapper who will not be looking kindly on this. (4/1)

4055 Drift, who has dropped 7lb since the beginning of the season, showed in front at the top of the hill but, collared over a quarter of a mile from home, was left standing by the winner. (16/1)

4063 Ellway Lady (IRE) picked up ground over a quarter of a mile from home but was then made to look very pedestrian. (6/1: op 4/1)

3211 Es Go was stepping up markedly in distance after an eyecatching run last time out but was made to look woefully one-paced in the straight. (3/1: op 5/1)

3329 Bellagrana, who went down very early, got outpaced at the top of the hill and could only struggle on in her own time once in line for home. (7/1)

4336 Alagna was already back-pedalling when done no favours on two occasions in the straight. (11/1)

4504 STEYNING H'CAP (0-60) (3-Y.O+) (Class F)

4-25 (4-26) **1m 1f 209y** £2,277.00 (£627.00: £297.00) Stalls: High GOING minus 0.39 sec per fur (F)

				SP	RR	SF
4371*	**Harlequin Walk (IRE) (39)** (RJO'Sullivan) **6-8-7** 5x SSanders(12) (hdwy over 4f out: led over 2f out: clr over 1f out: easily)	—	**1**	11/2[2]	54+	36
3849*	**Muara Bay (48)** (GLewis) **3-8-8**(3) RFfrench(4) (hdwy over 2f out: chsd wnr over 1f out: r.o one pce)	3½	**2**	7/2[1]	57	34
4449[4]	**Roman Reel (USA) (52)** (GLMoore) **6-9-6** CandyMorris(5) (hdwy over 2f out: one pce)	3½	**3**	7/1	56	38
4371[6]	**Without Friends (IRE) (46)** (JFfitch-Heyes) **3-8-9** RCochrane(8) (stdy hdwy fnl 3f: nvr nrr)	2	**4**	14/1	47	24
4323[6]	**Cheek To Cheek (59)** (CACyzer) **3-9-8** AClark(14) (led 2f: rdn over 4f out: chsd wnr 2f out tl over 1f out: wknd fnl f)	½	**5**	16/1	59	36
4172[11]	**Here's To Howie (USA) (60)** (RHannon) **3-9-9** WJO'Connor(15) (a.p: rdn over 3f out: wknd over 1f out)	5	**6**	25/1	52	29
3849[4]	**Rocky Waters (USA) (38)** (MDIUsher) **8-8-3v**(3)ow6 DSweeney(17) (s.s: hdwy over 2f out: nvr nrr)	1	**7**	14/1	28	4
4179[2]	**Law Dancer (IRE) (48)** (TGMills) **4-8-9**(7) LisaHackett(3) (lw: s.s: nvr nr to chal)	½	**8**	10/1	37	19
3971[3]	**Colour Counsellor (43)** (RMFlower) **4-8-11b** MartinDwyer(16) (led 8f out to over 2f out: wknd over 1f out)	3½	**9**	12/1	27	9
4179[7]	**Dark Age (IRE) (57)** (RAkehurst) **4-9-4**(7) DDenby(1) (lw: prom over 5f)	1¼	**10**	20/1	39	21
4373*	**Mac Oates (49)** (PRHedger) **4-9-3** 5x AMcGlone(6) (nvr nrr)	4	**11**	6/1[3]	24	6
3627[16]	**Conic Hill (IRE) (32)** (JPearce) **6-8-0** GBardwell(2) (lw: bhd fnl 4f)	3½	**12**	25/1	2	—
4326[13]	**Forward Miss (34)** (CJBenstead) **3-7-4**(7)ow1 PDoe(9) (prom over 3f)	1¾	**13**	50/1	1	—
4179[17]	**Harvey White (IRE) (53)** (JPearce) **5-9-7** MWigham(10) (bhd fnl 3f)	1	**14**	20/1	18	—
3470[11]	**Gulf of Siam (33)** (EAWheeler) **4-7-8b**(7) SCarson(13) (prom over 7f)	4	**15**	33/1	—	—
4243[4]	**Tabasco Jazz (58)** (BJMeehan) **3-9-7** MTebbutt(11) (lw: a bhd)	s.h	**16**	12/1	17	—
4179[15]	**Double Gold (54)** (MBell) **3-9-3** MRoberts(7) (plld hrd: bhd fnl 4f)	14	**17**	14/1	—	—
				(SP 136.9%)	**17 Rn**	

2m 1.0 (2.70) CSF £23.43 CT £136.98 TOTE £4.90: £1.30 £1.30 £2.10 £3.80 (£8.20) Trio £18.90 OWNER Mrs R. J. Doorgachurn (WHITCOMBE) BRED Ronnie Boland in Ireland

LONG HANDICAP Forward Miss 6-11

WEIGHT FOR AGE 3yo-5lb

4371* Harlequin Walk (IRE) is in the form of her life at present and, leading over a quarter of a mile from home, shot clear to win with a ton in hand. (11/2)

3849* Muara Bay came through to take second place below the distance but, although pulling clear of the remainder, had absolutely no hope with the winner. (7/2)

4449 Roman Reel (USA), fourth here on Sunday, goes well on this switchback track but this was a better-class race than he is used to and he could only go up and down in the same place in the final quarter-mile. Claiming company is his best level. (7/1)
4371 Without Friends (IRE) is very moderate but he did stay on through the pack to show he does stay this longer trip. A return to claiming or selling company is desperately needed. (14/1)
4323 Cheek To Cheek, the early leader, showed in second place for a brief time in the straight but had run out of gas in the final furlong. (16/1)
3455 Here's To Howie (USA), whose only win to date came over this course and distance in April, was close up until coming to the end of his tether below the distance. He is out of form. (25/1)
3971 Colour Counsellor (12/1: 8/1-14/1)

4505 EASTBOURNE LIMITED STKS (0-65) (3-Y.O) (Class F)

4-55 (4-55) **7f 214y** £2,277.00 (£627.00: £297.00) Stalls: Low GOING minus 0.39 sec per fur (F)

				SP	RR	SF
4319[6]	**Matoaka (65)** (VSoane) **3-8-11** CRutter(7) (lw: hld up: led over 2f out: rdn out)	—	**1**	11/10[1]	77	17
3894[14]	**Kafil (USA) (65)** (GLMoore) **3-9-0** AClark(1) (nt clr run over 2f out: swtchd rt: hdwy over 1f out: r.o ins fnl f)	1	**2**	5/1[2]	78	18
4179[16]	**Ortelius (65)** (RHannon) **3-9-0** WJO'Connor(6) (lw: a.p: ev ch over 2f out: unable qckn)	1½	**3**	13/2[3]	75	15
4168[9]	**Daylight Dreams (61)** (CACyzer) **3-8-11** MRoberts(4) (plld hrd: rdn & hdwy over 2f out: r.o one pce fnl f)	nk	**4**	12/1	71	11
4326[4]	**Heart Full of Soul (60)** (PFICole) **3-9-0b** RCochrane(5) (led 3f: ev ch over 2f out: wknd over 1f out)	3	**5**	13/2[3]	68	8
4009[8]	**Love Venture (65)** (SPCWoods) **3-8-8**(3) RFfrench(3) (lw: hld up: nt clr run over 2f out: bmpd 2f out: sn wknd)	5	**6**	5/1[2]	55	—
	Surprise Event (58) (WGMTurner) **3-8-11**(3) DSweeney(2) (w ldr: led 5f out tl over 2f out: sn wknd)	1¼	**7**	33/1	56	—
				(SP 118.3%)		**7 Rn**

1m 35.4 (4.10) CSF £6.85 TOTE £1.70: £1.10 £5.50 (£9.10) OWNER The Stargazers (ASTON ROWANT) BRED Campbell Stud
4319 Matoaka at last had a trouble-free run and took full advantage of it, leading over a quarter of a mile from home and being rousted along to keep the runner-up at bay. (11/10)
2492 Kafil (USA) has to be considered unlucky. Happier with the drop in class, he failed to get a clear run at a critical stage and, when he did begin to pick up ground, the winner had already asserted. (5/1: 7/2-11/2)
3591 Ortelius has been in diabolical form this season apart from one decent run over this course and distance in August. A return visit to this tricky course seemed to suit him and he showed in front for a few strides over a quarter of a mile from home before tapped for toe. (13/2: 4/1-7/1)
Daylight Dreams nearly pulled Roberts' arms out of his sockets as the two of them had a wrestling match in the early stages. Picking up ground on the outside of the field over a quarter of a mile from home, she stayed on in the final furlong and only just failed to get into the prize money. (12/1: op 7/1)
4326 Heart Full of Soul, dropping back in distance having failed to stay a mile and quarter on his last two runs, had every chance over a quarter of a mile from home before tiring below the distance. (13/2)
3720 Love Venture was at the back of the field when given a nudge by Kafil a quarter of a mile from home but was going nowhere at the time. (5/1: 7/2-11/2)

4506 HANNINGTONS OF BRIGHTON MAIDEN STKS (3-Y.O+) (Class D)

5-25 (5-25) **1m 1f 209y** £3,422.65 (£1,019.20: £485.10: £218.05) Stalls: High GOING minus 0.39 sec per fur (F)

				SP	RR	SF
4223[3]	**Easy Song (USA) (73)** (RCharlton) **3-8-12v[1]** SSanders(3) (lw: hld up: hrd rdn over 3f out: edgd lft & led over 1f out: r.o wl)	—	**1**	Evens[1]	86	36
4378[2]	**Tough Act (75)** (MrsAJPerrett) **3-8-12** AClark(4) (hld up: chsd ldr 6f out: led over 2f out tl over 1f out: eased whn btn ins fnl f)	12	**2**	6/4[2]	67	17
2126[7]	**Bedouin Honda (73)** (CEBrittain) **3-8-12** MRoberts(1) (led over 7f)	6	**3**	13/2[3]	57	7
3850[6]	**Silver Marble (IRE)** (RHannon) **3-8-8ow1** WJO'Connor(2) (lw: chsd ldr 4f: wknd 4f out)	13	**4**	33/1	32	—
4070[14]	**Croft Sands** (RAkehurst) **4-9-3** AMcGlone(5) (lw: bhd fnl 5f)	7	**5**	33/1	25	—
				(SP 109.2%)		**5 Rn**

2m 1.6 (3.30) CSF £2.45 TOTE £2.10: £1.10 £1.10 (£1.30) OWNER Mr K. Abdulla (BECKHAMPTON) BRED Juddmonte Farms
WEIGHT FOR AGE 3yo-5lb
4223 Easy Song (USA), fitted with a visor for the first time, looks a very hard ride and was already being given reminders over three furlongs from home. He at last struggled to the front below the distance and kept on, but he does not look one to put a great deal of faith in. (Evens)
4378 Tough Act got to the front over a quarter of a mile from home but he carried his head rather high and quickly threw in the towel when collared below the distance. He looks one to leave alone. (6/4)
Bedouin Honda, given a three-month break, took the field along but, collared over two furlongs from home, was easily brushed aside. (13/2: 7/2-7/1)
Silver Marble (IRE), tailed off on her debut here, showed that she lacks ability for she was in trouble fully half a mile from home. (33/1)

T/Plpt: £164.60 (101.64 Tckts). T/Qdpt: £6.00 (189.71 Tckts) AK

3801-NEWCASTLE (L-H) (Good to firm)
Wednesday October 1st

Race 1 & 4: hand timd
WEATHER: sunny periods WIND: str half against

4507 E.B.F. HEBBURN MAIDEN STKS (2-Y.O) (Class D)

2-10 (2-10) **1m 3y (straight)** £3,452.50 (£1,045.00: £510.00: £242.50) Stalls: High GOING: 0.11 sec per fur (G)

				SP	RR	SF
41324	**Kahtan** (JLDunlop) **2-9-0** RHills(2) (in tch: hdwy over 2f out: led ins fnl f: styd on wl)	—	**1**	1/4[1]	80+	28
41747	**Bombastic** (BWHills) **2-9-0** KDarley(5) (lw: chsd ldrs: led wl over 3f out tl ins fnl f: kpt on wl)	nk	**2**	9/2[2]	79	27
4299[6]	**Royal Shock (IRE)** (DRLoder) **2-9-0** KFallon(4) (hld up: effrt over 2f out: styd on strly towards fin)	3	**3**	16/1	73	21
4212[7]	**Stone Beck** (JMJefferson) **2-8-9** JCarroll(3) (hld up: hdwy 2f out: kpt on wl: nvr able to chal)	hd	**4**	50/1	68	16
4384[8]	**Asset Manager** (MJohnston) **2-9-0** DHolland(1) (cl up tl grad wknd appr fnl f)	hd	**5**	9/1[3]	73	21
4384[10]	**Common View (IRE)** (NTinkler) **2-9-0** LCharnock(8) (in tch: outpcd over 2f out: nvr nr to chal)	4	**6**	100/1	65	13
4278[3]	**Lady Rachel (IRE)** (JLEyre) **2-8-9** MGallagher(6) (b.hind: chsd ldrs: rdn along ½-wy: wknd fnl 2f)	½	**7**	25/1	59	7
4384[12]	**Sledmere (IRE)** (NTinkler) **2-9-0** KimTinkler(7) (bit bkwd: led over 4f: wknd qckly & sn t.o)	dist	**8**	100/1	—	—
				(SP 121.9%)		**8 Rn**

1m 46.46 (7.86) CSF £1.96 TOTE £1.50: £1.00 £1.60 £2.20 (£1.80) OWNER Mr Hamdan Al Maktoum (ARUNDEL) BRED Shadwell Estate Company Limited

4132 Kahtan stays well which is important here, facing a very strong wind on this stiff track. (1/4)
Bombastic is a real stayer in the making and, after looking likely to get swamped here, he kept fighting back. (9/2)
4299 Royal Shock (IRE) is, at present, a rather weak-looking individual, but he certainly got better as the race progressed and finished with some purpose. Time looks to be the key. (16/1)
4212 Stone Beck put in a useful effort and looks to be learning fast. (50/1)
4384 Asset Manager put in another decent effort here and was not over-punished once beaten. (9/1)
Common View (IRE) was always being tapped for toe, but was not knocked about and next year should see plenty of improvement. (100/1)

4508 PRICE WATERHOUSE MAIDEN AUCTION STKS (I) (2-Y.O) (Class F)
2-40 (2-41) **7f** £2,249.50 (£632.00: £308.50) Stalls: High GOING: 0.11 sec per fur (G)

Form	Horse	Dist	Pos	SP	RR	SF
4285^{5}	**Shamwari Song (63)** (JAGlover) **2-8-6** JCarroll(4) (trckd ldrs: led 1½f out: qcknd 1f out: jst hld on)	—	1	$9/2^{2}$	63	11
	Flaxen Pride (IRE) (MrsMReveley) **2-8-5**^{ow1} ACulhane(9) (cmpt: hmpd after s: bhd tl hdwy 2f out: swtchd & styd on strly towards fin)	hd	2	12/1	62	9
4209^{15}	**Premium Quest** (RAFahey) **2-8-9** FNorton(3) (cl up: led 2f out: sn hdd: r.o one pce)	1¼	3	20/1	63	11
4159^{7}	**Another Wyn-Bank** (JGFitzGerald) **2-7-9**(3) PFessey(7) (dwlt: sn in tch: styd on u.p fnl f: nt pce to chal)	¾	4	10/1	50	—
4411^{8}	**Heathyards Sheik (71)** (RHollinshead) **2-8-6** FLynch(8) (lw: hmpd s: bhd: bdly hmpd wl over 1f out & appr fnl f: swtchd & fin fast)	s.h	5	$4/1^{1}$	58+	6
4166^{12}	**Starliner (IRE) (52)** (MBrittain) **2-7-11**(7) DMernagh(12) (chsd ldrs: nt clr run over 2f out: swtchd & styd on one pce)	1¼	6	12/1	53	1
4209^{11}	**Missed Domino** (MrsASwinbank) **2-7-12** EJohnson(10) (bhd: effrt over 2f out: nvr rchd ldrs)	1¼	7	8/1	44	—
4166^{11}	**Townville Cee Cee (49)** (JSWainwright) **2-8-1** JBramhill(2) (effrt ½-wy: ch over 2f out: sn wknd)	½	8	16/1	46	—
	Corpus Christi (IRE) (MJohnston) **2-8-9** DeanMcKeown(6) (tall: unf: scope: cl up tl rdn & wknd wl over 1f out)	1½	9	$9/2^{2}$	51	—
3563^{9}	**Wee Christy (IRE)** (WMcKeown) **2-8-9** JLowe(5) (prom tl wknd over 1f out)	3½	10	33/1	43	—
4209^{9}	**One To Go (IRE) (65)** (JBerry) **2-8-9** KDarley(1) (led 5f: wknd)	¾	11	$6/1^{3}$	41	—

(SP 119.8%) **11 Rn**

1m 32.14 (7.64) CSF £53.53 TOTE £5.20: £1.30 £2.80 £13.80 (£82.20) Trio £156.40; £180.70 to Newmarket 2/10/97 OWNER Mr W. H. Strawson (WORKSOP) BRED Mrs M. Perry
4285 Shamwari Song won this by getting first run on the opposition and stealing just enough to last home. (9/2)
Flaxen Pride (IRE), from a yard not noted for two-year-old success, put in a really useful first effort and, but for getting messed about, would have beaten the winner. (12/1)
Premium Quest, a purposeful walker, showed his first signs of form here and looks to be improving fast. (20/1)
4159 Another Wyn-Bank, stepping up in trip, ran better but does not look an easy ride. (10/1)
3821 Heathyards Sheik had a luckless run from start to finish and would probably have won with ease had he seen any daylight at all. (4/1)
1760 Starliner (IRE) has been disappointing of late but this was a much better effort. (12/1)
4209 Missed Domino was edgy and sweaty beforehand and this effort proved to be disappointing. (8/1)

4509 SV RUTTER STAYERS H'CAP (0-75) (3-Y.O) (Class D)
3-15 (3-16) **2m 19y** £3,598.75 (£1,090.00: £532.50: £253.75) Stalls: High GOING minus 0.30 sec per fur (GF)

Form	Horse	Dist	Pos	SP	RR	SF
4313^{9}	**Tommy Tortoise (70)** (MissGayKelleway) **3-9-7** KFallon(5) (lw: in tch: effrt appr st: styng on whn hmpd ins fnl f: kpt on towards fin: fin 2nd, hd: awrdd r)	—	1	$2/1^{1}$	78	38
3826^{4}	**Pen Friend (52)** (WJHaggas) **3-8-3** FLynch(8) (lw: cl up: led ½-wy to 2½f out: swtchd & styd on to ld wl ins fnl f: fin 1st: disq: plcd 2nd)	hd	2	$3/1^{2}$	60	20
4323^{10}	**Lighten Up (58)** (CEBrittain) **3-8-9** DHolland(2) (led to ½-wy: led 2½f out & edgd lft: no ex towards fin)	nk	3	14/1	66	26
4171^{3}	**Ginger Rogers (63)** (DWPArbuthnot) **3-9-0** JQuinn(12) (b: a.p: hdwy over 2f out: edgd lft appr fnl f: ev ch ins fnl f: nt qckn towards fin)	¾	4	$9/2^{3}$	70	30
3870*	**Monarch's Pursuit (58)** (TDEasterby) **3-8-9** JCarroll(11) (chsd ldrs: effrt 3f out: ch appr fnl f: r.o one pce)	½	5	12/1	64	24
4010^{4}	**Classical Dance (IRE) (46)** (MrsMReveley) **3-7-11** LCharnock(10) (chsd ldrs: effrt 4f out: outpcd fnl 2f)	4	6	9/1	48	8
4289^{4}	**Skelton Sovereign (IRE) (50)** (RHollinshead) **3-8-1** NCarlisle(9) (bhd: effrt appr st: n.d)	5	7	25/1	47	7
4287^{11}	**Dulas Bay (48)** (MWEasterby) **3-7-13** DaleGibson(4) (prom tl wknd over 3f out)	hd	8	10/1	45	5
4336^{9}	**Maremma (45)** (DonEnricoIncisa) **3-7-10** KimTinkler(7) (a bhd)	4	9	33/1	38	—
4287^{14}	**Straffan Gold (USA) (45)** (MrsMReveley) **3-7-10** JLowe(6) (a bhd)	18	10	20/1	20	—
4045^{9}	**Announcing (68)** (JHMGosden) **3-9-5** GHind(3) (prom tl wknd 3f out: eased & t.o)	dist	11	5/1	—	—
4336^{3}	***Arisaig (IRE) (56)*** (PCalver) **3-8-7v**^{1} KDarley(1) (Withdrawn not under Starter's orders: lame at s)		W	7/1	—	—

(SP 150.7%) **11 Rn**

3m 34.77 (9.27) CSF £8.69 CT £71.80 TOTE £2.70: £1.20 £1.40 £3.10 (£7.20) Trio £56.70 OWNER Mr Tommy Staunton (WHITCOMBE) BRED R. E. A. Bott (Wigmore Street) Ltd
LONG HANDICAP Maremma 7-8
2189 Tommy Tortoise, as his name suggests, does not do anything quickly, but he does stay and would have won this outright but for being hampered by the original winner. (2/1)
3826 Pen Friend just stays and was a shade unlucky to be disqualified here, as it was not entirely all his own fault, but he did hamper the second and the Stewards had no option. (3/1)
Lighten Up had shown next to nothing previously, but this big step up in trip certainly made the difference and her improvement should not continue. (14/1)
4171 Ginger Rogers is in tremendous form and had her chances again here, but she was inclined to edge left under pressure and the handicapper probably just has her measure. (9/2)
3870* Monarch's Pursuit, having his first run for over a month, put up a decent effort but was just short of any real turn of foot to seize the opportunity. Jumping could be the game for him. (12/1)
4010 Classical Dance (IRE), taking a big step up in trip, failed to last home. (9/1)
3781 Dulas Bay (10/1: 8/1-12/1)
3720 Announcing (5/1: 9/2-7/1)

4510 BOLLINGER CHAMPAGNE CHALLENGE SERIES GENTLEMEN'S H'CAP (0-70) (3-Y.O+) (Class E)
3-45 (3-55) **1m (round)** £3,022.00 (£916.00: £448.00: £214.00) Stalls: Low GOING minus 0.30 sec per fur (GF)

Form	Horse	Dist	Pos	SP	RR	SF
4225^{7}	**Xylem (USA) (69)** (LMCumani) **6-11-9**(4) MrCRanson(7) (bhd: hdwy & hmpd over 2f out: c wd & styd on strly to ld nr fin)	—	1	8/1	76	58

4410[8]	**Alpine Hideaway (IRE) (68)** (MWEasterby) **4-11-8**(4) MrKRO'Ryan(13) (lw: a.p: nt clr run & swtchd over 1f out: styd on to ld wl ins fnl f: nt qckn towards fin)	½	**2**	12/1	74	56
4324[7]	**Chinour (IRE) (45)** (EJAlston) **9-9-13**(4) MrBJCrawley(3) (bhd: effrt & swtchd over 2f out: hrd rdn & styd on: nrst fin)	½	**3**	8/1	50	32
4184[9]	**Birchwood Sun (49)** (MDods) **7-10-7b** MrTMcCarthy(15) (bhd: hdwy over 2f out: styd on wl: nrst fin)	hd	**4**	20/1	54	36
3476[11]	**Murphy's Gold (IRE) (52)** (RAFahey) **6-10-6**(4) MrCRussell(11) (chsd ldrs: styd on to ld appr fnl f: no ex towards fin)	s.h	**5**	14/1	57	39
3976[22]	**Needle Match (60)** (JJO'Neill) **4-11-4** MrCBonner(6) (rr div: hdwy 3f out: nt clr run over 1f out: styd on)	½	**6**	6/1[2]	64	46
3605[6]	**Keep Battling (48)** (JSGoldie) **7-10-6** MrOMcPhail(10) (a.p: effrt over 2f out: no ex ins fnl f)	1	**7**	14/1	50	32
4249[2]	**Mezzoramio (52)** (KAMorgan) **5-10-6v**(4) MrBRFoster(12) (b: mde most tl hdd appr fnl f: no ex)	nk	**8**	13/2[3]	53	35
4472[10]	**Miletrian City (43)** (MissLAPerratt) **4-9-11b**(4) MrDBShaw(1) (bhd tl sme late hdwy)	2	**9**	20/1	40	22
3627[14]	**Petrico (37)** (PBeaumont) **5-9-5**(4)ow2 MrJOwen(2) (w ldr: rdn over 3f out: wknd appr fnl f)	nk	**10**	50/1	34	14
3759[7]	**Thatched (IRE) (45)** (REBarr) **7-9-13**(4) MrTComerford(16) (chsd ldrs tl wknd fnl 2f)	4	**11**	8/1	34	16
4210*	**Euro Sceptic (IRE) (56)** (TDEasterby) **5-11-0b** MrABalding(8) (lw: mid div to wknd fnl 3f)	½	**12**	3/1[1]	44	26
444[17]	**Maple Bay (IRE) (70)** (BEllison) **8-11-10**(4) MrSDurack(4) (a rr div)	s.h	**13**	33/1	57	39
3854[5]	**Termon (35)** (MissLAPerratt) **4-9-3**(4) MrCWatson(5) (a bhd)	½	**14**	33/1	21	3
3261[6]	**King of Show (IRE) (38)** (RAllan) **6-9-6**(4) MrVLukaniuk(14) (a bhd)	2	**15**	33/1	20	2
2290[9]	**Jack Flush (IRE) (66)** (BSRothwell) **3-11-7** MrJGoldstein(9) (a in rr)	5	**16**	9/1	38	17

(SP 137.3%) **16 Rn**

1m 44.4 (5.40) CSF £96.16 CT £787.43 TOTE £8.60: £2.90 £3.60 £2.00 £5.60 (£45.40) Trio £489.60; £427.61 to Newmarket 2/10/97 OWNER Mr Christopher Ranson (NEWMARKET) BRED James Blackburn

LONG HANDICAP Termon 8-13 Petrico 9-0

WEIGHT FOR AGE 3yo-3lb

OFFICIAL EXPLANATION **Euro Sceptic (IRE): lost a shoe.**

4225 Xylem (USA) certainly gets the trip well and, suited by the very strong pace, came from way behind to snatch it. (8/1: 6/1-9/1)

3822* Alpine Hideaway (IRE), in this strongly-run event, always held a good position and, after staying on to gain the advantage, he had no answer to the winner's storming late burst. (12/1)

3269 Chinour (IRE), dropped out, was given some extra-strong assistance in the last two furlongs and was never any nearer than at the line. His rider's use of the whip has to be seen to be believed. (8/1)

1511 Birchwood Sun has never won over this far, but he was certainly putting in some useful late work here. (20/1)

3476 Murphy's Gold (IRE) had his chances but the final sprint just proved too much and he may have seen too much daylight too soon. (14/1)

3855* Needle Match ran well but was short of room at a vital stage and his chance had soon gone. (6/1: op 4/1)

4249 Mezzoramio set a break-neck pace which eventually found him out. (13/2)

4511 PRICE WATERHOUSE LIMITED STKS (0-85) (3-Y.O+) (Class D)

4-15 (4-20) **7f** £3,387.50 (£1,025.00: £500.00: £237.50) Stalls: High GOING: 0.11 sec per fur (G)

				SP	RR	SF
2894[5]	**Arruhan (IRE) (85)** (PTWalwyn) **3-8-9** RHills(5) (lw: hld up gng wl: rdn over 1f out: led jst ins fnl f: drvn out)	—	**1**	5/2[1]	91	65
4219[9]	**Shamanic (72)** (SPCWoods) **5-9-0** KFallon(4) (lw: trckd ldr: led over 2f out tl jst ins fnl f: no ex)	3	**2**	5/1[3]	87	63
4307[8]	**Young Bigwig (IRE) (81)** (JBerry) **3-8-12b** KDarley(2) (chsd ldrs: effrt over 2f out: nt qckn appr fnl f)	3	**3**	9/2[2]	80	54
4436[6]	**Mujova (IRE) (82)** (RHollinshead) **3-9-0** ACulhane(1) (sn outpcd & bhd: hdwy u.p over 2f out: nvr nr to chal)	nk	**4**	5/2[1]	82	56
4114*	**Rock Falcon (IRE) (85)** (LadyHerries) **4-9-4b** DeanMcKeown(3) (led tl over 2f out: sn wknd)	1¾	**5**	9/2[2]	80	56

(SP 110.2%) **5 Rn**

1m 27.63 (3.13) CSF £13.64 TOTE £2.30: £1.60 £2.20 (£6.20) OWNER Mr Hamdan Al Maktoum (LAMBOURN) BRED Shadwell Estate Company Limited

WEIGHT FOR AGE 3yo-2lb

2894 Arruhan (IRE), best in on official figures, was the pick of the paddock and showed a fluent action going to post. Confidently ridden, she was always going to do more than enough. (5/2)

3024 Shamanic had plenty on on official figures. Making the best of his way home, he was readily cut down by the winner inside the last. This was easily his best effort for some time. (5/1)

1403 Young Bigwig (IRE), wearing blinkers again, is from a stable struggling to find form at present. (9/2)

4436 Mujova (IRE) could never go the pace over this inadequate trip. (5/2)

4114* Rock Falcon (IRE), taken to post early, won over a furlong further last time. Trying to run his rivals ragged, he was easily cut down and, in truth, found precious little. (9/2)

4512 BERNARD HATHAWAY RETIREMENT H'CAP (0-85) (3-Y.O+) (Class D)

4-45 (4-51) **5f** £3,728.75 (£1,130.00: £552.50: £263.75) Stalls: High GOING: 0.11 sec per fur (G)

				SP	RR	SF
4414[12]	**Just Bob (72)** (SEKettlewell) **8-9-2** DeanMcKeown(6) (lw: dwlt: racd far side: hdwy over 1f out: led jst ins fnl f: readily)	—	**1**	14/1	82	61
4385*	**Mon Bruce (64)** (MDods) **3-8-8** 7x JCarroll(10) (trckd ldrs: ev ch ins fnl f: r.o)	1	**2**	14/1	71	50
4434[3]	**Squire Corrie (81)** (DWChapman) **5-9-11** KFallon(20) (lw: led stands' side: nt qckn ins fnl f)	hd	**3**	3/1[1]	88	67
4385[16]	**Camionneur (IRE) (54)** (TDEasterby) **4-7-12b** LCharnock(15) (s.i.s: hdwy over 1f out: styd on towards fin)	nk	**4**	10/1	60	39
4365[11]	**That Man Again (83)** (SCWilliams) **5-9-13b** KDarley(18) (a.p: styd on same pce fnl f)	s.h	**5**	12/1	88	67
4280[12]	**Daawe (USA) (76)** (JAGlover) **6-8-13v**(7) TPengkerego(14) (lw: a chsng ldrs: kpt on same pce fnl f)	1½	**6**	20/1	77	56
4385[2]	**Jucea (55)** (JLSpearing) **8-7-13** JQuinn(11) (lw: mid div: styd on appr fnl f: nt rch ldrs)	nk	**7**	8/1[3]	55	34
4233[8]	**Goretski (IRE) (80)** (NTinkler) **4-9-10** DHolland(12) (chsd ldrs: drvn along ½-wy: kpt on one pce)	nk	**8**	11/1	79	58
4365[3]	**Lady Sheriff (84)** (MWEasterby) **6-10-0b** TLucas(5) (racd far side: chsd ldrs: wknd towards fin)	s.h	**9**	14/1	83	62
4414*	**Johayro (59)** (JSGoldie) **4-8-3** TWilliams(17) (w ldrs tl wknd fnl f)	½	**10**	10/1	56	35
3481[7]	**Insider Trader (55)** (BSRothwell) **6-7-8be**(5) IonaWands(9) (chsd ldrs: wknd jst ins fnl f)	hd	**11**	25/1	52	31
4365[7]	**U-No-Harry (IRE) (56)** (RHollinshead) **4-8-0** NCarlisle(4) (racd far side: sn outpcd: styd on appr fnl f)	¾	**12**	25/1	50	29
4169[14]	**Dona Filipa (53)** (MissLCSiddall) **4-7-11**ow1 FNorton(19) (sn drvn along & outpcd: sme hdwy appr fnl f: n.d)	½	**13**	50/1	46	24
1571[4]	**Ballymote (77)** (JBerry) **3-9-4**(3) PFessey(3) (racd far side: led tl hdd jst ins fnl f: wknd)	nk	**14**	40/1	69	48
4414[2]	**Saint Express (76)** (MrsMReveley) **7-9-6** ACulhane(16) (lw: mid div: sn drvn along: n.d)	s.h	**15**	9/2[2]	67	46
4307[9]	**Bollin Harry (53)** (TDEasterby) **5-7-11v1** DWright(8) (racd far side: sn outpcd: sme hdwy fnl f: n.d)	s.h	**16**	16/1	44	23
4385[10]	**Just Dissident (IRE) (56)** (RMWhitaker) **5-7-7**(7) DMernagh(7) (b.nr fore: racd far side: chsd ldrs tl wknd 1f out)	hd	**17**	33/1	47	26
4385[5]	**Lillibella (53)** (MrsJRRamsden) **4-7-11** JLowe(1) (racd far side: w ldrs tl wknd ins fnl f)	hd	**18**	11/1	44	23
4233[5]	**Another Episode (IRE) (52)** (MissLAPerratt) **8-7-3**(7) JMcAuley(13) (lw: dwlt: a in rr)	5	**19**	20/1	27	6

				SP	RR	SF
4365^{4}	***Sharp Pearl (84)*** (PRWebber) **4-10-0b** FLynch(2) (Withdrawn not under Starter's orders: v.unruly in stalls).......		**W**	11/1	—	—
				(SP 155.6%)	**19 Rn**	

61.23 secs (2.83) CSF £188.01 CT £631.05 TOTE £21.90: £4.90 £5.00 £1.70 £2.10 (£136.70) Trio £368.20 OWNER Mr J. Fotherby (MIDDLEHAM) BRED Mrs D. Whittingham

LONG HANDICAP Dona Filipa 7-3 Another Episode (IRE) 7-8

4233* Just Bob, 8lb higher than when winning at Ayr, put his disappointing run at Redcar when ridden by a girl apprentice behind him. Missing the break slightly, he moved up travelling really well and scored in tremendous style. McKeown's record on him now reads ridden three, won three. (14/1)

4385* Mon Bruce, under a 7lb penalty, ran probably his best ever race on turf. Never giving up, it was always an unequal struggle. (14/1)

4434 Squire Corrie, who looked particularly well, was gambled on to capitalize on the highest draw of all. Showing his rivals a clean pair of heels on the stands side, in the end the first two home were on the other wing. (3/1: op 6/1)

4385 Camionneur (IRE) quickly put his poor effort at Pontefract behind him. Missing the break as usual, he stayed on in the closing stages to finish second best on the stands' side. (10/1)

4365 That Man Again had the blinkers on again. (12/1)

4280 Daawe (USA), ridden by an inexperienced boy, is probably better over six. (20/1)

3481* Goretski (IRE) looks to be a pound or two too high in the weights at present. (11/1: 8/1-12/1)

4513 E.B.F. CALDERPRINT MAIDEN STKS (2-Y.O) (Class D)

5-15 (5-18) **6f** £3,420.00 (£1,035.00: £505.00: £240.00) Stalls: High GOING: 0.11 sec per fur (G)

				SP	RR	SF
4298^{10}	**Lucayan Indian (IRE)** (DRLoder) **2-9-0** KFallon(3) (lw: chsd ldr: drvn along over 3f out: styd on to ld over 1f out: r.o wl)........	—	**1**	5/2 2	88	58
3726^{2}	**Elhabub** (BWHills) **2-9-0** RHills(4) (lw: led tl over 1f out: nt qckn)........	2	**2**	4/9 1	83	53
	Roi Brisbane (MJohnston) **2-9-0** DHolland(5) (w'like: bit bkwd: sn chsng ldrs: drvn along ½-wy: swtchd lft 2f out: kpt on same pce)........	1½	**3**	7/1 3	79+	49
4132^{8}	**Holy Smoke** (JLEyre) **2-8-9** KDarley(1) (trckd ldrs: wkng whn sltly hmpd over 2f out)........	11	**4**	25/1	44	14
4017^{14}	**Intuitive** (JLEyre) **2-8-2(7)** SBuckley(2) (sn outpcd: rdn ½-wy: lost pl over 2f out)........	3	**5**	100/1	36	6
				(SP 115.1%)	**5 Rn**	

1m 14.98 (3.48) CSF £3.83 TOTE £2.60: £1.10 £1.10 (£1.20) OWNER Lucayan Stud (NEWMARKET) BRED C. Corrigan

Lucayan Indian (IRE) had obviously learnt plenty from his initial outing. After taking time to get into top gear, in the end he took this in decisive fashion, and a step up to seven will be no problem. (5/2)

3726 Elhabub looked to have his rivals in trouble at halfway but, when the chips were down, the winner found far too much for him. He obviously has his limitations. (4/9)

Roi Brisbane, who is not the best of walkers, looked as if the outing would do him the power of good. Showing definite signs of inexperience, he kept on in encouraging fashion and there is surely better to come. (7/1)

Holy Smoke was on the retreat when pushed sideways by the third with over a quarter of a mile left to run. (25/1)

4514 PRICE WATERHOUSE MAIDEN AUCTION STKS (II) (2-Y.O) (Class F)

5-45 (5-47) **7f** £2,239.00 (£629.00: £307.00) Stalls: High GOING: 0.11 sec per fur (G)

				SP	RR	SF
4209^{4}	**Misalliance** (CFWall) **2-7-10(5)** RMullen(9) (lw: trckd ldrs: shkn up 2f out: qcknd to ld jst ins fnl f: sn clr).......	—	**1**	9/4 1	71+	32
	Megred (JHMGosden) **2-8-4** GHind(3) (leggy: scope: dwlt: hdwy ½-wy: edgd rt & styd on fnl f)........	2½	**2**	5/1 3	68	29
3973^{7}	**Adeste Fideles** (MBell) **2-8-4** DHolland(4) (chsd ldrs: shkn up & kpt on fnl 2f)........	3½	**3**	5/1 3	60	21
4236^{7}	**Arab Gold** (MissSEHall) **2-8-9** KFallon(10) (led: clr ½-wy: wknd & hdd jst ins fnl f: fin tired)........	1	**4**	100/30 2	63	24
4278^{5}	**Glory of Love** (JHetherton) **2-8-6** DeanMcKeown(8) (chsd ldr: outpcd ½-wy: styd on fnl f)........	s.h	**5**	8/1	60	21
	Strategic Air (EWeymes) **2-8-6** JQuinn(5) (cmpt: bit bkwd: dwlt: hdwy 2f out: kpt on: nvr nr to chal)........	½	**6**	16/1	59	20
3905^{12}	**Celestial Welcome** (MrsMReveley) **2-7-12** DaleGibson(6) (sn outpcd & drvn along)........	4	**7**	10/1	42	3
4052^{9}	**Zillion (IRE)** (JWPayne) **2-8-9** KDarley(11) (dwlt: a in rr)........	¾	**8**	33/1	51	12
3808^{4}	**Double Appeal (IRE) (43)** (CaptJWilson) **2-7-9(3)** PFessey(1) (chsd ldrs: outpcd ½-wy: sn lost pl)........	8	**9**	33/1	22	—
4231^{7}	**Saintes (62)** (WMcKeown) **2-8-9** JCarroll(7) (outpcd fr ½-wy)........	½	**10**	33/1	32	—
4215^{9}	**Ladyofdistinction (IRE) (50)** (JSWainwright) **2-8-3ow2** FLynch(2) (chsd ldrs tl lost pl ½-wy: sn bhd)........	5	**11**	50/1	14	—
				(SP 124.0%)	**11 Rn**	

1m 29.84 (5.34) CSF £13.04 TOTE £2.80: £1.80 £3.40 £1.40 (£5.90) Trio £7.40 OWNER The Lively Partners (NEWMARKET) BRED Rockwell Bloodstock

4209 Misalliance quickly confirmed the promise shown at Beverley. Confidently ridden, she showed a nice turn of foot and will be an interesting proposition in a nursery. (9/4)

Megred, who showed a poor action going down, ran a satisfactory first race after a sluggish start. (5/1: 7/2-11/2)

3973 Adeste Fideles was not knocked about at any stage and should be capable of something better. (5/1)

4236 Arab Gold showed with a clear lead at halfway but, into a strong head-wind, he became very leg-weary entering the final furlong and looked exhausted at the line. (100/30)

4278 Glory of Love, who gave problems going to the start, probably found this trip too short. A mile will suit him much better. (8/1)

Strategic Air, who looked in need of the outing, showed a glimmer of ability on his debut. (16/1)

T/Jkpt: Not won; £6,054.25 to Newmarket 2/10/97. T/Plpt: £249.00 (85.49 Tckts). T/Qdpt: £59.50 (22.24 Tckts) AA/WG

3979-SALISBURY (R-H) (Good, Good to firm patches)

Wednesday October 1st

All races: hand-timed

WEATHER: fine but cloudy WIND: fresh against

4515 E.B.F. AUTUMN MAIDEN STKS (2-Y.O) (Class D)

2-00 (2-03) **6f 212y** £4,425.50 (£1,334.00: £647.00: £303.50) Stalls: High GOING minus 0.12 sec per fur (G)

				SP	RR	SF
4318^{6}	**Lucky Double** (RHannon) **2-9-0** DaneO'Neill(4) (hld up & bhd: hdwy over 2f out: led wl ins fnl f: r.o)........	—	**1**	11/2 2	75	32
3636^{3}	**Gunzells (USA)** (HCandy) **2-8-9** CRutter(5) (hld up: hdwy & edgd rt over 2f out: led over 1f out: hdd wl ins fnl f)........	nk	**2**	9/2 1	69	26
	Gleaming Hill (USA) (MRStoute) **2-9-0** JReid(10) (unf: scope: bit bkwd: hld up: hdwy whn hmpd over 2f out: ev ch over 1f out: one pce)........	2½	**3**	6/1 3	69+	26

Ref	Horse / details	Dist	Pos	SP	RR	SF
4216[11]	**Magic Powers** (GBBalding) **2-9-0** SDrowne(3) (hld up & bhd: gd hdwy over 1f out: nrst fin)	1½	**4**	33/1	65	22
3687[12]	**La Lyonesse** (JWHills) **2-8-6**(3) MHenry(11) (mid div: rdn 2f out: r.o one pce)	1¾	**5**	20/1	56	13
4379[7]	**Arctic Star** (MRChannon) **2-9-0** RPerham(12) (hld up mid div: rdn 2f out: no hdwy)	½	**6**	20/1	60	17
	Honey Suckle (MissGayKelleway) **2-8-6**(3) AWhelan(16) (unf: a.p: led wl over 1f out: sn hdd: wknd ins fnl f)	s.h	**7**	14/1	55	12
	In The Sun (USA) (JLDunlop) **2-8-9** TQuinn(17) (w'like: bit bkwd: nvr nr to chal)	¾	**8**	13/2	53	10
	My Pledge (IRE) (CAHorgan) **2-9-0** MFenton(19) (bit bkwd: rdn & hdwy 3f out: n.m.r wl over 1f out: sn wknd)	hd	**9**	33/1	58	15
3136[8]	**Surpresa Cara** (GLewis) **2-8-9** TSprake(15) (a mid div)	1½	**10**	33/1	49	6
	Kitoph (IRE) (EALDunlop) **2-8-9** DO'Donohoe(2) (unf: bit bkwd: b.nr hind: dwlt: nvr nrr)	2½	**11**	14/1	44	1
	Hunt Hill (IRE) (SirMarkPrescott) **2-9-0** GDuffield(1) (w'like: bit bkwd: nvr nrr)	nk	**12**	11/2[2]	48	5
	Pressurise (SirMarkPrescott) **2-9-0** CNutter(9) (w'like: scope: a bhd)	1¼	**13**	25/1	45	2
3094[14]	**Long Island** (RHannon) **2-9-0** DBiggs(13) (prom: wkng whn n.m.r over 2f out)	nk	**14**	25/1	44	1
2781[9]	**Gaily Mill** (IABalding) **2-8-9** SWhitworth(20) (led over 5f out tl wl over 1f out: sn wknd)	1½	**15**	16/1	36	—
4107[8]	**Ivory League** (GLewis) **2-8-9** NDay(8) (a bhd)	2½	**16**	20/1	30	—
3686[9]	**Rhapsody In Blue (IRE)** (AndrewTurnell) **2-9-0** NAdams(6) (b.hind: bit bkwd: prom 5f)	nk	**17**	33/1	35	—
	Boreas Hill (IRE) (JRArnold) **2-8-9**(5) CLowther(14) (unf: bit bkwd: b.nr hind: a bhd: t.o fnl 3f)	13	**18**	50/1	5	—
4042[15]	**Heiress of Meath (IRE)** (MDIUsher) **2-8-9** JMarshall(18) (bit bkwd: prom 4f: t.o)	5	**19**	50/1	—	—
2388[10]	**Jonathan's Girl (46)** (JJBridger) **2-8-6**(3) ADaly(7) (led over 1f: wknd 3f out: t.o)	3	**20**	33/1	—	—
				(SP 136.4%)	**20 Rn**	

1m 30.9 (4.90) CSF £25.68 TOTE £7.10: £1.40 £2.00 £3.00 (£12.70) Trio £7.20 OWNER Mr Mohamed Suhail (MARLBOROUGH) BRED Gainsborough Stud Management Ltd

4318 Lucky Double, a half-brother to a mile and a half winner in Ireland, is out of an Italian Oaks winner. He needed every yard of this trip having run over a mile last time. (11/2)

3636 Gunzells (USA), a sister to seven-furlong juvenile scorer Impulsif, appreciated this step up from the minimum distance. (9/2)

Gleaming Hill (USA) is a half-brother to Hatta Sunshine and several winner in the States, including a Grade Two scorer. Done no favours by the runner-up when beginning his run, improvement can be expected. (6/1: op 3/1)

Magic Powers, a half-brother to the sprinter Coquito's Friend, has plenty of speed on the dam side. However, he looked much more at home over this longer trip and showed plenty of promise for the future. (33/1)

La Lyonesse, ran her best race so far and may be better suited by a mile. (20/1)

4231 Arctic Star a half-brother to Irish Oaks winner Bolas and One For Baileys, has plenty of stamina in his pedigree on the dam's side. (20/1)

Honey Suckle, a half sister to Phylida and Major Change, made a promising start to her career until tying up in the closing stages. (14/1)

In The Sun (USA), the first foal of a half-sister to the useful middle-distance performer Allegan, is bred to need further and will do better in due course. (13/2: op 4/1)

Kitoph (IRE) (14/1: 8/1-16/1)

4516 FONTHILL H'CAP (0-70) (3-Y.O+) (Class E)

2-30 (2-33) **1m 1f 209y** £3,463.75 (£1,045.00: £507.50: £238.75) Stalls: Low GOING minus 0.12 sec per fur (G)

Ref	Horse / details	Dist	Pos	SP	RR	SF
4319[5]	**Absolute Utopia (USA) (55)** (NEBerry) **4-8-13** LDettori(17) (hld up: hdwy on ins 3f out: led 1f out: drvn out)	—	**1**	7/1[3]	68	50
4324[13]	**Sea Danzig (51)** (JJBridger) **4-8-9** NAdams(13) (led: rdn & hdd 1f out: one pce)	2½	**2**	25/1	60	42
4297[15]	**Serendipity (FR) (62)** (BRMillman) **4-9-6** MFenton(7) (hld up & bhd: gd hdwy fnl 2f: r.o)	1½	**3**	10/1	69	51
4172[12]	**Bakers Daughter (59)** (JRArnold) **5-8-12**(5) CLowther(16) (a.p: one pce fnl 2f)	½	**4**	16/1	65	47
1233[4]	**Seattle Alley (USA) (65)** (PRWebber) **4-9-9** RPerham(11) (hdwy over 4f out: rdn over 3f out: one pce fnl 2f)	nk	**5**	25/1	70	52
4219[8]	**Ashby Hill (IRE) (60)** (RRowe) **6-9-4** GCarter(14) (dwlt: hld up: hdwy 3f out: one pce fnl 2f)	1½	**6**	9/2[2]	63	45
4219[15]	**Alfahaal (IRE) (55)** (RFJohnsonHoughton) **4-8-13** JReid(15) (b.hind: hdwy over 3f out: r.o one pce fnl 2f)	¾	**7**	10/1	57	39
4172[4]	**Thatchmaster (IRE) (65)** (CAHorgan) **6-9-9** DO'Donohoe(2) (mid div: rdn over 2f out: no hdwy)	hd	**8**	10/1	67	49
3573[10]	**Tissue of Lies (USA) (55)** (RAkehurst) **4-8-13** TQuinn(6) (prom: rdn over 4f out: wknd over 2f out)	3	**9**	12/1	52	34
4323[18]	**Absolutelystunning (50)** (MrsBarbaraWaring) **4-8-8** DeclanO'Shea(9) (b: b.hind: a bhd)	7	**10**	50/1	35	17
4323[3]	**Missfortuna (66)** (SirMarkPrescott) **3-9-5** GDuffield(4) (sn rdn: bhd fnl 2f)	¾	**11**	5/2[1]	50	27
4109[12]	**Pay Homage (68)** (IABalding) **9-9-5**(7) LeanneMasterson(3) (nvr nr ldrs)	¾	**12**	20/1	51	33
4069[4]	**Haroldon (IRE) (60)** (BPalling) **8-9-4** TSprake(1) (sme hdwy over 3f out: wknd over 2f out)	8	**13**	25/1	30	12
4109[11]	**Alarmist (70)** (RCharlton) **3-9-2**(7) KParsons(12) (dwlt: sme hdwy over 6f out: wknd over 2f out)	nk	**14**	25/1	40	17
4109[3]	**Monument (61)** (JSKing) **5-9-2**(3) RHavlin(5) (prom: rdn over 4f out: wknd 3f out)	nk	**15**	10/1	30	12
	Dtoto (50) (RJBaker) **5-8-8** VSlattery(8) (bhd fnl 3f)	¾	**16**	66/1	18	—
	Timothy George (IRE) (60) (GBBalding) **3-8-13** SDrowne(10) (a bhd)	1½	**17**	33/1	26	3
3202[9]	**Borrador (44)** (RCurtis) **3-7-11** NVarley(18) (a bhd: t.o)	12	**18**	50/1	—	—
				(SP 137.7%)	**18 Rn**	

2m 10.0 (4.70) CSF £172.87 CT £1,651.34 TOTE £7.80: £1.80 £6.20 £2.70 £2.90 (£180.10) Trio £472.30 OWNER Mr M. T. Lawrance (UPPER LAMBOURN) BRED Gainsborough Farm Inc

WEIGHT FOR AGE 3yo-5lb

OFFICIAL EXPLANATION **Missfortuna: was unsuited by the ground.**

4319 Absolute Utopia (USA), 2lb higher than when winning over a mile in August, was brought with a nicely-timed run. (7/1)

4109 Sea Danzig appeared to set quite a strong pace and put all doubts to rest that he stays this trip. (25/1)

3980 Serendipity (FR), stepping up in distance, ran a similar race to his effort over a mile here early last month. (10/1)

3496 Bakers Daughter remains on a mark 2lb higher than when winning at Windsor in July. (16/1)

1233 Seattle Alley (USA) should find this serving as a useful pipe-opener for a possible return to hurdles. (25/1)

1482 Ashby Hill (IRE), five times a winner last year, has found things much tougher this season and is now 5lb lower than the last of those victories. (9/2)

4059 Alfahaal (IRE) (10/1: 8/1-12/1)

4517 CRANBORNE CONDITIONS STKS (2-Y.O) (Class C)

3-00 (3-00) **6f** £4,460.80 (£1,667.20: £813.60: £348.00: £154.00: £76.40) Stalls: High GOING minus 0.12 sec per fur (G)

Ref	Horse / details	Dist	Pos	SP	RR	SF
4167*	**Deterrent (94)** (JHMGosden) **2-9-1** LDettori(5) (hld up: hdwy & nt clr run over 2f out: swtchd lft wl over 1f out: led ins fnl f: r.o)	—	**1**	5/6[1]	92	40
4106[6]	**Toblersong** (RAkehurst) **2-9-1** TQuinn(3) (hld up: rdn to ld 2f out: hdd 1f out: r.o)	¾	**2**	9/1	90	38
4293[5]	**Bold Edge (100)** (RHannon) **2-9-1** DaneO'Neill(4) (hld up: n.m.r 2f out: one pce)	5	**3**	4/1[3]	77	25
4293[7]	**Flaming Ember (IRE) (93)** (BJMeehan) **2-8-12b[1]** GDuffield(1) (sn chsng ldr: rdn 3f out: wknd 1f out)	1¾	**4**	16/1	69	17
3706[6]	**Social Charter (USA) (97)** (PWChapple-Hyam) **2-9-1** JReid(6) (prom: rdn over 2f out: wknd 1f out)	½	**5**	7/2[2]	71	19

				SP	RR	SF
4218[4]	**Pichon Baron (USA)** (BJMeehan) **2-8-13**(7) GHannon(2) (a bhd)	5	**6**	50/1	62	10
3314[8]	**Regalo (62)** (DMHyde) **2-8-9**(3) RHavlin(7) (led 4f)	8	**7**	100/1	33	—

(SP 115.6%) **7 Rn**

1m 16.6 (3.60) CSF £9.28 TOTE £1.90: £1.50 £2.70 (£5.10) OWNER Sheikh Mohammed (NEWMARKET) BRED Aylesfield Farms Stud
4167* Deterrent had to overcome traffic problems and needed to be kept right up to his work after striking the front. (5/6: evens-5/4)
4106 Toblersong put up his best performance to date and did not go down without a fight. He should soon be back in the winner's enclosure. (9/1)
4293 Bold Edge does seem at his best when the mud is flying. (4/1)
4146 Flaming Ember (IRE), sharpened up by the blinkers, might be worth a return to the minimum distance. (16/1)
3489* Social Charter (USA), disappointing in the Gimcrack, fared little better here. (7/2: 5/2-4/1)

4518 AXMINSTER 100 APPRENTICE H'CAP (0-70) (3-Y.O+) (Class F)

3-35 (3-37) **6f** £2,721.75 (£834.00: £414.50: £204.75) Stalls: High GOING minus 0.12 sec per fur (G)

				SP	RR	SF
4221[5]	**Robellion (47)** (DWPArbuthnot) **6-8-3**(3) JWilkinson(3) (racd stands' side: hdwy 2f out: edgd rt & led ins fnl f: r.o)	—	**1**	8/1	59	29
3982[12]	**Out Line (65)** (MMadgwick) **5-9-7**(3) AEddery(6) (lw: sn pushed along: gd hdwy over 1f out: r.o ins fnl f)	1	**2**	14/1	74	44
4243[19]	**Double March (50)** (KTIvory) **4-8-9** GFaulkner(4) (rdn & hdwy over 2f out: led over 1f out tl ins fnl f: r.o)	s.h	**3**	33/1	59	29
4370[14]	**Scissor Ridge (60)** (JJBridger) **5-9-0**(5) RBrisland(7) (a.p: ev ch 1f out: nt qckn)	¾	**4**	9/1	67	37
4333[15]	**Pointer (58)** (MrsPNDutfield) **5-9-3** AimeeCook(9) (hld up: hdwy over 1f out: n.m.r ins fnl f: one pce)	1¼	**5**	6/1[2]	62	32
4321[9]	**Walk the Beat (64)** (MartynMeade) **7-9-1**(8) ClaireAngell(15) (lw: rdn & no hdwy fnl 2f)	1¼	**6**	16/1	65	35
4370[2]	**Flying Harold (45)** (MRChannon) **4-8-4** APolli(18) (prom: ev ch over 1f out: wknd ins fnl f)	1¼	**7**	100/30[1]	42	12
3139[6]	**Always Grace (50)** (MissGayKelleway) **5-8-6**(3) JoHunnam(17) (hdwy 2f out: rdn over 1f out: one pce)	nk	**8**	11/1	46	16
4249[6]	**Mister Raider (48)** (EAWheeler) **5-7-11b**(10)ow5 BO'Leary(13) (led over 4f)	½	**9**	12/1	43	8
4248[10]	**Mellors (IRE) (46)** (MJHeaton-Ellis) **4-8-2**(3) ADaly(16) (bhd fnl 2f)	1¼	**10**	25/1	38	8
4370[11]	**Tart and a Half (61)** (MPitman) **5-9-1**(5) ANicholls(14) (n.d)	nk	**11**	14/1	52	22
	Corporal Nym (USA) (63) (MRBosley) **4-9-3**(5) RStudholme(12) (bit bkwd: a bhd)	2	**12**	40/1	49	19
3641[2]	**Dorado Beach (43)** (LGCottrell) **3-7-12v**(3) RWinston(11) (bhd fnl 3f)	nk	**13**	16/1	28	—
3642[12]	**Superlao (BEL) (48)** (JJBridger) **5-8-2**(5) DarrenWilliams(10) (prom 4f: eased whn btn ins fnl f)	1½	**14**	25/1	29	—
3984[16]	**Supreme Thought (61)** (LGCottrell) **5-9-6** GMilligan(2) (racd stands' side: a bhd)	nk	**15**	7/1[3]	41	11
4328[13]	**Xenophon of Cunaxa (IRE) (58)** (MJFetherston-Godley) **4-9-3b** CLowther(1) (s.s: racd alone centre: a bhd)	1½	**16**	20/1	34	4
4049[9]	**Tommy Tempest (38)** (REPeacock) **8-7-6v**(5) PFitzsimons(8) (w ldr tl wknd qckly over 2f out)	7	**17**	25/1	—	—
489[5]	**Prix de Clermont (IRE) (55)** (GLewis) **3-8-5**(8) JDennis(5) (a bhd)	3	**18**	20/1	4	—

(SP 138.5%) **18 Rn**

1m 16.8 (3.80) CSF £108.45 CT £1,913.02 TOTE £8.90: £1.70 £3.80 £10.80 £2.60 (£91.30) Trio £629.10; £629.19 to Newmarket 2/10/97
OWNER Mr George Thompson (COMPTON) BRED Pitts Farm Stud
WEIGHT FOR AGE 3yo-1lb
4221 Robellion, no less than 19lb lower than when winning at Newmarket in August last year, had shown signs of a return to form at Sandown last time. (8/1: op 12/1)
2833 Out Line came back to form over this stiff six. (14/1)
61 Double March, dropped 10lb, ran his best race for some time over this shorter distance. (33/1)
3765 Scissor Ridge was not beaten that far in a very competitive handicap over five at Goodwood last time. (9/1)
4115 Pointer, raised 3lb for his third at Chepstow, was 7lb above the highest mark off which he has won. (6/1)
3417* Walk the Beat was again 5lb higher than when scoring at Lingfield in August. (16/1)
4370 Flying Harold seemed to get found out by this testing six. (100/30)
3139 Always Grace (11/1: 7/1-12/1)

4519 HURDLERS CLAIMING H'CAP (0-60) (3-Y.O+) (Class F)

4-05 (4-05) **1m 6f** £2,626.00 (£736.00: £358.00) GOING minus 0.34 sec per fur (GF)

				SP	RR	SF
4222[12]	**Tarry (46)** (MissGayKelleway) **4-9-10** LDettori(1) (hld up: stdy hdwy 4f out: hrd rdn over 2f out: styd on to ld wl ins fnl f)	—	**1**	2/1[1]	60	41
4374[2]	**Wilkins (48)** (RJO'Sullivan) **8-9-12** JReid(13) (a.p: led on bit over 3f out: rdn over 1f out: hdd wl ins fnl f)	½	**2**	3/1[2]	61	42
4160[13]	**Kika (40)** (KRBurke) **4-9-4** DaneO'Neill(9) (hld up: hdwy over 4f out: wknd over 1f out)	11	**3**	14/1	41	22
3210[8]	**Doyenne (38)** (GLewis) **3-8-7b**[1] NDay(4) (plld hrd: w ldr: led 8f out to over 3f out: wknd over 1f out)	2	**4**	20/1	37	9
3865[5]	**Golden Melody (51)** (MJHeaton-Ellis) **3-9-6** RPerham(2) (lw: a.p: hrd rdn over 4f out: wknd over 2f out)	3½	**5**	20/1	46	18
4432[11]	**Rose of Glenn (45)** (BPalling) **6-9-9** TSprake(8) (w.r.s: hdwy over 4f out: wknd over 2f out)	1¼	**6**	14/1	38	19
4170[10]	**Nornax Lad (USA) (36)** (MartynMeade) **9-8-11b**(3) RHavlin(10) (hld up: wknd over 2f out)	1¼	**7**	14/1	28	9
	Mu-Tadil (38) (RJBaker) **5-9-2** VSlattery(12) (bit bkwd: rdn over 6f out: a bhd)	5	**8**	33/1	24	5
3858[3]	**Perlethorpe (49)** (MBell) **3-9-4** MFenton(7) (lw: bhd fnl 5f)	13	**9**	5/1[3]	20	—
4275[16]	**Strat's Legacy (36)** (DWPArbuthnot) **10-9-0** NAdams(6) (hld up: hdwy 7f out: sn rdn: wknd 4f out)	s.h	**10**	16/1	7	—
3617[3]	**Saltimbanco (32)** (RAkehurst) **3-7-12**(3)ow1 ADaly(5) (led 6f: rdn & wknd over 4f out)	nk	**11**	12/1	3	—
4222[10]	**Sovereign Crest (IRE) (48)** (CAHorgan) **4-9-12v** SWhitworth(11) (s.s: a bhd)	1½	**12**	9/1	17	—
4289[2]	**Ronquista d'Or (49)** (GAHam) **3-9-4** SDrowne(3) (a bhd)	¾	**13**	20/1	17	—

(SP 135.8%) **13 Rn**

3m 5.8 (7.10) CSF £7.73 CT £70.49 TOTE £3.60: £1.80 £1.50 £3.90 (£6.50) Trio £38.20 OWNER Mr John Purcell (WHITCOMBE) BRED Highclere Stud Ltd
WEIGHT FOR AGE 3yo-9lb
3792* Tarry, back into a claimer, eventually wore down the runner-up. (2/1)
4374 Wilkins had little option than to take it up when he did, but that turned out to be a long way from home. (3/1)
3694 Kika has yet to prove she stays beyond a mile and a half. (14/1)
Doyenne ran too freely in the first-time blinkers over this longer trip. (20/1)

4520 E.B.F. MARLBOROUGH MAIDEN STKS (2-Y.O) (Class D)

4-35 (4-37) **1m** £3,980.50 (£1,204.00: £587.00: £278.50) Stalls: High GOING minus 0.12 sec per fur (G)

				SP	RR	SF
3789[4]	**Courteous** (PFICole) **2-9-0** TQuinn(5) (chsd ldr: led over 2f out: edgd lft ins fnl f: r.o)	—	**1**	4/1[3]	84	21
	Majestic Hills (JLDunlop) **2-9-0** LDettori(2) (unf: scope: bit bkwd: dwlt: hld up: hdwy over 2f out: ev ch ins fnl f: nt qckn)	¾	**2**	2/1[1]	83	20

	Elhayq (IRE) (JLDunlop) **2-9-0** GCarter(9) (rangy: scope: s.s: gd hdwy 3f out: ev ch over 1f out: btn whn n.m.r ins fnl f)	4	**3**	11/2	75+	12
4237[5]	**Grand Slam (IRE)** (RHannon) **2-9-0** DaneO'Neill(7) (hld up: hdwy over 2f out: rdn over 1f out: one pce)	1½	**4**	3/1[2]	72	9
	Classic Impact (IRE) (PWChapple-Hyam) **2-9-0** JReid(10) (leggy: scope: hld up mid div: no hdwy fnl 2f)	1¼	**5**	8/1	69	6
4237[11]	**First Master** (MissGayKelleway) **2-8-11**(3) AWhelan(14) (b: prom 6f)	1	**6**	33/1	67	4
	Conical (RCharlton) **2-8-9** TSprake(4) (tall: scope: hld up: wknd over 2f out)	1¼	**7**	9/2	60	—
	Ballykissann (DJSffrenchDavis) **2-9-0** SDrowne(11) (w'like: s.s: nvr nrr)	hd	**8**	50/1	64	1
	Flying Clouds (MBlanshard) **2-8-6**(3) PPMurphy(3) (w'like: bit bkwd: a bhd)	6	**9**	33/1	47	—
4229[7]	**Lycian (IRE)** (SirMarkPrescott) **2-9-0** GDuffield(6) (led over 5f)	1¾	**10**	33/1	49	—
4111[7]	**Blue Monk (IRE)** (IABalding) **2-9-0** SWhitworth(8) (prom over 5f)	nk	**11**	14/1	48	—
	Topaz (JWHills) **2-8-11**(3) MHenry(13) (w'like: hld up mid div: wknd wl over 1f out)	2	**12**	33/1	44	—
4379[6]	**Twoforten** (MMadgwick) **2-9-0** NVarley(12) (bhd fnl 2f)	¾	**13**	50/1	43	—
				(SP 145.4%)	**13 Rn**	

1m 46.8 (6.80) CSF £13.61 TOTE £4.60: £2.00 £1.90 £2.30 (£9.90) Trio £22.20 OWNER H R H Prince Fahd Salman (WHATCOMBE) BRED Newgate Stud Co

3789 Courteous, entered in the Derby, had a stiffer mile this time and held on well. (4/1)

Majestic Hills, a 35,000gns half-brother to Deputy Governor who went on to be a very useful horse in the States, is out of a Canadian Oaks winner. He should not be hard to place. (2/1)

Elhayq (IRE), a half-brother to seven-furlong winner Musharak, is out of a mare from the same family as Al Hareb. He looks the type who could make up into a nice three-year-old. (11/2: 3/1-6/1)

4237 Grand Slam (IRE) was a bit disappointing on the face of it but is bred to need further and is probably a longer-term prospect. (3/1)

Classic Impact (IRE), a 65,000gns half-brother to mile winner Viva Verdi and a Group Two winner in Germany, did not live up to his name on this debut. (8/1: 6/1-10/1)

First Master, a half-brother to mile and a half winner Arabian Bold, is out of a mare who won over that trip and also a furlong further. (33/1)

Conical (9/2: 3/1-5/1)

T/Plpt: £118.40 (176.66 Tckts). T/Qdpt: £16.60 (69.92 Tckts) KH

4473-**NEWMARKET** (R-H) (Good to firm, St crse Good)

Thursday October 2nd

WEATHER: sunny and warm WIND: fresh behind

4521 PORT OF FELIXSTOWE CLAIMING STKS (3-Y.O+) (Class D)

1-30 (1-35) **1m 4f (Rowley)** £3,882.50 (£1,160.00: £555.00: £252.50) Stalls: High GOING minus 0.31 sec per fur (GF)

				SP	RR	SF
4108[8]	**Water Flower (66)** (JRFanshawe) **3-8-6** MHills(9) (chsd ldr: led 1f out: hld on gamely cl home)	—	**1**	10/1	64	46
4161[6]	**Durgams First (IRE) (49)** (MrsMReveley) **5-9-0** ACulhane(13) (a chsng ldrs: rdn over 2f out: kpt on wl fnl f)	½	**2**	16/1	64	53
	Royal Diversion (IRE) (MCPipe) **4-9-3** OPeslier(8) (a.p: hrd drvn 2f out: kpt on wl cl home)	nk	**3**	6/1[2]	67	56
3277[5]	**Naval Games** (SCWilliams) **4-8-12** KDarley(11) (a.p: hrd rdn 2f out: r.o one pce)	½	**4**	6/1[2]	61	50
4415[2]	**Filial (IRE) (60)** (BJMeehan) **4-8-12** MTebbutt(6) (trckd ldrs: effrt 2f out: rdn & one pce ins fnl f)	1¼	**5**	10/1	60	49
1478[12]	**Belmarita (IRE) (60)** (GAHubbard) **4-9-8** DO'Donohoe(5) (led to 1f out: eased whn btn ins fnl f)	½	**6**	33/1	69	58
3929*	**Statajack (IRE) (57)** (DRCElsworth) **9-9-1b** TQuinn(7) (b: mid div: rdn over 2f out: no imp)	1½	**7**	7/1[3]	60	49
3467[4]	**Dauphin (IRE) (42)** (WJMusson) **4-9-2** RCochrane(10) (hld up mid div: effrt & drvn along 3f out: no imp)	5	**8**	33/1	54	43
4450[4]	**At Liberty (IRE) (65)** (RHannon) **5-9-3** DaneO'Neill(12) (nvr nr to chal)	1¼	**9**	20/1	54	43
4264[2]	**Break the Rules (75)** (DNicholls) **5-9-11** AlexGreaves(4) (lw: hld up & bhd: effrt 3f out: hung rt & no imp)	s.h	**10**	7/2[1]	62	51
*285**	**Once More for Luck (IRE) (65)** (MrsMReveley) **6-8-12**(5) SCopp(3) (hld up: a in rr)	2	**11**	10/1	51	40
4072[5]	**Monacle (45)** (DMorris) **3-8-10** NDay(1) (s.s: a bhd: t.o)	30	**12**	50/1	11	—
4180[3]	**Go Hence (51)** (WJarvis) **3-8-7** WRyan(2) (lw: rdn 4f out: sn lost tch: t.o)	hd	**13**	12/1	8	—
1877[8]	**Spartan Royale (76)** (CEBrittain) **3-9-0** KFallon(14) (bit bkwd: a bhd: t.o)	¾	**14**	8/1	14	—
				(SP 127.9%)	**14 Rn**	

2m 33.46 (2.96) CSF £149.44 TOTE £12.90: £3.00 £5.60 £2.70 (£256.60) Trio £454.90 OWNER Mr W. J. Gredley (NEWMARKET) BRED Stetchworth Park Stud Ltd

WEIGHT FOR AGE 3yo-7lb

Water Flower clmd CBarnes £11,000. Naval Games clmd CBarnes £5,000. Filial (IRE) clmd CWilliams £5,000.

OFFICIAL EXPLANATION **Break The Rules: rider reported that the gelding continuously hung right under pressure.**

2952 Water Flower has taken time to get off the mark but, well suited by this step down in class, poked her head in front passing the furlong pole and refused to give best in a hard-fought duel to the finish. (10/1: 7/1-12/1)

4161 Durgams First (IRE), possibly better when plenty of use is made of him, battled on gamely on meeting the rising ground and made sure the winner knew she had been in a race. (16/1)

Royal Diversion (IRE), successful in a similar event when she last ran on the Flat over eleven months ago, failed to fire in a couple of races over hurdles. Looking as though the run was needed, she ran extremely well in the circumstances and this is her game. (6/1: 4/1-13/2)

3277 Naval Games, very short on experience, gave a first-class account of himself to fail narrowly and, as he has now joined Martin Pipe, his future could probably lie over hurdles. (6/1: 8/1-5/1)

4415 Filial (IRE) showed signs at Redcar that he is approaching his peak and, though he was out-pointed in the closing stages, was claimed for £5,000, and he could prove a cheap buy. (10/1)

Belmarita (IRE), a winner at the winter game, is struggling to make her mark on the Flat, but her front-running tactics almost paid off here and she is probably better than her form would suggest. (33/1)

4264 Break the Rules could have found the ground faster than he cares for, because he did nothing but hang throughout the race and was never within striking range of the principals. (7/2)

4522 BAILEYS HORSE FEEDS NURSERY H'CAP (2-Y.O) (Class C)

2-05 (2-05) **5f (Rowley)** £7,375.00 (£2,200.00: £1,050.00: £475.00) Stalls: High GOING minus 0.31 sec per fur (GF)

				SP	RR	SF
4173*	**Bliss (IRE) (71)** (MrsPNDutfield) **2-7-10** JQuinn(12) (trckd ldrs: squeezed thro on ins to ld ins fnl f: r.o)	—	**1**	6/1[2]	74	39
4247[2]	**Shawdon (96)** (SirMarkPrescott) **2-9-7** GDuffield(11) (w ldr: ev ch ins fnl f: rdn & no ex cl home)	½	**2**	7/1	97	62
4296*	**Ivory's Joy (73)** (KTIvory) **2-7-12** MartinDwyer(6) (b: lw: led: rdn over 1f out: hdd & unable qckn ins fnl f)	½	**3**	8/1	73	38
4103[12]	**Midsummer Night (IRE) (73)** (RHannon) **2-7-9**(3) RFfrench(2) (chsd ldrs: ev ch 1f out: hrd drvn: unable qckn)	½	**4**	9/1	71	36
4173[2]	**High Carry (87)** (NTinkler) **2-8-7**(5) CLowther(10) (a.p: rdn over 1f out: btn whn hmpd ins fnl f)	1	**5**	8/1	82	47

4419*	**Mighty Sure (IRE) (72)** (CREgerton) **2-7-6**(5)ow1 7x RMullen(1) (trckd ldrs: rdn & unable qckn fnl f)	hd	**6**	20/1	67	31
3774[3]	**Nuclear Debate (USA) (89)** (MrsJRRamsden) **2-9-0** JFortune(3) (hld up & bhd: effrt & hmpd over 1f out: swtchd rt: fin fast)	hd	**7**	7/2[1]	83+	48
4296[4]	**Eastern Lyric (75)** (JBerry) **2-8-0** NAdams(9) (lw: a in rr)	1¾	**8**	16/1	64	29
4103[4]	**Solo Spirit (80)** (JRJenkins) **2-8-5** JFEgan(4) (in tch 3f: sn outpcd: t.o)	5	**9**	10/1	53	18
3965[8]	**Folklore (93)** (DRLoder) **2-9-4** LDettori(8) (pushed along & lost pl ½-wy: sn outpcd)	3	**10**	13/2[3]	56	21
4232[7]	**Eleventh Duke (IRE) (94)** (RHannon) **2-9-5** OPeslier(7) (b.hind: hld up: a bhd)	5	**11**	11/1	41	6

(SP 122.6%) **11 Rn**

59.58 secs (0.88) CSF £45.42 CT £321.38 TOTE £6.00: £1.80 £3.10 £2.60 (£26.60) Trio £33.50 OWNER Mr W. A. Harrison-Allan (SEATON) BRED Mrs Margaret Sinanan
LONG HANDICAP Mighty Sure (IRE) 7-0

4173* Bliss (IRE) got the gap she needed to complete her hat-trick. She proved very game under strong pressure and this was thoroughly deserved. (6/1)

4247 Shawdon has won at this trip but he is more effective over an extra furlong, and the winner took full advantage of a considerable weight concession to beat him to the punch. (7/1)

4296* Ivory's Joy, much happier when she can get her toe in, had little chance of turning the tables on the winner on 2lb better terms but she ran her heart out and was only worn down in the latter stages. (8/1)

1970 Midsummer Night (IRE) turned in a fine display in her first handicap and was only tapped for speed inside the last hundred yards. (9/1: op 6/1)

4173 High Carry, half a length behind the winner on identical terms on her previous outing, was always breathing down the necks of the leaders but she was flat to the boards and held when impeded inside the final furlong. (8/1)

4419* Mighty Sure (IRE), falling out of the bottom of the handicap, has changed stables since her success six days ago. In the firing line from the break, she just lacked that bit extra when the pressure was really on. (20/1)

3774 Nuclear Debate (USA) does seem to lack the speed to win at this minimum trip, but his cause was not helped when he was forced to switch on meeting the rising ground and his sustained late rally was never quite going to get him there. (7/2)

4103 Solo Spirit (10/1: 7/1-11/1)

4232 Eleventh Duke (IRE) (11/1: 8/1-12/1)

4523 HEATH COURT HOTEL JOEL STKS (Listed) (3-Y.O+) (Class A)

2-35 (2-35) **1m (Rowley)** £10,471.40 (£3,872.60: £1,856.30: £756.50: £298.25: £114.95) Stalls: High GOING minus 0.31 sec per fur (GF)

				SP	RR	SF
4003*	**Intikhab (USA) (111)** (DMorley) **3-9-1** RHills(5) (lw: chsd ldr: led over 2f out: sn clr: drvn out)	—	**1**	11/4[2]	93	65
3764[2]	**Swiss Law (108)** (JHMGosden) **3-8-11** LDettori(4) (h.d.w: chsd ldrs: drvn along over 2f out: styd on fnl f)	2	**2**	4/1[3]	85	57
4319[2]	**Polish Rhythm (IRE) (66)** (GAHubbard) **4-8-9** JReid(6) (led tl over 2f out: kpt on u.p fnl f)	½	**3**	50/1	79?	54
4252a[2]	**Ramooz (USA) (107)** (BHanbury) **4-9-7** WRyan(3) (b: lw: hld up in rr: effrt & nt clr run over 1f out: r.o wl nr fin)	nk	**4**	11/1	90	65
4281[4]	**Weet-A-Minute (IRE) (103)** (RHollinshead) **4-9-0** TQuinn(2) (prom: rdn over 2f out: wknd over 1f out)	1½	**5**	16/1	80	55
4292*	**Bin Rosie (113)** (DRLoder) **5-9-0b** KFallon(1) (lw: hld up: effrt 3f out: sn drvn along: wknd appr fnl f)	nk	**6**	Evens[1]	80	55

(SP 112.8%) **6 Rn**

1m 38.09 (0.79) CSF £12.93 TOTE £3.80: £1.70 £1.90 (£5.60) OWNER Mr Hamdan Al Maktoum (NEWMARKET) BRED J. I. Racing Inc. and Marvin Little Jr
WEIGHT FOR AGE 3yo-3lb
OFFICIAL EXPLANATION Bin Rosie: found the ground too firm and would not let himself down.

4003* Intikhab (USA) has been in the form of his life this term and he had this won from the time he struck the front. His jockey said that he gets better all the time and he thinks that he could turn out to be some animal next year. (11/4)

3764 Swiss Law, not disgraced when tried in this company in the spring, was hard at work soon after passing the bushes but he kept persevering and certainly lost no caste in defeat. (4/1: 11/4-9/2)

4319 Polish Rhythm (IRE) continues to run well but she is being thrown in at the deep end in this company, and it might be wise to campaign her in handicaps. (50/1)

4252a Ramooz (USA) invariably finds trouble when trying to work his way through, but he was denied any run at all this time until the outcome had been virtually decided. (11/1: 7/1-12/1)

4281 Weet-A-Minute (IRE) is a trier but he just falls below this class and he is being called upon to do almost the impossible. (16/1)

4292* Bin Rosie lacks gears on this more lively ground, and she was fighting a lost cause as soon as she came under pressure passing the quarter-mile marker. (Evens)

4524 THOROUGHBRED CORPORATION MIDDLE PARK STKS (Gp 1) (2-Y.O C) (Class A)

3-10 (3-10) **6f (Rowley)** £64,480.49 (£23,899.50: £11,499.75: £4,736.25: £1,918.13: £790.88) Stalls: High GOING minus 0.31 sec per fur (GF)

				SP	RR	SF
4146[3]	**Hayil (USA) (100)** (DMorley) **2-8-11b[1]** RHills(4) (lw: a.p: led 2f out: rdn out)	—	**1**	14/1	103	61
4135[4]	**Carrowkeel (IRE) (100)** (BWHills) **2-8-11** MHills(8) (sn w ldrs: outpcd ½-wy: rallied towards fin)	¾	**2**	15/2[3]	101	59
4247[3]	**Designer (USA)** (JHMGosden) **2-8-11** OPeslier(7) (led to 2f out: rdn & one pce ins fnl f)	nk	**3**	25/1	100	58
4293*	**Arkadian Hero (USA) (100)** (LMCumani) **2-8-11** LDettori(2) (lw: hld up: hdwy over 2f out: rdn & one pce fnl f)	1¾	**4**	10/11[1]	96	54
2863*	**Victory Note (USA)** (PWChapple-Hyam) **2-8-11** JReid(1) (hld up: effrt u.p 2f out: nt pce to chal)	3	**5**	4/1[2]	88	46
3770*	**Bemsha Swing (IRE) (96)** (RHannon) **2-8-11** DaneO'Neill(3) (lw: hld up: effrt & drvn along 2f out: no imp)	2	**6**	12/1	82	40
4167[2]	**Captain Tim** (DRLoder) **2-8-11** KFallon(6) (lw: s.i.s: sn chsng ldrs & pushed along: wknd 2f out)	1¼	**7**	15/2[3]	79	37
4007[3]	**Celtic Pageant (95)** (RAkehurst) **2-8-11** TQuinn(5) (prom: sn pushed along: btn 2f out)	nk	**8**	50/1	78	36

(SP 116.1%) **8 Rn**

1m 12.39 (0.59) CSF £104.40 TOTE £16.80: £2.80 £1.90 £2.20 (£45.80) OWNER Mr Hamdan Al Maktoum (NEWMARKET) BRED Shadwell Farm Inc

4146 Hayil (USA) responded to his first-time blinkers with a comparatively comfortable success in what could prove a sub-standard Middle Park. (14/1)

4135 Carrowkeel (IRE) did not impress to post and he did look to be in trouble passing the Bushes, but he found his feet when faced with the hill and he could be the one to progress most in the future. (15/2)

4247 Designer (USA) had more use made of him and he stuck to the task in hand willingly, and it can only be a matter of time before this progressive colt opens his account. (25/1)

4293* Arkadian Hero (USA) had a very hard race when successful on more testing ground twelve days ago, and as he failed to get in a blow here it could be that he had not fully recovered. (10/11: 4/5-evens)

2863* Victory Note (USA) finished some way ahead of the favourite on his debut in July but he was very wound up here, both in the paddock and on the way to post. When asked for his effort the response was, to say the least, very limited. (4/1: 3/1-5/1)
3770* Bemsha Swing (IRE) adopted more patient tactics on this occasion, but they did not have the desired effect for he was never able to make his presence felt. (12/1)

4525 JRA NAKAYAMA ROUS STKS (Listed) (3-Y.O+) (Class A)

3-40 (3-40) **5f (Rowley)** £10,471.40 (£3,872.60: £1,856.30: £756.50: £298.25: £114.95) Stalls: High GOING minus 0.31 sec per fur (GF)

				SP	RR	SF
4239[2]	**Dashing Blue (110)** (IABalding) **4-8-12** LDettori(2) (hld up centre: hdwy 2f out: r.o u.p to ld cl home)	—	**1**	2/1[1]	114	67
4098[4]	**Bishops Court (104)** (MrsJRRamsden) **3-8-12** JFortune(6) (trckd ldrs: rdn to ld wl ins fnl f: sn hdd: r.o)	nk	**2**	11/2[3]	113	66
4239[7]	**Tipsy Creek (USA) (108)** (BHanbury) **3-8-12** RHills(8) (b.hind: led tl hdd wl ins fnl f: r.o)	hd	**3**	6/1	113	66
4239[4]	**Croft Pool (108)** (JAGlover) **6-9-7** GCarter(3) (chsd ldrs centre: hdwy 2f out: no imp fnl f)	1¾	**4**	12/1	116	69
4098[8]	**Bolshoi (IRE) (106)** (JBerry) **5-8-12b** EmmaO'Gorman(4) (hld up: hdwy appr fnl f: nt rch ldrs)	2	**5**	10/1	101	54
4239[14]	**Almaty (IRE) (111)** (WRMuir) **4-9-1** JReid(7) (w ldrs centre: rdn & outpcd appr fnl f)	1	**6**	8/1	101	54
4062*	**Blue Iris (99)** (MAJarvis) **4-8-7** MRoberts(5) (hld up: effrt & drvn along 2f out: no imp)	1¾	**7**	100/30[2]	87	40
4444[5]	**Hello Mister (94)** (TEPowell) **6-8-12** PMcCabe(1) (dwlt: a in rr)	1¾	**8**	20/1	86	39
				(SP 118.7%)	**8 Rn**	

58.86 secs (0.16) CSF £12.85 TOTE £2.70: £1.30 £2.50 £1.30 (£10.50) OWNER Mrs Duncan Allen (KINGSCLERE) BRED Mrs I. A. Balding
4239 Dashing Blue had plenty to do running into the Dip but he always looked to have the situation under control, even though he did have to really dig deep to land the spoils. (2/1: 5/4-5/2)
4098 Bishops Court is not being rewarded for his consistency, and he gave it all he had got to force his head in front inside the final fifty yards before the winner pounced and worried him out of it. His fortune could change in a big way at any time. (11/2)
4239 Tipsy Creek (USA) improved considerably on his seasonal reappearance at Newbury and, in failing so narrowly to make all, it is going to take something more than useful to deny him next time. (6/1)
4239 Croft Pool, winner of this event last year, had a 9lb Group Two penalty to overcome this time and, hard though he tried, it proved beyond him. (12/1)
4098 Bolshoi (IRE) has been out of sorts since the spring, and his staying-on rally up the hill was never quite producing the burst of finishing speed that he is renowned for. (10/1: 8/1-12/1)
4098 Almaty (IRE), who has changed stables since his last run, showed plenty of pace in the centre of the track until finding his measure taken in running into the Dip. (8/1)
4062* Blue Iris was the subject of plenty of support and the tactics that were successful at Leicester were tried again but, in this much hotter contest, she was always struggling to find the pace to get involved. (100/30: 5/1-3/1)

4526 E.B.F. EQUITY FINANCIAL COLLECTIONS WESTLEY MAIDEN STKS (2-Y.O) (Class D)

4-15 (4-17) **7f (Rowley)** £7,573.50 (£2,268.00: £1,089.00: £499.50) Stalls: High GOING minus 0.31 sec per fur (GF)

				SP	RR	SF
4274[2]	**Quiet Assurance (USA) (100)** (EALDunlop) **2-9-0** RHills(11) (b: lw: led 1f: led over 1f out: r.o wl)	—	**1**	Evens[1]	96+	53
	Connoisseur Bay (USA) (PWChapple-Hyam) **2-9-0** JReid(8) (neat: led after 1f tl over 1f out: kpt on: no ch w wnr)	1½	**2**	12/1	93	50
	Minivet (MBell) **2-9-0** MFenton(14) (neat: chsd ldrs: r.o one pce fnl 2f)	5	**3**	50/1	81	38
	Joint Regent (USA) (BWHills) **2-9-0** MHills(16) (w'like: scope: b.hind: in tch: effrt over 2f out: nvr nrr)	1¾	**4**	12/1	77	34
	Honest Borderer (JLDunlop) **2-9-0** TSprake(18) (leggy: unf: s.i.s: hdwy 2f out: r.o wl fnl f)	nk	**5**	50/1	77+	34
	White Scissors (USA) (HRACecil) **2-9-0** WRyan(9) (w'like: str: bkwd: gd spd 5f: grad wknd)	2½	**6**	20/1	71	28
4311[4]	**Wandering Wolf** (RHannon) **2-9-0** OPeslier(2) (lw: mid div: effrt 2f out: nt rch ldrs)	¾	**7**	11/1	69	26
	Zobaida (IRE) (MAJarvis) **2-8-9** SSanders(22) (w'like: unf: s.s: styd on fnl 2f: improve)	nk	**8**	33/1	63+	20
	Sinan (USA) (SbinSuroor) **2-9-0** LDettori(10) (w'like: scope: chsd ldrs tl wknd fnl 2f)	¾	**9**	11/2[2]	67	24
	Mondschein (JLDunlop) **2-8-9** TQuinn(6) (leggy: lt-f: unf: rapid hdwy over 1f out: hmpd & snatched up ins fnl f)	½	**10**	25/1	61	18
	High Noon (LMCumani) **2-8-11**(3) RFfrench(5) (neat: chsd ldrs 5f: sn outpcd)	hd	**11**	12/1	65	22
	Wayne Lukas (HRACecil) **2-9-0** KFallon(17) (lt-f: scope: chsd ldrs: hrd drvn 2f out: sn btn)	s.h	**12**	13/2[3]	65	22
4379[9]	**My Tyson (IRE)** (KMahdi) **2-9-0** MartinDwyer(12) (prom over 4f)	2½	**13**	50/1	59	16
	Empire State (IRE) (MHTompkins) **2-8-11**(3) MHenry(13) (cmpt: in tch over 4f)	hd	**14**	50/1	59	16
4237[15]	**Frankie Ferrari (IRE)** (DRLoder) **2-9-0** RCochrane(19) (s.i.s: n.d)	nk	**15**	25/1	59	16
	Richmond Hill (BWHills) **2-9-0** DHolland(7) (w'like: nvr trbld ldrs)	½	**16**	50/1	57	14
4309[8]	**Ambiguous** (DRLoder) **2-9-0** GCarter(1) (lw: s.s: a in rr)	¾	**17**	50/1	56	13
	Cromer Pier (MHTompkins) **2-9-0** DaleGibson(15) (w'like: a bhd)	¾	**18**	50/1	54	11
4067[14]	**Northern Lass (IRE)** (MHTompkins) **2-8-9** DBiggs(4) (bhd fnl 3f)	1	**19**	50/1	47	4
	Regal Patriarch (IRE) (JLDunlop) **2-9-0** KDarley(21) (w'like: leggy: bkwd: sn pushed along: a rr div)	1	**20**	25/1	49	6
4229[9]	**Rock Sounds** (NACallaghan) **2-9-0** GDuffield(3) (lw: dwlt: a bhd: t.o)	5	**21**	50/1	38	—
	Top Gear (IRE) (PHowling) **2-9-0** MRoberts(20) (w'like: scope: lw: lost tch fr ½-wy: t.o)	5	**22**	25/1	27	—
				(SP 150.9%)	**22 Rn**	

1m 26.13 (1.63) CSF £14.89 TOTE £2.40: £1.40 £5.50 £14.70 (£22.70) Trio £1,063.20; £748.78 to Lingfield 3/10/97 OWNER Maktoum Al Maktoum (NEWMARKET) BRED Maple Leaf Farm
4274 Quiet Assurance (USA), far more experienced that any of his rivals, is a very ungainly mover but he found this much easier than on his previous outings and won just as a good thing should win. (Evens)
Connoisseur Bay (USA), a well-bred colt who should progress as he strengthens up, was the only one able to give the winner any problem at all and, in finishing clear of the remainder, showed he has what it takes. (12/1: 9/2-16/1)
Minivet, bred to need a true test of stamina, may have trouble winning a race this season as he is just beginning to get his winter coat, but he showed promise and he can only get better. (50/1)
Joint Regent (USA), whose half-brother Snow Forest won on his debut, is a late April foal and, in showing plenty of promise, will certainly be one to watch for next season. (12/1)
Honest Borderer, out of a dam who was quite a useful racemare, has already been gelded. Sluggish leaving the stalls, he was noted staying on steadily in the latter stages and immediate improvement should follow. (50/1)
White Scissors (USA), who is built like a tank, was too backward to do himself justice on this debut but the promise is there and he could be useful next season. (20/1)
4311 Wandering Wolf, running over a more suitable trip, was never able to get himself into the action, but he was not knocked about and he is learning the ropes. (11/1)

Zobaida (IRE), a May foal who is bred to be useful, stayed on strongly after losing ground at the start and, with this badly-needed run under her belt, she can only get better. (33/1)
Mondschein, a lightly-made filly with plenty of stamina in her breeding, was really into her stride when stopped in her tracks inside the final furlong and does look to be a filly with a future. (25/1)
High Noon (12/1: op 5/1)
Wayne Lukas (13/2: 9/2-8/1)

4527 FITZWILLIAM H'CAP (0-80) (3-Y.O) (Class D)

4-45 (4-48) **5f (Rowley)** £4,854.00 (£1,452.00: £696.00: £318.00) Stalls: High GOING minus 0.31 sec per fur (GF)

				SP	RR	SF
4321²	**Dominant Air (77)** (SirMarkPrescott) **3-9-6** GDuffield(9) (a.p: rdn to ld wl ins fnl f)	—	**1**	5/1 ²	90	54
	Kram (53) (MrsPNDutfield) **3-7-10** JQuinn(8) (lw: bhd: hdwy wl over 1f out: r.o strly nr fin)	½	**2**	20/1	64	28
4431*	**Passionatti (60)** (SGollings) **3-8-3** 7x TWilliams(10) (led 1f: led 2f out tl wl ins fnl f)	½	**3**	25/1	70	34
4137²	**Shalstayholy (IRE) (78)** (GLMoore) **3-9-2**(5) CLowther(4) (a chsng ldrs: rdn & outpcd appr fnl f: rallied cl home)	s.h	**4**	6/1	88	52
4047*	**First Principle (77)** (CFWall) **3-9-6** SSanders(7) (hld up: hdwy over 1f out: r.o wl towards fin)	hd	**5**	11/2 ³	86	50
4370⁷	**Anokato (60)** (KTIvory) **3-8-3b** MartinDwyer(15) (chsd ldrs: rdn & no ex wl ins fnl f)	nk	**6**	8/1	68	32
2964³	**Sally Green (IRE) (75)** (CFWall) **3-9-4** RHills(14) (hld up: effrt 2f out: nt rch ldrs)	1	**7**	10/1	80	44
3500⁹	**Loganlea (IRE) (53)** (WJMusson) **3-7-10** DeclanO'Shea(16) (in tch: hdwy over 2f out: no ex ins fnl f)	nk	**8**	20/1	57	21
4414⁶	**Storyteller (IRE) (55)** (MrsJRRamsden) **3-7-9v**(3) RFfrench(2) (hld up & bhd: effrt over 1f out: nrst fin)	hd	**9**	7/1	59	23
4168¹³	**College Princess (53)** (SCWilliams) **3-7-3**(7) DarrenWilliams(13) (b: bhd: effrt 2f out: n.m.r: styd on fnl f)	1¼	**10**	33/1	53	17
4321⁷	**Bramble Bear (69)** (MBlanshard) **3-8-12** JReid(6) (a bhd & outpcd)	1	**11**	16/1	66	30
3871¹⁰	**Tinker's Surprise (IRE) (55)** (JBalding) **3-7-5**(7)ow2 JFowle(5) (led after 1f to 2f out: wknd appr fnl f)	s.h	**12**	50/1	52	14
4329¹⁰	**Ice Age (55)** (RJRWilliams) **3-7-12b** NCarlisle(3) (swtchd rt s: a in rr)	nk	**13**	25/1	51	15
4365²	**Caution (70)** (SGollings) **3-8-13** KFallon(12) (hld up & bhd: nt clr run fnl 2f: eased)	nk	**14**	4/1 ¹	65	29
3100¹⁰	**Eurolink Profile (73)** (LMCumani) **3-9-2** LDettori(11) (outpcd 2f out: nt clr run 1f out: eased)	½	**15**	10/1	66	30
4328¹⁶	**Divide And Rule (62)** (RHollinshead) **3-8-5** FLynch(1) (lw: a bhd)	nk	**16**	33/1	54	18
				(SP 139.1%)		**16 Rn**

60.05 secs (1.35) CSF £105.24 CT £2,189.21 TOTE £5.30: £1.70 £4.60 £4.90 £2.00 (£69.20) Trio £708.50 OWNER Mr Neil Greig (NEWMARKET) BRED W. N. Greig
LONG HANDICAP Tinker's Surprise (IRE) 6-13 Loganlea (IRE) 7-5 College Princess 7-4
4321 Dominant Air, from a stable in fine form, showed that sprinting is his game with a very hard-fought victory and he is capable of winning more races. (5/1)
Kram, a winner in Ireland six weeks ago, was having his first run in this country. Making progress from the rear inside the last couple of furlongs, he should probably have won this but, that said, it is possible he does need at least six furlongs. (20/1)
4431* Passionatti, stepping up in class, did her best to slip her field, but the final climb caught her out and she was run out of it nearing the line. (25/1)
4137 Shalstayholy (IRE), on the heels of the leaders until tapped for toe in the death, rallied gamely towards the finish and certainly went down fighting. She is much better suited to another furlong. (6/1)
4047* First Principle, who spent the early part of the year in Dubai, was taking on handicappers for the first time. Not enjoying the smoothest of passages, he was running on really well towards the finish and will benefit from another furlong. (11/2)
3194 Anokato, running one of his better races, was in the thick of the action until failing to quicken inside the last fifty yards. (8/1: op 16/1)
4365 Caution needs luck in running to make progress from the rear in such a big field, especially at this trip, but that fortune was denied her throughout the last couple of furlongs and her jockey had no option but to call it a day. (4/1: op 6/1)

T/Jkpt: Not won; £15,826.76 to Newmarket 3/10/97. T/Plpt: £453.60 (108.74 Tckts). T/Qdpt: £32.50 (94.3 Tckts) IM

4390a-CHANTILLY (France) (R-H) (Good)
Tuesday September 23rd

4528a PRIX LA ROCHETTE (Gp 3) (2-Y.O C & G)

2-20 (2-19) **1m** £24,691.00 (£8,979.00: £4,489.00: £2,694.00)

				SP	RR	SF
	Pinmix (FR) (AFabre,France) **2-8-12** AJunk	—	**1**		92	—
3995a*	**Trans Island** (IABalding) **2-8-12** KDarley	nk	**2**		91	—
	Arnaqueur (USA) (AFabre,France) **2-8-12** OPeslier	1½	**3**		88	—
	Prospectheus (USA) (MmeCHead,France) **2-8-12** ODoleuze	4	**4**		80	—
						4 Rn

1m 38.8 (2.30) P-M 4.90F: 3.50F 3.10F OWNER Mr J-L Lagardere (CHANTILLY) BRED SNC Lagardere Elevage
3995a* Trans Island took the field along and began to quicken up at the distance. Hard ridden inside the final furlong, he was soon headed and could find little more at the finish.

3178a-MAISONS-LAFFITTE (France) (Good)
Wednesday September 24th

4529a PRIX SOYA (2-Y.O F)

2-00 (2-06) **7f** £8,979.00

				SP	RR	SF
	Soeur Ti (FR) (RCollet,France) **2-8-0**(7) SJesus	—	**1**		73	—
	Hasene (FR) (France) **2-8-7** DBoeuf	s.h	**2**		73	—
	Happy Heart (FR) (France) **2-8-7** CAsmussen	¾	**3**		71	—
3994a*	**Friendly Warning (FR)** (JEBanks) **2-9-3** AJunk	2	**4**		77	—
						15 Rn

1m 27.4 (5.10) P-M 3.70F: 1.60F 7.70F 2.20F (125.70F) OWNER S. Vallin (CHANTILLY) BRED Haras d'Etreham
3994a* Friendly Warning (FR), who won a decent event at Clairefontaine last month, tracked the leaders but found little room from two furlongs out to one furlong out, and when ridden, could only keep on at the same pace.

4530a LA COUPE DE MAISONS-LAFFITTE (Gp 3) (4-Y.O+)
3-30 (3-36) **1m 2f** £24,691.00 (£8,979.00: £4,489.00: £2,694.00)

				SP	RR	SF
3878a*	**Turning Wheel (USA)** (DSepulchre,France) **4-8-8** CAsmussen	—	**1**		103	—
	Perfect Vintage (MmePBarbe,France) **7-8-11** ODoleuze	1½	**2**		104	—
	Milford Track (IRE) (HVandePoele,France) **4-8-11** SGuillot	1½	**3**		101	—
	Martiniquais (IRE) (AFabre,France) **4-8-11** OPeslier	s.h	**4**		101	—
						4 Rn

2m 6.7 (4.70) P-M 2.40F: 1.40F 2.50F OWNER Niarchos Family BRED Flaxman Holdings Ltd

3368a-COLOGNE (Germany) (R-H) (Good)
Saturday September 27th

4531a GROSSER KAUFHOF PREIS (Gp 2) (3-Y.O+)
3-43 (3-48) **1m** £27,462.00 (£10,985.00: £5,492.00: £3,409.00)

				SP	RR	SF
3369a*	**Power Flame (GER)** (AWohler,Germany) **4-9-3** ABoschert (sn led: set str pce tl hdd jst ins fnl f: rallied to ld again cl home)	—	**1**		121	—
2821a7	**Accento** (RSuerland,Germany) **4-9-1** ATylicki (broke wl: trckd ldrs to st: chal 1½f out: led jst ins fnl f: wnt lft u.p: ct cl home)	hd	**2**		119	—
	Fifire (GER) (PPietsch,Germany) **4-9-1** WJakovlev (mid div: 5th st: r.o wl fr 2f out: tk 3rd cl home)	6	**3**		107	—
	Orsetto (GER) (RSuerland,Germany) **3-8-10** PVandekeere (in rr early: 7th st: slt prog fnl 2f)	½	**4**		105	—
	Blue Chief (DEN) (WNeuroth,Norway) **5-9-1** FJohansson (mid div: 4th st: one pce)	nk	**5**		105	—
1550a3	**Jashin (IRE)** (ALowe,Germany) **4-9-1** ABest (6th st: n.d)	s.h	**6**		105	—
1915a2	**Fine Fellow (IRE)** (MmeCHead,France) **3-8-10** ODoleuze (s.s: drvn to join ldrs after 2f: last pl ½-wy: btn st)	1¾	**7**		101	—
1550a3	**Tajawall (USA)** (DRichardson,Germany) **5-9-1b1** KWoodburn (prom: trckd wnr fr 5f out to over 2f out: wknd)	2½	**8**		97	—
				(SP 100.0%)		**8 Rn**

1m 36.58 (6.58) TOTE 39DM: 19DM 29DM 36DM OWNER Rennstall Darboven BRED Gestut Idee
Power Flame (GER), stepping up in class, took the field along until losing the lead inside the final furlong. However, he kept on battling and regained the lead close home.

4397a-SAN SIRO (Milan, Italy) (R-H) (Good)
Saturday September 27th

4532a PREMIO MORENGO (2-Y.O)
2-35 (2-38) **1m** £9,642.00

				SP	RR	SF
	Clapham Common (IRE) (LMCumani) **2-8-6** FJovine	—	**1**		—	—
	Skywasser (IRE) (BGrizzetti,Italy) **2-9-0** EBotti	nse	**2**		—	—
3177a3	**Elcari (IRE)** (VBignami,Italy) **2-9-0** LSorrentino	1	**3**		—	—
						7 Rn

1m 39.9 (9.90) TOTE 27L: 20L 31L (145L) OWNER Anglia Bloodstock Ltd (NEWMARKET) BRED Ballysheehan Stud
Clapham Common (IRE), a newcomer receiving a generous allowance, justified favouritism in the very last stride. He was all at sea and well adrift of the field in the first half of the race, but eventually ran on to score in promising style.

4533a PREMIO COLORNO MAIDEN (2-Y.O)
3-05 (3-10) **7f** £9,642.00 (£4,243.00: £2,314.00)

				SP	RR	SF
	Sottvus (IRE) (LMCumani) **2-8-8** MDemuro	—	**1**		—	—
	Sikesting (FJovine,Italy) **2-8-11** FJovine	1¾	**2**		—	—
	Black Weasel (IRE) (JLDunlop) **2-8-8** CColombi	1¼	**3**		—	—
						11 Rn

1m 27.0 (8.10) TOTE 39L: 15L 17L 13L (130L) OWNER Scuderia Rencati (NEWMARKET) BRED Studcrown Ltd
Sottvus (IRE) was always in touch, then stayed on to lead a furlong from home and kept on steadily.
Black Weasel (IRE) was slowly away and had only one behind him at halfway, but saved ground by staying on the far rail. He finished in good style to take third on the line and will come on a lot for the experience.

4534a PREMIO FORCORA MAIDEN (2-Y.O F)
4-35 (4-45) **7f** £9,642.00

				SP	RR	SF
	Fiamma (IRE) (JLDunlop) **2-8-12**ow2 MTellini	—	**1**		—	—
	Cragreen (GMaggi,Italy) **2-8-11** LSorrentino	3½	**2**		—	—
	Hunky Punky (IRE) (GBotti,Italy) **2-8-11** EBotti	1½	**3**		—	—
	Spazaca (USA) (LMCumani) **2-8-8** MDemuro		**5**		—	—
						12 Rn

1m 26.4 (7.50) TOTE 25L: 13L 27L 15L (336L) OWNER Allevamento Annarosa (ARUNDEL) BRED Allevamento Annarosa di V Schirone
Fiamma (IRE) was an impressive winner and recorded a good time. Unhurried early, she came with a smooth run on the outside to take it up entering the final furlong and soon quickened clear. A sister to Folgore and a half-sister to Lancashire Oaks winner, Fanjica - both winners in Italy - she could prove better than either.
Spazaca (USA) made some progress in the final quarter-mile but never looked likely to take a hand.

4253a-CAPANNELLE (Rome, Italy) (R-H) (Good)
Sunday September 28th

4535a PREMIO LYDIA TESIO (Gp 2) (3-Y.O+ F & M)
3-30 (3-30) **1m 2f** £50,552.00 (£22,968.00: £12,740.00: £6,370.00)

				SP	RR	SF
4131a*	**Papering (IRE)** (LMCumani) **4-8-11** FJovine (mde all: qcknd over 2f out: drvn out)	—	1		105	—
1368a⁴	**Bedside Story** (GBotti,Italy) **3-8-6** OPeslier (trckd ldr: chal over 1f out: ev ch ins fnl f: unable qckn cl home)	½	2		105	—
	Nenna (IRE) (ERusso,Italy) **5-8-11** CAsmussen (3rd st: kpt on one pce fnl 2f)	5	3		96	—
	Veri's Game (IRE) (Md'Auria,Italy) **4-8-11** CFiocchi (nvr nr to chal)	3	4		91	—
1367a*	**Schwarz Fairy** (MGuarnieri,Italy) **3-8-8** CColombi (a bhd)	1¾	5		92	—
	Golden Kendall (IRE) (LBietolini,Italy) **3-8-6** GBietolini (a bhd)	4	6		83	—
1549a⁵	**Germignana (ITY)** (LCamici,Italy) **4-8-11** MCangiano (4th st: wknd 2f out)	1	7		81	—
						7 Rn

2m 0.5 TOTE 14L: 11L 13L (15L) OWNER Sheikh Mohammed (NEWMARKET) BRED Sheikh Mohammed bin Rashid al Maktoum
4131a* Papering (IRE) had the measure of all her rivals and made all for a reasonably comfortable win, having quickened the pace two furlongs from home.

4531a-COLOGNE (Germany) (R-H) (Good)
Sunday September 28th

4536a PREIS VON KOLN (Listed) (3-Y.O+ F & M)
2-10 (2-32) **1m** £22,727.00

				SP	RR	SF
4120*	**Aunty Jane** (JLDunlop) **4-9-5** SGuillot	—	1		110	—
	Big Flower (GER) (Germany) **4-9-3** AStarke	½	2		107	—
1202a¹²	**Alte Kunst (IRE)** (Germany) **3-8-11** GBocskai	3	3		99	—
						12 Rn

1m 36.74 (6.74) TOTE 24DM: 17DM 20DM 24DM (164DM) OWNER Mr Paul Locke (ARUNDEL) BRED P. Locke
4120* Aunty Jane put up a good performance and, making all, held off a late challenge from the runner-up. Connections now hope to go to Italy with her for the Premio Bagutta.

4537a EMS KURIERPOST EUROPA PRIES (Gp 1) (3-Y.O+)
3-25 (3-45) **1m 4f** £113,636.00 (£45,455.00)

				SP	RR	SF
4000a*	**Taipan (IRE)** (JLDunlop) **5-9-6** SGuillot (trckd ldr to st: qcknd to ld 2f out: r.o wl)	—	1		126	—
4127a²	**Luso** (CEBrittain) **5-9-6** RCochrane (set pce: hdd 2f out: rdn & r.o one pce)	2	2		123	—
3737a⁴	**Protektor (GER)** (ALowe,Germany) **8-9-6** ABest (hld up: hdwy st: one pce fr over 1f out)	1¼	3		122	—
3998a³	**Don't Worry (GER)** (HBlume,Germany) **8-8-11** 1x THellier (in rr whn hmpd appr st: r.o fnl 2f)	nse	4		113	—
4127a⁴	**Narrabeth (IRE)** (UweStoltefuss,Germany) **4-9-6** KWoodburn (last tl st: styd on: nvr able chal)	1¼	5		120	—
3555a³	**Happy Change (GER)** (AWohler,Germany) **3-8-11** ABoschert (3rd st: sn wknd)	2	6		116	—
						6 Rn

2m 31.88 (4.88) TOTE 29DM 17DM 15DM (43DM) OWNER Lord Swaythling (ARUNDEL) BRED C. H. Wacker III
4000a* Taipan (IRE) gets better and better with every performance. Even on ground that was probably a bit quick for him, he still had the class to take this Group One event. Tracking the leaders, he quickened to lead two furlongs out and ran on well to score by a comfortable two lengths. He will now probably head off to Italy for a tilt at another Group One.
4127a Luso once again ran a creditable race. In front from the word go, he couldn't reply to the quickening burst of the winner, but he did keep on well to hold second.

3884a-DIELSDORF (Zurich, Switzerland) (L-H) (Good)
Sunday September 28th

4538a GROSSER PREIS DES HOTEL EUROP DAVOS (2-Y.O)
1-00 **7f** £2,193.00 (£877.00)

				SP	RR	SF
	Dulcileme (GER) (MWeiss,Switzerland) **2-9-7** J-MBreux	—	1		84+	—
4209²	**Long Bond (IRE)** (MJohnston) **2-9-6** JWeaver	¾	2		81+	—
	Tennessee (SWI) (RStadelmann,Switzerland) **2-9-2** PCoppin	2	3		73	—
						14 Rn

1m 25.6 TOTE 4.50F: 1.30F 1.20F 1.30F (8.00F) OWNER R & V Zuger
4209 Long Bond (IRE), drawn two of fourteen on the narrow inner course, had to be pushed along early and ran wide on the first bend as a result. He had every chance inside the final furlong, but was no match in the closing stages for a rival who had also won his only previous race. He will probably step up to a mile next time.

4539a GRAND PRIX JOCKEY CLUB (3-Y.O+)
3-17 **1m 4f 68y** £21,053.00 (£4,211.00)

				SP	RR	SF
3365a³	**Trait De Genie (FR)** (ALyon,France) **5-9-13** TJarnet	—	1		111	—
3884a*	**Cloud Inspector (IRE)** (MJohnston) **6-9-13** JWeaver	6	2		103	—
	Henderson (GER) (KSchafflutzel,Switzerland) **7-9-9** FGrenet	1¾	3		97	—
						10 Rn

2m 34.3 TOTE 4.50F: 1.40F 1.30F 1.40F (15.20F) OWNER Mr J. Bouchara BRED Comtesse Bertrand de Tarragon
3884a* Cloud Inspector (IRE) put up a fine performance for a horse whose target is the Cesarewitch. After setting a good pace for ten furlongs, he was no match for a horse who was completing a hat-trick and had twice finished third in listed races in France this year. Though well beaten, he was far from disgraced.

4540a GROSSER PREIS DES TAGES - ANZEIGERS (3-Y.O+)
3-45 **1m** £3,289.00

				SP	RR	SF
3735a*	**Celestial Key (USA)** (MJohnston) **7-9-7** JWeaver	—	**1**		102	—
	Liftoff (FR) (USuter,Switzerland) **6-8-9** FGrenet	1¾	**2**		87	—
	Tom Dooly (SWI) (USuter,Switzerland) **4-9-0** PCoppin	1½	**3**		89	—
						8 Rn

1m 40.1 TOTE 2.00F: 1.40F 2.60F (19.10F) OWNER Mr Markus Graff (MIDDLEHAM) BRED Pillar Stud Inc
3735a* Celestial Key (USA) was penalised for his win here last month and was meeting several he had beaten then on much worse terms. However, he is in excellent form at present and a well-timed run took him to the front inside the final furlong.

4532a-SAN SIRO (Milan, Italy) (R-H) (Good)
Sunday September 28th

4541a PREMIO PERINO (3-Y.O+)
2-05 (2-10) **1m 2f** £7,174.00

				SP	RR	SF
3424[8]	**Scoss** (LMCumani) **3-8-6** MDemuro	—	**1**		96	—
	Brave Indigo (GBotti,Italy) **4-9-5** MTellini	2½	**2**		99	—
	Haig Point (USA) (GVerricelli,Italy) **5-9-5** SDettori	3¼	**3**		94	—
						6 Rn

2m 3.7 (9.70) TOTE 25L: 14L 12L (28L) OWNER Scuderia Rencati Srl (NEWMARKET) BRED The Overbury Stud
1852 Scoss gained a comfortable win against fairly moderate opposition. Racing in fourth, he switched to the outside approaching the straight and quickened nicely to hit the front at the distance. He kept on well all the way to the line and never looked in any danger.

4065-LINGFIELD (L-H) (Firm)
Friday October 3rd
WEATHER: warm WIND: almost nil

4542 E.B.F. BLOND MCINDOE MAIDEN STKS (2-Y.O) (Class D)
1-55 (1-56) **5f** £3,556.00 (£1,063.00: £509.00: £232.00) Stalls: Low GOING minus 0.45 sec per fur (F)

				SP	RR	SF
4286[3]	**Iris May (75)** (JBerry) **2-8-9b** JWeaver(2) (mde all: drvn out)	—	**1**	3/1[3]	74	30
4402[2]	**Missed The Cut (IRE)** (RHannon) **2-8-2**(7) PDobbs(6) (a.p: chsd wnr fnl f: unable qckn)	½	**2**	15/8[2]	72	28
4145[9]	**Sacchetti (IRE)** (MRChannon) **2-9-0** JCarroll(4) (chsd wnr 4f: one pce)	1	**3**	16/1	74	30
	Braganza (USA) (DRLoder) **2-9-0** OPeslier(5) (str: scope: chsd ldrs: rdn 4f out: r.o one pce fnl f)	s.h	**4**	7/4[1]	74	30
722[6]	**Royal Interview (IRE)** (MRChannon) **2-9-0** SSanders(1) (bit bkwd: a.p: rdn over 1f out: sn wknd)	4	**5**	20/1	61	17
	Newala (WJHaggas) **2-8-9** FLynch(3) (leggy: lt-f: s.s: a bhd)	1¼	**6**	8/1	52	8
				(SP 117.9%)		**6 Rn**

58.39 secs (1.39) CSF £8.82 TOTE £4.60: £1.70 £1.40 (£2.90) OWNER John Brown & Megan Dennis (COCKERHAM) BRED P. D. and Mrs Player
IN-FOCUS: **The stalls for this meeting were advertised as being on the stands side. However, Lingfield made the far from punter-friendly decision just before racing to switch them to the far rail, while moving the stands rail in five yards to doll off a patch of ground which had not recovered from recent drainage work.**
4286 Iris May, rather warm beforehand, appreciated the return to the minimum trip and finally got off the mark in this bad race with a pillar-to-post victory. (3/1: op 5/1)
4402 Missed The Cut (IRE), who has no substance, raced in the front rank throughout. Struggling into second place entering the final furlong, she was unable to quicken up to get on terms with the winner. She should be able to find a very small race. (15/8)
564 Sacchetti (IRE) ran better here and had every chance over a furlong out, before tapped for toe. (16/1)
Braganza (USA), an attractive, scopey individual who is a half-brother to Blue Goblin, stood head and shoulders above his dreadful rivals in the paddock, but he took a massive walk in the betting and did not live up to his paddock appearance in the race. (7/4: op 1/2)
722 Royal Interview (IRE) looked in need of this first run in five and months and so it proved, as he tired approaching the final furlong. (20/1)

4543 GUINEA PIG CLUB CLAIMING STKS (2-Y.O) (Class F)
2-25 (2-26) **6f** £2,277.00 (£627.00: £297.00) Stalls: Low GOING minus 0.45 sec per fur (F)

				SP	RR	SF
4106[9]	**Dernier Croise (FR) (86)** (BJMeehan) **2-9-7** MTebbutt(6) (lw: stdy hdwy over 2f out: led ins fnl f: r.o wl)	—	**1**	5/1[3]	80	33
3808[3]	**Circuiteer (IRE) (57)** (JBerry) **2-8-12**(5) CLowther(7) (a.p: led 3f out tl ins fnl f: r.o)	nk	**2**	9/1	75	28
3782[3]	**Impulsive Decision (IRE) (51)** (MartynMeade) **2-8-6** SSanders(3) (lost pl 3f out: swtchd rt 1f out: rallied fnl f: r.o wl)	½	**3**	6/1	63	16
4401[5]	**Pinup (60)** (GLewis) **2-7-12** NAdams(10) (rdn over 2f out: hdwy over 1f out: unable qckn fnl f)	½	**4**	16/1	54	7
4284[8]	**Lasham (64)** (NACallaghan) **2-8-2**(7) CherylNosworthy(2) (a.p: one pce fnl 2f)	¾	**5**	16/1	63	16
4401*	**Legal Lark (IRE) (65)** (PHowling) **2-9-3** PaulEddery(1) (led 3f: ev ch over 1f out: one pce)	1	**6**	7/2[1]	68	21
2419[5]	**Slim Prior** (KRBurke) **2-8-9** JFEgan(12) (a.p: ev ch over 1f out: sn wknd)	3	**7**	25/1	52	5
3742[5]	**Bermuda Triangle (IRE) (60)** (MJHaynes) **2-7-13**(5) RMullen(15) (racd stands' side: outpcd)	nk	**8**	11/2	46	—
4402[4]	**Sergeant Imp (IRE) (58)** (PMitchell) **2-8-13** OPeslier(14) (lw: racd stands' side: outpcd)	hd	**9**	4/1[2]	55	8
4064[15]	**Noble Patriot** (RHollinshead) **2-9-4**(3) DGriffiths(13) (a bhd)	2	**10**	20/1	58	11
4311[10]	**Lady Ralphina (45)** (JJBridger) **2-8-4** JQuinn(4) (a bhd)	1¼	**11**	33/1	37	—
	Whimoweh (APJarvis) **2-8-8** SDrowne(11) (unf: s.s: a bhd)	12	**12**	16/1	9	—
				(SP 127.8%)		**12 Rn**

1m 11.31 (2.31) CSF £47.89 TOTE £5.80: £2.20 £2.40 £2.30 (£26.80) Trio £48.80 OWNER E H Jones (Paints) Ltd (UPPER LAMBOURN) BRED B. Ferrand & Coolmore Stud
OFFICIAL EXPLANATION **Dernier Croise (FR): benefited from the drop in class.**
3925 Dernier Croise (FR) was at long last dropped in grade after being completely outclassed in far better events in this country, although he has appeared to run better in valuable races in France. Cruising into the action from halfway, he was bustled along to lead inside the final furlong and kept the runner-up at bay. (5/1: 3/1-11/2)

3808 Circuiteer (IRE) gave a good account of himself and, up with the pace, showed in front from halfway. Collared inside the final furlong, he was always just being held by the winner but kept on well to the bitter end nevertheless. (9/1)
3782 Impulsive Decision (IRE), who got outpaced at halfway, stayed on in good style inside the final furlong but found the line always coming too soon. Further improvement should come over another furlong. (6/1)
4401 Pinup ran a similar race to that at Folkestone a week ago for, after picking up ground below the distance, she failed to find another gear in the final furlong. (16/1)
3869 Lasham received no assistance from the saddle and could only go up and down in the same place in the final quarter-mile. (16/1)
4401* Legal Lark (IRE) still had every chance over a furlong out, before tapped for toe. (7/2)

4544 E.B.F. BILLY LEVITA MAIDEN STKS (2-Y.O) (Class D)
2-55 (2-57) **6f** £4,345.75 (£1,306.00: £630.50: £292.75) Stalls: Low GOING minus 0.45 sec per fur (F)

				SP	RR	SF
	Daring Derek (USA) (DRLoder) **2-9-0** OPeslier(9) (str: scope: lw: s.s: plld hrd: hdwy over 4f out: led over 2f out: comf)	—	1	$11/10^{1}$	74+	37
4167^{3}	**Jila (IRE)** (RWArmstrong) **2-9-0** GCarter(13) (lw: hdwy over 2f out: chsd wnr over 1f out: no imp)	2	2	$15/8^{2}$	69	32
4105^{9}	**Hever Golf Ranger** (TJNaughton) **2-9-0** JWeaver(15) (rdn over 2f out: hdwy over 1f out: unable qckn fnl f)	1¼	3	25/1	65	28
4298^{18}	**Muyassir (IRE)** (CJBenstead) **2-9-0** TWilliams(11) (a.p: swtchd rt over 2f out: one pce)	1	4	33/1	63	26
2693^{10}	**Anvil (USA) (85)** (GLewis) **2-9-0** PaulEddery(8) (lw: a.p: rdn over 2f out: one pce)	s.h	5	$13/2^{3}$	63	26
	Best Quest (JHMGosden) **2-9-0** GHind(3) (w'like: bit bkwd: s.s: outpcd: stdy hdwy over 1f out: r.o: bttr for r)	1¼	6	20/1	59+	22
	Easter Ogil (IRE) (IABalding) **2-9-0** MartinDwyer(1) (w'like: swtchd lft 2f out: hdwy & hmpd on ins over 1f out: nt rcvr)	hd	7	16/1	59+	22
	Dahomey (USA) (CEBrittain) **2-9-0** MRimmer(2) (w'like: outpcd: nvr nrr)	1¾	8	25/1	54	17
4056^{10}	**Lady Imza** (WJHaggas) **2-8-9** FLynch(10) (b.hind: hld up: rdn over 2f out: sn wknd)	½	9	40/1	48	11
3818^{4}	**Zero Three Fifteen (IRE)** (MartynMeade) **2-8-11**$^{(3)}$ RHavlin(12) (prom over 4f)	1	10	33/1	50	13
3613^{10}	**House On Fire (IRE)** (JBerry) **2-8-9**$^{(5)}$ CLowther(6) (led over 3f: wknd over 1f out)	hd	11	25/1	50	13
	Peaceful Sarah (PMooney) **2-8-9** WJO'Connor(4) (b: leggy: bhd fnl 3f)	2	12	40/1	40	3
	Primaticcio (IRE) (SirMarkPrescott) **2-9-0** SSanders(7) (wl grwn: s.s: a bhd)	1½	13	25/1	41	4
	Mach One (FR) (SirMarkPrescott) **2-9-0** CNutter(5) (w'like: scope: bit bkwd: s.s: a bhd)	1	14	33/1	38	1
				(SP 135.5%)	**14 Rn**	

1m 10.49 (1.49) CSF £2.95 TOTE £2.50: £1.40 £1.20 £3.70 (£2.10) Trio £43.40 OWNER Lucayan Stud (NEWMARKET) BRED Brereton C. Jones & Timothy C. Thornton
Daring Derek (USA), a good-looking, well-made individual, took a keen hold in the early stages, but nevertheless cruised to the front just before the two-furlong marker and had no problems asserting his authority for a decisive victory. He is described as a nice horse but a big baby by his trainer. (11/10: 5/4-evens)
4167 Jila (IRE) looked in good shape beforehand but, after coming through to take second place approaching the final furlong, had no hope with the winner. He should soon go one better. (15/8)
Hever Golf Ranger left his debut run well behind but, after coming through to take third place a furlong out, could then make no further impression. (25/1)
Muyassir (IRE), a half-brother to the useful miler Restructure and Champion Hurdle winner Alderbrook, left previous form well behind and was never far away if tapped for toe in the final quarter-mile. (33/1)
2057 Anvil (USA), who failed to stay seven furlongs on his last appearance three months ago, was never far away but could only go up and down in the same place in the last two furlongs. (13/2: 5/1-8/1)
Best Quest, a medium-sized colt, did not look fully wound up but showed promise for the future. His jockey gave him a couple of smacks and did a lot of knitting, and the combination stayed on in eye-catching style in the last furlong and a half. He should come on a lot for this. (20/1)

4545 CHAMPAGNE JACQUART NURSERY H'CAP (0-75) (2-Y.O) (Class E)
3-30 (3-34) **7f** £3,746.25 (£1,125.00: £542.50: £251.25) Stalls: Low GOING minus 0.45 sec per fur (F)

				SP	RR	SF
4368^{5}	**Lauren's Lad (48)** (GLewis) **2-7-10b** NAdams(5) (mde all: rdn over 2f out: clr over 1f out: eased wl ins fnl f)	—	1	$9/1^{2}$	57+	25
4318^{7}	**Up The Wall (60)** (JohnBerry) **2-8-8** JQuinn(1) (hld up: rdn over 2f out: r.o one pce)	3½	2	12/1	61	29
3215^{11}	**Mohawk (IRE) (69)** (JLDunlop) **2-9-3** GCarter(2) (a.p: rdn over 3f: chsd wnr over 2f out tl ins fnl f: one pce)	½	3	12/1	69	37
4185^{6}	**Miss Muffett (IRE) (52)** (PMooney) **2-8-0** FNorton(6) (s.s: rdn over 2f out: hdwy on ins over 1f out: swtchd rt 1f out: r.o one pce)	nk	4	25/1	51	19
4227^{4}	**Face-Off (67)** (CFWall) **2-9-1** SSanders(13) (hld up: rdn over 2f out: one pce)	2	5	12/1	62	30
4166^{8}	**Mountain Magic (61)** (DJSffrenchDavis) **2-8-9** JWeaver(18) (lw: hdwy 5f out: rdn over 2f out: wknd over 1f out)	3½	6	11/1	48	16
4065*	**Bahamian Melody (USA) (73)** (DRLoder) **2-9-7v** OPeslier(8) (lw: nt clr run 1f out: nvr nrr)	½	7	$8/11^{1}$	59	27
3924*	**Chief Blade (69)** (RAkehurst) **2-8-10**$^{(7)}$ DDenby(10) (lw: prom over 5f)	nk	8	$10/1^{3}$	54	22
4185^{7}	**Jato Dancer (IRE) (53)** (JRArnold) **2-7-8**$^{(7)}$ PDoe(3) (b.hind: a mid div)	s.h	9	40/1	38	6
4327^{8}	**Silent Pride (IRE) (51)** (MDIUsher) **2-7-6**$^{(7)}$ JFowle(9) (b: prom 5f)	s.h	10	16/1	36	4
4006^{6}	**Coolin River (IRE) (61)** (KRBurke) **2-8-9** JFEgan(7) (hld up: rdn & swtchd rt 2f out: wknd over 1f out)	s.h	11	20/1	45	13
3489^{10}	**Naayel (IRE) (67)** (CJBenstead) **2-9-1** TWilliams(15) (a bhd)	1	12	25/1	49	17
4152^{11}	**Memorial (IRE) (58)** (RHannon) **2-8-6b^{1}** CRutter(14) (lw: bhd fnl 4f)	4	13	16/1	31	—
4042^{8}	**Zamarra (65)** (MajorDNChappell) **2-8-13** MartinDwyer(12) (lw: s.s: a bhd)	¾	14	20/1	36	4
4230^{9}	**Cd Newsround (IRE) (57)** (MRChannon) **2-8-5v^{1}** JCarroll(16) (bhd fnl 2f)	2	15	40/1	24	—
4052^{10}	**Fung Shui (IRE) (56)** (RHannon) **2-8-4** DBiggs(11) (bhd fnl 5f)	9	16	40/1	2	—
				(SP 144.7%)	**16 Rn**	

1m 22.66 (1.46) CSF £113.68 CT £800.58 TOTE £11.50: £1.70 £3.60 £3.30 £3.90 (£55.40) Trio £514.30; £115.91 to Newmarket 4/10/97
OWNER Mrs Linda McCalla (EPSOM) BRED Miss L. Pearson
LONG HANDICAP Lauren's Lad 7-7
OFFICIAL EXPLANATION **Bahamian Melody (USA): no explanation offered.**
4368 Lauren's Lad was well in at the weights as he is due to rise a stone from tomorrow. Making every post a winning one, he forged clear below the distance and, with the race well and truly in the bag, was eased down in the closing stages. The blinkers have made all the difference according to connections. (9/1: 10/1-20/1)
1854 Up The Wall chased the leaders. He stayed on to take second place in the closing stages and a return to a mile may help. (12/1)
1760 Mohawk (IRE), who has disappointed on his last two outings, ran better here and showed in a definite second place over a quarter of a mile from home. Unable to reel in the winner, he was caught for the runner-up berth in the closing stages. (12/1: op 6/1)
Miss Muffett (IRE) ran her best race to date, staying on in the last furlong and a half and only just failing to take third prize. (25/1)

4227 Face-Off did not show any improvement for the step up in trip and was only treading water in the final quarter-mile. (12/1)
3927 Mountain Magic appeared to find this longer trip beyond her and had been hung out to dry approaching the final furlong. (11/1: 7/1-12/1)
4065* Bahamian Melody (USA) stood out in the paddock and was all the rage in the betting. Unfortunately, he never gave his supporters anything to cheer about. (8/11: op 6/4)
3924* Chief Blade (10/1: op 6/1)

4546 CABLE TECH H'CAP (0-70) (3-Y.O) (Class E)

4-00 (4-07) **7f** £3,746.25 (£1,125.00: £542.50: £251.25) Stalls: Low GOING minus 0.45 sec per fur (F)

				SP	RR	SF
4168[6]	**Bold Tina (IRE) (60)** (RHannon) **3-9-0**(5) CLowther(4) (a.p: led 2f out: rdn out)	—	**1**	2/1[1]	74	40
4370[9]	**Churchill's Shadow (IRE) (45)** (BAPearce) **3-8-4** DRMcCabe(5) (s.s: in rr over 4f: gd hdwy over 1f out: str run fnl f: fin wl)	1	**2**	12/1	57	23
3413[12]	**Loxley's Girl (IRE) (37)** (HAkbary) **3-7-5**(5) APolli(12) (racd stands' side: a.p: ev ch over 2f out: unable qckn)	2	**3**	25/1	44	10
4176[11]	**Hawksbill Henry (USA) (49)** (MrsAJPerrett) **3-8-8** GayeHarwood(3) (lw: a.p: led over 2f out: sn hdd: one pce)	s.h	**4**	20/1	56	22
1746[3]	**Aybeegirl (52)** (MrsJCecil) **3-8-11** MartinDwyer(1) (led over 4f: hrd rdn wl over 1f out: one pce)	1	**5**	12/1	57	23
4328[14]	**Whizz Kid (40)** (JJBridger) **3-7-13** GBardwell(9) (rdn & no hdwy fnl 2f)	½	**6**	20/1	44	10
4505[4]	**Daylight Dreams (61)** (CACyzer) **3-9-6** TWilliams(14) (racd stands' side: hld up: rdn & ev ch over 2f out: wknd fnl f)	s.h	**7**	14/1	65	31
4333[2]	**Maladerie (IRE) (58)** (MRChannon) **3-9-3** JCarroll(13) (lw: racd stands side': a.p: ev ch over 2f out: wknd fnl f)	½	**8**	4/1[2]	60	26
3930[15]	**Carlton (IRE) (54)** (GLewis) **3-8-13** PaulEddery(10) (lw: nvr nrr)	¾	**9**	14/1	55	21
4319[8]	**Chasetown Flyer (USA) (60)** (NEBerry) **3-9-5** RPerham(6) (outpcd)	1½	**10**	10/1	57	23
3040[6]	**Blue Cheese (37)** (JRJenkins) **3-7-10** DeclanO'Shea(8) (outpcd)	1¼	**11**	25/1	31	—
	By Jay (IRE) (55) (BJCurley) **3-9-0** JQuinn(2) (a bhd)	hd	**12**	14/1	49	15
3930[11]	**Masterpiece (62)** (RHannon) **3-9-7** WJO'Connor(7) (mid div over 5f)	½	**13**	12/1	55	21
3936[10]	**Aquatic Queen (55)** (CADwyer) **3-8-11**(3) TEDurcan(11) (lw: mid div over 5f)	½	**14**	14/1	47	13
4291*	**Lamorna (51)** (MRChannon) **3-8-10** CRutter(15) (racd stands' side: spd over 4f)	1½	**15**	15/2[3]	39	5
				(SP 141.1%)	**15 Rn**	

1m 23.16 (1.96) CSF £29.42 CT £496.46 TOTE £3.10: £1.30 £4.80 £20.90 (£88.50) Trio £1,472.20 OWNER Mrs Chris Harrington (MARLBOROUGH) BRED Mrs Chris Harrington
LONG HANDICAP Loxley's Girl (IRE) 7-7 Blue Cheese 7-7
4168 Bold Tina (IRE) appreciated the return to seven furlongs and, striking the front a quarter of a mile out, just managed to hold off the whirlwind finish of the runner-up. (2/1)
673 Churchill's Shadow (IRE) was held up in last place to get the trip but the exaggerated tactics meant he had an awful lot to do entering the final quarter-mile. Going into overdrive from below the distance, he stormed through but the line was always beating him. (12/1: 8/1-14/1)
513 Loxley's Girl (IRE), one of four who elected to race down the stands' side, ran her best race on this return to grass and was on level terms with the far-side group approaching the final quarter-mile, before tapped for toe. (25/1)
Hawksbill Henry (USA) ran his best race to date and poked his head in front over a quarter of a mile from home. Soon passed, he could then only struggle on at one pace. (20/1)
883 Aybeegirl, without a run since finishing tailed off at Goodwood four months ago, took the field along but, collared approaching the final quarter-mile, could then only go up and down in the same place. (12/1: op 8/1)
3637 Whizz Kid was making little impression on the principals in the final quarter-mile. She is a very moderate performer with just one win from twenty-eight starts. (20/1)
4505 Daylight Dreams (14/1: op 8/1)
1333 Carlton (IRE) (14/1: op 8/1)
By Jay (IRE) (14/1: op 7/1)
693 Masterpiece (12/1: 6/1-14/1)

4547 LEFA ENTERPRISES MAIDEN STKS (3-Y.O+) (Class D)

4-35 (4-36) **1m 6f** £3,836.70 (£1,146.60: £548.80: £249.90) Stalls: High GOING minus 0.45 sec per fur (F)

				SP	RR	SF
3412[9]	**Crystal Hills (IRE) (80)** (JHMGosden) **3-8-12** GHind(4) (mde all: clr over 2f out: hrd rdn: r.o)	—	**1**	4/1[2]	81	24
4360[2]	**Spartan Heartbeat (102)** (CEBrittain) **4-9-7** WJO'Connor(8) (b: swtg: chsd wnr over 12f out: ev ch over 3f out: hrd rdn over 2f out: unable qckn)	1¾	**2**	1/2[1]	79	31
	Bawara (IRE) (MRChannon) **3-8-12** JCarroll(6) (w'like: scope: bit bkwd: hdwy over 6f out: one pce fnl 4f)	4	**3**	8/1[3]	74	17
3413[11]	**Paddy Hurry (35)** (NACallaghan) **3-8-12** JFEgan(2) (nvr nr to chal)	5	**4**	50/1	69	12
3918[3]	**Double Star** (JLHarris) **6-9-7** DeanMcKeown(1) (lw: hld up: rdn 6f out: sn wknd)	½	**5**	9/1	68	20
	Corporate Image (RSimpson) **7-9-7** MGallagher(9) (prom 8f)	10	**6**	50/1	57	9
4060[14]	**Choice Lady** (JLHarris) **3-8-7** ACulhane(7) (a bhd)	9	**7**	50/1	41	—
	Steam on (MrsLCJewell) **6-9-7** SDrowne(3) (bit bkwd: plld hrd: prom over 7f: t.o fnl 5f)	29	**8**	50/1	13	—
				(SP 115.6%)	**8 Rn**	

3m 5.05 (6.75) CSF £5.85 TOTE £5.70: £1.10 £1.50 £1.20 (£1.80) Trio £5.70 OWNER Sheikh Mohammed (NEWMARKET) BRED Sheikh Mohammed Bin Rashid Al Maktoum
WEIGHT FOR AGE 3yo-9lb
2692 Crystal Hills (IRE), fitted with a Monty Roberts rug for stalls entry, made every post a winning one and forged clear from his only serious rival early in the straight. He did not look over-enthusiastic as the whip was produced but struggled on to win this dreadful race. (4/1: 5/2-9/2)
4360 Spartan Heartbeat was sweating buckets in the paddock and hardly covered himself with glory in this atrocious race. On level terms with the winner entering the straight, he was soon under pressure and failed to find the necessary turn of foot. He may have run with credit in races such as the Irish Derby and Goodwood Cup but the fact remains he is still a maiden and this performance does not bode well for the future. (1/2)
Bawara (IRE), a good-bodied gelding who was just beginning to go in his coat, was carrying condition and was made to look very slow in the straight. (8/1: 6/1-10/1)
3054 Paddy Hurry, racing at the back field, struggled on past some very bad horses to be nearest at the line. (50/1)
3918 Double Star looks incredibly slow. (9/1: 6/1-10/1)

4548 MCINDOE AMATEUR LIMITED STKS (0-65) (3-Y.O+) (Class F)

5-10 (5-11) **1m 3f 106y** £2,277.00 (£627.00: £297.00) Stalls: High GOING minus 0.45 sec per fur (F)

				SP	RR	SF
4295[12]	**Random Kindness (65)** (RIngram) **4-10-10**(4) MrLJefford(11) (lw: hdwy 6f out: led 2f out: rdn out)	—	**1**	12/1	68	47

				SP	RR	SF
4335*	**Civil Liberty (60)** (GLewis) **4-11-0** MrABalding(4) (hdwy & swtchd lft over 1f out: swtchd rt: str run fnl f: fin wl: too much to do)	¾	**2**	15/8 1	67	46
1372 4	**Laurel Seeker (USA) (63)** (MrsAJPerrett) **3-10-6** MrsAPerrett(2) (lw: a.p: rdn over 2f out: unable qckn)	1	**3**	15/2	64	37
3864 4	**Newport Knight (60)** (RAkehurst) **6-10-12** MrTMcCarthy(3) (b.hind: lost pl 4f out: rallied over 2f out: one pce)	1¼	**4**	3/1 2	62	41
4275 18	**Sheep Stealer (60)** (REPeacock) **9-10-6**(6) MrsCPeacock(1) (hdwy 6f out: led 5f out to 2f out: sn wknd: sddle slipped)	6	**5**	33/1	54	33
3971 5	**Royal Acclaim (27)** (KRBurke) **12-10-6v**(6) MissRJPatman(6) (hdwy over 3f out: wknd over 2f out)	½	**6**	20/1	53	32
4275 19	**Gold Blade (60)** (JPearce) **8-10-12** MrsLPearce(7) (lw: hdwy 5f out: wknd wl over 1f out)	1½	**7**	7/2 3	51	30
3971 11	**Patrita Park (32)** (WGMTurner) **3-9-11**(6) MissCStretton(5) (b.hind: led over 6f)	2½	**8**	50/1	44	17
4450 5	**Another Fiddle (IRE) (23)** (JELong) **7-10-6**(6) MrRBlyth(10) (b.hind: a.p: chsd ldr 5f out tl over 2f out: sn wknd)	4	**9**	33/1	42	21
4050 4	**Dragon's Back (IRE) (48)** (DCO'Brien) **4-10-6**(6) MrVLukaniuk(12) (lw: prom 8f)	15	**10**	25/1	21	—
3397 5	**Bon Guest (IRE) (56)** (MissBSanders) **3-10-0**(6) MissLSheen(8) (lw: a bhd)	8	**11**	16/1	10	—
				(SP 123.8%)	**11 Rn**	

2m 30.84 (6.14) CSF £31.96 TOTE £14.80: £3.00 £1.40 £1.90 (£17.90) Trio £39.90 OWNER 949 Racing (EPSOM) BRED Pendley Farm
WEIGHT FOR AGE 3yo-6lb
OFFICIAL EXPLANATION **Sheep Stealer: saddle slipped during the race.**

1122 Random Kindness struck the front a quarter of a mile out and was ridden along to gain his first success. However, if the runner-up had been given a better ride, he would surely have been second best. (12/1)

4335* Civil Liberty was given a dreadful ride by his experienced amateur rider, even allowing for the fact that he was trying to make sure the gelding got this longer trip, which he did. With just one behind him entering the straight, his rider was quite content to sit on him doing very little and only began to pick up ground below the distance. For some bizarre reason, Balding decided to switch his mount to the inside, which was hardly a sensible thing to do, and it was no surprise that he then had to switch him to the outside to get a better run. Absolutely flying in the final furlong, he would undoubtedly have prevailed under a better ride. (15/8: 7/4-11/4)

1372 Laurel Seeker (USA), given a four and a half month break, ran his best race to date under his very experienced and competent rider, if failing to quicken in the last two furlongs. (15/2: 10/1-6/1)

3864 Newport Knight, who lost his pitch turning for home, soon got back into it but could only struggle on at one insufficient pace in the final quarter-mile. He has done all his winning at this trip. (3/1: 2/1-7/2)

3277 Sheep Stealer went on running down the hill but, collared a quarter of a mile out, soon had bellows to mend. It was later reported that his saddle had slipped during the race. (33/1)

3971 Royal Acclaim made an effort early in the straight but it proved to be short-lived. He has just one win to his name in the last four and a half years. (20/1)

T/Plpt: £120.80 (145.83 Tckts). T/Qdpt: £19.90 (58.78 Tckts) AK

4521-NEWMARKET (R-H) (Good to firm)
Friday October 3rd
WEATHER: overcast WIND: fresh half behind

4549 RACING POST GODOLPHIN STKS (Listed) (3-Y.O+) (Class A)
2-05 (2-06) **1m 4f (Rowley)** £11,601.40 (£4,013.40: £1,926.70: £788.50) Stalls: High GOING minus 0.36 sec per fur (F)

				SP	RR	SF
1172 2	**Mons (118)** (LMCumani) **4-9-0** LDettori(2) (swtg: mde all: qcknd over 2f out: r.o wl)	—	**1**	3/1 2	118	48
4134 2	**Memorise (USA) (107)** (HRACecil) **3-8-7** KFallon(3) (trckd wnr: effrt 3f out: outpcd over 1f out: kpt on towards fin)	1½	**2**	7/2 3	116	39
4149 3	**The Fly (110)** (BWHills) **3-8-7** MHills(1) (lw: hld up: hdwy over 2f out: rdn over 1f out: kpt on: nt pce to chal)	s.h	**3**	10/11 1	116	39
4149 7	**Shaya (100)** (MajorWRHern) **3-8-7** RHills(4) (lw: trckd ldrs: hdwy over 2f out: rdn & nt qckn appr fnl f)	½	**4**	12/1	115	38
				(SP 107.3%)	**4 Rn**	

2m 33.65 (3.15) CSF £11.53 TOTE £3.50: (£4.30) OWNER Mrs E. H. Vestey (NEWMARKET) BRED Sir Eric Parker
WEIGHT FOR AGE 3yo-7lb

1172 Mons, returning here after almost four months off, got pretty warm beforehand but has certainly been edgy before. He stays further than this and was allowed his own way throughout, which proved decisive when he kicked in the last two and a half furlongs. (3/1: op 7/4)

4134 Memorise (USA) kept tabs on the winner but was tapped for toe when the pace increased approaching the last two furlongs and, despite staying on gallantly, had no further chance. He could be interesting over further. (7/2: 5/2-4/1)

4149 The Fly was held up in last place but the pace was not strong enough for these tactics and he lacked the speed to get in a blow, despite trying hard. (10/11)

4149 Shaya had plenty on here and ran reasonably, but never looked likely to make a real impression. (12/1)

4550 CHARLES WELLS BOMBARDIER BITTER RATED STKS H'CAP (0-100) (3-Y.O+) (Class B)
2-35 (2-37) **7f (Rowley)** £8,468.64 (£3,137.76: £1,508.88: £620.40: £250.20: £102.12) Stalls: Centre GOING minus 0.36 sec per fur (F)

				SP	RR	SF
4121 2	**Al Muallim (USA) (88)** (JWPayne) **3-8-7** AMcGlone(4) (plld hrd: a.p: rdn to ld ins fnl f: r.o wl)	—	**1**	4/1 1	100	57
4282 11	**Madly Sharp (86)** (JWWatts) **6-8-7** JFortune(13) (lw: hld up: effrt over 2f out: swtchd over 1f out: r.o towards fin)	1¾	**2**	7/1 3	94	53
4297 9	**Mr Sponge (USA) (86)** (IABalding) **3-8-5** MHills(7) (lw: led: qcknd over 2f out: hdd ins fnl f: kpt on)	hd	**3**	16/1	94	51
3975 12	**Triple Hay (94)** (RHannon) **3-8-13** DaneO'Neill(11) (hld up & bhd: hdwy 2f out: r.o: nrst fin)	1½	**4**	20/1	98	55
4276 4	**All Is Fair (90)** (SirMarkPrescott) **3-8-9** GDuffield(10) (chsd ldr: rdn over 2f out: btn appr fnl f)	nk	**5**	7/1 3	94	51
2774 2	**Serenity (99)** (JRFanshawe) **3-9-4** KFallon(12) (chsd ldrs: effrt over 2f out: r.o one pce)	½	**6**	10/1	102	59
4314 4	**Concer Un (93)** (SCWilliams) **5-9-0** KDarley(2) (b: rr div: effrt over 2f out: styd on: n.d)	hd	**7**	11/1	95	54
3888*	**Highborn (IRE) (100)** (PSFelgate) **8-9-4**(3) DSweeney(6) (lw: in tch: rdn over 2f out: no imp)	s.h	**8**	8/1	102	61
4148 2	**Hawait (IRE) (92)** (BWHills) **3-8-8b**(3) PFessey(9) (swtg: s.i.s: hdwy u.p 2f out: n.d)	s.h	**9**	8/1	94	51
4423 2	**Kayvee (86)** (MrsAJPerrett) **8-8-7** AClark(8) (bhd: effrt over 2f out: nvr rchd ldrs)	nk	**10**	13/2 2	87	46
4280 5	**Mr Bergerac (IRE) (86)** (BPalling) **6-8-7** TSprake(1) (mid div: rdn over 2f out: sn btn)	nk	**11**	20/1	87	46
4153 3	**Bachelors Pad (93)** (WJarvis) **3-8-12** WRyan(3) (chsd ldrs: drvn along over 2f out: sn wknd)	2	**12**	20/1	89	46

				SP	RR	SF
2525^{P}	**Prince of India (100)** (LordHuntingdon) **5-9-7** LDettori(5) (s.i.s: a bhd)	10	**13**	25/1	73	32
				(SP 122.0%)		**13 Rn**

1m 24.85 (0.35) CSF £27.07 CT £390.93 TOTE £4.90: £2.10 £2.50 £4.00 (£16.80) Trio £141.50 OWNER Al Muallim Partnership (NEWMARKET) BRED James T. Gottwald
LONG HANDICAP Mr Bergerac (IRE) 8-5 Mr Sponge (USA) 8-2
WEIGHT FOR AGE 3yo-2lb
4121 Al Muallim (USA), despite taking a fierce hold early on, was always going best and won in useful style. (4/1)
4282 Madly Sharp, without the blinkers this time, did not do anything quickly but did run on when it was all too late. He is really well handicapped just now. (7/1)
3901 Mr Sponge (USA) looked magnificent and tried to pinch this by quickening off a slowish pace but was never quite good enough. (16/1)
1634* Triple Hay tried the impossible coming from virtually last and did remarkably well to get so close in this messy event. These tactics were probably employed to make sure he got the trip. (20/1)
4276 All Is Fair always held a good position but was short of toe when the tempo really increased in the last couple of furlongs. (7/1)
2774 Serenity settled quite well this time but was found wanting for speed when the tap was really turned on. (10/1)
4314 Concer Un, given plenty to do, ran well in the circumstances. (11/1)
3888* Highborn (IRE) was getting warn by the time he left the paddock and did not give his running. (8/1)

4551 SOMERVILLE TATTERSALL STKS (Listed) (2-Y.O C & G) (Class A)

3-05 (3-05) **7f (Rowley)** £8,954.40 (£3,309.60: £1,584.80: £644.00: £252.00: £95.20) Stalls: Centre GOING minus 0.36 sec per fur (F)

				SP	RR	SF
3895^{3}	**Haami (USA) (100)** (JLDunlop) **2-8-9** RHills(2) (lw: trckd ldrs: smooth hdwy to ld appr fnl f: rdn & r.o)	—	**1**	5/1	110+	63
4146*	**Bintang (IRE)** (PFICole) **2-8-9** TQuinn(7) (plld hrd: trckd ldrs: rdn to disp ld appr fnl f: sn hdd: kpt on same pce)	1½	**2**	7/2^{3}	107	60
3602*	**Aix En Provence (USA) (97)** (MJohnston) **2-8-9** DHolland(5) (lw: a cl up: effrt over 2f out: kpt on wl)	1¾	**3**	33/1	103	56
3895^{2}	**Tracking (100)** (HRACecil) **2-8-9** KFallon(8) (led: qcknd over 2f out: hdd appr fnl f: r.o one pce)	¾	**4**	3/1^{2}	101	54
4299^{3}	**Wuxi Venture (79)** (SPCWoods) **2-8-9b^{1}** JReid(3) (s.i.s: hld up: effrt over 2f out: sme late hdwy)	2½	**5**	50/1	95?	48
4145*	**Iceband (USA)** (JHMGosden) **2-8-9** WRyan(1) (hld up: drvn along over 2f out: no imp)	2	**6**	9/1	91	44
4174*	**Abreeze (USA)** (SbinSuroor) **2-8-9** LDettori(6) (hld up: stdy hdwy ½-wy: chsng ldrs & rdn wl over 1f out: sn btn)	1	**7**	15/8^{1}	88	41
4143^{3}	**Who Nose (IRE) (74)** (BJMeehan) **2-8-9v^{1}** KDarley(4) (hld up & bhd: rdn over 2f out: sn btn)	2	**8**	66/1	84	37
				(SP 115.1%)		**8 Rn**

1m 24.52 (0.02) CSF £20.76 TOTE £5.80: £1.80 £1.40 £3.60 (£13.30) OWNER Mr Hamdan Al Maktoum (ARUNDEL) BRED Shadwell Farm Inc
OFFICIAL EXPLANATION Abreeze (USA): rider was unable to offer any explanation for the colt's poor performance.
3895 Haami (USA) came back to form here and in style, and there were apparently excuses for him last time, apart from the soft ground. (5/1: 3/1-11/2)
4146* Bintang (IRE), taking his customary strong hold, was really tested here and had his chances, but was found wanting when the chips were down. This would appear as good as he is. (7/2)
3602* Aix En Provence (USA) has improved no end and this was a splendid performance. Another year could see even better from him. (33/1)
3895 Tracking had the run of the race out in front and kept trying hard and his jockey never gave up, but his limitations were well exposed in the final furlong and a half. (3/1)
4299 Wuxi Venture had blinkers on for the first time but, coming from off the pace, the race was over by the time he showed anything. (50/1)
4145* Iceband (USA) was disappointing, failing to pick up at all when the pace increased over two furlongs out. (9/1)
4174* Abreeze (USA) looked the part, both going to post and most of the way back but, once off the bit approaching the final furlong, he ran out of fuel as though something was wrong. (15/8)

4552 JAMES LEVETT H'CAP (0-100) (3-Y.O) (Class C)

3-40 (3-40) **1m 2f (Rowley)** £6,160.00 (£1,840.00: £880.00: £400.00) Stalls: Centre GOING minus 0.36 sec per fur (F)

				SP	RR	SF
4109*	**Kewarra (78)** (BRMillman) **3-8-1** TSprake(3) (trckd ldrs gng wl: led wl over 1f out: r.o wl fnl f)	—	**1**	7/2^{1}	90	70
1146^{2}	**Silverani (IRE) (98)** (LMCumani) **3-9-7** KDarley(2) (lw: hld up: hdwy 4f out: chal 2f out: nt qckn ins fnl f)	3	**2**	5/1^{2}	105	85
3989^{5}	**Fantail (79)** (MHTompkins) **3-7-13**(3) MHenry(1) (prom: pushed along 3f out: styd on fnl f: nt pce to chal)	1	**3**	10/1	85	65
4294^{6}	**Titta Ruffo (81)** (BJMeehan) **3-8-4** GDuffield(7) (trckd ldrs: effrt over 2f out: nt qckn appr fnl f)	1¾	**4**	9/1	84	64
2850^{2}	**Deep Water (USA) (73)** (PFICole) **3-7-10** NCarlisle(9) (chsd ldrs: pushed along over 4f out: wl outpcd 2f out: styd on)	½	**5**	11/1	75	55
4276^{3}	**Blewbury Hill (IRE) (73)** (RFJohnsonHoughton) **3-7-7**(3) RFfrench(6) (lw: led: effrt 3f out: hdd wl over 1f out: sn btn)	2½	**6**	10/1	71	51
4151^{2}	**Ihtiyati (USA) (97)** (JLDunlop) **3-9-6** RHills(8) (lw: hld up: outpcd over 2f out: no imp after)	¾	**7**	7/2^{1}	94	74
4435^{7}	**My Valentina (74)** (BWHills) **3-7-8**(3) PFessey(5) (hld up & bhd: hdwy over 3f out: rdn & btn wl over 1f out)	4	**8**	7/1^{3}	64	44
				(SP 110.1%)		**8 Rn**

2m 3.05 (-1.65) CSF £17.55 CT £132.60 TOTE £5.50: £1.60 £2.00 £2.30 (£13.20) Trio £30.50 OWNER Mr G. Palmer (CULLOMPTON) BRED Mrs M. Palmer and G. Palmer
LONG HANDICAP Blewbury Hill (IRE) 7-7 Deep Water (USA) 7-9
4109* Kewarra is obviously in the form of his life and won in some style to land a gamble. (7/2)
1146 Silverani (IRE), after almost five months off and up 9lb in the weights, was probably better for this, ran a cracker and looks one to side with. (5/1: 3/1-11/2)
3989 Fantail, who has a moderate action, ran well, staying on at the end but finding this trip too sharp. (10/1: 8/1-12/1)
4294 Titta Ruffo had his chances but failed to pick up at the end, and either needs a bit of cut in the ground or further. (9/1)
2850 Deep Water (USA), dropping back in trip, was always short of speed at the business end but did keep staying on. (11/1: 8/1-12/1)
4276 Blewbury Hill (IRE), trying his longest trip to date, surprisingly made the running and then ran out of fuel late on. (10/1)
4151 Ihtiyati (USA) moved moderately to post and ran poorly. (7/2: op 2/1)

4553 NGK SPARK PLUGS RATED STKS H'CAP (0-105) (3-Y.O+ F & M) (Class B)

4-15 (4-16) **6f (Rowley)** £7,716.96 (£2,852.64: £1,366.32: £555.60: £217.80: £82.68) Stalls: Centre GOING minus 0.36 sec per fur (F)

				SP	RR	SF
4444^{4}	**Bowden Rose (90)** (MBlanshard) **5-8-4b**(3) DSweeney(4) (lw: hld up & bhd: smooth hdwy to ld 1½f out: sn clr: r.o wl)	—	**1**	14/1	101	61

4282[22]	**Plaisir d'Amour (IRE) (91)** (NACallaghan) **3-8-7** LDettori(5) (lw: trckd ldrs: effrt 2f out: r.o u.p fnl f: nrst fin)	1¼	**2**	100/30[1]	99	58
4280[2]	**Almasi (IRE) (90)** (CFWall) **5-8-2**(5) JoHunnam(6) (a.p: effrt & ch 2f out: nt qckn)	1½	**3**	11/2[3]	94	54
4307*	**Prends Ca (IRE) (90)** (WRMuir) **4-8-7** JReid(8) (trckd ldrs: effrt 2f out: hrd rdn & r.o one pce)	½	**4**	6/1	92	52
4282*	**Wildwood Flower (104)** (RHannon) **4-9-7** DaneO'Neill(3) (hld up: effrt over 2f out: styd on: nvr able chal)	hd	**5**	6/1	106	66
3709[7]	**Dancethenightaway (90)** (BJMeehan) **3-8-6** GDuffield(1) (cl up: led 2f out: hdd 1½f out: hung rt & wknd)	nk	**6**	33/1	91	50
4421[9]	**Lochangel (94)** (IABalding) **3-8-10** TQuinn(2) (led 4f: sn rdn & btn)	hd	**7**	7/2[2]	95	54
4434*	**Patsy Grimes (90)** (JSMoore) **7-8-4**(3) 3x PPMurphy(9) (cl up tl wknd wl over 1f out)	1¼	**8**	9/1	88	48
2677[7]	**Wellspring (IRE) (92)** (DRLoder) **3-8-8** KFallon(7) (prom 4f: wknd qckly)	16	**9**	16/1	47	6

(SP 114.7%) **9 Rn**

1m 11.84 (0.04) CSF £54.65 CT £267.99 TOTE £13.90: £2.50 £1.50 £1.50 (£33.80) Trio £52.70 OWNER G H S Bailey & N C D Hall (UPPER LAMBOURN) BRED E. A. Badger

LONG HANDICAP Almasi (IRE) 8-5 Bowden Rose 8-6 Prends Ca (IRE) 8-6 Dancethenightaway 8-2

WEIGHT FOR AGE 3yo-1lb

4444 Bowden Rose, dropped out this time, was then brought wide to challenge and won it in a few strides when quickening approaching the final furlong. When things go her way, she is certainly useful. (14/1)

4282 Plaisir d'Amour (IRE) travelled quite well but, by the time she got into her stride, the winner had stolen it. She is certainly better than this. (100/30)

4280 Almasi (IRE) does not seem to know how to run a bad race these days and she kept trying here when well held. (11/2)

4307* Prends Ca (IRE) travelled on the bridle but, on this occasion, she never found as much as looked likely. (6/1)

4282* Wildwood Flower moved scratchily to post and has not surprisingly shot up the handicap. She never really got into this and was wisely not over-punished when obviously beaten. (6/1: 4/1-13/2)

3194 Dancethenightaway showed plenty of speed but always gave her rider problems by hanging right. (33/1)

4155 Lochangel was disappointing here and she looks the type who might well do better next year as she strengthens. (7/2: 5/2-4/1)

4434* Patsy Grimes (9/1: 8/1-12/1)

4554 FURTHER FLIGHT LIMITED STKS (0-90) (3-Y.O+) (Class C)

4-50 (4-50) **1m (Rowley)** £5,640.00 (£1,680.00: £800.00: £360.00) Stalls: Centre GOING minus 0.36 sec per fur (F)

				SP	RR	SF
3712[7]	**Strazo (IRE) (90)** (LadyHerries) **4-9-0** RCochrane(4) (mde most: qcknd over 2f out: r.o wl)	—	**1**	6/4[1]	100	75
4282[29]	**Midyan Call (90)** (MBell) **3-8-13** MFenton(6) (lw: hld up: hdwy over 2f out: chsng wnr appr fnl f: hung lft & rt: nt qckn)	2	**2**	6/1[3]	98	70
3725[9]	**Great Child (88)** (MRStoute) **3-8-13** JReid(1) (a.p: effrt over 2f out: rdn & no ex)	4	**3**	6/1[3]	90	62
3391[2]	**Rapier (88)** (RHannon) **3-8-11** DaneO'Neill(7) (prom: effrt 3f out: one pce)	½	**4**	6/1[3]	87	59
4176[6]	**First Chance (IRE) (67)** (DRCElsworth) **3-8-5**(3) RFfrench(5) (chsd ldrs: outpcd 3f out: sn btn)	9	**5**	25/1	66	38
3463*	**Dr Martens (IRE) (84)** (LMCumani) **3-8-13** LDettori(2) (lw: disp ld tl ½-wy: rdn & btn over 2f out)	6	**6**	100/30[2]	59	31

(SP 109.8%) **6 Rn**

1m 36.69 (-0.61) CSF £9.52 TOTE £2.70: £1.40 £3.40 (£10.20) OWNER Mr E. Reitel (LITTLEHAMPTON) BRED Juddmonte Farms

WEIGHT FOR AGE 3yo-3lb

OFFICIAL EXPLANATION **Strazo (IRE): regarding the apparent improvement in form, the gelding may have hurt his back when jinking coming out of the stalls last time, and had since been seen by a chiropractor.**

3150 Strazo (IRE) is a poor mover, but he was always far too good for this bunch and won particularly well. (6/4)

3425* Midyan Call, taking a step up in trip, was the only one able to give the winner a race, but he spoiled his chances by hanging badly in both directions every time he was shown the whip. (6/1: 4/1-13/2)

3189 Great Child has had six weeks off and may just have needed this. (6/1: 7/2-13/2)

3391 Rapier, returning after two months off, showed up well but proved short of pace. (6/1)

4176 First Chance (IRE) looked to have plenty on here and was beaten someway out. (25/1)

3463* Dr Martens (IRE) took the eye in the paddock but he was most disappointing and may well have some sort of a problem, as this was also his first outing for almost two months. (100/30: 9/4-7/2)

T/Jkpt: £22,725.60 (0.1 Tckts); £28,807.16 to Newmarket 4/10/97. T/Plpt: £202.30 (254.6 Tckts). T/Qdpt: £27.50 (111.58 Tckts) AA

4549-NEWMARKET (R-H) (Good to firm)

Saturday October 4th

WEATHER: sunny WIND: fresh half bhd

4555 OH SO SHARP STKS (Listed) (2-Y.O F) (Class A)

1-50 (1-51) **7f (Rowley)** £9,360.40 (£3,463.60: £1,661.80: £679.00: £269.50: £105.70) Stalls: Low GOING minus 0.37 sec per fur (F)

				SP	RR	SF
4007*	**Name of Love (IRE)** (DRLoder) **2-8-9** KFallon(3) (prom: rdn to ld 1f out: r.o)	—	**1**	7/1	104	66
4119[2]	**Flawless** (SirMarkPrescott) **2-8-9** GDuffield(5) (a chsng ldrs: drvn along thrght: swtchd outside 2f out: kpt on)	2	**2**	6/4[1]	99	61
3723[9]	**Shuhrah (USA)** (SbinSuroor) **2-8-9** RHills(2) (lw: w ldrs: led over 2f out tl hdd 1f out: kpt on same pce)	½	**3**	6/1[3]	98	60
3981[3]	**Nanoushka (IRE)** (RHannon) **2-8-9** PaulEddery(4) (dwlt: hdwy over 2f out: btn appr fnl f)	3	**4**	14/1	91	53
3934*	**Dazilyn Lady (USA) (99)** (PWHarris) **2-8-9** KDarley(8) (led after 2f tl over 2f out: wknd)	1¼	**5**	7/1	89	51
4273*	**Amabel (USA) (96)** (IABalding) **2-8-9** MHills(7) (lw: w ldrs tl rdn & btn 2f out)	3	**6**	11/2[2]	82	44
3874a[8]	**Diamond White (100)** (GCBravery) **2-8-13** DRMcCabe(1) (dwlt: drvn along ½-wy: n.d)	nk	**7**	16/1	85	47
3934[2]	**Parisian Lady (IRE) (98)** (AGNewcombe) **2-8-9** GHind(6) (led 2f: cl up tl wknd over 2f out)	3	**8**	20/1	74	36

(SP 112.0%) **8 Rn**

1m 24.22 (-0.28) CSF £15.63 TOTE £6.10: £1.80 £1.10 £2.00 (£5.10) OWNER Mr William Fox (NEWMARKET) BRED Noel O'Callaghan

4007* Name of Love (IRE) is improving with every run and this was a sound effort. She was certainly better suited by this galloping track. (7/1: 5/1-15/2)

4119 Flawless never looked happy for some reason and, racing with her head at an angle, needed a lot of driving. To her credit she did keep staying on, albeit in vain, but would seem to have some sort of a problem. (6/4)

3009* Shuhrah (USA), after a decent effort last time, was back to form here, but this keen sort had given her best entering the final furlong. (6/1: op 3/1)

3981 Nanoushka (IRE) took a strong hold going to post and, after a slow start, was happy to be out the back but, when the pressure was on, she was never good enough to make a real impression. (14/1: 10/1-16/1)

3934* Dazilyn Lady (USA) had her chances but ran out of fuel too far from home to say that the trip beat her and something must have gone wrong. (7/1)
4273* Amabel (USA) won on soft ground last time and was always finding conditions too fast here. (11/2)

4556 E.B.F. EQUITY FINANCIAL COLLECTIONS MAIDEN STKS (2-Y.O F) (Class D)

2-20 (2-20) **6f (Rowley)** £5,208.00 (£1,554.00: £742.00: £336.00) Stalls: Low GOING minus 0.37 sec per fur (F)

				SP	RR	SF
4103^{11}	**Qilin (IRE)** (MHTompkins) **2-8-11** DBiggs(2) (a.p: hdwy 2f out: rdn to ld ins fnl f: edgd lft towards fin)	—	1	8/1	91	61
	Grazia (SirMarkPrescott) **2-8-11** GDuffield(6) (wl grwn: scope: w ldrs: rdn to ld over 1f out: hdd ins fnl f: btn whn sltly hmpd towards fin)	1¼	2	15/8^{1}	88	58
	Court Lane (USA) (DRLoder) **2-8-11** RCochrane(10) (neat: scope: led tl hdd over 1f out: kpt on same pce)	2	3	7/1^{3}	82	52
4097^{6}	**Jilted (IRE) (80)** (RHannon) **2-8-11b^{1}** DaneO'Neill(4) (cl up: drvn along over 2f out: btn over 1f out)	5	4	7/1^{3}	69	39
4103^{14}	**Sixpence** (GWragg) **2-8-11** MHills(7) (bit bkwd: outpcd & lost pl after 2f: styd on fnl 2f: no imp)	nk	5	20/1	68	38
	Enchant (MRStoute) **2-8-11** JReid(1) (w'like: leggy: bit bkwd: prom: outpcd over 2f out: no imp after)	¾	6	11/2^{2}	66	36
3717^{4}	**Sassy Lady (IRE)** (CADwyer) **2-8-11** JFortune(3) (dwlt: nvr trbld ldrs)	1¾	7	25/1	62	32
1031^{4}	**Sky Red** (MBell) **2-8-11** TQuinn(5) (bit bkwd: chsd ldrs tl wknd fnl 2f)	s.h	8	20/1	61	31
	Almurooj (BWHills) **2-8-11** RHills(8) (neat: bit bkwd: cl up tl wknd fnl 2 ½f)	3	9	11/2^{2}	53	23
	Worth The Effort (MHTompkins) **2-8-8**(3) MHenry(9) (lt-f: unf: bkwd: s.s: a wl bhd)	8	10	50/1	32	2
				(SP 117.0%)	**10 Rn**	

1m 12.04 (0.24) CSF £20.43 TOTE £18.40: £3.50 £1.80 £2.50 (£11.60) Trio £63.90 OWNER Mr Ian Lochhead (NEWMARKET) BRED Gestut Romerhof
Qilin (IRE) did this nicely despite edging left in the closing stages and is obviously improving fast. (8/1: 10/1-16/1)
Grazia, an excitable sort, needed two handlers in the paddock and failed to stride out going to post, but she ran well and should improve for the experience. (15/8: 7/4-11/4)
Court Lane (USA) showed plenty of pace from an outside draw and there would seem to be better to come. (7/1: 4/1-8/1)
4097 Jilted (IRE) looked really well and had blinkers on for the first time but, once asked to struggle, she soon decided it was not for her. (7/1)
Sixpence, needing this, ran green and found this trip too sharp but she did finish well, suggesting that over further she is one to watch. (20/1)
Enchant, a useful type, looked likely to be all the better for this and was not knocked about when obviously struggling. The kindness will no doubt be repaid. (11/2: 3/1-6/1)
Almurooj (11/2: 3/1-6/1)

4557 EQUITY FINANCIAL COLLECTIONS SUN CHARIOT STKS (Gp 2) (3-Y.O+ F & M) (Class A)

2-55 (2-55) **1m 2f (Rowley)** £33,024.00 (£12,216.00: £5,858.00: £2,390.00: £945.00: £367.00) Stalls: Low GOING minus 0.37 sec per fur (F)

				SP	RR	SF
3913*	**One So Wonderful** (LMCumani) **3-8-8** JReid(6) (mde most: r.o gamely fnl f)	—	1	5/2^{2}	122	82
3875a*	**Kool Kat Katie (IRE)** (DRLoder) **3-8-8** RCochrane(7) (trckd ldrs: hdwy over 2f out: disp ld 1f out: r.o wl)	nk	2	7/2^{3}	122	82
3704^{4}	**Reams of Verse (USA) (119)** (HRACecil) **3-9-0** KFallon(5) (lw: hld up: effrt over 2f out: sn chsng ldrs: nt qckn fnl f)	3½	3	9/4^{1}	122	82
4292^{2}	**Fatefully (USA) (104)** (EALDunlop) **4-8-13** MHills(2) (cl up: effrt over 2f out: one pce)	3	4	20/1	111	76
4177^{6}	**Mrs Miniver (USA) (89)** (PAKelleway) **3-8-8** JFortune(1) (lw: hld up & bhd: effrt 3f out: styd on: nvr able chal)	2	5	100/1	108?	68
4181^{4}	**Ukraine Venture (92)** (SPCWoods) **3-8-8** KDarley(3) (chsd ldrs: rdn over 3f out: wknd over 2f out)	8	6	40/1	95	55
4256a^{7}	**Dust Dancer (115)** (JLDunlop) **3-8-8** TQuinn(4) (swtg: w ldrs tl rdn & wknd over 2f out)	8	7	8/1	82	42
3803*	**Sarayir (USA) (100)** (MajorWRHern) **3-8-8** RHills(8) (prom tl rdn & wknd wl over 2f out)	5	8	8/1	74	34
				(SP 112.0%)	**8 Rn**	

2m 2.38 (-2.32) CSF £10.11 TOTE £3.50: £1.40 £1.10 £1.20 (£4.50) OWNER Helena Springfield Ltd (NEWMARKET) BRED Meon Valley Stud
WEIGHT FOR AGE 3yo-5lb
3913* One So Wonderful is a really game filly who goes on any ground. This was the longest trip she had tackled to date, but she got it particularly well and even further should suit. (5/2)
3875a* Kool Kat Katie (IRE) lost her unbeaten record here but there was no disgrace in that as this was a super effort against what looks like a really classy filly. (7/2)
3704 Reams of Verse (USA), edgy in the paddock, needed two handlers and was taken early to post. She did nothing wrong in the race and always kept her eye on the leaders but, when the pace was really on, she was never up to it. (9/4)
4292 Fatefully (USA) has rather lost her way this season and was stepping up in trip here. Although she ran pretty well, she was never good enough and the extra distance would seem no real help. (20/1)
4177 Mrs Miniver (USA) ran well in this company but was probably flattered she was coming from off the pace. (100/1)
4181 Ukraine Venture, who started the season in a blaze of glory, has been generally disappointing since. (40/1)
4256a Dust Dancer got in a terrible state in the preliminaries and not surprisingly did not give her running. (8/1)

4558 TOTE CAMBRIDGESHIRE H'CAP (3-Y.O+) (Class B)

3-35 (3-37) **1m 1f (Rowley)** £50,627.00 (£18,893.00: £9,196.50: £3,907.50: £1,703.75: £822.25) Stalls: Low GOING minus 0.37 sec per fur (F)

				SP	RR	SF
2710*	**Pasternak (91)** (SirMarkPrescott) **4-9-1** GDuffield(17) (lw: prom: hdwy over 2f out: led ins fnl f: rdn & r.o)	—	1	4/1^{1}	106+	79
4102^{3}	**Rudimental (84)** (SirMarkPrescott) **3-8-4** JLowe(9) (hdwy ½-wy: chsng wnr ins fnl f: r.o wl)	¾	2	20/1	98	67
4147^{13}	**Hunters of Brora (IRE) (88)** (JDBethell) **7-8-12** RHills(1) (hdwy 3f out: styd on wl fnl f: nrst fin)	1	3	14/1^{3}	100	73
4441*	**Gulf Shaadi (77)** (EJAlston) **5-8-1** 5x JFEgan(25) (mid div: hdwy over 1f out: r.o wl towards fin)	½	4	16/1	88	61
4281^{2}	**Sandmoor Chambray (97)** (TDEasterby) **6-9-7** 5x JCarroll(5) (a chsng ldrs: rdn 3f out: kpt on wl)	nk	5	14/1^{3}	108	81
4314^{3}	**Secret Spring (FR) (80)** (PRHedger) **5-8-1**(3) DSweeney(10) (lw: hdwy over 2f out: styd on strly fnl f: nrst fin)	½	6	40/1	90	63
4276^{7}	**Angel Chimes (74)** (JEBanks) **4-7-7v^{1}**(5) RMullen(24) (led after 2f & sn clr: wknd & hdd ins fnl f)	¾	7	66/1	82	55
	Zankle (USA) (86) (DKWeld,Ireland) **4-8-10b** DO'Donohoe(29) (lw: a chsng ldrs: effrt 3f out: ev ch appr fnl f: no ex)	1	8	25/1	93	66
4242^{5}	**Gift Token (82)** (MajorDNChappell) **3-8-2v** NCarlisle(14) (bhd: hdwy 2f out: r.o wl towards fin)	½	9	33/1	88	57
4386*	**Bubble Wings (FR) (72)** (SPCWoods) **5-7-10** MartinDwyer(3) (bhd: hdwy ½-wy: sn rdn & nvr able to chal)	nk	10	25/1	77	50
4294^{7}	**Palatial Style (76)** (PJMakin) **10-8-0** DBiggs(15) (styd on fnl 3f: nrst fin)	s.h	11	66/1	81	54
4314^{2}	**Silk St John (80)** (MJRyan) **3-8-0** GBardwell(33) (hdwy ½-wy: sn chsng ldrs & rdn: btn over 1f out)	½	12	20/1	84	53
4147*	**Epic Stand (83)** (MrsJRRamsden) **3-8-3** 5x FLynch(26) (lw: prom: effrt 3f out: wknd appr fnl f)	nk	13	16/1	87	56
4141^{2}	**King of Tunes (FR) (83)** (MJHaynes) **5-8-4**(3) PRoberts(8) (lw: sme hdwy 2f out: nvr able to chal)	½	14	28/1	86	59
3615^{8}	**Hurtleberry (IRE) (75)** (LordHuntingdon) **4-7-8**(5) AimeeCook(30) (nvr nr to chal)	½	15	50/1	77	50

4141^{15}	**Mihriz (IRE) (72)** (RAkehurst) **5-7-3**(7) PFitzsimons(27) (chsd ldrs tl wknd wl over 1f out)	1½	**16**	33/1	71	44
2729^{3}	**The Dilettanti (USA) (94)** (JARToller) **4-9-4** WJO'Connor(7) (bit bkwd: chsd ldrs tl wknd fnl 2½f)	hd	**17**	33/1	93	66
4148^{3}	**Al Azhar (90)** (IABalding) **3-8-10** KDarley(31) (lw: nvr bttr than mid div)	1	**18**	14/1^{3}	87	56
4141^{5}	**Barba Papa (IRE) (97)** (LMCumani) **3-9-3** KFallon(2) (bhd: effrt ½-wy: n.d)	1	**19**	14/1^{3}	92	61
4294^{14}	**Ball Gown (91)** (DTThom) **7-9-1** DRMcCabe(12) (nvr trbld ldrs)	1	**20**	40/1	85	58
3622^{4}	**Southerly Wind (87)** (MrsJRRamsden) **3-8-7** JFortune(20) (lw: effrt ½-wy: sn in tch & rdn: wknd 2f out)	¾	**21**	16/1	79	48
4423^{4}	**Russian Music (105)** (MissGayKelleway) **4-9-8**(7) 5x JWilkinson(4) (lw: outpcd ½-wy: n.d after)	hd	**22**	28/1	97	70
4423^{11}	**Philistar (76)** (KRBurke) **4-8-0** LCharnock(16) (lw: bhd: rdn ½-wy: n.d)	¾	**23**	25/1	67	40
3150^{17}	**Generous Libra (94)** (DRLoder) **3-9-0** RCochrane(23) (chsd ldrs tl outpcd fnl 2 ½f)	¾	**24**	50/1	83	52
4223^{4}	**Secret Aly (CAN) (79)** (CEBrittain) **7-8-0**(3) RFfrench(13) (nvr trbld ldrs)	½	**25**	25/1	68	41
4441^{14}	**Pride of Pendle (76)** (MartynWane) **8-7-11**(3) PFessey(28) (in tch tl wknd over 2f out)	nk	**26**	50/1	64	37
4297*	**Prince of Denial (88)** (DWPArbuthnot) **3-8-8** 5x TQuinn(19) (b: n.d)	2½	**27**	12/1^{2}	72	41
4238^{4}	**Sunbeam Dance (USA) (92)** (SbinSuroor) **3-8-12** DHolland(21) (led 2f: chsd ldrs tl wknd over 2f out)	d.h	**27**	25/1	80	49
4294^{8}	**Game Ploy (POL) (96)** (DHaydnJones) **5-9-6** PaulEddery(18) (bhd fr ½-wy)	1¾	**29**	33/1	76	49
4148^{10}	**Stanton Harcourt (USA) (97)** (JLDunlop) **3-9-3** GCarter(32) (chsd ldrs 6f: wknd)	1	**30**	25/1	76	45
4283^{7}	**Sue's Return (77)** (APJarvis) **5-8-1** DWright(11) (n.d)	nk	**31**	40/1	55	28
3773^{4}	**Another Time (93)** (SPCWoods) **5-9-3** JReid(36) (bhd fr ½-wy)	s.h	**32**	20/1	71	44
4297^{10}	**Sharp Shuffle (IRE) (81)** (RHannon) **4-8-5** DaneO'Neill(6) (b: n.d)	nk	**33**	50/1	59	32
4141^{13}	**Miracle Kid (USA) (86)** (JHMGosden) **3-8-6** GHind(34) (in tch tl wknd over 3f out)	3½	**34**	25/1	57	26
4308^{7}	**Sharp Temper (84)** (BWHills) **3-8-4**ow1 MHills(35) (n.d)	nk	**35**	40/1	55	23
3901^{9}	**Van Gurp (84)** (BAMcMahon) **4-8-8** AMackay(22) (spd 6f: wknd qckly)	18	**36**	66/1	23	—

(SP 154.0%) **36 Rn**

1m 49.43 (-1.07) CSF £78.03 CT £1,032.39 TOTE £5.80: £2.60 £7.00 £4.70 £3.80 (£77.00) Trio £934.30 OWNER Mr Graham Rock (NEWMARKET) BRED Hesmonds Stud Ltd

LONG HANDICAP Gulf Shaadi 7-4 Bubble Wings (FR) 7-5 Mihriz (IRE) 7-8

WEIGHT FOR AGE 3yo-4lb

2710* Pasternak again had connections squealing about the ground, but once again he turned up and, with incredible support, did the business in style. He is obviously improving no end and looks likely to take on better company in due course. (4/1)

4102 Rudimental, asked for an effort from halfway, stuck to his task in game style but always found his stable-companion too strong. He, like the winner, is well suited by further. (20/1)

4147 Hunters of Brora (IRE) again ran her socks off in this event and was eating up the ground late on. She is not easy to win with these days and her come from behind tactics make things even harder, but she is particularly well and, as she showed here, still had bags of ability. (14/1)

4441* Gulf Shaadi, despite being injured when winning at Ascot last week, ran another cracking race here and finished in grand style. (16/1)

4281 Sandmoor Chambray has a poor action but plenty of guts and, although off the bit someway out, he kept plugging on. (14/1)

4314 Secret Spring (FR) was again flying in the closing stages to show that he is in tremendous form. (40/1)

3801 Angel Chimes had a visor on for the first time and that really woke her up as she had a big lead from halfway but, not surprisingly over this trip, she failed to last it out. (66/1)

Zankle (USA), a good-actioned sort, ran a super race, but this trip probably just proved beyond him. (25/1)

4242 Gift Token is obviously in tremendous heart and finished like the proverbial train here, but always too late, and would seem to need further. (33/1)

4294 Palatial Style, despite his years, showed signs of coming back to form. (66/1)

4559 PORTLAND PLACE PROPERTIES JOCKEY CLUB CUP STKS (Gp 3) (3-Y.O+) (Class A)

4-10 (4-13) **2m** **(Rowley)** £19,710.00 (£7,290.00: £3,495.00: £1,425.00: £562.50: £217.50) Stalls: High GOING minus 0.37 sec per fur (F)

				SP	RR	SF
4241^{2}	**Grey Shot (107)** (IABalding) **5-9-5** TQuinn(1) (lw: mde all: r.o strly fnl 4f)	—	**1**	10/1	126	93
4130a^{2}	**Double Eclipse (IRE) (116)** (MJohnston) **5-9-3** JReid(4) (a chsng wnr: effrt 4f out: styd on wl: nvr able to chal)	2	**2**	11/4^{2}	122	89
4118^{3}	**Further Flight (110)** (BWHills) **11-9-0** MHills(7) (b.hind: hld up & bhd: hdwy 5f out: rdn over 2f out: no imp)	7	**3**	4/1^{3}	112	79
4241*	**Jiyush (108)** (EALDunlop) **4-9-0** RHills(2) (swtg: trckd ldrs: hdwy ½-wy: outpcd 4f out: no imp after)	1¼	**4**	5/2^{1}	111	78
4412*	**The Faraway Tree (104)** (GWragg) **3-8-2**ow2 PaulEddery(3) (chsd ldrs: drvn along 4f out: wknd fnl 2f)	4	**5**	11/2	106	60
4376*	**Georgia Venture (86)** (SPCWoods) **3-8-0** RFfrench(5) (lw: in tch tl rdn & wknd 4f out)	8	**6**	12/1	96	52
4118^{5}	**Old Rouvel (USA) (95)** (DJGMurraySmith) **6-9-0** KDarley(6) (outpcd & lost tch fnl 4f)	2	**7**	50/1	97	64

(SP 109.4%) **7 Rn**

3m 19.51 (3.61 under best) (-3.79) CSF £31.32 TOTE £12.40: £4.10 £2.10 (£17.40) OWNER Mr J. C. Smith (KINGSCLERE) BRED Littleton Stud

WEIGHT FOR AGE 3yo-11lb

4241 Grey Shot was right back to his very best here. Really enjoying this, he stepped on the gas fully four furlongs out and won in tremendous style, breaking the course record. (10/1)

4130a Double Eclipse (IRE) was having his final race here and certainly ran his heart out but, try as both he and his rider did, they were never good enough. (11/4: 2/1-3/1)

4118 Further Flight, trying for his sixth win in this event, did his best but this ground was always too fast for his liking and he failed to get in a real blow. (4/1: 3/1-9/2)

4241* Jiyush is good on his day but needs things to go just right and, with a tremendous pace on here, he was struggling someway out and was never doing enough. (5/2)

4412* The Faraway Tree, trying her longest trip to date, was found out in this strongly-run event. (11/2)

4376* Georgia Venture was up against class stayers here and his limitations were well exposed in the last half-mile. (12/1)

4118 Old Rouvel (USA) was always finding this too much of a struggle for his liking. (50/1)

4560 NGK SPARK PLUGS PERFORMANCE NURSERY H'CAP (2-Y.O) (Class C)

4-45 (4-49) **6f** **(Rowley)** £5,796.00 (£1,728.00: £824.00: £372.00) Stalls: Low GOING minus 0.37 sec per fur (F)

				SP	RR	SF
4296^{3}	**Monte Lemos (IRE) (89)** (RCharlton) **2-9-1** JReid(4) (lw: cl up: led 2f out: r.o wl fnl f)	—	**1**	6/1	91	67
4247*	**Raise A King (95)** (JWPayne) **2-9-7** GCarter(2) (lw: in tch: effrt over 2f out: styd on u.p: nt pce of wnr)	1¼	**2**	6/4^{1}	94	70
4006^{5}	**Blakeset (86)** (RHannon) **2-8-12** TQuinn(1) (in tch: pushed along & hdwy over 2f out: styd on fnl f: nt pce to chal)	½	**3**	10/1	83	59
3926*	**Hakeem (IRE) (85)** (RWArmstrong) **2-8-11** RHills(5) (lw: chsd ldrs: ev ch 2f out: rdn & r.o one pce)	1¾	**4**	4/1^{2}	78	54
4296^{10}	**Exbourne's Wish (USA) (84)** (BWHills) **2-8-10** MHills(3) (led 4f: sn rdn & btn)	3	**5**	11/1	69	45

				SP	RR	SF
4305*	**Risque Lady (94)** (PWHarris) **2-9-6** KFallon(7) (wnt rt s: bhd: effrt over 2f out: no imp)	nk	**6**	9/2[3]	78	54
4411[11]	**Princess Natalie (82)** (MWEasterby) **2-8-8** TLucas(6) (spd 4f: sn wknd)	1½	**7**	33/1	62	38

(SP 112.8%) **7 Rn**

1m 11.85 (0.05) CSF £13.70 TOTE £6.90: £2.80 £1.80 (£8.30) OWNER Mr S M De Zoete (BECKHAMPTON) BRED Rathasker Stud

4296 Monte Lemos (IRE) seemed happier on this fast ground, was always travelling best and won really well. (6/1: 4/1-13/2)

4247* Raise A King is a determined sort who keeps responding to pressure, but the winner was always too good. He looks likely to appreciate another furlong. (6/4)

4006 Blakeset kept staying on here and looks the type to improve when tried over further. (10/1)

3926* Hakeem (IRE) had his limitations exposed here but this did look a useful event. (4/1)

3899 Exbourne's Wish (USA) likes things to go all his own way and this was always too competitive for his liking. (11/1: 8/1-12/1)

4305* Risque Lady, who has given problems previously, had to be led to the start here and, after swerving leaving the stalls, could never really make her presence felt. If she would settle down, she certainly has plenty of ability. (9/2: 11/4-5/1)

4561 LINKS H'CAP (0-90) (3-Y.O+) (Class C)

5-20 (5-25) **7f (Rowley)** £7,668.00 (£2,304.00: £1,112.00: £516.00) Stalls: Low GOING minus 0.37 sec per fur (F)

				SP	RR	SF
4270[4]	**Royal Result (USA) (65)** (MWEasterby) **4-8-5** TLucas(2) (unruly in stalls: trckd ldrs stands' side: led over 2f out: r.o wl u.p)	—	**1**	7/1[3]	78	55
4441[7]	**Broughtons Turmoil (71)** (BRMillman) **8-8-11** KFallon(17) (hld up: hdwy to ld centre 2f out: kpt on fnl f)	2½	**2**	13/2[2]	78	55
4276[5]	**Primo Lara (83)** (PWHarris) **5-9-9** JReid(1) (lw: led stands' side tl hdd over 2f out: kpt on)	½	**3**	14/1	89	66
4270[6]	**Rymer's Rascal (65)** (EJAlston) **5-8-5** JFEgan(21) (in tch centre: hdwy u.p over 2f out: styd on)	nk	**4**	16/1	71	48
3476[2]	**Stackattack (IRE) (72)** (MrsJRRamsden) **4-8-12** FLynch(8) (lw: a chsng ldrs stands' side: hdwy over 1f out: no ex ins fnl f)	s.h	**5**	8/1	77	54
4280[18]	**Mr Teigh (73)** (MrsJRRamsden) **5-8-13** JFortune(7) (lw: chsd ldrs stands' side: kpt on u.p fnl f)	nk	**6**	10/1	78	55
4276[2]	**Marjaana (IRE) (77)** (PTWalwyn) **4-9-3** JCarroll(18) (chsd ldrs centre: effrt over 2f out: nt qckn)	¾	**7**	14/1	80	57
4175[4]	**Zelda Zonk (73)** (BJMeehan) **5-8-13** KDarley(16) (lw: a chsng ldrs centre: one pce appr fnl f)	1¼	**8**	20/1	73	50
4121[19]	**Mullitover (80)** (MJHeaton-Ellis) **7-9-6** RCochrane(23) (lw: effrt centre 3f out: styd on: nvr able to chal)	2½	**9**	33/1	74	51
4270[8]	**Myttons Mistake (66)** (ABailey) **4-8-3**(3)ow2 PRoberts(11) (chsd ldrs centre: no imp fnl 2 ½f)	s.h	**10**	16/1	60	35
2775[10]	**Zaretski (78)** (CEBrittain) **3-9-2** GHind(19) (bit bkwd: led centre 5f: grad wknd)	hd	**11**	33/1	72	47
4283[17]	**Tertium (IRE) (79)** (MartynWane) **5-9-5** JBramhill(3) (racd stands' side: effrt 3f out: nvr trbld ldrs)	nk	**12**	25/1	72	49
4228[4]	**Sandicliffe (USA) (59)** (JARToller) **4-7-10**(3)ow1 MHenry(15) (effrt centre ½-wy: n.d)	5	**13**	6/1[1]	41	17
4219[2]	**Taffs Well (72)** (RAkehurst) **4-8-12** TQuinn(13) (spd centre 5f)	½	**14**	8/1	53	30
4270[2]	**Weetman's Weigh (IRE) (78)** (RHollinshead) **4-9-1**(3) DGriffiths(9) (chsd ldrs stands' side 5f: wknd)	d.h	**14**	12/1	60	37
4225[13]	**Night Dance (73)** (KAMorgan) **5-8-10**(3) RFfrench(24) (lw: s.s: n.d)	hd	**16**	20/1	54	31
4155[10]	**Jeffrey Anotherred (84)** (KMcAuliffe) **3-9-8** MHills(22) (hdwy centre 3f out: sn btn)	nk	**17**	16/1	64	39
4121[18]	**Raaha (82)** (RWArmstrong) **3-9-6** RHills(5) (racd stands' side: a bhd)	5	**18**	16/1	50	25
	Cossack Count (85) (SDow) **4-9-11** WJO'Connor(20) (bkwd: effrt centre 3f out: sn wknd)	1½	**19**	50/1	50	27
4225[4]	**Gain Line (USA) (56)** (BobJones) **4-7-10v[1]** LCharnock(6) (unruly in stalls: cl up stands' side tl wknd qckly 3f out)	½	**20**	25/1	20	—
4301[13]	**Watch The Fire (64)** (JEBanks) **4-8-4** DBiggs(4) (in tch stands' side over 4f)	2½	**21**	33/1	22	—
3420[7]	**Rise Up Singing (56)** (WJMusson) **9-7-10b** DeclanO'Shea(10) (bit bkwd: gd spd centre 5f)	½	**22**	50/1	13	—
3128[7]	**Undercover Agent (IRE) (83)** (JLDunlop) **3-9-7** GCarter(14) (chsd ldrs centre 4 ½f: wknd)	1¼	**23**	25/1	37	12
2598[17]	**Saseedo (USA) (82)** (WAO'Gorman) **7-9-8** EmmaO'Gorman(12) (bkwd: s.s & swtchd stands' side: a bhd)	6	**24**	25/1	22	—

(SP 153.6%) **24 Rn**

1m 24.85 (0.35) CSF £50.55 CT £627.81 TOTE £15.20: £3.50 £2.30 £4.10 £4.80 (£59.30) Trio £433.80 OWNER Burke's 5th Family Settlement (SHERIFF HUTTON) BRED Dr. J. Fred Miller III

LONG HANDICAP Rise Up Singing 6-3 Gain Line (USA) 7-8

WEIGHT FOR AGE 3yo-2lb

4270 Royal Result (USA) got upset in the stalls but was obviously not affected by this and, always travelling well, had the edge from someway out. (7/1)

4297 Broughtons Turmoil is obviously in good heart and ought to pick up a race before long. (13/2)

4276 Primo Lara loves fast ground and likes to be out in front, and showed here he is in really fine form. (14/1)

4270 Rymer's Rascal, like many from this yard, is in super form and kept responding to pressure in game style. (16/1)

3476 Stackattack (IRE), despite a lengthy lay-off, looked and ran well, but just failed to pick up late on. (8/1)

4121 Mr Teigh was always well enough placed and kept plugging on under pressure, but was just short of the necessary turn of foot. (10/1)

4276 Marjaana (IRE) had her chances but her rise in the weights seems to have anchored her. (14/1)

4175 Zelda Zonk is running well just now. (20/1)

1770 Zaretski, having his first run for almost three months, obviously needed it and blew up late on. (33/1)

T/Jkpt: Not won; £45,832.24 to Leicester 5/10/97. T/Plpt: £36.60 (1,885.25 Tckts). T/Qdpt: £10.20 (319.82 Tckts) AA

4453-NOTTINGHAM (L-H) (Good to firm, Good patches)

Saturday October 4th

WEATHER: overcast WIND: mod half against

4562 FUN FAIR H'CAP (0-70) (3-Y.O+) (Class E)

2-15 (2-16) **1m 6f 15y** £4,016.00 (£1,208.00: £584.00: £272.00) Stalls: Low GOING minus 0.32 sec per fur (GF)

				SP	RR	SF
4313[6]	**Children's Choice (IRE) (50)** (WJMusson) **6-8-10** SWhitworth(3) (sn bhd & pushed along: hdwy & nt clr run 3f out: swtchd outside: led ins fnl f: jst hld on)	—	**1**	12/1	63	45
	Jawah (IRE) (65) (KMahdi) **3-8-11**(5) CLowther(7) (mid div: hdwy & n.m.r 3f out: hrd rdn & styd on fnl f: jst failed)	hd	**2**	16/1	78	51
4222*	**Veronica Franco (52)** (PRHedger) **4-8-12** AMcGlone(6) (hld up: hdwy 10f out: sn trckng ldrs: led 2f out tl ins fnl f: sn wknd)	3½	**3**	8/1[3]	61	43
4104[4]	**Taufan Boy (61)** (PWHarris) **4-9-7** MRimmer(17) (lw: chsd ldrs: drvn along over 5f out: led 3f out: sn hdd: one pce)	1	**4**	7/1[2]	69	51
3141[5]	**Salska (64)** (AStreeter) **6-9-3**(7) JFowle(10) (hld up & bhd: hdwy over 3f out: kpt on: nvr able to chal)	2½	**5**	20/1	69	51

Form	Horse / details	Dist	Pos	SP	RR	SF
4045^{3}	**Meilleur (IRE) (60)** (LadyHerries) **3-8-11** WRyan(5) (mid div: hdwy 3f out: n.m.r: kpt on same pce: nvr nr to chal)	2½	**6**	8/1^{3}	62	35
	Shift Again (IRE) (60) (OSherwood) **5-9-6b** SophieMitchell(4) (dwlt: drvn along ½-wy: sn chsng ldrs: wknd 2f out)	6	**7**	25/1	55	37
2035^{10}	**Mystic Quest (IRE) (67)** (KMcAuliffe) **3-9-4** MTebbutt(14) (bhd: kpt on fnl 3f: nvr nr ldrs)	1¼	**8**	16/1	61	34
4363^{6}	**New Inn (45)** (SGollings) **6-8-5** TWilliams(13) (mde most to 3f out: wknd over 1f out)	½	**9**	16/1	38	20
1565^{5}	**Mountaineer (IRE) (67)** (MBell) **3-8-13**$^{(5)}$ GFaulkner(18) (chsd ldrs: drvn along over 5f out: wknd & eased over 1f out)	1	**10**	16/1	59	32
4438^{2}	**Alpine Panther (IRE) (58)** (MrsMReveley) **4-9-4** ACulhane(16) (trckd ldrs: rdn over 3f out: wknd over 2f out)	2½	**11**	7/1^{2}	47	29
4222^{5}	**Casual Water (IRE) (60)** (AGNewcombe) **6-9-6** SDrowne(11) (mid div: pushed along 7f out: lost pl over 4f out)	½	**12**	5/2^{1}	49	31
4275^{4}	**The Roundsills (55)** (RFJohnsonHoughton) **3-8-6** JStack(12) (sn bhd & drvn along: n.d)	2	**13**	16/1	41	14
4222^{9}	**Copper Shell (65)** (APJones) **3-8-13**$^{(3)}$ PPMurphy(15) (chsd ldrs: drvn along 5f out: lost pl over 2f out)	1	**14**	25/1	50	23
4313^{3}	**Ela-Yie-Mou (IRE) (56)** (SDow) **4-8-9**$^{(7)}$ PDoe(1) (lw: chsd ldrs: disp ld 10f out tl lost pl over 3f out)	½	**15**	8/1^{3}	41	23
4172^{17}	**Rival Bid (USA) (52)** (MrsNMacauley) **9-8-12** SWebster(9) (sn bhd)	s.h	**16**	50/1	37	19
4304^{3}	**Mr Speculator (50)** (JEBanks) **4-8-10v** JQuinn(2) (lw: chsd ldrs tl lost pl over 2f out: eased)	13	**17**	20/1	20	2
4222^{7}	**Lime Street Blues (IRE) (55)** (TKeddy) **6-9-1** NDay(8) (mid div: sn drvn along: t.o fnl 4f)	dist	**18**	25/1	—	—
				(SP 147.0%)	**18 Rn**	

3m 2.8 (4.30) CSF £191.05 CT £1,540.81 TOTE £18.10: £3.60 £5.40 £2.40 £2.50 (£103.00) Trio £403.60; £289.97 to Longchamp 5/10/97
OWNER Mrs A. V. Totman (NEWMARKET) BRED M. J. Cassidy
WEIGHT FOR AGE 3yo-9lb
OFFICIAL EXPLANATION **Children's Choice (IRE): regarding the apparent improvement in form, the mare preferred today's left-handed track and slower pace.**

3579 Children's Choice (IRE) put two poor efforts behind her. Suited by the fast ground and a left-handed track, she had to overcome difficulties in running. (12/1)

Jawah (IRE), an ex-Irish gelding whose only previous win came on easy ground, stuck grimly to his task and in the end just failed to get there. (16/1)

4222* Veronica Franco, from a 3lb higher mark, weakened when collared inside the last. (8/1)

4104 Taufan Boy, who looked in good shape beforehand, has slipped right down the weights. (7/1)

3141 Salska was having her first outing for sixty-five days and will be better for it. (20/1)

4045 Meilleur (IRE) did not have the best of luck in running but it was his lack of pace that got him into trouble. (8/1)

4222 Casual Water (IRE), closely matched with the third on Sandown running, was gambled on but he ran very poorly, struggling to keep up soon after halfway and dropping right out going into the final turn. (5/2: op 5/1)

4563 ROLLER COASTER MAIDEN STKS (3-Y.O) (Class D)

2-45 (2-45) **6f 15y** £4,175.00 (£1,250.00: £600.00: £275.00) Stalls: High GOING minus 0.01 sec per fur (G)

Form	Horse / details	Dist	Pos	SP	RR	SF
4214^{3}	**Dark Mile (USA) (69)** (JHMGosden) **3-8-9** AMcGlone(2) (mde all: styd on fnl f: drvn out)	—	**1**	9/4^{1}	83	43
4214^{4}	**Nobalino (70)** (MrsNMacauley) **3-9-0** SDrowne(6) (sn trckng ldrs: kpt on same pce appr fnl f)	4	**2**	10/1	78	38
4047^{2}	**Tithcar (66)** (BHanbury) **3-8-4**$^{(5)}$ CLowther(10) (sn chsng ldrs: rdn over 2f out: kpt on same pce)	1	**3**	9/2^{3}	70	30
4316^{2}	**Silver Kristal (75)** (RAkehurst) **3-8-9** WRyan(8) (w ldrs tl wknd over 1f out)	2½	**4**	7/2^{2}	63	23
4316^{3}	**Mozambique (IRE)** (MrsJCecil) **3-9-0** JStack(4) (lw: sn chsng ldrs: drvn along ½-wy: hung lft: outpcd appr fnl f)	s.h	**5**	9/2^{3}	68	28
	Barrow Creek (GWragg) **3-9-0** AClark(5) (neat: scope: s.i.s: sme hdwy ½-wy: nvr nr ldrs)	½	**6**	14/1	67	27
4316^{12}	**Hamleys** (DMorris) **3-8-9** NDay(7) (lw: prom early: outpcd & hrd rdn ½-wy: edgd lft & hdwy over 1f out: n.d)	2½	**7**	50/1	55	15
	Democrat (SirMarkPrescott) **3-9-0** CNutter(9) (cmpt: bit bkwd: dwlt: a outpcd & bhd)	nk	**8**	20/1	59	19
3698^{4}	**Melbourne Princess (37)** (RMWhitaker) **3-8-9** DeanMcKeown(3) (hld up: effrt ½-wy: wknd over 1f out)	s.h	**9**	50/1	54	14
3202^{5}	**Beaucatcher (IRE) (52)** (MJHeaton-Ellis) **3-8-9** RPerham(1) (chsd ldrs tl wknd over 1f out)	2	**10**	50/1	49	9
				(SP 115.8%)	**10 Rn**	

1m 15.0 (3.50) CSF £23.08 TOTE £2.40: £1.10 £4.30 £2.10 (£10.10) Trio £11.90 OWNER Sheikh Mohammed (NEWMARKET) BRED Darley Stud Management Co Ltd

4214 Dark Mile (USA) had everything her own way this time. It was disconcerting the way she put her head in the air when driven clear in the final furlong. (9/4: 3/1-7/4)

4214 Nobalino had finished closer to the winner at Beverley last time. (10/1)

4047 Tithcar is finding it very hard to get her head in front. (9/2)

4316 Silver Kristal is probably better suited by seven. (7/2)

4316 Mozambique (IRE), whose action going to post left something to be desired, ran her Kempton form with the fourth to almost the pound. (9/2: 5/2-5/1)

Barrow Creek was making a belated debut. Green going to post, he showed some ability after a sluggish start. (14/1: 12/1-20/1)

4564 LEVY BOARD DODGEMS MAIDEN STKS (2-Y.O) (Class D)

3-15 (3-16) **6f 15y** £4,550.50 (£1,369.00: £662.00: £308.50) Stalls: High GOING minus 0.01 sec per fur (G)

Form	Horse / details	Dist	Pos	SP	RR	SF
4146^{2}	**Sky Rocket** (MRStoute) **2-9-0** WRyan(17) (mde all: comf)	—	**1**	1/7^{1}	75++	36
	Bedevilled (MJHeaton-Ellis) **2-9-0** SDrowne(13) (neat: a chsng wnr: kpt on wl fnl f)	¾	**2**	50/1	73+	34
4332^{9}	**Only In Dreams** (BJMeehan) **2-8-9** MTebbutt(11) (in tch: nt clr run over 2f out: hdwy over 1f out: styd on same pce towards fin)	1	**3**	33/1	65	26
4167^{10}	**Persiano** (JRFanshawe) **2-9-0** NDay(15) (a chsng ldrs: nt qckn fnl 2f)	1	**4**	14/1	68	29
	Gem (PJMakin) **2-8-9** AClark(16) (neat: unf: sn trckd ldrs: kpt on wl fnl f)	2½	**5**	40/1	56	17
4428^{6}	**Great Melody (IRE)** (JMPEustace) **2-9-0** JTate(10) (w ldrs: rdn over 2f out: one pce)	½	**6**	33/1	60	21
	Il Destino (PJMakin) **2-9-0** JQuinn(7) (cmpt: scope: chsd ldrs: wandered over 2f out: kpt on fnl f)	½	**7**	50/1	59	20
2336^{9}	**Prince Batshoof** (MBell) **2-9-0** ACulhane(3) (s.s: sme hdwy over 1f out: nvr nr ldrs)	hd	**8**	33/1	58	19
	Dog Watch (JHMGosden) **2-9-0** AMcGlone(12) (cmpt: scope: s.i.s: stdy hdwy over 2f out: nvr nr ldrs)	½	**9**	12/1^{3}	57	18
4216^{12}	**Algebra** (RHannon) **2-9-0** RPerham(5) (chsd ldrs: rdn over 2f out: hung lft: sn outpcd)	s.h	**10**	50/1	57	18
3458^{2}	**Ray of Sunshine (IRE)** (MrsJRRamsden) **2-9-0** OPears(1) (b.nr fore: chsd ldrs: hung lft over 2f out: sn lost pl)	½	**11**	11/1^{2}	56	17
	Priddy Green (HCandy) **2-8-9** CRutter(9) (neat: b.hind: s.i.s: a in rr)	¾	**12**	33/1	49	10
	The Woodcock (BWHills) **2-8-11**$^{(3)}$ JDSmith(8) (leggy: sn outpcd)	2	**13**	25/1	48	9
	Crofters Edge (APJarvis) **2-8-9**$^{(5)}$ CLowther(14) (neat: scope: sn drvn along & outpcd: a bhd)	1¾	**14**	50/1	44	5

4145[10] **Seven** (BSmart) **2-9-0** JStack(2) (chsd ldrs: sn drvn along: lost pl over 2f out) 1½ **15** 50/1 40 1
3619[8] **Have A Break** (CREgerton) **2-9-0** SWhitworth(6) (hld up: hung bdly lft over 2f out: n.d) ....s.h **16** 40/1 40 1
Girlie Set (IRE) (SirMarkPrescott) **2-8-9** CNutter(4) (leggy: bit bkwd: s.i.s: a bhd) ....nk **17** 20/1 34 —
(SP 145.2%) **17 Rn**

1m 15.9 (4.40) CSF £34.20 TOTE £1.10: £1.10 £7.50 £4.80 (£18.40) Trio £229.60; £164.96 to Longchamp 5/10/97 OWNER Mr Saeed Suhail (NEWMARKET) BRED Fittocks Stud

4146 Sky Rocket was found an easy opening and took this with the minimum of fuss. No doubt he will step up again in class. (1/7: op 2/9)
Bedevilled certainly took the eye in the paddock and ran a highly creditable first race. (50/1)
Only In Dreams ran much better than on her debut, and the way she finished after meeting trouble she will be suited by a step up to seven. (33/1)
3986 Persiano ran a pleasing race and significantly this was his third outing, qualifying him for a nursery mark. He is worth keeping an eye on. (14/1: op 25/1)
Gem, a narrow type, showed definite ability on her debut. (40/1)
4428 Great Melody (IRE), having his third outing and his second in a week, still looked to be carrying plenty of condition. (33/1)
Dog Watch, a small gelding, showed ability after a sluggish break and was by no means knocked about. (12/1: op 6/1)
3458 Ray of Sunshine (IRE), having his first outing for fifty-four days, was heavily bandaged on his near-fore. Showing a desperate action going down, on the way back all the wanted to do was hang left. (11/1: 8/1-12/1)

4565 AUTUMN H'CAP (0-80) (3-Y.O) (Class D)

3-50 (3-50) **6f 15y** £5,995.00 (£1,810.00: £880.00: £415.00) Stalls: High GOING minus 0.01 sec per fur (G)

SP RR SF

4214[2] **At Large (IRE) (74)** (JRFanshawe) **3-9-1** NDay(9) (lw: trckd ldrs: led over 1f out: sn rdn: hld on towards fin) .— **1** 5/1[3] 83 62
4321* **Distinctive Dream (IRE) (80)** (KTIvory) **3-9-2b**(5) CLowther(11) (s.i.s: hdwy & nt clr run ½-wy: str run over 1f out: r.o fnl f) ....nk **2** 4/1[2] 88 67
4452* **Levelled (73)** (MRChannon) **3-8-11**(3) PPMurphy(14) (hld up: nt clr run ½-wy: swtchd lft over 1f out: styd on wl towards fin) ....1¼ **3** 3/1[1] 78 57
4456[10] **Mouche (67)** (MrsJRRamsden) **3-8-8** DeanMcKeown(6) (hld up: effrt & n.m.r ½-wy: swtchd lft: styd on fnl f) .hd **4** 9/1 72 51
3418[8] **Roffey Spinney (IRE) (70)** (RHannon) **3-8-11** RPerham(8) (w ldrs: nt qckn appr fnl f) ....½ **5** 25/1 73 52
4365[6] **Swino (72)** (PDEvans) **3-8-13** ACulhane(4) (w ldrs: nt qckn appr fnl f) ....½ **6** 16/1 74 53
4527[14] **Caution (73)** (SGollings) **3-9-0** TWilliams(1) (prom: effrt over 2f out: kpt on same pce) ....½ **7** 7/1 74 53
3936[11] **Rum Lad (68)** (JJQuinn) **3-8-9** SDrowne(13) (prom: nt clr run ½-wy: kpt on same pce) ....½ **8** 16/1 67 46
3716[10] **Sylvan Dancer (IRE) (56)** (CFWall) **3-7-11** DaleGibson(7) (swtg: plld hrd: effrt & nt clr run over 1f out: nvr nr ldrs) 2 **9** 16/1 50 29
4441[17] **Zugudi (74)** (KMahdi) **3-9-1** MRimmer(5) (lw: sn outpcd & drvn along: n.d) ....½ **10** 20/1 67 46
4404[10] **Suite Factors (55)** (KRBurke) **3-7-10** JQuinn(3) (sn prom: effrt 2f out: sn wknd) 2 **11** 12/1 43 22
4321[15] **Loving And Giving (71)** (HCandy) **3-8-12b[1]** CRutter(2) (chsd ldrs: wkng whn hmpd over 1f out) 1¼ **12** 11/1 55 34
3326[9] **Chili Concerto (77)** (PJMakin) **3-9-4b[1]** WRyan(10) (swtg: led tl hdd & wknd over 1f out) 1¼ **13** 14/1 58 37
2835[14] **Frederick James (68)** (MJHeaton-Ellis) **3-8-9** AClark(12) (sn bhd) ....¾ **14** 20/1 47 26
(SP 137.9%) **14 Rn**

1m 14.1 (2.60) CSF £26.03 CT £70.45 TOTE £8.80: £2.90 £2.20 £2.40 (£13.00) Trio £6.20 OWNER Mr S. Hanson (NEWMARKET) BRED Barronstown Stud, John Horgan and Roncon Ltd

IN-FOCUS: **This was a very rough contest indeed and only the winner, amongst the first four home, had anything like a clear run.**
4214 At Large (IRE) gained an overdue first success but he had luck on his side and in the end it was a close call. (5/1)
4321* Distinctive Dream (IRE), from a 7lb higher mark, again missed the break. Meeting all the trouble going in what was a particularly rough race, in the end he was only just denied. He has a real will to win and deserves to find another opening. (4/1)
4452* Levelled, bidding for a quick follow up, was drawn fourteen of fourteen but saw no daylight at all and eventually had to switch to the middle to find any daylight. Hard ridden, he finished with a real purpose and must be accounted a shade unlucky. (3/1: tchd 9/2)
4168* Mouche was another one who had trouble finding room to make her run. (9/1)
459 Roffey Spinney (IRE), on his toes beforehand, was having his first outing for fifty-six days. This was easily his best effort on turf so far this year. (25/1)
4527 Caution, who has been kept busy, looked very hard-trained. (7/1)
3936 Rum Lad, another who did not have the best of runs, shaped as if on the verge of regaining his winning summer form. (16/1)

4566 MERRY-GO-ROUND NURSERY H'CAP (0-75) (2-Y.O) (Class E)

4-25 (4-27) **5f 13y** £3,470.00 (£1,040.00: £500.00: £230.00) Stalls: High GOING minus 0.01 sec per fur (G)

SP RR SF

4230* **Kettlesing (IRE) (67)** (MWEasterby) **2-9-0b**(3) GParkin(4) (sn drvn along: hdwy ½-wy: styd on u.p to ld nr fin) ....— **1** 8/1[3] 74 41
4178[4] **Rita's Rock Ape (65)** (RBrotherton) **2-9-1** SDrowne(6) (led tl hdd nr fin) 1 **2** 12/1 69 36
3926[8] **I Cried For You (IRE) (64)** (RHannon) **2-9-0** RPerham(1) (a chsng ldrs: styd on same pce fnl f) ....¾ **3** 20/1 66 33
3471[14] **Bala (65)** (HMorrison) **2-9-1** WRyan(13) (dwlt: hdwy 2f out: kpt on: nvr rchd ldrs) 3 **4** 11/1 57 24
3869[8] **Wishbone Alley (IRE) (64)** (MDods) **2-9-0** ACulhane(10) (chsd ldrs: rdn 2f out: one pce) ....s.h **5** 25/1 56 23
3433[5] **Kantone (IRE) (52)** (JMPEustace) **2-8-2b[1]** JTate(14) (s.i.s: bhd tl styd on appr fnl f) ....nk **6** 20/1 43 10
4327[13] **Mariana (58)** (RMWhitaker) **2-8-8v[1]** JStack(12) (s.i.s: hdwy ½-wy: nvr nr to chal) 1¼ **7** 14/1 45 12
4159* **Take A Risk (67)** (MJohnston) **2-9-3** DeanMcKeown(15) (lw: hld up: effrt & n.m.r 2f out: hung lft: nvr nr to chal) ....¾ **8** 100/30[1] 52 19
3556[3] **High Gain (71)** (PHowling) **2-9-7** CRutter(16) (in tch: rdn ½-wy: nvr nr to chal) ....nk **9** 9/2[2] 55 22
2147[7] **Wild Lilly (59)** (MJRyan) **2-8-9** AClark(11) (chsd ldrs tl lost pl ½-wy) 1½ **10** 16/1 38 5
3965[7] **Kathies Pet (60)** (RJHodges) **2-8-10** JQuinn(9) (chsd ldrs: rdn ½-wy: sn lost pl) ....hd **11** 9/1 39 6
4332[5] **Night Auction (IRE) (70)** (BPalling) **2-9-3**(3) RHavlin(3) (sn outpcd) ....1¾ **12** 8/1[3] 43 10
3471[9] **Mercury Falling (63)** (DWPArbuthnot) **2-8-13** SWhitworth(7) (b: b.hind: sn outpcd) ....2 **13** 16/1 30 —
4166[20] **Allasella (IRE) (65)** (BPalling) **2-9-1** NDay(2) (chsd ldrs tl wknd 2f out) ....1¾ **14** 25/1 26 —
(SP 125.2%) **14 Rn**

62.4 secs (3.50) CSF £90.01 CT £1,093.37 TOTE £10.10: £3.70 £2.80 £6.60 (£35.30) Trio £617.80; £182.74 to Longchamp 5/10/97 OWNER Mr I. Bray (SHERIFF HUTTON) BRED Liam Phelan

4230* Kettlesing (IRE), much improved by blinkers, was most capably handled to get up near the line. (8/1: op 5/1)
4178 Rita's Rock Ape, who has speed to burn, was only just worn down. (12/1: 16/1-10/1)
I Cried For You (IRE), a very keen type, appreciated the drop back in distance. (20/1)
2959 Bala stuck on after a slow break. She has a pronounced knee action and will appreciate six furlongs and easier ground. (11/1)
3260 Wishbone Alley (IRE), who looked badly handicapped, ran easily his best race so far. (25/1)

3084 Kantone (IRE), blinkered for the first time, showed his first signs of ability. (20/1)
4159* Take A Risk is clearly not an easy ride and all she wanted to do here was hang. (100/30)
3556 High Gain, in trouble at halfway, was reported afterwards to have finished in a distressed state. (9/2)
3324 Kathies Pet (9/1: op 20/1)

4567 E.B.F. HELTER SKELTER MAIDEN STKS (2-Y.O F) (Class D)

4-55 (5-00) **1m 54y** £4,597.50 (£1,380.00: £665.00: £307.50) Stalls: Low GOING minus 0.32 sec per fur (GF)

				SP	RR	SF
4119[4]	**Virtuous** (MRStoute) **2-8-11** WRyan(12) (trckd ldrs: shkn up to ld over 1f out: drvn clr ins fnl f)	—	**1**	1/2[1]	75+	29
4236[4]	**Relate (68)** (MartynMeade) **2-8-8**(3) RHavlin(7) (trckd ldrs: led 2f out: sn hdd: wknd towards fin)	3½	**2**	25/1	68	22
3920[4]	**Mareeba** (MJohnston) **2-8-11** DeanMcKeown(3) (chsd ldrs: drvn along over 2f out: styd on same pce)	¾	**3**	20/1	67	21
	Tajawuz (SbinSuroor) **2-8-11** AMcGlone(14) (cmpt: lw: sn led: hdd 2f out: kpt on same pce)	½	**4**	6/1[2]	66	20
2312[4]	**Migrate (USA)** (JHMGosden) **2-8-11** AGarth(9) (lw: unruly s: s.i.s: hdwy over 4f out: sn chsng ldrs: wknd over 1f out)	4	**5**	15/2[3]	58	12
4185[4]	**Ratiyya (IRE) (77)** (BHanbury) **2-8-11** JStack(1) (lw: led early: chsd ldr: rdn over 2f out: wknd over 1f out)	2½	**6**	25/1	53	7
4330[14]	**Kierans Bridge (IRE)** (APJarvis) **2-8-6**(5) CLowther(11) (lw: sn outpcd & pushed along: sme hdwy over 2f out: n.d)	1	**7**	50/1	51	5
	Absentee (WJarvis) **2-8-11** MTebbutt(4) (leggy: bit bkwd: unruly s: sn trckng ldrs: drvn along over 2f out: sn wknd)	½	**8**	11/1	50	4
	Rabea (USA) (JLDunlop) **2-8-11** MRimmer(13) (cmpt: sn outpcd: sme hdwy over 2f out: n.d)	½	**9**	20/1	49	3
4298[13]	**La Galleria** (JSMoore) **2-8-8**(3) PPMurphy(6) (sn bhd)	1¾	**10**	50/1	46	—
4330[11]	**On Call** (SirMarkPrescott) **2-8-11** CNutter(5) (s.s: a bhd)	10	**11**	16/1	27	—
4332[17]	**Perfect Lady** (JMPEustace) **2-8-11** JTate(8) (sn bhd & drvn along)	3	**12**	50/1	21	—
3717[7]	**Freckles** (MJRyan) **2-8-11b** AClark(10) (mid div: rdn over 3f out: sn lost pl)	4	**13**	66/1	13	—
				(SP 131.5%)	**13 Rn**	

1m 45.4 (4.10) CSF £25.17 TOTE £1.40: £1.10 £5.50 £4.60 (£29.90) Trio £64.30 OWNER Cheveley Park Stud (NEWMARKET) BRED Cheveley Park Stud Ltd

4119 Virtuous became slightly warm during the five-minute delay at the start. Found an easy option, in the end she took this modest event in decisive fashion. (1/2: op 1/3)
4236 Relate, stepping up to a mile, made the best of her way home but was firmly put in her place by the winner. Her stride was shortening markedly towards the line and seven might suit her better. (25/1)
3920 Mareeba seems to be improving with each outing. (20/1)
Tajawuz, who showed plenty of knee action going down, should come on for the outing. (6/1)
2312 Migrate (USA) gave real problems down at the start, rearing over backwards at one stage. (15/2: op 12/1)
Absentee (11/1: 8/1-12/1)

4568 CAROUSEL LIMITED STKS (0-65) (3-Y.O+) (Class F)

5-25 (5-27) **1m 1f 213y** £3,062.40 (£851.40: £409.20) Stalls: Low GOING minus 0.32 sec per fur (GF)

				SP	RR	SF
4172[14]	**Onefortheditch (USA) (60)** (JRFanshawe) **4-8-13** NVarley(1) (sn trckng ldrs: rdn to ld over 1f out: hld on towards fin)	—	**1**	13/2	67	11
4409[5]	**Passing Strangers (USA) (63)** (PWHarris) **4-9-5** AClark(10) (hdwy 4f out: led over 2f out tl over 1f out: rallied towards fin)	nk	**2**	6/1[3]	73	17
4176[12]	**Junikay (IRE) (62)** (RIngram) **3-8-11** AMcGlone(2) (in tch: outpcd 3f out: styd on wl fnl f)	1¾	**3**	14/1	67	6
3263[8]	**Hill Farm Blues (63)** (WMBrisbourne) **4-9-5** AGarth(8) (s.i.s: hdwy to chse ldrs 7f out: kpt on wl fnl 2f)	s.h	**4**	11/1	70	14
4323[2]	**Arletty (57)** (HRACecil) **3-8-8b**[1] WRyan(6) (in tch: hdwy over 3f out: edgd rt & lft: styd on fnl f)	1	**5**	5/1[1]	62	1
4172[8]	**Secret Ballot (IRE) (62)** (KMahdi) **3-9-0** MRimmer(14) (w ldrs: drvn along over 4f out: n.m.r over 2f out: kpt on fnl f)	2	**6**	6/1[3]	65	4
	Zaaleff (USA) (45) (KMahdi) **5-9-2** JTate(4) (mde most tl over 2f out: grad wknd)	3½	**7**	50/1	56	—
1826[14]	**Aficionado (IRE) (64)** (RJHodges) **3-8-11** JQuinn(3) (sn bhd: sme hdwy 3f out: nvr nr to chal)	¾	**8**	14/1	55	—
4335[3]	**Augustan (60)** (SGollings) **6-9-8** TWilliams(7) (lw: drvn along over 4f out: sme hdwy over 2f out: n.d)	1¾	**9**	10/1	58	2
4264*	**Falls O'Moness (IRE) (62)** (KRBurke) **3-8-6**(5) CLowther(5) (lw: trckd ldrs: effrt 3f out: sn wknd)	3	**10**	7/1	47	—
	Yaverland (IRE) (54) (JohnBerry) **5-9-2** MTebbutt(9) (sn bhd)	3	**11**	50/1	43	—
2884[3]	**Smart Spirit (IRE) (65)** (MrsMReveley) **3-8-8** ACulhane(12) (hld up: hdwy on outside over 3f out: sn rdn & wknd)	2	**12**	11/2[2]	36	—
4304[10]	**Polonaise Prince (USA) (45)** (VSoane) **4-9-2** CRutter(15) (w ldrs: ev ch tl wknd over 2f out)	1	**13**	50/1	38	—
4505[3]	**Ortelius (65)** (RHannon) **3-8-11** RPerham(11) (chsd ldrs tl wknd 3f out)	nk	**14**	8/1	37	—
				(SP 134.2%)	**14 Rn**	

2m 10.1 (7.60) CSF £46.06 TOTE £6.50: £2.20 £2.50 £2.60 (£36.80) Trio £200.10 OWNER Onefortheditch Partnership (NEWMARKET) BRED Linda L. Ramsey

WEIGHT FOR AGE 3yo-5lb

140* Onefortheditch (USA) has done well to come back after suffering a serious injury at Beverley in May. Showing a fluent action going down, at one stage she looked likely to win decisively but in the end she had to dig deep. (13/2)
4409 Passing Strangers (USA) rallied gamely and might have got back up with a little further to go. He will be suited by a little further. (6/1)
Junikay (IRE), a winner over six furlongs in Ireland, ran easily his best race in this country. (14/1)
2533* Hill Farm Blues, tailed off last time, as usual lost ground at the start and in the circumstances did well to finish so close. She looks on the way back. (11/1)
4323 Arletty, tried in blinkers, would not keep on a straight course under pressure. (5/1)
4264* Falls O'Moness (IRE) sweated up beforehand and proved much too keen both on the way to post and in the race itself. (7/1)

T/Plpt: £59.60 (339.13 Tckts). T/Qdpt: £21.60 (40.46 Tckts) WG

4479-WOLVERHAMPTON (L-H) (Standard)
Saturday October 4th
WEATHER: overcast WIND: almost nil

4569 PINK ICE MEDIAN AUCTION MAIDEN STKS (2-Y.O) (Class F)
7-00 (7-10) **6f (Fibresand)** £2,070.00 (£570.00: £270.00) Stalls: Low GOING: 0.20 sec per fur (SLW)

Form	Horse	Dist	Pos	SP	RR	SF
4103^{15}	**Arbenig (IRE) (65)** (BPalling) **2-8-6**(3) DSweeney(9) (mde all: edgd rt ins fnl f: drvn out)	—	1	8/1	77	40
4332^{10}	**Silken Dalliance** (LordHuntingdon) **2-8-9** DaneO'Neill(10) (hdwy 2f out: swtchd lft over 1f out: r.o wl ins fnl f)	hd	2	10/1	77	40
3783^{13}	**Third Cousin (IRE)** (MJHeaton-Ellis) **2-9-0** SDrowne(4) (a.p: ev ch ins fnl f: r.o)	nk	3	20/1	81	44
3892^{4}	**Bound To Please (75)** (PJMakin) **2-9-0** DHolland(6) (lw: a.p: r.o one pce fnl 2f)	1¼	4	$5/1^{2}$	78	41
4381^{11}	**Happy Wanderer** (PCHaslam) **2-9-0** DaleGibson(2) (s.i.s: hdwy over 1f out: nt rch ldrs)	2	5	50/1	72	35
4402^{8}	**Critical Air** (SirMarkPrescott) **2-9-0** GDuffield(3) (lw: nvr nr to chal)	nk	6	12/1	72	35
4061^{18}	**Press Ahead (54)** (BAMcMahon) **2-9-0** LNewton(13) (lw: prom tl wknd over 1f out)	1¾	7	50/1	67	30
4067^{4}	**Soft Touch (IRE) (81)** (MissGayKelleway) **2-8-9** DO'Donohoe(8) (s.i.s: nvr nr ldrs)	3	8	$5/4^{1}$	54	17
	Best of Our Days (CWThornton) **2-9-0** DeanMcKeown(12) (lw: bhd fnl 2f)	5	9	25/1	46	9
3985^{14}	**Mrs Pickles** (MDIUsher) **2-8-9** JMarshall(7) (a bhd)	2½	10	50/1	34	—
	Mamble's Pension (IRE) (ABailey) **2-8-9** DWright(11) (lt-f: unf: a bhd)	2	11	25/1	29	—
4361^{3}	**Rewardia (IRE) (70)** (PDEvans) **2-8-9** SWhitworth(1) (a bhd)	1½	12	$11/2^{3}$	25	—
4401^{3}	**Lady Almitra** (CJHill) **2-8-4**(5) RMullen(5) (a bhd)	1½	13	20/1	21	—

(SP 127.5%) **13 Rn**

1m 16.2 (5.00) CSF £76.58 TOTE £12.40: £2.50 £2.40 £6.60 (£62.80) Trio Not won; £113.34 to 6/10/97 OWNER Mr A Smallwood & Mr Alan Evans (COWBRIDGE) BRED John Mitchell and Dr John Waldron

3783 Arbenig (IRE) held on well, despite coming off a true line on this first try on the sand. (8/1)
Silken Dalliance had shown nothing in a much hotter race at Nottingham on her debut. (10/1: 7/1-11/1)
Third Cousin (IRE), a half-brother to Regal Reprimand, had been slowly away when twelve lengths behind the winner on his Windsor debut. (20/1)
3892 Bound To Please was stepping up to six for this first outing on an artificial surface. (5/1: 4/1-6/1)
4381 Happy Wanderer, a half-brother to a bumper winner, shaped as if he needed further. (50/1)
Critical Air, a half-brother to Dominant Air, is out of a five-furlong juvenile winner. (12/1)
4067 Soft Touch (IRE) had the best form credentials but it can be a totally different game on the sand. (5/4)

4570 AMETHYST CLAIMING STKS (3-Y.O+) (Class F)
7-30 (7-37) **7f (Fibresand)** £1,932.00 (£532.00: £252.00) Stalls: High GOING: 0.20 sec per fur (SLW)

Form	Horse	Dist	Pos	SP	RR	SF
4482^{5}	**Pericles (81)** (MJohnston) **3-9-6** DHolland(5) (chsd ldr: led over 4f out: clr whn edgd rt over 1f out: r.o wl)	—	1	$2/1^{1}$	91	61
4114^{10}	**Rock Island Line (IRE) (65)** (JBerry) **3-8-3**(5) CLowther(4) (s.i.s: sn prom: r.o ins fnl f: no ch w wnr)	8	2	16/1	61	31
3987^{19}	**Oberon's Dart (IRE) (65)** (PJMakin) **4-9-1**(3) RHavlin(6) (swtg: a.p: chsd wnr over 2f out: no imp)	s.h	3	$9/1^{3}$	69	41
4219^{10}	**Effervescence (87)** (RHannon) **3-9-6** DaneO'Neill(10) (lw: hdwy 3f out: r.o one pce fnl 2f)	nk	4	$7/1^{2}$	72	42
4071^{18}	**Just Loui (82)** (KRBurke) **3-9-1**(5) RMullen(7) (dwlt: gd hdwy over 3f out: wknd over 1f out)	6	5	14/1	58	28
3469^{4}	**Greatest (75)** (MissGayKelleway) **6-9-4b** GDuffield(2) (lw: led over 2f out: wknd over 2f out)	2½	6	$7/1^{2}$	49	21
4155^{25}	**Tea Party (USA) (66)** (KOCunningham-Brown) **4-9-3b** SDrowne(8) (bhd fnl 2f)	1¾	7	$7/1^{2}$	44	16
4051^{4}	**Bold Aristocrat (IRE) (64)** (RHollinshead) **6-8-10** ACulhane(9) (bhd fnl 3f)	¾	8	10/1	35	7
4059^{20}	**Countless Times (75)** (WRMuir) **3-8-1**(5) JoHunnam(11) (a bhd)	2½	9	16/1	27	—
3276^{16}	**Move With Edes (69)** (WGMTurner) **5-8-9**(3) DSweeney(12) (a bhd)	½	10	25/1	30	2
3561^{5}	**Crystal Heights (FR) (70)** (RJO'Sullivan) **9-8-8**ow2 SWhitworth(1) (b: dwlt: a bhd)	1½	11	12/1	23	—
4051^{13}	**My Godson (36)** (MDods) **7-8-7b**(3) CTeague(3) (a bhd: t.o fnl 3f)	26	12	33/1	—	—

(SP 122.8%) **12 Rn**

1m 29.7 (5.00) CSF £36.71 TOTE £3.50: £1.50 £3.30 £2.90 (£42.20) Trio £101.00; £129.48 to 6/10/97 OWNER Mr David Abell (MIDDLEHAM) BRED Elsdon Farms
WEIGHT FOR AGE 3yo-2lb
Pericles clmd Miss Gay Kelleway £12,000

4482 Pericles, dropped into a claimer, made no mistake back over the extra furlong. (2/1)
2517 Rock Island Line (IRE), on his sand debut, just got up to win the separate battle for second prize. (16/1)
3581* Oberon's Dart (IRE) was unable to go with the winner. (9/1)
2392 Effervescence failed to sparkle in the home straight. (7/1)
3189 Just Loui (14/1: op 8/1)
3561 Crystal Heights (FR) (12/1: op 8/1)

4571 CARL LLEWELLYN MEMORIAL H'CAP (0-70) (3-Y.O+) (Class E)
8-00 (8-04) **1m 1f 79y (Fibresand)** £3,101.00 (£861.00: £413.00) Stalls: Low GOING: 0.20 sec per fur (SLW)

Form	Horse	Dist	Pos	SP	RR	SF
4235^{17}	**Perpetual Light (55)** (JJQuinn) **4-8-13** SDrowne(4) (lw: a.p: rdn over 2f out: led ins fnl f: r.o wl)	—	1	20/1	69	43
*4485**	**Farmost (78)** (SirMarkPrescott) **4-10-8** 6x GDuffield(13) (lw: sn prom: led over 4f out: rdn over 2f out: hdd ins fnl f)	2½	2	$4/6^{1}$	88	62
4297^{18}	**Zermatt (IRE) (58)** (MDIUsher) **7-9-2** NAdams(2) (lw: rdn & hdwy over 3f out: one pce fnl f)	2	3	$14/1^{3}$	64	38
3937^{2}	**Legal Issue (IRE) (52)** (WWHaigh) **5-8-10** ACulhane(9) (lw: hld up & bhd: hdwy over 4f out: ev ch 2f out: one pce)	¾	4	$3/1^{2}$	57	31
4485^{7}	**Heighth of Fame (65)** (JHetherton) **6-9-9** MTebbutt(8) (bhd tl hdwy over 2f out: r.o one pce fnl f)	3	5	20/1	65	39
3585^{4}	**Bonne Ville (58)** (BPalling) **3-8-9**(3) RHavlin(5) (hdwy over 2f out: nt rch ldrs)	3	6	20/1	53	23
3762^{R}	**Grovefair Lad (IRE) (60)** (SRBowring) **3-8-11**(3) CTeague(3) (reluctant to r: wl bhd tl hdwy over 2f out: n.d)	5	7	50/1	46	16
2342^{8}	**Newbridge Boy (57)** (MGMeagher) **4-9-1** JFEgan(7) (led: hdd over 4f out: wknd over 2f out)	3	8	50/1	38	12
4161^{14}	**Thaleros (53)** (JSWainwright) **7-8-11** DeanMcKeown(10) (prom tl rdn & wknd 3f out)	1½	9	33/1	32	6
1441^{11}	**Captain's Day (56)** (HJCollingridge) **5-8-9**(5) GFaulkner(12) (lw: a bhd)	2½	10	16/1	30	4
4323^{20}	**Kristal Bridge (62)** (PWHarris) **3-9-2b** WJO'Connor(6) (prom tl wknd over 2f out)	10	11	16/1	19	—
3044^{10}	**Weet And See (65)** (RHollinshead) **3-9-2**(3) DGriffiths(11) (lw: a bhd: t.o)	15	12	40/1	—	—

2492^{14}	**Classic Form (IRE) (55)** (ICampbell) **4-8-13** AMackay(1) (a bhd: t.o)	dist	**13**	25/1	—	—
				(SP 130.9%)	**13 Rn**	

2m 4.2 (8.20) CSF £31.51 CT £228.78 TOTE £24.40: £5.30 £1.40 £2.20 (£24.40) Trio Not won; £142.83 to 6/10/97 OWNER The Four Point Partnership (MALTON) BRED Lord Matthews
WEIGHT FOR AGE 3yo-4lb

244 Perpetual Light bounced back to form off a mark 7lb lower than when successful over a mile at Southwell in June last year. (20/1)
4485* Farmost, only 2lb higher than when scoring over course and distance four days ago, was attempting to complete a hat-trick within a week. (4/6)
3980 Zermatt (IRE) has been very inconsistent on turf this season, but does like some give and was 8lb higher than when scoring at Chepstow in July. (14/1)
3937 Legal Issue (IRE) looked the likely winner until this slightly longer trip seemed to find him out. He looks well handicapped at the moment. (3/1)
2607 Heighth of Fame was again running over an inadequate distance. (20/1)
3585 Bonne Ville, without the blinkers this time, is another who requires a longer trip. (20/1)

4572 DIAMOND H'CAP (0-100) (3-Y.O+) (Class C)
8-30 (8-31) **1m 4f (Fibresand)** £5,494.90 (£1,640.20: £783.60: £355.30) Stalls: Low GOING: 0.20 sec per fur (SLW)

				SP	RR	SF
4108^{18}	**Polar Champ (75)** (SPCWoods) **4-8-12v** GDuffield(12) (a.p: rdn over 2f out: r.o to ld last strides)	—	**1**	7/1	85	55
3867^{3}	**Mister Aspecto (IRE) (75)** (MJohnston) **4-8-12v** DHolland(7) (chsd ldr: led over 4f out: hdd last strides)	s.h	**2**	$4/1^{2}$	85	55
4323^{8}	**Glow Forum (76)** (LMontagueHall) **6-8-10**(3) RFfrench(8) (a.p: rdn over 3f out: one pce fnl f)	2	**3**	5/1	83	53
4404*	**Master Millfield (IRE) (69)** (CJHill) **5-8-1**(5) RMullen(1) (bhd tl hdwy over 1f out: n.d)	9	**4**	$9/2^{3}$	64	34
4406*	**Opera Buff (IRE) (89)** (MissGayKelleway) **6-9-5**(7) JWilkinson(10) (bhd tl hdwy 3f out: one pce fnl 2f)	nk	**5**	$3/1^{1}$	84	54
4210^{7}	**Johnnie the Joker (73)** (JPLeigh) **6-8-7b**(3) CTeague(9) (led over 7f: wknd over 2f out)	5	**6**	16/1	61	31
1493^{3}	**Bonnie Lassie (69)** (CWThornton) **3-7-13** DaleGibson(2) (prom 9f)	3½	**7**	25/1	53	16
3584^{12}	**China Castle (82)** (PCHaslam) **4-8-12**(7) PGoode(3) (a bhd)	2½	**8**	10/1	62	32
4443^{14}	**Arctic Thunder (USA) (89)** (BPalling) **6-9-12** DaneO'Neill(11) (bhd fnl 3f)	11	**9**	20/1	55	25
	Classic Eagle (78) (ICampbell) **4-9-1** AMackay(6) (hld up: rdn & wknd over 4f out)	8	**10**	25/1	33	3
4281^{8}	**Night City (90)** (KRBurke) **6-9-10**(3) DSweeney(4) (bhd fnl 6f)	8	**11**	20/1	34	4
				(SP 124.5%)	**11 Rn**	

2m 41.1 (8.60) CSF £32.22 CT £142.98 TOTE £7.50: £2.50 £1.80 £2.90 (£21.20) Trio £50.90 OWNER Mr P. K. L. Chu (NEWMARKET) BRED High Point Bloodstock Ltd and Victor Sujanani
WEIGHT FOR AGE 3yo-7lb

3380 Polar Champ, successful for the first time over this trip, did take quite a while to wear down the runner-up. (7/1)
3867 Mister Aspecto (IRE), 6lb higher than when winning over two miles at Lingfield in August, ran his heart out but it was not quite enough. (4/1)
4323 Glow Forum, rated 20lb higher than on grass, was only 3lb above the mark off which he scored over course and distance in May. (5/1)
4404* Master Millfield (IRE) was rated no less than 22lb higher on sand than when dead-heating over seven at Folkestone last week. (9/2: 11/4-5/1)
4406* Opera Buff (IRE) was running off the same mark as when successful over course and distance back in January. (3/1)

4573 JACK KIRKLAND MEMORIAL (S) STKS (2-Y.O) (Class G)
9-00 (9-00) **5f (Fibresand)** £1,725.00 (£475.00: £225.00) Stalls: Low GOING: 0.20 sec per fur (SLW)

				SP	RR	SF
4159^{4}	**Rare Indigo (64)** (JBerry) **2-8-1**(5) CLowther(6) (mde all: r.o wl)	—	**1**	$7/2^{2}$	76	38
4065^{10}	**Poetto (70)** (BJMeehan) **2-8-11v¹** MTebbutt(9) (a.p: chsd wnr over 2f out: hung lft over 1f out: no imp)	4	**2**	5/1	68	30
*4054**	**Super Geil (56)** (CADwyer) **2-8-11** DHolland(4) (lw: a.p: bmpd over 1f out: one pce)	3½	**3**	$2/1^{1}$	57	19
4303^{5}	**Rock From The Sun (50)** (WGMTurner) **2-8-8b**(3) DSweeney(5) (lw: hdwy over 1f out: nt rch ldrs)	1¾	**4**	12/1	51	13
3932^{14}	**Russian Romeo (IRE) (56)** (BAMcMahon) **2-8-9b¹**(7) SRighton(8) (sn rdn along: chsd wnr over 2f: carried lft over 1f out: swtchd rt ins fnl f: one pce)	nk	**5**	8/1	55	17
4054^{14}	**I'm Not Sure (52)** (JBerry) **2-8-6** NAdams(2) (hld up: hdwy wl over 1f out: wknd fnl f)	5	**6**	10/1	29	—
4479^{8}	**Abstone Pet Girl** (PDEvans) **2-8-6** JFEgan(7) (a bhd)	½	**7**	20/1	28	—
4402^{10}	**Remember Frimley** (CJHill) **2-8-1**(5) RMullen(3) (a bhd)	4	**8**	20/1	15	—
4483^{2}	**Satis (IRE) (48)** (MRChannon) **2-8-6** ACulhane(1) (lw: chsd ldrs: nt clr run 3f out: sn wknd)	nk	**9**	$9/2^{3}$	14	—
				(SP 127.8%)	**9 Rn**	

63.0 secs (0.60 under 2y best) (4.10) CSF £21.97 TOTE £4.20: £1.60 £2.60 £2.00 (£8.60) Trio £23.00 OWNER Mrs B. C. Ansell (COCKERHAM) BRED Mrs D. R. Schreiber
Bt in 5,600 gns
OFFICIAL EXPLANATION **Satis (IRE): was inconvenienced at being drawn on the inside and resented the kick-back.**

4159 Rare Indigo was able to transfer her speed to this totally different type of surface. (7/2)
3742 Poetto, tried in a visor for this return to the minimum trip, caused some mayhem in behind the winner but was second best on merit. (5/1)
4054* Super Geil should not be considered unlucky. (2/1: op 7/2)
4303 Rock From The Sun found this shorter distance totally inadequate. (12/1)
3692* Russian Romeo (IRE) was certainly not a case of running too freely in the first-time headgear. (8/1)

4574 RUBY H'CAP (0-65) (3-Y.O+) (Class F)
9-30 (9-33) **6f (Fibresand)** £2,070.00 (£570.00: £270.00) Stalls: Low GOING: 0.20 sec per fur (SLW)

				SP	RR	SF
3583^{2}	**Thordis (60)** (PJMakin) **4-9-9v** DHolland(3) (mde all: rdn over 1f out: edgd rt ins fnl f: r.o wl)	—	**1**	$7/2^{1}$	71	53
3749^{5}	**Mike's Double (IRE) (64)** (MissGayKelleway) **3-9-7b**(5) CLowther(6) (hdwy 2f out: r.o ins fnl f)	¾	**2**	$7/1^{2}$	73	54
4301^{4}	**Hannah's Usher (58)** (CMurray) **5-9-7** NicolaHowarth(12) (hld up & plld hrd: hdwy over 3f out: ev ch over 1f out: one pce)	2	**3**	$7/1^{2}$	62	44
4280^{20}	**Gadge (65)** (ABailey) **6-9-11**(3) RFfrench(7) (b: lw: chsd ldrs: rdn & one pce fnl 2f)	3	**4**	$7/2^{1}$	61	43
3984^{4}	**Village Native (FR) (60)** (KOCunningham-Brown) **4-9-6b**(3) PPMurphy(8) (no hdwy fnl 2f)	¾	**5**	$8/1^{3}$	54	36
4169^{17}	**Croeso Cynnes (56)** (BPalling) **4-9-5** DaneO'Neill(13) (lw: prom tl wknd over 1f out)	4	**6**	14/1	39	21
79^{6}	**Hurgill Times (60)** (DShaw) **3-9-8** JFanning(10) (lw: nvr nr ldrs)	6	**7**	33/1	27	8
4164^{10}	**Don't Worry Mike (59)** (JLSpearing) **3-9-7** ACulhane(5) (prom over 3f)	nk	**8**	14/1	25	6
4115^{4}	**Will To Win (58)** (PGMurphy) **3-9-6** SDrowne(4) (b.hind: chsd ldr over 3f: sn wknd)	s.h	**9**	$8/1^{3}$	24	5
4301^{12}	**Leigh Crofter (56)** (PDCundell) **8-9-5** RPerham(11) (sn bhd)	1¾	**10**	20/1	17	—

				SP	RR	SF
4301[10]	**Little Ibnr (56)** (PDCundell) **6-9-5** JLowe(1) (a bhd)	nk	**11**	12/1	17	—
4051[7]	**Figlia (56)** (JLHarris) **3-9-4b** DeanMcKeown(2) (lw: bhd fnl 3f)	s.h	**12**	10/1	17	—
4047[11]	**Bicton Park (56)** (KCComerford) **3-9-4b** WJO'Connor(9) (lw: s.i.s: a bhd)	9	**13**	50/1	—	—
				(SP 131.4%)	**13 Rn**	

1m 16.2 (5.00) CSF £27.78 CT £165.51 TOTE £5.60: £1.90 £2.50 £2.70 (£13.00) Trio £166.00 OWNER Mr Barrie Whitehouse (MARLBOROUGH) BRED B. Whitehouse

WEIGHT FOR AGE 3yo-1lb

3583 Thordis found his front-running tactics paying off over this shorter distance. (7/2: 11/2-3/1)

3749 Mike's Double (IRE) was reverting to six, having won his maiden over course and distance in July. (7/1)

4301 Hannah's Usher put up a good effort, given the way he refused to settle. (7/1)

3273 Gadge, having shown tremendous improvement on grass, has gone up no less than 25lb since winning a mile seller at Lingfield in February, and is now rated another 17lb higher on turf. (7/2)

4649a Village Native (FR) was trying to prove that variety is the spice of life, having finished seventh at Maisons-Laffitte in a handicap over this trip four days earlier. (8/1)

102* Figlia (10/1: 8/1-12/1)

T/Plpt: £713.80 (24.86 Tckts). T/Qdpt: £10.70 (60.12 Tckts) KH

4324-**LEICESTER (R-H) (Good to firm)**
Sunday October 5th
WEATHER: sunny periods WIND: almost nil

4575 PLAYQUEST U.K. MAIDEN STKS (I) (2-Y.O) (Class D)
2-30 (2-30) **7f 9y** £3,225.00 (£975.00: £475.00: £225.00) Stalls: High GOING minus 0.45 sec per fur (F)

				SP	RR	SF
	Benin (USA) (HRACecil) **2-9-0** WRyan(12) (leggy: lt-f: unf: mde all: r.o wl fnl f)	—	**1**	7/4[1]	89+	42
	Rainbow Ways (BWHills) **2-9-0** JCarroll(4) (lt-f: unf: s.i.s: hld up: hdwy & swtchd rt 2f out: r.o wl fnl f)	½	**2**	6/1[3]	88+	41
	Pleasuredancer (USA) (WAO'Gorman) **2-9-0** EmmaO'Gorman(11) (small: lt-f: a chsng ldrs: one pce appr fnl f)	3	**3**	16/1	81	34
	La Tiziana (WJarvis) **2-8-9** MTebbutt(6) (lengthy: unf: bit bkwd: a chsng ldrs: rdn & one pce fnl f)	½	**4**	14/1	75	28
	Act Defiant (USA) (PFICole) **2-9-0** JFortune(5) (leggy: unf: bkwd: trckd ldrs: one pce fnl f)	2	**5**	5/1[2]	75	28
	Saleela (USA) (JLDunlop) **2-8-9** GCarter(3) (lt-f: unf: hld up: hdwy ½-wy: wknd wl over 1f out)	½	**6**	5/1[2]	69	22
	Mitch Passi (IRE) (SirMarkPrescott) **2-9-0** SSanders(8) (w'like: leggy: bkwd: s.i.s: nvr nr to chal)	2	**7**	10/1	70	23
3638[8]	**Coalminersdaughter (IRE)** (JWHills) **2-8-6**(3) MHenry(1) (rdn over 3f out: nvr nr ldrs)	1½	**8**	20/1	61	14
1744[7]	**Carouse** (MRChannon) **2-9-0** DaneO'Neill(9) (bkwd: chsd ldrs 4f)	½	**9**	16/1	65	18
	Master Caster (IRE) (DRLoder) **2-9-0** RCochrane(7) (unf: bkwd: prom tl wknd 2f out)	s.h	**10**	6/1[3]	65	18
2553[9]	**Glamorgan (IRE)** (CADwyer) **2-9-0** DO'Donohoe(10) (bit bkwd: a bhd & outpcd)	3½	**11**	25/1	57	10
2587[10]	**Lookingforlove Del (IRE)** (NACallaghan) **2-8-6**(3) RFfrench(2) (outpcd: t.o)	6	**12**	33/1	38	—
				(SP 137.3%)	**12 Rn**	

1m 24.7 (2.10) CSF £13.43 TOTE £2.50: £1.70 £2.80 £3.80 (£7.00) Trio £167.80 OWNER Baron G Von Ullmann (NEWMARKET) BRED Audley Farm Inc

Benin (USA), very lightly-made for a colt, was the only one anyone wanted to be on. Smartly into his stride to make all, he won with a shade more in hand than the margin might suggest. (7/4)

Rainbow Ways needs to strengthen but he ran a race full of promise on this debut and, if he takes after his dam, he will prove useful. (6/1)

Pleasuredancer (USA), a gelded, not over-big newcomer, made a very pleasing debut and looks sure to improve with this experience behind him. (16/1)

La Tiziana looked ill at ease cantering to post but she did not fare badly, and she could come into her own given time. (14/1)

Act Defiant (USA), a choicely-bred colt who is a late April foal, just needed this pipe-opener, but he would have learnt a lot and it will be surprising if he fails to make the grade. (5/1: op 3/1)

Saleela (USA), a half-sister to Arc winner Urban Sea, looks like a matchstick with the wood shaved off at present and she is also showing signs of getting her winter coat. Very free to post, she was only shaken off below the distance and she does look to need time. (5/1)

Master Caster (IRE) (6/1: op 4/1)

4576 ANDERSEN CONSULTING LEICESTER NURSERY H'CAP (0-75) (2-Y.O) (Class E)
3-00 (3-01) **1m 8y** £3,956.25 (£1,200.00: £587.50: £281.25) Stalls: High GOING minus 0.45 sec per fur (F)

				SP	RR	SF
4065[2]	**Tightrope (70)** (SirMarkPrescott) **2-9-5** SSanders(11) (lw: hld up in tch: hdwy to ld over 1f out: sn clr: comf)	—	**1**	13/8[1]	79+	43
4334[3]	**Narrogin (USA) (72)** (MRChannon) **2-9-7** JCarroll(3) (hld up: hdwy over 2f out: rdn & r.o wl fnl f)	4	**2**	10/1	73	37
4286[9]	**Saxon Victory (USA) (52)** (WJHaggas) **2-8-1** GBardwell(10) (lw: a.p: led over 3f out tl over 1f out: sn outpcd)	1¼	**3**	25/1	51	15
4208[6]	**Thecomebackking (57)** (SCWilliams) **2-8-6** AMcGlone(12) (swtg: a.p: hrd drvn over 1f out: one pce)	nk	**4**	33/1	55	19
4334[2]	**Iron Mountain (IRE) (71)** (NACallaghan) **2-9-3**(3) RFfrench(7) (lw: hld up: hdwy over 1f out: nrst fin)	2	**5**	6/1[2]	65	29
4447[6]	**Lobuche (IRE) (55)** (RHannon) **2-8-4** DaneO'Neill(5) (bhd: hrd rdn 2f out: nvr nr to chal)	¾	**6**	16/1	48	12
4265[14]	**Disco Tex (60)** (MWEasterby) **2-8-2**(7) SFinnamore(13) (a chsng ldrs: rdn wl over 1f out: sn outpcd)	nk	**7**	33/1	52	16
4208[4]	**Bint Nadia (54)** (JDBethell) **2-7-12**(5) CLowther(17) (swtg: prom tl rdn & wknd over 1f out)	nk	**8**	14/1	45	9
4007[12]	**King's Hussar (65)** (PFICole) **2-9-0** ACulhane(4) (lw: hld up: hdwy u.p 2f out: nt pce to chal)	½	**9**	10/1	55	19
4271[4]	**Frolicking (70)** (JLDunlop) **2-9-5** GCarter(14) (mid div: hdwy over 2f out: wknd over 1f out)	nk	**10**	14/1	60	24
4303[2]	**Pink Ticket (51)** (PDEvans) **2-8-0** JFEgan(15) (prom: rdn & wknd 2f out)	nk	**11**	12/1	40	4
4366[5]	**Opportune (GER) (62)** (CASmith) **2-8-11** DeanMcKeown(8) (effrt u.p over 2f out: no imp)	1½	**12**	12/1	48	12
4271[10]	**Daring News (68)** (RHannon) **2-9-3** RPerham(6) (chsd ldrs 5f: sn wknd: t.o)	7	**13**	14/1	40	4
4334[14]	**Fair Game (IRE) (61)** (JLDunlop) **2-8-10b[1]** KDarley(19) (racd far side: chsd ldrs: rdn & wknd 3f out: t.o)	1¼	**14**	33/1	31	—
4285[2]	**Supacalifragilistk (61)** (BWHills) **2-8-10** PaulEddery(1) (trckd ldrs tl rdn & wknd over 2f out: t.o)	1¾	**15**	7/1[3]	27	—
4152[16]	**Lambs Lane (65)** (TDEasterby) **2-9-0** LCharnock(20) (s.s: a bhd: t.o)	3	**16**	20/1	25	—
4334[8]	**Forgotten Star (IRE) (62)** (RFJohnsonHoughton) **2-8-11** TWilliams(2) (in tch stands' side: effrt & ev ch 3f out: sn wknd: t.o)	2½	**17**	16/1	17	—
3818[9]	**Stalwart Legion (IRE) (57)** (JWHills) **2-8-3**(3) MHenry(16) (a in rr: t.o)	6	**18**	20/1	—	—

3802^{15}	**Clermont City (IRE) (64)** (PWChapple-Hyam) **2-8-10b**$^{1(3)}$ RHavlin(18) (plld hrd: led over 4f: sn rdn & wknd: t.o)	14	**19**	16/1	—	—
				(SP 158.3%)		**19 Rn**

1m 37.1 (2.10) CSF £21.46 CT £360.92 TOTE £2.70: £1.20 £3.80 £5.30 £15.40 (£29.00) Trio £498.90; £632.45 to Pontefract 6/10/97 OWNER Mr W. E. Sturt (NEWMARKET) BRED Side Hill Stud and Floors Farming

4065 Tightrope found his true mark on this step up to a mile and won this with the minimum of fuss. With his stable in such good form, he should be able to defy a penalty. (13/8: op 3/1)

4334 Narrogin (USA) definitely needs more cut in the ground and, as at Nottingham, a stiffer test of stamina, but he performed with credit under top weight and his turn is close at hand. (10/1)

Saxon Victory (USA) has been waiting for this longer trip and, in running by far his best race yet, should not take long before he does open his account. (25/1)

4208 Thecomebackking is slowly but surely coming to hand and, over this more suitable trip, gave notice that his turn is near. (33/1)

4334 Iron Mountain (IRE) finished ahead of the runner-up on identical terms on his most recent outing, but he took much longer to warm up on this occasion and the race was over by the time he did get going. (6/1)

4068 Lobuche (IRE) is still struggling to get it together at this level, but he does appear to need all of this trip and must not be written off yet. (16/1)

4577 AC BPM MARITIME LIMITED STKS (0-90) (3-Y.O+) (Class C)

3-45 (3-45) **1m 1f 218y** £6,742.50 (£2,040.00: £995.00: £472.50) Stalls: High GOING minus 0.45 sec per fur (F)

				SP	RR	SF
4102*	**Mithali (87)** (BWHills) **4-9-6** RCochrane(7) (chsd ldr: disp ld 3f out: rdn to ld over 1f out: all out)	—	**1**	15/8^{2}	101	50
3648^{7}	**Zerpour (IRE) (90)** (LMCumani) **3-8-13** KDarley(5) (lw: hld up: hdwy to ld 3f out: hdd over 1f out: rallied u.p cl home)	½	**2**	6/4^{1}	98	42
4306^{3}	**Generous Gift (90)** (EALDunlop) **3-8-13** DO'Donohoe(3) (lw: hld up: hdwy over 3f out: sn ev ch: rdn & one pce fnl 2f)	3	**3**	11/2^{3}	93	37
4306^{5}	**Kuala Lipis (USA) (86)** (PFICole) **4-9-2b** JFortune(2) (led to 3f out: rdn over 3f out: one pce)	2½	**4**	11/2^{3}	87	36
4141^{17}	**Conspicuous (IRE) (88)** (LGCottrell) **7-9-1**$^{(3)}$ ADaly(4) (dwlt: a in rr)	3	**5**	14/1	85	34
1016^{14}	**Lionize (USA) (86)** (MrsJCecil) **4-9-2** JCarroll(6) (bkwd: chsd ldrs: rdn 4f out: sn lost tch: t.o)	29	**6**	25/1	36	—
	Marigliano (USA) (86) (KAMorgan) **4-9-2** OPears(1) (chsd ldng pair over 6f: sn rdn & wknd: t.o)	29	**7**	25/1	—	—
				(SP 119.9%)		**7 Rn**

2m 5.8 (2.10) CSF £4.99 TOTE £2.90: £2.00 £1.40 (£2.20) OWNER Mr Hamdan Al Maktoum (LAMBOURN) BRED Shadwell Estate Company Limited

WEIGHT FOR AGE 3yo-5lb

4102* Mithali showed that he does not have to make the running to win his races and, as he acts on all types of ground, he thoroughly deserved to succeed here. (15/8)

3648 Zerpour (IRE), taking a big step down in distance, did his best to put the emphasis on stamina when kicking on three furlongs out, but the winner had all his moves covered, and proved the strongest in a spirited duel to the finish. (6/4)

4306 Generous Gift, a winner over twelve furlongs, does seem to lack the pace to succeed at this trip for, after having every chance, he was tapped for toe when the principals took one another on. (11/2)

4306 Kuala Lipis (USA) set a very brisk pace, but he had been collared early in the straight and was found wanting when the battle to the line really got underway. (11/2)

3712* Conspicuous (IRE) (14/1: 8/1-16/1)

4578 LUCKY CHOICE H'CAP (0-85) (3-Y.O) (Class D)

4-20 (4-21) **1m 8y** £11,040.00 (£3,345.00: £1,635.00: £780.00) Stalls: High GOING minus 0.45 sec per fur (F)

				SP	RR	SF
4141^{8}	**Attitude (82)** (HCandy) **3-9-4** AMcGlone(3) (chsd ldrs: led 2f out: r.o wl)	—	**1**	20/1	92	58
4142^{4}	**Egoli (USA) (85)** (GWragg) **3-9-7** PaulEddery(2) (lw: hld up: hdwy 2f out: str run fnl f: r.o)	¾	**2**	14/1	94	60
4147^{7}	**High Spirits (IRE) (74)** (TDEasterby) **3-8-10b** LCharnock(9) (trckd ldrs: effrt & rdn wl over 1f out: kpt on wl towards fin)	1	**3**	7/2^{1}	81	47
3980*	**Dulcinea (68)** (IABalding) **3-8-4** MartinDwyer(6) (lw: hld up: hdwy wl over 1f out: kpt on u.p fnl f)	1	**4**	8/1	73	39
4223^{6}	**Can Can Lady (78)** (MJohnston) **3-9-0** DeanMcKeown(10) (led after 1f tl over 2f out: kpt on u.p)	2	**5**	12/1	79	45
3891^{9}	**Bevier (66)** (CEBrittain) **3-7-11**$^{(5)}$ RMullen(8) (b: prom: ev ch 2f out: one pce fnl f)	s.h	**6**	33/1	66	32
4297^{6}	**Mr Paradise (IRE) (70)** (TJNaughton) **3-8-6** DaneO'Neill(1) (nvr nr to chal)	nk	**7**	13/2	70	36
2695^{4}	**Wild Sky (IRE) (76)** (MJHeaton-Ellis) **3-8-12** AClark(11) (swtg: prom: hrd drvn wl over 1f out: sn btn)	3	**8**	14/1	70	36
4436*	**Nominator Lad (71)** (BAMcMahon) **3-8-7** AMackay(12) (lw: mid div: hrd rdn over 2f out: no imp)	nk	**9**	9/1	64	30
2015^{11}	**Premier (75)** (KTIvory) **3-8-11** RCochrane(5) (led 1f: prom tl wknd over 2f out)	nk	**10**	20/1	68	34
4121^{4}	**Cybertechnology (81)** (BWHills) **3-9-3** JCarroll(14) (prom tl rdn & wknd qckly wl over 1f out)	½	**11**	5/1^{2}	73	39
4410^{5}	**Sheer Face (77)** (WRMuir) **3-8-8**$^{(5)}$ CLowther(7) (a in rr)	1¼	**12**	6/1^{3}	66	32
3787^{13}	**Scarlet Crescent (67)** (PTWalwyn) **3-8-3** GHind(4) (a bhd: t.o)	3½	**13**	33/1	49	15
4408^{4}	**Present Chance (65)** (BAMcMahon) **3-8-1** LNewton(13) (lw: trckd ldrs: rdn over 3f out: sn wknd: t.o)	14	**14**	10/1	19	—
				(SP 133.1%)		**14 Rn**

1m 35.5 (0.50) CSF £266.02 CT £1,156.36 TOTE £20.70: £4.90 £3.90 £1.90 (£67.90) Trio £824.90 OWNER Girsonfield Ltd (WANTAGE) BRED Girsonfield Ltd

3243 Attitude, winner of his only previous race at this track twelve months ago, did well to return to form from so high in the handicap. Working his way to through to gain a narrow advantage entering the last quarter-mile, he had to put his best foot forward but always appeared likely to hold on. (20/1)

4142 Egoli (USA), taking on handicappers for the first time, began to pick up inside the last couple of furlongs and, responding willingly to pressure, did not fail for the want of trying. This was a better than average performance from the top of the handicap. (14/1)

4147 High Spirits (IRE) attracted all the support and ran on strongly in the closing stages, but the winner had got away and he always had far too much to do. (7/2)

3980* Dulcinea could have found the ground faster than she requires for she did stay on, but never really threatened to reach the leaders. (8/1)

4223 Can Can Lady, brought back to what is possibly her ideal trip, moved gingerly to post but helped force the pace until finding the task beyond her inside the distance. (12/1)

1688* Bevier pushed the pace on this return to a mile and disputed the lead two furlongs out, but was unable to increase his tempo when the race to the line developed. (33/1)

4121 Cybertechnology should have been the one to beat on recent form, but paddock inspection showed that he is getting his winter coat, and this disappointing run would suggest that he could be over the top. (5/1)

4408 Present Chance (10/1: op 33/1)

4579 LEICESTER MERCURY MAIDEN STKS (3-Y.O) (Class D)

4-50 (4-52) **1m 1f 218y** £3,761.25 (£1,140.00: £557.50: £266.25) Stalls: High GOING minus 0.45 sec per fur (F)

				SP	RR	SF
837^{2}	**Recourse (USA) (86)** (HRACecil) **3-9-0** WRyan(9) (lw: mde all: clr over 2f out: unchal)	—	**1**	4/9^{1}	87	30
2873^{11}	**Waterspout (USA) (78)** (MrsAJPerrett) **3-9-0** AClark(8) (hld up: hdwy on ins over 2f out: kpt on: no ch w wnr)	5	**2**	10/1^{3}	79	22
4378^{6}	**Balfour Lady (43)** (JARToller) **3-8-9** SSanders(10) (in tch: hdwy 3f out: rdn & one pce fnl 2f)	4	**3**	20/1	68	11
1866^{6}	**Flowing Fortune** (EALDunlop) **3-9-0** DO'Donohoe(1) (bit bkwd: s.i.s: sn rcvrd to chse wnr: rdn & btn over 2f out)	2½	**4**	5/1^{2}	69	12
4360^{4}	**Aeolina (FR)** (SEKettlewell) **3-8-9** JFortune(11) (chsd ldrs: hrd drvn 2f out: no imp)	1¾	**5**	10/1^{3}	61	4
	Lawfull Blue (IRE) (CADwyer) **3-8-9** NVarley(6) (bit bkwd: hld up: gd hdwy 4f out: rdn & wknd over 2f out)	3½	**6**	50/1	55	—
4290^{14}	**Damara** (CWFairhurst) **3-8-9** LCharnock(5) (nvr nr to chal)	½	**7**	50/1	54	—
	Cape Siren (MJRyan) **3-8-9** GCarter(4) (neat: drvn along ½-wy: a in rr)	s.h	**8**	20/1	54	—
4322^{6}	**Catchment** (MrsAJPerrett) **3-9-0** GayeHarwood(13) (plld hrd: prom 6f: sn lost tch)	4	**9**	25/1	53	—
4277^{6}	**Eider Hill** (DMorris) **3-8-9** NDay(3) (trckd ldrs over 6f: sn wknd)	¾	**10**	16/1	47	—
1272^{15}	**Blue Island (IRE)** (NPLittmoden) **3-9-0** TGMcLaughlin(12) (bit bkwd: chsd ldrs tl wknd over 3f out)	1	**11**	66/1	50	—
	Shanons Shinanigan (IRE) (MHTompkins) **3-9-0** DBiggs(7) (w'like: b: a bhd: t.o fr ½-wy)	10	**12**	25/1	34	—
	Tawny Artist (BRMillman) **3-8-9** MFenton(14) (small: lengthy: a bhd: t.o)	8	**13**	50/1	16	—
				(SP 134.6%)	**13 Rn**	

2m 7.7 (4.00) CSF £6.25 TOTE £1.50: £1.10 £3.00 £4.20 (£6.60) Trio £38.10 OWNER Mr K. Abdulla (NEWMARKET) BRED Juddmonte Farms

837 Recourse (USA) produced fresh and well for this first outing since the spring, appreciated this return to maiden company and opened his account in the easiest possible fashion. (4/9)

Waterspout (USA), in the same ownership as the winner but from different yards, is being brought along steadily and, though he was never going to be better than second best, this was certainly a step in the right direction. (10/1)

2491 Balfour Lady was fighting a losing battle for the final quarter-mile, but she stuck to the task in hand and she will find an opening one of these days. (20/1)

1866 Flowing Fortune, having only his third run in twelve months, is still as green as grass, and his attempt to hang onto the winner came to an end when he blew up over two furlongs out. (5/1)

3918 Aeolina (FR) has competed over longer trips in both her previous races and, hard at work someway out, could not raise her pace enough to trouble the winner. (10/1: op 16/1)

4580 ANDERSEN DERBY H'CAP (0-70) (3-Y.O+) (Class E)

5-20 (5-24) **5f 218y** £4,005.00 (£1,215.00: £595.00: £285.00) Stalls: High GOING minus 0.45 sec per fur (F)

				SP	RR	SF
4169^{2}	**Magic Lake (40)** (EJAlston) **4-8-0v**(3) MHenry(18) (hdwy 2f out: r.o u.p to ld cl home)	—	**1**	10/1	52	27
4249^{4}	**Southern Dominion (41)** (MissJFCraze) **5-8-4b** TWilliams(11) (lw: led: sn wl clr: hrd rdn & ct last stride)	hd	**2**	11/1	53	28
4248^{11}	**Rockcracker (IRE) (47)** (GGMargarson) **5-8-10b** GBardwell(9) (lw: a chsng ldrs: hrd drvn over 2f out: sustained chal fnl f: jst failed)	s.h	**3**	12/1	59	34
4333*	**Middle East (61)** (TDBarron) **4-9-10b** JCarroll(8) (hrd drvn ½-wy: hdwy 2f out: kpt on u.p towards fin)	2½	**4**	10/1	66	41
4512^{7}	**Jucea (57)** (JLSpearing) **8-9-6** JQuinn(12) (lw: hdwy over 1f out: r.o: nt pce to chal)	hd	**5**	10/1	62	37
4518^{7}	**Flying Harold (47)** (MRChannon) **4-8-7**(3) PPMurphy(10) (hdwy over 1f out: nrst fin)	1	**6**	12/1	49	24
4329^{9}	**Mindrace (57)** (KTIvory) **4-9-1**(5) GFaulkner(20) (hdwy appr fnl f: rdn & kpt on towards fin)	½	**7**	16/1	58	33
4249*	**Be Warned (50)** (JPearce) **6-8-13v** MWigham(17) (dwlt: hdwy appr fnl f: nvr nrr)	1¼	**8**	7/1^{3}	47	22
4404^{8}	**Don Pepe (59)** (RBoss) **6-9-8** KDarley(15) (lw: chsd ldrs: rdn over 1f out: one pce)	nk	**9**	16/1	56	31
4321^{6}	**Bayin (USA) (59)** (MDIUsher) **8-9-8** RStreet(14) (b: dwlt: nvr nr to chal)	¾	**10**	7/2^{1}	54	29
4329^{4}	**Here Comes a Star (45)** (JMCarr) **9-8-8** DWright(6) (in tch 3f)	¾	**11**	14/1	38	13
4518*	**Robellion (47)** (DWPArbuthnot) **6-8-3**(7) JWilkinson(16) (b: outpcd)	s.h	**12**	13/2^{2}	39	14
4333^{11}	**Souperficial (48)** (NTinkler) **6-8-11v** KimTinkler(1) (stumbled s: nt rcvr)	d.h	**13**	25/1	40	15
4169^{19}	**Deerly (44)** (RDickin) **4-8-0**(7) PMundy(2) (outpcd)	½	**13**	20/1	35	10
4112^{7}	**Mr Speaker (IRE) (58)** (CFWall) **4-9-7** SSanders(7) (bhd fnl 2f)	1¼	**15**	14/1	46	21
4385^{7}	**Bataleur (52)** (GWoodward) **4-8-12**(3) PRoberts(19) (lw: outpcd)	¾	**16**	20/1	38	13
4333^{3}	**Superbit (57)** (BAMcMahon) **5-9-6** LNewton(3) (lw: spd 3f)	s.h	**17**	10/1	43	18
4365^{12}	**Princely Sound (59)** (JEBanks) **4-9-8** WRyan(21) (outpcd)	5	**18**	25/1	31	6
4370^{22}	**Wychwood Sandy (40)** (HJCollingridge) **6-8-3**^{ow1} MFenton(4) (a outpcd)	2	**19**	50/1	7	—
3984^{13}	**Sharp Stock (49)** (RJHodges) **4-8-12** AMackay(22) (outpcd: t.o)	6	**20**	25/1	—	—
3038^{12}	**Five-O-Fifty (44)** (JJBirkett) **3-8-6** JLowe(5) (a outpcd: t.o)	¾	**21**	50/1	—	—
				(SP 158.2%)	**21 Rn**	

1m 11.6 (1.60) CSF £123.91 CT £1,316.25 TOTE £10.40: £2.50 £3.30 £5.70 £2.20 (£50.10) Trio £1,021.90; £331.06 to Pontefract 6/10/97
OWNER Peter Ebdon Racing (PRESTON) BRED Cheveley Park Stud Ltd
WEIGHT FOR AGE 3yo-1lb

4169 Magic Lake, finding the race run to suit her, made relentless progress from below the distance and stayed on strongly to get up right on the line. With her stable in such form, she is worth following now that she has got back to winning ways. (10/1)

4249 Southern Dominion soon had his field strung out like a line of washing and he held a three to four-length lead into the final furlong, but his stride shortened and he was most unfortunate to be touched off right on the line. (11/1)

3290 Rockcracker (IRE) was flat top the boards soon after halfway but he kept responding to a forceful ride and, finishing strongly with the winner, only just failed to gain the day. (12/1)

4333* Middle East was never able to land a blow, but he was far from disgraced with his bumper weight and there is still time for him to win another. (10/1)

4385 Jucea has only ever won once beyond five furlongs and, though she was ridden to get the trip, could not muster the pace to mount her challenge. She does win on this type of ground but her action to post would suggest that she would benefit from a drop of rain. (10/1)

4518 Flying Harold performs best when produced late but he has mistimed his efforts more than once, and that looked the case here. (12/1)

4249* Be Warned lost his chance when he missed the break but he did run on strongly to finish eighth and, if he can get the easier ground that he acts on best, then he could be worth waiting for. (7/1)

4321 Bayin (USA) should have been suited by this fast-run race, but he failed to fire at all and the fast ground could have had something to do with it. (7/2: op 6/1)

4581 PLAYQUEST U.K MAIDEN STKS (II) (2-Y.O) (Class D)
5-50 (5-51) **7f 9y** £3,208.75 (£970.00: £472.50: £223.75) Stalls: High GOING minus 0.45 sec per fur (F)

				SP	RR	SF
4174[6]	**Florazi** (JLDunlop) **2-9-0** GCarter(1) (lw: hld up: hdwy 2f out: led ins fnl f: edgd rt cl home)	—	**1**	10/1	75	29
4237[4]	**Misbah (USA)** (BHanbury) **2-9-0** WRyan(6) (lw: b.hind: hld up: hdwy 2f out: slt ld over 1f out: hdd & no ex fnl f)	1¼	**2**	5/4[1]	72	26
	Prospectress (USA) (LordHuntingdon) **2-8-4**(5) AimeeCook(9) (lt-f: unf: trckd ldrs: effrt over 1f out: no ex fnl f)	1¼	**3**	33/1	64	18
4237[16]	**Chrysolite (IRE)** (BWHills) **2-9-0** JCarroll(5) (a.p: rdn & one pce appr fnl f)	3½	**4**	33/1	61	15
3117[8]	**Guilsborough** (DMorris) **2-9-0** NDay(4) (hld up in rr: sme late hdwy: nrst fin)	1¾	**5**	20/1	57	11
4266[3]	**King of The River (USA)** (PWChapple-Hyam) **2-9-0** KDarley(10) (prom: led 3f out tl hdd & wknd over 1f out)	¾	**6**	7/4[2]	56	10
	Dashing Knight (IRE) (DRLoder) **2-9-0** RCochrane(7) (w'like: scope: bit bkwd: bhd: hdwy 3f out: wknd fnl 2f)	4	**7**	8/1[3]	47	1
4458[11]	**Miss Slender** (RHannon) **2-8-9** DaneO'Neill(3) (chsd ldrs: rdn 2f out: sn btn)	s.h	**8**	33/1	42	—
	Norski Lad (SirMarkPrescott) **2-9-0** SSanders(2) (unf: scope: s.s: a bhd)	4	**9**	11/1	37	—
3613[5]	**Campione (IRE)** (MHTompkins) **2-9-0** DBiggs(11) (chsd ldrs: rdn & wknd over 2f out)	3	**10**	40/1	31	—
4167[14]	**Dudley Allen** (TTClement) **2-9-0** JQuinn(8) (led 4f: wknd qckly: t.o)	10	**11**	50/1	8	—

(SP 127.3%) **11 Rn**

1m 25.2 (2.60) CSF £21.69 TOTE £11.30: £2.30 £1.40 £4.40 (£15.00) Trio £156.20 OWNER Mr Peter Winfield (ARUNDEL) BRED Sir Eric Parker

4174 Florazi put his previous experience to good use with a well-timed challenge to worry the favourite out if it inside the last two hundred yards. (10/1)
4237 Misbah (USA) got the gap he needed two furlongs out and struck the front approaching the final furlong but, hard as he tried, the winner had the legs of him in the sprint to the line. (5/4)
Prospectress (USA), an unfurnished filly bred in the States, gave a good account of herself on this racecourse debut and should not be too hard to place. (33/1)
Chrysolite (IRE) ran much better than he did on his racecourse debut last month, and he is learning the ropes. (33/1)
3117 Guilsborough, doing all his best work late on, is bred to need all of a mile, even at this early stage of his career. (20/1)
4266 King of The River (USA) had much more yielding ground to contend with on his debut last month and, though he was able to make his share of the running here, he was a spent force after being collared approaching the final furlong. (7/4: op 3/1)
Dashing Knight (IRE) (8/1: 9/2-9/1)

T/Jkpt: Not won; £56,863.44 to Pontefract 6/10/97. T/Plpt: £55.20 (465.92 Tckts). T/Qdpt: £20.30 (58.13 Tckts) IM

4381-PONTEFRACT (L-H) (Good to firm)
Monday October 6th
WEATHER: overcast & raining WIND: almost nil

4582 E.B.F. CLAXTON BAY MAIDEN STKS (2-Y.O) (Class D)
2-15 (2-17) **1m 2f 6y** £3,915.50 (£1,184.00: £577.00: £273.50) Stalls: Low GOING minus 0.16 sec per fur (GF)

				SP	RR	SF
4064[12]	**Dashing Chief (IRE) (70)** (MAJarvis) **2-9-0** SSanders(9) (dwlt: hdwy 5f out: pushed along over 2f out: nt clr run & swtchd 1½f out: r.o to ld wl ins fnl f)	—	**1**	16/1	87	37
4274[4]	**Glory of Grosvenor (IRE)** (PWChapple-Hyam) **2-9-0** JReid(8) (in tch: hdwy 4f out: rdn to ld ent fnl f: hdd wl ins fnl f: kpt on)	½	**2**	1/3[1]	86	36
4413[3]	**Paradise Soul (USA)** (DRLoder) **2-8-9** KFallon(3) (led: shkn up 3f out: hdd ent fnl f: one pce)	2½	**3**	5/1[2]	77	27
4165[4]	**Smiling Voter (IRE) (79)** (RHannon) **2-9-0** DaneO'Neill(1) (a chsng ldrs: effrt 3f out: nt qckn appr fnl f)	2½	**4**	20/1	78	28
4384[7]	**Konker** (WJHaggas) **2-9-0** FLynch(2) (cl up tl wknd appr fnl f)	11	**5**	16/1	61	11
4245[4]	**Festival Flyer (66)** (RBoss) **2-9-0** NDay(4) (swtg: bhd: sme hdwy over 2f out: nvr able chal)	nk	**6**	50/1	60	10
	Elabellou (IRE) (MJohnston) **2-8-9** JWeaver(6) (leggy: unf: scope: cl up tl wknd 3f out)	5	**7**	14/1[3]	47	—
	Announcing Peace (CADwyer) **2-8-9** DO'Donohoe(5) (w'like: unf: s.i.s: a bhd)	1¼	**8**	50/1	45	—
4470[5]	**Western Lord (46)** (CSmith) **2-9-0b** JFortune(7) (chsd ldrs tl wknd over 3f out)	17	**9**	200/1	23	—

(SP 119.3%) **9 Rn**

2m 15.9 (6.30) CSF £20.59 TOTE £30.80: £4.50 £1.10 £1.30 (£8.50) Trio £10.60 OWNER Lord Harrington (NEWMARKET) BRED Lord Harrington

IN-FOCUS: **This win completed a maiden century for Seb Sanders.**
3861 Dashing Chief (IRE) appreciated this trip, needed every yard of it and is obviously a stayer in the making. (16/1)
4274 Glory of Grosvenor (IRE) is a real stayer and is still learning, but he will always be susceptible to anything with a turn of foot. (1/3)
4413 Paradise Soul (USA) was made a lot more use of this time but was completely tapped for toe in the closing stages. (5/1)
4165 Smiling Voter (IRE) had his chances but he lacked any turn of foot to take them. (20/1)
4384 Konker, having his third run here, is still learning and ran out of fuel in the closing stages. (16/1)
4245 Festival Flyer got himself in a state beforehand and, not surprisingly, ran no sort of race. (50/1)
Elabellou (IRE) (14/1: 8/1-16/1)

4583 MARAVAL H'CAP (0-80) (3-Y.O) (Class D)
2-45 (2-46) **1m 4y** £5,936.00 (£1,778.00: £854.00: £392.00) Stalls: Low GOING minus 0.16 sec per fur (GF)

				SP	RR	SF
3087[4]	**Jay-Owe-Two (IRE) (71)** (RMWhitaker) **3-8-12v1** DeanMcKeown(3) (a chsng ldrs: chal over 1f out: styd on to ld wl ins fnl f)	—	**1**	20/1	83	57
4417[2]	**Barnburgh Boy (72)** (TDEasterby) **3-8-13** KFallon(7) (hld up: hdwy ½-wy: led 1½f out tl wl ins fnl f: no ex)	nk	**2**	11/4[1]	83	57
4176[9]	**Foot Battalion (IRE) (64)** (RHollinshead) **3-8-5** DaneO'Neill(5) (lw: bhd: hdwy over 1f out: fin wl)	5	**3**	14/1	65	39
4308[6]	**Night Chorus (67)** (BSRothwell) **3-8-8** LCharnock(11) (swtg: hmpd bnd after 1½f: hdwy 3f out: chsng ldrs appr fnl f: nt qckn)	1¼	**4**	16/1	66	40
3741[3]	**Dundel (IRE) (77)** (BWHills) **3-9-4** AClark(10) (bhd: styd in wl fnl 2f: nvr able chal)	1	**5**	11/1	74	48
4410[2]	**Jedi Knight (70)** (MWEasterby) **3-8-11** FNorton(15) (in tch: effrt over 2f out: styd on one pce)	1¼	**6**	7/1[2]	64	38
4472[4]	**Denton Lad (59)** (WTKemp) **3-8-0b** TWilliams(1) (lw: chsd ldrs: led over 2f to 1½f out: wknd)	1¼	**7**	12/1	51	25
4436[8]	**Cee-N-K (IRE) (70)** (MJohnston) **3-8-11b1** JWeaver(8) (chsd ldrs tl outpcd fnl 2f)	½	**8**	16/1	61	35

				SP	RR	SF
4385[8]	**Mungo Park (55)** (MrsJRRamsden) **3-7-7**(3) RFfrench(6) (lw: prom tl wknd fnl 2f)	1½	**9**	16/1	43	17
4408*	**Moonshiner (USA) (86)** (GWragg) **3-9-8v**(5) GMilligan(14) (led tl hdd & wknd over 2f out)	2½	**10**	9/1[3]	69	43
4308[8]	**Royale Rose (FR) (70)** (ABailey) **3-8-11** DWright(9) (rn wd bnd after 1½f & hmpd: sn bhd)	½	**11**	14/1	52	26
4175[8]	**Compatibility (IRE) (77)** (JHMGosden) **3-9-4** LDettori(4) (lw: hld up & bhd: nt clr run appr st: bdly hmpd over 1f out & ins fnl f: nt rcvr)	3	**12**	12/1	53	27
4102[6]	**Raivue (80)** (EWeymes) **3-9-7** KDarley(13) (chsd ldrs tl wknd over 2f out: t.o)	20	**13**	10/1	16	—
	Eastern Project (IRE) (76) (MDHammond) **3-9-3** JFortune(2) (lw: chsd ldrs 5f)	hd	**14**	33/1	12	—
				(SP 120.7%)	**14 Rn**	

1m 45.1 (2.70) CSF £67.82 CT £760.93 TOTE £37.70: £8.40 £1.10 £4.30 (£50.40) Trio £357.50 OWNER Mr R. M. Whitaker (LEEDS) BRED Thoroughbred Trust

LONG HANDICAP Mungo Park 7-9

3087 Jay-Owe-Two (IRE), after over two months off and wearing a visor for the first time, was back to something like his old form and stuck to his task in determined style. (20/1)

4417 Barnburgh Boy is proving extremely difficult to win with and it has to be said that this time he managed to snatch defeat from the jaws of victory. (11/4)

3457 Foot Battalion (IRE) was trying to come from behind, met with trouble aplenty and then finished like an express train but his chance had gone. He looks on good terms with himself but is never one to fully rely on. (14/1)

4308 Night Chorus was without the visor this time and ran reasonably but he did not have the best of runs. (16/1)

3741 Dundel (IRE) has had six weeks off but still left the impression that she does not really give it all she can. (11/1)

4410 Jedi Knight needs things to go just right and, in this messy race, they were never going to. (7/1)

4472 Denton Lad is running well and, with a bit more cut in the ground, can do better. (12/1)

3798 Compatibility (IRE) finished a long way behind here but found so much trouble in running, it is quite feasible that he could well have been in the shake-up. (12/1: 8/1-14/1)

4584 PONTEFRACT SERIES FINAL APPRENTICE H'CAP (0-60) (3-Y.O+) (Class F)

3-15 (3-19) **1m 4f 8y** £2,731.50 (£837.00: £416.00: £205.50) Stalls: Low GOING minus 0.16 sec per fur (GF)

				SP	RR	SF
4275[10]	**Siberian Mystic (35)** (PGMurphy) **4-8-3** JFowle(17) (hld up & bhd: hdwy on outside 4f out: led over 2f out: sn rdn clr)	—	**1**	12/1	49	28
4235[2]	**Mr Fortywinks (IRE) (47)** (JLEyre) **3-8-8** PDoe(5) (a cl up: one pce fnl 2f)	3½	**2**	13/2[2]	56	28
4432[10]	**Forzair (46)** (JJO'Neill) **5-9-0** CLowther(9) (lw: in tch: outpcd over 3f out: kpt on wl fnl f)	½	**3**	16/1	55	34
4415*	**Tart (FR) (44)** (DNicholls) **4-8-7**(5) ANicholls(4) (bhd: hdwy 4f out: styd on wl fnl f: nrst fin)	1¼	**4**	9/1[3]	51	30
4335[5]	**Essayeffsee (49)** (MrsMReveley) **8-9-3** PBradley(14) (lw: bhd: effrt 4f out: styd on fnl f: nrst fin)	½	**5**	14/1	55	34
3562[6]	**Admirals Secret (USA) (50)** (CFWall) **8-9-1**(3) DarrenWilliams(15) (swtg: bhd: hdwy 3f out: styd on: nvr able chal)	1¾	**6**	16/1	54	33
4160[3]	**Sushi Bar (IRE) (43)** (MrsMReveley) **6-8-11** RWinston(16) (bhd: effrt 4f out: hung lft & nt qckn appr fnl f)	1¾	**7**	5/1[1]	45	24
4432[2]	**Hasta la Vista (56)** (MWEasterby) **7-9-5b**(5) SFinnamore(3) (in tch: drvn along 5f out: no imp after)	1	**8**	9/1[3]	56	35
3026[6]	**Lookingforarainbow (IRE) (58)** (BobJones) **9-9-5**(7) GemmaJones(18) (bhd: hdwy 4f out: in tch 2f out: one pce after)	½	**9**	16/1	58	37
4429*	**Kingdom Pearl (54)** (MJCamacho) **3-9-1** TSiddall(10) (lw: trckd ldrs: effrt 3f out: wknd wl over 1f out)	1	**10**	10/1	52	24
4335[4]	**Tajar (USA) (41)** (TKeddy) **5-8-6**(3) PClarke(7) (cl up: led 7f out tl over 2f out: wknd)	nk	**11**	10/1	39	18
4453[6]	**Havana Heights (IRE) (36)** (JLEyre) **4-7-13**(5) RBrisland(11) (b.hind: effrt 5f out: n.d)	hd	**12**	20/1	34	13
3315[6]	**Bedazzle (36)** (MBrittain) **6-8-4** DMernagh(8) (bhd: effrt on ins 4f out: n.d)	½	**13**	20/1	33	12
3612[4]	**Brynkir (53)** (DJGMurraySmith) **3-9-0** RStudholme(2) (bhd: sme hdwy 4f out: sn wknd: t.o)	15	**14**	25/1	30	2
3413[9]	**Riscatto (USA) (48)** (WRMuir) **3-8-9** JWilkinson(12) (lost tch fnl 4f: t.o)	16	**15**	20/1	4	—
4453[8]	**Rock The Barney (IRE) (45)** (MDIUsher) **8-8-13b** SCarson(6) (gd hdwy on outside 8f out: sn chsng ldrs: wknd over 2f out: eased: t.o)	2	**16**	20/1	—	—
4432[6]	**My Millie (36)** (WStorey) **4-7-13**(5)ow1 CarolynBales(1) (chsd ldrs tl wknd qckly 4f out: t.o)	7	**17**	14/1	—	—
	Judge Advocate (IRE) (62) (JJO'Neill) **5-9-9**(7) SOlley(13) (bit bkwd: rdn & lost tch 5f out: t.o)	3½	**18**	50/1	1	—
				(SP 131.7%)	**18 Rn**	

2m 41.6 (7.30) CSF £77.11 CT £1,185.36 TOTE £11.60: £3.40 £1.60 £5.40 £2.30 (£46.40) Trio £595.30 OWNER Glenferry And Partners (BRISTOL) BRED Deerfield Farm

WEIGHT FOR AGE 3yo-7lb

OFFICIAL EXPLANATION **My Millie: was lame behind.**

3495 Siberian Mystic came from way off the pace to win this in some style and should obviously be kept in mind for a return to hurdling. (12/1: op 7/1)

4235 Mr Fortywinks (IRE) was the only one of the leading group to keep going and this was a fair performance after such a frenetic pace. (13/2)

3853 Forzair stays further than this and, after getting outpaced here, was staying on well at the end. (16/1)

4415* Tart (FR), having her first run for her new stable, is not the easiest of rides but she did struggle on well at the end. (9/1)

4335 Essayeffsee has his own ideas about the game and only ran on when it was all too late. (14/1: 12/1-20/1)

3562 Admirals Secret (USA) is a funny customer and was never fully co-operating on this occasion. (16/1)

4160 Sushi Bar (IRE) certainly has two ways of running and was never helping his rider here. (5/1: op 8/1)

4432 Hasta la Vista (9/1: 6/1-10/1)

4429* Kingdom Pearl travelled well on the leaders' heels but the pace was so strong that she was found out by the home turn. (10/1)

4585 TRINIDAD & TOBAGO H'CAP (0-70) (3-Y.O+) (Class E)

3-45 (3-47) **2m 1f 22y** £3,301.00 (£988.00: £474.00: £217.00) Stalls: Low GOING minus 0.16 sec per fur (GF)

				SP	RR	SF
4336[2]	**Sipowitz (53)** (CACyzer) **3-8-5** TWilliams(5) (lw: chsd ldrs: led wl over 1f out: styd on u.p)	—	**1**	3/1[2]	63	20
4438[6]	**Karisma (IRE) (42)** (DenysSmith) **4-8-0**(5)ow2 CLowther(2) (chsd ldrs: led wl over 2f out tl wl over 1f out: kpt on same pce)	¾	**2**	8/1	51	17
4160[2]	**Highfield Fizz (42)** (CWFairhurst) **5-8-5** LCharnock(8) (b.off hind: bhd: hdwy 5f out: styd on u.p fnl 2f: nrst fin)	1	**3**	9/2[3]	50	18
4438[12]	**Chimborazo (45)** (BJMcMath) **6-8-8** JWeaver(9) (swtg: rr div: styd on fnl 2f: nrst fin)	5	**4**	33/1	49	17
4432*	**Ranger Sloane (43)** (GFierro) **5-8-6** NCarlisle(6) (hld up: hdwy 6f out: sn trckng ldrs: effrt over 2f out: btn wl over 1f out)	nk	**5**	9/4[1]	46	14
4160[12]	**Dirab (64)** (TDBarron) **4-9-13** KDarley(7) (hdwy & prom ½-wy: sn drvn along: wknd fnl 3f)	5	**6**	9/2[3]	63	31
	Jelali (IRE) (55) (DJGMurraySmith) **4-9-4** DaneO'Neill(1) (in tch: wnt prom 6f out: wknd wl over 2f out)	¾	**7**	40/1	53	21
1624[13]	**Good Judge (IRE) (49)** (MDHammond) **3-7-12**(3) RFfrench(4) (hld up: shkn up 3f out: sn wknd)	4	**8**	20/1	43	—

				SP	RR	SF
	Rave-on-Hadley (IRE) (35) (NBycroft) **7-7-12** DWright(3) (b: bit bkwd: led & sn clr: wknd & hdd wl over 2f out)	16	**9**	100/1	14	—

(SP 114.4%) **9 Rn**

3m 52.1 (12.60) CSF £23.28 CT £96.31 TOTE £3.80: £1.10 £2.10 £1.30 (£14.40) Trio £16.10 OWNER Mr R. M. Cyzer (HORSHAM) BRED C. A. and R. M. Cyzer

WEIGHT FOR AGE 3yo-11lb

4336 Sipowitz, like his namesake, is certainly tough and he just stays and stays. (3/1)
4438 Karisma (IRE) appreciated this trip and had his chances, but again he failed to come up with the goods. (8/1)
4160 Highfield Fizz is proving difficult to win with this season and looks a funny customer but she was finishing well on this occasion. (9/2)
Chimborazo is a very warm individual. She showed signs of ability here after being set plenty to do. (33/1)
4432* Ranger Sloane travelled quite well but, once off the bit, he proved disappointing this time. (9/4)
4160 Dirab seems to have lost his way for the time being. (9/2)

4586 BUCCOO REEF CLAIMING STKS (3-Y.O) (Class F)

4-15 (4-19) **6f** £2,994.00 (£834.00: £402.00) Stalls: Centre GOING minus 0.16 sec per fur (GF)

				SP	RR	SF
3749[6]	**Nant Y Gamer (FR) (76)** (JBerry) **3-8-4**(5) CLowther(9) (a.p: styd on to wl ins fnl f)	—	**1**	13/2[3]	75	41
3206*	**Salty Behaviour (IRE) (80)** (RHannon) **3-8-11** DaneO'Neill(13) (in tch: effrt over 2f out: styd on wl fnl f: nrst fin)	nk	**2**	7/4[1]	76	42
4365[9]	**Top of The Form (IRE) (79)** (RAFahey) **3-8-1**(7) RWinston(11) (led: qcknd clr ent st: hdd & no ex wl ins fnl f)	1	**3**	4/1[2]	71	37
4324[15]	**Court House (54)** (MCChapman) **3-7-12**(7) SCarson(5) (outpcd & bhd tl hdwy 2f out: swtchd: styd on wl towards fin)	1	**4**	25/1	65	31
3088[13]	**C-Harry (IRE) (63)** (RHollinshead) **3-8-6** KFallon(12) (in tch: hdwy 2f out: nt clr run ent fnl f: kpt on one pce)	½	**5**	4/1[2]	65	31
3756[11]	**Moon Song (50)** (APJarvis) **3-8-2v** DWright(3) (chsd ldrs: effrt 2f out: btn appr fnl f)	½	**6**	25/1	59	25
3812[14]	**Mumkin (65)** (MrsLStubbs) **3-8-6b[1]** SWhitworth(10) (dwlt: bhd tl r.o wl fnl 2f)	1	**7**	20/1	61	27
3601[16]	**Petuntse (40)** (JGSmyth-Osbourne) **3-8-3** JLowe(4) (b.hind: swtg: dwlt: hdwy fnl 2f: nvr nrr)	d.h	**8**	50/1	53	19
4563[9]	**Melbourne Princess (37)** (RMWhitaker) **3-7-5**(7) DMernagh(7) (chsd ldrs tl wknd fnl 2f)	1¾	**8**	33/1	48	14
4328[9]	**Municipal Girl (IRE) (39)** (BPalling) **3-7-11**(3) RFfrench(15) (prom tl wknd appr fnl f)	5	**10**	16/1	37	3
4016[5]	**Fine Times (47)** (CWFairhurst) **3-8-5v** DeanMcKeown(17) (b.off hind: outpcd fr ½-wy)	4	**11**	16/1	31	—
3855[11]	**Skyers Tryer (60)** (RonaldThompson) **3-8-0** LCharnock(14) (in tch 4f: wknd)	3½	**12**	33/1	17	—
4115[16]	**Stock Hill Dancer (48)** (BJMeehan) **3-8-0** NCarlisle(6) (swtg: chsd ldrs over 4f: sn wknd)	1¾	**13**	66/1	12	—
3572[6]	**Joyful Joy (28)** (BPJBaugh) **3-7-13** NVarley(16) (in tch 4f)	s.h	**14**	250/1	11	—
3088[6]	**Sparkling Harry (48)** (MissLCSiddall) **3-8-6v[1]** KDarley(1) (bhd: hmpd appr st: t.o)	18	**15**	16/1	—	—
1864[12]	**Ohio Royale (48)** (MrsASwinbank) **3-8-3** EJohnson(2) (s.i.s: a outpcd & wl bhd: t.o)	4	**16**	66/1	—	—

(SP 131.0%) **16 Rn**

1m 18.0 (3.00) CSF £16.57 TOTE £7.90: £2.50 £1.50 £2.30 (£9.90) Trio £5.40 OWNER Mr J. Berry (COCKERHAM) BRED Mrs Carolyn Elwes

3749 Nant Y Gamer (FR) is one of those who is good on his day and this was certainly one of them. (13/2)
3206* Salty Behaviour (IRE) is usually in top form when fresh but, on this occasion, it took some time to find his stride and when he did, the line was always going to come too soon. (7/4)
3332* Top of The Form (IRE) did her utmost to burn her rivals off and almost achieved it but, in the end, the stiff six furlongs just proved beyond her. (4/1: 5/2-9/2)
3320 Court House found this trip too sharp but certainly finished with a flourish. (25/1)
2715* C-Harry (IRE) was always having problems in finding a clear run and that put paid to his chances. (4/1)
1690 Moon Song gave the impression that she is keeping something for herself. (25/1)
Mumkin, in blinkers for the first time, obviously has ability as he flew at the end, but in the early part of the race he looked none too enthusiastic. (20/1)

4587 CARONI MAIDEN STKS (3-Y.O) (Class D)

4-45 (4-49) **1m 4y** £3,550.00 (£1,075.00: £525.00: £250.00) Stalls: Low GOING minus 0.16 sec per fur (GF)

				SP	RR	SF
4177[2]	**Tonight's Prize (IRE) (82)** (CFWall) **3-9-0** SSanders(10) (lw: a.p: rdn to ld appr fnl f: r.o)	—	**1**	4/6[1]	78	39
3991[5]	**Macaribo** (JHMGosden) **3-9-0** LDettori(8) (hld up: effrt 2f out: r.o towards fin)	2	**2**	11/2[3]	74	35
4464[2]	**Faringdon Future (73)** (BWHills) **3-9-0** KFallon(7) (lw: cl up: led 2f out tl appr fnl f: no ex)	1¾	**3**	7/2[2]	71	32
4070[9]	**Ikram Boy (USA)** (ABailey) **3-9-0** DWright(1) (a chsng ldrs: drvn along over 2f out: one pce)	5	**4**	16/1	61	22
3917[10]	**Slieu Whallian** (RHannon) **3-8-9** DaneO'Neill(11) (a chsng ldrs: one pce fnl 2f)	3	**5**	20/1	50	11
	Job Rage (IRE) (ABailey) **3-9-0** FNorton(4) (leggy: unf: bit bkwd: bhd: hdwy over 1f out: nvr nr to chal)	4	**6**	66/1	47	8
4277[11]	**Pride of Narvik** (MRChannon) **3-9-0** KDarley(6) (led 6f: wknd)	nk	**7**	33/1	46	7
1415[9]	**Jaza** (NAGraham) **3-9-0** MRimmer(5) (a in rr)	3	**8**	25/1	40	1
	Salford Lad (GWragg) **3-9-0** AClark(12) (chsd ldrs tl wknd fnl 2f)	nk	**9**	33/1	39	—
4182[4]	**Shalaal (USA) (77)** (MCChapman) **3-8-7**(7) SCarson(9) (swtg: in tch tl wknd over 2f out)	nk	**10**	50/1	39	—
4417[9]	**Northern Accord** (MrsJRRamsden) **3-9-0** JFortune(3) (bit bkwd: a bhd)	½	**11**	25/1	38	—
	Barkston Warrior (DShaw) **3-8-11**(3) CTeague(2) (leggy: dwlt: a bhd: t.o)	15	**12**	100/1	8	—

(SP 126.3%) **12 Rn**

1m 47.2 (4.80) CSF £4.39 TOTE £1.80: £1.00 £1.90 £1.20 (£3.60) Trio £2.30 OWNER Mr Shunya Seki (NEWMARKET) BRED Shunya Seki

4177 Tonight's Prize (IRE) travelled really well and won in most convincing style. There would seem to be more to come. (4/6)
3991 Macaribo looks the type who has plenty more ability if he can be persuaded and this was not a bad effort. (11/2: 7/2-6/1)
4464 Faringdon Future was given a really good ride here and had no excuses, other than he simply was not good enough. (7/2)
Ikram Boy (USA) showed ability here and was given plenty of help from the saddle. (16/1)
Slieu Whallian improved on her debut here and looks likely to need a bit further. (20/1)
Job Rage (IRE) needed this and took time to realise what was required but was picking up at the end. (66/1)

4588 LEVY BOARD NURSERY H'CAP (0-75) (2-Y.O) (Class E)

5-15 (5-24) **6f** £3,665.00 (£1,100.00: £530.00: £245.00) Stalls: Low GOING minus 0.16 sec per fur (GF)

				SP	RR	SF
4231[4]	**Miss Vivien (72)** (MissLAPerratt) **2-9-5** LDettori(17) (racd alone & wd: mde all: clr 2f out: drvn out)	—	**1**	11/2[2]	75	26
4332[7]	**Moonstone (IRE) (72)** (APJarvis) **2-9-0**(5) CLowther(8) (a chsng ldrs: kpt on wl fnl f)	1	**2**	6/1[3]	72	23
4285*	**Petara (IRE) (66)** (JSWainwright) **2-8-13v** JReid(6) (lw: sn drvn along: hdwy 2f out: styd on wl towards fin)	nk	**3**	7/1	66	17
4419[6]	**Mr Fund Switch (49)** (DNicholls) **2-7-5**(5) IonaWands(16) (chsd ldrs: one pce fnl 2f)	6	**4**	50/1	33	—

2706^{11}	**Sharp Shooter (IRE) (61)** (MrsJRRamsden) **2-8-8** JFortune(2) (bhd: styd on fnl 2f: nrst fin)	2	**5**	12/1	39	—
4116^{13}	**Balance The Books (74)** (RHannon) **2-9-7** DaneO'Neill(14) (dwlt: bhd & nt clr run 2f out: r.o towards fin)	s.h	**6**	13/2	52	3
4327^{2}	**Dekelsmary (67)** (JBalding) **2-9-0** JEdmunds(4) (mid div: drvn along ½-wy: no imp)	½	**7**	$9/2^{1}$	44	—
4285^{16}	**The Cannie Rover (60)** (MWEasterby) **2-8-7** TLucas(3) (lw: nvr nr to chal)	1¾	**8**	25/1	32	—
4382^{4}	**Brookhouse Lady (IRE) (58)** (RHollinshead) **2-8-5** NCarlisle(1) (s.i.s: bhd tl sme late hdwy)	1	**9**	9/1	27	—
4056^{5}	**Lunchtime Girl (56)** (JDBethell) **2-8-3** LCharnock(5) (bhd: sme hdwy 2f out: n.d)	½	**10**	20/1	24	—
4381^{5}	**Strictly Rhythm (71)** (MrsSABramall) **2-9-1**(3) GParkin(12) (cl up tl wknd fnl 2f)	2½	**11**	16/1	32	—
4381^{9}	**Essandess (IRE) (60)** (JLEyre) **2-8-7** TWilliams(15) (sn chsng ldrs: wknd 2f out)	2	**12**	16/1	16	—
4433^{11}	**Maggice (56)** (RHollinshead) **2-8-3** DWright(7) (swtg: prom 4f)	nk	**13**	33/1	11	—
3031^{7}	**Balanita (IRE) (65)** (BPalling) **2-8-9**(3) DSweeney(10) (swtg: unruly s: chsd wnr 4f: wknd)	3	**14**	16/1	12	—
3212^{8}	**Ribble Assembly (59)** (RAFahey) **2-8-6** SSanders(9) (dwlt: a outpcd & bhd)	3½	**15**	10/1	—	—
4479^{5}	***Little Fizz (67)*** (BJMeehan) **2-9-0** KDarley(11) (Withdrawn not under Starter's order: veterinary advice)		**W**	20/1	—	—
4327^{3}	***Delciana (IRE) (66)*** (PWHarris) **2-8-13** KFallon(13) (Withdrawn not under Starter's orders: veterinary advice)		**W**	$6/1^{3}$	—	—
				(SP 150.7%)	**15 Rn**	

1m 19.9 (4.90) CSF £36.93 CT £230.78 TOTE £6.10: £2.40 £3.30 £2.60 (£22.50) Trio £64.80 OWNER Lostford Manor Stud (AYR) BRED Mrs V. E. Hughes

LONG HANDICAP Mr Fund Switch 6-12

4231 Miss Vivien, intelligently ridden, raced wide, getting the best ground on this wet afternoon, and had it sewn up entering the straight. (11/2)

3961a Moonstone (IRE) ran well at his first attempt at a nursery and ought to appreciate further. (6/1)

4285* Petara (IRE), full of himself beforehand, took a lot of driving to find his stride but certainly finished with a flourish and obviously needs a bit further. (7/1)

4054 Mr Fund Switch, from 12lb out of the handicap, ran pretty well. (50/1)

1492 Sharp Shooter (IRE) was gradually picking up as the race progressed, and time and further would seem to be the key. (12/1)

3387 Balance The Books never had any luck in running and he is better than this. (13/2)

T/Jkpt: Not won; £96,058.13 to Warwick 7/10/97. T/Plpt: £15.20 (2,017.5 Tckts). T/Qdpt: £5.70 (223.04 Tckts) AA

4569-WOLVERHAMPTON (L-H) (Standard)

Monday October 6th

WEATHER: overcast WIND: mod half bhd

4589 CORACLE NURSERY H'CAP (0-85) (2-Y.O) (Class E)

2-25 (2-26) **7f (Fibresand)** £3,148.25 (£941.00: £450.50: £205.25) Stalls: High GOING: 0.25 sec per fur (SLW)

				SP	RR	SF
3755^{9}	**Carambo (82)** (JLEyre) **2-9-4** MGallagher(4) (a.p: rdn to ld ins fnl f: r.o wl)	—	**1**	$9/1^{3}$	86	50
4468^{5}	**One Singer (85)** (MJohnston) **2-9-7** DHolland(12) (chsd ldrs: effrt over 1f out: ev ch ins fnl f: unable qckn)	1¼	**2**	10/1	86	50
3932^{12}	**Santa Faye (IRE) (75)** (BPalling) **2-8-11** TSprake(3) (led over 3f: rdn & ev ch ins fnl f: no ex)	¾	**3**	16/1	74	38
4362^{2}	**Montano (USA) (69)** (PFICole) **2-8-5** CRutter(1) (prom: led over 3f out tl hdd & no ex ins fnl f)	½	**4**	$5/1^{2}$	67	31
*4299**	**Pedro (IRE) (85)** (SirMarkPrescott) **2-9-7** GDuffield(9) (lw: plld hrd: prom: rdn over 2f out: sn btn)	2½	**5**	$11/10^{1}$	78	42
4315^{2}	**Kennet (77)** (PDCundell) **2-8-13** RPerham(5) (nvr gng pce of ldrs)	7	**6**	$9/1^{3}$	54	18
4458^{3}	**Fundance (75)** (MDods) **2-8-11** JCarroll(10) (lw: prom tl rdn & wknd 2f out)	¾	**7**	20/1	50	14
4265^{9}	**Chaska (64)** (ABailey) **2-7-7**(7) JBosley(11) (a bhd & outpcd)	hd	**8**	25/1	39	3
4068^{10}	**Won't Forget Me (IRE) (65)** (MHTompkins) **2-8-1** DBiggs(8) (outpcd)	2	**9**	14/1	35	—
4163*	**Kayo (70)** (TJEtherington) **2-8-6** SDrowne(6) (lw: in tch: rdn over 3f out: wknd)	1½	**10**	20/1	37	1
4299^{5}	**Gift of Gold (75)** (ICampbell) **2-8-11** AMackay(7) (s.i.s: effrt & rdn 3f out: no imp)	½	**11**	10/1	41	5
3610^{9}	**Dancing Rio (IRE) (70)** (PCHaslam) **2-8-6** DaleGibson(2) (lost tch 3f out: sn bhd)	¾	**12**	20/1	34	—
				(SP 133.1%)	**12 Rn**	

1m 30.8 (2.40 under 2y best) (6.10) CSF £92.63 CT £1,350.54 TOTE £9.00: £2.40 £2.40 £2.50 (£51.40) Trio £158.20 OWNER C H & D W Stephenson Ltd (HAMBLETON) BRED C. Stephenson

3042* Carambo had no trouble handling the seventh furlong and, repeating her success at this track in July, ran out a comfortable winner. (9/1: op 5/1)

4468 One Singer has done the majority of his racing over the minimum trip and he does not look quite up to carrying so much weight, but he gave it his best shot and certainly went down fighting. (10/1: 7/1-11/1)

3247* Santa Faye (IRE), in the firing line from the start, rallied gamely inside the distance but she had come to the end of her tether inside the last hundred yards. (16/1)

4362 Montano (USA) was able to gain revenge over the favourite, but he may have had just too much use made of him for he had shot his bolt when collared inside the final furlong. (5/1)

4299* Pedro (IRE), a grand-looking colt who holds engagements in Group races, proved a big disappointment in this first handicap and, even with top weight, should have won this if he is going to be as good as connections hope. (11/10: 6/4-evens)

4315 Kennet (9/1: op 6/1)

3967* Won't Forget Me (IRE) (14/1: 10/1-16/1)

4590 SKIFF AMATEUR H'CAP (0-60) (3-Y.O+) (Class G)

2-55 (2-57) **1m 6f 166y (Fibresand)** £1,984.50 (£547.00: £259.50) Stalls: Low GOING: 0.25 sec per fur (SLW)

				SP	RR	SF
*4302**	**Robbo (60)** (CWThornton) **3-10-9b**(5) MrJCrowley(7) (hld up: smooth hdwy 4f out: led wl over 1f out: rdn & r.o wl)	—	**1**	$5/2^{1}$	76	42
	Euro Forum (45) (GLewis) **5-10-4**(5) MrPO'Keeffe(4) (bit bkwd: hld up in tch: hdwy 4f out: ev ch ent fnl f: r.o one pce)	1¼	**2**	9/1	60	36
4010*	**Certain Magic (53)** (WRMuir) **3-10-7** MrTMcCarthy(8) (hld up: hdwy 5f out: ev ch over 1f out: sn rdn: one pce)	1½	**3**	$5/1^{2}$	66	32
4302^{6}	**Paradise Navy (57)** (CREgerton) **8-11-4b**(3) MissERamsden(11) (chsd ldr: ev ch 2f out: sn rdn & wknd)	6	**4**	$6/1^{3}$	64	40
4055^{3}	**Needwood Epic (52)** (BCMorgan) **4-10-9b**(7) MissSPhizacklea(2) (led tl hdd & wknd wl over 1f out)	½	**5**	14/1	58	34
4302^{5}	**Lake Dominion (44)** (KCComerford) **8-10-3**(5) MrJOwen(5) (b: s.s: a in rr)	16	**6**	14/1	33	9
3719^{4}	**Nosey Native (57)** (JPearce) **4-11-7** MrsLPearce(10) (hld up: a in rr)	4	**7**	14/1	41	17
2518^{3}	**Wesley's Lad (IRE) (60)** (DBurchell) **3-10-7**(7) MrGRichards(12) (bit bkwd: s.s: hdwy after 4f: wknd over 3f out)	5	**8**	16/1	39	5

				SP	RR	SF
4432[7]	**Arian Spirit (IRE) (50)** (JLEyre) **6-11-0v** MissDianaJones(3) (lw: lost pl after 6f: n.d afterwards)	3	**9**	6/1[3]	26	2
4481[7]	**Stalled (IRE) (53)** (PTWalwyn) **7-10-12**(5) MarchionessBlandford(9) (b: hld up: rdn & lost pl over 5f out)	5	**10**	16/1	23	—
4372[5]	**Herbshan Dancer (53)** (BRMillman) **3-10-4**(3) MrLJefford(1) (s.i.s: sn chsng ldrs: wknd ½-wy: t.o)	dist	**11**	14/1	—	—
	Maryjo (IRE) (48) (GLMoore) **8-10-5**(7) MrIMongan(6) (bkwd: a bhd: t.o fnl 4f)	5	**12**	20/1	—	—

(SP 127.0%) **12 Rn**

3m 26.7 (19.30) CSF £25.54 CT £103.09 TOTE £3.20: £1.10 £1.20 £3.70 (£9.50) Trio £8.20 OWNER Mr Guy Reed (MIDDLEHAM) BRED Godolphin Management Co Ltd

WEIGHT FOR AGE 3yo-10lb

4302* Robbo followed up his recent success over course and distance with another comfortable win, but he did have to fight a bit harder this time to make sure the prize was his. (5/2: 7/4-11/4)

Euro Forum, having his first outing on the Flat for two years, did try his luck between the flags last season and he looked well tuned up for this return to action. Making steady headway at the end of the back straight, he looked a live threat entering the final furlong, before the race-fit winner proved too strong. (9/1)

4010* Certain Magic failed in his bid to complete a hat-trick but he ran his race out to the finish, and he has time on his side. (5/1: 7/2-11/2)

4302 Paradise Navy runs well for his lady rider and he was in with every chance until finding demands too much once in line for home. (6/1)

4055 Needwood Epic adopted her usual front-running tactics and tried hard to hold the principals at bay, but she had been worn down soon after straightening up and had nothing more to give. (14/1: op 8/1)

3719 Nosey Native (14/1: op 8/1)

4591 MAN O'WAR H'CAP (0-85) (3-Y.O) (Class D)

3-25 (3-27) **7f (Fibresand)** £3,709.30 (£1,107.40: £529.20: £240.10) Stalls: High GOING: 0.25 sec per fur (SLW)

				SP	RR	SF
*3860**	**Bogan (IRE) (64)** (LordHuntingdon) **3-8-3v** JFEgan(10) (chsd ldrs: led 3f out: hld on wl cl home)	—	**1**	6/1[2]	72	35
4280[22]	**Silca Key Silca (78)** (MRChannon) **3-9-3** JCarroll(2) (bhd: hdwy over 2f out: rdn & r.o wl towards fin)	hd	**2**	10/1	86	49
4043[17]	**Molly Music (60)** (GGMargarson) **3-7-13** GBardwell(9) (lw: bhd & outpcd: gd hdwy appr fnl f: fin wl)	2	**3**	25/1	63	26
4328[8]	**Davis Rock (70)** (WRMuir) **3-8-9** TSprake(1) (hld up: hdwy on ins 2f out: kpt on u.p fnl f)	nk	**4**	14/1	73	36
3798[6]	**Swift (65)** (MJPolglase) **3-8-4** JTate(12) (lw: hld up: hdwy over 3f out: rdn & one pce appr fnl f)	½	**5**	6/1[2]	66	29
3790[3]	**Giko (63)** (JRPoulton) **3-8-2**[ow1] SDrowne(6) (swtg: trckd ldrs: rdn over 1f out: one pce)	1¼	**6**	8/1[3]	62	24
4482[3]	**Forcing Bid (80)** (SirMarkPrescott) **3-9-5** GDuffield(11) (lw: bhd: reminders 4f out: effrt ent st: rdn & wknd over 1f out)	s.h	**7**	11/4[1]	78	41
4316[7]	**Cuesta Rey (USA) (65)** (JWHills) **3-8-1**(3) MHenry(8) (sn drvn along: a bhd)	5	**8**	12/1	52	15
4436[5]	**Blooming Amazing (71)** (JLEyre) **3-8-10** WRyan(3) (b.hind: chsd ldr: led 4f out to 3f out: wknd wl over 1f out)	nk	**9**	6/1[2]	57	20
4307[12]	**Smart Kid (IRE) (82)** (PFICole) **3-9-0**(7) DavidO'Neill(5) (sn pushed along: a in rr)	½	**10**	14/1	67	30
3851[9]	**Goodbye Gatemen (IRE) (75)** (BAPearce) **3-9-0** DHolland(7) (unruly stalls: led 3f: rdn & wknd over 2f out: t.o)	16	**11**	33/1	24	—
3393[8]	**Tayovullin (IRE) (65)** (HMorrison) **3-8-4v**[1] CRutter(4) (prom: disp ld 3f out: wknd 2f out: t.o)	¾	**12**	16/1	12	—

(SP 123.4%) **12 Rn**

1m 30.9 (6.20) CSF £61.64 CT £1,311.02 TOTE £11.80: £3.20 £2.30 £4.30 (£24.60) Trio £203.10; £57.22 to Warwick 7/10/97 OWNER Mr G. Cosmelli (WEST ILSLEY) BRED Clare Dore Ltd

3860* Bogan (IRE) has certainly come good since the blinkers were fitted and, though he had to work hard here, he always looked to have the edge. (6/1)

3982 Silca Key Silca has done her winning at six furlongs and she was given a very patient ride. Set alight entering the straight, she battled on willingly but found the winner just too good for her at the weights. This was a very promising effort. (10/1)

2672 Molly Music, taken off her legs over this shorter trip, did not really get going until approaching the final furlong, and her sustained late challenge was always going to be too late. (25/1)

3691 Davis Rock, settled off the pace, stayed on well inside the distance and, had Molly Music not finished so strongly, she would have made the first three. (14/1)

3798 Swift, having his first run on this surface since the spring, could not summon the pace to get serious, but he did keep staying on and he has won in the autumn in the past. (6/1)

3790 Giko, running consistently well of late, was having his first try on the All-Weather. Awash with sweat, he waited on the leaders but did not find a lot when asked for his effort and was fighting a lost cause throughout the final quarter-mile. (8/1: op 5/1)

4482 Forcing Bid reserves his best for this surface but he was hard at work and in trouble halfway down the back straight and this was very much an off day. (11/4)

4592 LONGBOAT MAIDEN AUCTION STKS (2-Y.O) (Class E)

3-55 (3-56) **1m 100y (Fibresand)** £3,122.25 (£933.00: £446.50: £203.25) Stalls: Low GOING: 0.25 sec per fur (SLW)

				SP	RR	SF
4514[3]	**Adeste Fideles** (MBell) **2-8-2** MFenton(6) (lw: outpcd: rdn & hdwy 3f out: styd on to ld wl ins fnl f)	—	**1**	11/4[2]	61	28
4334[7]	**Gralmano (IRE) (64)** (NPLittmoden) **2-8-3** JQuinn(9) (lw: bhd: hdwy 4f out: jnd ldr 2f out: rdn to ld 1f out: hdd nr fin)	½	**2**	2/1[1]	61	28
	Diamond Drill (USA) (PJMakin) **2-8-11** GDuffield(3) (leggy: bit bkwd: led after 3f: hrd rdn & hdd 1f out: sn btn)	6	**3**	15/2	58	25
4245[8]	**Mamora Bay (IRE) (66)** (MHTompkins) **2-8-7b**[1] DBiggs(1) (lw: a.p: rdn 3f out: wknd appr fnl f)	1½	**4**	12/1	51	18
4265[12]	**Black Jet (55)** (NPLittmoden) **2-8-0**(3) ADaly(2) (led 3f: wknd over 2f out)	6	**5**	25/1	36	3
4433[7]	**Nuit d'Or (IRE)** (MJohnston) **2-8-11** DHolland(10) (bit bkwd: hdwy 5f out: rdn 2f out: eased whn btn over 1f out)	s.h	**6**	7/2[3]	43+	10
4334[13]	**Mary Lou (IRE) (48)** (MRChannon) **2-8-3v**[ow1] PaulEddery(11) (trckd ldrs: hrd rdn over 2f out: sn wknd)	1	**7**	33/1	34	—
4236[10]	**Rio (IRE) (60)** (JBerry) **2-8-0**(3) PFessey(5) (chsd ldrs 4f: sn rdn & lost tch: t.o)	14	**8**	8/1	7	—
3757[8]	**Swaybus** (MJohnston) **2-8-6** JFanning(7) (swtg: prom tl wknd over 2f out: t.o)	2	**9**	25/1	6	—
4064[18]	**Ziggy Stardust (IRE)** (MrsAJBowlby) **2-8-7** CandyMorris(4) (bit bkwd: prom 6f: sn rdn & wknd: t.o)	1¾	**10**	50/1	4	—
4163[9]	**Chardania (IRE) (49)** (CaptJWilson) **2-7-12** CRutter(8) (a bhd: t.o)	2½	**11**	33/1	—	—

(SP 128.3%) **11 Rn**

1m 53.3 (8.30) CSF £8.34 TOTE £4.00: £1.50 £1.50 £1.50 (£3.40) Trio £34.40 OWNER Capt B. W. Bell (NEWMARKET) BRED Sheikh Mohammed bin Rashid al Maktoum

OFFICIAL EXPLANATION **Nuit d'Or (IRE): Regarding the apparent tender handling, the rider reported that the colt became tired in the straight and had no more to give, so he held him together to the line.**

4514 Adeste Fideles was never travelling like a winner and her supporters must have felt like tearing up their tickets when she trailed the leaders by all of five lengths turning in, but stamina is obviously her strong suit, and she stayed on strongly to force her head in front close home. (11/4: 2/1-3/1)

3395 Gralmano (IRE), reverting a to a slightly shorter trip on this return to his home track, got the better of the long-time leader passing the furlong marker and did appear to have control until the winner took his measure within the shadow of the post. (2/1)
Diamond Drill (USA), a leggy debutant who looked as though he would benefit from the run, ran a race full of promise and he could be fancied to turn the tables on his conquerors with this outing under his belt. (15/2)
3067 Mamora Bay (IRE) is still not able to get it quite right, but he does seem to try hard enough and success will not come out of turn. (12/1: 7/1-14/1)
3265 Rio (IRE) (8/1: op 5/1)

4593 TRIREME (S) STKS (2-Y.O) (Class G)

4-25 (4-26) **6f (Fibresand)** £1,984.50 (£547.00: £259.50) Stalls: Low GOING: 0.25 sec per fur (SLW)

				SP	RR	SF
4054[3]	**Snappy Times (56)** (MDods) **2-8-12** DaleGibson(12) (in tch: hdwy over 2f out: led ent fnl f: all out)	—	1	15/2[2]	57	21
	Killarney Jazz (JWharton) **2-8-12** JQuinn(9) (leggy: scope: bit bkwd: s.s: bhd & outpcd: hdwy over 2f out: kpt on wl ins fnl f)	¾	2	20/1	55+	19
*4483**	**Malozza (62)** (PDEvans) **2-8-12** JFEgan(4) (mde most tl hdd 1f out: kpt on u.p)	hd	3	5/2[1]	55	19
4411[6]	**Miss Dangerous (56)** (MRChannon) **2-8-7** JCarroll(6) (prom tl rdn & wknd fnl 2f)	4	4	5/2[1]	39	3
4017[7]	**Little Risk** (KMcAuliffe) **2-8-7** TSprake(10) (b.hind: hdwy 3f out: rdn over 1f out: grad wknd)	2½	5	10/1[3]	32	—
4573[4]	**Rock From The Sun (50)** (WGMTurner) **2-8-5b**(7) DMcGaffin(11) (mid div: hdwy & rdn 2f out: nt rch ldrs)	2½	6	12/1	31	—
4178[8]	**River Frontier (IRE) (45)** (MDIUsher) **2-8-7** JMarshall(7) (nvr nr ldrs)	½	7	16/1	24	—
4379[8]	**Thomas O'Malley (62)** (RJO'Sullivan) **2-8-12** AProcter(13) (outpcd: a in rr)	s.h	8	10/1[3]	29	—
4458[7]	**Katies Treat (IRE) (45)** (DTThom) **2-8-7** DeclanO'Shea(8) (chsd ldrs over 3f)	½	9	20/1	23	—
4362[9]	**Aviva Lady (IRE) (48)** (CADwyer) **2-8-7** PaulEddery(5) (prom tl rdn & wknd over 1f out)	5	10	12/1	10	—
4014[10]	**City Dance** (PJMakin) **2-8-7** GDuffield(1) (dwlt: a bhd & outpcd)	4	11	10/1[3]	—	—
3629[8]	**Henry The Proud (IRE)** (JBerry) **2-8-9b**(3) TEDurcan(2) (lw: sn drvn along: a in rr)	½	12	14/1	3	—
4479[13]	**Precisely (IRE)** (JWharton) **2-8-12** JFanning(3) (bit bkwd: chsd ldrs: effrt over 3f out: wknd qckly over 1f out)	¾	13	33/1	1	—
				(SP 136.6%)		**13 Rn**

1m 18.1 (6.90) CSF £151.91 TOTE £6.00: £1.80 £10.70 £1.60 (£648.30) Trio £75.90 OWNER Mr J. A. Wynn-Williams (DARLINGTON) BRED Norton Grove Stud Ltd
No bid
4054 Snappy Times gained due rewards for consistency and it was more down to experience that enabled him to hold on. (15/2: 5/1-8/1)
Killarney Jazz, a half-brother to a couple of winners, is a May foal and he will strip fitter for the run. Flat-footed as the stalls opened and soon well outpaced, he began to make progress on the wide outside on the home turn and, maintaining his run, only just failed to make a winning debut. It has got to be doubtful if he continues in this grade. (20/1)
4483* Malozza did not give best without a struggle entering the last furlong and even renewed her effort to fail narrowly. (5/2)
4411 Miss Dangerous was well fancied to open her account on this step down in class but she had been made to work entering the straight and could do little more than stay on at the same pace. It is possible that she is not quite as effective on this surface. (5/2)
Little Risk ran at a mile on her debut and did not see it out, so she was given the chance to show what she was made of over this shorter trip. Taking closer order at halfway, she did promise to take a hand in the finish but she found little when pressure was applied and failed to make any impression. (10/1)
Thomas O'Malley (10/1: op 5/1)
3866 Aviva Lady (IRE) (12/1: 7/1-14/1)
City Dance (10/1: 8/1-12/1)
695 Henry The Proud (IRE) (14/1: op 8/1)

4594 YACHT LIMITED STKS (0-65) (3-Y.O+) (Class F)

4-55 (4-55) **1m 4f (Fibresand)** £2,277.00 (£627.00: £297.00) Stalls: Low GOING: 0.25 sec per fur (SLW)

				SP	RR	SF
4363[9]	**Rex Mundi (63)** (PDEvans) **5-9-6** JFEgan(3) (a chsng ldrs: rdn to ld ent fnl f: r.o strly)	—	1	9/1	72	52
4336[5]	**Indigo Dawn (65)** (MJohnston) **3-9-0b**[1] DHolland(2) (hld up: hdwy 6f out: rdn to ld wl over 1f out: sn hdd: one pce)	2½	2	9/2[3]	70	43
4279[10]	**Noufari (FR) (65)** (RHollinshead) **6-9-6** FLynch(8) (lw: hld up: rdn along over 5f out: hdwy over 1f out: nvr nrr)	4	3	9/2[3]	63	43
	Safecracker (65) (CPMorlock) **4-9-4** NAdams(6) (led tl wl over 1f out: sn rdn & wknd)	4	4	40/1	56	36
4288[2]	**Double Eight (IRE) (63)** (BWHills) **3-8-12** PaulEddery(7) (chsd ldr: ev ch & pushed along 2f out: sn rdn & wknd)	3½	5	9/4[1]	52	25
4481[9]	**English Invader (59)** (CADwyer) **6-9-3**(3) TEDurcan(4) (hld up in rr: effrt over 3f out: no imp fnl 2f)	1¼	6	8/1	52	32
4304[2]	**Royal Roulette (61)** (SPCWoods) **3-8-8v** NDay(1) (trckd ldrs on ins: rdn & wknd over 2f out)	hd	7	3/1[2]	47	20
4158[9]	**Shooting Star (IRE) (62)** (JHMGosden) **3-8-11v** JCarroll(5) (in tch: nudged along after 5f: wknd 4f out: t.o)	dist	8	12/1	—	—
				(SP 123.4%)		**8 Rn**

2m 43.4 (10.90) CSF £48.30 TOTE £11.90: £1.80 £1.20 £2.60 (£21.90) OWNER Mr J. W. Littler (WELSHPOOL) BRED J. W. Littler
WEIGHT FOR AGE 3yo-7lb
4235 Rex Mundi is a very versatile performer and all trips seem to come alike, and he was clearly the boss here from the time he had his head in front. (9/1)
4336 Indigo Dawn wore blinkers for the first time and worked hard to force her head in front on straightening up, but the winner took her measure without much trouble and, as she has gone in her coat, it might be wise to call it a day for this season. (9/2)
3412 Noufari (FR) stayed on well in the latter stages but he was never travelling fast enough to cause much concern to the principals. (9/2)
Safecracker is a poor selling plater over hurdles, but he came here fit from jumping and held the call until fading rather quickly after being collared turning in. (40/1)
4288 Double Eight (IRE) travelled well on the heels of the leader and always seemed to be well in control, but she came off the bridle on the home turn and stopped to nothing. She did not fire on her previous outing here eleven months ago but she is starting to go in her coat and may well have had enough for the time being. (9/4)
4304* English Invader made a token effort at the end of the back straight but it came to little and he was never a factor. (8/1: op 5/1)

T/Plpt: £242.90 (71.41 Tckts). T/Qdpt: £28.30 (37.2 Tckts) IM

4413-REDCAR (L-H) (Good to firm, Firm patches)
Tuesday October 7th
WEATHER: showers becoming fine WIND: fresh half bhd

4595 MALTON CLAIMING STKS (2-Y.O) (Class F)
2-10 (2-11) **7f** £2,570.00 (£720.00: £350.00) Stalls: High GOING minus 0.52 sec per fur (F)

Form	Horse / details	Dist	Pos	SP	RR	SF
4163^{2}	**Greenbrook (71)** (WGMTurner) **2-8-9**(7) DMcGaffin(2) (led after 1½f: hld on towards fin)	—	**1**	4/1^{2}	71	34
4230^{8}	**Pride of Bryn (46)** (DenysSmith) **2-7-8**(3) PFessey(12) (a chsng ldrs: kpt on wl towards fin)	½	**2**	10/1	51	14
4058^{4}	**Up The Clarets (IRE) (54)** (JJO'Neill) **2-8-8** JFEgan(4) (outpcd ½-wy: hdwy over 1f out: styd on towards fin)	4	**3**	12/1	53	16
4208^{10}	**Filgrave (IRE) (56)** (CADwyer) **2-8-8** JFortune(9) (a chsng ldrs: rdn over 2f out: kpt on same pce)	1¾	**4**	16/1	49	12
3186^{7}	**Bali Dance (62)** (CBBBooth) **2-8-7** KHodgson(15) (sn outpcd & drvn along: styd on appr fnl f)	2½	**5**	5/1^{3}	42	5
3751^{7}	**Wynbury Flyer (50)** (FMurphy) **2-8-7**ow1 KFallon(14) (chsd ldrs: outpcd ½-wy: styd on appr fnl f)	d.h	**6**	10/1	40	2
3395^{7}	**Percy (63)** (JHetherton) **2-8-8** LDettori(1) (b: chsd ldrs: one pce fnl 3f)	1	**6**	8/1	41	4
3808^{12}	**I'm Tef (45)** (TDEasterby) **2-8-6b** LCharnock(5) (hdwy to chse ldrs ½-wy: wknd 2f out)	3	**8**	50/1	32	—
4058^{7}	**Fanti Dancer (IRE) (62)** (BJMeehan) **2-8-3** KDarley(11) (lw: sn outpcd & drvn along: sme hdwy over 2f out: n.d)	s.h	**9**	11/4^{1}	29	—
4159^{9}	**Tigi (45)** (MrsMReveley) **2-8-3** DWright(7) (hld up: effrt ½-wy: hung rt & sn wknd)	2½	**10**	25/1	23	—
4163^{4}	**Docklands Dispatch (IRE) (54)** (NTinkler) **2-8-8** KimTinkler(10) (lw: chsd ldrs: rdn ½-wy: sn wknd)	5	**11**	16/1	17	—
3751^{15}	**Drain Doctor** (SEKettlewell) **2-8-6** JFanning(13) (bit bkwd: outpcd after 2f: sn bhd)	6	**12**	100/1	1	—
1045^{11}	**Robert's Daughter** (JBalding) **2-8-5** JEdmunds(3) (s.i.s: stumbled after 1f: n.d)	2	**13**	33/1	—	—
3857^{6}	**Classic Silver (IRE) (56)** (WWHaigh) **2-9-0** TWilliams(8) (s.i.s: bhd & drvn along ½-wy: n.d)	½	**14**	16/1	3	—
3062^{8}	**La Vaso Verdi** (RMWhitaker) **2-7-4v**^{1}(7) DMernagh(6) (led over 1f: lost pl ½-wy: sn bhd)	2	**15**	50/1	—	—

(SP 129.7%) **15 Rn**

1m 24.9 (1.90) CSF £41.89 TOTE £3.40: £2.00 £3.70 £6.10 (£32.90) Trio £209.80 OWNER Mrs L. P. Green (SHERBORNE) BRED B. E. Green

OFFICIAL EXPLANATION **Fanti Dancer (IRE): veterinary officer reported that on examination during routine testing after the race, the horse was coughing.**

4163 Greenbrook was suited by the slight drop back in distance and, well handled by the boy, was always doing just enough. (4/1)

3628 Pride of Bryn, who showed a very scratchy action going down, appreciated the step up in distance and, sticking to her guns, was just held at bay. (10/1: 7/1-12/1)

4058 Up The Clarets (IRE) seemed to run her best race so far. (12/1)

3639 Filgrave (IRE) put a very disappointing effort last time behind him. (16/1)

3067 Bali Dance seems to have lost completely the pace she showed in her first couple of outings. Here she was soon flat to the boards. (5/1)

3563 Wynbury Flyer will be an interesting proposition in a mile selling nursery. (10/1)

3076 Percy showed plenty of knee action going down and would appreciate easier ground. (8/1)

3819 Fanti Dancer (IRE), who looked to have a good chance at the weights, had the blinkers left off. Soon in trouble, she was found to be coughing after the race. (11/4)

4596 SCARBOROUGH H'CAP (0-70) (3-Y.O+) (Class E)
2-40 (2-44) **1m 1f** £3,190.75 (£961.00: £465.50: £217.75) Stalls: Low GOING minus 0.52 sec per fur (F)

Form	Horse / details	Dist	Pos	SP	RR	SF
4477^{3}	**Polar Prospect (56)** (BHanbury) **4-9-2** KDarley(15) (lw: b: chsd ldrs: hdwy to ld over 1f out: hld on wl)	—	**1**	5/1^{2}	66	41
4386^{10}	**Priolo Prima (68)** (SirMarkPrescott) **4-10-0** OPears(14) (s.i.s: hdwy over 4f out: styd on wl fnl f: nt rch wnr)	1¼	**2**	14/1	76	51
3937^{9}	**Mukhatab (65)** (JJQuinn) **5-9-11** TLucas(6) (lw: trckd ldrs: rdn & hung lft over 1f out: styd on towards fin)	¾	**3**	12/1	71	46
4210^{6}	**Bowcliffe (63)** (EJAlston) **6-9-9** JFEgan(10) (lw: hld up: effrt & nt clr run over 2f out: styd on fnl f)	hd	**4**	11/1	69	44
4386^{12}	**House of Dreams (55)** (GMMoore) **5-8-10**(5) CLowther(8) (bhd & pushed along: styd on wl fnl 2f)	1¾	**5**	40/1	58	33
4184*	**Gymcrak Premiere (68)** (GHolmes) **9-10-0** LDettori(3) (hdwy on outside over 3f out: styd on fnl f: nt rch ldrs)	½	**6**	11/2^{3}	70	45
4161^{7}	**Sparky (67)** (MWEasterby) **3-9-6b**(3) GParkin(9) (lw: b: mid div: hrd rdn & swtchd lft over 2f out: kpt on: nvr able to chal)	½	**7**	8/1	68	39
4210^{3}	**Java Red (IRE) (54)** (JGFitzGerald) **5-9-0** KFallon(4) (lw: bhd & drvn along over 4f out: nt clr run & swtchd outside over 1f out: kpt on: nvr nr to chal)	¾	**8**	4/1^{1}	54	29
3968^{8}	**Misty Rain (57)** (BWHills) **3-8-13** TSprake(12) (hld up: effrt & nt clr run over 2f out: swtchd outside: kpt on: no imp)	½	**9**	12/1	56	27
4324^{4}	**Forest Fantasy (56)** (JWharton) **4-9-2** JFortune(13) (lw: in tch: effrt 4f out: wknd over 2f out)	2	**10**	12/1	52	27
3330^{8}	**Lapu-Lapu (53)** (MJCamacho) **4-8-13** LCharnock(1) (trckd ldrs: led 4f out tl hdd & wknd over 1f out)	2½	**11**	12/1	44	19
4283^{18}	**Royal Ceilidh (IRE) (65)** (DenysSmith) **4-9-11** JWeaver(7) (hld up: effrt over 3f out: sn wknd)	½	**12**	14/1	55	30
4147^{24}	**No Cliches (68)** (DNicholls) **4-10-0v**^{1} AlexGreaves(5) (lw: led to 4f out: wknd 2f out)	3	**13**	12/1	53	28
2884^{5}	**Tilaal (USA) (62)** (MDHammond) **5-9-5**(3) PFessey(2) (in tch: drvn along 4f out: sn wknd)	2	**14**	50/1	43	18
4283^{11}	**Running Green (64)** (DMoffatt) **6-9-7v**(3) DarrenMoffatt(16) (b: w ldrs tl wknd 2f out)	1½	**15**	14/1	43	18
	Five Live (60) (MDHammond) **3-9-2** DaleGibson(11) (plld hrd: sn bhd: t.o)	30	**16**	66/1	—	—

(SP 135.8%) **16 Rn**

1m 52.5 (1.80) CSF £74.81 CT £796.94 TOTE £6.10: £1.40 £3.60 £2.00 £2.00 (£44.80) Trio £505.80 OWNER Ellway Racing (NEWMARKET) BRED C. H. Bothway

WEIGHT FOR AGE 3yo-4lb

4477 Polar Prospect, drawn on the outside, apparently had some difficulty handling the bend but, sent on coming to the final furlong, never looked in any real danger. (5/1)

4386 Priolo Prima, who presumably needed it last time, was given time to recover after a slow break. Staying on nicely inside the last, the impression was that with a little more help from the saddle, he would seriously have troubled the winner. Definitely something of an unlucky horse, he certainly has the ability to win better races than this. (14/1)

3937 Mukhatab, who has tumbled down the weights, was well backed both in the morning and on the track. After travelling strongly, he hung fire but was persuaded to put his best foot forward towards the finish. (12/1: op 8/1)

4210 Bowcliffe, as usual, travelled strongly, After running into trouble halfway up the straight, his rider showed a marked lack of urgency. Staying on at the finish, another prize is surely just around the corner. (11/1)

House of Dreams, a winning hurdler, was having only his second outing this time. Making up a lot of ground in the final quarter-mile, the outing will definitely have brought him on. (40/1)

4184* Gymcrak Premiere, who won a seller last time, found this company too tough. (11/2)
4210 Java Red (IRE), who must come from the back, was flat out turning in. With a wall of horses in front of him, he was switched outside over a furlong out and, although staying on, was never going to be a factor. A horse who has to be ridden like him needs everything to go just right, and he is better on tracks with an uphill finish. (4/1)

4597 E.B.F. PICKERING MAIDEN STKS (2-Y.O F) (Class D)

3-10 (3-13) **6f** £3,317.50 (£1,000.00: £485.00: £227.50) Stalls: High GOING minus 0.52 sec per fur (F)

				SP	RR	SF
4103[8]	**Sense of Wonder** (BJMeehan) **2-8-11** KDarley(7) (w ldr: disp ld ½-wy: hung lft: led over 1f out: jst hld on)	—	**1**	9/2[3]	80	41
4332[2]	**Final Tango** (JHMGosden) **2-8-11** LDettori(8) (trckd ldrs: chal fnl f: jst failed)	s.h	**2**	5/4[1]	80	41
2312[3]	**Light Step (USA)** (HRACecil) **2-8-11** KFallon(6) (lw: led: hung lft & hdd over 1f out: nt qckn)	2½	**3**	9/4[2]	73	34
3965[9]	**Sada (80)** (MajorWRHern) **2-8-11** TSprake(4) (trckd ldrs: effrt & swtchd outside over 2f out: nt qckn appr fnl f)	½	**4**	9/1	72	33
4267[13]	**Poetry In Motion (IRE)** (EJAlston) **2-8-11** JFEgan(1) (hld up & bhd: hdwy over 1f out: nvr nr to chal)	5	**5**	33/1	59+	20
	Jayess Elle (JGFitzGerald) **2-8-11** JWeaver(3) (neat: bit bkwd: sn outpcd & bhd: rn green: n.d)	½	**6**	33/1	57	18
2516[8]	**Phantom Ring** (ABailey) **2-8-11** SSanders(5) (b: chsd ldrs: rdn over 2f out: wknd over 1f out)	1	**7**	16/1	55	16
4212[5]	**Chimes of Peace** (JLEyre) **2-8-11** OPears(9) (s.i.s: a outpcd)	1¼	**8**	33/1	51	12
4227[5]	**Dublivia** (CADwyer) **2-8-11** JFortune(2) (sn outpcd & bhd)	4	**9**	20/1	41	2
				(SP 122.9%)	**9 Rn**	

1m 10.9 (0.70) CSF £9.94 TOTE £6.50: £1.80 £1.10 £1.40 (£10.20) Trio £6.10 OWNER Mr D. H. L. Thompson (UPPER LAMBOURN) BRED Godolphin Management Co Ltd

Sense of Wonder, poorly drawn on her debut, showed a good action going down. Tending to hang off the fence, in the end she hung on by the skin of her teeth. (9/2)
4332 Final Tango went down in smooth style. She had clearly learnt from her first outing and, after throwing down a strong challenge, was only just denied. Her turn is surely only delayed. (5/4)
2312 Light Step (USA), keen going to post, wanted to do nothing but hang left. (9/4)
3474 Sada, officially rated 80, is the true test of the value of the form. (9/1: 6/1-10/1)
Poetry In Motion (IRE), having her third outing, is still learning the ropes. Now qualified for a handicap mark, she is certainly capable of better. (33/1)
Jayess Elle, who looked in need of the run, showed a pronounced knee action going down and had not a clue on the way back. (33/1)

4598 WEATHERBYS BULLETIN MAGAZINE H'CAP (0-80) (3-Y.O+) (Class D)

3-40 (3-40) **1m 6f 19y** £3,532.00 (£1,066.00: £518.00: £244.00) Stalls: Centre GOING minus 0.52 sec per fur (F)

				SP	RR	SF
4372[4]	**Royal Castle (IRE) (74)** (MajorWRHern) **3-9-10** TSprake(1) (trckd ldrs: shkn up to ld over 3f out: rdn clr over 1f out: eased towards fin)	—	**1**	11/10[1]	86	43
4435[4]	**Ordained (52)** (EJAlston) **4-8-11** JFEgan(4) (lw: hld up: hdwy to chal 3f out: sn rdn & no imp)	7	**2**	11/4[3]	56	22
4466[6]	**Exactly (IRE) (55)** (JLEyre) **4-9-0** TWilliams(2) (trckd ldr: led 6f out tl over 3f out: sn btn)	8	**3**	5/2[2]	50	16
4288[7]	**Golden Hello (64)** (TDEasterby) **6-9-9** JFortune(3) (led to 6f out: wknd 3f out)	3½	**4**	14/1	55	21
				(SP 109.5%)	**4 Rn**	

3m 3.5 (4.20) CSF £4.08 TOTE £1.70 (£1.80) OWNER Lord Weinstock (LAMBOURN) BRED Ballymacoll Stud Farm Ltd
WEIGHT FOR AGE 3yo-9lb

4372 Royal Castle (IRE), shaken up to take charge, was ridden clear and is value for a ten-length success. (11/10: evens-6/5)
4435 Ordained, who has to be held up, made her challenge far too soon and in the end was readily shaken off. (11/4)
4466 Exactly (IRE), best forcing the pace, on this occasion was happy to get a lead. Trying to quicken up turning in, she was soon put well and truly in her place. (5/2)
4288 Golden Hello led on sufferance but he did not set a strong enough pace. Having trouble making the tight home turn, he dropped out without a struggle. (14/1)

4599 CASTLETON CONDITIONS STKS (3-Y.O+) (Class C)

4-10 (4-10) **7f** £4,784.37 (£1,737.50: £843.75: £356.25: £153.13) Stalls: High GOING minus 0.52 sec per fur (F)

				SP	RR	SF
4377[2]	**Restructure (IRE) (108)** (MrsJCecil) **5-9-6** JWeaver(4) (lw: b.off fore: led 1f: rdn to ld appr fnl f: styd on strly)	—	**1**	8/11[1]	115	74
4421[7]	**Rambling Bear (109)** (MBlanshard) **4-9-6** KDarley(1) (lw: led after 1f tl appr fnl f: no ex)	3	**2**	7/2[3]	108	67
4120[6]	**Well Warned (104)** (BWHills) **3-8-7** KFallon(3) (b.hind: trckd ldrs: effrt over 2f out: rdn: edgd rt & wknd over 1f out)	1¾	**3**	3/1[2]	93	50
4467[3]	**Venture Capitalist (92)** (DNicholls) **8-9-6** AlexGreaves(2) (stdd s: sn trckng ldrs: effrt over 2f out: wknd & eased over 1f out)	9	**4**	14/1	84	43
				(SP 111.8%)	**4 Rn**	

1m 21.8 CSF £3.47 TOTE £1.50 (£2.40) OWNER Mr Martin Myers (NEWMARKET) BRED J. H. Stone
WEIGHT FOR AGE 3yo-2lb

4377 Restructure (IRE), happy to get a lead, gained an overdue first success this year, eventually winning in fine style. (8/11)
4239 Rambling Bear, best coming from behind over five furlongs, surprisingly soon set the pace but, as expected, the winner brushed him aside in the final furlong. (7/2)
4120 Well Warned, best in on official figures, was keen going to post. Under pressure, she edged right and produced very little. (3/1)
4467 Venture Capitalist, who is off the boil at present, never settled and, with his stamina giving out, he was allowed to coast home. (14/1: 10/1-16/1)

4600 GUISBOROUGH MAIDEN STKS (3-Y.O) (Class D)

4-40 (4-40) **6f** £3,525.50 (£1,064.00: £517.00: £243.50) Stalls: High GOING minus 0.52 sec per fur (F)

				SP	RR	SF
4301[2]	**Beyond Calculation (USA) (68)** (PWHarris) **3-8-9**(5) CLowther(1) (lw: w ldr: led over 1f out: styd on u.p)	—	**1**	5/2[2]	80	46
4452[2]	**Listed Account (USA) (74)** (LMCumani) **3-8-9** LDettori(6) (lw: led: shkn up over 2f out: hdd over 1f out: nt qckn)	1¾	**2**	4/9[1]	70	36
4563[8]	**Democrat** (SirMarkPrescott) **3-9-0** SSanders(4) (dwlt: sme hdwy over 2f out: hung lft: nvr nr ldrs)	9	**3**	10/1[3]	51	17
4431[8]	**Woodetto (IRE) (51)** (EWeymes) **3-9-0** JFanning(5) (sn outpcd: sme hdwy ½-wy: n.d)	1½	**4**	66/1	47	13
3086[7]	**Mischievous Time (37)** (ASmith) **3-9-0** RLappin(3) (chsd ldrs: rdn ½-wy: sn lost pl)	14	**5**	150/1	10	—
				(SP 109.0%)	**5 Rn**	

1m 10.7 (0.50) CSF £3.53 TOTE £3.70: £1.20 £1.10 (£1.30) OWNER Abacus (BERKHAMSTED) BRED Pendley Farm

4301 Beyond Calculation (USA), who would have been 11lb worse off with the favourite in a handicap, showed by far the greater resolution. (5/2)
4452 Listed Account (USA) looked to have been found an easy opening to finally get off the mark but, after making the running travelling strongly, when shaken up she simply would not put her best foot forward. (4/9)
Democrat, who showed a very poor action going down, was having his second outing in three days after making a belated debut. Despite hanging, he kept on but clearly has a problem. (10/1: 6/1-11/1)

4601 SETTRINGTON H'CAP (0-70) (3-Y.O) (Class E)
5-10 (5-13) **7f** £3,190.75 (£961.00: £465.50: £217.75) Stalls: High GOING minus 0.52 sec per fur (F)

Form	Horse	Dist	Pos	SP	RR	SF
4410[15]	**Smokey From Caplaw (65)** (JJO'Neill) **3-9-2** JFEgan(13) (trckd ldrs: effrt over 1f out: r.o to ld nr fin)	—	**1**	8/1[3]	73	54
4546[8]	**Maladerie (IRE) (58)** (MRChannon) **3-8-9** SSanders(14) (sn trckng ldrs: led over 2f out tl nr fin)	½	**2**	9/1	65	46
4016*	**King Uno (53)** (MrsJRRamsden) **3-8-4v** TSprake(1) (trckd ldr far side gng wl: ev ch 1f out: kpt on same pce u.p)	2	**3**	10/1	55	36
4300[5]	**Kosevo (IRE) (45)** (MGMeagher) **3-7-7**(3) PFessey(3) (racd far side: w ldrs: nt qckn appr fnl f)	1¾	**4**	50/1	43	24
2004[5]	**Brave Envoy (60)** (MJHeaton-Ellis) **3-8-11** JWeaver(8) (mid div: hrd rdn ½-wy: styd on fnl 2f)	½	**5**	16/1	57	38
4220[5]	**Muscatana (57)** (BWHills) **3-8-8** JFortune(18) (plld hrd: sn trckng ldrs: kpt on same pce fnl 2f)	s.h	**6**	6/1[1]	54	35
4291[6]	**Polenka (IRE) (50)** (JWWatts) **3-8-1** LCharnock(12) (chsd ldrs: rdn over 2f out: one pce)	1	**7**	10/1	45	26
4164[2]	**Two On The Bridge (56)** (DenysSmith) **3-8-7**ow1 KFallon(2) (racd far side: hdwy over 2f out: edgd lft & wknd over 1f out)	1½	**8**	6/1[1]	47	27
4328*	**Petite Danseuse (62)** (DWChapman) **3-8-13** LDettori(15) (hld up: effrt over 2f out: sn rdn & hung lft: nvr nr to chal)	1	**9**	7/1[2]	51	32
4436[9]	**Sharpo Wassl (70)** (WJHaggas) **3-9-2**(5) JoHunnam(16) (lw: chsd ldrs: rdn over 2f out: sn btn)	3	**10**	8/1[3]	52	33
4436[10]	**Mystique Air (IRE) (59)** (EWeymes) **3-8-10** KDarley(23) (racd stands' side: chsd ldrs tl wknd 2f out)	s.h	**11**	10/1	41	22
3601[8]	**Bali-Pet (46)** (JParkes) **3-7-4b**(7)ow1 DMernagh(11) (nvr bttr than mid div)	1¾	**12**	100/1	24	4
4291[16]	**In Good Nick (46)** (MWEasterby) **3-7-8b**(3)ow1 DarrenMoffatt(19) (chsd ldr tl lost pl 3f out)	½	**13**	33/1	23	3
4049[11]	**Toss And Tumble (48)** (WWHaigh) **3-7-13** TWilliams(6) (swtchd rt s: n.d)	s.h	**14**	33/1	25	6
3868[8]	**Freedom of Troy (46)** (JLEyre) **3-7-6**(5)ow1 KimberleyHart(17) (hld up: effrt over 2f out: n.d)	s.h	**15**	50/1	23	3
3968[6]	**La Doyenne (IRE) (46)** (CBBBooth) **3-7-11**ow1 FNorton(9) (chsd ldrs tl lost pl over 2f out)	1¼	**16**	11/1	20	—
1756[9]	**Why O Six (49)** (RAFahey) **3-7-7**(7)ow4 RWinston(4) (racd far side: chsd ldrs tl wknd over 2f out)	2	**17**	33/1	18	—
4214[11]	**Alisadara (45)** (NBycroft) **3-7-3**(7) JennyBenson(21) (sn outpcd & bhd)	1¼	**18**	100/1	11	—
4290[7]	**Imperial Line (IRE) (46)** (ABMulholland) **3-7-11b**ow1 NCarlisle(7) (b: led tl over 2f out: sn wknd)	s.h	**19**	50/1	12	—
4049[13]	**Redspet (45)** (SRBowring) **3-7-5**(5) IonaWands(24) (racd stands' side: outpcd fr ½-wy)	¾	**20**	100/1	10	—
3088[9]	**Mill End Boy (46)** (MWEasterby) **3-7-11** DaleGibson(10) (mid div: hrd rdn ½-wy: sn bhd)	½	**21**	25/1	9	—
1580[9]	**Highly Respected (IRE) (60)** (ABailey) **3-8-11** DWright(20) (sn bhd & rdn along)	1¾	**22**	20/1	19	—
1423[14]	**Victoria House (IRE) (45)** (MJHeaton-Ellis) **3-7-10** NVarley(22) (racd stands' side: outpcd fr ½-wy)	hd	**23**	50/1	4	—
4051[8]	**Superapparos (45)** (SRBowring) **3-7-10** JBramhill(5) (racd far side: chsd ldrs over 4f: sn wknd)	½	**24**	33/1	3	—

(SP 146.0%) **24 Rn**

1m 23.2 (0.20) CSF £75.41 CT £714.35 TOTE £10.30: £2.10 £2.10 £4.70 £10.50 (£85.70) Trio £214.00 OWNER Mr G. P. Bernacchi (PENRITH) BRED Gino P. Bernacchi
LONG HANDICAP In Good Nick 7-9 Kosevo (IRE) 6-12 La Doyenne (IRE) 7-8 Bali-Pet 6-7 Imperial Line (IRE) 6-13 Redspet 6-4 Alisadara 6-3 Freedom of Troy 6-12 Victoria House (IRE) 7-5 Superapparos 7-0
3801 Smokey From Caplaw was 4lb lower in the weights than when winning at Thirsk in May. Under pressure, he certainly showed real determination. (8/1)
4333 Maladerie (IRE), who was poorly drawn when well beaten at Lingfield four days earlier, was only just collared. (9/1)
4016* King Uno, one of a handful to race on the far side, looked full of running but, kicking for home a furlong out, did not find as much as expected. he probably does better when able to be covered up longer. (10/1)
4300 Kosevo (IRE), who had shown nothing in three previous outings this year, did remarkably well considering he was 12lb out of the handicap. (50/1)
2004 Brave Envoy is a very hard ride who, one day, will get his jockey into trouble for his use of the whip. (16/1)
4220 Muscatana raced too keenly for her own good. She kept on surprisingly well and is probably better suited by a round track. (6/1)
4164 Two On The Bridge is not very consistent. (6/1)
3968 La Doyenne (IRE) (11/1: 8/1-12/1)

T/Plpt: £12.90 (1,598.46 Tckts). T/Qdpt: £2.10 (374.51 Tckts) WG

3814-WARWICK (L-H) (Good to firm)
Tuesday October 7th
WEATHER: sunny but cool WIND: fresh bhd

4602 POPPY BUS MAIDEN AUCTION STKS (2-Y.O) (Class E)
2-00 (2-02) **6f** £3,382.25 (£1,013.00: £486.50: £223.25) Stalls: Low GOING minus 0.26 sec per fur (GF)

Form	Horse	Dist	Pos	SP	RR	SF
4459[3]	**Grace Browning** (HCandy) **2-8-0** CRutter(7) (hld up: hdwy on ins ent st: led over 1f out: comf)	—	**1**	10/1	81+	30
4216[2]	**Bandbox (IRE) (78)** (SMellor) **2-8-8** JReid(8) (lw: led over 2f: led wl over 1f out: sn hdd: one pce)	1¾	**2**	15/8[1]	84	33
3228[9]	**Scene (IRE) (45)** (MartynMeade) **2-8-0** GDuffield(10) (swtg: a.p: kpt on u.p ins fnl f)	3	**3**	40/1	68	17
4216[6]	**Majalis** (RGuest) **2-8-5** PBloomfield(9) (in tch: outpcd 2f out: rallied u.p appr fnl f: r.o)	1	**4**	5/1[3]	71	20
	Ok Babe (JAkehurst) **2-8-1**ow2 DBiggs(4) (leggy: lt-f: bit bkwd: led over 3f out tl wl over 1f out: btn whn hmpd ent fnl f)	1¼	**5**	20/1	60	10
4298[4]	**Atlanta** (JLDunlop) **2-7-13** JQuinn(11) (plld hrd: trckd ldrs: rdn & wknd over 1f out)	¾	**6**	7/2[2]	56	8
1692[5]	**Blundell Lane (IRE)** (APJarvis) **2-8-9** SDrowne(12) (bkwd: bhd fnl 3f)	2½	**7**	16/1	59	12
3961a[25]	**Whacker-Do (IRE) (64)** (RHollinshead) **2-8-5** FLynch(2) (chsd ldrs 4f)	1¼	**8**	25/1	52	4
4402[3]	**Red Pepper (IRE) (68)** (PHowling) **2-8-7** SWhitworth(1) (sn pushed along: a bhd)	nk	**9**	14/1	53	6
	Casual Magic (MajorDNChappell) **2-8-10** NAdams(6) (w'like: leggy: bkwd: s.i.s: a bhd & outpcd: t.o)	9	**10**	33/1	32	—
3905[20]	**Benrock (IRE)** (CaptJWilson) **2-7-12**(7) AngelaHartley(5) (lw: s.s: a bhd: t.o)	2½	**11**	50/1	21	—
	Bon Sizzle (JRFanshawe) **2-8-7** NDay(3) (lengthy: unf: bkwd: s.s: a bhd & outpcd: t.o)	1¾	**12**	16/1	18	—

(SP 117.1%) **12 Rn**

1m 14.4 (2.40) CSF £24.78 TOTE £7.70: £2.00 £1.30 £22.80 (£11.80) Trio £132.10 OWNER Mrs Robert Langton (WANTAGE) BRED Mrs P. J. Fairbarns

4459 Grace Browning improved on her initial outing with a comfortably-gained success, and there should be no reason why she cannot continue to improve. (10/1)

4216 Bandbox (IRE), filling the runner-up spot for the fourth time, did not appear to do anything wrong but he once again found one too good, and that first success is taking time to come his way. (15/8)

1616 Scene (IRE) ran much better with stronger handling, and was still staying on at the finish to suggest that a longer trip cold bring out the best in her. (40/1)

4216 Majalis was poised to challenge turning in, but she then got tapped for speed as the tempo picked up, and her attempt to rally inside the last furlong was never quite going to succeed. (5/1)

Ok Babe, a lightly-made debutante whose dam was a prolific winner over the minimum trip, showed plenty of promise but she was already feeling the strain when the runner-up took her ground entering the final furlong. (20/1)

4298 Atlanta failed to produce her running on this much livelier ground, and she was under pressure and in trouble early in the straight. (7/2: op 7/4)

4402 Red Pepper (IRE) (14/1: op 8/1)

4603 E.B.F. BRINKLOW MAIDEN STKS (2-Y.O C & G) (Class D)

2-30 (2-32) **7f** £3,819.25 (£1,144.00: £549.50: £252.25) Stalls: Low GOING minus 0.26 sec per fur (GF)

				SP	RR	SF
3686[16]	**Komistar** (PWHarris) **2-8-11** AClark(13) (w ldrs: led 5f out tl over 3f out: led over 2f out: clr over 1f out: pushed out)	—	**1**	33/1	93+	51
3862[2]	**Zydeco (IRE)** (MCPipe) **2-8-11** WRyan(14) (hld up: hdwy over 2f out: chsd wnr fnl f: no imp)	5	**2**	100/30[2]	82	40
3887[2]	**Guaranteed (84)** (BWHills) **2-8-11** MHills(11) (hld up: hdwy 2f out: sn rdn & hung lft: one pce fnl f)	hd	**3**	11/4[1]	81	39
4113[9]	**Rhein Hill (IRE)** (PWHarris) **2-8-11** RHills(3) (hld up: hdwy 2f out: r.o one pce fnl f)	3½	**4**	33/1	73	31
4174[8]	**Mark of Prophet (IRE)** (JEBanks) **2-8-11** JQuinn(4) (trckd ldrs: outpcd 2f out: styd on fnl f)	hd	**5**	20/1	73	31
4384[3]	**Fly By Night (IRE) (85)** (MRStoute) **2-8-11** RCochrane(12) (trckd ldrs tl wknd over 2f out)	1½	**6**	6/1	70	28
	Desert Mirage (PWChapple-Hyam) **2-8-11** JReid(8) (leggy: w ldrs: led over 3f out tl over 2f out: wknd qckly over 1f out)	s.h	**7**	4/1[3]	70	28
4237[17]	**Beauchamp Magic** (JLDunlop) **2-8-11** MRimmer(6) (nvr nr ldrs)	5	**8**	33/1	58	16
4428[4]	**Howies Choice (IRE) (75)** (KMcAuliffe) **2-8-11** JCarroll(16) (prom over 4f)	¾	**9**	20/1	56	14
4379[4]	**Torrent (80)** (PFICole) **2-8-11** TQuinn(5) (hld up: wknd over 2f out)	1½	**10**	8/1	53	11
3686[21]	**Porthilly Buoy** (MJHaynes) **2-8-4**(7) MCornally(1) (a bhd)	nk	**11**	50/1	52	10
4157[8]	**Final Settlement (IRE)** (JRJenkins) **2-8-11** NDay(9) (led 2f: wknd 3f out)	3½	**12**	40/1	44	2
	Omar's Odyssey (IRE) (PMitchell) **2-8-11** DaneO'Neill(7) (unf: scope: s.s: a bhd)	2	**13**	50/1	40	—
4515[12]	**Hunt Hill (IRE)** (SirMarkPrescott) **2-8-11** CNutter(15) (lw: a bhd)	s.h	**14**	25/1	40	—
4515[13]	**Pressurise** (SirMarkPrescott) **2-8-11** GDuffield(10) (a bhd)	1	**15**	12/1	37	—
4298[9]	**Browning** (LordHuntingdon) **2-8-11** RPerham(2) (w ldrs over 4f)	s.h	**16**	20/1	37	—
				(SP 136.1%)	**16 Rn**	

1m 26.5 (1.90) CSF £131.50 TOTE £36.60: £4.60 £2.00 £1.60 (£201.70) Trio £91.30 OWNER Class Act (BERKHAMSTED) BRED Mrs S. Pepper

OFFICIAL EXPLANATION **Komistar: Regarding the improvement in form, the colt had appreciated today's extra furlong and easier ground.**

Komistar, the first foal of a mile and a half winner, had shown nothing on his debut but there was plenty to like about this performance over an extra furlong. (33/1)

3862 Zydeco (IRE), who has changed stables, was only playing for the places here and may do better over a mile. (100/30: 9/4-7/2)

3887 Guaranteed is proving difficult to win with and all he wanted to do was lean on the runner-up in the closing stages. (11/4)

Rhein Hill (IRE), a half-brother to Ascot Gold Cup and Irish St Leger second Tyrone Bridge, is certainly bred to stay, being out of a Lancashire Oaks winner. (33/1)

Mark of Prophet (IRE) is a half-brother to seven furlong and mile scorer-cum-hurdler Cointosser. (20/1)

4384 Fly By Night (IRE) did not adopt his front-running tactics on this return to seven. (6/1: 4/1-13/2)

Desert Mirage, a half-brother to three winners at up to seven furlongs, tied up badly and may do better sprinting. (4/1)

4604 E.B.F. MAIDEN STKS (2-Y.O F) (Class D)

3-00 (3-06) **7f** £3,848.50 (£1,153.00: £554.00: £254.50) Stalls: Low GOING minus 0.26 sec per fur (GF)

				SP	RR	SF
4317[5]	**Red Leggings** (JWHills) **2-8-11** MHills(13) (a.p: led over 1f out: clr fnl f)	—	**1**	9/2[2]	76	38
4103[10]	**Spree Rose** (KOCunningham-Brown) **2-8-11** MartinDwyer(14) (led tl hdd over 1f out: r.o one pce)	3	**2**	33/1	69	31
4332[6]	**Oare Kite** (PTWalwyn) **2-8-11** JCarroll(10) (a.p: ev ch over 1f out: sn rdn & outpcd)	1½	**3**	10/1	66	28
	Zany Lady (RJHodges) **2-8-11** SDrowne(11) (wl grwn: bkwd: hld up: hdwy over 2f out: kpt on ins fnl f)	1¼	**4**	10/1	63	25
	Moonshadow (IRE) (HRACecil) **2-8-11** WRyan(2) (lt-f: bit bkwd: trckd ldrs: no hdwy fnl 2f)	2½	**5**	9/4[1]	57	19
	Grosvenor Spirit (IRE) (PWChapple-Hyam) **2-8-11** JReid(1) (w'like: scope: bit bkwd: b.off hind: s.i.s: sn chsng ldrs: drvn along & wknd 2f out)	1½	**6**	6/1[3]	54	16
4298[17]	**Baby Spice** (MRChannon) **2-8-11** DaneO'Neill(5) (hld up & bhd: rdn & hdwy 2f out: nvr nrr)	½	**7**	33/1	53	15
4317[12]	**Savoury** (JLDunlop) **2-8-11** GCarter(7) (trckd ldrs tl wknd 2f out)	1	**8**	12/1	50	12
4479[9]	**Dorton Grange** (KCComerford) **2-8-4**(7) JBosley(4) (hld up: hdwy ½-wy: wknd fnl 2f)	3½	**9**	50/1	42	4
	Treasure Island (SirMarkPrescott) **2-8-11** GDuffield(6) (lt-f: unf: trckd ldrs 4f)	3	**10**	12/1	35	—
	Flicker (LordHuntingdon) **2-8-11** RPerham(15) (lt-f: unf: a in rr)	3	**11**	25/1	29	—
	Scapestrata (USA) (PFICole) **2-8-11** TQuinn(9) (lengthy: unf: s.i.s: a bhd)	nk	**12**	8/1	28	—
	Ivy Bird (IRE) (WJarvis) **2-8-11** JQuinn(3) (lt-f: unf: bit bkwd: mid div: pushed along ½-wy: sn lost tch)	2½	**13**	16/1	22	—
	Cool Waters (JRArnold) **2-8-11** AClark(12) (b.hind: leggy: a bhd & outpcd: t.o)	20	**14**	25/1	—	—
	The Robe (BJMeehan) **2-8-11** MTebbutt(8) (Withdrawn not under Starter's orders: unruly at s)		**W**	25/1	—	—
				(SP 133.2%)	**14 Rn**	

1m 27.6 (3.00) CSF £149.47 TOTE £4.50: £1.80 £7.30 £3.70 (£126.80) Trio £323.70; £227.97 to York 8/10/97 OWNER Mrs Claire Smith (LAMBOURN) BRED Ford Farm Bloodstock

4317 Red Leggings, much the wiser for the experience gained at Kempton, stepped up a gear to take command below the distance and quickly put the issue beyond doubt. She still left the impression that she will be a better filly next year. (9/2)

Spree Rose had far more use made of her than she did on her debut and only the winner was able to get past her. She is out of a middle-distance winner and she should be able to pay her way. (33/1)

4332 Oare Kite posed a serious threat when almost upsides the winner inside the last quarter-mile, but she was unable to increase her pace and was soon fighting a losing battle. (10/1: op 4/1)

Zany Lady, a well-grown half-sister to a couple of winning hurdlers, and very much in need of the run, was surprisingly nibbled at in the market. She has gone completely in her coat and, in the circumstances, performed with credit, and it would be wise to put her away until next year. (10/1: op 33/1)
Moonshadow (IRE), a very uneasy favourite, is a sparely-made filly who looks as though she could improve with time. Never able to land a blow, she will be all the better for the experience. (9/4: op 5/4)
Grosvenor Spirit (IRE), a May foal with plenty of scope, recovered from her sluggish start to track the leaders, but she was being nudged along entering the straight and could do little more than stay on at the one pace. (6/1: op 3/1)
Scapestrata (USA) (8/1: 4/1-9/1)

4605 MOSELEY RUGBY CLUB NURSERY H'CAP (0-85) (2-Y.O) (Class D)
3-30 (3-33) **1m** £3,848.50 (£1,153.00: £554.00: £254.50) Stalls: Low GOING minus 0.26 sec per fur (GF)

				SP	RR	SF
3990[6]	**Carry The Flag (84)** (PFICole) **2-9-7** TQuinn(11) (lw: a.p: rdn to ld ins fnl f: r.o wl)	—	**1**	100/30[1]	91	43
3904[5]	**Opposition Leader (76)** (BWHills) **2-8-13** MHills(12) (a.p: r.o one pce fnl f)	2½	**2**	7/1	78	30
4508[5]	**Heathyards Sheik (69)** (RHollinshead) **2-8-6** FLynch(13) (lw: hld up & bhd: hdwy over 2f out: edgd lft over 1f out: edgd rt fnl f: r.o)	s.h	**3**	7/1	71	23
4299[4]	**Casino Ace (IRE) (77)** (PWChapple-Hyam) **2-9-0** JReid(7) (led: hrd rdn over 1f out: hdd ins fnl f)	¾	**4**	13/2[3]	77	29
4334[10]	**Naked Oat (68)** (BSmart) **2-8-2**(3) RFfrench(3) (hld up: swtchd lft & hdwy over 1f out: nt rch ldrs)	¾	**5**	20/1	67	19
4330[7]	**Nisaba (IRE) (66)** (MJohnston) **2-8-3** GHind(6) (prom over 6f)	7	**6**	12/1	51	3
4427[3]	**The Honorable Lady (60)** (MRChannon) **2-7-11** JQuinn(2) (lw: prom over 5f)	2½	**7**	9/1	40	—
4334[9]	**After Dawn (IRE) (59)** (MrsPNDutfield) **2-7-10** GBardwell(8) (nvr trbld ldrs)	2	**8**	50/1	35	—
4368[7]	**Czar Wars (70)** (PTDalton) **2-8-4**(3) RHavlin(10) (lw: prom over 6f)	½	**9**	8/1	45	—
4111[3]	**Green Jacket (82)** (JLDunlop) **2-9-5** GCarter(9) (bhd fnl 3f)	1¾	**10**	11/2[2]	53	5
4271[7]	**Generous Embrace (74)** (MBell) **2-8-6**(5) RMullen(1) (prom: rdn over 3f out: sn wknd)	3½	**11**	8/1	38	—
4361[6]	**Elba Magic (IRE) (61)** (CADwyer) **2-7-12**[ow1] AMackay(4) (lw: a bhd)	3½	**12**	20/1	18	—
				(SP 128.2%)	**12 Rn**	

1m 40.3 (3.90) CSF £25.94 CT £132.67 TOTE £5.00: £2.00 £2.90 £2.50 (£20.90) Trio £47.70 OWNER Mr Athos Christodoulou (WHATCOMBE) BRED A. Christodoulou
LONG HANDICAP After Dawn (IRE) 7-0
3990 Carry The Flag, a half-brother to Posidonas, showed just how well he stays on this faster ground. (100/30)
3904 Opposition Leader appreciated the mile, but it was the winner who was at the dispatch box. (7/1)
4508 Heathyards Sheik had an extra furlong this time but rather caused his own problems by wandering about in the home straight. (7/1: 5/1-8/1)
4299 Casino Ace (IRE) is bred for stamina rather then speed and it shows. (13/2)
4044 Naked Oat, dropped a total of 5lb, had been tried over a mile and a quarter since his reasonable effort at Bath. (20/1)
4427 The Honorable Lady (9/1: op 14/1)
4111 Green Jacket (11/2: 3/1-6/1)
3859* Generous Embrace (8/1: op 5/1)

4606 'PAUSE TO REMEMBER' LIMITED STKS (0-70) (3-Y.O+) (Class E)
4-00 (4-01) **1m** £3,122.25 (£933.00: £446.50: £203.25) Stalls: Low GOING minus 0.26 sec per fur (GF)

				SP	RR	SF
4552[6]	**Blewbury Hill (IRE) (70)** (RFJohnsonHoughton) **3-8-12** JReid(6) (mde all: clr whn edgd rt fnl 2f: rdn out)	—	**1**	9/4[1]	66	60
4455[3]	**May Queen Megan (41)** (MrsALMKing) **4-8-12** NAdams(7) (bhd: hdwy 3f out: rdn & kpt on ins fnl f: no ch w wnr)	6	**2**	33/1	51	48
4225[8]	**Defined Feature (IRE) (69)** (DrJDScargill) **4-8-12** JQuinn(8) (hdwy 2f out: rdn & hung lft fnl f: r.o)	nk	**3**	8/1	50	47
4071[9]	**Prime Light (68)** (GWragg) **4-9-1b** MHills(2) (sn chsng wnr: rdn 2f out: wknd fnl f)	½	**4**	6/1	52	49
4319[14]	**Lucky Archer (70)** (JMBradley) **4-9-1** SDrowne(12) (bkwd: hld up in tch: effrt ½-wy: hrd rdn 2f out: one pce)	2	**5**	16/1	48	45
4319[13]	**The Stager (IRE) (68)** (JRJenkins) **5-9-1** NDay(5) (bkwd: hdwy over 3f out: hrd rdn 2f out: no imp)	1¾	**6**	14/1	45	42
4449[5]	**City Gambler (69)** (GCBravery) **3-9-1** MRimmer(9) (nvr nr ldrs)	hd	**7**	7/1	48	42
4220[4]	**Calypso Lady (IRE) (68)** (RHannon) **3-8-9** DaneO'Neill(4) (hdwy 5f out: sn prom: wknd wl over 1f out)	hd	**8**	11/2[3]	42	36
4480[3]	**Lady Silk (28)** (MissJFCraze) **6-8-12** SWebster(11) (sn rdn along: a in rr)	7	**9**	33/1	28	25
4375[4]	**Irtifa (68)** (PTWalwyn) **3-8-9v** RHills(10) (swtg: prom: pushed along 4f out: wknd over 2f out)	2½	**10**	4/1[2]	23	17
4324[5]	**Saltando (IRE) (43)** (PatMitchell) **6-9-1** PBloomfield(1) (a bhd)	4	**11**	33/1	18	15
4221[17]	**Tashkent (60)** (RSimpson) **5-9-1** MGallagher(3) (a bhd: t.o)	16	**12**	40/1	—	—
				(SP 127.9%)	**12 Rn**	

1m 37.8 (1.40) CSF £91.79 TOTE £3.30: £1.80 £4.40 £2.70 (£34.70) Trio £204.90 OWNER Mr Anthony Pye-Jeary (DIDCOT) BRED Tullamaine Castle Stud and Partners
WEIGHT FOR AGE 3yo-3lb
4552 Blewbury Hill (IRE), having his second outing in five days, was taking a big step down in class. Soon bowling along at the head of affairs, Reid booted him clear early in the straight and, though he continued to drift right, was never given the chance to shirk the issue. (9/4)
4455 May Queen Megan came from way off the pace in the closing stages and stayed on to make sure of the runner-up prize nearing the line. (33/1)
3718 Defined Feature (IRE) continues to show promise but she is only just beginning to feel her way at a mile and, though she did stay on in the latter stages, was inclined to hang left. One could not learn a lot from this. (8/1: 6/1-9/1)
2845 Prime Light was the only one able to make a race of it, but he was getting nowhere when put under pressure entering the last quarter-mile and he lost second prize inside the final fifty yards. (6/1)
Lucky Archer still needed this despite a run fifteen days ago, but he showed he is gradually getting back to something like his best. (16/1)
The Stager (IRE) usually runs well when fresh and he attracted support in the ring, but his paddock appearance suggested he was far from the finished article, and he was never able to give his supporters much hope. (14/1)
4449 City Gambler (7/1: op 3/1)

4607 BRITISH LEGION CLAIMING H'CAP (0-60) (I) (3-Y.O+) (Class F)
4-30 (4-31) **1m 2f 169y** £2,596.90 (£718.40: £342.70) Stalls: Low GOING minus 0.26 sec per fur (GF)

				SP	RR	SF
4453*	**Fighting Times (47)** (CASmith) **5-9-1v** DeanMcKeown(20) (b: lw: hld up: hdwy over 4f out: led over 2f out: clr ins fnl f: jst hld on)	—	**1**	3/1[1]	58	30
4477[9]	**Guesstimation (USA) (60)** (JPearce) **8-9-9**(5) RMullen(4) (s.s: stdy hdwy over 2f out: n.m.r over 1f out: rdn & r.o wl ins fnl f: jst failed)	hd	**2**	5/1[2]	71	43
4275[20]	**Krayyan Dawn (40)** (JAkehurst) **7-8-8** GCarter(17) (a.p: one pce fnl 2f)	8	**3**	33/1	39	11

3897^{10}	**Miskin Heights (IRE) (40)** (KRBurke) **3-8-2** MartinDwyer(14) (lw: hdwy over 4f out: ev ch over 2f out: swtchd lft wl over 1f out: one pce)	¾	**4**	33/1	38	4
4519^{4}	**Doyenne (38)** (GLewis) **3-8-0b** NAdams(3) (hld up: hdwy 2f out: nvr nr to chal)	¾	**5**	16/1	35	1
3027^{7}	**Dino's Mistral (30)** (KAMorgan) **4-7-5**(7) PDoe(15) (prom tl wknd over 1f out)	s.h	**6**	33/1	27	—
4465^{10}	**Sharp Deed (IRE) (55)** (PJMakin) **3-9-3v** DHolland(11) (hld up: hdwy over 4f out: wknd wl over 1f out)	2½	**7**	9/1	48	14
4324^{16}	**Rambo Tango (39)** (BRCambidge) **3-8-1** JLowe(2) (hdwy over 2f out: n.d)	½	**8**	33/1	31	—
4484^{8}	**Windswept (IRE) (46)** (MCPipe) **4-9-0b** WRyan(19) (led: hdd over 2f out: sn wknd)	1¼	**9**	12/1	36	8
4373^{14}	**Deevee (37)** (CJBenstead) **8-8-5** GDuffield(5) (bhd fnl 3f)	3½	**10**	14/1	22	—
4453^{4}	**Explosive Power (53)** (GCBravery) **6-9-7** MRimmer(16) (prom tl wknd wl over 1f out)	5	**11**	7/1 3	31	3
4562^{16}	**Rival Bid (USA) (52)** (MrsNMacauley) **9-9-6** SDrowne(18) (b: prom over 6f)	3½	**12**	33/1	25	—
2522^{9}	**Gold Clipper (34)** (MJRyan) **3-7-10** GBardwell(7) (bkwd: plld hrd: sn prom: wknd over 3f out)	2½	**13**	12/1	3	—
4450^{3}	**Kirov Protege (IRE) (36)** (GLMoore) **5-8-4v** JQuinn(1) (a bhd)	4	**14**	8/1	—	—
4224^{11}	**Generous Present (40)** (JWPayne) **4-8-1b**(7) JacquelineCoppard(6) (hdwy 7f out: wknd over 3f out)	½	**15**	33/1	2	—
4415^{8}	**Weet A Bit (IRE) (47)** (RHollinshead) **3-8-6b1**(3) DGriffiths(9) (lw: eased whn no ch fnl 2f)	15	**16**	16/1	—	—
1441^{6}	**Northern Grey (45)** (AWCarroll) **5-8-6**(7)ow1 RStudholme(13) (b: bkwd: a bhd: t.o)	nk	**17**	20/1	—	—
1088^{12}	**Miss Imp (IRE) (37)** (PMitchell) **3-7-10**(3)ow3 RFfrench(10) (b: a bhd: t.o)	15	**18**	50/1	—	—
1632^{20}	**Tauten (IRE) (33)** (AJChamberlain) **7-8-1**ow1 DBiggs(12) (bkwd: a bhd: p.u lame ins fnl f)		**P**	33/1	—	—
				(SP 136.4%)	**19 Rn**	

2m 20.5 (6.50) CSF £15.11 CT £420.32 TOTE £4.10: £1.80 £2.00 £3.10 £9.20 (£7.10) Trio £341.40 OWNER Julian Graves Ltd (HANLEY SWAN) BRED C. Hitchings

LONG HANDICAP Miss Imp (IRE) 7-6 Gold Clipper 7-9

WEIGHT FOR AGE 3yo-6lb

OFFICIAL EXPLANATION **Guesstimation (USA): Trainer reported that the gelding is a tricky ride who needs to hit the front as late as possible, and that the rider only just got it wrong here.**

4453* Fighting Times, raised 8lb, stole this entering the final furlong because he rather caught the runner-up's rider napping, and left him with too much to do. (3/1)

4224 Guesstimation (USA) ideally needs to be produced as late as possible, but the winner's tactics meant the post came a fraction too soon. (5/1)

Krayyan Dawn, having come down a total of 7lb, ran by far his best race since returning after a lengthy lay-off. (33/1)

Miskin Heights (IRE) showed her first signs of ability. (33/1)

4519 Doyenne settled much better in the blinkers this time but unfortunately did not have such a stiff test of stamina. (16/1)

2911 Dino's Mistral has changed stables. (33/1)

3134 Sharp Deed (IRE) (9/1: op 6/1)

4450 Kirov Protege (IRE) (8/1: op 16/1)

4608 BRITISH LEGION CLAIMING H'CAP (0-60) (II) (3-Y.O+) (Class F)

5-00 (5-03) **1m 2f 169y** £2,573.80 (£711.80: £339.40) Stalls: Low GOING minus 0.26 sec per fur (GF)

				SP	RR	SF
3601^{6}	**Misterton (34)** (JAGlover) **3-7-5**(5) APolli(18) (trckd ldrs: hrd rdn to ld wl ins fnl f: all out)	—	**1**	20/1	45	13
4504^{14}	**Harvey White (IRE) (53)** (JPearce) **5-9-7** AClark(7) (hld up: hdwy ent st: str chal fnl f: jst failed)	hd	**2**	8/1 3	64	38
3767^{3}	**Oozlem (IRE) (33)** (LMontagueHall) **8-7-12b**(3) RFfrench(17) (hld up in rr: hdwy over 2f out: fin strly)	1¼	**3**	8/1 3	42	16
3626^{8}	**Daira (50)** (JDBethell) **4-9-4** TQuinn(2) (lw: hld up: hdwy 4f out: effrt & rdn over 1f out: nt qckn)	hd	**4**	8/1 3	59	33
*2164**	**State Approval (58)** (PEccles) **4-9-7**(5) GFaulkner(5) (bit bkwd: led: rdn 2f out: hdd & no ex wl ins fnl f)	s.h	**5**	5/1 1	67	41
4472^{12}	**Jimjareer (IRE) (33)** (CaptJWilson) **4-8-1** AMackay(6) (a chsng ldrs: rdn over 2f out: sn btn)	2½	**6**	33/1	38	12
4373^{6}	**Fancy Design (IRE) (40)** (PMitchell) **4-8-8** DaneO'Neill(11) (hld up: effrt 3f out: nt rch ldrs)	5	**7**	8/1 3	38	12
3919^{14}	**Erlking (IRE) (46)** (SMellor) **7-9-0b** MWigham(16) (chsd ldrs: rdn over 2f out: grad wknd)	3½	**8**	7/1 2	38	12
4224^{7}	**Runic Symbol (35)** (MBlanshard) **6-8-3** CRutter(14) (sme late hdwy: nvr nrr)	2	**9**	14/1	25	—
4453^{5}	**Dannistar (45)** (WMBrisbourne) **5-8-13** AGarth(13) (b.off hind: trckd ldrs: hrd rdn over 2f out: sn btn)	1	**10**	10/1	33	7
4373^{10}	**Velvet Jones (37)** (GFHCharles-Jones) **4-8-5** SWhitworth(15) (hld up: hdwy 4f out: rdn & wknd over 2f out)	2½	**11**	12/1	21	—
2916^{13}	**Northern Saga (IRE) (32)** (CJDrewe) **4-8-0** NAdams(4) (bit bkwd: s.s: hdwy 8f out: wknd 3f out)	4	**12**	25/1	10	—
4371^{13}	**Little Pilgrim (28)** (TMJones) **4-7-10** GBardwell(3) (sn prom: rdn & wknd ent st)	2	**13**	20/1	3	—
4453^{12}	**Blazer's Baby (45)** (MrsNMacauley) **3-8-7** SDrowne(9) (b: bhd fnl 4f: t.o)	6	**14**	20/1	11	—
4045^{17}	**Cashtal Lace (30)** (BJLlewellyn) **4-7-5**(7) PDoe(10) (s.s: a in rr: t.o)	7	**15**	50/1	—	—
4465^{11}	**Saxon Bay (42)** (KOCunningham-Brown) **5-8-10** MartinDwyer(8) (trckd ldrs 7f: sn lost tch: t.o)	9	**16**	25/1	—	—
3074^{9}	**Charcol (30)** (JEBanks) **4-7-12** JQuinn(1) (swtg: prom tl wknd over 3f out: t.o)	¾	**17**	20/1	—	—
4043^{18}	**Risking (41)** (RJPrice) **4-8-9** MFenton(19) (a bhd: t.o)	dist	**18**	33/1	—	—
173^{4}	**Double Crest (IRE) (53)** (MJohnston) **3-9-1** DHolland(12) (bit bkwd: t.o 5f out: p.u over 3f out)		**P**	9/1	—	—
				(SP 141.6%)	**19 Rn**	

2m 20.5 (6.50) CSF £160.37 CT £1,317.22 TOTE £29.30: £4.90 £3.40 £1.50 £1.90 (£106.40) Trio £425.80; £299.91 to York 8/10/97 OWNER Mr B. H. Farr (WORKSOP) BRED Worksop Manor Stud Farm

LONG HANDICAP Misterton 7-6

WEIGHT FOR AGE 3yo-6lb

OFFICIAL EXPLANATION **Double Crest (IRE): lost her action approximately four furlongs from the finish before pulling up lame.**

3601 Misterton has been very disappointing but he was in a better frame of mind without the blinkers and, responding to a forceful ride, deservedly held on to break his duck. (20/1)

2150* Harvey White (IRE) looked sure to get the better of the winner when delivering a determined last-furlong challenge, but the concession of 30lb proved just too much. (8/1: op 5/1)

3767 Oozlem (IRE) has got into a nasty habit of throwing away races and this was the third consecutive time that he has done just that. He is one of those animals that could make a champion jockey look a fool. (8/1)

3626 Daira, full of running on the heels of the leaders turning for home, was unable to respond when set alight and, though she did look as though she failed to go through with her effort, it is more than possible this shorter trip was the main cause. (8/1)

2164* State Approval, much better on the All-Weather and over a slightly longer trip, ran extremely well after three months out of action, only being forced to give best halfway through the final furlong. With this run to sharpen him up, he could be a different proposition next time. (5/1)

3570 Jimjareer (IRE) barely lasts this trip when ridden with the pace and he was treading ground inside the distance. (33/1)

4373 Fancy Design (IRE) (8/1: op 5/1)

4114 Runic Symbol (14/1: 10/1-16/1)

173 Double Crest (IRE) (9/1: op 6/1)

4609 'GOODLUCK AGAINST BEDFORD' APPRENTICE H'CAP (0-70) (3-Y.O+) (Class F)
5-30 (5-30) **2m 20y** £2,715.90 (£752.40: £359.70) Stalls: Low GOING minus 0.26 sec per fur (GF)

				SP	RR	SF
86[6]	**Theme Arena (47)** (MCPipe) **4-9-4v** FLynch(4) (a.p: led over 6f out: clr over 4f out: rdn over 3f out: r.o wl)	—	**1**	9/2[2]	55	34
4363[7]	**Drama King (35)** (BJLlewellyn) **5-8-6** DSweeney(7) (hld up: hdwy & c wd over 2f out: styd on fnl f: nt rch wnr)	1¼	**2**	33/1	42	21
1114[2]	**Fortunes Course (IRE) (50)** (JSKing) **8-9-7** RFfrench(3) (lw: hld up: hdwy over 3f out: styd on fnl f)	1	**3**	4/1[1]	56	35
3896[4]	**Nick of Time (64)** (JLDunlop) **3-9-10** GMilligan(6) (hld up & bhd: hdwy 7f out: chsd wnr 3f out: no imp)	1¾	**4**	9/2[2]	68	36
4432[3]	**Welcome Lu (26)** (JLHarris) **4-7-11** RMullen(5) (hld up: hdwy 6f out: hmpd on ins over 3f out: one pce fnl 2f)	2½	**5**	10/1	28	7
4171[6]	**Moving Out (50)** (MissHCKnight) **9-9-7** RHavlin(9) (led 5f: rdn over 6f out: wknd over 3f out)	¾	**6**	12/1	51	30
4170[4]	**Keen Waters (36)** (MrsSDWilliams) **3-7-6**(4) DarrenWilliams(2) (plld hrd: prom tl wknd over 2f out)	hd	**7**	9/1	37	5
2511*	**Bridie's Pride (50)** (GAHam) **6-9-7** JFowle(1) (bhd fnl 5f)	½	**8**	11/2[3]	50	29
4405[3]	**Coh Sho No (48)** (SDow) **4-9-5** PDoe(8) (plld hrd: led 11f out tl over 6f out: wknd over 2f out)	3	**9**	4/1[1]	45	24
4374[10]	**Ginka (28)** (JWMullins) **6-7-13** SRighton(10) (a bhd: t.o)	dist	**10**	14/1	—	—
	Spencer Stallone (50) (GraemeRoe) **4-9-3**(4) CCogan(11) (a bhd: t.o whn shied & uns rdr 1f out)		**U**	50/1	—	—
				(SP 130.1%)	**11 Rn**	

3m 35.3 (9.80) CSF £140.66 CT £611.27 TOTE £6.70: £2.10 £6.70 £1.70 (£115.50) Trio £430.10; £139.34 to York 8/10/97 OWNER Mr Antony Sofroniou (WELLINGTON) BRED Halevale Ltd
WEIGHT FOR AGE 3yo-11lb

86 Theme Arena, visored for the first time on the Flat, was nicely backed and some enterprising riding tactics paid off. (9/2)
Drama King stays well but found himself with a little too much to do because of the winner's tactics. (33/1)
1114 Fortunes Course (IRE) was another left with plenty on her plate after Theme Arena set sail for home. (4/1: 3/1-9/2)
3896 Nick of Time, up 4lb, wants soft ground to be seen at her best. (9/2)
4432 Welcome Lu has certainly improved since being stepped up considerably in trip. (10/1)
4171 Moving Out did strip fitter after his run last month. (12/1)
2175 Ginka (14/1: 10/1-16/1)

T/Jkpt: Not won; £127,794.32 to York 8/10/97. T/Plpt: £86.90 (342.65 Tckts). T/Qdpt: £46.50 (24.99 Tckts) KH/IM

4610a - 4615a (Irish Racing) - See Computer Raceform

4353a-CURRAGH (Newbridge, Ireland) (R-H) (Good to yielding)
Saturday October 4th

4616a BLENHEIM STKS (Listed) (2-Y.O)
3-00 (3-01) **6f** IR £12,900.00 (IR £3,700.00: IR £1,700.00: IR £500.00) GOING minus 0.10 sec per fur (G)

				SP	RR	SF
4093a[9]	**Karakorum (IRE)** (APO'Brien,Ireland) **2-8-7** JAHeffernan (hld up in rr: swtchd rt 1½f out: last 1f out: rdn & r.o (on outside) to ld last strides)	—	**1**	8/1	99	14
4267[8]	**Cloudberry** (BJMeehan) **2-8-7** PShanahan (cl up: rdn & effrt over 1½f out: r.o u.p to ld nr fin: hdd last strides)	s.h	**2**	7/1[3]	99	14
4357a[8]	**Sideman (IRE)** (APO'Brien,Ireland) **2-9-0** MJKinane (hld up: hdwy over 2f out: chal 1f out: r.o u.p)	hd	**3**	8/1	106	21
3962a[4]	**The King Of Cloyne (USA)** (JSBolger,Ireland) **2-8-10** KJManning (a.p: led 2f out: hdd u.p nr fin)	hd	**4**	2/1[2]	101	16
4203a[2]	**Hopping Higgins (IRE)** (APO'Brien,Ireland) **2-8-12** CRoche (hld up: plld hrd: rdn 1½f out: nt trble ldrs nt trble ldrs 1f out: kpt on)	2½	**5**	7/4[1]	97	12
4357a[9]	**Galahad (IRE)** (TStack,Ireland) **2-8-10** JPMurtagh (led hdd 2f out: no ex over 1f out: wknd)	2	**6**	7/1[3]	89	4
				(SP 116.9%)	**6 Rn**	

1m 15.5 (5.00) OWNER Mrs John Magnier (PILTOWN)

Karakorum (IRE), successful in an auction maiden race at Listowel previously, stepped up in class here. She appeared to have no chance at all a furlong and a half out but, switched to the wide outside, found a turn of foot that saw her lead in the last couple of strides. She could be anything. (8/1)
4267 Cloudberry battled here way up the field to get her head in front close home, but was then thwarted by the winner's late burst. (7/1)
4357a Sideman (IRE), dropped back in trip, came close to finding his best form. He put in a sustained challenge on the outer inside the final furlong and might get another turn before the season is out. (8/1: op 4/1)
3962a The King Of Cloyne (USA), in front and disputing the lead for most of the way, battled on well. (2/1)
4203a Hopping Higgins (IRE) was not allowed to stride out and appeared to resent the restraint. She is better over five furlongs but was not given much chance here to demonstrate her speed. (7/4: op Evens)
4357a Galahad (IRE) ran much more prominently here than he had done in the National stakes, showing plenty of speed until dropping out with over a furlong to race. (7/1)

4617a - 4618a (Irish Racing) - See Computer Raceform

4619a C.L. WELD PARK STKS (Gp 3) (2-Y.O F)
4-30 (4-31) **7f** IR £19,500.00 (IR £5,700.00: IR £2,700.00: IR £900.00) GOING minus 0.10 sec per fur (G)

				SP	RR	SF
4212*	**Alborada** (SirMarkPrescott) **2-8-9** SSanders (cl up: led 2f out: rdn clr over 1f out: r.o.)	—	**1**	3/1[1]	101	48
4093a[10]	**Winona (IRE)** (JOxx,Ireland) **2-8-9** JPMurtagh (hld up in rr: hdwy over 2f out: 5th over 1f out: rdn & r.o. ins last: nt trble wnr)	2	**2**	11/2[3]	96	43
4267[4]	**Hoh Chi Min** (MBell) **2-8-9** MFenton (chsd ldrs ½-wy: 3rd & effrt over 1f out: kpt on: nt trble 1st 2)	s.h	**3**	7/1	96	43
4093a[3]	**Shahtoush (IRE)** (APO'Brien,Ireland) **2-8-10**ow1 CRoche (hld up in rr: rdn over 2f out: r.o u.p ins last)	s.h	**4**	4/1[2]	97	43
3839a[5]	**Susun Kelapa (USA)** (APO'Brien,Ireland) **2-8-9** JAHeffernan (led: hdd 2f out: 2nd & no ex over 1f out: kpt on same pce)	1½	**5**	14/1	93	40
3839a[2]	**Viola Royale (IRE)** (CCollins,Ireland) **2-8-9** PShanahan (hld up: hdwy 2f out: 4th, rdn & no ex over 1f out: kpt on same pce)	¾	**6**	7/1	91	38
4090a[2]	**Kitza (IRE)** (APO'Brien,Ireland) **2-8-9b[1]** WJSupple (hld up in rr: rdn & nt trble ldrs 1½f out: kpt on ins last)	¾	**7**	12/1	89	36

3839a[6] **Attractive Crown (USA)** (KPrendergast,Ireland) **2-8-9** SCraine (disp ld tl over 2f out: no imp over 1f out)....2½ **8** 12/1 84 31
Screen Idol (IRE) (DKWeld,Ireland) **2-8-9** MJKinane (hld up in tch: 6th ½-wy: rdn 2f out: btn 1½f out) ....3½ **9** 4/1[2] 76 23
Obvious Appeal (IRE) (DKWeld,Ireland) **2-8-9** DPMcDonogh (dwlt: towards rr: n.d last 2f) 5 **10** 14/1 64 11
(SP 134.1%) **10 Rn**

1m 26.1 (3.10) OWNER Miss K. Rausing (NEWMARKET) BRED Miss K. Rausing
IN-FOCUS: The winner's three-parts sister, Last Second, took this race for the stable in 1995.
4212* Alborada, well backed, stepped up successfully from Beverley maiden class to take this quite easily. She got to the front a furlong and a half out and dominated from there on. (3/1)
4093a Winona (IRE) came from behind to snatch second place close home. (11/2)
4267 Hoh Chi Min, always close up, was totally outpaced by the winner despite keeping on well. (7/1: op 4/1)
4093a Shahtoush (IRE) is still a maiden but stayed on well after switching two furlongs out. (4/1)
3839a Susun Kelapa (USA) led and disputed the way until being headed by the winner. (14/1)
3534a Attractive Crown (USA) (12/1: op 8/1)
Screen Idol (IRE) proved a real disappointment. Light in the market, she was eased right up inside the last furlong when her chance had gone. (4/1: op 7/4)

4620a IRISH CESAREWITCH H'CAP (0-110) (3-Y.O+)
5-00 (5-00) **2m** IR £13,000.00 (IR £3,800.00: IR £1,800.00: IR £600.00) GOING minus 0.10 sec per fur (G)

SP RR SF

Winged Hussar (JOxx,Ireland) **4-8-9** JPMurtagh (a.p: wnt 2nd st: came wde: led 2f out: styd on wl) ....— **1** 9/1 103+ 41
Torn Silk (JOxx,Ireland) **3-7-12**ow1 NGMcCullagh (hld up in tch: chsd ldrs st: 3rd & effrt over 1f out: styd on ins last) 2 **2** 8/1 101 27
Sirinndi (IRE) (JOxx,Ireland) **3-8-7** PShanahan (hld up towards rr: hdwy over 4f out: came wd st: styd on wl: nrst fin) 1 **3** 12/1 109 36
4191a[4] **Theatreworld (IRE)** (APO'Brien,Ireland) **5-9-10** 3x CRoche (hld up: hdwy 4f out: rdn 1½f out: styd on wl: nrst fin) .....hd **4** 7/2[1] 115 53
Broken Rites (IRE) (WMRoper,Ireland) **4-7-8**(8) GDPower (hld up in tch: sn chal & ev ch: 2nd & no ex over 1f out: kpt on) .....s.h **5** 16/1 93 31
Time for a Run (EJO'Grady,Ireland) **10-7-10**(6)ow3 JPSpencer (hld up towards rr: hdwy 4f out: rdn 1½f out: styd on ins last) .....nk **6** 13/2[3] 93 28
Metastasio (DGMcArdle,Ireland) **5-7-6b**(8)ow4 BAHunter (hld up in tch: hdwy ½-wy: chsd ldrs st: 7th & rdn 1½f out: styd on: nt rch ldrs).....1 **7** 16/1 90 24
3974[2] **Turgenev (IRE)** (RBastiman) **8-7-12** FNorton (hld up towards rr: hdwy over 4f out: styd on last 2f: nrst fin) 1 **8** 10/1 87 25
Generosa (JLHassett,Ireland) **4-8-8** JAHeffernan (led: jnd over 2f out: sn hdd: 4th & no ex over 1f out: one pce) 2 **9** 9/1 95 33
Space Trucker (IRE) (MrsJHarrington,Ireland) **6-8-1** WJSmith (hld up: hdwy to chse ldrs over 2f out: nt rch ldrs over 1f out: kpt on).....s.h **10** 5/1[2] 88 26
Antapoura (IRE) (APO'Brien,Ireland) **5-7-4b**1(6) SWKelly (sn chsng ldr: disp ld briefly over 2f out: no ex 1½f out: one pce).....s.h **11** 14/1 82 20
Bolino Star (IRE) (SJTreacy,Ireland) **6-8-12** SCraine (hld up towards rr: no imp fr 3f out: kpt on) 2½ **12** 14/1 96 34
Dasharan (IRE) (JOxx,Ireland) **4-7-11**(2) EAhern (hld up towards rr: sme hdwy appr st: no imp over 2f out: kpt on) 1 **13** 12/1 82 20
Rainbow Frontier (IRE) (APO'Brien,Ireland) **3-7-11** WJSupple (hld up towards rr: no imp over 2f out)............2 **14** 10/1 89 16
Darbela (IRE) (JOxx,Ireland) **3-8-8** DHogan (in tch: rdn st: 6th & nt trble ldrs over 2f out: no imp) ....s.h **15** 14/1 100 27
Reasilvia (IRE) (EJO'Grady,Ireland) **7-7-7**(6)ow3 DPMcDonogh (hmpd early: sn mid div: 9th 5f out: chsd ldrs: no imp in st).....nk **16** 20/1 80 15
Cockney Lad (IRE) (NMeade,Ireland) **8-8-6** MFenton (mid div: no imp fr over 2f out).....½ **17** 14/1 86 24
Smarts Castle (IRE) (JGCoogan,Ireland) **5-7-10b** AJNolan (mid div: hdwy ½-wy & 4f out: wknd st: sn bhd: t.o) .....25 **18** 20/1 51 —
Layik (IRE) (DKWeld,Ireland) **4-9-7b** MJKinane (plld hrd: hld up in tch: chsd ldrs 4f out: no imp early st: wknd & eased: t.o).....6 **19** 20/1 70 8
Taklif (IRE) (MJPO'Brien,Ireland) **5-8-9** KJManning (in tch: chsd ldrs 5f out: wknd appr st: sn bhd: t.o) ....5 **20** 14/1 53 —
(SP 176.3%) **20 Rn**

3m 33.1 (9.10) OWNER Dundalk Racing Club (CURRABEG)
IN-FOCUS: Responsible for the first three home, John Oxx was winning this handicap for the sixth time.
Winged Hussar successful in a maiden at Lyons when trained in France last season, didn't wear blinkers this time. He led over two furlongs out and his stamina saw him through comfortably. (9/1)
Torn Silk chased the winner throughout the last furlong without ever looking likely to get on terms. (8/1)
Sirinndi (IRE) was a back-marker early on and, coming wide into the straight, stayed on better than anything. (12/1)
4191a Theatreworld (IRE), under top-weight, put up a brave showing and stayed on well without ever really looking a possibility. One wonders if he is quite as effective over this trip on the Flat, and he might be better suited by a shorter distance. (7/2)
Time for a Run ran well for a ten-year-old and looks all set for a successful National Hunt season. (13/2)
3974 Turgenev (IRE) got himself well behind but was staying on strongly over the last quarter-mile to be nearest at the finish. (10/1)
Generosa (9/1: op 6/1)
Space Trucker (IRE) possibly found the ground, slower than the official good to yielding on the round course, too sticky for him. (5/1)

4621a - 4624a (Irish Racing) - See Computer Raceform

0506a-TIPPERARY (Ireland) (L-H) (Good)
Sunday October 5th

4625a COOLMORE STUD HOME OF CHAMPIONS CONCORDE STKS (Gp 3) (3-Y.O+)
3-00 (3-04) **7f** IR £19,500.00 (IR £5,700.00: IR £2,700.00: IR £900.00)

SP RR SF

4344a* **Wizard King** (SirMarkPrescott) **6-9-4** GDuffield (hld up early: sn prom: led after 3f: rdn clr 2f out: kpt on: hld on).....— **1** Evens[1] 127 —
2447a[4] **Orange Grouse (IRE)** (LBrowne,Ireland) **4-8-8** JPSpencer (hld up in tch: rdn ½-wy: hdwy on ins st: hmpd over 1½f out: r.o wl: jst failed) .....s.h **2** 14/1 117 —

4344a[5]	**Azra (IRE)** (JSBolger,Ireland) **3-8-6b** NGMcCullagh (hld up: rdn & hdwy st: r.o u.p ins last)	1½	**3**	14/1	114	—
4204a[5]	**Dangerous Diva (IRE)** (APO'Brien,Ireland) **3-8-6** JAHeffernan (cl up early: rdn & chsd ldrs whn edgd lft over 1½f out: r.o u.p ins last)	s.h	**4**	10/1	113	—
2816a[2]	**Burden Of Proof (IRE)** (CO'Brien,Ireland) **5-9-1** PJSmullen (hld up in tch: 4th ½-wy: effrt early st: nt trble wnr 1f out: kpt on)	¾	**5**	7/1[3]	119	—
4203a[4]	**Poker-B (IRE)** (DGillespie,Ireland) **3-8-9** PShanahan (led 3f: 3rd & rdn st: nt trble wnr fr 1½f out: kpt on)	1	**6**	14/1	112	—
4344a[4]	**Theano (IRE)** (APO'Brien,Ireland) **4-8-8** WJSupple (dwlt: hld up: 6th ½-wy: effrt early st: nt rch ldrs over 1f out: kpt on)	½	**7**	9/1	108	—
4240[2]	**Hidden Meadow** (IABalding) **3-8-9** TSprake (dwlt: hdwy after 2f: 2nd after ½-wy: rdn & chsd wnr bef st: btn 1½f out)	1½	**8**	11/4[2]	108	—
	Nagnagnag (IRE) (MJPO'Brien,Ireland) **5-8-8** EAhern (dwlt: towards rr: n.d)	8	**9**	16/1	87	—
				(SP 134.1%)		**9 Rn**

1m 33.9 OWNER Sheikh Ahmed Bin Saeed Al Maktoum (NEWMARKET) BRED Sheikh Mohammed bin Rashid al Maktoum

4344a* Wizard King, successful in this race last year, brought his Irish count to seven wins from nine attempts. Clear into the straight, he had to pull out all the stops to resist the challenge of the runner-up. He may be looking for an invitation to Hong Kong, but the Knockaire at Leopardstown in November is available for another repeat success. (Evens)

2079a Orange Grouse (IRE) had no chance here on paper, but ran here best race so far and looked a shade unlucky, having an altercation with Dangerous Diva under two furlongs out. (14/1: op 8/1)

4344a Azra (IRE) had only one behind here turning in but kept on doggedly. (14/1)

4204a Dangerous Diva (IRE) met with interference over a furlong and a half out, but still kept on well. (10/1)

2816a Burden Of Proof (IRE) (7/1: op 7/2)

4203a Poker-B (IRE) (14/1: op 8/1)

4240 Hidden Meadow missed the break but was soon chasing the leaders. Travelling in second place at halfway, he dropped right away in the straight. Obviously this was not his true running. (11/4)

4626a (Irish Racing) - See Computer Raceform

4562-NOTTINGHAM (L-H) (Good becoming Good to soft becoming Soft)

Wednesday October 8th

WEATHER: heavy rain WIND: almost nil

4627 SECOND ROW (S) STKS (2-Y.O) (Class G)

2-10 (2-13) **1m 54y** £1,984.50 (£547.00: £259.50) Stalls: Low GOING: 0.40 sec per fur (GS)

				SP	RR	SF
1812[13]	**Blue Desert** (MBell) **2-8-6**(5) RMullen(10) (mde virtually all: clr over 1f out: unchal)	—	**1**	8/1[3]	85	44
4366[3]	**Royal Ground (IRE) (69)** (MRChannon) **2-8-11** GHind(14) (hld up: hdwy 5f out: jnd wnr 4f out: rdn & one pce fnl 2f)	8	**2**	7/4[1]	70	29
4303[9]	**Little Cracker** (AGNewcombe) **2-8-6** SDrowne(11) (trckd ldrs: rdn over 2f out: kpt on)	2	**3**	50/1	61	20
4163[3]	**Cherished (IRE) (56)** (NTinkler) **2-8-6b** GDuffield(8) (hld up in tch: hdwy u.p over 2f out: nvr able to chal)	½	**4**	8/1[3]	60	19
4303[3]	**Emperor's Gold (64)** (ICampbell) **2-8-11** AMackay(5) (hld up: hdwy over 2f out: nrst fin)	2½	**5**	12/1	60	19
4303[4]	**Sharp Monkey** (MrsNMacauley) **2-8-11** SWebster(2) (lw: bhd: styd on fnl 2f: nvr nrr)	¾	**6**	12/1	58	17
	Compassionate (WGMTurner) **2-8-8**(3) DSweeney(9) (lt-f: bit bkwd: hld up: hdwy over 2f out: nt rch ldrs)	¾	**7**	14/1	57	16
4502[8]	**Total Tropix** (WJHaggas) **2-8-6** FLynch(16) (mid div: effrt 4f out: rdn & wknd over 2f out)	¾	**8**	25/1	50	9
4459[11]	**Blanche The Almond** (CASmith) **2-8-7**ow1 ACulhane(1) (bit bkwd: s.s: wl bhd tl sme late hdwy)	2	**9**	50/1	48	6
4500[2]	**High Money (67)** (GLewis) **2-8-11** PaulEddery(13) (hdwy ent st: rdn & wknd 2f out)	1½	**10**	4/1[2]	49	8
4159[10]	**Crystal Waters (IRE)** (GROldroyd) **2-8-6** KHodgson(6) (chsd ldrs over 5f)	1¾	**11**	66/1	40	—
4366[8]	**Muja's Magic (IRE) (50)** (KTIvory) **2-8-5**(5)ow4 GFaulkner(3) (b: prom 4f: wknd & eased wl over 1f out)	4	**12**	16/1	37	—
4209[16]	**Itsnotyetnamed** (ASmith) **2-8-11** NAdams(7) (w wnr: rdn ent st: sn wknd)	4	**13**	40/1	30	—
4454[14]	**Windspeed** (BPJBaugh) **2-8-8**(3) PRoberts(15) (bit bkwd: s.s: a bhd: t.o)	9	**14**	50/1	12	—
4366[12]	**Pride of Fashion** (SGKnight) **2-8-11** SophieMitchell(4) (bkwd: a bhd: t.o)	7	**15**	50/1	—	—
4064[17]	**Perfect Way** (MrsNMacauley) **2-8-11** PBloomfield(12) (s.i.s: a bhd: t.o)	2	**16**	33/1	—	—
				(SP 125.1%)		**16 Rn**

1m 49.8 (8.50) CSF £19.74 TOTE £7.80: £2.30 £1.30 £8.30 (£14.10) Trio £118.10 OWNER Billion in Mind Partnership (NEWMARKET) BRED Catridge Farm and Stud Ltd and Trickledown Stud

Sold GLewis 11,000 gns

993 Blue Desert has been crying out for a test of stamina and, looking well tuned up after a four-month break, simply outclassed the opposition. (8/1: op 5/1)

4366 Royal Ground (IRE) promised to make a race of it when joining forces soon after straightening up, but once the winner lengthened his stride, the writing was on the wall. (7/4)

Little Cracker was struggling to hold on when ridden over two furlongs out and her attempt to stay this longer trip looked done for but, rather surprisingly, she began to pick up again inside the final furlong and kept on to run into the prizes. (50/1)

4163 Cherished (IRE), asked for her effort approaching the last quarter-mile, did look assured of third prize, but her stride shortened inside the distance and she finished very leg-weary. (8/1)

4303 Emperor's Gold, ridden to get the trip, did stay on to reach his final placing, but he was beaten quite a way and he would seem only moderate at present. (12/1: op 8/1)

4303 Sharp Monkey was once again doing all his best work late on and he is getting experience all the time. (12/1)

4500 High Money (4/1: op 5/2)

4628 FLY HALF H'CAP (0-70) (I) (3-Y.O+) (Class E)

2-40 (2-43) **1m 54y** £3,005.25 (£897.00: £428.50: £194.25) Stalls: Low GOING: 0.40 sec per fur (GS)

				SP	RR	SF
4471[2]	**Katie Komaite (39)** (CaptJWilson) **4-8-0v** AMackay(4) (hld up: hdwy wl over 1f out: r.o strly to ld nr fin)	—	**1**	8/1[3]	51	33
3759[9]	**Kass Alhawa (60)** (DWChapman) **4-9-7** ACulhane(5) (hld up & bhd: hdwy over 2f out: led over 1f out: hrd rdn & hdd nr fin)	1¼	**2**	12/1	70	52
2546[14]	**Up in Flames (IRE) (46)** (SRBowring) **6-8-4**(3) CTeague(1) (a.p: rdn over 1f out: kpt on)	2½	**3**	20/1	51	33
4471[13]	**Scenicris (IRE) (49)** (RHollinshead) **4-8-10** FLynch(11) (hld up: hdwy & nt clr run over 2f out: r.o wl towards fin)	nk	**4**	10/1	53	35

Entry	Dist	Pos	SP	RR	SF
4510^{6} **Needle Match (60)** (JJO'Neill) **4-9-2**(5) CLowther(12) (hld up: hdwy over 2f out: ev ch ent fnl f: no ex ins fnl f)	1¼	**5**	$5/1^{1}$	62	44
4291^{2} **Delight of Dawn (51)** (EAWheeler) **5-8-5b**(7) SCarson(3) (in tch: effrt over 2f out: nvr nrr)	¾	**6**	$13/2^{2}$	51	33
2915^{14} **Sharp Return (50)** (MJRyan) **3-8-5**(3) PMcCabe(9) (mid div: no hdwy fnl 2f)	hd	**7**	20/1	50	29
4510^{5} **Murphy's Gold (IRE) (52)** (RAFahey) **6-8-13** MartinDwyer(7) (mid div: effrt over 2f out: no imp)	4	**8**	12/1	44	26
4319^{4} **Sis Garden (59)** (JCullinan) **4-9-6** DO'Donohoe(17) (prom: led 3f out: rdn & edgd lft: hdd & wknd over 1f out)	1¾	**9**	$8/1^{3}$	48	30
4210^{10} **Ochos Rios (IRE) (53)** (BSRothwell) **6-9-0** GDuffield(13) (in tch: effrt centre over 3f out: sn rdn: no imp)	2	**10**	10/1	38	20
4371^{17} **Soaking (40)** (MDIUsher) **7-8-1** JQuinn(2) (chsd ldrs: effrt & swtchd rt over 2f out: wknd qckly)	1½	**11**	16/1	22	4
4016^{9} **Densben (45)** (DenysSmith) **13-8-6** WRyan(16) (a bhd)	1¾	**12**	16/1	24	6
4518^{12} **Corporal Nym (USA) (63)** (MRBosley) **4-9-3**(7) RStudholme(10) (trckd ldrs over 5f: sn wknd)	½	**13**	40/1	41	23
2533^{9} **Star of Ring (IRE) (60)** (MJHeaton-Ellis) **4-9-7** SDrowne(8) (prom tl wknd over 2f out: t.o)	6	**14**	25/1	26	8
4243^{5} **Godmersham Park (55)** (PSFelgate) **5-8-13**(3) DSweeney(14) (led to 3f out: sn lost pl: t.o)	6	**15**	10/1	10	—
			(SP 122.5%)	**15 Rn**	

1m 49.9 (8.60) CSF £87.90 CT £1083.71 TOTE £6.60: £2.20 £9.50 £7.50 (£37.70) Trio £181.20; £232.31 to York 9/10/97 OWNER Red Rose Partnership (PRESTON) BRED J. O'Neill

WEIGHT FOR AGE 3yo-3lb

4471 Katie Komaite has been knocking at the door in recent races and, taking advantage of a substantial weight difference, stayed on strongly to win her first race. (8/1: op 5/1)

3630 Kass Alhawa looked to have recovered his form when taking command into the final furlong but, on this ever-softening ground, stamina appeared to desert him and he was run out of it nearing the line. (12/1)

1384 Up in Flames (IRE) has not won a race for over two years but he was in contention all the way on this return to action and only got left behind in the closing stages. (20/1)

3937 Scenicris (IRE), denied a clear passage when trying to improve over two furlongs out, was into her stride again nearing the finish but by then she had given herself just too much to do. (10/1)

4510 Needle Match made smooth progress and looked to have timed it right when putting in his bid approaching the final furlong but a lack of stamina again appeared the problem and he failed to last home. (5/1)

4291 Delight of Dawn was not helped by the constant downpour and she was unable to land a blow. (13/2)

4629 FLY HALF H'CAP (0-70) (II) (3-Y.O+) (Class E)

3-10 (3-10) **1m 54y** £2,979.25 (£889.00: £424.50: £192.25) Stalls: Low GOING: 0.40 sec per fur (GS)

Entry	Dist	Pos	SP	RR	SF
4139^{3} **Ca'd'oro (58)** (GBBalding) **4-9-8** SDrowne(7) (hld up: rdn over 3f out: hdwy over 2f out: r.o to ld nr fin)	—	**1**	$9/2^{1}$	70	42
4319^{12} **Duello (60)** (MBlanshard) **6-9-10** WRyan(5) (hld up: hdwy over 2f out: led ins fnl f: ct cl home)	nk	**2**	10/1	71	43
4471^{3} **Winston (48)** (JDBethell) **4-8-7**(5) CLowther(1) (lw: hld up: hdwy on ins 3f out: nt clr run over 2f out: r.o ins fnl f)	1¾	**3**	$8/1^{3}$	56	28
4270^{16} **Impulsive Air (IRE) (60)** (EWeymes) **5-9-10** JQuinn(14) (lw: a.p: led 3f out tl ins fnl f: one pce)	1½	**4**	16/1	65	37
2828^{10} **Nkapen Rocks (SPA) (49)** (CaptJWilson) **4-8-13** AClark(13) (a.p: jnd ldr over 1f out: unable qckn ins fnl f)	s.h	**5**	16/1	54	26
4504^{6} **Here's To Howie (USA) (60)** (RHannon) **3-9-7** WJO'Connor(4) (prom: drvn along over 3f out: rdn & btn over 1f out)	¾	**6**	20/1	64	33
4371^{4} **Lord Oberon (IRE) (46)** (JAkehurst) **9-8-10** GCarter(9) (hld up: effrt 2f out: nvr nrr)	nk	**7**	10/1	49	21
4465* **The Green Grey (42)** (WRMuir) **3-8-3** MartinDwyer(2) (prom: rdn over 1f out: one pce)	nk	**8**	$7/1^{2}$	44	13
4243^{7} **Great Chief (40)** (BobJones) **4-8-4** FNorton(15) (in tch tl wknd over 2f out)	2	**9**	12/1	39	11
3759^{16} **Al Reet (IRE) (52)** (SRBowring) **6-8-13**(3) CTeague(12) (s.s: a in rr)	1¾	**10**	$8/1^{3}$	47	19
4455^{11} **Princess of Hearts (59)** (MCPipe) **3-9-6b** GDuffield(11) (bhd: sn rdn along: n.d)	2	**11**	16/1	50	19
4510^{8} **Mezzoramio (52)** (KAMorgan) **5-8-13v**(3) RFfrench(17) (b: chsd ldrs tl rdn & wknd over 2f out)	2	**12**	12/1	39	11
4472^{11} **Axeman (IRE) (40)** (MartynWane) **5-8-1**(3) AWhelan(6) (s.i.s: rdn along after 2f: n.d)	3½	**13**	14/1	21	—
4331^{4} **Occam (IRE) (57)** (GWragg) **3-9-4** PaulEddery(3) (in tch tl rdn & wknd over 3f out)	5	**14**	$7/1^{2}$	28	—
4385^{13} **Ned's Bonanza (46)** (MDods) **8-8-10** SWhitworth(8) (lw: sn led: hdd 3f out: sn wknd: t.o)	7	**15**	20/1	3	—
4448^{8} **Mislemani (IRE) (48)** (AGNewcombe) **7-8-9**(3) DGriffiths(10) (a bhd: t.o)	6	**16**	16/1	—	—
			(SP 138.7%)	**16 Rn**	

1m 51.1 (9.80) CSF £51.16 CT £340.42 TOTE £6.20: £2.10 £1.40 £1.80 £2.40 (£14.40) Trio £34.70 OWNER Miss B. Swire (ANDOVER) BRED Miss B. Swire

WEIGHT FOR AGE 3yo-3lb

4139 Ca'd'oro takes a long time to really find his stride but when he does, especially on this soft ground, he is really on song and he proved the stronger in an all out battle to the line. (9/2)

3392 Duello has found his form in the past at this time of year and he struck the front two hundred yards out, but the winner was also in top gear at the same time and he was worried out of it nearing the finish. (10/1)

4471 Winston persisted in making his run on the inside and in the end it probably cost him the race, but he is in form and probably deserves a change of fortune. (8/1)

3921 Impulsive Air (IRE), much better when he can hear his feet rattle, made his challengers fight hard to take his advantage inside the final furlong. (16/1)

2546 Nkapen Rocks (SPA) continues to run well and that elusive first success can not be far away. (16/1)

4504 Here's To Howie (USA), hard at work early in the straight, kept plugging away but over a trip short of his best he had to admit the principals too sharp for him. (20/1)

2913 Al Reet (IRE) (8/1: op 16/1)

4630 PROP FORWARD MAIDEN STKS (2-Y.O) (Class D)

3-40 (3-42) **5f 13y** £3,834.80 (£1,147.40: £550.20: £251.60) Stalls: High GOING: 0.17 sec per fur (G)

Entry	Dist	Pos	SP	RR	SF
4305^{4} **Shalford's Honour (IRE)** (WJarvis) **2-9-0** GHind(10) (a.p: shkn up to ld ins fnl r.o)	—	**1**	$15/8^{1}$	83+	48
4446^{3} **Territory (IRE)** (GLewis) **2-9-0** PaulEddery(17) (lw: led tl rdn & hdd ins fnl f)	1	**2**	$5/1^{3}$	80	45
4211^{3} **Odette** (SirMarkPrescott) **2-8-9** GDuffield(6) (a.p: rdn over 1f out: kpt on one pce ins fnl f)	1½	**3**	$7/2^{2}$	70	35
4167^{5} **Eminent** (LordHuntingdon) **2-9-0** WRyan(8) (bhd: hdwy over 1f out: kpt on ins fnl f)	3½	**4**	6/1	64	29
4311^{12} **Royal Blue** (MDIUsher) **2-9-0** JMarshall(4) (b.hind: hld up: hdwy & r.o over 1f out)	1	**5**	33/1	61	26
4515^{4} **Magic Powers** (GBBalding) **2-9-0** SDrowne(14) (sn outpcd: hdwy over 1f out: r.o)	1¼	**6**	12/1	57	22
4298^{5} **St Lucia (IRE)** (BJMeehan) **2-8-9** GCarter(13) (swtg: chsd ldrs tl rdn & wknd over 1f out)	½	**7**	6/1	50	15
4402^{5} **Ballasilla** (BPalling) **2-8-6**(3) DSweeney(11) (chsd ldrs 3f)	1	**8**	20/1	47	12
1031^{5} **Jewel (IRE)** (RHannon) **2-8-9** DaneO'Neill(1) (bit bkwd: veered lft leaving stalls: trckd ldrs 3f)	2½	**9**	12/1	39	4

4542[6] **Newala** (WJHaggas) **2-8-9** FLynch(5) (bit bkwd: outpcd) ....1½ **10** 16/1 35 —
2917[13] **College Rose** (SCWilliams) **2-8-9** PBloomfield(15) (b.hind: swtg: sn rdn along & bhd) ....hd **11** 50/1 34 —
3965[10] **Captain Brady (IRE) (57)** (WGMTurner) **2-8-7b[1](7)** DMcGaffin(9) (outpcd) ....hd **12** 33/1 39 4
4428[8] **Pabella Bluebird (IRE)** (GROldroyd) **2-8-9** KHodgson(12) (chsd ldrs to ½-wy: sn wknd) ....nk **13** 50/1 33 —
Quite Happy (IRE) (DrJDScargill) **2-8-9** JQuinn(16) (b.hind: w'like: scope: in tch stands' side tl wknd 2f out) ....1¼ **14** 33/1 29 —
Scurrilous (MBell) **2-8-9** ACulhane(7) (lt-f: bit bkwd: s.s: a bhd & outpcd) ....1¼ **15** 20/1 25 —
4428[10] **Crystal Lough (IRE)** (GROldroyd) **2-8-6(3)** RFfrench(3) (in tch to ½-wy: wknd qckly: t.o) .... **16** 50/1 — —
(SP 147.7%) **16 Rn**

62.7 secs (3.80) CSF £12.18 TOTE £2.80: £1.70 £2.50 £1.90 (£9.90) Trio £4.10 OWNER The Honourable Partnership (NEWMARKET) BRED K. Molloy

4305 Shalford's Honour (IRE) proved the stronger when the chips were down and opened his account a shade easier than the margin suggests. (15/8: 7/4-11/4)

4446 Territory (IRE) did his utmost to gallop his rivals into the ground on this step down to the minimum trip, but the winner kept him within his sights and took his measure halfway through the final furlong. (5/1)

4211 Odette may not have benefited from this changed ground and, though she was in the firing line from the break, was found wanting when a turn of speed was called for. She is a trier and deserves to get a break. (7/2)

4167 Eminent was never close enough to be concerned in the outcome, but he did stay on promisingly in the last furlong and he is learning all the time. (6/1: op 4/1)

Royal Blue ran so much better than he did on his debut and he does seem to be getting it together. (33/1)

4515 Magic Powers, brought back to the minimum trip, was always struggling with the pace and, unless he can find a stiff five furlongs, it would seem he would have to campaign over further. (12/1)

4298 St Lucia (IRE), subject of some inspired support, chased the leaders, but she was hard at work approaching the final furlong and was well short of the necessary acceleration. (6/1)

1031 Jewel (IRE) (12/1: 8/1-14/1)

4631 DYNASTY INTERNATIONAL MAIDEN STKS (3-Y.O) (Class D)

4-10 (4-11) **1m 1f 213y** £3,993.30 (£1,193.40: £571.20: £260.10) Stalls: Low GOING: 0.62 sec per fur (GS)

			SP	RR	SF
4005[5] **Basman (IRE) (102)** (BSmart) **3-9-0** JStack(9) (lw: mde all: clr ent st: unchal)	—	**1**	2/9[1]	107	48
4177[5] **Lysandros (IRE)** (JHMGosden) **3-9-0** GHind(10) (b: swtg: in tch: chsd wnr over 2f out: no imp)	18	**2**	5/1[2]	78	19
4319[16] **Quibbling (56)** (HCandy) **3-8-9** CRutter(6) (prom tl btn 3f out)	8	**3**	20/1	60	1
4378[9] **Mutabari (USA) (70)** (KMahdi) **3-9-0** PaulEddery(7) (chsd ldrs: rdn over 4f out: no imp)	2½	**4**	14/1[3]	61	2
4277[10] **Bob Knows** (RFJohnsonHoughton) **3-9-0** AClark(1) (lost pl & drvn 4f out: no imp)	2½	**5**	25/1	57	—
4579[8] **Cape Siren** (MJRyan) **3-8-9** GCarter(3) (prom: rdn over 3f out: wknd qckly)	1¼	**6**	33/1	50	—
4322[9] **Pleasure Boat** (NAGraham) **3-9-0** MRimmer(8) (bhd fr ½-wy: t.o)	10	**7**	50/1	39	—
Hiblaze (IRE) (KMcAuliffe) **3-9-0** DaneO'Neill(5) (w'like: str: bkwd: s.i.s: a bhd: t.o)	17	**8**	25/1	12	—
4290[13] **Six Shooter** (EWeymes) **3-8-9** JQuinn(4) (a bhd: t.o)	dist	**9**	66/1	—	—
2532[11] **Daniel's Mascot** (AGNewcombe) **3-9-0** GDuffield(2) (a bhd: t.o)	dist	**10**	50/1	—	—
			(SP 126.0%)	**10 Rn**	

2m 14.8 (12.30) CSF £1.72 TOTE £1.30: £1.10 £1.50 £1.10 (£1.70) Trio £5.90 OWNER Mr Alvarez Cervera (LAMBOURN) BRED L A C

4005 Basman (IRE) had little more than a public workout to break his duck and it should boost his confidence no end. He goes for the St. Simon Stakes at Newbury next, but looks the type to make up into a Triumph Hurdle possible. (2/9)

4177 Lysandros (IRE), the selected of the stable's four entries at the declaration stage, ran his best race yet to chase up the winner but he was beaten almost a furlong so what hope is there for the rest. (5/1: 3/1-6/1)

700 Mutabari (USA) (14/1: op 8/1)

4632 HOOKER H'CAP (0-70) (3-Y.O) (Class E)

4-40 (4-41) **1m 1f 213y** £3,486.25 (£1,045.00: £502.50: £231.25) Stalls: Low GOING: 0.62 sec per fur (GS)

			SP	RR	SF
4568[6] **Secret Ballot (IRE) (62)** (KMahdi) **3-8-13** WJO'Connor(4) (lw: hld up: rdn along after 3f: hdwy 3f out: chal & hung lft wl over 1f out: led ins fnl f: faltered nr fin)	—	**1**	6/1[2]	70	41
4472[7] **Tipperary Sunset (IRE) (50)** (JJQuinn) **3-7-8(7)** PBradley(17) (hld up: hdwy 3f out: led over 1f out tl ins fnl f: rdn & veered lft: rallied cl home)	s.h	**2**	13/2[3]	58	29
3937[12] **Doc Ryan's (62)** (MJRyan) **3-8-10b[1](3)** PMcCabe(2) (s.i.s: hdwy 4f out: disp ld 2f out tl rdn over 1f out: one pce ins fnl f)	4	**3**	14/1	64	35
4015[13] **Flying Flip (52)** (BCMorgan) **3-8-3ow1** GHind(14) (b.hind: s.i.s: bhd: hdwy 2f out: fin wl)	s.h	**4**	33/1	53	23
4455[7] **Go For Green (55)** (DrJDScargill) **3-8-6** JQuinn(7) (hld up: hdwy 4f out: ev ch over 2f out: one pce appr fnl f)	¾	**5**	20/1	55	26
4504[16] **Tabasco Jazz (58)** (BJMeehan) **3-8-9** WRyan(10) (hld up: hdwy on ins over 3f out: led over 2f out tl over 1f out: sn wknd)	2½	**6**	20/1	54	25
4326* **Rare Talent (61)** (SGollings) **3-8-9(3)** RFfrench(6) (in tch: rdn & one pce fr over 1f out)	nk	**7**	10/1	57	28
4472[6] **Il Falco (FR) (52)** (SirMarkPrescott) **3-8-3** GDuffield(9) (prom: rdn to ld over 3f out tl over 2f out: grad wknd)	½	**8**	7/1	47	18
4176[16] **Praeditus (70)** (RHannon) **3-9-7** DaneO'Neill(13) (in tch: effrt over 3f out: wknd over 2f out)	½	**9**	25/1	64	35
4010[3] **Foolish Flutter (IRE) (47)** (RBastiman) **3-7-12** NAdams(8) (chsd ldrs: rdn 6f out: wknd 3f out)	1	**10**	9/1	40	11
4438[7] **Beach Buoy (IRE) (50)** (CaptJWilson) **3-8-1** AMackay(5) (in rr: effrt over 2f out: sn no imp)	¾	**11**	14/1	41	12
4323[7] **Fantasy Girl (IRE) (58)** (JLDunlop) **3-8-9** GCarter(18) (mid div: effrt over 3f out: no imp)	6	**12**	16/1	40	11
4171[4] **Gallant Heights (55)** (GCBravery) **3-8-3(3)** AWhelan(15) (prom tl wknd qckly over 2f out)	1	**13**	14/1	35	6
4176[14] **Who's That Man (57)** (SCWilliams) **3-8-8** SDrowne(12) (chsd ldrs tl drvn & wknd over 2f out: t.o)	22	**14**	16/1	2	—
4323[13] **Made Bold (65)** (HCandy) **3-9-2** CRutter(3) (a bhd: hrd rdn 5f out: no imp: t.o)	¾	**15**	14/1	9	—
4242[8] **Noble Dane (IRE) (66)** (PWHarris) **3-9-3** ACulhane(1) (lw: mde most tl hdd & wknd over 3f out: t.o)	nk	**16**	9/2[1]	9	—
3021[6] **Chandler's Hall (58)** (MJHeaton-Ellis) **3-8-9** AClark(11) (b: trckd ldrs tl wknd over 3f out: t.o)	s.h	**17**	14/1	1	—
			(SP 138.8%)	**17 Rn**	

2m 15.5 (13.00) CSF £44.28 CT £513.43 TOTE £5.30: £1.50 £2.40 £6.00 £27.40 (£42.70) Trio £117.50 OWNER Mr Waleed Al-Mutawa (NEWMARKET) BRED Godolphin Management Co Ltd

OFFICIAL EXPLANATION **Noble Dane (IRE): rider reported that the horse was never travelling well and hung throughout the race.**

4063 Secret Ballot (IRE) followed up his course and distance win here in July with a performance that would have been more clear cut had he not faltered and almost lost his footing twenty yards from the line. (6/1)

3813* Tipperary Sunset (IRE) struck the front over a furlong out in the centre of the track, but the winner, wide of him, took his measure one hundred yards out. He veered left nearing the line and was caught close home. (13/2)

840 Doc Ryan's performed mush better in his first-time blinkers and was fighting for the lead until failing to quicken inside the last furlong. (14/1)
Flying Flip stayed on strongly to reach her finishing position after forfeiting ground at the start. (33/1)
3442 Go For Green failed to see this longer trip out but she ran a respectable race and it is now back to the drawing board. (20/1)
4243 Tabasco Jazz got to the front over two furlongs out and set sail for home, but as in her previous race, had to admit this trip just too far. (20/1)
4472 Il Falco (FR) (7/1: 5/1-8/1)

4633 FULL BACK H'CAP (0-60) (3-Y.O+) (Class E)

5-10 (5-11) **2m 9y** £3,362.70 (£937.20: £452.10) Stalls: Low GOING: 0.62 sec per fur (GS)

Form	Horse	Dist	Pos	SP	RR	SF
2511[2]	**Contrarie (37)** (MJRyan) **4-8-7**(3) PMcCabe(9) (lw: hld up in rr: hdwy 6f out: led 3f out: styd on strly)	—	**1**	10/1	50	32
4432[5]	**Course Fishing (32)** (BAMcMahon) **6-8-2**(3) RFfrench(12) (hld up: hdwy 5f out: rdn over 2f out: nvr able to chal)	2	**2**	14/1	43	25
4374[3]	**Palaemon (57)** (GBBalding) **3-9-5** SDrowne(5) (trckd ldrs: effrt over 2f out: rdn & one pce appr fnl f)	1½	**3**	7/2[1]	67	38
4519[5]	**Golden Melody (51)** (MJHeaton-Ellis) **3-8-6**(7) JFowle(14) (hld up & bhd: hdwy ½-wy: rdn over 4f out: kpt on)	1¾	**4**	16/1	59	30
4323[12]	**Keepsake (IRE) (52)** (MDIUsher) **3-9-0** RStreet(17) (bhd: hdwy over 4f out: nvr nrr)	nk	**5**	10/1	60	31
4055[5]	**Charlie Bigtime (43)** (ICampbell) **7-9-2** AMackay(6) (bhd tl styd on fnl 3f)	5	**6**	20/1	46	28
2908[2]	**Philosophic (54)** (SirMarkPrescott) **3-9-2** GDuffield(7) (bit bkwd: prom: hrd drvn 3f out: wknd fnl 2f)	9	**7**	5/1[2]	48	19
4170[7]	**Spa Lane (43)** (MPBielby) **4-8-13**(3) RHavlin(10) (prom: led ½-wy to 3f out: sn wknd)	7	**8**	8/1[3]	30	12
2910[5]	**Arif (IRE) (37)** (JohnHarris) **5-8-10** PaulEddery(8) (bit bkwd: in tch: rdn & effrt 5f out: wknd over 3f out)	13	**9**	12/1	11	—
3865[3]	**Rear Window (53)** (LordHuntingdon) **3-9-1v** WRyan(3) (trckd ldrs: wknd qckly over 2f out: eased whn btn)	6	**10**	8/1[3]	21	—
4336[7]	**Madison Welcome (IRE) (55)** (MrsJRRamsden) **3-9-3v** OPears(15) (mid div: pushed along ½-wy: wknd 5f out: t.o)	13	**11**	16/1	10	—
	Sir Pageant (30) (KSBridgwater) **8-8-3** JBramhill(13) (bkwd: chsd ldrs tl wknd over 4f out: t.o)	2	**12**	33/1	—	—
4222[14]	**Beauchamp Lion (57)** (JLDunlop) **3-9-5** GCarter(2) (led: rdn & hdd 8f out: wknd 4f out: t.o)	¾	**13**	14/1	9	—
3992[21]	**Dazzling Stone (49)** (LadyHerries) **3-8-11** DeclanO'Shea(18) (dwlt: a bhd: t.o)	22	**14**	20/1	—	—
4213[6]	**Welcome Home (45)** (PTDalton) **3-8-7** JQuinn(11) (chsd ldrs tl wknd qckly over 3f out: t.o)	18	**15**	25/1	—	—
4302[3]	**Salsee Lad (58)** (JRFanshawe) **3-9-6** AClark(4) (bhd: drvn along 6f out: t.o)	½	**16**	10/1	—	—

(SP 137.5%) **16 Rn**

3m 45.7 (22.70) CSF £140.09 CT £556.98 TOTE £12.60: £2.10 £1.40 £2.00 £10.90 (£57.00) Trio £162.40 OWNER Mr M. J. Ryan (NEWMARKET) BRED A. G. Martin
WEIGHT FOR AGE 3yo-11lb
2511 Contrarie fresh and well after a mid-summer break, had this won some way out and it is surprising that she has taken so long to get off the mark. (10/1)
4432 Course Fishing, given a very patient ride, always looked to prove a threat from the time he went in pursuit of the winner but he was the first to come under pressure and it would seem two miles is just beyond him. (14/1)
4374 Palaemon promises so much but fails to deliver, though it must be admitted he is high enough in the handicap for a maiden. (7/2)
3865 Golden Melody, flat to the boards on straightening up, did stay on in her own time without ever threatening to get on terms. (16/1)
4222 Keepsake (IRE), still to prove she stays two miles, was given no help by the soft ground and, though she did stay on, was only passing beaten animals inside the distance. (10/1)
2908 Philosophic had plenty of use made of him and, struggling to hold his pitch three furlongs out, would seem to have done too much too soon. (5/1)
2316 Spa Lane (8/1: op 12/1)

T/Plpt: £68.50 (267.08 Tckts). T/Qdpt: £8.00 (113.11 Tckts) IM

3986-YORK (L-H) (Good becoming Good to soft becoming Soft)
Wednesday October 8th

WEATHER: overcast & raining WIND: slt half behind

4634 EQUITY FINANCIAL COLLECTIONS NURSERY H'CAP (2-Y.O) (Class C)

2-00 (2-05) **6f** £6,576.00 (£1,968.00: £944.00: £432.00) Stalls: High GOING: 0.18 sec per fur (G)

Form	Horse	Dist	Pos	SP	RR	SF
4418*	**Special Treat (82)** (DRLoder) **2-9-4b** KFallon(15) (drvn along thrght: hdwy ½-wy: chal over 1f out: styd on to ld wl ins fnl f)	—	**1**	11/2[1]	82	53
4473[3]	**Inchalong (71)** (MBrittain) **2-8-0**(7) DMernagh(5) (mde most tl ct cl home)	hd	**2**	14/1	71	42
4411[5]	**Classy Cleo (IRE) (73)** (PDEvans) **2-8-9** JFEgan(1) (swtg: unruly gng to s: chsd ldrs: hdwy 2f out: nt qckn ins fnl f)	3½	**3**	11/1	63	34
4468[3]	**Pierpoint (IRE) (73)** (RAFahey) **2-8-2**(7) RWinston(11) (lw: outpcd & bhd tl styd on wl fnl 2f)	3½	**4**	14/1	54	25
3755*	**Grand Estate (74)** (TDEasterby) **2-8-10** RCochrane(3) (gd spd over 4f)	nk	**5**	7/1[3]	54	25
4236*	**Desert Sand (75)** (MissSEHall) **2-8-11** EJohnson(2) (bhd: effrt ½-wy: nrst fin)	1½	**6**	11/1	51	22
3774[11]	**Lido (IRE) (85)** (BWHills) **2-9-7** MHills(6) (bhd: hdwy ½-wy: wknd wl over 1f out)	½	**7**	12/1	60	31
4411[2]	**Branston Berry (IRE) (84)** (JLEyre) **2-9-6** RLappin(13) (cl up tl wknd appr fnl f)	1	**8**	9/1	56	27
4403[4]	**Escudo (IRE) (79)** (JHMGosden) **2-9-1** LDettori(10) (prom: rdn ½-wy: grad wknd)	¾	**9**	6/1[2]	49	20
3237[12]	**Composition (84)** (MAJarvis) **2-9-6** JReid(9) (nvr wnt pce)	5	**10**	14/1	41	12
4014[14]	**Really Done It Now (IRE) (60)** (KRBurke) **2-7-10** LCharnock(8) (chsd ldrs tl wknd over 2f out)	3	**11**	33/1	9	—
4284[4]	**Angel Hill (77)** (TDBarron) **2-8-13** JFortune(12) (nvr wnt pce)	2	**12**	14/1	21	—
4381*	**Prompt Delivery (USA) (84)** (MRStoute) **2-9-6** KDarley(4) (lw: chsd ldrs over 4f)	3½	**13**	6/1[2]	18	—
4014[16]	**Two Williams (83)** (MWEasterby) **2-9-5** TLucas(7) (swtg: unruly s: s.s: a bhd)	¾	**14**	33/1	15	—
3990[12]	**Deeceebee (80)** (WStorey) **2-9-2** SSanders(14) (nvr nr ldrs)	nk	**15**	20/1	12	—

(SP 128.1%) **15 Rn**

1m 14.99 (4.49) CSF £77.84 CT £780.46 TOTE £6.20: £2.40 £3.40 £3.70 (£81.70) Trio £248.30 OWNER Cheveley Park Stud (NEWMARKET) BRED David John Brown
OFFICIAL EXPLANATION Prompt Delivery (USA): no explanation offered.
4418* Special Treat was never happy at any stage here but Fallon's considerable strength made her mind up for her. (11/2)
4473 Inchalong ran her socks off yet again but in the end she met one more determined. (14/1)
4014* Classy Cleo (IRE) was certainly edgy and sweating beforehand and gave problems going to the start, but she still ran well which was amazing in the circumstances. (11/1)
4468 Pierpoint (IRE), normally up with the pace, got left behind here but certainly finished strongly and he still looks particularly well. (14/1)

3755* Grand Estate, off the track for almost seven weeks, ran as though he needed this. (7/1)
4236* Desert Sand could never get into this but was staying on and might well appreciate further. (11/1)
4403 Escudo (IRE) is a rather edgy sort who was never really co-operating. (6/1)
4381* Prompt Delivery (USA), again taken to post early, was certainly getting stirred up before the race and used up most of his energy before it all began. (6/1)

4635 WALMGATE H'CAP (0-85) (3-Y.O+) (Class D)

2-30 (2-37) **1m 2f 85y** £6,680.00 (£2,000.00: £960.00: £440.00) Stalls: Low GOING: 0.18 sec per fur (G)

Form	Horse	Dist	Pos	SP	RR	SF
4386^{7}	**Mcgillycuddy Reeks (IRE) (68)** (DonEnricoIncisa) **6-8-12** KimTinkler(5) (hld up: hdwy 4f out: led wl over 1f out: hld on wl)	—	**1**	16/1	77	47
4410^{9}	**Master Beveled (71)** (PDEvans) **7-9-1** JFEgan(7) (bhd: hdwy over 3f out: chsng wnr fnl f: nt qckn towards fin)	1	**2**	13/2	79	49
4449^{6}	**Kamin (USA) (71)** (RWArmstrong) **3-8-10** RHills(12) (lw: chsd ldrs: led 2½f out tl wl over 1f out: one pce)	2½	**3**	6/1 ^{3}	75	40
4210^{17}	**Pekay (64)** (MJohnston) **4-8-8** DHolland(11) (hld up & bhd: brought wd & hdwy 4f out: styd on: nvr able to chal)	½	**4**	14/1	67	37
	Wellaki (USA) (82) (JHMGosden) **3-9-7** LDettori(8) (a.p: brought wd & racd alone stands' side: rdn & no imp fnl 2½f)	1¼	**5**	13/2	83	48
4063^{12}	**Princess Danielle (66)** (WRMuir) **5-8-10** JReid(9) (bhd: hdwy 4f out: sn chsng ldrs: btn over 1f out)	2½	**6**	11/1	63	33
3853^{3}	**Golden Thunderbolt (FR) (63)** (NTinkler) **4-8-7** KDarley(6) (prom tl wknd fnl 3f)	8	**7**	20/1	48	18
4449^{2}	**Tallulah Belle (63)** (NPLittmoden) **4-8-7** JWeaver(1) (lw: hld up & bhd: n.d)	7	**8**	9/2 ^{1}	37	7
4378^{4}	**Dick Turpin (USA) (74)** (LordHuntingdon) **3-8-13** TQuinn(3) (chsd ldrs tl wknd fnl 3½f)	1¾	**9**	7/1	45	10
4306^{7}	**Bend Wavy (IRE) (80)** (THCaldwell) **5-9-10** JCarroll(4) (trckd ldrs: ev ch 3f out: wknd 2f out)	2½	**10**	50/1	47	17
4449^{3}	**Supreme Sound (72)** (PWHarris) **3-8-11** KFallon(10) (lw: led tl hdd & wknd 2½f out)	7	**11**	5/1 ^{2}	29	—
4383^{9}	**Jack The Lad (IRE) (79)** (JHetherton) **3-9-4** MTebbutt(2) (lost tch & wl bhd fnl 4f)	7	**12**	16/1	25	—
				(SP 121.8%)	**12 Rn**	

2m 17.2 (8.20) CSF £108.97 CT £648.94 TOTE £26.90: £3.90 £2.30 £2.10 (£59.00) Trio £395.30 OWNER Don Enrico Incisa (MIDDLEHAM) BRED Noel Sweeney
WEIGHT FOR AGE 3yo-5lb

3906 Mcgillycuddy Reeks (IRE), normally a fast-ground specialist, revelled in ground which was getting softer by the minute. She showed fine courage in the closing stages and may yet find another race. (16/1)
1979 Master Beveled loves easy ground and is obviously on his way back to his best. (13/2)
4449 Kamin (USA) had his chances but in the softening conditions he did not seem to get home. (6/1)
3630 Pekay has not raced in soft ground previously this season and by the way he stayed on, he could well appreciate a bit further. (14/1)
Wellaki (USA), having his first race of the season, certainly likes the soft but, taken on a tour of the track, was never good enough and might well have just needed this. (13/2)
3824 Princess Danielle had her chances but she is still 5lb higher than her last winning mark and that seemed to anchor her. (11/1)
4449 Tallulah Belle never got into this and was not knocked about unduly. She seems much better on faster ground. (9/2)

4636 NEWINGTON HOTEL YORK RACEGOERS H'CAP (0-80) (3-Y.O+) (Class D)

3-00 (3-05) **5f** £6,680.00 (£2,000.00: £960.00: £440.00) Stalls: High GOING: 0.32 sec per fur (G)

Form	Horse	Dist	Pos	SP	RR	SF
4280^{17}	**Canovas Heart (79)** (BobJones) **8-10-0** NDay(13) (chsd ldrs: led ins fnl f: r.o)	—	**1**	10/1	92	75
4365^{5}	**Polly Golightly (54)** (MBlanshard) **4-8-3b** DaleGibson(11) (led tl hdd ins fnl f: r.o)	¾	**2**	16/1	65	48
4329^{5}	**Pleasure Time (62)** (CSmith) **4-8-11v** JTate(19) (w ldrs: edgd lft 2f out: kpt on)	2½	**3**	20/1	65	48
4527^{2}	**Kram (53)** (MrsPNDutfield) **3-8-2** JFEgan(18) (hdwy stands' side 2f out: hung rt: styd on)	½	**4**	8/1 ^{2}	54	37
4456^{14}	**Palo Blanco (67)** (GLMoore) **6-9-2** CandyMorris(22) (s.i.s: racd stands' side: styd on fnl 2f: hmpd ins fnl f: nrst fin)	nk	**5**	20/1	67	50
4370^{4}	**Songsheet (68)** (MSSaunders) **4-9-0(3)** PPMurphy(20) (s.i.s: styd on u.p fnl 2f: nrst fin)	nk	**6**	12/1	67	50
4370*	**Beau Venture (USA) (70)** (BPalling) **9-9-5** TSprake(15) (lw: outpcd tl hdwy over 1f out: r.o)	s.h	**7**	16/1	69	52
4518^{5}	**Pointer (56)** (MrsPNDutfield) **5-8-5** SSanders(1) (racd alone far side: gd spd 4f)	1¼	**8**	20/1	51	34
4512*	**Just Bob (78)** (SEKettlewell) **8-9-13** 7x DeanMcKeown(7) (s.i.s: hdwy fnl 2f: nrst fin)	nk	**9**	8/1 ^{2}	72	55
4280^{27}	**Samwar (76)** (MRChannon) **5-9-11v¹** TQuinn(9) (b: chsd ldrs: ev ch 2f out: wknd fnl f)	s.h	**10**	16/1	70	53
4321^{12}	**White Emir (72)** (BJMeehan) **4-9-7** MTebbutt(8) (prom tl wknd appr fnl f)	hd	**11**	16/1	66	49
1219^{7}	**Stylish Ways (IRE) (62)** (JPearce) **5-8-11** GBardwell(10) (s.i.s: nvr nr ldrs)	1¾	**12**	25/1	50	33
4512^{4}	**Camionneur (IRE) (53)** (TDEasterby) **4-8-2b** LCharnock(21) (dwlt: swtchd lft after s: n.d)	nk	**13**	9/1 ^{3}	40	23
4414^{8}	**Shadow Jury (53)** (DWChapman) **7-8-2b** TWilliams(12) (w ldrs: outpcd whn bdly hmpd 1½f out: sn btn)	1	**14**	25/1	37	20
4321^{5}	**Silent Miracle (IRE) (66)** (MBell) **3-9-1** MFenton(14) (bhd fr ½-wy)	nk	**15**	16/1	49	32
4233^{11}	**William's Well (59)** (MWEasterby) **3-8-8b**ow1 KFallon(4) (lw: prom: drvn along ½-wy: sn wknd)	3½	**16**	14/1	31	13
4385^{11}	**Royal Dome (IRE) (67)** (MartynWane) **5-9-2** DHolland(17) (in tch to ½-wy: sn wknd)	2½	**17**	20/1	31	14
3443^{8}	**Bee Health Boy (65)** (MWEasterby) **4-8-11b(3)** GParkin(5) (lw: sn outpcd & bhd)	2	**18**	25/1	22	5
4512^{2}	**Mon Bruce (61)** (MDods) **3-8-10** JCarroll(3) (lw: spd to ½-wy: sn wknd)	¾	**19**	13/2 ^{1}	16	—
4385^{3}	**Brecongill Lad (65)** (MissSEHall) **5-9-0v** AMcGlone(23) (dwlt: a bhd)	nk	**20**	14/1	19	2
4370^{6}	**Sweet Magic (63)** (PHowling) **6-8-12** KDarley(6) (bhd most of wy)	12	**21**	14/1	—	—
4434^{7}	***Swynford Dream (70)*** (JHetherton) **4-9-5b¹** JLowe(16) (Withdrawn not under Starter's orders: unruly in stalls)		**W**	14/1	—	—
				(SP 149.0%)	**21 Rn**	

61.41 secs (3.71) CSF £142.69 CT £2558.56 TOTE £12.40: £3.10 £6.00 £6.70 £2.80 (£281.60) Trio £779.20 OWNER Mr M J Osborne and Mrs J Woods (NEWMARKET) BRED M. J. Hall

3604 Canovas Heart loves cut in the ground. After two races over six furlongs, he was happy back at the minimum trip and did all that was required. (10/1)
4365 Polly Golightly has never won in soft, but put up a gallant effort here and is obviously in really good heart. (16/1)
4329 Pleasure Time is running well just now and deserves to pick up a race. (20/1)
4527 Kram likes the ground but gave the impression that another furlong might well suit him better. (8/1)
4221* Palo Blanco, from a poor draw, ran well in this soft ground after a bad start and is certainly off a fair mark. (20/1)
4370 Songsheet, not well drawn, ran well in the conditions. (12/1)
4370* Beau Venture (USA), who normally helps force the pace, could not go in this soft ground until picking up really well in the closing stages. (16/1)

4518 Pointer ploughed a lone furrow on the far side and showed bags of speed, which probably burst him as all his wins have been over further. (20/1)
4512* Just Bob is off a mark here 2lb higher than he previously won off and that seemed to steady him somewhat. (8/1)
3900 Samwar, tried in a visor this time, showed something until calling it a day with a furlong left. (16/1)

4637 CHARLES HEIDSIECK CHAMPAGNE RATED STKS H'CAP (0-100) (3-Y.O+) (Class B)

3-30 (3-36) **7f 202y** £9,855.00 (£3,645.00: £1,747.50: £712.50: £281.25: £108.75) Stalls: Low GOING: 0.53 sec per fur (GS)

Form	Horse	Dist	Pos	SP	RR	SF
4283*	**Solar Storm (89)** (MBell) **3-8-10** MFenton(3) (trckd ldrs: smooth hdwy to ld 1f out: rdn & r.o)	—	1	4/1[2]	101	53
3810[3]	**Mawingo (IRE) (83)** (GWragg) **4-8-2**(5) GMilligan(2) (lw: sn cl up: led 2f out to 1f out: kpt on)	1¼	2	6/1[3]	93	48
2525[6]	**Sharp Rebuff (86)** (PJMakin) **6-8-10** SSanders(1) (a chsng ldrs: effrt over 2f out: kpt on one pce)	3½	3	14/1	88	43
4147[3]	**Kala Sunrise (90)** (CSmith) **4-9-0** JFortune(6) (lw: prom: effrt 2f out: r.o one pce)	hd	4	8/1	92	47
4424[8]	**Queens Consul (IRE) (88)** (BSRothwell) **7-8-12** RCochrane(11) (led tl hdd 2f out: grad wknd)	2	5	10/1	86	41
4554[3]	**Great Child (88)** (MRStoute) **3-8-9v[1]** JReid(5) (trckd ldrs: shkn up over 2f out: no rspnse)	½	6	9/1	85	37
4540a*	**Celestial Key (USA) (97)** (MJohnston) **7-9-7** JWeaver(12) (hld up: effrt 3f out: wknd & eased appr fnl f)	20	7	12/1	54	9
4148[9]	**Mukaddar (USA) (92)** (CJBenstead) **3-8-13** RHills(9) (cl up tl wknd 2f out)	7	8	20/1	35	—
3725[13]	**Hi Nod (96)** (MJCamacho) **7-9-6** LCharnock(10) (lw: lost tch over 4f out: sn t.o)	8	9	12/1	22	—
4423[8]	**Speedball (IRE) (95)** (IABalding) **3-9-2** LDettori(8) (lw: prom to ½-wy: sn wknd)	hd	10	8/1	21	—
4308*	**Shawm (98)** (DRLoder) **3-9-5** KFallon(7) (shkn up ½-wy: sn bhd: t.o)	5	11	100/30[1]	14	—
*4314**	***Yalta (IRE) (84)*** (RCharlton) **4-8-8b** TSprake(4) (Withdrawn not under Starter's orders: uns rdr & bolted leaving paddock)		W	9/1	—	—
				(SP 135.5%)	**11 Rn**	

1m 45.22 (8.22) CSF £25.61 CT £191.61 TOTE £4.20: £2.00 £1.70 £4.80 (£17.30) Trio £113.90 OWNER Mr T. F. Harris (NEWMARKET) BRED Cheveley Park Stud Ltd
WEIGHT FOR AGE 3yo-3lb
4283* Solar Storm loves soft ground and travels particularly well. Although not finding quite as much as expected when let down, he was always doing enough. (4/1)
3810 Mawingo (IRE), who has done all his racing on fast ground this season, took to these soft conditions particularly well. (6/1)
2525 Sharp Rebuff, after three months off, ran a smashing race here, despite being 7lb higher than his last win. (14/1)
4147 Kala Sunrise won this last year but was off a 6lb higher mark on this occasion and that seemed to make the difference. (8/1)
4147 Queens Consul (IRE) has shot up the weights with some splendid performances this season and is now 9lb higher than her last win. (10/1)
4554 Great Child was tried in a visor here for the first time, with no apparent help. (9/1)
4540a* Celestial Key (USA) has been winning some ordinary races in Switzerland this season and this ground tested his stamina to the limit. He was eased a great deal when beaten. (12/1)
4308* Shawm has won with cut in the ground but on this occasion he was never firing at any stage and ran miserably. (100/30)

4638 CONSTANT SECURITY MEDIAN AUCTION MAIDEN STKS (2-Y.O) (Class E)

4-00 (4-04) **7f 202y** £6,524.00 (£1,952.00: £936.00: £428.00) Stalls: Low GOING: 0.53 sec per fur (GS)

Form	Horse	Dist	Pos	SP	RR	SF
4057[5]	**Chim Chiminey** (BWHills) **2-8-9** MHills(2) (chsd ldrs: disp ld over 3f out tl led ins fnl f: styd on gamely)	—	1	10/1	86	42
4367[2]	**Achilles** (RAkehurst) **2-9-0** JWeaver(5) (lw: a.p: disp ld over 3f out tl ins fnl f: kpt on)	nk	2	3/1[2]	90	46
4237[10]	**Guildhall** (BJMeehan) **2-9-0** MTebbutt(14) (lw: effrt over 4f out: racd stands' side & styd on: nvr able to chal)	6	3	20/1	78	34
4007[2]	**Distinctive Dance (USA)** (LordHuntingdon) **2-9-0** LDettori(12) (effrt ½-wy: racd stands' side & styd on: no imp)	4	4	13/8[1]	70	26
	Double Edged (MJohnston) **2-9-0** DHolland(11) (w'like: mid div: effrt 4f out: no imp)	11	5	14/1	48	4
	Benjamin Frank (SPCWoods) **2-9-0** KFallon(6) (w'like: bhd: t.o over 2f out: shkn up & r.o)	3½	6	14/1	41	—
4231[6]	**Fearless Brave** (CWThornton) **2-9-0** DeanMcKeown(13) (sn bhd: sme hdwy fnl 3f: n.d)	nk	7	25/1	40	—
4107[7]	**St Clair Shores (USA)** (MRStoute) **2-8-9** JReid(15) (racd wd & led tl over 3f out: grad wknd)	½	8	14/1	34	—
4318[16]	**General Monck** (DMorley) **2-9-0** RHills(7) (hdwy & in tch ½-wy: wknd fnl 3f)	3	9	25/1	33	—
4113[6]	**Jollyhack** (JGMO'Shea) **2-9-0** JCarroll(9) (effrt ½-wy: n.d)	¾	10	33/1	32	—
4209[13]	**Joli Fille (49)** (JSWainwright) **2-8-9** TWilliams(1) (chsd ldrs: stumbled wl over 5f out: wknd over 3f out)	1	11	33/1	25	—
4107[4]	**Goldtune** (MAJarvis) **2-8-9** EmmaO'Gorman(8) (sn bhd & drvn along: n.d)	2	12	7/1[3]	21	—
4381[2]	**Nunthorpe** (JAGlover) **2-8-9** NDay(3) (trckd ldrs tl wknd over 3f out)	1¾	13	8/1	17	—
4236[9]	**Pas de Memoires (IRE)** (MHTompkins) **2-9-0** TQuinn(16) (dwlt: sn rcvrd to chse ldrs: wknd & eased fnl 2½f)	5	14	16/1	12	—
	Manufan (RFJohnsonHoughton) **2-9-0** KDarley(10) (lengthy: unf: s.i.s: hmpd appr st: t.o)	13	15	20/1	—	—
				(SP 144.8%)	**15 Rn**	

1m 46.2 (9.20) CSF £40.60 TOTE £14.50: £2.60 £1.60 £8.20 (£28.90) Trio £412.40 OWNER Mr W. J. Gredley (LAMBOURN) BRED Stetchworth Park Stud Ltd
4057 Chim Chiminey revelled in the soft ground. She certainly stays well and is as game as they come. (10/1)
4367 Achilles is a real staying type and he is game enough but, after a battle-royal, just met one too determined. (3/1)
Guildhall showed his first signs of form here but coming over to the stands rails may have been a disadvantage and he failed to get in a blow. (20/1)
4007 Distinctive Dance (USA) came towards the stands side which appeared no apparent help and, failing to offer a threat, this is best ignored. (13/8: 5/4-2/1)
Double Edged needed this and looks the type to do much better in time. (14/1)
Benjamin Frank never got into this but showed definite signs of ability and is one to watch. (14/1)
4231 Fearless Brave is weak as yet and is still learning. (25/1)

4639 STONEGATE LIMITED STKS (0-85) (3-Y.O+) (Class D)

4-30 (4-33) **1m 3f 195y** £6,004.00 (£1,792.00: £856.00: £388.00) Stalls: Low GOING: 0.53 sec per fur (GS)

Form	Horse	Dist	Pos	SP	RR	SF
4409[8]	**Celestial Choir (85)** (JLEyre) **7-9-1** KFallon(3) (outpcd & drvn along appr st: bhd & hmpd wl over 3f out: hdwy 2f out: styd on u.p to ld ins fnl f)	—	1	4/1[1]	96	45
3689[6]	**Hoh Express (85)** (MrsJRRamsden) **5-9-4** JFortune(6) (b.off hind: bhd: hdwy 4f out: led over 1f out: no ex ins fnl f)	3½	2	10/1	94	43
4476[10]	**Mister Pink (82)** (RFJohnsonHoughton) **3-8-9** KDarley(13) (chsd ldrs: chal 4f out: one pce appr fnl f)	5	3	14/1	86	28
4177*	**Flagship (80)** (MajorWRHern) **3-8-8** TSprake(12) (hld up: hdwy ent st: chal over 3f out: rdn & btn appr fnl f)	nk	4	11/2[2]	84	26
	Merit (IRE) (83) (PFICole) **5-9-2** TQuinn(9) (bit bkwd: hld up: hdwy 4f out: hung bdly lft fnl 2f: nvr able to chal)	¾	5	8/1	84	33

				SP	RR	SF
4320^{4}	**Patriot Games (IRE) (83)** (MRStoute) **3-8-11** JReid(2) (in tch: chal 4f out: wknd over 1f out)	5	**6**	6/1 ^{3}	79	21
4409^{2}	**Billy Bushwacker (82)** (MrsMReveley) **6-9-2** RCochrane(5) (bhd: effrt 4f out: btn 2f out)	2	**7**	6/1 ^{3}	75	24
3705^{U}	**Colour Code (81)** (MrsASwinbank) **5-9-2** SSanders(4) (chsd ldrs: rdn 4f out: wknd 2f out)	1¾	**8**	7/1	72	21
3916^{15}	**Khawafi (82)** (EALDunlop) **3-8-8** RHills(8) (cl up: led over 2f out tl over 1f out: wknd)	nk	**9**	12/1	71	13
4151^{19}	**Royal Crusade (USA) (85)** (WJHaggas) **3-8-9** MHills(11) (chsd ldrs: led over 4f out tl over 2f out: wknd wl over 1f out)	14	**10**	20/1	53	—
	Filmore West (85) (DWPArbuthnot) **4-9-2** LDettori(1) (b: bit bkwd: effrt over 4f out: wknd 3f out)	2½	**11**	16/1	50	—
4466^{12}	**Happy Minstral (USA) (85)** (MJohnston) **3-8-9b^{1}** DHolland(7) (led tl hdd over 4f out: sn wknd: t.o)	22	**12**	16/1	20	—
				(SP 127.5%)		**12 Rn**

2m 42.04 (14.24) CSF £44.34 TOTE £4.60: £1.80 £4.20 £4.90 (£32.30) Trio £187.00 OWNER Mrs Carole Sykes (HAMBLETON) BRED J. L. Eyre
WEIGHT FOR AGE 3yo-7lb
OFFICIAL EXPLANATION **Merit (IRE): reported that the horse hung badly left and he was unable to ride out.**
4136 Celestial Choir is the type of mare who runs when it suits her. Although she never looked happy here, she had the right man aboard to persuade her. (4/1: 3/1-9/2)
3689 Hoh Express has changed stables and looked to have got it right here when coming from way off the pace, but probably hit the front too soon. (10/1)
788 Mister Pink goes in the ground and seems to stay well enough but lacks that final dash when a struggle develops. (14/1)
4177* Flagship had her chances but this longer trip and the soft ground found her out. (11/2: 4/1-6/1)
Merit (IRE) has a lot more ability but all he wanted to do was hang left here and his rider just had to sit and hang on. (8/1)

4640 E.B.F. SANCTON MAIDEN STKS (2-Y.O) (Class D)
5-00 (5-09) **6f** £5,744.00 (£1,712.00: £816.00: £368.00) Stalls: High GOING: 0.53 sec per fur (GS)

				SP	RR	SF
3602^{2}	**Mihnah (IRE)** (DMorley) **2-8-9** RHills(4) (mde most: qcknd over 1f out: easily)	—	**1**	5/2 ^{1}	85+	42
2112^{4}	**Love Academy** (MJohnston) **2-9-0** DHolland(6) (trckd ldrs: hdwy 2f out: no ch w wnr)	5	**2**	7/2 ^{3}	77	34
4145^{7}	**Masha-Il (IRE)** (JHMGosden) **2-9-0** LDettori(3) (hld up: shkn up over 1f out: nvr nr to chal)	2½	**3**	100/30 ^{2}	70	27
4286^{4}	**Asyaad (USA)** (BWHills) **2-9-0** MHills(2) (trckd ldrs: nt qckn fnl 2f)	nk	**4**	9/2	69	26
3986^{2}	**Wolfhunt** (PJMakin) **2-9-0** SSanders(7) (w ldrs tl wknd fnl 2f)	nk	**5**	7/1	68	25
	Dancing Dervish (IABalding) **2-9-0** KDarley(8) (w'like: spd to ½-wy: sn btn & eased: t.o)	20	**6**	11/1	15	—
	All Our Blessings (IRE) (PCHaslam) **2-8-9** JFortune(1) (lengthy: scope: bit bkwd: sn outpcd & bhd: t.o)	4	**7**	20/1	—	—
4236^{2}	***Ryefield*** (MissLAPerratt) **2-9-0** JWeaver(5) (Withdrawn not under Starter's orders: spread both hind plates in paddock)		**W**	11/2	—	—
				(SP 133.0%)		**7 Rn**

1m 17.3 (6.80) CSF £11.00 TOTE £2.70: £1.90 £2.50 (£6.10) OWNER Mr Hamdan Al Maktoum (NEWMARKET) BRED Shadwell Estate Company Limited
3602 Mihnah (IRE) loved this testing ground and, always on the bridle, won with plenty in hand. (5/2)
2112 Love Academy is learning and was not knocked about once well beaten. (7/2)
Masha-Il (IRE) had an educational here and should improve for the run. (100/30)
4286 Asyaad (USA) showed something here and was not knocked about and time should see improvement. (9/2)
3986 Wolfhunt showed fair speed and he could be interesting when trying faster ground. (7/1)

T/Jkpt: Not won; £177,839.79 to York 9/10/97. T/Plpt: £1,476.70 (34.33 Tckts). T/Qdpt: £93.40 (25.79 Tckts) AA

4634-YORK (L-H) - Thursday October 9th
4641 Abandoned-Waterlogged

4529a-MAISONS-LAFFITTE (France) (Good)
Tuesday September 30th

4647a CRITERIUM DES YVELINES (Listed) (2-Y.O)
2-20 (2-32) **6f** £15,713.00 (£5,387.00: £4,040.00)

				SP	RR	SF
4106^{3}	**Merlin's Ring** (IABalding) **2-8-11** OPeslier	—	**1**		95	—
$3366a^{3}$	**Uninhibited (IRE)** (SWattel,France) **2-8-8** DBoeuf	2½	**2**		85	—
	Alliteration (France) **2-8-11** TJarnet	3	**3**		80	—
						11 Rn

1m 11.5 (1.80) P-M 5.00F: 2.30F 2.90F 2.10F (26.50F) OWNER Mrs Richard Plummer & Partners (KINGSCLERE) BRED Mrs A. Plummer
4106 Merlin's Ring was prominent throughout but, after taking the advantage at halfway, had the race won before the last furlong, and had something in hand at the end. He will not run again this season.

4648a PRIX D'ESTIMAUVILLE H'CAP (3-Y.O)
3-20 (3-29) **6f** £7,859.00

				SP	RR	SF
	Vassia (USA) (DBoulard,France) **3-8-10** ODoleuze	—	**1**		76	—
	Samarinka (FR) (France) **3-8-11** CAsmussen	2½	**2**		70	—
	Pistole Bliss (FR) (France) **3-8-4** FSanchez	d.h	**2**		63	—
2605^{5}	**Village Pub (FR)** (KOCunningham-Brown) **3-8-4** OPeslier (btn approx 9½l)		**9**		39	—
						9 Rn

1m 12.3 (2.60) P-M 4.50F: 1.90F 1.70F S 3.40F PB (3.70F S 18.40F PB) OWNER Mme A. Head BRED Yolande Seydoux
2300 Village Pub (FR) set the pace until ridden and headed a quarter of a mile from home.

4649a PRIX DU TIBBE H'CAP (4-Y.O+)
4-50 (4-54) **6f** £6,173.00

				SP	RR	SF
	Port-Lao (BEL) (HdeWaele,France) **6-8-8** OPeslier	—	**1**		69	—
	Leading Edge (FR) (France) **6-8-9(3)** ABouleau	¾	**2**		71	—
	Kaymadi (FR) (France) **6-8-13** GMosse	hd	**3**		72	—

				SP	RR	SF
3984[4]	**Village Native (FR)** (KOCunningham-Brown) **4-8-9** SGuillot (btn approx 3l)		7		65	—

15 Rn

1m 13.5 (3.80) P-M 4.30F: 2.10F 9.70F 2.30F (152.90F) OWNER H de Waele BRED Haras Flying Horse
3984 Village Native (FR) was in mid-division throughout.

3555a-HOPPEGARTEN (Berlin, Germany) (R-H) (Good)
Friday October 3rd

4650a PRIX ZINO DAVIDOFF - PREIS DER DEUTSCHEN EINHEIT (Gp 3) (3-Y.O+)
2-30 **1m 2f** £32,576.00 (£13,636.00: £6,818.00)

				SP	RR	SF
3998a*	**March Groom (USA)** (OGervai,Germany) **3-9-0** StephenDavies	—	1		121	—
4396a[9]	**Kalatos (GER)** (AWohler,Germany) **5-9-7** ABoschert	4	2		117	—
	Autriche (IRE) (HBlume,Germany) **3-8-12** THellier	¾	3		111	—

7 Rn

2m 8.7 TOTE 30DM: 20DM 30DM 27DM OWNER Stall MAGRO BRED Albert P. Coppola
March Groom (USA) who had become the first Hungarian-trained Group winner at Baden-Baden in August, followed up in style for his new trainer.

4395a-BELMONT PARK (New York, USA) (L-H) (Firm)
Saturday October 4th

4651a FLOWER BOWL INVITATIONAL (Gp 1) (3-Y.O+ F & M)
10-19 **1m 2f** £142,857.00 (£47,619.00: £26,190.00)

				SP	RR	SF
2814a[2]	**Yashmak (USA)** (HRACecil) **3-8-2** CNakatani	—	1		123	—
3879a[2]	**Maxzene (USA)** (USA) **4-8-11** MESmith	½	2		126	—
3879a*	**Memories Of Silver (USA)** (JToner,USA) **4-8-11** JBailey	hd	3		126	—

8 Rn

1m 59.3 TOTE $8.90: (1-2) $5.20 $3.70 (1-2-3) $2.70 $2.30 $2.20 OWNER Mr K. Abdullah (NEWMARKET) BRED Juddmonte Farms
2814a Yashmak (USA), held up, came wide off the bend to pass several rivals in the stretch. She has now been retired.

KEENELAND (Lexington, USA) (L-H) (Firm)
Saturday October 4th

4652a QUEEN ELIZABETH 11 CHALLENGE CUP (Gp 1) (3-Y.O F)
9-26 **1m 1f (Turf)** £147,619.00 (£47,619.00: £23,809.00)

				SP	RR	SF
3216*	**Ryafan (USA)** (JHMGosden) **3-8-9** ASolis	—	1		116	—
	Auntie Mame (USA) (USA) **3-8-9** JVelasquez	1½	2		113	—
3007a*	**Golden Arches (FR)** (USA) **3-8-9** CMcCarron	nk	3		113	—

8 Rn

1m 46.6 TOTE $7.60: (1-2) $4.60 $3.60 (1-2-3) $3.20 $2.60 $2.80 OWNER Mr K. Abdullah (NEWMARKET) BRED Juddmonte Farms
3216* Ryafan (USA) initiated a notable double for her owner in her usual brave style, bursting through late-on to score. She may go for the Yellow Ribbon at Santa Anita.

3373a-KLAMPENBORG (Copenhagen, Denmark) (R-H) (Good)
Saturday October 4th

4653a DANSK KRITERIUM (2-Y.O)
2-38 **7f** £14,896.00 (£4,965.00: £3,476.00)

				SP	RR	SF
	Grey Express (DEN) (SJensen,Denmark) **2-8-9** SMeacock	—	1		—	—
	Pfizer Ascot (DEN) (Denmark) **2-9-0** OLarsen	1	2		—	—
3887*	**O'Kelly (DEN)** (RGuest) **2-8-9** PBloomfield	3	3		—	—

12 Rn

1m 26.6 TOTE 68.6OKr: 18Kr 13Kr 15Kr (267Kr) OWNER Stall Lambada BRED Lone & Finn Pederson
3887* O'Kelly (DEN) put up a fair performance to finish third. He was always prominent and, third entering the straight, had every chance over a furlong out but ran on at the one pace. He will now go for another two-year-old race in Denmark later in the month.

4391a-LONGCHAMP (Paris, France) (R-H) (Good)
Saturday October 4th
WEATHER: very warm and sunny WIND: almost nil

4654a PRIX DU CADRAN (Gp 1) (4-Y.O+)
1-25 (1-21) **2m 4f** £56,117.00 (£22,447.00: £11,223.00: £5,612.00) GOING minus 0.02 sec per fur (G)

				SP	RR	SF
4130a[3]	**Chief Contender (IRE)** (PWChapple-Hyam) **4-9-2** ODoleuze (rdn in 3rd: effrt over 2f out: styd on to ld ins fnl f)	—	1	114/10	127	95
3645[4]	**Celeric** (DMorley) **5-9-2** LDettori (hld up bhd: 5th ent st: hrd rdn over 1f out: styd on cl home)	nk	2	4/5[1]	127	95
4346a[2]	**Persian Punch (IRE)** (DRCElsworth) **4-9-2** CAsmussen (broke wl: led tl hdd ins fnl f: styd on one pce)	¾	3	27/10[2]	126	94
	Always Earnest (USA) (MmeMBollack-Badel,France) **9-9-2** ABadel (hld up in rr: nvr plcd to chal)	2	4	88/10	125	93
4118[4]	**Double Trigger (IRE)** (MJohnston) **6-9-2** TJarnet (prom: lost pl & rdn ent st: one pce)	½	5	47/10[3]	124	92
	Leonard Quercus (FR) (FBedouret,Spain) **5-9-2** OPeslier (in rr: hdwy st: wknd wl over 1f out)	6	6	141/10	119	87

	Toba (IRE) (RMartin-Sanchez,Spain) **8-9-2** SGuillot (n.d)	dist	7	55/1	—	—
				(SP 126.8%)		**7 Rn**

4m 16.4 (1.40) P-M 12.40F: 3.30F 1.40F OWNER Mrs J. Magnier (MARLBOROUGH) BRED Jayeff 'B' Stables and Calogo Bloodstock A G

4130a Chief Contender (IRE) raced in third place before starting his challenge up the centre of the track two furlongs out. He ran on in the gamest of manners and took the lead with one hundred yards left to run. He stayed the two and a half miles well and is a really tough individual. His future has yet to be decided, but he could go to the Horses in Training Sale. (114/10)

3645 Celeric was held up and was going really well as he entered the straight. He started his challenge one and a half out, but just failed to find that bit extra in the closing stages. There were no excuses and he will now be rested for the season. (4/5)

4346a Persian Punch (IRE) attempted to make all the running and he stuck to his guns right up to the post. He attempted to draw the sting from his rivals and lost nothing in defeat. He will stay in training next year, but is now finished for the season. (27/10)

4118 Double Trigger (IRE) was without his intended rider, Michael Roberts, who was held up by travel problems. He was never allowed to dominate and seemed to lose interest back in second place. Under pressure four, out he was very one-paced. He is better than this. (47/10)

4655a PRIX DE ROYALLIEU (Gp 2) (3-Y.O+ F & M)

2-25 (2-24) **1m 4f 110y** £33,670.00 (£13,468.00: £6,734.00: £3,367.00) GOING minus 0.02 sec per fur (G)

				SP	RR	SF
2513^{2}	**Tulipa (USA)** (SbinSuroor) **4-9-1** LDettori (mde all: jst hld on)	—	1	$2/5^{1}$	117	66
	Dame Kiri (FR) (MmeCHead,France) **3-8-7** ODoleuze (a in tch: qcknd wl ins fnl f: jst failed)	s.h	2	$6/1^{3}$	116	58
$3370a^{4}$	**Kassana (IRE)** (AdeRoyerDupre,France) **3-8-7** GMosse (hld up: prog st: styd on ins fnl f)	1	3	$23/10^{2}$	115	57
	Annaba (IRE) (JHMGosden) **4-9-1** OPeslier (mid div: rdn over 2f out: styd on fnl f)	1½	4	$2/5^{1}$	114	53
	Muscadel (AFabre,France) **3-8-7** TJarnet (hld up: u.p 2f out: prog over 1f out: one pce cl home)	3	5	$2/5^{1}$	109	53
$1916a^{11}$	**Darashandeh (IRE)** (AdeRoyerDupre,France) **3-8-7** CAsmussen (prom: wknd over 1f out)	nk	6	$23/10^{2}$	109	52
	Averring (USA) (JCunnington,France) **4-9-1** FSanchez (a bhd)	4	7	131/10	104	55
	Rosabella (H-APantall,France) **3-8-7** SGuillot (in rr: n.d)	¾	8	$2/5^{1}$	102	44
$1366a^{5}$	**Gracie Lady (IRE)** (RCollet,France) **3-8-7** DBoeuf (trckd ldr: wknd 2f out: eased)	20	9	261/1	77	19
				(SP 368.1%)		**9 Rn**

2m 39.4 (4.90) P-M 1.40F: 1.30F 2.00F 1.50F (16.20F) OWNER Godolphin (NEWMARKET) BRED Fares Farm Inc

IN FOCUS: For betting purposes Tulipa (USA), Annaba (IRE), Muscadel and Rosabella were coupled.

2513 Tulipa (USA) ran the bravest of races. She went from pillar to post and showed a lot of courage to hold off the runner-up by a matter of inches. This was her second Group Two event as she also won the Ribblesdale Stakes at Ascot last year. She now goes to stud and should make an excellent broodmare. (2/5)

Dame Kiri (FR) raced in third place and attacked Tulipa at the furlong marker. Hard as she tried, she was not quite able to peg back the winner. She has a consistent record and this was her best effort to date. (6/1)

3370a Kassana (IRE), held up, made late progress but she never threatened the first two. (23/10)

Annaba (IRE) came back after the race with a horrible cut on her off-fore. She had apparently been struck into after just a hundred yards of the race. This was a great pity as it was her first run since winning the Prix de Conseil de Paris just under a year ago. She looked very well in the paddock, but this was just not to be her day as she also hard no luck in running in the straight. (2/5)

4656a PRIX DOLLAR (Gp 2) (3-Y.O+)

2-55 (2-56) **1m 1f 165y** £33,670.00 (£13,468.00: £6,734.00: £3,367.00) GOING minus 0.02 sec per fur (G)

				SP	RR	SF
$4204a^{3}$	**Alhaarth (IRE)** (SbinSuroor) **4-9-4** LDettori (set gd pce: mde all: qcknd 2f out: r.o strly)	—	1	$8/5^{2}$	123	96
$3730a^{4}$	**Lord Cromby (IRE)** (RCollet,France) **3-8-9** DBoeuf (mid div st: outpcd 1f out: rallied: r.o wl)	1	2	122/10	117	85
$1725a^{4}$	**Visionary (FR)** (AFabre,France) **3-8-9** TJarnet (4th st: hdwy 2f out: one pce fnl f)	2½	3	$47/10^{3}$	113	81
$1726a^{3}$	**Astarabad (USA)** (AdeRoyerDupre,France) **3-8-9** GMosse (bhd st: prog u.p 1f out: styd on)	½	4	$Evens^{1}$	112	80
4154^{2}	**Desert Story (IRE)** (MRStoute) **3-8-9** OPeslier (prom: ev ch: sn btn)	1½	5	$8/5^{2}$	110	78
$4392a^{3}$	**Handsome Ridge** (JHMGosden) **3-8-9** SGuillot (trckd wnr: 2nd st: wknd 2f out)	1½	6	104/10	108	76
	Mannenberg (IRE) (PDemercastel,France) **3-8-9** VVion (a bhd)	1½	7	40/1	105	73
	Bello (ARG) (FBedouret,Spain) **5-9-0** CAsmussen (n.d)	10	8	325/10	89	62
				(SP 166.2%)		**8 Rn**

1m 59.2 (0.70) P-M 2.60F: 2.10F 3.00F 2.10F (46.20F) OWNER Godolphin (NEWMARKET) BRED Shadwell Estate Company Limited

4204a Alhaarth (IRE) made every yard of the running and was still a comfortable length clear of the runner-up at the post. He was giving 9lb to his younger rivals and it was a really fine effort. He will now stand at the Derrinstown Stud. (8/5)

3730a Lord Cromby (IRE) raced in mid division before putting in a sustained late challenge in the straight. He was sold soon after this event and will now race in the States. (122/10)

1725a Visionary (FR) moved into second position halfway up the straight and then stayed on at one pace to the line. This distance seemed to be a little too long for him. (47/10)

1726a Astarabad (USA), held up, never really looked like getting on terms in the straight. He was probably a little rusty after a break of four months, and will come on a lot for the outing. (Evens)

4154 Desert Story (IRE) was prominent until halfway up the straight where he began to fade out of contention. (8/5)

4392a Handsome Ridge prominent for most of the way, was in trouble with a furlong and a half left to run. He has travelled to France a lot recently and may appreciate a rest. (104/10)

4657a PRIX DE CONDE (Gp 3) (2-Y.O C & G)

3-25 (3-25) **1m 1f** £24,691.00 (£8,979.00: £4,489.00: £2,694.00) GOING minus 0.02 sec per fur (G)

				SP	RR	SF
	Thief Of Hearts (IRE) (AFabre,France) **2-9-2** OPeslier	—	1		—	76
	Special Quest (FR) (MmeCHead,France) **2-9-2** ODoleuze	1	2		—	74
	Daymarti (IRE) (AdeRoyerDupre,France) **2-9-2** GMosse	hd	3		—	74
	Silic (FR) (PBary,France) **2-9-2** SGuillot	s.nk	4		—	74
	Quel Senor (FR) (FDoumen,France) **2-9-2** DBoeuf	6	5		—	63
$3874a^{2}$	**Milligan (FR)** (JEPease,France) **2-9-2** FSanchez	4	6		—	56
	Season Of Love (FR) (PDemercastel,France) **2-9-2** TJarnet	6	7		—	45
						7 Rn

1m 50.5 (2.50) P-M 4.10F 2.20F 2.00F OWNER No Owner (CHANTILLY)

Thief Of Hearts (IRE) races in similar fashion to his half-brother Swain, and he too is likely to improve as he gets older. Held up, he came with a steady run before taking the advantage inside the final furlong. Softer ground might suit him a little better and he now goes for the Criterium de Saint-Cloud.

Special Quest (FR) was asked to make all the running, but he was unable to hold off the tough winner in the final furlong.

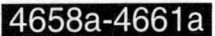

Daymarti (IRE) ran a strange race. He was coltish in the paddock and did not seem all that interested until coming into the straight. Suddenly he took hold of his bit and ran on really well in the closing stages. This half-brother to Daylami is a bit of a character, but he has definite talent.
Silic (FR) was a rather disappointing favourite. He was the first to attack Special Quest in the straight but his effort was short-lived.

4658a PRIX DE LUTECE 'TROPHEE SIR PETER O'SULLEVAN' (Gp 3) (3-Y.O)

3-55 (3-54) **1m 7f** £24,691.00 (£8,979.00: £4,489.00: £2,694.00) GOING minus 0.02 sec per fur (G)

				SP	RR	SF
2596*	**Three Cheers (IRE)** (JHMGosden) **3-8-11** LDettori	—	**1**		116	80
4392a[2]	**Bonapartiste (FR)** (PDemercastel,France) **3-8-11** GMosse	2	**2**		114	78
3000a[3]	**Warbler** (PBary,France) **3-8-8** SGuillot	½	**3**		110	74
4101*	**Sausalito Bay** (IABalding) **3-8-9** CAsmussen	s.h	**4**		111	75
	Heavenly Calm (USA) (AdeRoyerDupre,France) **3-8-6** OPeslier	s.nk	**5**		108	72
3763*	**Pentad (USA)** (RCharlton) **3-8-9** MRoberts	5	**6**		106	70
4257a[4]	**New Frontier (IRE)** (AFabre,France) **3-9-0** TJarnet	6	**7**		104	68
4191a*	**Aliya (IRE)** (JOxx,Ireland) **3-8-6** PJSmullen	1½	**8**		95	59
	Big Ander (SPA) (RMartin-Sanchez,Spain) **3-8-9** DBoeuf	20	**9**		76	40

9 Rn

3m 8.7 (2.70) P-M 2.60F: 1.40F 2.00F 2.70F (16.10F) OWNER No Owner (NEWMARKET) BRED Sheikh Mohammed Bin Rashid Al Maktoum
2596* Three Cheers (IRE) looked to have no chance of winning this race until halfway up the straight. He was virtually refusing to race and his jockey nearly gave up and pulled him up, but, taken wide and hard ridden, he began to advance. He took the lead a furlong out and was going right from the others at the post.
4392a Bonapartiste (FR) was held up for a late challenge and was putting in his best work at the end.
3000a Warbler was also held up and, making headway from one and a half furlongs out, fought on well to the line.
4101* Sausalito Bay, racing in mid-division, was perfectly placed to challenge in the straight. Although running on, he was one-paced in the closing stages.
3763* Pentad (USA) raced just behind the leaders and was second into the straight, but was a spent force soon after.

4541a-SAN SIRO (Milan, Italy) (R-H) (Good to firm)
Saturday October 4th

4659a PREMIO DUCA D'AOSTA (Listed) (3-Y.O+)

12-40 (12-40) **1m 7f** £23,142.00 (£10,183.00: £5,554.00)

				SP	RR	SF
4346a[6]	**Samraan (USA)** (JLDunlop) **4-9-1** TSprake	—	**1**		117+	—
	Upper Class (GER) (Italy) **4-9-1** THellier	1½	**2**		115	—
	Belsalazie (Italy) **4-8-12** CColombi	2¾	**3**		110	—

5 Rn

3m 12.8 (14.80) TOTE 12L: 10L 11L (13L) OWNER Mr K. M. Al-Mudhaf (ARUNDEL) BRED Mrs Afaf A. Al Essa
4346a Samraan (USA) never looked in any real danger once he hit the front with two furlongs to run, and this was a very convincing performance.

4660a PREMIO VITTORIO DI CAPUA (Gp 1) (3-Y.O+ C & F)

2-50 (2-56) **1m** £68,849.00 (£31,387.00: £19,382.00: £9,691.00)

				SP	RR	SF
3993a*	**Devil River Peek (USA)** (BSchutz,Germany) **5-8-12** AStarke (hld up: 4th st: hdwy to ld 1½f out: r.o wl)	—	**1**		127	—
1728a[4]	**Kierkegaard** (DDucci,Italy) **4-8-12** FJovine (hld up: 8th st: hdwy 1½f out: fin wl)	1¼	**2**		125	—
2453a[4]	**Wixim (USA)** (RCharlton) **4-8-12** TSprake (hld up: hdwy to chse ldrs ½-wy: trckd ldr gng wl 2½f out: rdn 1½f out: fnd nil)	3	**3**		119	—
1200a[3]	**Taxi de Nuit (USA)** (AVerdesi,Italy) **5-8-12** MMonteriso (hld up: styd on fnl 2f: nvr able to chal)	1¾	**4**		115	—
4122a[3]	**Gothenberg (IRE)** (MJohnston) **4-8-12** JWeaver (set fast pce: hdd & wknd 1½f out)	4¾	**5**		106	—
1728a[3]	**Morigi** (ITellini,Italy) **6-8-12** MTellini (5th st: sn n.d)	9	**6**		88	—
	Soleil Trompeur (IRE) (PGuarsegnati,Italy) **3-8-9** ACorniani (nvr bttr than mid div)	3½	**7**		81	—
3996a[2]	**Parfait Glace (FR)** (JEHammond,France) **5-8-12** MBoutin (prom early: wnt clr w ldr: wknd 3f out)	s.h	**8**		80	—
	Attimo Fuggente (IRE) (APeraino,Italy) **4-8-12** AParravani (a bhd)	10	**9**		60	—

9 Rn

1m 36.3 (6.30) TOTE 102L: 20L 22L 13L (672L) OWNER Stall Hoppegarten BRED Fares Farm Inc.
2453a Wixim (USA) had no reply to the finishing bursts of the first two. Held up, he made headway at the halfway stage and looked to be going really well two and a half furlongs out. Unfortunately he found very little when asked the question and could only keep on at the one pace.
4122a Gothenberg (IRE) led until headed and weakening with a furlong and a half to run.

2272a-DORTMUND (Germany) (R-H) (Good)
Sunday October 5th

4661a BMW DEUTSCHES ST LEGER (Gp 2) (3-Y.O C & F)

3-55 (3-57) **1m 6f** £45,455.00 (£18,182.00: £9,091.00: £4,545.00)

				SP	RR	SF
4127a[6]	**Ungaro (GER)** (HBlume,Germany) **3-9-2** THellier (racd in 5th: hdwy ½-wy: 3rd st: led 2f out: r.o strly)	—	**1**		118	—
3737a[7]	**Asolo (GER)** (BSchutz,Germany) **3-9-2** AStarke (hld up in rr: 5th st: styd on wl fnl 2f: no ch w wnr)	3½	**2**		114	—
2641a*	**Maceo (GER)** (HJentzsch,Germany) **3-9-2** PSchiergen (cl up: wnt 2nd 5f out: ev ch 2f out: one pce)	2½	**3**		111	—
4251a*	**Palio Sky** (JLDunlop) **3-9-2** WNewnes (led after 1f: rdn & hdd 2f out: unable qckn)	1	**4**		110	—
1545a[3]	**Damus (GER)** (AWohler,Germany) **3-9-2b1** ABoschert (hld up in rr: hdwy ½-wy: 4th st: rdn & btn over 2f out)	8	**5**		101	—
	Lonango (GER) (MHofer,Germany) **3-9-2** ABest (6th st: sn btn)	6	**6**		94	—
2642a[7]	**Penalty (GER)** (UOstmann,Germany) **3-9-2** GBocskai (racd 4th: lost pl ½-wy: 8th & btn st)	14	**7**		78	—
	All Blade (GER) (RSuerland,Germany) **3-9-2** ATylicki (led 1f: in 2nd tl lost pl ½-wy: 7th & wkng st)	21	**8**		54	—
	Periannath (GER) (CSprengel,Germany) **3-9-2** TMundry (a in rr: p.u 2f out: lame)		**P**		—	—

9 Rn

2m 53.0 TOTE 59DM: 15DM 20DM 12DM OWNER Gestut Rottgen BRED Gestut Rottgen
4251a* Palio Sky soon took up the running but, joined by Ungaro and Maceo two furlongs out, he was soon in trouble.

4654a-LONGCHAMP (Paris, France) (R-H) (Good to firm)
Sunday October 5th
WEATHER: very warm and sunny WIND: almost nil

4662a EUROSTAR - PRIX DU ROND-POINT (Gp 2) (3-Y.O)
1-30 (1-28) **1m** £44,893.00 (£17,957.00: £8,979.00: £4,489.00) GOING minus 0.08 sec per fur (G)

				SP	RR	SF
4377*	**Decorated Hero** (JHMGosden) **5-9-1** LDettori (trckd ldr: rdn ent st: r.o strly: led over 1f out: r.o strly)	—	**1**	12/10[2]	117	84
3002a[6]	**Kaldou Star** (ELellouche,France) **3-8-12** TThulliez (3rd ent st: rdn over 1f out: r.o & wnt 2nd cl home)	¾	**2**	7/10[1]	116	80
3996a*	**Marathon (USA)** (MmeCHead,France) **3-8-12** ODoleuze (led: hdd over 1f out: no ex)	hd	**3**	102/10	115	79
4122a[2]	**Eden Rock (GER)** (BSchutz,Germany) **3-8-12** KFallon (a bhd: outpcd fnl 2f)	1½	**4**	6/1[3]	112	76
				(SP 127.5%)	**4 Rn**	

1m 35.9 (0.90) P-M 2.20F: 2.20F 2.70F OWNER Exors of the late Mr Herbert Allen (NEWMARKET) BRED Reg Griffin and Jim McGrath

4377* Decorated Hero is continuing to improve with age, and won this race with a little in hand despite being under strong pressure early in the straight. He is now likely to run in the Challenge Stakes at Newmarket. (12/10)

1915a* Kaldou Star was putting in his best work at the finish, and took second place close home. He is not quite up to Group Two class, and prefers more cut in the ground. (7/10)

3996a* Marathon (USA) was a disappointing favourite. He tried to make all, but ran very freely and consequently had little in reserve when challenged by the winner. He has had little racing due to various problems, including a virus which kept him off the track for three months earlier in the season, and so he not surprisingly stays in training next year. He could well make the top grade and is one for the note book. (102/10)

Eden Rock (GER) was held up at the back, but just stayed on in the straight. (6/1)

4663a PRIX MARCEL BOUSSAC (Gp 1) (2-Y.O F)
2-05 (2-04) **1m** £89,787.00 (£35,915.00: £17,957.00: £8,979.00) GOING minus 0.08 sec per fur (G)

				SP	RR	SF
	Loving Claim (USA) (MmeCHead,France) **2-8-12** ODoleuze (broke wl: set gd pce: mde all: drvn out)	—	**1**	37/10[3]	98	62
	Isle De France (USA) (AFabre,France) **2-8-12** AJunk (mid div st: outpcd 2f out: r.o wl cl home)	1½	**2**	118/10	95	59
	Plasir Des Yeux (FR) (PDemercastel,France) **2-8-12** TGillet (hld up in rr: swtchd lft over 1f out: r.o ins fnl f)	¾	**3**	517/10	94	58
3882a[4]	**Khumba Mela (IRE)** (AFabre,France) **2-8-12** TJarnet (mid div st: r.o wl u.p cl home)	nk	**4**	77/10	93	57
	Desert Drama (IRE) (RCollet,France) **2-8-12** SGuillot (a.p: 3rd st: no ex u.p)	s.h	**5**	227/10	93	57
4259a*	**Silent Tribute (IRE)** (MBell) **2-8-12** LDettori (trckd ldr: 2nd st: rdn over 1f out: no ex)	s.h	**6**	91/10	93	57
3744*	**Ashraakat (USA)** (JLDunlop) **2-8-12** RHills (prom: rdn over 1f out: one pce)	s.h	**7**	33/10[2]	93	57
3874a*	**Saralea (FR)** (DSmaga,France) **2-8-12** DBoeuf (a bhd: n.d)	4	**8**	162/10	85	49
4250a*	**Anna Palariva (IRE)** (AFabre,France) **2-8-12** OPeslier (s s: a bhd: eased st)	¾	**9**	5/2[1]	83	47
	Noemie (FR) (GSandor,France) **2-8-12b[1]** GGuignard (n.d)	½	**10**	59/1	82	46
				(SP 115.9%)	**10 Rn**	

1m 37.6 (2.60) P-M 4.70F: 2.20F 3.30F 6.80F (35.10F) OWNER Maktoum Al Maktoum (CHANTILLY) BRED Gainsborough Farm Inc

Loving Claim (USA) put up a terrific effort on only her second outing. She led throughout and won with something in hand. A good-actioned filly, she will either be aimed at the 1,000 Guineas or the Pouliches, depending on plans for her owner's other fillies. (37/10)

Isle De France (USA) raced in mid-division, and was left struggling when the pace quickened, but finished really well. She is sure to benefit from the experience, and may prefer a longer trip in time. (118/10)

Plasir Des Yeux (FR) must have had an off-day when fifth to Anna Palariva in the d'Aumale. However, she ran up to her best this time, coming with a storming late run up the centre of the track. She can win a Group Three at least on this form, possibly the Prix des Reservoirs. (517/10)

3882a Khumba Mela (IRE) was on her toes in the paddock, and played-up at the start. She was held up early on, and put in her best work at the finish. She is not the easiest of fillies to deal with, but has plenty of talent. (77/10)

4259a* Silent Tribute (IRE) tracked the winner for much of the race but, despite battling on well, did not look up to this class. (91/10)

3744* Ashraakat (USA) had an outside draw and ran freely early on. She was under pressure soon after entering the straight, and could not quicken up in the last furlong. This was a little disappointing but, as things did not go her way, she should be given another chance (33/10)

4250a* Anna Palariva (IRE) never had a chance after missing the break, and this run should be ignored. (5/2)

4664a PRIX DE L'ABBAYE DE LONGCHAMP (Gp 1)
2-40 (2-41) **5f** £56,117.00 (£22,447.00: £11,223.00: £5,612.00) GOING minus 0.08 sec per fur (G)

				SP	RR	SF
4098[3]	**Carmine Lake (IRE)** (PWChapple-Hyam) **3-9-8** JReid (a cl up: rdn over 1f out: r.o wl to ld cl home)	—	**1**	168/10	124	55
4001a*	**Pas De Reponse (USA)** (MmeCHead,France) **3-9-8** ODoleuze (broke wl: w ldr: led over 3f out: hrd rdn over 1f out: no ex cl home)	½	**2**	9/5[1]	122	53
4011*	**Royal Applause** (BWHills) **4-9-11** MHills (rn 5th: hrd rdn ins fnl f: unable qckn cl home)	nse	**3**	122/10	125	56
4390a[3]	**Kistena (FR)** (MmeCHead,France) **4-9-8** DBoeuf (bhd early: hdwy 2f out: sltly hmpd: r.o strly)	hd	**4**	9/5[1]	122	53
4421[3]	**Averti (IRE)** (WRMuir) **6-9-11** MJKinane (mid div: rdn over 1f out: styd on one pce)	1½	**5**	134/10	120	51
4124a[5]	**Titus Livius (FR)** (JEPease,France) **4-9-11** CAsmussen (mid div: nvr plcd to chal)	s.nk	**6**	122/10	120	51
4239[15]	**Hever Golf Rose** (TJNaughton) **6-9-8** JWeaver (rdn in rr: hdwy over 1f out: hmpd: styd on)	¾	**7**	498/10	114	45
4124a*	**Don't Worry Me (IRE)** (GHenrot,France) **5-9-8** OPeslier (mid div: nvr any ch)	½	**8**	98/10[3]	113	44
3882a[7]	**Zelding (IRE)** (RCollet,France) **2-8-4** TJarnet (a bhd)	1½	**9**	219/10	109?	21
4239[16]	**Deep Finesse** (MAJarvis) **3-9-11** MRoberts (prom tl wknd wl over 1f out)	1½	**10**	964/10	106	37
4239*	**Eveningperformance** (HCandy) **6-9-8** CRutter (led over 1f: wknd 2f out)		**11**	91/10[2]	—	—
	Late Parade (IRE) (ARenzoni,Italy) **6-9-11** OFancera (bhd: one pce st)		**12**	138/10	—	—
				(SP 132.4%)	**12 Rn**	

56.9 secs (2.40) P-M 17.80F: 2.90F 1.40F 1.50F (33.20F) OWNER Mr R. E. Sangster (MARLBOROUGH) BRED Swettenham Stud

IN FOCUS: For betting purposes Pas De Reponse and Kistena (FR) were coupled.

4098 Carmine Lake (IRE) put up a fine effort on only her second run of the season. She is difficult to train due to arthritis, but her trainer had her spot-on this time. She was superbly ridden to get her head in front in the closing stages and, in an open year, may still take the sprinters' title. It is undecided as to whether she remains in training. (168/10)

4001a* Pas De Reponse (USA) broke quickly and tried to make all. She stuck to her task well when headed, and is likely to go for the Breeders' Cup Sprint. Connections were not happy about the way she was ridden, and perhaps she may be held up next time. (9/5)

4011* Royal Applause missed the break but was on terms below the distance. He ran on bravely over a trip short of his ideal. No plans for his future have been announced. (122/10)

4390a Kistena (FR) ran a cracking race on only her second outing since winning this last year. She was last just after halfway, but weaved her way through, and was finishing best of all. She will now go for the Prix de Petit Couvert if she comes out of this race in good order. (9/5)

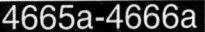

4421 Averti (IRE) was putting in his best work at the finish without ever looking like catching the principals. (134/10)
4260a Hever Golf Rose made some late progress, but was never really in the hunt. She has lost a little of her sparkle this term. (498/10)
3111 Deep Finesse was well up for much of the race, but could not sustain the effort. (964/10)
4239* Eveningperformance was quickly away as usual but, taken on by the runner-up, failed to give her running. She has been retired. (91/10)

4665a PRIX DE L'ARC DE TRIOMPHE (Gp 1) (3-Y.O+ C & F)

3-20 (3-20) **1m 4f** £448,934.00 (£179,574.00: £89,787.00: £44,893.00: £22,447.00) GOING minus 0.08 sec per fur (G)

				SP	RR	SF
4257a[2]	**Peintre Celebre (USA)** (AFabre,France) **3-8-11** OPeslier (mid div: hdwy 2f out: led appr fnl f: qcknd clr)	—	**1**	22/10[1]	141	100
4204a*	**Pilsudski (IRE)** (MRStoute) **5-9-5** MJKinane (7th st: hdwy 2f out: styd on strly)	5	**2**	38/10[3]	135	101
4127a*	**Borgia (GER)** (BSchutz,Germany) **3-8-8** KFallon (hld up bhd tl st: rdn over 2f out: r.o wl)	2½	**3**	162/10	128	87
4346a*	**Oscar Schindler (IRE)** (KPrendergast,Ireland) **5-9-5** CAsmussen (mid div: styd on fnl 2f)	s.h	**4**	123/10	132	98
4127a[3]	**Predappio** (SbinSuroor) **4-9-5** JReid (a bhd ldrs: 4th st: hrd rdn ins fnl f: styd on)	s.h	**5**	94/10	132	98
4129a[2]	**Helissio (FR)** (ELellouche,France) **4-9-5** DBoeuf (led after 2f tl over 1f out: no ex fnl f)	s.nk	**6**	5/2[2]	132	98
4238[3]	**Swain (IRE)** (SbinSuroor) **5-9-5** LDettori (a.p: ev ch: one pce fnl f)	nk	**7**	94/10	131	97
3737a[3]	**Que Belle (USA)** (HRemmert,Germany) **3-8-8** KWoodburn (last st: hdwy 2f out: styd on)	1½	**8**	681/10	125	84
4238*	**Posidonas** (PFICole) **5-9-5** TQuinn (prom: 5th st: one pce fnl 2f)	2½	**9**	912/10	126	92
4134*	**Busy Flight** (BWHills) **4-9-5** MHills (led for 2f: 2nd st: btn over 1f out)	½	**10**	65/1	125	91
3704*	**My Emma** (RGuest) **4-9-2** DHolland (hld up: u.p ins fnl f: sn wknd)	2½	**11**	161/10	119	85
2814a*	**Ebadiyla (IRE)** (JOxx,Ireland) **3-8-8** JPMurtagh (a bhd)	½	**12**	544/10	117	76
4256a[2]	**Gazelle Royale (FR)** (JEHammond,France) **3-8-8** MRoberts (prom: 8th st: sn wknd)	nk	**13**	106/1	117	76
1917a*	**Steward (FR)** (DSepulchre,France) **4-9-5** SGuillot (a bhd)	5	**14**	105/1	114	80
4256a*	**Queen Maud (IRE)** (JdeRoualle,France) **3-8-8** TJarnet (mid div: 10th st: sn btn)	1½	**15**	315/10	108	67
4258a[3]	**Le Destin (FR)** (PDemercastel,France) **4-9-5** TGillet (hld up: hdwy over 3f out: outpcd)	2½	**16**	462/10	109	75
4258a[2]	**Nothin' Leica Dane (AUS)** (JEHammond,France) **5-9-5** GMosse (in tch over 8f)	½	**17**	578/10	108	74
4258a*	**Yokohama (USA)** (MmeCHead,France) **6-9-5** ODoleuze (in tch: 6th st: sn btn)	1½	**18**	437/10	106	72
				(SP 135.9%)	**18 Rn**	

2m 24.6 (-1.40) P-M 3.20F: 1.60F 2.20F 3.30F (7.80F) OWNER Mr D. Wildenstein (CHANTILLY) BRED Allez France Stables

4257a Peintre Celebre (USA) put up a magnificent performance. He looked hemmed in on the rail coming into the straight but, once a gap appeared, he had the class and the speed to go ahead and dominate the final stages of the race. He smashed the course record by 1.7 seconds and came home alone, five lengths clear of his nearest rival. Peintre Celebre is the outstanding three-year-old colt in Europe this season and is in a class of his own. His connections would not be tempted to run him in either the Breeders' Cup or the Japan Cup as they have his four-year-old career very much in mind. He is likely to be seen in England next year as the King George VI is one of the targets being considered before another run in the Arc, followed by retirement to the Coolmore Stud. (22/10)
4204a* Pilsudski (IRE) was beaten five lengths for the second consecutive year. He was in front of Peintre Celebre for much of the race, but could not go with the winner when he burst for home two out. He ran his usual genuine race, but he could just be a better horse over ten to eleven furlongs. He now goes for the Champion Stakes and will hopefully receive an invitation for the Japan Cup. (38/10)
4127a* Borgia (GER) was outpaced early in the race, and had plenty to do at the entrance to the straight. However, she came through strongly, and took third place close home. She lacks the speed required at the very top level, but nevertheless this was a fine effort. She is in the Japan Cup, and remains in training next year. (162/10)
4346a* Oscar Schindler (IRE) raced alongside the winner from before halfway. He had a clear run in the straight but, despite lacking acceleration, his courage and stamina earned him fourth place. (123/10)
4127a Predappio was given every possible chance. He was always well up and raced in fourth place for much of the time. He battled on gamely in the straight, and only lost third place by two short-heads. He is likely to race in Italy for the rest of the season. (94/10)
4129a Helissio (FR) tried to repeat last year's success in similar style but, on this ground, was unable to get his rivals into trouble, and was beaten for speed in the last furlong and a half. (5/2)
4238 Swain (IRE) was always close to the pace. He battled on well in the straight, but lacked acceleration in the closing stages, and would have preferred more cut in the ground. He is to be aimed at the Japan Cup. (94/10)
4238* Posidonas was always up with the pace, but could not sustain his effort in the closing stages. (912/10)
4134* Busy Flight led early, but then settled in behind Helissio, and was still there entering the straight. However, he had nothing left in the closing stages, and is not really up to this class. (65/1)
3704* My Emma was waited with at the back of the field but, after making an effort two out, ran out of gas in the closing stages. Her recent setback may have taken its toll, and she will retire to the paddocks. (161/10)

4666a SUNSET & VINE PRIX DE L'OPERA (Gp 2) (3-Y.O+ F & M)

4-00 (4-12) **1m 1f 55y** £44,893.00 (£17,957.00: £8,979.00: £4,489.00) GOING minus 0.08 sec per fur (G)

				SP	RR	SF
3003a[2]	**Clodora (FR)** (AFabre,France) **3-8-9** TJarnet (7th st: rdn to qckn over 2f out: hdwy to ld ins fnl f: pushed out)	—	**1**	209/10	117	97
3704[6]	**Squeak** (JHMGosden) **3-8-9** GMosse (a bhd ldrs: 4th st: rdn 2f out: chal ldr ins fnl f: styd on)	1	**2**	96/10	115	95
3376a[5]	**La Blue (GER)** (BSchutz,Germany) **4-8-12** CAsmussen (hld up in rr: hdwy fr 2f out: r.o)	hd	**3**	44/10[2]	114	98
3988[3]	**Balalaika** (LMCumani) **4-8-12** JReid (5th st: u.p 2f out: r.o one pce)	½	**4**	213/10	113	97
4117[3]	**Samara (IRE)** (JLDunlop) **4-8-12** TQuinn (prom: led briefly over 2f out: one pce fnl f)	1	**5**	82/10	112	96
4181*	**Entice (FR)** (SbinSuroor) **3-8-9** LDettori (9th st: nvr plcd to chal)	nk	**6**	13/10[1]	112	92
1916a[6]	**Always Loyal (USA)** (MmeCHead,France) **3-9-0** ODoleuze (6th st: rdn & r.o one pce)	1½	**7**	13/10[1]	114	94
1727a[3]	**Veiled Threat (IRE)** (RCollet,France) **3-8-9** DBoeuf (hld up bhd: prog over 2f out: n.d)	s.nk	**8**	61/10[3]	109	89
3552a*	**Tenuous** (PBary,France) **3-8-9** SGuillot (n.d)	½	**9**	75/10	108	88
1202a[9]	**Genevra (IRE)** (HRemmert,Germany) **3-8-9** KWoodburn (hld up in rr: nt clr run over 1f out: hmpd 1f out: nt rcvr)	1½	**10**	122/10	106	86
4094a*	**Clerio** (H-APantall,France) **3-8-9** MJKinane (mid div: u.p over 1f out: n.d)		**11**	13/10[1]	—	—
1728a[8]	**Sensation** (JHMGosden) **4-8-12** OPeslier (8th st: one pce)		**12**	13/10[1]	—	—
3552a[2]	**Majinskaya (FR)** (SWattel,France) **3-8-9** FSanchez (prom: 5th st: outpcd)		**13**	23/1	—	—
4094a[2]	**Supercal** (DRCElsworth) **3-8-9** SDrowne (a bhd)		**14**	28/1	—	—
4181[2]	**Meshhed (USA)** (BHanbury) **3-8-9** RHills (3rd st: sn wknd)		**15**	45/1	—	—
3552a[3]	**Enigma (GER)** (BSchutz,Germany) **3-8-9** KFallon (n.d)		**16**	46/1	—	—
3878a[3]	**Camille (FR)** (PDemercastel,France) **4-8-12** VVion (led: hdd over 2f out: sn btn)		**17**	59/1	—	—
				(SP 268.8%)	**17 Rn**	

1m 51.1 (-0.90) P-M 21.80F: 4.50F 3.20F 2.30F (137.40F) OWNER Mr J-L Lagardere (CHANTILLY)

IN FOCUS: For betting purposes Entice (FR), Always Loyal (USA), Clerio and Sensation were coupled.

Clodora (FR) was given an enterprising ride. In mid-division until the straight, she produced a good turn of foot to lead entering the last furlong. This was her first Group success, and she will now be retired to stud. (209/10)
3704 Squeak put up a genuine performance. Always well placed on the rail, she stuck to her task until the end, despite not having the speed of the winner in the last half-furlong. She is still considered immature by her trainer, and is probably better suited by further. She may stay in training next year. (96/10)
1550a* La Blue (GER) had a rotten run, as she was given plenty to do by her jockey, and was twice hampered in the final quarter-mile. She was the moral winner. (44/10)
3988 Balalaika was putting in her best work at the finish, but lacked acceleration. (213/10)
4117 Samara (IRE) looked the winner when bursting into the lead at the two-furlong marker. However, she had nothing in reserve in the closing stages. (82/10)
4181* Entice (FR) was held up and made some late progress without ever looking a serious threat. (13/10)
Sensation was beaten a furlong and a half out. (13/10)
4094a Supercal was never seen with a chance. (28/1)
4181 Meshhed (USA) was prominent for a long way, but dropped out quickly in the straight. (45/1)

4439-ASCOT (R-H) (Heavy)
Friday October 10th

WEATHER: fair WIND: mod half against

4667 BOLLINGER CHAMPAGNE CHALLENGE SERIES FINAL GENTLEMEN'S H'CAP (0-80) (3-Y.O+) (Class E)

2-00 (2-00) **1m 4f** £4,318.50 (£1,308.00: £639.00: £304.50) Stalls: High GOING: 0.45 sec per fur (GS)

				SP	RR	SF
4521^{8}	**Dauphin (IRE) (46)** (WJMusson) **4-9-4**$^{(4)ow1}$ MrSDurack(1) (hld up: led over 1f out: r.o wl)	—	**1**	12/1	58	38
4562^{9}	**New Inn (47)** (SGollings) **6-9-9**^{ow2} MrRWakley(2) (led over 5f: led over 3f out tl over 1f out: unable qckn)	1¼	**2**	25/1	57	36
4426^{11}	**Whitechapel (USA) (80)** (LordHuntingdon) **9-12-0** MrABalding(7) (a.p: rdn over 2f out: ev ch over 1f out: one pce)	1½	**3**	15/8^{1}	88	69
4548^{2}	**Civil Liberty (64)** (GLewis) **4-10-12** MrTMcCarthy(3) (hdwy over 2f out: rdn over 1f out: one pce)	1½	**4**	13/2^{3}	70	51
3593^{4}	**Running Free (IRE) (55)** (MJFetherston-Godley) **3-9-10** MrJGoldstein(6) (lw: a.p: rdn over 2f out: sn wknd)	7	**5**	20/1	52	26
	Granby Bell (48) (PHayward) **6-9-6**$^{(4)}$ MrVLukaniuk(4) (bit bkwd: swtg: a.p: led over 6f out tl over 3f out: wknd 2f out)	½	**6**	20/1	44	25
4371^{12}	**Country Thatch (45)** (CAHorgan) **4-9-3**$^{(4)}$ MrJCrowley(5) (lost pl 10f out: no hdwy fnl 2f)	4	**7**	25/1	36	17
	World Express (IRE) (54) (BRMillman) **7-10-2** MrKGoble(9) (lw: nvr nr to chal)	½	**8**	20/1	44	25
3739^{4}	**Koraloona (IRE) (60)** (GBBalding) **4-10-8** MrLJefford(10) (lw: a bhd)	2	**9**	11/2^{2}	48	29
4435^{10}	**Rasayel (USA) (72)** (PDEvans) **7-11-2**$^{(4)}$ MrAEvans(12) (hdwy 10f out: wknd over 6f out)	16	**10**	16/1	38	19
4108^{10}	**Fourdaned (IRE) (56)** (SDow) **4-10-4** MrOMcPhail(11) (hdwy 10f out: wknd over 6f out)	25	**11**	16/1	—	—
4510*	**Xylem (USA) (74)** (LMCumani) **6-11-8** ^{5x} MrCRanson(8) (swtg: sme hdwy on ins 3f out: sn wknd)	6	**12**	15/2	—	—
				(SP 116.7%)	**12 Rn**	

2m 45.54 (15.54) CSF £257.26 CT £737.77 TOTE £16.50: £3.10 £5.20 £1.10 (£106.20) Trio £85.10 OWNER Mrs Rita Brown (NEWMARKET)
BRED Patrick H. Dillon
LONG HANDICAP Dauphin (IRE) 9-4
WEIGHT FOR AGE 3yo-7lb

3467 Dauphin (IRE) stalked the leaders and, striking the front approaching the final furlong, kept on too well for the runner-up. (12/1: 8/1-14/1)
4363 New Inn regained the advantage over three furlongs from home, but collared below the distance was unable to match the winner. (25/1)
1208* Whitechapel (USA), had ground and trip in his favour, but he was conceding an awful lot of weight to the first two, and although still having every chance below the distance, looked very tired as he struggled on at one pace. (15/8)
4548 Civil Liberty was given a much better ride this time, but after taking closer order entering the straight could then only go up and down in the same place. (13/2: 4/1-7/1)
3593 Running Free (IRE) played an active role until tiring in the ground early in the straight. (20/1)
Granby Bell goes well in the mud. Moving to the front running out of Swinley Bottom, he was collared over three furlongs from home and tired a quarter of a mile out as lack of race fitness took its toll, having been off the course for nearly a year. (20/1)
4510* Xylem (USA) (15/2: 4/1-8/1)

4668 TRIPLEPRINT MAIDEN STKS (UNRACED 2-Y.O) (Class D)

2-30 (2-30) **6f** £6,775.00 (£2,050.00: £1,000.00: £475.00) Stalls: Low GOING: 0.87 sec per fur (S)

			SP	RR	SF
Wiston Cheese (USA) (JLDunlop) **2-9-0** TSprake(7) (w'like: scope: bit bkwd: shkn up & hdwy over 1f out: led nr fin)	—	**1**	8/1^{3}	94 t	55
Tussle (MBell) **2-9-0** MFenton(2) (w'like: scope: lw: hld up: rdn over 1f out: ev ch fnl f: r.o)	½	**2**	9/4^{1}	93 t	54
Late Night Out (WJarvis) **2-9-0** JReid(5) (w'like: a.p: led over 1f out: rdn: hdd nr fin)	hd	**3**	5/1^{2}	92 t	53
Courageous (IRE) (PFICole) **2-9-0** TQuinn(1) (w'like: scope: bit bkwd: led over 4f: wknd ins fnl f)	3	**4**	9/4^{1}	84 t	45
Miss Money Spider (IRE) (RHannon) **2-8-9** DaneO'Neill(4) (neat: a.p: ev ch over 1f out: sn wknd)	3½	**5**	5/1^{2}	70 t	31
Russian Delight (IRE) (RHannon) **2-8-9** RPerham(3) (w'like: chsd ldr over 3f)	10	**6**	14/1	43 t	4
Maylan (IRE) (DMHyde) **2-8-9** SSanders(6) (w'like: s.s: rdn 4f out: bhd fnl 3f)	9	**7**	33/1	19 t	—
			(SP 115.6%)	**7 Rn**	

1m 22.4 (8.40) CSF £24.58 TOTE £9.20: £3.00 £2.10 (£16.00) OWNER Mr Robin Scully (ARUNDEL) BRED Clovelly Farms

Wiston Cheese (USA), a good-looking, scopey newcomer, had leg problems earlier in the year and gave the impression that the run was needed which makes this performance even more commendable. Needing only to be woken up to pick up ground approaching the final furlong, he came through to snatch the spoils near the line. (8/1: 6/1-9/1)
Tussle, an attractive, good-bodied colt with plenty of scope, certainly looked tuned up for this. Throwing down a very determined challenge in the final furlong, he may have got his head in front for a couple of strides in the closing stages before the winner went by. He should have no problems in finding a race. (9/4)
Late Night Out, a medium-sized colt, gained control approaching the final furlong but he was given no peace whatsoever, and was worried out of it near the line. He should soon be winning. (5/1: 3/1-11/2)
Courageous (IRE), an attractive, deep-girthed chestnut, was carrying condition for this debut and ran accordingly, for after taking the field along until below the distance, he tired inside the last two-hundred yards. He will do better over middle distances next year. (9/4: 6/4-5/2)
Miss Money Spider (IRE) had far less substance than any of her rivals in the paddock, but still had every chance approaching the final furlong before tiring. (5/1)

4669 BONUSPRINT OCTOBER STKS (Listed) (3-Y.O+ F & M) (Class A)
3-05 (3-05) **1m (round)** £17,181.25 (£5,200.00: £2,537.50: £1,206.25) Stalls: High GOING: 0.45 sec per fur (GS)

				SP	RR	SF
3913^{4}	**Jafn (95)** (BHanbury) **3-8-8** RHills(11) (s.s: n.m.r over 2f out: hdwy over 1f out: hrd rdn: led wl ins fnl f: r.o wl)	—	**1**	5/1^{1}	106	56
4153^{2}	**Dancing Drop (100)** (RHannon) **3-8-8** DaneO'Neill(6) (hdwy over 2f out: led 1f out tl wl ins fnl f: unable qckn)	1¼	**2**	6/1^{3}	104	54
3875a^{0}	**Blessed Spirit (80)** (CFWall) **4-8-11** SSanders(4) (hld up: led wl over 1f out to 1f out: ev ch ins fnl f: one pce)	nk	**3**	8/1	103	56
4013^{8}	**Fiametta (84)** (CEBrittain) **3-8-8** LDettori(8) (bhd whn nt clr run over 2f out: hdwy over 1f out: r.o)	2	**4**	11/1	99	49
4331*	**Northern Blessing** (PWHarris) **3-8-8** JReid(1) (a.p: led over 2f out tl wl over 1f out: sn wknd)	2½	**5**	10/1	94	44
1499*	**Heavenly Ray (USA) (80)** (JRFanshawe) **3-8-8** TQuinn(2) (hld up: rdn over 2f out: wknd over 1f out)	2½	**6**	20/1	89	39
4226^{4}	**Palisade (USA)** (HRACecil) **3-8-8** KFallon(3) (hdwy over 3f out: wknd over 2f out)	12	**7**	5/1^{1}	65	15
4421^{11}	**Dame Laura (IRE) (99)** (HMorrison) **3-8-8** TSprake(10) (prom 6f)	4	**8**	20/1	57	7
4424^{2}	**Priena (IRE) (91)** (DRLoder) **3-8-8v^{1}** RCochrane(9) (lw: hdwy over 3f out: sn wknd)	hd	**9**	13/2	57	7
4306*	**Marilaya (IRE) (90)** (LMCumani) **3-8-8** KDarley(5) (lw: led over 5f)	10	**10**	11/2^{2}	37	—
				(SP 114.4%)	**10 Rn**	

1m 48.1 (7.30) CSF £30.95 TOTE £4.50: £1.70 £2.70 £2.30 (£11.50) Trio £40.80 OWNER Mr Hamdan Al Maktoum (NEWMARKET) BRED P. and Mrs Venner

WEIGHT FOR AGE 3yo-3lb

3913 Jafn loves this ground and demonstrated at Goodwood back in May where she had a nightmare run that she was up to winning a race of this nature. Covered up until as late as possible, she began her effort from below the distance and, responding to pressure, got up in the closing stages. (5/1)

4153 Dancing Drop gave a good account of herself, but having hit the front a furlong from home was worried out of it in the closing stages. She is having a lot of difficulty in getting her head in front this year. (6/1)

3875a Blessed Spirit certainly had no easy task at the weights, but she likes this ground and proved co-operative on this occasion. Striking the front early in the final quarter-mile, she was headed a furlong out but still held on until tapped for toe in the last one hundred yards. (8/1)

4013 Fiametta had a lot more on her plate here but nevertheless stayed on well in the last furlong and a half. (11/1)

4331* Northern Blessing was taking a step up in class but acquitted herself well, showing in front early in the straight before overhauled well over a furlong from home. (10/1)

1499* Heavenly Ray (USA), without a run in four and a half months, chased the leaders. She looked in trouble turning for home but held on grimly until tiring below the distance. (20/1)

4306* Marilaya (IRE) (11/2: 4/1-6/1)

4670 SCOTTISH EQUITABLE/JOCKEYS ASSOCIATION NURSERY H'CAP (2-Y.O) (Class C)
3-40 (3-40) **7f** £8,949.00 (£2,712.00: £1,326.00: £633.00) Stalls: Low GOING: 0.87 sec per fur (S)

				SP	RR	SF
4113*	**Smart Squall (USA) (83)** (LordHuntingdon) **2-9-1** JReid(2) (nt clr run over 2f out: hdwy over 1f out: led ins fnl f: rdn out)	—	**1**	8/1^{3}	95+	54
3067^{4}	**Indian Missile (83)** (JLDunlop) **2-9-1** RHills(13) (lw: hdwy 2f out: rdn over 1f out: unable qckn)	2½	**2**	14/1	89	48
3802^{5}	**Pay On Red (USA) (75)** (PFICole) **2-8-7** TQuinn(9) (rdn over 2f out: hdwy 1f out: r.o)	1½	**3**	12/1	78	37
4215*	**Scent of Success (USA) (80)** (MRStoute) **2-8-12v** KDarley(12) (lw: a.p: led 3f out tl ins fnl f: sn wknd)	¾	**4**	7/1^{2}	81	40
4368^{2}	**Titan (77)** (SDow) **2-8-9** KFallon(8) (lw: hdwy 2f out: hrd rdn over 1f out: wknd fnl f)	1¾	**5**	8/1^{3}	74	33
4576*	**Tightrope (75)** (SirMarkPrescott) **2-8-7** 5x SSanders(1) (lw: nvr nr to chal)	2½	**6**	11/4^{1}	66	25
4113^{3}	**Chief Cashier (77)** (GBBalding) **2-8-9** SDrowne(10) (swtg: hdwy over 2f out: sn wknd)	3	**7**	14/1	62	21
4411^{4}	**Cool Secret (77)** (ABMulholland) **2-8-9** TLucas(5) (nvr nrr)	5	**8**	20/1	50	9
4271^{6}	**Water Force (70)** (GBBalding) **2-8-2** NVarley(7) (lw: prom over 5f)	hd	**9**	20/1	43	2
4065^{4}	**Signatory (69)** (RHannon) **2-8-1** JQuinn(6) (lw: prom 5f)	½	**10**	14/1	41	—
4551^{8}	**Who Nose (IRE) (74)** (BJMeehan) **2-8-6b** MTebbutt(15) (hld up: rdn 2f out: sn wknd)	9	**11**	20/1	25	—
4315^{8}	**Moontabeh (84)** (PTWalwyn) **2-9-2v^{1}** DHolland(14) (a bhd)	3	**12**	20/1	28	—
4468^{2}	**Demolition Jo (77)** (PDEvans) **2-8-9v** JFEgan(4) (prom 5f)	1¼	**13**	12/1	19	—
4362^{6}	**Balaclava (IRE) (72)** (EALDunlop) **2-8-4** GCarter(11) (prom 4f)	4	**14**	20/1	4	—
4265^{10}	**Take A Turn (80)** (MRChannon) **2-8-12v** JFortune(3) (led 4f)	10	**15**	10/1	—	—
				(SP 129.7%)	**15 Rn**	

1m 37.2 (10.00) CSF £102.08 CT £1,225.78 TOTE £9.70: £3.50 £4.30 £3.60 (£35.70) Trio £579.90 OWNER Mr George Ward (WEST ILSLEY) BRED Centaur Farms Inc.

4113* Smart Squall (USA), who has a problem with starting stalls, had someone down at the start with him. Beginning to get into top gear from below the distance, he swept into the lead inside the final furlong, and was rousted along to put daylight between himself and his rivals. He would not be inconvenienced by further. (8/1)

3067 Indian Missile goes in the ground, but after moving up on the outside of the field a quarter of a mile from home, then failed to find another gear from below the distance despite winning the battle for second prize. (14/1)

3802 Pay On Red (USA) at last found his stride a furlong from home but by then it was all over. He is well worth another try at a mile. (12/1)

4215* Scent of Success (USA) struck the front three furlongs from home, but she probably made her bid for glory too early because she tired in the testing ground inside the final furlong. (7/1)

4368 Titan took closer order a quarter of a mile from home but had run out of steam in the final furlong. (8/1)

4576* Tightrope was encountering soft ground for the first time and never threatened to get in a blow. (11/4)

4671 RACING CHANNEL CONDITIONS STKS (3-Y.O+) (Class C)
4-15 (4-15) **1m (straight)** £4,755.70 (£1,733.20: £846.60: £363.00: £161.50) Stalls: Low GOING: 0.87 sec per fur (S)

				SP	RR	SF
4277*	**Ghalib (IRE)** (MajorWRHern) **3-9-0** RHills(4) (lw: hld up: led over 1f out: shkn up: r.o wl)	—	**1**	11/8^{1}	90	68
451^{5}	**Chai-Yo** (JABOld) **7-8-12** SSanders(1) (bkwd: swtchd rt & hdwy over 1f out: one pce)	2	**2**	25/1	81?	62
4523^{5}	**Weet-A-Minute (IRE) (103)** (RHollinshead) **4-8-12** TQuinn(3) (chsd ldr 1f: ev ch over 1f out: unable qckn)	nk	**3**	9/4^{2}	80	61
4312^{4}	**Royal Philosopher (96)** (JWHills) **5-8-12** MHills(2) (led over 6f)	16	**4**	4/1^{3}	48	29
	Stories To Tell (USA) (HRACecil) **3-8-9** KFallon(5) (lw: chsd ldr 7f out tl over 1f out: wknd qckly)	6	**5**	11/2	36	14
				(SP 112.1%)	**5 Rn**	

1m 49.92 (9.92) CSF £27.04 TOTE £2.40: £1.50 £2.60 (£23.90) OWNER Mr Hamdan Al Maktoum (LAMBOURN) BRED Shadwell Estate Company Limited

WEIGHT FOR AGE 3yo-3lb

4277* Ghalib (IRE) showed at Newbury on his debut that he enjoys this ground, and put up a polished display in this much better company, leading approaching the final furlong and needing only to be shaken up for a very convincing victory. When stabled with Tom Jones last year he broke a bone in his knee, which had to have a screw put in it, and then suffered a stress fracture on his opposite leg this year, hence his late arrival on the scene. He is described as a nice horse in the making by the Major, and plenty more will be heard of this attractive colt who should certainly be making up for lost time next year. (11/8: 11/10-7/4)
451 Chai-Yo, winner of three races over hurdles last winter, was carrying plenty of surplus flesh for this first run since March. However, he ran surprisingly well and managed to win the battle for second prize. This should have helped get him right for a successful National Hunt campaign. (25/1)
4523 Weet-A-Minute (IRE) had an easier task here, but he was unable to take advantage of it, and after having every chance below the distance was tapped for toe. He has not won for two years. (9/4)
4312 Royal Philosopher had ground and trip in his favour but he continues to run poorly, and after setting the pace until below the distance tamely dropped away. (4/1)
Stories To Tell (USA) looked in really good shape for this belated reappearance and was certainly fit. However, the heavy ground proved his downfall for after having every chance in the final-quarter-mile then stopped as if shot. (11/2)

4672 LITTLETON STUD H'CAP (0-90) (3-Y.O+) (Class C)

4-45 (4-45) **1m 4f** £7,490.00 (£2,270.00: £1,110.00: £530.00) Stalls: High GOING: 0.45 sec per fur (GS)

				SP	RR	SF
4443^{7}	**Taunt (90)** (DMorley) **3-9-10** MHills(1) (hld up: led over 1f out: rdn out)	—	1	7/1	103	78
4176^{4}	**Mantles Prince (73)** (GLewis) **3-8-7** PaulEddery(9) (lw: rdn & hdwy over 2f out: chsd wnr over 1f out: r.o)	1¼	2	14/1	84	59
4477^{2}	**Mattimeo (IRE) (80)** (APJarvis) **4-9-2**(5) CLowther(5) (rdn over 2f out: hdwy over 1f out: r.o one pce)	6	3	8/1	83	65
4242^{11}	**Happy Go Lucky (74)** (RJO'Sullivan) **3-8-8** SSanders(6) (a.p: led over 2f out tl over 1f out: sn wknd)	3½	4	33/1	73	48
3748^{3}	**Wild Rita (80)** (WRMuir) **5-9-7** JReid(2) (lw: rdn & hdwy over 2f out: wknd over 1f out)	2	5	12/1	76	58
3434^{4}	**Veridian (80)** (PWHarris) **4-9-7** KFallon(8) (s.s: rdn & hdwy over 2f out: 5th & btn whn nt clr run on ins over 1f out)	1¼	6	$11/2^{3}$	74	56
2776^{5}	**Premier Generation (IRE) (71)** (DWPArbuthnot) **4-8-12** DHolland(4) (rdn & hdwy over 2f out: wknd over 1f out)	2½	7	10/1	62	44
	Tiger Lake (70) (SDow) **4-8-11** JFEgan(13) (lw: s.s: rdn & sme hdwy 2f out: sn wknd)	1½	8	20/1	59	41
4521^{3}	**Royal Diversion (IRE) (75)** (MCPipe) **4-9-2** KDarley(7) (a.p: hrd rdn & ev ch over 1f out: sn wknd)	1¼	9	$9/2^{1}$	62	44
4378*	**Bel Canto (IRE) (78)** (JHMGosden) **3-8-12** LDettori(12) (lw: rdn over 2f out: sme hdwy on ins wl over 1f out: sn wknd)	8	10	$5/1^{2}$	55	30
3918*	**Double Alleged (USA) (88)** (MJohnston) **3-9-8** JWeaver(11) (b: w ldr: led 8f out tl over 2f out: sn wknd)	½	11	14/1	64	39
4369^{5}	**Lonely Heart (82)** (DRCElsworth) **3-9-2** TQuinn(3) (swtg: prom over 8f: t.o)	dist	12	20/1	—	—
4136^{16}	**Magic Combination (IRE) (73)** (BJCurley) **4-9-0** JQuinn(10) (lw: led 4f: wknd over 3f out: t.o)	3	13	16/1	—	—

(SP 122.3%) **13 Rn**

2m 39.85 (9.85) CSF £91.75 CT £741.30 TOTE £8.20: £2.50 £4.60 £3.90 (£49.60) Trio £210.30 OWNER Lord Hartington (NEWMARKET)
BRED Side Hill Stud
WEIGHT FOR AGE 3yo-7lb
2572* Taunt loves the mud and, swinging off the bridle entering the straight, led below the distance and was rousted along to assert. (7/1)
4176 Mantles Prince saw out this longer trip and, taking second place approaching the final furlong, pulled well clear of the remainder if unable to get on level terms with the winner. He has still to get his head in front. (14/1)
4477 Mattimeo (IRE) has never won beyond a mile and a quarter but stayed on in the last furlong and a half to take third prize. (8/1: 6/1-10/1)
2594 Happy Go Lucky bounced back to form and gained control early in the straight. Collared below the distance, she had little more to offer. (33/1)
3748 Wild Rita made an effort early in the straight but had shot her bolt below the distance. (12/1)
3434 Veridian took closer order early in the straight, but was already held when done no favours along the inside rail below the distance.(11/2)
4521 Royal Diversion (IRE) appeared to be absolutely hacking over her rivals entering the straight, but she had been racing up with the fast early pace, and that proved her downfall, for although still holding every chance below the distance she was then out on her feet. (9/2: 7/1-4/1)

4673 WYNDHAM H'CAP (0-90) (3-Y.O+) (Class C)

5-20 (5-20) **2m 45y** £9,441.25 (£2,860.00: £1,397.50: £666.25) Stalls: High GOING: 0.45 sec per fur (GS)

				SP	RR	SF
4426*	**Jaseur (USA) (82)** (JHMGosden) **4-9-10v** LDettori(6) (lw: a.p: led 2f out: clr over 1f out: easily)	—	1	$4/1^{1}$	93+	52
4426^{12}	**Galapino (67)** (MissGayKelleway) **4-8-9** JReid(4) (swtg: hdwy & n.m.r over 2f out: rdn over 1f out: r.o ins fnl f)	1¼	2	6/1	77	36
4235^{4}	**Bold Buster (69)** (IABalding) **4-8-11** MHills(3) (b.off hind: hdwy over 2f out: hrd rdn over 1f out: unable qckn)	hd	3	$9/2^{2}$	79	38
4461*	**City Hall (IRE) (78)** (MRStoute) **3-8-9v** 3x TQuinn(2) (led to 2f out: one pce)	s.h	4	13/2	88	36
4426^{9}	**Thornby Park (80)** (JLDunlop) **3-8-11b1** TSprake(5) (b: lw: hdwy over 6f out: hrd rdn over 1f out: one pce)	nk	5	$5/1^{3}$	89	37
3383*	**Arcady (62)** (JLHarris) **4-7-13**(5) RMullen(1) (b: hdwy on ins 3f out: wknd over 2f out)	7	6	10/1	64	23
4002^{8}	**Royal Seaton (67)** (MrsPNDutfield) **8-8-6**(3) RHavlin(10) (a bhd)	13	7	25/1	57	16
4426^{10}	**Story Line (80)** (DWPArbuthnot) **4-9-5**(3) RFfrench(8) (lw: prom 13f)	½	8	25/1	69	28
4426^{6}	**Sea Victor (73)** (JLHarris) **5-9-1** DHolland(9) (lw: chsd ldr tl over 2f out: sn wknd)	s.h	9	12/1	62	21
4313^{7}	**Hal Hoo Yaroom (77)** (RAkehurst) **4-9-5** JWeaver(7) (lw: swtchd rt & hdwy on ins over 3f out: wknd over 2f out)	12	10	25/1	54	13

(SP 110.8%) **10 Rn**

3m 45.88 (18.68) CSF £23.35 CT £95.92 TOTE £3.20: £1.80 £2.10 £1.60 (£12.80) Trio £19.10 OWNER Sheikh Mohammed (NEWMARKET)
BRED Darley Stud Management Co Ltd
WEIGHT FOR AGE 3yo-11lb
4426* Jaseur (USA) looks an improving performer, and had no problems with an 8lb rise in the weights as he completed the hat-trick in impressive style, leading a quarter of a mile from home and being eased considerably in the closing stages. He was value for six lengths. (4/1: op 5/2)
4222 Galapino, who met traffic problems at the last meeting here, took closer order early in the straight but appeared to be going nowhere below the distance. However, he found another gear in the closing stages and came between horses to snatch second prize right on the line. (6/1)
4235 Bold Buster began a forward move early in the straight but, under pressure below the distance, was then only fighting for minor honours. (9/2)
4461* City Hall (IRE) took the field along but, collared two furlongs from home, could then only struggle on at the one insufficient pace. (13/2)
3763 Thornby Park, fitted with blinkers for the first time, made a forward move running out of Swinley Bottom but could only go up and down in the same place in the final quarter-mile. (5/1)

3383* Arcady does not go on this ground, and an effort along the inside rail turning for home proved to be short-lived. (10/1)

T/Jkpt: £238,492.50 (0.29 Tckts); £238,492.58 to Ascot 11/10/97. T/Plpt: £910.50 (78.31 Tckts). T/Qdpt: £119.00 (29.35 Tckts) AK

4667-ASCOT (R-H) (Race 1 Soft, remainder Heavy)
Saturday October 11th
WEATHER: raining WIND: almost nil

4674 MCGEE GROUP AUTUMN STKS (Listed) (2-Y.O) (Class A)
2-00 (2-00) **1m (round)** £12,429.00 (£3,762.00: £1,836.00: £873.00) Stalls: High GOING: 0.62 sec per fur (GS)

				SP	RR	SF
4237*	**Dr Fong (USA)** (HRACecil) **2-8-11** KFallon(1) (lw: hld up: c centre st: chsd ldr 2f out: hrd rdn & led 1f out: r.o wl)	—	**1**	9/4[2]	95?	60
4278*	**Equity Princess (87)** (MJohnston) **2-8-6** DHolland(3) (lw: led over 2f: led 3f out: hrd rdn & edgd lft over 1f out: hdd 1f out: r.o)	½	**2**	9/2[3]	89?	54
4116[2]	**Rabah (93)** (JLDunlop) **2-8-11** RHills(4) (lw: hld up: rdn over 2f out: sn wknd)	12	**3**	9/2[3]	70	35
4274[3]	**Evening World (FR)** (PFICole) **2-8-11** TQuinn(2) (lw: plld hrd: led over 5f out to 3f out: wknd 2f out)	7	**4**	7/4[1]	56	21
				(SP 103.5%)	**4 Rn**	

1m 49.31 (8.51) CSF £9.62 TOTE £2.70 (£4.40) OWNER The Thoroughbred Corporation (NEWMARKET) BRED Prestonwood Farm Inc

4237* Dr Fong (USA), who made an impressive debut at Newbury last month on a fast surface, was not suited by the heavy ground according to Fallon, which makes this performance even more commendable, as he was rousted along in the straight and managed to get on top entering the final furlong. He has all the makings of a high-class three-year-old. (9/4: op 5/4)

4278* Equity Princess regained the advantage turning for home and, although collared a furlong out, lost nothing in defeat, keeping on really well to the bitter end. (9/2)

4116 Rabah flopped in the mud and was in trouble early in the straight. (9/2: 3/1-5/1)

4274 Evening World (FR) may have won in the mud but he refused to settle and had soon pulled his way to the front. Collared turning for home, he had run out of puff early in the straight. (7/4)

4675 WILLMOTT DIXON CORNWALLIS STKS (Gp 3) (2-Y.O) (Class A)
2-30 (2-30) **5f** £23,239.99 (£8,800.75: £4,312.88: £1,971.38) Stalls: Low GOING: 0.62 sec per fur (GS)

				SP	RR	SF
4232*	**Halmahera (IRE) (100)** (IABalding) **2-8-12** MartinDwyer(4) (a.p: led 2f out: rdn out)	—	**1**	8/1	111?	84
3706[4]	**Lord Kintyre (100)** (BRMillman) **2-8-12** OPeslier(3) (lw: rdn over 2f out: hdwy to chse wnr over 1f out: unable qckn)	4	**2**	6/1[3]	98	71
4387a[5]	**Ella (IRE)** (LordHuntingdon) **2-8-7** LDettori(9) (rdn over 2f out: hdwy over 1f out: r.o one pce)	5	**3**	8/1	77	50
4150*	**Land of Dreams (100)** (MJohnston) **2-8-13** DHolland(10) (hdwy 2f out: rdn over 1f out: wknd fnl f)	2	**4**	4/1[1]	77	50
4267[3]	**Thanksgiving (IRE) (100)** (MajorDNChappell) **2-8-7** MHills(6) (lw: a.p: rdn over 2f out: one pce)	½	**5**	14/1	69	42
4093a[7]	**Lady Alexander (IRE)** (CCollins,Ireland) **2-8-10** PShanahan(2) (lw: w ldr: led over 2f out: sn hdd & wknd)	2½	**6**	9/2[2]	64	37
4305[2]	**Pure Coincidence (100)** (GLewis) **2-8-12** PaulEddery(8) (led over 2f: wknd over 1f out)	¾	**7**	16/1	64	37
4150[2]	**Tippitt Boy (100)** (KMcAuliffe) **2-9-1** JReid(11) (swtchd rt & hdwy over 1f out: wknd fnl f)	s.h	**8**	14/1	67	40
2584[4]	**Blueridge Dancer (IRE) (100)** (BJMeehan) **2-8-12b** KFallon(7) (rdn 3f out: bhd fnl 2f)	2	**9**	20/1	57	30
4517[3]	**Bold Edge (100)** (RHannon) **2-8-12** DaneO'Neill(12) (lw: prom 3f)	4	**10**	14/1	44	17
4293[6]	**Banningham Blade (99)** (KTIvory) **2-8-7** JQuinn(13) (swtg: prom over 3f)	1½	**11**	16/1	35	8
3629[2]	**Legs Be Frendly (IRE) (86)** (KMcAuliffe) **2-8-12** SSanders(5) (lw: s.s: a bhd)	½	**12**	33/1	38	11
4428*	**Mrs Malaprop (85)** (MRChannon) **2-8-7** TQuinn(1) (lw: bhd fnl 2f)	12	**13**	10/1	—	—
				(SP 123.2%)	**13 Rn**	

64.06 secs (3.86) CSF £52.10 TOTE £8.30: £3.10 £2.50 £2.20 (£16.80) Trio £82.70 OWNER Robert & Exors Late Elizabeth Hitchins (KINGSCLERE) BRED Mrs John McEnery

4232* Halmahera (IRE) is an improving individual who had his first run way back in March. He goes well with plenty of give underfoot and, leading a quarter of a mile out, forged clear from below the distance for a decisive victory. (8/1)

3706 Lord Kintyre has shown himself to be a very useful juvenile and seemed to cope on this first encounter with soft ground. Taking second place approaching the final furlong, he had no hope with the winner, but still finished well clear of the remainder. (6/1)

4387a Ella (IRE) has gained both her wins to date on soft ground but, despite staying on in the last furlong and a half to take third prize, found the front two were already home and dry. (8/1)

4150* Land of Dreams began her effort a quarter of a mile from home, but tired in this energy-sapping ground in the final furlong. A sound surface is needed for her. (4/1: 9/4-9/2)

4267 Thanksgiving (IRE) was never far away but could only struggle on at the one insufficient pace in the final quarter-mile. (14/1)

4093a Lady Alexander (IRE) appreciated the return to a shorter trip, but the soft ground was not in her favour and, although she showed in front over a quarter of a mile from home, she was soon headed and in trouble. (9/2)

4676 PRINCESS ROYAL STKS (Gp 3) (3-Y.O+ F & M) (Class A)
3-00 (3-00) **1m 4f** £31,400.00 (£11,882.50: £5,816.25: £2,651.25) Stalls: High GOING: 0.95 sec per fur (S)

				SP	RR	SF
4445[4]	**Delilah (IRE) (95)** (MRStoute) **3-8-7v** OPeslier(2) (rdn over 5f out: hdwy over 2f out: led over 1f out: r.o wl)	—	**1**	4/1[2]	110	65
4099[4]	**Snow Princess (IRE) (98)** (LordHuntingdon) **5-9-0** MJKinane(7) (led over 9f: hrd rdn over 1f out: unable qckn)	3	**2**	5/2[1]	106	68
4435*	**Saafeya (IRE) (88)** (JHMGosden) **3-8-7** LDettori(4) (lw: chsd ldr: led over 2f out tl over 1f out: one pce)	nk	**3**	11/2	106	61
3370a[5]	**Reine Wells (IRE)** (PBary,France) **4-9-0** TJarnet(6) (hld up: rdn over 2f out: one pce)	3½	**4**	9/2[3]	101	63
4181[3]	**Bombazine (IRE) (96)** (LMCumani) **3-8-7** JReid(1) (rdn over 2f out: nvr nr to chal)	1¼	**5**	6/1	99	54
4445[2]	**Graceful Lass (97)** (DRLoder) **3-8-7** TQuinn(5) (b.nr hind: a bhd)	20	**6**	9/1	73	28
3917[4]	**Alcalali (USA) (80)** (PAKelleway) **3-8-7** KFallon(3) (lw: plld hrd: hdwy over 10f out: wknd over 2f out)	18	**7**	25/1	49	4
				(SP 110.3%)	**7 Rn**	

2m 45.33 (15.33) CSF £12.15 TOTE £3.40: £1.90 £1.60 (£3.40) OWNER Highclere Thoroughbred Racing Ltd (NEWMARKET) BRED Tullamaine Castle Stud

WEIGHT FOR AGE 3yo-7lb

4445 Delilah (IRE) was given a masterly ride by the French ace on ground she loves. The signs did not look at all good as she was being pushed along soon after Swinley Bottom, but she picked up nicely in the straight and, striking the front approaching the final furlong, in the end won with a bit in hand. She will now go to the sales. (4/1)

4099 Snow Princess (IRE) certainly wants further but the heavy ground which she loves brought her stamina into play. Bowling along in front, she was collared over a quarter of a mile from home and, although dropping back to third place, struggled on again to regain the runner-up berth in the last few strides. (5/2)
4435* Saafeya (IRE) appeared to be cruising as she moved to the front over a quarter of a mile from home but, headed below the distance, she was then struggling. This longer trip in these very testing conditions appeared to be a bit too much for her. (11/2)
1199a Reine Wells (IRE) needs this ground but, when an effort was called for, she could only plod on at the one pace. (9/2: 3/1-5/1)
4181 Bombazine (IRE) faced her stiffest task to date and in these energy-sapping conditions could never figure. (6/1: op 4/1)
4445 Graceful Lass failed to handle the heavy ground. (9/1: 5/1-10/1)

4677 WILLMOTT DIXON H'CAP (0-110) (3-Y.O+) (Class B)

3-35 (3-35) **5f** £18,237.50 (£5,525.00: £2,700.00: £1,287.50) Stalls: Low GOING: 0.95 sec per fur (S)

				SP	RR	SF
4553⁶	**Dancethenightaway (89)** (BJMeehan) **3-8-7** JReid(5) (a.p: led 2f out tl over 1f out: led ins fnl f: rdn out)	—	**1**	20/1	99	81
4434²	**Ansellman (84)** (JBerry) **7-7-13b**(3) PFessey(4) (hld up: rdn over 1f out: ev ch ins fnl f: r.o)	nk	**2**	10/1	93	75
4553⁸	**Patsy Grimes (89)** (JSMoore) **7-8-4**(3) PPMurphy(2) (rdn over 2f out: hdwy over 1f out: r.o wl ins fnl f)	1¼	**3**	13/2 2	94	76
4100¹⁴	**Repertory (84)** (MSSaunders) **4-8-2** SDrowne(8) (a.p: led over 1f out tl ins fnl f: unable qckn)	1½	**4**	20/1	84	66
4100²⁰	**Surprise Mission (89)** (MrsJRRamsden) **5-8-7** JFortune(3) (a.p: ev ch over 1f out: one pce)	½	**5**	7/2 1	88	70
4565²	**Distinctive Dream (IRE) (84)** (KTIvory) **3-8-2b** MartinDwyer(6) (lw: s.s: hdwy over 1f out: wknd fnl f)	3	**6**	14/1	73	55
4280⁹	**Rudi's Pet (IRE) (90)** (RHannon) **3-8-3b**(5) CLowther(11) (b.off hind: outpcd: nvr nrr)	2½	**7**	14/1	71	53
4565³	**Levelled (78)** (MRChannon) **3-7-7**(3) RFfrench(13) (lw: a.p: ev ch wl over 1f out: sn wknd)	6	**8**	20/1	40	22
4525⁴	**Croft Pool (108)** (JAGlover) **6-9-12** GCarter(9) (lw: a bhd)	1¼	**9**	20/1	66	48
4444*	**Tedburrow (110)** (EJAlston) **5-10-0** KFallon(10) (lw: hld up: rdn over 2f out: wknd over 1f out)	¾	**10**	8/1 3	65	47
2872⁶	**Gone Savage (83)** (WJMusson) **9-8-1** TSprake(12) (a bhd)	½	**11**	10/1	37	19
4282⁴	**Azizzi (98)** (CREgerton) **5-9-2** LDettori(1) (led 3f)	8	**12**	13/2 2	26	8
4527⁴	**Shalstayholy (IRE) (80)** (GLMoore) **3-7-12** JQuinn(7) (prom 2f)	8	**13**	11/1	—	—
				(SP 118.9%)	**13 Rn**	

65.59 secs (5.39) CSF £178.79 CT £900.57 TOTE £16.10: £2.60 £2.90 £2.00 (£76.30) Trio £92.70 OWNER Mr G. A. Bosley (UPPER LAMBOURN) BRED G. A. Bosley and H. Clarkin
LONG HANDICAP Levelled 7-8
4553 Dancethenightaway gained her only other success this year on soft ground and, obviously at home on this surface, regained the advantage inside the final furlong and held on well. (20/1)
4434 Ansellman ran another fine race and, throwing down his challenge from below the distance, only just failed. He has done all his winning at five furlongs. (10/1)
4434* Patsy Grimes, racing at the back of the field, ran on in really good style in the last furlong and a half but found the line always beating her. (13/2)
3914 Repertory ran another sound race on testing ground, and showed with a narrow advantage below the distance before being worried out of it inside the final furlong. (20/1)
3011 Surprise Mission, 6lb higher than he has won off before, was swinging off the bridle entering the final quarter-mile, but once let down could only go up and down in the same place. (7/2)
4565 Distinctive Dream (IRE) has been in cracking form this year, winning six times, but this heavy ground was against him, and an effort below the distance proved to be short-lived. (14/1: 10/1-16/1)
4282 Azizzi (13/2: 9/2-7/1)
4527 Shalstayholy (IRE) (11/1: 8/1-12/1)

4678 FINANCIAL DYNAMICS RATED STKS H'CAP (0-105) (3-Y.O+) (Class B)

4-10 (4-20) **1m 2f** £12,613.60 (£4,722.40: £2,311.20: £996.00: £448.00: £228.80) Stalls: High GOING: 0.95 sec per fur (S)

				SP	RR	SF
4133²	**Alezal (100)** (WJarvis) **3-8-11** SSanders(11) (chsd ldr: led over 2f out: wandered over 1f out: hung bdly rt ins fnl f: all out)	—	**1**	4/1 2	108	49
4110²	**Cugina (91)** (GBBalding) **3-8-2** SDrowne(2) (hdwy over 2f out: chsd wnr over 1f out: hrd rdn: r.o)	½	**2**	9/2 3	98	39
4294²	**Lomberto (91)** (VSoane) **4-8-4**(3) RFfrench(1) (lw: rdn & hdwy over 2f out: r.o)	2	**3**	14/1	95	41
849³	**Greenstead (USA) (98)** (JHMGosden) **4-9-0** LDettori(5) (rdn & hdwy over 2f out: sn wknd)	13	**4**	10/1	81	27
4312³	**Wilcuma (100)** (PJMakin) **6-9-2b** KFallon(4) (rdn over 2f out: nvr nr to chal)	5	**5**	9/2 3	75	21
4383⁴	**Premier Bay (95)** (PWHarris) **3-8-6b** GCarter(8) (led over 7f)	17	**6**	10/1	43	—
4281³	**Winter Romance (104)** (EALDunlop) **4-9-6** MHills(7) (lw: a bhd)	nk	**7**	3/1 1	52	—
4558³²	**Another Time (93)** (SPCWoods) **5-8-9** JReid(9) (lw: a bhd)	5	**8**	14/1	33	—
*4369**	***Danish Rhapsody (IRE) (105)*** (LadyHerries) **4-9-7** PaulEddery(3) (Withdrawn not under Starter's orders: state of the ground)		**W**	8/1	—	—
				(SP 124.0%)	**8 Rn**	

2m 20.75 (15.25) CSF £19.77 CT £204.23 TOTE £5.90: £1.90 £1.30 £2.90 (£10.30) Trio £49.10 OWNER Mr Howard Spooner (NEWMARKET) BRED Godolphin Management Co Ltd
LONG HANDICAP Lomberto 7-13 Cugina 7-13
WEIGHT FOR AGE 3yo-5lb
IN-FOCUS: **Following steady rain during the afternoon the Stewards called an inspection before this race, but after a lengthy deliberation allowed racing to continue.**
4133 Alezal has done all his winning with some cut in the ground, and moved to the front over a quarter of a mile from home, but he was punch drunk in these extremely testing conditions and, wandering all over the shop, had nothing in reserve come the line. (4/1: 5/2-9/2)
4110 Cugina had a stiff task at the weights - 3lb out of the handicap making her 13lb higher than when last successful - but this is her ground and, moving into second place approaching the final furlong, she made sure the winner had a very hard race. (9/2)
4294 Lomberto had a stiff task at the weights - he was still carrying 5lb more than his long handicap weight despite his talented apprentice's claim - but he does act on this ground and stayed on nicely in the straight to finish well clear of the remainder. (14/1)
849 Greenstead (USA), whose only previous run this season was back in April, closed with the pack turning for home but was in trouble early in the straight. (10/1: 8/1-12/1)
4312 Wilcuma had the ground in his favour but never threatened to play a part. (9/2)
4383 Premier Bay had the ground to his liking, but after setting the pace stopped to nothing when collared over two furlongs from home. (10/1)
4281 Winter Romance ran no race at all on ground he loves. (3/1)
3773 Another Time (14/1: 12/1-20/1)

4679 HYPERION CONDITIONS STKS (2-Y.O) (Class B)

4-40 (4-48) **7f** £7,365.60 (£2,685.60: £1,312.80: £564.00: £252.00) Stalls: Low GOING: 0.95 sec per fur (S)

				SP	RR	SF
3644^{7}	**La-Faah (IRE)** (BWHills) **2-8-11** RHills(4) (lw: bmpd s: hld up: led over 1f out: pushed out)	—	**1**	$7/4^{1}$	87+	49
4232^{8}	**Batswing (82)** (MartynMeade) **2-8-11b** KFallon(3) (chsd ldr: hrd rdn & ev ch over 1f out: unable qckn)	3	**2**	10/1	80	42
$4391a^{7}$	**Chips (IRE) (100)** (DRCElsworth) **2-9-5** OPeslier(5) (lw: jinked lft s: led over 5f: wknd fnl f)	7	**3**	$5/2^{2}$	72	34
4218^{3}	**Smooth Sailing (90)** (KMcAuliffe) **2-8-11b^{1}** JReid(1) (a bhd)	5	**4**	6/1	53	15
3644^{6}	**Jazz Club (USA)** (PFICole) **2-8-13** TQuinn(2) (lw: bhd fnl 4f)	28	**5**	$7/2^{3}$	—	—
				(SP 110.5%)	**5 Rn**	

1m 37.86 (10.66) CSF £16.76 TOTE £2.40: £1.70 £2.40 (£8.70) OWNER Mr Hamdan Al Maktoum (LAMBOURN) BRED Shadwell Estate Company Limited

3047* La-Faah (IRE) is certainly suited by give underfoot and, moving to the front below the distance, needed only to be nudged along in the testing conditions to win in decisive style. (7/4)

3142 Batswing ran much better, and may have showed in front for a few strides below the distance before tapped for toe. (10/1: 8/1-12/1)

4391a Chips (IRE) took the field along but, collared over a furlong out, had nothing in reserve. (5/2)

3644 Jazz Club (USA) was all at sea on this ground. (7/2: 5/2-4/1)

4680 DUKE OF EDINBURGH H'CAP (0-90) (3-Y.O+) (Class C)

5-15 (5-21) **1m (straight)** £9,378.00 (£2,844.00: £1,392.00: £666.00) Stalls: Low GOING: 0.95 sec per fur (S)

				SP	RR	SF
4511^{5}	**Rock Falcon (IRE) (80)** (LadyHerries) **4-9-4b** DeanMcKeown(15) (mde virtually all: rdn out)	—	**1**	14/1	97	48
4121^{12}	**Q Factor (81)** (DHaydnJones) **5-9-5** SDrowne(18) (hld up: chsd wnr over 2f out: hrd rdn: r.o)	2	**2**	$7/1^{2}$	94	45
4404*	**Zurs (IRE) (60)** (JRPoulton) **4-7-7**(5)ow1 RMullen(16) (s.s: hdwy over 4f out: hrd rdn over 2f out: wknd wl over 1f out)	10	**3**	11/1	53	3
4308^{4}	**Sycamore Boy (USA) (74)** (LordHuntingdon) **3-8-9** OPeslier(13) (lw: rdn & hdwy over 2f out: one pce)	1	**4**	12/1	65	13
4523^{3}	**Polish Rhythm (IRE) (84)** (GAHubbard) **4-9-8** JReid(17) (lw: lost pl 6f out: rallied 2f out: one pce)	nk	**5**	14/1	74	25
4558^{16}	**Mihriz (IRE) (70)** (RAkehurst) **5-8-8** TQuinn(10) (lw: prom 5f)	17	**6**	$7/1^{2}$	26	—
4121^{20}	**Musick House (IRE) (85)** (MissGayKelleway) **4-9-9b** KFallon(6) (prom over 5f)	½	**7**	$8/1^{3}$	40	—
4319*	**Myrtle Quest (78)** (RCharlton) **5-9-2** TSprake(3) (nvr nr to chal)	1¾	**8**	$4/1^{1}$	30	—
4319^{10}	**Prenonamoss (58)** (DWPArbuthnot) **9-7-10** MartinDwyer(4) (b.hind: a mid div)	2	**9**	25/1	6	—
1016^{15}	**Polar Eclipse (75)** (BJMeehan) **4-8-13** MTebbutt(11) (prom over 4f)	5	**10**	33/1	13	—
4283^{14}	**Test The Water (IRE) (79)** (RHannon) **3-9-0** DaneO'Neill(14) (lw: bhd fnl 3f)	2	**11**	9/1	13	—
3976^{11}	**Phonetic (73)** (GBBalding) **4-8-8**(3) PPMurphy(12) (a bhd)	nk	**12**	9/1	6	—
3605^{5}	**Plan For Profit (IRE) (80)** (MJohnston) **3-9-1** DHolland(19) (lw: a bhd)	18	**13**	20/1	—	—
4112^{15}	**Caudillo (IRE) (58)** (MrsPNDutfield) **4-7-10** JQuinn(8) (bhd fnl 3f)	2½	**14**	14/1	—	—
	Zygo (USA) (75) (RTPhillips) **5-8-13** RPerham(1) (lw: bhd fnl 3f)	½	**15**	33/1	—	—
4308^{5}	**Abajany (77)** (MRChannon) **3-8-12** JFortune(5) (prom over 4f)	3	**16**	10/1	—	—
				(SP 135.7%)	**16 Rn**	

1m 52.99 (12.99) CSF £106.17 CT £707.56 TOTE £30.20: £5.60 £2.20 £2.60 £3.10 (£230.80) Trio £424.50 OWNER Mr E. Reitel (LITTLEHAMPTON) BRED Juddmonte Farms

LONG HANDICAP Caudillo (IRE) 7-9 Prenonamoss 7-5

WEIGHT FOR AGE 3yo-3lb

4511 Rock Falcon (IRE) was well-suited by the mud and, allowed to do his own thing in front, was ridden along to keep his only serious rival at bay in the final quarter-mile. (14/1)

3888 Q Factor goes well in this ground. Moving into second place over a quarter of a mile out, he was unable to get on terms with the winner but still pulled well clear of the remainder. (7/1: 5/1-8/1)

4404* Zurs (IRE) took closer order at halfway, but was left for dead by the front two in the final quarter-mile. (11/1)

4308 Sycamore Boy (USA) passed tired rivals over a quarter of a mile from home, but needed binoculars to see the front two. (12/1)

4523 Polish Rhythm (IRE), a massive 24lb higher than when winning a Yarmouth handicap back in July, was only treading water in the final quarter-mile. (14/1)

3392* Mihriz (IRE) had been seen off fully three furlongs from home. (7/1)

4319* Myrtle Quest (4/1: 3/1-9/2)

3894 Test The Water (IRE) (9/1: 6/1-10/1)

2508 Phonetic (9/1: 6/1-10/1)

4308 Abajany (10/1: 8/1-12/1)

T/Jkpt: £55,894.90 (6.23 Tckts). T/Plpt: £691.10 (127.9 Tckts). T/Qdpt: £57.30 (55.76 Tckts) AK

4641-YORK (L-H) - Saturday October 11th

4681 Abandoned-Waterlogged

4278-AYR (L-H) (Soft)

Monday October 13th

Race 6: hand timed.

WEATHER: sunny periods - very cool WIND: mod across

4688 E.B.F. KIRKOSWALD MAIDEN STKS (2-Y.O F) (Class D)

2-20 (2-20) **6f** £3,259.00 (£982.00: £476.00: £223.00) Stalls: High GOING: 0.54 sec per fur (GS)

				SP	RR	SF
4556^{3}	**Court Lane (USA)** (DRLoder) **2-8-11** KFallon(5) (lw: mde all: rdn clr over 1f out: eased towards fin)	—	**1**	$1/3^{1}$	75+	39
4437^{7}	**Esse (40)** (EWeymes) **2-8-11** JQuinn(1) (a chsng wnr: no ch fnl 2f)	9	**2**	50/1	51	15
	Splendid (IRE) (SirMarkPrescott) **2-8-11** GDuffield(6) (w'like: scope: bit bkwd: a chsng ldrs: outpcd over 2f out: no imp after)	1¾	**3**	$3/1^{2}$	46	10
4470^{6}	**Anka Lady (47)** (DMoffatt) **2-8-8**(3) DarrenMoffatt(4) (prom: effrt over 2f out: no imp)	½	**4**	100/1	45	9
4327^{6}	**Lady From Limerick (IRE) (64)** (JBerry) **2-8-8b^{1}**(3) PFessey(3) (s.s: sn rcvrd & prom: wknd fnl 2f)	3	**5**	$20/1^{3}$	37	1

3312[9]	**E B Treasure** (NBycroft) **2-8-11** LCharnock(2) (outpcd & hung lft ½-wy: sn t.o)	dist	**6**	100/1	—	—

(SP 108.7%) **6 Rn**

1m 16.96 (7.16) CSF £23.33 TOTE £1.20: £1.10 £12.50 (£20.90) OWNER Sheikh Mohammed (NEWMARKET) BRED Darley Stud Management Inc

4556 Court Lane (USA) never found this easy, and had to really knuckle down to gain command, but in the end she did it well, and will certainly appreciate further. (1/3)

Esse had shown nothing previously but ran quite well. However, apart from the winner the quality of the remainder would seem very ordinary. (50/1)

Splendid (IRE), is a really nice-looking sort, but she did need this and was laid back to the point of almost being asleep, and not surprisingly showed no spark in the race. If looks mean anything she will do a deal better in time. (3/1: op 7/4)

4470 Anka Lady ran a shade better this time but was short of any change of gear. (100/1)

4327 Lady From Limerick (IRE) had blinkers on for the first time and they seemed to have an adverse effect. (20/1)

4689 ARRAN CONDITIONS STKS (3-Y.O) (Class C)

2-50 (2-51) **1m** £4,583.97 (£1,657.10: £798.55: £330.25: £135.13) Stalls: High GOING: 0.54 sec per fur (GS)

				SP	RR	SF
4463[3]	**Right Wing (IRE) (95)** (MajorWRHern) **3-9-5** KDarley(2) (lw: trckd ldr: led on bit 2f out: shkn up appr fnl f: kpt on)	—	**1**	2/1[1]	104+	40
	The Wild Widow (JMPEustace) **3-8-4** JTate(3) (w'like: bhd: hdwy over 2f out: styd on wl towards fin)	1¾	**2**	66/1	86	22
4417*	**Ricky Ticky Tavie (USA)** (DRLoder) **3-9-3** KFallon(4) (lw: chsd ldrs: ev ch 2f out: rdn & r.o one pce)	¾	**3**	4/1[3]	97	33
1314*	**Bea's Ruby (IRE) (92)** (ABailey) **3-9-3** GDuffield(1) (led tl hdd 2f out: sn rdn & btn)	7	**4**	4/1[3]	83	19
4316*	**Musharak (95)** (JLDunlop) **3-9-3** DHolland(5) (plld hrd: effrt 3f out: rdn & no rspnse)	19	**5**	9/4[2]	45	—

(SP 105.6%) **5 Rn**

1m 47.85 (10.45) CSF £50.55 TOTE £2.40: £1.20 £5.20 (£25.00) OWNER The Earl Cadogan (LAMBOURN) BRED Tarworth Bloodstock Investments Ltd and J. J. Melk

OFFICIAL EXPLANATION **Musharak: rider reported that the colt was never moving well and found nothing when off the bridle.**

4463 Right Wing (IRE), all the better for his recent run and on the soft ground he loves, was always going best but needed shaking up to put it beyond doubt. (2/1)

The Wild Widow put in a useful first effort, and got better as the race progressed. She will obviously improve for the experience, and should appreciate further. (66/1)

4417* Ricky Ticky Tavie (USA) had his chances and kept trying hard, but this would seem as good as he is. (4/1: 3/1-9/2)

1314* Bea's Ruby (IRE), returning after almost five months off, failed to impress on looks and probably blew up. (4/1)

4316* Musharak, is a big, awkward-looking individual with a high head-carriage and, after racing freely, he disappointed once the button was pressed. He looks the type who, after a visit from the vet, would delight any National Hunt trainer. (9/4)

4690 MINISHANT NURSERY H'CAP (0-85) (2-Y.O) (Class E)

3-20 (3-20) **1m** £3,073.75 (£925.00: £447.50: £208.75) Stalls: High GOING: 0.54 sec per fur (GS)

				SP	RR	SF
4589[10]	**Kayo (67)** (TJEtherington) **2-7-13**(5) CLowther(3) (lw: hld up & bhd: hmpd 6f out: gd hdwy 2f out: led ins fnl f: edgd lft: r.o)	—	**1**	25/1	71	15
4361[4]	**Prince Ashleigh (74)** (PCHaslam) **2-8-11** LCharnock(5) (cl up: led over 2f out tl ins fnl f: kpt on wl)	¾	**2**	15/2	77	21
4265[5]	**Flow By (77)** (JLDunlop) **2-9-0** KDarley(9) (a chsng ldrs: ev ch 1f out: nt qckn)	nk	**3**	8/1	79	23
3961a[11]	**Miquelon (83)** (RHollinshead) **2-9-6** MWigham(8) (rr div & rdn appr st: styd on wl fnl f: nrst fin)	1	**4**	20/1	83	27
4265*	**Fashion Victim (82)** (THCaldwell) **2-9-5** ACulhane(1) (lw: hld up & bhd: hmpd 6f out: hdwy to chse ldrs 2f out: one pce fnl f)	hd	**5**	13/2[3]	82	26
4265[2]	**Tearaway (75)** (JWWatts) **2-8-12** JCarroll(10) (lw: s.i.s: sn prom: effrt over 2f out: n.m.r & r.o one pce)	nk	**6**	5/1[2]	74	18
3707[9]	**Bollinger Rose (IRE) (59)** (JJO'Neill) **2-7-7**(3) PFessey(4) (led tl hdd over 2f out: wknd appr fnl f)	2½	**7**	16/1	53	—
4382*	**Naskhi (84)** (MJohnston) **2-9-7** DHolland(12) (b.hind: chsd ldrs: ev ch 3f out: rdn & wknd fnl 2f)	3	**8**	9/2[1]	72	16
3545[6]	**Winsome George (83)** (CWFairhurst) **2-9-6** NKennedy(11) (s.i.s: a bhd)	3	**9**	20/1	65	9
4362*	**Burnt Yates (IRE) (75)** (MWEasterby) **2-8-9**(3) GParkin(7) (lw: bhd: effrt over 3f out: sn rdn & btn)	hd	**10**	13/2[3]	57	1
4468[9]	**Baylham (62)** (JSGoldie) **2-7-13** JQuinn(2) (lost pl appr st: n.d after)	2	**11**	25/1	40	—
3887[4]	**Durar (72)** (JLDunlop) **2-8-9** KFallon(6) (wnt prom 6f out: wknd over 2f out)	1¼	**12**	7/1	47	—
4384[6]	**Dentardia (IRE) (75)** (JMPEustace) **2-8-12** JTate(14) (in tch: rdn 3f out: sn wknd)	5	**13**	14/1	40	—
2714[5]	**Falkenberg (FR) (70)** (MJohnston) **2-8-7** JFanning(15) (cl up tl wknd qckly over 2f out)	½	**14**	20/1	34	—
4208[3]	**Tom (60)** (JHetherton) **2-7-8v**(3)ow1 DarrenMoffatt(13) (s.i.s: hdwy ½-wy: wknd over 2f out)	½	**15**	33/1	23	—

(SP 134.4%) **15 Rn**

1m 48.95 (11.55) CSF £187.98 CT £1572.96 TOTE £49.30: £9.70 £2.40 £3.40 (£119.10) Trio £460.30; £90.78 to Leicester 14/10/97 OWNER Mr David Abell (MALTON) BRED Bridge End Bloodstock

LONG HANDICAP Bollinger Rose (IRE) 7-8 Tom 7-5

OFFICIAL EXPLANATION **Kayo: regarding the improvement in form, the colt had been unsuited by the All-Weather last time.**

4163* Kayo likes the soft and loves to come from off the pace and, when things go his way, he is as he showed here quite useful. (25/1)

4361 Prince Ashleigh is improving all the time, and obviously appreciated this step up in trip. (15/2)

4265 Flow By, who looked short of pace at the previous meeting, had her chances this time, but again lacked that vital change of gear. (8/1)

3961a Miquelon, after six weeks off, never looked happy but, given plenty of assistance, he was staying on strongly at the end. He seems to be the type that runs when in the mood. (20/1)

4265* Fashion Victim, 8lb higher this time, again ran well but this was always just beyond him. (13/2)

4265 Tearaway had his chances, but gives the impression that he needs things to go all his own way. (5/1)

3070 Bollinger Rose (IRE), stepping up in trip, went well on this soft surface but then just ran out of stamina. (16/1)

4362* Burnt Yates (IRE) (13/2: 9/2-7/1)

4691 ERICA'S 50TH ANNIVERSARY H'CAP (0-80) (3-Y.O+) (Class D)

3-50 (3-52) **1m 2f 192y** £4,055.00 (£1,220.00: £590.00: £275.00) Stalls: High GOING: 0.54 sec per fur (GS)

				SP	RR	SF
4635[4]	**Pekay (64)** (MJohnston) **4-8-13** DHolland(6) (hld up & bhd: gd hdwy whn bdly hmpd 1½f out: swtchd & r.o wl to ld post)	—	**1**	10/1	75	46
4279[5]	**Shaffishayes (68)** (MrsMReveley) **5-9-3** DeanMcKeown(9) (trckd ldrs: led 2½f out & qcknd clr: no ex nr fin: hdd post)	s.h	**2**	5/1[2]	79	50
4435[2]	**Ajayib (USA) (79)** (JLDunlop) **3-9-8b** KDarley(7) (chsd ldrs: drvn along over 3f out: hung lft 1½f out: kpt on)	2½	**3**	9/2[1]	86	51
4235*	**Philmist (50)** (MissLAPerratt) **5-7-13b** NKennedy(3) (swtg: bhd: hdwy 3f out: styd on u.p: nvr able to chal)	1½	**4**	11/2[3]	55	26

4568^{4}	**Hill Farm Blues (63)** (WMBrisbourne) **4-8-12** KFallon(5) (lw: bhd: hdwy 3f out: n.m.r over 1f out: kpt on)	¾	**5**	6/1	67	38
4471^{5}	**Stormless (56)** (JSGoldie) **6-8-5** TWilliams(8) (lw: trckd ldrs: ev ch & rdn over 2f out: one pce)	s.h	**6**	5/1^{2}	60	31
4471^{8}	**Sing And Dance (47)** (EWeymes) **4-7-7**$^{(3)}$ PFessey(1) (chsd ldrs: led over 3f out tl hdd 2½f out: sn outpcd)	3½	**7**	20/1	46	17
4466^{13}	**Manful (73)** (MissLAPerratt) **5-9-8b** GDuffield(2) (lw: prom: outpcd whn hmpd over 1f out: nt rcvr)	hd	**8**	20/1	72	43
3242^{3}	**Albaha (USA) (75)** (JEBanks) **4-9-10** JQuinn(10) (lw: led tl hdd over 3f out: sn wknd)	30	**9**	15/2	29	—
2045^{7}	**Zaahir (IRE) (74)** (WStorey) **3-9-3** JFanning(4) (outpcd & bhd fr ½-wy)	5	**10**	33/1	21	—

(SP 114.5%) **10 Rn**

2m 28.69 (12.79) CSF £51.61 CT £235.48 TOTE £9.10: £2.20 £1.50 £2.60 (£27.20) Trio £32.40 OWNER Mr T G & Mrs M E Holdcroft (MIDDLEHAM) BRED Bearstone Stud

LONG HANDICAP Sing And Dance 7-4

WEIGHT FOR AGE 3yo-6lb

4635 Pekay appreciated this extra furlong and, after running into serious trouble, showed an incredible turn of foot to make it. (10/1)

4279 Shaffishayes looked to have stolen this when kicking clear early in the straight but, when the chips were down, he found little and was just worried out of it. (5/1)

4435 Ajayib (USA) has the ability but just gives the impression that he is not always giving it his best shot. (9/2)

4235* Philmist was sweating on this very cool afternoon, and needed a stronger pace. (11/2)

4568 Hill Farm Blues looked on good terms with herself, but lacked the pace to get into this. (6/1)

4471 Stormless looked the part and travelled well, but failed to pick up when ridden and was a shade disappointing. (5/1)

1992 Manful gives the impression on looks that he is coming back to form, and did not have the run of the race. (20/1)

4692 FAILFORD (S) STKS (3-Y.O+) (Class F)

4-20 (4-20) **1m 5f 13y** £2,637.00 (£732.00: £351.00) Stalls: High GOING: 0.54 sec per fur (GS)

				SP	RR	SF
4521^{11}	**Once More for Luck (IRE) (64)** (MrsMReveley) **6-9-4** ACulhane(1) (hld up: hdwy on bit appr st: led ins fnl f: shkn up & qcknd)	—	**1**	9/4^{2}	59+	29
4584^{3}	**Forzair (46)** (JJO'Neill) **5-9-4**$^{(5)}$ CLowther(5) (chsd ldrs: led 6f out tl ins fnl f: one pce)	4	**2**	7/1	59	29
721^{12}	**Flyaway Blues (42)** (MrsMReveley) **5-8-13**$^{(5)}$ SCopp(6) (mid div: effrt 3f out: styd on: no imp)	9	**3**	16/1	43	13
4415^{10}	**Eurolink Windsong (IRE) (39)** (MartynWane) **3-8-5** LCharnock(8) (hdwy ½-wy: prom appr st: one pce fnl 2f)	4	**4**	16/1	33	—
	Speculative (WStorey) **3-8-10** KFallon(11) (w'like: lw: dwlt: outpcd & bhd tl gd hdwy 7f out: ev ch & rdn over 3f out: hung lft & wknd wl over 1f out)	2	**5**	2/1^{1}	36	—
4015^{16}	**Northern Flash (64)** (FMurphy) **3-8-10b^{1}** DeanMcKeown(4) (cl up tl outpcd fnl 3½f)	2	**6**	6/1^{3}	33	—
4469^{4}	**Sweet Note (IRE) (27)** (MissLAPerratt) **3-7-12**$^{(7)}$ JMcAuley(9) (bhd: hdwy ½-wy: in tch appr st: one pce after)	2	**7**	20/1	26	—
3919^{10}	**Cois Na Farraige (IRE) (26)** (MissLAPerratt) **4-9-1**$^{(3)}$ PFessey(3) (in tch to ½-wy: n.d after)	1	**8**	100/1	30	—
4466^{17}	**Grog (IRE) (47)** (BMactaggart) **8-9-4** JCarroll(12) (led tl hdd 6f out: ev ch tl wknd 3f out)	1¼	**9**	100/1	28	—
4466^{9}	**Craigary (42)** (MrsASwinbank) **6-9-9** GDuffield(7) (prom tl wknd fnl 3f)	3½	**10**	12/1	29	—
4415^{6}	**Golden Fish (24)** (EJAlston) **5-9-4** JQuinn(10) (bhd fnl 7f)	9	**11**	25/1	13	—
4429^{5}	**Showstopper (28)** (TJEtherington) **3-8-3**$^{(7)}$ PBradley(2) (a rr div)	½	**12**	100/1	12	—
4466^{16}	**Prophits Pride (IRE) (40)** (PMonteith) **5-9-4** OPears(14) (in tch to ½-wy)	13	**13**	50/1	—	—
2503^{12}	**Silver Pearl (30)** (MrsAMNaughton) **6-9-9v^{1}** JSupple(13) (b: outpcd & bhd fr ½-wy)	9	**14**	16/1	—	—

(SP 129.8%) **14 Rn**

3m 4.02 (19.22) CSF £17.94 TOTE £4.20: £1.10 £2.70 £7.90 (£8.30) Trio £39.10 OWNER The Mary Reveley Racing Club (SALTBURN) BRED Kerr and Co Ltd

WEIGHT FOR AGE 3yo-8lb

Bt in 7,000 gns, Northern Flash clmd JHaynes £6,000

285* Once More for Luck (IRE) revelled in this strongly-run event and, always on the bridle, it was a question of when and how far. (9/4)

4584 Forzair went well on this soft ground, but found the winner far too good in the closing stages. (7/1)

721 Flyaway Blues showed some ability, staying on at the end, and is obviously in good heart. (16/1)

3781 Eurolink Windsong (IRE) has ability but has generally been disappointing. (16/1)

Speculative looked the part beforehand, but he proved very green in the race, and needed all Fallon's strength to get him into contention, but then cried enough entering the last couple of furlongs. (2/1)

2330 Northern Flash had blinkers on for the first time, but they did not appear to be much help. (6/1: op 4/1)

4693 AYR AUTUMN H'CAP (0-70) (3-Y.O) (Class E)

4-50 (4-50) **1m 1f** £2,995.75 (£901.00: £435.50: £202.75) Stalls: High GOING: 0.54 sec per fur (GS)

				SP	RR	SF
4485^{6}	**Zorba (60)** (JHetherton) **3-8-13** NKennedy(1) (hld up & bhd: gd hdwy to ld appr fnl f: r.o)	—	**1**	12/1^{3}	70	54
2226^{3}	**Gadroon (43)** (PCHaslam) **3-7-10** LCharnock(2) (in tch: hdwy 3f out: styd on fnl f: nt pce of wnr)	1	**2**	12/1^{3}	51	35
4583^{3}	**Foot Battalion (IRE) (64)** (RHollinshead) **3-9-3** KFallon(8) (lw: hld up: hdwy appr st: ev ch over 1f out: nt qckn)	nk	**3**	11/4^{1}	72	56
4400*	**Dellua (IRE) (67)** (RGuest) **3-9-1**$^{(5)}$ CLowther(11) (lw: trckd ldrs: led wl over 2f out tl appr fnl f: sn btn)	3½	**4**	11/4^{1}	69	53
1465^{5}	**Tycoon Tina (53)** (WMBrisbourne) **3-8-6** JCarroll(6) (bhd: effrt ent st: kpt on: nvr able to chal)	4	**5**	16/1	47	31
4323^{4}	**Hidden Agenda (FR) (51)** (RCharlton) **3-8-4b^{1}** KDarley(10) (lw: trckd ldrs: disp ld over 2f out: wknd wl over 1f out)	5	**6**	5/1^{2}	37	21
3225^{7}	**Biff-Em (IRE) (50)** (MissLAPerratt) **3-8-3** GDuffield(9) (plld hrd: bhd: effrt 3f out: sn btn)	s.h	**7**	50/1	35	19
4572^{7}	**Bonnie Lassie (68)** (CWThornton) **3-9-7** DeanMcKeown(4) (led tl hdd & wknd wl over 2f out)	1½	**8**	25/1	51	35
4586^{11}	**Fine Times (47)** (CWFairhurst) **3-7-11v**$^{(3)}$ PFessey(5) (b.off hind: prom tl wknd fnl 3f)	1	**9**	25/1	28	12
4235^{9}	**Beau Roberto (43)** (JSGoldie) **3-7-10** JQuinn(7) (prom tl wknd over 3f out)	hd	**10**	16/1	24	8
4269^{13}	**Belle Bijou (53)** (MJohnston) **3-8-6** DHolland(3) (cl up tl wknd qckly 6f out: sn bhd)	16	**11**	12/1^{3}	5	—

(SP 114.5%) **11 Rn**

2m 0.1 (9.60) CSF £127.80 CT £471.77 TOTE £16.60: £3.70 £2.30 £1.70 (£43.00) Trio £110.70 OWNER Mr C. D. Barber-Lomax (MALTON) BRED B. Freiha

LONG HANDICAP Gadroon 7-6 Beau Roberto 7-7

4485 Zorba has run his races from the front previously, but this time the opposite tactics were employed, and he did it really well. (12/1: op 8/1)

2226 Gadroon put in another useful effort, and ran as though he should get further. If he tries hurdling, he would be one to keep on the right side of. (12/1)

4583 Foot Battalion (IRE) has the ability when things go just right, but the struggle on this occasion was just beyond him. (11/4)

4400* Dellua (IRE), on soft ground for the first time, proved disappointing when the pressure was applied. (11/4)

1465 Tycoon Tina likes cut in the ground but, after over four months off, was ring-rusty and only ran on when it was too late. She looks well worth another chance. (16/1)

4323 Hidden Agenda (FR) had blinkers on for the first time and, racing too freely, failed to get home. (5/1)
2030 Biff-Em (IRE) is a very hard puller indeed, but seems to have ability if he would channel it in the right direction. (50/1)

T/Plpt: £137.10 (163.34 Tckts). T/Qdpt: £41.50 (40.83 Tckts) AA

4575-LEICESTER (R-H) (Soft)
Monday October 13th
WEATHER: Cloudy with sunny periods WIND: mod against

4694 E.B.F. HARE MAIDEN STKS (I) (2-Y.O F) (Class D)
1-30 (1-33) **7f 9y** £3,249.00 (£972.00: £466.00: £213.00) Stalls: High GOING: 0.39 sec per fur (GS)

Form	Horse	Dist	Pos	SP	RR	SF
4564[3]	**Only In Dreams** (BJMeehan) **2-8-11** MTebbutt(10) (hld up: hdwy over 2f out: led appr fnl f: r.o wl)	—	**1**	5/1[2]	79	30
4425[5]	**Astrapi** (MRStoute) **2-8-11** JReid(4) (hld up: hdwy to ld over 2f out: hdd appr fnl f: one pce)	1½	**2**	11/10[1]	76	27
	Chocolate Box (WJHaggas) **2-8-11** FLynch(9) (w'like: leggy: bit bkwd: dwlt: sn rcvrd: r.o one pce appr fnl f)	1½	**3**	14/1	72	23
4103[7]	**Tajmil (IRE) (75)** (MajorWRHern) **2-8-11** RHills(6) (a.p: rdn over 1f out: kpt on)	nk	**4**	8/1	72	23
4227[7]	**Water's Edge** (GWragg) **2-8-11** MHills(7) (hld up & bhd: hdwy over 1f out: nrst fin)	1¼	**5**	12/1	69	20
4317[8]	**Caledonian Express** (JLDunlop) **2-8-11** TSprake(3) (bit bkwd: hld up: hdwy over 2f out: r.o ins fnl f)	½	**6**	11/2[3]	68	19
4317[9]	**Robanna** (RAkehurst) **2-8-11** SSanders(5) (mid div: rdn over 3f out: no hdwy fnl 2f)	1¾	**7**	25/1	64	15
4066[7]	**Pixielated (IRE)** (DRLoder) **2-8-11** RCochrane(11) (hld up: effrt over 1f out: nvr nrr)	nk	**8**	10/1	63+	14
2875[12]	**Wrought Iron (USA)** (MBell) **2-8-11** MFenton(2) (bit bkwd: hld up: effrt & pushed along 2f out: no imp)	½	**9**	25/1	62	13
4332[16]	**Our Molly Malone** (DMorley) **2-8-11** JStack(13) (s.i.s: sn prom: wknd over 2f out)	1	**10**	25/1	60	11
	Swingtime (AGFoster) **2-8-11** RPerham(12) (w'like: str: bkwd: hld up: rdn & effrt over 2f out: wknd appr fnl f)	1½	**11**	33/1	56	7
4178[12]	**Hot Topic (IRE)** (PAKelleway) **2-8-11** JWeaver(14) (w ldr tl wknd qckly over 2f out: t.o)	11	**12**	50/1	31	—
3099[5]	**Woodlands Pride (IRE)** (MCChapman) **2-8-4**(7) SCarson(8) (led tl hdd over 2f out: sn wknd: t.o)	2½	**13**	50/1	25	—
	Precision Finish (JCullinan) **2-8-11** WJO'Connor(1) (w'like: scope: bkwd: s.s: a bhd & outpcd: t.o)	s.h	**14**	50/1	25	—

(SP 134.6%) **14 Rn**

1m 30.8 (8.20) CSF £10.52 TOTE £10.30: £3.30 £1.00 £5.00 (£3.50) Trio £47.80 OWNER Mascalls Stud (UPPER LAMBOURN) BRED Mascalls Stud
OFFICIAL EXPLANATION Pixielated (IRE): rider's instructions were to sit in behind and give the filly every chance. She travelled well until losing her action at halfway, and returned with a cut on her off-fore.
4564 Only In Dreams took full advantage of the extra furlong, and won going away. She is likely to follow-up before the season ends. (5/1: 4/1-6/1)
4425 Astrapi gained command under the stand rail entering the last quarter-mile and looked to have the measure of her rivals. However, the winner found extra when set alight and she had to admit she had met one too good. (11/10: 4/5-5/4)
Chocolate Box, a May foal closely related to several winners, ran a fine race after missing a beat at the start, and she is not likely to let the family name down. (14/1)
1927 Tajmil (IRE), having her first run over this slightly longer trip, was placed to challenge all the way but, when the pressure was on, she did little more than stay on at the one pace. (8/1: op 5/1)
Water's Edge stayed on steadily inside the distance and, although she was not born until May 12th, she would seem to have learned a lot from her debut. (12/1: op 7/1)
Caledonian Express, a filly with plenty of scope who should come into her own as a three-year-old, caught the eye staying on pleasingly in the latter stages. She looks to have ability. (11/2)
Pixielated (IRE) (10/1: op 6/1)

4695 SHELDUCK H'CAP (0-70) (3-Y.O+ F & M) (Class E)
2-00 (2-03) **1m 8y** £3,561.00 (£1,068.00: £514.00: £237.00) Stalls: High GOING: 0.39 sec per fur (GS)

Form	Horse	Dist	Pos	SP	RR	SF
4451[4]	**Literary (66)** (JHMGosden) **3-9-10** LDettori(17) (hld up & bhd: gd hdwy to ld over 1f out: r.o wl)	—	**1**	7/1[2]	80	57
4628*	**Katie Komaite (46)** (CaptJWilson) **4-8-7v** 6x AMackay(3) (hld up: hdwy 2f out: r.o fnl f: nt rch wnr)	2	**2**	7/1[2]	56	36
4324[11]	**Mayflower (48)** (MHTompkins) **3-8-6v** DBiggs(8) (hld up & bhd: hdwy fnl 2f: r.o)	1½	**3**	33/1	55	32
4455[4]	**Bold Faith (47)** (WJMusson) **4-8-8** RCochrane(18) (hld up & bhd: hdwy over 1f out: nt rch ldrs)	1½	**4**	5/1[1]	51	31
4480[12]	**Tael of Silver (45)** (ABailey) **5-8-6** FNorton(12) (prom: outpcd over 2f out: styd on fnl f)	2	**5**	20/1	45	25
4371[9]	**Oxbane (51)** (CADwyer) **3-8-4**(5) RMullen(19) (a.p: led over 2f out tl over 1f out: wknd fnl f)	nk	**6**	16/1	51	28
*4571**	**Perpetual Light (43)** (JJQuinn) **4-8-4** SDrowne(7) (no hdwy fnl 2f)	1	**7**	10/1	41	21
3787[4]	**Queen's Insignia (USA) (57)** (PFICole) **4-9-4** TQuinn(14) (prom 6f)	3½	**8**	12/1	48	28
4568[12]	**Smart Spirit (IRE) (60)** (MrsMReveley) **3-9-4** JFortune(6) (nvr nrr)	hd	**9**	14/1	50	27
3452[6]	**Racing Heart (56)** (PJMakin) **3-9-0** RHills(11) (s.i.s: no hdwy fnl 2f)	2½	**10**	16/1	41	18
4554[5]	**First Chance (IRE) (67)** (DRCElsworth) **3-9-6**(5) APolli(10) (w ldrs: led over 4f out tl over 2f out: wknd over 1f out)	1	**11**	20/1	50	27
4431[2]	**Misty Point (62)** (IABalding) **3-9-6** MHills(5) (lw: mid div: rdn over 3f out: wknd over 2f out)	1¼	**12**	9/1	43	20
4629[10]	**Al Reet (IRE) (52)** (SRBowring) **6-8-10**(3) CTeague(20) (prom over 6f)	nk	**13**	12/1	32	12
3316[3]	**Viva Verdi (IRE) (65)** (JLDunlop) **3-9-9** TSprake(4) (trckd ldrs: wknd 2f out)	3	**14**	8/1[3]	39	16
4404[13]	**Primelta (45)** (RAkehurst) **4-8-6** SSanders(2) (lw: bhd fnl 2f)	½	**15**	20/1	18	—
3452[4]	**Rumbustious (49)** (RHannon) **3-8-7** DaneO'Neill(9) (led 6f out tl over 4f out: wknd over 2f out)	½	**16**	20/1	21	—
4291[4]	**Crissem (IRE) (49)** (RHollinshead) **4-8-10** FLynch(15) (hld up: hdwy over 2f out: hrd rdn & wknd qckly over 1f out)	nk	**17**	20/1	21	1
2731[11]	**Flying Colours (IRE) (63)** (CJBenstead) **3-9-7** AMcGlone(16) (a bhd)	nk	**18**	33/1	34	11
4220[8]	**Eliza (62)** (LordHuntingdon) **3-9-6** JReid(1) (prom over 5f)	nk	**19**	20/1	33	10
3777[8]	**Snowy Mantle (47)** (JDBethell) **4-8-8** JWeaver(13) (plld hrd: led 2f: wknd 3f out)	2½	**20**	20/1	13	—

(SP 144.9%) **20 Rn**

1m 42.9 (7.90) CSF £50.12 CT £1498.04 TOTE £7.90: £2.60 £2.40 £20.70 £1.50 (£23.10) Trio £494.90; £418.27 to Leicester 14/10/97
OWNER Sheikh Mohammed (NEWMARKET) BRED Sheikh Mohammed Bin Rashid Al Maktoum
WEIGHT FOR AGE 3yo-3lb
4451 Literary,down 4lb, found the combination of a mile and soft ground enabling her to get off the mark at the twelfth attempt. (7/1)
4628* Katie Komaite did not mind the soft and stuck to her task under the stand rail, but the winner was home and dry in the centre of the course. (7/1)

Mayflower, 22lb lower than when last in a handicap, has been struggling to find the right trip and was rather late in setting sail for home. (33/1)
4455 Bold Faith was given quite a bit to do and clearly finds this trip on the short side. (5/1)
4448 Tael of Silver is certainly a lot better on grass than sand. (20/1)
4248 Oxbane likes this ground but does not seem to get a mile in it. (16/1)

4696 BADGER LIMITED STKS (0-60) (3-Y.O+) (Class F)

2-30 (2-31) **1m 8y** £3,183.00 (£888.00: £429.00) Stalls: High GOING: 0.39 sec per fur (GS)

Form	Horse / details	Btn	Pos	SP	RR	SF
4516[7]	**Alfahaal (IRE) (54)** (RFJohnsonHoughton) **4-9-5** JReid(13) (b.hind: plld hrd: hld up: stdy hdwy 2f out: led on bit fnl 50y: hld on)	—	**1**	8/1[3]	69	56
4008[5]	**Star Turn (IRE) (60)** (MBell) **3-9-0** MFenton(19) (lw: a.p: led over 2f out tl wl ins fnl f: rallied cl home)	s.h	**2**	7/1[2]	67	51
4335[11]	**Tulsa (IRE) (44)** (BGubby) **3-9-0** JFortune(12) (hld up: hdwy over 3f out: ev ch over 1f out: unable qckn)	1¼	**3**	33/1	64	48
4485[8]	**Penlop (55)** (ACStewart) **3-9-2b** LDettori(15) (a.p: ev ch 2f out: hrd rdn: one pce)	1¼	**4**	10/1	64	48
4601[5]	**Brave Envoy (60)** (MJHeaton-Ellis) **3-9-0** JWeaver(7) (chsd ldrs: rdn over 1f out: one pce)	1¼	**5**	12/1	59	43
1826[16]	**Ardent (59)** (CJBenstead) **3-9-0** CRutter(9) (lw: hld up: hdwy over 1f out: nrst fin)	½	**6**	33/1	58	42
4139[19]	**Witchfinder (USA) (50)** (MrsLStubbs) **5-9-3** SWhitworth(5) (lw: hld up: hdwy 3f out: one pce fnl 2f)	nk	**7**	25/1	58	45
4629[2]	**Duello (60)** (MBlanshard) **6-9-3** WRyan(1) (hld up: hdwy 2f out: rdn over 1f out: no imp)	hd	**8**	9/4[1]	58	45
4472[9]	**Warrior King (IRE) (51)** (CADwyer) **3-8-13**(3) TEDurcan(14) (hld up mid div: no imp fnl 2f)	1¼	**9**	20/1	57	41
2868[9]	**Saratoga Red (USA) (60)** (WAO'Gorman) **3-9-0b** EmmaO'Gorman(4) (bkwd: s.i.s: n.d)	2½	**10**	16/1	50	34
4571[3]	**Zermatt (IRE) (58)** (MDIUsher) **7-9-5** NAdams(10) (lw: prom: wkng whn n.m.r 2f out)	1½	**11**	12/1	49	36
3695*	**Phylida (56)** (PJMakin) **3-9-1** SSanders(6) (a in rr)	2½	**12**	7/1[2]	43	27
4233[25]	**Nightingale Song (57)** (MartynMeade) **3-8-11** TSprake(2) (led over 3f: wknd 2f out)	1½	**13**	20/1	36	20
2835[15]	**Davids Revenge (60)** (MajorDNChappell) **3-9-0** AClark(8) (trckd ldrs 5f: grad wknd)	¾	**14**	12/1	38	22
2353[4]	**Kristopher (53)** (JWHills) **3-8-11**(3) MHenry(17) (bkwd: prom: led 3f out: sn hdd & wknd)	1¾	**15**	16/1	34	18
4485[11]	**Genuine John (IRE) (60)** (JParkes) **4-9-3** JBramhill(11) (rdn along 3f out: sn bhd)	s.h	**16**	25/1	34	21
1011[9]	**Mac's Delight (53)** (HAkbary) **3-8-9**(5) APolli(18) (b.hind: prom: led over 4f out to 3f out: sn rdn along & wknd)	nk	**17**	50/1	34	18
4527[16]	**Divide And Rule (58)** (RHollinshead) **3-8-11**(3) DGriffiths(3) (a bhd: t.o)	dist	**18**	33/1	—	—
4568[7]	**Zaaleff (USA) (45)** (KMahdi) **5-9-3** WJO'Connor(16) (lw: s.i.s: sn chsng ldrs: wknd 3f out: virtually p.u appr fnl f)	dist	**19**	33/1	—	—

(SP 141.8%) **19 Rn**

1m 42.6 (7.60) CSF £58.93 TOTE £8.80: £2.80 £4.20 £13.30 (£61.70) Trio £397.00; £335.50 to Leicester 14/10/97 OWNER Mr C. W. Sumner (DIDCOT) BRED Airlie Stud
WEIGHT FOR AGE 3yo-3lb

4059 Alfahaal (IRE) made amends for the race he threw away when he last ran here just over a month ago. He looked as though he would trot up when cruising to the front on the bridle fifty yards out, but in the end the line only just arrived in time. He obviously has plenty of ability and eight flights of hurdles could make a man of him. He is entered at the Horses-In-Training sale at Newmarket next month. (8/1)
4008 Star Turn (IRE), returning to a mile, raced in the firing line all the way, and rallied so strongly late on that he all but pulled the prize out of the fire. (7/1)
3897 Tulsa (IRE) is still striving to find a correct trip, but ran up to his best and that initial success could arrive before the season closes. (33/1)
1217 Penlop had the easy ground that he needs and had plenty of use made of him, but he was at full stretch entering the final furlong and lacked the necessary speed to take a hand in the outcome. (10/1: 7/1-12/1)
4601 Brave Envoy has barely lasted this trip when tried in the past, and though he was close enough to land a blow approaching the final furlong found an extra effort beyond him. (12/1)
1088 Ardent looked well tuned-up despite having had a four-month break, and the way he was staying on in the closing stages suggests he could be about to find his way. (33/1)
4629 Duello tried to get himself into the action on the approach to the final furlong, but failed to respond to strong pressure and could not deliver a challenge. He is beginning to get his winter coat. (9/4)
4571 Zermatt (IRE) (12/1: op 8/1)

4697 KENNETH MANN CONDITIONS STKS (2-Y.O) (Class C)

3-00 (3-00) **1m 1f 218y** £5,182.80 (£1,654.80: £792.40) Stalls: High GOING: 0.21 sec per fur (G)

Form	Horse / details	Btn	Pos	SP	RR	SF
4165*	**Asakir** (SbinSuroor) **2-9-1** LDettori(3) (mde all: qcknd 3f out: r.o wl)	—	**1**	5/4[1]	88+	43
4460*	**St Helensfield** (MJohnston) **2-9-1** JWeaver(2) (lw: chsd wnr: rdn & wandered over 1f out & ins fnl f: nt qckn)	1½	**2**	9/4[3]	86+	41
3912[2]	**Abuhail (USA)** (DMorley) **2-9-1** RHills(1) (lw: hld up: rdn over 2f out: eased whn btn over 1f out)	20	**3**	2/1[2]	54	9

(SP 108.5%) **3 Rn**

2m 12.7 (9.00) CSF £3.82 TOTE £1.80: (£2.60) OWNER Godolphin (NEWMARKET) BRED Shadwell Estate Company Limited

4165* Asakir, thought by his trainer to have preferred better ground, still did it well and connections are now thinking in terms of the Zetland Stakes at Newmarket. (5/4)
4460* St Helensfield ran around quite a bit under pressure and, in fact, the only time he seemed to keep straight was when he was directly behind the winner. (9/4)
3912 Abuhail (USA) is probably not at his best when the ground rides soft . (2/1)

4698 STOAT (S) STKS (2-Y.O) (Class G)

3-30 (3-31) **1m 1f 218y** £2,595.00 (£720.00: £345.00) Stalls: High GOING: 0.21 sec per fur (G)

Form	Horse / details	Btn	Pos	SP	RR	SF
4265[4]	**Hiding Place (66)** (MBell) **2-8-6** MFenton(17) (a.p: led 3f out: hrd rdn: all out)	—	**1**	9/4[1]	65	22
4334[5]	**Pianist (IRE) (55)** (GLewis) **2-8-11b[1]** PaulEddery(3) (hld up: hdwy u.p 3f out: styd on strly towards fin)	hd	**2**	7/1[3]	70	27
4334[4]	**Red Maple (USA) (62)** (PFICole) **2-8-11b** TQuinn(9) (led to 3f out: hrd rdn & no ex ins fnl f)	2	**3**	9/4[1]	67	24
4303[8]	**Lady Eil** (BSmart) **2-8-6** JStack(10) (a.p: chal 3f out: sn rdn: wknd ins fnl f)	4	**4**	33/1	55	12
4595[11]	**Docklands Dispatch (IRE) (54)** (NTinkler) **2-9-1** KimTinkler(18) (trckd ldrs: outpcd 3f out: styd on ins fnl f)	1¼	**5**	20/1	62	19
4592[7]	**Mary Lou (IRE) (48)** (MRChannon) **2-8-6** AMackay(1) (hdwy 2f out: kpt on u.p ins fnl f)	d.h	**5**	33/1	53	10
4113[11]	**Carlasanta (IRE)** (AGNewcombe) **2-8-6** FNorton(6) (hld up & bhd: hdwy wl over 1f out: nvr nrr)	½	**7**	14/1	52	9
4627[2]	**Royal Ground (IRE) (69)** (MRChannon) **2-8-11** JFortune(7) (in tch: rdn & hdwy over 3f out: sn outpcd)	½	**8**	3/1[2]	57	14
4627[7]	**Compassionate** (WGMTurner) **2-8-8**(3) DSweeney(8) (bkwd: bhd fnl 3f)	11	**9**	14/1	39	—
4265[11]	**Reach For A Star (55)** (CWThornton) **2-8-11** EJohnson(12) (lw: nvr nr ldrs)	3	**10**	25/1	34	—
4384[13]	**Silver Hope (IRE) (55)** (RHollinshead) **2-8-11** WRyan(2) (a bhd)	hd	**11**	33/1	34	—

				SP	RR	SF
4299^{8}	**Lascensa (USA)** (PAKelleway) **2-8-6** SSanders(15) (chsd ldrs 7f: sn lost pl)	1¼	**12**	33/1	27	—
4462^{4}	**Son of Good Times** (PGMurphy) **2-8-11** SDrowne(11) (a in rr)	hd	**13**	50/1	32	—
2935^{11}	**Gay Abandon (42)** (KMcAuliffe) **2-8-6b^{1}** JFEgan(13) (plld hrd: hld up: a bhd)	1½	**14**	33/1	25	—
4593^{5}	**Little Risk** (KMcAuliffe) **2-8-7**^{ow1} JReid(5) (prom to 3f out: wknd qckly: t.o)	10	**15**	12/1	10	—
4208^{8}	**Tilburg (48)** (MrsNMacauley) **2-8-1**$^{(5)}$ JoHunnam(16) (bhd fnl 3f: t.o)	19	**16**	33/1	—	—
				(SP 148.3%)		**16 Rn**

2m 14.3 (10.60) CSF £20.21 TOTE £3.40: £1.30 £1.80 £1.60 (£22.70) Trio £27.30 OWNER Cheveley Park Stud (NEWMARKET)
Sold AStafford 10,000 gns, Pianist (IRE) clmd GHeywood £6,000

4265 Hiding Place found this step down to selling company over an extended trip made-to-measure, but after having to work hard to shake off Red Maple, she had little more to give and the line arrived only just in time. (9/4)

4334 Pianist (IRE) needs a lot of driving and, even though equipped with blinkers, he did not get going until far too late and he was still a stride down at the line. (7/1)

4334 Red Maple (USA) attempted to gallop his rivals into the ground, but he had been collared early in the straight and, though he battled on under a strong ride, had shot his bolt on reaching the final furlong. (9/4)

Lady Eil will need this sort of trip and she showed her first glimpse of form, but she has gone in her coat and had had enough once into the final furlong. (33/1)

4163 Docklands Dispatch (IRE) lost his pitch when the pace lifted three furlongs out, but he was back into his stride in the latter stages and was still galloping on at the finish. (20/1)

1997 Mary Lou (IRE) was beginning to find her feet in the closing stages, as she is bred to need this sort of trip. Maybe she is about to strike form. (33/1)

4699 RABBIT H'CAP (0-85) (3-Y.O) (Class D)

4-00 (4-00) **1m 3f 183y** £3,873.00 (£1,164.00: £562.00: £261.00) Stalls: High GOING: 0.21 sec per fur (G)

				SP	RR	SF
4632*	**Secret Ballot (IRE) (67)** (KMahdi) **3-8-6**$^{ow1\ 5x}$ WJO'Connor(6) (lw: a.p: led 3f out: rdn out)	—	**1**	8/1	77	52
3893^{3}	**Dovedon Star (75)** (PAKelleway) **3-9-0** JWeaver(13) (hld up & bhd: hdwy over 2f out: r.o wl ins fnl f)	hd	**2**	7/1^{3}	85	61
4552^{5}	**Deep Water (USA) (72)** (PFICole) **3-8-11** TQuinn(3) (chsd ldr: led over 3f out: sn hdd: wknd fnl f)	5	**3**	8/1	75	51
4234^{3}	**Tarxien (70)** (KRBurke) **3-8-9** JFEgan(7) (lw: a.p: rdn over 2f out: one pce)	hd	**4**	5/1^{2}	73	49
4568^{3}	**Junikay (IRE) (60)** (RIngram) **3-7-10**$^{(3)}$ MHenry(2) (lw: hld up: hdwy 2f out: nvr nr to chal)	2½	**5**	10/1	60	36
4469*	**Tyrolean Dream (IRE) (77)** (MHTompkins) **3-9-2** LDettori(5) (lw: hld up: stdy hdwy 5f out: one pce fnl 2f)	nk	**6**	7/2^{1}	76	52
4046^{8}	**Harmony Hall (66)** (JRFanshawe) **3-8-5**^{ow1} MHills(10) (lw: b: b.hind: hld up & bhd: hdwy over 2f out: n.d)	4	**7**	10/1	60	35
2574^{7}	**Tom Tailor (GER) (76)** (DRCElsworth) **3-9-1** JFortune(1) (dwlt: nvr nr ldrs)	1¼	**8**	14/1	68	44
3907^{8}	**In The Genes (62)** (IPWilliams) **3-8-1** DaleGibson(11) (prom: hrd rdn over 4f out: wknd over 3f out)	1¾	**9**	20/1	52	28
4372^{6}	**Pennys From Heaven (79)** (HCandy) **3-9-4** CRutter(4) (prom tl wknd over 2f out)	6	**10**	12/1	61	37
4310^{6}	**Island Sanctuary (IRE) (82)** (PJMakin) **3-9-7** SSanders(12) (lw: bhd most of wy)	11	**11**	11/1	49	25
4213^{2}	**Scarrots (69)** (SCWilliams) **3-8-8** DaneO'Neill(14) (prom over 5f: t.o)	10	**12**	12/1	22	—
4477^{12}	**Absolute Liberty (USA) (64)** (SPCWoods) **3-8-3b^{1}** AClark(8) (plld hrd: led over 8f: sn wknd: t.o)	7	**13**	20/1	8	—
4378^{3}	**Quiet Venture (74)** (EALDunlop) **3-8-13** JReid(15) (hld up mid div: rdn over 3f out: sn bhd: t.o)	1¾	**14**	10/1	15	—
				(SP 140.8%)		**14 Rn**

2m 36.7 (8.20) CSF £67.56 CT £446.41 TOTE £11.80: £2.70 £3.80 £1.70 (£57.50) Trio £241.50 OWNER Mr Waleed Al-Mutawa(NEWMARKET) BRED Godolphin Management Co Ltd

4632* Secret Ballot (IRE) looked particularly well on a cold day and, relishing the give in the ground, was in front plenty soon enough over this longer trip. (8/1)

3893 Dovedon Star out of a ten-furlong juvenile winner, stayed on well towards the finish and stamina was certainly not a problem. (7/1)

4552 Deep Water (USA) was back to a more suitable trip, but not even soft ground could offset his lack of finishing pace. (8/1)

4234 Tarxien back to a mile and a half, was still off an 8lb higher mark following his two back-to-back wins. (5/1)

4568 Junikay (IRE) has been plummeting down the ratings, and seemed to be ridden as if he was not guaranteed to stay. It would be interesting to see if he reverts to a mile and a quarter next time. (10/1)

4469* Tyrolean Dream (IRE), upped in distance on this handicap debut, never gave his supporters much cause to yodel. (7/2)

4310 Island Sanctuary (IRE) (11/1: 8/1-12/1)

4700 DORMOUSE MAIDEN APPRENTICE STKS (3-Y.O) (Class G)

4-30 (4-31) **7f 9y** £2,679.00 (£744.00: £357.00) Stalls: High GOING: 0.39 sec per fur (GS)

				SP	RR	SF
4587^{10}	**Shalaal (USA) (77)** (MCChapman) **3-8-9**$^{(3)}$ SCarson(3) (hld up: rdn to ld over 1f out: drvn clr)	—	**1**	33/1	84	63
	Saguaro (JHMGosden) **3-8-12** PDoe(5) (lengthy: scope: a.p: led over 3f out tl over 1f out: shkn up & rn green fnl f: sn btn)	2	**2**	7/1	80	59
4578^{8}	**Wild Sky (IRE) (75)** (MJHeaton-Ellis) **3-8-9v^{1}**$^{(3)}$ JFowle(11) (hdwy over 3f out: one pce fnl 2f)	5	**3**	3/1^{2}	68	47
4316^{5}	**Star Invader** (MRStoute) **3-8-12** JoHunnam(1) (hld up: outpcd 3f out: styd on appr fnl f)	2	**4**	2/1^{1}	64	43
4480^{2}	**Van Chino (47)** (BAMcMahon) **3-8-9**$^{(3)}$ SRighton(8) (plld hrd: led over 4f out tl over 3f out: wknd 2f out)	1¾	**5**	10/1	60	39
4600^{3}	**Democrat** (SirMarkPrescott) **3-8-5**$^{(7)}$ ClareLund(10) (trckd ldrs: rdn over 2f out: sn wknd)	4	**6**	20/1	51	30
3396^{5}	**Bustopher Jones** (CREgerton) **3-8-7**$^{(5)}$ LeanneMasterson(9) (a in rr)	2½	**7**	33/1	45	24
4563^{6}	**Barrow Creek** (GWragg) **3-8-12** RWinston(7) (trckd ldrs: rdn over 3f out: wknd over 2f out)	4	**8**	5/1	36	15
4047^{4}	**Persevere (63)** (LordHuntingdon) **3-8-2**$^{(5)}$ CCogan(2) (a in rr)	2	**9**	9/2^{3}	26	5
4587^{7}	**Pride of Narvik** (MRChannon) **3-8-12** AEddery(13) (in tch 4f: sn outpcd)	3½	**10**	50/1	23	2
2591^{12}	**Falcon Ridge (42)** (JCFox) **3-8-7**$^{(5)}$ GMcDonald(12) (bkwd: chsd ldrs 4f: sn wknd)	5	**11**	50/1	12	—
3043^{7}	**Dyce** (JBalding) **3-8-7** JWilkinson(6) (bkwd: led over 2f: wknd 3f out: t.o)	17	**12**	50/1	—	—
	Lucayan Beach (BGubby) **3-8-9**$^{(3)}$ DMcGaffin(4) (bkwd: s.s: sn prom: wknd 3f out: t.o)	6	**13**	16/1	—	—
				(SP 137.2%)		**13 Rn**

1m 28.1 (5.50) CSF £248.32 TOTE £41.60: £4.70 £2.10 £1.50 (£39.60) Trio £170.60 OWNER Mr Eric Knowles (MARKET RASEN) BRED W. G. Lyster III

Shalaal (USA) seemed to appreciate the easier ground. He was always travelling comfortably, and quickened up readily to leave the runner-up standing. (33/1)

Saguaro looked as though he would benefit from the run, but he had to force the pace and, had he not edged left when shown the whip inside the last furlong, would have made a race of it. (7/1)

2695 Wild Sky (IRE), visored for the first time, promised to get into the action entering the last quarter-mile, but he found very little when given the office and was unable to go through with his effort. (3/1)

4316 Star Invader, although he stayed on well towards the finish, always had far too much to do. He does look to have come to himself but may well need stronger handling. (2/1)

4480 Van Chino intended to do as he did on his previous outing and adopt catch-me-if-you-can tactics, but he had company in the early stages and, losing his lead over three furlongs out, was very soon fighting a lost cause. (10/1)
4600 Democrat, a very poor mover having his third outing of the month, was never in a position to cause concern and he is not yet getting it together. (20/1)

4701 E.B.F. HARE MAIDEN STKS (II) (2-Y.O F) (Class D)
5-00 (5-03) **7f 9y** £3,223.00 (£964.00: £462.00: £211.00) Stalls: High GOING: 0.39 sec per fur (GS)

				SP	RR	SF
	La Nuit Rose (FR) (SbinSuroor) **2-8-11** LDettori(6) (lt-f: unf: a.gng wl: led wl over 1f out: sn qcknd clr: easily)	—	1	7/4[2]	89+	38
4317[3]	**Yanabi (USA) (83)** (PTWalwyn) **2-8-11** RHills(5) (tk keen hold: hdwy over 2f out: chsd wnr fnl f: no imp)	4	2	6/4[1]	80	29
	Pursuit Venture (SPCWoods) **2-8-11** NDay(9) (leggy: a.p: ev ch 2f out: one pce)	1¾	3	16/1	76	25
4317[7]	**Blue Dawn (IRE)** (EALDunlop) **2-8-11** WRyan(10) (hld up: hdwy over 2f out: ev ch wl over 1f out: wknd fnl f)	3	4	14/1	69	18
4515[8]	**In The Sun (USA)** (JLDunlop) **2-8-11** TQuinn(1) (no hdwy fnl 2f)	2	5	14/1	65	14
	Sure Quest (DWPArbuthnot) **2-8-11** SWhitworth(2) (lt-f: unf: bit bkwd: nvr nr to chal)	1¼	6	50/1	62	11
4567[2]	**Relate (75)** (MartynMeade) **2-8-8**(3) RHavlin(7) (led over 5f: sn wknd)	1½	7	10/1[3]	58	7
3926[9]	**Midnight Sting** (MAJarvis) **2-8-11** JFortune(4) (b: tk keen hold: rdn over 3f out: sn bhd)	hd	8	20/1	58	7
4515[16]	**Ivory League** (GLewis) **2-8-11** PaulEddery(8) (hld up & bhd: sme hdwy wl over 1f out: nvr plcd to chal)	1¼	9	33/1	55+	4
	Lineage (NAGraham) **2-8-11** AMcGlone(3) (scope: bkwd: hld up: hdwy 3f out: sn rdn & wknd)	3	10	10/1[3]	48	—
4317[13]	**Glitter Princess (63)** (MajorDNChappell) **2-8-11** MHills(11) (w ldrs tl wknd over 2f out)	2½	11	33/1	43	—
	Linguistic Dancer (AGNewcombe) **2-8-11** SDrowne(13) (lt-f: bit bkwd: s.s: hdwy over 2f out: wknd wl over 1f out)	5	12	50/1	31	—
	Shambles (GGMargarson) **2-8-8**(3) MHenry(12) (lt-f: prom: rdn 3f out: sn wknd)	1	13	50/1	29	—
				(SP 130.3%)	**13 Rn**	

1m 30.1 (7.50) CSF £4.52 TOTE £3.30: £2.40 £1.10 £17.30 (£2.10) Trio £24.10 OWNER Godolphin (NEWMARKET) BRED Kaichi Nitta
OFFICIAL EXPLANATION **Ivory League: rider reported that the filly is nervy and temperamental, and that his instructions were to drop her in and ride a finish on her.**
La Nuit Rose (FR) is out of a mare who, after finishing second in the Prix Marcel Boussac to Shadayid as a juvenile, went on to win the French Oaks the following year. Certainly no oil painting, her trainer's worries about the ground turned out to be totally unfounded, and she is likely to have one more outing before wintering in Dubai. (7/4)
4317 Yanabi (USA) probably came up against an above-average sort in the winner, but she is beginning to look like one who has had plenty of chances. (6/4)
Pursuit Venture, a half-sister to Soviet Express and the stayer Pearl Venture, is a full-sister to the three-year-old maiden Love Venture. (16/1)
3117 Blue Dawn (IRE), a half-sister to a mile Listed scorer in Germany, and a mile and a quarter winner in France, did not get home in the soft ground. (14/1)
4515 In The Sun (USA) should be a different proposition over longer distances next season. (14/1: op 8/1)
Sure Quest, a half-sister to several winners, including Strat's Quest and Quest Again, was given a nice introduction to the game. (50/1)
Ivory League, out of a sister to a Cherry Hinton winner, caught the eye of the Stewards but the explanations were accepted. (33/1)
Lineage (10/1: 25/1-8/1)

T/Jkpt: Not won; £4,128.31 to Leicester 14/10/97. T/Plpt: £272.20 (82.05 Tckts). T/Qdpt: £75.00 (12.13 Tckts) IM/KH

4688-AYR (L-H) (Soft)
Tuesday October 14th
WEATHER: overcast & raining WIND: mod across

4702 LOCH ENOCH NURSERY H'CAP (0-85) (2-Y.O) (Class E)
2-20 (2-23) **6f** £3,015.25 (£907.00: £438.50: £204.25) Stalls: High GOING: 0.50 sec per fur (GS)

				SP	RR	SF
4231[10]	**Daybreak (62)** (JWWatts) **2-7-9**(3) PFessey(11) (hld up & bhd: hdwy over 1f out: r.o to ld wl ins fnl f)	—	1	12/1	64	5
4566*	**Kettlesing (IRE) (74)** (MWEasterby) **2-8-7b**(3) GParkin(10) (hld up & bhd: hdwy & swtchd 2f out: led 1f out: wandered: hdd & nt qckn towards fin)	¾	2	5/1[1]	74	15
2473[7]	**Liberte Bell (IRE) (60)** (SirMarkPrescott) **2-7-10** NVarley(3) (s.i.s: drvn along & bhd tl hdwy 2f out: ch ins fnl f: styd on)	½	3	7/1[3]	59	—
4267[11]	**Selkirk Rose (IRE) (78)** (MissLAPerratt) **2-9-0** KDarley(1) (lw: wnt lft s: sn trckng ldrs: ev ch appr fnl f: nt qckn)	2	4	10/1	71	12
4419[4]	**Rhinefield Beauty (IRE) (60)** (JSGoldie) **2-7-10** JQuinn(12) (hld up & bhd: hdwy over 1f out: swtchd ins fnl f: nrst fin)	1½	5	10/1	49	—
4634[15]	**Deeceebee (80)** (WStorey) **2-9-2v[1]** JCarroll(5) (cl up tl rdn & btn appr fnl f)	nk	6	16/1	69	10
4588*	**Miss Vivien (78)** (MissLAPerratt) **2-9-0** 6x DHolland(8) (lw: led: qcknd 2f out: hdd 1f out: wknd)	1¼	7	6/1[2]	63	4
3571[6]	**Happy Days (74)** (DMoffatt) **2-8-7**(3) DarrenMoffatt(2) (outpcd ½-wy: n.d after)	1½	8	10/1	55	—
4042[13]	**Perfect Harmony (IRE) (72)** (BJMeehan) **2-8-8** SSanders(6) (lw: in tch: hrd drvn ½-wy: no imp after)	½	9	10/1	52	—
4284[12]	**Suivez La Trace (80)** (JJO'Neill) **2-9-2** RCochrane(9) (chsd ldrs 4f: sn wknd)	1½	10	14/1	56	—
4566[5]	**Wishbone Alley (IRE) (61)** (MDods) **2-7-11** TWilliams(4) (prom 4f: sn rdn & btn)	2½	11	16/1	30	—
4305[5]	**First Village (IRE) (85)** (JBerry) **2-9-2**(5) CLowther(7) (s.i.s: a bhd)	7	12	10/1	36	—
				(SP 115.0%)	**12 Rn**	

1m 18.34 (8.54) CSF £62.65 CT £422.75 TOTE £17.00: £4.40 £2.60 £2.90 (£110.80) Trio £411.30; £417.10 to Haydock 15/10/97 OWNER Duke of Sutherland (RICHMOND) BRED The Duke of Sutherland
LONG HANDICAP Liberte Bell (IRE) 7-8 Rhinefield Beauty (IRE) 7-9
OFFICIAL EXPLANATION **Daybreak: regarding the improved form, the filly failed to settle from an outside draw over a furlong further last time.**
3806 Daybreak, dropped back in trip, came from some way off the pace and had to weave her way through and finished strongly, suggesting that longer trips would also suit. (12/1)
4566* Kettlesing (IRE) has plenty of ability but is certainly not a straightforward individual, although extra furlong was no real problem. (5/1)
2473 Liberte Bell (IRE) had plenty to do from her draw, but it was lack of early pace that was the real problem and she will no doubt do better over further. (7/1)
3265* Selkirk Rose (IRE) had her chances but, when a struggle really developed, she was never doing enough. (10/1)
4419 Rhinefield Beauty (IRE), a free-running sort, was anchored out the back and then met with trouble in running and failed to get in a blow. (10/1)

3990 Deeceebee had the visor on for the first time which certainly sharpened him up, but he called it a day when a serious effort was required. (16/1)
4588* Miss Vivien, again attempting to make all, ran out of fuel in these testing conditions. (6/1)

4703 LOCH DEE CLAIMING STKS (3 & 4-Y.O) (Class E)

2-50 (2-51) **1m 2f 192y** £2,742.25 (£823.00: £396.50: £183.25) Stalls: High GOING: 0.77 sec per fur (S)

				SP	RR	SF
4283[8]	**Begorrat (IRE) (68)** (DMoffatt) **3-8-13b**(3) DarrenMoffatt(1) (hld up: hdwy appr st: wnt 2nd over 2f out: hung rt over 1f out: r.o to ld post)	—	**1**	11/4[3]	75	46
4415[7]	**Grate Times (58)** (EWeymes) **3-8-4b** SSanders(4) (led: qcknd clr 3f out: hrd rdn ins fnl f: jst ct)	s.h	**2**	13/2	63	34
4264[6]	**Deadline Time (IRE) (68)** (MrsMReveley) **4-8-10** KDarley(5) (hld up: hdwy over 3f out: sn rdn & no imp)	6	**3**	13/8[1]	54	31
2523[10]	**Imperial Or Metric (IRE) (54)** (JJO'Neill) **3-7-13**(5) CLowther(2) (chsd ldr tl outpcd fnl 2½f)	4	**4**	25/1	48	19
2328[6]	**Foxes Tail (73)** (MissSEHall) **3-9-2** DHolland(3) (hld up: effrt over 3f out: sn btn)	4	**5**	9/4[2]	54	25
				(SP 112.7%)	**5 Rn**	

2m 31.65 (15.75) CSF £18.06 TOTE £3.30: £1.90 £3.20 (£7.00) OWNER Mr Mike Flynn (CARTMEL) BRED C. Crowley
WEIGHT FOR AGE 3yo-6lb
STEWARDS' ENQUIRY Sanders susp: 23-24/10/97 (excessive use of whip)
3976 Begorrat (IRE) is not the easiest of rides but has ability and needed every yard of this longer trip. (11/4: 2/1-3/1)
3870 Grate Times was given a brilliant tactical ride and all but pinched it, and is obviously in good heart. (13/2)
4264 Deadline Time (IRE) looked a cut above these but, when asked a question, his response was disappointing to say the least. (13/8)
1994 Imperial Or Metric (IRE) has been disappointing and has changed stables again, but perhaps hurdling might change his attitude. (25/1)
2328 Foxes Tail, having his first run for over three months, showed little. (9/4)

4704 ALLOA PUBS AND RESTAURANTS 'BUDGET BEATERS' H'CAP (0-95) (3-Y.O+) (Class C)

3-20 (3-20) **1m 5f 13y** £5,169.25 (£1,549.00: £744.50: £342.25) Stalls: High GOING: 0.77 sec per fur (S)

				SP	RR	SF
4416[2]	**Wahiba Sands (94)** (JLDunlop) **4-10-0** KDarley(9) (hld up: stdy hdwy 3f out: shkn up over 1f out: led ins fnl f: qcknd)	—	**1**	4/1[2]	105	64
4691[5]	**Hill Farm Blues (63)** (WMBrisbourne) **4-7-6**(5) IonaWands(6) (lw: hdwy to trck ldrs 8f out: led over 3f out & qcknd: hdd ins fnl f: no ex)	4	**2**	14/1	69	28
4279[4]	**Ledgendry Line (69)** (MrsMReveley) **4-8-3** ACulhane(2) (lw: hld up: stdy hdwy over 3f out: sn rdn & prom: no imp fnl 2f)	8	**3**	3/1[1]	65	24
4242[13]	**Nightlark (IRE) (82)** (DRLoder) **3-8-8** RCochrane(4) (lw: cl up: led 5f out tl over 3f out: sn outpcd)	4	**4**	3/1[1]	73	24
3974[11]	**One For Baileys (80)** (MJohnston) **3-8-6** DHolland(7) (chsd ldrs: racd wd: ev ch 5f out tl wknd fnl 3f)	10	**5**	9/1	59	10
4288[4]	**Tycooness (IRE) (77)** (MJohnston) **3-8-3b[1]** JFanning(1) (sn drvn along & wl bhd: sme late hdwy)	hd	**6**	6/1[3]	56	7
4466[2]	**Lord Advocate (62)** (DANolan) **9-7-7b**(3) PFessey(5) (chsd ldrs: led 7f to 5f out: outpcd fnl 3½f)	6	**7**	33/1	34	—
4466[10]	**Sioux (72)** (CWThornton) **3-7-12** JQuinn(8) (chsd ldrs tl rdn & wknd 4f out)	2½	**8**	14/1	41	—
4405[6]	**Classic Flyer (IRE) (64)** (ICampbell) **4-7-12** AMackay(3) (led tl hdd 7f out: sn wknd)	30	**9**	8/1	—	—
				(SP 121.7%)	**9 Rn**	

3m 2.56 (17.76) CSF £55.78 CT £178.00 TOTE £4.10: £1.60 £4.80 £1.60 (£25.90) Trio £50.40 OWNER Lord Swaythling (ARUNDEL) BRED Fares Stables Ltd
LONG HANDICAP Lord Advocate 7-1
WEIGHT FOR AGE 3yo-8lb
4416 Wahiba Sands ran as though he has a problem and was on and off the bit at various stages, but he did win nicely in the end. (4/1)
4691 Hill Farm Blues, having her second run in consecutive days, put up a useful effort but always found the winner too strong. (14/1)
4279 Ledgendry Line needs a strong pace and got a reasonable one here but, once he came off the bit early in the straight, the struggle was always too much for his liking. (3/1)
3903* Nightlark (IRE) helped force the pace, but proved most disappointing when the pressure was applied once into the home straight. (3/1)
1230* One For Baileys has just had six weeks off and ran as though this was needed. (9/1)
4288 Tycooness (IRE), a moody customer, had blinkers on this time and wanted nothing to do with it. (6/1)

4705 ALLIED DOMECQ INNS 'BUDGET BEATERS' MAIDEN STKS (3-Y.O+) (Class D)

3-50 (3-51) **1m 2f** £3,447.50 (£1,040.00: £505.00: £237.50) Stalls: High GOING: 0.77 sec per fur (S)

				SP	RR	SF
	Taberann (IRE) (LMCumani) **3-9-0** KDarley(8) (w'like: scope: in tch: drvn along 3f out: hdwy over 1f out: r.o to ld wl ins fnl f)	—	**1**	6/1[3]	85	51
3738[2]	**Ricardo** (RCharlton) **3-9-0** SSanders(4) (hld up: hdwy appr st: rdn to ld 1f out: hrd rdn & hdd towards fin)	2	**2**	6/4[1]	82	48
4331[3]	**Waterwave (USA)** (JHMGosden) **4-9-5** JCarroll(7) (lw: b.hind: a.p: rdn to ld 2f out: hdd 1f out: kpt on)	1¼	**3**	5/2[2]	80	51
2008[5]	**Classic Jenny (IRE)** (ICampbell) **4-9-0** AMackay(5) (chsd ldr: led over 2f out: sn hdd: rdn & btn appr fnl f)	3½	**4**	8/1	69	40
4469[7]	**The Munro's** (JSGoldie) **3-9-0** JQuinn(3) (trckd ldrs tl edgd lft & grad wknd fnl 3f)	15	**5**	100/1	50	16
	Fairy Fingers (JLEyre) **3-8-9** TWilliams(1) (leggy: racd alone on ins: led tl hdd & wknd over 2f out)	2	**6**	50/1	42	8
2555[6]	**Isabella Gonzaga** (JLDunlop) **3-8-9** DHolland(6) (in tch: effrt ent st: wknd & eased fnl 2f)	1½	**7**	8/1	40	6
4469[6]	**San Francisco** (CWThornton) **3-9-0** DeanMcKeown(2) (lw: outpcd & bhd fnl 7f)	nk	**8**	100/1	44	10
	Golden Saddle (IRE) (MissLAPerratt) **3-8-9** RCochrane(9) (wl bhd fnl 4f: t.o)	21	**9**	50/1	6	—
				(SP 111.0%)	**9 Rn**	

2m 19.37 (13.57) CSF £13.22 TOTE £4.40: £1.10 £1.10 £1.10 (£5.10) Trio £6.00 OWNER H H Aga Khan (NEWMARKET) BRED His Highness the Aga Khan's Studs S.C.
WEIGHT FOR AGE 3yo-5lb
Taberann (IRE), a most attractive newcomer, took time to realise what was needed but, as the race progressed, he warmed up. In the end he won really well, suggesting that further will see even better. (6/1: op 3/1)
3738 Ricardo has been gelded and did little wrong, only to meet a useful opponent. (6/4)
2008 Classic Jenny (IRE), a most attractive sort, had her chances, but lacked a change of gear in this very testing ground. (8/1)
The Munro's gave a hint of ability and was not knocked about. (100/1)
Fairy Fingers had plenty of use made of her for a debutante, and this should have taught her something. (50/1)
2555 Isabella Gonzaga, a plain-looking individual, was stepping up in trip, but was struggling some way out and was then given a very easy time. (8/1: 5/1-9/1)

4706 E.B.F. LINFERN MAIDEN STKS (2-Y.O) (Class D)
4-20 (4-23) **7f** £3,376.00 (£1,018.00: £494.00: £232.00) Stalls: High GOING: 0.77 sec per fur (S)

				SP	RR	SF
4231^{2}	**Set Trail (IRE) (83)** (JHanson) **2-8-9** EJohnson(8) (b.hind: led tl hdd ins fnl f: sn led again: kpt on)	—	**1**	11/4^{1}	81	16
4382^{9}	**Chocolate (IRE) (85)** (JLDunlop) **2-8-9b** KDarley(5) (lw: a.p: hdwy to ld ins fnl f: sn hdd: hrd rdn & kpt on)	s.h	**2**	4/1^{3}	81	16
	North Ofthe Border (MJohnston) **2-9-0** JFanning(6) (w'like: chsd ldrs: pushed along ½-wy: r.o one pce fnl f)	1½	**3**	16/1	83	18
	Culcraggie (JLEyre) **2-9-0** TWilliams(4) (leggy: unf: hdwy ½-wy: sn chsng ldrs & rdn: kpt on fnl f: nvr able chal)	s.h	**4**	16/1	82	17
3127^{5}	**Royal Rights** (DRLoder) **2-9-0** RCochrane(1) (chsd ldrs: rdn & one pce fnl 2f)	13	**5**	9/2	53	—
	Amazonian (CWThornton) **2-9-0** DeanMcKeown(10) (leggy: scope: outpcd & bhd ½-wy: n.d)	½	**6**	33/1	52	—
4544^{6}	**Best Quest** (JHMGosden) **2-9-0** JCarroll(7) (chsd ldrs tl wknd fnl 3f)	8	**7**	3/1^{2}	33	—
4381^{10}	**Brave Maple** (JMPEustace) **2-9-0** JTate(9) (prom tl outpcd 3f out: sn wknd)	dist	**8**	25/1	—	—
	Rangatira (IRE) (MJohnston) **2-9-0** DHolland(3) (Withdrawn not under Starter's orders: inj in stalls)		**W**	5/1	—	—
4231^{14}	***Ryefield Star*** (JBerry) **2-9-0** SSanders(2) (Withdrawn not under Starter's orders: inj in stalls)		**W**	33/1	—	—
				(SP 128.0%)	**8 Rn**	

1m 36.39 (11.99) CSF £10.70 TOTE £3.50: £1.30 £1.10 £3.40 (£4.20) Trio £14.20 OWNER Mr J. Hanson (WETHERBY) BRED Cyclades Farming Co

4231 Set Trail (IRE) looked a real handful in the paddock, but did nothing wrong in the race and showed a fine attitude under pressure. (11/4)
4382 Chocolate (IRE) looked to have been given the perfect ride as she came to win it inside the final furlong, but in the end she found the effort required just too much. (4/1)
North Ofthe Border put in a useful first effort, and there should be a fair amount of improvement to come. (16/1)
Culcraggie, an angular sort, showed definite signs of ability and was staying on particularly well. (16/1)
3127 Royal Rights was stepping up in trip and that, coupled with the testing ground, proved all too much. (9/2)
Amazonian looked short of toe throughout the race. (33/1)
4544 Best Quest ran poorly, and looks the type that will do better when everything goes his way. (3/1)

4707 LOCH VALLEY H'CAP (0-70) (3-Y.O+) (Class E)
4-50 (4-55) **5f** £3,112.75 (£937.00: £453.50: £211.75) Stalls: High GOING: 0.50 sec per fur (GS)

				SP	RR	SF
4580^{2}	**Southern Dominion (45)** (MissJFCraze) **5-8-11b** SWebster(13) (lw: mde all: kpt on wl fnl f)	—	**1**	10/1	60	42
4512^{19}	**Another Episode (IRE) (49)** (MissLAPerratt) **8-8-8**(7) JMcAuley(5) (lw: a chsng wnr: hrd rdn & no ex ins fnl f)	.2	**2**	25/1	58	40
4047^{10}	**Hiltons Executive (IRE) (35)** (EJAlston) **3-8-1** JQuinn(3) (in tch: hdwy u.p over 1f out: kpt on towards fin)	s.h	**3**	14/1	43	25
4434^{5}	**Gold Edge (58)** (MRChannon) **3-9-10** AMackay(6) (lw: chsd ldrs: rdn 2f out: kpt on same pce)	1½	**4**	13/2^{2}	62	44
4233^{16}	**Pallium (IRE) (52)** (DANolan) **9-9-4b** RCochrane(2) (hdwy 2f out: styd on: nrst fin)	nk	**5**	16/1	55	37
3761^{9}	**Soaked (35)** (DWChapman) **4-8-1b** DaleGibson(17) (hdwy ½-wy: styd on: nvr able chal)	1½	**6**	8/1^{3}	33	15
4385^{15}	**Rich Glow (46)** (NBycroft) **6-8-12** KDarley(14) (lw: bhd tl hdwy 2f out: r.o u.p: nrst fin)	1¼	**7**	5/1^{1}	40	22
4512^{13}	**Dona Filipa (45)** (MissLCSiddall) **4-8-11** EJohnson(11) (lw: s.i.s: hdwy 2f out: nvr rchd ldrs)	¾	**8**	25/1	37	19
4329^{3}	**Young Ben (IRE) (47)** (JSWainwright) **5-8-10b**(3) GParkin(10) (b.hind: chsd ldrs tl rdn & btn over 1f out)	nk	**9**	12/1	38	20
4233^{22}	**Leading Princess (IRE) (43)** (MissLAPerratt) **6-8-9b** DHolland(4) (chsd ldrs over 3f: grad wknd)	hd	**10**	20/1	33	15
4472^{2}	**Seconds Away (35)** (JSGoldie) **6-8-1** TWilliams(12) (sn drvn along: nvr nr ldrs)	½	**11**	14/1	24	6
4233^{18}	**Six for Luck (45)** (DANolan) **5-8-6**(5) CLowther(19) (rdn ½-wy: n.d)	1¼	**12**	25/1	30	12
3871^{13}	**Blazing Imp (USA) (40)** (MrsJJordan) **4-8-3**(3) DarrenMoffatt(9) (sn outpcd & bhd: n.d)	1	**13**	12/1	21	3
4291^{12}	**Naissant (52)** (MartynWane) **4-9-4** DeanMcKeown(16) (sn drvn along: n.d)	hd	**14**	8/1^{3}	33	15
4168^{2}	**Pathaze (39)** (NBycroft) **4-8-5** ACulhane(20) (nvr wnt pce)	1¼	**15**	12/1	16	—
4370^{3}	**Lucy In The Sky (IRE) (41)** (BJMeehan) **3-8-7** JTate(1) (in tch 3f: wknd)	½	**16**	10/1	17	—
3871^{14}	**Sunset Harbour (IRE) (42)** (SEKettlewell) **4-8-8** JCarroll(8) (s.i.s: a bhd)	2	**17**	20/1	11	—
4164^{13}	**Hostile Native (43)** (RGuest) **4-8-9b** SSanders(15) (spd 3f: wknd)	1	**18**	25/1	9	—
4471^{15}	**Another Nightmare (IRE) (44)** (RMMcKellar) **5-8-10** NVarley(7) (lw: s.i.s: a bhd)	5	**19**	33/1	—	—
3922^{4}	**Hajat (46)** (JBerry) **3-8-9**(3) PFessey(18) (s.i.s: a bhd)	nk	**20**	8/1^{3}	—	—
				(SP 151.7%)	**20 Rn**	

62.51 secs (5.51) CSF £247.30 CT £3,333.39 TOTE £14.10: £3.10 £6.10 £3.80 £2.30 (£631.40) Trio £831.30; £948.45 to Haydock 15/10/97 OWNER Mrs Angela Wilson (YORK) BRED A. Wilkinson and J. W. Brown

4580 Southern Dominion has been threatening to do this all season and showed a good attitude this time. This seems a particularly good effort from his draw. (10/1)
4233 Another Episode (IRE) left his dismal effort last time way behind but, try as he might, the winner was always too good. (25/1)
3606 Hiltons Executive (IRE), from a yard going well, put in some determined late work but is yet to win a race. (14/1)
4434 Gold Edge won her only race over six furlongs and, although trying hard, was always just short of the necessary toe. (13/2)
3922 Pallium (IRE), normally a top of the ground performer, ran well in these conditions. (16/1)
3625 Soaked ran well from his draw. (8/1)
4329 Rich Glow had plenty to do both from his draw and after a poor start, and did well to get so close in the end. (5/1)
4329 Young Ben (IRE) (12/1: op 8/1)

T/Plpt: £46.00 (526.83 Tckts). T/Qdpt: £12.70 (126.64 Tckts) AA

4694-LEICESTER (R-H) (Good to soft)
Tuesday October 14th
WEATHER: cloudy, rain later WIND: nil

4708 E.B.F. REFERENCE POINT MAIDEN STKS (I) (2-Y.O C & G) (Class D)
1-30 (1-31) **7f 9y** £3,379.00 (£1,012.00: £486.00: £223.00) Stalls: Low GOING: 0.01 sec per fur (G)

				SP	RR	SF
	Brave Reward (USA) (MRStoute) **2-8-11** JReid(10) (lt-f: unf: hmpd s: sn trckng ldrs: qcknd to ld ins fnl f: r.o wl)	—	**1**	3/1^{2}	87+	54
4524^{8}	**Celtic Pageant (95)** (RAkehurst) **2-8-11** LDettori(9) (led tl hdd ins fnl f: sn rdn & no ex)	1½	**2**	5/4^{1}	84	51
4167^{13}	**Krisamba** (BJMeehan) **2-8-11** MTebbutt(5) (hld up: hdwy over 2f out: one pce fnl f)	1¾	**3**	25/1	80	47
	Kings Arrow (IRE) (MBell) **2-8-11** MFenton(2) (leggy: lt-f: bit bkwd: hdwy over 3f out: wknd fnl f)	4	**4**	5/1^{3}	71	38

				SP	RR	SF
3687^{9}	**Mashab** (NAGraham) **2-8-11** RHills(4) (prom: pushed along over 2f out: outpcd fnl f)	¾	**5**	20/1	69	36
	Ritual (HCandy) **2-8-11** CRutter(11) (leggy: lt-f: dwlt: plld hrd: hld up: r.o ins fnl f)	2½	**6**	20/1	63	30
4581^{7}	**Dashing Knight (IRE)** (DRLoder) **2-8-11** GCarter(13) (bkwd: in tch: no hdwy fnl 2f)	1	**7**	12/1	61	28
3783^{14}	**Academy (IRE)** (AndrewTurnell) **2-8-11** NAdams(8) (bit bkwd: bhd tl sme late hdwy)	½	**8**	50/1	60	27
4061^{10}	**Saudi** (PFICole) **2-8-11** TQuinn(7) (chsd ldrs tl wknd 2f out)	4	**9**	14/1	51	18
	Brave Noble (USA) (EALDunlop) **2-8-11** MRimmer(12) (w'like: leggy: scope: s.s: effrt & rdn over 3f out: wknd fnl 2f)	2	**10**	12/1	46	13
	Abu Camp (MJHeaton-Ellis) **2-8-8**$^{(3)}$ ADaly(14) (w'like: leggy: bkwd: chsd ldrs: rdn 3f out: grad wknd)	hd	**11**	33/1	46	13
	Silent Warning (SirMarkPrescott) **2-8-11** GDuffield(6) (w'like: leggy: lw: s.s: a bhd)	¾	**12**	10/1	44	11
	Longbowman (MrsLStubbs) **2-8-11** SWhitworth(3) (unf: scope: bit bkwd: a bhd)	3	**13**	50/1	37	4
				(SP 137.5%)	**13 Rn**	

1m 26.1 (3.50) CSF £7.08 TOTE £6.20: £1.20 £1.70 £18.30 (£6.40) Trio £43.60 OWNER Mr Saeed Suhail (NEWMARKET) BRED Warner L. Jones Farm, Inc. & W. S. Farnish III

Brave Reward (USA), a lightly-made debutant who can be fitter, quickened impressively to leave the favourite in his wake inside the final furlong and, with the winter months to strengthen up, he could be anything come next year. (3/1: op 2/1)

4007 Celtic Pageant looked something to bet on back in his own class, and he appeared to be in control until the winner did him for a turn of foot in a sprint to the line. (5/4: evens-11/8)

Krisamba, very keen to post, improved considerably on his only previous outing and was only shaken off inside the last 200 yards. He could be an interesting proposition next term. (25/1)

Kings Arrow (IRE), a leggy colt who comes from a winning family, did not really stretch out, but he can improve as he strengthens up, and this was a pleasing start to his career. (5/1)

Mashab had more of a trouble-free run than he did on his debut, but he was being nudged along some way out and had met his match before reaching the final furlong. (20/1)

Ritual, who has already been gelded, looks to need time. Keen to get on with it after losing ground at the start, he was doing all his best work inside the final furlong and should be able to make his mark next season. (20/1)

Silent Warning (10/1: op 6/1)

4709 WYMESWOLD CONDITIONS STKS (2-Y.O) (Class C)

2-00 (2-01) **7f 9y** £4,517.80 (£1,670.20: £800.10: £325.50: £127.75: £48.65) Stalls: High GOING: 0.01 sec per fur (G)

				SP	RR	SF
4517^{5}	**Social Charter (USA) (93)** (PWChapple-Hyam) **2-9-2** JReid(5) (mde all: drvn out)	—	**1**	10/1	94	52
4458*	**Swing Sister** (PRWebber) **2-8-8** KFallon(7) (s.i.s: hdwy over 2f out: r.o ins fnl f)	½	**2**	10/1	85	43
2524^{4}	**Mulahen** (DMorley) **2-8-10** RHills(4) (hld up: chsd wnr over 2f out: ev ch fnl f: nt qckn)	½	**3**	2/1^{1}	86	44
4439^{5}	**Absolutly Sparklin** (LMCumani) **2-9-2** LDettori(1) (chsd wnr over 4f: wknd over 1f out)	2½	**4**	9/4^{2}	86	44
4146^{4}	**Harmonic Way** (RCharlton) **2-9-2** TSprake(2) (hld up: hdwy over 2f out: one pce fnl f)	nk	**5**	9/2^{3}	85	43
4501^{3}	**Beware (82)** (RWArmstrong) **2-8-7**$^{(3)}$ RFfrench(6) (hld up: rdn 2f out: wknd over 1f out)	5	**6**	20/1	68	26
4364^{4}	**Kawafil (IRE) (90)** (PTWalwyn) **2-8-11** GHind(3) (hld up: hdwy over 2f out: hung bdly lft over 1f out: sn wknd)	3½	**7**	7/1	61	19
				(SP 117.7%)	**7 Rn**	

1m 26.6 (4.00) CSF £94.88 TOTE £9.70: £2.40 £5.00 (£32.50) OWNER Mr R. E. Sangster (MARLBOROUGH) BRED Swettenham Stud

4517 Social Charter (USA) had finished second on his debut in worse conditions than he encountered here, and was able to dictate matters on this step-up in distance. (10/1: op 5/1)

4458* Swing Sister, a half-sister to the stayer Ptoto and good middle-distance performer Bob's Ploy, confirmed that stamina is not a problem and gave a good account of herself in this better class. (10/1)

2524 Mulahen, a half-sister to the useful middle-distance performer Lemhill, should not be long losing her maiden tag. (2/1: 6/4-9/4)

4439 Absolutly Sparklin is a half-brother to the stayer Doddington Flyer out of a mile and a quarter winner from the family of Teenoso. He may already need a stiffer test of stamina. (9/4)

4146 Harmonic Way, having his first run on soft ground, failed to pick up after seeming to travel well. (9/2: 3/1-5/1)

4501 Beware needs better ground to see out seven furlongs. (20/1)

4364 Kawafil (IRE) showed her old wayward tendencies under pressure. (7/1)

4710 E.B.F. REFERENCE POINT MAIDEN STKS (II) (2-Y.O C & G) (Class D)

2-30 (2-33) **7f 9y** £3,379.00 (£1,012.00: £486.00: £223.00) Stalls: Low GOING: 0.01 sec per fur (G)

				SP	RR	SF
4113^{10}	**Goodwood Cavalier** (JLDunlop) **2-8-11** MRimmer(14) (a.p: led over 2f out: clr ent fnl f: r.o wl)	—	**1**	50/1	86	32
4507^{2}	**Bombastic** (BWHills) **2-8-11** TQuinn(10) (a.p: led wl over 2f out: sn hdd: rallied u.p nr fin)	1¼	**2**	6/5^{1}	83	29
	Russian Party (IRE) (ACStewart) **2-8-11** WRyan(5) (wl grwn: bkwd: plld hrd: hdwy 3f out: kpt on one pce fnl f)	2½	**3**	10/1^{3}	78	24
	Mudalal (USA) (DMorley) **2-8-11** RHills(8) (lt-f: bit bkwd: s.i.s: sn rcvrd: outpcd 3f out: styd on again fnl f)	¾	**4**	11/1	76	22
	Empire Gold (USA) (HRACecil) **2-8-11** KFallon(9) (leggy: lt-f: prom: one pce fnl 2f)	hd	**5**	11/4^{2}	76	22
4244^{4}	**Desert Spa (USA)** (PWHarris) **2-8-11** AClark(3) (led over 4f: sn drvn along: lost tch)	7	**6**	14/1	60	6
3686^{15}	**After Eight** (RWArmstrong) **2-8-11** FNorton(6) (mid div: bhd fnl 3f)	nk	**7**	33/1	59	5
2842^{11}	**Balla d'Aire (IRE)** (RBoss) **2-8-11** JFortune(2) (plld hrd: a in rr)	1¾	**8**	12/1	55	1
	Stormy Blue (IRE) (SPCWoods) **2-8-11** NDay(4) (lengthy: lt-f: a bhd)	1¼	**9**	20/1	52	—
4603^{14}	**Hunt Hill (IRE)** (SirMarkPrescott) **2-8-11** CNutter(12) (a bhd)	2½	**10**	33/1	47	—
4603^{15}	**Pressurise** (SirMarkPrescott) **2-8-11** GDuffield(13) (a in rr)	½	**11**	25/1	45	—
	Brooksie (JWHills) **2-8-8**$^{(3)}$ MHenry(7) (unf: scope: bkwd: rdn 4f out: sn lost tch)	3	**12**	20/1	39	—
4575^{10}	**Master Caster (IRE)** (DRLoder) **2-8-11** GCarter(1) (bit bkwd: a bhd: outpcd)	1¾	**13**	20/1	35	—
				(SP 129.9%)	**13 Rn**	

1m 27.9 (5.30) CSF £102.95 TOTE £78.60: £8.40 £1.10 £2.60 (£60.00) Trio £217.90; £248.65 to Haydock 15/10/97 OWNER Goodwood Racehorse Owners Group (Three) (ARUNDEL) BRED Fulling Mill Farm and Stud

Goodwood Cavalier put his previous experience to good use on this more suitable ground and, in winning comfortably, caused quite an upset. (50/1)

4507 Bombastic could have found this step down in trip his undoing. He was coming back for more at the finish after getting tapped for toe below the distance (6/5)

Russian Party (IRE), far from fully wound up and looking more like a three-year-old, showed plenty of promise on this first look at a racecourse, and, as he is bred to need a test of stamina, should certainly be one for the future. (10/1: op 6/1)

Mudalal (USA), beginning to look wintery, still needs time to fill his frame. Finding the pace too hot for him soon after halfway, he was starting to pick up again towards the finish and he has time on his side. (11/1: 8/1-12/1)

Empire Gold (USA), a sparely-made colt who is a poor mover in his slower paces, pressed the leaders until feeling the strain on the run to the final furlong. (11/4: 5/4-3/1)
4244 Desert Spa (USA) has run over slightly longer trips in his outings to date but, forcing the pace this time until over two furlongs out, he was soon struggling and is not yet getting his act together (14/1)

4711 WHISSENDINE (S) H'CAP (0-60) (3-Y.O+) (Class G)

3-00 (3-03) **7f 9y** £2,889.00 (£804.00: £387.00) Stalls: High GOING: 0.01 sec per fur (G)

				SP	RR	SF
4373^{8}	**Scathebury (47)** (KRBurke) **4-9-2** KFallon(13) (lw: hdwy over 3f out: led wl over 1f out: sn clr: r.o)	—	**1**	11/2^{2}	60	45
4510^{4}	**Birchwood Sun (47)** (MDods) **7-9-2b** JWeaver(6) (lw: hld up: hdwy over 2f out: r.o ins fnl f)	1½	**2**	10/1	57	42
3860^{11}	**Ed's Folly (IRE) (53)** (SDow) **4-9-8** JFEgan(9) (a.p: ev ch 2f out: r.o one pce)	1½	**3**	12/1	59	44
4249^{9}	**Ocker (IRE) (56)** (MHTompkins) **3-9-9** DBiggs(3) (s.s: hdwy & swvd rt over 1f out: hung rt fnl f: fin wl)	1¼	**4**	16/1	59	42
4570^{6}	**Greatest (53)** (MissGayKelleway) **6-9-5b**$^{(3)}$ RFfrench(17) (chsd ldr: led over 4f out tl over 2f out: one pce)	½	**5**	9/1	55	40
4016^{2}	**Halmanerror (55)** (MrsJRRamsden) **7-9-10** JFortune(14) (hld up: stdy hdwy 3f out: rdn 2f out: one pce)	1½	**6**	11/2^{2}	54	39
4112^{5}	**Queen of Shannon (IRE) (51)** (AWCarroll) **9-8-13**$^{(7)}$ RStudholme(15) (dwlt: nvr nrr)	nk	**7**	5/1^{1}	49	34
4629^{7}	**Lord Oberon (IRE) (46)** (JAkehurst) **9-9-1** GCarter(11) (b: hdwy over 3f out: hrd rdn & wknd over 2f out)	s.h	**8**	12/1	44	29
4333^{6}	**Shashi (IRE) (46)** (PatMitchell) **5-9-1** PBloomfield(19) (nvr trbld ldrs)	2½	**9**	20/1	38	23
4628^{10}	**Ochos Rios (IRE) (53)** (BSRothwell) **6-9-8** GDuffield(7) (prom: led over 2f out tl wl over 1f out: sn wknd)	½	**10**	7/1^{3}	44	29
4324^{12}	**Fearless Cavalier (50)** (RHollinshead) **3-9-3** FLynch(2) (a bhd)	2½	**11**	20/1	36	19
1423^{11}	**Sure To Dream (IRE) (50)** (RTPhillips) **4-9-5** RPerham(16) (plld hrd: bhd fnl 2f)	hd	**12**	33/1	35	20
4059^{11}	**Oneknight With You (49)** (MJFetherston-Godley) **3-9-2** JReid(4) (b: sme hdwy over 3f out: rdn & wknd over 2f out)	1	**13**	16/1	32	15
4371^{8}	**Mr Rough (47)** (DMorris) **6-9-2v** NDay(5) (prom over 4f)	s.h	**14**	16/1	30	15
4570^{12}	**My Godson (48)** (MDods) **7-9-3v** RLappin(8) (prom over 4f)	nk	**15**	33/1	30	15
4243*	**Shark (IRE) (47)** (KAMorgan) **4-9-2** OPears(10) (led over 2f: wknd over 2f out)	2	**16**	7/1^{3}	25	10
4628^{7}	**Sharp Return (50)** (MJRyan) **3-9-0**$^{(3)}$ PMcCabe(1) (bhd fnl 2f)	6	**17**	14/1	14	—
	Hopperetta (50) (BPalling) **3-9-3** AClark(18) (bkwd: hld up & plld hrd: bhd fnl 3f: t.o)	16	**18**	33/1	—	—
4546^{12}	**By Jay (IRE) (48)** (BJCurley) **3-9-1** LDettori(12) (prom 3f: t.o)	2½	**19**	8/1	—	—
				(SP 160.7%)	**19 Rn**	

1m 27.2 (4.60) CSF £67.84 CT £651.97 TOTE £7.90: £2.10 £1.90 £5.70 £7.10 (£45.20) Trio £684.90 OWNER Mr Nigel Shields (WANTAGE) BRED The Duke Of Marlborough
WEIGHT FOR AGE 3yo-2lb
Bt in 5,000 gns
3290 Scathebury, having slipped a total of 10lb in the ratings, does not mind this sort of ground and took advantage of a return to selling company. (11/2)
4510 Birchwood Sun, down 2lb, handles all sorts of ground and was dropping back to seven. (10/1)
3561 Ed's Folly (IRE), dropped 2lb, is another who seems to act on most types of going. (12/1)
3969 Ocker (IRE), down 13lb since his handicap debut, was in a seller for the first time. He did not look an easy ride and must have gone close had he kept straight. (16/1)
3469 Greatest scored on similar ground at Chepstow and did not appear to have any excuses. (9/1: 12/1-8/1)
4016 Halmanerror (11/2: op 3/1)
3310 Ochos Rios (IRE) (7/1: op 9/2)

4712 EDGE & ELLISON CONDITIONS STKS (3-Y.O F) (Class C)

3-30 (3-30) **1m 8y** £5,424.00 (£1,734.00: £832.00) Stalls: Low GOING: 0.01 sec per fur (G)

				SP	RR	SF
2869^{9}	**Star Precision (99)** (GBBalding) **3-8-9** SDrowne(3) (mde all: drvn & qcknd 1f out: r.o wl)	—	**1**	3/1^{3}	100	33
3499^{4}	**Keyboogie (USA) (95)** (RCharlton) **3-8-13** JReid(2) (lw: a chsng wnr: effrt over 1f out: sn rdn: unable qckn)	1½	**2**	13/8^{2}	101	34
4669^{9}	**Priena (IRE) (91)** (DRLoder) **3-8-9v** KFallon(1) (hld up: pushed along over 2f out: kpt on u.p fnl f)	nk	**3**	11/8^{1}	96	29
				(SP 105.2%)	**3 Rn**	

1m 40.8 (5.80) CSF £6.82 TOTE £4.20: (£3.30) OWNER Miss B. Swire (ANDOVER) BRED Miss B. Swire
2513 Star Precision, tackling a mile for the first time in her career, adopted new tactics in an attempt to put the emphasis on stamina and it worked a treat. (3/1)
3499 Keyboogie (USA), fresh and well after a two-month break, was quite happy to accept the lead and she looked able to take over but, when the pressure was really on, she just could not summon the speed to match strides with the winner. (13/8)
4424 Priena (IRE), settled in the rear, was caught flat-footed as the pace lifted over two furlongs out and she was soon made to work. Staying on without being able to quicken, she was never nearer than at the finish. (11/8)

4713 PADDOCK CLAIMING STKS (3-Y.O+) (Class F)

4-00 (4-01) **1m 3f 183y** £2,994.00 (£834.00: £402.00) Stalls: High GOING: 0.01 sec per fur (G)

				SP	RR	SF
3284^{5}	**Swan Hunter (60)** (DJSCosgrove) **4-8-11**$^{(5)}$ RMullen(14) (lw: hld up: hdwy over 3f out: led over 2f out: sn clr: r.o wl)	—	**1**	9/2^{3}	68	47
4521^{4}	**Naval Games** (MCPipe) **4-8-13** FLynch(1) (chsd ldr: hung bdly lft & c stands' side st: led 3f out: sn hdd: one pce)	5	**2**	2/1^{1}	58	37
4521^{7}	**Statajack (IRE) (57)** (DRCElsworth) **9-9-11b** TQuinn(5) (b: dwlt: hdwy over 3f out: styd on fnl f)	1½	**3**	8/1	68	47
4590^{4}	**Paradise Navy (70)** (CREgerton) **8-9-11b** LDettori(18) (s.s: stdy hdwy 4f out: one pce fnl 2f)	1¼	**4**	7/2^{2}	67	46
	Anjou (56) (JPearce) **5-9-2** KFallon(15) (hdwy over 1f out: nvr nrr)	2½	**5**	10/1	54	33
4481^{12}	**Armston** (JWharton) **5-8-13**$^{(3)}$ DGriffiths(3) (bit bkwd: a.p: ev ch over 2f out: wknd over 1f out)	3½	**6**	33/1	49	28
4594^{7}	**Royal Roulette (54)** (SPCWoods) **3-8-10v** NDay(16) (hdwy over 3f out: ev ch over 2f out: sn wknd)	1½	**7**	10/1	48	20
4633^{9}	**Arif (IRE) (37)** (JohnHarris) **5-8-13** PaulEddery(2) (lw: prom: ev ch over 2f out: sn wknd)	1½	**8**	20/1	42	21
3929^{4}	**Bobby's Dream (28)** (MHTompkins) **5-8-8** DBiggs(17) (hld up mid div: wknd over 2f out)	7	**9**	14/1	28	7
2067^{3}	**Champagne Warrior (IRE) (51)** (MJCamacho) **4-8-11** LCharnock(12) (swtg: bkwd: prom tl wknd over 2f out)	s.h	**10**	12/1	31	10
4224^{4}	**Bobbitt (44)** (WJarvis) **3-7-12b**$^{(3)}$ RFfrench(9) (hld up mid div: rdn & wknd over 2f out)	s.h	**11**	12/1	28	—
	Nocatchim (KAMorgan) **8-9-8v** OPears(13) (a bhd)	7	**12**	33/1	32	11
2662^{5}	**Miami Moon (43)** (GFJohnsonHoughton) **3-8-4** DaneO'Neill(8) (bkwd: plld hrd: led 9f: sn wknd)	5	**13**	16/1	15	—
4373^{11}	**Racing Telegraph (37)** (CNAllen) **7-9-5** MartinDwyer(4) (hld up & plld hrd: a bhd)	6	**14**	33/1	14	—
4587^{12}	**Barkston Warrior** (DShaw) **3-8-3** SDrowne(11) (b: bit bkwd: a bhd)	6	**15**	50/1	—	—

				SP	RR	SF
4453[13]	**African Sun (IRE) (35)** (MCChapman) **4-9-2** FNorton(7) (prom: sddle slipped early: wknd over 4f out: virtually p.u)	dist	**16**	33/1	—	—
2537[10]	**Halavadream** (MJBolton) **3-8-6**(3) MHenry(6) (plld hrd: sn bhd: t.o fnl 6f)	dist	**17**	50/1	—	—

(SP 151.4%) **17 Rn**

2m 36.5 (8.00) CSF £15.08 TOTE £5.90: £1.70 £2.20 £2.80 (£17.80) Trio £23.20 OWNER Mr Derrick Yarwood (NEWMARKET) BRED The Arrow Farm and Stud

WEIGHT FOR AGE 3yo-7lb

Naval Games clmd Stuart Glanmore-Martin £4,000

3284 Swan Hunter, given injections for problems with his knees, has been waiting for some soft ground. (9/2)

4521 Naval Games, who did not handle the home turn at all well and eventually ended up alone on the stand rails, was in trouble once the winner was launched. (2/1: 6/4-5/2)

3929* Statajack (IRE) could not overhaul the runner-up, let alone bother the winner. (8/1)

4590 Paradise Navy had not run over a distance as short as this since 1993. (7/2)

Anjou, lightly-raced of late, shaped well on this comeback and was staying on when most had cried enough. (10/1)

Armston fared much better than on his comeback race at Wolverhampton a fortnight ago. (33/1)

4304 Royal Roulette (10/1: op 16/1)

4714 STEWARDS H'CAP (0-70) (3-Y.O+) (Class E)

4-30 (4-32) **1m 1f 218y** £3,795.00 (£1,140.00: £550.00: £255.00) Stalls: Low GOING: 0.01 sec per fur (G)

				SP	RR	SF
4596[2]	**Priolo Prima (68)** (SirMarkPrescott) **4-9-12** GDuffield(4) (lw: hld up: hdwy 4f out: rdn wl over 1f out: r.o to ld last stride)	—	**1**	4/1[1]	78	58
3329*	**Bonanza Peak (USA) (64)** (MrsJCecil) **4-9-8** MartinDwyer(5) (hld up: hdwy 5f out: led over 2f out: hrd rdn: hdd last stride)	s.h	**2**	13/2[3]	74	54
4406[4]	**North Reef (IRE) (64)** (JPearce) **6-9-8** JReid(12) (a.p: rdn over 1f out: one pce)	3	**3**	9/1	69	49
2876[2]	**Calendula (64)** (DMorley) **4-9-8** GCarter(14) (bit bkwd: hld up: hmpd on ins 6f out: hdwy over 3f out: one pce appr fnl f)	2	**4**	6/1[2]	66	46
4466[11]	**Slasher Jack (IRE) (62)** (RAFahey) **6-8-13**(7) RWinston(19) (chsd ldrs: rdn 3f out: sn btn)	7	**5**	20/1	53	33
4268[6]	**Step N Go (IRE) (66)** (MrsJRRamsden) **3-9-5** JFortune(1) (lw: hld up: hdwy 4f out: sn rdn: no imp)	2½	**6**	14/1	53	28
4223[8]	**Maradi (IRE) (66)** (MBell) **3-9-5** MFenton(7) (led tl hdd over 2f out: sn wknd)	1¼	**7**	16/1	51	26
4386[5]	**Muhassil (IRE) (64)** (KAMorgan) **4-9-8** OPears(17) (lw: prom tl wknd over 2f out)	2½	**8**	12/1	45	25
4275[7]	**Punkah (USA) (65)** (GMMcCourt) **4-9-2**(7) RStudholme(2) (hld up & bhd: hdwy over 4f out: wknd fnl 2f)	nk	**9**	12/1	45	25
	Star Witness (IRE) (65) (AGNewcombe) **5-9-9** GHind(3) (bkwd: nvr nr to chal)	12	**10**	14/1	26	6
3453[4]	**Massyar Seventeen (65)** (HJCollingridge) **3-9-4** TQuinn(10) (bdly hmpd & checked 6f out: nt rcvr)	½	**11**	12/1	25	—
	Designer Lines (70) (CJames) **4-10-0** CRutter(13) (hld up: stdy hdwy 5f out: wknd over 2f out)	2	**12**	33/1	27	7
	Blaze of Song (62) (RHannon) **5-9-6** DaneO'Neill(11) (bkwd: a in rr)	3	**13**	16/1	14	—
4109[9]	**Kings Assembly (70)** (PWHarris) **5-10-0** KFallon(6) (hld up: hdwy ent st: eased whn btn fnl 2f)	4	**14**	13/2[3]	16	—
2867[10]	**Classic Find (USA) (67)** (PatMitchell) **4-9-11** PBloomfield(16) (bit bkwd: s.i.s: a bhd)	¾	**15**	14/1	12	—
4516[4]	**Bakers Daughter (59)** (JRArnold) **5-9-3** AClark(9) (a in rr)	3	**16**	8/1	—	—
	Classic Colours (USA) (65) (GHYardley) **4-9-9** VSlattery(8) (bkwd: prom to ½-wy: sn lost tch: t.o)	9	**17**	33/1	—	—
3768[2]	**Shining Example (69)** (PJMakin) **5-9-13** PaulEddery(15) (s.i.s: hmpd on ins 6f out: racd alone st: t.o)	¾	**18**	12/1	—	—
	El Bailador (IRE) (60) (JDBethell) **6-9-4** JWeaver(18) (lw: prom tl wknd 3f out: t.o)	½	**19**	20/1	—	—

(SP 160.0%) **19 Rn**

2m 10.2 (6.50) CSF £32.84 CT £234.25 TOTE £3.90: £2.50 £4.90 £2.50 £1.70 (£13.90) Trio £88.70 OWNER Petra Bloodstock (NEWMARKET) BRED P. D. and Mrs Player

WEIGHT FOR AGE 3yo-5lb

4596 Priolo Prima, much happier when he can get his toe in, had it all to do from below the distance, but he is not short on stamina and, answering his jockey's every call, stayed on to nose ahead right on the line. (4/1)

3329* Bonanza Peak (USA) has had a light season, and he promised to follow up his success at Bath when gaining a healthy lead into the final furlong, but the winner's determined late challenge proved just too strong and he was touched off in the last stride. (13/2)

4406 North Reef (IRE) returning to a more suitable trip, ran well, and as he has not been over-raced, there could be better to come. (9/1)

2876 Calendula, one of several stopped in their tracks before turning out of the back straight, began to look dangerous when poised to challenge two furlongs out, but four months out of action began to take its toll and she could do little more than stay on at the one pace. There is still time for her to get back to winning ways. (6/1: op 7/2)

Slasher Jack (IRE) finds this trip inadequate and he was in trouble when the pace lifted fully three furlongs out, but he never stopped trying and all is not lost yet. (20/1)

4268 Step N Go (IRE) won a couple of races in the spring, but has shown little since she returned from the break, and she was never able to get close enough to cause concern. (14/1)

Star Witness (IRE) (14/1: 10/1-16/1)

2475 Classic Find (USA) (14/1: op 25/1)

4516 Bakers Daughter (8/1: 6/1-9/1)

4715 E.B.F. SOAR MAIDEN STKS (2-Y.O) (Class D)

5-00 (5-04) **1m 8y** £4,198.00 (£1,264.00: £612.00: £286.00) Stalls: High GOING: 0.01 sec per fur (G)

				SP	RR	SF
4318[2]	**Mantusis (IRE)** (PWHarris) **2-9-0** CRutter(15) (dwlt: hdwy over 3f out: led wl ins fnl f: r.o)	—	**1**	4/1[2]	87	27
	Ta Aruf (USA) (DMorley) **2-8-9** GCarter(12) (str: cmpt: bkwd: dwlt: wl bhd tl rapid hdwy to ld over 2f out: sn rdn & edgd lft: hdd wl ins fnl f)	1½	**2**	16/1	79+	19
4229[2]	**Brimming** (HRACecil) **2-9-0** KFallon(4) (lw: led over 5f: one pce)	4	**3**	6/4[1]	76	16
3862[3]	**Muhib (USA)** (MRStoute) **2-9-0** RHills(17) (a.p: ev ch over 2f out: one pce)	2	**4**	5/1[3]	72	12
	All Made Up (USA) (MBell) **2-9-0** MFenton(20) (wl grwn: scope: bkwd: dwlt: rdn & hdwy 2f out: one pce appr fnl f)	1¼	**5**	25/1	70	10
4237[6]	**Pelagos (FR)** (RCharlton) **2-9-0** TSprake(3) (no hdwy fnl 2f)	1	**6**	12/1	68	8
4520[2]	**Majestic Hills** (JLDunlop) **2-9-0** LDettori(14) (hdwy 4f out: eased whn btn fnl f)	2	**7**	4/1[2]	64	4
4237[14]	**Rainmaker** (MAJarvis) **2-9-0** PaulEddery(18) (bkwd: s.i.s: sn prom: wknd over 2f out)	5	**8**	33/1	54	—
4318[10]	**Salford** (LMCumani) **2-8-11**(3) RFfrench(8) (bit bkwd: bhd fnl 2f)	1¼	**9**	20/1	51	—
	Secrecy (PFICole) **2-9-0** TQuinn(19) (gd sort: bkwd: prom: rdn over 4f out: sn wknd)	nk	**10**	10/1	51	—
4520[5]	**Classic Impact (IRE)** (PWChapple-Hyam) **2-9-0** JReid(1) (lw: bhd fnl 2f)	nk	**11**	10/1	50	—
4526[17]	**Ambiguous** (DRLoder) **2-9-0** JFortune(16) (a bhd)	nk	**12**	33/1	49	—

Form	Horse / details	Dist	Pos	SP	RR	SF
4526[15]	**Frankie Ferrari (IRE)** (DRLoder) **2-8-11**(3) MHenry(5) (a bhd)	1½	**13**	50/1	46	—
4545[2]	**Up The Wall (63)** (JohnBerry) **2-8-11**(3) ADaly(6) (lw: hld up: rdn 4f out: bhd fnl 2f)	¾	**14**	33/1	45	—
	Cool Spray (USA) (EALDunlop) **2-8-9** MRimmer(11) (str: bkwd: plld hrd: prom tl wknd over 2f out)	3½	**15**	20/1	33	—
1607[12]	**Sabre Butt** (MHTompkins) **2-9-0** DBiggs(9) (bkwd: a bhd)	4	**16**	33/1	30	—
	Rolling High (IRE) (DJGMurraySmith) **2-9-0** JFEgan(13) (lengthy: a bhd: t.o)	dist	**17**	40/1	—	—
	Ivorian (MrsAJPerrett) **2-9-0** AClark(2) (Withdrawn not under Starter's orders: ref to ent stalls)		**W**	25/1	—	—
				(SP 161.8%)		**17 Rn**

1m 41.9 (6.90) CSF £72.88 TOTE £4.70: £1.40 £17.10 £1.10 (£125.70) Trio £78.00 OWNER The Romantics (BERKHAMSTED) BRED Anamoine Ltd

IN-FOCUS: **Brimming and Up The Wall started from each other's stalls; resulting in both jockeys being fined £125 under Rule G1.**

4318 Mantusis (IRE) justified market support and eventually gained the upper hand in ground that had become quite testing because of the rain. (4/1)

Ta Aruf (USA), closely related to Tajar, is out of a half-sister to Magic Of Life. Despite looking in need of the run she ran quite an extraordinary race on her debut, and seems a ready-made future winner. (16/1)

4229 Brimming deserves another chance on better ground. (6/4: tchd 9/4)

3862 Muhib (USA), out of a mare that won at up to nine furlongs in the States, could not raise his game in the rain-softened ground. (5/1)

All Made Up (USA), out of a winner of three races in the States, seems sure to come on for the outing. (25/1)

4237 Pelagos (FR) had totally different ground conditions this time, but again showed signs of ability. (12/1: op 7/1)

4520 Majestic Hills probably needs a sounder surface. (4/1: op 5/2)

Secrecy (10/1: 7/1-12/1)

T/Jkpt: Not won; £8,344.91 to Haydock 15/10/97. T/Plpt: £421.00 (49.34 Tckts). T/Qdpt: £19.90 (62.8 Tckts) IM/KH

4716a - 4730a : (Irish Racing) - See Computer Raceform

4433-HAYDOCK (L-H) (Soft becoming Heavy)
Wednesday October 15th

Poor visibility Race 7
WEATHER: cloudy, heavy drizzle later WIND: almost nil

4731 HORNBEAM H'CAP (0-80) (3-Y.O F) (Class D)

2-00 (2-01) **1m 2f 120y** £3,647.50 (£1,105.00: £540.00: £257.50) Stalls: High GOING: 0.63 sec per fur (GS)

Form	Horse / details	Dist	Pos	SP	RR	SF
4268[3]	**Topatori (IRE) (71)** (MHTompkins) **3-9-0** DBiggs(13) (lw: hld up in rr: hdwy over 3f out: led 2f out: rdn & edgd lft fnl f: r.o)	—	**1**	10/1	81	44
2507[3]	**Top Jem (75)** (MJRyan) **3-9-4** GBardwell(11) (bit bkwd: hld up in rr: drvn along 3f out: hdwy over 1f out: r.o wl fnl f)	1¼	**2**	9/2[2]	83	46
4407*	**Sunny Isle (75)** (CFWall) **3-9-4** JReid(4) (hld up & bhd: hdwy over 2f out: hrd rdn whn hmpd & swtchd ins fnl f)	½	**3**	8/1	82	45
4568[10]	**Falls O'Moness (IRE) (60)** (KRBurke) **3-8-3** JFEgan(8) (swtg: bhd: hdwy over 2f out: r.o wl ins fnl f)	1½	**4**	20/1	67	30
3453[3]	**Boss Lady (IRE) (78)** (RCharlton) **3-9-7** KDarley(6) (lw: a chsng ldrs: rdn & one pce appr fnl f)	1¾	**5**	7/1[3]	82	45
4242[12]	**Come Together (67)** (DWPArbuthnot) **3-8-5**(5) CLowther(10) (lw: bhd: effrt & rdn 3f out: no imp fnl 2f)	12	**6**	14/1	53	16
4144[4]	**Leading Note (USA) (74)** (LMCumani) **3-9-3** JWeaver(9) (led after 2f to 3f out: rdn & wknd over 1f out)	3	**7**	9/1	55	18
4435[3]	**Agony Aunt (76)** (MrsJCecil) **3-9-5** MartinDwyer(5) (led 2f: wknd over 2f out)	½	**8**	10/1	56	19
3439*	**Karakia (IRE) (75)** (JHMGosden) **3-9-4** LDettori(7) (trckd ldrs: led 3f out to 2f out: wknd qckly appr fnl f)	4	**9**	5/2[1]	49	12
3089[2]	**Understudy (57)** (RHollinshead) **3-8-0** JQuinn(2) (lw: a bhd: t.o)	15	**10**	25/1	9	—
4158*	**Silvery (66)** (JARToller) **3-8-9** SSanders(1) (chsd ldrs: rdn 3f out: sn wknd: t.o)	3	**11**	10/1	13	—
3432[10]	**Dizzy Tilly (65)** (TJNaughton) **3-8-8** DHolland(12) (hdwy 6f out: hrd drvn ent st: wknd 3f out: t.o)	nk	**12**	16/1	12	—
4070[10]	**Sharkiyah (IRE) (70)** (RWArmstrong) **3-8-13** MHills(3) (dropped rr ½-wy: sn bhd: t.o)	dist	**13**	20/1	—	—
				(SP 133.6%)		**13 Rn**

2m 25.19 (13.69) CSF £54.34 CT £366.77 TOTE £17.80: £3.40 £1.70 £3.00 (£23.80) Trio £114.30 OWNER Mr M. P. Bowring (NEWMARKET) BRED Frank Dunne

OFFICIAL EXPLANATION **Sharkiyah (IRE): was found to be lame after the race.**

4268 Topatori (IRE) showed she was about to strike form with a good performance at Ayr and, handling the testing ground really well, she proved too strong for a host of persistent challengers. (10/1)

2507 Top Jem gave the impression that she would be all the better for this first run in over three months, but she has shown a liking for soft ground in the past, and gave the winner something to think about in the closing stages (9/2)

4407* Sunny Isle, a lightly-made filly taking on handicappers for the first time, does not look the type to act in this bottomless ground, but she ran extremely well and her heart is in the right place. (8/1)

4568 Falls O'Moness (IRE) performs best when ridden with restraint and, staying on strongly inside the last furlong, only just failed to make the frame. (20/1)

3453 Boss Lady (IRE), unproven on this ground, did not fail for the want of trying under her welter burden and she may be best put away until conditions come in her favour. (7/1)

4732 NEWTON INVESTMENT MANAGEMENT CONDITIONS STKS (3-Y.O+) (Class C)

2-30 (2-30) **1m 3f 200y** £4,750.80 (£1,777.20: £868.60: £373.00: £166.50: £83.90) Stalls: High GOING: 0.63 sec per fur (GS)

Form	Horse / details	Dist	Pos	SP	RR	SF
4295[5]	**Rainwatch (100)** (JLDunlop) **3-8-9** JReid(3) (lw: mde all: drvn clr over 2f out: unchal)	—	**1**	5/2[2]	115?	65
4241[7]	**State Fair (92)** (BWHills) **3-8-9** MHills(4) (hld up in rr: hdwy over 3f out: chsd wnr fnl 2f: no imp)	20	**2**	10/1	88	38
3191[7]	**Medaille Militaire (106)** (MCPipe) **5-9-2** KDarley(7) (bit bkwd: hld up: styd on fnl 2f: nvr rchd ldrs)	10	**3**	6/1	75	32
4149[10]	**Besiege (111)** (HRACecil) **3-8-9** WRyan(1) (lw: chsd ldrs: rdn over 2f out: sn btn)	1¼	**4**	7/2[3]	73	23
4412[2]	**Poltarf (USA) (108)** (JHMGosden) **6-9-2** LDettori(5) (lw: racd wd: chsd wnr: rdn 4f out: sn wknd & eased)	12	**5**	2/1[1]	57	14
4635[10]	**Bend Wavy (IRE) (80)** (THCaldwell) **5-9-2** JCarroll(6) (hld up: hdwy 5f out: wknd 3f out: eased whn btn: t.o)	5	**6**	66/1	50	7
4281[5]	**Star Selection (95)** (JMackie) **6-9-2** JQuinn(2) (lw: prom tl lost pl 4f out: sn t.o)	1¼	**7**	14/1	49	6
				(SP 115.7%)		**7 Rn**

2m 41.07 (11.67) CSF £25.20 TOTE £3.20: £1.90 £3.30 (£20.30) OWNER Hesmonds Stud (ARUNDEL) BRED Hesmonds Stud Ltd

WEIGHT FOR AGE 3yo-7lb

4295 Rainwatch had everything in his favour and, happy to be bowling along in front, showed no signs of stopping and left his rivals floundering inside the last quarter-mile. (5/2)
2596 State Fair, taking a step down in distance, improved to chase the winner throughout the last couple of furlongs but, try as he might, he could not muster the speed to get within striking range. (10/1)
1960 Medaille Militaire, very lightly-raced this season, began to stay on in the later stages but the winner had gone beyond recall and he was never able to give his supporters much hope. He may just have needed the spin. (6/1)
4149 Besiege did not really relish this softer ground, and he was hard at work and in trouble over two furlongs out. (7/2)
4412 Poltarf (USA), returning to a shorter trip, picked his ground down the back straight but he was uneasy soon after straightening up for home and faded rather tamely. (2/1)
4281 Star Selection (14/1: 10/1-16/1)

4733 MAPLE H'CAP (0-80) (3-Y.O+) (Class D)

3-00 (3-01) **6f** £3,875.00 (£1,175.00: £575.00: £275.00) Stalls: High GOING: 0.63 sec per fur (GS)

				SP	RR	SF
2560[9]	**Alumisiyah (USA) (76)** (RWArmstrong) **3-9-9** MHills(5) (racd far side: led over 3f out: drvn clr appr fnl f)	—	**1**	16/1	88	70
4482[6]	**First Maite (75)** (SRBowring) **4-9-6b**(3) CTeague(1) (chsd ldrs far side: hrd rdn 2f out: kpt on fnl f: nt pce of wnr)	2½	**2**	20/1	80	63
4563*	**Dark Mile (USA) (78)** (JHMGosden) **3-9-11** LDettori(23) (chsd ldrs stands' side: led over 2f out: rdn & r.o)	½	**3**	5/1[2]	82	64
4565[6]	**Swino (70)** (PDEvans) **3-9-3** JFEgan(18) (a chsng ldrs stands' side: rdn & one pce fnl 2f)	1½	**4**	12/1	70	52
4280[6]	**Always Alight (75)** (KRBurke) **3-9-8** MartinDwyer(3) (lw: prom far side: rdn 2f out: wknd ins fnl f)	¾	**5**	12/1	73	55
4482[8]	**Garnock Valley (66)** (JBerry) **7-9-0b** JWeaver(12) (hdwy appr fnl f: kpt on wl towards fin)	2½	**6**	14/1	57	40
4456[6]	**Corniche Quest (IRE) (64)** (MRChannon) **4-8-5**(7) AEddery(13) (racd centre: chsd ldrs: rdn over 1f out: one pce)	1	**7**	16/1	53	36
3984[3]	**Nineacres (69)** (NMBabbage) **6-9-3v** JReid(17) (lw: led stands' side 3f out: sn hdd: rdn & one pce appr fnl f)	s.h	**8**	16/1	58	41
4456[17]	**Dovebrace (74)** (TDBarron) **4-9-8** WRyan(16) (outpcd stands' side tl r.o fnl f)	½	**9**	40/1	61	44
4456[11]	**Benzoe (IRE) (78)** (MrsJRRamsden) **7-9-12** MTebbutt(9) (lw: hdwy 2f out: hrd rdn over 1f out: nvr nrr)	s.h	**10**	12/1	65	48
4565[8]	**Rum Lad (66)** (JJQuinn) **3-8-13** JQuinn(15) (chsd ldrs stands' side: rdn 2f out: sn btn)	5	**11**	9/1[3]	40	22
4321[8]	**Montendre (79)** (MJHeaton-Ellis) **10-9-13** SSanders(11) (lw: nvr trbld ldrs)	s.h	**12**	14/1	53	36
4219[12]	**Fayik (67)** (AGNewcombe) **3-9-0** GHind(19) (a bhd)	hd	**13**	12/1	40	22
4636[10]	**Samwar (76)** (MRChannon) **5-9-10v** JCarroll(7) (b: trckd ldrs far side over 3f)	½	**14**	14/1	48	31
4482[13]	**Spaniards Close (77)** (PJMakin) **9-9-11** DHolland(10) (rdn 2f out: no imp)	¾	**15**	25/1	47	30
4307[7]	**Mary Magdalene (72)** (MBell) **3-9-5** MFenton(24) (overall ldr stands' side to ½-wy: wknd over 1f out)	1	**16**	9/2[1]	39	21
4467[6]	**Natural Key (73)** (DHaydnJones) **4-9-7** AMackay(14) (lw: trckd ldrs stands' side 4f)	½	**17**	16/1	39	22
4600*	**Beyond Calculation (USA) (74)** (PWHarris) **3-9-2**(5) 6x CLowther(8) (lw: effrt over 2f out: sn hrd rdn & wknd)	2½	**18**	14/1	33	15
4636[18]	**Bee Health Boy (65)** (MWEasterby) **4-8-10b**(3) GParkin(21) (lw: prom stands' side over 3f)	nk	**19**	14/1	24	7
4417[4]	**Speedboat (USA) (65)** (JLEyre) **3-8-12** OPears(4) (led far side 2f: wknd over 2f out)	3	**20**	25/1	16	—
3923[6]	**Samsung Spirit (74)** (EWeymes) **3-9-7** JFanning(6) (swtg: chsd ldrs far side over 3f)	3½	**21**	16/1	15	—
2377[12]	**Bajan Rose (73)** (MBlanshard) **5-9-7** KDarley(2) (swtg: early spd: bhd fnl 3f)	nk	**22**	20/1	13	—
				(SP 158.0%)	**22 Rn**	

1m 16.8 (5.10) CSF £323.97 CT £1,749.19 TOTE £23.00: £3.80 £7.80 £2.90 £2.50 (£346.20) Trio £2,240.60 OWNER Mr Hamdan Al Maktoum (NEWMARKET) BRED Shadwell Farm Inc
WEIGHT FOR AGE 3yo-1lb
STEWARDS' ENQUIRY Holland susp. 24-25 & 27-28/10/97 (excessive use of whip)
1243 Alumisiyah (USA) has been highly tried in a limited number of outings this year, but she showed she can act on this ground and, electing to stay on the far side, had the prize safely under wraps entering the final furlong. If seen out again she could well defy a penalty . (16/1)
4482 First Maite battled on under strong pressure inside the distance, but had to admit the winner just too good for him. (20/1)
4563* Dark Mile (USA) won the race on the stands' side in her first handicap and, as she had it all to do at the weights, this can be classed as a very promising effort. (5/1)
4365 Swino ran up to his best, and there was much to be said about the way he stuck to his task after looking to be in trouble at least two furlongs out. (12/1)
4280 Always Alight ran much better than his final placings might suggest, as he was head to head with the winner from halfway which left him legless when an extra spurt was needed. (12/1)
2326 Garnock Valley has not won a race for twelve months but, with the going in his favour, he was pegging back the leaders at the finish. (14/1)
4385 Corniche Quest (IRE) won her only race on heavy ground and she was fancied to get back to winning ways, but her front-running tactics had come to an end at halfway and she was down to a walk below the distance. (16/1)

4734 CHESTNUT CONDITIONS STKS (2-Y.O) (Class C)

3-30 (3-31) **1m 30y** £4,870.40 (£1,702.40: £831.20: £356.00) Stalls: Low GOING: 0.63 sec per fur (GS)

				SP	RR	SF
4384*	**Close Up (IRE) (92)** (JLDunlop) **2-9-1** KDarley(2) (lw: chsd ldrs: effrt & drvn along 3f out: led wl over 1f out: hld on gamely cl home)	—	**1**	7/4[2]	85	41
4454*	**Giveaway** (HRACecil) **2-9-1** WRyan(1) (lw: chsd ldr: ev ch over 1f out: rallied u.p cl home)	hd	**2**	13/8[1]	85	41
3760*	**Alberich (IRE)** (MJohnston) **2-9-1** DHolland(4) (racd wd bk st: led over 6f: sn rdn & wknd)	9	**3**	11/2	67	23
4575[5]	**Act Defiant (USA)** (PFICole) **2-8-11** LDettori(3) (lw: stdd s: swtchd rt & effrt over 2f out: no imp: t.o)	17	**4**	5/1[3]	30	—
				(SP 106.5%)	**4 Rn**	

1m 51.57 (10.97) CSF £4.39 TOTE £2.60: (£2.70) OWNER Mr Ian Cameron (ARUNDEL) BRED Lowquest Ltd
4384* Close Up (IRE) has really found his form now and, having no difficulty handling the ground, he showed the right commitment when strongly pressed close home. (7/4)
4454* Giveaway, very weak in the market, had the verdict go against him this time, but he lost no caste in defeat and could turn out to be a useful three-year-old. (13/8: evens-7/4)
3760* Alberich (IRE) attempted to put the emphasis on stamina to see if there were any weak links in his rivals, but the tactics backfired somewhat and he was well outpaced inside the distance. (11/2)
4575 Act Defiant (USA), steadied leaving the stalls, was pulled out to deliver his challenge during the last quarter-mile but he was unable to make the slightest impression and was soon well outpaced. (5/1)

4735 E.B.F. HAWTHORN MAIDEN STKS (2-Y.O) (Class D)
4-00 (4-02) **7f 30y** £3,810.00 (£1,155.00: £565.00: £270.00) Stalls: Low GOING: 0.63 sec per fur (GS)

				SP	RR	SF
4174^{2}	**Dark Moondancer (95)** (PWChapple-Hyam) **2-9-0** JReid(9) (bhd: hdwy over 2f out: r.o to ld ins fnl f)	—	**1**	11/8^{1}	83	42
	Pass The Rest (IRE) (JLEyre) **2-9-0** TWilliams(6) (w'like: scope: a.p: led over 2f out tl hdd & no ex ins fnl f)	1½	**2**	33/1	80	39
4212^{4}	**Akarita (IRE)** (BAMcMahon) **2-8-9** SSanders(10) (bhd: rdn along 3f out: styd on ins fnl f)	1¼	**3**	20/1	72	31
3013^{4}	**Rainbow High** (BWHills) **2-9-0** MHills(3) (led tl over 2f out: rdn & wknd fnl f)	1¾	**4**	5/1^{3}	73	32
4507^{4}	**Stone Beck** (JMJefferson) **2-8-9** JCarroll(13) (mid div tl styd on appr fnl f)	5	**5**	33/1	57	16
4017^{3}	**Adjutant** (BJMeehan) **2-9-0** MTebbutt(8) (lw: prom: jnd ldrs 3f out: rdn & hung lft wl over 1f out: wknd fnl f)	hd	**6**	9/2^{2}	62	21
	Polska Modelle (FR) (JHMGosden) **2-9-0** LDettori(2) (w'like: scope: bkwd: s.s: a in rr)	9	**7**	5/1^{3}	41	—
3117^{13}	**Bay of Delight** (EALDunlop) **2-8-9** WRyan(4) (s.i.s: hdwy ent st: wknd over 2f out)	nk	**8**	16/1	36	—
	Love Kiss (IRE) (MJohnston) **2-9-0** DHolland(11) (w'like: leggy: bkwd: chsd ldrs tl wknd over 2f out)	2½	**9**	10/1	35	—
	King Priam (IRE) (WJarvis) **2-9-0** JQuinn(1) (lengthy: scope: bit bkwd: trckd ldrs 5f: sn pushed along & wknd)	¾	**10**	14/1	33	—
	Paddy Deux (VSoane) **2-9-0** GHind(7) (lt-f: lw: bhd: effrt 3f out: sn drvn along & no imp)	1¼	**11**	33/1	31	—
	Breakin Even (JLEyre) **2-9-0** RLappin(12) (w'like: leggy: bkwd: b.off hind: s.i.s: a bhd: t.o)	8	**12**	33/1	13	—
4508^{9}	**Corpus Christi (IRE)** (MJohnston) **2-9-0** JWeaver(5) (plld hrd: prom to ½-wy: sn wknd: t.o)	s.h	**13**	14/1	13	—
				(SP 138.5%)	**13 Rn**	

1m 37.39 (9.39) CSF £72.10 TOTE £2.40: £1.20 £11.80 £3.10 (£90.40) Trio £384.30; £406.01 to Newmarket 16/10/97 OWNER Dr Anne J F Gillespie & Mr John Wilson (MARLBOROUGH) BRED Dr A. Gillespie

4174 Dark Moondancer, ridden with more restraint over the slightly longer trip, made up a lot of ground in the closing stages and timed it just right to have his head in front where it mattered. (11/8)

Pass The Rest (IRE) poked his head in front entering the last quarter-mile, but the sustained late challenge of the winner proved just too strong in the final hundred yards. (33/1)

4212 Akarita (IRE), a late-May foal, showed her appreciation for this easier ground and stayed on from way off the pace to reach her final placing. (20/1)

3013 Rainbow High has filled this spot in all his outings so far, but he is not getting beaten for the want of trying and he certainly deserves to find an opening. (5/1)

4507 Stone Beck, who was staying on when it was all over, obviously has plenty of stamina in her breeding and she is continuing to progress. (33/1)

4017 Adjutant, a good mover in his slower places, posed a serious threat when joining issue three furlongs out but he was getting the worst of the battle when he hung left below the distance, and that was the beginning of the end. He will probably be better-suited by a sounder surface. (9/2)

4736 HOLLY MAIDEN STKS (3-Y.O+) (Class D)
4-30 (4-33) **1m 3f 200y** £3,696.25 (£1,120.00: £547.50: £261.25) Stalls: High GOING: 0.63 sec per fur (GS)

				SP	RR	SF
4322^{2}	**Sabadilla (USA) (80)** (JHMGosden) **3-8-12** LDettori(2) (racd wd bk st: hdwy 6f out: rdn to ld over 1f out: r.o wl)	—	**1**	5/1^{3}	89	35
3977^{2}	**Shadiann (IRE) (83)** (LMCumani) **3-8-12** JWeaver(3) (led tl rdn & hdd over 1f out: one pce)	3	**2**	6/4^{1}	85	31
683^{2}	**Reggie Buck (USA)** (RJO'Sullivan) **3-8-12** SSanders(4) (b: bit bkwd: s.i.s: hdwy over 4f out: hrd rdn over 2f out: sn btn)	13	**3**	9/1	68	14
4177^{3}	**Messina (IRE)** (RCharlton) **3-8-7** KDarley(8) (bit bkwd: sn chsng ldr: rdn along 3f out: sn wknd)	5	**4**	15/8^{2}	56	2
4587^{6}	**Job Rage (IRE)** (ABailey) **3-8-12** DWright(6) (bhd: hrd drvn 4f out: styd on)	3	**5**	25/1	57	3
4579^{4}	**Flowing Fortune** (EALDunlop) **3-8-12** JReid(10) (chsd ldrs tl lost tch 3f out: eased: t.o)	26	**6**	10/1	22	—
4407^{5}	**Taborite (USA)** (EJAlston) **3-8-12** JFEgan(1) (trckd ldrs: pushed along over 5f out: grad wknd: t.o)	6	**7**	50/1	14	—
	Among Islands (RLee) **6-9-0** OPears(5) (bkwd: chsd ldrs tl wknd 4f out: sn t.o)	5	**8**	66/1	2	—
4360^{7}	**Sostenuto** (RHollinshead) **4-8-11**(3) DGriffiths(9) (unruly stalls: a wl bhd: t.o)	26	**9**	66/1	—	—
				(SP 119.3%)	**9 Rn**	

2m 46.15 (16.75) CSF £12.07 TOTE £5.00: £1.70 £1.10 £2.40 (£4.30) Trio £10.70 OWNER Sheikh Mohammed (NEWMARKET) BRED Mr and Mrs John C. Mabee

WEIGHT FOR AGE 3yo-7lb

4322 Sabadilla (USA) gained his revenge over the runner-up, but he had to work to assert his superiority. (5/1: 7/2-11/2)

3977 Shadiann (IRE) decided on more forceful tactics and, for most of the way, did look to hold all the aces but, with the ground getting more testing with each race, he was forced to give best on the approach to the final furlong. (6/4)

683 Reggie Buck (USA), off the track since the spring and attempting the trip for the first time, improved to reach the heels of the leaders over two furlongs out, but lack of a recent run took its toll and he gradually faded. He can improve considerably with this run under his belt and he should be able to win races. (9/1)

4177 Messina (IRE), who still looked to have a bit left to work on, struggled in this testing ground and she had shot her bolt halfway up the straight. She will show this was not her true running. (15/8)

4587 Job Rage (IRE) stayed on past beaten rivals in the latter stages, but may well be flattered to have finished as close as he eventually did. (25/1)

4737 SYCAMORE NURSERY H'CAP (2-Y.O) (Class D)
5-00 (5-01) **5f** £3,550.00 (£1,075.00: £525.00: £250.00) Stalls: High GOING: 0.41 sec per fur (GS)

				SP	RR	SF
4296^{6}	**Supreme Angel (75)** (MPMuggeridge) **2-8-6** DHolland(10) (lw: hdwy 2f out: swtchd lft ent fnl f: r.o u.p to ld cl home)	—	**1**	11/2^{3}	81	50
4634^{3}	**Classy Cleo (IRE) (73)** (PDEvans) **2-8-4** JFEgan(4) (lw: chsd ldrs: rdn to ld over 1f out: ct nr fin)	nk	**2**	4/1^{1}	78	47
4411^{7}	**Quiz Master (68)** (EWeymes) **2-7-13b^{1}** JQuinn(1) (lw: a.p: led 2f out: sn hdd: one pce fnl f)	2	**3**	14/1	67	36
4566^{8}	**Take A Risk (67)** (MJohnston) **2-7-12** NAdams(7) (b.hind: bhd: hdwy 2f out: r.o ins fnl f)	8	**4**	7/1	40	9
4517^{7}	**Regalo (65)** (DMHyde) **2-7-10** NKennedy(5) (prom tl rdn & wknd over 1f out)	nk	**5**	25/1	37	6
2931^{3}	**Tempus Fugit (88)** (BRMillman) **2-9-5** MFenton(12) (bit bkwd: led: hung lft & hdd 2f out: sn wknd)	2	**6**	7/1	54	23
4381^{4}	**Sorridar (66)** (JLEyre) **2-7-11** TWilliams(3) (w ldrs over 3f)	hd	**7**	12/1	31	—
3892^{9}	**Dancing Icon (IRE) (75)** (RHannon) **2-8-6** MartinDwyer(6) (a bhd)	2	**8**	7/1	34	3
4634^{14}	**Two Williams (83)** (MWEasterby) **2-9-0** TLucas(9) (a in rr)	1¾	**9**	16/1	36	5
3811^{4}	**Marton Moss (SWE) (90)** (TDEasterby) **2-9-7** KDarley(8) (lw: trckd ldrs: drvn along ½-wy: sn btn)	nk	**10**	9/2^{2}	42	11
4589^{7}	**Fundance (75)** (MDods) **2-8-6** JCarroll(2) (lw: prom tl wknd 2f out)	1½	**11**	14/1	23	—

Form	Horse	Dist	Pos	SP	RR	SF
3699^{4}	**Risky Whisky (65)** (JBerry) **2-7-7b**(3) PFessey(11) (chsd ldrs to ½-wy: wknd qckly: t.o)	7	**12**	8/1	—	—

(SP 132.9%) **12 Rn**

63.92 secs (4.42) CSF £28.63 CT £291.02 TOTE £8.50: £2.80 £1.60 £4.20 (£14.60) Trio £146.80 OWNER Least Moved Partners (LAMBOURN) BRED K. J. and Mrs Sims

LONG HANDICAP Regalo 7-7 Risky Whisky 7-8

IN-FOCUS: **Darryll Holland reached his first domestic century in this race, having ridden his 500th winner on Pekay two days earlier.**

4296 Supreme Angel had to put her best foot forward to land this, and a lot of credit must go to her never say die partner. (11/2)

4634 Classy Cleo (IRE) looked to have stolen a march when leading into the final furlong, but the winner came fresh on the scene and wore her down in the dying strides. (4/1)

3265 Quiz Master struck the front passing the quarter-mile marker and set sail for home, but the runner-up was onto him in next to no time, and he was short of pace in the battle to the finish. (14/1)

4566 Take A Risk came from a long way off the pace to reach her finishing position, but she was beaten fair and square and not too much can be read into this. (7/1)

2781 Regalo tried hard enough and rarely runs a bad race, but he is yet to start paying his way and he may have to step down in class to do so. (25/1)

2931 Tempus Fugit, a speedy filly not ideally suited by this softer ground, did her usual and forced the pace until she began to drift out into the centre of the track and forfeited her lead two furlongs out. This was her first outing since July and she did look on the burly side. (7/1)

4381 Sorridar (12/1: op 8/1)

T/Jkpt: £10,987.90 (0.1 Tckts); £13,928.37 to Newmarket 16/10/97. T/Plpt: £285.50 (106.62 Tckts). T/Qdpt: £27.30 (49.38 Tckts) IM

4627-NOTTINGHAM (L-H) (Soft, Heavy patches, Good in st on Rnd crse)
Wednesday October 15th

WEATHER: overcast WIND: almost nil

4738 KEGWORTH LIMITED STKS (0-60) (3-Y.O+) (Class F)

2-10 (2-11) **6f 15y** £2,277.00 (£627.00: £297.00) Stalls: High GOING: 0.35 sec per fur (G)

Form	Horse	Dist	Pos	SP	RR	SF
4580^{4}	**Middle East (60)** (TDBarron) **4-9-4b** TSprake(4) (mde virtually all far side: hld on fnl f)	—	1	13/2^{1}	72	49
4518^{15}	**Supreme Thought (59)** (LGCottrell) **5-9-1** NCarlisle(10) (prom: led stands' side ins fnl f: unable qckn nr fin)	hd	2	14/1	69	46
4319^{7}	**Akalim (57)** (LGCottrell) **4-8-12**(3) MHenry(14) (prom: led stands' side over 2f out: one pce ins fnl f)	¾	3	12/1^{3}	67	44
4574^{2}	**Mike's Double (IRE) (60)** (MissGayKelleway) **3-9-3b** KFallon(12) (rdn & hdwy 3f out: kpt on fnl f)	3	4	13/2^{1}	62	38
4601^{2}	**Maladerie (IRE) (58)** (MRChannon) **3-9-0** JFortune(1) (lw: chsd ldrs far side: one pce appr fnl f)	¾	5	7/1^{2}	57	33
4112*	**Mybotye (59)** (RBastiman) **4-9-4** DeanMcKeown(6) (racd far side: hdwy over 2f out: one pce fnl f)	¾	6	13/2^{1}	58	35
4333^{16}	**Marengo (55)** (JAkehurst) **3-9-0** AMcGlone(13) (led stands' side over 3f: sn btn)	2	7	20/1	50	26
4565^{9}	**Sylvan Dancer (IRE) (53)** (CFWall) **3-8-11** GDuffield(8) (racd far side: prom 4f)	1¾	8	20/1	42	18
4112^{16}	**Macgillycuddy (IRE) (53)** (MrsPNDutfield) **8-9-1** CRutter(20) (lw: effrt over 2f out: nt rch ldrs)	s.h	9	16/1	45	22
4570^{5}	**Just Loui (60)** (KRBurke) **3-8-11**(3) DSweeney(2) (dwlt: swtchd rt after 2f: n.d)	3	10	20/1	37	13
4290^{6}	**Marylebone (IRE) (60)** (JBerry) **3-8-11**(3) PRoberts(19) (sn bhd)	2	11	20/1	32	8
4563^{7}	**Hamleys (53)** (DMorris) **3-8-11v^{1}** NDay(18) (sn pushed along: nvr nr ldrs)	¾	12	33/1	27	3
4518^{16}	**Xenophon of Cunaxa (IRE) (56)** (MJFetherston-Godley) **4-9-1b** ACulhane(11) (outpcd)	¾	13	20/1	28	5
4512^{12}	**U-No-Harry (IRE) (53)** (RHollinshead) **4-9-1** FLynch(7) (b.nr fore: racd far side: outpcd)	½	14	25/1	26	3
4451^{10}	**Mazeed (IRE) (60)** (PDEvans) **4-9-1b^{1}** AClark(5) (racd far side: sn wl bhd)	3	15	25/1	19	—
3398^{2}	**Aljaz (60)** (MissGayKelleway) **7-9-1** DaneO'Neill(3) (w wnr far side 3f)	5	16	16/1	5	—
4155^{28}	**Heavenly Miss (IRE) (55)** (JJBridger) **3-8-11** RCochrane(16) (chsd ldrs 3f)	¾	17	12/1^{3}	—	—
4580^{9}	**Don Pepe (58)** (RBoss) **6-9-4b^{1}** GCarter(17) (chsd ldrs over 3f)	5	18	16/1	—	—
4329^{8}	**Barranak (IRE) (58)** (GMMcCourt) **5-9-0**(7) RStudholme(15) (s.i.s: a bhd)	7	19	12/1^{3}	—	—

(SP 134.3%) **19 Rn**

1m 17.4 (5.90) CSF £82.04 TOTE £11.00: £3.40 £7.10 £3.90 (£432.30) Trio £422.30; £475.84 to Newmarket 16/10/97 OWNER Mrs J. Hazell (THIRSK) BRED Miss M. Grantmyre

WEIGHT FOR AGE 3yo-1lb

IN-FOCUS: **Round course races were run on the old National Hunt course, where the ground seemed faster in the home straight than the back. The first race was run on the normal track.**

4580 Middle East, on ground softer than seemed ideal, was clear of the far side group from halfway, and battled on well. (13/2)

3393* Supreme Thought came back to form and clearly loves plenty of cut in the ground. (14/1)

4112 Akalim, who seems as able over a little further, was rightly made plenty of use of. (12/1: op 8/1)

4574 Mike's Double (IRE), outpaced to halfway, then responded to a typical Fallon ride all the way to the line. He could certainly win a similar race over seven. (13/2)

4601 Maladerie (IRE) raced wide apart from the winner when second to him here last month, but this time was beaten fair and square by the furlong pole. (7/1)

4112* Mybotye again wore the pricker, but could not get going in time over this shorter trip. (13/2)

4739 E.B.F. MAIDEN STKS (I) (2-Y.O) (Class D)

2-40 (2-41) **1m 54y** £4,045.00 (£1,210.00: £580.00: £265.00) Stalls: Low GOING: 0.20 sec per fur (G)

Form	Horse	Dist	Pos	SP	RR	SF
	Decisive Action (USA) (PFICole) **2-9-0** TQuinn(1) (w'like: leggy: in tch: hdwy to ld over 1f out: rdn & r.o strly)	—	1	12/1	96+	46
4318^{5}	**Jaazim (USA)** (MRStoute) **2-9-0** RHills(7) (led over 4f: led 2f out: sn hdd & one pce)	4	2	7/1^{3}	88	38
4165^{3}	**Wadi** (HRACecil) **2-9-0** KFallon(12) (chsd ldrs: led 4f out to 2f out: sn btn)	3½	3	5/6^{1}	81	31
4526^{5}	**Honest Borderer** (JLDunlop) **2-9-0** TSprake(11) (prom: rdn 3f out: one pce)	1¾	4	5/1^{2}	78	28
4604^{11}	**Flicker** (LordHuntingdon) **2-8-9** RPerham(10) (bhd: rdn 3f out: kpt on: nvr nr to chal)	2½	5	50/1	68	18
4209^{6}	**Piccadilly** (TJEtherington) **2-8-9** DaleGibson(2) (prom tl wknd 3f out)	1½	6	25/1	65	15
4111^{5}	**Mutafarij (USA)** (EALDunlop) **2-9-0** MRimmer(5) (plld hrd: prom: pushed along 4f out: btn over 1f out)	1¼	7	8/1	68	18
	On The Right Side (JWHills) **2-8-11**(3) MHenry(4) (w'like: unf: bkwd: hld up & plld hrd: sme hdwy fnl 3f: nvr nr ldrs)	hd	8	40/1	68	18
4174^{12}	**Petruchio (IRE) (63)** (MajorDNChappell) **2-9-0** RCochrane(8) (n.d)	12	9	50/1	44	—
4520^{9}	**Flying Clouds** (MBlanshard) **2-8-6**(3) PPMurphy(9) (a bhd)	nk	10	50/1	39	—
	Caradoc (SCWilliams) **2-9-0** SDrowne(6) (leggy: unf: bkwd: stdd s: sn in tch: btn 3f out)	½	11	20/1	43	—

				SP	RR	SF
	Travelling Clock (BAMcMahon) **2-9-0** JFortune(3) (lengthy: unf: bit bkwd: s.i.s: a bhd)	4	**12**	33/1	35	—
	Norcroft Joy (MJRyan) **2-8-9** AClark(13) (leggy: unf: dwlt: sn in tch: wknd over 3f out)	1¼	**13**	50/1	28	—
				(SP 124.3%)	**13 Rn**	

1m 48.2 (6.90) CSF £82.29 TOTE £21.90: £3.30 £2.10 £1.10 (£46.40) Trio £21.30 OWNER Mr Christopher Wright (WHATCOMBE) BRED Dr Hiram Polk & Dr J. David Richardson

Decisive Action (USA), by Alleged out of a winning mare, relished this soft ground and won in fine style. He is an interesting prospect. (12/1: 8/1-14/1)
4318 Jaazim (USA) has been gradually getting his act together, and forcing the pace seemed to bring about further improvement. (7/1)
4165 Wadi probably found the ground less than ideal, bur did not pick up significantly when his chance was there. (5/6)
4526 Honest Borderer, a tall, rangy type, does have ability and plenty of stamina, but does not look a straightforward ride. (5/1: op 3/1)
Flicker, running again just eight days after her debut, found her stamina coming into play in the straight, keeping on past beaten horses. Middle distances should suit eventually. (50/1)
4209 Piccadilly got worked up at the start and was again easily left behind once the tempo picked up. (25/1)

4740 E.B.F. MAIDEN STKS (II) (2-Y.O) (Class E)

3-10 (3-11) **1m 54y** £4,012.50 (£1,200.00: £575.00: £262.50) Stalls: Low GOING: 0.20 sec per fur (G)

				SP	RR	SF
4460[2]	**Corniche (IRE)** (PFICole) **2-9-0** TQuinn(5) (led over 6f: rdn & hung lft fnl f: led fnl stride)	—	**1**	11/10[1]	85	30
	Edwardian (MrsAJPerrett) **2-9-0** AClark(9) (wl grwn: bit bkwd: plld hrd: trckd ldrs: led over 1f out: rdn & edgd rt: jst ct)	s.h	**2**	20/1	85+	30
4165[5]	**Ei Ei** (BWHills) **2-9-0** PaulEddery(11) (a.p: led 2f out: sn hdd: n.m.r fnl f: one pce)	2	**3**	11/1[3]	81	26
4520[3]	**Elhayq (IRE)** (JLDunlop) **2-9-0** RHills(1) (in tch: outpcd 4f out: styd on wl fnl 2f)	s.h	**4**	2/1[2]	81	26
	Needwood Spirit (BCMorgan) **2-9-0** DeanMcKeown(12) (leggy: unf: bit bkwd: sn outpcd: hdwy 3f out: r.o)	2½	**5**	50/1	76	21
	Eliza Acton (PWHarris) **2-8-9** ACulhane(4) (w'like: unf: dwlt: hdwy over 1f out: styd on wl fnl f)	1¼	**6**	25/1	69	14
	Bridge (DMorley) **2-8-9** RCochrane(2) (unf: scope: bit bkwd: dwlt: hdwy fnl 2f: nrst fin)	4	**7**	16/1	61	6
	Slip Venture (SPCWoods) **2-9-0** NDay(8) (unf: b.nr fore: bhd fnl 3f)	1½	**8**	14/1	63	8
4229[6]	**Hastate** (WJarvis) **2-9-0** KFallon(6) (b.off hind: chsd ldrs tl rdn & btn 3f out)	3½	**9**	20/1	56	1
	Cadmax (IRE) (KRBurke) **2-9-0** DaneO'Neill(7) (leggy: bkwd: in tch over 4f)	4	**10**	50/1	48	—
4165[17]	**Fleet Lady (IRE) (50)** (MrsPNDutfield) **2-8-9** CRutter(10) (plld hrd: w wnr 5f: sn btn)	2½	**11**	100/1	39	—
4318[15]	**Red Brook Lad** (SDow) **2-8-7**(7) PDoe(3) (chsd ldrs tl wknd 3f out)	4	**12**	50/1	36	—
				(SP 122.1%)	**12 Rn**	

1m 49.9 (8.60) CSF £29.69 TOTE £1.80: £1.10 £3.10 £2.30 (£20.60) Trio £76.80 OWNER H R H Prince Fahd Salman (WHATCOMBE) BRED Hadi al Tajir

4460 Corniche (IRE) apparently does not have to lead, but it was a good job he did this time, for stamina won him the race in the shadow of the post when all looked lost. In truth, his previous defeats had promised more. (11/10)
Edwardian, a big colt out of a mare from a speedy family, looked all set to score when hitting the front, but blew up and, hard as he tried, was just touched off. He will surely gain compensation, but whether he will stay further is open to question. (20/1)
4165 Ei Ei, taken down at a trot, settled better and showed further progress. (11/1)
4520 Elhayq (IRE), a very long-backed colt who flashed his tail, has plenty of stamina judged by the way he finished. (2/1: 6/4-5/2)
Needwood Spirit hardly looks bred for the Flat, but his dam is a half-sister to Mareth Line, who was not a bad staying handicapper. He showed plenty of stamina himself, sticking on in fine style towards the finish. Not a great deal to look at, he showed promise, but his proximity to the winner does put a question mark against the form. (50/1)
Eliza Acton, a full-sister to Top Cees, missed the break and was only beginning to get going when the race was over. (25/1)

4741 THURGATON H'CAP (0-70) (3-Y.O+) (Class E)

3-40 (3-46) **1m 54y** £3,824.25 (£1,149.00: £554.50: £257.25) Stalls: Low GOING: 0.20 sec per fur (G)

				SP	RR	SF
4139[4]	**Sovereigns Court (56)** (LGCottrell) **4-9-3** KFallon(5) (lw: hld up: hdwy 3f out: led over 1f out: sn drvn clr)	—	**1**	4/1[1]	77	53
4112[4]	**Welcome Heights (55)** (MJFetherston-Godley) **3-8-13** FNorton(13) (hld up: hdwy over 2f out: styd on fnl f)	5	**2**	6/1[2]	66	39
4632[3]	**Doc Ryan's (62)** (MJRyan) **3-9-3b**(3) PMcCabe(10) (chsd ldrs: led 2f out: sn hdd: one pce fnl f)	½	**3**	6/1[2]	72	45
4591[5]	**Swift (70)** (MJPolglase) **3-10-0** MRimmer(3) (lw: unruly s: led over 6f: one pce)	5	**4**	16/1	71	44
4139[7]	**Swinging The Blues (IRE) (58)** (RAkehurst) **3-9-2** TQuinn(16) (lw: chsd ldrs: rdn 3f out: no imp)	¾	**5**	12/1	57	30
4448[6]	**Mr Cube (IRE) (52)** (JMBradley) **7-8-6b**(7) RThomas(18) (hld up & plld hrd: hdwy & n.m.r 2f out: r.o ins fnl f)	1	**6**	16/1	49	25
3980[12]	**Parsa (USA) (52)** (JLDunlop) **4-8-13** TSprake(14) (chsd ldrs: rdn & btn over 2f out)	6	**7**	16/1	38	14
1436[5]	**Truly Parched (USA) (69)** (PWChapple-Hyam) **3-9-10**(3) RHavlin(8) (rdn over 3f out: nvr nr to chal)	hd	**8**	14/1	54	27
4580[15]	**Mr Speaker (IRE) (57)** (CFWall) **4-9-4** GDuffield(1) (chsd ldrs over 4f)	2½	**9**	16/1	38	14
4477[11]	**Golden Ace (IRE) (54)** (RCSpicer) **4-9-1** DeanMcKeown(12) (prom tl wknd over 2f out)	1¼	**10**	16/1	32	8
4335[17]	**Flashtalkin' Flood (64)** (CADwyer) **3-9-8** DO'Donohoe(9) (hld up & bhd: sme hdwy fnl 2f)	3½	**11**	10/1[3]	35	8
3329[6]	**Epworth (70)** (JAGlover) **3-10-0** GCarter(17) (w ldr over 4f)	3	**12**	20/1	36	9
4578[10]	**Premier (70)** (KTIvory) **3-10-0** RCochrane(7) (unruly s: hld up: a bhd)	½	**13**	25/1	35	8
4059[17]	**Tal-Y-Llyn (IRE) (65)** (BWHills) **3-9-9** PaulEddery(6) (prom 3f)	½	**14**	12/1	29	2
4510[16]	**Jack Flush (IRE) (64)** (BSRothwell) **3-9-8v**[1] JFortune(15) (prom tl wknd over 3f out)	1¼	**15**	16/1	25	—
4596[3]	***Mukhatab (65)*** (JJQuinn) **5-9-12** NDay(11) (Withdrawn not under Starter's orders: unruly in stalls)		**W**	12/1	—	—
				(SP 131.3%)	**15 Rn**	

1m 47.8 (6.50) CSF £23.19 CT £121.54 TOTE £3.50: £1.60 £2.30 £2.70 (£13.20) Trio £19.90 OWNER Mr E. Gadsden (CULLOMPTON) BRED Mrs D. O. Joly

WEIGHT FOR AGE 3yo-3lb

4139 Sovereigns Court, considered to have not gone through with his effort last time, had the right man for the job on top, and there was no shirking allowed, as he cruised up to the leaders with plenty in hand before being bullied clear. He is a more impressive horse in behind than once he strikes the front. (4/1: 3/1-9/2)
4112 Welcome Heights remains in good form and, held up to get the trip, followed the winner through, but was never going nearly as well as that rival. (6/1)
4632 Doc Ryan's again seemed suited by blinkers and soft ground, but failed to quicken over the shorter trip. (6/1)
4591 Swift, with the ground no longer fast, ran a good race, unusually from the front, but the Handicapper seems to have his measure. (16/1)
3281 Swinging The Blues (IRE) has had an easy season, but needs to find improvement to win a race. (12/1: op 8/1)
3442 Mr Cube (IRE) found plenty of trouble when still looking to be travelling well, and is worth looking out for when there is cut in the ground. (16/1)
864 Parsa (USA), with her tongue tied down, ran a little better but has failed to recapture her form this season. (16/1)

4742 RAINWORTH CLAIMING STKS (3-Y.O+) (Class F)
4-10 (4-13) **1m 54y** £2,277.00 (£627.00: £297.00) Stalls: Low GOING: 0.20 sec per fur (G)

			SP	RR	SF
4264^{8}	**Brighstone (79)** (MCPipe) **4-8-11** AMcGlone(2) (t: mde virtually all: hrd rdn & edgd lft over 2f out: hld on towards fin) ——	**1**	7/2 1	66	32
4264^{5}	**Scaraben (72)** (SEKettlewell) **9-8-13** JFortune(18) (lw: s.i.s: hdwy over 3f out: ev ch & hung lft ins fnl f: nt qckn nr fin) s.h	**2**	4/1 2	68	34
4291^{8}	**Dispol Diamond (45)** (GROldroyd) **4-8-10** KHodgson(5) (chsd ldrs: hmpd & lost pl appr st: hdwy over 2f out: styd on wl towards fin) ¾	**3**	33/1	63	29
3584^{16}	**Muhandam (IRE) (70)** (PAKelleway) **4-9-0**(3) AWhelan(4) (trckd ldrs: ev ch 2f out: hung lft: nt qckn ins fnl f) hd	**4**	11/1	70	36
4172^{3}	**Zidac (65)** (PJMakin) **5-9-7** KFallon(11) (b: reard s: hdwy over 2f out: sn ev ch: nt qckn fnl f) s.h	**5**	13/2	74	40
4373^{5}	**Gresatre (46)** (CADwyer) **3-8-8v** SDrowne(17) (in tch: effrt over 2f out: sn ev ch: one pce) ¾	**6**	16/1	63	26
3897^{8}	**Orontes (USA) (64)** (RHannon) **3-9-4** DaneO'Neill(6) (bhd: hdwy & swtchd lft over 3f out: hrd rdn & ev ch 2f out: styd on one pce) 1½	**7**	20/1	70	33
4607^{15}	**Generous Present (40)** (JWPayne) **4-7-12**(7) JacquelineCoppard(9) (sn chsng ldrs: lost pl over 3f out) 11	**8**	33/1	32	—
4386^{11}	**Rhapsody In White (IRE) (60)** (MAJarvis) **3-9-4b** RCochrane(15) (racd wd: sn drvn along: sn chsng ldrs: wknd over 2f out) nk	**9**	14/1	48	11
4224^{10}	**Hadadabble (26)** (PatMitchell) **4-8-6** DeanMcKeown(12) (bhd & drvn along over 4f out: n.d) s.h	**10**	40/1	33	—
4484^{3}	**Eastleigh (27)** (RHollinshead) **8-8-4**(7) LisaWatson(16) (bhd: hdwy on outside over 4f out: wknd over 2f out) ¾	**11**	33/1	36	2
3822^{2}	**Special-K (53)** (EWeymes) **5-8-3**(5) GFaulkner(3) (chsd ldrs: rdn over 4f out: sn lost pl) 3½	**12**	9/2 3	27	—
2463^{8}	**First Gold (36)** (JWharton) **8-8-9** AClark(14) (bit bkwd: dwlt: hdwy over 2f out: sn ev ch: wknd over 1f out) 1	**13**	33/1	26	—
4570^{2}	**Rock Island Line (IRE) (65)** (JBerry) **3-8-11**(3) PRoberts(7) (sn chsng ldrs: rdn 3f out: sn wknd) nk	**14**	10/1	33	—
3399^{5}	**Malsisio (21)** (NPLittmoden) **5-8-8** TGMcLaughlin(13) (sn bhd) 3	**15**	50/1	18	—
4606^{11}	**Saltando (IRE) (43)** (PatMitchell) **6-8-11** PBloomfield(8) (lw: hdwy u.p over 3f out: sn chsng ldrs: wknd over 2f out) 1½	**16**	50/1	18	—
429^{13}	**Island Prince (49)** (NMBabbage) **3-8-10** TSprake(1) (trckd ldrs: hmpd & lost pl appr st: sn wl bhd) 6	**17**	50/1	9	—

(SP 128.6%) **17 Rn**

1m 49.4 (8.10) CSF £14.87 TOTE £3.70: £2.00 £1.60 £7.60 (£7.50) Trio £132.00 OWNER Richard Green (Fine Paintings) (WELLINGTON) BRED Michael Poland

WEIGHT FOR AGE 3yo-3lb

4264 Brighstone, who had 9lb in hand on official figures, made amends for his poor effort at Ayr last time. Straightened by the running rail, he held on by the skin of his teeth. (7/2)

4264 Scaraben, who found the ground no problem, bounced back to his very best and in the end was only just denied. (4/1)

2937 Dispol Diamond, who would have been meeting the winner on no less than 33lb better terms in a handicap, was unlucky. Knocked right back on the home turn, she was overhauling the first two at the line. (33/1)

2313* Muhandam (IRE), who would have been over a stone better off with the winner in a handicap, ran easily his best race for his present trainer after two poor efforts but he hung violently and gave the boy real problems. (11/1: 8/1-12/1)

4172 Zidac, who would have been meeting the winner on 24lb better terms in a handicap, is better suited by a mile and a quarter. (13/2)

4373 Gresatre, who would have been 33lb better off with the winner in a handicap, ran above himself and is no doubt being primed for an All-Weather campaign. (16/1)

2508 Orontes (USA), who would have met the winner on 25lb better terms in a handicap, ran his best race for some time. (20/1)

4743 CALVERTON MAIDEN STKS (3-Y.O+) (Class D)
4-40 (4-40) **1m 6f 15y** £4,207.50 (£1,260.00: £605.00: £277.50) Stalls: Low GOING: 0.20 sec per fur (G)

			SP	RR	SF
4046^{2}	**Moon Colony (66)** (LadyHerries) **4-9-7** PaulEddery(4) (hdwy ½-wy: led over 2f out: edgd lft: jst hld on) ——	**1**	5/1 2	87	59
4234^{2}	**Royal Crown (IRE) (87)** (PWChapple-Hyam) **3-8-9**(3) RHavlin(16) (sn trckng ldrs: led over 3f out: hung lft & hdd over 2f out: kpt on wl ins fnl f: jst failed) hd	**2**	evens 1	87	50
4234^{9}	**Toi Toi (IRE) (74)** (DWPArbuthnot) **3-8-7** SWhitworth(2) (b.hind: bhd: hdwy appr st: chal over 2f out: sn hung lft & wknd) 8	**3**	12/1	73	36
3133^{5}	**Viburnum (50)** (AGFoster) **3-8-7** TSprake(6) (hld up: hdwy over 3f out: wknd fnl 2f) 1¼	**4**	16/1	71	34
4360^{3}	**Aboo Hom (73)** (ACStewart) **3-8-12** KFallon(11) (sn outpcd & drvn along: hdwy ½-wy: one pce fnl 3f) 2½	**5**	11/2 3	74	37
1276^{4}	**Big Target (IRE) (75)** (MRStoute) **3-8-12** TQuinn(3) (led to 8f out: ev ch over 3f out: wkng whn hmpd 2f out) 2½	**6**	6/1	71	34
3390^{4}	**Puteri Wentworth (66)** (MissGayKelleway) **3-8-4**(3) AWhelan(12) (chsd ldrs: drvn along ½-wy: wknd over 2f out) 11	**7**	11/1	53	16
4547^{6}	**Corporate Image** (RSimpson) **7-9-7** MGallagher(7) (chsd ldrs: led 8f out tl over 3f out: sn wknd) 13	**8**	50/1	43	15
4312^{5}	**Dunabrattin** (DTThom) **4-9-7** MWigham(5) (lw: wl bhd fr ½-wy) s.h	**9**	50/1	43	15
4521^{12}	**Monacle (42)** (DMorris) **3-8-12** NDay(10) (hdwy u.p on outside appr st: sn lost pl) 2½	**10**	33/1	41	4
4547^{3}	**Bawara (IRE)** (MRChannon) **3-8-12** JFortune(9) (sn trckng ldrs: rdn & wknd over 2f out) 5	**11**	9/1	35	—
	Starlight Waltzer (KSBridgwater) **4-9-7** SDrowne(8) (plld hrd: w ldrs tl wknd 7f out) 1½	**12**	33/1	33	5
	Boat O'Brig (JGSmyth-Osbourne) **4-9-7** DaneO'Neill(13) (s.v.s: a wl bhd) 7	**13**	33/1	25	—
4322^{5}	**Lark's Rise** (HCandy) **3-8-7** CRutter(1) (sn chsng ldrs: hmpd after 3f: lost pl 4f out) 3	**14**	20/1	17	—
4072^{9}	**Dutch** (GPEnright) **5-9-7** RCochrane(15) (bit bkwd: s.i.s: t.o fnl 5f) 30	**15**	50/1	—	—
2879^{9}	**Such Presence (45)** (KSBridgwater) **3-8-12** JBramhill(14) (chsd ldrs tl lost pl over 6f out: t.o) 1½	**16**	33/1	—	—

(SP 150.7%) **16 Rn**

3m 9.4 (10.90) CSF £11.16 TOTE £9.00: £3.20 £1.00 £4.00 (£6.80) Trio £15.90 OWNER Mrs Berta Lazarus (LITTLEHAMPTON) BRED Juddmonte Farms

WEIGHT FOR AGE 3yo-9lb

4046 Moon Colony, who would have been meeting the favourite on 21lb better terms in a handicap, was given a much more patient ride and in the end held scraped home. Connections will no doubt be keen to turn him out under a small penalty. (5/1)

4234 Royal Crown (IRE), who has a pronounced knee action, contributed to his own downfall, hanging left for the boy and into the winner. (evens)

3815 Toi Toi (IRE), a very poor mover, had plenty to find with the favourite on Ayr running. (12/1: op 8/1)

3133 Viburnum, having her first outing for seventy-seven days, ran as if just needing it. (16/1)

4360 Aboo Hom, who is a very poor mover, is very slow. (11/2: op 3/1)

1276 Big Target (IRE), having his first outing for one hundred and forty-nine days, probably needed it and his chance was already slipping when he was hampered in a shemozzle two furlongs from home. (6/1: 4/1-13/2)

3390 Puteri Wentworth (11/1: 8/1-12/1)

4547 Bawara (IRE) (9/1: op 6/1)

4744 WOODBOROUGH H'CAP (0-80) (3-Y.O+) (Class D)
5-10 (5-11) **2m 9y** £4,565.00 (£1,370.00: £660.00: £305.00) Stalls: Low GOING: 0.20 sec per fur (G)

				SP	RR	SF
4609*	**Theme Arena (48)** (MCPipe) **4-7-10v**$^{(3)ow1}$ MHenry(2) (mde all: hld on wl fnl f)	—	**1**	9/1	61	42
4673^{4}	**City Hall (IRE) (75)** (MRStoute) **3-9-1v** TQuinn(1) (lw: a chsng ldrs: chal over 3f out: nt qckn fnl f)	1¾	**2**	5/1^{2}	86	57
4633*	**Contrarie (47)** (MJRyan) **4-7-7**$^{(5)ow2\ 5x}$ RMullen(4) (lw: hld up: stdy hdwy ½-wy: effrt over 2f out: kpt on: no imp)	3½	**3**	4/1^{1}	55	35
4269^{4}	**Classic Line (67)** (JLDunlop) **3-8-7b** GCarter(5) (a chsng ldrs: hrd rdn over 3f out: wknd over 1f out)	8	**4**	10/1	67	38
4269*	**Selmeston (IRE) (52)** (SCWilliams) **5-8-0**$^{(3)}$ RFfrench(9) (bhd: hdwy u.p over 3f out: kpt on: nvr nr ldrs)	½	**5**	7/1^{3}	51	33
4269^{2}	**Opaque (70)** (WStorey) **5-9-7** JFortune(13) (lw: bhd: hdwy appr st: sn chsng ldrs: wknd & eased over 1f out)	10	**6**	8/1	59	41
3928^{11}	**Silvretta (IRE) (55)** (RCSpicer) **4-8-6** PaulEddery(14) (bhd: hdwy u.p appr st: nvr nr ldrs)	4	**7**	33/1	40	22
4336^{12}	**Woody's Boy (IRE) (63)** (MJHeaton-Ellis) **3-8-0**$^{(3)}$ ADaly(11) (bhd: kpt on u.p fnl 3f: n.d)	3	**8**	20/1	45	16
4620a^{8}	**Turgenev (IRE) (74)** (RBastiman) **8-9-11** DeanMcKeown(6) (lw: sn chsng ldrs: hrd rdn over 3f out: sn wknd)	3	**9**	5/1^{2}	53	35
1260^{9}	**Kadastrof (FR) (70)** (RDickin) **7-9-7** DaneO'Neill(8) (bit bkwd: s.i.s: sn chsng ldrs: lost pl 4f out)	2½	**10**	16/1	47	29
4562^{7}	**Shift Again (IRE) (56)** (OSherwood) **5-8-7b** SophieMitchell(7) (chsd ldrs tl lost pl 7f out: t.o 4f out)	5	**11**	33/1	28	10
4269^{11}	**Ambuscade (USA) (45)** (MrsJJordan) **11-7-3**$^{(7)}$ ANicholls(16) (sn bhd & drvn along: t.o 4f out)	10	**12**	50/1	7	—
2198^{3}	**Golden Hadeer (57)** (MJRyan) **6-8-8** AClark(3) (b: sn drvn along: chsd ldrs tl lost pl 7f out: t.o fnl 4f)	dist	**13**	14/1	—	—
4461^{6}	**Height of Heights (IRE) (74)** (LadyHerries) **4-9-11** TSprake(17) (w ldrs: lost pl over 5f out: sn wl bhd)	4	**14**	14/1	—	—
				(SP 127.9%)	**14 Rn**	

3m 34.6 (11.60) CSF £50.25 CT £198.99 TOTE £10.30: £2.10 £2.00 £3.00 (£22.60) Trio £98.30 OWNER Mr Antony Sofroniou (WELLINGTON) BRED Halevale Ltd

LONG HANDICAP Ambuscade (USA) 7-0 Contrarie 7-2

WEIGHT FOR AGE 3yo-11lb

OFFICIAL EXPLANATION **Height of Heights (IRE) reportedly had a breathing problem in the race.**

4609* Theme Arena, who wore a tongue-strap, is as tough as old boots and she would not be denied. (9/1: 6/1-10/1)

4673 City Hall (IRE), suited by the trip and the soft ground, was the only one to make a real race of it with the winner but, hard as he tried, he could not get his head in front. (5/1)

4633* Contrarie was racing from an 8lb higher mark. (4/1: op 6/1)

4269 Classic Line, a poor mover, does not do anything in a hurry. (10/1)

4269* Selmeston (IRE), from a 5lb higher mark, was ridden with much more restraint than usual. (7/1)

4269 Opaque ran a rather stale race and was possibly just remembering the very hard race he was given last time at Ayr. (8/1)

4745 HORSERACE BETTING LEVY BOARD MEDIAN AUCTION MAIDEN STKS (2-Y.O) (Class F)
5-40 (5-43) **1m 1f 213y** £2,715.90 (£752.40: £359.70) Stalls: Low GOING: 0.20 sec per fur (G)

				SP	RR	SF
4454^{4}	**Wave Rock (78)** (JLDunlop) **2-9-0** MRimmer(10) (in tch: effrt 3f out: styd on u.p to ld ins fnl f: hld on towards fin)	—	**1**	4/1^{3}	82	—
4478^{3}	**Jamorin Dancer** (MAJarvis) **2-9-0** RCochrane(9) (led: hdd ins fnl f: styd on)	nk	**2**	100/30^{1}	82	—
4605^{4}	**Casino Ace (IRE) (77)** (PWChapple-Hyam) **2-8-6**$^{(3)}$ RHavlin(8) (chsd ldrs: chal 3f out: sn rdn: one pce fnl f)	2½	**3**	7/2^{2}	73	—
4605^{3}	**Heathyards Sheik (67)** (RHollinshead) **2-9-0** FLynch(13) (hld up: hdwy over 2f out: sn chsng ldrs: one pce appr fnl f)	4	**4**	12/1	71	—
	Tokay (PFICole) **2-8-9** TQuinn(7) (cmpt: mid div: effrt 3f out: nvr nr to chal)	6	**5**	16/1	57	—
4582^{4}	**Smiling Voter (IRE) (79)** (RHannon) **2-9-0** DaneO'Neill(6) (lw: in tch: hdwy to chal over 3f out: wknd over 1f out)	1½	**6**	9/2	59	—
3607^{8}	**Magic Falls (IRE)** (MJPolglase) **2-9-0** JTate(3) (chsd ldrs: ev ch tl wknd over 3f out)	3	**7**	50/1	54	—
4044^{9}	**Oisin (IRE) (68)** (MrsPNDutfield) **2-9-0** CRutter(4) (in tch: hdwy & ev ch over 3f out: sn wknd)	4	**8**	33/1	48	—
	Cutting Anshake (MRChannon) **2-9-0** JFortune(2) (lengthy: unf: bkwd: s.s: hdwy over 3f out: hung bdly lft & sn lost pl)	½	**9**	33/1	47	—
	Spirito (LordHuntingdon) **2-9-0** TSprake(5) (s.s: hdwy over 4f out: sn rdn & wknd)	1½	**10**	12/1	45	—
4627^{6}	**Sharp Monkey** (MrsNMacauley) **2-9-0** SDrowne(11) (trckd ldrs: lost pl over 3f out)	½	**11**	33/1	44	—
	Were Not Stoppin (RBastiman) **2-8-13**$^{(5)ow4}$ HBastiman(12) (Withdrawn not under Starter's orders: v.unruly & ref to ent stalls)		**W**	33/1	—	—
				(SP 118.5%)	**11 Rn**	

2m 17.0 (14.50) CSF £15.35 TOTE £4.60: £1.10 £1.50 £1.60 (£8.70) Trio £13.40 OWNER The Earl Cadogan (ARUNDEL) BRED Pinfold Stud and Farms Ltd

4454 Wave Rock appreciated the extra quarter-mile and in the end took this run of the mill auction event with not an ounce to spare. (4/1)

4478 Jamorin Dancer, who looked very fit, is obviously regarded as a stayer because his rider set off in front taking no prisoners, and in the end they were only just worn down. (100/30)

4605 Casino Ace (IRE), who looked very light beforehand, was best on official figures but had no obvious excuse. (7/2: op 9/4)

4605 Heathyards Sheik stayed the trip alright but had his limitations ruthlessly exposed. (12/1)

Tokay, who ran a satisfactory first race, lacks size and substance. (16/1)

4582 Smiling Voter (IRE), who looked very fit indeed, is not progressing at all. (9/2)

Spirito (12/1: op 6/1)

T/Plpt: £14.30 (1,513.87 Tckts). T/Qdpt: £3.20 (381.18 Tckts) Dk/WG

4427-CATTERICK (L-H) (Soft, Good to soft patches)
Thursday October 16th
WEATHER: drizzle WIND: mod half bhd

4746 OCTOBER NURSERY H'CAP (0-85) (2-Y.O) (Class E)
2-10 (2-11) **5f** £3,096.25 (£925.00: £442.50: £201.25) Stalls: Low GOING: 0.33 sec per fur (G)

				SP	RR	SF
4311*	**Refined (IRE) (85)** (LMCumani) **2-9-7** KDarley(10) (lw: b.off hind: chsd ldr: led 2f out: r.o wl: comf)	—	**1**	2/1^{1}	93+	52
4428^{3}	**Carol Singer (USA) (68)** (MJohnston) **2-8-4** DHolland(8) (chsd ldrs: outpcd & rdn ½-wy: hdwy over 1f out: styd on: no ch w wnr)	3	**2**	8/1	66	25

3932⁷ **Summerseat (60)** (GHolmes) **2-7-10** LCharnock(6) (sn outpcd: hdwy 2f out: styd on ins fnl f)..........5	**3**	12/1	42	1
4542* **Iris May (74)** (JBerry) **2-8-7b**(3) TEDurcan(3) (w ldrs tl wknd over 1f out)..........¾	**4**	7/1 3	54	13
4566⁴ **Bala (64)** (HMorrison) **2-8-0** CRutter(4) (s.i.s: hdwy ½-wy: styng on whn nt clr run ins fnl f)..........3	**5**	12/1	34	—
4522³ **Ivory's Joy (75)** (KTIvory) **2-8-11** GDuffield(9) (b: led: hung lft thrght: hdd 2f out: sn wknd)..........7	**6**	9/4 2	23	—
4542³ **Sacchetti (IRE) (75)** (MRChannon) **2-8-11** JCarroll(5) (chsd ldrs tl outpcd ½-wy: sn lost pl)..........4	**7**	7/1 3	10	—
4468¹² **Makahu Don (61)** (WTKemp) **2-7-11b**ow1 TWilliams(1) (sn chsng ldrs: rdn & lost pl ½-wy)..........2½	**8**	50/1	—	—
3707¹⁸ **Dibola (60)** (JSWainwright) **2-7-7**(3) PFessey(7) (sn wl outpcd & bhd)..........¾	**9**	33/1	—	—
3932¹⁶ **Wait'n'see (80)** (MWEasterby) **2-9-2** TLucas(2) (bit bkwd: sn outpcd & drvn along: bhd fr ½-wy)..........4	**10**	25/1	—	—

(SP 124.3%) **10 Rn**

62.4 secs (4.70) CSF £18.48 CT £150.14 TOTE £2.60: £1.40 £2.50 £3.80 (£9.00) Trio £61.70 OWNER Sheikh Mohammed (NEWMARKET) BRED W. Maxwell Ervine

LONG HANDICAP Makahu Don 7-2 Dibola 6-11

4311* Refined (IRE) looked a cut above her rivals in the paddock. With the best ground on the stands-side rail, as it turned out she had the plum draw and she proved much too good for this lot. The handicapper has obviously underestimated her, putting her on 85 for her handicap debut.(2/1)

4428 Carol Singer (USA) on this occasion was badly tapped for foot at halfway. Despite sticking on, the winner was much too good. (8/1)

3932 Summerseat presumably needed her Pontefract outing, her first for four months. Sticking on at the finish, six on the All-Weather should be no problem. (12/1)

4542* Iris May raced on the slower ground towards the centre. (7/1)

4566 Bala, who didn't have the best of luck in running, is crying out for six furlongs. (12/1)

1860* Wait'n'see, who looked some way short of peak fitness, wore a tongue strap and was mounted on the track and taken to post early. (25/1)

4747 E.B.F. RIPLEY MAIDEN STKS (I) (2-Y.O) (Class D)

2-45 (2-46) **5f 212y** £3,034.50 (£906.00: £433.00: £196.50) Stalls: Low GOING: 0.69 sec per fur (GS)

		SP	RR	SF
4298¹⁴ **Robin Goodfellow** (PTWalwyn) **2-9-0** JCarroll(4) (led 2f: led ½-wy: styd on wl appr fnl f)..........—	**1**	5/1 3	83	45
4544⁷ **Easter Ogil (IRE)** (IABalding) **2-9-0** SWhitworth(6) (chsd ldrs: outpcd ½-wy: styd on appr fnl f)..........2½	**2**	3/1 2	76	38
4332⁸ **Implicitly** (WJarvis) **2-8-9** GHind(7) (chsd ldrs: outpcd & rdn over 2f out: kpt on one pce)..........2½	**3**	9/1	65	27
4381⁷ **My Lost Love** (MJohnston) **2-9-0** DHolland(3) (led after 2f to 3f out: wknd over 1f out)..........5	**4**	9/1	56	18
Orange Bush (IRE) (PCHaslam) **2-9-0** LCharnock(2) (leggy: scope: bkwd: s.i.s: outpcd over 2f out: kpt on appr fnl f)..........s.h	**5**	33/1	56	18
4502³ **Palmetto Bay (IRE) (79)** (MRStoute) **2-9-0** KDarley(8) (chsd ldrs: effrt 3f out: wknd over 1f out)..........10	**6**	9/4 1	29	—
Shipley Glen (SirMarkPrescott) **2-9-0** GDuffield(9) (cmpt: bkwd: chsd ldrs: hung bdly rt & lost pl bnd after 2f: sn bhd & eased)..........18	**7**	7/1	—	—
Appian Dame (IRE) (DJGMurraySmith) **2-8-9** CRutter(1) (leggy: unf: bit bkwd: dwlt s: sn bhd)..........4	**8**	14/1	—	—

(SP 114.5%) **8 Rn**

1m 18.8 (7.90) CSF £18.61 TOTE £7.40: £1.20 £1.60 £2.00 (£9.20) Trio £38.00 OWNER Mr Michael Gough (LAMBOURN) BRED Major and Mrs R. B. Kennard and Whitsbury Manor St

OFFICIAL EXPLANATION **Palmetto Bay (IRE) was reportedly unsuited by the soft ground.**

Robin Goodfellow, who moved very short going to post, proved well suited by the testing ground, and getting the plum stand side position in the home straight, in the end scored in decisive fashion. (5/1)

Easter Ogil (IRE), who showed plenty of knee action going down, will be suited by a step up to seven. (3/1)

4332 Implicitly, very keen going to post, ran as if seven would not come amiss. (9/1: op 5/1)

4381 My Lost Love, having his third outing, was still noisy in the paddock. Showing a fluent action going down, he should do better in handicap company at three. (9/1: op 5/1)

Orange Bush (IRE), a backward-looking newcomer, showed a very round action going down, very inexperienced he will surely improve on this next year, (33/1)

4502 Palmetto Bay (IRE), who wore a tongue strap, ran no race at all in the soft ground and his rider gave up. (9/4: evens-5/2)

Shipley Glen (7/1: 9/2-8/1)

Appian Dame (IRE) (14/1: op 25/1)

4748 NORTHALLERTON RATING RELATED MAIDEN STKS (0-65) (3-Y.O) (Class F)

3-20 (3-21) **1m 3f 214y** £2,784.00 (£774.00: £372.00) Stalls: Low GOING: 0.69 sec per fur (GS)

		SP	RR	SF
4336¹⁷ **Alakdar (CAN) (64)** (ACStewart) **3-8-12** SWhitworth(8) (hld up: hdwy 6f out: led over 3f out: drvn clr over 1f out)..........—	**1**	9/1	84	32
4429² **Back Row (64)** (LMCumani) **3-8-9** KDarley(9) (mid div: drvn along 7f out: hdwy 4f out: kpt on fnl 2f: no ch w wnr)..........8	**2**	4/1 2	70	18
4568⁵ **Arletty (57)** (HRACecil) **3-8-9** AMcGlone(1) (chsd ldrs: one pce fnl 3f)..........2	**3**	13/2 3	68	16
4562¹⁰ **Mountaineer (IRE) (64)** (MBell) **3-8-12** MFenton(5) (chsd ldrs: drvn along 6f out: one pce)..........5	**4**	8/1	64	12
4378⁵ **Pradesh (65)** (JHMGosden) **3-8-9** GHind(7) (lw: sn trckng ldrs: led over 4f out tl over 3f out: sn wknd)..........3	**5**	2/1 1	57	5
4336¹⁴ **Classic Fan (USA) (57)** (MRChannon) **3-8-9** JCarroll(6) (sn drvn along: hdwy 6f out: nvr nr to chal)..........3	**6**	25/1	53	1
3495¹¹ **Savu Sea (IRE) (55)** (CFWall) **3-8-9v¹** GDuffield(4) (s.i.s: sn drvn along: reminders 7f out: sme hdwy over 4f out: n.d)..........4	**7**	20/1	48	—
Hustle An Bustle (USA) (56) (GFierro) **3-8-9** NCarlisle(12) (b. hind: hld up: effrt over 5f out: sn lost pl)..........6	**8**	14/1	40	—
2114⁶ **Autumn Time (IRE) (65)** (PWChapple-Hyam) **3-8-6**(3) RHavlin(2) (bhd & drvn along 7f out: t.o)..........dist	**9**	10/1	—	—
4579³ **Balfour Lady (58)** (JARToller) **3-8-9** WJO'Connor(11) (rr div: sme hdwy 4f out: sn wknd: t.o)..........5	**10**	8/1	—	—
3696¹¹ **Monaco (IRE) (65)** (RAllan) **3-8-12** ACulhane(10) (sn trckng ldr: led 6f out tl over 4f out: sn wknd: t.o)..........7	**11**	20/1	—	—
2902³ **Ingleborough (49)** (DMoffatt) **3-8-9**(3) DarrenMoffatt(3) (led to 6f out: sn lost pl: wl t.o whn p.u 2f out)..........	**P**	100/1	—	—

(SP 129.0%) **12 Rn**

2m 49.4 (18.00) CSF £43.00 TOTE £10.20: £2.50 £1.70 £2.70 (£11.90) Trio £55.30 OWNER Mr Hamdan Al Maktoum (NEWMARKET) BRED Huntingdon Stud Farm Inc

4104 Alakdar (CAN), who showed a pronounced knee action going down, did not stay the two-mile trip last time. Given a positive ride, he pinched the stands' side rail in the home straight, and in the end proved much too good for this field of mainly disappointing individuals. (9/1: op 5/1)

4429 Back Row, whose rider was hard at work a long way from home, proved painfully one-paced. (4/1: op 5/2)

4568 Arletty, had the blinkers left off this time, and kept straight. (13/2)

1565 Mountaineer (IRE) has a very round action. (8/1)

4378 Pradesh, who looked really well, showed plenty of knee action going down, but she dropped out, beaten, on the turn for home. (2/1)

4579 Balfour Lady (8/1: 12/1-20/1)

4749 DARLINGTON H'CAP (0-80) (3-Y.O) (Class D)

3-50 (3-51) **1m 7f 177y** £3,717.00 (£1,116.00: £538.00: £249.00) Stalls: Low GOING: 0.69 sec per fur (GS)

Form	Horse / details	Dist	Pos	SP	RR	SF
4279^{6}	**Jazz Track (IRE) (78)** (PWChapple-Hyam) **3-9-2**(3) RHavlin(6) (lw: sn trckng ldrs: effrt over 3f out: styd on u.p to ld nr fin)	—	**1**	$9/2^{3}$	86	32
3865^{7}	**Sad Mad Bad (USA) (55)** (MrsMReveley) **3-7-10** LCharnock(2) (sn trckng ldrs: led over 2f out to last 50y)	hd	**2**	10/1	63	9
*4590**	**Robbo (60)** (CWThornton) **3-8-1b** 4x GDuffield(5) (hld up: effrt 5f out: led over 3f out: hdd over 2f out: nt qckn fnl f)	1¼	**3**	$4/1^{2}$	67	13
3890*	**Vicki Romara (79)** (MJohnston) **3-9-6** DHolland(4) (chsd ldr: led 5f out tl over 3f out: wknd & eased over 1f out)	17	**4**	$6/4^{1}$	68	14
4547*	**Crystal Hills (IRE) (80)** (JHMGosden) **3-9-7** GHind(7) (led to 5f out: lost pl over 3f out: virtually p.u)	dist	**5**	7/1	—	—
4633^{7}	**Philosophic (55)** (SirMarkPrescott) **3-7-10** JLowe(3) (trckd ldrs: drvn along & lost pl 8f out: t.o 5f out: virtually p.u)	¾	**6**	$9/2^{3}$	—	—

(SP 118.0%) **6 Rn**

3m 47.4 (25.40) CSF £43.03 TOTE £5.70: £3.00 £1.90 (£19.40) OWNER Mr Richard Santulli and Mrs J Magnier (MARLBOROUGH) BRED Jayeff 'B' Stables and Calogo Bloodstock A G

LONG HANDICAP Philosophic 7-9

4279 Jazz Track (IRE), full of himself in the paddock, was travelling best some way from home, but in the end it was a close haul. He certainly stayed the trip all right. (9/2)

3623 Sad Mad Bad (USA), who has a pronounced round action, proved well suited by the rain-softened ground and in a three-way battle came off just second best. (10/1)

4590* Robbo, a proven All-Weather performer, proved well suited by the mud. Pinching the favoured stands-side rail in the home straight, he had no more to offer in the final furlong. (4/1)

3890* Vicki Romara, who acts in the mud, was having her first outing for forty-eight days and almost certainly needed it. (6/4)

4547* Crystal Hills (IRE), loaded into the stalls with the help of a Monty Roberts rug, ran a tame race. Sticking to the far side in the home straight he was virtually pulled up. (7/1)

4633 Philosophic was never happy on this ground and was in trouble with a circuit to go. In the end, his rider simply hacked him home. (9/2)

4750 E.B.F. ZETLAND MEDIAN AUCTION MAIDEN STKS (2-Y.O F) (Class E)

4-25 (4-28) **7f** £3,122.25 (£933.00: £446.50: £203.25) Stalls: Low GOING: 0.69 sec per fur (GS)

Form	Horse / details	Dist	Pos	SP	RR	SF
4425^{3}	**Shfoug (USA)** (BWHills) **2-8-11** KDarley(7) (sn trckng ldrs: effrt over 2f out: led ins fnl f: eased nr fin: jst hld on)	—	**1**	$6/5^{1}$	77	37
4468^{7}	**Sharp Cracker (IRE) (75)** (MJohnston) **2-8-11** DHolland(4) (led to 4f out: led 3f out: edgd rt 1f out: sn hdd: rallied nr fin)	s.h	**2**	10/1	77	37
4575^{4}	**La Tiziana** (WJarvis) **2-8-11** GHind(5) (w ldrs: led 4f out to 3f out: styng on same pce whn nt clr run 1f out)	2½	**3**	$7/2^{2}$	71	31
4545^{5}	**Face-Off (66)** (CFWall) **2-8-11** GDuffield(10) (w ldrs: ev ch tl wknd fnl f)	5	**4**	$8/1^{3}$	60	20
	Forest Fire (SWE) (PMooney) **2-8-11** WJO'Connor(6) (unf: bkwd: s.s: bhd tl styd on fnl f)	6	**5**	33/1	46	6
4362^{8}	**Positive Air (77)** (BAMcMahon) **2-8-11** JBramhill(3) (chsd ldrs: rdn & one pce fnl 2f)	1½	**6**	10/1	43	3
4382^{8}	**Ida Lupino (IRE) (50)** (BWHills) **2-8-8**(3) PFessey(2) (hld up: hdwy ½-wy: edgd rt & wknd over 2f out)	1¼	**7**	50/1	40	—
4564^{12}	**Priddy Green** (HCandy) **2-8-11** CRutter(12) (b.off hind: chsd ldrs tl wknd over 2f out)	½	**8**	14/1	39	—
4597^{8}	**Chimes of Peace** (JLEyre) **2-8-11** OPears(13) (s.i.s: bhd tl sme hdwy fnl 2f)	½	**9**	25/1	38+	—
4097^{5}	**Robin Lane (73)** (IABalding) **2-8-11** SWhitworth(9) (sn outpcd)	2	**10**	$8/1^{3}$	33	—
4332^{15}	**Shotley Marie (IRE)** (NBycroft) **2-8-11** LCharnock(1) (bit bkwd: s.i.s: a outpcd & sn rdn along)	1¼	**11**	100/1	30	—
4470^{3}	**Ngaere Princess (48)** (WTKemp) **2-8-11** TWilliams(11) (in tch to ½-wy: sn bhd: virtually p.u 2f out)	dist	**12**	200/1	—	—
4604^{7}	**Baby Spice** (MRChannon) **2-8-11** JCarroll(8) (lost pl ½-wy: sn bhd: virtually p.u 2f out)	dist	**13**	20/1	—	—

(SP 129.7%) **13 Rn**

1m 33.3 (9.70) CSF £14.72 TOTE £2.00: £1.10 £2.90 £2.00 (£9.20) Trio £6.80 OWNER Mr Hilal Salem (LAMBOURN) BRED Gainsborough Farm Inc

4425 Shfoug (USA), who showed a very scratchy action going down, proved well suited by the give underfoot. Taking time to get into full stride, she was value for a neck win. She will be seen to better effect on a more orthodox track. (6/5: evens-11/8)

3307 Sharp Cracker (IRE), who was fully exposed, stuck on, despite coming off a true line, and in the end, almost gave the winner a fright. (10/1)

4575 La Tiziana, was messed about by Sharp Cracker, but would still only have finished third at best. (7/2)

4545 Face-Off is fully exposed . (8/1)

Forest Fire (SWE), a backward-looking newcomer, showed a very round action going down. After a slow start, she did show some ability. (33/1)

4362 Positive Air, who is only small, showed a pronounced knee action going to post. Given a very quiet ride, she is now qualified for a handicap mark. (10/1)

4097 Robin Lane (8/1: op 5/1)

4751 HORNBY CASTLE H'CAP (0-75) (3-Y.O+) (Class D)

5-00 (5-01) **1m 3f 214y** £4,003.00 (£1,204.00: £582.00: £271.00) Stalls: Low GOING: 0.69 sec per fur (GS)

Form	Horse / details	Dist	Pos	SP	RR	SF
4438^{8}	**Whitley Grange Boy (46)** (JLEyre) **4-7-13** LCharnock(12) (sn chsng ldrs: led over 2f out: drvn clr 1f out: eased towards fin)	—	**1**	20/1	61	26
4406^{8}	**Pietro Bembo (IRE) (65)** (SirMarkPrescott) **3-8-11** GDuffield(13) (a chsng ldrs: kpt on same pce appr fnl f)	5	**2**	14/1	73	31
4596^{5}	**House of Dreams (55)** (GMMoore) **5-8-8** JCarroll(5) (bhd: hdwy over 4f out: styd on same pce appr fnl f)	2	**3**	$7/1^{3}$	61	26
4335^{2}	**Riccarton (53)** (PCalver) **4-8-6** KDarley(2) (hdwy 5f out: sn chsng ldrs: kpt on same pce appr fnl f)	¾	**4**	$6/1^{2}$	58	23
4279^{2}	**Gold Desire (60)** (MBrittain) **7-8-8**(5) SCopp(9) (a chsng ldrs: hrd rdn & one pce fnl 2f)	2½	**5**	$11/2^{1}$	61	26
4521^{10}	**Break the Rules (72)** (DNicholls) **5-9-11** AlexGreaves(4) (lw: hdwy 8f out: effrt over 3f out: kpt on: nvr able chal)	s.h	**6**	10/1	73	38
4571^{8}	**Newbridge Boy (49)** (MGMeagher) **4-7-13**(3) PFessey(18) (led tl over 2f out: wknd appr fnl f)	s.h	**7**	25/1	50	15
4248^{13}	**Ocean Stream (IRE) (51)** (JLEyre) **4-8-4** RLappin(6) (hld up: hdwy 4f out: kpt on fnl 2f: nvr nr to chal)	1¾	**8**	33/1	50	15
4584^{8}	**Hasta la Vista (56)** (MWEasterby) **7-8-6b**(3) GParkin(1) (chsd ldrs: rdn 3f out: wknd over 1f out)	8	**9**	8/1	44	9
4510^{7}	**Keep Battling (46)** (JSGoldie) **7-7-13**ow1 AMackay(10) (bhd: sme hdwy over 4f out: n.d)	1½	**10**	16/1	32	—
4108^{6}	**Tappeto (71)** (HCandy) **5-9-10** CRutter(14) (mid div: drvn along over 4f out: sn lost pl)	nk	**11**	$11/2^{1}$	57	22
4438^{4}	**Alzotic (IRE) (44)** (JNorton) **4-7-11**ow1 NKennedy(17) (sn bhd & drvn along: t.o 2f out)	23	**12**	16/1	—	—
	Salinger (43) (JParkes) **9-7-10** NCarlisle(15) (b: hld up: a bhd)	½	**13**	66/1	—	—
4235^{20}	**Westminster (IRE) (57)** (MHTompkins) **5-8-10v** DaleGibson(8) (hld up: effrt over 5f out: sn wknd)	5	**14**	14/1	5	—

			SP	RR	SF
4466[5] **Summerhill Special (IRE) (64)** (DWBarker) **6-9-3** TWilliams(11) (chsd ldrs: rdn over 5f out: lost pl & eased over 3f out)	nk	**15**	10/1	11	—
2399[11] **Baranov (IRE) (52)** (DJGMurraySmith) **4-8-5** SWhitworth(7) (hld up: a bhd: t.o 3f out)	7	**16**	50/1	—	—
4063[11] **Temptress (63)** (JohnHarris) **4-9-2** MFenton(3) (bhd & drvn along 6f out: t.o 2f out)	12	**17**	10/1	—	—
3813[12] **Swynford Charmer (50)** (JHetherton) **3-7-10** JLowe(16) (b.hind: in tch tl lost pl 6f out: t.o 3f out: virtually p.u)	dist	**18**	66/1	—	—
			(SP 137.5%)	**18 Rn**	

2m 48.5 (17.10) CSF £267.98 CT £2,002.02 TOTE £16.10: £2.60 £2.50 £1.90 £1.50 (£319.80) Trio £332.40; £285.64 to Newmarket 17/10/97
OWNER Mrs Carole Sykes (HAMBLETON) BRED J. L. Eyre
LONG HANDICAP Salinger 7-4 Alzotic (IRE) 6-12 Swynford Charmer 6-9
WEIGHT FOR AGE 3yo-7lb
IN-FOCUS: **This was Lindsay Charnock's (age 42) maiden half-century.**
4053 Whitley Grange Boy, who has plenty of size and scope, revelled in the ground and, getting the plum stands-side position in the home straight, was eventually able to win easing up. (20/1)
4108 Pietro Bembo (IRE), with the headgear again left off, looked to run his best race this year. (14/1)
4596 House of Dreams proved well suited by the step up in distance, and will no doubt soon be seen in action over hurdles. (7/1)
4335 Riccarton possibly found this trip and these conditions testing his stamina to the very limit. (6/1: op 4/1)
4279 Gold Desire who should have been suited by the underfoot conditions, made the mistake of sticking up the middle in the home straight.(11/2)
4108 Tappeto was in trouble turning out of the back straight and soon beat a retreat. (11/2)

4752 E.B.F. RIPLEY MAIDEN STKS (II) (2-Y.O) (Class D)

5-30 (5-30) **5f 212y** £3,008.50 (£898.00: £429.00: £194.50) Stalls: Low GOING: 0.69 sec per fur (GS)

			SP	RR	SF
3770[3] **Obsessed (84)** (MRStoute) **2-8-9** KDarley(3) (chsd ldrs: rdn & edgd lft over 1f out: led post)	—	**1**	8/11[1]	81	32
4575[7] **Mitch Passi (IRE)** (SirMarkPrescott) **2-9-0** GDuffield(1) (s.i.s: hdwy to ld after 1½f: rdn over 1f out: edgd lft & jst ct)	s.h	**2**	7/2[2]	86	37
4311[11] **Polish Pilot (IRE)** (WRMuir) **2-9-0** ACulhane(2) (hdwy ½-wy: sn chsng ldrs: outpcd appr fnl f)	7	**3**	20/1	67	18
4544[12] **Peaceful Sarah** (PMooney) **2-8-9** WJO'Connor(7) (in tch: effrt over 2f out: nvr nr to chal)	5	**4**	10/1	49	—
3717[6] **Dangerus Precedent (IRE)** (CREgerton) **2-9-0** CRutter(5) (sn outpcd & bhd: sme hdwy over 1f out: n.d)	3	**5**	10/1	46	—
4231[11] **Repton** (MrsASwinbank) **2-8-11**(3) GParkin(9) (stdd s: bhd tl sme hdwy fnl 2f)	5	**6**	66/1	32	—
4211[7] **Detroit City (IRE) (69)** (JBerry) **2-8-11**(3) TEDurcan(4) (chsd ldrs tl outpcd 2f out)	1¼	**7**	16/1	29	—
4428[5] **Anditz (IRE)** (JLEyre) **2-8-10**ow1 OPears(8) (led 1½f: chsd ldrs tl wknd 2f out)	nk	**8**	7/1[3]	24	—
Runadrum (WWHaigh) **2-9-0** JBramhill(6) (leggy: lt-f: unf: s.i.s: a bhd)	18	**9**	100/1	—	—
			(SP 123.9%)	**9 Rn**	

1m 19.4 (8.50) CSF £3.51 TOTE £1.80: £1.10 £1.40 £3.10 (£3.10) Trio £13.60 OWNER Cheveley Park Stud (NEWMARKET) BRED Cheveley Park Stud Ltd
3770 Obsessed looked to have been found an easy opening, but in the end, in this ground, it was a desperate call. (8/11: 1/2-4/5)
Mitch Passi (IRE), a backward-looking type, who looks likely to improve at three, stepped up considerably on his debut effort and in the end was just denied. (7/2)
Polish Pilot (IRE), having his third outing, showed his first worthwhile form. (20/1)
Peaceful Sarah, who on breeding should have been suited by the mud, could never take a hand. (10/1)
3717 Dangerus Precedent (IRE), still carrying condition, showed a round action going to post. Unable completely to go the pace, he is obviously of limited ability but looks potentially a real stayer. (10/1)

T/Plpt: £434.20 (47.78 Tckts). T/Qdpt: £55.30 (21.78 Tckts) WG

4555-NEWMARKET (R-H) (St Good to Soft, Remainder Good)
Thursday October 16th

WEATHER: overcast, damp WIND: mod half against

4753 EQUITY FINANCIAL COLLECTIONS (S) STKS (2-Y.O) (Class E)

1-30 (1-31) **7f (Rowley)** £6,027.50 (£1,820.00: £885.00: £417.50) Stalls: High GOING: 0.33 sec per fur (G)

			SP	RR	SF
4068[8] **Mari-Ela (IRE) (57)** (JRArnold) **2-8-1**(5) CLowther(13) (a.p: rdn to ld ins fnl f: all out)	—	**1**	20/1	62	27
4285[10] **Tom Dougal (67)** (CSmith) **2-8-11** JFEgan(11) (lw: hdwy over 2f out: chsng ldrs ins fnl f: kpt on wl towards fin)	nk	**2**	33/1	66	31
4366[4] **Arm And A Leg (IRE) (62)** (CADwyer) **2-9-2** JReid(15) (lw: in tch: hdwy over 2f out: ev ch 1f out: kpt on)	nk	**3**	20/1	71	36
4315[3] **Oh So Easy (70)** (BJMeehan) **2-8-11** JWeaver(19) (led tl hdd ins fnl f: no ex)	2	**4**	10/1	61	26
3257[5] **Frankie Fair (IRE) (67)** (MAJarvis) **2-8-6** RCochrane(8) (hld up: gd hdwy ½-wy: sn chsng ldrs: kpt on ins fnl f)	½	**5**	10/1	55	20
4602[3] **Scene (IRE) (45)** (MartynMeade) **2-8-6** TSprake(9) (in tch: outpcd & nt clr run 2f out: kpt on wl fnl f)	nk	**6**	20/1	54	19
4299[7] **Flying Bold (IRE)** (WRMuir) **2-8-11** MartinDwyer(17) (lw: bhd: hdwy 2f out: r.o wl towards fin)	½	**7**	20/1	58+	23
4368[3] **Madame Jones (IRE) (70)** (BJMeehan) **2-8-6** MTebbutt(29) (in tch: effrt u.p 2f out: nvr able chal)	s.h	**8**	6/1[1]	53	18
4459[4] **Dilly Lane (USA) (61)** (PRWebber) **2-8-6** RPerham(27) (lw: hdwy over 2f out: rdn & no imp)	hd	**9**	14/1	53	18
Primary Colours (WJHaggas) **2-8-6** MHills(26) (w'like: chsd ldrs over 4f)	1¼	**10**	8/1[3]	50	15
4543[3] **Impulsive Decision (IRE) (53)** (MartynMeade) **2-8-6** DeanMcKeown(20) (w ldrs 5f: wknd)	¾	**11**	14/1	48	13
Opening Night (RSimpson) **2-8-11** MGallagher(12) (leggy: lt-f: chsd ldrs tl wknd appr fnl f)	s.h	**12**	25/1	53	18
4209[3] **Blue Zola (IRE) (72)** (MBell) **2-8-1**(5) RMullen(18) (chsd ldrs: effrt over 2f out: nt qckn)	nk	**13**	13/2[2]	47	12
4595[9] **Fanti Dancer (IRE) (62)** (BJMeehan) **2-7-13**(7) GHannon(2) (bhd: sme hdwy 2f out: n.d)	s.h	**14**	20/1	47	12
4380[5] **Ringleader (70)** (PFICole) **2-8-11b** TQuinn(5) (cl up over 5f: wknd)	s.h	**15**	10/1	52	17
4366[7] **Five Fairies (58)** (NACallaghan) **2-8-3**(3) RFfrench(25) (a.p: effrt 2f out: no imp)	½	**16**	14/1	46	11
4266[6] **Mr Miyagi (62)** (ABailey) **2-8-11b1** DWright(7) (in tch tl outpcd ½-wy: styd on fnl f)	nk	**17**	14/1	50	15
4058[5] **Patricia Olive (IRE) (51)** (MHTompkins) **2-8-3v**(3) MHenry(1) (chsd ldrs 5f)	3	**18**	20/1	39	4
4592[4] **Mamora Bay (IRE) (66)** (MHTompkins) **2-8-11b** DBiggs(14) (a bhd)	¾	**19**	20/1	42	7
2943[15] **Vicky Jazz** (JSMoore) **2-8-6** JQuinn(21) (n.d)	s.h	**20**	33/1	37	2
4401[7] **Zimzie (55)** (MJHaynes) **2-8-11** GCarter(28) (nvr wnt pce)	1	**21**	25/1	39	4
4526[21] **Rock Sounds** (NACallaghan) **2-8-11** SDrowne(6) (b.hind: a bhd)	nk	**22**	20/1	39	4
631[5] **Shindium** (CADwyer) **2-8-8**ow2 KFallon(16) (mid div: pushed along ½-wy: eased whn btn appr fnl f)	hd	**23**	10/1	35	—

3497[7]	**Prince Oxley** (GLMoore) **2-8-11** AClark(23) (bkwd: bhd fr ½-wy)	1½	**24**	33/1	35	—
4595[4]	**Filgrave (IRE) (56)** (CADwyer) **2-8-11** JFortune(10) (in tch 5f: wknd)	2½	**25**	20/1	29	—
4178[13]	**Resurrection (IRE) (57)** (RHannon) **2-8-6** DaneO'Neill(4) (a bhd)	2	**26**	16/1	20	—
4507[8]	**Sledmere (IRE)** (NTinkler) **2-8-11** WRyan(22) (a bhd)	5	**27**	33/1	13	—
4066[11]	**Fair Sonia (65)** (KMcAuliffe) **2-8-6** DO'Donohoe(30) (n.d)	9	**28**	33/1	—	—
4459[7]	**The Druidess (IRE) (43)** (GCBravery) **2-8-6** NDay(24) (bkwd: bhd fr ½-wy)	13	**29**	33/1	—	—

(SP 175.8%) **29 Rn**

1m 32.22 (7.72) CSF £568.66 TOTE £120.60: £25.90 £11.50 £5.80 (£982.50) Trio Not won; £666.39 to Newmarket 17/10/97 OWNER Mr J. K. Gale (UPPER LAMBOURN) BRED Jim Murphy

No bid

OFFICIAL EXPLANATION **Flying Bold (IRE): became upset on the way to the start last time and hung badly in the race. Here, the rider's orders were to hold up the colt and get him settled, but the colt again hung to the left. The trainer reported that subsequent to the colt's return to the yard, he was found to have a large abscess on his off-fore.**

2565 Mari-Ela (IRE), who has been generally disappointing, found her form here and showed a good attitude. (20/1)

3905 Tom Dougal gave his best performance to date and was staying on really well at the end, suggesting that even stiffer tasks are needed. (33/1)

4366 Arm And A Leg (IRE) keeps running well but is just short of a real turn of foot to take it. (20/1)

4315 Oh So Easy, trying his longest trip to date, put up a useful performance but just failed to last it out. (10/1)

3257 Frankie Fair (IRE) certainly has an engine, but is a shade disappointing off the bit. If the key can be found, there is better to come. (10/1)

4602 Scene (IRE) got messed about at a vital stage and had no further chance despite finishing well. She obviously stays, should improve further yet and is one to watch. (20/1)

4052 Flying Bold (IRE), having his first run on turf, is learning fast. By the way he finished, he should certainly get further and looks well worth another chance. (20/1)

Primary Colours (8/1: 6/1-10/1)

4754 FAKENHAM RATED STKS H'CAP (0-100) (3-Y.O+) (Class B)

2-05 (2-09) **1m 4f (Rowley)** £8,607.84 (£3,190.56: £1,535.28: £632.40: £256.20: £105.72) Stalls: High GOING: 0.33 sec per fur (G)

				SP	RR	SF
4552[7]	**Ihtiyati (USA) (96)** (JLDunlop) **3-8-11** RHills(17) (hld up: hdwy 4f out: led ins fnl f: hld on wl cl home)	—	**1**	16/1	106	76
4476[3]	**Dance So Suite (93)** (PFICole) **5-9-1** RCochrane(6) (hld up mid div: hdwy 3f out: rdn & r.o wl cl home)	hd	**2**	10/1	103	80
4476*	**Solo Mio (IRE) (98)** (BWHills) **3-8-13** MHills(11) (led: rdn wl over 1f out: hdd ins fnl f: rallied towards fin)	nk	**3**	7/1[1]	108	78
3989[7]	**Heritage (92)** (JHMGosden) **3-8-7** LDettori(7) (hld up: effrt whn hmpd 3f out: styd on wl ins fnl f)	½	**4**	15/2[2]	101	71
4476[6]	**Papua (87)** (IABalding) **3-8-2** MartinDwyer(3) (hld up: hdwy 3f out: kpt on u.p fnl f)	1	**5**	20/1	95	65
4672[11]	**Double Alleged (USA) (88)** (MJohnston) **3-8-3** DeanMcKeown(15) (hld up in tch: effrt & rdn over 3f out: wknd fnl f)	5	**6**	33/1	89	59
4558[24]	**Generous Libra (93)** (DRLoder) **3-8-8** KFallon(9) (trckd ldrs: chal 3f out: sn rdn: wknd over 1f out)	6	**7**	20/1	86	56
4004[6]	**Present Arms (USA) (99)** (PFICole) **4-9-7** TQuinn(8) (hld up in tch: hdwy 4f out: ev ch 2f out: rdn & wknd appr fnl f)	1½	**8**	12/1	90	67
4443[4]	**Better Offer (IRE) (95)** (MrsAJPerrett) **5-9-3** PaulEddery(1) (lost pl ½-wy: styd on again fnl 2f)	4	**9**	9/1[3]	81	58
4141[9]	**Calypso Grant (IRE) (92)** (PWHarris) **3-8-7**ow1 JReid(10) (nvr nr to chal)	nk	**10**	20/1	77	46
4639*	**Celestial Choir (88)** (JLEyre) **7-8-10v1** 3x JFortune(12) (drvn along & bhd over 4f out: n.d)	2	**11**	12/1	70	47
4409[3]	**Aerleon Pete (IRE) (88)** (MRStoute) **3-8-3** TSprake(5) (hdwy 5f out: rdn & wknd 3f out)	3	**12**	15/2[2]	66	36
4004[4]	**Yarob (IRE) (87)** (RAkehurst) **4-8-9** JWeaver(18) (chsd ldrs tl wknd fnl 4f)	3½	**13**	16/1	61	38
4558[17]	**The Dilettanti (USA) (93)** (JARToller) **4-9-1** SSanders(14) (chsd ldr tl wknd 4f out)	2½	**14**	16/1	63	40
4476[4]	**Forza Figlio (86)** (RAkehurst) **4-8-8** DaneO'Neill(2) (prom tl rdn & wknd over 3f out)	¾	**15**	12/1	55	32
4443[8]	**Rokeby Bowl (93)** (IABalding) **5-9-1** WRyan(19) (a in rr)	4	**16**	16/1	57	34
4443[5]	**Willie Conquer (94)** (RAkehurst) **5-9-2** AClark(13) (a in rr)	4	**17**	12/1	53	30
4477[13]	**Blurred (IRE) (85)** (MHTompkins) **4-8-4**(3) MHenry(4) (wl bhd fr ½-wy: t.o)	2	**18**	33/1	41	18
680[13]	**Song Of The Sword (85)** (JABOld) **4-8-4**(3) RFfrench(16) (t.o fnl 6f)	5	**19**	50/1	34	11
1595[10]	**Asas (97)** (JLDunlop) **3-8-12** GCarter(20) (lost pl 5f out: t.o)	12	**20**	25/1	30	—

(SP 135.4%) **20 Rn**

2m 37.38 (6.88) CSF £152.16 CT £1,150.30 TOTE £20.90: £4.50 £2.90 £2.20 £2.20 (£249.80) Trio £333.60 OWNER Mr Hamdan Al Maktoum (ARUNDEL) BRED John F. and Kirsten B. Swift

LONG HANDICAP Blurred (IRE) 7-13 Song Of The Sword 8-6

WEIGHT FOR AGE 3yo-7lb

4552 Ihtiyati (USA), a winner at this time last year, has been lightly raced since. Patiently ridden on this step up to twelve furlongs, he stayed on strongly up the hill and should not be hard pressed to win again, even with a penalty. (16/1)

4476 Dance So Suite edged closer three furlongs out but did not really find top gear until he met the rising ground, and his determined late challenge only just failed. He has not had a busy season and there is still time for him to score again. (10/1)

4476* Solo Mio (IRE) did his best to follow up his course and distance win last month with an all-the-way performance, but he was hard at work when faced with the hill and was forced to give best nearing the line. A very much improved colt, we have not seen the best of him yet. (7/1)

3989 Heritage, impeded when about to deliver his challenge three furlongs out, got outpaced when running down into the dip, but he picked up on the rising ground and though he drifted right stayed on strongly to the finish. He could be an ideal type for the November Handicap. (15/2)

4476 Papua has had a disappointing year but the handicapper gave him a bit of a chance here and, although unable to land a blow, he was not beaten far and he could be about to strike. (20/1)

3918* Double Alleged (USA) sat behind the leaders travelling comfortably, but he was made to work passing the Bushes and had to admit the task beyond him. (33/1)

4004 Present Arms (USA), possibly better over a slightly shorter trip, did not fare badly under top weight, and was only shaken off up the hill. He is fresher than many at this late stage of the season. (12/1)

4755 NGK SPARK PLUGS NURSERY H'CAP (2-Y.O) (Class C)

2-35 (2-41) **6f (Rowley)** £6,836.00 (£2,048.00: £984.00: £452.00) Stalls: High GOING: 0.33 sec per fur (G)

				SP	RR	SF
4670[13]	**Demolition Jo (77)** (PDEvans) **2-8-8v** JFEgan(12) (hld up & bhd: hdwy ½-wy: led ins fnl f: r.o)	—	**1**	20/1	81	54
4458[5]	**The Downtown Fox (78)** (BAMcMahon) **2-8-9** SSanders(2) (a chsng ldrs: hdwy 2f out: kpt on wl towards fin)	1	**2**	25/1	79	52
4634[2]	**Inchalong (71)** (MBrittain) **2-7-9**(7) DMernagh(1) (a cl up: led over 1f out tl ins fnl f: no ex)	½	**3**	5/1[2]	71	44

				SP	RR	SF
4564^{4}	**Persiano (74)** (JRFanshawe) **2-8-5** NDay(17) (lw: mid div: drvn along: hdwy over 1f out: styd on strly: edgd lft: nrst fin)	s.h	**4**	4/1^{1}	74	47
4522^{7}	**Nuclear Debate (USA) (89)** (MrsJRRamsden) **2-9-6** JFortune(10) (hld up: hdwy on bit 2f out: effrt & ch appr fnl f: rdn & fnd nil)	1	**5**	15/2^{3}	86	59
4411*	**Kheyrah (USA) (90)** (EALDunlop) **2-9-7** RHills(13) (chsd ldrs: wkng whn sltly hmpd ins fnl f)	5	**6**	5/1^{2}	74	47
3925^{4}	**Contrary Mary (90)** (GLewis) **2-9-7** PaulEddery(9) (in tch: effrt over 2f out: nvr able chal)	1¼	**7**	25/1	71	44
4479^{2}	**Love Again (75)** (MBell) **2-8-1**$^{(5)}$ RMullen(5) (chsd ldrs tl rdn 2f out: grad wknd)	1	**8**	16/1	53	26
4311^{3}	**Dancing Wolf (IRE) (77)** (MissGayKelleway) **2-8-8** JReid(7) (b.hind: stdd s: effrt ½-wy: nvr rchd ldrs)	nk	**9**	8/1	54	27
*4479**	**Blue Kite (87)** (NPLittmoden) **2-9-4** JWeaver(8) (hld up & bhd: effrt ½-wy: n.d)	1¼	**10**	14/1	61	34
4419^{2}	**Swanmore Lady (IRE) (65)** (SCWilliams) **2-7-3**$^{(7)}$ DarrenWilliams(18) (led tl hdd & wknd over 1f out)	nk	**11**	25/1	38	11
4462*	**Lady Charlotte (85)** (DRCElsworth) **2-9-2** TQuinn(4) (in tch: rdn ½-wy: grad wknd)	nk	**12**	14/1	57	30
4284^{2}	**Premium Pursuit (85)** (RAFahey) **2-9-2** RCochrane(16) (lw: in tch tl outpcd fr ½-wy)	hd	**13**	12/1	57	30
4146^{6}	**Sara Moon Classic (IRE) (68)** (KMcAuliffe) **2-7-10v**$^{1(3)}$ RFfrench(11) (spd 4f: wknd)	nk	**14**	25/1	39	12
3892^{11}	**Means Business (IRE) (67)** (BJMeehan) **2-7-12b** MartinDwyer(6) (lw: racd alone stands' side: bhd fr ½-wy)	2	**15**	33/1	33	6
4544^{4}	**Muyassir (IRE) (75)** (CJBenstead) **2-8-6** JQuinn(14) (sn bhd)	9	**16**	20/1	17	—
4173^{3}	**Golden Strategy (IRE) (80)** (RHannon) **2-8-11** DaneO'Neill(15) (b.nr hind: a bhd)	s.h	**17**	16/1	22	—

(SP 136.8%) **17 Rn**

1m 16.55 (4.75) CSF £423.70 CT £2,727.28 TOTE £25.80: £4.00 £3.50 £1.50 £2.00 (£300.70) Trio £465.00 OWNER Mr John Pugh (WELSHPOOL) BRED Bylon Farmers Ltd

LONG HANDICAP Swanmore Lady (IRE) 7-9

4468 Demolition Jo is tough beyond belief and, having her thirteenth race of the season, showed as much enthusiasm as ever. (20/1)

4458 The Downtown Fox keeps running well and this, his first attempt in handicaps, gives the impression that there is a race to be found, and he should get a bit further. (25/1)

4634 Inchalong, as usual, ran her heart out, but was never quite good enough. (5/1)

4564 Persiano ran well at his first attempt in handicap company, but he did leave the impression that longer trips would bring improvement. (4/1)

4522 Nuclear Debate (USA) travelled so well it looked a question of 'how far? 'when produced approaching the final furlong but, when asked, the response was extremely disappointing. He has so much ability if he can ever be persuaded to use it fully. (15/2: 9/2-8/1)

4411* Kheyrah (USA) had her chances but was back-pedalling when the fourth hampered her inside the last furlong. (5/1)

3925 Contrary Mary has ability but looks a bit of a funny customer. (25/1)

4756 OLIVIER DOUIEB MEMORIAL RATED STKS H'CAP (0-105) (3-Y.O+) (Class B)

3-10 (3-13) **5f (Rowley)** £9,668.96 (£3,580.64: £1,720.32: £705.60: £282.80: £113.68) Stalls: Low GOING: 0.33 sec per fur (G)

				SP	RR	SF
4100^{15}	**The Puzzler (IRE) (98)** (BWHills) **6-9-5** MHills(7) (stdd s: hdwy 2f out: r.o strly to ld last stride)	—	**1**	20/1	105	65
4280^{15}	**The Gay Fox (86)** (BAMcMahon) **3-8-7** LDettori(18) (led far side tl ct post)	s.h	**2**	11/1	93	53
4677^{2}	**Ansellman (86)** (JBerry) **7-8-2b**$^{(5)}$ CLowther(11) (a.p: hrd rdn & ev ch ins fnl f: r.o)	hd	**3**	8/1^{2}	93	53
4457^{2}	**Crofters Ceilidh (94)** (BAMcMahon) **5-9-1** SSanders(4) (a.p: ev ch 1f out: r.o)	s.h	**4**	14/1	100	60
4525^{8}	**Hello Mister (90)** (TEPowell) **6-8-8**$^{(3)}$ PMcCabe(13) (a chsng ldrs: ev ch fr 2f out: rdn & r.o towards fin)	nk	**5**	16/1	95	55
4677^{4}	**Repertory (86)** (MSSaunders) **4-8-7** SDrowne(15) (chsd ldrs far side: kpt on u.p ins fnl f)	hd	**6**	20/1	91	51
4444^{8}	**Twice as Sharp (88)** (PWHarris) **5-8-9** TQuinn(9) (trckd ldrs: hrd drvn appr fnl f: unable qckn)	¾	**7**	11/1	91	51
4430*	**Gaelic Storm (90)** (MJohnston) **3-8-11** JWeaver(12) (bhd: effrt 2f out: nvr nrr)	nk	**8**	9/2^{1}	92	52
4100^{5}	**Lago Di Varano (86)** (RMWhitaker) **5-8-7b** DeanMcKeown(3) (hdwy over 1f out: kpt on u.p ins fnl f)	s.h	**9**	14/1	88	48
4457*	**Tadeo (100)** (MJohnston) **4-9-7** RHills(6) (trckd ldrs centre over 3f)	nk	**10**	16/1	101	61
4677^{5}	**Surprise Mission (89)** (MrsJRRamsden) **5-8-10** JFortune(16) (hld up: effrt 2f out: rdn & one pce fnl f)	hd	**11**	8/1^{2}	89	49
4226^{3}	**Double Splendour (IRE) (95)** (PSFelgate) **7-8-13**$^{(3)}$ AWhelan(10) (nvr nr to chal)	¾	**12**	20/1	93	53
4282^{27}	**Bold Effort (FR) (94)** (KOCunningham-Brown) **5-9-1b** KFallon(8) (outpcd)	½	**13**	14/1	90	50
4467^{5}	**Indian Spark (97)** (JSGoldie) **3-9-4** RCochrane(17) (lost tch fr ½-wy)	1	**14**	20/1	90	50
4553*	**Bowden Rose (96)** (MBlanshard) **5-9-0b**$^{(3)}$ DSweeney(1) (racd centre: hdwy 2f out: rdn over 1f out: sn wknd)	hd	**15**	14/1	89	49
4677*	**Dancethenightaway (92)** (BJMeehan) **3-8-13** ^{3x} JReid(5) (w ldrs tl rdn & wknd over 1f out)	2	**16**	10/1^{3}	78	38
4423^{22}	**Ursa Major (86)** (PAKelleway) **3-8-7** JQuinn(2) (outpcd)	13	**17**	66/1	31	—
4155^{5}	**March Crusader (86)** (BHanbury) **3-8-7** WRyan(14) (uns rdr leaving stalls)		**U**	12/1	—	—

(SP 132.8%) **18 Rn**

62.54 secs (3.84) CSF £207.52 CT £1,823.87 TOTE £14.50: £4.80 £2.20 £2.60 £4.40 (£137.80) Trio £722.90 OWNER Lady Richard Wellesley (LAMBOURN)

LONG HANDICAP Ansellman 8-5 Repertory 8-5 The Gay Fox 8-6 Ursa Major 8-4

3975 The Puzzler (IRE), much more effective when he can get his toe in, only got up in the final stride, but he gave the impression he was only asked to do just enough. He can strike again whilst the iron is hot. (20/1)

3975 The Gay Fox forced the pace at the far rail and looked to be holding a host of challengers inside the final furlong, but to the surprise of many, the line had arrived a stride too late. (11/1)

4677 Ansellman turned in another sparkling display and once again just failed to gain the day. This was the third successive time that the photo-finish verdict has gone against him. (8/1)

4457 Crofters Ceilidh prefers a sounder surface but she is in the form of her life just now and certainly deserves to win another race. (14/1)

4444 Hello Mister seems to need a slightly stiffer test of stamina now but he was fighting for supremacy throughout the last quarter-mile and did not fail for the want of trying. (16/1)

4677 Repertory is not enjoying the success he deserves for he is performing to the best of his ability just now, and fortunes should favour him before long. (20/1)

3600 Twice as Sharp, very free to post, was never far away and, battling on under pressure inside the final furlong, could make amends before the season closes. (11/1)

4430* Gaelic Storm has got plenty of speed as he showed at Epsom, but he was given just too much to do on this occasion and, in this company, ridden this way, would need all of six furlongs. (9/2)

4757 MILCARS H'CAP (0-85) (3-Y.O+) (Class D)

3-40 (3-48) **1m (Rowley)** £8,032.00 (£2,416.00: £1,168.00: £544.00) Stalls: High GOING: 0.33 sec per fur (G)

				SP	RR	SF
4583*	**Jay-Owe-Two (IRE) (77)** (RMWhitaker) **3-9-3v** ^{6x} DeanMcKeown(8) (sn trckng ldrs: led 2f out: rdn clr: styd on wl)	—	**1**	16/1	87	64
4441^{15}	**Comanche Companion (63)** (TJNaughton) **7-8-6** AClark(15) (hdwy ½-wy: kpt on wl fnl f: nrst fin)	nk	**2**	33/1	72	52
4441^{2}	**Consort (84)** (MrsAJPerrett) **4-9-13** KFallon(21) (s.s: hdwy ½-wy: chsng ldrs 1f out: kpt on wl u.p)	½	**3**	8/1^{2}	92	72
4578^{11}	**Cybertechnology (81)** (BWHills) **3-9-7** MHills(10) (hdwy over 2f out: kpt on wl fnl f: nrst fin)	½	**4**	25/1	88	65

4635[2]	**Master Beveled (71)** (PDEvans) **7-9-0** JFEgan(30) (in tch: outpcd over 3f out: kpt on wl fnl 2f)	1¼	**5**	6/1[1]	76	56
4410[14]	**Grand Musica (78)** (IABalding) **4-9-7** MartinDwyer(19) (in tch: ev ch 2f out: wknd ins fnl f)	½	**6**	33/1	82	62
1670[8]	**No More Pressure (IRE) (80)** (MrsJRRamsden) **3-9-6** JFortune(6) (bhd: hdwy u.p 3f out: styd on: nrst fin)	3	**7**	20/1	78	55
4375[6]	**Refuse To Lose (78)** (JMPEustace) **3-9-4** RCochrane(26) (chsd ldrs tl wknd fnl 2½f)	1½	**8**	20/1	73	50
*4570**	**Pericles (73)** (MissGayKelleway) **3-8-13** JReid(9) (effrt 3f out: styd on: no imp)	1½	**9**	11/1	65	42
4606[3]	**Defined Feature (IRE) (69)** (DrJDScargill) **4-8-12b** JQuinn(14) (b.hind: in tch: drvn along 3f out: no imp)	¾	**10**	40/1	59	39
3976[18]	**Trading Aces (70)** (MBell) **3-8-5v(5)** RMullen(24) (effrt ½-wy: styd on: n.d)	1¼	**11**	40/1	58	35
2775[9]	**Sky Dome (IRE) (80)** (MHTompkins) **4-9-6(3)** MHenry(23) (a chsng ldrs: one pce fnl 2f)	2½	**12**	25/1	63	43
4423[17]	**Young Precedent (83)** (PWHarris) **3-9-4(5)** CLowther(17) (lw: led tl hdd 2f out: wknd)	2	**13**	14/1	62	39
4158[4]	**Arco Colora (60)** (DRCElsworth) **3-7-11(3)** RFfrench(12) (cl up tl wknd fnl 2f)	nk	**14**	33/1	38	15
4631[4]	**Mutabari (USA) (70)** (KMahdi) **3-8-10** RHills(13) (chsd ldrs tl wknd fnl 3f)	nk	**15**	50/1	48	25
4277[3]	**Mount Holly (USA) (75)** (JHMGosden) **3-9-1** LDettori(20) (hld up: effrt ½-wy: btn & eased fnl 2f)	nk	**16**	6/1[1]	52	29
4637[W]	**Yalta (IRE) (84)** (RCharlton) **4-9-13b** TSprake(27) (w ldr tl wknd fnl 2½f)	3	**17**	16/1	55	35
4680[10]	**Polar Eclipse (75)** (BJMeehan) **4-9-4** MTebbutt(22) (n.d)	s.h	**18**	33/1	46	26
4304[12]	**Young Butt (57)** (BAPearce) **4-8-0** GBardwell(16) (b: n.d)	1¾	**19**	66/1	25	5
3976[21]	**Jibereen (60)** (PHowling) **5-8-3** PaulEddery(3) (b: led stands' side: rdn 3f out: sn no ch)	s.h	**20**	20/1	27	7
4591[6]	**Giko (62)** (JRPoulton) **3-8-2** SDrowne(18) (n.d)	1½	**21**	33/1	26	3
4558[12]	**Silk St John (82)** (MJRyan) **3-9-8** GCarter(2) (racd stands' side: effrt ½-wy: eased whn no ch fnl f)	½	**22**	9/1[3]	45	22
3320[5]	**Manikato (USA) (57)** (DJSCosgrove) **3-7-11v** NAdams(25) (in tch over 5f)	nk	**23**	50/1	20	—
4015[6]	**Interdream (77)** (RHannon) **3-9-3** DaneO'Neill(7) (b.nr hind: n.d)	3	**24**	20/1	34	11
4210[9]	**Monte Cavo (55)** (MBrittain) **6-7-5(7)** DMernagh(29) (nvr trbld ldrs)	1	**25**	25/1	10	—
4308[3]	**Green Power (83)** (JRFanshawe) **3-9-9** TQuinn(1) (lw: racd stands' side: outpcd & bhd fr ½-wy)	8	**26**	25/1	22	—
4410[4]	**Sualtach (IRE) (70)** (RHollinshead) **4-8-13** WRyan(4) (lw: racd stands' side: outpcd & bhd fnl 3f)	¾	**27**	20/1	7	—
3888[12]	**Double-J (IRE) (78)** (KMcAuliffe) **3-9-4** SSanders(11) (racd alone centre: spd 5f: wknd)	1½	**28**	33/1	12	—
1833[4]	**Stellar Line (USA) (69)** (MJPolglase) **4-8-12** JWeaver(5) (racd stands' side: bhd fr ½-wy)	3	**29**	40/1	—	—
3248[2]	**Waikiki Beach (USA) (64)** (GLMoore) **6-8-7** CandyMorris(28) (bhd fr ½-wy: t.o)	17	**30**	33/1	—	—

(SP 149.0%) **30 Rn**

1m 43.55 (6.25) CSF £441.83 CT £4,172.67 TOTE £22.20: £4.80 £6.20 £2.50 £5.80 (£158.80) Trio £3,078.60; £2,601.69 to Newmarket 17/10/97 OWNER Mr R. M. Whitaker (LEEDS) BRED Thoroughbred Trust

WEIGHT FOR AGE 3yo-3lb

4583* Jay-Owe-Two (IRE), having his second run in the visor, showed just as much enthusiasm as the first time, and once in front he was not going to stop. (16/1)

4262a Comanche Companion, despite her years, is in good form and she was certainly sticking gamely to her task. (33/1)

4441 Consort has plenty of ability but is certainly not an easy ride, although he always has to be considered in such events. (8/1)

4578 Cybertechnology likes to come from off a strong pace and was eating up the ground late on, but needed another half-furlong to make it. (25/1)

4635 Master Beveled found this trip just a shade too sharp on this occasion, and after getting well outpaced, was sticking on doggedly at the finish. (6/1)

Grand Musica showed his first signs of form this season here, and looks to be coming right. (33/1)

853 No More Pressure (IRE), having only his second run for his new stable, has also had over four months off, and was noted picking up heaps of ground in the last three furlongs. (20/1)

1245 Trading Aces, after six weeks off, showed a little and should be all the better for it. (40/1)

4758 E.B.F. CHESTERTON MAIDEN STKS (2-Y.O) (Class D)

4-15 (4-24) **1m (Rowley)** £8,334.00 (£2,502.00: £1,206.00: £558.00) Stalls: High GOING: 0.33 sec per fur (G)

				SP	RR	SF
	Border Arrow (IABalding) **2-9-0** RCochrane(10) (neat: unf: hld up & bhd: hdwy 2f out: led ins fnl f: sn clr: impressive)	—	**1**	33/1	95++	58
	Albarahin (USA) (SbinSuroor) **2-9-0** LDettori(7) (gd sort: wl grwn: a.p: led wl over 1f out: hdd & one pce fnl f)	3	**2**	7/4[1]	89+	52
3978[3]	**Bering Gifts (IRE)** (PFICole) **2-9-0** TQuinn(9) (lw: a.p: led over 2f out: sn hdd: one pce fnl f)	3½	**3**	10/1	82	45
4575[2]	**Rainbow Ways** (BWHills) **2-9-0** MHills(16) (a w ldrs: ev ch & rdn 2f out: one pce fnl f)	½	**4**	2/1[2]	81	44
4439[6]	**Sherganzar** (MSalaman) **2-9-0** DaneO'Neill(12) (a chsng ldrs: ev ch 2f out: rdn over 1f out: one pce)	3½	**5**	33/1	74	37
	La Rochelle (IRE) (CEBrittain) **2-8-9** JFortune(8) (w'like: mid div: went prom ½-wy: styd on one pce appr fnl f)	1½	**6**	50/1	66	29
3688[4]	**Eagle's Cross (USA)** (RCharlton) **2-9-0** TSprake(1) (hld up: hdwy over 3f out: wknd fnl 2f)	1¾	**7**	12/1	68	31
4526[20]	**Regal Patriarch (IRE)** (JLDunlop) **2-9-0** GCarter(3) (bhd tl styd on fnl 2f)	s.h	**8**	33/1	67	30
	Silver Sun (DRCElsworth) **2-8-9** SDrowne(5) (lt-f: leggy: bhd: hdwy ½-wy: nvr rchd ldrs)	1¼	**9**	50/1	60	23
	Baffin Bay (HRACecil) **2-9-0** KFallon(13) (gd sort: chsd ldrs over 5f: sn rdn & outpcd)	s.h	**10**	9/1[3]	65	28
	Generous Terms (HCandy) **2-9-0** JReid(6) (w'like: nvr nr to chal)	1	**11**	20/1	63	26
	Tartan Lass (RGuest) **2-8-9** PBloomfield(19) (leggy: scope: hld up in rr: hdwy fnl 2f: nvr nrr)	1¼	**12**	50/1	55	18
	Lemon Bridge (IRE) (JWHills) **2-9-0** RHills(4) (lt-f: nvr nrr)	½	**13**	33/1	59	22
4384[2]	**Free Option (IRE)** (BHanbury) **2-9-0** WRyan(23) (lw: led tl over 2f out: sn rdn & wknd)	nk	**14**	14/1	59	22
4514[5]	**Glory of Love** (JHetherton) **2-9-0** MTebbutt(15) (prom: pushed along 3f out: grad wknd)	s.h	**15**	33/1	59	22
	Scorned (GER) (IABalding) **2-9-0** MartinDwyer(17) (leggy: scope: s.s: a in rr)	hd	**16**	33/1	58	21
	High And Mighty (JHMGosden) **2-8-11(3)** RFfrench(14) (neat: dwlt: a in rr)	¾	**17**	25/1	57	20
4367[5]	**Allgrit (USA)** (EALDunlop) **2-9-0** DO'Donohoe(22) (prom over 5f)	1¾	**18**	50/1	53	16
	Franklin Lakes (CAHorgan) **2-9-0** PaulEddery(11) (cmpt: bkwd: prom early: sn lost tch: t.o)	3½	**19**	50/1	46	9
4556[7]	**Sassy Lady (IRE)** (CADwyer) **2-8-9** AClark(2) (bhd fr ½-wy: t.o)	5	**20**	50/1	31	—
	U K Magic (IRE) (JEBanks) **2-9-0** JQuinn(18) (neat: hmpd after 2f: sn lost pl: t.o)	10	**21**	50/1	16	—
	Rajati (USA) (MrsJCecil) **2-9-0** JWeaver(20) (gd sort: bit bkwd: a bhd: t.o)	9	**22**	33/1	—	—

(SP 146.1%) **22 Rn**

1m 43.82 (6.52) CSF £87.07 TOTE £124.60: £14.90 £1.70 £2.90 (£298.40) Trio £245.90 OWNER R P B Michaelson & Wafic Said (KINGSCLERE) BRED Lord Halifax

Border Arrow has still to fill to his frame but he is out of a middle-distance winner, and the way he lengthened to draw clear up the hill stamps him as a very useful stayer in the making. (33/1)

Albarahin (USA), a useful-looking newcomer, related to winners abroad, looked to have this in safe keeping when showing with a two-length advantage into the final furlong, but the winner brushed him aside with ease, and, as he is considered up with the best, how good is his conqueror? (7/4)

3978 Bering Gifts (IRE) showed much more promise on this better ground but the leading pair shot right away from him in the closing stages, and he could not do a lot about it. (10/1: 5/1-12/1)
4575 Rainbow Ways broke well and was with the pace, holding every chance until feeling the strain when faced with the hill. (2/1)
4439 Sherganzar again ran a race full of promise and, as in the past, showed he has plenty of speed, and it might be worth taking a chance with him over six furlongs. (33/1)
La Rochelle (IRE), a May foal, bred to need middle-distances, was given a nice introduction to the game, and she should be able to improve on this. (50/1)
3688 Eagle's Cross (USA) (12/1: 5/1-14/1)
Regal Patriarch (IRE), a half-brother to St Leger winner Silver Patriarch, performed much better than he did on his debut, and he is getting to realise what is required. (33/1)
Baffin Bay (9/1: 6/1-12/1)

4759 SEVERALS CONDITIONS STKS (3-Y.O+) (Class B)
4-50 (4-53) **1m 2f (Rowley)** £7,953.60 (£2,942.40: £1,411.20: £576.00: £228.00: £88.80) Stalls: High GOING: 0.33 sec per fur (G)

				SP	RR	SF
	Santillana (USA) (112) (JHMGosden) **4-9-0** LDettori(6) (lw: hld up: qcknd to ld 1½f out: r.o)	—	**1**	6/1	109	70
4565[10]	**Zugudi (71)** (KMahdi) **3-8-9** RCochrane(5) (plld hrd: trckd ldrs: effrt 2f out: styd on wl towards fin)	¾	**2**	100/1	108?	64
4558[5]	**Sandmoor Chambray (101)** (TDEasterby) **6-9-0** SSanders(2) (lw: a chsng ldrs: pushed along over 3f out: kpt on wl)	1½	**3**	7/2[2]	105	66
4312*	**Barnum Sands (105)** (JLDunlop) **3-9-0** TQuinn(1) (led: rdn over 2f out: hdd 1 1/2f out: r.o one pce)	½	**4**	9/2[3]	110	66
1771[8]	**Rocky Oasis (USA) (97)** (MRStoute) **4-9-3** JReid(7) (trckd ldrs: n.m.r 2f out: swtchd & r.o towards fin)	s.h	**5**	14/1	108	69
4552[2]	**Silverani (IRE) (100)** (LMCumani) **3-8-12** KFallon(3) (s.s: in tch after 2f: outpcd over 2f out: kpt on towards fin)	nk	**6**	7/4[1]	107	63
4377[5]	**Oh Nellie (USA) (110)** (NACallaghan) **3-8-4** SDrowne(4) (cl up tl wknd fnl 2f)	8	**7**	6/1	86	42
				(SP 113.0%)		**7 Rn**

2m 11.52 (6.82) CSF £248.12 TOTE £4.20: £2.60 £6.40 (£116.30) OWNER Sheikh Mohammed (NEWMARKET) BRED Mr David Caldwell
WEIGHT FOR AGE 3yo-5lb
Santillana (USA), returning after well over a year off with injury, looked as good as ever and, although he had to battle to hold on, defeat was never on the cards. (6/1: 3/1-13/2)
3615 Zugudi, stepping up in trip, obviously has plenty of ability as he spent most of the race pulling too hard, but then kept on really well when ridden in the closing stages. (100/1)
4558 Sandmoor Chambray was one of the first off the bit, but this game and consistent sort kept battling away, if never quite up to it. (7/2)
4312* Barnum Sands tried his best to pinch this, by quickening from the front approaching the last two furlongs, but was never quite good enough. (9/2)
1476 Rocky Oasis (USA), has plenty of ability when things go his way but, short of room here, was certainly not knocked about. The kindness should be repaid. (14/1)
4552 Silverani (IRE), showed signs of temperament, by missing the break by many lengths. This was certainly not his true running. (7/4)
4377 Oh Nellie (USA) found this trip stretching her stamina. (6/1: 5/1-8/1)

T/Jkpt: Not won; £20,735.50 to Newmarket 17/10/97. T/Plpt: £7,336.30 (6.54 Tckts). T/Qdpt: £88.10 (53.32 Tckts) IM/AA

4659a-SAN SIRO (Milan, Italy) (R-H) (Good to soft)
Saturday October 11th

4760a PREMIO QUADERNA (3-Y.O+)
1-05 (1-05) **1m 2f** £11,571.00 (£5,091.00: £2,777.00)

				SP	RR	SF
1553a[5]	**Risiat (IRE)** (EBorromeo,Italy) **3-9-0** MDemuro	—	**1**		111	—
	Strachin (LMCumani) **3-8-9** CFiocchi	4½	**2**		99	—
4541a[2]	**Brave Indigo** (Italy) **4-9-2** EBotti	1¾	**3**		98	—
						4 Rn

2m 6.8 (12.80) Tote 13L: 12L 18L (33L) OWNER Scuderia Rencati Srl BRED Azienda Agricola Francesca
Strachin made a decent debut, but was no match for the winner. Held up in the rear, he quickened nicely in the last furlong but could not get on terms.

4761a PREMIO TESERO (2-Y.O)
1-30 (1-33) **7f 110y** £9,642.00 (£4,243.00: £2,314.00)

				SP	RR	SF
4379[2]	**Chief Whip (USA)** (LMCumani) **2-8-9** FJovine	—	**1**		90	—
	Elmortero Derufino (IRE) (Italy) **2-8-8** GForte	2½	**2**		84	—
	Golden Spanish (USA) (Italy) **2-8-6** GBietolini	¾	**3**		80	—
						6 Rn

1m 34.1 (9.60) Tote 15L: 12L 19L (39L) OWNER Mr Michael Kerr-Dineen (NEWMARKET) BRED Vinery & Ben P. Walden, Sr.
4379 Chief Whip (USA) was too good for his rivals and, making all the running, never looked likely to be caught.

3182a-DUSSELDORF (Germany) (R-H) (Soft)
Sunday October 12th

4762a GROSSER PREIS VON DUSSELDORF (Gp 2) (3-Y.O+)
3-25 (3-27) **1m 110y** £30,303.00 (£12,121.00: £6,061.00: £3,030.00)

				SP	RR	SF
4463*	**Crimson Tide (IRE)** (JWHills) **3-8-9** MHills (trckd ldr: led 2f out: sn clr: hung lft ins fnl f)	—	**1**		115	—
4124a[10]	**Lagarto (GER)** (HJentzsch,Germany) **5-9-0** PSchiergen (led: rn wde ent st: hdd 2f out: one pace)	6	**2**		106	—
4396a[6]	**Sambakonig (GER)** (HHorwart,Germany) **4-9-0** PHarley (hld up in rr: r.o fnl 2f)	1½	**3**		103	—
3998a[2]	**Ferrari (GER)** (PLautner,Germany) **3-8-8** WNewnes (mid-div: hdwy st: no imp)	1	**4**		98	—
4122a*	**Waky Nao** (BSchutz,Germany) **4-9-0** AStarke (hld up: hdwy st: no imp)	1½	**5**		98	—
	Tres Heureux (GER) (FrauEMader,Germany) **7-9-0** LMader (a bhd)	3½	**6**		92	—

					SP	RR	SF
4650a[2]	**Kalatos (GER)** (AWohler,Germany) **5-9-2** ABoschert (prom tl wknd over 3f out)	12	**7**			71	—
	Lanelly (GER) (HBlume,Germany) **3-8-4** ABest (cl up tl wknd after ½-way)	8	**8**			47	—

8 Rn

1m 47.35 Tote 71DM: 27DM 28DM 25DM (1340DM) OWNER Mr Christopher Wright (LAMBOURN) BRED Barronstown Stud and Roncon Ltd
4463* Crimson Tide (IRE), stepped up in class, produced a fine effort to win by six lengths. After stalking the leader he went for home a quarter of a mile out and quickly opened up a gap. He hung badly in the closing stages but had the race won by then. He may well go to Italy next.

4760a-SAN SIRO (Milan, Italy) (R-H) (Good to firm)
Sunday October 12th

4763a PREMIO IRISH NATIONAL STUD (3-Y.O+)
3-05 (3-10) **1m 2f** £11,571.00 (£5,091.00: £2,777.00)

				SP	RR	SF
3005a[2]	**Viscoumtess Brave (IRE)** (LordHuntingdon) **3-8-9** CColombi	—	**1**		100+	—
	Windy Day (IRE) (Italy) **3-8-9** EBotti	3¾	**2**		94	—
	Pershex (IRE) (Italy) **5-9-0** GForte	s.h	**3**		94	—

8 Rn

2m 5.2 (11.20) Tote 16L: 11L 17L 18L (69L) OWNER Scuderia San Pancrazio (WEST ILSLEY)
3005a Viscoumtess Brave (IRE) was the first leg of a Lord Huntingdon double. After racing in mid-division, she moved through to hit the front two furlongs out and ran out a very comfortable winner.

4764a PREMIO DORMELLO (Gp 3) (2-Y.O)
4-05 (4-17) **1m** £33,387.00 (£15,475.00: £8,671.00)

				SP	RR	SF
3872a*	**Wren (IRE)** (LordHuntingdon) **2-8-11** FJovine	—	**1**		100+	—
4397a*	**Sopran Londa (IRE)** (LCamici,Italy) **2-8-11** MDemuro	4¾	**2**		91	—
2996b*	**Andoya (FR)** (ARenzoni,Italy) **2-8-11** OFancera	hd	**3**		90	—

9 Rn

1m 39.6 (9.60) Tote 17L: 12L 15L 20L (36L) OWNER Anglia Bloodstock Ltd (WEST ILSLEY) BRED Barnane Partnership
3008a* Wren (IRE) produced a very good turn of foot and spreadeagled her rivals. Racing in fifth, she made headway to lead two furlongs out and soon put daylight between herself and her pursuers. She is on the upgrade.

4765a PREMIO OMENONI (Gp 3) (3-Y.O+)
4-35 (4-45) **5f** £32,831.00 (£15,058.00: £8,393.00)

				SP	RR	SF
2102a[2]	**Armando Carpio** (ARenzoni,Italy) **4-8-10** OFancera	—	**1**		116	—
	Grey Perri (JPotempa,Italy) **4-8-4** RKalmus	1	**2**		107	—
1201a[3]	**Nil (IRE)** (SBenedetti,Italy) **4-8-7** PPerlanti	2½	**3**		102	—

10 Rn

58.4 secs (3.20) Tote 36L: 14L 14L 22L (43L) OWNER Scuderia Jerome BRED Super King Srl

4662a-LONGCHAMP (Paris, France) (R-H) (Very soft)
Sunday October 12th

4766a GRAND CRITERIUM (Gp 1) (2-Y.O C & F)
2-30 (4-54) **1m** £112,233.00 (£44,893.00: £22,447.00: £11,223.00)

				SP	RR	SF
4255a*	**Second Empire (IRE)** (APO'Brien,Ireland) **2-9-0** MJKinane (trckd ldr: rdn over 2f out: led 1½f out: r.o strly)	—	**1**	4/5[1]	116	—
4391a[2]	**Charge D'Affaires** (AdeRoyerDupre,France) **2-9-0** GMosse (hld up: hdwy st: hrd rdn 2f out: r.o wl)	1½	**2**	23/10[2]	113	—
4140*	**Alboostan** (DMorley) **2-9-0** RHills (led tl hdd 1½f out: no ex)	3	**3**	102/10	107	—
4524[2]	**Carrowkeel (IRE)** (BWHills) **2-9-0** LDettori (3rd early: rdn over 2f out: one pce)	3	**4**	33/10[3]	101	—
	Worms (IRE) (HVandePoele,France) **2-9-0** OPeslier (a rr: n.d)	2½	**5**	109/10	96	—

(SP 126.4%) **16 Rn**

1m 47.7 (12.70) P-M 1.80F: 1.10F 1.10F (SF 4.30F) OWNER Mr M. Tabor (PILTOWN)
4255a* Second Empire (IRE), a fine-looking colt with a good action, put up a really decent effort on dead ground which would have not been in his favour. He never looked like being beaten once in front, and beat a good yardstick in the runner-up. He was made favourite for the 2,000 Guineas after this, and that may be his next race, as he will not run again this year and is unlikely to have a previous run before Newmarket. He gives the impression that he may get further than a mile in time. (4/5)
4391a Charge D'Affaires looked dangerous two furlongs out, but could never land a serious blow. Another who was probably unsuited by the testing ground, he nevertheless ran his race. He has performed consistently in the highest grade this season, with his victory in the Morny his best effort. He will be entered in the 2,000 Guineas and the Poulains, with the latter probably his best chance of avoiding Xaar and Second Empire. (23/10)
4140* Alboostan took the field along, but was outclassed by the front two. He will not run again this year, but is likely to run over longer distances in 1998. (102/10)
4524 Carrowkeel (IRE) was never really seen with a chance. He did not appear to act on the surface, and was probably out of his depth. (33/10)

4746-CATTERICK (L-H) (Soft, Good to soft patches)
Friday October 17th
WEATHER: Unsettled WIND: moderate, half behind

4767 RICHMONDSHIRE NURSERY H'CAP (0-85) (2-Y.O) (Class E)
2-10 (2-13) **7f** £3,460.25 (£1,037.00: £498.50: £229.25) Stalls: Low GOING: 0.64 sec per fur (GS)

				SP	RR	SF
4564[11]	**Ray of Sunshine (IRE) (70)** (MrsJRRamsden) **2-8-11** JFortune(2) (b.nr fore: s.i.s: hdwy ½-wy: hrd rdn to ld over 1f out: hld on towards fin)	—	**1**	8/1[2]	73	28

				SP	RR	SF
4690^{2}	**Prince Ashleigh (74)** (PCHaslam) **2-8-10**(5) CLowther(14) (lw: sn trckng ldrs: barged thro & ev ch ins fnl f: nt qckn nr fin)	½	**2**	11/2^{1}	76	31
4502^{4}	**Rubamma (79)** (PTWalwyn) **2-9-6** RPerham(7) (hld up: hdwy far side 2f out: edgd rt: ev ch & hmpd ins fnl f)	1¼	**3**	12/1	78	33
3932^{6}	**Sandmoor Tartan (63)** (TDEasterby) **2-8-4** LCharnock(5) (trckd ldrs: led 2f out: sn hdd & nt qckn)	1¾	**4**	8/1^{2}	58	13
4588^{3}	**Petara (IRE) (66)** (JSWainwright) **2-8-7v** FLynch(6) (bhd: hdwy & ev ch over 1f out: styng on sme pce whn hmpd ins fnl f: eased nr fin)	s.h	**5**	12/1	61+	16
4427^{4}	**Marske Machine (62)** (NTinkler) **2-8-3b** KimTinkler(11) (sn bhd & drvn along: styd on fnl 2f: nt rch ldrs)	nk	**6**	10/1^{3}	56	11
3755^{10}	**Barrelbio (IRE) (60)** (JJO'Neill) **2-8-1** GBardwell(12) (sn bhd & drvn along: styd on fnl 2f: nt rch ldrs)	1¾	**7**	12/1	50	5
4514*	**Misalliance (80)** (CFWall) **2-9-7** GDuffield(15) (bhd & drvn along ½-wy: hdwy 2f out: kpt on same pce: nvr nr to chal)	2	**8**	8/1^{2}	66	21
3932^{8}	**Fast Franc (IRE) (62)** (SCWilliams) **2-8-3** TWilliams(3) (w ldrs: edgd rt & led over 2f out: sn hdd: wknd over 1f out)	2	**9**	20/1	43	—
4265^{6}	**Miss Salsa Dancer (66)** (DenysSmith) **2-8-4**(3) PFessey(16) (sn chsng ldrs: outpcd fnl 2f)	1	**10**	20/1	45	—
4702^{6}	**Deeceebee (80)** (WStorey) **2-9-7** OPears(10) (swtg: bhd & drvn along ½-wy: n.d)	s.h	**11**	20/1	59	14
4433^{9}	**Laramania (70)** (PDEvans) **2-8-11** JFEgan(4) (sn bhd & drvn along)	1¼	**12**	33/1	46	1
4560^{7}	**Princess Natalie (76)** (MWEasterby) **2-9-3** TLucas(9) (led to ½-wy: sn wknd)	½	**13**	16/1	51	6
3186^{8}	**Respond (74)** (GLMoore) **2-9-1** AClark(17) (rr div: effrt whn bdly hmpd over 2f out: nt rcvr)	3	**14**	8/1^{2}	42+	—
3802^{7}	**Suggest (71)** (WStorey) **2-8-12** JFanning(1) (sn chsng ldrs: wkng whn hmpd over 2f out)	nk	**15**	20/1	38	—
4542^{5}	**Royal Interview (IRE) (68)** (MRChannon) **2-8-9** ACulhane(13) (hdwy on outside to ld ½-wy: hdd over 2f out: sn wknd)	nk	**16**	16/1	34	—
4501^{2}	**Counsel (63)** (CEBrittain) **2-7-13**(5) RMullen(8) (plld hrd: w ldrs tl wknd over 2f out)	2½	**17**	12/1	24	—

(SP 133.4%) **17 Rn**

1m 33.7 (10.10) CSF £47.04 CT £522.15 TOTE £13.00: £4.60 £1.80 £3.40 £3.70 (£56.90) Trio £119.90 OWNER Charlton Bloodstock Ltd (THIRSK) BRED Knocktoran Stud

STEWARDS' ENQUIRY Lowther susp 27-28/10/97 (careless riding).

4564 Ray of Sunshine (IRE) again showed a poor action going to post, and was well suited by the give underfoot. Getting cover this time, he responded to strong pressure to scrape home with nothing at all to spare. He was kicked pulling up and it is doubtful if he will reappear this year. (8/1)

4690 Prince Ashleigh looked to be full of running when his young rider decided to press the panic button and barge his way through. Not quite able to get there, he ought to have taken this. (11/2)

4502 Rubamma has a round action, and proved well suited by the ground. Surprisingly sticking to the far side at first turning in, he edged right under pressure, contributing to the runner-up's misfortune. (12/1)

3932 Sandmoor Tartan made the best of his way home, but this trip and this ground seemed to tax his stamina beyond the limit. (8/1)

4588 Petara (IRE) was the meat in the sandwich, but he was only sticking on at the same pace. Even so he would have finished fourth had his rider not dropped his hands near the line. (12/1)

4427 Marske Machine was staying on when it was all over, and will be suited by either a stiffer track or a mile. (10/1)

2762 Barrelbio (IRE) was well-supported at long odds on his first outing for eight weeks. Only getting going late in the day, he is worth a try over a mile. (12/1: op 33/1)

4514* Misalliance looked very fit. The handicapper was taking no chances rating her 80 and, after being slightly messed about, she was not given a hard time of it. She almost certainly needs a more galloping track. (8/1)

2595 Respond was hampered and struck the heels of a horse in front once in line for home, and her rider immediately called it a day.(8/1: op 12/1)

4768 PLODMIRE WOOD APPRENTICE CLAIMING STKS (3-Y.O+) (Class G)

2-45 (2-47) **1m 3f 214y** £2,228.50 (£626.00: £305.50) Stalls: Low GOING: 0.64 sec per fur (GS)

				SP	RR	SF
4713*	**Swan Hunter (60)** (DJSCosgrove) **4-8-8**(3) RMullen(11) (lw: hld up: stdy hdwy 6f out: qcknd to ld 3f out: smoothly)	—	**1**	10/11^{1}	63+	33
4572^{11}	**Night City (84)** (KRBurke) **6-9-4** DSweeney(4) (lw: set str pce: hdd 3f out: kpt on wl: no ch w wnr)	1	**2**	11/2^{2}	69	39
4289*	**Ziggy's Viola (IRE) (50)** (MrsMReveley) **3-7-9**(7) ANicholls(12) (lw: hld up: hdwy over 3f out: remained far side st: edgd rt & kpt on same pce appr fnl f)	1¼	**3**	6/1^{3}	58	21
4109^{16}	**Hillzah (USA) (75)** (RBastiman) **9-9-0**(3) HBastiman(7) (hld up: sme hdwy over 2f out: nvr nr ldrs)	16	**4**	13/2	45	15
4608^{6}	**Jimjareer (IRE) (25)** (CaptJWilson) **4-8-4**(7) AngelaHartley(6) (chsd ldrs: remained far side st: wknd 2f out)	2½	**5**	100/1	35	5
3919^{8}	**Peep O Day (33)** (JLEyre) **6-8-3v**^{1}(7)ow3 SBuckley(3) (b.hind: chsd ldrs: wknd fnl 3f)	2	**6**	16/1	32	—
4692^{5}	**Speculative** (WStorey) **3-8-2**(7) CarolynBales(10) (lw: outpcd & drvn along 5f out: styd far side st: n.d)	2	**7**	6/1^{3}	35	—
3565^{9}	**Stolen Music (IRE) (24)** (REBarr) **4-8-1**(5) IonaWands(5) (s.i.s: bhd: sme hdwy over 3f out: sn wknd)	2½	**8**	66/1	22	—
4453^{10}	**Oakbury (IRE) (34)** (MissLCSiddall) **5-8-6**(5) TSiddall(8) (mid div: drvn along 7f out: sn wl bhd)	5	**9**	100/1	20	—
4609^{5}	**Welcome Lu (26)** (JLHarris) **4-8-8** PPMurphy(9) (trckd ldrs: drvn along 5f out: sn wknd)	7	**10**	14/1	8	—
4407^{5}	**All Girls Forget** (JDBethell) **3-8-0**(3)ow4 CLowther(1) (hld up: bhd & rdn 6f out)	6	**11**	66/1	2	—
4415^{12}	**Raased (33)** (FWatson) **5-8-12v**^{1} PFessey(2) (lw: plld hrd: trckd ldr tl wknd 3f out)	8	**12**	66/1	—	—

(SP 128.7%) **12 Rn**

2m 48.6 (17.20) CSF £6.60 TOTE £2.10: £1.10 £2.50 £2.50 (£5.90) Trio £13.90 OWNER Mr Derrick Yarwood (NEWMARKET) BRED The Arrow Farm and Stud

WEIGHT FOR AGE 3yo-7lb

4713* Swan Hunter, who has a history of bad knees, showed a dreadful action going to post, but once underway it was a different story, and he won this without hardly coming off the bridle. There were eight claims for him, but as far as connections were concerned the right one came out of the hat. (10/11)

4264 Night City had 17lb in hand of the winner on official figures. A keen-going sort, he kept on surprisingly well after setting a very strong pace in this ground. (11/2)

4289* Ziggy's Viola (IRE), who had plenty to do on official figures, surprisingly elected to stay on the far side turning in. At this meeting the only place to race was on the stands-side rail. Doing herself a favour by edging right towards the first two under pressure, this was a creditable effort because she had plenty on at the weights. (6/1)

Hillzah (USA) possibly still needed this. (13/2)

4609 Welcome Lu (14/1: 10/1-16/1)

4769 E.B.F. PROSPECT HILL MAIDEN STKS (2-Y.O) (Class D)

3-20 (3-21) **5f** £3,671.50 (£1,102.00: £531.00: £245.50) Stalls: Low GOING: 0.28 sec per fur (G)

				SP	RR	SF
4428^{R}	**Arjan (IRE)** (JBerry) **2-8-6**(3) TEDurcan(7) (mde all: drvn out)	—	**1**	16/1	75	45
4630^{3}	**Odette** (SirMarkPrescott) **2-8-9** GDuffield(3) (chsd ldrs: rdn ½-wy: styd on ins fnl f)	2½	**2**	7/4^{1}	67	37

				SP	RR	SF
4630^{7}	**St Lucia (IRE)** (BJMeehan) **2-8-9b^{1}** MTebbutt(12) (chsd wnr: rdn ½-wy: kpt on same pce)	½	**3**	3/1^{2}	65	35
4593^{2}	**Killarney Jazz** (JWharton) **2-9-0** TLucas(11) (hdwy ½-wy: kpt on wl: nvr nr to chal)	4	**4**	11/1	58	28
4211^{W}	**Anstand** (MrsJRRamsden) **2-9-0** JFortune(5) (sn outpcd: hdwy 2f out: styd on towards fin)	3	**5**	5/1^{3}	48+	18
	Hit The Spot (IRE) (WJHaggas) **2-8-9** FLynch(13) (cmpt: bkwd: b: sn bhd: stdy hdwy & nt clr run jst ins fnl f: nvr nr ldrs)	6	**6**	12/1	24	—
4544^{11}	**House On Fire (IRE)** (JBerry) **2-8-9**(5) CLowther(6) (sn bhd: sme hdwy 2f out: n.d)	2	**7**	20/1	22	—
	Shocker (IRE) (WJHaggas) **2-8-4**(5) JoHunnam(8) (unf: bkwd: s.i.s: bhd tl stdy hdwy fnl f)	hd	**8**	14/1	17	—
2037^{15}	**Ashangem** (BobJones) **2-9-0** MWigham(10) (outpcd & bhd fr ½-wy)	¾	**9**	25/1	20	—
4630^{15}	**Scurrilous** (MBell) **2-8-9** ACulhane(4) (dwlt: a outpcd)	3½	**10**	16/1	4	—
	Sable Cloak (JLHarris) **2-8-9** LCharnock(14) (lt-f: unf: unruly in stalls: dwlt: a bhd)	6	**11**	25/1	—	—
4428^{9}	**Westcourt Ruby** (MWEasterby) **2-8-6**(3) GParkin(1) (sn drvn along & outpcd: a bhd)	8	**12**	33/1	—	—
4470^{10}	**The Other Risk** (DANolan) **2-8-11**(3) PFessey(2) (chsd ldrs: hung lft & outpcd ½-wy: sn lost pl)	6	**13**	200/1	—	—

(SP 128.4%) **13 Rn**

61.9 secs (4.20) CSF £41.47 TOTE £38.00: £5.50 £1.10 £1.10 (£30.70) Trio £41.20 OWNER Mr W. J. Kelly (COCKERHAM) BRED Ballinacurra Stud

Arjan (IRE), who had refused to race last time, got the favoured stands-side rail, and pulled clear inside the last. This was probably a very modest event. (16/1)

4630 Odette had to use her early speed to overcome a poor draw. In real trouble at halfway, she was sticking on willingly at the end. (7/4)

4630 St Lucia (IRE), who showed a very scratchy action going down, had blinkers on this time. About six lengths behind the runner-up at Nottingham last time, she certainly seemed to show improved form. (3/1)

4593 Killarney Jazz, who was carrying plenty of condition, ran a highly satisfactory race over a furlong-shorter trip and in stronger company. His future will eventually lie in handicaps over further. (11/1)

Anstand, who was withdrawn when kicked at the start at Beverley, looked to have a slightly enlarged near-fore knee. Soon run off his legs, he showed ability, staying on in resolute fashion towards the finish. He obviously needs further, and more significantly one more run before he is qualified for a handicap mark. (5/1: 6/1-10/1)

Hit The Spot (IRE), a backward-looking newcomer, showed a glimmer of ability. but she is a good way off the finished article yet. (12/1: op 5/1)

Shocker (IRE), who showed a scratchy action going down, hinted at better to come in time. (14/1)

4770 CROW HOLE BANK H'CAP (0-85) (3-Y.O+) (Class D)

3-55 (3-57) **5f** £4,003.00 (£1,204.00: £582.00: £271.00) Stalls: Low GOING: 0.28 sec per fur (G)

				SP	RR	SF
4636^{2}	**Polly Golightly (54)** (MBlanshard) **4-7-11b** DaleGibson(19) (chsd ldrs: styd on wl to ld ins fnl f)	—	**1**	4/1^{1}	66	54
4512^{3}	**Squire Corrie (81)** (DWChapman) **5-9-10** ACulhane(12) (lw: w ldrs: led 2f out tl ins fnl f: no ex)	1¼	**2**	8/1^{3}	89	77
4527^{3}	**Passionatti (62)** (SGollings) **3-8-5** TWilliams(11) (led to 2f out: nt qckn appr fnl f)	2½	**3**	9/1	62	50
4527*	**Dominant Air (84)** (SirMarkPrescott) **3-9-13** GDuffield(16) (a chsng ldrs: rdn 2f out: kpt on same pce)	1¼	**4**	11/2^{2}	80	68
4414^{7}	**Palacegate Touch (74)** (JBerry) **7-8-12b**(5) CLowther(3) (chsd ldr far side: kpt on wl appr fnl f)	s.h	**5**	20/1	70	58
4707^{5}	**Pallium (IRE) (53)** (DANolan) **9-7-10b** NKennedy(20) (a in tch: kpt on wl appr fnl f)	nk	**6**	14/1	48	36
4636^{3}	**Pleasure Time (62)** (CSmith) **4-8-5v** JTate(13) (a chsng ldrs: kpt on same pce fnl 2f)	nk	**7**	9/1	56	44
4580^{6}	**Flying Harold (54)** (MRChannon) **4-7-11**^{ow1} FNorton(1) (swtchd rt s: hdwy over 1f out: styd on towards fin)	¾	**8**	33/1	46	33
4636^{11}	**White Emir (72)** (BJMeehan) **4-9-1b** MTebbutt(15) (a in tch: one pce fnl 2f)	¾	**9**	16/1	61	49
4636^{9}	**Just Bob (77)** (SEKettlewell) **8-9-6** JFortune(5) (lw: dwlt: sn wl bhd: hdwy & edgd lft over 1f out: nvr nr ldrs)	1	**10**	9/1	63	51
4414^{16}	**Lennox Lewis (55)** (DNicholls) **5-7-5**(7) ANicholls(14) (bhd: hdwy u.p over 1f out: n.d)	1	**11**	40/1	38	26
4482^{7}	**Pride of Brixton (72)** (CWThornton) **4-9-1** PaulEddery(18) (outpcd ½-wy: sme hdwy over 1f out: n.d)	1	**12**	16/1	52	40
4512^{8}	**Goretski (IRE) (79)** (NTinkler) **4-9-8** LCharnock(17) (mid div: drvn along ½-wy: n.d)	2½	**13**	9/1	51	39
4434^{4}	**Kira (81)** (JLEyre) **7-9-10** OPears(7) (b: led far side over 3f: sn wknd)	nk	**14**	14/1	52	40
4512^{9}	**Lady Sheriff (83)** (MWEasterby) **6-9-12b** TLucas(9) (bhd fr ½-wy)	½	**15**	16/1	52	40
473^{4}	**Miletrian Refurb (IRE) (58)** (MRChannon) **4-8-1** AMackay(8) (a in rr)	5	**16**	40/1	11	—
4270^{12}	**Treasure Touch (IRE) (85)** (DNicholls) **3-10-0** AlexGreaves(10) (bhd fr ½-wy)	1½	**17**	33/1	33	21
2354^{7}	**Keen To Please (53)** (JParkes) **3-7-10** GBardwell(2) (racd far side: a outpcd)	1¼	**18**	100/1	—	—
4512^{14}	**Ballymote (73)** (JBerry) **3-8-13**(3) PFessey(4) (mid div: rdn ½-wy: sn bhd)	nk	**19**	25/1	16	4

(SP 137.8%) **19 Rn**

60.7 secs (3.00) CSF £33.61 CT £276.27 TOTE £5.60: £1.30 £3.60 £3.30 £2.20 (£49.30) Trio £148.70 OWNER Mr David Sykes (UPPER LAMBOURN) BRED Aston Park Stud and T. R. Lock

LONG HANDICAP Pallium (IRE) 7-9 Flying Harold 7-3 Keen To Please 7-0

4636 Polly Golightly, well drawn and ideally suited by sharp tracks such as this, was on this occasion happy to get a lead. In the end she did it in good style. (4/1)

4512 Squire Corrie got the favoured stands-side rail, but in the end the winner proved simply too good. (8/1)

4527 Passionatti, with two handlers in the paddock and racing with her tongue tied down, does not lack early pace. (9/1)

4527* Dominant Air, from a 7lb higher mark, ran well, but he is only small and is probably better suited by carrying less weight in better company. (11/2)

3566 Palacegate Touch, an in-and-out performer, gave a creditable account of himself considering he was one of three to race on the unfavoured far side. (20/1)

4580 Flying Harold, in effect 8lb wrong at the weights, ran well from a poor draw. Though by no means reliable, there is no doubt he is capable of winning again from his proper handicap mark. (33/1)

4434 Kira (14/1: 10/1-16/1)

4771 THIEVES GILL LIMITED STKS (0-60) (3-Y.O+) (Class F)

4-25 (4-26) **1m 5f 175y** £2,889.00 (£804.00: £387.00) Stalls: Low GOING: 0.64 sec per fur (GS)

				SP	RR	SF
4400^{2}	**Priluki (57)** (CEBrittain) **3-8-1**(5) RMullen(15) (s.i.s: hdwy over 6f out: sn chsng ldrs: styd on wl to ld jst ins fnl f: drvn clr)	—	**1**	12/1	68	24
4287^{8}	**Uncle Doug (60)** (MrsMReveley) **6-9-4** ACulhane(5) (lw: chsd ldrs: rdn to ld 3f out: hdd jst ins fnl f: nt qckn)	3½	**2**	9/1	67	32
4562^{4}	**Taufan Boy (60)** (PWHarris) **4-9-4** AClark(12) (lw: hld up: hdwy 7f out: led over 5f out to 3f out: one pce fnl 2f)	½	**3**	4/1^{1}	66	31
4304^{6}	**Brecon (56)** (WRMuir) **4-8-13**(5) CLowther(7) (bhd: hdwy over 3f out: styd on fnl f)	½	**4**	14/1	66	31
4432^{8}	**Finestatetobein (28)** (FWatson) **4-8-12v**(3) PFessey(2) (hmpd & lost pl 6f out: hdwy 4f out: one pce fnl 2f)	1¾	**5**	100/1	61	26
4579^{5}	**Aeolina (FR) (52)** (SEKettlewell) **3-8-6** JFortune(4) (sn chsng ldrs: outpcd over 3f out: kpt on one pce)	½	**6**	4/1^{1}	60	16
4015^{8}	**Sefton Blake (57)** (MGMeagher) **3-8-9** FNorton(14) (sn trckng ldrs: effrt over 2f out: no imp)	2½	**7**	20/1	60	16

Form	Horse / details	Dist	Pos	SP	RR	SF
4287^{4}	**Good Reputation (56)** (BWHills) **3-8-6** PaulEddery(10) (s.i.s: hdwy to chse ldrs after 3f: outpcd over 4f out: wknd 2f out)	3½	**8**	9/2^{2}	53	9
4503^{2}	**Drift (59)** (SirMarkPrescott) **3-8-9** GDuffield(11) (chsd ldrs: rdn over 4f out: lost pl over 2f out)	7	**9**	6/1^{3}	48	4
*4594**	**Rex Mundi (60)** (PDEvans) **5-9-8** JFEgan(13) (hld up & bhd: hdwy 6f out: rdn over 4f out: sn lost pl)	1	**10**	4/1^{1}	51	16
	Claireswan (IRE) (58) (MHTompkins) **5-9-4** DaleGibson(6) (w ldrs: drvn along 7f out: lost pl 5f out)	½	**11**	20/1	46	11
4323^{11}	**Sun Alert (USA) (52)** (MJPolglase) **3-8-8** JTate(9) (mid div: drvn along 8f out: lost pl 3f out)	3	**12**	20/1	42	—
4584^{12}	**Havana Heights (IRE) (36)** (JLEyre) **4-8-8**(7) SBuckley(8) (sn outpcd & rdn along: wl bhd fnl 3f)	1¾	**13**	33/1	38	3
	Ginger Flower (45) (GPKelly) **8-8-12**(3) GParkin(3) (led tl over 5f out: wknd qckly: t.o whn p.u 2f out)		**P**	50/1	—	—

(SP 137.0%) **14 Rn**

3m 16.7 (20.70) CSF £111.91 TOTE £21.00: £5.10 £2.30 £1.60 (£76.90) Trio £123.00 OWNER Mr C. E. Brittain (NEWMARKET) BRED Sheikh Marwan al Maktoum
WEIGHT FOR AGE 3yo-9lb
OFFICIAL EXPLANATION **Rex Mundi: was reportedly unsuited by the soft ground.**
4400 Priluki proved well suited by the step up in distance and, getting the favoured stands side rail, in the end took this in decisive fashion. (12/1)
4287 Uncle Doug looked back to his best in the paddock, and proved it in the race. (9/1)
4562 Taufan Boy probably ran up to the best he is now capable of. (4/1)
4304 Brecon, a keen-going sort, put a poor run over hurdles last time behind him. (14/1)
4287 Finestatetobein, who had a bundle to find on official figures, belied his odds, and looked to run out of his skin. Whether this effort turns out to be a fluke remains to be seen. (100/1)
4579 Aeolina (FR), a big buzz on the racetrack, was well supported including one individual wager of £27,000 to £6,000. Showing a very choppy action going down, she did not seem to handle the downhill run to the turn too well, but to her credit kept on all the way to the line. Presumably she had been showing better at home. (4/1: tchd 6/1)
4594* Rex Mundi was beaten a long way out, and his rider was inclined to blame the soft ground. (4/1)

4772 SOUR BECK CONDITIONS STKS (2-Y.O) (Class D)

4-55 (4-56) **5f** £3,177.50 (£950.00: £455.00: £207.50) Stalls: Low GOING: 0.28 sec per fur (G)

Form	Horse / details	Dist	Pos	SP	RR	SF
*4573**	**Rare Indigo (65)** (JBerry) **2-8-5**(5) CLowther(4) (swtg: led to ½-wy: led ins nl f: kpt on wl)	—	**1**	16/1	86	46
4178^{6}	**Happy Days Again (IRE) (82)** (JWharton) **2-8-5b^{1}**(5) RMullen(2) (s.i.s: sn chsng ldrs: led ½-wy tl ins fnl f: no ex)	1¼	**2**	7/2^{2}	82	42
4630^{2}	**Territory (IRE)** (GLewis) **2-8-11** PaulEddery(5) (lw: chsd ldrs: drvn along & outpcd ½-wy: hdwy & swtchd lft over 1f out: kpt on: nvr able to chal)	hd	**3**	11/8^{1}	83	43
4403^{2}	**Arian Da (85)** (BPalling) **2-8-12** JFortune(3) (chsd ldrs: rdn 2f out: one pce)	3	**4**	4/1^{3}	74	34
3237^{15}	**Whisky Mack (IRE) (89)** (RHannon) **2-9-3** WJO'Connor(1) (wl outpcd after 2f: n.d after)	2½	**5**	9/2	71	31
4500*	**Private Seal (67)** (GLMoore) **2-9-1** AClark(6) (sn outpcd)	hd	**6**	20/1	69	29

(SP 113.2%) **6 Rn**

61.9 secs (4.20) CSF £64.74 TOTE £11.20: £2.10 £1.60 (£45.80) OWNER Mrs B. C. Ansell (COCKERHAM) BRED Mrs D. R. Schreiber
4573* Rare Indigo was in a muck-sweat down at the start and at one stage it looked as though she might be withdrawn. Racing with plenty of dash, she pulled off a surprise win, but there was certainly no fluke about it. (16/1)
4178 Happy Days Again (IRE), tried in blinkers, missed the break slightly. Getting the favoured stands side, she had to give best inside the last. (7/2)
4630 Territory (IRE) was always finding this downhill five furlongs too sharp, even on the rain-soaked ground. He definitely needs six at least. (11/8)
4403 Arian Da, taken to post early, had no excuse and was simply not good enough. (4/1: 11/4-9/2)
2786* Whisky Mack (IRE), taken to post early, found this much too sharp. (9/2)
4500* Private Seal, a keen-going sort, simply found the opposition much too good. (20/1)

4773 'CLOSE OF PLAY' H'CAP (0-70) (3-Y.O+) (Class E)

5-25 (5-27) **7f** £3,772.25 (£1,133.00: £546.50: £253.25) Stalls: Low GOING: 0.64 sec per fur (GS)

Form	Horse / details	Dist	Pos	SP	RR	SF
4410^{3}	**Night of Glass (61)** (JLEyre) **4-9-6b^{1}** MGallagher(6) (b: sn chsng ldrs: led over 2f out: hld on towards fin)	—	**1**	6/1^{2}	71	53
4071^{13}	**Halowing (USA) (69)** (JGSmyth-Osbourne) **3-9-12** GDuffield(2) (sn outpcd: hdwy on ins ½-wy: styd on far side: edgd rt & ev ch fnl f: nt qckn nr fin)	¾	**2**	20/1	77	57
4636^{12}	**Stylish Ways (IRE) (62)** (JPearce) **5-9-7** GBardwell(3) (bhd: gd hdwy on ins ½-wy: sn ev ch: one pce appr fnl f)	4	**3**	16/1	61	43
4628^{2}	**Kass Alhawa (60)** (DWChapman) **4-9-5** ACulhane(11) (hld up: gd hdwy ½-wy: ev ch & hrd rdn 2f out: one pce)	2	**4**	9/1	55	37
2845^{9}	**Antonias Melody (61)** (SRBowring) **4-9-3**(3) CTeague(5) (w ldrs: led over 4f out tl over 2 out: nt clr run over 1f out: kpt on towards fin)	1¾	**5**	20/1	52	34
4601^{6}	**Muscatana (57)** (BWHills) **3-9-0** PaulEddery(4) (hld up: hdwy over 2f out: sn rdn: no imp)	3	**6**	8/1^{3}	41	21
4414^{13}	**Gipsy Princess (54)** (MWEasterby) **3-8-8**(3) GParkin(7) (reminders after s: w ldrs: led over 2f out: sn hdd: wknd over 1f out)	1¼	**7**	20/1	35	15
4404^{3}	**Mukhlles (USA) (62)** (BobJones) **4-9-7** FNorton(10) (sn bhd: kpt on u.p fnl 2f)	½	**8**	14/1	42	24
3936^{3}	**Depreciate (63)** (CJames) **4-9-8** TLucas(15) (lw: chsd ldrs: drvn along ½-wy: lost pl over 2f out)	4	**9**	14/1	34	16
4601^{11}	**Mystique Air (IRE) (59)** (EWeymes) **3-8-13**(3) PFessey(16) (chsd ldrs tl wknd over 2f out)	¾	**10**	16/1	28	8
4301^{5}	**Barrack Yard (50)** (ACStewart) **4-8-9** SWhitworth(12) (chsd ldrs: drvn along ½-wy: sn lost pl)	2½	**11**	10/1	13	—
3987^{6}	**Deeply Vale (IRE) (64)** (GLMoore) **6-9-9** MWigham(1) (s.i.s: hdwy ½-wy: lost pl over 2f out)	hd	**12**	10/1	27	9
4601*	**Smokey From Caplaw (71)** (JJO'Neill) **3-9-9**(5) 6x CLowther(8) (in tch: styd far side & lost pl over 2f out)	nk	**13**	10/1	33	13
4464^{3}	**Finarts Bay (65)** (MrsJCecil) **3-9-8** JFortune(13) (sn bhd)	1	**14**	16/1	25	5
4561^{4}	**Rymer's Rascal (65)** (EJAlston) **5-9-10** JFEgan(17) (hdwy on outside ½-wy: lost pl over 2f out)	2½	**15**	4/1^{1}	19	1
4228^{11}	**Allinson's Mate (IRE) (59)** (TDBarron) **9-8-11b**(7) VictoriaAppleby(14) (s.i.s: a wl bhd)	½	**16**	11/1	12	—
4467^{7}	**Scharnhorst (65)** (ARDicken) **5-9-10** AMackay(9) (b: led over 2f: lost pl over 2f out: virtually p.u)	dist	**17**	40/1	—	—

(SP 138.7%) **17 Rn**

1m 32.3 (8.70) CSF £125.02 CT £1105.76 TOTE £8.80: £2.20 £4.70 £4.00 £2.30 (£92.80) Trio Not won; £1179.68 to Newmarket 18/10/97
OWNER Mr K Silvester and Mr B Silvester (HAMBLETON) BRED Brian Silvester and Kenneth Paul Silvester
WEIGHT FOR AGE 3yo-2lb
4410 Night of Glass, who wore blinkers instead of a visor, looked miserable in the paddock, but in the race he showed plenty of dash and, getting the stands' side rail, did just enough. (6/1)

2705 Halowing (USA), at last shown some mercy by the handicapper, from his low draw made his effort towards the far side once in line for home. Edging right and racing alongside the winner, in the end she was just denied. (20/1)
610 Stylish Ways (IRE), a keen-going sort, ran his best race for a long time. (16/1)
4628 Kass Alhawa, who raced towards the stands side, had every chance. (9/1)
1765 Antonias Melody, reappearing after a three-month absence, was handled sympathetically and is no doubt being primed for another All-Weather campaign. (20/1)
4561 Rymer's Rascal, asked to make headway on the wide-outside from his high draw on the turn for home, had nothing left in reserve on straightening up. (4/1)

T/Plpt: £106.00 (204.95 Tckts). T/Qdpt: £60.10 (17.9 Tckts) WG

4753-NEWMARKET (R-H) (Good to soft)
Friday October 17th
WEATHER: Sunny periods WIND: fresh, half against

4774 EQUITY FINANCIAL COLLECTIONS H'CAP (0-95) (3-Y.O) (Class C)
1-30 (1-31) **1m 6f (Rowley)** £6,212.00 (£1,856.00: £888.00: £404.00) Stalls: High GOING: 0.04 sec per fur (G)

				SP	RR	SF
4699^{2}	**Dovedon Star (75)** (PAKelleway) **3-8-7** KFallon(4) (hld up & bhd: hdwy 4f out: led 2f out: styd on strly)	—	**1**	6/1^{2}	87	60
3974^{15}	**Mithak (USA) (83)** (BWHills) **3-9-1** RHills(2) (hld up & bhd: smooth hdwy over 4f out: sn ev ch: kpt on u.p fnl f)	1½	**2**	9/1	93	66
4598*	**Royal Castle (IRE) (79)** (MajorWRHern) **3-8-11** 5x TSprake(1) (trckd ldrs: drvn along ½-wy: outpcd over 2f out: styd on ins fnl f)	4	**3**	11/2^{1}	85	58
4476^{2}	**Kilma (USA) (89)** (LMCumani) **3-9-7** LDettori(7) (trckd ldrs: led on bit over 4f out: hdd 2f out: one pce)	3½	**4**	8/1	91	64
4562^{2}	**Jawah (IRE) (70)** (KMahdi) **3-8-2** MartinDwyer(5) (b.hind: hld up: hdwy 4f out: ev ch 3f out: rdn & wandered: sn btn)	11	**5**	13/2^{3}	59	32
4673^{5}	**Thornby Park (80)** (JLDunlop) **3-8-9**(3) RFfrench(12) (lw: b: nvr nr to chal)	4	**6**	8/1	65	38
4639^{3}	**Mister Pink (79)** (RFJohnsonHoughton) **3-8-11** JReid(11) (nvr rchd ldrs)	5	**7**	16/1	58	31
3242^{2}	**Rheinbold (78)** (TJEtherington) **3-8-10** CRutter(10) (prom tl wknd over 3f out)	1¼	**8**	14/1	55	28
4426^{2}	**Princess Topaz (79)** (CACyzer) **3-8-11** KDarley(3) (hld up: hdwy ½-wy: ev ch 3f out: sn rdn & wknd)	3	**9**	8/1	53	26
4372*	**Zibeth (65)** (SDow) **3-7-4**(7)ow1 PDoe(9) (prom: led 5f out: sn hdd: grad wknd)	5	**10**	25/1	33	5
2423*	**Foreign Rule (IRE) (78)** (JRJenkins) **3-8-10** TQuinn(6) (b.hind: chsd ldrs tl wknd over 3f out: t.o)	29	**11**	20/1	13	—
4509^{11}	**Announcing (65)** (JHMGosden) **3-7-11v^{1}** JQuinn(8) (lw: led to 5f out: sn drvn along & wknd: t.o)	2	**12**	25/1	—	—
4476^{5}	**Assured Gamble (81)** (CEBrittain) **3-8-13** MJKinane(14) (in tch on ins tl rdn & wknd 4f out: t.o)	5	**13**	16/1	8	—
700*	**Hurgill Dancer (72)** (JWWatts) **3-8-4** JCarroll(13) (chsd ldrs tl wknd 5f out: sn t.o)	dist	**14**	20/1	—	—
				(SP 122.0%)	**14 Rn**	

3m 2.04 (6.04) CSF £51.50 CT £288.80 TOTE £5.60: £1.50 £3.20 £2.30 (£26.40) Trio £51.90 OWNER Mr Michael Whatley (NEWMARKET)
BRED Stud-On-The-Chart
LONG HANDICAP Zibeth 7-3
OFFICIAL EXPLANATION Princess Topaz: rider reported that the filly was unable to handle the loose ground.
IN-FOCUS: This was the final winner and runner for Paul Kelleway, who has retired after a twenty-year training career.
4699 Dovedon Star, having her second outing of the week, and trying this extended trip for the first time, landed quite a touch for connections with a going-away success, and now that she has proved that she does stay, there should be more glory to follow. (6/1)
3648 Mithak (USA) was travelling better than anything when delivering his challenge in the Dip, but the winner found extra when set alight, and he had to admit that he had met his match. (9/1)
4598* Royal Castle (IRE) takes a lot of driving, but he does keep responding, and he was coming back for more nearing the finish. (11/2: op 7/2)
4476 Kilma (USA) has yet to prove she stays this trip, but she took it up plenty soon enough travelling strongly, and in hindsight may well have delayed her challenge until the final furlong. (8/1: op 5/1)
4562 Jawah (IRE) made smooth progress, and was on the heels of the leaders two furlongs out, but he drifted both left and right when asked to quicken, and soon gave away what chance he had. (13/2: 9/2-7/1)
4673 Thornby Park, waiting on the leaders, got outpaced when the tempo picked up passing the Bushes, and though she did stay on again up the hill, the damage had been done. (8/1)
3242 Rheinbold (14/1: op 8/1)
4426 Princess Topaz, who is starting to get her winter coat, looked a live threat three furlongs out, but she found little when pressure was applied, and her jockey said she did not relish the loose ground. (8/1)

4775 HOUGHTON CONDITIONS STKS (2-Y.O) (Class B)
2-05 (2-05) **7f (Rowley)** £6,454.00 (£2,386.00: £1,143.00: £465.00: £182.50: £69.50) Stalls: High GOING: 0.21 sec per fur (G)

				SP	RR	SF
4513*	**Lucayan Indian (IRE)** (DRLoder) **2-9-1** KFallon(3) (lw: a.p: rdn along 3f out: led 1f out: styd on strly)	—	**1**	13/8^{1}	91	41
4298^{3}	**Astrologer** (WRMuir) **2-8-12** JReid(5) (plld hrd: led after 2f to 1f out: kpt on u.p cl home)	1	**2**	9/2^{3}	86	36
	Cloud Castle (CEBrittain) **2-8-7** MJKinane(6) (w'like: led 1f: drvn along 2f out: r.o strly towards fin)	nk	**3**	6/1	80	30
4551^{7}	**Abreeze (USA)** (SbinSuroor) **2-9-1** LDettori(1) (lw: led after 1f: sn hdd: chal 1f out: unable qckn)	hd	**4**	11/4^{2}	88	38
	Louis Philippe (USA) (JHMGosden) **2-8-12** GHind(4) (w'like: scope: bkwd: hld up: effrt over 2f out: nt pce to chal)	3	**5**	25/1	78?	28
	Al-Fateh (IRE) (JLDunlop) **2-8-12** TQuinn(7) (w'like: unf: dwlt: a bhd & outpcd)	4	**6**	14/1	69?	19
				(SP 107.7%)	**6 Rn**	

1m 30.91 (6.41) CSF £7.69 TOTE £2.30: £1.70 £1.90 (£4.10) OWNER Lucayan Stud (NEWMARKET) BRED C. Corrigan
4513* Lucayan Indian (IRE) got stronger the further he went, and in the last two hundred yards he began to assert his superiority. He looks set to go a long way. (13/8)
4298 Astrologer finished some way ahead of the winner last month when they were both making their racecourse debuts, but he raced a bit too keenly over this extra furlong, and the hill caught him out. He is a promising colt and he will win his share of prizes. (9/2)
Cloud Castle is bred to be a high-class filly, and she showed plenty of promise on this racecourse debut. Once she tackles an extra furlong, she will always be the one to beat. (6/1: 3/1-10/1)
4551 Abreeze (USA), in the firing-line all the way, may have led briefly inside the final furlong, but he was unable to sustain his effort, and was losing out in the final one hundred yards. (11/4: op 11/10)
Louis Philippe (USA), an attractive colt who did look to need the run, could not muster the pace to mount a challenge, but he was not disgraced against these proven performers, and he will be all the sharper next time. (25/1)

Al-Fateh (IRE) (14/1: 8/1-16/1)

4776 BARING INTERNATIONAL DARLEY STKS (Listed) (3-Y.O+) (Class A)

2-35 (2-36) **1m 1f (Rowley)** £11,169.00 (£4,131.00: £1,980.50: £807.50: £318.75: £123.25) Stalls: High GOING: 0.21 sec per fur (G)

				SP	RR	SF
4420[4]	**Fahris (IRE) (115)** (BHanbury) **3-9-3** RHills(1) (lw: mde all: shkn up & styd on strly fnl f)	—	**1**	11/10[1]	125	73
4154[4]	**Amid Albadu (USA) (107)** (JLDunlop) **3-8-10b** GCarter(7) (stdd s: hdwy over 2f out: ev ch ent fnl f: unable qckn)	3	**2**	15/2[3]	113	61
4369[2]	**Proper Blue (USA) (104)** (TGMills) **4-9-0** TQuinn(3) (lw: hld up: hdwy over 2f out: one pce ins fnl f)	1½	**3**	8/1	110	62
4396a[8]	**Musalsal (IRE) (112)** (BWHills) **3-8-10** MHills(2) (trckd ldrs: chal 3f out: rdn & btn appr fnl f)	hd	**4**	13/2[2]	110	58
4154[3]	**Green Card (USA) (107)** (SPCWoods) **3-8-10** JReid(5) (hld up: effrt 3f out: hrd rdn & one pce appr fnl f)	1¾	**5**	9/1	107	55
4671[3]	**Weet-A-Minute (IRE) (103)** (RHollinshead) **4-9-0** MJKinane(6) (prom: effrt over 2f out: sn rdn & outpcd: eased: t.o)	15	**6**	20/1	80	32
4557[4]	**Fatefully (USA) (103)** (EALDunlop) **4-8-9** LDettori(4) (chsd wnr 6f: sn rdn & btn: eased: t.o)	10	**7**	9/1	57	9
				(SP 108.6%)		**7 Rn**

1m 55.43 (4.93) CSF £7.93 TOTE £1.90: £1.40 £2.50 (£5.50) OWNER Mr Hamdan Al Maktoum (NEWMARKET) BRED Shadwell Estate Company Limited

WEIGHT FOR AGE 3yo-4lb

4420 Fahris (IRE), a very attractive individual, showed his class on this return to a more suitable trip, and won doing handsprings. (11/10: 5/4-evens)

4154 Amid Albadu (USA) had a 7lb pull in the weights with the winner from when they last clashed, and he did his best to make a race of it, but when push came to shove, he quite simply had no answer. (15/2)

4369 Proper Blue (USA), successful over course and distance in the autumn last year, has run well in all his outings this term, but he is still struggling for an opening, and that was never going to happen here. (8/1)

4396a Musalsal (IRE) joined the winner three furlongs out, and looked to be travelling just as well, but he had been worried out of it in the Dip, and this trip could be a bit short for him now. (13/2)

4154 Green Card (USA) moved into the action passing the Bushes, and briefly posed a threat, but he was soon flat to the boards, and had shot his bolt before reaching the final furlong. (9/1)

4557 Fatefully (USA) (9/1: 5/1-10/1)

4777 BEDFORD LODGE HOTEL BENTINCK STKS (Listed) (3-Y.O+) (Class A)

3-10 (3-11) **6f (Rowley)** £13,287.60 (£4,928.40: £2,374.20: £981.00: £400.50: £168.30) Stalls: High GOING: 0.21 sec per fur (G)

				SP	RR	SF
4421[12]	**My Best Valentine (103)** (VSoane) **7-8-12** RCochrane(3) (lw: hld up & bhd: hdwy 2f out: rdn to ld ins fnl f: r.o wl)	—	**1**	14/1	110	72
4239[3]	**Bollin Joanne (107)** (TDEasterby) **4-8-7** KFallon(1) (lw: b: hld up: hdwy 2f out: qcknd to ld appr fnl f: hdd & kpt on ins fnl f)	nk	**2**	100/30[2]	104	66
4344a[2]	**Snow Kid (110)** (DRLoder) **3-8-11** LDettori(7) (lw: a.p: ev ch ent fnl f: kpt on u.p)	½	**3**	3/1[1]	108	69
4553[4]	**Prends Ca (IRE) (89)** (WRMuir) **4-8-7** JReid(12) (a chsng ldrs: effrt over 1f out: unable qckn fnl f)	¾	**4**	25/1	101	63
4421[10]	**Cretan Gift (105)** (NPLittmoden) **6-9-2b** JWeaver(5) (hld up & bhd: nt clr run over 1f out: swtchd lft: r.o wl)	s.h	**5**	33/1	110	72
4424[5]	**Divina Luna (85)** (JWHills) **4-8-7** MHills(9) (in tch: drvn along & hdwy 2f out: nvr able to chal)	½	**6**	66/1	99	61
4421[14]	**Daring Destiny (105)** (KRBurke) **6-8-7b** DHolland(10) (hld up: hdwy & nt clr run ins fnl f: swtchd rt: r.o)	¾	**7**	50/1	97	59
3975[15]	**Za-Im (105)** (BWHills) **3-8-11** KDarley(11) (led tl hdd appr fnl f: one pce)	hd	**8**	25/1	102	63
4553[5]	**Wildwood Flower (103)** (RHannon) **4-8-7** DaneO'Neill(16) (trckd ldrs: effrt 2f out: sn rdn: one pce)	nk	**9**	8/1	96	58
4456[5]	**Rififi (77)** (RIngram) **4-8-12** DO'Donohoe(4) (b: effrt over 2f out: nt pce to chal)	½	**10**	66/1	100	62
4444[6]	**Superior Premium (103)** (RAFahey) **3-8-11** JCarroll(14) (prom 4f)	1¾	**11**	16/1	95	56
4664a[7]	**Hever Golf Rose (107)** (TJNaughton) **6-8-11** TQuinn(8) (b.hind: in tch: rdn & outpcd 2f out: sn btn)	s.h	**12**	10/1	94	56
4677[9]	**Croft Pool (108)** (JAGlover) **6-9-5** GCarter(17) (trckd ldrs far side over 4f)	nk	**13**	33/1	101	63
4423[14]	**Omaha City (IRE) (103)** (BGubby) **3-8-11** MFenton(15) (prom over 4f)	½	**14**	50/1	93	54
4525[3]	**Tipsy Creek (USA) (104)** (BHanbury) **3-8-11** RHills(2) (b.hind: bhd fnl 3f)	4	**15**	15/2	82	43
4553[2]	**Plaisir d'Amour (IRE) (94)** (NACallaghan) **3-8-6** MJKinane(6) (chsd ldrs: pushed along ½-wy: sn wknd)	3½	**16**	7/1[3]	68	29
				(SP 125.6%)		**16 Rn**

1m 14.81 (3.01) CSF £53.38 TOTE £20.10: £4.10 £1.90 £2.10 (£42.10) Trio £55.20 OWNER The Valentines (ASTON ROWANT) BRED Ridgecourt Stud

WEIGHT FOR AGE 3yo-1lb

4100 My Best Valentine was a seven-furlong specialist a few years back, but his last victory was gained over the minimum trip at Sandown. Getting black type against his name for winning this Listed event, he has proved a real star throughout his career. (14/1)

4239 Bollin Joanne has had some hard races of late, and she did look to be showing signs of going over the top, but she is as courageous as they come, and in just failing to hold the determined late challenge of the winner, she certainly lost no caste in defeat. (100/30)

4344a Snow Kid, rather surprisingly for the son of an Ayr Gold Cup and Portland Handicap winner having his first try at sprinting, raced with the pace from the start. He had every chance on meeting the rising ground, but just could not match strides in an all-out dash to the finish. Had the ground been as he needs, he would have taken all the beating. (3/1)

4553 Prends Ca (IRE) possibly sat closer to the pace than she usually does, but she gave a good account of herself in this higher-grade event, and this performance must rank as her best yet. (25/1)

3535a* Cretan Gift, forced to switch when in full flight in the Dip, kept on strongly up the hill, and may have been a shade unlucky not to have made the frame. (33/1)

4424 Divina Luna has done all her racing over longer trips, and despite battling on all the way to the line, she was just short of a turn of speed to mount a challenge. (66/1)

961 Daring Destiny was just beginning to find her stride when denied a clear run just inside the last furlong, and though she did run on once switched, her chance by then was long gone. (50/1)

4553 Wildwood Flower (8/1: op 5/1)

4664a Hever Golf Rose (10/1: 6/1-11/1)

4778 NGK SPARK PLUGS NURSERY H'CAP (2-Y.O) (Class C)

3-45 (3-47) **1m (Rowley)** £7,564.00 (£2,272.00: £1,096.00: £508.00) Stalls: High GOING: 0.21 sec per fur (G)

				SP	RR	SF
4116[3]	**The Glow-Worm (IRE) (89)** (BWHills) **2-9-1** MHills(15) (lw: hld up: hdwy 3f out: swtchd lft over 1f out: rdn to ld wl ins fnl f)	—	**1**	8/1[2]	89	57

Form	Horse / details	Dist	Pos	SP	RR	SF
3990*	**Noble Demand (USA) (81)** (MrsJRRamsden) **2-8-7** DO'Donohoe(10) (lw: bhd: hdwy u.p 2f out: swtchd lft: styd on strly towards fin)	nk	**2**	16/1	80	48
4064[11]	**Dutch Lad (70)** (MHTompkins) **2-7-10** DWright(9) (hld up: hdwy 2f out: fin wl)	1¼	**3**	50/1	67	35
4454[3]	**Canadian Puzzler (USA) (81)** (PWHarris) **2-8-7**ow1 JReid(13) (hld up: hdwy over 2f out: r.o wl cl home)	hd	**4**	20/1	78	45
4116[5]	**Monsajem (USA) (84)** (SbinSuroor) **2-8-10** LDettori(8) (a chsng ldrs: rdn & outpcd over 1f out)	5	**5**	4/1[1]	71	39
4576[5]	**Iron Mountain (IRE) (72)** (NACallaghan) **2-7-5**(7)ow1 PDoe(27) (chsd ldrs: led over 1f out tl hdd & wknd wl ins fnl f)	¾	**6**	20/1	57	24
4384[4]	**After The Rain (85)** (BWHills) **2-8-11** DHolland(4) (hld up in tch: hdwy 3f out: rdn & unable qckn appr fnl f)	3	**7**	20/1	64	32
4044[7]	**Al's Fella (IRE) (72)** (PFICole) **2-7-12** CRutter(24) (sme hdwy fnl 2f: nvr nrr)	s.h	**8**	33/1	51	19
3920*	**Generosity (79)** (PFICole) **2-8-5** TQuinn(16) (a chsng ldrs: one pce fnl 2f)	s.h	**9**	10/1[3]	58	26
3686[14]	**Petane (IRE) (70)** (JRArnold) **2-7-10** MartinDwyer(6) (nvr nrr)	nk	**10**	33/1	48	16
4627*	**Blue Desert (72)** (GLewis) **2-7-9**(3) 5x RFfrench(14) (lw: mde most tl hdd & wknd over 1f out)	1¼	**11**	10/1[3]	48	16
3750[6]	**Roborant (79)** (JLDunlop) **2-8-5** MJKinane(5) (outpcd tl styd on u.p fnl 2f)	½	**12**	10/1[3]	54	22
4116[15]	**Tensile (IRE) (82)** (LMCumani) **2-8-8** KDarley(3) (hdwy ½-wy: no imp fnl 2f)	hd	**13**	16/1	57	25
3990[2]	**Ben Rinnes (82)** (RFJohnsonHoughton) **2-8-5**(3) ADaly(12) (prom: drvn along over 2f out: sn outpcd)	2½	**14**	20/1	52	20
3750[2]	**Ron's Pet (85)** (RHannon) **2-8-11** DaneO'Neill(17) (wnt lft s: sn chsng ldrs: wknd 2f out)	hd	**15**	20/1	55	23
3650[2]	**Alconleigh (95)** (MJohnston) **2-9-7** JWeaver(22) (lw: prom tl wknd fnl 2f)	hd	**16**	16/1	64	32
3402*	**Nautical Star (85)** (JWHills) **2-8-8**(3) MHenry(25) (prom tl wknd 2f out)	s.h	**17**	14/1	54	22
3569[4]	**Legend of Love (80)** (JAGlover) **2-8-6** GCarter(2) (sn hdwy over 2f out: eased whn btn appr fnl f)	½	**18**	25/1	48	16
4266[4]	**Buzz (85)** (CWThornton) **2-8-11** DeanMcKeown(19) (trckd ldrs: rdn & wknd 2f out)	1¼	**19**	25/1	51	19
4271[5]	**Kim's Brave (86)** (BJMeehan) **2-8-12b** KFallon(23) (chsd ldrs 5f)	1¼	**20**	16/1	49	17
4433[5]	**Lord Warford (76)** (GBBalding) **2-8-2**ow1 SDrowne(21) (a in rr)	hd	**21**	25/1	39	6
3924[11]	**Moothyeb (USA) (71)** (NAGraham) **2-7-11b1** JLowe(7) (in tch 5f)	3	**22**	25/1	28	—
4447[3]	**Leofric (70)** (MJPolglase) **2-7-10** NAdams(26) (b.hind: a bhd)	1	**23**	33/1	25	—
4427[6]	**Zena (74)** (WJarvis) **2-8-0b1** JQuinn(28) (t.o fr ½-wy)	9	**24**	25/1	11	—
4271[12]	**Master Mac (USA) (83)** (RAkehurst) **2-8-9** SSanders(1) (bhd fr ½-wy)	6	**25**	20/1	8	—
*4052**	**Mister Benjamin (IRE) (81)** (SPCWoods) **2-8-7** NDay(18) (cl up 5f: sn rdn & wknd)	½	**26**	16/1	5	—
3750[4]	**Minetta (79)** (MBell) **2-8-5** MFenton(20) (a bhd)	¾	**27**	25/1	2	—
4217*	**Nebl (85)** (MajorWRHern) **2-8-11** RHills(11) (lw: lost tch fnl 3f)	nk	**28**	10/1[3]	7	—
				(SP 166.0%)		**28 Rn**

1m 43.08 (5.78) CSF £123.32 CT £5674.48 TOTE £11.40: £2.60 £6.90 £11.80 £5.00 (£238.60) Trio £9997.00; £2956.89 to Newmarket 18/10/97 OWNER Mrs J. M. Corbett (LAMBOURN) BRED Dr J. Ryan and Rozelle Bloodstock

LONG HANDICAP Leofric 7-9 Dutch Lad 7-6 Petane (IRE) 7-9

4116 The Glow-Worm (IRE), successful on the July course earlier in the year, showed his appreciation for this stiff uphill finish with a finely-timed effort that saw him win a shade cleverly. (8/1)

3990* Noble Demand (USA) did not have such testing ground as he won on at York, but he was getting down to some serious work nearing the finish, and he could turn out a promising stayer next season. (16/1)

1396 Dutch Lad, showing his first signs of form, is bred to need all of this trip, and he is weighted to take advantage in the near future. (50/1)

4454 Canadian Puzzler (USA), in his first handicap, tried hard to make his presence felt in the closing stages, but he was outpointed up the hill despite staying on, and he is not quite there yet. (20/1)

4116 Monsajem (USA), poised to challenge for most of the trip, was unable to respond when the pace lifted in the Dip, and was floundering in the race to the line. (4/1)

4576 Iron Mountain (IRE) is running well enough to win a nursery, but on this occasion he may have got there too soon, for he was a spent force once the winner had taken his measure. (20/1)

4384 After The Rain ran much better than his finishing position might suggest, but he got well outpointed in the closing stages, and it is possible he needs an even longer trip, even at this early stage of his career. (20/1)

4217* Nebl (10/1: 8/1-12/1)

4779 E.B.F. SNAILWELL MAIDEN STKS (2-Y.O) (Class D)

4-15 (4-18) **6f (Rowley)** £6,391.00 (£1,918.00: £924.00: £427.00) Stalls: High GOING: 0.21 sec per fur (G)

Form	Horse / details	Dist	Pos	SP	RR	SF
4425[2]	**Atuf (USA)** (SbinSuroor) **2-8-9** LDettori(7) (lw: hdwy ½-wy: led wl over 1f out: hrd drvn: all out)	—	**1**	2/1[1]	86	40
	Swing Along (CFWall) **2-8-9** SSanders(12) (w'like: lw: a.p: str chal ins fnl f: jst failed)	hd	**2**	50/1	86	40
4309[3]	**Shart (IRE)** (JHMGosden) **2-9-0** RHills(6) (hld up: hdwy 2f out: r.o wl cl home)	nk	**3**	9/2[2]	90	44
3219[8]	**Golden Reprimand (IRE)** (RHannon) **2-9-0** MJKinane(10) (hdwy over 2f out: rdn & r.o wl ins fnl f)	1½	**4**	12/1	86	40
	Jocasta (CFWall) **2-8-9** JReid(4) (neat: lw: bhd: stdy hdwy appr fnl f: r.o)	1¾	**5**	33/1	76+	30
4145[6]	**Dilkusha (IRE)** (BJMeehan) **2-9-0** DHolland(1) (in tch: hdwy u.p 2f out: one pce appr fnl f)	¾	**6**	14/1	79	33
	Splendid Isolation (USA) (LMCumani) **2-9-0** KDarley(5) (leggy: scope: hdwy over 2f out: styd on fnl f: nvr able to chal)	1½	**7**	8/1[3]	75	29
	Fairy Rock (IRE) (BWHills) **2-8-9** MHills(19) (w'like: scope: bhd: hdwy over 1f out: nrst fin)	1¾	**8**	12/1	66	20
	Rush Off (RAkehurst) **2-9-0** JWeaver(11) (lt-f: scope: bhd: hrd rdn 2f out: kpt on wl ins fnl f)	1¼	**9**	33/1	67	21
2556[6]	**Surprise Present (IRE)** (RHannon) **2-9-0** DaneO'Neill(20) (in tch tl grad wknd fnl 2f)	½	**10**	10/1	66	20
	Ribblesdale (JLDunlop) **2-8-9** TQuinn(15) (w'like: scope: nvr trbld ldrs)	1¾	**11**	20/1	56	10
4526[14]	**Empire State (IRE)** (MHTompkins) **2-8-11**(3) MHenry(14) (prom: rdn 3f out: grad wknd)	s.h	**12**	50/1	61	15
2875[11]	**Touchanova** (AHide) **2-8-4**(5) GMilligan(13) (led & sn clr: wknd & hdd wl over 1f out)	¾	**13**	50/1	54	8
	Hetra Heights (USA) (WJMusson) **2-8-9** RCochrane(9) (leggy: scope: bhd: hmpd over 1f out: n.d)	1	**14**	33/1	52	6
4526[13]	**My Tyson (IRE)** (KMahdi) **2-9-0** MartinDwyer(18) (mid div: drvn along over 2f out: sn btn)	s.h	**15**	50/1	56	10
4231[9]	**Nautical Warning** (MHTompkins) **2-9-0** DBiggs(8) (lw: prom over 4f)	4	**16**	33/1	46	—
	Society King (IRE) (JEBanks) **2-9-0** JQuinn(3) (w'like: lost tch fnl 3f)	4	**17**	20/1	35	—
	Magic Morning (WJMusson) **2-9-0** KFallon(2) (cmpt: hld up in tch: wkng whn hmpd 2f out)	hd	**18**	16/1	35	—
4459[9]	**Eiffel Tiger (IRE)** (BobJones) **2-9-0** NDay(16) (in tch 4f)	1½	**19**	50/1	31	—
	Toffolux (HJCollingridge) **2-8-9** DeclanO'Shea(17) (leggy: s.s: a wl bhd: t.o)	24	**20**	50/1	—	—
				(SP 132.7%)		**20 Rn**

1m 16.89 (5.09) CSF £137.12 TOTE £2.30: £1.40 £11.00 £1.90 (£99.80) Trio £97.40 OWNER Godolphin (NEWMARKET) BRED Shadwell Farm Inc

4425 Atuf (USA) put her previous experience to good use, but she needed to dig deep to hang on close home. (2/1)

Swing Along comes from a winning family, and in turning in such an encouraging performance on this debut, it is possible she could turn out best of the lot. (50/1)

4309 Shart (IRE), stepping down to six furlongs, finished best of all, and it would seem he will eventually fare better over a longer trip. (9/2: 7/2-11/2)
Golden Reprimand (IRE), a half-brother to useful sprinter Espartero, showed considerable improvement on his initial outing, and he does appear to be getting it together. (12/1: 7/1-14/1)
Jocasta was beginning to realise what was needed in the latter stages, and she looks to have ability. (33/1)
4145 Dilkusha (IRE) picked up when given a reminder entering the last quarter-mile, but he was unable to maintain his run, and may possibly still have needed this spin. (14/1: 12/1-20/1)
Splendid Isolation (USA), an American-bred colt with plenty of scope, was doing all his best work late on, and he will be much wiser next time. (8/1: 5/1-10/1)
Fairy Rock (IRE) (12/1: op 6/1)
Rush Off needed a lot of driving to get him to extend himself, but he was getting the message late on, and he should be able to win races. (33/1)

4780 NEWMARKET CHALLENGE CUP (MAIDEN 2-Y.O) (Class G)
4-45 (4-45) **7f (Rowley)** Stalls: High GOING: 0.21 sec per fur (G)

				SP	RR	SF
4564^{9}	**Dog Watch** (JHMGosden) **2-9-0** LDettori(3) (lw: chsd ldr: led 2f out: clr fnl f)	—	**1**	$1/2^{1}$	84?	19
4605^{10}	**Green Jacket (82)** (JLDunlop) **2-9-0** GCarter(1) (led to 2f out: sn rdn & outpcd)	2½	**2**	$5/2^{2}$	78?	13
	Highly Pleased (USA) (EALDunlop) **2-9-0** KFallon(2) (w'like: s.s: hdwy to chal over 2f out: eased whn btn)	10	**3**	$9/2^{3}$	55?	—
				(SP 113.4%)	**3 Rn**	

1m 32.79 (8.29) CSF £2.08 TOTE £1.50: (£1.50) OWNER Lord Hartington (NEWMARKET) BRED Side Hill Stud and John Warren
4564 Dog Watch, content to be given a lead, took over entering the last quarter-mile, and did not need to get serious to open his account. (1/2: 1/3-4/7)
4111 Green Jacket, far more experienced than his rivals, held the call for five furlongs, but the winner proved much too good for him, and had his measure throughout the last couple of furlongs. (5/2: 2/1-3/1)
Highly Pleased (USA), flat-footed as the stalls opened, moved up and posed a serious threat passing the Bushes, but lack of a recent outing took it's toll, and he was eased right down once his measure had been taken. (9/2)

T/Jkpt: £24,082.90 (0.1 Tckts); £30,527.74 to Newmarket 18/10/97. T/Plpt: £54.30 (985.59 Tckts). T/Qdpt: £12.90 (201.58 Tckts) IM

4774-NEWMARKET (R-H) (Good)
Saturday October 18th
WEATHER: sunny & v.warm WIND: slt half against

4781 ROTHMANS ROYALS NORTH SOUTH CHALLENGE SERIES FINAL H'CAP (3-Y.O+) (Class B)
1-40 (1-41) **1m (Rowley)** £37,612.50 (£11,400.00: £5,575.00: £2,662.50) Stalls: Low GOING minus 0.13 sec per fur (G)

				SP	RR	SF
4558^{4}	**Gulf Shaadi (82)** (EJAlston) **5-9-3** SSanders(3) (hdwy over 2f out: led ins fnl f: r.o u.p)	—	**1**	$7/1^{1}$	96	79
4441^{9}	**For Your Eyes Only (78)** (TDEasterby) **3-8-3b**(7) RWinston(2) (lw: a chsng ldrs: led 1½f tl ins fnl f: kpt on wl)	½	**2**	20/1	91	71
4596^{4}	**Bowcliffe (63)** (EJAlston) **6-7-12** JQuinn(12) (hld up: hdwy 3f out: ev ch appr fnl f: sn btn)	4	**3**	33/1	68	51
4297^{8}	**Ben Gunn (69)** (PTWalwyn) **5-8-4** TSprake(4) (swtg: in tch: hdwy 2f out: kpt on ins fnl f)	nk	**4**	33/1	73	56
4441^{5}	**Antarctic Storm (69)** (RAFahey) **4-8-4** FNorton(5) (led tl hdd 1½f out: kpt on)	½	**5**	25/1	72	55
4558^{27}	**Prince of Denial (89)** (DWPArbuthnot) **3-9-7** TQuinn(27) (b: bhd: hdwy 2f out: styd on wl towards fin)	¾	**6**	14/1	91	71
4147^{8}	**Shinerolla (76)** (CParker) **5-8-11b** RCochrane(10) (swtg: hdwy & in tch ½-wy: chsng ldrs appr fnl f: nt qckn)	hd	**7**	20/1	78	61
4558^{13}	**Epic Stand (82)** (MrsJRRamsden) **3-9-0** JFortune(15) (lw: swtg: hdwy u.p 2f out: wandered appr fnl f: nvr able to chal)	nk	**8**	14/1	83	63
4583^{2}	**Barnburgh Boy (76)** (TDEasterby) **3-8-8** WRyan(1) (hld up & bhd: effrt over 2f out: n.m.r: nrst fin)	½	**9**	$11/1^{2}$	76	56
4441^{12}	**Cashmere Lady (74)** (JLEyre) **5-8-9** LDettori(6) (swtg: drvn along & bhd ½-wy: hdwy 2f out: styd on)	nk	**10**	$12/1^{3}$	74	57
4578^{3}	**High Spirits (IRE) (75)** (TDEasterby) **3-8-7b** GBardwell(26) (lw: bhd: swtchd rt 2f out: styd on: nvr nrr)	s.h	**11**	25/1	74	54
4558^{3}	**Hunters of Brora (IRE) (91)** (JDBethell) **7-9-12** RHills(13) (bhd: effrt over 2f out: nvr rchd ldrs)	1	**12**	$11/1^{2}$	88	71
4558^{26}	**Pride of Pendle (73)** (MartynWane) **8-8-3**(5) RMullen(24) (hld up & bhd: effrt 3f out: sme hdwy 2f out: n.d)	1	**13**	33/1	68	51
4637^{4}	**Kala Sunrise (90)** (CSmith) **4-9-11** AClark(16) (lw: bhd: hdwy 2f out: n.d)	¾	**14**	33/1	84	67
4441^{10}	**Present Situation (64)** (LordHuntingdon) **6-7-13** MartinDwyer(28) (effrt on outside over 3f out: n.d)	1½	**15**	33/1	55	38
4441^{4}	**Therhea (IRE) (81)** (BRMillman) **4-8-13**(3) AWhelan(22) (chsd ldrs tl wknd appr fnl f)	½	**16**	20/1	71	54
4297^{13}	**Apache Star (96)** (GWragg) **3-10-0v** MHills(25) (in tch tl wknd fnl 2f)	½	**17**	25/1	85	65
4578^{7}	**Mr Paradise (IRE) (70)** (TJNaughton) **3-7-13**(3) RFfrench(19) (nvr trbld ldrs)	½	**18**	33/1	58	38
4297^{14}	**Artful Dane (IRE) (74)** (MJHeaton-Ellis) **5-8-9v** SDrowne(7) (chsd ldrs tl wknd 2f out)	½	**19**	33/1	61	44
4441^{8}	**Mo-Addab (IRE) (66)** (ACStewart) **7-8-1** TWilliams(17) (swtg: n.d)	2	**20**	16/1	49	32
4558^{33}	**Sharp Shuffle (IRE) (79)** (RHannon) **4-9-0** OPeslier(23) (b: a rr div)	nk	**21**	25/1	61	44
4297^{12}	**Family Man (78)** (JRFanshawe) **4-8-13** JReid(29) (prom tl wknd wl over 1f out)	1½	**22**	25/1	57	40
4410*	**Duraid (IRE) (82)** (DenysSmith) **5-8-12**(5) CLowther(21) (chsd ldrs tl rdn & wknd over 1f out)	nk	**23**	16/1	61	44
4637^{5}	**Queens Consul (IRE) (88)** (BSRothwell) **7-9-9** JWeaver(11) (chsd ldrs 6f)	1	**24**	33/1	65	48
4410^{6}	**Suez Tornado (IRE) (68)** (EJAlston) **4-8-3v** JFEgan(18) (prom over 5f: wknd)	2	**25**	33/1	41	24
4441^{19}	**Anonym (IRE) (61)** (JLEyre) **5-7-10b** DWright(30) (lost tch fr ½-wy)	1¾	**26**	50/1	30	13
4410^{7}	**Band on the Run (77)** (BAMcMahon) **10-8-12** GCarter(14) (chsd ldrs tl wknd qckly wl over 2f out)	1½	**27**	40/1	43	26
4297^{3}	**La Modiste (82)** (MissGayKelleway) **4-9-3** KFallon(9) (prom 5f: wknd)	3½	**28**	14/1	41	24
4297^{4}	**Saifan (86)** (DMorris) **8-9-7v** NDay(8) (swtg: chsd ldrs tl rdn & wknd 2f out: b.b.v)	6	**29**	16/1	33	16
4441^{3}	**Sweet Wilhelmina (74)** (LordHuntingdon) **4-8-9** MJKinane(20) (prom over 5f: sn wknd)	3½	**30**	$11/1^{2}$	14	—
				(SP 147.2%)	**30 Rn**	

1m 38.44 (1.14) CSF £133.68 CT £4,100.13 TOTE £9.60: £2.50 £8.20 £9.40 £5.90 (£175.20) Trio £2,371.40; £2,171.08 to Pontefract 20/10/97 OWNER The Bibby Halliday Partnership (PRESTON) BRED Sheikh Mohammed bin Rashid al Maktoum
WEIGHT FOR AGE 3yo-3lb
OFFICIAL EXPLANATION **Saifan: the trainer's representative reported that the gelding bled from the nose.**
4558 Gulf Shaadi has been in brilliant form and has, not surprisingly, shot up the weights. The Handicapper will not easily forgive him for this, as the first two were well clear. (7/1)
4147 For Your Eyes Only ran his best race of the season, and this was much more encouraging. (20/1)
4596 Bowcliffe is another who has improved tremendously this season but, after looking dangerous, he was found out in the closing stages. (33/1)
2557* Ben Gunn likes these competitive events, but is high enough in the weights at the moment, and that seemed to blunt his finishing speed. (33/1)

4441 Antarctic Storm keeps running well, but trying to dictate throughout in this really competitive race was virtually impossible, and he just helped set the race up. (25/1)
4297* Prince of Denial finished best of all and, with a better draw, must have gone close. (14/1)
4147 Shinerolla, despite sweating up badly beforehand, travelled particularly well during the race, but just failed to pick up at the end. He is obviously in good heart just now. (20/1)
4583 Barnburgh Boy was trying to come from way off the pace and needed all the luck going, but never got into it and was certainly not over-punished. (11/1)
4578 High Spirits (IRE) ran well from his draw, and was putting in some fine late work. (25/1)

4782 CHALLENGE STKS (Gp 2) (3-Y.O+) (Class A)

2-15 (2-16) **7f (Rowley)** £53,059.49 (£19,660.50: £9,455.25: £3,888.75: £1,569.38: £641.63) Stalls: Low GOING minus 0.13 sec per fur (G)

				SP	RR	SF
4142*	**Kahal (109)** (SbinSuroor) **3-8-12** LDettori(4) (hld up & bhd: swtchd & effrt wl over 1f out: qcknd to ld ins fnl f: r.o)	—	**1**	9/2 2	120	75
4422 2	**Rebecca Sharp (113)** (GWragg) **3-8-13** MHills(3) (b.hind: trckd ldrs: nt clr run 2f out: swtchd appr fnl f: r.o wl)	nk	**2**	9/2 2	120	75
4421 6	**Muchea (110)** (MRChannon) **3-8-12** TQuinn(6) (in tch: drvn along over 2f out: styd on wl towards fin)	1¾	**3**	33/1	115	70
4421*	**Elnadim (USA) (113)** (JLDunlop) **3-9-2** RHills(10) (cl up: chal 1½f out: sn hrd drvn: kpt on)	hd	**4**	9/4 1	119	74
4662a*	**Decorated Hero (113)** (JHMGosden) **5-9-4** WRyan(12) (trckd ldrs: led 1½f out tl ins fnl f: no ex)	nk	**5**	5/1 3	118	75
2677 6	**Elegant Warning (IRE) (106)** (BWHills) **3-8-9** JReid(11) (swtg: hld up & bhd: hdwy over 2f out: styd on: nvr able chal)	hd	**6**	33/1	111	66
4441 16	**Law Commission (96)** (DRCElsworth) **7-9-0** SDrowne(9) (hld up & bhd: effrt 2f out: nvr able chal)	hd	**7**	100/1	114	71
4421 5	**Dazzle (112)** (MRStoute) **3-8-9** KFallon(8) (swtg: in tch: hdwy over 2f out: sn hrd drvn: btn whn hmpd wl ins fnl f)	1	**8**	13/2	109	64
4344a 7	**Almushtarak (IRE) (110)** (KMahdi) **4-9-0** RCochrane(1) (chsd ldrs: rdn over 2f out: wknd appr fnl f)	1½	**9**	25/1	108	65
4421 8	**Swift Gulliver (IRE)** (JSBolger,Ireland) **3-8-12b** JWeaver(2) (lw: led tl hdd & wknd 1½f out)	2	**10**	33/1	104	59
4625a 4	**Dangerous Diva (IRE)** (APO'Brien,Ireland) **3-8-9** MJKinane(7) (lt-f: chsd ldrs: rdn along 3f out: sn wknd)	s.h	**11**	33/1	101	56
4344a 3	**Deadly Dudley (IRE) (114)** (RHannon) **3-8-12** OPeslier(5) (bhd: effrt over 2f out: n.d)	nk	**12**	14/1	103	58
				(SP 120.4%)	**12 Rn**	

1m 25.38 (0.88) CSF £21.82 TOTE £5.00: £1.40 £1.80 £7.80 (£11.50) Trio £160.50 OWNER Godolphin (NEWMARKET) BRED Shadwell Estate Company Limited
WEIGHT FOR AGE 3yo-2lb
4142* Kahal is useful when things go his way, and loves coming from off a strong pace. Getting first run made all the difference. (9/2: op 7/1)
4422 Rebecca Sharp was most unlucky yet again, and should have won this. (9/2)
4421 Muchea, from a yard that has not been firing this season, showed he is coming right with a game effort, and was getting stronger as the race progressed. (33/1)
4421* Elnadim (USA), stepping up a furlong, got it well enough but, surprisingly, got caught for speed at a vital stage and, although running on at the end, could not get back up. Now connections know he stays, he will no doubt be ridden even more positively. (9/4)
4662a* Decorated Hero is as tough as they come, and he ran a smashing race, only to get tapped for toe in the closing stages. (5/1)
2677 Elegant Warning (IRE), after three months off, put in a fair effort, but was never quite good enough to make it. (33/1)
4153* Law Commission had the race run to suit, and performed surprisingly well in this class, but was still never able to get into it. (100/1)
4421 Dazzle needs everything to go her way, and had her limitations well exposed. (13/2)

4783 TOTE CESAREWITCH H'CAP (3-Y.O+) (Class B)

2-55 (2-58) **2m 2f (Rowley)** £73,350.00 (£22,050.00: £10,650.00: £4,950.00) Stalls: High GOING minus 0.13 sec per fur (G)

				SP	RR	SF
4363 2	**Turnpole (IRE) (74)** (MrsMReveley) **6-7-10** LCharnock(6) (hld up: hdwy gng wl 5f out: led over 3f out: r.o strly)	—	**1**	16/1	91	57
4279*	**Top Cees (90)** (MrsJRRamsden) **7-8-12** JFortune(15) (hld up: hdwy over 3f out: chsd wnr fnl 2f: r.o: nvr able to chal)	1¾	**2**	5/1 1	105	71
3748*	**Mawared (IRE) (90)** (JLDunlop) **4-8-12** RHills(24) (b: hld up: effrt & n.m.r over 4f out: hdwy 3f out: styd on: no imp)	3½	**3**	12/1	102	68
4118*	**Canon Can (USA) (106)** (HRACecil) **4-10-0** 4x KFallon(16) (hld up: hdwy ½-wy: chsng ldrs 4f out: kpt on same pce)	3	**4**	10/1 3	116	82
2834*	**Captain Jack (87)** (MCPipe) **7-8-9** OPeslier(19) (a chsng ldrs: effrt 4f out: styd on same pce)	1¾	**5**	12/1	95	61
3896*	**Siege Perilous (IRE) (76)** (SCWilliams) **4-7-12** MartinDwyer(17) (hdwy ½-wy: sn chsng ldrs: one pce fnl 3f)	1½	**6**	33/1	83	49
3896 13	**Shadirwan (IRE) (74)** (RAkehurst) **6-7-3**(7) PFitzsimons(12) (swtg: styd on fnl 4f: nrst fin)	s.h	**7**	40/1	81	47
	Ivor's Flutter (80) (DRCElsworth) **8-8-2** TSprake(5) (lw: hdwy ½-wy: sn chsng ldrs: one pce fnl 3f)	1	**8**	50/1	86	52
3122 5	**Transom (USA) (85)** (MrsAJPerrett) **6-8-7** JReid(7) (chsd ldrs tl wknd fnl 2½f)	½	**9**	33/1	90	56
4363 3	**Etterby Park (USA) (74)** (MJohnston) **4-7-10** NCarlisle(31) (in tch: effrt over 4f out: grad wknd)	2½	**10**	50/1	77	43
4101 15	**Valagalore (85)** (BWHills) **3-7-7**(3) PFessey(13) (hdwy & prom 7f out: wknd fnl 3½f)	nk	**11**	25/1	88	43
4269 8	**Great Easeby (IRE) (78)** (WStorey) **7-8-0** ow4 JFanning(23) (nvr trbld ldrs)	4	**12**	50/1	77	39
4639 5	**Merit (IRE) (83)** (PFICole) **5-8-5** TQuinn(8) (racd wd: prom: rdn along 6f out: wknd 4f out)	¾	**13**	12/1	82	48
4269 6	**Shirley Sue (75)** (MJohnston) **4-7-11** NAdams(9) (nvr trbld ldrs)	1	**14**	33/1	73	39
4269 9	**Grand Cru (74)** (JCullinan) **6-7-10** DWright(14) (hld up & bhd: shkn up 6f out: n.d)	4	**15**	100/1	68	34
4466*	**Totem Dancer (74)** (JLEyre) **4-7-5**(5) RMullen(30) (hdwy ½-wy: led over 4f out tl over 3f out: wknd)	5	**16**	20/1	64	30
4426 4	**Star Rage (IRE) (79)** (MJohnston) **7-8-1** JFEgan(32) (hdwy ½-wy: sn chsng ldrs: wknd fnl 3f)	1	**17**	40/1	68	34
4673 9	**Sea Victor (74)** (JLHarris) **5-7-10** JLowe(25) (chsd ldrs tl wknd fnl 4f)	2½	**18**	25/1	61	27
4476 7	**Inchcailloch (IRE) (82)** (JSKing) **8-8-1**(3) RFfrench(29) (lw: n.d)	3	**19**	16/1	66	32
4246*	**Motet (85)** (GWragg) **3-7-10** JQuinn(10) (lw: hld up: hdwy 7f out: wknd fnl 3½f)	½	**20**	7/1 2	69	24
3383 3	**Here Comes Herbie (74)** (WStorey) **5-7-10** EJohnson(26) (n.d)	5	**21**	40/1	53	19
4099 5	**Sweetness Herself (101)** (MJRyan) **4-9-9** GCarter(27) (in tch: hdwy & ev ch over 3f out: sn rdn & wknd)	hd	**22**	20/1	80	46
*4481**	**Onefourseven (75)** (JLEyre) **4-7-11** TWilliams(28) (chsd ldrs tl wknd fnl 4f)	s.h	**23**	16/1	54	20
4481 6	**Nigel's Lad (IRE) (80)** (PCHaslam) **5-8-2** SDrowne(2) (racd wd: prom tl wknd fnl 6f)	1	**24**	50/1	58	24
4269 5	**Aztec Flyer (USA) (75)** (CEBrittain) **4-7-6**(5)ow1 APolli(22) (swtg: chsd ldrs tl wknd 5f out)	½	**25**	100/1	53	18
4376 2	**Media Star (USA) (93)** (JHMGosden) **4-9-1v** LDettori(1) (lw: racd wd: chsd ldrs tl wknd fnl 6f)	nk	**26**	7/1 2	70	36
4539a 2	**Cloud Inspector (IRE) (88)** (MJohnston) **6-8-10** JWeaver(11) (chsd ldrs tl wknd fnl 4f)	½	**27**	33/1	65	31
4562 5	**Salska (74)** (AStreeter) **6-7-3**(7) JFowle(4) (racd wd: chsd ldrs: led over 5f out tl over 4f out: wknd)	½	**28**	100/1	51	17

				SP	RR	SF
4509*	**Tommy Tortoise (85)** (MissGayKelleway) **3-7-3**(7) PDoe(21) (lost tch fr ½-wy)	1¼	**29**	33/1	60	15
4241[3]	**Go Britannia (90)** (DRLoder) **4-8-12** RCochrane(3) (racd wd: effrt ½-wy: n.d)	nk	**30**	20/1	65	31
3318[4]	**The Flying Phantom (74)** (MHTompkins) **6-7-10** GBardwell(18) (b: led tl hdd & wknd over 5f out)	dist	**31**	50/1	—	—

(SP 148.3%) **31 Rn**

3m 53.56 (3.16) CSF £79.49 CT £973.52 TOTE £18.40: £3.70 £2.80 £3.80 £3.60 (£65.20) Trio £892.50 OWNER Mr & Mrs W J Williams (SALTBURN) BRED Old Meadow Stud

LONG HANDICAP Sea Victor 7-7 Here Comes Herbie 7-2 Shadirwan (IRE) 7-4 Totem Dancer 7-5 Etterby Park (USA) 7-6 Aztec Flyer (USA) 6-9 Valagalore 7-9 Great Easeby (IRE) 6-13 Salska 7-0 Tommy Tortoise 6-12 Grand Cru 7-1 The Flying Phantom 7-7

WEIGHT FOR AGE 3yo-11lb

4363 Turnpole (IRE) came here pretty fresh after a quiet season and, from the moment he came sailing through on the bridle to lead over three furlongs out, there were never any doubts about the result. He is obviously still improving, and will no doubt continue that over hurdles. (16/1)

4279* Top Cees did everything right, but just found one too good. To his credit he kept trying hard. (5/1)

3748* Mawared (IRE) has improved no end as he has tried longer distances, and this was his longest trip to date. After having problems when beginning his run, he certainly finished well. (12/1)

4118* Canon Can (USA) was 22lb higher than when finishing third last year, but this game sort again put up a super performance, albeit in vain. (10/1)

2834* Captain Jack stays forever and ran his heart out, but was well short of pace in the last half-mile. (12/1)

3896* Siege Perilous (IRE) is a good staying type and he has been consistent all season, but it would seem he is now high enough in the weights. (33/1)

3122 Shadirwan (IRE), from 6lb out of the handicap, was putting in his best work when it was all over, showing he still has the ability when in the mood. (40/1)

Ivor's Flutter had his last outing in this event last year, and ran surprisingly well in the circumstances. (50/1)

Great Easeby (IRE), from 11lb out of the handicap, put up another 4lb overweight, but did show something. (50/1)

4784 THOROUGHBRED CORPORATION DEWHURST STKS (Gp 1) (2-Y.O C & F) (Class A)

3-30 (3-31) **7f (Rowley)** £117,674.00 (£43,766.00: £21,183.00: £8,865.00: £3,732.50: £1,679.50) Stalls: Low GOING minus 0.13 sec per fur (G)

				SP	RR	SF
4391a*	**Xaar** (AFabre,France) **2-9-0** OPeslier(1) (nice colt: lw: hld up: pushed along & hdwy 3f out: qcknd to ld 1f out: r.o wl: impressive)	—	**1**	11/8[1]	127+	84
4474*	**Tamarisk (IRE)** (RCharlton) **2-9-0** TSprake(7) (led tl hdd 1f out: r.o: no ch w wnr)	7	**2**	9/2[3]	111	68
3962a*	**Impressionist (IRE)** (APO'Brien,Ireland) **2-9-0** MJKinane(2) (gd sort: chsd ldrs: effrt over 2f out: kpt on same pce)	2½	**3**	20/1	105	62
3882a[5]	**Desert Prince (IRE)** (DRLoder) **2-9-0** LDettori(6) (h.d.w: hld up: hdwy over 2f out: shkn up over 1f out: nt qckn)	nk	**4**	14/1	105	62
4439[2]	**Pegnitz (USA)** (CEBrittain) **2-9-0** JReid(4) (plld hrd: hdwy over 2f out: rdn & btn over 1f out)	2	**5**	50/1	100?	57
4135*	**Daggers Drawn (USA) (100)** (HRACecil) **2-9-0** KFallon(3) (lw: swtg: chsd ldr: drvn along over 2f out: wknd appr fnl f)	9	**6**	3/1[2]	80	37
3123*	**Central Park (IRE) (100)** (PFICole) **2-9-0** TQuinn(5) (lw: chsd ldrs: rdn 3f out: sn wknd & eased)	9	**7**	11/2	59	16

(SP 114.1%) **7 Rn**

1m 24.81 (0.31) CSF £7.26 TOTE £2.40: £1.50 £2.20 (£5.30) OWNER Mr K. Abdulla (CHANTILLY) BRED Juddmonte Farms

OFFICIAL EXPLANATION Daggers Drawn (USA): the trainer reported that the colt had gone over the top.
Central Park (IRE): no explanation was offered.

4391a* Xaar without doubt put up one of the best performances ever seen from a two-year old and has now dropped to a prohibitive price for next year's Two Thousand Guineas but, unless something unforeseen happens, the rest will be only be playing for places and then the Derby awaits. (11/8)

4474* Tamarisk (IRE) is an improving colt who ran a cracking race in defeat but was plain and simply outclassed. (9/2)

3962a* Impressionist (IRE) ran well and will no doubt give connections a good clue to their faint chance of beating the winner next year. (20/1)

3882a Desert Prince (IRE), who finished just over a couple of lengths behind the winner at Deauville, had his chances for revenge but was firmly put in his place. (14/1)

4439 Pegnitz (USA) had a lot to find on his previous run and did not help matters by refusing to settle but it would seem that with experience there is better to come. (50/1)

4135* Daggers Drawn (USA) ran too badly to be true here and would seem to have gone over the top. (3/1)

3123* Central Park (IRE) has looked the type to appreciate further but that was not the problem here as he was beaten so far out. At present connections cannot find anything physically wrong but obviously he had a problem. (11/2)

4785 DUBAI CHAMPION STKS (Gp 1) (3-Y.O+) (Class A)

4-10 (4-11) **1m 2f (Rowley)** £233,014.00 (£86,026.00: £41,113.00: £16,615.00: £6,407.50: £2,324.50) Stalls: Low GOING minus 0.13 sec per fur (G)

				SP	RR	SF
4665a[2]	**Pilsudski (IRE) (135)** (MRStoute) **5-9-2** MJKinane(1) (lw: b.nr hind: hld up: nt clr run & swtchd 2f out: qcknd to ld ins fnl f: r.o wl)	—	**1**	Evens[1]	131	84
4392a*	**Loup Sauvage (USA)** (AFabre,France) **3-8-11** OPeslier(2) (gd sort: unf: trckd ldrs: led wl over 1f out: hdd ins fnl f: r.o)	2	**2**	6/1[3]	128	76
4422[4]	**Bahhare (USA) (116)** (JLDunlop) **3-8-11** RHills(4) (lw: hld up & bhd: hdwy over 2f out: sn chsng ldrs: nt qckn fnl f)	2	**3**	9/1	125	73
3647*	**Stowaway** (SbinSuroor) **3-8-11** LDettori(3) (led 3f: stdd: effrt & stltly hmpd 2f out: styd on: no imp)	1½	**4**	8/1	122	70
4422[8]	**Revoque (IRE) (122)** (PWChapple-Hyam) **3-8-11** JReid(6) (hld up: hdwy to trck ldrs ½-wy: effrt 2f out: nt qckn)	1¼	**5**	9/2[2]	120	68
3646[3]	**Benny The Dip (USA) (126)** (JHMGosden) **3-8-11** WRyan(7) (lw: swtg: cl up: led over 3f out tl wl over 1f out: sn rdn & btn)	¾	**6**	7/1	119	67
4422[5]	**Bijou d'Inde (116)** (MJohnston) **4-9-2** JWeaver(5) (led after 3f tl over 3f out: sn wknd)	9	**7**	25/1	105	58

(SP 119.9%) **7 Rn**

2m 5.46 (0.76) CSF £7.61 TOTE £2.20: £1.60 £2.80 (£5.60) OWNER Lord Weinstock (NEWMARKET) BRED Ballymacoll Stud Co

WEIGHT FOR AGE 3yo-5lb

4665a Pilsudski (IRE) is a smashing horse who, on all known form, was way above this lot and, despite a hard race in the Arc only days previously, he won this in style without having the clearest of runs. This was his final race in this country and he now goes for the Japan Cup. (Evens)

4392a* Loup Sauvage (USA), who is a poor mover, was one of the few perfectly relaxed on this very warm afternoon and he ran a super race but had to admit he had met a class rival. (6/1)
4422 Bahhare (USA), held up as usual, had his chances and ran well over this his longest trip to date but he was found out in the final furlong. (9/1)
3647* Stowaway found this a messy event and his rider, despite the trip being well short of his best, seemed eager to anchor him and he had no chance in the final sprint. This is best put down to experience as he is much better. (8/1)
4422 Revoque (IRE) is certainly not improving at the moment and was well tapped for speed late on. (9/2)
3646 Benny The Dip (USA), with no real pace on in the early stages, should have been helping force the pace sooner and was left wanting for speed in the last couple of furlongs. (7/1)
4422 Bijou d'Inde put in a lifeless display here and was beaten a long way out. (25/1)

4786 OWEN BROWN ROCKFEL STKS (Gp 3) (2-Y.O F) (Class A)

4-45 (4-56) **7f (Rowley)** £16,860.00 (£6,240.00: £2,995.00: £1,225.00: £487.50: £192.50) Stalls: Low GOING minus 0.13 sec per fur (G)

				SP	RR	SF
4555*	**Name of Love (IRE) (100)** (DRLoder) **2-8-12** KFallon(5) (lw: hld up: hdwy 3f out: rdn to ld ins fnl f: r.o wl)	—	**1**	9/4[1]	103	63
4267[9]	**Tadwiga (98)** (RHannon) **2-8-9** JReid(8) (trckd ldrs: nt clr rn 1½f out: swtchd lft & styd on wl)	1¼	**2**	25/1	97	57
3926[3]	**Statua (IRE) (90)** (PJMakin) **2-8-9** JFortune(4) (hld up & bhd: hdwy 2f out: styd on wl fnl f: nrst fin)	s.h	**3**	40/1	97	57
4555[2]	**Flawless (100)** (SirMarkPrescott) **2-8-9** SSanders(11) (trckd ldrs: chal 2f out: nt qckn ins fnl f)	1	**4**	11/2[3]	95	55
3740[3]	**Elshamms** (ACStewart) **2-8-9** RHills(9) (cl up: led 2f out tl ins fnl f: no ex)	hd	**5**	4/1[2]	95	55
4442[4]	**Expect To Shine (95)** (BWHills) **2-8-9** MHills(6) (hld up & bhd: hdwy 3f out: ev ch 1f out: sn rdn & btn)	1½	**6**	10/1	91	51
4567*	**Virtuous (97)** (MRStoute) **2-8-9** MJKinane(2) (lw: swtg: chsd ldrs tl wknd fnl f)	¾	**7**	12/1	89	49
4534a*	**Fiamma (IRE)** (JLDunlop) **2-8-9** TQuinn(7) (bhd & outpcd 3f out: r.o wl towards fin)	½	**8**	10/1	88	48
4556*	**Qilin (IRE)** (MHTompkins) **2-8-9** DBiggs(12) (chsd ldrs: drvn along over 2f out: wknd over 1f out)	s.h	**9**	9/1	88	48
4317*	**Elsurur (USA) (88)** (SbinSuroor) **2-8-9** LDettori(1) (lw: hld up: effrt 3f out: sn rdn & n.d)	4	**10**	8/1	79	39
4473[2]	**Belle de Nuit (IRE) (83)** (BJMeehan) **2-8-9** JWeaver(3) (led tl hdd 2f out: sn wknd)	2½	**11**	33/1	73	33
4425*	**Wenda (IRE)** (CEBrittain) **2-8-9** OPeslier(10) (hld up: effrt 3f out: sn btn)	nk	**12**	9/1	73	33
				(SP 132.4%)	**12 Rn**	

1m 26.42 (1.92) CSF £70.21 TOTE £3.00: £1.70 £8.20 £8.60 (£71.20) Trio £428.30 OWNER Mr William Fox (NEWMARKET) BRED Noel O'Callaghan
STEWARDS' ENQUIRY Sanders susp. 27-29/10/97 (excessive use of whip)
IN-FOCUS: There was a false start to this race. Stalls eleven and twelve failed to open and the rest of the field were recalled after two furlongs.
4555* Name of Love (IRE), who looked absolutely magnificent, looks as though she is improving with every run. Although she had to fight for this, she did it really well. (9/4)
4267 Tadwiga was back to form after a dismal effort last time and, had she not been blocked at a vital stage, would have given the winner plenty more to think about. (25/1)
3926 Statua (IRE) showed her previous runs to be no fluke, and got this extra furlong particularly well. She deserves to find a decent race. (40/1)
4555 Flawless, despite being 3lb better in with the winner, was beaten further this time and seems to have her problems. (11/2)
3740 Elshamms had her chances, and there was no apparent excuse, other than she was not good enough on the day. (4/1)
4442 Expect To Shine has not progressed since her early races, and seems to be the type of filly that beats herself. (10/1)
4567* Virtuous, despite having the confidence-booster of an easy win last time, again sweated up and proved disappointing when a real effort was required. (12/1: op 8/1)
4534a* Fiamma (IRE) won what appeared a moderate race in Italy last time, and found things happening too quickly. However, she picked up in the closing stages and in another half-furlong would have been in the shake-up. She looks one to keep an eye on. (10/1)

4787 NGK SPARK PLUGS H'CAP (0-95) (3-Y.O+) (Class C)

5-20 (5-29) **7f (Rowley)** £9,176.00 (£2,768.00: £1,344.00: £632.00) Stalls: Low GOING minus 0.13 sec per fur (G)

				SP	RR	SF
4308[2]	**Desert Beauty (IRE) (82)** (MRStoute) **3-9-2** LDettori(12) (hdwy stands' side over 2f out: led ins fnl f: r.o wl)	—	**1**	9/4[1]	93	64
4423[7]	**Return of Amin (85)** (JDBethell) **3-9-5** MJKinane(22) (racd centre: in tch: hdwy & ch 1f out: kpt on)	1¾	**2**	12/1	92	63
4270[5]	**Sheltering Sky (IRE) (85)** (JLDunlop) **3-9-5** TQuinn(7) (b: in tch stands' side: hdwy over 1f out: styd on)	1	**3**	9/1[2]	90	61
4565*	**At Large (IRE) (80)** (JRFanshawe) **3-9-0** OPeslier(6) (lw: chsd ldrs stands' side: outpcd 2f out: swtchd & styd on strly fnl f)	nk	**4**	12/1	84	55
4423[20]	**Safio (78)** (ABailey) **4-9-0** DWright(18) (in tch stands' side: hdwy 2f out: ch 1f out: kpt on one pce)	s.h	**5**	16/1	82	55
4456[12]	**Top Banana (81)** (HCandy) **6-8-10**(7) BarrySmith(10) (cl up stands' side: rdn 2f out: nt qckn ins fnl f)	1	**6**	25/1	83	56
4436[3]	**Style Dancer (IRE) (76)** (RMWhitaker) **3-8-10v** NDay(9) (in tch stands' side: hdwy 2f out: nvr able chal)	½	**7**	20/1	77	48
4456[7]	**Pleading (74)** (HCandy) **4-8-10** NAdams(11) (swtg: in tch stands' side: hdwy over 2f out: one pce fnl f)	nk	**8**	20/1	74	47
4561[3]	**Primo Lara (84)** (PWHarris) **5-9-6** JReid(27) (racd centre: led tl hdd & no ex ins fnl f)	2	**9**	14/1	79	52
4550[2]	**Madly Sharp (86)** (JWWatts) **6-9-8** JFortune(28) (chsd ldr: ch 1f out: nt qckn)	s.h	**10**	10/1[3]	81	54
4307[4]	**Nomore Mr Niceguy (82)** (EJAlston) **3-9-2** LCharnock(17) (lw: w ldrs stands' side tl rdn & btn ins fnl f)	nk	**11**	20/1	76	47
4561[9]	**Mullitover (75)** (MJHeaton-Ellis) **7-8-11** RCochrane(13) (sme hdwy over 2f out: nvr trbld ldrs)	s.h	**12**	16/1	69	42
4307[11]	**Bacchus (76)** (ACStewart) **3-8-10** WRyan(5) (prom stands' side tl rdn & btn appr fnl f)	hd	**13**	20/1	70	41
4558[7]	**Angel Chimes (73)** (JEBanks) **4-8-4v**(5) RMullen(16) (swtg: sn pushed along: nvr trbld ldrs)	1	**14**	11/1	65	38
4456[9]	**Tiler (IRE) (79)** (MJohnston) **5-9-1** JWeaver(15) (cl up centre tl rdn & wknd ins fnl f)	nk	**15**	14/1	70	43
3423[13]	**Master Boots (90)** (DRLoder) **4-9-12** KFallon(8) (hdwy u.p stands' side 2f out: n.d)	½	**16**	14/1	80	53
4282[18]	**Persian Fayre (87)** (JBerry) **5-9-4**(5) CLowther(3) (lw: led stands' side tl rdn & btn appr fnl f)	s.h	**17**	25/1	77	50
4182*	**Mr Majica (81)** (BJMeehan) **3-8-8**(7) GHannon(4) (chsd ldrs stands' side tl wknd over 1f out)	¾	**18**	20/1	69	40
4375[8]	**Salty Jack (IRE) (79)** (VSoane) **3-8-13** RPerham(1) (chsd ldr stands' side tl wknd qckly fnl 2f)	2½	**19**	40/1	61	32
2216[12]	**Stoppes Brow (77)** (GLMoore) **5-8-13v** AClark(23) (racd centre: prom: pushed along ½-wy: sn wknd)	4	**20**	40/1	50	23
4561[19]	**Cossack Count (80)** (SDow) **4-9-2** MartinDwyer(20) (racd centre: n.d)	nk	**21**	50/1	53	26
4241[9]	**Fletcher (82)** (HMorrison) **3-9-2** MHills(21) (racd centre: a bhd)	s.h	**22**	50/1	55	26
4554[2]	**Midyan Call (90)** (MBell) **3-9-5**(5) GFaulkner(24) (gd spd centre 5f: wknd qckly)	¾	**23**	20/1	61	32
3772[5]	**Jawhari (85)** (JLDunlop) **3-9-5** GCarter(26) (chsd ldrs centre 5f)	1¼	**24**	20/1	53	24
4680[7]	**Musick House (IRE) (82)** (MissGayKelleway) **4-9-1**(3) AWhelan(30) (racd centre: n.d)	½	**25**	25/1	49	22
3984[17]	**Lough Erne (75)** (CFWall) **5-8-11** SSanders(14) (nvr trbld ldrs)	1	**26**	33/1	40	13
4511*	**Arruhan (IRE) (85)** (PTWalwyn) **3-9-5** RHills(29) (unruly in stalls: racd centre: in tch 5f)	2½	**27**	16/1	44	15
2679[5]	**General Song (IRE) (88)** (KMcAuliffe) **3-9-8** JLowe(19) (swtg: racd centre: a bhd)	½	**28**	50/1	46	17

	High Priority (IRE) (83) (MJHaynes) **4-9-5** DBiggs(2) (wl bhd fnl 3f)	3½	**29**	50/1	33	6
				(SP 171.8%)		**29 Rn**

1m 26.66 (2.16) CSF £29.35 CT £241.56 TOTE £3.20: £1.40 £4.50 £2.80 £4.70 (£43.70) Trio £143.80 OWNER Lord Weinstock(NEWMARKET) BRED Ballymacoll Stud Farm Ltd
WEIGHT FOR AGE 3yo-2lb
4308 Desert Beauty (IRE) was supported as though defeat was out of the question in this very open-looking handicap, and she did the business in good style, getting stronger as the race progressed. (9/4: 4/1-2/1)
4423 Return of Amin ran particularly well from his draw and is obviously in top form. (12/1)
4270 Sheltering Sky (IRE) again ran well and is obviously coming back to top form. (9/1)
4565* At Large (IRE) looked a shade unlucky, getting blocked at one stage and, ridden with more dash, left the impression that he would have been in the shake-up. (12/1)
4283 Safio ran well again, and is obviously not finished with yet. (16/1)
1309 Top Banana has yet to win this season, and has never won over this trip, but he is well-handicapped and is showing plenty just now. (25/1)
4436 Style Dancer (IRE) is running particularly well at the moment. (20/1)
4561 Primo Lara looks a picture, and ran a superb race from an impossible draw. He has done all his winning on fast ground and, on over-watered tracks at the end of the season, such conditions are virtually impossible to find. (14/1)
4550 Madly Sharp ran well from a no-hope draw. (10/1)
4558 Angel Chimes, back to a proper trip, wanted nothing to do with it on her second run in a visor. (11/1)

T/Jkpt: £36,326.10 (0.2 Tckts); £40,930.83 to Pontefract 20/10/97. T/Plpt: £255.50 (337.23 Tckts). T/Qdpt: £13.80 (329.92 Tckts) AA

4595-REDCAR (L-H) (Good to firm, Good patches)
Saturday October 18th
WEATHER: sunny & warm WIND: almost nil

4788 LESLIE PETCH MEMORIAL H'CAP (0-85) (3-Y.O+) (Class D)
2-15 (2-17) **1m 2f** £3,805.00 (£1,150.00: £560.00: £265.00) Stalls: Low GOING minus 0.28 sec per fur (GF)

				SP	RR	SF
4435^{9}	**Ganga (IRE) (83)** (WJarvis) **3-9-9** GHind(16) (hld up: hdwy over 3f out: rdn over 1f out: r.o to ld last strides)	—	**1**	10/1	92	69
4383^{3}	**Infatuation (83)** (LadyHerries) **4-10-0** KDarley(3) (lw: hld up: gd hdwy over 3f out: rdn to ld over 1f out: hdd nr fin)	nk	**2**	3/1 ^{1}	92	74
4383^{10}	**The In-Laws (IRE) (81)** (SirMarkPrescott) **3-9-7** GDuffield(9) (sn bhd & pushed along: hdwy on outside 3f out: hrd rdn over 1f out: nt qckn ins fnl f)	¾	**3**	10/1	88	65
4691*	**Pekay (70)** (MJohnston) **4-9-1** 6x DHolland(15) (bhd: hdwy over 2f out: styd on wl towards fin)	2	**4**	8/1 ^{2}	74	56
4757^{5}	**Master Beveled (74)** (PDEvans) **7-9-5** ACulhane(14) (hdwy 4f out: hrd rdn & nt qckn appr fnl f)	1½	**5**	8/1 ^{2}	76	58
4591^{9}	**Blooming Amazing (70)** (JLEyre) **3-8-10** MGallagher(4) (chsd ldrs: ev ch over 1f out: kpt on sme pace)	s.h	**6**	20/1	72	49
4751^{6}	**Break the Rules (72)** (DNicholls) **5-9-3** AlexGreaves(5) (bhd: hdwy & nt clr rn over 3f out: styng on same pce whn nt clr run ins fnl f)	nk	**7**	14/1	73	55
4635*	**Mcgillycuddy Reeks (IRE) (73)** (DonEnricoIncisa) **6-9-4** KimTinkler(6) (mid div: hdwy & rdn whn nt clr run over 1f out: styng on whn n.m.r towards fin)	1¼	**8**	12/1	72	54
4477^{6}	**Time for Action (IRE) (73)** (MHTompkins) **5-9-4** WJO'Connor(10) (trckd ldr: chal over 3f out: wknd appr fnl f)	1½	**9**	11/1	70	52
4583^{13}	**Raivue (80)** (EWeymes) **3-9-6** DeanMcKeown(8) (trckd ldrs: led over 3f out tl hdd & wknd over 1f out)	2	**10**	20/1	74	51
4579^{2}	**Waterspout (USA) (72)** (MrsAJPerrett) **3-8-12** PaulEddery(11) (mid div: drvn along 4f out: wknd & eased 2f out)	8	**11**	9/1 ^{3}	53	30
4635^{5}	**Wellaki (USA) (82)** (JHMGosden) **3-9-8** DO'Donohoe(13) (sn bhd & drvn along: n.d)	2	**12**	9/1 ^{3}	60	37
431^{4}	**Selberry (82)** (PCHaslam) **3-9-8** DaleGibson(1) (mid div: hdwy appr st: lost pl over 3f out)	7	**13**	20/1	48	25
3445^{4}	**Tangshan (CAN) (75)** (MRStoute) **3-9-1** FLynch(12) (chsd ldrs: rdn over 3f out: sn wknd)	4	**14**	10/1	35	12
4558^{34}	**Miracle Kid (USA) (84)** (JHMGosden) **3-9-10v^{1}** AMcGlone(2) (led tl over 3f out: sn lost pl & eased)	6	**15**	12/1	34	11
4506^{3}	**Bedouin Honda (69)** (CEBrittain) **3-8-9** MRimmer(17) (racd wd: in tch: drvn along over 4f out: wknd over 3f out)	¾	**16**	25/1	18	—
				(SP 143.0%)		**16 Rn**

2m 5.4 (1.80) CSF £40.66 CT £313.58 TOTE £16.40: £3.20 £1.60 £2.60 £2.70 (£36.70) Trio £86.80 OWNER Cuadra Africa (NEWMARKET) BRED Cambremont Ltd Partnership
WEIGHT FOR AGE 3yo-5lb
OFFICIAL EXPLANATION **Ganga (IRE): the Stewards considered the improvement in form compared with her previous run at Haydock on 27/9/97. After hearing from the trainer who reported that the filly had run too freely in a falsely-run race at Haydock, they decided not to hold an enquiry.**
3906* Ganga (IRE) settled much better in this strongly-run race and did just enough to get up near the line. (10/1)
4383 Infatuation, as usual taken to post early, had the race run to suit him but he possibly hit the front too soon and was jut shaded near the line. (3/1: op 5/1)
4383 The In-Laws (IRE) put a poor effort last time behind her, struggling to go the pace but sticking to her guns in the closing stages. (10/1)
4691* Pekay, under a 6lb penalty, stayed on strongly late in the day but just too late to be seriously involved in the final action. (8/1)
4757 Master Beveled gets no respite. Having his second outing in three days, he did as well as could be expected on ground too fast for him. (8/1)
4436 Blooming Amazing gave a good account of himself, considering he raced up with the leaders in what looked a strongly-run race. (20/1)
4635* Mcgillycuddy Reeks (IRE), from a 5lb higher mark, was under pressure but closing when running completely out of room over a furlong out. (12/1)
3445 Tangshan (CAN), absent for 69 days after running herself into the ground last time, wore a net-muzzle in the paddock and, taken to post last, went to the start very gently. After chasing the leaders she found nothing at all under pressure. (10/1)

4789 E.B.F. MAIDEN STKS (2-Y.O F) (Class D)
2-45 (2-47) **7f** £3,395.50 (£1,024.00: £497.00: £233.50) Stalls: High GOING minus 0.28 sec per fur (GF)

				SP	RR	SF
4597^{2}	**Final Tango** (JHMGosden) **2-8-11** GHind(10) (trckd ldrs: led over 2f out: hld on wl towards fin)	—	**1**	13/8 ^{1}	86	52
4526^{10}	**Mondschein** (JLDunlop) **2-8-11** KDarley(2) (sn chsng ldrs: ev ch fnl 2f: nt qckn nr fin)	nk	**2**	7/2 ^{2}	85	51
	Ranna (ACStewart) **2-8-11** SWhitworth(8) (unf: s.i.s: sn outpcd: hdwy & hung lft over 2f out: kpt on appr fnl f)	4	**3**	11/1	76	42
4556^{4}	**Jilted (IRE) (76)** (RHannon) **2-8-11** DaneO'Neill(7) (chsd ldrs: rdn & outpcd ½-wy: styd on appr fnl f)	3	**4**	10/1	69	35

4425[7]	**Tabasco (IRE)** (MRChannon) **2-8-11** JCarroll(6) (led tl over 2f out: grad wknd)	1¾	**5**	12/1	65	31
4526[8]	**Zobaida (IRE)** (MAJarvis) **2-8-11** PaulEddery(5) (chsd ldrs: drvn along ½-wy: wknd 2f out)	7	**6**	11/2[3]	49	15
4515[2]	**Gunzells (USA) (78)** (HCandy) **2-8-11** CRutter(9) (w ldrs tl wknd 2f out)	6	**7**	7/1	36	2
	Anita Marie (IRE) (MJohnston) **2-8-11** DHolland(4) (tall: unf: s.i.s: sn chsng ldrs: rdn over 2f out: sn wknd)	½	**8**	14/1	35	1
4597[6]	**Jayess Elle** (JGFitzGerald) **2-8-11** WJO'Connor(12) (bit bkwd: s.i.s: sn w ldrs: rdn 3f out: sn wknd)	¾	**9**	25/1	33	—
4567[11]	**On Call** (SirMarkPrescott) **2-8-11** GDuffield(3) (sn bhd & rdn along)	1½	**10**	33/1	29	—
	Flamboyant Belle (MrsAJPerrett) **2-8-11** AMcGlone(11) (wl grwn: bkwd: sn outpcd & drvn along)	½	**11**	20/1	28	—
	Tiller Girl (IRE) (MJCamacho) **2-8-11** TLucas(1) (unf: scope: bkwd: reminders after s: sn wl outpced & hd)	1	**12**	33/1	26	—
				(SP 134.5%)	**12 Rn**	

1m 24.6 (1.60) CSF £7.22 TOTE £2.50: £1.30 £1.80 £4.70 (£5.20) Trio £35.90 OWNER Mrs C. A. Waters (NEWMARKET) BRED Satwa Farm

4597 Final Tango gained a well-deserved first success and always looked to just have the upper hand. (13/8: op 5/2)

4526 Mondschein, a confirmed tail-swisher, showed the benefit of her initial outing. Throwing down a strong challenge, she always looked likely to come off second best. (7/2)

Ranna, a narrow type, hung as if feeling the ground and will be suited by a step up to a mile. (11/1: 6/1-12/1)

4556 Jilted (IRE), with the blinkers left off, stuck on after being outpaced at halfway. She seems thoroughly exposed. (10/1)

Tabasco (IRE), who took a fierce grip going to the start, seemed to run herself into the ground. (12/1)

4515 Gunzells (USA), loaded with the help of a Monty Roberts-type blanket, was beaten a long way from home. (7/1)

4790 COMCAST TEESSIDE TWO-YEAR-OLD TROPHY STKS (2-Y.O) (Class B)

3-15 (3-19) **6f** £69,249.60 (£25,646.40: £12,323.20: £5,056.00: £2,028.00: £816.80) Stalls: High GOING minus 0.28 sec per fur (GF)

				SP	RR	SF
4556[2]	**Grazia** (SirMarkPrescott) **2-8-2** GDuffield(3) (lw: trckd ldrs: led over 1f out: drvn out)	—	**1**	7/2[1]	97+	50
4293[4]	**Mijana (IRE) (100)** (JHMGosden) **2-8-10** AMcGlone(19) (trckd ldrs stands' side: styd on wl ins fnl f: nt rch wnr)	1	**2**	9/1	102	55
4387a[2]	**Shudder** (WJHaggas) **2-8-4** FLynch(2) (chsd ldrs far side: styd on same pce fnl f)	½	**3**	6/1[2]	95	48
4402*	**Call To Order (82)** (CFWall) **2-8-4** SWhitworth(16) (lw: led stands' side tl ins fnl f)	1½	**4**	33/1	91	44
4266[2]	**Ho Leng (IRE)** (MissLAPerratt) **2-8-7** NKennedy(1) (hdwy 2f out: hung lft: styd on wl towards fin)	¾	**5**	20/1	92	45
4616a[5]	**Hopping Higgins (IRE)** (APO'Brien,Ireland) **2-8-8** DHolland(9) (led tl over 1f out: wknd towards fin)	hd	**6**	8/1[3]	93	46
4293[3]	**Pool Music (100)** (RHannon) **2-8-10** DaneO'Neill(26) (lw: w ldrs stands' side: nt qckn appr fnl)	hd	**7**	10/1	95	48
3905[2]	**Cease Fire (IRE) (79)** (MrsJCecil) **2-8-5** JCarroll(11) (b.hind: mid div: rdn ½-wy: styd on appr fnl f)	1	**8**	33/1	87	40
4468*	**Jacmar (IRE) (90)** (MissLAPerratt) **2-8-7** MRimmer(14) (lw: hdwy centre over 2f out: kpt on: nvr nr ldrs)	1¼	**9**	20/1	86	39
4231[3]	**Requestor (85)** (JGFitzGerald) **2-8-7** WJO'Connor(13) (w ldrs centre: edgd lft ½-wy: outpcd fnl 2f)	1	**10**	25/1	83	36
4473[5]	**Occhi Verdi (IRE) (81)** (MJohnston) **2-8-5** DeanMcKeown(12) (mid div: drvn along ½-wy: no imp)	1	**11**	50/1	78	31
3688[3]	**Mantles Star (95)** (GLewis) **2-8-4** PaulEddery(18) (mid div: rdn ½-wy: n.m.r: n.d)	hd	**12**	9/1	77	30
4253a[7]	**Bay Prince (IRE) (100)** (MRChannon) **2-8-13** AMackay(20) (chsd ldrs over 4f: sn wknd)	hd	**13**	20/1	86	39
4679[3]	**Chips (IRE) (100)** (DRCElsworth) **2-8-13** PPMurphy(5) (chsd ldrs: rdn over 2f out: sn wknd)	nk	**14**	25/1	85	38
4473[7]	**Pacifica (88)** (RBoss) **2-8-5** DSweeney(21) (mid div: effrt over 2f out: n.d)	½	**15**	50/1	76	29
4379*	**Young Josh** (JHMGosden) **2-8-12** GHind(25) (lw: sn chsng ldrs: drvn along ½-wy: sn wknd)	½	**16**	20/1	81	34
4143[7]	**Roi de Danse (79)** (JWHills) **2-8-4** MHenry(10) (mid div: sme hdwy over 2f out: sn wknd)	¾	**17**	50/1	71	24
4305[3]	**Star (85)** (MAJarvis) **2-7-13** DO'Donohoe(7) (in tch: rdn over 2f out: sn wknd)	2½	**18**	11/1	60	13
4630*	**Shalford's Honour (IRE)** (WJarvis) **2-8-7** MTebbutt(23) (lw: hld up: sme hdwy 2f out: sn wknd)	nk	**19**	14/1	67	20
4675[9]	**Blueridge Dancer (IRE) (100)** (BJMeehan) **2-8-10b** KDarley(4) (chsd ldrs over 3f: sn wknd)	hd	**20**	33/1	69	22
4468[4]	**Friar Tuck (95)** (MissLAPerratt) **2-8-7** RLappin(17) (s.i.s: a in rr)	¾	**21**	33/1	64	17
4042[6]	**Mysticism (81)** (CEBrittain) **2-7-13** DaleGibson(24) (chsd ldrs over 3f: sn lost pl)	½	**22**	50/1	55	8
4589[2]	**One Singer (85)** (MJohnston) **2-8-4** JTate(6) (sn bhd)	4	**23**	40/1	49	2
4411[3]	**Peter's Imp (IRE) (80)** (JBerry) **2-8-7** TEDurcan(8) (bhd fnl 2f)	½	**24**	40/1	51	4
3817[3]	**Rejected (83)** (RHannon) **2-8-1** CRutter(15) (prom over 3f: sn wknd)	¾	**25**	25/1	43	—
4211*	**Lord Lieutenant** (MBell) **2-8-10** ACulhane(22) (chsd ldrs: hrd rdn ½-wy: sn lost pl & eased)	9	**26**	20/1	28	—
				(SP 151.5%)	**26 Rn**	

1m 11.1 (0.90) CSF £28.95 TOTE £6.20: £2.70 £4.40 £3.90 (£64.10) Trio £103.40 OWNER Mr Cyril Humphris (NEWMARKET) BRED Cyril Humphris

4556 Grazia was backed almost to the exclusion of her rivals and the confidence was certainly justified. Ridden with more patience this time, she could be named the winner over a furlong out. Still inexperienced, she should prove very useful at three. (7/2: op 6/1)

4293 Mijana (IRE) had the strong-run race he needs. Staying on in determined fashion inside the last, he was first home on the stands' side but the winner was always containing his challenge. (9/1)

4387a Shudder, who does not look a straightforward ride, stuck on under pressure against the far rail without ever looking like finding sufficient. (6/1)

4402* Call To Order showed bags of toe on the stands' side and finished second best of that group. (33/1)

4266 Ho Leng (IRE) gave his rider problems hanging left. Putting in some good work at the finish, seven furlongs and easier ground will suit this useful sort even better. (20/1)

4616a Hopping Higgins (IRE), allowed to get on with it this time, showed her rivals on the far side a clean pair of heels for over four furlongs. (8/1)

4791 COMCAST TEESSIDE LIMITED STKS (0-70) (3-Y.O+) (Class E)

3-45 (3-49) **5f** £2,917.75 (£877.00: £423.50: £196.75) Stalls: High GOING minus 0.28 sec per fur (GF)

				SP	RR	SF
4733[4]	**Swino (70)** (PDEvans) **3-8-12** ACulhane(8) (lw: hdwy 2f out: hrd rdn & styd on to ld nr fin)	—	**1**	11/4[1]	72	54
4636[17]	**Royal Dome (IRE) (65)** (MartynWane) **5-9-4** JCarroll(9) (chsd ldrs: rdn & outpcd ½-wy: styd on & ev ch ins fnl f: nt qckn)	1	**2**	8/1	75	57
4452[4]	**Another Batchworth (61)** (EAWheeler) **5-8-2b(7)** SCarson(7) (dwlt s: swtchd lft after 1f: hdwy 2f out: led ins fnl f: wknd & hdd towards fin)	1¼	**3**	6/1[3]	62	44
4365[13]	**Palacegate Jack (IRE) (66)** (JBerry) **6-9-7b(3)** TEDurcan(6) (led: clr 2f out: wknd & hdd ins fnl f)	1¼	**4**	6/1[3]	73	55
4636[6]	**Songsheet (68)** (MSSaunders) **4-8-12(3)** PPMurphy(1) (lw: hdwy ½-wy: kpt on same pce appr fnl f)	hd	**5**	3/1[2]	64	46
3417[9]	**Master of Passion (61)** (JMPEustace) **8-8-12b** JTate(13) (b.hind: racd stands' side: chsd ldrs: hrd rdn & outpcd ½-wy: styd on ins fnl f)	1	**6**	10/1	57	39
4707[13]	**Blazing Imp (USA) (40)** (MrsJJordan) **4-9-1** MRimmer(3) (sn outpcd & rdn along: styd on appr fnl f)	2½	**7**	33/1	52	34
4414[17]	**Antithesis (IRE) (40)** (JSHaldane) **4-8-9** KDarley(5) (chsd ldr tl wknd over 1f out)	2	**8**	40/1	40	22
3898[10]	**Mutasawwar (68)** (MSSaunders) **3-8-12** AMackay(4) (s.i.s: a outpcd)	hd	**9**	14/1	43	25
3271[W]	**Superfrills (35)** (MissLCSiddall) **4-8-9** DeanMcKeown(12) (nvr wnt pce)	hd	**10**	33/1	39	21

4370^{16}	**Windrush Boy (42)** (MRBosley) **7-8-12** CRutter(10) (sn outpcd & drvn along)	1¼	**11**	20/1	38	20
4430^{4}	**Ohnonotagain (37)** (NTinkler) **5-8-9** KimTinkler(11) (sn outpcd)	¾	**12**	33/1	33	15
4214^{9}	**Fancy Clancy (34)** (MissLCSiddall) **4-8-10**ow1 OPears(2) (s.v.s: a t.o)	25	**13**	50/1	—	—
				(SP 125.1%)	**13 Rn**	

58.5 secs (1.00) CSF £22.73 TOTE £3.70: £1.40 £2.30 £2.30 (£19.40) Trio £28.40 OWNER Swinnerton Transport Ltd (WELSHPOOL) BRED Mrs F. A. Veasey

4733 Swino was best in on official figures and had to work hard but got there in the end. (11/4)

3146 Royal Dome (IRE) is obviously right back to his best. (8/1)

4452 Another Batchworth, attempting to repeat last year's victory in this event, looked very light in the paddock. Normally a speedy sort, she lost ground at the start and, forced to switch to the centre to get a run, had no more to offer in the closing stages. (6/1)

4051* Palacegate Jack (IRE) had it all to do on official figures under a penalty, but he showed all his old speed to establish a clear lead soon after halfway. (6/1)

4636 Songsheet ran a very flat race indeed. (3/1)

4792 STANLEY RACING H'CAP (0-85) (3-Y.O+) (Class D)

4-15 (4-18) **1m** £5,030.00 (£1,520.00: £740.00: £350.00) Stalls: High GOING minus 0.28 sec per fur (GF)

				SP	RR	SF
2873*	**Desert Track (85)** (JHMGosden) **3-10-0** GHind(12) (lw: chsd ldrs: edgd lft & led over 1f out: drvn out)	—	**1**	5/1^{1}	103	74
4583^{8}	**Cee-N-K (IRE) (68)** (MJohnston) **3-8-11b** DHolland(10) (mde most centre: clr over 2f out: hdd over 1f out: kpt on)	2½	**2**	20/1	81	52
4059^{19}	**Oriole (51)** (DonEnricoIncisa) **4-7-11** KimTinkler(6) (hdwy ½-wy: styd on one pce appr fnl f)	5	**3**	20/1	54	28
4583^{6}	**Jedi Knight (70)** (MWEasterby) **3-8-13** DO'Donohoe(18) (in tch: effrt over 2f out: kpt on same pce)	¾	**4**	10/1^{2}	72	43
3087^{5}	**Magic Mill (IRE) (77)** (JLEyre) **4-9-9** RLappin(11) (swtg: chsd ldrs: rdn & outpcd ½-wy: styd on fnl f)	nk	**5**	14/1	78	52
4147^{22}	**Knave's Ash (USA) (73)** (DNicholls) **6-9-5** AlexGreaves(13) (hld up: effrt over 2f out: kpt on fnl f)	¾	**6**	11/1^{3}	72	46
4511^{4}	**Mujova (IRE) (81)** (RHollinshead) **3-9-10** ACulhane(16) (s.i.s: hdwy over 2f out: kpt on fnl f: nvr nr to chal)	½	**7**	14/1	79	50
4455^{6}	**Gymcrak Flyer (66)** (GHolmes) **6-8-12** DeanMcKeown(2) (b.hind: hld up: hdwy over 2f out: hung lft: nvr nr to chal)	½	**8**	12/1	63	37
4456^{13}	**Thwaab (66)** (FWatson) **5-8-12v** NKennedy(15) (mid div: effrt over 2f out: no imp: eased over 1f out)	nk	**9**	14/1	63	37
4629^{4}	**Impulsive Air (IRE) (58)** (EWeymes) **5-8-4** GDuffield(19) (chsd ldrs stands side tl outpcd fnl 3f)	5	**10**	10/1^{2}	45	19
4561^{12}	**Tertium (IRE) (75)** (MartynWane) **5-9-7** JBramhill(17) (sn chsng ldrs: effrt 3f out: sn wknd)	½	**11**	11/1^{3}	61	35
4472^{3}	**Spanish Verdict (51)** (DenysSmith) **10-7-4**(7)ow1 PBradley(7) (w ldrs tl wknd 3f out)	¾	**12**	14/1	35	8
	Diamond Beach (70) (GMMoore) **4-9-2** PaulEddery(9) (sn bhd)	hd	**13**	40/1	54	28
4628^{8}	**Murphy's Gold (IRE) (54)** (RAFahey) **6-8-0**ow4 AMackay(20) (dwlt s: a in rr)	4	**14**	16/1	30	—
2045^{2}	**No Grousing (IRE) (79)** (PCHaslam) **3-9-8** DaleGibson(5) (chsd ldrs: rdn ½-wy: sn wknd)	¾	**15**	12/1	54	25
4436^{3}	**Nor-Do-I (70)** (JMPEustace) **3-8-13** JTate(1) (racd alone far side: w ldrs whn lost pl over 2f out)	½	**16**	11/1^{3}	44	15
4283^{2}	**Somerton Boy (IRE) (71)** (PCalver) **7-9-3** JCarroll(8) (chsd ldrs: rdn ½-wy: sn wknd & eased)	½	**17**	5/1^{1}	44	18
4639^{10}	**Royal Crusade (USA) (82)** (WJHaggas) **3-9-11** KDarley(3) (w ldrs: rdn ½-wy: lost pl & eased 2f out)	5	**18**	20/1	45	16
2160^{5}	**Doctor Bravious (IRE) (60)** (BEllison) **4-8-6** AMcGlone(4) (prom: rdn ½-wy: sn lost pl)	2½	**19**	33/1	18	—
4410^{16}	***Mountgate (60)*** (MPBielby) **5-8-6** MTebbutt(14) (Withdrawn not under Starter's orders: uns rdr (rdr sltly inj))		**W**	33/1	—	—
				(SP 147.1%)	**19 Rn**	

1m 36.3 (1.30) CSF £114.45 CT £1,791.73 TOTE £5.40: £2.20 £4.30 £8.00 £2.70 (£102.90) Trio Not won; £491.57 to Pontefract 20/10/97

OWNER Sheikh Mohammed (NEWMARKET) BRED Sheikh Mohammed Bin Rashid Al Maktoum

LONG HANDICAP Spanish Verdict 7-9

WEIGHT FOR AGE 3yo-3lb

2873* Desert Track, fresh and well after an absence of 91 days, took this in decisive fashion despite a marked tendency to hang left, giving Gary Hind a three-timer on what he regards as his local and lucky track. (5/1)

3262 Cee-N-K (IRE), with the blinkers on again, showed in a clear lead with over two furlongs left to run, but in the end he was comprehensively beaten by the winner. (20/1)

3777 Oriole, having his first outing for 39 days, gave a sound account and should be sharper as a result. (20/1)

4583 Jedi Knight looks in the grip of the Handicapper at present. (10/1)

3087 Magic Mill (IRE), having his first outing for 82 days, was very warm beforehand. Sticking on after being outpaced, he is worth a try over a mile and a quarter. (14/1)

3801 Knave's Ash (USA), who has won off a 21lb higher mark, was by no means knocked about, and no doubt will succeed some day for his new connections. (11/1)

4283 Somerton Boy (IRE) seems to reserve his best for Ayr and, under pressure at halfway, his rider sensibly soon gave up. (5/1)

4793 TYNE & WEAR MEDIAN AUCTION MAIDEN STKS (2-Y.O) (Class E)

4-50 (4-51) **1m** £3,073.75 (£925.00: £447.50: £208.75) Stalls: High GOING minus 0.28 sec per fur (GF)

				SP	RR	SF
2688^{5}	**Herminius (IRE) (82)** (JLDunlop) **2-9-0** KDarley(4) (in tch: drvn along & edgd rt ½-wy: led 1f out: drvn clr)	—	**1**	5/1^{3}	80	41
4017^{2}	**Eco Friendly** (BWHills) **2-9-0** PaulEddery(10) (swtg: chsd ldrs: drvn along ½-wy: nt qckn fnl f)	2	**2**	2/1^{1}	76	37
4460^{4}	**O' Higgins (IRE) (56)** (RBoss) **2-9-0** MTebbutt(5) (trckd ldrs: effrt over 2f out: styd on same pce appr fnl f)	1¼	**3**	16/1	74	35
4638^{5}	**Double Edged** (MJohnston) **2-9-0** DHolland(12) (lw: w ldrs: kpt on sme pce appr fnl f)	s.h	**4**	11/2	73	34
4382^{3}	**Campari (IRE) (75)** (MAJarvis) **2-8-9** DeanMcKeown(8) (swtg: mde most tl hdd & wknd 1f out)	1	**5**	9/2^{2}	66	27
4638^{8}	**St Clair Shores (USA)** (MRStoute) **2-8-9** FLynch(14) (chsd ldrs: rdn over 3f out: wknd 2f out)	6	**6**	12/1	54	15
4413^{5}	**Little Brave** (JMPEustace) **2-9-0** JTate(15) (in tch: rdn ½-wy: sn outpcd)	5	**7**	10/1	49	10
4483^{9}	**Gaelic Quinie (IRE) (52)** (GROldroyd) **2-8-9** KHodgson(7) (chsd ldrs: outpcd fnl 3f)	1½	**8**	50/1	41	2
	Coded Message (IRE) (JAGlover) **2-9-0** CRutter(3) (unf: bkwd: sn outpcd: sme hdwy 2f out: n.d)	s.h	**9**	25/1	46	7
4309^{W}	**Manila Moon (USA)** (JJO'Neill) **2-8-11**(3) TEDurcan(1) (wl grwn: bit bkwd: dwlt s: hdwy ½-wy: sn wknd)	5	**10**	33/1	36	—
4581^{9}	**Norski Lad** (SirMarkPrescott) **2-9-0** GDuffield(6) (sn bhd & pushed along)	1½	**11**	12/1	33	—
4514^{6}	**Strategic Air** (EWeymes) **2-9-0** AMcGlone(13) (plld hrd: outpcd ½-wy: sn bhd)	½	**12**	16/1	32	—
4507^{6}	**Common View (IRE) (68)** (NTinkler) **2-9-0** KimTinkler(9) (sn outpcd)	nk	**13**	40/1	32	—
4433^{12}	**College Mount** (MPBielby) **2-9-0** ACulhane(2) (w ldrs tl wknd over 3f out: sn bhd)	1¼	**14**	50/1	29	—
	Bahia Blanca Sun (IRE) (JLEyre) **2-9-0** OPears(11) (leggy: unf: bit bkwd: chsd ldrs tl ½-wy: sn lost pl)	2½	**15**	25/1	24	—
				(SP 136.8%)	**15 Rn**	

1m 38.2 (3.20) CSF £15.11 TOTE £4.90: £1.60 £1.30 £7.10 (£4.60) Trio £52.10 OWNER Mr D. R. Hunnisett (ARUNDEL) BRED Rathasker Stud

2688 Herminius (IRE), who showed plenty of promise first-time, put two rather disappointing efforts behind him. Edging right and straightened by the running rail, he eventually took this run-of-the-mill event in convincing fashion. (5/1)

4017 Eco Friendly, who has changed stables, was warm beforehand. Under pressure at halfway, he soon had every chance, but the winner proved much too strong in the closing stages. (2/1)
4460 O' Higgins (IRE) was banging his head against a brick wall on official figures, but he seemed to give a good account of himself, casting doubt on the value of the form. (16/1)
4638 Double Edged, who has a pronounced round action, looks in need of more time. (11/2: 4/1-6/1)
4382 Campari (IRE), an edgy type, led on sufferance, but she weakened towards the finish. (9/2)
St Clair Shores (USA), a pronounced tail-swisher, is only moderate and looks to have little room for improvement. (12/1)

4794 LEVY BOARD H'CAP (0-70) (3-Y.O+) (Class E)

5-25 (5-25) **1m 6f 19y** £3,463.75 (£1,045.00: £507.50: £238.75) Stalls: Centre GOING minus 0.28 sec per fur (GF)

	Horse / details	Dist	Pos	SP	RR	SF
	Outset (IRE) (56) (MDHammond) **7-9-4** JCarroll(6) (sn chsng ldrs: led over 2f out: styd on wl fnl f)	—	1	33/1	68	47
4585³	**Highfield Fizz (43)** (CWFairhurst) **5-8-2**(3) DarrenMoffatt(1) (b.off hind: bhd: hdwy on outside 3f out: nt qckn appr fnl f)	3½	2	14/1	51	30
4438*	**Devilish Charm (USA) (68)** (MrsAJPerrett) **3-9-7** PaulEddery(11) (hdwy 8f out: hmpd over 5f out: hdwy to chse ldrs over 2f out: styd on same pce)	1¼	3	13/2 2	75	45
4235⁸	**Spick And Span (51)** (CWThornton) **3-8-4** DeanMcKeown(5) (in tch: hdwy over 3f out: sn chsng ldrs: one pce fnl 2f)	s.h	4	16/1	58	28
3974⁴	**Midyan Blue (IRE) (62)** (JMPEustace) **7-9-10v¹** JTate(12) (trckd ldrs: led & hung lft over 3f out: hdd over 2f out: wknd over 1f out)	1¼	5	8/1 3	67	46
4633⁸	**Spa Lane (38)** (MPBielby) **4-8-0** NKennedy(4) (hld up: hdwy over 2f out: sn rdn & no imp)	4	6	14/1	39	18
430⁶	**Parrot's Hill (IRE) (45)** (MHTompkins) **4-8-7** DaleGibson(15) (hld up: hdwy over 3f out: sn rdn & hung lft: no imp)	2½	7	16/1	43	22
*4481*¹⁰	**Shakiyr (FR) (43)** (RHollinshead) **6-8-5** FLynch(8) (hld up: hdwy on outside 3f out: nvr nr ldrs)	3½	8	33/1	37	16
4432⁴	**Fullopep (61)** (MrsMReveley) **3-9-0** ACulhane(16) (hdwy 7f out: rdn over 2f out: nvr nr to chal)	2	9	10/1	53	23
4405⁴	**Duncombe Hall (38)** (CACyzer) **4-8-0** AMackay(13) (hdwy 8f out: sn prom: drvn along over 3f out: wknd over 2f out)	5	10	16/1	24	3
4509³	**Lighten Up (59)** (CEBrittain) **3-8-12** MRimmer(2) (swtg: trckd ldrs: ev ch whn hmpd over 3f out: wknd over 2f out)	2½	11	8/1 3	42	12
*4572*²	**Mister Aspecto (IRE) (59)** (MJohnston) **4-9-7v** DHolland(10) (sn chsng ldrs: led over 4f out tl over 3f out: sn lost pl)	¾	12	12/1	41	20
3931³	**Polenista (55)** (JLDunlop) **3-8-8** KDarley(9) (sn prom: rdn over 3f out: lost pl over 2f out)	5	13	3/1 1	31	1
4235³	**Farfields Prince (43)** (DNicholls) **5-8-5** GDuffield(7) (led tl over 4f out: sn wknd)	11	14	8/1 3	7	—
*4481*¹¹	**Broughtons Formula (44)** (WJMusson) **7-8-3b**(3) PMcCabe(14) (sn wl bhd)	26	15	12/1	—	—

(SP 133.0%) **15 Rn**

3m 5.1 (5.80) CSF £437.32 CT £3,093.36 TOTE £50.50: £5.50 £3.00 £4.40 (£183.80) Trio £419.50; £472.78 to Pontefract 20/10/97 OWNER Mr Mark Kilner (MIDDLEHAM) BRED Lexington Thoroughbreds Ltd
WEIGHT FOR AGE 3yo-9lb

Outset (IRE), no doubt having a warm-up outing before recommencing his hurdling campaign, pulled off a shock result, but there was no fluke about this, as he stayed on in determined fashion to pull clear in the final furlong. (33/1)
4585 Highfield Fizz invariably seems to get placed, but is finding it very hard to get her head in front. (14/1)
4438* Devilish Charm (USA), from a 3lb higher mark, had to be snatched up turning in. Driven up onto the heels of the leaders three furlongs from home, he then looked woefully one-paced. (13/2)
4235 Spick And Span seemed to appreciate the extra half-mile, without ever looking likely to prove a danger. (16/1)
3974 Midyan Blue (IRE), in a visor for the first time, hung violently left when hitting the front, causing real problems for Lighten Up on his inside. (8/1)
2316 Spa Lane, well backed at long odds, travelled strongly off the pace but, when picked up, he showed precious little interest. (14/1)
4509 Lighten Up, warm beforehand, raced keenly, but looked to have little more to give when hampered by Midyan Blue just under half-a-mile from home. (8/1)
3931 Polenista, flat-out once in line for home, never looked a threat, and her rider called it a day with over two furlongs left to run. She is proving expensive to follow. (3/1: 9/4-4/1)
351 Broughtons Formula (12/1: op 8/1)

T/Plpt: £26.60 (982.04 Tckts). T/Qdpt: £15.70 (65.12 Tckts) WG

4589-WOLVERHAMPTON (L-H) (Standard)

Saturday October 18th

Visibility races 3, 4, 5, fair: race 6 mod.
WEATHER: fine WIND: nil

4795 ATHENA MEDIAN AUCTION MAIDEN STKS (3-Y.O) (Class F)

7-00 (7-01) **7f (Fibresand)** £2,070.00 (£570.00: £270.00) Stalls: High GOING: 0.05 sec per fur (STD)

	Horse / details	Dist	Pos	SP	RR	SF
4518¹³	**Dorado Beach (39)** (LGCottrell) **3-8-9** NCarlisle(10) (trckd ldrs: ev ch over 1f out: rdn to ld nr fin)	—	1	12/1	59	25
4070¹⁵	**Fonteyn (78)** (ACStewart) **3-8-9** SWhitworth(8) (lw: a.p: led over 1f out: rdn & edgd lft fnl f: ct nr fin)	nk	2	4/5 1	58	24
4601²⁴	**Superapparos (35)** (SRBowring) **3-8-11**(3) CTeague(1) (led over 5f: one pce)	2	3	33/1	59	25
*4574*⁸	**Don't Worry Mike (56)** (JLSpearing) **3-8-11**(3) PFessey(3) (sn wl bhd: c wd & hdwy over 2f out: nrst fin)	3½	4	10/1 3	51	17
4221¹⁴	**Amelia Jane** (LMontagueHall) **3-8-2**(7) MHarfield(11) (chsd ldrs: rdn 3f out: sn no imp)	3½	5	33/1	38	4
4601¹⁴	**Toss And Tumble (40)** (WWHaigh) **3-8-9** DaneO'Neill(7) (chsd ldrs over 4f)	4	6	14/1	29	—
4290¹¹	**Who Dealt (40)** (RHollinshead) **3-8-9** JQuinn(12) (dwlt: effrt 3f out: nvr rchd ldrs)	1	7	25/1	26	—
4601²⁰	**Redspet (25)** (SRBowring) **3-8-6**(3) DSweeney(9) (chsd ldrs tl rdn & wknd wl over 1f out)	½	8	33/1	25	—
	Ellamine (DHaydnJones) **3-8-9** SDrowne(4) (lt-f: unf: dwlt: a bhd)	¾	9	20/1	24	—
4586¹⁴	**Joyful Joy (28)** (BPJBaugh) **3-8-6**(3) PRoberts(2) (chsd ldrs tl wknd 2f out)	½	10	33/1	22	—
3850⁵	**Passion** (TGMills) **3-8-9v¹** TWilliams(6) (w ldr 4f)	14	11	11/2 2	—	—
	Verity (LordHuntingdon) **3-8-9** JFEgan(5) (unf: s.i.s: a bhd)	5	12	11/2 2	—	—

(SP 130.1%) **12 Rn**

1m 30.9 (6.20) CSF £20.78 TOTE £10.20: £2.20 £1.50 £6.70 (£6.50) Trio £60.10 OWNER Mr Ray Richards (CULLOMPTON) BRED Berkshire Equestrian Services Ltd

3641 Dorado Beach, not inconvenienced by the step back up to seven furlongs, carried her head rather high in the straight, but stayed on well enough to lead where it matters. (12/1: op 7/1)
2580 Fonteyn seemed to have found an easy race to break her run of bad luck in close finishes, but is an edgy sort and, hanging away from the whip in the last furlong, caused her jockey to have to stop riding in the last fifty yards, costing her the race. (4/5)
412 Superapparos had a low draw, which seemed to be an advantage to front-runners on this particular night, and did his best to use it. (33/1)
3702 Don't Worry Mike, who usually races close to the pace, had lost his pitch completely after a furlong and, only staying on late, is almost certainly better than this. (10/1: op 6/1)
3425 Amelia Jane, stepping up in trip on her All-Weather debut, was easily left behind on the home turn. (33/1)
3807 Toss And Tumble, a good mover, was losing her pitch leaving the back straight. (14/1)

4796 HERA CLAIMING STKS (2-Y.O) (Class F)

7-30 (7-32) **6f (Fibresand)** £1,932.00 (£532.00: £252.00) Stalls: Low GOING: 0.05 sec per fur (STD)

Form	Horse	Dist	Pos	SP	RR	SF
4573^{5}	**Russian Romeo (IRE) (56)** (BAMcMahon) **2-8-4b**(7) SRighton(1) (mde all: rdn & edgd rt fnl f: r.o)	—	1	16/1	74	28
4595*	**Greenbrook (69)** (WGMTurner) **2-8-8**(7) DMcGaffin(2) (chsd wnr: rdn & no imp appr fnl f)	2½	2	4/1^{2}	71	25
4593^{3}	**Malozza (65)** (PDEvans) **2-8-2** JFEgan(13) (lw: chsd ldrs: rdn over 2f out: kpt on ins fnl f)	1¾	3	7/2^{1}	54	8
4403^{5}	**Always Lucky (67)** (JBerry) **2-8-7**(3) PRoberts(11) (prom: no imp appr fnl f)	½	4	6/1	60	14
4545^{13}	**Memorial (IRE) (56)** (RHannon) **2-8-11** DaneO'Neill(4) (lw: bhd: rdn 3f out: styd on wl fnl 2f: nvr able to chal)	1½	5	20/1	57	11
4401^{4}	**Shannon (IRE) (52)** (CADwyer) **2-8-0** JQuinn(12) (chsd ldrs: rdn 2f out: no imp)	1¼	6	12/1	43	—
4573^{3}	**Super Geil (56)** (CADwyer) **2-7-11**(3) RFfrench(6) (lw: hdwy 2f out: nvr nr ldrs)	¾	7	11/2^{3}	41	—
4543^{6}	**Legal Lark (IRE) (70)** (PHowling) **2-9-1** SWhitworth(9) (chsd ldrs tl wknd over 1f out)	nk	8	8/1	55	9
4543^{10}	**Noble Patriot** (RHollinshead) **2-9-1** MWigham(10) (chsd ldrs 3f)	1½	9	33/1	51	5
4362^{11}	**Junior Muffin (IRE) (73)** (JBerry) **2-8-12**(3) PFessey(3) (dwlt: a bhd)	¾	10	9/1	49	3
4178^{7}	**Safabee (55)** (JCullinan) **2-7-12** NCarlisle(5) (a bhd)	2	11	25/1	27	—
4595^{13}	**Robert's Daughter** (JBalding) **2-8-5** JEdmunds(8) (rdn over 2f out: sn bhd)	4	12	50/1	23	—
				(SP 120.1%)	**12 Rn**	

1m 16.3 (5.10) CSF £70.36 TOTE £18.80: £4.40 £1.70 £1.80 (£57.20) Trio £84.70; £41.79 to Pontefract 20/10/97 OWNER Mr R. L. Bedding (TAMWORTH) BRED Peadar Devereux
4573 Russian Romeo (IRE), who had not been able to get to the front in either of his races since his selling race win, broke well from the inside stall and proved game in the straight. (16/1)
4595* Greenbrook, drawn outside the winner, would have liked to lead himself but was always going second-best. (4/1)
4593 Malozza did her best, but the writing was on the wall, with her pilot hard at work some way out. (7/2)
4403 Always Lucky could not dominate and jinked as a rival crossed in front of her early in the straight. (6/1)
1251 Memorial (IRE), blindfolded for stalls entry, stayed on as if another furlong was needed. (20/1)
4401 Shannon (IRE) was coming back for more at the finish, and should get seven well on this surface. (12/1)
4543 Legal Lark (IRE), on his toes and taken down early, could not get to the front and had done his running by the home turn. (8/1)
4178 Junior Muffin (IRE) (9/1: 6/1-10/1)

4797 VALLEY PADDOCKS RACING FAT BOYS ON TOUR H'CAP (0-95) (3-Y.O+) (Class C)

8-00 (8-01) **6f (Fibresand)** £5,589.80 (£1,669.40: £798.20: £362.60) Stalls: Low GOING: 0.05 sec per fur (STD)

Form	Horse	Dist	Pos	SP	RR	SF
*4482**	**State of Caution (88)** (DShaw) **4-9-13v** JFanning(1) (w ldr: led ins fnl f: rdn out)	—	1	8/1^{3}	96	65
4282^{26}	**Zuhair (75)** (DMcCain) **4-8-11**(3) PFessey(7) (b: mde most tl ins fnl f: unable qckn)	nk	2	20/1	82	51
4280^{8}	**Double Oscar (IRE) (80)** (DNicholls) **4-8-12b**(7) ANicholls(9) (hld up: hdwy over 1f out: r.o wl fnl f)	3	3	10/1	79	48
4013^{4}	**Sir Joey (USA) (82)** (PGMurphy) **8-9-7** SDrowne(8) (chsd ldrs: rdn 2f out: kpt on fnl f)	s.h	4	9/1	81	50
4423^{12}	**Waypoint (80)** (RCharlton) **4-9-5** TSprake(5) (in tch: hdwy over 1f out: r.o)	nk	5	5/1^{1}	78	47
4456^{16}	**The Happy Fox (IRE) (88)** (BAMcMahon) **5-9-13b** LNewton(4) (w ldrs tl rdn & wknd over 1f out)	hd	6	11/1	86	55
4467^{4}	**Ziggy's Dancer (USA) (86)** (EJAlston) **6-9-11** JFEgan(11) (hdwy over 1f out: nt rchd ldrs)	½	7	10/1	83	52
4591^{7}	**Forcing Bid (80)** (SirMarkPrescott) **3-9-4** MWigham(2) (lw: sn pushed along: chsd ldrs: btn over 2f out)	1¼	8	6/1^{2}	73	41
4276^{10}	**Golden Pound (USA) (75)** (MissGayKelleway) **5-8-11v^{1}**(3) RFfrench(6) (lw: chsd ldrs: rdn 2f out: sn btn)	¾	9	5/1^{1}	66	35
4550^{11}	**Mr Bergerac (IRE) (87)** (BPalling) **6-9-9**(3) DSweeney(12) (lw: hld up: effrt 2f out: nvr nr ldrs)	nk	10	9/1	78	47
4482^{10}	**Robo Magic (USA) (78)** (LMontagueHall) **5-9-3** DaneO'Neill(13) (b: s.i.s: nvr trbld ldrs)	2	11	14/1	63	32
4280^{25}	**Iblis (IRE) (76)** (GWragg) **5-9-1v^{1}** JQuinn(3) (chsd ldrs 3f: sn wl bhd)	5	12	10/1	48	17
				(SP 125.8%)	**12 Rn**	

1m 14.7 (3.50) CSF £151.14 CT £1,515.24 TOTE £11.40: £2.80 £6.20 £3.90 (£88.50) Trio £99.00; £111.58 to Pontefract 20/10/97 OWNER Mr J. C. Fretwell (NEWARK) BRED C. Wiggins
WEIGHT FOR AGE 3yo-1lb
IN-FOCUS: **Unusually for the track, being on the inside and drawn low was not a disadvantage. Front-runners had an excellent nightwith the often-successful tactics of coming wide on the home bend to deliver a late challenge proving fruitless.**
4482* State of Caution took full advantage of a good draw and was never out of the first two. (8/1: 6/1-9/1)
3508a Zuhair, better on the All-Weather than on turf, ran a cracker and deserves to find a similar race. (20/1)
4280 Double Oscar (IRE) has yet to win beyond six furlongs, but recent evidence suggests he is worth another try over further. (10/1)
4013 Sir Joey (USA), with his tongue tied down for his All-Weather debut, did not perform at all badly considering the Handicapper made no allowance for the old boy's inexperience of the surface. (9/1)
2835* Waypoint, up a stone on the All-Weather without running on the surface, did not do badly in the straight, but seven is probably her ideal trip. (5/1)
4137 The Happy Fox (IRE), beaten eight times on turf since winning over course and distance in June, was the first of the three trailblazers to crack. (11/1)
3604 Golden Pound (USA) (5/1: 4/1-6/1)

4798 S.J. DIXON H'CAP (0-60) (3-Y.O+) (Class F)

8-30 (8-31) **1m 100y (Fibresand)** £2,070.00 (£570.00: £270.00) Stalls: Low GOING: 0.05 sec per fur (STD)

Form	Horse	Dist	Pos	SP	RR	SF
3696^{2}	**Sea Ya Maite (58)** (SRBowring) **3-9-8**(3) CTeague(12) (b: hdwy over 4f out: chal 2f out: led & edgd rt ins fnl f: shkn up & r.o)	—	1	13/2^{3}	71	56
3608^{7}	**Phoenix Princess (53)** (BAMcMahon) **3-9-6** JFortune(4) (a.p: led over 3f out: hdd & hung lft ins fnl f)	2	2	10/1	62	47

*4591*³ **Molly Music (60)** (GGMargarson) **3-9-13** GBardwell(7) (chsd ldrs: rdn 5f out: one pce fnl 2f)	5	**3**	7/1	60	45
3759⁶ **Heathyards Lady (USA) (49)** (RHollinshead) **6-9-5** JQuinn(13) (b: bhd: hdwy over 3f out: nvr nrr)	1¼	**4**	11/1	46	34
4580⁸ **Be Warned (55)** (JPearce) **6-9-11v** MWigham(8) (sn pushed along: in tch: no hdwy fnl 2f)	1¼	**5**	8/1	50	38
*4571*⁴ **Legal Issue (IRE) (52)** (WWHaigh) **5-9-8** ACulhane(11) (lw: dwlt: hdwy over 4f out: nt clr run over 1f out: no ch after)	s.h	**6**	3/1 1	47	35
4448³ **Homestead (51)** (RHannon) **3-9-4** DaneO'Neill(9) (bhd: hdwy 5f out: hmpd wl over 1f out: nvr plcd to chal)	5	**7**	7/2 2	37	22
Holloway Melody (49) (BAMcMahon) **4-9-5** JBramhill(3) (bit bkwd: chsd ldrs: rdn 3f out: btn 2f out)	6	**8**	20/1	23	11
*4050*¹⁶ **Live Project (IRE) (56)** (RCraggs) **5-9-9**(3) RFfrench(6) (prom over 4f)	hd	**9**	25/1	30	18
*1786*⁵ **Jigsaw Boy (55)** (PGMurphy) **8-9-11** SDrowne(10) (pushed along 4f out: nvr nr to chal)	2½	**10**	12/1	24	12
4580¹³ **Deerly (50)** (RDickin) **4-8-13**(7) PMundy(5) (prom 6f)	1	**11**	33/1	17	5
4010⁷ **Red Embers (55)** (RCSpicer) **3-9-8** AClark(2) (s.i.s: a bhd)	1¼	**12**	33/1	20	5
*4574*⁷ **Hurgill Times (53)** (DShaw) **3-9-6v** JFanning(1) (led 5f: sn wknd)	1½	**13**	25/1	15	—

(SP 127.6%) **13 Rn**

1m 50.9 (5.90) CSF £63.73 CT £451.84 TOTE £6.10: £1.70 £2.60 £2.40 (£30.10) Trio £80.70; £35.28 to Pontefract 20/10/97 OWNER Mr S. R. Bowring (EDWINSTOWE) BRED S. R. Bowring

WEIGHT FOR AGE 3yo-3lb

OFFICIAL EXPLANATION **Legal Issue: the trainer was unable to offer any explanation for the horse's poor performance.**

3696 Sea Ya Maite confirmed recent promise in fine style, but is a tricky ride and, though travelling much the best from some way out, was kidded along to take the prize. (13/2)

2912 Phoenix Princess got a lead to past halfway, and this seemed to bring the best out of her. (10/1)

4591 Molly Music back over her ideal trip, ran a fine race as she is hardly built to carry big weights. (7/1)

3759 Heathyards Lady (USA), a frustrating mare on a losing run of twenty-six, should not be completely written off as this was not a night to try coming fast and late. (11/1)

4580 Be Warned had a good draw when winning at Yarmouth, but is a tail-flasher and does not seem as good as he was a couple of years back. (8/1)

4571 Legal Issue (IRE), with everything looking set-up for him, missed the break and, although quite close to the leaders, was booked for a place at best when hampered straightening up for the finish. (3/1)

4448 Homestead, making his debut on the surface, caught the eye courtesy of some rather odd tactics, and is worth bearing in mind. (7/2)

4799 ARTEMIS (S) STKS (2-Y.O F) (Class G)

9-00 (9-01) **1m 100y (Fibresand)** £1,725.00 (£475.00: £225.00) Stalls: Low GOING: 0.05 sec per fur (STD)

			SP	RR	SF
4576¹¹ **Pink Ticket (51)** (PDEvans) **2-8-7** JFEgan(10) (led 3f: rallied over 2f out: led over 1f out: rdn out)	—	**1**	7/2 2	62	17
2893⁹ **Dance To The Beat** (MartynMeade) **2-8-7** TSprake(4) (hmpd after 1f: sn in tch: hdwy 2f out: r.o wl ins fnl f)	2	**2**	7/2 2	58	13
4627⁴ **Cherished (IRE) (56)** (NTinkler) **2-8-7** SSanders(7) (prom: led over 3f out: clr over 2f out: hdd over 1f out: one pce)	1	**3**	2/1 1	56	11
*4573*⁷ **Abstone Pet Girl** (PDEvans) **2-8-0**(7) AMcCarthy(3) (chsd ldrs: no imp fnl 3f)	10	**4**	25/1	37	—
4627⁸ **Total Tropix** (WJHaggas) **2-8-7** FLynch(5) (b: b.hind: bhd: hdwy 2f out: edgd lft fnl f: nvr rchd ldrs)	¾	**5**	16/1	36	—
*3072*⁷ **Ruby Bear** (WMBrisbourne) **2-8-4**(3) RFfrench(2) (b.hind: bhd tl some hdwy appr fnl f)	8	**6**	33/1	21	—
*4593*⁶ **Rock From The Sun (51)** (WGMTurner) **2-8-9b**(3) DSweeney(8) (hdwy 5f out: wknd 2f out)	¾	**7**	11/1	24	—
*4483*⁴ **Rosewood Lady (IRE) (49)** (KRBurke) **2-8-12** AClark(6) (hdwy 4f out: sn chsng ldr: wknd over 1f out)	1¾	**8**	11/2 3	21	—
4604⁹ **Dorton Grange (52)** (KCComerford) **2-8-0**(7) JBosley(1) (s.i.s: a bhd)	½	**9**	33/1	15	—
4627⁹ **Blanche The Almond** (CASmith) **2-8-7v¹** SDrowne(9) (reard s: a bhd)	2	**10**	12/1	11	—
4208⁷ **Candy Twist (48)** (RonaldThompson) **2-8-7** VHalliday(13) (chsd ldr tl led over 5f out: hdd over 3f out: wknd 2f out)	9	**11**	14/1	—	—

(SP 131.5%) **11 Rn**

1m 53.3 (8.30) CSF £16.54 TOTE £4.30: £1.50 £2.10 £1.40 (£11.30) Trio £7.10 OWNER Mr John Pugh (WELSHPOOL) BRED Mrs F. A. Veasey

Bt in 4000 gns

4303 Pink Ticket found unexpected reserves of stamina, but was hugging the inside rail on the home turn when it would have been easier to pull wide, and that probably made the difference. (7/2)

2306 Dance To The Beat, having her first run on the surface, had little chance of a clear passage on the first bend as she appeared to find the turns too sharp. Bred to stay, she was staying on well at the post and can be considered rather unlucky. (7/2)

4627 Cherished (IRE) looked to have taken the winner's measure when going clear early on the home turn, but the complexion changed dramatically on straightening up. Finishing so far clear of the fourth it is hard to say she definitely did not stay, but she would have been mighty hard to beat over seven. (2/1: op 3/1)

Abstone Pet Girl stuck to the favoured inside but was easily left behind. (25/1)

Total Tropix, pulled out to make progress on the home turn, might have got a good deal closer but for the way the track was riding. (16/1)

Ruby Bear looked sure to finish just about last until staying on up the inside past beaten horses. (33/1)

3628 Candy Twist (14/1: op 8/1)

4800 APOLLO H'CAP (0-70) (3-Y.O+ F & M) (Class E)

9-30 (9-30) **1m 4f (Fibresand)** £2,671.00 (£751.00: £367.00) Stalls: Low GOING: 0.05 sec per fur (STD)

			SP	RR	SF
4633¹⁵ **Welcome Home (43)** (PTDalton) **3-7-12**ow2 NKennedy(7) (mde all: clr 4f out: hld on wl ins fnl f)	—	**1**	33/1	56	20
*4484*² **Portite Sophie (43)** (MBrittain) **6-7-12**(7) DMernagh(5) (chsd wnr: outpcd 4f out: rdn 2f out: unable qckn ins fnl f)	1¾	**2**	7/1	54	27
4584⁴ **Tart (FR) (56)** (DNicholls) **4-8-11**(7) ANicholls(11) (hld up: hdwy 5f out: r.o fnl f)	nk	**3**	13/2 3	66	39
*4484*⁵ **Madam Lucy (43)** (JLSpearing) **3-7-9**(3) PFessey(4) (chsd ldrs: outpcd 4f out: rallied over 1f out: r.o wl fnl f)	s.h	**4**	16/1	53	19
4466³ **Classic Ballet (FR) (66)** (RGuest) **4-9-9**(5) CLowther(1) (chsd ldrs: rdn 3f out: one pce)	½	**5**	9/4 1	76	49
4632¹² **Fantasy Girl (IRE) (54)** (JLDunlop) **3-8-9** JFortune(6) (lw: chsd ldrs: no hdwy fnl 3f)	2½	**6**	10/1	60	26
4667¹⁰ **Rasayel (USA) (50)** (PDEvans) **7-8-5**(7) AMcCarthy(10) (hld up: hdwy 7f out: wknd over 2f out)	4	**7**	6/1 2	51	24
4213⁴ **Shilling (IRE) (60)** (ACStewart) **3-9-1** SWhitworth(2) (prom tl wknd 2f out)	¾	**8**	6/1 2	60	26
4060⁹ **Minster Star (60)** (JLSpearing) **3-9-1** SDrowne(3) (dwlt: nvr nr to chal)	5	**9**	25/1	53	19
4465¹⁴ **Ilandra (IRE) (39)** (GLMoore) **5-7-8**(7) PDoe(9) (a bhd)	11	**10**	14/1	18	—
2727* **Nubile (52)** (WJMusson) **3-8-7** JQuinn(8) (lw: hld up: effrt 5f out: wknd over 3f out)	6	**11**	12/1	23	—
4608¹⁰ **Dannistar (41)** (WMBrisbourne) **5-8-3** JFEgan(12) (b.hind: rdn 5f out: a bhd)	1	**12**	8/1	10	—

(SP 132.4%) **12 Rn**

2m 42.7 (10.20) CSF £252.49 CT £1,588.97 TOTE £31.40: £6.00 £2.70 £1.90 (£110.00) Trio £118.70; £133.83 to Pontefract 20/10/97 OWNER Messinger Stud Ltd (BURTON-ON-TRENT) BRED Messinger Stud Ltd

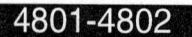

LONG HANDICAP Welcome Home 7-9
WEIGHT FOR AGE 3yo-7lb

OFFICIAL EXPLANATION Welcome Home: the Stewards considered the improvement in form compared with her previous run at Nottingham on 8/10/97 and, after hearing from her trainer who reported that the mare was unable to dominate on the very soft ground at Nottingham and seemed to relish this All-Weather surface, the Stewards decided not to hold an enquiry.

3992 Welcome Home, able to dominate over a suitable trip at last, proved very game as she began to tie up inside the final furlong. (33/1)
4484 Portite Sophie, back up in trip, looked to have a chance inside the final furlong, but has always found winning difficult and the winner proved too strong. (7/1)
4584 Tart (FR) kept plugging away, and stayed on quite well late in the day when her pilot eventually switched his stick. (13/2)
4484 Madam Lucy appeared to stay this trip, and this sort of work does give her a chance of finding another race. (16/1)
4466 Classic Ballet (FR), drawn on the inside, stayed close to the rail which seemed favoured on this occasion, but was beaten by the weight. (9/4)
1301 Fantasy Girl (IRE) could not make much impact, but raced wide for most of the race and is not a lost cause quite yet. (10/1)
4453 Dannistar (8/1: op 14/1)

T/Plpt: £193.70 (92.35 Tckts). T/Qdpt: £89.20 (6.94 Tckts) Dk

4582-PONTEFRACT (L-H) (Good to soft)
Monday October 20th
WEATHER: overcast WIND: fresh against

4801 JONJO FAREWELL MAIDEN AUCTION STKS (I) (2-Y.O) (Class F)
2-30 (2-35) **6f** £2,248.00 (£628.00: £304.00) Stalls: Low GOING: 0.23 sec per fur (G)

				SP	RR	SF
4750^{2}	**Sharp Cracker (IRE) (75)** (MJohnston) **2-8-6** DMcKeown(1) (mde all: all out)	—	**1**	8/11^{1}	74	22
4017^{12}	**Bless 'im** (RHannon) **2-8-10** DaneO'Neill(4) (outpcd tl hdwy u.p 2 out: styd on wl towards fin)	1	**2**	15/2^{2}	75	23
4753^{6}	**Scene (IRE) (56)** (MartynMeade) **2-8-1**ow1 GDuffield(12) (swtg: racd wd: a cl up: kpt on u.p fnl f)	½	**3**	9/1	65	12
4402^{7}	**Cape Hope (59)** (RBoss) **2-8-8** KFallon(8) (lw: chsd ldrs: rdn over 2f out: kpt on one pce)	2	**4**	16/1	67	15
3905^{14}	**Moy (IRE) (57)** (MBrittain) **2-7-8**(7) DMernagh(3) (chsd ldrs: rdn 2f out: styd on same pce)	1¾	**5**	25/1	55	3
4479^{4}	**Just Testing** (JLEyre) **2-8-4** TWilliams(14) (racd wd: cl up: hung lft 2f out: wknd ins fnl f)	¾	**6**	8/1^{3}	56	4
4459^{8}	**Nordic Pirjo** (MrsJRRamsden) **2-8-1** DO'Donohoe(7) (s.i.s: nvr nr to chal)	1¼	**7**	25/1	50	—
	Albrighton (BSRothwell) **2-8-7** MFenton(6) (w'like: str: bkwd: s.i.s: nvr trbld ldrs)	hd	**8**	50/1	55	3
	Tie Break (IRE) (WJHaggas) **2-8-7** FLynch(13) (gd sort: bkwd: s.i.s: n.d)	½	**9**	20/1	54	2
4592^{8}	**Rio (IRE) (65)** (JBerry) **2-8-6** KDarley(5) (chsd ldrs tl wknd wl over 1f out)	4	**10**	14/1	42	—
4602^{12}	**Bon Sizzle** (JRFanshawe) **2-8-9** NDay(11) (bit bkwd: in tch 4f: sn wknd)	3	**11**	25/1	37	—
	Crystal Craze (CACyzer) **2-7-13** DWright(9) (b.off hind: lt-f: bit bkwd: s.s: sn outpcd & wl t.o: sme late hdwy)	7	**12**	33/1	9	—
	Cool Affair (IRE) (ABMulholland) **2-8-8** TLucas(2) (w'like: scope: bkwd: prom to ½-wy: wknd qckly)	6	**13**	33/1	2	—
				(SP 127.5%)	**13 Rn**	

1m 21.6 (6.60) CSF £5.84 TOTE £1.60: £1.10 £2.10 £2.20 (£4.60) Trio £14.50 OWNER Mrs I. Bird (MIDDLEHAM) BRED Barnane Partnership

4750 Sharp Cracker (IRE), who on all known form looked a cut above these, did it determinedly despite running on what appeared the slower ground on the rail. (8/11: evens-5/4)
3489 Bless 'im, flat to the boards for most of the race, looked likely to benefit from a longer distance. (15/2: op 5/1)
4753 Scene (IRE), unlucky in a seller last time, was given an intelligent ride here and ran well, but despite keeping on was never quite good enough. She will surely do better over further. (9/1: 7/1-12/1)
2466 Cape Hope, a moderate mover, had his chances but lacked the toe to ever take them. (16/1)
2739 Moy (IRE) has speed and has been tried in blinkers to no effect. She again failed to see it out. (25/1)
4479 Just Testing did the right thing and raced wide, but then threw chances away by hanging left in the straight. (8/1)

4802 CLAYTON BIGLEY PARTNERSHIP H'CAP (0-70) (3-Y.O+) (Class E)
3-00 (3-06) **1m 2f 6y** £4,207.50 (£1,260.00: £605.00: £277.50) Stalls: Low GOING: 0.23 sec per fur (G)

				SP	RR	SF
4485^{2}	**Rutland Chantry (USA) (60)** (LordHuntingdon) **3-9-0** KDarley(15) (chsd ldrs: led 3f out: hld on wl)	—	**1**	11/2^{2}	72	54
4714^{2}	**Bonanza Peak (USA) (64)** (MrsJCecil) **4-9-9** MartinDwyer(17) (lw: a.p: hdwy over 2f out: sn chsng wnr: kpt on: nt pce to chal)	1	**2**	4/1^{1}	74	61
4632^{2}	**Tipperary Sunset (IRE) (54)** (JJQuinn) **3-8-8** JQuinn(10) (trckd ldrs: effrt wl over 1f out: hung lft & nt qckn fnl f)	2	**3**	10/1	61	43
4516^{3}	**Serendipity (FR) (62)** (BRMillman) **4-9-7** RCochrane(3) (bhd: hdwy 3f out: styd on wl towards fin)	5	**4**	6/1^{3}	61	48
4568^{2}	**Passing Strangers (USA) (66)** (PWHarris) **4-9-11** JReid(19) (a chsng ldrs: kpt on one pce fnl 2f)	nk	**5**	14/1	65	52
4471^{4}	**Raindeer Quest (49)** (JLEyre) **5-8-8** RLappin(9) (bhd: gd hdwy 4f out: ch 2f out: btn appr fnl f)	1½	**6**	20/1	47	34
4632^{7}	**Rare Talent (60)** (SGollings) **3-9-0** TWilliams(4) (lw: hdwy over 2f out: nvr nrr)	2½	**7**	20/1	54	36
4449^{8}	**Wentbridge Lad (IRE) (59)** (ABailey) **7-9-4v** DWright(13) (b: b.hind: effrt 4f out: sn rdn & nvr trbld ldrs)	¾	**8**	14/1	52	39
3890^{3}	**Suga Hawk (IRE) (64)** (EJAlston) **5-9-4**(5) RMullen(16) (in tch: effrt over 3f out: btn wl over 1f out)	hd	**9**	14/1	57	44
4596^{8}	**Java Red (IRE) (54)** (JGFitzGerald) **5-8-13** KFallon(11) (bhd: gd hdwy 4f out: sn chsng ldrs & rdn: wknd fnl 2f)	1¾	**10**	8/1	44	31
4714^{17}	**Classic Colours (USA) (65)** (GHYardley) **4-9-10** VSlattery(6) (bit bkwd: nvr trbld ldrs)	1½	**11**	100/1	52	39
4109^{6}	**Danegold (IRE) (58)** (MRChannon) **5-9-3v** JFortune(7) (s.i.s: nvr nr ldrs)	1	**12**	12/1	44	31
4046^{15}	**Verdi (IRE) (60)** (KMcAuliffe) **3-9-0v^{1}** JCarroll(8) (led tl hdd 3f out: sn wknd)	6	**13**	25/1	36	18
4415^{5}	**Pickens (USA) (53)** (DonEnricoIncisa) **5-8-12** KimTinkler(2) (b: sn wl bhd: n.d)	5	**14**	25/1	21	8
4287^{12}	**Bold Top (47)** (BSRothwell) **5-8-6be** GDuffield(1) (bhd: effrt 5f out: n.d)	1¼	**15**	33/1	13	—
4568^{11}	**Yaverland (IRE) (50)** (JohnBerry) **5-8-9** MTebbutt(14) (bit bkwd: in tch tl wknd fnl 3f)	1¾	**16**	40/1	14	1
4466^{8}	**Kathryn's Pet (63)** (MrsMReveley) **4-9-8** ACulhane(5) (lw: chsd ldrs tl wknd qckly 1½f out)	6	**17**	12/1	17	4
4632^{17}	**Chandler's Hall (54)** (MJHeaton-Ellis) **3-8-8**ow1 JWeaver(18) (chsd ldrs tl wknd & eased fnl 2f)	½	**18**	33/1	7	—
4596^{13}	**No Cliches (65)** (DNicholls) **4-9-10** AlexGreaves(12) (bhd fnl 4f)	5	**19**	20/1	10	—
				(SP 136.5%)	**19 Rn**	

2m 17.6 (8.00) CSF £24.57 CT £213.63 TOTE £8.30: £2.90 £1.50 £2.00 £1.80 (£20.50) Trio £37.00 OWNER The Queen (WEST ILSLEY) BRED Queen Elizabeth
WEIGHT FOR AGE 3yo-5lb

4485 Rutland Chantry (USA) went for home some way out and, getting the trip well, showed fine courage to hold on. (11/2)

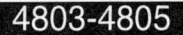

4714 Bonanza Peak (USA) is a most determined sort who is in tremendous form but, try as he might, he had met one just too tough. (4/1)
4632 Tipperary Sunset (IRE) looked the likely winner for a long way, but just wanted to hang left when ridden and proved a shade disappointing. (10/1)
4516 Serendipity (FR) looks a funny customer, but he has plenty of ability if he can be persuaded. (6/1)
4568 Passing Strangers (USA) put up a reasonable effort under top weight, but he was treading water in the last couple of furlongs. (14/1)
4471 Raindeer Quest is in good form at the moment, but she is a moody mare who needs things to go just right, and the struggle was always just beyond her on this occasion. (20/1)
4326* Rare Talent is the type who is probably better in a lower class, and seems to keep a bit for himself, but this was a reasonably encouraging effort for his new stable. (20/1)

4803 TOTE SILVER TANKARD STKS (Listed) (2-Y.O) (Class A)

3-30 (3-31) **1m 4y** £12,929.00 (£4,811.00: £2,330.50: £977.50: £413.75: £188.25) Stalls: Low GOING: 0.23 sec per fur (G)

				SP	RR	SF
4096²	**Gulland** (GWragg) **2-8-11** MHills(5) (lw: trckd ldrs gng wl: led 2f out: sn qckrd clr)	—	1	10/11¹	102+	59
4330*	**Rambling Rose (90)** (MRStoute) **2-8-7**ow1 KFallon(3) (b.nr hind: sn pushed along: a in tch: r.o wl fnl 2f: nrst fin)	2½	2	9/2²	93	49
4532a*	**Clapham Common (IRE)** (LMCumani) **2-9-0** KDarley(7) (a.p: effrt over 2f out: r.o one pce)	7	3	20/1	86	43
4433²	**The Gene Genie** (MJHeaton-Ellis) **2-8-11** JWeaver(8) (plld hrd: in tch: effrt over 2f out: r.o one pce)	¾	4	20/1	82	39
4364³	**Confirmation (98)** (SirMarkPrescott) **2-9-0** GDuffield(4) (lw: led tl hdd 2f out: wknd over 1f out)	2½	5	7/1³	80	37
4638*	**Chim Chiminey (88)** (BWHills) **2-8-6** RCochrane(1) (chsd ldrs tl rdn & btn 1½f out)	3	6	10/1	66	23
4690⁵	**Fashion Victim (82)** (THCaldwell) **2-8-11** ACulhane(2) (stdd s: a bhd)	9	7	100/1	53	10
4551³	**Aix En Provence (USA) (100)** (MJohnston) **2-8-11** JReid(6) (lw: cl up tl wknd qckly 2f out)	16	8	7/1³	21	—
				(SP 115.2%)	**8 Rn**	

1m 47.9 (5.50) CSF £4.67 TOTE £1.80: £1.20 £1.10 £2.80 (£3.30) OWNER Mollers Racing (NEWMARKET) BRED Stowell Hill Ltd
4096 Gulland looked really useful, and this confidence booster should have done him no end of good. Next year he could be a very interesting individual. (10/11: evens-4/5)
4330* Rambling Rose is certainly not an easy ride, but staying is the name of the game with her, and she finished particularly well. (9/2)
4532a* Clapham Common (IRE), who won what appeared a modest race in Italy on his debut, had his limitations exposed and looked short of toe. (20/1)
4433 The Gene Genie is a real free-running sort and will have to learn to settle, otherwise he will continue to beat himself. (20/1)
4364 Confirmation keeps leaving the impression that, next season over longer distances, he will really come into his own. (7/1)
4638* Chim Chiminey had a hard race last time, and that probably found her out. (10/1)
4551 Aix En Provence (USA) was extremely disappointing this time, but this can probably be put down to a hard race at Newmarket just over a fortnight ago. (7/1: op 9/2)

4804 BLUFF COVE H'CAP (0-70) (3-Y.O+) (Class E)

4-00 (4-03) **2m 1f 216y** £3,275.00 (£980.00: £470.00: £215.00) Stalls: Centre GOING: 0.23 sec per fur (G)

				SP	RR	SF
4585*	**Sipowitz (56)** (CACyzer) **3-8-8** JWeaver(2) (hdwy 6f out: led 2f out: styd on gamely)	—	1	11/2¹	70	37
4794²	**Highfield Fizz (43)** (CWFairhurst) **5-8-6** LCharnock(4) (b.off hind: hdwy 6f out: chal 2f out: nt qckn ins fnl f)	1¼	2	9/1	56	34
3309⁵	**All On (54)** (JHetherton) **6-9-3** GDuffield(6) (trckd ldrs: led over 3f tl hdd 2f out: sn rdn & btn)	14	3	11/2¹	54	32
4749²	**Sad Mad Bad (USA) (55)** (MrsMReveley) **3-8-7** WJO'Connor(7) (a chsng ldrs: drvn along 7f out: one pce)	6	4	8/1³	50	17
4519⁷	**Nornax Lad (USA) (33)** (MartynMeade) **9-7-3b**(7) RBrisland(13) (hdwy & in tch ½-wy: one pce fnl 3f)	4	5	25/1	25	3
4609²	**Drama King (38)** (BJLlewellyn) **5-8-1** JBramhill(18) (hdwy ½-wy: sn in tch: one pce fnl 3f)	1	6	10/1	29	7
3401⁷	**Black Ice Boy (IRE) (41)** (RBastiman) **6-8-4b**ow2 DeanMcKeown(9) (chsd ldrs tl wknd over 2f out)	9	7	16/1	24	—
4667²	**New Inn (48)** (SGollings) **6-8-11** TWilliams(15) (chsd ldrs: led 8f out tl over 3f out: sn btn)	5	8	8/1³	26	4
4585²	**Karisma (IRE) (44)** (DenysSmith) **4-8-7** RCochrane(12) (hdwy ½-wy: drvn along 6f out: btn over 3f out)	16	9	6/1²	8	—
	Harbet House (FR) (55) (RJO'Sullivan) **4-9-4** KDarley(11) (bkwd: prom tl wknd fnl 6f)	11	10	16/1	9	—
4438¹³	**What Jim Wants (IRE) (33)** (JJO'Neill) **4-7-10** JQuinn(1) (drvn along ½-wy: n.d)	nk	11	33/1	—	—
	Dr Bones (IRE) (60) (FMurphy) **4-9-9** JFortune(16) (nvr bttr than mid div)	s.h	12	16/1	14	—
4585⁹	**Rave-on-Hadley (IRE) (34)** (NBycroft) **7-7-11**ow1 DWright(17) (b: bkwd: led tl hdd 8f out: wknd qckly)	17	13	100/1	—	—
4426⁸	**Tawafek (USA) (65)** (SDow) **4-10-0** RPerham(5) (lw: bhd: effrt ½-wy: sn btn)	1	14	12/1	3	—
4744¹²	**Ambuscade (USA) (35)** (MrsJJordan) **11-7-7**(5) APolli(3) (n.d)	2½	15	50/1	—	—
4585⁷	**Jelali (IRE) (50)** (DJGMurraySmith) **4-8-13** DaneO'Neill(10) (bhd fr ½-wy)	1	16	20/1	—	—
4583⁷	**Denton Lad (57)** (WTKemp) **3-8-9b** JCarroll(8) (a bhd)	s.h	17	50/1	—	—
4632¹³	**Gallant Heights (53)** (GCBravery) **3-8-5** NDay(14) (hdwy & prom ½-wy: wknd 6f out: t.o)	dist	18	12/1	—	—
				(SP 135.9%)	**18 Rn**	

4m 9.0 (17.00) CSF £51.86 CT £276.83 TOTE £5.60: £1.90 £1.80 £1.60 £2.20 (£14.30) Trio £40.00 OWNER Mr R. M. Cyzer (HORSHAM) BRED C. A. and R. M. Cyzer
LONG HANDICAP What Jim Wants (IRE) 7-9 Nornax Lad (USA) 7-9 Rave-on-Hadley (IRE) 7-2
WEIGHT FOR AGE 3yo-11lb
4585* Sipowitz did his usual and outbattled the opposition. (11/2: 9/2-7/1)
4794 Highfield Fizz keeps looking likely to win a race, but never quite comes up with the goods, and her rider had his whip knocked out of his hand entering the final furlong, which did not help matters. (9/1)
3309 All On ran a smashing race after over two months off, but appeared to blow up. (11/2)
4749 Sad Mad Bad (USA) stays well, but just looks slow. (8/1)
4170 Nornax Lad (USA) was never quick enough to make his presence felt. (25/1)
4585 Karisma (IRE) showed just what an unpredictable sort he is, and downed tools once ridden approaching the last half-mile. (6/1)

4805 WHITE SWAN H'CAP (0-80) (3-Y.O+) (Class D)

4-30 (4-31) **5f** £4,207.50 (£1,260.00: £605.00: £277.50) Stalls: Low GOING: 0.23 sec per fur (G)

				SP	RR	SF
3910²²	**Afaan (IRE) (62)** (RFMarvin) **4-8-10v** TGMcLaughlin(18) (b: cl up: led ½-wy: sn qcknd clr: all out)	—	1	33/1	73	46
4456⁸	**Bowlers Boy (74)** (JJQuinn) **4-9-8** JFortune(15) (bhd: hdwy wl over 1f out: styd on wl: nrst fin)	1	2	9/2¹	82	55
4580¹²	**Robellion (53)** (DWPArbuthnot) **6-8-1** MartinDwyer(11) (b: a chsng ldrs: kpt on u.p fnl f)	½	3	25/1	59	32
4512¹⁸	**Lillibella (54)** (MrsJRRamsden) **4-8-2** DO'Donohoe(14) (lw: bhd: hdwy 2f out: styd on: nrst fin)	1	4	16/1	57	30
3936¹⁷	**Night Harmony (IRE) (53)** (MissSJWilton) **4-8-1** LCharnock(16) (b: a chsng ldrs: rdn 2f out: kpt on one pce)	nk	5	33/1	55	28
4733⁷	**Corniche Quest (IRE) (64)** (MRChannon) **4-8-5**(7) AEddery(12) (bhd tl styd on wl appr fnl f)	½	6	16/1	64	37
4733²	**First Maite (75)** (SRBowring) **4-9-6b**(3) CTeague(4) (chsd ldrs tl rdn & btn over 1f out)	1	7	11/2²	72	45

				SP	RR	SF
4770^{10}	**Just Bob (77)** (SEKettlewell) **8-9-11** DeanMcKeown(6) (s.i.s: hdwy 2f out: nvr rchd ldrs)	¾	**8**	15/2	72	45
4546^{7}	**Daylight Dreams (58)** (CACyzer) **3-8-6**ow2 AMorris(5) (bhd: hdwy over 1f out: nvr rchd ldrs)	1½	**9**	25/1	48	19
4365^{10}	**Gi La High (61)** (MartynMeade) **4-8-9** JReid(13) (mid div: rdn ½-wy: no imp)	1¼	**10**	14/1	46	19
4580^{5}	**Jucea (56)** (JLSpearing) **8-8-4** JQuinn(17) (chsd ldrs tl wknd wl over 1f out)	nk	**11**	14/1	40	13
4183^{6}	**Cross The Border (80)** (DNicholls) **4-10-0** AlexGreaves(8) (lw: led to ½-wy: wknd wl over 1f out)	2	**12**	12/1	58	31
4636^{8}	**Pointer (55)** (MrsPNDutfield) **5-8-3** CRutter(2) (rdn ½-wy: nvr trbld ldrs)	½	**13**	14/1	31	4
4636^{16}	**William's Well (57)** (MWEasterby) **3-8-5b** TLucas(3) (a bhd)	nk	**14**	16/1	32	5
4527^{7}	**Sally Green (IRE) (75)** (CFWall) **3-9-9** GDuffield(7) (chsd ldrs tl wknd 1½f out)	1¼	**15**	6/1 3	46	19
4586^{3}	**Top of The Form (IRE) (77)** (RAFahey) **3-9-4**(7) RWinston(9) (mid div & rdn ½-wy: sn wknd)	3	**16**	16/1	39	12
4565^{7}	**Caution (71)** (SGollings) **3-9-5** TWilliams(1) (bhd: effrt on ins 2f out: sn btn)	3½	**17**	10/1	22	—
				(SP 133.5%)	**17 Rn**	

65.8 secs (4.10) CSF £169.02 CT £3,657.88 TOTE £51.20: £11.40 £2.30 £6.40 £6.10 (£177.60) Trio £1,109.00 OWNER Mr E. Gray (NEWARK) BRED Shadwell Estate Company Limited

1977 Afaan (IRE) had the required wide draw, and showed a splendid turn of foot halfway through the race which saw him clear, and that was all that was needed. (33/1)

4048 Bowlers Boy needs things to go just right and, despite finishing well, the effort was always too late. (9/2)

4518* Robellion had his chances, but lacked a change of gear to take them. (25/1)

4385 Lillibella is running quite well, and just needs to drop another few pounds in the handicap. (16/1)

3327 Night Harmony (IRE) is not an easy ride, and has only won once in twenty-one outings. (33/1)

4733 Corniche Quest (IRE), off a 4lb higher mark than when he won at this track earlier in the season, stayed on, but never had a hope. (16/1)

4183 Cross The Border had speed to burn early on but, after five weeks off, obviously needed the blow out. (12/1)

4806 FEATHERS HOTEL NURSERY H'CAP (0-75) (2-Y.O) (Class E)

5-00 (5-03) **1m 4y** £3,925.00 (£1,180.00: £570.00: £265.00) Stalls: Low GOING: 0.23 sec per fur (G)

				SP	RR	SF
4508^{3}	**Premium Quest (66)** (RAFahey) **2-8-13** FNorton(20) (bhd: hdwy over 2f out: c wd: led ins fnl f: r.o)	—	**1**	14/1	70	33
4767^{6}	**Marske Machine (62)** (NTinkler) **2-8-9b** RCochrane(16) (bhd: hdwy on outside over 1f out: r.o wl towards fin)	nk	**2**	10/1	65	28
4380^{8}	**Polo Venture (67)** (SPCWoods) **2-9-0** NDay(17) (hdwy 3f out: led over 1f out tl ins fnl f: no ex)	¾	**3**	16/1	69	32
4576^{2}	**Narrogin (USA) (74)** (MRChannon) **2-9-7** JCarroll(7) (bhd: hdwy on outside 2f out: ev ch ins fnl f: kpt on)	1½	**4**	8/1 2	73	36
4330^{13}	**Loubin Lane (55)** (AGNewcombe) **2-8-2** JQuinn(4) (mid div: hdwy u.p 2f out: sn chsng ldrs: nt qckn fnl f)	¾	**5**	25/1	52	15
4285^{7}	**Bawsian (65)** (JLEyre) **2-8-12** OPears(2) (b.hind: hmpd after 1½f: shkn up ½-wy: hdwy whn hmpd 2f out: r.o towards fin)	hd	**6**	13/2 1	62+	25
4334^{17}	**Danzig Flyer (IRE) (71)** (PWHarris) **2-9-4** JReid(6) (lw: chsd ldrs: effrt over 2f out: r.o one pce)	1	**7**	20/1	66	29
4334^{6}	**Jonas Nightengale (70)** (CACyzer) **2-9-3** AMorris(19) (mid div: hdwy u.p 2f out: no imp)	1¼	**8**	20/1	63	26
3859^{6}	**Mystagogue (58)** (RHannon) **2-8-5** DaneO'Neill(18) (chsd ldrs: led wl over 1f out: sn hdd: grad wknd)	hd	**9**	16/1	51	14
4057^{8}	**Chlo-Jo (70)** (AGFoster) **2-8-10**(7) DMernagh(13) (chsd ldrs tl wknd wl over 1f out)	4	**10**	20/1	55	18
4595^{5}	**Bali Dance (60)** (CBBBooth) **2-8-7b** KHodgson(1) (in tch: outpcd 3f out: n.d after)	¾	**11**	20/1	43	6
4576^{4}	**Thecomebackking (56)** (SCWilliams) **2-8-3** MartinDwyer(8) (mid div: rdn over 3f out: n.d)	3½	**12**	20/1	32	—
4285^{4}	**Impulse (IRE) (63)** (MrsJRRamsden) **2-8-10** JFortune(14) (lw: outpcd & bhd after 3f: n.d)	3	**13**	8/1 2	33	—
4366^{6}	**Francesca's Folly (57)** (JWHills) **2-8-1**(3) MHenry(5) (chsd ldrs 6f: wknd)	nk	**14**	20/1	27	—
4690*	**Kayo (73)** (TJEtherington) **2-9-6** 6x ACulhane(3) (hld up & bhd: effrt 3f out: n.d)	2	**15**	10/1	39	2
4361^{8}	**Genius (IRE) (66)** (PFICole) **2-8-13b1** KDarley(12) (led tl hdd & wknd wl over 1f out)	3½	**16**	10/1	25	—
4605^{5}	**Naked Oat (67)** (BSmart) **2-9-0** JWeaver(11) (lw: hdwy ½-wy: sn chsng ldrs: wknd over 1f out)	¾	**17**	16/1	24	—
4588^{5}	**Sharp Shooter (IRE) (57)** (MrsJRRamsden) **2-8-4** DO'Donohoe(15) (s.i.s: a outpcd & bhd)	9	**18**	9/1 3	—	—
4185^{8}	**Risada (IRE) (71)** (DRLoder) **2-9-4** GDuffield(9) (cl up tl wknd fnl 3f: eased considerably)	dist	**19**	9/1 3	—	—
				(SP 139.6%)	**19 Rn**	

1m 50.8 (8.40) CSF £134.86 CT £1,261.81 TOTE £22.80: £4.50 £2.50 £4.10 £2.50 (£150.90) Trio £578.10 OWNER Mr J. C. Parsons (MALTON) BRED Simon and Helen Plumbly

OFFICIAL EXPLANATION **Risada (IRE): the trainer's representative was unable to offer any explanation for the horse's poor performance.**

4508 Premium Quest, like most of the principals, came from off the pace. He raced slightly wide on the better ground, and stayed particularly well. (14/1)

4767 Marske Machine is a real stayer, and the stiffer the task the better she likes it. (10/1)

4056 Polo Venture is improving, but this stiff finish just found him out. (16/1)

4576 Narrogin (USA) keeps running well, and came from a long way off the pace. He had his chances, only then to be anchored by his weight. (8/1)

Loubin Lane showed her first signs of form, but she seemed to lack a turn of speed. (25/1)

4285 Bawsian had no luck at all in running, and is a good deal better than this. (13/2: 10/1-6/1)

4285 Impulse (IRE) (8/1: op 5/1)

4690* Kayo (10/1: op 6/1)

4588 Sharp Shooter (IRE) (9/1: 12/1-8/1)

4807 JONJO FAREWELL MAIDEN AUCTION STKS (II) (2-Y.O) (Class F)

5-30 (5-31) **6f** £2,248.00 (£628.00: £304.00) Stalls: Low GOING: 0.23 sec per fur (G)

				SP	RR	SF
4479^{10}	**Itch** (RBastiman) **2-8-7** DeanMcKeown(6) (chsd ldrs: styd on to ld 1f out: hld on wl)	—	**1**	40/1	75	23
4458^{2}	**Premium Princess (65)** (JJQuinn) **2-7-13** DaleGibson(7) (in tch: gd hdwy over 1f out: rdn to chal ins fnl f: hung lft & no ex)	nk	**2**	7/2 2	66	14
4458^{4}	**Recognition (74)** (WJarvis) **2-8-11** JReid(10) (a.p: hdwy 2f out: one pce fnl f)	7	**3**	9/2 3	60	8
4627^{13}	**Itsnotyetnamed (44)** (ASmith) **2-7-10**(7) RWinston(2) (sn outpcd & bhd: brought wd & racd stands' side st: r.o towards fin)	nk	**4**	50/1	51	—
4159^{W}	**Sun Dancing (IRE)** (JBerry) **2-8-0** JQuinn(12) (w'like: bit bkwd: cl up: led 2f out: sn rdn & put head in air: hdd & wknd 1f out)	½	**5**	11/1	46	—
4514^{7}	**Celestial Welcome** (MrsMReveley) **2-8-0** LCharnock(8) (outpcd & bhd ½-wy: sme late hdwy)	3½	**6**	25/1	37	—
4459^{2}	**Julies Jewel (IRE) (70)** (MCChapman) **2-8-3**(7) SCarson(4) (led tl hdd 2f out: grad wknd)	nk	**7**	9/1	46	—
3459^{8}	**Stephangeorge** (MBrittain) **2-7-11**(7) DMernagh(3) (outpcd & bhd tl sme late hdwy)	1	**8**	50/1	38	—
4508^{10}	**Wee Christy (IRE) (44)** (WMcKeown) **2-8-10** JCarroll(13) (chsd ldrs: rdn ½-wy: wknd wl over 1f out)	hd	**9**	50/1	43	—
	Samata One (IRE) (WJHaggas) **2-8-8** FLynch(1) (lt-f: unf: s.s: n.d)	1¾	**10**	9/1	37	—
4514^{4}	**Arab Gold** (MissSEHall) **2-8-9** AMcGlone(5) (chsd ldrs over 4f: wknd qckly)	9	**11**	5/1	14	—

4564[7] **Il Destino** (PJMakin) **2-8-7** JFortune(11) (lost pl after 3f: sn p.u) .... **P** 100/30[1] — —
Licketysplit (NBycroft) **2-8-1** MartinDwyer(9) (Withdrawn not under Starter's orders: unruly in paddock: rdr inj) .... **W** 50/1 — —
(SP 122.6%) **12 Rn**

1m 21.6 (6.60) CSF £160.13 TOTE £44.40: £6.60 £1.40 £2.10 (£146.20) Trio £69.70 OWNER Mr Charles Castle (WETHERBY) BRED S. V. Wadsworth

OFFICIAL EXPLANATION **Il Destino: the rider reported that the colt had felt wrong in his action.**

Itch won this well, and had far too much determination for the runner-up. (40/1)

4458 Premium Princess came bursting through looking likely to swamp the winner but, once she saw the front, she cried enough., (7/2)

4458 Recognition is proving disappointing, and failed to pick up at all when ridden in the straight. (9/2)

Itsnotyetnamed ran as though further is needed, but his rider did the intelligent thing and brought him wide into the straight, which may well have been a big advantage. (50/1)

Sun Dancing (IRE) sailed along on the bridle but, once in front, she looked none too keen and flashed her tail violently under pressure. (11/1)

Celestial Welcome does not do anything quickly, but she was keeping on at the finish. (25/1)

Il Destino appeared to have a problem, and was pulled up after halfway, but was later found to be perfectly sound. (100/30)

T/Jkpt: Not won; £51,877.61 to Folkestone 21/10/97. T/Plpt: £32.00 (1,062.22 Tckts). T/Qdpt: £26.70 (38.84 Tckts) AA

4049-SOUTHWELL (L-H) (Standard)
Monday October 20th

WEATHER: dry, cold & windy WIND: str half against

4808 LAGERFELD NURSERY H'CAP (0-85) (2-Y.O) (Class E)
2-10 (2-10) **6f (Fibresand)** £2,966.25 (£885.00: £422.50: £191.25) Stalls: Low GOING minus 0.20 sec per fur (FST)

				SP	RR	SF
4589[3]	**Santa Faye (IRE) (76)** (BPalling) **2-9-7** TSprake(1) (trckd ldrs: led over 1f out: hld on wl towards fin)	—	1	5/2[1]	74	42
4595[8]	**I'm Tef (51)** (TDEasterby) **2-7-10** LCharnock(3) (a chsng ldrs: ev ch over 1f out: nt qckn nr fin)	½	2	50/1	48?	16
4543[5]	**Lasham (60)** (NACallaghan) **2-8-2**(3) RFfrench(4) (swtg: sn chsng ldrs: outpcd over 2f out: styd on same pce appr fnl f)	2½	3	8/1	50	18
4702*	**Daybreak (69)** (JWWatts) **2-8-11**(3) 7x PFessey(6) (sn outpcd: hdwy ½-wy: styd on fnl 2f: nvr nr to chal)	1¾	4	7/2[2]	54	22
4271[14]	**Island Girl (IRE) (59)** (DWPArbuthnot) **2-8-1**(3) MHenry(5) (sn bhd & drvn along: kpt on fnl 2f: n.d)	3	5	12/1	36	4
4411[10]	**Forty Love (IRE) (59)** (JEBanks) **2-8-1v**[1](3) DSweeney(8) (racd wd: in tch: sn drvn along: outpcd fr ½-wy)	nk	6	10/1	36	4
4634[11]	**Really Done It Now (IRE) (56)** (KRBurke) **2-8-1** JFEgan(9) (swtchd lft after s: led tl over 1f out: sn wknd)	1¾	7	14/1	28	—
4592[6]	**Nuit d'Or (IRE) (64)** (MJohnston) **2-8-9** JFanning(10) (racd wd: outpcd ½-wy: sn bhd)	6	8	9/2[3]	20	—
4588[4]	**Mr Fund Switch (51)** (DNicholls) **2-7-5**(5) IonaWands(7) (sn chsng ldrs: wknd fnl 2f)	1½	9	25/1	3	—
4473[10]	**Tullich Refrain (62)** (WRMuir) **2-8-7** AClark(2) (s.i.s: sn drvn along & a bhd)	½	10	9/2[3]	13	—

(SP 127.5%) **10 Rn**

1m 16.9 (3.40) CSF £134.20 CT £717.32 TOTE £4.40: £1.10 £6.90 £2.60 (£42.20) Trio £187.00 OWNER Mrs R. M. Williams (COWBRIDGE) BRED Martyn J. McEnery

LONG HANDICAP Mr Fund Switch 6-12 I'm Tef 7-0

4589 Santa Faye (IRE), a weak-looking filly who needs give underfoot on turf, proved very willing. (5/2)

2904 I'm Tef, 10lb wrong at the weights, certainly seemed to show vastly improved form on this surface but, hard as he tried, he was always going to be just denied. (50/1)

4543 Lasham, warm beforehand on a very cold day, stuck on after being outpaced. (8/1)

4702* Daybreak, under a 7lb penalty, was completely run off her legs. Sticking on in the final quarter-mile, she was never doing anything quickly enough to get involved. On this surface, she will almost certainly need seven furlongs or a mile. (7/2)

2196 Island Girl (IRE) (12/1: op 6/1)

4809 CERUTTI MEDIAN AUCTION MAIDEN STKS (3-Y.O) (Class F)
2-40 (2-41) **6f (Fibresand)** £2,277.00 (£627.00: £297.00) Stalls: Low GOING minus 0.20 sec per fur (FST)

				SP	RR	SF
4370[8]	**Dancing Mystery (44)** (EAWheeler) **3-8-11b**(3) ADaly(9) (chsd ldrs: styd on to ld over 1f out: sn clr: all out)..	—	1	16/1	69	44
4563[5]	**Mozambique (IRE)** (MrsJCecil) **3-8-11**(3) RFfrench(14) (racd wd: sn bhd: nt clr run 2f out: swtchd: fin fast)	2	2	5/1[2]	64	39
4431[4]	**Daintree (IRE) (47)** (HJCollingridge) **3-8-9v** JFEgan(8) (mid div: styd on appr fnl f: nvr nr to chal)	1½	3	14/1	55	30
4563[2]	**Nobalino (70)** (MrsNMacauley) **3-9-0** SDrowne(5) (led tl over 1f out: wknd ins fnl f)	¾	4	6/4[1]	58	33
4248[17]	**Magic Fizz (50)** (TJEtherington) **3-9-0b** JLowe(2) (w ldr: ev ch over 2f out: wknd ins fnl f)	1¾	5	14/1	53	28
4333[10]	**Hype Superior (IRE) (55)** (ABailey) **3-9-0** PaulEddery(7) (prom tl outpcd ½-wy: kpt on fnl f)	1¼	6	8/1[3]	50	25
3698[6]	**Flo's Choice (IRE) (37)** (JO'Reilly) **3-8-9** JO'Reilly(3) (chsd ldrs: wl outpcd over 2f out: kpt on appr fnl f)	nk	7	33/1	44	19
4586[15]	**Sparkling Harry (48)** (MissLCSiddall) **3-9-1**ow1 MWigham(12) (s.i.s: rn wd & hdwy on outside over 2f out: n.d)	2	8	33/1	45	19
3299[7]	**Millpet (44)** (RGuest) **3-8-4b**[1](5) CLowther(13) (sn outpcd & bhd: sme hdwy on outside 2f out: wandered: n.d)	1¼	9	16/1	35	10
4695[19]	**Eliza (62)** (LordHuntingdon) **3-8-9** WRyan(4) (mid div: effrt over 2f out: sn wknd)	2½	10	8/1[3]	29	4
3500[7]	**Badrinath (IRE) (37)** (HJCollingridge) **3-9-0** JTate(11) (racd wd: sme hdwy & edgd lft over 2f out: sn wknd)	1¼	11	8/1[3]	30	5
4431[3]	**Pardan (42)** (BPalling) **3-9-0** TSprake(6) (chsd ldrs tl lost pl over 2f out)	¾	12	8/1[3]	28	3
4600[4]	**Woodetto (IRE) (51)** (EWeymes) **3-8-11**(3) PFessey(10) (racd wd: mid div: hrd rdn & edgd lft over 2f out: sn wknd)	1¾	13	33/1	24	—
	Snow Cloud (DCO'Brien) **3-8-9** GBardwell(1) (leggy: unf: s.s: a bhd)	10	14	20/1	—	—

(SP 139.8%) **14 Rn**

1m 16.3 (2.80) CSF £96.47 TOTE £27.90: £8.40 £1.50 £3.60 (£91.60) Trio £69.70 OWNER Austin Stroud & Co Ltd (PANGBOURNE) BRED Mrs D. Price

3280 Dancing Mystery took a decisive advantage over a furlong out but, with the second finishing like a train, although the winning margin was two lengths the post came just in time. (16/1)

4563 Mozambique (IRE), who does not have the best of actions, proved well-suited by this surface. Drawn worst of all, he ran out of room when still well off the pace two furlongs out. After being switched, he made up ten or twelve lengths in the final furlong and would definitely have won with a little further to go. (5/1: op 5/2)

4431 Daintree (IRE), picking up ground late in the day, needs seven furlongs or a mile. (14/1)
4563 Nobalino seemed to run out of stamina in the closing stages. (6/4)
1401 Magic Fizz, who has shown no pop at all on his last four starts, ran better this time. (14/1)
3040 Badrinath (IRE) (8/1: 10/1-16/1)

4810 ROUGE LIMITED STKS (0-60) (3-Y.O+) (Class F)
3-10 (3-11) **1m 4f (Fibresand)** £2,277.00 (£627.00: £297.00) Stalls: Low GOING minus 0.20 sec per fur (FST)

				SP	RR	SF
4275*	**Montecristo (60)** (RGuest) **4-9-1**$^{(5)}$ CLowther(7) (hld up: hdwy over 3f out: led 2f out: drvn out)	—	1	4/6^{1}	57	31
4480^{6}	**Avanti Blue (42)** (KMcAuliffe) **3-8-11** JFEgan(5) (trckd ldrs: led over 2f out: sn hdd: kpt on same pce)	1½	2	16/1	53	20
4213^{12}	**Wildmoor (54)** (JDBethell) **3-8-13** AClark(8) (trckd ldr: ev ch & edgd rt over 2f out: grad wknd)	9	3	9/2^{2}	43	10
4235^{18}	**Domino Flyer (60)** (MrsASwinbank) **4-9-4** PaulEddery(6) (lw: led tl over 2f out: grad wknd)	¾	4	6/1^{3}	40	14
4606^{9}	**Lady Silk (37)** (MissJFCraze) **6-9-1** SWebster(9) (chsd ldrs: rdn & outpcd over 3f out: n.d after)	1	5	16/1	36	10
4480^{9}	**Grey Again (40)** (DShaw) **5-9-1v** JFanning(3) (hld up: hdwy on outside 6f out: lost pl 3f out)	19	6	12/1	10	—
4579^{11}	**Blue Island (IRE) (40)** (NPLittmoden) **3-8-4**$^{(7)}$ KPierrepont(10) (s.i.s: hdwy on outside 6f out: hrd rdn & lost pl over 3f out)	1¾	7	20/1	11	—
4607^{12}	**Rival Bid (USA) (50)** (MrsNMacauley) **9-9-4** SDrowne(2) (lw: b: hld up: effrt over 4f out: sn wknd & eased: fin lame)	13	8	16/1	—	—
	Kenilworth Dancer (33) (BRCambidge) **4-9-4** NAdams(4) (sn chsng ldrs: drvn along over 7f out: sn lost pl: t.o 4f out)	½	9	50/1	—	—

(SP 124.5%) **9 Rn**

2m 41.8 (8.80) CSF £15.18 TOTE £1.50: £1.10 £2.00 £1.70 (£9.40) Trio £18.90 OWNER Mr Rae Guest (NEWMARKET) BRED Lord Matthews
WEIGHT FOR AGE 3yo-7lb

4275* Montecristo, ideally suited by the strongly-run race, was well-handled and took this with the minimum of fuss. (4/6)
4480 Avanti Blue never gave up trying. He would have been meeting the winner on 16lb better terms in a handicap. (16/1)
2757 Wildmoor seemed to appreciate the switch to this surface but, edging right once in line for home, soon found the first two leaving him for dead. (9/2)
552 Domino Flyer, who has been bang out of form, set a strong gallop. (6/1)
4480 Lady Silk, as usual, misbehaved coming out on to the track. This trip is surely well beyond her optimum. (16/1)

4811 ALEX LAWRIE H'CAP (0-70) (3-Y.O+) (Class E)
3-40 (3-42) **1m 6f (Fibresand)** £3,252.25 (£973.00: £466.50: £213.25) Stalls: Low GOING minus 0.20 sec per fur (FST)

				SP	RR	SF
4590^{5}	**Needwood Epic (48)** (BCMorgan) **4-8-9b** SWhitworth(7) (mde all: clr 6f out: hrd rdn: edgd rt & styd on fnl 2f: all out)	—	1	14/1	64	15
4336^{8}	**Trooper (65)** (RAkehurst) **3-9-3** AClark(11) (a chsng ldrs: kpt on u.p fnl 2f: no imp)	7	2	8/1	73	15
2874^{9}	**Ijab (CAN) (35)** (JParkes) **7-7-10b** GBardwell(6) (bhd: hdwy u.p 6f out: kpt on appr fnl f)	1¼	3	12/1	42	—
1940^{4}	**Evezio Rufo (49)** (NPLittmoden) **5-8-7b**$^{(3)}$ PRoberts(9) (sn bhd & drvn along: hdwy 9f out: one pce fnl 3f)	¾	4	20/1	55	6
4302^{2}	**La Menorquina (USA) (47)** (DMarks) **7-8-5**$^{(3)}$ RFfrench(12) (sn bhd: sme hdwy over 3f out: styd on appr fnl f)	2	5	4/1^{2}	50	1
4287^{7}	**Alwarqa (43)** (NPLittmoden) **4-8-1**$^{(3)}$ AWhelan(10) (chsd ldrs: drvn along 8f out: one pce fnl 4f)	¾	6	7/1^{3}	46	—
4302^{8}	**Signed And Sealed (USA) (48)** (CACyzer) **3-7-7**$^{(7)ow3}$ JFowle(1) (bhd: sme hdwy 3f out: nvr nr to chal)	3½	7	14/1	47	—
4417^{11}	**Notation (IRE) (44)** (DWChapman) **3-7-7**$^{(3)}$ PFessey(14) (s.i.s: sn in tch: rdn & lost pl over 5f out: n.d)	6	8	33/1	36	—
4768^{10}	**Welcome Lu (35)** (JLHarris) **4-7-10** JLowe(15) (bhd: sme hdwy 3f out: n.d)	1¾	9	20/1	25	—
2725^{3}	**Tellion (68)** (MajorWRHern) **3-9-6** PaulEddery(5) (chsd ldrs: wnt 2nd over 3f out: wknd qckly over 1f out)	hd	10	8/1	58	—
4170^{17}	**Big Bang (64)** (MBlanshard) **3-8-13**$^{(3)}$ DSweeney(2) (a rr div)	hd	11	11/1	54	—
3102^{4}	**Digital Option (IRE) (44)** (JLSpearing) **3-7-3**$^{(7)}$ PBradley(3) (mid div & drvn along: sme hdwy 5f out: sn wknd)	10	12	40/1	22	—
4571^{5}	**Heighth of Fame (63)** (JHetherton) **6-9-10** NKennedy(4) (sn bhd: t.o 4f out)	9	13	14/1	31	—
4594^{2}	**Indigo Dawn (62)** (MJohnston) **3-9-0b** NAdams(8) (kicked s: chsd ldrs: drvn along 6f out: sn lost pl & eased: fin lame)	10	14	5/2^{1}	18	—
4055^{11}	**El Nido (40)** (DWChapman) **9-8-1** NCarlisle(13) (bit bkwd: chsd ldrs tl wknd over 7f out: t.o 4f out)	½	15	33/1	—	—

(SP 137.2%) **15 Rn**

3m 9.4 (11.40) CSF £118.89 CT £1,311.85 TOTE £21.60: £4.30 £3.30 £3.30 (£33.00) Trio £340.50; £335.72 to Folkestone 21/10/97 OWNER Needwood Racing Ltd (BURTON-ON-TRENT) BRED Barrettstown Stud Farms Ltd
LONG HANDICAP Welcome Lu 7-6 Digital Option (IRE) 7-1 Ijab (CAN) 7-7 Notation (IRE) 7-6
WEIGHT FOR AGE 3yo-9lb
OFFICIAL EXPLANATION **Indigo Dawn: the veterinary officer reported that the filly was lame on her near-fore.**

4590 Needwood Epic got off the mark at her 16th attempt. Given a most enterprising ride, she stuck on grimly under pressure and was never going to be caught. (14/1)
4336 Trooper, who apparently did not stay two miles on turf last time, kept on in pursuit of the winner, but was never doing anything like enough to get in a blow. (8/1)
2539 Ijab (CAN), having his first race for 79 days, got his second wind coming to the final furlong. He really needs the full two miles. (12/1)
1287 Evezio Rufo was having his first outing for 129 days. He seemed to stay alright. (20/1)
4302 La Menorquina (USA) stayed on late in the day and is better-suited by two miles. (4/1)
2725 Tellion (8/1: 6/1-9/1)
4594 Indigo Dawn was kicked at the start. It must have upset her because she was in trouble soon after halfway and, dropping right out, was virtually pulled up. She was later found to be lame on her near-fore leg, the one she looked to be kicked on at the start. (5/2)

4812 COCO (S) STKS (2-Y.O) (Class G)
4-10 (4-14) **7f (Fibresand)** £1,984.50 (£547.00: £259.50) Stalls: Low GOING minus 0.20 sec per fur (FST)

				SP	RR	SF
4427^{8}	**Smooth Princess (IRE) (56)** (JGFitzGerald) **2-8-1**$^{(5)}$ BenedichteHalvorsen(7) (mde all: qcknd clr over 1f out: easily)	—	1	11/1	78+	19
4595^{6}	**Percy (64)** (JHetherton) **2-8-8**$^{(3)}$ DSweeney(4) (b: a chsng ldrs: kpt on u.p fnl 2f: no ch w wnr)	9	2	9/1	62	3
4753^{25}	**Filgrave (IRE) (54)** (CADwyer) **2-8-11v** WRyan(14) (racd wd: chsd ldrs: rdn & hung lft 2f out: kpt on one pce)	1½	3	12/1	59	—
4543^{7}	**Slim Prior (46)** (KRBurke) **2-8-11** AClark(1) (sn chsng ldrs: one pce fnl 2f)	s.h	4	33/1	59	—
4567^{13}	**Freckles (40)** (MJRyan) **2-8-4v**$^{1(3)ow1}$ PMcCabe(2) (s.i.s: hdwy ½-wy: hrd rdn: hung lft: one pce fnl 2f)	s.h	5	33/1	55	—
4690^{7}	**Bollinger Rose (IRE) (57)** (JJO'Neill) **2-8-1**$^{(5)}$ CLowther(9) (a chsng ldrs: rdn 3f out: one pce)	1¼	6	6/1^{3}	51	—

3258^{10} **Ellenber (52)** (WMcKeown) **2-8-8**(3) PFessey(15) (racd wd: nvr rchd ldrs)....2 **7** 25/1 51 —
4753^{16} **Five Fairies (58)** (NACallaghan) **2-8-3**(3) RFfrench(13) (racd wd: chsd ldrs: edgd lft & grad wknd fnl 2f)....½ **8** 7/2^{2} 45 —
4627^{10} **High Money (65)** (GLewis) **2-8-11b** PaulEddery(5) (lw: chsd ldrs: wknd & eased over 1f out)....3 **9** 3/1^{1} 43 —
4698^{15} **Little Risk** (KMcAuliffe) **2-8-6** TSprake(10) (mid div: drvn along ½-wy: sn lost pl)....17 **10** 16/1 — —
4483^{6} **Shanthi (46)** (PJMakin) **2-8-3**(3) RHavlin(11) (bhd & rdn ½-wy)....1½ **11** 6/1^{3} — —
4401^{10} **Aries Boy** (DCO'Brien) **2-8-11** GBardwell(3) (sn chsng ldrs & drvn along: lost pl over 2f out)....2 **12** 33/1 — —
4483^{12} **Miss Beveled (36)** (MBrittain) **2-8-6b** NCarlisle(6) (s.i.s: sme hdwy over 2f out: sn wknd)....2½ **13** 33/1 — —
2664^{6} **Inner Key** (PDEvans) **2-8-11** JFEgan(12) (b.hind: bhd after 2f)....hd **14** 16/1 — —
4627^{14} **Windspeed** (BPJBaugh) **2-8-8**(3) PRoberts(16) (sn outpcd & bhd)....12 **15** 40/1 — —
4413^{10} **Sixth Avenue (IRE) (35)** (RMWhitaker) **2-8-6v^{1}** VHalliday(8) (sn bhd)....4 **16** 33/1 — —
(SP 134.6%) **16 Rn**

1m 31.4 (4.90) CSF £101.11 TOTE £20.60: £5.40 £2.70 £3.20 (£83.70) Trio £114.60 OWNER Mr J. G. FitzGerald (MALTON) BRED L T K Meat Processors
Bt in 11,200 gns

Smooth Princess (IRE) turned this into a procession, and connections had to dig deep to retain her at the auction. (11/1)
4595 Percy stuck on to finish second-best, but the winner was in a totally different league. (9/1)
4595 Filgrave (IRE) gave his rider problems, persisting in hanging left. (12/1: op 8/1)
2191 Slim Prior seemed to appreciate the step up in distance. (33/1)
4690 Bollinger Rose (IRE) (6/1: op 4/1)
4500 High Money possibly ran out of stamina. Though only moderate, six might turn out to be his best trip. (3/1)
4483 Shanthi (6/1: op 4/1)

4813 MINOTAUR APPRENTICE H'CAP (0-70) (3-Y.O+) (Class G)
4-40 (4-46) **1m (Fibresand)** £1,984.50 (£547.00: £259.50) Stalls: Low GOING minus 0.20 sec per fur (FST)

SP RR SF

3992^{4} **Jona Holley (47)** (GLMoore) **4-8-6** GParkin(9) (trckd ldrs: led over 1f out: rdn clr)....— **1** 100/30^{1} 58 40
4485^{5} **Bentico (66)** (MrsNMacauley) **8-9-8v**(3) GMilligan(13) (b: trckd ldrs: led over 2f out: hdd over 1f out: kpt on: no ch w wnr)....2½ **2** 14/1 72 54
4164^{14} **Zalotto (IRE) (60)** (TJEtherington) **3-8-13b**(3) PRoberts(12) (racd wd: a chsng ldrs: kpt on same pce fnl 2f)....½ **3** 9/1 65 44
514^{8} **Yeoman Oliver (69)** (BAMcMahon) **4-9-9b**(5) SRighton(15) (racd wd: trckd ldrs: edgd lft & wknd over 1f out)...5 **4** 10/1 64 46
3064^{6} **Sweet Supposin (IRE) (65)** (CADwyer) **6-9-10v** TEDurcan(10) (a chsng ldrs: effrt over 2f out: edgd lft & no imp)....2 **5** 16/1 56 38
4471* **Shontaine (57)** (MJohnston) **4-8-9**(7) IGrantham(3) (lw: sn bhd: hdwy & swtchd over 1f out: styd on: nvr nr to chal)....1¼ **6** 5/1^{2} 46 28
4571^{7} **Grovefair Lad (IRE) (57)** (SRBowring) **3-8-13** AWhelan(8) (s.s: bhd tl hdwy on outside 2f out: styd on towards fin)....½ **7** 33/1 45 24
4059^{8} **Surf City (48)** (WWHaigh) **4-8-7** RFfrench(7) (in tch: effrt 3f out: nvr rchd ldrs)....1¾ **8** 6/1^{3} 32 14
3627^{10} **Tinklers Folly (49)** (RMWhitaker) **5-8-5**(3) CLowther(6) (mde most tl over 2f out: wknd over 1f out)....1¾ **9** 20/1 30 12
*4480** **Colins Choice (51)** (JLSpearing) **3-8-7** PFessey(5) (bhd: sme hdwy 2f out: n.d)....1 **10** 6/1^{3} 30 9
4477^{8} **Fancy A Fortune (IRE) (60)** (DNicholls) **3-8-9**(7) ANicholls(1) (in tch: drvn along 3f out: grad wknd)....3 **11** 10/1 33 12
4628^{6} **Delight of Dawn (50)** (EAWheeler) **5-8-6b**(3) ADaly(11) (chsd ldrs tl wknd over 2f out)....3½ **12** 10/1 16 —
4301^{6} **Desert Invader (IRE) (67)** (DWChapman) **6-9-12** DSweeney(14) (w ldrs tl wknd 2f out)....½ **13** 16/1 32 14
2471^{4} **Chadleigh Lane (USA) (57)** (ABMulholland) **5-8-11**(5) PDoe(4) (sn outpcd & bhd)....1 **14** 25/1 20 2
*4300** **Gablesea (51)** (BPJBaugh) **3-8-7** PPMurphy(16) (racd wd: sn outpcd & pushed along)....hd **15** 12/1 13 —
4696^{16} **Genuine John (IRE) (65)** (JParkes) **4-9-5**(5) TSiddall(2) (hld up: a in rr)....1½ **16** 50/1 24 6
(SP 145.2%) **16 Rn**

1m 42.4 (3.40) CSF £56.98 CT £394.70 TOTE £3.00: £1.10 £3.20 £2.60 £3.50 (£37.00) Trio £114.60 OWNER Joe Bates (Bloodstock) Ltd (BRIGHTON) BRED I. A. Balding
WEIGHT FOR AGE 3yo-3lb

IN-FOCUS: **This was a winner on her first ride in this country for twenty-four year old Benedichte Halvorsen, who has thirty six winners to her credit in Scandinavia and has twice been champion apprentice in Norway.**
3992 Jona Holley, a winner on soft ground at Folkestone in July, landed quite a gamble. Well handled, nothing was left to chance. (100/30: 8/1-5/2)
4485 Bentico probably ran up to his best, but had met a tartar. (14/1)
4050 Zalotto (IRE), as usual, gave problems being loaded into the stalls. (9/1)
257 Yeoman Oliver began to tread water coming to the final furlong. This was his first outing for 205 days and he almost certainly needed it. (10/1)
3064 Sweet Supposin (IRE) has won thirteen races, but significantly they have all come on the different surfaces at Lingfield and Wolverhampton. (16/1)
4471* Shontaine has been in good form on turf. Dropped behind not getting the run of the race, he was staying on in his own time at the finish. He should do better soon with a more experienced rider aboard. (5/1: 4/1-6/1)

T/Plpt: £1,334.50 (11.94 Tckts). T/Qdpt: £208.00 (4.28 Tckts) WG

4400-FOLKESTONE (R-H) (Good)
Tuesday October 21st
WEATHER: sunny WIND: str half against

4814 WESTENHANGER MAIDEN AUCTION STKS (I) (2-Y.O) (Class D)
1-30 (1-32) **6f 189y** £3,167.50 (£940.00: £445.00: £197.50) Stalls: Low GOING: 0.28 sec per fur (G)

SP RR SF

4135^{5} **Stone of Destiny (92)** (BJMeehan) **2-8-10** KFallon(7) (lw: a.p: chsd ldr 2f out: led 1f out: rdn out)....— **1** 11/10^{1} 91 43
4446^{2} **The Boy John (USA) (79)** (RHannon) **2-8-7** DaneO'Neill(9) (lw: led 6f out to 1f out: edgd lft: unable qckn)....3 **2** 4/1^{2} 81 33
4097^{15} **Fire Goddess (67)** (JSMoore) **2-7-9**(3) RFfrench(6) (rdn over 2f out: hdwy on ins over 1f out: one pce)....3 **3** 10/1 65 17
4361^{5} **The Magistrate (IRE) (73)** (MBlanshard) **2-8-2**(3) PPMurphy(2) (hld up: rdn 3f out: edgd rt ins fnl f: one pce) s.h **4** 6/1^{3} 72 24
4209^{5} **Hobart Junction (IRE)** (SCWilliams) **2-8-5** PBloomfield(5) (rdn over 2f out: hdwy over 1f out: nvr nrr)....2½ **5** 12/1 66 18
4638^{14} **Pas de Memoires (IRE)** (MHTompkins) **2-8-5** DBiggs(4) (lw: nvr nr to chal)....¾ **6** 16/1 64 16

4544^{10}	**Zero Three Fifteen (IRE) (65)** (MartynMeade) **2-8-3** GDuffield(3) (lw: led 1f: rdn over 2f out: wknd over 1f out)	5	**7**	20/1	51	3
4592^{3}	**Diamond Drill (USA)** (PJMakin) **2-8-7** SSanders(1) (lw: prom 5f)	3½	**8**	10/1	47	—
4564^{10}	**Algebra** (RHannon) **2-8-5** JQuinn(8) (a bhd)	s.h	**9**	25/1	44	—

(SP 122.3%) **9 Rn**

1m 27.5 (6.10) CSF £5.48 TOTE £1.90: £1.10 £1.50 £3.60 (£2.60) Trio £8.50 OWNER Mr P. Heath (UPPER LAMBOURN) BRED Mrs G. C. Stanley

4135 Stone of Destiny, out of his league against Daggers Drawn last time out, had a much simpler task and, leading a furlong from home, was rousted along to assert his authority. (11/10)

4446 The Boy John (USA) saw out this longer trip but he is having a real problem getting his head in front and, for the fifth time this season, had to settle for second-best. (4/1: 3/1-9/2)

3774 Fire Goddess had less on her plate but, after picking up ground along the inside rail below the distance, was then only fighting for third prize. (10/1: 8/1-12/1)

4361 The Magistrate (IRE) was rousted along three furlongs from home but, judged on this, looks rather one-paced. (6/1: op 10/1)

4209 Hobart Junction (IRE), racing towards the back of the field, passed a few tired horses. (12/1: op 6/1)

4592 Diamond Drill (USA) (10/1: op 6/1)

4815 WESTENHANGER MAIDEN AUCTION STKS (II) (2-Y.O) (Class D)

2-00 (2-00) **6f 189y** £3,167.50 (£940.00: £445.00: £197.50) Stalls: Low GOING: 0.28 sec per fur (G)

				SP	RR	SF
4520^{6}	**First Master** (MissGayKelleway) **2-8-4**(3) AWhelan(1) (b: lw: led 1f: led over 1f out: rdn out)	—	**1**	13/2^{3}	74	18
2688^{6}	**Three Angels (IRE)** (MHTompkins) **2-8-3** DBiggs(7) (hdwy over 2f out: hrd rdn over 1f out: unable qckn)	1¾	**2**	5/1^{2}	66	10
4564^{8}	**Prince Batshoof** (MBell) **2-8-5** MFenton(3) (a.p: swtchd lft over 2f out: hrd rdn over 1f out: one pce)	1	**3**	11/4^{1}	66	10
	Dancing Dervish (IABalding) **2-8-10** RCochrane(4) (lw: led 6f out tl over 1f out: wknd ins fnl f)	2	**4**	5/1^{2}	66	10
4668^{6}	**Russian Delight (IRE)** (RHannon) **2-7-12** JQuinn(8) (lw: hld up: rdn over 2f out: one pce)	nk	**5**	5/1^{2}	53	—
	Courage Under Fire (DWPArbuthnot) **2-8-3** TSprake(6) (w'like: dwlt: nvr nr to chal)	3	**6**	16/1	51	—
3926^{6}	**Persian Sabre (71)** (VSoane) **2-7-12** CRutter(5) (b: hld up: n.m.r over 2f out: sn wknd)	s.h	**7**	5/1^{2}	46	—
4066^{13}	**Ombra di Nube (FR)** (CJames) **2-7-9**(3) RFfrench(2) (hld up: nt clr run over 2f out: sn wknd)	3½	**8**	25/1	38	—
4602^{10}	**Casual Magic** (MajorDNChappell) **2-8-5** NAdams(9) (lw: a bhd)	5	**9**	20/1	33	—

(SP 121.2%) **9 Rn**

1m 29.4 (8.00) CSF £37.32 TOTE £6.90: £1.50 £2.40 £1.70 (£29.60) Trio £35.70 OWNER Three's Lucky Partnership (WHITCOMBE) BRED Kirtlington Stud Ltd

4520 First Master coped with the drop in trip in this bad event and, leading over a furlong from home, was ridden along to win in a time almost two seconds slower than the first division. (13/2)

2688 Three Angels (IRE), off the course for three and a half months since his debut, took closer order turning for home but, under pressure below the distance, could only struggle on at one insufficient pace. (5/1: 7/2-6/1)

2336 Prince Batshoof ran better and was never far away, if tapped for toe in the last furlong and a half. (11/4)

Dancing Dervish ran better over this extra furlong and took the field along, but he was collared below the distance and had nothing left to offer inside the final furlong. (5/1: op 5/2)

Russian Delight (IRE) failed to negotiate the downhill run, and was only going up and down in the same place once in line for home. (5/1)

4816 BIDDENDEN (S) STKS (3-Y.O) (Class F)

2-30 (2-31) **6f 189y** £2,277.00 (£627.00: £297.00) Stalls: Low GOING: 0.28 sec per fur (G)

				SP	RR	SF
4591^{4}	**Davis Rock (61)** (WRMuir) **3-8-9** MartinDwyer(5) (lw: a.p: led 2f out: rdn out)	—	**1**	7/2^{2}	58	34
4546^{15}	**Lamorna (50)** (MRChannon) **3-9-0** TQuinn(13) (chsd ldr: led over 2f out: sn hdd: unable qckn)	1½	**2**	9/1	60	36
4738^{4}	**Mike's Double (IRE) (60)** (MissGayKelleway) **3-9-5b** KFallon(9) (nt clr run over 2f out: hdwy wl over 1f out: hrd rdn & wandered ins fnl f: one pce)	s.h	**3**	5/2^{1}	64	40
4711^{17}	**Sharp Return (46)** (MJRyan) **3-8-11**(3) PMcCabe(10) (lw: rdn & hdwy over 1f out: r.o ins fnl f)	1	**4**	25/1	57	33
4326^{9}	**Gunners Glory (46)** (MrsLStubbs) **3-9-0** RCochrane(14) (lw: nt clr run over 2f out: hdwy over 1f out: r.o one pce)	s.h	**5**	12/1	57	33
3382^{9}	**Italian Symphony (IRE) (38)** (PDEvans) **3-9-0v1** JFEgan(11) (a.p: rdn over 2f out: one pce)	1¼	**6**	16/1	54	30
4184^{11}	**Glen Ogil (47)** (MRChannon) **3-8-7**(7) AEddery(1) (rdn over 2f out: hdwy over 1f out: nvr nrr)	hd	**7**	25/1	54	30
4565^{13}	**Chili Concerto (72)** (PJMakin) **3-8-9** SSanders(16) (prom 4f)	5	**8**	6/1^{3}	37	13
4316^{6}	**Madame Maxi** (PRHedger) **3-8-9** SDrowne(8) (nvr nr to chal)	3	**9**	9/1	30	6
3851^{8}	**Ginny Wossername (33)** (WGMTurner) **3-8-6b**(3) DSweeney(6) (lw: sme hdwy 3f out: wknd over 2f out)	4	**10**	16/1	21	—
4328^{17}	**Class Distinction (IRE) (51)** (RHannon) **3-9-0** DaneO'Neill(7) (lw: prom 3f)	½	**11**	20/1	25	1
4546^{6}	**Whizz Kid (37)** (JJBridger) **3-8-9** GBardwell(12) (a bhd)	d.h	**11**	20/1	20	—
2730^{16}	**Don't Forget Shoka (IRE) (31)** (JSMoore) **3-8-9b1** JQuinn(15) (led over 4f)	½	**13**	25/1	19	—
4221^{19}	**Copenhagen** (JAkehurst) **3-8-9** AClark(4) (a bhd)	2	**14**	33/1	14	—
2852^{12}	**Beveled Crystal (40)** (CJames) **3-8-9** CRutter(3) (hld up: rdn over 2f out: sn wknd)	2½	**15**	25/1	8	—
4504^{13}	**Forward Miss (20)** (CJBenstead) **3-8-9** GDuffield(2) (prom over 4f)	1¼	**16**	33/1	5	—

(SP 135.3%) **16 Rn**

1m 28.2 (6.80) CSF £31.87 TOTE £6.40: £1.90 £2.60 £1.10 (£24.50) Trio £17.90 OWNER Mr J. Jannaway (LAMBOURN) BRED Hesmonds Stud Ltd

No bid

4591 Davis Rock, a leading light throughout, struck the front a quarter of a mile from home and proved too strong for her rivals. (7/2)

4291* Lamorna showed in front turning for home, but she was soon passed by the winner and put in her place. (9/1: 6/1-10/1)

4738 Mike's Double (IRE) began to pick up ground early in the straight, but he did not look over-enthusiastic inside the final furlong, and failed to find the required acceleration. (5/2)

1107 Sharp Return, who has shown nothing so far this season, ran better this time, keeping on in the last furlong and a half to be nearest at the line. (25/1)

4184 Gunners Glory, who failed to stay a mile and a quarter last time, did not have the best of runs turning for home, but stayed on from below the distance. (12/1)

3213 Italian Symphony (IRE), given a ten-week break, was never far away, but could only struggle on in his own time once in line for home. He remains a maiden after sixteen attempts. (16/1)

1294 Chili Concerto (6/1: 4/1-13/2)

Madame Maxi (9/1: 6/1-10/1)

4817 HARDRES H'CAP (0-60) (3-Y.O) (Class F)

3-00 (3-02) **1m 1f 149y** £3,470.00 (£1,040.00: £500.00: £230.00) Stalls: Low GOING: 0.28 sec per fur (G)

Form	Horse	Dist	Pos	SP	RR	SF
4222^{6}	**Star Entry (54)** (MajorDNChappell) **3-9-2** KFallon(15) (a.p: led wl over 1f out: rdn: r.o wl)	—	**1**	6/1^{2}	69	42
4798^{7}	**Homestead (51)** (RHannon) **3-8-13** DaneO'Neill(13) (lw: hdwy 2f out: chsd wnr over 1f out: unable qckn)	4	**2**	5/1^{1}	59	32
4713^{7}	**Royal Roulette (54)** (SPCWoods) **3-9-2v** NDay(4) (lw: swtchd lft 2f out: hrd rdn & hdwy over 1f out: r.o)	3½	**3**	8/1	57	30
4465^{2}	**Ron's Round (53)** (CADwyer) **3-9-1** JFEgan(7) (lw: hld up: rdn over 3f out: one pce)	3½	**4**	6/1^{2}	50	23
4629^{6}	**Here's To Howie (USA) (57)** (RHannon) **3-9-5** WJO'Connor(3) (a.p: led over 2f out tl wl over 1f out: sn wknd)	nk	**5**	20/1	53	26
4696^{6}	**Ardent (59)** (CJBenstead) **3-9-7** CRutter(9) (lw: hrd rdn over 2f out: nvr nr to chal)	4	**6**	16/1	49	22
4693^{5}	**Tycoon Tina (53)** (WMBrisbourne) **3-9-1** RCochrane(2) (lw: dwlt: nvr nrr)	5	**7**	7/1	34	7
4632^{6}	**Tabasco Jazz (57)** (BJMeehan) **3-9-5** MTebbutt(8) (nvr nrr)	s.h	**8**	16/1	38	11
4648a^{9}	**Village Pub (FR) (47)** (KOCunningham-Brown) **3-8-9** JWeaver(12) (led over 1f: wknd over 2f out)	2	**9**	16/1	25	—
4169^{13}	**Inclination (58)** (MBlanshard) **3-9-6** JQuinn(11) (lw: led 8f out tl over 2f out: sn wknd)	nk	**10**	12/1	36	9
4300^{3}	**Jolly Jackson (51)** (RAkehurst) **3-8-13** TQuinn(1) (bhd fnl 4f)	7	**11**	13/2^{3}	17	—
4546^{2}	**Churchill's Shadow (IRE) (45)** (BAPearce) **3-8-7** TSprake(10) (s.s: a bhd)	3	**12**	6/1^{2}	6	—
2407^{7}	**Sidney The Kidney (55)** (MJRyan) **3-9-3** AClark(6) (bhd fnl 2f)	8	**13**	20/1	3	—
4177^{11}	**After Hours (49)** (DJSffrenchDavis) **3-8-11** RPerham(5) (s.s: a wl bhd)	12	**14**	25/1	—	—
				(SP 135.2%)	**14 Rn**	

2m 7.2 (9.50) CSF £36.22 CT £236.90 TOTE £8.90: £2.70 £2.10 £4.90 (£22.20) Trio £201.40 OWNER Mr J. H. Widdows (PULBOROUGH) BRED D. F. Bradstock

4222 Star Entry, may never have been far away, but Fallon was nudging her along fully a mile from home. She got to the front early in the final quarter-mile and, once there, soon asserted for a decisive victory. (6/1)

4798 Homestead, making a quick reappearance, came through to take second place over a furlong out but, despite pulling clear of the remainder, had no hope with the winner. (5/1: 4/1-6/1)

4304 Royal Roulette found the drop in trip against her and, although running on in the last furlong and a half, found the front two already home and dry. (8/1)

4465 Ron's Round is certainly in the Handicapper's grip at present, having been hiked up a massive 14lb since his last run, and could only struggle on at one insufficient pace in the last three furlongs. (6/1: op 10/1)

4629 Here's To Howie (USA) ran better, and showed in front turning for home. Collared early in the final quarter mile, he had soon shot his bolt. (20/1)

3968 Inclination (12/1: op 8/1)

4818 CLIFF MEDIAN AUCTION MAIDEN STKS (2-Y.O) (Class F)

3-30 (3-32) **5f** £2,277.00 (£627.00: £297.00) Stalls: Low GOING: 0.28 sec per fur (G)

Form	Horse	Dist	Pos	SP	RR	SF
4569^{3}	**Third Cousin (IRE)** (MJHeaton-Ellis) **2-9-0** SDrowne(4) (a.p: led over 1f out: r.o wl)	—	**1**	14/1	82	34
4602^{2}	**Bandbox (IRE) (78)** (SMellor) **2-9-0** MWigham(6) (lw: bmpd over 4f out: rdn over 2f out: hdwy wl over 1f out: r.o one pce)	2½	**2**	5/2^{1}	74	26
4602^{6}	**Atlanta** (JLDunlop) **2-8-9** TQuinn(7) (rdn & hdwy over 1f out: r.o one pce)	hd	**3**	8/1	69	21
4296^{2}	**Emperor Naheem (IRE) (77)** (BJMeehan) **2-9-0** KFallon(2) (lw: led over 3f: one pce)	½	**4**	100/30^{2}	72	24
2829^{5}	**Double Brandy** (IABalding) **2-9-0** RCochrane(12) (lw: a.p: rdn over 2f out: one pce)	s.h	**5**	9/2^{3}	72	24
4602^{5}	**Ok Babe** (JAkehurst) **2-8-9** DBiggs(3) (b: a.p: ev ch over 1f out: one pce)	s.h	**6**	25/1	67	19
4515^{14}	**Long Island** (RHannon) **2-9-0** DaneO'Neill(13) (lw: hld up: rdn over 2f out: one pce)	1½	**7**	25/1	67	19
	Mystical Song (RGuest) **2-8-9** MartinDwyer(9) (neat: bkwd: shkn up over 1f out: hdwy fnl f: r.o: bttr for r)	s.h	**8**	16/1	62+	14
3638^{13}	**Tough Nell (IRE)** (BobJones) **2-8-9** NDay(8) (lw: prom over 2f)	2½	**9**	40/1	54	6
4630^{5}	**Royal Blue** (MDIUsher) **2-9-0** JMarshall(10) (b.hind: lw: bhd fnl 3f)	1½	**10**	25/1	54	6
3711^{3}	**Dover Soul (70)** (PJMakin) **2-8-9** SSanders(5) (lw: bmpd over 4f out: prom 3f)	½	**11**	7/1	47	—
	Batchworth Belle (EAWheeler) **2-8-6**(3) ADaly(11) (leggy: bit bkwd: s.s: a bhd)	2½	**12**	40/1	39	—
4311^{5}	**Game Bird** (JLSpearing) **2-8-9** JWeaver(1) (a bhd)	½	**13**	12/1	38	—
				(SP 130.1%)	**13 Rn**	

62.7 secs (5.10) CSF £46.49 TOTE £16.50: £2.80 £1.10 £4.50 (£31.50) Trio £145.90 OWNER Mr P. G. Lowe (WROUGHTON) BRED John McKay

4569 Third Cousin (IRE), never far away, struck the front approaching the final furlong and, rousted along, kept his rivals at bay. (14/1)

4602 Bandbox (IRE) is becoming seriously frustrating, and has now finished second in five of his last six runs. (5/2)

4602 Atlanta stayed on from below the distance, but never looked like posing a serious threat. (8/1: 9/2-9/1)

4296 Emperor Naheem (IRE) took the field along but, collared over a furlong out, could only struggle along in his own time. (100/30)

2829 Double Brandy, off the track for three months since an encouraging debut, was strangely taking a drop in distance, so it was no surprise that that vital turn of foot was missing in the last furlong and a half. (9/2)

4602 Ok Babe had every chance over a furlong out, but was then tapped for toe. (25/1)

Mystical Song is not that big, and appeared to be carrying plenty of surplus flesh. Nevertheless, she caught the eye on this debut, grasping the hang of things in the final furlong and running on nicely to be nearest at the finish. She will have learnt from this. (16/1)

3711 Dover Soul (7/1: 9/2-8/1)

4819 LEVY BOARD RATING RELATED MAIDEN STKS (0-60) (2-Y.O) (Class F)

4-00 (4-02) **6f** £2,808.30 (£778.80: £372.90) Stalls: Low GOING: 0.28 sec per fur (G)

Form	Horse	Dist	Pos	SP	RR	SF
4753^{11}	**Impulsive Decision (IRE) (53)** (MartynMeade) **2-8-11** KFallon(3) (hld up: rdn over 2f out: led 1f out: drvn out)	—	**1**	6/1^{2}	63	41
4566^{11}	**Kathies Pet (57)** (RJHodges) **2-8-11** RCochrane(4) (rdn & hdwy 2f out: r.o ins fnl f)	½	**2**	12/1	62	40
4143^{9}	**Flame Tower (IRE) (59)** (RHannon) **2-9-0** DaneO'Neill(10) (lw: led: rdn 2f out: hdd 1f out: unable qckn)	2	**3**	7/1^{3}	59	37
4569^{6}	**Critical Air (60)** (SirMarkPrescott) **2-9-0** GDuffield(9) (a.p: hrd rdn & ev ch over 1f out: wknd ins fnl f)	2	**4**	7/2^{1}	54	32
4178^{11}	**Corsecan (52)** (SDow) **2-8-7**(7) PDoe(7) (lw: rdn & hdwy 2f out: one pce)	2	**5**	20/1	49	27
4152^{14}	**Life Sentence (55)** (JGSmyth-Osbourne) **2-9-0b** TSprake(13) (lw: rdn & hdwy over 1f out: nvr nr to chal)	4	**6**	20/1	38	16
3859^{3}	**Petaling (IRE) (60)** (BJMeehan) **2-8-11b** MTebbutt(6) (spd over 4f)	1¾	**7**	6/1^{2}	30	8
4545^{10}	**Silent Pride (IRE) (46)** (MDIUsher) **2-8-4**(7) JFowle(1) (b: nvr nrr)	¾	**8**	16/1	28	6
4545^{6}	**Mountain Magic (59)** (DJSffrenchDavis) **2-8-11** JWeaver(15) (nvr nrr)	1½	**9**	10/1	24	2
3312^{2}	**Courtney Gym (IRE) (59)** (MRChannon) **2-9-0** TQuinn(11) (a mid div)	1¾	**10**	8/1	23	1

4566^{6}	**Kantone (IRE) (50)** (JMPEustace) **2-9-0v^{1}** JTate(14) (lw: a mid div)	nk	**11**	20/1	22	—
4327^{14}	**Blarney Park (50)** (CADwyer) **2-8-11v^{1}** DO'Donohoe(8) (mid div over 4f)	2	**12**	20/1	14	—
4381^{12}	**Goldmaster (57)** (WAO'Gorman) **2-9-0b^{1}** EmmaO'Gorman(16) (lw: bhd fnl 2f)	3½	**13**	16/1	7	—
4566^{10}	**Wild Lilly (55)** (MJRyan) **2-8-11** GCarter(2) (bhd fnl 2f)	nk	**14**	14/1	3	—
4566^{13}	**Mercury Falling (60)** (DWPArbuthnot) **2-8-11** SWhitworth(5) (b: b.nr hind: gd spd over 3f)	3½	**15**	12/1	—	—
4068^{9}	**Miss Skye (IRE) (60)** (TJNaughton) **2-8-11** SSanders(12) (prom over 3f)	1¼	**16**	14/1	—	—

(SP 143.0%) **16 Rn**

1m 15.7 (5.50) CSF £77.77 TOTE £6.70: £1.90 £5.20 £2.80 (£36.40) Trio £317.80; £268.57 to Newcastle 22/10/97 OWNER Ladyswood Racing Club (MALMESBURY) BRED Loualin Bloodstock

4543 Impulsive Decision (IRE) chased the leaders. Striking the front a furlong out, she responded to pressure and kept on well. (6/1)

3324 Kathies Pet began a forward move a quarter of a mile from home and, easing her way towards the stands' side a furlong out, ran on to make sure the winner did not have things all her own way. (12/1)

2681 Flame Tower (IRE), attempting to make every post a winning one, was collared a furlong from home, then found another turn of foot lacking. (7/1)

4569 Critical Air, in a handy position throughout, had every chance below the distance before running out of gas. (7/2)

2784 Corsecan, racing at the back of the field, came through the pack two furlongs from home, but could then make no further impression. (20/1)

3859 Petaling (IRE) (6/1: op 4/1)

4820 HERSTMONCEUX LIMITED STKS (0-70) (3-Y.O+) (Class E)

4-30 (4-32) **6f** £3,226.25 (£965.00: £462.50: £211.25) Stalls: Low GOING: 0.28 sec per fur (G)

				SP	RR	SF
4290^{2}	**Topton (IRE) (70)** (IABalding) **3-8-11v** SWhitworth(3) (hdwy 3f out: led over 1f out: drvn out)	—	**1**	10/1	80	62
4280^{16}	**Mister Jolson (70)** (RJHodges) **8-9-1b** RCochrane(15) (b.nr fore: s.s & swtchd lft s: hrd rdn & hdwy over 1f out: ev ch wl ins fnl f: r.o wl)	hd	**2**	9/1 3	83	66
4565^{5}	**Roffey Spinney (IRE) (69)** (RHannon) **3-8-11** DaneO'Neill(2) (lw: led over 4f: unable qckn)	1¾	**3**	8/1 2	75	57
4375^{5}	**Braveheart (IRE) (70)** (MRChannon) **3-8-11** TQuinn(1) (lost pl 3f out: rallied over 1f out: r.o one pce)	1¾	**4**	13/2 1	70	52
4773^{2}	**Halowing (USA) (69)** (JGSmyth-Osbourne) **3-8-5(3)** DSweeney(4) (lw: a.p: rdn over 2f out: wknd fnl f)	1¼	**5**	10/1	64	46
3107^{3}	**Broadstairs Beauty (IRE) (66)** (DShaw) **7-8-9b(3)** CTeague(14) (b: lw: racd far side: a.p: ev ch over 1f out: eased whn btn ins fnl f)	hd	**6**	10/1	67	50
4321^{4}	**Kentucky Fall (FR) (69)** (LadyHerries) **4-8-12** AClark(13) (racd far side: hld up: ev ch over 1f out: eased whn btn ins fnl f)	2½	**7**	9/1 3	60	43
4518^{2}	**Out Line (66)** (MMadgwick) **5-8-8(7)** AEddery(5) (s.s: nvr nrr)	hd	**8**	16/1	63	46
4328^{2}	**Mystical (64)** (MrsLStubbs) **3-9-0v** KFallon(11) (a mid div)	½	**9**	11/1	62	44
4791*	**Swino (70)** (PDEvans) **3-9-0 3x** JFEgan(10) (hdwy over 2f out: wknd wl over 1f out)	nk	**10**	13/2 1	61	43
4290^{4}	**Warning Express (70)** (RWArmstrong) **3-8-8** FNorton(8) (b: hdwy over 3f out: wknd 2f out)	¾	**11**	12/1	53	35
2481^{3}	**Nopalea (68)** (TJNaughton) **3-8-11** TSprake(9) (lw: bhd fnl 2f)	¾	**12**	14/1	54	36
4797^{8}	**Forcing Bid (69)** (SirMarkPrescott) **3-9-3** GDuffield(6) (lw: prom 4f)	4	**13**	12/1	49	31
4563^{3}	**Tithcar (65)** (BHanbury) **3-8-8** MRimmer(7) (prom 3f)	5	**14**	20/1	27	9
2698^{15}	**Sharp 'n Smart (65)** (BSmart) **5-8-12** MTebbutt(16) (lw: racd far side: bhd fnl 2f)	1¾	**15**	20/1	25	8
4451^{2}	**Bubbly (66)** (JLDunlop) **3-8-11** SSanders(12) (bhd fnl 2f)	4	**16**	9/1 3	14	—

(SP 140.8%) **16 Rn**

1m 14.2 (4.00) CSF £102.09 TOTE £19.30: £4.00 £2.80 £4.10 (£60.20) Trio £365.90 OWNER Mr George Strawbridge (KINGSCLERE) BRED George Strawbridge

WEIGHT FOR AGE 3yo-1lb

4290 Topton (IRE) at last came good. Striking the front approaching the final furlong, he responded to pressure and just managed to hold off the very serious challenge of the runner-up. (10/1: 8/1-12/1)

3326 Mister Jolson has been a grand servant over the years and appreciated this easier company. Throwing down his challenge inside the final furlong, he gave it his all, and only just failed. (9/1)

4565 Roffey Spinney (IRE), attempted to make all the running but, collared over a furlong out, failed to find another turn of foot. (8/1: 6/1-9/1)

4375 Braveheart (IRE) was outpaced at halfway, but did stay on again below the distance. (13/2)

4773 Halowing (USA), never far away, had run out of steam in the final furlong. (10/1: 6/1-12/1)

3107 Broadstairs Beauty (IRE), without a run in nearly three months, was one of three who elected to run on the far rails. He was certainly up with the pace approaching the final furlong but, when his chance had gone inside the last two hundred yards, his jockey was not hard on him. Despite some good efforts this season, he has not won for nearly two years. (10/1: op 6/1)

4321 Kentucky Fall (FR) (9/1: 5/1-10/1)

4328 Mystical (11/1: 6/1-12/1)

4290 Warning Express (12/1: 7/1-14/1)

4451 Bubbly (9/1: 6/1-10/1)

4821 LEEDS H'CAP (0-60) (3-Y.O+) (Class F)

5-00 (5-01) **1m 4f** £2,415.00 (£665.00: £315.00) Stalls: Low GOING: 0.28 sec per fur (G)

				SP	RR	SF
4572^{3}	**Glow Forum (56)** (LMontagueHall) **6-9-10** KFallon(7) (hld up: led over 2f out: clr over 1f out: r.o wl)	—	**1**	9/2 2	66	48
4562^{3}	**Veronica Franco (52)** (PRHedger) **4-9-3(3)** RFfrench(13) (hdwy & hmpd on ins over 2f out: lost pl: swtchd lft over 1f out: rallied fnl f: r.o wl)	½	**2**	3/1 1	61	43
4771^{9}	**Drift (59)** (SirMarkPrescott) **3-9-6** GDuffield(4) (rdn over 6f out: hdwy over 3f out: unable qckn fnl 2f)	1½	**3**	14/1	66	41
4562^{6}	**Meilleur (IRE) (56)** (LadyHerries) **3-9-3** RCochrane(14) (lost pl 5f out: rallied over 2f out: one pce)	½	**4**	9/1	63	38
4516^{2}	**Sea Danzig (53)** (JJBridger) **4-9-7** NAdams(12) (lw: led over 9f: wknd ins fnl f)	1¾	**5**	14/1	57	39
4699^{5}	**Junikay (IRE) (60)** (RIngram) **3-9-7** AMcGlone(5) (a.p: rdn over 2f out: one pce)	1¼	**6**	7/1 3	63	38
4179^{8}	**Reimei (55)** (KCComerford) **8-9-9b** WJO'Connor(15) (hdwy over 2f out: wknd 1f out)	1¼	**7**	50/1	56	38
4584^{6}	**Admirals Secret (USA) (49)** (CFWall) **8-9-3** SSanders(1) (lw: hdwy 6f out: wknd 2f out)	½	**8**	8/1	49	31
4322^{10}	**My Roland (IRE) (51)** (JFfitch-Heyes) **3-8-12** JWeaver(17) (lw: nvr nrr)	3½	**9**	50/1	47	22
4590^{11}	**Herbshan Dancer (53)** (BRMillman) **3-8-11(3)** AWhelan(10) (lw: prom 10f)	10	**10**	20/1	35	10
4743^{4}	**Viburnum (50)** (AGFoster) **3-8-11** TSprake(2) (bhd fnl 5f)	nk	**11**	8/1	32	7
4667*	**Dauphin (IRE) (49)** (WJMusson) **4-9-3** MWigham(3) (bhd fnl 4f)	s.h	**12**	7/1 3	31	13
3970^{7}	**Persian Blue (59)** (RHannon) **3-9-6** DaneO'Neill(18) (prom 10f)	nk	**13**	14/1	41	16
4590^{12}	**Maryjo (IRE) (48)** (GLMoore) **8-9-2** CandyMorris(11) (lw: a bhd)	9	**14**	20/1	18	—
4631^{5}	**Bob Knows (56)** (RFJohnsonHoughton) **3-9-3** AClark(9) (hmpd s: a bhd)	11	**15**	25/1	11	—

4562[17] **Mr Speculator (50)** (JEBanks) **4-9-4v** GBardwell(16) (lw: bhd fnl 5f)..........3 **16** 33/1 1 —
(SP 140.6%) **16 Rn**

2m 43.6 (12.40) CSF £18.19 CT £179.52 TOTE £4.60: £1.90 £1.10 £4.30 £2.10 (£8.90) Trio £156.70 OWNER Miss J D Anstee & Partners (EPSOM) BRED Forum Bloodstock Ltd
WEIGHT FOR AGE 3yo-7lb
4572 Glow Forum struck the front over a quarter of a mile from home and forged clear to win her fifth race of the year. (9/2: 6/1-7/2)
4562 Veronica Franco had no luck in running. Hampered as she picked up ground along the inside rail turning for home, she lost her place and was only tenth entering the final quarter-mile. Switched left, she really found her feet in the final furlong and came sweeping through only to find the line beating her. (3/1)
4503 Drift, off the bridle early in the back straight, took closer order running down the hill, but failed to find that vital turn of foot once in line for home. (14/1: 10/1-16/1)
4562 Meilleur (IRE), outpaced at the top of the hill, got back into it turning for home, but could then only struggle on at one insufficient pace. (9/1: 6/1-10/1)
4516 Sea Danzig, moving up in trip, set the pace. Collared over two furlongs from home, he grimly held on until tiring inside the last two hundred yards. (14/1)
4699 Junikay (IRE) was never far away, but never looked like finding that vital turn of foot in the last two furlongs. (7/1)
4667* Dauphin (IRE) (7/1: op 4/1)

T/Jkpt: Not won; £71,823.29 to Newcastle 22/10/97. T/Plpt: £55.10 (493.26 Tckts). T/Qdpt: £22.70 (55.81 Tckts) AK

4822a - 4833a : (Irish Racing) - See Computer Raceform

4615a-CURRAGH (Newbridge, Ireland) (R-H) (Soft)
Saturday October 18th

4834a WATERFORD TESTIMONIAL STKS (Listed) (3-Y.O+)
2-50 (2-51) **6f** IR £12,900.00 (IR £3,700.00: IR £1,700.00: IR £500.00) GOING: 0.95 sec per fur (S)

				SP	RR	SF
4625a[5]	**Burden Of Proof (IRE)** (CO'Brien,Ireland) **5-9-3** PJSmullen (hld up in tch: 4th ½-wy: chal 2f out: led wl over 1f out: rdn & kpt on fnl f)	—	**1**	5/2[1]	119+	47
	Alarme Belle (DKWeld,Ireland) **3-8-6** PShanahan (towards rr: hdwy to 5th & chsd ldrs 1½f out: r.o u.p ins last)	nk	**2**	12/1	108	35
4625a[2]	**Orange Grouse (IRE)** (LBrowne,Ireland) **4-8-7** JPSpencer (dwlt: chsd ldrs ½-wy: effrt & nt clr run over 1f out: swtchd rt jst ins last: r.o u.p)	hd	**3**	5/2[1]	108	36
3508a[9]	**Tinker Amelia** (JGMcDonnell,Ireland) **5-8-8**ow1 SCraine (hld up towards rr: cld 2f out: 6th over 1f out: rdn & r.o.)	hd	**4**	20/1	109	36
4625a[6]	**Poker-B (IRE)** (DGillespie,Ireland) **3-8-13** JPMurtagh (led: jnd under 2f out: sn hdd & no ex: wknd ins last)	2½	**5**	8/1	108	35
2815a[7]	**Royal Affinity (IRE)** (APO'Brien,Ireland) **3-8-9b** JAHeffernan (cl up: 3rd ½-wy: ev ch 2f out: 2nd u.p & no ex over 1f out: wknd ins last)	1½	**6**	5/1[2]	100	27
1533a[10]	**Royale (IRE)** (APO'Brien,Ireland) **3-8-10b** NGMcCullagh (in tch: rdn ½-wy: btn over 2f out)	9	**7**	7/1[3]	77	4
2078a[5]	**Mosconi (IRE)** (JSBolger,Ireland) **3-8-9b** KJManning (chsd ldr: 2nd ½-wy: rdn & n.m.r over 2f out: btn & wknd over 1½f out)	2½	**8**	12/1	69	—

(SP 117.6%) **8 Rn**

1m 20.0 (9.50) OWNER M. V. O'Brien BRED Lyonstown Stud in Ireland
2816a Burden Of Proof (IRE), on his favourite track, had things very much to suit. Successful in this race two years ago and runner-up last season, he cruised into the lead a furlong out and held on well. This was probably his last appearance. (5/2: op 6/4)
Alarme Belle ran well for an ordinary handicapper and goes up 7lb. (12/1)
4625a Orange Grouse (IRE) could not confirm her previous form with the winner and was squeezed up a furlong out. (5/2)
Tinker Amelia was another to run above herself, as indeed she did in the race last year. She has also gone up 7lb. (20/1)
2078a Mosconi (IRE) (12/1: op 8/1)

4835a : (Irish Racing) - See Computer Raceform

4836a JUDDMONTE BERESFORD STKS (Gp 3) (2-Y.O)
3-50 (3-52) **1m (New)** IR £19,500.00 (IR £5,700.00: IR £2,700.00: IR £900.00) GOING: 0.95 sec per fur (S)

				SP	RR	SF
4135[3]	**Saratoga Springs (CAN)** (APO'Brien,Ireland) **2-8-12**ow1 CRoche (rn 2nd: chal early st: led 2f out: rdn clr ins last)	—	**1**	7/4[1]	93+	43
	Hanzanar (IRE) (JOxx,Ireland) **2-8-11** JPMurtagh (rn 3rd: effrt over 2f out: wnt 2nd wl ins last)	4	**2**	13/2[3]	84	35
4128a[2]	**Timekeeper (USA)** (MBell) **2-8-11** MFenton (led: rdn & hdd 2f out: no ex over 1f out)	½	**3**	8/1	83	34
4619a[8]	**Attractive Crown (USA)** (KPrendergast,Ireland) **2-8-8** SCraine (plld hrd: hld up: rdn over 1f out: kpt on same pce)	1½	**4**	11/1	77	28
	Catch The Dragon (IRE) (LBrowne,Ireland) **2-8-11** PShanahan (hld up: last & rdn 2f out: kpt on u.p ins last)	1	**5**	14/1	78	29
	Stopwatch (IRE) (TStack,Ireland) **2-8-11** PJSmullen (dwlt: towards rr: rdn & effrt 2f out: no imp over 1f out)	2	**6**	11/1	74	25
	Sabre Mountain (USA) (JSBolger,Ireland) **2-8-11** KJManning (hld up: 4th st: sn chal: wknd 1½f out)	1½	**7**	2/1[2]	71	22

(SP 117.5%) **7 Rn**

1m 47.7 (12.70) OWNER Michael Tabor (PILTOWN)
4135 Saratoga Springs (CAN), without the visor that he wore at Doncaster and York, made this look very easy. Surprisingly easy to back, he went to the front well over one furlong out and drew clear under gentle pressure. There are five above him in the known pecking order at Ballydoyle but his trainer still thinks he might mature into a Derby horse. (7/4: op 4/5)
Hanzanar (IRE), whose stamina saw him move into second place inside the last, never looked like getting on terms. (13/2: op 4/1)
4128a Timekeeper (USA) made the running but was left behind once the winner went by. (8/1: op 5/1)
3534a Attractive Crown (USA) plugged on at the one pace without ever looking a possibility. (11/1)
Catch The Dragon (IRE) is a maiden and ran well enough here to suggest that he will lose that status before long. (14/1)
Sabre Mountain (USA) was ridden up on the outer to go third turning in but dropped out quickly over one furlong out, and was found to be "distressed and slightly lame" afterwards. (2/1)

4837a BLANDFORD STKS (Gp 2) (3-Y.O+)
4-20 (4-24) **1m 3f** IR £32,500.00 (IR £9,500.00: IR £4,500.00: IR £1,500.00) GOING: 0.95 sec per fur (S)

Form	Horse / details	Pos	SP	RR	SF
4356a*	**Quws** (KPrendergast,Ireland) **3-8-8** SCraine (hld up towards rr: clsd st: chal fr 2f out: led ins last: rdn & r.o.)—	1	5/2[2]	109	30
	Spirit Of Tara (IRE) (MJGrassick,Ireland) **3-8-5** WJSupple (rn 3rd: chal st: rdn to ld 1½f out: hdd u.p ins last: no ex) 1½	2	14/1	104	25
4191a[2]	**Vivo (IRE)** (JOxx,Ireland) **4-9-0** JPMurtagh (rn 4th: effrt over 2f out: no ex ins last) 1	3	9/2[3]	105	32
	Khairabar (IRE) (JOxx,Ireland) **3-8-8** DHogan (sn led & disp ld: hdd u.p 1½f out: no ex) 2	4	7/1	103	24
4204a[4]	**Rayouni (IRE)** (JOxx,Ireland) **3-8-8** PJSmullen (hld up: 5th ½-wy: chal on outside over 2f out: btn 1½f out) ..nk	5	7/4[1]	102	23
2814a[11]	**Absolute Glee (USA)** (DKWeld,Ireland) **3-8-5** PShanahan (led early: 2nd & disp ld: ev ch st: btn over 2f out).8	6	9/1	87	8

(SP 112.3%) **6 Rn**

2m 32.9 (18.90) OWNER Mr Hamdan Al Maktoum (FRIARSTOWN)

4356a* Quws gained a nice reward for his consistency and the Cambridgeshire winner saw this trip out well. He looked like winning a lot easier than he eventually did, cruising a furlong and a half out but not doing a lot when he got his head in front inside the last. A winter in Dubai beckons. (5/2)

Spirit Of Tara (IRE), a sister to Salsabil, gained a bit of black type on her final racecourse appearance and now visits Gone West. (14/1: op 8/1)

4191a Vivo (IRE) is strictly a handicapper and found this trip a bit too much. (9/2: op 3/1)

Khairabar (IRE) (7/1: op 3/1)

4204a Rayouni (IRE), uneasy in the market, came under pressure early in the straight and was subsequently found to be in "respiratory distress". (7/4: op Evens)

2814a Absolute Glee (USA) (9/1: op 5/1)

(NR)

4838a - 4839a : (Irish Racing) - See Computer Raceform

4507-NEWCASTLE (L-H) (Good to firm, Good patches)
Wednesday October 22nd
Races 4, 6, 7 & 8: hand-timed

WEATHER: sunny periods WIND: slt half against

4840 E.B.F. MAIDEN STKS (2-Y.O) (Class D)
2-00 (2-00) **6f** £3,436.25 (£1,040.00: £507.50: £241.25) Stalls: High GOING minus 0.11 sec per fur (G)

Form	Horse / details	Pos	SP	RR	SF
4640[2]	**Love Academy** (MJohnston) **2-9-0** SSanders(12) (lw: mde all: rdn & hung lft over 1f out: r.o) ....—	1	10/11[1]	86	40
4640[W]	**Ryefield** (MissLAPerratt) **2-9-0** GCarter(11) (lw: trckd ldrs: effrt over 1f out: kpt on: nt pce of wnr) 1¾	2	11/2[3]	81	35
4544[5]	**Anvil (USA) (80)** (GLewis) **2-9-0b[1]** PaulEddery(2) (lw: chsd ldrs: effrt 2f out: r.o one pce) 2	3	9/2[2]	76	30
4433[8]	**The Blues Academy (IRE)** (MJohnston) **2-9-0v** JFortune(13) (sn chsng ldrs: kpt on one pce appr fnl f) ....hd	4	20/1	76	30
4236[12]	**Snowballs** (MissLAPerratt) **2-9-0** JFEgan(9) (outpcd tl r.o fnl 2f) 1½	5	25/1	72	26
4211[6]	**Lake Taal** (MJCamacho) **2-8-9** LCharnock(7) (hld up: hdwy 2f out: styd on) 2	6	12/1	61	15
3869[10]	**Inshallah (57)** (MartinTodhunter) **2-8-9** JCarroll(3) (chsd ldrs tl outpcd fnl 2f) 1½	7	33/1	57	11
	Pipe Music (IRE) (PCHaslam) **2-9-0** JWeaver(8) (cmpt: scope: bit bkwd: s.i.s: nvr nr to chal) 4	8	11/1	52	6
	Caplaw Skeen (JLEyre) **2-9-0** MGallagher(1) (unf: scope: sn outpcd & bhd: n.d) 1	9	20/1	49	3
4286[6]	**Bolshaya** (JBerry) **2-8-9** KDarley(5) (hld up: nvr nr to chal) 3	10	14/1	36	—
4750[11]	**Shotley Marie (IRE)** (NBycroft) **2-8-9b[1]** ACulhane(4) (s.i.s: a bhd) ....¾	11	50/1	34	—
	Taj Mahal (IRE) (CWThornton) **2-9-0** DeanMcKeown(6) (cmpt: s.i.s: a bhd) ....nk	12	20/1	38	—
	Mac's Type (IRE) (WStorey) **2-8-9** JFanning(10) (neat: bkwd: sn outpcd & bhd) 12	13	50/1	1	—

(SP 133.6%) **13 Rn**

1m 15.01 (3.51) CSF £5.94 TOTE £1.80: £1.20 £1.60 £1.80 (£4.30) Trio £3.20 OWNER Mr M. Doyle (MIDDLEHAM) BRED Highclere Stud Ltd

4640 Love Academy was always too good for these but he did not help matters by hanging left and his rider needed to work to keep him going. (10/11: tchd evens)

4236 Ryefield travelled well and responded to pressure in good style but the winner was always too good. Easier opportunities will surely be found. (11/2)

4544 Anvil (USA) had blinkers on for the first time and, although they sharpened him up early on, they made little difference when the race began in earnest. (9/2)

4309 The Blues Academy (IRE) put in his best effort to date and is obviously learning. (20/1)

3857 Snowballs has the looks but also gives the impression that he might have his own ideas about the game, although he should appreciate further. (25/1)

4211 Lake Taal gives the impression that she is still learning and should do better as she tries further yet. (12/1)

Pipe Music (IRE), a reasonable sort, needed this both fitness and-experience-wise. (11/1)

4841 ALNWICK MAIDEN STKS (2-Y.O F) (Class D)
2-35 (2-36) **7f** £3,225.00 (£975.00: £475.00: £225.00) Stalls: High GOING minus 0.11 sec per fur (G)

Form	Horse / details	Pos	SP	RR	SF
4066[3]	**Frond** (LMCumani) **2-8-11** KDarley(3) (hld up: nt clr run over 2f out & over 1f out: swtchd outside jst ins fnl f: qcknd to ld nr fin) ....—	1	6/1	84+	54
4694[2]	**Astrapi** (MRStoute) **2-8-11** FLynch(6) (trckd ldrs: rdn to ld jst ins fnl f: hdd & no ex nr fin) ....½	2	13/8[1]	83	53
4382[2]	**Summer Deal (USA) (81)** (PFICole) **2-8-11** TQuinn(4) (w ldrs: led over 1f out: hdd & nt qckn jst ins fnl f) 2	3	9/2[2]	78	48
4567[4]	**Tajawuz** (SbinSuroor) **2-8-11** GHind(7) (trckd ldrs: led over 2f out tl over 1f out: one pce) 1½	4	5/1[3]	75	45
	Kameez (IRE) (MJohnston) **2-8-11** JWeaver(5) (small: unf: s.i.s: sn chsng ldrs: sn drvn along: kpt on one pce fnl 2f) 3	5	14/1	68	38
4508[8]	**Townville Cee Cee (49)** (JSWainwright) **2-8-11** JFortune(9) (in tch: effrt ½-wy: sn outpcd) 7	6	100/1	52	22
4508[2]	**Flaxen Pride (IRE)** (MrsMReveley) **2-8-11** ACulhane(2) (hld up: effrt over 2f out: sn wknd) ....½	7	10/1	51	21
4688[3]	**Splendid (IRE)** (SirMarkPrescott) **2-8-11** SSanders(8) (led tl over 2f out: sn btn) 2½	8	7/1	45	15
	Ellerbeck (JMJefferson) **2-8-11** JCarroll(1) (leggy: unf: bit bkwd: dwlt s: sn drvn along & outpcd: sn wl bhd) ...9	9	100/1	25	—
	Second Term (IRE) (WStorey) **2-8-11** JFanning(10) (leggy: unf: bit bkwd: s.i.s: sn drvn along & a outpcd) ..1¾	10	100/1	21	—

(SP 118.5%) **10 Rn**

1m 27.24 (2.74) CSF £15.00 TOTE £8.30: £2.20 £1.50 £1.40 (£11.40) Trio £13.80 OWNER Fittocks Stud (NEWMARKET)

4066 Frond would have been a most unlucky loser. Denied an opening several times whn switched outside, she showed a nice turn of foot to get up near the line. (6/1: op 7/2)
4694 Astrapi, rather keen going to post, looked to have it in the bag when going over a length up inside the last but she had no answer to the winner's late burst. (13/8)
4382 Summer Deal (USA) is officially rated 81 and it should be an accurate guide to the value of the form. (9/2: 3/1-5/1)
4567 Tajawuz looked to be walking stiffly on her near-hind in the paddock. Showing plenty of knee action going down, she raced keenly but, off the bit, could do no more than stick on at the one pace. (5/1)
Kameez (IRE), a daughter of Arazi, lacks size and substance but she ran a satisfactory first race. (14/1: op 8/1)
4508 Flaxen Pride (IRE) looks the type to do better at three years. (10/1)
4688 Splendid (IRE) (7/1: 12/1-6/1)

4842 DURANT OF DUNSTALL HEALTH FOOD HOLDINGS WHOLESALE PRODUCTS H'CAP (0-85) (3-Y.O+) (Class D)

3-05 (3-07) **6f** £3,858.75 (£1,170.00: £572.50: £273.75) Stalls: High GOING minus 0.11 sec per fur (G)

				SP	RR	SF
4733^{5}	**Always Alight (75)** (KRBurke) **3-9-3** JFEgan(16) (lw: in tch stands' side: hdwy to ld over 1f out: r.o wl)	—	**1**	11/1	84	62
4565^{4}	**Mouche (69)** (MrsJRRamsden) **3-8-11** JFortune(18) (hdwy stands' side 2f out: r.o fnl f: nrst fin)	nk	**2**	14/1	77	55
4733*	**Alumisiyah (USA) (83)** (RWArmstrong) **3-9-11** ^{7x} GCarter(10) (racd stands' side: hdwy ½-wy: ch 1f out: kpt on)	1½	**3**	$11/2^{2}$	87	65
4601^{3}	**King Uno (54)** (MrsJRRamsden) **3-7-10v** LCharnock(15) (lw: racd stands' side: hdwy 2f out: kpt on: nvr able chal)	½	**4**	$8/1^{3}$	57	35
4456^{3}	**Double Bounce (84)** (PJMakin) **7-9-13** SSanders(5) (b: racd far side: hdwy whn nt clr over 1f out: swtchd ins fnl f: nvr able chal)	1¼	**5**	$5/1^{1}$	84	63
4773^{5}	**Antonias Melody (61)** (SRBowring) **4-8-4** DaleGibson(3) (chsd ldrs far side: nt qckn fnl f)	1½	**6**	20/1	57	36
4321^{11}	**Eastern Prophets (73)** (GLewis) **4-9-2** PaulEddery(20) (lw: a cl up stands' side: rdn 2f out: r.o one pce)	hd	**7**	33/1	68	47
4738^{14}	**U-No-Harry (IRE) (53)** (RHollinshead) **4-7-10** NCarlisle(4) (b.nr fore: racd far side: chsd ldrs: n.m.r over 1f out: kpt on)	½	**8**	33/1	47	26
4574^{4}	**Gadge (79)** (ABailey) **6-9-8** DWright(7) (b: bhd far side: stdy hdwy over 1f out: hmpd ins fnl f: nt rcvr)	nk	**9**	16/1	72	51
4512^{10}	**Johayro (67)** (JSGoldie) **4-8-7**$^{(3)ow3}$ DGriffiths(17) (racd stands' side: led tl hdd & wknd appr fnl f)	s.h	**10**	14/1	60	36
4280^{24}	**Knotty Hill (70)** (RCraggs) **5-8-13** JFanning(2) (led far side tl wknd ins fnl)	s.h	**11**	25/1	63	42
4805^{2}	**Bowlers Boy (74)** (JJQuinn) **4-9-3** SDrowne(8) (racd far side: bhd: effrt ½-wy: n.d)	1¼	**12**	10/1	64	43
4512^{15}	**Saint Express (80)** (MrsMReveley) **7-9-9** ACulhane(14) (chsd ldrs stands' side tl btn over 1f out)	½	**13**	14/1	68	47
4280^{13}	**Grey Kingdom (71)** (MBrittain) **6-8-7**$^{(7)}$ DMernagh(11) (chsd ldrs stands' side tl outpcd fnl 2f)	1¼	**14**	16/1	56	35
4787^{15}	**Tiler (IRE) (79)** (MJohnston) **5-9-8** JWeaver(1) (cl up far side tl wknd ent fnl f)	s.h	**15**	14/1	64	43
4472*	**Pine Ridge Lad (IRE) (56)** (JLEyre) **7-7-13** TWilliams(6) (lw: in tch far side tl rdn 2f out)	s.h	**16**	12/1	41	20
3922^{7}	**Don't Care (IRE) (60)** (MissLAPerratt) **6-7-10b**$^{(7)}$ JMcAuley(9) (racd alone centre: outpcd fr ½-wy)	1	**17**	33/1	42	21
4482^{12}	**Takhlid (USA) (64)** (DWChapman) **6-8-7** JCarroll(13) (lw: prom stands' side over 4f)	s.h	**18**	16/1	46	25
4748^{11}	**Monaco (IRE) (65)** (RAllan) **3-8-7** KDarley(12) (dwlt: a bhd stands' side)	2½	**19**	33/1	40	18
4414^{4}	**French Grit (IRE) (71)** (MDods) **5-9-0** FLynch(19) (prom stands' side to ½-wy: sn rdn & btn)	9	**20**	10/1	22	1
				(SP 142.1%)	**20 Rn**	

1m 13.61 (2.11) CSF £151.23 CT £896.99 TOTE £16.00: £2.70 £4.50 £2.50 £2.40 (£60.60) Trio £112.40 OWNER Mr M. Nelmes-Crocker (WANTAGE) BRED Bylon Farmers Ltd
LONG HANDICAP King Uno 7-9
WEIGHT FOR AGE 3yo-1lb
4733 Always Alight appreciated this stiff track and, once he hit the front, he was certainly not going to stop. (11/1)
4565 Mouche, who needed a visor to win her previous race, was without the headgear this time but finished strongly, if always that few strides too late. (14/1)
4733* Alumisiyah (USA) was not helped by a middle draw but she still had a chance and this was not a bad effort. (11/2)
4601 King Uno is a funny customer and stayed on in the closing stages but was never doing enough to make an impression. (8/1)
4456 Double Bounce won the race up the far side despite not getting a clear run and is obviously in really good form. (5/1)
4773 Antonias Melody has the ability and ran quite well here but she is very difficult to weigh up. (20/1)
4574 Gadge was given little chance here and also met with trouble and it would seem he is not done with yet. (16/1)

4843 MILBURN HEALTH FOODS MISTLETOE ROAD JESMOND CLAIMING H'CAP (0-60) (I) (3-Y.O+) (Class F)

3-35 (3-37) **1m (round)** £2,346.00 (£656.00: £318.00) Stalls: Low GOING minus 0.11 sec per fur (G)

				SP	RR	SF
4228^{17}	**On The Green (36)** (AHide) **4-8-4b**^{1} DaleGibson(5) (lw: trckd ldrs: led jst ins fnl f: drvn clr)	—	**1**	12/1	49	27
4373^{16}	**Southern Memories (IRE) (34)** (WJMusson) **7-8-2**^{ow1} SDrowne(13) (chsd ldrs: hung lft & led over 1f out: sn hdd & nt qckn)	2	**2**	14/1	43	20
4455^{2}	**Bella's Legacy (39)** (KRBurke) **4-8-4**$^{(3)}$ DSweeney(7) (a in tch: styd on same pce fnl 2f)	3½	**3**	$13/2^{2}$	41	19
4455^{9}	**Dispol Gem (60)** (PCalver) **4-10-0** KDarley(9) (hld up: hdwy over 2f out: styd on fnl f: nt rch ldrs)	½	**4**	$7/1^{3}$	61	39
4711^{7}	**Queen of Shannon (IRE) (51)** (AWCarroll) **9-8-12v**$^{(7)}$ RStudholme(15) (s.s: bhd tl hdwy 2f out: styd on wl towards fin)	nk	**5**	8/1	51	29
4414^{15}	**Trojan Hero (SAF) (58)** (MrsMReveley) **6-9-12** ACulhane(1) (mde most tl over 1f out: sn wknd)	s.h	**6**	$9/2^{1}$	58	36
3919^{5}	**Diamond Crown (IRE) (36)** (MartynWane) **6-8-4**^{ow4} JCarroll(2) (hld up: hdwy on ins whn hmpd appr st: kpt on fnl 2f: nt rch ldrs)	1½	**7**	9/1	33	7
4415^{9}	**Bison Belting (33)** (JAGlover) **3-7-7**$^{(5)}$ APolli(4) (lw: w ldr tl wknd over 1f out)	½	**8**	16/1	29	4
4693^{9}	**Fine Times (43)** (CWFairhurst) **3-8-8** DeanMcKeown(8) (b.off hind: sn bhd & drvn along: sme hdwy 2f out: n.d)	½	**9**	33/1	38	13
4290^{10}	**Dance Melody (31)** (GROldroyd) **3-7-10** LCharnock(11) (chsd ldrs: hrd rdn over 2f out: sn wknd)	3½	**10**	33/1	19	—
4768^{8}	**Stolen Music (IRE) (28)** (REBarr) **4-7-5**$^{(5)}$ IonaWands(16) (sn bhd & drvn along)	2	**11**	33/1	12	—
4711^{15}	**My Godson (48)** (MDods) **7-9-2** RLappin(10) (sn bhd & drvn along)	2	**12**	33/1	28	6
4510^{14}	**Termon (29)** (MissLAPerratt) **4-7-4**$^{(7)ow1}$ JMcAuley(17) (a in rr)	1¾	**13**	20/1	6	—
3453^{8}	**Majal (IRE) (44)** (JSWainwright) **8-8-9**$^{(3)}$ GParkin(12) (chsd ldrs: sn pushed along: lost pl over 2f out)	1½	**14**	20/1	18	—
4742^{12}	**Special-K (53)** (EWeymes) **5-9-2**$^{(5)}$ CLowther(3) (chsd ldrs: drvn along appr st: lost pl 3f out)	1¾	**15**	$7/1^{3}$	23	1
4707^{11}	**Seconds Away (35)** (JSGoldie) **6-8-3** TWilliams(14) (bhd: sme hdwy on outside 3f out: sn wknd)	hd	**16**	15/2	5	—
				(SP 130.9%)	**16 Rn**	

1m 44.3 (5.30) CSF £152.98 CT £1,131.44 TOTE £15.50: £3.40 £3.50 £1.70 £2.00 (£164.80) Trio £348.70 OWNER Mrs C. T. Bletsoe (NEWMARKET) BRED C. T. and Mrs Bletsoe

LONG HANDICAP Termon 7-9 Dance Melody 7-8 Stolen Music (IRE) 7-6
WEIGHT FOR AGE 3yo-3lb

3718 On The Green was tried in blinkers and they certainly had the desired effect, giving her trainer, who calls it a day at the end of the season, her first success this time. (12/1)
Southern Memories (IRE), who had shown nothing on his two previous outings, gave his rider problems by hanging, as if feeling something. (14/1)
4455 Bella's Legacy, from a 4lb higher mark, is still a maiden after fourteen attempts. (13/2)
2546* Dispol Gem ran much better than of late. (7/1)
4112 Queen of Shannon (IRE), who has apparently had wind problems, wore a cross-noseband and had her tongue tied down. Considering she gave away ground at the start and was badly drawn, it was not a bad effort. (8/1: 6/1-9/1)
3855 Trojan Hero (SAF), best drawn, made the running but had no excuse whatsoever. (9/2)
3919 Diamond Crown (IRE), carrying 4lb overweight, was knocked right back on the turn for home. (9/1)

4844 SEVEN SEAS SLUMBER CUP H'CAP (0-70) (3-Y.O+) (Class E)

4-10 (4-13) **5f** £2,986.25 (£905.00: £442.50: £211.25) Stalls: High GOING minus 0.11 sec per fur (G)

				SP	RR	SF
4583[9]	**Mungo Park (53)** (MrsJRRamsden) **3-8-11** JFortune(20) (lw: trckd ldrs stands' side: led over 1f out: sn clr: drvn out)	—	**1**	8/1[3]	66	56
1613[13]	**Sue Me (IRE) (55)** (DNicholls) **5-8-13** AlexGreaves(18) (bhd stands' side: hdwy over 1f out: r.o: nt rch wnr)	3	**2**	12/1	58	48
4636[19]	**Mon Bruce (64)** (MDods) **3-9-8** JCarroll(14) (lw: a chsng ldrs stands' side: nt qckn appr fnl f)	2	**3**	6/1[1]	61	51
4707*	**Southern Dominion (52)** (MissJFCraze) **5-8-10b** 7x SWebster(3) (dwlt: racd far side: sn chsng ldrs: kpt on fnl f)	s.h	**4**	6/1[1]	49	39
4414[10]	**Plum First (51)** (MAPeill) **7-8-9** JFanning(1) (b.hind: racd far side: dwlt: hdwy over 1f out: r.o)	nk	**5**	20/1	47	37
4333[7]	**Archello (IRE) (57)** (GROldroyd) **3-9-1** KDarley(17) (lw: racd stands' side: outpcd & bhd tl styd on appr fnl f)	1	**6**	14/1	50	40
4512[11]	**Insider Trader (53)** (BSRothwell) **6-8-4be**(7) RWinston(13) (chsd ldrs stands' side tl wknd over 1f out)	hd	**7**	16/1	45	35
4707[2]	**Another Episode (IRE) (49)** (MissLAPerratt) **8-8-7** JWeaver(2) (lw: led far side tl wknd fnl f)	1¼	**8**	10/1	37	27
4233[12]	**Manolo (FR) (60)** (JBerry) **4-8-13b**(5) CLowther(8) (dwlt: nrst fin)	s.h	**9**	12/1	48	38
4636[14]	**Shadow Jury (51)** (DWChapman) **7-8-9b** LCharnock(5) (gd spd far side tl btn appr fnl f)	s.h	**10**	25/1	39	29
4051[9]	**Super Rocky (47)** (RBastiman) **8-8-2b**(3) DSweeney(9) (racd stands' side: nvr trbld ldrs)	½	**11**	33/1	33	23
4016[18]	**Sound the Trumpet (IRE) (48)** (RCSpicer) **5-8-6** JBramhill(10) (racd stands' side: no imp fr ½-wy)	hd	**12**	25/1	34	24
4707[9]	**Young Ben (IRE) (47)** (JSWainwright) **5-8-5b** FLynch(16) (b.hind: spd stands' side over 3f: wknd)	1¾	**13**	14/1	28	18
4636[W]	**Swynford Dream (70)** (JHetherton) **4-10-0b** JLowe(19) (racd stands' side: led tl hdd & wknd over 1f out)	hd	**14**	13/2[2]	50	40
4385[14]	**Panther (IRE) (51)** (PDEvans) **7-8-9b** JFEgan(7) (racd far side: nvr wnt pce)	nk	**15**	16/1	30	20
4707[7]	**Rich Glow (47)** (NBycroft) **6-8-5**ow1 DeanMcKeown(6) (racd far side: n.d)	nk	**16**	12/1	25	14
4629[15]	**Ned's Bonanza (46)** (MDods) **8-8-4** TWilliams(15) (racd stands' side: in tch: sn drvn along: wknd fnl 2f)	nk	**17**	16/1	23	13
20[11]	**Colston-C (51)** (PDEvans) **5-8-9** ACulhane(4) (racd far side: a outpcd)	1	**18**	33/1	25	15
4049[14]	**General Equation (55)** (JBalding) **4-8-13** JEdmunds(11) (racd stands' side: spd 3f: wknd)	2	**19**	66/1	23	13
2313[13]	**Play The Tune (47)** (AWCarroll) **4-8-0**(5) APolli(12) (racd stands' side: sn bhd)	nk	**20**	33/1	14	4
				(SP 138.9%)	**20 Rn**	

60.13 secs (1.73) CSF £95.35 CT £590.85 TOTE £8.70: £2.10 £3.50 £2.10 £2.00 (£66.90) Trio £148.90 OWNER Mrs H. M. Carr (THIRSK) BRED Hyde Park Racing

4385 Mungo Park looked absolutely magnificent and was given a cracking ride as he is, without doubt, a moody sort. Once in front, his jockey made his mind up for him. (8/1: op 12/1)
1269 Sue Me (IRE), having his first run for almost five months, put in a tremendous effort and certainly finished to some purpose. She seems to go particularly well after a lay-off. (12/1)
4512 Mon Bruce, happier on this faster ground, ran pretty well. (6/1)
4707* Southern Dominion won the race up the far side but he marginally missed the kick, which made this a useful effort. (6/1)
3936 Plum First has not won a race for well over two years, but the way he finished here would suggest that he still has the ability. (20/1)
3606* Archello (IRE) found these experienced sprinters too sharp early on but she did finish well and should certainly appreciate further. (14/1)
4707 Another Episode (IRE) had no excuses this time, other than the stiff track probably found him out. (10/1)
3856 Manolo (FR) threw all chances away at the start. (12/1)
4434 Swynford Dream showed that when in the mood, he still has the ability and had blistering pace here to lead the field, until crying enough approaching the last furlong. (13/2)

4845 NATURE'S STORE CONVERLEAN H'CAP (0-60) (I) (3-Y.O+) (Class F)

4-40 (4-46) **1m 2f 32y** £2,430.00 (£680.00: £330.00) Stalls: Low GOING minus 0.11 sec per fur (G)

				SP	RR	SF
	Vanadium Ore (48) (WMcKeown) **4-9-3** JWeaver(10) (lw: hld up: nt clr run over 2f out: swtchd rt over 1f out: r.o wl to ld ins fnl f)	—	**1**	25/1	58	33
4584[5]	**Essayeffsee (49)** (MrsMReveley) **8-9-4** KDarley(12) (lw: hld up: effrt & nt clr run over 2f out: swtchd outside over 1f out: styd on strly towards fin)	1¼	**2**	15/2[3]	57	32
4472[16]	**Broctune Line (41)** (MrsMReveley) **3-8-5**ow1 ACulhane(2) (led tl ins fnl f: no ex)	nk	**3**	25/1	49	18
4335[8]	**Clued Up (51)** (PDEvans) **4-9-6v** JFEgan(8) (hdwy & hung lft over 2f out: hrd rdn: kpt on same pce fnl f)	s.h	**4**	16/1	59	34
4504[2]	**Muara Bay (50)** (GLewis) **3-9-0** PaulEddery(17) (lw: a in tch: chal over 1f out: sn rdn & nt qckn)	½	**5**	11/4[1]	57	27
4731[4]	**Falls O'Moness (IRE) (60)** (KRBurke) **3-9-7**(3) DSweeney(5) (plld hrd: hdwy on ins over 2f out: nt clr run: kpt on ins fnl f: nvr rchd ldrs)	1½	**6**	14/1	64	34
4632[4]	**Flying Flip (51)** (BCMorgan) **3-9-1** DeanMcKeown(3) (chsd ldrs: nt clr run fnl 2f: kpt on wl towards fin)	s.h	**7**	16/1	55	25
4695[2]	**Katie Komaite (45)** (CaptJWilson) **4-9-0v** JFortune(4) (hdwy over 2f out: nt clr run: styd on fnl f)	hd	**8**	15/2[3]	49	24
4693[2]	**Gadroon (39)** (PCHaslam) **3-8-3** LCharnock(15) (trckd ldrs: chal 2f out: wknd ins fnl f)	hd	**9**	10/1	43	13
4691[7]	**Sing And Dance (41)** (EWeymes) **4-8-5**(5) CLowther(20) (prom early: bhd ½-wy: sme hdwy on outside 2f out: n.d)	2½	**10**	16/1	41	16
4802[8]	**Wentbridge Lad (IRE) (59)** (ABailey) **7-10-0v** JCarroll(18) (b: hld up & bhd: sme hdwy on outside 2f out: n.d)	nk	**11**	20/1	59	34
4608[2]	**Harvey White (IRE) (57)** (JPearce) **5-9-12** SSanders(1) (hld up: effrt & n.m.r over 1f out: n.d)	1¾	**12**	7/1[2]	54	29
3601[2]	**Gymcrak Gorjos (44)** (GHolmes) **3-8-8b** TLucas(7) (lw: b.hind: plld hrd: trckd ldrs: rdn & hmpd over 3f out: wkng whn hmpd over 1f out)	1½	**13**	14/1	38	8
4584[13]	**Bedazzle (33)** (MBrittain) **6-7-9**(7) DMernagh(14) (b: chsd ldrs tl wknd 2f out)	hd	**14**	20/1	27	2
870[10]	**Dancing Destiny (43)** (RBastiman) **5-8-12** NCarlisle(6) (sn trckng ldrs: wknd & eased 2f out)	6	**15**	25/1	28	3
4417[10]	**Distant King (37)** (GPKelly) **4-7-13**(7)ow7 SFinnamore(11) (b: chsd ldrs tl lost pl 3f out: sn bhd)	3½	**16**	50/1	16	—

				SP	RR	SF
2845[12]	**Energy Man (45)** (MDods) **4-9-0** DaleGibson(13) (plld hrd: trckd ldrs: wkng whn hmpd over 1f out)	1	**17**	33/1	23	—
4798[9]	**Live Project (IRE) (48)** (RCraggs) **5-9-3** JFanning(9) (lw: dwlt: hdwy on outside over 5f out: wknd & eased over 1f out)	1¾	**18**	50/1	23	—
4579[7]	**Damara (47)** (CWFairhurst) **3-8-8**(3) PFessey(19) (unruly: dwlt: sn chsng ldrs: drvn along: lost pl over 3f out)	16	**19**	20/1	—	—
4741[10]	***Golden Ace (IRE) (54)*** (RCSpicer) **4-9-9** FLynch(16) (Withdrawn not under Starter's orders: lame at s)		**W**	16/1	—	—
				(SP 141.3%)	**19 Rn**	

2m 14.3 (7.60) CSF £182.55 CT £4,361.80 TOTE £30.70: £3.60 £1.50 £11.50 £3.80 (£281.90) Trio £525.10; £591.73 to Brighton 23/10/97 OWNER Mr Garth Ormond (NEWCASTLE-UPON-TYNE) BRED Mrs Christine Ormond

WEIGHT FOR AGE 3yo-5lb

IN-FOCUS: With a maximum field and just a modest pace, there was a deal of trouble in the final two and a half furlongs and more than one horse looked unlucky not to be more closely involved.

Vanadium Ore, who has been gelded and who was having his first outing since changing stables, was turned out in good trim. Full of running but with nowhere to go early in the straight, when pulled to the outside he showed a nice turn of foot to get up near the line. (25/1)

4584 Essayeffsee is on a losing run of seventeen but, a come-from-the-back horse, he is always liable to find trouble and essentially needs a strong gallop that he did not get and, after meeting plenty of trouble, he was reeling in the winner at the line. (15/2)

581* Broctune Line, who presumably needed it last time after a break, was well-drawn on the inner and had the run of the race, being allowed to set his own pace. (25/1)

2375* Clued Up looked the villain of the piece, making her move towards the outer and, with her rider persisting in using his whip in his right hand, the filly hung left, tightening up all those on the inner. (16/1)

4504 Muara Bay, one of the few to enjoy a trouble-free run, had every chance and so had no excuse. (11/4)

4731 Falls O'Moness (IRE), settled off the pace, went for an ambitious run up the inner. Meeting all the trouble going, she did well to finish so close. (14/1)

4632 Flying Flip, who wore a tongue-strap, had no room at all to manoeuvre in the final quarter-mile. (16/1)

4695 Katie Komaite is in the form of her life at present. After meeting trouble, she was staying on at the finish and the extended trip was certainly no problem. (15/2)

4846 MILBURN HEALTH FOODS MISTLETOE ROAD JESMOND CLAIMING H'CAP (0-60) (II) (3-Y.O+) (Class F)

5-10 (5-16) **1m (round)** £2,346.00 (£656.00: £318.00) Stalls: Low GOING minus 0.11 sec per fur (G)

				SP	RR	SF
3853[4]	**Monis (IRE) (30)** (BEllison) **6-7-12** NKennedy(16) (lw: bhd: hdwy over 2f out: led over 1½f out: hld on wl)	—	**1**	9/1	43	21
4510[3]	**Chinour (IRE) (43)** (EJAlston) **9-8-11** JFEgan(5) (dwlt: hdwy 2f out: r.o: nrst fin)	¾	**2**	4/1[1]	55	33
4326[7]	**Inkwell (34)** (AHide) **3-7-13** DaleGibson(8) (lw: a.p: chal 1½f out: rdn & r.o one pce)	nk	**3**	12/1	45	20
3454[9]	**Patina (43)** (RHollinshead) **3-8-8** FLynch(14) (mid div: nt clr run fr 3f out to 2f out: r.o fnl f)	¾	**4**	16/1	52	27
4469[9]	**Al Ava Consonant (36)** (JDBethell) **3-7-8**(7)ow5 RWinston(15) (mid div: hdwy 3f out: styd on: no imp)	1½	**5**	25/1	42	12
3987[21]	**Raed (59)** (MrsASwinbank) **4-9-13** JSupple(4) (trckd ldrs: effrt 2f out: hrd rdn fnl f: no imp)	s.h	**6**	12/1	65	43
4711[2]	**Birchwood Sun (47)** (MDods) **7-9-1b** JWeaver(17) (lw: bhd: effrt 3f out: nvr trbld ldrs)	1¾	**7**	9/2[2]	50	28
4438[14]	**Most Wanted (IRE) (30)** (WMcKeown) **4-7-12** JBramhill(6) (in tch: effrt 3f out: sn outpcd: styd on appr fnl f)	½	**8**	33/1	32	10
4693[10]	**Beau Roberto (40)** (JSGoldie) **3-8-5b** ACulhane(10) (bhd: hrd drvn over 2f out: styd on n.d)	6	**9**	16/1	30	5
1482[9]	**Kriscliffe (60)** (GLewis) **4-10-0** PaulEddery(1) (mid div: nt clr run over 2f out: n.d)	1¾	**10**	6/1[3]	46	24
3477[13]	**Celia's Rainbow (29)** (RMWhitaker) **4-7-11**ow1 NCarlisle(9) (a rr div)	2	**11**	50/1	11	—
	Gresham Flyer (36) (MrsSLamyman) **4-8-4** JFanning(12) (plld hrd: bhd: hmpd over 2f out: n.d)	½	**12**	66/1	17	—
4324[8]	**French Ginger (47)** (LRLloyd-James) **6-9-1** TWilliams(7) (led: clr ent st: hdd 1½f out: eased whn btn ins fnl f)	½	**13**	15/2	27	5
4471[11]	**Great Bear (33)** (DWChapman) **5-7-12**(3) PFessey(2) (chsd ldrs tl wknd fnl 3f)	6	**14**	14/1	1	—
4472[13]	**Samspet (39)** (RAFahey) **3-8-4** DeanMcKeown(11) (chsd ldr tl wknd fnl 3f)	nk	**15**	12/1	7	—
3405[3]	**Tom Pladdey (31)** (RBastiman) **3-7-10** LCharnock(3) (chsd ldrs tl wknd fnl 2½f)	s.h	**16**	12/1	—	—
2203[8]	**Express Girl (51)** (MartinTodhunter) **3-9-2** JCarroll(13) (in tch tl wknd fnl 3f)	7	**17**	16/1	5	—
				(SP 139.6%)	**17 Rn**	

1m 44.3 (5.30) CSF £45.47 CT £442.27 TOTE £12.20: £2.90 £1.10 £3.10 £4.40 (£14.60) Trio £81.20 OWNER Mr C. E. Sherry (LANCHESTER) BRED Mrs S. O'Riordan

LONG HANDICAP Celia's Rainbow 7-2 Tom Pladdey 7-8 Al Ava Consonant 7-7

WEIGHT FOR AGE 3yo-3lb

3853 Monis (IRE) looked in tremendous condition. Dropped back in trip here, he was well suited by the strong pace and, once in front, he showed fine courage to hold on. (9/1: op 6/1)

4510 Chinour (IRE) last won over two years ago and has slipped way down the handicap. He obviously still has the ability but he is, to say the least, a bit of a monkey and even his in-form stable is having trouble in getting his head in front. (4/1: 3/1-9/2)

3601 Inkwell looks tremendously well and has ability but is short of any turn of foot. (12/1: op 8/1)

3268 Patina has yet to win a race but would have been a shade closer here with any luck in running. (16/1)

4429 Al Ava Consonant ran her best race for a long time but she is inconsistent. (25/1)

2937 Raed travels well but, once serious pressure is applied, never finds as much as looks likely. (12/1: op 8/1)

4164* French Ginger (15/2: 5/1-8/1)

2733 Samspet (12/1: 8/1-14/1)

3405 Tom Pladdey (12/1: 8/1-14/1)

4847 NATURE'S STORE CONVERLEAN H'CAP (0-60) (II) (3-Y.O+) (Class F)

5-40 (5-45) **1m 2f 32y** £2,430.00 (£680.00: £330.00) Stalls: Low GOING minus 0.11 sec per fur (G)

				SP	RR	SF
4335[6]	**Brambles Way (45)** (MrsMReveley) **8-8-9**(5) SCopp(5) (lw: trckd ldrs: led over 2f out: hld on wl fnl f)	—	**1**	9/1	59	41
4691[6]	**Stormless (56)** (JSGoldie) **6-9-11** JBramhill(9) (hld up: hdwy over 2f out: styd on wl ins fnl f: nt rch wnr)	1	**2**	12/1	68	50
4596[11]	**Lapu-Lapu (51)** (MJCamacho) **4-9-6** LCharnock(6) (hld up: hdwy over 2f out: sn chsng ldrs: nt qckn appr fnl f)	nk	**3**	6/1[2]	63	45
4607*	**Fighting Times (49)** (CASmith) **5-9-4v** ACulhane(8) (b: hdwy over 4f out: sn prom: kpt on same pce appr fnl f)	nk	**4**	11/4[1]	61	43
4802[6]	**Raindeer Quest (49)** (JLEyre) **5-8-11**(7) SBuckley(10) (sn bhd: styd on fnl 2f: nt rch ldrs)	2	**5**	8/1[3]	57	39
3487[3]	**Bernard Seven (IRE) (33)** (MDods) **5-8-2**ow1 JFEgan(11) (lw: plld hrd: hdwy over 3f out: rdn 2f out: one pce)	nk	**6**	14/1	41	22
4800[2]	**Portite Sophie (39)** (MBrittain) **6-8-1**(7) DMernagh(3) (a chsng ldrs: one pce fnl 3f)	1½	**7**	11/1	45	27
4628[4]	**Scenicris (IRE) (48)** (RHollinshead) **4-9-3** FLynch(13) (s.i.s: hld up & bhd: swtchd outside & hdwy 2f out: nvr nr ldrs)	3	**8**	11/1	49	31
4510[11]	**Thatched (IRE) (43)** (REBarr) **7-8-9**(3) PFessey(7) (hld up & bhd: styd on fnl 2f: nvr nr to chal)	1	**9**	16/1	42	24
4608*	**Misterton (39)** (JAGlover) **3-7-12**(5) APolli(19) (lw: chsd ldrs: led 4f out tl over 2f out: wknd over 1f out)	1	**10**	11/1	37	14

4771[P]	**Ginger Flower (45)** (GPKelly) **8-8-11**(3) GParkin(2) (bit bkwd: prom tl lost pl appr st)	1¾	**11**	50/1	40	22
4386[13]	**Silent Valley (53)** (MissLCSiddall) **3-9-3v** OPears(12) (s.v.s: wl bhd tl sme hdwy 2f out: n.d)	1	**12**	25/1	46	23
4628[3]	**Up in Flames (IRE) (45)** (SRBowring) **6-8-11**(3) CTeague(16) (w ldrs: ev ch tl wknd 2f out)	2½	**13**	10/1	34	16
4472[5]	**Tarradale (38)** (CBBBooth) **3-8-2** JLowe(1) (plld v.hrd: led 3f: wknd & eased 2f out)	1	**14**	16/1	26	3
4053[8]	**Hanajir (IRE) (44)** (CWThornton) **3-8-8** DeanMcKeown(4) (bhd fnl 5f)	6	**15**	20/1	22	—
3762[5]	**Junior Ben (IRE) (32)** (MESowersby) **5-7-8**(7)ow2 NPollard(14) (w ldrs: led after 3f to after 4f out: sn wknd)	8	**16**	25/1	—	—
	Whitegate's Son (46) (BEllison) **3-8-10** JCarroll(20) (bit bkwd: s.s: hdwy on outside appr st: sn wknd)	1½	**17**	50/1	9	—
4748[P]	**Ingleborough (49)** (DMoffatt) **3-8-10**(3) DarrenMoffatt(18) (plld v.hrd: in tch tl lost pl over 3f out)	3	**18**	25/1	8	—
3696[12]	**Maraud (60)** (LRLloyd-James) **3-9-10** TWilliams(15) (w ldrs: edgd rt & wknd over 2f out)	11	**19**	25/1	1	—
4584[18]	**Judge Advocate (IRE) (57)** (JJO'Neill) **5-9-5**(7) SOlley(17) (bit bkwd: w ldrs tl wknd 4f out: p.u lame 2f out)		**P**	33/1	—	—
				(SP 149.3%)	**20 Rn**	

2m 12.8 (6.10) CSF £113.34 CT £676.28 TOTE £11.50: £2.10 £2.90 £1.50 £2.20 (£79.90) Trio £305.90 OWNER Mr Nigel Jones (SALTBURN) BRED W. P. S. Johnson

WEIGHT FOR AGE 3yo-5lb

4335 Brambles Way, 5lb lower than when successful at Beverley in April, was given an enterprising ride and was always going to do just enough. (9/1)

4691 Stormless, racing off a rating 3lb higher than he has ever won off, stuck on in willing fashion but had given the winner too much rope. (12/1)

3330 Lapu-Lapu, who won this a year ago from a 1lb higher mark, looked wintry in her coat. (6/1)

4607* Fighting Times was 10lb higher than when successful at Nottingham two outings ago. (11/4)

4802 Raindeer Quest is a frustrating individual, putting her best foot forward far too late in the day. (8/1)

3487 Bernard Seven (IRE) has been in action over hurdles but, on his return to the level, he showed his usual lack of urgency. (14/1)

4800 Portite Sophie (11/1: 8/1-12/1)

4628 Scenicris (IRE), who has won off a 12lb higher mark, really needs softer ground and, after missing the break slightly, she certainly did not have the run of the race here. If she gets the mud between now and the close, she is certainly capable of popping up again. (11/1)

4608* Misterton (11/1: op 7/1)

T/Jkpt: Not won; £92,237.27 to Brighton 23/10/97. T/Plpt: £200.50 (148.66 Tckts). T/Qdpt: £179.50 (6.48 Tckts) WG/AA

4243-YARMOUTH (L-H) (Good)
Wednesday October 22nd

WEATHER: sunny WIND: fresh across

4848 RUNHAM MAIDEN STKS (3-Y.O) (Class D)

2-10 (2-11) **1m 3y** £3,900.40 (£1,166.20: £558.60: £254.80) Stalls: Low GOING minus 0.56 sec per fur (F) TF 81

				SP	RR	SF
4757[16]	**Mount Holly (USA) (75)** (JHMGosden) **3-9-0** LDettori(3) (mde all far side: hld on wl cl home)	—	**1**	4/1[3]	91	43
	Marozia (USA) (JHMGosden) **3-8-9** AGarth(6) (still unf: a chsng wnr: r.o wl towards fin)	hd	**2**	33/1	86	38
4283[13]	**Regal Thunder (USA) (67)** (MRStoute) **3-9-0** MHills(10) (lw: racd stands'-side group: chsd ldrs: kpt on ins fnl f)	5	**3**	16/1	81	33
963[5]	**Assailable** (ACStewart) **3-9-0** WRyan(7) (bit bkwd: w ldrs stands' side: rdn over 1f out: one pce)	nk	**4**	13/8[1]	80	32
4757[15]	**Mutabari (USA) (65)** (KMahdi) **3-9-0** DHolland(4) (s.i.s: sn trckng ldrs far side: styd on ins fnl f)	¾	**5**	33/1	79	31
4760a[2]	**Strachin** (LMCumani) **3-9-0** JReid(9) (racd stands' side: effrt 3f out: sn hrd drvn: no imp)	1½	**6**	7/2[2]	76	28
4579[10]	**Eider Hill** (DMorris) **3-8-9** NDay(11) (nvr trbld ldrs)	6	**7**	50/1	59	11
4671[5]	**Stories To Tell (USA) (80)** (HRACecil) **3-9-0** KFallon(14) (racd stands' side: hdwy 3f out: wknd appr fnl f)	2½	**8**	6/1	59	11
4408[2]	**Kawa-Ib (IRE) (70)** (PTWalwyn) **3-8-9** RHills(12) (mde most stands' side over 6f)	½	**9**	6/1	53	5
4579[6]	**Lawfull Blue (IRE)** (CADwyer) **3-8-9** DaneO'Neill(13) (trckd ldrs stands' side 5f)	3	**10**	33/1	47	—
	Inspirational (IRE) (CACyzer) **3-8-9** GDuffield(1) (lt-f: unf: bkwd: racd far side: a bhd & outpcd)	3½	**11**	33/1	40	—
	Milky Way (AHide) **3-8-9** AMcGlone(8) (w'like: leggy: bit bkwd: a in rr)	2	**12**	50/1	36	—
	Sugar Reef (MJRyan) **3-8-11**(3) PMcCabe(2) (leggy: lt-f: s.s: a t.o)	14	**13**	50/1	13	—
4631[6]	**Cape Siren** (MJRyan) **3-8-9** AClark(5) (racd far side: bhd fr ½-wy: t.o)	2½	**14**	50/1	3	—
				(SP 134.4%)	**14 Rn**	

1m 36.8 (0.80) CSF £133.41 TOTE £4.60: £1.30 £7.00 £5.60 (£178.40) Trio £240.80 OWNER Sheikh Mohammed (NEWMARKET) BRED Darley Stud Management Inc

4277 Mount Holly (USA), one of five to remain over on the far side, made all the running and it needed all Dettori's strength to hold on in the dying strides. (4/1)

Marozia (USA), a still unfurnished filly making a belated seasonal debut, ran on extremely well inside the distance after tracking the winner from the start, and even at this late stage is only just coming to herself. (33/1)

3937 Regal Thunder (USA), taking a step down in class and running without a visor, finished ahead of the stands' side group but the leading pair had got away. (16/1)

963 Assailable did not look fully wound-up on this return to action, but he helped push the pace under the stands' rail until finding no extra inside the final furlong. (13/8: 5/4-15/8)

700 Mutabari (USA), sluggish leaving the stalls, soon recovered to chase the leaders and, staying on strongly inside the last furlong, does seem to need further. (33/1)

4760a Strachin, who made his debut in Italy earlier in the month, was always struggling with the pace on the stands' side and was never able to mount a challenge. (7/2)

4671 Stories To Tell (USA), a grand-looking colt still short of peak fitness, took closer order three furlongs out but, unable to maintain the run, was not knocked about once held. (6/1)

4408 Kawa-Ib (IRE) (6/1: op 10/1)

4849 BILLOCKBY NURSERY H'CAP (0-85) (2-Y.O) (Class D)

2-45 (2-45) **1m 3y** £3,585.25 (£1,072.00: £513.50: £234.25) Stalls: Low GOING minus 0.56 sec per fur (F)

				SP	RR	SF
4245*	**Sick As A Parrot (75)** (CADwyer) **2-8-12v** MHills(2) (led tl over 1f out: rallied to ld ins fnl f: hld on)	—	**1**	9/2[2]	79	40
2768[4]	**Middle Temple (75)** (EALDunlop) **2-8-12** WRyan(4) (bit bkwd: trckd ldrs: rdn to ld over 1f out: hdd ins fnl f: rallied u.p cl home)	hd	**2**	9/1	79	40
4380[3]	**Elakik (84)** (JLDunlop) **2-9-7b** RHills(6) (lw: hld up in tch: effrt wl over 1f out: hrd rdn: unable qckn)	2½	**3**	6/1[3]	83	44
4690[4]	**Miquelon (83)** (RHollinshead) **2-9-6** MWigham(12) (hld up & bhd: hdwy u.p 2f out: styd on wl nr fin)	2½	**4**	12/1	77	38

4567[3] **Mareeba (73)** (MJohnston) **2-8-10** DHolland(9) (chsd ldrs over 6f) 3 **5** 7/1 61 22
4589[11] **Gift of Gold (77)** (ICampbell) **2-9-0** AMackay(1) (lw: chsd ldrs: drvn along over 2f out: sn outpcd) 1 **6** 16/1 63 24
4380[6] **Ballet Rambert (71)** (MJHeaton-Ellis) **2-8-8** LDettori(5) (trckd ldrs: rdn over 2f out: grad fdd) 1½ **7** 9/1 54 15
4382[11] **No Shame (59)** (JGSmyth-Osbourne) **2-7-10** GBardwell(8) (chsd ldrs: rdn over 2f out: sn lost tch) ....s.h **8** 33/1 42 3
4670[15] **Take A Turn (78)** (MRChannon) **2-9-1v** DaneO'Neill(7) (a in rr) 1¼ **9** 20/1 58 19
4545[7] **Bahamian Melody (USA) (75)** (DRLoder) **2-8-12v** KFallon(10) (lw: sn in rr & rdn along: effrt over 2f out: no imp) ....1¼ **10** 3/1[1] 53 14
4366* **Siena (GER) (63)** (MRChannon) **2-8-0** JQuinn(3) (in tch: hrd rdn over 2f out: sn btn) ....5 **11** 12/1 31 —
4165[12] **Rude Shock (62)** (MHTompkins) **2-7-10**(3)ow2 MHenry(11) (hld up: a in rr) ....s.h **12** 14/1 30 —
(SP 125.6%) **12 Rn**

1m 36.9 (0.90) CSF £43.60 CT £232.16 TOTE £4.20: £1.50 £2.90 £1.50 (£37.80) Trio £54.60 OWNER Mrs Shelley Dwyer (NEWMARKET) BRED Helshaw Grange Farms Ltd, Miss Powner & A. Hampton

4245* Sick As A Parrot is becoming something of a course specialist and, in winning his third race this season, had to pull out all the stops to retain his advantage close home. (9/2)
2768 Middle Temple, tackling a mile for the first time on his handicap debut, showed he is knocking at the door with by far his best performance yet, and looks a ready-made winner. (9/1: 6/1-10/1)
4380 Elakik delivered a determined challenge below the distance, but could not muster the pace to match strides with the principals as top-weight took its toll. (6/1: op 3/1)
4690 Miquelon was once again doing all his best work when it was too late, and he deserves to find another race. (12/1: op 8/1)
4567 Mareeba showed plenty of promise in this first handicap, but she was hard at work below the distance and unable to hold her pitch. (7/1: 6/1-9/1)
4299 Gift of Gold has been running on the All-Weather recently and he may have found this surface just too fast for him, but he did not fare badly and there is a race in him. (16/1)
4545 Bahamian Melody (USA) never took hold of his bit and was one of the first beaten. (3/1: tchd 9/2)
Rude Shock (14/1: 10/1-16/1)

4850 MARTHAM (S) H'CAP (0-60) (3-Y.O+) (Class G)

3-15 (3-15) **1m 3f 101y** £2,427.00 (£672.00: £321.00) Stalls: High GOING minus 0.56 sec per fur (F)

SP RR SF

4713[5] **Anjou (56)** (JPearce) **5-10-0** KFallon(3) (hld up: drvn along 3f out: hdwy over 1f out: rdn to ld fnl 50y) ....— **1** 5/2[1] 67 21
4713[8] **Arif (IRE) (32)** (JohnHarris) **5-8-1**(3) RFfrench(4) (lw: led tl over 4f out: rdn to ld over 1f out: hdd & no ex wl ins fnl f) ....1¼ **2** 4/1[2] 41 —
4633[6] **Charlie Bigtime (40)** (ICampbell) **7-8-12b** AMackay(2) (dwlt: hld up & bhd: gd hdwy appr fnl f: fin wl) ....3½ **3** 12/1 44 —
4607[7] **Sharp Deed (IRE) (50)** (PJMakin) **3-9-2v** DHolland(5) (lw: hld up in rr: hdwy over 2f out: nrst fin) ....hd **4** 11/2[3] 54 2
4713[6] **Armston (47)** (JWharton) **5-9-5** JQuinn(1) (lw: a.p: rdn over 2f out: kpt on sme pce) ....¾ **5** 12/1 50 4
4713[16] **African Sun (IRE) (35)** (MCChapman) **4-8-7** GDuffield(8) (plld hrd: hld up: hdwy 3f out: rdn over 1f out: one pce) ....½ **6** 20/1 38 —
4184[14] **Persephone (26)** (CNAllen) **4-7-7**(5)ow2 RMullen(9) (hld up: effrt 3f out: nt pce to chal) ....¾ **7** 33/1 27 —
4743[10] **Monacle (42)** (DMorris) **3-8-8b[1]** NDay(6) (lw: hld up: hdwy 4f out: hrd drvn over 2f out: sn btn) ....nk **8** 14/1 43 —
4224[5] **Reeds (49)** (JRFanshawe) **3-9-1** MHills(11) (racd wd bk st: trckd ldrs tl wknd fnl 2f) ....2 **9** 6/1 47 —
4607[6] **Dino's Mistral (27)** (KAMorgan) **4-7-6**(7)ow1 PDoe(10) (lw: chsd ldr: led over 4f out: rdn & hdd over 1f out: sn btn) ....1¼ **10** 14/1 24 —
4465[9] **D J Cat (32)** (WRMuir) **4-8-4** MartinDwyer(7) (chsd ldr 6f: grad lost tch: t.o) ....8 **11** 14/1 17 —
(SP 121.3%) **11 Rn**

2m 28.4 (6.60) CSF £11.36 CT £94.88 TOTE £3.20: £2.00 £2.30 £2.20 (£5.50) Trio £25.40 OWNER Mr G. H. Tufts (NEWMARKET) BRED Sheikh Mohammed bin Rashid al Maktoum
LONG HANDICAP Persephone 7-3
WEIGHT FOR AGE 3yo-6lb
No bid

4713 Anjou looked to be in serious trouble entering the last quarter-mile but, with stamina coming into play, and with the assistance of a never-say-die jockey, he produced a telling burst of speed to settle the issue nearing the finish. (5/2)
2910 Arif (IRE) has only ever won on soft ground, but he did nothing wrong and he may be the type to turn his attention to hurdles. (4/1)
4055 Charlie Bigtime can handle faster ground than this, but he did not impress with his action. Last to exit from the stalls, he was putting in some good, late work and should be noted when he returns to the All-Weather. (12/1: 8/1-14/1)
3134 Sharp Deed (IRE) has been disappointing, but he was staying on as good as any inside the final furlong and he has more ability than he cares to show. (11/2: 4/1-6/1)
4713 Armston, always pressing the leaders, was unable to quicken when the battle to the line got under way. He may well need more yielding ground. (12/1)
2174 African Sun (IRE), restrained under a keen hold, closed up early in the straight but could never find the speed to get involved. (20/1)
3320 Monacle (14/1: op 8/1)
4224 Reeds (6/1: op 4/1)

4851 MAUTBY CONDITIONS STKS (2-Y.O) (Class C)

3-45 (3-46) **6f 3y** £4,532.00 (£1,688.00: £819.00: £345.00: £147.50: £68.50) Stalls: Low GOING minus 0.56 sec per fur (F)

SP RR SF

4517[2] **Toblersong (100)** (RAkehurst) **2-9-2** LDettori(4) (lw: hld up: hdwy 2f out: rdn to ld wl ins fnl f) ....— **1** 2/1[1] 93 37
4543* **Dernier Croise (FR) (78)** (BJMeehan) **2-8-11** MTebbutt(7) (a.p: led over 1f out tl wl ins fnl f) ....½ **2** 20/1 87 31
3740[5] **Half-Hitch (USA)** (DRLoder) **2-8-11** KFallon(1) (hld up: effrt & nt clr run over 2f out: outpcd over 1f out: r.o wl u.p towards fin) ....1¼ **3** 9/2[3] 83+ 27
4286* **Title Bid (USA)** (MRStoute) **2-9-2** JReid(6) (lw: led tl hdd over 1f out: one pce) ....nk **4** 5/2[2] 88 32
4403* **Mantles Pride (85)** (GLewis) **2-8-8**(3) RFfrench(5) (b: hld up: hdwy over 1f out: r.o wl cl home) 1¼ **5** 7/1 79 23
3060* **Darwell's Folly (USA)** (MJohnston) **2-9-0** MHills(2) (lw: disp ld: rdn 2f out: sn wknd) 7 **6** 13/2 64 8
Lead Singer (JMPEustace) **2-8-11** JTate(3) (w'like: str: bkwd: dwlt: a bhd & outpcd: t.o) ....29 **7** 25/1 — —
(SP 114.5%) **7 Rn**

1m 12.0 (1.10) CSF £37.87 TOTE £2.80: £1.40 £4.10 (£35.80) OWNER The Fairy Story Partnership (EPSOM) BRED Deepwood Farm Stud

4517 Toblersong, whose only previous win was gained on the soft, landed quite a touch under a very cool ride from Dettori. (2/1)
4543* Dernier Croise (FR) had little chance of turning the tables on the winner despite a 5lb turnaround in the weights, but he ran possibly his best race yet and could still be on the up-grade. (20/1)
3740 Half-Hitch (USA) did not enjoy the best of luck in running and she has got to be regarded as a slightly unlucky loser. (9/2: 5/2-5/1)

4286* Title Bid (USA) adopted more forceful tactics and did his best to make it all, but he was tapped for finishing speed after being collared entering the final furlong. (5/2)
4403* Mantles Pride usually races with the pace but he attempted to come from behind on this occasion. His finishing position was as close as he could manage. (7/1)

4852 WICKHAMPTON MAIDEN STKS (I) (2-Y.O) (Class D)
4-20 (4-21) **7f 3y** £3,172.50 (£945.00: £450.00: £202.50) Stalls: Low GOING minus 0.56 sec per fur (F)

				SP	RR	SF
4544[2]	**Jila (IRE)** (RWArmstrong) **2-9-0** RHills(11) (lw: a.p: jnd ldr ent fnl f: rdn to ld cl home)	—	**1**	7/2[3]	84	43
	Timbervati (USA) (HRACecil) **2-8-9** WRyan(13) (leggy: lt-f: dwlt: hdwy ½-wy: led 2f out tl wl ins fnl f)	s.h	**2**	10/1	79	38
4105[4]	**Close Shave** (MRStoute) **2-9-0** JReid(10) (trckd ldrs: shkn up & swtchd rt over 1f out: kpt on one pce)	1¾	**3**	7/4[1]	80	39
4381[8]	**Captain Logan (IRE)** (DRLoder) **2-9-0** KFallon(8) (bit bkwd: a.p: hrd rdn over 1f out: unable qckn)	½	**4**	9/4[2]	79	38
4229[4]	**Sconced (USA)** (GWragg) **2-9-0** MHills(12) (hld up: effrt 3f out: styd on ins fnl f)	3	**5**	16/1	72	31
	Ten Bob (IRE) (MHTompkins) **2-9-0** DBiggs(2) (w'like: bkwd: hld up: hdwy on ins & nt clr run 3f out: styd on fnl f)	½	**6**	40/1	71	30
4507[5]	**Asset Manager** (MJohnston) **2-9-0** DHolland(5) (lw: swvd rt s: sn chsng ldrs: pushed along whn nt clr run over 2f out: sn btn)	¾	**7**	20/1	69	28
	Laa Jadeed (IRE) (ACStewart) **2-9-0** SWhitworth(1) (unf: scope: bkwd: trckd ldrs: pushed along 4f out: outpcd over 2f out)	1¾	**8**	20/1	65	24
4278[10]	**Tornado Prince (IRE)** (NACallaghan) **2-9-0** GDuffield(6) (lw: hmpd s: a in rr)	nk	**9**	33/1	64	23
4603[5]	**Mark of Prophet (IRE)** (JEBanks) **2-9-0** JQuinn(7) (a bhd)	hd	**10**	50/1	64	23
3783[4]	**Main Street** (WJHaggas) **2-9-0** RCochrane(9) (lw: led tl hdd 2f out: sn wknd)	2	**11**	14/1	60	19
	Dearie Me (MAJarvis) **2-8-6**(3) RFfrench(3) (lt-f: unf: chsd ldrs 4f: sn wknd)	½	**12**	25/1	53	12
3450[14]	**Lady Rockstar** (MJRyan) **2-8-9b[1]** AClark(4) (a bhd: t.o)	13	**13**	50/1	24	—

(SP 133.7%) **13 Rn**

1m 24.9 (0.70) CSF £36.87 TOTE £5.30: £1.70 £2.10 £1.40 (£16.00) Trio £18.50 OWNER Mr Hamdan Al Maktoum (NEWMARKET) BRED Shadwell Estate Company Limited
4544 Jila (IRE) has improved with each run and, with the help of an extra furlong, just found sufficient to wear down the gallant runner-up. (7/2)
Timbervati (USA), a lightly-made, fit-looking newcomer, ran really well on this first look at a racecourse, and it will come as a big surprise if she does not make her mark. (10/1: 5/1-11/1)
4105 Close Shave sat much closer to the pace than he did on his debut, but he still took time to really find top gear and the principals had got away. (7/4: 5/4-2/1)
4381 Captain Logan (IRE) still looked as though he had a bit left to work on, and his effort to match strides inside the last furlong proved just too much. (9/4)
4229 Sconced (USA) had allowed the leading quartet too much leeway and, although he did stay on, was never able to get within striking range. (16/1)
Ten Bob (IRE), a workmanlike newcomer who looked too backward to do himself justice, did not fare badly after losing ground at the start and the experience should prove beneficial. (40/1)
3783 Main Street (14/1: 12/1-25/1)

4853 WICKHAMPTON MAIDEN STKS (II) (2-Y.O) (Class D)
4-50 (4-54) **7f 3y** £3,172.50 (£945.00: £450.00: £202.50) Stalls: Low GOING minus 0.56 sec per fur (F)

				SP	RR	SF
4581[2]	**Misbah (USA)** (BHanbury) **2-9-0** RHills(10) (b.hind: mde all: hrd drvn over 1f out: r.o strly)	—	**1**	7/2[3]	91	56
2693[3]	**Chattan** (BWHills) **2-9-0** RCochrane(12) (chsd ldrs: kpt on u.p fnl f: nt rch wnr)	1½	**2**	10/1	88	53
4524[7]	**Captain Tim** (DRLoder) **2-9-0** KFallon(1) (a.p: rdn 2f out: r.o one pce)	4	**3**	11/8[1]	79	44
	Capital Prince (FR) (SbinSuroor) **2-9-0** LDettori(13) (lt-f: a.p: chal wl over 1f out: one pce fnl f)	1¾	**4**	5/2[2]	75	40
	Teroom (ACStewart) **2-9-0** SWhitworth(11) (lt-f: unf: bit bkwd: hld up: hdwy 2f out: nrst fin)	3½	**5**	25/1	67+	32
	Bryony Brind (IRE) (JRFanshawe) **2-8-9** NDay(2) (w'like: leggy: nvr nr to chal)	6	**6**	33/1	48	13
	Knife Edge (USA) (MRStoute) **2-9-0** JReid(4) (leggy: lt-f: unf: bkwd: nvr bttr than mid div)	½	**7**	14/1	52	17
4739[13]	**Norcroft Joy** (MJRyan) **2-8-9** AClark(5) (trckd ldrs over 4f)	2	**8**	50/1	42	7
	Golden Lyric (IRE) (GWragg) **2-9-0** MHills(3) (w'like: scope: bit bkwd: hld up: effrt & drvn along over 2f out: no imp)	5	**9**	20/1	36	1
	Qismat (HAkbary) **2-8-9** DO'Donohoe(8) (b: lt-f: s.s: a bhd)	nk	**10**	50/1	30	—
4708[12]	**Silent Warning** (SirMarkPrescott) **2-9-0** GDuffield(7) (prom to ½-wy: sn lost tch)	1	**11**	25/1	33	—
4526[19]	**Northern Lass (IRE)** (MHTompkins) **2-8-9** DBiggs(9) (a bhd & outpcd)	hd	**12**	50/1	28	—
	Charlie's Gold (ICampbell) **2-9-0** AMackay(6) (lt-f: bit bkwd: outpcd: a bhd: t.o)	11	**13**	50/1	7	—

(SP 131.9%) **13 Rn**

1m 23.8 (-0.40) CSF £35.72 TOTE £5.40: £2.00 £2.00 £1.10 (£16.70) Trio £13.70 OWNER Mr Hamdan Al Maktoum (NEWMARKET) BRED J. D. Squires
4581 Misbah (USA) made sure the emphasis was on stamina, and that was what won him the race. Well in command inside the final furlong, he will, on this evidence, stay further. (7/2)
2693 Chattan has enjoyed a long break since making his debut in July, but he did look well tuned-up and stuck on willingly right to the end. (10/1)
4167 Captain Tim, thought good enough to take his chance in the Group One Middle Park Stakes, was pushed to challenge all the way but, off the bridle inside the last quarter-mile, it did seem as though the seventh furlong caught him out. (11/8)
Capital Prince (FR), a sparely-made debutant, waited on the leaders and delivered his challenge below the distance but failed to quicken when set alight and, with his measure taken, was allowed to come home in his own time. (5/2)
Teroom, bred for stamina, still needs to fill to his frame, but he was really into his stride inside the distance and will not be hard to place. (25/1)
Bryony Brind (IRE), never going the pace of the leaders, began to stay on late on and the experience should prove beneficial. (33/1)
Knife Edge (USA) (14/1: 6/1-16/1)

4854 THRIGBY H'CAP (0-85) (3-Y.O+) (Class D)
5-20 (5-20) **1m 2f 21y** £3,995.95 (£1,195.60: £573.30: £262.15) Stalls: High GOING minus 0.56 sec per fur (F)

				SP	RR	SF
4441[13]	**Fahs (USA) (75)** (RAkehurst) **5-9-10** AClark(3) (hld up: hdwy wl over 1f out: hrd rdn to ld cl home)	—	**1**	9/1	85	24
4635[3]	**Kamin (USA) (71)** (RWArmstrong) **3-9-1** RHills(12) (chsd ldrs: rdn to ld ent fnl f: ct post)	s.h	**2**	7/1	81	15
4759[2]	**Zugudi (71)** (KMahdi) **3-9-1** RCochrane(6) (hld up in rr: gd hdwy appr fnl f: fin wl)	2½	**3**	7/2[1]	77	11
4386[4]	**Florentino (IRE) (69)** (BWHills) **4-9-4** MHills(7) (a chsng ldrs: rdn to ld over 1f out: sn hdd: no ex fnl f)	hd	**4**	11/1	75	14

				SP	RR	SF
2485^{3}	**Kailey Senor (USA) (71)** (RWArmstrong) **4-9-6** FNorton(5) (bit bkwd: chsd ldrs: drvn along 3f out: ev ch over 1f out: one pce)	¾	**5**	14/1	76	15
4558^{11}	**Palatial Style (75)** (PJMakin) **10-9-10** KFallon(2) (b.off hind: hld up mid div: hdwy over 2f out: rdn & one pce appr fnl f)	½	**6**	11/2^{2}	79	18
4731^{2}	**Top Jem (75)** (MJRyan) **3-9-5** GBardwell(8) (trckd ldrs: no hdwy fnl 2f)	½	**7**	6/1^{3}	78	12
4788^{16}	**Bedouin Honda (69)** (CEBrittain) **3-8-13** DaneO'Neill(10) (led tl rdn & hdd over 1f out)	¾	**8**	33/1	71	5
4552^{3}	**Fantail (79)** (MHTompkins) **3-9-6**$^{(3)}$ MHenry(4) (in tch: hrd drvn over 1f out: grad wknd)	1	**9**	10/1	79	13
4568*	**Onefortheditch (USA) (61)** (JRFanshawe) **4-8-10** NVarley(13) (hld up: hdwy over 4f out: wknd over 2f out)	1¼	**10**	7/1	59	—
4572^{10}	**Classic Eagle (72)** (ICampbell) **4-9-7** AMackay(9) (hld up: hdwy over 3f out: wknd fnl 2f)	2½	**11**	50/1	66	5
4578^{13}	**Scarlet Crescent (62)** (PTWalwyn) **3-8-3v**$^{1(3)}$ RFfrench(11) (s.s: hdwy ½-wy: rdn over 3f out: wknd 2f out)	4	**12**	33/1	50	—
4672^{13}	**Magic Combination (IRE) (70)** (BJCurley) **4-9-5b**^{1} LDettori(1) (chsd ldr: rdn over 3f out: sn wknd: t.o)	7	**13**	7/1	47	—

(SP 131.3%) **13 Rn**

2m 8.6 (4.80) CSF £70.25 CT £250.50 TOTE £8.90: £4.50 £2.70 £1.60 (£35.10) Trio £74.50 OWNER City Industrial Supplies Ltd (EPSOM) BRED Shadwell Farm Inc

WEIGHT FOR AGE 3yo-5lb

4151 Fahs (USA), back in his own class, defied top weight with a determined late challenge that enabled him to get up in the shadow of the post. One of three from his stable entered in the November Handicap, he escapes a penalty but, at only 7st 3lb in the long handicap, he may not make the cut. (9/1)

4635 Kamin (USA) failed by the minimum distance to open his account, but he gave all he had and was not beaten for the want of trying. He is a winner without a penalty. (7/1)

4759 Zugudi, twice a winner over sprint distances, was restrained in the rear. Sent about his work, he ran on well in the closing stages but had been given just too much to do. He appeared to stay this trip and is capable of adding to his score. (7/2)

4386 Florentino (IRE) worked hard to poke his nose in front on the approach to the final furlong but, taken on and headed in next to no time, found an extra effort beyond him. (11/1)

2485 Kailey Senor (USA), a winner on his only start as a two-year-old in the French Provinces, is still struggling to make his mark in this country. Restrained on the heels of the leaders, he battled on willingly in the latter stages but was always finding the task just beyond him. He deserves a change of fortune. (14/1: 10/1-16/1)

4558 Palatial Style, at the veteran stage now, has struggled to regain his form of yesteryear and he is still high enough in the handicap but, without having the run of the race, he showed that has the ability to pick up another small prize. (11/2)

4552 Fantail (10/1: op 6/1)

T/Plpt: £73.20 (281.18 Tckts). T/Qdpt: £5.00 (205.85 Tckts) IM

4500-**BRIGHTON** (L-H) (Good to firm)
Thursday October 23rd

WEATHER: sunny WIND: almost nil

4855 PYECOMBE MEDIAN AUCTION MAIDEN STKS (2-Y.O) (Class E)
2-10 (2-11) **6f 209y** £3,486.25 (£1,045.00: £502.50: £231.25) Stalls: Low GOING minus 0.31 sec per fur (GF)

				SP	RR	SF
4670^{10}	**Signatory (67)** (RHannon) **2-9-0** DaneO'Neill(11) (lw: a.p: led over 2f out: shkn up: comf)	—	**1**	13/2^{3}	75+	46
3613^{2}	**Silversmith (FR)** (SDow) **2-9-0** JFEgan(12) (lw: a.p: chsd wnr 2f out: edgd lft over 1f out: no imp)	5	**2**	2/1^{1}	64	35
	Absalom's Lad (PWHarris) **2-9-0** TQuinn(9) (w'like: bit bkwd: rdn over 3f out: hdwy 2f out: r.o ins fnl f)	1½	**3**	2/1^{1}	60	31
4603^{16}	**Browning** (LordHuntingdon) **2-9-0** JReid(2) (lw: rdn over 3f out: hdwy over 1f out: r.o ins fnl f)	¾	**4**	20/1	58	29
3847^{2}	**Jus'chillin' (IRE) (68)** (CADwyer) **2-8-9** KFallon(8) (prom over 4f)	5	**5**	6/1^{2}	42	13
4630^{8}	**Ballasilla** (BPalling) **2-8-9** TSprake(7) (led over 4f)	2	**6**	20/1	37	8
	Chi-Lin (JFfitch-Heyes) **2-8-6**$^{(3)}$ AWhelan(4) (w'like: s.s: nvr nrr)	2½	**7**	33/1	31	2
4278^{9}	**Arcane Star (IRE) (70)** (APJarvis) **2-9-0** SDrowne(5) (lw: prom over 4f)	1½	**8**	14/1	33	4
	Dancing Grey (PWHarris) **2-9-0** AClark(1) (str: bkwd: s.s: a bhd)	1	**9**	20/1	31	2
4454^{11}	**Citrus Express (SWE)** (PMooney) **2-9-0** AMcGlone(3) (s.s: a bhd)	¾	**10**	50/1	29	—
3613^{11}	**Danzino (IRE)** (APJarvis) **2-9-0** MHills(6) (a bhd)	11	**11**	25/1	4	—
4446^{7}	**Fiercely Ginger** (EAWheeler) **2-8-11**$^{(3)}$ ADaly(10) (chsd ldr over 4f)	8	**12**	50/1	—	—

(SP 125.9%) **12 Rn**

1m 22.0 (2.00) CSF £17.82 TOTE £8.50: £1.80 £1.30 £1.10 (£6.60) Trio £24.40 OWNER The Winning Team (MARLBOROUGH) BRED B. E. Green

4065 Signatory, from a stable that is going through a very lean spell at present, put up a very convincing display, leading over two furlongs from home and needing only to be bustled along for a decisive victory. (13/2: op 4/1)

3613 Silversmith (FR), off the course for ten weeks, went in pursuit of the winner two furlongs from home but he drifted left on the camber and could make no impression on his rival. He can find a race before long. (2/1)

Absalom's Lad, a medium-sized half-brother to middle-distance handicapper Rising Spray, looked as though he would benefit from this but still ran on encouragingly in the final quarter-mile if never remotely looking likely to trouble the winner. (2/1)

Browning showed his first sign of form, running on in the last furlong and a half to be nearest at the line. (20/1)

3847 Jus'chillin' (IRE) was close up until calling it a day over two furlongs from home. (6/1)

4402 Ballasilla took the field along but, collared over two furlongs out, she soon had bellows to mend. (20/1)

4236 Arcane Star (IRE) (14/1: 8/1-16/1)

4856 ALDRINGTON NURSERY H'CAP (0-75) (2-Y.O) (Class E)
2-40 (2-41) **6f 209y** £3,356.25 (£1,005.00: £482.50: £221.25) Stalls: Low GOING minus 0.31 sec per fur (GF)

				SP	RR	SF
4588^{14}	**Balanita (IRE) (60)** (BPalling) **2-8-9** TSprake(7) (mde all: rdn 3f out: clr over 2f out: r.o wl)	—	**1**	33/1	67	40
4318^{12}	**Radar (IRE) (66)** (MAJarvis) **2-9-1** RCochrane(2) (s.s: rdn & hdwy 2f out: r.o wl ins fnl f)	1½	**2**	5/1^{1}	70	43
4589^{4}	**Montano (USA) (69)** (PFICole) **2-9-4** TQuinn(4) (a.p: chsd wnr over 3f out: rdn over 2f out: unable qckn)	hd	**3**	6/1^{2}	72	45
4520^{10}	**Lycian (IRE) (50)** (SirMarkPrescott) **2-7-13** GBardwell(10) (rdn over 3f out: hdwy over 1f out: nvr nrr)	5	**4**	8/1^{3}	42	15
4753^{18}	**Patricia Olive (IRE) (51)** (MHTompkins) **2-7-11v**$^{(3)}$ MHenry(8) (rdn & hdwy over 2f out: one pce)	½	**5**	25/1	42	15
4545*	**Lauren's Lad (62)** (GLewis) **2-8-11b** PaulEddery(18) (no hdwy fnl 2f)	1¼	**6**	5/1^{1}	50	23
4767^{17}	**Counsel (63)** (CEBrittain) **2-8-7**$^{(5)}$ RMullen(11) (rdn over 2f out: hdwy & n.m.r over 1f out: nvr nrr)	½	**7**	20/1	50	23
4459*	**Praetorian Gold (72)** (RHannon) **2-9-7** DaneO'Neill(1) (lw: hdwy on ins 2f out: mid div whn hmpd wl over 1f out)	½	**8**	8/1^{3}	58	31

				SP	RR	SF
4715[14]	**Up The Wall (63)** (JohnBerry) **2-8-12** JQuinn(14) (nvr nrr)	4	**9**	12/1	39	12
4543[9]	**Sergeant Imp (IRE) (65)** (PMitchell) **2-8-11**(3) AWhelan(9) (lw: prom 4f)	½	**10**	25/1	40	13
4271[15]	**Argumentative (55)** (SDow) **2-8-4** JFEgan(15) (hdwy 2f out: mid div whn hmpd over 1f out)	1¾	**11**	20/1	26	—
4605[7]	**The Honorable Lady (58)** (MRChannon) **2-8-7** CandyMorris(3) (prom 4f)	1	**12**	16/1	27	—
4380[9]	**Little Tumbler (IRE) (59)** (SWoodman) **2-8-8**ow1 KFallon(12) (bhd fnl 4f)	1¼	**13**	14/1	25	—
4767[16]	**Royal Interview (IRE) (68)** (MRChannon) **2-9-3** RPerham(6) (s.s: a bhd)	1	**14**	25/1	32	5
4185[5]	**Sassy (IRE) (61)** (APJarvis) **2-8-10** SDrowne(13) (a bhd)	hd	**15**	25/1	24	—
4545[4]	**Miss Muffett (IRE) (53)** (PMooney) **2-8-2** MartinDwyer(17) (prom 4f)	¾	**16**	11/1	15	—
4575[9]	**Carouse (69)** (MRChannon) **2-9-4** JReid(5) (a bhd)	½	**17**	16/1	30	3
4753[4]	**Oh So Easy (70)** (BJMeehan) **2-9-5b**[1] MTebbutt(16) (lw: chsd wnr over 4f)	½	**18**	12/1	29	2

(SP 139.8%) **18 Rn**

1m 22.1 (2.10) CSF £182.42 CT £1,086.85 TOTE £59.40: £13.70 £2.20 £2.10 £1.60 (£114.30) Trio £468.10 OWNER Merthyr Motor Auctions (COWBRIDGE) BRED Humphrey Okeke

OFFICIAL EXPLANATION **Balanita (IRE): Stewards enquired into the improvement of this horse's form compared with his run at Pontefract on 6/10/97. The trainer's representative reported that the horse had settled better on this occasion as a result of being taken to the start early, and the Stewards accepted this explanation.**

2388 Balanita (IRE), who went down early, had his stable girl down at the start aswell and, as a result, was much better behaved this time. Well suited by the step up in trip, he made every post a winning one and forged clear in the straight to win in good style. (33/1)

2336 Radar (IRE) ran much better on this handicap debut but, although running on strongly inside the final furlong to snatch second prize in the last couple of strides, was not going to get to the winner in time. (5/1)

4589 Montano (USA) moved into second place early in the straight but he was unable to make any impression on the winner and was caught for second prize in the last few strides. (6/1)

Lycian (IRE) ran better here, staying on in the last furlong and a half to be nearest at the line. (8/1)

3692 Patricia Olive (IRE) made an effort over a quarter of a mile from home but could then only go up and down in the same place. (25/1)

4857 E.B.F. GARDEN AWARD MAIDEN STKS (2-Y.O) (Class D)

3-10 (3-10) **7f 214y** £3,614.50 (£1,081.00: £518.00: £236.50) Stalls: Low GOING minus 0.31 sec per fur (GF)

				SP	RR	SF
3013[7]	**Angstrom (IRE)** (MRStoute) **2-9-0** JReid(2) (bkwd: mde all: rdn over 1f out: r.o wl)	—	**1**	20/1	84+	39
4165[2]	**Hadith** (DMorley) **2-9-0** RHills(5) (lw: bmpd s: hld up: chsd wnr over 2f out: hrd rdn over 1f out: no imp)	4	**2**	4/9[1]	76	31
4367[4]	**High Tension (USA)** (PFICole) **2-9-0** TQuinn(6) (lw: rdn 4f out: hdwy over 1f out: r.o)	2½	**3**	3/1[2]	71	26
4061[11]	**Wintertime** (GLewis) **2-9-0** PaulEddery(3) (bmpd s: a.p: rdn 3f out: one pce: fin 4th, hd: disq: plcd last)	hd	**4d**	16/1[3]	71	26
	Stage Whisper (LordHuntingdon) **2-9-0** DaneO'Neill(7) (w'like: rdn & hdwy 3f out: wknd wl over 1f out: fin 5th, 2l: plcd 4th)	2	**4**	25/1	67	22
4520[8]	**Ballykissann** (DJSffrenchDavis) **2-9-0** SDrowne(1) (lw: prom 5f: fin 6th: plcd 5th)	1½	**5**	40/1	64	19
4515[18]	**Boreas Hill (IRE)** (JRArnold) **2-9-0** MartinDwyer(8) (b.nr hind: prom 5f: fin 7th: plcd 6th)	14	**6**	66/1	36	—
	Little Charmer (RRowe) **2-8-9** GBardwell(4) (neat: a wl bhd: fin 8th: plcd 7th)	2½	**7**	66/1	26	—
2768[14]	**Zada** (GLMoore) **2-9-0** AClark(9) (bit bkwd: swvd rt & uns rdr s)		**U**	50/1	—	—

(SP 116.1%) **9 Rn**

1m 34.2 (2.90) CSF £26.82 TOTE £16.30: £2.60 £1.10 £1.20 (£7.00) Trio £2.40 OWNER Sheikh Mohammed (NEWMARKET) BRED Godolphin Management Co Ltd

STEWARDS' ENQUIRY Obj. to Wintertime by Clerk of the Scales sustained. Eddery susp.1 & 3/11/97 (failure to weigh-in)

OFFICIAL EXPLANATION **Angstrom (IRE): Stewards considered the improvement in form of this horse compared with his previous run at Ascot on 25/7/97. The trainer reported that, due the the horse showing no interest in racing on that occasion, he has since been gelded which appears to have brought about improvement.**

Angstrom (IRE), a half-brother to the classy Annus Mirabilis, has been gelded since his appalling debut at Ascot three months ago and appeared to have nothing going for him here. He looked as fat as a pig in the paddock, was extremely woolly in his coat and was totally friendless in the betting. Appearances can be deceptive and he proved a complete revelation as he made all the running and asserted his authority in the final quarter-mile for a decisive victory. (20/1)

4165 Hadith once again had to settle for being the bridesmaid and although travelling well early in the straight, proved no match for the winner in the final quarter-mile. (4/9)

4367 High Tension (USA) looked in tremendous shape in the paddock but this tall individual may well not have been suited by this extremely difficult switchback track and was off the bridle at the top of the hill. Only finding his feet from below the distance, he did manage to take third prize but found it all over bar the shouting. (3/1)

Wintertime, always close up, was only going up and down in the same place in the last three furlongs. The colt was later disqualified after Eddery failed to weigh-in. (16/1)

Stage Whisper, a medium-sized colt, took closer order early in the straight but had shot his bolt early in the final quarter-mile. (25/1)

4858 RACE HILL (S) H'CAP (0-60) (3-Y.O+) (Class G)

3-40 (3-43) **1m 1f 209y** £2,070.00 (£570.00: £270.00) Stalls: High GOING minus 0.31 sec per fur (GF)

				SP	RR	SF
4371[3]	**Cabcharge Blue (36)** (TJNaughton) **5-8-4** TSprake(4) (s.s: hdwy on ins over 2f out: n.m.r & swtchd lft over 1f out: led ins fnl f: r.o wl)	—	**1**	13/2[2]	54	28
4465[8]	**Jubilee Scholar (IRE) (33)** (GLMoore) **4-8-1** FNorton(6) (hld up: led wl over 1f out tl ins fnl f: unable qckn)	1	**2**	16/1	49	23
4504[4]	**Without Friends (IRE) (41)** (JFfitch-Heyes) **3-8-1**(3) AWhelan(5) (lost pl 4f out: swtchd rt & rallied wl over 1f out: nt run on ins fnl f)	1¼	**3**	8/1	55	24
4139[14]	**Piquant (48)** (LordHuntingdon) **10-9-2** JReid(19) (rdn over 3f out: hdwy over 1f out: r.o wl ins fnl f)	1¾	**4**	12/1	60	34
4448[4]	**Multi Franchise (42)** (RMFlower) **4-8-10** DaneO'Neill(11) (rdn over 3f out: hdwy over 1f out: r.o)	¾	**5**	10/1	52	26
4415[3]	**Lochlass (IRE) (43)** (SPCWoods) **3-8-6b** NDay(3) (rdn over 3f out: n.m.r 2f out: hdwy over 1f out: nvr nrr)	3	**6**	8/1	49	18
4596[9]	**Misty Rain (55)** (BWHills) **3-9-4** MHills(12) (rdn over 3f out: hdwy over 1f out: nvr nrr)	2½	**7**	15/2[3]	57	26
4505[7]	**Surprise Event (53)** (WGMTurner) **3-8-9**(7) DMcGaffin(17) (nvr nrr)	6	**8**	33/1	45	14
4228[15]	**Blowing Away (IRE) (60)** (MHTompkins) **3-9-9v**[1] DBiggs(15) (nvr nrr)	hd	**9**	20/1	52	21
4608[7]	**Fancy Design (IRE) (35)** (PMitchell) **4-8-3** JFEgan(2) (hld up: hrd rdn over 1f out: sn wknd)	1	**10**	12/1	25	—
4607[4]	**Miskin Heights (IRE) (37)** (KRBurke) **3-8-0** DO'Donohoe(1) (led over 8f)	nk	**11**	10/1	27	—
4607[10]	**Deevee (32)** (CJBenstead) **8-8-0** CRutter(16) (nvr nrr)	¾	**12**	14/1	20	—
4371[14]	**Memory's Music (34)** (MMadgwick) **5-8-2** NVarley(18) (prom over 7f)	s.h	**13**	25/1	22	—
4607[14]	**Kirov Protege (IRE) (31)** (GLMoore) **5-7-10v**(3) MHenry(9) (nvr nrr)	¾	**14**	14/1	18	—
3814[4]	**Select Star (IRE) (41)** (APJarvis) **3-8-4v** SDrowne(8) (prom over 5f)	1	**15**	14/1	27	—
3929[6]	**Soda Pop (IRE) (48)** (GLMoore) **3-8-11v**[1] CandyMorris(14) (prom over 7f)	3	**16**	15/2[3]	29	—

				SP	RR	SF
3432[11]	**Passage Creeping (IRE) (60)** (SDow) **4-10-0** TQuinn(7) (prom over 7f)	2	**17**	12/1	38	12
4594[4]	**Safecracker (60)** (CPMorlock) **4-10-0v[1]** NAdams(13) (a bhd)	21	**18**	25/1	4	—
	Narbonne (40) (BJMcMath) **6-8-8** MTebbutt(20) (bhd fnl 3f)	12	**19**	16/1	—	—
4441[20]	**Dances With Hooves (54)** (DJSffrenchDavis) **5-9-8** KFallon(10) (a bhd)	15	**20**	6/1[1]	—	—
				(SP 161.8%)	**20 Rn**	

2m 2.4 (4.10) CSF £121.84 CT £839.25 TOTE £8.50: £2.90 £6.40 £3.50 £3.60 (£331.70) Trio £1,649.00; £255.48 to Newbury 24/10/97
OWNER Mr J. J. Wise (EPSOM) BRED Dullingham House Stud
WEIGHT FOR AGE 3yo-5lb
No bid

4371 Cabcharge Blue has slumped in the weights - she started the season on 60 but was rated just 36 here - and took full advantage of it, coming through to lead inside the final furlong and win her first race over this trip. (13/2)
2748 Jubilee Scholar (IRE) struck the front early in the final quarter-mile but was unable to cope with the winner inside the final furlong. This was a good effort but he remains a maiden after twenty-four attempts. (16/1)
4504 Without Friends (IRE) was at last dropped into his proper class. However, he has looked a dodgy customer in the past and that was once again demonstrated here for, after launching his challenge in the final furlong, he looked far from enthusiastic as he carried his head rather high and was certainly not putting it all in. (8/1)
1588 Piquant, who has run badly since finishing third at Kempton back in May, was taking a drop in class and ran on nicely in the last furlong and a half to be nearest at the line. Well into the veteran stage, he has not won for over two years and this is surely his level now. (12/1)
4448 Multi Franchise stayed on from below the distance but never threatened to get into it. This is his level. (10/1)
4415 Lochlass (IRE) (8/1: 6/1-9/1)

4859 HANNINGTONS OF BRIGHTON LIMITED STKS (0-80) (3-Y.O+) (Class D)

4-10 (4-11) **7f 214y** £3,645.60 (£1,087.80: £519.40: £235.20) Stalls: Low GOING minus 0.31 sec per fur (GF)

				SP	RR	SF
4558[6]	**Secret Spring (FR) (80)** (PRHedger) **5-8-11**(3) DSweeney(5) (stdy hdwy on bit over 2f out: hrd rdn over 1f out: led last strides)	—	**1**	11/8[1]	91	41
4561[23]	**Undercover Agent (IRE) (80)** (JLDunlop) **3-8-8** TQuinn(6) (a.p: chsd ldr 2f out: led over 1f out: hrd rdn: hdd last strides)	hd	**2**	9/2[2]	88	35
4375[7]	**Sword Arm (80)** (RCharlton) **3-9-3v** TSprake(2) (hrd rdn & hdwy over 1f out: r.o wl ins fnl f)	s.h	**3**	15/2[3]	97	44
3445[3]	**Vanishing Trick (USA) (77)** (HRACecil) **3-8-8b** KFallon(1) (a.p: rdn over 4f out: r.o one pce fnl f)	1	**4**	9/2[2]	86	33
4448*	**Toujours Riviera (78)** (JPearce) **7-9-6** GBardwell(3) (lw: led: rdn over 2f out: hdd over 1f out: wknd ins fnl f)	2	**5**	8/1	91	41
4511[2]	**Shamanic (80)** (SPCWoods) **5-9-0** JReid(8) (chsd ldr 6f: wknd 1f out)	2	**6**	14/1	81	31
4583[5]	**Dundel (IRE) (77)** (BWHills) **3-8-11** MHills(4) (a bhd)	½	**7**	8/1	80	27
3930[14]	**Muhandis (65)** (GLMoore) **4-9-0** CandyMorris(9) (bhd fnl 2f)	8	**8**	33/1	64	14
4175[13]	**Galibis (FR) (75)** (RHannon) **3-8-11** DaneO'Neill(7) (a bhd)	16	**9**	20/1	32	—
				(SP 126.8%)	**9 Rn**	

1m 34.0 (2.70) CSF £8.02 TOTE £2.40: £1.60 £2.00 £3.70 (£9.90) Trio £37.10 OWNER Mr M. K. George (CHICHESTER) BRED Timothy D. Rootes
WEIGHT FOR AGE 3yo-3lb

4558 Secret Spring (FR) appeared to be absolutely cruising in the straight but he has only one short run and, although both his Flat wins have been over a mile, this is his minimum trip. He looked in trouble when off the bridle and under pressure below the distance, but he eventually managed to struggle to the front in the last couple of strides. He looks set for a successful hurdling campaign. (11/8)
2331 Undercover Agent (IRE), who ran poorly on her last two starts, had 3lb or more to spare over her rivals on official adjusted ratings and only just failed. Gaining control over a furlong out, she did little wrong as she was challenged on all sides and only lost out in the last couple of strides. (9/2)
3712 Sword Arm, winner of three races this year, appeared to be travelling well in behind the leaders below the distance. Under pressure a furlong from home, he ran on really strongly and only just failed. (15/2)
3445 Vanishing Trick (USA) was being scrubbed along in typical Fallon style from the top of the hill and her rider's efforts did pay off to some extent as she stayed on in the final furlong. Lack of acceleration is her downfall. (9/2)
4448* Toujours Riviera did a good job of pacemaking but he was collared below the distance and had little more to offer inside the final furlong. (8/1: 6/1-9/1)
4511 Shamanic found this trip beyond him for, after racing in second place to the two-furlong marker, he had run out of gas entering the final furlong. He has not won for over two and a half years. (14/1)
4583 Dundel (IRE) (8/1: op 5/1)

4860 FRIENDS OF QUEEN'S PARK APPRENTICE H'CAP (0-80) (3-Y.O+) (Class E)

4-40 (4-41) **1m 3f 196y** £2,830.25 (£857.00: £418.50: £199.25) Stalls: High GOING minus 0.31 sec per fur (GF)

				SP	RR	SF
4503*	**Be True (53)** (GLMoore) **3-7-5**(5) RBrisland(3) (swtg: hdwy over 1f out: hrd rdn & hung bdly lft 1f out: led ins fnl f: r.o wl)	—	**1**	4/1[1]	62	37
4548*	**Random Kindness (65)** (RIngram) **4-8-12**(3) JFowle(6) (hld up: led over 2f out: hrd rdn over 1f out: hdd ins fnl f: unable qckn)	1½	**2**	6/1	72	54
4572[5]	**Opera Buff (IRE) (75)** (MissGayKelleway) **6-9-11** JWilkinson(8) (lw: hdwy over 3f out: hrd rdn over 2f out: ev ch ins fnl f: one pce)	1¼	**3**	5/1[2]	80	62
4466[4]	**Ciro's Pearl (IRE) (77)** (MHTompkins) **3-9-1**(5) PClarke(2) (led over 9f: wknd over 1f out)	4	**4**	5/1[2]	77	52
3559[2]	**Sapphire Son (IRE) (53)** (PCClarke) **5-8-0**(3) SCarson(1) (lw: hdwy over 3f out: wknd 2f out)	12	**5**	5/1[2]	37	19
4450[2]	**Bewitching Lady (53)** (DWPArbuthnot) **3-7-10** KimberleyHart(5) (lw: chsd ldr over 9f)	½	**6**	14/1	36	11
4584[9]	**Lookingforarainbow (IRE) (55)** (BobJones) **9-7-12**(7) GemmaJones(7) (lw: hld up: rdn over 3f out: sn wknd)	1¼	**7**	12/1	36	18
4548[4]	**Newport Knight (60)** (RAkehurst) **6-8-5**(5) PFitzsimons(9) (b.hind: lw: bhd fnl 5f)	s.h	**8**	11/2[3]	41	23
				(SP 114.0%)	**8 Rn**	

2m 30.4 (2.80) CSF £25.41 CT £110.16 TOTE £4.00: £1.60 £2.60 £1.60 (£19.40) Trio £23.90 OWNER Mr F. L. Hill (BRIGHTON) BRED J. A. E. Hobby
LONG HANDICAP Bewitching Lady 7-5 Be True 7-2
WEIGHT FOR AGE 3yo-7lb

4503* Be True followed up his recent victory here but appeared to have an awful lot to do at the top of the hill. With his jockey doing little on him, the combination did pick up ground on the outside below the distance. His jockey decided to go for his whip and gave the gelding a couple of reminders, the result of which was the gelding hanging badly to his left. It was very lucky that no interference was caused but Brisland did manage to straighten up the gelding and, leading inside the final furlong, the combination ran on for a decisive victory. (4/1)

4548* Random Kindness, in good heart this year, moved to the front over a quarter of a mile from home but proved no match for the winner when collared inside the final furlong. (6/1)
4572 Opera Buff (IRE), twice successful over this course and distance this year, was 10lb higher than the last of those victories. Taking closer order early in the straight, he was battling for the lead inside the final furlong before tapped for toe. (5/1)
4466 Ciro's Pearl (IRE), on the same mark as when last successful, took the field along but she was collared over two furlongs from home and was soon hung out to dry. (5/1)
3559 Sapphire Son (IRE) made an effort early in the straight but had shot his bolt two furlongs out. (5/1: 4/1-6/1)
4450 Bewitching Lady (14/1: 8/1-16/1)
4548 Newport Knight (11/2: 4/1-6/1)

T/Jkpt: Not won; £170,749.36 to Newbury 24/10/97. T/Plpt: £30.80 (1,171.12 Tckts). T/Qdpt: £13.00 (108.84 Tckts) AK

4388a-SAINT-CLOUD (France) (L-H) (Very soft)
Friday October 17th

4861a PRIX ECLIPSE (Gp 3) (2-Y.O)
1-50 (1-48) **6f 110y** £24,691.00 (£8,979.00: £4,489.00)

					SP	RR	SF
4647a*	**Merlin's Ring** (IABalding) **2-8-11** OPeslier	—	**1**			101	—
3882a[6]	**Roi Gironde (IRE)** (MmeCHead,France) **2-8-11** GMosse	3	**2**			94	—
3873a[3]	**Gold Away (IRE)** (MmeCHead,France) **2-8-11** ODoleuze	4	**3**			84	—

4 Rn

1m 25.6 P-M 1.80FF: 1.50FF 2.00FF (SF 10.40FF) OWNER Mrs Richard Plummer & Partners (KINGSCLERE) BRED Mrs A. Plummer
4647a* Merlin's Ring, despite the sticky ground, came through to take the advantage early in the straight and stayed on bravely to hold off the challenge of the runner-up. This was his last race of the season and he is a possible for next year's French 2,000 Guineas.

4651a-BELMONT PARK (New York, USA) (L-H) (Fast)
Saturday October 18th

4862a KELSO H'CAP (Gp 2) (3-Y.O+)
20-39 (20-41) **1m (Turf)** £71,429.00 (£23,810.00: £13,095.00)

				SP	RR	SF
	Lucky Coin (RNieminski,USA) **4-8-7** RobbieDavis	—	**1**		122	—
4117[6]	**Hawksley Hill (IRE)** (NDrysdale,USA) **4-8-5**ow1 GaryStevens	4	**2**		112	—
	Colcon (USA) (USA) **4-8-0** JBailey	1¼	**3**		105	—
4523[6]	**Bin Rosie** (DRLoder) **5-8-5** MESmith (btn over 10½l)		**11**		—	—

12 Rn

1m 33.72 P-M $3.70: PL $3.30 $10.20: SHOW $2.60 $6.70 $3.90 (SF $55.50) OWNER E. I. Kelly BRED Mrs M. Brittain and Mrs J. M. Khan
4523 Bin Rosie put up a very disappointing display to trail in last of the finishers. Held up towards the rear, he had to be scrubbed along after three furlongs and, short of room in the straight, could only run on at one pace.

4766a-LONGCHAMP (Paris, France) (R-H) (Very soft)
Sunday October 19th

4863a PRIX DU CONSEIL DE PARIS (Gp 2) (3-Y.O+)
2-50 (2-50) **1m 4f** £33,670.00 (£13,468.00: £6,734.00: £3,367.00)

				SP	RR	SF
4389a*	**Majorien** (MmeCHead,France) **3-8-9** ODoleuze (trckd ldr: qcknd st: led over 2f out: r.o wl)	—	**1**		120	—
4258a[5]	**Tamure (IRE)** (JHMGosden) **5-9-2** LDettori (racd 3rd: u.p over 2f out: chsd ldr fr wl over 1f out: no ex fnl f)	1	**2**		119	—
3006a[4]	**For Valour (USA)** (AFabre,France) **4-9-4** TJarnet (hld up: hrd rdn over 1f out: one pce fnl f)	3	**3**		117	—
4665a[16]	**Le Destin (FR)** (PDemercastel,France) **4-9-2** TGillet (hld up rr: qcknd over 1f out: outpcd fnl stages)	½	**4**		114	—
	Missing Link (FR) (PDemercastel,France) **4-9-2** AJunk (ted tl over 2f out: one pce)	6	**5**		106	—
4420[6]	**Mongol Warrior (USA)** (LordHuntingdon) **4-9-2** DHolland (racd 4th: wknd st: no ex)	5	**6**		99	—

6 Rn

2m 37.2 (11.20) P-M 2.20FF: 1.70FF 2.40FF (SF 8.80FF) OWNER Maktoum Al Maktoum (CHANTILLY) BRED Francois Geffroy
Majorien displayed his true colours over a mile and a half at Longchamp. He raced in second place for most of the race, before taking up the running early in the straight. Tamure chased him to the line but he galloped on strongly to win by a length. He stayed well on the heavy ground and is being aimed at the Breeders' Cup Turf race at Hollywood Park. He is likely to stay in training as a four-year-old.
4258a Tamure (IRE) acted well on the soft ground and showed his characteristic tenacity. Racing in third place, he made some headway over one furlong out to challenge the leader but he did not have enough in hand. He may get one more run in before going off to Australia to become a stallion.
2270a* For Valour (USA) was held up behind early on and then hard ridden in the last one and a half furlongs. He was never placed to challenge the leader and this step up in class may not have suited his ability.
4420 Mongol Warrior (USA) never really showed and the soft going and opposition may have proved too testing.

4864a PRIX DE LA FORET (Gp 1) (3-Y.O+)
3-20 (3-22) **7f** £56,117.00 (£22,447.00: £11,223.00: £5,612.00)

				SP	RR	SF
3554a*	**Occupandiste (IRE)** (MmeCHead,France) **4-8-13** ODoleuze (mde all: qcknd clr st: r.o wl: easily)	—	**1**	7/5[1]	128	—
4660a[5]	**Gothenberg (IRE)** (MJohnston) **4-9-2** DHolland (trckd ldr: 3rd 3f out: prog over 1f out: r.o)	6	**2**	44/1	117	—
4011[2]	**Tomba** (BJMeehan) **3-9-0** MTebbutt (mid div: hdwy 3f out: chal 2f out: one pce)	¾	**3**	87/10	116	—
4393a[3]	**Keos (USA)** (JEHammond,France) **3-9-0** CAsmussen (mid div: swtchd lft st: hrd rdn over 1f out: styd on)	2	**4**	37/10[2]	111	—
4129a[4]	**Daneskaya** (AFabre,France) **4-8-13** AJunk (hld up bhd: u.p 2f out: one pce)	1	**5**	46/10[3]	106	—
4421[4]	**Russian Revival (USA)** (JHMGosden) **4-9-2** LDettori (racd 3rd: prog st: wknd over 1f out)	s.h	**6**	63/10	109	—
4390a[2]	**Linoise (FR)** (AFabre,France) **5-8-13** TJarnet (racd 4th: sn btn)	¾	**7**	46/10[3]	104	—
4662a[2]	**Kaldou Star** (ELellouche,France) **3-9-0** TThulliez (mid div: u.p over 2f out: sn btn)	¾	**8**	11/1	105	—

4664a[8]	**Don't Worry Me (IRE)** (GHenrot,France) **5-8-13** TGillet (hld up bhd: n.d)	2¼	9	35/1	97	—
4129a[5]	**Classic Park** (APO'Brien,Ireland) **3-8-11** SCraine (a bhd: n.d)	6	10	12/1	83	—
				(SP 143.7%)		10 Rn

1m 21.4 (2.40) P-M 2.40FF: 1.30FF 7.20FF 2.40FF (44.80FF) OWNER Wertheimer Brothers (CHANTILLY) BRED J. Wertheimer & Frere
IN-FOCUS: For betting purposes, Daneskaya and Linoise (FR) were coupled.
3554a* Occupandiste (IRE) produced a magnificent turn of foot to win by an impressive six lengths. Relishing the soft ground, she quickened easily into the straight to finish very strongly. She is now at full maturity and will probably be kept in training next year. (7/5)
4660a Gothenberg (IRE) showed excellent form on the testing ground which he acts best on, and never put a foot wrong throughout the race. He is normally a front-running horse but, on this occasion, could not get anywhere near the winner. The colt will now go to Rome for a race next month and is likely to stay in training next year. (44/1)
4011 Tomba ran bravely against the four-year-old leaders, giving a very pleasing performance. He will stay in training next year and connections are looking forward to a promising season. (87/10)
Keos (USA) was disappointing on soft ground which does not suit him at all, staying on at one pace in the final stages and finding no extra. He will probably stay in training next year and could make a good miler as a four-year-old. (37/10)
4421 Russian Revival (USA) probably did not appreciate the going and weakened in the straight against opposition too strong for him. (63/10)

4763a-SAN SIRO (Milan, Italy) (R-H) (Good)
Sunday October 19th

4865a GRAN CRITERIUM (Gp 1) (2-Y.O C & F)
3-10 (3-15) **1m** £72,204.00 (£33,904.00: £21,060.00: £10,530.00)

				SP	RR	SF
4116*	**Lend A Hand** (MJohnston) **2-8-11** JWeaver (a.p: led over 2f out: sn clr: impressive)	—	1		115+	—
4357a[4]	**Mowbray (USA)** (PFICole) **2-8-11** RCochrane (mid-div: hdwy fr 2f out: r.o wl)	7½	2		104	—
	Boldini (IRE) (APO'Brien,Ireland) **2-8-11** JAHeffernan (hld up: hdwy 2f out: r.o)	nk	3		103	—
4244*	**Dower House** (WJarvis) **2-8-11** WRyan (trckd ldrs: r.o one pce fnl 2f)	1	4		101	—
4128a*	**Special Nash (IRE)** (PGuarsegnati,Italy) **2-8-11** ACorniani (led over 6f out tl hdd over 2f out: wknd)	1¼	5		99	—
	Mac Black (BAgriformi,Italy) **2-8-11** GBietolini (chsd ldrs tl wknd 2f out)	nk	6		98	—
4397a[2]	**Bardonecchia (ITY)** (LCamici,Italy) **2-8-8** MCangiano (led early: prom tl wknd over 2f out)	nse	7		95	—
	Bold Raparee (IRE) (DKWeld,Ireland) **2-8-11** MJKinane (a rr)	s.nk	8		98	—
2822a[3]	**Diamond Snake (IRE)** (GColleo,Italy) **2-8-11** MLatorre (prom tl wknd st)	2	9		94	—
3178a[5]	**Della Scala (IRE)** (BGrizzetti,Italy) **2-8-11** GForte (a bhd)	2½	10		89	—
						10 Rn

1m 37.2 (7.20) Tote 35L: 12L 11L 20L (21L) OWNER Maktoum Al Maktoum (MIDDLEHAM) BRED Gainsborough Stud Management Ltd
4116* Lend A Hand proved far too strong for his opponents. Moving to the front over two furlongs out, he soon showed his rivals a clean pair of heels to win in a very impressive style. He may return for the Italian 2,000 Guineas.
4357a Mowbray (USA) was no match for the winner but nevertheless put up a solid performance. Slightly hampered after two furlongs, he made late headway to take second from Boldini in the dying strides.
Boldini (IRE) made good progress in the straight and was unlucky not to hold on to second place, just losing out on the line.
4244* Dower House pleased his connections with his performance, despite not being able to challenge the leaders. Racing in fourth place, he kept on steadily in the final two furlongs.
Bold Raparee (IRE) was always towards the rear of the field and was never able to land a blow.

4866a GRAN PREMIO DEL JOCKEY CLUB (Gp 1) (3-Y.O+ C & F)
3-40 (3-51) **1m 4f** £160,146.00 (£84,238.00: £49,988.00: £24,994.00)

				SP	RR	SF
4127a[5]	**Caitano** (BSchutz,Germany) **3-8-13** AStarke (hld up: hdwy fr 2f out: led ins fnl f: r.o wl)	—	1		128	—
4537a[2]	**Luso** (CEBrittain) **5-9-4** MJKinane (trckd ldr: chal & hung rt 2f out: sn led: hdd ins fnl f: r.o one pce)	1¾	2		124	—
4549*	**Mons** (LMCumani) **4-9-4** JWeaver (led: hmpd 2f out: sn hdd: r.o fnl f)	½	3		123	—
4537a*	**Taipan (IRE)** (JLDunlop) **5-9-4** JReid (a.p: no ex fr 2f out)	1¼	4		121	—
4655a[4]	**Annaba (IRE)** (JHMGosden) **4-9-1** FJovine (trckd ldrs: one pce fnl 2f)	nk	5		118	—
4257a[3]	**Ivan Luis (FR)** (MBell) **3-8-13** RCochrane (hld up rr st: nvr nrr)	1½	6		121	—
4537a[4]	**Don't Worry (GER)** (HBlume,Germany) **3-8-13** THellier (mid-div: one pce st)	¾	7		120	—
4398a*	**War Declaration (IRE)** (BGrizzetti,Italy) **3-8-13** GForte (a bhd)	8	8		109	—
4398a[2]	**Honey Colour (IRE)** (ACalchetti,Italy) **3-8-13** OFrancera (a bhd: t.o)	11	9		95	—
						9 Rn

2m 26.2 (6.20) Tote 86L: 25L 18L 22L (169L) OWNER Stall Blauer Reiter
2097a* Caitano survived a Stewards' enquiry to take this, after hanging into Mons two furlongs out. He made headway to lead inside the final furlong and kept on well all the way to the line. He may go for the Japan Cup and is likely to stay in training next season.
4537a Luso put up his usual game performance, leading inside the final furlong before hanging right and being headed by the winner. The Hong Kong International Vase in December is his likely target.
4549* Mons tried to make all the running and, despite being hampered two furlongs out, rallied again close home but could not quite get up to take second spot.
4537a* Taipan (IRE), on ground too fast, had every chance on the run for home but was unable to quicken inside the final two furlongs.
4655a Annaba (IRE) was unable to conjure up any real finishing speed and ran on at the one pace in the final quarter-mile.
4257a Ivan Luis (FR) was given a fair amount to do. Held up in rear and last entering the straight, he was unable to get in a challenge.

4867a PREMIO BAGUTTA MEMORIAL SERGIO CUMANI (Gp 3) (3-Y.O+ F & M)
4-10 (4-40) **1m** £33,973.00 (£15,914.00: £8,964.00)

				SP	RR	SF
815a[6]	**She Bat** (VCaruso,Italy) **3-8-7** CFiocchi	—	1		110	—
1919a*	**Karla Wyller (ITY)** (AAiello,Italy) **4-8-9** CColombi	1½	2		106	—
4424*	**Kenmist** (LMCumani) **3-8-7** FJovine	s.h	3		107	—
4536a*	**Aunty Jane** (JLDunlop) **4-8-9** JReid (btn approx. 4l)		6		—	—
4424[9]	**Unconditional Love (IRE)** (MJohnston) **4-8-9** JWeaver (btn approx. 4¼l)		7		—	—
						16 Rn

1m 37.4 (7.40) Tote 101L: 30L 57L 19L (1252L) OWNER G. B. Benvenuto

4424* Kenmist fared best of the English raiders and lost second spot right on the line. In touch turning for home, she made good headway to go second inside the final furlong but was unable to hold on to that position.
4536a* Aunty Jane tried to make all the running but did not quite have the stamina to hold on.
3913 Unconditional Love (IRE) never really got in a blow and was unable to quicken when asked.

4868a PREMIO EUPILI (Listed) (2-Y.O)
5-10 (5-45) **6f** £23,142.00 (£10,183.00: £5,554.00)

				SP	RR	SF
4619a3	**Hoh Chi Min** (MBell) **2-8-6** JReid	—	1		96	—
	Hollywood Paradise (IRE) (Italy) **2-8-8** FJovine	2½	2		91	—
	Nobledil (IRE) (Italy) **2-8-8** FSpanu	1	3		89	—

9 Rn

1m 10.14 (2.14) Tote 20L: 14L 32L 17L (217L) OWNER Mr D. F. Allport (NEWMARKET) BRED Christian Marner
IN-FOCUS: **This race was run under floodlights.**
4619a Hoh Chi Min put up a useful display that proved too good for her rivals. Always prominent, she showed a good turn of foot on the outside to lead just over a furlong out, and was pushed out by her jockey.

4394a-WOODBINE (Toronto, Canada) (L-H) (Firm)
Sunday October 19th

4869a E P TAYLOR STKS (Gp 2) (3-Y.O+)
19-26 (19-26) **1m 2f (Turf)** £89,377.00 (£29,792.00: £16,386.00)

				SP	RR	SF
45572	**Kool Kat Katie (IRE)** (DRLoder) **3-8-6** OPeslier	—	1		120	—
4256a4	**Mousse Glacee (FR)** (JLesbordes,France) **3-8-6** GMosse	1¼	2		118	—
3878a2	**L'Annee Folle (FR)** (FDoumen,France) **4-8-11** PDay	s.h	3		118	—
32164	**Grey Way (USA)** (JLDunlop) **4-8-11** TQuinn (btn approx 6½l)		6		—	—

9 Rn

2m 2.0 P-M $6.80: PL $4.00 $4.90 SHOW $4.20 $4.30 $8.00 (SF $26.90) OWNER Augustin Stables (NEWMARKET) BRED Lucayan Stud Ltd
4557 Kool Kat Katie (IRE) showed her rivals what a tough and genuine filly she is. Tracking the leaders for the majority of the race, she got squeezed for room in the straight and had to switch right but, once she got some daylight, she put in a finishing burst to land the spoils. She now leaves Loder and joins the stable of Jonathan Sheppard.
3216 Grey Way (USA) lacked the finish of the winner, but nevertheless gave a reasonable account of herself. Held up, she made some headway to go fourth half a mile out but, when the pace quickened, she was unable to respond.

4870a CANADIAN INTERNATIONAL (Gp 1) (3-Y.O+)
21-35 (21-35) **1m 4f (Turf)** £259,740.00 (£86,580.00: £47,619.00: £25,974.00)

				SP	RR	SF
	Chief Bearhart (CAN) (MFrostad,Canada) **4-9-0** JSantos	—	1		128	—
	Down The Aisle (USA) (WMott,USA) **4-9-0** PDay	2¼	2		125	—
44202	**Romanov (IRE)** (PWChapple-Hyam) **3-8-7** OPeslier	3¼	3		121	—
4263a*	**Strategic Choice (USA)** (PFICole) **6-9-0** TQuinn	8½	4		109	—

6 Rn

2m 29.0 (-2.50) P-M $3.30: PL $2.30 $3.70 SHOW $2.10 $2.50 $3.20 (SF $8.10) OWNER Sam-Son Farm BRED R. Maynard
4420 Romanov (IRE) disputed the lead but was unable to pick up on the fast ground, and was headed three furlongs out.
4263a* Strategic Choice (USA) was unable to go with the winner when the pace quickened and he weakened from two furlongs out.

4146-DONCASTER (L-H) (Good)
Friday October 24th
WEATHER: fine & sunny WIND: almost nil

4871 E. B. F. WHEATLEY PARK MAIDEN STKS (2-Y.O) (Class D)
2-00 (2-01) **7f** £4,243.50 (£1,278.00: £619.00: £289.50) Stalls: Low GOING minus 0.32 sec per fur (GF)

				SP	RR	SF
	Zaya (SbinSuroor) **2-9-0** PaulEddery(10) (tall: unf: led: qcknd clr 1f out: v.easily)	—	1	9/4 2	89++	32
	Legal Lunch (USA) (PWHarris) **2-9-0** ACulhane(6) (w'like: leggy: scope: hld up: hdwy over 2f out: styd on fnl f: no ch w wnr)	2	2	16/1	84	27
	Kilcullen (IRE) (JHMGosden) **2-9-0** GHind(5) (unf: scope: s.i.s: drvn along & hung lft ½-wy: styd on fnl 2f)	1¼	3	9/1	82	25
47359	**Love Kiss (IRE)** (MJohnston) **2-9-0** DeanMcKeown(1) (trckd ldrs: drvn along over 2f out: kpt on same pce)	s.h	4	25/1	82	25
	Rayik (RWArmstrong) **2-9-0** GCarter(11) (w'like: bit bkwd: s.i.s: shkn up & hdwy ½-wy: stdy hdwy fnl f: improve)	hd	5	9/1	81+	24
45264	**Joint Regent (USA)** (BWHills) **2-9-0** KFallon(8) (sn drvn along & outpcd: styd on fnl 2f: nvr nr to chal)	2	6	2/1 1	77	20
42315	**Gypsy Passion (IRE)** (MJohnston) **2-9-0** JFortune(7) (chsd ldrs: drvn along ½-wy: wandered: kpt on same pce)	nk	7	16/1	76	19
479311	**Norski Lad** (SirMarkPrescott) **2-9-0** GDuffield(4) (sn drvn along: chsd ldrs: outpcd ½-wy: sn wknd)	8	8	33/1	58	1
	Bold Legacy (IRE) (WRMuir) **2-9-0** MartinDwyer(9) (leggy: bit bkwd: s.i.s: a outpcd)	½	9	33/1	57	—
471012	**Brooksie** (JWHills) **2-8-11(3)** MHenry(2) (chsd ldrs: drvn along & outpcd ½-wy: sn wknd)	½	10	50/1	55	—
39868	**Alrabyah (IRE)** (PTWalwyn) **2-9-0** JCarroll(12) (chsd ldrs: drvn along over 2f out: sn wknd)	nk	11	8/1 3	55	—
44788	**Pinsharp (IRE)** (PHowling) **2-9-0** JQuinn(3) (b: w ldrs tl wknd over 2f out)	8	12	50/1	36	—

(SP 120.6%) **12 Rn**

1m 27.95 (3.45) CSF £33.63 TOTE £3.10: £1.20 £3.80 £2.70 (£63.70) Trio £123.30 OWNER Godolphin (NEWMARKET) BRED Sheikh Mohammed bin Rashid al Maktoum
Zaya, a tall, narrow, athletic type, was yet another promising two-year-old by the first-season sire Zafonic. Never out of second gear here, he would have learnt a lot more had his rider pushed him out. (9/4)
Legal Lunch (USA), a quite attractive son of Alleged, looks the type to do better at three. (16/1)

Kilcullen (IRE), a narrow type, was a shade excitable in the paddock. Showing a round action going down, he hung left and looked some way off the finished object yet. (9/1: op 6/1)
Love Kiss (IRE), who raced keenly, should do better next year. (25/1)
Rayik, a medium-sized, attractive type, was very green going to post. After missing the break, he was handled with kid gloves in the final furlong and might have finished second had he been more vigorously ridden. (9/1: op 6/1)
4526 Joint Regent (USA) looked absolutely paceless. In a moderately-run race, he was soon off the bridle. (2/1)
4231 Gypsy Passion (IRE) tended to run about under pressure and will do better in handicap company next year. (16/1)

4872 SPROTBOROUGH CLAIMING STKS (3, 4 & 5-Y.O) (Class E)
2-30 (2-33) **7f** £3,512.25 (£1,053.00: £506.50: £233.25) Stalls: Low GOING minus 0.32 sec per fur (GF)

			SP	RR	SF
4586*	**Nant Y Gamer (FR) (75)** (JBerry) **3-8-7**(5) CLowther(10) (chsd ldrs stands' side: led over 2f out: styd on wl)..—	**1**	7/1	80	36
4816*	**Davis Rock (61)** (WRMuir) **3-8-4** MartinDwyer(4) (chsd ldrs far side: led over 2f out: r.o: no ex wl ins fnl f) .....¾	**2**	8/1	70	26
4680[14]	**Caudillo (IRE) (56)** (MrsPNDutfield) **4-8-3** JQuinn(2) (racd far side: hdwy 3f out: styd on wl) ....½	**3**	16/1	66	24
4680[13]	**Plan For Profit (IRE) (79)** (MJohnston) **3-8-12** JWeaver(21) (swtchd & hdwy stands' side over 2f out: styd on wl towards fin) 1	**4**	4/1[1]	75	31
4742[3]	**Dispol Diamond (45)** (GROldroyd) **4-8-5** KHodgson(7) (hdwy far side 3f out: styd on: nvr able chal) 3	**5**	16/1	59	17
4586[2]	**Salty Behaviour (IRE) (77)** (RHannon) **3-8-8**(3) PFessey(18) (lw: hdwy u.p stands' side 2f out: nvr nrr) ....½	**6**	9/2[2]	66	22
526[18]	**Gold Lining (IRE) (28)** (EJAlston) **4-8-2** GDuffield(3) (chsd ldrs far side: outpcd over 2f out: no imp after) 5	**7**	33/1	43	1
4373[2]	**Rawi (46)** (MissGayKelleway) **4-8-8b** JCarroll(12) (lw: chsd ldrs stands's side tl wknd fnl 2f) 3	**8**	25/1	43	1
4587[4]	**Ikram Boy (USA)** (ABailey) **3-8-6** DWright(22) (b: racd stands' side: effrt ½-wy: no imp) ....nk	**9**	16/1	42	—
4816[5]	**Gunners Glory (46)** (MrsLStubbs) **3-8-3v**(3) RFfrench(8) (prom far side: effrt 3f out: no imp) ....½	**10**	25/1	41	—
4742[4]	**Muhandam (IRE) (70)** (PAKelleway) **4-8-10v**[1] KFallon(9) (chsd ldrs far side: led ½-wy tl over 2f out: wknd)..1¼	**11**	6/1[3]	40	—
4586[7]	**Mumkin (61)** (MrsLStubbs) **3-8-6b** ACulhane(5) (chsd ldrs far side over 4f) 3	**12**	20/1	31	—
4373[15]	**Belzao (46)** (RSimpson) **4-8-7b**[1] MGallagher(17) (racd stands' side: no ch fnl 3f) ....½	**13**	50/1	29	—
1603[10]	**Sheraz (IRE) (36)** (NTinkler) **5-8-7b** KimTinkler(1) (led far side to ½-wy: wknd) ....¾	**14**	33/1	27	—
4570[3]	**Oberon's Dart (IRE) (63)** (PJMakin) **4-8-12** JFortune(20) (lw: chsd ldrs stands' side tl wknd over 2f out) ....½	**15**	10/1	31	—
4586[4]	**Court House (58)** (MCChapman) **3-7-13**(7) SCarson(13) (bolted gng to s: racd stands' side: n.d) 1½	**16**	14/1	24	—
4224[13]	**Bright Desert (28)** (MartynWane) **4-8-7** DeanMcKeown(11) (racd stands' side: wl outpcd fr ½-wy) 3½	**17**	66/1	15	—
	Risky Missile (DMorris) **3-8-5** NDay(6) (racd far side: sn bhd) 2	**18**	20/1	10	—
4601[16]	**La Doyenne (IRE) (41)** (CBBBooth) **3-7-9**(7) RWinston(16) (led stands' side tl wknd over 2f out) 1½	**19**	33/1	4	—
	Allemande (IRE) (RonaldThompson) **5-9-4** VHalliday(15) (chsd ldrs stands' side over 4f: wknd) ....nk	**20**	25/1	17	—
3822[13]	**Lomond Lassie (USA) (25)** (TKersey) **4-8-2** NKennedy(19) (racd stands' side: sn wl bhd) 5	**21**	100/1	—	—
2492[17]	**Milton Abbot** (MSSaunders) **4-8-9**(3) PPMurphy(14) (dwlt: racd stands' side: n.d) ....¾	**22**	100/1	—	—
			(SP 144.8%)	**22 Rn**	

1m 27.42 (2.92) CSF £57.89 TOTE £9.10: £3.50 £2.90 £8.60 (£28.20) Trio £121.40 OWNER Mr J. Berry (COCKERHAM) BRED Mrs Carolyn Elwes
WEIGHT FOR AGE 3yo-2lb
4586* Nant Y Gamer (FR) has been in tremendous form of late and he gets this seven furlongs really well. (7/1)
4816* Davis Rock, in top form just now, was on the opposite side of the track to the winner which may have been a slight disadvantage. (8/1)
2418 Caudillo (IRE) has yet to win in this country but this was a decent effort and she would seem to need a bit further. (16/1)
3605 Plan For Profit (IRE), who got bogged down in the Ascot mud last time, showed he is in good heart and was finishing strongly. (4/1)
4742 Dispol Diamond ran well up the far side making useful late progress. (16/1)
4586 Salty Behaviour (IRE), trying a longer trip, was again running on when it was all too late and he does not look an easy ride. (9/2)
428 Gold Lining (IRE) spends most of her time on the All-Weather these days and also this trip was short of her best. (33/1)

4873 E. B. F. FLAXTON MAIDEN STKS (2-Y.O F) (Class D)
3-00 (3-05) **1m (round)** £3,931.50 (£1,182.00: £571.00: £265.50) Stalls: High GOING minus 0.32 sec per fur (GF)

			SP	RR	SF
	Merciless (SbinSuroor) **2-8-11** JCarroll(13) (leggy: unf: scope: mde all: edgd rt & styd on fnl f)....—	**1**	11/2[3]	88	38
	Silver Rhapsody (USA) (HRACecil) **2-8-11** KFallon(3) (w'like: lengthy: chsd ldrs: nt qckn appr fnl f)....1½	**2**	2/1[1]	85	35
4474[3]	**Putuna** (IABalding) **2-8-11** MartinDwyer(1) (trckd ldrs: styd on appr fnl f: nvr able chal) 3½	**3**	3/1[2]	78	28
4425[6]	**Niki (IRE)** (JHMGosden) **2-8-11** AGarth(9) (trckd ldrs: styd on same pce fnl 2f) ....nk	**4**	12/1	77	27
4462[2]	**Taalluf (USA) (83)** (MajorWRHern) **2-8-11** GDuffield(2) (trckd ldrs: effrt & edgd lft 2f out: one pce)....1	**5**	7/1	75	25
4212[5]	**Slipper** (LMCumani) **2-8-8**(3) RFfrench(10) (mid div: hdwy over 2f out: styd on fnl f) ....nk	**6**	20/1	75	25
	Trigger Happy (IRE) (MJohnston) **2-8-11** JWeaver(11) (leggy: unf: chsd ldrs: drvn along ½-wy: sn outpcd: kpt on fnl f) 1	**7**	20/1	73	23
	Careful Timing (MRStoute) **2-8-11** FLynch(4) (lengthy: b.hind: s.i.s: hdwy over 4f out: shkn up & wknd over 1f out) ....nk	**8**	16/1	72	22
4217[2]	**Sahara** (PFICole) **2-8-11** JFortune(18) (racd wd: w ldrs tl wknd over 1f out)....1½	**9**	14/1	69	19
	Beacon Blaze (DRLoder) **2-8-11** GCarter(12) (w'like: lengthy: scope: bit bkwd: sn outpcd & bhd: n.d) 6	**10**	20/1	57	7
4367[7]	**Santarene (IRE)** (PHowling) **2-8-11** DWright(8) (s.i.s: a in rr)....1	**11**	66/1	55	5
4215[5]	**Tugela (USA)** (BWHills) **2-8-8**(3) JDSmith(17) (sn outpcd & bhd) ....nk	**12**	25/1	55	5
4507[7]	**Lady Rachel (IRE)** (JLEyre) **2-8-11** MGallagher(5) (a bhd)....¾	**13**	50/1	53	3
4567[9]	**Rabea (USA)** (JLDunlop) **2-8-11** MRimmer(16) (mid div: pushed along over 3f out: sn wknd) 1¾	**14**	25/1	50	—
4067[9]	**Hippocracy** (BWHills) **2-8-11** PaulEddery(6) (mid div: drvn along ½-wy: sn lost pl) 5	**15**	25/1	40	—
	Lady of The Dance (MAJarvis) **2-8-11** GHind(15) (w'like: unf: sn bhd & drvn along) 5	**16**	33/1	30	—
4779[20]	**Toffolux** (HJCollingridge) **2-8-11** JQuinn(7) (sn bhd) 10	**17**	50/1	10	—
	My Floosie (PJBevan) **2-8-11** GBardwell(14) (unf: rn green: sn bhd) 10	**18**	66/1	—	—
			(SP 142.1%)	**18 Rn**	

1m 41.55 (3.15) CSF £15.76 TOTE £11.30: £3.30 £1.70 £1.90 (£14.90) Trio £8.80 OWNER Godolphin (NEWMARKET) BRED Gainsborough Stud Management Ltd
Merciless, a long-backed, narrow filly, was tending to edge to her right from the home turn. Even so, she still won this in decisive fashion. She looks a real stayer. (11/2: 7/2-6/1)
Silver Rhapsody (USA), who showed a pronounced round action going down, stuck to her guns but was always second best. The form is nothing out of the ordinary but she is sure to improve and find an opening. (2/1)
4474 Putuna, who showed a round action going down, raced keenly. Short of room over a furlong out, she was staying on in her own time at the finish. She should do better with stronger handling. (3/1)
4425 Niki (IRE) was not knocked about and should be able to make her mark in handicap company at three. (12/1)

4462 Taalluf (USA) tended to edge left leaving Putuna short of room on her inner. (7/1)
4212 Slipper, on edge beforehand, stayed on late in the day. She should do better in handicap company over further next year. (20/1)
Trigger Happy (IRE), a leggy, narrow type, ran a highly satisfactory first race. A sister to the stable's ill-fated three-year-old, Eldorado, she will probably need at least a mile and a half at three. (20/1)

4874 RACING CHANNEL RUSSBOROUGH H'CAP (0-85) (3-Y.O+) (Class D)

3-30 (3-36) **1m 6f 132y** £4,435.00 (£1,330.00: £640.00: £295.00) Stalls: Low GOING minus 0.32 sec per fur (GF)

				SP	RR	SF
4774[5]	**Jawah (IRE) (70)** (KMahdi) **3-7-13**(5) CLowther(4) (b.hind: hld up: gd hdwy on outside 4f out: hung lft: led over 2f out: sn clr)	—	1	10/1[3]	81	32
	Silence in Court (IRE) (85) (ABailey) **6-10-0** AMackay(2) (b: hld up & bhd: hdwy over 3f out: r.o fnl f: nrst fin)	¾	2	25/1	95	55
4804[3]	**All On (54)** (JHetherton) **6-7-8**(3) RFfrench(7) (led early: a chsng ldrs: effrt 3f out: r.o one pce fnl 2f)	3	3	14/1	61	21
4363[8]	**Campaspe (74)** (JGFitzGerald) **5-9-3** KFallon(11) (bhd: hdwy 4f out: chsng ldrs 2f out: r.o one pce)	¾	4	10/1[3]	80	40
4363*	**Forgie (IRE) (77)** (PCalver) **4-9-6** NDay(12) (prom: chal over 3f out: one pce fnl 2f)	½	5	13/2[2]	83	43
4743*	**Moon Colony (70)** (LadyHerries) **4-8-13** 4x PaulEddery(3) (lw: hld up & bhd: gd hdwy whn hmpd over 2f out: one pce after)	1	6	100/30[1]	74	34
4222[3]	**Lookout (71)** (BWHills) **3-8-5** JCarroll(9) (chsd ldrs: ev ch 4f out: wknd over 2f out: eased whn btn)	7	7	10/1[3]	68	19
4631[2]	**Lysandros (IRE) (74)** (JHMGosden) **3-8-8** GHind(6) (b.hind: bhd: effrt 4f out: styd on: nvr rchd ldrs)	1½	8	12/1	69	20
4547[2]	**Spartan Heartbeat (78)** (CEBrittain) **4-9-7** GDuffield(5) (swtg: hld up & bhd: hdwy 3f out: nvr rchd ldrs)	nk	9	16/1	73	33
4594[3]	**Noufari (FR) (65)** (RHollinshead) **6-8-8** FLynch(16) (hdwy to ld 10f out: hdd & wknd over 2f out)	3½	10	20/1	56	16
4673[7]	**Royal Seaton (62)** (MrsPNDutfield) **8-8-5** JQuinn(10) (mid div: effrt appr st: n.d)	2	11	33/1	51	11
3805[8]	**Rusk (80)** (JPearce) **4-9-2**(7) RWinston(18) (chsd ldrs tl wknd fnl 3½f)	½	12	12/1	68	28
4568[9]	**Augustan (60)** (SGollings) **6-8-3** TWilliams(15) (effrt 4f out: n.d)	1¼	13	25/1	47	7
4426[5]	**Shining Dancer (58)** (SDow) **5-8-1** MartinDwyer(8) (dwlt: hdwy to jn ldrs appr st: wknd 3f out)	2½	14	10/1[3]	42	2
4704[6]	**Tycooness (IRE) (77)** (MJohnston) **3-8-11b** JWeaver(17) (sn led tl hdd 2f out: wknd 4f out)	1¾	15	20/1	59	10
3826*	**Amiarge (53)** (MBrittain) **7-7-10b** GBardwell(14) (s.i.s: hdwy 8f out: chsng ldrs ent st: sn wknd)	16	16	20/1	18	—
4584[11]	**Tajar (USA) (53)** (TKeddy) **5-7-10** NKennedy(1) (lw: hld up & bhd: n.d)	1¼	17	50/1	16	—
4673[10]	**Hal Hoo Yaroom (70)** (RAkehurst) **4-8-13** GCarter(13) (chsd ldrs tl wknd fnl 4f)	hd	18	20/1	33	—

(SP 132.3%) **18 Rn**

3m 9.45 (5.85) CSF £231.16 CT £3,215.02 TOTE £12.10: £2.20 £8.60 £2.30 £2.80 (£327.70) Trio £748.40; £316.26 to Doncaster 25/10/97
OWNER Sheik Ahmad Yousuf Al Sabah (NEWMARKET)
LONG HANDICAP Amiarge 7-8 Tajar (USA) 6-12
WEIGHT FOR AGE 3yo-9lb

4774 Jawah (IRE) has a good turn of foot but is inclined to hang and does not want to see the front too soon. (10/1)
Silence in Court (IRE), who last ran almost two and a half years ago, showed here he still has plenty of ability and just needed a bit further to make it. (25/1)
4804 All On is running particularly well but was just tapped for foot over this shorter trip. (14/1)
4363 Campaspe ran well and got into this halfway up the straight but her limitations were exposed in the last couple of furlongs. (10/1)
4363* Forgie (IRE) had his chances but basically he needs a stiffer test and was done for toe in the last two and a half furlongs. (13/2)
4743* Moon Colony likes to come from off the pace and got stopped in his run approaching the last two furlongs and quickly lost all interest. (100/30)

4875 DANUM NURSERY H'CAP (2-Y.O) (Class D)

4-00 (4-05) **1m (round)** £3,983.50 (£1,198.00: £579.00: £269.50) Stalls: High GOING minus 0.32 sec per fur (GF)

				SP	RR	SF
4116[16]	**Panama House (73)** (TDEasterby) **2-8-6** GDuffield(2) (chsd ldrs: led over 5f out: edgd rt & hld on wl fnl f)	—	1	20/1	81	32
4778[3]	**Dutch Lad (66)** (MHTompkins) **2-7-13** DaleGibson(6) (hld up: stdy hdwy 3f out: ev ch over 1f out: sn rdn: nt qckn ins fnl f)	½	2	11/4[1]	73	24
4437[3]	**Winsa (USA) (83)** (JLDunlop) **2-9-2** GCarter(8) (sn pushed along: hdwy over 3f out: styd on one pce appr fnl f)	3½	3	13/2[3]	83	34
4334[11]	**Lord of Love (66)** (TDEasterby) **2-7-13** DWright(4) (a chsng ldrs: one pce fnl 2f)	1¼	4	16/1	64	15
4245[4]	**Captain McCloy (USA) (63)** (MrsJRRamsden) **2-7-7**(3) RFfrench(7) (hld up: effrt & n.m.r 2f out: styd on towards fin)	3	5	8/1	55	6
4806[9]	**Mystagogue (63)** (RHannon) **2-7-7**(3) PFessey(13) (lw: sn chsng ldrs: hrd rdn & hung lft over 2f out: one pce)	s.h	6	25/1	54	5
4605[2]	**Opposition Leader (77)** (BWHills) **2-8-10** KFallon(10) (chsd ldrs: rdn & outpcd 3f out: kpt on fnl 2f)	hd	7	7/1	68	19
4767[2]	**Prince Ashleigh (74)** (PCHaslam) **2-8-2**(5) CLowther(11) (lw: chsd ldrs tl lost pl over 2f out)	2	8	11/2[2]	61	12
4698[8]	**Royal Ground (IRE) (66)** (MRChannon) **2-7-13** AMackay(1) (sn wl bhd & drvn along: hdwy over 3f out: n.d)	½	9	20/1	52	3
4690[9]	**Winsome George (83)** (CWFairhurst) **2-9-2** NKennedy(14) (sn outpcd & drvn along: sme hdwy 3f out: n.d)	1½	10	20/1	66	17
4157[9]	**Lift The Offer (IRE) (73)** (RHannon) **2-8-6** PaulEddery(12) (bhd: hdwy u.p over 3f out: sn lost pl)	5	11	12/1	46	—
4745[8]	**Oisin (IRE) (68)** (MrsPNDutfield) **2-8-1** JQuinn(9) (in tch: hrd rdn 4f out: sn wknd)	1¼	12	33/1	39	—
4265[3]	**Flower O'Cannie (IRE) (88)** (MWEasterby) **2-9-7** TLucas(5) (swtg: chsd ldrs: wkng whn hmpd over 2f out: eased)	hd	13	16/1	59	10
4702[10]	**Suivez La Trace (80)** (JJO'Neill) **2-8-13** JWeaver(3) (led tl over 2f out: lost pl & eased)	16	14	20/1	19	—

(SP 124.3%) **14 Rn**

1m 41.66 (3.26) CSF £64.38 CT £396.67 TOTE £21.50: £3.40 £1.80 £2.20 (£63.00) Trio £129.40 OWNER Mr P. England (MALTON) BRED R. B. Warren
LONG HANDICAP Captain McCloy (USA) 7-9 Mystagogue 7-5

3458* Panama House put two poor efforts behind him. He showed real spirit to hold off the runner-up and there was definitely no fluke at all about this. (20/1)
4778 Dutch Lad travelled strongly off the pace. After moving up and looking all over a winner, he could not get his head in front. A son of a Cesarewitch winner, he looks an out and out stayer who will be suited by strongly-run races. (11/4)
4437 Winsa (USA), who is well related, stuck on after getting behind. A lengthy filly, she looks sure to train on. (13/2)
3973 Lord of Love proved much better suited by the shorter trip and faster ground. (16/1)
4245 Captain McCloy (USA), tucked away on the inside, did not get the run of the race but he would not have finished any better than fifth in any case. (8/1)
2893 Mystagogue, 5lb wrong at the weights, wanted to do nothing but hang left. (25/1)
4767 Prince Ashleigh, who showed a pronounced round action going down, was having his third race in quick succession and found this surface too lively. (11/2)

4876 WESTWOODSIDE H'CAP (0-80) (3-Y.O) (Class D)

4-30 (4-34) **1m 2f 60y** £4,467.50 (£1,340.00: £645.00: £297.50) Stalls: Low GOING minus 0.32 sec per fur (GF)

				SP	RR	SF
3424^{7}	**American Whisper (75)** (PWHarris) **3-8-11**(5) CLowther(6) (prom: hdwy to ld over 2f out: r.o)	—	**1**	12/1	89	48
4699*	**Secret Ballot (IRE) (72)** (KMahdi) **3-8-10**(3) 5x RFfrench(14) (lw: hld up: hdwy 4f out: hung lft: chsd wnr fnl 1½f: no imp)	3	**2**	4/1^{1}	81	40
4147^{21}	**Night Mirage (USA) (76)** (MJohnston) **3-9-3** JWeaver(13) (bhd: effrt over 4f out: styd on wl: nrst fin)	4	**3**	9/1	79	38
4477^{4}	**Zoom Up (IRE) (80)** (MJHeaton-Ellis) **3-9-7v^{1}** GCarter(11) (lw: hld up & bhd: effrt 4f out: styd on: nvr able chal)	1¾	**4**	8/1^{3}	80	39
4693*	**Zorba (65)** (JHetherton) **3-8-6** 5x NKennedy(1) (hld up & bhd: effrt over 1f out: r.o: nrst fin)	2½	**5**	10/1	62	21
4632^{9}	**Praeditus (67)** (RHannon) **3-8-8** KFallon(17) (led after 1f tl over 2f out: sn btn)	2	**6**	10/1	60	19
4268^{4}	**Fantastic Flame (IRE) (77)** (PJMakin) **3-9-4** JFortune(8) (lw: hld up: hdwy ent st: chsng ldrs 3f out: rdn & one pce fnl 2f)	3	**7**	9/1	66	25
4693^{3}	**Foot Battalion (IRE) (64)** (RHollinshead) **3-8-5** FLynch(16) (lw: hld up & bhd: c wd & effrt 4f out: nvr trbld ldrs)	nk	**8**	10/1	52	11
4703^{5}	**Foxes Tail (73)** (MissSEHall) **3-8-7**(7) RWinston(12) (prom: rdn & hung lft 4f out: btn over 2f out)	6	**9**	33/1	52	11
4632^{14}	**Who's That Man (57)** (SCWilliams) **3-7-12** JQuinn(5) (chsd ldrs: rdn over 4f out: wknd over 2f out)	1¾	**10**	25/1	33	—
4699^{13}	**Absolute Liberty (USA) (64)** (SPCWoods) **3-8-5v^{1}** NDay(10) (mid div: drvn along over 3f out: sn btn)	2½	**11**	25/1	36	—
4386^{3}	**Ile Distinct (IRE) (73)** (MrsASwinbank) **3-9-0** GDuffield(7) (a chsng ldrs: effrt over 3f out: sn wknd)	1¼	**12**	9/2^{2}	43	2
4635^{12}	**Jack The Lad (IRE) (75)** (JHetherton) **3-8-9**(7) TSiddall(9) (hld up & bhd: n.d)	nk	**13**	25/1	45	4
	Danka (66) (PTWalwyn) **3-8-7** JCarroll(2) (prom tl rdn & wknd over 3f out)	¾	**14**	25/1	35	—
4802^{7}	**Rare Talent (60)** (SGollings) **3-8-1** TWilliams(15) (cl up tl wknd 3f out)	nk	**15**	25/1	28	—
471^{8}	**Head Gardener (IRE) (63)** (NPLittmoden) **3-8-4** DWright(4) (led 1f: chsd ldrs tl rdn & wknd over 4f out)	10	**16**	33/1	16	—
				(SP 129.4%)	**16 Rn**	

2m 11.22 (3.42) CSF £52.96 CT £432.92 TOTE £12.30: £2.80 £1.60 £2.60 £2.40 (£33.70) Trio £112.80 OWNER The Confederates (BERKHAMSTED) BRED Cambremont Ltd Partnership

OFFICIAL EXPLANATION **Ile Distinct (IRE): no explanation offered**

3424 American Whisper keeps going up the weights but also keeps improving and this was a most emphatic victory, particularly after two and a half months off. (12/1)

4699* Secret Ballot (IRE) looked absolutely superb and ran well but, when put under pressure, he was always tending to hang left which did not help matters. (4/1: 3/1-9/2)

4015 Night Mirage (USA), returning here after almost six weeks off, put up a useful effort to show she is as well as ever. (9/1)

4477 Zoom Up (IRE) had the visor on instead of blinkers and, although taking time to warm to his task, he was responding to pressure in the closing stages. (8/1: 6/1-10/1)

4693* Zorba, given a lot to do, did well to finish so close and is obviously in really good heart. (10/1: op 6/1)

1238 Praeditus, who won a maiden when making all, tried a return to these tactics here but either did not stay or is not doing it these days. (10/1)

4693 Foot Battalion (IRE) (10/1: 8/1-12/1)

4386 Ile Distinct (IRE) (9/2: op 8/1)

4877 OCTOBER APPRENTICE H'CAP (0-70) (3-Y.O) (Class E)

5-00 (5-05) **7f** £3,642.25 (£1,093.00: £526.50: £243.25) Stalls: High GOING minus 0.32 sec per fur (GF)

				SP	RR	SF
4417^{3}	**Colway Ritz (65)** (JWWatts) **3-9-3** PFessey(10) (swtchd rt s: stdy hdwy over 2f out: styd on wl to ld ins fnl f)	—	**1**	16/1	75	34
3583^{3}	**Legend of Aragon (45)** (JAGlover) **3-7-11** APolli(5) (racd far side: in tch: edgd rt & styd on wl appr fnl f)	1¾	**2**	20/1	51	10
4842^{4}	**King Uno (53)** (MrsJRRamsden) **3-8-5v** CLowther(2) (racd far side: hld up: hdwy to ld over 1f out: hdd & no ex ins fnl f)	½	**3**	4/1^{1}	58	17
4813^{11}	**Fancy A Fortune (IRE) (60)** (DNicholls) **3-8-7**(5) ANicholls(16) (a chsng ldrs: styd on same pce appr fnl f)	hd	**4**	20/1	65	24
4636^{4}	**Kram (57)** (MrsPNDutfield) **3-8-9** TEDurcan(7) (racd far side: chsd ldrs: edgd rt & kpt on same pce appr fnl f)	1	**5**	13/2^{3}	59	18
4695^{6}	**Oxbane (51)** (CADwyer) **3-8-3** AWhelan(19) (chsd ldr stands' side: kpt on same pce fnl 2f)	½	**6**	12/1	52	11
4700*	**Shalaal (USA) (73)** (MCChapman) **3-9-6**(5) 6x SCarson(18) (swtg: unruly s: chsd ldrs tl outpcd ½-wy: kpt on appr fnl f)	hd	**7**	12/1	74	33
4738^{5}	**Maladerie (IRE) (63)** (MRChannon) **3-9-1** PPMurphy(15) (chsd ldrs: drvn along 3f out: no imp)	nk	**8**	8/1	63	22
2733^{14}	**Loch-Hurn Lady (48)** (KWHogg) **3-7-9**(5) DMernagh(14) (chsd ldrs: outpcd fnl 2f)	nk	**9**	25/1	48	7
3898^{11}	**Batsman (52)** (WJMusson) **3-8-4**^{ow2} JDSmith(11) (lw: s.i.s: bhd tl sme hdwy fnl 2f)	nk	**10**	20/1	51	8
*4798**	**Sea Ya Maite (54)** (SRBowring) **3-8-6** 6x CTeague(6) (b: chsd ldrs far side: led over 2f out tl over 1f out: sn wknd)	hd	**11**	6/1^{2}	53	12
4328^{3}	**Nervous Rex (55)** (WRMuir) **3-8-4**(3) JoHunnam(12) (chsd ldrs centre: hrd rdn ½-wy: wknd over 2f out)	1½	**12**	14/1	50	9
4565^{11}	**Suite Factors (51)** (KRBurke) **3-7-12**(5) SRighton(20) (s.i.s: n.d)	3	**13**	14/1	39	—
4773^{7}	**Gipsy Princess (54)** (MWEasterby) **3-8-1b**(5) SFinnamore(8) (dwlt: racd far side: sn chsng ldrs: wknd over 2f out)	nk	**14**	33/1	42	1
4696^{9}	**Warrior King (IRE) (51)** (CADwyer) **3-7-12**(5) AMcCarthy(1) (racd far side: chsd ldrs tl lost pl 3f out)	nk	**15**	25/1	38	—
4586^{5}	**C-Harry (IRE) (62)** (RHollinshead) **3-9-0** FLynch(22) (trckd ldrs: effrt over 2f out: sn wknd)	½	**16**	16/1	48	7
4436^{12}	**Cantina (69)** (ABailey) **3-9-7** RFfrench(21) (led stands' side tl wknd over 2f out)	1½	**17**	8/1	52	11
4546^{5}	**Aybeegirl (49)** (MrsJCecil) **3-8-1** MartinDwyer(3) (led far side tl over 2f out: sn wknd)	1½	**18**	14/1	28	—
4601^{17}	**Why O Six (46)** (RAFahey) **3-7-9**(3)^{ow2} RWinston(9) (racd far side: outpcd fr ½-wy)	nk	**19**	33/1	24	—
4436^{15}	**Unshaken (55)** (EJAlston) **3-8-0v**(7) MelanieWorden(4) (w ldrs far side 4f: sn wknd)	½	**20**	33/1	32	—
3968^{9}	**Warring (56)** (MSSaunders) **3-8-8** DarrenMoffatt(17) (swtg: outpcd fr ½-wy)	2½	**21**	33/1	28	—
4591^{8}	**Cuesta Rey (USA) (60)** (JWHills) **3-8-12** MHenry(13) (chsd ldrs tl lost pl ½-wy)	3½	**22**	33/1	24	—
				(SP 153.7%)	**22 Rn**	

1m 28.03 (3.53) CSF £307.55 CT £1,444.86 TOTE £18.30: £3.40 £5.70 £1.70 £7.80 (£265.40) Trio £286.60 OWNER Mr R. Coleman (RICHMOND) BRED R. P. Williams

LONG HANDICAP Why O Six 7-7

4417 Colway Ritz, who has slipped down the weights, opened his account at his eleventh attempt. Given a confident ride and switched to race towards the main group on the stands' side, he was persuaded to put his best foot forward in the closing stages. (16/1)

3583 Legend of Aragon, without any headgear, stuck on strongly under his inexperienced and weak-looking boy. (20/1)

4842 King Uno, having his second outing in three days, possibly hit the front too soon on the far side. (4/1: tchd 6/1)

3457 Fancy A Fortune (IRE) stuck on again at the death and a mile might turn out to be his best trip. (20/1)

4636 Kram was racing over an extended distance and on totally different ground. (13/2)

4695 Oxbane appreciated the drop back in distance. (12/1)
4700* Shalaal (USA), who had plenty to do under his 6lb penalty, proved very difficult to load into the stalls. (12/1)

T/Plpt: £397.90 (58.61 Tckts). T/Qdpt: £43.90 (36.68 Tckts) WG

4292-NEWBURY (L-H) (Good, Good to soft bk st)
Friday October 24th
WEATHER: sunny WIND: almost nil

4878 VODAFONE BRITISH AND NORTHERN RACING SCHOOLS APPRENTICE H'CAP (0-80) (3-Y.O+) (Class F)
2-10 (2-12) **7f (straight)** £3,230.00 (£905.00: £440.00) Stalls: High GOING minus 0.01 sec per fur (G)

				SP	RR	SF
4071[3]	**Victory Team (IRE) (75)** (GBBalding) **5-9-4**(5) RStudholme(23) (s.s: stdy hdwy over 1f out: led ins fnl f: rdn out)	—	**1**	11/1[3]	87	59
4680[3]	**Zurs (IRE) (59)** (JRPoulton) **4-8-4**(3) AEddery(12) (s.s: hdwy 2f out: hrd rdn over 1f out: ev ch ins fnl f: r.o)	½	**2**	8/1[1]	70	42
4561[14]	**Taffs Well (71)** (RAkehurst) **4-9-2**(3) DDenby(19) (b.off fore: led tl ins fnl f: r.o)	hd	**3**	8/1[1]	82	54
4518[4]	**Scissor Ridge (59)** (JJBridger) **5-8-2**(5) RBrisland(21) (a.p: rdn over 2f out: unable qckn)	3½	**4**	20/1	62	34
4561[17]	**Jeffrey Anotherred (80)** (KMcAuliffe) **3-9-12** DSweeney(10) (hdwy over 2f out: hrd rdn over 1f out: wknd ins fnl f)	½	**5**	11/1[3]	82	52
4456[15]	**Intiaash (IRE) (66)** (DHaydnJones) **5-8-7**(7) JoeleneRichards(14) (lw: hdwy over 1f out: r.o ins fnl f)	1¾	**6**	14/1	64	36
4546*	**Bold Tina (IRE) (64)** (RHannon) **3-8-5**(5) RSmith(15) (lw: hdwy over 2f out: wknd ins fnl f)	nk	**7**	10/1[2]	61	31
4561[16]	**Night Dance (70)** (KAMorgan) **5-8-13**(5) DMcGaffin(11) (lw: hld up: rdn over 2f out: wknd over 1f out)	1¾	**8**	20/1	63	35
2374[9]	**Proud Monk (60)** (GLMoore) **4-8-3b**[1](5) DarrenWilliams(24) (bkwd: s.s: nvr nrr)	nk	**9**	14/1	52	24
4319[3]	**Veni Vidi Vici (IRE) (64)** (MJHeaton-Ellis) **4-8-7**(5) JFowle(3) (lw: nvr nrr)	2	**10**	14/1	52	24
4787[13]	**Bacchus (76)** (ACStewart) **3-9-5**(3) PDoe(13) (hrd rdn & hdwy over 2f out: sn wknd)	hd	**11**	20/1	63	33
4574[10]	**Leigh Crofter (48)** (PDCundell) **8-7-5b**(5) CCogan(18) (prom over 3f)	1½	**12**	33/1	32	4
4757[21]	**Giko (62)** (JRPoulton) **3-8-3**(5) PBradley(8) (hdwy 3f out: wknd over 2f out)	1¼	**13**	20/1	43	13
3092*	**Ella Lamees (60)** (WJMusson) **3-8-3**(3) JWilkinson(16) (a mid div)	3½	**14**	12/1	33	3
4276[6]	**Strat's Quest (60)** (DWPArbuthnot) **3-8-3**(3) KimberleyHart(17) (prom over 4f)	1¼	**15**	25/1	30	—
4175[9]	**Nordinex (IRE) (70)** (DRCElsworth) **5-9-4** DGriffiths(5) (b: lw: bhd fnl 2f)	3	**16**	33/1	33	5
4375[10]	**Gee Bee Dream (74)** (APJarvis) **3-9-1**(5) CCarver(20) (prom over 4f)	½	**17**	16/1	36	6
146[8]	**Tom Morgan (53)** (PTWalwyn) **6-7-10**(5)ow3 RCody-Boutcher(1) (bkwd: bhd fnl 2f)	¾	**18**	50/1	14	—
4561[8]	**Zelda Zonk (72)** (BJMeehan) **5-9-6** RHavlin(2) (lw: bhd fnl 2f)	1¼	**19**	20/1	30	2
4175[11]	**Summer Queen (74)** (SPCWoods) **3-9-6** GMilligan(9) (bhd fnl 2f)	s.h	**20**	20/1	32	2
	Arantxa (75) (MBell) **3-9-7** RMullen(4) (bhd fnl 2f)	5	**21**	20/1	21	—
	Sawlajan (USA) (80) (TRWatson) **6-10-0** SCopp(7) (lw: dwlt: bhd fnl 3f)	s.h	**22**	50/1	26	—
1620[15]	**Wild Nettle (50)** (JCFox) **3-7-3**(7) KelliPhillips(6) (swtg: dwlt: bhd fnl 2f)	8	**23**	50/1	—	—

(SP 130.5%) **23 Rn**

1m 28.06 (3.96) CSF £73.32 CT £705.53 TOTE £12.90: £2.70 £1.50 £2.20 £2.80 (£27.60) Trio £43.10 OWNER Mr R. J. Lavelle (ANDOVER) BRED Barronstown and Swettenham Studs and Ron Con Ltd
LONG HANDICAP Leigh Crofter 7-8 Wild Nettle 7-0
WEIGHT FOR AGE 3yo-2lb

4071 Victory Team (IRE), who has gained his two previous turf wins at Folkestone over this trip, came with a steady run to lead inside the final furlong and, ridden along, held off his rivals. (11/1: 8/1-12/1)
4680 Zurs (IRE) is in fine form at present and ran another solid race. Throwing down his challenge from below the distance, he gave his all but found the winner a little bit too strong. (8/1)
4219 Taffs Well showed his Newmarket run at the beginning of the month to be all wrong and, taking the field along, was only overhauled inside the final furlong. (8/1)
4518 Scissor Ridge, never far away, failed to quicken in the last two furlongs. Both his turf wins have come at Goodwood. (20/1)
3975 Jeffrey Anotherred, dropped 4lb by the Handicapper since his last run, took closer order over a quarter of a mile from home but had run out of steam inside the final furlong. (11/1: 8/1-12/1)
4221 Intiaash (IRE), racing at the back of the field, did not have a great deal of assistance but ran on in pleasing style in the last furlong and a half to be nearest at the line. (14/1: 8/1-16/1)
4546* Bold Tina (IRE) (10/1: 8/1-12/1)
2117 Proud Monk (14/1: op 25/1)

4879 VODAFONE GROUP H'CAP (0-90) (3-Y.O+) (Class C)
2-40 (2-40) **2m** £6,232.00 (£1,876.00: £908.00: £424.00) Stalls: Low GOING minus 0.01 sec per fur (G)

				SP	RR	SF
4667[3]	**Whitechapel (USA) (79)** (LordHuntingdon) **9-9-3** TQuinn(6) (hdwy 5f out: rdn over 3f out: led over 2f out tl over 1f out: led ins fnl f: all out)	—	**1**	10/1	88	46
4673*	**Jaseur (USA) (90)** (JHMGosden) **4-10-0v** LDettori(10) (lw: hdwy 5f out: led over 1f out: wandered & hdd ins fnl f: r.o)	nk	**2**	7/4[1]	99	57
4783[10]	**Etterby Park (USA) (75)** (MJohnston) **4-8-13** MHills(1) (hrd rdn over 4f out: swtchd rt over 2f out: hdwy over 1f out: r.o wl ins fnl f)	s.h	**3**	25/1	84	42
4743[2]	**Royal Crown (IRE) (87)** (PWChapple-Hyam) **3-8-12**(3) RHavlin(4) (lw: rdn 7f out: hdwy on ins 5f out: hrd rdn over 2f out: r.o)	1	**4**	12/1	95	43
4156[4]	**Nanton Point (USA) (68)** (LadyHerries) **5-8-6** RCochrane(7) (nvr nr to chal)	15	**5**	8/1[3]	61	19
4461[2]	**Prospero (69)** (MrsAJPerrett) **4-8-7** AClark(9) (lw: plld hrd: a.p: led over 3f out tl over 2f out: wknd over 1f out)	¾	**6**	12/1	61	19
4744*	**Theme Arena (58)** (MCPipe) **4-7-10v** 4x NCarlisle(3) (prom over 12f)	nk	**7**	8/1[3]	50	8
4609[4]	**Nick of Time (68)** (JLDunlop) **3-7-3**(7) PDoe(8) (a bhd)	8	**8**	20/1	52	—
4783[5]	**Captain Jack (86)** (MCPipe) **7-9-10b** DaneO'Neill(2) (led over 11f: wknd over 3f out)	2½	**9**	6/1[2]	67	25
4673[2]	**Galapino (69)** (MissGayKelleway) **4-8-2**(5) RMullen(11) (lw: plld hrd: a.p: led over 4f out tl over 3f out: sn wknd)	4	**10**	8/1[3]	46	4

Atours (USA) (70) (DRCElsworth) **9-8-8** SDrowne(5) (b.off hind: bit bkwd: a bhd)..........7 **11** 25/1 40 —
(SP 120.9%) **11 Rn**

3m 35.43 (11.23) CSF £25.41 CT £403.21 TOTE £12.80: £3.10 £1.30 £5.00 (£12.00) Trio £48.40 OWNER The Queen (WEST ILSLEY) BRED The Queen
LONG HANDICAP Theme Arena 7-4 Nick of Time 7-6
WEIGHT FOR AGE 3yo-10lb
4667 Whitechapel (USA) gained a narrow lead over a quarter of a mile from home. Marginally headed approaching the final furlong he had a tremendous ding-dong battle and just managed to prevail, to gain his first victory beyond one mile five and a half furlongs. (10/1: 7/1-11/1)
4673* Jaseur (USA) looked all set to complete the four-timer as he went about a neck up approaching the final furlong but he has risen 21lb since the first of those victories and that told as he was worried out of it in the closing stages. (7/4)
4363 Etterby Park (USA), under pressure early in the straight, at last found his feet from below the distance and, running on really strongly inside the final furlong, would surely have prevailed with a little further to go. (25/1)
4743 Royal Crown (IRE) moved up along the inside rail turning into the straight and, responding to pressure, ran on willingly to finish a mile clear of the remainder. (12/1)
4156 Nanton Point (USA) never threatened to get into it. (8/1: 6/1-9/1)
4461 Prospero moved to the front over three furlongs from home but, carrying his head high and looking far from enthusiastic, was collared over a quarter of a mile from home and soon decided he had done enough. (12/1)
4744* Theme Arena (8/1: 6/1-9/1)
4673 Galapino (8/1: 5/1-9/1)

4880 VODAFONE HORRIS HILL STKS (Gp 3) (2-Y.O C & G) (Class A)
3-10 (3-10) **7f 64y (round)** £19,799.99 (£7,451.25: £3,613.13: £1,610.63) Stalls: Low GOING minus 0.01 sec per fur (G)

				SP	RR	SF
4679*	**La-Faah (IRE) (96)** (BWHills) **2-8-9** RHills(3) (nt clr run over 2f out tl wl over 1f out: hdwy to ld over 1f out: shkn up: comf)	—	**1**	9/1	108+	48
4064*	**Sensory** (BWHills) **2-8-9** MHills(4) (chsd ldr: led over 2f out tl over 1f out: unable qckn ins fnl f)	1¾	**2**	10/1	104	44
4524[5]	**Victory Note (USA) (100)** (PWChapple-Hyam) **2-8-9** JReid(5) (lw: a.p: rdn 2f out: one pce)	1	**3**	9/2[3]	102	42
4229*	**Naughty Blue (USA)** (SbinSuroor) **2-8-9** LDettori(2) (a.p: rdn & n.m.r 2f out: swtchd rt over 1f out: one pce)	1½	**4**	4/1[2]	99	39
4670*	**Smart Squall (USA) (90)** (LordHuntingdon) **2-8-9** TQuinn(8) (lw: rdn over 3f out: hdwy over 2f out: r.o one pce)	hd	**5**	15/2	99	39
4274*	**Duck Row (USA)** (JARToller) **2-8-9** AClark(1) (s.s: rdn & hdwy on ins over 3f out: wknd over 1f out)	3½	**6**	7/4[1]	91	31
4368*	**Imshishway (IRE) (84)** (BJMeehan) **2-8-9** MTebbutt(7) (hld up: rdn 3f out: wknd over 1f out)	3½	**7**	33/1	83	23
4679[2]	**Batswing (90)** (MartynMeade) **2-8-9b** TSprake(6) (led 5f)	5	**8**	66/1	72	12

(SP 109.8%) **8 Rn**

1m 32.06 (3.96) CSF £78.26 TOTE £8.00: £2.20 £2.20 £2.00 (£19.30) OWNER Mr Hamdan Al Maktoum (LAMBOURN) BRED Shadwell Estate Company Limited
OFFICIAL EXPLANATION **Duck Row (USA): the trainer reported that the colt ran a lifeless race.**
4679* La-Faah (IRE) did not have the mud that he seems to enjoy but still put up an impressive display especially considering he did not have the best of runs. However, he showed a fine turn of foot to quicken into the lead at the distance and won with plenty in hand. He is certainly a progressive youngster. (9/1)
4064* Sensory moved to the front over a quarter of a mile from home but, when collared by the winner at the distance, was well and truly put in his place. (10/1)
4524 Victory Note (USA), a leading player throughout, failed to find that vital turn of foot in the final quarter-mile. (9/2)
4229* Naughty Blue (USA) was never far away and, although he did not have a great deal of room a quarter of a mile from home, was already tapped for toe at the time. (4/1)
4670* Smart Squall (USA) found this trip in this class on good ground too sharp for him and, although staying on, never threatened to get into it. He needs further. (15/2)
4274* Duck Row (USA) ran a lifeless race and with Clark not looking happy on him early in the straight, the combination tamely dropped away below the distance. (7/4)

4881 GARDNER MERCHANT RATED STKS H'CAP (0-110) (3-Y.O+) (Class B)
3-40 (3-42) **6f 8y** £8,681.20 (£3,230.80: £1,565.40: £657.00: £278.50: £127.10) Stalls: High GOING minus 0.01 sec per fur (G)

				SP	RR	SF
4777*	**My Best Valentine (106)** (VSoane) **7-9-7** 3x RCochrane(2) (lw: hdwy over 1f out: led ins fnl f: pushed out)	—	**1**	10/1[3]	117	70
4467*	**Brave Edge (101)** (RHannon) **6-9-2** DaneO'Neill(1) (a.p: led over 3f out tl ins fnl f: unable qckn)	1¾	**2**	20/1	107	60
4777[4]	**Prends Ca (IRE) (92)** (WRMuir) **4-8-4**(3) PRoberts(4) (a.p: rdn over 1f out: r.o one pce)	½	**3**	8/1[2]	97	50
4282[2]	**Double Action (101)** (TDEasterby) **3-9-1** LCharnock(3) (lw: a.p: rdn over 1f out: ev ch ins fnl f: one pce)	1	**4**	5/1[1]	103	55
4282[19]	**Astrac (IRE) (93)** (NTinkler) **6-8-8**ow1 LDettori(10) (led over 2f: rdn 2f out: one pce)	½	**5**	16/1	94	46
4756[15]	**Bowden Rose (96)** (MBlanshard) **5-8-8b**(3) DSweeney(5) (hld up: hrd rdn 2f out: ev ch ins fnl f: one pce)	nk	**6**	25/1	96	49
4677[3]	**Patsy Grimes (92)** (JSMoore) **7-8-7** TQuinn(12) (lost pl over 3f out: r.o one pce fnl f)	1¾	**7**	10/1[3]	88	41
4467[2]	**Open Credit (92)** (HRACecil) **3-8-6** AMcGlone(8) (hld up: rdn 2f out: wknd over 1f out)	hd	**8**	16/1	87	39
2329[5]	**Carranita (IRE) (105)** (BPalling) **7-9-6** TSprake(9) (prom over 4f)	¾	**9**	20/1	98	51
4677[6]	**Distinctive Dream (IRE) (92)** (KTIvory) **3-8-6b** JFEgan(17) (s.s: rdn & hdwy on ins over 2f out: one pce)	½	**10**	40/1	84	36
4700[13]	**Lucayan Beach (92)** (BGubby) **3-8-6** MFenton(15) (s.s: hdwy 2f out: wknd over 1f out)	s.h	**11**	100/1	84	36
4756*	**The Puzzler (IRE) (101)** (BWHills) **6-9-2** 3x MHills(11) (nvr nrr)	nk	**12**	10/1[3]	92	45
4756[5]	**Hello Mister (92)** (TEPowell) **6-8-4**(3) PMcCabe(16) (nvr nrr)	hd	**13**	12/1	83	36
4423[15]	**No Extras (IRE) (92)** (GLMoore) **7-8-4**(3) GParkin(13) (a bhd)	½	**14**	10/1[3]	82	35
4525[5]	**Bolshoi (IRE) (106)** (JBerry) **5-9-7** EmmaO'Gorman(6) (lw: bhd fnl 2f)	¾	**15**	25/1	94	47
4756[13]	**Bold Effort (FR) (94)** (KOCunningham-Brown) **5-8-9b** SDrowne(7) (prom over 4f)	6	**16**	20/1	66	19
2775[6]	**Shock Value (IRE) (94)** (MRStoute) **3-8-8** JReid(14) (prom over 2f)	½	**17**	12/1	64	16
4777[7]	**Daring Destiny (104)** (KRBurke) **6-9-5b** RHills(18) (a bhd)	5	**18**	12/1	61	14

(SP 124.4%) **18 Rn**

1m 14.27 (2.47) CSF £184.65 CT £971.32 TOTE £8.90: £2.10 £6.00 £2.20 £1.70 (£128.50) Trio £378.70 OWNER The Valentines (ASTON ROWANT) BRED Ridgecourt Stud
LONG HANDICAP Patsy Grimes 8-5 Prends Ca (IRE) 8-4 Astrac (IRE) 8-5 No Extras (IRE) 8-5 Hello Mister 8-5 Lucayan Beach 6-13 Open Credit 8-5 Distinctive Dream (IRE) 7-12
WEIGHT FOR AGE 3yo-1lb
4777* My Best Valentine, the paddock pick, continues in tremendous heart and, sweeping through to lead inside the final furlong, was nudged along to win readily. (10/1)

4467* Brave Edge, 11lb higher than when last successful in a handicap, moved to the front just before halfway but, collared by the winner inside the final furlong, was firmly put in his place. (20/1)
4777 Prends Ca (IRE), 9lb better off with the winner, not including her rider's allowance, for a one and a half length beating at Newmarket last week, failed to reverse the placings but did stay on from below the distance. (8/1)
4282 Double Action, a leading light throughout, threatened to take the lead a furlong from home but was tapped for toe in the last one hundred yards. (5/1)
3975 Astrac (IRE) has proved very disappointing this year but did run better here, showing in front until just before halfway and then keeping on at one pace. (16/1)
4553* Bowden Rose came to have every chance inside the final furlong before tapped for toe. She has yet to win on ground worse than good. (25/1)

4882 ROUND OAK H'CAP (0-90) (3-Y.O+) (Class C)

4-10 (4-13) **1m 2f 6y** £6,320.00 (£1,910.00: £930.00: £440.00) Stalls: Low GOING minus 0.01 sec per fur (G)

				SP	RR	SF
4577[5]	**Conspicuous (IRE) (86)** (LGCottrell) **7-9-11**(3) ADaly(2) (hld up: rdn over 2f out: led ins fnl f: drvn out)	—	**1**	25/1	97	49
4854[7]	**Top Jem (75)** (MJRyan) **3-8-9**(3) PMcCabe(14) (a.p: led over 3f out tl ins fnl f: r.o)	hd	**2**	12/1	86	33
4294*	**Sharp Consul (IRE) (85)** (HCandy) **5-9-13** CRutter(12) (plld hrd: stdy hdwy over 2f out: rdn over 1f out: r.o)	2½	**3**	13/2[1]	92	44
4558[10]	**Bubble Wings (FR) (72)** (SPCWoods) **5-9-0** JReid(4) (n.m.r over 3f out: nt clr run over 2f out: hdwy over 1f out: str run fnl f: fin wl)	1¼	**4**	9/1[2]	77	29
4788[5]	**Master Beveled (74)** (PDEvans) **7-9-2v** JFEgan(5) (rdn over 2f out: hdwy over 1f out: r.o wl ins fnl f)	hd	**5**	9/1[2]	79	31
1869[4]	**Sophomore (86)** (BWHills) **3-9-9** LDettori(10) (a.p: rdn over 2f out: wknd ins fnl f)	½	**6**	10/1[3]	90	37
3263[5]	**Hachiyah (IRE) (89)** (DMorley) **3-9-12** RHills(8) (lw: a.p: rdn over 2f out: one pce)	hd	**7**	20/1	93	40
4672[4]	**Happy Go Lucky (72)** (RJO'Sullivan) **3-8-9** DBiggs(20) (led over 6f: wknd 1f out)	2	**8**	33/1	73	20
4672[7]	**Premier Generation (IRE) (70)** (DWPArbuthnot) **4-8-12** SWhitworth(1) (b: hdwy over 1f out: wknd ins fnl f)	s.h	**9**	20/1	71	23
4552*	**Kewarra (85)** (BRMillman) **3-9-8** TSprake(9) (lw: prom over 7f)	½	**10**	9/1[2]	85	32
4477[7]	**Mutadarra (IRE) (67)** (WJMusson) **4-8-6**(3) DSweeney(16) (nvr nrr)	¾	**11**	14/1	66	18
4294[4]	**Star Manager (USA) (83)** (PFICole) **7-9-11** TQuinn(11) (s.s: a mid div)	2	**12**	10/1[3]	78	30
4558[9]	**Gift Token (82)** (MajorDNChappell) **3-9-5v** NCarlisle(13) (a mid div)	nk	**13**	10/1[3]	77	24
4606[8]	**Calypso Lady (IRE) (67)** (RHannon) **3-8-4** DaneO'Neill(19) (prom over 7f)	1½	**14**	33/1	59	6
4558[14]	**King of Tunes (FR) (85)** (MJHaynes) **5-9-13** RCochrane(7) (a bhd)	1¾	**15**	25/1	75	27
3705[9]	**Prairie Falcon (IRE) (85)** (BWHills) **3-9-8** MHills(21) (mid div over 8f)	hd	**16**	14/1	75	22
4680[15]	**Zygo (USA) (70)** (RTPhillips) **5-8-12** RPerham(6) (lw: a bhd)	9	**17**	50/1	45	—
1277[3]	**Natural Eight (IRE) (83)** (RWArmstrong) **3-9-6** AClark(17) (a bhd)	1½	**18**	33/1	56	3
4680[4]	**Sycamore Boy (USA) (73)** (LordHuntingdon) **3-8-10** DO'Donohoe(18) (a bhd)	¾	**19**	20/1	45	—
4572[9]	**Arctic Thunder (USA) (83)** (BPalling) **6-9-11** SDrowne(3) (bhd fnl 2f)	½	**20**	50/1	54	6
4297[11]	**Koathary (USA) (72)** (LGCottrell) **6-9-0** MFenton(15) (hld up: rdn over 3f out: wknd over 2f out)	7	**21**	25/1	32	—

(SP 130.2%) **21 Rn**

2m 11.71 (7.71) CSF £252.57 CT £2,013.05 TOTE £64.50: £8.50 £2.40 £1.80 £2.70 (£332.50) Trio £204.20 OWNER Mrs Jenny Hopkins (CULLOMPTON) BRED Gerry Canavan
WEIGHT FOR AGE 3yo-5lb

3712* Conspicuous (IRE) chased the leaders and, responding to pressure, eventually managed to get on top inside the final furlong and just held on. (25/1)
4731 Top Jem showed no ill-effects from her race at Yarmouth on Thursday and gained control over three furlongs from home. Collared inside the last two hundred yards, she kept on well to the bitter end. (12/1)
4294* Sharp Consul (IRE) steadily cruised into the action over a quarter of a mile from home and kept on nicely to the end. (13/2)
4386* Bubble Wings (FR) did not have the smoothest of passages as she had to come through the entire field. However, she really found her feet in the final furlong and finished best of all. (9/1)
4788 Master Beveled began a forward move below the distance and, running on strongly inside the final furlong, only just lost out in the prize money. (9/1)
1869 Sophomore, without a run in four and a half months, was close up until lack of a previous run took its toll inside the final furlong. (10/1)
4558 Gift Token (10/1: 8/1-12/1)

4883 ENBOURNE MAIDEN STKS (3-Y.O) (Class D)

4-40 (4-46) **1m 2f 6y** £3,938.00 (£1,184.00: £572.00: £266.00) Stalls: Low GOING minus 0.01 sec per fur (G)

				SP	RR	SF
4407[3]	**Mowelga** (LadyHerries) **3-9-0** DeclanO'Shea(13) (rdn & hdwy over 3f out: led over 1f out: r.o wl)	—	**1**	12/1	67	32
4705[2]	**Ricardo** (RCharlton) **3-9-0** WJO'Connor(1) (lw: a.p: rdn 3f out: ev ch fnl f: r.o wl)	s.h	**2**	100/30[3]	67	32
4503[8]	**Mary Culi (40)** (HCandy) **3-8-9** NAdams(14) (hld up: led over 3f out tl over 1f out: unable qckn)	2½	**3**	50/1	58	23
4736[2]	**Shadiann (IRE) (83)** (LMCumani) **3-9-0** MTebbutt(8) (a.p: led over 5f out tl over 3f out: one pce)	3½	**4**	11/10[1]	57	22
4587[5]	**Slieu Whallian** (RHannon) **3-8-9** JTate(11) (a.p: rdn over 3f out: one pce)	hd	**5**	33/1	52	17
4736[3]	**Reggie Buck (USA)** (RJO'Sullivan) **3-9-0** AProcter(2) (hld up: rdn over 3f out: sn wknd)	13	**6**	7/1	36	1
3998b[4]	**Polska Princess (GER) (70)** (LordHuntingdon) **3-8-9** DO'Donohoe(4) (rdn & hdwy over 3f out: wknd over 2f out)	3	**7**	16/1	27	—
4277[7]	**Lawz (IRE) (69)** (CJBenstead) **3-9-0** JLowe(7) (plld hrd: lost pl over 4f out: no hdwy fnl 2f)	1¾	**8**	12/1	29	—
	Storm Command (DWPArbuthnot) **3-9-0** CandyMorris(9) (leggy: unf: nvr nrr)	1	**9**	50/1	27	—
4322[7]	**Joli Flyers** (MJHaynes) **3-9-0** DBiggs(5) (led over 4f)	¾	**10**	50/1	26	—
3891[10]	**Danzas (73)** (RCharlton) **3-9-0** RPerham(16) (hld up: rdn over 4f out: wknd over 2f out)	10	**11**	20/1	10	—
3389[10]	**Cherrymentary** (KOCunningham-Brown) **3-8-9** FNorton(10) (bhd fnl 5f)	3	**12**	50/1	—	—
	Jester Minute (BAPearce) **3-9-0** LeesaLong(6) (lt-f: bkwd: bhd fnl 7f: t.o fnl 3f)	dist	**13**	50/1	—	—
	Angel One Five (PRHedger) **3-8-9** NVarley(12) (leggy: a wl bhd: t.o fnl 5f)	6	**14**	50/1	—	—
1415[10]	***Prinia*** (RTPhillips) **3-8-9** NCarlisle(15) (Withdrawn not under Starter's orders: ref to ent stalls)		**W**	50/1	—	—
4060[3]	***Serpentara (73)*** (HRACecil) **3-8-9** AMcGlone(3) (Withdrawn not under Starter's orders: spread a plate at s)		**W**	3/1[2]	—	—

(SP 150.9%) **14 Rn**

2m 12.22 (8.22) CSF £46.32 TOTE £11.90: £2.80 £1.40 £17.70 (£20.00) Trio £455.00; £448.60 to Doncaster 25/10/97 OWNER Hesmonds Stud (LITTLEHAMPTON) BRED Hesmonds Stud Ltd

IN-FOCUS: This looked a very bad maiden by Newbury standards. It was confined to full jockeys who had not ridden more than thirty winners this year.

4407 Mowelga, pushed along to take closer order in the straight, eventually got on top below the distance but was given no peace by the runner-up and only just prevailed. (12/1: 10/1-20/1)

4705 Ricardo threw down his challenge in the final quarter-mile and, engaged in a ding-dong battle with the winner, only just failed. Having now finished second on his last three outings, he deserves a change of luck. (100/30)
2848 Mary Culi ran much better here and moved to the front in the centre of the course over three furlongs from home. Collared below the distance, she then failed to find another gear. (50/1)
4736 Shadiann (IRE) moved to the front turning into the straight but he was collared over three furlong from home and made to look very pedestrian. (11/10: evens-5/4)
4587 Slieu Whallian, never far away, could only struggle on at one very insufficient pace in the last three furlongs. (33/1)
4736 Reggie Buck (USA) chased the leaders but had been hung out to dry fully three furlong from home. (7/1: 6/1-10/1)

4884 E. B. F. THEALE MAIDEN STKS (2-Y.O) (Class D)
5-10 (5-17) **6f 8y** £4,276.00 (£1,288.00: £624.00: £292.00) Stalls: High GOING minus 0.01 sec per fur (G)

				SP	RR	SF
	Mister Rambo (BJMeehan) **2-9-0** MTebbutt(9) (gd sort: hld up: hrd rdn over 1f out: swtchd rt: str run ins fnl f: led last strides)	—	**1**	20/1	87	49
	Fa-Eq (IRE) (SbinSuroor) **2-9-0** LDettori(16) (lengthy: a.p: led over 1f out: shkn up: hdd last strides)	nk	**2**	11/10[1]	86+	48
4379[2]	**Uplifting** (LGCottrell) **2-8-9** RCochrane(14) (led over 4f: unable qckn ins fnl f)	1½	**3**	15/2[3]	77	39
	Caernarfon Bay (IRE) (PFICole) **2-9-0** TQuinn(3) (w'like: a.p: rdn over 2f out: wknd over 1f out)	5	**4**	12/1	69	31
	Moon Gorge (WJarvis) **2-8-9** AMcGlone(22) (w'like: a.p: rdn over 2f out: wknd over 1f out)	hd	**5**	20/1	64	26
	Lucy Glitters (USA) (IABalding) **2-8-6**(3) DGriffiths(4) (small: hld up: rdn over 2f out: wknd over 1f out)	½	**6**	20/1	62	24
	Squabble (RFJohnsonHoughton) **2-8-9** JReid(5) (lengthy: bkwd: nvr nr to chal)	1¼	**7**	12/1	59	21
	Riot (JHMGosden) **2-9-0** RHills(21) (gd sort: lw: s.s: swtchd lft over 2f out: stdy hdwy over 1f out: nvr nrr: bttr for r)	s.h	**8**	10/1	64	26
	Sheila-B (PJMakin) **2-8-9** TSprake(24) (cmpt: bit bkwd: a.p: rdn over 1f out: sn wknd)	¾	**9**	33/1	57	19
	Alarming Motown (IABalding) **2-8-6**(3) DSweeney(20) (lt-f: a mid div)	hd	**10**	20/1	57	19
4113[12]	**Desert Valentine** (LGCottrell) **2-9-0** MFenton(8) (lw: a mid div)	1¼	**11**	50/1	58	20
4298[7]	**Waff's Folly** (GFHCharles-Jones) **2-8-9** CRutter(1) (a mid div)	hd	**12**	33/1	53	15
4298[11]	**Mantello** (MajorDNChappell) **2-9-0** NAdams(12) (nvr nrr)	2	**13**	50/1	53	15
	Primordial (FR) (SDow) **2-9-0** RPerham(17) (b.hind: w'like: s.s: nvr nrr)	1¼	**14**	33/1	50	12
	Bomb Alaska (GBBalding) **2-9-0** DBiggs(10) (lengthy: unf: nvr nrr)	hd	**15**	50/1	49	11
	Tanimbar (IRE) (DHaydnJones) **2-9-0** SDrowne(6) (w'like: a mid div)	nk	**16**	25/1	48	10
4513[3]	**Roi Brisbane** (MJohnston) **2-9-0** MHills(15) (prom over 3f)	½	**17**	13/2[2]	47	9
4298[6]	**Aganon** (MRChannon) **2-9-0** JFEgan(19) (bhd fnl 2f)	nk	**18**	20/1	46	8
	Fields of Omagh (USA) (IABalding) **2-9-0** SWhitworth(18) (scope: bit bkwd: bhd fnl 2f)	1	**19**	16/1	44	6
4753[24]	**Prince Oxley** (GLMoore) **2-9-0** CandyMorris(23) (bhd fnl 2f)	hd	**20**	33/1	43	5
	Buzzing (IRE) (RHannon) **2-9-0** DaneO'Neill(2) (w'like: s.s: a bhd)	s.h	**21**	20/1	43	5
4747[7]	**Shipley Glen** (SirMarkPrescott) **2-9-0** CNutter(7) (a bhd)	5	**22**	16/1	30	—
4694[8]	**Pixielated (IRE)** (DRLoder) **2-8-9** AClark(11) (a bhd)	1¼	**23**	33/1	22	—
2181[24]	**Highland Lord** (MJFetherston-Godley) **2-9-0** FNorton(13) (bhd fnl 3f)	12	**24**	50/1	—	—
				(SP 163.9%)	**24 Rn**	

1m 15.28 (3.48) CSF £42.36 TOTE £52.20: £10.80 £1.40 £2.90 (£109.10) Trio £167.30 OWNER Abbott Racing Ltd (UPPER LAMBOURN) BRED R. S. A. Urquhart

Mister Rambo, a well-made individual who has already been gelded, stalked the leaders. Switched right a furlong from home, he came with a real rattle to snatch the spoils in the last strides. (20/1)
Fa-Eq (IRE), an attractive, lengthy individual who has reportedly been showing promise at home, looked all set to make a winning debut as he poked his head in front approaching the final furlong. Asserting inside the last two hundred yards and with Dettori doing little more than nudging him along, the combination got caught in the last couple of strides. Losses are only lent. (11/10)
4379 Uplifting again adopted a front-running role but she was collared approaching the final furlong and failed to find another gear. (15/2: 5/1-8/1)
Caernarfon Bay (IRE), a medium-sized colt, was never far away but was getting left behind approaching the final furlong. (12/1: op 5/1)
Moon Gorge, a half-sister to Welsh Guide who won a Group One race in Europe, was close up until tiring approaching the final furlong. (20/1)
Lucy Glitters (USA) is not very big but chased the leaders until calling it a day over a furlong out. (20/1)
Riot, an attractive, good-bodied colt, certainly caught the eye under sympathetic handling, staying on encouragingly once shaken up in the final quarter-mile. He is sure to have learnt a great deal from this and a lot of improvement can be expected. (10/1: 6/1-12/1)
4513 Roi Brisbane (13/2: 4/1-7/1)

T/Jkpt: Not won; £233,260.94 to Doncaster 25/10/97. T/Plpt: £368.20 (158.07 Tckts). T/Qdpt: £63.50 (34.1 Tckts) AK

4871-DONCASTER (L-H) (Good)
Saturday October 25th
WEATHER: overcast WIND: almost nil

4885 'JOCK MURRAY MEMORIAL' NURSERY H'CAP (2-Y.O) (Class C)
1-40 (1-41) **7f** £6,163.50 (£1,848.00: £889.00: £409.50) Stalls: High GOING minus 0.07 sec per fur (G)

				SP	RR	SF
4581*	**Florazi (86)** (JLDunlop) **2-9-7** MJKinane(1) (hld up: hdwy ½-wy: led over 1f out: r.o u.p)	—	**1**	4/1[1]	90	56
4634[7]	**Lido (IRE) (81)** (BWHills) **2-9-2** RHills(14) (lw: hld up & bhd: swtchd & hdwy ½-wy: chal over 1f out: r.o)	nk	**2**	12/1	84	50
4755[3]	**Inchalong (73)** (MBrittain) **2-8-1**(7) DMernagh(12) (a chsng ldrs: ev ch over 1f out: r.o one pce)	2	**3**	6/1[2]	72	38
3597[3]	**Sea Magic (IRE) (86)** (BWHills) **2-9-7** KFallon(3) (hdwy ½-wy: sn chsng ldrs: nt qckn fnl f)	hd	**4**	8/1[3]	85	51
4265[15]	**Naviasky (IRE) (74)** (MrsJRRamsden) **2-8-9** JFortune(9) (hld up & bhd: hdwy & n.m.r over 1f out: rdn & no imp fnl f)	1¾	**5**	8/1[3]	69	35
4690[10]	**Burnt Yates (IRE) (75)** (MWEasterby) **2-8-10** JReid(7) (trckd ldrs: outpcd 2f out: nt clr run over 1f out: kpt on towards fin)	¾	**6**	9/1	68	34
4767[4]	**Sandmoor Tartan (61)** (TDEasterby) **2-7-10** LCharnock(4) (prom: outpcd 2f out: grad wknd)	3	**7**	16/1	47	13
4753[5]	**Frankie Fair (IRE) (62)** (MAJarvis) **2-7-11**ow1 TWilliams(10) (cl up: led wl over 2f out tl appr fnl f: wknd)	s.h	**8**	14/1	48	13
4597*	**Sense of Wonder (85)** (BJMeehan) **2-9-6** JWeaver(13) (lw: hld up & bhd: effrt & n.m.r over 2f out: n.d)	1¾	**9**	6/1[2]	67	33
4271[17]	**Welcome Sunset (74)** (JWharton) **2-8-4**(5) CLowther(2) (in tch: effrt over 2f out: sn wknd)	1½	**10**	20/1	52	18
4767[13]	**Princess Natalie (72)** (MWEasterby) **2-8-7** TLucas(6) (gd spd over 4f: grad lost pl)	6	**11**	20/1	37	3
4767[12]	**Laramania (64)** (PDEvans) **2-7-13** DWright(8) (bhd: effrt ½-wy: n.d)	1¼	**12**	33/1	26	—
4690[14]	**Falkenberg (FR) (65)** (MJohnston) **2-8-0** NAdams(11) (cl up over 4f: wknd)	4	**13**	25/1	18	—

				SP	RR	SF
2904[5]	**Penniless (IRE) (70)** (NTinkler) **2-8-5** KimTinkler(5) (led tl hdd wl over 2f out: wknd)	1	**14**	33/1	20	—
				(SP 120.3%)		**14 Rn**

1m 28.13 (3.63) CSF £44.70 CT £268.48 TOTE £5.20: £2.20 £3.30 £1.30 (£28.70) Trio £83.70 OWNER Mr Peter Winfield (ARUNDEL) BRED Sir Eric Parker

4581* Florazi has now settled down and improved a good deal and, well-handled, he did it in game style. (4/1)
3204 Lido (IRE), running over his longest trip to date, came from way off the pace and had to switch round the whole field but ran by far his best race for a while and there may well be another opportunity before the season ends. (12/1)
4755 Inchalong has had an incredibly busy season and this was her twenty-second race. This sparely-made individual keeps running amazingly well. (6/1)
3597 Sea Magic (IRE) is in the shake-up every time but she never seems to quite come up with the goods. (8/1)
4116 Naviasky (IRE), whose come from behind tactics seem to continually find him in trouble, certainly has plenty more ability but he also may have his own ideas. (8/1)
4362* Burnt Yates (IRE) was short of a room at a vital stage and that was enough for him. (9/1: 12/1-8/1)
4597* Sense of Wonder, dropped out, ran no sort of race and this is best completely ignored. (6/1)
2314* Princess Natalie keeps dropping down the handicap and next year should see plenty more from her. (20/1)

4886 CORN EXCHANGE CLAIMING STKS (3-Y.O+) (Class D)

2-10 (2-11) **1m 2f 60y** £4,077.50 (£1,220.00: £585.00: £267.50) Stalls: Low GOING minus 0.07 sec per fur (G)

				SP	RR	SF
4788[9]	**Time for Action (IRE) (73)** (MHTompkins) **5-9-1** JWeaver(8) (trckd ldr: led over 2f out: r.o strly: sn clr)	—	**1**	10/1	87	69
4598[2]	**Ordained (52)** (EJAlston) **4-8-8** KFallon(5) (in tch: effrt over 3f out: styd on: no ch w wnr)	9	**2**	10/1	66	48
4639[7]	**Billy Bushwacker (82)** (MrsMReveley) **6-9-7** JReid(14) (dwlt: hld up: effrt 3f out: nt clr run: r.o appr fnl f: nrst fin)	1½	**3**	3/1[1]	77	59
4788[7]	**Break the Rules (72)** (DNicholls) **5-9-1**(3) PRoberts(12) (lw: a in tch: hdwy over 3f out: styd on: nt pce to chal)	nk	**4**	10/1	73	55
2528[8]	**Gone for a Burton (IRE) (84)** (PJMakin) **7-9-3** JFortune(15) (hld up & bhd: nt clr run 2f out: hdwy over 1f out: nvr rchd ldrs)	1¾	**5**	7/1[3]	70	52
4691[8]	**Manful (73)** (MissLAPerratt) **5-9-4b** NKennedy(9) (lw: chsd ldrs: rdn over 3f out: one pce)	hd	**6**	20/1	70	52
4742*	**Brighstone (79)** (MCPipe) **4-8-8** AMcGlone(7) (t: led tl hdd over 2f out: sn outpcd)	½	**7**	9/2[2]	60	42
4802[14]	**Pickens (USA) (53)** (DonEnricoIncisa) **5-8-6** KimTinkler(2) (b: hld up & bhd: hdwy 4f out: sn rdn: btn 2f)	½	**8**	50/1	57	39
3274[6]	**Juggler (70)** (LordHuntingdon) **3-8-10** LDettori(10) (mid div: effrt over 3f out: sn btn)	1¼	**9**	10/1	64	41
4742[5]	**Zidac (65)** (PJMakin) **5-9-1** GDuffield(13) (trckd ldrs: effrt over 2f out: wknd qckly)	1½	**10**	12/1	62	44
4243[10]	**Miss Riviera Rose (44)** (GWragg) **3-8-6** MJKinane(6) (hld up: effrt 4f out: n.d)	1¾	**11**	25/1	55	32
1207[14]	**Prince of Bhutan (IRE)** (RAkehurst) **3-8-7**[ow1] OPeslier(4) (chsd ldrs tl wknd fnl 3f)	6	**12**	14/1	46	22
4845[6]	**Falls O'Moness (IRE) (60)** (KRBurke) **3-8-5** JFEgan(1) (hld up: gd hdwy 4f out: sn chsng ldrs: wknd over 2f out)	2½	**13**	12/1	41	18
	Appleton's Fancy (35) (ABailey) **3-8-4** DWright(11) (hld up & bhd: n.d)	25	**14**	50/1	1	—
				(SP 126.6%)		**14 Rn**

2m 10.93 (3.13) CSF £98.60 TOTE £12.10: £3.40 £2.20 £1.50 (£67.90) Trio £89.90 OWNER Mrs G. A. E. Smith (NEWMARKET) BRED J. C. Condon

WEIGHT FOR AGE 3yo-5lb

4477 Time for Action (IRE) showed here that when things go his way, he is quite useful, and fairly trotted up. (10/1)
4598 Ordained has yet to win this season but she is running consistently well just now. (10/1)
4409 Billy Bushwacker has plenty more ability, but he got messed about in trying to come from off the pace and never had a hope of getting into it. (3/1)
4521 Break the Rules is now running better after two moderate efforts earlier this month. (10/1)
Gone for a Burton (IRE) never saw daylight until too late and should have finished a lot closer. (7/1)
4691 Manful again looked superb but, after having his chances, he also looked very one-paced. (20/1)
4742* Brighstone (9/2: op 3/1)

4887 DONCASTER WRITERS RATED STKS H'CAP (0-100) (3-Y.O+) (Class B)

2-40 (2-43) **5f** £8,266.49 (£3,073.50: £1,486.75: £621.25: £260.63: £116.38) Stalls: High GOING minus 0.07 sec per fur (G)

				SP	RR	SF
4677[7]	**Rudi's Pet (IRE) (88)** (RHannon) **3-8-11b** OPeslier(15) (lw: hmpd s: bhd tl hdwy 2f out: led ins fnl f: r.o wl)	—	**1**	20/1	103	60
4280*	**Perryston View (90)** (PCalver) **5-8-13v** LDettori(14) (hmpd s: hdwy ½-wy: ev ch ins fnl f: kpt on)	2½	**2**	7/1[2]	97	54
4423[10]	**Faraway Lass (85)** (LordHuntingdon) **4-8-8** MJKinane(6) (bhd: hdwy over 1f out: styd on wl)	s.h	**3**	16/1	92	49
4756[6]	**Repertory (86)** (MSSaunders) **4-8-9** SDrowne(4) (lw: led tl hdd & no ex ins fnl f)	nk	**4**	20/1	92	49
4444[2]	**Crowded Avenue (95)** (PJMakin) **5-9-4** KFallon(19) (hld up & bhd: effrt over 1f out: r.o)	½	**5**	5/1[1]	99	56
4636*	**Canovas Heart (86)** (BobJones) **8-8-9** NDay(18) (chsd ldrs: rdn 2f out: kpt on)	nk	**6**	12/1	89	46
4756[7]	**Twice as Sharp (87)** (PWHarris) **5-8-10** GHind(11) (chsd ldrs: kpt on u.p fnl f)	½	**7**	16/1	89	46
4756[8]	**Gaelic Storm (89)** (MJohnston) **3-8-12** JWeaver(21) (lw: hld up: effrt 2f out: nrst fin)	½	**8**	11/1	89	46
4756[14]	**Indian Spark (93)** (JSGoldie) **3-8-13**(3) DGriffiths(20) (lw: chsd ldrs: rdn 2f out: r.o one pce)	nk	**9**	50/1	92	49
4770[14]	**Kira (84)** (JLEyre) **7-8-0**(7) RWinston(17) (b: b.hind: in tch: hdwy over 1f out: styd on)	½	**10**	20/1	82	39
4756[10]	**Tadeo (98)** (MJohnston) **4-9-7** DeanMcKeown(5) (chsd ldrs tl rdn & btn over 1f out)	½	**11**	16/1	94	51
3217[24]	**Sea-Deer (84)** (CADwyer) **8-8-7** AMcGlone(8) (in tch: effrt ½-wy: no imp)	nk	**12**	25/1	79	36
4452[8]	**Spender (84)** (PWHarris) **8-8-7** GDuffield(12) (gd spd tl wknd appr fnl f)	1¼	**13**	33/1	75	32
4280[23]	**Westcourt Magic (87)** (MWEasterby) **4-8-10** LCharnock(10) (drvn along ½-wy: nvr trbld ldrs)	hd	**14**	25/1	78	35
4756[11]	**Surprise Mission (86)** (MrsJRRamsden) **5-8-9** JFortune(7) (lw: trckd ldrs: effrt 2f out: sn btn)	½	**15**	12/1	75	32
4756[9]	**Lago Di Varano (85)** (RMWhitaker) **5-8-8v** FLynch(2) (chsd ldrs tl rdn & wknd appr fnl f)	2½	**16**	20/1	66	23
4770[2]	**Squire Corrie (84)** (DWChapman) **5-8-4**(3) PFessey(22) (lw: spd over 3f)	½	**17**	14/1	64	21
1980[16]	**Cadeaux Cher (84)** (BWHills) **3-8-7** RHills(3) (lw: chsd ldrs: ch over 1f out: wknd qckly)	nk	**18**	20/1	63	20
4797[7]	**Ziggy's Dancer (USA) (89)** (EJAlston) **6-8-12** JFEgan(9) (lw: hld up: effrt ½-wy: sn btn)	s.h	**19**	25/1	67	24
4756[3]	**Ansellman (88)** (JBerry) **7-8-6b**(5) CLowther(1) (chsd ldrs tl rdn & btn over 1f out)	1½	**20**	10/1[3]	62	19
4677[12]	**Azizzi (98)** (CREgerton) **5-9-7** DO'Donohoe(16) (hmpd s: n.d after)	s.h	**21**	20/1	71	28
4434[6]	**Lord High Admiral (CAN) (84)** (MJHeaton-Ellis) **9-8-4v**(3) ADaly(13) (wnt bdly rt s: spd over 3f)	4	**22**	20/1	45	2
				(SP 136.1%)		**22 Rn**

60.1 secs (1.70) CSF £126.44 CT £2,188.87 TOTE £24.90: £5.70 £2.60 £4.00 £5.30 (£116.20) Trio £634.00 OWNER The Broadgate Partnership (MARLBOROUGH) BRED Declan MacPartlin

LONG HANDICAP Spender 8-5 Kira 8-2 Lord High Admiral (CAN) 8-4

3914* Rudi's Pet (IRE) got knocked over at the start and then came from last to first to win this in splendid style. (20/1)
4280* Perryston View, like the winner, got murdered leaving the stalls and then ran really well, but he was no match in the closing stages and this trip may just be too sharp these days. (7/1)
3765 Faraway Lass came from way off the pace to finish in determined style. This trip would seem short of her best. (16/1)
4756 Repertory has the speed, is in good heart and is off a useful mark, if he can be persuaded. (20/1)
4444 Crowded Avenue was given the perfect ride to beat all those around him but, by the time he made his move, the centre to far side had the race sewn up. (5/1)
4636* Canovas Heart ran well here off a mark 7lb higher than he has previously won off. (12/1)
4756 Twice as Sharp ran well again and is obviously in good heart. (16/1)
4756 Gaelic Storm keeps setting himself too stiff a task and another year will obviously improve him. (11/1)
4434 Kira, although never seriously getting into it, still put up a reasonable effort from 5lb out of the handicap. (20/1)

4888 RACING POST CONDITIONS STKS (3-Y.O+) (Class B)

3-10 (3-10) **7f** £7,843.25 (£2,837.00: £1,368.50: £567.50: £233.75) Stalls: High GOING minus 0.07 sec per fur (G)

			SP	RR	SF
4423*	**Jo Mell (105)** (TDEasterby) **4-8-12** OPeslier(2) (lw: mde all: shkn up over 2f out: r.o wl) ....—	**1**	11/8[1]	110	70
4523[2]	**Swiss Law (106)** (JHMGosden) **3-9-0** LDettori(6) (swtg: hld up: hdwy to chal 2f out: rdn & nt qckn appr fnl f) 1¾	**2**	2/1[2]	110	68
4282[15]	**Nigrasine (100)** (JLEyre) **3-8-10v** KFallon(1) (trckd ldrs: outpcd over 2f out: kpt on appr fnl f) ....½	**3**	8/1	105	63
4550[13]	**Prince of India (90)** (LordHuntingdon) **5-8-12** MJKinane(3) (hld up: hdwy 3f out: sn rdn & outpcd) 4	**4**	20/1	96	56
4344a[6]	**Cool Edge (IRE) (111)** (MHTompkins) **6-9-4** NDay(4) (cl up tl outpcd over 2f out: sn btn) 1¾	**5**	9/2[3]	98	58
			(SP 109.5%)		**5 Rn**

1m 26.2 (1.70) CSF £3.94 TOTE £2.30: £1.40 £1.40 (£1.80) OWNER C H Newton Jnr Ltd (MALTON) BRED D.B. Lamplough
WEIGHT FOR AGE 3yo-2lb
4423* Jo Mell continues his improvement. Out in front as he likes to be, he kept responding when asked and, in the end, won it nicely. (11/8)
4523 Swiss Law was sweating profusely beforehand but still travelled well in the race, only to find the winner too strong when the pressure was applied. (2/1)
2517* Nigrasine was stepping back up in trip after a generally disappointing season, and this was a better effort. (8/1)
Prince of India, after some very disappointing efforts, ran slightly more encouragingly. (20/1)
4344a Cool Edge (IRE) has been running well in Ireland this year but there was none of his spark in this performance. (9/2)

4889 RACING POST TROPHY STKS (Gp 1) (2-Y.O C & F) (Class A)

3-40 (3-41) **1m (round)** £94,096.49 (£34,993.50: £16,934.25: £7,083.75: £2,979.38: £1,337.63) Stalls: High GOING minus 0.07 sec per fur (G)

			SP	RR	SF
4836a*	**Saratoga Springs (CAN)** (APO'Brien,Ireland) **2-9-0** MJKinane(4) (lw: prom: hdwy to ld wl over 1f out: hrd rdn & hld on wl) ....—	**1**	9/2[2]	113	73
4439*	**Mudeer** (SbinSuroor) **2-9-0** LDettori(7) (lw: trckd ldrs: hdwy over 2f out: hung lft: sn ev ch: r.o towards fin)...s.h	**2**	9/2[2]	113	73
4364*	**Mutamam** (ACStewart) **2-9-0** RHills(1) (lw: hld up: hdwy whn hmpd & swtchd lft wl over 1f out: r.o).......1	**3**	13/2	111+	71
4440[6]	**Craigsteel (100)** (HRACecil) **2-9-0** KFallon(5) (cl up: led over 3f out tl wl over 1f out: one pce) 4	**4**	13/2	103	63
4526*	**Quiet Assurance (USA) (100)** (EALDunlop) **2-9-0** GCarter(2) (lw: b: hld up: gd hdwy on ins to chal 2f out: sn rdn & btn).......2½	**5**	14/1	98	58
4440[4]	**Kilimanjaro (100)** (MRStoute) **2-9-0** JReid(6) (lw: chsd ldrs: rdn over 3f out: sn outpcd) 5	**6**	7/2[1]	88	48
3895*	**Little Indian (100)** (SPCWoods) **2-9-0** OPeslier(8) (bhd: effrt over 3f out: no imp) ....¾	**7**	6/1[3]	86	46
4357a[3]	**Mountain Song (100)** (SirMarkPrescott) **2-9-0** GDuffield(3) (led tl hdd over 3f out: wknd over 2f out) 10	**8**	9/1	66	26
			(SP 116.2%)		**8 Rn**

1m 40.36 (1.96) CSF £23.20 TOTE £4.40: £2.10 £1.80 £2.50 (£11.50) OWNER Mr M Tabor & Mrs John Magnier (PILTOWN)
STEWARDS' ENQUIRY Obj. to Saratoga Springs (CAN) & Mudeer by Hills overruled.
4836a* Saratoga Springs (CAN), without the visor again, did little wrong and had the right man on top to keep him going when he looked in trouble. He is going to need to improve to take a hand in next year's Classics. (9/2)
4439* Mudeer was the pick on looks and another year will see him strengthen. Over further, he is likely to be the best of these. (9/2)
4364* Mutamam, dropped out, got squeezed out between the front pair when beginning his run. That cost him any chance and he may well have gone pretty close. (13/2)
4440 Craigsteel was always in the right place if good enough, but his lack of pace was well exposed in the last furlong and a half. (13/2)
4526* Quiet Assurance (USA) has a useful turn of foot, but his limitations were well exposed in this company, once off the bit. (14/1)
4440 Kilimanjaro was most disappointing here and he had a hard race last time which would seem to have taken its toll. (7/2)
3895* Little Indian did not impress on looks and ran poorly. (6/1)
4357a Mountain Song was never racing on an even keel and something was obviously wrong. (9/1)

4890 CHARLES SIDNEY MERCEDES BENZ DONCASTER STKS (Listed) (2-Y.O) (Class A)

4-15 (4-15) **6f** £9,227.49 (£3,422.50: £1,648.75: £681.25: £278.13: £116.88) Stalls: High GOING minus 0.07 sec per fur (G)

			SP	RR	SF
4332*	**Ikhteyaar (USA) (93)** (RWArmstrong) **2-8-4** RHills(8) (lw: hld up & bhd: nt clr run & swtchd 2f out: r.o u.p to ld ins fnl f) ....—	**1**	9/4[1]	91+	42
4634*	**Special Treat (88)** (DRLoder) **2-8-6b**ow2 KFallon(3) (hld up & bhd: swtchd & hdwy ½-wy: chal ins fnl f: r.o) ....½	**2**	10/1	92	41
4517*	**Deterrent (100)** (JHMGosden) **2-8-9** LDettori(2) (hld up & bhd: stdy hdwy ½-wy: ev ch 1f out: r.o).......s.h	**3**	4/1[2]	95	46
4296[5]	**Yorkies Boy (96)** (BAMcMahon) **2-8-9** JFortune(5) (w ldrs: led ½-wy: hrd rdn fnl f: hdd wl ins fnl f: no ex)......nk	**4**	25/1	94	45
4851*	**Toblersong (100)** (RAkehurst) **2-8-9** JWeaver(1) (a.p: effrt 2f out: kpt on: nvr able to chal).......4	**5**	10/1	83	34
4560*	**Monte Lemos (IRE) (96)** (RCharlton) **2-8-9** JReid(4) (plld hrd: disp ld to ½-wy: wknd over 1f out).......nk	**6**	7/1[3]	82	33
4755*	**Demolition Jo (76)** (PDEvans) **2-8-4v** JFEgan(6) (prom: rdn ½-wy: wknd 2f out) 4	**7**	25/1	67	18
4284*	**Hujoom (IRE) (93)** (JLDunlop) **2-8-9** MJKinane(7) (lw: in tch: effrt over 2f out: btn over 1f out).......nk	**8**	10/1	71	22
4522[2]	**Shawdon (99)** (SirMarkPrescott) **2-8-9** GDuffield(10) (lw: led to ½-wy: sn rdn: btn over 2f out) 2½	**9**	10/1	64	15
4616a[2]	**Cloudberry (96)** (BJMeehan) **2-8-7b**ow3 OPeslier(9) (chsd ldrs over 3f: sn btn) 19	**10**	14/1	12	—
			(SP 114.0%)		**10 Rn**

1m 13.85 (2.85) CSF £22.96 TOTE £3.00: £1.60 £2.40 £1.50 (£14.50) Trio £17.40 OWNER Mr Hamdan Al Maktoum (NEWMARKET) BRED Shadwell Farm Inc
4332* Ikhteyaar (USA) should have won this easily but her rider managed to find all the trouble going and, in the end, she had an unnecessarily hard race. (9/4: op 7/2)
4634* Special Treat, because of switching in good time, got the first run on the winner but, despite a gallant effort, was never quite good enough. (10/1)

4517* Deterrent went well for a long way but just got tapped for toe when it mattered and may well appreciate a bit further. (4/1: op 5/2)
4296 Yorkies Boy ran his heart out and was given some fine assistance but, basically, this is as good as he is. (25/1)
4851* Tobiersong was reappearing very quickly after his win only three days earlier and that may well have made the difference. (10/1)
4560* Monte Lemos (IRE) pulled too hard for his own good this time. (7/1)

4891 LADBROKE H'CAP (0-100) (3-Y.O+) (Class C)

4-45 (4-47) **1m 4f** £13,012.50 (£3,900.00: £1,875.00: £862.50) Stalls: Low GOING minus 0.07 sec per fur (G)

			SP	RR	SF
4558[18]	**Al Azhar (91)** (IABalding) **3-9-1** AMcGlone(18) (lw: hld up: gd hdwy on ins 2f out: led ins fnl f: r.o wl) —	1	8/1[2]	102	62
4672[6]	**Veridian (80)** (PWHarris) **4-8-11** OPeslier(5) (lw: hld up & bhd: hdwy on outside 3f out: chal ins fnl f: kpt on) 1½	2	11/1	89	56
4788[4]	**Pekay (69)** (MJohnston) **4-8-0** JFEgan(12) (hld up & bhd: hdwy over 2f out: r.o towards fin) hd	3	16/1	78	45
4151[16]	**Oops Pettie (85)** (MrsJCecil) **4-9-2** JWeaver(15) (hld up & bhd: hdwy on outside 3f out: ev ch ins fnl f: kpt on) ¾	4	12/1	93	60
4577[2]	**Zerpour (IRE) (92)** (LMCumani) **3-9-2** JReid(4) (lw: a.p: led 2f out tl ins fnl f: no ex) hd	5	11/4[1]	100	60
4788[8]	**Mcgillycuddy Reeks (IRE) (72)** (DonEnricoIncisa) **6-8-3** KimTinkler(11) (hld up & bhd: hdwy over 3f out: nt clr run over 2f out: styd on wl fnl f) 4	6	20/1	74	41
4268*	**Capilano Princess (90)** (DHaydnJones) **4-9-7** SDrowne(13) (prom: ev ch over 2f out: wknd appr fnl f) hd	7	11/1	92	59
4754[6]	**Double Alleged (USA) (85)** (MJohnston) **3-8-9** DeanMcKeown(14) (cl up: led 2½f out: sn hdd & grad wknd) s.h	8	12/1	87	47
4383[2]	**Pinchincha (FR) (84)** (DMorris) **3-8-8** NDay(9) (uns rdr & bolted bef s: rr div: effrt 4f out: n.d) 2½	9	20/1	83	43
4704[2]	**Hill Farm Blues (65)** (WMBrisbourne) **4-7-5(5)** IonaWands(10) (in tch tl rdn & wknd 4f out) 1¾	10	25/1	62	29
4295[7]	**Debutante Days (78)** (ACStewart) **5-8-4(5)** CLowther(1) (lw: rr div: effrt & nt clr run 2f out: kpt on fnl f) s.h	11	14/1	75	42
4288*	**Tessajoe (90)** (MJCamacho) **5-9-7** LCharnock(6) (b.hind: mid div: hdwy 3f out: sn chsng ldrs: btn over 1f out) hd	12	14/1	86	53
4699[6]	**Tyrolean Dream (IRE) (76)** (MHTompkins) **3-8-0** DBiggs(7) (chsd ldrs tl wknd over 2f out) nk	13	20/1	72	32
4667[4]	**Civil Liberty (65)** (GLewis) **4-7-7(3)** PFessey(8) (in tch: rdn ent st: sn lost pl) 2½	14	12/1	58	25
4639[11]	**Filmore West (83)** (DWPArbuthnot) **4-9-0** JFortune(16) (b: prom tl wknd fnl 3f) 1¼	15	50/1	74	41
4678[4]	**Greenstead (USA) (97)** (JHMGosden) **4-10-0** LDettori(2) (swtg: hld up & bhd: effrt 4f out: n.d) 5	16	10/1[3]	81	48
4279[12]	**Stakis Casinos Boy (IRE) (75)** (MJohnston) **3-7-13** NAdams(17) (led tl hdd & wknd qckly 2½f out) 3½	17	25/1	55	15
			(SP 129.8%)		**17 Rn**

2m 34.68 (4.68) CSF £81.18 CT £1,289.18 TOTE £9.90: £2.00 £2.00 £3.50 £2.10 (£30.20) Trio £225.20 OWNER Al Muallim Partnership (KINGSCLERE) BRED P. D. and Mrs Player
LONG HANDICAP Hill Farm Blues 7-8 Civil Liberty 7-9
WEIGHT FOR AGE 3yo-7lb

4148 Al Azhar, stepping up in trip, really appreciated it and won this in good style. (8/1)
4672 Veridian came from off the pace as he likes to and had his chances, only to find the winner too determined. (11/1)
4788 Pekay, stepping up in distance, again put up a useful effort and he has certainly improved of late, using his come from behind tactics. (16/1)
3722 Oops Pettie is yet to win over this trip but she does seem to get it well enough. (12/1)
4577 Zerpour (IRE) looked to have done everything right when kicking on two furlongs out but, in the end, was well tapped for speed and perhaps more use should be made of him. (11/4)
4788 Mcgillycuddy Reeks (IRE) ran another useful race over this longer trip and, without meeting trouble, would have finished a good deal closer. She is obviously not done with yet. (20/1)
4268* Capilano Princess did not appear to see this trip out. (11/1)

T/Jkpt: £255,534.10 (0.99 Tckts); £3,599.07 to Leicester 27/10/97. T/Plpt: £61.80 (1,230.2 Tckts). T/Qdpt: £11.20 (266.9 Tckts) AA

4878-NEWBURY (L-H) (Good to soft)

Saturday October 25th

WEATHER: sunny WIND: almost nil

4892 FURLONG CLUB RADLEY STKS (Listed) (2-Y.O F) (Class A)

1-30 (1-31) **7f 64y (round)** £10,495.00 (£3,160.00: £1,530.00: £715.00) Stalls: Low GOING: 0.10 sec per fur (G)

			SP	RR	SF
3774[10]	**Ffestiniog (IRE) (85)** (PFICole) **2-8-8** TQuinn(10) (led 2f: led over 3f out: edgd lft ins fnl f: rdn out) —	1	14/1	94	50
4555[6]	**Amabel (USA) (94)** (IABalding) **2-8-11** MartinDwyer(2) (a.p: rdn over 2f out: unable qckn) 1	2	11/1	95	51
4107[3]	**Leggera (IRE)** (JLDunlop) **2-8-8** TSprake(3) (lw: s.s: hrd rdn over 2f out: hdwy over 1f out: r.o wl ins fnl f) hd	3	8/1[3]	92	48
4057*	**Bristol Channel** (BWHills) **2-8-8** MHills(8) (a.p: rdn over 2f out: one pce) 4	4	100/30[1]	83	39
4604*	**Red Leggings (82)** (JWHills) **2-8-8** AClark(9) (hld up: rdn over 2f out: wknd over 1f out) 3½	5	16/1	75	31
4709[2]	**Swing Sister** (PRWebber) **2-8-8** DaneO'Neill(13) (rdn over 3f out: nvr nr to chal) 3½	6	20/1	67	23
4688*	**Court Lane (USA)** (DRLoder) **2-8-8** RCochrane(11) (rdn over 3f out: nvr nrr) 1	7	9/2[2]	65	21
4231*	**Arctic Air** (EWeymes) **2-8-8** SSanders(5) (hld up: hrd rdn over 2f out: wknd over 1f out) 1½	8	10/1	62	18
4529a[4]	**Friendly Warning (FR)** (JEBanks) **2-8-8** JQuinn(4) (hld up: rdn over 2f out: wknd over 1f out) ½	9	14/1	61	17
	Midsummer Romance (IRE) (BJMeehan) **2-8-8** MTebbutt(12) (leggy: unf: scope: a bhd) ¾	10	25/1	59	15
4640*	**Mihnah (IRE) (85)** (DMorley) **2-8-8** JCarroll(7) (led over 5f out tl over 3f out: wknd over 2f out) 1¾	11	9/2[2]	55	11
4119[9]	**Admire (89)** (MissGayKelleway) **2-8-8** SWhitworth(6) (lw: prom over 4f) 12	12	20/1	29	—
4668[7]	**Maylan (IRE)** (DMHyde) **2-8-8** RHavlin(1) (s.s: a wl bhd) 25	13	66/1	—	—
			(SP 122.1%)		**13 Rn**

1m 32.54 (4.44) CSF £141.74 TOTE £11.80: £2.30 £5.30 £2.70 (£85.00) Trio £279.30 OWNER Elite Racing Club (WHATCOMBE) BRED Theo Waddington

OFFICIAL EXPLANATION **Ffestiniog (IRE): the Stewards considered the apparent improvement in form compared with her previous run at Newmarket on 23/8/97. They interviewed the trainer and noted his explanation that her previous poor run may have been due to a ringworm infection which only appeared three days after the race.**

3774 Ffestiniog (IRE), whose poor run last time out was put down to a ringworm infection which was only discovered three days after the race, coped with this extra furlong. Regaining the advantage at halfway, she was rousted along to keep her rivals at bay. (14/1: op 8/1)
4555 Amabel (USA), always close up, was one of two who stayed on the far side early in the straight as the other runners came down the centre of the course. Rousted along over a quarter of a mile from home, she kept on for second prize but was unable to find that vital turn of foot. (11/1: 7/1-12/1)

4107 Leggera (IRE) is crying out for further for, although putting in sterling work in the last furlong and a half, the line was always going to beat her. (8/1)
4057* Bristol Channel was never far away but failed to find that vital turn of foot in the final quarter-mile. (100/30)
4604* Red Leggings chased the leaders until coming to the end of her tether over a furlong out. (16/1)
4688* Court Lane (USA) (9/2: 3/1-5/1)

4893 RECRUIT EMPLOYMENT SERVICES RATED STKS H'CAP (0-100) (3-Y.O+) (Class B)

2-00 (2-02) **1m 1f** £8,484.00 (£3,156.00: £1,528.00: £640.00: £270.00: £122.00) Stalls: GOING: 0.10 sec per fur (G)

				SP	RR	SF
4781[6]	**Prince of Denial (89)** (DWPArbuthnot) **3-8-6** SWhitworth(11) (hdwy 2f out: chsd ldr 1f out: led wl ins fnl f: drvn out)	—	**1**	4/1[1]	100	56
4554*	**Strazo (IRE) (92)** (LadyHerries) **4-8-13** RCochrane(10) (led: hrd rdn over 1f out: hdd wl ins fnl f: r.o)	½	**2**	13/2[2]	102	62
4110[3]	**Zalitzine (USA) (91)** (MRStoute) **3-8-8** MFenton(12) (lw: stdy hdwy 3f out: chsd ldr over 2f out to 1f out: unable qckn)	2	**3**	11/1	98	54
	Crazy Chief (86) (PFICole) **4-8-7** TQuinn(15) (a.p: rdn 2f out: wknd over 1f out)	5	**4**	33/1	84	44
1146[6]	**Polar Flight (89)** (MJohnston) **3-8-6** JCarroll(8) (a.p: rdn over 4f out: wknd over 2f out)	2	**5**	25/1	83	39
4294[13]	**Grief (IRE) (92)** (DRCElsworth) **4-8-10**(3) RFfrench(4) (b: rdn over 3f out: hdwy over 1f out: nvr nrr)	hd	**6**	16/1	86	46
4577*	**Mithali (95)** (BWHills) **4-9-2** MHills(7) (b.hind: lw: chsd ldr over 6f)	2	**7**	7/1[3]	85	45
4678[8]	**Another Time (92)** (SPCWoods) **5-8-13** MartinDwyer(2) (lw: rdn over 3f out: hdwy over 2f out: wknd 1f out)	1½	**8**	20/1	80	40
4689*	**Right Wing (IRE) (95)** (MajorWRHern) **3-8-12** TSprake(5) (lw: hld up: rdn over 2f out: sn wknd)	nk	**9**	13/2[2]	82	38
4550[7]	**Concer Un (91)** (SCWilliams) **5-8-12** JQuinn(13) (b: s.s: nvr nrr)	nk	**10**	11/1	78	38
2598[14]	**Welton Arsenal (90)** (KBishop) **5-8-11** PaulEddery(9) (lw: a bhd)	8	**11**	33/1	62	22
4757[3]	**Consort (86)** (MrsAJPerrett) **4-8-7** CRutter(3) (lw: mid div over 7f)	½	**12**	9/1	58	18
4554[4]	**Rapier (87)** (RHannon) **3-8-4** DaneO'Neill(6) (hld up: rdn over 3f out: wknd over 2f out)	s.h	**13**	25/1	58	14
4671[2]	**Chai-Yo (90)** (JABOld) **7-8-11** SSanders(14) (plld hrd: bhd fnl 3f)	nk	**14**	16/1	61	21
4678[5]	**Wilcuma (100)** (PJMakin) **6-9-7b** AClark(1) (hdwy over 4f out: wknd over 2f out)	5	**15**	14/1	62	22
				(SP 122.6%)	**15 Rn**	

1m 54.94 (4.64) CSF £24.25 CT £245.79 TOTE £5.00: £1.90 £2.50 £4.30 (£20.00) Trio £112.70 OWNER Mr J. S. Gutkin (COMPTON) BRED R. E. Crutchley
LONG HANDICAP Consort 8-6 Crazy Chief 8-3
WEIGHT FOR AGE 3yo-4lb
4781 Prince of Denial appreciated the extra furlong and, responding to pressure, managed to get on top in the closing stages. (4/1)
4554* Strazo (IRE) attempted to make all the running and appeared to be travelling well early in the straight. Responding well to pressure from below the distance, he was only worried out of it in the closing stages. (13/2)
4110 Zalitzine (USA) cruised into the action in the straight and was certainly close enough if good enough over a furlong out, before tapped for toe. (11/1: 8/1-12/1)
Crazy Chief, making a very belated seasonal debut, was close up until lack of a recent run took its toll approaching the final furlong. (33/1)
1146 Polar Flight, off the course for five and a half months, was a leading player until calling it a day over two furlongs out. (25/1)
3916 Grief (IRE) found the drop in distance all against him and, by the time he was staying on, it was all far too late. A return to a mile and a half is needed. (16/1)

4894 PERPETUAL ST SIMON STKS (Gp 3) (3-Y.O+) (Class A)

2-30 (2-31) **1m 4f 5y** £21,300.00 (£7,980.00: £3,840.00: £1,680.00) Stalls: Low GOING: 0.10 sec per fur (G)

				SP	RR	SF
4256a[5]	**Kaliana (IRE) (111)** (LMCumani) **3-8-4** RFfrench(6) (hdwy over 2f out: led over 1f out: qcknd: easily)	—	**1**	7/2[2]	120+	54
3902[2]	**Kutta (110)** (RWArmstrong) **5-9-0** AClark(2) (hld up: rdn over 3f out: chsd wnr ins fnl f: no imp)	3	**2**	11/2[3]	119	60
4665a[10]	**Busy Flight (116)** (BWHills) **4-9-0** MHills(5) (led: rdn 2f out: hdd over 1f out: one pce)	1¼	**3**	9/4[1]	117	58
4443[2]	**Taufan's Melody (109)** (LadyHerries) **6-9-0** RCochrane(11) (racd far side bk st: hdwy 6f out: rdn over 2f out: one pce)	hd	**4**	6/1	117	58
4658a[6]	**Pentad (USA) (111)** (RCharlton) **3-8-7** TSprake(8) (lw: hld up: rdn over 3f out: one pce)	nk	**5**	11/1	117	51
4312[2]	**Haltarra (USA) (108)** (SbinSuroor) **3-8-7** JCarroll(3) (lw: a.p: rdn over 3f out: wknd over 2f out)	5	**6**	9/1	110	44
4191a[5]	**Buddy Marvel (IRE)** (JJMcLoughlin,Ireland) **3-8-7** NGMcCullagh(7) (rdn over 3f out: sme hdwy 2f out: wknd over 1f out)	1¾	**7**	25/1	108	42
2638a[8]	**Lord Jim (IRE) (97)** (LordHuntingdon) **5-9-0v** DaneO'Neill(9) (chsd ldr 11f out to 4f out: sn wknd)	5	**8**	50/1	101	42
	Suplizi (IRE) (98) (PBowen) **6-9-0** MFenton(1) (bit bkwd: a bhd)	13	**9**	50/1	84	25
4420[7]	**Salmon Ladder (USA) (110)** (PFICole) **5-9-3** TQuinn(10) (racd far side bk st: hld up: rdn over 3f out: sn wknd)	4	**10**	12/1	82	23
				(SP 116.5%)	**10 Rn**	

2m 36.38 (6.38) CSF £20.76 TOTE £4.60: £1.80 £1.80 £1.80 (£11.10) Trio £9.10 OWNER H H Aga Khan (NEWMARKET) BRED His Highness the Aga Khan's Studs S.C.
WEIGHT FOR AGE 3yo-7lb
4256a Kaliana (IRE) put up a scintillating performance to land her first Group race, leading over a furlong out and showing a fine turn of foot to sprint away from her rivals and win in emphatic style. (7/2)
3902 Kutta hunted up the leaders. He managed to win the battle for second prize early inside the final furlong, but had absolutely no hope with the winner. (11/2)
4665a Busy Flight attempted to make all the running and appeared to be going best of all early in the straight, with the majority of the runners off the bridle. Pushed along a quarter of a mile out, he was headed below the distance and was then only scrapping for minor honours. (9/4)
4443 Taufan's Melody took closer order three-quarters of a mile from home but, try as he might, failed to find the necessary turn of foot in the last two furlongs. (6/1)
4658a Pentad (USA) chased the leaders but never looked like finding another gear in the last three furlongs. He is probably better suited by a mile and three-quarters. (11/1: 8/1-12/1)
4312 Haltarra (USA) was disappointing, for the writing was on the wall halfway up the straight. (9/1)

4895 STAFFORD KNIGHT CONDITIONS STKS (2-Y.O) (Class C)

3-00 (3-00) **1m** £4,501.75 (£1,633.00: £791.50: £332.50: £141.25) Stalls: High GOING: 0.10 sec per fur (G)

				SP	RR	SF
4237[2]	**Distant Mirage (IRE)** (PWChapple-Hyam) **2-8-8**(3) RHavlin(2) (lw: hld up: led wl over 1f out: all out)	—	**1**	4/7[1]	90	54
	Evander (IRE) (PFICole) **2-8-8** TQuinn(4) (leggy: scope: hld up: rdn 2f out: r.o wl ins fnl f)	hd	**2**	7/1[3]	87	51
4603*	**Komistar** (PWHarris) **2-9-0** AClark(3) (lw: plld hrd: led 6f out tl wl over 1f out: rdn: r.o)	hd	**3**	7/2[2]	93	57

				SP	RR	SF
	Stingray (IRE) (MJohnston) **2-8-8** MHills(1) (leggy: a bhd)	28	**4**	7/1 ^{3}	31	—
2860^{5}	**Alazan** (DMHyde) **2-8-11** SSanders(5) (led 2f: wknd over 3f out)	9	**5**	40/1	16	—
				(SP 113.3%)		**5 Rn**

1m 41.79 (4.79) CSF £5.13 TOTE £1.50: £1.10 £2.30 (£4.60) OWNER Mr R Sangster Mr R Kaster Cypress Farms (MARLBOROUGH) BRED Tullamaine Castle Stud and Partners

STEWARDS' ENQUIRY Havlin susp 3-4, 6-8, 10 & 13/11/97 (excessive use of whip).

4237 Distant Mirage (IRE) appeared to be travelling sweetly. However, pushed along over a quarter of a mile from home, the picture began to change. His jockey was determined to get him home which was great news for punters but not for the horse, who received no fewer than nineteen reminders as the combination scrambled home in front. It was absolutely no surprise that Havlin was handed a seven-day suspension. (4/7)

Evander (IRE), a tall angular colt, made a very pleasing debut. One of three in contention a quarter of a mile from home, he did not pick up immediately but certainly found his feet in the final furlong and, running on strongly, may well have succeeded with a little further to go. He should not be difficult to win with. (7/1)

4603* Komistar showed his Warwick run to be no flash in the pan and had soon pulled his way to the front. Collared early in the final quarter-mile, he refused to lie down and made sure the winner had a very hard race. (7/2: 5/2-4/1)

Stingray (IRE) (7/1: op 4/1)

4896 JOHN COALES 70TH BIRTHDAY CLAIMING STKS (3-Y.O+) (Class D)

3-30 (3-31) **1m 4f 5y** £3,756.00 (£1,128.00: £544.00: £252.00) Stalls: Low GOING: 0.10 sec per fur (G)

				SP	RR	SF
2521*	**Raise A Prince (FR) (71)** (SPCWoods) **4-9-3** SSanders(3) (hld up: led wl over 1f out: shkn up: comf)	—	**1**	6/1	87+	39
3633^{5}	**Protocol (IRE) (67)** (JWHills) **3-8-5** TQuinn(4) (lw: a.p: rdn over 2f out: ev ch wl over 1f out: unable qckn)	4	**2**	100/30 ^{2}	77	22
4673^{8}	**Story Line (75)** (DWPArbuthnot) **4-8-8**(3) RFfrench(8) (lw: led over 10f: one pce fnl f)	hd	**3**	7/2 ^{3}	76	28
4692*	**Once More for Luck (IRE) (60)** (MrsMReveley) **6-8-10** ACulhane(7) (hdwy over 3f out: hrd rdn over 1f out: sn wknd)	5	**4**	3/1 ^{1}	68	20
4794^{5}	**Midyan Blue (IRE) (60)** (JMPEustace) **7-8-10v** RCochrane(1) (nvr nr to chal)	5	**5**	7/2 ^{3}	61	13
4521^{9}	**At Liberty (IRE) (57)** (RHannon) **5-8-10** DaneO'Neill(2) (lw: a bhd)	21	**6**	8/1	33	—
519^{11}	**Funchal Way** (BRMillman) **5-8-11** TSprake(9) (chsd ldr over 6f)	d.h	**7**	25/1	13	—
	Clonoe (RIngram) **3-8-11** RPerham(5) (w'like: bkwd: bhd fnl 3f)	16	**7**	33/1	20	—
4748^{4}	***Mountaineer (IRE) (60)*** (MBell) **3-8-3** MFenton(6) (Withdrawn not under Starter's orders: broken sddle)		**W**	10/1	—	—
				(SP 133.8%)		**8 Rn**

2m 40.55 (10.55) CSF £26.32 TOTE £8.40: £2.50 £1.50 £1.70 (£13.10) Trio £50.80 OWNER Dr Frank Chao (NEWMARKET) BRED S. Niarchos

WEIGHT FOR AGE 3yo-7lb

2521* Raise A Prince (FR) put up a polished display as he made a winning debut for his new stable, despite a four-month absence, leading early in the final quarter-mile and needing only to be shaken up for a very convincing victory. (6/1)

3633 Protocol (IRE), a leading player throughout, had every chance early in the final quarter-mile, before the winner was given the office. (100/30)

3915 Story Line has been disappointing this year apart from one run at Sandown in August. She ran better here as she took the field along, until collared early in the final quarter-mile. She grimly tried to hold on but the writing was on the wall in the final furlong. (7/2)

4692* Once More for Luck (IRE) eased his way into the action early in the straight but punters knew their fate over a furlong from home. He has gained five of his six wins in either claiming or selling company. (3/1)

4794 Midyan Blue (IRE) found the drop in class doing nothing for him and he could never get into it. (7/2)

4897 DICK DAWSON NURSERY H'CAP (2-Y.O) (Class C)

4-00 (4-00) **6f 8y** £5,345.00 (£1,610.00: £780.00: £365.00) Stalls: High GOING: 0.10 sec per fur (G)

				SP	RR	SF
4709^{6}	**Beware (81)** (RWArmstrong) **2-9-1** AClark(2) (hld up: led 2f out: edgd rt ins fnl f: drvn out)	—	**1**	14/1	84	36
4670^{11}	**Who Nose (IRE) (74)** (BJMeehan) **2-8-1b**(7) GHannon(14) (lw: hdwy 2f out: ev ch whn edgd lft & hmpd ins fnl f: r.o)	½	**2**	33/1	76	28
4315^{7}	**Hill Magic (84)** (DRCElsworth) **2-9-1**(3) RFfrench(4) (lw: hdwy over 1f out: stumbled ins fnl f: nt rcvr)	1¼	**3**	20/1	82	34
4808^{10}	**Tullich Refrain (62)** (WRMuir) **2-7-10** MartinDwyer(16) (rdn over 2f out: hdwy over 1f out: r.o)	hd	**4**	25/1	60	12
4576^{10}	**Frolicking (67)** (JLDunlop) **2-8-1** TSprake(10) (nt clr run over 2f out: hmpd wl over 1f out: hdwy over 1f out: r.o)	1¾	**5**	10/1	61+	13
4630^{9}	**Jewel (IRE) (63)** (RHannon) **2-7-11** JQuinn(3) (s.s: hdwy over 1f out: nvr nrr)	6	**6**	16/1	41	—
4589^{6}	**Kennet (77)** (PDCundell) **2-8-11** RPerham(18) (lw: nvr nr to chal)	3½	**7**	14/1	45	—
4479^{6}	**Elleysanta (63)** (AGNewcombe) **2-7-11**ow1 FNorton(15) (nvr nrr)	nk	**8**	33/1	31	—
4501*	**Truth Teller (70)** (RHannon) **2-8-4** DaneO'Neill(13) (lw: nvr nrr)	nk	**9**	12/1	37	—
4425^{8}	**Poly Blue (IRE) (79)** (MissGayKelleway) **2-8-10**(3) AWhelan(11) (lw: nvr nrr)	nk	**10**	8/1 ^{2}	45	—
4545^{3}	**Mohawk (IRE) (71)** (JLDunlop) **2-8-5** PaulEddery(5) (prom over 3f)	3	**11**	10/1	29	—
4640^{5}	**Wolfhunt (79)** (PJMakin) **2-8-13** SSanders(9) (lw: prom over 4f)	2	**12**	10/1	32	—
4747*	**Robin Goodfellow (83)** (PTWalwyn) **2-9-3** JCarroll(19) (lw: s.s: hdwy over 1f out: mid div whn hmpd ins fnl f)	2½	**13**	7/2 ^{1}	29	—
4737^{6}	**Tempus Fugit (85)** (BRMillman) **2-9-5** MFenton(17) (lw: led over 3f: bhd whn hmpd ins fnl f)	¾	**14**	16/1	29	—
4767^{9}	**Fast Franc (IRE) (63)** (SCWilliams) **2-7-4**(7)ow1 DarrenWilliams(1) (mid div over 4f)	2½	**15**	20/1	—	—
4679^{4}	**Smooth Sailing (87)** (KMcAuliffe) **2-9-7b** ACulhane(12) (prom 4f: bhd whn hmpd ins fnl f)	dist	**16**	16/1	—	—
4702^{9}	**Perfect Harmony (IRE) (67)** (BJMeehan) **2-8-1** CRutter(7) (lw: a.p: led over 2f out: sn hdd: ev ch 1f out: 4th whn hmpd & b.d ins fnl f)		**B**	16/1	—	—
4814^{2}	**The Boy John (USA) (79)** (RHannon) **2-8-13** WJO'Connor(8) (lw: hld up: ev ch 1f out: 3rd whn hmpd & b.d ins fnl f)		**B**	8/1 ^{2}	81?	—
4588^{2}	**Moonstone (IRE) (74)** (APJarvis) **2-8-8** TQuinn(6) (mid div tl b.d ins fnl f)		**B**	9/1 ^{3}	72?	—
				(SP 145.5%)		**19 Rn**

1m 16.91 (5.11) CSF £420.72 CT £8,343.13 TOTE £20.50: £4.40 £3.20 £5.10 £10.50 (£112.30) Trio £1,126.40; £1,427.90 to 27/10/97 OWNER Wyck Hall Stud (NEWMARKET) BRED Wyck Hall Stud Ltd

LONG HANDICAP Fast Franc (IRE) 7-7 Elleysanta 7-8

STEWARDS' ENQUIRY Clark susp. 3-4 & 6-8/11/97 (careless riding). Hannon susp. 3-4, 6-8, 13-15/11/97 (careless riding).

4709 Beware moved to the front a quarter of a mile from home and, although he did edge slightly to his right inside the final furlong, Clark had his whip in his correct hand and the combination just held on. However, the Stewards harshly banned Clark for five days for careless riding over the melee that took place inside the final furlong. (14/1)

4143 Who Nose (IRE), who has gained both his wins in sellers, threw down a very determined challenge from below the distance but, although Hannon had his whip in his correct hand, the gelding drifted left inside the final furlong and got hampered in the melee which certainly did his cause no good. Hannon was harshly found guilty of careless riding and was banned for nine days. (33/1)
2863 Hill Magic cruised into the action below the distance and was right on the heels of the winner, which caused him to stumble as that rival drifted right inside the final furlong. Not surprisingly, he was unable to recover. (20/1)
4042 Tullich Refrain began a forward move along the inside rail below the distance and, running on, only just failed to take third prize. (25/1)
4271 Frolicking had absolutely no luck in running and she did very well to finish as close as she did. (10/1: 8/1-12/1)
1031 Jewel (IRE) stayed on in the last furlong and a half to be nearest at the line. (16/1)
4640 Wolfhunt (10/1: 8/1-12/1)
2356 Perfect Harmony (IRE) moved to the front over a quarter of a mile from home but was soon headed by the winner. Refusing to give way, she was still battling for honours when badly hampered and brought down inside the final furlong. (16/1)
4814 The Boy John (USA), making a quick reappearance, appeared to be travelling really well below the distance, but he does have trouble getting his head in front and, although still battling inside the final furlong, was probably just getting the worst of the argument when badly hampered and brought down. (8/1)

4898 LEVY BOARD NURSERY H'CAP (0-85) (2-Y.O) (Class D)

4-30 (4-37) **7f 64y (round)** £3,649.00 (£1,102.00: £536.00: £253.00) Stalls: Low GOING: 0.10 sec per fur (G)

				SP	RR	SF
4753^{7}	**Flying Bold (IRE) (63)** (WRMuir) **2-8-0** MartinDwyer(12) (rdn & hdwy 2f out: led ins fnl f: r.o wl)	—	**1**	10/1	71	37
4217^{4}	**Acebo Lyons (IRE) (71)** (APJarvis) **2-8-1**$^{(7)}$ DarrenWilliams(8) (lw: rdn over 2f out: hdwy over 1f out: hung lft 1f out: r.o one pce)	2	**2**	10/1	75	41
4368^{8}	**Bettron (84)** (RHannon) **2-9-7** DaneO'Neill(9) (plld hrd: stdy hdwy over 3f out: led over 1f out tl ins fnl f: one pce)	hd	**3**	12/1	87	53
4515^{6}	**Arctic Star (68)** (MRChannon) **2-8-5** RPerham(6) (swtg: plld hrd: hdwy over 2f out: nt clr run 1f out: r.o ins fnl f)	nk	**4**	12/1	71	37
4753*	**Mari-Ela (IRE) (61)** (JRArnold) **2-7-9**$^{(3)}$ RFfrench(1) (a.p: led 4f out tl over 1f out: one pce)	1	**5**	11/2^{1}	62	28
4767^{14}	**Respond (72)** (GLMoore) **2-8-9** AClark(14) (rdn & hdwy 2f out: one pce)	2	**6**	12/1	68	34
4569^{4}	**Bound To Please (73)** (PJMakin) **2-8-10** SSanders(11) (stdy hdwy over 3f out: wknd 2f out)	5	**7**	14/1	58	24
4502^{7}	**Priors Moor (67)** (RWArmstrong) **2-8-4** FNorton(7) (prom 4f)	s.h	**8**	16/1	52	18
4284^{9}	**Anita At Dawn (IRE) (79)** (BPalling) **2-9-2** TSprake(3) (led over 3f: wknd over 2f out)	3	**9**	15/2^{3}	58	24
4694^{4}	**Tajmil (IRE) (75)** (MajorWRHern) **2-8-12** PaulEddery(5) (a bhd)	5	**10**	11/2^{1}	43	9
4362^{10}	**Shannon's Secret (IRE) (70)** (BJMeehan) **2-8-7b**^{ow6} MTebbutt(4) (prom 5f)	1½	**11**	20/1	34	—
4814^{3}	**Fire Goddess (67)** (JSMoore) **2-8-4** MFenton(2) (prom 5f)	7	**12**	12/1	16	—
4315^{6}	**Sampower Lady (60)** (WJMusson) **2-7-11** JQuinn(13) (a bhd)	1¾	**13**	16/1	5	—
2363^{4}	**Night Vigil (IRE) (76)** (BWHills) **2-8-13** MHills(10) (styd far side st: a bhd)	5	**14**	6/1^{2}	10	—
				(SP 129.0%)	**14 Rn**	

1m 33.03 (4.93) CSF £103.84 CT £1,135.59 TOTE £11.40: £2.20 £5.10 £4.50 (£45.70) Trio £622.70 OWNER Mrs H. Levy (LAMBOURN) BRED P. Hardy
STEWARDS' ENQUIRY Obj to Acebo Lyons (IRE) by Perham overruled.
OFFICIAL EXPLANATION Flying Bold (IRE): had an abscess following his last run.
4753 Flying Bold (IRE), who caught the eye of the Newmarket Stewards last week, was subsequently found to have an abscess on his off-fore. However, he proved to be fully recovered from that here and, picking up ground a quarter of a mile from home, got on top inside the final furlong. (10/1: 8/1-12/1)
4217 Acebo Lyons (IRE) began a forward move from the back of the field below the distance but, with his jockey having his whip in his incorrect hand, the filly drifted badly left. Despite this handicap, she managed to take second prize. (10/1: 8/1-12/1)
3780 Bettron, who took a keen hold early on, showed in front below the distance but was unable to find another gear when collared inside the final furlong. (12/1: op 8/1)
4515 Arctic Star began to take closer order over a quarter of a mile from home and was done no favours by Acebo Lyons when that rival came across him a furlong out. He did run on in the closing stages and only just failed to take third prize. His jockey rather optimistically objected to the second, and it was no surprise the Stewards turned his objection down. (12/1: 8/1-14/1)
4753* Mari-Ela (IRE) went on half a mile from home but, collared below the distance, could only go up and down in the same place. (11/2)
4767 Respond began a forward move a quarter of a mile from home but was then only treading water. (12/1)
4814 Fire Goddess (12/1: op 8/1)

T/Plpt: £1,338.10 (31.48 Tckts). T/Qdpt: £57.50 (36.92 Tckts) AK

4708-LEICESTER (R-H) (Good)

Monday October 27th

WEATHER: fine & sunny WIND: slt half against

4899 SEAGRAVE APPRENTICE CLAIMING H'CAP (0-70) (3 & 4-Y.O) (Class G)

1-30 (1-31) **1m 8y** £2,207.00 (£627.00: £311.00) Stalls: High GOING: 0.00 sec per fur (G)

				SP	RR	SF
4561^{10}	**Myttons Mistake (62)** (ABailey) **4-9-2**$^{(7)}$ JBosley(3) (in tch: hdwy to ld wl over 1f out: edgd rt: sn clr)	—	**1**	11/2^{2}	84?	66
4228^{18}	**Silver Harrow (58)** (AGNewcombe) **4-9-5** RStudholme(2) (a.p: kpt on fnl f: nt pce of wnr)	8	**2**	6/1^{3}	64	46
4711*	**Scathebury (53)** (KRBurke) **4-8-9**$^{(5)}$ ANicholls(13) (lw: a.p: hdwy to chal & hung rt over 1f out: one pce)	½	**3**	9/2^{1}	58	40
4742^{6}	**Gresatre (50)** (CADwyer) **3-8-5v**$^{(3)ow4}$ RichardSmith(11) (chsd ldr: rdn & one pce fnl 2f)	1	**4**	8/1	53	28
4798^{8}	**Holloway Melody (50)** (BAMcMahon) **4-8-11** SRighton(5) (chsd ldrs: one pce fnl 2f)	2½	**5**	16/1	48	30
4607^{9}	**Windswept (IRE) (41)** (MCPipe) **4-8-2b** JDennis(8) (led: sn clr: drifted rt 3f out: hdd wl over 1f out)	3½	**6**	11/2^{2}	32	14
4214^{7}	**Skelton Countess (IRE) (41)** (RHollinshead) **4-7-11**$^{(5)}$ DHayden(12) (hdwy fnl 2f: nvr nrr)	½	**7**	20/1	31	13
4795^{4}	**Don't Worry Mike (47)** (JLSpearing) **3-8-5** PBradley(16) (nvr nr to chal)	1	**8**	14/1	35	14
4809^{8}	**Sparkling Harry (48)** (MissLCSiddall) **3-8-6** TSiddall(1) (nvr trbld ldrs)	½	**9**	20/1	35	14
4798^{11}	**Deerly (42)** (RDickin) **4-7-10**$^{(7)}$ PMundy(10) (a chsng ldrs: grad wknd fnl 2f)	3½	**10**	20/1	22	4
4404^{12}	**Prince Zizim (35)** (RCSpicer) **4-7-7**$^{(3)}$ DarrenWilliams(14) (a in rr)	2½	**11**	25/1	10	—
4606^{5}	**Lucky Archer (65)** (JMBradley) **4-9-5**$^{(7)}$ RThomas(9) (bit bkwd: bhd fr ½-wy)	1	**12**	14/1	38	20
4465^{3}	**One In The Eye (36)** (JRPoulton) **4-7-11**^{ow1} JFowle(6) (a bhd)	½	**13**	12/1	8	—
4843^{8}	**Bison Belting (40)** (JAGlover) **3-7-12**^{ow2} SCarson(15) (bhd fr ½-wy: t.o)	11	**14**	20/1	—	—

				SP	RR	SF
4757[29]	**Stellar Line (USA) (67)** (MJPolglase) **4-10-0** VictoriaAppleby(4) (a in rr)	hd	**15**	14/1	17	—
				(SP 130.8%)		**15 Rn**

1m 38.8 (3.80) CSF £34.74 CT £158.36 TOTE £7.40: £2.00 £1.80 £1.90 (£18.90) Trio £12.60 OWNER Mr Gordon Mytton (TARPORLEY) BRED R. S. A. Urquhart
LONG HANDICAP Prince Zizim 7-7 One In The Eye 7-4 Bison Belting 7-5
WEIGHT FOR AGE 3yo-3lb
Myttons Mistake clmd RHodges £7,000
4270 Myttons Mistake, winning for the first time at a mile, appreciated this step down in class, and supplied his young jockey with his initial success. (11/2)
4043 Silver Harrow, never far away, kept on willingly inside the distance, but the winner always had his measure and proved a class apart. (6/1)
4711* Scathebury has shown a tendency to edge right in the past, and his attempt to match strides with the winner in the closing stages proved way beyond him. (9/2)
4742 Gresatre appeared to find this trip just beyond him but he was in the action all the way until feeling the strain inside the final furlong. (8/1)
Holloway Melody ran extremely well for one having only her second outing of the season and, as she won at this time last year, perhaps she will have the opportunity to repeat the feat. (16/1)
3787 Windswept (IRE), brought back to a more suitable trip, soon had a healthy advantage, but she veered badly right from three furlongs out and, once headed, had little more to give. (11/2)

4900 JOHN O'GAUNT NURSERY H'CAP (0-85) (2-Y.O) (Class E)
2-00 (2-01) **7f 9y** £3,353.00 (£1,004.00: £482.00: £221.00) Stalls: High GOING: 0.00 sec per fur (G)

				SP	RR	SF
3635*	**Caversfield (75)** (RHannon) **2-9-1** DaneO'Neill(2) (lw: a.p: led 2f out: hrd rdn: hld on gamely)	—	**1**	7/1	76	40
3862[9]	**Zuryaf (IRE) (64)** (BJMeehan) **2-8-4b[1]** JFEgan(5) (hld up & bhd: hdwy u.p over 2f out: str chal wl ins fnl f: jst failed)	hd	**2**	20/1	65	29
4361*	**Pure Nobility (IRE) (81)** (BWHills) **2-9-7** MHills(8) (lw: a.p: led over 3f out to 2f out: rallied u.p fnl f)	hd	**3**	9/4[1]	82	46
4309[4]	**Former Love (USA) (73)** (PRWebber) **2-8-13** KFallon(3) (bhd: hdwy over 2f out: ev ch ins fnl f: kpt on)	hd	**4**	11/2[3]	73	37
4427[2]	**Katah (74)** (JHMGosden) **2-9-0** LDettori(10) (b.hind: hld up: hdwy & rdn over 2f out: hung rt: wknd appr fnl f)	4	**5**	3/1[2]	65	29
4808[6]	**Forty Love (IRE) (59)** (JEBanks) **2-7-8**(5) RMullen(11) (led over 3f: rdn 2f out: sn btn)	¾	**6**	14/1	49	13
4380[10]	**Dawn Treader (USA) (56)** (RHannon) **2-7-10** JLowe(6) (nvr nr to chal)	¾	**7**	33/1	44	8
4508*	**Shamwari Song (67)** (JAGlover) **2-8-7** JCarroll(4) (prom tl wknd over 1f out)	nk	**8**	12/1	54	18
3783[7]	**Chayanee's Arena (IRE) (65)** (AGNewcombe) **2-8-5** SDrowne(1) (prom over 4f: eased whn btn over 1f out)	3	**9**	11/1	45	9
3979[3]	**Cantonese (USA) (78)** (RCharlton) **2-9-4** GCarter(9) (lw: in tch tl wknd fnl 2f)	5	**10**	8/1	47	11
4514[8]	**Zillion (IRE) (63)** (JWPayne) **2-8-3** AMackay(7) (dwlt: a in rr)	¾	**11**	20/1	30	—
				(SP 129.9%)		**11 Rn**

1m 27.5 (4.90) CSF £136.63 CT £392.83 TOTE £7.00: £1.50 £6.20 £1.20 (£351.90) Trio £136.80 OWNER Mr William Kelly (MARLBOROUGH) BRED Stud-On-The-Chart
3635* Caversfield had been brought along steadily and, in following up the success of his previous outing ten weeks ago, stayed this trip well and hung on grimly right to the finish. (7/1)
Zuryaf (IRE) performed much better in his first-time blinkers and battling on gamely only just failed to wear down the winner. He gets this trip well and should be able to make his mark next year even if time runs out this term. (20/1)
4361* Pure Nobility (IRE) had to force the pace and rallied under strong pressure inside the last furlong to go down fighting. A winner on slightly easier ground at Chester, he moved rather short to post. (9/4)
4309 Former Love (USA) ran much better with less use made of her and, as she is bred to need all of this trip, she seems to be getting better as she gains experience. (11/2: 4/1-6/1)
4427 Katah,showing signs of going in her coat, did her best to mount a challenge over a furlong out but, she hung off a true line inside the distance and that quickly put paid to what chance remained. (3/1)
4068 Forty Love (IRE) shows plenty of knee action and, under strong pressure passing the quarter-mile pole, had to admit his measure taken. (14/1)

4901 E.B.F. WIDMERPOOL MAIDEN STKS (2-Y.O) (Class D)
2-30 (2-37) **7f 9y** £3,782.00 (£1,136.00: £548.00: £254.00) Stalls: High GOING: 0.00 sec per fur (G)

				SP	RR	SF
	Altibr (USA) (SbinSuroor) **2-9-0** LDettori(9) (wl grwn: a.p: led over 2f out: rn green: r.o wl)	—	**1**	8/11[1]	101++	57
	Lonesome Dude (CAN) (MRStoute) **2-9-0** JCarroll(5) (cmpt: lw: hld up in tch: hdwy 2f out: r.o fnl f: no ch w wnr)	2	**2**	7/1[3]	97+	53
4710[4]	**Mudalal (USA)** (DMorley) **2-9-0** GCarter(11) (trckd ldrs: rdn & outpcd fnl 2f)	6	**3**	6/1[2]	83	39
4706[3]	**North Ofthe Border** (MJohnston) **2-9-0** DeanMcKeown(1) (a chsng ldrs: rdn wl over 1f out: one pce)	¾	**4**	7/1[3]	81	37
	Willa Wooster (PGMurphy) **2-8-9** SDrowne(7) (w'like: unf: bkwd: s.i.s: stdy hdwy fnl 2f: nvr nrr)	6	**5**	50/1	63	19
	Play Safe (BWHills) **2-9-0** RCochrane(10) (unf: b.hind: bhd tl styd on fnl 2f)	2	**6**	16/1	63	19
4209[10]	**Cultured King (IRE)** (JGSmyth-Osbourne) **2-8-11**(3) RHavlin(2) (nvr rchd ldrs)	hd	**7**	66/1	63	19
	Alzahra (JGSmyth-Osbourne) **2-8-9** JLowe(6) (unf: chsd ldrs tl wknd over 2f out)	¾	**8**	33/1	56	12
4708[8]	**Academy (IRE)** (AndrewTurnell) **2-9-0** DaleGibson(8) (chsd ldrs over 4f)	½	**9**	50/1	60	16
4779[15]	**My Tyson (IRE) (65)** (KMahdi) **2-9-0** DaneO'Neill(12) (prom tl rdn & wknd over 2f out)	½	**10**	50/1	59	15
4694[10]	**Our Molly Malone (63)** (DMorley) **2-8-9** MFenton(14) (dwlt: a bhd: t.o)	13	**11**	33/1	24	—
4801[13]	**Cool Affair (IRE)** (ABMulholland) **2-9-0** TLucas(13) (b.hind: in tch over 4f: t.o)	1¼	**12**	100/1	26	—
4604[2]	**Spree Rose** (KOCunningham-Brown) **2-8-9** KFallon(3) (led tl hdd & wknd over 2f out: t.o)	1¼	**13**	10/1	19	—
4237[12]	***Incepta*** (BWHills) **2-9-0** MHills(4) (Withdrawn not under Starter's orders: burst out of stalls)		**W**	10/1	—	—
				(SP 135.5%)		**13 Rn**

1m 26.0 (3.40) CSF £6.16 TOTE £1.70: £1.10 £2.20 £1.70 (£4.90) Trio £11.70 OWNER Godolphin (NEWMARKET) BRED Hint At Love Partnership, C. McGaughey III, et al
Altibr (USA) a well-grown full-brother to the very sharp Keen Hunter amongst others, is more like a three-year-old already. He is a fluent mover and, despite moving very green, won this in a time that was faster than more experienced older horses in the following event. He does look decidedly useful. (8/11)
Lonesome Dude (CAN) did not look fully wound up for this racecourse debut, but he turned in a very promising performance and time may show he was taking on a much better than average rival. (7/1)
4710 Mudalal (USA) had much faster ground to contend with on this occasion and, when the winner stepped up the tempo, he quite simply had no answer. (6/1)

4706 North Ofthe Border was certainly not disgraced in this better-class event, but he too had raced on much softer ground on his debut and was tapped for speed when the pace lifted. He will win races. (7/1)
Willa Wooster,an unfurnished filly closely related to two winners, did well after finding taking time to find her stride, and with this experience behind her she should be able to make a name for herself. (50/1)
Play Safe doing all his best work inside the distance, will know more next time he appears. (16/1)

4902 WYSALL CONDITIONS STKS (3-Y.O+) (Class C)
3-00 (3-01) **7f 9y** £4,889.00 (£1,811.00: £870.50: £357.50: £143.75: £58.25) Stalls: High GOING: 0.00 sec per fur (G)

				SP	RR	SF
4666a[15]	**Meshhed (USA) (100)** (BHanbury) **3-8-11** KFallon(7) (mde all: hrd rdn over 1f out: r.o)	—	**1**	9/4[2]	99	45
2761[6]	**Groom's Gordon (FR) (94)** (JLDunlop) **3-8-10** RCochrane(4) (hld up: hdwy 2f out: rdn & r.o ins fnl f)	¾	**2**	7/1	96	42
4669[2]	**Dancing Drop (98)** (RHannon) **3-8-5** DaneO'Neill(2) (lw: a.p: rdn 2f out: styd on same pce)	½	**3**	13/8[1]	90	36
4797[10]	**Mr Bergerac (IRE) (84)** (BPalling) **6-8-9**(3) DSweeney(8) (trckd ldrs: chal over 1f out: hrd rdn: unable qckn)	s.h	**4**	16/1	95	43
4792[7]	**Mujova (IRE) (80)** (RHollinshead) **3-9-0** ACulhane(6) (hld up: effrt & rdn 2f out: nt pce to chal)	2½	**5**	25/1	93	39
3189[12]	**Fun Galore (USA) (88)** (BWHills) **3-8-10** MHills(5) (hld up: hdwy 2f out: rdn & wknd appr fnl f)	1¼	**6**	10/1	87	33
4154[5]	**Acharne (104)** (CEBrittain) **4-8-12** LDettori(1) (cl up over 4f)	5	**7**	4/1[3]	75	23
	Isit Izzy (BAMcMahon) **5-8-7** LNewton(3) (chsd ldrs: rdn 3f out: sn wknd: t.o)	12	**8**	100/1	43?	—

(SP 121.2%) **8 Rn**

1m 26.7 (4.10) CSF £18.14 TOTE £3.10: £2.00 £1.10 £1.10 (£12.00) OWNER Mr Hamdan Al Maktoum (NEWMARKET) BRED Shadwell Farm Inc
WEIGHT FOR AGE 3yo-2lb
4666a Meshhed (USA) ended her racing career with a well deserved, all the way success, and she needed to show all her better qualities to keep her head in front in an all-out battle to the line. (9/4)
2761 Groom's Gordon (FR) has worn blinkers in his last couple of races but, given a three-month break, he ran on strongly in the closing stages. Over a slightly longer trip it is possible he would have won. (7/1)
4669 Dancing Drop has only ever won at sprint distances, and though she has been narrowly beaten over longer trips of late does seem to lack that little bit extra when the whips are cracking. (13/8)
4280 Mr Bergerac (IRE) had too much use made of him over this longer trip and, when a final effort was called for, he was unable to produce the finishing speed that has won him so many races at sprint distances. (16/1)
4511 Mujova (IRE) had an impossible task trying to give weight all round, and it came as no surprise that he was unable to land a blow. (25/1)
1170 Fun Galore (USA), who has not found his true form this year, delivered a challenge below the distance which petered out as lack of a recent run took its toll. (10/1)
4154 Acharne (4/1: 3/1-9/2)

4903 SQUIRREL CONDITIONS STKS (3-Y.O+) (Class C)
3-30 (3-30) **1m 3f 183y** £4,975.60 (£1,795.60: £862.80: £354.00: £142.00) Stalls: High GOING: 0.00 sec per fur (G)

				SP	RR	SF
4704*	**Wahiba Sands (100)** (JLDunlop) **4-9-0** LDettori(2) (hld up: hdwy on bit to chal 2f out: led ins fnl f: sn clr)	—	**1**	4/6[1]	94	53
4732[4]	**Besiege (105)** (HRACecil) **3-8-7** KFallon(1) (lw: led tl hdd wl over 1f out: rallied cl home)	2	**2**	2/1[2]	91	43
4876[2]	**Secret Ballot (IRE) (73)** (KMahdi) **3-8-7** RCochrane(3) (lw: a.p: slt ld wl over 1f out: hrd rdn & hdd ins fnl f)	s.h	**3**	13/2[3]	91	43
	Edipo Re (PJHobbs) **5-9-0** MHills(5) (b: bit bkwd: hld up & bhd: hdwy over 3f out: wknd over 1f out)	4	**4**	16/1	86	45
3014[8]	**Primero (IRE)** (ABarrow) **3-8-7** SDrowne(4) (bit bkwd: prom tl rdn & wknd over 2f out: t.o)	dist	**5**	100/1	—	—

(SP 113.5%) **5 Rn**

2m 35.1 (6.60) CSF £2.16 TOTE £1.60: £1.40 £1.40 (£1.50) OWNER Lord Swaythling (ARUNDEL) BRED Fares Stables Ltd
WEIGHT FOR AGE 3yo-7lb
4704* Wahiba Sands, at his best at this time of year, could be named the winner from some way out, but his jockey did not let him hit the front too soon and in the end he lengthened up to win cleverly. (4/6)
4732 Besiege has certainly not produced the form he showed in the autumn of last year and, though he has been highly tried, this was a real chance for him to show what he is made of. Although he did stay on at the finish, he should have been able to pick these rivals up. (2/1)
4876 Secret Ballot (IRE) has been kept busy but he is in form, and the faster ground as much as anything else could have prevented him from winning this. (13/2: op 10/1)
Edipo Re, a class individual who may possibly need further, was making a belated seasonal debut. He was very much in need of the run and under the circumstances probably did not shape badly. (16/1)

4904 E.B.F. FLECKNEY MAIDEN STKS (2-Y.O F) (Class D)
4-00 (4-02) **5f 218y** £3,938.00 (£1,184.00: £572.00: £266.00) Stalls: High GOING: 0.00 sec per fur (G)

				SP	RR	SF
4522[9]	**Solo Spirit (80)** (JRJenkins) **2-8-11** JFEgan(18) (a w ldrs: led over 1f out: rdn out)	—	**1**	20/1	81	38
4750[6]	**Positive Air (74)** (BAMcMahon) **2-8-11** LNewton(15) (a.p: led ½-wy tl over 1f out: one pce fnl f)	2	**2**	16/1	76	33
3114[6]	**Empirical (USA)** (JHMGosden) **2-8-11** LDettori(22) (lw: a chsng ldrs: rdn 2f out: kpt on towards fin)	hd	**3**	5/2[1]	75	32
4779[8]	**Fairy Rock (IRE)** (BWHills) **2-8-11** JCarroll(4) (hld up: hdwy ½-wy: r.o wl fnl f)	¾	**4**	8/1	73	30
	De-Wolf (PJMakin) **2-8-8**(3) DSweeney(5) (leggy: hld up: stdy hdwy over 2f out: swtchd appr fnl f: r.o)	1¼	**5**	33/1	70	27
4418[3]	**Lindesberg** (MJohnston) **2-8-11** DeanMcKeown(8) (a.p: rdn over 1f out: one pce)	1¼	**6**	8/1	67	24
4012[7]	**Treble Term** (PJMakin) **2-8-11** JFortune(3) (trckd ldrs: ev ch over 2f out: one pce appr fnl f)	¾	**7**	10/1	65	22
4066[15]	**Clouds of Glory** (RCharlton) **2-8-11** GCarter(16) (prom: rdn over 1f out: grad wknd)	nk	**8**	33/1	64	21
4818[9]	**Tough Nell (IRE)** (BobJones) **2-8-11** DBiggs(12) (chsd ldrs tl wknd over 1f out)	hd	**9**	50/1	64	21
3574[6]	**Gandoura (USA)** (JHMGosden) **2-8-11** DaleGibson(10) (mid div: shkn up over 2f out: no imp)	½	**10**	12/1	62	19
4556[8]	**Sky Red** (MBell) **2-8-11** MFenton(21) (chsd ldrs far side over 4f)	¾	**11**	20/1	60	17
4769[6]	**Hit The Spot (IRE)** (WJHaggas) **2-8-11** FLynch(17) (b: bkwd: nvr bttr than mid div)	¾	**12**	25/1	58	15
	Citadel (JGSmyth-Osbourne) **2-8-11** JLowe(14) (lt-f: bkwd: dwlt: a in rr)	s.h	**13**	33/1	58	15
	Margone (USA) (GWragg) **2-8-11** ACulhane(6) (neat: bit bkwd: nvr nr to chal)	s.h	**14**	14/1	58	15
4556[5]	**Sixpence** (GWragg) **2-8-11** MHills(7) (nvr trbld ldrs)	½	**15**	5/1[3]	57	14
4597[3]	**Light Step (USA)** (HRACecil) **2-8-11** KFallon(13) (led to ½-wy: sn rdn along & wknd)	4	**16**	3/1[2]	46	3
4779[14]	**Hetra Heights (USA)** (WJMusson) **2-8-11** RCochrane(9) (s.s: a bhd)	nk	**17**	33/1	45	2
4227[8]	**Jolly Harbour** (WJHaggas) **2-8-6**(5) JoHunnam(2) (s.s: a bhd)	¾	**18**	33/1	43	—
	Just Deserts (PJMakin) **2-8-8**(3) RHavlin(11) (leggy: prom 4f)	hd	**19**	33/1	43	—
	Needwood Spitfire (BCMorgan) **2-8-11** SDrowne(20) (lt-f: unf: a bhd & outpcd)	2½	**20**	50/1	36	—
	Scotland Bay (RHannon) **2-8-11** DaneO'Neill(19) (w'like: bit bkwd: swvd lft s: effrt ½-wy: wnt lft: sn lost tch)	½	**21**	25/1	35	—

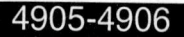

Efodos (GWragg) **2-8-6**(5) GMilligan(1) (unf: bkwd: sn drvn along: a bhd: t.o)..12 **22** 20/1 3 —

(SP 165.3%) **22 Rn**

1m 14.0 (4.00) CSF £324.46 TOTE £26.00: £7.40 £6.10 £2.40 (£266.10) Trio £333.70; £14.10 to Redcar 28/10/97 OWNER Mrs I. Hampson (ROYSTON) BRED Miss E. Colver

4103 Solo Spirit has been knocking at the door so this success should not have been such a surprise as her price suggests, and she had things sewn up inside the last furlong. (20/1)

4750 Positive Air has had more experience than all her rivals put together but she is finding it hard to get off the mark, although it certainly is not for the want of trying. (16/1)

3114 Empirical (USA) found the three-month break she had just enjoyed costing her dearly inside the final furlong, and she may now have to wait until next year to make her mark. (5/2)

Fairy Rock (IRE) still gave the impression that the run was needed but she was really into her stride in the latter stages and, if seen out again, could make it third time lucky. (8/1)

De-Wolf,a lightly-made half-sister to three winners, showed plenty of promise on this debut and should have little trouble in winning a race or two. (33/1)

4418 Lindesberg, fighting for the lead, was unable to step up the pace when shaken up approaching the final furlong and she may have done too much too soon. (8/1)

Treble Term had a chance as good as any entering the last quarter-mile but the quickening tempo proved just too strong and she was unable to hold her pitch. She has run well on both outings to date and she will win races. (10/1: op 16/1)

4556 Sixpence (5/1: op 8/1)

4905 THRUSSINGTON H'CAP (0-70) (3-Y.O+) (Class E)

4-30 (4-32) **5f 218y** £3,665.00 (£1,100.00: £530.00: £245.00) Stalls: High GOING: 0.00 sec per fur (G)

				SP	RR	SF
4375^{9}	**Midnight Shift (IRE) (60)** (RGuest) **3-9-3** KFallon(4) (chsd ldrs: outpcd 2f out: rdn to ld wl ins fnl f)	—	**1**	10/1	69	54
4820^{6}	**Broadstairs Beauty (IRE) (66)** (DShaw) **7-9-7v**(3) CTeague(15) (b: chsd ldrs: outpcd 2f out: rdn & r.o wl towards fin)	¾	**2**	8/1	73	59
4580^{16}	**Bataleur (49)** (GWoodward) **4-8-7b** GCarter(9) (hdwy over 2f out: rdn to ld ins fnl f: sn hdd: r.o)	s.h	**3**	33/1	56	42
4580^{17}	**Superbit (57)** (BAMcMahon) **5-9-1** LNewton(8) (led over 3f: led over 1f out tl wl ins fnl f)	¾	**4**	16/1	62	48
4248*	**Gay Breeze (49)** (PSFelgate) **4-8-0**(7) JFowle(2) (w ldrs: led over 2f out tl over 1f out: outpcd ins fnl f)	1½	**5**	13/2 2	50	36
4805^{6}	**Corniche Quest (IRE) (63)** (MRChannon) **4-9-0**(7) AEddery(14) (hdwy appr fnl f: nrst fin)	hd	**6**	10/1	64	50
4791^{2}	**Royal Dome (IRE) (71)** (MartynWane) **5-10-1** JCarroll(22) (chsd ldrs: effrt 2f out: rdn & one pce ins fnl f)	nk	**7**	7/1 3	71	57
4385^{4}	**General Sir Peter (IRE) (52)** (NACallaghan) **5-8-10b** AmandaSanders(5) (bhd: hdwy 2f out: nt rch ldrs)	nk	**8**	13/2 2	51	37
4773^{9}	**Depreciate (63)** (CJames) **4-9-7** TLucas(1) (hdwy ½-wy: rdn & wknd over 1f out)	½	**9**	20/1	61	47
4820^{3}	**Roffey Spinney (IRE) (69)** (RHannon) **3-9-12** DaneO'Neill(11) (prom tl wknd wl over 1f out)	½	**10**	10/1	65	50
4518^{3}	**Double March (50)** (KTIvory) **4-8-3**(5) GFaulkner(10) (b: b.hind: trckd ldrs: rdn & btn over 1f out)	s.h	**11**	10/1	46	32
4842^{8}	**U-No-Harry (IRE) (53)** (RHollinshead) **4-8-11** FLynch(16) (bhd tl sme hdwy fnl 2f)	2½	**12**	14/1	43	29
4695^{13}	**Al Reet (IRE) (50)** (SRBowring) **6-8-8** DaleGibson(20) (sn drvn along: a in rr)	s.h	**13**	20/1	39	25
4321^{13}	**Tinker Osmaston (62)** (RJHodges) **6-9-6** SDrowne(6) (effrt ½-wy: styd on: nt rch ldrs)	s.h	**14**	16/1	51	37
4482^{9}	**Ramsey Hope (58)** (CWFairhurst) **4-9-2v** NKennedy(12) (w ldrs: effrt over 1f out: sn rdn & wknd)	1¼	**15**	25/1	44	30
4168^{5}	**Newlands Corner (57)** (JAkehurst) **4-9-1b** DBiggs(17) (a bhd & outpcd)	2½	**16**	12/1	36	22
4580^{3}	**Rockcracker (IRE) (53)** (GGMargarson) **5-8-8b**(3) MHenry(7) (drvn along ½-wy: a in rr)	nk	**17**	10/1	31	17
4580^{10}	**Bayin (USA) (58)** (MDIUsher) **8-9-2** RStreet(3) (effrt ½-wy: no imp)	2	**18**	5/1 1	31	17
4561^{21}	**Watch The Fire (62)** (JEBanks) **4-9-6** RCochrane(13) (a bhd & outpcd)	½	**19**	14/1	34	20
2416^{5}	**Statoyork (59)** (DShaw) **4-9-3** JFanning(19) (hld up: stdy hdwy ½-wy: wknd wl over 1f out: t.o)	13	**20**	16/1	—	—
3801^{14}	**Sailormaite (65)** (SRBowring) **6-9-9** SWebster(18) (virtually ref to r: a t.o)	4	**21**	20/1	—	—
904^{8}	**Bonyalua Mill (52)** (AStreeter) **3-8-6**(3) RHavlin(21) (outpcd & lost tch fr ½-wy: t.o)	2½	**22**	40/1	—	—

(SP 174.6%) **22 Rn**

1m 13.3 (3.30) CSF £102.05 CT £2,542.78 TOTE £16.90: £5.10 £3.20 £2.60 £4.00 (£158.90) Trio £3,088.10; £3,523.06 to Redcar 28/10/97 OWNER Mr C. J. Mills (NEWMARKET) BRED A. Steigenberger

WEIGHT FOR AGE 3yo-1lb

IN-FOCUS: **Depreciate was the last runner sent out by trainer Charlie James, who has handed over the licence to his son Ed.**

4059 Midnight Shift (IRE), brought back to sprinting, looked to have shot her bolt when losing her prominent position two furlongs out but, responding to a forceful ride, came back strongly and, leading inside the final hundred yards, had gained enough lead to hold on. (10/1)

4820 Broadstairs Beauty (IRE) has been out of sorts for the past couple of years and he was in trouble when tapped for toe two furlongs out but, galvanised into action, he finished with a flourish. He still has the ability to win races. (8/1)

Bataleur, lightly-raced this year, showed his first glimpse of form, and as he handles the soft maybe the All-Weather could suit him. (33/1)

4333 Superbit made the majority of the running and was only shaken off inside the final furlong. It is possible he will be seen out again and unless the company is hot he will be worth supporting. (16/1)

4248* Gay Breeze went with the pace and had every chance until having to admit his measure taken inside the last two hundred yards. (13/2)

4805 Corniche Quest (IRE) continues to run well, but if it is possible she does need things to go her own way and her fast-finishing effort here was always going to be too late. (10/1)

4791 Royal Dome (IRE) does all his winning over five furlongs, but he ran well here under top weight, only getting tapped for speed inside the final furlong. (7/1)

4385 General Sir Peter (IRE) has plenty of speed for he has already won five times at the minimum trip, but he was never able to get competitive on this occasion and is capable of better. (13/2)

4580 Bayin (USA) (5/1: op 8/1)

T/Jkpt: Not won; £8,092.01 to Leicester 28/10/97. T/Plpt: £11.40 (1,933.55 Tckts). T/Qdpt: £4.20 (255 Tckts) IM

4542-LINGFIELD (L-H) (Turf Good, AWT Standard)

Monday October 27th

WEATHER: fine WIND: almost nil

4906 GRAHAM POTTER ASSOCIATES H'CAP (0-70) (3-Y.O) (Class E)

12-50 (12-51) **1m 2f (Equitrack)** £2,966.25 (£885.00: £422.50: £191.25) Stalls: Low GOING minus 0.50 sec per fur (FST)

				SP	RR	SF
4481^{4}	**Castles Burning (USA) (65)** (CACyzer) **3-9-3** JWeaver(2) (hdwy 4f out: rdn over 2f out: led wl ins fnl f: drvn out)	—	**1**	7/1	73	42

4505^{2}	**Kafil (USA) (65)** (GLMoore) **3-9-3** AClark(3) (a.p: rdn 2f out: ev ch ins fnl f: r.o wl)	s.h	**2**	$9/4^{1}$	73	42
4810^{2}	**Avanti Blue (44)** (KMcAuliffe) **3-7-10** MartinDwyer(5) (w ldr: led 6f out tl wl ins fnl f: unable qckn)	¾	**3**	$9/2^{2}$	51	20
4705^{7}	**Isabella Gonzaga (58)** (JLDunlop) **3-8-10** TQuinn(11) (stumbled s: rdn over 3f out: hdwy over 2f out: r.o one pce)	3	**4**	7/1	60	29
4485^{3}	**Soden (IRE) (69)** (TGMills) **3-9-7** TWilliams(7) (a.p: chsd ldr 5f out tl over 1f out: sn wknd)	hd	**5**	$13/2^{3}$	71	40
4323^{17}	**Dancing Feather (60)** (BWHills) **3-8-12** RHills(8) (rdn over 2f out: hdwy over 1f out: one pce)	8	**6**	12/1	49	18
4795^{11}	**Passion (50)** (TGMills) **3-7-9**(7) LisaHackett(4) (nvr nr to chal)	1½	**7**	20/1	37	6
4243^{17}	**Shaded (IRE) (53)** (SDow) **3-7-12e**(7) PDoe(6) (b: b.hind: lw: prom 6f)	5	**8**	25/1	32	1
4858^{6}	**Lochlass (IRE) (53)** (SPCWoods) **3-8-5b** NDay(10) (bhd fnl 4f)	2½	**9**	14/1	28	—
4429^{4}	**Erinrinca (IRE) (45)** (JEBanks) **3-7-11v¹** JQuinn(9) (lw: hld up: rdn over 4f out: sn wknd)	8	**10**	25/1	7	—
4465^{7}	**Trevor Mitchell (44)** (JJBridger) **3-7-10** NAdams(1) (led 4f)	12	**11**	50/1	—	—
				(SP 116.1%)	**11 Rn**	

2m 6.67 (2.37) CSF £19.81 CT £72.81 TOTE £6.50: £1.80 £1.60 £1.60 (£10.90) Trio £10.10 OWNER Mr R. M. Cyzer (HORSHAM) BRED Robert S. West Jr.

LONG HANDICAP Avanti Blue 7-8 Trevor Mitchell 6-7

4481 Castles Burning (USA), who failed to stay one mile seven furlongs last time out, is well suited by this surface and coped with the big drop in distance, managing to get up in the closing stages. (7/1)

4505 Kafil (USA), making his All-Weather debut, had no problems with the surface or the longer trip and had every chance inside the final furlong, and only just lost out in a very tight finish. (9/4)

4810 Avanti Blue seems better suited by the All-Weather and this may well be his optimum trip. In front three-quarters of a mile from home, he grimly tried to fend off his rivals and was only worried out of it in the closing stages. (9/2)

4705 Isabella Gonzaga began a forward move over a quarter of a mile from home but she looked an awkward ride in the straight and never threatened to get to the principals in time. (7/1: op 4/1)

4485 Soden (IRE), successful over this course and distance in August, moved into second place at halfway but, collared for that position approaching the final furlong, soon had bellows to mend. (13/2)

3903 Dancing Feather picked up early in the short straight but could then make no further impression. (12/1: op 6/1)

4415 Lochlass (IRE) (14/1: op 8/1)

4907 E.B.F. MONICA BARNES BIRTHDAY MAIDEN STKS (I) (2-Y.O F) (Class D)

1-20 (1-21) **7f** £3,143.25 (£936.00: £445.50: £200.25) Stalls: High GOING: 0.16 sec per fur (G)

				SP	RR	SF
	Housekeeper (IRE) (RCharlton) **2-8-11** TSprake(5) (leggy: dwlt: stdy hdwy over 2f out: led over 1f out: qcknd ins fnl f: comf)	—	**1**	8/1	85+	37
4217^{5}	**Red Rabbit** (BWHills) **2-8-11** RHills(1) (plld hrd: hld up: rdn over 1f out: chsd wnr ins fnl f: unable qckn)	3½	**2**	$3/1^{2}$	77	29
	Confidante (USA) (MRStoute) **2-8-11** WRyan(10) (b.nr hind: unf: scope: dwlt: stdy hdwy over 1f out: r.o wl ins fnl f: bttr for r)	nk	**3**	$3/1^{2}$	76+	28
	Sharera (IRE) (LMCumani) **2-8-11** JWeaver(9) (neat: led over 5f: one pce)	1½	**4**	$5/1^{3}$	73	25
3187^{10}	**Magic Spring (IRE)** (KMcAuliffe) **2-8-11** GHind(6) (rdn over 2f out: nvr nr to chal)	2½	**5**	20/1	67	19
4706^{2}	**Chocolate (IRE) (84)** (JLDunlop) **2-8-11b** TQuinn(3) (a.p: chsd ldr over 2f out tl over 1f out: sn wknd)	1¼	**6**	$9/4^{1}$	64	16
3574^{13}	**Azulino (IRE)** (JWHills) **2-8-11** JReid(2) (bit bkwd: bhd fnl 2f)	4	**7**	20/1	55	7
	Mothers Help (HCandy) **2-8-11** NAdams(7) (leggy: unf: reard s: a bhd)	1	**8**	33/1	53	5
4694^{11}	**Swingtime** (AGFoster) **2-8-11** RPerham(4) (chsd ldr over 4f)	2½	**9**	33/1	47	—
4604^{14}	**Cool Waters** (JRArnold) **2-8-11** AClark(8) (b.hind: prom over 4f)	13	**10**	25/1	18	—
				(SP 127.8%)	**10 Rn**	

1m 27.09 (5.89) CSF £30.37 TOTE £10.90: £2.20 £1.70 £1.30 (£15.40) Trio £20.70 OWNER Anglia Bloodstock Syndicate (BECKHAMPTON) BRED Michael Morrin

Housekeeper (IRE), a tall filly who looked very woolly in her coat, swept into the lead over a furlong out and quickened away inside the final furlong for a very polished display. (8/1: 5/1-10/1)

4217 Red Rabbit once again pulled too hard. Nevertheless, she managed to take second place inside the final furlong, if having no hope with the winner. Once she learns to settle, she can find a race. (3/1: 2/1-7/2)

Confidante (USA), quite a nice-looking filly who still needs time to develop, was the subject of encouraging home reports and there was plenty to like about this debut. Given considerate handling, she crept closer below the distance and, grasping what was required inside the final furlong, ran on in really pleasing style, only just failing to take second prize. She will not be difficult to win with. (3/1: 7/4-7/2)

Sharera (IRE), by Derby winner Kahyasi out of a half-sister to Shahrastani, is not very big. Taking the field along, she was collared below the distance and then tapped for toe. She will be better suited by middle distances next year. (5/1)

Magic Spring (IRE), off the course since the beginning of August, never threatened to get into it. (20/1)

4706 Chocolate (IRE) moved into second place over a quarter of a mile from home but she was collared for that position below the distance and then melted away. She has had plenty of chances. (9/4)

4908 E.B.F. TAUBER MAIDEN STKS (I) (2-Y.O C & G) (Class D)

1-50 (1-52) **7f** £3,143.25 (£936.00: £445.50: £200.25) Stalls: High GOING: 0.16 sec per fur (G)

				SP	RR	SF
3489^{7}	**Derryquin** (RCharlton) **2-8-11** TSprake(10) (swtg: s.s: hdwy over 2f out: rdn over 1f out: led wl ins fnl f: r.o wl)	—	**1**	12/1	81	41
4758^{14}	**Free Option (IRE) (82)** (BHanbury) **2-8-11** WRyan(2) (lw: stdy hdwy 3f out: led over 1f out: hrd rdn: hdd wl ins fnl f: r.o)	nk	**2**	$8/1^{3}$	80	40
4581^{4}	**Chrysolite (IRE)** (BWHills) **2-8-11** RHills(4) (chsd ldr over 4f: rdn: unable qckn)	7	**3**	$6/1^{2}$	64	24
1932^{4}	**Ellway Prince** (IABalding) **2-8-11** MartinDwyer(6) (b.off hind: bit bkwd: rdn over 2f out: hdwy over 1f out: one pce)	1¾	**4**	$6/1^{2}$	60	20
4708^{2}	**Celtic Pageant (91)** (RAkehurst) **2-8-11** TQuinn(8) (led tl hung lft & hdd over 1f out: sn wknd)	2	**5**	$4/6^{1}$	56	16
4446^{6}	**Hopeful Star (IRE)** (MissGayKelleway) **2-8-8**(3) AWhelan(7) (b.hind: rdn 3f out: nvr nr to chal)	3	**6**	20/1	49	9
	Mister Tricky (PMitchell) **2-8-11** NDay(1) (b: w'like: s.s: wl bhd over 5f: nvr nrr)	1¼	**7**	50/1	46	6
4857^{U}	**Zada** (GLMoore) **2-8-11** AClark(3) (bit bkwd: bhd fnl 2f)	2	**8**	33/1	42	2
2948^{8}	**Hickory (IRE)** (MJHaynes) **2-8-8**(3) RFfrench(9) (prom over 3f)	3	**9**	25/1	35	—
4735^{11}	**Paddy Deux** (VSoane) **2-8-11** JReid(5) (prom over 3f)	9	**10**	33/1	14	—
				(SP 123.8%)	**10 Rn**	

1m 26.7 (5.50) CSF £92.84 TOTE £13.20: £3.50 £1.90 £1.40 (£45.10) Trio £32.60 OWNER Lady Bland (BECKHAMPTON) BRED Lady Bland

OFFICIAL EXPLANATION **Celtic Pageant: the rider reported that the colt hung left.**

Derryquin, who has been off the course since his debut in August with sore shins, was a different proposition this time and, moving into contention over a quarter of a mile from home, eventually got on top in the closing stages. (12/1: 8/1-14/1)

4384 Free Option (IRE) had less use made of him here and ran better as a result. Creeping closer from halfway, he gained the initiative from below the distance but, despite doing little wrong, was worried out of it in the last fifty yards. (8/1)
4581 Chrysolite (IRE), in second place until over two furlongs from home, was then only scrapping for minor honours. (6/1)
1932 Ellway Prince looked in need of this first run in four and a half months and drifted ominously in the betting. He did make a forward move below the distance but was then making no further impression. (6/1: op 9/4)
4708 Celtic Pageant is proving expensive to follow. Once again setting the pace, he did not look an easy ride as he hung left and was headed below the distance and tamely dropped away. He may be worth trying to hold up. (4/6: 4/5-evens)

4909 E.B.F. MONICA BARNES BIRTHDAY MAIDEN STKS (II) (2-Y.O F) (Class D)
2-20 (2-21) **7f** £3,114.00 (£927.00: £441.00: £198.00) Stalls: High GOING: 0.16 sec per fur (G)

				SP	RR	SF
	Madjamila (IRE) (LMCumani) **2-8-8**(3) RFfrench(8) (leggy: unf: hld up: shkn up to ld over 1f out: comf)	—	**1**	9/2 2	84+	40
4701^{3}	**Pursuit Venture** (SPCWoods) **2-8-11** NDay(3) (lw: a.p: led 2f out tl over 1f out: unable qckn)	3½	**2**	5/2 1	76	32
4067^{10}	**Hever Golf Passion (IRE)** (TJNaughton) **2-8-11** AMcGlone(9) (rdn & hdwy over 1f out: r.o ins fnl f)	2	**3**	20/1	71	27
4132^{7}	**Shantung (IRE)** (KMcAuliffe) **2-8-11** MartinDwyer(1) (a.p: rdn over 2f out: one pce)	nk	**4**	25/1	71	27
4701^{6}	**Sure Quest** (DWPArbuthnot) **2-8-11** SWhitworth(2) (rdn & swtchd lft 2f out: nvr nr to chal)	3½	**5**	12/1	63	19
4582^{8}	**Announcing Peace** (CADwyer) **2-8-11b¹** AGarth(6) (rdn 3f out: no hdwy fnl 2f)	3	**6**	33/1	56	12
4694^{6}	**Caledonian Express** (JLDunlop) **2-8-11** TSprake(7) (a.p: ev ch 2f out: wknd over 1f out)	s.h	**7**	6/1 3	56	12
	Secret Bourne (USA) (BWHills) **2-8-11** RHills(5) (w'like: bit bkwd: a.p: led over 3f out to 2f out: wknd over 1f out)	1½	**8**	6/1 3	52	8
4604^{6}	**Grosvenor Spirit (IRE)** (PWChapple-Hyam) **2-8-11** JReid(10) (led over 3f: wknd over 2f out)	2	**9**	6/1 3	48	4
	Peridot (JHMGosden) **2-8-11** GHind(4) (b.hind: w'like: s.s: a bhd)	1¼	**10**	7/1	45	1

(SP 121.4%) **10 Rn**

1m 26.81 (5.61) CSF £15.03 TOTE £4.30: £1.60 £1.40 £2.30 (£14.80) Trio £63.70 OWNER H H Aga Khan (NEWMARKET) BRED His Highness the Aga Khan's Studs S.C.
Madjamila (IRE), whose dam is from the family of Slip Anchor, has been too backward to run before now but certainly knew what was required of her and made an impressive debut, leading over a furlong out and forging clear for a very decisive victory. A tall, weak-looking filly, she will be far more the finished article next year. (9/2)
4701 Pursuit Venture poked a nostril in front a quarter of a mile from home but, headed approaching the final furlong, found the winner had far too many guns for her. (5/2)
Hever Golf Passion (IRE) showed the benefit of her initial run here and, staying on in the last furlong and a half, just managed to snatch third prize. (20/1)
Shantung (IRE) ran much better here and was never far away, if failing to quicken in the last two furlongs. (25/1)
4701 Sure Quest, who looked woolly in the paddock, never threatened to get into it. (12/1)
4604 Grosvenor Spirit (IRE) (6/1: 4/1-7/1)
Peridot (7/1: op 4/1)

4910 E.B.F. TAUBER MAIDEN STKS (II) (2-Y.O C & G) (Class D)
2-50 (2-51) **7f** £3,143.25 (£936.00: £445.50: £200.25) Stalls: High GOING: 0.16 sec per fur (G)

				SP	RR	SF
4111^{2}	**Khalas (90)** (BWHills) **2-8-11** RHills(3) (a.p: led on bit over 1f out: shkn up: comf)	—	**1**	4/11 1	78+	12
2534^{9}	**Storm Cry (USA)** (MajorDNChappell) **2-8-11** AMcGlone(6) (stdy hdwy over 1f out: unable qckn ins fnl f)	1¼	**2**	14/1	75	9
	King Slayer (BSmart) **2-8-11** JStack(9) (leggy: unf: a.p: nt clr run on ins wl over 1f out: rdn: one pce)	3	**3**	20/1	68	2
4758^{19}	**Franklin Lakes** (CAHorgan) **2-8-11** PaulEddery(1) (s.s: rdn over 2f out: hdwy over 1f out: wknd ins fnl f)	1¼	**4**	25/1	65	—
	Divvinayshan (IRE) (RWArmstrong) **2-8-11** FNorton(7) (leggy: a.p: rdn over 2f out: wknd over 1f out)	3	**5**	9/2 2	59	—
	Rising Mane (DRCElsworth) **2-8-11** TSprake(8) (w'like: s.s: a bhd)	7	**6**	25/1	43	—
4603^{13}	**Omar's Odyssey (IRE)** (PMitchell) **2-8-11** AClark(2) (lw: led over 5f)	1	**7**	33/1	40	—
	Prince of Salsa (KMcAuliffe) **2-8-11** GHind(4) (unf: w ldr over 5f)	2½	**8**	33/1	35	—
	Red Shift (IRE) (RHannon) **2-8-11** JReid(5) (str: bit bkwd: s.s: a bhd: lame)	23	**9**	10/1 3	—	—

(SP 125.6%) **9 Rn**

1m 29.17 (7.97) CSF £7.16 TOTE £1.40: £1.10 £3.20 £1.20 (£10.50) Trio £22.10 OWNER Mr Hamdan Al Maktoum (LAMBOURN) BRED Shadwell Estate Company Limited
OFFICIAL EXPLANATION **Red Shift (IRE): the veterinary officer reported that the horse was lame on its near-fore.**
IN-FOCUS: **This contest was run at a crawl and was over two seconds slower than the other three races run at this distance.**
4111 Khalas, who lost out in a photo in his last two outings, made no mistake here, cruising into the lead on the bridle approaching the final furlong and needing only to be woken up to win with plenty to spare. (4/11)
Storm Cry (USA) cruised into the action appearing to be travelling really well below the distance, but found the winner was only toying with him inside the final furlong. (14/1: op 8/1)
King Slayer, a tall, weak-looking colt, was never far away and, although he did not have a great deal of room along the inside rail early in the final quarter-mile, could only plod on at one pace when daylight appeared. (20/1)
Franklin Lakes made a forward move on the outside of the field below the distance but had shot his bolt inside the final furlong. (25/1)
Divvinayshan (IRE), a tall, angular colt who is a half-brother to several winners, was close up until feeling the pinch below the distance. (9/2)

4911 BURR CONDITIONS STKS (2-Y.O) (Class C)
3-20 (3-21) **5f** £4,653.36 (£1,722.24: £826.62: £338.10: £134.55: £53.13) Stalls: High GOING: 0.16 sec per fur (G)

				SP	RR	SF
4675^{12}	**Legs Be Frendly (IRE) (86)** (KMcAuliffe) **2-8-11b¹** JReid(1) (lw: hld up: rdn over 1f out: led ins fnl f: r.o wl)	—	**1**	10/1	89	51
4772^{*}	**Rare Indigo (81)** (JBerry) **2-8-7**(3) PFessey(6) (led: rdn over 2f out: hdd ins fnl f: r.o)	½	**2**	5/1 3	86	48
4737^{5}	**Regalo (59)** (DMHyde) **2-8-11** AMcGlone(2) (chsd ldr over 2f: unable qckn)	1¼	**3**	100/1	83?	45
4150^{3}	**Titanic (IRE) (100)** (JHMGosden) **2-9-7** GHind(3) (lw: hld up: rdn 2f out: one pce)	½	**4**	9/4 2	92	54
4851^{5}	**Mantles Pride (84)** (GLewis) **2-8-11** PaulEddery(5) (b: rdn thrght: a.p: one pce fnl 2f)	nk	**5**	9/1	81	43
3148^{6}	**Cortachy Castle (IRE) (100)** (BJMeehan) **2-9-1** MTebbutt(7) (lw: a.p: rdn over 2f out: one pce)	¾	**6**	7/4 1	82	44
4796^{7}	**Super Geil (53)** (CADwyer) **2-8-6** DO'Donohoe(4) (lost pl over 3f out: r.o one pce fnl f)	½	**7**	50/1	72?	34
1235^{2}	**English Lady (IRE)** (MJHaynes) **2-8-1**(7)ow2 MCornally(8) (b.hind: a bhd)	21	**8**	25/1	7	—

(SP 109.7%) **8 Rn**

60.31 secs (3.31) CSF £48.95 TOTE £7.00: £1.20 £1.50 £10.10 (£10.90) OWNER BABK Racing (LAMBOURN) BRED Mrs Janet Murray
3629 Legs Be Frendly (IRE) found the application of blinkers working the oracle for, after finishing second in six of his previous nine starts, he at long last came good, gaining control inside the final furlong. He lacks concentration according to connections. (10/1: 8/1-12/1)
4772* Rare Indigo attempted to make all the running and, although passed inside the final furlong, kept on well to the bitter end. (5/1)

4737 Regalo, in second place to halfway, could then only go up and down in the same place. (100/1)
4150 Titanic (IRE) was all at sea in the final quarter-mile and could only plod on in his own time. Although both his wins have come over this trip, he needs further. (9/4)
4851 Mantles Pride, off the bridle virtually throughout, could only go up and down in the same place in the final quarter-mile. (9/1)
3148 Cortachy Castle (IRE), without a run in three months, was rather disappointing as he failed to quicken in the last two furlongs. (7/4)

4912 ELM H'CAP (0-70) (3-Y.O+) (Class E)

3-50 (3-50) **1m 4f (Equitrack)** £3,356.25 (£1,005.00: £482.50: £221.25) Stalls: Low GOING minus 0.50 sec per fur (FST)

				SP	RR	SF
4562^{8}	**Mystic Quest (IRE) (70)** (KMcAuliffe) **3-9-10v** JReid(8) (lw: mde virtually all: drvn out)	—	**1**	10/1	83	36
4275^{14}	**Rehaab (46)** (MissBSanders) **4-8-7v** AClark(6) (hdwy over 2f out: chsd wnr fnl f: r.o)	1¾	**2**	12/1	57	17
4607^{3}	**Krayyan Dawn (38)** (JAkehurst) **7-7-10**(3) RFfrench(7) (stdy hdwy on ins over 2f out: nt clr run over 1f out: r.o ins fnl f)	¾	**3**	$7/1^{3}$	48	8
4504*	**Harlequin Walk (IRE) (47)** (RJO'Sullivan) **6-8-8** JQuinn(14) (hld up: rdn over 5f out: chsd wnr wl over 1f out to 1f out: sn wknd)	2½	**4**	$7/4^{1}$	53	13
4504^{9}	**Colour Counsellor (35)** (RMFlower) **4-7-10b** MartinDwyer(10) (chsd wnr over 10f out tl wl over 1f out: sn wknd)	¾	**5**	9/1	40	—
4609^{7}	**Keen Waters (42)** (MrsSDWilliams) **3-7-5**(5) APolli(2) (a.p: rdn over 4f out: wknd wl over 1f out)	2½	**6**	14/1	44	—
4516^{13}	**Haroldon (IRE) (55)** (BPalling) **8-9-2** TSprake(1) (b: nvr nrr)	3	**7**	$4/1^{2}$	53	13
1156^{11}	**Awesome Power (48)** (JWHills) **11-8-9** RHills(5) (prom over 10f)	1¼	**8**	14/1	44	4
4050^{13}	**Charlie Chang (IRE) (42)** (BJLlewellyn) **4-8-3** TWilliams(9) (prom 10f)	1¼	**9**	20/1	37	—
4594^{6}	**English Invader (59)** (CADwyer) **6-9-6** DO'Donohoe(4) (dwlt: bhd fnl 4f)	1¼	**10**	10/1	52	12
4335^{16}	**Strength of Vision (42)** (CREgerton) **3-7-7**(3) PFessey(13) (lw: bhd fnl 8f)	13	**11**	16/1	18	—
381^{8}	**Uoni (40)** (PButler) **4-8-1** JBramhill(3) (bhd fnl 6f)	12	**12**	20/1	—	—
4743^{9}	**Dunabrattin (55)** (DTThom) **4-9-2** MWigham(12) (lw: s.s: a bhd)	1¾	**13**	25/1	12	—
				(SP 137.3%)	**13 Rn**	

2m 34.81 (4.81) CSF £126.95 CT £849.01 TOTE £12.00: £2.80 £4.70 £1.70 (£92.10) Trio £328.40; £379.36 to Redcar 28/10/97 OWNER Delamere Cottage Racing Partners (1996) (LAMBOURN) BRED John O'Connor and Jeremiah Aherne
LONG HANDICAP Strength of Vision 7-8 Keen Waters 7-4
WEIGHT FOR AGE 3yo-7lb

2035 Mystic Quest (IRE), who has winning form on Fibresand, was making his Equitrack debut. He made virtually all the running and, responding to pressure, held on well. (10/1: 6/1-11/1)
3848 Rehaab ran much better here. Picking up ground over a quarter of a mile from home, she came through to take second place entering the final furlong and kept on well to make sure the winner did not have things all his own way. (12/1)
4607 Krayyan Dawn was not given a hard time. Catching the eye as he edged closer along the inside rail over a quarter of a mile from home, he then met traffic problems early in the straight but did run on nicely in the closing stages. (7/1)
4504* Harlequin Walk (IRE) has been in tremendous heart of late, winning her last three races on the Flat and scoring over hurdles recently. However, those races may be taking their toll for, after showing in second place early in the short straight, she was collared for that position a furlong out and soon dropped away. (7/4)
3971 Colour Counsellor, soon racing in second place, was collared for that position entering the straight and soon had bellows to mend. He has yet to win away from Brighton. (9/1)
4170 Keen Waters was close up until calling it a day entering the short straight. (14/1)

4913 FALLING LEAF LIMITED STKS (0-65) (3-Y.O+) (Class F)

4-20 (4-23) **7f (Equitrack)** £2,277.00 (£627.00: £297.00) Stalls: Low GOING minus 0.50 sec per fur (FST)

				SP	RR	SF
4453^{2}	**Pegasus Bay (56)** (MissAEEmbiricos) **6-9-2** JQuinn(5) (b: s.s: stdy hdwy on ins over 2f out: rdn over 1f out: led last strides)	—	**1**	10/1	70	28
3240^{22}	**Everset (FR) (62)** (ABailey) **9-9-0b** DWright(1) (b: lw: s.s: hdwy on ins over 5f out: led over 1f out: hrd rdn fnl f: hdd last strides)	hd	**2**	20/1	68	26
4738^{3}	**Akalim (59)** (LGCottrell) **4-8-11**(3) ADaly(4) (a.p: rdn over 2f out: r.o ins fnl f)	¾	**3**	10/1	66	24
4485^{9}	**Invocation (60)** (GLMoore) **10-9-2** AClark(10) (lw: chsd ldrs: rdn over 4f out: r.o ins fnl f)	1¼	**4**	16/1	65	23
4805^{9}	**Daylight Dreams (56)** (CACyzer) **3-8-9** MTebbutt(3) (a.p: hrd rdn over 1f out: one pce)	hd	**5**	12/1	60	16
4741^{4}	**Swift (63)** (MJPolglase) **3-9-2** JTate(9) (lw: hdwy over 1f out: r.o ins fnl f)	hd	**6**	$11/2^{2}$	67	23
4505*	**Matoaka (65)** (VSoane) **3-8-11** JReid(7) (lw: plld hrd: hld up: rdn over 1f out: one pce)	1¾	**7**	$7/2^{1}$	58	14
4373^{7}	**Step On Degas (65)** (MJFetherston-Godley) **4-8-10**(3) RFfrench(11) (lw: hdwy over 1f out: nvr nrr)	s.h	**8**	$7/2^{1}$	58	16
4527^{6}	**Anokato (61)** (KTIvory) **3-9-0** MartinDwyer(13) (nvr nr to chal)	¾	**9**	16/1	59	15
4404^{9}	**Ivor's Deed (63)** (MissGayKelleway) **4-8-13**(3) AWhelan(2) (b: b.hind: led over 5f out tl over 1f out: sn wknd)	hd	**10**	12/1	59	17
4009^{7}	**Palisander (IRE) (62)** (SDow) **3-8-5e**(7) PDoe(8) (prom 5f)	1½	**11**	33/1	53	9
4452^{7}	**The Fugative (57)** (PMitchell) **4-9-3** NDay(16) (bhd fnl 2f)	5	**12**	20/1	45	3
4410^{17}	**Orange Place (IRE) (65)** (BJLlewellyn) **6-9-0** TWilliams(12) (led over 1f: wknd 2f out)	2½	**13**	$13/2^{3}$	36	—
4527^{13}	**Ice Age (51)** (RJRWilliams) **3-8-12** NCarlisle(15) (hdwy over 3f out: wknd over 2f out)	2	**14**	25/1	32	—
2491^{8}	**Misconduct (50)** (GLMoore) **3-8-9** SWhitworth(14) (a bhd)	¾	**15**	20/1	27	—
4328^{5}	**Polgwynne (53)** (BSmart) **3-8-9** JStack(6) (lw: prom over 2f)	1¼	**16**	20/1	24	—
				(SP 144.3%)	**16 Rn**	

1m 27.04 (2.64) CSF £198.46 TOTE £9.00: £3.30 £7.80 £3.60 (£101.90) Trio £161.60 OWNER Mr Don Cantillon (NEWMARKET) BRED R. P. Dineen
WEIGHT FOR AGE 3yo-2lb

4453 Pegasus Bay nearly got caught out by the drop in distance. Picking up ground along the inside rail over a quarter of a mile from home, he nevertheless ran on strongly to get up in the last couple of strides. (10/1: op 6/1)
2302 Everset (FR), given a three-month break, is at his best on the sand where he has gained nine of his eleven victories. He nearly added to that score here as he moved to the front below the distance but, despite doing nothing wrong, was collared in the last couple of strides. (20/1)
4738 Akalim was never far away and, rousted along in the short straight, kept on well. He has not won for two years. (10/1: 6/1-12/1)
3058* Invocation, pushed along before halfway, kept on in the closing stages. He is a real Equitrack specialist who has gained eight of his nine victories here - four coming this year. (16/1)
4505 Daylight Dreams was never far away but could only go up and down in the same place in the short home straight. (12/1)
4741 Swift stayed on in the short straight but was never going to get there in time. (11/2)

T/Plpt: £223.00 (66.45 Tckts). T/Qdpt: £38.80 (24.12 Tckts) AK

4899-LEICESTER (R-H) (Good)

Tuesday October 28th

WEATHER: sunny WIND: fresh against

4914 E.B.F. MANNY BERNSTEIN TRADE DIVISION MAIDEN STKS (I) (2-Y.O) (Class E)

1-00 (1-05) **1m 8y** £3,327.00 (£996.00: £478.00: £219.00) Stalls: High GOING minus 0.09 sec per fur (G)

				SP	RR	SF
4758^{10}	**Baffin Bay** (HRACecil) **2-9-0** KFallon(9) (led tl hdd over 3f out: shkn up to ld fnl f: hld on)	—	1	$5/1^{3}$	91	29
4478^{6}	**Banker Dwerry (FR)** (SPCWoods) **2-9-0** NDay(6) (bit bkwd: a chsng ldrs: pushed along 3f out: r.o u.p cl home)	½	2	33/1	90	28
4709^{3}	**Mulahen (86)** (DMorley) **2-9-0** RHills(7) (lw: prom: led over 3f out to 1f out: unable qckn fnl f)	2	3	$11/10^{1}$	86	24
4739^{8}	**On The Right Side** (JWHills) **2-9-0** MHills(10) (prom: rdn along 3f out: r.o one pce fnl f)	¾	4	25/1	85	23
	Ferghana Ma (SCWilliams) **2-8-9** SDrowne(1) (lt-f: unf: in tch: rdn 2f out: styd on ins fnl f)	2½	5	33/1	75	13
	Telalanjon (TGMills) **2-9-0** SWhitworth(5) (leggy: lt-f: bit bkwd: s.s: hdwy 2f out: nt rch ldrs)	½	6	33/1	79	17
	Tereyna (RFJohnsonHoughton) **2-8-9** WRyan(12) (leggy: lt-f: unf: hld up: effrt over 2f out: wknd appr fnl f)	1¾	7	25/1	70	8
4715^{10}	**Secrecy** (PFICole) **2-9-0** TQuinn(14) (nvr nr to chal)	2½	8	14/1	70	8
	Still Waters (RCharlton) **2-9-0** TSprake(4) (w'like: leggy: bit bkwd: plld hrd: trckd ldrs: drvn along 3f out: sn btn)	1	9	$7/2^{2}$	68	6
4715^{8}	**Rainmaker** (MAJarvis) **2-9-0** RCochrane(3) (trckd ldrs: hrd drvn 3f out: sn lost tch: t.o)	9	10	25/1	50	—
	Spanish Eyes (JARToller) **2-8-9** AClark(13) (neat: unf: s.i.s: sn in tch: wknd qckly over 2f out: t.o)	2	11	33/1	41	—
4367^{6}	**St Enodoc (FR)** (JLDunlop) **2-9-0** GCarter(2) (sn outpcd: t.o)	10	12	20/1	26	—
4698^{9}	**Compassionate** (WGMTurner) **2-8-7(7)** DMcGaffin(11) (chsd ldrs: rdn & btn over 2f out: t.o)	3	13	40/1	20	—
	Rudi Knight (MJFetherston-Godley) **2-9-0** DaneO'Neill(8) (Withdrawn not under Starter's orders: ref to ent stalls)		W	33/1	—	—
				(SP 126.6%)	**13 Rn**	

1m 40.9 (5.90) CSF £149.57 TOTE £6.10: £1.70 £8.10 £1.10 (£79.60) Trio £23.70 OWNER Mr L. B. Holliday (NEWMARKET) BRED Cleaboy Farms Co

Baffin Bay, much sharper for the run at Newmarket earlier in the month, adopted more forceful tactics and, seeing the trip out well, was always going to hold on. (5/1)

Banker Dwerry (FR) was unable to make his presence felt on his debut but he knew what was needed this time and, in failing narrowly, gave notice that he will need to be watched next year. (33/1)

4709 Mulahen has not run a bad race yet and this longer trip did seem ideal but, after being in the firing line from the start, was found wanting when a final effort was called for. (11/10)

On The Right Side looked to be in trouble when driven along three furlongs out, but he responded and only really got shaken off inside the last furlong. (25/1)

Ferghana Ma, a lightly-made, unfurnished, late April foal who has got her winter coat, did not fare badly on this racecourse debut and, once she has filled out a bit, she could prove a useful stayer. (33/1)

Telalanjon, quite an attractive individual who was colty in the preliminaries, was flat-footed as the stalls opened but was noted putting in all his best work in the closing stages and the experience will prove beneficial. (33/1)

4915 E.B.F. MANNY BERNSTEIN TRADE DIVISION MAIDEN STKS (II) (2-Y.O) (Class D)

1-30 (1-32) **1m 8y** £3,301.00 (£988.00: £474.00: £217.00) Stalls: High GOING minus 0.09 sec per fur (G)

				SP	RR	SF
	Himself (USA) (HRACecil) **2-9-0** KFallon(3) (unf: scope: bhd: pushed along 5f out: plld out over 2f out: led over 1f out: sn clr)	—	1	$7/2^{2}$	93+	33
3576^{5}	**Speaker's Chair** (RCharlton) **2-9-0** TSprake(10) (trckd ldrs: led over 2f out tl over 1f out: one pce)	3	2	$9/4^{1}$	87	27
4708^{10}	**Brave Noble (USA)** (EALDunlop) **2-9-0** SWhitworth(13) (mid div: swtchd lft ½-wy: rdn to chal over 1f out: one pce fnl f)	1½	3	33/1	84	24
4740^{5}	**Needwood Spirit** (BCMorgan) **2-9-0** RCochrane(11) (bhd tl r.o fnl 2f)	4	4	16/1	76	16
	Emerald Heights (JRFanshawe) **2-9-0** NDay(5) (tall: unf: in tch: effrt 2f out: nt pce to chal)	hd	5	12/1	76	16
	Cold Front (JWHills) **2-8-11(3)** MHenry(8) (str: scope: prom tl rdn & wknd wl over 1f out)	2	6	20/1	72	12
4739^{11}	**Caradoc** (SCWilliams) **2-9-0** SDrowne(12) (prom: rdn over 2f out: r.o one pce)	¾	7	16/1	70	10
	Tutankhamun (MRStoute) **2-9-0** WRyan(4) (tall: scope: bit bkwd: trckd ldrs: chal 2f out: sn wknd)	2½	8	$9/1^{3}$	65	5
4526^{9}	**Sinan (USA)** (SbinSuroor) **2-9-0** RHills(2) (led tl over 2f out: wknd appr fnl f)	hd	9	$9/4^{1}$	65	5
4715^{5}	**All Made Up (USA)** (MBell) **2-9-0** MFenton(14) (a in rr)	3	10	12/1	59	—
	Spirit of Love (USA) (MJohnston) **2-9-0** MHills(1) (leggy: scope: s.s: a bhd: t.o)	7	11	12/1	45	—
4753^{28}	**Fair Sonia (53)** (KMcAuliffe) **2-8-9b1** AClark(6) (bhd fnl 3f: t.o)	11	12	100/1	18	—
1927^{9}	**Idaho (IRE)** (BGubby) **2-8-9** JTate(9) (b.hind: prom over 4f: sn wknd: t.o)	nk	13	50/1	18	—
4111^{W}	**Gunboat Diplomacy** (MJFetherston-Godley) **2-9-0** DaneO'Neill(7) (prom tl wknd wl over 1f out: t.o)	7	14	50/1	9	—
				(SP 141.2%)	**14 Rn**	

1m 40.5 (5.50) CSF £12.51 TOTE £3.80: £2.00 £1.20 £9.90 (£11.70) Trio £112.20 OWNER Scrope, Scott Partners (NEWMARKET) BRED Poole Investments

Himself (USA), a full-brother to a seven-furlong winner, took a long time to grasp what was needed but, once he did get into his stride, drew clear impressively, and he could turn out a decent colt. (7/2)

3576 Speaker's Chair has had a ten-week break since he last ran and he took quite a tug to post. Settled just behind the leaders, he struck the front over two furlongs out and promised to extend his advantage, but the winner brushed him aside with ease in the closing stages and he had to admit he had met one too good. (9/4)

Brave Noble (USA), drawn on the far side, somehow worked his way over to deliver his challenge on the stands' side but the leading pair proved just too strong and he was galloping on the spot throughout the final furlong. (33/1)

4740 Needwood Spirit has shown in both his outings so far that stamina is his strong suit for, once again, he was only finding his stride once the race was all but over. (16/1)

Emerald Heights needs time to strengthen to his frame but he showed promise and, with the winter months to develop, he will be a name to remember come next season. (12/1)

Cold Front, a strong colt with a choppy action, pressed the leaders but he was beginning to feel the strain entering the last quarter-mile and the position was quite rightly accepted. (20/1)

Sinan (USA) settled down in the lead under the stands' rail but did not find much once overtaken and he was on the retreat approaching the final furlong. (9/4)

4916 MANNY BERNSTEIN 20TH ANIVERSARY CLAIMING STKS (3-Y.O) (Class F)

2-00 (2-01) **1m 8y** £2,868.00 (£798.00: £384.00) Stalls: High GOING minus 0.09 sec per fur (G)

				SP	RR	SF
4858[9]	**Blowing Away (IRE) (60)** (MHTompkins) **3-8-0** DBiggs(15) (hld up: hdwy 2f out: shkn up to ld wl ins fnl f)	—	**1**	11/1	60	16
4696[10]	**Saratoga Red (USA) (60)** (WAO'Gorman) **3-9-3v[1]** KFallon(11) (chsd ldrs: rdn to ld over 2f out: hdd wl ins fnl f)	¾	**2**	5/2[1]	76	32
4043[15]	**Rochea (35)** (MrsNMacauley) **3-8-2v** SDrowne(17) (lw: led over 5f: kpt on u.p fnl f)	3	**3**	25/1	55	11
4319[11]	**Briska (IRE) (60)** (RAkehurst) **3-8-8** TQuinn(9) (trckd ldrs: outpcd 2f out: styd on ins fnl f)	1¼	**4**	7/1[3]	58	14
4846[3]	**Inkwell (34)** (AHide) **3-7-13**(5)ow1 GMilligan(6) (lw: bhd: hdwy fnl 2f: nrst fin)	4	**5**	14/1	46	1
4696[3]	**Tulsa (IRE) (51)** (BGubby) **3-9-7** MFenton(14) (reard s: hdwy u.p 2f out: nt rch ldrs)	½	**6**	8/1	62	18
4700[11]	**Falcon Ridge (34)** (JCFox) **3-9-3** DaneO'Neill(10) (in rr tl sme hdwy fnl 2f)	s.h	**7**	50/1	58	14
4484[10]	**Bollero (IRE) (52)** (JBerry) **3-8-4** GCarter(3) (chsd ldrs stands' side: rdn over 2f out: sn btn)	2½	**8**	9/1	40	—
4600[5]	**Mischievous Time (37)** (ASmith) **3-8-3** NAdams(18) (trckd ldrs: no hdwy fnl 3f)	2½	**9**	25/1	34	—
4608[14]	**Blazer's Baby (40)** (MrsNMacauley) **3-7-12** FNorton(20) (b: chsd ldrs: nt clr run 3f out: grad wknd)	2	**10**	25/1	25	—
4696[15]	**Kristopher (48)** (JWHills) **3-8-13** MHills(2) (cl up tl wknd wl over 1f out)	¾	**11**	10/1	39	—
4179[12]	**Blush (49)** (MCPipe) **3-7-12v[1]** MartinDwyer(19) (trckd ldrs tl wknd & eased over 2f out)	s.h	**12**	14/1	24	—
4816[9]	**Madame Maxi** (PRHedger) **3-8-4** NVarley(7) (nvr bttr than mid div)	2	**13**	12/1	26	—
4713[15]	**Barkston Warrior** (DShaw) **3-8-0**(3) AWhelan(8) (b: in tch to ½-wy: sn wknd)	5	**14**	50/1	15	—
4795[10]	**Joyful Joy (23)** (BPJBaugh) **3-8-0** AMackay(12) (prom tl rdn & wknd over 2f out)	4	**15**	50/1	4	—
1167[13]	**Not Out Lad (39)** (PButler) **3-8-7** JBramhill(16) (bit bkwd: a in rr)	3	**16**	33/1	5	—
4505[6]	**Love Venture (60)** (SPCWoods) **3-8-6** NDay(1) (prom 4f: sn drvn along & wknd)	3½	**17**	6/1[2]	—	—
876[10]	**Our Drowsy Maggie** (WMBrisbourne) **3-8-12** AGarth(4) (a bhd: t.o)	7	**18**	50/1	—	—
1876[11]	**How Bizarre** (RSimpson) **3-8-7b[1]** MGallagher(13) (bit bkwd: prom: rdn & lost tch 3f out: eased whn btn: t.o)	17	**19**	50/1	—	—
				(SP 139.2%)		**19 Rn**

1m 40.9 (5.90) CSF £36.61 TOTE £10.90: £3.10 £1.80 £5.10 (£42.70) Trio £346.10; £292.54 to Yarmouth 29/10/97 OWNER Mark Tompkins Racing (NEWMARKET) BRED Mrs D. Davison

3135 Blowing Away (IRE), making a quick return to action without the visor, showed much-improved form to open her account and the manner of this victory would suggest that she is just coming to herself. (11/1)

2645 Saratoga Red (USA), well supported to get off the mark with the help of the champion elect, did look to hold all the aces when leading into the final furlong, but the winner had not read the script and had far too much pace for him in the battle to the line. (5/2: op 5/1)

2941 Rochea decided on more forceful tactics in an attempt to record her first success, but she had nothing left when the runner-up took her measure and she just had to accept the inevitable. (25/1)

Briska (IRE) turned in her best performance of the year on this step down in class but she did seem to run her race in snatches and she is not yet getting it together. (7/1)

4846 Inkwell has been promising to win a race, but he got outpaced at halfway and did not begin to stay on again until it was far too late. (14/1)

4696 Tulsa (IRE), messing about as the stalls were released, did try hard to get into the action inside the last quarter-mile, but top weight took its toll and he was never able to mount a challenge. (8/1)

4917 MANNY BERNSTEIN EARLY PRICE MEDIAN AUCTION MAIDEN STKS (2-Y.O) (Class F)

2-30 (2-32) **5f 218y** £2,952.00 (£822.00: £396.00) Stalls: High GOING minus 0.09 sec per fur (G)

				SP	RR	SF
4818[2]	**Bandbox (IRE) (78)** (SMellor) **2-9-0** MWigham(10) (a.p: rdn over 1f out: r.o to ld wl ins fnl f)	—	**1**	6/1[3]	78	49
4818[5]	**Double Brandy** (IABalding) **2-9-0** SWhitworth(21) (a.p: led 3f out tl wl ins fnl f)	½	**2**	6/1[3]	77	48
4564[2]	**Bedevilled** (MJHeaton-Ellis) **2-9-0** SDrowne(18) (lw: a chsng ldrs: ev ch 1f out: unable qckn)	1¾	**3**	7/2[1]	72	43
4569[2]	**Silken Dalliance** (LordHuntingdon) **2-8-9** WRyan(12) (led stands' side fr ½-wy: no ch w ldrs)	¾	**4**	9/1	65	36
4758[5]	**Sherganzar (83)** (MSalaman) **2-9-0** DBiggs(15) (hdwy over 2f out: sn hrd rdn: nt pce to chal)	1	**5**	5/1[2]	67	38
4779[11]	**Ribblesdale** (JLDunlop) **2-8-9** TQuinn(7) (dwlt: r.o fnl 2f: nvr nrr)	4	**6**	8/1	52	23
	Internal Affair (USA) (WJHaggas) **2-9-0** RHills(3) (scope: trckd ldrs: no hdwy fnl 2f)	¾	**7**	5/1[2]	55	26
4801[11]	**Bon Sizzle** (JRFanshawe) **2-9-0** MHills(13) (led 3f: wknd over 1f out)	nk	**8**	25/1	54	25
4701[13]	**Shambles** (GGMargarson) **2-8-6**(3) MHenry(19) (nvr nr ldrs)	3½	**9**	100/1	40	11
	Blazing Billy (CADwyer) **2-9-0** KFallon(20) (leggy: bit bkwd: w ldrs 4f: eased whn btn fnl f)	1¾	**10**	11/1	40	11
4564[5]	**Gem** (PJMakin) **2-8-9** AClark(2) (nvr rchd ldrs)	¾	**11**	10/1	33	4
4753[12]	**Opening Night** (RSimpson) **2-9-0** MGallagher(9) (n.d)	3½	**12**	33/1	29	—
2693[13]	**Minjara** (APJones) **2-9-0** MartinDwyer(1) (s.s: a in rr)	nk	**13**	100/1	28	—
594[14]	**Burnden Days (IRE)** (MissJFCraze) **2-9-0** SWebster(16) (bit bkwd: a in rr)	3	**14**	50/1	20	—
4515[17]	**Rhapsody In Blue (IRE)** (AndrewTurnell) **2-9-0** NAdams(6) (b.hind: prom over 3f)	2½	**15**	33/1	13	—
	Regal Arrow (AGFoster) **2-9-0** TSprake(8) (b: unf: scope: bkwd: a in rr)	1¼	**16**	33/1	10	—
4818[7]	**Long Island** (RHannon) **2-9-0** DaneO'Neill(4) (a in rr)	½	**17**	20/1	8	—
	Maas (IRE) (PJMakin) **2-9-0** JTate(11) (wl grwn: bit bkwd: s.s: nvr nr ldrs)	1½	**18**	20/1	4	—
4807[10]	**Samata One (IRE)** (WJHaggas) **2-9-0** FLynch(17) (lw: s.s: a bhd)	nk	**19**	20/1	4	—
4769[9]	**Ashangem** (BobJones) **2-9-0** NDay(5) (outpcd: t.o)	12	**20**	50/1	—	—
4017[8]	**Grecian Prince** (JGSmyth-Osbourne) **2-9-0** GCarter(14) (bit bkwd: bhd fr ½-wy: t.o)	2½	**21**	25/1	—	—
				(SP 159.4%)		**21 Rn**

1m 12.9 (2.90) CSF £44.14 TOTE £7.80: £2.20 £2.30 £2.60 (£15.60) Trio £10.60 OWNER The Bandbox Brigade (SWINDON) BRED Mrs Carole Burns

4818 Bandbox (IRE), not winning out of turn on this return to six furlongs, had only one serious rival to contend with inside the distance and this was to be his day. (6/1)

4818 Double Brandy, less than a length behind the winner over the minimum trip, promised to defy him success yet again but he could not maintain his run and was forced to give best inside the last hundred yards. (6/1)

4564 Bedevilled appears to lack a turn of finishing speed at present, but he is still in the process of learning and his turn will come. (7/2)

4569 Silken Dalliance, back on turf, was with the pace all the way on the stands' side but the principals racing on the much faster ground in the centre of the track were always ahead. (9/1)

4758 Sherganzar did not have the speed to hold his pitch on this step down in distance and, though he did attempt to get himself into the action, he was always short of pace. (5/1)

Ribblesdale missed the beat at the start and, deciding to race on the stands' side, did stay on without ever threatening to reach the leaders. Experience will improve her. (8/1)

Internal Affair (USA) (5/1: op 8/1)

4918 MANNY BERNSTEIN IN RUNNING H'CAP (0-70) (3-Y.O+) (Class E)

3-00 (3-02) **1m 1f 218y** £3,509.00 (£1,052.00: £506.00: £233.00) Stalls: High GOING minus 0.09 sec per fur (G)

				SP	RR	SF
4714^{4}	**Calendula (64)** (DMorley) **4-9-10** GCarter(14) (bhd: hdwy 5f out: led ins fnl f: rdn out)	—	**1**	6/1^{2}	74	56
4584^{16}	**Rock The Barney (IRE) (40)** (MDIUsher) **8-7-7b**(7) ANicholls(9) (hld up & bhd: hdwy 3f out: led 2f out tl ins fnl f: r.o)	nk	**2**	12/1	50	32
4699^{9}	**In The Genes (58)** (IPWilliams) **3-8-10**(3) MHenry(13) (chsd ldrs: led over 2f out: sn hdd: kpt on fnl f)	2	**3**	25/1	64	41
4802^{9}	**Suga Hawk (IRE) (64)** (EJAlston) **5-9-10** KFallon(6) (a.p: one pce fnl 2f)	1¾	**4**	12/1	68	50
4714^{13}	**Blaze of Song (57)** (RHannon) **5-9-3** DaneO'Neill(4) (in tch: lost pl after 3f: r.o wl fnl 2f)	4	**5**	20/1	54	36
4845^{8}	**Katie Komaite (48)** (CaptJWilson) **4-8-8v** AMackay(18) (trckd ldrs: rdn over 3f out: wknd over 2f out)	3½	**6**	7/1^{3}	40	22
4714^{16}	**Bakers Daughter (58)** (JRArnold) **5-9-4** MartinDwyer(17) (led after 2f: racd along far side st: hdd over 3f out: eased whn btn)	5	**7**	14/1	42	24
4800^{9}	**Minster Star (60)** (JLSpearing) **3-8-8**(7) SRighton(5) (chsd ldrs 7f)	¾	**8**	33/1	42	19
842^{12}	**Needwood Legend (45)** (BCMorgan) **4-8-5** SDrowne(8) (bhd tl some hdwy fnl 3f)	hd	**9**	50/1	27	9
4731^{6}	**Come Together (65)** (DWPArbuthnot) **3-9-6** SWhitworth(19) (plld hrd: nvr nr to chal)	¾	**10**	16/1	46	23
4714^{3}	**North Reef (IRE) (64)** (JPearce) **6-9-10** MWigham(12) (lw: chsd ldrs: rdn 6f out: btn 4f out)	½	**11**	100/30^{1}	44	26
	El Presidente (44) (GPEnright) **4-8-4** NDay(1) (bit bkwd: prom tl wknd over 3f out)	1½	**12**	50/1	22	4
4741^{5}	**Swinging The Blues (IRE) (54)** (RAkehurst) **3-8-9** AClark(7) (in tch 6f)	3½	**13**	9/1	26	3
1660^{8}	**Northern Fan (IRE) (58)** (NTinkler) **5-9-4** FLynch(2) (lw: led 2f: led over 3f out tl over 2f out: sn wknd)	2	**14**	25/1	27	9
4406^{3}	**Nobel Lad (63)** (MCPipe) **3-9-4** TQuinn(11) (prom 7f)	½	**15**	6/1^{2}	31	8
4711^{19}	**By Jay (IRE) (45)** (BJCurley) **3-8-0** JBramhill(15) (trckd ldrs: rdn over 3f out: sn wknd)	½	**16**	16/1	12	—
4714^{10}	**Star Witness (IRE) (62)** (AGNewcombe) **5-9-8** JStack(10) (lw: hld up: nvr nr ldrs)	1½	**17**	20/1	27	9
4516^{17}	**Timothy George (IRE) (53)** (GBBalding) **3-8-8** WRyan(16) (prom: rdn 5f out: sn wknd)	15	**18**	33/1	—	—
4844^{20}	**Play The Tune (47)** (AWCarroll) **4-8-2**(5) APolli(3) (prom 5f)	3	**19**	33/1	—	—

(SP 137.9%) **19 Rn**

2m 9.1 (5.40) CSF £69.22 CT £1,599.74 TOTE £6.30: £3.10 £3.50 £4.90 £3.20 (£52.40) Trio £372.60 OWNER Mr Christopher Spence (NEWMARKET) BRED Chieveley Manor Enterprises

WEIGHT FOR AGE 3yo-5lb

OFFICIAL EXPLANATION **North Reef (IRE): the trainer's representative reported that the horse had lost a shoe and suffered an overreach.**

4714 Calendula, fresher than most, was settled some way off the fast early pace, which brought her stamina into play in the closing stages. (6/1)

4179* Rock The Barney (IRE), back on the mark he won off just three outings ago, bounced back to form on a track where he often runs well. Had he not got to the front so quickly when starting his move, he might well have won. (12/1)

2888 In The Genes, made plenty of use of over this shorter trip, lacked the pace to respond in the last furlong but kept plugging away. (25/1)

3890 Suga Hawk (IRE) raced close to the lead, but the fast early pace had found him out in the closing stages. (12/1)

Blaze of Song, who contested the major handicaps last year, has plummeted in the weights and really caught the eye in the home straight having been last but one on the home turn. Off this mark, a return to form is yet possible. (20/1)

4845 Katie Komaite raced rather too keenly and close to the pace, eventually paying the penalty. (7/1)

4714 North Reef (IRE) may have found this an insufficient test of stamina and was in trouble a long way out but apparently lost a shoe. (100/30)

4919 MANNY BERNSTEIN CREDIT DIVISION LIMITED STKS (0-70) (3-Y.O) (Class E)

3-35 (3-35) **1m 3f 183y** £2,833.00 (£844.00: £402.00: £181.00) Stalls: High GOING minus 0.09 sec per fur (G)

				SP	RR	SF
4234^{4}	**Nichol Fifty (70)** (MHTompkins) **3-9-2** DBiggs(3) (hld up & bhd: rdn & swtchd rt over 1f out: r.o to ld ins fnl f)	—	**1**	4/1^{3}	79	24
4699^{4}	**Tarxien (70)** (KRBurke) **3-9-0** KFallon(1) (lw: prom: led over 1f out: hdd ins fnl f: unable qckn)	1½	**2**	11/10^{1}	75	20
4743^{3}	**Toi Toi (IRE) (65)** (DWPArbuthnot) **3-8-11** SWhitworth(2) (hld up: effrt over 2f out: no ex fnl f)	¾	**3**	8/1	71	16
4896^{2}	**Protocol (IRE) (67)** (JWHills) **3-9-2** TQuinn(5) (led after 3f tl over 1f out: sn btn)	hd	**4**	3/1^{2}	76	21
4714^{11}	**Massyar Seventeen (63)** (HJCollingridge) **3-9-0** GCarter(4) (led 3f: bhd fnl 2f)	21	**5**	12/1	45	—

(SP 111.4%) **5 Rn**

2m 38.8 (10.30) CSF £8.23 TOTE £6.00: £1.90 £1.10 (£4.20) OWNER Mr Lloyd Bedack (NEWMARKET) BRED Sheikh Mohammed Obaid Al Maktoum

4234 Nichol Fifty, dropped back to his winning trip, was unlikely to be suited by the slow early pace but found much the best turn of foot when the chips were down. (4/1)

4699 Tarxien, weighted to win on official marks, had beaten the winner over further last month but, after winning a protracted battle for supremacy with Protocol, had no more to give near the finish. (11/10: 5/4-evens)

4743 Toi Toi (IRE) again moved poorly and, with the Nottingham form not working out at all, did little to change things, finding little once off the bridle. (8/1)

4896 Protocol (IRE), having a second run very hastily after two months off, has the action of one who would prefer softer ground and did not excel. (3/1)

3453 Massyar Seventeen, taken down steadily, ran poorly and would seem to have had enough for the moment. (12/1: op 8/1)

4920 MANNY BERNSTEIN DOUBLE RESULT H'CAP (0-85) (3-Y.O+) (Class D)

4-10 (4-10) **1m 8y** £3,743.00 (£1,124.00: £542.00: £251.00) Stalls: High GOING minus 0.09 sec per fur (G)

				SP	RR	SF
4577^{6}	**Lionize (USA) (80)** (MrsJCecil) **4-10-0b^{1}** RHills(5) (prom: led 3f out: rdn & hld on wl fnl f)	—	**1**	33/1	90	55
4175^{3}	**Howaida (IRE) (78)** (MRStoute) **3-9-9** WRyan(14) (plld hrd: trckd ldrs: ev ch 2f out: styd on ins fnl f)	1¼	**2**	5/1^{2}	86	48
4360^{6}	**Midnight Watch (USA) (75)** (HRACecil) **3-9-6** KFallon(8) (lw: hld up: rdn over 2f out: n.m.r over 1f out: r.o ins fnl f)	½	**3**	5/1^{2}	82	44
4667^{12}	**Xylem (USA) (72)** (LMCumani) **6-8-13**(7) DYoung(12) (lw: hld up: hdwy over 3f out: one pce ins fnl f)	s.h	**4**	12/1	78	43
4606*	**Blewbury Hill (IRE) (69)** (RFJohnsonHoughton) **3-9-0** TQuinn(13) (w ldrs: ev ch 2f out: wknd fnl f)	1¼	**5**	5/1^{2}	73	35
4695*	**Literary (74)** (JHMGosden) **3-9-5** AGarth(7) (hld up: hdwy over 2f out: rdn over 1f out: no imp)	nk	**6**	9/4^{1}	77	39
4781^{25}	**Suez Tornado (IRE) (66)** (EJAlston) **4-8-11**(3) MHenry(6) (in tch: n.m.r over 2f out: no imp fnl f)	5	**7**	16/1	59	24
4781^{20}	**Mo-Addab (IRE) (64)** (ACStewart) **7-8-12** SWhitworth(11) (hld up: rdn & hdwy 3f out: wknd fnl f)	1¼	**8**	9/1	55	20
4705^{4}	**Classic Jenny (IRE) (69)** (ICampbell) **4-9-3** AMackay(3) (dropped rr after 2f: n.d afterwards)	3	**9**	20/1	54	19
4121^{16}	**Final Stab (IRE) (73)** (PWHarris) **4-9-7** MRimmer(2) (in tch: rdn 3f out: sn btn)	½	**10**	20/1	57	22
4680^{12}	**Phonetic (72)** (GBBalding) **4-8-13**(7) FTynan(9) (in tch: pushed along 3f out: sn wknd)	3½	**11**	20/1	49	14
4757^{7}	**No More Pressure (IRE) (78)** (MrsJRRamsden) **3-9-9** DaneO'Neill(10) (chsd ldrs: rdn & wknd over 2f out)	½	**12**	8/1^{3}	54	16
4792^{2}	**Cee-N-K (IRE) (72)** (MJohnston) **3-9-3b** MHills(4) (led 5f: sn wknd: eased whn btn)	7	**13**	8/1^{3}	34	—

				SP	RR	SF
4768^{2}	**Night City (65)** (KRBurke) **6-8-13** DeclanO'Shea(1) (sn wl bhd)	dist	**14**	16/1	—	—
				(SP 149.7%)	**14 Rn**	

1m 39.6 (4.60) CSF £205.49 CT £966.10 TOTE £33.20: £8.10 £3.30 £3.10 (£339.20) Trio £469.90; £132.37 to Yarmouth 29/10/97 OWNER Lord Howard de Walden (NEWMARKET) BRED Bloomsbury Stud
WEIGHT FOR AGE 3yo-3lb

Lionize (USA), off a stone lower mark than when making his seasonal debut in the Newbury Spring Cup, changed yards in the summer and was galvanized into action by a tongue-strap and first-time blinkers. (33/1)
4175 Howaida (IRE), a tail-flasher who takes a good hold, got slightly outpaced below the distance and may well get further. (5/1)
4360 Midnight Watch (USA), dropped in trip in an attempt to find a race, stayed on as if needing further. (5/1)
4510* Xylem (USA), who failed to stay when stepped up considerably in trip last time, made smooth progress to challenge towards the centre of the track at the distance but was always being held. He ought to stay a little further. (12/1)
4606* Blewbury Hill (IRE), unable to dominate in this tougher race, had done his running entering the final furlong. (5/1)
4695* Literary, who came good on soft ground, found her turn of foot not nearly so potent on this faster surface. (9/4: op 5/1)

T/Jkpt: £8,914.40 (0.1 Tckts); £11,300.03. T/Plpt: £48.20 (408.51 Tckts). T/Qdpt: £17.40 (60.42 Tckts) Dk/IM

4788-REDCAR (L-H) (Good to firm)
Tuesday October 28th
WEATHER: sunny & cold WIND: slt half bhd

4921 E.B.F. WILTON MEDIAN AUCTION MAIDEN STKS (2-Y.O) (Class F)
1-05 (1-07) **5f** £2,598.00 (£728.00: £354.00) Stalls: High GOING minus 0.47 sec per fur (F)

				SP	RR	SF
4479^{3}	**Mary Jane** (JBerry) **2-8-6**(3) PFessey(1) (mde all: all out)	—	**1**	7/1^{2}	68	42
4630^{14}	**Quite Happy (IRE)** (DrJDScargill) **2-8-9** JQuinn(15) (lw: b.hind: trckd ldrs: effrt over 1f out: styd on wl towards fin)	½	**2**	20/1	66	40
4737^{3}	**Quiz Master (70)** (EWeymes) **2-9-0b** GHind(9) (chsd ldrs: effrt 2f out: hung lft & r.o one pce)	1½	**3**	8/1^{3}	67	41
4569^{9}	**Best of Our Days** (CWThornton) **2-9-0** DeanMcKeown(4) (a chsng ldrs: nt qckn fnl f)	nk	**4**	7/1^{2}	66	40
4500^{3}	**Glass River (55)** (PDEvans) **2-9-0** JFEgan(7) (a.p: kpt on fnl f: nvr able chal)	s.h	**5**	20/1	66	40
4769^{5}	**Anstand** (MrsJRRamsden) **2-9-0** JFortune(18) (bhd: hdwy 2f out: r.o towards fin)	nk	**6**	8/1^{3}	65+	39
4569^{5}	**Happy Wanderer** (PCHaslam) **2-9-0** LCharnock(16) (styd on fnl 2f: nvr nr to chal)	2½	**7**	14/1	57	31
3821^{2}	**Cool Prospect (75)** (ABMulholland) **2-9-0** TLucas(5) (lw: chsd ldrs over 3f: sn btn)	1¾	**8**	9/2^{1}	51	25
4167^{7}	**Redswan** (SCWilliams) **2-9-0** PBloomfield(3) (s.i.s: outpcd & bhd tl sme late hdwy)	hd	**9**	10/1	51	25
4801^{4}	**Cape Hope (59)** (RBoss) **2-9-0** MTebbutt(8) (hdwy ½-wy: rdn & wknd wl over 1f out)	1½	**10**	8/1^{3}	46	20
4159^{8}	**Clanblue Chick** (JBerry) **2-8-6**(3) PRoberts(12) (chsd ldrs over 3f)	nk	**11**	12/1	40	14
3753^{11}	**Mystical Rodge** (MDods) **2-9-0** DaleGibson(14) (nvr wnt pce)	1½	**12**	33/1	40	14
4640^{7}	**All Our Blessings (IRE)** (PCHaslam) **2-8-9** JWeaver(17) (bit bkwd: s.i.s: a bhd)	1½	**13**	10/1	30	4
4752^{6}	**Repton** (MrsASwinbank) **2-8-11**(3) GParkin(11) (s.s: a bhd)	s.h	**14**	66/1	35	9
4630^{16}	**Crystal Lough (IRE)** (GROldroyd) **2-8-9** ACulhane(6) (prom 3f: wknd)	¾	**15**	100/1	28	2
4630^{13}	**Pabella Bluebird (IRE) (55)** (GROldroyd) **2-8-9v**^{1} KHodgson(10) (s.i.s: n.d)	2	**16**	50/1	21	—
				(SP 126.0%)	**16 Rn**	

58.1 secs (0.60) CSF £138.42 TOTE £8.00: £2.40 £7.20 £3.10 (£183.20) Trio £153.50 OWNER Mr W. R. Milner (COCKERHAM) BRED Aramstone Stud Co

4479 Mary Jane, after two previous efforts, was now fully fit and certainly knew her job. She has plenty of speed and that won the day. (7/1)
Quite Happy (IRE) travelled well but it was lack of experience that made the difference and she should know plenty more next time. (20/1)
4737 Quiz Master, as usual, had his chances but he failed to respond sufficiently when ridden. (8/1)
Best of Our Days looked particularly well and is obviously on the upgrade. (7/1)
4500 Glass River has never fully got it together this season but again showed here he has ability, and may well be worth trying over a little further. (20/1)
4769 Anstand, having his third run here over a trip that would appear too short, showed plenty and the Handicapper cannot over-punish him for this. (8/1)
4569 Happy Wanderer was picking up ground at the end, suggesting that longer trips will see better. (14/1)
3821 Cool Prospect, after two months off, went very free to post and ran poorly. (9/2)
4167 Redswan (10/1: op 6/1)
Clanblue Chick (12/1: op 8/1)

4922 LEVY BOARD NURSERY H'CAP (0-75) (2-Y.O) (Class E)
1-35 (1-37) **6f** £3,171.25 (£955.00: £462.50: £216.25) Stalls: High GOING minus 0.47 sec per fur (F)

				SP	RR	SF
4602^{7}	**Blundell Lane (IRE) (69)** (APJarvis) **2-9-1** AMcGlone(12) (lw: a.p: hdwy to ld ins fnl f: r.o wl)	—	**1**	7/1^{2}	76	60
4097^{7}	**Rich Choice (66)** (JDBethell) **2-8-12** PaulEddery(4) (led tl hdd ins fnl f: nt qckn)	2	**2**	7/1^{2}	68	52
4807^{2}	**Premium Princess (65)** (JJQuinn) **2-8-11** JFortune(2) (a.p: effrt 2f out: kpt on: nvr able chal)	hd	**3**	8/1^{3}	66	50
4508^{11}	**One To Go (IRE) (60)** (JBerry) **2-8-3**(3) PFessey(3) (chsd ldrs tl wknd appr fnl f)	5	**4**	20/1	48	32
*4569**	**Arbenig (IRE) (66)** (BPalling) **2-8-9**(3) DSweeney(9) (trckd ldrs: bmpd 2f out: nvr nr to chal after)	2	**5**	13/2^{1}	49	33
4362^{5}	**Sing For Me (IRE) (52)** (RHollinshead) **2-7-12** NCarlisle(14) (hdwy ½-wy: bmpd 2f out: styd on: nvr nrr)	hd	**6**	16/1	35	19
4750^{9}	**Chimes of Peace (61)** (JLEyre) **2-8-0**(7) RWinston(16) (pushed along thrght: nvr able rch ldrs)	s.h	**7**	7/1^{2}	43	27
4710^{7}	**After Eight (66)** (RWArmstrong) **2-8-12b**^{1} JWeaver(1) (gd spd over 4f: sn rdn & btn)	hd	**8**	13/2^{1}	48	32
4796^{3}	**Malozza (57)** (PDEvans) **2-8-3** JFEgan(10) (chsd ldrs: hung rt u.p 2f out: sn btn)	1	**9**	11/1	36	20
4468^{10}	**Cosmic Case (64)** (JSGoldie) **2-8-10** JQuinn(7) (effrt ½-wy: nvr trbld ldrs)	3	**10**	25/1	35	19
3306^{17}	**Good On Yer (55)** (SEKettlewell) **2-7-12**(3) RFfrench(11) (sn bhd)	1¾	**11**	11/1	22	6
4737^{9}	**Two Williams (72)** (MWEasterby) **2-9-4** TLucas(5) (trckd ldrs 4f: grad lost pl)	1	**12**	25/1	36	20
4746^{10}	**Wait'n'see (72)** (MWEasterby) **2-9-1**(3) GParkin(6) (nvr nr ldrs)	½	**13**	25/1	35	19
4419^{5}	**Mill End Quest (57)** (MWEasterby) **2-8-3** DaleGibson(13) (sn bhd)	3	**14**	20/1	12	—
4807^{8}	**Stephangeorge (54)** (MBrittain) **2-7-7**(7) DMernagh(15) (sn drvn along: bhd fr ½-wy)	½	**15**	50/1	7	—
4702^{2}	**Kettlesing (IRE) (75)** (MWEasterby) **2-9-7b** DO'Donohoe(8) (b: reard s: a wl bhd)	6	**16**	7/1^{2}	12	—
				(SP 133.3%)	**16 Rn**	

1m 10.1 (-0.10) CSF £50.54 CT £399.75 TOTE £7.50: £1.10 £2.00 £1.70 £4.70 (£45.90) Trio £99.90 OWNER Mr N. Coverdale (ASTON UPTHORPE) BRED Mrs Kathleen Reynolds

1692 Blundell Lane (IRE), having his first run in a handicap, did it well and really looks to be going the right way. (7/1: op 4/1)
4097 Rich Choice has been dropped 7lb since her previous effort and tried here but was well out-pointed late on. (7/1)
4807 Premium Princess again had her chances but she was never doing enough when it mattered. (8/1)
3819 One To Go (IRE) has speed but, as yet, is failing to see it out. (20/1)
4569* Arbenig (IRE) ran pretty well without getting into this and was not given too hard a time. She will obviously find other opportunities on the All-Weather. (13/2)
4362 Sing For Me (IRE) was staying on at the end, suggesting that this trip is short of her best. (16/1)

4923 BRASS CASTLE CLAIMING STKS (3-Y.O+) (Class F)

2-10 (2-11) **1m 3f** £2,598.00 (£728.00: £354.00) Stalls: Low GOING minus 0.47 sec per fur (F)

				SP	RR	SF
4886[8]	**Pickens (USA) (53)** (DonEnricoIncisa) **5-8-7** KimTinkler(8) (b: a.p: led 2f out: r.o u.p)	—	**1**	9/1	47	27
2961[14]	**Trojan Risk (74)** (GLewis) **4-9-7** PaulEddery(12) (hld up & bhd: hdwy 4f out: ev ch wl over 1f out: nt qckn)	1½	**2**	3/1[2]	59	39
4288[3]	**Mad Militant (IRE) (62)** (AStreeter) **8-8-13** JWeaver(9) (hld up: hdwy over 3f out: chsng ldrs over 1f out)	2	**3**	5/2[1]	48	28
4521[2]	**Durgams First (IRE) (54)** (MrsMReveley) **5-9-1** ACulhane(14) (lw: hld up & bhd: hdwy 4f out: chsng ldrs 2f out: r.o one pce)	1¾	**4**	100/30[3]	47	27
4843[7]	**Diamond Crown (IRE) (32)** (MartynWane) **6-8-7** JCarroll(2) (hld up & bhd: styd on fnl 3f: nrst fin)	5	**5**	25/1	32	12
4768[12]	**Raased (33)** (FWatson) **5-8-9** NKennedy(7) (chsd clr ldr: led over 2f out: sn hdd & btn)	2	**6**	100/1	31	11
3486[9]	**Chancancook (20)** (JLEyre) **4-8-4** RLappin(6) (mid div: effrt 3f out: no imp)	1	**7**	100/1	25	5
2854[7]	**Maurangi (24)** (BWMurray) **6-8-11b** JFortune(10) (lw: s.i.s: nvr trbld ldrs)	¾	**8**	33/1	31	11
4768[7]	**Speculative** (WStorey) **3-8-11** JFanning(4) (nvr nr ldrs)	½	**9**	33/1	36	10
4519[3]	**Kika (36)** (KRBurke) **4-8-6** JFEgan(3) (chsd ldrs tl wknd 3f out)	2	**10**	8/1	22	2
4692[3]	**Flyaway Blues (41)** (MrsMReveley) **5-8-8**(5) SCopp(5) (a rr div)	1½	**11**	20/1	27	7
4324[19]	**Banneret (USA) (40)** (JO'Reilly) **4-8-9b** JO'Reilly(13) (led & sn wl clr: wknd & hdd over 2f out)	5	**12**	100/1	16	—
4768[11]	**All Girls Forget** (JDBethell) **3-7-12** TWilliams(1) (chsd ldrs tl rdn & wknd 4f out)	1	**13**	100/1	9	—
4692[11]	**Golden Fish (24)** (EJAlston) **5-8-7** JQuinn(11) (hdwy ent st: sn in tch: wknd over 2f out)	2½	**14**	200/1	9	—
3929[W]	**Key To** (APJarvis) **3-8-6** AMcGlone(15) (in tch to st: sn bhd)	12	**15**	33/1	—	—
				(SP 119.6%)	**15 Rn**	

2m 20.7 (3.70) CSF £30.74 TOTE £12.80: £4.20 £1.10 £1.90 (£40.40) Trio £26.20 OWNER Don Enrico Incisa (MIDDLEHAM) BRED Allen E. Paulson
WEIGHT FOR AGE 3yo-6lb
Trojan Risk clmd PDavidson-Brown £10,000
4415 Pickens (USA), for once, kept tabs on the leaders and, after striking the front two furlongs out, he was not going to stop. (9/1)
2528* Trojan Risk likes to come from off the pace and looked to have done everything right here, but he just met one too determined. (3/1: op 2/1)
4288 Mad Militant (IRE) ran well but the effort was always just beyond him and he is obviously in good form for the All-Weather season. (5/2)
4521 Durgams First (IRE) needs things to go just right and, over this shorter trip, he was always having to struggle just too much for his liking. (100/30)
4843 Diamond Crown (IRE) has to come from way behind, needs all the luck going and was never doing things fast enough to get into this. (25/1)
Raased had his chances but decided it was not for him when the struggle really began in the last two furlongs. (100/1)

4924 ELLERBY H'CAP (0-75) (3-Y.O+) (Class D)

2-40 (2-46) **1m** £4,091.00 (£1,238.00: £604.00: £287.00) Stalls: High GOING minus 0.47 sec per fur (F)

				SP	RR	SF
4757[27]	**Sualtach (IRE) (69)** (RHollinshead) **4-9-5**(3) DGriffiths(7) (lw: hdwy over 3f out: led appr fnl f: rdn out)	—	**1**	20/1	80	63
4792[4]	**Jedi Knight (69)** (MWEasterby) **3-9-5** LCharnock(15) (hdwy 3f out: chsng ldrs 1f out: styd on wl towards fin)	hd	**2**	14/1	80	60
4510[2]	**Alpine Hideaway (IRE) (68)** (MWEasterby) **4-9-4**(3) GParkin(9) (b.hind: mde most tl hdd over 1f out: wknd)	¾	**3**	14/1	77	60
4847[9]	**Thatched (IRE) (43)** (REBarr) **7-7-7**(3) PFessey(20) (in tch: effrt over 2f out: sn chsng ldrs: kpt on fnl f)	½	**4**	16/1	51	34
4781[3]	**Bowcliffe (63)** (EJAlston) **6-9-2** JFEgan(22) (lw: hld up: hdwy & ev ch 2f out: nt qckn)	1	**5**	5/2[1]	69	52
4792[5]	**Magic Mill (IRE) (75)** (JLEyre) **4-9-7**(7) SBuckley(18) (chsd ldrs: effrt & ev ch 2f out: btn appr fnl f)	½	**6**	33/1	80	63
4596[6]	**Gymcrak Premiere (67)** (GHolmes) **9-9-6** ACulhane(11) (b.hind: bhd: n.m.r & swtchd over 1f out: styd on strly towards fin)	½	**7**	12/1[3]	71	54
4773[13]	**Smokey From Caplaw (71)** (JJO'Neill) **3-9-7** GHind(6) (mid div & n.m.r over 3f out: hdwy 2f out: nvr able chal)	hd	**8**	20/1	75	55
4283[19]	**Moscow Mist (IRE) (73)** (BPalling) **6-9-9**(3) DSweeney(17) (trckd ldrs: disp ld over 2f out tl wknd over 2f out)	nk	**9**	33/1	77	60
4813[6]	**Shontaine (57)** (MJohnston) **4-8-10** JWeaver(25) (lw: prom: rdn ½-wy: btn whn n.m.r over 1f out)	1	**10**	14/1	59	42
4596[15]	**Running Green (62)** (DMoffatt) **6-9-1v** DeanMcKeown(3) (b: mid div: hdwy & ch 2f out: sn rdn & btn)	s.h	**11**	25/1	63	46
4628[5]	**Needle Match (58)** (JJO'Neill) **4-8-11** OPears(26) (bhd: effrt 3f out: rdn & no imp)	½	**12**	12/1[3]	58	41
4792[3]	**Oriole (50)** (DonEnricoIncisa) **4-8-3** KimTinkler(21) (in tch: edgd lft over 2f out: sn btn)	½	**13**	16/1	49	32
4629[3]	**Winston (48)** (JDBethell) **4-7-12**(3) RFfrench(8) (outpcd ½-wy: no imp)	hd	**14**	11/1[2]	47	30
4243[3]	**Forest Robin (47)** (MrsJRRamsden) **4-8-0** DO'Donohoe(19) (lw: nvr nr to chal)	½	**15**	14/1	45	28
4845[16]	**Distant King (54)** (GPKelly) **4-8-0**(7)ow11 SFinnamore(14) (b: chsd ldrs 6f)	hd	**16**	100/1	52	24
4842[16]	**Pine Ridge Lad (IRE) (56)** (JLEyre) **7-8-9** RLappin(16) (disp ld to ½-wy: sn rdn & grad wknd)	3	**17**	16/1	48	31
4792[17]	**Somerton Boy (IRE) (71)** (PCalver) **7-9-10** JCarroll(10) (dwlt: effrt 3f out: no imp)	1	**18**	20/1	61	44
4583[4]	**Night Chorus (67)** (BSRothwell) **3-8-10**(7) RWinston(12) (lw: chsd ldrs over 5f)	s.h	**19**	14/1	57	37
4225[9]	**Court Express (67)** (TJEtherington) **3-9-3** MTebbutt(4) (bhd fr ½-wy)	3½	**20**	33/1	50	30
4139[13]	**Chairmans Choice (55)** (APJarvis) **7-8-8** AMcGlone(2) (prom 5f: sn btn)	2½	**21**	16/1	33	16
4845[17]	**Energy Man (45)** (MDods) **4-7-12** DaleGibson(24) (sn bhd)	2½	**22**	50/1	18	1
4792[19]	**Doctor Bravious (IRE) (55)** (BEllison) **4-8-8** NKennedy(13) (sn bhd)	nk	**23**	100/1	27	10
4410[13]	**Celebration Cake (IRE) (66)** (MissLAPerratt) **5-9-5** TWilliams(5) (drvn along ½-wy: sn lost tch)	1½	**24**	16/1	35	18
4628[12]	**Densben (43)** (DenysSmith) **13-7-10** JQuinn(1) (wl bhd fr ½-wy)	4	**25**	33/1	4	—
4742[2]	***Scaraben (70)*** (SEKettlewell) **9-9-9** JFortune(23) (Withdrawn not under Starter's orders: ref to ent stalls)		**W**	16/1	—	—
				(SP 154.8%)	**25 Rn**	

1m 35.3 (0.30) CSF £267.15 CT £3,768.56 TOTE £42.20: £6.90 £4.40 £5.90 £3.80 (£213.60) Trio £1,297.60 OWNER Mr Noel Sweeney (UPPER LONGDON) BRED Brownstown Stud
LONG HANDICAP Distant King 6-11

WEIGHT FOR AGE 3yo-3lb

OFFICIAL EXPLANATION Sualtach (IRE): regarding the improvement in form compared with his previous run at Newmarket on 16/10/97, the Stewards accepted the trainer's explanation that the colt had been coming down the handicap, and last time had raced on the unfavoured side of the course.

4410 Sualtach (IRE) has proved difficult to win with this year but this was a determined effort and was also his first victory over this trip. (20/1)
4792 Jedi Knight likes to come from off the pace and finished strongly but always that couple of strides too late. (14/1)
4510 Alpine Hideaway (IRE) likes it out in front and kept battling away but was a lost cause in the last furlong and a half. (14/1)
3264 Thatched (IRE) is difficult to predict but is obviously in good form just now as this was one of his better efforts. (16/1)
4781 Bowcliffe keeps having his chances but he just lacks that finishing dash at the moment. (5/2: op 5/1)
4792 Magic Mill (IRE) has been generally disappointing this year and is beginning to slip down the handicap. This was not too bad an effort. (33/1)
4596 Gymcrak Premiere takes a bit of knowing but finished like an express train here and is obviously in really good heart. (12/1: op 8/1)

4925 CAPTAIN COOK CONDITIONS STKS (2-Y.O) (Class D)

3-10 (3-11) **7f** £3,122.50 (£940.00: £455.00: £212.50) Stalls: High GOING minus 0.47 sec per fur (F)

				SP	RR	SF
4851[2]	**Dernier Croise (FR) (78)** (BJMeehan) **2-9-1** MTebbutt(1) (lw: trckd ldrs: slt ld 3f out: hld on wl)	—	1	2/1[3]	87	31
4775[5]	**Louis Philippe (USA)** (JHMGosden) **2-8-11** GHind(2) (lw: hld up: smooth hdwy to disp ld 2f out: rn green: no ex wl ins fnl f)	½	2	6/4[1]	82	26
4735[2]	**Pass The Rest (IRE)** (JLEyre) **2-8-11** TWilliams(4) (cl up: chal 3f out: outpcd fnl 2f)	5	3	15/8[2]	70	14
4841[10]	**Second Term (IRE)** (WStorey) **2-8-6** JFanning(3) (led 4f: sn rdn & btn)	11	4	150/1	40	—
				(SP 108.8%)	**4 Rn**	

1m 25.4 (2.40) CSF £4.93 TOTE £2.80: (£2.50) OWNER E H Jones (Paints) Ltd (UPPER LAMBOURN) BRED B. Ferrand & Coolmore Stud

4851 Dernier Croise (FR) won this through sheer experience as the runner-up threw it away through greenness. (2/1)
4775 Louis Philippe (USA) looked to be going best for much of the trip and probably put his head in front at one stage, but then proved very green and his rider could do nothing about it. (6/4)
4735 Pass The Rest (IRE) ran reasonably but found the front pair too classy when the pace was really on. (15/8)
Second Term (IRE) was quickly put in his place once this hotted up from halfway. (150/1)

4926 TELEPROMPTER LIMITED STKS (0-65) (3-Y.O+) (Class F)

3-45 (3-45) **1m 2f** £2,542.00 (£712.00: £346.00) Stalls: Low GOING minus 0.47 sec per fur (F)

				SP	RR	SF
4635[8]	**Tallulah Belle (63)** (NPLittmoden) **4-9-2** JWeaver(7) (lw: hld up & bhd: hdwy over 3f out: chal over 1f out: rdn to ld wl ins fnl f)	—	1	6/4[1]	74	46
4714[15]	**Classic Find (USA) (64)** (PatMitchell) **4-9-3** PBloomfield(5) (a.p: hdwy to ld 2f out: sn rdn & r.o: hdd & nt qckn towards fin)	½	2	6/1[3]	74	46
4751[14]	**Westminster (IRE) (55)** (MHTompkins) **5-9-0**(5) RMullen(8) (in tch: rdn over 2f out: no imp)	6	3	8/1	67	39
3455[5]	**Gee Bee Boy (64)** (APJarvis) **3-9-0** AMcGlone(6) (hdwy on outside 4f out: rdn over 2f out: nt pce to chal)	s.h	4	7/1	67	34
2416[4]	**Terdad (USA) (62)** (MrsMReveley) **4-9-5** DeanMcKeown(2) (lw: trckd ldrs: rdn over 2f out: one pce)	½	5	5/2[2]	66	38
4733[20]	**Speedboat (USA) (63)** (JLEyre) **3-8-12** LCharnock(1) (led after 2f: sn clr: hdd & wknd 2f out)	6	6	16/1	54	21
4847[11]	**Ginger Flower (40)** (GPKelly) **8-8-11**(3) GParkin(4) (in tch tl rdn & btn 3f out)	6	7	66/1	42	14
4469[5]	**Fantasy Flight (27)** (MAPeill) **3-8-9** JCarroll(3) (led 2f: chsd ldrs tl rdn & wknd 4f out: sn t.o)	dist	8	33/1	—	—
				(SP 116.8%)	**8 Rn**	

2m 5.6 (2.00) CSF £10.57 TOTE £2.40: £1.10 £2.20 £2.40 (£7.50) OWNER Trojan Racing (WOLVERHAMPTON) BRED Bowler (Presswork) Services Ltd

WEIGHT FOR AGE 3yo-5lb

4635 Tallulah Belle, back on the ground she loves, showed the right attitude under pressure. (6/4)
2475 Classic Find (USA) won his only race on this track last season and has lost his way since, but there was enough in this to suggest that he can regain winning ways. (6/1)
3200 Westminster (IRE), from a yard in form, ran quite well but is better coming from off a strong pace. (8/1)
3455 Gee Bee Boy was having his first run here for over two months and it was not too bad an effort in the circumstances. (7/1)
2416 Terdad (USA), twice a winner over hurdles this season, was stepped up in trip here and proved a shade disappointing. (5/2: 7/4-11/4)
4417 Speedboat (USA), stepping up in distance, pulled too hard out in front and failed to get home. (16/1)

4927 GANTON H'CAP (0-85) (3-Y.O+) (Class D)

4-15 (4-17) **7f** £3,701.00 (£1,118.00: £544.00: £257.00) Stalls: High GOING minus 0.47 sec per fur (F)

				SP	RR	SF
4842[13]	**Saint Express (80)** (MrsMReveley) **7-9-10** ACulhane(7) (hld up: hdwy over 2f out: r.o to ld wl ins fnl f)	—	1	14/1	89	65
4842[10]	**Johayro (64)** (JSGoldie) **4-8-8** AMcGlone(6) (led: qcknd ½-wy: hdd wl ins fnl f: kpt on)	½	2	20/1	72	48
4842[15]	**Tiler (IRE) (79)** (MJohnston) **5-9-9** JWeaver(2) (reard s: hdwy 3f out: r.o fnl f: nrst fin)	½	3	15/2[3]	86	62
4878[19]	**Zelda Zonk (72)** (BJMeehan) **5-9-2** MTebbutt(11) (lw: trckd ldrs: ev ch 2f out: rdn & r.o one pce)	2	4	8/1	74	50
4561*	**Royal Result (USA) (73)** (MWEasterby) **4-9-3** TLucas(9) (trckd ldrs: hdwy u.p to chse ldr over 1f out: sn btn)	nk	5	9/4[1]	75	51
4844[5]	**Plum First (52)** (MAPeill) **7-7-10** JQuinn(13) (b.hind: hld up: effrt over 2f out: styd on towards fin)	1½	6	16/1	50	26
4561[14]	**Weetman's Weigh (IRE) (78)** (RHollinshead) **4-9-5**(3) DGriffiths(4) (lw: in tch tl n.m.r & outpcd over 2f out: n.d after)	½	7	7/1[2]	75	51
4792[8]	**Gymcrak Flyer (65)** (GHolmes) **6-8-9** JFortune(12) (b.hind: bhd: hdwy 2f out: nvr nr to chal)	hd	8	14/1	62	38
4733[6]	**Garnock Valley (63)** (JBerry) **7-8-7b** JCarroll(10) (bhd: effrt over 2f out: no imp)	1¾	9	14/1	56	32
3484[3]	**Mister Westsound (52)** (MissLAPerratt) **5-7-10b** NKennedy(8) (dwlt: hdwy 3f out: chsng ldrs 2f out: sn btn)	hd	10	14/1	44	20
4787[7]	**Style Dancer (IRE) (75)** (RMWhitaker) **3-9-3b[1]** DeanMcKeown(15) (trckd ldrs tl wknd fnl 2f)	1	11	8/1	65	39
3937[10]	**Pleasure Trick (USA) (52)** (DonEnricoIncisa) **6-7-10** KimTinkler(14) (hld up & bhd: n.d)	½	12	50/1	41	17
4792[6]	**Knave's Ash (USA) (71)** (DNicholls) **6-8-12**(3) PRoberts(3) (chsd ldrs: rdn over 2f out: sn wknd)	1	13	8/1	58	34
4792[W]	**Mountgate (60)** (MPBielby) **5-8-4** JFEgan(1) (hld up: effrt over 2f out: sn btn & eased)	nk	14	14/1	46	22
4291[7]	**Komlucky (57)** (ABMulholland) **5-7-8v**(7)ow5 RWinston(5) (spd 4f: sn rdn & wknd)	8	15	50/1	25	—
				(SP 136.3%)	**15 Rn**	

1m 23.2 (0.20) CSF £266.83 CT £2,091.49 TOTE £22.40: £5.00 £8.60 £4.90 (£158.10) Trio £52.90 OWNER Mr D. S. Hall (SALTBURN) BRED R. M. Whitaker

LONG HANDICAP Mister Westsound 7-8 Pleasure Trick (USA) 7-3 Plum First 7-9 Komlucky 6-11

WEIGHT FOR AGE 3yo-2lb

4414 Saint Express at last got it right and this was his first win here for well over two years. (14/1)
4414* Johayro was allowed to dictate things at his own pace and almost stole it. (20/1)

4280 Tiler (IRE) was up to his old tricks at the start but then ran really well, finishing strongly, but he is beginning to look like an unreliable customer. (15/2)
4561 Zelda Zonk likes fast ground and also this track and is running well just now. (8/1)
4561* Royal Result (USA), up 8lb for his recent win, was never going as well this time but did still have his chances, only to look short of finishing pace. (9/4)
4844 Plum First ran well but would have been happier with a stronger gallop. (16/1)
4787 Style Dancer (IRE) had blinkers on instead of a visor this time and raced too freely. (8/1: op 5/1)
3105 Pleasure Trick (USA), returning here after almost two months off, had a quiet run and should improve for it. (50/1)

T/Plpt: £245.10 (63.44 Tckts). T/Qdpt: £45.60 (31.48 Tckts) AA

4928a - 4945a (Irish Racing) - See Computer Raceform

4848-YARMOUTH (L-H) (Firm)
Wednesday October 29th
WEATHER: sunny & cold WIND: slt against

4946 NEWPORT CLAIMING STKS (3-Y.O+) (Class F)
1-20 (1-20) **1m 6f 17y** £2,692.80 (£745.80: £356.40) Stalls: Low GOING minus 0.44 sec per fur (F)

				SP	RR	SF
4713[4]	**Paradise Navy (63)** (CREgerton) **8-9-7b** LDettori(3) (mde all: hrd rdn fnl f: jst hld on)	—	1	9/4[1]	62	44
4850*	**Anjou (55)** (JPearce) **5-9-6** KFallon(5) (hld up: hdwy over 2f out: hrd rdn fnl f: r.o)	s.h	2	5/2[2]	61	43
4607[5]	**Doyenne (34)** (GLewis) **3-7-11b**(3) RFfrench(9) (a.p: effrt & n.m.r fnl 2f: r.o strly nr fin)	nk	3	12/1[3]	50	23
4519[6]	**Rose of Glenn (40)** (BPalling) **6-8-9** JQuinn(2) (chsd wnr: rdn over 2f out: one pce)	1½	4	20/1	48	30
4850[8]	**Monacle (42)** (DMorris) **3-8-7b** NDay(1) (lost pl ½-wy: rallied appr fnl f: kpt on)	3½	5	40/1	51	24
4171[2]	**Batabanoo (53)** (MrsMReveley) **8-9-2** JReid(8) (hld up: effrt 3f out: grad wknd: fin lame)	¾	6	9/4[1]	50	32
	Clinking (MrsAJPerrett) **6-9-4** AClark(4) (hld up: hdwy over 3f out: wknd over 1f out)	1½	7	14/1	50	32
4846[12]	**Gresham Flyer (36)** (MrsSLamyman) **4-8-12** DHolland(7) (bit bkwd: a bhd: t.o)	26	8	66/1	15	—
4053[12]	**So Keen (40)** (ABailey) **4-8-13**(3) PRoberts(6) (trckd ldrs tl wknd 3f out: t.o)	3	9	50/1	15	—
				(SP 115.1%)	**9 Rn**	

3m 2.7 (4.70) CSF £7.18 TOTE £3.40: £1.60 £1.10 £2.80 (£4.60) Trio £17.00 OWNER Elite Racing Club (CHADDLEWORTH) BRED Stetchworth Park Stud Ltd
WEIGHT FOR AGE 3yo-9lb
OFFICIAL EXPLANATION **Batabanoo: the trainer's representative reported that the gelding finished lame.**
4713 Paradise Navy, a winner over course and distance in August, had far more use made of him this time and defied his rivals to wear him down. He is a character but this was his fourth success this term. (9/4)
4850* Anjou finished behind the winner on better terms earlier in the month so he can be said to have run a fine race in only just failing to get up. (5/2)
4607 Doyenne showed she truly stays this trip with a determined, last-furlong challenge after being tightened up on the rail throughout the last couple of furlongs. (12/1: 7/1-14/1)
3623 Rose of Glenn has been out of sorts for quite some time now but she showed something of a return to form with a pleasing display. She does win on the All-Weather so perhaps that will be where her immediate future lies. (20/1)
3320 Monacle dropped out of contention halfway down the back straight and looked out of it but he began to stay on again under strong pressure without ever threatening to reach the leaders. (40/1)
4171 Batabanoo ran a very lacklustre race here but he was lame on pulling up and that was sure to have been the reason. (9/4)
Clinking (14/1: 7/1-16/1)

4947 CORTON CONDITIONS STKS (3-Y.O+) (Class C)
1-55 (1-56) **1m 2f 21y** £5,176.00 (£1,666.00: £808.00) Stalls: High GOING minus 0.44 sec per fur (F)

				SP	RR	SF
4759[6]	**Silverani (IRE) (100)** (LMCumani) **3-9-0** LDettori(2) (lw: stdd s: hdwy 3f out: led 2f out: rdn & qcknd nr fin)	—	1	Evens[1]	108	30
4867a[7]	**Unconditional Love (IRE) (96)** (MJohnston) **4-8-11** DHolland(3) (chsd ldr: outpcd over 2f out: rallied appr fnl f: r.o)	¾	2	4/1[3]	99	26
3634[5]	**Behaviour (101)** (MrsJCecil) **5-9-2** JReid(4) (bit bkwd: led to 2f out: rdn & ev ch wl ins fnl f: no ex cl home)	nk	3	7/4[2]	103	30
				(SP 106.4%)	**3 Rn**	

2m 7.9 (4.10) CSF £4.23 TOTE £1.70 (£2.30) OWNER Mr Paul Silver (NEWMARKET) BRED J. Bowdren
WEIGHT FOR AGE 3yo-5lb
4759 Silverani (IRE), prepared to be given a lead, made smooth progress to nose ahead passing the quarter-mile marker and, finding more when set alight inside the last furlong, won readily. (Evens)
4867a Unconditional Love (IRE), having her first try at ten furlongs, was tapped for toe when the tempo lifted two furlongs out but she renewed her effort inside the final furlong and, given slightly easier ground, should be able to win at this trip. (4/1: 3/1-9/2)
3634 Behaviour did not look in tip-top condition after a lengthy rest and he was forced into setting the pace. Taken on and headed by the winner two furlongs out, he rallied in fine style and it was only in the final one hundred yards that he did eventually get shaken off. (7/4)

4948 LOUND NURSERY H'CAP (0-85) (2-Y.O) (Class E)
2-30 (2-30) **5f 43y** £2,961.00 (£882.00: £420.00: £189.00) Stalls: High GOING minus 0.44 sec per fur (F)

				SP	RR	SF
4737[2]	**Classy Cleo (IRE) (79)** (PDEvans) **2-9-1** JFEgan(2) (a.p: led over 1f out: rdn out)	—	1	5/1[2]	86	39
4746[2]	**Carol Singer (USA) (72)** (MJohnston) **2-8-8** DHolland(4) (hld up: swtchd lft & hdwy over 1f out: r.o)	2	2	10/1	73	26
4772[4]	**Arian Da (82)** (BPalling) **2-9-4** TSprake(1) (lw: led to 2f out: sn led again: hdd appr fnl f: one pce)	s.h	3	6/1	83	36
4772[2]	**Happy Days Again (IRE) (80)** (JWharton) **2-9-2b** KFallon(5) (hld up: effrt & rdn 2f out: nvr able to chal)	3½	4	11/2[3]	70	23
4746[6]	**Ivory's Joy (75)** (KTIvory) **2-8-11** MartinDwyer(9) (w ldrs: slt ld 2f out: sn hdd: wknd ins fnl f)	nk	5	12/1	64	17
4597[7]	**Phantom Ring (64)** (ABailey) **2-7-11**(3) RFfrench(8) (prom over 3f: sn rdn along & outpcd)	2½	6	6/1	45	—
4779[13]	**Touchanova (62)** (AHide) **2-7-7**(5) RMullen(3) (bhd: rdn ½-wy: no rspnse)	nk	7	20/1	42	—
4675[13]	**Mrs Malaprop (85)** (MRChannon) **2-9-7** JCarroll(6) (prom over 3f)	hd	8	7/2[1]	65	18

4755[11]	**Swanmore Lady (IRE) (61)** (SCWilliams) **2-7-11** JQuinn(7) (sn pushed along: nvr gng pce of ldrs)	5	**9**	13/2	26	—
				(SP 117.7%)		**9 Rn**

62.4 secs (1.40) CSF £49.90 CT £281.60 TOTE £5.00: £1.80 £2.30 £2.80 (£10.80) Trio £13.70 OWNER Mr J. E. Abbey (WELSHPOOL) BRED Rathasker Stud

4737 Classy Cleo (IRE) has certainly paid her way and, though she is beginning to get her winter coat, it did not prevent her from storming clear after taking command on the approach to the final furlong. (5/1)

4746 Carol Singer (USA) continues to perform well but she is not getting the success she deserves and, though she won the battle for the runner-up prize, the winner proved much too sharp. (10/1)

4772 Arian Da did her utmost to make it all and, not failing for the want of trying, had met her match inside the final furlong. (6/1)

4772 Happy Days Again (IRE) found this ground much too lively and she could never find the speed to launch a bid. (11/2: 4/1-6/1)

4522 Ivory's Joy, fighting for the lead from the start, did manage to poke her nose in front but she was being pestered all the time and her run had come to an end two hundred yards out. (12/1: 8/1-14/1)

2212 Phantom Ring (6/1: op 14/1)

4428* Mrs Malaprop looked ill at ease on this firm ground and she was in trouble soon after entering the last quarter-mile. (7/2)

4949 E.B.F. HERRINGFLEET MAIDEN STKS (2-Y.O) (Class D)

3-05 (3-07) **7f 3y** £4,071.60 (£1,216.80: £582.40: £265.20) Stalls: High GOING minus 0.44 sec per fur (F)

				SP	RR	SF
	Asad (SbinSuroor) **2-9-0** LDettori(3) (wl grwn: bit bkwd: mde all: shkn up appr fnl f: r.o wl)	—	**1**	5/2[2]	89++	38
	Great Dane (IRE) (HRACecil) **2-9-0** KFallon(5) (w'like: a chsng wnr: rdn & rn green 2f out: one pce fnl f)	1½	**2**	4/6[1]	86+	35
4454[5]	**Double Classic (USA)** (MRStoute) **2-9-0** JReid(8) (trckd ldrs: rdn 2f out: no imp)	7	**3**	7/1[3]	70	19
	Raffaello (IRE) (MRChannon) **2-9-0** JCarroll(1) (cmpt: bkwd: trckd ldrs: hrd drvn over 1f out: sn outpcd)	1¾	**4**	14/1	66	15
	Kimberley (GWragg) **2-9-0** MHills(4) (wl grwn: bit bkwd: nvr nr to chal)	3½	**5**	12/1	58	7
	Tigullio (IRE) (CFWall) **2-9-0** GHind(2) (leggy: lt-f: s.i.s: sn chsng ldrs: rdn 2f out: sn wknd)	1¼	**6**	50/1	55	4
4780[3]	**Highly Pleased (USA)** (EALDunlop) **2-9-0** DO'Donohoe(6) (dwlt: a in rr)	s.h	**7**	50/1	55	4
	Verocity (FR) (GWragg) **2-9-0** AClark(7) (lt-f: unf: bit bkwd: s.s: a bhd: t.o)	17	**8**	50/1	16	—
				(SP 121.3%)		**8 Rn**

1m 26.2 (2.00) CSF £4.36 TOTE £3.50: £1.40 £1.10 £1.60 (£2.40) OWNER Godolphin (NEWMARKET) BRED Sheikh Mohammed bin Rashid al Maktoum

Asad, a powerful-looking colt who covers a lot of ground, did look as though he would benefit from the run but, dictating from the front, was always going much too well for the hard-driven favourite. (5/2)

Great Dane (IRE), a plain-looking May foal, raced with his head high and gave the impression he disliked the fast ground, but he also changed his legs several times throughout the race and ran green so perhaps this was not a bad effort after all. (4/6)

4454 Double Classic (USA) still has a bit left to work on and though he stayed on to make the frame, the leading pair were a class apart. (7/1)

Raffaello (IRE), another May foal who looked far from fully wound up, ran well until having to admit his measure taken before reaching the final furlong. (14/1: 7/1-16/1)

Kimberley, bred to need middle-distances, was always struggling to lay up but he does look a nice type and more will be heard of him next year. (12/1: 8/1-14/1)

4950 RANWORTH MAIDEN STKS (2-Y.O) (Class D)

3-40 (3-42) **1m 3y** £4,173.00 (£1,248.00: £598.00: £273.00) Stalls: High GOING minus 0.44 sec per fur (F)

				SP	RR	SF
	Publisher (USA) (JRFanshawe) **2-9-0** TSprake(4) (w'like: leggy: bit bkwd: stdd s: hdwy 2f out: str run to ld cl home)	—	**1**	12/1	88++	32
	Star Crystal (IRE) (HRACecil) **2-8-9** KFallon(3) (leggy: lt-f: mde most: rdn over 1f out: hdd cl home)	nk	**2**	5/2[2]	82+	26
	Un Melodie (SbinSuroor) **2-8-9** LDettori(8) (unf: scope: bit bkwd: disp ld: pushed along over 1f out: unable qckn)	1¼	**3**	2/1[1]	80+	24
4229[3]	**Highwayman (IRE)** (MRStoute) **2-9-0** JReid(2) (hdwy ½-wy: effrt & rdn wl over 1f out: unable qckn ins fnl f)	s.h	**4**	4/1[3]	85	29
4734[4]	**Act Defiant (USA)** (PFICole) **2-9-0** AClark(5) (chsd ldrs: one pce appr fnl f)	1¾	**5**	10/1	81	25
	There Be Demons (USA) (GWragg) **2-9-0** MHills(1) (w'like: scope: bkwd: in tch: rdn along over 2f out: sn btn)	3	**6**	8/1	75	19
	Sternsinger (USA) (HRACecil) **2-9-0** WRyan(9) (neat: scope: trckd ldrs: pushed along over 2f out: grad wknd)	2	**7**	12/1	71	15
4740[8]	**Slip Venture** (SPCWoods) **2-9-0** NDay(6) (s.s: rdn 3f out: a bhd)	4	**8**	25/1	63	7
	Battle Warning (HRACecil) **2-9-0** AMcGlone(7) (lt-f: a bhd: t.o)	13	**9**	14/1	37	—
4244[7]	**Ardleigh Charmer** (CADwyer) **2-9-0** DO'Donohoe(10) (trckd ldrs: rdn along ½-wy: sn lost tch: t.o)	6	**10**	100/1	25	—
				(SP 129.0%)		**10 Rn**

1m 38.9 (2.90) CSF £42.60 TOTE £15.70: £3.80 £1.20 £1.60 (£49.90) Trio £54.60 OWNER Mr Joseph Allen (NEWMARKET) BRED Joseph Allen

Publisher (USA), a tall colt who looked the most backward of the lot, brought up the rear for the majority of the way but he began to stay on inside the distance and, maintaining his run, timed it just right. (12/1: op 8/1)

Star Crystal (IRE), a leggy half-sister to two Group Three winners, came out on top in her duel with the favourite but, after thinking she had the prize sewn up, the winner came from out of the blue to wear her down in the dying strides. (5/2)

Un Melodie, an unfurnished filly with plenty of scope, had a head to head with Star Crystal which she eventually lost and was not knocked about when held. She is sure to be a much better and stronger individual next season. (2/1: 6/4-9/4)

4229 Highwayman (IRE) continues to progress and it was only her inability to quicken that was beating him inside the last furlong. (4/1)

4734 Act Defiant (USA) has not run on ground as fast as he had here but he sat on the tails of the leaders and had every chance until getting tapped for toe entering the final furlong. Tenderly handled when beaten, we have not seen the best of this fellow yet. (10/1: op 5/1)

There Be Demons (USA) comes from a useful winning family but he does look to need more time and this experience will stand him in good stead. (8/1)

Sternsinger (USA), quite an attractive newcomer, ran much better than his final placing might suggest and he should be capable of making the grade. (12/1: op 7/1)

4951 CALIFORNIA H'CAP (0-70) (3-Y.O+) (Class E)

4-10 (4-12) **7f 3y** £3,659.75 (£1,097.00: £527.50: £242.75) Stalls: High GOING minus 0.44 sec per fur (F)

				SP	RR	SF
4404[5]	**Speedy Classic (USA) (53)** (MJHeaton-Ellis) **8-8-12** AClark(20) (a.p stands' side: led 2f out: all out)	—	**1**	14/1	66	43
4451*	**Lord Olivier (IRE) (69)** (WJarvis) **7-10-0** JReid(19) (chsd ldrs stands' side: rdn & r.o wl fnl f)	nk	**2**	8/1[3]	81	58

				SP	RR	SF
4738^{6}	**Mybotye (59)** (RBastiman) **4-9-4** WRyan(6) (racd far side: led wl over 1f out: rdn & r.o)	2	**3**	$5/1^{1}$	67	44
4404^{7}	**Lunch Party (40)** (DNicholls) **5-7-8**(5) IonaWands(5) (led far side after 2f: rdn, edgd rt & hdd wl over 1f out)	nk	**4**	$7/1^{2}$	47	24
4601^{4}	**Kosevo (IRE) (42)** (MGMeagher) **3-7-10**(3) PFessey(2) (chsd ldrs far side: ev ch 1f out: unable qckn)	nk	**5**	12/1	48	23
4741^{9}	**Mr Speaker (IRE) (55)** (CFWall) **4-8-9**(5) RMullen(8) (trckd ldrs far side: styd on ins fnl f)	s.h	**6**	20/1	61	38
4561^{20}	**Gain Line (USA) (54)** (BobJones) **4-8-13** NDay(14) (nvr nrr)	¾	**7**	14/1	59	36
3910^{7}	**Lachesis (45)** (MrsSLamyman) **4-8-4** JQuinn(18) (hdwy stands' side over 1f out: nrst fin)	nk	**8**	25/1	49	26
4629^{12}	**Mezzoramio (50)** (KAMorgan) **5-8-4v**(5) JoHunnam(7) (led far side 2f: rdn 2f out: wknd appr fnl f)	nk	**9**	$8/1^{3}$	53	30
4333^{5}	**Shining Cloud (55)** (MBell) **4-9-0b^{1}** MFenton(13) (led stands' side 5f: sn rdn & grad wknd)	1¼	**10**	$8/1^{3}$	55	32
4695^{5}	**Tael of Silver (43)** (ABailey) **5-8-2** DWright(16) (in tch stands' side over 4f)	s.h	**11**	9/1	43	20
4738^{15}	**Mazeed (IRE) (58)** (PDEvans) **4-9-3** KFallon(4) (s.s: hdwy 5f out: rdn & wknd over 2f out)	1	**12**	20/1	56	33
4404^{6}	**Dark Menace (45)** (EAWheeler) **5-7-11b**(7) SCarson(1) (racd far side: nvr nr to chal)	1½	**13**	25/1	40	17
4798^{5}	**Be Warned (50)** (JPearce) **6-8-9** GBardwell(3) (nvr nr ldrs)	s.h	**14**	$8/1^{3}$	44	21
4872^{16}	**Court House (58)** (MCChapman) **3-9-1** LNewton(9) (nvr trbld ldrs)	¾	**15**	25/1	51	26
3476^{7}	**Super Park (38)** (JPearce) **5-7-6**(5) APolli(17) (bkwd: a bhd)	2	**16**	33/1	26	3
4773^{14}	**Finarts Bay (57)** (MrsJCecil) **3-9-0** JWeaver(15) (chsd ldrs stands' side over 4f)	5	**17**	20/1	34	9
4333^{12}	**Aegean Sound (46)** (KTIvory) **3-8-3** MartinDwyer(12) (trckd ldrs over 4f)	nk	**18**	33/1	22	—
4606^{2}	**May Queen Megan (43)** (MrsALMKing) **4-8-2** NAdams(11) (prom: rdn along ½-wy: sn lost tch)	hd	**19**	9/1	19	—
	Absolutely Abstone (45) (PDEvans) **3-8-2**ow1 JFEgan(10) (t.o)	18	**20**	33/1	—	—
				(SP 149.3%)	**20 Rn**	

1m 25.6 (1.40) CSF £117.61 CT £623.74 TOTE £14.20: £3.20 £2.10 £1.70 £5.20 (£58.40) Trio £167.80 OWNER South Wales Shower S Faucets (WROUGHTON) BRED Lagrange Chance Partnership & Overbrook Farm
WEIGHT FOR AGE 3yo-2lb

4404 Speedy Classic (USA) took command under the stands' rail two furlongs out and, though he was strongly pressed right to the finish, always looked likely to hold on. (14/1)
4451* Lord Olivier (IRE) put in a sustained last-furlong challenge but the winner was up to it and the line was always going to arrive too soon for him. (8/1)
4738 Mybotye forged ahead of the far side below the distance and set sail for home but the leading pair, racing away from him, just beat him to the punch. (5/1)
4228* Lunch Party made the majority of the running on the far side and, if he had not drifted off a true line over a furlong out, it is possible he could have held on. (7/1: 6/1-10/1)
4601 Kosevo (IRE) is improving in leaps and bounds now that he is tackling a more suitable trip and success is only delayed. (12/1: op 8/1)
3690 Mr Speaker (IRE), in behind the leaders on the far side, battled on willingly in the closing stages but the season could end too soon for him. (20/1)
4225 Gain Line (USA) usually runs well here and, though he was unable to make his presence felt on this occasion, he did finish on the heels of the pack. (14/1)
4510 Mezzoramio (8/1: op 12/1)

T/Jkpt: Not won; £21,816.97 to Nottingham 30/10/97. T/Plpt: £12.70 (1,713.54 Tckts). T/Qdpt: £6.10 (309.56 Tckts) IM

4738-NOTTINGHAM (L-H) (Good, Good to soft patches)
Thursday October 30th
WEATHER: overcast and showery WIND: nil

4952 E.B.F. NETHERFIELD MAIDEN STKS (I) (2-Y.O) (Class D)
1-00 (1-00) **1m 54y** £3,460.00 (£1,030.00: £490.00: £220.00) Stalls: Low GOING: 0.02 sec per fur (G)

				SP	RR	SF
4478^{5}	**Almandab (IRE)** (JHMGosden) **2-9-0** GHind(4) (sn chsng ldr: led 3f out: drvn clr)	—	**1**	12/1	96+	50
4478^{4}	**Free As The Wind (IRE)** (PWChapple-Hyam) **2-9-0** JReid(5) (lw: led to 3f out: sn hrd drvn & outpcd)	9	**2**	10/1	79	33
4668^{4}	**Courageous (IRE)** (PFICole) **2-9-0** TQuinn(1) (lw: chsd ldrs: r.o one pce fnl 2f)	2	**3**	$7/2^{2}$	75	29
4715^{2}	**Ta Aruf (USA)** (DMorley) **2-8-9** RHills(10) (hld up: styd on one pce fnl 2f)	1¾	**4**	$5/2^{1}$	66	20
4701^{5}	**In The Sun (USA)** (JLDunlop) **2-8-9** GCarter(12) (swtg: in tch: rdn over 3f out: styd on one pce)	¾	**5**	25/1	65	19
	Kadir (SbinSuroor) **2-9-0** LDettori(9) (w'like: lengthy: bit bkwd: hld up: nvr nr to chal)	1	**6**	$4/1^{3}$	68	22
	Moratorium (USA) (HRACecil) **2-9-0** AMcGlone(7) (w'like: leggy: scope: chsd ldrs tl wknd over 2f out)	1	**7**	$7/2^{2}$	66	20
4710^{3}	**Russian Party (IRE)** (ACStewart) **2-9-0** SWhitworth(8) (hld up: effrt 3f out: sn wknd)	1	**8**	10/1	64	18
	Sunstreak (CFWall) **2-9-0** GDuffield(11) (leggy: unf: dwlt: a in rr)	3½	**9**	33/1	57	11
3494^{13}	**High Jinks** (BSmart) **2-9-0** JStack(13) (w ldrs: rdn 3f out: wknd fnl 2f)	s.h	**10**	50/1	57	11
	Cadillac Jukebox (USA) (JWHills) **2-8-11**(3) MHenry(6) (unf: trckd ldrs: sn drvn along: lost tch over 3f out)	1¾	**11**	16/1	54	8
4852^{13}	**Lady Rockstar** (MJRyan) **2-8-9** AClark(2) (mid div: drvn along over 3f out: sn lost tch)	3	**12**	50/1	43	—
4575^{11}	**Glamorgan (IRE)** (CADwyer) **2-9-0** DHolland(3) (a bhd)	2½	**13**	50/1	43	—
				(SP 137.4%)	**13 Rn**	

1m 46.3 (5.00) CSF £127.96 TOTE £16.80: £3.10 £3.90 £1.50 (£76.40) Trio £42.40 OWNER Sheikh Ahmed Al Maktoum (NEWMARKET) BRED Tony O'Callaghan
IN-FOCUS: **The races on the round course were run on the old hurdles track, only the second time this has happened.**
4478 Almandab (IRE) showed how much he had improved with a race under his belt, and the way he spread-eagled these rivals he could be something to go to work with next year. (12/1)
4478 Free As The Wind (IRE) finished upsides the winner when they were both making their racecourse debut last month, but he got well and truly thrashed this time although he did beat the rest easily enough. (10/1)
4668 Courageous (IRE), tackling a longer trip, still looked as though he could be made fitter. His lack of pace in the closing stages would suggest that he has been brought along steadily and we should see the real thing next season. (7/2: 5/2-4/1)
4715 Ta Aruf (USA), content to lob along in mid-division, did not pick up as readily as expected in the straight but she did stay on, if never able to get herself into contention. (5/2)
4701 In The Sun (USA), always tracking the leaders, failed to respond when driven along early in the straight, and her one pace was never going to enable her to take a hand in proceedings. (25/1)
Moratorium (USA), quite an impressive-looking colt, almost took charge on the way to the start but he settled better once in action and chased the leaders until feeling the strain before reaching the final quarter-mile. He should be able to make his mark as a three-year-old. (7/2: op 6/4)

4953 RUSHCLIFFE NURSERY H'CAP (2-Y.O) (Class E)

1-30 (1-30) **1m 54y** £3,330.25 (£997.00: £478.50: £219.25) Stalls: Low GOING: 0.02 sec per fur (G)

				SP	RR	SF
4856[2]	**Radar (IRE) (70)** (MAJarvis) **2-7-8**(3)ow1 RFfrench(7) (lw: a.p: led 2f out: eased nr fin)	—	**1**	11/8[1]	79+	23
4778[8]	**Al's Fella (IRE) (69)** (PFICole) **2-7-10** JQuinn(1) (led tl over 2f out: styd on again ins fnl f)	2	**2**	6/1	74	19
4856[8]	**Praetorian Gold (73)** (RHannon) **2-8-0**ow1 DBiggs(8) (s.i.s: hld up: hdwy over 2f out: nt rch ldrs)	1¾	**3**	11/2[3]	75	19
4778[16]	**Alconleigh (94)** (MJohnston) **2-9-7** DHolland(4) (prom: led over 2f out: sn hdd: wknd fnl f)	1¼	**4**	9/2[2]	93	38
4806[4]	**Narrogin (USA) (74)** (MRChannon) **2-8-1** AMackay(5) (bhd: outpcd over 2f out: styd on u.p fnl f)	hd	**5**	6/1	73	18
4803[7]	**Fashion Victim (81)** (THCaldwell) **2-8-8** ACulhane(6) (bhd: effrt over 2f out: no imp)	3	**6**	9/1	74	19
4566[12]	**Night Auction (IRE) (70)** (BPalling) **2-7-8**(3)ow1 PFessey(3) (lw: trckd ldrs tl wknd fnl 2f)	2	**7**	10/1	59	3
3078[2]	**Wedding Band (70)** (AGFoster) **2-7-4**(7)ow1 PDoe(2) (bkwd: sn outpcd & pushed along: t.o)	16	**8**	40/1	28	—
				(SP 125.8%)	**8 Rn**	

1m 47.5 (6.20) CSF £10.73 CT £36.35 TOTE £2.20: £1.10 £1.80 £2.20 (£5.90) OWNER Mr John Sims (NEWMARKET) BRED Samoth Bloodstock

LONG HANDICAP Radar (IRE) 7-7 Night Auction (IRE) 7-9 Wedding Band 6-8

4856 Radar (IRE), supported to the exclusion of the rest on this return to a mile, won this with quite a bit in hand and it is doubtful if he will be so well handicapped again. (11/8)

3794 Al's Fella (IRE) attempted to make all, but the winner was always in his slipstream and when he said go the race was all but over. (6/1)

4459* Praetorian Gold, a persistent tooth grinder, had little chance of turning the tables on the winner on these identical terms, but he did battle on right to the end and he stays this trip well enough. (11/2)

3650 Alconleigh, a big, strong colt, has in his most recent races given the impression that he has had enough for this season and, with top weight taking its toll, he had reached the end of his tether inside the distance. (9/2)

4806 Narrogin (USA) has had some hard races in the past month and in this instance he never really got going until it was far too late. (6/1)

4954 SNEINTON CONDITIONS STKS (3-Y.O+) (Class C)

2-00 (2-01) **6f 15y** £4,963.60 (£1,842.40: £888.70: £368.50: £151.75: £65.05) Stalls: High GOING: 0.02 sec per fur (G)

				SP	RR	SF
4881[9]	**Carranita (IRE) (105)** (BPalling) **7-8-7** TSprake(11) (lw: a.p: effrt 2f out: r.o to ld towards fin)	—	**1**	3/1[1]	102	61
4797[2]	**Zuhair (83)** (DMcCain) **4-8-9**(3) PFessey(12) (b: lw: led & sn wl clr: rdn over 1f out: hdd wl ins fnl f)	¾	**2**	33/1	105	64
4756[4]	**Crofters Ceilidh (95)** (BAMcMahon) **5-8-7** TQuinn(10) (hld up: hdwy 2f out: styd on u.p ins fnl f)	1¼	**3**	7/1[3]	97	56
4881[2]	**Brave Edge (101)** (RHannon) **6-9-3** DaneO'Neill(6) (a.p: rdn 2f out: kpt on wl)	s.h	**4**	4/1[2]	107	66
4777[6]	**Divina Luna (92)** (JWHills) **4-8-7**(3) MHenry(9) (hdwy over 2f out: kpt on ins fnl f)	1¼	**5**	8/1	96	55
4240[5]	**Soviet State (USA) (105)** (PWChapple-Hyam) **3-9-2** JReid(2) (lw: trckd ldrs: rdn over 2f out: nt pce to chal)	½	**6**	7/1[3]	102	60
4777[10]	**Rififi (86)** (RIngram) **4-9-1** DO'Donohoe(5) (b: hld up & bhd: effrt over 2f out: wknd appr fnl f)	1¼	**7**	20/1	97	56
4756[12]	**Double Splendour (IRE) (92)** (PSFelgate) **7-8-9**(3) DSweeney(3) (bhd: effrt & shkn up 2f out: no imp)	hd	**8**	9/1	93	52
4881[6]	**Bowden Rose (96)** (MBlanshard) **5-8-12b** JQuinn(7) (hld up & bhd: effrt 2f out: no imp)	s.h	**9**	8/1	93	52
4881[7]	**Patsy Grimes (90)** (JSMoore) **7-8-4**(3) RFfrench(1) (outpcd fnl 3f)	3½	**10**	7/1[3]	79	38
4787[6]	**Top Banana (80)** (HCandy) **6-8-5**(7) BarrySmith(8) (a in rr)	s.h	**11**	20/1	84	43
4805[5]	**Night Harmony (IRE) (53)** (MissSJWilton) **4-8-12** SWhitworth(4) (b: outpcd fr ½-wy: t.o)	6	**12**	100/1	45 t	27
				(SP 128.2%)	**12 Rn**	

1m 13.8 (2.30) CSF £114.28 TOTE £5.00: £1.70 £9.10 £1.90 (£83.40) Trio £69.00 OWNER Mr Humphrey Okeke & Mrs Rena Davies (COWBRIDGE) BRED Mrs Anita Quinn

WEIGHT FOR AGE 3yo-1lb

2329 Carranita (IRE) has taken time to get off the mark this term but she landed quite a touch here with a readily-gained success and, she has certainly lost none of her ability. (3/1)

4797 Zuhair had the favoured stand-side rail to race against and, setting a scorching pace in the conditions, was only pegged back while inside the last furlong. When these tactics are adopted he will always take some catching. (33/1)

4756 Crofters Ceilidh much more effective over the minimum trip on faster ground, ran well in the circumstances but she just could not summon the pace to deliver her challenge. (7/1)

4881 Brave Edge has from time to time beaten most of these rivals, but not on these terms, and the winner for one was able to gain her revenge. (4/1: 3/1-9/2)

4777 Divina Luna did not have the hill that she had when running over this trip on her previous outing, and though she was gaining ground all the way to the line the post was always going to arrive to soon. She is in good heart at present. (8/1)

4240 Soviet State (USA), the only three-year-old in the field, had plenty on his plate trying to concede weight to older horses and, unable to pick up when given the office, his chance had soon disappeared. (7/1)

4955 'JACK JENNINGS' CONDITIONS STKS (2-Y.O) (Class D)

2-30 (2-30) **6f 15y** £3,785.00 (£1,130.00: £540.00: £245.00) Stalls: High GOING: 0.02 sec per fur (G)

				SP	RR	SF
4668[3]	**Late Night Out** (WJarvis) **2-8-11** JReid(1) (hld up in tch: effrt & shkn up over 1f out: led appr fnl f: r.o wl)	—	**1**	2/1[1]	88+	53
3905*	**Ring Dancer** (PJMakin) **2-9-3** DHolland(5) (lw: w ldrs: drvn along & hung lft over 2f out: kpt on)	1½	**2**	11/4[2]	90+	55
4755[2]	**The Downtown Fox (80)** (BAMcMahon) **2-8-11** SSanders(7) (led tl hdd over 1f out: kpt on u.p nr fin)	1¾	**3**	4/1[3]	79	44
4211[2]	**Sarah Stokes (IRE) (75)** (RGuest) **2-8-3**(3) RFfrench(3) (chsd ldrs: kpt on one pce fnl 2f)	¾	**4**	11/2	73	38
4755[10]	**Blue Kite (84)** (NPLittmoden) **2-9-1** JWeaver(4) (sn outpcd & a bhd)	7	**5**	10/1	63	28
2286[5]	**Piped Aboard (IRE)** (JLDunlop) **2-8-11** GCarter(6) (bit bkwd: s.i.s: a outpcd)	5	**6**	10/1	46	11
				(SP 113.6%)	**6 Rn**	

1m 14.6 (3.10) CSF £7.20 TOTE £2.70: £1.70 £1.80 (£4.20) OWNER Mr J. M. Greetham (NEWMARKET) BRED J. M. Greetham

4668 Late Night Out found this not-so-testing ground more to his liking and, always travelling comfortably, won with a shade to spare, despite showing signs of greenness when sent about his work. (2/1)

3905* Ring Dancer had a 6lb penalty to contend with after making a winning debut and he hung left when bustled along on the approach to the final furlong, but he did keep staying on and lost no caste in defeat. (11/4: op 6/4)

4755 The Downtown Fox, a very edgy individual in the paddock, held the call until the winner wore him down, and his one pace from then on was just not good enough. He is just beginning to get his winter coat. (4/1)

4211 Sarah Stokes (IRE) had a slightly longer trip and the softer ground that she looks to need, but despite running another genuine race she was short of the necessary speed at the business end. She will win races when she gets it all together. (11/2)

4479* Blue Kite (10/1: 6/1-12/1)

2286 Piped Aboard (IRE) (10/1: 7/1-11/1)

4956 COLWICK PARK H'CAP (0-80) (3-Y.O+) (Class D)

3-00 (3-01) **1m 6f 15y** £4,175.00 (£1,250.00: £600.00: £275.00) Stalls: Low GOING: 0.02 sec per fur (G)

			SP	RR	SF
4874*	**Jawah (IRE) (75)** (KMahdi) **3-8-11**(3) 5x CLowther(3) (b.hind: hld up & bhd: hdwy 4f out: led 1f out: r.o strly)..—	**1**	7/4[1]	87+	60
4783[28]	**Salska (60)** (AStreeter) **6-8-5**(3) RHavlin(11) (hld up: hdwy over 4f out: led 2f out to 1f out: one pce) 2½	**2**	10/1[3]	69	51
4363[5]	**Beaumont (IRE) (74)** (JEBanks) **7-9-8** JQuinn(9) (sn chsng ldrs: ev ch over 1f out: styd on one pce)...............2	**3**	7/1[2]	81	63
4744[4]	**Classic Line (65)** (JLDunlop) **3-8-4b** GCarter(7) (a chsng ldrs: rdn & one pce fnl 2f)..........................½	**4**	10/1[3]	71	44
4874[15]	**Tycooness (IRE) (75)** (MJohnston) **3-9-0b** JWeaver(12) (hld up & bhd: hdwy 3f out: hung lft: nt rch ldrs).......nk	**5**	20/1	81	54
4874[9]	**Spartan Heartbeat (78)** (CEBrittain) **4-9-12b** DaneO'Neill(14) (swtg: hld up & bhd: hdwy 3f out: styd on).........2	**6**	20/1	82	64
4783[17]	**Star Rage (IRE) (80)** (MJohnston) **7-10-0** JReid(13) (lw: bhd: sme hdwy fnl 2f: nvr nrr) 2	**7**	10/1[3]	81	63
4279[9]	**The Butterwick Kid (60)** (RAFahey) **4-8-1**(7) RWinston(15) (bit bkwd: hld up in tch: hdwy over 3f out: wknd wl over 1f out)..........nk	**8**	14/1	61	43
4891[10]	**Hill Farm Blues (63)** (WMBrisbourne) **4-8-11** AGarth(1) (chsd ldr: led 7f out to 2f out: wknd qckly appr fnl f) ...4	**9**	16/1	60	42
4751[9]	**Hasta la Vista (55)** (MWEasterby) **7-8-3b** LCharnock(4) (trckd ldrs tl wknd over 2f out) 1¼	**10**	16/1	50	32
4860[2]	**Random Kindness (65)** (RIngram) **4-8-13** AMcGlone(6) (chsd ldrs: rdn & wknd over 2f out) 1½	**11**	7/1[2]	58	40
3579[4]	**Thaljanah (IRE) (78)** (BSmart) **5-9-12** JStack(10) (lw: sn in tch: wknd 3f out)..nk	**12**	12/1	71	53
	Influence Pedler (59) (JABOld) **4-8-4**(3) RFfrench(8) (bit bkwd: sn prom: wknd 3f out) ....¾	**13**	12/1	51	33
4313[5]	**Artic Courier (78)** (DJSCosgrove) **6-9-12** MRimmer(2) (b: hld up: effrt on ins over 3f out: sn wknd: t.o) 11	**14**	16/1	58	40
4794[12]	**Mister Aspecto (IRE) (59)** (MJohnston) **4-8-7v** DHolland(16) (racd wd: led to 7f out: lost pl over 3f out: t.o) 3	**15**	16/1	35	17
			(SP 143.7%)	**15 Rn**	

3m 5.6 (7.10) CSF £22.72 CT £109.37 TOTE £2.90: £2.10 £3.20 £2.10 (£25.80) Trio £158.10 OWNER Mr H. Al-Mutawa (NEWMARKET)
WEIGHT FOR AGE 3yo-9lb

4874* Jawah (IRE) was the only one anyone wanted to be on, and he defied his penalty with the minimum of fuss. He has clearly come to himself now but it is feared that, even with his penalties, he might have trouble surviving the cut for the November Handicap. (7/4)

4562 Salska is a pretty consistent mare and she is a trier, but the very much improved winner brushed her aside without much difficulty inside the distance. (10/1)

3805 Beaumont (IRE) sat closer to the pace than he normally does and delivered his determined challenge entering the final furlong, but the weight concession was just too much and he was forced to admit that this was not going to be his day. (7/1)

4744 Classic Line won her only race at this trip and she was always pushed to challenge on the heels of the leaders, but she does not do things quickly once off the bridle, and she was tapped for toe in the closing stages. (10/1)

4704 Tycooness (IRE), restrained in the rear, showed a tendency to hang left when staying on inside the last half-mile and was never able to make her presence felt. (20/1)

4547 Spartan Heartbeat, who was colty in the preliminaries, has his mind on other things now and, though he was doing all his best work late on, he has still not fulfilled the promise he has always shown he has. (20/1)

4957 E.B.F. NETHERFIELD MAIDEN STKS (II) (2-Y.O) (Class D)

3-30 (3-36) **1m 54y** £3,460.00 (£1,030.00: £490.00: £220.00) Stalls: Low GOING: 0.02 sec per fur (G)

			SP	RR	SF
4740[6]	**Eliza Acton** (PWHarris) **2-8-9** ACulhane(10) (lw: hld up: hdwy over 4f out: led wl ins fnl f: gamely)..............—	**1**	13/2[3]	74	27
	Capri (HRACecil) **2-9-0** AMcGlone(2) (w'like: leggy: scope: chsd ldrs: rdn over 1f out: r.o wl) ....hd	**2**	9/4[1]	79+	32
4638[9]	**General Monck** (DMorley) **2-9-0** MFenton(11) (lw: w ldr: led over 3f out tl ins fnl f: r.o u.p)...........................s.h	**3**	33/1	79	32
	Sea Wave (IRE) (SbinSuroor) **2-9-0** LDettori(5) (w'like: bit bkwd: hld up: hdwy over 3f out: rdn 2f out: kpt on)..........1¼	**4**	5/2[2]	76	29
4758[8]	**Regal Patriarch (IRE)** (JLDunlop) **2-9-0** GCarter(12) (a chsng ldrs: r.o one pce fnl 3f) 5	**5**	14/1	67	20
4244[8]	**Shohra Wa Jaah** (MAJarvis) **2-9-0** PaulEddery(3) (led tl over 3f out: wknd over 1f out) ....nk	**6**	33/1	66	19
4758[21]	**U K Magic (IRE)** (JEBanks) **2-9-0** JQuinn(13) (hdwy ½-wy: wknd 3f out) 2½	**7**	50/1	61	14
4853[8]	**Norcroft Joy** (MJRyan) **2-8-9** AClark(6) (trckd ldrs: effrt 3f out: wknd wl over 1f out) 3	**8**	50/1	50	3
	Inchahoy (JGSmyth-Osbourne) **2-8-9** TSprake(4) (unf: bit bkwd: s.i.s: a in rr) ....s.h	**9**	33/1	50	3
4715[16]	**Sabre Butt** (MHTompkins) **2-9-0** DBiggs(9) (a bhd: t.o) 15	**10**	33/1	26	—
4789[12]	**Tiller Girl (IRE)** (MJCamacho) **2-8-9** LCharnock(8) (bit bkwd: chsd ldrs: pushed along ½-wy: grad wknd: t.o)..........1¼	**11**	50/1	19	—
	Swallow Warrior (IRE) (TJEtherington) **2-8-11**(3) CLowther(1) (small: str: bkwd: sn t.o) 8	**12**	50/1	8	—
4758[3]	***Bering Gifts (IRE)*** (PFICole) **2-9-0** TQuinn(7) (Withdrawn not under Starter's orders: ref to ent stalls)	**W**	9/4[1]	—	—
			(SP 129.7%)	**12 Rn**	

1m 48.2 (6.90) CSF £11.15 TOTE £5.00: £1.10 £1.10 £7.30 (£5.40) Trio £50.30 OWNER Mrs P. W. Harris (BERKHAMSTED) BRED Pendley Farm

4740 Eliza Acton, much sharper this time, knew full well what was needed and, showing her true battling qualities in a hectic battle to the line, was always going to hold on. Her stable continues to turn out an impressive number of winners every year. (13/2: op 12/1)

Capri, a May foal who could prove useful over middle-distances next term, showed the right commitment in a hard fought head-to-head to the finish and it took a very fit winner to edge him out. (9/4: op evens)

General Monck, improving as he gains experience, left his previous form behind with a very pleasing display, and if seen out again this season he may well take all the beating. (33/1)

Sea Wave (IRE), from a family who comes into their own over middle-distances and includes two Group winners, did look as though he would benefit from this experience. Given reminders early in the straight, he battled on willingly and will be all the sharper if he should appear again this year. (5/2: 2/1-3/1)

4758 Regal Patriarch (IRE) is gradually progressing with every run and the experience should stand him in good stead next season. (14/1)

Shohra Wa Jaah, who has gone in his coat, forced the pace until past halfway and called enough below the distance. (33/1)

4958 WOODTHORPE H'CAP (0-70) (3-Y.O) (Class E)

4-00 (4-01) **1m 54y** £3,226.25 (£965.00: £462.50: £211.25) Stalls: Low GOING: 0.02 sec per fur (G)

			SP	RR	SF
4696[5]	**Brave Envoy (57)** (MJHeaton-Ellis) **3-8-8**ow1 JWeaver(15) (hld up: hdwy over 3f out: rdn to ld ins fnl f: r.o)...—	**1**	14/1	71	35
4788[6]	**Blooming Amazing (70)** (JLEyre) **3-9-7** MGallagher(10) (b.hind: plld hrd: w ldrs: styd on wl fnl f).....................1	**2**	10/1	82	47
4741[3]	**Doc Ryan's (61)** (MJRyan) **3-8-9b**(3) PMcCabe(16) (bhd: hdwy over 2f out: styd on strly fnl f) 1	**3**	8/1	71	36
4848[5]	**Mutabari (USA) (65)** (KMahdi) **3-9-2** DHolland(17) (swtg: racd wd: led after 1f tl hdd ins fnl f)........................s.h	**4**	16/1	75	40
4696[2]	**Star Turn (IRE) (57)** (MBell) **3-8-8** MFenton(13) (hld up: hdwy over 2f out: one pce fnl f) ....¾	**5**	15/2	66	31
4277[9]	**Bestemor (54)** (HCandy) **3-8-5** NAdams(14) (hdwy 3f out: hung lft & kpt on fnl f) ....hd	**6**	20/1	62	27

4741^{2}	**Welcome Heights (55)** (MJFetherston-Godley) **3-8-6** FNorton(1) (sn pushed along: prom: one pce fnl 3f)	hd	**7**	7/2^{1}	63	28
4695^{18}	**Flying Colours (IRE) (56)** (CJBenstead) **3-8-7**^{ow1} SSanders(4) (hld up: hdwy over 2f out: nt rch ldrs)	3½	**8**	33/1	57	21
4210^{18}	**With A Will (63)** (HCandy) **3-8-7**$^{(7)}$ SarahJackson(7) (chsd ldrs tl wknd wl over 1f out)	3	**9**	20/1	59	24
4817^{2}	**Homestead (51)** (RHannon) **3-7-13**$^{(3)}$ RFfrench(2) (trckd ldrs: pushed along ent st: wknd wl over 1f out)	hd	**10**	6/1^{2}	46	11
3793^{14}	**Haydn James (USA) (56)** (PWHarris) **3-8-7** ACulhane(3) (hld up: effrt over 2f out: n.d)	3	**11**	25/1	46	11
4632^{5}	**Go For Green (54)** (DrJDScargill) **3-8-5** JQuinn(9) (chsd ldrs tl wknd over 2f out)	nk	**12**	10/1	43	8
4220^{6}	**Shoshaloza (USA) (63)** (PRWebber) **3-9-0** LDettori(18) (racd wd: chsd ldrs tl rdn & wknd over 2f out)	hd	**13**	8/1	52	17
4877*	**Colway Ritz (65)** (JWWatts) **3-8-13**$^{(3)}$ PFessey(5) (s.i.s: hld up: hdwy over 3f out: n.d)	1	**14**	13/2^{3}	52	17
4700^{9}	**Persevere (60)** (LordHuntingdon) **3-8-11** JReid(8) (led 1f: chsd ldrs tl wknd over 2f out)	1¼	**15**	8/1	44	9
4817^{6}	**Ardent (55)** (CJBenstead) **3-8-6** DBiggs(12) (sn t.o)	26	**16**	20/1	—	—
2546^{15}	**Cairn Dhu (52)** (DWBarker) **3-8-3** TWilliams(6) (lw: prom tl wknd 3f out: t.o)	10	**17**	25/1	—	—
4877^{11}	**Sea Ya Maite (56)** (SRBowring) **3-8-4**$^{(3)ow1}$ CTeague(11) (b: sn wl bhd: t.o fr ½-wy)	10	**18**	11/1	—	—
				(SP 158.9%)	**18 Rn**	

1m 47.3 (6.00) CSF £158.02 CT £1,156.51 TOTE £23.20: £3.40 £4.00 £2.90 £3.40 (£118.60) Trio £501.30 OWNER Mr Tom Burge (WROUGHTON) BRED Robert Courtney

4696 Brave Envoy responded to a more patient ride and produced a well-timed run to take command two hundred yards out and win going away. (14/1)

4788 Blooming Amazing stays this trip well, but he ran a bit too freely with all his weight and in the end only succeeded in beating himself. (10/1: 8/1-12/1)

4741 Doc Ryan's, buried in the pack, really found his stride inside the distance but by then he had given himself just too much to do. (8/1)

4848 Mutabari (USA) has not added to his stable score as yet but he is running well, and as he is still a maiden there is a race waiting to be picked up. (16/1)

4696 Star Turn (IRE) finished ahead of the winner when they clashed earlier in the month and he looked the one to beat when mounting a challenge approaching the final furlong, but he was unable to go through with his effort and could only plug on at the same pace. (15/2)

3917 Bestemor produced her best performance in this first handicap and, had she not drifted out towards the centre of the track, could have finished much closer. (20/1)

4741 Welcome Heights was unable to take advantage of his plum draw as he likes to come from behind and, nudged along from some way out, could not muster the speed to get involved. (7/2)

T/Jkpt: Not won; £34,584.36 to Newmarket 31/10/97. T/Plpt: £49.40 (531.03 Tckts). T/Qdpt: £6.60 (284.79 Tckts) IM

3999a-**DEAUVILLE (France)** (R-H) (Very soft)
Monday October 20th

4959a PRIX DE CAEN (2-Y.O C & G)
1-00 (12-58) **7f** £10,101.00 (£4,040.00)

				SP	RR	SF
	Diableneyev (USA) (MmeCHead,France) **2-8-9** ODoleuze	—	**1**		63	—
4544^{3}	**Hever Golf Ranger** (TJNaughton) **2-9-0** CAsmussen	1½	**2**		65	—
	Danakil (France) **2-9-0** TJarnet	2½	**3**		59	—
						7 Rn

1m 33.9 (9.90) P-M 4.20FF: 2.20FF 2.30FF (SF 18.60FF) OWNER Wertheimer et Frere (CHANTILLY)

4544 Hever Golf Ranger was given every chance but had no answer to the winner's late challenge. He handled the ground and is likely to return for the Prix Zeddaan (Listed) in November.

4960a PRIX DE SAINT-CYR (Listed) (3-Y.O F)
3-00 (2-58) **7f** £15,713.00 (£5,387.00: £4,040.00)

				SP	RR	SF
	Woven Silk (USA) (AFabre,France) **3-8-11** TJarnet	—	**1**		109	—
	Primrose Place (USA) (France) **3-8-11** DBoeuf	½	**2**		108	—
3007a^{D}	**Cunning Vixen (IRE)** (France) **3-9-2** CAsmussen	1½	**3**		109	—
4550^{5}	**All Is Fair** (SirMarkPrescott) **3-8-11** SSanders (btn approx. 6½l)		**6**		—	—
						9 Rn

1m 28.8 (4.80) P-M 7.60FF: 2.90FF 3.20FF 2.20FF (44.10FF) OWNER Sheikh Mohammed (CHANTILLY)

4550 All Is Fair never really got into the race, making a half-hearted effort two out before gradually fading.

4959a-**DEAUVILLE (France)** (R-H) (Very soft)
Tuesday October 21st

4961a PRIX DES RESERVOIRS (Gp 3) (2-Y.O F)
2-10 (2-07) **1m (round)** £24,691.00 (£8,979.00: £4,489.00: £2,694.00)

				SP	RR	SF
	Zalaiyka (FR) (AdeRoyerDupre,France) **2-8-9** GMosse	—	**1**		109	—
	Insight (FR) (JEHammond,France) **2-8-9** CAsmussen	¾	**2**		108	—
	Cyrillic (USA) (MZilber,France) **2-8-9** DBoeuf	2½	**3**		103	—
4437*	**Muhaba (USA)** (SbinSuroor) **2-8-9** LDettori	1½	**4**		100	—
						7 Rn

1m 48.8 P-M 6.40FF: 3.00FF 4.50FF (26.00FF) OWNER Aga Khan (CHANTILLY)

Zalaiyka (FR), racing in second place, took the lead a furlong out and ran on really well to the line. Her trainer reported that she has always been highly regarded and can improve on better ground. Considered to be one of the best in her stable, she could be Classic material and will be aimed at the Prix de la Grotte and Poule d'Essai des Pouliches in 1998.

Insight (FR) ran a decent race considering the big step up in class. Making a forward move early in the straight, she did not have the pace to go with the winner inside the final furlong, but is still inexperienced and will improve for the outing.
Cyrillic (USA), held up for a late run and putting in her best work at the finish, looked a little inexperienced but is surely a decent filly in the making.
4437* Muhaba (USA) tried to make all the running but had no answer when challenged halfway up the straight. She stayed on at one pace, and may not have been suited by the sticky ground.

3736a-GELSENKIRCHEN-HORST (Gelsenkirchen, Germany) (R-H) (Soft)
Saturday October 25th

4962a NEREIDE-RENNEN (Listed) (3-Y.O+ F & M)
3-43 (3-49) **1m 2f** £7,576.00 (£3,030.00: £1,515.00)

				SP	RR	SF
	Evening Breeze (GER) (BSchutz,Germany) **3-8-9** AStarke	—	1		100	—
	Personal Best (IRE) (JEPease,France) **3-8-9** WNewnes	1¾	2		97	—
	Lea (HSteguweit,Germany) **4-8-10** AHelfenbein	1	3		92	—
4435⁶	**Arriving** (JWHills) **3-8-13** MHenry (btn approx 6l)		7		—	—
2389*	**Spartan Girl (IRE)** (LordHuntingdon) **3-8-5** StephenDavies (btn over 20l)		12		—	—

12 Rn

2m 2.9 Tote 36DM: 18DM 27DM 81DM (SF 243DM) OWNER Stall Gamshof
4435 Arriving disappointed connections with her performance and, racing in mid-division, she was unable to quicken in the final quarter-mile.
2389* Spartan Girl (IRE) totally bemused her connections with this lacklustre display. In touch early on, she dropped right out from halfway and this performance is best ignored.

4762a-DUSSELDORF (Germany) (R-H) (Good to soft)
Sunday October 26th

4963a PREIS DER SPIELBANKEN DES LANDES NORDRHEIN-WESTFALEN (Gp 3) (3-Y.O+)
3-25 (3-42) **1m 4f** £18,939.00 (£7,576.00: £4,545.00: £3,030.00)

				SP	RR	SF
2642a¹⁸	**Saugerties (USA)** (HJentzsch,Germany) **3-8-8** PSchiergen	—	1		118	—
4863a⁶	**Mongol Warrior (USA)** (LordHuntingdon) **4-9-2** WNewnes	¾	2		118	—
4537a³	**Protektor (GER)** (ALowe,Germany) **8-9-2** ABest	hd	3		118	—
4661a²	**Asolo (GER)** (BSchutz,Germany) **3-8-8** AStarke	2½	4		114	—
4420⁵	**Poseidon** (MRChannon) **3-8-6** SSanders	1½	5		110	—

9 Rn

2m 35.95 Tote 71DM: 21DM 23DM 13DM (569DM) OWNER Baron G Von Ullmann BRED John C. Oxley
4863a Mongol Warrior (USA), with his tongue tied down for the first time, put last week's disappointing performance behind him with a much better display. Tracking the leader into the straight, he moved into the lead just past the two-furlong pole, but was unable to hold off the winner's late challenge.
4420 Poseidon, racing in mid-division for most of the way, was never able to challenge.

4863a-LONGCHAMP (Paris, France) (R-H) (Soft)
Sunday October 26th

4964a PRIX DU PETIT COUVERT (Gp 3) (3-Y.O+)
1-35 (1-34) **5f** £24,691.00 (£8,979.00: £4,489.00: £2,694.00)

				SP	RR	SF
4777¹²	**Hever Golf Rose** (TJNaughton) **6-9-10** CAsmussen	—	1		116	—
4664a⁴	**Kistena (FR)** (MmeCHead,France) **4-9-7** ODoleuze	1½	2		108	—
4239⁹	**Midnight Escape** (CFWall) **4-10-0** JReid	nk	3		114	—
4525²	**Bishops Court** (MrsJRRamsden) **3-9-10** JFortune	½	4		109	—

8 Rn

59.3 secs (4.80) P-M 13.60FF: 1.10FF 1.10FF 1.30FF (7.00FF) OWNER Hever Racing Club (EPSOM) BRED Ronald Popely
4664a Hever Golf Rose was given a lovely ride and won this sprint with some authority, taking the advantage a furlong out and dominating in the final stages. Despite the sticky ground, she put up a good time and looked as fresh as ever. She may now go to the Breeders' Cup but is likely to retire at the end of this season.
4664a Kistena (FR) ran on well in the final furlong but never looked like catching the winner. Six furlongs appears to be her best distance now and she could be aimed at the Sprinters' Stakes in Japan in December, before being retired to stud where she will be covered by Danzig.
4203a* Midnight Escape was quickly into his stride and led until the furlong marker, before being outpaced in the final stages. He is now finished for the season but, all being well, will stay in training next year.
4525 Bishops Court was another well away and he held second place until just inside the final furlong, battling on well to dead-heat for fourth place.

4965a PRIX ROYAL-OAK (Gp 1) (3-Y.O+)
2-40 (2-38) **1m 7f 110y** £44,893.00 (£17,957.00: £8,979.00: £4,489.00)

				SP	RR	SF
4665a¹²	**Ebadiyla (IRE)** (JOxx,Ireland) **3-8-7** GMosse (hld up bhd: hdwy over 3f out: c wd to ld 1f out: qcknd clr: r.o wl)	—	1	7/1 ²	123	—
4676²	**Snow Princess (IRE)** (LordHuntingdon) **5-9-1** KFallon (hld up in rr: hdwy fr over 1f out to take 2nd ins fnl f)	6	2	54/1	116	—
4665a⁴	**Oscar Schindler (IRE)** (KPrendergast,Ireland) **5-9-4** CAsmussen (a in tch: ev ch over 1f out: no ex cl home)	¾	3	7/10 ¹	118	—
4256a⁹	**Silver Fun (FR)** (MmeCHead,France) **3-8-7** ODoleuze (a cl up: led 3f out tl over 1f out: one pce)	1½	4	20/1	115	—
4559²	**Double Eclipse (IRE)** (MJohnston) **5-9-4** JWeaver (trckd ldrs: rdn to ld 5f out: hdd & wknd 3f out)	3	5	9/1 ³	113	—
4000a²	**Camporese (IRE)** (PWChapple-Hyam) **4-9-1** JReid (5th st: outpcd over 2f out: hrd rdn & one pce fnl f)	hd	6	18/1	110	—
4665a¹⁷	**Nothin' Leica Dane (AUS)** (JEHammond,France) **5-9-4** TJarnet (prom: 4th & rdn st: ev ch: one pce fnl f)	2½	7	12/1	111	—
3883a⁷	**Stretarez (FR)** (DSepulchre,France) **4-9-4** FSanchez (mid div: n.d)	5	8	11/1	106	—

4559[3]	**Further Flight** (BWHills) **11-9-4** MHills (hld up bhd: 7th st: sn btn)	s.h	**9**	45/1	106	—
4559*	**Grey Shot** (IABalding) **5-9-4** JFortune (led to 5f out: wknd appr st: t.o fnl 2f)	15	**10**	7/1[2]	90	—
4134[3]	**Bahamian Knight (CAN)** (RAkehurst) **4-9-4** OPeslier (prom tl over 4f out: t.o)		**11**	24/1	—	—
				(SP 127.9%)		**11 Rn**

3m 26.5 (10.50) P-M 8.30FF: 1.90FF 5.70FF 1.10FF (362.50FF) OWNER Aga Khan (CURRABEG)

2814a* Ebadiyla (IRE) was held up and coasting. Making progress before the home turn, she took the lead with a furlong left to run and, drawing clear most impressively, made her rivals look extremely ordinary. After winning the Irish Oaks, she suffered a setback and was disappointing in the Arc but, with another Group One win under her belt, she now goes to stud where she should have considerable success as a broodmare. (7/1)

4676 Snow Princess (IRE) was another held up for a late run. Staying on well, she still had plenty left to do entering the straight and never looked likely to catch the winner. This was a decent last performance by a mare who is also destined for stud duties. (54/1)

4665a Oscar Schindler (IRE) was given every chance but appeared not to stay in a race run at a decent pace on testing ground. He led halfway up the straight but had no answer when tackled by the winner and the second. The Japan Cup is his likely target. (7/10)

2275a* Silver Fun (FR) raced just in behind the leaders and looked extremely dangerous when taking the lead on entering the straight. Despite enjoying the soft ground, the filly did not stay the distance and was beaten at the furlong pole. (20/1)

4559 Double Eclipse (IRE), tracking the leaders, made a forward move with over half a mile to run but weakened in the straight. His trainer was pleased with the run but the horse's leg problem means he will now be retired to stud. (9/1)

4000a Camporese (IRE), racing in mid-division, made some late progress in the straight but never looked likely to finish in the frame. (18/1)

4559 Further Flight, always behind, was beaten before the straight. (45/1)

4559* Grey Shot set a lively pace until reaching the straight where he began to fade right out of contention. He finished a tired horse, but will be back again next season. (7/1)

4134 Bahamian Knight (CAN) raced prominently for a long time before dropping right out in the straight to finish plumb last. He did not appear to enjoy this experience over a longer distance. (24/1)

4781-**NEWMARKET** (R-H) (Good to firm)
Friday October 31st
WEATHER: sunny WIND: almost nil

4966 E.B.F. RED LODGE MAIDEN STKS (2-Y.O) (Class D)
12-50 (12-50) **6f (Rowley)** £4,077.50 (£1,220.00: £585.00: £267.50) Stalls: High GOING minus 0.24 sec per fur (GF)

				SP	RR	SF
4668[2]	**Tussle** (MBell) **2-9-0** MFenton(13) (mde all: drew clr fnl f: comf)	—	**1**	5/4[1]	95+	52
	Baajil (LMCumani) **2-9-0** LDettori(12) (neat: b.nr fore: dwlt: hld up: swtchd lft & hdwy over 2f out: rdn & hung rt ins fnl f: r.o)	2	**2**	5/1[2]	90+	47
4779[7]	**Splendid Isolation (USA)** (LMCumani) **2-8-11**(3) RFfrench(8) (lw: plld hrd: trckd ldrs: kpt on wl fnl f)	¾	**3**	7/1[3]	88	45
4315[4]	**Storm Fromthe East (85)** (RHannon) **2-9-0** JReid(11) (trckd ldrs: hmpd & lost pl over 2f out: r.o wl fnl f)	1½	**4**	7/1[3]	84	41
	Abusamrah (USA) (RWArmstrong) **2-9-0** RHills(10) (w'like: unf: plld hrd: w wnr: wkng whn hmpd ins fnl f)	1¾	**5**	12/1	79	36
3825[9]	**Spring Fever** (BWHills) **2-9-0** MHills(4) (lw: prom: ev ch 2f out: no ex whn hmpd ins fnl f)	1¼	**6**	25/1	76	33
4752[4]	**Peaceful Sarah** (PMooney) **2-8-9** DaneO'Neill(3) (trckd ldrs tl wknd appr fnl f)	3½	**7**	50/1	61	18
4901[10]	**My Tyson (IRE) (65)** (KMahdi) **2-9-0** JFortune(6) (hld up: bhd tl stdy hdwy fnl f)	nk	**8**	66/1	66	23
	Arry Martin (WRMuir) **2-9-0** MartinDwyer(5) (w'like: cmpt: plld hrd: rdn over 2f out: n.d)	hd	**9**	33/1	65	22
	Generous Rosi (DRLoder) **2-9-0** GCarter(9) (wl grwn: bkwd: s.i.s: nvr nr ldrs)	1	**10**	8/1	63	20
4526[22]	**Top Gear (IRE)** (PHowling) **2-9-0** PaulEddery(14) (b: trckd ldrs over 4f)	1½	**11**	66/1	59	16
4236[6]	**Muji** (APJarvis) **2-8-6**(3) CLowther(7) (b.nr hind: prom 3f)	1¼	**12**	33/1	50	7
4779[19]	**Eiffel Tiger (IRE)** (BobJones) **2-9-0** NDay(2) (a bhd)	¾	**13**	66/1	53	10
4779[18]	**Magic Morning** (WJMusson) **2-9-0** MWigham(1) (sn pushed along: bhd fnl 2f)	7	**14**	33/1	35	—
				(SP 124.0%)		**14 Rn**

1m 13.64 (1.84) CSF £6.47 TOTE £2.00: £1.40 £2.20 £2.00 (£4.90) Trio £17.10 OWNER Mr T. F. Harris (NEWMARKET) BRED Stratford Place Stud

STEWARDS' ENQUIRY Dettori referred to Portman Square on 13/11/97 under totting-up procedure (careless riding), and was susp. for 21 days, 14 days 18/11-1/12/97 on worldwide basis, and further 7days suspended & would come into effect should he re-offend before 13/5/98.

IN-FOCUS: **The far rail seemed fast all afternoon and a couple of the results appeared to be affected in favour of horses racing against it.**

4668 Tussle comes out of a very fast female line, his grand-dam being Crime of Passion, and looks keen and quick on this evidence. The only surprise was that, given his marvellous action, he did so well in dreadful ground first time out. (5/4)

Baajil didn't move down terribly well and proved a tricky ride, even so Dettori can have few excuses. Pulled out to begin his run at the Bushes, he did Storm Fromthe East no favours but when pressure was applied on meeting the rising ground he picked up, but not in a straight line, causing more trouble. He has ability but much to learn. (5/1)

4779 Splendid Isolation (USA), a nice mover who moved down with his head a little high, had the far rails to race against but certainly did some good running in the last furlong. He should stay further. (7/1)

4315 Storm Fromthe East the most experienced of the party, was knocked back at the bushes but came home really strongly. He has given one or two problems on occasions and connections seem to have concentrated on getting him settled this season rather than finding his trip, which is surely around a mile. (7/1)

Abusamrah (USA), a full-brother to two-year-old Listed winner Watani, is a taller, weaker sort. Taking quite a hold early on, he could not match strides with the winner from the Dip but was still in with a place chance when hampered. (12/1: 7/1-14/1)

3464 Spring Fever, poorly drawn when flopping at Ripon, has had nine weeks off and ran very much better here, being involved in a battle for third when hampered. (25/1)

My Tyson (IRE), a keen sort, was settled in the rear this time and the way he finished, this may prove the answer to getting the best out of him. A cheap buy, there is a little race to be found. (66/1)

Generous Rosi (8/1: 5/1-9/1)

4967 NGK SPARK PLUGS SOHAM HOUSE CONDITIONS STKS (2-Y.O) (Class C)
1-20 (1-20) **1m (Rowley)** £5,330.20 (£1,703.20: £816.60) Stalls: High GOING minus 0.24 sec per fur (GF)

				SP	RR	SF
4674[3]	**Rabah (94)** (JLDunlop) **2-8-13** RHills(1) (led 6f: rallied to ld wl ins fnl f)	—	**1**	5/1[3]	94	56
4758[2]	**Albarahin (USA)** (SbinSuroor) **2-8-11** LDettori(2) (lw: trckd wnr: qcknd to ld 2f out: rdn 1f out: ct wl ins fnl f)	nk	**2**	8/11[1]	91	53
4708*	**Brave Reward (USA)** (MRStoute) **2-8-13** JReid(4) (stdd s: plld hrd: plld out over 2f out: no imp)	4	**3**	2/1[2]	85	47
				(SP 107.9%)		**3 Rn**

1m 39.41 (2.11) CSF £8.37 TOTE £4.50 (£2.20) OWNER Mr Hamdan Al Maktoum (ARUNDEL) BRED Shadwell Estate Company Limited

4674 Rabah, who got hopelessly stuck in the mud last time, proved a winner for the adage that the best place to be, when there is a false pace, is in front. Tackled by the favourite at the two pole, that rival initially looked in complete charge but, with the benefit of the rail, he kept plugging away to get on top near the finish. (5/1: 9/4-11/2)
4758 Albarahin (USA), a hugely impressive individual who shows a bit of knee action, may have outgrown his strength for the moment for, having looked in charge when quickening to the front, he failed to sustain the effort to the line. (8/11)
4708* Brave Reward (USA), a narrow colt, moved down well if somewhat keenly. He didn't take to being held up in last place and, by the time he got into his stride, the whole trio were quickening and his efforts came to zero. (2/1)

4968 JAMES SEYMOUR STKS (Listed) (3-Y.O+) (Class A)

1-55 (1-56) **1m 2f (Rowley)** £10,378.60 (£3,837.40: £2,587.20: £2,587.20: £294.25: £112.55) Stalls: High GOING minus 0.24 sec per fur (GF)

				SP	RR	SF
4676^{3}	**Saafeya (IRE) (96)** (JHMGosden) **3-8-4** LDettori(3) (prom: led 3f out: hld on wl fnl f)	—	**1**	$7/2^{2}$	107+	59
4759^{3}	**Sandmoor Chambray (101)** (TDEasterby) **6-9-0** SSanders(5) (lw: led: hdd 3f out: r.o fnl f)	1	**2**	$7/1^{3}$	110	67
4776^{3}	**Proper Blue (USA) (104)** (TGMills) **4-9-0** TQuinn(9) (hld up: hdwy over 2f out: rdn & r.o fnl f)	¾	**3**	$7/2^{2}$	109	66
4671*	**Ghalib (IRE)** (MajorWRHern) **3-8-9** RHills(4) (trckd ldrs: rdn over 1f out: one pce fnl f)	d.h	**3**	$11/4^{1}$	109	61
761^{2}	**Sheer Danzig (IRE) (105)** (RWArmstrong) **5-9-0** MHills(8) (in tch: rdn over 2f out: nvr able to chal)	3	**5**	8/1	104	61
4557^{6}	**Ukraine Venture (94)** (SPCWoods) **3-8-4** NDay(7) (prom tl wknd over 1f out)	1	**6**	16/1	98	50
	Baron Ferdinand (RCharlton) **7-9-0** TSprake(2) (b: lw: hld up: hdwy over 2f out: btn appr fnl f)	1¼	**7**	14/1	101	58
4854^{3}	**Zugudi (90)** (KMahdi) **3-8-9** DHolland(6) (lw: plld hrd: trckd ldrs tl rdn & outpcd fnl 2f)	½	**8**	20/1	100	52
4669^{4}	**Fiametta (88)** (CEBrittain) **3-8-4** DaneO'Neill(1) (chsd ldrs tl rdn & wknd over 3f out)	7	**9**	25/1	84	36

(SP 115.9%) **9 Rn**

2m 5.95 (1.25) CSF £25.83 TOTE £4.00: £1.60 £2.00 PB £0.70 G £0.80 (£12.70) Trio S, SC & PB £6.90; S, SC & G £8.70 OWNER Sheikh Ahmed Al Maktoum (NEWMARKET) BRED Sheikh Ahmed Bin Rashid Al Maktoum
WEIGHT FOR AGE 3yo-5lb
STEWARDS' ENQUIRY R. Hills susp. 10-11 & 13-15/11/97 (failure to ensure best possible placing).
IN-FOCUS: Major Dick Hern sent out the final runner of a marvellous forty-year career in this race.
4676 Saafeya (IRE), dropped back in trip, continued her progress, taking this with something in hand, despite looking a little warm and on edge beforehand. (7/2)
4759 Sandmoor Chambray is a real trier and never gave up, the far rail proving an asset as he battled back in the last furlong. (7/1)
4776 Proper Blue (USA) couldn't repeat his win of twelve months ago, having had a harder campaign this time. Once again he didn't have much daylight in the Dip, but stayed on for a share of third place. (7/2)
4671* Ghalib (IRE), a final runner for one of the great post-war trainers, had impressed over a shorter trip on softer ground but could not quite handle this step up in class although he battled well and would have been third outright but for Hills dropping his hands a couple of strides from the line. (11/4)
761 Sheer Danzig (IRE), off since April, looked big but really well. Outpaced as the field quickened up, he looked ring rusty but really needs further. (8/1)
4557 Ukraine Venture, already clipped, travelled well enough until dropping away tamely. (16/1)
Baron Ferdinand, who looked exceptionally well in his coat for the time of the year if slightly on the burly side, looked the winner briefly at the two-furlong pole before blowing up. Clearly a nightmare to train, he looks to retain a fair bit of ability. (14/1)

4969 GEORGE STUBBS RATED STKS H'CAP (0-105) (Listed) (3-Y.O+) (Class A)

2-30 (2-30) **2m (Rowley)** £10,391.16 (£3,583.96: £1,711.98: £690.90) Stalls: High GOING minus 0.24 sec per fur (GF)

				SP	RR	SF
4376^{4}	**Lady of The Lake (91)** (JLDunlop) **3-7-11** RFfrench(4) (trckd ldrs: led over 3f out: rdn & hld on gamely fnl f)	—	**1**	7/1	102	43
4783^{3}	**Mawared (IRE) (91)** (JLDunlop) **4-8-7** RHills(1) (b: lw: hld up: hdwy over 4f out: chal on bit 3f out: rdn over 1f out: unable qckn fnl f)	½	**2**	$8/15^{1}$	102	53
4783^{22}	**Sweetness Herself (98)** (MJRyan) **4-9-0** GCarter(3) (led after 1f: edgd lft & hdd over 3f out: sn btn: eased fnl f)	11	**3**	$5/1^{2}$	98	49
4732^{5}	**Poltarf (USA) (105)** (JHMGosden) **6-9-7** LDettori(2) (led 1f: pushed along 5f out: wknd & eased over 3f out)	dist	**4**	$11/2^{3}$	—	—

(SP 109.8%) **4 Rn**

3m 23.08 (-0.22) CSF £10.74 TOTE £5.80 (£2.60) OWNER Capt J. Macdonald-Buchanan (ARUNDEL) BRED The Lavington Stud
LONG HANDICAP Mawared (IRE) 8-6 Lady of The Lake 7-7
WEIGHT FOR AGE 3yo-10lb
4376 Lady of The Lake looked in tremendous shape and really happy to be racing after five weeks away, judged by the way she got on her toes when mounted. Her stable companion seemed to be cantering all over her when beginning his challenge but she is not short on courage and battled her heart out. (7/1)
4783 Mawared (IRE) might have been suited by a stronger pace and further, but odds-on layers were still counting their winnings as he moved alongside his stable companion. Possibly edging fractionally ahead going into the Dip, he could never get on top and the situation became increasingly desperate, as Hills threw everything at him. (8/15)
4099 Sweetness Herself doesn't move too badly on fast ground, but only excels when the mud is flying and tended to hang once at full stretch. (5/1)
4732 Poltarf (USA) found the ground too fast and ran exactly the same as he had in last year's Jockey Club Cup. (11/2)

4970 EQUITY FINANCIAL COLLECTIONS NURSERY H'CAP (2-Y.O) (Class D)

3-05 (3-05) **5f (Rowley)** £3,492.50 (£1,040.00: £495.00: £222.50) Stalls: High GOING minus 0.24 sec per fur (GF)

				SP	RR	SF
4948^{4}	**Happy Days Again (IRE) (80)** (JWharton) **2-8-0b**(5) RMullen(5) (b.hind: mde all: clr whn rdn 1f out: hld on)	—	**1**	6/1	84	40
4948*	**Classy Cleo (IRE) (86)** (PDEvans) **2-8-11** 7x JFEgan(3) (bhd: gd hdwy 1f out: n.m.r & swtchd lft ins fnl f: r.o wl: nt rch wnr)	1¼	**2**	$3/1^{2}$	86	42
3908^{2}	**Atlantic Viking (IRE) (96)** (MJohnston) **2-9-7** DHolland(1) (lw: chsd wnr: rdn over 1f out: no imp fnl f)	s.h	**3**	$6/4^{1}$	96	52
4566^{9}	**High Gain (72)** (PHowling) **2-7-11**ow1 FNorton(2) (bhd tl styd on appr fnl f)	¾	**4**	16/1	69	24
4522^{4}	**Midsummer Night (IRE) (74)** (RHannon) **2-7-13** JQuinn(4) (prom over 3f: nt run on)	3½	**5**	$4/1^{3}$	60	16

(SP 105.2%) **5 Rn**

60.41 secs (1.71) CSF £19.70 TOTE £7.80: £2.20 £1.60 (£10.30) OWNER Mrs S. M. Moore (MELTON MOWBRAY) BRED William Flood
LONG HANDICAP High Gain 7-9

4948 Happy Days Again (IRE) has one prime asset, tremendous early pace and, with the rails draw, a good break saw her have the whole field in trouble with two furlongs left. Something of a short runner, she was treading water near the line but had enough to hold on. These are tactics to use on her, the only mystery being why they were abandoned in the first place. (6/1: 4/1-13/2)
4948* Classy Cleo (IRE), unable to confirm form of a couple of days ago with the winner, was taken off her feet this time before finishing in fine style. (3/1)
3908 Atlantic Viking (IRE) would have been expected to lead from the off but not many are able to give the winner a stone and a lead. Not able to dominate and hard at work two furlongs out, he kept plugging on but never looked like getting to the front. (6/4)
4566 High Gain had no trouble in getting a lead and her effort leaving the Dip ultimately came to little. (16/1)
4522 Midsummer Night (IRE) may have had enough for the season but her head came up when she dropped away, as if she was feeling something. (4/1: 3/1-9/2)

4971 NGK SPARK PLUGS H'CAP (0-70) (3-Y.O+ F & M) (Class E)

3-40 (3-42) **1m 4f (Rowley)** £4,532.50 (£1,360.00: £655.00: £302.50) Stalls: High GOING minus 0.51 sec per fur (F)

				SP	RR	SF
4886^{2}	**Ordained (52)** (EJAlston) **4-9-3** AMackay(26) (hdwy 5f out: led over 2f out: rdn out)	—	**1**	10/1^{2}	66	51
4519*	**Tarry (52)** (MissGayKelleway) **4-9-3** SSanders(27) (lw: a.p: rdn over 1f out: r.o wl fnl f)	1½	**2**	16/1	64	49
4748^{2}	**Back Row (60)** (JHetherton) **3-9-4** LDettori(24) (chsd ldrs: styd on fnl f)	1¼	**3**	12/1^{3}	70	48
4821^{2}	**Veronica Franco (52)** (PRHedger) **4-9-3** DaneO'Neill(13) (chsd ldrs: wnt 2nd over 1f out: wknd wl ins fnl f)	¾	**4**	7/2^{1}	61	46
4731^{12}	**Dizzy Tilly (63)** (TJNaughton) **3-9-7** DHolland(22) (in tch: effrt 5f out: no imp fnl f)	2	**5**	33/1	70	48
4821*	**Glow Forum (61)** (LMontagueHall) **6-9-9**$^{(3)}$ 5x RFfrench(12) (b: chsd ldrs: one pce fnl 3f)	½	**6**	16/1	67	52
4817*	**Star Entry (59)** (MajorDNChappell) **3-9-3** 5x JReid(5) (prom tl wknd over 2f out)	3½	**7**	12/1^{3}	60	38
4322^{4}	**Eternity (56)** (JRFanshawe) **3-9-0** MHills(23) (trckd ldrs: rdn & btn 3f out)	½	**8**	33/1	57	35
4562*	**Children's Choice (IRE) (56)** (WJMusson) **6-9-7** JQuinn(9) (sme hdwy fnl 2f: nvr rchd ldrs)	3	**9**	12/1^{3}	53	38
4503^{6}	**Alagna (46)** (SCWilliams) **3-8-4v** GCarter(28) (chsd ldrs: led over 3f out: hung lft & hdd over 2f out: sn btn)	1¾	**10**	50/1	40	18
4633^{5}	**Keepsake (IRE) (50)** (MDIUsher) **3-8-8** RStreet(19) (b: bhd: hdwy fnl 2f: nvr rchd ldrs)	2	**11**	25/1	42	20
4751^{17}	**Temptress (61)** (JohnHarris) **4-9-12** DeanMcKeown(16) (led: hdd over 3f out: sn btn)	4	**12**	33/1	47	32
4804^{18}	**Gallant Heights (53)** (GCBravery) **3-8-11** NDay(4) (nvr nr to chal)	nk	**13**	33/1	39	17
4802^{17}	**Kathryn's Pet (63)** (MrsMReveley) **4-10-0** ACulhane(10) (bhd tl sme hdwy fnl 2f)	hd	**14**	33/1	49	34
4771*	**Priluki (62)** (CEBrittain) **3-9-1**$^{(5)}$ RMullen(11) (chsd ldrs 8f)	¾	**15**	14/1	47	25
4584*	**Siberian Mystic (43)** (PGMurphy) **4-8-8** SDrowne(3) (in tch: rdn over 5f out: sn bhd)	hd	**16**	10/1^{2}	28	13
4631^{3}	**Quibbling (59)** (HCandy) **3-9-3** PaulEddery(21) (in tch 8f)	½	**17**	50/1	43	21
4800^{11}	**Nubile (52)** (WJMusson) **3-8-10** SWhitworth(20) (s.i.s: effrt over 3f out: nvr trbld ldrs)	hd	**18**	33/1	36	14
4771^{12}	**Sun Alert (USA) (52)** (MJPolglase) **3-8-10** NAdams(7) (in tch: rdn & wknd over 4f out)	1¼	**19**	33/1	34	12
4800^{6}	**Fantasy Girl (IRE) (54)** (JLDunlop) **3-8-12** TQuinn(25) (lw: prom 9f)	½	**20**	25/1	36	14
4400^{3}	**Miss Vita (USA) (56)** (RJRWilliams) **3-9-0** MartinDwyer(2) (in tch 8f)	5	**21**	33/1	31	9
4798^{12}	**Red Embers (38)** (RCSpicer) **3-7-10** NVarley(8) (b: swtg: a bhd)	½	**22**	50/1	12	—
4800^{3}	**Tart (FR) (44)** (DNicholls) **4-8-9** JWeaver(6) (prom: ev ch over 3f out: sn wknd)	5	**23**	14/1	12	—
4429^{3}	**Silver Whirl (USA) (65)** (RCharlton) **3-9-9** TSprake(15) (prom tl rdn & wknd over 4f out)	2	**24**	20/1	30	8
4503^{5}	**Bellagrana (53)** (MJFetherston-Godley) **3-8-11** JFortune(14) (pushed along 6f out: sn bhd)	1	**25**	33/1	17	—
4323^{5}	**Laguna Bay (IRE) (56)** (APJarvis) **3-9-0** DBiggs(1) (a bhd)	½	**26**	33/1	19	—
4800^{5}	**Classic Ballet (FR) (62)** (RGuest) **4-9-10**$^{(3)}$ CLowther(17) (prom 7f)	¾	**27**	25/1	24	9
4748^{3}	**Arletty (57)** (HRACecil) **3-9-1b** AMcGlone(18) (lw: prom 6f)	1¼	**28**	20/1	17	—
4744^{7}	**Silvretta (IRE) (50)** (RCSpicer) **4-8-12b**$^{(3)}$ PFessey(29) (ref to r: t.n.p)		**R**	33/1	—	—
				(SP 147.9%)	**29 Rn**	

2m 31.88 (1.38) CSF £134.86 CT £1,834.24 TOTE £11.40: £2.50 £6.30 £3.40 £1.50 (£116.10) Trio £147.60 OWNER Peter Ebdon Racing (PRESTON) BRED Sheikh Mohammed Bin Rashid Al Maktoum
LONG HANDICAP Red Embers 7-7
WEIGHT FOR AGE 3yo-7lb
4886 Ordained, whose dipped back has become even more pronounced with time, found this trip ideal and improved her modest win-to-run ratio with a game success. (10/1)
4519* Tarry, well drawn and relatively fresh, made great strides in the last furlong but couldn't get to the winner. (16/1)
4748 Back Row, still a maiden, didn't seem inconvenienced by this fast ground but wasn't good enough despite racing close to the far rail. (12/1)
4821 Veronica Franco, well supported, followed the winner through but was beaten by the three better-drawn horses. She should not be written off yet. (7/2)
3256 Dizzy Tilly, keen going down, never got near the front and could make little impact at the business end. (33/1)
4821* Glow Forum not drawn as high as those who beat her, was always racing wide and must have run creditably to finish so close. (16/1)
4817* Star Entry did very well from an awful draw and deserves another chance. (12/1)
4562* Children's Choice (IRE) (12/1: op 7/1)
4584* Siberian Mystic under pressure a long way out, couldn't overcome her draw. (10/1: 8/1-12/1)

4972 AVENUE APPRENTICE H'CAP (0-70) (3-Y.O) (Class E)

4-15 (4-17) **1m 1f (Rowley)** £3,655.00 (£1,090.00: £520.00: £235.00) Stalls: High GOING minus 0.24 sec per fur (GF)

				SP	RR	SF
4802^{3}	**Tipperary Sunset (IRE) (54)** (JJQuinn) **3-8-11** PRoberts(4) (trckd ldrs: led over 1f out: rdn out)	—	**1**	9/4^{1}	64	41
4816^{7}	**Glen Ogil (47)** (MRChannon) **3-8-1**$^{(3)}$ AEddery(2) (b: prom: ev ch 3f out tl over 1f out: r.o fnl f)	¾	**2**	14/1	56	33
4010^{2}	**Protaras Bay (39)** (PLGilligan) **3-7-10** APolli(8) (hld up: hdwy 3f out: ev ch over 1f out: one pce ins fnl f)	nk	**3**	14/1	47	24
4584^{2}	**Mr Fortywinks (IRE) (49)** (JLEyre) **3-8-1**$^{(5)}$ SBuckley(5) (prom: rdn & outpcd 4f out: styd on fnl 2f)	s.h	**4**	11/4^{2}	57	34
4695^{9}	**Smart Spirit (IRE) (57)** (MrsMReveley) **3-9-0** SCopp(11) (rdn & hdwy over 2f out: ev ch over 1f out: sn btn)	1¾	**5**	13/2^{3}	62	39
3316^{4}	**Twin Time (64)** (JSKing) **3-9-7** GFaulkner(7) (led 1f: rdn over 2f out: ev ch over 1f out: wknd fnl f)	2½	**6**	8/1	65	42
2554^{13}	**Pointelle (54)** (AHide) **3-8-8**$^{(3)}$ JoHunnam(1) (plld hrd: led after 1f tl hdd & wknd over 1f out)	1½	**7**	16/1	52	29
4846^{5}	**Al Ava Consonant (40)** (JDBethell) **3-7-8**$^{(3)ow1}$ RWinston(6) (plld hrd: rdn & dropped rr 6f out: sme hdwy & hung rt appr fnl f)	hd	**8**	33/1	38	14
2523^{2}	**Linden's Lad (IRE) (50)** (JRJenkins) **3-8-4v**$^{(3)}$ JWilkinson(9) (bhd fnl 2f)	5	**9**	10/1	39	16
4563^{10}	**Beaucatcher (IRE) (47)** (MJHeaton-Ellis) **3-7-13**$^{(5)}$ JFowle(3) (b: chsd ldrs over 5f)	5	**10**	33/1	27	4
4243^{18}	**Verinder's Gift (49)** (DrJDScargill) **3-8-6b**^{1} RMullen(10) (lw: hld up: hdwy 4f out: wknd 2f out)	¾	**11**	33/1	28	5
				(SP 119.0%)	**11 Rn**	

1m 54.34 (3.84) CSF £32.52 CT £329.87 TOTE £3.30: £1.20 £2.50 £3.30 (£38.80) Trio £287.00 OWNER Mr Harold Bray (MALTON) BRED M. G. Masterson

LONG HANDICAP Protaras Bay 7-7 Al Ava Consonant 6-13

4802 Tipperary Sunset (IRE), taken down very steadily, kept pretty straight on this faster ground and won in decent style. (9/4)

3966 Glen Ogil, stepping up in trip, was always in the firing line and stayed on well inside the final furlong as if staying every inch of the trip. (14/1)

4010 Protaras Bay is still lightly raced and ought to find a race at this sort of trip. (14/1: 10/1-16/1)

4584 Mr Fortywinks (IRE), caught out by the quickening pace, did really well to get back onto the heels of the leaders in the Dip but needs further on such quick ground. (11/4)

2884 Smart Spirit (IRE) had the advantage of the far rail when starting her move but it petered out as quickly as it started. (13/2)

3316 Twin Time, a really good mover, seemed to be found out by stepping up a furlong in trip. (8/1)

2523 Linden's Lad (IRE) (10/1: 7/1-11/1)

T/Jkpt: £47,929.50 (0.2 Tckts); £54,005.17 to Newmarket 1/11/97. T/Plpt: £307.60 (85.38 Tckts). T/Qdpt: £53.30 (36.59 Tckts) Dk

4966-NEWMARKET (R-H) (Good to firm)
Saturday November 1st

WEATHER: sunny WIND: nil

4973 E.B.F. BALATON LODGE MAIDEN STKS (2-Y.O F) (Class D)

1-00 (1-05) **7f (Rowley)** £4,077.50 (£1,220.00: £585.00: £267.50) Stalls: High GOING minus 0.24 sec per fur (GF)

				SP	RR	SF
	Pontoon (HRACecil) **2-8-11** KFallon(10) (leggy: unf: chsd ldrs: sn pushed along: styd on wl fnl f: led nr fin)	—	**1**	3/1[2]	84	53
	Lovers Knot (DRLoder) **2-8-11** GCarter(14) (cmpt: bkwd: a.p: str run ins fnl f: jst failed: knocked over after post)	s.h	**2**	5/4[1]	84	53
	Spanish Fern (USA) (RCharlton) **2-8-11** TSprake(2) (gd sort: lw: a.p: r.o wl ins fnl f)	s.h	**3**	12/1	84	53
4397a[3]	**Lea Grande** (LMCumani) **2-8-11** JWeaver(16) (w'like: scope: led: edgd lft over 1f out & ins fnl f: ct nr fin)	s.h	**4**	10/1[3]	84	53
	Cruinn A Bhord (ACStewart) **2-8-11** SWhitworth(3) (leggy: scope: lw: hdwy over 3f out: rdn over 2f out: one pce fnl f)	3	**5**	40/1	77	46
	Genoa (BWHills) **2-8-11** DHolland(7) (w'like: scope: plld hrd: in tch: effrt over 2f out: nt trble ldrs)	4	**6**	16/1	68	37
	Meniatarra (USA) (SbinSuroor) **2-8-8**(3) RFfrench(17) (w'like: chsd ldr tl wknd over 1f out)	2	**7**	11/1	63	32
	Miss Bussell (BWHills) **2-8-11** JCarroll(4) (small: unf: bhd: rdn & styd on fnl 2f: nvr rchd ldrs)	¾	**8**	50/1	61	30
4758[12]	**Tartan Lass** (RGuest) **2-8-11** JQuinn(18) (stdd s: bhd tl r.o strly fnl f)	nk	**9**	50/1	61	30
	Playgroup (MrsJCecil) **2-8-11** GHind(12) (w'like: scope: chsd ldrs over 4f)	2½	**10**	25/1	55	24
	Ivory Crown (IRE) (EALDunlop) **2-8-11** JFortune(9) (neat: s.s: nvr nr ldrs)	1¾	**11**	25/1	51	20
	Mockery (MRStoute) **2-8-11** JReid(5) (w'like: dwlt: plld hrd: a bhd)	1½	**12**	20/1	48	17
	Certain Danger (IRE) (RHannon) **2-8-11** DaneO'Neill(1) (lt-f: unf: in tch: sn pushed along: wknd over 2f out)	hd	**13**	40/1	47	16
	Milling (IRE) (RGuest) **2-8-11** MartinDwyer(19) (w'like: wl bhd fnl 2f)	nk	**14**	50/1	47	16
	June Bounty (USA) (GWragg) **2-8-11** MHills(6) (w'like: unf: sn outpcd)	3½	**15**	33/1	39	8
	Natayig (JLDunlop) **2-8-11** RHills(13) (leggy: unf: s.i.s: a bhd)	hd	**16**	25/1	38	7
	Pleasure (RWArmstrong) **2-8-11** FNorton(11) (cmpt: bit bkwd: in tch: rdn 4f out: sn wknd)	1	**17**	50/1	36	5
	In Charge (HCandy) **2-8-11** AMcGlone(8) (w'like: scope: a bhd)	15	**18**	50/1	2	—
				(SP 134.4%)	**18 Rn**	

1m 26.41 (1.91) CSF £6.18 TOTE £3.80: £1.80 £1.30 £3.50 (£3.40) Trio £17.90 OWNER Mr K. Abdulla (NEWMARKET) BRED Juddmonte Farms

Pontoon, a half-sister to Wharf who started second favourite for Zafonic's Guineas, was taken to post very steadily after the others. Never looking to be travelling that well, she kept on finding when Fallon asked but, although she was finishing well, the photo verdict came as something of a surprise. Unfortunately, after the line she swerved violently towards the paddock exit, knocking one of her rivals for six. (3/1: 6/4-100/30)

Lovers Knot, the first foal of a modest half-sister to the useful stayer-then-hurdler Muir Station, found her stamina really coming into play in the last furlong and looked from the stands as if she might have got there but the post had come a stride too soon. On pulling up she was sent crashing to the ground by the veering winner but, if she is not too badly hurt, there are races to be won with her. (5/4: op 9/4)

Spanish Fern (USA), probably the paddock pick, was a little on the keen side going down but picked up in great style on meeting the rising ground. Out of a sister to Al Bahathri, she looks sure to progress from this. (12/1: op 7/1)

4397a Lea Grande, who showed plenty of ability on her debut in Italy - both of those who beat her have subsequently performed well in Italian Group races - adopted different tactics this time and it almost worked. She should not be too hard to place. (10/1: 6/1-12/1)

Cruinn A Bhord, whose dam is a full sister to Teleprompter, still has some growing to do but looked well. Quite keen going down, she came with a good run towards the outside which only petered out inside the final furlong. Not a bad start. (40/1)

Genoa, the first foal of the impeccably-bred Yawl - by an Arc winner out of an Oaks winner who was herself placed in an Oaks trial - took a keen hold going down and was very keen once the stalls opened. To her credit, she stayed on to the line but she is going to need to learn to settle better to live up to her pedigree. (16/1)

Meniatarra (USA), out of Snow Bride, is therefore a half-sister to Lammtarra and closely related to a host of other good horses. A rangy, eye-catching filly, she began to fade in the Dip but should come on a lot for the outing. (11/1: 5/1-12/1)

Tartan Lass, a likeable half-sister to several winners including the sprinter Tedburrow, was steadied at the start and raced in a hopeless position until flying through the last furlong. She has ability if it can be tapped. (50/1)

Mockery, a quite sparely-made filly, moved down very well but missed the break. She looked green and achieved little but, being out of a half-sister to Percy's Lass and Braiswick, could easily do better next year. (20/1)

4974 NGK SPARK PLUGS (S) STKS (2-Y.O) (Class E)

1-30 (1-35) **1m (Rowley)** £4,110.00 (£1,230.00: £590.00: £270.00) Stalls: High GOING minus 0.24 sec per fur (GF)

				SP	RR	SF
4753[15]	**Ringleader (64)** (PFICole) **2-8-11** JFortune(11) (a.p: led over 3f out tl over 1f out: styd on wl to ld nr fin)	—	**1**	8/1	70	38
4753[13]	**Blue Zola (IRE) (67)** (MBell) **2-8-1**(5) RMullen(8) (chsd ldrs: ev ch whn hung rt over 2f out: led over 1f out: rdn & ct nr fin)	hd	**2**	9/1	65	33
4753[10]	**Primary Colours** (WJHaggas) **2-8-6** MHills(13) (hld up & plld hrd: swtchd rt & hdwy over 5f out: rdn over 1f out: kpt on)	3½	**3**	7/1[3]	58	26
4604[W]	**The Robe** (BJMeehan) **2-7-13**(7) GHannon(7) (w'like: scope: led over 4f: wknd ins fnl f)	s.h	**4**	20/1	58	26
4778[11]	**Blue Desert (74)** (GLewis) **2-8-11**(3) RFfrench(17) (hdwy over 2f out: kpt on fnl f)	½	**5**	5/1[2]	65	33
4875[6]	**Mystagogue (58)** (RHannon) **2-8-11** DaneO'Neill(1) (hdwy over 2f out: edgd rt over 1f out: no ex ins fnl f)	3	**6**	12/1	56	24
4806[11]	**Bali Dance (60)** (CBBBooth) **2-8-6** KHodgson(4) (lw: chsd ldrs: no imp fnl 3f)	2	**7**	14/1	47	15
4856[9]	**Up The Wall (63)** (JohnBerry) **2-8-11** JQuinn(20) (prom 6f)	2½	**8**	14/1	47	15

				SP	RR	SF
4576[12]	**Opportune (GER) (62)** (CASmith) **2-8-11** MWigham(9) (dwlt: styd on fnl 3f: nvr nr ldrs)	3	**9**	16/1	41	9
4856[17]	**Carouse (67)** (MRChannon) **2-8-11** SSanders(3) (in tch 5f)	2½	**10**	16/1	36	4
4855[10]	**Citrus Express (SWE)** (PMooney) **2-8-11** MartinDwyer(18) (s.i.s: hdwy 4f out: wknd 2f out)	hd	**11**	33/1	36	4
4853[13]	**Charlie's Gold** (ICampbell) **2-8-11** AMackay(6) (lw: s.i.s: hdwy over 2f out: wknd fnl f)	nk	**12**	33/1	35	3
4753[20]	**Vicky Jazz** (JSMoore) **2-8-0**(7)ow1 PaulCleary(10) (b.off hind: plld hrd: trckd ldrs over 4f)	1¼	**13**	33/1	28	—
4799[10]	**Blanche The Almond (42)** (CASmith) **2-8-6** DeanMcKeown(2) (prom 5f)	3	**14**	20/1	21	—
4740[7]	**Bridge** (DMorley) **2-8-7**ow1 KFallon(19) (stdd s: plld hrd: sn chsng ldrs: wknd over 2f out)	nk	**15**	4/1[1]	22	—
	Capercaillie (DMorris) **2-8-11** NDay(12) (w'like: bit bkwd: outpcd after 4f: rdn over 2f out: eased whn btn)	nk	**16**	8/1	25	—
4470[2]	**Always Trying** (MJohnston) **2-8-11** DHolland(15) (lw: hmpd over 5f out: sn pushed along: bhd fnl 3f)	¾	**17**	10/1	24	—
2588[9]	**Donegal Sean** (NACallaghan) **2-8-11** SDrowne(14) (lw: plld hrd: chsd ldrs 5f)	8	**18**	20/1	8	—
4575[12]	**Lookingforlove Del (IRE)** (NACallaghan) **2-8-6** GCarter(5) (lw: a bhd)	2½	**19**	33/1	—	—
4745[9]	**Cutting Anshake** (MRChannon) **2-8-11** JCarroll(16) (w ldr over 4f: sn wknd & eased)	13	**20**	20/1	—	—
				(SP 154.1%)	**20 Rn**	

1m 40.93 (3.63) CSF £80.16 TOTE £14.10: £3.60 £3.80 £2.60 (£37.20) Trio £61.50 OWNER Axom (WHATCOMBE) BRED W. P. Jenks
Bt in 7,500 gns

4380 Ringleader, well beaten in a similar race at the last meeting, appreciated this step back up to a mile and stamina and toughness ended up deciding the issue. (8/1)

4209 Blue Zola (IRE), taken down first, looked to be travelling best from some way out but did hang and didn't quite see out the trip. (9/1)

Primary Colours, rather keen going down, was held up at the back but still looked hard to settle and appeared to strike into the back of a rival before halfway. Coming home well, she is bred to get further but needs to settle down. (7/1: 4/1-8/1)

The Robe consented to go near the stalls this time and showed a fair bit of ability, only running out of steam in the last one hundred yards. (20/1)

4627* Blue Desert seems best when front-running and these tactics did not suit. (5/1: 7/2-11/2)

4875 Mystagogue, taken down steadily and held up, looked for a moment as if the drop in class might pay dividends, but he again failed to keep straight. (12/1)

Bridge soon pulled her way on to the heels of the leaders and had burnt herself out long before the finish. (4/1)

Capercaillie (8/1: op 16/1)

4975 EQUITY FINANCIAL COLLECTIONS CONDITIONS STKS (2 & 3-Y.O) (Class C)

2-05 (2-06) **6f (Rowley)** £5,070.40 (£1,873.60: £896.80: £364.00: £142.00: £53.20) Stalls: High GOING minus 0.24 sec per fur (GF)

				SP	RR	SF
4155[16]	**Always On My Mind (85)** (PJMakin) **3-9-3** SSanders(6) (mde all: r.o wl)	—	**1**	5/2[2]	92	66
4881[10]	**Distinctive Dream (IRE) (84)** (KTIvory) **3-9-5b** MartinDwyer(7) (chsd ldrs: wnt 2nd over 1f out: r.o fnl f)	1¼	**2**	8/1	91	65
4790[3]	**Shudder** (WJHaggas) **2-8-8** MHills(2) (chsd ldrs: rdn & one pce appr fnl f)	2	**3**	6/4[1]	93	48
4733[3]	**Dark Mile (USA) (79)** (JHMGosden) **3-9-3** GHind(4) (b: stdd s: hdwy over 2f out: rdn & no imp appr fnl f)	1	**4**	4/1[3]	81	55
4787[19]	**Salty Jack (IRE) (72)** (VSoane) **3-9-5** RPerham(1) (prom: rdn over 1f out: edgd rt & wknd fnl f)	5	**5**	25/1	69	43
4451[9]	**Impulsif (USA) (70)** (DJSffrenchDavis) **3-9-5** KFallon(5) (lw: rdn 3f out: sn btn)	7	**6**	20/1	51	25
4881[11]	**Lucayan Beach (80)** (BGubby) **3-9-5** MFenton(3) (s.i.s: sn chsng wnr: wknd 2f out)	10	**7**	33/1	24	—
				(SP 111.2%)	**7 Rn**	

1m 12.88 (1.08) CSF £18.62 TOTE £3.40: £1.70 £3.90 (£12.20) OWNER Mascalls Stud (MARLBOROUGH) BRED Mascalls Stud Farm
WEIGHT FOR AGE 2yo-19lb

3145* Always On My Mind, beaten by the draw last time, made it four wins in five starts by jumping out in front and dictating matters. She responded willingly to some hard riding to seal the issue. (5/2)

4677 Distinctive Dream (IRE) broke on terms for a change and was always chasing the winner along the far rail. Pulled out in the Dip, he could make little impression. (8/1: op 4/1)

4790 Shudder was something of a letdown, finding little when coming off the bridle from the Dip. (6/4)

4733 Dark Mile (USA) didn't get out very well, although it did seem intentional, and could make little impression from the Dip as, once again, her head went up under pressure. (4/1: 5/2-5/1)

Salty Jack (IRE), dropped back to this trip for the first time since breaking his duck as a two-year-old, hung right as the leaders got away from him in the Dip, as he did on his final appearance last year. (25/1)

3710 Impulsif (USA) broke with the field but was hard at work and losing his pitch by halfway. (20/1)

4976 BEN MARSHALL STKS (Listed) (3-Y.O+) (Class A)

2-40 (2-40) **1m (Rowley)** £10,555.95 (£3,802.20: £1,821.10: £740.50: £290.25) Stalls: High GOING minus 0.24 sec per fur (GF)

				SP	RR	SF
4666a[5]	**Samara (IRE) (106)** (JLDunlop) **4-8-10** KFallon(4) (set stdy pce: qcknd 4f out: rdn & r.o wl appr fnl f)	—	**1**	13/8[1]	114	72
4666a[4]	**Balalaika (108)** (LMCumani) **4-8-10** JReid(2) (lw: trckd ldrs: rdn over 2f out: r.o ins fnl f)	¾	**2**	2/1[2]	113	71
4787*	**Desert Beauty (IRE) (89)** (MRStoute) **3-8-5** RHills(3) (trckd ldrs: pushed along over 2f out: effrt over 1f out: one pce ins fnl f)	¾	**3**	5/2[3]	108	64
4669[6]	**Heavenly Ray (USA) (80)** (JRFanshawe) **3-8-5** MHills(5) (lw: hld up: effrt 2f out: no imp)	2½	**4**	20/1	103?	59
4782[7]	**Law Commission (100)** (DRCElsworth) **7-8-12** SDrowne(1) (hld up: a bhd)	5	**5**	12/1	98	56
				(SP 112.5%)	**5 Rn**	

1m 37.59 (0.29) CSF £4.88 TOTE £2.30: £1.40 £1.50 (£3.20) OWNER Aylesfield Farms Stud Ltd (ARUNDEL) BRED Mount Coote Stud
WEIGHT FOR AGE 3yo-2lb

IN-FOCUS: **From this point onwards, the emphasis seemed to switch to racing towards the centre of the course, for no obvious reason.**

4666a Samara (IRE), dropped in trip, was given a cracking ride and was always finding too much for the others once asked to lengthen. (13/8)

4666a Balalaika, in front of Samara last time, made no attempt to make use of her superior stamina and paid the price. (2/1)

4787* Desert Beauty (IRE) didn't seem to be feeling the faster ground but this was a considerable step back up in class and she could not get to the winner, flagging nearing the line. She is proven in more truly-run races and is no lost cause. (5/2: 7/4-11/4)

4669 Heavenly Ray (USA), who missed much of last season, moved poorly to post and didn't appear up to this company. (20/1)

4782 Law Commission, using the tactics which saw him run surprisingly well last time, found the slow early pace against him, as the others quickened at the same time as he did and he never looked likely to improve his position. (12/1: 8/1-14/1)

4977 NGK SPARK PLUGS ZETLAND STKS (Listed) (2-Y.O) (Class A)

3-10 (3-10) **1m 2f (Rowley)** £9,035.60 (£3,340.40: £1,600.20: £651.00: £255.50: £97.30) Stalls: High GOING minus 0.24 sec per fur (GF)

				SP	RR	SF
4873[7]	**Trigger Happy (IRE)** (MJohnston) **2-8-6** JCarroll(7) (lost pl 3f out: hdwy over 2f out: led over 1f out: rdn & r.o wl)	—	**1**	20/1	85	61

4330[3]	**Night Rule** (BHanbury) **2-8-7**ow1 KFallon(4) (s.i.s: hdwy 6f out: rdn & outpcd 3f out: swtchd rt over 1f out: r.o wl fnl f)	1¾	**2**	5/2[1]	83	58
4697[2]	**St Helensfield** (MJohnston) **2-8-11** JReid(2) (lw: outpcd over 4f out: shkn up & hdwy over 2f out: unable qckn fnl f)	s.h	**3**	100/30[3]	87	63
4803[4]	**The Gene Genie** (MJHeaton-Ellis) **2-8-11** SDrowne(5) (lw: led tl hdd over 1f out: sn rdn: one pce)	hd	**4**	10/1	87	63
4582*	**Dashing Chief (IRE) (85)** (MAJarvis) **2-8-11** SSanders(1) (hld up: hdwy 3f out: rdn & one pce ins fnl f)	hd	**5**	11/2	87	63
4413*	**Sinon (IRE)** (MJohnston) **2-8-11** DHolland(3) (chsd ldrs: pushed along over 3f out: sn wl outpcd: styd on strly ins fnl f)	½	**6**	3/1[2]	86	62
4778[20]	**Kim's Brave (84)** (BJMeehan) **2-8-11b** MTebbutt(6) (chsd ldr 7f: hrd drvn over 2f out: sn outpcd)	1½	**7**	25/1	84	60
				(SP 109.7%)	**7 Rn**	

2m 6.02 (1.32) CSF £58.58 TOTE £21.20: £4.80 £1.80 (£46.00) OWNER Mr R. W. Huggins (MIDDLEHAM) BRED Joseph Kruger II

4873 Trigger Happy (IRE), in a race her trainer has won twice in recent years, was the least fancied of the three runners representing him this time. Relishing the step up in trip, she showed what she is made of with a very gutsy performance. (20/1)

4330 Night Rule, driven along to keep in touch some way out, did not begin to stay on until she was switched right in the Dip and her determined, last-furlong challenge was always being matched. Showing signs of getting her winter coat, she will be worth waiting for next season. (5/2)

4697 St Helensfield could not go the pace entering the last half-mile but he responded when shaken up passing the Bushes and had a chance as good as any until failing to quicken in the battle to the line. (100/30)

4803 The Gene Genie was allowed to stride on from the start but he was forced to give best in the Dip and, though he did rally, he was being held in the final one hundred yards. (10/1: 8/1-12/1)

4582* Dashing Chief (IRE) closed up three furlongs out and was soon poised to challenge but he was tapped for speed when the tempo increased entering the final furlong and could only stay on at the same pace. (11/2: 4/1-6/1)

4413* Sinon (IRE), pushed along over three furlongs out, lost more ground when the leaders quickened away from him running into the Dip but he really found his stride again on meeting the rising ground and was gaining hand over fist at the finish. (3/1: op 2/1)

4978 LADBROKE AUTUMN H'CAP (0-100) (3-Y.O+) (Class C)

3-45 (3-46) **1m (Rowley)** £24,234.00 (£9,006.00: £4,353.00: £1,815.00: £757.50: £334.50) Stalls: High GOING minus 0.24 sec per fur (GF)

				SP	RR	SF
4893[12]	**Consort (84)** (MrsAJPerrett) **4-9-0** KFallon(14) (lw: a chsng ldrs: drvn along over 2f out: r.o to ld wl ins fnl f)	—	**1**	15/2[2]	95	67
4781[2]	**For Your Eyes Only (85)** (TDEasterby) **3-8-6b**(7) RWinston(10) (trckd ldrs: hdwy & ev ch ins fnl f: r.o)	nk	**2**	12/1[3]	95	65
4441[6]	**Brilliant Red (89)** (PRHedger) **4-9-5** AMcGlone(8) (lw: led tl wl ins fnl f)	nk	**3**	20/1	99	71
4781[19]	**Artful Dane (IRE) (73)** (MJHeaton-Ellis) **5-8-3v** SDrowne(6) (hld up: hdwy 3f out: r.o wl ins fnl f)	1¼	**4**	50/1	80	52
3764[9]	**Chewit (84)** (GLMoore) **5-9-0** CandyMorris(4) (s.s: bhd: hdwy over 4f out: r.o wl ins fnl f)	½	**5**	33/1	90	62
4787[17]	**Persian Fayre (85)** (JBerry) **5-8-12**(3) TEDurcan(13) (disp ld: rdn & one pce appr fnl f)	hd	**6**	33/1	91	63
4550[10]	**Kayvee (90)** (MrsAJPerrett) **8-9-6** AClark(3) (chsd ldrs: rdn over 2f out: wknd fnl f)	¾	**7**	20/1	95	67
4424[4]	**Pomona (87)** (PJMakin) **4-9-3** JFortune(17) (bhd: hdwy 3f out: r.o strly ins fnl f)	s.h	**8**	20/1	92	64
4558[15]	**Hurtleberry (IRE) (73)** (LordHuntingdon) **4-8-3** JFEgan(25) (hdwy over 4f out: styd on fnl f)	hd	**9**	40/1	77	49
4558[30]	**Stanton Harcourt (USA) (97)** (JLDunlop) **3-9-11** MRimmer(9) (plld hrd: prom tl outpcd over 1f out)	s.h	**10**	25/1	101	71
4757[6]	**Grand Musica (76)** (IABalding) **4-8-6** MartinDwyer(15) (in tch: no hdwy fnl 2f)	¾	**11**	20/1	79	51
4893*	**Prince of Denial (94)** (DWPArbuthnot) **3-9-8** SWhitworth(26) (bhd: effrt 4f out: btn 2f out)	s.h	**12**	12/1[3]	97	67
4757[22]	**Silk St John (80)** (MJRyan) **3-8-8** GBardwell(27) (bhd tl styd on appr fnl f)	nk	**13**	14/1	82	52
4757*	**Jay-Owe-Two (IRE) (82)** (RMWhitaker) **3-8-10v** DeanMcKeown(1) (lw: prom tl outpcd over 2f out)	¾	**14**	14/1	83	53
4680[5]	**Polish Rhythm (IRE) (83)** (GAHubbard) **4-8-13** DO'Donohoe(2) (racd alone: rdn over 3f out: sn lost tch)	2	**15**	50/1	80	52
4424[7]	**Irish Light (USA) (87)** (MRStoute) **3-9-1** JReid(24) (hld up: n.d)	hd	**16**	16/1	83	53
4893[11]	**Welton Arsenal (90)** (KBishop) **5-9-3**(3) RFfrench(7) (in tch over 5f)	hd	**17**	50/1	86	58
4792*	**Desert Track (94)** (JHMGosden) **3-9-8** GHind(11) (prom: wknd & eased over 1f out)	½	**18**	4/1[1]	89	59
4703*	**Begorrat (IRE) (71)** (DMoffatt) **3-7-10b**(3)ow3 DarrenMoffatt(5) (nvr nr to chal)	nk	**19**	40/1	66	33
4306[6]	**Boojum (84)** (BWHills) **3-8-12** MHills(16) (chsd ldrs 5f)	hd	**20**	25/1	78	48
2735[5]	**Rainbow Rain (USA) (77)** (SDow) **3-8-5** DaneO'Neill(12) (trckd ldrs 5f)	2	**21**	50/1	67	37
4550[8]	**Highborn (IRE) (98)** (PSFelgate) **8-9-11**(3) DSweeney(22) (chsd ldrs 5f: sn lost pl)	2½	**22**	33/1	83	55
4637[3]	**Sharp Rebuff (86)** (PJMakin) **6-9-2** SSanders(21) (in tch 5f: sn bhd)	1¼	**23**	20/1	69	41
4558[23]	**Philistar (76)** (KRBurke) **4-8-3**(3) CLowther(18) (a in rr)	1¾	**24**	20/1	55	27
4888[4]	**Prince of India (90)** (LordHuntingdon) **5-9-6** JWeaver(19) (mid div tl wknd over 2f out)	2	**25**	33/1	65	37
4680[8]	**Myrtle Quest (78)** (RCharlton) **5-8-8** TSprake(20) (prom over 4f)	s.h	**26**	20/1	53	25
4781[24]	**Queens Consul (IRE) (86)** (BSRothwell) **7-9-2** MFenton(23) (chsd ldrs over 5f: sn wknd: t.o)	7	**27**	40/1	47	19
4781[29]	**Saifan (86)** (DMorris) **8-9-2b** NDay(28) (a in rr: t.o)	22	**28**	20/1	3	—
				(SP 139.1%)	**28 Rn**	

1m 38.39 (1.09) CSF £65.24 CT £1,627.89 TOTE £9.20: £2.20 £2.60 £6.20 £9.40 (£32.20) Trio £440.30 OWNER Mrs S. L. Whitehead (PULBOROUGH) BRED Crest Stud Ltd

WEIGHT FOR AGE 3yo-2lb

4757 Consort, a lightly-raced colt, has been promising to do this for some time and, under a very forceful ride, had his head in front where it mattered. (15/2)

4781 For Your Eyes Only, from a stable in terrific form, just failed yet again to pick up a very decent prize. Battling long and hard, he may have poked his nose in front briefly inside the last furlong but the winner proved just too strong for him in a thrilling duel to the line. He is back to his best now and success will not come out of turn. (12/1)

4441 Brilliant Red made a brave attempt to make all and he was only collared inside the final one hundred yards. He has been running consistently well without a great deal of success and, from a very shrewd yard, deserves better. (20/1)

2117 Artful Dane (IRE), winner of a competitive handicap in the spring, has been in the doldrums since but he really found his stride on the hill here and has certainly lost none of his ability. (50/1)

3615 Chewit, last to leave the start, probably by choice, edged closer at halfway but did not begin to stay on until well inside the last furlong. He has still to win at this trip. (33/1)

3403 Persian Fayre enjoyed a very successful Autumn last year but he has trouble getting the mile on such a stiff track and his effort was petering out towards the finish. There is still time for him to open his account for this season. (33/1)

4423 Kayvee was always in a challenging position but the pace never slackened and he was found wanting for a turn of finishing speed up the hill. (20/1)

4424 Pomona gave herself just too much to do for she finished like a train, and is still in good heart. (20/1)

4893* Prince of Denial (12/1: 8/1-14/1)

4792* Desert Track was all the rage to complete his hat-trick but he was taking a big step up in class here and was just not up to it. (4/1)

4979 BURROUGH GREEN H'CAP (0-80) (3-Y.O+) (Class D)

4-15 (4-20) **7f (Rowley)** £5,361.00 (£1,608.00: £774.00: £357.00) Stalls: High GOING minus 0.24 sec per fur (GF)

				SP	RR	SF
4700[3]	**Wild Sky (IRE) (72)** (MJHeaton-Ellis) **3-9-5** AClark(4) (lw: bhd: hdwy over 3f out: led ent fnl f: rdn out)	—	**1**	25/1	82	60
4820[4]	**Braveheart (IRE) (69)** (MRChannon) **3-9-2** SSanders(11) (a.p: rdn & ev ch over 1f out: unable qckn)	1	**2**	20/1	77	55
4787[5]	**Safio (78)** (ABailey) **4-9-12** DWright(5) (hld up: hdwy over 2f out: fin wl)	s.h	**3**	7/1[2]	86	65
4757[20]	**Jibereen (60)** (PHowling) **5-8-8** KFallon(14) (b: hdwy over 2f out: sn hrd drvn: no ex ins fnl f)	½	**4**	6/1[1]	67	46
4219[7]	**Dummer Golf Time (66)** (LordHuntingdon) **4-9-0v** JReid(18) (hld up: hdwy 2f out: kpt on u.p fnl f)	3	**5**	11/1	66	45
4951[7]	**Gain Line (USA) (54)** (BobJones) **4-8-2** DBiggs(8) (lw: prom tl rdn & btn appr fnl f)	s.h	**6**	25/1	54	33
4877[6]	**Oxbane (49)** (CADwyer) **3-7-7**(3) RFfrench(21) (led tl wknd & hdd 1f out)	s.h	**7**	16/1	48	26
4436[2]	**Al Masroor (USA) (75)** (JWPayne) **3-9-8** DeanMcKeown(7) (b.off hind: hdwy ½-wy: rdn & no imp fnl f)	½	**8**	6/1[1]	73	51
4927[11]	**Style Dancer (IRE) (75)** (RMWhitaker) **3-9-8** ACulhane(22) (chsd ldrs: rdn over 4f out: no imp fnl 2f)	¾	**9**	25/1	72	50
4580*	**Magic Lake (51)** (EJAlston) **4-7-10v**(3)ow3 MHenry(2) (hld up: hdwy over 3f out: no imp appr fnl f)	¾	**10**	16/1	46	22
4773*	**Night of Glass (65)** (JLEyre) **4-8-13b** MGallagher(16) (b: in tch over 4f)	nk	**11**	16/1	59	38
4878[4]	**Scissor Ridge (57)** (JJBridger) **5-7-12**(7) RBrisland(23) (prom over 4f)	nk	**12**	25/1	50	29
4913[6]	**Swift (67)** (MJPolglase) **3-9-0** JTate(13) (n.d)	s.h	**13**	25/1	60	38
4270*	**Knobbleeneeze (66)** (MRChannon) **7-9-0v** JCarroll(20) (lw: trckd ldrs over 4f)	hd	**14**	16/1	59	38
4757[18]	**Polar Eclipse (68)** (BJMeehan) **4-9-2** MTebbutt(15) (prom 4f)	nk	**15**	40/1	60	39
4773[3]	**Stylish Ways (IRE) (60)** (JPearce) **5-8-8** GBardwell(17) (hrd rdn 2f out: sn wknd)	hd	**16**	20/1	52	31
4859[2]	**Undercover Agent (IRE) (76)** (JLDunlop) **3-9-9** AMcGlone(1) (in tch over 4f)	hd	**17**	10/1[3]	68	46
4518[6]	**Walk the Beat (61)** (MartynMeade) **7-8-9** TSprake(10) (chsd ldrs over 4f)	1	**18**	25/1	51	30
4878[2]	**Zurs (IRE) (63)** (JRPoulton) **4-8-6**(5) RMullen(3) (s.i.s: hdwy over 5f out: wknd 2f out)	s.h	**19**	12/1	53	32
4878[14]	**Ella Lamees (60)** (WJMusson) **3-8-7** JQuinn(12) (s.s: a bhd)	hd	**20**	16/1	49	27
3146[5]	**Awassi (IRE) (65)** (KMahdi) **4-8-10**(3) MBaird(19) (prom to ½-wy)	¾	**21**	25/1	53	32
4155[29]	**Youdontsay (79)** (TJNaughton) **5-9-13** DaneO'Neill(9) (a bhd)	s.h	**22**	33/1	67	46
4842[6]	**Antonias Melody (58)** (SRBowring) **4-8-6** DaleGibson(6) (in tch: hrd rdn over 2f out: sn btn)	1½	**23**	20/1	42	21
4878*	**Victory Team (IRE) (80)** (GBBalding) **5-9-7**(7) RStudholme(24) (prom 4f)	1¼	**24**	20/1	61	40
4711[10]	**Ochos Rios (IRE) (53)** (BSRothwell) **6-7-8**(7)ow3 RWinston(25) (racd alone far side: prom over 4f)	2½	**25**	25/1	29	5
				(SP 150.8%)		**25 Rn**

1m 26.4 (1.90) CSF £429.61 CT £3,591.54 TOTE £38.20: £8.20 £4.90 £3.30 £2.90 (£130.40) Trio £2,514.50; £1,168.71 to Nottingham 3/11/97 OWNER The Gold Partnership (WROUGHTON) BRED Morven Stud

WEIGHT FOR AGE 3yo-1lb

4700 Wild Sky (IRE) had the visor left off and, ridden with more restraint, produced a determined run under strong pressure to fend off a host of challengers. Breaking his duck, he could hardly have chosen a more competitive handicap to do so. (25/1)

4820 Braveheart (IRE) is not quite lasting home at this trip on such a demanding track but he ran a first-class race in defeat and deserves a change of luck. (20/1)

4787 Safio has done all his winning on easier tracks and, though he sprouted wings inside the final furlong, the post was always going to arrive too soon. (7/1)

2868* Jibereen, twice a winner on the July course this year, needed a lot of hard driving to get him to put his best foot forward and, when he did, he could not quite produce the pace to reach the principals. (6/1: 10/1-5/1)

3987 Dummer Golf Time, sent about his work passing the Bushes, took time to respond and was never able to quicken sufficiently to get involved. (11/1)

4951 Gain Line (USA) pushed the pace and had every chance until the final hill caught him out. (25/1)

4877 Oxbane, still struggling to find an opening, proved a tough nut to wear down and it was only late on that she was forced to give best. These tactics will pay off one of these days. (16/1)

4436 Al Masroor (USA) made an effort running into the Dip but he was unable to maintain the run and was never a serious threat. (6/1: op 10/1)

T/Jkpt: £58,955.70 (0.5 Tckts); £41,518.12 to Nottingham 3/11/97. T/Plpt: £445.90 (112.51 Tckts). T/Qdpt: £61.70 (39.14 Tckts) Dk

4795-WOLVERHAMPTON (L-H) (Standard)

Saturday November 1st

WEATHER: drizzly WIND: almost nil

4980 CHARLECOTE MEDIAN AUCTION MAIDEN STKS (3-Y.O) (Class E)

7-00 (7-00) **1m 100y (Fibresand)** £2,427.00 (£672.00: £321.00) Stalls: High GOING: 0.35 sec per fur (SLW)

				SP	RR	SF
4176[15]	**Villarica (IRE) (70)** (PWChapple-Hyam) **3-8-6**(3) RHavlin(8) (a.p: led on bit wl over 1f out: sn clr: easily)	—	**1**	5/4[1]	63+	52
4899[8]	**Don't Worry Mike (50)** (JLSpearing) **3-8-11**(3) PFessey(2) (chsd ldrs: kpt on u.p to take 2nd over 1f out: no ch w wnr)	6	**2**	12/1	57	46
874[8]	**Concer Arall** (SCWilliams) **3-9-0** DaneO'Neill(12) (a.p: led over 2f out: hdd wl over 1f out: sn btn)	3½	**3**	16/1	50	39
3213[7]	**Presentiment (48)** (SRBowring) **3-8-11**(3) CTeague(1) (mid div: drvn over 2f out: sn chsng ldrs: no imp over 1f out)	nk	**4**	16/1	50	39
4587[11]	**Northern Accord** (MrsJRRamsden) **3-9-0** JFortune(3) (hld up in rr: effrt & hdwy over 3f out: no imp fnl 2f)	4	**5**	20/1	42	31
4817[9]	**Village Pub (FR) (43)** (KOCunningham-Brown) **3-9-0** TSprake(13) (led: rdn & hdd over 2f out: sn wknd)	2	**6**	20/1	38	27
4736[5]	**Job Rage (IRE)** (ABailey) **3-9-0** SSanders(9) (mid div: rdn 3f out: sn btn)	2	**7**	14/1	34	23
4872[9]	**Ikram Boy (USA) (60)** (ABailey) **3-9-0** DWright(7) (b: a in rr: rdn over 3f out: n.d)	4	**8**	4/1[2]	27	16
4795[9]	**Ellamine** (DHaydnJones) **3-8-9** SDrowne(5) (mid div: lost pl ½-wy: sn bhd)	1½	**9**	33/1	19	8
4848[10]	**Lawfull Blue (IRE)** (CADwyer) **3-8-9** SWhitworth(4) (prom: ev ch over 2f out: sn wknd)	1½	**10**	10/1[3]	16	5
4848[12]	**Milky Way** (AHide) **3-8-9** DaleGibson(10) (trckd ldrs: rdn ½-wy: wknd over 2f out)	1¼	**11**	20/1	14	3
	Lance's Pet (DCO'Brien) **3-8-9** GBardwell(6) (bkwd: dwlt: a bhd)	5	**12**	33/1	4	—
4795[7]	**Who Dealt (32)** (RHollinshead) **3-8-9** ACulhane(11) (a bhd: struggling after 2f: t.o)	9	**13**	33/1	—	—
				(SP 122.8%)		**13 Rn**

1m 52.3 (7.30) CSF £14.92 TOTE £1.80: £1.30 £1.70 £4.10 (£7.10) Trio £91.00; £102.57 to Nottingham 3/11/97 OWNER Mr R. E. Sangster (MARLBOROUGH) BRED Swettenham Stud

4015 Villarica (IRE) finally broke her maiden tag when cruising clear on the bridle inside the final furlong to trounce inferior rivals. (5/4: 4/7-6/4)

4795 Don't Worry Mike is now eighteen starts without a victory but, in all honest, met a far superior rival in the winner. (12/1)

588 Concer Arall, a half-brother to the useful Concer Un, looked fit enough to do himself justice after a long lay-off but could find no reserves once collared by the winner over a furlong from home. (16/1)
3088 Presentiment could never make any impression on the principals. (16/1)
Northern Accord might find a race over a longer trip in the depths of winter. (20/1)
4648a Village Pub (FR) ran on empty in the straight. (20/1)

4981 SHIFNAL CLAIMING STKS (3-Y.O+) (Class F)

7-30 (7-30) **1m 4f (Fibresand)** £1,932.00 (£532.00: £252.00) Stalls: High GOING: 0.35 sec per fur (SLW)

				SP	RR	SF
4521[5]	**Filial (IRE) (82)** (JPearce) **4-9-9** KFallon(1) (chsd clr ldr: improved to ld over 2f out: drvn out ins fnl f)	—	**1**	5/2[2]	78	58
4608[5]	**State Approval (70)** (PEccles) **4-9-0**(5) GFaulkner(5) (led: clr 7f out: hdd over 2f out: kpt on u.p)	¾	**2**	2/1[1]	73	53
1122[3]	**Greenspan (IRE) (72)** (WRMuir) **5-9-11** AClark(11) (mid div: effrt to chse ldrs 4f out: kpt on one pce fr over 1f out)	3	**3**	8/1	75	55
4771[10]	**Rex Mundi (65)** (PDEvans) **5-9-5** JFEgan(9) (in tch: rdn to chal over 3f out: one pce over 1f out)	nk	**4**	7/1[3]	69	49
4213[9]	**Nikita's Star (IRE) (70)** (DJGMurraySmith) **4-9-6**(3) CLowther(6) (bhd: styd on u.p fnl 2f: nvr nrr)	2	**5**	10/1	70	50
4571[6]	**Bonne Ville (55)** (BPalling) **3-8-8** TSprake(10) (prom: lost pl after 3f: pushed along & hdwy to chse ldrs over 4f out: wknd over 2f out)	2	**6**	12/1	58	32
4800[4]	**Madam Lucy (43)** (JLSpearing) **3-8-3**(3) PFessey(2) (chsd ldrs: rdn & wknd over 2f out)	3	**7**	20/1	52	26
3972[7]	**White Plains (IRE) (75)** (KRBurke) **4-9-9** DaneO'Neill(3) (mid div: tk closer order after 3f: rdn & wknd over 2f out)	5	**8**	16/1	57	37
4811[4]	**Evezio Rufo (47)** (NPLittmoden) **5-9-2b**(3) PRoberts(8) (in rr: rdn 7f out: n.d)	8	**9**	25/1	42	22
3074[3]	**Mystic Strand (44)** (WGMTurner) **4-8-9**(7) DMcGaffin(7) (s.i.s: a bhd: t.o)	dist	**10**	16/1	—	—
4912[10]	**English Invader (59)** (CADwyer) **6-9-5** JFortune(4) (bhd: sn pushed along: t.o)	6	**11**	25/1	—	—
2544[14]	**Lena's Pride** (GBarnett) **4-8-2** NCarlisle(12) (swtg: mid div: bhd after 4f: t.o)	dist	**12**	66/1	—	—

(SP 128.0%) **12 Rn**

2m 44.1 (11.60) CSF £7.56 TOTE £3.70: £2.50 £1.60 £3.20 (£4.00) Trio £9.30 OWNER Mr D. Leech (NEWMARKET) BRED Juddmonte Farms
WEIGHT FOR AGE 3yo-6lb
IN-FOCUS: **Kieren Fallon's victory made him only the eighth jockey in history to ride 200 winners in a season. His tally includes six winners on the sand before the start of the turf season, which do not count towards the championship.**
4521 Filial (IRE), sent on over a quarter of a mile from home, was made to keep up to his work inside the final furlong to hold the determined runner-up and, in doing so, provided his pilot with his two hundredth winner of a memorable year. The Danehill gelding, who has recently changed stables, had plummeted down the weights from the start of the season. (5/2)
4608 State Approval set the pace but, once headed, kept on admirably to ensure the winner did not have it all easy inside the final furlong. This front-runner is sure to taste success again. (2/1: 5/2-6/4)
1122 Greenspan (IRE) looked well on this first outing since May. He could only plug on at one pace in the straight, and it may pay to go jumping again with this five-year-old. (8/1: 6/1-9/1)
4771 Rex Mundi, who was edgy in the preliminaries, mounted a promising effort over three furlongs out but struggled to change gear once in line for home. (7/1)
299 Nikita's Star (IRE) came from way off the pace here without being a great threat to the leaders. (10/1: 8/1-12/1)
4571 Bonne Ville ran out of gas in the closing stages. (12/1: op 8/1)

4982 PENDEFORD MEDIAN AUCTION MAIDEN STKS (2-Y.O) (Class F)

8-00 (8-00) **6f (Fibresand)** £2,070.00 (£570.00: £270.00) Stalls: High GOING: 0.35 sec per fur (SLW)

				SP	RR	SF
4884[17]	**Roi Brisbane** (MJohnston) **2-9-0** DHolland(7) (towards rr: hdwy after 2f: sn chsng ldrs: r.o to ld ins fnl f: sn clr)	—	**1**	3/1[1]	79+	42
4852[11]	**Main Street** (WJHaggas) **2-9-0** FLynch(5) (in rr: hdwy over 2f out: styd on to chse wnr wl ins fnl f: no imp)	4	**2**	6/1[3]	68	31
4917[17]	**Long Island** (RHannon) **2-9-0** DaneO'Neill(13) (chsd ldrs: rdn over 2f out: sn one pce)	½	**3**	14/1	67	30
4855[6]	**Ballasilla** (BPalling) **2-8-9** TSprake(11) (prom: led over 4f out: rdn & hdd ins fnl f: no ex)	nk	**4**	14/1	61	24
4897[7]	**Kennet (72)** (PDCundell) **2-9-0** RPerham(2) (outpcd: styd on u.p fnl f: nvr nrr)	1¼	**5**	9/2[2]	63	26
4755[14]	**Sara Moon Classic (IRE) (62)** (KMcAuliffe) **2-9-0** JFEgan(4) (b.hind: bhd: late hdwy: nt trble ldrs)	2	**6**	12/1	58	21
4483[5]	**Maedaley (47)** (RonaldThompson) **2-8-9** VHalliday(12) (cl up: rdn ½-wy: wknd 2f out)	½	**7**	25/1	51	14
4769[8]	**Shocker (IRE)** (WJHaggas) **2-8-4**(5) JoHunnam(9) (s.i.s: a rr div)	1½	**8**	33/1	47	10
3847[4]	**Lady Laphroaig (FR)** (WRMuir) **2-8-9** KFallon(8) (outpcd: hdwy to chse ldrs after 2f: wknd over 2f out)	hd	**9**	7/1	47	10
2959[6]	**Sharp Fellow** (IABalding) **2-9-0** MartinDwyer(10) (led: hdd over 4f out: wknd qckly over 1f out)	½	**10**	13/2	51	14
4855[8]	**Arcane Star (IRE) (67)** (APJarvis) **2-8-11**(3) CLowther(3) (chsd ldrs tl wknd ½-wy)	6	**11**	12/1	35	—
4588[13]	**Maggice (50)** (RHollinshead) **2-8-9** ACulhane(6) (bhd after 2f)	½	**12**	50/1	28	—
4812[12]	**Aries Boy** (DCO'Brien) **2-9-0** GBardwell(1) (b: gd spd: pushed along over 3f out: wknd qckly over 2f out: t.o)	27	**13**	50/1	—	—

(SP 122.7%) **13 Rn**

1m 17.3 (6.10) CSF £18.88 TOTE £3.80: £1.90 £2.20 £8.20 (£6.60) Trio £30.30 OWNER Mr John Hodge (MIDDLEHAM) BRED Green Ireland Properties Ltd
4513 Roi Brisbane, looking super-fit, asserted his superiority inside the final furlong. (3/1: 2/1-7/2)
3783 Main Street, dropping down in distance, came from off the pace but failed to land a blow at the winner. There could be a race for this colt in a similar grade this winter. (6/1)
Long Island failed to quicken at a vital time. (14/1)
4855 Ballasilla had no answer to the winner's finishing kick inside the closing stages. (14/1: 12/1-20/1)
4315 Kennet may appreciate a step up in trip. (9/2)

4983 GODFREY MYTTON H'CAP (0-100) (3-Y.O+) (Class C)

8-30 (8-31) **7f (Fibresand)** £5,732.15 (£1,713.20: £820.10: £373.55) Stalls: Low GOING: 0.35 sec per fur (SLW)

				SP	RR	SF
*4797**	**State of Caution (95)** (DShaw) **4-9-9v** JFanning(7) (a.p: led 3f out: r.o ins fnl f)	—	**1**	9/2[2]	102	67
4797[4]	**Sir Joey (USA) (82)** (PGMurphy) **8-8-10** SDrowne(2) (swtg: led 1f: remained prom: ev ch over 1f out: unable qckn ins fnl f)	1½	**2**	7/1[3]	86	51
4777[5]	**Cretan Gift (100)** (NPLittmoden) **6-10-0v** TGMcLaughlin(12) (hld up: rapid hdwy on outside 4f out: ev ch 2f out: r.o cl home)	¾	**3**	11/4[1]	102	67
4787[20]	**Stoppes Brow (85)** (GLMoore) **5-8-13v** AClark(1) (mid div: effrt 4f out: sn chsng ldrs: styd on one pce fnl f)	s.h	**4**	16/1	87	52
4881[5]	**Astrac (IRE) (92)** (NTinkler) **6-9-6** SSanders(10) (prom: led over 4f out: hdd 3f out: no ex ins fnl f)	¾	**5**	10/1	92	57

4872^{4}	**Plan For Profit (IRE) (80)** (MJohnston) **3-8-7** DHolland(5) (in rr: styd on fnl f: nvr nrr)	½	**6**	20/1	79	43
4905^{21}	**Sailormaite (82)** (SRBowring) **6-8-10** SWebster(3) (chsd ldrs: rdn over 2f out: wknd over 1f out)	3	**7**	33/1	74	39
4881^{16}	**Bold Effort (FR) (98)** (KOCunningham-Brown) **5-9-12** TSprake(11) (mid div: hdwy to go prom 4f out: ev ch 2f out: wknd over 1f out)	¾	**8**	12/1	88	53
4550^{3}	**Mr Sponge (USA) (86)** (IABalding) **3-8-13** MartinDwyer(6) (s.s: a bhd)	2½	**9**	8/1	71	35
4902^{4}	**Mr Bergerac (IRE) (84)** (BPalling) **6-8-9**$^{(3)}$ DSweeney(4) (a bhd)	½	**10**	12/1	68	33
4757^{9}	**Pericles (85)** (MissGayKelleway) **3-8-12** JFortune(8) (a outpcd)	1½	**11**	11/1	65	29
4430^{2}	**Albert The Bear (87)** (JBerry) **4-8-12b**$^{(3)}$ PFessey(9) (led after 1f: hdd over 4f out: sn rdn: wknd over 2f out)	7	**12**	8/1	51	16

(SP 126.0%) **12 Rn**

1m 30.5 (5.80) CSF £35.24 CT £98.39 TOTE £6.30: £2.30 £3.40 £2.10 (£21.90) Trio £35.00 OWNER Mr J. C. Fretwell (NEWARK) BRED C. Wiggins

WEIGHT FOR AGE 3yo-1lb

4797* State of Caution, back over seven furlongs, made light of his 7lb hike in the handicap to land a hat-trick of wins here. He certainly thrives on the West Midlands air. (9/2)

4797 Sir Joey (USA) was a reluctant leader for the first furlong here but remained prominent throughout. This tough eight-year-old has never won over the trip. (7/1)

4777 Cretan Gift gave the impression he was going to collect before the straight. However, he stuck to his task well over this foreign trip and he is sure to taste further success. (11/4)

1658 Stoppes Brow ran a game race in defeat. (16/1)

4881 Astrac (IRE) had no more to give inside the final furlong but it was still a solid performance. (10/1)

4872 Plan For Profit (IRE) may appreciate a step up in trip on this surface. (20/1)

4550 Mr Sponge (USA) missed the break and never looked at ease on the surface. (8/1)

4570* Pericles (11/1: 8/1-12/1)

4984 MIDLAND BAR (S) NURSERY H'CAP (0-65) (2-Y.O) (Class G)

9-00 (9-00) **1m 100y (Fibresand)** £1,725.00 (£475.00: £225.00) Stalls: High GOING: 0.35 sec per fur (SLW)

				SP	RR	SF
4627^{5}	**Emperor's Gold (58)** (ICampbell) **2-9-0** AMackay(2) (cl up: led 1f out: sn rdn clr)	—	**1**	10/1^{3}	64	31
4698^{4}	**Lady Eil (51)** (BSmart) **2-8-7** JStack(3) (led: hdd 1f out: nt pce of wnr ins fnl f)	5	**2**	12/1	48	15
4808^{5}	**Island Girl (IRE) (56)** (DWPArbuthnot) **2-8-12** SWhitworth(4) (a.p: drvn over 1f out: one pce ins fnl f)	2½	**3**	12/1	48	15
4698^{5}	**Mary Lou (IRE) (48)** (MRChannon) **2-8-4** AClark(9) (in tch: rdn 4f out: one pce fnl 2f)	1¾	**4**	14/1	37	4
4806^{12}	**Thecomebackking (54)** (SCWilliams) **2-8-10** KFallon(7) (chsd ldrs tl wknd over 3f out)	4	**5**	3/1^{1}	35	2
4745^{11}	**Sharp Monkey (53)** (MrsNMacauley) **2-8-9v^{1}** SDrowne(5) (prom: pushed along over 3f out: wknd over 1f out)	2	**6**	16/1	30	—
*4799**	**Pink Ticket (59)** (PDEvans) **2-9-1** JFEgan(6) (sn pushed along & bhd)	¾	**7**	7/2^{2}	35	2
4799^{4}	**Abstone Pet Girl (45)** (PDEvans) **2-7-8**$^{(7)}$ AMcCarthy(1) (nvr nr to chal)	2	**8**	16/1	17	—
4799^{3}	**Cherished (IRE) (55)** (NTinkler) **2-8-11** SSanders(11) (chsd ldrs: drvn & wknd qckly ½-wy)	2	**9**	3/1^{1}	23	—
4796^{11}	**Safabee (50)** (JCullinan) **2-8-6** NCarlisle(12) (wl bhd: t.o)	30	**10**	33/1	—	—
2018^{11}	**Monopoly (IRE) (58)** (MJohnston) **2-9-0** DHolland(8) (in tch: drvn & lost pl qckly 5f out: sn n.d: t.o)	21	**11**	10/1^{3}	—	—

(SP 127.2%) **11 Rn**

1m 55.0 (10.00) CSF £121.79 CT £910.82 TOTE £13.80: £2.70 £5.00 £3.90 (£279.30) Trio Not won; £175.23 to Nottingham 3/11/97 OWNER Classic Gold (NEWMARKET) BRED R. and Mrs Lockhart

No bid

4627 Emperor's Gold reversed earlier form with some of these rivals when striding clear inside the final furlong. (10/1)

4698 Lady Eil, stepping down in trip, could do nothing to stop the winner inside the closing stages. However, she may be capable of tasting glory this winter. (12/1: op 8/1)

2196 Island Girl (IRE) had no more to give inside the closing stages on this step up in distance. (12/1)

4698 Mary Lou (IRE) could make no impression on the leaders. (14/1)

4799* Pink Ticket was never going a yard. (7/2)

4799 Cherished (IRE) was a spent force a long way from home. (3/1)

4985 WEST MIDLANDS H'CAP (0-60) (3-Y.O+) (Class F)

9-30 (9-33) **6f (Fibresand)** £1,932.00 (£532.00: £252.00) Stalls: High GOING: 0.35 sec per fur (SLW)

				SP	RR	SF
4816^{6}	**Italian Symphony (IRE) (55)** (PDEvans) **3-9-2v**$^{(7)}$ AMcCarthy(11) (a.p: led over 2f out: hld on wl cl home)	—	**1**	16/1	68	50
4574^{3}	**Hannah's Usher (57)** (CMurray) **5-9-11** NicolaHowarth(1) (hld up: hdwy over 3f out: r.o ins fnl f)	nk	**2**	11/2^{2}	69	51
4570^{8}	**Bold Aristocrat (IRE) (60)** (RHollinshead) **6-10-0** FLynch(12) (in tch: drvn to cl over 2f out: styd on ins fnl f)	1	**3**	14/1	70	52
4049^{3}	**Silk Cottage (54)** (RMWhitaker) **5-9-8** DeanMcKeown(10) (led: hdd over 2f out: no ex wl ins fnl f)	¾	**4**	7/1^{3}	62	44
4574^{5}	**Village Native (FR) (57)** (KOCunningham-Brown) **4-9-11** TSprake(5) (in rr: styd on fnl 2f: nvr nrr)	1½	**5**	11/1	61	43
4733^{8}	**Nineacres (54)** (NMBabbage) **6-9-8v** DaneO'Neill(4) (cl up: outpcd ent fnl 2f)	½	**6**	11/2^{2}	56	38
4452^{3}	**Pharaoh's Joy (58)** (AGNewcombe) **4-9-12** AMackay(7) (b: bhd: sme late hdwy u.p: nt rch ldrs)	3	**7**	7/1^{3}	52	34
4844^{10}	**Shadow Jury (59)** (DWChapman) **7-9-13v** JFortune(9) (chsd ldrs: checked sltly over 3f out: sn outpcd)	1½	**8**	12/1	49	31
4844^{11}	**Super Rocky (56)** (RBastiman) **8-9-5b**$^{(5)}$ HBastiman(2) (in tch: drvn & wknd ½-wy)	1½	**9**	20/1	42	24
4518^{10}	**Mellors (IRE) (60)** (MJHeaton-Ellis) **4-10-0** SDrowne(13) (in tch: drvn 4f out: sn wknd)	2	**10**	14/1	41	23
3910^{21}	**Amy Leigh (IRE) (57)** (CaptJWilson) **4-9-4v**$^{(7)}$ AngelaHartley(3) (s.s: a bhd)	nk	**11**	16/1	37	19
4574^{9}	**Will To Win (55)** (PGMurphy) **3-9-9** KFallon(8) (b.hind: prom tl wknd ½-wy)	4	**12**	4/1^{1}	24	6
2305^{10}	**Hoh Majestic (IRE) (60)** (RonaldThompson) **4-10-0v** VHalliday(6) (sn bhd)	8	**13**	20/1	8	—

(SP 126.4%) **13 Rn**

1m 17.3 (6.10) CSF £97.87 CT £1,215.64 TOTE £32.30: £5.80 £1.90 £3.00 (£310.30) Trio £169.70; £215.23 to Nottingham 3/11/97 OWNER Mr J. E. Abbey (WELSHPOOL) BRED Howard Kaskel

4816 Italian Symphony (IRE), dropping down in distance, kicked on before the straight and held on well as the post beckoned to record a first-ever victory. (16/1)

4574 Hannah's Usher came from off the pace here and, with a few more yards, would have prevailed. This five-year-old is overdue a victory. (11/2)

4051 Bold Aristocrat (IRE), a Southwell specialist, was certainly finishing to some effect. (14/1)

4049 Silk Cottage, as per usual, showed blistering speed from the gate, but had to give way before the straight. (7/1)

4574 Village Native (FR) came from the rear without making any real impression. (11/1: 7/1-12/1)

3984 Nineacres seemed to lack a finishing kick. (11/2: 4/1-6/1)

512 Mellors (IRE) (14/1: 25/1-40/1)
4115 Will To Win (4/1: 6/1-7/2)

T/Plpt: £238.10 (83.85 Tckts). T/Qdpt: £94.90 (5.67 Tckts) DO

4952-NOTTINGHAM (L-H) (Good, Good to soft patches)
Monday November 3rd
WEATHER: overcast WIND: slt bhd

4986 'LAST CHANCE AT NOTTINGHAM' AMATEUR LIMITED STKS (0-70) (3-Y.O+) (Class G)
1-10 (1-10) **1m 6f 15y** £1,984.50 (£547.00: £259.50) Stalls: Low GOING: minus 0.08 sec per fur (G)

Form	Horse	Dist	Pos	SP	RR	SF
*4810**	**Montecristo (70)** (RGuest) **4-11-5**(4) MissRFlynn(1) (lw: trckd ldrs: effrt over 1f out: led ins fnl f: r.o)	—	1	3/1 2	80	61
4673^{3}	**Bold Buster (70)** (IABalding) **4-11-7** MrABalding(2) (lw: led after 4f tl hdd & no ex ins fnl f)	¾	2	6/4 1	77	58
4800^{7}	**Rasayel (USA) (70)** (PDEvans) **7-10-12**(4) MrAEvans(15) (s.i.s: racd wd: hdwy ½-wy: rdn over 2f out: one pce)	10	3	8/1	61	42
2927^{2}	**Charming Admiral (IRE) (54)** (MrsASwinbank) **4-11-5** MrPScott(7) (bit bkwd: sn prom: rdn 3f out: outpcd appr fnl f)	¾	4	8/1	63	44
4548^{3}	**Laurel Seeker (USA) (61)** (MrsAJPerrett) **3-10-11** MrsAPerrett(14) (led 4f: drvn along 3f out: wknd wl over 1f out)	1	5	11/2 3	62	35
1162^{12}	**Campaign (70)** (MDHammond) **6-11-5** MrCBonner(5) (bit bkwd: sn bhd & pushed along styd on fnl 2f: nvr nrr)	6	6	16/1	55	36
4912^{13}	**Dunabrattin (55)** (DTThom) **4-11-1**(4) MrJCrowley(9) (lw: chsd ldrs tl rdn & wknd over 3f out)	2½	7	50/1	52	33
2577^{11}	**Aquavita (46)** (JSMoore) **3-10-4**(4) MrsSMoore(12) (bhd: sme late hdwy: n.d)	¾	8	40/1	48	21
4811^{15}	**El Nido (30)** (DWChapman) **9-10-12**(7) MrRClark(13) (plld hrd: sn chsng ldrs: lost pl 7f out)	8	9	50/1	42	23
4850^{4}	**Sharp Deed (IRE) (49)** (PJMakin) **3-10-7v**(4) MrLBaker(16) (lw: wnt prom after 4f: hung rt 3f out: sn btn)	1	10	16/1	41	14
4751^{13}	**Salinger (37)** (JParkes) **9-10-12**(7) MrTComerford(4) (b: s.s: a in rr)	1½	11	50/1	39	20
4360^{8}	**Single Man (IRE) (34)** (BPJBaugh) **4-10-12**(7) MissSRodman(3) (a rr div: t.o)	7	12	50/1	31	12
4713^{13}	**Miami Moon (43)** (GFJohnsonHoughton) **3-10-8** MissEJohnsonHoughton(6) (plld hrd: sn trckng ldrs: wknd 3f out)	2½	13	25/1	26	—
86^{13}	**Impending Danger (38)** (KSBridgwater) **4-11-5** MrOMcPhail(10) (bkwd: a bhd: t.o fnl 4f)	10	14	50/1	17	—
	Texas Scramble (55) (BPJBaugh) **8-10-12**(7) MissSMPotts(8) (b: bkwd: in tch tl lost pl 7f out: t.o)	3½	15	50/1	13	—

(SP 132.4%) **15 Rn**

3m 10.1 (11.60) CSF £7.55 TOTE £4.20: £1.60 £1.10 £3.00 (£3.10) Trio £7.00 OWNER Mr Rae Guest (NEWMARKET) BRED Lord Matthews
WEIGHT FOR AGE 3yo-8lb

4810* Montecristo, given a very confident over this longer trip, completed a four-timer with another smoothly-gained success. He can handle all surfaces and has not not stopped winning yet. (3/1: 7/4-100/30)
4673 Bold Buster may have found the drying ground livelier than he really needs but he was only forced to give best inside the final furlong and he did finish clear of the remainder. (6/4)
3886* Rasayel (USA) has had a longish season but she is game and once more gave it her best. (8/1: op 5/1)
2927 Charming Admiral (IRE), on the heels of the leaders, was being made to work three furlongs out and found lack of peak fitness taking its toll in the closing stages. He will be all the better for this first run in over three months. (8/1: op 14/1)
4548 Laurel Seeker (USA), beginning to get his winter coat, helped share the lead and remained a serious contender until fading inside the last quarter-mile. (11/2: op 3/1)
Campaign, having only his second run on the Flat in two years, has tasted success over hurdles in the past and this badly needed pipe-opener should have helped put him right for a return to the winter game. (16/1)

4987 END OF SEASON (S) STKS (3-Y.O+) (Class G)
1-40 (1-41) **1m 1f 213y** £1,984.50 (£547.00: £259.50) Stalls: Low GOING minus 0.08 sec per fur (G)

Form	Horse	Dist	Pos	SP	RR	SF
4713^{3}	**Statajack (IRE) (60)** (DRCElsworth) **9-9-2b** TQuinn(1) (b: s.i.s: hdwy 7f out: effrt over 3f out: styd on to ld nr fin)	—	1	13/2 3	64	33
4886^{7}	**Brighstone (68)** (MCPipe) **4-9-7** AMcGlone(8) (t: led tl wl ins fnl f)	¾	2	7/2 2	68	37
2911^{4}	**Esperto (52)** (JPearce) **4-9-2** GBardwell(2) (sn trckng ldrs: effrt over 2f out: hrd rdn & hung lft: nvr able chal)	4	3	12/1	56	25
4924^{7}	**Gymcrak Premiere (67)** (GHolmes) **9-9-7** KFallon(11) (b.hind: hld up: hdwy over 3f out: rdn 2f out: no imp)	2	4	11/8 1	58	27
4923^{5}	**Diamond Crown (IRE) (32)** (MartynWane) **6-9-2** JCarroll(16) (swtg: s.i.s: bhd hdwy over 2f out: hrd rdn & styd on fnl f)	1½	5	50/1	51	20
4858^{2}	**Jubilee Scholar (IRE) (36)** (GLMoore) **4-9-2** JQuinn(12) (bhd tl sme hdwy fnl 2f)	½	6	25/1	50	19
4886^{12}	**Prince of Bhutan (IRE) (50)** (RAkehurst) **3-8-12** DHolland(3) (chsd ldrs tl wknd over 1f out)	hd	7	20/1	50	15
4810^{5}	**Lady Silk (30)** (MissJFCraze) **6-9-2b**1 SWebster(10) (mid div: drvn along over 3f out: n.d)	6	8	33/1	40	9
4817^{13}	**Sidney The Kidney (49)** (MJRyan) **3-8-5**(3)ow1 PMcCabe(15) (trckd ldr: wknd over 2f out)	nk	9	33/1	36	—
4179^{5}	**Arzani (USA) (58)** (DJSCosgrove) **6-9-2** MRimmer(14) (b: hld up & bhd: sme hdwy over 2f out: n.d)	nk	10	10/1	39	8
2512^{7}	**Burundi (IRE) (68)** (AWCarroll) **3-8-12** MTebbutt(4) (hld up & bhd: effrt over 2f out: wandered: n.d)	2	11	14/1	36	1
4568^{8}	**Aficionado (IRE) (60)** (RJHodges) **3-8-9**(3) RFfrench(6) (bhd: sme hdwy 3f out: sn wknd)	1	12	10/1	34	—
4608^{13}	**Little Pilgrim (23)** (TMJones) **4-9-2** RPerham(17) (bhd: sme hdwy on outside appr st: sn wknd)	½	13	50/1	34	3
4843^{3}	**Bella's Legacy (39)** (KRBurke) **4-8-8**(3) DSweeney(18) (plld hrd: hdwy on outside 6f out: lost pl over 2f out)	¾	14	16/1	27	—
4114^{18}	**Baba Sadhu** (PJMakin) **3-8-12** JFortune(7) (sn bhd & drvn along: edgd rt 2f out: sn wknd)	6	15	33/1	23	—
4711^{18}	**Hopperetta (43)** (BPalling) **3-8-7** DaneO'Neill(5) (chsd ldrs tl wknd over 3f out)	3½	16	33/1	12	—
4742^{16}	**Saltando (IRE) (33)** (PatMitchell) **6-9-2** PBloomfield(13) (mid div: drvn along 7f out: lost pl over 3f out)	3½	17	33/1	12	—
4742^{11}	**Eastleigh (27)** (RHollinshead) **8-9-0**(7) SClarke(9) (b.nr hind: trckd ldrs: effrt over 3f out: sn wknd)	nk	18	50/1	16	—

(SP 145.3%) **18 Rn**

2m 9.9 (7.40) CSF £29.39 TOTE £5.60: £2.50 £1.90 £2.70 (£21.30) Trio £26.10 OWNER Mrs M. E. Slade (WHITCOMBE) BRED Princess Oettingen-Spielberg
WEIGHT FOR AGE 3yo-4lb
Bt in 4,200 gns

4713 Statajack (IRE), last away, was persuaded to do just enough to record his eleventh career win. He had recently run in a charity race at Wincanton, finishing a close second to Pay Homage. (13/2)

4742* Brighstone led his rivals a merry dance. Looking to be going best halfway up the straight, in the end he was just worn down. (7/2)
2911 Esperto, an excitable type, was having his first outing for one hundred and five days. Under pressure, all he wanted to do was hang left. (12/1)
4924 Gymcrak Premiere tried to come from off the pace. Flat out two furlongs from home, on this occasion he was never going to find sufficient to take a hand. (11/8)
4923 Diamond Crown (IRE), who had an impossible task on official figures, ran his usual sort of race, staying on from off the pace. (50/1)
2512 Burundi (IRE) (14/1: op 8/1)

4988 MANNY BERNSTEIN BOOKMAKERS H'CAP (0-70) (3-Y.O+) (Class E)

2-10 (2-10) **1m 1f 213y** £3,242.50 (£970.00: £465.00: £212.50) Stalls: Low GOING minus 0.08 sec per fur (G)

				SP	RR	SF
4741*	**Sovereigns Court (65)** (LGCottrell) **4-9-11** KFallon(1) (hld up: hdwy over 1f out: qckned to ld 200y out: sn clr)	—	**1**	7/2^{2}	79	21
4773^{4}	**Kass Alhawa (62)** (DWChapman) **4-9-8** ACulhane(4) (lw: hld up: effrt over 2f out: kpt on fnl f: no ch w wnr)	5	**2**	11/1^{3}	68	10
4802^{2}	**Bonanza Peak (USA) (68)** (MrsJCecil) **4-10-0** MartinDwyer(12) (lw: s.i.s: sn chsng ldrs: ev ch over 2f out: unable qckn fnl f)	nk	**3**	2/1^{1}	74	16
4798^{6}	**Legal Issue (IRE) (57)** (WWHaigh) **5-9-3** TSprake(8) (hld up: hdwy appr fnl f: nrst fin)	½	**4**	14/1	62	4
4918^{9}	**Needwood Legend (45)** (BCMorgan) **4-8-5** LCharnock(3) (prom: rdn over 2f out: wknd appr fnl f)	2½	**5**	50/1	46	—
4899*	**Myttons Mistake (62)** (RJHodges) **4-9-5**$^{(3)}$ RFfrench(2) (hld up: effrt 3f out: hrd drvn whn not clr run over 2f out)	hd	**6**	7/2^{2}	63	5
4854^{8}	**Bedouin Honda (65)** (CEBrittain) **3-9-7b^{1}** DaneO'Neill(5) (plld hrd: chsd ldrs: chal over 2f out: wknd appr fnl f)	hd	**7**	20/1	65	3
4810^{4}	**Domino Flyer (65)** (MrsASwinbank) **4-9-11** GDuffield(9) (swtg: led tl hdd & wknd ins fnl f)	½	**8**	14/1	65	7
4845^{7}	**Flying Flip (50)** (BCMorgan) **3-8-6** DeanMcKeown(10) (b.hind: in tch: effrt & drvn along 3f out: sn lost tch)	1¼	**9**	14/1	48	—
3466^{4}	**The Negotiator (58)** (MJHeaton-Ellis) **3-9-0** SDrowne(11) (lw: plld hrd: effrt over 3f out: sn wknd)	3	**10**	14/1	51	—
4469^{2}	**Slipstream Star (70)** (IABalding) **3-9-12** JReid(6) (trckd ldr: ev ch tl wknd fnl 2f)	hd	**11**	12/1	63	1
4927^{14}	**Mountgate (60)** (MPBielby) **5-9-6** JFEgan(7) (s.s: a bhd)	4	**12**	33/1	46	—
				(SP 130.1%)	**12 Rn**	

2m 12.6 (10.10) CSF £41.87 CT £93.51 TOTE £4.20: £1.90 £4.50 £1.60 (£76.90) Trio £31.50 OWNER Mr E. Gadsden (CULLOMPTON) BRED Mrs D. O. Joly
WEIGHT FOR AGE 3yo-4lb
IN-FOCUS: **A number of trainers were caught unawares by a late decision to change the distance of this race from seven to ten furlongs.**
4741* Sovereigns Court made his first appearance over this longer trip a winning one with a runaway success and for him it will be a pity the season ends so soon. (7/2)
4773 Kass Alhawa made relentless progress in the latter stages and kept staying on but the winner had too much pace for him and the runner-up prize was the only issue at stake. He has an engagement later in the week and if he turns out he is sure to give a good account of himself. (11/1)
4802 Bonanza Peak (USA) has been running consistently well this season and has steadily crept to the top of the handicap and that as much as anything was holding him when the race to the finish really developed. (2/1)
4798 Legal Issue (IRE) needed to be ridden with restraint in an attempt to get this slightly longer trip and he caught the eye doing all his best work late on. A winner on the All-Weather, he should be able to improve on this before too long. (14/1)
Needwood Legend has now run two identical races over this trip inside the past week and, though this run probably came much too soon, he does look capable of winning if lowered slightly in class. (50/1)
4899* Myttons Mistake, having his first run since changing stables, would seem to find this trip beyond him but was not without a chance when he was denied a clear passage approaching the final furlong. (7/2)

4989 CENTENARY CONFERENCE FACILITY NURSERY H'CAP (2-Y.O) (Class E)

2-40 (2-41) **6f 15y** £3,665.00 (£1,100.00: £530.00: £245.00) Stalls: High GOING: minus 0.08 sec per fur (G)

				SP	RR	SF
4284^{7}	**Five of Spades (IRE) (77)** (RAFahey) **2-8-6**$^{(7)}$ RWinston(11) (lw: mde all stands' side: r.o wl fnl f)	—	**1**	9/1	79	51
4885^{3}	**Inchalong (73)** (MBrittain) **2-8-2**$^{(7)}$ DMernagh(7) (racd far side: chsd ldr: led over 2f out: edgd bdly rt ins fnl f: r.o)	1	**2**	7/2^{1}	72	44
4890^{7}	**Demolition Jo (82)** (PDEvans) **2-9-4v** JFEgan(16) (racd stands' side: chsd wnr: kpt on same pce fnl 2f)	3	**3**	6/1^{3}	74	46
4818*	**Third Cousin (IRE) (82)** (MJHeaton-Ellis) **2-9-4** SDrowne(14) (racd stands' side: hdwy 2f out: styd on ins fnl f)	1	**4**	8/1	71	43
4922*	**Blundell Lane (IRE) (76)** (APJarvis) **2-8-9**$^{(3)}$ 7x CLowther(6) (lw: racd far side: sn outpcd: hdwy ½-wy: styd on one pce appr fnl f: eased inside fnl f)	¾	**5**	4/1^{2}	63	35
4885^{9}	**Sense of Wonder (85)** (BJMeehan) **2-9-7** KFallon(9) (racd stands' side: hdwy over 2f out: nvr nr to chal)	nk	**6**	10/1	71	43
4922^{6}	**Sing For Me (IRE) (60)** (RHollinshead) **2-7-10** NCarlisle(12) (racd stands' side: hdwy 2f out: kpt on: nvr nr ldrs)	2½	**7**	33/1	40	12
4814^{9}	**Algebra (62)** (RHannon) **2-7-9**$^{(3)ow2}$ RFfrench(8) (b.hind: racd far side: outpcd ½-wy: hdwy 2f out: kpt on fnl f)	nk	**8**	16/1	41	11
4779^{16}	**Nautical Warning (62)** (MHTompkins) **2-7-7**$^{(5)ow2}$ RMullen(1) (s.i.s: racd far side: bhd tl styd on appr fnl f)	hd	**9**	12/1	40	10
4851^{6}	**Darwell's Folly (USA) (80)** (MJohnston) **2-9-2** DHolland(15) (swtg: racd stands' side: sn bhd)	1¼	**10**	10/1	55	27
4755^{17}	**Golden Strategy (IRE) (79)** (RHannon) **2-9-1** DaneO'Neill(10) (racd stands' side: chsd ldrs tl rdn & wknd 2f out)	1	**11**	12/1	52	24
4296^{9}	**Fast Tempo (IRE) (76)** (BPalling) **2-8-12** TSprake(3) (led far side tl hdd over 2f out: sn wknd & eased)	2½	**12**	16/1	42	14
4885^{14}	**Penniless (IRE) (66)** (NTinkler) **2-8-2** KimTinkler(5) (chsd ldrs far side tl wknd over 2f out)	1	**13**	25/1	29	1
4167^{15}	**Dragon Boy (67)** (IPWilliams) **2-8-3** MartinDwyer(13) (s.i.s: racd stands' side: a bhd)	3½	**14**	25/1	21	—
3825^{10}	**Stately Favour (68)** (MJCamacho) **2-8-4** LCharnock(4) (b.hind: racd far side: chsd ldrs tl lost pl over 2f out)	3½	**15**	20/1	13	—
4982^{11}	**Arcane Star (IRE) (60)** (APJarvis) **2-7-10** JQuinn(2) (racd far side: prom to ½-wy: sn lost pl)	1¼	**16**	33/1	2	—
				(SP 141.3%)	**16 Rn**	

1m 14.3 (2.80) CSF £40.49 CT £211.44 TOTE £7.90: £1.80 £1.10 £2.10 £1.80 (£29.40) Trio £23.50 OWNER Mr B. L. Cassidy (MALTON) BRED N. and D. Wallace and Co
LONG HANDICAP Algebra 7-9 Sing For Me (IRE) 7-2 Arcane Star (IRE) 7-7
3932* Five of Spades (IRE), who really took the eye beforehand, appreciated getting his toe in. Making all on the stands' side, he provided his promising young rider with his twentieth success of the year, reducing his allowance to 5lb. (9/1)
4885 Inchalong, having her twenty-third outing of the year, showed ahead on the far side soon after halfway. Edging badly right and ending up almost alongside the winner on the stands' side at the line, had she kept straight she must have gone very close indeed. (7/2)

4755* Demolition Jo was having her fifteenth outing this time. (6/1)
4818* Third Cousin (IRE), who looked very fit, looked to have been pitched in a pound or two too high on his Folkestone win. (8/1)
4922* Blundell Lane (IRE) struggled to go the pace on the far side. Staying on the same pace coming to the final furlong, he was disputing third place when he was eased up near the line. (4/1)
4885 Sense of Wonder, who looked to have plenty on at the weights, was very edgy beforehand. (10/1)

4990 NOVEMBER CONDITIONS STKS (3-Y.O+) (Class C)
3-10 (3-10) **1m 54y** £5,550.20 (£2,061.80: £995.90: £414.50: £172.25: £75.35) Stalls: Low GOING minus 0.08 sec per fur (G)

				SP	RR	SF
4893^{2}	**Strazo (IRE) (96)** (LadyHerries) **4-9-4** DeanMcKeown(6) (mde all: clr over 2f out: unchal)	—	**1**	4/1^{3}	110	66
4781^{14}	**Kala Sunrise (89)** (CSmith) **4-8-13** JTate(7) (lw: chsd ldrs: styd on u.p ins fnl f: no ch w wnr)	3½	**2**	7/1	98	54
4978^{7}	**Kayvee (90)** (MrsAJPerrett) **8-8-13** KFallon(1) (lw: hld up: hdwy over 2f out: rdn & one pce fnl f)	nk	**3**	3/1^{1}	98	54
4902^{2}	**Groom's Gordon (FR) (94)** (JLDunlop) **3-8-11** TQuinn(8) (lw: a chsng ldrs: hrd rdn 3f out: one pce)	3	**4**	7/2^{2}	92	46
4947^{2}	**Unconditional Love (IRE) (96)** (MJohnston) **4-8-8** DHolland(11) (trckd ldrs: hrd drvn over 3f out: kpt on)	2½	**5**	5/1	82	38
4550^{12}	**Bachelors Pad (90)** (WJarvis) **3-8-11** JReid(4) (hld up: hdwy over 2f out: nt rch ldrs)	nk	**6**	14/1	86	40
4423^{23}	**Chickawicka (IRE) (89)** (BPalling) **6-8-13** TSprake(5) (lw: hld up & bhd: effrt over 2f out: nt rch ldrs)	nk	**7**	12/1	86	42
4637^{7}	**Celestial Key (USA) (94)** (MJohnston) **7-8-10**(3) MHenry(12) (sn bhd & drvn along: effrt over 3f out: wknd appr fnl f)	4	**8**	12/1	78	34
4689^{4}	**Bea's Ruby (IRE) (89)** (ABailey) **3-8-12v^{1}** JFortune(9) (b: chsd wnr tl wknd wl over 2f out: t.o)	13	**9**	14/1	54	8
	Stamp (IRE) (BSmart) **3-8-11** JStack(2) (b: bkwd: chsd ldrs tl wknd over 3f out: t.o)	1¾	**10**	20/1	49	3
4506^{5}	**Croft Sands** (RAkehurst) **4-8-13** AMcGlone(10) (bit bkwd: sn wl outpcd: t.o fnl 3f)	5	**11**	66/1	40	—
				(SP 131.4%)	**11 Rn**	

1m 44.3 (3.00) CSF £33.35 TOTE £6.40: £1.80 £2.10 £1.40 (£27.50) Trio £21.50 OWNER Mr E. Reitel (LITTLEHAMPTON) BRED Juddmonte Farms
WEIGHT FOR AGE 3yo-2lb
4893 Strazo (IRE) has fared much better since being allowed to stride on from the start and, though he is beginning to look woolly in his coat, galloped these rivals into the ground. (4/1)
4637 Kala Sunrise, a winner in the Autumn last year, stayed on particularly well inside the final furlong without having a hope of reaching the winner. (7/1)
4978 Kayvee, having his second outing in three days, tried hard to reel in the winner but that rival had got away and he was even denied the runner-up prize nearing the line. (3/1)
4902 Groom's Gordon (FR) ran a fine race a week ago after a longish break and, though the extra furlong may not have been in his favour, he did perform as if he had not fully recovered. (7/2)
4947 Unconditional Love (IRE) has failed to win a race this year but she had been knocking at the door in some decent races and, though brought back a couple of furlongs, she ran a bit too free and was struggling to hang on throughout the last quarter-mile. (5/1)
4153 Bachelors Pad, settled in rear to conserve his stamina, did make a forward move early in the straight but, with the pace being maintained, could not get close enough to mount a challenge. (14/1)
2390 Chickawicka (IRE) likes to force the pace but he was denied that role here and was anchored towards the rear under a strong hold. When asked for his effort two furlongs out, he was unable to respond and these tactics did not suit. (12/1: 8/1-14/1)
4637 Celestial Key (USA) (12/1: op 8/1)

4991 'SEE YOU NEXT MARCH' H'CAP (0-60) (I) (3-Y.O+) (Class F)
3-40 (3-47) **1m 54y** £1,927.00 (£527.00: £247.00) Stalls: Low GOING minus 0.08 sec per fur (G)

				SP	RR	SF
4847^{13}	**Up in Flames (IRE) (43)** (SRBowring) **6-8-9**(3) CTeague(4) (hld up: gd hdwy over 3f out: led over 1f out: hld on wl)	—	**1**	12/1	52	34
4847^{8}	**Scenicris (IRE) (46)** (RHollinshead) **4-9-1** FLynch(8) (hdwy over 3f out: sn chsng ldrs: ev ch ins fnl f: no ex)	1¼	**2**	5/1^{1}	53	35
3315^{12}	**Grooms Gold (IRE) (53)** (PWHarris) **5-9-8** ACulhane(3) (led tl over 1f out: kpt on same pce)	1¼	**3**	20/1	57	39
4958^{10}	**Homestead (51)** (RHannon) **3-9-4** DaneO'Neill(14) (hld up: hdwy over 2f out: styd on same pce fnl f)	s.h	**4**	8/1^{3}	55	35
4877^{2}	**Legend of Aragon (46)** (JAGlover) **3-8-8**(5) APolli(9) (hld up: hdwy 3f out: edgd lft: styd on appr fnl f)	1	**5**	11/2^{2}	48	28
4695^{7}	**Perpetual Light (41)** (JJQuinn) **4-8-10** SDrowne(5) (a chsng ldrs: one pce fnl 2f)	hd	**6**	10/1	43	25
4741^{7}	**Parsa (USA) (48)** (JLDunlop) **4-9-3v^{1}** TQuinn(7) (hld up: hdwy over 2f out: kpt on fnl f)	2½	**7**	12/1	45	27
4899^{5}	**Holloway Melody (50)** (BAMcMahon) **4-9-5** LNewton(2) (w ldrs: one pce fnl 2f)	1¼	**8**	12/1	45	27
4802^{11}	**Classic Colours (USA) (58)** (GHYardley) **4-9-13** NAdams(1) (w ldr tl wknd 2f out)	nk	**9**	33/1	52	34
4927^{12}	**Pleasure Trick (USA) (45)** (DonEnricoIncisa) **6-9-0** KimTinkler(16) (bhd: rdn over 3f out: styd on fnl f)	s.h	**10**	14/1	39	21
4813^{15}	**Gablesea (45)** (BPJBaugh) **3-8-12** JFEgan(18) (plld hrd: hdwy on outside 3f out: hung lft: nvr rchd ldrs)	hd	**11**	20/1	39	19
3449^{2}	**Lucky Begonia (IRE) (52)** (WJMusson) **4-9-7** AMcGlone(12) (prom: effrt 4f out: wknd over 1f out)	3½	**12**	8/1^{3}	39	21
4924^{15}	**Forest Robin (47)** (MrsJRRamsden) **4-9-2** JFortune(13) (lw: hld up: effrt over 3f: n.d)	1¾	**13**	8/1^{3}	31	13
4629^{5}	**Nkapen Rocks (SPA) (47)** (CaptJWilson) **4-9-2** AMackay(6) (plld hrd: trckd ldrs tl wknd 2f out)	2½	**14**	9/1	26	8
1576^{W}	**Ethbaat (USA) (47)** (MJHeaton-Ellis) **6-8-13**(3) ADaly(17) (plld v.hrd: racd wd: trckd ldrs tl lost pl over 3f out)	s.h	**15**	12/1	26	8
4843^{5}	**Queen of Shannon (IRE) (49)** (AWCarroll) **9-8-11v**(7) AHall(11) (reluctant to r: hdwy appr st: lost pl over 2f out)	hd	**16**	9/1	27	9
	Saltz (IRE) (55) (PTDalton) **5-9-7**(3) RFfrench(10) (Withdrawn not under Starter's orders: burst out of stalls)		**W**	25/1	—	—
				(SP 148.2%)	**16 Rn**	

1m 47.0 (5.70) CSF £74.74 CT £1,164.42 TOTE £16.40: £2.20 £1.60 £11.10 £1.90 (£30.60) Trio £777.70; £547.72 to Redcar 4/11/97 OWNER Mr Mark Kilner (EDWINSTOWE) BRED Mrs D. Hutch
WEIGHT FOR AGE 3yo-2lb
4628 Up in Flames (IRE) ended a long losing sequence in this low-grade handicap. (12/1: op 8/1)
4847 Scenicris (IRE), on her favourite track and with the ground to suit, looked to have been found a golden opportunity but when the cards were played the winner showed more determination. (5/1)
Grooms Gold (IRE), having only his third outing in two years, tried hard to make all. (20/1)
4817 Homestead, who has been kept busy, put a poor run last time behind him. (8/1)
4877 Legend of Aragon proved a bit of a handful for her inexperienced rider. (11/2)
4741 Parsa (USA) (12/1: 8/1-14/1)
3449 Lucky Begonia (IRE) (8/1: 6/1-9/1)

4992 'SEE YOU NEXT MARCH' H'CAP (0-60) (II) (3-Y.O+) (Class F)

4-10 (4-20) **1m 54y** £1,927.00 (£527.00: £247.00) Stalls: Low GOING minus 0.08 sec per fur (G)

				SP	RR	SF
4695^{4}	**Bold Faith (47)** (WJMusson) **4-9-2** KFallon(5) (s.i.s: hdwy over 3f out: led ins fnl f: r.o wl)	—	**1**	$11/4^{1}$	61	41
4951^{11}	**Tael of Silver (43)** (ABailey) **5-8-12** DWright(13) (w ldrs: led 1f out: sn hdd: unable qckn)	1½	**2**	16/1	54	34
4905^{13}	**Al Reet (IRE) (50)** (SRBowring) **6-9-5** DeanMcKeown(8) (hld up in tch: effrt 3f out: hrd drvn 2f out: kpt on u.p)	1½	**3**	16/1	58	38
4918^{6}	**Katie Komaite (48)** (CaptJWilson) **4-9-3v** AMackay(16) (bhd: hdwy 3f out: rdn, edgd lft & kpt on fnl f)	s.h	**4**	$10/1^{3}$	56	36
4813^{4}	**Yeoman Oliver (59)** (BAMcMahon) **4-9-7b**(7) SRighton(9) (plld hrd: a.p: led over 3f out to 1f out: one pce)	½	**5**	12/1	66	46
4858*	**Cabcharge Blue (41)** (TJNaughton) **5-8-10** TSprake(14) (b.off hind: mid div: styd on u.p appr fnl f)	s.h	**6**	$10/1^{3}$	48	28
1020^{20}	**Girl of My Dreams (IRE) (41)** (MJHeaton-Ellis) **4-8-10** SDrowne(18) (bkwd: bhd: sme hdwy fnl 2f: n.d)	5	**7**	20/1	38	18
4484^{7}	**Cats Bottom (40)** (AGNewcombe) **5-8-9** JQuinn(12) (trckd ldrs: rdn along 3f out: styd on fnl f)	s.h	**8**	20/1	37	17
4813^{12}	**Delight of Dawn (50)** (EAWheeler) **5-8-12b**(7) SCarson(4) (in tch: effrt over 2f out: nt pce to chal)	s.h	**9**	$10/1^{3}$	47	27
4813^{2}	**Bentico (50)** (MrsNMacauley) **8-9-0v**(5) GMilligan(10) (b: led tl hdd over 3f out: sn hrd drvn & wknd)	s.h	**10**	$7/1^{2}$	47	27
4916*	**Blowing Away (IRE) (60)** (MHTompkins) **3-9-13** 5x DBiggs(3) (chsd ldrs tl wknd over 2f out)	d.h	**10**	14/1	57	35
4846^{7}	**Birchwood Sun (48)** (MDods) **7-9-3b** ACulhane(15) (bhd: sn drvn along: no imp)	4	**12**	12/1	37	17
4846^{2}	**Chinour (IRE) (45)** (EJAlston) **9-9-0** JFEgan(11) (in tch: effrt over 3f out: sn wknd)	½	**13**	$7/1^{2}$	33	13
3321*	**Welsh Mountain (43)** (KAMorgan) **4-8-12** JReid(17) (chsd ldrs: drvn along & lost pl over 3f out)	½	**14**	16/1	30	10
4277^{8}	**Evidently (IRE) (54)** (IABalding) **3-9-7** MartinDwyer(6) (prom tl wknd over 3f out)	3	**15**	12/1	36	14
4802^{16}	**Yaverland (IRE) (43)** (JohnBerry) **5-8-12** MTebbutt(2) (bit bkwd: bhd: drvn along over 2f out: no imp)	½	**16**	33/1	24	4
4695^{20}	**Snowy Mantle (44)** (JDBethell) **4-8-8**(5) RMullen(1) (trckd ldrs tl wknd fnl 2f)	4	**17**	20/1	17	—
	Dr Caligari (IRE) (49) (SGollings) **5-9-4** TWilliams(7) (bkwd: w ldrs over 4f: sn wknd)	4	**18**	33/1	14	—
				(SP 146.5%)	**18 Rn**	

1m 46.6 (5.30) CSF £53.12 CT £633.61 TOTE £4.40: £1.90 £3.20 £4.20 £2.80 (£56.70) Trio £528.60 OWNER Jumbo Ltd (NEWMARKET) BRED Juddmonte Farms

WEIGHT FOR AGE 3yo-2lb

4695 Bold Faith, allowed to freewheel in the rear, edged closer three furlongs out and, set alight to lead two hundred yards out, was driven out firmly to the post. (11/4)

4695 Tael of Silver, in the action from the start, poked her head in front for a few strides entering the last furlong but the winner pounced almost immediately and she was unable to respond. (16/1)

2913 Al Reet (IRE), who runs with her tongue tied down, turned in one of her best performances and she only lost out in the battle to the line. She appreciates getting her toe in and this ground could have been just that bit too lively. (16/1)

4918 Katie Komaite should have had the beating of most of these rivals but she has been kept very busy lately and in the circumstances this was a very game effort. (10/1)

4813 Yeoman Oliver does the majority of his racing and only ever wins on the All-Weather so this better than average performance suggests he is ready to score again. (12/1)

4858* Cabcharge Blue seems to find this trip short for her nowadays and she was only finding top gear when it was all too late. She does win on the All-Weather and is worth bearing in mind. (10/1)

4916* Blowing Away (IRE) (14/1: op 6/1)

4711 Birchwood Sun (12/1: op 8/1)

Evidently (IRE) (12/1: op 6/1)

T/Jkpt: Not won; £56,766.84 to Redcar 4/11/97. T/Plpt: £13.90 (1,965.83 Tckts). T/Qdpt: £6.20 (244.69 Tckts) WG/

4921-REDCAR (L-H) (Good, Good to firm patches)

Tuesday November 4th

WEATHER: overcast WIND: mod half bhd

4993 E.B.F BIRCH MAIDEN STKS (2-Y.O) (Class D)

1-30 (1-30) **7f** £3,493.00 (£1,054.00: £512.00: £241.00) Stalls: High GOING minus 0.37 sec per fur (F)

				SP	RR	SF
4871^{7}	**Gypsy Passion (IRE)** (MJohnston) **2-9-0** JFortune(1) (lw: led after 2f: rdn & r.o wl fnl 2f)	—	**1**	14/1	85+	49
4780*	**Dog Watch** (JHMGosden) **2-9-0** GHind(6) (sn pushed along & in tch: hdwy 2f out: r.o)	2	**2**	$3/1^{2}$	80	44
4908^{2}	**Free Option (IRE) (82)** (BHanbury) **2-9-0** WRyan(13) (lw: trckd ldrs: effrt over 2f out: r.o one pce)	nk	**3**	$100/30^{3}$	80	44
	Chist (USA) (MHTompkins) **2-9-0** DBiggs(8) (leggy: unf: in tch: outpcd over 2f out: kpt on wl fnl f)	1¼	**4**	11/2	77+	41
4708^{3}	**Krisamba** (BJMeehan) **2-9-0** TQuinn(18) (lw: in tch: drvn along 3f out: sn chsng ldrs: one pce fnl 2f)	1	**5**	$9/4^{1}$	75	39
	Shaveling (MrsJCecil) **2-9-0** KDarley(7) (leggy: unf: scope: s.i.s: hdwy & prom ½-wy: nt qckn appr fnl f)	¾	**6**	7/1	73+	37
4735^{13}	**Corpus Christi (IRE)** (MJohnston) **2-9-0** DeanMcKeown(2) (s.i.s: hdwy & prom ½-wy: grad wknd fnl 2f)	5	**7**	100/1	62	26
4841^{7}	**Flaxen Pride (IRE)** (MrsMReveley) **2-8-9** ACulhane(16) (hld up: stdy hdwy over 2f out: nvr plcd to chal)	1¾	**8**	25/1	53+	17
	Trojan Wolf (MHTompkins) **2-8-11**(3) MHenry(12) (tall: unf: bit bkwd: outpcd tl sme late hdwy)	2½	**9**	33/1	52	16
4735^{12}	**Breakin Even** (JLEyre) **2-9-0b¹** RLappin(5) (gd spd over 4f)	hd	**10**	100/1	52	16
4793^{12}	**Strategic Air** (EWeymes) **2-9-0** JQuinn(10) (s.i.s: wl bhd tl sme late hdwy)	1¾	**11**	66/1	48	12
4706^{W}	**Ryefield Star** (JBerry) **2-9-0** OPears(4) (plld hrd: in tch over 4f)	2	**12**	50/1	43	7
4752^{9}	**Runadrum** (WWHaigh) **2-9-0** JBramhill(3) (chsd ldrs over 4f: wknd)	4	**13**	500/1	34	—
4841^{9}	**Ellerbeck** (JMJefferson) **2-8-9** JCarroll(15) (early spd: sn rdn & bhd)	2	**14**	100/1	24	—
	Accystan (PCHaslam) **2-9-0** LCharnock(11) (str: cmpt: bkwd: dwlt: a bhd)	½	**15**	100/1	28	—
4925^{4}	**Second Term (IRE)** (WStorey) **2-8-9** JFanning(14) (led 2f: cl up tl wknd wl over 2f out)	½	**16**	100/1	22	—
4921^{13}	**All Our Blessings (IRE)** (PCHaslam) **2-8-2**(7) PGoode(17) (sn outpcd & bhd)	2½	**17**	200/1	16	—
	Florence Asher (DonEnricoIncisa) **2-8-9** KimTinkler(9) (lt-f: unf: dwlt: a bhd)	3	**18**	200/1	9	—
				(SP 129.8%)	**18 Rn**	

1m 24.5 (1.50) CSF £53.31 TOTE £21.10: £3.40 £1.80 £1.40 (£37.10) Trio £21.20 OWNER Mr P. D. Savill (MIDDLEHAM) BRED Dr M. V. O'Brien

4871 Gypsy Passion (IRE) made plenty of use of, did this particularly well and should have no difficulty in staying further. (14/1)

4780* Dog Watch won a poor race last time and apparently learnt little as he needed plenty of help from the saddle here, but despite running on was never good enough. (3/1)

4908 Free Option (IRE) travels quite well, but then didn't find as much as looked likely. (100/30)

Chist (USA) put up a useful first effort here, and next year over further there should be plenty of improvement. (11/2)

4708 Krisamba looked ultra-fit, but found this ground a shade too quick and could never make any serious impression. (9/4)
Shaveling, very green early on, should improve a fair bit for the experience. (7/1)
Corpus Christi (IRE) showed his first real signs of form here, and next season over further should see plenty more improvement. (100/1)
4841 Flaxen Pride (IRE) had another educational, showed plenty and will be very interesting in handicaps. (25/1)
Trojan Wolf, a big, backward sort, gave signs of ability without getting into it. Time is obviously the key. (33/1)

4994 BEECH NURSERY H'CAP (0-75) (2-Y.O) (Class E)

2-00 (2-02) **1m** £3,424.75 (£1,033.00: £501.50: £235.75) Stalls: High GOING minus 0.37 sec per fur (F)

			SP	RR	SF
4806[6] **Bawsian (65)** (JLEyre) **2-8-12** TWilliams(20) (b.hind: a chsng ldrs: rdn to ld ins fnl f: all out)	—	**1**	5/1[1]	72	37
4814[6] **Pas de Memoires (IRE) (65)** (MHTompkins) **2-8-12** KDarley(22) (a chsng ldrs: led over 2f out: hung lft: hdd ins fnl f: rallied)	s.h	**2**	11/1	72	37
4113[8] **Ocean Line (IRE) (57)** (APJarvis) **2-8-1**(3) CLowther(21) (mde most tl hdd over 2f out: no ex)	4	**3**	14/1	56	21
4806[2] **Marske Machine (64)** (NTinkler) **2-8-11b** DeanMcKeown(10) (hdwy 3f out: styd on u.p: nrst fin)	1	**4**	8/1[3]	61	26
4380[7] **Bronzino (65)** (GBBalding) **2-8-12** SDrowne(2) (in tch: hdwy ½-wy: ch 2f out: kpt on)	½	**5**	12/1	61	26
4898[4] **Arctic Star (69)** (MRChannon) **2-9-2** RPerham(3) (s.i.s: hdwy ½-wy: hmpd over 2f out: kpt on wl towards fin)	1	**6**	6/1[2]	63	28
4576[15] **Supacalifragilistk (61)** (BWHills) **2-8-8** DHolland(12) (trckd ldrs: effrt over 2f out: rdn & btn over 1f out)	nk	**7**	20/1	54	19
4871[8] **Norski Lad (59)** (SirMarkPrescott) **2-8-6** GDuffield(1) (a.p: outpcd 3f out: styd on appr fnl f)	1¾	**8**	20/1	49	14
4588[15] **Ribble Assembly (56)** (RAFahey) **2-8-3**ow2 GHind(19) (s.i.s: styd on fnl 3f: nrst fin)	s.h	**9**	20/1	46	9
4767[5] **Petara (IRE) (67)** (JSWainwright) **2-9-0v** JFortune(8) (s.i.s: hdwy ½-wy: sn in tch & rdn: no imp fnl 2f)	2½	**10**	14/1	52	17
4812[7] **Ellenber (50)** (WMcKeown) **2-7-11** JBramhill(4) (w ldrs tl wknd over 2f out)	3	**11**	100/1	29	—
4885[12] **Laramania (56)** (PDEvans) **2-8-3** DWright(13) (s.i.s: bhd tl styd on fnl 3f)	s.h	**12**	50/1	35	—
4595[3] **Up The Clarets (IRE) (56)** (JJO'Neill) **2-8-3**ow1 JFEgan(15) (hld up: effrt ½-wy: no imp)	s.h	**13**	16/1	35	—
4885[11] **Princess Natalie (67)** (MWEasterby) **2-8-11**(3) GParkin(9) (w ldrs tl rdn & wknd fnl 2½f)	s.h	**14**	50/1	45	10
4690[11] **Baylham (53)** (JSGoldie) **2-8-0** JQuinn(26) (nvr trbld ldrs)	nk	**15**	16/1	31	—
4698* **Hiding Place (62)** (WStorey) **2-8-9** JFanning(11) (in tch over 5f)	½	**16**	10/1	39	4
4381[13] **Antonio Joli (52)** (PFICole) **2-7-8**(5) RMullen(27) (effrt ½-wy: no imp)	1½	**17**	20/1	26	—
4807[9] **Wee Christy (IRE) (49)** (WMcKeown) **2-7-10** NCarlisle(6) (bhd: effrt ½-wy: n.d)	1¼	**18**	50/1	20	—
4885[6] **Burnt Yates (IRE) (74)** (MWEasterby) **2-9-7** TLucas(24) (lw: plld hrd: sddle slipped & lost tch fr ½-wy)	½	**19**	16/1	44	9
4508[4] **Another Wyn-Bank (54)** (JGFitzGerald) **2-7-12**(3) PFessey(7) (s.i.s: n.d)	1¾	**20**	12/1	21	—
4806* **Premium Quest (69)** (RAFahey) **2-9-2** FNorton(25) (prom 5f: grad wknd)	½	**21**	11/1	35	—
4922[11] **Good On Yer (55)** (SEKettlewell) **2-7-13**(3) RFfrench(16) (n.d)	1	**22**	33/1	19	—
4752[8] **Anditz (IRE) (55)** (JLEyre) **2-8-2** LCharnock(14) (outpcd & lost tch fr ½-wy)	s.h	**23**	33/1	19	—
4413[9] **Durgams Delight (IRE) (57)** (BWMurray) **2-8-1**(3) DSweeney(17) (outpcd & bhd fr ½-wy)	hd	**24**	33/1	21	—
4215[4] **Priolette (IRE) (63)** (JGFitzGerald) **2-8-5**(5) BenedichteHalvorsen(23) (a bhd)	1	**25**	50/1	25	—
4767[11] **Deeceebee (73)** (WStorey) **2-9-6** JCarroll(5) (prom 5f: wknd)	11	**26**	33/1	13	—
4807[6] **Celestial Welcome (52)** (MrsMReveley) **2-7-13** DaleGibson(18) (hrd rdn & wl bhd fr ½-wy)	15	**27**	20/1	—	—

(SP 158.6%) **27 Rn**

1m 37.7 (2.70) CSF £57.27 CT £737.07 TOTE £4.80: £1.40 £2.90 £8.30 £2.50 (£26.80) Trio £578.00; £569.95 to Haydock 5/11/97 OWNER Mr David Scott (HAMBLETON) BRED Shadwell Estate Company Limited
LONG HANDICAP Wee Christy (IRE) 7-5

4806 Bawsian, given plenty of help from the saddle, did just enough in a desperate finish. (5/1: op 3/1)
Pas de Memoires (IRE) is learning fast, and but for greenness would have won this. (11/1)
Ocean Line (IRE) had shown little previously, but this was his first ever run in a handicap and he is obviously improving, particularly after almost two months off. (14/1)
4806 Marske Machine just stays, and needs either further or softer ground to help. (8/1)
Bronzino, drawn out in the wilderness, ran well. He is obviously getting his act together and will stay further. (12/1)
4898 Arctic Star would have finished a bit closer with a better run here, and will obviously appreciate longer trips. (6/1)
4285 Supacalifragilistk went well for much of the race, but was a shade disappointing when the button was pressed. (20/1)
Norski Lad ran as though he is going to need further. (20/1)

4995 ASH H'CAP (0-95) (3-Y.O+) (Class C)

2-30 (2-34) **6f** £6,011.25 (£1,815.00: £882.50: £416.25) Stalls: High GOING minus 0.37 sec per fur (F)

			SP	RR	SF
4787[9] **Primo Lara (84)** (PWHarris) **5-9-6** TQuinn(24) (led after 2f: hrd rdn & hld on wl)	—	**1**	10/1	93	62
4954[8] **Double Splendour (IRE) (92)** (PSFelgate) **7-9-11**(3) DSweeney(15) (hdwy & prom ½-wy: kpt on fnl f: nrst fin)	¾	**2**	12/1	99	68
4842* **Always Alight (80)** (KRBurke) **3-9-2** JFEgan(1) (lw: chsd ldr far side: hdwy 2f out: r.o)	1	**3**	12/1	84	53
4887[18] **Cadeaux Cher (81)** (BWHills) **3-9-3** WRyan(13) (b: trckd ldrs: hdwy 2f out: sn rdn: r.o towards fin)	hd	**4**	25/1	85	54
4842[5] **Double Bounce (84)** (PJMakin) **7-9-6** GDuffield(17) (effrt ½-wy: styd on strly fnl 2f: nrst fin)	s.h	**5**	11/2[2]	88	57
4887[8] **Gaelic Storm (88)** (MJohnston) **3-9-10** DHolland(19) (b.hind: bhd: hdwy 2f out: hung lft: r.o wl)	hd	**6**	8/1[3]	92	61
4905* **Midnight Shift (IRE) (67)** (RGuest) **3-8-3**ow1 6x GHind(4) (racd far side: cl up: kpt on fnl f)	hd	**7**	16/1	70	38
4927[2] **Johayro (64)** (JSGoldie) **4-8-0** JQuinn(22) (led 2f: chsd wnr: rdn over 2f out: btn over 1f out)	½	**8**	16/1	66	35
4983[10] **Mr Bergerac (IRE) (84)** (BPalling) **6-9-6** DaneO'Neill(21) (lw: styd on fnl 2f: nrst fin)	s.h	**9**	16/1	86	55
4842[2] **Mouche (72)** (MrsJRRamsden) **3-8-8** JFortune(18) (bhd: effrt over 2f out: n.d)	2	**10**	11/1	69	38
4887[12] **Sea-Deer (82)** (CADwyer) **8-9-1**(3) GParkin(14) (bhd tl sme late hdwy)	nk	**11**	20/1	78	47
4456[2] **Mallia (64)** (TDBarron) **4-8-0** LCharnock(6) (cl up tl wknd ent fnl f)	¾	**12**	14/1	58	27
4787[26] **Lough Erne (69)** (CFWall) **5-8-0**(5) RMullen(8) (sn outpcd)	¾	**13**	25/1	61	30
4797[3] **Double Oscar (IRE) (80)** (DNicholls) **4-9-2b** AlexGreaves(25) (in tch: outpcd ½-wy: no imp after)	hd	**14**	16/1	72	41
4887[10] **Kira (80)** (JLEyre) **7-9-2** RLappin(9) (b: b.hind: cl up tl wknd 3f out)	¾	**15**	16/1	70	39
4927[3] **Tiler (IRE) (77)** (MJohnston) **5-8-10**(3) MHenry(12) (reard s: n.d)	1½	**16**	5/1[1]	63	32
4733[9] **Dovebrace (70)** (TDBarron) **4-8-6** KDarley(2) (sn bhd)	hd	**17**	14/1	55	24
4770[17] **Treasure Touch (IRE) (83)** (DNicholls) **3-9-0**(5) IonaWands(23) (prom 4f)	nk	**18**	33/1	68	37
4905[7] **Royal Dome (IRE) (71)** (MartynWane) **5-8-7** JCarroll(20) (spd over 4f)	s.h	**19**	20/1	55	24
4733[10] **Benzoe (IRE) (75)** (MrsJRRamsden) **7-8-11** OPears(3) (a bhd)	s.h	**20**	20/1	59	28
4887[16] **Lago Di Varano (83)** (RMWhitaker) **5-9-5v** DeanMcKeown(5) (in tch: rdn ½-wy: sn btn)	1¼	**21**	33/1	64	33
4887[14] **Westcourt Magic (84)** (MWEasterby) **4-9-6** TLucas(7) (chsd ldrs 4f: wknd qckly)	hd	**22**	33/1	65	34
4805[16] **Top of The Form (IRE) (76)** (RAFahey) **3-8-5**(7) DEgan(10) (cl up 4f: wknd)	1	**23**	50/1	54	23

4511^{3} **Young Bigwig (IRE) (80)** (DWChapman) **3-9-2** ACulhane(16) (sn bhd) 3½ **24** 33/1 49 18
3273^{12} **Charlie Sillett (85)** (BWHills) **5-9-4**(3) JDSmith(11) (dwlt: a bhd) ....hd **25** 25/1 53 22
(SP 158.3%) **25 Rn**

1m 10.9 (0.70) CSF £123.68 CT £1,423.46 TOTE £11.00: £2.30 £4.80 £4.10 £11.10 (£222.70) Trio £2,032.80 OWNER Thanet Leasing Ltd (BERKHAMSTED) BRED Pendley Farm
4787 Primo Lara got his ground but had to take a step back in trip. He had the courage and that made the difference. (10/1)
4226 Double Splendour (IRE) has drawn a blank this season, but this was a fine effort to show he still has the ability. (12/1)
4842* Always Alight is running his socks off just now, and from his draw this was a super run. (12/1)
1609 Cadeaux Cher has obviously had problems as this was a much-improved effort, and he looks worth bearing in mind. (25/1)
4842 Double Bounce found the early pace too strong, and only picked up when it was all over. (11/2)
4887 Gaelic Storm continually sets himself impossible tasks and made up a tremendous amount of ground here, but always too late. He needs to learn to jump off on terms and he could then make up into a really good sprinter. (8/1: 6/1-9/1)
4905* Midnight Shift (IRE) went well up the unfavoured far side. (16/1)
4842 Mouche (11/1: 8/1-12/1)

4996 SYCAMORE H'CAP (0-80) (3-Y.O) (Class D)

3-00 (3-04) **1m 3f** £3,623.00 (£1,094.00: £532.00: £251.00) Stalls: Low GOING minus 0.37 sec per fur (F)

Form	Horse	Dist	Pos	SP	RR	SF
4854^{9}	**Fantail (78)** (MHTompkins) **3-9-6** DBiggs(11) (trckd ldrs: led on bit wl over 1f out: shkn up: sn clr)	—	1	7/1^{2}	90+	53
4876^{3}	**Night Mirage (USA) (75)** (MJohnston) **3-9-3** DHolland(16) (a chsng ldrs: sn pushed along: led 3f out tl wl over 1f out: edgd lft & nt qckn)	3	2	15/2^{3}	83	46
4771^{6}	**Aeolina (FR) (55)** (SEKettlewell) **3-7-8**(3)ow1 RFfrench(8) (bhd: hdwy 4f out: kpt on: nvr able chal)	1¾	3	12/1	60	22
4748^{5}	**Pradesh (62)** (JHMGosden) **3-8-4v^{1}** GHind(4) (bhd: effrt 4f out: styd on wl fnl 2f: nrst fin)	hd	4	16/1	67	30
4771^{7}	**Sefton Blake (55)** (MGMeagher) **3-7-8**(3)ow1 PFessey(6) (in tch: effrt over 3f out: sn rdn: styd on: no imp)	1	5	33/1	59	21
4691^{3}	**Ajayib (USA) (79)** (JLDunlop) **3-9-7b** KDarley(9) (cl up: chal 4f out: one pce fnl 2f)	s.h	6	9/2^{1}	82	45
4310^{4}	**Vain Tempest (79)** (PWChapple-Hyam) **3-9-7** SWhitworth(2) (lw: in tch: effrt over 3f out: one pce)	½	7	10/1	82	45
4774^{8}	**Rheinbold (78)** (TJEtherington) **3-9-6** ACulhane(17) (hdwy & prom appr st: one pce fnl 4f)	4	8	20/1	75	38
4731^{5}	**Boss Lady (IRE) (77)** (RCharlton) **3-9-5** TSprake(15) (bhd: effrt on outside 4f out: no imp)	1¾	9	8/1	71	34
4748*	**Alakdar (CAN) (73)** (RChampion) **3-9-1** AMcGlone(10) (bhd: effrt 4f out: n.d)	1	10	10/1	66	29
4926^{4}	**Gee Bee Boy (64)** (APJarvis) **3-8-3**(3) CLowther(5) (bhd: effrt over 4f out: n.d)	nk	11	16/1	56	19
4774^{14}	**Hurgill Dancer (72)** (JWWatts) **3-9-0** JCarroll(1) (lw: chsd ldrs: effrt over 3f out: grad wknd)	1½	12	20/1	62	25
4883^{5}	**Slieu Whallian (60)** (RHannon) **3-8-2** JFEgan(3) (bhd & pushed along: sme hdwy 4f out: sn wknd)	9	13	10/1	37	—
*1421**	**Smart Boy (IRE) (70)** (PFICole) **3-8-12** TQuinn(13) (lw: chsd ldrs tl wknd fnl 3f)	1	14	16/1	46	9
2005^{3}	**Mystic Ridge (79)** (BJCurley) **3-9-7** JQuinn(12) (hld up & bhd: n.d)	1½	15	20/1	53	16
2468^{9}	**Glorious Dancer (54)** (JHetherton) **3-7-10** NCarlisle(14) (t: a bhd)	nk	16	100/1	27	—
4883^{W}	**Serpentara (73)** (HRACecil) **3-9-1** WRyan(7) (lw: led tl hdd 3f out: sn wknd)	11	17	7/1^{2}	30	—

(SP 136.9%) **17 Rn**

2m 19.9 (2.90) CSF £56.40 CT £599.33 TOTE £10.70: £2.30 £2.40 £2.90 £5.00 (£51.30) Trio £244.90 OWNER Pamela, Lady Nelson of Stafford (NEWMARKET) BRED Skyline Racing Limited
LONG HANDICAP Sefton Blake 7-6 Glorious Dancer 6-1 Aeolina (FR) 7-8
IN-FOCUS: Hurgill Dancer was the last runner sent out by Bill Watts, who has retired after thirty years as a trainer.
4552 Fantail won this in very useful style, and should he get into the November Handicap on the softer ground he really likes he should be seriously considered. (7/1: op 9/2)
4876 Night Mirage (USA) is not an easy ride but does keep responding, and was always second best despite a valiant attempt. (15/2)
4771 Aeolina (FR) if anything found this trip a bit on the sharp side, but she was gradually warming to her task. (12/1)
4748 Pradesh had the visor on for the first time, and finished well, suggesting that further is needed. (16/1)
2046 Sefton Blake ran reasonably from 4lb out of the handicap, and seems to stay really well. (33/1)
4691 Ajayib (USA) again had his chances, but failed yet again to come up with the goods. (9/2)

4997 OAK LIMITED STKS (0-75) (3-Y.O+) (Class D)

3-30 (3-31) **5f** £3,350.00 (£1,010.00: £490.00: £230.00) Stalls: High GOING minus 0.37 sec per fur (F)

Form	Horse	Dist	Pos	SP	RR	SF
4805*	**Afaan (IRE) (68)** (RFMarvin) **4-9-4v** TGMcLaughlin(4) (b: trckd ldr: led 2f out: shkn up & r.o wl)	—	1	4/1^{3}	85	68
4809^{4}	**Nobalino (70)** (MrsNMacauley) **3-8-12** SDrowne(6) (lw: chsd ldrs: effrt ½-wy: kpt on: nt pce to chal)	3	2	5/1	69	52
4733^{22}	**Bajan Rose (70)** (MBlanshard) **5-8-9** KDarley(7) (a chsng ldrs: rdn over 2f out: kpt on: nvr able chal)	1¼	3	3/1^{2}	62	45
4805^{8}	**Just Bob (75)** (SEKettlewell) **8-9-7** DeanMcKeown(8) (dwlt: effrt 2f out: nvr rchd ldrs)	2½	4	11/4^{1}	66	49
4770^{19}	**Ballymote (68)** (JBerry) **3-8-9**(3) PFessey(1) (led 3f: rdn & grad wknd)	1¾	5	6/1	52	35
4791^{7}	**Blazing Imp (USA) (40)** (MrsJJordan) **4-9-1** MFenton(2) (outpcd ½-wy: no imp after)	¾	6	33/1	52	35
4707^{8}	**Dona Filipa (43)** (MissLCSiddall) **4-8-12** OPears(5) (lw: effrt ½-wy: rdn & no imp)	hd	7	50/1	49	32
4927^{6}	**Plum First (50)** (MAPeill) **7-8-7**(5) KimberleyHart(3) (b.hind: s.i.s: nvr wnt pce)	hd	8	20/1	49	32

(SP 112.3%) **8 Rn**

57.6 secs (0.10) CSF £21.00 TOTE £3.60: £2.10 £1.50 £1.10 (£11.00) OWNER Mr E. Gray (NEWARK) BRED Shadwell Estate Company Limited
4805* Afaan (IRE) is a typical sprinter in form, and was always going to win this. Should he return to the All-Weather, he could well continue his winning ways. (4/1)
4809 Nobalino is running well, and ought to break his duck on the All-Weather this winter. (5/1)
2232 Bajan Rose has the ability but is not producing it these days, and only ran on here when it was all over. (3/1)
4636 Just Bob has had his purple patch and never showed any real spark this time. (11/4)
1571 Ballymote has the speed but is not seeing it out at present. (6/1: op 4/1)
2934 Blazing Imp (USA) had plenty on here and ran well enough in the circumstances. (33/1)

4998 POPLAR H'CAP (0-70) (3-Y.O+) (Class E)

4-00 (4-00) **1m 2f** £3,249.25 (£979.00: £474.50: £222.25) Stalls: Low GOING minus 0.37 sec per fur (F)

Form	Horse	Dist	Pos	SP	RR	SF
4924^{2}	**Jedi Knight (69)** (MWEasterby) **3-9-9** LCharnock(10) (trckd ldrs: smooth hdwy 3f out: led 1½f out: r.o)	—	1	7/1^{3}	80	55
4845^{2}	**Essayeffsee (50)** (MrsMReveley) **8-8-8** KDarley(13) (bhd tl hdwy over 2f out: styd on strly towards fin)	nk	2	9/2^{1}	61	40
4926^{2}	**Classic Find (USA) (64)** (PatMitchell) **4-9-8** PBloomfield(12) (lw: hld up: effrt over 3f out: styd on: nt pce of wnr)	½	3	8/1	74	53
4751^{7}	**Newbridge Boy (47)** (MGMeagher) **4-8-2**(3) PFessey(14) (led tl hdd 1½f out: kpt on)	½	4	14/1	56	35
4845*	**Vanadium Ore (52)** (WMcKeown) **4-8-10** JCarroll(11) (lw: hld up & bhd: styd on wl fnl 3f: nrst fin)	1	5	12/1	59	38

				SP	RR	SF
4802[10]	**Java Red (IRE) (53)** (JGFitzGerald) **5-8-11** JFortune(8) (hld up: effrt 4f out: styd on u.p: nvr rchd ldrs)	½	**6**	16/1	60	39
4918[3]	**In The Genes (58)** (IPWilliams) **3-8-9**(3) MHenry(1) (chsd ldrs: outpcd over 2f out: styd on fnl f)	¾	**7**	9/1	63	38
4845[4]	**Clued Up (51)** (PDEvans) **4-8-9v** JFEgan(17) (in tch: effrt 4f out: no imp)	¾	**8**	10/1	55	34
4847[5]	**Raindeer Quest (49)** (JLEyre) **5-8-0**(7)ow1 SBuckley(3) (swtg: trckd ldrs: chal 3f out: btn appr fnl f)	½	**9**	14/1	52	30
4751[10]	**Keep Battling (45)** (JSGoldie) **7-8-0**(3)ow1 CLowther(7) (hld up & bhd: effrt 3f out: n.d)	hd	**10**	20/1	48	26
4691[2]	**Shaffishayes (70)** (MrsMReveley) **5-10-0** DeanMcKeown(15) (lw: trckd ldrs tl wknd fnl 2½f)	3	**11**	11/2[2]	68	47
4714[7]	**Maradi (IRE) (63)** (BJCurley) **3-9-3** JQuinn(5) (in tch tl grad wknd fnl 3f)	4	**12**	33/1	55	30
4923*	**Pickens (USA) (54)** (DonEnricoIncisa) **5-8-12** 6x KimTinkler(2) (b: chsd ldrs tl wknd fnl 2½f)	½	**13**	16/1	45	24
3992[20]	**Versatility (62)** (RFJohnsonHoughton) **4-9-6** DHolland(6) (a bhd)	1¼	**14**	20/1	51	30
4912[7]	**Haroldon (IRE) (59)** (BPalling) **8-9-3** DaneO'Neill(9) (b: dwlt: n.d)	5	**15**	20/1	40	19
2187[2]	**Missile Toe (IRE) (57)** (DMorris) **4-9-1** NDay(4) (plld hrd early: effrt over 4f out: n.d)	2	**16**	10/1	35	14
4571[9]	**Thaleros (44)** (JSWainwright) **7-8-2** RLappin(16) (s.s: a bhd)	10	**17**	33/1	6	—

(SP 138.3%) **17 Rn**

2m 6.3 (2.70) CSF £36.95 CT £252.63 TOTE £6.70: £1.90 £1.50 £2.60 £4.30 (£12.80) Trio £48.90 OWNER Mr K. Hodgson (SHERIFF HUTTON) BRED E. J. B. Maude
WEIGHT FOR AGE 3yo-4lb
4924 Jedi Knight is not the easiest of rides but his present jockey handles him particularly well, and he was always doing just enough. (7/1)
4845 Essayeffsee runs when he is in the mood, and his effort was always that couple of strides too late here. (9/2)
4926 Classic Find (USA) ran well and kept plugging away, but he is short of any real turn of foot. (8/1)
Newbridge Boy is obviously in good form and stays well. He is worth keeping in mind for a return to the All-Weather. (14/1)
4845* Vanadium Ore tried to come from way off the pace again but just set himself too much to do. (12/1: 9/1-14/1)
4596 Java Red (IRE) had the required strong assistance but was never good enough. (16/1)
4847 Raindeer Quest normally held up, saw too much daylight too soon this time. (14/1)

T/Jkpt: Not won; £68,512.02 to Haydock 5/11/97. T/Plpt: £223.50 (141.33 Tckts). T/Qdpt: £70.20 (26.17 Tckts) AA

4999a - 5001a (Irish Racing) - See Computer Raceform

1094a-LEOPARDSTOWN (Dublin, Ireland) (L-H) (Good to yielding)
Monday October 27th

5002a BORD GAIS KILLAVULLAN STKS (Gp 3) (2-Y.O)
2-15 (2-21) **7f** IR £19,500.00 (IR £5,700.00: IR £2,700.00: IR £900.00) GOING: 0.18 sec per fur (G)

				SP	RR	SF
	Kincara Palace (IRE) (APO'Brien,Ireland) **2-8-7** JAHeffernan (dwlt: hld up towards rr: swtchd to outside 2f out: r.o. to ld last 100 yds)	—	**1**	10/1	101+	29
	Musk Lime (USA) (APO'Brien,Ireland) **2-8-7** NGMcCullagh (s.s: hld up towards rr: hdwy over 2f out: chal 1½f out: led briefly ins last: r.o.)	nk	**2**	12/1	100	29
4357a[6]	**Takarian (IRE)** (JOxx,Ireland) **2-8-10** JPMurtagh (in tch: 5th ½-wy: chal 2f out: r.o u.p fnl f)	hd	**3**	8/1[3]	103	31
4357a[7]	**Natalis (IRE)** (JOxx,Ireland) **2-8-10** PShanahan (sn chsng ldr: ev ch 1½f out: rdn & kpt on ins last)	hd	**4**	8/1[3]	103	31
4619a[2]	**Winona (IRE)** (JOxx,Ireland) **2-8-7** PJSmullen (hld up in tch: chal st: led over 1f out: hdd ins last: no ex)	¾	**5**	4/1[2]	98	27
	Queen Of Silk (IRE) (DKWeld,Ireland) **2-8-7** MJKinane (cl up early: 8th ½-wy: rdn 1½f out: kpt on ins last)	¾	**6**	10/1	96	25
	Matter Of Trust (IRE) (TDoyle,Ireland) **2-8-10** JPSpencer (hld up towards rr: hdwy over 2f out: rdn 1½f out: kpt on ins last)	s.h	**7**	20/1	99	28
	Chateau Royal (USA) (APO'Brien,Ireland) **2-8-10** CRoche (s.s: hld up: rdn 2f out: kpt on u.p)	s.h	**8**	4/5[1]	99	28
	Have Merci (MrsJHarrington,Ireland) **2-8-7** WJSmith (sn led: hdd u.p over 1f out: no ex ins last)	5½	**9**	20/1	84	14
	Amravati (IRE) (JSBolger,Ireland) **2-8-7** EAhern (cl up: 4th ½-wy: rdn & effrt over 2f out: btn wl over 1f out)	¾	**10**	20/1	82	13

(SP 137.9%) **10 Rn**

1m 31.6 (6.60) OWNER Mrs John Magnier (PILTOWN)
Kincara Palace (IRE), successful in her maiden a fortnight previously, followed up with a win off 87 in a Navan nursery and sprang a little surprise here in a race where the stable's odds-on chance proved a real disappointment. She only got on top close home but her sustained effort on the outer was always going to prove a winning one. (10/1: op 5/1)
Musk Lime (USA), successful off 77 in a nursery the previous week, also appeared to run above herself. (12/1)
Takarian (IRE) could make up into a useful middle-distance performer next season but he rather had his limitations underlined here. (8/1: op 5/1)
4357a Natalis (IRE) looked the likely winner from one and a half furlongs out but just could not quicken close home. (8/1: op 4/1)
4619a Winona (IRE), runner-up to Alborada in a Curragh Group Three earlier in the month, ran a similar race here, finding her inability to quicken a real problem. (4/1)
Queen Of Silk (IRE) (10/1: op 5/1)
Chateau Royal (USA), heavily-backed, came away slowly and never appeared happy on this turning track. He should not be written off. (4/5: op 7/4)

5003a - 5016a (Irish Racing) - See Computer Raceform

4906-LINGFIELD (L-H) (Standard)
Thursday November 6th
WEATHER: overcast WIND: slight half behind

5017 NATIONAL MAGAZINES NURSERY H'CAP (0-75) (2-Y.O) (Class E)
1-40 (1-40) **5f (Equitrack)** £2,914.25 (£869.00: £414.50: £187.25) Stalls: High GOING minus 0.51 sec per fur (FST)

				SP	RR	SF
4737[12]	**Risky Whisky (63)** (JBerry) **2-8-13b**(3) PRoberts(8) (b.hind: a.p: led 3f out: drvn out)	—	**1**	4/1[2]	64	27
4948[9]	**Swanmore Lady (IRE) (61)** (SCWilliams) **2-9-0** DHolland(5) (lw: hdwy over 2f out: chsd wnr over 1f out: r.o ins fnl f)	½	**2**	4/1[2]	60	23
4403[8]	**Blue Shadow (63)** (RHannon) **2-9-2** DaneO'Neill(7) (hdwy over 3f out: rdn over 1f out: r.o one pce)	¾	**3**	9/2[3]	60	23
4588[12]	**Essandess (IRE) (54)** (JLEyre) **2-8-7** SDrowne(2) (lost pl 2f out: r.o one pce fnl f)	1¾	**4**	10/1	45	8

4403^{6}	**Rapid Reliance (66)** (RIngram) **2-9-5** AMcGlone(1) (led 2f: 3rd & btn whn n.m.r on ins 2f out)	¾	**5**	7/2^{1}	55	18
4753^{29}	**The Druidess (IRE) (45)** (GCBravery) **2-7-5b^{1}**$^{(7)ow2}$ PDoe(4) (bhd fnl 3f)	3	**6**	40/1	24	—
4819^{15}	**Mercury Falling (52)** (DWPArbuthnot) **2-8-5b^{1}** MartinDwyer(3) (b: b.hind: bhd fnl 3f)	2½	**7**	16/1	23	—
4602^{9}	**Red Pepper (IRE) (68)** (PHowling) **2-9-7** SWhitworth(9) (prom over 2f)	2	**8**	7/1	33	—
				(SP 110.3%)	**8 Rn**	

59.95 secs (1.75) CSF £17.16 CT £62.38 TOTE £3.40: £1.60 £1.20 £1.80 (£7.80) Trio £7.70 OWNER Mr W. J. Kelly (COCKERHAM) BRED Roldvale Ltd

LONG HANDICAP The Druidess (IRE) 7-6

3699 Risky Whisky, winner of two sellers and an auction race this year - one coming on the All-Weather at Wolverhampton - was soon at the head of affairs and responded well to pressure to keep his rivals at bay. (4/1)

4419 Swanmore Lady (IRE) moved into second place over a furlong out and for a while was making little impression on the winner. However she got a second wind in the closing stages and was cutting back the leeway nearing the line. Her only success this year came over six furlongs and a return to that trip might help her find a small race. (4/1)

3783 Blue Shadow was racing over his optimum trip, but failed to find that vital turn of foot in the short straight despite staying on. (9/2)

2538 Essandess (IRE), who got outpaced turning for home, struggled on again in the closing stages. A drop to selling company is needed. (10/1: op 6/1)

4178* Rapid Reliance, the early leader, was already feeling the pinch when tightened up for room turning for home. A drop to claiming company would help. (7/2)

5018 MAIL NEWSPAPERS H'CAP (0-70) (3-Y.O+) (Class E)

2-10 (2-10) **5f (Equitrack)** £2,992.25 (£893.00: £426.50: £193.25) Stalls: High GOING minus 0.51 sec per fur (FST)

				SP	RR	SF
4913^{9}	**Anokato (61)** (KTIvory) **3-9-5b** MartinDwyer(5) (a.p: chsd ldr over 2f out: hrd rdn over 1f out: led ins fnl f: r.o wl)	—	**1**	10/1	71	43
4791^{4}	**Palacegate Jack (IRE) (66)** (JBerry) **6-9-7b**$^{(3)}$ TEDurcan(10) (a.p: led over 3f out: clr over 1f out: hdd ins fnl f: unable to qckn)	2	**2**	11/2^{3}	70	42
4791^{3}	**Another Batchworth (67)** (EAWheeler) **5-9-8b**$^{(3)}$ ADaly(8) (s.s: wl bhd over 2f: hdwy over 1f out: r.o wl ins fnl f)	1¾	**3**	15/2	65	37
4791^{5}	**Songsheet (59)** (MSSaunders) **4-9-0**$^{(3)}$ PPMurphy(1) (lw: rdn over 3f out: hdwy fnl f: r.o one pce)	1¾	**4**	5/1^{2}	51	23
4770^{3}	**Passionatti (61)** (SGollings) **3-9-5** SSanders(7) (led over 1f: rdn over 2f out: one pce)	s.h	**5**	9/2^{1}	53	25
4301^{3}	**Napier Star (67)** (MrsNMacauley) **4-9-11v** SWebster(6) (b.hind: nvr nr to chal)	¾	**6**	7/1	57	29
4820^{9}	**Mystical (63)** (MrsLStubbs) **3-9-7v** SWhitworth(3) (a.p: rdn over 2f out: wknd fnl f)	½	**7**	10/1	51	23
2780^{4}	**Lucky Dip (59)** (DRCElsworth) **3-9-3** DaneO'Neill(4) (prom 2f)	s.h	**8**	7/1	47	19
638^{9}	**Lift Boy (USA) (62)** (GLMoore) **8-9-6** CandyMorris(9) (swtg: bit bkwd: bhd fnl 3f)	¾	**9**	16/1	48	20
4905^{8}	**General Sir Peter (IRE) (70)** (NACallaghan) **5-10-0b** AmandaSanders(2) (s.s: a wl bhd)	3	**10**	10/1	46	18
				(SP 120.2%)	**10 Rn**	

59.13 secs (0.93) CSF £60.21 CT £414.74 TOTE £10.60: £2.90 £2.10 £2.10 (£44.80) Trio £97.00 OWNER Mr K. T. Ivory (RADLETT) BRED Mrs P. A. Brown

4527 Anokato, reverting back to the minimum trip, was due to drop 6lb in future handicaps, but that was not needed here as he responded to pressure to get up inside the final furlong. (10/1)

4791 Palacegate Jack (IRE) was soon adopting his usual straight, but front-running roll and had a useful advantage early in the straight, however he was reeled in inside the final furlong. Ten of his twelve victories have come at this trip. (11/2)

4791 Another Batchworth likes to make the running so did extremely well considering a slow start saw her soon out with the washing. Finding her feet in the short straight, she ran on strongly but the line was always coming far too soon. (15/2)

4791 Songsheet stayed on in the final furlong but by then it was all too late. She has done all her winning at this trip. (5/1)

4770 Passionatti, who was in the firing line throughout, could only go up and down in the same place in the final quarter-mile. (9/2)

4301 Napier Star did not look enthusiastic and it was surprising to see her get as close as she did. (7/1)

4905 General Sir Peter (IRE) (10/1: 6/1-12/1)

5019 MIRROR SELECT CLAIMING STKS (3-Y.O+) (Class F)

2-40 (2-41) **1m 4f (Equitrack)** £2,646.60 (£732.60: £349.80) Stalls: Low GOING minus 0.51 sec per fur (FST)

				SP	RR	SF
4920^{14}	**Night City (65)** (KRBurke) **6-9-9**$^{(3)}$ DSweeney(4) (lw: led over 8f: led over 1f out: rdn out)	—	**1**	9/1	74	63
4987*	**Statajack (IRE) (68)** (DRCElsworth) **9-9-12b** TQuinn(2) (b: stdy hdwy over 4f out: ev ch over 1f out: rdn: fnd nil)	2½	**2**	5/2^{1}	71	60
4896^{6}	**At Liberty (IRE) (70)** (RHannon) **5-8-11** DaneO'Neill(1) (lw: a.p: chsd ldr over 6f out: led over 3f out tl over 1f out: one pce)	3½	**3**	3/1^{2}	51	40
	Yacht (75) (AGNewcombe) **5-8-9**$^{(5)}$ JoHunnam(14) (no hdwy fnl 4f)	9	**4**	20/1	42	31
4858^{18}	**Safecracker (53)** (CPMorlock) **4-8-8** NAdams(13) (lw: chsd ldr over 5f: wknd over 3f out)	hd	**5**	20/1	36	25
4912^{3}	**Krayyan Dawn (38)** (JAkehurst) **7-9-6** DHolland(8) (b: lw: nvr nr to chal)	22	**6**	8/1	19	8
4607^{11}	**Explosive Power (65)** (GCBravery) **6-9-6** MRimmer(9) (nvr nrr)	1¾	**7**	13/2^{3}	16	5
4916^{5}	**Inkwell (34)** (GLMoore) **3-9-0** MFenton(7) (lw: bhd fnl 6f)	3	**8**	25/1	12	—
4845^{12}	**Harvey White (IRE) (50)** (JPearce) **5-9-12** MWigham(10) (bhd fnl 5f)	6	**9**	10/1	10	—
4850^{11}	**D J Cat (28)** (WRMuir) **4-8-11** MartinDwyer(6) (bhd fnl 4f)	15	**10**	50/1	—	—
3970^{11}	**Classic Dame (FR) (63)** (SDow) **4-9-1e** SSanders(5) (b.hind: plld hrd: prom over 7f)	5	**11**	14/1	—	—
4872^{22}	**Milton Abbot** (MSSaunders) **4-9-0**$^{(3)}$ PPMurphy(11) (s.s: a bhd: t.o fnl 5f)	24	**12**	40/1	—	—
4221^{20}	**Logie Pert Lad (25)** (JJBridger) **5-8-11** GBardwell(12) (s.s: a bhd: t.o fnl 6f)	dist	**13**	50/1	—	—
4608^{3}	***Oozlem (IRE) (38)*** (LMontagueHall) **8-9-3b** WRyan(3) (Withdrawn not under Starter's orders: lame at s)		**W**	14/1	—	—
				(SP 130.2%)	**13 Rn**	

2m 30.89 (0.89) CSF £27.84 TOTE £14.00: £3.70 £1.30 £1.10 (£14.40) Trio £13.60 OWNER Mr Nigel Shields (WANTAGE)

WEIGHT FOR AGE 3yo-6lb

OFFICIAL EXPLANATION **Night City: the Stewards enquired into the improvement in form compared to his previous run at Leicester 28/10/97, and accepted the trainer's explanation that the horse likes to dominate, which he was unable to do over a mile in his previous race, but on this occasion he was and he was also suited by the longer trip.**

4768 Night City found a mile too sharp for him last time out and was much happier being allowed to dictate. Collared over three furlongs from home, he refused to lie down and, battling his way back to the front approaching the final furlong, kept on really well. (9/1)

4987* Statajack (IRE) has been in good heart this Autumn, but he is no easy ride and is not one to trust. That was well demonstrated here for although he had a nice, strong pace to come off, when he was asked to take the lead over a furlong out, he threw in the towel. (5/2)

4450 At Liberty (IRE) is not easy to win with, and although moving to the front over three furlongs from home was passed approaching the final furlong. (3/1)
3640 Classic Dame (FR) (14/1: 10/1-16/1)

5020 JOHNSONS INTERNATIONAL MAIDEN STKS (3-Y.O) (Class D) TF 69

3-10 (3-11) **7f (Equitrack)** £3,613.75 (£1,078.00: £514.50: £232.75) Stalls: Low GOING minus 0.51 sec per fur (FST)

				SP	RR	SF
4916[2]	**Saratoga Red (USA) (57)** (WAO'Gorman) **3-9-0v** DHolland(4) (lw: a.p: hrd rdn over 2f out: led wl ins fnl f: r.o wl)	—	1	11/4[2]	71	46
4455[8]	**Blushing Desert (61)** (RHannon) **3-8-9** DaneO'Neill(10) (lw: a.p: led over 2f out: edgd lft over 1f out: hrd rdn: hdd wl ins fnl f: unable qckn)	¾	2	8/1[3]	64	39
4848[2]	**Marozia (USA)** (JHMGosden) **3-8-9** GHind(1) (lw: hdwy over 1f out: r.o ins fnl f)	2	3	4/5[1]	60	35
4757[23]	**Manikato (USA) (50)** (DJSCosgrove) **3-9-0** MRimmer(3) (lw: a.p: one pce fnl 2f)	3	4	25/1	58	33
4951[17]	**Finarts Bay (57)** (MrsJCecil) **3-8-9b[1]** MartinDwyer(9) (led over 4f)	5	5	12/1	41	16
4791[9]	**Mutasawwar (66)** (MSSaunders) **3-8-11**(3) PPMurphy(5) (prom over 5f)	¾	6	16/1	45	20
4896[7]	**Clonoe** (RIngram) **3-9-0** AMcGlone(2) (bit bkwd: s.s: a bhd)	5	7	66/1	33	8
	Tierra Del Fuego (HJCollingridge) **3-8-9** NAdams(8) (w'like: bkwd: s.s: a bhd)	¾	8	33/1	27	2
2372[10]	**Kilmeena Lady (42)** (JCFox) **3-8-9** SDrowne(7) (dwlt: a bhd)	3	9	50/1	20	—
4878[23]	**Wild Nettle (40)** (JCFox) **3-8-9** DeclanO'Shea(6) (a bhd)	8	10	66/1	1	—
				(SP 118.6%)	**10 Rn**	

1m 25.2 (0.80) CSF £22.14 TOTE £3.10: £1.10 £3.00 £1.10 (£12.80) Trio £5.80 OWNER Mr T. Mohan (NEWMARKET) BRED Scott D. Quire
4916 Saratoga Red (USA), never far away, responded to pressure and eventually got up in the closing stages to lose his maiden tag in this bad race at the fourteenth attempt. (11/4)
4070 Blushing Desert moved to the front over a quarter of a mile from home, but she drifted left approaching the final furlong and was worried out of it in the closing stages. She can find a small maiden. (8/1: 6/1-10/1)
4848 Marozia (USA), uneasy in the market, had far less to do her following her eye-catching Yarmouth run, but she did not look very happy on the sand and although running on in the last furlong and a half, never threatened. A step up in trip would help. (4/5: 2/5-evens)
3320 Manikato (USA) looked very short on acceleration in the straight so it is no surprise that he remains a maiden after eighteen attempts. (25/1)
4464 Finarts Bay found the application of blinkers for the first time not working and, after setting the pace, found little more to offer when collared approaching the last two furlongs. (12/1: op 6/1)

5021 A.C.E. H'CAP (0-80) (3-Y.O+) (Class D)

3-40 (3-44) **7f (Equitrack)** £3,900.40 (£1,166.20: £558.60: £254.80) Stalls: Low GOING minus 0.51 sec per fur (FST)

				SP	RR	SF
4482[4]	**Twin Creeks (74)** (VSoane) **6-9-9** RPerham(3) (lw: a.p: chsd ldr over 2f out: led over 1f out: r.o wl)	—	1	11/2[3]	83	66
4770[5]	**Palacegate Touch (72)** (JBerry) **7-9-4b**(3) TEDurcan(6) (lw: a.p: led over 3f out tl over 1f out: unable qckn)	3½	2	14/1	73	56
4071[11]	**Northern Angel (IRE) (73)** (PWHarris) **3-9-7** DHolland(9) (lw: gd hdwy over 1f out: r.o wl ins fnl f)	3½	3	7/2[2]	66	48
4451[6]	**Barbason (69)** (GLMoore) **5-9-4** CandyMorris(10) (hdwy over 2f out: r.o one pce)	5	4	3/1[1]	51	34
4370[10]	**Friendly Brave (USA) (67)** (MissGayKelleway) **7-8-13**(3) AWhelan(4) (b: b.hind: a.p: chsd ldrs over 3f out tl over 2f out: wknd over 1f out)	hd	5	12/1	48	31
4628[15]	**Godmersham Park (53)** (PSFelgate) **5-8-2** SDrowne(2) (led 2f: wknd over 2f out)	1½	6	14/1	31	14
4324[18]	**Las Vistas (49)** (HJCollingridge) **3-7-11**ow1 NAdams(11) (nvr nr to chal)	5	7	33/1	16	—
4905[6]	**Corniche Quest (IRE) (62)** (MRChannon) **4-8-4**(7) AEddery(14) (nvr nrr)	hd	8	12/1	28	11
3860[5]	**Lancashire Legend (68)** (SDow) **4-8-10e**(7) PDoe(1) (b.hind: a.p: led 5f out tl over 3f out: wknd over 2f out)	1¼	9	12/1	31	14
4591[11]	**Goodbye Gatemen (IRE) (68)** (BAPearce) **3-9-2** MartinDwyer(15) (bhd fnl 3f)	2½	10	33/1	26	8
4905[10]	**Roffey Spinney (IRE) (75)** (RHannon) **3-9-9** DaneO'Neill(16) (lw: a bhd)	7	11	12/1	17	—
4328[11]	**Kings Harmony (IRE) (75)** (PJMakin) **4-9-10** SSanders(7) (prom 3f)	nk	12	12/1	16	—
4896[7]	**Funchal Way (48)** (BRMillman) **5-7-11** FNorton(8) (bhd fnl 4f)	9	13	33/1	—	—
2050[9]	**Mijas (74)** (LMontagueHall) **4-9-9** WRyan(13) (lw: bhd fnl 4f)	nk	14	25/1	—	—
	Retoto (52) (BJMcMath) **3-8-0** GBardwell(12) (a bhd)	12	15	33/1	—	—
				(SP 130.0%)	**15 Rn**	

1m 24.28 (-0.12) CSF £74.82 CT £284.81 TOTE £5.90: £2.80 £3.10 £2.30 (£30.80) Trio £15.20 OWNER The Armchair Jockeys-Four Seasons Racing (ASTON ROWANT) BRED Crest Stud Ltd
WEIGHT FOR AGE 3yo-1lb
STEWARDS' ENQUIRY Whelan susp. 15 & 17/11/97 under Rule 151 (failure to ensure best possible placing)
4482 Twin Creeks has gained five of his seven previous victories on the All- Weather, and, striking the front approaching the final furlong, scooted clear to win with plenty in hand. (11/2)
4770 Palacegate Touch moved to the front at half way but, collared below the distance, was then firmly put in his place by the winner. (14/1: 10/1-16/1)
3715* Northern Angel (IRE), formerly with Julie Cecil, put in some really good work in the last furlong and a half, but found the front two were all ready home and dry. (7/2)
4451 Barbason, already 5lb higher than when last successful, was not given a hard time but did stay on to snatch fourth place. Well suited by this surface where he has won four times, he should soon regain the winning thread. (3/1)
3590 Friendly Brave (USA) was never far away but he was at the end of his tether below the distance and was caught for fourth place in the last couple of strides. His jockey was later harshly suspended for two days for failing to ride out. (12/1: op 8/1)
4243 Godmersham Park the early leader, had shot his bolt over two furlongs from home. He remains a maiden after twenty attempts. (14/1)

5022 TELEGRAPH NEWSPAPERS AMATEUR H'CAP (0-80) (3-Y.O+) (Class F)

4-10 (4-12) **1m 2f (Equitrack)** £2,739.00 (£759.00: £363.00) Stalls: Low GOING minus 0.51 sec per fur (FST)

				SP	RR	SF
4821[5]	**Sea Danzig (67)** (JJBridger) **4-10-6**(5) MissRIllman(13) (lw: led over 7f: led ins fnl f: r.o wl)	—	1	16/1	75	56
4924[6]	**Magic Mill (IRE) (75)** (JLEyre) **4-11-5** MissDianaJones(8) (chsd ldr: led over 2f out tl ins fnl f: unable qckn)	1½	2	6/1[3]	81	62
4882[5]	**Master Beveled (66)** (PDEvans) **7-10-5v**(5) MrAEvans(2) (a.p: hrd rdn over 2f out: one pce)	½	3	5/1[2]	71	52
4913[11]	**Palisander (IRE) (62)** (SDow) **3-9-11e**(5) MrRGuest(4) (b.hind: a.p: rdn over 1f out: one pce)	nk	4	20/1	66	43
*4913**	**Pegasus Bay (61)** (MrsAJohnson) **6-10-5** 5x MrsLPearce(7) (b: stdy hdwy over 3f out: r.o one pce fnl f)	¾	5	6/1[3]	64	45
*4906**	**Castles Burning (USA) (70)** (CACyzer) **3-10-10** 5x MrsSBosley(11) (hdwy over 1f out: nvr nrr)	1¾	6	7/1	70	47
4504[3]	**Roman Reel (USA) (55)** (GLMoore) **6-9-13** MrsJMoore(12) (prom 5f)	¾	7	13/2	54	35
4781[21]	**Sharp Shuffle (IRE) (77)** (RHannon) **4-11-7** MrCVigors(1) (b: b.hind: hld up: rdn over 2f out: sn wknd)	2½	8	9/2[1]	72	53

4548^{5} **Sheep Stealer (60)** (REPeacock) **9-9-13**(5) MrsCPeacock(9) (nvr nrr) 7 **9** 33/1 44 25
*4912** **Mystic Quest (IRE) (75)** (KMcAuliffe) **3-11-1v** 5x MrTMcCarthy(10) (bhd fnl 4f) ....11 **10** 6/1^{3} 41 18
4335^{12} **Montone (IRE) (58)** (JRJenkins) **7-10-2** DrMMannish(3) (dwlt: a bhd) ....s.h **11** 20/1 24 5
3864^{9} **Shahik (USA) (60)** (KCComerford) **7-9-13**(5) DrAKimber(14) (b: bhd fnl 5f) 1½ **12** 20/1 24 5
3581^{7} **Bagshot (65)** (GLMoore) **6-10-4**(5) MrIMongan(6) (b: bhd fnl 4f) ....11 **13** 14/1 11 —
Copperbeech (IRE) (63) (KCComerford) **3-9-12**(5) MrJOwen(5) (dwlt: hdwy over 8f out: wknd over 5f out: t.o)dist**14** 33/1 — —
(SP 136.3%) **14 Rn**

2m 7.35 (3.05) CSF £105.52 CT £525.65 TOTE £16.40: £3.50 £3.50 £2.20 (£38.00) Trio £98.10 OWNER Mr P. Cook (LIPHOOK) BRED Theobalds Stud
WEIGHT FOR AGE 3yo-4lb
STEWARDS' ENQUIRY Pearce susp. 15, 17-18 & 21/11/97 under Rule 151 (riding an ill-judged race)
IN-FOCUS: A winner on her first ride for Rachel Illman.
4821 Sea Danzig,whose two previous victories came over seven furlongs, took the field along until collared over a quarter of a mile from home. Although his rider did not do a great deal on him, the combination got back in front inside the final furlong and kept on well. (16/1)
4924 Magic Mill (IRE) made his bid for glory over two furlongs from home, but, collared inside the final furlong, then failed to find another gear. (6/1)
4882 Master Beveled, 8lb lower than on turf, was never far away but failed to find that vital turn of foot once in line for home. (5/1)
268a Palisander (IRE) ran his best race to date and was never far away if failing to quicken in the final quarter-mile. (20/1)
4913* Pegasus Bay was given a poor ride by his experienced jockey who looked extremely weak. Creeping closer running down the hill, his jockey was of little assistance in the straight although the combination did struggle on. The stewards took a dim view of Mrs Pearce's riding and suspended her for four days for riding an ill-judged race. (6/1)
4906* Castles Burning (USA) stayed on in the last furlong and a half but never threatened to get there in time. (7/1)
3581 Bagshot (14/1: 10/1-16/1)

T/Plpt: £37.80 (496.83 Tckts). T/Qdpt: £10.60 (126.55 Tckts) AK

4159-MUSSELBURGH (R-H) (Good to soft)
Thursday November 6th
WEATHER: overcast WIND: almost nil

5023 LADBROKE ON-COURSE H'CAP (0-70) (I) (3-Y.O+) (Class E)
12-30 (12-31) **1m 16y** £3,135.50 (£944.00: £457.00: £213.50) Stalls: High GOING: 0.27 sec per fur (G)

SP RR SF

4781^{5} **Antarctic Storm (69)** (RAFahey) **4-9-9**(5) RWinston(2) (mde all far side: racd alone in st: hld on towards fin) ....— **1** 11/2^{2} 79 52
4696* **Alfahaal (IRE) (57)** (CADwyer) **4-9-2** JFortune(10) (lw: hld up: stdy hdwy over 2f out: led stands' side ins fnl f: r.o) ....hd **2** 3/1^{1} 67 40
4899^{3} **Scathebury (53)** (KRBurke) **4-8-12** LCharnock(7) (lw: trckd ldrs: led stands' side over 2f out tl ins fnl f: no ex) 1¼ **3** 10/1 60 33
4988^{2} **Kass Alhawa (62)** (DWChapman) **4-9-7** GDuffield(5) (lw: chsd ldr: led stands' side over 3f out: hdd over 2f out: nt qckn appr fnl f) 1¾ **4** 8/1 66 39
4951^{12} **Mazeed (IRE) (58)** (PDEvans) **4-9-3v**[1] JFEgan(3) (hld up: effrt over 3f out: kpt on appr fnl f: nvr rchd ldrs)....1 **5** 25/1 60 33
3143^{12} **The Barnsley Belle (IRE) (46)** (JLEyre) **4-8-5** TWilliams(9) (a chsng ldrs: ev ch & rdn over 2f out: outpcd over 1f out) 1¾ **6** 14/1 44 17
4924^{11} **Running Green (62)** (DMoffatt) **6-9-7v** DeanMcKeown(4) (b: bhd: hdwy whn hmpd 3f out: nvr nr to chal) 1 **7** 16/1 58 31
4924^{4} **Thatched (IRE) (41)** (REBarr) **7-7-11**(3) PFessey(8) (bhd: hdwy over 2f out: nvr nr ldrs) 2½ **8** 8/1 33 6
4813^{16} **Genuine John (IRE) (50)** (JParkes) **4-8-9b** NDay(6) (chsd ldrs: ev ch tl wknd over 1f out) ....hd **9** 25/1 41 14
4979^{14} **Knobbleeneeze (66)** (MRChannon) **7-9-11v** ACulhane(1) (hld up: effrt & hmpd 3f out: n.d) ....3 **10** 6/1^{3} 51 24
4991^{13} **Forest Robin (47)** (MrsJRRamsden) **4-8-6b**[1] FLynch(12) (lw: a in rr) ....¾ **11** 14/1 31 4
4804^{17} **Denton Lad (57)** (WTKemp) **3-9-0** JCarroll(14) (mid div: drvn along 4f out: sn lost pl) 1½ **12** 25/1 38 9
4842^{19} **Monaco (IRE) (59)** (RAllan) **3-9-2** JQuinn(13) (s.i.s: plld hrd: a bhd) 2 **13** 14/1 36 7
4707^{12} **Six for Luck (44)** (DANolan) **5-8-3** AMackay(11) (plld hrd: hmpd after 1f: sn bhd: t.o fnl 3f) ....20 **14** 66/1 — —
(SP 124.9%) **14 Rn**

1m 47.0 (8.00) CSF £20.30 CT £157.95 TOTE £6.50: £1.50 £1.80 £3.10 (£10.40) Trio £40.60 OWNER Northumbria Leisure Ltd (MALTON) BRED N. and Mrs Bryce-Smith
WEIGHT FOR AGE 3yo-2lb
4781 Antarctic Storm was the only one to stay on the far side in the home straight. Connections were chancing their arm but, in truth they had little option as, in the past, this horse has shown a marked tendency to hang to his right. (11/2)
4696* Alfahaal (IRE), who changed hands for 17,000gns, came with a perfectly-timed challenge to lead on the stands' side inside the last but, at the line, the winner on the opposite wing was just ahead. He could prove a shrewd purchase. Potentially well-handicapped, he is worth watching out for on the All-Weather at Lingfield. (3/1)
4899 Scathebury, who raced keenly, possibly hit the front too soon for his own good. (10/1)
4988 Kass Alhawa was another who had a lot of use made of him. He is surely better suited by more patient tactics. (8/1)
Mazeed (IRE) looked to run his best race so far this year. (25/1)
2892 The Barnsley Belle (IRE), having her first race for 98 days, acquitted herself well and is no doubt being prepared for an All-Weather campaign this winter. (14/1)

5024 SUPPORTERS CARE H'CAP (0-65) (I) (3-Y.O+) (Class F)
1-00 (1-01) **1m 4f 31y** £3,213.50 (£968.00: £469.00: £219.50) Stalls: High GOING: 0.27 sec per fur (G)

SP RR SF

4958^{3} **Doc Ryan's (61)** (MJRyan) **3-9-5b**(3) PMcCabe(13) (lw: hld up & bhd: hdwy 3f out: styd on to ld wl ins fnl f)..— **1** 4/1^{2} 73 49
4714^{5} **Slasher Jack (IRE) (59)** (RAFahey) **6-9-7**(5) RWinston(2) (hld up: hdwy ent st: led ins fnl f: hrd rdn, hdd & nt qckn towards fin) ....½ **2** 6/1 70 52
4055^{15} **Moonraking (40)** (TJEtherington) **4-8-7** DaleGibson(6) (bhd: rdn ent st: styd on wl: nrst fin) 3 **3** 16/1 47 29
4584^{10} **Kingdom Pearl (50)** (MJCamacho) **3-8-11** LCharnock(3) (hld up: hdwy ½-wy: led 3f out tl ins fnl f: no ex) ....s.h **4** 11/1 57 33
4972^{3} **Protaras Bay (36)** (PLGilligan) **3-7-6**(5) APolli(8) (lw: chsd ldrs: effrt over 3f out: one pce) ....6 **5** 11/2^{3} 35 11
4847^{4} **Fighting Times (50)** (CASmith) **5-9-3v** DeanMcKeown(11) (b: chsd ldrs: effrt 4f out: r.o one pce) 4 **6** 6/1 44 26
4704^{7} **Lord Advocate (53)** (DANolan) **9-9-3b**(3) PFessey(12) (led: racd alone far side st: wknd fnl 3f) 1½ **7** 10/1 45 27

				SP	RR	SF
4971[3]	**Back Row (60)** (JHetherton) **3-9-7** GDuffield(4) (trckd ldrs: chal ent st: wknd over 2f out)	2½	**8**	100/30[1]	49	25
4923[6]	**Raased (33)** (FWatson) **5-8-0** TWilliams(9) (trckd ldrs tl wknd fnl 3f)	1½	**9**	20/1	20	2
4771[13]	**Havana Heights (IRE) (33)** (JLEyre) **4-8-0** JQuinn(5) (prom tl ½-wy: sn lost pl)	9	**10**	33/1	8	—
4923[8]	**Maurangi (30)** (BWMurray) **6-7-11b**[ow1] DWright(1) (a bhd)	11	**11**	20/1	—	—

(SP 122.8%) **11 Rn**

2m 45.5 (12.00) CSF £26.35 CT £326.24 TOTE £3.90: £1.20 £2.80 £5.40 (£18.00) Trio £207.40 OWNER Mr P. J. Flavin (NEWMARKET) BRED Mrs M. A. Ryan

LONG HANDICAP Maurangi 7-5

WEIGHT FOR AGE 3yo-6lb

4958 Doc Ryan's appreciated the step up in trip and proved most determined in a driving finish. (4/1)

4714 Slasher Jack (IRE) travelled particularly well but did not find as much as looked likely when let down, and is obviously keeping something for himself. (6/1)

3867 Moonraking, who has always looked better on the All-Weather, showed his well-being here, staying on strongly in the last half-mile. (16/1)

4584 Kingdom Pearl ran much better than last time and has plenty of ability when things go her way. (11/1: 6/1-12/1)

4972 Protaras Bay both looked and ran well but is short of any turn of speed. (11/2)

4847 Fighting Times had really gone in his coat and this longer trip might just have found him out. (6/1: op 4/1)

4971 Back Row (100/30: 9/4-7/2)

5025 COCKATOO E.B.F. MAIDEN STKS (2-Y.O) (Class D)

1-30 (1-30) **1m 16y** £3,629.50 (£1,096.00: £533.00: £251.50) Stalls: High GOING: 0.27 sec per fur (G)

				SP	RR	SF
4852[6]	**Ten Bob (IRE)** (MHTompkins) **2-9-0** DBiggs(1) (lw: hld up: gd hdwy 4f out: shkn up to ld over 2f out: clr whn eased ins fnl f)	—	**1**	3/1[2]	91+	34
4551[5]	**Wuxi Venture (95)** (SPCWoods) **2-9-0v**[1] NDay(7) (b.nr hind: led tl over 2f out: kpt on: no ch w wnr)	1¾	**2**	2/1[1]	81	31
4841[5]	**Kameez (IRE)** (MJohnston) **2-8-9** DeanMcKeown(8) (chsd ldrs: drvn along over 3f out: one pce fnl 2f)	4	**3**	5/1[3]	68	18
4871[3]	**Kilcullen (IRE)** (JHMGosden) **2-9-0** JCarroll(3) (s.i.s: hdwy over 4f out: sn rdn: kpt on: no imp)	5	**4**	2/1[1]	63	13
4690[15]	**Tom (53)** (JHetherton) **2-9-0b**[1] LCharnock(4) (chsd ldrs tl wknd 3f out)	9	**5**	100/1	45	—
4909[6]	**Announcing Peace** (CADwyer) **2-8-9** JQuinn(6) (trckd ldrs: drvn along over 4f out: wknd 3f out)	1	**6**	50/1	38	—
4840[9]	**Caplaw Skeen** (JLEyre) **2-9-0** OPears(5) (chsd ldrs: drvn along ½-wy: sn lost pl)	4	**7**	200/1	35	—
4067[16]	**Zeptepi (IRE)** (RSimpson) **2-8-9** MGallagher(2) (sn bhd)	8	**8**	100/1	14	—

(SP 112.8%) **8 Rn**

1m 47.6 (8.60) CSF £8.35 TOTE £4.70: £1.40 £1.10 £2.10 (£6.10) OWNER Mrs M. H. Tompkins (NEWMARKET) BRED Dullingham House Stud

4852 Ten Bob (IRE), who carries plenty of condition, was easily the pick of the paddock. Travelling strongly, he proved much too good for this lot and would have won by about five lengths, but for being eased considerably inside the last. (3/1)

4551 Wuxi Venture, in a visor, set out to make all but in the winner he had caught a tartar. (2/1)

4841 Kameez (IRE) is on the small side and still looks weak. This easy ground proved just too much for her and she will need another year over her head. (5/1)

4871 Kilcullen (IRE), who still does not look the finished article, was in trouble as far out as the home turn. (2/1: op 11/10)

5026 COCKATOO (S) NURSERY H'CAP (0-65) (2-Y.O) (Class F)

2-00 (2-00) **5f** £3,395.50 (£1,024.00: £497.00: £233.50) Stalls: Low GOING: 0.27 sec per fur (G)

				SP	RR	SF
4767[7]	**Barrelbio (IRE) (57)** (JJO'Neill) **2-9-7** KDarley(5) (in tch: effrt over 1f out: rdn to ld wl ins fnl f)	—	**1**	8/1[3]	64	32
4573[9]	**Satis (IRE) (48)** (MRChannon) **2-8-12** ACulhane(7) (lw: mde most tl hdd wl ins fnl f)	¾	**2**	10/1	53	21
2904[11]	**Glenstal Lad (43)** (RHollinshead) **2-8-7** FLynch(3) (lw: s.i.s: swtchd & hdwy ½-wy: styd on: nvr able to chal)	3	**3**	25/1	38	6
4808[2]	**I'm Tef (41)** (TDEasterby) **2-8-5** LCharnock(1) (a chsng ldrs: hrd rdn ½-wy: r.o one pce)	2	**4**	5/2[1]	30	—
4921[5]	**Glass River (55)** (PDEvans) **2-9-5** JFEgan(8) (lw: chsd ldrs: hrd rdn ½-wy: btn appr fnl f)	2	**5**	7/2[2]	37	5
4688[2]	**Esse (48)** (JBerry) **2-8-9**(3) PFessey(9) (cl up tl rdn & btn appr fnl f)	nk	**6**	5/2[1]	29	—
4840[7]	**Inshallah (57)** (MartinTodhunter) **2-9-7** JCarroll(2) (outpcd & bhd fr ½-wy)	2½	**7**	14/1	30	—
4750[12]	**Ngaere Princess (48)** (WTKemp) **2-8-12** TWilliams(4) (lw: trckd ldrs: effrt ½-wy: sn btn)	3½	**8**	20/1	10	—
4746[9]	**Dibola (46)** (JSWainwright) **2-8-10b**[1] DeanMcKeown(6) (w ldr tl rdn & wknd wl over 1f out)	s.h	**9**	50/1	8	—

(SP 116.8%) **9 Rn**

63.3 secs (5.60) CSF £75.15 CT £1,742.36 TOTE £10.90: £1.50 £2.20 £1.90 (£35.90) Trio £127.20; £39.44 to Doncaster 7/11/97 OWNER Mr A Sweeney and Mr I Cross (PENRITH) BRED E. C. Gowing and Michael Hickey

No bid

4767 Barrelbio (IRE), gambled on over seven furlongs last time, showed what a frustrating character he is here by winning well over this minimum trip to show that, when in the mood, he has the ability. (8/1: 5/1-10/1)

4483 Satis (IRE) showed plenty of toe from a poor draw and looks in good heart for a return to the All-Weather. (10/1)

2304 Glenstal Lad, having his first run for over three months, has certainly not grown much but he did run quite well, staying on as though further might help. (25/1)

4808 I'm Tef was always being taken off his legs here and may do better back on the sand. (5/2)

4921 Glass River, poorly drawn, burnt himself out trying to lay up with the pace. (7/2)

4688 Esse, looks-wise she would pick this lot up and carry them, but she has yet to give a performance to match. (5/2)

3628 Inshallah (14/1: 10/1-16/1)

5027 OLIVER HOMES NOVEMBER H'CAP (0-75) (3-Y.O+) (Class D)

2-30 (2-30) **2m** £7,298.00 (£2,204.00: £1,072.00: £506.00) Stalls: High GOING: 0.27 sec per fur (G)

				SP	RR	SF
4794*	**Outset (IRE) (63)** (MDHammond) **7-9-2** JCarroll(12) (lw: chsd ldrs: led over 3f out: styd on wl fnl f)	—	**1**	11/1	74	—
4783[21]	**Here Comes Herbie (66)** (WStorey) **5-9-5** JFEgan(15) (hld up: gd hdwy 6f out: wnt 2nd 3f out: kpt on: nt qckn fnl f)	2	**2**	9/1	75	—
4919*	**Nichol Fifty (75)** (MHTompkins) **3-9-5** 5x DBiggs(2) (lw: hld up: stdy hdwy 7f out: effrt over 3f out: hung rt: styd on same pce appr fnl f)	2½	**3**	6/1[2]	82	—
4956[8]	**The Butterwick Kid (60)** (RAFahey) **4-8-8**(5) RWinston(7) (hdwy over 3f out: kpt on appr fnl f)	s.h	**4**	12/1	66	—
4971[9]	**Children's Choice (IRE) (56)** (WJMusson) **6-8-6**(3) CLowther(16) (lw: bhd & pushed along: styd on one pce fnl 4f: nvr nr to chal)	4	**5**	9/1	58	—
4971[2]	**Tarry (52)** (MissGayKelleway) **4-8-5** GDuffield(3) (lw: hld up: hdwy 6f out: rdn 3f out: nvr nr to chal)	2½	**6**	7/1[3]	52	—

4562[11] **Alpine Panther (IRE) (58)** (MrsMReveley) **4-8-11** KDarley(17) (lw: prom: ev ch over 3f out: wknd over 1f out) ....5 **7** 25/1 53 —
4879[7] **Theme Arena (54)** (MCPipe) **4-8-7v** FLynch(4) (sn chsng ldrs: led over 4f out tl over 3f out: wknd 2f out) ......hd **8** 5/1[1] 49 —
4874[3] **All On (54)** (JHetherton) **6-8-4**(3) RFfrench(11) (swtg: led tl over 4f out: wknd & eased over 1f out) ....5 **9** 6/1[2] 44 —
4751[5] **Gold Desire (60)** (MBrittain) **7-8-6**(7) DMernagh(13) (bhd: sme hdwy over 3f out: n.d) ....5 **10** 20/1 45 —
4783[18] **Sea Victor (70)** (JLHarris) **5-9-9** DeanMcKeown(8) (prom: effrt over 4f out: sn wknd) ....½ **11** 20/1 54 —
4956[2] **Salska (60)** (AStreeter) **6-8-13** LNewton(10) (mid div: drvn along 6f out: lost pl 4f out) ....15 **12** 10/1 29 —
2682[8] **Northern Motto (50)** (JSGoldie) **4-8-3** JQuinn(14) (a bhd) ....11 **13** 20/1 8 —
4691[4] **Philmist (49)** (MissLAPerratt) **5-8-2b** LCharnock(5) (hdwy ½-wy: rdn & lost pl over 3f out: eased) ....7 **14** 25/1 — —
4744[13] **Golden Hadeer (55)** (MJRyan) **6-8-5**(3) PMcCabe(1) (prom: sn pushed along: lost pl 7f out) ....2½ **15** 25/1 4 —
Shonara's Way (75) (PMonteith) **6-10-0** OPears(6) (bkwd: prom tl wknd ½-wy: sn t.o) ....dist **16** 66/1 — —
4744[5] **Selmeston (IRE) (50)** (SCWilliams) **5-8-3** TWilliams(9) (chsd ldrs: lost pl 4f out: sn wknd & eased: virtually p.u) ....dist **17** 12/1 — —
(SP 137.9%) **17 Rn**

3m 41.2 CSF £100.01 CT £620.45 TOTE £17.40: £3.90 £1.30 £2.70 £4.70 (£53.70) Trio £206.80 OWNER Mr Mark Kilner (MIDDLEHAM) BRED Lexington Thoroughbreds Ltd
WEIGHT FOR AGE 3yo-9lb
4794* Outset (IRE), from a 7lb higher mark, was kept wide to get the better ground. In the end, he took this in decisive fashion and is clearly in great heart for when he reverts to hurdles. (11/1)
3383 Here Comes Herbie, who had an impossible task at the weights in the Cesarewitch, moved up on the bridle going into the home turn. Keeping on in pursuit of the winner, he will be interesting when he goes back over timber. (9/1)
4919* Nichol Fifty, under a 5lb penalty, gave his rider problems, persisting in hanging right out towards the centre. (6/1)
4279 The Butterwick Kid, 6lb higher in the weights than when winning his third race this year here in the spring, ran much better and looked very much like a horse on the way back to form. (12/1)
4562* Children's Choice (IRE), over a trip short of her best, lacked the pace to join issue. (9/1)
4971 Tarry, who is only a pony, possibly ran out of stamina. (7/1)
4744* Theme Arena, 6lb higher in the weights than when winning at Nottingham two outings ago, helped force the pace but, when taken on by the winner and the second, she soon capitulated. (5/1)

5028 SUPPORTERS CARE H'CAP (0-65) (II) (3-Y.O+) (Class F)

3-00 (3-00) **1m 4f 31y** £3,194.00 (£962.00: £466.00: £218.00) Stalls: High GOING: 0.27 sec per fur (G)

SP RR SF

4743[7] **Puteri Wentworth (60)** (MissGayKelleway) **3-9-7** JFortune(1) (lw: bhd: hdwy 3f out: led over 1f out: styd on wl) ....— **1** 9/2[1] 74 46
4817[7] **Tycoon Tina (50)** (WMBrisbourne) **3-8-11** JBramhill(8) (lw: a.p: led over 2f out tl appr fnl f: no ex) ....6 **2** 5/1[2] 56 28
4692[2] **Forzair (50)** (JJO'Neill) **5-9-0**(3) CLowther(3) (cl up: rdn over 3f out: one pce) ....6 **3** 9/2[1] 48 26
4872[13] **Belzao (40)** (RSimpson) **4-8-7** MGallagher(2) (led after 4f tl over 2f out: sn rdn & btn) 1 **4** 33/1 37 15
4768[6] **Peep O Day (33)** (JLEyre) **6-8-0** TWilliams(10) (b: b.hind: a chsng ldrs: rdn 4f out: one pce) ....3 **5** 7/1[3] 26 4
4768[5] **Jimjareer (IRE) (31)** (CaptJWilson) **4-7-12**ow1 AMackay(13) (sme hdwy over 3f out: nvr rchd ldrs) ....½ **6** 16/1 23 —
4607[13] **Gold Clipper (37)** (MJRyan) **3-7-9b**[1](3)ow2 RFfrench(12) (led 4f: chsd ldrs tl wknd over 2f out) ....4 **7** 25/1 24 —
4811[8] **Notation (IRE) (38)** (DWChapman) **3-7-10**(3) PFessey(5) (a rr div) ....7 **8** 20/1 16 —
*4800** **Welcome Home (40)** (PTDalton) **3-8-1** LCharnock(9) (cl up tl wknd fnl 3f) ....s.h **9** 5/1[2] 18 —
4926[3] **Westminster (IRE) (55)** (MHTompkins) **5-9-8v** DBiggs(4) (hld up: effrt appr st: sn btn) ....3 **10** 9/2[1] 29 7
4845[18] **Live Project (IRE) (42)** (RCraggs) **5-8-9** ACulhane(6) (swtg: a bhd: t.o) ....30 **11** 33/1 — —
1761[14] **Tickntima (65)** (MDHammond) **3-9-12** JCarroll(11) (chsd ldrs tl wknd ent st: t.o) ....5 **12** 50/1 — —
(SP 122.7%) **12 Rn**

2m 45.8 (12.30) CSF £24.04 CT £100.70 TOTE £6.80: £1.80 £3.10 £2.20 (£24.30) Trio £36.50 OWNER H R H Sultan Ahmad Shah (WHITCOMBE) BRED West Blagdon Stud and Calogo Bloodstock A.G.
LONG HANDICAP Gold Clipper 7-4
WEIGHT FOR AGE 3yo-6lb
3390 Puteri Wentworth obviously needs a strong gallop as she was going nowhere until three furlongs out, from which point she fairly flew. (9/2)
4693 Tycoon Tina did everything right this time, only to meet one just too useful. (5/1)
4692 Forzair had his chances but was always short of any change of pace. (9/2)
Belzao put in his best effort of the season and either hurdling or the All-Weather might see more of him. (33/1)
Peep O Day won this last year but, off a 2lb lower mark, was left struggling some way out his time. (7/1)
2159 Gold Clipper went off far too fast in the first-time blinkers. (25/1)

5029 OLIVER HOMES E.B.F. MEDIAN AUCTION MAIDEN STKS (2-Y.O) (Class E)

3-30 (3-30) **7f 30y** £3,551.50 (£1,072.00: £521.00: £245.50) Stalls: High GOING: 0.27 sec per fur (G)

SP RR SF

4849[6] **Gift of Gold (73)** (ICampbell) **2-9-0** AMackay(6) (lw: w ldr: led over 2f out: styd on strly fnl 2f) ....— **1** 6/1[3] 76 23
4922[4] **One To Go (IRE) (60)** (JBerry) **2-8-11**(3) PFessey(5) (chsd ldrs: wnt 2nd 4f out: kpt on: no imp) 6 **2** 33/1 63 10
4815[2] **Three Angels (IRE)** (MHTompkins) **2-9-0** DBiggs(4) (lw: hdwy 4f out: sn rdn & outpcd: styd on fnl 2f) ....2 **3** 3/1[2] 58 5
4694[3] **Chocolate Box** (WJHaggas) **2-8-9** FLynch(10) (sn bhd: hdwy over 3f out: kpt on fnl 2f: nvr nr ldrs) ....4 **4** 11/8[1] 44 —
4688[4] **Anka Lady (42)** (DMoffatt) **2-8-6**(3) DarrenMoffatt(2) (hld up: hdwy over 4f out: sn chsng ldrs: wknd over 2f out) ....8 **5** 100/1 26 —
4706[4] **Culcraggie** (JLEyre) **2-9-0** TWilliams(8) (chsd ldrs: drvn along over 4f out: wandered: hrd rdn & wknd 2f out) ....s.h **6** 3/1[2] 31 —
4984[8] **Abstone Pet Girl** (PDEvans) **2-8-9** JFEgan(9) (mde most tl over 4f out: wknd over 2f out) ....9 **7** 100/1 6 —
Minster Moorgate (MWEasterby) **2-8-6**(3) GParkin(1) (lengthy: unf: bkwd: s.s: a wl bhd) ....8 **8** 33/1 — —
4840[13] **Mac's Type (IRE)** (WStorey) **2-8-9** JFanning(7) (sn wl outpcd & bhd) ....4 **9** 100/1 — —
(SP 115.2%) **9 Rn**

1m 34.5 (8.50) CSF £141.11 TOTE £9.90: £1.40 £2.10 £1.20 (£16.10) Trio £23.60 OWNER Classic Gold (NEWMARKET) BRED David John Brown
4849 Gift of Gold, who looked really well beforehand. revelled in this ground and, making the most of his stamina, came right away coming to the final furlong. (6/1: 5/1-8/1)
4922 One To Go (IRE), who has plenty of size and scope, was taken quietly to post. He went second four furlongs out but it was soon clear the winner was much too good. (33/1)

4815 Three Angels (IRE), who carried plenty of condition beforehand, was tapped for foot early in the straight. Keeping on in his own time towards the finish, he should do better in handicap company over further next year. (3/1)
4694 Chocolate Box, a lean sort, seemed unable to go the pace. Picking up ground halfway up the straight, her effort was a short-lived one. Presumably she will do better next year. (11/8)
4706 Culcraggie, a very narrow type, had a hard race in vain. He looks as though he will need another winter over his head before he is anything like the finished article. (3/1: 9/4-7/2)

5030 LADBROKE ON COURSE H'CAP (0-70) (II) (3-Y.O+) (Class E)
4-00 (4-01) **1m 16y** £3,116.00 (£938.00: £454.00: £212.00) Stalls: High GOING: 0.27 sec per fur (G)

				SP	RR	SF
4951[4]	**Lunch Party (40)** (DNicholls) **5-7-8**(5) IonaWands(2) (bhd: swtchd & gd hdwy over 1f out: qcknd to ld ins fnl f)	—	**1**	10/1	55	23
4972[2]	**Glen Ogil (42)** (MRChannon) **3-7-13** AMackay(4) (lw: rr div: hdwy 3f out: hrd rdn & led 1f out: sn hdd & nt qckn)	1¾	**2**	7/1 3	54	20
4991[14]	**Nkapen Rocks (SPA) (47)** (CaptJWilson) **4-8-3**(3) RFfrench(9) (bhd: hdwy over 2f out: styd on wl)	1	**3**	16/1	57	25
4924[17]	**Pine Ridge Lad (IRE) (56)** (JLEyre) **7-9-1** RLappin(5) (mde most tl hdd & btn 1f out)	hd	**4**	12/1	65	33
4924[10]	**Shontaine (57)** (MJohnston) **4-9-2** DeanMcKeown(10) (lw: mid div: effrt over 3f out: kpt on: nvr able to chal)	3	**5**	10/1	60	28
4924[12]	**Needle Match (58)** (JJO'Neill) **4-9-0**(3) CLowther(3) (bhd: hdwy ½-wy: chsng ldrs 2f out: nt qckn)	½	**6**	10/1	60	28
4471[6]	**Principal Boy (IRE) (45)** (TJEtherington) **4-8-4** DaleGibson(1) (bhd: hdwy u.p over 2f out: nvr rchd ldrs)	1½	**7**	14/1	44	12
4924[14]	**Winston (48)** (JDBethell) **4-8-7** JCarroll(11) (in tch: hdwy over 3f out: wknd fnl 2f)	10	**8**	12/1	28	—
4876[5]	**Zorba (63)** (JHetherton) **3-9-6** GDuffield(7) (bhd: effrt ent st: n.d)	4	**9**	8/1	35	1
4924[3]	**Alpine Hideaway (IRE) (68)** (MWEasterby) **4-9-10**(3) GParkin(12) (cl up: sn drvn along: wknd over 3f out: eased)	3	**10**	7/2 1	34	2
4843[6]	**Trojan Hero (SAF) (56)** (MrsMReveley) **6-9-1** ACulhane(6) (chsd ldrs tl wknd 2f out)	6	**11**	16/1	10	—
4843[4]	**Dispol Gem (57)** (PCalver) **4-9-2** KDarley(14) (in tch tl wknd fnl 3f)	3	**12**	13/2 2	5	—
2216[8]	**Kingchip Boy (54)** (MJRyan) **8-8-10v**(3) PMcCabe(8) (disp ld 5f: sn wknd)	3½	**13**	10/1	—	—
4291[14]	**Anetta (54)** (MissSEHall) **3-8-11** LCharnock(13) (b.nr hind: chsd ldrs tl st: wknd qckly)	11	**14**	14/1	—	—
				(SP 136.0%)	**14 Rn**	

1m 47.2 (8.20) CSF £80.79 CT £1,084.64 TOTE £14.70: £4.00 £3.10 £4.00 (£27.80) Trio £314.20 OWNER Mr S. Aitken (THIRSK) BRED Aston Park Stud
WEIGHT FOR AGE 3yo-2lb
4951 Lunch Party came from off the pace over this longer trip and it suited him well as he produced an amazing turn of foot to win it. (10/1)
4972 Glen Ogil looked particularly well and, given some strong assistance, ran his heart out but was well tapped for speed late on. (7/1)
4629 Nkapen Rocks (SPA) is basically his own worst enemy as he certainly has the ability, if he can be persuaded. (16/1)
4472* Pine Ridge Lad (IRE) ran well and may well be worth keeping in mind for a return to the All-Weather. (12/1)
4813 Shontaine still looks in good condition and, after two disappointing efforts, ran much better this time. (10/1)
4876 Zorba (8/1: op 12/1)
4924 Alpine Hideaway (IRE) could never gain command, did not like it at all and dropped tamely away once into the straight. (7/2)

T/Jkpt: Not won; £2,858.18 to Doncaster 7/11/97. T/Plpt: £1,457.40 (13.27 Tckts). T/Qdpt: £136.30 (8.55 Tckts) AA/

4861a-SAINT-CLOUD (France) (L-H) (Soft)
Tuesday October 28th

5031a PRIX DE LA FLORE (Gp 3) (3-Y.O+ F & M)
2-40 (2-36) **1m 2f 110y** £24,691.00 (£8,979.00: £4,489.00)

				SP	RR	SF
1916a[10]	**Palme D'Or (IRE)** (AFabre,France) **3-8-7** OPeslier	—	**1**		116	—
4254a*	**Lomita (GER)** (BSchutz,Germany) **3-8-10** AStarke	1	**2**		118	—
1916a[5]	**La Nana (FR)** (DSepulchre,France) **3-8-7** FSanchez	5	**3**		107	—
4676[5]	**Bombazine (IRE)** (LMCumani) **3-8-7** CAsmussen (btn 14½l)		**6**		—	—
						10 Rn

2m 16.9 (6.90) P-M 1.80FF: 1.20FF 2.50FF 1.80FF (12.20FF) OWNER Mr D. Wildenstein (CHANTILLY)
Palme D'Or (IRE) was always going well in a race which she dominated from soon after entering the straight. Although chased home by Lomita in the closing stages, she stayed on to win with plenty in hand and will now be retired to stud.
4254a* Lomita (GER) was held up for a late challenge and, although running on well in the last furlong and a half, she was unable to reel in the winner. This was her last run of the season, but she is likely to stay in training next year.
813a La Nana (FR), another held up for a late challenge, was outpaced early on in the straight but did stay on in the final stages.
4676 Bombazine (IRE) ran well in third for much of the race, but was beaten soon after entering the straight.

3872a-BORDEAUX (France) (R-H) (Very soft)
Wednesday October 29th

5032a PRIX ANDRE BABOIN GRAND PRIX DES PROVINCES (Gp 3) (3-Y.O+)
2-30 (2-43) **1m 1f 110y** £24,691.00 (£8,979.00: £4,489.00)

				SP	RR	SF
4656a[4]	**Astarabad (USA)** (AdeRoyerDupre,France) **3-8-9** GMosse	—	**1**		117	—
3729a[3]	**Keep Playing (FR)** (J-CRouget,France) **3-8-6** J-RDubosc	1½	**2**		112	—
4656a[3]	**Visionary (FR)** (AFabre,France) **3-8-9** TJarnet	½	**3**		114	—
						11 Rn

No Time Taken P-M 3.70FF: 1.20FF 2.20FF 1.10FF (15.80FF) OWNER Aga Khan (CHANTILLY) BRED H H The Aga Khans Studs
4656a Astarabad (USA) made virtually all the running and, with the race sewn up at the furlong marker, won with plenty in hand. He may go for the Japan Cup in December and could stay in training next year.

Keep Playing (FR) was held up for a late run and put in his best work at the finish. He is very much an improving colt and, if he is kept in training next year, he should continue to hold his own at this level.
4656a Visionary (FR) was another who finished well but this distance probably tested his stamina to the limit. He should be able to win a Group race if he stays in training next year.

4865a-SAN SIRO (Milan, Italy) (R-H) (Good)
Friday October 31st

5033a PREMIO ABETONE MAIDEN (2-Y.O)
2-43 (2-43) **1m 110y** £9,642.00 (£4,242.00: £2,314.00)

				SP	RR	SF
	Priwings (IRE) (ITellini,Italy) **2-8-12** MTellini	—	1		—	—
	Ego Night (IRE) (MBell) **2-8-12** FJovine	1½	2		—	—
	Saddler's Cove (FR) (Italy) **2-8-12** EBotti	nk	3		—	—
						9 Rn

1m 48.2 Tote 58L: 14L 11L 14L (50L) OWNER Razza Giallorosso
Ego Night (IRE) put up a promising display on his debut. Making the running, he was headed a furlong out and could only keep on at the same pace. He should improve for the outing.

5031a-SAINT-CLOUD (France) (L-H) (Good to soft)
Saturday November 1st

5034a CRITERIUM DE SAINT-CLOUD (Gp 1) (2-Y.O C & F)
1-40 (1-39) **1m 2f** £44,893.00 (£17,957.00: £8,979.00: £4,489.00)

				SP	RR	SF
4657a[2]	**Special Quest (FR)** (MmeCHead,France) **2-9-0b[1]** ODoleuze (led: qcknd 2f out: r.o wl)	—	1	44/10[3]	97	—
4697*	**Asakir** (SbinSuroor) **2-9-0** LDettori (prom: chal ldrs over 1f out: ev ch ins fnl f: no ex cl home)	nk	2	22/10[2]	97	—
4657a[3]	**Daymarti (IRE)** (AdeRoyerDupre,France) **2-9-0** GMosse (hld up bhd: c wd st: prog over 2f out: r.o)	hd	3	21/10[1]	96	—
	Croco Rouge (IRE) (PBary,France) **2-9-0** SGuillot (mid div: u.p st: nvr plcd to chal)	hd	4	67/10	96	—
4895*	**Distant Mirage (IRE)** (PWChapple-Hyam) **2-9-0** OPeslier (trckd ldr: rdn 2f out: one pce)	4	5	83/10	90	—
4157*	**Wales** (PFICole) **2-9-0** TQuinn (a cl up: u.p & wknd st: n.d)	1½	6	59/10	87	—
	Abbatiale (FR) (DSepulchre,France) **2-8-11** TJarnet (a in rr: sn btn)	6	7	143/10	75	—
				(SP 126.8%)		7 Rn

2m 11.3 (7.80) P-M 5.40FF: 2.70FF 2.10FF OWNER Wertheimer Brothers (CHANTILLY)
4657a Special Quest (FR) made virtually every yard of the running and battled on gamely when challenged by three of his rivals early in the straight. He is a nervous colt and is therefore fitted with blinkers so tight that he can hardly see the track. He has a lovely flowing action and should improve both mentally and physically during the winter, with the Prix du Jockey-Club being next season's main target. (44/10)
4697* Asakir ran a decent race despite his inexperience and was given every possible chance. Always prominent, he battled on gamely in the straight and will have learnt a lot from the outing. Dettori reported that the colt took a long time to balance and that cost them the race. Asakir will now be wintered in Dubai before being aimed at the top middle-distance events next season. (22/10)
4657a Daymarti (IRE) ran almost pound for pound with the winner and his attitude is improving with every race. He would have been suited by a stronger pace but is reported to be a very good horse in the making, and may even be Classic material. (21/10)
Croco Rouge (IRE) did not settle too well in the back straight and showed his inexperience. He got pushed back by some of his rivals in the straight and still has a lot to learn about the game, but he could prove to be the best of this field in the future. A colt with considerable scope, he will be aimed at either the English or French Derby next year. (67/10)
4895* Distant Mirage (IRE) raced in second place but was in trouble at the two-furlong marker before finishing a remote fifth. He does not really look up to this class. (83/10)
4157* Wales disappointed connections with a lacklustre display. With every chance turning for home, he weakened in the straight, dropping right away. This was not his true form. (59/10)

5033a-SAN SIRO (Milan, Italy) (R-H) (Good)
Saturday November 1st

5035a PREMIO GIOVANNI FALCK (Listed) (3-Y.O+ F & M)
2-10 (2-14) **1m 4f** £23,142.00 (£10,183.00: £5,554.00)

				SP	RR	SF
3005a[3]	**Open Air (GER)** (WHaustein,Germany) **3-8-6** StephenDavies	—	1		104	—
4445*	**Puce** (LMCumani) **4-9-0** FJovine	s.h	2		106	—
4445[5]	**Tempting Prospect** (LordHuntingdon) **3-8-6** WNewnes	1	3		103	—
						6 Rn

2m 30.9 (10.90) Tote 249L: 41L 13L (177L) OWNER Gestut Ittlingen
4445* Puce put up a brave performance and only just failed to land the spoils. Tracking the leaders, she moved up to take the advantage with a furlong and a half to run, only to be caught on the line.
4445 Tempting Prospect took the field along but had no answer when challenged in the straight.

5036a PREMIO MIRANDOLA MAIDEN (2-Y.O F)
3-10 (3-28) **7f 110y** £9,642.00 (£4,243.00: £2,314.00)

				SP	RR	SF
4534a[5]	**Spazaca (USA)** (LMCumani) **2-8-11** MDemuro	—	1		—	—
	Totom (LordHuntingdon) **2-8-8** WNewnes	1	2		—	—
	Welsh Poppy (Italy) **2-8-11** OFrancera	8	3		—	—
	Kelang (MrsJCecil) **2-8-8** FJovine (btn over a dist)		7		—	—
						7 Rn

1m 34.4 (9.90) Tote 39L: 19L 15L (67L) OWNER Scuderia Rencati (NEWMARKET)
4534a Spazaca (USA) made every post a winning one and, along with the runner-up, was a class above her rivals. She will now remain in Italy and will be trained by Giuseppe Botti.

Totom was held up in the early stages and finished in promising style. He will have benefited from this run.
Kelang was a most reluctant participant. Unseating her rider on the way to post, she dug her toes in as the gates opened and was soon a long way behind her rivals.

5037a PREMIO CHIUSURA (Gp 3)
3-40 (4-01) **7f** £33,109.00 (£15,266.00: £8,532.00: £4,266.00)

Form	Horse	Dist	Pos	SP	RR	SF
1552a[3]	**Robins (IRE)** (ACalchetti,Italy) **5-9-7** OFrancera	—	1		114	—
4531a[2]	**Accento** (RSuerland,Germany) **4-9-7** ATylicki	1½	2		111	—
4124a[11]	**Nautiker (GER)** (PRemmert,Germany) **6-9-7** MissMGloor	s.h	3		111	—
4523[4]	**Ramooz (USA)** (BHanbury) **4-10-0** FJovine	1¼	4		115	—
						7 Rn

1m 23.3 (4.40) Tote 72L: 25L 14L (90L) OWNER San Paolo Agricola Stud
Robins (IRE), trying to give 7lb all round, ran creditably but was unable to quicken in the closing stages.

AQUEDUCT (New York, USA) (L-H) (Sloppy)
Sunday November 2nd

5038a LONG ISLAND H'CAP (3-Y.O+ F & M)
21-00 (21-07) **1m 3f** **(Dirt)** £53,571.00 (£17,857.00: £9,821.00: £5,357.00)

Form	Horse	Dist	Pos	SP	RR	SF
	Sweetzie (USA) (RitaNash,USA) **5-8-3** JChavez	—	1		118?	—
	Sweet Sondra (USA) (USA) **4-8-2** FLovato	2½	2		113	—
	Scenic Point (USA) (USA) **4-8-8** JSantos	3½	3		114	—
4655a*	**Tulipa (USA)** (SbinSuroor) **4-8-2** JBravo	5¾	4		100	—
						6 Rn

2m 16.66 P-M $20.20: PL $11.80 $14.60: SHOW $4.00 $4.70 $2.60 (SF $150.00) OWNER R Hamilton & Rita Nash
IN-FOCUS: **This race was due to be run on Turf but because of the condition of the track, it was moved to the dirt.**
4655a* Tulipa (USA) ran well for a long way in a race that was switched to a surface that was unfamiliar to her. She was eased when beaten and may get a further opportunity before retiring to stud.

0393a-SANTA ANITA (Los Angeles, USA) (L-H) (Firm)
Sunday November 2nd

5039a YELLOW RIBBON STKS (GRADE 1) (Gp 1) (3-Y.O+ F & M)
23-45 (23-48) **1m 2f** £178,571.00 (£59,524.00: £35,714.00: £17,857.00)

Form	Horse	Dist	Pos	SP	RR	SF
4652a*	**Ryafan (USA)** (JHMGosden) **3-8-6** ASolis	—	1		123	—
	Fanjica (IRE) (USA) **5-8-10** CNakatani	1¼	2		121	—
4651a[3]	**Memories Of Silver (USA)** (USA) **4-8-10** JBailey	1½	3		119	—
4666a[2]	**Squeak** (JHMGosden) **3-8-6** GaryStevens	1	4		117	—
3879a[3]	**Dance Design (IRE)** (DKWeld,Ireland) **4-8-10** MJKinane (btn 7l)		7		—	—
						8 Rn

2m 3.69 P-M $7.20: PL $4.80 $7.20: SHOW $3.00 $3.20 $2.40 (SF $40.60) OWNER Juddmonte Farms (NEWMARKET) BRED Juddmonte Farms
4652a* Ryafan (USA) supplemented her victory in the Queen Elizabeth Cup at Keeneland with a typically brave victory in a rough race. Held up just off the pace, she took the lead below the distance and ran on strongly to hold off the challenge of the ex-English runner-up. She was responsible for some of the trouble in the straight but survived a Stewards' enquiry, and now goes for the Matriarch Stakes at Hollywood Park.
4666a Squeak was held up at the back and came through the trouble in the straight. She is likely to continue her career in America.
3879a Dance Design (IRE) was the chief sufferer from the scrimmaging which took place in the straight. Having led until headed by the winner, she was bumped and stumbled inside the last furlong and then came home in her own time. She came back none the worse for the experience and is still on course for the Breeders' Cup Turf.

4885-DONCASTER (L-H) (Good)
Friday November 7th
WEATHER: fine and sunny WIND: almost nil

5040 E.B.F. COOPERATIVE BANK MAIDEN STKS (I) (2-Y.O) (Class D)
12-30 (12-32) **7f** £3,494.25 (£1,044.00: £499.50: £227.25) Stalls: High GOING: 0.33 sec per fur (G)

Form	Horse	Dist	Pos	SP	RR	SF
4758[16]	**Scorned (GER)** (IABalding) **2-9-0** SWhitworth(12) (trckd ldrs: led 2f out: rdn & kpt on wl fnl f)	—	1	14/1[3]	88	54
	High And Low (BWHills) **2-8-9** DHolland(14) (str: cmpt: bit bkwd: mid div: effrt & hdwy 3f out: swtchd lft: kpt on fnl f: nt rch wnr)	2½	2	7/1[2]	77	43
4105[10]	**Anemos (IRE)** (MAJarvis) **2-9-0** WRyan(15) (bit bkwd: n tch: hdwy over 2f out: one pce fnl f)	4	3	16/1	73	39
4925[3]	**Pass The Rest (IRE)** (JLEyre) **2-9-0** TWilliams(2) (lw: cl up: led 4f out tl hdd 2f out: wknd fnl f)	¾	4	7/1[2]	71	37
4884[15]	**Bomb Alaska** (GBBalding) **2-9-0** SDrowne(18) (bit bkwd: mid div: sme hdwy 2f out: nvr rchd ldrs)	4	5	50/1	62	28
4955[6]	**Piped Aboard (IRE)** (JLDunlop) **2-9-0** KDarley(7) (chsd ldrs: drvn along over 3f out: no ex fr over 1f out)	nk	6	14/1[3]	62	28
	Masamadas (CFWall) **2-9-0** SSanders(13) (leggy: scope: bit bkwd: mid div: pushed along & hung lft fr ½-wy: n.d)	¾	7	25/1	60	26
	Tankersley (AHide) **2-9-0** TQuinn(9) (wl grwn: scope: bit bkwd: chsd ldrs: rdn & wknd fnl 2f)	2½	8	33/1	54	20
4758[17]	**High And Mighty** (JHMGosden) **2-9-0** GHind(3) (cl up tl wknd fr 2f out)	¾	9	7/1[2]	53	19
4265[7]	**Clarity (IRE) (75)** (APJarvis) **2-8-6**(3) CLowther(19) (hdwy fnl 2f: nvr trbld ldrs)	¾	10	14/1[3]	46	12
	Billionaire (DRLoder) **2-9-0** GCarter(10) (lt-f: unf: s.s: rdn along ½-wy: nvr nr ldrs)	5	11	3/1[1]	39	5
	Lutine Bell (JEBanks) **2-9-0** JStack(16) (leggy: unf: s.i.s: a in rr)	hd	12	20/1	39	5
4564[17]	**Girlie Set (IRE)** (SirMarkPrescott) **2-8-9** GDuffield(11) (bit bkwd: s.i.s: nvr plcd to chal)	1¼	13	20/1	31	—
	Hot Spot (IABalding) **2-9-0** MartinDwyer(8) (lengthy: bit bkwd: chsd ldrs 4f)	1½	14	16/1	33	—

	Musalse (PCHaslam) **2-8-7**(7) PGoode(17) (w'like: bit bkwd: s.s: a in rr)	10	**15**	25/1	10	—
4871[9]	**Bold Legacy (IRE)** (WRMuir) **2-9-0** DaneO'Neill(1) (chsd ldrs tl wknd over 2f out)	½	**16**	33/1	9	—
	Jaati (IRE) (JHMGosden) **2-9-0** AGarth(6) (w'like: scope: prom to ½-wy: sn lost pl: eased whn btn)	nk	**17**	14/1[3]	8	—
	Puiwee (PTDalton) **2-8-9** LCharnock(5) (cmpt: bkwd: s.i.s: a rr div)	nk	**18**	50/1	2	—
4904[20]	**Needwood Spitfire** (BCMorgan) **2-8-9** DBiggs(4) (led 3f: wknd qckly: t.o)	5	**19**	25/1	—	—
				(SP 131.8%)	**19 Rn**	

1m 30.54 (6.04) CSF £93.54 TOTE £31.50: £5.70 £2.50 £10.20 (£82.40) Trio £234.40; £99.05 to Doncaster 8/11/97 OWNER Mr George Strawbridge (KINGSCLERE) BRED I. A. Balding

IN-FOCUS: **The stalls on the straight course were placed on the stands' side and the low numbers racing down the centre of the track always had a considerable advantage, especially over five and six furlongs, and it was quite obvious where the fastest ground was.**

Scorned (GER) had clearly benefited from his Newmarket debut and won this average contest in splendid style. (14/1)

High And Low, a likeable individual, took time to grasp what was required and never got in a blow at the winner, but she will surely improve further and win races next year. (7/1: op 9/2)

Anemos (IRE) stepped up considerably on his Kempton debut and is clearly not without some ability. (16/1)

4925 Pass The Rest (IRE) put in a determined effort but had nothing more to give in the closing stages. (7/1)

Bomb Alaska, stepping up to seven furlongs, showed signs of ability. He will do better in time. (50/1)

2286 Piped Aboard (IRE), stepping up in distance, was struggling to hold his place fully three furlongs out. He will probably do better in handicaps next year. (14/1)

Masamadas, despite being burly and green, showed some promise. (25/1)

Tankersley, in need of the race, ran well to the two-furlong pole. (33/1)

High And Mighty (7/1: op 9/2)

Billionaire missed the break and never got in the hunt. He is probably capable of better. (3/1)

Girlie Set (IRE), a big filly, never showed here but is likely to do better in time when she strengthens and matures. (20/1)

5041 E.B.F. COOPERATIVE BANK MAIDEN STKS (II) (2-Y.O) (Class D)
1-00 (1-02) **7f** £3,494.25 (£1,044.00: £499.50: £227.25) Stalls: High GOING: 0.33 sec per fur (G)

				SP	RR	SF
	High-Rise (IRE) (LMCumani) **2-8-11**(3) RFfrench(10) (lt-f: unf: a.p: nt clr run & sltly outpcd over 1f out: str run fnl f to ld cl home)	—	**1**	8/1	87+	43
	Volontiers (FR) (PWHarris) **2-9-0** ACulhane(13) (lt-f: hld up: hdwy over 2f out: led ent fnl f tl ct last stride)	s.h	**2**	7/1[3]	87	43
4775[6]	**Al-Fateh (IRE)** (JLDunlop) **2-9-0** KDarley(2) (lw: a.p centre: chal 1f out: unable qckn cl home)	1½	**3**	8/1	84	40
4901[4]	**North Ofthe Border** (MJohnston) **2-9-0** DeanMcKeown(18) (lw: mde most tl hdd & no ent ex fnl f)	2	**4**	6/1[2]	79	35
	Olive The Twist (USA) (JHMGosden) **2-8-9** AGarth(1) (leggy: unf: b.hind: swvd lft s: bhd: hdwy fnl 2f: nrst fin)	hd	**5**	14/1	74+	30
4884[19]	**Fields of Omagh (USA)** (IABalding) **2-9-0** SWhitworth(3) (lw: in tch: effrt 2f out: sn rdn: nt pce to chal)	2	**6**	16/1	74	30
	Mole Creek (JRFanshawe) **2-8-9** NDay(4) (leggy: pushed along ½-wy: sme late hdwy: n.d)	3	**7**	20/1	62	18
	Celebration (IABalding) **2-8-9** MartinDwyer(5) (w'like: leggy: bkwd: trckd ldrs: drvn along & outpcd fnl 2f)	¾	**8**	20/1	61	17
	Temeraire (USA) (MrsAJPerrett) **2-9-0** TQuinn(8) (gd sort: bkwd: dwlt: hdwy appr fnl f: nvr nrr)	hd	**9**	14/1	65	21
	Mystic Flight (USA) (RCharlton) **2-8-9** TSprake(14) (lt-f: unf: s.s: a in rr)	1¼	**10**	10/1	57	13
	Ethereal (DRLoder) **2-9-0** GCarter(12) (w'like: scope: chsd ldrs: hrd drvn 2f out: grad wknd)	nk	**11**	5/1[1]	62	18
4706[7]	**Best Quest** (JHMGosden) **2-9-0** GHind(11) (trckd ldrs: drvn along over 2f out: sn btn)	1¼	**12**	8/1	59	15
	Elbarree (IRE) (MAJarvis) **2-9-0** WRyan(9) (unf: scope: bkwd: prom tl wknd over 2f out)	4	**13**	20/1	50	6
4853[9]	**Golden Lyric (IRE)** (GWragg) **2-8-9**(5) GMilligan(6) (prom over 5f)	¾	**14**	14/1	48	4
4604[10]	**Treasure Island** (SirMarkPrescott) **2-8-9** GDuffield(17) (a bhd)	1¾	**15**	20/1	39	—
4907[5]	**Magic Spring (IRE)** (KMcAuliffe) **2-8-9** JFEgan(16) (swtg: prom tl wknd over 2f out)	2	**16**	25/1	35	—
4871[12]	**Pinsharp (IRE)** (PHowling) **2-9-0** JQuinn(7) (b: prom tl rdn & wknd 2f out)	3	**17**	25/1	33	—
	Janet Lindup (BWHills) **2-8-9** DHolland(15) (lt-f: s.s: a bhd)	3	**18**	8/1	21	—
				(SP 149.6%)	**18 Rn**	

1m 31.42 (6.92) CSF £63.47 TOTE £12.40: £3.60 £2.60 £3.00 (£81.60) Trio £164.10 OWNER Sheikh Mohammed Obaid Al Maktoum (NEWMARKET) BRED Sheikh Mohammed Obaid al Maktoum

High-Rise (IRE), a sparely-made colt, closely related to three winners, looked done for when denied a clear run below the distance but he responded willingly when sent about his work, and stayed on to lead right on the line. (8/1)

Volontiers (FR), a lean-looking debutant who attracted support in the ring, kicked for home approaching the final furlong and, battling on bravely, did not deserve to be touched off in the last stride. (7/1)

Al-Fateh (IRE), not quite so highly-tried as he was on his debut, showed with the pace all the way but, when an extra effort was called for, he was unable to deliver. Out of a very useful racemare, he will come into his own next season. (8/1: op 5/1)

4901 North Ofthe Border set a brisk pace under the slower stands' rail and, forced to give best entering the last furlong, found another effort beyond him. He would probably have won had he been drawn towards the middle. (6/1: op 4/1)

Olive The Twist (USA), a leggy, unfurnished filly whose dam won three Group races, swerved violently left when the stalls opened. Switched right almost immediately to race in the pack, she was really staying on strongly nearing the finish and could be a better than average contender next season. (14/1)

Fields of Omagh (USA) could well need more time, but he shaped much better than he did on his debut two weeks ago, and he is progressing in the right direction. (16/1)

Mole Creek, a leggy filly who comes from a good winning family, was struggling with the pace at halfway but she began to stay on as stamina came into play, and she will benefit considerably from the experience. (20/1)

Temeraire (USA), an attractive newcomer who was colty in the preliminaries, was getting into his stride in the latter stages after a tardy strata and it will come as a surprise if he does not win his share of prizes. (14/1)

5042 E.B.F GIBSON BOOTH MAIDEN STKS (2-Y.O) (Class D)
1-30 (1-32) **6f** £4,053.25 (£1,216.00: £585.50: £270.25) Stalls: High GOING: 0.33 sec per fur (G)

				SP	RR	SF
4640[3]	**Masha-Il (IRE)** (JHMGosden) **2-9-0** RHills(10) (lw: in tch: effrt 2f out: styd on to ld ins fnl f: r.o)	—	**1**	7/4[1]	79	32
4904[6]	**Lindesberg** (MJohnston) **2-8-9** DHolland(11) (lw: disp ld tl led ½-wy: rdn wl over 1f out: hdd ins fnl f: kpt on wl)	1	**2**	9/2[2]	71	24
	Fabrice (HCandy) **2-9-0** NAdams(12) (wl grwn: bit bkwd: chsd ldrs: drvn along over 2f out: nt qckn fnl f)	1½	**3**	16/1	72	25
	Shaji (IRE) (CJBenstead) **2-9-0** TWilliams(15) (w'like: scope: bit bkwd: s.i.s: hdwy 2f out: kpt on wl fnl f)	nk	**4**	33/1	72	25
4884[18]	**Aganon** (MRChannon) **2-9-0** RPerham(9) (hld up: stdy hdwy fnl 2f: nvr plcd to chal)	nk	**5**	20/1	71+	24
	Rachaels North (IRE) (RWArmstrong) **2-9-0** SLanigan(8) (leggy: scope: bit bkwd: in tch: effrt & hdwy 2f out: rn green: nt qckn fnl f)	½	**6**	33/1	69	22

				SP	RR	SF
4564[15]	**Seven** (BSmart) **2-9-0b[1]** JStack(18) (disp ld tl rdn wl over 2f out: no ex appr fnl f)	½	**7**	33/1	68	21
	Prima Facie (DRLoder) **2-8-9** JFortune(6) (neat: scope: chsd ldrs: rdn & one pce fr over 1f out)	1	**8**	6/1[3]	60	13
4779[12]	**Empire State (IRE)** (MHTompkins) **2-9-0** DBiggs(3) (s.i.s: bhd tl hdwy 2f out: kpt on fnl f)	hd	**9**	20/1	65	18
	Bow Bells (CFWall) **2-8-9** SSanders(1) (unf: bit bkwd: hdwy over 2f out: styd on fnl f: nvr nrr)	½	**10**	16/1	59	12
4840[8]	**Pipe Music (IRE)** (PCHaslam) **2-9-0** LCharnock(13) (bit bkwd: in tch: drvn along 3f out: wknd)	4	**11**	33/1	53	6
	Briery Mec (HJCollingridge) **2-9-0** JQuinn(19) (unf: bit bkwd: dwlt: hld up: nvr nr ldrs)	hd	**12**	33/1	53	6
4909[4]	**Shantung (IRE)** (KMcAuliffe) **2-8-9** JFEgan(21) (rdn along in mid div ½-wy: outpcd fnl 2f)	s.h	**13**	10/1	48	1
4871[10]	**Brooksie** (JWHills) **2-8-11**(3) MHenry(16) (in tch tl wknd fnl 2f)	1	**14**	33/1	50	3
4564[14]	**Crofters Edge** (APJarvis) **2-8-11**(3) CLowther(2) (outpcd fr ½-wy)	½	**15**	33/1	49	2
4884[16]	**Tanimbar (IRE)** (DHaydnJones) **2-9-0** AMackay(5) (prom tl rdn & wknd fnl 2f)	hd	**16**	20/1	49	2
4841[8]	**Splendid (IRE)** (SirMarkPrescott) **2-8-9** GDuffield(20) (rdn along ½-wy: sn lost pl)	nk	**17**	12/1	43	—
4801[8]	**Albrighton** (BSRothwell) **2-9-0** MFenton(17) (sn rdn along & outpcd)	½	**18**	33/1	46	—
	Fifth Emerald (CFWall) **2-8-9** AMcGlone(14) (lengthy: bkwd: bhd fr ½-wy)	½	**19**	20/1	40	—
4884[22]	**Shipley Glen** (SirMarkPrescott) **2-9-0** CNutter(7) (hld up & a bhd)	nk	**20**	33/1	44	—
4917[16]	**Regal Arrow** (AGFoster) **2-9-0** TSprake(4) (sn pushed along: outpcd fr ½-wy)	hd	**21**	33/1	44	—
				(SP 145.8%)		**21 Rn**

1m 17.73 (6.73) CSF £7.62 TOTE £2.70: £1.50 £2.80 £7.20 (£7.50) Trio £267.60 OWNER Mr Hamdan Al Maktoum (NEWMARKET) BRED Miss Audrey F. Thompson

4640 Masha-Il (IRE) fulfilled earlier promise with a battling success in what was nothing more than an average race. (7/4)

4904 Lindesberg made a gallant attempt, being in the front rank all the way. This half-sister to Gothenberg should come into her own next year. (9/2)

Fabrice looked burly and green beforehand but shaped with distinct promise. He can only improve. (16/1)

Shaji (IRE), a likeable individual who looked in need of the race, took time to grasp what was required but came home in fine style. Races will surely be won with him next year. (33/1)

4298 Aganon, having his third run, came home in eye-catching style under a noticeably sympathetic ride. Better things are surely in store. (20/1)

Rachaels North (IRE) made a promising debut and will do better with further experience and a winter on his back. (33/1)

Prima Facie (6/1: op 3/1)

Empire State (IRE), having his third run, was doing all his best work in the closing stages. (20/1)

Shipley Glen, having his third outing, was always out the back but should not be written off as being without some ability. (33/1)

5043 CPL INDUSTRIES CONDITIONS STKS (3-Y.O+) (Class C)

2-00 (2-01) **1m 6f 132y** £4,884.00 (£1,806.00: £865.50: £352.50: £138.75: £53.25) Stalls: Low GOING: 0.33 sec per fur (G)

				SP	RR	SF
4969[3]	**Sweetness Herself (98)** (MJRyan) **4-9-2** GCarter(1) (swtg: hld up: hdwy over 2f out: led appr fnl f: drvn clr)	—	**1**	6/1	107	58
4443[9]	**Elbaaha (87)** (MAJarvis) **3-8-4** SSanders(8) (hld up: hdwy to chse ldr 8f out: led over 3f out tl over 1f out: nt pce of wnr)	3	**2**	11/2[3]	100	43
4903*	**Wahiba Sands (100)** (JLDunlop) **4-9-5** KDarley(4) (b: dwlt: hld up: hdwy 6f out: rdn over 1f out: one pce)	1½	**3**	7/2[2]	105	56
4322*	**Carisbrooke** (HRACecil) **3-8-9** WRyan(5) (lw: led tl over 3f out: rdn & one pce appr fnl f)	nk	**4**	100/30[1]	103	46
4295[2]	**Beauchamp Jade (98)** (HCandy) **5-8-9** AMcGlone(2) (hld up: hdwy over 4f out: hrd drvn over 2f out: sn btn)	9	**5**	7/2[2]	85	36
4712*	**Star Precision (99)** (GBBalding) **3-8-6** SDrowne(7) (chsd ldr over 6f: pushed along over 3f out: sn lost tch: t.o)	13	**6**	7/1	76	19
1630[5]	**Mount Genius (USA)** (BobJones) **4-9-0** NDay(3) (bkwd: prom tl lost tch 7f out: sn t.o)	dist	**7**	66/1	—	—
4281[6]	***Sacho (IRE) (94)*** (JHMGosden) **4-9-3** GHind(6) (Withdrawn not under Starter's orders: veterinary advice)		**W**		—	—
				(SP 111.2%)		**7 Rn**

3m 16.16 (12.56) CSF £32.91 TOTE £5.50: £2.40 £2.50 (£15.00) OWNER Mrs M. J. Lavell (NEWMARKET) BRED Stud-On-The-Chart
WEIGHT FOR AGE 3yo-8lb

4969 Sweetness Herself, given a more patient ride and restrained as late as possible, showed her rivals a clean pair of heels when set alight and, though she has won in the spring, this is her time of year. (6/1)

4136 Elbaaha, having her first try at such an extended trip, struck the front some way out and did look to have control but, once the winner appeared on the scene, she must have wondered what had hit her. (11/2)

4903* Wahiba Sands made steady headway before reaching the turn into the straight and then sat on the tails of the leaders waiting to pounce, but he was tapped for speed when the winner quickened things up and had soon met his match. (7/2)

4322* Carisbrooke settled down in the lead but he had been collared over three furlongs out and, though he did not lose his pitch approaching the final furlong, found this company much stronger than he had met to date. (100/30)

4295 Beauchamp Jade has had a rather disappointing season and, though her trainer was at pains to prove she did not act on the ground, the times throughout the day suggested the going was probably little different to that on which she failed narrowly at Newbury on her previous outing. (7/2)

5044 RJB MINING LIONHEART CONDITIONS STKS (3-Y.O+ F & M) (Class C)

2-30 (2-30) **1m 2f 60y** £4,753.49 (£1,756.50: £840.75: £341.25: £133.13: £49.88) Stalls: Low GOING: 0.33 sec per fur (G)

				SP	RR	SF
4891[4]	**Oops Pettie (85)** (MrsJCecil) **4-8-12** MartinDwyer(2) (b: lw: trckd ldr: led wl over 1f out: drvn clr ent fnl f)	—	**1**	5/2[1]	99	72
4990[5]	**Unconditional Love (IRE) (96)** (MJohnston) **4-8-12** DHolland(7) (chsd ldrs: effrt over 2f out: kpt on fnl f: no ch w wnr)	5	**2**	9/2[3]	91	64
4268[7]	**Sweet Contralto (87)** (DRLoder) **3-8-12** JFortune(3) (led: rdn over 2f out: hdd wl over 1f out: no ex)	2½	**3**	5/1	91	60
4891[6]	**Mcgillycuddy Reeks (IRE) (72)** (DonEnricoIncisa) **6-8-12** KimTinkler(4) (lw: dwlt: hld up: effrt over 2f out: kpt on one pce fnl f: nvr trbld ldrs)	10	**4**	12/1	72	45
4859[4]	**Vanishing Trick (USA) (75)** (HRACecil) **3-8-8b** WRyan(5) (in tch: rdn 3f out: btn 2f out)	3	**5**	7/1	67	36
4882[7]	**Hachiyah (IRE) (88)** (DMorley) **3-8-12** RHills(6) (in tch: effrt 3f out: hung lft & wknd 2f out: eased fnl f)	7	**6**	7/2[2]	60	29
4990[9]	**Bea's Ruby (IRE) (89)** (ABailey) **3-9-2** GCarter(1) (b: lw: chsd ldrs tl rdn & btn 3f out: eased fnl 2f)	20	**7**	14/1	33	2
4516[10]	**Absolutelystunning (45)** (MrsBarbaraWaring) **4-9-1ow3** EByrne(8) (s.s: a bhd: lost tch fnl 3f: t.o)	8	**8**	50/1	16	—
				(SP 114.5%)		**8 Rn**

2m 14.3 (6.50) CSF £12.76 TOTE £2.80: £1.20 £1.40 £2.10 (£3.70) OWNER Mrs D. MacRae (NEWMARKET) BRED D. Macrae
WEIGHT FOR AGE 3yo-4lb

4891 Oops Pettie fulfilled the promise of her recent effort over this course and distance by winning in emphatic style. She now goes to the paddocks. (5/2)

4990 Unconditional Love (IRE) was no match for the winner and, although keeping on to finish a clear second best, swished her tail under pressure. (9/2)

3741* Sweet Contralto, off the course for seven weeks since her last run, was easily brushed aside by the winner inside the final quarter-mile. (5/1)
4891 Mcgillycuddy Reeks (IRE) had little chance at the weights here and ran as well as could be expected. (12/1)
4859 Vanishing Trick (USA) was on the retreat fully three furlongs out. (7/1)
3263 Hachiyah (IRE) proved disappointing and faded tamely when pressure was applied. (7/2)

5045 AMCO CORPORATION NURSERY H'CAP (0-85) (2-Y.O) (Class D)
3-00 (3-02) **5f** £3,526.75 (£1,054.00: £504.50: £229.75) Stalls: High GOING: 0.33 sec per fur (G)

				SP	RR	SF
4634[9]	**Escudo (IRE) (77)** (JHMGosden) **2-9-1** GHind(8) (b.hind: in tch: rdn 2f out: hdwy appr fnl f: r.o to ld post)	—	**1**	7/1	81	29
4566[2]	**Rita's Rock Ape (68)** (RBrotherton) **2-8-6** AMackay(1) (led: clr ½-wy: rdn fnl f: ct last stride)	s.h	**2**	8/1	72	20
4970[2]	**Classy Cleo (IRE) (86)** (PDEvans) **2-9-10** 7x JFEgan(7) (sn bhd & outpcd: hdwy u.p appr fnl f: fin wl)	1¼	**3**	5/1[2]	86	34
4875[14]	**Suivez La Trace (67)** (JJO'Neill) **2-8-2**(3) PFessey(6) (a chsng ldrs: kpt on u.p fnl f)	1	**4**	20/1	64	12
4911[2]	**Rare Indigo (81)** (JBerry) **2-9-2**(3) CLowther(3) (chsd ldr: rdn along wl over 1f out: one pce)	nk	**5**	4/1[1]	77	25
4897[16]	**Smooth Sailing (83)** (KMcAuliffe) **2-9-7** JFortune(2) (trckd ldrs: rdn over 2f out: kpt on fnl f)	nk	**6**	20/1	78	26
4948[5]	**Ivory's Joy (75)** (KTIvory) **2-8-6**(7) SCarson(5) (trckd ldrs: outpcd 2f out: sn btn)	½	**7**	16/1	68	16
3791[3]	**Dim Ots (82)** (BPalling) **2-9-6** TSprake(11) (a bhd & outpcd)	hd	**8**	10/1	75	23
4948[7]	**Touchanova (62)** (AHide) **2-8-0** JLowe(9) (outpcd)	2½	**9**	33/1	47	—
4921[8]	**Cool Prospect (75)** (ABMulholland) **2-8-13** TLucas(4) (lw: rdn along ½-wy: nvr on terms)	3	**10**	12/1	50	—
4818[13]	**Game Bird (66)** (JLSpearing) **2-8-4** SDrowne(10) (outpcd: rdn 2f out: no imp)	1¼	**11**	20/1	37	—
4948[2]	**Carol Singer (USA) (72)** (MJohnston) **2-8-10** DHolland(12) (outpcd)	4	**12**	11/2[3]	30	—
4796[8]	**Legal Lark (IRE) (70)** (PHowling) **2-8-8** JQuinn(13) (outpcd)	1¾	**13**	16/1	23	—

(SP 121.4%) **13 Rn**

64.15 secs (5.75) CSF £54.19 CT £293.11 TOTE £8.00: £1.90 £4.10 £1.90 (£50.30) Trio £109.90 OWNER Sheikh Mohammed (NEWMARKET) BRED Miss Rita B. Kennedy
4634 Escudo (IRE), back over her ideal trip, had to work hard to score and she looked unlikely to succeed until the leader tied up a bit in the dying strides. (7/1)
4566 Rita's Rock Ape blazed the trail and looked to have gone beyond recall but the more testing ground took its toll and she was shaded right on the line. (8/1)
4970 Classy Cleo (IRE) had it all to do under a 7lb penalty and for most of the way looked more likely to finish last than first, but she is as game as they come and, struggling on under strong pressure, took third place close home. (5/1)
3899 Suivez La Trace, taking a big step down in distance, tracked the leaders all the way and, though he battled on gamely inside the last couple of furlongs, could not muster the pace to deliver his challenge. (20/1)
4911 Rare Indigo has got plenty of speed but she was unable to match strides with the tearaway leader and, driven along from halfway, was certainly far from disgraced in defeat. (4/1: 3/1-9/2)
4218 Smooth Sailing, returning to the minimum trip, was having trouble holding his pitch at halfway but he did keep persevering, and was gradually getting back into it at the finish. (20/1)

5046 DRANSFIELD NOVELTY COMPANY CONDITIONS STKS (2-Y.O) (Class C)
3-30 (3-30) **1m (straight)** £4,428.20 (£1,593.20: £761.60: £308.00: £119.00) Stalls: High GOING: 0.33 sec per fur (G)

				SP	RR	SF
4908*	**Derryquin** (RCharlton) **2-9-1** TSprake(1) (lw: trckd ldrs gng wl: led over 1f out: drvn out)	—	**1**	5/2[2]	95	44
4857*	**Angstrom (IRE)** (MRStoute) **2-9-1** TQuinn(3) (swtchd & racd alone stands' side: led tl hung bdly lft 3f out: kpt on u.p fnl f)	1¾	**2**	5/4[1]	92	41
4871[4]	**Love Kiss (IRE)** (MJohnston) **2-8-11** DHolland(4) (led centre: rdn over 2f out: hdd over 1f out: no ex)	3	**3**	6/1	82	31
4892[6]	**Swing Sister (85)** (PRWebber) **2-8-8** DaneO'Neill(5) (chsd ldrs: rdn along & outpcd wl over 2f out: kpt on fnl f)	nk	**4**	9/2[3]	78	27
4895[4]	**Stingray (IRE)** (MJohnston) **2-8-11** DeanMcKeown(2) (lw: a bhd & outpcd fr ½-wy)	3	**5**	16/1	75	24

(SP 111.4%) **5 Rn**

1m 45.22 (8.02) CSF £5.59 TOTE £3.70: £1.30 £1.30 (£2.10) OWNER Lady Bland (BECKHAMPTON) BRED Lady Bland
4908* Derryquin stepped up on his Lingfield success over this extra furlong, and looks the type to progress further as a three-year-old. (5/2)
4857* Angstrom (IRE), whose rider elected to race close to the stands' rail on his own, hung badly left to join the other runners in the centre of the course three furlongs out. Considering how much ground he forfeited, he ran well in the circumstances. (5/4: 10/11-11/8)
4871 Love Kiss (IRE), a grand stamp of an individual, did much of the donkey work before being tapped for toe in the closing stages. Better will be seen of him next year. (6/1)
4709 Swing Sister clearly stays well and, after becoming outpaced when the tempo increased, stuck on well again inside the final furlong. (9/2)
Stingray (IRE) was never really at the races here but was not beaten all that far in the end. An imposing-looking colt, it will be disappointing if he does not show marked improvement as a three-year-old. (16/1)

5047 C.I.S.W.O. H'CAP (0-80) (3-Y.O+) (Class D)
4-00 (4-01) **5f** £4,240.00 (£1,270.00: £610.00: £280.00) Stalls: High GOING: 0.33 sec per fur (G)

				SP	RR	SF
4844[4]	**Southern Dominion (51)** (MissJFCraze) **5-7-13b** TWilliams(6) (mde all: rdn fnl f: r.o wl)	—	**1**	9/1[2]	62	38
4636[5]	**Palo Blanco (67)** (GLMoore) **6-9-1** CandyMorris(7) (a.p: jnd wnr appr fnl f: rdn & no ex cl home)	½	**2**	14/1	76	52
4844*	**Mungo Park (62)** (MrsJRRamsden) **3-8-10** JFortune(13) (hdwy over 2f out: kpt on u.p ins fnl f)	1	**3**	7/1[1]	68	44
4770*	**Polly Golightly (61)** (MBlanshard) **4-8-9b** DaleGibson(17) (a.p: rdn & ev ch over 1f out: unable qckn fnl f)	hd	**4**	9/1[2]	67	43
4820[10]	**Swino (68)** (PDEvans) **3-9-2v** JFEgan(1) (a.p: rdn over 1f out: r.o)	nk	**5**	16/1	73	49
4878[5]	**Jeffrey Anotherred (78)** (MDods) **3-9-12** FLynch(2) (chsd ldrs: rdn & unable qckn fnl f)	1	**6**	14/1	80	56
4842[12]	**Bowlers Boy (76)** (JJQuinn) **4-9-10** SDrowne(14) (lw: sn trckng ldrs: kpt on one pce fnl f)	½	**7**	14/1	76	52
4844[2]	**Sue Me (IRE) (56)** (DNicholls) **5-7-11**(7) ANicholls(3) (hdwy appr fnl f: nvr nrr)	s.h	**8**	12/1	56	32
4997[4]	**Just Bob (75)** (SEKettlewell) **8-9-9** ACulhane(8) (hdwy 2f out: nvr nrr)	½	**9**	14/1	73	49
4696[18]	**Divide And Rule (53)** (RHollinshead) **3-7-12**(3) RFfrench(4) (wnt rt s: sn in tch: rdn over 1f out: one pce)	1	**10**	33/1	48	24
4770[6]	**Pallium (IRE) (51)** (DANolan) **9-7-10b**(3) PFessey(9) (b.hind: chsd ldrs: no hdwy fnl 2f)	¾	**11**	25/1	44	20
4905[2]	**Broadstairs Beauty (IRE) (66)** (DShaw) **7-8-11v**(3) CTeague(12) (b: lw: drvn along 2f out: no imp)	1	**12**	7/1[1]	56	32
4995[15]	**Kira (80)** (JLEyre) **7-9-7**(7) SBuckley(16) (b: b.hind: drvn along ½-wy: nvr trbld ldrs)	½	**13**	14/1	68	44
4770[13]	**Goretski (IRE) (77)** (NTinkler) **4-9-11** LCharnock(10) (prom tl wknd appr fnl f)	½	**14**	20/1	63	39
4385[12]	**Tropical Beach (53)** (JPearce) **4-8-1** GBardwell(11) (a in rr)	1½	**15**	33/1	35	11
4770[12]	**Pride of Brixton (66)** (CWThornton) **4-9-0** DeanMcKeown(22) (w ldrs: rdn & hung lft 2f out: btn appr fnl f)	nk	**16**	25/1	47	23
4787[8]	**Pleading (72)** (WJMusson) **4-9-6** MWigham(21) (a bhd & outpcd)	¾	**17**	16/1	50	26

			SP	RR	SF
4365*	**Swan At Whalley (68)** (RAFahey) **5-8-11**(5) RWinston(19) (swtchd lft s: a in rr)	2½ **18**	11/1[3]	38	14
4844[14]	**Swynford Dream (68)** (JHetherton) **4-9-2** JLowe(20) (sn outpcd)	hd **19**	14/1	38	14
4636[21]	**Sweet Magic (62)** (PHowling) **6-8-10** KDarley(15) (outpcd)	1 **20**	20/1	29	5
4844[3]	**Mon Bruce (63)** (MDods) **3-8-11** JCarroll(18) (lw: prom over 3f)	½ **21**	12/1	28	4
4248[16]	**Captain Carat (58)** (RonaldThompson) **6-8-6**bow[3] VHalliday(5) (bmpd s: a bhd: t.o)	7 **22**	25/1	1	—
			(SP 147.4%)	**22 Rn**	

62.72 secs (4.32) CSF £126.42 CT £905.97 TOTE £13.90: £3.10 £6.80 £1.80 £2.60 (£181.20) Trio £716.00 OWNER Mrs Angela Wilson (YORK) BRED A. Wilkinson and J. W. Brown

4844 Southern Dominion was drawn on the correct side on this occasion and, showing his usual blistering speed, deservedly held on to the end. (9/1)

4636 Palo Blanco possibly needs a sounder surface than she had here, but she pressed the winner all the way, and the 16lb weight difference must have been telling in the all-out sprint to the finish. (14/1)

4844* Mungo Park edged closer over two furlongs out but did not really find top gear until the race was virtually over. (7/1)

4770* Polly Golightly had a chance second to none entering the final furlong but, hard as she tried, an extra burst of pace was missing when it was most needed. (9/1)

4791* Swino, always pushing the pace out in the centre of the track, never once stopped trying but, with the tempo not dropping, just could not summon the speed to get to terms. (16/1)

4878 Jeffrey Anotherred has had a barren year and, though he did win at this time last season at this track, he was always fighting a lost cause. (14/1)

4805 Bowlers Boy was sluggish leaving the stalls and, although soon recovering to track the leaders, could never find the speed to land a blow. Nonetheless this was a very promising performance and he could well win another if he tries his luck on the All-Weather. (14/1)

4844 Sue Me (IRE) came out of the pack and finished best of all, but he finds this trip just too sharp, and needs at least another furlong. (12/1)

4905 Broadstairs Beauty (IRE) usually goes with the pace but he was soon being bustled along, and was never able to get himself into the action. (7/1)

T/Jkpt: Not won; £6,603.64 to Doncaster 8/11/97. T/Plpt: £1,331.40 (16.4 Tckts). T/Qdpt: £26.30 (84.06 Tckts) IM/O'R

5040-DONCASTER (L-H) (Good to soft becoming Soft)
Saturday November 8th
WEATHER: sunny periods WIND: fresh against

5048 B.O.C. SUREFLOW MEDIAN AUCTION MAIDEN STKS (2-Y.O) (Class E)
12-50 (12-56) **1m (straight)** £3,665.00 (£1,100.00: £530.00: £245.00) Stalls: High GOING: 0.86 sec per fur (S)

			SP	RR	SF
4793[2]	**Eco Friendly (77)** (BWHills) **2-9-0** DHolland(16) (chsd ldrs: nt clr run & swtchd lft over 1f out: rdn to ld nr fin)	— **1**	7/1[2]	83	43
4793[4]	**Double Edged** (MJohnston) **2-9-0** JFEgan(9) (lw: chsd ldrs: led over 2f out: rdn, wandered & hdd wl ins fnl f)	½ **2**	9/1	82	42
4638[2]	**Achilles (92)** (RAkehurst) **2-9-0** SSanders(12) (a w ldrs: chal over 2f out: one pce fnl f)	3 **3**	6/4[1]	76	36
4917[6]	**Ribblesdale** (JLDunlop) **2-8-9** TQuinn(19) (trckd ldrs: rdn wl over 1f out: styd on)	1½ **4**	9/1	68	28
	Zomaradah (LMCumani) **2-8-6**(3) RFfrench(15) (w'like: scope: bit bkwd: dwlt: bhd: nt clr run & swtchd 2f out: styd on strly fnl f)	2 **5**	8/1[3]	64+	24
4917[5]	**Sherganzar (81)** (MSalaman) **2-9-0** DaneO'Neill(17) (mid div: effrt & nt clr run 2f out: styd on fnl f)	s.h **6**	10/1	69	29
4914[6]	**Telalanjon** (TGMills) **2-9-0** SWhitworth(14) (bit bkwd: hdwy over 2f out: nt rch ldrs)	2½ **7**	16/1	64	24
4855[3]	**Absalom's Lad** (PWHarris) **2-9-0** ACulhane(7) (mid div: styd on one pce fnl 2f)	nk **8**	8/1[3]	63	23
4950[8]	**Slip Venture** (SPCWoods) **2-9-0** NDay(4) (trckd ldrs over 6f)	s.h **9**	33/1	63	23
4974[4]	**The Robe** (BJMeehan) **2-8-9** MTebbutt(8) (cl up: led ½-wy tl over 2f out)	4 **10**	16/1	50	10
	Formation Dancer (PWHarris) **2-9-0** JFortune(22) (leggy: scope: s.s: a in rr)	½ **11**	20/1	54	14
	She's A Gem (MrsNMacauley) **2-8-9** SDrowne(6) (lt-f: unf: chsd ldrs over 5f)	hd **12**	50/1	49	9
4111[10]	**Lady Felix (55)** (SMellor) **2-8-9** RPerham(13) (bit bkwd: a in rr)	nk **13**	50/1	48	8
4952[9]	**Sunstreak** (CFWall) **2-9-0** GDuffield(3) (bkwd: edgy in stalls: nvr trbld ldrs)	1¾ **14**	33/1	50	10
4793[10]	**Manila Moon (USA)** (JJO'Neill) **2-8-11**(3) PFessey(2) (bit bkwd: led to ½-wy: grad wknd)	3½ **15**	33/1	43	3
	Bank On Him (GLMoore) **2-9-0** MWigham(11) (lt-f: a bhd)	s.h **16**	33/1	43	3
	Ornamental (JRFanshawe) **2-8-9** TSprake(5) (neat: bkwd: prom over 5f: wknd qckly)	4 **17**	12/1	30	—
4567[7]	**Kierans Bridge (IRE)** (APJarvis) **2-8-6**(3) CLowther(10) (a bhd)	1¾ **18**	33/1	26	—
	Gold Hawk (BSmart) **2-9-0** JStack(20) (cmpt: bkwd: chsd ldrs over 5f: sn lost tch)	1¼ **19**	20/1	29	—
4873[16]	**Lady of The Dance** (MAJarvis) **2-8-9** RCochrane(18) (lost tch ½-wy: t.o)	7 **20**	33/1	10	—
4949[6]	**Tigullio (IRE)** (CFWall) **2-9-0** GHind(21) (bit bkwd: spd over 4f: t.o)	nk **21**	33/1	14	—
4908[8]	**Zada** (GLMoore) **2-9-0** CandyMorris(1) (cl up 5f: sn wknd: t.o)	4 **22**	50/1	6	—
			(SP 159.3%)	**22 Rn**	

1m 49.46 (12.26) CSF £71.87 TOTE £5.70: £2.30 £3.70 £1.10 (£30.20) Trio £20.10 OWNER Mr W. J. Gredley (LAMBOURN) BRED Stetchworth Park Stud Ltd

4793 Eco Friendly, not winning out of turn, is certainly not short on stamina and on this rain-saturated ground it was only his superior strength that got him home. (7/1)

4793 Double Edged finished closer to the winner than he did when they last clashed, and if he had not run about a bit under strong pressure inside the distance it is more than possible he would have held on. (9/1: op 6/1)

4638 Achilles, supported to the exclusion of the rest, has proved he can act in testing ground and he was always going to be the one to beat, but his stride shortened rapidly inside the last furlong and he finished tired. (6/4)

4917 Ribblesdale seemed well suited by the step up to a mile, and though she was unable to find the pace to get to terms, she kept battling on and looks an interesting prospect for next season. (9/1: op 6/1)

Zomaradah, a strongly-made, good quartered filly, who should have no trouble staying twelve furlongs, did not enjoy the run of the race but she was noted staying on strongly nearing the finish and she could make a name for herself next term. (8/1: 6/1-9/1)

4917 Sherganzar, restrained just behind the leaders, was denied a clear passage entering the final quarter-mile but he did stay on once into the final furlong and is forever knocking at the door. (10/1)

5049 TOTE LADY RIDERS' CHAMPIONSHIP H'CAP (0-80) (3-Y.O+) (Class E)

1-20 (1-28) **1m (straight)** £4,272.50 (£1,280.00: £615.00: £282.50) Stalls: High GOING: 1.12 sec per fur (S)

Form	Horse / details	Dist	Pos	SP	RR	SF
4972*	**Tipperary Sunset (IRE) (56)** (JJQuinn) **3-10-0** MrsLPearce(4) (lw: hdwy ½-wy: styd on wl to ld ins fnl f)	—	**1**	7/1[2]	70	50
4629*	**Ca'd'oro (62)** (GBBalding) **4-10-3**(5) MissSNewby-Vincent(11) (lw: trckd ldrs: led over 1f out tl ins fnl f: no ex)	½	**2**	11/1	75	57
4848*	**Mount Holly (USA) (75)** (JHMGosden) **3-11-5** MissERamsden(14) (mid div: outpcd 3f out: hdwy over 1f out: hung bdly lft: styd on wl)	2	**3**	6/1[1]	84	64
4979[4]	**Jibereen (61)** (PHowling) **5-10-2**(5) MissIFoustok(8) (b: in tch: hdwy over 2f out: styd on wl towards fin)	2½	**4**	11/1	65	47
4951[3]	**Mybotye (59)** (RBastiman) **4-10-0**(5) MissRBastiman(21) (a chsng ldrs: rdn over 2f out: one pce)	1¾	**5**	12/1	60	42
4924[21]	**Chairmans Choice (53)** (APJarvis) **7-9-8**(5) MissSSamworth(1) (led: sn clr: hdd & wknd over 1f out)	½	**6**	20/1	53	35
4920[4]	**Xylem (USA) (72)** (LMCumani) **6-10-13**(5) MissLAndersen(13) (wl bhd tl hdwy 2f out: styd on wl)	2	**7**	12/1	68	50
4842[18]	**Takhlid (USA) (60)** (DWChapman) **6-10-6** MissRClark(12) (in tch tl outpcd fnl 2½f)	2½	**8**	16/1	51	33
4997*	**Afaan (IRE) (73)** (RFMarvin) **4-11-0**(5) 5x MissRFlynn(20) (b: hdwy fnl 2f: n.d)	½	**9**	12/1	63	45
4979[11]	**Night of Glass (64)** (JLEyre) **4-10-10b** MissJAllison(9) (b: drvn along over 3f out: n.d)	1	**10**	14/1	52	34
4781[26]	**Anonym (IRE) (59)** (JLEyre) **5-10-5b** MissPRobson(15) (outpcd ½-wy: n.d)	1	**11**	20/1	45	27
4732[6]	**Bend Wavy (IRE) (75)** (THCaldwell) **5-11-2**(5) MrsPWharfe(3) (chsd ldrs tl outpcd fnl 2½f)	¾	**12**	33/1	59	41
4920[7]	**Suez Tornado (IRE) (64)** (EJAlston) **4-10-5v**(5) MissKimJones(10) (nvr bttr than mid div)	½	**13**	20/1	47	29
4410[10]	**Sycamore Lodge (IRE) (63)** (MAPeill) **6-10-4**(5) MrsAHammond(18) (s.i.s: hdwy 3f out: nvr rchd ldrs)	nk	**14**	20/1	45	27
4781[10]	**Cashmere Lady (74)** (JLEyre) **5-11-6** MissDianaJones(16) (in tch: effrt 3f out: grad wknd)	hd	**15**	11/1	56	38
4978[11]	**Grand Musica (74)** (IABalding) **4-11-1**(5) MissSHiggins(5) (lw: outpcd & no ch fr ½-wy)	4	**16**	11/1	48	30
4920[12]	**No More Pressure (IRE) (75)** (MrsJRRamsden) **3-11-0**(5) MissADeniel(19) (n.d)	2	**17**	16/1	45	25
4979[2]	**Braveheart (IRE) (71)** (MRChannon) **3-11-1** MissEJohnsonHoughton(17) (prom: effrt over 2f out: sn wknd)	½	**18**	9/1	40	20
4504[10]	**Dark Age (IRE) (52)** (RAkehurst) **4-9-7**(5) MrsKHills(2) (outpcd fr ½-wy)	1½	**19**	33/1	18	—
4441[11]	**Rebel County (IRE) (71)** (ABailey) **4-11-3v** MissAElsey(24) (a bhd)	hd	**20**	8/1[3]	37	19
4842[11]	**Knotty Hill (67)** (RCraggs) **5-10-8**(5) MissNicolaCraggs(6) (spd 5f: wknd)	8	**21**	33/1	17	—
4628[9]	**Sis Garden (58)** (JCullinan) **4-9-13**(5) MissEmmaGarley(22) (spd stands' side over 5f)	1	**22**	25/1	6	—
4757[30]	**Waikiki Beach (USA) (62)** (GLMoore) **6-10-8** MrsJMoore(23) (spd stands' side over 4f: wknd qckly: sddle slipped)	6	**23**	20/1	—	—

(SP 159.2%) **23 Rn**

1m 52.1 (14.90) CSF £82.91 CT £489.47 TOTE £6.80: £1.60 £3.50 £1.60 £4.70 (£67.40) Trio £56.10 OWNER Mr Harold Bray (MALTON) BRED M. G. Masterson

WEIGHT FOR AGE 3yo-2lb

4972* Tipperary Sunset (IRE) has improved no end and, despite again showing a tendency to hang left, he did the business well enough. (7/1)

4629* Ca'd'oro had the ground and the trip in his favour, but despite a gallant effort was just outbattled. (11/1)

4848* Mount Holly (USA) was racing on the slower ground towards the stands' side, but in the end he hung badly left and finished up on the far rails, making useful late progress. He is certainly not a straightforward ride. (6/1)

4979 Jibereen is in good heart for a return to the All-Weather. (11/1)

4951 Mybotye had his chances, but this trip was probably just stretching things enough. (12/1)

3153 Chairmans Choice showed bags of toe here and this was his best effort for a while. (20/1)

4920 Xylem (USA) came from a mile behind to finish twice as fast as any and was probably racing in the slower ground. (12/1)

4283 Rebel County (IRE) (8/1: op 12/1)

5050 CLUB MEMBERS FINANCIAL SERVICES NURSERY H'CAP (2-Y.O) (Class D)

1-50 (1-56) **7f** £4,370.00 (£1,310.00: £630.00: £290.00) Stalls: High GOING: 1.12 sec per fur (S)

Form	Horse / details	Dist	Pos	SP	RR	SF
4801[3]	**Scene (IRE) (66)** (MartynMeade) **2-7-10** LCharnock(2) (mde all: rdn & hld on gamely towards fin)	—	**1**	20/1	70	22
4953[4]	**Alconleigh (91)** (MJohnston) **2-9-7** DHolland(3) (lw: a.p: ev ch ins fnl f: hrd rdn: kpt on)	¾	**2**	10/1	93	45
4566[3]	**I Cried For You (IRE) (66)** (RHannon) **2-7-10** DWright(1) (a chsng ldrs: effrt over 2f out: kpt on u.p fnl f)	½	**3**	14/1	67	19
4974[7]	**Bali Dance (67)** (CBBBooth) **2-7-8**(3)ow1 PFessey(7) (a.p: rdn & styd on fnl 2f)	1¼	**4**	33/1	65?	16
3932[9]	**Rioja (74)** (TPTate) **2-8-4**ow1 TLucas(5) (in tch: effrt & rdn over 2f out: one pce)	1½	**5**	25/1	69	20
4588[9]	**Brookhouse Lady (IRE) (66)** (RHollinshead) **2-7-3**(7) PMQuinn(16) (styd on appr fnl f: nvr on terms)	½	**6**	33/1	60?	12
4989[2]	**Inchalong (73)** (MBrittain) **2-7-10**(7) DMernagh(22) (cl up stands' side: rdn & outpcd over 2f out: styd on ins fnl f)	nk	**7**	4/1[1]	66	18
4900[2]	**Zuryaf (IRE) (67)** (BJMeehan) **2-7-11b** TWilliams(14) (sn drvn along: nvr trbld ldrs)	2	**8**	16/1	56	8
4634[8]	**Branston Berry (IRE) (82)** (JLEyre) **2-8-5**(7) SBuckley(8) (lw: prom: rdn 2f out: one pce)	d.h	**8**	10/1	71	23
4778[18]	**Legend of Love (74)** (JAGlover) **2-8-4** NDay(9) (trckd ldrs centre over 5f)	2½	**10**	20/1	57	9
4989*	**Five of Spades (IRE) (84)** (RAFahey) **2-8-9**(5) 7x RWinston(10) (prom: effrt over 2f out: sn wknd)	hd	**11**	7/1[2]	67	19
4885[5]	**Naviasky (IRE) (72)** (MrsJRRamsden) **2-8-2** GDuffield(4) (chsd ldrs far side: rdn over 2f out: grad wknd)	1	**12**	7/1[2]	52	4
4807*	**Itch (77)** (RBastiman) **2-8-7** TQuinn(12) (lost tch fnl 3f)	1½	**13**	14/1	54	6
4806[10]	**Chlo-Jo (66)** (AGFoster) **2-7-10** GBardwell(6) (a in rr)	nk	**14**	25/1	42	—
4897[B]	**Moonstone (IRE) (74)** (APJarvis) **2-8-1**(3) CLowther(15) (a in rr)	¾	**15**	14/1	48	—
4989[3]	**Demolition Jo (82)** (PDEvans) **2-8-5v**(7) AMcCarthy(18) (trckd ldrs centre: hrd rdn over 1f out: sn wknd)	nk	**16**	9/1	56	8
4897[3]	**Hill Magic (84)** (DRCElsworth) **2-8-11**(3) RFfrench(21) (lw: racd stands' side: nvr nr ldrs)	s.h	**17**	8/1[3]	58	10
4362[13]	**Boulevard Rouge (USA) (77)** (MJohnston) **2-8-7** DeanMcKeown(20) (a bhd)	3½	**18**	14/1	43	—
4767*	**Ray of Sunshine (IRE) (74)** (MrsJRRamsden) **2-8-4** DO'Donohoe(13) (b.nr fore: in tch 4f)	1¾	**19**	7/1[2]	36	—
3904[6]	**Out Like Magic (81)** (PDEvans) **2-8-11** JFEgan(17) (a bhd: t.o)	15	**20**	14/1	8	—
4922[13]	**Wait'n'see (69)** (MWEasterby) **2-7-13** DaleGibson(11) (bhd fr ½-wy: t.o)	10	**21**	25/1	—	—
4922[12]	**Two Williams (66)** (MWEasterby) **2-7-10** JQuinn(19) (a bhd: t.o)	nk	**22**	25/1	—	—

(SP 166.8%) **22 Rn**

1m 37.32 (12.82) CSF £225.46 CT £1,594.59 TOTE £35.20: £7.50 £2.30 £5.60 £21.20 (£178.00) Trio £361.10 OWNER Mr Paul Dixon (MALMESBURY) BRED T. E. Fitzsimons

LONG HANDICAP Brookhouse Lady (IRE) 6-13 Scene (IRE) 7-7 Chlo-Jo 7-8 Bali Dance 6-10 I Cried For You (IRE) 7-9

4801 Scene (IRE) decided on more forceful tactics on ground she has proved she acts on and, defying her rivals to catch her, showed the right attitude when strongly pressed throughout the final furlong. (20/1)

4953 Alconleigh, brought back to seven furlongs, was in the action all the way but the concession of 25lb in this bottomless ground was certainly asking a lot. There is no disgrace in this defeat. (10/1)

4566 I Cried For You (IRE) ran well in this step up in distance, and the way he battled on in the closing stages would suggest that this is what he needs. (14/1)
4595 Bali Dance ran possibly her best race yet and, with stamina appearing not to be a problem, especially at this trip, she could come in to her own as a three-year-old. (33/1)
3270 Rioja travelled well and always looked assured of taking a hand in the outcome, but he failed to pick up inside the final furlong and may need more time. (25/1)
4382 Brookhouse Lady (IRE) performed best of the higher-number stalls but she was only finding her stride when it was all to late. (33/1)
4989 Inchalong was never happy on this rain-softened ground, but she is as brave as they come and she did not fail for the want of trying. (4/1: op 6/1)

5051 CIU INJURED JOCKEYS FUND SERLBY STKS (Listed) (3-Y.O+) (Class A)

2-25 (2-29) **1m 4f** £11,102.00 (£4,118.00: £1,984.00: £820.00: £335.00: £141.00) Stalls: Low GOING: 0.89 sec per fur (S)

				SP	RR	SF
4894⁴	**Taufan's Melody (109)** (LadyHerries) **6-8-13** RCochrane(8) (racd wd: mde most: rdn clr fnl 2½f)	—	**1**	11/4 2	120	79
4863a²	**Tamure (IRE) (110)** (JHMGosden) **5-8-13** WRyan(7) (chsd ldrs: effrt 4f out: styd on: no ch w wnr)	13	**2**	3/1 3	103	62
4968⁸	**Zugudi (80)** (KMahdi) **3-8-7** JFortune(4) (lw: chsd ldrs: outpcd ent st: kpt on fnl 2f: no imp)	5	**3**	33/1	96	49
4866a⁵	**Annaba (IRE) (113)** (JHMGosden) **4-8-8** GHind(1) (led on ins: rdn 4f out: wknd fnl 2½f)	1	**4**	11/8 1	90	49
4893⁶	**Grief (IRE) (91)** (DRCElsworth) **4-8-13** RFfrench(6) (b: outpcd tl styd on fnl 4f: n.d)	3½	**5**	20/1	90	49
4882⁴	**Bubble Wings (FR) (72)** (SPCWoods) **5-8-8** NDay(5) (outpcd ½-wy: n.d)	10	**6**	25/1	72	31
4631*	**Basman (IRE) (102)** (BSmart) **3-8-7** JStack(9) (racd wd: chsd wnr tl wknd fnl 4f)	8	**7**	11/1	66	19
4894⁹	**Suplizi (IRE) (98)** (PBowen) **6-8-13** MFenton(2) (in tch: pushed along 7f out: sn wknd & t.o)	dist	**8**	33/1	—	—
4971*	**Ordained (59)** (EJAlston) **4-8-8** AMackay(10) (lw: racd wd: chsd ldrs tl wknd fnl 4f: t.o)	2½	**9**	50/1	—	—
4903³	**Secret Ballot (IRE) (78)** (KMahdi) **3-8-7** MBaird(3) (lw: chsd ldrs tl wknd fnl 4f: t.o)	3	**10**	25/1	—	—

(SP 122.4%) **10 Rn**

2m 43.52 (13.52) CSF £10.13 TOTE £4.60: £1.60 £1.50 £7.30 (£6.90) Trio £352.00 OWNER All At Sea (LITTLEHAMPTON) BRED Midhurst Farm Inc
WEIGHT FOR AGE 3yo-6lb
4894 Taufan's Melody picked his way around the wide outside finding the better ground, and drew right away in the last three furlongs. Full credit for this should go to his rider. (11/4)
4863a Tamure (IRE) finished up best of those racing on the inside but he had no chance with the winner. (3/1)
4854 Zugudi looked to have little chance in this event but he ran pretty well to show just what a frustrating character he is. (33/1)
4866a Annaba (IRE) was getting slightly warm beforehand and ran poorly on ground that should have been right up her street. (11/8: evens-6/4)
4893 Grief (IRE) had plenty on here and only got going once the race was over. (20/1)
4882 Bubble Wings (FR) was always finding this company far too hot. (25/1)

5052 COALITE DRAGON H'CAP (0-95) (3-Y.O+) (Class C)

2-55 (2-56) **2m 110y** £8,090.00 (£2,420.00: £1,160.00: £530.00) Stalls: Low GOING: 0.89 sec per fur (S)

				SP	RR	SF
4744⁶	**Opaque (68)** (WStorey) **5-8-6** JFortune(3) (hld up: hdwy 4f out: led wl over 1f out: edgd lft: sn clr: styd on strly)	—	**1**	14/1	81	50
4879¹⁰	**Galapino (69)** (MissGayKelleway) **4-8-2**(5) RMullen(14) (s.s: hdwy 6f out: swtchd ins 3f out: nt clr run 2f out: rdn & r.o wl fnl f)	1¾	**2**	14/1	80	49
4874⁶	**Moon Colony (75)** (LadyHerries) **4-8-13** RCochrane(17) (hld up & bhd: hdwy 7f out: chsng ldrs 3f out: kpt on one pce)	2	**3**	10/1	84	53
4956*	**Jawah (IRE) (82)** (KMahdi) **3-8-8**(3) CLowther(13) (b.hind: hld up & bhd: hdwy 5f out: chsng ldrs appr fnl f: no imp)	2½	**4**	4/1 1	89	49
4956³	**Beaumont (IRE) (75)** (JEBanks) **7-8-10**(3) RFfrench(4) (lw: chsd ldrs: lost pl over 4f out: styd on appr fnl f)	3	**5**	12/1	79	48
4783¹³	**Merit (IRE) (80)** (PFICole) **5-9-4** TQuinn(9) (a chsng ldrs: ev ch fnl 3f: hrd rdn & wknd appr fnl f)	s.h	**6**	8/1	84	53
4956¹²	**Thaljanah (IRE) (75)** (BSmart) **5-8-13** JStack(5) (lw: hdwy 8f out: led over 4f out tl over 2f out: wknd over 1f out)	3½	**7**	16/1	76	45
4783¹⁴	**Shirley Sue (70)** (MJohnston) **4-8-8** RHills(10) (hld up: hdwy 4f out: rdn & no imp fnl 2f)	7	**8**	16/1	64	33
4783⁷	**Shadirwan (IRE) (68)** (RAkehurst) **6-8-6** SSanders(7) (lw: chsd ldr tl wknd fnl 3f)	½	**9**	8/1	61	30
4879³	**Etterby Park (USA) (76)** (MJohnston) **4-9-0** JFanning(16) (hld up: hdwy ½-wy: wknd over 3f out)	1¾	**10**	10/1	68	37
4874⁵	**Forgie (IRE) (77)** (PCalver) **4-9-1** NDay(1) (hld up: hdwy ent st: led over 2f out tl wl over 1f out: sn wknd)	1¾	**11**	15/2 3	67	36
4744⁹	**Turgenev (IRE) (74)** (RBastiman) **8-8-12** WRyan(2) (led tl hdd over 4f out: sn lost tch: t.o)	18	**12**	14/1	47	16
4783⁸	**Ivor's Flutter (77)** (DRCElsworth) **8-9-1** TSprake(18) (hld up: a bhd: t.o)	27	**13**	8/1	23	—
4854¹³	**Magic Combination (IRE) (65)** (BJCurley) **4-8-3** JQuinn(15) (a in rr: t.o)	9	**14**	25/1	3	—
4783⁶	**Siege Perilous (IRE) (75)** (SCWilliams) **4-8-13** DHolland(12) (prom: outpcd ½-wy: sn bhd: t.o)	1¼	**15**	13/2 2	11	—
4903⁴	**Edipo Re (78)** (PJHobbs) **5-9-2** MFenton(8) (bit bkwd: prom tl wknd 5f out: t.o)	12	**16**	25/1	3	—
4874²	***Silence in Court (IRE) (88)*** (ABailey) **6-9-12** AMackay(11) (Withdrawn not under Starter's orders: due to the ground)		**W**		—	—

(SP 143.8%) **16 Rn**

3m 53.14 (23.14) CSF £210.08 CT £1,916.53 TOTE £29.70: £4.80 £4.30 £2.10 £1.90 (£231.20) Trio £962.60 OWNER Mr G. J. Keary (CONSETT) BRED Snailwell Stud Co Ltd
WEIGHT FOR AGE 3yo-9lb
4744 Opaque has not been the easiest animal to place, but he does stay well and, with everything in his favour here, opened his seasonal account on the very last day. (14/1)
4673 Galapino, poised on the heels of the leaders full of running entering the last couple of furlongs, was being tightened up when he switched towards the inside rail, and he did not really get the opening he was looking for until far too late. With the winner staying on relentlessly, he may not have been able to wear him down even with an uninterrupted run. (14/1)
4874 Moon Colony had reached a challenging position early in the straight and he did pose a serious threat but, when a final effort was called for, he was unable to respond. It is possible that this trip could be stretching his stamina to the limit. (10/1)
4956* Jawah (IRE) delivered his challenge from out of the pack from below the distance, but failed to make any further progress inside the final furlong, and on such testing ground gave the impression he did not see the trip out. (4/1)
4956 Beaumont (IRE) dropped out of contention on the approach to the straight and looked to have called it a day, but he stayed on strongly in the latter stages and is a law unto himself. (12/1)
4639 Merit (IRE), very lightly raced this season and the winner of this corresponding race two years ago, was fighting for the lead throughout the last three furlongs and, though he did receive a bump when the winner delivered his challenge, he was in the end beaten on merit. (8/1)

4783 Ivor's Flutter (8/1: op 12/1)
4903 Edipo Re did not fare so well over this extended trip as he had done on his seasonal debut two weeks ago, and he did eventually finish tailed off, but he could be getting ready for a return for hurdles and is worth bearing in mind. (25/1)

5053 TOTE CREDIT NOVEMBER H'CAP (3-Y.O+) (Class B)

3-30 (3-32) **1m 4f** £26,391.60 (£9,824.40: £4,762.20: £2,001.00: £850.50: £390.30) Stalls: Low GOING: 0.89 sec per fur (S)

				SP	RR	SF
4736*	**Sabadilla (USA) (84)** (JHMGosden) **3-7-8**(3) 4x RFrench(22) (lw: hld up: stdy hdwy 6f out: led 2f out: rdn clr)	—	**1**	10/1	100+	76
4672*	**Taunt (97)** (DMorley) **3-8-10** DHolland(12) (a chsng ldrs: kpt on u.p fnl 3f)	8	**2**	11/2[1]	102	80
4241^{5}	**Shaft of Light (94)** (LordHuntingdon) **5-8-13v** WRyan(19) (led tl hdd 2f out: kpt on same pce)	¾	**3**	20/1	98	82
4310^{2}	**Invermark (85)** (JRFanshawe) **3-7-9**(3) PFessey(15) (hdwy on ins ent st: styd on fnl 2f: nt pce to chal)	½	**4**	28/1	89	66
4891*	**Al Azhar (99)** (IABalding) **3-8-12** 8x AMcGlone(20) (lw: hdwy 6f out: sn in tch: kpt on fnl 3f: nvr able to chal)	4	**5**	10/1	97	75
3190*	**Future Perfect (95)** (PFICole) **3-8-8** TQuinn(17) (lw: hdwy 7f out: chsng ldrs 3f out: one pce fnl 2f)	2½	**6**	20/1	90	68
4754^{17}	**Willie Conquer (94)** (RAkehurst) **5-8-13** SSanders(7) (hld up: hdwy 7f out: sn prom: rdn 4f out: styd on: no imp)	2	**7**	33/1	86	71
4754^{11}	**Celestial Choir (88)** (JLEyre) **7-8-7** TWilliams(23) (prom: rdn over 4f out: no imp after)	5	**8**	20/1	74	59
4443*	**Ridaiyma (IRE) (99)** (LMCumani) **3-8-12** KDarley(11) (prom: effrt 4f out: btn wl over 2f out)	3	**9**	7/1[3]	81	60
4383^{5}	**Wafir (IRE) (82)** (PCalver) **5-7-12**(3) DarrenMoffatt(8) (bhd after 3f: rdn ent st: n.d)	3½	**10**	33/1	59	46
4886^{5}	**Gone for a Burton (IRE) (84)** (PJMakin) **7-8-3** TSprake(13) (bhd tl styd on fnl 3f: n.d)	2	**11**	50/1	58	45
4136*	**Dantesque (IRE) (94)** (GWragg) **4-8-8**(5) GMilligan(21) (lw: w ldrs tl grad wknd fnl 3f)	2	**12**	9/1	66	52
4639^{2}	**Hoh Express (87)** (MrsJRRamsden) **5-8-6** JFortune(2) (bhd: effrt appr st: n.d)	7	**13**	20/1	49	37
4672^{3}	**Mattimeo (IRE) (84)** (APJarvis) **4-8-0**(3)ow2 CLowther(6) (rdn 5f out: sn btn)	1	**14**	25/1	45	33
4134^{5}	**Key to My Heart (IRE) (103)** (JLEyre) **7-9-8** RCochrane(10) (w ldrs tl wknd fnl 3f)	1	**15**	16/1	63	50
4891^{7}	**Capilano Princess (90)** (DHaydnJones) **4-8-9** SDrowne(16) (nvr trbld ldrs)	2½	**16**	25/1	46	35
4956^{6}	**Spartan Heartbeat (78)** (CEBrittain) **4-7-11** MartinDwyer(14) (swtg: a rr div)	1¼	**17**	50/1	33	22
4754^{4}	**Heritage (92)** (JHMGosden) **3-8-5** GHind(1) (hld up: effrt ent st: n.d)	1¼	**18**	7/1[3]	45	28
4891^{9}	**Pinchincha (FR) (84)** (DMorris) **3-7-11** FNorton(5) (chsd ldrs tl wknd 5f out)	3	**19**	33/1	33	17
4882^{10}	**Kewarra (85)** (BRMillman) **3-7-12** LCharnock(9) (lw: chsd ldrs tl wknd fnl 4f)	1	**20**	25/1	33	17
4443^{3}	**Arctic Owl (95)** (JRFanshawe) **3-8-8** NDay(18) (a outpcd & bhd)	1½	**21**	13/2[2]	41	24
4854*	**Fahs (USA) (79)** (RAkehurst) **5-7-12** 4x JQuinn(4) (bhd fnl 5f)	22	**22**	25/1	—	—
3434^{3}	**Bit on the Side (IRE) (82)** (NEBerry) **8-8-1** GBardwell(24) (a bhd)	2½	**23**	25/1	—	—
4968^{5}	**Sheer Danzig (IRE) (105)** (RWArmstrong) **5-9-10** RHills(3) (lw: cl up tl wknd over 5f out)	24	**24**	25/1	—	—
				(SP 146.1%)	**24 Rn**	

2m 41.68 (11.68) CSF £53.92 CT £1,055.72 **TOTE** £11.90: £2.70 £2.20 £4.20 £12.70 (£34.20) Trio £278.80 OWNER Sheikh Mohammed (NEWMARKET) BRED Mr and Mrs John C. Mabee
WEIGHT FOR AGE 3yo-6lb
4736* Sabadilla (USA) loves the ground and is obviously improving fast. He turned this into a procession from the two-furlong marker. (10/1)
4672* Taunt was off his highest mark to date, but he does love the soft ground and ran his heart out, only to be well outpointed by the winner. (11/2)
4241 Shaft of Light made full use of his obvious stamina but he was tapped for speed when it mattered. This was nevertheless a tremendous effort. (20/1)
4310 Invermark certainly stays well and acted on this soft ground but his effort was always too late. (28/1)
4891* Al Azhar ran a useful race and on faster ground would have really taken a hand in proceedings. (10/1)
3190* Future Perfect, returning here after three months off and trying a longer trip, travelled well but didn't appear to stay. (20/1)
4443 Willie Conquer, on ground softer than he would normally prefer, had his chances, but was well held when the pressure was on halfway up the straight. (33/1)
4136* Dantesque (IRE) looked absolutely fantastic beforehand, but this soft ground found him out with over two furlongs to go. (9/1)
4754 Heritage never gave supporters the slightest signs of hope. (7/1)

5054 SAAB JOCKEYS' CHAMPIONSHIP WENTWORTH STKS (Listed) (3-Y.O+) (Class A)

4-05 (4-06) **6f** £10,928.00 (£4,052.00: £1,951.00: £805.00: £327.50: £136.50) Stalls: High GOING: 1.12 sec per fur (S)

				SP	RR	SF
4777^{3}	**Snow Kid (108)** (DRLoder) **3-8-11** JFortune(12) (lw: mde all: clr 2f out: hld on wl cl home)	—	**1**	5/1[2]	117	74
4881*	**My Best Valentine (113)** (VSoane) **7-9-0** RCochrane(5) (lw: hld up in rr: hdwy 2f out: rdn & r.o wl towards fin)	nk	**2**	5/1[2]	119	76
4864a^{3}	**Tomba (116)** (BJMeehan) **3-9-3** MTebbutt(1) (lw: sn pushed along in tch: hung b.rt 2f out: r.o one pce)	4	**3**	9/4[1]	112	69
4777^{11}	**Superior Premium (101)** (RAFahey) **3-9-0** JCarroll(8) (a chsng ldrs: rdn 2f out: kpt on same pce)	3	**4**	25/1	101	58
4881^{3}	**Prends Ca (IRE) (98)** (WRMuir) **4-8-6** PRoberts(14) (hdwy ½-wy: sn chsng ldrs: rdn & one pce appr fnl f)	1¼	**5**	16/1	89	46
4983^{3}	**Cretan Gift (107)** (NPLittmoden) **6-9-3b** SWhitworth(6) (lw: chsd ldrs: hmpd 2f out: one pce)	1¼	**6**	12/1	97	54
4983^{5}	**Astrac (IRE) (92)** (NTinkler) **6-8-11** SSanders(10) (lw: chsd ldrs over 4f)	5	**7**	33/1	78	35
4954^{2}	**Zuhair (83)** (DMcCain) **4-8-11** PFessey(4) (b: lw: disp ld to ½-wy: wknd 2f out)	½	**8**	33/1	76	33
4881^{12}	**The Puzzler (IRE) (101)** (BWHills) **6-8-11** DHolland(11) (b: swvd rt s: a bhd)	¾	**9**	16/1	74	31
2677^{8}	**Queen's Pageant (88)** (JLSpearing) **3-8-6** SDrowne(7) (bit bkwd: outpcd)	½	**10**	50/1	68	25
4954*	**Carranita (IRE) (102)** (BPalling) **7-8-6** TSprake(13) (lw: s.i.s: outpcd fr ½-wy: t.o)	8	**11**	13/2	47	4
4954^{4}	**Brave Edge (103)** (RHannon) **6-8-11** DaneO'Neill(3) (prom: rdn whn hmpd 2f out: sn btn)	hd	**12**	11/1	51	8
4842^{3}	**Alumisiyah (USA) (84)** (RWArmstrong) **3-8-6** RHills(2) (lw: prom: drvn along & outpcd whn hmpd 2f out: sn bhd)	1¼	**13**	6/1[3]	43	—
				(SP 131.2%)	**13 Rn**	

1m 19.26 (8.26) CSF £29.68 **TOTE** £6.10: £2.00 £2.20 £1.80 (£22.10) Trio £10.40 OWNER Mr Ali Saeed (NEWMARKET) BRED Raymond Clive Tooth
4777 Snow Kid was able to deliver the goods with ground conditions in his favour, but he did need to find extra when strongly pressed in the last hundred yards. (5/1)
4881* My Best Valentine just failed to peg back the winner after looking to have timed his effort just right, but he went down fighting and has enjoyed a very rewarding season. (5/1)
4864a Tomba, a very powerful colt, did look something to bet on after showing up so well in Group races recently but, nudged along from the break, he continually hung right and found the principals running away from him inside the distance. (9/4)
4444 Superior Premium performs best when he can get his toe in, and he gave a good account of himself in this company, but a turn of finishing speed was missing when it was most needed. (25/1)

4881 Prends Ca (IRE) was staying on under strong pressure inside the last couple of furlongs but in this company she was lacking the pace to mount a challenge. (16/1)
4983 Cretan Gift, one of several knocked out of their stride by the handy Tomba, could never fully recover and was never a factor. (12/1)
4954 Brave Edge (11/1: 8/1-12/1)

T/Jkpt: Not won; £14,912.71 to 10/11/97. T/Plpt: £1,060.20 (51 Tckts). T/Qdpt: £352.20 (7.34 Tckts) AA/IM

0437a-FLEMINGTON (Melbourne, Australia) (L-H) (Good)
Tuesday November 4th

5055a FOSTER'S MELBOURNE CUP H'CAP (Gp 1) (3-Y.O+)
4-20 (4-20) **2m** £668,224.00 (£203,271.00: £91,121.00: £42,056.00: £23,364.00)

				SP	RR	SF
	Might And Power (NZ) (JDenham,Australia) **4-8-11b1** JCassidy (led: rdn 2f out: r.o wl: jst hld on)	—	**1**		125	—
	Doriemus (NZ) (DLFreedman,Australia) **7-9-0b** GHall (hld up in rr: prog over 2f out: r.o wl: nt rch wnr)	s.h	**2**		128	—
	Markham (AUS) (CBrown,Australia) **4-8-4** LDittman (mid div: rdn over 2f out: styd on wl)	½	**3**		117	—
4261a*	**Harbour Dues** (LadyHerries) **4-8-6** RCochrane (racd in rr early: hmpd appr st: rdn & r.o wl: nrst fin)	½	**4**		119	—
	Linesman (NZ) (MrsGWaterhouse,Australia) **6-8-4** LCassidy (trckd ldrs: ev ch over 2f out: one pce fr over 1f out)	s.h	**5**		117	—
4238²	**Arabian Story** (LordHuntingdon) **4-8-6** LDettori (mid div: styd on wl fr over 2f out)	2¼	**6**		117	—
						22 Rn

3m 18.33 Tote A$5.70: A$2.90 A$3.70 A$8.90 (A$29.10) (SF A$46.40) OWNER N. Moraitis BRED Windsor Park Stud Ltd
Might And Power (NZ) became the first horse to make all the running to win this race since Lord Fury in 1961. Headed by the runner-up in the closing stages, he managed to get back up right on the line. He will now be given a well-earned rest.
Doriemus (NZ), trying to win the race for the second time, battled on gamely in the straight. He did manage to get his head in front at one stage, but just lost it in a photo on the line.
4261a* Harbour Dues got hampered on the bend approaching the straight when the runner-up cut across him. That cost him about three lengths, delayed his late run and, despite finishing at blistering speed, he could only manage fourth place. Connections were delighted by the run and will consider bringing him back for a second attempt in 1998.
4238 Arabian Story missed the break after getting flustered in the stalls. Although never in a good position, he got the trip well and could return for the race again next year.

HOLLYWOOD PARK (Los Angeles, USA) (L-H) (Firm)
Friday November 7th

5056a MATIARA H'CAP (3-Y.O F)
23-11 (23-11) **1m 110y (Turf)** £30,238.00 (£8,929.00: £5,357.00: £2,679.00)

				SP	RR	SF
	I Ain't Bluffing (USA) (REllis,USA) **3-8-6** MESmith	—	**1**		118	—
	Corona Lake (USA) (USA) **3-8-5** GaryStevens	2	**2**		113	—
	Kalosca (FR) (USA) **3-8-8ow2** EDelahoussaye	s.h	**3**		116	—
4424³	**Noisette** (JHMGosden) **3-8-3** LDettori	½	**4**		110	—
						9 Rn

1m 40.0 P-M $17.20: PL: $7.40 $4.00 SHOW: $4.00 $2.60 $3.60 ($22.20) (SF $52.40) OWNER J, M & S Siegel BRED Rolling Hills Farm
4424 Noisette raced in mid-division and, although running on well in the straight, never troubled the winner.

4647a-MAISONS-LAFFITTE (France) (Soft)
Friday November 7th

5057a CRITERIUM DE MAISONS-LAFFITTE (Gp 2) (2-Y.O)
1-40 (1-38) **7f** £39,282.00 (£15,713.00: £7,856.00: £3,928.00)

				SP	RR	SF
4861a²	**Roi Gironde (IRE)** (MmeCHead,France) **2-8-11** OPeslier (mde all: drvn out fnl f)	—	**1**		101	—
4959a*	**Diableneyev (USA)** (MmeCHead,France) **2-8-11** DBoeuf (trckd ldr: hrd rdn to chal over 1f out: nt rch wnr)	s.h	**2**		101	—
4663a⁵	**Desert Drama (IRE)** (RCollet,France) **2-8-8** TJarnet (trckd ledrs: hdwy 1½f out: ev ch fnl f: wknd)	2	**3**		93	—
	Last Mecene (FR) (PDemercastel,France) **2-8-8** GMosse (a bhd)	1½	**4**		90	—
						4 Rn

1m 27.5 (5.20) P-M 2.60FF: 1.10FF 1.10FF (SF 5.20FF) OWNER Mr P. D. Savill (CHANTILLY)
3178a Roi Gironde (IRE) made all to deny his stable companion and win this in good style. The son of Fairy King is up for sale, although the price has risen after this win.

5034a-SAINT-CLOUD (France) (L-H) (Holding)
Saturday November 8th

5058a PRIX THOMAS BRYON (Gp 3) (2-Y.O)
1-15 (1-18) **1m** £24,691.00 (£8,979.00: £4,489.00)

				SP	RR	SF
4861a³	**Gold Away (IRE)** (MmeCHead,France) **2-9-2** OPeslier	—	**1**		90+	—
4529a*	**Soeur Ti (FR)** (RCollet,France) **2-8-13** TGillet	1½	**2**		84	—
	Fontevrault (FR) (AFabre,France) **2-9-2** TJarnet	6	**3**		75	—
						5 Rn

1m 49.4 (10.90) P-M 2.80FF: 2.50FF 2.50FF (26.90FF) OWNER Wertheimer Brothers (CHANTILLY)
Gold Away (IRE), running over his correct distance, dictated the race from start to finish to win in impressive style.
Soeur Ti (FR) was held up at the back of the field for much of the race and, although making late progress in the straight, was never able to reach the winner.

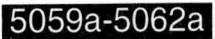

5059a PRIX PERTH (Gp 3) (3-Y.O+)
3-20 (3-19) **1m** £24,691.00 (£8,979.00: £4,489.00)

Form	Horse	Dist	Pos	SP	RR	SF
	Jim And Tonic (FR) (FDoumen,France) **3-8-11** GMosse	—	1		115	—
4662a3	**Marathon (USA)** (MmeCHead,France) **3-9-1** DBoeuf	2	2		115	—
4660a8	**Parfait Glace (FR)** (JEHammond,France) **5-9-0** TGillet	2	3		108	—
						8 Rn

1m 47.8 (9.30) P-M 9.60FF: 3.70FF 1.90FF 3.70FF (13.00FF) OWNER Haras D'Ecouves
Jim And Tonic (FR) was held up towards the rear of the field before being asked to quicken in the last quarter-mile. Responding in good style, he ran on well to win this fairly comfortably.
4662a Marathon (USA) disputed the lead over two furlongs out but, once the winner passed him, he had no answer.

5056a-HOLLYWOOD PARK (Los Angeles, USA) (L-H) (Dirt Fast, Turf Firm)
Saturday November 8th

5060a BREEDERS' CUP JUVENILE FILLIES (GRADE 1) (2-Y.O F)
18-55 (19-01) **1m 110y (Dirt)** £340,476.00 (£130,952.00: £78,571.00: £36,667.00: £13,095.00) GOING minus 0.57 sec per fur (FST)

Horse	Dist	Pos	SP	RR	SF
Countess Diana (USA) (PByrne,USA) **2-8-7** SSellers (trckd ldr: led 4f out: qcknd clr 1f out: impressive)	—	1	2/1 1	—	73
Career Collection (USA) (WDollase,USA) **2-8-7** CNakatani (a.p: wnt 2nd 3f out: rdn & nt qckn 1f out)	8½	2	3/1 2	—	57
Primaly (CAN) (RAttfield,Canada) **2-8-7** MESmith (outpcd early: gd hdwy 3f out: r.o)	4	3	17/1	—	50
Marie J (USA) (BBaffert,USA) **2-8-7b** GaryStevens (bhd early: hdwy 3f out: styd on)	2	4	15/1	—	46
Kirby's Song (CAN) (TAttard,Canada) **2-8-7** TKabel (in tch: hdwy 3f out: wknd over 1f out)	nk	5	46/1	—	45
Vivid Angel (USA) (BBaffert,USA) **2-8-7** EDelahoussaye (hdwy 2f out: one pce st)	1	6	5/1 3	—	43
Diamond On The Run (USA) (SHough,USA) **2-8-7** RobbieDavis (a mid-div)	3	7	31/1	—	38
Carrielle (USA) (HJBond,USA) **2-8-7** JChavez (a bhd)	nk	8	27/1	—	37
Love Lock (USA) (DWLukas,USA) **2-8-7** PDay (a bhd)	1¾	9	7/1	—	34
Beautiful Pleasure (USA) (JWardJnr,USA) **2-8-7** JBailey (hdwy 3f out: rdn st: sn wknd)	hd	10	7/1	—	34
Balisian Beauty (USA) (CDominguez,USA) **2-8-7b** KDesormeaux (wl bhd fnl 3f)	6½	11	17/1	—	21
Nancy's Glitter (USA) (FKnibbs,USA) **2-8-7** PARodriguez (chsd ldrs tl wknd 2f out)	2½	12	34/1	—	17
Lily O'Gold (USA) (VickieFoley,USA) **2-8-7** CMcCarron (a rr)	10	13	17/1	—	—
Bay Harbor (USA) (DWLukas,USA) **2-8-7** ASolis (led to 4f out: wknd over 2f out: eased)	7½	14	31/1	—	—
			(SP 137.7%)		**14 Rn**

1m 42.11 (-2.89) P-M $6.00: PL: $3.60 $4.20 SHOW: $3.00 $3.80 $4.80 (SF $29.40) OWNER N & R Kaster
IN-FOCUS: **For betting purposes, Primaly (CAN), Balisian Beauty (USA) & Lily O'Gold (USA) were coupled.**
Countess Diana (USA) cruised into the lead before the last turn, and drew right away when asked to score in impressive fashion. (2/1)
Career Collection (USA) looked a big danger turning in, but could find no answer when the winner stretched. (3/1)
Primaly (CAN) stayed on to take third place in the straight. (17/1)

5061a BREEDERS' CUP SPRINT (GRADE 1) (3-Y.O+)
19-30 (19-37) **6f (Dirt)** £364,881.00 (£140,476.00: £84,286.00: £39,333.00: £14,048.00) GOING minus 0.57 sec per fur (FST)

Form	Horse	Dist	Pos	SP	RR	SF
	Elmhurst (USA) (JenineSahadi,USA) **7-9-0** CNakatani (bhd: hdwy 2f out: qcknd ins fnl f: led cl hme)	—	1	166/10	130	99
	Hesabull (USA) (MikeChambers,USA) **4-9-0b** GaryStevens (a.p: led ½-wy: r.o wl u.p: hdd cl hme)	½	2	154/10	129	98
	Bet On Sunshine (USA) (PMcGee,USA) **5-9-0** PDay (rr early: hdwy 2f out: r.o wl)	nk	3	154/10	128	97
	Exotic Wood (USA) (REllis,USA) **5-8-11** CMcCarron (a.p: rdn over 1f out: no ex)	1	4	67/10 2	122	91
	Confide (USA) (BWPerkins,USA) **3-8-12b** MESmith (hdwy over 2f out: one pce)	2	5	33/1	118	87
	Men's Exclusive (USA) (WWard,USA) **4-9-0** LPincay (prom: 6th st: no ex)	nse	6	34/10 1	120	89
	Northern Afleet (USA) (DHofmans,USA) **4-9-0** JBailey (nvr nrr)	5½	7	159/10	115	74
	Trafalger (USA) (DWLukas,USA) **3-8-12** KDesormeaux (prom tl wknd st)	5	8	158/10	90	59
4664a*	**Carmine Lake (IRE)** (PWChapple-Hyam) **3-8-9** JReid (trckd ldrs tl rdn & outpcd 2f out)	hd	9	158/10	87	56
	Track Gal (USA) (JSadler,USA) **6-8-11** DFlores (led over 2f: 4th & wknd st)	1½	10	115/10	85	54
4664a2	**Pas De Reponse (USA)** (MmeCHead,France) **3-8-9** ODoleuze (trckd ldrs: rdn 2f out: sn bhd)	½	11	158/10	81	50
	Crafty Friend (USA) (WDollase,USA) **4-9-0b** ASolis (a bhd)	1¾	12	85/10 3	82	51
	Richter Scale (USA) (PByrne,USA) **3-8-12** SSellers (bhd fr ½-wy)	2¾	13	34/10 1	72	41
4664a3	**Royal Applause** (BWHills) **4-9-0** MHills (dwlt: a rr)	5½	14	225/10	60	29
				(SP 125.8%)		**14 Rn**

1m 8.01 (-3.39) P-M $35.20: PL: $15.80 $13.20 SHOW: $10.40 $8.20 $6.00 (SF $395.60) OWNER Evergreen Farm & J Sahadi
IN-FOCUS: **For betting purposes, Trafalger (USA), Carmine Lake (IRE) & Pas De Reponse (USA) were coupled.**
Elmhurst (USA) emulated stable-companion Lit de Justice by producing a terrific burst to secure victory in the dying strides. (166/10)
Hesabull (USA), up with the pace throughout, ran on gamely, and was a little unlucky to be deprived of the prize close home. (154/10)
Bet On Sunshine (USA), behind early on, finished well but lacked the acceleration of the winner. (154/10)
4664a* Carmine Lake (IRE) was well enough placed at halfway, but had nothing left before the straight. (158/10)
4664a Pas De Reponse (USA) broke well, and was stride for stride with Carmine Lake for most of the way. (158/10)
4664a Royal Applause missed the break and never got into the race. (225/10)

5062a BREEDERS' CUP DISTAFF (GRADE 1) (3-Y.O+ F & M)
20-05 (20-10) **1m 1f (Dirt)** £309,524.00 (£119,048.00: £71,429.00: £33,333.00: £11,905.00) GOING minus 0.57 sec per fur (FST)

Horse	Dist	Pos	SP	RR	SF
Ajina (USA) (WMott,USA) **3-8-8** MESmith (a.p: led st: drvn out)	—	1	48/10 3	118	86
Sharp Cat (USA) (DWLukas,USA) **3-8-8b** ASolis (led over 7f out tl over 1f out: nt qckn u.p)	2	2	Evens 1	114	82
Escena (USA) (WMott,USA) **4-8-11** JBailey (a.p: one pce fnl f)	3½	3	48/10 3	108	79
Radu Cool (USA) (JShirreffs,USA) **5-8-11** CMcCarron (led over 1f: 4th st: one pce)	1	4	165/10	106	77
Minister's Melody (USA) (DHofmans,USA) **3-8-8b** GaryStevens (in tch: 5th & btn st)	7½	5	301/10	93	61
Clear Mandate (USA) (GArnold,USA) **5-8-11** PDay (a bhd)	4	6	135/10	86	57
Hidden Lake (USA) (JKimmel,USA) **4-8-11** RMigliore (bhd fnl 2f)	4	7	17/10 2	79	50

				SP	RR	SF
	Jewel Princess (USA) (WDollase,USA) **5-8-11** CNakatani (in rr: hdwy 3f out: wknd qckly st)	11	**8**	Evens [1]	59	30

(SP 187.3%) **8 Rn**

1m 47.3 (-4.30) P-M $11.60: PL: $3.80 $2.40 SHOW: $3.80 $2.20 $3.80 (SF $23.60) OWNER Mr Allen Paulson
IN-FOCUS: **For betting purposes, Ajina (USA) & Escena (USA) were coupled, as were Sharp Cat (USA) & Jewel Princess (USA).**
Ajina (USA) battled on well to outstay the favourite in the straight (48/10)
Sharp Cat (USA) made a lot of the running, as she likes to do, but found little and swished her tail when headed. (Evens)
Escena (USA), the winner's stable-companion, could not match the front two in the final furlong. (48/10)

5063a BREEDERS' CUP MILE (GRADE 1) (3-Y.O+)
20-40 (20-44) **1m (Turf)** £340,476.00 (£130,952.00: £78,571.00: £36,667.00: £13,095.00) GOING minus 0.74 sec per fur (HD)

				SP	RR	SF
4129a*	**Spinning World (USA)** (JEPease,France) **4-9-0** CAsmussen (trckd ldrs: hdwy 3f out: chal to ld ins fnl f: comf)	—	**1**	2/1 [1]	132	98
	Geri (USA) (WMott,USA) **5-9-0** JBailey (in rr: hdwy 3f out: r.o wl)	2	**2**	6/1 [3]	128	94
4782[5]	**Decorated Hero** (JHMGosden) **5-9-0** LDettori (dwlt: hdwy 4f out: rdn st: r.o wl)	nk	**3**	40/1	127	93
	Lucky Coin (USA) (RNieminski,USA) **4-9-0** RobbieDavis (led tl hdd ins fnl f: no ex)	nse	**4**	29/10 [2]	127	93
	Magellan (USA) (NDrysdale,USA) **4-9-0** EDelahoussaye (bhd: hdwy 2f out: nvr nrr)	5	**5**	13/1	117	83
	El Angelo (USA) (JenineSahadi,USA) **5-9-0** ASolis (bhd early: sme late hdwy)	hd	**6**	15/2	117	83
	Soviet Line (IRE) (KPMcLaughlin,USA) **7-9-0** PDay (prom 5f: rdn & btn st)	1¼	**7**	39/1	115	81
1767[8]	**Fantastic Fellow (USA)** (DWLukas,USA) **3-8-11** KDesormeaux (prom tl rdn & wknd 2f out)	hd	**8**	33/1	113	77
	Wild Event (USA) (LGoldfine,USA) **4-9-0** MGuidry (bhd: hdwy over 2f out: hmpd over 2f out: no ex)	hd	**9**	21/1	114	80
	Helmsman (USA) (WDollase,USA) **5-9-0b** CNakatani (bhd: hdwy 3f out: no imp st)	hd	**10**	15/1	114	80
	Pinfloron (USA) (WGreenman,USA) **5-9-0** DFlores (a rr)	½	**11**	12/1	113	79
	Naninja (USA) (MAMitchell,USA) **4-9-0** CMcCarron (mid-div tl wknd st)	nk	**12**	42/1	112	78

(SP 120.9%) **12 Rn**

1m 32.77 (-5.73) P-M $6.20: PL: $4.00 $5.60 SHOW: $2.80 $4.40 $10.20 (SF $71.60) OWNER Flaxman Holdings Ltd (CHANTILLY)
4129a* Spinning World (USA) adapted to the track and the going with little difficulty, and outclassed his rivals. It is hard to disagree with Asmussen's assertion that he is the best miler in the world. (2/1)
Geri (USA) reproduced his Woodbine effort, but was no match for the winner. (6/1)
4782 Decorated Hero deserves medals for his efforts this year, and once again excelled himself. He may go to Hong Kong next month, and will no doubt be back next year. (40/1)
Lucky Coin (USA) set a strong pace, but had nothing in hand when challenged. (29/10)

5064a BREEDERS' CUP JUVENILE (GRADE 1) (2-Y.O C & G)
21-15 (21-18) **1m 110y (Dirt)** £309,524.00 (£119,048.00: £71,429.00: £33,333.00: £11,905.00) GOING minus 0.57 sec per fur (FST)

			SP	RR	SF
Favorite Trick (USA) (PByrne,USA) **2-8-10** PDay (a.p: led 3f out: rdn clr over 1f out: easily)	—	**1**	6/5 [1]	—	82
Dawson's Legacy (USA) (MsRSchnitzler,USA) **2-8-10** TKabel (a.p: 3rd st: r.o one pce)	5½	**2**	78/1	—	72
Nationalore (USA) (MyungKwonCho,Japan) **2-8-10b** EDelahoussaye (wl bhd tl gd hdwy fr 2f out: fin wl)	nk	**3**	407/10	—	71
Souvenir Copy (USA) (BBaffert,USA) **2-8-10** CMcCarron (in tch: 4th st: one pce)	¾	**4**	28/10 [3]	—	70
Johnbill (USA) (BBaffert,USA) **2-8-10** DFlores (mid-div: 5th st: no imp)	hd	**5**	139/10	—	70
Double Honor (USA) (DWLukas,USA) **2-8-10** ASolis (bhd tl sme hdwy st: no imp)	3	**6**	378/10	—	64
Time Limit (USA) (DWLukas,USA) **2-8-10** SSellers (led over 5f: 2nd st: sn wknd)	2	**7**	346/10	—	60
Grand Slam (USA) (DWLukas,USA) **2-8-10** GaryStevens (hdwy ½-wy: btn st)	28	**8**	2/1 [2]	—	7

(SP 120.9%) **8 Rn**

1m 41.47 (-3.53) P-M $4.40: PL: $3.40 $30.80 SHOW: $2.60 $9.20 $6.40 (SF $190.60) OWNER La Combe
Favorite Trick (USA) was never in trouble once he hit the front, and completed a notable double for London-born trainer Patrick Byrne. (6/5)
Dawson's Legacy (USA) was up with the pace throughout, but was unable to answer the winner's surge. (78/1)
Nationalore (USA) was tailed off going into the home turn, but ran on through beaten horses and almost snatched second place. (407/10)

5065a BREEDERS' CUP TURF (GRADE 1) (3-Y.O+)
21-50 (21-54) **1m 4f (Turf)** £619,048.00 (£238,095.00: £142,857.00: £66,667.00: £23,809.00) GOING minus 0.74 sec per fur (HD)

				SP	RR	SF
4870a*	**Chief Bearhart (CAN)** (MFrostad,Canada) **4-9-0b** JSantos (hld up: hdwy 3f out: chal to ld ins fnl f: r.o wl)	—	**1**	19/10 [1]	129	95
4665a[3]	**Borgia (GER)** (BSchutz,Germany) **3-8-7** KFallon (mid-div: hdwy st: chal ins fnl f: r.o wl u.p)	¾	**2**	4/1 [2]	127	87
	Flag Down (CAN) (CClement,USA) **7-9-0** JBailey (in tch: hdwy st: led over 1f out: rdn & hdd ins fnl f)	½	**3**	14/1	127	93
	Buck's Boy (USA) (NHickey,USA) **4-9-0** MGuidry (led tl hdd over 1f out: no ex)	4	**4**	35/1	122	88
	Big Sky Chester (USA) (BHone,USA) **5-9-0** GaryStevens (hld up: hdwy 2f out: nrst fin)	½	**5**	29/1	121	87
4257a*	**Rajpoute (FR)** (RMcAnally,USA) **3-8-10** CMcCarron (trckd ldr tl wknd over 1f out)	3	**6**	6/1 [3]	119	79
	Ops Smile (USA) (WilliamBoniface,USA) **5-9-0b** J-LSamyn (bhd: hdwy 3f out: one pce st)	nk	**7**	15/1	117	83
4395a[2]	**Val's Prince (USA)** (JPicou,USA) **5-9-0** MESmith (prom tl wknd st)	4	**8**	7/1	112	78
4395a[3]	**Awad (USA)** (DDonk,USA) **7-9-0b** PDay (a rr)	hd	**9**	7/1	112	78
4863a*	**Majorien** (MmeCHead,France) **3-8-10** ODoleuze (trckd ldrs tl wknd 2f out)	¾	**10**	11/1	113	73
5039a[7]	**Dance Design (IRE)** (DKWeld,Ireland) **4-8-11** MJKinane (prom tl wknd over 3f out)	4	**11**	27/1	102	68

(SP 124.7%) **11 Rn**

2m 23.92 (-8.18) P-M $5.80: PL: $3.60 $5.00 SHOW $3.20 $3.80 $6.20 (SF $26.80) OWNER Sam-Son Farm BRED R. Maynard
Chief Bearhart (CAN) came from well off a good pace, and this consistent colt battled on well to gain a first Breeders' Cup victory for his trainer. (19/10)
4665a Borgia (GER), a game third in the Arc, again put up a terrific performance. Given a fine ride, she looked the winner for a moment when making her challenge, but found the older colt just too tough. She remains in training, and will be aimed at big races across the world next autumn. (4/1)
Flag Down (CAN), held up early, burst through entering the straight, and looked the winner until caught in the last hundred yards. (14/1)
4257a* Rajpoute (FR), who beat the Arc winner before being sold to race in America, once again ran well, but probably went too fast too soon. (6/1)
4863a* Majorien ran well for a long way, but may have found this ground too fast. (11/1)
5039a Dance Design (IRE) tracked the leaders for a long way, but once again failed to get home. (27/1)

5066a BREEDERS' CUP CLASSIC (GRADE 1) (3-Y.O+)

22-35 (22-38) **1m 2f** **(Dirt)** £1,361,905.00 (£523,810.00: £314,286.00: £314,286.00: £52,381.00) GOING minus 0.57 sec per fur (FST)

				SP	RR	SF
	Skip Away (USA) (HHine,USA) **4-9-0b** MESmith (a.p: led over 3f out: sn clr: unchal)	—	**1**	18/10 [1]	134	100
	Deputy Commander (USA) (WDollase,USA) **3-8-10** CNakatani (led 7f out tl over 3f out: rdn & r.o st)	6	**2**	4/1 [3]	124	86
	Dowty (USA) (WMott,USA) **5-9-0** GaryStevens (outpcd early: gd hdwy over 2f out: hmpd over 1f out: fin 4th, 3l: plcd 3rd)	¾	**3**	46/1	123	89
	Whiskey Wisdom (CAN) (RAttfield,Canada) **4-9-0** PDay (led 3f: a.p: 3rd st: rdn & hng rt: r.o one pce: fin 3rd, 3/4l: disq: plcd 4th)	3	**4**	11/1	118	84
	Savinio (USA) (WGreenman,USA) **7-9-0** ASolis (in tch: 5th & btn st)	12	**5**	81/1	99	65
	Taiki Blizzard (USA) (KFujisawa,Japan) **6-9-0b** YOkabe (in tch: rdn wl over 3f out: sn bhd)	2	**6**	32/1	96	62
	Behrens (USA) (HJBond,USA) **3-8-10** JBailey (prom 7f)	1	**7**	/1	94	56
3881a*	**Honor Glide (USA)** (JDay,Canada) **3-8-10** SSellers (prom: led over 8f out tl 7f out: sn wknd)	12	**8**	76/1	75	37
*1912a**	**Touch Gold (USA)** (DHofmans,USA) **3-8-10** CMcCarron (prom 7f: sn bhd)	nk	**9**	2/1 [2]	75	37
				(SP 205.1%)		**9 Rn**

1m 59.16 (-5.74) P-M $5.60: PL: $3.20 $4.60 SHOW: $2.80 $4.00 $7.60 (SF $25.00) OWNER Mrs Carolyn Hine BRED Marie Anna Bamhart

Skip Away (USA), supplemented for $480,000, rewarded the gamble in style. Bursting into the lead before the home turn, he lived up to his name and came home on his own. (18/10)

Deputy Commander (USA) was always up with the pace, but had no answer when the winner kicked for home. (4/1)

Dowty (USA) was tailed off for a long way and, despite running on, seemed a little fortunate to be awarded third after being bumped by Whisky Wisdom. (46/1)

Whiskey Wisdom (CAN) put in a game effort and looked third on merit, but was put down for interference. (11/1)

KEY TO RACEREADERS' INITIALS

AA	Alan Amies	KH	Keith Hewitt
AK	Anthony Kemp	LM	Louise Mackinlay
AR	Ashley Rumney	LMc	Lee McKenzie
CR	Colin Roberts	Mk	Iain Mackenzie
Dk	David Dickinson	NB	Nicky Bowen
DB	David Bellingham	NR	Neville Ring
DO	Darren Owen	O'R	Tom O'Ryan
DS	Desmond Stoneham	P	John Penney
GB	Gordon Brown	RL	Richard Lowther
Hn	John Hanmer	SC	Steven Clarke
IM	Ivor Markham	SM	Stephen Mellish
J	Mike Jones	T	Mary Truman
KC	Kate Corbett	WG	Walter Glynn

INDEX TO MEETINGS

ABU DHABI 308a,
AQUEDUCT 5038a,
ARLINGTON 3879a-3881a,
ASCOT 890, 2133, 3009, 3047, 3183, 4420, 4439, 4667, 4674,
AYR 721, 1310, 1557, 2109, 2140, 2713, 2854, 2898, 3401, 4230, 4264, 4278, 4688, 4702
BADEN-BADEN 1548a, 1550a, 1551a, 1720a, 1723a, 1724a, 3993a, 3997a-3998b, 4122a-4124a, 4126a-4127a,
BATH 875, 1108, 1272, 1563, 1951, 2306, 2531, 2777, 2928, 3324, 3469, 4042, 4460,
BELMONT 1912a, 4395a, 4651a, 4862a,
BETTOLE 3367a,
BEVERLEY 570, 631, 792, 1095, 1115, 1298, 1651, 1682, 1828, 2463, 2493, 2733, 2904, 3102, 3476, 3540, 3757, 4208,
BORDEAUX 3872a, 5032a,
BRIGHTON 637, 750, 1007, 1370, 1504, 1638, 1984, 2740, 2746, 2953, 3078, 3294, 3556, 3588, 3847, 3965, 4446, 4500, 4855,
CAGNES-SUR-MER 148a, 149a, 189a, 190a, 267a, 270a, 310a,
CAPANNELLE 815a, 917a, 1200a, 1201a, 1549a, 1552a, 1553a, 4253a, 4535a,
CARLISLE 822, 1076, 1510, 1860, 2202, 2233, 2500, 3264, 3853,
CASCINE 4128a,
CATTERICK 466, 779, 1569, 1581, 1729, 2412, 2752, 2934, 3282, 3562, 4285, 4427, 4746, 4767,
CHANTILLY 1070a, 1358a, 1359a, 1721a, 1722a, 1725a, 1726a, 1727a, 1915a, 1916a, 1917a, 2268a, 2457a, 2819a, 2996a, 4250a-4251a, 4387a, 4390a, 4528a,
CHEPSTOW 1434, 1920, 2375, 2506, 2645, 3015, 3245, 3788, 4109,
CHESTER 1013, 1025, 1031, 1657, 2209, 2651, 2681, 3252, 3886, 3899, 4360,
CHURCHILL DOWNS 1071a,
CLAIREFONTAINE 3994a,
COLOGNE 440a, 1072a, 1073a, 1074a, 1544a, 2097a, 3368a, 3369a, 4531a, 4536a - 4537a,
CORK 3362a,
CURRAGH 713a, 1058a, 1060a, 1062a, 1531a, 1532a, 1533a, 1538a, 1540a, 1541a, 1542a, 1896a, 2439a, 2441a, 2446a, 2447a, 2451a, 2453a, 2454a, 2456a, 2811a, 2814a, 2815a, 2816a, 3172a, 3672a, 3674a-3675a, 3961a, 3962a, 4090a, 4093a-4094a, 4834a, 4836a-4837a,
DEAUVILLE 2639a, 2820a, 3000a, 3001a, 3003a, 3366a, 3370a, 3371a, 3372a, 3552a, 3554a, 3729a-3734a, 3873a-3878a, 3882a-3883a, 3995a-3996a, 3999a-4001a, 4959a-4961a,
DIELSDORF 918a, 3735a, 3884a, 4538a - 4540a,
DONCASTER 430, 441, 447, 971, 1019, 1395, 1760, 2312, 2338, 2758, 3116, 3141, 4096, 4116, 4132, 4146, 4871, 4885, 5040, 5048,
DORTMUND 2272a, 4661a,
DOWN ROYAL 2967a,
DUSSELDORF 816a, 1202a, 3182a, 4963a,
EPSOM 786, 1735, 1766, 2215, 2388, 2571, 3300†, 3432, 3794, 4002, 4018†,
FLEMINGTON 437a, 5055a,
FOLKESTONE 472, 601, 765, 1479, 1663, 2276, 2394, 2577, 2719, 3288, 3638, 3924, 4400, 4814,
FRANKFURT 920a, 3004a, 4396a,
GALWAY 4191a,
GELSENKIRCHEN-HORST 719a, 3736a-3737a, 4962a,
GOODWOOD 1304, 1316, 1322, 1742, 1866, 1926, 2115, 2282, 2344, 3109, 3122, 3147, 3189, 3214, 3738, 3763, 4139, 4153, 4366, 4374,
GOWRAN PARK 2267a,
HAMBURG 2458a, 2459a, 2637a, 2638a, 2640a, 2641a, 2642a,
HAMILTON 548, 608, 950, 1037, 1227, 1613, 1835, 2029, 2221, 2382, 2469, 2657, 3221, 3483, 3626, 3918, 4466,
HANOVER 4254a,
HAYDOCK 498, 978, 1376†, 1402, 1748, 1773, 2418, 2475, 2512, 3377, 3407, 3568, 4010, 4023†, 4305, 4407, 4433, 4731,
HOLLYWOOD PARK 5056a, 5060a-5066a,
HOPPEGARTEN 817a, 2821a, 3553a, 3555a, 4650a,
JEBE ALI 392a,
KEENELAND 4652a,
KEMPTON 504, 517, 985, 1409, 1587, 3685, 4103, 4311, 4317,
KLAMPENBORG 3373a, 3374a, 4653a,
KREFELD 3005a,
LEICESTER 479, 554, 835, 1440, 1460, 1619, 1958, 2783, 2941, 3450, 3691, 4057, 4324, 4575, 4694, 4708, 4899, 4914,
LEOPARDSTOWN 806a, 807a, 809a, 1192a, 1193a, 1195a, 1198a, 1698a, 1880a, 1881a, 2078a, 2079a, 2081a, 2987a, 2989a, 3506a, 3508a, 3510a, 3511a, 3534a, 3535a, 3837a, 3839a, 3842a, 4203a-4204a, 5002a,
LES LANDES 624a, 2997a, 2998a, 2999a,
LINGFIELD 8*, 20*, 43*, 57*, 73*, 92*, 104*, 116*, 128*, 141*, 158*, 170*, 183*, 197*, 210*, 223*, 236*, 248*, 261*, 278*, 290*, 302*, 319*, 334*, 347*, 361*, 379*, 401*, 454*, 486*, 564, 1082, 1101, 1151*, 1233, 1416, 1593, 1964, 2146, 2190, 2318, 2590, 2663, 2687, 3054, 3227, 3413, 3613, 3859, 4065, 4542, 4906, 5017,
LONGCHAMP 625a, 629a, 630a, 818a, 916a, 921a, 1203a, 1204a, 1205a, 1206a, 1361a, 1362a, 1365a, 1366a, 1554a, 1719a, 2270a, 2273a, 2274a, 2275a, 4129a-4130a, 4255a-4258a, 4389a, 4391a-4393a, 4654a-4658a, 4662a-4666a, 4766a, 4863a-4864a, 4964a-4965a,
MAIA 3176a, 3177a,
MAISONS-LAFFITTE 717a, 718a, 811a, 1913a, 2096a, 2269a, 2818a, 3006a, 3007a, 3178a, 3179a, 3180a, 3181a, 4529a - 4530a, 4647a-4649a, 5057a,
MULHEIM 1918a,
MUNICH 1545a, 3375a, 3376a,
MUSSELBURGH 492, 664, 924, 1280, 1600, 1990, 2165, 2350, 2538, 2823, 3697, 3866, 4159, 5023,
NAPLES 2643a,
NAD AL SHEBA 309a, 408a, 409a, 438a, 626a, 627a, 628a,
NEWBURY 722, 735, 1207, 1239, 1260, 1486, 1872, 2829, 2860, 3574, 3594, 4237, 4271, 4292, 4878, 4892,
NEWCASTLE 460, 524, 993, 1328, 1669, 2288, 2324, 3060, 3084, 3258, 3306, 3801, 4507, 4840,
NEWMARKET 670, 677, 690, 930, 937, 957, 1213, 1606, 1779, 1841, 2121, 2294,2331, 2556, 2583, 2596, 2836, 2867, 3021, 3196, 3233, 3383, 3419, 3744, 3770, 4473, 4521, 4555, 4753, 4774, 4781, 4966, 4973,
NOTTINGHAM 530, 582, 644, 757, 882, 1089, 1246, 1383, 1791, 2035, 2171, 2518, 2874, 3027, 3129, 3312, 4165, 4330, 4453, 4562, 4627, 4738, 4952, 4986,
OVREVOLL 3885a,
PARILLY 1199a, 2271a,
PIMLICO 1364a,
PONTEFRACT 684, 772, 861, 1389, 1645, 1797, 1997, 2356, 2564, 2842, 3330, 3619, 3931, 4381, 4582, 4801,
REDCAR 896, 1126, 1447, 1466, 1815, 2127, 2152, 2400, 2880, 3066, 3426, 3438, 3776, 4413, 4595, 4788, 4921, 4993,
RIPON 594, 697, 843, 1266, 1492, 2041, 2059, 2544, 2886, 3270, 3601, 3808, 3821, 3905,
ROYAL ASCOT 2009, 2023, 2053, 2103,
SAINT-CLOUD 439a, 716a, 813a, 1067a, 1360a, 1363a, 1546a, 1547a, 2460a, 3002a, 4125a, 4388a, 4861a, 5031a, 5034a, 5058a, 5059a,
SALISBURY 964, 1163, 1821, 1847, 2227, 2240, 2693, 2848, 3202, 3389, 3489, 3710, 3979, 4515,
SANDOWN 828, 850, 1453, 1473, 1932, 1970, 2481, 2524, 2764, 2947, 2959, 3135, 3496, 3546, 3892, 3911, 4173, 4216,
SAN SIRO 812a, 814a, 821a, 1068a, 1069a, 1075a, 1367a, 1368a, 1369a, 1555a, 1556a, 1728a, 1911a, 1919a, 2098a, 2099a, 2100a, 2101a, 2102a, 2461a, 2462a, 2644a, 2822a, 3008a, 4131a, 4259a, 4397a-4399a, 4532a - 4534a, 4541a, 4659a-4660a, 4760a-4761a, 4762a, 4763a-4765a, 4865a-4868a, 5033a, 5035a-5037a,
SANTA ANITA 393a, 5039a,
SAN ROSSORE 64a,
SHA TIN 720a,
SOUTHWELL 1*, 14*, 36*, 65*, 85*, 110*, 122*, 150*, 164*, 191*, 203*, 230*, 242*, 272*, 284*, 326*, 355*, 373*, 410*, 423*, 542*, 576*, 867*, 1043*, 1132*, 1286*, 1754*, 1939*, 2066*, 2363*, 2602*, 2910*, 3072*, 3581*, 4049*, 4808*,
ST-MORITZ 229a, 271a, 311a, 353a, 354a,
TABY 1909a, 1910a, 4260a-4262a,
THIRSK 729, 743, 944, 1220, 1253, 1626, 2015, 3033, 3208, 3239, 3456, 3751, 4029†,
TIPPERARY 1186a,
VELIEFENDI 4252a, 4263a,
VICHY 3364a, 3365a,
WARWICK 536, 651, 999, 1422, 1675, 1803, 2196, 2487, 2700, 2892, 3814, 4602,
WINDSOR 1139, 1292, 1632, 1809, 2003, 2178, 2369, 2550, 2727, 2916, 3090, 3276, 3462, 3632, 3782,
WOLVERHAMPTON 28*, 49*, 79*, 98*, 135*, 176*, 217*, 254*, 296*, 312*, 341*, 367*, 385*, 394*, 417*, 511*, 588*, 658*, 855*, 902*, 1121*, 1428*, 1575*, 1785*, 2047*, 2159*, 2300*, 2669, 3040*, 3395*, 3607*, 4036*†, 4299*, 4479*, 4569*, 4589*, 4795*, 4980*,
WOODBINE 4394a, 4869a-4870a,
YARMOUTH 1498, 1688, 1853, 2184, 2406, 2424, 2770, 2922, 3096, 3318, 3444, 3716, 4180, 4223, 4243, 4848, 4946,
YORK 1145, 1157, 1170, 1945, 1977, 2675, 2706, 3644, 3703, 3722, 3972, 3986, 4634, 4641†, 4681†,

† abandoned * all-weather

INDEX TO FLAT RACING

Figure following the horses name indicates its **age**. The figures following the pedigree refer to the numbers of the races (*all-weather are in italics*) in which the horse has run; parentheses () indicate a win; small figures [2,3,4] etc denote other placings. Foreign races are denoted by the suffix 'a'. Horses withdrawn (not under orders) are shown with the suffix 'w'. The figure within arrows eg. **>100<** indicate Raceform Private Handicap MASTER rating. The ratings are based on a scale of 0-140. The following symbols are used: 'a' all-weather rating, 'f' turf rating, '+' on the upgrade, 'd' disappointing, '?' questionable form, 't' tentative rating based on time.

A

Aardwolf 6 b g Dancing Brave (USA)-Pretoria (Habitat) 865[2] 1252[3] 2108[5] **>82?f<**
Abajany 3 b g Akarad (FR)-Miss Ivory Coast (USA) (Sir Ivor) 495[3] 742[9] 958[3] 1078[2] 1164[5] 1272[5] (3696) 3894[5] (4176) 4308[5] 4680[16] **>83f<**
Abandonment (IRE) 2 b f Caerleon (USA)-Fermoy (USA) (Irish River (FR)) 2987a[2] 3839a[10] **>88f<**
Abbatiale (FR) 2 5034a[7] **>75f<**
Abbey Theatre (IRE) 3 b c Sadler's Wells (USA)-Altiyna (Troy) 2008[19] 2311[8] 2537[8] 3325[4] **>38f<**
Abduction 4 ch g Risk Me (FR)-Spirit Away (Dominion) 3249[14] **>29f<**
Aberkeen 2 ch c Keen-Miss Aboyne (Lochnager) 1557[4] (1801) 2060[5] 2500[2] 3258[2] **>82f<**
Able Choice (IRE) 7 b g Taufan (USA)-Great Land (USA) (Friend's Choice (USA)) **1996:** *5120[11]* **>79da 54f<**
Able Lass (IRE) 3 ch f Classic Music (USA)-Miami Life (Miami Springs) 3641[5] 4009[9] **>38f<**
Able Player (USA) 10 b or br g Solford (USA)-Grecian Snow (CAN) (Snow Knight) 2208[3] 3401[5] **>40f<**
Able Sheriff 5 br g Doulab (USA)-Rich Lass (Broxted) 464[9] 666[2] 772[2] 1223[B] **>23a 67f<** **(DEAD)**
Aboo Hom 3 b c Sadler's Wells (USA)-Maria Waleska (Filiberto (USA)) 1023[10] 1846[5] 2410[4] 3021[9] 4360[3] 4743[5] **>78f<**
Abou Lahab 3 1544a[9] 2642a[20] **>96f<**
Abou Zouz (USA) 3 b c Miswaki (USA)-Bold Jessie (Never so Bold) 1455[10] 2334[6] (3118) 3535a[5] 3747[11] **>104f<**
Above Board 2 b c Night Shift (USA)-Bundled Up (USA) (Sharpen Up) 2588[7] 3031[3] **>63f<**
A Breeze 3 br g Precocious-Wasimah (Caerleon (USA)) *180[7]* *307[8]* 448[7] 694[7] 977[4] 1392[8] 1691[4] 2002[10] **>38a 76df<**
Abreeze (USA) 2 b c Danzig (USA)-Priceless Pearl (USA) (Alydar (USA)) (4174) 4551[7] 4775[4] **>94f<**
Absalom's Lad 2 ch c Absalom-Rose Bouquet (General Assembly (USA)) 4855[3] 5048[8] **>63f<**
Absentee 2 br f Slip Anchor-Meliora (Crowned Prince (USA)) 4567[8] **>50f<**
Absolute Charlie 3 ch g Prince Daniel (USA)-Absolutely Blue (Absalom) 997[9] 1130[12] **>23f<**
Absolute Glee (USA) 3 gr f Kenmare (FR)-Looking Brill 2814a[11] 4837a[6] **>100f<**
Absolute Liberty (USA) 3 ch g Gold Alert (USA)-Mutterfly (USA) (Muttering (USA)) *(1121)* 1629[5] (2195) 3135[4] *3397[2]* 3992[17] 4477[12] 4699[13] 4876[11] **>80a 65?f<**
Absolutely Abstone 3 gr f Petong-Odilese (Mummy's Pet) 4951[20] **>46?f<**
Absolutely Fayre 6 ch g Absalom-June Fayre (Sagaro) 1463[9] 1800[5] 2174[15] 2576[4] 3091[13] **>42a 43f<**
Absolutelystunning 4 br f Aragon-Dramatic Mood (Jalmood (USA)) **1996:** *5094[4]* *(5223)* *5247[8]* **1997:** *134[9]* *186[5]* *305[7]* 647[2] 887[7] 3091[14] 4063[17] 4179[14] 4323[18] 4516[10] 5044[8] **>35a 35f<**
Absolute Magic 7 b g Doulab (USA)-Trickster (Major Portion) **1996:** *5106[5]* **1997:** *14[7]* *273[12]* **>84da 84f<**
Absolute Ruler (IRE) 6 ch g Absalom-Princess Biddy (Sun Prince) **1996:** *5115[13]* **>33a 55f<**
Absolute Utopia (USA) 4 b g Mr Prospector (USA)-Magic Gleam (USA) (Danzig (USA)) 1273[12] 1588[4] 1878[10] 2848[2] (3470) 3793[4] 4319[5] (4516) **>68f<**
Absolutly Sparklin 2 b c Midyan (USA)-Tino-Ella (Bustino) (3978) 4439[5] 4709[4] **>92+f<**
Abstone Pet Girl 2 b f Absalom-Peters Pet Girl (Norwick (USA)) *4479[8]* *4573[7]* *4799[4]* *4984[8]* 5029[7] **>37a 6f<**
Abstone Queen 3 b f Presidium-Heavenly Queen (Scottish Reel) *225[4]* *307[6]* *372[5]* (467) 535[16] 785[4] 896[6] 997[7] 1284[6] 1573[7] 3285[7] 3405[2] **>44a 56f<**
Abtaal 7 b g Green Desert (USA)-Stufida (Bustino) 848[4] 1005[2] 1422[8] 1483[9] (1965) 2282[8] 2573[8] 2723[5] 2852[3] 3249[4] 4112[12] **>69a 53f<**
Abu Camp 2 b c Indian Ridge-Artistic Licence (High Top) 4708[11] **>46f<**
Abuhail (USA) 2 b br c Silver Hawk (USA)-Bank Key (USA) (Key To The Mint (USA)) (2881) 3912[2] 4697[3] **>101f<**
Abusamrah (USA) 2 b c Riverman (USA)-Azayim (Be My Guest (USA)) 4966[5] **>79f<**
Academy (IRE) 2 ch g Archway (IRE)-Dream Academy (Town And Country) 3783[14] 4708[8] 4901[9] **>60f<**
Academy House (IRE) 4 b c Sadler's Wells (USA)-Shady Leaf (IRE) (Glint of Gold) 1478[13] 2014[17] **>79f<**
Academy Star 3 b f Royal Academy (USA)-Startino (Bustino) 992[4] 3720[U] 4158[5] **>69f<**
Accento 4 b c Midyan (USA)-Daleside Ladybird (Tolomeo) 1067a[3] 2821a[7] 4531a[2] 5037a[2] **>119f<**
Access Adventurer (IRE) 6 b g Al Hareb (USA)-Olwyn (Relko) 3134[10] 4386[9] **>79a 66f<**
Accommodate You 4 br f Precocious-Time for Joy (Good Times (ITY)) 4114[13] 4224[12] **>13f<**
Accystan 2 ch g Efisio-Amia (CAN) (Nijinsky (CAN)) 4993[15] **>28f<**
Acebo Lyons (IRE) 2 b f Waajib-Etage (Ile de Bourbon (USA)) 3009[5] 3450[6] 4217[4] 4898[2] **>85f<**
Acerbis (GER) 3 f 1918a[4] **>104f<**
Acerbus Dulcis 6 ch g Hadeer-Current Pattie (USA) (Little Current (USA)) **1996:** *5116[11]* *5181[14]* **1997:** *2[10]* *16[9]* *86[2]* *122[5]* *232[6]* *284[15]* *544[5]* 1248[13] 1503[4] 1694[3] 1779[3] 2430[7] 2927[4] (3449) 3719[8] **>40a 37f<**
Acharne 4 ch c Pharly (FR)-Sibley (Northfields (USA)) 678[5] 830[5] 1210[7] 1542a[4] 2010[5] 2656[5] 3634[4] 3988[4] 4154[5] 4902[7] **>104df<**
Achilles 2 ch c Deploy-Vatersay (USA) (Far North (CAN)) 2720[3] 4367[2] 4638[2] 5048[3] **>90f<**
Acid Test 2 ch c Sharpo-Clunk Click (Star Appeal) 1812[11] 2037[7] 2306[10] (2664) 3237[8] (3387) 3597[2] 4044[5] 4271[2] 4411[9] **>72f<**
Acquittal (IRE) 5 b g Danehill (USA)-Perfect Alibi (Law Society (USA)) 1383[3] 1441[2] 1796[11] 2701[7] 4415[17] **>55a 49f<**
Across The Water 3 b f Slip Anchor-Stara (Star Appeal) 1420[5] 1742[6] 2190[7] **>53f<**
Acrow Line 12 b g Capricorn Line-Miss Acrow (Comedy Star (USA)) **1996:** *5143[9]* **>49da 34f<**
Act Defiant (USA) 2 br c Nureyev (USA)-Alydariel (USA) (Alydar (USA)) 4575[5] 4734[4] 4950[5] **>81f<**
Action Jackson 5 ch g Hadeer-Water Woo (USA) (Tom Rolfe) 461[16] 843[2-] 1246[2] 1441[3] 1665[4] 3026[12] 3134[5] 3588[3] 3719[2] 3928[12] **>39a 64f<**
Action Replay 4 ch g Fearless Action (USA)-Pentland Beauty (Remainder Man) **1996:** *5169[7]*
Action Stations 3 b g High Estate-Toast (IRE) (Be My Guest (USA)) 599[16] 1742[4] 2190[5] *2910[4]* 4372[9] 4503[10] **>48a 57df<**
Act Of Defiance (IRE) 3 b c Caerleon (USA)-Trusted Partner (USA) (Affirmed (USA)) 713a[5] **>98f<**
Act of Folly 2 b f Midyan (USA)-Height of Folly (Shirley Heights) 4317[10] **>59f<**
Adamton 5 b g Domynsky-Berwyn (Sharpo) **1996:** *(5123)* *5181[2]* *(5281)* **>75a 51f<**
Adeste Fideles 2 b f Groom Dancer (USA)-Decided Air (IRE) (Sure Blade (USA)) 3973[7] 4514[3] *(4592)* **>61a 65f<**
Adilov 5 b g Soviet Star (USA)-Volida (Posse (USA)) **1996:** *5247[7]* *5255[5]* *5277[4]* **1997:** *73[7]* **>41a 53f<**
Adjutant 2 b c Batshoof-Indian Love Song (Be My Guest (USA)) 3569[3] 4017[3] 4735[6] **>73f<**
Admirals Flame (IRE) 6 b g Doulab (USA)-Fan The Flame (Grundy) 895[19] 1782[5] 2201[12] 2778[4] 3786[10] **>56a 80df<**
Admirals Secret (USA) 8 ch g Secreto (USA)-Noble Mistress (USA) (Vaguely Noble) 1636[9] 1844[10] 2279[5] 2843[5] (3093) 3283[7] 3562[6] 4584[6] 4821[8] **>63a 54f<**
Admire 2 b f Last Tycoon-Belle Isis (USA) (Sir Ivor) 3638[7] (3788) 4119[9] 4892[12] **>74f<**
Adorea (GER) 3 f 1202a[7] **>81f<**
Adrenalin 2 ch c Risk Me (FR)-High Cairn (FR) (Ela-Mana-Mou) 948[3] 1019[5] 1298[7] 2016[8] 2712[7] **>54df<**
Advance East 5 b g Polish Precedent (USA)-Startino (Bustino) 900[6] 1128[13] 1560[7] 1795[6] 2114[4] 2199[4] **>45+a 54f<**
Advance Repro 3 b f Risk Me (FR)-Sunday Sport Gem (Lomond (USA)) **1996:** *5278[6]* **1997:** *103[6]* *181[7]* *212[3]* *399[4]* *(546)* 882[13] *1047[5]* *1786[8]* **>67da 48f<**
Aegean 3 b g Rock Hopper-Sayulita (Habitat) 1508[4] 2532[9] 2952[7] 3643[6] *3865[12]* **>23f<**
Aegean Breeze 2 b g Pharly (FR)-Rich Pickings (Dominion) 2917[14] 3103[13] 3295[8] **>24f<**
Aegean Dawn 2 ch f Anshan-Midnight Owl (FR) (Ardross) 2746[2] 2953[11] **>71f<**
Aegean Sound 3 b f Distant Relative-Imperatrice (USA) (Kings Lake (USA)) **1996:** *5083[10]* **1997:** 694[14] 2691[13] 2918[10] 3297[7] 4184[7] 4333[12] 4951[18] **>48a**

43f<

Aeolina (FR) 3 b br f Kaldoun (FR)-Folia (Sadler's Wells (USA)) 3918^{2} 4360^{4} 4579^{5} 4771^{6} 4996^{3} **>61f<**

Aerleon Pete (IRE) 3 b c Caerleon (USA)-Bristle (Thatch (USA)) 1006^{6} 1741^{8} 2328^{12} 3277^{2} (3632) (4144) 4409^{3} 4754^{12} **>98f<**

Afaan (IRE) 4 ch c Cadeaux Genereux-Rawaabe (USA) (Nureyev (USA)) 14^{5} 87^{2} 135^{2} 423^{2} 545^{3} 593^{8} 1080^{2} 1385^{3} (1467) 1759^{8} 1977^{2} 2915^{11} 3582^{9} 3771^{9} 3910^{22} (4805) (4997) 5049^{9} **>50++a 85f<**

Afarka (IRE) 4 b f Kahyasi-Afasara 2967a^{6} **>86f<**

Aficionado (IRE) 3 b g Marju (IRE)-Haneena (Habitat) 644^{2} 771^{2} 1140^{9} 1568^{11} 1826^{14} 4568^{8} 4987^{12} **>64a 57f<**

Afon Alwen 4 ch f Henbit (USA)-Brenig (Horage) 881^{9} 1623^{3} 1996^{3} 3080^{4} 3931^{2} **>49a 69f<**

African-Pard (IRE) 5 b g Don't Forget Me-Petite Realm (Realm) **1996:** 5237^{11} **1997:** 72^{11} 140^{8} 284^{2} 360^{3} 1463^{12} 2164^{3} (2876) 3315^{11} (3793) 4109^{10} **>52a 75f<**

African Sun (IRE) 4 b g Mtoto-Nuit D'Ete (USA) (Super Concorde (USA)) 328^{7} 373^{11} 896^{20} 1024^{2} 1145^{11} 1632^{17} 1694^{11} 2152^{10} 2174^{6} 2411^{9} 4453^{13} 4713^{16} 4850^{6} **>32a 38f<**

After Dawn (IRE) 2 b f Brief Truce (USA)-Faakirah (Dragonara Palace (USA)) 648^{11} 828^{14} 1664^{6} 2394^{11} 2697^{8} 4334^{9} 4605^{8} **>61f<**

After Eight 2 b c Presidium-Vickenda (Giacometti) 2943^{9} 3686^{15} 4710^{7} 4922^{8} **>59f<**

After Hours 3 b f Polar Falcon (USA)-Tarasova (USA) (Green Forest (USA)) 1207^{10} 1567^{6} 4177^{11} 4817^{14} **>49f<**

After The Rain 2 ch c Sanglamore (USA)-Rainy Sky (Rainbow Quest (USA)) 1174^{6} 2699^{4} 3253^{4} 3802^{2} 4116^{17} 4384^{4} 4778^{7} **>84f<**

Against The Clock 5 b g Puissance-Sara Sprint (Formidable (USA)) 3467^{10}

Agami (USA) 2 b f Nureyev (USA)-Agacerie (USA) (Exclusive Native (USA)) 4330^{12} **>40f<**

Aganon 2 b c Aragon-Plain Tree (Wolver Hollow) 4298^{6} 4884^{18} 5042^{5} **>71+f<**

Agent 4 ch g Anshan-Maria Cappuccini (Siberian Express (USA)) **1996:** 5267^{3} **1997:** (306) 1583^{9} 1944^{13} 2342^{9} 2502^{8} 2912^{7} **>69a 60df<**

Agent Mulder 3 b g Kylian (USA)-Precious Caroline (IRE) (The Noble Player (USA)) 576^{5} 868^{7} 1164^{2} (1633) 1826^{4} **>37a 67f<**

Agift 3 b f Cadeaux Genereux-Aspark (Sparkler) 778^{6} 989^{8} 1423^{9} 2510^{11} **>59f<**

Agony Aunt 3 b f Formidable (USA)-Loch Clair (IRE) (Lomond (USA)) 533^{4} 887^{4} 1270^{5} (2952) 3906^{7} 4144^{3} 4435^{3} 4731^{8} **>86f<**

Agwa 8 b g Local Suitor (USA)-Meissarah (USA) (Silver Hawk (USA)) **1996:** 5099^{11} **1997:** 2751^{6} 2958^{8} 3327^{9} 3469^{12} 3969^{8} **>45a 40f<**

Ailleacht (USA) 5 b or br m Chief's Crown (USA)-Poster Beauty (USA) (Codex (USA)) 1186a^{3} 1881a^{2} 2056^{23} 2815a^{5} 3535a^{3} 4203a^{3} **>103f<**

Air Attache (USA) 2 b c Sky Classic (CAN)-Diplomatic Cover (USA) (Roberto (USA)) 3745^{2} 4111^{4} **>76f<**

Airborne Harris (IRE) 4 ch g Persian Heights-Excuse Slip (USA) (Damascus (USA)) **1996:** 5208^{12} **1997:** 243^{12} 3469^{15} 3608^{9} 3762^{14} 4069^{13} **>27a 32f<**

Air Express (IRE) 3 b c Salse (USA)-Ibtisamm (USA) (Caucasus (USA)) 692^{4} (917a) (1544a) 2011^{2} 3124^{7} (4422) **>128f<**

Air Of Distinction (IRE) 3 br f Distinctly North (USA)-Kaysama (FR) (Kenmare (FR)) 1532a^{6} **>99f<**

Airport (USA) 6 b h Lear Fan (USA)-Vague Prospect (USA) (Vaguely Noble) 308a^{3} **>107a 116f<**

Air Quest 4 b c Rainbow Quest (USA)-Aryenne (FR) (Green Dancer (USA)) 736^{13} 1319^{3} **>107f<**

Aix En Provence (USA) 2 b c Geiger Counter (USA)-Low Hill (Rousillon (USA)) (2110) 2584^{7} 2863^{4} (3602) 4551^{3} 4803^{8} **>103?f<**

Ajano (GER) 3 b c Kings Lake (USA)-Anona (GER) (Arratos (FR)) 920a^{3} (1545a) 3555a^{4} **>115f<**

Ajayib (USA) 3 b f Riverman (USA)-Maplejinsky (USA) (Nijinsky (CAN)) 797^{2} 1435^{5} 4268^{10} 4435^{2} 4691^{3} 4996^{6} **>88f<**

Ajcombe (IRE) 4 b g Ajraas (USA)-Whichcombe (Huntercombe) 2311^{7} 2692^{7} 2853^{3} 4104^{8} 4374^{11} **>72f<**

Ajeebah (IRE) 3 b f Mujtahid (USA)-Saffron (FR) (Fabulous Dancer (USA)) 2184^{5} 2770^{6} 2941^{9} **>57f<**

Ajig Dancer 2 b f Niniski (USA)-Gloire (Thatching) 1240^{2} 2057^{7} 2558^{10} (4042) 4267^{14} **>93f<**

Ajina (USA) 3 b f Strawberry Road (AUS)-Winglet (USA) Alydar (USA) (5062a) **>118a f<**

Ajkuit (IRE) 4 b g Persian Heights-Hazar (IRE) (Thatching) **1996:** 5227^{7} **1997:** 319^{6} 401^{8} **>37a 55f<**

Akalim 4 b g Petong-Tiszta Sharok (Song) 1317^{10} 2529^{13} 2933^{4} 3642^{4} 4112^{3} 4319^{7} 4738^{3} 4913^{3} **>66a 68f<**

Akarita (IRE) 2 b f Akarad (FR)-Safita (Habitat) 3985^{6} 4212^{4} 4735^{3} **>72f<**

Akdariya (IRE) 3 b f Shirley Heights-Akishka (Nishapour (FR)) 2053^{2} 2967a^{5} **>102f<**

Al Abraq (IRE) 4 b g Reprimand-Dazzling Maid (IRE) (Tate Gallery (USA)) 738^{13} 1085^{7} 1473^{3} **>78df<**

Alaflak (IRE) 6 b h Caerleon (USA)-Safe Haven (Blakeney) 1092^{4} 2930^{4} **>80f<**

Alagna 3 b f Unfuwain (USA)-Spica (USA) (Diesis) 306^{6} 395^{7} 606^{4} 1299^{3} 1469^{2} 1785^{2} 2068^{7} 2397^{5} 3400^{6} 4336^{4} 4503^{6} 4971^{10} **>48da 53f<**

Alakdar (CAN) 3 ch c Green Dancer (USA)-Population (General Assembly (USA)) 2315^{7} 2846^{3} 3277^{13} 3714^{U} 4104^{3} 4336^{17} (4748) 4996^{10} **>79f<**

Alakhluki 4 b f Aragon-Hawaiian Bloom (USA) (Hawaii) **1996:** 5088^{7} **>18a 58f<**

Alamein (USA) 4 ch g Roi Danzig (USA)-Pollination (Pentotal) 450^{6} 1874^{2} 2105^{17} 2775^{4} 2894^{10} 3822^{7} **>88f<**

Alamo Bay (USA) 4 b c Nureyev (USA)-Albertine (FR) (Irish River (FR)) (2818a) 4393a^{2} **>114f<**

Alamode 3 b f Statoblest-Alo Ez (Alzao (USA)) (1401) 2001^{6} 4329^{15} **>68+f<**

Alana's Ballad (IRE) 4 b f Be My Native (USA)-Radalgo (Ballad Rock) 2^{9} 54^{11} 85^{7} 150^{11} 290^{11} **>23a 10f<**

Alaraby (IRE) 5 b m Caerleon (USA)-Circo (High Top) 3069^{6} **>35f<**

Alarico (FR) 4 ch g Kadrou (FR)-Calabria (FR) (Vitiges (FR)) (173) 250^{3} 1974^{6} 2218^{9} 2694^{3} 3137^{2} 3318^{8} **>80a 73f<**

Alarme Belle 3 b f Warning-Dazzlingly Radiant (Try My Best (USA)) 4834a^{2} **>108f<**

Alarming Motown 2 b f Warning-Sweet Soul Dream (USA) (Conquistador Cielo (USA)) 4884^{10} **>57f<**

Alarmist 3 b c Warning-Wryneck (Niniski (USA)) 1866^{3} 2287^{3} 2731^{8} 3475^{10} 3864^{8} 4109^{11} 4516^{14} **>74f<**

Al Ava Consonant 3 b f Reprimand-Dragonist (Dragonara Palace (USA)) 547^{7} 1096^{14} 1333^{9} 1820^{11} 4429^{6} 4469^{9} 4846^{5} 4972^{8} **>19a 42f<**

Alazan 2 ch c Risk Me (FR)-Gunnard (Gunner B) 2057^{12} 2860^{5} 4895^{5} **>25f<**

Al Azhar 3 b c Alzao (USA)-Upend (Main Reef) 1982^{6} 3190^{15} 3741^{2} 4148^{3} 4558^{18} (4891) 5053^{5} **>102f<**

Albaha (USA) 4 br g Woodman (USA)-Linda's Magic (USA) (Far North (CAN)) **1996:** (5259) **1997:** 39^{2} (70) (389) 680^{18} 2839^{9} 3242^{3} 4691^{9} **>88a 78f<**

Albarahin (USA) 2 b c Silver Hawk (USA)-My Dear Lady (USA) (Mr Prospector (USA)) 4758^{2} 4967^{2} **>91f<**

Albaran (GER) 4 b c Sure Blade (USA)-Araqueen (GER) (Konigsstuhl (GER)) 3885a^{3} **>108f<**

Alberich (IRE) 2 b c Night Shift (USA)-Tetradonna (IRE) (Teenoso (USA)) 3479^{5} (3760) 4734^{3} **>80+f<**

Albert The Bear 4 b g Puissance-Florentynna Bay (Aragon) 953^{3} (1035) 1324^{12} (1658) 2105^{14} 2478^{5} 2666^{4} 3220^{6} 3615^{2} 3888^{8} 3901^{7} 4147^{20} 4282^{5} 4430^{2} 4983^{12} **>51a 92f<**

Alboostan 2 b c Sabrehill (USA)-Russian Countess (USA) (Nureyev (USA)) (3103) 3688^{2} (4140) 4766a^{3} **>107f<**

Alborada 2 gr f Alzao (USA)-Alouette (Darshaan) 2875^{3} 3151^{3} (4212) (4619a) **>101f<**

Albrighton 2 b g Terimon-Bright-One (Electric) 4801^{8} 5042^{18} **>55f<**

Alcalali (USA) 3 ch f Septieme Ciel (USA)-Princess Verna (USA) (Al Hattab (USA)) 833^{2} 1147^{6} 1316^{8} 1646^{4} 2053^{4} 2513^{8} 3188^{4} 3704^{7} 3917^{4} 4676^{7} **>81f<**

Alcayde 2 ch c Alhijaz-Lucky Flinders (Free State) 4433^{4} **>72f<**

Alcian Blue 6 b h Tina's Pet-Rhiannon (Welsh Pageant) 632^{6} 865^{9} **>52a 44f<**

Alconleigh 2 ch c Pursuit of Love-Serotina (IRE) (Mtoto) 1076^{3} (1267) 2343^{2} 2758^{2} (3036) 3650^{2} 4778^{16} 4953^{4} 5050^{2} **>93f<**

Aldino (GER) 3 b c Dashing Blade-Alabama (GER) (Surumu (GER)) 3553a^{3} **>110f<**

Aldo Piccolo (IRE) 3 b c Danehill (USA)-Aztec Princess (Indian King (USA)) **1996:** 5196a^{2}

Aldwych Arrow (IRE) 2 ch g Rainbows For Life (CAN)-Shygate (Shy Groom (USA)) 1842^{6} 2320^{9} 2953^{6} 4044^{11} 4334^{12} **>67f<**

Alekos (USA) 3 b c Irish River (USA)-Tanapa (FR) (Luthier) 1070a^{3} 2274a^{4} 3002a^{5} **>110f<**

Alessiass (IRE) 3 **1996:** 5283a^{3}

Alezal 3 b c Anshan-Dance On The Stage (Dancing Brave (USA)) 740^{2} (1041) (1404) 2013^{20} 4133^{2} (4678) **>108f<**

Alfa Daisy (IRE) 3 1368a^{8} **>62f<**

Alfahaal (IRE) 4 b c Green Desert (USA)-Fair of the Furze (Ela-Mana-Mou) 763^{9} 895^{12} 1385^{5} 2006^{10} (2760) 3115^{7} 3328^{5} 4059^{3} 4219^{15} 4516^{7} (4696) 5023^{2} **>69f<**

Alfannan 3 b c Lear Fan (USA)-Connecting Link (USA) (Linkage (USA)) 683^{13} **>68f<**

Al-Fateh (IRE) 2 b c Caerleon (USA)-Filia Ardross (Ardross) 4775^{6} 5041^{3} **>84f<**

Alfayza 4 b f Danehill (USA)-Dahlawise (IRE) (Caerleon (USA)) **1996:** 5094^{3} **>36a 51f<**

Alfiglia 2 b f Alhijaz-Saraswati (Mansingh (USA)) (1635) 2103^{5} 2648^{3} 3379^{6} 4143^{10} **>87f<**

Alfredo Alfredo (USA) 5 b g Miswaki (USA)-Alleged Queen (USA) (Alleged (USA)) 647^{7} **>68+f<**

Algaleb 2 ch c Alhijaz-Brise de Mer (USA) (Bering) 3686^{12} 4056^{4} 4458^{10} **>70a 34f<**

Algebra 2 b g Statoblest-Alghabrah (Lomond (USA)) 4216^{12} 4564^{10} 4814^{9} 4989^{8} **>57f<**

Al Haal (USA) 8 b g Northern Baby (CAN)-Kit's Double (USA) (Spring Double) **1996:** 5244^{11} 5277^{5} **1997:** 22^{5} 78^{7} 101^{7} 183^{6} **>42a f< (DEAD)**

Alhaarth (IRE) 4 b c Unfuwain (USA)-Irish Valley

(USA) (Irish River (FR)) 2010^{2} (2453a) 3124^{9} 4204a^{3} (4656a) **>128f<**
Alharir (USA) 2 b br f Zafonic (USA)-Thawakib (IRE) (Sadler's Wells (USA)) 2840^{3} (3426) 4119^{5} **>92+f<**
Alhawa (USA) 4 ch c Mt Livermore (USA)-Petrava (NZ) (Imposing (AUS)) 832^{4} 987^{15} 3052^{3} 3150^{16} **>82f<**
Al Helal 5 b h In The Wings-Rosia Bay (High Top) *18^{6} 43^{3} 104^{4} 147^{2} 183^{2} 216^{P}* **>52a 70f< (DEAD)**
Alhosaam 3 b c Belmez (USA)-Leipzig (Relkino) 725^{10} 1144^{8} 1434^{7} 2373^{3} (4108) 4363^{4} **>84f<**
Alicia Lea (IRE) 5 b m Cyrano de Bergerac-Sasha Lea (Cawston's Clown) **1996:** *5099^{12}*
Alifandango (IRE) 3 b f Alzao (USA)-Fandangerina (USA) (Grey Dawn II) 833^{7} (2184) 3128^{8} 3633^{6} **>77f<**
Alignment (IRE) 2 b f Alzao (USA)-Scots Lass (Shirley Heights) 3547^{2} 3740^{2} 4442^{7} **>89f<**
Alikhlas 3 b br f Lahib (USA)-Mathaayl (USA) (Shadeed (USA)) 935^{3} 1316^{5} 1656^{2} (3079) 3752^{3} 3930^{8} 4175^{6} 4436^{13} **>78f<**
Alimerjam 3 b f Thowra (FR)-Sicilian Vespers (Mummy's Game) **1996:** *5087^{6} 5147^{8}* **1997:** *26^{6} 239^{4}* 539^{4} 1094^{17} 1502^{5} **>53a 49df<**
Aliprod (IRE) 3 **1996:** (5283a)
Ali-Royal (IRE) 4 b c Royal Academy (USA)-Alidiva (Chief Singer) (678) 852^{3} 1210^{2} 2009^{3} (2679) (3124) **>129f<**
Alisadara 3 b f Nomination-Nishara (Nishapour (FR)) 1451^{4} 1730^{11} 2017^{8} 2171^{10} 2715^{11} 3038^{4} 3405^{4} 3601^{7} 4214^{11} 4601^{18} **>34f<**
Alisura 4 br f Lead on Time (USA)-Iosifa (Top Ville) **1996:** *5244^{12}* **1997:** *1086^{11}* 1779^{23} 2175^{9} 3421^{11} 3719^{7} **>19a 14f<**
Aliya (IRE) 3 b f Darshaan-Alannya (FR) (Relko) 2267a^{5} 2814a^{9} 3511a^{2} 3842a^{2} (4191a) 4658a^{8} **>107f<**
Aljaz 7 b g Al Nasr (FR)-Santa Linda (USA) (Sir Ivor) **1996:** *5173^{2} 5268^{5}* **1997:** *20^{3} 79^{2} 107^{6} 318^{6} 391^{2} 459^{7} 593^{10} 3398^{2}* 4738^{16} **>53a 23f<**
Al Jinn 6 ch g Hadeer-Mrs Musgrove (Jalmood (USA)) *157^{7}* **>9a 40?f<**
Allandro (GER) 3 4396a^{7} **>103f<**
Allasella (IRE) 2 b f Persian Bold-Silks Princess (Prince Tenderfoot (USA)) 1293^{5} 1806^{9} 2227^{10} 2534^{8} 3094^{4} 3965^{5} 4166^{20} 4566^{14} **>67f<**
Allaton (IRE) 2 ch g Shalford (IRE)-Confirmed Friend (Wolverlife) 2181^{26} 2520^{6} 3861^{7} **>59f<**
All Blade (GER) 4 c 4661a^{8} **>54f<**
All Done 4 ch f Northern State (USA)-Doogali (Doon) 944^{9} 1434^{10} **>42f<**
Allemande (IRE) 5 b h Nashwan (USA)-Dance Festival (Nureyev (USA)) 4872^{20} **>77a 109f<**
Allez Cyrano (IRE) 6 b g Alzao (USA)-Miss Bergerac (Bold Lad (IRE)) *219^{5} 254^{7} 359^{6}* **>46a 74?f<**
Allez Pablo 7 b g Crisp-Countess Mariga (Amboise) *381^{9}* **>24f<**
All Girls Forget 3 ch f Rock Hopper-Happydrome (Ahonoora) 4407^{5} 4768^{11} 4923^{13} **>32f<**
Allgrit (USA) 2 b c Shadeed (USA)-Arsaan (USA) (Nureyev (USA)) 4061^{8} 4367^{5} 4758^{18} **>74f<**
Allied Academy 3 ch g Royal Academy (USA)-Tsungani (Cure The Blues (USA)) *341^{5}* 535^{6} 1470^{5} 2132^{8} **>59a 64df<**
Allied Forces (USA) 4 ch c Miswaki (USA)-Mangala (USA) (Sharpen Up) (2009) 2527^{4} 3124^{3} 3880a^{6} 4422^{6} **>126f<**
All In Leather 3 b f Saddlers' Hall (IRE)-Ivana (IRE) (Taufan (USA)) *(3396)* 3551^{4} 3897^{11} **>78?a 61f<**
Allinson's Mate (IRE) 9 b g Fayruz-Piney Pass (Persian Bold) **1996:** *5082^{3} 5165^{9}* **1997:** *382^{6}* 468^{5} 1020^{8} (1077) 1315^{6} (1395) 1511^{4} 1761^{2} 2204^{3} 2325^{11} 3143^{18} 3420^{2} 3759^{12} 3855^{6} 4059^{4} 4228^{11} 4773^{16} **>64a 64f<**
All Is Fair 3 b f Selkirk (USA)-Allegra (Niniski (USA)) 2945^{2} 4120^{5} 4276^{4} 4550^{5} 4960a^{6} **>96f<**
Alliteration 2 b c Polish Precedent (USA)-African Peace (USA) (Roberto (USA)) 4647a^{3} **>80f<**
All Made Up (USA) 2 b c Sheikh Albadou-Mascara Miss (USA) (Fio Rito (USA)) 4715^{5} 4915^{10} **>70f<**
Allmaites 2 b c Komaite (USA)-Darling Miss Daisy (Tina's Pet) 948^{W} 1447^{10} 1657^{5} 3806^{14} 3986^{7} 4162^{3} **>72f<**
All On 6 ch m Dunbeath (USA)-Fresh Line (High Line) **1996:** *5177^{10}* **1997:** 465^{3} *542^{7} 858^{2}* (865) (928) 1039^{3} (1081) *1125^{3}* 3309^{5} 4804^{3} 4874^{3} 5027^{9} **>70a 62f<**
All Our Blessings (IRE) 2 b f Statoblest-Zenga (Try My Best (USA)) 4640^{7} 4921^{13} 4993^{17} **>30f<**
All Stand 4 ch f Dominion-Now In Session (USA) (Diesis) 1139^{16} **>59f<**
Allstars Dancer 4 b f Primo Dominie-Danzig Harbour (USA) (Private Account (USA)) *24^{5} 128^{2} 172^{4} 223^{2} 304^{7} 339^{6}* 3083^{9} 3299^{6} **>42a 21f<**
Allstars Express 4 b g Rambo Dancer (CAN)-Aligote (Nebbiolo) 607^{7} **>69a 69f<**
Allurement (IRE) 3 b f Sadler's Wells (USA)-Alydaress (USA) (Alydar (USA)) (1360a) **>106f<**
Allwight Then (IRE) 6 gr g Dancing Dissident (USA)-Abergwrle (Absalom) 1627^{13} 2061^{12} **>48a 56df<**
Al Mabrook (IRE) 2 b c Rainbows For Life (CAN)-Sky Lover (Ela-Mana-Mou) 2870^{10} 3131^{6} 3235^{5} 3589^{2} **>80f<**
Almandab (IRE) 2 b br c Last Tycoon-Fortune Teller (Troy) 4478^{5} (4952) **>96+f<**
Almasi (IRE) 5 b m Petorius-Best Niece (Vaigly Great) 759^{7} 1020^{7} 1385^{2} (1765) (2244) 2841^{2} 3195^{2} (3580) (4013) 4280^{2} 4553^{3} **>96f<**
Al Masroor (USA) 3 b c Red Ransom (USA)-Gaye's Delight (USA) (Imperial Falcon (CAN)) 675^{10} 1238^{5} 1958^{10} (2062) 2290^{2} 2868^{6} 3138^{3} 3392^{3} 3894^{11} 4176^{13} 4436^{2} 4979^{8} **>82f<**
Almaty (IRE) 4 b c Dancing Dissident (USA)-Almaaseh (IRE) (Dancing Brave (USA)) 877^{3} (1590) 2106^{15} 3111^{15} 3724^{15} 4098^{2} 4239^{14} 4525^{6} **>119df<**
Almazhar (IRE) 2 b c Last Tycoon-Mosaique Bleue (Shirley Heights) 4318^{11} **>52f<**
Almond Rock 5 b g Soviet Star (USA)-Banket (Glint of Gold) 738^{4} 987^{8} 1261^{3} 3243^{11} 3901^{5} 4297^{19} **>98f<**
Almost Skint (IRE) 3 b f Last Tycoon-Rich Relation (Golden Act) 806a^{3} 1533a^{7} **>99f<**
Al Muallim (USA) 3 b c Theatrical-Gerri N Jo Go (USA) (Top Command (USA)) 3198^{4} (3614) 3772^{3} 4121^{2} (4550) **>100f<**
Almuhimm (USA) 5 b g Diesis-Abeesh (USA) (Nijinsky (CAN)) 1214^{9} 1397^{5} (2857) 3185^{5} 3649^{17} 4121^{11} **>91f<**
Almuhtaram 5 b g Rambo Dancer (CAN)-Mrs Mainwaring (FR) (Home Guard (USA)) 430^{16} 598^{7} 770^{3} 1036^{11} 1393^{7} 1641^{3} 2154^{7} 2592^{5} 3229^{5} **>79a 58f<**
Almurooj 2 b f Zafonic (USA)-Al Bahathri (USA) (Blushing Groom (FR)) 4556^{9} **>53f<**
Almushtarak (IRE) 4 b c Fairy King (USA)-Exciting (Mill Reef (USA)) 1767^{5} 2056^{8} 2334^{2} 2766^{8} 3577^{5} 3747^{3} 4003^{2} (4117) 4344a^{7} 4782^{9} **>120f<**
Almutawakel 2 b c Machiavellian (USA)-Elfaslah (IRE) (Green Desert (USA)) (2524) (3233) 4140^{2} 4440^{5} **>105f<**
Alonso De Castillo (IRE) 3 b c Classic Secret (USA)-Stage Deli (ITY) (Prince Tenderfoot (USA)) 1555a^{2} **>82f<**
Alosaili 10 ch g Kris-Vaison la Romaine (Arctic Tern (USA)) *116^{12}*
Alpen Wolf (IRE) 2 ch c Wolfhound (USA)-Oatfield (Great Nephew) 850^{5} 1143^{6} 1760^{8} 1954^{5} 3094^{7} 3288^{3} 3774^{7} 4065^{7} **>71f<**
Alphabet 3 b f Saddlers' Hall (IRE)-A-to-Z (IRE) (Ahonoora) 930^{9} (3281) 3786^{4} 4121^{17} **>86f<**
Alpha Whisky (GER) 2 gr f Wolfhound (USA)-Alsiba (Northfields (USA)) 1970^{5} 2534^{3} 2831^{5} 3817^{2} 4166^{7} 4462^{3} **>73f<**
Alpheton Prince 4 b g Prince of Cill Dara-Batsam Lady (Battle Hymn) *235^{13}* 1246^{6} **>21a 34f<**
Alpina (USA) 3 b f El Prado (IRE)-Aspara (USA) (Crimson Satan) 1784^{6} 2046^{6} 2389^{5} 3234^{15} **>67f<**
Alpine Hideaway (IRE) 4 b g Tirol-Arbour (USA) (Graustark) 1021^{3} 1308^{8} 1606^{3} 1782^{8} 2325^{13} *(2603)* 2922^{3} *3075^{14}* 3418^{6} (3822) 4213^{13} 4410^{8} 4510^{2} 4924^{3} 5030^{10} **>72a 77f<**
Alpine Music (IRE) 3 b g Tirol-Holy Devotion (Commanche Run) 1090^{7} 1388^{14} 1925^{12} 2310^{18} 2510^{6} 3018^{12} **>31f<**
Alpine Panther (IRE) 4 b g Tirol-Kentucky Wildcat (Be My Guest (USA)) 3491^{5} 3777^{6} 3937^{14} 4235^{7} 4438^{2} 4562^{11} 5027^{7} **>69f<**
Alpine Time (IRE) 3 b f Tirol-Millie Musique (Miller's Mate) 1453^{4} 2133^{12} 2601^{13} **>92df<**
Alrabyah (IRE) 2 br c Brief Truce (USA)-Bean Siamsa (Solinus) 3986^{8} 4871^{11} **>55f<**
Al Reet (IRE) 6 b m Alzao (USA)-Reet Petite (Thatching) *545^{8}* 883^{10} *1046^{6}* 1385^{7} 1761^{10} *2069^{3}* (2317) 2569^{2} *2913^{5} 3582^{7}* 3759^{16} 4629^{10} 4695^{13} 4905^{13} 4992^{3} **>61a 58f<**
Alsahib (USA) 4 b g Slew O' Gold (USA)-Khwlah (USA) (Best Turn (USA)) 755^{6} 895^{14} 1262^{6} *(1788) 2161^{6}* 2374^{3} 2512^{8} 3200^{10} **>82a 69f<**
Al's Alibi 4 b c Alzao (USA)-Lady Kris (IRE) (Kris) 499^{4} 680^{8} 984^{2} 1260^{6} 2122^{12} (3267) 3689^{10} 3907^{4} 4279^{7} 4443^{12} **>84f<**
Al's Fella (IRE) 2 br c Alzao (USA)-Crystal Cross (USA) (Roberto (USA)) 1293^{3} 2336^{4} 2693^{6} 3794^{6} 4044^{7} 4778^{8} 4953^{2} **>74f<**
Al Shaati (FR) 7 b m Lead on Time (USA)-With You All (Free Round (USA)) **1996:** *5144^{11} 5215^{9}* **1997:** *57^{12}* **>5a 35f< (DEAD)**
Altamura (USA) 4 b f El Gran Senor (USA)-Narwala (Darshaan) **1996:** 5198a^{9} **>115f<**
Alte Kunst (IRE) 3 1202a^{12} 4536a^{3} **>99f<**
Althib (IRE) 2 ch c Wolfhound (USA)-Sure Enough (IRE) (Diesis) 2409^{2} 2856^{4} 3899^{6} 4173^{5} **>76f<**
Altibr (USA) 2 ch c Diesis-Love's Reward (Nonoalco (USA)) (4901) **>101++f<**
Altitude (IRE) 2 b c Alzao (USA)-Elevate (Ela-Mana-Mou) 4064^{19} 4244^{6} 4413^{8} **>61f<**
Altor 5 gr h Kendor (FR)-Ramonda 630a^{3} **>105f<**
Alumisiyah (USA) 3 b br f Danzig (USA)-Mathkurh (USA) (Riverman (USA)) 1243^{2} 1609^{11} 2560^{9} (4733) 4842^{3} 5054^{13} **>88f<**
Alvilde 3 b f Alzao (USA)-Volida (Posse (USA)) *145^{2} 185^{2} 215^{4} 368^{4} 456^{5}* 644^{6} **>55a 63f<**
Alwarqa 4 b f Old Vic-Ostora (USA) (Blushing Groom (FR)) 846^{7} 2000^{8} 2589^{6} 2882^{4} 3010^{7} 3317^{7} 3461^{5} 4213^{5} 4287^{7} *4811^{6}* **>46a 53f<**
Always Alight 3 ch g Never so Bold-Fire Sprite (Mummy's Game) 483^{9} 649^{2} 845^{2} 1090^{8} 1243^{4} (1488) 1673^{2} (2347) 2833^{3} 3189^{10} 3923^{3} 4280^{6} 4733^{5} (4842) 4995^{3} **>24a 84f<**
Always Earnest (USA) 9 b g Alleged (USA)-Nettie Cometti (USA) (Giacometti) **1996:** 5125a^{2} 5199a^{2}

1997: 4654a^{4} **>125f<**

Always Grace 5 b m Never so Bold-Musical Sally (USA) (The Minstrel (CAN)) 1666^{6} 2751^{4} 2958^{4} 3139^{6} 4518^{8} **>50a 57f<**

Always Happy 4 ch f Sharrood (USA)-Convivial (Nordance (USA)) *187^{2} 226^{6}* 1373^{6} **>80da 71f<**

Always Loyal (USA) 3 b f Zilzal (USA)-Balbonella (FR) (Gay Mecene (USA)) (818a) (1203a) 1916a^{6} 4666a^{7} **>115f<**

Always Lucky 2 gr f Absalom-Petitesse (Petong) 536^{3} 897^{5} *(1286)* 1729^{2} 2140^{3} 2823^{2} *(3076)* 3544^{2} 4403^{5} *4796^{4}* **>76a 65f<**

Always On My Mind 3 b f Distant Relative-Fleur Rouge (Pharly (FR)) 1587^{7} 1967^{2} (2491) (2841) (3145) 4155^{16} (4975) **>94+f<**

Always Trying 2 b c Always Fair (USA)-Bassita (Bustino) 4236^{14} 4470^{2} 4974^{17} **>46f<**

Alzahra 2 ch f Interrex (CAN)-Flirty Lady (Never so Bold) 4901^{8} **>56f<**

Alzotic (IRE) 4 b g Alzao (USA)-Exotic Bride (USA) (Blushing Groom (FR)) 3826^{9} 4438^{4} 4751^{12} **>70a 42f<**

Amabel (USA) 2 b f Silver Hawk (USA)-Routilante (Rousillon (USA)) 3574^{9} 3979^{7} (4273) 4555^{6} 4892^{2} **>95f<**

Amadour (IRE) 4 b g Contract Law (USA)-Truly Flattering (Hard Fought) *(334)* 430^{17} 510^{9} *1421^{5}* 1636^{5} **>72a 57f<**

Amany (IRE) 5 b m Waajib-Treeline (High Top) 550^{9} 1385^{16} **>48?f<**

Amarella (IRE) 3 ch f Soviet Lad (USA)-Eight Mile Rock (Dominion) 3550^{6} 3787^{15} 4316^{11} **>43f<**

Amaryllis (IRE) 3 b f Sadler's Wells (USA)-Heartbreak (USA) (Stage Door Johnny) **1996:** *(5103)* **>68a 72f<**

Amazing Bay 4 b f Mazilier (USA)-Petriece (Mummy's Pet) 726^{11} 941^{9} 1158^{14} 1766^{8} **>93f<**

Amazing Sail (IRE) 4 b g Alzao (USA)-Amazer (USA) (Vaguely Noble) *86^{12} 167^{13}* **>34a 65f<**

Amazonian 2 b c Formidable (USA)-Red Rose Garden (Electric) 4706^{6} **>52f<**

Ambassadori (USA) 4 b c Lear Fan (USA)-Czar's Bride (USA) (Northern Dancer) **1996:** *(5088)* **>62a 50f<**

Amber Fort 4 gr g Indian Ridge-Lammastide (Martinmas) *398^{10}* 832^{9} 987^{5} 1166^{2} 1456^{13} 1739^{17} 1878^{3} (2282) **>66a 83f<**

Amber Regent 2 ch g King's Signet (USA)-Silly Sally (Music Boy) 3821^{9} 4211^{8} 4428^{11} **>45f<**

Amber Valley (USA) 6 ch g Bering-Olatha (USA) (Miswaki (USA)) *82^{10}* **>42a 69f<**

Ambidextrous (IRE) 5 b h Shareef Dancer (USA)-Amber Fizz (USA) (Effervescing (USA)) *123^{6} 260^{3} 315^{2} 516^{5}* 574^{8} 1281^{3} 1660^{5} (1992) 2351^{3} 2512^{2} (2686) 2890^{8} 3380^{4} 3886^{6} 4161^{5} **>53a 63f<**

Ambiguous 2 ch c Arazi (USA)-Vaguely (Bold Lad (IRE)) 4309^{8} 4526^{17} 4715^{12} **>56f<**

Ambitious 2 b f Ardkinglass-Ayodhya (IRE) (Astronef) 1812^{9} 3416^{2} 3926^{4} **>69f<**

Ambuscade (USA) 11 ch g Roberto (USA)-Gurkhas Band (USA) (Lurullah) 3935^{5} 4269^{11} 4744^{12} 4804^{15} **>66da 23f<**

Ameena (USA) 2 b f Irish River (FR)-London Pride (USA) (Lear Fan (USA)) 4066^{9} **>67f<**

Ameer Alfayaafi (IRE) 4 b g Mujtahid (USA)-Sharp Circle (IRE) (Sure Blade (USA)) 477^{9} 587^{15} **>55f<**

Amelia Jane 3 ch f Efisio-Blue Jane (Blue Cashmere) 3425^{9} 4221^{14} *4795^{5}* **>38a 20f<**

American Cousin 2 b c Distant Relative-Zelda (USA) (Sharpen Up) 2181^{18} 2388^{3} 2571^{3} *3042^{3}* 3635^{10} **>58a 58f<**

American Hero 9 ch g Persian Bold-American Winter (USA) (Lyphard (USA)) 950^{10} **>27f<**

American Whisper 3 b c Dixieland Band (USA)-Only A Rumour (Ela-Mana-Mou) 599^{11} 1256^{11} (1747) (2187) 3424^{7} (4876) **>89f<**

Amiarge 7 b g Reference Point-Scotia Rose (Tap On Wood) **1996:** *5116^{9}* **1997:** 1494^{5} 1654^{5} 1795^{9} (2316) 2498^{4} 2867^{9} 3309^{4} 3543^{5} (3826) 4874^{16} **>24a 56f<**

Amiasapphire 2 ch f Safawan-Amethystine (USA) (Barachois (CAN)) 1954^{12} 2306^{15} 2700^{W} **>31f<**

Amico 3 b c Efisio-Stormswept (USA) (Storm Bird (CAN)) **1996:** *5111^{5} 5238^{W}* **1997:** *230^{2} (292) 366^{2}* 471^{3} **>73a 61f<**

Amid Albadu (USA) 3 b c Sheikh Albadou-Dream Play (USA) (Blushing Groom (FR)) (723) 1412^{2} 1767^{4} 2217^{2} 3172a^{5} (3797) 4154^{4} 4776^{2} **>113f<**

Amid The Stars 3 b f Midyan (USA)-Celebrity (Troy) 3244^{3} 3488^{4} **>57f<**

A Million Watts 6 b g Belfort (FR)-Peters Pet Girl (Norwick (USA)) **1996:** *5211^{10}* **1997:** *23^{10} 123^{13}* **>29a 31f<**

Amington Girl 2 b f Tragic Role (USA)-Millfields House (Record Token) 1860^{5} 2233^{3} 2784^{6} 3451^{14} 3564^{6} **>48f<**

Amington Lass 4 ch f Cree Song-Millfields House (Record Token) **1996:** *(5268)* **1997:** *32^{4} 53^{8}* **>62da 68f<**

Amnesty Bay 5 b m Thatching-Sanctuary Cove (Habitat) *169^{11} 260^{9} 390^{8}* 1279^{8} 1620^{16} 1951^{9} 2121^{4} 2310^{17} 2848^{14} **>31f<**

Amoeba (IRE) 4 b f Distinctly North (USA)-Lady Ingrid (Taufan (USA)) 901^{5} *1046^{10} 1428^{4}* 1828^{6} 2418^{7} **>34a 46f<**

Among Islands 6 b m Jupiter Island-Queen of The Nile (Hittite Glory) 4736^{8} **>43?f<**

Among Men (USA) 3 b c Zilzal (USA)-Questionablevirtue (USA) (Key To The Mint (USA)) (963) (1412) (2023) 3124^{4} (3766) **>124f<**

Amrak Ajeeb (IRE) 5 b h Danehill (USA)-Noble Dust (USA) (Dust Commander (USA)) 433^{4} 678^{3} 1323^{5} 2009^{8} 2338^{3} 2766^{15} 3051^{8} 3797^{5} 4272^{5} **>94f<**

Amravati (IRE) 2 ch f Project Manager-Smaoineamh (Tap On Wood) 5002a^{10} **>96f<**

Amron 10 b g Bold Owl-Sweet Minuet (Setay) (464) 527^{6} 827^{2} 977^{6} 1079^{2} 1259^{9} 1561^{2} 2505^{6} 2900^{3} 3208^{8} 3406^{4} 3910^{17} 4233^{15} **>66f<**

Amy 3 b f Timeless Times (USA)-Rion River (IRE) (Taufan (USA)) *19^{8} 41^{7}* **>2a 35f<**

Amyas (IRE) 3 b c Waajib-Art Duo (Artaius (USA)) (853) 1404^{6} 2013^{9} 2585^{4} 3190^{13} (3703) **>111f<**

Amy Leigh (IRE) 4 b f Imperial Frontier (USA)-Hollyberry (IRE) (Runnett) **1996:** *5131^{6} 5173^{4} 5241^{12} 5268^{6}* **1997:** *(32) 152^{4} 222^{8} (421)* 2177^{19} *2674^{2}* 3287^{18} *3398^{6}* 3910^{21} *4985^{11}* **>61a 46f<**

Anakela Bay (IRE) 2 b f Fairy King (USA)-Natuschka (Authi) 3151^{11}

Anak-Ku 4 ch g Efisio-City Link Lass (Double Jump) *(566)* 735^{5} 1016^{16} 1588^{2} (1923) (2065) 2533^{2} (2920) 3246^{2} 4004^{8} **>80a 91f<**

Anaxagoras 7 b g Mtoto-I'll Try (Try My Best (USA)) **1996:** *5114^{6} 5132^{10}* **>33a 35f<**

Anchored In Love 3 b f Alzao (USA)-Lyndonville (IRE) (Top Ville) 727^{9} 992^{5} 1316^{7} 2005^{6} **>64f<**

Anchorena 5 b m Slip Anchor-Canna (Caerleon (USA)) 470^{7} 632^{4} 669^{2} 950^{6} 1100^{11} 1494^{3} 1515^{4} 2154^{5} 3754^{8} 3826^{10} **>50a 50f<**

Anchor Venture 4 b g Slip Anchor-Ski Michaela (USA) (Devil's Bag (USA)) 770^{10} 1022^{9} *1153^{3}* 1574^{5} (1798) 2430^{3} **>62a 57f<**

Ancient Quest 4 b g Rainbow Quest (USA)-Racquette (Ballymore) 962^{13} 1215^{4} 1491^{5} (1844) (2218) 2373^{4} **>90f<**

Andalish 2 b f Polish Precedent (USA)-Risanda (Kris) 4067^{13} **>47f<**

Anditz (IRE) 2 b f Soviet Lad (USA)-Miss Fortunate (IRE) (Taufan (USA)) 4211^{13} 4428^{5} 4752^{8} 4994^{23} **>51f<**

Andoya 2 b f Sagal Wells-Sharrara (CAN) (Blushing Groom (FR)) 4259a^{2} **>90f<**

Andoya (FR) 2 b f Exit To Nowhere (USA)-Clear Sound (Bellypha) (2996b) 4764a^{3} **>90f<**

Andreyev (IRE) 3 ch c Presidium-Missish (Mummy's Pet) 679^{4} (1216) 2023^{17} 2861^{8} **>106f<**

Anemos (IRE) 2 ch c Be My Guest (USA)-Frendly Persuasion (General Assembly (USA)) 4105^{10} 5040^{3} **>73f<**

Anetta 3 ch f Aragon-Pronetta (USA) (Mr Prospector (USA)) 792^{9} 995^{17} 1496^{11} 2169^{3} (3132) 3316^{6} 4291^{14} 5030^{14} **>58f<**

Aneysar (IRE) 3 b c Darshaan-Aneyza (USA) (Blushing Groom (FR)) 1361a^{2} 1915a^{3} 3180a^{2} **>107f<**

Angel Chimes 4 ch f Most Welcome-Bell Toll (High Line) 892^{20} 1459^{15} 3801^{6} 4276^{7} 4558^{7} 4787^{14} **>82f<**

Angel Face (USA) 4 b f Zilzal (USA)-Touching Love (Touching Wood (USA)) **1996:** *(5145) 5175^{2} 5206^{2} (5210) 5281^{9}* **1997:** *(422)* 435^{15} (657) (749) 947^{7} *1123^{3}* 1450^{3} *1575^{W}* **>89a 93f<**

Angel Hill 2 ch f King's Signet (USA)-Tawny (Grey Ghost) (993) 1447^{2} 1653^{3} 2758^{4} 3823^{3} 4152^{5} 4284^{4} 4634^{12} **>78f<**

Angelina 2 b f Most Welcome-Mystic Crystal (IRE) (Caerleon (USA)) 3411^{5} 3927^{3} **>58f<**

Angelique 2 ch f Soviet Star (USA)-Lady Habitat (Habitat) 985^{5} 1295^{5} 2138^{10} **>51f<**

Angel One Five 3 b f Allazzaz-Watch Her Go (Beldale Flutter (USA)) 4883^{14}

Angie Minor 2 b f Mazilier (USA)-Angelica Park (Simply Great (FR)) *1286^{6} 1577^{6}* 2022^{9} **>44a 8f<**

Anglesey Sea View 8 gr m Seymour Hicks (FR)-Lexham View (Abwah) **1996:** *5213^{10}* **1997:** *101^{3} 167^{4}* **>54a 66f<**

Angry Albert 2 ch c Clantime-Croft Original (Crofthall) *1045^{12}* 1251^{13} 2186^{5} 2412^{4} 2784^{5} 3451^{9} **>46f<**

Angstrom (IRE) 2 b g Alzao (USA)-Anna Petrovna (FR) (Wassl) 3013^{7} (4857) 5046^{2} **>92f<**

Angus-G 5 br g Chief Singer-Horton Line (High Line) (680) (1145) **>99+f<**

Anistop 5 b h Nomination-Pounelta (Tachypous) *356^{6}* 574^{10} 721^{16} *867^{9}* **>36a 45f<**

Anita At Dawn (IRE) 2 br f Anita's Prince-Dawn is Breaking (Import) 1791^{3} (2176) 3904^{2} 4284^{9} 4898^{9} **>80f<**

Anita Marie (IRE) 2 b f Anita's Prince-Fandangerina (USA) (Grey Dawn II) 4789^{8} **>35f<**

Anita's Contessa (IRE) 5 b m Anita's Prince-Take More (GER) (Frontal) **1996:** *5112^{2} 5170^{5} 5264^{5}* **1997:** *4^{5} (65) 113^{4} 209^{3} 275^{3} 349^{3}* **>60a 52f<**

Anjou 5 b g Saumarez-Bourbon Topsy (Ile de Bourbon (USA)) 4713^{5} (4850) 4946^{2} **>61a 67f<**

Anka Lady 2 b f Precocious-Hicklam Millie (Absalom) 460^{6} 611^{3} 1557^{7} 4470^{6} 4688^{4} 5029^{5} **>45f<**

Anna 2 b f Ela-Mana-Mou-Anna Rella (IRE) (Danehill (USA)) 2719^{3} **>64f<**

Annaba (IRE) 4 ch f In The Wings-Anna Matrushka (Mill Reef (USA)) 4655a^{4} 4866a^{5} 5051^{4} **>118f<**

Annaletta 3 b f Belmez (USA)-A Priori (GER) (Prince Ippi (GER)) 2131^{W} 2940^{3} **>75f<**

Anna Palariva (IRE) 2 ch f Caerleon (USA)-Anna of Saxony (Ela-Mana-Mou) (4250a) 4663a^{9} **>83f<**

Anna Thea (IRE) 3 f 1202a^{4} 1916a^{8} (2458a)

(3005a) 4254a^3 **>111f<**
Annie Hall 2 b f Saddlers' Hall (IRE)-Rainbow Fleet (Nomination) 2243^{12} **>4f<**
Anniemitchellslass 2 b f Noble Patriarch-Fair Janet (Feelings (FR)) 2383^6 2827^2 4163^6 **>44f<**
Anno Luce 4 ch f Old Vic-Anna Paola (GER) (Prince Ippi (GER)) 2099a^5 2333^3 (2869) 4099^7 **>112f<**
Announcing 3 b br c Old Vic-D'Azy (Persian Bold) 2783^7 3319^3 3720^2 4045^9 4509^{11} 4774^{12} **>72df<**
Announcing Peace 2 b f Danehill (USA)-Remoosh (Glint of Gold) 4582^8 4909^6 5025^6 **>56f<**
Ann's Music 4 b f Clantime-An-Go-Look (Don't Look) **1996:** *5112^{15}* **1997:** *88^{14} 125^{13}* **>36f<**
Annus Mirabilis (FR) 5 b h Warning-Anna Petrovna (FR) (Wassl) 720a^3 (3388) (3785) 4395a^5 **>87a 128f<**
Anokato 3 b g Tina's Pet-High Velocity (Frimley Park) 652^4 879^8 1113^6 1294^7 (1375) 1644^3 1792^6 2590^6 2779^3 2964^6 3194^4 3614^7 3851^7 4183^{11} 4370^7 4527^6 *4913^9 (5018)* **>71a 68f<**
Anonym (IRE) 5 b g Nashamaa-Bonny Bertha (Capistrano) **1996:** *5264^7* **1997:** *(1) (82) 136^2 179^9 398^{12}* 947^5 1097^{15} *(1575) 1788^3* 2340^5 2708^2 3476^{12} 4441^{19} 4781^{26} 5049^{11} **>80da 45f<**
Anotheranniversary 4 gr f Emarati (USA)-Final Call (Town Crier) 573^6 877^7 1766^3 2872^4 3436^6 **>93f<**
Another Batchworth 5 b m Beveled (USA)-Batchworth Dancer (Ballacashtal (CAN)) **1996:** *5096^3 5184^6* **1997:** 1327^7 1479^8 2197^5 2895^{10} 3032^5 4329^2 4452^4 4791^3 *5018^3* **>65a 66f<**
Another Episode (IRE) 8 b g Drumalis-Pasadena Lady (Captain James) 3856^{17} 4233^5 4512^{19} 4707^2 4844^8 **>56a 58f<**
Another Fantasy (IRE) 2 b f Danehill (USA)-Ariadne (Bustino) (985) 1211^4 1411^3 1735^2 3049^7 3464^5 (3961a) **>102f<**
Another Fiddle (IRE) 7 b g Waajib-Elmar (Lord Gayle (USA)) **1996:** *5149^{11}* **1997:** 755^{11} 1011^{10} 2195^6 2577^{12} 2916^{14} 3617^4 3929^7 4450^5 4548^9 **>53f<**
Another Night (IRE) 3 ch c Waajib-Little Me (Connaught) 1589^8 (1777) 2137^5 2574^{10} 3012^6 4102^9 4310^9 **>90df<**
Another Nightmare (IRE) 5 b m Treasure Kay-Carange (Known Fact (USA)) **1996:** *5112^{11}* **1997:** *(385) 423^8* 494^7 *663^6* 827^{17} 1227^5 1613^{12} 2033^4 2221^W (2382) 2472^5 2657^4 2826^6 2899^{13} (3240) 3406^{11} 3771^6 3910^{12} 4016^{11} 4233^{20} 4471^{15} 4707^{19} **>48a 35f<**
Anotherone to Note 6 ch g Beveled (USA)-Dame Nellie (Dominion) 1951^{11} 2310^{13} **>28a 29f<**
Another Quarter (IRE) 4 b f Distinctly North (USA)-Numidia (Sallust) **1996:** *5177^5* **1997:** *276^4 360^{10} 580^{10} 1133^5* 2000^6 2154^{14} **>39a 57f<**
Another Sky-Lark (IRE) 9 b g Muscatite-Another Deb 2815a^6 **>91f<**
Another Time 5 ch g Clantime-Another Move (Farm Walk) (776) 939^5 1456^5 2026^{17} 2710^{12} (2866) 3112^2 3773^4 4558^{32} 4678^8 4893^8 **>99f<**
Another Victim 3 ch g Beveled (USA)-Ragtime Rose (Ragstone) 1272^{17}
Another Wyn-Bank 2 b f Presidium-Wyn-Bank (Green God) 3857^4 4159^7 4508^4 4994^{20} **>50f<**
Ansellman 7 gr g Absalom-Grace Poole (Sallust) **1996:** *5131^3* **1997:** *397^4* (698) *905^4* 1269^8 1402^2 1608^{11} 2289^9 2377^5 *2663^2* 2933^3 3326^2 3481^9 (4329) 4434^2 4677^2 4756^3 4887^{20} **>88a 93f<**
Anstand 2 b c Anshan-Pussy Foot (Red Sunset) 4012^{12} 4211^W 4769^5 4921^6 **>65+f<**
Answers-To-Thomas 4 b g Komaite (USA)-Launde Abbey (Absalom) *87^6 127^5 288^6 318^{11} 429^6* 924^7 1080^8 1603^{14} 2738^8 2899^6 **>53da 30f<**
Antapoura (IRE) 5 b m Bustino-Aneyza (USA) (Blushing Groom (FR)) 4620a^{11} **>96+f<**
Antarctic Storm 4 b g Emarati (USA)-Katie Scarlett (Lochnager) 1259^{11} 1468^3 1977^{18} 2759^4 3034^5 3254^3 (3403) 3622^2 (3921) 4147^{25} 4441^5 4781^5 (5023) **>79f<**
Antares 3 b g Governor General-Eucharis (Tickled Pink) *546^7* 758^8 **>10a 34f<**
Antartictern (USA) 7 b g Arctic Tern (USA)-False Image (USA) (Danzig (USA)) 595^{15} 1503^{12} **>38a 41f<**
Antiguan Jane 4 b f Shirley Heights-Dabbiana (CAN) (Fappiano (USA)) 1414^{16} *2049^4* 2279^{11} 2582^7 **>45a 44f<**
Antithesis (IRE) 4 b f Fairy King (USA)-Music of The Night (USA) (Blushing Groom (FR)) 698^4 1037^{10} 1332^6 1572^5 1835^{13} 1993^5 4414^{17} 4791^8 **>40f<**
Antonia's Choice 3 ch f Music Boy-Mainly Sunset (Red Sunset) 901^9 3194^{10} 3614^5 4168^7 **>61f<**
Antonia's Double 2 ch f Primo Dominie-Mainly Sunset (Red Sunset) 525^4 730^3 1031^6 **>71f<**
Antonias Melody 4 b f Rambo Dancer (CAN)-Ayodessa (Lochnager) **1996:** *5131^{10} 5235^{10}* **1997:** *(275) (286) 301^8* 942^{17} 1269^6 1765^6 1977^{11} 2197^8 2339^9 2845^9 4773^5 4842^6 4979^{23} **>83a 57f<**
Antonio Joli 2 b g Prince Sabo-Revisit (Busted) *4056^{12}* 4165^8 4381^{13} 4994^{17} **>21a 49f<**
Antrim Coast 2 ch c Mujtahid (USA)-Tarsa (Ballad Rock) 1538a^8 **>81f<**
Anvil (USA) 2 ch g Strike The Gold (USA)-Matilda The Hun (USA) (Young Bob (USA)) 696^5 1263^2 2057^6 2693^{10} 4544^5 4840^3 **>76f<**
Anyar Reem 6 b g Slip Anchor-Alruccaba (Crystal Palace (FR)) *2067^2* (2342) *3073^4* **>74da 89?f<**
Anzio (IRE) 6 b g Hatim (USA)-Highdrive (Ballymore) **1996:** *5203^8* **>78a 111f<**
Apache Chief (IRE) 3 bb c Doyoun-Amerindian (Commanche Run) 2081a^4 **>74f<**
Apache Park (USA) 4 b g Alleged (USA)-Fairly Magic (USA) (Raise A Native) *867^7* **>46a f<**
Apache Red (IRE) 2 ch c Indian Ridge-Moonlight Partner (IRE) (Red Sunset) 1531a^{10} 4474^9 **>92f<**
Apache Star 3 b f Arazi (USA)-Wild Pavane (Dancing Brave (USA)) 741^4 1028^3 1875^8 2380^3 2894^3 (3128) (3622) 3913^3 4297^{13} 4781^{17} **>92f<**
Apartments Abroad 4 b f Prince Sabo-La Graciosa (Comedy Star (USA)) 1246^{10} **>52a 42f<**
Apiculate (IRE) 3 b c Exactly Sharp (USA)-Reine de Chypre (FR) (Habitat) *277^6 355^5 547^6* 1115^{11} **>35a 25f<**
Apollono 5 b g Cyrano de Bergerac-Daima (Dominion) **1996:** *5274^{11}* **1997:** 1371^9 **>4a 79f<**
Apollo Red 8 ch g Dominion-Woolpack (Golden Fleece (USA)) **1996:** *(5095) (5209)* **1997:** *21^4 48^4 121^3 (214) 253^3 323^2 364^3 459^2 (569)* 643^2 766^3 (1009) 1317^{14} 1599^3 2006^9 2743^7 3056^2 3296^5 4448^5 **>85a 80f<**
Appeal Again (IRE) 4 br g Mujtahid (USA)-Diva Encore (Star Appeal) *111^5 195^6 421^9* 864^{12} *1132^7* **>41a 46f<**
Appearance Money (IRE) 6 b m Dancing Dissident (USA)-Fussy Budget (Wolver Hollow) **1996:** *5136^{13}* **1997:** *99^9* 848^{15} **>15f<**
Appian Dame (IRE) 2 b f Mukaddamah (USA)-Apapa Port (My Swanee) 4747^8 **>32a f<**
Apple Sauce 2 b f Prince Sabo-Mrs Bacon (Balliol) 1564^{11} 3136^4 3497^5 3823^{15} 4068^{13} **>53f<**
Appleton's Fancy 3 ch g Thowra (FR)-Rota (Reliance II) 4886^{14} **>42f<**
Apprehension 3 b c In The Wings-First Kiss (Kris) 1159^6 1399^3 3647^4 4261a^{10} **>115f<**
Appyabo 2 ch c Never so Bold-Cardinal Palace (Royal Palace) 1872^{16} 2719^4 2953^5 3306^2 3701^3 **>70f<**
April In Paris 3 b f Inca Chief (USA)-Plectrum (Adonijah) 2878^8 **>23f<**
April Jackson 3 b f Petong-Raintree Venture (Good Times (ITY)) 436^8 883^{17} **>37f<**
Aquado 8 b g Green Desert (USA)-Meliora (Crowned Prince (USA)) 779^{13} 956^{15} *1132^R* **>44da 48df<**
Aquarela 2 b f Shirley Heights-Mardi Gras Belle (USA) (Masked Dancer (USA)) 4066^8 **>69+f<**
Aquatic Queen 3 b f Rudimentary (USA)-Aquarula (Dominion) **1996:** *5187^6* **1997:** *247^7* 485^7 584^6 759^3 889^5 1089^5 1680^6 1963^5 2177^2 (2891) 3290^3 3716^7 3936^{10} 4546^{14} **>32a 60f<**
Aquavita 3 b gr f Kalaglow-Aigua Blava (USA) (Solford (USA)) 841^{13} 992^{10} 1507^4 2039^{13} 2577^{11} 4986^8 **>53df<**
Arab Gold 2 b g Presidium-Parklands Belle (Stanford) 4236^7 4514^4 4807^{11} **>68f<**
Arabian King 9 b h Sayf El Arab (USA)-New Edition (Great Nephew) 1726a^{12} **>94f<**
Arabian Story 4 gr c Sharrood (USA)-Once Upon a Time (Teenoso (USA)) 1261^6 (1771) (2864) 3374a^2 4238^2 5055a^6 **>119f<**
Araboybill 6 b g Aragon-Floral (Floribunda) 1441^{12} 1642^3 3792^4 3928^{15} **>52a 53f<**
Arantxa 3 b f Sharpo-Amalancher (USA) (Alleged (USA)) 4878^{21} **>71+f<**
Arapi (IRE) 3 b f Arazi (USA)-Princess Pati (Top Ville) **1996:** *(5133) 5229^5* **>83a 75f<**
Arawak Cay (IRE) 2 b c Common Grounds-Alaroos (IRE) (Persian Bold) (1842) 2054^3 2600^3 3123^4 **>96f<**
Arbatax (IRE) 4 br c Mtoto-Caprarola (FR) (Bellypha) 625a^6 **>116f<**
Arbenig (IRE) 2 b f Anita's Prince-Out On Her Own (Superlative) 3314^5 3783^3 4103^{15} *(4569)* 4922^5 **>77a 68f<**
Arboreal (USA) 3 b f Green Forest (USA)-Saddle Bow (Sadler's Wells (USA)) 436^6 475^{12} 862^6 1095^4 1282^4 1441^{17} **>50f<**
Arcady 4 b f Slip Anchor-Elysian (Northfields (USA)) **1996:** *(5139)* **1997:** 607^{12} 762^{10} 888^8 1100^{17} 1252^2 (1478) 2014^3 2589^4 3122^9 (3383) 4673^6 **>68a 71f<**
Arcane Star (IRE) 2 b c Arcane (USA)-Chatsworth Bay (IRE) (Fairy King (USA)) 4111^{11} 4236^5 4278^9 4855^8 *4982^{11}* 4989^{16} **>35a 71df<**
Arcatura 5 b g Beveled (USA)-Bar Gold (Lucky Brief) **1996:** *5149^4 (5271)* **1997:** *(76)* 1093^6 1473^8 *2160^4* 2488^{17} **>68a 49f< (DEAD)**
Arch Angel (IRE) 4 ch f Archway (IRE)-Saintly Guest (What A Guest) *1152^6* **>33a 28f<**
Archello (IRE) 3 b f Archway (IRE)-Golden Room (African Sky) 636^3 792^3 1119^2 1687^2 2157^2 2496^4 3146^3 (3606) 4137^{10} 4333^7 4844^6 **>57f<**
Archiduque (SPA) 6 ch h Chamartin (FR)-Quin Rock (FR) (Quinault (FR)) (3181a) **>90f<**
Archway Belle (IRE) 4 ch f Archway (IRE)-Quilting (Mummy's Pet) 2447a^7 **>61f<**
Arco Colora 3 b f Rainbow Quest (USA)-Bella Colora (Bellypha) 2773^7 3917^7 4158^4 4757^{14} **>70f<**
Arc of The Diver (IRE) 4 ch g Archway (IRE)-Inner Pearl (Gulf Pearl) **1996:** *5116^5* **>62a 61f<**
Arctic Air 2 br f Polar Falcon (USA)-Breadcrumb (Final Straw) 3426^2 (4231) 4892^8 **>76f<**
Arctic Fancy (USA) 4 ch g Arctic Tern (USA)-Fit And Fancy (USA) (Vaguely Noble) 1162^{11} 1478^3 1947^5 2327^{11} 2867^8 3915^3 4313^{10} **>79f<**

Arctic Owl 3 b g Most Welcome-Short Rations (Lorenzaccio) (1637) 2292[4] 3689[2] (3989) 4443[3] 5053[21] **>102f<**

Arctic Star 2 b c Polar Falcon (USA)-Three Stars (Star Appeal) 4231[8] 4379[7] 4515[6] 4898[4] 4994[6] **>71f<**

Arctic Starry (FR) 5 ch m Star Maite (FR)-Arrow Blue (FR) (Gairloch) (2096a) 3876a[3] **>88f<**

Arctic Thunder (USA) 6 b g Far North (CAN)-Flying Cloud (USA) (Roberto (USA)) 4443[14] *4572[9]* 4882[20] **>55a 99?f<**

Arctic Triumph 6 b g Arctic Lord-Borotown (Treboro (USA)) 2692[6] **>47f<**

Arctiid (USA) 4 b br g Silver Hawk (USA)-Arctic Eclipse (USA) (Northern Dancer) 1414[9] 2136[8] 4004[7] **>78f<**

Arcus (IRE) 4 ch g Archway (IRE)-Precision Chop (Hard Fought) **1996:** *5095[7] 5129[10] 5237[10]* **1997:** *203[9]* **>47a 66f<**

Ardarroch Prince 6 b g Chief Singer-Queen's Eyot (Grundy) 1230[5] 1558[4] 2046[15] 2662[W] 3567[2] **>65f<**

Ardent 3 b c Aragon-Forest of Arden (Tap On Wood) 1088[5] 1587[9] 1826[16] 4696[6] 4817[6] 4958[16] **>58f<**

Ardleigh Charmer 2 ch c Theatrical Charmer-Miss Adventure (Adonijah) 4244[7] 4950[10] **>25f<**

Areish (IRE) 4 b f Keen-Cool Combination (Indian King (USA)) **1996:** *5210[11]* **1997:** *76[8]* 3848[6] 4503[9] **>42a 36f<**

Arethusa 3 ch f Primo Dominie-Downeaster Alexa (USA) (Red Ryder (USA)) 724[8] 1112[2] 1610[5] **>102f<**

Are Yer There 2 gr g Terimon-Indian Swallow (FR) (Shirley Heights) 1120[12] 1492[13] 1829[8] 2018[10] 2493[9] 3212[11] **>48f<**

Argumentative 2 b g Mujadil (USA)-Dusky Nancy (Red Sunset) 1321[8] 2181[20] 2388[7] 3799[9] 3924[4] 4271[15] 4856[11] **>51f<**

Ar Hyd Y Knos 3 b f Alzao (USA)-Top Table (Shirley Heights) 889[8] 1164[13] 1483[2] 1988[7] *2319[8]* **>28a 62f<**

Arian Da 2 ch f Superlative-Nell of The North (USA) (Canadian Gil (CAN)) 557[2] 739[2] 1425[11] 1619[3] 1821[4] 3480[2] 3711[7] 4042[2] (4216) 4403[2] 4772[4] 4948[3] **>83f<**

Arian Spirit (IRE) 6 b m High Estate-Astral Way (Hotfoot) **1996:** *5139[10]* **1997:** 1424[11] 1585[5] 2000[10] 2350[5] (2737) *3046[3]* 3141[2] (3401) 3623[7] 4269[3] 4432[7] *4590[9]* **>49a 53f<**

Ariant (USA) 2 ch c Mr Prospector (USA)-Six Months Long (USA) (Northern Dancer) (2829) 3706[7] **>85+f<**

Aries Boy 2 ch c Risk Me (FR)-Fancy Pages (Touch Paper) 3094[16] 4401[10] *4812[12] 4982[13]* **>25f<**

Arif (IRE) 5 bb g Try My Best (USA)-Sable Royale (USA) (Real Value (USA)) 1732[6] (2279) 2430[8] (2518) *2910[5]* 4633[9] 4713[8] 4850[2] **>22a 42f<**

Ariosta (GER) 3 f 1202a[11] **>53f<**

Arisaig (IRE) 3 ch g Ela-Mana-Mou-Glasson Lady (GER) (Priamos (GER)) 528[6] 826[3] 1469[6] 2207[2] 2908[7] 3317[5] 4336[3] 4509[W] **>63f<**

Aristid (GER) 4 b c Daun (GER)-Anstandige (GER) (Star Appeal) 4263a[2] **>114f<**

Arjan (IRE) 2 gr f Paris House-Forest Berries (IRE) (Thatching) 3247[8] 4012[9] 4428[R] (4769) **>75f<**

Arkadian Hero (USA) 2 ch c Trempolino (USA)-Careless Kitten (USA) (Caro) 2556[5] (3127) (3811) (4293) 4524[4] **>104+f<**

Arkady (IRE) 6 ch h Tate Gallery (USA)-Veruschka (Lorenzaccio) (2997a) **>74a 68f<**

Arletty 3 b f Rainbow Quest (USA)-Mixed Applause (USA) (Nijinsky (CAN)) 978[6] 1625[4] 2532[5] 3495[8] 3906[11] 4323[2] 4568[5] 4748[3] 4971[28] **>63f<**

Arm And A Leg (IRE) 2 ch c Petardia-Ikala (Lashkari) 557[6] 836[8] 1330[5] (1498) 1815[2] 2681[6] 3025[7] 3228[5] 3911[6] 4058[3] 4366[4] 4753[3] **>71f<**

Armando Carpio 4 b c Warning-Melodic (Song) (1201a) 2102a[2] (4765a) **>116f<**

Armston 5 ch g Rock City-Silka (ITY) (Lypheor) *4481[12]* 4713[6] 4850[5] **>66?a 50f<**

Armungia 3 b f Shareef Dancer (USA)-Arbela (IRE) (Persian Bold) 1367a[2]

Arnaqueur (USA) 2 b c Miswaki (USA)-All Along (FR) (Targowice (USA)) 4528a[3] **>88f<**

Arnie (IRE) 5 b g Double Schwartz-The Moneys Gone (Precocious) 473[5] *855[5]* 1012[7] 1236[16] 1279[13] 1483[13] (2115) 2424[8] 2721[12] 3394[4] **>22a 48?f<**

Around Fore Alliss 3 b g Reprimand-Artistic Licence (High Top) **1996:** *5248[2]* **1997:** *26[7] 292[4] 350[2] 568[3]* 764[4] 1164[18] 1633[5] *(2151)* 2523[11] 2957[5] **>75a 68df<**

Arpeggio 2 b c Polar Falcon (USA)-Hilly (Town Crier) 696[2] 1321[2] 1607[4] **>79f<**

Arpista (GER) 3 b f Chief Singer-Areole (GER) (Mister Rock's (GER)) 1551a[3] **>93f<**

Arrasas Lady 7 ch m Arrasas (USA)-Sharelle (Relko) *2070[3] 2602[3] 2913[3]* 3248[13] *4300[2] 4480[8]* **>41a 31f<**

Arriving 3 br f Most Welcome-Affirmation (Tina's Pet) 885[6] 1272[6] (1938) 2194[2] 2652[3] 3234[4] 3455[3] 4172[2] (4242) 4435[6] 4962a[7] **>77f<**

Arruhan (IRE) 3 b f Mujtahid (USA)-Wakayi (Persian Bold) 694[6] 968[3] 1170[15] 1453[2] 2561[3] 2894[5] (4511) 4787[27] **>91f<**

Arry Martin 2 b c Aragon-Bells of St Martin (Martinmas) 4966[9] **>65f<**

Artan (IRE) 5 b h Be My Native (USA)-Cambridge Lodge (Tower Walk) (1200a) 1724a[5] **>125f<**

Arterxerxes 4 b g Anshan-Hanglands (Bustino) 560[2] 892[4] 1308[5] 2026[27] 2678[12] 3138[6] (3718) **>87f<**

Artful Dane (IRE) 5 b h Danehill (USA)-Art Age (Artaius (USA)) (444) 987[10] 1166[5] 1442[10] 2117[2] 3150[18] 3976[14] 4297[14] 4781[19] 4978[4] **>55a 80f<**

Arthur's Seat 3 b c Salse (USA)-Abbey Strand (USA) (Shadeed (USA)) 875[6] 1487[6] 2245[8] **>49f<**

Artic Courier 6 gr g Siberian Express (USA)-La Reine de France (Queen's Hussar) 789[3] 962[7] 1771[4] 2391[4] 3434[6] 3689[11] 4002[3] 4313[5] 4956[14] **>85f<**

Arzani (USA) 6 ch h Shahrastani (USA)-Vie En Rose (USA) (Blushing Groom (FR)) **1996:** *(5094) 5123[7] 5210[7] 5247[6]* **1997:** *10[4] 140[4] 187[4]* 476[4] 587[13] 838[3] *1156[8]* (1441) 2039[2] 2399[4] (2701) 2896[2] 2916[10] *3413[7]* 4179[5] 4987[10] **>56a 66f<**

Asad 2 ch c Lion Cavern (USA)-Negligent (Ahonoora) (4949) **>89++f<**

Asakir 2 ch c Nashwan (USA)-Yaqut (USA) (Northern Dancer) (4165) (4697) 5034a[2] **>97f<**

Asas 3 b c Nashwan (USA)-Oumaldaaya (USA) (Nureyev (USA)) 1173[6] 1595[10] 4754[20] **>86f<**

Asbestaswecan 2 ch g Faustus (USA)-Lady Chaser (Posse (USA)) 3306[13] 3707[5] 4007[13] **>57f<**

Ascot Cyclone (USA) 2 ch f Rahy (USA)-Dabaweyaa (Shareef Dancer (USA)) (1564) 2024[8] 2600[4] 4097[2] 4267[6] **>92f<**

Asef Alhind 3 ch c Indian Ridge-Willowbed (Wollow) 963[8] 1207[5] (1682) 2013[8] 2528[9] 2951[3] 3435[6] **>90f<**

Asfurah (USA) 2 b br f Dayjur (USA)-Mathkurh (USA) (Riverman (USA)) 1619[2] (2103) (2558) 3534a[2] **>101f<**

Ashangem 2 ch c Risk Me (FR)-Dancing Belle (Dance In Time (CAN)) 2037[15] 4769[9] 4917[20] **>20f<**

Ashby Hill (IRE) 6 ch m Executive Perk-Petite Deb (Cure The Blues (USA)) 735[3] 933[6] 1262[5] 1482[5] 3982[11] 4219[8] 4516[6] **>65f<**

Ashgore 7 b g Efisio-Fair Atlanta (Tachypous) **1996:** *5106[12]* **1997:** *89[7] 1786[2] 2603[9]* **>52a 67f<**

Ashjajon 2 b f Lugana Beach-Dondale Rose (Nishapour (FR)) 767[8] 1498[6] **>38f<**

Ashkernazy (IRE) 6 ch m Salt Dome (USA)-Eskaroon (Artaius (USA)) **1996:** *5220[6]* **1997:** 1814[6] 2536[10] 2732[5] (3016) 3280[14] 4370[21] **>43a 53f<**

Ashley Park (IRE) 3 b c Sadler's Wells (USA)-Maiden Concert (Condorcet (FR)) (1195a) 3675a[6] **>98f<**

Ashraakat (USA) 2 b f Danzig (USA)-Elle Seule (USA) (Exclusive Native (USA)) 3009[2] (3744) 4663a[7] **>94+f<**

Asinbox (IRE) 2 ch c Persian Bold-Traveling Dancer (FR) (Lomond (USA)) 3490[9] 3861[10] 4174[10] **>51f<**

As-Is 3 b g Lomond (USA)-Capriati (USA) (Diesis) *7[5] (130) 162[2] (249) 314[2] (347)* 431[6] 539[2] (665) *1043[10]* 1299[2] 1465[6] 1853[7] **>69a 70f<**

A S Jim 6 b g Welsh Captain-Cawston's Arms (Cawston's Clown) *54[8] 114[8]* **>6a f<**

Askern 6 gr g Sharrood (USA)-Silk Stocking (Pardao) 657[7] 1427[11] 1831[2] 2030[8] 2533[4] (2660) 2920[5] 3246[7] 3380[2] **>69f<**

Asking 5 b g Skyliner-Ma Famille (Welsh Saint) 1803[9] 2246[6] 2398[6] **>37a 33f<**

Ask Speedy Snaps 2 ch g Librate-Miss Moody (Jalmood (USA)) 2784[12] 3090[7] 3312[10] **>12f<**

Asmara (USA) 4 b f Lear Fan (USA)-Anaza (Darshaan) **1996:** 5154a[4] 5198a[6] **>109f<**

Asolo (GER) 3 1545a[4] 2642a[19] 3737a[7] 4661a[2] 4963a[4] **>114f<**

Aspecto Lad (IRE) 3 ch g Imp Society (USA)-Thatcherite (Final Straw) **1996:** *5166[3] 5212[8]* **1997:** *(41) 90[2] 124[2] 240[3] 298[7] 370[2] 414[2]* 4335[13] *4485[12]* **>68a 42f<**

Aspen (IRE) 2 br f Scenic-All In White (FR) (Carwhite) 1564[6] 1997[3] **>69f<**

Aspirant Dancer 2 b c Marju (IRE)-Fairy Ballerina (Fairy King (USA)) 3745[9] 4064[13] 4381[16] **>52f<**

Asprilla (IRE) 2 b g Sharp Victor (USA)-Aspire (Nebbiolo) 993[13] 1126[7] 1510[13] 4419[8] **>41f<**

Assailable 3 b c Salse (USA)-Unsuitable (Local Suitor (USA)) 963[5] 4848[4] **>80f<**

Asset Manager 2 b c Night Shift (USA)-Hud Hud (USA) (Alydar (USA)) 4384[8] 4507[5] 4852[7] **>73f<**

Assignment 11 b g Known Fact (USA)-Sanctuary (Welsh Pageant) 1127[7] 1514[11] **>43a 44f<**

Assos (USA) 3 b c Alleged (USA)-Myth to Reality (FR) (Sadler's Wells (USA)) 1913a[2] **>106f<**

Assume (USA) 3 br c Known Fact (USA)-Free Spirit (USA) (Avatar (USA) *(455)* 1737[14] **>82+a 69+f<**

Assured Gamble 3 b c Rock Hopper-Willowbank (Gay Fandango (USA)) 670[3] (1218) 2027[9] 2514[16] 2963[7] 3125[10] 4476[5] 4774[13] **>85f<**

Astarabad (USA) 3 b c Alleged (USA)-Anaza (Darshaan) 819a[2] 1205a[4] 1726a[3] 4656a[4] (5032a) **>119f<**

Asterix 9 ch g Prince Sabo-Gentle Gael (Celtic Ash) 687[11] 848[9] 1128[15] 1483[4] 1677[8] 1920[3] 2375[6] 2646[9] 2785[12] 3248[5] 3276[17] 3456[15] **>19a 37f<** **(DEAD)**

Astrac (IRE) 6 b g Nordico (USA)-Shirleen (Daring Display (USA)) **1996:** (5155a) **1997:** 452[8] 980[6] 2105[23] 2526[13] 3118[3] 3975[9] 4100[22] 4282[19] 4881[5] *4983[5]* 5054[7] **>92a 94f<**

Astral Crown (IRE) 3 b f Astronef-Current Bay (Tyrant (USA)) 531[7] 1119[19] 1401[8] 1681[4] 2167[9] 2354[10] **>29f<**

Astral Invader (IRE) 5 ch g Astronef-Numidia

(Sallust) **1996:** *5266[7]* **1997:** *11[7] 59[4] 214[3] 278[8] 335[5] 385[2] 429[9]* (484) 601[9] 752[8] 1620[9] *2070[5]* 2424[6] 2536[9] **>41ta 42f<**

Astral Invasion (USA) 6 ch g Risen Star (USA)-Santiki (Be My Guest (USA)) *80[7]* **>11a 66f<**

Astral Weeks (IRE) 6 ch g Astronef-Doon Belle (Ardoon) 1169[14] 2373[8] **>49f<**

Astrapi 2 b f Last Tycoon-Graecia Magna (USA) (Private Account (USA)) 4425[5] 4694[2] 4841[2] **>83f<**

Astrojoy (IRE) 5 ch m Astronef-Pharjoy (FR) (Pharly (FR)) 4045[15] **>33a 44f<**

Astrolabe 5 b g Rainbow Quest (USA)-Sextant (Star Appeal) 843[12] 1220[12] 1507[9] **>39f<**

Astrolfell (IRE) 2 ch f River Falls-Indian Starlight (Kafu) 530[8]

Astrologer 2 b c Soviet Star (USA)-Taalif (Last Tycoon) 4298[3] 4775[2] **>86f<**

Asyaad (USA) 2 b c Zilzal (USA)-Shihama (USA) (Shadeed (USA)) 3490[3] 4286[4] 4640[4] **>74+f<**

Ath Cheannaithe (FR) 5 ch g Persian Heights-Pencarreg (Caerleon (USA)) *589[12]* **>4f<**

Atienza (USA) 4 ch f Chief's Crown (USA)-Hattab Voladora (USA) (Dewan (USA)) 769[8] **>30a 57f<**

Atlanta 2 b f Rock City-Olympic Run (Salse (USA)) 4298[4] 4602[6] 4818[3] **>77f<**

Atlantic Desire (IRE) 3 b f Ela-Mana-Mou-Bold Miss (Bold Lad (IRE)) 597[5] 1670[2] 1869[2] 2133[3] (2292) 2585[8] 2871[12] 3190[3] (3274) (3391) **>100f<**

Atlantic Mist 4 ch g Elmaamul (USA)-Overdue Reaction (Be My Guest (USA)) 647[6] 986[2] 1169[3] 1805[9] 2650[9] **>57f<**

Atlantic Viking (IRE) 2 b c Danehill (USA)-Hi Bettina (Henbit (USA)) 1174[7] (1669) 3178a[6] 3908[2] 4970[3] **>97+f<**

At Large (IRE) 3 b g Night Shift (USA)-Lady Donna (Dominion) 792[4] 970[2] 1119[3] 2563[17] 3898[3] 4214[2] (4565) 4787[4] **>84f<**

At Liberty (IRE) 5 b h Danehill (USA)-Music of The Night (USA) (Blushing Groom (FR)) *100[10] 365[4]* 444[15] *(486)* 680[11] *867[2]* 1036[7] 1371[4] 1686[4] 1809[3] 2218[W] 4450[4] 4521[9] 4896[6] *5019[3]* **>72da 57f<**

Atnab (USA) 3 b br f Riverman (USA)-Magic Slipper (Habitat) 1587[8] 2380[7] (2763) 3210[3] 3549[4] 3928[5] **>66f<**

Atomic Shell (CAN) 4 ch c Geiger Counter (USA)-In Your Sights (USA) (Green Dancer (USA)) 1023[8] 1437[4] 1811[14] **>73f<**

Atours (USA) 9 b g Chief's Crown (USA)-Ataire (USA) (What A Pleasure (USA)) 4879[11] **>86f<**

Attarikh (IRE) 4 b g Mujtahid (USA)-Silly Tune (IRE) (Coquelin (USA)) 443[21] 560[7] 1436[6] 1800[16] 2313[10] 2505[5] 2760[10] 2785[8] 4043[3] 4243[14] 4465[5] **>53f<**

Attimo Fuggente (IRE) 4 b c Roi Danzig (USA)-Pepi Image (USA) (National) 4660a[9] **>60f<**

Attitre (FR) 3 b f Mtoto-Aquaglow (Caerleon (USA)) 724[10] 959[2] 1368a[2] 1738[10] 2513[3] 3704[8] 4445[6] **>107f<**

Attitude 3 b g Priolo (USA)-Parfum D'Automne (FR) (Sharpen Up) 1399[9] 2601[3] 3243[5] 3894[8] 4141[8] (4578) **>92f<**

Attractive Crown (USA) 2 b f Chief's Crown (USA)-Attirance (FR) (Crowned Prince (USA)) 1880a[3] 3534a[8] 3839a[6] 4619a[8] 4836a[4] **>88f<**

Attribute 3 b f Warning-Victoriana (USA) (Storm Bird (CAN)) *49[4] 145[7]* **>54a 73f<**

Atuf (USA) 2 b f Danzig (USA)-Alchaasibiyeh (USA) (Seattle Slew (USA)) 4103[6] 4425[2] (4779) **>86f<**

Auchinleck Judge 4 b g Precious Metal-Pharly Rose (Pharly (FR)) **1996:** *5132[12]* **1997:** 484[9] 896[15] 1247[7] 1689[16] **>23f<**

Audeen 2 ch f Keen-Aude la Belle (FR) (Ela-Mana-Mou) 3788[8]

Augustan 6 b g Shareef Dancer (USA)-Krishnagar (Kris) 574[4] 866[3] (1022) 1145[8] 1398[4] 1628[2] 1832[3] 2015[6] 2316[10] 2843[3] 3015[2] 3197[6] (3330) 3779[3] 3796[4] 4213[3] 4335[3] 4568[9] 4874[13] **>64da 67f<**

Augustus Rex (IRE) 3 1545a[5] **>96f<**

Aunt Daphne 3 b f Damister (USA)-Forbearance (Baim (USA)) 1731[2] 2386[6] **>59f<**

Auntie Mame (USA) 3 b f Theatrical-Lady Vixen (USA) (Sir Ivor) 4652a[2] **>113f<**

Aunt Sadie 2 ch f Pursuit of Love-Piney River (Pharly (FR)) 1783[6] 2181[7] 2534[2] **>69f<**

Aunty Jane 4 b f Distant Relative-Aloha Jane (USA) (Hawaii) 1456[10] 2525[2] (3052) 3875a[7] (4120) (4536a) 4867a[6] **>110f<**

Aurelian 3 ch g Ron's Victory (USA)-Rive-Jumelle (IRE) (M Double M (USA)) 838[13] 1140[14] (1469) (1853) 2189[4] 3057[S] 3309[7] 3781[3] 4336[11] **>68f<**

Aurigny 2 b f Timeless Times (USA)-Dear Glenda (Gold Song) 836[3] (1007) 1109[6] 2103[3] 2370[3] 2484[3] 3178a[2] (3595) 4150[7] **>91f<**

Aurora Bay (IRE) 3 b f Night Shift (USA)-Dimmer (Kalaglow) 1409[8] *1787[8]* 2183[14] 3452[11] **>5a 47f<**

Autriche (IRE) 3 b f Acatenango (GER)-Aminata (GER) (Local Suitor (USA)) 4650a[3] **>111f<**

Autumn Cover 5 gr g Nomination-Respray (Rusticaro (FR)) **1996:** *5210[13]* **1997:** (987) 1768[6] 2866[13] 3112[18] 3786[7] **>60a 80f<**

Autumn Time (IRE) 3 b f Last Tycoon-Cochineal (USA) (Vaguely Noble) 670[6] 1150[5] 1742[2] 2114[6] 4748[9] **>62f<**

Avant Huit 5 ch m Clantime-Apres Huit (Day Is Done) **1996:** *5093[9] 5178[9] 5220[10] 5268[13]* **1997:** *97[6]* **>20a 12f<**

Avanti Blue 3 b g Emarati (USA)-Dominion Blue (Dominion) *868[9] 1151[5]* 1401[4] *1939[5] 4480[6] 4810[2] 4906[3]* **>53a 58f<**

Averham Star 2 ch g Absalom-Upper Sister (Upper Case (USA)) 1120[13] *1286[8]* 1461[5] *1758[8]* **>42a 32f<**

Averring (USA) 4 b f Alleged (USA)-Chinguetti (Green Dancer (USA)) 4655a[7] **>106f<**

Averti (IRE) 6 b h Warning-Imperial Jade (Lochnager) (877) 1171[4] 1881a[4] 2106[4] 2861[5] (3111) 3724[3] 4011[4] 4421[3] 4664a[5] **>121f<**

Aviva Lady (IRE) 2 ch f Mac's Imp (USA)-Flying Beauty (Super Concorde (USA)) 3324[5] 3636[13] 3866[4] 4362[9] *4593[10]* **>10a 47f<**

Avro Avian 3 b f Ardross-Tremellick (Mummy's Pet) 1130[9] 1497[10] 2020[10] 2908[9] **>46f<**

Awad (USA) 7 b h Caveat (USA)-Dancer's Candy (USA) **1996:** 5159a[5] **1997:** 4395a[3] 5065a[9] **>128f<**

Awafeh 4 b g Green Desert (USA)-Three Piece (Jaazeiro (USA)) *71[10] 321[7]* **>31a 48f<**

Awasha (IRE) 5 b m Fairy King (USA)-Foliage (Thatching) 2563[18] **>65a 65f<**

Awassi (IRE) 4 b c Fairy King (USA)-Phantom Row (Adonijah) 2173[7] 2491[2] 2704[3] 2868[10] 3146[5] 4979[21] **>65f<**

Awesome Power 11 b g Vision (USA)-Majestic Nurse (On Your Mark) **1996:** *(5081) 5145[5]* **1997:** *10[2] 160[2] 290[4] (487) 566[9] 1156[11] 4912[8]* **>44a 31f<**

Awesome Venture 7 b g Formidable (USA)-Pine Ridge (High Top) *3[2] 15[7] 89[2] 113[11] 127[6] 274[10] 870[16]* 972[5] *1291[8]* 1799[11] *1944[4] 2069[5] 2368[11]* 3143[17] 3456[5] 3822[8] *4050[7]* **>50a 39f<**

Awesome Wells (IRE) 3 b c Sadler's Wells (USA)-Shadywood (Habitat) 1218[5] 1612[2] 2046[2] 2924[2] (4072) 4320[5] **>84f<**

Awestruck 7 b g Primo Dominie-Magic Kingdom (Kings Lake (USA)) *139[8] 2048[5]* **>12a 33?f<**

Axeman (IRE) 5 b g Reprimand-Minnie Tudor (Tudor Melody) 1020[21] 2019[10] 3759[15] 3910[16] 4184[10] 4228[2] 4472[11] 4629[13] **>48f<**

Aybeegirl 3 b f Mazilier (USA)-So it Goes (Free State) 477[7] 883[11] *1151[12]* 1746[3] 4546[5] 4877[18] **>31a 61f<**

Aydigo 4 b g Aydimour-Briglen (Swing Easy (USA)) **1996:** *5213[9]* **>17a 41f<**

Aye Ready 4 ch g Music Boy-Cindy's Princess (Electric) 2221[W] 2382[9] 2659[10] 2854[13] **>12f<**

Ayunli 6 b m Chief Singer-Tsungani (Cure The Blues (USA)) **1996:** 5125a[7] 5199a[7] **>70a 82f<**

Azelna (FR) 2 ch f Tropular-La Miserable (FR) (Miswaki (USA)) 3872a[3]

Azizzi 5 ch g Indian Ridge-Princess Silca Key (Grundy) 2329[2] 2598[15] 3535a[2] 4282[4] 4677[12] 4887[21] **>103f<**

Azores 3 b c Polish Precedent (USA)-Shirley Superstar (Shirley Heights) 1866[7] 2131[4] 2731[5] 3633[3] (3897) 4144[5] **>85f<**

Azra (IRE) 3 b f Danehill (USA)-Easy to Please (What A Guest) 806a[8] 1062a[2] 4094a[5] 4344a[5] 4625a[3] **>114f<**

Aztec Flyer (USA) 4 b g Alwasmi (USA)-Jetta J (USA) (Super Concorde (USA)) *400[5]* 838[4] 2199[5] (2927) (3317) (3815) 4269[5] 4783[25] **>37a 63f<**

Aztec Traveller 3 b g Timeless Times (USA)-Chief Dancer (Chief Singer) **1996:** *5100[9]* **>8a 69f<**

Azulino (IRE) 2 gr f Bluebird (USA)-Page Blanche (USA) (Caro) 3574[13] 4907[7] **>55f<**

B

Baaheth (USA) 3 ch g Seeking the Gold (USA)-Star Glimmer (USA) (General Assembly (USA)) **1996:** *5228[7]* **1997:** *96[2] 173[3]* 533[10] 926[3] 2487[15] 3068[4] 3321[7] 3762[11] *4069[8]* **>56a 43f<**

Baajil 2 b c Marju (IRE)-Arctic River (FR) (Arctic Tern (USA)) 4966[2] **>90+f<**

Baba Au Rhum (IRE) 5 b g Baba Karam-Spring About (Hard Fought) 1248[2] 1422[9] (1972) 2485[4] 3115[10] (3382) **>77f<**

Babanina 2 b f Night Shift (USA)-Babita (Habitat) 2597[6] 2926[6] 3925[7] **>71f<**

Baba Sadhu 3 b g Mazilier (USA)-La Jambalaya (Reform) 2228[7] 4114[18] 4987[15] **>42tf<**

Babe (IRE) 3 b f Treasure Kay-Nujoom (USA) (Halo (USA)) 1650[9] **>54f<**

Babsy Babe 4 b f Polish Patriot (USA)-Welcome Break (Wollow) 677[15] 980[8] 2900[6] 3273[4] 3604[14] 4013[6] **>90df<**

Baby Grand (IRE) 2 b f Mukaddamah (USA)-Samriah (IRE) (Wassl) 897[3] 1280[4] (1569) (1729) (2140) 2712[5] (3209) 3595[9] (3908) 4232[5] **>95f<**

Baby Jane 3 b f Old Vic-Sutosky (Great Nephew) *395[3] 456[6] 662[2]* (862) (926) 1329[4] 1863[8] 2224[2] 2855[7] **>59a 68f<**

Baby Spice 2 ch f Then Again-Starawak (Star Appeal) 4298[17] 4604[7] 4750[13] **>34f<**

Baby's Tiara (IRE) 2 b f Chief's Crown (USA)-Baby Diamonds (Habitat) 1806[6] 2181[11] 2597[9] **>64f<**

Bacchus 3 b c Prince Sabo-Bonica (Rousillon (USA)) 2491[4] (2838) 3614[6] 4307[11] 4787[13] 4878[11] **>86f<**

Bachelors Pad 3 b c Pursuit of Love-Note Book (Mummy's Pet) 973[6] 1462[4] 1737[15] 4153[3] 4550[12] 4990[6] **>96f<**

Backhander (IRE) 5 b g Cadeaux Genereux-Chevrefeuille (Ile de Bourbon (USA)) *422[12]* 480[2] 638[8] 3249[6] *3608[8]* 4404[14] 4465[13] **>12a 42f<**

Back Row 3 b f In The Wings-Temple Row (Ardross) 2008[13] 3188[5] 4060[7] 4429[2] 4748[2] 4971[3] 5024[8] **>70f<**

Backview 5 ch g Backchat (USA)-Book Review

(Balidar) **1996:** 5167^{8} 5205^{11} **1997:** 315^{5} **>81?a 65f<**

Backwoods 4 ch g In The Wings-Kates Cabin (Habitat) **1996:** 5108^{4} 5171^{7} **>58a 71f<**

Badawi (FR) 7 ch g Script Ohio (USA)-Beautiful Bedouin (USA) (His Majesty (USA)) 1424^{5} (1808) 2198^{4} **>54a 49f<**

Bad Bertrich Again (IRE) 4 b c Dowsing (USA)-Ajuga (USA) (The Minstrel (CAN)) $2459a^{5}$ $3182a^{6}$ $3737a^{8}$ **>115f<**

Badenoch (IRE) 3 br br c Ela-Mana-Mou-Highland Ball (Bold Lad (IRE)) 1434^{3} 3809^{5} **>76f<**

Badge of Fame (IRE) 3 gr c Caerleon (USA)-Infamy (Shirley Heights) 1239^{11} (1846) 2230^{W} 3498^{4} 3974^{7} **>91f<**

Badger Bay (IRE) 4 b f Salt Dome (USA)-Legit (IRE) (Runnett) 1843^{11} 2177^{18} 2569^{9} 2772^{9} **>53a 40f<**

Badila (IRE) 2 b f Doyoun-Badaraya (USA) $3839a^{8}$ **>80f<**

Badlesmere (USA) 3 b c Geiger Counter (USA)-Arising (USA) (Secreto (USA)) (991) (1165) $1553a^{4}$ **>106f<**

Bad News 5 ch m Pharly (FR)-Phylae (Habitat) 313^{11} 1128^{10} 1388^{12} 1694^{9} 2041^{11} **>26a 31f<**

Badrinath (IRE) 3 b g Imperial Frontier (USA)-Badedra (Kings Lake (USA)) 511^{7} 576^{8} 2704^{13} 3040^{4} 3500^{7} 4809^{11} **>39a 38f<**

Baffin Bay 2 b c Bustino-Surf Bird (Shareef Dancer (USA)) 4758^{10} (4914) **>91f<**

Bag And A Bit 4 b f Distant Relative-Vaigrant Wind (Vaigly Great) 480^{4} **>49f<**

Bagshot 6 b h Rousillon (USA)-Czar's Bride (USA) (Northern Dancer) **1996:** 5149^{2} 5209^{5} 5271^{2} **1997:** 47^{6} (160) (280) 352^{2} 476^{15} 578^{3} 1128^{11} 1965^{14} 3581^{7} 5022^{13} **>70a 42f<**

Bahamian Beauty (USA) 3 b f Lord At War (ARG)-Ever (USA) (What Luck (USA)) 2838^{5} (3086) (3709) 4013^{3} 4183^{10} **>92f<**

Bahamian Bounty 3 ch c Cadeaux Genereux-Clarentia (Ballad Rock) $1204a^{6}$ 2599^{4} **>115f<**

Bahamian Knight (CAN) 4 b br c Ascot Knight (CAN)-Muskoka Command (USA) (Top Command (USA)) 2765^{6} 3191^{6} 4005^{6} 4134^{3} $4965a^{11}$ **>106f<**

Bahamian Melody (USA) 2 b c Rubiano (USA)-Song of Syria (USA) (Damascus (USA)) 2588^{6} 3022^{7} 3619^{7} (4065) 4545^{7} 4849^{10} **>75f<**

Bahamian Sunshine (USA) 6 ch g Sunshine Forever (USA)-Pride of Darby (USA) (Danzig (USA)) 1319^{2} 2108^{12} (3191) 3983^{3} **>107f<**

Baher (USA) 8 b g Damister (USA)-Allatum (USA) (Alleged (USA)) **1996:** 5177^{7} **>39a f<**

Bahhare (USA) 3 b c Woodman (USA)-Wasnah (USA) (Nijinsky (CAN)) 4138^{2} 4422^{4} 4785^{3} **>125f<**

Bahia Blanca Sun (IRE) 2 b c Tirol-Wild Applause (IRE) (Sadler's Wells (USA)) 4793^{15} **>24f<**

Bahr 2 ch f Generous (IRE)-Lady of the Sea (Mill Reef (USA)) (2312) (3576) **>97+f<**

Bahr Alsalaam (USA) 3 b br f Riverman (USA)-Trolley Song (USA) (Caro) 847^{8} **>27f<**

Bailieborough Boy (IRE) 3 ch g Shalford (IRE)-Salique (Sallust) **1996:** 5257^{4} **1997:** 38^{7} 156^{2} 168^{2} (234) (300) (329) 362^{3} 414^{6} **>73a 65f<**

Bailiwick 4 b g Dominion-Lady Barkley (Habitat) 516^{10} 580^{5} 857^{13} **>48a 46f<**

Bairn Atholl 4 ch f Bairn (USA)-Noble Mistress (Lord Gayle (USA)) 1567^{10} 1925^{10} 2197^{2} 2536^{8} 3327^{4} 3470^{12} 3637^{2} 4169^{8} **>44f<**

Bajan (IRE) 6 b g Taufan (USA)-Thatcherite (Final Straw) 141^{5} **>56a 70df<**

Bajan Rose 5 b m Dashing Blade-Supreme Rose (Frimley Park) 942^{23} 1021^{6} 1402^{8} 1824^{5} 2232^{4} 2377^{12} 4733^{22} 4997^{3} **>75f<**

Baked Alaska 3 b f Green Desert (USA)-Snowing (USA) (Icecapade (USA)) 672^{6} 1101^{2} 1740^{5} 2133^{6} 2561^{11} **>95f<**

Bakers Daughter 5 ch m Bairn (USA)-Tawnais (Artaius (USA)) **1996:** 5242^{3} 5274^{10} **1997:** 74^{7} 245^{4} 340^{2} 380^{7} 1244^{2} 1632^{4} 2281^{2} 2668^{4} (3091) 3496^{6} 4172^{12} 4516^{4} 4714^{16} 4918^{7} **>47a 65f<**

Bakio (FR) 6 b g Caerwent-Chester County (Realm) $189a^{3}$ $269a^{3}$ **>78f<**

Bala 2 ch f Casteddu-Baladee (Mummy's Pet) 2553^{6} 2959^{3} 3471^{14} 4566^{4} 4746^{5} **>64f<**

Balaclava (IRE) 2 b c Balla Cove-Little Cynthia (Wolver Hollow) 2693^{11} 3084^{2} 3687^{3} 4116^{20} 4362^{6} 4670^{14} **>72f<**

Balaitini (IRE) 2 b f Lion Cavern (USA)-Balwa (USA) (Danzig (USA)) 4067^{6} **>76+f<**

Balal (GR) 4 $627a^{11}$ **>81a f<**

Balalaika 4 b f Sadler's Wells (USA)-Bella Colora (Bellypha) (934) 1326^{4} 2010^{6} 3988^{3} $4666a^{4}$ 4976^{2} **>113f<**

Balance of Power 5 b g Ballacashtal (CAN)-Moreton's Martha (Derrylin) 639^{5} 791^{11} 1166^{15} 1459^{14} 1972^{9} 2573^{4} 2745^{F} **>59f< (DEAD)**

Balance The Books 2 b f Elmaamul (USA)-Psylla (Beldale Flutter (USA)) (1149) 2057^{11} 2516^{7} 3387^{5} 4116^{13} 4588^{6} **>83f<**

Balanita (IRE) 2 b g Anita's Prince-Ballybannon (Ballymore) 1251^{8} 1932^{6} 2388^{6} 3031^{7} 4588^{14} (4856) **>67f<**

Baleno (GER) 3 b c Heraldiste (USA)-Blumme (GER) (Jadar (GER)) $920a^{2}$ $2642a^{6}$ $4396a^{2}$ **>109f<**

Baleriena (BEL) 4 br f Bacalao (USA)-Regendinoa (FR) (Prince Regent (FR)) 2492^{15}

Balfour Lady 3 gr f Absalom-Pearl Cove (Town And Country) 1088^{6} 2183^{12} 2491^{5} 2730^{15} 3800^{8} 4378^{6} 4579^{3} 4748^{10} **>68f<**

Bali Dance 2 br f Rambo Dancer (CAN)-Baliana (Midyan (USA)) 1330^{3} 1821^{5} 2288^{3} 2587^{3} 3067^{3} 3186^{7} 4595^{5} 4806^{11} 4974^{7} 5050^{4} **>65?f<**

Balinsky (IRE) 4 b f Skyliner-Ballinacurra (King's Troop) **1996:** 5122^{5} 5267^{6} **1997:** 65^{7} 275^{4} **>43a 58f<**

Bali Paradise (USA) 3 b g Red Ransom (USA)-Dream Creek (USA) (The Minstrel (CAN)) 646^{4} 1146^{5} 1595^{5} 2328^{4} 2601^{6} 3190^{5} 3575^{2} 4294^{5} 4476^{9} **>101f<**

Bali-Pet 3 b g Tina's Pet-Baligay (Balidar) **1996:** (5166) 5202^{2} **1997:** 6^{5} 41^{5} 600^{11} 785^{15} 1095^{8} 1584^{6} 2171^{14} 2364^{3} 2670^{7} 3038^{7} 3477^{14} 3601^{8} 4601^{12} **>35a 29f<**

Balisian Beauty (USA) 2 f $5060a^{11}$

Balla d'Aire (IRE) 2 b br c Balla Cove-Silius (Junius (USA)) 1842^{4} 2842^{11} 4710^{8} **>74f<**

Balladara (IRE) 3 b c Ballad Rock-Mochara (Last Fandango) 1394^{5} 1851^{9} 1976^{6} 2510^{12} 3205^{8} 4243^{13} 4480^{13} **>58f<**

Ballantrae Boy 3 ch g Safawan-Romany Home (Gabitat) 2143^{8} 4290^{15} 4469^{10} **>30f<**

Ballard Lady (IRE) 5 ch m Ballad Rock-First Blush (Ela-Mana-Mou) **1996:** 5109^{3} **1997:** (4) 152^{5} 203^{5} 423^{10} 749^{8} 883^{6} 1250^{4} 1332^{2} 1765^{8} 2418^{2} 2651^{3} 3039^{5} (3224) 3761^{10} 4169^{18} **>52a 51f<**

Ballasilla 2 b f Puissance-Darussalam (Tina's Pet) 4402^{5} 4630^{8} 4855^{6} 4982^{4} **>61a 59f<**

Balla Sola (IRE) 2 ch c Simply Great (FR)-Dance Alone (USA) (Monteverdi) $3961a^{5}$ **>97+f<**

Ballerina's Dream 3 b f Suave Dancer (USA)-Our Reverie (USA) (J O Tobin (USA)) 221^{5} 259^{6} 513^{9} **>30a 49f<**

Ballet de Cour 4 b g Thowra (FR)-Chaleureuse (Final Straw) 16^{14} 122^{8} 312^{3} 367^{9} 490^{11} 687^{16} 900^{11} 1229^{3} 1605^{9} 2034^{8} 2518^{4} 2662^{3} 2874^{8} **>34a 30f<**

Ballet Prince (IRE) 7 b h Sadler's Wells (USA)-Sun Princess (English Prince) $2638a^{3}$ **>99f<**

Ballet Rambert 2 b f Rambo Dancer (CAN)-Kind Thoughts (Kashmir II) (880) 1675^{6} 2286^{4} 2688^{8} 3474^{9} 3750^{7} 4271^{8} 4380^{6} 4849^{7} **>73f<**

Ball Gown 7 b m Jalmood (USA)-Relatively Smart (Great Nephew) 1157^{3} 1323^{9} 2710^{16} 2869^{7} 4294^{14} 4558^{20} **>92f<**

Ballpoint 4 ch g Indian Ridge-Ballaquine (Martinmas) (781) 994^{5} 1672^{4} 2236^{9} 3283^{4} 3603^{P} **>83?f<**

Ballydinero (IRE) 3 b g Ballacashtal (CAN)-Nutwood Emma (Henbit (USA)) 862^{8} 1043^{5} 1229^{14} 2357^{9} 2673^{3} 3068^{9} 3572^{7} **>36a 33f<**

Ballykissangel 4 ro g Hadeer-April Wind (Windjammer (USA)) **1996:** 5262^{11} **1997:** 65^{11} **>30a 25f<**

Ballykissann 2 ch g Ballacashtal (CAN)-Mybella Ann (Anfield) 4520^{8} 4857^{5} **>64f<**

Ballymote 3 b g Chilibang-Be My Honey (Bustino) 434^{5} 783^{2} 1254^{4} 1571^{4} 4512^{14} 4770^{19} 4997^{5} **>69f<**

Ballyranter 8 ch g Bold Owl-Whipalash (Stephen George) 1244^{6} 1632^{23} **>59a 53f<**

Bally Souza (IRE) 3 b f Alzao (USA)-Cheese Soup (USA) (Spectacular Bid (USA)) 1392^{6} 1999^{2} 2194^{4} 2421^{3} (2885) (3035) 3259^{3} 3377^{3} 3989^{4} **>90f<**

Bally Wonder 5 b m Music Boy-Salacious (Sallust) 3691^{10} 3992^{11} **>39a 8f<**

Baltic State (USA) 2 b c Danzig (USA)-Kingscote (Kings Lake (USA)) (1692) (2600) 3123^{5} **>99f<**

Banbury (USA) 3 b c Silver Hawk (USA)-Sugar Hollow (USA) (Val de L'Orne (FR)) 503^{3} 847^{3} (1130) 2058^{18} 3263^{7} **>100f<**

Bandbox (IRE) 2 ch c Imperial Frontier (USA)-Dublah (USA) (Private Account (USA)) 1293^{8} 1635^{5} 2520^{3} 2942^{9} 3131^{2} 3497^{4} 3791^{2} 4216^{2} 4602^{2} 4818^{2} (4917) **>84f<**

Bandira (GER) 3 ch f Nityo (USA)-Brigantin (Arratos (FR)) (1551a) **>100f<**

Band on the Run 10 ch h Song-Sylvanecte (FR) (Silver Shark) 433^{3} 738^{18} 947^{9} 1495^{7} (1775) 1979^{14} 2478^{6} 2678^{4} 3408^{8} 3901^{11} 4147^{10} 4410^{7} 4781^{27} **>66a 81f<**

Bandore (IRE) 3 ch g Salse (USA)-Key Tothe Minstrel (USA) (The Minstrel (CAN)) 1242^{9} 1482^{10} 1831^{4} 3864^{11} 4336^{10} **>63f<**

Banker Dwerry (FR) 2 b c Unfuwain (USA)-Tartique Twist (USA) (Arctic Tern (USA)) 4478^{6} 4914^{2} **>90f<**

Bankers Order 3 b c Prince Sabo-Bad Payer (Tanfirion) 4049^{16} 4214^{13} **>6a 30f<**

Bank On Him 2 b g Elmaamul (USA)-Feather Flower (Relkino) 5048^{16} **>43f<**

Banneret (USA) 4 b g Imperial Falcon (CAN)-Dashing Partner (Formidable (USA)) 1230^{13} 2487^{20} 3758^{15} 4324^{19} 4923^{12} **>16f<**

Banningham Blade 2 b f Sure Blade (USA)-High Velocity (Frimley Park) 447^{8} (564) (637) (750) 893^{3} (1143) 1475^{2} 1735^{4} 2024^{4} 2335^{6} 2862^{3} 3192^{4} 3595^{2} 3908^{3} 4150^{5} 4293^{6} 4675^{11} **>94f<**

Banzhaf (USA) 4 ch g Rare Performer (USA)-Hang On For Effer (USA) (Effervescing (USA)) 363^{9} 567^{7} 1082^{2} 1320^{10} 1745^{5} 3056^{5} (3139) 3465^{12} 3930^{2} 4404^{4} 4451^{3} **>88a 78f<**

Bapsford 3 b g Shalford (IRE)-Bap's Miracle (Track Spare) 1151^{11} 1589^{11} 2151^{4} 2670^{5} 3054^{3} (3413) (4484) **>66a 45f<**

Baptismal Rock (IRE) 3 ch g Ballad Rock-Flower From Heaven (Baptism) 288^{9} 367^{10} 556^{9} 644^{9} 759^{15} 1083^{12} 1730^{8} **>17a 26f<**

Baranov (IRE) 4 b g Mulhollande (USA)-Silojoka (Home Guard (USA)) *291^{10}* 1001^{18} 2399^{11} 4751^{16} **>48a 23f<**

Barato 6 ch g Efisio-Tentraco Lady (Gay Fandango (USA)) 443^{9} 527^{10} 702^{12} 863^{12} **>61f< (DEAD)**

Barba Papa (IRE) 3 b c Mujadil (USA)-Baby's Smile (Shirley Heights) (765) 1099^{3} (1555a) (2101a) 2338^{5} 3190^{10} 4141^{5} 4558^{19} **>98f<**

Barbara's Jewel 5 b g Rakaposhi King-Aston Lass (Headin' Up) *203^{7} 367^{3} (511) 578^{8} 589^{10} 858^{U}* 955^{5} *1125^{2}* 1562^{5} 1748^{4} **>67a 62df< (DEAD)**

Barbason 5 ch g Polish Precedent (USA)-Barada (USA) (Damascus (USA)) **1996:** *5079^{3} 5182^{4} 5221^{4} 5249^{3}* **1997:** *24^{3} 109^{4} 128^{7} (349) (458) (490)* (567) (752) 1107^{W} 1640^{5} 2721^{3} (2745) 4451^{6} *5021^{4}* **>74a 74f<**

Barbrallen 5 b m Rambo Dancer (CAN)-Barrie Baby (Import) **1996:** *5093^{8} 5110^{9}* **1997:** 1473^{12} 1484^{7} 2281^{8} 2395^{14} 3292^{8} **>27a 35f<**

Barbury Ballad (IRE) 3 b c Ballad Rock-Eeduff (Auction Ring (USA)) 1087^{12} 1297^{16} 1508^{3} 2747^{10} 2946^{3} 3299^{13} 3641^{4} 4249^{17} **>50f<**

Bardonecchia (ITY) 2 ch f Indian Ridge-Rosa de Caerleon (Caerleon (USA)) 4397a^{2} 4865a^{7} **>95f<**

Bardon Hill Boy (IRE) 5 br g Be My Native (USA)-Star With A Glimer (Montekin) *176^{3} 299^{6} 405^{4}* 1016^{12} 1300^{5} 1768^{8} 2122^{W} 2296^{4} 2653^{3} 2961^{2} 3238^{7} **>88a 91f<**

Bargash 5 ch g Sharpo-Anchor Inn (Be My Guest (USA)) **1996:** *5209^{3}* **1997:** *27^{4}* **>47a 65f<**

Barings (FR) 3 629a^{5} **>103f<**

Baritone 3 b c Midyan (USA)-Zinzi (Song) 483^{6} 699^{2} 930^{7} 1170^{12} 1977^{8} 2214^{5} 2415^{5} **>68f<**

Barkston Warrior 3 b g Totem (USA)-Bold Difference (Bold Owl) 4587^{12} 4713^{15} 4916^{14} **>15f<**

Barlovento (GER) 4 b c Dowsing (USA)-Bebe Eliza (GER) (Esclavo (FR)) (3736a) **>103f<**

Barnata (FR) 3 b f Diamond Prospect (USA)-Tanny (FR) (Gift Card (FR)) 718a^{2}

Barnburgh Boy 3 ch g Shalford (IRE)-Tuxford Hideaway (Cawston's Clown) 1792^{3} 2044^{5} 2547^{4} 3037^{2} 3211^{2} 3457^{2} 3622^{3} 3937^{3} 4147^{14} 4417^{2} 4583^{2} 4781^{9} **>83f<**

Barnum Sands 3 b c Green Desert (USA)-Circus Plume (High Top) 691^{4} 1032^{2} 2345^{2} 3388^{5} (4312) 4759^{4} **>110f<**

Barnwood Crackers 3 ch g Be My Chief (USA)-Tartique Twist (USA) (Arctic Tern (USA)) **1996:** *5212^{7}* **1997:** *8^{5} 46^{4}* 2916^{12} 3116^{3} 3643^{P} **>58a 48f<**

Baroness Noble 2 b f Noble Patriarch-Baroness Gymcrak (Pharly (FR)) 1626^{9} **>20f< (DEAD)**

Baron Ferdinand 7 ch g Ferdinand (USA)-In Perpetuity (Great Nephew) 4968^{7} **>121?f<**

Baroon 3 c 2097a^{9} 2642a^{2} (3555a) **>120f<**

Barossa Valley (IRE) 6 b g Alzao (USA)-Night of Wind (Tumble Wind (USA)) **1996:** *5099^{2} 5186^{3} 5227^{2} (5250) (5274)* **1997:** *131^{6}* 450^{21} 1166^{18} 1745^{9} **>86a 55f<**

Baroud d'Honneur (FR) 4 gr c Highest Honor (FR)-Petite Soeur (FR) (Lyphard (USA)) 625a^{3} 1554a^{4} (3364a) **>120f<**

Barrack Yard 4 b c Forzando-Abbotswood (Ahonoora) *(663)* 1020^{5} 1489^{15} 3987^{22} *4301^{5}* 4773^{11} **>73a 61df<**

Barranak (IRE) 5 b g Cyrano de Bergerac-Saulonika (Saulingo) 473^{6} 702^{18} 1003^{5} 1250^{11} 1514^{2} (1848) (2148) 2321^{2} 2529^{4} 3032^{2} 3126^{15} 3500^{5} 3898^{4} 4137^{15} 4329^{8} 4738^{19} **>66f<**

Barrelbio (IRE) 2 b g Elbio-Esther (Persian Bold) 2140^{4} 2356^{9} 2762^{6} 3755^{10} 4767^{7} (5026) **>64f<**

Barrel of Hope 5 b g Distant Relative-Musianica (Music Boy) **1996:** *5161^{3} (5206) 5262^{3}* **1997:** *56^{4} 175^{2} 194^{6} 254^{6}* 444^{9} 863^{17} 1225^{20} **>74a 67f<**

Barresbo 3 b g Barrys Gamble-Bo' Babbity (Strong Gale) **1996:** *5083^{5} 5133^{12} 5176^{11}* **1997:** 535^{4} 609^{3} 886^{5} 1129^{9} 1603^{2} 1820^{9} 2169^{2} 2543^{7} (3088) 3457^{4} 4436^{14} **>37a 73f<**

Barrier Ridge 3 ch c Lycius (USA)-Star Ridge (USA) (Storm Bird (CAN)) 645^{2} 1271^{3} (1630) **>90f<**

Barrow Creek 3 ch c Cadeaux Genereux-Breadcrumb (Final Straw) 4563^{6} 4700^{8} **>67f<**

Bartex (FR) 3 b c Groom Dancer (USA)-Belisonde (FR) (Gay Mecene (USA)) 1358a^{2} **>99f<**

Barwell Boy 3 b g Clantime-Kasu (Try My Best (USA)) *230^{8} 287^{4} 412^{2}* 469^{5} *588^{5} 871^{6}* **>46a 43tf<**

Basanta (IRE) 4 b c Sadler's Wells (USA)-La Meilleure (Lord Gayle (USA)) 2967a^{8} **>92f<**

Bashful Brave 6 ch g Indian Ridge-Shy Dolly (Cajun) **1996:** *5096^{6} 5220^{9}* **1997:** 1572^{8} 1667^{2} 2540^{11} (3271) 3871^{6} *4051^{3}* 4385^{6} **>63a 58f<**

Basic Style 2 b c Alhijaz-Turbo Rose (Taufan (USA)) 850^{10} 1084^{6} 1321^{7} 2215^{5} **>50f<**

Basman (IRE) 3 b c Persian Heights-Gepares (IRE) (Mashhor Dancer (USA)) 725^{2} 1103^{3} 3501^{2} 4005^{5} (4631) 5051^{7} **>110?f<**

Basood (USA) 4 b f Woodman (USA)-Basoof (USA) (Believe It (USA)) **1996:** *(5119) 5148^{2} 5222^{12}* **>60da 61f<**

Basse Besogne (IRE) 3 b f Pursuit of Love-Baiser Vole (USA) (Foolish Pleasure (USA)) 1727a^{2} 3371a^{7} 3875a^{2} **>110f<**

Bataan (USA) 6 b h Manila (USA)-Comtesse de Loir (FR) (Val de Loir) 607^{10} **>67?f<**

Batabanoo 8 ch g Bairn (USA)-For Instance (Busted) *867^{3} 1152^{4}* 1570^{3} 1795^{5} 2737^{3} (3309) 3754^{4} 4171^{2} 4946^{6} **>69a 58f<**

Bataleur 4 b g Midyan (USA)-Tinkerbird (Music Boy) 827^{6} 1089^{15} 1385^{15} 3936^{14} 4385^{7} 4580^{16} 4905^{3} **>56f<**

Batchworth Belle 2 b f Interrex (CAN)-Treasurebound (Beldale Flutter (USA)) 4818^{12} **>39f<**

Bathe In Light (USA) 3 ch f Sunshine Forever (USA)-Ice House (Northfields (USA)) 475^{6} 990^{10} 1624^{3} 2782^{2} 3298^{W} 3495^{6} 3970^{2} **>67f<**

Bath Knight 4 b g Full Extent (USA)-Mybella Ann (Anfield) *76^{12} 129^{5} 183^{11}* **>24a 59f<**

Batoutoftheblue 4 br g Batshoof-Action Belle (Auction Ring (USA)) 982^{11} 1162^{13} 3069^{7} 3309^{8} 3543^{9} *4481^{2}* **>73a 52f<**

Batsman 3 b c Batshoof-Lady Bequick (Sharpen Up) 474^{10} 694^{17} 1141^{22} 2004^{12} 2554^{2} 3898^{11} 4877^{10} **>58f<**

Batswing 2 b c Batshoof-Magic Milly (Simply Great (FR)) 850^{8} 938^{W} 1492^{2} 1744^{8} (2320) 2863^{6} 3142^{4} 3597^{11} 4232^{8} 4679^{2} 4880^{8} **>80f<**

Battle Dore (USA) 4 ch c Sanglamore (USA)-Nashmeel 1914a^{2} **>115f<**

Battle Green 4 b g Old Vic-Sword Lily (UAE) (Mr Prospector (USA)) *626a^{2}* **>96a f<**

Battle Ground (IRE) 3 b g Common Grounds-Last Gunboat (Dominion) **1996:** *5098^{4}* **1997:** 556^{5} *662^{5}* 1689^{5} 1965^{15} 2171^{5} 2399^{3} (2577) **>43a 57f<**

Battleship Bruce 5 b g Mazilier (USA)-Quick Profit (Formidable (USA)) **1996:** *5211^{9}* **1997:** 2369^{9} **>49a 60f<**

Battle Spark (USA) 4 b g Gold Seam (USA)-Flick Your Bick (USA) (Bicker (USA)) *457^{9}* **>36a 72f<**

Battle Warning 2 b c Warning-Royal Ballet (IRE) (Sadler's Wells (USA)) 4950^{9} **>37f<**

Baubigny (USA) 3 b g Shadeed (USA)-Pearl Essence (USA) (Conquistador Cielo (USA)) 431^{8} 533^{6} 886^{8} 2182^{6} 2853^{5} 3299^{4} 3685^{4} 4243^{11} **>54f<**

Bawara (IRE) 3 b g Slip Anchor-Alwatar (USA) (Caerleon (USA)) 4547^{3} 4743^{11} **>74f<**

Bawsian 2 b c Persian Bold-Bawaeth (USA) (Blushing Groom (FR)) 3619^{3} 3806^{7} 4061^{14} 4285^{7} 4806^{6} (4994) **>72f<**

Bayford Thrust 3 ro g Timeless Times (USA)-Gem of Gold (Jellaby) 1018^{8} 1468^{10} 1661^{3} 2044^{2} 2192^{2} 2547^{3} 2779^{5} 3332^{2} 3709^{11} 3923^{7} 4328^{19} **>55f<**

Bay Harbor (USA) 2 f *5060a^{14}*

Bayin (USA) 8 b g Caro-Regatela (USA) (Dr Fager) 520^{9} 643^{7} 835^{7} 977^{12} 1488^{6} 1977^{13} (2308) 2711^{6} 2950^{8} 3198^{10} 3417^{7} 4048^{2} 4155^{18} 4248^{6} 4321^{6} 4580^{10} 4905^{18} **>62f<**

Bayleaf 2 ch f Efisio-Bayonne (Bay Express) (2831) 4150^{4} **>87f<**

Baylham 2 b g Risk Me (FR)-So Beguiling (USA) (Woodman (USA)) 3402^{4} 3628^{2} 3920^{5} 4284^{10} 4468^{9} 4690^{11} 4994^{15} **>67f<**

Bay of Delight 2 ch f Cadeaux Genereux-Zawaahy (USA) (El Gran Senor (USA)) 3117^{13} 4735^{8} **>54f<**

Bay of Islands 5 b g Jupiter Island-Lawyer's Wave (USA) (Advocator) 735^{9} 933^{5} 1244^{5} (1660) 2155^{3} 2710^{8} 3238^{4} **>88f<**

Bay Prince (IRE) 2 b c Mujadil (USA)-Kingston Rose (Tudor Music) 2917^{8} (3619) (3708) 4126a^{4} 4253a^{7} 4790^{13} **>95f<**

Bayrak (USA) 7 b g Bering-Phydilla (FR) (Lyphard (USA)) *23^{9} 908^{10}* **>16a 56df<**

Bay Watch (IRE) 2 ch c Priolo (USA)-Life Watch (USA) (Highland Park (USA)) 3019^{6} **>49f<**

Bazelle (FR) 4 b f Fabulous Dancer (USA)-Copy Cat (FR) (King Of Macedon) 1369a^{3} 1919a^{2} **>98f<**

Beach Buoy (IRE) 3 ch g Orchestra-Seapoint (Major Point) 2888^{3} 3211^{8} 3624^{2} 4161^{9} 4438^{7} 4632^{11} **>59f<**

Beacon Blaze 2 ch f Rudimentary (USA)-Beacon Hill (Bustino) 4873^{10} **>57f<**

Beacon Silver 3 b f Belmez (USA)-Nettle (Kris) 3389^{5} 3820^{3} 4177^{4} 4407^{2} **>78?f<**

Beano Script 4 b g Prince Sabo-Souadah (USA) (General Holme (USA)) 1991^{2} 2239^{4} 2546^{12} 2785^{10} 2884^{4} 3330^{5} **>60f<**

Bear Hug 4 b g Polar Falcon (USA)-Tender Loving Care (Final Straw) 1106^{4} 1477^{11} 3293^{2} 4063^{16} 4477^{10} **>78df<**

Bear To Dance 4 b f Rambo Dancer (CAN)-Pooh Wee (Music Boy) 1501^{13} 1843^{8} 2406^{5} **>39a 41f<**

Bea's Ruby (IRE) 3 b f Fairy King (USA)-Beautiful Secret (USA) (Secreto (USA)) (1030) (1314) 4689^{4} 4990^{9} 5044^{7} **>91f<**

Beat of Drums 6 b h Warning-Nyoka (USA) (Raja Baba (USA)) **1996:** 5127a^{2} **>118f<**

Beau Bruno 4 b g Thatching-Lady Lorelei (Derring-Do) *135^{4} 215^{7}* **>75da 73df<**

Beaucatcher (IRE) 3 b f Thatching-Gale Warning (IRE) (Last Tycoon) 2491^{11} 2704^{6} 3202^{5} 4563^{10} 4972^{10} **>53f<**

Beauchamp Jade 5 gr m Kalaglow-Beauchamp Buzz (High Top) 736^{12} 2869^{3} 3191^{5} 3902^{5} 4295^{2} 5043^{5} **>105f<**

Beauchamp King 4 gr c Nishapour (FR)-Afariya (FR) (Silver Shark) 830^{6} 1210^{9} 2009^{7} (3144) 3674a^{8} **>111f<**

Beauchamp Knight 4 ch g Chilibang-Beauchamp Cactus (Niniski (USA)) 762^{14} 2932^{8} **>38f<**

Beauchamp Lion 3 ch c Be My Chief (USA)-Beauchamp Cactus (Niniski (USA)) 1140^{11} 1465^{4} 3455^{4} 3781^{8} 4222^{14} 4633^{13} **>68f<**

Beauchamp Magic 2 b c Northern Park (USA)-

Beauchamp Buzz (High Top) 3598^{12} 4237^{17} 4603^{8} **>58f<**

Beauman 7 b g Rainbow Quest (USA)-Gliding (Tudor Melody) **1996:** *5240^{5}* **1997:** *34^{4} 82^{11} 88^{6}* **>59a 68f<**

Beau Matelot 5 ch g Handsome Sailor-Bellanoora (Ahonoora) *37^{7}* **>34?a 58f<**

Beaumont (IRE) 7 br g Be My Native (USA)-Say Yes (Junius (USA)) *55^{5} 542^{6}* (2867) 3805^{4} 4363^{5} 4956^{3} 5052^{5} **>72a 81f<**

Beau Roberto 3 b g Robellino (USA)-Night Jar (Night Shift (USA)) 840^{13} 1078^{7} 1449^{W} 1838^{3} 2715^{3} 2903^{6} 3225^{5} 3430^{5} 3992^{6} 4235^{9} 4693^{10} 4846^{9} **>41f<**

Beautiful Fire (IRE) 3 ro c Selkirk (USA)-Beautiful France (Sadler's Wells (USA)) 807a^{4} 2441a^{9} **>103f<**

Beautiful Pleasure (USA) 2 f *5060a^{10}*

Beau Tudor (IRE) 3 b g Aragon-Sunley Silks (Formidable (USA)) 2420^{11} 2838^{9} 3086^{6} 3606^{12} 4214^{12} 4331^{6} **>31f<**

Beau Venture (USA) 9 ch h Explodent (USA)-Old Westbury (USA) (Francis S) **1996:** *5138^{7} 5246^{10}* **1997:** 585^{2} (604) 879^{11} 1250^{9} 1662^{4} 2006^{16} 2703^{2} 2788^{17} 2933^{6} 3016^{2} 3280^{8} 3473^{7} 3693^{4} 4329^{6} (4370) 4636^{7} **>48a 75f<**

Beau Vienna 2 b f Superpower-Waltz on Air (Doc Marten) 3701^{6} **>45f<**

Beckenham Insight 3 b f Efisio-Capel Lass (The Brianstan) 1587^{17} *3043^{6}* **>14a f<**

Bedazzle 6 b g Formidable (USA)-Wasimah (Caerleon (USA)) 526^{12} 587^{2} 668^{2} 848^{3} 1005^{7} 1231^{7} 1472^{10} 1802^{2} 2041^{2} 2362^{4} 2660^{5} 2876^{7} 3315^{6} 4584^{13} 4845^{14} **>31a 43f<**

Bedevilled 2 ch c Beveled (USA)-Putout (Dowsing (USA)) 4564^{2} 4917^{3} **>78f<**

Bedouin Honda 3 b br c Mtoto-Bedouin Veil (USA) (Shareef Dancer (USA)) 676^{8} 2126^{7} 4506^{3} 4788^{16} 4854^{8} 4988^{7} **>71f<**

Bedouin Prince (USA) 10 b g Danzig (USA)-Regal Heiress (English Prince) *302^{3} 381^{4} 486^{3}* 570^{2} 753^{2} 1010^{7} 1222^{5} *(2322)* 2874^{6} *3415^{8}* **>52a 45f<**

Bedside Story 3 b f Mtoto-Biograph (USA) (Riverman (USA)) (1075a) 1368a^{4} 4535a^{2} **>105f<**

Beechwood Quest (IRE) 2 b f River Falls-Egalite (IRE) (Fools Holme (USA)) *1137^{3}* 1997^{12} 2288^{7} 2412^{2} *(2606)* 3209^{3} *(3586)* 3776^{4} 3823^{13} **>75?a 59f<**

Bee Dee Best (IRE) 6 b g Try My Best (USA)-Eloquent Charm (USA) (Private Account (USA)) 3271^{9} 3590^{12} **>40a 44f<**

Bee Health Boy 4 b g Superpower-Rekindle (Relkino) 949^{2} 1227^{6} 1402^{3} *1942^{10}* 2129^{3} 2326^{6} 2422^{3} 2711^{13} 3034^{11} 3143^{5} 3443^{8} 4636^{18} 4733^{19} **>30a 70f<**

Begorrat (IRE) 3 ch g Ballad Rock-Hada Rani (Jaazeiro (USA)) 795^{4} 990^{8} 1144^{12} 2695^{3} 2897^{5} 3132^{4} (3572) 3976^{4} 4283^{8} (4703) 4978^{19} **>75f<**

Beguine (USA) 3 br f Green Dancer (USA)-La Papagena (Habitat) 3211^{11} 4060^{13} 4323^{16} **>58f<**

Behaviour 5 b h Warning-Berry's Dream (Darshaan) 678^{4} 787^{3} 3388^{6} 3634^{5} 4947^{3} **>103f<**

Behind The Scenes 3 ch c Kris-Free Guest (Be My Guest (USA)) 683^{20} 1014^{9} (1322) 1747^{8} 2058^{19} 2850^{4} 2963^{10} *3231^{2}* **>79a 55f<**

Behind The Veil 2 ch f Forzando-Karonga (Main Reef) 1447^{12} 2153^{8} 2383^{9} **>24f<**

Behold 2 ch f Prince Sabo-Be My Lass (IRE) (Be My Guest (USA)) (1466) 2429^{2} **>80f<**

Behrens (USA) 3 *5066a^{7}* **>94a f<**

Belbay Star 4 b f Belfort (FR)-Gavea (African Sky) **1996:** *5183^{6}* **1997:** 1467^{6} 1733^{7} 2237^{5} 2657^{2} 2891^{12} **>37a 37f<**

Bel Canto (IRE) 3 b c Sadler's Wells (USA)-Fair of the Furze (Ela-Mana-Mou) 3977^{3} 4177^{7} (4378) 4672^{10} **>79f<**

Beldray Park (IRE) 4 b br g Superpower-Ride Bold (USA) (J O Tobin (USA)) 823^{11} 1446^{8} 2002^{12} 4016^{20} 4219^{14} 4453^{11} **>38f<**

Belinda Blue 5 b m Belfort (FR)-Carrula (Palm Track) **1996:** *5178^{6}* **1997:** *4^{4} 79^{3} 137^{11}* **>38a 49f<**

Bella Daniella 3 br f Prince Daniel (USA)-Danse D'Esprit (Lidhame) 1217^{6} *1785^{9} 2068^{9}* 2357^{7} **>26f<**

Belladera (IRE) 2 b f Alzao (USA)-Reality (Known Fact (USA)) (1174) 2558^{8} 3036^{2} 3422^{6} 4119^{8} **>84f<**

Bellagrana 3 ch f Belmez (USA)-Nafis (USA) (Nodouble (USA)) 727^{13} 1297^{5} 1823^{11} 2832^{8} 3133^{2} 3329^{2} 3864^{7} 4503^{5} 4971^{25} **>61f<**

Bella Michela (IRE) 4 ch f Superpower-Lumiere (USA) (Northjet) **1996:** 5127a^{3} **>102f<**

Bellaphento 4 b f Lyphento (USA)-Nautical Belle (Kind of Hush) **1996:** *5101^{5} 5185^{9}* **>46a 54f<**

Bellara 5 b m Thowra (FR)-Sicilian Vespers (Mummy's Game) 498^{5} *660^{12}* 982^{3} 1162^{10} **>57a 62f<**

Bellarula 3 gr f Belfort (FR)-Carrula (Palm Track) 462^{7} 556^{3} 758^{10} 1467^{19} 2235^{7} **>52df<**

Bellas Gate Boy 5 b g Doulab (USA)-Celestial Air (Rheingold) *211^{8} 401^{5}* 848^{6} (1599) 1779^{2} 1920^{4} *2302^{10}* 2430^{4} 2564^{9} 3248^{11} 3432^{2} 3971^{6} **>37a 55f<**

Bella's Legacy 4 b f Thowra (FR)-Miss Lawsuit (Neltino) 2852^{11} 3590^{9} 4169^{20} 4455^{2} 4843^{3} 4987^{14} **>47f<**

Bellateena 5 b m Nomination-Bella Travaille (Workboy) **1996:** *5081^{3} 5242^{12}* **>49da 38f<**

Belle Bijou 3 ch f Midyan (USA)-Pushkar (Northfields (USA)) *(239)* 600^{7} 1837^{6} 2224^{3} 2387^{2} 3485^{3} 4269^{13} 4693^{11} **>67a 63f<**

Belle Dancer 3 b f Rambo Dancer (CAN)-Warning Bell (Bustino) **1996:** *5180^{9}*

Belle de Montfort 2 b f Presidium-Judys Girl (IRE) (Simply Great (FR)) 2534^{13} 2893^{10} 3967^{11} **>38f<**

Belle de Nuit (IRE) 2 b f Statoblest-Elminya (IRE) (Sure Blade (USA)) 2831^{6} 3471^{12} (3783) 4097^{9} (4185) 4473^{2} 4786^{11} **>85f<**

Bello (ARG) 5 h 4656a^{8} **>89f<**

Bellow (IRE) 2 b g Petorius-Kristen Belle (Viking (USA)) 648^{10} 2378^{5} (2587) 3215^{8} **>78f<**

Bellroi (IRE) 6 b g Roi Danzig (USA)-Balela (African Sky) 2411^{11} **>56f<**

Belmarita (IRE) 4 ch f Belmez (USA)-Congress Lady (General Assembly (USA)) 888^{18} 1478^{12} 4521^{6} **>69f<**

Belsalazie 4 b f Belmez (USA)-Salazie (Ile de Bourbon (USA)) 4659a^{3} **>110f<**

Belushi 3 b f Risk Me (FR)-Trigamy (Tribal Chief) *90^{8} 156^{3} 234^{6}* **>33a f<**

Belzao 4 b g Alzao (USA)-Belle Enfant (Beldale Flutter (USA)) 2006^{23} 4373^{15} 4872^{13} 5028^{4} **>58a 37f<**

Bemsha Swing (IRE) 2 b br c Night Shift (USA)-Move It Baby (IRE) (Thatching) 1411^{6} 1744^{2} 1978^{5} 3127^{2} (3770) 4524^{6} **>101f<**

Be My Girl 2 ch f Be My Guest (USA)-Kaprisky (IRE) (Red Sunset) 3613^{7} 3979^{12} 4227^{6} **>56f<**

Be My Wish 2 b f Be My Chief (USA)-Spinner (Blue Cashmere) 1031^{3} 1306^{4} 1806^{4} 2862^{8} **>78f<**

Benatom (USA) 4 gr g Hawkster (USA)-Dance Til Two (USA) (Sovereign Dancer (USA)) 1319^{5} 1947^{4} 2327^{16} (2709) 3110^{3} **>103f<**

Bend Wavy (IRE) 5 ch g Kefaah (USA)-Prosodie (FR) (Relko) *344^{8}* 4306^{7} 4635^{10} 4732^{6} 5049^{12} **>59f<**

Beneventus 2 b c Most Welcome-Dara Dee (Dara Monarch) 2699^{3} 3806^{4} 4174^{4} **>77f<**

Ben Gunn 5 b g Faustus (USA)-Pirate Maid (Auction Ring (USA)) **1996:** *5130^{3} 5209^{9} 5247^{2}* **1997:** *10^{3} 131^{5}* (1166) 1489^{6} 2036^{4} 2369^{2} (2557) 3115^{9} 3622^{8} 4297^{8} 4781^{4} **>60a 73f<**

Benicia Boy 5 ch g Grey Desire-Fabia (FR) (Faunus (FR)) 3249^{13} 4114^{17}

Benin (USA) 2 b c Sky Classic (CAN)-Battle Drum (USA) (Alydar (USA)) (4575) **>89+f<**

Benjamin Frank 2 b c Tragic Role (USA)-Flower Princess (Slip Anchor) 4638^{6} **>41f<**

Benjamins Law 6 b or br g Mtoto-Absaloute Service (Absalom) *870^{3}* 1233^{2} 1463^{13} 2146^{2} 2564^{2} 3010^{2} 3579^{3} 3890^{7} **>73a 60f<**

Benny The Dip (USA) 3 b br c Silver Hawk (USA)-Rascal Rascal (USA) (Ack Ack (USA)) 851^{2} (1159) (1769) 2527^{2} 3646^{3} 4785^{6} **>130f<**

Ben Rinnes 2 ch c Ardkinglass-Magical Veil (Majestic Light (USA)) 1263^{7} 1480^{10} (2181) 2689^{9} 3474^{11} 3990^{2} 4778^{14} **>84f<**

Benrock (IRE) 2 ch c Ballad Rock-Madame Champvert (IRE) (Cardinal Flower) *1136^{5}* 3905^{20} 4602^{11} **>37a 21f<**

Ben's Ridge 3 b c Indian Ridge-Fen Princess (IRE) (Trojan Fen) **1996:** *5141^{6}* **1997:** *12^{4} 44^{5}* **>60a 80f<**

Bentico 8 b g Nordico (USA)-Bentinck Hotel (Red God) **1996:** *5106^{3} 5182^{2} 5231^{5} 5269^{11}* **1997:** *243^{4} 274^{9} 297^{5} 578^{6} 857^{4}* 1093^{10} *1291^{3} 1754^{3} (1786) 1969^{2} 2161^{2} (2193)* 2369^{5} *3584^{9} 4485^{5} 4813^{2}* 4992^{10} **>72a 53f<**

Bentnose 3 b c Saddlers' Hall (IRE)-Blonde Prospect (USA) (Mr Prospector (USA)) **1996:** *5228^{8}* **1997:** *6^{8}* 582^{15} **>48a 52f<**

Bent Raiwand (USA) 4 b f Cadeaux Genereux-Raiwand (Tap On Wood) **1996:** *5112^{5}* **1997:** *1289^{12} 1759^{9}* 1828^{12} 2313^{11} *2602^{11}* 3241^{8} 3488^{3} 3854^{9} 4214^{W} **>38a 32f<**

Benzoe (IRE) 7 b g Taufan (USA)-Saintly Guest (What A Guest) 596^{15} 835^{12} 977^{8} 1225^{3} 1259^{3} (1627) 1977^{14} 2129^{6} 2339^{8} 2711^{2} (3034) 3208^{3} 3649^{5} 4280^{19} 4456^{11} 4733^{10} 4995^{20} **>85f<**

Bequeath 5 ch h Rainbow Quest (USA)-Balabina (USA) (Nijinsky (CAN)) 852^{5} 1241^{5} 1490^{3} 1762^{3} **>111f<**

Bergen (IRE) 2 b c Ballad Rock-Local Custom (IRE) (Be My Native (USA)) (2842) 4266^{5} **>86+f<**

Bering Gifts (IRE) 2 b c Bering-Bobbysoxer (Valiyar) 3013^{W} 3978^{3} 4758^{3} 4957^{W} **>82f<**

Berlin Blue 4 b g Belmez (USA)-Blue Brocade (Reform) 846^{6} 1145^{4} 2028^{18} 2475^{7} 3805^{7} 4101^{6} **>79f<**

Bermuda Boy 2 b g Robellino (USA)-Bermuda Lily (Dunbeath (USA)) 2849^{2} 3193^{7} (3711) **>91f<**

Bermuda Triangle (IRE) 2 b f Conquering Hero (USA)-Bermuda Princess (Lord Gayle (USA)) 1480^{2} 1827^{6} 2719^{6} 2923^{5} (3228) 3451^{2} 3742^{5} 4543^{8} **>57f<**

Bernardo Bellotto (IRE) 2 b c High Estate-Naivity (IRE) (Auction Ring (USA)) 504^{2} 583^{2} 684^{4} *2047^{2}* 2349^{2} 2571^{2} (3433) 3650^{8} 4006^{3} **>72a 78f<**

Bernard Seven (IRE) 5 b g Taufan (USA)-Madame Nureyev (USA) (Nureyev (USA)) *14^{3} 140^{3} 213^{3} 294^{7}* 733^{13} 1024^{13} *1291^{16}* 1631^{15} 2019^{16} 2200^{4} 2544^{3} 2887^{6} 3487^{3} 4847^{6} **>72a 49f<**

Bernie's Star (IRE) 3 b br g Arcane (USA)-Abaca (USA) (Manila (USA)) 983^{12} 2143^{5} 2315^{18} 3336^{10} 4336^{15} **>33f<**

Beryllium 3 b g Tragic Role (USA)-Flower Princess (Slip Anchor) 966^{6} 1773^{7} 2601^{15} 3897^{2} **>69f<**

Be Satisfied **4** ch g Chilibang-Gentalyn (Henbit (USA)) **1996:** *5081[9] 5188[8] 5253[9]* **1997:** *322[8]* **>31a 34f<**

Besiege **3** b c Rainbow Quest (USA)-Armeria (USA) (Northern Dancer) 851[6] 4149[10] 4732[4] 4903[2] **>101df<**

Best Attempt **2** ch c Beveled (USA)-Sheznice (IRE) (Try My Best (USA)) 2579[6] **>37f<**

Best Before Dawn (IRE) **6** b g Try My Best (USA)-Pistol Petal (Pitskelly) 2105[9] 2815a[8] 3508a[3] 4203a[6] **>106f<**

Bestelina **3** b f Puissance-Brittle Grove (Bustino) **1996:** *5142[4] 5202[6]* **1997:** 1375[4] 1644[7] 2732[16] **>47a 46f<**

Bestemor **3** b f Selkirk (USA)-Lillemor (Connaught) 3917[6] 4070[12] 4277[9] 4958[6] **>62f<**

Best Kept Secret **6** b g Petong-Glenfield Portion (Mummy's Pet) **1996:** *5161[7]* **1997:** *1433[10]* 1748[12] 2177[7] 2488[8] 2651[5] 3378[5] **>41a 46f<**

Best of All (IRE) **5** b m Try My Best (USA)-Skisette (Malinowski (USA)) **1996:** *(5132) 5200[7]* **1997:** 608[6] 749[3] 951[9] *1135[9]* (1818) (1994) 2355[2] 2660[4] 3153[16] 3428[6] 4268[8] 4283[9] **>67a 77f<**

Best of Our Days **2** b c Clantime-Uptown Girl (Caruso) *4569[9]* 4921[4] **>46a 66f<**

Best Quest **2** b c Salse (USA)-Quest for the Best (Rainbow Quest (USA)) 4544[6] 4706[7] 5041[12] **>59f<**

Besweetome **4** b f Mtoto-Actraphane (Shareef Dancer (USA)) *(322)* **>76a 19++f<**

Bet On Sunshine (USA) **5** *5061a[3]* **>128a f<**

Be True **3** b g Robellino (USA)-Natchez Trace (Commanche Run) *225[6] 362[6]* 2722[7] 2956[6] 3592[7] 3929[3] (4503) (4860) **>46a 64f<**

Better Offer (IRE) **5** b g Waajib-Camden's Gift (Camden Town) 2028[13] 2709[6] 3191[4] 3705[14] 4443[4] 4754[9] **>104f<**

Bettron **2** b g Alnasr Alwasheek-Aigua Blava (USA) (Solford (USA)) 1418[U] (2741) 3780[2] 4368[8] 4898[3] **>87f<**

Be Valiant **3** gr g Petong-Fetlar (Pharly (FR)) 1297[12] **>41f<**

Beveled Crystal **3** ro f Beveled (USA)-Countess Mariga (Amboise) 1485[8] 1921[6] 2244[5] 2665[13] 2852[12] 4816[15] **>41f<**

Beveled Mill **3** b f Beveled (USA)-Lonely Shore (Blakeney) **1996:** *5166[6] 5180[8]* **>12a 40f<**

Bevier **3** b c Nashwan (USA)-Bevel (USA) (Mr Prospector (USA)) 937[6] 1477[7] (1688) 2013[23] 2585[15] 3891[9] 4578[6] **>66f<**

Beware **2** br c Warning-Dancing Spirit (IRE) (Ahonoora) 2295[6] 2870[3] 3479[6] 3794[4] 4286[2] 4501[3] 4709[6] (4897) **>84f<**

Be Warned **6** b g Warning-Sagar (Habitat) *424[6]* 529[4] 610[4] 863[2] 1020[14] 1315[16] 2002[8] *2603[11]* 2847[7] 3261[4] 3310[7] *3581[2] 4050[5]* (4249) 4580[8] *4798[5]* 4951[14] **>52a 55f<**

Bewitching Lady **3** ch f Primo Dominie-Spirit of India (Indian King (USA)) 748[4] 1116[11] 1624[8] 1859[6] 2667[2] 3234[11] 3495[9] 3593[3] *3865[9]* (4180) 4450[2] 4860[6] **>26a 57f<**

Beyond Calculation (USA) **3** ch c Geiger Counter (USA)-Placer Queen (Habitat) 517[4] 674[10] 3037[3] 3548[5] *4301[2]* (4600) 4733[18] **>73a 80f<**

Bianca Cappello (IRE) **4** b f Glenstal (USA)-Idara (Top Ville) **1996:** *5223[14]* **>26a 33f<**

Bianca Nera **3** b f Salse (USA)-Birch Creek (Carwhite) 724[6] 960[11] **>107f<**

Biba (IRE) **3** ch f Superlative-Fahrenheit (Mount Hagen (FR)) 532[12] *1086[10]* **>13a 49f<**

Bicton Park **3** b c Distant Relative-Merton Mill (Dominion) 2687[8] 2920[8] 4047[11] *4574[13]* **>70f<**

Biff-Em (IRE) **3** ch g Durgam (USA)-Flash The Gold (Ahonoora) 953[8] 1243[12] 2030[6] 2382[7] 2715[9] 3225[7] 4693[7] **>54f<**

Big Ander (SPA) **3** c 4658a[9] **>76f<**

Big Bang **3** b g Superlative-Good Time Girl (Good Times (ITY)) *341[3] (417)* 537[10] *857[9]* 1140[18] *(2068) 2365[3]* 4170[17] *4811[11]* **>71a 56f<**

Big Ben **3** ch c Timeless Times (USA)-Belltina (Belfort (FR)) 506[7] 1029[10] 1217[3] (1746) 1958[15] *(2319) 2605[4]* 2921[5] 3139[4] 3420[3] *3860[7]* **>67a 68f<**

Big Erotavlas (ITY) **3** **1996:** 5128a[8] **>80f<**

Big Flower (GER) **4** b f Big Shuffle (USA)-Bowl Of Flower's (GER) (Sir Ivor) 4536a[2] **>107f<**

Big Pat **8** b g Backchat (USA)-Fallonetta (Tachypous) 2039[12] 2479[6] **>57a 40f<**

Big Sky Chester (USA) **5** h 5065a[5] **>121f<**

Big Target (IRE) **3** b g Suave Dancer (USA)-Prima Domina (FR) (Dominion) 683[9] 1004[5] 1276[4] 4743[6] **>73f<**

Bigwig (IRE) **4** ch c Thatching-Sabaah (USA) (Nureyev (USA)) **1996:** *5091[8] 5185[8]* **>37a 28f<**

Bijou d'Inde **4** ch c Cadeaux Genereux-Pushkar (Northfields (USA)) *409a[4] 628a[B]* 4129a[8] 4422[5] 4785[7] **>113a 123f<**

Bilko **3** gr c Risk Me (FR)-Princess Tara (Prince Sabo) 506[5] 854[10] 1662[8] **>86f<**

Billaddie **4** b g Touch of Grey-Young Lady (Young Generation) *396[6] 458[6]* **>55a 60f<**

Billionaire **2** b c Distant Relative-Miss Plum (Ardross) 5040[11] **>39f<**

Billy Bushwacker **6** b g Most Welcome-Secret Valentine (Wollow) 775[2] 974[3] 1450[5] 2155[2] 2292[2] 3542[4] 3822[5] 4102[7] 4409[2] 4639[7] 4886[3] **>91df<**

Billycan (IRE) **3** b c Mac's Imp (USA)-Sassalin (Sassafras (FR)) *6[9] 41[8]* **>28a 13f<**

Billy Nomaite **3** ch g Komaite (USA)-Lucky Monashka (Lucky Wednesday) 1630[3] 2059[2] 2783[2] 3430[6] 3813[10] **>73f<**

Billy Owl (IRE) **2** ch c Shalford (IRE)-Ounavarra (Homeric) 3701[7] **>50f<**

Bimsey (IRE) **7** b h Horage-Cut It Out (Cut Above) 2767[6] 3137[4] 3705[12] **>89f<**

Bina Gardens **3** b f Shirley Heights-Balabina (USA) (Nijinsky (CAN)) 2410[6] 3014[4] 3419[4] (3909) (4110) **>103f<**

Bin Cyclone (USA) **3** b c Shadeed (USA)-Dubian (High Line) 3144[7] 3463[4] 3715[3] 4008[16] 4319[15] **>71f<**

Bin Rosie **5** b g Distant Relative-Come on Rosi (Valiyar) 830[3] 1210[8] 2009[6] 2821a[6] 3577[2] (3790) (4292) 4523[6] 4862a[11] **>124f<**

Bint Albaadiya (USA) **3** ch f Woodman (USA)-Pixie Erin (Golden Fleece (USA)) (1021) (2299) (2677) 4240[4] **>116f<**

Bintang (IRE) **2** ch c Soviet Star (USA)-Brush Away (Ahonoora) (3726) (4146) 4551[2] **>107f<**

Bintang Timor (USA) **3** ch c Mt Livermore (USA)-Frisky Kitten (USA) (Isopach (USA)) 693[4] 842[4] 1589[7] **>78f<**

Bint Baladee **3** b f Nashwan (USA)-Sahara Baladee (USA) (Shadeed (USA)) (992) 1738[7] (2180) 3017[2] 3492[4] **>108f<**

Bint Kaldoun (IRE) **2** b f Kaldoun (FR)-Shy Danceuse (FR) (Groom Dancer (USA)) 4317[4] **>74f<**

Bint Nadia **2** b f Deploy-Faisalah (Gay Mecene (USA)) 1645[6] 2288[5] 2493[W] 2935[3] (3563) 3802[10] 4208[4] 4576[8] **>57f<**

Bint Rosie **3** b f Exit To Nowhere (USA)-Butterfly Rose (USA) (Iron Ruler (USA)) 725[18] 1168[14] 2397[11] 3183[6] 3495[7] **>43f<**

Bint Shihama (USA) **3** b f Cadeaux Genereux-Shihama (USA) (Shadeed (USA)) 1499[4] 1976[3] 2184[2] (2506) 2774[5] 3982[16] **>95?f<**

Birchwood Sun **7** b g Bluebird (USA)-Shapely Test (USA) (Elocutionist (USA)) 529[13] 827[5] (1079) 1395[7] 1511[12] 3936[15] 4059[13] 4184[9] 4510[4] 4711[2] 4846[7] 4992[12] **>57f<**

Bird Island **6** gr g Jupiter Island-Roybirdie (Mansingh (USA)) (2998a) **>67f<**

Bishops Court **3** ch g Clantime-Indigo (Primo Dominie) 434[3] 854[3] (1029) 1158[3] 1980[3] 2134[2] 2683[2] 4098[4] 4525[2] 4964a[4] **>113f<**

Bismarck (IRE) **2** b c Common Grounds-Family At War (USA) (Explodent (USA)) 1538a[4] 2451a[5] **>79f<**

Bison Belting **3** b g Full Extent (USA)-Sylvan Song (Song) *576[4] 874[5]* 1090[12] *1754[15]* 4415[9] 4843[8] 4899[14] **>46a 29f<**

Bisquet-de-Bouche **3** ch f Most Welcome-Larive (Blakeney) 670[7] 1094[4] 1387[3] 2397[6] 2702[12] **>54f<**

Bit on the Side (IRE) **8** b m Vision (USA)-Mistress (USA) (Damascus (USA)) 1414[3] 1934[4] 3434[3] 5053[23] **>91f<**

Biya (IRE) **5** ch g Shadeed (USA)-Rosie Potts (Shareef Dancer (USA)) *80[5] 157[3] (188) 401[4] 589[9] 908[12]* **>51da 48f<**

Black Ice Boy (IRE) **6** b g Law Society (USA)-Hogan's Sister (USA) (Speak John) 865[11] (2207) (2498) 2737[6] *3046[4]* 3401[7] 4804[7] **>42a 40f<**

Black Jet **2** b c Durgam (USA)-Blazing Sunset (Blazing Saddles (AUS)) 822[8] 2243[8] *2604[4] 3042[6]* 4265[12] *4592[5]* **>61a 30f<**

Blackpatch Hill **8** br g Efisio-Myrtlegrove (Scottish Rifle) **1996:** *5136[12]* **>47f<**

Black Pidgeon (IRE) **2** b f Paris House-Isla Bonita (Kings Lake (USA)) 3961a[26] **>67f<**

Black Rock City **2** b c Rock City-Jomel Amou 3961a[28] **>59f<**

Black Weasel (IRE) **2** b c Lahib (USA)-Glowlamp (IRE) (Glow (USA)) 4533a[3]

Blakeset **2** ch c Midyan (USA)-Penset (Red Sunset) 583[3] (695) 1924[2] 4006[5] 4560[3] **>83f<**

Blanche The Almond **2** ch f Northern Park (USA)-Gaucherie (USA) (Sharpen Up) 4165[15] 4459[11] 4627[9] *4799[10]* 4974[14] **>11a 48f<**

Blane Water (USA) **3** b f Lomond (USA)-Triode (USA) (Sharpen Up) 507[6] 1326[9] 2561[6] 4121[10] 4424[10] **>86f<**

Blarney Park **2** b f Never so Bold-Walking Saint (Godswalk (USA)) 828[12] *2066[5]* 2684[5] 3106[11] 3314[3] 3742[3] 4162[11] 4327[14] 4819[12] **>26a 56f<**

Blasket Island (IRE) **3** bg c Kenmare (FR)-Starring Role 3180a[3] **>106f<**

Blatant Outburst **7** b g War Hero-Miss Metro (Upper Case (USA)) 761[5] 982[10] 3317[11] **>66df<**

Blaze of Oak (USA) **6** ch g Green Forest (USA)-Magic Robe (USA) (Grey Dawn II) 763[4] 900[9] 1383[8] 1507[11] 1825[16] **>51f<**

Blaze of Song **5** ch g Jester-Intellect (Frimley Park) **1996:** *5088[6]* **1997:** 4714[13] 4918[5] **>51a 60f<**

Blazer's Baby **3** ch f Norton Challenger-Qualitair Blazer (Blazing Saddles (AUS)) 1587[13] 1858[5] 2332[9] 2770[4] (3027) 3320[8] 4453[12] 4608[14] 4916[10] **>34f<**

Blazing Billy **2** ch c Anshan-Worthy Venture (Northfields (USA)) 4917[10] **>46f<**

Blazing Castle **3** gr g Vague Shot-Castle Cary (Castle Keep) 448[22] *569[10]* 757[4] 882[7] 1566[6] 1667[4] 1921[5] 2954[9] **>57a 52f<**

Blazing Imp (USA) **4** ch g Imp Society (USA)-Marital (USA) (Marine Patrol (USA)) 1733[8] (2167) 2540[7] 2754[7] 2934[6] 3287[12] 3871[13] 4707[13] 4791[7] 4997[6] **>52f<**

Blenheim Terrace **4** b g Rambo Dancer (CAN)-Boulevard Girl (Nicholas Bill) 612[2] 1022[8] 1763[11] 3700[4] (4161) 4409[4] **>48a 71?f<**

Blessed Spirit **4** ch f Statoblest-Kukri (Kris) 749[2] 934[6] 1813[2] 2331[6] 2868[4] (3048) 3548[3] 3875a[0]

4669^{3} **>103f<**

Bless 'im 2 b c Presidium-Saint Systems (Uncle Pokey) 3489^{5} 4017^{12} 4801^{2} **>75f<**

Blessingindisguise 4 b g Kala Shikari-Blowing Bubbles (Native Admiral (USA)) 464^{8} 744^{18} 863^{14} 1098^{2} 1225^{2} (1468) 1977^{12} (2061) 2289^{2} (2480) (2717) (3011) 3410^{3} 3649^{3} 4098^{U} 4282^{8} 4444^{3} **>104f<**

Blewbury Hill (IRE) 3 gr c Kenmare (FR)-Greatest Pleasure (Be My Guest (USA)) 740^{W} 1207^{11} 1587^{4} 1876^{4} 2347^{6} 2778^{2} 3236^{9} 3894^{12} 4276^{3} 4552^{6} (4606) 4920^{5} **>81f<**

Bliss (IRE) 2 b f Statoblest-Moira My Girl (Henbit (USA)) 472^{6} 648^{7} 880^{6} 1293^{4} 2578^{6} 2942^{7} (3965) (4173) (4522) **>74f<**

Blitz 2 b f Casteddu-Lake Mistassiu (Tina's Pet) 572^{6} 1569^{11} 2545^{14} 3106^{12} 3544^{5} 3751^{9} *4054^{16}* **>5a 35f<**

Blockade (USA) 8 b g Imperial Falcon (CAN)-Stolen Date (USA) (Sadair) 864^{9} 1219^{10} (1503) 1678^{8} (1796) 2187^{4} 2430^{5} 2776^{6} **>67f<**

Blomberg (IRE) 5 b h Indian Ridge-Daniella Drive (USA) (Shelter Half (USA)) **1996:** *5204^{10}* **>86a 113f< (DEAD)**

Blondane 4 b g Danehill (USA)-Whos The Blonde (Cure The Blues (USA)) **1996:** *5129^{9} 5174^{8}* **>36a f<**

Blood Orange 3 ch c Ron's Victory (USA)-Little Bittern (USA) (Riva Ridge (USA)) 693^{6} 1238^{10} **>65f<**

Blooming Amazing 3 b g Mazilier (USA)-Cornflower Blue (Tyrnavos) (575) 699^{3} 998^{4} 1392^{5} 3801^{10} 4436^{5} *4591^{9}* 4788^{6} 4958^{2} **>57a 82f<**

Blot 3 b c Warning-Rattle Along (Tap On Wood) 1221^{3} 1611^{8} 2960^{3} (3211) **>88f<**

Blowing Away (IRE) 3 b br f Last Tycoon-Taken By Force (Persian Bold) 1499^{3} 2116^{3} 2772^{5} 3135^{6} 3787^{11} 4228^{15} 4858^{9} (4916) 4992^{10} **>60f<**

Blu Carillon (IRE) 2 ch c Love the Groom (USA)-Carillon Miss (USA) (The Minstrel (CAN)) 2098a^{3} (4253a) **>106+f<**

Blue Anchor 2 b c Robellino (USA)-Fair Seas (General Assembly (USA)) 1330^{9} 1961^{8} 2165^{4} 2565^{8} 3869^{6} **>55f<**

Blue And Royal (IRE) 5 b g Bluebird (USA)-Cat Girl (USA) (Grey Dawn II) *147^{5} 252^{4} 375^{7}* 986^{6} *1156^{7}* 1636^{10} 1825^{10} **>40da 49f<**

Bluebell Miss 3 b f High Kicker (USA)-Mio Mementa (Streak) 1622^{10} 2029^{3} 2200^{2} 2577^{2} (2770) *3073^{3}* **>66a 68f<**

Blueberry 2 b f Batshoof-Always a Lady (Dominion) 2371^{7} 2728^{14} 2953^{4} 3215^{12} **>66f<**

Blue Calvine 3 b g Silver Kite (USA)-Calvanne Miss (Martinmas) 1272^{16} 1437^{8} *2300^{7}* 4465^{12} **>29a 31f<**

Blue Cheese 3 gr f Mystiko (USA)-Legal Sound (Legal Eagle) 1090^{13} *1787^{10} 2603^{10} 3040^{6}* 4546^{11} **>37a 31f<**

Blue Chief (DEN) 5 4531a^{5} **>105f<**

Blue Dawn (IRE) 2 ch f Bluebird (USA)-Spring Carnival (USA) (Riverman (USA)) 3117^{5} 4317^{7} 4701^{4} **>69f<**

Blue Desert 2 ch g Elmaamul (USA)-Shehana (USA) (The Minstrel (CAN)) 836^{5} 993^{5} 1812^{13} (4627) 4778^{11} 4974^{5} **>65f<**

Blue Domain 6 b g Dominion-Blue Rag (Ragusa) **1996:** *5174^{11}* **1997:** *18^{8}* 574^{7} **>10a 43f<**

Blue Duster (USA) 4 b f Danzig (USA)-Blue Note (FR) (Habitat) 1171^{3} 2056^{7} **>115f<**

Blue Flyer (IRE) 4 b g Bluebird (USA)-Born to Fly (IRE) (Last Tycoon) **1996:** *5186^{4} 5249^{14}* **1997:** *(121) 238^{6} 323^{8} 363^{8}* 2576^{7} 2835^{3} 3138^{14} 3423^{5} 3615^{10} 3718^{2} 4225^{11} 4441^{22} **>83da 74f<**

Blue Gentian (USA) 2 b f Known Fact (USA)-Caithness (USA) (Roberto (USA)) (3985) 4273^{3} **>84f<**

Blue Goblin (USA) 3 gr c Trempolino (USA)-Blue Daisy (USA) (Shahrastani (USA)) 518^{4} 675^{3} 942^{3} (1237) (1609) 2056^{2} 2599^{8} 3747^{9} **>113f<**

Blue Havana 5 br m Cigar-Welsh Bluebell (Manado) *2160^{8}* 3816^{12} 3969^{9}

Blue Hopper 3 b f Rock Hopper-Kimble Blue (Blue Refrain) 998^{9} 1140^{7} 1820^{17} 1971^{4} **>57f<**

Blue Imperial (FR) 3 gr c Bluebird (USA)-Real Gold (Yankee Gold) 765^{9} (1164) (1568) 1955^{2} (2929) 3153^{15} 3712^{9} **>80f<**

Blue Iris 4 b f Petong-Bo' Babbity (Strong Gale) 1112^{3} 1766^{5} 2683^{8} 3011^{11} (4062) 4525^{7} **>96f<**

Blue Island (IRE) 3 br g Contract Law (USA)-Bluebutton (Blue Cashmere) 795^{11} 1272^{15} 4579^{11} *4810^{7}* **>11a 50f<**

Blue Jay (IRE) 3 b br g Bluebird (USA)-Alpine Spring (Head for Heights) 2941^{12} 3454^{11} **>7f<**

Blue Jumbo (IRE) 4 b f Bluebird (USA)-Finalist (Star Appeal) *125^{11} 236^{6}* 1441^{4} **>11a 47f<**

Blue Kite 2 ch c Silver Kite (USA)-Gold And Blue (IRE) (Bluebird (USA)) *902^{2} 1045^{2} 3610^{2}* 3811^{6} 4152^{2} 4232^{6} *(4479)* 4755^{10} 4955^{5} **>74a 81f<**

Blue Lamp (USA) 3 ch f Shadeed (USA)-Matter of Time (Habitat) 1110^{5} 1316^{11} 1681^{2} 2001^{10} 2496^{8} 2747^{5} 3086^{4} 3606^{4} 4115^{11} **>59f<**

Blue Lugana 5 b g Lugana Beach-Two Friendly (Be Friendly) *36^{5} 69^{2} 127^{2} 172^{3} 287^{2} 318^{9} 429^{8}* 469^{6} *855^{7}* **>45a 43tf<**

Blue Marine (GER) 2 b f Lagunas-Bowl Of Flower's (GER) (Sir Ivor) 3368a^{3} **>83f<**

Blue Monk (IRE) 2 ch c Bluebird (USA)-High Habit (Slip Anchor) 3598^{10} 4111^{7} 4520^{11} **>75f<**

Blueprint (IRE) 2 b c Generous (IRE)-Highbrow (Shirley Heights) 3598^{9} 4274^{5} **>80f<**

Blue Ridge 3 ch c Indian Ridge-Souadah (USA) (General Holme (USA)) 2861^{12} 3863^{5} 4100^{21} **>94?f<**

Blueridge Dancer (IRE) 2 gr c Bluebird (USA)-Maraquiba (FR) (Kenmare (FR)) (432) (893) 1475^{5} 2012^{12} 2584^{4} 4675^{9} 4790^{20} **>96df<**

Blue River (IRE) 3 ch c River Falls-Royal Resident (Prince Regent (FR)) 690^{5} 1146^{3} 1962^{2} 2135^{5} 3109^{10} **>102df<**

Blue Shadow 2 gr c Pips Pride-Lingdale Lass (Petong) 1263^{12} 1486^{6} 1954^{11} 3783^{5} 4065^{8} 4403^{8} *5017^{3}* **>60a 67f<**

Blue Sky (IRE) 3 b/ c Marignan (USA)-Belle Bleue (Blazing Saddles (AUS)) 4125a^{3} **>103f<**

Blues Magic (IRE) 3 ch g Imp Society (USA)-Fairy Folk (IRE) (Fairy King (USA)) *118^{2} 251^{4} 282^{2} 320^{3} 379^{2}* **>67a f<**

Blues Queen 3 b f Lahib (USA)-Queens Welcome (Northfields (USA)) 724^{9} 988^{6} 1634^{5} 2211^{6} 2517^{5} 2925^{6} 3092^{7} 3207^{5} 3327^{11} 3710^{9} *4049^{7}* **>50a 79f<**

Bluewain Lady 2 b f Unfuwain (USA)-Blue Guitar (Cure The Blues (USA)) 3547^{3} 4057^{4} 4317^{6} **>89df<**

Blueygreen 3 b f Green Desert (USA)-Bluebook (USA) (Secretariat (USA)) 1316^{2} 1823^{2} (2773) 3147^{8} 4377^{6} **>81f<**

Blue Zola (IRE) 2 b f Alzao (USA)-Lady of Shalott (Kings Lake (USA)) 2728^{8} 3295^{2} *3607^{4}* 3794^{5} 4209^{3} 4753^{13} 4974^{2} **>66a 72f<**

Blundell Lane (IRE) 2 ch c Shalford (IRE)-Rathbawn Realm (Doulab (USA)) 1418^{2} 1692^{5} 4602^{7} (4922) 4989^{5} **>76f<**

Blurred (IRE) 4 ch g Al Hareb (USA)-I'll Take Paris (USA) (Vaguely Noble) 933^{15} 4477^{13} 4754^{18} **>51f<**

Blush 3 b f Gildoran-Rather Warm (Tribal Chief) (1809) 2178^{6} 2744^{4} 3793^{7} 4179^{12} 4916^{12} **>55f<**

Blushing Desert 3 b f Green Desert (USA)-Blushing Storm (USA) (Blushing Groom (FR)) 1030^{10} 4070^{3} 4455^{8} *5020^{2}* **>64a 66f<**

Blushing Grenadier (IRE) 5 ch g Salt Dome (USA)-La Duse (Junius (USA)) **1996:** *5237^{2}* **1997:** *69^{3} 128^{11} 319^{2}* 1965^{17} 2179^{8} 2395^{9} 2646^{14} 3276^{11} **>59a 39f<**

Blushing Minstrel (IRE) 3 b f Nicholas (USA)-Motley (Rainbow Quest (USA)) 3508a^{12} **>70f<**

Blushing Victoria 2 b f Weldnaas (USA)-Bollin Victoria (Jalmood (USA)) (583) 884^{5} 2697^{6} 3131^{W} 3416^{4} *3610^{8}* 3707^{10} **>47a 76f<**

Boater 3 b g Batshoof-Velvet Beret (IRE) (Dominion) **1996:** *5121^{3}* **1997:** (642) 794^{4} 1256^{2} 1670^{3} 2062^{5} **>81a 82f<**

Boat O'Brig 4 b g Slip Anchor-Advie Bridge (High Line) 4743^{13} **>25f<**

Boat Strand (IRE) 2 b g Distinctly North (USA)-Gorgeous Twist 3961a^{24} **>87f<**

Bobbitt 3 b f Reprimand-Pleasuring (Good Times (ITY)) 864^{6} 1503^{7} 2392^{3} 2878^{6} *4053^{6}* 4224^{4} 4713^{11} **>33a 49f<**

Bobbydazzle 2 ch f Rock Hopper-Billie Blue (Ballad Rock) 1440^{8} 2018^{2} 2562^{6} 3025^{4} (3802) 4116^{9} **>78f<**

Bobby's Dream 5 b m Reference Point-Kiralyi (FR) (Kings Lake (USA)) 1570^{7} 2175^{10} 2539^{8} 3617^{2} 3929^{4} 4713^{9} **>57f<**

Bob Knows 3 br g Robellino (USA)-Snowline (Bay Express) 3991^{7} 4277^{10} 4631^{5} 4821^{15} **>57f<**

Bob's Saintly Aim 3 b f Mazilier (USA)-Great Aim (Great Nephew) 4224^{15}

Bob The Broker (IRE) 3 b c Bob Back (USA)-Java Jive (Hotfoot) 1541a^{8} **>96f<**

Boccolino 2 b g Robellino (USA)-Brockton Dancer (Fairy King (USA)) 1791^{5} 2412^{10} *2914^{7}* **>36f<**

Bodantree 6 b g Rambo Dancer (CAN)-Snow Tree (Welsh Pageant) 3245^{3} **>34a 43f<**

Bodfaridistinction (IRE) 2 b f Distinctly North (USA)-Brave Louise (Brave Shot) 730^{4} (1031) 1211^{5} 2024^{16} 3257^{6} 3889^{6} **>77f<**

Bodfari Pride (IRE) 2 b c Pips Pride-Renata's Ring (IRE) (Auction Ring (USA)) 2477^{3} 3253^{8} **>68f<**

Bodfari Wren 3 b f Handsome Sailor-My Valentine Card (USA) (Forli (ARG)) 3624^{4} 3820^{6} **>52f<**

Bodyguard 2 ch c Zafonic (USA)-White Wisteria (Ahonoora) (938) (1161) 2054^{4} (2484) 3148^{3} **>103f<**

Boffy (IRE) 4 ch c Mac's Imp (USA)-No Dowry (Shy Groom (USA)) **1996:** *5163^{11} 5230^{11} 5234^{11} 5268^{2}* **1997:** *32^{3} 58^{7} 79^{4} 137^{6} 178^{4} 222^{5} 371^{4} 391^{10} 593^{4}* 779^{11} 956^{12} *1759^{10}* **>41a 34f<**

Bogan (IRE) 3 b c Caerleon (USA)-Belize Tropical (IRE) (Baillamont (USA)) *350^{4}* 2126^{8} 2566^{10} 3205^{4} *(3860) (4591)* **>72a 70f<**

Bogart 6 gr g Belfort (FR)-Larnem (Meldrum) **1996:** *5237^{9}* **1997:** *136^{3} 176^{9} 297^{3} 349^{6} 424^{11}* 574^{14} **>49a 62df<**

Bold Appeal (IRE) 5 b g Caerleon (USA)-La Bella Fontana (Lafontaine (USA)) 2330^{6} 2549^{6} 3061^{8} **>22a 47f<**

Bold Aristocrat (IRE) 6 b g Bold Arrangement-Wyn Mipet (Welsh Saint) **1996:** *5163^{3} 5174^{2} 5236^{8} 5258^{3}* **1997:** *65^{5} 87^{3} 113^{2} 192^{5} 233^{10} (332) 421^{6} 429^{2} 512^{4} 907^{5} 1047^{3} 1132^{2} 1754^{10} (2069) 2603^{3} 3075^{6} 3583^{4} 4051^{4} 4570^{8} 4985^{3}* **>70a 47f<**

Bold Becky 3 b f Never so Bold-Princess Silca Key (Grundy) 1567^{3} **>72f<**

Bold Brief 3 b g Tina's Pet-Immodest Miss (Daring Display (USA)) 529^{14} 785^{14} 995^{14} 1496^{5}

1730^{9} 2206^{2} 2504^{2} 3266^{4} **>59f<**

Bold Buster 4 b g Bustino-Truly Bold (Bold Lad (IRE)) 2853^{4} 3277^{10} (3864) 4235^{4} 4673^{3} 4986^{2} **>79f<**

Bold Charlie 5 ch g Weldnaas (USA)-Flirty Lady (Never so Bold) 18^{7} **>10a 2f<**

Bold Demand 3 b c Rainbow Quest (USA)-Dafrah (USA) (Danzig (USA)) 937^{2} (1477) 1769^{9} 2515^{6} **>100f<**

Bold Edge 2 ch c Beveled (USA)-Daring Ditty (Daring March) (1263) 2012^{13} 2863^{3} 3148^{5} 4293^{5} 4517^{3} 4675^{10} **>98f<**

Bold Effort (FR) 5 b g Bold Arrangement-Malham Tarn (Riverman (USA)) **1996:** (5246) **1997:** 254^{2} 357^{6} 394^{2} 443^{6} 726^{15} 892^{24} 1317^{12} (1578) 2105^{25} 2393^{2} 2818a^{10} 3372a^{5} 3876a^{D} 4100^{4} 4282^{27} 4756^{13} 4881^{16} 4983^{8} **>100a 102f<**

Bold Elect 9 b g Electric-Famous Band (USA) (Banderilla (USA)) 2682^{9} 2825^{2} 3122^{6} **>19a 64f<**

Bold Engagement 3 b f Never so Bold-Diamond House (Habitat) 774^{10} 896^{18} **>21f<**

Bold Et Noir 3 b c Never so Bold-Mill D'Art (Artaius (USA)) 874^{7} 1144^{15} 1297^{11} 1633^{14} 2577^{6} 2874^{14} 3413^{8} **>20a 48f<**

Bold Fact (USA) 2 b c Known Fact (USA)-Sookera (USA) (Roberto (USA)) (1744) 2012^{3} (2584) 3706^{2} **>102f<**

Bold Faith 4 b f Warning-Bold and Beautiful (Bold Lad (IRE)) 213^{4} 297^{7} 1139^{7} (2281) 4455^{4} 4695^{4} (4992) **>61a 61f<**

Bold Frontier 5 gr g Chief Singer-Mumtaz Flyer (USA) (Al Hattab (USA)) **1996:** 5246^{7} **1997:** 137^{5} 233^{2} 318^{3} 357^{2} (394) **>79a 57f<**

Bold Gayle 3 ch f Never so Bold-Storm Gayle (IRE) (Sadler's Wells (USA)) 531^{3} 685^{8} 845^{17} **>59f<**

Bold Habit 12 ch g Homing-Our Mother (Bold Lad (IRE)) **1996:** 5242^{5} 5260^{4} **1997:** (141) 210^{2} 319^{3} 333^{3} 385^{5} 407^{8} 587^{9} 668^{4} 2067^{8} **>45a 37f<**

Boldini (IRE) 2 b c Sadler's Wells (USA)-Green Leaf (USA) (Alydar (USA)) 4865a^{3} **>103f<**

Bold Joker 6 b g Jester-Bold Difference (Bold Owl) **1996:** 5136^{9} **1997:** 122^{6} 243^{W} 313^{10} **>3f<**

Bold King 2 br c Anshan-Spanish Heart (King of Spain) 1961^{2} 2509^{2} 2856^{2} 3597^{7} **>70f<**

Bold Legacy (IRE) 2 ch c Mujtahid (USA)-Lagrion (USA) (Diesis) 4871^{9} 5040^{16} **>57f<**

Bold Oriental (IRE) 3 b g Tirol-Miss Java (Persian Bold) 509^{7} 690^{8} (878) 990^{3} 1175^{17} 2013^{10} 2296^{5} 2585^{6} 2839^{7} **>89f<**

Bold Patriot (IRE) 4 b c Polish Patriot (USA)-Don't Be Cruel (Persian Bold) 1266^{10} **>78?f<**

Bold Pilot (TUR) 4 b c Persian Bold-Bold Palumbo (TUR) (Imperial Fling (USA)) 4263a^{3} **>112f<**

Bold Raparee (IRE) 2 ch c Bob Back (USA)-Shagudine (USA) 4865a^{8} **>98f<**

Bold Saint (IRE) 3 b c Persian Bold-St Clair Star (Sallust) 742^{13} 1024^{14} 1568^{12} 1796^{4} 2246^{15} 3044^{5} 3449^{3} (3612) 3865^{8} **>46a 51f<**

Bold Spring (IRE) 3 b c Never so Bold-Oasis (Valiyar) **1996:** 5214^{2} 5224^{3} **1997:** 970^{5} 1237^{5} 1573^{6} 1781^{5} 1988^{3} 2510^{13} 2669^{3} **>78da 68df<**

Bold Street (IRE) 7 ch g Shy Groom (USA)-Ferry Lane (Dom Racine (FR)) **1996:** 5095^{4} **1997:** 610^{13} 953^{6} 2033^{5} 2463^{10} 2915^{9} 3581^{3} 4050^{14} **>58a 56f<**

Bold Tina (IRE) 3 b f Persian Bold-Tinas Image (He Loves Me) 964^{3} 1141^{18} 1439^{11} 2918^{9} 3202^{6} 3642^{2} (3968) 4168^{6} (4546) 4878^{7} **>74f<**

Bold Top 5 ch g Bold Owl-Whirlygigger (Taufan (USA)) **1996:** 5115^{10} **1997:** 689^{8} 1222^{3} 1686^{5} 1798^{2} 2564^{3} 3330^{3} 3540^{7} (3620) 3933^{9} 4287^{12} 4802^{15} **>11a 52df<**

Bold Tycoon (IRE) 3 b f Last Tycoon-Bold-E-Be (Persian Bold) 2447a^{3} **>92f<**

Bold Words (CAN) 3 ch c Bold Ruckus (USA)-Trillium Woods (CAN) (Briartic (CAN)) (597) 691^{5} 1456^{2} 2026^{25} 2766^{4} 3369a^{10} **>117f<**

Bolero Kid 2 b c Rambo Dancer (CAN)-Barrie Baby (Import) 836^{12} 1045^{4} 1447^{6} 1941^{3} (3067) 3545^{2} **>64a 86f<**

Bolino Star (IRE) 6 b m Stalker-Gobolino (Don) 4620a^{12} **>96f<**

Bolivar (IRE) 5 b g Kahyasi-Shuss (USA) (Princely Native (USA)) 728^{8} 1413^{8} (2139) 3010^{6} 3383^{6} **>77f<**

Bollero (IRE) 3 b f Topanoora-Charo (Mariacci (FR)) 1096^{6} 1390^{8} 1820^{6} 2021^{8} (2376) (2501) 2659^{6} 2734^{2} 2913^{4} 3038^{5} 3572^{2} 3854^{6} 4291^{13} 4484^{10} 4916^{8} **>54a 64f<**

Bollin Ann 2 b f Anshan-Bollin Zola (Alzao (USA)) 3569^{9} 4017^{9} 4215^{6} **>56+f<**

Bollin Dorothy 4 b f Rambo Dancer (CAN)-Bollin Harriet (Lochnager) 468^{11} 779^{5} 901^{4} 1079^{10} 1765^{2} 2422^{2} 2708^{14} 3143^{4} 3431^{3} 3565^{3} 3936^{6} 4059^{9} 4291^{15} **>49f<**

Bollin Ethos 2 b c Precocious-Bollin Harriet (Lochnager) 4012^{20} **>30f<**

Bollin Frank 5 b h Rambo Dancer (CAN)-Bollin Emily (Lochnager) 1495^{4} 1775^{2} 2205^{2} 2465^{6} 3243^{6} 3810^{5} 4147^{11} 4283^{16} **>75f<**

Bollinger Rose (IRE) 2 b f Fayruz-Gobolino (Don) 1466^{8} 3070^{4} 3265^{8} 3707^{9} 4690^{7} 4812^{6} **>51a 65f<**

Bollin Harry 5 b h Domynsky-Bollin Harriet (Lochnager) 596^{4} 863^{13} 1799^{8} 2129^{4} 2326^{13} 2788^{16} 3621^{10} 4137^{6} 4307^{9} 4512^{16} **>55f<**

Bollin Joanne 4 b f Damister (USA)-Bollin Zola (Alzao (USA)) (1148) 2105^{3} 2677^{2} 3747^{2} (4098) 4239^{3} 4777^{2} **>115f<**

Bollin Terry 3 b c Terimon-Bollin Zola (Alzao (USA)) 448^{4} 654^{2} 1017^{3} 1175^{10} (1670) **>85f<**

Bolshaya 2 gr f Cadeaux Genereux-Mainly Dry (The Brianstan) 3411^{7} 4286^{6} 4840^{10} **>54f<**

Bolshoi (IRE) 5 br g Royal Academy (USA)-Mainly Dry (The Brianstan) (573) 941^{4} 1455^{3} 1881a^{3} 2106^{8} 2526^{11} 2683^{5} 3111^{4} 3724^{8} 4098^{8} 4525^{5} 4881^{15} **>110f<**

Bomb Alaska 2 br g Polar Falcon (USA)-So True (So Blessed) 4884^{15} 5040^{5} **>62f<**

Bombastic 2 ch c Polish Precedent (USA)-Fur Hat (Habitat) 4174^{7} 4507^{2} 4710^{2} **>83f<**

Bombazine (IRE) 3 ch f Generous (IRE)-Brocade (Habitat) 1611^{2} (2126) 4181^{3} 4676^{5} 5031a^{6} **>104f<**

Bonanza Peak (USA) 4 b c Houston (USA)-Bunnicula (USA) (Shadeed (USA)) 1477^{12} 1811^{11} 2187^{6} 2876^{3} (3329) 4714^{2} 4802^{2} 4988^{3} **>74f<**

Bonapartiste (FR) 3 b c Kendor-Fab's Melody (FR) 1726a^{9} 4392a^{2} 4658a^{2} **>115f<**

Bongo 3 b g Efisio-Boo Hoo (Mummy's Pet) 1451^{2} **>71f<**

Bon Guest (IRE) 3 ch c Kefaah (USA)-Uninvited Guest (Be My Guest (USA)) 193^{4} 251^{3} 361^{6} 577^{2} 659^{4} 757^{5} 876^{9} 1008^{5} (1388) 1506^{11} 1639^{6} 1929^{5} 2160^{2} 2318^{5} 2670^{2} 2878^{3} 3044^{3} 3320^{3} 3397^{5} 4548^{11} **>63a 62f<**

Bon Jovi (GER) 4 bl c Konigsstuhl (GER)-Book Of Love (GER) (Formidable (USA)) **1996:** 5126a^{3} **1997:** 1073a^{6} **>111f<**

Bon Luck (IRE) 5 ch g Waajib-Elle Va Bon (Tanfirion) 766^{4} 1097^{19} 2036^{15} **>76f<**

Bonne Ville 3 gr f Good Times (ITY)-Ville Air (Town Crier) **1996:** 5160^{2} **1997:** 581^{3} 1043^{4} 1465^{10} 2068^{2} 2607^{5} 3390^{7} 3585^{4} 4571^{6} 4981^{6} **>58a 56df<**

Bonnie Lassie 3 gr f Efisio-Normanby Lass (Bustino) 227^{5} 329^{2} 1493^{3} 4572^{7} 4693^{8} **>70a 75f<**

Bon Secret (IRE) 5 b g Classic Secret (USA)-Bon Retour (Sallust) **1996:** (5208) 5254^{3} 5271^{3} **1997:** 54^{3} 76^{2} 210^{7} 335^{4} 601^{13} 997^{3} 1965^{7} **>62a 49f<**

Bonsiel 3 b f Skyliner-Shawiniga (Lyphard's Wish (FR)) 1843^{7} 2554^{8} 2721^{W} **>45a 43f< (DEAD)**

Bon Sizzle 2 b c Sizzling Melody-Bonne de Berry (Habitat) 4602^{12} 4801^{11} 4917^{8} **>54f<**

Bonyalua Mill 3 gr f Chilibang-Candesco (Blushing Scribe (USA)) (412) 466^{4} 904^{8} 4905^{22} **>37a 55f<**

Boojum 3 b f Mujtahid (USA)-Haboobti (Habitat) 959^{7} 1209^{3} 3913^{13} 4306^{6} 4978^{20} **>79f<**

Book At Bedtime (IRE) 3 b f Mtoto-Akila (FR) (Top Ville) 833^{4} 1102^{2} 1738^{8} 2027^{3} (2486) 2596^{3} 3179a^{2} 3727^{3} 3763^{3} (4099) 4149^{4} **>119f<**

Bookcase 10 b g Siberian Express (USA)-Colourful (FR) (Gay Mecene (USA)) 657^{5} **>71?f<**

Borani 2 b c Shirley Heights-Ower (IRE) (Lomond (USA)) 3576^{6} 4157^{3} **>75f<**

Border Arrow 2 ch c Selkirk (USA)-Nibbs Point (IRE) (Sure Blade (USA)) (4758) **>95++f<**

Border Falcon 3 ch c Polar Falcon (USA)-Tender Loving Care (Final Straw) 742^{8} **>61f<**

Boreas Hill (IRE) 2 b c Petardia-Salonniere (FR) (Bikala) 4515^{18} 4857^{6} **>36f<**

Borgia (GER) 3 b f Acatenango (GER)-Britannia (GER) (Tarim) 1918a^{2} (2642a) 3555a^{2} (4127a) 4665a^{3} 5065a^{2} **>128f<**

Born A Lady 4 ch f Komaite (USA)-Lucky Candy (Lucky Wednesday) 415^{9} 470^{13} 896^{7} 1127^{4} 1289^{4} 1395^{11} 1818^{5} 2463^{12} 2913^{9} 3456^{12} **>42a 31f<**

Born On The Wild 4 b f Golden Lahab (USA)-First Born (Be My Native (USA)) 463^{7} 2152^{9} **>46f<**

Borrador 3 b g Full Extent (USA)-Wild Jewel (Great Heron (USA)) 2183^{11} 2591^{9} 3202^{9} 4516^{18} **>49f<**

Bosra Sham (USA) 4 ch f Woodman (USA)-Korveya (USA) (Riverman (USA)) (1476) (2010) 2527^{3} 3646^{4} **>131f<**

Boss Lady (IRE) 3 b f Last Tycoon-Queen Helen (Troy) 989^{6} 1297^{2} (1567) 2832^{2} 3453^{3} 4731^{5} 4996^{9} **>83f<**

Boston Tea Party 4 b f Rambo Dancer (CAN)-Tea-Pot (Ragstone) **1996:** 5242^{10} **>50a 27f<**

Boulevard Rouge (USA) 2 b f Red Ransom (USA)-Beetwentysix (USA) (Buckaroo (USA)) 2127^{3} 2713^{3} 3331^{5} 3869^{2} 4362^{13} 5050^{18} **>78f<**

Bound To Please 2 b c Warrshan (USA)-Hong Kong Girl (Petong) 1959^{5} 2181^{14} 2917^{2} 3546^{U} 3892^{4} 4569^{4} 4898^{7} **>78a 78f<**

Bout 3 br f Batshoof-Reyah (Young Generation) 387^{8} 425^{10} 524^{10} 608^{12} 1469^{14} 2145^{9} 2502^{13} 3919^{17} **>27f<**

Bow Bells 2 b f Absalom-Dancing Chimes (London Bells (CAN)) 5042^{10} **>59f<**

Bowcliffe 6 b g Petoski-Gwiffina (Welsh Saint) 951^{12} 1389^{3} 1560^{3} (1800) 2205^{5} (2502) 2828^{6} 3153^{2} 3605^{3} 4147^{6} 4210^{6} 4596^{4} 4781^{3} 4924^{5} **>69f<**

Bowcliffe Court (IRE) 5 b g Slip Anchor-Res Nova (USA) (Blushing Groom (FR)) (655) 1027^{12} 2530^{3} 2767^{9} **>84f<**

Bowcliffe Grange (IRE) 5 b g Dominion Royale-Cala-Vadella (Mummy's Pet) 304^{4} 348^{4} 391^{7} 406^{7} 1627^{7} 1865^{5} 2754^{6} 3287^{10} 3756^{3} 3871^{16} 4329^{14} **>52a 54f<**

Bowden Rose 5 ch m Dashing Blade-Elegant Rose (Noalto) 726^{10} 1034^{3} 1317^{11} 1608^{9} 1975^{9} (2590) 2872^{10} (3130) (3436) 3604^{4} 3765^{12} 4100^{16}

4444[4] (4553) 4756[15] 4881[6] 4954[9] **>101f<**

Bowled Over 4 b g Batshoof-Swift Linnet (Wolver Hollow) 521[12] 680[4] 888[17] *1156[10]* 1371[8] 1481[7] **>49a 75df<**

Bowlers Boy 4 ch g Risk Me (FR)-Snow Wonder (Music Boy) 744[20] 863[4] 1269[7] 1446[5] 1799[13] 2001[2] (2497) 2567[2] 2844[12] 3066[3] 3208[9] 3481[6] 3761[5] (3910) 3922[2] 4048[2] 4456[8] 4805[2] 4842[12] 5047[7] **>43a 82f<**

Bow Peep (IRE) 2 b br f Shalford (IRE)-Gale Force Seven (Strong Gale) 1569[5] 1829[4] *2066[4]* 3209[4] **>46a 65f<**

Bradbury Falls (IRE) 2 ch f River Falls-Asturiana (Julio Mariner) 2003[10] 2396[3] *2606[8]* 3097[7] **>56f<**

Braes'O'Shieldhill 4 ch f Music Maestro-Dalchroy (Hotfoot) **1996:** *5267[11]* **>13a 18f<**

Braganza (USA) 2 ch c Rahy (USA)-Blue Daisy (USA) (Shahrastani (USA)) 4542[4] **>74f<**

Bramble Bear 3 b f Beveled (USA)-Supreme Rose (Frimley Park) 652[7] (1294) (1571) 2134[15] 2655[4] 2964[5] 3121[2] 3460[4] 3984[14] 4321[7] 4527[11] **>69f<**

Brambles Way 8 ch g Clantime-Streets Ahead (Ovid) **1996:** *5181[11]* **1997:** (574) 898[7] 1040[6] 3779[5] 4235[19] 4335[6] (4847) **>59f<**

Brand New Dance 3 b g Gildoran-Starawak (Star Appeal) *(658)* 1491[4] 2423[6] 3218[8] 3549[2] **>71a 83f<**

Brandon Frank 2 ch g Beveled (USA)-Island Desert (IRE) (Green Desert (USA)) 880[8] 1593[3] 1812[2] (2306) 2862[14] 3131[9] **>79f<**

Brandon Jack 3 ch c Cadeaux Genereux-Waitingformargaret (Kris) 654[10] 990[9] 1175[13] 1595[7] 1973[5] (2285) 2686[5] 2961[6] (3551) 3891[3] 4141[12] **>85f<**

Brandon Magic 4 ch c Primo Dominie-Silk Stocking (Pardao) 1016[6] 1176[7] 1947[2] 2284[3] 2676[12] 3333[4] 3796[2] **>90f<**

Brandonville 4 b c Never so Bold-Enduring (Sadler's Wells (USA)) *860[11]* (1315) 1560[6] 2019[9] (2418) **>32a 66f<**

Branston Abby (IRE) 8 ch m Risk Me (FR)-Tuxford Hideaway (Cawston's Clown) **1996:** 5155a[7] **>113f< (DEAD)**

Branston Berry (IRE) 2 ch f Mukaddamah (USA)-Food of Love (Music Boy) *872[2]* (1120) 1328[3] 1729[3] 2466[2] 3823[11] (4097) 4411[2] 4634[8] 5050[8] **>55a 79f<**

Brave Edge 6 b g Beveled (USA)-Daring Ditty (Daring March) 573[3] 941[11] 1455[2] 1590[6] 2106[16] 2526[10] 3001a[4] 3023[3] 3372a[4] 4001a[5] 4062[6] 4098[6] 4239[11] (4467) 4881[2] 4954[4] 5054[12] **>107f<**

Brave Envoy 3 b g High Estate-Restless Anna (Thatching) (556) 785[2] 1164[11] 1568[5] 2004[5] 4601[5] 4696[5] (4958) **>71f<**

Braveheart (IRE) 3 br g Mujadil (USA)-Salonniere (FR) (Bikala) 502[7] 723[13] 1243[8] 3900[10] 4375[5] 4820[4] 4979[2] 5049[18] **>77f<**

Brave Indigo 4 b c Rainbow Quest (USA)-Nyoka (USA) (Raja Baba (USA)) 4541a[2] 4760a[3] **>99f<**

Brave Kris (IRE) 3 b f Kris-Famosa (Dancing Brave (USA)) 688[8] (958) (2133) 2690[6] **>102f<**

Brave Maple 2 b c Petong-Hazy Kay (IRE) (Treasure Kay) 4381[10] 4706[8] **>53f<**

Brave Montgomerie 3 ch c Most Welcome-Just Precious (Ela-Mana-Mou) 1314[2] 1670[4] 2113[4] 2855[6] **>77f<**

Brave Noble (USA) 2 ch c Woodman (USA)-Badge of Courage (USA) (Well Decorated (USA)) 4708[10] 4915[3] **>84f<**

Brave Reward (USA) 2 b c Lear Fan (USA)-A Tad Better (USA) (Northern Prospect (USA)) (4708) 4967[3] **>87+f<**

Brave Spy 6 b g Law Society (USA)-Contralto (Busted) **1996:** *5222[14]* **1997:** *43[11]* **>37a 65f<**

Brawling Springs 3 b g Belfort (FR)-Oyster Gray (Tanfirion) 3287[19] **>37f<**

Break For Peace (IRE) 2 b f Brief Truce (USA)-Run Bonnie (Runnett) 4103[20] **>37f<**

Breakin Even 2 ch g Chilibang-Bee Dee Dancer (Ballacashtal (CAN)) 4735[12] 4993[10] **>52f<**

Break the Rules 5 b g Dominion-Surf Bird (Shareef Dancer (USA)) (435) (1016) 1981[4] (2209) 2528[6] 2729[7] 2889[7] 4151[14] 4264[2] 4521[10] 4751[6] 4788[7] 4886[4] **>73f<**

Brecon 4 b br c High Estate-No Can Tell (USA) (Clev Er Tell (USA)) **1996:** *5227[9]* *5267[4]* **1997:** 4046[4] *4304[6]* 4771[4] **>64a 66f<**

Brecongill Lad 5 b g Clantime-Chikala (Pitskelly) 1468[7] 1734[3] 1977[6] 2339[10] 3130[2] 3334[2] 3481[3] 3761[3] 4233[14] 4385[3] 4636[20] **>72f<**

Breezed Well 11 b g Wolverlife-Precious Baby (African Sky) 763[7] *1575[8]* *2302[12]* (2494) 3104[9] 3248[3] 3432[4] 3476[D] 4275[9] **>15a 51f<**

Breffni (IRE) 3 b f Mac's Imp (USA)-Bon Retour (Sallust) 1681[6] 1810[13] 2197[13] *3399[6]* **>43a 28f<**

Bresil (USA) 8 ch g Bering-Clever Bidder (USA) (Bold Bidder) 769[6] 1507[10] 2531[8] 2896[9] **>29a 32f<**

Breydon 4 ch g Be My Guest (USA)-Palmella (USA) (Grundy) 552[12] 669[3] 955[13] 2170[7] 2352[6] 2825[10] 3223[4] **>46a 39f<**

Bricviste (FR) 5 b h Bricassar (USA)-Recidiviste (FR) (Native Guile (USA)) 149a[3]

Bride's Reprisal 3 b f Dunbeath (USA)-Matching Lines (Thatching) 853[10] 1112[7] **>80df<**

Bridge 2 b f Batshoof-The Strid (IRE) (Persian Bold) 4740[7] 4974[15] **>61f<**

Bridie's Pride 6 b g Alleging (USA)-Miss Monte Carlo (Reform) *660[9]* 1114[3] 1413[5] 2139[6] 2381[2] (2511) 4609[8] **>41a 58f<**

Bridlington Bay 4 b g Roscoe Blake-City Sound (On Your Mark) 526[20] **>33a 19f<**

Briery Mec 2 b c Ron's Victory (USA)-Briery Fille (Sayyaf) 5042[12] **>53f<**

Brigand (IRE) 3 b g Common Grounds-Strike It Rich (FR) (Rheingold) 3991[2] 4277[2] (4464) **>87f<**

Briggs Turn 3 b g Rudimentary (USA)-Turnabout (Tyrnavos) 1130[8] 2924[8] **>55f<**

Brighstone 4 ch c Cadeaux Genereux-High Fountain (High Line) 1323[10] (1951) 2574[5] (3462) (3972) 4264[8] (4742) 4886[7] 4987[2] **>68f<**

Bright Desert 4 b g Green Desert (USA)-Smarten Up (Sharpen Up) 528[P] 4224[13] 4872[17] **>18f<**

Brighter Byfaah (IRE) 4 ch g Kefaah (USA)-Bright Landing (Sun Prince) **1996:** *5084[7]* **1997:** 650[11] 1795[7] (2932) **>53a 56f<**

Bright Fountain (IRE) 3 ch f Cadeaux Genereux-High Fountain (High Line) 1276[6] 3897[6] 4114[4] 4326[3] **>57f<**

Bright Gold 3 ch g Clantime-Miss Brightside (Crofthall) 2738[19] 2941[10] 3241[14] 3606[11] **>21f<**

Bright Heritage (IRE) 4 b g Ela-Mana-Mou-Mother of The Wind (Tumble Wind (USA)) 2008[4] 2566[5] 2960[2] (3335) 3786[5] **>82f<**

Bright Paragon (IRE) 8 b or br g Treasure Kay-Shining Bright (USA) (Bold Bidder) **1996:** *5280[6]* **1997:** *107[8]* *159[7]* *199[5]* *319[9]* 756[4] 879[6] (1236) 1419[5] 1857[4] 2148[7] 2536[2] 2732[12] 3083[2] 3500[3] 3852[5] 4248[5] 4370[13] **>29a 46f<**

Bright Sapphire 11 b g Mummy's Pet-Bright Era (Artaius (USA)) *1964[8]* **>21a f<**

Bright Water 4 b c Caerleon (USA)-Shining Water (Kalaglow) (2656) 3191[2] 3578[3] **>115f<**

Brilliance (FR) 3 b f Priolo (USA)-Briesta (FR) (Cresta Rider (USA)) (813a) (1366a) 1916a[3] 2814a[3] 4256a[3] **>116f<**

Brilliant Red 4 b g Royal Academy (USA)-Red Comes Up (USA) (Blushing Groom (FR)) *250[2]* 2346[3] (2666) 3150[6] 3391[4] 3764[7] 4441[6] 4978[3] **>87a 99f<**

Brimming 2 ch c Generous (IRE)-Rainbow Lake (Rainbow Quest (USA)) 4229[2] 4715[3] **>76f<**

Brimstone (IRE) 2 ch c Ballad Rock-Blazing Glory (IRE) (Glow (USA)) 1842[9] 2370[6] (3136) 3474[2] **>81f<**

Brin-Lodge (IRE) 4 b f Doubletour (USA)-Nordico's Dream (Nordico (USA)) 1681[3] 1963[11] 2197[10] *2300[6]* 2895[9] **>34a 38f<**

Briska (IRE) 3 b f River Falls-Calash (Indian King (USA)) 2705[10] 3930[12] 4319[11] 4916[4] **>60f<**

Bristol Channel 2 b f Generous (IRE)-Shining Water (Kalaglow) (4057) 4892[4] **>84+f<**

Bristol Gold 4 b g Golden Heights-The Bristol Flyer (True Song) 1570[10]

Britannia Mills 6 gr m Nordico (USA)-May Fox (Healaugh Fox) *18[13]* *111[12]* **>13?a 17f<**

Broadgate Flyer (IRE) 3 b g Silver Kite (USA)-Fabulous Pet (Somethingfabulous (USA)) **1996:** *5239[4]* **1997:** *44[2]* *94[2]* *181[8]* *279[4]* 556[6] 952[4] 1115[5] 2132[6] **>63a 52f<**

Broad River (USA) 3 b c Broad Brush (USA)-Monture Creek (USA) (Stop The Music (USA)) 674[5] (899) 1305[6] 2044[8] 2557[15] **>79f<**

Broadstairs Beauty (IRE) 7 ch g Dominion Royale-Holy Water (Monseigneur (USA)) *89[11]* *166[2]* *301[4]* *357[3]* *397[6]* 527[2] 834[3] 1223[2] 1402[5] *2162[8]* 2339[6] *3077[2]* 3107[3] 4820[6] 4905[2] 5047[12] **>80a 73f<**

Broadway Melody 3 b f Beveled (USA)-Broadway Stomp (USA) (Broadway Forli (USA)) 1302[5] *(2669)* 2921[4] 3121[11] 3206[11] *3398[5]* **>61a 63f<**

Broctune Gold 6 b g Superpower-Golden Sunlight (Ile de Bourbon (USA)) 823[2] 1077[5] 1285[2] 1631[9] (1993) 2355[3] (2542) *2912[5]* 3477[2] 3718[9] **>51a 74f<**

Broctune Line 3 ch g Safawan-Ra Ra (Lord Gayle (USA)) **1996:** *5164[4]* **1997:** *(124)* *298[5]* 471[4] *(581)* *1043[13]* 4472[16] 4845[3] **>64a 49f<**

Brodessa 11 gr g Scallywag-Jeanne du Barry (Dubassoff (USA)) 570[8] 777[7] 950[2] 1452[6] (2175) 2350[3] 2874[2] 3540[2] **>66da 67f<**

Broken Detraeh (IRE) 6 1200a[7] **>103f<**

Broken Rites (IRE) 4 b g Broken Hearted-Lady Wise (Lord Gayle (USA)) 4620a[5] **>93f<**

Bronhallow 4 b g Belmez (USA)-Grey Twig (Godswalk (USA)) *908[11]* *2071[9]* 2174[4] 2398[2] 2650[8] 3491[11] 4222[13] 4438[11] **>5a 35f<**

Bronze Maquette (IRE) 7 b m Ahonoora-Working Model (Ile de Bourbon (USA)) 881[5] 1042[4] 1371[7] **>37a 43f<**

Bronzino 2 ch c Midyan (USA)-Indubitable (Sharpo) 3489[8] 3861[6] 4105[7] 4380[7] 4994[5] **>68f<**

Brookhouse Lady (IRE) 2 b f Polish Patriot (USA)-Honagh Lee (Main Reef) 861[4] 1645[10] 2736[8] 3823[8] 4152[7] 4382[4] 4588[9] 5050[6] **>60?f<**

Brooksie 2 b c Efisio-Elkie Brooks (Relkino) 4710[12] 4871[10] 5042[14] **>55f<**

Brother Roy 4 b c Prince Sabo-Classic Heights (Shirley Heights) *13[10]* *108[8]* **>26a 70f<**

Broughtons Champ 5 b g Dowsing (USA)-Knees Up (USA) (Dancing Champ (USA)) **1996:** *5145[10]* **>13a 42f<**

Broughtons Error 3 ch c Most Welcome-Eloquent Charm (USA) (Private Account (USA)) **1996:** *5100[4]* **1997:** 1219[6] 1633[13] 1972[13] **>60a 68+f<**

Broughtons Formula 7 b g Night Shift (USA)-Forward Rally (Formidable (USA)) **1996:** *5084[6]* *5148[4]* *5213[2]* *5277[2]* **1997:** *63[6]* *(133)* *(252)* *351[6]* *4302[10]* *4481[11]* 4794[15] **>46a 43f<**

Broughtons Lure (IRE) 3 ch f Archway (IRE)-Vaal

Salmon (IRE) (Salmon Leap (USA)) 2555[10] 2873[10] 3095[10] **>42f<**

Broughtons Mill 2 ch c Ron's Victory (USA)-Sandra's Desire (Grey Desire) 2870[6] **>58f<**

Broughton's Pride (IRE) 6 b m Superpower-French Quarter (Ile de Bourbon (USA)) *(36) 91[2] 125[10] 245[2] (333) 428[4] 578[7]* 951[2] 1442[4] 1994[6] 2569[3] *3041[4]* **>59a 60f<**

Broughtons Relish 4 b f Nomination-Mosso (Ercolano (USA)) **1996:** *5211[12] 5253[8]* **1997:** *14[12] 104[7] 183[9] 262[6]* **>25a f<**

Broughtons Turmoil 8 b g Petorius-Rustic Stile (Rusticaro (FR)) 484[2] 653[11] (895) 1111[3] *2161[3]* 2557[20] 3392[10] 3712[10] 4297[5] 4441[7] 4561[2] **>73a 78f<**

Brown Fairy (USA) 9 b m Northern Baby (CAN)-Chepstow Vale (USA) (Key To The Mint (USA)) (2999a) **>64f<**

Browning 2 b g Warrshan (USA)-Mossy Rose (King of Spain) 4298[9] 4603[16] 4855[4] **>58f<**

Brume La Voile 4 b g Puissance-Bali Lady (Balidar) 1809[14] *2301[8]* 2511[10] **>33a f<**

Brumon (IRE) 6 b g Sadler's Wells (USA)-Loveliest (USA) (Tibaldo) 442[7] 613[12] **>52f<**

Brutal Fantasy (IRE) 3 b g Distinctly North (USA)-Flash Donna (USA) (Well Decorated (USA)) *(17) 89[5] (258)* (434) (783) 1254[8] 1980[12] 2044[3] 2655[6] 3194[2] 3604[11] **>80a 90f<**

Bruz 6 b g Risk Me (FR)-My Croft (Crofter (USA)) 493[5] 1229[6] 1601[8] 2145[2] 2207[12] 3486[8] 4287[9] **>43a 37f<**

Brynkir 3 b g Batshoof-Felinwen (White Mill) 886[9] 1164[15] *3612[4]* 4584[14] **>47a 66f<**

Bryony Brind (IRE) 2 ch f Kris-Bayadere (USA) (Green Dancer (USA)) 4853[6] **>48f<**

Bubble Wings (FR) 5 b m In The Wings-Bubble Prospector (USA) (Miswaki (USA)) *1086[6]* 1802[5] 2593[4] 3026[9] 4109[2] (4386) 4558[10] 4882[4] 5051[6] **>52a 77f<**

Bubbly 3 b c Rudimentary (USA)-Champagne Season (USA) (Vaguely Noble) 479[4] (606) 990[11] 1958[12] 3200[4] 4176[8] 4451[2] 4820[16] **>74f<**

Buck's Boy (USA) 4 5065a[4] **>122f<**

Buddy Marvel (IRE) 3 b c Law Society (USA)-Rosa Van Fleet (Sallust) 1195a[5] 1698a[6] 3842a[3] 4191a[5] 4894[7] **>108f<**

Buddy's Friend (IRE) 9 ch h Jester-Hasta (Skymaster) *111[8] 150[9] 213[7]* **>35a 42f<**

Buena Vista 3 b f Be My Chief (USA)-Florentynna Bay (Aragon) *287[7]* **>8a f< (DEAD)**

Buffalo River 7 b g Robellino (USA)-Strapless (Bustino) 647[17]

Bukett (GER) 4 ch f Turfkonig (GER)-Bella Figura (GER) (Surumu (GER)) 3736a[2] **>97f<**

Bulington (FR) 5 br h Sicyos (USA)-Barbra (FR) (Le Fabuleux) 922a[6] 2270a[3] 3364a[2] **>122f<**

Bullfinch 4 b g Anshan-Lambay (Lorenzaccio) 1852[6] **>84f<**

Bullion 2 b f Sabrehill (USA)-High and Bright (Shirley Heights) 3450[5] (4017) 4271[3] **>82f<**

Bulsara 5 b g Dowsing (USA)-Taiga (Northfields (USA)) 824[5] 1472[12] 1683[10] 1862[4] 2205[10] 2828[8] 3061[6] **>1a 61f<**

Burberry (GER) 3 b c Fairy King (USA)-Bourrette (GER) (Experte (GER)) 1072a[3] **>103f<**

Burden Of Proof (IRE) 5 b h Fairy King (USA)-Belle Passe (Be My Guest (USA)) (1198a) (1532a) 2056[17] 2816a[2] 4625a[5] (4834a) **>119+f<**

Burlesque 3 b g Old Vic-Late Matinee (Red Sunset) 599[14] 1024[16] 1284[9] 3486[12] **>47df<**

Burnden Days (IRE) 2 ch g Fayruz-Monaco Lady (Manado) 594[14] 4917[14] **>20f<**

Burning (USA) 5 b g Bering-Larnica (USA) (Alydar (USA)) 2776[2] 3110[11] 3559[5] 3864[14] **>84f<**

Burning Cost 7 br m Lochnager-Sophie Avenue (Guillaume Tell (USA)) **1996:** *5167[10] 5177[13] 5232[8]* **1997:** *1138[5]* 2146[12] 2696[14] 3240[11] *3581[5]* 3971[10] **>23a 32f<**

Burning Flame 4 b f Robellino (USA)-No Islands (Lomond (USA)) **1996:** *5118[7]* **1997:** *16[6] 88[10]* 1011[6] 1441[9] 1689[20] **>26a 45f<**

Burning Love 2 b f Forzando-Latest Flame (IRE) (Last Tycoon) 739[9] 1240[13] 1821[10] **>45f<**

Burning Truth (USA) 3 ch c Known Fact (USA)-Galega (Sure Blade (USA)) 436[3] 599[3] 853[2] 1234[2] 2877[3] 4331[2] **>84f<**

Burnley Belle 5 b m Dominion-Ulla Laing (Mummy's Pet) 3820[7] 4331[8] **>27f<**

Burn Out 5 b g Last Tycoon-Obertura (USA) (Roberto (USA)) 944[6] 1372[5] 1477[16] 2014[7] 2589[13] **>73f<**

Burnt Offering 4 b c Old Vic-Burnt Amber (Balidar) 787[8] 974[6] 1478[2] 2014[18] 2327[7] 3010[9] 3734a[7] **>59a 73f<**

Burnt Yates (IRE) 2 b g Distinctly North (USA)-Ibda (Mtoto) 594[9] 684[5] 1839[3] 2202[5] 2473[5] 3438[4] 3707[8] 3932[10] 4230[4] (4362) 4690[10] 4885[6] 4994[19] **>72f<**

Bursul Lady 4 b f Be My Chief (USA)-Neverdown (Never so Bold) **1996:** *5084[8]* **1997:** 4072[8] **>34a 8f<**

Burundi (IRE) 3 b g Danehill (USA)-Sofala (Home Guard (USA)) 517[8] 1025[6] 2058[17] 2512[7] 4987[11] **>69f<**

Bushwhacker 3 b g Green Desert (USA)-Missed Again (High Top) 2420[4] **>67f<**

Bustingoutallover (USA) 3 ch f Trempolino (USA)-June Bride (USA) (Riverman (USA)) *287[8] 1787[12]* 2156[11]

Bustopher Jones 3 b g Robellino (USA)-Catkin (USA) (Sir Ivor) 2420[7] *3396[5]* 4700[7] **>33a 47f<**

Busy Flight 4 br c Pharly (FR)-Bustling Nelly (Bustino) 932[2] 1363a[3] 2104[10] (3578) (4134) 4665a[10] 4894[3] **>121f<**

Butrinto 3 ch g Anshan-Bay Bay (Bay Express) 683[14] 970[3] 1237[6] 2838[6] (3202) 3709[4] 4048[16] **>77f<**

Buzz 2 b c Anshan-Ryewater Dream (Touching Wood (USA)) 1839[4] (2168) 3908[5] 4116[18] 4266[4] 4778[19] **>88f<**

Buzzby Babe 3 b f Presidium-Aposse Ad Esse (Record Run) **1996:** *5214[7]* **1997:** *26[9] 124[9] 168[6] 277[4]* 1809[10] 2307[9] **>39a 21f<**

Buzzing (IRE) 2 ch c Ballad Rock-Buzzing Around (Prince Bee) 4884[21] **>43f<**

Buzz The Agent 2 b c Prince Sabo-Chess Mistress (USA) (Run The Gantlet (USA)) 2842[15] 3282[6] 3821[11] 4285[14] **>50f<**

Bybus (FR) 6 gr h Courtroom (FR)-Belle Caro (FR) (Caro) 148a[3] **>89f<**

Byhookorbycrook (IRE) 5 b m Cardinal Flower-Frisky Matron (On Your Mark) 2692[8]

By Jay (IRE) 3 b f Last Tycoon-Tomona (Linacre) 4546[12] 4711[19] 4918[16] **>49f<**

By The Bay 5 b m Shareef Dancer (USA)-Beryl's Jewel (Siliconn) **1996:** *5123[5]* **>39a 56f<**

Byzantium 3 b c Shirley Heights-Dulceata (IRE) (Rousillon (USA)) (1415) 2229[6] 3012[11] 3575[12] **>77f<**

C

Cabaret (IRE) 4 b f Sadler's Wells (USA)-Chamonis (USA) (Affirmed (USA)) **1996:** 5157a[2] 5198a[4] **1997:** 2869[10] 3878a[9] **>104f<**

Cabcharge Blue 5 b m Midyan (USA)-Mashobra (Vision (USA)) 2369[16] 2947[12] 3316[7] *4069[9]* 4371[3] (4858) 4992[6] **>33a 54f<**

Cabcharge Glory 3 ch f Executive Man-Clipsall (Petitioner) 1643[4] 1858[6] 2183[13] 2750[11] 3129[7] **>34f<**

Cadbury Castle 3 b f Midyan (USA)-Orange Hill (High Top) 889[9] 1140[15] 1387[5] 1623[7] 2397[3] 3028[7] *3587[8]* **>4a 48f<**

Caddy's First 5 b g Petong-Love Scene (Carwhite) **1996:** *5151[10]* **1997:** *42[4]* **>44a 47f<**

Cadeaux Cher 3 ch g Cadeaux Genereux-Home Truth (Known Fact (USA)) (453) 854[4] 1609[6] 1980[16] 4887[18] 4995[4] **>85f<**

Cadeaux Tryst 5 b h Cadeaux Genereux-Trystero (Shareef Dancer (USA)) 738[10] 892[9] 1214[3] 2026[3] (2690) 3577[7] **>112f<**

Cadford Jewel 4 gr g Distant Relative-Fast Car (FR) (Carwhite) 638[11] *1047[14]*

Cadillac Jukebox (USA) 2 b br c Alleged (USA)-Symphonic Music (USA) (Al Nasr (FR)) 4952[11] **>54f<**

Cadmax (IRE) 2 b g Second Set (IRE)-Stella Ann (Ahonoora) 4740[10] **>48f<**

Ca'd'oro 4 ch g Cadeaux Genereux-Palace Street (USA) (Secreto (USA)) 608[10] 1273[9] (1878) (2117) 2346[7] 2868[5] 3248[4] 3496[5] 3980[7] 4139[3] (4629) 5049[2] **>75f<**

Caerfilly Dancer 3 ch f Caerleon (USA)-Darnelle (Shirley Heights) 672[10] 988[5] 2134[7] **>90f<**

Caernarfon Bay (IRE) 2 ch c Royal Academy (USA)-Bay Shade (USA) (Sharpen Up) 4884[4] **>69f<**

Cage Aux Folles (IRE) 2 b c Kenmare (FR)-Ivory Thread (USA) (Sir Ivor) 2693[12] 2948[3] 3253[6] 3802[14] **>73f<**

Cairn Dhu 3 ch g Presidium-My Precious Daisy (Sharpo) 649[8] (757) 995[12] 1573[4] 2505[4] 2546[15] 4958[17] **>58f<**

Caiseal Ros (IRE) 3 b f Roi Danzig (USA)-Scapa (USA) 809a[3] 1533a[3] 2267a[4] 2446a[3] 2814a[8] (3172a) **>107f<**

Caitano 3 b c Niniski (USA)-Eversince (USA) (Foolish Pleasure (USA)) 1545a[2] (2097a) 2642a[4] (3737a) 4127a[5] (4866a) **>128f<**

Calamander (IRE) 3 b f Alzao (USA)-Local Custom (IRE) (Be My Native (USA)) 886[7] 1245[3] 1500[2] 2040[2] 2730[3] 3207[7] 3849[13] 4324[10] **>44f<**

Calandrella 4 b f Sizzling Melody-Maravilla (Mandrake Major) 1439[10] 1849[10] 2244[7] 2491[7] 2730[14] **>37f<**

Calchas (IRE) 2 b c Warning-Nassma (IRE) (Sadler's Wells (USA)) *(2047)* (2215) 2584[8] 2905[2] 3142[3] **>88+a 93f<**

Calchou 3 bl f Barrys Gamble-Ping Pong (Petong) **1996:** *5176[15]* **1997:** *25[8] 75[4] 222[10]* **>55da 55f<**

Calder King 6 ch g Rakaposhi King-Name the Game (Fair Season) *18[5] (114) (195) 426[2]* 550[3] **>71a 71f<**

Caledonian Express 2 b f Northern Park (USA)-New Edition (Great Nephew) 4317[8] 4694[6] 4909[7] **>68f<**

Calendula 4 b f Be My Guest (USA)-Sesame (Derrylin) *16[7] 115[5] (196) 261[2] (346) 400[3] 566[7] 1086[2] 1156[6]* 1463[3] 1623[4] (2430) 2876[2] 4714[4] (4918) **>63a 74f<**

Callaloo 4 b g Mtoto-Catawba (Mill Reef (USA)) **1996:** *5206[12]* **1997:** *280[6]* 4453[W] **>27?a 59f<**

Calliram 2 b f Petardia-Sheesha (USA) (Shadeed (USA)) 767[4] 1019[10] 1370[3] 1856[3] 2191[4] 2664[5] 3055[3] 3692[8] 3782[5] 3967[16] **>62f<**

Callisthene (FR) 5 dk h Garde Royale-Canne Ma Mie (FR) (Emerson) **1996:** 5216a[3] **>101f<**

Call Me Vera 2 ch f Beveled (USA)-Cee Beat (Bairn (USA)) 2917[9] 3247[7] 3636[9] 4402[9] **>54f<**

Callonescy (IRE) 5 b g Royal Academy (USA)-Take Your Mark (USA) (Round Table) **1996:** *5118[13]*

1997: *9^{10} 104^{10} 143^{8}* **>14a 4f<**

Call To Order 2 b c Reprimand-Gena Ivor (USA) (Sir Ivor) 2917^{4} 3926^{2} 4216^{3} (4402) 4790^{4} **>91f<**

Calypso Grant (IRE) 3 b f Danehill (USA)-Why so Silent (Mill Reef (USA)) (507) 724^{7} 1147^{9} 1875^{10} 3190^{4} 3725^{6} 4141^{9} 4754^{10} **>97f<**

Calypso Lady (IRE) 3 ch f Priolo (USA)-Taking Steps (Gay Fandango (USA)) 966^{5} 1175^{11} 1813^{7} 2380^{8} 4220^{4} 4606^{8} 4882^{14} **>74f<**

Cambridge Ball (IRE) 3 b f Royal Academy (USA)-Boat Race (USA) (Seattle Slew (USA)) 1859^{8} 3721^{6} *4053^{10}* **>60f<**

Cambridge Blue (USA) 3 gr g Sheikh Albadou-Fit And Ready (USA) (Fit To Fight (USA)) 565^{4} 792^{7} 964^{8} 1566^{8} 2552^{11} **>70f<**

Camille (FR) 4 b f Bikala-Jemifa (FR) (Fabulous Dancer (USA)) $3878a^{3}$ $4666a^{17}$ **>105f<**

Camionneur (IRE) 4 b g Cyrano de Bergerac-Fact of Time (Known Fact (USA)) 527^{4} 827^{9} 949^{6} 1098^{6} 1627^{2} 1734^{10} 2497^{3} 2738^{6} 2844^{2} 3034^{3} 3208^{2} 3334^{5} (3431) 3625^{2} 3756^{2} 3910^{5} 4233^{2} 4385^{16} 4512^{4} 4636^{13} **>60f<**

Campaign 6 b g Sure Blade (USA)-Just Cause (Law Society (USA)) 1162^{12} 4986^{6} **>64f<**

Campari (IRE) 2 b f Distinctly North (USA)-Foolish Flight (IRE) (Fools Holme (USA)) 2394^{4} 3322^{3} 4017^{4} 4382^{3} 4793^{5} **>67f<**

Campaspe 5 b m Dominion-Lady River (FR) (Sir Gaylord) 1118^{2} (1452) 1617^{3} 2236^{2} (3272) 3482^{3} (3867) (4213) 4363^{8} 4874^{4} **>22a 80f<**

Camp David (GER) 7 b h Surumu (GER)-Capitolina (FR) (Empery (USA)) (1548a) 2055^{10} $4123a^{2}$ **>123f<**

Camp Follower 4 b g Warrshan (USA)-House Maid (Habitat) 1292^{15} 1592^{12} **>76df<**

Camphar 4 ch f Pharly (FR)-Camomilla (Targowice (USA)) *322^{7} 403^{9}* 2550^{12} **>20f<**

Campione (IRE) 2 b c Common Grounds-Kyrenia (Zino) 1418^{7} 3613^{5} 4581^{10} **>50f<**

Camporese (IRE) 4 b f Sadler's Wells (USA)-Campestral (USA) (Alleged (USA)) (1199a) 2513^{5} $4000a^{2}$ $4965a^{6}$ **>116f<**

Canadian Fantasy 3 b g Lear Fan (USA)-Florinda (CAN) (Vice Regent (CAN)) *511^{2}* 944^{8} 1230^{11} *(1939) 2052^{2}* (2385) 2660^{13} 3115^{18} *3397^{8}* **>80a 82f<**

Canadian Jive 4 b f Dominion-Ural Dancer (Corvaro (USA)) 1105^{12} 1276^{11} 2246^{14} **>31f<**

Canadian Puzzler (USA) 2 gr c With Approval (CAN)-Puzzle Book (USA) (Text (USA)) 3687^{4} 4064^{4} 4454^{3} 4778^{4} **>78f<**

Canary Falcon 6 ch g Polish Precedent (USA)-Pumpona (USA) (Sharpen Up) **1996:** *(5270)* **1997:** *30^{3} 182^{12}* **>69a 56f<**

Can Can Charlie 7 gr g Vaigly Great-Norton Princess (Wolver Hollow) **1996:** *5223^{5} 5244^{7}* **1997:** *61^{2} 188^{8}* **>63a 53f<**

Can Can Lady 3 ch f Anshan-Agama (USA) (Nureyev (USA)) 794^{3} (998) 1301^{2} (2113) 2285^{7} 2760^{11} 3061^{5} 4223^{6} 4578^{5} **>87f<**

Candereli (IRE) 3 b c Darshaan-Calounia $1195a^{6}$ **>86f<**

Candy Twist 2 b f Deploy-Simply Candy (IRE) (Simply Great (FR)) 684^{9} 1860^{6} 2412^{5} 3106^{14} 3312^{3} 3628^{4} 4208^{7} *4799^{11}* **>49f<**

Canny Chronicle 9 b or br g Daring March-Laisser Aller (Sagaro) 4466^{15} **>57f<**

Canon Can (USA) 4 ch g Green Dancer (USA)-Lady Argyle (USA) (Don B (USA)) (728) 1027^{4} (2108) 3149^{7} (4118) 4783^{4} **>120f<**

Canonize (IRE) 2 b f Alzao (USA)-Cecina (Welsh Saint) 3278^{3} 3711^{17} 4381^{6} **>80f<**

Canovas Heart 8 b g Balidar-Worthy Venture (Northfields (USA)) (1269) 2289^{8} 3011^{9} 3604^{6} 4280^{17} (4636) 4887^{6} **>59a 92f<**

Can She Can Can 5 b m Sulaafah (USA)-Dominance (Dominion) 2737^{9} **>1a 36f<**

Cantina 3 b f Tina's Pet-Real Claire (Dreams to Reality (USA)) *3396^{3}* (4290) 4436^{12} 4877^{17} **>54a 68f<**

Cantonese (USA) 2 b f Easy Goer (USA)-Queen of Song (USA) (His Majesty (USA)) 2840^{7} 3638^{5} 3979^{3} 4900^{10} **>68f<**

Canton Ron 3 ch g Ron's Victory (USA)-Briery Fille (Sayyaf) **1996:** *5113^{12}* **1997:** 840^{19} 1238^{11} 1467^{25} 1988^{8} *2151^{5} 2669^{4}* 3449^{4} 3640^{11} **>49a 27f<**

Canton Venture 5 ch g Arctic Tern (USA)-Ski Michaela (USA) (Devil's Bag (USA)) *(1156) 1431^{5}* 2015^{2} 2749^{6} 3035^{2} 3242^{6} 4288^{6} **>85a 82f<**

Can't Say (IRE) 5 br g Gallic League-Mixed Feelings (Junius (USA)) 3248^{14} **>23?f<**

Cantsaynowt 3 b f Rambo Dancer (CAN)-Petiller (Monsanto (FR)) **1996:** *5107^{10}* **>56f<**

Canyon Creek (IRE) 4 b c Mr Prospector (USA)-River Memories (USA) (Riverman (USA)) (433) $716a^{8}$ **>107+f<**

Cape Cross (IRE) 3 b c Green Desert (USA)-Park Appeal (Ahonoora) 692^{3} 940^{8} 3048^{2} (3214) 3499^{2} 3766^{D} **>126?f<**

Cape Hope 2 b c Risk Me (FR)-Bernstein Bette (Petong) 2037^{12} 2466^{3} 3278^{9} 3821^{8} 4402^{7} 4801^{4} 4921^{10} **>67f<**

Cape Pigeon (USA) 12 ch g Storm Bird (CAN)-Someway Somehow (USA) (What Luck (USA)) 1292^{8} (2228) 2748^{3} 3465^{6} **>72?f<**

Capercaillie 2 ch g Deploy-Tee Gee Jay (Northern Tempest (USA)) 4974^{16} **>25f<**

Cape Siren 3 b f Warning-Cape Race (USA) (Northern Dancer) 4579^{8} 4631^{6} 4848^{14} **>54f<**

Cape Verdi (IRE) 2 b f Caerleon (USA)-Afrique Bleu Azur (USA) (Sagace (FR)) (1607) 2057^{2} (3723) 4475^{4} **>99f<**

Capilano Princess 4 b f Tragic Role (USA)-Lady Capilano (Nebbiolo) 887^{5} (1092) 1308^{10} 2346^{10} (2507) (3120) (4268) 4891^{7} 5053^{16} **>61a 95f<**

Capital Prince (FR) 2 b c Alzao (USA)-Sudah (USA) (Rainbow Quest (USA)) 4853^{4} **>75f<**

Cap Juluca (IRE) 5 b h Mtoto-Tabyan (USA) (Topsider (USA)) 894^{3} (1490) 1767^{3} (2217) **>114f<**

Caplaw Skeen 2 b g Sure Blade (USA)-Mary From Dunlow (Nicholas Bill) 4840^{9} 5025^{7} **>49f<**

Capri 2 ch c Generous (IRE)-Island Jamboree (USA) (Explodent (USA)) 4957^{2} **>79+f<**

Capsoff (IRE) 4 b f Mazaad-Minerstown (IRE) (Miner's Lamp) 1477^{13} 2008^{11} 2410^{3} 2568^{7} 3915^{12} 4323^{9} **>60f<**

Captain Bliss 2 b g Rambo Dancer (CAN)-Edwin's Princess (Owen Dudley) 492^{4} 631^{3} 743^{4} 927^{4} 2153^{4} 2425^{2} (2827) 3097^{4} 3639^{4} 3967^{5} *4303^{6}* **>44a 64f<**

Captain Bodgit (USA) 3 b c Saint Ballado (USA)-Answering Echo (USA) (Greek Answer (USA)) $1071a^{2}$ *$1364a^{3}$* **>125a 124f<**

Captain Brady (IRE) 2 ch g Soviet Lad (USA)-Eight Mile Rock (Dominion) 447^{7} 611^{4} *1286^{3} 1941^{8}* 3965^{10} 4630^{12} **>59a 63f<**

Captain Carat 6 gr g Handsome Sailor-Gem of Gold (Jellaby) **1996:** *5268^{4}* **1997:** *11^{3} 51^{7} 127^{4} 233^{7}* 464^{4} 527^{5} 744^{8} 949^{3} 1223^{4} 1385^{11} (1572) 1671^{5} 2754^{5} 2844^{13} 3481^{12} 3566^{4} 3761^{2} 4115^{6} 4248^{16} 5047^{22} **>64a 58f<**

Captain Carparts 3 b c Hubbly Bubbly (USA)-Choir (High Top) *287^{3} 378^{2}* 785^{3} 929^{5} 1385^{13} 1733^{3} 2017^{6} (2238) 2546^{16} **>47a 64f<**

Captain Collins (IRE) 3 gr c El Gran Senor (USA)-Kanmary (FR) (Kenmare (FR)) (693) (1305) 2023^{4} 3063^{3} 3577^{4} 4117^{8} **>112f<**

Captain Flint 3 b br g Bedford (USA)-Sun Yat Chen (Chou Chin Chow) **1996:** *5113^{10} 5160^{7}* **1997:** 582^{8} 862^{13} (2357) **>4a 56f<**

Captain Horatius (IRE) 8 b h Taufan (USA)-One Last Glimpse (Relko) 522^{4} 1323^{8} 2837^{3} 3784^{4} **>108f<**

Captain Jack 7 b g Salse (USA)-Sanctuary (Welsh Pageant) 728^{4} (2834) 4783^{5} 4879^{9} **>95f<**

Captain Jones (IRE) 2 ch c Imp Society (USA)-Thatcherite (Final Straw) 884^{11} 1749^{3} 2018^{8} *2595^{6}* **>20a 61f<**

Captain Logan (IRE) 2 b c Fairy King (USA)-Heaven High (High Line) 4381^{8} 4852^{4} **>79f<**

Captain Marmalade 8 ch g Myjinski (USA)-Lady Seville (Orange Bay) *22^{4} 116^{6} 147^{8} 188^{4} 381^{7}* 465^{13} 721^{2} 1383^{5} 2430^{9} 3026^{7} 3200^{7} *3413^{5}* 4264^{7} 4453^{3} **>45a 43f<**

Captain McCloy (USA) 2 ch g Lively One (USA)-Fly Me First (USA) (Herbager) 1801^{3} 2680^{6} 2905^{6} 3307^{9} 3755^{5} 4245^{4} 4875^{5} **>63f<**

Captain Picard 3 b c Today and Tomorrow-Nimble Dancer (Northern Wizard) 2954^{13} **>4f<**

Captain Scott (IRE) 3 b g Polar Falcon (USA)-Camera Girl (Kalaglow) *(425)* 688^{3} 1175^{5} (2855) 3901^{17} **>76+a 90f<**

Captain's Day 5 ch g Ballacashtal (CAN)-Seymour Ann (Krayyan) *194^{3} 294^{6} (340) (380)* 476^{11} *857^{6}* 1233^{11} 1441^{11} *4571^{10}* **>54a 41f<**

Captain's Guest (IRE) 7 b g Be My Guest (USA)-Watership (USA) (Foolish Pleasure (USA)) 1325^{6} 2867^{3} **>91f<**

Captain Sinbad 5 b g Welsh Captain-Lane Patrol (Hopton Lane) 656^{2} 760^{12} 1572^{7} *2050^{7}* 2703^{7} 2895^{8} **>28a 53f<**

Captain Tandy (IRE) 8 ch g Boyne Valley-Its All A Dream (Le Moss) **1996:** *5110^{11}* **1997:** *16^{12} 1755^{8}* **>4a 48?f<**

Captain Tim 2 ch c Lion Cavern (USA)-Monaiya (Shareef Dancer (USA)) 4167^{2} 4524^{7} 4853^{3} **>79f<**

Captivating (IRE) 2 b f Wolfhound (USA)-Winning Appeal (FR) (Law Society (USA)) 2227^{7} 3151^{8} 3638^{6} **>67f<**

Captive Fact (USA) 2 ch c Known Fact (USA)-Bold Captive (USA) (Boldnesian) 2720^{13} **>40f<**

Caradoc 2 ch c Bustino-Hathaway (Connaught) 4739^{11} 4915^{7} **>70f<**

Carambo 2 b f Rambo Dancer (CAN)-Light the Way (Nicholas Bill) 525^{2} 684^{6} 1255^{2} 1990^{2} 2565^{9} *(3042)* 3755^{9} *(4589)* **>86a 69f<**

Carati 3 b f Selkirk (USA)-Clytie (USA) (El Gran Senor (USA)) 507^{7} 988^{4} 1610^{9} 2925^{5} 3621^{12} 3772^{12} **>76f<**

Caraway 2 b f Shadeed (USA)-Massorah (FR) (Habitat) 3806^{10} 3985^{11} **>44f<**

Carbon 2 b c Batshoof-Reyah (Young Generation) (1978) 2343^{4} 3258^{3} 3650^{5} **>87f<**

Carburton 4 b c Rock City-Arminda (Blakeney) **1996:** *5203^{12}* **1997:** *358^{12}* 450^{17} 596^{12} 1020^{11} 1442^{2} (1632) 1811^{2} 2065^{2} **>53a 82f<**

Career Collection (USA) 2 f *$5060a^{2}$*

Careful Timing 2 b f Caerleon (USA)-By Charter (Shirley Heights) 4873^{8} **>72f<**

Carhue Lass (IRE) 3 b f Common Grounds-Return Journey (1186a) $3535a^{4}$ $4203a^{7}$ **>91f<**

Caribbean Monarch (IRE) 2 b c Fairy King (USA)-Whos The Blonde (Cure The Blues (USA)) 3687^{13} **>41f<**

Caribbean Star 3 b f Soviet Star (USA)-Whos The Blonde (Cure The Blues (USA)) 958^{10} 1458^{8} 2705^{3} (3037) 3418^{4} 4219^{4} 4436^{7} **>81f<**

Caribbee Beach (IRE) 3 ch f Magical Strike

(USA)-Madam John (Ballad Rock) 1499^{10} 1804^{7} 2395^{16} **>12f<**

Carinthia (IRE) 2 br f Tirol-Hot Lavender (CAN) (Shadeed (USA)) 3783^{2} **>71f<**

Carisbrooke 3 b c Kahyasi-Dayanata (Shirley Heights) 3809^{2} (4322) 5043^{4} **>103f<**

Carlasanta (IRE) 2 ch f Imp Society (USA)-Ski Slope (Niniski (USA)) 3783^{16} 4113^{11} 4698^{7} **>52f<**

Carling (FR) 5 b m Garde Royale-Corraleja (FR) (Carvin (FR)) *627a^{13}* **>73a 121f<**

Carlisle Bay (IRE) 3 b c Darshaan-My Potters (USA) 4356a^{7} **>83f<**

Carlton (IRE) 3 ch g Thatching-Hooray Lady (Ahonoora) 535^{7} 840^{4} (1096) 1333^{3} *1754^{8}* 1958^{11} 3930^{15} 4546^{9} **>47a 55f<**

Carlys Quest 3 ch g Primo Dominie-Tuppy (USA) (Sharpen Up) 755^{3} 900^{5} 1164^{3} 1482^{6} 1747^{4} 1852^{5} 2174^{9} **>57a 78f<**

Carmine Lake (IRE) 3 ch f Royal Academy (USA)-Castilian Queen (USA) (Diesis) 4098^{3} (4664a) *5061a^{9}* **>87a 124f<**

Carmosa (USA) 4 ch f Blushing John (USA)-Bobbinette (Whitstead) *54^{5} 71^{14} 125^{14} 177^{12}* **>20a 60df<**

Carnabrae (IRE) 2 ch c Superlative-Rainbow Brite (BEL) (Captain's Treasure) 3961a^{W} **>75f<**

Carnation King 2 b c King's Signet (USA)-Primrose Way (Young Generation) 743^{12} *859^{W}* **>1f< (DEAD)**

Carnelly (IRE) 3 ch f Priolo (USA)-Pennine Drive 2989a^{2} 3511a^{5} 4191a^{P} **>101f<**

Carnival of Light 5 b m Squill (USA)-June Fayre (Sagaro) **1996:** *5183^{11}* **1997:** *275^{8}* **>17a 30f<**

Carol Again 5 b m Kind of Hush-Lady Carol (Lord Gayle (USA)) **1996:** *5181^{9} 5260^{2}* **1997:** *15^{11} 88^{5} 115^{8} 196^{2} (284) 360^{4} 410^{5}* 553^{5} 598^{12} *1138^{6}* 1618^{4} *1943^{4}* 2145^{11} **>55a 33f<**

Carol Grimes 2 b f Beveled (USA)-Come to Good (Swing Easy (USA)) 447^{6} 472^{3} **>64f<**

Caroline's Pet (IRE) 2 b f Contract Law (USA)-Princess Roxanne (Prince Tenderfoot (USA)) 2516^{10} 3411^{11} 3569^{8} 4433^{10} **>46f<**

Carol's Dream (USA) 5 ch h Risen Star (USA)-Merle Halton (USA) (Rattle Dancer) 657^{12} *869^{5} 1152^{3}* 1481^{8} 1601^{5} 2307^{11} **>76a 60f<**

Carol Singer (USA) 2 b f Geiger Counter (USA)-Wake Up Noel (USA) (Nureyev (USA)) 4012^{19} 4230^{3} 4428^{3} 4746^{2} 4948^{2} 5045^{12} **>73f<**

Carouse 2 br c Petong-Merry Rous (Rousillon (USA)) 1321^{5} 1744^{7} 4575^{9} 4856^{17} 4974^{10} **>65f<**

Carranita (IRE) 7 b m Anita's Prince-Take More (GER) (Frontal) **1996:** 5155a^{4} **1997:** 540^{2} 671^{4} 961^{3} 1171^{9} 2329^{5} 4881^{9} (4954) 5054^{11} **>112?f<**

Carreamia 4 b f Weldnaas (USA)-Carribean Tyme (Tyrnavos) 748^{11} 1586^{4} 2177^{13} 2313^{4} 2659^{5} 3213^{3} **>50da 54df<**

Carrick View (IRE) 2 b c Posen (USA)-Linda's Fantasy (Raga Navarro (ITY)) 3060^{10} 3753^{4} 3905^{11} 4285^{15} **>49f<**

Carrielle (USA) 2 f *5060a^{8}*

Carrie's Fantasy 3 ch f Formidable (USA)-Caress (Godswalk (USA)) *546^{8}* 1807^{13}

Carrolls Marc (IRE) 9 b g Horage-Rare Find (Rarity) **1996:** *5244^{8}* **1997:** *104^{12} 295^{9} 302^{4} 418^{9} 516^{8} (867) 1133^{6} 1287^{6} (1417) 2322^{5}* **>58a 57f<**

Carrowkeel (IRE) 2 b c Waajib-Par Un Nez (IRE) (Cyrano de Bergerac) (1293) 3464^{4} (3706) 4135^{4} 4524^{2} 4766a^{4} **>101f<**

Carry The Flag 2 b c Tenby-Tamassos (Dance In Time (CAN)) 1744^{4} (2018) 3990^{6} (4605) **>91f<**

Cartouche 3 gr g Terimon-Emblazon (Wolver Hollow) *874^{2}* 1078^{11} *1939^{2}* (2323) 2667^{8} **>76a 75f<**

Carver Doone 2 b c Tragic Role (USA)-Miss Milton (Young Christopher) 3927^{9} 4298^{16} **>39f<**

Carver John 2 ch g Sure Blade (USA)-Dawn Ditty (Song) 1274^{5} **>34f<**

Carwyn's Choice 4 b f Then Again-Over My Head (Bay Express) **1996:** *5118^{12}* **>24a 24f<**

Casa Rosa 2 b f Casteddu-Kasarose (Owen Dudley) 472^{10} 530^{5} 1984^{4} **>42f<**

Cascatelle Bleue (IRE) 4 b f Bluebird (USA)-Wuthering Falls (Wind And Wuthering (USA)) 1574^{8} 1802^{10} 1993^{8} 2109^{10} **>61df<**

Casey Tibbs (IRE) 3 b c Sadler's Wells (USA)-Fleur Royale (Mill Reef (USA)) (809a) 1195a^{2} 1726a^{11} 2454a^{7} 3172a^{2} 3881a^{2} **>113f<**

Cashaplenty 4 ch g Ballacashtal (CAN)-Storm of Plenty (Billion (USA)) *(218) 516^{9}* 1093^{13} **>50+a 20f<**

Cashmere Lady 5 b m Hubbly Bubbly (USA)-Choir (High Top) *376^{9}* 444^{10} 749^{12} *1123^{4}* 1390^{4} 1628^{5} (2021) *(2161)* 2340^{2} 2678^{9} 3403^{4} (3777) 3976^{17} 4147^{19} 4441^{12} 4781^{10} 5049^{15} **>95a 74f<**

Cashmirie 5 b m Domynsky-Betrothed (Aglojo) 595^{18} 898^{3} (2362) (2564) 2763^{2} 3104^{2} **>36a 55f<**

Cashtal Lace 4 ch f Ballacashtal (CAN)-Chantilly Lace (FR) (Carwhite) 4045^{17} 4608^{15}

Casino Ace (IRE) 2 b f Scenic-Aces Full (USA) (Round Table) 3788^{2} 4017^{5} *4299^{4}* 4605^{4} 4745^{3} **>68a 77f<**

Casino King (IRE) 2 b c Fairy King (USA)-Justsayno (USA) (Dr Blum (USA)) (4111) 4439^{3} **>85+f<**

Caspian Morn 3 b f Lugana Beach-Parijoun (Manado) 1644^{4} 1828^{9} *2671^{7} 3040^{5}* 3590^{8} **>42a 52f<**

Castel Rosselo 7 br h Rousillon (USA)-On The House (FR) (Be My Guest (USA)) 1273^{3} 1584^{5} (2019) 2395^{3} **>88a 71f<**

Castle Ashby Jack 3 gr g Chilibang-Carly-B (IRE) (Commanche Run) *204^{3} 251^{2} 320^{2}* 434^{9} 531^{5} *1151^{4}* 1691^{5} *2151^{10} 2300^{2} 2669^{2} 3043^{3}* 3313^{4} 3641^{7} **>59a 53f<**

Castle Courageous 10 b g Castle Keep-Peteona (Welsh Saint) 728^{7} 969^{4} 1400^{4} 1778^{5} 1871^{4} 3137^{6} 3472^{3} 3896^{5} **>77f<**

Castle Friend 2 b g Durgam (USA)-Furry Friend (USA) (Bold Bidder) 697^{7} 2288^{9} 3628^{6} 4285^{11} **>55f<**

Castlerea Lad 8 b h Efisio-Halo (Godswalk (USA)) **1996:** *5105^{8} 5144^{4} 5230^{7} 5249^{7}* **>47a 68f<**

Castles Burning (USA) 3 b br g Minshaanshu Amad (USA)-Major Overhaul (Known Fact (USA)) **1996:** *5147^{2} 5214^{3}* **1997:** *(456)* 600^{4} 886^{16} *1154^{4} 1788^{4} 2672^{5}* 2956^{3} 3200^{15} (3593) 4222^{11} *4481^{4} (4906) 5022^{6}* **>73a 60f<**

Castle Secret 11 b g Castle Keep-Baffle (Petingo) *660^{8}* 865^{5} *(1122) 2048^{2} 3046^{5} 4481^{5}* **>63a 66f<**

Casual Magic 2 ch c Magic Ring (IRE)-Unsuitable (Local Suitor (USA)) 4602^{10} 4815^{9} **>33f<**

Casual Water (IRE) 6 b g Simply Great (FR)-Top Nurse (High Top) 969^{5} 1478^{4} 1805^{6} 2198^{12} 2865^{5} 3333^{8} 3796^{9} 4222^{5} 4562^{12} **>68f<**

Catawampus 6 ch h Beveled (USA)-Second Flower (Indian Ruler (USA)) 624a^{3} **>34f<**

Catchable 3 b c Pursuit of Love-Catawba (Mill Reef (USA)) 725^{5} 1242^{5} (1930) 2596^{6} 4136^{7} 4416^{4} **>90f<**

Catchment 3 ch g Persian Bold-Cachou (USA) (Roberto (USA)) 4158^{8} 4322^{6} 4579^{9} **>59f<**

Catch The Blues (IRE) 5 b m Bluebird (USA)-Dear Lorraine (FR) (Nonoalco (USA)) 1532a^{2} (1881a) 2056^{3} **>114f<**

Catch The Dragon (IRE) 2 b c Sharp Victor (USA)-Roblanna (Roberto (USA)) 4836a^{5} **>78f<**

Catch The Lights 4 b f Deploy-Dream Chaser (Record Token) 1813^{5} **>75+a 80f<**

Catch The Rainbow 2 ch f Deploy-Sing a Rainbow (IRE) (Rainbow Quest (USA)) 1251^{5} 1510^{8} 2196^{8} *3072^{3}* 3911^{3} 4334^{16} **>40a 61f<**

Catfoot Lane 2 b f Batshoof-T Catty (USA) (Sensitive Prince (USA)) 2467^{15} *3076^{4}* 3859^{11} *4483^{8}* **>51a 32f<**

Cathedral (IRE) 3 b g Prince Sabo-Choire Mhor (Dominion) 531^{2} (792) 2106^{13} 2526^{3} 3111^{2} 3863^{2} **>114f<**

Catherines Song 2 b f Aragon-Songstead (Song) 1760^{14} (2186) 2578^{4} 2862^{15} 3692^{2} **>66f<**

Catherston Lucky 3 b f Liboi (USA)-Buckhurst (Gulf Pearl) 1823^{13} 2492^{16} 3095^{14}

Catienus (USA) 3 b br c Storm Cat (USA)-Diamond City (USA) (Mr Prospector (USA)) (1257) 2656^{4} 3675a^{4} 3988^{6} **>117df<**

Catoki (USA) 4 b c Storm Cat (USA)-Matoki (USA) (Hail To Reason) 1074a^{2} 3736a^{3} **>110f<**

Catria (IRE) 3 br f Caerleon (USA)-Embla (Dominion) **1996:** *5133^{6}* **1997:** 2491^{13} **>61a 61f<**

Cats Bottom 5 ch m Primo Dominie-Purple Fan (Dalsaan) **1996:** *5237^{6} (5256)* **1997:** *15^{3} 29^{2} 125^{8} (428) 579^{3} 870^{7} 1135^{7}* 1640^{8} 2310^{5} 2730^{9} 3421^{6} 3787^{11} *4484^{7}* 4992^{8} **>54a 44f<**

Catumbella (USA) 4 ch f Diesis-Benguela (USA) (Little Current (USA)) **1996:** *5117^{2}* **>64a 74f<**

Catwalk Girl 4 b f Skyliner-Pokey's Pet (Uncle Pokey) 2569^{10} 3143^{19} 3627^{17} **>24f<**

Cauda Equina 3 gr g Statoblest-Sea Fret (Habat) (876) (1275) 2134^{16} 2377^{4} (2547) 2779^{D} 2833^{7} 3194^{6} 3410^{15} 3812^{11} **>82f<**

Caudillo (IRE) 4 b f Nordico (USA)-Over Swing (FR) (Saint Cyrien (FR)) *398^{6}* 444^{19} 521^{15} 728^{12} 1292^{2} 1632^{9} 1920^{2} 2244^{2} 2418^{4} 2698^{11} 4112^{15} 4680^{14} 4872^{3} **>59a 66f<**

Caution 3 b f Warning-Fairy Flax (IRE) (Dancing Brave (USA)) 1175^{12} (1661) (2734) 3145^{4} 3199^{3} 3604^{16} 3888^{10} 4365^{2} 4527^{14} 4565^{7} 4805^{17} **>74f<**

Caversfield 2 ch c Tina's Pet-Canoodle (Warpath) 1274^{2} 1425^{8} 1872^{10} 2689^{7} (3635) (4900) **>76f<**

Caviar Royale (IRE) 3 ch c Royal Academy (USA)-Petite Liqueurelle (IRE) (Shernazar) 747^{3} 1146^{10} 1404^{3} 2013^{27} 2601^{10} (3243) 3725^{14} 3901^{13} **>106df<**

Cavina 7 b m Ardross-Royal Yacht (USA) (Riverman (USA)) **1996:** *5255^{8}* **>65da 61f<**

Cayman Kai (IRE) 4 ch c Imperial Frontier (USA)-Safiya (USA) (Riverman (USA)) 671^{5} 980^{2} 1210^{10} 2056^{16} 2476^{3} 2830^{5} **>103f<**

Cayo Guillermo (IRE) 3 64a^{2} **>53f<**

Cd Newsround (IRE) 2 b f Mujadil (USA)-Coffee Bean (Doulab (USA)) 3471^{17} 3711^{16} 4042^{10} 4230^{9} 4545^{15} **>57f<**

Ceanothus (IRE) 3 ch f Bluebird (USA)-Golden Bloom (Main Reef) 1967^{6} 2353^{2} 2956^{4} 3430^{4} *3612^{2} 4053^{4} 4302^{7}* **>62a 62f<**

Cease Fire (IRE) 2 b f Brief Truce (USA)-Lisa's Favourite (Gorytus (USA)) 3411^{3} 3711^{2} 3905^{2} 4790^{8} **>87f<**

Cedez le Passage (FR) 6 b h Warning-Microcosme (Golden Fleece (USA)) **1996:** *5120^{5} (5137) 5231^{6} 5250^{3} 5269^{4}* **1997:** *56^{6} 160^{5} 182^{8} 207^{9}* 789^{6} 1016^{7} 1142^{3} 1547a^{8} **>65a 78f<**

Cee-Jay-Ay 10 gr g Free State-Raffinrula (Raffingora) 468^{9} 733^{11} 824^{4} 1005^{9} 1128^{12} 1511^{7} 1677^{3} 1830^{7} 2204^{10} 2651^{9} 3248^{8} 3476^{3} 4471^{10} **>62a 40f<**

Cee-N-K (IRE) 3 b c Thatching-Valois (Lyphard (USA)) **1996:** *5083^{6} 5111^{2} (5212)* **1997:** *388^{8} 420^{4}* 634^{4} 1296^{10} 2043^{6} (2735) 2906^{12} 3262^{5} 4270^{7} 4436^{8} 4583^{8} 4792^{2} 4920^{13} **>76a 81f<**

Ceilidh Star (IRE) 4 b f Soviet Star (USA)-Highland Ball (Bold Lad (IRE)) **1996:** *5119[5]* **>63a 70f<**
Celandine 4 b f Warning-Silly Bold (Rousillon (USA)) 1446[10] 1761[12] 2557[13] 2958[6] 3393[2] 3710[3] 4059[6] 4291[3] **>69a 58f<**
Celebrant 3 b f Saddlers' Hall (IRE)-Cathedra (So Blessed) 3184[7] 4063[14] 4323[14] **>58f<**
Celebration 2 br f Selkirk (USA)-No Restraint (Habitat) 5041[8] **>61f<**
Celebration Cake (IRE) 5 b g Mister Majestic-My Louise (Manado) 633[8] 824[10] 1837[9] 3630[6] 4270[11] 4283[6] 4410[13] 4924[24] **>71f<**
Celeric 5 b g Mtoto-Hot Spice (Hotfoot) 932[4] (1172) 1454[2] (2055) 2559[5] 3645[4] 4654a[2] **>127f<**
Celestial Bay (IRE) 2 b f Star de Naskra (USA)-Kandara (FR) (Dalsaan) 2482[3] 2768[7] 3204[3] 3638[4] **>69f<**
Celestial Choir 7 b m Celestial Storm (USA)-Choir (High Top) *52[2]* *100[6]* 1981[10] 2292[3] 2514[14] (3333) 3722[12] 4136[5] 4409[8] (4639) 4754[11] 5053[8] **>91a 96f<**
Celestial Key (USA) 7 br g Star de Naskra (USA)-Casa Key (USA) (Cormorant (USA)) **1996:** *5204[13]* **1997:** 229a[3] 271a[2] 311a[7] 919a[5] 1074a[5] 1160[12] 2026[21] (3735a) (4540a) 4637[7] 4990[8] **>70a 102df<**
Celestial Ridge (IRE) 3 ch f Indian Ridge-Orion Dream (Skyliner) 4408[6]
Celestial Welcome 2 b f Most Welcome-Choral Sundown (Night Shift (USA)) 3905[12] 4514[7] 4807[6] 4994[27] **>42f<**
Celia's Rainbow 4 gr f Belfort (FR)-Mrs Skinner (Electric) 636[9] 1818[9] 2828[13] 3477[13] 4846[11] **>11f<**
Celtic Cavalier (IRE) 2 b c Caerleon (USA)-Irish Arms (FR) (Irish River (FR)) 3895[5] 4357a[2] **>106f<**
Celtic Comfort 2 ch g Executive Man-Annacando (Derrylin) 1797[7] 2240[2] (2500) *3395[3]* *3610[10]* 3750[10] **>72a 72f<**
Celtic Cross 2 b f Selkirk (USA)-Abbey Strand (USA) (Shadeed (USA)) 3574[4] 4107[2] **>95f<**
Celtic Pageant 2 b c Tenby-Certain Story (Known Fact (USA)) 1418[6] 3013[2] 4007[3] 4524[8] 4708[2] 4908[5] **>96df<**
Celtic Venture 2 ch c Risk Me (FR)-Celtic River (IRE) (Caerleon (USA)) 3324[9] 3782[6] 3808[2] **>66f<**
Censor 4 b g Kris-Mixed Applause (USA) (Nijinsky (CAN)) 947[17] *1788[7]* 1979[16] 2890[10] 3242[7] 3622[11] **>32a 73f<**
Central Committee (IRE) 2 ch c Royal Academy (USA)-Idle Chat (USA) (Assert) (4209) 4368[4] **>88+f<**
Central Park (IRE) 2 ch c In The Wings-Park Special (Relkino) 1411[4] (1749) (2057) (3123) 4784[7] **>111df<**
Centre Court 2 ch f Second Set (IRE)-Raffle (Balidar) 2320[4] (2553) 3152[8] 4296[11] **>76+f<**
Centre Stalls (IRE) 4 b c In The Wings-Lora's Guest (Be My Guest (USA)) 830[7] (1160) 1476[3] 2009[2] 4240[3] 4422[9] **>123f<**
Cerbera 8 b g Caruso-Sealed Contract (Runnymede) *285[8]* 480[10] **>43a f<**
Cerisette (IRE) 2 b f Polar Falcon (USA)-Crimson Conquest (USA) (Diesis) (2688) **>85f<**
Certain Danger (IRE) 2 b f Warning-Please Believe Me (Try My Best (USA)) 4973[13] **>47f<**
Certain Magic 3 ch c Faustus (USA)-Dependable (Formidable (USA)) 537[7] 837[4] 1140[12] 1568[10] 2182[7] 2398[10] *(3400)* (4010) *4590[3]* **>66a 55f<**
Certain Surprise 3 b f Grey Desire-Richesse (FR) (Faraway Son (USA)) 1272[12] 1637[9] 2952[5] 3495[10] **>66f<**
Certainty 3 br f Belmez (USA)-La Carlotta (USA) (J O Tobin (USA)) *1939[10]* 2059[10] 2428[7] **>17f<**
Chabrol (CAN) 4 b c El Gran Senor (USA)-Off The Record (USA) (Chas Conerly (USA)) 430[5] 650[3] 888[3] 1260[4] 1693[2] 2014[13] 2490[2] 2837[5] 3279[10] **>71f<**
Chadleigh Lane (USA) 5 ch g Imp Society (USA)-Beauty Hour (USA) (Bold Hour) **1996:** *(5129)* **1997:** *14[6]* *(85)* *111[2]* *248[W]* *358[3]* *422[2]* 461[17] *578[10]* *1291[10]* *1576[6]* *2071[6]* 2471[4] *4813[14]* **>55da 49?f<**
Chadwell Hall 6 b h Kala Shikari-Cherrywood Blessin (Good Times (ITY)) **1996:** *5131[7]* *(5163)* *5236[2]* **1997:** *89[4]* *137[12]* *301[5]* *357[9]* *545[2]* 585[5] 702[3] 772[8] 1223[F] **>78a 72f< (DEAD)**
Chain Reaction (IRE) 3 b f Fayruz-Timiya (High Top) 1589[14] 1810[12] 2369[10] 2957[3] 3292[7] **>58f<**
Chairmans Choice 7 ch g Executive Man-Revida Girl (Habat) 521[16] 951[5] 2121[11] 2743[3] 3029[3] 3153[3] 4139[13] 4924[21] 5049[6] **>84a 63f<**
Chairmans Daughter 3 b f Unfuwain (USA)-Ville Sainte (FR) (Saint Estephe (FR)) 3210[6] (3643) **>69f<**
Chai-Yo 7 b h Rakaposhi King-Ballysax Lass (Main Reef) 451[5] 4671[2] 4893[14] **>81?f<**
Chakra 3 gr g Mystiko (USA)-Maracuja (USA) (Riverman (USA)) 674[11] 991[17] 1237[14] 2192[7] 2554[12] (3083) 3296[7] 4115[13] **>54f<**
Chalice 4 b f Governor General-Eucharis (Tickled Pink) 2501[6] 2755[7] 3240[23] **>48a 46f<**
Chalky Dancer 5 br g Adbass (USA)-Tiny Feet (Music Maestro) **1996:** *5086[7]* *5208[9]* *5264[10]* **1997:** 526[15] 653[6] 1388[2] 1639[12] 2041[3] 2577[5] 3476[10] 3822[11] **>25a 36f<**
Challenger (IRE) 4 b g Nordico (USA)-Sweet Miyabi (JPN) (Royal Ski (USA)) 476[14] 1139[14] 1809[11] 1926[13] 3617[6] 3767[7] 4222[8] 4374[14] **>40f<**
Challenger Two (IRE) 2 b c Petorius-Blue Elver (Kings Lake (USA)) 3961a[7] **>89f<**
Chaluz 3 b g Night Shift (USA)-Laluche (USA) (Alleged (USA)) **1996:** *5141[2]* **1997:** 600[3] 771[10] 1256[14] 3685[7] 3852[7] 4228[13] *4480[4]* **>52a 37f<**
Chameli 2 b f Nordico (USA)-Try Vickers (USA) (Fuzzbuster (USA)) 2519[4] 3131[8] **>63f<**
Champagne Gold 10 ch g Bairn (USA)-Halkissimo (Khalkis) 3015[15] **>16f<**
Champagne N Dreams 5 b m Rambo Dancer (CAN)-Pink Sensation (Sagaro) 1128[14] 1683[9] 2828[4] 3064[3] 3264[5] **>50f<**
Champagne On Ice 3 b f Efisio-Nip In The Air (USA) (Northern Dancer) 497[3] 644[5] 1077[7] *1580[4]* *1757[4]* *2052[6]* **>47a 53f<**
Champagne Prince 4 b c Prince Sabo-Champagne Season (USA) (Vaguely Noble) 633[4] 787[2] (933) 1176[W] (1450) (1768) 3112[3] 3703[7] 4294[11] **>104f<**
Champagne Warrior (IRE) 4 b f Waajib-Late Swallow (My Swallow) (570) 595[6] *(869)* 1222[7] *1943[2]* *2067[3]* 4713[10] **>62a 56f<**
Chancancook 4 ch f Hubbly Bubbly (USA)-Majuba Road (Scottish Rifle) **1996:** *5177[12]* *5260[9]* **1997:** 3429[5] 3486[9] 4923[7] **>25f<**
Chandler's Hall 3 b c Saddlers' Hall (IRE)-Queen's Visit (Top Command (USA)) 1322[5] 2287[4] 3021[6] 4632[17] 4802[18] **>60f<**
Change 3 b c North Briton-Karminski (Pitskelly) 1207[16] 1464[7] **>46f<**
Changed To Baileys (IRE) 3 b g Distinctly North (USA)-Blue Czarina (Sandhurst Prince) 656[5] 1573[9] 1864[10] **>58df<**
Change For A Buck (USA) 3 ch f Time For A Change (USA)-Pearl Bracelet (USA) (Lyphard (USA)) 681[3] (885) **>81f<**
Chania (IRE) 3 ch f In The Wings-Chalon (Habitat) 806a[2] 1062a[3] 2446a[2] 2989a[3] 4356a[4] **>101f<**
Chanson d'Amour (IRE) 3 b f High Estate-Wind of Change (FR) (Sicyos (USA)) 2145[15] 2226[8] 2543[11] 2715[10] 2859[4] 3223[7] 3405[6] 3488[5] 3918[4] 4264[10] **>23f<**
Charbertsam 4 b g Rabdan-Harts Mead (Posse (USA)) 3277[15] 3617[7] **>8f<**
Charcol 4 b f Nicholas Bill-Dutch Princess (Royalty) 841[15] 2492[13] *3074[9]* 4608[17] **>15f<**
Chardania (IRE) 2 ch f Rainbows For Life (CAN)-Far From Home (Habitat) 780[4] *902[8]* *1137[6]* 3062[7] 3451[4] 3699[6] 4014[6] 4163[9] *4592[11]* **>25a 47f<**
Charge D'Affaires 2 b c Kendor-Lettre de Cachet (FR) (Secreto (USA)) 2639a[3] 3366a[2] (3882a) 4391a[2] 4766a[2] **>113f<**
Charisse Dancer 4 b f Dancing Dissident (USA)-Cadisa (Top Ville) 1603[7] 2502[7] *2602[4]* 2854[6] **>37a 44f<**
Charita (IRE) 3 ch f Lycius (USA)-Seme de Lys (USA) (Slew O' Gold (USA)) 2267a[9] **>90f<**
Charity Crusader 6 b g Rousillon (USA)-Height of Folly (Shirley Heights) 570[5] 1081[5] 1605[2] 2154[3] 2352[2] 2825[4] (3429) 3778[2] **>51f<**
Charlie Bigtime 7 b g Norwick (USA)-Sea Aura (Roi Soleil) **1996:** *5233[7]* **1997:** *2910[7]* 3626[3] 3919[6] *4055[5]* 4633[6] 4850[3] **>30a 46f<**
Charlie Chang (IRE) 4 b g Don't Forget Me-East River (FR) (Arctic Tern (USA)) 3853[5] 3933[3] *4050[13]* *4912[9]* **>37a 56f<**
Charlie's Gold 2 b g Shalford (IRE)-Ballet (Sharrood (USA)) 4853[13] 4974[12] **>35f<**
Charlie Sillett 5 ch g Handsome Sailor-Bystrouska (Gorytus (USA)) 443[15] 892[22] 1148[10] 1317[8] (2211) 2326[16] 2833[13] 3273[12] 4995[25] **>54a 73f<**
Charlies Lad (IRE) 2 b g Petardia-Brigadina (Brigadier Gerard) 938[3] *1136[2]* 2538[4] 2862[17] (3097) 3228[2] *3586[3]* 3967[2] **>63a 68f<**
Charlotte Corday 4 b f Kris-Dancing Rocks (Green Dancer (USA)) 894[2] 1157[2] 1740[2] 2217[3] 2586[7] **>109f<**
Charlton Imp (USA) 4 b f Imp Society (USA)-Percentage (USA) (Vaguely Noble) 554[3] 848[19] 1273[15] 1794[3] 2150[10] 2488[19] 2646[7] 2852[4] 3248[7] 3469[9] 4043[6] **>47f<**
Charlton Spring (IRE) 3 ch f Masterclass (USA)-Relankina (IRE) (Broken Hearted) 556[7] 757[6] 3558[7] 3968[7] 4168[20] **>55f<**
Charming Admiral (IRE) 4 b g Shareef Dancer (USA)-Lilac Charm (Bustino) 2592[11] 2927[2] 4986[4] **>67f<**
Charming Bride 4 b f Charmer-Loredana (Grange Melody) **1996:** *5124[13]* *5134[14]* **>55a 52f<**
Charnwood Jack (USA) 4 ch c Sanglamore (USA)-Hyroglyph (USA) (Northern Dancer) 559[5] 770[2] 888[4] 1371[6] (1693) 2411[4] 2694[4] **>73f<**
C-Harry (IRE) 3 ch c Imperial Frontier (USA)-Desert Gale (Taufan (USA)) **1996:** *5133[2]* *5164[2]* *5238[4]* **1997:** *17[8]* *(217)* *(372)* 532[6] 652[5] 845[5] 1096[10] 1573[3] 1661[2] 1931[2] (2715) 3088[13] 4586[5] 4877[16] **>73a 70f<**
Charsy (IRE) 3 (64a) **>57f<**
Charter 6 b g Reference Point-Winter Queen (Welsh Pageant) *205[9]* *315[11]* 1224[9] 1494[6] 1763[8] 1981[7] 2316[4] 2535[2] 3309[12] 3754[2] 4287[6] **>22a 68f<**
Chasetown Cailin 2 b f Suave Dancer (USA)-Kilvarnet (Furry Glen) 1657[6] *2047[5]* **>58a 40f<**
Chasetown Flyer (USA) 3 b c Thorn Dance (USA)-Thought Provoker (USA) (Exceller (USA)) **1996:** *5111[6]* *5160[3]* *5202[10]* *5261[2]* **1997:** *6[4]* *90[5]* *132[6]* *181[4]* *458[2]* 649[6] *1151[9]* (1826) (2004) 2552[3] 3980[8] 4139[9] 4319[8] 4546[10] **>64?a 60f<**
Chaska 2 b f Reprimand-Royal Passion (Ahonoora) 2176[9] 3033[4] 3306[5] (3628) 3990[10]

4265^9 *4589^8* **>39a 68f<**

Chateau Country (USA) 2 b c Lear Fan (USA)-Mt Morna (USA) (Mt Livermore (USA)) 3874a^3 **>82f<**

Chateauherault (IRE) 3 b g Contract Law (USA)-Secret Hideaway (USA) (Key To The Mint (USA)) *(46) 84^2 174^3 249^3* 3485^4 3781^{12} **>67a 63f<**

Chateau Royal (USA) 2 ch c Personal Hope (USA)-Petroleuse (Habitat) 5002a^8 **>99f<**

Chatham Island 9 ch g Jupiter Island-Floreal (Formidable (USA)) 789^{16} 1841^6 2411^{10} 3318^6 **>93a 62f<**

Chattan 2 b c Lycius (USA)-Chanzi (USA) (El Gran Senor (USA)) 2693^3 4853^2 **>88f<**

Chauncy Lane (IRE) 3 b f Sadler's Wells (USA)-Broadway Joan (USA) (Bold Arian (USA)) 1540a^5 **>88f<**

Chayanee's Arena (IRE) 2 b f High Estate-Arena (Sallust) 2038^5 2699^8 3783^7 4900^9 **>60f<**

Check The Band (USA) 3 gr c Dixieland Band (USA)-Check Bid (USA) (Grey Dawn II) 1186a^2 1881a^5 2106^{14} **>111f<**

Cheek To Cheek 3 b f Shavian-Intoxication (Great Nephew) 885^9 1316^{13} 1859^2 2194^5 2744^2 3080^3 4323^6 4504^5 **>66f<**

Cheeky Chappy 6 b g Sayf El Arab (USA)-Guilty Guest (USA) (Be My Guest (USA)) **1996:** *5097^8 5138^5 5161^{14} 5220^4 5230^3 5241^8 5268^9 5280^8* **1997:** *79^{12} 545^{11}* **>25a 71f< (DEAD)**

Cheerful Groom (IRE) 6 ch g Shy Groom (USA)-Carange (Known Fact (USA)) *40^{11} 69^6 113^{12} 159^4 203^8 241^8 332^6 423^3* 468^{13} **>30a 40f<**

Chemcast 4 ch g Chilibang-Golden October (Young Generation) **1996:** *(5097) 5184^4* **1997:** *53^2 137^2 170^6 301^{11} 397^5* (494) 744^{16} 1158^{13} 1627^{10} 2061^4 2675^{13} 2759^7 3287^{11} 3871^{15} **>73a 54f<**

Cherished (IRE) 2 b f Distinctly North (USA)-Key Partner (Law Society (USA)) 1564^5 1806^7 2038^4 3750^9 4058^8 4163^3 4627^4 *4799^3 4984^9* **>56a 60f<**

Cherokee Band (USA) 2 b br c Dixieland Band (USA)-Cherokee Darling (USA) (Alydar (USA)) 4064^9 4361^7 **>67f<**

Cherokee Charlie 2 ch g Interrex (CAN)-Valentine Song (Pas de Seul) 2042^6 2202^8 2886^7 **>46f<**

Cherokee Flight 3 b g Green Desert (USA)-Totham (Shernazar) 1000^7 1458^4 1589^6 1958^5 2201^{13} *2671^6 (3044)* 3236^3 3496^3 *(3609)* 4063^2 **>70a 80f<**

Cherry Blossom (IRE) 3 br f Primo Dominie-Varnish (Final Straw) 694^{10} 1018^{11} 1594^{10} **>76f< (DEAD)**

Cherrymentary 3 b f Rudimentary (USA)-Beaute Fatale (Hello Gorgeous (USA)) 1823^W 3389^{10} 4883^{12}

Chester House (USA) 2 b c Mr Prospector (USA)-Toussaud (USA) (El Gran Senor (USA)) (3193) 3644^2 **>106f<**

Chevalier (USA) 5 b br h Danzig (USA)-Royal Touch (Tap On Wood) **1996:** *5181^F* **>65a 73f< (DEAD)**

Cheval Roc 3 ch c Keen-Gentle Gain (Final Straw) **1996:** *5100^8* **1997:** *361^2 458^4* 1167^{15} 2573^{11} *4484^{12}* **>58a 42f<**

Chewit 5 gr g Beveled (USA)-Sylvan Song (Song) **1996:** *5203^3* **1997:** *363^2 514^2* 892^5 1085^3 2649^2 (3185) 3615^6 3764^9 4978^5 **>104a 90f<**

Chez Catalan 6 b h Niniski (USA)-Miss Saint-Cloud (Nonoalco (USA)) **1996:** *5244^9* **1997:** *93^2 202^5 324^6* 1665^9 3080^8 4405^7 **>46a 39f<**

Chicago's Best 10 br g Try My Best (USA)-Maryville Bick (Malacate (USA)) 2702^{11} **>26f<**

Chickawicka (IRE) 6 b h Dance of Life (USA)-Shabby Doll (Northfields (USA)) **1996:** *5203^{11}* **1997:** (677) 892^7 1214^5 1658^6 2390^2 3185^7 3423^7 3764^8 4282^{10} 4423^{23} 4990^7 **>54a 89f<**

Chief Bearhart (CAN) 4 ch c Chief's Crown (USA)-Amelia Beaarhart (CAN) (Bold Hour) (4870a) (5065a) **>129f<**

Chief Blade 2 ch c Be My Chief (USA)-Nagida (Skyliner) 1812^{18} 2948^5 3613^8 (3924) 4545^8 **>65f<**

Chief Cashier 2 b c Persian Bold-Kentfield (Busted) 1872^6 3494^{12} 4113^3 4670^7 **>76f<**

Chief Connections 4 b c Inca Chief (USA)-Ballafort (Ballacashtal (CAN)) 1023^{15} 1221^{12} 1656^5 2313^{22} 2546^{17} **>42f<**

Chief Contender (IRE) 4 b c Sadler's Wells (USA)-Minnie Hauk (USA) (Sir Ivor) 736^8 3883a^3 4130a^3 (4654a) **>127f<**

Chief Monarch 3 b c Be My Chief (USA)-American Beauty (Mill Reef (USA)) 740^8 991^3 1277^2 1741^5 2242^5 (3140) 3575^5 4151^{12} **>88f<**

Chief Mouse 4 b g Be My Chief (USA)-Top Mouse (High Top) 2834^6 3412^6 **>77?a 45f<**

Chief Predator (USA) 3 ch c Chief's Crown (USA)-Tsavorite (USA) (Halo (USA)) **1996:** *5087^3 5212^2* **1997:** *491^3* 537^8 771^{11} 1139^4 1426^3 1825^4 1971^2 2218^7 3462^4 3928^8 **>69a 60f<**

Chief's Lady 5 b m Reprimand-Pussy Foot (Red Sunset) *386^8* 760^3 1467^{15} 1620^2 1676^W 1848^9 2197^6 2536^W 2780^7 3240^{19} **>53a 33f<**

Chief's Song 7 b g Chief Singer-Tizzy (Formidable (USA)) 4374^8 **>44f<**

Chief's Spirit 3 b g Inca Chief (USA)-Country Spirit (Sayf El Arab (USA)) 2234^6 3313^2 3572^8 **>61f<**

Chieftain (IRE) 2 b c Indian Ridge-Legit (IRE) (Runnett) 696^4 3192^3 3414^2 3708^7 **>95f<**

Chieftain's Crown (USA) 6 ch g Chief's Crown (USA)-Simple Taste (USA) (Sharpen Up) *116^{10}* 1632^{16} **>47f<**

Chief Whip (USA) 2 b c Premiership (USA)-Merci Mouillet (USA) (Bob's Dusty (USA)) 3177a^{10} 3743^4 4145^4 4379^2 (4761a) **>90f<**

Chikal 2 b g Nalchik (USA)-Ty-With-Belle (Pamroy) 2720^{10} 3312^4 4017^{11} 4334^{18} **>50f<**

Chikapenny 2 b f Mon Tresor-Arabian Nymph (Sayf El Arab (USA)) 1569^{12} 1860^3 2538^3 3106^6 3265^4 3416^3 3847^3 4159^3 4402^6 **>60f<**

Chika Shan (IRE) 2 ch c Archway (IRE)-Judy's Pinch (Ballymore) 1370^6 *1758^5* 2191^8 2741^5 **>33a 40f<**

Chik's Secret 4 ch f Nalchik (USA)-Lana's Secret (Most Secret) **1996:** *5116^{10}* **>51a 58f<**

Child Prodigy (IRE) 2 br f Ballad Rock-Minnie Habit (Habitat) 1149^3 2024^7 (2713) 3595^{10} **>80f<**

Children's Choice (IRE) 6 b m Taufan (USA)-Alice Brackloon (USA) (Melyno) *202^8* 1252^7 2411^3 2592^U (3096) 3317^2 3579^5 4313^6 (4562) 4971^9 5027^5 **>40a 63f<**

Chilibang Bang 4 b f Chilibang-Quenlyn (Welsh Pageant) **1996:** *5170^8 5235^8* **1997:** *3^8 169^5* **>42a 51f<**

Chili Bouchier (USA) 3 br f Stop The Music (USA)-Low Approach (Artaius (USA)) 1823^{12} 2229^5 3715^9 *4300^8* **>33a 56f<**

Chili Concerto 3 ro f Chilibang-Whirling Words (Sparkler) *904^7* 1294^2 2134^8 2655^7 3326^9 4565^{13} 4816^8 **>39a 70f<**

Chi-Lin 2 b f Precocious-Cool Combination (Indian King (USA)) 4855^7 **>31f<**

Chilled Wine 3 gr f Chilibang-Persian Joy (Persian Bold) 779^{14} 896^{19} 1220^{13} 1451^7 1572^9 **>8a 25f<**

Chilli Boom 3 gr f Chilibang-Silent Sun (Blakeney) 4326^5 **>41f<**

Chilling 3 gr f Chilibang-Appealing (Star Appeal) **1996:** *5172^3* **1997:** *51^4 (181) 247^5 (345) 399^5 427^4 462^9 659^5 856^4 (1047)* 1332^3 1496^8 1661^{10} **>68a 57f<**

Chill Wind 8 gr or gr g Siberian Express (USA)-Springwell (Miami Springs) 3267^7 3626^6 4170^{16} **>30f<**

Chilly Lad 6 ch g High Kicker (USA)-Miss Poll Flinders (Swing Easy (USA)) **1996:** *5149^5 5181^8* **1997:** *18^{10} 80^9* **>43a 51f<**

Chiltern Emerald 2 b f Thowra (FR)-Treasure Time (IRE) (Treasure Kay) 999^9 1425^{13} 2875^{15} 3228^8 **>13f<**

Chimborazo 6 ch g Salse (USA)-Pale Gold (FR) (New Chapter) 4104^{11} 4438^{12} 4585^4 **>64?a 49f<**

Chim Chiminey 2 b f Sabrehill (USA)-William's Bird (USA) (Master Willie) 3744^6 4057^5 (4638) 4803^6 **>86f<**

Chimes of Peace 2 b f Magic Ring (IRE)-Leprechaun Lady (Royal Blend) 4212^5 4597^8 4750^9 4922^7 **>56f<**

Chinaberry 3 b f Soviet Star (USA)-Crimson Conquest (USA) (Diesis) 1316^4 1621^5 2654^4 3119^{11} **>63f<**

China Castle 4 b g Sayf El Arab (USA)-Honey Plum (Kind of Hush) **1996:** *5200^4* **1997:** *(39) (88) (115) 244^2 299^4 389^3 426^5 3584^{12} 4572^8* **>85da 60f<**

China Girl (IRE) 3 b f Danehill (USA)-Chamonis (USA) (Affirmed (USA)) 2056^{19} 2677^5 3436^4 **>97df<**

Chinaider (IRE) 2 b f Mujadil (USA)-We Two (Glenstal (USA)) *(2367) 2606^3* (3427) (3707) 4014^2 4116^6 4473^8 **>65+a 73f<**

China Mail (IRE) 5 b g Slip Anchor-Fenney Mill (Levmoss) 1808^5 2511^7 2874^7 **>41f<**

China Red (USA) 3 br c Red Ransom (USA)-Akamare (FR) (Akarad (FR)) (645) 2013^{26} 2666^5 2866^{11} 4410^{12} **>86f<**

Chingachgook 3 b g Superlative-Petomania (Petong) 532^8 1633^2 2004^{11} 2408^8 2957^6 **>40f<**

Chinour (IRE) 9 b g Dalsaan-Chishtiya (Try My Best (USA)) *288^7* 467^{10} 653^4 925^7 1583^4 2355^6 2937^7 3039^6 3269^5 4324^7 4510^3 4846^2 4992^{13} **>59?a 55f<**

Chips (IRE) 2 ch c Common Grounds-Inonder (Belfort (FR)) 722^3 (965) 1143^2 (1411) 2012^{11} (3997a) 4391a^7 4679^3 4790^{14} **>93f<**

Chirac 3 b c Belmez (USA)-Vivienda (Known Fact (USA)) 1909a^2 **>83f<**

Chist (USA) 2 b br c Lear Fan (USA)-Morna (Blakeney) 4993^4 **>77+f<**

Chloe Nicole (USA) 3 b f Personal Flag (USA)-Balakhna (FR) (Tyrant (USA)) 889^7 988^9 1375^5 1925^{13} **>54f<**

Chloe's Anchor 4 b f Slip Anchor-Mademoiselle Chloe (Night Shift (USA)) 2172^5 **>56f<**

Chlo-Jo 2 b f Belmez (USA)-Shaadin (USA) (Sharpen Up) 2728^{10} 3450^4 4057^8 4806^{10} 5050^{14} **>73f<**

Chocolate (IRE) 2 b f Brief Truce (USA)-Vian (USA) (Far Out East (USA)) 1927^5 2349^6 3411^2 4185^2 4382^9 4706^2 4907^6 **>81f<**

Chocolate Box 2 ch f Most Welcome-Short Rations (Lorenzaccio) 4694^3 5029^4 **>72f<**

Chocolate Ice 4 b g Shareef Dancer (USA)-Creake (Derring-Do) **1996:** *5213^7* **1997:** *13^6* 2487^{10} **>55a 67f<**

Choice Lady 3 b f Shavian-Elarrih (USA) (Sharpen Up) 4060^{14} 4547^7 **>47f<**

Cholas 3 b c Shirley Heights-Chevisaunce (Fabulous Dancer (USA)) (1911a)

Chopin (IRE) 3 b g Classic Music (USA)-La Toulzanie (FR) (Sanctus II) 1008^4 1383^{16} 2748^8 2954^7 3297^4 3560^3 **>50f<**

Chorus Song (USA) 3 b f Alleged (USA)-Performing Arts (The Minstrel (CAN)) 749^{4} 1012^{8} 1373^{11} 1820^{7} **>67f<**

Chris's Lad 6 b g Thowra (FR)-Stockline (Capricorn Line) 650^{8} 865^{14} 1100^{6} 1478^{9} (1779) 1974^{9} 2530^{7} 2696^{10} 2865^{8} 3015^{3} 3197^{3} 3719^{6} 4104^{10} **>56a 60f<**

Chrysalis 2 b f Soviet Star (USA)-Vivienda (Known Fact (USA)) 739^{3} 1007^{3} 1440^{5} **>69f<**

Chrysolite (IRE) 2 ch c Kris-Alamiya (IRE) (Doyoun) 4237^{16} 4581^{4} 4908^{3} **>64f<**

Chucklestone 14 b g Chukaroo-Czar's Diamond (Queen's Hussar) 1953^{6} **>43f<**

Chunito 2 b c Beveled (USA)-Wasimah (Caerleon (USA)) 722^{5} 1026^{3} 1425^{6} **>70f<**

Churchill's Shadow (IRE) 3 b c Polish Precedent (USA)-Shy Princess (USA) (Irish River (FR)) 673^{5} 1265^{8} 2591^{11} 4047^{9} 4370^{9} 4546^{2} 4817^{12} **>57f<**

Churlish Charm 2 b c Niniski (USA)-Blushing Storm (USA) (Blushing Groom (FR)) 3598^{15} **>38f<**

Chynna 3 b f Golden Heights-What A Present (Pharly (FR)) **1996:** *5207^{6} 5248^{8}* **>14a 57f<**

Cim Bom Bom (IRE) 5 b h Dowsing (USA)-Nekhbet (Artaius (USA)) **1996:** *(5144) (5203)* **1997:** *257^{2} (343)* 520^{4} 834^{8} 1324^{14} *1578^{2}* 1799^{7} (2567) 2844^{3} **>100a 81f<**

Cimmerian 3 ch f Aragon-Relatively Easy (Relkino) 1449^{7} 1689^{9} 2171^{2} 2569^{8} *2911^{9}* 3931^{10} **>61f<**

Cinder Hills 2 ch f Deploy-Dame du Moulin (Shiny Tenth) 836^{7} 1492^{15} *2066^{9}* **>25a 56f<**

Cinders Girl 7 b m Presidium-Salinas (Bay Express) 901^{10} 1266^{13}

Cindy Kate (IRE) 4 br f Sayf El Arab (USA)-Marton Maid (Silly Season) *135^{6} 209^{10}* 883^{14} **>50da 59f<**

Cinema Paradiso 3 b c Polar Falcon (USA)-Epure (Bellypha) 973^{3} 1170^{5} 1739^{13} (2242) 2585^{16} 3125^{12} 3575^{10} 4308^{10} **>85f<**

Cinnamon Stick (IRE) 4 ch g Don't Forget Me-Gothic Lady (Godswalk (USA)) 587^{10} 896^{17} 1246^{8} **>44a 31f<**

Circled (USA) 4 gr f Cozzene (USA)-Hold The Hula (USA) (Hawaii) *70^{2} 182^{7}* **>73a 67f<**

Circle of Magic 3 gr f Midyan (USA)-Miss Witch (High Line) **1996:** *5142^{11}* **1997:** 1167^{5} 2171^{8} 2646^{5} (2941) **>38a 58f<**

Circuiteer (IRE) 2 ch c Pips Pride-Day Dress (Ashmore (FR)) 971^{7} 1819^{6} 2288^{11} 3427^{3} 3808^{3} 4543^{2} **>75f<**

Circus 2 b c Caerleon (USA)-Circo (High Top) 2524^{10} 3322^{4} 4474^{10} **>74f<**

Circus Colours 7 b g Rainbow Quest (USA)-Circus Plume (High Top) *487^{7} 1417^{8}* **>37a 81f<**

Cirino (USA) 3 c 1725a^{5} **>104f<**

Ciro's Pearl (IRE) 3 b f Petorius-Cut it Fine (USA) (Big Spruce (USA)) 889^{3} (1416) (1868) 2058^{3} 2647^{4} 3648^{10} 3916^{12} 4466^{4} 4860^{4} **>83f<**

Ciste (IRE) 3 b f Treasure Kay-Mothers Blessing (Wolver Hollow) 1193a^{4} **>85f<**

Citadel 2 b f Emarati (USA)-Round Tower (High Top) 4904^{13} **>58f<**

Citrus Express (SWE) 2 br c Mango Express-Thilda (IRE) (Roi Danzig (USA)) 4454^{11} 4855^{10} 4974^{11} **>36f<**

Cittern 7 b g Ela-Mana-Mou-Seattle Serenade (USA) (Seattle Slew (USA)) 2386^{8} *2910^{8}* 3309^{6} 4160^{4} **>32a 63f<**

City Dance 2 b br f Rock City-Fen Dance (IRE) (Trojan Fen) 4014^{10} *4593^{11}* **>37f<**

City Gambler 3 b f Rock City-Sun Street (Ile de Bourbon (USA)) 690^{11} 1002^{3} 1415^{3} 1784^{4} 1973^{8} (3230) (3452) 3696^{4} 4297^{17} 4449^{5} 4606^{7} **>78f<**

City Girl (ITY) 3 b f Nordance (USA)-Inly Mine (ITY) (Grundy) **1996:** 5195a^{2}

City Hall (IRE) 3 b c Generous (IRE)-City Fortress (Troy) 1866^{10} 3096^{2} 3549^{3} 4246^{3} (4461) 4673^{4} 4744^{2} **>88f<**

City Honours (USA) 2 b c Darshaan-Ikebana (IRE) (Sadler's Wells (USA)) 3576^{4} (4132) 4440^{3} **>105f<**

City Run (USA) 5 b h Mehmet (USA)-Sable Sham (USA) (Sham (USA)) *63^{10} 235^{11}* **>61f<**

Civil Liberty 4 b g Warning-Libertine (Hello Gorgeous (USA)) 1745^{8} 2124^{11} 2390^{8} 2835^{11} 3712^{8} 3798^{8} 4071^{5} (4335) 4548^{2} 4667^{4} 4891^{14} **>70f<**

Claireswan (IRE) 5 ch g Rhoman Rule (USA)-Choclate Baby (Kashiwa) 4771^{11} **>70a 62f<**

Clan Ben (IRE) 5 ch h Bluebird (USA)-Trina's Girl (Nonoalco (USA)) 939^{6} 1176^{4} 1450^{9} (2525) 2766^{14} 3112^{16} (4272) **>111f<**

Clanblue Chick 2 b f Clantime-Lavenham Blue (Streetfighter) 4159^{8} 4921^{11} **>40a 40f<**

Clan Chief 4 b g Clantime-Mrs Meyrick (Owen Dudley) 1772^{4} 2529^{5} 2769^{9} 3217^{29} 3600^{8} **>83f<**

Clapham Common (IRE) 2 b c Common Grounds-West of Eden (Crofter (USA)) (4532a) 4803^{3} **>86f<**

Claque 5 ch g Kris-Mixed Applause (USA) (Nijinsky (CAN)) **1996:** *5167^{7} 5222^{4} 5240^{6}* **1997:** *338^{3}* 721^{19} **>54a 42f<**

Clara House 3 b f Shirley Heights-Mountain Lodge (Blakeney) 814a^{2} 1368a^{7} **>79f<**

Clarity (IRE) 2 b f Scenic-Cristalga (High Top) 3117^{3} 3547^{8} 3744^{7} 4265^{7} 5040^{10} **>82f<**

Clash of Swords 4 b g Shaadi (USA)-Swept Away (Kris) 1232^{5} 1605^{7} 3283^{6} (3567) **>56f<**

Class Distinction (IRE) 3 ch c Masterclass (USA)-Brook's Dilemma (Known Fact (USA)) 1141^{25} 2921^{16} 3420^{6} 3710^{12} 4328^{17} 4816^{11} **>58f<**

Classic Account 9 ch g Pharly (FR)-Money Supply (Brigadier Gerard) *101^{4} 167^{5} 252^{5} 315^{3} 384^{5}* **>42a f<**

Classic Affair (USA) 4 ch f Trempolino (USA)-Coupole (USA) (Vaguely Noble) **1996:** *5108^{6}* **>54a 71f<**

Classical Dance (IRE) 3 b g Classic Music (USA)-Eyre Square (IRE) (Flash of Steel) 1646^{10} 2059^{7} 2315^{17} 3486^{3} 4010^{4} 4509^{6} **>53f<**

Classic Ballet (FR) 4 b f Fabulous Dancer (USA)-Tyranesque (USA) (Key To The Mint (USA)) **1996:** *5104^{4}* **1997:** 1248^{9} 1463^{8} 2036^{6} 2471^{2} (2824) *(3074)* 3085^{2} *3232^{3} (3585)* 3867^{4} 4161^{2} 4466^{3} *4800^{5}* 4971^{27} **>76a 69f<**

Classic Beauty (IRE) 4 b f Fairy King (USA)-Working Model (Ile de Bourbon (USA)) 796^{3} *1086^{9}* **>50a 54f<**

Classic Cliche (IRE) 5 b h Salse (USA)-Pato (High Top) 1172^{9} 2055^{2} 3149^{2} (3883a) 4346a^{7} **>130f<**

Classic Colours (USA) 4 ch g Blushing John (USA)-All Agleam (USA) (Gleaming (USA)) 4714^{17} 4802^{11} 4991^{9} **>52f<**

Classic Daisy 4 b f Prince Sabo-Bloom of Youth (IRE) (Last Tycoon) **1996:** *5260^{12}* **1997:** *67^{12}* **>38a 43f<**

Classic Dame (FR) 4 gr f Highest Honor (FR)-Reem El Fala (FR) (Fabulous Dancer (USA)) 647^{16} 3640^{4} 3970^{11} *5019^{11}* **>69f<**

Classic Defence (IRE) 4 b g Cyrano de Bergerac-My Alanna (Dalsaan) 4477^{14} **>82?f<**

Classic Eagle 4 b g Unfuwain (USA)-La Lutine (My Swallow) *4572^{10}* 4854^{11} **>33a 66f<**

Classic Fan (USA) 3 b f Lear Fan (USA)-Miss Boniface (Tap On Wood) 3277^{8} 3501^{5} 3903^{2} 4336^{14} 4748^{6} **>53f<**

Classic Find (USA) 4 b br g Lear Fan (USA)-Reve de Reine (USA) (Lyphard (USA)) 680^{9} 962^{11} 1398^{6} 2122^{7} 2475^{3} 2867^{10} 4714^{15} 4926^{2} 4998^{3} **>74f<**

Classic Flyer (IRE) 4 b f Alzao (USA)-Sea Harrier (Grundy) 3100^{12} 3630^{3} 3906^{3} 4161^{3} 4405^{6} 4704^{9} **>78a 74df<**

Classic Form (IRE) 4 b f Alzao (USA)-Formulate (Reform) 2492^{14} *4571^{13}* **>49f<**

Classic Impact (IRE) 2 ch c Generous (IRE)-Vaison la Romaine (Arctic Tern (USA)) 4520^{5} 4715^{11} **>69f<**

Classic Jenny (IRE) 4 b f Green Desert (USA)-Eileen Jenny (IRE) (Kris) *511^{4}* 2008^{5} 4705^{4} 4920^{9} **>58a 69f<**

Classic Leader 4 b c Thatching-Tenderetta (Tender King) *514^{9} 661^{11}* 824^{11} 1139^{13} 1925^{2} 2157^{5} 2313^{15} **>54a 70f<**

Classic Line 3 b f Last Tycoon-Classic Beam (Cut Above) 1140^{5} (2154) 2498^{3} 3714^{5} 4269^{4} 4744^{4} 4956^{4} **>71f<**

Classic Manoeuvre (USA) 2 ch c Sky Classic (CAN)-Maid of Honor (USA) (Blushing Groom (FR)) 1872^{4} 2057^{4} 2482^{2} 3494^{7} **>81f<**

Classic Mystery (IRE) 3 ch g Classic Secret (USA)-Mystery Bid (Auction Ring (USA)) 478^{3} 700^{P} 1140^{17} **>20a 69?f<**

Classic Parisian (IRE) 4 b f Persian Bold-Gay France (FR) (Sir Gaylord) 1142^{7} 1278^{5} 2782^{10} **>73df<**

Classic Park 3 b f Robellino (USA)-Wanton (Kris) (806a) (1533a) 2025^{4} 3124^{5} 4129a^{5} 4864a^{10} **>119f<**

Classic Ribbon (IRE) 4 b f Persian Bold-House Tie (Be Friendly) 1297^{9} **>66f<**

Classic Romance 4 b f Cadeaux Genereux-What A Pity (Blakeney) **1996:** *5136^{5}* **>54a 54f<**

Classic Silver (IRE) 2 b c Silver Kite (USA)-Classic Ring (IRE) (Auction Ring (USA)) 1774^{5} 2739^{9} 3857^{6} 4595^{14} **>53f<**

Classic Victory 4 b g Puissance-Seattle Mama (USA) (Seattle Song (USA)) *411^{10}* 823^{13} **>26a 26f<**

Classy Chief 4 b g Be My Chief (USA)-Jalopy (Jalmood (USA)) *(73) 202^{6} 261^{3}* 607^{8} 4374^{P} **>62a 58f<**

Classy Cleo (IRE) 2 b f Mujadil (USA)-Sybaris (Crowned Prince (USA)) 447^{2} 500^{3} (572) (861) 1391^{3} 2103^{7} 2371^{2} 2919^{5} 3707^{17} (4014) 4411^{5} 4634^{3} 4737^{2} (4948) 4970^{2} 5045^{3} **>86f<**

Clean Swop (IRE) 3 b g Astronef-Sauvignon (IRE) (Alzao (USA)) 729^{8} 843^{11} **>6f<**

Clear Mandate (USA) 5 ch m Deputy Minister (CAN)-Dream Deal (USA) (Sharpen Up) *5062a^{6}* **>95a f<**

Clear The Air 3 ch f Salse (USA)-Belle Enfant (Beldale Flutter (USA)) 1094^{14} 1426^{6} **>44f<**

Clear View 2 b g Beveled (USA)-Scenic Villa (Top Ville) 1593^{10} 1812^{15} 3078^{3} 3451^{8} 3782^{9} **>48f<**

Clef of Silver 2 b c Indian Ridge-Susquehanna Days (USA) (Chief's Crown (USA)) 1932^{2} 2324^{2} 2926^{2} 3237^{2} (3564) **>85f<**

Clemency (IRE) 5 ch m Kefaah (USA)-Supreme Crown (USA) (Chief's Crown (USA)) *3608^{12}* 3814^{5} **>49?a 50f<**

Clerio 3 b f Soviet Star (USA)-Lady of the Sea (Mill Reef (USA)) (4094a) 4666a^{11} **>106f<**

Clerkenwell (USA) 4 b c Sadler's Wells (USA)-Forlene (Forli (ARG)) (3983) 4238^{5} **>121f<**

Clermont City (IRE) 2 b c Royal Academy (USA)-Diamond Spring (USA) (Vaguely Noble) 1873^{4} 2112^{5} 3019^{5} *(3395)* 3802^{15} 4576^{19} **>66a 63f<**

Clever Caption (IRE) 3 b c Topanoora-Fundraiser

(Welsh Saint) 941[3] **>111f<**
Clever Cliche 4 b c Danehill (USA)-Beacon Hill (Bustino) *(626a)* **>112a 107f<**
Cliburnel News (IRE) 7 b m Horage-Dublin Millennium (Dalsaan) 3694[9] 3992[10] (4171) **>55a 65f<**
Clifton Beat (USA) 6 b h Danzatore (CAN)-Amenity (FR) (Luthier) 1016[9] 1208[5] **>66f<**
Clifton Game 7 b g Mummy's Game-Brave Maiden (Three Legs) 640[4] **>49a 49f<**
Clifton Wood (IRE) 2 b c Paris House-Millie's Lady (IRE) (Common Grounds) 3806[17]
Clinking 6 b g Glint of Gold-Kai (Kalamoun) 4946[7] **>50f<**
Cloak of Darkness (IRE) 2 b c Thatching-Madame Nureyev (USA) (Nureyev (USA)) 4105[6] 4174[5] 4454[6] **>69f<**
Clodora (FR) 3 b f Linamix (FR)-Cloche D'Or (Good Times (ITY)) 3003a[2] (4666a) **>117f<**
Clonoe 3 b g Syrtos-Anytime Anywhere (Daring March) 4896[7] *5020[7]* **>33a 20f<**
Close Shave 2 b c Warning-La Barberina (USA) (Nijinsky (CAN)) 4105[4] 4852[3] **>80+f<**
Close Up (IRE) 2 ch c Cadeaux Genereux-Zoom Lens (IRE) (Caerleon (USA)) 2693[5] 3494[4] 4061[2] (4384) (4734) **>85f<**
Cloudberry 2 b f Night Shift (USA)-Chatterberry (Aragon) 682[7] 880[2] 2831[2] (2959) 3595[4] 4267[8] 4616a[2] 4890[10] **>81f<**
Cloud Castle 2 b f In The Wings-Lucayan Princess (High Line) 4775[3] **>80f<**
Cloudings (IRE) 3 b c Sadler's Wells (USA)-Ispahan (Rusticaro (FR)) (1205a) 1769[10] **>111f<**
Cloud Inspector (IRE) 6 b g Persian Bold-Timbale d'Argent (Petingo) 1585[2] 1871[2] 2475[2] 2589[3] (3122) (3884a) 4539a[2] 4783[27] **>103?f<**
Clouds Hill (FR) 4 b g Sarhoob (USA)-Dana Dana (FR) (Pharly (FR)) 986[10] 1459[13] 1985[4] 2246[6] 2552[5] 3115[2] 3153[8] 3496[13] 3849[2] 3980[5] 4243[2] **>63f<**
Clouds of Glory 2 b f Lycius (USA)-Dance a Jig (Dance In Time (CAN)) 3711[9] 4066[15] 4904[8] **>64f<**
Club Elite 5 b m Salse (USA)-Little Bittern (USA) (Riva Ridge (USA)) 1222[9] *1417[7] 1940[9]* 2518[9] **>26a 22f<**
Clued Up 4 b f Beveled (USA)-Scharade (Lombard (GER)) 574[6] 653[2] 721[5] (1040) 1233[3] 1422[6] 1748[S] *2302[11]* (2375) 2876[9] 3330[6] 4335[8] 4845[4] 4998[8] **>21a 59f<**
Clytha Hill Lad 6 b g Domitor (USA)-Quae Supra (On Your Mark) 1483[3] 1689[2] 2152[4] 2646[6] (2880) (3018) 3227[2] (3443) (3573) 3718[4] 4112[11] 4225[10] **>41a 62f<**
Coalminersdaughter (IRE) 2 b f Dynaformer (USA)-Sportin' Notion (USA) (Sportin' Life (USA)) 3187[8] 3638[8] 4575[8] **>61f<**
Coastal Bluff 5 gr g Standaan (FR)-Combattente (Reform) 2599[5] (3023) 3217[11] (3724) 4011[8] **>121f<**
Coastguards Hero 4 ch g Chilibang-Aldwick Colonnade (Kind of Hush) 1003[11] 1320[15] 1920[8] 2115[11] 2485[8] 2745[8] 3138[7] 3465[11] **>51a 48f<**
Coble 3 b c Slip Anchor-Main Sail (Blakeney) 683[8] 963[10] 1239[7] 2692[4] 2927[6] 3452[10] 3793[15] **>50f<**
Cochiti 3 b f Kris-Sweet Jaffa (Never so Bold) 524[9] 1221[11] 1497[9] 1863[7] *2068[8]* 3102[3] 3308[4] 3486[7] 4289[6] **>46f<**
Cockney Lad (IRE) 8 ch g Camden Town-Big Bugs Bomb (Skymaster) 4620a[17] **>86f<**
Cocksure (IRE) 2 b c Nomination-Hens Grove (Alias Smith (USA)) 1819[5] 2181[6] **>70f<**
Coded Message (IRE) 2 b g Deploy-Princess Carmen (IRE) (Arokar (FR)) 4793[9] **>46f<**
Code Red 4 b g Warning-For Action (USA) (Assert) **1996:** *5108[3] 5136[4] 5177[3] 5255[7]* **1997:** *78[6] 1964[7]* **>54a 72f<**
Cohiba 4 b g Old Vic-Circus Ring (High Top) *284[14] 369[8]* 435[16] 650[9] 763[10] *1133[7]* 1779[18] 2174[12] (2874) **>45a 48f<**
Coh Sho No 4 b f Old Vic-Castle Peak (Darshaan) **1996:** *5084[4] 5255[3] 5277[8]* **1997:** (603) 1114[4] 1974[3] 2198[7] 2932[4] 3203[U] 3826[5] 3928[3] 4170[2] 4405[3] 4609[9] **>62a 59f<**
Coincidence 3 ch f Niniski (USA)-Baino Fit (USA) (Fit To Fight (USA)) 875[10] **>14f<**
Cointosser (IRE) 4 b f Nordico (USA)-Sure Flyer (IRE) (Sure Blade (USA)) 2848[8] **>56a 72f<**
Cois Na Farraige (IRE) 4 b g Nashamaa-Persian Sparkler (Persian Bold) 430[19] 613[15] 955[12] 1281[9] 1601[6] 1618[3] 1840[5] 2208[4] 2661[3] 2825[8] 3223[6] 3485[9] 3626[7] 3919[10] 4692[8] **>30f<**
Colcon (USA) 4 b f Pleasant Colony (USA)-Continental Girl (USA) (Transworld (USA)) 4862a[3] **>105f<**
Cold Front 2 br c Polar Falcon (USA)-Chandni (IRE) (Ahonoora) 4915[6] **>72f<**
Cold Lazarus 3 br g Warning-Indian Pink (USA) (Seattle Slew (USA)) 1976[5] 2492[11] 3048[7] 3800[5] 4008[12] 4326[12] **>56df<**
Cold Steel 3 b c Warrshan (USA)-Rengaine (FR) (Music Boy) *(50) 420[7]* 1238[15] 2836[3] 3200[17] 3558[6] 3749[8] **>77?a 53f<**
Coleridge 9 gr g Bellypha-Quay Line (High Line) **1996:** *5084[2] 5116[2] 5213[6]* **1997:** *133[7] 205[3] 252[6] (324) 375[2] 381[3] 660[4]* 831[5] 1252[4] 1424[6] 1665[5] 1953[4] 2932[6] **>65a 47f<**
Colins Choice 3 ch f Risk Me (FR)-Give Me a Day (Lucky Wednesday) **1996:** *5103[2] 5142[3]* **1997:** 2201[11] *2671[9] (3041) 3608[4] (4480) 4813[10]* **>58a 41f<**
Collacar 2 b c Man Among Men (IRE)-Safety First (Wassl) 684[10] 1298[6] 1581[7] *1941[14] 2051[5]* **>43a 39f<**
College Clipper 2 b c Sizzling Melody-Mawaddah (USA) (Topsider (USA)) 1492[18]
College Mount 2 b c Merdon Melody-Young Whip (Bold Owl) 4433[12] 4793[14] **>29f<**
College Night (IRE) 5 b m Night Shift (USA)-Gertrude Lawrence (Ballymore) 473[3] 585[15] (1012) 1131[5] 1374[4] 1479[6] 2665[6] 2788[6] **>43f<**
College Princess 3 b f Anshan-Tinkers Fairy (Myjinski (USA)) **1996:** *5080[7]* **1997:** *345[3] 399[7]* 602[9] 1566[4] 1995[2] 2354[3] (2883) 3083[5] 3323[3] 4168[13] 4527[10] **>52a 53f<**
College Rose 2 b f Prince Sabo-Tinkers Fairy (Myjinski (USA)) 2917[13] 4630[11] **>34f<**
Colleville 2 gr f Pharly (FR)-Kibitka (FR) (Baby Turk) 2953[8] (3450) 3912[3] 4245[3] **>86f<**
Collier Bay 7 b g Green Desert (USA)-Cockatoo Island (High Top) 498[4] **>85?f<**
Colonel Custer 2 ch c Komaite (USA)-Mohican (Great Nephew) 2467[9] *(2604)* 3650[13] **>76a 33f<**
Colonel's Pride 3 ch g Superpower-Yankeedoodledancer (Mashhor Dancer (USA)) 1226[8] 1496[15] 2002[11] 2313[21] 2891[10] 3121[9] 3606[9] *4300[10]* 4431[7] **>10a 39f<**
Colosse 5 b m Reprimand-French Cutie (USA) (Vaguely Noble) **1996:** *5189[6] 5240[2] 5270[8]* **1997:** *104[8] 236[2] 302[2]* **>55a 50f<**
Colour Code 5 ch g Polish Precedent (USA)-Reprocolor (Jimmy Reppin) 1230[2] 1558[2] 2315[3] 2867[4] 3705[U] 4639[8] **>88f<**
Colour Counsellor 4 gr g Touch of Grey-Bourton Downs (Philip of Spain) *13[4] 106[10]* 640[5] 1010[8] 1641[2] 2318[3] 3080[5] 3229[3] (3297) 3588[6] 3971[3] 4504[9] *4912[5]* **>40a 50f<**
Colour Key (USA) 3 b g Red Ransom (USA)-Trend (USA) (Ray's Word (USA)) 1409[10] 2126[10] **>65f<**
Colours To Gold (IRE) 2 ch f Rainbows For Life (CAN)-Brave Ivy (Decoy Boy) (1228) 2439a[10] **>67+f<**
Colston-C 5 gr g Belfort (FR)-Grand Occasion (Great Nephew) **1996:** *5188[3] 5280[7]* **1997:** *20[11]* 4844[18] **>56a 44f<**
Columella (ITY) 3 b c Law Society (USA)-Canadian Guest (Be My Guest (USA)) **1996:** 5263a[3]
Colway Ritz 3 b g Rudimentary (USA)-Million Heiress (Auction Ring (USA)) 453[5] 636[5] 792[2] 1170[17] 2567[3] 2857[10] 3443[3] 3812[6] 4270[17] 4417[3] (4877) 4958[14] **>75f<**
Comanche Companion 7 b m Commanche Run-Constant Companion (Pas de Seul) 2485[7] (2730) 2918[3] 3254[2] 3435[5] 3982[7] 4262a[3] 4441[15] 4757[2] **>66a 72f<**
Come Dancing 3 b f Suave Dancer (USA)-Cominna (Dominion) **1996:** *5080[8]* **1997:** *19[7] 97[4]* 1000[15] **>25a 49f<**
Comedy River 10 br g Comedy Star (USA)-Hopeful Waters (Forlorn River) **1996:** *5118[3]* **1997:** 1093[18] **>56?a 56?f< (DEAD)**
Comeonup 6 b g Most Welcome-Scarlet Veil (Tyrnavos) **1996:** *5137[7]* **>26a 41f<**
Come Together 3 b f Mtoto-Pfalz (Pharly (FR)) 886[13] (2487) 3390[3] 4242[12] 4731[6] 4918[10] **>68f<**
Come Too Mamma's 3 ch f La Grange Music-Purchased by Phone (IRE) (Wolverlife) **1996:** *5092[8]* **1997:** *75[2] 102[8] 158[5]* 756[8] *1428[11]* **>60da 58f<**
Comic's Future (USA) 4 b c Carnivalay (USA)-Destiny's Hour (USA) (Fit To Fight (USA)) 1230[15] 1615[7] 2539[9] **>12f<**
Commander Charlie 2 ch c Alnasr Alwasheek-Bentinck Hotel (Red God) 1872[5] 2286[2] (2768) 3186[6] **>80f<**
Commin' Up 4 b f Primo Dominie-Ridalia (Ridan (USA)) **1996:** *5122[6] 5223[8]* **1997:** *143[4] 273[8] 870[4] 1132[4]* 1467[18] 2488[18] *2602[10]* **>53da 47f<**
Common Rock (IRE) 3 b f Common Grounds-Quatre Femme (Petorius) *168[11]* **>46a f<**
Common View (IRE) 2 b g Scenic-Stony Ground (Relko) 4165[13] 4384[10] 4507[6] 4793[13] **>65f<**
Compact Disc (IRE) 3 b f Royal Academy (USA)-Sharp Circle (IRE) (Sure Blade (USA)) **1996:** *(5135) 5160[4] 5180[11]* **1997:** *8[8]* **>58da 58f<**
Companys Gamble 2 b f Barrys Gamble-Pleasant Company (Alzao (USA)) 572[9] 780[8] 1019[9] **>32f<**
Compassionate 2 b g Seymour Hicks (FR)-Snow Child (Mandrake Major) 4627[7] 4698[9] 4914[13] **>57f<**
Compass Pointer 4 gr c Mazilier (USA)-Woodleys (Tyrnavos) **1996:** *(5136) 5213[U]* **1997:** *360[10]* 613[7] 1408[6] 1636[7] 2316[3] (2411) **>69a 61f<**
Compatibility (IRE) 3 b c Common Grounds-Nikki's Groom (Shy Groom (USA)) 446[5] 784[3] 1587[5] (2234) 2517[3] 3145[5] 3798[5] 4175[8] 4583[12] **>79f<**
Composition 2 ch f Wolfhound (USA)-Tricky Note (Song) 682[6] 999[3] 1927[3] (2565) 3237[12] 4634[10] **>83f<**
Compradore 2 b f Mujtahid (USA)-Keswa (Kings Lake (USA)) 1163[2] (1486) 2024[9] 3192[12] **>76f<**
Compromise (IRE) 3 b c Soviet Star (USA)-Lower The Tone (USA) (Master Willie) 503[4] 983[5] (1423) 1813[3] 2340[12] **>88f<**
Compton Place 3 ch c Indian Ridge-Nosey (Nebbiolo) 1590[2] 2106[12] (2599) 3724[14] **>128f<**
Comtec's Legend 7 ch m Legend of France (USA)-Comtec Princess (Gulf Pearl) *3074[10]* 3297[6] 3562[2] 3700[2] **>36a 39f<**
Concepcion (GER) 7 br h Acatenango (GER)-

Comprida (GER) (Windwurf (GER)) 4399a^{3} **>119f<**
Concer Arall 3 ch g Ron's Victory (USA)-Drudwen (Sayf El Arab (USA)) *588^{4} 874^{8} 4980^{3}* **>50a f<**
Concer Un 5 ch g Lord Bud-Drudwen (Sayf El Arab (USA)) 677^{5} 987^{9} 1160^{8} 1456^{9} *2161^{5}* 2598^{13} 2766^{13} 3198^{6} (3725) 3888^{2} 4314^{4} 4550^{7} 4893^{10} **>81a 100f<**
Condition Red 4 b f Sayf El Arab (USA)-Forever Mary (Red Alert) **1996:** *5267^{9}* **1997:** *387^{7}* **>11a 18f<**
Conectis (IRE) 2 b f River Falls-Christle Mill (Pas de Seul) 472^{2} 648^{5} 893^{2} 1735^{6} 2037^{2} (2286) 2558^{5} 3961a^{6} 4267^{10} **>88?f<**
Coneybury (IRE) 7 b h Last Tycoon-Jackie Berry (Connaught) 3885a^{2} **>113?f<**
Confidante (USA) 2 b f Dayjur (USA)-Won't She Tell (USA) (Banner Sport (USA)) 4907^{3} **>76+f<**
Confide (USA) 3 *5061a^{5}* **>118a f<**
Confirmation 2 b c Polar Falcon (USA)-Blessed Event (Kings Lake (USA)) 3235^{10} *(4056)* (4266) 4364^{3} 4803^{5} **>98+a 104f<**
Confronter 8 ch g Bluebird (USA)-Grace Darling (USA) (Vaguely Noble) 149a^{2} 189a^{7} 269a^{12} 755^{7} 1005^{10} 1320^{7} 1640^{4} (1955) 2201^{8} 2743^{4} 3115^{6} 3768^{6} 3980^{13} **>53a 63f<**
Conical 2 b f Zafonic (USA)-De Stael (USA) (Nijinsky (CAN)) 4520^{7} **>60f<**
Conic Hill (IRE) 6 ch g Lomond (USA)-Krisalya (Kris) 1384^{14} 1845^{8} 3627^{16} 4504^{12} **>51a 24f<**
Connemara (IRE) 3 b f Mujadil (USA)-Beechwood (USA) (Blushing Groom (FR)) 672^{7} 941^{12} 1112^{4} 1403^{3} 1609^{2} 2056^{12} 2677^{3} 3111^{13} 3747^{10} 4062^{5} 4226^{6} **>97df<**
Connoisseur Bay (USA) 2 b c Nureyev (USA)-Feminine Wiles (IRE) (Ahonoora) 4526^{2} **>93f<**
Conon Falls (IRE) 3 b c Sadler's Wells (USA)-Cocotte (Troy) (1014) 1307^{4} 2135^{3} 2642a^{12} 3634^{3} 4272^{3} **>109f<**
Considerable Charm 5 ch m Charmer-Leap in Time (Dance In Time (CAN)) **1996:** *5222^{13}* **>36a 36f<**
Consort 4 b c Groom Dancer (USA)-Darnelle (Shirley Heights) 2894^{4} 3615^{4} 4441^{2} 4757^{3} 4893^{12} (4978) **>95f<**
Conspicuous (IRE) 7 b g Alzao (USA)-Mystery Lady (USA) (Vaguely Noble) 1308^{9} 1768^{4} 2136^{2} 2528^{10} 3112^{14} (3712) 4141^{17} 4577^{5} (4882) **>60+a 97f<**
Conspiracy 3 b f Rudimentary (USA)-Roussalka (Habitat) 1112^{6} 1610^{6} 2561^{9} 3199^{2} 3765^{16} **>92f<**
Constant Attention 2 ch f Royal Academy (USA)-Impudent Miss (Persian Bold) 2519^{2} 2943^{13} 3295^{6} 3707^{12} 4058^{2} 4366^{2} 4473^{4} **>74f<**
Contentment (IRE) 3 b c Fairy King (USA)-Quality Of Life (Auction Ring (USA)) 509^{9} 723^{9} 1637^{5} (2005) 2328^{10} 2855^{4} 3551^{3} 4141^{18} 4386^{8} **>80f<**
Context 2 ch f Zafonic (USA)-Twixt (Kings Lake (USA)) 2996b^{2}
Contract Bridge (IRE) 4 b f Contract Law (USA)-Mystery Bid (Auction Ring (USA)) 1435^{8} 1779^{20} 3015^{11} 3714^{12} 3792^{10} 3971^{14} **>29a 36f<**
Contrafire (IRE) 5 b g Contract Law (USA)-Fiery Song (Ballad Rock) 746^{8} 1118^{6} **>76a 65f<**
Contrarie 4 b f Floose-Chanita (Averof) 481^{11} 1100^{2} 1232^{7} 1795^{8} 2411^{5} 2511^{2} (4633) 4744^{3} **>11a 55f<**
Contrary Mary 2 b f Mujadil (USA)-Love Street (Mummy's Pet) 1109^{2} (1593) 2103^{10} 3595^{5} 3925^{4} 4755^{7} **>82+f<**
Contravene (IRE) 3 b f Contract Law (USA)-Vieux Carre (Pas de Seul) *110^{5} 259^{5} 300^{5} 317^{4} 399^{6}* **>42a 66f<**
Control Freak 3 b f Inca Chief (USA)-Forest Nymph (Native Bazaar) 484^{7} 582^{13} **>35f<**
Conwy 4 ch f Rock City-Degannwy (Caerleon (USA)) **1996:** *5137^{4} 5233^{10}* **>34a 53f<**
Cool Affair (IRE) 2 ch g Statoblest-Ukraine's Affair (USA) (The Minstrel (CAN)) 4801^{13} 4901^{12} **>2f<**
Cool Edge (IRE) 6 ch g Nashamaa-Mochara (Last Fandango) (713a) 2078a^{2} 3674a^{4} 4344a^{6} 4888^{5} **>114f<**
Cool Fire 4 b c Colmore Row-Into the Fire (Dominion) **1996:** *5120^{8}* **>73a 56f<**
Cool Grey 3 gr f Absalom-Crisp Air (Elegant Air) **1996:** *5135^{3} 5202^{4}* **1997:** 2662^{8} **>54a 31f<**
Coolin River (IRE) 2 b c River Falls-The Coolin (Don) 1812^{5} 2571^{4} 3127^{7} 4006^{6} 4545^{11} **>65f<**
Cool Luke (IRE) 8 b g Red Sunset-Watet Khet (FR) (Wittgenstein (USA)) 781^{10} **>74?f<**
Cool Mystery 2 ro c Mystiko (USA)-Romantic Saga (Prince Tenderfoot (USA)) 2477^{12} 3407^{4} 3905^{10} 4152^{10} 4419^{7} **>62f<**
Cool Prospect 2 b c Mon Tresor-I Ran Lovely (Persian Bold) 3060^{5} 3306^{3} 3821^{2} 4921^{8} 5045^{10} **>71f<**
Cool Secret 2 gr c Petong-Cool Run (Deep Run) 861^{7} 2500^{6} 2893^{4} 3258^{5} (3438) 3650^{14} 4411^{4} 4670^{8} **>80f<**
Cool Spray (USA) 2 b f Hansel (USA)-Kissogram Girl (USA) (Danzig (USA)) 4715^{15} **>33f<**
Cool Waters 2 b f Puissance-Keep Cool (FR) (Northern Treat (USA)) 4604^{14} 4907^{10} **>18f<**
Copenhagen 3 b f Midyan (USA)-Crymlyn (Welsh Pageant) 3206^{10} 4221^{19} 4816^{14} **>14f<**
Copernicus 2 b c Polish Precedent (USA)-Oxslip (Owen Dudley) 4064^{5} *4299^{2}* **>75a 71f<**
Copperbeech (IRE) 3 ch f Common Grounds-Caimanite (Tap On Wood) *5022^{14}* **>68f<**
Copper Shell 3 ch g Beveled (USA)-Luly My Love (Hello Gorgeous (USA)) 875^{4} 1144^{7} 1434^{11} 4222^{9} 4562^{14} **>71f<**
Coral Island 3 b g Charmer-Misowni (Niniski (USA)) (1513) 1796^{12} 2158^{6} 2757^{8} 3196^{5} 3336^{8} **>55f<**
Coral Strand 3 ch f Indian Ridge-Sea Venture (FR) (Diatome) 998^{10} 1651^{4} **>51f<**
Cordate (IRE) 3 b f Lahib (USA)-La Romance (USA) (Lyphard (USA)) 1415^{5} 1823^{4} 2184^{3} **>75f<**
Coretta (IRE) 3 b f Caerleon (USA)-Free At Last (Shirley Heights) 1682^{2} 2315^{4} (3453) 3803^{3} 4445^{3} **>103f<**
Corinchili 3 ch f Chilibang-Corinthia (USA) (Empery (USA)) 531^{4} 584^{7} *871^{4} 1046^{3} 1428^{5}* 1730^{7} *2305^{5}* **>61a 55f<**
Corniche (IRE) 2 b br c Marju (IRE)-Far But Near (USA) (Far North (CAN)) 4278^{2} 4460^{2} (4740) **>85f<**
Corniche Quest (IRE) 4 b f Salt Dome (USA)-Angel Divine (Ahonoora) 883^{3} 956^{2} (1080) (1385) 1584^{9} 1613^{10} 1816^{5} 2001^{4} 2244^{6} 2751^{2} 2958^{3} 3290^{4} (3625) 3642^{6} 3898^{6} 3984^{7} 4385^{9} 4456^{6} 4733^{7} 4805^{6} 4905^{6} *5021^{8}* **>28a 69f<**
Corona Lake (USA) 3 f b Storm Cat (USA)-Aziyah (USA) (Alleged (USA)) 5056a^{2} **>113f<**
Corporal Nym (USA) 4 gr g Cozzene (USA)-Fiji Fan (USA) (Danzig (USA)) 4518^{12} 4628^{13} **>49f<**
Corporate Image 7 ch g Executive Man-Robis (Roan Rocket) 4547^{6} 4743^{8} **>57f<**
Corpus Christi (IRE) 2 b g Royal Academy (USA)-Christi Dawn (USA) (Grey Dawn II) 4508^{9} 4735^{13} 4993^{7} **>62f<**
Corradini 5 b h Rainbow Quest (USA)-Cruising Height (Shirley Heights) 761^{4} 1454^{4} (2837) 3149^{10} 3645^{6} **>119df<**
Corsecan 2 ch g Phountzi (USA)-Sagareina (Sagaro) 1235^{5} 2534^{11} 2784^{3} 3556^{6} 3859^{10} 4178^{11} 4819^{5} **>36a 60f<**
Cortachy Castle (IRE) 2 ch c Pips Pride-Maricica (Ahonoora) 1486^{4} (1791) 2103^{2} 2639a^{2} 3148^{6} 4911^{6} **>102f<**
Cortona (IRE) 2 b f Caerleon (USA)-Olbia (Mill Reef (USA)) 4250a^{3}
Coscoroba (IRE) 3 ch f Shalford (IRE)-Tameeza (USA) (Shahrastani (USA)) *546^{W} 907^{3}* 1077^{2} **>40a 59f<**
Cosmic Case 2 b f Casteddu-La Fontainova (IRE) (Lafontaine (USA)) 948^{6} 1038^{6} 2168^{6} 2827^{3} 3062^{6} 3226^{4} 3438^{7} 3699^{3} 4284^{3} 4468^{10} 4922^{10} **>62f<**
Cosmic Countess (IRE) 2 b f Lahib (USA)-Windmill Princess (Gorytus (USA)) 2597^{8} 3187^{5} 3799^{3} 4068^{4} (4446) **>72f<**
Cosmic Prince (IRE) 3 b c Teenoso (USA)-Windmill Princess (Gorytus (USA)) 654^{3} 1170^{W} (1737) 2766^{9} 3150^{W} 3423^{10} 4153^{W} 4423^{21} **>95?f<**
Cossack Count 4 ch c Nashwan (USA)-Russian Countess (USA) (Nureyev (USA)) 4561^{19} 4787^{21} **>89f<**
Cottage Prince (IRE) 4 b g Classic Secret (USA)-Susan's Blues (Cure The Blues (USA)) 574^{18} (898) 1118^{9} (1732) 1844^{12} 2154^{12} **>25a 55f<**
Cotteir Chief (IRE) 6 b g Chief Singer-Hasty Key (USA) (Key To The Mint (USA)) *591^{5}* 1261^{10} **>103a 107?f<**
Couchant (IRE) 6 b g Petoski-Be Easy (Be Friendly) 1424^{12} **>55?f<**
Counsel 2 ch c Most Welcome-My Polished Corner (IRE) (Tate Gallery (USA)) 938^{7} 3927^{5} 4165^{14} 4501^{2} 4767^{17} 4856^{7} **>60f<**
Counterplot (IRE) 3 f 815a^{13} **>75f<**
Countess Diana (USA) 2 fDeerhound(USA)-T V Countess (USA) T V Commercial (USA) *(5060a)*
Count Keni 2 ch g Formidable (USA)-Flying Amy (Norwick (USA)) 3117^{16} 3760^{7} 3973^{15} **>46f<**
Countless Times 3 ch g Timeless Times (USA)-Arroganza (Crofthall) **1996:** *5202^{9} 5251^{3} 5279^{2}* **1997:** *25^{7} (118) (132) 227^{4} 307^{5}* 3614^{10} 4059^{20} *4570^{9}* **>67a 50?f<**
Country Garden 2 b f Selkirk (USA)-Totham (Shernazar) 1109^{3} 1569^{3} 1760^{2} (2719) (3186) 3802^{4} **>77f<**
Country Thatch 4 b g Thatching-Alencon (Northfields (USA)) 476^{7} 1273^{16} 1632^{13} 1825^{12} 2577^{3} (3293) 3640^{3} 4371^{12} 4667^{7} **>51f<**
Count Tony 3 ch g Keen-Turtle Dove (Gyr (USA)) (537) 826^{5} 976^{4} 1371^{10} *2668^{2}* 3200^{12} (3721) **>71a 71f<**
Courageous (IRE) 2 ch c Generous (IRE)-Legend of Arabia (Great Nephew) 4668^{4} 4952^{3} **>84tf<**
Courageous Knight 8 gr g Midyan (USA)-Little Mercy (No Mercy) 838^{12} 1632^{10} 1825^{2} 2218^{3} 2696^{5} 3015^{12} 3203^{3} 3475^{6} 3714^{9} **>64da 49f<**
Courage Under Fire 2 b g Risk Me (FR)-Dreamtime Quest (Blakeney) 4815^{6} **>51f<**
Courbaril 5 b g Warrshan (USA)-Free on Board (Free State) 3203^{6} 3714^{6} 3896^{2} **>60a 66f<**
Course Fishing 6 ch g Squill (USA)-Migoletty (Oats) 1732^{3} *2164^{7}* 2843^{7} 3272^{4} 3931^{6} 4170^{13} 4432^{5} 4633^{2} **>17?a 43f<**
Courteous 2 b c Generous (IRE)-Dayanata (Shirley Heights) 3789^{4} (4520) **>84f<**
Court Express 3 b g Then Again-Moon Risk (Risk Me (FR)) 1096^{12} 1470^{9} (1864) (2206) 2505^{2} 4225^{9} 4924^{20} **>74f<**
Court House 3 b g Reprimand-Chalet Girl (Double Form) 1807^{10} (1998) 3320^{7} 4324^{15} 4586^{4} 4872^{16} 4951^{15} **>44a 65f<**
Courting Danger 4 b g Tina's Pet-Court Town (Camden Town) 895^{27} 1139^{12} **>28f<**
Courting Newmarket 9 b g Final Straw-Warm Wind (Tumble Wind (USA))653^{14} 1003^{13} **>57a 47df<**

Court Lane (USA) 2 b f Machiavellian (USA)-Chicarica (USA) (The Minstrel (CAN)) 4556^3 (4688) 4892^7 **>82f<**
Courtly Times 2 ch f Machiavellian (USA)-Dancing Moon (IRE) (Dancing Brave (USA)) 2948^4 **>65f<**
Court Minstrel 8 br g Hadeer-Sheer Bliss (St Paddy) 2395^{10} **>63?f<**
Court Nap (IRE) 5 ch g Waajib-Mirhar (FR) (Sharpen Up) *29^3* **>58a 64f<**
Courtney Gym (IRE) 2 ch c Shalford (IRE)-Fair Or Foul (Patch) 1635^{11} 1812^{23} 3090^2 3312^2 4819^{10} **>65f<**
Court Shareef 2 b c Shareef Dancer (USA)-Fairfields Cone (Celtic Cone) 2556^9 **>47f<**
Courtship 3 b c Groom Dancer (USA)-Dance Quest (FR) (Green Dancer (USA)) 646^5 776^2 2137^6 2601^{14} **>93f<**
Cowtharee 3 ch f Arazi (USA)-Hawait Al Barr (Green Desert (USA)) 875^7 **>62f<**
Crackerbox 3 b f Lochnager-Festival Flame (Blakeney) *204^4 361^5 874^4* 1388^{15} 1500^5 1690^6 1966^8 *2300^9* 2554^{16} **>44da 40f<**
Crafty Friend (USA) 4 *5061a^{12}* **>82a f<**
Crafty Pet (IRE) 2 ch f Petardia-Frans Cap (Captain James) 743^7 1280^3 1990^4 3106^{16} 3480^6 **>52f<**
Cragreen 2 b f Green Desert (USA)-Croda Alta (Caro) 4534a^2
Craigary 6 b g Dunbeath (USA)-Velvet Pearl (Record Token) 1229^8 1570^8 2386^4 2564^4 3223^3 3486^2 (3919) 4466^9 4692^{10} **>47f<**
Craigie Boy 7 b g Crofthall-Lady Carol (Lord Gayle (USA)) **1996:** *5134^6 5165^7 5258^2* **1997:** *40^3 69^8 113^8 233^4 332^8* 527^{11} 1315^{14} 1613^2 *1944^{15}* 2033^9 2384^9 2497^8 **>36a 48df<**
Craigievar 3 b c Mujadil (USA)-Sweet Home (Home Guard (USA)) 449^3 (981) 1719a^4 2273a^8 4153^8 **>106f<**
Craignairn 4 b g Merdon Melody-Bri-Ette (Brittany) **1996:** *5258^9* **>50f<**
Craigsteel 2 b c Suave Dancer (USA)-Applecross (Glint of Gold) 1933^2 (2556) 4440^6 4889^4 **>104f<**
Craven Hill (IRE) 3 gr g Pursuit of Love-Crodelle (IRE) (Formidable (USA)) 645^{13} 1105^{13} 2171^{16} **>30f<**
Crazee Mental 2 b f Magic Ring (IRE)-Corn Futures (Nomination) 1228^3 (1839) 2024^2 2558^2 4475^2 **>99f<**
Crazy Chief 4 b c Indian Ridge-Bizarre Lady (Dalsaan) 4893^4 **>85f<**
Credit Call (IRE) 9 br g Rhoman Rule (USA)-Maiacourt (Malacate (USA)) *68^{16}*
Credite Risque 4 b f Risk Me (FR)-Lompoa (Lomond (USA)) 759^{18} 887^{15} **>43f<**
Credit Squeeze 7 ch g Superlative-Money Supply (Brigadier Gerard) 1592^7 2198^{10} (2696) 3475^9 **>74a 69f<**
Crees Sqaw 5 b m Cree Song-Elsocko (Swing Easy (USA)) *4049^{12}* 4214^8 **>36a 60?f<**
Crescent's Whisper (IRE) 3 gr c Shalford (IRE)-Checkers (Habat) 1297^{15} 1409^7 1688^4 **>60f<**
Crest Wing (USA) 4 b g Storm Bird (CAN)-Purify (USA) (Fappiano (USA)) 1636^{15} **>52f<**
Cretan Gift 6 ch g Cadeaux Genereux-Caro's Niece (USA) (Caro) **1996:** *5203^5* **1997:** *(357) 397^2* 443^8 573^2 745^2 892^{11} 1148^6 2105^{12} (2326) 2598^5 2861^4 3252^4 (3535a) 4282^{20} 4421^{10} 4777^5 *4983^3* 5054^6 **>103a 111f<**
Crimson Tide (IRE) 3 b c Sadler's Wells (USA)-Sharata (IRE) (Darshaan) 691^3 1159^9 3499^3 4003^3 4272^2 (4463) (4762a) **>115f<**
Crissem (IRE) 4 b f Thatching-Deer Emily (Alzao (USA)) 749^{15} 1816^7 2204^5 2422^5 2788^{13} 3573^{14} 3936^8 4291^4 4695^{17} **>57f<**
Critical Air 2 b g Reprimand-Area Girl (Jareer (USA)) 3926^{10} 4402^8 *4569^6* 4819^4 **>72a 54f<**
Croa (IRE) 4 b f Alzao (USA)-Crodas (Shirley Heights) (1369a) **>68f<**
Croagh Patrick 5 b g Faustus (USA)-Pink Pumpkin (Tickled Pink) **1996:** *5237^{12}* **1997:** 964^7 **>5a 44f<**
Croco Rouge (IRE) 2 5034a^4 **>96f<**
Croeso Cynnes 4 ch f Most Welcome-Miss Taleca (Pharly (FR)) 1089^8 3251^7 3580^9 3910^{18} 4048^{17} 4169^{17} *4574^6* **>39a 46f<**
Crofters Ceilidh 5 ch m Scottish Reel-Highland Rowena (Royben) 1608^4 1946^2 2299^5 2675^2 3011^8 3410^{11} 3600^6 4062^2 4457^2 4756^4 4954^3 **>100f<**
Crofters Edge 2 ch c Beveled (USA)-Zamindara (Crofter (USA)) 4564^{14} 5042^{15} **>49f<**
Croft Pool 6 b g Crofthall-Blackpool Belle (The Brianstan) (1455) 2106^9 3001a^7 3111^{14} 3724^{11} 4098^9 4239^4 4525^4 4677^9 4777^{13} **>84a 116f<**
Croft Sands 4 ch g Crofthall-Sannavally (Sagaro) 4070^{14} 4506^5 4990^{11} **>40f<**
Cromer Pier 2 b c Reprimand-Fleur du Val (Valiyar) 4526^{18} **>54f<**
Crompton Lights 3 br c Sylvan Express-Ela-Yianni-Mou (Anfield) 2172^9 2410^9 2731^{15} **>49f<**
Crosby Don 2 b c Alhijaz-Evening Star (Red Sunset) 2112^6 2499^5 3780^5 **>38f<**
Crosby Nod 3 b g Shalford (IRE)-Kirkby Belle (Bay Express) 462^5 1998^{12} 2171^{17} **>54f<**
Cross of Valour 4 b g Never so Bold-X-Data (On Your Mark) **1996:** *5234^{13}* **1997:** *175^6* 1220^{14} 2121^W 2337^5 2428^9 **>26a 23f<**
Cross Talk (IRE) 5 b g Darshaan-Liaison (USA) (Blushing Groom (FR)) **1996:** *5177^4 5244^6* **1997:** *13^7 261^6* **>45a 68f<**
Cross The Border 4 b g Statoblest-Brave Advance (USA) (Bold Laddie (USA)) 464^{13} 585^{18} 744^9 1311^6 2480^7 2717^2 (2759) (2934) 3637^6 (3756) (3761) 3795^3 (3871) 4137^3 4183^6 4805^{12} **>84f< (DEAD)**
Crowded Avenue 5 b g Sizzling Melody-Lady Bequick (Sharpen Up) 877^5 1309^3 1721a^6 1975^2 2675^{10} 3111^8 3410^{12} 4444^2 4887^5 **>106f<**
Crown Attorney (USA) 4 b/c Silver Deputy (CAN)-Key To Khartoum (CAN) (Key to the Moon (CAN)) 4394a^3 **>127f<**
Crown Court (USA) 4 b c Chief's Crown (USA)-Bold Courtesan (USA) (Bold Bidder) 1085^2 2026^2 2598^9 **>102f<**
Crown of Light 3 b f Mtoto-Russian Countess (USA) (Nureyev (USA)) 959^4 (1102) 1738^3 2053^3 3704^3 4099^6 **>119df<**
Crown of Thorns (USA) 3 b g Diesis-Mystery Play (IRE) (Sadler's Wells (USA)) 2492^5 (2960) **>84f<**
Crown Point 2 gr f Mystiko (USA)-Milne's Way (The Noble Player (USA)) 1538a^5 **>71f<**
Crown Regent (IRE) 3 b c Fairy King (USA)-Sronica (Midsummer Night II) 2078a^3 **>109f<**
Cruinn A Bhord 2 b f Inchinor-Selection Board (Welsh Pageant) 4973^5 **>77f<**
Crumpton Hill (IRE) 5 b g Thatching-Senane (Vitiges (FR)) 892^{16} 1456^4 2026^8 2598^{10} 3150^2 3725^5 4423^3 **>104f<**
Cruz Santa 4 b f Lord Bud-Linpac Mapleleaf (Dominion) 1390^{10} 1818^4 *2602^6* **>31a 52f<**
Cryhavoc 3 b c Polar Falcon (USA)-Sarabah (IRE) (Ela-Mana-Mou) 968^2 1551a^4 2023^{18} 3764^5 4155^{23} **>98f<**
Crystal Craze 2 b f Warrshan (USA)-Single Gal (Mansingh (USA)) 4801^{12} **>9f<**
Crystal Crossing (IRE) 3 b f Royal Academy (USA)-Never so Fair (Never so Bold) 1610^7 **>102+f<**
Crystal Falls (IRE) 4 b r Alzao (USA)-Honourable Sheba (USA) (Roberto (USA)) 2015^5 2236^7 **>83f<**
Crystal Gold 3 ch g Arazi (USA)-Crystal Land (Kris) 599^2 795^2 *(1123)* 1773^2 2155^9 **>96a 94f<**
Crystal Hearted 3 b c Broken Hearted-Crystal Fountain (Great Nephew) 508^5 646^2 (1032) 1769^{12} (2901) 3730a^2 (4396a) **>112f<**
Crystal Heights (FR) 9 ch g Crystal Glitters (USA)-Fahrenheit (Mount Hagen (FR)) 444^{23} 643^6 879^7 1374^{12} 2745^7 2954^2 3249^8 3417^3 3561^5 *4570^{11}* **>75a 65f<**
Crystal Hills (IRE) 3 b g Darshaan-Lustre (USA) (Halo (USA)) 2410^{10} 2692^2 2963^{11} 3412^9 (4547) 4749^5 **>81f<**
Crystal Lough (IRE) 2 b f Maelstrom Lake-Holy Water (Monseigneur (USA)) 4428^{10} 4630^{16} 4921^{15} **>36f<**
Crystal Waters (IRE) 2 b f River Falls-Annie's Glen (IRE) (Glenstal (USA)) 4159^{10} 4627^{11} **>40f<**
Cuban Nights (USA) 5 b g Our Native (USA)-Havana Moon (USA) (Cox's Ridge (USA)) *660^2* 769^3 *1288^3 1579^2 1755^3 2048^4* **>68da 62f< (DEAD)**
Cuban Reef 5 b m Dowsing (USA)-Cox's Pippin (USA) (Cox's Ridge (USA)) *141^6 295^8* 574^{13} 1024^4 (1233) 1748^2 1926^2 2550^4 2782^6 3200^6 3330^2 **>32a 55f<**
Cue Man (IRE) 2 b c Dancing Dissident (USA)-Albona (Neltino) 1492^{17} **>19f<**
Cuesta Rey (USA) 3 ch g Lord At War (ARG)-Ms Hobby (USA) (Northern Prospect (USA)) 3775^9 4009^5 4316^7 *4591^8* 4877^{22} **>52a 66f<**
Cuff Link (IRE) 7 ch g Caerleon (USA)-Corinth Canal (Troy) 2108^4 2709^3 3255^3 4123a^3 4241^4 **>111?f<**
Cugina 3 b f Distant Relative-Indubitable (Sharpo) 1437^2 (2380) (3916) 4110^2 4678^2 **>98f<**
Cuillin Caper 5 b m Scottish Reel-That Space (Space King) 2207^{10} **>17f<**
Culcraggie 2 b c Weldnaas (USA)-Strathrusdale (Blazing Saddles (AUS)) 4706^4 5029^6 **>82?f<**
Culrain 6 b g Hadeer-La Vie En Primrose (Henbit (USA)) *356^5* **>36a 36f<**
Culsyth Flyer 6 b g Nomination-Polly Worth (Wolver Hollow) 1676^7 2002^{15} **>19a 55f<**
Cultural Role 2 ch f Night Shift (USA)-Bright Spells (Salse (USA)) 4093a^{11} **>86f<**
Cultured King (IRE) 2 b g Imp Society (USA)-Regina St Cyr (IRE) (Doulab (USA)) 4064^{16} 4209^{10} 4901^7 **>63f<**
Cumbrian Cadet 2 br g Handsome Sailor-City Sound (On Your Mark) 1255^8 1447^3 1797^5 2127^4 2538^2 2739^2 3209^6 3707^2 (3821) 4284^6 **>73f<**
Cumbrian Caruso 2 b c Primo Dominie-Conquista (Aragon) 979^8 (1819) 2060^2 2359^2 **>80f<**
Cunning Vixen (IRE) 3 b f Machiavellian (USA)-Sailor's Mate (Shirley Heights) 3007a^D 4960a^3 **>109f<**
Curiously 3 b f Warning-Last Exit (Dominion) 4191a^9 **>92f<**
Currer Bell 4 b f Belmez (USA)-Hello Cuddles (He Loves Me) *173^7*
Curriculus (IRE) 2 ch c Sharp Victor (USA)-Felsen (IRE) (Ballad Rock) 2886^W
Curtelace 7 ch g Nishapour (FR)-Khandjar (Kris) 3272^8 3477^6 3933^{14} **>11f<**
Curzon Street 3 b f Night Shift (USA)-Pine Ridge (High Top) 1810^{14} 1988^2 2665^{12} 3389^7 3495^4 3893^2 3970^3 4378^7 **>76f<**
Cut Diamond 2 ch c Keen-Diamond Princess

(Horage) 1744[6] 2022[7] 2181[17] **>51f<**
Cutthroat Kid (IRE) 7 b g Last Tycoon-Get Ahead (Silly Season) *256[4]* **>66a 72df<**
Cutting Anshake 2 gr g Anshan-Golden Scissors (Kalaglow) 4745[9] 4974[20] **>51f<**
Cybertechnology 3 b c Environment Friend-Verchinina (Star Appeal) 775[4] 1949[2] 2292[5] 3238[9] (3772) 4121[4] 4578[11] 4757[4] **>89f<**
Cyrano's Lad (IRE) 8 b or br g Cyrano de Bergerac-Patiala (Crocket) 677[6] (961) 1148[4] (1596) 2056[18] 3724[4] 4239[13] 4421[13] **>118f<**
Cyrian (IRE) 3 b c Persian Bold-Regina St Cyr (IRE) (Doulab (USA)) *(395)* 1092[2] (1242) 2514[10] 3125[8] 3648[6] **>72+a 91f<**
Cyrillic (USA) 2 b f Irish River (USA)-Polemic (USA) (Roberto (USA)) 4961a[3] **>103f<**
Czarna (IRE) 6 b g Polish Precedent (USA)-Noble Dust (USA) (Dust Commander (USA)) **1996:** *5079[7] 5206[8]* **1997:** *295[4] 338[10] 401[9]* 755[2] 866[9] 1248[8] **>46da 74f<**
Czar Wars 2 b c Warrshan (USA)-Dutch Czarina (Prince Sabo) 2752[5] 3458[4] (3819) 4368[7] 4605[9] **>83f<**
Czech Maite 2 b f Komaite (USA)-Miss Mint (Music Maestro) 4458[12] **>2f<**

D

Daaniera (IRE) 7 gr g Standaan (FR)-Right Cash (Right Tack) **1996:** *5225[5] 5280[4]* **1997:** *95[3] 223[9] 593[11]* **>31a 23f<**
Daawe (USA) 6 b h Danzig (USA)-Capo Di Monte (Final Straw) *357[5]* 443[5] *(545)* 977[7] 1303[3] 1948[3] (2129) 2326[11] 2711[5] 2872[2] 3065[5] 3410[6] 3649[19] 4137[8] 4280[12] 4512[6] **>81a 79f<**
Da Boss 2 ch c Be My Chief (USA)-Lady Kris (IRE) (Kris) 2181[3] 2524[6] 3686[6] 4111[6] 4361[9] **>76f<**
Daffodil Dale (IRE) 3 b f Cyrano de Bergerac-Supreme Crown (USA) (Chief's Crown (USA)) 1062a[6] **>80f<**
Daffodil Express (IRE) 4 b f Skyliner-Miss Henry (Blue Cashmere) **1996:** *5109[15]* **1997:** 887[16] 1229[15] **>14f<**
Daggers Drawn (USA) 2 ch c Diesis-Sun and Shade (Ajdal (USA)) (2588) (3148) (4135) 4784[6] **>114df<**
Dahiyah (USA) 6 b g Ogygian (USA)-Sticky Prospect (USA) (Mr Prospector (USA)) *(3) 87[5] 243[3] 385[8]* 484[5] *1047[8]* **>58a 57f<**
Dahlidya 2 b f Midyan (USA)-Dahlawise (IRE) (Caerleon (USA)) 1997[14] 3384[6] 3742[4] **>42f<**
Dahomey (USA) 2 b br c Dayjur (USA)-Dish Dash (Bustino) 4544[8] **>54f<**
Daily Sport Girl 8 b m Risk Me (FR)-Net Call (Song) *68[8] 151[6]* 1278[4] 1435[6] **>28a 50f<**
Daintree (IRE) 3 b f Tirol-Aunty Eileen (Ahonoora) 792[12] 1083[10] 1633[7] 2040[4] 2756[3] 3088[3] 3292[3] 3868[3] 4008[9] 4431[4] *4809[3]* **>55a 55f<**
Dainty Damsel 4 b f Good Times (ITY)-Classy Lassy (Class Distinction) 3439[3] 3624[5] **>35?f<**
Daira 4 br f Daring March-Ile de Reine (Ile de Bourbon (USA)) 781[9] 1036[9] 1628[3] 2015[3] 2503[4] 3085[3] 3283[9] 3626[8] 4608[4] **>43a 66f<**
Daisy Bates (IRE) 4 b f Danehill (USA)-Martha Stevens (USA) (Super Concorde (USA)) **1996:** *5112[9] 5183[8]* **>55a 65f<**
Dallai (IRE) 6 b g Dance of Life (USA)-Wavetree (Realm) 2350[7] *3046[11]* **>29?a f<**
Dalliance (IRE) 3 ch g Arazi (USA)-Lastcomer (USA) (Kris) 742[7] 1130[5] *(1430) 1788[2]* 1973[3] 2525[7] **>104a 96f<**
Dalwhinnie 4 b f Persian Bold-Land Line (High Line) 1393[8] 1844[3] 2122[6] 2421[5] 2927[5] **>63f<**
Damancher 5 b h Damister (USA)-Amalancher (USA) (Alleged (USA)) 1542a[5] 1698a[2] 2456a[3] **>107+f<**
Damanka (IRE) 3 b f Slip Anchor-Doumayna (Kouban (FR)) 1423[15] 1820[12] 2178[8] **>31f<**
Damara 3 b f Damister (USA)-Gem-May (Mansingh (USA)) 3037[6] 4290[14] 4579[7] 4845[19] **>54f<**
Dame Kiri (FR) 3 f 4655a[2] **>116f<**
Dame Laura (IRE) 3 b f Royal Academy (USA)-Aunty (FR) (Riverman (USA)) 672[8] 1147[10] (3199) 4421[11] 4669[8] **>103f<**
Damus (GER) 3 b c Surumu (GER)-Dawn Side (GER) (Bold Forbes (USA)) 1545a[3] 4661a[5] **>101f<**
Danakil 2 b c Warning-Danilova (FR) (Lyphard (USA)) 4959a[3] **>59f<**
Dance Design (IRE) 4 b f Sadler's Wells (USA)-Elegance in Design (Habitat) (1058a) (1542a) (2446a) 3376a[2] 3879a[3] 5039a[7] 5065a[11] **>122+f<**
Dance Melody 3 b f Rambo Dancer (CAN)-Cateryne (Ballymoss) 748[10] 1998[6] *2602[12]* 3068[7] 4290[10] 4843[10] **>15a 44f<**
Dance Model 4 b f Unfuwain (USA)-Bourgeonette (Mummy's Pet) **1996:** *5139[7]* **>12a 50f<**
Dance of Joy 5 b m Shareef Dancer (USA)-Lady Habitat (Habitat) **1996:** *5281[6]* **>18a 39f<**
Dance Parade (USA) 3 ch f Gone West (USA)-River Jig (USA) (Irish River (FR)) (724) 960[12] **>111f<**
Dancer Mitral 4 c Shareef Dancer (USA)-Almitra (Targowice (USA)) 1200a[6] 1549a[6] **>114f<**
Dance So Suite 5 b g Shareef Dancer (USA)-Three Piece (Jaazeiro (USA)) 787[10] 2729[4] 3053[7] 3599[5] 3796[3] (4002) 4476[3] 4754[2] **>58a 103f<**
Dances With Dreams 3 b f Be My Chief (USA)-Oh So Well (IRE) (Sadler's Wells (USA)) **1996:** 5153a[2] **1997:** 1203a[4] 1916a[12] 3017[3] 3913[10] **>113df<**
Dances With Hooves 5 b h Dancing Dissident (USA)-Princesse Legere (USA) (Alleged (USA)) *(108) 226[7] 363[7]* 1262[17] 1588[10] 3135[5] 3392[12] 4219[13] 4441[20] 4858[20] **>63a 48f<**
Dancethenightaway 3 gr f Efisio-Dancing Diana (Raga Navarro (ITY)) 555[4] *904[3]* (1018) 1212[6] 1608[6] 1766[10] 2134[10] 2779[2] 3194[3] 3709[7] 4553[6] (4677) 4756[16] **>80a 99f<**
Dance To The Beat 2 b f Batshoof-Woodleys (Tyrnavos) 1954[10] 2306[5] 2562[8] 2893[9] *4799[2]* **>58a 63f<**
Dance Treat (USA) 5 ch m Nureyev (USA)-Office Wife (USA) (Secretariat (USA)) **1996:** 5154a[2] **>119f<**
Dance Trick (USA) 2 ch f Diesis-Performing Arts (The Minstrel (CAN)) (1240) (1735) **>93f<**
Dancing Al 2 br c Alnasr Alwasheek-Lyne Dancer (Be My Native (USA)) 1607[11] 2240[8] 3078[7] 3294[5] **>54f<**
Dancing-Alone 5 ch g Adbass (USA)-Lady Alone (Mr Fluorocarbon) *242[2]* **>58a f<**
Dancing Cavalier 4 b g Nalchik (USA)-Miss Admington (Double Jump) *70[7] 182[5] 244[3] 299[8] 374[2]* 430[4] (470) *542[4]* (650) 728[5] 762[4] 888[6] 1036[W] 1408[10] 1778[6] (2035) (2198) 2316[7] 2682[6] 3108[4] 3283[3] 3543[6] 3815[3] **>60a 74f<**
Dancing Cormorant 4 b g Shareef Dancer (USA)-Cormorant Creek (Gorytus (USA)) 2386[5] **>44f<**
Dancing Dervish 2 b g Shareef Dancer (USA)-Taj Victory (Final Straw) 4640[6] **>15f<**
Dancing Destiny 5 b m Dancing Brave (USA)-Tender Loving Care (Final Straw) *870[10]* 4845[15] **>42a 49f<**
Dancing Drop 3 b f Green Desert (USA)-Moon Drop (Dominion) 1453[3] 2133[2] 2561[8] 3913[9] 4153[2] 4669[2] 4902[3] **>104f<**
Dancing Em 2 b f Rambo Dancer (CAN)-Militia Girl (Rarity) 730[7] 1267[9] 2022[8] 2493[3] 3307[5] 4382[7] **>42f<**
Dancing Feather 3 ch f Suave Dancer (USA)-English Spring (USA) (Grey Dawn II) 1477[5] 1922[4] 3903[3] 4046[11] 4323[17] *4906[6]* **>49a 48f<**
Dancing Grey 2 gr c Petong-Mountain Harvest (FR) (Shirley Heights) 4855[9] **>31f<**
Dancing Icon (IRE) 2 b f Mujtahid (USA)-Babushka (IRE) (Dance of Life (USA)) 2138[7] 2862[23] (3407) 3892[9] 4737[8] **>83f<**
Dancing Image 4 ch g Salse (USA)-Reflection (Mill Reef (USA)) 1324[2] 2026[4] 2766[6] (3220) 3764[3] 4003[4] 4423[16] **>107f<**
Dancing Jack 4 ch c Clantime-Sun Follower (Relkino) **1996:** *5188[12] 5210[14] 5225[10] 5280[9]* **1997:** *57[11]* 1814[9] 2536[13] 2848[15] 3417[12] 3637[9] **>62da 26f<**
Dancing Lawyer 6 b g Thowra (FR)-Miss Lawsuit (Neltino) **1996:** *5095[9] 5151[11]* **1997:** 1505[5] 1599[5] 1878[11] 1965[10] 3227[6] 3469[7] 3848[10] 4114[3] 4371[2] **>42a 58f<**
Dancing Mystery 3 b g Beveled (USA)-Batchworth Dancer (Ballacashtal (CAN)) *588[7]* 1279[11] 1814[10] 2179[14] 2481[5] 2732[2] 2946[2] 3280[5] 3500[8] 4047[7] 4370[8] *(4809)* **>69a 67f<**
Dancing Phantom 2 b c Darshaan-Dancing Prize (IRE) (Sadler's Wells (USA)) 3861[2] **>83+f<**
Dancing Queen (IRE) 3 b f Sadler's Wells (USA)-Bay Shade (USA) (Sharpen Up) 841[5] 1470[3] 1844[14] 2468[6] 3101[4] *3400[3]* 4161[15] **>54a 58f<**
Dancing Rio (IRE) 2 ch g Roi Danzig (USA)-Tameen (FR) (Pharly (FR)) 2356[5] 2842[5] 3131[5] *3610[9] 4589[12]* **>48a 80f<**
Dancing Sioux 5 b g Nabeel Dancer (USA)-Sutosky (Great Nephew) *333[8] 386[2] 903[2]* 1285[4] *1575[3] 1944[6]* 3240[3] **>70a 56f<**
Dancing Wolf (IRE) 2 b f Wolfhound (USA)-Aigue (High Top) 3636[10] 3981[4] 4311[3] 4755[9] **>72f<**
Dancing Zena (IRE) 7 b h Dancing Brave (USA)-Princess Zena (Habitat) 308a[7] **>101a 89f<**
Dande Flyer 4 b br c Clantime-Lyndseylee (Swing Easy (USA)) *53[5] 214[5] 301[9]* 473[2] 744[10] 834[12] 1098[11] 1374[11] 1419[7] 2590[9] 2769[5] 2950[4] 3126[4] 3326[4] 3500[6] 3642[7] 3852[3] **>71a 60f<**
Dande Times 2 ch c Timeless Times (USA)-Miss Merlin (Manacle) 880[5] 1370[5] 3097[3] 3446[3] 3692[6] 3859[5] *4054[4]* **>50a 56f<**
Dandy Regent 3 b g Green Desert (USA)-Tahilla (Moorestyle) 517[9] 693[7] 1012[5] 1238[4] 4375[2] **>70f<**
Danegold (IRE) 5 b g Danehill (USA)-Cistus (Sun Prince) 482[3] 866[7] 1244[22] 3475[10] 3916[8] 4109[6] 4802[12] **>67a 60f<**
Danehill Dancer (IRE) 4 b c Danehill (USA)-Mira Adonde (USA) (Sharpen Up) 1171[7] **>121f<**
Danehill Princess (IRE) 3 b f Danehill (USA)-Top Glad (USA) (I'm Glad (ARG)) **1996:** *5113[7] 5265[3]* **1997:** *84[7]* 2420[10] 2945[11] 3336[4] 3854[7] 4169[15] **>41a 53f<**
Dane River (IRE) 2 b c Danehill (USA)-Allegheny River (USA) (Lear Fan (USA)) 2987a[3] **>87f<**
Daneskaya 4 b f Danehill (USA)-Boubskaia (FR) (Niniski (USA)) (3371a) 4129a[4] 4864a[5] **>120f<**
Danesman (IRE) 4 b g Danehill (USA)-Vernonhills (Hard Fought) 4295[8] **>82f<**
Danetime (IRE) 3 b c Danehill (USA)-Allegheny River (USA) (Lear Fan (USA)) 449[12] 930[11] 1317[7] 2105[2] (2560) (3217) 4011[3] **>120f<**
Dangerman (IRE) 2 ch g Pips Pride-Two Magpies (Doulab (USA)) 1267[7] 2127[2] 2356[4] **>70+f<**
Dangerous Diva (IRE) 3 ch f Royal Academy (USA)-Loveliest (USA) (Tibaldo) (1062a) 3674a[2] 4094a[3] 4204a[5] 4625a[4] 4782[11] **>113f<**

Dangerus Precedent (IRE) 2 ch c Polish Precedent (USA)-Circus Feathers (Kris) 3331^{6} 3717^{6} 4752^{5} **>46f<**

Daniel's Mascot 3 b g Sharpo-Kirby's Princess (Indian King (USA)) 2532^{11} 4631^{10}

Danish Rhapsody (IRE) 4 b g Danehill (USA)-Ardmelody (Law Society (USA)) 1105^{3} (1482) 1981^{9} (2594) (3112) 3703^{12} 4004^{2} (4141) (4369) 4678^{W} **>111f<**

Danjing (IRE) 5 b g Danehill (USA)-Beijing (USA) (Northjet) 1027^{10} **>97f<**

Danka 3 gr g Petong-Angel Drummer (Dance In Time (CAN)) 4876^{14} **>68f<**

Dannistar 5 br m Puissance-Loadplan Lass (Nicholas Bill) 687^{7} 1001^{6} 1441^{8} 4453^{5} 4608^{10} *4800^{12}* **>42a 52f<**

Dantesque (IRE) 4 b c Danehill (USA)-I Want My Say (USA) (Tilt Up (USA)) 1630^{2} 2156^{2} 2566^{2} (3089) (3444) 3722^{5} (4136) 5053^{12} **>97f<**

Danyross (IRE) 2 b f Danehill (USA)-Rosita (Bold Lad (IRE)) 1475^{4} 2451a^{2} 2558^{4} 3534a^{6} **>99f<**

Danzas 3 b g Polish Precedent (USA)-Dancing Rocks (Green Dancer (USA)) 1437^{5} 2183^{3} 2532^{3} 2930^{3} 3891^{10} 4883^{11} **>79f<**

Danzig Flyer (IRE) 2 b c Roi Danzig (USA)-Fenland Express (IRE) (Reasonable (FR)) 2018^{4} *2595^{2}* 2943^{4} 3545^{3} 3904^{7} 4334^{17} 4806^{7} **>73a 71f<**

Danzino (IRE) 2 b g Roi Danzig (USA)-Luvi Ullmann (Thatching) 2324^{9} 2771^{8} 3094^{13} 3613^{11} 4855^{11} **>40f<**

Darapour (IRE) 3 b g Fairy King (USA)-Dawala (IRE) (Lashkari) 2287^{8} (2537) 2961^{13} 3773^{3} 3989^{3} (4295) **>98+f<**

Darashandeh (IRE) 3 b f Darshaan-Daralinsha (USA) (Empery (USA)) 813a^{2} 1366a^{4} 1916a^{11} 4655a^{6} **>110f<**

Daratown 4 b g Tragic Role (USA)-Darakah (Doulab (USA)) **1996:** *5122^{8}* **1997:** *61^{14}* 1005^{15} 3299^{11} **>36a f<**

Daraydan (IRE) 5 b g Kahyasi-Delsy (FR) (Abdos) 2108^{3} 3705^{18} **>85f<**

Darazari (IRE) 4 fb c Sadler's Wells (USA)-Darara (Top Ville) 1363a^{4} 1917a^{3} 2460a^{4} **>122f<**

Darb Alola (USA) 3 b c Nureyev (USA)-Kristana (Kris) (656) 968^{10} 2134^{11} 2655^{5} 3065^{6} **>84f<**

Darbela (IRE) 3 br f Doyoun-Darata (IRE) (Vayrann) 4620a^{15} **>100f<**

Darcy 3 ch c Miswaki (USA)-Princess Accord (USA) (D'Accord (USA)) 683^{7} (1271) 1962^{4} 2180^{3} 3722^{14} 3989^{10} **>101df<**

Dare 2 b g Beveled (USA)-Run Amber Run (Run The Gantlet (USA)) 4459^{6} **>33f<**

Dargo 3 b c Formidable (USA)-Mountain Memory (High Top) 983^{8} **>75f<**

Darien 3 b c Sadler's Wells (USA)-Aryenne (FR) (Green Dancer (USA)) 725^{15} 2572^{3} 3419^{6} 3754^{7} 4046^{7} **>79f<**

Daring Derek (USA) 2 ch c Naevus (USA)-Gatap (USA) (Buckfinder (USA)) (4544) **>74+f<**

Daring Destiny 6 b m Daring March-Raunchy Rita (Brigadier Gerard) 961^{7} 4421^{14} 4777^{7} 4881^{18} **>99f<**

Daring Flight (USA) 3 b c Danzig (USA)-Life At the Top (Habitat) *341^{4}* 2149^{6} **>64a 68f<**

Daring Hen (IRE) 7 b m Henbit (USA)-Daring Glen (Furry Glen) *68^{13}*

Daring News 2 b c Risk Me (FR)-Hot Sunday Sport (Star Appeal) 2243^{5} 2693^{7} 2768^{10} 4271^{10} 4576^{13} **>72f<**

Dario's Girl 4 b f Good Times (ITY)-Our Krystle (Tender King) 686^{9} 1266^{8} 1838^{10} 2386^{9} **>27f<**

Dark Age (IRE) 4 b c Darshaan-Sarela (USA) (Danzig (USA)) *250^{4}* 1809^{6} 1975^{8} 2285^{9} 2528^{14} 3796^{10} 4179^{7} 4504^{10} 5049^{19} **>50a 56f<**

Dark Green (USA) 3 ch c Green Dancer (USA)-Ardisia (USA) (Affirmed (USA)) 528^{2} 1930^{2} 2311^{5} **>86f<**

Dark Menace 5 br g Beveled (USA)-Sweet and Sure (Known Fact (USA)) **1996:** *5089^{7} 5188^{5} 5215^{2}* **1997:** *21^{8} 199^{7}* 1483^{6} (1639) 1965^{18} 2745^{14} 2954^{4} 3249^{7} 3590^{5} 4404^{6} 4951^{13} **>50a 58df<**

Dark Midnight (IRE) 8 br g Petorius-Gaelic Jewel (Scottish Rifle) 1674^{6} **>29f<**

Dark Mile (USA) 3 b f Woodman (USA)-Fateful (USA) (Topsider (USA)) 4047^{5} 4214^{3} (4563) 4733^{3} 4975^{4} **>83f<**

Dark Moondancer 2 b c Anshan-Oh So Well (IRE) (Sadler's Wells (USA)) 2860^{3} 3494^{2} 4174^{2} (4735) **>83f<**

Dark Waters (IRE) 4 b g Darshaan-Grecian Sea (FR) (Homeric) *858^{4}* 1260^{5} *(1964)* 2530^{8} *3231^{3}* **>69a 75f<**

Darling Clover 5 ch m Minster Son-Lady Clementine (He Loves Me) 2546^{19} 3029^{9} 3491^{9} 4210^{13} **>61a 62f<**

Darnaway 3 b c Green Desert (USA)-Reuval (Sharpen Up) 674^{3} 1221^{2} (4070) **>93+f<**

Daru (USA) 8 gr g Caro-Frau Daruma (ARG) (Frari (ARG)) *205^{14}* **>83f<**

Darwell's Folly (USA) 2 ch c Blushing John (USA)-Hispanolia (FR) (Kris) (3060) 4851^{6} 4989^{10} **>79f<**

Daryabad (IRE) 5 b h Thatching-Dayanata (Shirley Heights) **1996:** *5106^{9}* **1997:** *21^{5} 241^{12}* **>61a 79f<**

Dasharan (IRE) 4 b c Shahrastani (USA)-Delsy (FR) (Abdos) 4620a^{13} **>82f<**

Dashing Blue 4 ch g Dashing Blade-Blubella (Balidar) 726^{14} 877^{2} 1148^{8} 1590^{5} 1766^{2} (2675) 3217^{3} 3863^{3} (4100) 4239^{2} (4525) **>118f<**

Dashing Chief (IRE) 2 b c Darshaan-Calaloo Sioux (USA) (Our Native (USA)) 1607^{8} 3861^{4} 4064^{12} (4582) 4977^{5} **>87f<**

Dashing Dancer (IRE) 6 ch g Conquering Hero (USA)-Santa Maria (GER) (Literat) *429^{14}* 467^{8} 585^{12} 774^{2} 1003^{10} *1134^{6}* **>25a 51f<**

Dashing Invader (USA) 4 ch g Pirate Army (USA)-Cherie's Hope (USA) (Flying Paster (USA)) 598^{9} 1022^{5} 1452^{7} 1779^{9} 2154^{6} *(2607) 2910^{3} 3415^{2}* 3719^{5} *4055^{7}* **>52a 40f<**

Dashing Knight (IRE) 2 b c Night Shift (USA)-Hastening (Shirley Heights) 4581^{7} 4708^{7} **>61f<**

Daughter In Law (IRE) 4 b f Law Society (USA)-Colonial Line (USA) (Plenty Old (USA)) 1236^{U} *1428^{6}* **>15a 39f<**

Daunting Lady (IRE) 2 b f Mujadil (USA)-Dauntess (Formidable (USA)) (828) (1013) 2024^{3} 2484^{2} 2862^{13} 3961a^{3} **>97f<**

Dauntless Fort 6 gr m Belfort (FR)-Dauntless Flight (Golden Mallard) 2939^{7} **>20a 28f<**

Dauphin (IRE) 4 b br g Astronef-Va Toujours (Alzao (USA)) 607^{2} (1001) 1445^{13} 1632^{19} 2344^{3} 3135^{3} 3467^{4} 4521^{8} (4667) 4821^{12} **>53a 58f<**

David James' Girl 5 b m Faustus (USA)-Eagle's Quest (Legal Eagle) *333^{7} 390^{3} 411^{4} 428^{5}* 687^{17} *1135^{3} 1291^{7}* 2109^{8} 2237^{7} 2488^{15} 2651^{11} **>49a 36f<**

Davids Revenge 3 b g Reprimand-Tribal Lady (Absalom) 1265^{9} 1876^{3} 2554^{10} 2835^{15} 4696^{14} **>60f<**

Davis Rock 3 ch f Rock City-Sunny Davis (USA) (Alydar (USA)) **1996:** *5100^{5} 5176^{6} 5238^{9}* **1997:** 1661^{6} 1966^{2} 2214^{7} 2665^{3} 3268^{2} 3454^{2} 3691^{4} 4328^{8} *4591^{4}* (4816) 4872^{2} **>73a 70f<**

Davoski 3 b gr c Niniski (USA)-Pamela Peach (Habitat) *(568)* 1025^{7} 1868^{8} 2749^{3} (3381) 3570^{3} 4383^{8} **>77a 86f<**

Dawalib (USA) 7 ch g Danzig Connection (USA)-Centavos (USA) (Scout Leader (USA)) *31^{8} 72^{7} 113^{5} (203) (241) 257^{6} 316^{3} 349^{2} 514^{4}* 892^{21} *1048^{6} 1433^{2}* 1830^{P} 2395^{15} *3583^{5} 3860^{2}* 4112^{18} **>68a 43f<**

Dawam Allail (IRE) 3 b g Night Shift (USA)-Veronica (Persian Bold) 634^{8} 1092^{3} *1430^{2}* 1678^{2} 2190^{3} 2492^{2} (2859) *3584^{14}* **>16a f<**

Dawn Patrol 2 ch f Weldnaas (USA)-Silverdale Rose (Nomination) 557^{8} 583^{4} 651^{4} 1645^{5} 1749^{7} 1860^{4} 3258^{6} 3427^{8} **>56f<**

Dawn Summit 3 ch c Salse (USA)-Bereeka (Main Reef) 825^{6} *1043^{15}* 1299^{6} (1502) 1853^{9} 2189^{10} 2531^{6} **>57f<**

Dawn Treader (USA) 2 gr c El Prado (IRE)-Marie de La Ferte (Amber Rama (USA)) 3278^{10} 3686^{18} *4056^{6}* 4380^{10} 4900^{7} **>58a 60f<**

Dawson's Legacy (USA) 2 c *5064a^{2}*

Daybreak 2 ch f Komaite (USA)-Lady Day (FR) (Lightning (FR)) 3084^{4} 3806^{6} 4231^{10} (4702) *4808^{4}* **>54a 64f<**

Daydream Island 4 ch f Never so Bold-La Belle Vie (Indian King (USA)) *172^{8}* **>3f<**

Daylami (IRE) 3 gr c Doyoun-Daltawa (IRE) (Miswaki (USA)) (820a) (1204a) 2011^{3} 3733a^{2} 4129a^{3} **>127f<**

Daylight Dreams 3 b f Indian Ridge-Singing Nelly (Pharly (FR)) 1002^{4} 3056^{8} 3418^{10} 4168^{9} 4505^{4} 4546^{7} 4805^{9} *4913^{5}* **>60a 71f<**

Daymarti (IRE) 2 c 4657a^{3} 5034a^{3} **>96f<**

Daynabee 2 b f Common Grounds-Don't Wary (FR) (Lomond (USA)) 572^{7} 743^{6} *872^{3} 1758^{4} 2367^{2} 2606^{2}* (2784) (3062) (3314) 3438^{3} 3823^{6} 4162^{7} 4327^{10} **>59a 68f<**

Dayrella 3 ch f Beveled (USA)-Divissima (Music Boy) *590^{6} 873^{3} (1151) 1580^{3}* (1810) 2179^{10} 2554^{17} 3092^{5} 3614^{8} 4333^{13} **>56a 63f<**

Days of Grace 2 gr f Wolfhound (USA)-Inshirah (USA) (Caro) 432^{5} 564^{4} 682^{4} (897) 2138^{6} 2648^{4} 2851^{3} 3226^{6} 3414^{3} **>69f<**

Dayville (USA) 3 b f Dayjur (USA)-Chain Fern (USA) (Blushing Groom (FR)) (685) 1112^{5} 1610^{8} 1980^{15} (2649) 2894^{8} 3273^{11} 4013^{7} **>69a 84f<**

Dazilyn Lady (USA) 2 ch f Zilzal (USA)-Jetbeeah (IRE) (Lomond (USA)) 2312^{2} (2875) 3723^{7} (3934) 4555^{5} **>96f<**

Dazla's Double 3 b f Golden Heights-Dazla (Dublin Taxi) 1322^{8} 2389^{6} **>48f<**

Dazzle 3 b br f Gone West (USA)-Belle et Deluree (USA) (The Minstrel (CAN)) 960^{3} 1533a^{9} (3147) 3577^{6} 4120^{2} 4421^{5} 4782^{8} **>114f<**

Dazzling 4 b f Rambo Dancer (CAN)-Azaiyma (Corvaro (USA)) 1010^{9} **>38a 75?f<**

Dazzling Stone 3 b g Mujtahid (USA)-Lady In Green (Shareef Dancer (USA)) 2287^{7} 2532^{7} *2912^{8}* 3470^{13} 3992^{21} 4633^{14} **>35a 58f<**

Dead Aim (IRE) 3 b g Sadler's Wells (USA)-Dead Certain (Absalom) 2285^{3} 2897^{2} (3633) 4015^{3} 4234^{5} **>84f<**

Deadline Time (IRE) 4 b g Fayruz-Cut it Fine (USA) (Big Spruce (USA)) 3972^{6} 4264^{6} 4703^{3} **>91a 54f<**

Deadly Dudley (IRE) 3 gr c Great Commotion (USA)-Renzola (Dragonara Palace (USA)) 3554a^{5} 4344a^{3} 4782^{12} **>113f<**

Deardaw 5 b m Tina's Pet-Faw (Absalom) *391^{13}* 469^{8} *515^{6}* 774^{12} **>20a 31tf<**

Dear Drue 3 b f Jupiter Island-Top and Tail (USA) (Tilt Up (USA)) **1996:** *5087^{9}* **>24a 20f< (DEAD)**

Dearie Me 2 b f Batshoof-Cos I Do (IRE) (Double Schwartz) 4852^{12} **>53f<**

Dear John (IRE) **4** b g Caerleon (USA)-Alligatrix (USA) (Alleged (USA)) 4114[19]
Debutante Days **5** ch m Dominion-Doogali (Doon) 1968[9] (2421) (3085) (3694) 4295[7] 4891[11] **>84f<**
Decision Maker (IRE) **4** b g Taufan (USA)-Vain Deb (Gay Fandango (USA)) *369[11]* 430[14] **>54a 72f<**
Decisive Action (USA) **2** br c Alleged (USA)-Maria Balastiere (USA) (Majestic Light (USA)) (4739) **>100+f<**
Decorated Hero **5** b g Warning-Bequeath (USA) (Lyphard (USA)) **1996:** *5204[2]* **1997:** 1210[6] (1776) (2830) 3063[6] (3577) 4117[2] (4377) (4662a) 4782[5] 5063a[3] **>113a 127f<**
Deeceebee **2** b g Rudimentary (USA)-Do Run Run (Commanche Run) 1669[8] 2168[3] (2324) 2685[6] 3990[12] 4634[15] 4702[6] 4767[11] 4994[26] **>75f<**
Dee-Lady **5** b m Deploy-Bermuda Lily (Dunbeath (USA)) **1996:** *5231[8]* **>51a 87f<**
Dee Pee Tee Cee (IRE) **3** b g Tidaro (USA)-Silver Glimpse (Petingo) 1096[8] 1496[9] (1830) 2019[7] (2158) (2239) (2495) (2543) 3262[3] 3777[4] 3901[15] **>81f<**
Deep Finesse **3** b c Reprimand-Babycham Sparkle (So Blessed) 501[6] (941) 2106[11] 3001a[8] 3111[6] 4239[16] 4664a[10] **>112f<**
Deeply Vale (IRE) **6** b g Pennine Walk-Late Evening (USA) (Riverman (USA)) **1996:** *(5099) 5150[5] 5249[15]* **1997:** *3[5] 241[5] 325[4] 382[5] 2069[6]* 2390[5] *(3583)* 3987[6] 4773[12] **>69a 69f<**
Deep Magic (USA) **2** b f Gone West (USA)-Nimble Folly (USA) (Cyane) 3717[5] **>45f<**
Deep Space (IRE) **2** br c Green Desert (USA)-Dream Season (USA) (Mr Prospector (USA)) 3047[4] 4298[12] **>76tf<**
Deep Water (USA) **3** b c Diesis-Water Course (USA) (Irish River (FR)) *425[3]* 565[3] 1437[7] 2230[5] 2850[2] 4552[5] 4699[3] **>48a 75f<**
Deerly **4** b f Hadeer-Grafitti Gal (USA) (Pronto) 1279[5] (1439) 1666[14] 2177[17] *3398[4]* 3746[8] 4169[19] 4580[13] *4798[11]* 4899[10] **>39a 41f<**
Deevee **8** b h Hallgate-Lady Woodpecker (Tap On Wood) 1244[19] 1845[5] 3465[17] 4373[14] 4607[10] 4858[12] **>26f<**
Defiance **2** b c Warning-Princess Athena (Ahonoora) 2534[6] 2856[3] 3433[3] **>75+f<**
Defined Feature (IRE) **4** ch f Nabeel Dancer (USA)-Meissarah (USA) (Silver Hawk (USA)) *343[2]* 450[23] 677[17] 934[7] 1300[8] 1658[13] 3718[3] 4225[8] 4606[3] 4757[10] **>89a 76f<**
Deflagration (FR) **3** ch f Pistolet Bleu (IRE)-Dansoline (FR) (Trempolino (USA)) 1360a[3] **>105f<**
Degree **4** b f Warning-Krill (Kris) *28[4] 163[7] 245[8]* 1470[8] *1757[2]* (1991) 2399[12] **>59a 59f<**
Deilginis **2** b c Ardkinglass-Greenhill Lass (Upper Case (USA)) 3961a[13] **>81f<**
Dekelsmary **2** b f Komaite (USA)-Final Call (Town Crier) 2706[13] 3459[4] 3619[5] 4166[3] 4327[2] 4588[7] **>68f<**
Deki (USA) **2** b br c Mujtahid (USA)-Glamorous Bride (FR) (Baillamont (USA)) (1418) 2060[3] 2936[2] (3545) **>87f<**
Delayed Reaction **2** b c Theatrical Charmer-Pingin (Corvaro (USA)) 2870[12] 3799[7] 4165[9] **>46f<**
Delciana (IRE) **2** b f Danehill (USA)-Delvecchia (Glint of Gold) 1997[4] 3033[3] 3278[11] 3597[6] 3924[12] 4327[3] 4588[W] **>66f<**
Delight of Dawn **5** b m Never so Bold-Vogos Angel (Song) 864[11] 1009[11] 1273[8] 1680[3] 1849[7] 2004[4] 2237[8] 2552[2] 2785[6] 3018[7] 3227[4] 3394[2] 3787[7] 4228[12] 4291[2] 4628[6] *4813[12]* 4992[9] **>16a 59f<**
Delilah (IRE) **3** b f Bluebird (USA)-Courtesane (USA) (Majestic Light (USA)) 681[2] 890[3] 1146[4] 3803[2] (3977) 4445[4] (4676) **>110f<**
Delirious Tantrum (IRE) **2** b f Taufan (USA)-Shrewd Girl (USA) (Sagace) 2987a[5] 3961a[19] **>77f<**
Della Scala (IRE) **2** b c Marju (IRE)-Blue Sticks (ITY) (Bluebird (USA)) (2644a) 3178a[5] 4865a[10] **>91f<**
Dellen Walker (IRE) **4** b g Pennine Walk-Lady Ellen (Horage) *424[13]*
Dellua (IRE) **3** b f Suave Dancer (USA)-Joma Kaanem (Double Form) 681[8] 989[4] 1611[7] 3793[2] 4046[6] (4400) 4693[4] **>75f<**
Delphic Way **2** b f Warning-Palace Street (USA) (Secreto (USA)) 2831[8] 3471[6] **>57f<**
Delrob **6** b m Reprimand-Stoneydale (Tickled Pink) **1996:** *5144[6] 5170[11]* **1997:** *233[8] 275[2] 318[10] 429[5] 663[7]* 883[5] *1046[4] 1289[6] 1428[2]* 1666[11] *1759[12]* 2536[6] 2780[6] (2899) 3016[7] 3327[7] **>49a 45f<**
Delta Soleil (USA) **5** b h Riverman (USA)-Sunny Roberta (USA) (Robellino (USA)) 520[8] 1035[12] 1410[6] 1824[2] 2129[5] 2708[9] 3130[4] 3580[7] 4071[2] 4225[6] **>72a 83f<**
Democrat **3** b g Selkirk (USA)-Land of Ivory (USA) (The Minstrel (CAN)) 4563[8] 4600[3] 4700[6] **>59f<**
Demolition Jo **2** gr f Petong-Fire Sprite (Mummy's Game) *902[4]* 1031[2] 1440[2] 1616[2] 1997[2] 2038[2] (3701) 3889[4] 4325[2] 4362[4] 4468[2] 4670[13] (4755) 4890[7] 4989[3] 5050[16] **>41a 81f<**
Denbrae (IRE) **5** b g Sure Blade (USA)-Fencing (Viking (USA)) 520[3] 942[28] 1107[8] 1666[W] 2372[3] 2788[5] 3146[4] 3417[4] (3691) 4270[13] **>69a 74f<**
Densben **13** b g Silly Prices-Eliza de Rich (Spanish Gold) 863[7] 1225[9] 1448[4] 1511[6] 1816[3] 4016[9] 4628[12] 4924[25] **>51f<**
Dentardia (IRE) **2** br c Petardia-Modena (Sassafras (FR)) 1842[10] 2196[12] 4384[6] 4690[13] **>73f<**
Denton Lad **3** b g Prince Sabo-Dahlawise (IRE) (Caerleon (USA)) (845) 1225[23] 2044[10] 2547[11] 3262[7] 3976[5] 4472[4] 4583[7] 4804[17] 5023[12] **>62f<**
Depreciate **4** ch c Beveled (USA)-Shiny Penny (Glint of Gold) 726[18] 1021[4] 1410[9] 1957[9] *2162[4]* 2422[12] 2895[7] 3936[3] 4773[9] 4905[9] **>72a 68f<**
Deputy Commander (USA) **3** *5066a[2]* **>124a f<**
De Quest **5** b h Rainbow Quest (USA)-De Stael (USA) (Nijinsky (CAN)) 1363a[2] **>120f<**
Derby Darbak (USA) **4** b c Lyphard (USA)-Joy Returned (USA) (Big Spruce (USA)) 1497[4] **>74f<**
Deri Fach **2** b f Warrshan (USA)-Cwm Deri (IRE) (Alzao (USA)) 1444[2] **>56f<**
Derisbay (IRE) **9** b g Gorytus (USA)-Current Bay (Tyrant (USA)) *93[6]* **>19?a f<**
Dernier Croise (FR) **2** ch c Royal Academy (USA)-Guardian Spirit (USA) (Lyphard (USA)) 1657[8] 2268a[4] 2212[6] 3366a[5] 3873a[4] 3925[5] 4106[9] (4543) 4851[2] (4925) **>87f<**
Derrymoyle (IRE) **8** b g Callernish-Luminous Lady (Girandole) 1005a[4]
Derryquin **2** b c Lion Cavern (USA)-Top Berry (High Top) 3489[7] (4908) (5046) **>95f<**
Desert Arrow (USA) **2** b c Gone West (USA)-Afaff (USA) (Nijinsky (CAN)) 2699[12] **>28f<**
Desert Beauty (IRE) **3** b f Green Desert (USA)-Hellenic (Darshaan) 1028[4] 2537[2] (3389) 4308[2] (4787) 4976[3] **>108f<**
Desert Calm (IRE) **8** br g Glow (USA)-Lancette (Double Jump) *294[4] 338[5]* **>54a 58f<**
Desert Cat (IRE) **4** b g Green Desert (USA)-Mahabba (USA) (Elocutionist (USA)) 823[4] 1020[19] 1470[10] 1674[3] 1830[11] 2876[11] 3442[4] **>64f<**
Desert Drama (IRE) **2** f 4663a[5] 5057a[3] **>93f<**
Desert Dunes **4** b g Unfuwain (USA)-Palm Springs (Top Ville) 969[2] 1841[4] **>80f< (DEAD)**
Desert Ease (IRE) **3** bb f Green Desert (USA)-Easy to Copy (USA) (Affirmed (USA)) 3510a[7] **>101+f<**
Desert Fighter **6** b g Green Desert (USA)-Jungle Rose (Shirley Heights) 435[3] (746) (994) 1628[4] **>83?a 82f<**
Desert Green (FR) **8** b g Green Desert (USA)-Green Leaf (USA) (Alydar (USA)) 1874[8] 3969[2] **>61a 68f<**
Desert Horizon **3** b c Danehill (USA)-Sand Grouse (USA) (Arctic Tern (USA)) 931[4] 2345[4] 2761[4] 3190[6] **>100f<**
Desert Invader (IRE) **6** br g Lead on Time (USA)-Aljood (Kris) **1996:** *5144[2] 5165[4] 5230[2] 5264[3]* **1997:** *15[2] 40[4] 81[3] 127[3] 166[7] 243[6] 274[6] 288[3] 359[3] 385[4] 415[3] 579[2] (907) 1047[2] (1132)* 1225[19] *1575[5] 1944[12]* 2019[15] *(2305)* 2567[15] *3075[3] 3583[6] 4301[6] 4813[13]* **>76da 30f<**
Desert King (IRE) **3** b c Danehill (USA)-Sabaah (USA) (Nureyev (USA)) 713a[2] (1060a) (1541a) 2011[4] (2454a) 3646[2] 4204a[2] **>133f<**
Desert Lady (IRE) **2** b f Danehill (USA)-Hooray Lady (Ahonoora) (1847) 2314[2] (2851) 3152[2] 3595[6] **>88f<**
Desert Lore **6** b g Green Desert (USA)-Chinese Justice (USA) (Diesis) *29[8] 54[13]* **>40a 44f<**
Desert Lynx (IRE) **4** b f Green Desert (USA)-Sweeping (Indian King (USA)) 2201[10] (2422) 2833[8] 3130[7] **>78f<**
Desert Mirage **2** b c Green Desert (USA)-Anodyne (Dominion) 4603[7] **>70f<**
Desert Mountain (IRE) **4** b g Alzao (USA)-Curie Point (USA) (Sharpen Up) 451[6] **>85f<**
Desert Native **2** b f Formidable (USA)-Desert Nomad (Green Desert (USA)) 1425[9] 1959[4] 2181[21] 3474[10] 3924[9] 4166[15] **>56f<**
Desert Prince (IRE) **2** b c Green Desert (USA)-Flying Fairy (Bustino) (1396) 2012[2] 3882a[5] 4784[4] **>105f<**
Desert Sand **2** b f Tragic Role (USA)-Miss Suntan (Bruni) 3806[9] (4236) 4634[6] **>76f<**
Desert Shot **7** b g Green Desert (USA)-Out of Shot (Shirley Heights) *627a[5]* **>108a 114f<**
Desert Skimmer (USA) **4** ch f Shadeed (USA)-Massorah (FR) (Habitat) **1996:** *5183[12]* **>25a 49f<**
Desert Spa (USA) **2** b c Sheikh Albadou-Healing Waters (USA) (Temperence Hill (USA)) 3861[5] 4244[4] 4710[6] **>64f<**
Desert Story (IRE) **3** b c Green Desert (USA)-Aliysa (Darshaan) (692) 940[6] 1159[2] 4154[2] 4656a[5] **>112f<**
Desert Time **7** b or br g Green Desert (USA)-Supper Time (Shantung) 1459[12] 1972[2] 3115[19] 3153[18] 3849[8] 4139[18] 4449[10] **>55f<**
Desert Track **3** b c Green Desert (USA)-Mill Path (Mill Reef (USA)) 2330[3] (2873) (4792) 4978[18] **>103f<**
Desert Valentine **2** b c Midyan (USA)-Mo Ceri (Kampala) 4113[12] 4884[11] **>58f<**
Desert Warrior (IRE) **3** b c Fairy King (USA)-Highland Girl (USA) (Sir Ivor) 2172[6] 2492[6] **>60f<**
Desert Zone (USA) **8** ch g Affirmed (USA)-Deloram (CAN) (Lord Durham (CAN)) **1996:** *5114[2] 5179[3] (5200)* **1997:** *4050[15] 4485[10]* **>67a 60f<**
Designer (USA) **2** b c Danzig (USA)-Classy Women (USA) (Relaunch (USA)) 3219[3] 3726[W] 4247[3] 4524[3] **>100f<**
Designer Lines **4** ch g Beveled (USA)-Parrot Fashion (Pieces of Eight) 4714[12] **>81?f<**
Desire's Gold **2** br g Grey Desire-Glory Gold (Hittite Glory) 993[9] 3458[6] 3905[16] **>31f<**
Despina **3** ch f Waajib-Staiconme (USA) (Pancho Villa (USA)) 1144[14] 2873[8] 3470[17] 4277[12] **>43f<**

Deterrent 2 b c Warning-Delve (IRE) (Shernazar) 1872^{12} 2295^{2} 2588^{2} (4167) (4517) 4890^{3} **>95f<**

Detroit City (IRE) 2 b c Distinctly North (USA)-Moyhora (IRE) (Nashamaa) 2842^{12} 3459^{9} 4211^{7} 4752^{7} **>61f<**

Deux Carr (USA) 4 b c Carr de Naskra (USA)-Deux Chance (USA) (Vaguely Noble) *218^{8}*

Deva Lady 2 b f Prince Sabo-Known Line (Known Fact (USA)) 2306^{6} 2534^{4} 3019^{3} 3278^{14} 3707^{3} 4065^{5} 4185^{U} **>77f<**

De-Veers Currie (IRE) 5 b m Glenstal (USA)-Regent Star (Prince Regent (FR)) **1996:** *5130^{16}* **>59df<**

Devilish Charm (USA) 3 ch g Devil's Bag (USA)-Popularity (USA) (Blushing Groom (FR)) 2537^{5} 2924^{6} 4045^{5} (4438) 4794^{3} **>78f<**

Devil River Peek (USA) 5 h Silver Hawk (USA)-Black Tulip (FR) (Fabulous Dancer (USA)) 1067a^{4} 1550a^{2} 1728a^{7} (3004a) (3993a) (4660a) **>127f<**

Dewi Sant 3 ch g Nalchik (USA)-Secret Ingredient (Most Secret) 2311^{10} 2537^{9} **>37f<**

De-Wolf 2 gr f Petong-Doppio (Dublin Taxi) 4904^{5} **>70f<**

Dhes-C 4 b f Lochnager-Keep Cool (FR) (Northern Treat (USA)) **1996:** *5138^{13} 5234^{9}* **1997:** *29^{7} 136^{5} 275^{7}* 480^{8} **>37a 31f<**

Diableneyev (USA) 2 b c Nureyev (USA)-La Pitie (USA) (Devil's Bag (USA)) (4959a) 5057a^{2} **>101f<**

Dia Georgy 6 b h Reesh-Carpadia (Icecapade (USA)) **1996:** *5086^{6} 5124^{11}* **1997:** *34^{7} 128^{8} 216^{11}* 1011^{7} 1501^{10} **>22a 37f<**

Diamond Beach 4 b g Lugana Beach-Cannon Boy (USA) (Canonero (USA)) 4792^{13} **>74f<**

Diamond Crown (IRE) 6 ch g Kris-State Treasure (USA) (Secretariat (USA)) 1283^{2} 1383^{7} 1603^{5} 1798^{3} (2039) 2544^{9} 2716^{5} 3315^{10} 3456^{6} 3758^{9} 3919^{5} 4843^{7} 4923^{5} 4987^{5} **>17a 51f<**

Diamond Drill (USA) 2 b c Geiger Counter (USA)-Decollete (USA) (Al Nasr (FR)) *4592^{3}* 4814^{8} **>58a 47f<**

Diamond Eyre 3 ch f Then Again-Renira (Relkino) **1996:** *5135^{8}* **1997:** *6^{2} 90^{3} 240^{4} (317)* 749^{5} 1129^{5} 1999^{5} 2238^{4} **>62a 54f<**

Diamond On The Run (USA) 2 f *5060a^{7}*

Diamond Pro 6 b h Diamond Prospect (USA)-French Cutie (311a) **>98f<**

Diamonds Are 3 b f Touch of Grey-H R Micro (High Award) **1996:** *5111^{14} 5135^{13} 5166^{4} 5180^{7}* **>40a f<**

Diamond Snake (IRE) 2 b c Thatching-Dorothy Harding (ITY) (Chief Singer) 2822a^{3} 4865a^{9} **>94f<**

Diamond Steve 2 b g Rambo Dancer (CAN)-Shoot to Kill (Posse (USA)) 594^{12} (743) *859^{4}* 1019^{7} 1815^{8} 2031^{4} 2493^{7} 2935^{10} **>38a 59f<**

Diamond White 2 b f Robellino (USA)-Diamond Wedding (USA) (Diamond Shoal) 1213^{2} 1607^{9} 3022^{3} 3237^{3} (3422) 3874a^{8} 4555^{7} **>95f<**

Dibola 2 ch g Dilum (USA)-Bella Bambola (IRE) (Tate Gallery (USA)) 1492^{11} 1684^{8} 2739^{10} 2904^{9} 3707^{18} 4746^{9} 5026^{9} **>43f<**

Dicentra 4 b f Rambo Dancer (CAN)-Be Noble (Vaguely Noble) 3272^{7} **>46a 43f<**

Dick Turpin (USA) 3 br g Red Ransom (USA)-Turn To Money (USA) (Turn To Mars (USA)) 1587^{12} 4158^{3} 4378^{4} 4635^{9} **>79f<**

Dictation (USA) 5 b g Dayjur (USA)-Mofida (Right Tack) **1996:** *5241^{7}* **1997:** *1^{11} 326^{3} 421^{11}* 467^{4} 687^{3} 925^{2} 1220^{2} 1603^{3} 1800^{4} 2019^{8} 2144^{2} **>50a 63f<**

Dieci Anno (IRE) 4 b f Classic Music (USA)-Moira My Girl (Henbit (USA)) **1996:** *5105^{13} 5173^{7}* **>60a 70f<**

Diego 4 b g Belmez (USA)-True Queen (USA) (Silver Hawk (USA)) *1138^{4}* 1648^{2} 2139^{5} (2592) **>71a 76f<**

Diet 11 b g Starch Reduced-Highland Rossie (Pablond) 496^{13} 668^{9} 823^{8} 1613^{6} 1835^{17} 1993^{6} 2032^{4} 2221^{3} 2355^{5} 2472^{6} 2659^{9} 3406^{12} 3484^{6} 3922^{15} **>23f<**

Diffident (FR) 5 b h Nureyev (USA)-Shy Princess (USA) (Irish River (FR)) 1171^{5} 1720a^{5} 2273a^{6} **>126f<**

Dig For Gold 4 ch g Digamist (USA)-Formidable Task (Formidable (USA)) 3933^{10} **>2f<**

Digital Option (IRE) 3 b g Alzao (USA)-Elevated (Shirley Heights) 899^{5} 1449^{8} 1798^{7} 2357^{2} 2564^{15} 3102^{4} *4811^{12}* **>22a 38df<**

Digpast (IRE) 7 ch g Digamist (USA)-Starlit Way (Pall Mall) *291^{6} 380^{2} 405^{9} 566^{8}* 1422^{20} 1677^{13} 1926^{11} 2282^{6} 2892^{4} 3465^{8} 3768^{9} **>74a 45f<**

Digwana (IRE) 4 b g Digamist (USA)-Siwana (IRE) (Dom Racine (FR)) 1507^{8} **>50a 26f<**

Dijon 3 ro g Chilibang-Princess Fair (Crowned Prince (USA)) 1780^{13}

Diktat 2 br c Warning-Arvola (Sadler's Wells (USA)) 4061^{7} **>72f<**

Diktys (GER) 5 b h Kamiros II-Danae (GER) (Nebos (GER)) (2638a) **>113f<**

Dil 2 b c Primo Dominie-Swellegant (Midyan (USA)) 2562^{10} 2720^{2} 3094^{6} 4012^{4} **>72f<**

Diligence (IRE) 2 b c Dilum (USA)-Florinda (CAN) (Vice Regent (CAN)) 1026^{2} (1306) 2012^{4} **>85f<**

Diligent Dodger (IRE) 6 b g Posen (USA)-Crannog (Habitat) 3508a^{10} **>95f<**

Dilkusha (IRE) 2 b g Indian Ridge-Crimson Glen (Glenstal (USA)) 4145^{6} 4779^{6} **>79f<**

Dilly Lane (USA) 2 ch f Personal Hope (USA)-Trickily (USA) (Trempolino (USA)) 4064^{10} 4309^{7} 4459^{4} 4753^{9} **>53f<**

Di Matteo (IRE) 2 ch c Emarati (USA)-Piney Lake (Sassafras (FR)) 3084^{3} 3686^{10} *4056^{2}* **>73a 55f<**

Diminsky (IRE) 2 b c Danehill (USA)-Schwanensee (USA) (Mr Leader (USA)) 3177a^{2}

Diminutive (USA) 4 b g Diesis-Graceful Darby (USA) (Darby Creek Road (USA)) 735^{22} 3444^{3} 3773^{13} 4223^{7} **>83df<**

Dim Ots 2 b f Alhijaz-Placid Pet (Mummy's Pet) (648) 971^{2} (1274) 1593^{2} 3791^{3} 5045^{8} **>81f<**

Dina Line (USA) 3 ch f Diesis-Lajna (Be My Guest (USA)) 1239^{6} 2045^{6} 2330^{4} **>62f<**

Dino's Mistral 4 b g Petong-Marquessa d'Howfen (Pitcairn) *177^{4} 313^{4}* 595^{12} *1287^{7}* 1798^{14} *2911^{5}* 3027^{7} 4607^{6} 4850^{10} **>30a 24f<**

Dirab 4 ch g Groom Dancer (USA)-Double Celt (Owen Dudley) *410^{3}* 470^{6} 846^{4} (1100) 1224^{4} 2142^{5} 2327^{15} 2882^{10} 3069^{3} 3309^{3} 3543^{4} 3826^{3} 3890^{2} 4160^{12} 4585^{6} **>80a 72f<**

Disallowed (IRE) 4 b f Distinctly North (USA)-Miss Allowed (USA) (Alleged (USA)) 4335^{9} **>62da 76f<**

Disco Boy 7 b g Green Ruby (USA)-Sweet And Shiny (Siliconn) **1996:** *5178^{8} 5230^{8}* **>56a 46f<**

Disco Tex 2 b g Rambo Dancer (CAN)-Andbracket (Import) 2493^{13} 3212^{5} 3458^{5} 4265^{14} 4576^{7} **>66f<**

Dishy Diamond 4 b f Prince Daniel (USA)-My Diamond Ring (Sparkling Boy) *2^{6} 98^{8}* 4045^{16} **>18a f<**

Dispol Conqueror (IRE) 4 b g Conquering Hero (USA)-Country Niece (Great Nephew) *42^{7}* **>41f<**

Dispol Dancer 6 ch g Salse (USA)-High Quail (USA) (Blushing Groom (FR)) *16^{10}* **>6a 24f<**

Dispol Diamond 4 b f Sharpo-Fabulous Rina (FR) (Fabulous Dancer (USA)) 526^{11} (896) 1448^{2} 1655^{4} 2002^{7} 2317^{9} 2937^{4} 3285^{13} 4291^{8} 4742^{3} 4872^{5} **>63f<**

Dispol Emerald 2 b f Emarati (USA)-Double Touch (FR) (Nonoalco (USA)) 2042^{5} 2412^{6} 2823^{5} **>51f<**

Dispol Gem 4 b f Rambo Dancer (CAN)-Andbracket (Import) 599^{6} 733^{2} 848^{13} 1116^{12} (1472) 1674^{2} 2021^{4} (2546) 2890^{7} 3064^{8} 3428^{8} 3810^{7} 4455^{9} 4843^{4} 5030^{12} **>63f<**

Dispol Lass 2 b f Mazilier (USA)-Hen Night (Mummy's Game) *1136^{13}* 1626^{4} 2016^{14} 2658^{4} 2904^{7} 3451^{10} 3808^{11} **>42f<**

Dispol Prince 4 b g Risk Me (FR)-Gemma Kaye (Cure The Blues (USA)) 484^{11} 997^{10} 1247^{9} 2544^{12} 2874^{15}

Dissentor (IRE) 5 b g Dancing Dissident (USA)-Helen's Dynasty (Habitat) **1996:** *5130^{15} 5178^{13}* **1997:** *65^{3} 127^{12} 545^{4}* 702^{8} 772^{5} *1134^{5}* **>43a 44f<**

Dissington Times 3 ch g Timeless Times (USA)-Zam's Slave (Zambrano) 1582^{7} 1820^{14} 2351^{4} **>43f<**

Distant Dynasty 7 br g Another Realm-Jianna (Godswalk (USA)) **1996:** *5089^{14} 5183^{13} 5220^{8}* **1997:** *95^{6} 128^{10} 907^{9}* 1236^{17} **>11a 33f<**

Distant King 4 b g Distant Relative-Lindfield Belle (IRE) (Fairy King (USA)) 4214^{10} 4417^{10} 4845^{16} 4924^{16} **>52f<**

Distant Mirage (IRE) 2 b c Caerleon (USA)-Desert Bluebell (Kalaglow) 4237^{2} (4895) 5034a^{5} **>90f<**

Distant Storm 4 ch g Pharly (FR)-Candle in the Wind (Thatching) *375^{12}* **>9a 45f<**

Distinctive Dance (USA) 2 b c Distinctive Pro (USA)-Allison's Dance (USA) (Storm Bird (CAN)) 4007^{2} 4638^{4} **>94f<**

Distinctive Dream (IRE) 3 b g Distinctly North (USA)-Green Side (USA) (Green Dancer (USA)) 532^{4} 649^{7} *871^{5} 1044^{11}* 1638^{5} 2125^{4} 2332^{8} 2407^{2} (2554) (2852) (2921) *(3077)* (3280) 3385^{2} 3709^{6} 4155^{15} (4321) 4565^{2} 4677^{6} 4881^{10} 4975^{2} **>72a 91f<**

Distinctly Lillie (IRE) 2 b br f Distinctly North (USA)-Richmond Lillie (Fairbairn) 722^{7} 1240^{7} 1675^{R} 2240^{7} 2719^{7} **>58f<**

Distinct Vintage (IRE) 2 b c Distinctly North (USA)-Princess Raisa (Indian King (USA)) 938^{5} (2740) 3192^{13} 4126a^{5} **>78+f<**

Ditty Box 3 b f Northern State (USA)-Upholder (Young Generation) **1996:** *5239^{12}* **1997:** *130^{5}* **>8a f<**

Divide And Rule 3 b c Puissance-Indivisible (Remainder Man) 434^{7} 555^{6} 731^{7} 1018^{3} 1275^{4} 3816^{8} 4328^{16} 4527^{16} 4696^{18} 5047^{10} **>54f<**

Divina Luna 4 b f Dowsing (USA)-Famosa (Dancing Brave (USA)) 1874^{5} 2325^{14} 2690^{5} (2894) 3150^{13} 3220^{3} 3736a^{5} 4424^{5} 4777^{6} 4954^{5} **>99f<**

Divine Miss-P 4 ch f Safawan-Faw (Absalom) (729) 883^{16} 953^{7} 1225^{14} 1743^{8} 2372^{6} 2745^{10} 2852^{W} (3323) 3637^{7} (3816) 4233^{6} **>65f<**

Divinity 3 ch f Lycius (USA)-Heavenly Abode (FR) (Habitat) 833^{9} 2188^{3} 2410^{8} **>70?f<**

Divvinayshan (IRE) 2 b c Darshaan-Sharaniya (USA) (Alleged (USA)) 4910^{5} **>59f<**

Dixie Crossroads 2 b f Efisio-Moments Joy (Adonijah) 739^{8} 1293^{6} 1438^{5} 2003^{5} 3228^{4} 3493^{11} **>55f<**

Dixie d'Oats 2 b f Alhijaz-Helsanon (Hello Gorgeous (USA)) 4330^{6} **>57f<**

Dixie Dynamo (USA) 2 bb c Dixie Brass (USA)-Far Out Nurse (USA) 1531a^{3} 2451a^{3} **>94f<**

Dixie Eyes Blazing (USA) 3 ch f Gone West (USA)-Mariakova (USA) (The Minstrel (CAN)) **1996:** *5168^{6}* **1997:** *145^{4}* **>47a f<**

Dizzy Tilly 3 b f Anshan-Nadema (Artaius (USA)) 1140^{3} (1636) 1938^{5} (2374) 2582^{4} 3256^{2} 3432^{10} 4731^{12} 4971^{5} **>35a 73f<**

D J Cat 4 b g Ballad Rock-Four-Legged Friend

(Aragon) **1996:** *5101^{6}* **1997:** 3470^{7} 4043^{4} *4300^{11}* 4465^{9} 4850^{11} *5019^{10}* **>47a 43f<**

D'Marti 2 b f Emarati (USA)-Hellene (Dominion) 2042^{2} 2314^{3} 3070^{3} 3407^{6} **>76f<**

Doating (IRE) 2 b f Doyoun-Hayat (IRE) (Sadler's Wells (USA)) 2840^{9} 4437^{5} **>79f<**

Dockland Executive 2 b c Nomination-Khadino (Relkino) 4165^{16} **>30f<**

Docklands Carriage (IRE) 3 b g Anita's Prince-Zestino (Shack (USA)) 532^{11} 634^{5} 785^{6} 995^{18} (1573) 1807^{7} 2755^{10} 3132^{7} 3336^{9} 3572^{5} **>56f<**

Docklands Courier 5 b g Dominion-High Quail (USA) (Blushing Groom (FR)) *108^{7}* **>54a 50f<**

Docklands Dispatch (IRE) 2 b g Distinctly North (USA)-Frantesa (Red Sunset) 1253^{8} 1444^{6} 1614^{5} 2016^{12} 2587^{6} *(2914)* 3751^{10} 4058^{11} 4163^{4} 4595^{11} 4698^{5} **>63a 62f<**

Docklands Limo 4 b c Most Welcome-Bugle Sound (Bustino) 521^{17} 735^{7} 1268^{3} 2028^{10} 2136^{3} (2967a) 3705^{7} 4136^{14} **>65a 96f<**

Docksider (USA) 2 ch c Diesis-Pump (USA) (Forli (ARG)) 2123^{5} (2699) 3123^{2} 4135^{2} **>108f<**

Doc Ryan's 3 b c Damister (USA)-Jolimo (Fortissimo) 483^{11} 840^{3} 990^{14} 2408^{10} 3463^{7} 3937^{12} 4632^{3} 4741^{3} 4958^{3} (5024) **>73f<**

Doctor Bravious (IRE) 4 b g Priolo (USA)-Sharp Slipper (Sharpo) *52^{7}* 755^{5} 895^{4} 1248^{7} 1606^{10} *2160^{5}* 4792^{19} 4924^{23} **>48a 59f<**

Doctor Leckter (USA) 3 b c Key to the Kingdom (USA)-Clothes Horse (ITY) (Proudest Roman (USA)) 917a^{11} **>90f<**

Doctor's Remedy 11 br g Doc Marten-Champagne Party (Amber Rama (USA)) *285^{7}* **>33?f<**

Dodo (IRE) 2 b f Alzao (USA)-Dead Certain (Absalom) 1847^{5} 2227^{4} 2728^{2} 3187^{2} 3411^{4} **>84f<**

Dog Watch 2 ch g Night Shift (USA)-Abet (USA) (Alleged (USA)) 4564^{9} (4780) 4993^{2} **>84?f<**

Dojima Muteki (JPN) 7 b h Tudenham King (HK)-Dojima Victory (HK) (Clever Fella) **1996:** 5218a^{2} **>119f<**

Dokos (USA) 3 b c Nureyev (USA)-Pasadoble (USA) (Prove Out (USA)) (683) 973^{2} **>101f<**

Dolliver (USA) 5 b g Northern Baby (CAN)-Mabira (Habitat) **1996:** *5102^{7} 5200^{12}* **1997:** *147^{10}* **>32a 64df<**

Domappel 5 b g Domynsky-Appelania (Star Appeal) 962^{8} 1452^{2} **>76f<**

Dominant Air 3 b g Primo Dominie-Area Girl (Jareer (USA)) **1996:** *5146^{9} (5176)* **1997:** *(38) 180^{3}* (2779) 3066^{2} 4175^{5} 4321^{2} (4527) 4770^{4} **>81a 90f<**

Dominant Duchess 3 b f Old Vic-Andy's Find (USA) (Buckfinder (USA)) (539) (764) 2210^{6} 2551^{2} 3218^{2} **>88f<**

Dominelle 5 b m Domynsky-Gymcrak Lovebird (Taufan (USA)) 702^{19} 1223^{5} 1514^{5} 1627^{6} 1828^{3} 2738^{13} 3034^{16} 3240^{18} 3481^{2} 3761^{13} 3856^{8} 4016^{10} **>32a 51f<**

Domino Flyer 4 b g Warrshan (USA)-Great Dilemma (Vaigly Great) **1996:** *(5114) 5175^{3}* **1997:** *(15) 72^{3} 207^{6}* (461) 552^{13} *870^{12} 4050^{11}* 4235^{18} *4810^{4}* 4988^{8} **>42a 78df<**

Domino Style 3 b f Primo Dominie-Corman-Style (Ahonoora) 2549^{5} **>55f<**

Domulla 7 br h Dominion-Ulla Laing (Mummy's Pet) 2476^{7} **>102f<**

Dona Filipa 4 ch f Precocious-Quisissanno (Be My Guest (USA)) 1020^{18} 1390^{14} 1511^{13} 1764^{4} 1963^{10} 2496^{3} 2732^{7} 2891^{5} 3086^{3} 3606^{7} (3698) 3761^{15} 3871^{11} 4169^{14} 4512^{13} 4707^{8} 4997^{7} **>49f<**

Donegal Sean 2 ch c Alhijaz-Malzeta (IRE) (Alzao (USA)) 1675^{5} 2196^{11} 2588^{9} 4974^{18} **>47f<**

Donna's Dancer (IRE) 3 ch g Magical Wonder (USA)-Ice On Fire (Thatching) 1572^{3} 1861^{3} 2032^{2} 2417^{7} 2883^{13} 3121^{8} 3405^{7} **>37f<**

Donna's Double 2 ch c Weldnaas (USA)-Shadha (Shirley Heights) 447^{11} 684^{8} 2018^{9} 2493^{6} **>51f<**

Don Pepe 6 br g Dowsing (USA)-Unique Treasure (Young Generation) **1996:** *5089^{9}* **1997:** 1279^{16} (1857) 2424^{2} 2847^{4} 3100^{4} 3417^{10} 3746^{7} 4228^{14} 4404^{8} 4580^{9} 4738^{18} **>50a 67f<**

Don Sebastian 3 b c Indian Ridge-Sunley Stars (Sallust) *(255) 388^{4}* 509^{8} 2043^{7} 2309^{4} 2392^{2} 2836^{6} *3397^{11}* **>81a 74f<**

Don't Care (IRE) 6 b m Nordico (USA)-Eyeliner (USA) (Raise A Native) 529^{5} 953^{9} 1131^{8} 1561^{7} 1977^{15} 2717^{8} 3224^{2} 3406^{13} 3922^{7} 4842^{17} **>67f<**

Don't Drop Bombs (USA) 8 ch g Fighting Fit (USA)-Promised Star (USA) (Star de Naskra (USA)) **1996:** *5189^{3} 5210^{3}* **1997:** *116^{7} 188^{6} 210^{3} 261^{4} 384^{2} (407)* 1779^{14} 2146^{6} 3197^{9} 3421^{4} 3562^{8} 3971^{7} *4069^{3}* **>49a 41f<**

Don't Forget Mikie (IRE) 4 b g Don't Forget Me-Sokolova (Red Regent) 601^{3} **>56a 64f<**

Don't Forget Shoka (IRE) 3 br f Don't Forget Me-Shoka (FR) (Kaldoun (FR)) 644^{8} 1483^{5} 2730^{16} 4816^{13} **>44a 41f<**

Dont Shoot Fairies 5 ch h Vague Shot-Fairy Fans (Petingo) *244^{6}* **>56a 76f<**

Don't Worry (GER) 3 b c Windwurf (GER)-Danae (GER) (Nebos (GER)) 3998a^{3} 4537a^{4} 4866a^{7} **>120f<**

Don't Worry Me (IRE) 5 b m Dancing Dissident (USA)-Diva Encore (Star Appeal) 1721a^{4} (2106) 3111^{7} 3724^{9} (4124a) 4664a^{8} 4864a^{9} **>116f<**

Don't Worry Mike 3 ch g Forzando-Hat Hill (Roan Rocket) *588^{2} 855^{3}* 1096^{7} 2522^{7} 2828^{9} 3029^{13} 3269^{2} 3702^{2} 4164^{10} *4574^{8} 4795^{4}* 4899^{8} *4980^{2}* **>57a 54f<**

Doodle 2 b f Green Desert (USA)-Quillotern (USA) (Arctic Tern (USA)) 3636^{12} 4211^{12} **>41f<**

Doomna (IRE) 2 b f Machiavellian (USA)-Just a Mirage (Green Desert (USA)) 3151^{2} **>82+f<**

Dooze (IRE) 2 b br f Marju (IRE)-Angelus Chimes (Northfields (USA)) 1645^{12} 2123^{6} 2728^{16} **>47f<**

Dorado Beach 3 b f Lugana Beach-Cannon Boy (USA) (Canonero (USA)) 446^{8} 1485^{10} 1925^{11} 2244^{10} 2724^{8} 3206^{4} 3641^{2} 4518^{13} *(4795)* **>59a 54f<**

Doraid (IRE) 2 b c Danehill (USA)-Quiche (Formidable (USA)) 4433^{3} **>79f<**

Doreg (IRE) 7 br h Fools Holme (USA)-Sally St Clair (Sallust) *(409a) 627a^{4}* **>123a f<**

Doriemus (NZ) 7 ch g Norman Pentaquad (NZ)-Golden Woods (Zamazaan) 5055a^{2} **>128f<**

Dormy Three 7 b g Morston (FR)-Dominant (Behistoun) 838^{7} 1114^{8} *1287^{8}* **>20a 60df<**

Dorton Grange 2 ch f Absalom-Stranger to Fear (Never so Bold) 648^{8} 954^{7} *4479^{9}* 4604^{9} *4799^{9}* **>19a 47f<**

Dot 2 b f Reprimand-Summer Eve (Hotfoot) 1821^{12} 2587^{9} 3090^{4} **>54f<**

Double Action 3 br g Reprimand-Final Shot (Dalsaan) 596^{14} 1018^{5} 1254^{7} 1980^{2} (2044) 2560^{4} 3065^{7} 3273^{7} 3604^{9} (3975) 4282^{2} 4881^{4} **>110f<**

Double Alleged (USA) 3 b br c Alleged (USA)-Danseuse Etoile (USA) (Buckpasser) 847^{2} 1165^{2} 1558^{3} (3918) 4672^{11} 4754^{6} 4891^{8} **>89f<**

Double Appeal (IRE) 2 b f Waajib-Leaping Salmon (Salmon Leap (USA)) 2477^{14} 3060^{7} *3586^{6}* 3808^{4} 4514^{9} **>42a 38f<**

Double Blade 2 b c Kris-Sesame (Derrylin) 4132^{5} 4413^{2} **>82f<**

Double Blue 8 ch g Town And Country-Australia Fair (AUS) (Without Fear (FR)) **1996:** *5150^{10} 5182^{3}* **>71a 89f<**

Double Bounce 7 b g Interrex (CAN)-Double Gift (Cragador) 1317^{6} 2105^{10} 2598^{12} 3217^{13} 3423^{6} 3765^{17} 4456^{3} 4842^{5} 4995^{5} **>92f<**

Double Brandy 2 ch c Elmaamul (USA)-Brand (Shareef Dancer (USA)) 2829^{5} 4818^{5} 4917^{2} **>83f<**

Double Classic (USA) 2 br c Riverman (USA)-Adam's Angel (USA) (Halo (USA)) 4454^{5} 4949^{3} **>70f<**

Double Crest (IRE) 3 b f Royal Academy (USA)-Sweetbird (Ela-Mana-Mou) **1996:** *5142^{5} 5228^{5}* **1997:** *60^{4} 173^{4}* 4608^{P} **>68da f<**

Double Dash (IRE) 4 gr g Darshaan-Safka (USA) (Irish River (FR)) 465^{14} **>49a 63f<**

Double Eclipse (IRE) 5 b h Ela-Mana-Mou-Solac (FR) (Gay Lussac (ITY)) 2055^{6} 3149^{3} (3645) 4130a^{2} 4559^{2} 4965a^{5} **>123f<**

Double Edged 2 ch c Sabrehill (USA)-Island Lake (Kalaglow) 4638^{5} 4793^{4} 5048^{2} **>82f<**

Double-E-I-B-A 3 br g Reprimand-Doppio (Dublin Taxi) 2407^{9} 2748^{10} **>45f<**

Double Eight (IRE) 3 b f Common Grounds-Boldabsa (Persian Bold) **1996:** *5103^{7}* **1997:** 1985^{2} 2468^{3} (2744) (3256) 3970^{12} 4288^{2} *4594^{5}* **>52a 78f<**

Double Espresso (IRE) 3 b f Taufan (USA)-Kilcoy (USA) (Secreto (USA)) **1996:** *(5100) 5141^{3}* **1997:** *46^{2} 250^{5}* 4002^{7} **>84a 75f<**

Double Flight 3 b f Mtoto-Sariah (Kris) 1270^{4} 1624^{11} 2030^{4} 2576^{5} 3272^{2} 3478^{2} 3631^{6} 4172^{5} **>68f<**

Double Gold 3 b f Statoblest-Adriya (Vayrann) 448^{19} 654^{9} 793^{2} (1426) (1487) 1624^{7} (1971) 2569^{5} 2785^{16} 3448^{6} 4179^{15} 4504^{17} **>32f<**

Double Honor (USA) 2 c *5064a^{6}*

Double Indemnity (IRE) 4 b g Doubletour (USA)-Splendid Pleasure (Dunphy) *28^{11} 73^{13}* **>10a 52f<**

Double-J (IRE) 3 b g Fayruz-Farriers Slipper (Prince Tenderfoot (USA)) 1029^{2} 1170^{8} 1673^{4} 1980^{7} 2478^{3} 3888^{12} 4757^{28} **>83f<**

Double March 4 b g Weldnaas (USA)-Double Gift (Cragador) **1996:** *5221^{7} 5235^{4}* **1997:** *10^{5} 61^{6} 120^{5}* 4112^{17} 4243^{19} 4518^{3} 4905^{11} **>63a 59f<**

Double Matt (IRE) 5 b g Double Schwartz-Kasarose (Owen Dudley) 1225^{24} 2179^{13} 2788^{3} 3146^{6} 3417^{8} **>62f<**

Double-O 3 b c Sharpo-Ktolo (Tolomeo) **1996:** *5111^{3} (5207) 5238^{5}* **1997:** *17^{6} (413)* 845^{18} 1029^{7} *1578^{8}* **>79+a 49f<**

Double Or Bust 4 ch f Presidium-Defy Me (Bustino) 2732^{15} 3083^{12} *3399^{8}* **>25a 9f<**

Double Oscar (IRE) 4 ch g Royal Academy (USA)-Broadway Rosie (Absalom) *51^{6} 87^{9} 178^{2} 214^{7} 223^{4} 263^{4} 303^{3}* 702^{9} (760) 896^{2} 956^{4} 1127^{14} 1671^{4} 1857^{3} 2542^{2} (2721) 2900^{5} 3126^{2} (3287) (3334) 3481^{8} 3604^{12} 3649^{22} (3856) 4155^{6} 4280^{8} *4797^{3}* 4995^{14} **>79a 87f<**

Double Power 2 ch f Superpower-Double Decree (Sayf El Arab (USA)) 2037^{10} 3459^{3} 3821^{4} 4159^{6} **>63f<**

Double Rush (IRE) 5 b g Doulab (USA)-Stanza Dancer (Stanford) **1996:** *(5086) (5118) 5281^{7}* **1997:** 1093^{7} *1421^{4}* 1632^{14} 1968^{7} 2218^{4} 2550^{8} 3297^{8} **>67a 45f<**

Double Splendour (IRE) 7 b g Double Schwartz-Princess Pamela (Dragonara Palace (USA)) 1148^{5} 1948^{4} 2326^{9} 2775^{7} 3975^{7} 4226^{3} 4756^{12} 4954^{8} 4995^{2} **>45a 99f<**

Double Star 6 b g Soviet Star (USA)-Startino (Bustino) 3720^{4} 3918^{3} 4547^{5} **>68f<**

Double Trigger (IRE) 6 ch h Ela-Mana-Mou-Solac (FR) (Gay Lussac (ITY)) 891^{8} 2055^{8} (3149) 4118^{4} 4654a^{5} **>126f<**

Double Vintage (IRE) 4 b g Double Schwartz-Great Alexandra (Runnett) 114^{11} 1222^{12} **>14f<**

Doubling Dice 6 b g Jalmood (USA)-Much Too Risky (Bustino) 553^{7} **>33f<**

Doubly Sharp (USA) 3 ch c Diesis-Nijana (USA) (Nijinsky (CAN)) 2046^{11} 2572^{4} 2902^{2} 3283^{5} **>63f<**

Dougs Dream (IRE) 2 ch f Mac's Imp (USA)-Lomond Heights (IRE) (Lomond (USA)) 2202^{9} 2500^{7} 2752^{6} 3426^{8} 4052^{12} **>16a 44f<**

Dovebrace 4 b g Dowsing (USA)-Naufrage (Main Reef) 4307^{13} 4456^{17} 4733^{9} 4995^{17} **>65f<**

Dovedon Star 3 b f Unfuwain (USA)-Whitstar (Whitstead) 2126^{4} 2389^{3} 2583^{4} 3021^{3} 3893^{3} 4699^{2} (4774) **>87f<**

Dover Soul 2 ch f Absalom-Whirling Words (Sparkler) 2781^{3} 3247^{3} 3711^{3} 4818^{11} **>67f<**

Dowdency 5 b m Dowsing (USA)-Tendency (Ballad Rock) **1996:** 5182^{7} **>55a 60f<**

Dower House 2 ch c Groom Dancer (USA)-Rose Noble (USA) (Vaguely Noble) 3047^{5} 3322^{2} 3874a^{4} (4244) 4865a^{4} **>101f<**

Downclose Duchess 2 ch f King's Signet (USA)-Lucky Love (Mummy's Pet) 1924^{4} 2509^{7} 2849^{6} 3474^{7} 4166^{18} 4483^{10} **>46f<**

Down Hearted (IRE) 3 b g Broken Hearted-Italian Cashmere (Taufan (USA)) 1331^{5} 1731^{5} 1838^{8} 3697^{7} **>52f<**

Down The Aisle (USA) 4 gr c Runaway Groom (CAN)-That's My Hon (CAN) (L'Enjoleur (CAN)) 4870a^{2} **>125f<**

Down The Yard 4 b f Batshoof-Sequin Lady (Star Appeal) **1996:** 5178^{5} 5262^{8} **1997:** (42) 85^{6} 125^{9} 169^{4} 206^{7} 245^{5} 1048^{8} 1135^{12} 1689^{18} **>42a 39f<**

Dowty (USA) 5 5066a^{3} **>123a f<**

Doyella (IRE) 3 b f Doyoun-Santella Bell (Ballad Rock) 1316^{3} 1591^{2} (2116) 2380^{5} 3128^{13} 3906^{10} **>81df<**

Doyenne 3 gr f Mystiko (USA)-No Chili (Glint of Gold) 727^{16} 885^{10} 1110^{12} 1568^{W} 2399^{7} 3210^{8} 4519^{4} 4607^{5} 4946^{3} **>50f<**

Dozen Roses 3 b f Rambo Dancer (CAN)-Andbracket (Import) **1996:** 5226^{8} **1997:** 765^{11} 1292^{17} 3641^{6} 4221^{18} **>5a 30f<**

Dragonada (USA) 3 b f Nureyev (USA)-Don't Sulk (USA) (Graustark) (2219) 2586^{4} 3214^{2} 3492^{2} 3913^{2} 4388a^{3} **>108f<**

Dragon Boy 2 b c Bustino-Safe House (Lyphard (USA)) 2849^{5} 3322^{6} 4167^{15} 4989^{14} **>57f<**

Dragon Green 6 gr g Green Desert (USA)-Dunoof (Shirley Heights) **1996:** 5230^{13} 5254^{4} 5271^{10} **>54a 50f<**

Dragonjoy 4 b g Warrshan (USA)-Nazakat (Known Fact (USA)) **1996:** 5114^{9} 5140^{2} 5200^{5} 5235^{11} **1997:** 342^{2} 369^{3} 422^{7} 512^{9} (589) 860^{4} 1005^{8} 1291^{6} 1433^{9} 2160^{3} 2671^{8} 2887^{7} **>55a 61df<**

Dragon's Back (IRE) 4 ch g Digamist (USA)-Classic Choice (Patch) 3054^{10} 3293^{7} 4050^{4} 4548^{10} **>47a 52?f<**

Drain Doctor 2 b g State Diplomacy (USA)-Stilvella (Camden Town) 3212^{12} 3751^{15} 4595^{12} **>2f<**

Drama King 5 b g Tragic Role (USA)-Consistent Queen (Queen's Hussar) **1996:** 5136^{10} 5169^{5} **1997:** 4363^{7} 4609^{2} 4804^{6} **>33a 42f<**

Dramatic Moment 4 b f Belmez (USA)-Drama School (Young Generation) 838^{11} 1822^{2} 2118^{6} 2483^{6} 4108^{13} 4323^{15} **>66f<**

Dramatic Pass (IRE) 8 ch g Coquelin (USA)-Miss Flirt (Welsh Pageant) 1118^{10} 2518^{5} **>1a 13f<** **(DEAD)**

Dr Bones (IRE) 4 bb g Durgam (USA)-Rose Deer (Whistling Deer) 4804^{12} **>71f<**

Dr Caligari (IRE) 5 b g My Generation-Mallabee (Pall Mall) 4992^{18} **>8a 14f<**

Dream Carrier (IRE) 9 b g Doulab (USA)-Dream Trader (Auction Ring (USA)) 15^{12} 211^{5} 280^{3} 327^{3} 386^{4} 401^{2} 490^{4} 1575^{7} (1944) 2302^{3} 2651^{4} 3018^{4} 3608^{5} 4050^{3} **>51a 46f<**

Dream of Nurmi 3 ch g Pursuit of Love-Finlandaise (FR) (Arctic Tern (USA)) 797^{4} 1331^{2} 1741^{3} (2676) 3125^{2} **>75a 96f<**

Dreams End 9 ch h Rainbow Quest (USA)-Be Easy (Be Friendly) 521^{3} 678^{6} (1979) 2026^{20} 2514^{5} 2866^{4} 3705^{16} 4151^{20} **>87f<**

Dr Edgar 5 b g Most Welcome-African Dancer (Nijinsky (CAN)) 61^{7} 144^{3} 216^{2} 295^{5} 418^{3} 598^{10} **>64a 60f<**

Dress Design (IRE) 2 b f Brief Truce (USA)-Lady President 1880a^{5} 3506a^{4} **>88f<**

Dr Fong (USA) 2 ch c Kris S (USA)-Spring Flight (USA) (Miswaki (USA)) (4237) (4674) **>95?f<**

Drift 3 b g Slip Anchor-Norgabie (Northfields (USA)) 3291^{5} 4055^{10} 4300^{9} 4503^{2} 4771^{9} 4821^{3} **>23a 66f<**

Drimard (IRE) 6 ch g Ela-Mana-Mou-Babilla (USA) **1996:** 5177^{14} **>40a 33f<**

Drive Assured 3 gr c Mystiko (USA)-Black Ivor (USA) (Sir Ivor) 505^{3} 837^{3} **>80f<**

Dr Johnson (USA) 3 ch c Woodman (USA)-Russian Ballet (USA) (1540a) (2081a) 2454a^{2} (3842a) **>123+f<**

Dr Martens (IRE) 3 b c Mtoto-Suyayeb (USA) (The Minstrel (CAN)) 2583^{11} 2873^{2} (3463) 4554^{6} **>90f<**

Dr Massini (IRE) 4 b c Sadler's Wells (USA)-Argon Laser (Kris) (522) 1542a^{R} **>116+f<**

Druzus (POL) 4 4127a^{9} **>46f<**

Dr Woodstock 3 br g Rock City-Go Tally-Ho (Gorytus (USA)) 765^{7} 876^{6} 1164^{14} 2151^{9} 2415^{6} 2646^{2} 2892^{3} 3269^{9} 3849^{6} 4043^{7} **>31a 45f<**

Dry Lightning 2 b f Shareef Dancer (USA)-Valkyrie (Bold Lad (IRE)) 1760^{6} 2196^{5} **>60f<**

Dtoto 5 b g Mtoto-Deposit (Thatch (USA)) 4516^{16} **>43f<**

Dubai Dolly (IRE) 4 b f Law Society (USA)-Lola Sharp (Sharpen Up) 2701^{5} **>34?f<**

Dubelle 7 b m Dubassoff (USA)-Flopsy Mopsy (Full of Hope) 4045^{8} **>44f<**

Dublivia 2 b f Midyan (USA)-Port Isaac (USA) (Seattle Song (USA)) 3744^{11} 4227^{5} 4597^{9} **>41f<**

Duck Row (USA) 2 ch c Diesis-Sunny Moment (USA) (Roberto (USA)) (4274) 4880^{6} **>100f<**

Dudley Allen 2 ch c Superlative-Smooth Flight (Sandhurst Prince) 4167^{14} 4581^{11} **>39f<**

Duello 6 b g Sure Blade (USA)-Royal Loft (Homing) 661^{4} 895^{11} 1035^{14} 1262^{4} 1489^{5} 1745^{6} 2465^{4} 2835^{5} 3138^{2} 3392^{4} 3690^{9} 3987^{12} 4219^{11} 4319^{12} 4629^{2} 4696^{8} **>71?a 71f<**

Due South 2 b f Darshaan-Island Wedding (USA) (Blushing Groom (FR)) 2524^{7} 3103^{4} (3479) 3802^{3} 4140^{3} **>93f<**

Duffertoes 5 ch g High Kicker (USA)-Miss Poll Flinders (Swing Easy (USA)) 91^{8} 209^{8} 869^{6} 1001^{12} **>41a 49f<**

Duke of Flight (USA) 4 b c Alleged (USA)-Stage Flight (ITY) (Lord Durham (CAN)) **1996:** (5158a) **>118f<**

Duke Valentino 5 br h Machiavellian (USA)-Aldhabyih (General Assembly (USA)) **1996:** (5106) 5150^{3} **1997:** 56^{5} 82^{7} 146^{2} (179) 220^{6} 254^{4} (297) 363^{6} 398^{8} 444^{21} 661^{6} 947^{14} 1154^{7} 1830^{2} 2465^{7} 2672^{2} 2906^{10} 3105^{10} 3382^{10} **>80a 58f<**

Dukhan (USA) 3 b c Silver Hawk (USA)-Azayim (Be My Guest (USA)) 1499^{5} 4060^{6} 4177^{10} **>82f<**

Dulas Bay 3 b g Selkirk (USA)-Ivory Gull (USA) (Storm Bird (CAN)) 840^{14} 944^{5} 1138^{11} 1299^{13} 3430^{3} 3781^{2} 4287^{11} 4509^{8} **>22a 56f<**

Dulcileme (GER) 2 b c Katoleme (SWI)-Dulcikalle (SWI) (Kaldoun (FR)) (4538a) **>84+f<**

Dulcinea 3 ch f Selkirk (USA)-Ahohoney (Ahonoora) 992^{8} 1587^{6} (2231) 2695^{2} 2835^{13} (3980) 4578^{4} **>74f<**

Dummer Golf Time 4 ch c Clantime-Chablisse (Radetzky) 895^{10} 1745^{7} 2416^{6} 2785^{4} 3143^{2} 3328^{3} (3690) 3987^{2} 4219^{7} 4979^{5} **>61+a 72f<**

Dunabrattin 4 b c Blakeney-Relatively Smart (Great Nephew) 2008^{W} 4072^{4} 4312^{5} 4743^{9} 4912^{13} 4986^{7} **>12a 52f<**

Duncombe Hall 4 b g Salse (USA)-Springs Welcome (Blakeney) 487^{3} 640^{2} 1010^{3} 1665^{3} 1964^{4} 2398^{12} 2592^{10} (3928) 4170^{11} 4405^{4} 4794^{10} **>54a 51f<**

Dundel (IRE) 3 gr f Machiavellian (USA)-Dunoof (Shirley Heights) 1028^{5} 1318^{7} 1866^{4} (2143) 2894^{7} 3119^{4} 3403^{3} 3741^{3} 4583^{5} 4859^{7} **>86f<**

Dunmebrains (IRE) 4 ch f Rich Charlie-Branch Out (Star Appeal) **1996:** 5234^{12} **>17a 54f<**

Dunrowan 4 b f Dunbeath (USA)-Sun Lamp (Pall Mall) 1281^{11} 1996^{10} 2541^{6} **>58f<**

Dunston Bill 3 b g Sizzling Melody-Fardella (ITY) (Molvedo) 2544^{10} 2783^{8} **>42f<**

Dunston Gold 3 ch g Risk Me (FR)-Maria Whittaker (Cure The Blues (USA)) 2670^{9} **>10a 36f<**

Dunston Star (IRE) 4 b g Poet's Dream (IRE)-Cherry Glory (Final Straw) 2673^{5} **>2a f<**

Durable George 3 ch g Durandal-Sun Follower (Relkino) 1088^{9} 1237^{16} 1967^{9} 2231^{9} 2481^{9} 2663^{6} 2954^{11} 3437^{7} **>34a 40f<**

Duraid (IRE) 5 ch g Irish River (FR)-Fateful Princess (USA) (Vaguely Noble) 528^{4} 599^{7} 686^{5} 1145^{10} 1802^{4} (2290) 2678^{10} 3105^{2} 3605^{4} 3810^{4} 3976^{13} 4147^{4} (4410) 4781^{23} **>88f<**

Durar 2 ch c Wolfhound (USA)-Mashair (USA) (Diesis) 1749^{5} 3490^{4} 3887^{4} 4690^{12} **>69f<**

Durgams Delight (IRE) 2 b f Durgam (USA)-Miromaid (Simply Great (FR)) 2110^{U} 3806^{13} 4056^{8} 4413^{9} 4994^{24} **>38a 54f<**

Durgams First (IRE) 5 ch g Durgam (USA)-Miromaid (Simply Great (FR)) 580^{8} 843^{4} 1222^{6} (1515) 1779^{13} 2236^{4} 2413^{6} 2753^{2} 3116^{2} 3429^{2} (3853) 4161^{6} 4521^{2} 4923^{4} **>68?a 64f<**

Durham 6 ch g Caerleon (USA)-Sanctuary (Welsh Pageant) 986^{11} 1491^{8} 1795^{10} 2284^{5} 2490^{6} 2592^{4} 2867^{2} 3203^{2} (3318) 3748^{5} 4104^{2} 4374^{7} **>62a 76f<**

Durham Flyer 2 b c Deploy-Hyde Princess (Touch Paper) 594^{7} 993^{6} 1819^{2} 2168^{4} 2936^{4} 3306^{7} 4265^{13} **>71f<**

Dushyantor (USA) 4 b c Sadler's Wells (USA)-Slightly Dangerous (USA) (Roberto (USA)) 1736^{2} 2104^{6} 2559^{6} (3596) 4005^{2} **>121f<**

Dust 3 b f Green Desert (USA)-Storm Warning (Tumble Wind (USA)) 1876^{5} 3715^{4} 4070^{5} 4333^{19} **>62f<**

Dust Dancer 3 ch f Suave Dancer (USA)-Galaxie Dust (USA) (Blushing Groom (FR)) (485) 1318^{5} 1875^{5} (2348) 2869^{4} (3492) (3877a) 4256a^{7} 4557^{7} **>116f<**

Dutch 5 ch g Nicholas Bill-Dutch Princess (Royalty) 4072^{9} 4743^{15}

Dutch Dyane 4 b f Midyan (USA)-Double Dutch (Nicholas Bill) **1996:** 5101^{8} 5149^{8} **1997:** 73^{6} 356^{7} 1417^{6} 2279^{2} **>36da 42f<**

Dutch Lad 2 b c Alnasr Alwasheek-Double Dutch (Nicholas Bill) 1396^{8} 3745^{7} 4064^{11} 4778^{3} 4875^{2} **>73f<**

Dutch Patriarch 2 b f Noble Patriarch-Dunnington

(Risk Me (FR)) 1626^{5} 2493^{11} **>29f<**

Duty Time 6 b h Night Shift (USA)-Moorish Idol (Aragon) 4261a^{2} **>104f<**

Dyanko 4 b g Midyan (USA)-Regain (Relko) **1996:** *5269^{10}* **>32df<**

Dyce 3 b f Green Ruby (USA)-Miss Display (Touch Paper) *3043^{7}* 4700^{12} **>8a f<**

Dyhim (USA) 6 b h Polish Navy (USA)-Savage Bunny (USA) (Never Bend) *392a^{3}* **>104a f<**

Dyhim Diamond (IRE) 3 ch c Night Shift (USA)-Happy Landing (FR) (Homing) 3372a^{2} 4124a^{2} (4390a) **>118f<**

E

Eager Hero 2 ch c Keen-Honour and Glory (Hotfoot) 1819^{13} 2016^{13} 3751^{13} **>42f<**

Eager To Please 3 ch g Keen-Ackcontent (USA) (Key To Content (USA)) **1996:** *5224^{9} 5245^{4} 5278^{3}* **1997:** *12^{2} 103^{5} (212) 237^{2} (379)* 434^{8} *(489)* 649^{10} 1238^{6} 1375^{8} (1807) 2169^{7} **>80a 65f<**

Eagle Canyon (IRE) 4 b br g Persian Bold-Chrism (Baptism) *182^{11} 426^{8}* 866^{4} 1036^{5} 1329^{2} 1685^{3} 2297^{5} 2653^{7} (2787) **>78a 81f<**

Eagle Dancer 5 b g Persian Bold-Stealthy (Kind of Hush) 1105^{4} *1430^{5}* **>67a 81f<**

Eagle's Cross (USA) 2 b c Trempolino (USA)-Shining Bright (Rainbow Quest (USA)) 3688^{4} 4758^{7} **>84f<**

Earl Of March 3 b c Caerleon (USA)-Homage (Ajdal (USA)) 1719a^{2} **>112f<**

Early Memory (USA) 2 ch f Devil's Bag (USA)-Grenzen (USA) (Grenfall (USA)) 4093a^{12} **>48f<**

Early Peace (IRE) 5 b g Bluebird (USA)-Everything Nice (Sovereign Path) 2035^{3} 2352^{5} 2539^{4} *2607^{7}* 3620^{3} **>55f<**

Eastbury Rose 3 ch f Beveled (USA)-Shapina (Sharp Edge) 1434^{12} **>30f<**

Eastern Eagle (IRE) 3 b g Polish Patriot (USA)-Lady's Turn (Rymer) 475^{5} 1023^{14} *4485^{13}* **>61f<**

Eastern Firedragon (IRE) 3 b f Shalford (IRE)-Doobie Do (Derring-Do) 634^{9} **>58f<**

Eastern Glory (USA) 2 ch c Eastern Echo (USA)-Brattice Cloth (USA) (L'Enjoleur (CAN)) 2905^{5} **>50f<**

Eastern Lyric 2 gr f Petong-Songlines (Night Shift (USA)) (999) 1149^{5} 1635^{4} 3152^{9} 3571^{3} 3817^{4} 3965^{11} 4296^{4} 4522^{8} **>75f<**

Eastern Project (IRE) 3 b c Project Manager-Diandra (Shardari) 4583^{14} **>82f<**

Eastern Prophets 4 b g Emarati (USA)-Four Love (Pas de Seul) (520) 726^{3} 834^{4} 1772^{12} 3198^{9} 3771^{11} 3984^{10} 4321^{11} 4842^{7} **>68f<**

Eastern Purple (IRE) 2 b c Petorius-Broadway Rosie (Absalom) 2842^{8} (3306) 3706^{5} 3774^{4} 4232^{4} **>89f<**

Easter Ogil (IRE) 2 ch g Pips Pride-Piney Pass (Persian Bold) 4544^{7} 4747^{2} **>76f<**

Eastleigh 8 b g Efisio-Blue Jane (Blue Cashmere) **1996:** *5086^{2} 5149^{6} 5223^{7} 5254^{6} 5271^{7}* **1997:** *104^{5} 195^{4} 211^{6} 290^{7} (352) 407^{2} 490^{8}* 848^{12} *1125^{6} 1576^{2}* 1802^{9} *2070^{6}* 2488^{12} *3413^{13}* 3933^{11} *4484^{3}* 4742^{11} 4987^{18} **>50a 36f<**

Eastwell Hall 2 b c Saddlers' Hall (IRE)-Kinchenjunga (Darshaan) 1744^{9} 2588^{8} 2917^{19} 4044^{16} 4334^{15} **>55f<**

Eastwell Minstrel 2 ch c Risk Me (FR)-Ramz (IRE) (The Minstrel (CAN)) 2003^{14} (2396) 2936^{8} **>65?f<**

Easycall 3 b c Forzando-Up And Going (FR) (Never so Bold) 1455^{8} 2106^{5} 2599^{6} 3023^{2} 3724^{12} 4098^{5} 4239^{6} **>110f<**

Easy Dollar 5 ch g Gabitat-Burglars Girl (Burglar) 452^{2} 671^{2} 1720a^{3} 2056^{9} 2830^{6} **>108f<**

Easy Listening (USA) 5 b g Easy Goer (USA)-Queen of Song (USA) (His Majesty (USA)) 4295^{10} **>93?f<**

Easy Nomi 7 b g Nomination-Muna (Thatch (USA)) 2496^{11} *2603^{15}*

Easy Risk 2 ch f Risk Me (FR)-Egnoussa (Swing Easy (USA)) 3628^{8}

Easy Song (USA) 3 b c Easy Goer (USA)-Queen of Song (USA) (His Majesty (USA)) 1207^{9} 1611^{3} 3277^{4} 4009^{2} 4223^{3} (4506) **>86f<**

Eaton Park (IRE) 3 ch c Mac's Imp (USA)-Pepilin (Coquelin (USA)) 1375^{10} 2167^{10} **>43f<**

Eat Your Pear 3 ch f Dunbeath (USA)-Track Angel (Ardoon) 3807^{6} **>22f<**

Eau Benite 6 br g Monsanto (FR)-Hopeful Waters (Forlorn River) *2301^{12}*

Eau Secours (FR) 5 ch m Lesotho (USA)-Nomina (USA) (Northjet) *1943^{8}*

Ebadiyla (IRE) 3 b f Sadler's Wells (USA)-Ebaziya (IRE) (Darshaan) 1195a^{3} 1738^{6} (2814a) 4665a^{12} (4965a) **>123f<**

Eben Albadou (USA) 3 b c Sheikh Albadou-Stealthy Lady (USA) (J O Tobin (USA)) 991^{16}

Ebony Boy 4 bl g Sayf El Arab (USA)-Actress (Known Fact (USA)) **1996:** *5134^{5} 5179^{4}* **>48a 38f<** **(DEAD)**

E B Treasure 2 b f Precocious-Petite Elite (Anfield) *1758^{10}* 2233^{7} 2412^{9} *2914^{6}* 3106^{13} 3312^{9} 4688^{6} **>31f<**

Ebullisante (IRE) 3 br f Lead on Time (USA)-Bubbling Danseuse (USA) (Arctic Tern (USA)) 3876a^{2} **>85f<**

Eccentric Dancer 4 b f Rambo Dancer (CAN)-Lady Eccentric (IRE) (Magical Wonder (USA)) **1996:** *5130^{12}* **1997:** *28^{12} 111^{9} 192^{10} 312^{11}* **>2a 47f<**

Eco Friendly 2 ch c Sabrehill (USA)-Flower Girl (Pharly (FR)) 3201^{10} 4017^{2} 4793^{2} (5048) **>83f<**

Ecoute (USA) 4 b f Manila (USA)-Soundings (USA) (Mr Prospector (USA)) **1996:** (5192a) **>105f<**

Edan Heights 5 b g Heights of Gold-Edna (Shiny Tenth) 735^{15} 933^{8} 1414^{11} 2118^{2} 2341^{7} 2574^{6} 2839^{8} 3616^{3} 3916^{5} (4063) 4151^{8} 4294^{10} **>81f<**

Eddie Rombo 2 b g Aragon-Jolimo (Fortissimo) 1760^{20} 2356^{7} 2881^{9} 3212^{10} **>49f<**

Eden Dancer 5 b g Shareef Dancer (USA)-Dash (Connaught) 1686^{7} 2170^{4} 3758^{14} **>41f<**

Eden Rock (GER) 3 b c Dashing Blade-Eriphyle (GER) (Surumu (GER)) (817a) 1544a^{5} 2097a^{7} 2821a^{3} 3376a^{3} 4122a^{2} 4662a^{4} **>116f<**

Edgar Kirby 6 ch g Caerleon (USA)-Martha Stevens (USA) (Super Concorde (USA)) 571^{8} **>43a 65f<**

Edipo Re 5 b h Slip Anchor-Lady Barrister (Law Society (USA)) 4903^{4} 5052^{16} **>86f<**

Edna's Gift (IRE) 2 b f Cyrano de Bergerac-Glenstal Priory (Glenstal (USA)) (1626) *1789^{2}* 2016^{7} 2378^{3} 2681^{10} *2914^{2} 3395^{6}* 3563^{6} *4483^{11}* **>62da 57f<**

Ed's Folly (IRE) 4 b g Fayruz-Tabriya (Nishapour (FR)) 601^{11} 1012^{3} 1250^{7} 1446^{2} 1666^{10} 2216^{11} 2747^{3} 3082^{5} 3299^{2} 3561^{4} *3860^{11}* 4711^{3} **>35a 59f<**

Edwardian 2 ch c Sanglamore (USA)-Woodwardia (USA) (El Gran Senor (USA)) 4740^{2} **>85+f<**

Edward Seymour (USA) 10 b g Northern Baby (CAN)-Regal Leader (USA) (Mr Leader (USA)) *139^{10}*

Effectual 4 b g Efisio-Moharabuiee (Pas de Seul) *(336) 661^{3} 1123^{2}* (1268) (1414) 1482^{3} 1934^{6} **>92a 93f<**

Effervescence 3 ch c Efisio-Petite Elite (Anfield) **1996:** *5113^{2} 5228^{4} 5238^{2} (5252) (5272)* **1997:** *(12)* 448^{20} 1017^{16} *1154^{5}* 1921^{2} 2125^{7} 2392^{5} 4219^{10} *4570^{4}* **>91a 76df<**

Efficacious (IRE) 4 ch f Efisio-Bushti Music (Bustino) **1996:** *5117^{5} 5145^{3} 5189^{8} 5244^{5} 5254^{7}* **1997:** *43^{7} 104^{11} 256^{8} 313^{6} 390^{5} 418^{8} 487^{3}* 753^{5} *1086^{5}* 1507^{12} 3248^{16} **>36a 39f<**

Efficacy 6 b m Efisio-Lady Killane (Reform) *172^{7} 512^{3} 593^{12} 3399^{7}* **>50a 40f<**

Efipetite 4 ch f Efisio-Petite Elite (Anfield) **1996:** *5175^{8} 5256^{6}* **1997:** *42^{3} 85^{10} 125^{5} 169^{6} 245^{3} 286^{5} 428^{6}* 526^{16} *1135^{4} 1433^{7} 1580^{7} 1754^{14}* 2109^{7} 2317^{12} *2368^{9}* 3039^{11} 3316^{9} *3581^{11}* **>38a 17f<**

Efodos 2 ch f Pursuit of Love-Sariza (Posse (USA)) 4904^{22} **>3f<**

Efra 8 b g Efisio-Ra Ra (Lord Gayle (USA)) 520^{14} 643^{9} **>58f<**

Egoli (USA) 3 ch f Seeking the Gold (USA)-Krisalya (Kris) (3550) 3913^{14} 4142^{4} 4578^{2} **>94f<**

Ego Night (IRE) 2 c b Night Shift (USA)-Sharp Ego (USA) (Sharpen Up) 5033a^{2}

Eider Hill 3 b f Alawir (FR)-Matrah (Northfields (USA)) 4277^{6} 4579^{10} 4848^{7} **>55f<**

Ei Ei 2 b c North Briton-Branitska (Mummy's Pet) 2870^{11} 4165^{5} 4740^{3} **>81f<**

Eiffel Tiger (IRE) 2 b br c Paris House-Rosa Bengala (Balidar) 4459^{9} 4779^{19} 4966^{13} **>53f<**

Eileen's Lady 3 b f Mtoto-Laughsome (Be My Guest (USA)) *568^{5}* 889^{13} **>57a 27f<**

Ejeer (IRE) 3 b g Jareer (USA)-Precious Egg (Home Guard (USA)) *300^{4} 329^{4} 427^{5}* 462^{6} **>61a 53f<**

Ekaterini Paritsi 3 b f Timeless Times (USA)-Wych Willow (Hard Fought) **1996:** *5098^{2} 5135^{9} 5187^{3} 5279^{4}* **1997:** *45^{3} 102^{6} 158^{6} 212^{5}* **>45a 60f<**

Ela Agapi Mou (USA) 4 b g Storm Bird (CAN)-Vaguar (USA) (Vaguely Noble) **1996:** *5185^{7}* **1997:** *13^{9}* 770^{7} **>38a 60f<**

Ela-Aristokrati (IRE) 5 b h Danehill (USA)-Dubai Lady (Kris) 736^{2} 1736^{4} 2104^{5} 2559^{4} 3374a^{3} **>119f<**

Elabellou (IRE) 2 b f Ela-Mana-Mou-Salabella (Sallust) 4582^{7} **>47f<**

Elakik 2 b c Green Desert (USA)-Narjis (USA) (Blushing Groom (FR)) 1872^{3} 2286^{3} (3253) 4044^{12} 4380^{3} 4849^{3} **>83f<**

Ela Man Howa 6 b g Mtoto-Top Treat (USA) (Topsider (USA)) *78^{4} 116^{4} 183^{7} 236^{5} 262^{4}* **>59a 56f<**

Ela-Ment (IRE) 5 b g Ela-Mana-Mou-Dorado Llave (USA) (Well Decorated (USA)) **1996:** *5084^{10}* **>26a 23f<**

Elanaaka 2 ch f Lion Cavern (USA)-Mousaiha (USA) (Shadeed (USA)) 3757^{3} 4215^{2} **>78+f<**

El Angelo (USA) 5 El Gran Senor (USA)-Angela Serra (Arctic Tern (USA)) 5063a^{6} **>117f<**

Ela-Yie-Mou (IRE) 4 ch g Kris-Green Lucia (Green Dancer (USA)) 190a^{14} 267a^{8} 3053^{8} 3392^{11} 3815^{5} 4104^{5} 4313^{3} 4562^{15} **>69f<**

Elaysha (USA) 3 ch f Gulch (USA)-Key Flyer (USA) (Nijinsky (CAN)) 2687^{9}

Elbaaha 3 ch f Arazi (USA)-Gesedeh (Ela-Mana-Mou) 1591^{4} 2389^{4} 2924^{4} (3319) 3694^{2} 4136^{2} 4443^{9} 5043^{2} **>100f<**

El Bailador (IRE) 6 b g Dance of Life (USA)-Sharp Ego (USA) (Sharpen Up) 4714^{19} **>62a 71?f<**

Elba Magic (IRE) 2 b f Faustus (USA)-Dependable (Formidable (USA)) 2394^{8} 3322^{7} 4361^{6} 4605^{12} **>63f<**

El Bardador (IRE) 4 b g Thatching-Osmunda (Mill Reef (USA)) *54^{7}* 1001^{8} *1287^{9}* **>18a 61f<**

Elbarree (IRE) 2 b g Green Desert (USA)-Walimu (IRE) (Top Ville) 5041^{13} **>50f<**

Elcari (IRE) 2 b c Merdon Melody-Earles-Field (Wolverlife) 3177a^{3} 4532a^{3}

El Don 5 b g High Kicker (USA)-Madam Gerard (Brigadier Gerard) **1996:** *5260^{10}* **1997:** *16^{8}* **>16a 44f<**

Eldorado (IRE) 3 b c Ela-Mana-Mou-Happy Tidings (Hello Gorgeous (USA)) 3842a^{6} **>104f< (DEAD)**

Election Day (IRE) 5 b h Sadler's Wells (USA)-Hellenic (Darshaan) 736^{5} 891^{3} 1033^{6} 2055^{3} 3149^{4} 3645^{5} **>126f<**

Elegant Dance 3 ch f Statoblest-Furry Dance (USA) (Nureyev (USA)) 989^{5} 1272^{10} **>64f<**

Elegant Warning (IRE) 3 b f Warning-Dance It (USA) (Believe It (USA)) 672^{3} 960^{7} 1610^{2} 2677^{6} 4782^{6} **>113f<**

Eleonora d'Arborea 2 b f Prince Sabo-Kala Rosa (Kalaglow) 1806^{2} 2024^{17} 2335^{5} 2875^{6} (3070) 3468^{6} 3932^{5} **>84f<**

Eleos 3 c 1205a^{5} **>99f<**

Eleventh Duke (IRE) 2 b c Imperial Frontier (USA)-Disregard That (IRE) (Don't Forget Me) 648^{4} 1812^{4} 2697^{7} 2942^{3} (3474) (3791) 3925^{2} 4232^{7} 4522^{11} **>89f<**

Elfland (IRE) 6 b g Fairy King (USA)-Ridge The Times (USA) (Riva Ridge (USA)) 1166^{D} (2124) 2598^{3} 3975^{5} 4121^{7} 4282^{25} **>95f<**

Elhabub 2 b c Lion Cavern (USA)-Million Heiress (Auction Ring (USA)) 3219^{2} 3726^{2} 4513^{2} **>83f<**

Elhafid (USA) 3 ch c Nureyev (USA)-Shy Dame (USA) (Damascus (USA)) 3864^{10} **>66f<**

Elhayq (IRE) 2 b c Nashwan (USA)-Mahasin (USA) (Danzig (USA)) 4520^{3} 4740^{4} **>81f<**

Elite Bliss (IRE) 5 b m Tirol-Krismas River (Kris) **1996:** *5115^{4} 5167^{3}* **1997:** *5^{8} 232^{8}* 465^{6} 595^{9} **>49da 49df<**

Elite Force (IRE) 4 b g Fairy King (USA)-La Petruschka (Ballad Rock) *290^{10}* **>76f<**

Elite Hope (USA) 5 ch m Moment of Hope (USA)-Chervil (USA) (Greenough (USA)) **1996:** *5112^{8} (5170) 5249^{9} (5266)* **1997:** *(35) 81^{2} 254^{3} 316^{4}* 1035^{15} 1453^{9} **>79+a 53f<**

Eliza 3 ch f Shavian-One Degree (Crooner) *118^{6}* 1851^{3} 2491^{10} 4220^{8} 4695^{19} *4809^{10}* **>29a 47f<**

Eliza Acton 2 b f Shirley Heights-Sing Softly (Luthier) 4740^{6} (4957) **>74f<**

Eljjanah (USA) 2 b c Riverman (USA)-True Celebrity (USA) (Lyphard (USA)) 1933^{10} 2336^{3} 2881^{2} **>71f<**

Ella (IRE) 2 b f Brief Truce (USA)-The Queen of Soul (Chief Singer) (2370) 2862^{6} (3368a) 4387a^{5} 4675^{3} **>85+f<**

Ella Falls (IRE) 2 ch f Dancing Dissident (USA)-Over Swing (FR) (Saint Cyrien (FR)) 1466^{4} 1760^{9} 2288^{6} **>67f<**

Ella Lamees 3 b f Statoblest-Lamees (USA) (Lomond (USA)) 778^{7} 1248^{12} 1843^{6} 2921^{2} (3092) 4878^{14} 4979^{20} **>66f<**

Ellamine 3 b f Warrshan (USA)-Anhaar (Ela-Mana-Mou) *4795^{9} 4980^{9}* **>24a f<**

Elle Mac 4 b f Merdon Melody-Tripolitaine (FR) (Nonoalco (USA)) **1996:** *5161^{10}* **1997:** *16^{13}* **>8a 31?f<**

Ellenber 2 ch g Risk Me (FR)-Brig of Ayr (Brigadier Gerard) 1228^{8} *1941^{13}* 2153^{5} 2383^{3} 2714^{6} 3258^{10} *4812^{7}* 4994^{11} **>51a 55f<**

Ellenbrook (IRE) 2 b f Petorius-Short Stay (Be My Guest (USA)) 572^{5} 743^{2} 927^{2} *1137^{2} (1290) (1432)* 1829^{3} (2031) (2165) 4162^{2} 4419^{3} 4468^{8} **>65+a 74f<**

Ellens Lad (IRE) 3 b c Polish Patriot (USA)-Lady Ellen (Horage) 434^{2} 694^{5} 834^{6} 1158^{9} 1294^{4} 2517^{6} **>89f<**

Ellerbeck 2 b f Priolo (USA)-Cadisa (Top Ville) 4841^{9} 4993^{14} **>25f<**

Elle Shaped (IRE) 7 b g Treasure Kay-Mamie's Joy (Prince Tenderfoot (USA)) 949^{17} **>24a 89?f<**

Elleysanta 2 b f Warrshan (USA)-Sophisticated Baby (Bairn (USA)) *1136^{4}* 1827^{4} 2306^{4} 2689^{10} 3794^{8} *4479^{6}* 4897^{8} **>30a 64f<**

Ellway Lady (IRE) 3 br f Be My Native (USA)-Scaravie (IRE) (Drumalis) 2374^{11} 2782^{12} 4063^{5} 4503^{3} **>62f<**

Ellway Prince 2 b c Prince Sabo-Star Arrangement (Star Appeal) 1932^{4} 4908^{4} **>64f<**

Elly Fleetfoot (IRE) 5 b m Elmaamul (USA)-Fleetwood Fancy (Taufan (USA)) *418^{7}* 1093^{2} (1247) 1435^{4} 1636^{P} **>50a 60f<**

El Maimoun 2 b c Royal Academy (USA)-Tootsiepop (USA) (Robellino (USA)) (1723a) (4126a) **>101f<**

Elmhurst (USA) 7 b/br g Wild Again (USA)-Mimbet(USA) Raise A Native(USA)*(5061a)***>130a f<**

Elmortero Derufino (IRE) 2 b c In The Wings-Cresilla (IRE (Fabulous Dancer (USA))4761a^{2} **>84f<**

Elnadim (USA) 3 b br c Danzig (USA)-Elle Seule (USA) (Exclusive Native (USA)) (1650) 2560^{2} (2925) (3747) (4421) 4782^{4} **>128+f<**

El Nido 9 ch g Adonijah-Seleter (Hotfoot) **1996:** *5177^{2}* **1997:** *(68) 139^{5} 157^{4} (205) 231^{3} 242^{4} 272^{7} 356^{4} 543^{4} 580^{6}* 1100^{16} *1133^{9}* 1494^{9} *2910^{13}* 3540^{9} *4055^{11} 4811^{15}* 4986^{9} **>19a 42f<**

El Opera (IRE) 4 b f Sadler's Wells (USA)-Ridge The Times (USA) (Riva Ridge (USA)) 839^{5} 1101^{7} 1610^{4} 1776^{4} **>94f<**

Eloquent 2 b f Polar Falcon (USA)-Lady Barrister (Law Society (USA)) (2202) 2962^{2} 3422^{7} **>94f<**

El Presidente 4 b g Presidium-Spanish Princess (King of Spain) 4918^{12} **>39f<**

Elraas (USA) 5 b g Gulch (USA)-Full Card (USA) (Damascus (USA)) **1996:** *5268^{7}* **1997:** *177^{6}* **>32a 5f<**

Elsaayoura (IRE) 2 b f Indian Ridge-Pursue (Auction Ring (USA)) 3638^{10} **>52f<**

Elshamms 2 ch f Zafonic (USA)-Gharam (USA) (Green Dancer (USA)) (3201) 3740^{3} 4786^{5} **>95f<**

Elsinore (IRE) 2 b f Danehill (USA)-Park Heiress (IRE) (Sadler's Wells (USA)) 1645^{7} 2202^{4} 2842^{9} 3258^{8} 3545^{9} 4162^{9} **>68f<**

Elsurur (USA) 2 ch f Storm Cat (USA)-Ajfan (USA) (Woodman (USA)) 2597^{4} 3114^{4} (4317) 4786^{10} **>84+f<**

Elton Ledger (IRE) 8 b g Cyrano de Bergerac-Princess of Nashua (Crowned Prince (USA)) **1996:** *5129^{2}* **1997:** *1^{2} 71^{2} (89) 127^{8} 166^{8} (208) 288^{2} 1047^{6}* **>77a 53f<**

El Zulia (GER) 3 b f Primo Dominie-Espada (GER) (Surumu (GER)) 1202a^{2} **>100f<**

E-Mail (IRE) 3 b c High Estate-Water Pixie (IRE) (Dance of Life (USA)) **1996:** *5201^{2}* **1997:** 2922^{16} 3987^{17} **>50a 69f<**

Embassy 2 b f Cadeaux Genereux-Pass the Peace (Alzao (USA)) (2597) (3049) 3723^{2} (4475) **>106f<**

Ember 4 b f Nicholas (USA)-Cinderwench (Crooner) 3091^{10} 3491^{10} **>46f<**

Embody 2 b c Indian Ridge-Kamakha (ITY) (Natroun (FR)) 3367a^{2} **>74f<**

Embroidered 4 br f Charmer-Emblazon (Wolver Hollow) *43^{9} 295^{14}* 2748^{9} 3327^{3} 3816^{6} 4169^{11} **>22a 47f<**

Embryonic (IRE) 5 b g Prince Rupert (FR)-Belle Viking (FR) (Riverman (USA)) 470^{3} 655^{2} 777^{5} 1224^{7} (1400) (1672) 3255^{5} **>89f<**

Emei Shan 4 br f Inca Chief (USA)-Tricata (Electric) **1996:** *5093^{7} 5129^{12}* **1997:** *2^{4} 54^{6} 108^{10} 390^{9}* **>39a 26f<**

Emerald Heights 2 b c Shirley Heights-Lady In Green (Shareef Dancer (USA)) 4915^{5} **>76f<**

Emerging Market 5 b g Emarati (USA)-Flitteriss Park (Beldale Flutter (USA)) 677^{3} 892^{6} 2105^{18} 2598^{16} 3150^{W} 3604^{2} 4282^{14} 4423^{13} **>105f<**

Emily-Jayne 3 b f Absalom-Tearful Reunion (Pas de Seul) 1078^{10} 1333^{10} 2145^{10} 3068^{8} 3870^{4} **>36f<**

Eminent 2 ch c Alnasr Alwasheek-Vague Lass (Vaigly Great) 4167^{5} 4630^{4} **>67f<**

Emmajoun 2 b f Emarati (USA)-Parijoun (Manado) 3574^{12} 3926^{5} 4232^{9} **>66f<**

Emmas Breeze 3 ch f Anshan-Baby Flo (Porto Bello) 883^{15} 1236^{18} 2883^{8} 3321^{14} 4184^{19} **>26f<**

Emma's Risk 3 b f Risk Me (FR)-Lana's Pet (Tina's Pet) *282^{6} 361^{7} 1944^{16}* **>21a 42f<**

Emperor Naheem (IRE) 2 b g Imperial Frontier (USA)-Desert Gale (Taufan (USA)) 695^{5} 850^{4} 3094^{5} 3265^{7} 4296^{2} 4818^{4} **>80f<**

Emperor's Gold 2 gr g Petong-Tarnside Rosal (Mummy's Game) 1593^{7} 3629^{3} 3905^{15} 4163^{5} *4303^{3}* 4627^{5} *(4984)* **>64a 60f<**

Empire Gold (USA) 2 ch c Strike The Gold (USA)-Careless Halo (USA) (Sunny's Halo (CAN)) 4710^{5} **>76f<**

Empire Park 2 b c Tragic Role (USA)-Millaine (Formidable (USA)) 2202^{3} 2706^{9} 3402^{3} **>74f<**

Empire State (IRE) 2 b c High Estate-Palm Dove (USA) (Storm Bird (CAN)) 4526^{14} 4779^{12} 5042^{9} **>65f<**

Empirical (USA) 2 b f Miswaki (USA)-Louisville (FR) (Val de L'Orne (FR)) 3114^{6} 4904^{3} **>75f<**

Enavius (IRE) 3 b c Lycius (USA)-Enaya (Caerleon (USA)) 2173^{9} **>56df<**

Enchant 2 ch f Lion Cavern (USA)-Belle et Deluree (USA) (The Minstrel (CAN)) 4556^{6} **>66f<**

Enchanted Guest (IRE) 4 ch f Be My Guest (USA)-Last Blessing (Final Straw) 835^{16} 946^{10} **>77f<**

Enchantica 3 ch f Timeless Times (USA)-North Pine (Import) **1996:** *5080^{5} 5107^{2} 5162^{8}* **1997:** *25^{6} 79^{11} 158^{3} 198^{2} 345^{6}* **>63da 68f<**

Enchanting Eve 3 ch f Risk Me (FR)-Red Sails (Town And Country) **1996:** *5133^{7} 5176^{4}* **1997:** *17^{3} 103^{3} 138^{6} 217^{5} (237) 286^{2} (362) 420^{5} 489^{2}* 694^{18} *871^{10} 1153^{2} 1421^{3}* 2040^{13} *2193^{3}* **>70a 66f<**

Encore 3 b f Be My Guest (USA)-Lucia Tarditi (FR) (Crystal Glitters (USA)) 3030^{4} 3917^{11} 4316^{10} **>60f<**

Encore M'Lady (IRE) 6 b m Dancing Dissident (USA)-Diva Encore (Star Appeal) **1996:** *5134^{11} 5170^{2} 5241^{5} 5258^{7}* **>55a 59f<**

Energy Man 4 b g Hadeer-Cataclysmic (Ela-Mana-Mou) 925^{6} 1472^{7} 1615^{8} 2845^{12} 4845^{17} 4924^{22} **>23f<**

English Invader 6 b h Rainbow Quest (USA)-Modica (Persian Bold) *129^{4} (236) 285^{3} 324^{4} (384) (418) 516^{4}* 680^{14} 753^{4} *2365^{6}* 2787^{5} 3197^{8} 3467^{8} *4069^{7} (4304) 4481^{9} 4594^{6} 4912^{10} 4981^{11}* **>52a 57df<**

English Lady (IRE) 2 b f Fayruz-Paradise Regained (North Stoke) 1084^{4} 1235^{2} 4911^{8} **>65f<**

Enigma (GER) 3 f 1202a^{14} 1918a^{3} 2458a^{2} 3552a^{3} 4666a^{16} **>105f<**

Enlisted (IRE) 3 b f Sadler's Wells (USA)-Impudent Miss (Persian Bold) **1996:** *5228^{2}* **1997:** *60^{3}* 885^{3} (2832) 3071^{2} **>79a 85f<**

Enrica (GER) 3 f 3998b^{2} **>95f<**

Enthrone (USA) 3 b f Diesis-Crowning Ambition (USA) (Chief's Crown (USA)) 1409^{11} 4070^{8} **>51f<**

Entice (FR) 3 b f Selkirk (USA)-Loure (USA) (Lyphard (USA)) 1147^{4} 3216^{2} 3727^{7} (4181) 4666a^{6} **>116f<**

Entrepreneur 3 b c Sadler's Wells (USA)-Exclusive Order (USA) (Exclusive Native (USA))

(940) 1769^{4} 4422^{7} **>127?f<**

Epic Stand 3 b g Presidium-Surf Bird (Shareef Dancer (USA)) 763^{2} 864^{2} 1129^{3} (1333) (2854) 3428^{2} 3801^{11} (4147) 4558^{13} 4781^{8} **>90f<**

Eponine 3 ch f Sharpo-Norska (Northfields (USA)) 878^{9} 1140^{16} 1301^{3} 1487^{4} (1731) 1853^{3} 1956^{5} 2225^{3} 2397^{10} **>66f<**

Epsilon 3 b f Environment Friend-Girette (USA) (General Assembly (USA)) 2184^{9} **>48f<**

Epsom Cyclone (USA) 2 ch c Rahy (USA)-Aneesati (Kris) 4298^{8} **>60+f<**

Epworth 3 b f Unfuwain (USA)-Positive Attitude (Red Sunset) 586^{4} 885^{2} 1271^{2} 1773^{6} 2328^{2} 2551^{3} 3071^{5} 3329^{6} 4741^{12} **>80df<**

Equerry 6 b g Midyan (USA)-Supreme Kingdom (Take A Reef) 1389^{10} **>68a 81f<**

Equity Princess 2 b f Warning-Hawait Al Barr (Green Desert (USA)) 3411^{6} 3806^{3} 3978^{2} (4278) 4674^{2} **>89?f<**

Eric's Bett 4 b g Chilibang-Mira Lady (Henbit (USA)) 1273^{17} 1463^{18} 1951^{8} 2310^{10} **>45f<**

Erika's Young Man 2 b c Unfuwain (USA)-Tearful Reunion (Pas de Seul) 1812^{24} 2482^{4} 3598^{18} 4366^{10} **>18f<**

Erinrinca (IRE) 3 ch f Waajib-Rivulet (USA) (Irish River (FR)) 3281^{6} 3463^{11} 3807^{4} 4429^{4} *4906^{10}* **>7a 43f<**

Erlking (IRE) 7 b g Fairy King (USA)-Cape of Storms (Fordham (USA)) 3792^{3} 3919^{14} 4608^{8} **>45a 57df<**

Erosion (IRE) 3 b c Green Desert (USA)-Swept Away (Kris) **1996:** *(5113) 5133^{4}* **>78a 76f<**

Errant 5 b h Last Tycoon-Wayward Lass (USA) (Hail the Pirates (USA)) **1996:** *5088^{8} 5151^{6} 5227^{3}* **1997:** 1093^{14} 1606^{5} 2150^{12} **>67a 42f<**

Erro Codigo 2 b g Formidable (USA)-Home Wrecker (DEN) (Affiliation Order (USA)) 697^{4} 971^{5} 2288^{2} 2565^{D} 2936^{3} 3427^{2} 3804^{2} **>65f<**

Ertlon 7 b g Shareef Dancer (USA)-Sharpina (Sharpen Up) **1996:** *5221^{5}* **1997:** *241^{2} 294^{2} 330^{4} (403)* 567^{2} 752^{3} *1154^{2}* 1501^{3} 1739^{15} 3548^{7} 3718^{7} 3930^{6} 4225^{2} 4448^{7} **>82a 74f<**

Erupt 4 b g Beveled (USA)-Sparklingsovereign (Sparkler) 520^{6} 1035^{5} 1977^{5} 2347^{5} 2698^{2} 3251^{6} 3580^{6} 3710^{10} *4301^{7}* **>36a 70f<**

Escena (USA) 4 f *5062a^{3}* **>108a f<**

Escudo (IRE) 2 ch f Indian Ridge-Eskaroon (Artaius (USA)) 2926^{3} (4012) 4403^{4} 4634^{9} (5045) **>81f<**

Es Go 4 ch g Dunbeath (USA)-Track Angel (Ardoon) 2315^{12} 2549^{8} 3211^{6} 4503^{4} **>52f<**

E Sharp (USA) 3 b f Diesis-Elvia (USA) (Roberto (USA)) 606^{2} 2184^{8} 2510^{W} **>51f<**

Eshtiaal (USA) 3 b br c Riverman (USA)-Lady Cutlass (USA) (Cutlass (USA)) 1105^{2} 1331^{3} (2902) (3380) (3542) (4383) **>105f<**

Eskimo Nel (IRE) 6 ch m Shy Groom (USA)-North Lady (Northfields (USA)) 499^{2} **>24a 82f<**

Esperto 4 b g Risk Me (FR)-Astrid Gilberto (Runnett) (1246) 1383^{2} 1503^{3} *2301^{4}* 2577^{4} *2673^{2} 2911^{4}* 4987^{3} **>51a 60f<**

Espla 6 b g Sure Blade (USA)-Morica (Moorestyle) *907^{8}* **>17a 73?f<**

Espresso 2 br c Faustus (USA)-Shikabell (Kala Shikari) 1251^{12} 2893^{13} 3078^{4} 3493^{6} **>59f<**

Essandess (IRE) 2 b f Casteddu-Ra Ra (Lord Gayle (USA)) 2538^{5} 4012^{16} 4381^{9} 4588^{12} *5017^{4}* **>45a 53f<**

Essayeffsee 8 b g Precocious-Floreal (Formidable (USA)) 1024^{9} 1268^{10} 1683^{3} 2564^{7} 2824^{4} 3308^{2} 3620^{2} 3779^{2} 3933^{4} 4335^{5} 4584^{5} 4845^{2} 4998^{2} **>61f<**

Esse 2 ch f Rudimentary (USA)-School Concert (Music Boy) 3753^{8} 3905^{17} 4437^{7} 4688^{2} 5026^{6} **>51f<**

Esta Maria (IRE) 4 b f High Estate-Maria Stuarda (Royal And Regal (USA)) 1481^{10} **>42a 29f<**

Estopped (IRE) 2 b g Case Law-Action Belle (Auction Ring (USA)) 1026^{4} 1760^{15} 1819^{12} 2425^{3} 2741^{7} **>56f<**

Eternal Host (IRE) 3 b g Be My Guest (USA)-To The Limit (Junius (USA)) **1996:** *5168^{9} 5228^{10}* **1997:** *1241^{2}* 2059^{8} 2213^{3} **>12a 39f<**

Eternal Joy 3 b c Fairy King (USA)-Prosperous Lady (Prince Tenderfoot (USA)) 2441a^{10} 2816a^{3} **>105f<**

Eternally Grateful 4 b f Picea-Carpadia (Icecapade (USA)) 2424^{10} 2730^{17} 3081^{6} 3299^{12}

Eternity 3 b f Suave Dancer (USA)-Chellita (Habitat) 989^{10} 1168^{11} 4322^{4} 4971^{8} **>59f<**

Ethbaat (USA) 6 b or br g Chief's Crown (USA)-Alchaasibiyeh (USA) (Seattle Slew (USA)) *382^{4} 422^{3} 457^{7}* 653^{7} 1273^{10} *1576^{W}* 4991^{15} **>73a 54f<**

Ethereal 2 b c Fairy King (USA)-Secret Seeker (USA) (Mr Prospector (USA)) 5041^{11} **>62f<**

Etmal 3 1545a^{8} **>78f<**

Etoile (FR) 3 gr f Kris-La Luna (USA) (Lyphard (USA)) 1147^{3} 1738^{5} 2814a^{6} 3216^{6} **>113f<**

Etoile du Nord 5 b or br g Tragic Role (USA)-Daisy Topper (Top Ville) **1996:** *5222^{7} 5255^{10}* **1997:** *63^{4} 147^{13} 183^{15}* **>33a f<**

Etterby Park (USA) 4 b g Silver Hawk (USA)-Bonita Francita (CAN) (Devil's Bag (USA)) *591^{3}* 655^{3} (831) 1027^{2} *1288^{2}* 1400^{5} 2014^{16} 2327^{14} 3255^{6} 4246^{2} 4363^{3} 4783^{10} 4879^{3} 5052^{10} **>77a 84f<**

Eudoxe (IRE) 4 ch g Be My Guest (USA)-Violence (USA) (Riverman (USA)) (1547a) **>96f<**

Eulogy (FR) 10 b or br g Esprit du Nord (USA)-Louange (Green Dancer (USA)) *80^{8} 195^{5}* **>64da 44f<**

Euphoric Illusion 6 ch g Rainbow Quest (USA)-High and Bright (Shirley Heights) 1497^{7} 2000^{4} 2207^{11} 2682^{10} 3108^{7} 3935^{3} **>53?f<**

Eurobox Boy 4 ch g Savahra Sound-Princess Poquito (Hard Fought) 476^{2} (587) 733^{6} 1489^{8} 1878^{4} 1979^{2} 2155^{5} *2672^{4}* (2848) 3039^{2} 3153^{9} (3496) 3616^{7} 4063^{8} **>56a 78f<**

Eurofen 2 br c Goldneyev (USA)-Mineramare (IRE) (Kenmare (FR)) 880^{7} 993^{10} 1498^{2} 1797^{9} *2051^{8}* 2186^{6} 3312^{5} 3563^{10} 4014^{12} **>12a 61f<**

Euro Forum 5 ch g Deploy-Unique Treasure (Young Generation) *4590^{2}* **>60a 67f<**

Eurolink Profile 3 b f Prince Sabo-Taiga (Northfields (USA)) (1690) 2119^{6} 2691^{4} 3100^{10} 4527^{15} **>74f<**

Eurolink Shadow 5 b g Be My Chief (USA)-Miss Top Ville (FR) (Top Ville) *2051^{3}* **>76f<**

Eurolink the Lad 10 b g Burslem-Shoshoni Princess (Prince Tenderfoot (USA)) *99^{2} 192^{2} 415^{7} (857)* **>59a f<**

Eurolink Windsong (IRE) 3 ch f Polish Patriot (USA)-Delvecchia (Glint of Gold) 551^{7} 1230^{14} 2874^{5} 3129^{2} 3567^{6} 3781^{6} 4171^{10} 4415^{10} 4692^{4} **>33f<**

Euroquest 3 b g Ron's Victory (USA)-Raaya (Be My Guest (USA)) *154^{6} (287)* 785^{13} 1496^{13} 1513^{5} *1756^{3}* 2903^{4} 3266^{6} **>49a 37f<**

Euro Sceptic (IRE) 5 ch g Classic Secret (USA)-Very Seldom (Rarity) 571^{12} 733^{8} 848^{11} 1285^{6} 1511^{10} 1655^{5} 1830^{4} 1994^{3} 2204^{4} 2502^{2} 2906^{2} 3105^{7} (3264) 3476^{4} 3759^{2} (4210) 4510^{12} **>63f<**

Euro Singer 5 br g Chief Singer-Crystal Gael (Sparkler) **1996:** *5148^{13}* **1997:** 1677^{10} 3245^{7} **>26a 41f<**

Euro Superstar (FR) 3 b g Rock City-Douceur (USA) (Shadeed (USA)) 840^{9} 1296^{12} 1506^{10} 1971^{3} 2228^{6} 2577^{10} 2785^{11} **>41f<**

Eurotwist 8 b g Viking (USA)-Orange Bowl (General Assembly (USA)) 553^{10} 595^{10} **>40a 41f<**

Euro Venture 2 b c Prince Sabo-Brave Advance (USA) (Bold Laddie (USA)) 971^{3} 1255^{5} 3239^{6} 3755^{4} **>78f<**

Eurynome (GER) 4 ch f Acatenango (GER)-Eidothea (GER) (Teotepec (GER)) 3883a^{4} **>110f<**

Eva Luna (USA) 5 b m Alleged (USA)-Media Luna (Star Appeal) 1033^{5} 1454^{3} (1960) **>123f<**

Evander (IRE) 2 ch c Indian Ridge-Heavenly Hope (Glenstal (USA)) 4895^{2} **>87f<**

Evan 'elp Us 5 ch g Executive Man-Recent Events (Stanford) *242^{6}* 864^{17} **>46da 64df<**

Evaporate 5 b m Insan (USA)-Mona (Auction Ring (USA)) *544^{3} 1138^{9}* (1445) **>35a 40f<**

Evdokimova 3 b f Adonijah-Heil (Star Appeal) 814a^{3}

Evening Breeze (GER) 3 ch f Surumu (GER)-Evening Kiss (Kris) (4962a) **>100f<**

Evening In Paris 4 ch f Be My Chief (USA)-Photo Call (Chief Singer) **1996:** *5282^{4}* **1997:** *98^{2} 216^{8} 416^{2}* 496^{11} 796^{P} **>50a 11f<**

Eveningperformance 6 b m Night Shift (USA)-Classic Design (Busted) 2526^{8} 3111^{10} 3724^{5} (4239) 4664a^{11} **>116f<**

Evening Set (GER) 2 b f Second Set (IRE)-Evening Ballad (GER) (Windwurf (GER)) 4126a^{3} **>92f<**

Evening World (FR) 2 ch c Bering-Pivoine (USA) (Nureyev (USA)) 2996b^{3} (3973) 4274^{3} 4674^{4} **>100df<**

Even Top (IRE) 4 br c Topanoora-Skevena (Niniski (USA)) *628a^{7}* 1210^{3} 2010^{4} 2901^{3} 3785^{2} 4394a^{11} **>113a 114f<**

Everglades (IRE) 9 b g Green Desert (USA)-Glowing With Pride (Ile de Bourbon (USA)) 981^{5} 1309^{5} 1874^{7} **>108df<**

Everset (FR) 9 b g Green Desert (USA)-Eversince (USA) (Foolish Pleasure (USA)) 1422^{19} *1575^{4}* 1920^{7} *2162^{7} 2302^{4}* 2937^{13} 3240^{22} *4913^{2}* **>68a 43f<**

Every Penny 2 b f Interrex (CAN)-Shiny Penny (Glint of Gold) 3493^{5} 4057^{10} **>50f<**

Evezio Rufo 5 b g Blakeney-Empress Corina (Free State) *30^{6} 55^{6}* 442^{8} 1001^{7} *(1138) 1287^{3}* 1660^{9} *1940^{4} 4811^{4} 4981^{9}* **>55a 50f<**

Evidently (IRE) 3 b f Slip Anchor-Evocatrice (Persepolis (FR)) 3095^{8} 3632^{10} 4277^{8} 4992^{15} **>52f<**

Ewar Arrangement 3 b c Bold Arrangement-Emily Allan (IRE) (Shirley Heights) **1996:** *5187^{5} 5238^{8}* **>40a 57f<**

Ewar Bold 4 b c Bold Arrangement-Monaneigue Lady (Julio Mariner) **1996:** *5270^{10}* **1997:** 603^{5} **>53f<**

Ewar Snowflake 3 b f Snow Chief (USA)-Petillante (Petong) 2323^{5} 2853^{6} 3281^{7} 3557^{4} **>29f<**

Exactly (IRE) 4 b f Taufan (USA)-Not Mistaken (USA) (Mill Reef (USA)) 2015^{12} 2763^{5} 3035^{5} 3931^{4} 4287^{3} 4466^{6} 4598^{3} **>41a 64f<**

Exbourne's Wish (USA) 2 b c Exbourne (USA)-Social Wish (USA) (Lyphard's Wish (FR)) 1263^{4} 2057^{10} 3489^{3} (3753) 3899^{4} 4296^{10} 4560^{5} **>85f<**

Excelled (IRE) 8 gr m Treasure Kay-Excelling Miss (USA) (Exceller (USA)) 2307^{5} 2531^{3} 2896^{3} 3245^{8} **>28a 37f<**

Exclusive 2 ch f Polar Falcon (USA)-Exclusive Order (USA) (Exclusive Native (USA)) (4107) 4442^{3} **>99+f<**

Executive Design 5 b g Unfuwain (USA)-Seven Seas (FR) (Riverman (USA)) 982^{4} 1162^{W} **>74f<**

Executive Officer 4 b g Be My Chief (USA)-Caro's Niece (USA) (Caro) *86^{10}* 770^{9} 1445^{12} 1968^{11} 2246^{9} *2668^{8} 3054^{2}* 3293^{6} 3971^{13} **>39a 35f<**
Exit To Somewhere (IRE) 2 b c Exit To Nowhere (USA)-Zivania (IRE) (Shernazar) 2336^{6} 3103^{2} **>82f<**
Exotic Wood (USA) 5 *5061a^{4}* **>122a f<**
Expectation (IRE) 3 b f Night Shift (USA)-Phantom Row (Adonijah) 1089^{18} **>63f<**
Expect To Shine 2 b f Fairy King (USA)-Anjaab (USA) (Alydar (USA)) 2597^{2} (3114) 3723^{8} 4442^{4} 4786^{6} **>91f<**
Expialiodoocius 3 b c Environment Friend-Rainbow Ring (Rainbow Quest (USA)) 1144^{11} 1477^{9} 1804^{2} 2487^{17} 3721^{4} 4243^{12} **>70f<**
Explosive Power 6 br h Prince Sabo-Erwarton Seabreeze (Dunbeath (USA)) **1996:** *5106^{4} 5189^{5} 5231^{9}* **1997:** *34^{6}* 3980^{9} 4453^{4} 4607^{11} *5019^{7}* **>68a 60f<**
Express Gift 8 br g Bay Express-Annes Gift (Ballymoss) 552^{6} 1215^{3} (1408) 1832^{4} 2063^{4} 2475^{5} **>57f<**
Express Girl 3 b f Sylvan Express-Oh My Oh My (Ballacashtal (CAN)) 464^{10} 685^{7} 845^{7} 1269^{3} 1673^{8} 2044^{7} 2203^{8} 4846^{17} **>34f<**
Express Routing 5 b g Aragon-San Marguerite (Blakeney) *855^{9}* 1006^{11} **>24a 57f<**
Extra Hour (IRE) 4 b g Cyrano de Bergerac-Renzola (Dragonara Palace (USA)) **1996:** *5273^{5}* **>22a 50f<**
Extremely Friendly 4 ch g Generous (IRE)-Water Woo (USA) (Tom Rolfe) *104^{13}* **>9a 16f<**

F

Fable 3 ch f Absalom-Fiction (Dominion) 970^{8} 1508^{2} 1987^{6} 3592^{10} **>47f<**
Fabled Light (IRE) 3 b c Alzao (USA)-Fabled Lifestyle (Kings Lake (USA)) 676^{13} 1014^{5} (1270) **>89+f<**
Fabrice 2 b g Pursuit of Love-Parfum D'Automne (FR) (Sharpen Up) 5042^{3} **>72f<**
Fabulous La Fouine (FR) 4 gr f Fabulous Dancer (USA)-Mercalle (FR) (Kaldoun (FR)) **1996:** 5159a^{2} **>128f<**
Fabulous Mtoto 7 b h Mtoto-El Fabulous (FR) (Fabulous Dancer (USA)) **1996:** *5270^{7}* **1997:** *63^{7} (144) 216^{5} 295^{2} 340^{6} 402^{2}* 430^{7} 481^{2} 640^{6} 1811^{5} 2533^{6} 2696^{8} 2843^{12} 3015^{4} 3203^{8} **>50a 59f<**
Face It 3 b f Interrex (CAN)-Facetious (Malicious) **1996:** *5172^{5}* **>40a 47f<**
Face-Off 2 b f Aragon-Rock Face (Ballad Rock) 739^{6} 1240^{5} 1961^{6} 4227^{4} 4545^{5} 4750^{4} **>74f<**
Facile Tigre 2 gr c Efisio-Dancing Diana (Raga Navarro (ITY)) 2320^{7} 2720^{11} 3589^{4} 3892^{8} 4296^{8} 4501^{4} **>78f<**
Facsimile 2 b f Superlative-Just Julia (Natroun (FR)) 2520^{2} 3070^{W} **>71f<**
Fa-Eq (IRE) 2 ch c Indian Ridge-Searching Star (Rainbow Quest (USA)) 4884^{2} **>86f<**
Fahris (IRE) 3 ch c Generous (IRE)-Janbiya (IRE) (Kris) (691) 1769^{6} 2901^{2} 3409^{3} 3785^{3} (4154) 4420^{4} (4776) **>125f<**
Fahs (USA) 5 b br g Riverman (USA)-Tanwi (Vision (USA)) 1262^{13} (1459) 1768^{3} 2710^{20} 3112^{11} 3616^{6} 3798^{3} 4151^{6} 4441^{13} (4854) 5053^{22} **>85f<**
Failed To Hit 4 b g Warrshan (USA)-Missed Again (High Top) **1996:** *5264^{6}* **1997:** *81^{7} 140^{7} 579^{6} 857^{5}* 1001^{14} 1292^{12} *2302^{2}* 2785^{15} *3041^{2} 3608^{3}* 3849^{10} **>65a 38df<**
Fair and Fancy (FR) 6 b g Always Fair (USA)-Fancy Star (FR) (Bellypha) *542^{9}* **>48da 66?f<**
Fair Deal (USA) 2 b f Zilzal (USA)-Fadetta (USA) (Fappiano (USA)) 2919^{3} 3479^{3} **>75f<**
Fairelaine 5 b m Zalazl (USA)-Blue and White (Busted) 721^{18} **>34a 42f<**
Fair Ella (IRE) 5 ch m Simply Great (FR)-Dance Or Burst (Try My Best (USA)) **1996:** *5247^{9}* **1997:** *59^{11}* **>18a 43?f<**
Fair Game (IRE) 2 b c Bluebird (USA)-Blonde Goddess (IRE) (Godswalk (USA)) 1872^{13} 2768^{11} *3607^{10}* 4334^{14} 4576^{14} **>45a 67f<**
Fairhonor (FR) 4 b c Hero's Honor (USA)-Fairolan (FR) (Olantengy (FR)) **1996:** (5125a) **1997:** 1365a^{5} 2819a^{3} **>114f<**
Fairly Grey (FR) 2 gr f Linamix (FR)-Fairlee Wild (FR) (Wild Again (USA)) 4250a^{2}
Fairly Sharp (IRE) 4 b f Glenstal (USA)-Bengala (FR) (Hard To Beat) 1953^{7} **>80?f<**
Fairly Sure (IRE) 4 b f Red Sunset-Mirabiliary (USA) (Crow (FR)) 1005^{16} 2228^{12} 2892^{11} 3227^{5} 4451^{8} **>5a 49f<**
Fair Sonia 2 b f Efisio-Ausonia (Beldale Flutter (USA)) 3019^{7} 3547^{13} 4066^{11} 4753^{28} 4915^{12} **>64f<**
Fairy Domino 2 ch f Primo Dominie-Fairy Fortune (Rainbow Quest (USA)) 993^{3} 1228^{2} 1498^{4} 1600^{3} **>64f<**
Fairy Fingers 3 b f Treasure Kay-Nellie Moss (Le Moss) 4705^{6} **>42f<**
Fairy Flight (IRE) 2 b f Fairy King (USA)-Rising Tide (Red Alert) 3839a^{7} 4090a^{4} **>86f<**
Fairy Knight 5 b h Fairy King (USA)-Vestal Flame (Habitat) *380^{4}* 430^{18} 538^{8} 746^{2} (984) 1233^{5} 1632^{7} 1844^{6} 2344^{4} 3796^{11} **>66a 71f<**
Fairy Lake (IRE) 4 b f Fairy King (USA)-Inisfree (USA) (Hoist The Flag (USA)) 1198a^{5} **>88f<**
Fairy Prince (IRE) 4 b g Fairy King (USA)-Danger Ahead (Mill Reef (USA)) 585^{14} 827^{7} 1799^{2} 2006^{2} 2698^{4} (2847) (3032) (3146) 3410^{10} 3621^{5} 4048^{12} 4155^{26} **>72f<**
Fairy Rock (IRE) 2 b f Fairy King (USA)-Safe Home (Home Guard (USA)) 4779^{8} 4904^{4} **>73f<**
Faith Alone 4 b f Safawan-Strapless (Bustino) **1996:** *5089^{8} 5152^{10}* **1997:** 1446^{4} (1963) 2179^{5} (2424) (2769) 3273^{3} 3600^{5} **>74a 84f<**
Faithful Son (USA) 3 b g Zilzal (USA)-Carduel (USA) (Round Table) (1207) (1462) 1767^{2} 3214^{5} (4133) 4422^{3} **>124f<**
Fakhr (USA) 2 b br c Riverman (USA)-Roseate Tern (Blakeney) (2693) 3912^{4} **>91++f<**
Falak (USA) 3 b c Diesis-Tafrah (IRE) (Sadler's Wells (USA)) 741^{2} (1399) (2135) 3109^{8} **>114f<**
Falcon Ridge 3 ch g Seven Hearts-Glen Kella Manx (Tickled Pink) 964^{9} 2591^{12} 4700^{11} 4916^{7} **>58f<**
Falkenberg (FR) 2 ch c Polish Precedent (USA)-Mithi Al Gamar (USA) (Blushing Groom (FR)) 1228^{7} 1684^{7} *2363^{3}* 2714^{5} 4690^{14} 4885^{13} **>63a 65f<**
Falls O'Moness (IRE) 3 b f River Falls-Sevens Are Wild (Petorius) 503^{8} 685^{3} 765^{4} 1245^{5} 1573^{8} 2313^{12} *2669^{5}* 3336^{6} 3696^{6} 3854^{4} 4164^{3} (4264) 4568^{10} 4731^{4} 4845^{6} 4886^{13} **>40a 67f<**
Fame Again 5 b m Then Again-Starawak (Star Appeal) 468^{8} 585^{8} (883) (1020) 1799^{6} 2358^{2} 2567^{8} 3034^{6} 3310^{6} (3621) **>75f<**
Family Man 4 ch g Indian Ridge-Auntie Gladys (Great Nephew) 895^{2} 1097^{5} (1606) 2557^{12} 4297^{12} 4781^{22} **>84df<**
Family Tradition (IRE) 3 b f Sadler's Wells (USA)-Sequel 1366a^{7} 2267a^{3} 2814a^{5} (3511a) 4346a^{4} **>115f<**
Fan (GER) 3 1544a^{7} 2097a^{10} **>73f<**
Fanadiyr (IRE) 5 b g Kahyasi-Fair Fight (Fine Blade (USA)) 955^{14} 1042^{5} 2114^{5} **>41f<**
Fancy A Fortune (IRE) 3 b g Fools Holme (USA)-Fancy's Girl (FR) (Nadjar (FR)) 2546^{3} 2888^{2} 3039^{3} (3213) 3457^{3} 4308^{9} 4477^{8} *4813^{11}* 4877^{4} **>33a 65f<**
Fancy Clancy 4 b f Clantime-Bold Sophie (Bold Owl) *1046^{12}* 1332^{10} 1604^{6} 1764^{7} 2167^{8} 2496^{7} 3261^{9} 4214^{9} 4791^{13} **>36f<**
Fancy Design (IRE) 4 b f Cyrano de Bergerac-Crimson Robes (Artaius (USA)) **1996:** *5082^{6} 5117^{6} 5253^{5}* **1997:** *32^{7} 59^{8} 134^{4} 169^{12} 303^{5} 352^{8}* 484^{10} 1088^{8} 1236^{14} 1484^{13} 2550^{6} 2730^{2} 2918^{2} 3143^{13} 3465^{10} 3496^{7} 3787^{9} 4373^{6} 4608^{7} 4858^{10} **>30a 48f<**
Fancy Heights 4 b f Shirley Heights-Miss Fancy That (USA) (The Minstrel (CAN)) 2638a^{2} **>97f<**
Fanjica (IRE) 5 b m Law Society (USA)-Florie (FR) (Gay Mecene (USA)) 5039a^{2} **>121f<**
Fan of Vent-Axia 3 b c Puissance-Miss Milton (Young Christopher) 649^{15} 1012^{6} 1988^{4} 2310^{14} 2745^{11} 3038^{13} **>35a 47f<**
Fantail 3 b c Taufan (USA)-Eleganza (IRE) (Kings Lake (USA)) 690^{10} 990^{6} (1449) (2224) (3071) 3989^{5} 4552^{3} 4854^{9} (4996) **>90+f<**
Fantastic Fellow (USA) 3 b c Lear Fan (USA)-Chateaubaby (USA) (Nureyev (USA)) (717a) 1204a^{5} 1541a^{5} 1767^{8} 5063a^{8} **>114f<**
Fantastic Flame (IRE) 3 b f Generous (IRE)-Gay Fantastic (Ela-Mana-Mou) 727^{6} 992^{6} 1276^{2} 1747^{10} 2832^{5} (3277) 3803^{10} 4268^{4} 4876^{7} **>84f<**
Fantasy Flight 3 b f Forzando-Ryewater Dream (Touching Wood (USA)) 3313^{W} 4290^{9} 4469^{5} 4926^{8} **>35f<**
Fantasy Girl (IRE) 3 br f Marju (IRE)-Persian Fantasy (Persian Bold) 875^{5} 1301^{6} 4323^{7} 4632^{12} *4800^{6}* 4971^{20} **>60a 55f<**
Fantasy Island (IRE) 2 b c Zafonic (USA)-Um Lardaff (Mill Reef (USA)) (3745) **>84++f<**
Fantasy Night (IRE) 2 b c Night Shift (USA)-Gay Fantasy (Troy) 2336^{10} 2849^{3} 4454^{8} **>55+f<**
Fanti Dancer (IRE) 2 b f Anshan-Maiden Way (Shareef Dancer (USA)) 2700^{7} 3099^{3} 3493^{2} 3819^{3} 4058^{7} 4595^{9} 4753^{14} **>75f<**
Far Ahead 5 b g Soviet Star (USA)-Cut Ahead (Kalaglow) **1996:** *5205^{8}* **1997:** *70^{4} 182^{6}* (1685) 2028^{14} 2676^{11} 3412^{2} (3705) **>71a 98f<**
Farasan (IRE) 4 b c Fairy King (USA)-Gracieuse Majeste (FR) (Saint Cyrien (FR)) 678^{7} **>114f<**
Far Atlantic 4 b f Phardante (FR)-Atlantic View (Crash Course) 3335^{3} **>28f<**
Faraway Lass 4 b f Distant Relative-Vague Lass (Vaigly Great) 1594^{9} 1824^{4} (2711) 3217^{4} 3765^{5} 4423^{10} 4887^{3} **>97f<**
Farewell My Love (IRE) 3 b f Waajib-So Long Boys (FR) (Beldale Flutter (USA)) *904^{6}* 1141^{8} 1661^{5} 1989^{6} 2376^{3} 2847^{9} 3088^{11} 3454^{10} **>31a 37f<**
Farfields Prince 5 b g Weldnaas (USA)-Coca (Levmoss) 1683^{12} 2843^{2} 3486^{5} 3762^{2} 4235^{3} 4794^{14} **>51f<**
Farhan (USA) 3 b c Lear Fan (USA)-Mafatin (IRE) (Sadler's Wells (USA)) 1144^{5} 1647^{7} **>80f<**
Farhana 4 b f Fayruz-Fahrenheit (Mount Hagen (FR)) (811a) 1171^{2} 1455^{7} 2056^{14} **>116df<**
Faringdon Future 3 b g Distant Relative-Lady Dowery (USA) (Manila (USA)) 723^{10} 2309^{6} 4176^{10} 4464^{2} 4587^{3} **>76f<**
Farley Green 3 b f Pharly (FR)-Ring Cycle (Auction Ring (USA)) 1090^{3} (1485) 2705^{7} 3092^{2} 3690^{6} **>76f<**
Farley Mount 3 b g Pharly (FR)-Mossy Rose (King of Spain) *455^{3} 568^{4}* 1443^{3} 1956^{4} 2667^{12} **>72a 71f<**
Farmost 4 ch g Pharly (FR)-Dancing Meg (USA) (Marshua's Dancer (USA)) *1082^{11} 2672^{9}* (2930) 3424^{4} 4144^{6} (4449) *(4485) 4571^{2}* **>90a 91f<**
Farndon Princess 2 b f Nomination-Ankara's Princess (USA) (Ankara (USA)) 2684^{3} 3416^{7} 3889^{5}

>55f<

Far Removed (IRE) 2 b c Distant Relative-Cormorant Creek (Gorytus (USA)) 3239[13] 3459[2] 3619[4] 3823[2] (4152) **>79f<**

Farringdon Hill 6 b g Minster Son-Firgrove (Relkino) 1142[5] 1748[3] 2344[6] (3467) (3779) 4335[15] **>78f<**

Far-So-La 2 b g Absalom-Fara (Castle Keep) 432[15] 648[13] 1480[9] 3742[8] 4366[11] **>31f<**

Fascinating Rhythm 3 b f Slip Anchor-Pick of the Pops (High Top) 2869[5] 4181[7] **>93f<**

Fashion Victim 2 b c High Estate-Kirkby Belle (Bay Express) 2500[5] (2736) 3131[10] 3602[5] 3932[4] (4265) 4690[5] 4803[7] 4953[6] **>82f<**

Fasil (IRE) 4 ch g Polish Patriot (USA)-Apple Peel (Pall Mall) 4320[6] **>75?f<**

Fasta (USA) 4 b f Seattle Song (USA)-Aspern (FR) (Riverman (USA)) **1996:** 5156a[2] **>111f<**

Fast Franc (IRE) 2 ch g Paris House-Elle Va Bon (Tanfirion) 2003[3] 2186[3] (2276) (2383) 2681[8] *3042[7]* 3932[8] 4767[9] 4897[15] **>43a 70+f<**

Fast Spin 3 b g Formidable (USA)-Topwinder (USA) (Topsider (USA)) **1996:** *(5261)* **1997:** *7[4] 33[5] (156) 317[3] 424[3]* **>61a 61f<**

Fast Tempo (IRE) 2 b f Statoblest-Bellinzona (Northfields (USA)) 828[4] 999[2] (1235) 1635[3] 2370[5] 2931[2] 3152[11] 3892[3] 4296[9] 4989[12] **>74f<**

Fatal Baraari 3 b g Green Desert (USA)-Possessive (Posse (USA)) 1409[W] 2960[4] 3211[7] 3624[3] **>73f<**

Fatal Sahra (IRE) 3 ch c Caerleon (USA)-Ploy (Posse (USA)) 847[9] **>70df<**

Fatefully (USA) 4 b f Private Account (USA)-Fateful (USA) (Topsider (USA)) *627a[10]* 1740[4] 4292[2] 4557[4] 4776[7] **>92a 111f<**

Fatehalkhair (IRE) 5 ch g Kris-Midway Lady (USA) (Alleged (USA) 461[12] 608[5] 3562[3] **>48a 43f<**

Father Dan (IRE) 8 ch g Martin John-Sonia John (Main Reef) **1996:** *5123[3] 5223[2] (5247) 5274[3]* **1997:** *74[4] 216[7] 248[3]* 435[8] 476[6] 689[2] 838[6] 1233[6] 1632[12] 3588[2] 3793[5] *4069[5] 4304[7]* (4450) **>58a 66f<**

Father Eddie 3 b g Aragon-Lady Philippa (IRE) (Taufan (USA)) *235[12] 373[12]* 609[5] *868[8]* (1095) 1281[6] 1683[13] 1820[10] **>34a 58f<**

Father Sky 6 b g Dancing Brave (USA)-Flamenco Wave (USA) (Desert Wine (USA)) (4374) **>84?f<**

Faugeron 8 ch g Niniski (USA)-Miss Longchamp (Northfields (USA)) 1022[10] 1224[10] 1452[8] 1605[8] *1755[2] 1940[6]* **>62a 50f<**

Fauna (IRE) 3 b f Taufan (USA)-Labwa (USA) (Lyphard (USA)) 701[5] 1078[4] 1301[7] **>67f<**

Favorite Trick (USA) 2 b/br g Phone Trick (USA)-Evil Elaine (USA) Medieval Man (USA) *(5064a)*

Fawning 2 b f Alnasr Alwasheek-Flattering (USA) (Nodouble (USA)) 2394[3] 2953[9] 3927[6] 4271[13] **>63f<**

Fayez 2 ch c Interrex (CAN)-Forest Nymph (Native Bazaar) 4174[9] **>54f<**

Fayik 3 ch c Arazi (USA)-Elfaslah (IRE) (Green Desert (USA)) 1437[3] 2045[5] 3425[4] 3936[13] 4219[12] 4733[13] **>71?f<**

Faym (IRE) 3 b f Fayruz-Lorme (Glenstal (USA)) **1996:** *5239[5] 5257[2]* **1997:** *49[3] 217[3] 255[4] 590[2] 1757[5]* 2523[6] 2945[7] 3452[5] **>72a 61f<**

Fayrana (IRE) 2 b f Fayruz-Paryiana (IRE) (Shernazar) 648[6] 828[7] 1466[2] 1821[2] (2700) 3215[4] 3635[5] 3961a[10] 4473[6] **>80f<**

Fearless Brave 2 b c Aragon-Siouan (So Blessed) 4231[6] 4638[7] **>56+f<**

Fearless Cavalier 3 b g Bold Arrangement-Gold Belt (IRE) (Bellypha) 3132[3] 3702[3] 4059[16] 4324[12] 4711[11] **>52a 47f<**

Fearless Sioux 3 b f Formidable (USA)-Washita (Valiyar) **1996:** *5111[4] 5147[7]* **1997:** *289[2] 368[2]* 609[6] 1449[10] 2357[6] **>52a 33f<**

Fear Not (IRE) 2 b f Alzao (USA)-Fear Naught (Connaught) 3978[6] 4278[4] **>55f<**

Feather Bed (IRE) 3 b f Fools Holme (USA)-Piffle (Shirley Heights) **1996:** *(5248)* **1997:** *46[7]* **>61a 71f<**

Featherstone Lane 6 b g Siberian Express (USA)-Try Gloria (Try My Best (USA)) **1996:** *5097[4] 5184[7] 5225[3] 5268[10]* **1997:** *69[7] 127[9] 178[3] 222[3] 263[6] 303[6] 371[2] 391[8] 421[4] 515[2] 593[9]* 760[8] *856[2]* 1514[4] 1671[2] 1865[3] 2759[5] 2899[9] *(3399)* 3625[4] *4051[2]* 4221[3] **>70a 59f<**

Febrar (ITY) 4 b c Saumarez-Scuretada (ITY) (Kris) 1549a[3] **>114f<**

February 4 b f Full Extent (USA)-Foligno (Crofter (USA)) 2938[9] 3271[12] **>32a 23f<**

Feel A Line 3 b g Petong-Cat's Claw (USA) (Sharpen Up) 535[13] 771[14] 1333[6] 1633[11] 1807[4] 1921[W] (1988) 2171[3] (2407) 2723[6] 3268[4] (3405) 3868[6] **>56f<**

Feel Free (IRE) 2 b f Generous (IRE)-As You Desire Me (Kalamoun) 4330[10] **>41f<**

Feel No Fear 4 b f Fearless Action (USA)-Charm Bird (Daring March) 3250[3] 3550[3] 4070[13] **>51f<**

Feliciano (SWI) 3 br c Pennine Walk-Finger Lake (Kings Lake (USA)) 918a[2] **>105f<**

Felony (IRE) 2 ch c Pharly (FR)-Scales of Justice (Final Straw) 2943[14] **>14f<**

Fengari 8 ch g Formidable (USA)-Foreseen (Reform) 2947[8] *3413[14]* **>10a 51f<**

Fenian Court (IRE) 6 b m John French-Penny Maes (Welsh Saint) *18[14] 68[15]* 1601[7] **>38f<**

Fen Warrior 2 b g Pursuit of Love-Kennedys Prima (Primo Dominie) 2409[5] **>52f<**

Ferghana Ma 2 br f Mtoto-Justine (GER) (Luciano) 4914[5] **>75f<**

Fern's Governor 5 b m Governor General-Sharp Venita (Sharp Edge) 647[5] 933[3] 1244[11] 1811[9] 2331[U] 2557[5] 2918[6] 3315[3] (3787) 4335[7] **>67f<**

Ferny Hill (IRE) 3 b c Danehill (USA)-Miss Allowed (USA) (Alleged (USA)) 2855[2] (3259) 4136[3] (4320) (4416) **>80a 96f<**

Ferrari (GER) 3 2642a[9] 3998a[2] 4762a[4] **>104f<**

Festival Flyer 2 b g Alhijaz-Odilese (Mummy's Pet) 938[4] 1760[10] 3386[8] 4245[4] 4582[6] **>62f<**

Festival Song (USA) 2 b f Irish River (FR)-Amirati (USA) (Danzig (USA)) 1880a[2] 2451a[4] 2811a[5] **>98f<**

Fey Rouge (IRE) 2 ch f Fayruz-Isa (Dance In Time (CAN)) 536[11] 884[8] 4332[13] **>43f<**

Ffestiniog (IRE) 2 b f Efisio-Penny Fan (Nomination) 1457[9] (1664) (2138) 3774[10] (4892) **>94f<**

Fiaba 9 b m Precocious-Historia (Northfields (USA)) **1996:** *5179[5]* **1997:** *126[3] 209[4] 245[6] 326[6] 415[8]* **>41a 35f<**

Fiametta 3 ch f Primo Dominie-Monaiya (Shareef Dancer (USA)) (2278) 4013[8] 4669[4] 4968[9] **>99f<**

Fiamma (IRE) 2 b f Irish River (FR)-Florie (FR) (Gay Mecene (USA)) (4534a) 4786[8] **>88f<**

Fiasco 4 ch f Dunbeath (USA)-Rainbow Trout (Comedy Star (USA)) *206[8] 272[4]* **>37a 52f<**

Fiddler's Rock (IRE) 2 b c Ballad Rock-Rockbourne (Midyan (USA)) 1531a[9] **>86f<**

Field of Vision (IRE) 7 b g Vision (USA)-Bold Meadows (Persian Bold) 470[5] **>75a 81f<**

Fieldridge 8 ch g Rousillon (USA)-Final Thought (Final Straw) 1114[5] 1413[6] 1808[4] **>67f<**

Fields of Omagh (USA) 2 b g Pleasant Tap (USA)-Brave And True (USA) (Fappiano (USA)) 4884[19] 5041[6] **>74f<**

Fiercely Ginger 2 ch c Interrex (CAN)-Broadway Stomp (USA) (Broadway Forli (USA)) 4105[11] 4446[7] 4855[12] **>13f<**

Fier Danseur (FR) 3 1070a[6] 1726a[10] **>106f<**

Fiery Footsteps 5 ro m Chilibang-Dancing Daughter (Dance In Time (CAN)) *76[14]* 484[12] **>31a 7f<**

Fife Major (USA) 3 b c Gone West (USA)-Fife (IRE) (Lomond (USA)) 1876[6] 2183[7] *2671[3] 3044[U]* 3721[2] 3971[4] 4172[7] 4503[7] **>67a 66f<**

Fifire (GER) 5 4531a[3] **>107f<**

Fifth Emerald 2 b f Formidable (USA)-Glossary (Reference Point) 5042[19] **>40f<**

Figawin 2 b c Rudimentary (USA)-Dear Person (Rainbow Quest (USA)) 1007[5] 1330[4] *(1758)* 2016[4] 2240[4] 2489[5] 2904[3] **>59a 69f<**

Fighting Times 5 b g Good Times (ITY)-Duellist (Town Crier) 2843[11] 3108[6] 3486[6] *4053[2]* (4453) (4607) 4847[4] 5024[6] **>49a 61f<**

Figlia 3 b f Sizzling Melody-Fiorini (Formidable (USA)) **1996:** *5107[7]* **1997:** *38[2] (102) 4051[7] 4574[12]* **>57a 73f<**

Fiji 3 b f Rainbow Quest (USA)-Island Jamboree (USA) (Explodent (USA)) (3017) **>110f<**

Filey Brigg 2 b f Weldnaas (USA)-Dusty's Darling (Doyoun) 432[9] 492[3] 548[3] (611) 844[2] 1013[6] 1149[4] (1653) 2024[15] 3049[3] 3740[6] 4267[12] 4442[8] **>86f<**

Filfilah 2 ch f Cadeaux Genereux-El Rabab (USA) (Roberto (USA)) 1645[2] (1927) 3049[5] 4097[10] **>83f<**

Filgrave (IRE) 2 b c Petardia-Party Guest (What A Guest) 1251[11] 2553[11] 2904[10] 3384[3] 3639[3] 4208[10] 4595[4] 4753[25] *4812[3]* **>59a 57f<**

Filial (IRE) 4 b g Danehill (USA)-Sephira (Luthier) **1996:** *5120[6] (5189)* **1997:** 2028[17] 2533[8] 3053[W] 3689[12] 3916[9] 4139[17] 4415[2] 4521[5] *(4981)* **>92a 69f<**

Filmore West 4 b c In The Wings-Sistabelle (Bellypha) 4639[11] 4891[15] **>63+a 83f<**

Final Claim 2 b c Absalom-For Gold (Tina's Pet) 1581[2] 2016[11] **>66f<**

Final Settlement (IRE) 2 b c Soviet Lad (USA)-Tender Time (Tender King) 3783[12] 4157[8] 4603[12] **>48f<**

Final Stab (IRE) 4 b g Kris-Premier Rose (Sharp Edge) 2929[7] (3328) 3496[10] 4121[16] 4920[10] **>80df<**

Final Stage (IRE) 3 ch g Shalford (IRE)-Alpine Symphony (Northern Dancer) 676[14] 1239[4] 2486[4] **>69f<**

Final Tango 2 b f Danehill (USA)-Sombre Lady (Sharpen Up) 4332[2] 4597[2] (4789) **>86f<**

Final Trial (IRE) 3 b c Last Tycoon-Perfect Alibi (Law Society (USA)) 524[3] **>83f<**

Final Warning 3 b g Warning-Lovely Lagoon (Mill Reef (USA)) 586[6] 1234[8] 1499[8] 3465[18] **>63f<**

Finarts Bay 3 b f Aragon-Salinas (Bay Express) 4316[4] 4464[3] 4773[14] 4951[17] *5020[5]* **>41a 67f<**

Fine Fellow (IRE) 3 b c Bluebird (USA)-Majieda (Kashmir II) 820a[3] 1544a[3] 1915a[2] 4531a[7] **>111f<**

Fine Quill 3 ch f Unfuwain (USA)-Quillotern (USA) (Arctic Tern (USA)) 3021[11] **>18f<**

Finestatetobein 4 ch f Northern State (USA)-Haywain (Thatching) 493[12] 1222[10] 1574[7] 1996[5] *2910[14]* 3429[4] 3567[3] 3778[4] 4287[5] 4432[8] 4771[5] **>61f<**

Fine Times 3 b c Timeless Times (USA)-Marfen (Lochnager) *871[8]* 1119[9] 1496[2] *1790[6]* 2017[9] 2203[4] 2547[7] 4016[5] 4586[11] 4693[9] 4843[9] **>44a 46f<**

Finisterre (IRE) 4 b g Salt Dome (USA)-Inisfail (Persian Bold) **1996:** *5138[9] 5235[2]* **1997:** 774[3] 1315[10] *1754[13]* **>61a 62f<**

Finnegan's Hollow (IRE) 7 b g Bulldozer-Amber

Goer (Amber Rama (USA)) 1005a[F]

Finsbury Flyer (IRE) 4 ch g Al Hareb (USA)-Jazirah (Main Reef) 843[10] 1139[6] (1292) 1473[5] 1920[5] 2369[6] 2646[12] 4043[13] **>49f<**

Fionn de Cool (IRE) 6 b g Mazaad-Pink Fondant (Northfields (USA)) 1262[11] 1640[6] 2216[5] 2485[6] 3115[15] (3435) 4139[8] **>70f<**

Fire Goddess 2 ch f Magic Ring (IRE)-Into the Fire (Dominion) 1418[4] 1593[4] 1827[3] 2138[3] 3468[8] 3774[6] 4097[15] 4814[3] 4898[12] **>65f<**

First Bite (IRE) 5 b g Be My Native (USA)-Saga's Humour (Bustino) 2362[6] 2880[11] 3283[16] **>39f<**

First Chance (IRE) 3 b f Lahib (USA)-Honagh Lee (Main Reef) *(215) 293[5]* 535[3] 642[2] 791[12] 1164[10] 1826[3] 2730[4] 3685[2] 4176[6] 4554[5] 4695[11] **>64a 72f<**

First Consul (USA) 2 ch c Rubiano (USA)-Sunflower Fields (USA) (Fit To Fight (USA)) 3201[4] **>70f<**

First Dance 2 b f Primo Dominie-Soviet Swan (USA) (Nureyev (USA)) 999[4] 1440[4] 1664[2] 2181[4] 2831[7] (3742) >70f<

First Frame 2 b c Mukaddamah (USA)-Point of Law (Law Society (USA)) 2324[5] **>38f<**

First Gallery 4 b f Charmer-Hound Song (Jukebox) **1996:** *5085[6]*

First Gold 8 gr g Absalom-Cindys Gold (Sonnen Gold) **1996:** *5161[2] 5175[5]* **1997:** *15[6] 71[5] 411[2]* (480) *579[8]* 1077[3] 1220[6] 1389[6] 1483[8] *2070[9]* 2463[8] 4742[13] **>59a 41f<**

First Idea 2 b f Primo Dominie-Good Thinking (USA) (Raja Baba (USA)) 3090[8] 3289[5] 3782[12] **>47f<**

First Island (IRE) 5 ch h Dominion-Caymana (FR) (Bellypha) **1996:** (5219a) **1997:** 830[2] (1210) **>131f< (DEAD)**

First Maite 4 b g Komaite (USA)-Marina Plata (Julio Mariner) *376[10]* 698[5] *(856)* 942[6] (1098) 1402[4] 1799[5] *2162[6]* 2844[9] *3075[9] 4482[6]* 4733[2] 4805[7] **>79a 80f<**

First Man 3 b g Man Among Men (IRE)-Sharp Thistle (Sharpo) **1996:** *5103[9] 5160[8] 5201[9]* **1997:** 875[8] 1094[16] 1565[7] 1920[11] **>46f<**

First Master 2 ch c Primo Dominie-Bodham (Bustino) 4237[11] 4520[6] (4815) **>74f<**

First Option 7 ch g Primo Dominie-Merrywren (Julio Mariner) 2887[9] 3240[16] **>62a 30f<**

First Principle 3 b c Rudimentary (USA)-Revoke (USA) (Riverman (USA)) 3202[2] (4047) 4527[5] **>86f<**

First Village (IRE) 2 b f Danehill (USA)-L-Way First (IRE) (Vision (USA)) 1645[3] 2467[14] 2831[11] (3471) 3791[4] 4305[5] 4702[12] **>80f<**

Fisiostar 4 b g Efisio-Sweet Colleen (Connaught) 823[7] 896[5] 1128[9] 1467[10] 2109[11] 2234[3] 2542[4] 2659[2] 2891[15] 3261[2] 3431[15] 4164[7] **>54df<**

Fit For The Job (IRE) 3 ch g Mac's Imp (USA)-Jolly Dale (IRE) (Huntingdale) **1996:** *5107[3] 5162[3] (5201)* **1997:** *38[4] 102[4] 181[6] 293[4] 372[7]* 556[8] 758[6] 1250[16] 1566[14] 3266[11] *3582[12] 4049[15]* 4328[20] **>61a 16f<**

Five Fairies 2 ch f Sabrehill (USA)-Fiveofive (IRE) (Fairy King (USA)) 3201[14] 4066[12] 4366[7] 4753[16] *4812[8]* **>45a 63f<**

Five Live 3 b f Pharly (FR)-Manageress (Mandamus) 4596[16] **>64?f<**

Fiveo'clock Shadow (IRE) 2 b br c Magical Strike (USA)-U-Can Do It (Ballad Rock) 750[3] 1007[2] 1411[5] 2243[10] (2425) 2588[4] 2863[7] 3237[14] **>78f<**

Five-O-Fifty 3 b br g Anshan-Wyns Vision (Vision (USA)) 1730[12] 3038[12] 4580[21] **>28f<**

Five of Spades (IRE) 2 b g Roi Danzig (USA)-Hellicroft (High Line) 432[11] 594[6] 954[2] 1616[9] 2565[11] (3932) 4284[7] (4989) 5050[11] **>79f<**

Fizzed 2 ch f Efisio-Clicquot (Bold Lad (IRE)) 3239[4] (3541) 4267[7] **>84f<**

Fizzy Boy (IRE) 4 b g Contract Law (USA)-Generation Gap (Young Generation) 2143[6] 2352[7] 2716[10] **>28f<**

Flag Down (CAN) 7 b h **1996:** 5159a[9] **1997:** 5065a[3] **>127f<**

Flag Fen (USA) 6 b br g Riverman (USA)-Damascus Flag (USA) (Damascus (USA)) *359[2] 411[5]* 461[8] (1266) 1495[10] 2546[6] **>62da 71df<**

Flagship 3 ch f Rainbow Quest (USA)-Bireme (Grundy) 1168[10] (4177) 4639[4] **>87f<**

Flagstaff (USA) 4 b g Personal Flag (USA)-Shuffle Up (USA) (Raja Baba (USA)) **1996:** *5237[7] 5271[8]* **1997:** *83[6] 144[7] 313[2] 390[4]* 755[9] 1266[5] 1388[5] 2041[5] 2195[4] 2399[8] 2646[15] 3421[12] **>46a 42df<**

Flamboyance (USA) 3 b f Zilzal (USA)-Bridal Wreath (USA) (Stop The Music (USA)) *(49)* 890[2] 1875[6] 2133[10] 3391[3] 3772[2] 4120[4] 4423[6] **>85+a 98f<**

Flamboyant Belle 2 b f Lahib (USA)-Mainmast (Bustino) 4789[11] **>28f<**

Flame Tower (IRE) 2 ch c Archway (IRE)-Guantanamera (USA) (El Gran Senor (USA)) 1026[7] 1791[4] 2037[11] *2604[2]* 2681[4] 4143[9] 4819[3] **>73a 59f<**

Flame Violet (IRE) 2 b f Fairy King (USA)-Really Sharp (Sharpen Up) 1531a[6] (2987a) 3534a[7] 4093a[6] **>109f<**

Flaming Ember (IRE) 2 b c Fayruz-Embustera (Sparkler) 564[3] (1425) 1504[2] 1735[3] 4146[5] 4293[7] 4517[4] **>88f<**

Flamingo Queen (GER) 3 f (3998b) 4254a[2] **>114f<**

Flash d'Or (IRE) 2 b f Shalford (IRE)-Gulf Craft (IRE) (Petorius) (780) 1253[6] 1330[7] 1581[8] 2153[11] 2233[8] *2367[7]* **>9a 47f<**

Flashfeet 7 b g Rousillon (USA)-Miellita (King Emperor (USA)) 1599[11] **>42a 40f<**

Flash In The Pan (IRE) 4 ch f Bluebird (USA)-Tomona (Linacre) 435[13] **>45a 54f<**

Flashnight (FR) 5 ch h Hero's Honor (USA)-Sweetbird (FR) (Gyr (USA)) (189a) **>75f<**

Flash of Realm (FR) 11 b g Super Moment (USA)-Light of Realm (Realm) 2539[7] 2661[7] **>38f<**

Flashtalkin' Flood 3 ch g Then Again-Linguistic (Porto Bello) *568[6]* 670[9] 963[13] 1568[3] 1820[5] (2171) 4335[17] 4741[11] **>30a 76f<**

Flawless 2 b f Warning-Made of Pearl (USA) (Nureyev (USA)) (3979) 4119[2] 4555[2] 4786[4] **>99f<**

Flaxen Pride (IRE) 2 ch f Pips Pride-Fair Chance (Young Emperor) 4508[2] 4841[7] 4993[8] **>62f<**

Flea In Your Ear 2 b f Young Senor (USA)-Lowrianna (IRE) (Cyrano de Bergerac) 743[11]

Fleet Cadet 6 ch h Bairn (USA)-Pirogue (Reliance II) *54[12]* **>16?a 38f<**

Fleeting Footsteps 5 b h Komaite (USA)-Hyperion Palace (Dragonara Palace (USA)) 1250[18] *1289[16]* **>21f<**

Fleeting Glimpse 3 b f Rainbow Quest (USA)-Flit (USA) (Lyphard (USA)) 1366a[2] **>105f<**

Fleet Lady (IRE) 2 b f Don't Forget Me-Yavarro (Raga Navarro (ITY)) 651[5] 828[9] 1425[10] 1827[9] 4165[17] 4740[11] **>46f<**

Fleet River (USA) 3 b f Riverman (USA)-Nimble Feet (USA) (Danzig (USA)) 4003[7] **>87f<**

Fleetwood (IRE) 2 ch c Groom Dancer (USA)-Up Anchor (IRE) (Slip Anchor) (4309) **>95++f<**

Flemensfirth (USA) 5 b h Alleged (USA)-Etheldreda (USA) (Diesis) *628a[10]* **>100a 128f<**

Fletcher 3 b g Salse (USA)-Ballet Classique (USA) (Sadler's Wells (USA)) 735[18] 1165[3] 1850[3] 2027[6] 2596[5] 3110[13] 3599[6] 4101[10] 4241[9] 4787[22] **>90f<**

Fleur-de-Lys 2 ch f King's Signet (USA)-Kind of Cute (Prince Sabo) 1019[4] 1444[7] 2003[8] 3451[5] **>42f<**

Fleuve d'Or (IRE) 3 gr f Last Tycoon-Aldern Stream (Godswalk (USA)) **1996:** *5103[6]* **>41a 39f<**

Flibbertigibbet 2 b f Almoojid-Stella Royale (Astronef) 1438[7]

Flickan 2 ch f Superpower-Spark (IRE) (Flash of Steel) *902[5] 1286[2]* 1664[5] **>70a 66f<**

Flicker 2 b f Unfuwain (USA)-Lovers Light (Grundy) 4604[11] 4739[5] **>68f<**

Flight 2 ch g Night Shift (USA)-Caspian Tern (USA) (Arctic Tern (USA)) 3201[15] 3386[5] 3717[3] **>77f<**

Flight For Freedom 2 b f Saddlers' Hall (IRE)-Anatroccolo (Ile de Bourbon (USA)) 3973[4] **>66+f<**

Flint And Steel 4 b g Rock City-Brassy Nell (Dunbeath (USA)) *18[11]* **>58f<**

Flint Knapper 3 ch c Kris-Circe's Isle (Be My Guest (USA)) 1004[3] 3463[6] (3820) 4223[2] (4477) **>89f<**

Flirtation 3 b f Pursuit of Love-Eastern Shore (Sun Prince) 503[5] **>53f<**

Flirtina 2 b f Tina's Pet-Immodest Miss (Daring Display (USA)) 536[10] 780[6] 1581[6] 1856[6] **>43f<**

Flirting Around (USA) 3 b c Silver Hawk (USA)-Dancing Grass (USA) (Northern Dancer) 524[4] 1025[2] (1150) 2027[7] 2327[6] 3218[12] **>100f<**

Floating Charge 3 b g Sharpo-Poyle Fizz (Damister (USA)) 3775[7] 4070[2] **>76f<**

Floating Devon 3 br g Simply Great (FR)-Devon Dancer (Shareef Dancer (USA)) 600[6] 826[8] **>45a 56df< (DEAD)**

Flood's Hot Stuff 3 gr f Chilibang-Tiszta Sharok (Song) *33[6] 102[7] 181[13] 2669[7]* 2878[2] 3132[6] (3557) 3848[8] 4043[12] **>19a 46f<**

Floral Park 2 b f Northern Park (USA)-Whitchurch Silk (IRE) (Runnett) 2227[9] 2489[4] 2693[14] 3493[12] **>42f<**

Florazi 2 b c Arazi (USA)-Flo Russell (USA) (Round Table) 3745[5] 4174[6] (4581) (4885) **>90f<**

Florence Asher 2 b f Shardari-Filicaia (Sallust) 4993[18] **>9f<**

Florentino (IRE) 4 b br g Machiavellian (USA)-Helens Dreamgirl (Caerleon (USA)) 680[15] 1371[2] 1481[5] 2065[3] (2570) 2718[2] 3053[6] 4386[4] 4854[4] **>81f<**

Floristan (IRE) 3 b c Fairy King (USA)-Le Melody (Levmoss) 3463[14] 3991[3] **>72f<**

Florrie'm 4 ch f Tina's Pet-Rosie Dickins (Blue Cashmere) **1996:** *5109[5] 5165[12]* **>24a 42df<**

Flo's Choice (IRE) 3 b f Dancing Dissident (USA)-Miss Siddons (Cure The Blues (USA)) 2354[4] 2883[12] 3332[5] 3698[6] *4809[7]* **>44a 31f<**

Flotilla 3 b g Saddlers' Hall (IRE)-Aim for the Top (USA) (Irish River (FR)) 1166[14] 1588[9] 2036[14] 2523[8] 2876[4] 3234[10] **>59a 61f<**

Flourishing Way 3 b f Sadler's Wells (USA)-Darayna (IRE) (Shernazar) 784[4] 1237[2] 2278[3] 2491[9] **>78f<**

Flow Back 5 gr g Royal Academy (USA)-Flo Russell (USA) (Round Table) **1996:** *5102[6] 5148[14] 5181[7]* **1997:** *13[13]* **>48da 44f<**

Flow By 2 b f Formidable (USA)-Lobinda (Shareef Dancer (USA)) 1440[7] 2394[2] (2953) 3387[4] 4265[5] 4690[3] **>79f<**

Flower Hill Lad (IRE) 3 b g Sizzling Melody-Persian Tapestry (Tap On Wood) **1996:** *5121[11]* **>50a 76f<**

Flower Miller 4 b g Formidable (USA)-Sunflower Seed (Mummy's Pet) 3211[9] 3822[14] 4264[11] **>28f<**

Flower O'Cannie (IRE) 2 b f Mujadil (USA)-Baby's Smile (Shirley Heights) 460[2] 525[3] 844[6] 1466[5] 1997[9] (2222) (2499) 2714[3] 3650[3] 3802[12] 4265[3] 4875[13] **>85f<**

Flowing Fortune 3 b g Kenmare (FR)-Green Flower (USA) (Fappiano (USA)) 1866[6] 4579[4] 4736[6] **>69f<**

Flowing Ocean 7 ch h Forzando-Boswellia (Frankincense) **1996:** *5260[13]* **>8a 65?f< (DEAD)**

Flush (FR) 2 b br f Warning-Garden Pink (FR) (Bellypha) 3187[9] 4067[8] 4502[5] **>72f<**

Flyaway Blues 5 b g Bluebird (USA)-Voltigeuse (USA) (Filiberto (USA)) 574[5] 721[12] 4692[3] 4923[11] **>47f<**

Flyaway Hill (FR) 3 b f Danehill (USA)-Flyaway Bride (USA) (Blushing Groom (FR)) 1567[5] 1826[8] 2239[3] **>62f<**

Fly By Night (IRE) 2 b br c Night Shift (USA)-Fatah Flare (USA) (Alydar (USA)) 3887[7] 4064[3] 4384[3] 4603[6] **>79f<**

Fly by North (USA) 9 b g Northern Horizon (USA)-Lazy E (CAN) (Meadow Court) *66[P]* **(DEAD)**

Fly High 3 b f Wing Park-Nahawand (High Top) 1780[6] 1998[4] 2407[6] 2941[11] **>52df<**

Flying Angel 3 br f Almoojid-Silvie (Kind of Hush) 2727[10]

Flying Bold (IRE) 2 ch c Persian Bold-Princess Reema (USA) (Affirmed (USA)) *4052[2] 4299[7]* 4753[7] (4898) **>62+a 71f<**

Flying Clouds 2 b f Batshoof-Fleeting Rainbow (Rainbow Quest (USA)) 4520[9] 4739[10] **>47f<**

Flying Colours (IRE) 3 b f Fairy King (USA)-Crazed Rainbow (USA) (Graustark) 1087[7] 1316[9] 1823[10] 2731[11] 4695[18] 4958[8] **>48a 57f<**

Flying Esprit 3 ch g High Kicker (USA)-Sport Lady (USA) (Sportin' Life (USA)) *874[12]* 1144[16] 1443[10] 2397[13] **>6f<**

Flying Flip 3 b f Rolfe (USA)-Needwood Sprite (Joshua) 2704[7] 2960[8] *3396[4]* 4015[13] 4632[4] 4845[7] 4988[9] **>40a 55f<**

Flying Harold 4 b g Gildoran-Anytime Anywhere (Daring March) 477[6] 879[2] 1012[4] 1079[4] 1279[3] 1743[2] (1925) 2179[6] 2384[4] 3693[8] 4115[5] 4233[19] 4370[2] 4518[7] 4580[6] 4770[8] **>53f<**

Flying High (IRE) 2 b c Fayruz-Shayista (Tap On Wood) 1038[5] 1860[7] 2127[7] **>48f<**

Flying North (IRE) 4 b g Distinctly North (USA)-North Kildare (USA) (Northjet) 1268[7] (1831) 2528[5] 3061[7] 4151[18] **>88f<**

Flying Pennant (IRE) 4 ch c Waajib-Flying Beckee (IRE) (Godswalk (USA)) 734[10] 1035[13] 1599[4] 1920[6] 2508[8] 3718[10] 4228[5] 4448[10] **>56f<**

Flying Singer 2 b f Bluebird (USA)-Singer on the Roof (Chief Singer) 1806[10] 2371[5] 2740[4] 3474[8] 3924[7] 4285[12] **>65f<**

Fly To The Stars 3 b c Bluebird (USA)-Rise and Fall (Mill Reef (USA)) (436) 807a[2] 1060a[5] 1741[4] (2013) 2766[16] (3150) 3729a[2] 4252a[3] **>118f<**

Flyway (FR) 4 b c Priolo (USA)-Flying Circus (FR) (Gay Mecene (USA)) (630a) 916a[4] (1363a) 1917a[4] **>123f<**

Foist 5 b g Efisio-When The Saints (Bay Express) (468) 529[3] (610) 734[2] (953) 1259[4] 1734[9] 1977[20] 2422[10] 2711[17] 3034[8] 3431[16] 3936[16] **>64+a 43f<**

Foleys Quest (IRE) 3 b f River Falls-Katie's Delight (Relko) 1637[6] 1850[5] 3462[2] 3758[6] 4275[15] **>58f<**

Folgore (USA) 3 ch f Irish River (FR)-Florie (FR) (Gay Mecene (USA)) 4110[5] **>58f<**

Folklore 2 b f Fairy King (USA)-Falsoola (Kris) 1457[2] 1653[7] 2024[11] 3541[2] (3823) 3965[8] 4522[10] **>93+f<**

Folle Tempete (FR) 4 dk f Fabulous Dancer (USA)-Belle Tempete (FR) 2818a[3] **>102f<**

Folling (FR) 2 b f Take Risks (FR)-Folle Angoisse (ITY) (Amber Rama (USA)) 3008a[2]

Folly Foot Fred 3 b g Crisp-Wessex Kingdom (Vaigly Great) 535[17] 1167[14] 1566[11] 1849[8] 2554[14] **>47f<**

Fond Embrace 4 b f Emarati (USA)-Detente (Dominion) 1975[5] 2377[6] 3011[13] **>93f<**

Fontcaudette (IRE) 3 b f River Falls-Lune de Miel (Kalamoun) *873[14]* 1500[9] 2407[5] **>40f<**

Fontevrault (FR) 2 c b Subotica (FR)-Touville (FR) (Shadeed (USA)) 5058a[3] **>75f<**

Fonteyn 3 b f Aragon-Trull (Lomond (USA)) 681[9] 935[2] 2278[2] 2580[3] 4070[15] *4795[2]* **>58a 79df<**

Fonzy 3 b g Phountzi (USA)-Diavalezza (Connaught) 2204[9] *2605[7]* 3261[7] 3936[18] **>54?a 50f<**

Fooled You (USA) 3 br c Wild Again (USA)-Foolish Miz (USA) (Foolish Pleasure (USA)) 599[4] 1239[14] **>74f<**

Foolish Flutter (IRE) 3 b br f Fools Holme (USA)-Thornbeam (Beldale Flutter (USA)) 582[11] 1095[6] 2488[6] 2701[2] (3102) *3585[2]* 4010[3] 4632[10] **>49a 53f<**

Fools Honor (IRE) 3 b c Fools Holme (USA)-Honorine (USA) (Blushing Groom (FR)) 812a[2] **>71f<**

Foot Battalion (IRE) 3 b c Batshoof-Roxy Music (IRE) (Song) **1996:** *5229[2]* **1997:** *(103) 138[7] 343[3] 388[2] (396)* 449[7] 597[6] 1017[8] 1175[7] 1773[4] 2062[8] 2328[9] 2585[12] 3236[8] 3457[6] 4176[9] 4583[3] 4693[3] 4876[8] **>97?a 72f<**

Forbes (ITY) 3 b c Sikeston (USA)-Strolega (ITY) (Cure The Blues (USA)) 1068a[2] **>86f<**

Forcing Bid 3 b g Forzando-Cox's Pippin (USA) (Cox's Ridge (USA)) *(855) (871)* 2925[8] *3075[7]* 4071[17] *4482[3] 4591[7] 4797[8]* 4820[13] **>83a 50f<**

Forecast 4 b g Formidable (USA)-Princess Matilda (Habitat) 1127[8] 1861[5] 2203[14] 3431[22] **>32a 45f<**

Foreign Judgement (USA) 4 b g El Gran Senor (USA)-Numeral (USA) (Alleged (USA)) 2039[16] 2487[19] **>23f<**

Foreign Relation (IRE) 4 b f Distant Relative-Nicola Wynn (Nicholas Bill) **1996:** *5170[10]* **>18a 57f<**

Foreign Rule (IRE) 3 b g Danehill (USA)-Guida Centrale (Teenoso (USA)) 518[3] 740[6] 996[2] 1372[2] 1805[4] (2423) 4774[11] **>83f<**

Forest Boy 4 b g Komaite (USA)-Khadine (Astec) *(29) 140[9] 179[5]* **>76a 76f<**

Forest Buck (USA) 4 ch c Green Forest (USA)-Perlee (FR) (Margouillat (FR)) 943[2] **>114f<**

Forest Fantasy 4 b f Rambo Dancer (CAN)-Another Treat (Derring-Do) 1390[7] 1796[3] 2174[8] (3316) 3573[12] 4324[4] 4596[10] **>62f<**

Forest Fire (SWE) 2 b f Never so Bold-Mango Sampaquita (SWE) (Colombian Friend (USA)) 4750[5] **>46f<**

Forest Robin 4 ch g Formidable (USA)-Blush Rambler (IRE) (Blushing Groom (FR)) 435[14] 647[13] 776[3] 987[11] 1397[8] 1583[7] 1800[6] 2152[3] 2313[9] 2546[9] 2880[5] 3091[7] 3605[9] 3777[13] 3937[7] 4243[3] 4924[15] 4991[13] 5023[11] **>56f<**

Forestry 3 b g Highest Honor (FR)-Arboretum (IRE) (Green Desert (USA)) 1637[13] 2591[8] 2873[7] 4179[19] **>52f<**

Forest Signal 3 ch c Indian Forest (USA)-Telegraph Callgirl (Northern Tempest (USA)) 793[7] 1656[3] 1834[7] 2313[14] 2546[20] **>60f<**

Forest Treasure (IRE) 2 b f Brief Truce (USA)-In The Clover (Meadow Mint (USA)) (1255) 1653[2] 2024[5] 2558[3] 3049[6] **>89f<**

Forget Paris (IRE) 4 gr f Broken Hearted-Miss Deauville (Sovereign Path) **1996:** *5179[16]* **1997:** *66[6]* **>48a 43f<**

Forget To Remindme 3 b f Forzando-Sandy Looks (Music Boy) (1167) 1458[13] 1668[6] 2245[9] *2670[8]* 4371[20] **>20a 39f<**

Forgie (IRE) 4 b g Don't Forget Me-Damia (Vision (USA)) 650[5] 888[5] 1118[3] (1996) (2352) 2882[9] 3440[4] 3754[5] (3974) (4363) 4874[5] 5052[11] **>83f<**

Forgotten Dancer (IRE) 6 ch g Don't Forget Me-Dancing Diana (Raga Navarro (ITY)) **1996:** *5082[8] 5145[13] 5271[13]* **1997:** *59[7]* **>24a 51f<**

Forgotten Star (IRE) 2 b br f Don't Forget Me-Sterna Star (Corvaro (USA)) 3450[8] 3818[6] 3973[3] 4334[8] 4576[17] **>66f<**

Forgotten Times (USA) 3 ch f Nabeel Dancer (USA)-Etoile D'Amore (USA) (The Minstrel (CAN)) **1996:** *5187[4] 5272[3]* **1997:** *12[3] 62[2] (97) 214[2] 293[2] (339)* 506[10] 649[13] 2372[9] 2554[5] 2665[9] 2921[6] 3968[11] **>77a 58f<**

Formal Gold (CAN) 4 b br c Black Tie Affair-Ingoldsby (USA) (Screen King (USA)) *628a[5]* **>121a 125f<**

Formation Dancer 2 ch c Groom Dancer (USA)-Golden Form (Formidable (USA)) 5048[11] **>54f<**

Former Love (USA) 2 b f Dynaformer (USA)-Love and Legend (USA) (Lyphard's Wish (FR)) 3117[7] 4007[5] 4309[4] 4900[4] **>73f<**

Formidable Flame 4 ch g Formidable (USA)-Madiyla (Darshaan) *544[W]* 1244[12] 1844[11] 2297[6] **>36df<**

Formidable Liz 7 ch m Formidable (USA)-Areej (Rusticaro (FR)) 1583[10] 1765[7] 2061[14] 2358[4] 2567[7] 3285[9] **>52a 37f<**

Formidable Spirit 3 ch g Formidable (USA)-Hicklam Millie (Absalom) **1996:** *5187[10] 5226[6]* **1997:** *132[4]* 1375[6] 1730[13] *2151[11]* 2554[19] 2747[8] **>31a 32f<**

For the Present 7 b g Then Again-Axe Valley (Royben) 744[3] 1468[8] 1772[9] 2129[7] 2675[9] 2844[10] 3034[13] 3130[3] 3385[4] 3604[10] 4307[5] **>80f<**

Fort Knox (IRE) 6 b g Treasure Kay-Single Viking (Viking (USA)) **1996:** *5249[4]* **1997:** *27[2] 121[6] 146[7] 211[4]* 1506[5] 1639[7] 2743[5] 3056[9] 3421[7] 3561[W] **>64da 56f<**

Fortune Hopper 3 br g Rock Hopper-Lots of Luck (Neltino) 862[3] 1217[5] 1502[3] 2357[4] 2531[5] 2727[8] 3129[3] **>55f<**

Fortune Hunter (IRE) 3 ch g Lycius (USA)-Cardomine (Dom Racine (FR)) 1023[13] 1167[11] 1493[5] 4335[18] **>61f<**

Fortunes Course (IRE) 8 b m Crash Course-Night Rose (Sovereign Gleam) 1114[2] 4609[3] **>56f<**

Fortune's Way (IRE) 3 b f Distinctly North (USA)-Shanliss (Blazing Saddles (AUS)) 2020[8] *2300[8] 3396[8]* **>23a 40f<**

Forty Love (IRE) 2 b g Second Set (IRE)-Pharjoy (FR) (Pharly (FR)) 3201[9] 3613[9] (3808) 4068[5] 4411[10] *4808[6]* 4900[6] **>36a 66f<**

Forum 2 b f Lion Cavern (USA)-Top Society (High Top) 2138[2] 2558[6] 2962[3] 3547[4] (4502) **>86f<**

For Valour (USA) 4 b c Trempolino (USA)-Glitter (FR) (Reliance II) (2270a) 3006a[4] 4863a[3] **>118f<**

Forward Miss 3 b f Bold Arrangement-Maiden Bidder (Shack (USA)) 2580[8] 3230[9] 4114[15] 4326[13] 4504[13] 4816[16] **>19a 12f<**

For Your Eyes Only 3 b g Pursuit of Love-Rivers Rhapsody (Dominion) 1170[10] 1980[10] 2326[10] 2857[3] 3254[7] 3622[6] 3801[2] 3976[3] 4147[16] 4441[9] 4781[2] 4978[2] **>95f<**

Forza Figlio 4 b c Warning-Wish You Well (Sadler's Wells (USA)) 738[7] 939[2] 1261[5] 1745[3] 2026[9] 2764[2] 3112[13] 4476[4] 4754[15] **>93f<**

Forzair 5 b g Forzando-Persian Air (Persian Bold)

1996: 5115[3] 5143[3] 5232[4] **1997:** 18[2] 114[2] 231[4] (276) 315[8] 375[4] 542[3] 595[5] 721[3] 867[6] 1125[4] 1288[6] 1579[3] 1748[10] 2145[4] 2479[2] 2824[7] (3284) 3540[10] 3853[2] 4235[16] 4432[10] 4584[3] 4692[2] 5028[3] **>55a 59f<**

Forzara 4 ch f Risk Me (FR)-Valldemosa (Music Boy) 956[14] 2197[11] 2536[12] 3327[12] **>18f<**

Foundry Lane 6 b g Mtoto-Eider (Niniski (USA)) 3705[10] 3974[5] 4295[4] **>81f<**

Fourdaned (IRE) 4 b g Danehill (USA)-Pro Patria (Petingo) 435[5] 544[8] 763[11] 1244[16] 2398[4] 2696[2] 3093[3] 4108[10] 4667[11] **>48a 65f<**

Four of Spades 6 ch g Faustus (USA)-Fall To Pieces (USA) (Forli (ARG)) 1433[12] 1796[13] 2004[14] **>62a 59f<**

Foxes Tail 3 gr g Batshoof-Secret Gill (Most Secret) 699[8] 2043[5] 2328[6] 4703[5] 4876[9] **>76df<**

Foxford Lad 3 b g Akid (USA)-Spring Rose (Blakeney) **1996:** 5243[7] **1997:** 26[11] 228[4] 347[5] 534[4] 1565[6] 2397[12] **>45a 43f<**

Foxie Lady 2 ch f Wolfhound (USA)-Final Thought (Final Straw) 3806[8] **>47f<**

Fox Sparrow 7 b g Sharpo-Wryneck (Niniski (USA)) 2034[9] 2753[7] 3429[6] **>43f<**

Fragrant Mix (FR) 3 gr c Linamix (FR)-Fragrant Hill (Shirley Heights) (629a) 1726a[4] **>113f<**

Francesca's Folly 2 b f Efisio-Nashville Blues (IRE) (Try My Best (USA)) 1564[10] 2227[11] 3493[4] 3911[9] (4058) 4366[6] 4806[14] **>57f<**

Frandickbob 3 b g Statoblest-Crimson Ring (Persian Bold) **1996:** 5111[W] 5162[11] 5239[13] **1997:** 757[11] **>19a 27f<**

Frankie 3 b g Shalford (IRE)-Twilight Secret (Vaigly Great) 1804[4] 2008[15] 2662[6] 3234[12] **>56df<**

Frankie Fair (IRE) 2 b f Red Sunset-Animate (IRE) (Tate Gallery (USA)) 1970[4] 2147[3] 2604[3] 3257[5] 4753[5] 4885[8] **>62a 62f<**

Frankie Ferrari (IRE) 2 b c Common Grounds-Miss Kelly (Pitskelly) 4237[15] 4526[15] 4715[13] **>59f<**

Franklin Lakes 2 ch c Sanglamore (USA)-Eclipsing (IRE) (Baillamont (USA)) 4758[19] 4910[4] **>65f<**

Frans Lad 5 ch g Music Boy-Moberry (Mossberry) 1576[9] **>42a 47f<**

Freckles 2 b f High Kicker (USA)-Ship of Gold (Glint of Gold) 3450[19] 3717[7] 4567[13] 4812[5] **>55a 32f<**

Freddie Mac (IRE) 2 b c River Falls-Golden Thread (Glint of Gold) 4478[7] **>39f<**

Frederick James 3 b c Efisio-Rare Roberta (USA) (Roberto (USA)) 1090[2] 1764[3] 2130[6] 2422[9] 2835[14] 4565[14] **>75df<**

Fredrik The Fierce (IRE) 3 b g Puissance-Hollia (Touch Boy) 1018[13] 1254[11] **>92df<**

Fred's Delight (IRE) 6 b g Law Society (USA)-Madame Nureyev (USA) (Nureyev (USA)) 15[9] 151[5] 206[6] **>32a 20f<**

Fred's In The Know 2 ch g Interrex (CAN)-Lady Vynz (Whitstead) 1007[6] 1854[5] 2425[7] **>38f<**

Free 2 ch c Gone West (USA)-Bemissed (USA) (Nijinsky (CAN)) 1872[9] 4165[7] **>74f<**

Free As A Bird 3 b f Robellino (USA)-Special Guest (Be My Guest (USA)) 1690[2] 1976[4] 2231[8] 2705[6] 3205[5] **>60f<**

Free As The Wind (IRE) 2 b c Brief Truce (USA)-Skhiza (Targowice (USA)) 4478[4] 4952[2] **>79f<**

Freedom Chance (IRE) 3 ch g Lahib (USA)-Gentle Guest (IRE) (Be My Guest (USA)) **1996:** 5090[5] **1997:** (535) 764[9] 1421[8] 1833[3] 2158[4] 2650[4] 3080[2] 3593[2] 4002[9] 4406[7] **>62a 79f<**

Freedom of Troy 3 b g Puissance-Wing of Freedom (Troy) 2733[11] 3868[8] 4601[15] **>32f<**

Freedom Quest (IRE) 2 b c Polish Patriot (USA)-Recherchee (Rainbow Quest (USA)) 4361[2] 4502[2] **>84f<**

Free House (USA) 3 ro c Smokester (USA)-Fountain Lake (USA) (Vigors (USA)) 1071a[3] 1364a[2] 1912a[3] **>125a 118f<**

Free Option (IRE) 2 ch c Indian Ridge-Saneena (Kris) 3235[9] 4384[2] 4758[14] 4908[2] 4993[3] **>80f<**

Freequent 4 ch c Rainbow Quest (USA)-Free Guest (Be My Guest (USA)) 3703[8] 4004[5] (4399a) **>116f<**

Free To Speak (IRE) 5 ch g Be My Guest (USA)-Love For Poetry (Lord Gayle (USA)) 1058a[4] 1542a[6] 3362a[6] **>100f<**

French Ballerina (IRE) 4 b f Sadler's Wells (USA)-Filia Ardross (Ardross) (1698a) 2267a[2] 2456a[5] **>108+f<**

French Connection 2 b c Tirol-Heaven-Liegh-Grey (Grey Desire) 3253[7] 3701[2] 3973[2] **>78f<**

French Ginger 6 ch m Most Welcome-French Plait (Thatching) 3822[4] 4050[12] (4164) 4324[8] 4846[13] **>28a 60f<**

French Grit (IRE) 5 b g Common Grounds-Charbatte (FR) (In Fijar (USA)) (596) 942[13] 1259[8] 1561[9] (1799) 2129[9] 2900[14] 3087[7] 3621[13] 4414[4] 4842[20] **>77f<**

French Holly (USA) 6 b g Sir Ivor-Sans Dot (Busted) 2108[11]

French Ivy (USA) 10 ch g Nodouble (USA)-Lierre (USA) (Gummo (USA)) 632[11] 1100[12] 1494[4] 2139[7] **>72f<**

French Kiss (IRE) 3 b g Petorius-Cerosia (Pitskelly) **1996:** 5265[4] **1997:** 26[10] **>18a f<**

French Mist 3 b f Mystiko (USA)-Flambera (FR) (Akarad (FR)) 975[3] 1147[7] 1649[6] 2189[2] 2411[6] 2726[3] 3279[11] **>72f<**

French Pride (IRE) 2 b f Pips Pride-Reasonably French (Reasonable (FR)) 3222[5] **>45f<**

French Project (IRE) 5 b m Project Manager-Malia (Malacate (USA)) 612[7] 950[14]

Fresh Fruit Daily 5 b m Reprimand-Dalmally (Sharpen Up) **1996:** 5114[8] **1997:** (2) 66[4] 284[9] 418[4] (607) 763[5] (1125) 1233[U] 2164[4] 3104[8] 3432[8] 4302[4] **>58a 75df<**

Fret (USA) 7 b g Storm Bird (CAN)-Windy and Mild (USA) (Best Turn (USA)) 2166[6] **>46?f<**

Friar's Oak 5 b g Absalom-Sunset Ray (Hotfoot) 607[11] 753[8] **>25?a 33?f<**

Friar Tuck 2 ch c Inchinor-Jay Gee Ell (Vaigly Great) 2473[4] (2856) 3379[3] 4232[3] 4468[4] 4790[21] **>90f<**

Friendly Brave (USA) 7 b g Well Decorated (USA)-Companionship (USA) (Princely Native (USA)) **1996:** 5096[5] 5150[6] **1997:** 520[16] 569[4] 643[8] 731[5] 835[10] 1848[5] 2115[9] 2308[2] 2581[7] 2698[5] 3280[6] 3590[4] 4370[10] 5021[5] **>71a 68f<**

Friendly Coast 11 b g Blakeney-Noreena (Nonoalco (USA)) 195[7]

Friendly Knight 7 b g Horage-Be A Dancer (Be Friendly) 1040[5] **>24f<**

Friendly Warning (FR) 2 b f Warning-Dedara (Head for Heights) 3235[2] (3994a) 4529a[4] 4892[9] **>77f<**

Frisky Lady 2 b f Magic Ring (IRE)-Epithet (Mill Reef (USA)) 1328[6] 1569[6] 2222[3] 3042[4] **>51a 51f<**

Fritton (IRE) 2 br c Petardia-Calash (Indian King (USA)) 2771[6] 3235[11] 3783[15] **>44f<**

Frolicking 2 b f Mujtahid (USA)-Perfect Desire (USA) (Green Forest (USA)) 2227[8] 2534[5] 3489[4] 3924[15] 4271[4] 4576[10] 4897[5] **>72f<**

Frond 2 b f Alzao (USA)-Fern (Shirley Heights) 2098a[5] 3744[5] 4066[3] (4841) **>84+f<**

Front View 3 b g Backchat (USA)-Book Review (Balidar) **1996:** 5207[7] **1997:** 255[10]

Frost King 3 gr g Northern State (USA)-Celtic Image (Welsh Saint) **1996:** 5243[9] **1997:** 2667[10] 3057[5] 3643[5] **>13a 44f<**

Frozen Sea (USA) 6 ch h Diesis-Ocean Ballad (Grundy) 510[6] 789[8] 4108[17] 4275[12] 4406[6] **>46f<**

Frugal 4 b g Dunbeath (USA)-Sum Music (Music Boy) 1220[10] 1448[7] 2156[8] **>40f<**

Fruitana (IRE) 3 b g Distinctly North (USA)-Tadjnama (USA) (Exceller (USA)) **1996:** 5146[8] **>85a 73f<**

Fruitie O'Flarety 3 gr c Environment Friend-Dame Margot (USA) (Northern Dancer) **1996:** 5121[8] **>54a 68f<**

Fruits of Love (USA) 2 b c Hansel (USA)-Vallee Secrete (USA) (Secretariat (USA)) (3260) 3576[3] 3962a[2] **>97f<**

Frundin 2 ch f Anshan-Freudenau (Wassl) 651[6] 872[W] 1045[8] **>38a 26f<**

Fuenji (FR) 3 f 3371a[9] **>97f<**

Full Moon 2 b g Almoojid-High Time (FR) (Adonijah) 2361[9] 2827[7] **>32f<**

Fullopep 3 b g Dunbeath (USA)-Suggia (Alzao (USA)) 448[15] 575[12] 785[9] (1574) 2189[9] 2757[4] 4432[4] 4794[9] **>70f<**

Full Throttle 4 br g Daring March-Wheatley (Town Crier) 1215[7] 1811[12] 2464[4] **>54f<**

Full Traceability (IRE) 3 b f Ron's Victory (USA)-Miss Petella (Dunphy) **1996:** 5239[9] **1997:** 19[5] 314[10] **>32a 58df<**

Fully Booked 3 b f Midyan (USA)-Vielle (Ribero) 2731[14] 3133[9] **>34f<**

Funchal Way 5 b g One Man Band-Dusky Nancy (Red Sunset) 519[11] 4896[7] 5021[13] **>58?f<**

Fundance 2 b g Rambo Dancer (CAN)-Having Fun (Hard Fought) 1819[4] 2110[3] 2477[7] 3307[12] 4458[3] 4589[7] 4737[11] **>50a 72f<**

Fun Galore (USA) 3 b c Gone West (USA)-Ma Petite Jolie (USA) (Northern Dancer) 1170[9] 2426[5] 3189[12] 4902[6] **>89f<**

Fung Shui (IRE) 2 b c Night Shift (USA)-Isola (GER) (Konigsstuhl (GER)) 2579[7] 3493[10] 4052[10] 4545[16] **>39a 51f<**

Fun Harbour (FR) 4 ch c Funambule (USA)-Clef des Ondes (269a) **>82f<**

Funky 4 ch f Classic Music (USA)-Foreno (Formidable (USA)) 286[7] 496[9] 668[6] **>12a 31f<**

Funny Howithappens 2 b f Forzando-Girl's Brigade (Brigadier Gerard) 1213[7]

Furnish 3 b f Green Desert (USA)-Eternal (Kris) 1406[4] (1764) 2141[2] 2517[9] **>89f<**

Further Flight 11 gr g Pharly (FR)-Flying Nelly (Nelcius) 1033[2] 1241[2] 2709[4] 3705[4] (3902) 4118[3] 4559[3] 4965a[9] **>120f<**

Further Outlook (USA) 3 gr c Zilzal (USA)-Future Bright (USA) (Lyphard's Wish (FR)) 851[5] 1307[6] 2013[19] **>96f<**

Fur Will Fly 3 br f Petong-Bumpkin (Free State) 727[12] 964[2] 1265[6] 1967[5] **>66f<**

Future Perfect 3 b g Efisio-True Ring (High Top) (688) 958[6] 1404[2] 2013[17] 2729[2] (3190) 5053[6] **>97f<**

Fuwala 3 b f Unfuwain (USA)-Lobela (Lorenzaccio) 3909[6] 4060[17] **>52f<**

G

Gablesea 3 b g Beveled (USA)-Me Spede (Valiyar) 503[6] 845[12] 2020[5] 2214[9] 2651[12] 3030[9] (4300) 4813[15] 4991[11] **>53a 39f<**

Gadge 6 br g Nomination-Queenstyle (Moorestyle) **1996:** 5206[6] 5233[11] **1997:** 31[6] 153[5] 188[7] 211[3] (321) 407[3] 490[3] (526) 608[2] 721[9] 864[3] (947) (1111) (1324) (1561) 1658[5] 2211[3] 2326[5] 3273[2] 3604[13] 3765[18] 3888[7] 4280[20] 4574[4] 4842[9] **>61a 78f<**

Gadroon 3 ch g Cadeaux Genereux-Greensward Blaze (Sagaro) 1119^{14} *2159^{5}* 2226^{3} 4693^{2} 4845^{9} **>8a 51f<**

Gad Yakoun 4 ch g Cadeaux Genereux-Summer Impressions (USA) (Lyphard (USA)) **1996:** *(5085) 5144^{7} 5266^{9}* **1997:** *31^{5} 79^{7}* **>57a 73f<**

Gaelic Quinie (IRE) 2 b f River Falls-Eliza Wooding (Faustus (USA)) 3106^{5} 3808^{6} *4483^{9}* 4793^{8} **>3a 54f<**

Gaelic Storm 3 b c Shavian-Shannon Princess (Connaught) 2044^{6} 3194^{8} (3460) (3795) 4282^{5} (4430) 4756^{8} 4887^{8} 4995^{6} **>92f<**

Gagajulu 4 b f Al Hareb (USA)-Rion River (IRE) (Taufan (USA)) 702^{17} 924^{9} **>59a 37f<**

Gaily Mill 2 b f Keen-Island Mill (Mill Reef (USA)) 2227^{5} 2781^{9} 4515^{15} **>70f<**

Gain Line (USA) 4 b c Dayjur (USA)-Safe Play (USA) (Sham (USA)) 517^{10} 838^{16} 1501^{4} 1845^{2} 2121^{3} 2891^{8} (3100) 4225^{4} 4561^{20} 4951^{7} 4979^{6} **>59f<**

Gajan (IRE) 3 b g Ela-Mana-Mou-Delightful Time (Manado) 1876^{10} 2173^{6} 2379^{6} **>42f<**

Galacia (IRE) 5 br m Gallic League-Little Wild Duck (Great Heron (USA)) **1996:** *5132^{5}* **>43a 46f<**

Galahad (IRE) 2 b c Alzao (USA)-Maimiti (Goldhill) 4357a^{9} 4616a^{6} **>89f<**

Gala Miss 2 b f Sizzling Melody-Luckifosome (Smackover) 1253^{10} 1581^{9} 2904^{8} **>26f<**

Galapino 4 b g Charmer-Carousella (Rousillon (USA)) *54^{2} (99) 129^{2}* (430) 598^{4} 680^{2} 1036^{8} 1592^{9} (1805) 3915^{2} 4222^{2} 4426^{12} 4673^{2} 4879^{10} 5052^{2} **>72a 80f<**

Galaxy Flight 3 ch f Superlative-Glide Path (Sovereign Path) 2960^{6} 3230^{5} **>54f<**

Galibis (FR) 3 b g Groom Dancer (USA)-Damasquine (USA) (Damascus (USA)) *(145)* 505^{5} 4175^{13} 4859^{9} **>66+a 78f<**

Galine 4 b f Most Welcome-Tarasova (USA) (Green Forest (USA)) 942^{12} 2529^{9} 2841^{6} **>78a 85f<**

Gallaash (USA) 2 b c Gulch (USA)-In View (USA) (In Reality) 2948^{6} 3687^{8} **>56f<**

Gallant Heights 3 b f Anshan-Marie Galante (Shirley Heights) 1784^{5} 3021^{5} 3419^{7} 3928^{7} 4171^{4} 4632^{13} 4804^{18} 4971^{13} **>60f<**

Game Bird 2 b f Absalom-Mistral's Dancer (Shareef Dancer (USA)) 4012^{14} 4311^{5} 4818^{13} 5045^{11} **>60f<**

Game Ploy (POL) 5 b g Deploy-Guestimate (FR) (Be My Guest (USA)) 1016^{5} 1176^{3} 1934^{2} 2136^{5} 2710^{3} 3051^{2} 3703^{4} 4294^{8} 4558^{29} **>104f<**

Gandoura (USA) 2 b f Sheikh Albadou-Alqwani (USA) (Mr Prospector (USA)) 2597^{12} 3574^{6} 4904^{10} **>66f<**

Ganga (IRE) 3 ch f Generous (IRE)-Congress Lady (General Assembly (USA)) (2330) 2495^{7} 3119^{6} (3906) 4435^{9} (4788) **>92f<**

Garlandhayes 5 b m Adbass (USA)-Not Alone (Pas de Seul) *80^{10}*

Garnock Valley 7 b g Dowsing (USA)-Sunley Sinner (Try My Best (USA)) **1996:** *5105^{3}* **1997:** 443^{7} 731^{9} 953^{4} 1259^{2} 1561^{4} 2033^{8} 2111^{4} 2326^{7} 2422^{11} 3406^{9} 4270^{10} *4482^{8}* 4733^{6} 4927^{9} **>70a 65f<**

Garolo (FR) 7 b g Garde Royale-Valgoya (FR) (Valdingran (FR)) 891^{6} **>106f<**

Garrys Lock (IRE) 8 b g Fools Holme (USA)-Tale of Intrigue (USA) (Alleged (USA)) 1005a^{3}

Garuda (IRE) 3 b c Danehill (USA)-Ardmelody (Law Society (USA)) 676^{4} (1239) 1762^{5} 2515^{3} 3647^{5} **>104f<**

Gates (USA) 4 ch g Jade Hunter (USA)-Royal Herat (USA) (Herat (USA)) 2026^{30} **>88f<**

Gaultier Gale (IRE) 3 b c Ajraas (USA)-David's Pleasure (Welsh Saint) 2078a^{4} **>98f<**

Gautama 2 b c Batshoof-Actress (FR) (Arctic Tern (USA)) 3176a^{2}

Gay Abandon 2 ch f Risk Me (FR)-School Dinners (Sharpo) 1933^{12} 2394^{10} 2752^{4} 2935^{11} 4698^{14} **>46f<**

Gay Breeze 4 b g Dominion-Judy's Dowry (Dragonara Palace (USA)) 585^{10} 1089^{3} 1467^{2} 2313^{2} 2891^{2} (3693) (4248) 4905^{5} **>54f<**

Gay da Cheen (IRE) 2 b f Tenby-Gaychimes (Steel Heart) 1626^{7} 2827^{9} 3751^{8} **>27f<**

Gay's Best Boy (USA) 10 b h Nataraja (USA)-Gay Timer (USA) 3842a^{7}

Gazelle Royale (FR) 3 b f Garde Royale-Beautywal (FR) (Magwal (FR)) 1366a^{3} 1738^{2} 3877a^{3} 4256a^{2} 4665a^{13} **>117f<**

Gee Bee Boy 3 ch c Beveled (USA)-Blue and White (Busted) 725^{W} 1234^{5} 1742^{5} (2132) 2291^{5} 2570^{5} 3455^{5} 4926^{4} 4996^{11} **>67f<**

Gee Bee Dream 3 ch f Beveled (USA)-Return to Tara (Homing) (1238) 1737^{2} 2325^{4} 2691^{5} 3189^{13} 4220^{9} 4375^{10} 4878^{17} **>76f<**

Geimhriuil (IRE) 3 b c Distinctly North (USA)-Ventry (Stanford) 1406^{2} (1870) 2346^{9} (3024) **>91+f<**

Gelosia 3 ch f Old Vic-Ghanayim (USA) (Sharpen Up) 1911a^{2}

Gem 2 b f Most Welcome-Miss Top Ville (FR) (Top Ville) 4564^{5} 4917^{11} **>56f<**

Gemolly (IRE) 4 b f Be My Native (USA)-Hayhurst (Sandhurst Prince) 4114^{8} **>40f<**

General Academy (IRE) 4 g Royal Academy (USA)-Hastening (Shirley Heights) **1996:** *5204^{9}* **1997:** 1214^{8} 1456^{8} 2026^{26} 2341^{5} **>82a 97f<**

General Assembly (IRE) 5 b h Pharly (FR)-Hastening (Shirley Heights) 962^{5} 1319^{9} 1778^{4} 2108^{8} **>100f<**

General Equation 4 b g Governor General-Logarithm (King of Spain) **1996:** *5173^{10} 5225^{6}* **1997:** *4049^{14}* 4844^{19} **>34a 24f<**

General Glow 4 b g Presidium-Glow Again (The Brianstan) 430^{12} 650^{10} 1281^{7} *2164^{6}* 2824^{9} 3467^{5} 3570^{5} **>24a 49f<**

General Hastie 3 b g Cadeaux Genereux-Fast Car (FR) (Carwhite) 2020^{7} 2420^{14} 3037^{7} **>46f<**

General Haven 4 ch g Hadeer-Verchinina (Star Appeal) **1996:** *5189^{2} 5222^{2}* **1997:** *23^{2} (74) 133^{4}* 789^{17} 1001^{2} *1156^{4}* 1678^{7} 1934^{3} 2118^{9} 2961^{7} 3184^{6} 3616^{10} **>86a 74f<**

General Joey 2 b g Governor General-Joie de Patina (Forzando) 631^{9} 743^{9} *1290^{5}* 2016^{15} 2233^{4} 2412^{13} **>41f<**

General Klaire 2 b br f Presidium-Klairover (Smackover) 2519^{6} 3031^{10} 3819^{5} 3973^{14} **>71f<**

General Monck 2 ch g Formidable (USA)-Merton Mill (Dominion) 4318^{16} 4638^{9} 4957^{3} **>79f<**

General Monty 5 b g Vague Shot-State Free (Free State) 1512^{9} 1630^{4} 2226^{10} 2651^{7} 2880^{6} 3456^{9} **>44f<**

General Mouktar 7 ch g Hadeer-Fly The Coop (Kris) 1408^{3} 2014^{11} 2381^{3} 2682^{7} 2949^{6} **>53f<**

General Sir Peter (IRE) 5 br g Last Tycoon-Nashya (Rousillon (USA)) 520^{18} *(659)* 760^{2} *905^{8}* 972^{3} 1250^{13} 2006^{14} 2177^{8} 2563^{15} *3399^{U}* 3871^{12} (4115) 4385^{4} 4905^{8} *5018^{10}* **>79a 59f<**

General Song (IRE) 3 b c Fayruz-Daybreaker (Thatching) 2679^{5} 4787^{28} **>95?f<**

Genereux 4 ch g Generous (IRE)-Flo Russell (USA) (Round Table) 2131^{5} **>22f<**

Generosa 4 b f Generous (IRE)-Hotel Street (USA) (Alleged (USA)) 4620a^{9} **>95+f<**

Generosity 2 ch c Generous (IRE)-Pageantry (Welsh Pageant) 3193^{6} (3920) 4778^{9} **>69f<**

Generous Embrace 2 b f Cadeaux Genereux-Hug Me (Shareef Dancer (USA)) 3471^{5} (3859) 4271^{7} 4605^{11} **>74a 74f<**

Generous Gift 3 ch c Generous (IRE)-Barari (USA) (Blushing Groom (FR)) 690^{2} 1015^{5} (1742) 2058^{10} 3190^{8} 3703^{15} 4306^{3} 4577^{3} **>95f<**

Generous Lady 3 ch f Generous (IRE)-Northern Blossom (CAN) (Snow Knight) 3842a^{4} **>94f<**

Generous Libra 3 b g Generous (IRE)-Come on Rosi (Valiyar) 1207^{3} (1656) 2013^{18} 2478^{2} 2871^{3} 3150^{17} 4558^{24} 4754^{7} **>102df<**

Generous Present 4 ch g Cadeaux Genereux-Dance Move (Shareef Dancer (USA)) 477^{14} 925^{9} 1800^{13} 4224^{11} 4607^{15} 4742^{8} **>42f<**

Generous Rosi 2 b c Generous (IRE)-Come on Rosi (Valiyar) 4966^{10} **>63f<**

Generous Terms 2 ch c Generous (IRE)-Time Charter (Saritamer (USA)) 4758^{11} **>63f<**

Genevra (IRE) 3 b f Danehill (USA)-Astra Adastra (Mount Hagen (FR)) 1202a^{9} 4666a^{10} **>106f<**

Genius (IRE) 2 b c Lycius (USA)-Once in My Life (IRE) (Lomond (USA)) 3726^{6} 4111^{9} 4361^{8} 4806^{16} **>66f<**

Genoa 2 b f Zafonic (USA)-Yawl (Rainbow Quest (USA)) 4973^{6} **>68f<**

Gentilesse 3 gr f Generous (IRE)-As You Desire Me (Kalamoun) (1106) **>78f<**

Gentleman Sid 7 b g Brotherly (USA)-Eugenes Chance (Flashback) 769^{5} 865^{10} 1114^{11} **>32a 37f< (DEAD)**

Gentlemen (ARG) 5 ch h Robin Des Bois (USA)-Elegant Glance (USA) (Loose Cannon (IRE)) 393a^{3} **>124f<**

Genuine John (IRE) 4 b g High Estate-Fiscal Folly (USA) (Foolish Pleasure (USA)) **1996:** *5132^{3} 5235^{9}* **1997:** *123^{7} 150^{3} 207^{5} 322^{2} 358^{2} (416)* 468^{4} 571^{3} 734^{12} 776^{7} 1097^{14} 1395^{3} 1674^{5} 1993^{7} *4485^{11}* 4696^{16} *4813^{16}* 5023^{9} **>24a 41f<**

Geordie Lad 3 ch g Tina's Pet-Edraianthus (Windjammer (USA)) 531^{6} 765^{8} 1989^{8} 2878^{7} 3241^{7} 3710^{6} 4047^{12} 4373^{20} **>39f<**

George (IRE) 2 b c Distinctly North (USA)-Heather Lark (Red Alert) 2439a^{7} **>79f<**

Georgia Venture 3 b f Shirley Heights-Georgica (USA) (Raise A Native) 683^{11} 978^{2} 1258^{4} 2194^{3} (2767) 3218^{3} 3648^{5} 4101^{2} (4376) 4559^{6} **>98f<**

Georgie Boy (USA) 4 b br g Zilzal (USA)-Stealthy Lady (USA) (J O Tobin (USA)) **1996:** *5253^{7}* **>17a 31f<**

Georgina (IRE) 3 b f Lycius (USA)-Princess Nawaal (USA) (Seattle Slew (USA)) 3632^{3} 4009^{P} **>74f< (DEAD)**

Geri (USA) 5 ch h Theatrical-Garimpeiro (CAN) (Mr Prospector (USA)) (4394a) 5063a^{2} **>130f<**

Germano 4 b c Generous (IRE)-Gay Fantastic (Ela-Mana-Mou) 522^{2} (943) (1323) 2864^{2} 3409^{2} 3993a^{4} **>119f<**

Germignana (ITY) 4 b f Miswaki Tern (USA)-Guida Centrale (Teenoso (USA)) 1200a^{U} 1549a^{5} 4535a^{7} **>106f<**

Ger's Royale (IRE) 6 ch g Dominion Royale-Sister Dympna (Grundy) 1532a^{5} 2079a^{7} **>111f<**

Get A Life 4 gr f Old Vic-Sandstream (Sandford Lad) 558^{4} 761^{6} 1230^{7} 2065^{8} 2541^{3} 2824^{11} 3333^{10} 3700^{5} **>54f<**

Get The Point 3 b c Sadler's Wells (USA)-Tolmi (Great Nephew) 436^{4} 502^{6} 575^{4} 699^{4} 842^{5} 1014^{7} 1302^{6} 1833^{2} 2238^{6} 2879^{6} 3381^{4} 3697^{2} 3968^{5} 4172^{13} 4417^{5} **>59f<**

Ghali (USA) 2 b c Alleged (USA)-Kareema (USA) (Coastal (USA)) 4439^{4} **>77f<**

Ghalib (IRE) 3 ch c Soviet Star (USA)-Nafhaat

(USA) (Roberto (USA)) (4277) (4671) 4968^{3} >109f<

Gharib (USA) 3 b c Dixieland Band (USA)-The Way We Were (USA) (Avatar (USA)) 795^{5} 1087^{4} 2495^{2} 2877^{6} 3606^{2} (4214) >79f<

Ghataas 3 b c Sadler's Wells (USA)-Harmless Albatross (Pas de Seul) (725) 1015^{4} (1962) 2864^{4} 3785^{4} (4281) >113f<

Ghayah (IRE) 3 ch f Night Shift (USA)-Blinding (IRE) (High Top) 992^{12} >16f<

Ghayyur (USA) 3 ch f Riverman (USA)-New Trends (USA) (Lyphard (USA)) 754^{3} 1110^{4} 1436^{4} >70f<

Ghillies Ball 3 ch g Groom Dancer (USA)-Highbrow (Shirley Heights) 2566^{3} (3188) >96f<

Ghorapani (IRE) 2 b f Fairy King (USA)-Kates Cabin (Habitat) 1440^{10} 2312^{7} 2728^{15} 3541^{7} 3859^{7} >38a 48f<

Ghostly Apparition 4 gr g Gods Solution-Tawny (Grey Ghost) 2043^{8} >40a 32f<

Gianky Gioffry (IRE) 3 ch c Primo Dominie-Annamaria Pacificus (Niniski (USA)) 917a^{3} 1728a^{5} >109f<

Giddy 4 b br f Polar Falcon (USA)-Spin Turn (Homing) **1996:** *5179^{13}* **1997:** *14^{4} 125^{3} 273^{10} 428^{7}* >46a 55f<

Giftbox (USA) 5 b h Halo (USA)-Arewehavingfunyet (USA) (Sham (USA)) 461^{14} 552^{9} 608^{13} 898^{10} 3264^{11} 3631^{3} >61a 35f<

Gifted Bairn (IRE) 2 b f Casteddu-Latin Mass (Music Boy) 730^{6} *1045^{9} 1286^{4} 1789^{6} 2051^{2}* 2545^{18} >54a 31f<

Gift of Gold 2 ch c Statoblest-Ellebanna (Tina's Pet) 1396^{11} 1842^{8} 3825^{4} 3920^{2} *4299^{5} 4589^{11}* 4849^{6} (5029) >64a 76f<

Gift Token 3 b f Batshoof-Visible Form (Formidable (USA)) (1823) 2133^{9} 2729^{9} 3575^{9} 3773^{5} 4242^{5} 4558^{9} 4882^{13} >88+f<

Giko 3 b g Arazi (USA)-Gayane (Nureyev (USA)) 1087^{2} 1587^{11} 1851^{8} 2231^{3} 2510^{3} 2835^{10} (3250) 3790^{3} *4591^{6}* 4757^{21} 4878^{13} >62a 77f<

Gi La High 4 gr f Rich Charlie-Gem of Gold (Jellaby) **1996:** *5097^{9} 5163^{2}* **1997:** *4^{3} 20^{5} (137) 222^{2} 301^{6} (391) 406^{3}* 494^{2} 541^{3} 1957^{2} *2050^{6}* 3600^{12} 3637^{12} 4169^{4} 4365^{10} 4805^{10} >68a 67f<

Gildersleve 2 ch f Gildoran-Fragrant Hackette (Simply Great (FR)) 2736^{2} 3106^{10} 3905^{8} 4230^{6} >59df<

Gilding The Lily (IRE) 3 b f High Estate-Millingdale Lillie (Tumble Wind (USA)) *1121^{7}* 1246^{5} >42a 54f<

Gilling Dancer (IRE) 4 b g Dancing Dissident (USA)-Rahwah (Northern Baby (CAN)) *153^{7} 235^{9}* 824^{7} 1495^{5} 1800^{8} 2205^{8} 2876^{8} 3315^{13} >41a 49f<

Ginas Girl 4 gr f Risk Me (FR)-Grey Cree (Creetown) *423^{14} 545^{13}* >20da 48f<

Ginger Flower 8 ch m Niniski (USA)-Monterana (Sallust) 4771^{P} 4847^{11} 4926^{7} >61?a 42f<

Ginger Rogers 3 ch f Gildoran-Axe Valley (Royben) **1996:** *5147^{10}* **1997:** 1096^{11} 1487^{5} 1853^{2} (2189) (3028) (3325) 4171^{3} 4509^{4} >5a 70f<

Gingersnap 3 ch f Salse (USA)-Humble Pie (Known Fact (USA)) 681^{6} 4182^{2} >80f< **(DEAD)**

Ginka 6 b m Petoski-Pine (Supreme Sovereign) 603^{3} 1114^{9} 1665^{8} 2175^{4} 3714^{U} 3983^{4} 4374^{10} 4609^{10} >31a 39f<

Ginner Morris 2 b g Emarati (USA)-Just Run (IRE) (Runnett) 4236^{11} >62f<

Ginnieshope 2 ch f Never so Bold-Sweet Home (Home Guard (USA)) 2509^{14} 2781^{12} 3847^{6} >22f<

Ginny Wossername 3 br f Prince Sabo-Leprechaun Lady (Royal Blend) 1167^{12} 1921^{4} 2310^{16} 3266^{3} 3851^{8} 4816^{10} >33a 36f<

Ginzbourg 3 b g Ferdinand (USA)-Last Request (Dancers Image (USA)) 646^{7} 966^{2} 2058^{11} 2574^{9} 3120^{5} >92f<

Gipsy Moth 2 b f Efisio-Rock the Boat (Slip Anchor) 1240^{8} 1970^{6} 2370^{9} 2728^{7} (2926) 3192^{10} (3571) 4173^{6} >91f<

Gipsy Princess 3 b f Prince Daniel (USA)-Gypsy's Barn Rat (Balliol) 845^{11} 1496^{14} 2062^{12} 2317^{5} 2733^{3} 2906^{7} 3285^{5} 3565^{4} 3812^{4} 3910^{6} 4291^{10} 4414^{13} 4773^{7} 4877^{14} >61f<

Girlie Set (IRE) 2 b f Second Set (IRE)-Heavenward (USA) (Conquistador Cielo (USA)) 4564^{17} 5040^{13} >34f<

Girl of My Dreams (IRE) 4 b f Marju (IRE)-Stylish Girl (USA) (Star de Naskra (USA)) 1020^{20} 4992^{7} >39f<

Giveaway 2 ch c Generous (IRE)-Radiant Bride (USA) (Blushing Groom (FR)) (4454) 4734^{2} >85f<

Give Me A Ring (IRE) 4 b g Be My Guest (USA)-Annsfield Lady (Red Sunset) 832^{2} (1176) 1771^{6} >74a 100f<

Gladys Althorpe (IRE) 4 b f Posen (USA)-Gortadoo (USA) (Sharpen Up) 1097^{18} 1450^{11} 3039^{7} 4147^{23} >66f<

Glamorgan (IRE) 2 b c Petardia-Presentable (Sharpen Up) 2553^{9} 4575^{11} 4952^{13} >57f<

Glass River 2 b c Ardkinglass-Rion River (IRE) (Taufan (USA)) *1045^{10}* 1614^{4} 1860^{9} 3097^{6} 3314^{4} 3571^{7} 4500^{3} 4921^{5} 5026^{5} >26a 66f<

Gleaming Hill (USA) 2 b c Marquetry (USA)-Mountain Sunshine (USA) (Vaguely Noble) 4515^{3} >69+f<

Glen Garnock (IRE) 5 gr g Danehill (USA)-Inanna (Persian Bold) *1579^{4}* >49a 56f<

Glen Ogil 3 ch g Thatching-Cormorant Bay (Don't Forget Me) 3206^{3} 3966^{6} 4184^{11} 4816^{7} 4972^{2} 5030^{2} >56f<

Glen Parker (IRE) 4 ch c Bluebird (USA)-Trina's Girl (Nonoalco (USA)) 3786^{3} 4314^{5} >87f<

Glenstal Lad 2 b c Nomination-Glenstal Princess (Glenstal (USA)) *2051^{4} 2304^{3}* 2904^{11} 5026^{3} >48a 38f<

Glenturret (GER) 3 f 1202a^{15}

Glide Path (USA) 8 ch g Stalwart (USA)-Jolly Polka (USA) (Nice Dancer (CAN)) *205^{8}* 789^{19} >32a 61f<

Glimmering Hope (IRE) 3 b g Petorius-Angevin (English Prince) *287^{5} 412^{9}* 532^{13} >31a 32f<

Glittering (USA) 3 b c Local Talent (USA)-Glitter (FR) (Reliance II) 2360^{5} 2687^{5} 2924^{7} 3230^{3} 3465^{9} 3732a^{5} >63f<

Glitter Princess 2 ch f Prince Sabo-Maritime Lady (USA) (Polish Navy (USA)) 3009^{4} 4103^{19} 4317^{13} 4701^{11} >73?f<

Glivana (FR) 3 b/f Highest Honor (FR)-Glifahda (FR) (Bolkonski) (3876a) >96f<

Global Player 4 b c Tirol-Guest Performer (Be My Guest (USA)) (2640a) 3553a^{2} 4124a^{3} >120f<

Global Risk 2 b g Risk Me (FR)-Georgina Park (Silly Season) 1812^{17} 2664^{7} 3639^{6} >36f<

Globe Raider 2 b g Safawan-Polola (Aragon) 2110^{7} 2500^{12} >47f<

Globe Runner 4 b c Adbass (USA)-Scenic Villa (Top Ville) **1996:** *5240^{9}* **1997:** *15^{10}* (553) 3267^{3} (3626) 4279^{3} >45a 69f<

Globetrotter (IRE) 3 b g Polish Patriot (USA)-Summer Dreams (CAN) (Victoria Park) *(33) (96) (119) (155) 281^{3} 298^{2} (388)* 575^{7} 1238^{8} *(1576)* >86a 64f<

Glok (USA) 3 b c Theatrical-Gozo Baba (USA) (Raja Baba (USA)) 3881a^{3} >106f<

Gloria Imperator (IRE) 4 b g Imperial Frontier (USA)-English Lily (Runnett) **1996:** *5173^{9}* **1997:** *164^{12} 327^{9} 429^{15} 577^{4}* 729^{9} >32a 43f<

Glorious Dancer 3 b f Past Glories-Precious Ballerina (Ballacashtal (CAN)) 795^{9} 1023^{12} 1271^{9} *1757^{9}* 2040^{9} 2468^{9} 4996^{16} >37f<

Glorosia (FR) 2 ch f Bering-Golden Sea (FR) (Saint Cyrien (FR)) (2840) 4119^{3} (4442) >100f<

Glory of Grosvenor (IRE) 2 ch c Caerleon (USA)-Abury (IRE) (Law Society (USA)) 4274^{4} 4582^{2} >88f<

Glory of Love 2 b c Belmez (USA)-Princess Lieven (Royal Palace) 4278^{5} 4514^{5} 4758^{15} >65f<

Glow Forum 6 b m Kalaglow-Beau's Delight (USA) (Lypheor) **1996:** *5205^{7}* **1997:** *23^{3} 163^{2} (187) 283^{2} (1431)* 2218^{2} (2318) 2398^{3} (2650) 3183^{5} 3915^{6} 4323^{8} *4572^{3}* (4821) 4971^{6} >83a 67f<

Glowing Mantle (IRE) 9 ch m Glow (USA)-Dismantle (Aureole) *1133^{16}*

Glowing Moon 4 b f Kalaglow-Julia Flyte (Drone) 842^{14} 1372^{6} >45?f<

Go Britannia 4 b g Machiavellian (USA)-Chief Celebrity (USA) (Chief's Crown (USA)) 738^{15} 1400^{3} 2327^{13} 3122^{4} 3805^{3} 4241^{3} 4783^{30} >99f<

God Knows (IRE) 2 b f Elbio-Sweet Accord (Balidar) 1959^{7} 2700^{11} 3819^{11} 4058^{14} >39f<

Godmersham Park 5 b g Warrshan (USA)-Brown Velvet (Mansingh (USA)) 571^{13} 733^{4} 900^{2} 947^{11} 1248^{5} 1501^{5} 2019^{14} 4243^{5} 4628^{15} *5021^{6}* >31a 62f<

Go For Green 3 br f Petong-Guest List (Be My Guest (USA)) 1690^{5} *2151^{6}* 2772^{2} 3236^{12} 3442^{7} 4455^{7} 4632^{5} 4958^{12} >53a 59f<

Go For Salt (USA) 3 b f Hawkster (USA)-Wall St Girl (USA) (Rich Cream (USA)) 833^{3} 1102^{4} 2533^{5} (2783) >82f<

Go Green Flag 3 b c Salse (USA)-One Last Glimpse (Relko) 944^{10} 1218^{6} >42f<

Go Hence 3 b c Be My Chief (USA)-Hence (USA) (Mr Prospector (USA)) 683^{15} 963^{9} 2846^{4} 3108^{5} 3567^{10} 4180^{3} 4521^{13} >60f<

Going For Broke 3 b g Simply Great (FR)-Empty Purse (Pennine Walk) **1996:** *5238^{7}* **1997:** *(7) 46^{5} 331^{3}* (793) (952) *(1429)* 2294^{2} >77a 72f<

Going Green 3 b f Environment Friend-Pacific Gull (USA) (Storm Bird (CAN)) 681^{11} *874^{3}* 1008^{2} 1485^{9} >33a 63f<

Going Places 2 b f Risk Me (FR)-Spring High (Miami Springs) 536^{5} 682^{3} 844^{3} 1235^{4} (1295) 1653^{9} 3892^{10} >70f<

Golborne Lad 4 ch g Jester-Taskalady (Touching Wood (USA)) *855^{13}* >32a 32f<

Gold Away (IRE) 2 ch c Goldneyev-Blushing Away (FR) (Blushing Groom (FR)) 3873a^{3} 4861a^{3} (5058a) >90+f<

Gold Blade 8 ch g Rousillon (USA)-Sharp Girl (FR) (Sharpman) **1996:** *5167^{6} 5210^{5}* **1997:** *384^{4}* 435^{7} 763^{12} 1748^{P} 2146^{4} 2494^{2} 2854^{2} 4275^{19} 4548^{7} >62a 68f<

Goldbridge (IRE) 2 b c Distinctly North (USA)-Bold Kate 3961a^{27} >64f<

Gold City (NZ) 6 br m Gold and Ivory (USA)-Teton Moss (AUS) (Twig Moss (FR)) 437a^{2} >114f<

Gold Clipper 3 b c High Kicker (USA)-Ship of Gold (Glint of Gold) 586^{17} 842^{13} 1284^{4} 1624^{4} 1803^{8} *2159^{2}* 2522^{9} 4607^{13} 5028^{7} >45a 39f<

Gold Desire 7 b g Grey Desire-Glory Gold (Hittite Glory) 1024^{7} 1117^{3} 1231^{5} (1313) 1459^{4} 1463^{7} 1831^{3} 2043^{3} 2293^{4} 2660^{8} 2889^{2} 3026^{4} (3183) 3333^{11} 3603^{2} 3907^{3} (3992) 4108^{7} 4279^{2} 4751^{5} 5027^{10} >18a 69f<

Gold Edge 3 ch f Beveled (USA)-Golden October (Young Generation) 466^{3} 1375^{2} 1604^{2} 1730^{3} 1963^{3} 2167^{5} 2510^{2} 2747^{4} (3251) 3417^{5} 3851^{5} 4016^{17} 4155^{22} 4233^{4} 4434^{5} 4707^{4} >63f<

Golden Ace (IRE) 4 ch c Archway (IRE)-Gobolino

(Don) 943[6] 1261[4] 1414[12] 2228[14] *2603[13]* 2947[3] (3196) 3691[7] 3992[3] 4319[9] 4477[11] 4741[10] 4845[W] **>36a 64df<**

Goldenacres 2 b c Desert Splendour-Normanby Damsel (High Line) 1438[6] *1758[6]* 2240[5] 2741[P] 3090[6] **>32a 54f<**

Golden Arches (FR) 3 b f Common Grounds-Echoes Of Eternity (FR) 1916a[7] (3007a) 4652a[3] **>113f<**

Golden Aventura (IRE) 3 1996: (5128a) **1997:** 917a[8] **>104f<**

Golden Biscayne 3 c 917a[4] **>104f<**

Golden Dice (USA) 2 ch c Diesis-Fariedah (USA) (Topsider (USA)) 3235[4] (3806) 4096[4] 4364[2] **>98f<**

Golden Fact (USA) 3 b g Known Fact (USA)-Cosmic Sea Queen (USA) (Determined Cosmic (USA)) 723[12] 958[13] 1238[2] 3249[3] **>71df<**

Golden Fawn 4 ch f Crowning Honors (CAN)-Hill of Fare (Brigadier Gerard) *516[6]* 1093[16] **>44a 38f<**

Golden Fish 5 b g Efisio-Fishpond (Homing) 2152[11] 2686[7] 3264[14] 3382[8] 3456[10] 3933[8] 4415[6] 4692[11] 4923[14] **>22a 30f<**

Golden Fortune 2 ch f Forzando-Short And Sharp (Sharpen Up) 2842[6] 3094[9] 3636[11] (4166) (4473) **>78f<**

Golden Glory 4 b g Grey Desire-Glory Gold (Hittite Glory) 2046[18] 2156[7] 2549[7] **>43f<**

Golden Hadeer 6 ch h Hadeer-Verchinina (Star Appeal) **1996:** *(5167) 5240[3]* **1997:** *(5) (55) (101) 115[3] 205[2] (232) 261[5]* 493[2] (1039) 1100[3] (1252) (1424) 1491[2] 2034[6] 2198[3] 4744[13] 5027[15] **>83a 62f<**

Golden Hanoof (USA) 5 ch m Slew O' Gold (USA)-Hanoof (USA) (Northern Dancer) **1996:** *5259[4]* **1997:** *37[2] 218[4]* **>32a f<**

Golden Hawk (USA) 2 ch c Silver Hawk (USA)-Crockadore (USA) (Nijinsky (CAN)) 4318[3] **>81f<**

Golden Hello 6 b g Glint of Gold-Waltz (Jimmy Reppin) 4136[13] 4288[7] 4598[4] **>60f<**

Golden Kendall (IRE) 3 4535a[6] **>83f<**

Golden Lyric (IRE) 2 ch c Lycius (USA)-Adjala (Northfields (USA)) 4853[9] 5041[14] **>48f<**

Golden Melody 3 b f Robellino (USA)-Rose Chanelle (Welsh Pageant) 1853[4] 2189[6] 2535[4] 3028[6] *3865[5]* 4519[5] 4633[4] **>45a 59f<**

Golden Mirage (IRE) 2 b f Green Desert (USA)-Please Widd (IRE) (Thatching) 844[5] (954) 1143[3] (1531a) **>96f<**

Golden Oriental (USA) 3 b c Glitterman (USA)-Oriental Silk (ITY) (Far Out East (USA)) **1996:** (5127a) **>111f<**

Golden Pound (USA) 5 b g Seeking the Gold (USA)-Coesse Express (USA) (Dewan (USA)) 1824[6] 1948[6] 2232[6] 2393[4] 2649[4] 2950[5] (3296) 3604[5] 4155[14] 4276[10] *4797[9]* **>77a 86f<**

Golden Reprimand (IRE) 2 b c Reprimand-Elabella (Ela-Mana-Mou) 3219[8] 4779[4] **>86f<**

Golden Saddle (IRE) 3 b f Waajib-Flying Beckee (IRE) (Godswalk (USA)) 4705[9] **>6f<**

Golden Saddle (USA) 3 bb c Riverman (USA)-Rossard (DEN) (Glacial (DEN)) 742[11] 970[6] 1237[15] 1938[7] 2132[7] 2750[4] 3093[6] 3695[5] **>64f<**

Golden Silver 4 b f Precious Metal-Severals Princess (Formidable (USA)) *21[9] 59[12]* **>2a 42f< (DEAD)**

Golden Spanish (USA) 2 b c Robin Des Pins (USA)-Tomorrow's Image (USA) (Tom Rolfe) 4761a[3] **>80f<**

Golden Strategy (IRE) 2 b c Statoblest-Lady Taufan (IRE) (Taufan (USA)) 2477[8] (2917) 3774[5] 3965[2] 4173[3] 4755[17] 4989[11] **>78f<**

Golden Thunderbolt (FR) 4 b g Persian Bold-Carmita (Caerleon (USA)) 463[5] 633[7] 1097[2] 1300[4] (1389) 1622[7] 1686[2] 2065[5] 3286[3] 3477[8] 3853[3] 4635[7] **>61f<**

Golden Touch (USA) 5 ch h Elmaamul (USA)-Tour D'Argent (USA) (Halo (USA)) **1996:** *5118[5] 5200[2] 5262[10]* **1997:** *56[3] 140[6] 422[13]* 538[7] 647[13] 1001[3] 1384[3] 1459[7] 1694[5] 2281[6] 3200[8] 3432[7] **>58a 55f<**

Golden Tyke (IRE) 4 b g Soviet Lad (USA)-Golden Room (African Sky) *273[14]* **>52a 33f<**

Goldfill 2 b f Marju (IRE)-Briggsmaid (Elegant Air) *4052[3]* 4244[3] 4413[4] **>53+a 69f<**

Gold Hawk 2 ch c Weldnaas (USA)-Bel Esprit (Sagaro) 5048[19] **>29f<**

Gold Lance (USA) 4 ch g Seeking the Gold (USA)-Lucky State (USA) (State Dinner (USA)) **1996:** *5282[2]* **1997:** *98[3] 120[8] 241[11] 321[4]* (687) 1093[11] 1273[4] 1506[3] 2488[7] (2646) 3227[3] (3465) (4139) **>52a 66f<**

Gold Lining (IRE) 4 ch f Magical Wonder (USA)-Muntaz (ARG) (Search Tradition (USA)) *177[3] 286[3] (313) 428[3]* 526[18] 4872[7] **>43a 43f<**

Goldman (IRE) 2 br c Statoblest-Adamparais 3961a[16] **>83f<**

Goldmaster 2 b g Most Welcome-Miss Gorgeous (IRE) (Damister (USA)) *4056[11]* 4229[5] 4381[12] 4819[13] **>28a 50f<**

Gold Millenium (IRE) 3 gr g Kenmare (FR)-Gold Necklace (Golden Fleece (USA)) 1415[7] **>64f<**

Gold Radiance 2 ch c Dilum (USA)-Three Lucky (IRE) (Final Straw) 3961a[21] **>70f<**

Gold Spats (USA) 4 b c Seeking the Gold (USA)-Foot Stone (USA) (Cyane) 987[3] (1308) 2026[19] 2766[3] **>103f<**

Goldtune 2 b f Damister (USA)-Tantalizing Song (CAN) (The Minstrel (CAN)) 3744[8] 4107[4] 4638[12] **>85f<**

Gollaccia 3 gr f Mystiko (USA)-Millie Grey (Grey Ghost) 900[10] 1469[11] **>36f<**

Gomanta 3 ch Bustino-Golden Glint (Vitiges (FR)) 1556a[6]

Gone for a Burton (IRE) 7 ch g Bustino-Crimbourne (Mummy's Pet) 2528[8] 4886[5] 5053[11] **>88f<**

Gone Savage 9 b g Nomination-Trwyn Cilan (Import) 698[2] (834) 1158[7] 1608[3] 1937[4] 2529[7] (2563) 2872[6] 4677[11] **>85f<**

Gone To Press 2 b c Aragon-Casamurrae (Be My Guest (USA)) 3926[P]

Gonzaga (IRE) 3 ro c Pistolet Bleu (IRE)-Gay Spring (FR) (Free Round (USA)) (1546a) **>79f<**

Goodbye Gatemen (IRE) 3 gr g Soviet Lad (USA)-Simple Love (Simply Great (FR)) *1155[2]* 1485[2] 1638[2] 1967[7] 2277[2] (2946) 3280[13] 3642[11] 3851[9] *4591[11] 5021[10]* **>76da 52f<**

Good Catch (IRE) 2 br f Last Tycoon-Good Reference (IRE) (Reference Point) 2842[3] 3547[5] 3788[5] 4217[3] 4382[6] **>85f<**

Good Day 3 gr g Petong-Courtesy Call (Northfields (USA)) **1996:** *5164[7]* **1997:** *191[5] 328[5] 355[2] 1043[7]* (1312) *4304[11]* 4472[15] **>54a 71f<**

Good For You 2 ch c Ron's Victory (USA)-To Oneiro (Absalom) 492[6] 3483[5]

Good Hand (USA) 11 ch g Northjet-Ribonette (USA) (Ribot) 1817[2] (3778) 4416[5] **>67f<**

Good Judge (IRE) 3 b g Law Society (USA)-Cuirie (Main Reef) 1624[13] 4585[8] **>53f<**

Good News (IRE) 3 ch f Ajraas (USA)-Blackeye (Busted) (1008) 1373[W] 1987[4] 3207[W] **>67f<**

Good On Yer 2 b f Reprimand-Princess Eurolink (Be My Guest (USA)) 1997[7] 2752[3] 3306[17] 4922[11] 4994[22] **>58f<**

Good Reputation 3 ch f Bluebird (USA)-Reputation (Tower Walk) 742[12] 1322[3] 3439[2] 4045[6] 4287[4] 4771[8] **>57a 64f<**

Good To Talk 4 b g Weldnaas (USA)-Kimble Blue (Blue Refrain) 1586[6] 1687[6] 2061[8] 2167[3] 2480[9] 2540[16] 2934[14] 3271[5] 3606[6] **>49f<**

Goodwood Cavalier 2 b g Efisio-Brassy Nell (Dunbeath (USA)) 1744[11] 4113[10] (4710) **>86f<**

Goodwood Lass (IRE) 3 b f Alzao (USA)-Cutleaf (Kris) 878[10] 1387[8] *(2049) 2365[9]* **>73a 64f<**

Gopi 3 b f Marju (IRE)-Chandni (IRE) (Ahonoora) *489[3]* 685[4] 2575[5] 3378[6] 3816[7] **>72a 44f<**

Gordi (USA) 4 ch c Theatrical-Royal Alydar (USA) (Alydar (USA)) 2081a[3] 2456a[4] (2989a) 3705[20] **>103+f<**

Gore Hill 3 b f Be My Chief (USA)-Hollow Heart (Wolver Hollow) 989[11] 1277[10] 2182[10] **>13f<**

Goretski (IRE) 4 b g Polish Patriot (USA)-Celestial Path (Godswalk (USA)) 494[4] 585[13] 744[11] (1227) 1311[2] *(1759) (1942)* 2221[W] (2536) (2754) 2826[2] (3481) 4233[8] 4512[8] 4770[13] 5047[14] **>73a 79f<**

Gorgeous 2 b f Prince Sabo-Crackerjill (Sparkler) 1657[7] *2066[8] 3045[4]* 3451[12] **>33a 36f<**

Gormire 4 ro f Superlative-Lady of the Lodge (Absalom) *275[9]* 734[11] 929[11] 2317[10] 2899[7] 3271[13] **>38a 33f<**

Gothenberg (IRE) 4 b c Polish Patriot (USA)-Be Discreet (Junius (USA)) *309a[4] 408a[3] 438a[4] 627a[6]* 830[4] 1210[5] (1728a) 2009[11] 2453a[2] (2821a) 3124[6] 3674a[7] 4122a[3] 4660a[5] 4864a[2] **>113a 119f<**

Got It Wrong Again 4 b g Reprimand-Fine Asset (Hot Spark) 3463[16] **>39f<**

Go Too Moor (IRE) 4 b g Posen (USA)-Gulistan (Sharpen Up) **1996:** *5101[2]* **>71a 53f<**

Go With The Wind 4 b c Unfuwain (USA)-Cominna (Dominion) 2142[3] 2352[4] **>49a 71f<**

Gracco (IRE) 3 ch c Archway (IRE)-Grecian Hill (Ela-Mana-Mou) (821a) 1555a[3] **>81f<**

Grace 3 b f Buzzards Bay-Bingo Bongo (Petong) 1921[10] 2376[5] 2506[5] 3092[9] 3716[9] 3923[4] 4168[11] **>55f<**

Grace Browning 2 b f Forzando-Queen Angel (Anfield) 4459[3] (4602) **>81+f<**

Graceful Lass 3 b f Sadler's Wells (USA)-Hi Lass (Shirley Heights) 1477[6] 1784[2] (2194) (2647) 3727[6] 4445[2] 4676[6] **>103f<**

Gracie Lady (IRE) 3 f 1366a[5] 4655a[9] **>77f<**

Gracious Gretclo 4 gr f Common Grounds-Gratclo (Belfort (FR)) **1996:** *5173[11] 5282[10]* **>18a 38f<**

Gracious Imp (USA) 4 ch f Imp Society (USA)-Lady Limbo (USA) (Dance Spell (USA)) 790[10] 1139[15] 1237[17] 1779[25] *1964[6]* 2279[12] 2896[10] *3054[7]* **>38a 6f<**

Graduated (IRE) 5 b g Royal Academy (USA)-Saviour (USA) (Majestic Light (USA)) 2441a[6] **>97f<**

Gralmano (IRE) 2 b c Scenic-Llangollen (IRE) (Caerleon (USA)) *1136[11] 1577[3]* 2196[10] 2681[9] *3395[2]* 4334[7] *4592[2]* **>65a 45f<**

Granby Bell 6 b g Ballacashtal (CAN)-Betbellof (Averof) 4667[6] **>46f<**

Grand Applause (IRE) 7 gr g Mazaad-Standing Ovation (Godswalk (USA)) 2146[3] 2307[4] **>62a 40f<**

Grand Chapeau (IRE) 5 b g Ballad Rock-All Hat (Double Form) 464[14] 527[8] 779[7] *1759[6]* 1865[7] 2934[4] 3034[2] (3208) (3431) 3625[5] 3936[4] 4155[3] 4307[6] **>48a 75f<**

Grand Crack (IRE) 5 b g Runnett-Foston Bridge (Relkino) *177[10] 213[9]* **>34a 48f<**

Grand Cru 6 ch g Kabour-Hydrangea (Warpath) *(356) (580) 869[3]* (1260) 1413[3] 2014[21] 2530[6] 4269[9] 4783[15] **>73a 68f<**

Grand Estate 2 b g Prince Sabo-Ultimate Dream (Kafu) 1267[10] 2060[4] 2324[4] 2712[3] 3258[4] (3755) 4634[5] **>75f<**

Grand Hotel (IRE) 3 ch c Be My Guest (USA)-State Treasure (USA) (Secretariat (USA)) 683^{17} 1023^{11} 1297^{13} 1624^{10} *(2159)* 2399^{13} *3609^{2}* 4010^{5} **>57a 45f<**

Grand Lad (IRE) 3 ch c Mujtahid (USA)-Supportive (IRE) (Nashamaa) (555) **>110f<**

Grand Musica 4 b g Puissance-Vera Musica (USA) (Stop The Music (USA)) 450^{15} 738^{16} 1775^{13} 4410^{14} 4757^{6} 4978^{11} 5049^{16} **>82f<**

Grand Ovation (IRE) 3 b c Green Desert (USA)-Fitnah (Kris) 1409^{5} **>64f<**

Grand Slam (IRE) 2 b c Second Set (IRE)-Lady In The Park (IRE) (Last Tycoon) 4237^{5} 4520^{4} **>72+f<**

Grand Slam (USA) 2 c *5064a^{8}*

Grand Splendour 4 b f Shirley Heights-Mayaasa (FR) (Green Desert (USA)) 735^{17} 986^{8} 1244^{20} 1683^{4} 2118^{3} 2494^{4} (3720) 4144^{7} 4435^{8} **>80f<**

Granny's Pet 3 ch c Selkirk (USA)-Patsy Western (Precocious) 679^{2} 917a^{5} 1216^{3} 1403^{4} 1609^{12} 2517^{4} 3189^{9} **>101f<**

Grapeshot (USA) 3 b c Hermitage (USA)-Ardy Arnie (USA) (Hold Your Peace (USA)) 692^{2} (1307) **>114+f<**

Grapevine (IRE) 3 b f Sadler's Wells (USA)-Gossiping (USA) (Chati (USA)) 725^{6} 1028^{2} **>84f<**

Grasshopper 4 b g Petoski-Mistral's Dancer (Shareef Dancer (USA)) **1996:** *5208^{8}* **>22a f<**

Grate Times 3 b g Timeless Times (USA)-Judys Girl (IRE) (Simply Great (FR)) *1044^{7}* 1629^{4} 2130^{8} 2415^{8} 2909^{3} 3478^{7} 3870^{2} 4415^{7} 4703^{2} **>14a 63f<**

Grazia 2 b f Sharpo-Dance Machine (Green Dancer (USA)) 4556^{2} (4790) **>97+f<**

Great Bear 5 ch g Dominion-Bay Bay (Bay Express) **1996:** *5242^{11} 5281^{8}* **1997:** 4371^{18} 4415^{11} 4471^{11} 4846^{14} **>30a 31f<**

Great Chief 4 ch g Be My Chief (USA)-Padelia (Thatching) *233^{13}* 598^{14} 1273^{13} 4008^{3} 4243^{7} 4629^{9} **>49f<**

Great Child 3 b c Danehill (USA)-Charmina (FR) (Nonoalco (USA)) 675^{11} (1017) 1175^{2} 1737^{9} 3189^{2} 3725^{9} 4554^{3} 4637^{6} **>93f<**

Great Dane (IRE) 2 b c Danehill (USA)-Itching (IRE) (Thatching) 4949^{2} **>86+f<**

Great Easeby (IRE) 7 ch g Caerleon (USA)-Kasala (USA) (Blushing Groom (FR)) 4269^{8} 4783^{12} **>77f<**

Greatest 6 b g Superlative-Pillowing (Good Times (ITY)) **1996:** *5079^{2} 5152^{6} 5186^{6} (5215) 5249^{8}* **1997:** *121^{12} 171^{4} (224) (335) 403^{2}* 477^{10} 2144^{13} 2573^{10} 2937^{6} (3249) 3469^{4} *4570^{6}* 4711^{5} **>80a 62f<**

Great Hall 8 gr g Hallgate-Lily of France (Monsanto (FR)) 1089^{4} 1395^{13} **>39a 45f<**

Great Lyth Lass (IRE) 2 b f Waajib-Global Princess (USA) (Transworld (USA)) 1425^{3} 1657^{4} *2047^{8}* 2875^{8} 3869^{5} 4230^{7} **>21a 65f<**

Great Melody (IRE) 2 ch c Pips Pride-Unbidden Melody (USA) (Chieftain II) 1854^{4} 4428^{6} 4564^{6} **>60f<**

Great Oration (IRE) 8 b or br g Simply Great (FR)-Spun Gold (Thatch (USA)) (777) 1224^{5} 1672^{3} 2014^{24} 2682^{3} 2882^{6} 3255^{4} (3623) 4363^{11} **>27a 79f<**

Great Tern 5 b m Simply Great (FR)-La Neva (FR) (Arctic Tern (USA)) 4156^{7} **>37a 63f<**

Grecian Prince 2 ch c Risk Me (FR)-Troyes (Troy) 3322^{5} 4017^{8} 4917^{21} **>57f<**

Greeba 2 b f Fairy King (USA)-Guanhumara (Caerleon (USA)) 3235^{12} 3574^{8} 4012^{5} 4166^{10} **>62f<**

Greek Dance (IRE) 2 b c Sadler's Wells (USA)-Hellenic (Darshaan) 4105^{2} **>84f<**

Greek Night Out (IRE) 6 b m Ela-Mana-Mou-Ce Soir (Northern Baby (CAN)) **1996:** *5136^{6} 5213^{11}* **>55a 54f<**

Greek Palace (IRE) 3 b c Royal Academy (USA)-Grecian Sea (FR) (Homeric) 740^{3} 1173^{3} (1497) **>95f<**

Greenacres Goddess 3 ch f River God (USA)-Greenacres Girl (Tycoon II) 1426^{5} 1998^{13} 3268^{6} *3611^{10}* **>39f<**

Greenaway Bay (USA) 3 ch c Green Dancer (USA)-Raise 'n Dance (USA) (Raise A Native) (518) 829^{6} 1399^{10} 2062^{10} 2601^{11} **>88f<**

Greenback (BEL) 6 b g Absalom-Batalya (BEL) (Boulou) 1413^{9} **>78a 58?f<**

Green Bopper (USA) 4 b g Green Dancer (USA)-Wayage (USA) (Mr Prospector (USA)) 735^{19} 1292^{9} **>70f<**

Green Boulevard (USA) 3 ch f Green Forest (USA)-Assez Cuite (USA) (Graustark) **1996:** *5201^{5} 5279^{3}* **1997:** *(45) 142^{6}* **>55a 52f<**

Greenbrook 2 b g Greensmith-Comedy Lady (Comedy Star (USA)) 1370^{8} *1577^{9}* 1815^{3} 2153^{2} (2493) *3610^{7}* 3911^{4} 4163^{2} (4595) *4796^{2}* **>71a 71f<**

Green Card (USA) 3 br c Green Dancer (USA)-Dunkellin (USA) (Irish River (FR)) (599) 940^{9} 1412^{3} 3172a^{4} 3634^{2} 4154^{3} 4776^{5} **>113f<**

Green Dolphin 2 gr f Greensmith-Jane Herring (Nishapour (FR)) 2746^{6}

Greenflag Princess (IRE) 6 b m Executive Perk-Greencloyne Girl 1005a^{5}

Green Golightly (USA) 6 b g Green Dancer (USA)-Polly Daniels (USA) (Clever Trick (USA)) **1996:** *5174^{7}* **1997:** *40^{5} 113^{7} 197^{7}* 2228^{13} *2663^{7}* **>32a 4f<**

Green Jacket 2 b c Green Desert (USA)-Select Sale (Auction Ring (USA)) 2699^{9} 3687^{15} 4111^{3} 4605^{10} 4780^{2} **>78?f<**

Green Jewel 3 gr f Environment Friend-Emeraude (Kris) (930) 1305^{4} 1782^{6} 1869^{3} **>94f<**

Green Lady (IRE) 3 b f Green Desert (USA)-Fawaayid (USA) (Vaguely Noble) 818a^{3} 3371a^{5} **>106f<**

Greenlander 2 b c Green Desert (USA)-Pripet (USA) (Alleged (USA)) (2409) (3178a) 4391a^{4} **>95f<**

Green Power 3 b g Green Desert (USA)-Shaft of Sunlight (Sparkler) 645^{5} (1297) 2062^{2} 3894^{13} 4308^{3} 4757^{26} **>90f<**

Greenspan (IRE) 5 b g Be My Guest (USA)-Prima Ballerina (FR) (Nonoalco (USA)) **1996:** *5115^{2} (5143) 5205^{4} (5269)* **1997:** *39^{8} 99^{4} (231) 285^{2} (374) 426^{3} 591^{4} 869^{2} 1122^{3} 4981^{3}* **>81a 78f<**

Greenstead (USA) 4 b c Green Dancer (USA)-Evening Air (USA) (J O Tobin (USA)) 849^{3} 4678^{4} 4891^{16} **>83f<**

Greenwich Fore 3 b g Formidable (USA)-What a Challenge (Sallust) **1996:** *5147^{4} 5212^{3}* **1997:** *46^{6}* 986^{12} *1964^{5} 4055^{16}* **>69da 75f<**

Gresatre 3 gr c Absalom-Mild Deception (IRE) (Glow (USA)) *(378) 547^{2} 581^{7} 871^{9}* 1115^{10} 1781^{9} 2017^{5} 2125^{5} 2836^{5} 3321^{5} *3582^{4}* 3749^{4} 4184^{13} 4373^{5} 4742^{6} 4899^{4} **>64a 63f<**

Gresham Flyer 4 b g Clantime-Eleanor Cross (Kala Shikari) 4846^{12} 4946^{8} **>28f<**

Gretel 3 ch f Hansel (USA)-Russian Royal (USA) (Nureyev (USA)) 1209^{4} 1326^{7} 1740^{6} 3017^{8} **>95f<**

Grey Again 5 gr m Unfuwain (USA)-Grey Goddess (Godswalk (USA)) 4291^{11} 4455^{10} *4480^{9} 4810^{6}* **>39a 46f<**

Grey Express (DEN) 2 gr f Grey Desire-Belle Express (Music Boy) (4653a)

Grey Kingdom 6 gr g Grey Desire-Miss Realm (Realm) **1996:** *5161^{9}* **1997:** 585^{3} (759) (827) 863^{3} (929) 1324^{13} 1761^{3} (1977) 2124^{3} 2326^{3} (2390) 2708^{4} 2857^{4} 2900^{2} 3024^{3} 3198^{5} 3254^{6} 3649^{18} 3987^{4} 4147^{18} 4280^{13} 4842^{14} **>17a 79f<**

Grey Legend 4 gr g Touch of Grey-Northwold Star (USA) (Monteverdi) *59^{6} 321^{12} 338^{9}* 770^{11} **>33a 14f<**

Grey Perri 4 ch f Siberian Express (USA)-Martin-Lavell Post (Tina's Pet) 4765a^{2} **>107f<**

Grey Prospect 3 b g Grey Desire-Nicky Mygirl (Chief Singer) 997^{11} 1582^{8} **>35f<**

Grey Risk (FR) 4 gr c Kendor (FR)-Swiss Risk (FR) (Last Tycoon) 1067a^{5} **>124f<**

Grey Shot 5 gr g Sharrood (USA)-Optaria (Song) 891^{4} 1365a^{2} 2055^{13} 3149^{8} 3902^{3} 4241^{2} (4559) 4965a^{10} **>126f<**

Grey Way (USA) 4 gr ro f Cozzene (USA)-Northern Naiad (FR) (Nureyev (USA)) 1200a^{5} 3216^{4} 4869a^{6} **>108f<**

Grief (IRE) 4 ch g Broken Hearted-Crecora (Royal Captive) 2729^{5} 3112^{7} (3434) 3916^{2} 4294^{13} 4893^{6} 5051^{5} **>90f<**

Grindstone (FR) 5 b g Comrade in Arms-Maple Sugar (Northern Treat (USA)) 3884a^{3} **>83f<**

Grinkov (IRE) 2 b br c Soviet Lad (USA)-Tallow Hill (Dunphy) 1872^{15} **>56f<**

Grisellito (FR) 4 b c Galetto (FR)-Grisellina (FR) (River River (FR)) **1996:** 5157a^{3} **>106f<**

Grog (IRE) 8 b g Auction Ring (USA)-Any Price (Gunner B) 4466^{17} 4692^{9} **>28f<**

Grooms Gold (IRE) 5 ch g Groom Dancer (USA)-Gortynia (FR) (My Swallow) 3315^{12} 4991^{3} **>57f<**

Groom's Gordon (FR) 3 b c Groom Dancer (USA)-Sonoma (FR) (Habitat) 508^{2} 679^{5} 1544a^{11} 2023^{10} 2761^{6} 4902^{2} 4990^{4} **>97f<**

Grosvenor Miss (IRE) 2 b f Tirol-Somnifere (USA) (Nijinsky (CAN)) 536^{13} 3416^{8} 4007^{14} **>45f<**

Grosvenor Spirit (IRE) 2 b br f Fairy King (USA)-La Koumia (FR) (Kaldoun (FR)) 4604^{6} 4909^{9} **>48f<**

Groucho (USA) 3 b c Lyphard (USA)-Alvernia (USA) (Alydar (USA)) 676^{11} **>74f<**

Ground Game 4 b f Gildoran-Running Game (Run The Gantlet (USA)) *1123^{5} 1431^{2}* 2028^{12} **>92a 90f<**

Grovefair Dancer (IRE) 3 ch f Soviet Lad (USA)-Naval Artiste (Captain's Gig (USA)) 4114^{14} 4289^{5} **>55a 50f<**

Grovefair Lad (IRE) 3 b g Silver Kite (USA)-Cienaga (Tarboosh (USA)) 900^{4} 1129^{11} 1469^{13} 1820^{13} 2041^{4} 2226^{5} 2701^{10} 2887^{5} 3068^{6} 3405^{5} 3601^{4} 3762^{R} *4571^{7} 4813^{7}* **>46a 36?f<**

Grovefair Venture 3 ch c Presidium-Miramede (Norwick (USA)) 2873^{6} 3200^{14} 3591^{6} 3968^{10} **>57f<**

Guaranteed 2 b c Distant Relative-Pay the Bank (High Top) 2829^{9} 3253^{2} *3607^{2}* 3887^{2} 4603^{3} **>80a 81f<**

Guard A Dream (IRE) 3 ch g Durgam (USA)-Adarenna (FR) (Mill Reef (USA)) 862^{11} 1095^{7} 1312^{2} 4336^{16} **>29f<**

Guenivite (USA) 2 ch f St Jovite (USA)-Gueniviere (USA) (Prince John) 3201^{13} **>41f<**

Guesstimation (USA) 8 b g Known Fact (USA)-Best Guess (USA) (Apalachee (USA)) 1383^{10} 1632^{15} 1689^{6} 2128^{3} (2200) 2544^{2} (2716) 2770^{5} 3200^{13} (3814) (3848) 4224^{2} 4477^{9} 4607^{2} **>51a 71f<**

Guest Alliance (IRE) 5 ch g Zaffaran (USA)-Alhargah (Be My Guest (USA)) **1996:** *(5084) 5148^{6} 5213^{5} 5255^{2}* **1997:** *78^{3} 106^{6} 252^{2} 324^{5}* 769^{4} **>70a 54f<**

Guest Envoy (IRE) 2 b f Paris House-Peace Mission (Dunbeath (USA)) 3450^{18} **>4f<**

Guildhall 2 b c Saddlers' Hall (IRE)-Queen's Visit (Top Command (USA)) 4237^{10} 4638^{3} **>78f<**

Guilsborough 2 br c Northern Score (USA)-Super Sisters (AUS) (Call Report (USA)) 3117^{8} 4581^{5} **>68f<**

Gulf Harbour (IRE) 3 b c Caerleon (USA)-Jackie Berry (Connaught) 1014^{6} **>78f<**

Gulf of Siam 4 ch g Prince Sabo-Jussoli (Don) *544^{10}* 1463^{16} 2174^{16} 2892^{13} 3470^{11} 4504^{15} **>17a 30f<**

Gulf Shaadi 5 b g Shaadi (USA)-Ela Meem (USA) (Kris) **1996:** *5206^{9} 5237^{3} 5266^{4}* **1997:** *31^{4} (72) (91) 153^{9} 176^{4} 207^{3} 257^{4} 274^{5} 316^{6}* 468^{2} (571) 734^{4} 947^{2} 1035^{4} 1583^{6} 1775^{11} 2760^{4} 3254^{13} (3548) 3901^{2} 4147^{12} (4441) 4558^{4} (4781) **>73a 96f<**

Gulland 2 b c Unfuwain (USA)-Spin (High Top) 3745^{4} 4096^{2} (4803) **>102+f<**

Gulliver 4 b g Rainbow Quest (USA)-Minskip (USA) (The Minstrel (CAN)) *70^{3}* 639^{3} 766^{5} (1631) 2290^{13} 3064^{5} 3262^{6} 3428^{10} 3777^{7} 3937^{15} 4210^{12} **>51a 57f<**

Gumair (USA) 4 ch g Summer Squall (USA)-Finisterre (AUS) (Biscay (AUS)) 1169^{7} 1481^{3} 1795^{4} 2381^{7} **>75f<**

Gunboat Diplomacy 2 b br c Mtoto-Pepper Star (IRE) (Salt Dome (USA)) 1872^{17} 4111^{W} 4915^{14} **>54f<**

Gunfire (IRE) 3 ch c Great Commotion (USA)-West Chazy (USA) (Gone West (USA)) 809a^{7} **>90f<**

Gunmaker 8 ch g Gunner B-Lucky Starkist (Lucky Wednesday) *68^{6} 232^{3}* **>48a 34f<**

Gunner B Special 4 ch g Gunner B-Sola Mia (Tolomeo) *1132^{6}* 1247^{6} *1287^{10}* 2531^{7} **>21a 42f<**

Gunners Glory 3 b g Aragon-Massive Powder (Caerleon (USA)) 434^{11} 506^{9} 758^{3} 882^{6} 2192^{8} 2481^{6} 2883^{2} 3206^{2} 3749^{3} 3969^{7} 4184^{5} 4326^{9} 4816^{5} 4872^{10} **>57f<**

Gunzells (USA) 2 ch f Diesis-High Sevens (Master Willie) 3471^{13} 3636^{3} 4515^{2} 4789^{7} **>69f<**

Gurkha 2 b c Polish Precedent (USA)-Glendera (Glenstal (USA)) 3598^{7} (3986) **>91f<**

Guscott (IRE) 2 b c Distinctly North (USA)-Midnight Patrol (Ashmore (FR)) 3961a^{14} **>85f<**

Guy's Gamble 4 ch g Mazilier (USA)-Deep Blue Sea (Gulf Pearl) **1996:** *5130^{10}* **1997:** *71^{4} 209^{12} 332^{7} 1289^{13} 1576^{11}* 2041^{14} *3581^{6}* **>42da 39f<**

Gwespyr 4 ch g Sharpo-Boozy (Absalom) 863^{6} 1374^{7} 1505^{3} 1977^{16} *2671^{11}* 2958^{7} 3394^{7} 3856^{11} 4329^{13} **>15a 45f<**

Gymcrak Cyrano (IRE) 8 b m Cyrano de Bergerac-Sun Gift (Guillaume Tell (USA)) 1100^{9} 2000^{5} 2154^{10} 2413^{5} 2825^{11} **>35f<**

Gymcrak Flyer 6 b m Aragon-Intellect (Frimley Park) 734^{8} (864) 1003^{3} (1131) 1501^{7} 2906^{14} 3937^{8} 4059^{5} (4225) 4455^{6} 4792^{8} 4927^{8} **>54a 74f<**

Gymcrak Gorjos 3 b br f Rock Hopper-Bit O' May (Mummy's Pet) 1258^{6} 2156^{4} 2757^{9} 3068^{2} 3601^{2} 4845^{13} **>50f<**

Gymcrak Jester 3 b g Derrylin-Emerin (King Emperor (USA)) **1996:** *5166^{7}* **>6f<**

Gymcrak Mystery 2 br f Ballacashtal (CAN)-Little Unknown (Known Fact (USA)) 1120^{6} *1758^{3} 2367^{5}* **>47a 29f<**

Gymcrak Premiere 9 ch g Primo Dominie-Oraston (Morston (FR)) (633) 1117^{4} 1268^{12} 1450^{8} 2293^{5} 2686^{4} 2890^{4} 3428^{4} 3801^{4} 3921^{7} (4184) 4596^{6} 4924^{7} 4987^{4} **>75f<**

Gymcrak Tiger (IRE) 7 b g Colmore Row-Gossip (Sharp Edge) 762^{8} 1100^{18} 2413^{3} 2825^{5} **>55f<**

Gymcrak Watermill (IRE) 3 b br f River Falls-Victorian Pageant (Welsh Pageant) **1996:** *5162^{9}* **1997:** *49^{8} 193^{8}* 2171^{13} **>38a 11f<**

Gypsy Hill 2 ch f Theatrical Charmer-Mirkan Honey (Ballymore) 536^{14} (1109) 1386^{3} 1952^{2} 2371^{4} 3215^{6} **>78f<**

Gypsy Passion (IRE) 2 ch c Woodman (USA)-Rua D'Oro (USA) (El Gran Senor (USA)) 4231^{5} 4871^{7} (4993) **>85+f<**

H

Haami (USA) 2 b c Nashwan (USA)-Oumaldaaya (USA) (Nureyev (USA)) (2562) (3142) 3895^{3} (4551) **>110+f<**

Habeta (USA) 11 ch h Habitat-Prise (Busted) 848^{8} 1472^{3} 1800^{11} 2880^{9} 3630^{7} 4471^{7} **>40f<**

Hachiyah (IRE) 3 b br f Generous (IRE)-Himmah (USA) (Habitat) 1106^{2} 1477^{3} (2190) 2574^{2} 3263^{5} 4882^{7} 5044^{6} **>98f<**

Hadabet 5 b g Hadeer-Betsy Bay (FR) (Bellypha) 4108^{19} **>54?f<**

Hadadabble 4 ch f Hadeer-Magnifica (Sandy Creek) **1996:** *5114^{10}* **1997:** 748^{7} *1135^{10}* 1501^{8} 1689^{4} 2121^{8} 2246^{12} *2602^{5}* 2947^{7} 3321^{9} 4224^{10} 4742^{10} **>27a 33f<**

Hadawah (USA) 3 ch f Riverman (USA)-Sajjaya (USA) (Blushing Groom (FR)) 535^{14} 1164^{6} 1826^{9} 2750^{9} **>67f<**

Hadayik 2 b f Unfuwain (USA)-Almarai (USA) (Vaguely Noble) 3151^{4} (3769) 4119^{6} **>86f<**

Haddit 4 b g Thowra (FR)-Ocean Hound (Main Reef) **1996:** *5084^{14}* **>13f<**

Hadid (USA) 2 b c Irish River (FR)-Top Corsage (USA) (Topsider (USA)) 1486^{2} 2012^{14} 3193^{4} 4167^{11} **>79f<**

Hadidi 3 b c Alzao (USA)-Sesame (Derrylin) 1846^{6} 2189^{5} 2757^{3} 2908^{12} **>67f<**

Hadith 2 ch c Nashwan (USA)-Azyaa (Kris) 3479^{2} 4165^{2} 4857^{2} **>82f<**

Hahnio (IRE) 3 1553a^{13} **>90f<**

Haig Point (USA) 5 b h Dahar (USA)-Fourty Glories (ITY) (Nonoalco (USA)) 4541a^{3} **>94f<**

Hajat 3 ch f Mujtahid (USA)-Nur (USA) (Diesis) 475^{7} 1096^{17} 1843^{5} 2510^{10} *(3040) 3398^{11}* 3922^{4} 4707^{20} **>48a 51f<**

Hajr (IRE) 3 b c Rainbow Quest (USA)-Dance by Night (Northfields (USA)) (1876) 2229^{4} 3115^{11} (3424) 3773^{2} 4294^{12} 4476^{8} **>93f<**

Hakeem (IRE) 2 ch c Kefaah (USA)-Masarrah (Formidable (USA)) 3235^{3} (3926) 4560^{4} **>78f<**

Hakiki (IRE) 5 b h Ballad Rock-Salvationist (Mill Reef (USA)) 1910a^{2} 4124a^{4} 4260a^{3} **>109f<**

Hakkaniyah 3 b f Machiavellian (USA)-Mousaiha (USA) (Shadeed (USA)) 2426^{6} 2691^{12} **>85f<**

Halavadream 3 b c Mon Tresor-Hala (Persian Bold) 1322^{9} 2537^{10} 4713^{17}

Halbert 8 b g Song-Stoneydale (Tickled Pink) **1996:** *5144^{10} (5188)* **1997:** *24^{11} 107^{10} 152^{8}* 638^{6} 1009^{14} 1236^{13} 1509^{9} **>50a 44f<**

Half A Knicker 2 b g Weldnaas (USA)-Queen of the Quorn (Governor General) 1510^{5} *1941^{10}* 2739^{3} 3650^{9} **>33a 62+f<**

Half An Inch (IRE) 4 gr g Petoski-Inch (English Prince) **1996:** *5276^{6}* **1997:** *160^{8}* **>42a 62f<**

Half-Hitch (USA) 2 b f Diesis-Marling (IRE) (Lomond (USA)) (3033) 3740^{5} 4851^{3} **>86f<**

Half Tone 5 gr h Touch of Grey-Demilinga (Nishapour (FR)) 834^{10} 1083^{9} (1327) 1419^{4} 1594^{7} 2115^{4} 2232^{3} 2321^{3} 2769^{4} 2950^{2} 3126^{6} (3500) 3898^{5} 4370^{5} **>71a 66f<**

Hal Hoo Yaroom 4 b c Belmez (USA)-Princess Nawaal (USA) (Seattle Slew (USA)) 4002^{14} 4313^{7} 4673^{10} 4874^{18} **>65f<**

Hallmark (IRE) 3 b c Shalford (IRE)-Cryptic Gold (Glint of Gold) **1996:** *5147^{6} 5202^{11} 5226^{3}* **>58a 71f<**

Halmahera (IRE) 2 b c Petardia-Champagne Girl (Robellino (USA)) 504^{4} 2320^{2} (2509) (3113) 3464^{3} 3774^{2} (4232) (4675) **>111?f<**

Halmanerror 7 gr g Lochnager-Counter Coup (Busted) 596^{13} 759^{8} (977) 1395^{15} 1761^{11} 1977^{17} 2422^{7} 2711^{16} 3431^{5} 3621^{6} 3936^{5} 4016^{2} 4711^{6} **>59f<**

Halowing (USA) 3 b f Danzatore (CAN)-Halo Ho (USA) (Halo (USA)) 654^{7} 853^{6} 1170^{13} 1958^{W} 2216^{3} 2705^{5} 2945^{8} 4071^{13} 4773^{2} 4820^{5} **>77f<**

Hal's Pal 4 br g Caerleon (USA)-Refinancing (USA) (Forli (ARG)) *(661)* 1456^{12} 2026^{5} 2525^{5} 3052^{5} **>103a 106f<**

Haltarra (USA) 3 ch c Zilzal (USA)-Snow Bride (USA) (Blushing Groom (FR)) 931^{2} (1936) 3784^{2} 4149^{9} 4312^{2} 4894^{6} **>113f<**

Hambye 3 1721a^{7} **>95f<**

Hamerra (IRE) 2 b f Hamas (IRE)-Sound Performance (IRE) (Ahonoora) 739^{12} 1019^{13} 1298^{5} 1444^{8} **>25f<**

Hamilton Gold 4 ch f Safawan-Golden Della (Glint of Gold) 2504^{8} 2759^{10} 3287^{13} **>7a 21f<**

Hamleys 3 ch f Superlative-Child's Play (USA) (Sharpen Up) 3715^{8} 4316^{12} 4563^{7} 4738^{12} **>58f<**

Hammerstein 4 b c Kris-Musical Bliss (USA) (The Minstrel (CAN)) *409a^{2}* 1160^{13} **>110a 111f<**

Hanajir (IRE) 3 b f Cadeaux Genereux-Muhit (USA) (El Gran Senor (USA)) 2156^{6} 2549^{4} 2859^{2} *4053^{8}* 4847^{15} **>4a 73f<**

Hanan (USA) 3 b f Twilight Agenda (USA)-Maikai (USA) (Never Bend) 2229^{7} 2491^{6} 3425^{6} **>58f<**

Hanbitooh (USA) 4 b g Hansel (USA)-Bitooh (Seattle Slew (USA)) 603^{7} **>74df<**

Hanby 5 b g Most Welcome-My Princess (King Emperor (USA)) 467^{6} 550^{5} 997^{5} 1231^{10} **>53f<**

Hancock 5 b g Jester-Fresh Line (High Line) **1996:** *5177^{11}* **1997:** 1779^{8} 2000^{7} 2207^{4} *3587^{4}* **>28a 38f<**

Handaza (IRE) 3 b f Be My Guest (USA)-Hazaradjat (IRE) (Darshaan) 4356a^{5} **>90f<**

Handley Cross (USA) 3 b br g Houston (USA)-Imaginary Lady (USA) (Marfa (USA)) 1804^{6} **>40f<**

Hand of Straw (IRE) 5 b g Thatching-Call Me Miss (Hello Gorgeous (USA)) **1996:** *5140^{6}* **1997:** 721^{4} **>34a 56f<**

Handsome Ridge 3 ch c Indian Ridge-Red Rose Garden (Electric) 449^{2} 597^{2} 2013^{11} (2345) (3180a) 3730a^{3} 4392a^{3} 4656a^{6} **>116f<**

Handson 5 ch g Out of Hand-My Home (Homing) 770^{6} **>20?a 45f<**

Hannah's Usher 5 b g Marching On-La Pepper (Workboy) *421^{5} 512^{2} 659^{3} 1047^{13}* 1857^{7} 1965^{12} 2788^{10} *3582^{3}* 4249^{10} *4301^{4} 4574^{3} 4985^{2}* **>69a 49f<**

Hannalou (FR) 4 b f Shareef Dancer (USA)-Litani River (USA) (Irish River (FR)) 1506^{6} 1985^{6} 2573^{9} 3470^{10} 4465^{4} **>16a 48f<**

Hanzanar (IRE) 2 b c Alzao (USA)-Hanzala (FR) 4836a^{2} **>84f<**

Happy (FR) 2 b f Hero's Honor (USA)-Serie Bleu Nuit (FR) (Devil's Bag (USA)) 3994a^{2} **>73f<**

Happy Brave 5 b g Daring March-Fille de Phaeton (Sun Prince) *312^{6} 367^{4} (544) 908^{6} 1138^{7}* **>43a 22f<**

Happy Change (GER) 3 ch c Surumu (GER)-Happy Gini (Ginistrelli (USA)) 817a^{2} 1544a^{6} 2097a^{8} 2642a^{3} 3555a^{3} 4537a^{6} **>116f<**

Happy Days 2 b g Primitive Rising (USA)-Miami Dolphin (Derrylin) 594^{2} 954^{4} 1174^{2} 1774^{3} 2713^{7} 3239^{2} 3571^{6} 4702^{8} **>77f<**

Happy Days Again (IRE) 2 b f Elbio-Tacheo (Tachypous) 1492^{4} *2066^{2}* (2545) 3237^{5} 4178^{6} 4772^{2} 4948^{4} (4970) **>68a 84f<**

Happy Go Lucky 3 ch f Teamster-Meritsu (IRE)

(Lyphard's Special (USA)) 505^{4} 1208^{7} (1679) 2594^{5} 3125^{14} 3916^{16} 4242^{11} 4672^{4} 4882^{8} **>79f<**

Happy Heart (FR) 2 b f Exit To Nowhere (USA)-Light of Hope (USA) (Lyphard (USA)) 4529a^{3} **>71f<**

Happy Medium (IRE) 4 b g Fairy King (USA)-Belle Origine (USA) (Exclusive Native (USA)) *266^{3} 373^{4}* 1277^{8} 2398^{13} **>56a 52f<**

Happy Minstral (USA) 3 b g Alleged (USA)-Minstrelete (USA) (Round Table) 782^{2} 837^{9} 3125^{5} 3333^{9} 3648^{12} 4466^{12} 4639^{12} **>85f<**

Happy Venturer (IRE) 4 br g Petorius-Primacara (Rusticaro (FR)) 1796^{W} **>43df<**

Happy Wanderer 2 ch g Clantime-Maha (Northfields (USA)) 4381^{11} *4569^{5}* 4921^{7} **>72a 57f<**

Harbet House (FR) 4 b g Bikala-Light of Hope (USA) (Lyphard (USA)) 4804^{10} **>66a 60f<**

Harbour Dues 4 b c Slip Anchor-Quillotern (USA) (Arctic Tern (USA)) (849) 1241^{4} 1771^{2} 2333^{2} (3374a) (4261a) 5055a^{4} **>119f<**

Harbour Master (FR) 2 b c Bluebird (USA)-Pharsala (FR) (Hello Gorgeous (USA)) 1531a^{7} (2012) 3534a^{3} 4391a^{5} **>100f<**

Hard Love 5 b m Rambo Dancer (CAN)-Djimbaran Bay (Le Levanstell) *205^{10} 232^{9}* 465^{11} 613^{17} **>61a 55f<**

Hard to Figure 11 gr g Telsmoss-Count On Me (No Mercy) **1996:** *5203^{10}* **1997:** 1317^{18} 1676^{5} 2216^{10} 2567^{9} (2780) (2933) (3327) 4280^{3} **>64a 94f<**

Hardy Dancer 5 ch g Pharly (FR)-Handy Dancer (Green God) 521^{5} 735^{16} 987^{13} 2118^{7} 2570^{3} 2920^{3} **>45a 71f<**

Harlequin Walk (IRE) 6 ch m Pennine Walk-Taniokey (Grundy) **1996:** *5151^{3} 5242^{6} 5281^{5}* **1997:** *47^{9} 74^{2} 163^{4} 216^{4} (283) 346^{5} 566^{4}* 1373^{13} 2577^{8} 2955^{5} *3232^{4} 3413^{2}* 3767^{2} *(4069)* (4371) (4504) *4912^{4}* **>54a 54+f<**

Harlestone Heath 4 gr f Aragon-Harlestone Lake (Riboboy (USA)) *114^{10}* **>45f<**

Harmonic Way 2 ch c Lion Cavern (USA)-Pineapple (Superlative) (3490) 4146^{4} 4709^{5} **>92f<**

Harmony Hall 3 ch g Music Boy-Fleeting Affair (Hotfoot) 2005^{8} 2557^{14} 3029^{4} 3455^{2} 3714^{3} 4046^{8} 4699^{7} **>74f<**

Harmony In Red 3 ch c Rock Hopper-Lucky Song (Lucky Wednesday) *45^{2} 118^{4} 161^{2} 225^{2}* **>64a 72f<**

Harnage (IRE) 2 b c Mujadil (USA)-Wilderness (Martinmas) 1174^{8} 1760^{12} 2191^{3} 2383^{4} 2664^{9} **>61f<**

Haroldon (IRE) 8 ch g Heraldiste (USA)-Cordon (Morston (FR)) 482^{9} *869^{7}* 1478^{10} 1805^{8} 2373^{6} (2550) 2920^{4} 3091^{11} 3246^{9} 3475^{5} 3814^{2} 3929^{5} *4069^{4}* 4516^{13} *4912^{7}* 4998^{15} **>63a 67f<**

Harry's Treat 5 b m Lochnager-Megara (USA) (Thatching) *169^{9} 296^{4}* 496^{3} 687^{12} 2041^{7} **>49a 50f<**

Harry Wolton 3 b c Distant Relative-Tashinsky (USA) (Nijinsky (CAN)) 829^{2} 1257^{4} (1793) 2766^{5} 3388^{3} 3703^{3} **>112f<**

Harvest Reaper 5 gr g Bairn (USA)-Real Silver (Silly Season) **1996:** *5140^{9}* **1997:** 896^{22} 1622^{9} **>43a 46f<**

Harvey's Future 3 b c Never so Bold-Orba Gold (USA) (Gold Crest (USA)) **1996:** *5162^{6}* **1997:** 1764^{6} 2496^{W} 2946^{4} 3280^{9} 4214^{14} **>48a 36f<**

Harvey White (IRE) 5 b or br g Petorius-Walkyria (Lord Gayle (USA)) 933^{13} 1472^{15} 1642^{9} 1968^{5} (2150) 3153^{11} 3315^{7} 4179^{17} 4504^{14} 4608^{2} 4845^{12} *5019^{9}* **>10a 64f<**

Hasene (FR) 2 b f Akarad (FR)-She's My Lovely (Sharpo) 4529a^{2} **>73f<**

Hasta la Vista 7 b g Superlative-Falcon Berry (FR) (Bustino) *410^{4}* 470^{4} 781^{2} 994^{3} *1133^{4}* 1494^{2} (1605) 1996^{2} (2034) 2166^{2} (2413) 2737^{5} 3069^{5} (3283) 3461^{3} 3754^{6} (3907) 4269^{7} 4432^{2} 4584^{8} 4751^{9} 4956^{10} **>46a 64f<**

Hastate 2 b c Persian Bold-Gisarne (USA) (Diesis) 3201^{11} 4229^{6} 4740^{9} **>56f<**

Hatimena 3 b f Hatim (USA)-Everingham Park (Record Token) 1998^{8} 2544^{15} 3477^{9} **>38f<**

Hattaafeh (IRE) 6 b m Mtoto-Monongelia (Welsh Pageant) *(78) (106) (261) 324^{3} 384^{7}* 510^{4} 1478^{8} **>78a 71f<**

Hattab (IRE) 3 b c Marju (IRE)-Funun (USA) (Fappiano (USA)) (854) 1212^{3} 1590^{8} (1855) (2861) 3728^{5} 4240^{7} **>110f<**

Hatta Sunshine (USA) 7 b g Dixieland Band (USA)-Mountain Sunshine (USA) (Vaguely Noble) **1996:** *5123^{6} 5149^{7} 5250^{4}* **1997:** *(143) 197^{6} 280^{4} 407^{6} 487^{2} 907^{6}* 1506^{14} 1639^{9} 1926^{12} 2577^{9} 2748^{7} 3249^{10} **>64a 35f<**

Haunt The Zoo 2 b f Komaite (USA)-Merryhill Maid (IRE) (M Double M (USA)) 3031^{9} 4167^{4} 4458^{6} **>63f<**

Haute Cuisine 4 b g Petong-Nevis (Connaught) *22^{8} 200^{3} 218^{6} 322^{3}* **>45a 53f<**

Havago 3 b c Risk Me (FR)-Sporting Lass (Blakeney) 1166^{13} 1458^{7} 1849^{8} 2395^{6} 2892^{7} 3558^{4} 3851^{4} **>58f<**

Havana Heights (IRE) 4 ch f Persian Heights-Havana Blade (USA) (Blade (USA)) **1996:** *5108^{5} 5213^{8}* **1997:** 2661^{4} 2753^{4} 3461^{7} 3758^{7} 3919^{2} *4055^{9}* 4453^{6} 4584^{12} 4771^{13} 5024^{10} **>34a 38f<**

Havana Miss 5 b m Cigar-Miss Patdonna (Starch Reduced) **1996:** *5110^{8} 5129^{7}* **1997:** *1^{4} 51^{11} 71^{11} 144^{4} 213^{8}* **>49a 49f<**

Have A Break 2 b c Most Welcome-Miss Tealeaf (USA) (Lear Fan (USA)) 3094^{10} 3619^{8} 4564^{16} **>59f<**

Have a Nightcap 8 ch g Night Shift (USA)-Final Orders (USA) (Prince John) **1996:** *5110^{5}* **>54a 39f< (DEAD)**

Have Merci 2 b f High Estate-Icecapped (Caerleon (USA)) 5002a^{9} **>86f<**

Hawaii Storm (FR) 9 b g Plugged Nickle (USA)-Slewvindaloo (USA) (Seattle Slew (USA)) **1996:** *5124^{3} 5152^{4} 5215^{3}* **1997:** *21^{3} (57) 121^{10} 134^{2} (197) 278^{5} 319^{4} 458^{5} 490^{9} 1082^{10}* 1639^{13} *1969^{5}* 2310^{11} 2724^{7} (2748) 3139^{5} 3469^{11} 3969^{3} 4139^{15} 4448^{9} **>51a 54f<**

Hawait (IRE) 3 gr c Green Desert (USA)-Hayati (Hotfoot) (794) 1017^{12} 2062^{7} 2735^{2} 3220^{5} 3712^{5} 4148^{2} 4550^{9} **>101f<**

Hawanafa 4 b f Tirol-Woodland View (Precipice Wood) 1142^{12} **>51df<**

Hawker Hunter (USA) 6 b or br g Silver Hawk (USA)-Glorious Natalie (USA) (Reflected Glory (USA)) 1763^{2} 2483^{5} 3434^{8} **>86df<**

Hawkers Deal 4 b g K-Battery-Boreen Geal (Boreen (FR)) 3624^{6}

Hawkish (USA) 8 b g Silver Hawk (USA)-Dive Royal (USA) (Inverness Drive (USA)) 1683^{5} 2063^{6} **>41a 57f<**

Hawksbill Henry (USA) 3 ch g Known Fact (USA)-Novel Approach (USA) (Codex (USA)) 3202^{8} 3425^{7} 3775^{8} 3980^{11} 4176^{11} 4546^{4} **>56f<**

Hawksley Hill (IRE) 4 ch g Rahy (USA)-Gaijin (Caerleon (USA)) 450^{2} (738) 2026^{14} (2766) 3112^{10} 3725^{2} 4117^{6} 4862a^{2} **>57a 112f<**

Haya Ya Kefaah 5 b g Kefaah (USA)-Hayat (IRE) (Sadler's Wells (USA)) 4275^{13} **>71a 72f<**

Hayburner 2 b c Mujadil (USA)-Kotsina (Top Ville) 993^{12} 1829^{7} 2153^{6} 2288^{10} 2412^{3} 3257^{4} 3571^{5} 3699^{2} 4162^{4} **>56f<**

Hay Dance 6 b g Shareef Dancer (USA)-Hay Reef (Mill Reef (USA)) 1803^{2} **>27a 57f<**

Haydn James (USA) 3 ch c Danzig Connection (USA)-Royal Fi Fi (USA) (Conquistador Cielo (USA)) 991^{15} 1297^{14} 2552^{16} 2876^{5} 3793^{14} 4958^{11} **>66f<**

Haydown (IRE) 5 b or br g Petorius-Hay Knot (Main Reef) 1445^{10} 1677^{9} *2302^{13}* 3329^{4} 3560^{2} 3814^{6} 4503^{11} **>38f<**

Hayes Way (IRE) 3 b c Lahib (USA)-Edgeaway (Ajdal (USA)) **1996:** *(5090)* **1997:** *(227)* 449^{4} 737^{6} 2871^{7} 3150^{19} **>93a 97f<**

Hayil (USA) 2 b c Dayjur (USA)-Futuh (USA) (Diesis) 1396^{2} 2012^{5} (2870) 3379^{2} 4146^{3} (4524) **>103f<**

Hayling-Billy 4 ch c Captain Webster-Mistress Royal (Royalty) *73^{8}* **>29a 60f< (DEAD)**

Hazama 7 b m Caerwent-Gerania (FR) (Arctic Tern (USA)) 270a^{3} **>71f<**

Hazard a Guess (IRE) 7 ch g Digamist (USA)-Guess Who (Be My Guest (USA)) 450^{11} 521^{4} 680^{3} 789^{13} 974^{5} 1145^{7} 1981^{13} 2890^{2} 3112^{15} 3542^{2} 3722^{8} 3796^{6} **>89f<**

Hazel 5 ro m Risk Me (FR)-Sir Tangs Gift (Runnett) **1996:** *5267^{8}* **1997:** *9^{3} 83^{3} 147^{9} 417^{6}* 748^{8} 1642^{7} *1964^{3}* (3617) **>52da 47f<**

Head Gardener (IRE) 3 b br g Be My Chief (USA)-Silk Petal (Petorius) *(191) 314^{5} 370^{3}* 431^{10} 471^{8} 4876^{16} **>77?a 73f<**

Head Girl (IRE) 3 ch f Masterclass (USA)-Rebecca's Girl (IRE) (Nashamaa) **1996:** *5135^{2} 5160^{6} (5180)* **1997:** *6^{3} 41^{2} 90^{6} (246) 414^{4}* **>66a 66f<**

Headhunter (IRE) 2 b c Last Tycoon-Erzsi (Caerleon (USA)) (2771) 3706^{3} 4474^{4} **>91f<**

Heart 4 ch f Cadeaux Genereux-Recipe (Bustino) **1996:** *5171^{5}* **>81a 88f<**

Heart Full of Soul 3 ch g Primo Dominie-Scales of Justice (Final Straw) 1249^{8} 2695^{7} 3894^{15} 3966^{3} 4180^{6} 4326^{4} 4505^{5} **>68f<**

Heart of Armor 3 b c Tirol-Hemline (Sharpo) 502^{4} 690^{15} 878^{6} (1296) 1592^{2} 1868^{7} 2230^{2} 2963^{6} 3377^{2} 4310^{10} **>88f<**

Heart of Gold (IRE) 3 ch c Broken Hearted-Originality (Godswalk (USA)) 701^{4} 996^{3} (1470) (2064) 2291^{2} 2676^{4} 3333^{12} (4234) **>94f<**

Heathyard's Flight 3 b c Statoblest-Jeanne Avril (Music Boy) *296^{11} 412^{7}* 453^{8} *546^{5}* 758^{7} **>20a 38f<**

Heathyards Lady (USA) 6 b m Mining (USA)-Dubiously (USA) (Jolie Jo (USA)) 468^{10} 554^{4} 864^{13} *1135^{5} 1788^{6}* 1818^{6} 2021^{5} 2418^{8} *2671^{10} 2913^{6}* 3759^{6} *4798^{4}* **>49a 39f<**

Heathyards Pearl (USA) 3 gr ro f Mining (USA)-Dance Dance Dance (IRE) (Dance of Life (USA)) **1996:** *5201^{6}* **1997:** *50^{8} 110^{7}* 1226^{7} 1864^{7} 2235^{8} 4047^{13} **>22a 52f<**

Heathyards Rock 5 br g Rock City-Prudence (Grundy) (1222) 1562^{2} 1779^{5} 2063^{5} *2301^{6}* **>73a 67f<**

Heathyards Sheik 2 b c Alnasr Alwasheek-Wilsonic (Damister (USA)) 1797^{8} 2706^{7} 3265^{5} 3569^{5} 3821^{5} 4411^{8} 4508^{5} 4605^{3} 4745^{4} **>75f<**

Heavenly Abstone 2 b f Interrex (CAN)-Heavenly Queen (Scottish Reel) 492^{2} 572^{2} (664) 750^{4} 1013^{2} (1310) 1653^{6} 2024^{12} 2500^{3} 2685^{2} 3257^{2} *3610^{3}* 3889^{2} 4014^{9} **>57a 80f<**

Heavenly Calm (USA) 3 f 4658a^{5} **>108f<**

Heavenly Dancer 3 b f Warrshan (USA)-High Halo (High Top) 644^{10} 757^{10} **>34a 57f<**

Heavenly Falls (IRE) 2 b c River Falls-Almost Heaven (Corvaro (USA)) *1136^{9}* 1418^{5} 1760^{16} (2191) 2565^{5} 3067^{5} (3312) 3755^{7} 4014^{15} 4285^{17} **>22a 73f<**

Heavenly Hand 3 ch f Out of Hand-My Home

(Homing) **1996:** *5098[7] 5248[10]* **1997:** *568[7]* **>24a f<**

Heavenly Miss (IRE) 3 b f Anita's Prince-Heavenly Blessed (Monseigneur (USA)) **1996:** *5224[12] (5245) 5251[5] 5278[4]* **1997:** *25[2] 162[4] 198[6] 279[3]* 506[11] 602[6] 988[8] 1141[2] 1294[10] 1566[12] 1810[5] 1931[7] 2554[9] 2921[7] 3327[10] 3500[2] 3984[6] 4155[28] 4738[17] **>74a 62f<**

Heavenly Ray (USA) 3 ch f Rahy (USA)-Highest Truth (USA) (Alydar (USA)) 485[2] (1499) 4669[6] 4976[4] **>103?f<**

Heaven's Command 3 b f Priolo (USA)-Heavenly Music (FR) (Seattle Song (USA)) **1996:** 5194a[2] **1997:** (3003a) 3371a[4] **>108f<**

Hebony 2 b f Sabrehill (USA)-Hebba (USA) (Nureyev (USA)) 4103[W]

Heed My Warning (IRE) 2 b f Second Set (IRE)-Warning Sound (Red Alert) 4093a[2] **>105f<**

Heeremandi (IRE) 2 b f Royal Academy (USA)-La Dame du Lac (USA) (Round Table) (1880a) 2024[6] 3882a[3] 4093a[4] 4475[5] **>103f<**

Heighth of Fame 6 b g Shirley Heights-Land of Ivory (USA) (The Minstrel (CAN)) **1996:** *(5148)* **1997:** *256[2] 384[3] 410[15]* 613[5] 762[13] 888[14] *1138[3]* 1683[7] *(1943)* 2208[2] *2607[3]* 3108[8] *4485[7] 4571[5] 4811[13]* **>65a 51f<**

Height of Heights (IRE) 4 b g Shirley Heights-Azallya (FR) (Habitat) 1106[3] 1477[14] 2311[6] (3203) 4461[6] 4744[14] **>79f<**

Heiress of Meath (IRE) 2 ch f Imperial Frontier (USA)-Rich Heiress (IRE) (Last Tycoon) 1425[12] 4042[15] 4515[19] **>43f<**

He Knows The Rules 5 b g Tirol-Falls of Lora (Scottish Rifle) 3469[14] 4426[13] **>44f<**

Helenes Hill 2 b f Sabrehill (USA)-Sea of Clouds (Soviet Star (USA)) 1619[10] 3707[13] *4479[11]* **>18a 36f<**

Helicon (IRE) 4 b c Nashwan (USA)-Hebba (USA) (Nureyev (USA)) 1490[2] 2765[5] **>109f<**

Helios 9 br g Blazing Saddles (AUS)-Mary Sunley (Known Fact (USA)) 2201[5] 2375[3] 2848[10] 4059[18] **>39a 66f<**

Helissio (FR) 4 b c Fairy King (USA)-Helice (USA) (Slewpy (USA)) **1996:** 5159a[3] **1997:** (922a) (2460a) 3050[3] 4129a[2] 4665a[6] **>133+f<**

Hello Dolly (IRE) 3 b f Mujadil (USA)-Great Leighs (Vaigly Great) **1996:** *(5141) 5212[4]* **1997:** *46[3] 138[8]* 665[2] **>69a 70f<**

Hello Mister 6 b h Efisio-Ginnies Petong (Petong) 726[19] 839[9] 942[19] 961[5] 1596[5] 2105[19] 2775[4] 2861[3] 3217[18] 3447[4] 3577[10] 4100[9] 4153[9] 4444[5] 4525[8] 4756[5] 4881[13] **>83a 95f<**

Hello There 3 b g Picea-Estonia (Kings Lake (USA)) 582[14] **>36f<**

Helmsman (USA) 5 El Gran Senor (USA)-Sacred Journey (USA) (King's Bishop (USA)) 5063a[10] **>114f<**

Henbury Princess 4 ch f Teamster-Record Flight (Record Token) 3277[14] 4045[12] **>9f<**

Henderson (GER) 7 4539a[3] **>97f<**

Hen Harrier 3 ch f Polar Falcon (USA)-Circus Feathers (Kris) (699) 794[6] 1595[4] (2155) 2676[8] 3803[7] 4181[6] **>98f<**

Henley (USA) 3 b c Salem Drive (USA)-Leap of The Heart (USA) (Nijinsky (CAN)) **1996:** *(5121)* **1997:** 837[5] (1595) 2058[12] 2574[11] 3120[4] **>90a 91f<**

Henry's Mother 3 b f Rock City-Sleepline Princess (Royal Palace) 989[3] (1443) 2120[3] **>82f<**

Henry The Fifth 4 b c Village Star (FR)-Microcosme (Golden Fleece (USA)) **1996:** *5182[8]* **1997:** 943[5] 1476[6] 1768[14] 2136[12] 2666[6] 3181a[9] **>18a 90df<**

Henry the Hawk 6 b g Doulab (USA)-Plum Blossom (USA) (Gallant Romeo (USA)) 772[3] 1037[4] 1227[4] (1613) 1816[4] 2002[14] 2659[7] 2755[3] 3240[6] 3271[6] 3484[5] *4049[5]* **>56a 43f<**

Henry The Proud (IRE) 2 ch g Shalford (IRE)-June Goddess (Junius (USA)) 695[6] 2842[10] 3629[8] *4593[12]* **>3a 71f<**

Herbshan Dancer 3 b g Warrshan (USA)-Herbary (USA) (Herbager) 478[2] 771[8] 1296[3] 1938[8] 2182[3] 2373[5] 4179[6] 4372[5] *4590[11]* 4821[10] **>56f<**

Here Comes a Star 9 b g Night Shift (USA)-Rapidus (Sharpen Up) 744[17] 949[12] 1250[14] 1514[9] 1671[3] 2061[5] 2203[5] 2738[9] 4329[4] 4580[11] **>49f<**

Here Comes Herbie 5 ch g Golden Lahab (USA)-Megan's Move (Move Off) (493) 553[2] 669[4] (846) 1224[3] 2682[2] 2882[3] (3069) 3383[3] 4783[21] 5027[2] **>76f<**

Here's To Howie (USA) 3 b c Hermitage (USA)-Choice Comment (USA) (Rich Cream (USA)) *455[2]* (641) 878[7] 1474[9] 2182[5] 3455[6] 4172[11] 4504[6] 4629[6] 4817[5] **>68a 64f<**

Heritage 3 b c Danehill (USA)-Misty Halo (High Top) 445[3] (1405) (2058) 2514[7] 3989[7] 4754[4] 5053[18] **>101f<**

Hermanus 3 b g Lugana Beach-Hitravelscene (Mansingh (USA)) 503[9] *576[9]* **>43f<**

Herminius (IRE) 2 b c Ballad Rock-Scotia Rose (Tap On Wood) 1396[4] 2243[4] 2688[5] (4793) **>80f<**

Heron Island (IRE) 4 b c Shirley Heights-Dalawara (IRE) (Top Ville) **1996:** (5199a) **1997:** 923a[3] 1454[5] 2055[4] **>122f<**

Herr Trigger 6 gr g Sharrood (USA)-Four-Legged Friend (Aragon) 2961[10] 3238[6] 3381[3] 3739[3] **>83?a 77f<**

Hershebar 7 ch h Stanford-Sugar Token (Record Token) *152[14] 203[13] 327[7] 423[13]* **>11?a f<**

Hesabull (USA) 4 *5061a[2]* **>129a f<**

He's Got Wings (IRE) 4 b g In The Wings-Mariella (Sir Gaylord) 430[8] 613[3] 888[7] 1100[7] 3623[10] **>34a 61f<**

Hetra Heights (USA) 2 b f Cox's Ridge (USA)-Top Hope (High Top) 4779[14] 4904[17] **>52f<**

Heubach Boy 3 b g Belmez (USA)-North Pacific (USA) (Hawaii) 899[6] 1271[7] 2020[9] 2474[3] 4405[8] **>55f<**

Hever Golf Angel (IRE) 3 b f Mujadil (USA)-Doon Belle (Ardoon) 701[8] 792[8] 1115[9] 1733[6] 4289[3] **>52f<**

Hever Golf Charger (IRE) 3 b g Silver Kite (USA)-Peace Carrier (IRE) (Doulab (USA)) **1996:** *5146[6]* **1997:** *118[5] 212[2] 259[2] (279) 337[2] 420[6] 489[4] 547[3] 1291[11]* 1505[6] 1746[2] *2319[7]* 2554[15] **>64a 65f<**

Hever Golf Charmer 3 b g Precocious-Callas Star (Chief Singer) *588[8]* 964[10] 1272[8] *1756[15]* 1991[3] 2487[9] 4213[11] **>23a 59f<**

Hever Golf Classic 4 b br g Bustino-Explosiva (USA) (Explodent (USA)) **1996:** *5259[7]* **>54f<**

Hever Golf Dancer 3 b g Distant Relative-Blue Rag (Ragusa) **1996:** *5207[4]* **1997:** *19[3] 154[8] 279[2]* 886[17] **>56a 65f<**

Hever Golf Eagle 4 b g Aragon-Elkie Brooks (Relkino) **1996:** *5253[3]* **1997:** *2[2] 86[11] (338) 422[10]* 1139[18] 2428[3] **>60a 58f<**

Hever Golf Glory 3 b c Efisio-Zaius (Artaius (USA)) 742[4] 1006[2] 1358a[3] (1909a) 2457a[6] 3373a[4] 3885a[7] **>96f<**

Hever Golf Lover (IRE) 3 b f Taufan (USA)-Anagall (USA) (Irish River (FR)) **1996:** *5226[2] (5279)* **1997:** *(75) 320[5]* 1966[11] 4115[17] 4249[15] **>63a 50f<**

Hever Golf Machine 2 ch c Rudimentary (USA)-Stop Press (USA) (Sharpen Up) 3136[3] 3619[10] **>31a 63f<**

Hever Golf Magic (IRE) 3 ch f Ballad Rock-Track Twenty Nine (IRE) (Standaan (FR)) **1996:** *5121[13]* **1997:** 768[4] 3980[17] **>25a 63f<**

Hever Golf Mover 3 ch f Efisio-Joyce's Best (Tolomeo) **1996:** *5224[7] 5243[3] 5252[4]* **1997:** *155[6]* (751) 995[2] *1151[10]* 1810[4] 2169[4] 2892[9] (3266) 3558[2] 3851[2] 4169[16] **>66a 73f<**

Hever Golf Passion (IRE) 2 b f Pips Pride-Base Camp (Derring-Do) 4067[10] 4909[3] **>71f<**

Hevergolf Princess (IRE) 2 ch f Petardia-High Profile (High Top) 4066[10] 4330[9] **>64f<**

Hever Golf Ranger 2 b c Efisio-Bold Green (FR) (Green Dancer (USA)) 4105[9] 4544[3] 4959a[2] **>65f<**

Hever Golf Rocket 3 b g Efisio-Truly Bold (Bold Lad (IRE)) 2278[4] (2580) 2964[9] 3406[3] 3614[3] **>77f<**

Hever Golf Rose 6 b m Efisio-Sweet Rosina (Sweet Revenge) 811a[6] 941[2] (1206a) 1455[9] 1721a[3] (1910a) 2106[3] 2640a[4] 3001a[9] 3724[6] 4001a[3] 4260a[5] 4239[15] 4664a[7] 4777[12] (4964a) **>111a 116f<**

Hever Golf Star 5 b g Efisio-Truly Bold (Bold Lad (IRE)) 604[3] **>79a 72f< (DEAD)**

Hever Golf Stormer (IRE) 3 b c Mujadil (USA)-Clogher Head (Sandford Lad) **1996:** *5261[4]* **1997:** *132[5] 378[9] 427[8]* 602[3] 758[9] 1236[15] 2723[13] **>47a 29f<**

Hey Up Mate (IRE) 2 b g River Falls-Damira (FR) (Pharly (FR)) *902[11]* 1510[14] 2477[13] 3239[7] *3610[12]* 4381[15] 4459[5] **>14a 69f<**

Hibernica (IRE) 3 b br f Law Society (USA)-Brave Ivy (Decoy Boy) 3389[4] 3715[6] 3917[8] 3982[13] **>60f<**

Hiblaze (IRE) 3 b c Lahib (USA)-Gezalle (Shareef Dancer (USA)) 4631[8] **>12f<**

Hickleton Miss 4 ch f Timeless Times (USA)-Honest Opinion (Free State) **1996:** *5112[12]* **>9a 55f<**

Hickory (IRE) 2 b c Fayruz-La Mortola (Bold Lad (IRE)) 893[5] 2012[9] 2948[8] 4908[9] **>77f<**

Hidden Agenda (FR) 3 b f Machiavellian (USA)-Ever Genial (Brigadier Gerard) 1823[6] 2315[9] 3463[5] 3931[8] 4323[4] 4693[6] **>56f<**

Hidden Lake (USA) 4 f *5062a[7]* **>79a f<**

Hidden Meadow 3 b c Selkirk (USA)-Spurned (USA) (Robellino (USA)) (679) 940[13] (1770) 2009[10] 2830[4] (3728) 4240[2] 4625a[8] **>125f<**

Hiding Place 2 b f Saddlers' Hall (IRE)-Sanctuary Cove (Habitat) 1251[7] 2181[5] 3450[9] 4265[4] (4698) 4994[16] **>65f<**

High And Low 2 b f Rainbow Quest (USA)-Cruising Height (Shirley Heights) 5040[2] **>77f<**

High And Mighty 2 b c Shirley Heights-Air Distingue (USA) (Sir Ivor) 4758[17] 5040[9] **>57f<**

Highborn (IRE) 8 b or br g Double Schwartz-High State (Free State) 596[11] 677[7] 1035[10] 1214[7] 1397[4] 1775[10] 2124[2] 2598[19] 3423[9] (3810) (3888) 4550[8] 4978[22] **>83a 106f<**

Highbury Legend 2 ch c Mazilier (USA)-Jans Contessa (Rabdan) 1084[8] 1267[8] *2595[4]* **>48a 38f<**

High Carry 2 b f Forzando-Carn Maire (Northern Prospect (USA)) 1806[8] 2181[23] (2904) 3480[5] 3755[3] (3892) 4006[2] 4173[2] 4522[5] **>87f<**

High Desire (IRE) 4 b f High Estate-Sweet Adelaide (USA) (The Minstrel (CAN)) 1169[12] 1592[10] 1825[6] 2039[4] 2246[5] 2916[7] **>24a 54f<**

High Domain (IRE) 6 b g Dominion Royale-Recline (Wollow) 834[9] 1848[3] 2061[11] 2308[5] 2497[5] 3130[11] 3334[12] 3984[15] 4115[14] **>56a 55f<**

Highfield Fizz 5 b m Efisio-Jendor (Condorcet (FR)) **1996:** *5108[9]* **1997:** 781[8] 1081[2] 1232[8] 1452[3] 2154[4] 2737[2] 2882[5] 3069[2] 3440[5] 3754[3] 3931[5] 4160[2] 4585[3] 4794[2] 4804[2] **>28a 56f<**

Highfield Pet 4 b g Efisio-Jendor (Condorcet (FR)) 2940[9] 3309[13] 3758[8] 4415[13] **>36f<**

High Five (IRE) 7 b g High Line-Finger Lake (Kings Lake (USA)) *295[12] 351[2] (381)* 865[3] (1114) *1133[2]* 2139[P] **>40a 53f<**

Highflying 11 br g Shirley Heights-Nomadic Pleasure (Habitat) 846^8 994^4 1494^8 2000^{13} 2882^{11} **>66f<**

High Gain 2 b f Puissance-Femme Formidable (Formidable (USA)) 1091^3 1295^2 1783^7 (2746) 3098^3 3556^3 4566^9 4970^4 **>72f<**

High Intrigue (IRE) 3 b br c Shirley Heights-Mild Intrigue (USA) (Sir Ivor) 1846^4 (2213) (2963) 3648^{11} (4156) **>92+f<**

High Jinks 2 b c High Estate-Waffling (Lomond (USA)) 2579^5 3494^{13} 4952^{10} **>57f<**

Highland Lord 2 b c Primo Dominie-Tarvie (Swing Easy (USA)) 2181^{24} 4884^{24} **>6f<**

Highland Pass (IRE) 3 b g Petorius-Whatawoman (Tumble Wind (USA)) *456^8* **>61f<**

High Low (USA) 9 b g Clever Trick (USA)-En Tiempo (USA) (Bold Hour) *99^8 136^8* 721^8 848^{18} 2063^2 2469^5 3104^7 **>25a 48f<**

Highly Pleased (USA) 2 b c Hansel (USA)-Bint Alfalla (USA) (Nureyev (USA)) 4780^3 4949^7 **>55?f<**

Highly Prized 3 b c Shirley Heights-On The Tiles (Thatch (USA)) 725^{16} 967^2 1242^8 1877^4 **>81f<**

Highly Respected (IRE) 3 b f High Estate-Respectfully (USA) (The Minstrel (CAN)) 446^4 676^{16} 784^8 1017^7 1030^8 *1580^9* 4601^{22} **>58a 62f<**

High Money 2 b c Dilum (USA)-Renira (Relkino) 1084^5 1391^5 2018^5 2720^7 3589^6 4500^2 4627^{10} *4812^9* **>43a 68f<**

High Noon 2 b c Shirley Heights-Hocus (High Top) 4526^{11} **>65f<**

High On Life 3 b c Mazilier (USA)-Tina Rosa (Bustino) 641^2 1282^2 1853^8 3108^3 3298^3 4010^8 **>69f<**

High Premium 9 b g Forzando-High Halo (High Top) **1996:** *5231^3* **1997:** *1^9* 444^5 (550) (823) 947^3 (1097) 1300^3 1979^4 2441a^4 2947^2 3822^3 3972^2 **>88a 84df<**

High Priority (IRE) 4 b c Marju (IRE)-Blinding (IRE) (High Top) 4787^{29} **>77?f<**

High Pyrenees 5 b g Shirley Heights-Twyla (Habitat) 2889^8 **>73f<**

High-Rise (IRE) 2 b c High Estate-High Tern (High Line) (5041) **>87+f<**

High Sheriff (IRE) 2 b g High Estate-Call Me Miss (Hello Gorgeous (USA)) 2388^2 (2893) **>83+f<**

High Shot 7 b g Darshaan-Nollet (High Top) 839^{10} **>77f<**

Highspeed (IRE) 5 ch g Double Schwartz-High State (Free State) 1560^{10} 1862^3 2239^7 3029^7 3573^{11} 3777^9 **>6a 53f<**

High Spirits (IRE) 3 b g Great Commotion (USA)-Spoilt Again (Mummy's Pet) 575^5 699^5 995^6 1256^{10} 1467^3 (1733) 2019^4 (2169) 2415^7 (2733) 2903^2 (3262) (3605) 4147^7 4578^3 4781^{11} **>81f<**

High Summer 7 b g Green Desert (USA)-Beacon Hill (Bustino) *1288^5* **>53a 36f<**

High Tension (USA) 2 b c Sadler's Wells (USA)-Very Confidential (USA) (Fappiano (USA)) 4367^4 4857^3 **>75f<**

Hightide 5 b m Lugana Beach-Moon Charter (Runnymede) **1996:** *5282^8* **1997:** *108^{11}* **>14a f<**

Highwayman (IRE) 2 b c Danehill (USA)-Millerette (Mill Reef (USA)) 3978^5 4229^3 4950^4 **>85f<**

Hi Hoh (IRE) 4 ch f Fayruz-Late Date (Goldhill) *1428^8 2674^7* **>13a 41f<**

Hill Farm Blues 4 b f Mon Tresor-Loadplan Lass (Nicholas Bill) (1383) 2174^2 *2301^{10}* (2533) 2782^{11} 3263^8 4568^4 4691^5 4704^2 4891^{10} 4956^9 **>43a 69f<**

Hill Farm Dancer 6 ch m Gunner B-Loadplan Lass (Nicholas Bill) **1996:** *(5104) 5169^2 5233^5* **1997:** *(182) 344^3 389^4* 482^4 *591^6* 657^{11} 881^3 *1431^3* 1803^5 **>84a 57f<**

Hill Magic 2 br c Magic Ring (IRE)-Stock Hill Lass (Air Trooper) 2123^2 (2534) 2863^5 4106^8 4315^7 4897^3 5050^{17} **>82f<**

Hillside Rose (IRE) 2 b f Danehill (USA)-Miss Belgravia (USA) (Smarten (USA)) 1538a^3 **>77f<**

Hill Society (IRE) 5 br g Law Society (USA)-Sun Screen (Caerleon (USA)) 2967a^3 **>82f<**

Hillswick 6 ch g Norwick (USA)-Quite Lucky (Precipice Wood) 1507^2 2702^2 3203^4 (3472) 3896^6 4170^5 4374^4 **>51f<**

Hillzah (USA) 9 ch g Blushing Groom (FR)-Glamour Girl (ARG) (Mysolo) 4109^{16} 4768^4 **>78?a 45f<**

Hiltons Executive (IRE) 3 b f Petorius-Theatral (Orchestra) 1096^9 1467^{13} 2354^2 2883^3 3266^7 3606^5 4047^{10} 4707^3 **>35a 50f<**

Himself (USA) 2 b c El Gran Senor (USA)-Celtic Loot (USA) (Irish River (FR)) (4915) **>93+f<**

Hi Mujtahid (IRE) 3 ch g Mujtahid (USA)-High Tern (High Line) 758^5 876^8 1127^{10} 1467^7 2169^6 2237^6 2415^3 2715^2 (2903) 3088^2 3269^3 3812^2 3868^2 4059^{10} **>60f<**

Hi Nod 7 b h Valiyar-Vikris (Viking (USA)) 1160^9 1397^7 2761^3 3052^4 (3252) 3725^{13} 4637^9 **>101f<**

Hint of Victory 3 ch g Ron's Victory (USA)-May Hinton (Main Reef) *50^4 (161) 264^3* 1464^5 1807^5 *2319^6* **>67a 56f<**

Hinton Rock (IRE) 5 ch g Ballad Rock-May Hinton (Main Reef) 1667^7 **>28a 74df<**

Hio Nod 3 b g Precocious-Vikris (Viking (USA)) **1996:** *5111^{13}* **1997:** *874^{11} 1044^{14}* 2502^{17} **>14a f<**

Hippios 3 b br g Formidable (USA)-Miss Doody (Gorytus (USA)) 475^{13} 1234^9 1465^8 2279^9 2397^8 2908^5 *3865^6* 4171^8 4336^{13} **>30a 44f<**

Hippocracy 2 b f Unfuwain (USA)-Marielou (FR) (Carwhite) 4067^9 4873^{15} **>65f<**

Hippy Chick 3 b f Ron's Victory (USA)-Enchanted Tale (USA) (Told (USA)) 768^7 1090^{11} 1500^6 **>47f<**

Hirasah (IRE) 3 b f Lahib (USA)-Mayaasa (USA) (Lyphard (USA)) (3499) 3913^6 4120^9 **>103?f<**

Hirst Bridge (IRE) 2 b c Mujadil (USA)-Mirabiliary (USA) (Crow (FR)) 697^2 (1076) 1255^3 1684^5 2712^4 3755^2 3990^4 **>83f<**

Hi Rudolf 2 b g Ballet Royal (USA)-Hi Darlin' (Prince de Galles) 2378^7

Hisar (IRE) 4 br g Doyoun-Himaya (IRE) (Mouktar) 3246^8 3548^{12} 3976^{12} 4386^2 **>78f<**

Hishi Natalie (USA) 4 **1996:** 5159a^7 **>124f<**

Hit The Spot (IRE) 2 b f Night Shift (USA)-Winning Feature (Red Alert) 4769^6 4904^{12} **>53a 58f<**

Hobart Junction (IRE) 2 ch c Classic Secret (USA)-Art Duo (Artaius (USA)) 3760^4 4209^5 4814^5 **>72f<**

Hobbs Choice 4 b f Superpower-Excavator Lady (Most Secret) 2564^{16} *3585^5* **>12a 50?f<**

Hobean 3 b f Rock Hopper-Beacon (High Top) 2461a^2 **>90f<**

Hogaif (IRE) 2 ch c Persian Bold-Camarat (Ahonoora) 1396^{10} 2112^2 **>70f<**

Hoh Chi Min 2 ch f Efisio-Special Guest (Be My Guest (USA)) (979) 1211^3 (2371) 3981^2 4267^4 4619a^3 (4868a) **>96f<**

Hoh Dancer 3 ch f Indian Ridge-Alteza Real (Mansingh (USA)) 656^3 792^{14} 2231^{10} **>44f<**

Hoh Down (IRE) 3 b f Fairy King (USA)-Tintomara (IRE) (Niniski (USA)) **1996:** *5168^5 5226^5* **1997:** *41^3 90^4 156^4 1785^{10}* 2701^6 **>58da 40f<**

Hoh Explorer (IRE) 3 ch c Shahrastani (USA)-Heart's Harmony (Blushing Groom (FR)) 725^{11} 967^6 2046^{12} 2548^3 2940^6 *4055^{12}* 4269^{10} **>63f<**

Hoh Express 5 b g Waajib-Tissue Paper (Touch Paper) 521^{14} 787^9 939^8 (1325) 1771^3 2028^7 2348^3 3110^6 3434^7 3689^6 4639^2 5053^{13} **>94f<**

Hoh Flyer (USA) 3 b f Northern Flagship (USA)-Beautiful Bedouin (USA) (His Majesty (USA)) 509^{10} 675^6 791^{13} *1135^{11}* 1449^5 **>35a 72df<**

Hoh Justice 2 b c Petardia-Cactus Road (FR) (Iron Duke (FR)) 850^7 1954^2 2196^3 2689^4 3295^4 3794^7 4216^5 **>74f<**

Hoh Majestic (IRE) 4 b g Soviet Lad (USA)-Sevens Are Wild (Petorius) **1996:** *5173^3* **1997:** *20^2 152^2 198^5 318^5 332^2 421^2 (429) 545^5 663^8* 997^8 *1289^5 (1790) 2069^9 2305^{10} 4985^{13}* **>56da 50f<**

Hoh Navigator (IRE) 2 ch c Common Grounds-Flying Diva (Chief Singer) 2007^3 **>74f<**

Hoh Returns (IRE) 4 b g Fairy King (USA)-Cipriani (Habitat) 726^6 1148^{11} 1948^9 2105^{30} 2769^6 3130^9 3420^5 3621^{11} 3777^{12} *4301^8* **>38a 73df<**

Hokuto Vega (JPN) 7 b m *628a^F* **>118f<**

Holders Hill (IRE) 5 b g Tirol-Delightful Time (Manado) **1996:** *5267^2* **1997:** *28^2 83^7* 864^{19} *2071^5* **>72da f<**

Ho Leng (IRE) 2 ch g Statoblest-Indigo Blue (IRE) (Bluebird (USA)) (3629) 4266^2 4790^5 **>101f<**

Holloway Melody 4 ch f Cree Song-Holloway Wonder (Swing Easy (USA)) **1996:** *5170^4 5241^{11} 5256^8* **1997:** *4798^8* 4899^5 4991^8 **>46a 48f<**

Hollow Haze (USA) 2 b br f Woodman (USA)-Libeccio (NZ) (Danzatore (CAN)) 4273^2 4442^6 **>85+f<**

Holly Hedge (IRE) 2 b c Petardia-Holly Bird (Runnett) 1192a^2 **>79+f<**

Hollywood Paradise (IRE) 2 gr c Cyrano de Bergerac-Fun Frolic (Sexton Blake) 4868a^2 **>91f<**

Holy Smoke 2 b f Statoblest-Native Flair (Be My Native (USA)) 3770^7 4132^8 4513^4 **>63f<**

Holy Wine (USA) 2 ch g Thorn Dance (USA)-Gloria Mundi (FR) (Saint Cyrien (FR)) 2870^9 3306^{10} 3783^9 (4068) 4265^8 **>77f<**

Hombre 2 ch c Shemazar-Delray Jet (USA) (Northjet) 3103^5 3760^5 4209^8 **>72f<**

Home Counties (IRE) 8 ch g Ela-Mana-Mou-Safe Home (Home Guard (USA)) 4432^9 **>66?f<**

Ho Mei Surprise 5 ch h Hadeer-By Surprise (Young Generation) *135^9* **>38a 4f<**

Homestead 3 ch g Indian Ridge-Bertrade (Homeboy) 1248^{17} 1506^7 1925^7 2554^6 (3299) (3592) 4448^3 *4798^7* 4817^2 4958^{10} 4991^4 **>37a 59f<**

Hondero (GER) 7 b h Damister (USA)-Hone (Sharpen Up) 2643a^3 4396a^3 **>115f<**

Honest Borderer 2 b g Selkirk (USA)-Tell No Lies (High Line) 4526^5 4739^4 **>78f<**

Honestly 4 ch f Weldnaas (USA)-Shadha (Shirley Heights) **1996:** *(5140) 5269^3* **1997:** *76^6 160^3 290^5 340^3 418^2* 4453^9 **>55a 39f<**

Honey Colour (IRE) 3 ch c Night Shift (USA)-Honey Stage (USA) (Stage Door Johnny) 1553a^7 2462a^2 4398a^2 4866a^9 **>105f<**

Honeyhall 4 b f Crofthall-Attila the Honey (Connaught) **1996:** *(5109) 5178^7* **1997:** *4^7 79^W 222^4 275^6 339^5* **>30a 38f<**

Honeyshan 5 b m Warrshan (USA)-Divissima (Music Boy) 790^7 **>43f<**

Honey Storm (IRE) 2 b f Mujadil (USA)-Milk And Honey (So Blessed) 3187^3 3743^3 3961a^9 4067^2 4437^4 **>80f<**

Honey Suckle 2 br f Petong-May the Fourteenth (Thatching) 4515^7 **>55f<**

Hong Kong Dollar 5 b g Superpower-Daleside Ladybird (Tolomeo) **1996:** *5079^{11} 5174^{13}* **>9a 42df<**

Hong Kong Express (IRE) 3 b f Distinctly North (USA)-North Kildare (USA) (Northjet) 748^5 1586^5 1733^5 1991^5 **>48f<**

Honiara Bay 3 b f Welsh Captain-Honiara

(Pitcairn) 2941[14] 3250[5] 3572[9] 3816[11] 4289[7] **>12f<**

Honor Glide (USA) 3 b c Honor Grades (USA)-Becky Branch (Run The Gantlet (USA)) (3881a) *5066a[8]* **>75a 120f<**

Honourable 3 ch g Old Vic-Integrity (Reform) 446[3] *576[3]* 784[6] 1392[2] (1999) 2291[3] 3120[2] (3722) 3989[2] 4443[10] **>58a 103f<**

Hoofprints (IRE) 4 b c Distinctly North (USA)-Sweet Reprieve (Shirley Heights) **1996:** *(5102) 5119[3]* **1997:** 3640[8] **>74a 70f<**

Hope Chest 3 ch f Kris-Hopeful Search (USA) (Vaguely Noble) 1372[3] 1646[W] 2389[8] 2879[5] **>71df<**

Hopeful Bid (IRE) 8 b g Auction Ring (USA)-Irish Kick (Windjammer (USA)) 1782[11] 1972[11] 2760[12] 2922[13] 4184[12] **>49f<**

Hopefully 2 b f Salse (USA)-Silver Maple (USA) (Silver Hawk (USA)) 441[4] 631[2] 780[2] 1298[2] 1581[3] 2016[9] 2186[4] **>63f<**

Hopeful Star (IRE) 2 ch c Pips Pride-Mijouter (IRE) (Coquelin (USA)) 4446[6] 4908[6] **>50a 56f<**

Hopesay 3 b f Warning-Tatouma (USA) (The Minstrel (CAN)) 2654[5] 2925[11] 3710[5] 4414[14] **>71f<**

Hope Value 2 b g Rock City-Folle Idee (USA) (Foolish Pleasure (USA)) 2018[7] 2419[3] *2604[6]* 4208[16] **>49a 67f<**

Hopperetta 3 b f Rock Hopper-Can Can Girl (Gay Fandango (USA)) **1996:** *5135[4] 5180[3]* **1997:** 4711[18] 4987[16] **>54a 52df<**

Hopping Higgins (IRE) 2 b f Brief Truce (USA)-Yellow Creek (Sandy Creek) 1531a[2] 2054[2] (3506a) 3534a[4] 4203a[2] 4616a[5] 4790[6] **>99f<**

Hornbeam 3 b c Rich Charlie-Thinkluckybelucky (Maystreak) (1265) 2023[3] 2766[12] **>108f<**

Hornpipe 5 b g Handsome Sailor-Snake Song (Mansingh (USA)) **1996:** *5132[8] 5181[6] 5259[3]* **1997:** *18[9] 37[3] 86[17] 177[2] 312[8] 367[5] 544[6]* **>39da f<** **(DEAD)**

Hostile Native 4 b g Formidable (USA)-Balatina (Balidar) 4008[14] 4164[13] 4707[18] **>18f<**

Hotcake 4 b g Sizzling Melody-Bold Cookie (Never so Bold) 1448[8] 1761[6] 2880[7] 3627[9] **>41f<**

Hot News 3 b c Sizzling Melody-In the Papers (Aragon) 1638[6] 2125[9] 2278[5] 2883[14] **>34f<**

Hot Shot 3 gr g Chilibang-Free Rein (Sagaro) 1487[P] 1929[7] *2319[10]* **>15a f<**

Hot Spot 2 ch g Bustino-Royal Seal (Privy Seal) 5040[14] **>33f<**

Hotstepper 4 ch f Never so Bold-Brilliant Timing (USA) (The Minstrel (CAN)) 3820[8] 4465[15] **>26f<**

Hot Topic (IRE) 2 ch f Desse Zenny (USA)-Sajanjal (Dance In Time (CAN)) 4178[12] 4694[12] **>31f<**

Housekeeper (IRE) 2 b f Common Grounds-Staff Approved (Teenoso (USA)) (4907) **>85+f<**

House of Dreams 5 b g Darshaan-Helens Dreamgirl (Caerleon (USA)) 4386[12] 4596[5] 4751[3] **>61f<**

House On Fire (IRE) 2 b g Paris House-La Fille de Feu (Never so Bold) 3613[10] 4544[11] 4769[7] **>55a 50f<**

Howaida (IRE) 3 b f Night Shift (USA)-Fear Naught (Connaught) 2873[U] (3095) 4175[3] 4920[2] **>86f<**

How Bizarre 3 b g Thatching-Relatively Sharp (Sharpen Up) 1876[11] 4916[19]

How Could-I (IRE) 4 br f Don't Forget Me-Shikari Rose (Kala Shikari) **1996:** *5250[5]* **>4a 52f< (DEAD)**

Howies Choice (IRE) 2 b g Petardia-Better Goods (IRE) (Glow (USA)) 2196[7] 2706[4] 4428[4] 4603[9] **>65f<**

How Long 4 b c Alzao (USA)-Fresh (High Top) 677[4] 961[2] 1552a[2] 2102a[3] 2598[2] 3063[2] **>112f<**

Howqua River 5 b g Petong-Deep Blue Sea (Gulf Pearl) **1996:** *5148[9]* **>46a 54f<**

How's Yer Father 11 b g Daring March-Dawn Ditty (Song) **1996:** *5138[2] 5230[6] 5241[9]* **>64a 65f<**

Hoyland Common (IRE) 2 ch f Common Grounds-Scoby Lass (Prominer) 2467[11] 2736[7] 3106[15] 3312[7] *3586[9]* **>32a 29f<**

Hugger-Mugger 2 br g Prince Sabo-Fair Eleanor (Saritamer (USA)) 1274[6] 1635[8] 2003[7] 2741[8] **>43f<**

Hujoom (IRE) 2 b c Fairy King (USA)-Maellen (River Beauty) 2123[3] (2849) 3186[2] 3774[12] (4284) 4890[8] **>91f<**

Hulal 3 b g Arazi (USA)-Almarai (USA) (Vaguely Noble) 645[11] 1004[6] 2158[3] 2415[2] **>69f<**

Hullbank 7 b g Uncle Pokey-Dubavarna (Dubassoff (USA)) 1100[15] (1654) 2000[2] 2882[2] **>57a 76f<**

Humbel (USA) 5 b h Theatrical-Claxton's Slew (USA) (Seattle Slew (USA)) 1073a[11] **>114f<**

Humourless 4 ch c Nashwan (USA)-Sans Blague (USA) (The Minstrel (CAN)) 1325[3] 2028[6] 2710[19] 3191[3] **>101f<**

Hung Jury 3 b c Night Shift (USA)-Chepstow Vale (USA) (Key To The Mint (USA)) 1546a[3] **>76f<**

Hunky Punky (IRE) 2 b f Petorius-Matouba (ITY) (Riverman (USA)) 4534a[3]

Hunters of Brora (IRE) 7 b m Sharpo-Nihad (Alleged (USA)) 450[9] 738[D] 934[4] 1456[11] 1768[13] 3112[8] 3901[4] 4147[13] 4558[3] 4781[12] **>100f<**

Hunt Hill (IRE) 2 b c High Estate-Royaltess (Royal And Regal (USA)) 4515[12] 4603[14] 4710[10] **>48f<**

Hunting Ground 9 b g Dancing Brave (USA)-Ack's Secret (USA) (Ack Ack (USA)) *5[7] 55[9]* 669[6] 2000[14] **>20f<**

Huntswood 2 b c Warning-Clarista (USA) (Riva Ridge (USA)) 1873[3] 2007[4] (2684) (3288) 4284[11] **>86f<**

Hurgill Dancer 3 b g Rambo Dancer (CAN)-Try Vickers (USA) (Fuzzbuster (USA)) 533[8] (700) 4774[14] 4996[12] **>60a 74f<**

Hurgill Lady 3 ch f Emarati (USA)-Gitee (FR) (Carwhite) 995[7] 1843[9] **>68f<**

Hurgill Times 3 b g Timeless Times (USA)-Crimson Dawn (Manado) *79[6] 4574[7] 4798[13]* **>42a 60f<**

Hurricane State (USA) 3 ch c Miswaki (USA)-Regal State (USA) (Affirmed (USA)) 917a[6] 1767[9] **>108f<**

Hurtleberry (IRE) 4 b f Tirol-Allberry (Alzao (USA)) **1996:** *5082[2]* **1997:** *(175) 363[3]* (1320) 3615[8] 4558[15] 4978[9] **>77a 77f<**

Hustle An Bustle (USA) 3 ch f Lomond (USA)-City Crowds (General Assembly (USA)) 4748[8] **>20a 60f<**

Husun (USA) 3 b f Sheikh Albadou-Tadwin (Never so Bold) 1650[3] 1967[4] 2358[5] 3092[11] 3930[10] **>65f<**

Hutchies Lady 5 b m Efisio-Keep Mum (Mummy's Pet) **1996:** *5115[8]* **1997:** 552[14] 608[11] 951[4] 1040[2] 1231[6] 1748[B] 2030[5] 2385[8] 2469[9] 2660[14] 2854[12] **>27a 25f<**

Huxleen 2 ch f Timeless Times (USA)-Bergliot (Governor General) 1438[2] 1626[3] (1815) 2489[W] 2827[W] **>66f<**

Hyde Park (IRE) 3 b c Alzao (USA)-Park Elect (Ahonoora) **1996:** *(5080)* **>71a 71f<**

Hype Energy 3 b f Tina's Pet-Stoneydale (Tickled Pink) 652[11] 1141[15] 2006[15] 2481[4] 2922[8] 3816[4] 4016[16] 4221[2] **>56f<**

Hype Superior (IRE) 3 ch g Mac's Imp (USA)-Katysue (King's Leap) 693[9] 792[5] 1014[10] 1119[7] 1650[7] 1781[10] 2496[2] 4333[10] *4809[6]* **>50a 58f<**

I

I Ain't Bluffing (USA) 3 f b Pine Bluff (USA)-Cup of Honey (USA) (Raise A Cup (USA)) (5056a) **>118f<**

Iamus 4 ch g Most Welcome-Icefern (Moorestyle) *330[6] 376[8]* 450[4] 974[7] 1442[3] 1782[3] 2026[22] 2678[8] (3064) 3243[3] **>67a 93f<**

Ibin St James 3 b c Salse (USA)-St James's Antigua (IRE) (Law Society (USA)) (600) 1025[4] 1649[5] 2328[3] 2890[5] 3242[9] **>69f<**

Iblis (IRE) 5 b g Danehill (USA)-In Unison (Bellypha) *376[4]* 1442[5] 1658[10] 2325[12] 2835[4] 3746[4] 4280[25] *4797[12]* **>84da 79df<**

Ibn Masirah 3 b g Crowning Honors (CAN)-Masirah (Dunphy) 2170[6] 2908[11] **>50f<**

I Can't Remember 3 br g Petong-Glenfield Portion (Mummy's Pet) *388[7]* 448[6] 654[6] 688[10] 699[6] 1017[4] 1175[9] 1658[12] 2214[6] 2877[9] 3901[14] **>70a 57f<**

Ice Age 3 gr c Chilibang-Mazarine Blue (Bellypha) 694[19] 1018[14] 1294[9] 1730[10] 1792[5] 2148[4] 2298[4] 2406[4] 2732[6] 3693[3] 4221[12] 4329[10] 4527[13] *4913[14]* **>32a 63df<**

Iceband (USA) 2 ch c Dixieland Band (USA)-Zero Minus (USA) (It's Freezing (USA)) 2870[2] (4145) 4551[6] **>98f<**

Icemoon (GER) 3 ch c Monsagem (USA)-Icena (Jimmy Reppin) 817a[3] 1544a[4] 2097a[6] 2642a[11] 4396a[4] **>107f<**

I Cried For You (IRE) 2 b c Statoblest-Fall of The Hammer (IRE) (Auction Ring (USA)) 2534[14] 2917[7] 3926[8] 4566[3] 5050[3] **>67f<**

Icy Guest (USA) 3 b br f Clever Trick (USA)-Minstrel Guest (Be My Guest (USA)) 1265[2] *1787[3]* 2192[5] 2427[3] *(2913) 3584[11]* **>80a 72f<**

Icy Love 3 b f Pursuit of Love-Ice Chocolate (USA) (Icecapade (USA)) (1556a)

Idaho (IRE) 2 ch f Common Grounds-Queen's Share (Main Reef) 1927[9] 4915[13] **>19f<**

Ida Lupino (IRE) 2 b f Statoblest-Alpine Symphony (Northern Dancer) 2860[6] 3450[16] 3598[16] 4382[8] 4750[7] **>40f<**

I Don't Think So 6 b m Mas Media-Misdevious (USA) (Alleged (USA)) *356[9]*

Idrica 3 b f Rainbow Quest (USA)-Idraak (Kris) (3377) 3974[10] **>91f<**

Iechyd-Da (IRE) 3 b g Sharp Victor (USA)-Key Partner (Law Society (USA)) 502[3] 597[3] 1242[6] 1949[4] 4102[12] **>91df<**

Ihtimaam (FR) 5 b g Polish Precedent (USA)-Haebeh (USA) (Alydar (USA)) **1996:** *(5115) 5181[3]* **1997:** *66[8] 231[6] 869[9]* 1229[11] 3284[6] **>67da 22f<**

Ihtiyati (USA) 3 ch c Chief's Crown (USA)-Native Twine (Be My Native (USA)) 690[3] 1025[3] 3773[10] 4151[2] 4552[7] (4754) **>106f<**

Ijab (CAN) 7 b g Ascot Knight (CAN)-Renounce (USA) (Buckpasser) 1996[11] 2539[3] 2874[9] *4811[3]* **>42a 40f<**

Ijtinab 3 b c Green Desert (USA)-Nahilah (Habitat) 517[3] 790[2] 991[9] 2951[5] 3551[5] 4071[10] 4375[11] **>71f<**

Ikaab (USA) 5 b g Danzig (USA)-Dazzling Concorde (USA) (Super Concorde (USA)) 308a[4] **>102df<**

Ikatania 3 b c Highest Honor (FR)-Lady Liska (USA) (Diesis) (533) 700[2] 1868[5] 2391[8] **>88f<**

Ikdam (USA) 3 b br f Dayjur (USA)-Orca (ARG) (Southern Halo (USA)) 988[11] **>95f<**

Ikhteyaar (USA) 2 b br f Mr Prospector (USA)-Linda's Magic (USA) (Far North (CAN)) 3770[2] 4103[2] (4332) (4890) **>95+f<**

Ikhtisar (USA) 3 b br f Slew O' Gold (USA)-Halholah (USA) (Secreto (USA)) 1646[5] 1922[3] 2423[3] 3020[3] **>79f<**

Ikram Boy (USA) 3 b g Salem Drive (USA)-Vast Domain (CAN) (Vice Regent (CAN)) 4070[9] 4587[4] 4872[9] *4980[8]* **>27a 61f<**

Ilandra (IRE) 5 b m Roi Danzig (USA)-Island Goddess (Godswalk (USA)) **1996:** *5079[5] 5247[4]* **1997:** *9[4] 85[2] 125[4] 202[7]* 7551[2] 4465[14] *4800[10]* **>45a 32f<**

Il Destino 2 b c Casteddu-At First Sight (He Loves Me) 4564[7] 4807[P] **>59f<**

Il Doria (IRE) 4 ch f Mac's Imp (USA)-Pasadena Lady (Captain James) 1419[9] 4008[10] 4370[20] **>8a 31f<**

Ile de Librate 3 b g Librate-Little Missile (Ile de Bourbon (USA)) 445[8] 3632[6] 4158[10] **>67f<**

Ile Distinct (IRE) 3 b g Dancing Dissident (USA)-Golden Sunlight (Ile de Bourbon (USA)) 2909[5] (3697) (4172) 4386[3] 4876[12] **>80f<**

Il Falco (FR) 3 ch g Polar Falcon (USA)-Scimitarlia (USA) (Diesis) 2773[6] 4070[11] 4182[5] 4472[6] 4632[8] **>52f<**

Illegally Yours 4 br f Be My Chief (USA)-Legal Precedent (Star Appeal) *183[3] 262[3] 351[5] 908[7] 1417[4] 2322[2]* 2727[9] *3074[5]* **>50a 36f<**

Illuminate 4 b g Marju (IRE)-Light Bee (USA) (Majestic Light (USA)) *(228) 324[8] 1138[10]* 1481[9] **>70a 70f<**

Illusion 3 b c Green Desert (USA)-Time Charter (Saritamer (USA)) 1415[2] (1983) 2761[2] 3703[11] **>108f<**

Ilonka (ITY) 3 f 815a[14] **>74f<**

Il Principe (IRE) 3 b g Ela-Mana-Mou-Seattle Siren (USA) (Seattle Slew (USA)) **1996:** *5090[8]* **1997:** 2158[7] 2750[5] (3486) 3626[2] (3700) *3865[2] (4055)* (4160) (4287) 4405[9] **>65a 71f<**

Il Trastevere (FR) 5 b g L'Emigrant (USA)-Ideas At Work (Persepolis (FR)) **1996:** *5269[8]* **1997:** *22[3] 76[7]* **>62a 81f<**

I'm a Dreamer (IRE) 7 b g Mister Majestic-Lady Wise (Lord Gayle (USA)) *410[14]* **>38a 67f<**

Image Maker (IRE) 4 gr f Nordico (USA)-Dream Trader (Auction Ring (USA)) *169[8] 235[8]* **>30a 52f<**

I'm a Nut Man 6 b h Shardari-Zahiah (So Blessed) 951[13] 1383[4] 1926[14] 2896[6] 3104[6] **>22a 41f<**

Imbackagain (IRE) 2 b g Mujadil (USA)-Ballinclogher (IRE) (Creative Plan (USA)) 697[9] 2295[8] *3607[7]* **>50a 40f<**

Imelda (USA) 2 ch f Manila (USA)-Rich And Riotous (USA) (Empery (USA)) 4215[8] **>43f<**

I'm Not Sure 2 gr f Petong-Glenfield Portion (Mummy's Pet) 441[6] 1019[11] 1600[5] *2051[3] 2367[3] 3586[4]* 3866[3] *4054[14] 4573[6]* **>54a 47f<**

Impala 3 ch g Interrex (CAN)-Raleigh Gazelle (Absalom) 1167[6] 1448[3] 1807[2] (2392) *3044[7]* 3392[9] **>44a 70f<**

Impending Danger 4 ch g Fearless Action (USA)-Crimson Sol (Crimson Beau) *37[5] 86[13]* 4986[14] **>18a 26f<**

Imperator (IRE) 2 b c Mac's Imp (USA)-Secret Hideaway (USA) (Key To The Mint (USA)) 2243[14]

Imperial Bid (FR) 9 b or br g No Pass No Sale-Tzaritsa (USA) (Young Emperor) 669[9] **>60a 54?f<**

Imperial Court (IRE) 2 b c Imperial Frontier (USA)-Fandikos (IRE) (Taufan (USA)) 3278[20]

Imperial Garden (IRE) 3 ch g Imperial Frontier (USA)-Spindle Berry (Dance In Time (CAN)) *25[4] 102[2] 142[3] (158) 181[3] 427[2]* **>70a 60f<**

Imperial Glen (IRE) 3 b f Imperial Frontier (USA)-Tribute to Viqueen (Furry Glen) 1423[10] 2287[5] 2555[12] 2921[12] 3470[9] 3643[3] **>45f<**

Imperial Honey (IRE) 2 b f Imperial Frontier (USA)-Indian Honey (Indian King (USA)) 1126[5] 1466[7] 1669[5] 3106[2] 3699[5] **>65f<**

Imperial Line (IRE) 3 ch g Mac's Imp (USA)-Ellaline (Corvaro (USA)) 1512[7] 2020[11] 3037[11] 3431[19] 4290[7] 4601[19] **>43f<**

Imperial Or Metric (IRE) 3 b g Prince Rupert (FR)-Caroline's Mark (On Your Mark) 764[3] 958[7] 1256[P] 1472[11] 1994[7] 2523[10] 4703[4] **>48f<**

Imperial Prince 2 b c Prince Sabo-Joli's Girl (Mansingh (USA)) 1109[7] **>66f<**

Imperial Scholar (IRE) 3 b f Royal Academy (USA)-Last Ball (IRE) (Last Tycoon) 672[5] 890[5] 1738[9] 2190[2] 2537[6] 3550[W] **>94df<**

Impetuosity (IRE) 3 ch f Imp Society (USA)-Catherine Clare (Sallust) 469[9] *576[6] 874[6]* 1229[7] **>24a 37f<**

Impetuous Lady (USA) 4 b f Imp Society (USA)-Urakawa (USA) (Roberto (USA)) 1632[22] 2199[9] 2730[8] 3101[6] 3291[6] 3540[11] **>34f<**

Impetus 3 b g Puissance-Cold Line (Exdirectory) 945[7] 1271[10] 1834[2] **>56f<**

Imp Express (IRE) 4 b g Mac's Imp (USA)-Fair Chance (Young Emperor) *40[13] 127[14] 152[6] 198[3] 223[6] 304[9]* 2203[11] 2754[4] 2899[4] 2934[3] 3271[2] 3287[6] 3566[5] 3756[4] 3871[8] **>54da 47f<**

Impish (IRE) 3 ch g Imp Society (USA)-Halimah (Be My Guest (USA)) *204[5] 247[6] 412[3]* 549[3] 652[3] 924[5] (1037) 1223[3] 1613[14] 1835[8] 1995[6] 2221[W] 2504[6] **>32a 52f<**

Impish Lady (IRE) 2 br f Mac's Imp (USA)-Wabarah (Shirley Heights) 1827[11] *2163[5]* **>1a f<**

Implicitly 2 ch f Lion Cavern (USA)-Pushkinia (FR) (Pharly (FR)) 4332[8] 4747[3] **>65f<**

Imposing Time 6 b g Music Boy-Jandell (NZ) (Shifnal) **1996:** *5105[2] 5150[9]* **1997:** 2372[8] 2422[13] 2895[5] 3016[8] 3642[9] 4016[13] 4221[10] **>76a 51f<**

Impressionist (IRE) 2 b c Royal Academy (USA)-Yashville (Top Ville) (3962a) 4784[3] **>105f<**

Impulse (IRE) 2 ch g Imp Society (USA)-Kristar (Kris) *1124[2]* 1251[4] 1480[6] 1959[6] 2565[7] *3395[5]* 3451[7] (3751) 4285[4] 4806[13] **>56a 66f<**

Impulsif (USA) 3 ch c Diesis-High Sevens (Master Willie) 990[15] 1305[5] 1737[8] 2691[2] 2951[4] 3614[4] 3710[2] 4071[8] 4451[9] 4975[6] **>72a 69f<**

Impulsive Air (IRE) 5 b g Try My Best (USA)-Tracy's Sundown (Red Sunset) 529[2] 895[13] 1035[6] 1560[8] 1775[5] 2290[8] 2546[4] 2890[9] 3134[2] 3262[2] (3442) (3702) 3921[6] 4270[16] 4629[4] 4792[10] **>66f<**

Impulsive Decision (IRE) 2 gr f Nomination-Siva (FR) (Bellypha) 2917[10] 3222[4] 3782[3] 4543[3] 4753[11] (4819) **>63f<**

Impy Fox (IRE) 3 ch f Imp Society (USA)-Rusty Goddess (Hard Fought) 1245[14] *2305[12]* **>65a 58f<**

Imroz (USA) 3 b f Nureyev (USA)-All At Sea (USA) (Riverman (USA)) 1460[2] 2426[2] (2774) 3147[4] 3728[3] 4226[2] **>105f<**

Imshishway (IRE) 2 b c Royal Academy (USA)-Mama Lucia (Workboy) 3047[8] 3235[7] (4368) 4880[7] **>83f<**

I'm Still Here 3 gr g Skyliner-Miss Colenca (Petong) (549) 785[12] **>50a 64f<**

I'm Tef 2 b g Noble Patriarch-Who's That Lady (Nordance (USA)) 1120[11] 1396[13] 2904[4] 3212[7] 3427[10] 3808[12] 4595[8] *4808[2]* 5026[4] **>48?a 42f<**

Inaminit 4 gr g Timeless Times (USA)-Dolly Bevan (Another Realm) **1996:** *5093[R]* **>44f<**

In A Tizzy 4 b f Sizzling Melody-Tizzy (Formidable (USA)) 1118[4] 1463[15] 2474[5] **>38a 38f<**

In Cahoots 4 gr c Kalaglow-Royal Celerity (USA) (Riverman (USA)) *92[4] 147[12]* 1233[15] **>39a 55f<**

Incantrice 4 ch f Faustus (USA)-Dependable (Formidable (USA)) 467[12] 550[10] 843[13] **>28f<**

Incatime 3 b g Inca Chief (USA)-Parrot Fashion (Pieces of Eight) **1996:** *5187[7] 5279[5]* **1997:** *45[5]* 3500[14] 3850[3] 4115[19] **>30a 27f<**

Incatinka 4 gr f Inca Chief (USA)-Encore L'Amour (USA) (Monteverdi) **1996:** *5082[11]* **>16a 65f<**

Incepta 2 b c Selkirk (USA)-Ringlet (USA) (Secreto (USA)) 4237[12] 4901[W] **>50f<**

Inchacooley (IRE) 5 b m Rhoman Rule (USA)-Blue Cashmere (USA) 2079a[6] 2441a[3] (3510a) **>100f<**

Inchahoy 2 ch f Inchinor-Ackcontent (USA) (Key To Content (USA)) 4957[9] **>50f<**

Inchalong 2 b f Inchinor-Reshift (Night Shift (USA)) 492[5] 572[3] 594[5] 927[3] 1253[2] 1466[6] 1829[5] 2016[2] (2288) 2658[2] 2786[5] 3438[2] 3480[3] 3755[6] (3869) 4152[4] 4285[3] 4362[3] 4473[3] 4634[2] 4755[3] 4885[3] 4989[2] 5050[7] **>72f<**

In Charge 2 ch f Be My Chief (USA)-Great Exception (Grundy) 4973[18] **>2f<**

Inchcailloch (IRE) 8 b g Lomond (USA)-Glowing With Pride (Ile de Bourbon (USA)) 442[6] (510) 1413[2] 2014[14] 2108[6] 4476[7] 4783[19] **>83f<**

Inchella 4 b f Inca Chief (USA)-Sandy Cap (Sandy Creek) 1567[9] *2301[11]* 2531[13] **>31f<**

Inchtina 2 b f Inchinor-Nikitina (Nijinsky (CAN)) 3490[2] 4317[2] **>80f<**

Inclination 3 b f Beveled (USA)-Pallomere (Blue Cashmere) 840[6] 1245[13] 1826[10] 2149[3] 2468[2] 2832[3] 3101[3] 3452[3] 3691[3] 3968[3] 4169[13] 4817[10] **>60f<**

In Command (IRE) 3 b c Sadler's Wells (USA)-Flying Melody (Auction Ring (USA)) 737[4] 2011[6] 4117[7] **>116f<**

Indiahra 6 b m Indian Ridge-Mavahra (Mummy's Pet) **1996:** *(5110) 5209[11] 5256[2]* **>65a 57f<**

Indian Affair 3 b f Indian Ridge-Steppey Lane (Tachypous) 2045[12] **>14f<**

Indiana Princess 4 b f Warrshan (USA)-Lovely Greek Lady (Ela-Mana-Mou) 1022[11] 4046[14] 4438[10] **>65f<**

Indian Blaze 3 ch g Indian Ridge-Odile (Green Dancer (USA)) 688[11] 983[7] 1589[9] 1958[13] 2395[12] 2956[2] **>61f<**

Indian Brave 3 b c Indian Ridge-Supreme Kingdom (Take A Reef) 1234[7] 1777[4] **>83df<**

Indian Missile 2 ch c Indian Ridge-Haitienne (FR) (Green Dancer (USA)) 1321[3] (1924) 2215[2] 3067[4] 4670[2] **>89f<**

Indian Nectar 4 b f Indian Ridge-Sheer Nectar (Piaffer (USA)) 482[8] 2487[7] 2782[5] **>2a 45f<**

Indian Rapture 3 ch f Be My Chief (USA)-Moments Joy (Adonijah) *6[7] 90[7] 191[7] 314[7]* **>44a 10f<**

Indian Relative 4 b f Distant Relative-Elegant Tern (USA) (Sea Bird II) 942[26] 1317[13] 1594[4] 2308[4] 2788[15] 3292[6] 3710[8] 4249[13] **>75a 65f<**

Indian Rocket 3 b c Indian Ridge-Selvi (Mummy's Pet) 2056[5] 2599[3] 3111[3] 3724[10] 4011[9] **>115f<**

Indian Serenade 6 ch g Mansingh (USA)-La Melodie (Silly Season) 1077[8] 1666[9] *2302[5]* 2646[18] **>46a 31f<**

Indian Silver 2 b f Indian Ridge-Ovideo (Domynsky) 985[2] 1149[2] 1619[5] 3799[5] **>79f<**

Indian Spark 3 ch c Indian Ridge-Annes Gift (Ballymoss) 4491[0] 555[2] (968) 1171[10] 1596[6] 2476[2] 3447[6] 4100[17] 4467[5] 4756[14] 4887[9] **>95f<**

Indian Wolf 4 ch c Indian Ridge-Red Riding Hood (FR) (Mummy's Pet) **1996:** *5161[13]* **1997:** *20[9] 69[9]* 541[11] 879[10] 1920[12] **>5a 27f<**

Indigo Dawn 3 b f Rainbow Quest (USA)-Dame Ashfield (Grundy) 463[3] 825[3] 1258[5] 1574[3] 2114[3] (2474) (2702) *(2910)* 3309[2] 3896[8] 4336[5] *4594[2] 4811[14]* **>75a 70f<**

Indimaaj 2 b c Mtoto-Fairy Feet (Sadler's Wells (USA)) 2556[3] 3103[3] 3760[2] **>77+f<**

Indiscreet (CAN) 3 b c St Jovite (USA)-Imprudent Love (USA) (Foolish Pleasure (USA)) (1099) 1307[5]

2023^{16} **>106f<**

Indium 3 b c Groom Dancer (USA)-Gold Bracelet (Golden Fleece (USA)) 878^{5} 1747^{5} **>83f<**

Indonesian (IRE) 5 b or br g Alzao (USA)-Miss Garuda (Persian Bold) 1601^{2} 2063^{7} 2503^{9} 3758^{12} **>35f<**

Indrapura (IRE) 5 b g Gallic League-Stella Ann (Ahonoora) 4109^{15} 4219^{16} **>74a 47f<**

Indulgent Toto 3 b c Mtoto-Indulgence (USA) (Raise A Cup (USA)) $812a^{3}$ **>71f<**

Indy Knight (IRE) 2 ch f Indian Ridge-Bag Lady (Be My Guest (USA)) 3687^{14} 4231^{13} **>35f<**

Infamous (USA) 4 ch g Diesis-Name And Fame (USA) (Arts And Letters) *100^{3} 176^{6}* **>74a 89f<**

Infatuation 4 b g Music Boy-Fleeting Affair (Hotfoot) 1244^{15} 1459^{8} (1832) 2889^{4} 3197^{2} (4151) 4383^{3} 4788^{2} **>92f<**

Infiel 4 b f Luge-Indocina (Indian King (USA)) $1919a^{4}$ **>96f<**

Inflation 3 b f Primo Dominie-Fluctuate (Sharpen Up) 1090^{5} **>76f<**

Influence Pedler 4 b g Keen-La Vie En Primrose (Henbit (USA)) 4956^{13} **>11a 69?f<**

Influent (CAN) 6 b/ h Ascot Knight (CAN)-Katerina Key (USA) (Key To The Mint (USA)) (4395a) **>131f<**

Ingleborough 3 b g Barrys Gamble-Dreamy Desire (Palm Track) 2045^{8} 2420^{8} 2902^{3} 4748^{P} 4847^{18} **>47f<**

Ingle Boy 2 b g Barrys Gamble-Maydrum (Meldrum) 2827^{8} 3628^{7} 3920^{7} **>39f<**

In Good Faith 5 b g Beveled (USA)-Dulcidene (Behistoun) **1996:** *5256^{3}* **1997:** *36^{2}* 1040^{9} 1268^{8} 1802^{6} *2071^{7}* 3105^{9} **>61a 58f<**

In Good Nick 3 b f Nicholas (USA)-Better Still (IRE) (Glenstal (USA)) 634^{7} 748^{3} 1096^{2} 1226^{6} 1582^{4} 2313^{20} 2891^{11} 3241^{9} 4291^{16} 4601^{13} **>38f<**

Inimitable 3 b f Polish Precedent (USA)-Saveur (Ardross) 1168^{6} 1938^{9} (2246) 2763^{4} **>69f<**

Injazaat (USA) 3 b br f Dayjur (USA)-Basma (USA) (Grey Dawn II) 4070^{4} 4316^{9} **>76df<**

Inkatha (FR) 3 gr c Double Bed (FR)-Majuba (FR) (Mendez (FR)) $717a^{3}$ **>107f<**

Inkwell 3 b g Relief Pitcher-Fragrant Hackette (Simply Great (FR)) 1807^{8} 2245^{4} 3038^{2} 3321^{6} 3601^{3} 3897^{9} 4326^{7} 4846^{3} 4916^{5} *5019^{8}* **>12a 46f<**

Inner Key 2 b g Interrex (CAN)-Key to Enchantment (Key To Content (USA)) 2191^{6} 2664^{6} *4812^{14}* **>41f<**

Inn On The Park 2 b c Northern Park (USA)-Hotel California (IRE) (Last Tycoon) 3022^{6} 3613^{12} 4157^{11} **>38f<**

Inovar 7 b g Midyan (USA)-Princess Cinders (King of Spain) *360^{13}* **>35a 34f<**

In Question 3 br b c Deploy-Questionable (Rainbow Quest (USA)) 773^{3} 1144^{3} (1804) (2142) 2589^{12} 3805^{11} **>95df<**

Insatiable (IRE) 4 b c Don't Forget Me-Petit Eclair (Major Portion) 1160^{3} (1456) **>111+f<**

Inshallah 2 ch f Durgam (USA)-Kaliala (FR) (Pharly (FR)) 1328^{7} 1669^{6} 2110^{4} 2886^{W} 3257^{7} 3628^{3} 3869^{10} 4840^{7} 5026^{7} **>64df<**

Insider Trader 6 b g Dowsing (USA)-Careless Whisper (Homing) 464^{11} 744^{7} 949^{8} 1098^{9} 1269^{9} 1468^{4} 1627^{3} 1662^{6} 1835^{3} 2061^{7} 2657^{8} 2934^{9} 3481^{7} 4512^{11} 4844^{7} **>63a 52f<**

Insight (FR) 2 f $4961a^{2}$ **>108f<**

Inspirational (IRE) 3 ch f Lahib (USA)-Sun Breiz (FR) (Boran) 4848^{11} **>36f<**

Interaction 3 ch g Interrex (CAN)-Kimbolton Katie (Aragon) 462^{8} 774^{7} 896^{12} 1467^{14} 2208^{7} 3038^{8} **>29f<**

Interdream 3 b g Interrex (CAN)-Dreamtime Quest (Blakeney) *366^{8}* 533^{5} 642^{3} 886^{2} 1164^{4} 1392^{3} 1633^{4} 1972^{12} 2750^{2} (2956) 3382^{2} (3685) 4015^{6} 4757^{24} **>80f<**

Internal Affair (USA) 2 b g Nicholas (USA)-Gdynia (USA) (Sir Ivor) 4917^{7} **>61f<**

Interregnum 3 ch f Interrex (CAN)-Lillicara (FR) (Caracolero (USA)) 742^{15} 2190^{8} 3129^{9} **>17f<**

In The Band 4 b f Sharrood (USA)-Upper Caen (High Top) *334^{4} 418^{5}* **>50a 47f<**

In The Genes 3 b g Syrtos-Ruby's Vision (Balinger) 1282^{3} 2315^{6} 2888^{4} 3907^{8} 4699^{9} 4918^{3} 4998^{7} **>64f<**

In the Money (IRE) 8 b h Top Ville-Rensaler (USA) (Stop The Music (USA)) **1996:** *5233^{4} 5270^{2}* **1997:** *30^{7} 80^{3} 106^{4} (147) (216) 295^{3} (315) (402)* (481) *591^{8} 908^{9} 1156^{3}* 1515^{3} 2015^{4} *2164^{10}* 3035^{3} **>59a 59f<**

In The Sun (USA) 2 b f Alleged (USA)-Pandysia (USA) (Storm Bird (CAN)) 4515^{8} 4701^{5} 4952^{5} **>65f<**

Intiaash (IRE) 5 br m Shaadi (USA)-Funun (USA) (Fappiano (USA)) *376^{11} 406^{6} 459^{6} 569^{3}* (879) *905^{7}* (1113) *2162^{2}* 2377^{11} *2603^{2} (2663) 3075^{4}* 3217^{25} 3326^{8} 3566^{8} 4048^{9} 4221^{6} 4456^{15} 4878^{6} **>75?a 76f<**

Intikhab (USA) 3 b c Red Ransom (USA)-Crafty Example (USA) (Crafty Prospector (USA)) 747^{2} 957^{2} 1257^{2} (2761) (4003) (4523) **>114+f<**

Intisab 4 b f Green Desert (USA)-Ardassine (Ahonoora) (565) 894^{5} 1453^{6} 1935^{6} 2331^{2} 2775^{2} **>93f<**

Into Debt 4 b f Cigar-Serious Affair (Valiyar) **1996:** *5099^{7}* **1997:** *24^{10} 109^{9} (134) 197^{9} 241^{4} 278^{3} 352^{6}* 585^{16} 1009^{13} *1969^{7}* 3393^{7} 3590^{11} 4328^{12} **>37a 41f<**

Intrepid Fort 8 gr g Belfort (FR)-Dauntless Flight (Golden Mallard) *86^{15}* 526^{8} 2041^{8} 2152^{7} 3213^{5} 3762^{13} **>28a 13f<**

Intuitive 2 b f Teenoso (USA)-Hasland (Aragon) 3753^{9} 4017^{14} 4513^{5} **>36f<**

Invermark 3 b g Machiavellian (USA)-Applecross (Glint of Gold) 933^{12} (2924) 3424^{5} 4310^{2} 5053^{4} **>89f<**

Invest Wisely 5 ch g Dashing Blade-Saniette (Crystal Palace (FR)) 442^{5} 777^{P} **>73f<**

Invigilate 8 ch g Viking (USA)-Maria da Gloria (St Chad) 1374^{10} 1620^{18} 1857^{8} **>37f<**

Invocation 10 ch g Kris-Royal Saint (USA) (Crimson Satan) **1996:** *5124^{5} 5183^{7}* **1997:** *(20) 107^{9} 117^{2} (171) 213^{2} (294) 403^{7} 490^{5} 1969^{6}* 2115^{7} 2347^{8} 2552^{10} *(3058) 3860^{8}* 4371^{10} *4485^{9} 4913^{4}* **>67a 48f<**

In Waiting (IRE) 5 b m In The Wings-Arousal (Rousillon (USA)) (4262a) **>91f<**

Iota 8 b or br m Niniski (USA)-Iosifa (Top Ville) **1996:** *5116^{3} 5139^{5}* **>61a 59f<**

Ioulios 3 ch c Shavian-Touch of White (Song) 1119^{17} 1401^{6} 2703^{9} *4051^{14}* **>6a 41f<**

Ipoh (FR) 5 ch m Funambule (USA)-Irish Sea (Irish River (FR)) $189a^{2}$ **>83f<**

Irish Accord (USA) 3 b br c Cahill Road (USA)-Dimples (USA) (Smile (USA)) 555^{3} 853^{7} 1175^{19} 1775^{4} 2013^{22} 2708^{5} 3150^{10} **>96f<**

Irish Fiction (IRE) 3 b g Classic Music (USA)-Wasmette (IRE) (Wassl) **1996:** *5100^{7}* **1997:** 477^{15} 642^{8} 1009^{15} 2005^{9} 2200^{F} **>28a 59f<**

Irish Fighter (IRE) 3 $1545a^{6}$ **>94f<**

Irish Groom 10 b g Shy Groom (USA)-Romany Pageant (Welsh Pageant) 3814^{8} **>42da 52f<**

Irish Kinsman 4 b g Distant Relative-Inesdela (Wolver Hollow) 1001^{20} 1093^{9} 1383^{11} **>17a 38f<**

Irish Light (USA) 3 ch f Irish River (FR)-Solar Star (USA) (Lear Fan (USA)) (1110) 2137^{9} (4220) 4424^{7} 4978^{16} **>92f<**

Irish Oasis (IRE) 4 b g Mazaad-Alpenwind (Tumble Wind (USA)) 595^{14} 2544^{8} 3477^{12} **>32a 42f<**

Irish Sea (USA) 4 b g Zilzal (USA)-Dunkellin (USA) (Irish River (FR)) **1996:** *5256^{11}* **>64df<**

Irish Stainy (IRE) 3 $2642a^{14}$ **>98f<**

Irish Stamp (IRE) 8 b g Niniski (USA)-Bayazida (Bustino) 4171^{12} **>26f<**

Iris May 2 b f Brief Truce (USA)-Choire Mhor (Dominion) 1657^{2} 1978^{2} 2222^{2} 3031^{6} 3564^{4} 4286^{3} (4542) 4746^{4} **>74f<**

Iron Mountain (IRE) 2 b g Scenic-Merlannah (IRE) (Shy Groom (USA)) 1933^{15} 2320^{5} 2388^{4} 3794^{3} 4006^{9} 4334^{2} 4576^{5} 4778^{6} **>70f<**

Irsal 3 ch c Nashwan (USA)-Amwag (USA) (El Gran Senor (USA)) 645^{6} 875^{3} 1230^{3} 1868^{6} 2537^{3} (2850) 3125^{4} 3549^{6} **>80f<**

Irtifa 3 ch f Lahib (USA)-Thaidah (CAN) (Vice Regent (CAN)) 1589^{4} 3448^{4} 3894^{10} 4220^{3} 4375^{4} 4606^{10} **>73f<**

Isabella 2 ch f Primo Dominie-Scossa (USA) (Shadeed (USA)) 1457^{10} 1806^{11} 3282^{7} **>50f<**

Isabella Gonzaga 3 b f Rock Hopper-Lawful (Law Society (USA)) 2183^{5} 2555^{6} 4705^{7} *4906^{4}* **>60a 56f<**

Isca Maiden 3 b f Full Extent (USA)-Sharp N' Easy (Swing Easy (USA)) 840^{16} 1110^{13} 2178^{5} 2695^{9} 3205^{6} **>34f<**

I See You Sydney (AUS) 3 ch g Al Hareb (USA)-Sorrento (AUS) (Best Western (AUS)) 3991^{8} 4322^{8} 4450^{7} **>53f<**

Ishmael 4 b g Prionsaa-Pert (Sayf El Arab (USA)) 2116^{6}

Isis Honda (IRE) 3 ch f Archway (IRE)-Ceann-Na-Bann (Doulab (USA)) *292^{2} 341^{7} 868^{4} 1135^{2}* 1503^{2} 1668^{5} 2281^{3} 2487^{4} 3101^{5} **>62a 69f<**

Isit Izzy 5 b m Crofthall-Angie's Girl (Dubassoff (USA)) 4902^{8} **>43?f<**

Isitoff 4 b g Vague Shot-Plum Blossom (USA) (Gallant Romeo (USA)) 1001^{16} 1371^{D} (1481) 1678^{6} 2297^{3} 3279^{2} (3824) 4294^{3} **>56a 85f<**

Islamabad 2 gr c Petong-Kinlacey (Aragon) 1635^{2} (1952) (2685) 3708^{4} **>90f<**

Island Girl (IRE) 2 br f Elbio-Miss Java (Persian Bold) 536^{6} (1438) 2196^{4} 2689^{8} 3186^{9} 4271^{14} *4808^{5} 4984^{3}* **>48a 66f<**

Island Lore (IRE) 3 ch f Polish Precedent (USA)-Island Wedding (USA) (Blushing Groom (FR)) 727^{2} **>96f<**

Island Prince 3 ch g Prince Sabo-Island Mead (Pharly (FR)) **1996:** *(5251) 5272^{4}* **1997:** *225^{9} 429^{13}* 4742^{17} **>49a 54f<**

Island Race 2 b f Common Grounds-Lake Isle (IRE) (Caerleon (USA)) 4103^{16} **>46f<**

Island Sanctuary (IRE) 3 ch c Fools Holme (USA)-Church Light (Caerleon (USA)) 742^{6} *(874)* (1249) 2285^{2} 3184^{2} 3689^{3} 4310^{6} 4699^{11} **>77a 90f<**

Isle De France (USA) 2 b f Nureyev (USA)-Stella Madrid (FR) (Alydar (USA)) $4663a^{2}$ **>95f<**

Isle of Man (USA) 3 b c Manila (USA)-Princess of Man (Green God) 1399^{6} 1741^{7} 3599^{3} 3989^{9} 4320^{3} **>94f<**

Ismaros 3 ch c Selkirk (USA)-Trikymia (Final Straw) (2008) 2765^{4} **>106f<**

Ismeno 6 b g Ela-Mana-Mou-Seattle Siren (USA) (Seattle Slew (USA)) *78^{W}* **>37a 67f<**

Istidaad (USA) 5 b h Chief's Crown (USA)-Mazzei Mood (USA) (Roberto (USA)) $437a^{4}$ **>117f<**

Is Tirol (IRE) 3 b c Tirol-Islande (Gift Card (FR)) $1544a^{2}$ $2272a^{2}$ $2642a^{17}$ **>113f<**

Italian Rose 2 ch f Aragon-Cayla (Tumble Wind

(USA)) 2037^3 2545^{10} 3407^3 3892^5 4152^6 4327^5 **>35a 61f<**
Italian Symphony (IRE) 3 b g Royal Academy (USA)-Terracotta Hut (Habitat) *425^2* 497^6 *1044^6* 1312^4 1998^7 2501^5 2878^5 3213^2 3382^9 4816^6 *(4985)* **>68a 54f<**
Itatinga (USA) 3 b f Riverman (USA)-Ivrea (Sadler's Wells (USA)) 1168^9 (2414) 2582^6 **>68+f<**
Itch 2 b c Puissance-Panienka (POL) (Dom Racine (FR)) *4479^{10}* (4807) 5050^{13} **>24a 75f<**
Ithaca 3 b c Groom Dancer (USA)-Ionian Sea (Slip Anchor) 2996a^2 3179a^5 **>105f<**
Ithaki (IRE) 3 b c Sadler's Wells (USA)-Idyllic (USA) (Foolish Pleasure (USA)) 1070a^3 1726a^5 2274a^2 3730a^6 4257a^5 **>119f<**
Its All Relative 2 gr f Distant Relative-Sharp Anne (Belfort (FR)) 1569^4 (1990) (2931) 3192^7 3595^{11} 4232^2 **>89f<**
Itsinthepost 4 b f Risk Me (FR)-Where's the Money (Lochnager) 1003^8 1279^{10} *1790^2 2069^4* (2395) *(2671)* **>70a 63f<**
Its My Pleasure 3 b f Rock Hopper-The Fink Sisters (Tap On Wood) 4469^3 **>36f<**
Itsnotyetnamed 2 b c Kasakov-Wych Willow (Hard Fought) 2467^{12} 4209^{16} 4627^{13} 4807^4 **>51f<**
Ivan Luis (FR) 3 b c Lycius (USA)-Zivania (IRE) (Shernazar) (782) 1015^2 1553a^5 (2515) 3109^3 4257a^3 4866a^6 **>121f<**
Ivorian 2 b g Slip Anchor-Ivorine (USA) (Blushing Groom (FR)) 4715^W
Ivor's Deed 4 b g Shadeed (USA)-Gena Ivor (USA) (Sir Ivor) **1996:** *5095^3* **1997:** 779^3 929^3 (1484) 3980^{14} 4404^9 *4913^{10}* **>61a 59f<**
Ivor's Flutter 8 b g Beldale Flutter (USA)-Rich Line (High Line) 4783^8 5052^{13} **>86f<**
Ivory Charm 2 b f Batshoof-Amazing Journey (USA) (Spectacular Bid (USA)) 3278^{17} 3598^{19} 4216^{14} **>23f<**
Ivory Crown (IRE) 2 b f Chief's Crown (USA)-Royal Myth (USA) (Sir Ivor) 4973^{11} **>51f<**
Ivory Dawn 3 b f Batshoof-Cradle of Love (USA) (Roberto (USA)) 448^{14} 506^2 685^9 930^8 1141^5 1410^8 1781^2 (1931) 2134^{13} 2298^2 2691^3 2925^3 3189^{11} 3418^2 3604^{19} 3987^{13} 4155^{24} 4328^{15} **>64f<**
Ivory Girl (IRE) 2 ch f Sharp Victor (USA)-Nordic Dance (USA) (Graustark) *4303^{11}* 4454^{13} **>6a 7f<**
Ivory League 2 b f Last Tycoon-Ivory Lane (USA) (Sir Ivor) 4107^8 4515^{16} 4701^9 **>69f<**
Ivory's Grab Hire 4 b g Shavian-Knees Up (USA) (Dancing Champ (USA)) **1996:** *5209^{10}* **1997:** *159^5 199^2 (223) 263^5 304^2 348^5 (406) 459^4 488^3 569^8* 604^7 1279^7 (1374) (1509) 2006^{21} 2220^6 2563^{16} 2922^4 3082^8 3296^2 3600^4 (3852) 4048^{10} 4183^7 4452^5 **>56a 68f<**
Ivory's Joy 2 b f Tina's Pet-Jacqui Joy (Music Boy) 648^{14} *1290^4* 1635^6 (1867) 2186^2 (2283) 2689^2 4173^4 (4296) 4522^3 4746^6 4948^5 5045^7 **>73f<**
Ivy Bird (IRE) 2 b f Contract Law (USA)-Hollyberry (IRE) (Runnett) 4604^{13}

J

Jaati (IRE) 2 b c Alzao (USA)-Majestic Amber (USA) (Majestic Light (USA)) 5040^{17} **>8f<**
Jaazim 7 ch g Night Shift (USA)-Mesmerize (Mill Reef (USA)) **1996:** *5215^8* **1997:** 752^7 1320^{12} 1484^9 2228^9 2721^{11} **>43a 39f<**
Jaazim (USA) 2 b c Silver Hawk (USA)-Alvear (USA) (Seattle Slew (USA)) 4061^{12} 4318^5 4739^2 **>88f<**
Jabaroot (IRE) 6 b g Sadler's Wells (USA)-Arctic Heroine (USA) (Arctic Tern (USA)) 553^{14} **>38f<**
Jack Doyle (IRE) 6 ch g Be My Native (USA)-Sister Ida (Bustino) 1221^6 1558^5 **>70f<**
Jackerin (IRE) 2 b c Don't Forget Me-Meanz Beanz (High Top) (441) (971) 1161^3 2786^{12} 3307^{13} 3571^2 3823^{14} **>79f<**
Jack Flush (IRE) 3 b g Broken Hearted-Clubhouse Turn (IRE) (King of Clubs) 448^{11} 733^{10} 1024^6 1128^3 (1256) 1513^2 2062^4 2290^9 4510^{16} 4741^{15} **>70f<**
Jackies Webb 2 b f Selkirk (USA)-Hawayah (IRE) (Shareef Dancer (USA)) 1564^9 1821^8 3471^7 **>48f<**
Jackmanii 5 b g Most Welcome-Blue Flower (FR) (Carwhite) 570^6 **>48f<**
Jack-N-Jilly (IRE) 2 b f Anita's Prince-Little Club (King of Clubs) 472^5 *592^6 859^2 1124^3 1432^2 1789^3 2163^2* 2396^4 **>52a 50f<**
Jack Ruby 2 b c Risk Me (FR)-Atisayin (USA) (Al Nasr (FR)) 3306^{15} 3686^5 4012^{15} **>49f<**
Jack Says 3 b g Rambo Dancer (CAN)-Madam Cody (Hot Spark) *38^5 110^4 168^3 234^3 289^3 546^4* 649^{12} **>51a 57f<**
Jackson Falls 3 ch g Dunbeath (USA)-Hysteria (Prince Bee) 797^7 1333^{12} 1631^{16} **>41df<**
Jackson's Panther (IRE) 5 ch m Jackson's Drift (USA)-Pitiless Panther (No Mercy) *313^9* **>2a 43f<**
Jack The Lad (IRE) 3 b g Shalford (IRE)-Indian Honey (Indian King (USA)) **1996:** *5228^9* **1997:** *317^6 377^2 415^4 513^8* 575^6 826^4 (900) 1024^{10} (1078) (1129) (1300) 1416^2 1773^8 1982^4 4383^9 4635^{12} 4876^{13} **>57a 78f<**
Jacmar (IRE) 2 br c High Estate-Inseyab (Persian Bold) 1038^2 (1616) 2168^2 2714^2 (3226) 3961a^4 (4468) 4790^9 **>93+f<**
Jacobina 2 b f Magic Ring (IRE)-Mistitled (USA) (Miswaki (USA)) 1447^8 1669^3 2037^8 2565^3 **>65f<**
Jades Shadow 4 gr g General Wade-Gellifawr (Saulingo) 3202^{10}
Jafn 3 ch f Sharpo-Harold's Girl (FR) (Northfields (USA)) 727^5 (935) 1326^5 2598^{20} 3913^4 (4669) **>106f<**
Jago 2 b c Salse (USA)-Wanda (Taufan (USA)) 2881^7 3103^{10} 3282^8 **>47f<**
Jalb (IRE) 3 b g Robellino (USA)-Adjacent (IRE) (Doulab (USA)) 647^{11} 998^3 1955^6 2521^7 **>73f<**
Jamaica Bridge 7 b g Doulab (USA)-Mill Hill (USA) (Riva Ridge (USA)) 4471^{16} **>55a 34f<**
Jamaican Flight (USA) 4 b c Sunshine Forever (USA)-Kalamona (USA) (Hawaii) 831^2 1100^5 3383^5 3543^2 3826^2 3935^2 4246^6 **>78f<**
Jameel Asmar 5 br g Rock City-Barsham (Be My Guest (USA)) 1979^7 2710^{14} **>81f<**
Jamorin Dancer 2 b c Charmer-Geryea (USA) (Desert Wine (USA)) 4478^3 4745^2 **>82f<**
Jamrat Jumairah (IRE) 4 b f Polar Falcon (USA)-Coryana (Sassafras (FR)) 3144^2 3875a^{10} **>91f<**
Janara 3 b f Aragon-Aimee Jane (USA) (Our Native (USA)) 4070^7 **>54f<**
Jandal 3 ch c Arazi (USA)-Littlefield (Bay Express) 1936^5 **>68f<**
Janet Lindup 2 b f Sabrehill (USA)-Tartan Pimpernel (Blakeney) 5041^{18} **>21f<**
Janglynyve 3 ch f Sharpo-Wollow Maid (Wollow) *590^5 873^7* (1217) (1464) 1780^2 (2294) **>30a 67f<**
Janie's Boy 3 b c Persian Bold-Cornelian (Great Nephew) (1226) 1427^7 1845^6 2214^8 **>37a 67f<**
Jar (IRE) 2 b c Niniski (USA)-Mistral's Collette (Simply Great (FR)) (3177a)
Jareer Do (IRE) 5 b m Jareer (USA)-Shining Bright (USA) (Bold Bidder) **1996:** *5095^6 5161^8 5282^5* **1997:** *71^{13}* **>39a 67f<**
Jarnail (FR) 2 c 3178a^7 **>38f<**
Jarrayan 2 ch f Machiavellian (USA)-Badrah (USA) (Private Account (USA)) 2720^6 3613^4 **>59f<**
Jarrow 6 ch g Jalmood (USA)-Invite (Be My Guest (USA)) 950^9 1229^{10} 1570^5 **>18a 34f<**
Jaseur (USA) 4 b g Lear Fan (USA)-Spur Wing (USA) (Storm Bird (CAN)) 2924^5 3277^{12} 3864^5 (4046) (4426) (4673) 4879^2 **>99f<**
Jashin (IRE) 4 c 1550a^3 4531a^6 **>110f<**
Jasmine Tea 2 ch f Alhijaz-Come To Tea (IRE) (Be My Guest (USA)) 1760^{19} 2240^6 **>41f<**
Jato Dancer (IRE) 2 b f Mukaddamah (USA)-Que Tranquila (Dominion) 2700^8 (3078) 3911^{10} 4185^7 4545^9 **>49f<**
Jaunty Jack 3 b c Midyan (USA)-Juliette Marny (Blakeney) 686^2 (1069a) (1741) (2462a) 4398a^3 **>109f<**
Java Bay 3 b f Statoblest-Flopsy (Welsh Pageant) 1249^7 1633^{15} 1966^{10} 2376^4 **>48f<**
Java Red (IRE) 5 b g Red Sunset-Coffee Bean (Doulab (USA)) 687^9 1511^5 (1655) 2019^5 2463^4 2845^6 3382^3 3477^3 (3933) 4210^3 4596^8 4802^{10} 4998^6 **>57?a 60f<**
Java Shrine (USA) 6 b g Java Gold (USA)-Ivory Idol (USA) (Alydar (USA)) 2344^7 2646^3 2928^6 3276^5 **>62f<**
Jawah (IRE) 3 br g In The Wings-Saving Mercy (Lord Gayle (USA)) 4562^2 4774^5 (4874) (4956) 5052^4 **>89f<**
Jawhari 3 b c Lahib (USA)-Lady of the Land (Wollow) (2591) 3189^{15} 3772^5 4787^{24} **>86f<**
Jayannpee 6 ch g Doulab (USA)-Amina (Brigadier Gerard) 1309^2 1596^4 2056^{15} 2476^4 2861^9 3747^5 3975^{14} 4444^{11} **>106f<**
Jaybee Silver 2 gr f Mystiko (USA)-Pipistrelle (Shareef Dancer (USA)) 1091^8 2425^6 3097^2 3294^4 3782^{10} 4327^9 4401^8 **>53f<**
Jay-Em-Bee 4 b g Double Schwartz-Kasarose (Owen Dudley) 1004^8 2311^{11} 2780^{10} **>3f<**
Jayess Elle 2 b f Sabrehill (USA)-Sorayah (Persian Bold) 4597^6 4789^9 **>57f<**
Jay Gee (IRE) 2 b f Second Set (IRE)-Polynesian Goddess (IRE) (Salmon Leap (USA)) 1143^5 1457^6 2024^{18} 2728^3 (2919) (3237) 3422^8 4097^{17} **>92f<**
Jayir (IRE) 2 b g Mujtahid (USA)-Arylh (USA) (Lyphard (USA)) 3978^4 4446^5 **>67f<**
Jay-Owe-Two (IRE) 3 b g Distinctly North (USA)-Fiery Song (Ballad Rock) **1996:** *5111^9 5207^2 (5257)* **1997:** *17^7* 448^2 (634) 699^7 1170^{19} 2062^{13} 2340^{13} 2735^7 3087^4 (4583) (4757) 4978^{14} **>79a 87f<**
Jaza 3 b c Pursuit of Love-Nordica (Northfields (USA)) 983^9 1415^9 4587^8 **>57f<**
Jazz Club (USA) 2 b c Dixieland Band (USA)-Hidden Garden (USA) (Mr Prospector (USA)) (3379) 3644^6 4679^5 **>90f<**
Jazz King 4 br g Kalaglow-Sabrine (Mount Hagen (FR)) 1145^{12} (2551) (2865) 3110^4 4101^{16} 4295^9 **>92f<**
Jazz Singer 2 b f Prince Sabo-Blues Player (Jaazeiro (USA)) 2394^6 3384^4 3967^3 **>55f<**
Jazz Track (IRE) 3 b c Sadler's Wells (USA)-Minnie Hauk (USA) (Sir Ivor) 2046^7 2940^2 3419^3 3809^3 4279^6 (4749) **>86f<**
J B Quick 3 b c Simply Great (FR)-Quick J (Jim J (USA)) 2566^7 **>76f<**
Jeanne Cutrona 4 b f Risk Me (FR)-Veuve Perrin (Legend of France (USA)) *18^{12}* **>4f<**
Jeanne D'Arc 2 gr f Highest Honor (FR)-Fight Right (FR) (Crystal Glitters (USA)) 1880a^6 **>56f<**
Jean Pierre 4 b g Anshan-Astolat (Rusticaro (FR)) 574^2 689^3 933^{13} 1093^3 1574^6 1617^2 2199^8 2521^6 3329^5 **>51f<**
Jedi Knight 3 b g Emarati (USA)-Hannie Caulder (Workboy) 434^{10} 783^7 998^5 1225^{22} 1584^2 (1761) (1862) 1994^2 2029^4 2546^7 2906^8 3310^4 (3457) 3901^{12} 3976^9 4410^2 4583^6 4792^4 4924^2 (4998) **>80f<**

Jeffrey Anotherred **3** b g Emarati (USA)-First Pleasure (Dominion) **1996:** *5113^{9}* **1997:** 449^{11} 1017^{2} 1170^{16} 1737^{7} 2325^{6} 3189^{7} 3436^{3} 3975^{6} 4155^{10} 4561^{17} 4878^{5} 5047^{6} **>54a 87f<**

Jelali (IRE) **4** b g Last Tycoon-Lautreamont (Auction Ring (USA)) 4585^{7} 4804^{16} **>53f<**

Jendali Princess **4** ro f Jendali (USA)-Hyperion Princess (Dragonara Palace (USA)) **1996:** *5115^{16}* **1997:** 2787^{8}

Jennelle **3** b f Nomination-Its A Romp (Hotfoot) 501^{7} 877^{6} 1018^{9} 1590^{9} 2299^{4} 2560^{7} 2872^{11} 3198^{13} **>83df<**

Jen's In The Know **2** br f Presidium-Lurking (Formidable (USA)) *1286^{9} 1941^{12} 2066^{7}* 2784^{13} **>25a 3f<**

Jenzsoph (IRE) **6** br m Glow (USA)-Taken By Force (Persian Bold) 1808^{6} **>26f<**

Jester Minute **3** gr g Jester-Jealous Lover (Alias Smith (USA)) 4883^{13}

Jet Set Sarah (USA) **2** b f Digression (USA)-Little Jet Setter (USA) (Star de Naskra (USA)) 2935^{5} 3312^{6} 3751^{14} 3967^{7} 4163^{7} **>52f<**

Jewel (IRE) **2** b f Cyrano de Bergerac-Renzola (Dragonara Palace (USA)) 682^{5} 1031^{5} 4630^{9} 4897^{6} **>60f<**

Jewel Fighter **3** br f Good Times (ITY)-Duellist (Town Crier) 2783^{11} 4114^{12} **>19f<**

Jewel Princess (USA) **5** b m Key To The Mint (USA)-Jewell Ridge (USA) (Melyno) *5062a^{8}* **>118a f<**

Jhazi **3** b c Arazi (USA)-Shoot Clear (Bay Express) 745^{7} 1460^{4} **>101df<**

Jibe (USA) **2** b f Danzig (USA)-Slightly Dangerous (USA) (Roberto (USA)) 3744^{4} (4066) 4442^{2} **>99f<**

Jibereen **5** b g Lugana Beach-Fashion Lover (Shiny Tenth) **1996:** *(5178) 5236^{4}* **1997:** *(87) (136) 207^{4} 376^{5} 424^{2} (578)* 1292^{7} 1501^{6} 2004^{8} (2337) 2557^{7} (2868) *3584^{10}* 3976^{21} 4757^{20} 4979^{4} 5049^{4} **>81a 67f<**

Jib Jab **3** br g Jendali (USA)-No Rejection (Mummy's Pet) 882^{11} 1388^{10} 1624^{14} **>46f<**

Jigsaw Boy **8** ch g Homeboy-Chiparia (Song) **1996:** *5144^{7} 5237^{5} 5264^{9}* **1997:** *136^{4} 297^{2} 342^{3} 579^{4} 860^{8} (1134)* 1422^{13} *1754^{9}* 1786^{5} *4798^{10}* **>55a 45f<**

Jila (IRE) **2** ch c Kris-Enaya (Caerleon (USA)) 4167^{3} 4544^{2} (4852) **>84f<**

Jilly Beveled **5** b m Beveled (USA)-Karens Valentine (Daring March) **1996:** *5169^{6}* **1997:** *3^{7} 71^{P} 164^{6} (312) 428^{8}* 526^{19} *579^{7} 867^{8} 1135^{14} 1291^{9} 1786^{3}* 2463^{9} *2603^{7} 2915^{5} 3583^{7}* **>42a 16f<**

Jilly Woo **3** gr f Environment Friend-William's Bird (USA) (Master Willie) **1996:** *5092^{5} 5142^{8}* **1997:** 2332^{7} 2724^{6} 2947^{4} 3081^{5} *3415^{7}* 4009^{4} **>41a 61f<**

Jilted (IRE) **2** b f Pursuit of Love-What A Pity (Blakeney) 1293^{2} 1457^{8} 1927^{2} 2349^{7} 3114^{2} 3471^{2} 4097^{6} 4556^{4} 4789^{4} **>80f<**

Jilvarra **2** b f Desert Splendour-Charlotte Daughter (Brigadier Gerard) 2741^{6} 2935^{9} *3586^{12}* 3782^{7} **>10a 40f<**

Jim And Tonic (FR) **3** g c Double Bed (FR)-Jimka (FR) (Jim French (USA)) (5059a) **>115f<**

Jim Dore (IRE) **2** b br c Mac's Imp (USA)-Secret Assignment (Vitiges (FR)) 447^{4} **>69f<**

Jimjareer (IRE) **4** br g Jareer (USA)-Onthecomet (Chief Singer) **1996:** *5179^{12}* **1997:** 3570^{7} 3886^{8} 4472^{12} 4608^{6} 4768^{5} 5028^{6} **>49a 35f<**

Jimmy The Greek (IRE) **2** b c Tenby-Some Fun (Wolverlife) 1538a^{2} **>95f<**

Jimmy the Skunk (IRE) **6** b g Fayruz-Very Seldom (Rarity) **1996:** *5165^{8}* **1997:** (624a) **>44a 70f<**

Jimmy Too **2** b br c Nomination-Cutlass Princess (USA) (Cutlass (USA)) 1657^{3} (2212) 2685^{3} (3899) 4293^{2} **>98?f<**

Jingoist (IRE) **3** b f Polish Patriot (USA)-Hot Curry (USA) (Sharpen Up) *1151^{14}* 1483^{14} 2407^{8} **>51a 57df<**

Jive Boogie **3** b br g Nomination-Jive Music (Music Boy) 3211^{12} 3335^{6} **>10f<**

Jiyush **4** b c Generous (IRE)-Urjwan (USA) (Seattle Slew (USA)) 891^{7} (1319) 2055^{7} 2819a^{5} (4241) 4559^{4} **>115f<**

Jobie **7** b g Precocious-Lingering (Kind of Hush) *458^{8}* 601^{15} **>5a 55f<**

Job Rage (IRE) **3** b br g Yashgan-Snatchingly (Thatch (USA)) 4587^{6} 4736^{5} *4980^{7}* **>34a 57f<**

Jocasta **2** b f Warning-Breed Reference (Reference Point) 4779^{5} **>76+f<**

Jockweiler (IRE) **2** b c Night Shift (USA)-Johara (USA) (Exclusive Native (USA)) 2324^{8} 2762^{7} 3808^{7} *4054^{11}* **>25a 61f<**

Johan Cruyff **3** b c Danehill (USA)-Teslemi (USA) (Ogygian (USA)) (1896a) 2454a^{4} **>113+f<**

Johayro **4** ch g Clantime-Arroganza (Crofthall) 494^{6} (666) (702) (779) 949^{4} 1223^{7} 1602^{5} 1835^{10} 2111^{5} 2717^{6} 2754^{2} 2934^{8} 3208^{4} 3287^{3} 3406^{2} 3756^{5} 4233^{9} (4414) 4512^{10} 4842^{10} 4927^{2} 4995^{8} **>68a 72f<**

Johnbill (USA) **2** c *5064a^{5}*

John Bowdler Music **2** b c Soviet Star (USA)-Arianna Aldini (Habitat) 1616^{11} **>39f<**

John Emms (IRE) **3** ch c Shalford (IRE)-Miss Lee Ann (Tumble Wind (USA)) 474^{2} 694^{3} 768^{2} 1029^{6} 3385^{3} (3710) 3812^{15} **>83f<**

John Ferneley **2** b c Polar Falcon (USA)-I'll Try (Try My Best (USA)) 1486^{7} **>52f<**

John Lee Hooker **5** b g Superlative-Aunt Jemima (Busted) 1562^{6} 3096^{4} **>56f<**

Johnnie the Joker **6** gr g Absalom-Magic Tower (Tower Walk) **1996:** *5106^{11}* **1997:** *358^{10} 410^{13} 578^{11} 860^{3} 1048^{7} (1291) 1754^{2} (2071) (2302) 2672^{3} 3075^{8} 3584^{3}* 4210^{7} *4572^{6}* **>74a 56f<**

Johnny Staccato **3** b g Statoblest-Frasquita (Song) 1212^{4} 1403^{7} 1855^{3} (1975) 2526^{14} 2861^{10} 3011^{12} 3594^{10} 4430^{3} **>80f<**

John O'Dreams **12** b g Indian King (USA)-Mississipi Shuffle (Steel Heart) 698^{6} 879^{3} 1083^{4} 1279^{12} 1743^{10} 2480^{6} 2759^{11} 3280^{10} 3693^{11} 4221^{13} **>34f<**

Johns Act (USA) **7** b g Late Act (USA)-Deluxe Type (USA) (Singh (USA)) **1996:** *5119^{6} 5270^{12}* **>31a 62f<**

Joint Regent (USA) **2** br c St Jovite (USA)-Ice Fantasy (USA) (It's Freezing (USA)) 4526^{4} 4871^{6} **>77f<**

Joli Fille **2** b f Merdon Melody-Thabeh (Shareef Dancer (USA)) 3070^{7} 3427^{11} 4209^{13} 4638^{11} **>53f<**

Joli Flyers **3** gr c Joli Wasfi (USA)-Hagen's Bargain (Mount Hagen (FR)) 4322^{7} 4883^{10} **>53f<**

Joli's Prince **3** b g Superlative-Joli's Girl (Mansingh (USA)) 693^{11} 1012^{11} 1238^{9} 4243^{15} **>48f<**

Joli's Son **4** gr c Joli Wasfi (USA)-Hagen's Bargain (Mount Hagen (FR)) 1105^{7} 1477^{15} 2180^{4} 3434^{9} **>54f<**

Jollyhack **2** b c Mon Tresor-Spiritofaffection (Raga Navarro (ITY)) 3783^{8} 4113^{6} 4638^{10} **>61f<**

Jolly Harbour **2** b f Rudimentary (USA)-Ask Mama (Mummy's Pet) 4227^{8} 4904^{18} **>48f<**

Jolly Jackson **3** br c Primo Dominie-Pounelta (Tachypous) **1996:** *5248^{4}* **1997:** *60^{2} 161^{5} 341^{2}* 840^{15} 1423^{13} 1633^{8} 1826^{5} 2245^{2} 2645^{8} 3056^{7} 3470^{18} *4300^{3}* 4817^{11} **>68a 53f<**

Jo Maximus **5** b g Prince Sabo-Final Call (Town Crier) **1996:** *5211^{6} 5246^{9}* **1997:** *27^{3} 121^{11} 201^{6}* 638^{3} 1009^{17} 1761^{5} 2006^{11} **>66a 67f<**

Jo Mell **4** b g Efisio-Militia Girl (Rarity) 443^{10} 529^{8} 835^{8} 1583^{8} 1977^{19} (2325) (2478) (2678) 3725^{7} 4148^{6} (4423) (4888) **>110f<**

Jona Holley **4** b g Sharpo-Spurned (USA) (Robellino (USA)) 1005^{14} 1292^{5} 1473^{4} *2071^{2}* 2310^{2} (2399) 3200^{2} 3793^{9} 3992^{4} *(4813)* **>58a 59f<**

Jonas Nightengale **2** b g Deploy-Springs Welcome (Blakeney) 3295^{3} 3789^{5} 4132^{6} 4334^{6} 4806^{8} **>74f<**

Jonathan's Girl **2** b f Thowra (FR)-Sicilian Vespers (Mummy's Game) 1847^{8} *2163^{4}* 2388^{10} 4515^{20} **>36a 17f<**

Jonny's Joker **3** b g Precocious-Mardessa (Ardross) 3030^{7} 3313^{5} 3697^{6} **>50f<**

Jorrocks (USA) **3** b g Rubiano (USA)-Perla Fina (USA) (Gallant Man) 1876^{2} 2172^{3} 2704^{2} (2951) (3189) 3772^{6} (4276) 4463^{4} **>100f<**

Joseph's Wine (IRE) **8** b g Smile (USA)-Femme Gendarme (USA) (Policeman (FR)) **1996:** *5129^{8}* **1997:** *(14) 39^{7} 176^{5} (213) 273^{7}* **>86+a 76f<**

Joust **3** b g Keen-Tudorealm (USA) (Palace Music (USA)) 2960^{5} 3720^{6} 4072^{7} **>66f<**

Jovian **3** gr f Petong-What A Pet (Mummy's Pet) 3820^{4} **>51f<**

Jovie King (IRE) **5** ch g Salt Dome (USA)-Jovial Josie (USA) (Sea Bird II) **1996:** *5099^{10}* **>43a 39f<**

Jovine (USA) **2** ch f St Jovite (USA)-Big E Dream (USA) 3839a^{11} **>78f<**

Joyful Joy **3** b f River God (USA)-Joyfulness (FR) (Cure The Blues (USA)) **1996:** *5239^{8}* **1997:** *38^{6} 181^{11} 259^{8}* 644^{7} 785^{7} 1272^{11} 1661^{7} 2171^{7} 2523^{9} 2756^{4} 3038^{10} 3572^{6} 4586^{14} *4795^{10}* 4916^{15} **>22a 38f<**

Joyrider **6** b g Risk Me (FR)-Villajoyosa (FR) (Satingo) *68^{10}* **>6a 31f<**

Juba **5** b m Dowsing (USA)-Try the Duchess (Try My Best (USA)) **1996:** *5112^{3} 5165^{10} 5174^{5} 5258^{8}* **1997:** *4^{10}* **>35a 45?f<**

Jubilee Scholar (IRE) **4** b g Royal Academy (USA)-Jaljuli (Jalmood (USA)) **1996:** *5221^{10}* **1997:** *28^{9} 61^{12} 109^{10} 424^{4} 512^{5} 579^{14}* 2723^{7} 2748^{4} 2954^{10} 3276^{12} 3561^{7} 4373^{12} 4465^{8} 4858^{2} 4987^{6} **>49a 50f<**

Jubran (USA) **11** b g Vaguely Noble-La Vue (USA) (Reviewer (USA)) 846^{5} 1281^{5} 1992^{7} 2293^{6} 2503^{6} 3758^{11} **>45f<**

Jucea **8** b m Bluebird (USA)-Appleby Park (Bay Express) 3326^{7} 3500^{13} 3898^{12} 4385^{2} 4512^{7} 4580^{5} 4805^{11} **>62f<**

Jucinda **3** gr f Midyan (USA)-Catch The Sun (Kalaglow) 665^{5} 1094^{2} 1387^{2} 1853^{5} 2189^{7} 3028^{5} 3567^{7} *3865^{13}* **>59f<**

Juddy **3** ch c Clantime-Two's Up (Double Jump) 758^{2} 1394^{7} 2755^{9} **>54df<**

Jude **3** b f Darshaan-Alruccaba (Crystal Palace (FR)) 1168^{8} 1420^{4} 1922^{5} 4046^{12} **>63f<**

Judge Advocate (IRE) **5** b g Contract Law (USA)-Brigadina (Brigadier Gerard) 4584^{18} 4847^{P} **>1f<**

Judicial Supremacy **3** b c Warning-Song Test (USA) (The Minstrel (CAN)) 674^{7} 963^{6} 1320^{4} 2296^{6} **>82f<**

Juggler **3** b g Soviet Star (USA)-Wily Trick (USA) (Clever Trick (USA)) *1155^{3}* 1637^{4} 2537^{7} 3274^{6} 4886^{9} **>63a 67f<**

Juggler (AUS) **5** br g Jugah (AUS)-Kashalyn (AUS) (Shy Rambler (USA)) 437a^{3} *628a^{6}* **>117a 117f<**

Juicy Ting **3** ch g Hatim (USA)-Floating Note (Music Boy) 1998^{11} 2544^{11} 2937^{15} *3611^{4}* **>46a 34f<**

Jukebox Jive 3 ch f Scottish Reel-My Sweet Melody (Music Boy) 474[7] 602[4] 751[5] *873[8]* 1484[5] 2125[2] (2332) 2564[8] **>16a 64f<**
Julia's Relative 3 b f Distant Relative-Alkion (Fordham (USA)) *135[3] 265[3] 317[2] 378[6] 399[2] 546[2] (577) 873[10] 2070[14] 4049[8]* **>47da 47f<**
Julies Jewel (IRE) 2 ch g Simply Great (FR)-Melungeon (Ardoon) 1174[9] 2037[14] 3117[14] 3717[9] 3905[6] 4459[2] 4807[7] **>64f<**
Julietta Mia (USA) 3 ch f Woodman (USA)-Just Juliet (USA) (What A Pleasure (USA)) 1845[9] 2832[11] 3381[5] **>61f<**
Jump The Lights 4 b g Siberian Express (USA)-Turtle Dove (Gyr (USA)) 481[10] 762[9] *908[3] 1133[10]* 1445[15] *2301[3]* **>57a 56f<**
Junction City (USA) 3 b c Forty Niner (USA)-Key Witness (USA) (Key To The Mint (USA)) 1936[8] **>38f<**
Junction Twentytwo 7 ch g Local Suitor (USA)-Pollinella (Charlottown) 2518[10]
June Bounty (USA) 2 b f Red Ransom (USA)-June Bride (USA) (Riverman (USA)) 4973[15] **>39f<**
Jungle Fresh 4 b g Rambo Dancer (CAN)-Report 'em (USA) (Staff Writer (USA)) 848[14] 1118[8] 1383[15] 1817[4] **>42f<**
Jungle Story (IRE) 2 b f Alzao (USA)-Jungle Jezebel (Thatching) 2728[6] 3099[4] 3711[5] 4143[2] (4427) **>74f<**
Junie (IRE) 3 ch f Astronef-Numidia (Sallust) 474[8] 642[6] 1500[11] **>60f<**
Junikay (IRE) 3 b g Treasure Kay-Junijo (Junius (USA)) 807a[7] 3548[13] 3798[11] 4176[12] 4568[3] 4699[5] 4821[6] **>67f<**
Junior Ben (IRE) 5 b g Tirol-Piney Pass (Persian Bold) 1222[2] 1393[5] 1654[6] 2154[9] 2362[2] 3540[6] 3762[5] 4847[16] **>36f<**
Junior Muffin (IRE) 2 b c Paris House-Clodianus (Bay Express) 1228[5] 2127[5] 2823[7] (3324) (3804) 4178[3] 4362[11] *4796[10]* **>49a 77f<**
Jupiter (IRE) 3 b g Astronef-Native Flower (Tumble Wind (USA)) 532[5] 649[4] 1000[6] 1972[15] 3024[9] 3548[14] 3968[12] **>65a 52f<**
Jus'chillin' (IRE) 2 b f Elbio-Not Mistaken (USA) (Mill Reef (USA)) 1854[2] *2363[6]* 2771[7] 3387[7] 3847[2] 4855[5] **>27a 63f<**
Just Alex (IRE) 3 b c River Falls-Picnic Basket (Pharly (FR)) 3014[5] 3419[5] **>80f<**
Just Another Time 2 ch c Mazilier (USA)-Entourage (Posse (USA)) 1616[3] *2047[4]* 2684[6] 3314[2] 3859[2] 4006[7] 4401[2] 4468[6] **>67a 67f<**
Just A Stroll 2 ch g Clantime-Willow Walk (Farm Walk) 2276[2] *3076[8]* 3312[11] **>44?f<**
Just Blink (IRE) 4 b f Fairy King (USA)-Cooliney Princess (Bruni) 2496[10] 3420[11] **>1f<**
Just Bob 8 b g Alleging (USA)-Diami (Swing Easy (USA)) 744[19] 949[16] 1227[2] 1311[3] 1561[3] 1835[7] 1977[7] 2504[4] 2717[9] 3107[4] 3334[10] 3406[8] 3642[10] (4137) (4233) 4414[12] (4512) 4636[9] 4770[10] 4805[8] 4997[4] 5047[9] **>56a 73f<**
Just Deserts 2 b f Alhijaz-What A Pet (Mummy's Pet) 4904[19] **>43f<**
Just Dickens 3 b f Robellino (USA)-Lucy Manette (Final Straw) 2555[11] 2960[10] 3140[7] **>43f<**
Just Dissident (IRE) 5 b g Dancing Dissident (USA)-Betty Bun (St Chad) 1584[10] 1734[5] 2001[8] 2738[7] (2844) 3130[6] 3334[9] 3481[10] 3625[7] 3856[6] 4048[18] 4183[9] 4385[10] 4512[17] **>58f<**
Just Flamenco 6 ch g Scorpio (FR)-Suzannah's Song (Song) *333[9]* 1142[10] 1809[16] **>33a 46f<**
Justfortherecord 5 br m Forzando-Classical Vintage (Stradavinsky) *35[7] 2301[2]* **>28?a 42?f<**
Just For Tina 2 b f Presidium-Mushy Boff (Tina's Pet) 2003[11] **>10f<**
Just Grand (IRE) 3 b c Green Desert (USA)-Aljood (Kris) 446[7] 1256[3] 2005[4] (2236) 2647[5] **>86f<**
Just Harry 6 ch h High Kicker (USA)-Dorame (Music Boy) **1996:** *5106[2] 5137[3]* **>81da 58f<**
Justin Hope 2 b g Prince Sabo-Affirmation (Tina's Pet) 3314[6] 3707[19] **>49f<**
Justinianus (IRE) 5 ch h Try My Best (USA)-Justitia (Dunbeath (USA)) **1996:** *5095[8] 5236[10] 5254[9]* **1997:** *128[4] 184[4] (303) 319[5] 404[3] 459[8]* 638[2] 756[3] 1009[2] 1374[3] 1509[6] 1849[4] 2115[2] 2220[3] 2393[5] 2852[5] 3082[3] 3280[11] 3436[5] 3852[4] 4221[16] 4451[7] **>50a 64tf<**
Just In Time 2 b c Night Shift (USA)-Future Past (USA) (Super Concorde (USA)) 3193[2] **>80f<**
Just Lead (FR) 6 b h Lead on Time (USA)-Just A Beauty (FR) (Kenmare (FR)) 3181a[2] **>103f<**
Just Loui 3 gr g Lugana Beach-Absaloui (Absalom) **1996:** *(5092) 5146[2] (5229) (5278)* **1997:** *(62) 180[4]* 1107[4] *1578[9]* 1957[4] 1989[5] *2319[2] 2663[5]* 3189[6] 3604[21] 3765[11] 4071[18] *4570[5]* 4738[10] **>71a 65f<**
Just Nick 3 b c Nicholas (USA)-Just Never Know (USA) (Riverman (USA)) 675[2] 930[3] 1170[2] 1305[3] 2013[5] 3189[14] 3594[4] 3894[2] 4423[9] **>89f<**
Just Nobby 2 b g Totem (USA)-Loving Doll (Godswalk (USA)) 631[7] 993[11] 2383[7] 3973[13] 4470[4] **>41f<**
Just Rachel 3 ch f Primitive Rising (USA)-Glendyne (Precipice Wood) **1996:** *5228[11]* **1997:** *49[9] 228[5]* **>6a f<**
Just Sidium 3 b f Nicholas (USA)-Frimley Dancer (Northern Tempest (USA)) 1921[9] *2300[3]* **>44a 7f<**
Just Testing 2 br f Sharpo-Antoinette Jane (Ile de Bourbon (USA)) 3905[5] *4479[4]* 4801[6] **>39a 60f<**
Just Typical 3 ch f Timeless Times (USA)-Mayor (Laxton) 1119[12] 1401[7] *1757[7]* **>36f<**
Just Visiting 3 b f Superlative-Just Julia (Natroun (FR)) 2517[8] 2900[12] 3273[13] 3812[8] 4410[11] **>60a 67f<**
Just Whistle 5 gr m Absalom-Aunt Blue (Blue Refrain) 1838[4] **>11a 55f<**
Juvenilia (IRE) 3 ch f Masterclass (USA)-Amtico (Bairn (USA)) 1485[3] 1690[3] **>61f<**
Juwwi 3 ch c Mujtahid (USA)-Nouvelle Star (AUS) (Luskin Star (AUS)) 679[10] 3118[4] **>104df<**

K

Kabcast 12 b g Kabour-Final Cast (Saulingo) 2934[5] 3271[7] 3756[7] 3871[3] 3922[14] 4370[19] **>13a 41f<**
Kaberlaba (ITY) 3 b f Sikeston (USA)-Odette de Crecy (ITY) 1367a[3] 2461a[3] **>91f<**
Kadastrof (FR) 7 ch h Port Etienne (FR)-Kadastra (FR) (Stradavinsky) 1260[9] 4744[10] **>54?f<**
Kadeena 3 b f Never so Bold-Alencon (Northfields (USA)) 1670[6] **>75f<**
Kadir 2 b br c Unfuwain (USA)-Rafif (USA) (Riverman (USA)) 4952[6] **>68f<**
Kafaf (USA) 3 b br f Zilzal (USA)-Alqwani (USA) (Mr Prospector (USA)) 575[W] 2773[2] (3244) 3741[9] **>84++f<**
Kafil (USA) 3 b br c Housebuster (USA)-Alchaasibiyeh (USA) (Seattle Slew (USA)) 1207[7] 1813[4] 2492[3] 3496[12] 3894[14] 4505[2] *4906[2]* **>73a 78f<**
Kagsi 2 br f King's Signet (USA)-Azaiyma (Corvaro (USA)) *1136[10]* 1593[11] **>4a f<**
Kahal 3 b c Machiavellian (USA)-Just a Mirage (Green Desert (USA)) 2023[2] 2679[4] 3554a[4] (4142) (4782) **>120f<**
Kahir Almaydan (IRE) 4 b c Distinctly North (USA)-Kilfenora (Tribal Chief) 308a[6] **>116f<**
Kahtan 2 b c Nashwan (USA)-Harmless Albatross (Pas de Seul) 4132[4] (4507) **>94+f<**
Kailey Goddess (USA) 4 b c Nureyev (USA)-Gay Senorita (USA) (Raise A Native) 2172[8] 2566[13] 2704[4] 3138[11] **>61f<**
Kailey Senor (USA) 4 ch c Woodman (USA)-Sex Appeal (USA) (Buckpasser) 849[4] 1108[4] 1597[4] 1972[7] 2187[7] 2485[3] 4854[5] **>59a 76f<**
Kaiser Kache (IRE) 3 b c Treasure Kay-Poka Poka (FR) (King Of Macedon) **1996:** *5100[3]* **1997:** 509[5] 575[2] 930[4] 1175[18] (1589) 1935[10] 2013[24] 2894[9] **>81a 89df<**
Kaitak (IRE) 6 ch g Broken Hearted-Klairelle (Klairon) 746[6] **>46a 79f<**
Kaizen (FR) 3 b c Saumarez-Karannja (USA) (Shahrastani (USA)) 4389a[3] **>108f<**
Kajostar 7 ch m Country Classic-Rasimareem (Golden Mallard) **1996:** *5138[8] 5211[11]* **1997:** *3[6] 71[7] 113[10]* **>30a 25f<**
Kalabo (USA) 5 b h Trempolino (USA)-Kalikala (Darshaan) *627a[8]* **>97a 117f<**
Kalakate 12 gr g Kalaglow-Old Kate (Busted) *262[7]* **>7a 33f<**
Kalamata 5 ch h Kalaglow-Good Try (Good Bond) **1996:** *5270[9]* **1997:** *196[4] (242) 360[5]* 430[20] *(543) 660[3]* 888[11] *(1133) (1288) (1940)* 2154[8] **>85+a 46f<**
Kalar 8 b g Kabour-Wind And Reign (Tumble Wind (USA)) **1996:** *(5096) 5131[16] 5184[2] 5225[4] (5258)* **1997:** *51[2] 126[2] (178) (198) 394[4]* 464[2] 527[7] 702[5] *856[5] 903[6]* 1269[4] 1627[15] 2061[6] 2540[17] 2934[15] 3240[15] *4051[5]* 4370[18] **>58a 22f<**
Kala Sunrise 4 ch c Kalaglow-Belle of the Dawn (Bellypha) 450[5] 738[17] 1097[3] 1300[2] 2026[29] 2338[2] 2679[6] 3063[7] 3408[5] 4147[3] 4637[4] 4781[14] 4990[2] **>98f<**
Kalatos (GER) 5 ch h Big Shuffle (USA)-Kardia (GER) (Mister Rock's (GER)) (2272a) 2821a[4] 3369a[2] 4396a[9] 4650a[2] 4762a[7] **>117f<**
Kaldoun Choice (FR) 3 3179a[4] **>94f<**
Kaldou Star 3 ch c Kaldoun (FR)-Loisaida (FR) (Sicyos (USA)) (1358a) (1915a) 3002a[6] 4662a[2] 4864a[8] **>116f<**
Kaliana (IRE) 3 b f Slip Anchor-Kadissya (USA) (Blushing Groom (FR)) (2379) 2869[2] (3727) 4256a[5] (4894) **>120+f<**
Kalimat 3 b f Be My Guest (USA)-Kantado (Saulingo) 641[3] 976[6] *2602[2] 2912[2]* 3591[4] 3855[2] 4008[4] 4455[5] **>69a 68f<**
Kalimisik (FR) 3 gr c Linamix (FR)-Karmisyn (Baldric II (FR)) 1205a[3] **>106f<**
Kalinini (USA) 3 ch c Seattle Dancer (USA)-Kaiserfahrt (GER) (Frontal) 533[11] 1427[9] 2408[4] **>76f<**
Kalinka (IRE) 3 b f Soviet Star (USA)-Tralthee (USA) (Tromos) 853[4] 1175[4] 2133[4] 3128[4] 3803[6] 4242[9] **>91f<**
Kalisz (IRE) 3 b f Polish Precedent (USA)-Housefull (Habitat) 1558[6] **>20?f<**
Kalmoojid 3 b g Almoojid-Skerryvore (Kalaglow) 2731[16] 2941[13] 3230[8] 4326[W] **>15f<**
Kalosca (FR) 3 f b Kaldoun (FR)-Shangrila (FR) (Riverman (USA)) 5056a[3] **>116f<**
Kalousion 3 b g K-Battery-Louise Moulton (Moulton) 1582[6] 1820[15] 2226[9] 2503[10] 3038[6] 3488[8] **>21f<**
Kamanev (IRE) 3 b c Soviet Star (USA)-Konigsrose (GER) (Cortez (GER)) 2731[3] 2952[2] (3404) 3891[7] **>90f<**
Kameez (IRE) 2 ch f Arazi (USA)-Kalikala (Darshaan) 4841[5] 5025[3] **>68f<**
Kamin (USA) 3 b c Red Ransom (USA)-Sweet Rhapsody (USA) (Sea Bird II) 3140[3] 3772[4] 4176[5] 4449[6] 4635[3] 4854[2] **>81f<**

Kammtarra (USA) **4** ch c Zilzal (USA)-Snow Bride (USA) (Blushing Groom (FR)) *(309a) (438a) 628a*^{8} 1767^{6} **>113a 111f<**

Kanat Lee (IRE) **6** b m Salse (USA)-Badiya (USA) (Sir Ivor) **1996:** *5110*^{14} **>43f<**

Kanawa **3** b f Beveled (USA)-Kiri Te (Liboi (USA)) 1110^{7} 1485^{6} 1826^{15} *2368*^{16} 2747^{9} 3083^{10} 3327^{8} **>28f<**

Kantone (IRE) **2** ch c Petardia-Green Life (Green Desert (USA)) 884^{9} 3084^{6} 3433^{5} 4566^{6} 4819^{11} **>43f<**

Kapatchi (FR) **6** b g River Mist (USA)-Montagne d'Or (FR) (Hauban) 1547a^{2} **>99f<**

Karachi **7** b g Nishapour (FR)-Lady Dacre (Queen's Hussar) 3229^{6} 3640^{9} 4373^{22} **>51a 46f<**

Karakia (IRE) **3** b f Sadler's Wells (USA)-Kissagram (USA) (Alysheba (USA)) 2173^{2} 2555^{3} 3095^{2} (3439) 4731^{9} **>79f<**

Karakorum (IRE) **2** b f Fairy King (USA)-Sable Lake (Thatching) 4093a^{9} (4616a) **>99f<**

Kara-Lovo **2** ch f Rock City-Lariston Gale (Pas de Seul) 1253^{9} 1466^{10} **>24f<**

Kara Queen **3** ch f Silver Kite (USA)-Darakah (Doulab (USA)) 1110^{14} 1437^{6} **>28f<**

Karatisa (IRE) **3** bg f Nishapour (FR)-Kathouda 2447a^{10} **>93f<**

Karawan **3** ch f Kris-Sweetly (FR) (Lyphard (USA)) (2020) 3207^{2} **>85f<**

Karaylar (IRE) **5** b g Kahyasi-Karamana (Habitat) 2413^{7} 3283^{10} 3826^{6} **>35f<**

Karenaragon **2** b f Aragon-Rosy Sunset (IRE) (Red Sunset) 993^{15} *1290*^{3} *1789*^{4} *2304*^{4} *2606*^{9} **>34a f<**

Karinska **7** b m Master Willie-Kaiserchronik (GER) (Cortez (GER)) *327*^{6} *358*^{8} 947^{10} 2036^{7} 2408^{5} (2427) 2922^{5} 3039^{4} (3101) 3448^{2} 3721^{3} 3906^{5} 3976^{8} 4181^{8} 4228^{16} (4455) **>55a 69f<**

Karisma (IRE) **4** b g Tirol-Avra (FR) (Mendez (FR)) 470^{11} 613^{2} 721^{7} 1039^{4} 3992^{7} 4161^{8} 4438^{6} 4585^{2} 4804^{9} **>51f<**

Kariver (FR) **6** b g River Mist (USA)-The Equal Skies (USA) (Sir Gaylord) 310a^{3} **>108f<**

Karla Wyller (ITY) **4** ch f Salse (USA)-Calder Hall (Grundy) (1919a) 4867a^{2} **>106f<**

Kart Star (IRE) **3** b f Soviet Star (USA)-Karmiska (FR) (Bikala) 4388a^{2} **>108f<**

Kashan (IRE) **9** b g Darshaan-Kamanika (FR) (Amber Rama (USA)) 481^{6} 1114^{7} **>36f<**

Kashwan (SPA) **3** b c Unfuwain (USA)-Kalawelsh (FR) (Kalaglow) 819a^{3} 1726a^{8} 2996a^{3} **>106f<**

Kass Alhawa **4** b g Shirley Heights-Silver Braid (USA) (Miswaki (USA)) *150*^{8} 467^{9} 668^{3} *1291*^{4} 1603^{4} 1800^{3} (2152) 2237^{10} 2543^{2} 2760^{7} (3285) 3630^{4} 3759^{9} 4628^{2} 4773^{4} 4988^{2} 5023^{4} **>30a 68f<**

Kassana (IRE) **3** ch f Shernazar-Kassiyda (Mill Reef (USA)) 1722a^{2} 2275a^{3} (3000a) 3370a^{4} 4655a^{3} **>115f<**

Kassbaan (USA) **7** b g Alydar (USA)-Ma Biche (USA) (Key to the Kingdom (USA)) (308a) *309a*^{2} **>104a 105f<**

Katah **2** ch f Arazi (USA)-Kadwah (USA) (Mr Prospector (USA)) 1486^{5} 1970^{3} 3636^{7} 4427^{2} 4900^{5} **>72f<**

Katatonic (IRE) **4** b c Waajib-Miss Kate (FR) (Nonoalco (USA)) **1996:** *5182*^{5} *5273*^{3} **>47a f<**

Kate Lane (IRE) **2** b f Petardia-Splendid Yankee (Yankee Gold) 1821^{7} 2699^{5} 2943^{11} 3961a^{12} **>79f<**

Katherine **3** ch f Chilibang-Kaasiha (Kings Lake (USA)) **1996:** *5135*^{10} **1997:** *239*^{5} **>23a f<**

Kathies Pet **2** b f Tina's Pet-Unveiled (Sayf El Arab (USA)) 1954^{7} 3324^{2} 3636^{8} 3965^{7} 4566^{11} 4819^{2} **>62f<**

Kathryn's Pet **4** b f Blakeney-Starky's Pet (Mummy's Pet) (495) 689^{4} 1042^{2} 1281^{2} 1562^{3} (2210) 2421^{4} 4466^{8} 4802^{17} 4971^{14} **>70f<**

Katie Komaite **4** b f Komaite (USA)-City to City (Windjammer (USA)) *423*^{9} 848^{W} 2226^{2} 2488^{10} 2887^{4} 3488^{2} 3759^{5} 4164^{4} 4471^{2} (4628) 4695^{2} 4845^{8} 4918^{6} 4992^{4} **>28?a 56f<**

Katie's Cracker **2** b f Rambo Dancer (CAN)-Tea-Pot (Ragstone) 1440^{9} *1758*^{2} 1815^{W} 2493^{5} *3045*^{2} 3563^{3} 3751^{2} 3967^{13} **>52a 55f<**

Katie's Kid **7** br g Balidar-Khahmens Delight (Come On Grey) 3432^{5} **>15a 44f<**

Katies Treat (IRE) **2** ch f Superpower-Fancied (Dominion) 750^{8} *2066*^{12} 2425^{9} 3384^{5} 4065^{11} 4458^{7} *4593*^{9} **>23a 39f<**

Katun (FR) **4** c 3734a^{2} **>95f<**

Katy's Lad **10** b g Camden Town-Cathryn's Song (Prince Tenderfoot (USA)) **1996:** *5260*^{11} **>40a 77f<**

Katy Thomas **2** b f Puissance-Indian Summer (Young Generation) (948) 2042^{4} 2314^{6} 4284^{13} **>55f<**

Katyushka (IRE) **2** b f Soviet Star (USA)-Welsh Note (USA) (Sharpen Up) 2553^{7} 3278^{13} 4042^{4} 4403^{7} **>74f<**

Kawafil (IRE) **2** b f Warning-Nur (USA) (Diesis) 1847^{4} (2227) 2558^{12} 3474^{4} 4044^{3} 4364^{4} 4709^{7} **>95f<**

Kawa-Ib (IRE) **3** b f Nashwan (USA)-Awayed (USA) (Sir Ivor) 1591^{3} 1823^{3} 3715^{2} 4175^{10} 4408^{2} 4848^{9} **>77df<**

Kayesam **3** b br g Failiq (FR)-Another-Kaye (Jimmy The Singer) 3720^{8} 4060^{18} **>21f<**

Kaye's Secret **4** b f Failiq (FR)-Another-Kaye (Jimmy The Singer) *86*^{9} **>13a 8f<**

Kayfiyah (IRE) **3** b br f Marju (IRE)-Princess Sucree (USA) (Roberto (USA)) 1130^{7} 1497^{3} 2046^{3} 2410^{5} 2885^{3} 3457^{5} **>69f<**

Kayf Tara **3** b c Sadler's Wells (USA)-Colorspin (FR) (High Top) 2731^{2} (3014) **>97+f<**

Kay-Jay **3** b f Be My Chief (USA)-Greenhil Jazz Time (Music Boy) 485^{8} **>8f<**

Kaymadi (FR) **6** b/ h Lashkari-Kaysama (FR) (Kenmare (FR)) 4649a^{3} **>72f<**

Kayo **2** b c Superpower-Shiny Kay (Star Appeal) 3060^{4} 3306^{14} *4052*^{4} (4163) *4589*^{10} (4690) 4806^{15} **>57a 71f<**

Kayvee **8** gr g Kaldoun (FR)-Secret Life (USA) (Elocutionist (USA)) 892^{15} 1456^{14} 2026^{15} 2525^{8} 3052^{6} 3185^{8} 3435^{3} 3594^{3} 3798^{7} 4423^{2} 4550^{10} 4978^{7} 4990^{3} **>98f<**

Kayzee (IRE) **3** b f River Falls-Northern Amber (Shack (USA)) *185*^{3} *307*^{7} 1965^{16} *3611*^{3} *4069*^{14} *4484*^{13} **>49da 38f<**

Kazimiera (IRE) **4** b f Polish Patriot (USA)-Cartier Bijoux (Ahonoora) **1996:** *5117*^{3} *5165*^{11} **>65a 73f<**

Kaziranga (USA) **3** b f Lear Fan (USA)-Kazoo (Shareef Dancer (USA)) 681^{5} 935^{4} 1777^{2} 2832^{9} 3906^{6} **>70f<**

Kedwick (IRE) **8** b g Be My Guest (USA)-Lady Pavlova (Ballymore) **1996:** *5081*^{8} *5152*^{5} *(5242)* *5274*^{7} **1997:** *10*^{8} (476) 657^{10} 2118^{5} 3153^{12} **>55a 64f<**

Keen Alert **3** b g Keen-Miss Coco (Swing Easy (USA)) 768^{8} *(868)* 1238^{12} 2004^{17} **>65a 51f<**

Keen Companion **4** b f Keen-Constant Companion (Pas de Seul) **1996:** *5101*^{3} **1997:** 1088^{10} 1297^{3} *1757*^{8} 2246^{10} *3054*^{6} **>58a 61f<**

Keen Dancer **3** ch g Keen-Royal Shoe (Hotfoot) 784^{7} 1272^{4} 1624^{9} *1939*^{4} 2374^{5} **>46a 70f<**

Keenest Reluctance **3** gr f Environment Friend-Baharlilys (Green Dancer (USA)) 676^{18} 1011^{11} **>38f<**

Keen Lady **2** b f Keen-Bizarre Lady (Dalsaan) *1432*^{5} *3045*^{7} 3450^{12} 3692^{5} 3808^{9} 3967^{14} **>20a 48f<**

Keen To Please **3** ch f Keen-Tasseled (USA) (Tate Gallery (USA)) 466^{8} 779^{4} 1127^{15} 1995^{7} 2354^{7} 4770^{18} **>37f<**

Keen Waters **3** b f Keen-Miss Oasis (Green Desert (USA)) 473^{11} 649^{16} 1245^{10} 1484^{4} 1966^{7} 2750^{3} 2956^{7} 3081^{2} (3560) *3865*^{4} 4170^{4} 4609^{7} *4912*^{6} **>44a 48f<**

Keep Battling **7** b g Hard Fought-Keep Mum (Mummy's Pet) 898^{5} 1268^{13} 1313^{4} 1559^{4} 1992^{5} 2293^{7} 2686^{2} 3061^{2} 3380^{5} 3605^{6} 4510^{7} 4751^{10} 4998^{10} **>51f<**

Keep Playing (FR) **3** ch c Highest Honor (FR)-Playing for Keeps (FR) (Royal Match) 3729a^{3} 5032a^{2} **>113f<**

Keepsake (IRE) **3** b f Distinctly North (USA)-Souveniers (Relko) 840^{10} 1164^{9} 1449^{6} 1938^{2} 2182^{4} 2725^{5} 3028^{3} 3234^{2} (3495) 3781^{4} 4222^{4} 4323^{12} 4633^{5} 4971^{11} **>60f<**

Kelang **2** Kris-Ebbing Tide (USA) (His Majesty (USA)) 5036a^{7}

Kellaire Girl (IRE) **5** b m Gallic League-Frensham Manor (Le Johnstan) **1996:** *5093*^{11} **>55a 46f<**

Kemo Sabo **5** b g Prince Sabo-Canoodle (Warpath) 823^{3} 997^{2} 1077^{4} **>78df<**

Kenilworth Dancer **4** br g Shareef Dancer (USA)-Reltop (High Top) *4810*^{9} **>5a 46f<**

Kenkan (IRE) **2** b f Kenmare (FR)-Farewell Song (USA) (The Minstrel (CAN)) 2227^{3} 2831^{10} 4067^{15} **>74f<**

Kenmist **3** gr f Kenmare (FR)-Mistral's Collette (Simply Great (FR)) (2461a) 2774^{3} 3214^{3} 3492^{5} (4424) 4867a^{3} **>110f<**

Kennemara Star (IRE) **3** ch g Kenmare (FR)-Dawn Star (High Line) (840) 1175^{15} 2013^{28} 2557^{2} (3937) 4283^{10} **>96f<**

Kennet **2** b g Kylian (USA)-Marwell Mitzi (Interrex (CAN)) 722^{2} 836^{6} 1480^{U} 1872^{8} *3042*^{2} 3237^{4} 3597^{8} 4315^{2} *4589*^{6} 4897^{7} *4982*^{5} **>63a 74f<**

Kentavrus Way (IRE) **6** b g Thatching-Phantom Row (Adonijah) *76*^{13} **>50a 55f<**

Kentucky Dreams **7** b g Dreams to Reality (USA)-Kentucky Tears (USA) (Cougar (CHI)) 3565^{12} 3856^{16} **>23f<**

Kentucky Fall (FR) **4** b f Lead on Time (USA)-Autumn Tint (USA) (Roberto (USA)) 1262^{14} 1640^{2} 2119^{5} 2918^{4} (3716) 3930^{4} 4071^{7} 4321^{4} 4820^{7} **>79f<**

Keos (USA) **3** dk c Riverman (USA)-Konafa (USA) (Damascus (USA)) 4393a^{3} 4864a^{4} **>117f<**

Kepster (USA) **3** b c Royal Academy (USA)-Zarissa (USA) (Lyphard (USA)) 2457a^{2} **>97f<**

Kernof (IRE) **4** b g Rambo Dancer (CAN)-Empress Wu (High Line) 866^{10} 1393^{4} 1779^{19} (2170) 2824^{2} (3108) 3485^{6} **>66f<**

Keroub (FR) **3** 629a^{4} 1913a^{3} **>106f<**

Keston Pond (IRE) **7** b g Taufan (USA)-Maria Renata (Jaazeiro (USA)) 468^{18} 529^{10} 776^{9} 974^{9} 1761^{8} *2069*^{8} 3087^{6} 3443^{7} 3702^{5} **>60a 50f<**

Kettlesing (IRE) **2** b f Mujadil (USA)-Icefern (Moorestyle) 979^{5} 2467^{5} 3070^{9} 3331^{8} 3804^{4} (4230) (4566) 4702^{2} 4922^{16} **>74f<**

Kevasingo **5** b g Superpower-Katharina (Frankincense) 587^{14} **>55a 57f<**

Kewarra **3** b g Distant Relative-Shalati (FR) (High Line) 483^{7} 1166^{8} 1436^{2} 1663^{3} 2309^{5} 2645^{3} 3012^{3} (3246) 3616^{9} (4109) (4552) 4882^{10} 5053^{20} **>90+f<**

Keyboogie (USA) **3** b f Lyphard (USA)-Key Dancer (USA) (Nijinsky (CAN)) 727^{7} 1318^{3} (1784) 2446a^{4} 3499^{4} 4712^{2} **>101f<**

Key Change (IRE) **4** b f Darshaan-Kashka (USA)

(The Minstrel (CAN)) 1363a^{5} **>118f<**

Key of Luck (USA) 6 b or br h Chief's Crown (USA)-Balbonella (FR) (Gay Mecene (USA)) *409a^{3} 628a^{4}* **>131a 107f<**

Keyser Soze 2 b g Petong-Lamees (USA) (Lomond (USA)) 564^{7} **>12f<**

Key To 3 b f Interrex (CAN)-Key to Enchantment (Key To Content (USA)) 3695^{6} 3929^{W} 4923^{15} **>29f<**

Key to My Heart (IRE) 7 b h Broken Hearted-Originality (Godswalk (USA)) **1996:** *5204^{12}* **1997:** 761^{3} 1172^{6} 1960^{4} 2710^{15} 3409^{5} 3902^{8} 4134^{5} 5053^{15} **>70a 105f<**

Khabar 4 b g Forzando-Ella Mon Amour (Ela-Mana-Mou) 574^{19} 2399^{14} **>49df<**

Khafaaq 3 b c Green Desert (USA)-Ghanimah (Caerleon (USA)) 742^{10} 991^{5} 1320^{3} 1851^{2} 2420^{2} (3418) 3801^{3} 4121^{6} (4375) **>91f<**

Khairabar (IRE) 3 gr c Shernazar-Khairkana 4837a^{4} **>103f<**

Khairun Nisaa 3 b f Never so Bold-Sea Clover (IRE) (Ela-Mana-Mou) **1996:** *5142^{10} 5275^{2}* **1997:** 532^{18} **>43a 68f< (DEAD)**

Khalas 2 b c Wolfhound (USA)-Absaar (USA) (Alleged (USA)) 3598^{8} 3806^{2} 4111^{2} (4910) **>84f<**

Khalik (IRE) 3 br c Lear Fan (USA)-Silver Dollar (Shirley Heights) 963^{7} 1271^{4} 1870^{2} **>75f<**

Khamsin (IRE) 3 b f River Falls-Burren Breeze (IRE) (Mazaad) 1272^{9} 1563^{5} **>45f<**

Khassah 3 b f Green Desert (USA)-Kadwah (USA) (Mr Prospector (USA)) 960^{8} 2025^{5} 2586^{5} 3913^{8} **>110f<**

Khatara (IRE) 3 b f Green Desert (USA)-Khanata (USA) (Riverman (USA)) 3510a^{2} 4094a^{10} **>95f<**

Khatir (CAN) 6 gr g Alwasmi (USA)-Perfect Poppy (USA) (Poppy Jay) *106^{8}* **>33a 72f<**

Khattaff (IRE) 2 ch c Hamas (IRE)-Coven (Sassafras (FR)) 1961^{10} 2181^{15} 3253^{5} 4113^{4} 4362^{12} **>73f<**

Khattat (USA) 7 ch g El Gran Senor (USA)-Don't Joke (USA) (Shecky Greene (USA)) **1996:** *5236^{W}* **>69f<**

Khawafi 3 b f Kris-Tabdea (USA) (Topsider (USA)) 935^{5} 1316^{6} (1866) 2764^{3} 3125^{7} 3916^{15} 4639^{9} **>84f<**

Khayal (USA) 3 b g Green Dancer (USA)-Look Who's Dancing (USA) (Affirmed (USA)) 436^{7} 991^{13} 1297^{4} 1877^{7} 2374^{12} **>63df<**

Khayali (IRE) 3 b c Unfuwain (USA)-Coven (Sassafras (FR)) 841^{6} 1331^{4} 1625^{3} (2846) 3238^{3} 4151^{17} **>97f<**

Khazinat El Dar (USA) 3 b br f Slew O' Gold (USA)-Alghuzaylah (Habitat) 3095^{3} 3281^{2} 3917^{3} 4242^{17} **>75f<**

Kheyrah (USA) 2 b br f Dayjur (USA)-Khwlah (USA) (Best Turn (USA)) 3235^{6} (3717) (4411) 4755^{6} **>83f<**

Khumba Mela (IRE) 2 f Chief III- 3882a^{4} 4663a^{4} **>102f<**

Ki Chi Saga (USA) 5 ch g Miswaki (USA)-Cedilla (USA) (Caro) *21^{7} 59^{2} 248^{7} (383) 407^{4} 490^{2}* 755^{13} *1082^{6}* 1473^{10} 1965^{11} 2310^{12} 2369^{17} **>70a 39f<**

Kickonsun (IRE) 3 b g High Estate-Damezao (Alzao (USA)) 467^{13} 582^{6} *1043^{9}* 1469^{4} **>13a 35f<**

Kid Ory 6 ch g Rich Charlie-Woomargama (Creetown) **1996:** *5230^{5} 5266^{6}* **1997:** *209^{13} 333^{5}* 526^{7} 734^{7} 827^{4} 1079^{6} *1289^{3}* 1511^{11} 1816^{2} 2002^{4} 2221^{W} 2382^{5} 2721^{9} 3431^{12} 3443^{10} **>41a 37f<**

Kierans Bridge (IRE) 2 ch f Arcane (USA)-Rhein Valley (IRE) (Kings Lake (USA)) 4330^{14} 4567^{7} 5048^{18} **>51f<**

Kierans Maiden 3 b f Inca Chief (USA)-Donosa (Posse (USA)) 475^{10} 644^{11} **>45f< (DEAD)**

Kierkegaard 4 1728a^{4} 4660a^{2} **>125f<**

Kika 4 gr f Niniski (USA)-Goeswell (Roan Rocket) 2777^{3} (3116) 3694^{6} 4160^{13} 4519^{3} 4923^{10} **>42f<**

Kilbride Lad (IRE) 3 b c Mac's Imp (USA)-Cordon (Morston (FR)) 3362a^{2} **>93f<**

Kilcora (IRE) 2 b f Mujadil (USA)-Miss Audimar (USA) (Mr Leader (USA)) 682^{2} 1013^{3} (1457) 1653^{5} 2024^{14} **>80f< (DEAD)**

Kilcullen (IRE) 2 b br c In The Wings-Liffey Lass (USA) (Irish River (FR)) 4871^{3} 5025^{4} **>82f<**

Kilcullen Lad (IRE) 3 b c Fayruz-Royal Home (Royal Palace) **1996:** *(5146) (5224) 5278^{5}* **1997:** 1419^{2} (1594) 1975^{4} 2134^{17} 2590^{8} 2769^{8} 2964^{2} 3217^{30} 4183^{4} 4456^{18} **>77a 85f<**

Kildee Boy 3 b g Interrex (CAN)-National Time (USA) (Lord Avie (USA)) 1237^{W} 1485^{11} 1851^{10} 2278^{6} 2732^{14} **>31f<**

Kildee Lad 7 b g Presidium-National Time (USA) (Lord Avie (USA)) 443^{20} *569^{7}* 835^{14} 1113^{2} 1317^{15} 1594^{5} 1957^{6} 2220^{5} 2581^{6} 2933^{5} 3082^{9} 3469^{5} 3849^{12} **>69a 67df<**

Kilernan 6 ch g K-Battery-Lekuti (Le Coq d'Or) (3242) **>56f<**

Kilimanjaro 2 b c Shirley Heights-Darara (Top Ville) 3598^{4} (3912) 4440^{4} 4889^{6} **>105df<**

Killarney Jazz 2 b c Alhijaz-Killarney Belle (USA) (Irish Castle (USA)) *4593^{2}* 4769^{4} **>55+a 58f<**

Killernan Kilmaine (IRE) 2 b c Sure Blade (USA)-Rio Piedras (Kala Shikari) 500^{10} **>15f<**

Killgham (IRE) 6 b m Law Society (USA)-Stockrose (FR) (Horage) **1996:** 5199a^{3} **>101f<**

Kilma (USA) 3 b f Silver Hawk (USA)-Nikishka (USA) (Nijinsky (CAN)) 1168^{4} (1625) (2291) 3218^{9} 4101^{11} 4476^{2} 4774^{4} **>96f<**

Kilmeena Lady 3 b f Inca Chief (USA)-Kilmeena Glen (Beveled (USA)) 970^{9} 1237^{12} 1966^{9} 2372^{10} *5020^{9}* **>20a 44f<**

Kilnamartyra Girl 7 b m Arkan-Star Cove (Porto Bello) *67^{3} 123^{3} (151) 206^{3} 272^{8} 360^{2} 410^{2}* 430^{9} 574^{12} *867^{4} 1138^{2}* 1390^{2} 1683^{6} *2365^{4}* (2541) *2910^{11}* 3283^{12} **>54a 48f<**

Kilshanny 3 b f Groom Dancer (USA)-Kiliniski (Niniski (USA)) 885^{4} 1226^{2} (1623) 1928^{5} **>78f<**

Kilvine 4 b g Shaadi (USA)-Kilavea (USA) (Hawaii) 726^{16} 2649^{7} 2954^{12} 3139^{3} 3690^{3} 3849^{14} **>74f<**

Kimberley 2 b c Shareef Dancer (USA)-Willowbank (Gay Fandango (USA)) 4949^{5} **>58f<**

Kimberley Boy 7 b g Mtoto-Diamond House (Habitat) 2063^{10} **>49?f<**

Kim's Brave 2 b g Deploy-Princess Dina (Huntercombe) 1263^{8} (1984) 2429^{4} 3025^{5} 3750^{5} (4044) 4116^{4} 4271^{5} 4778^{20} 4977^{7} **>86f<**

Kincara Palace (IRE) 2 b f Fairy King (USA)-Haughty Manner (High Top) (5002a) **>101+f<**

Kind of Light 4 b f Primo Dominie-Kind Thoughts (Kashmir II) 942^{29} 2216^{13} 2841^{8} 3024^{2} 3224^{4} 3323^{5} (3746) 3982^{6} 4155^{8} **>69a 75f<**

Kindred Greeting 5 b g Most Welcome-Red Berry (Great Nephew) 2518^{8} 2874^{13} 3540^{8} 3562^{5} 3778^{3} **>23a 40f<**

King Alex 4 b c Rainbow Quest (USA)-Alexandrie (USA) (Val de L'Orne (FR)) (1108) 1323^{2} 2104^{7} (3675a) **>118f<**

King Athelstan (USA) 9 b g Sovereign Dancer (USA)-Wimbledon Star (USA) (Hoist The Flag (USA)) 653^{3} 776^{8} (1005) 1584^{7} 2205^{15} (2892) 3421^{5} 3759^{17} **>61f<**

King Chestnut 6 ch g Efisio-Sweet Colleen (Connaught) 1285^{12} 1560^{13} 1800^{14} 2174^{14} 2543^{10} 2847^{8} **>45f<**

Kingchip Boy 8 b g Petong-Silk St James (Pas de Seul) **1996:** *5152^{2} 5209^{7} 5262^{2}* **1997:** *15^{14} (113) (207) (274) 330^{8} 358^{4}* 791^{5} 895^{9} 1040^{4} 1422^{17} 1677^{5} 2036^{17} 2216^{8} 5030^{13} **>85a 62f<**

King Cobra 8 ch h Ardross-Sibley (Northfields (USA)) 3365a^{2} **>103f<**

King Darius (IRE) 2 ch c Persian Bold-Valiant Friend (USA) (Shahrastani (USA)) 722^{8} 1812^{14} 2306^{7} (2378) 2786^{4} 3215^{3} 3650^{6} 4044^{4} **>79f<**

Kingdom Emperor 3 b g Forzando-Wrangbrook (Shirley Heights) 600^{2} 900^{15} 1999^{7} 3068^{3} **>46f<**

Kingdom Pearl 3 ch f Statoblest-Sunfleet (Red Sunset) **1996:** *5257^{8}* **1997:** *154^{5} 230^{7}* 471^{2} 665^{4} 1863^{3} *2068^{6}* 2757^{2} 3210^{5} (4429) 4584^{10} 5024^{4} **>48a 58f<**

Kingdom Princess 4 br f Forzando-Song of Hope (Chief Singer) **1996:** *5256^{10}* **1997:** *125^{12}* **>68da 70f<**

Kingdom Queen (IRE) 2 b f Night Shift (USA)-Yashina (FR) (Tennyson (FR)) 4215^{3} 4413^{7} **>61+f<**

Kingfisher Mill (USA) 3 ch c Riverman (USA)-Charming Life (NZ) (Sir Tristram) (676) 1159^{4} (2107) 3050^{8} 3647^{3} (4420) **>125f<**

King Kato 4 b g Unfuwain (USA)-Sharmood (USA) (Sharpen Up) 842^{3} (2726) 3053^{4} 3689^{9} **>96f<**

King of Dance 2 ch c King's Signet (USA)-Times (Junius (USA)) 1126^{4} 1447^{7} 2361^{8} 3755^{11} **>59f<**

King of Heights (GER) 5 271a^{3} 3735a^{3}

King Of Kings (IRE) 2 b c Sadler's Wells (USA)-Zummerudd (Habitat) (1538a) (2451a) 2811a^{2} (3672a) (4357a) **>107+f<**

King of Peru 4 b c Inca Chief (USA)-Julie's Star (IRE) (Thatching) 452^{3} 540^{3} 677^{14} 961^{4} 1148^{9} 2105^{7} 2329^{4} 2683^{6} 3217^{6} 3764^{11} 4282^{28} **>107f<**

King of Show (IRE) 6 b g Green Desert (USA)-Don't Rush (USA) (Alleged (USA)) 956^{10} 1311^{5} 1835^{12} 2203^{6} 2828^{12} 3261^{6} 4510^{15} **>27a 32f<**

King of the Horse (IRE) 6 ch g Hatim (USA)-Milly Whiteway (Great White Way (USA)) 669^{8} **>55a 18?f<**

King of The River (USA) 2 b c Kingmambo (USA)-La Favorita (FR) (Nikos) 4266^{3} 4581^{6} **>87f<**

King of Tunes (FR) 5 b h Chief Singer-Marcotte (Nebos (GER)) 895^{3} 1308^{6} (1782) 2026^{16} 2866^{6} 3150^{5} 3773^{6} 4141^{2} 4558^{14} 4882^{15} **>78a 92f<**

King Parrot (IRE) 9 br g King of Spain-Red Lory (Bay Express) 1878^{14} 2848^{5} 3056^{4} 3849^{11} 4373^{13} **>63da 57f<**

King Priam (IRE) 2 b c Priolo (USA)-Barinia (Corvaro (USA)) 4735^{10} **>33f<**

King Protea 3 b c Shareef Dancer (USA)-Bright Crocus (USA) (Clev Er Tell (USA)) 2783^{10} **>20f<**

King Rat (IRE) 6 ch g King of Clubs-Mrs Tittlemouse (Nonoalco (USA)) *254^{8}* **>77da 81f<**

Kings Arrow (IRE) 2 b c Mujadil (USA)-Great Leighs (Vaigly Great) 4708^{4} **>71f<**

Kings Assembly 5 b h Presidium-To The Point (Sharpen Up) 3916^{17} 4109^{9} 4714^{14} **>69f<**

Kings Check 2 b c Komaite (USA)-Ski Baby (Petoski) 2886^{5} 3629^{6} *4052^{5}* **>54a 54f<**

Kingsdown Trix (IRE) 3 b g Contract Law (USA)-Three of Trumps (Tyrnavos) **1996:** 5243^{5} **1997:** *8^{4} 96^{6} (240) 314^{4} (454) 581^{6} (906)* 1416^{5} 1825^{15} *2668^{10}* 2750^{7} 3560^{4} **>63+a 48f<**

Kings Harmony (IRE) 4 b g Nordico (USA)-Kingston Rose (Tudor Music) **1996:** *5150^{2} 5246^{13}* **1997:** 752^{4} 2006^{4} (2954) 3296^{4} 3746^{2} 3930^{5} 4328^{11} *5021^{12}* **>78a 77f<**

King's Hussar 2 b c Be My Chief (USA)-Croire (IRE) (Lomond (USA)) 2768^{8} *3607^{6}* 4007^{12} 4576^{9} **>59a 57f<**

King Slayer 2 b c Batshoof-Top Sovereign (High Top) 4910^{3} **>68f<**

King's Mistress 2 ch f King's Signet (USA)-

Rectory Maid (Tina's Pet) *4052[8]* **>38a f<**
King Sound **3** br c Caerleon (USA)-Flood (USA) (Riverman (USA)) 741[3] 3109[5] (3784) 4420[3] **>118f<**
King's Shilling (USA) **10** b g Fit To Fight (USA)-Pride's Crossing (USA) (Riva Ridge (USA)) *67[10]* **>30da 47f<**
Kingston Bay (NZ) **8** b g Kingdom Bay (HK)-Cook Strait (HK) (My Call (HK)) **1996:** 5219a[3] **>124f<**
Kings Vision **5** gr g Absalom-Eye Sight (Roscoe Blake) 653[12] **>18f<**
King Uno **3** b g Be My Chief (USA)-The Kings Daughter (Indian King (USA)) 535[12] 1078[8] 1333[4] (2002) 2237[2] 2417[3] 3266[5] 3484[9] (4016) 4601[3] 4842[4] 4877[3] **>27a 58f<**
Kinlochewe **4** b f Old Vic-Reuval (Sharpen Up) 3492[10] **>105f<**
Kinnescash (IRE) **4** ch g Persian Heights-Gayla Orchestra (Lord Gayle (USA)) **1996:** *5143[2] 5240[8]* **1997:** *67[4]* (838) (2373) 2512[3] 2865[2] **>53a 74f<**
Kinoko **9** ch g Bairn (USA)-Octavia (Sallust) (465) (632) 1100[8] 1252[6] 2498[5] 4170[15] 4287[10] **>46f<**
Kintavi **7** b g Efisio-Princess Tavi (Sea Hawk II) 762[3] 1039[2] (1232) 1445[2] 1763[7] **>61f<**
Kintwyn **7** b g Doulab (USA)-Harriet Emma (USA) (Secretariat (USA)) **1996:** *5120[12] 5200[9]* **>76a 51f<**
Kippilaw **3** ch f Selkirk (USA)-Contralto (Busted) 1333[8] 1733[4] 1864[11] **>42f<**
Kira **7** b m Starry Night (USA)-Irish Limerick (Try My Best (USA)) *316[5] 394[3]* (443) 596[2] (901) 1158[5] *1578[5]* 1772[2] 2289[10] 2675[11] 3795[5] 4280[4] 4434[4] 4770[14] 4887[10] 4995[15] 5047[13] **>72a 87f<**
Kiratas **3** b c Primo Dominie-Kausalya (ITY) (Top Ville) **1996:** 5193a[3]
Kirby's Song (CAN) **2** f *5060a[5]*
Kirkham **3** ch g Golden Lahab (USA)-Topcliffe (Top Ville) 2128[8] *2364[6]* 3286[5] **>23f<**
Kirkie Cross **5** b m Efisio-Balgownie (Prince Tenderfoot (USA)) **1996:** *5167[9]* **>42f<**
Kirkwall **3** ch c Selkirk (USA)-Kamkova (USA) (Northern Dancer) (1361a) 1725a[3] (3002a) 3730a[5] **>119f<**
Kirov Protege (IRE) **5** b g Dancing Dissident (USA)-Still River (Kings Lake (USA)) **1996:** *5081[5] 5118[6] 5183[10] 5208[7] 5223[11]* **1997:** *334[5] 381[5]* 603[6] 769[7] 1011[5] 1507[6] 1665[10] (1803) 2121[5] 2195[3] 2281[9] 2955[9] 3229[8] 3966[10] 4450[3] 4607[14] 4858[14] **>36a 53?f<**
Kismetim **7** b g Dowsing (USA)-Naufrage (Main Reef) **1996:** *5143[11]* **>32a 12f<**
Kissandy **3** b f Batshoof-Amazing Journey (USA) (Spectacular Bid (USA)) *355[7]* 528[5] 773[11] 1469[15] 3283[15]
Kissavos **11** ch g Cure The Blues (USA)-Hairbrush (USA) (Sir Gaylord) **1996:** *5081[7] 5223[13]* **1997:** *42[6] 150[10]* **>31a 37f<**
Kissel **5** b m Warning-Ice Chocolate (USA) (Icecapade (USA)) 2021[7] 2416[3] *2913[7]* 3264[10] 3906[9] **>49a 57f<**
Kistena (FR) **4** ro f Miswaki (USA)-Mabrova (Prince Mab (FR)) 4390a[3] 4664a[4] 4964a[2] **>125f<**
Kite **2** ch f Thatching-Melaka (Kris) 2295[7] 2587[5] 2923[3] 3307[4] 4058[6] 4327[4] *4483[3]* **>33a 55f<**
Kitoph (IRE) **2** b f Night Shift (USA)-Soxoph (Hotfoot) 4515[11] **>44f<**
Kitty Kitty Cancan **4** b f Warrshan (USA)-Kittycatoo Katango (USA) (Verbatim (USA)) **1996:** *5281[3]* **1997:** *61[11]* **>65da 76f<**
Kitza (IRE) **2** b f Danehill (USA)-Pitmarie 3839a[4] 4090a[2] 4619a[7] **>90f<**
Klipspinger **4** ch f Formidable (USA)-Distant Relation (Great Nephew) **1996:** *5109[14] 5178[12]* **1997:** *4[2] 69[5] 89[10] 332[5] 1047[10]* 1250[12] 2463[14] **>59a 33f<**
Klondike Charger (USA) **3** b c Crafty Prospector (USA)-Forever Waving (USA) (Hoist The Flag (USA)) 840[12] 1226[3] 1470[2] 2064[2] 3141[3] 3440[2] 3826[11] **>77f<**
Klosters **5** ch m Royal Match-Snowy Autumn (Deep Run) **1996:** *5208[10]* **>9a f<**
Knave **4** b g Prince Sabo-Royal Agnes (Royal Palace) 496[4] 668[13] 721[20] 2542[5] 2716[8] 3221[6] 3487[9] **>58a 31f<**
Knave's Ash (USA) **6** ch g Miswaki (USA)-Quiet Rendezvous (USA) (Nureyev (USA)) 3034[9] 3273[6] 3801[5] 3901[10] 4147[22] 4792[6] 4927[13] **>72f<**
Knife Edge (USA) **2** b br c Kris S (USA)-My Turbulent Miss (USA) (My Dad George (USA)) 4853[7] **>52f<**
Knightcracker **2** b f Cadeaux Genereux-Top Treat (USA) (Topsider (USA)) 3819[12]
Knobbleeneeze **7** ch g Aragon-Proud Miss (USA) (Semi-Pro) 444[20] (848) 1035[2] 1111[8] 1324[3] 1489[10] 1658[9] 1920[10] 3254[8] 3418[7] 3690[11] 3987[5] 4139[5] (4270) 4979[14] 5023[10] **>75f<**
Knotty Hill **5** b g Green Ruby (USA)-Esilam (Frimley Park) *(230) 358[7] 376[2]* 529[11] 835[2] 3410[9] 3621[3] 3987[18] 4280[24] 4842[11] 5049[21] **>85a 63f<**
Koathary (USA) **6** b g Capote (USA)-Jeffo (USA) (Ridan (USA)) 1262[10] 1813[6] 2242[2] 2508[3] 3052[8] 4141[11] 4297[11] 4882[21] **>73f<**
Kolby **2** b c Superpower-Abrasive (Absalom) 2003[2] 2419[4] **>61f<**
Komaseph **5** b g Komaite (USA)-Starkist (So Blessed) *1047[11] 1134[2]* 1650[6] *2366[7] 3582[11]* 3691[11] **>43a 58f<**
Komasta **3** b g Komaite (USA)-Sky Fighter (Hard Fought) **1996:** *5133[13] 5201[8] (5265)* **1997:** *33[2] 103[7] 420[2]* 532[9] *871[14] 3397[10]* **>70a 59f<**
Komi **3** b g Soviet Star (USA)-Home Address (Habitat) 674[2] 829[3] (1221) 2013[2] 2710[11] **>102f<**
Komiamaite **5** b g Komaite (USA)-Mia Scintilla (Blazing Saddles (AUS)) **1996:** *5140[10]* **>63a 52f<**
Komistar **2** ch c Komaite (USA)-Rosie's Gold (Glint of Gold) 3686[16] (4603) 4895[3] **>93f<**
Komlucky **5** b m Komaite (USA)-Sweet And Lucky (Lucky Wednesday) **1996:** *5170[6]* **1997:** *423[11] 579[15]* 734[9] 896[3] (1220) 1584[3] 2317[7] 2384[5] 3285[14] 3565[14] 4291[7] 4927[15] **>45a 45f<**
Komodo (USA) **5** ch g Ferdinand (USA)-Platonic Interest (USA) (Drone) **1996:** *5086[3] 5186[8] 5242[9] 5271[12]* **1997:** *236[7] 290[9] 338[8] 487[8]* 1484[6] 2723[11] **>18a 33f<**
Konker **2** ch g Selkirk (USA)-Helens Dreamgirl (Caerleon (USA)) 3825[6] 4384[7] 4582[5] **>73f<**
Kool Kat Katie (IRE) **3** gr f Fairy King (USA)-Miss Toot (Ardross) (727) (3875a) 4557[2] (4869a) **>122f<**
Koordinaite **3** b f Komaite (USA)-Fair Dino (Thatch (USA)) *1756[14]* **>21f<**
Koraloona (IRE) **4** b g Archway (IRE)-Polynesian Charm (USA) (What A Pleasure (USA)) 1244[9] 1384[2] 1926[4] (2118) (2344) 2961[5] (3279) 3739[4] 4667[9] **>66f<**
Kosevo (IRE) **3** b g Shareef Dancer (USA)-Kallista (Zeddaan) 2059[11] 2492[10] *4300[5]* 4601[4] 4951[5] **>23a 48f<**
Kota **4** b c Kris-Lady Be Mine (USA) (Sir Ivor) (558) 1142[11] 1463[10] **>74f<**
Krabloonik (FR) **3** b g Bering-Key Role (Be My Guest (USA)) 1297[7] *1430[8] 1787[6] 2052[4]* 2521[13] **>60a 56f<**
Kram **3** ch g Kris-Balenare (Pharly (FR)) 4527[2] 4636[4] 4877[5] **>67f<**
Krayyan Dawn **7** ch g Krayyan-Tana Mist (Homeboy) 3279[8] 3640[10] 4275[20] 4607[3] *4912[3] 5019[6]* **>48a 42f<**
Krisamba **2** ch c Kris-Lia's Dance (Lead on Time (USA)) 4167[13] 4708[3] 4993[5] **>80f<**
Kriscliffe **4** ch c Kris-Lady Norcliffe (USA) (Norcliffe (CAN)) *457[5]* 647[15] 895[28] 1244[17] 1482[9] 4846[10] **>76a 46f<**
Kris Green (IRE) **3** ch c Kris-Green Lucia (Green Dancer (USA)) 1698a[4] 4136[15] **>94f<**
Krispy Knight **2** ch c Kris-Top Table (Shirley Heights) 2588[3] (3022) 3494[3] 3962a[5] **>81f<**
Krissante (USA) **4** b f Kris-Vallee Dansante **1996:** 5198a[3] **>102f<**
Kristal Breeze **5** ch m Risk Me (FR)-Mistral's Dancer (Shareef Dancer (USA)) 476[10] 1093[8] 1390[9] 1632[3] 1968[6] 2174[3] 2373[7] (2582) **>19a 61+f<** **(DEAD)**
Kristal Bridge **3** ch f Kris-Connaught Bridge (Connaught) 1591[6] 1936[W] 2731[6] 3014[6] 3392[6] 3787[14] *4053[3]* 4323[20] *4571[11]* **>61a 65f<**
Kristopher **3** ch c Kris-Derniere Danse (Gay Mecene (USA)) 645[8] *1155[6]* 1633[10] *2151[3]* 2353[4] 4696[15] 4916[11] **>64a 63df<**
Krizevac **2** b c Royal Academy (USA)-Onesixnine (IRE) (Trojan Fen) (3176a)
Krosno **3** ch g Kris-Pastorale (Nureyev (USA)) *185[5] 255[7] 387[5]* 497[2] (667) 878[2] 1140[2] 1449[4] 1853[6] (2667) 3229[4] 4108[15] 4406[9] **>50a 75f<**
Krystal Davey (IRE) **3** b g Classic Music (USA)-Robin Red Breast (Red Alert) **1996:** *5162[7] 5257[7]* **1997:** *(25) 193[5] 379[6]* **>62a 56f<**
Krystal Max (IRE) **4** b g Classic Music (USA)-Lake Isle (IRE) (Caerleon (USA)) **1996:** *5163[7] 5203[9]* **1997:** *32[2] 51[3] (58) 117[5] 201[7] 253[8] 323[9]* 1410[11] 1676[9] **>73a 75f<**
K S Sunshine (USA) **3** b f Sunshine Forever (USA)-Lake Worth (USA) (Cure The Blues (USA)) *412[4] 588[3]* **>53a f<**
Kuala Lipis (USA) **4** b c Lear Fan (USA)-Caerna (USA) (Caerleon (USA)) *398[4]* (450) 738[11] 1016[2] 1456[7] 2028[15] 2710[10] 3051[4] 3703[5] 4151[11] 4306[5] 4577[4] **>88a 95f<**
Kulepopsie (IRE) **4** b f Contract Law (USA)-Flight Fantasy (USA) (Air Forbes Won (USA)) **1996:** *5137[6]* **1997:** *83[10] 112[4]* 3308[3] 3540[12] 3992[15] 4287[15] **>17a 50f<**
Kumait (USA) **3** b br c Danzig (USA)-Colour Chart (USA) (Mr Prospector (USA)) 1766[9] 3144[3] 3725[10] 4138[3] **>94f<**
Kustom Kit Kate **2** b f Tragic Role (USA)-Wing of Freedom (Troy) *3072[4] 3610[11]* 3821[3] 4166[9] **>40a 58f<**
Kustom Kit Klassic **3** b c Chilibang-Norvi (Viking (USA)) **1996:** *5111[12] 5168[4]* **1997:** *1134[3]* 1465[9] *1756[6] 2068[3]* 2487[16] *2670[4]* **>53a 34f<**
Kustom Kit Xpres **3** gr f Absalom-Miss Serlby (Runnett) **1996:** *5133[14] 5176[13]* **1997:** *154[7] 204[7]* 532[16] 1248[16] *1785[6]* 2040[12] 2171[11] **>22a 41f<**
Kutbeya (USA) **6** ch m Diesis-Antartica (FR) (Arctic Tern (USA)) 4261a[3] **>100f<**
Kutta **5** b h Old Vic-Ardassine (Ahonoora) 736[3] 932[8] 1172[5] 1454[6] (2333) 3006a[2] 3902[2] 4894[2] **>120f<**
Kweilo **3** b g Mtoto-Hug Me (Shareef Dancer (USA)) 1226[5] 1449[9] 1820[4] 2132[4] **>59f<**
Kwikpoint **3** ch g Never so Bold-Try the Duchess (Try My Best (USA)) 1512[4] 3807[5] 4290[5] **>56f<**
Kyle Rhea **3** b f In The Wings-Rynechra (Blakeney) (686) (1028) 1722a[6] **>99+f<**

L

Laa Jadeed (IRE) **2** b c Petorius-Sea Mistress (Habitat) 4852[8] **>65f<**
Laazim Afooz **4** b g Mtoto-Balwa (USA) (Danzig (USA)) 1803[7] **>64f<**
La Belle Dominique **5** b m Dominion-Love Street

(Mummy's Pet) **1996:** *5173^{12} 5184^{9}* **>49?a 59f<**
La Belle Otero (USA) 3 ch f Nureyev (USA)-Part Time Lover (USA) (Proud Clarion) 3917^{5} **>56f<**
Labeq (IRE) 3 b c Lycius (USA)-Ahbab (IRE) (Ajdal (USA)) (2687) 3190^{18} (3773) **>95+f<**
La Blue (GER) 4 dk f Bluebird (USA)-La Luganese (Surumu (GER)) $1074a^{3}$ (1550a) $2821a^{2}$ $3376a^{5}$ $4666a^{3}$ **>120f<**
La Brief 5 b m Law Society (USA)-Lady Warninglid (Ela-Mana-Mou) 465^{2} 846^{P} **>77a 65f< (DEAD)**
Lab Test (IRE) 5 ch g Doulab (USA)-Princess Reema (USA) (Affirmed (USA)) 2887^{P} **>57f<**
Labudd (USA) 7 ch h Deputy Minister (CAN)-Delightful Vie (USA) (Barbs Delight) **1996:** *5185^{6}* **1997:** *104^{2}* **>63a 54f<**
Lacandona (USA) 4 b f Septieme Ciel (USA)-Grand Luxe (USA) (Sir Ivor) **1996:** *5117^{7}* **>1a 68f<**
La Chatelaine 3 b f Then Again-La Domaine (Dominion) 656^{4} 992^{11} 1639^{4} 1843^{2} 2121^{2} 2573^{5} 3018^{11} (3558) 3787^{10} 4373^{17} **>54f<**
Lachesis 4 ch f Lycius (USA)-Chance All (FR) (Glenstal (USA)) **1996:** *5112^{7} 5175^{9}* **1997:** *36^{4} 134^{5} 273^{5} 319^{7}* 571^{6} 733^{18} 883^{4} *1135^{13}* 2177^{20} *2602^{9}* (2788) *2915^{10}* 3693^{9} 3910^{7} 4951^{8} **>29a 51f<**
La Curamalal (IRE) 3 b f Rainbow Quest (USA)-North Telstar (Sallust) 833^{6} 1784^{3} 2726^{2} **>76f<**
La Dolce Vita 3 b f Mazilier (USA)-Actress (Known Fact (USA)) *62^{5} 155^{3} 180^{8} (377)* 448^{21} 685^{5} 785^{11} 995^{4} 1131^{2} 1285^{10} 1385^{6} 1781^{8} 2130^{4} 2317^{6} (2945) 3207^{6} 3443^{5} (3749) 4071^{15} **>77+a 72f<**
La Doyenne (IRE) 3 ch f Masterclass (USA)-Sainthill (St Alphage) 792^{10} 1119^{11} 1604^{5} 2354^{5} 3313^{3} 3572^{3} (3850) 3968^{6} 4601^{16} 4872^{19} **>60df<**
Lady Alexander (IRE) 2 ch f Night Shift (USA)-Sandhurst Goddess (Sandhurst Prince) (2811a) (3192) $4093a^{7}$ 4675^{6} **>101f<**
Lady Almitra 2 b br f Presidium-Armaiti (Sayf El Arab (USA)) 2003^{6} 4401^{3} *4569^{13}* **>21a 55f<**
Lady Anna 2 b f Anshan-Minteen (Teenoso (USA)) 1091^{9} **>5f<**
Lady Arpel (IRE) 5 b m Phardante (FR)-La Maree (Tumble Wind (USA)) $1698a^{7}$ **>80f<**
Lady Assassin (IRE) 3 ch f Polish Patriot (USA)-Jambo Jambo (IRE) (Kafu) $4203a^{5}$ **>80f<**
Lady Bi (IRE) 3 b f Alzao (USA)-Kallopina (ITY) (Targowice (USA)) $815a^{5}$ $1368a^{6}$ **>91f<**
Ladybower (IRE) 5 b m Pennine Walk-Eimkar (Junius (USA)) *1048^{12}* 1484^{2} 1987^{5} 2395^{11} 2723^{12} 2848^{11} *3413^{10}* 3966^{9} **>26a 31f<**
Lady Carla 4 b f Caerleon (USA)-Shirley Superstar (Shirley Heights) 2104^{9} 2559^{7} **>107f<**
Lady Caroline Lamb (IRE) 4 b f Contract Law (USA)-Tuft Hill (Grundy) 3287^{2} 3500^{11} 3900^{11} **>42a 68f<**
Lady Charlotte 2 b f Night Shift (USA)-Circulate (High Top) 3636^{5} 4311^{7} (4462) 4755^{12} **>82f<**
Lady d'Abo 2 b f Ron's Victory (USA)-Lady Sabo (Prince Sabo) *872^{7}* 4012^{22} 4311^{R}
Lady Diesis (USA) 3 b f Diesis-Sedulous (Tap On Wood) 507^{8} 968^{12} 2358^{3} 2833^{12} 3130^{10} 3580^{10} 4155^{9} **>76f<**
Lady Eclat 4 b f Nomination-Romantic Saga (Prince Tenderfoot (USA)) **1996:** *5109^{11} 5137^{9}* **1997:** *14^{13} 111^{7}* **>9a 50f<**
Lady Eil 2 ch f Elmaamul (USA)-Oakbrook Tern (USA) (Arctic Tern (USA)) 3493^{9} *4303^{8}* 4698^{4} *4984^{2}* **>48a 55f<**
Lady Emral 2 br f Handsome Sailor-Precious Jay (Hotfoot) 3804^{5} 4428^{13} **>21f<**
Lady Felix 2 br f Batshoof-Volcalmeh (Lidhame) 3490^{8} 3861^{11} 4111^{10} 5048^{13} **>50f<**
Lady From Limerick (IRE) 2 ch f Rainbows For Life (CAN)-Coshlea (Red Alert) 1749^{2} 3114^{7} 3541^{3} 4097^{11} 4327^{6} 4688^{5} **>65df<**
Lady Godiva 3 b f Keen-Festival Fanfare (Ile de Bourbon (USA)) 431^{7} 1782^{12} 2122^{11} 2285^{8} 2552^{6} 2735^{6} 3143^{16} 3561^{6} **>58f<**
Lady Imza 2 b f Polar Falcon (USA)-Blade of Grass (Kris) *4056^{10}* 4544^{9} **>28a 48f<**
Lady In Waiting 2 b f Kylian (USA)-High Savannah (Rousillon (USA)) 1240^{4} (1619) 1945^{2} (2335) **>92f<**
Lady Komaite 4 b f Komaite (USA)-Hyperion Girl (Royal Palm) *164^{13}* 480^{12}
Lady Laphroaig (FR) 2 ch f Elmaamul (USA)-Venerate (IRE) (Ahonoora) 3711^{6} 3847^{4} *4982^{9}* **>47a 59f<**
Lady Leprechaun (IRE) 3 ch f Ela-Mana-Mou-Lady Alcea (ITY) (On Your Mark) **1996:** $5197a^{3}$
Lady Magician 3 ch f Lord Bud-Miss Merlin (Manacle) 3068^{5} 3308^{8} 3695^{7} **>35f<**
Lady Moll 2 b f King's Signet (USA)-Simply Style (Bairn (USA)) (472) (844) 1653^{4} 2103^{14} 2862^{21} 3589^{3} 3823^{16} **>79f<**
Ladyofdistinction (IRE) 2 b f Distinctly North (USA)-Lady Anna Livia (Ahonoora) 3070^{10} 3426^{5} 4215^{9} 4514^{11} **>44f<**
Lady of Glendowan 4 b f Teenoso (USA)-Mearlin (Giolla Mear) 3820^{9} 4060^{19} 4400^{7} **>4f<**
Lady of The Dance 2 b f Tragic Role (USA)-Waltz (Jimmy Reppin) 4873^{16} 5048^{20} **>30f<**
Lady of The Lake 3 b f Caerleon (USA)-Llyn Gwynant (Persian Bold) 764^{2} 1299^{12} 1822^{5} (2535) (3020) (3543) 4156^{2} 4376^{4} (4969) **>102f<**
Lady Rachel (IRE) 2 b f Priolo (USA)-Alpine Spring (Head for Heights) 4278^{3} 4507^{7} 4873^{13} **>59f<**
Lady Ralphina 2 b f General Wade-Lady Regent (Wolver Hollow) 1867^{5} 2919^{6} 3094^{U} 3471^{14} 3742^{6} 4065^{12} 4311^{10} 4543^{11} **>44f<**
Lady Rochelle 2 b f Noble Patriarch-Panic Button (IRE) (Simply Great (FR)) 2881^{8} 3084^{5} 3427^{7} 4208^{11} **>44f<**
Lady Rockstar 2 b f Rock Hopper-Silk St James (Pas de Seul) 3450^{14} 4852^{13} 4952^{12} **>43f<**
Lady Salome 3 gr f Absalom-Lady River (FR) (Sir Gaylord) 1299^{14} 1820^{16} **>48f<**
Lady Shannon (USA) 3 gr f Mr Prospector (USA)-Flowing (USA) (El Gran Senor (USA)) $1186a^{5}$ $2815a^{3}$ **>89f<**
Lady Sheriff 6 b m Taufan (USA)-Midaan (Sallust) 702^{11} 901^{2} *(1046)* 1269^{2} (1332) 1602^{2} 1946^{3} 2289^{4} 2497^{2} 2675^{4} 3065^{2} (3126) 3795^{4} 4100^{6} 4233^{7} 4365^{3} 4512^{9} 4770^{15} **>70a 89f<**
Lady Shirl (IRE) 3 b f Fayruz-Christmas Show (Petorius) **1996:** *5080^{2}* **>65a 65f<**
Lady Silk 6 ch m Prince Sabo-Adduce (USA) (Alleged (USA)) **1996:** *5110^{15}* **1997:** *40^{10} (69) 127^{11} 152^{3} 203^{6}* 827^{18} 925^{11} *1048^{11} 1289^{15}* 1993^{3} 2317^{11} 2542^{6} 2753^{5} *3074^{6}* 4168^{15} *4480^{3}* 4606^{9} *4810^{5}* 4987^{8} **>43a 40f<**
Lady So Bold 2 ch f Bold Arrangement-Lady Blues Singer (Chief Singer) 2153^{10} 2493^{12} 3967^{9} **>50f<**
Lady Swift 6 ch m Jalmood (USA)-Appealing (Star Appeal) 1081^{8} **>39f<**
Lady Westbury (IRE) 6 b m Superpower-Fleur-de-Luce (Tumble Wind (USA)) *273^{13} 306^{5} 512^{8}* 638^{10} 1385^{17} **>29a 15f<**
Lady Yavanna 2 ch f Lycius (USA)-Isotonic (Absalom) 1619^{6} 1933^{7} 2842^{4} 3932^{13} 4116^{11} **>74f<**
La-Faah (IRE) 2 ch c Lahib (USA)-Rawaabe (USA) (Nureyev (USA)) (3047) 3644^{7} (4679) (4880) **>108+f<**
Laffah (USA) 2 b c Silver Hawk (USA)-Sakiyah (USA) (Silver Hawk (USA)) 2336^{8} 2699^{7} **>65f<**
L'Affranchi (FR) 4 b c Caerwent-Perle de Culture (FR) (Dictus (FR)) $148a^{2}$ **>66f<**
L'Africain Bleu (FR) 4 b c Saint Cyrien (FR)-Afrique Bleu Azur (USA) (Sagace (FR)) (2271a) $4000a^{4}$ **>115f<**
La Galleria 2 ch f Royal Academy (USA)-Two and Sixpence (USA) (Chief's Crown (USA)) 4298^{13} 4567^{10} **>46f<**
Lagan 4 b g Shareef Dancer (USA)-Lagta (Kris) 2662^{2} **>42a 44f<**
Lagarto (GER) 5 $4124a^{10}$ $4762a^{2}$ **>106f<**
Lago Di Varano 5 b g Clantime-On the Record (Record Token) 596^{10} 953^{5} 1158^{2} 1608^{7} 1946^{7} 2339^{7} 2675^{8} 2872^{9} (3065) 3410^{13} 3649^{23} 4100^{5} 4756^{9} 4887^{16} 4995^{21} **>92f<**
Laguna Bay (IRE) 3 b f Arcane (USA)-Meg Daughter (IRE) (Doulab (USA)) 791^{6} 952^{2} 1299^{7} 1938^{4} 2582^{5} (3320) 3767^{4} 4180^{2} 4323^{5} 4971^{26} **>64f<**
Lahab Nashwan 3 ch c Nashwan (USA)-Shadha (USA) (Devil's Bag (USA)) 967^{5} 1239^{10} **>73f<**
Lahik (IRE) 4 b g Lycius (USA)-Sangala (FR) (Jim French (USA)) **1996:** *5122^{4} 5145^{12} 5211^{8} 5247^{11}* **1997:** *105^{4} 144^{5} 230^{5} 290^{3} 338^{4} 418^{6} 486^{4}* **>52a 41f<**
Lake Aria 4 b f Rambo Dancer (CAN)-Hinge (Import) 1512^{10} 1798^{13} 2143^{7} *2674^{6}* **>4a f<**
Lake Dominion 8 b g Primo Dominie-Piney Lake (Sassafras (FR)) *(3046)* 4170^{9} *4302^{5} 4590^{6}* **>52a 38f<**
Lakeland Pride (IRE) 2 gr c Pips Pride-Divine Apsara (Godswalk (USA)) 1076^{5} 1174^{5} 1510^{3} 1978^{3} 2112^{3} 2786^{10} 3650^{10} 3904^{4} 3990^{5} **>70f<**
Lake Taal 2 ch f Prince Sabo-Calachuchi (Martinmas) 4211^{6} 4840^{6} **>61f<**
Lake Wobegone (IRE) 2 ch c Inchinor-Westerlake (Blakeney) 1984^{5} 2784^{8} **>31f<**
Lakota Brave 3 ch c Anshan-Pushkinia (FR) (Pharly (FR)) 1443^{8} **>42f<**
Lakota Dance (GER) 3 $1545a^{7}$ **>83f<**
Lalindi (IRE) 6 b m Cadeaux Genereux-Soemba (General Assembly (USA)) 607^{5} 888^{12} 1233^{8} (2464) **>79a 80?f<**
Lallans (IRE) 4 b c Old Vic-Laluche (USA) (Alleged (USA)) 2327^{9} 3110^{10} 3599^{7} **>94f<**
La Lyonesse 2 b f Lion Cavern (USA)-Princess Sioux (Commanche Run) 3151^{10} 3687^{12} 4515^{5} **>56f<**
Lamarita 3 b f Emarati (USA)-Bentinck Hotel (Red God) 474^{4} 584^{2} (731) 1018^{10} 1294^{3} (1792) 2298^{3} **>83f<**
Lambrini Lad (IRE) 2 b c Shalford (IRE)-Swift Reply (He Loves Me) 2680^{10} **>28f<**
Lambs Lane 2 b c Petoski-Collison Lane (Reesh) 3239^{11} 3459^{5} 3825^{7} 4152^{16} 4576^{16} **>63f<**
La Menorquina (USA) 7 b m Woodman (USA)-Hail The Lady (USA) (Hail the Pirates (USA)) *272^{2} 375^{3} (660)* 3928^{10} *4055^{2} 4302^{2} 4811^{5}* **>58a 40?f<**
La Modiste 4 b f Most Welcome-Dismiss (Daring March) *238^{4} 291^{9} 335^{3}* (791) 987^{14} (1473) 1739^{12} 2346^{11} *(2668)* 3616^{2} 3798^{2} (3982) 4297^{3} 4781^{28} **>69a 89f<**
Lamorna 3 ch f Shavian-Malibasta (Auction Ring (USA)) 1000^{9} 1245^{11} 1810^{6} 1931^{5} 2852^{7} 3266^{2} 3716^{3} 4169^{7} (4291) 4546^{15} 4816^{2} **>60f<**
Lamoura 2 ch f Executive Man-Armalou (Ardoon) *902^{12}* 1564^{13} 2003^{12} 3090^{9}
Lamsaat (IRE) 2 b f Thatching-Fair Shirley (IRE) (Shirley Heights) 4317^{11} **>59f<**

La Nana (FR) 3 b f Homme de Loi (IRE)-Leslina (FR) (In Fijar (USA)) 813a^3 1916a^5 5031a^3 **>115f<**
Lanara 2 b f Formidable (USA)-Alnasr Jewel (USA) (Al Nasr (FR)) 2519^7 2943^{16} 3312^{12}
Lancashire Knight 3 b g High Estate-Just a Treat (IRE) (Glenstal (USA)) 2190^6 2550^{11} **>55f<**
Lancashire Legend 4 gr g Belfort (FR)-Peters Pet Girl (Norwick (USA)) **1996:** *5089^4 5152^{11}* **1997:** *57^9 109^3 146^5 241^3 278^4 325^2* 1374^5 1680^{10} 2724^2 2937^8 3139^7 3590^{13} *3860^5 5021^9* **>73a 50f<**
Lance's Pet 3 b f Warning-Snub (Steel Heart) *4980^{12}* **>4a f<**
Landler 4 b g Shareef Dancer (USA)-Les Dancelles (Pas de Seul) 2131^6 **>4f<**
Landlord 5 b g Be My Chief (USA)-Pubby (Doctor Wall) 1001^{17} 1424^4 (1665) 2932^9 **>44a 59f<**
Land of Dreams 2 b f Cadeaux Genereux-Sahara Star (Green Desert (USA)) (1645) 2335^2 2558^9 3811^2 (4150) 4675^4 **>98f<**
Landsuitor (GER) 5 b h Local Suitor (USA)-Landfrau (GER) (Frontal) (1074a) 3373a^2 **>113f<**
Lanelly (GER) 3 f 4762a^8 **>47f<**
Langara Heights 3 br c Golden Heights-Cushina (Sparkler) 2941^8 3463^{12} 3632^9 *4053^9* 4170^{14} **>2a 58f<**
L'Annee Folle (FR) 4 b f Double Bed (FR)-3878a^2 4869a^3 **>118f<**
La Nuit Rose (FR) 2 b f Rainbow Quest (USA)-Caerlina (IRE) (Caerleon (USA)) (4701) **>89+f<**
La Perdoma 3 b f Sylvan Express-Oratava Valley (Mansingh (USA)) 2234^5 2756^5 3268^5 3601^9 3853^U **>37f<**
La Perruche (IRE) 4 b f Cyrano de Bergerac-Red Lory (Bay Express) *383^7* **>46a f<**
La Petite Fusee 6 br m Cigar-Little Missile (Ile de Bourbon (USA)) 450^{14} 835^{15} 1107^2 1439^{12} 2833^{11} 3092^3 3615^3 4155^{12} 4321^{13} **>78a 84f<**
Lapimi 2 b f Lapierre-Miami Pride (Miami Springs) *3076^7*
Lapon (USA) 6 b h Bering-Erin Go Rose (USA) (Sensitivo) 1547a^3 **>108?f<**
Lapu-Lapu 4 b f Prince Sabo-Seleter (Hotfoot) 633^9 1024^{12} 1390^3 1559^2 1732^5 (2471) 2907^5 3330^8 4596^{11} 4847^3 **>53a 63f<**
Laramania 2 ch g Safawan-Lara's Baby (IRE) (Valiyar) 3569^7 3887^8 4433^9 4767^{12} 4885^{12} 4994^{12} **>62f<**
Largesse 3 b c Cadeaux Genereux-Vilanika (FR) (Top Ville) 501^8 3274^4 3777^{11} (4015) 4223^5 (4310) **>83f<**
Lark's Rise 3 b f Niniski (USA)-Line of Cards (High Line) 2783^6 4322^5 4743^{14} **>54f<**
La Rochelle (IRE) 2 b f Salse (USA)-Lagta (Kris) 4758^6 **>66f<**
Larrylukeathugh 4 b g Prince Sabo-Hidden Asset (Hello Gorgeous (USA)) **1996:** *5110^{13}* **>41f<**
Lascensa (USA) 2 ch f Lord At War (ARG)-Trattoria (USA) (Alphabatim (USA)) *4299^8* 4698^{12} **>15a 27f<**
Lasham 2 ch g Presidium-Travel Myth (Bairn (USA)) (767) 1444^4 1856^2 3237^{10} 3635^2 3869^4 4284^8 4543^5 *4808^3* **>50a 72f<**
La Spagna 6 ch m Aragon-Ringed Aureole (Aureole) 1327^8 *1580^{11}* 2281^7 2518^7 2916^8 **>25a 30f<**
Last Ambition (IRE) 5 b m Cadeaux Genereux-Fabulous Rina (FR) (Fabulous Dancer (USA)) 4248^{15} **>30f<**
Last Chance 3 b c River Falls-Little Red Hut (Habitat) **1996:** *5092^9* **1997:** 483^2 654^{12} 958^8 1167^3 2407^4 *2663^8* 3100^7 3145^6 3454^7 **>28a 56f<**
Last Christmas 2 b c Salse (USA)-State Ball (Dance In Time (CAN)) 4061^3 (4433) **>83f<**
Last Dance (DEN) 6 gr h Shahdji-What A Meeting (DEN) (Jammed Red (DEN)) 3373a^3 **>93f<**
Last Dream (IRE) 3 b f Alzao (USA)-Last Tango (FR) (Luthier) 4191a^8 **>84f<**
Last Frontier (IRE) 3 f **1996:** (5263a)
Last Knight (IRE) 2 b g Distinctly North (USA)-Standing Ovation (Godswalk (USA)) 460^4 594^{11} 1306^6 **>61f<**
Last Lap 2 b f Noble Patriarch-Warning Bell (Bustino) 1815^4 2153^7 2493^4 2935^6 *3045^3* **>44a 54f<**
Last Laugh (IRE) 5 b m Last Tycoon-Little Me (Connaught) (881) **>69f<**
Last Mecene (FR) 2 5057a^4 **>90f<**
Last Second (IRE) 4 gr f Alzao (USA)-Alruccaba (Crystal Palace (FR)) 922a^7 3216^5 **>121?f<**
Las Vistas 3 b f Tina's Pet-Maravista (Swing Easy (USA)) 1423^7 1638^3 2704^8 2945^3 3299^5 3850^4 4324^{18} *5021^7* **>16a 49f<**
Latalomne (USA) 3 ch c Zilzal (USA)-Sanctuary (Welsh Pageant) (586) 829^5 4142^2 4463^2 **>102f<**
Late Night Out 2 b c Lahib (USA)-Chain Dance (Shareef Dancer (USA)) 4668^3 (4955) **>92tf<**
Late Parade (IRE) 6 b h Astronef-Skisette (Malinowski (USA)) 4664a^{12} **>116f<**
Latin Bay 2 b c Superlative-Hugging (Beveled (USA)) 500^{11} 836^{11} 1760^W 2196^{14} 2719^5 3818^{11} 4068^{11} **>53f<**
Latin Nexus (USA) 2 b f Roman Diplomat (USA)-Miami Game (USA) (Crozier) 1440^3 2394^5 3450^7 **>74f<**
La Tiziana 2 b f Rudimentary (USA)-Tizona (Pharly (FR)) 4575^4 4750^3 **>75f<**
L A Touch 4 b f Tina's Pet-Silvers Era (Balidar) 1098^{18} 1627^9 1865^8 1963^{12} 2899^{11} 3240^2 3431^{17} **>19a 45f<**
Latvian 10 gr g Rousillon (USA)-Lorelene (FR) (Lorenzaccio) (1601) 1992^4 2170^3 2661^2 3308^6 **>63f<**
Laurel Delight 7 ch m Presidium-Foudroyer (Artaius (USA)) 1766^7 2111^7 **>92df<**
Laurel Pleasure 2 ch f Selkirk (USA)-Laurel Delight (Presidium) 594^8 (1253) **>69f<**
Laurel Seeker (USA) 3 b g Mining (USA)-L'On Vite (USA) (Secretariat (USA)) 605^5 875^9 1372^4 4548^3 4986^5 **>71?f<**
Lauren's Lad 2 ch c Tachyon Park-Glory Isle (Hittite Glory) 2243^{11} 3295^7 4007^{15} 4368^5 (4545) 4856^6 **>69f<**
La Vaso Verdi 2 b f Ardkinglass-Emerald Gulf (IRE) (Wassl) 948^8 2827^{11} 3062^8 4595^{15} **>28f<**
Lavender Della (IRE) 4 gr f Shernazar-All In White (FR) (Carwhite) **1996:** *5101^4 5233^9* **1997:** 1968^8 2199^3 2865^7 **>49a 67f<**
Lavernock Lady 2 b f Don't Forget Me-Danissa (Dancing Brave (USA)) 2700^{12} 3060^9 4470^8 **>27f<**
La Vizelle (IRE) 2 b f Distinctly North (USA)-Queen of Erin (IRE) (King of Clubs) 2196^{13} 2425^8 2587^{11} 3278^{19} **>29f<**
La Volta 4 b f Komaite (USA)-Khadino (Relkino) 444^{13} 571^{10} 749^{14} *1048^{14}* 1514^{10} 1861^4 *2915^{12}* 3271^4 3625^{10} (4169) 4291^9 **>31a 54f<**
Lawahik 3 b c Lahib (USA)-Lightning Legacy (USA) (Super Concorde (USA)) 528^3 (847) 1399^4 1982^3 2676^6 **>103f<**
Law Commission 7 ch g Ela-Mana-Mou-Adjala (Northfields (USA)) 1111^6 1308^7 2026^{11} 2242^7 2598^{11} 2833^6 3024^6 3185^2 3594^2 (4153) 4441^{16} 4782^7 4976^5 **>114?f<**
Law Dancer (IRE) 4 b g Alzao (USA)-Judicial (USA) (Law Society (USA)) *131^{10} 179^4 226^5 291^8* 791^7 1011^2 1503^5 2150^7 *2193^2 2668^6* 4179^2 4504^8 **>64a 60f<**
Lawful Contract (IRE) 2 br g Contract Law (USA)-Lucciola (FR) (Auction Ring (USA)) *1286^7* 1961^9 *2604^8* 4428^{12} **>45a 32f<**
Lawfull Blue (IRE) 3 b f Bluebird (USA)-Maraquiba (FR) (Kenmare (FR)) 4579^6 4848^{10} *4980^{10}* **>16a 55f<**
Lawful Love (IRE) 7 b g Law Society (USA)-Amata (USA) (Nodouble (USA)) 650^4 1100^{19} **>41f<**
Lawless Bridget 2 b f Alnasr Alwasheek-Geoffrey's Sister (Sparkler) *859^5* **>2a f<**
Law Library (IRE) 2 ch c Case Law-Ukud (USA) 1531a^8 3506a^2 3961a^2 (4090a) **>98+f<**
Lawn Lothario 3 ch g Pursuit of Love-Blade of Grass (Kris) *119^3 (174) (281) (331) (370)* **>94a 67f< (DEAD)**
Lawsimina 4 b f Silly Prices-Star of the Sea (Absalom) **1996:** *5093^6 5097^5 5144^5 5178^{11}* **1997:** *1428^7* 1620^W **>29a 34f<**
Lawz (IRE) 3 br c Lahib (USA)-Sea Port (Averof) 2183^2 2591^6 4009^3 4277^7 4883^8 **>71f<**
Layik (IRE) 4 b c Be My Guest (USA)-Forest Lair (Habitat) 4620a^{19} **>100f<**
Lay The Blame 4 b c Reprimand-Rose And The Ring (Welsh Pageant) 1495^3 1782^{10} 2043^2 2205^9 2890^6 3061^3 3242^{10} **>79f<**
Lea 4 ch f Persian Bold-Lady Ambassador (General Assembly (USA)) 4962a^3 **>92f<**
Leading Edge (FR) 6 b g Script Ohio (USA)-Just In Front (FR) (Alias Smith (USA)) 4649a^2 **>71f<**
Leading Note (USA) 3 ch f Blushing John (USA)-Beat (USA) (Nijinsky (CAN)) 833^5 2776^3 4144^4 4731^7 **>82f<**
Leading Princess (IRE) 6 gr m Double Schwartz-Jenny Diver (USA) (Hatchet Man (USA)) **1996:** *5109^7* **1997:** 494^8 666^5 (956) 1227^7 1311^8 1835^{11} 2032^3 2111^9 2384^3 2472^3 2659^3 2899^{10} 3224^7 4233^{22} 4707^{10} **>41a 33f<**
Leading Spirit (IRE) 5 b g Fairy King (USA)-Shopping (FR) (Sheshoon) *(299) 426^4* **>85a 93f<**
Lead Singer 2 b g Ballad Rock-Parisana (FR) (Gift Card (FR)) 4851^7
Lea Grande 2 ch f Highest Honor (FR)-Lovely Rita (USA) (Topsider (USA)) 4397a^3 4973^4 **>84f<**
Leap for Joy 5 ch m Sharpo-Humble Pie (Known Fact (USA)) **1996:** 5127a^5 **>111f<**
Lear Jet (USA) 4 b g Lear Fan (USA)-Lajna (Be My Guest (USA)) 3640^5 4104^6 **>76f<**
Learmont (USA) 7 b h Lear Fan (USA)-Wistoral (USA) (Exceller (USA)) *438a^3 627a^{12}* **>98a 100f<**
Lear Spear (USA) 2 b c Lear Fan (USA)-Golden Gorse (USA) (His Majesty (USA)) 3494^6 4105^3 4367^3 **>83f<**
Lear White (USA) 6 b h Lear Fan (USA)-White Water (FR) (Pharly (FR)) **1996:** 5158a^2 **>119f<**
Leather And Scrim (IRE) 2 b f Imperial Frontier (USA)-Yola (IRE) (Last Tycoon) 1126^6 1253^5 2545^7 3707^{11} **>45f<**
Leatherneck (IRE) 4 b g Sadler's Wells (USA)-Louveciennes (USA) (Super Concorde (USA)) 605^6 842^9 1106^8 1445^{11} 1636^{11} **>62f<**
Le Bam Bam 5 ch h Emarati (USA)-Lady Lustre (On Your Mark) *3860^9* 4008^{11} **>55a 44f<**
Le Battant (GER) 3 b c Konigsstuhl (GER)-Lerma (GER) (Surumu (GER)) 1072a^2 **>100f<**
Lebedinski (IRE) 4 ch f Soviet Lad (USA)-Excavate (Nishapour (FR)) *67^8 114^5* **>26a 48f<**
Le Chevalier (GER) 3 b c Heraldiste (USA)-La Chapelle (SWI) (Rocket) (918a) **>105f<**
Le Conquet (FR) 9 b h Pink (FR)-Miss Kit (FR) (Tourangeau (FR)) **1996:** 5216a^2 **>113f<**
Leconte (GER) 6 b h Homing-Las Palmas (GER) (Experte (GER)) (440a) 1073a^7 **>110f<**

Le Destin (FR) 4 b c Zayyani-My Darling (Ela-Mana-Mou) 439a[2] 922a[2] 1736[3] 4258a[3] 4665a[16] 4863a[4] **>125f<**

Ledgendry Line 4 b g Mtoto-Eider (Niniski (USA)) 984[3] 1398[2] 1763[10] (2114) 2291[4] 3440[7] 3907[6] 4279[4] 4704[3] **>78f<**

Legal Brief 5 b g Law Society (USA)-Ahonita (Ahonoora) 3213[9] **>29df<**

Legal Issue (IRE) 5 b h Contract Law (USA)-Natuschka (Authi) **1996:** *5134[4] 5165[5]* **1997:** 1020[9] 1248[6] *1433[5]* 1655[2] 1761[7] 2416[2] 2828[5] 3285[6] *(3608)* 3937[2] *4571[4] 4798[6]* 4988[4] **>58a 67f<**

Legal Lark (IRE) 2 ro g Case Law-Park Silver (Beldale Flutter (USA)) 3497[9] 3770[9] 4178[5] (4401) 4543[6] *4796[8]* 5045[13] **>55a 68f<**

Legal Lunch (USA) 2 b c Alleged (USA)-Dinner Surprise (USA) (Lyphard (USA)) 4871[2] **>84f<**

Legal Right (USA) 4 b c Alleged (USA)-Rose Red (USA) (Northern Dancer) 625a[7] 849[5] **>105df<**

Legat de France (FR) 3 gr c Always Fair (USA)-Luna Maya (FR) (Gay Mecene (USA)) 1546a[2] **>78f<**

Leg Beforum (IRE) 3 b g Distinctly North (USA)-Paulines Girl (Hello Gorgeous (USA)) *26[8] 161[4] 185[4] 249[2] 347[4] 366[3]* 478[6] *662[4]* 1011[4] 1642[10] *2151[7]* **>64a 46f<**

Legendary Lover (IRE) 3 b c Fairy King (USA)-Broken Romance (IRE) (Ela-Mana-Mou) 740[13] 1276[3] 2126[6] 2568[4] 4015[9] **>86f<**

Legend Maker (IRE) 3 b f Sadler's Wells (USA)-High Spirited (Shirley Heights) (1722a) 2275a[5] 3370a[3] 4256a[8] **>109f<**

Legend of Aragon 3 b f Aragon-Legendary Dancer (Shareef Dancer (USA)) 587[11] 749[10] 883[12] 1096[5] *1433[8] 1580[6]* 2002[9] 2206[4] 2463[7] *2915[4] 3583[3]* 4877[2] 4991[5] **>52a 51f<**

Legend of Love 2 b g Pursuit of Love-Legendary Dancer (Shareef Dancer (USA)) 2359[3] 2842[7] 3569[4] 4778[18] 5050[10] **>73f<**

Leggera (IRE) 2 b f Sadler's Wells (USA)-Lady Ambassador (General Assembly (USA)) (3547) 4107[3] 4892[3] **>92f<**

Le Grand Gousier (USA) 3 ch c Strawberry Road (AUS)-Sandy Baby (USA) (Al Hattab (USA)) 1094[11] 1296[11] 1574[4] 1809[5] *1964[2]* 2535[7] 2727[2] (2896) 3870[5] 4180[4] **>58a 63f<**

Legs Be Frendly (IRE) 2 b c Fayruz-Thalssa (Rusticaro (FR)) 938[2] 1263[3] *1941[2]* 2243[2] 2565[2] 3113[4] 3278[2] 3629[2] 4675[12] (4911) **>89f<**

Leguard Express (IRE) 9 b g Double Schwartz-All Moss (Prince Tenderfoot (USA)) 2892[12] 3328[9] **>11a 34?f<**

Leif the Lucky (USA) 8 ch g Lemhi Gold (USA)-Corvine (USA) (Crow (FR)) **1996:** *5200[3]* **1997:** 550[4] 689[6] 1472[5] 2030[3] 2342[2] 2512[4] 3330[4] 3992[8] **>61a 61f<**

Leigh Crofter 8 ch g Son of Shaka-Ganadora (Good Times (ITY)) **1996:** *(5134) 5174[4] (5237) 5264[4]* **1997:** *(31) 65[4] 113[9] 220[5] 257[7] 316[2] 385[9] 578[12] 663[11] 1048[9]* 1089[9] *4301[12] 4574[10]* 4878[12] **>55a 62df<**

Lemon Bridge (IRE) 2 b c Shalford (IRE)-Sharply (Sharpman) 4758[13] **>59f<**

Lena's Pride 4 b f Precious Metal-Lucky Lena (Leander) 2544[14] *4981[12]*

Lend A Hand 2 b c Great Commotion (USA)-Janaat (Kris) 1557[2] (2571) (2752) (2905) (4116) (4865a) **>119f<**

Lennox Lewis 5 b g Superpower-Song's Best (Never so Bold) **1996:** *5095[5]* **1997:** 443[19] 520[15] 2934[12] 3034[12] *4051[6]* 4233[21] 4414[16] 4770[11] **>57a 52f<**

Leofric 2 b c Alhijaz-Wandering Stranger (Petong) 1492[3] 2553[4] 2886[3] 3237[11] 3650[7] 3823[9] 4065[3] 4381[3] 4447[3] 4778[23] **>68f<**

Leonard Quercus (FR) 5 h 4654a[6] **>119f<**

Leonato (FR) 5 b g Law Society (USA)-Gala Parade (Alydar (USA)) *389[8]* **>109f<**

Le Rastaquouere (USA) 6 ro g Alwasmi (USA)-Icy Dial (USA) (Banderilla (USA)) (354a) 816a[3] **>98f<**

Leros (FR) 3 f 2275a[4] **>100f<**

Le Shuttle 3 b f Presidium-Petitesse (Petong) **1996:** *5107[6]* **1997:** *102[5] 193[7] 329[3]* 1008[8] 1483[11] **>44a 30f<**

Lesley's Adventure (IRE) 2 b br f Petardia-Island Adventure (Touching Wood (USA)) 2477[9] 2842[16] 3701[8] **>42f<**

Le Sport 4 b g Dowsing (USA)-Tendency (Ballad Rock) *111[4] 179[6] 194[4] 248[2] 274[2] 325[5]* **>75a 57f<**

Lets Be Fair 2 b f Efisio-Play the Game (Mummy's Game) 2545[4] (2739) (3222) **>91+f<**

Lettyfak (FR) 3 br c Akarad (FR)-Lettyfana (USA) (Fappiano (USA)) 2241[2] 2596[9] **>99f<**

Levelled 3 b g Beveled (USA)-Baino Charm (USA) (Diesis) 448[16] (602) 845[10] 995[3] (1989) 2141[5] 2563[12] 3473[4] 3614[2] 3765[7] 4183[5] 4321[3] (4452) 4565[3] 4677[8] **>81f<**

Leviticus (IRE) 3 b g Law Society (USA)-Rubbiera (IRE) (Pitskelly) 1268[2] 1981[6] 2494[3] 2889[3] 3267[4] (3754) **>86f<**

Lia Fail (IRE) 4 b f Soviet Lad (USA)-Sympathy (Precocious) **1996:** *5109[12] 5170[9] 5241[4] 5269[5]* **1997:** *35[3]* **>40a 43f<**

Liathach 6 b g Shirley Heights-Reuval (Sharpen Up) *1940[7]* 2175[7] 2518[2] 3540[4] 3929[9] **>7a 40f<**

Liberalis 2 ch f Interrex (CAN)-Hello Lady (Wolverlife) 836[16] 1425[14] 2003[13]

Liberte Bell (IRE) 2 b f Petorius-Ransomed (IRE) (Ballad Rock) *1286[10] 1941[9]* 2473[7] 4702[3] **>29a 59f<**

Libria (IRE) 3 b f Bering-L'Americaine (USA) (Verbatim (USA)) 3003a[3] 3875a[3] **>106f<**

Licketysplit 2 b f Rock City-Constant Companion (Pas de Seul) 4807[W]

Lidanna 4 b f Nicholas (USA)-Shapely Test (USA) (Elocutionist (USA)) 1881a[6] **>109f<**

Lido (IRE) 2 ch c Waajib-Licimba (GER) (Konigsstuhl (GER)) 1675[3] 2477[2] (2781) 3204[4] 3774[11] 4634[7] 4885[2] **>85f<**

Life of Riley 3 ch c Caerleon (USA)-Catina (Nureyev (USA)) 1239[3] (1646) 2122[4] 4002[15] 4295[13] **>92df<**

Life On The Street 3 b f Statoblest-Brave Advance (USA) (Bold Laddie (USA)) 3868[9] 4115[18] 4333[17] **>37f<**

Life Sentence 2 ch c Timeless Times (USA)-Marfen (Lochnager) *1136[8]* 2739[4] 2959[U] 3295[5] 3817[5] 4152[14] 4819[6] **>26a 61f<**

Liffey Ballad (IRE) 2 ch f Ballad Rock-Liffey Reef (Main Reef) 3961a[20] **>71f<**

Liffre (IRE) 3 b f Sadler's Wells (USA)-Liffey Lass (USA) (Irish River (FR)) 1846[3] 2410[2] (3218) 3648[3] 4234[8] **>88f<**

Lift Boy (USA) 8 b g Fighting Fit (USA)-Pressure Seat (USA) (Ginistrelli (USA)) **1996:** *5246[11]* **1997:** *11[4] 58[3] 117[8] 224[3] (278) 335[2] 512[6]* 638[9] *5018[9]* **>66a 51f<**

Liftoff (FR) 6 ch h Sharpo-Lighted Glitter 4540a[2] **>111f<**

Lift The Offer (IRE) 2 ch c Ballad Rock-Timissara (USA) (Shahrastani (USA)) 2699[6] 2943[2] 3887[3] 4157[9] 4875[11] **>68f<**

Lighted Rainbow (FR) 8 b h Rainbow Quest (USA)-Lighted Glory (USA) (270a) **>72?f<**

Lighten Up 3 b f Nashwan (USA)-Lagta (Kris) 683[10] 3738[4] 3977[7] 4323[10] 4509[3] 4794[11] **>66f<**

Lightning Bolt (IRE) 3 b f Magical Strike (USA)-Killyhevlin (Green God) **1996:** *5146[4] 5172[2] (5202) 5239[11]* **>58a 68f<**

Lightning Rebel 3 b g Rambo Dancer (CAN)-Ozra (Red Alert) *425[6]* 1470[7] 3487[7] 3870[6] **>17a 51f<**

Lightning Star (USA) 2 b c El Gran Senor (USA)-Cuz's Star (USA) (Galaxy Libra) 3962a[7] **>81f<**

Light Programme 3 b c El Gran Senor (USA)-Nashmeel (USA) (Blushing Groom (FR)) 2126[2] (2583) **>93f<**

Light Reflections 4 b g Rainbow Quest (USA)-Tajfah (USA) (Shadeed (USA)) 1108[5] 1276[9] 2199[11] **>58tf<**

Lights of Home 3 b c Deploy-Dream Chaser (Record Token) **1996:** *5121[7]* **1997:** *126[7] 181[9] 289[4]* **>36a 18f<**

Light Step (USA) 2 b f Nureyev (USA)-Nimble Feet (USA) (Danzig (USA)) 2312[3] 4597[3] 4904[16] **>76f<**

Likely Story (IRE) 2 b f Night Shift (USA)-Perfect Alibi (Law Society (USA)) 1783[3] 2516[2] 3033[2] 3595[7] (3799) 4106[5] 4267[5] **>85f<**

Lilanita 2 b f Anita's Prince-Jimlil (Nicholas Bill) 2571[5] 2875[13] **>41f<**

Lila Pedigo (IRE) 4 b f Classic Secret (USA)-Miss Goldie Locks (Dara Monarch) *340[8]* 574[15] 864[15] 1093[15] 2039[10] 2564[12] **>41a 51f<**

Lilian Marks (IRE) 2 gr f Astronef-Alicia Markova (Habat) 1997[16] 2306[12] 2587[7] 2923[7] **>48f<**

Lillibella 4 b f Reprimand-Clarandal (Young Generation) 749[6] 929[6] 1395[14] (1816) (2540) 3287[9] 3756[8] 4169[12] 4385[5] 4512[18] 4805[4] **>62f<**

Lilli Claire 4 ch f Beveled (USA)-Lillicara (FR) (Caracolero (USA)) (1085) 1326[2] **>104f<**

Lil's Boy (USA) 3 b c Danzig (USA)-Kentucky Lill (USA) (Raise A Native) (807a) 1060a[3] 2816a[4] **>100f<**

Lily Jaques 3 b f Petong-Scossa (USA) (Shadeed (USA)) **1996:** *5239[7] 5252[2]* **1997:** *8[3] 77[2] 124[13] 350[5]* 1233[12] **>53a 64f<**

Lily O'Gold (USA) 2 f *5060a[13]*

Limelight 3 b f Old Vic-Nellie Dean (Song) 989[7] 1563[4] 2008[10] 2374[7] 3133[3] *4053[7]* 4378[8] **>16a 60f<**

Lime Street Blues (IRE) 6 b g Digamist (USA)-Royal Daughter (High Top) 1422[18] 2198[6] 2589[9] 2949[3] 3283[2] 4104[12] 4222[7] 4562[18] **>64f<**

Limni (USA) 3 ch c Gone West (USA)-Lightning Fire (Kris) 3275[3] 4277[4] 4407[4] **>70f<**

Lincolnshire (USA) 2 b c Shadeed (USA)-Linkit (USA) (Linkage (USA)) 1163[5] 1933[5] 2349[4] 3402[2] **>74f<**

Linda 2 b f Risk Me (FR)-Farrh Nouriya (IRE) (Lomond (USA)) 3022[8] *4052[7] 4303[7] 4483[7]* **>46a 24f<**

Linden Heights 2 b c Distinctly North (USA)-Enaam (Shirley Heights) 1842[2] (2295) 2584[2] 3148[4] **>97f<**

Linden's Lad (IRE) 3 b c Distinctly North (USA)-Make Or Mar (Daring March) 509[13] 675[14] 1458[9] 1633[9] 1988[5] 2523[2] 4972[9] **>56f<**

Lindesberg 2 b f Doyoun-Be Discreet (Junius (USA)) 4418[3] 4904[6] 5042[2] **>71+f<**

Lindrick Lady (IRE) 3 b f Broken Hearted-Fiodoir (Weavers' Hall) 862[2] (1115) (1299) 1390[15] 1999[8] (2468) 2907[4] 3242[5] 3543[7] 3992[18] 4213[10] **>51f<**

Linea-G 3 ch f Keen-Horton Line (High Line) 996[5] 1282[5] 1630[7] **>48f<**

Lineage 2 b f Distant Relative-Hymne D'Amour (USA) (Dixieland Band (USA)) 4701[10] **>48f<**

Linesman (NZ) 6 5055a^5 **>117f<**

Linguistic Dancer 2 ch f Aragon-Linguistic (Porto Bello) 4701^{12} **>31f<**

Linnetsong 2 b f Rambo Dancer (CAN)-Blue Linnet (Habitat) 861^9 1310^7 (2153) 2499^4 3307^7 3990^{15} **>62f<**

Linoise (FR) 5 b m Caerwent-LiNeo (Gift Card (FR)) **1996:** 5155a^2 **1997:** 3372a^3 4001a^2 4390a^2 4864a^7 **>113f<**

Lionel 2 ch c Lion Cavern (USA)-Degannwy (Caerleon (USA)) 3176a^3 4253a^3 **>95?f<**

Lionels Lucky Lady 2 ch f Emarati (USA)-Gaynor Goodman (IRE) (Fayruz) 2003^9 2784^{11} 4500^7 **>19f<**

Lionize (USA) 4 ch c Storm Cat (USA)-Pedestal (High Line) 738^{12} 1016^{14} 4577^6 (4920) **>90f<**

Liquid Gold (IRE) 3 b br c Fairy King (USA)-Heavenward (USA) (Conquistador Cielo (USA)) 1322^6 (2173) 2760^6 3236^6 *(3584)* 3824^4 **>88+a 77+f<**

Lisa's Pride (IRE) 2 ch f Pips Pride-Brazilian Princess (Absalom) 828^{13} 985^8 (1827) 2138^{11} 2578^8 4447^5 **>73f<**

Listed Account (USA) 3 b f Private Account (USA)-Sypharina (FR) (Lyphard (USA)) 1110^6 1647^4 2427^2 2838^2 3425^3 4452^2 4600^2 **>82df<**

Literary 3 b f Woodman (USA)-Book Collector (USA) (Irish River (FR)) 1643^3 2143^2 2415^4 2772^8 3293^5 3787^3 4063^{13} 4451^4 (4695) 4920^6 **>80f<**

Literary Society (USA) 4 ch c Runaway Groom (CAN)-Dancing Gull (USA) (Northern Dancer) 834^2 1113^5 (1608) 1772^7 2563^3 (2833) 3198^{12} 4183^2 **>90f<**

Lithe Spirit (IRE) 5 b m Dancing Dissident (USA)-Afternoon Nap (USA) (Key To Content (USA)) **1996:** *5112^{10} 5134^{10}* **>24a 37f<**

Little Acorn 3 b g Unfuwain (USA)-Plaything (High Top) **1996:** *5103^5* **1997:** *387^2* (471) (826) 928^2 1877^3 2391^2 2963^2 4234^7 **>66a 93f<**

Little Annie 3 b f Syrtos-Anne's Bank (IRE) (Burslem) 565^6 768^9 1087^{10} **>42f<**

Little Brave 2 b c Kahyasi-Littlemisstrouble (USA) (My Gallant (USA)) 4413^5 4793^7 **>73f<**

Little Charmer 2 b f Theatrical Charmer-Saysana (Sayf El Arab (USA)) 4857^7 **>26f<**

Little Cracker 2 ch f Tina's Pet-All That Crack (Stanford) 3574^{15} *4303^9* 4627^3 **>11a 61f<**

Little Egypt (SWE) 3 ch c Diaglyphard (USA)-Saqqara (SWE) (Persian Bold) 1909a^3 **>80f<**

Little Emily 2 gr f Zafonic (USA)-Petillante (Petong) 2394^{12} **>10f<**

Little Fizz 2 b f Efisio-Apprila (Bustino) 2553^3 2740^5 4042^5 *4479^5* 4588^W **>52a 67f<**

Little Ibnr 6 b g Formidable (USA)-Zalatia (Music Boy) **1996:** *5236^7* **1997:** *1^6 31^3 51^5 (81) 89^3 126^4 136^6 233^{12} (371) 386^7 421^3 515^3 663^{10} 856^7 907^2 4301^{10} 4574^{11}* **>47a 54f<**

Little Indian 2 ch c Little Missouri (USA)-Both Sides Now (USA) (Topsider (USA)) 1842^3 (2477) 3123^3 (3895) 4889^7 **>102f<**

Little Luke (IRE) 6 b h Somethingfabulous (USA)-Yours Sincerely (USA) (Stalwart (USA)) *78^{10}* **>20da 36f<**

Little Miss Huff (IRE) 2 b f Anita's Prince-Regal Charmer (Royal And Regal (USA)) 2840^5 (3818) **>73+f<**

Little Miss Lucy 3 b f Petoski-Puki Puki (Roselier (FR)) 3133^4 3695^4 4045^P **>57f<**

Little Miss Rocker 3 b f Rock Hopper-Drama School (Young Generation) 1563^3 1986^2 2487^8 2787^4 (3298) 4161^{12} **>67f<**

Little Murray 4 b g Mon Tresor-Highland Daisy (He Loves Me) *98^7* **>49f<**

Little Papoose 4 b f Cree Song-Little Tich (Great Nephew) *659^7 856^{10} 1134^8 1428^{10}* 2203^{13} **>32a 16f<**

Little Pilgrim 4 b g Precocious-Bonny Bright Eyes (Rarity) **1996:** *5227^8 5253^6* **1997:** *76^{11} 160^7 224^6* 2488^{13} 2723^2 2947^{10} 3227^{13} 4371^{13} 4608^{13} 4987^{13} **>39a 34f<**

Little Progress 3 b g Rock City-Petite Hester (Wollow) **1996:** *5224^8* **1997:** 652^{12} *874^9* 1292^{13} **>23a 62f<**

Little Risk 2 b f Risk Me (FR)-Little Preston (IRE) (Pennine Walk) 4017^7 *4593^5* 4698^{15} *4812^{10}* **>32a 44f<**

Littlestone Rocket 3 ch c Safawan-Miss Hocroft (Dominion) 474^6 602^7 876^7 1236^6 1566^{10} (1667) 1848^4 1937^5 2581^3 2732^{10} *3398^{12}* 4115^{12} 4221^{11} **>19a 59f<**

Little Tolerance 2 ch f Weldnaas (USA)-Beau Dada (IRE) (Pine Circle (USA)) 3416^9

Little Tucker 3 ch g Hadeer-Fly The Coop (Kris) *255^{11}*

Little Tumbler (IRE) 2 b f Cyrano de Bergerac-Glass Minnow (IRE) (Alzao (USA)) 2664^2 2923^2 3289^4 4143^5 4380^9 4856^{13} **>59f<**

Live Project (IRE) 5 b g Project Manager-Saturday Live (Junius (USA)) *35^4 82^{13} 152^6 (209) 274^7 321^2 (382) 411^3* 526^9 608^8 *4050^{16} 4798^9* 4845^{18} 5028^{11} **>63a 49f<**

Livingstone 2 b c Dilum (USA)-Batra (USA) (Green Dancer (USA)) 447^9 938^6 **>48f<**

Livius (IRE) 3 b c Alzao (USA)-Marie de Beaujeu (FR) (Kenmare (FR)) 2532^2 **>80f<**

Lizium 5 b m Ilium-Lizaway (Casino Boy) 1779^{24} 3432^9 3792^8 **>37f<**

Llanasa 2 br f Petong-Chasing Moonbeams (Final Straw) 954^3 1407^3 1839^9 3070^7 3628^U **>65f<**

Lloc 5 b m Absalom-Nosey (Nebbiolo) **1996:** *5096^9 5173^6* **>50a 52f<**

Lobkov 5 ch m Dunbeath (USA)-Lucy Manette (Final Straw) 1237^{10} **>24f<**

Lobuche (IRE) 2 b c Petardia-Lhotse (IRE) (Shernazar) 836^{13} 1007^4 1370^2 3597^9 3924^8 4068^6 4447^6 4576^6 **>65f<**

Lochangel 3 ch f Night Shift (USA)-Peckitts Well (Lochnager) 1101^3 4155^4 4421^9 4553^7 **>108?f<**

Loch Bering (USA) 5 ch h Bering-Passerine (USA) (Dr Fager) **1996:** *5204^6* **>105a 92f<**

Lochdene (IRE) 2 b c Robellino (USA)-Cat's Claw (USA) (Sharpen Up) 954^5 1510^4 **>69f<**

Loch-Hurn Lady 3 b f Lochnager-Knocksharry (Palm Track) (466) 652^8 1029^{12} 1098^{15} 1250^{17} 2547^{10} 2733^{14} 4877^9 **>48f<**

Loch Laird 2 b g Beveled (USA)-Daisy Loch (Lochnager) 564^2 2553^2 3497^3 **>73f<**

Lochlass (IRE) 3 b f Distinctly North (USA)-Littleton Song (Song) **1996:** *5090^3 5147^5 5248^3* **1997:** *26^3* 2468^8 2956^8 3133^6 3592^6 *3860^{15}* 4243^6 4415^3 4858^6 *4906^9* **>58a 51f<**

Lochon 6 br g Lochnager-Sky Mariner (Julio Mariner) *263^{12} 349^7 386^3 421^8 545^7 593^6* 779^{10} 1089^6 *1289^8* 1620^{14} *1759^{11} 1944^5 2305^9* **>25a 37f<**

Loch Patrick 7 b g Beveled (USA)-Daisy Loch (Lochnager) 519^4 961^6 3217^{23} 3594^8 3914^7 4155^{17} **>94f<**

Loch Style 4 b g Lochnager-Simply Style (Bairn (USA)) **1996:** *5110^6* **1997:** *(54) 194^{10} 294^{10} 316^7 422^5* 467^2 687^8 *860^9 1786^6* 2755^5 3269^6 *3608^{11} 4480^5* **>48a 48f<**

Locksill 3 b c Silly Prices-Steelock (Lochnager) 1119^8 1394^8 1582^9 4214^{18} **>46?f<**

Loganlea (IRE) 3 br f Petong-White's Pet (Mummy's Pet) 1409^6 1587^{16} 2121^W 2332^{11} 3500^9 4527^8 **>57f<**

Logie Pert Lad 5 b g Green Ruby (USA)-Rhazya (Rousillon (USA)) **1996:** *5093^{10} 5149^{10} 5183^4 5215^{10} 5234^{10} 5282^9* **1997:** *58^8 97^5 199^6 223^5 282^5 304^8* 4221^{20} *5019^{13}* **>42a 28f<**

Loki (IRE) 9 ch g Thatching-Sigym (Lord Gayle (USA)) *384^9 402^4* **>66a 63f<**

Lombardic (USA) 6 b h Private Account (USA)-If Winter Comes (USA) (Dancing Champ (USA)) 1771^9 **>95f<**

Lomberto 4 b c Robellino (USA)-Lamees (USA) (Lomond (USA)) 1456^{16} (1852) 2296^2 2676^9 3773^{14} 3916^7 4294^2 4678^3 **>95f<**

Lomita (GER) 3 b f Niniski (USA)-La Luganese (Surumu (GER)) (4254a) 5031a^2 **>118f<**

Lomond Lassie (USA) 4 b f Lomond (USA)-Herbivorous (USA) (Nashua) *428^{11}* 3822^{13} 4872^{21} **>23f<**

Lonango (GER) 3 c 4661a^6 **>94f<**

London Lights 3 b c Slip Anchor-Pageantry (Welsh Pageant) 523^3 4060^5 **>84f<**

London News (SAF) 5 ch h Bush Telegraph (SAF)-Soho Secret (SAF) (Regent Street (ARG)) (720a) 2010^3 2453a^5 **>120f<**

London's Heart (USA) 3 b f Woodman (USA)-Seattle Belle (USA) (Seattle Slew (USA)) 559^3 686^8 841^{12} 1245^6 **>67f<**

Lonely Heart 3 b f Midyan (USA)-Take Heart (Electric) 989^2 1168^2 1591^5 1822^3 2507^4 2832^4 3389^9 (3738) 4369^5 4672^{12} **>88f<**

Lonely Leader (IRE) 4 ch c Royal Academy (USA)-Queen To Conquer (USA) (King's Bishop (USA)) 433^6 738^2 987^2 1323^7 2026^6 2766^{10} 3052^9 3150^{14} **>111df<**

Lone Piper 2 b c Warning-Shamisen (Diesis) 2429^3 3123^6 3644^9 **>92f<**

Lonesome Dude (CAN) 2 b c With Approval (CAN)-Local Lass (Local Suitor (USA)) 4901^2 **>97+f<**

Long Bond (IRE) 2 ch c Kris-Compton Lady (USA) (Sovereign Dancer (USA)) 4209^2 4538a^2 **>81+f<**

Longbowman 2 ch g Prince Sabo-Nuit de Lune (FR) (Crystal Palace (FR)) 4708^{13} **>37f<**

Longcroft 5 ch m Weldnaas (USA)-Najariya (Northfields (USA)) 493^{11} 1817^3 2000^9 2175^5 2932^7 **>12a 49f<**

Long Island 2 ch c Elmaamul (USA)-Ginny Binny (Ahonoora) 3094^{14} 4515^{14} 4818^7 4917^{17} *4982^3* **>67a 67f<**

Longmore Boy (IRE) 7 b g Bustomi-Ringford Lass 1005a^P

Long Siege (IRE) 2 ch c Brief Truce (USA)-Sugarbird (Star Appeal) 2588^5 **>72f<**

Longwick Lad 4 ro c Chilibang-Bells of St Martin (Martinmas) 520^{17} 834^7 (949) 1410^{13} 2950^7 3126^8 3326^6 3600^{10} **>72f<**

Lookingforarainbow (IRE) 9 ch g Godswalk (USA)-Bridget Folly (Crofter (USA)) 521^7 746^3 1118^5 1844^5 2744^3 3026^6 4584^9 4860^7 **>78a 58f<**

Lookingforlove Del (IRE) 2 ch f Be My Guest (USA)-Debenham (Formidable (USA)) 2587^{10} 4575^{12} 4974^{19} **>38f<**

Lookout 3 b f Salse (USA)-Sea Pageant (Welsh Pageant) 2008^6 2315^5 2652^6 (3455) 3694^5 (4104) 4222^3 4874^7 **>78f<**

Look Who's Calling (IRE) 4 b g Al Hareb (USA)-House Call (Artaius (USA)) 729^6 899^2 1406^3 1761^{15} 2760^{14} 3476^6 3910^{20} 4417^7 **>64f<**

Lord Advocate 9 br g Law Society (USA)-Kereolle (Riverman (USA)) 493^4 552^2 669^7 955^6 1039^5 1232^2 1281^8 (1618) (1840) 2034^5 2469^7 2824^5

3485^{7} 3631^{2} 3867^{5} 3921^{8} 4235^{11} 4279^{8} 4466^{2} 4704^{7} 5024^{7} **>32a 60f<**

Lordan Velvet (IRE) 5 br g Lord Americo-Danny's Miracle (Superlative) *415^{6} 543^{7}* 653^{8} *869^{8}* **>30a 37f<**

Lord Cornelious 4 b c Lochnager-Title (Brigadier Gerard) 1311^{9} 1604^{8} 2540^{15} 2657^{10} 2899^{12} **>10f<**

Lord Cromby (IRE) 3 ch c Risen Star (USA)-Havinia 3730a^{4} 4656a^{2} **>117f<**

Lord Discord 3 b g Primo Dominie-Busted Harmony (Busted) 2495^{6} 3071^{4} 3430^{2} 3813^{5} 4010^{9} **>68f<**

Lord Ellangowan (IRE) 4 ch c Astronef-Gossip (Sharp Edge) *141^{7} 295^{13}* **>48a 48f<**

Lord Esker (IRE) 5 b g Glacial Storm (USA)-April Rhapsody 1005a^{6}

Lord Eurolink (IRE) 3 b c Danehill (USA)-Lady Eurolink (Kala Shikari) 683^{3} (1023) 1399^{8} 2137^{3} 3190^{7} **>93f<**

Lord Hastie (USA) 9 b g Affirmed (USA)-Sheika (USA) (Minnesota Mac) 552^{8} 613^{6} 950^{5} 1081^{6} 1329^{3} 1452^{5} 2342^{7} 2503^{8} **>23a 51f<**

Lord High Admiral (CAN) 9 b g Bering-Baltic Sea (CAN) (Danzig (USA)) 443^{16} 834^{16} 972^{2} 1402^{6} 2289^{7} 2769^{10} 3410^{5} (3984) 4137^{18} 4434^{6} 4887^{22} **>91df<**

Lord High Emperor 3 b g High Estate-The Last Empress (IRE) (Last Tycoon) *90^{10} 156^{5} 191^{9}* **>23a f<**

Lord Jim (IRE) 5 b g Kahyasi-Sarah Georgina (Persian Bold) 736^{9} 891^{5} 1548a^{3} 2638a^{8} 4894^{8} **>89a 108f<**

Lord Kintyre 2 b c Makbul-Highland Rowena (Royben) 1109^{4} (1812) 2103^{4} (2862) 3148^{2} 3706^{4} 4675^{2} **>110f<**

Lord Lieutenant 2 b c Primo Dominie-Danzig Harbour (USA) (Private Account (USA)) 4012^{18} (4211) 4790^{26} **>79f<**

Lord Naskra (USA) 8 b g Naskra (USA)-Corvallis (USA) (Sir Ivor) *3583^{10}* 3933^{15} **>11?a f<**

Lord Oberon (IRE) 9 b g Fairy King (USA)-Vaguely Jade (Corvaro (USA)) 3392^{5} 3690^{10} 4179^{11} 4371^{4} 4629^{7} 4711^{8} **>57f<**

Lord of Love 2 b c Noble Patriarch-Gymcrak Lovebird (Taufan (USA)) 1510^{9} 1760^{7} 2168^{5} 2500^{4} 2681^{3} 3067^{8} 3869^{3} 3973^{6} 4334^{11} 4875^{4} **>69f<**

Lord of Men 4 ch c Groom Dancer (USA)-Upper Strata (Shirley Heights) (2338) (2765) (3731a) 4000a^{3} **>116f<**

Lord Olivier (IRE) 7 b g The Noble Player (USA)-Burkina (African Sky) (786) 942^{9} 1259^{7} 1772^{11} 2833^{9} 3130^{12} 3378^{2} 3765^{8} (4451) 4951^{2} **>81f<**

Lord Sky 6 b g Emarati (USA)-Summer Sky (Skyliner) **1996:** *5138^{4} 5230^{12}* **1997:** *53^{7} (117) 170^{2} 214^{9} 304^{6} 323^{3} 348^{2} 364^{7} (488) 905^{10}* 956^{3} 1037^{9} 1402^{10} 1957^{5} **>72a 57df<**

Lord Smith 2 ch g Greensmith-Lady Longmead (Crimson Beau) 441^{2} (530) 861^{5} (1330) (2240) (2489) (2681) (3025) **>89f<**

Lord Warford 2 b c Bustino-Jupiter's Message (Jupiter Island) 2768^{9} 3789^{6} 4433^{5} 4778^{21} **>68f<**

Lorins Gold 7 ch g Rich Charlie-Woolcana (Some Hand) 1089^{13} 1374^{9} (1677) 2281^{4} 2785^{2} (3227) **>48f<**

Lost In The Post (IRE) 4 ch g Don't Forget Me-Postie (Sharpo) *164^{9} 230^{6} 273^{9}* 595^{11} **>40a 39f<**

Lost Lagoon (USA) 5 ch h Riverman (USA)-Lost Virtue (USA) (Cloudy Dawn (USA)) 1809^{9} **>33f<**

Lostris (IRE) 6 b m Pennine Walk-Herila (FR) (Bold Lad (USA)) 465^{15} **>46f<**

Loubin Lane 2 b f Deploy-Another Lane (Tina's Pet) 3574^{16} 3979^{10} 4330^{13} 4806^{5} **>52f<**

Lough Erne 5 b m Never so Bold-Laugharne (Known Fact (USA)) 3984^{17} 4787^{26} 4995^{13} **>61f<**

Louis Philippe (USA) 2 b c El Gran Senor (USA)-Naqiyah (USA) (In Reality) 4775^{5} 4925^{2} **>82f<**

Loup Sauvage (USA) 3 ch c Riverman (USA)-Louveterie (USA) (Nureyev (USA)) 820a^{2} 1204a^{2} 2454a^{3} (4392a) 4785^{2} **>128f<**

Love Academy 2 b c Royal Academy (USA)-Quiet Week-End (Town And Country) 2112^{4} 4640^{2} (4840) **>86f<**

Love Again 2 br f Reprimand-Town Lady (Town Crier) 3857^{2} 4159^{2} *4479^{2}* 4755^{8} **>66a 62f<**

Love Has No Pride (USA) 3 gr c El Prado (IRE)-Chili Lee (USA) (Belted Earl (USA)) 431^{2} 690^{17} 990^{4} 1146^{12} 1482^{4} 1852^{4} 2551^{5} **>85f<**

Love Kiss (IRE) 2 b c Brief Truce (USA)-Pendulina (Prince Tenderfoot (USA)) 4735^{9} 4871^{4} 5046^{3} **>82f<**

Love Legend 12 ch g Glint of Gold-Sweet Emma (Welsh Saint) *401^{3}* 1599^{6} 1920^{9} **>36a 30f<**

Love Lock (USA) 2 f *5060a^{9}*

Lovely Morning 4 b f Thowra (FR)-Sweet Pleasure (Sweet Revenge) *322^{6}* **>10a 57f<**

Love Me Do (USA) 3 b g Minshaanshu Amad (USA)-I Assume (USA) (Young Emperor) *26^{5} 154^{3} 191^{2} 228^{3} (328)* 471^{6} 2352^{3} 2469^{6} 2737^{4} 3623^{6} (3781) **>76?a 73f<**

Love Over Gold 3 ch f Primo Dominie-Salacious (Sallust) *41^{10} 156^{6} 377^{8}* 1119^{16} 1858^{F} *2364^{5}* 3271^{14} 4326^{P}

Lovers Knot 2 b f Groom Dancer (USA)-Nemea (USA) (The Minstrel (CAN)) 4973^{2} **>84f<**

Love Venture 3 b f Pursuit of Love-Our Shirley (Shirley Heights) 1304^{4} 1646^{8} 2184^{4} 3132^{2} 3720^{3} 4009^{8} 4505^{6} 4916^{17} **>61f<**

Loveyoumillions (IRE) 5 b g Law Society (USA)-Warning Sound (Red Alert) **1996:** *5231^{10}* **1997:** *176^{10} 207^{7}* 435^{6} 570^{11} **>33a 62f<**

Loving And Giving 3 b f Sharpo-Pretty Poppy (Song) 506^{8} 1975^{7} 2833^{4} 3385^{5} 3984^{8} 4321^{15} 4565^{12} **>66f<**

Loving Claim (USA) 2 b f Hansel (USA)-Ville D'Amore (USA) (Irish River (FR)) (4663a) **>98f<**

Loxley's Girl (IRE) 3 b f Lahib (USA)-Samnaun (USA) (Stop The Music (USA)) *367^{6} 513^{4} 2368^{14} 3413^{12}* 4546^{3} **>44a 44f<**

Lucayan Beach 3 gr g Cyrano de Bergerac-Mrs Gray (Red Sunset) 4700^{13} 4881^{11} 4975^{7} **>84?f<**

Lucayan Indian (IRE) 2 ch c Indian Ridge-Eleanor Antoinette (IRE) (Double Schwartz) 4298^{10} (4513) (4775) **>91f<**

Lucayan Prince (USA) 4 br c Fast Play (USA)-Now That's Funny (USA) (Saratoga Six (USA)) 1532a^{3} 1776^{2} 2056^{11} 2599^{9} 3063^{8} **>118df<**

Lucky Archer 4 b g North Briton-Preobrajenska (Double Form) 4319^{14} 4606^{5} 4899^{12} **>56f<**

Lucky Bea 4 b g Lochnager-Knocksharry (Palm Track) 633^{5} **>47a 51f<**

Lucky Begonia (IRE) 4 br f Simply Great (FR)-Hostess (Be My Guest (USA)) 1262^{16} 1463^{11} 2036^{5} 2593^{2} 3101^{2} 3449^{2} 4991^{12} **>57f<**

Lucky Blue 10 b g Blue Cashmere-Cooling (Tycoon II) 481^{7} **>38f<**

Lucky Coin 5 b m Hadeer-Lucky Omen (Queen's Hussar) (4862a) **>122f<**

Lucky Coin (USA) 4 5063a^{4} **>127f<**

Lucky Dip 3 b f Tirol-Miss Loving (Northfields (USA)) 765^{6} 970^{4} (1566) 1848^{2} 2308^{6} *2663^{4}* 2780^{4} *5018^{8}* **>53a 73f<**

Lucky Double 2 b c Green Desert (USA)-Lady Bentley (Bellypha) 2388^{8} 4318^{6} (4515) **>75f<**

Lucky Hoof 4 b f Batshoof-Lucky Omen (Queen's Hussar) 632^{9} 1693^{5} **>53df<**

Lucky Myst 2 b c Mystiko (USA)-Lucky Omen (Queen's Hussar) 2893^{3} **>66f<**

Lucky Revenge 4 b f Komaite (USA)-Sweet And Lucky (Lucky Wednesday) *137^{9} 166^{5} 214^{6} 223^{8}* 774^{6} 997^{13} **>54a 59f<**

Lucy Glitters (USA) 2 b f Cryptoclearance (USA)-Way of The World (USA) (Dance of Life (USA)) 4884^{6} **>62f<**

Lucy In The Sky (IRE) 3 b f Lycius (USA)-Nazwa (Tarboosh (USA)) 4370^{3} 4707^{16} **>46f<**

Lucy of Arabia (IRE) 3 b f Mujadil (USA)-Fleur-de-Luce (Tumble Wind (USA)) *142^{5} 251^{5} 320^{7} 378^{4} 873^{4} 1151^{6}* 1373^{9} **>56a 56f<**

Lucy Tufty 6 b m Vin St Benet-Manor Farm Toots (Royalty) **1996:** *5139^{9}* **1997:** *63^{11}* 640^{7} *1417^{3} 2322^{4}* 2518^{6} **>40a 50df<**

Ludere (IRE) 2 ch c Desse Zenny (USA)-White Jasmin (Jalmood (USA)) 1819^{10} 2493^{8} 2827^{5} 2935^{7} **>37f<**

Ludo 3 br gr c Petong-Teacher's Game (Mummy's Game) 649^{14} 1012^{12} 1139^{2} 1487^{2} (1624) 1747^{7} 1956^{2} 2374^{6} 2667^{11} 3455^{8} 3792^{12} **>58f<**

Lunar Mist 4 b f Komaite (USA)-Sugar Token (Record Token) 731^{2} 942^{22} 1113^{3} 1446^{3} 1765^{5} 2377^{3} 2563^{14} **>79f<**

Lunar Music 3 b f Komaite (USA)-Lucky Candy (Lucky Wednesday) *158^{2} 247^{4} 379^{4} 427^{3}* 434^{6} 759^{11} 886^{14} 1080^{9} 1514^{8} 1730^{4} 2001^{9} 2883^{5} 3121^{10} **>64a 45f<**

Lunch Party 5 b g Beveled (USA)-Crystal Sprite (Crystal Glitters (USA)) 494^{10} 610^{8} 2567^{12} 3143^{11} (4228) 4404^{7} 4951^{4} (5030) **>55f<**

Lunchtime Girl 2 ch f Cadeaux Genereux-Thewaari (USA) (Eskimo (USA)) 2127^{8} 2467^{13} *4056^{5}* 4588^{10} **>54a 35f<**

Luso 5 b h Salse (USA)-Lucayan Princess (High Line) **1996:** (5217a) **1997:** *628a^{9}* 932^{5} (1549a) 2100a^{2} (3182a) 3737a^{2} 4127a^{2} 4537a^{2} 4866a^{2} **>100a 130f<**

Lutine Bell 2 b g Fairy King (USA)-Bell Toll (High Line) 5040^{12} **>39f<**

Lycian (IRE) 2 b c Lycius (USA)-Perfect Time (IRE) (Dance of Life (USA)) 4111^{12} 4229^{7} 4520^{10} 4856^{4} **>49f<**

Lycility (IRE) 3 b f Lycius (USA)-She's the Tops (Shernazar) 507^{2} 815a^{7} 1102^{5} 1318^{6} 3989^{8} 4383^{7} **>80f<**

Lycius Touch 3 b f Lycius (USA)-Homely Touch (Touching Wood (USA)) *19^{6} 124^{14}* 1503^{8} *1756^{11}* **>31a 47f<**

Lynton Lad 5 b g Superpower-House Maid (Habitat) 1085^{4} 1219^{4} 1473^{9} 2036^{2} 2390^{4} 2835^{16} **>71f<**

Lyphielo (USA) 3 b f Lyphard (USA)-Miss Concielo (USA) (Conquistador Cielo (USA)) 2873^{12} 3211^{13} 4400^{5} **>46f<**

Lysandros (IRE) 3 b c Lycius (USA)-Trojan Relation (Trojan Fen) 3095^{9} 4177^{5} 4631^{2} 4874^{8} **>78f<**

M

Maas (IRE) 2 br c Elbio-Payne's Grey (Godswalk (USA)) 4917^{18} **>10f<**

Maazoom (IRE) 2 b br c Be My Guest (USA)-Lancette (Double Jump) 2556^{7} **>48f<**

Mabli 2 b f Dilum (USA)-Eastwood Heiress (Known Fact (USA)) 1253^{12} **>18f<**

Macari 3 gr g Arzanni-View Halloa (Al Sirat (USA)) **1996:** *5160^{5}* **1997:** 1998^{4} 2171^{12} *2670^{6}* 3027^{3} 3601^{5} 3919^{16} 4415^{16} **>40a 48f<**

Macaribo 3 ch c Machiavellian (USA)-Sweet Mover (USA) (Nijinsky (CAN)) 3775^{3} 3991^{5} 4587^{2} **>74f<**

Macaroni Beach 3 ch f Jupiter Island-Real

Princess (Aragon) **1996:** *5090^{9} 5228^{12}* **>5a 58f<**
Mac Black 2 c 4865a^{6} **>98f<**
Macca Luna (IRE) 2 b f Kahyasi-Medicosma (USA) (The Minstrel (CAN)) 4057^{6} (4470) **>62+f<**
Maceo (GER) 3 ch c Acatenango (GER)-Metropolitan Star (USA) (Lyphard (USA)) (2641a) 4661a^{3} **>111f<**
Macgillycuddy (IRE) 8 bb g Petorius-My Bonnie (Highland Melody) 1446^{7} 1848^{6} 2232^{7} 2422^{6} 4112^{16} 4738^{9} **>57f<**
Machiavelli 3 b c Machiavellian (USA)-Forest Blossom (USA) (Green Forest (USA)) 841^{3} 1477^{4} 2046^{4} (2568) 3599^{4} 4101^{17} **>95f<**
Mach One (FR) 2 b g Sanglamore (USA)-Douceur (USA) (Shadeed (USA)) 4544^{14} **>38f<**
Macnamarasband (IRE) 8 b g Orchestra-Susan McCann (Furry Glen) 1005a^{2}
Mac Oates 4 b g Bairn (USA)-Bit of a Lass (Wassl) 4043^{9} (4373) 4504^{11} **>57f<**
Mac's Back (USA) 2 br c Momsfurrari (USA)-Peace Sister (USA) (Hold Your Peace (USA)) 2758^{5} **>12f<**
Mac's Delight 3 b g Machiavellian (USA)-Bashoosh (USA) (Danzig (USA)) 523^{6} 763^{16} 1011^{9} 4696^{17} **>55f<**
Mac's Type (IRE) 2 b f Mac's Imp (USA)-Pass No Problem (Pas de Seul) 4840^{13} 5029^{9} **>1f<**
Mad Alex 4 b g Risk Me (FR)-Princess Mona (Prince Regent (FR)) **1996:** *5101^{9} 5208^{11}* **1997:** *9^{9} 128^{5} 197^{8}* 1139^{3} 2281^{5} 2947^{14} **>20a 57f<**
Madame Chinnery 3 b f Weldnaas (USA)-Bel Esprit (Sagaro) 1474^{2} 2058^{20} 2421^{6} **>84f<**
Madame Claude (IRE) 2 b f Paris House-Six Penny Express (Bay Express) 2831^{9} 3288^{2} 3925^{6} (4227) 4473^{14} **>78f<**
Madame Jones (IRE) 2 ch f Lycius (USA)-Gold Braisim (IRE) (Jareer (USA)) 3711^{13} 4014^{3} 4368^{3} 4753^{8} **>68f<**
Madame Maxi 3 ch f Ron's Victory (USA)-New Pastures (Formidable (USA)) 4316^{6} 4816^{9} 4916^{13} **>62f<**
Madame Steinlen 4 b f Steinlen-Equadif (FR) (Abdos) **1996:** *5148^{11}* **>57a 72f<**
Madam Lucy 3 ch f Efisio-Our Aisling (Blakeney) *544^{7}* 826^{6} *1044^{3} 1429^{2} 1756^{4}* 2128^{4} *(2670) 3041^{5}* 3432^{3} 3562^{7} *4484^{5} 4800^{4} 4981^{7}* **>53a 49f<**
Madam Zando 4 ch f Forzando-Madam Trilby (Grundy) 1332^{7} 1734^{11} 1963^{13} 2891^{4} 3241^{12} 3431^{10} 3484^{12} 4417^{8} **>31a 37f<**
Maddie 5 b m Primitive Rising (USA)-Dubavarna (Dubassoff (USA)) *1755^{7}* 3089^{4} 3429^{3} 3858^{9} **>51f<**
Made Bold 3 b f Never so Bold-Classical Vintage (Stradavinsky) 2506^{3} 2704^{9} 4323^{13} 4632^{15} **>58df<**
Madge's Pet 3 b f Precious Metal-Lucky Lena (Leander) 2420^{12} 2704^{12} **>13f<**
Madison Mist 3 gr f Mystiko (USA)-Hi-Li (High Top) 645^{4} 899^{4} 1221^{9} 1470^{6} 1818^{10} **>70f<**
Madison's Touch 4 b f Touch of Grey-Cabinet Shuffle (Thatching) **1996:** *5085^{5} 5149^{9}* **1997:** 1689^{17} **>31a 4f<**
Madison Welcome (IRE) 3 b g Be My Guest (USA)-Subtle Change (IRE) (Law Society (USA)) 431^{14} 533^{3} 975^{5} 1449^{3} 2342^{4} 2469^{2} 3197^{7} 3779^{4} 4010^{6} 4336^{7} 4633^{11} **>59f<**
Madjamila (IRE) 2 b f Doyoun-Madaniyya (USA) (Shahrastani (USA)) (4909) **>84+f<**
Madler (IRE) 3 b c Saddlers' Hall (IRE)-Matahina (Moorestyle) **1996:** 5128a^{3} **>101f<**
Madly Sharp 6 ch g Sharpo-Madison Girl (Last Fandango) 677^{11} 1948^{8} 2211^{8} 3423^{8} 3649^{10} 4282^{11} 4550^{2} 4787^{10} **>94f<**
Madman's Mirage (FR) 2 b c Green Desert (USA)-Layaali (USA) (Diesis) 3629^{7} 3825^{8} 4278^{8} **>50f<**
Mad Militant (IRE) 8 b g Vision (USA)-Ullapool (Dominion) **1996:** *5233^{3} 5270^{3}* **1997:** *114^{3}* (538) 1427^{5} (1678) 2015^{9} 2686^{3} 3467^{3} 3886^{9} 4288^{3} 4923^{3} **>71a 67f<**
Madonna da Rossi 4 b f Mtoto-Granny's Bank (Music Boy) *59^{5} 128^{3} 143^{9} 209^{9} 321^{11}* **>33a 48f<**
Madrina 4 b f Waajib-Mainly Sunset (Red Sunset) **1996:** *(5093) 5112^{4} 5246^{8} 5268^{11}* **1997:** *58^{2} 170^{4} 301^{2} 391^{6}* **>71a 67f<**
Maduka (IRE) 2 ch f Paris House-Topseys Tipple 3506a^{3} **>92f<**
Maedaley 2 b f Charmer-Carousella (Rousillon (USA)) 780^{3} *1137^{7}* 2545^{11} 3451^{3} 4208^{2} 4427^{7} *4483^{5} 4982^{7}* **>51a 55f<**
Maenad 6 gr m Sharrood (USA)-Now In Session (USA) (Diesis) 3501^{4} **>68f<**
Maftool 3 ch c Machiavellian (USA)-Majmu (USA) (Al Nasr (FR)) (463) 723^{8} 2137^{4} 2328^{7} **>88f<**
Maftun (USA) 5 ch h Elmaamul (USA)-Allesheny (Be My Guest (USA)) *39^{3} 88^{2} 123^{2} 206^{2} 242^{3} (360) 410^{12}* 598^{3} **>68a 56f<**
Magaona (FR) 3 b f Slip Anchor-Movieland (USA) (Nureyev (USA)) 978^{5} 1420^{8} 1823^{9} **>53f<**
Magazine Gap 4 ch g Weldnaas (USA)-Divissima (Music Boy) **1996:** *5282^{3}* **1997:** *215^{5} 306^{4}* 585^{11} 759^{13} 792^{13} 1967^{10} *2193^{4}* 2246^{11} 2744^{5} *2912^{6}* 3321^{12} *4069^{2}* 4324^{9} **>53a 46f<**
Magellan (USA) 4 Hansel (USA)-Dabaweyaa (Shareef Dancer (USA)) 5063a^{5} **>117f<**
Magellano (USA) 3 b c Miswaki (USA)-Mount Holyoke (Golden Fleece (USA)) (1362a) 2460a^{2} **>125f<**
Maggice 2 b f Magic Ring (IRE)-Ice Chocolate (USA) (Icecapade (USA)) 2477^{5} 2842^{17} 3411^{12} 4433^{11} 4588^{13} *4982^{12}* **>28a 50f<**
Magical 2 b c Magic Ring (IRE)-Cal Norma's Lady (IRE) (Lyphard's Special (USA)) (3019) 3811^{5} **>76f<**
Magical Baba (IRE) 2 b c Magical Wonder (USA)-Mystery Treat 1531a^{5} 2439a^{9} 2987a^{4} **>86f<**
Magical Cliche (USA) 3 b f Affirmed (USA)-Talking Picture (USA) (Articulate) 1193a^{3} **>83f<**
Magical Colours (IRE) 2 b f Rainbows For Life (CAN)-Immediate Impact (Caerleon (USA)) 3490^{6} 4067^{11} **>62f<**
Magical Dancer (IRE) 2 b f Magical Wonder (USA)-Diva Encore (Star Appeal) 583^{5} 739^{10} 1091^{7} 1593^{8} 1954^{6} 2693^{9} 2917^{6} 3965^{6} 4166^{17} **>59f<**
Magical Minty (IRE) 2 b c Magical Wonder (USA)-Zany (Junius (USA)) 3962a^{6} 4357a^{5} **>102f<**
Magication 7 b m Nomination-Gundreda (Gunner B) *14^{9} 67^{9}* **>19a 42f<**
Magic Combination (IRE) 4 b g Scenic-Etage (Ile de Bourbon (USA)) 442^{9} 728^{11} 962^{12} 1215^{8} 2122^{5} (2483) 3010^{3} 3110^{9} 4136^{16} 4672^{13} 4854^{13} 5052^{14} **>78df<**
Magic Falls (IRE) 2 b c River Falls-Simply Inch (Simply Great (FR)) *3607^{8}* 4745^{7} **>46a 54f<**
Magic Fizz 3 gr c Efisio-Strawberry Pink (Absalom) **1996:** *5111^{11} 5162^{5} 5257^{3}* **1997:** *193^{6} 372^{3} 855^{2}* 1119^{15} 1401^{3} *1942^{8} 2305^{8}* 3088^{10} 4248^{17} *4809^{5}* **>53a 52df<**
Magic Hill 3 b f Danehill (USA)-Magic Flute (USA) (The Minstrel (CAN)) 727^{14} 2045^{4} **>72f<**
Magic Lahr (GER) 4 ch g Dashing Blade-Miraflores (GER) (Esclavo (FR)) 2008^{9} 2315^{11} 2492^{7} 2848^{12} 3470^{4} 3793^{3} **>61f<**
Magic Lake 4 b f Primo Dominie-Magic Kingdom (Kings Lake (USA)) 464^{12} *5931^{3}* 1131^{6} 1315^{13} 2651^{10} 2906^{3} 3393^{6} 4043^{14} 4169^{2} (4580) 4979^{10} **>48a 52f<**
Magic Melody 4 b f Petong-Miss Rossi (Artaius (USA)) 585^{19} 951^{11} *2070^{12} 2368^{12}* **>5a 21f<**
Magic Mill (IRE) 4 b c Simply Great (FR)-Rosy O'Leary (Majetta) 529^{12} 635^{6} 1583^{3} 2326^{12} 3087^{5} 4792^{5} 4924^{6} *5022^{2}* **>81a 80f<**
Magic Morning 2 ch g Magic Ring (IRE)-Incarnadine (Hot Spark) 4779^{18} 4966^{14} **>35f<**
Magic of Aloha (IRE) 2 ch f Diesis-Satz (USA) (The Minstrel (CAN)) 4474^{5} **>77f<**
Magic Powers 2 ch c Magical Wonder (USA)-Kissin' Cousin (Be Friendly) 4216^{11} 4515^{4} 4630^{6} **>65f<**
Magic Rainbow 2 b c Magic Ring (IRE)-Blues Indigo (Music Boy) 1425^{4} (1959) 2689^{5} **>76f<**
Magic Spring (IRE) 2 ch f Persian Bold-Oasis (Valiyar) 3187^{10} 4907^{5} 5041^{16} **>67f<**
Magic Surprise 3 f 815a^{15} **>64f<**
Maginot (USA) 2 gr c St Jovite (USA)-Gardien du Jour (USA) (Grey Dawn II) 2720^{8} **>55f<**
Magni Momenti 2 b f King's Signet (USA)-Halka (Daring March) 2306^{16} **>10f<**
Magyar Titok (IRE) 3 b c Treasure Kay-Aliyna (FR) (Vayrann) **1996:** *5092^{6}* **1997:** *132^{7}* **>47a 63f<**
Mahab (USA) 2 b f Nureyev (USA)-Personal Business (USA) (Private Account (USA)) 4332^{4} **>69f<**
Mahboob (IRE) 2 b br c Marju (IRE)-Miss Gris (USA) (Hail the Pirates (USA)) 2688^{2} (3598) 4096^{3} **>101f<**
Maiden Castle 4 b g Darshaan-Noble Destiny (Dancing Brave (USA)) 1176^{8} **>101f<**
Maid of Camelot 3 br f Caerleon (USA)-Waterfowl Creek (IRE) (Be My Guest (USA)) 676^{6} (875) (1318) 2053^{8} 2513^{6} 3216^{7} 3803^{4} 4181^{5} **>105f<**
Maiella 2 ch f Salse (USA)-Forelino (USA) (Trempolino (USA)) 3574^{11} 3973^{10} **>52f<**
Mail Shot (IRE) 2 b c Maledetto (IRE)-Pallachine (FR) (Lichine (USA)) 3489^{11} 4064^{14} 4379^{10} **>54f<**
Main Street 2 b c Emarati (USA)-I'm Yours (Forzando) 3783^{4} 4852^{11} *4982^{2}* **>68a 68f<**
Mai Tai (IRE) 2 b f Scenic-Oystons Propweekly (Swing Easy (USA)) 651^{3} 1109^{5} **>64f<**
Maiteamia 4 ch g Komaite (USA)-Mia Scintilla (Blazing Saddles (AUS)) 527^{3} 596^{3} 835^{13} 2422^{8} 2567^{13} *3075^{15}* 3761^{14} **>79?a 57f<**
Majaari 2 b br c Marju (IRE)-Ahbab (IRE) (Ajdal (USA)) 3489^{2} (3825) 4106^{4} **>94f<**
Majal (IRE) 8 b g Caerleon (USA)-Park Special (Relkino) 1472^{6} 1732^{2} 2170^{5} 2716^{7} 3453^{8} 4843^{14} **>60a 51f<**
Majalis 2 b br f Mujadil (USA)-Rose Barton (Pas de Seul) 4042^{3} 4216^{6} 4602^{4} **>74f<**
Majestic Hills 2 b c Shirley Heights-Regent Miss (CAN) (Vice Regent (CAN)) 4520^{2} 4715^{7} **>83f<**
Majesty (IRE) 3 b c Sadler's Wells (USA)-Princesse Timide (USA) (Blushing Groom (FR)) 479^{3} 3738^{3} 3977^{6} **>81f<**
Majinskaya (FR) 3 gr f Marignan (USA)-Makarova (FR) (Nijinsky (CAN)) 3552a^{2} 4666a^{13} **>107f<**
Major Ballaby (IRE) 2 b c Balla Cove-Surreal (Bustino) 3973^{11} 4209^{14} 4384^{5} **>75f<**
Major Change 5 gr h Sharrood (USA)-May the Fourteenth (Thatching) 310a^{10} *389^{2}* 451^{3} 499^{7} (787) 1176^{2} 1456^{6} 1768^{5} 2710^{21} 2839^{6} 3263^{3} 3703^{16} **>95a 93f<**
Major Dundee (IRE) 4 b g Distinctly North (USA)-Indigo Blue (IRE) (Bluebird (USA)) 2014^{19} **>81f<**
Majorien 3 ch c Machiavellian (USA)-Green Rosy (USA) (Green Dancer (USA)) (4389a) (4863a) 5065a^{10} **>120f<**
Major Mouse 9 ch g All Systems Go-Tzu-Hsi (Songedor) *71^{9} 153^{10} 194^{7} 273^{6} 359^{5} 415^{2} 578^{9}* 687^{13} 1472^{9} 2128^{5} 2544^{7} *2912^{4} 3609^{8}* **>57a**

44f<
Major Quality **4** b g Sizzling Melody-Bonne de Berry (Habitat) 726[20] **>95df<**
Major Twist (IRE) **3** b g Dancing Dissident (USA)-Kafsa (IRE) (Vayrann) *362[2]* 535[15] 1008[9] **>74a 39f<**
Makahu Don **2** ch g Derrylin-Rockalong (Native Bazaar) 1228[6] (1600) 1614[2] 2165[2] 2288[4] 2714[7] 2827[4] 3062[5] 3258[9] 3699[7] *4054[17]* 4468[12] 4746[8] **>9a 58df<**
Makati **3** b g Efisio-Seleter (Hotfoot) 599[W] 899[7] 1119[18] 1451[8] 2502[14] **>28f<**
Make Believe **2** ch f Caerleon (USA)-Sleeping Beauty (Mill Reef (USA)) 1564[7] 2038[3] **>57f<**
Make It So **2** ch f Henbit (USA)-H and K Gambler (Rheingold) 1664[7] 2893[W] **>14f<**
Make Ready **3** b f Beveled (USA)-Prepare (IRE) (Millfontaine) *871[12] 1046[7]* 1439[3] 1963[8] 2179[4] 2536[5] 3016[9] 3121[7] 3693[5] 4016[22] 4328[18] **>57a 56f<**
Makidarti **2** ch f Akid (USA)-Middletown Girl (Steel City) 3808[10] **>17f<**
Malabi (USA) **3** b c Danzig (USA)-Gmaasha (IRE) (Kris) 565[2] 1967[3] 2704[10] **>82f<**
Maladerie (IRE) **3** b g Thatching-Native Melody (Tudor Music) 723[15] 930[12] 1589[10] 1973[9] 3236[11] 3548[9] 3923[2] 4048[11] 4112[6] 4248[3] 4333[2] 4546[8] 4601[2] 4738[5] 4877[8] **>65f<**
Male-Ana-Mou (IRE) **4** ch g Ela-Mana-Mou-Glasson Lady (GER) (Priamos (GER)) 1108[3] 1319[7] 1934[7] 4002[5] 4156[5] 4376[3] **>90f<**
Malibu Man **5** ch g Ballacashtal (CAN)-National Time (USA) (Lord Avie (USA)) (473) 731[3] *905[3]* 1223[6] 1743[7] *(2050)* 2339[4] 2590[3] 3126[9] (3326) 3771[12] 3900[7] 4137[5] *4482[2]* **>84a 81f<**
Mallia **4** b g Statoblest-Pronetta (USA) (Mr Prospector (USA)) 942[14] 1259[10] 1799[14] 1946[9] 2326[17] 2711[9] 2900[11] 3756[17] 3910[2] 4155[19] 4414[11] 4456[2] 4995[12] **>72f<**
Malozza **2** b f Michelozzo (USA)-Lis Na Mon (Gleason (USA)) *(1136)* 1675[7] 1945[5] *3395[8] (4483) 4593[3] 4796[3]* 4922[9] **>59a 36f<**
Malsisio **5** b m Efisio-Moonlight Fling (Imperial Fling (USA)) *3399[5]* 4742[15] **>22a 18f<**
Mamalik (USA) **3** b c Diesis-Have It Out (USA) (Roberto (USA)) (742) 1725a[2] 2011[8] 4142[3] **>108f<**
Mamble's Pension (IRE) **2** ch f Elmaamul (USA)-Chance All (FR) (Glenstal (USA)) *4569[11]* **>29a f<**
Mambo Music (FR) **3** gr f Rusticaro (FR)-Musical Soul (USA) (Youth (USA)) *239[6]* **>9a f<**
Mamma Luigi (IRE) **3** b f Classic Music (USA)-Second Movement (Music Boy) 727[17] 989[12] 1316[15] **>14f<**
Mamma's Boy **2** b g Rock City-Henpot (IRE) (Alzao (USA)) 548[2] 684[3] 861[3] 1038[4] 3226[3] 3379[5] 3869[7] 4236[3] **>73f<**
Mamora Bay (IRE) **2** b c High Estate-Amenaide (Known Fact (USA)) 695[3] 861[6] 1842[7] 2689[3] 3067[2] 3237[13] 3990[14] 4245[8] *4592[4]* 4753[19] **>51a 70f<**
Manabar **5** b g Reprimand-Ring of Pearl (Auction Ring (USA)) **1996:** *5132[2] 5223[6] 5242[3]* **1997:** *10[6] 81[4] 113[6] 120[7] 319[8] 490[10]* 653[9] *2071[8]* 3420[8] **>37a 42f<**
Manaloj (USA) **4** ch c Gone West (USA)-Deviltante (USA) (Devil's Bag (USA)) 939[7] 1264[4] 2743[8] 3135[8] **>71f<**
Manazil (IRE) **3** ch f Generous (IRE)-Stay Sharpe (USA) (Sharpen Up) (889) 1462[5] 1973[7] 2210[2] 2585[6] (2839) (3012) 3492[9] **>99f<**
Mandellicht (IRE) **3** f 1202a[5] **>92f<**
Mandhar (IRE) **2** b c Scenic-Clonross Lady (Red Alert) 4007[11] 4318[14] **>60f<**
Mandilak (USA) **3** b c El Gran Senor (USA)-Madiriya (Diesis) 1793[2] 2180[2] 2515[4] 3125[6] **>102f<**
Manful **5** b g Efisio-Mandrian (Mandamus) **1996:** *(5181) 5233[2]* **1997:** *88[4] 196[7]* 435[4] (552) 781[7] (955) 1313[2] 1992[3] 2293[9] 2676[10] 4279[W] 4466[13] 4691[8] 4886[6] **>75a 72f<**
Mangus (IRE) **3** b c Mac's Imp (USA)-Holly Bird (Runnett) *204[2] 258[2]* (652) 1018[2] 1294[11] 2134[5] 2377[13] 2779[6] **>71a 75df<**
Manhattan Diamond **3** ch f Primo Dominie-June Fayre (Sagaro) **1996:** *5133[9] 5164[8]* **1997:** *395[5]* 497[4] 1284[8] 1467[5] 2237[13] **>48a 54f<**
Man Howa (IRE) **3** ch c Lycius (USA)-Almuhtarama (IRE) (Rainbow Quest (USA)) 980[3] 1403[2] 2023[14] **>102f<**
Manikato (USA) **3** b c Clever Trick (USA)-Pasampsi (USA) (Crow (FR)) 509[11] 766[2] 1226[4] 1505[4] 2246[8] 2722[6] 3320[5] 4757[23] *5020[4]* **>58a 53f<**
Manila Moon (USA) **2** b c Manila (USA)-Sign Language (USA) (Silent Screen (USA)) 4309[W] 4793[10] 5048[15] **>43f<**
Manileno **3** ch g K-Battery-Andalucia (Rheingold) 445[7] 551[3] 793[3] (1507) (2146) (2490) 2932[3] **>71+f<**
Mannenberg (IRE) **3** c 4656a[7] **>105f<**
Mannequin (IRE) **2** b f In The Wings-Pretty Lady (High Top) 3479[4] **>69+f<**
Mann o Mann (GER) **3** c 2097a[12] **>67f<**
Manolo (FR) **4** b g Cricket Ball (USA)-Malouna (FR) (General Holme (USA)) 666[4] (772) 949[7] 1627[8] *2050[2]* 2221[5] 2563[2] 2717[4] 2844[4] 3107[5] 3856[4] 4233[12] 4844[9] **>61a 63f<**
Mansab (USA) **4** b g Housebuster (USA)-Epitome (USA) (Summing (USA)) *(152) (233) (254)* 443[11] 1977[23] 3548[15] 3690[13] **>83+a 61f<**
Mansa Musa (IRE) **2** br c Hamas (IRE)-Marton Maid (Silly Season) 4446[4] **>70f<**
Mans Passion **5** gr g Jupiter Island-Roybirdie (Mansingh (USA)) 2998a[2] **>42f<**
Mantello **2** ch c Mon Tresor-Laena (Roman Warrior) 3770[11] 4298[11] 4884[13] **>56f<**
Mantles Pride **2** b c Petong-State Romance (Free State) 504[5] 3686[2] 4145[8] (4403) 4851[5] 4911[5] **>83f<**
Mantles Prince **3** ch g Emarati (USA)-Miami Mouse (Miami Springs) 509[4] 690[6] 958[4] 1249[2] 1739[5] 3153[6] 3741[4] 3897[4] 4176[4] 4672[2] **>84f<**
Mantles Star **2** ch c Beveled (USA)-Nosey (Nebbiolo) 2295[5] *(2595)* 3215[2] 3688[3] 4790[12] **>74a 92+f<**
Mantusis (IRE) **2** ch c Pursuit of Love-Mana (GER) (Windwurf (GER)) 4318[2] (4715) **>87f<**
Manuetti (IRE) **3** b f Sadler's Wells (USA)-Rosefinch (USA) (Blushing Groom (FR)) 978[3] 2389[2] **>83f<**
Manufan **2** b c Sabrehill (USA)-The Last Empress (IRE) (Last Tycoon) 4638[15]
Mapengo **6** b g Salse (USA)-Premiere Cuvee (Formidable (USA)) **1996:** *5130[14] 5232[2] 5255[6]* **1997:** *43[10] 167[3] 256[9] 272[3]* 950[8] *1288[4]* 2874[11] 2955[7] 3792[7] **>37a 45f<**
Maple Bay (IRE) **8** b g Bold Arrangement-Cannon Boy (USA) (Canonero (USA)) **1996:** *5106[10]* **1997:** 444[17] 4510[13] **>86a 66f<**
Maradata (IRE) **5** ch m Shardari-Maridana (USA) (Nijinsky (CAN)) **1996:** *5118[2] 5206[3] 5274[8]* **1997:** *140[2] 219[4]* 2570[7] 3570[8] **>71a 58f<**
Maradi (IRE) **3** b g Marju (IRE)-Tigora (Ahonoora) *(355)* 690[9] 1002[2] *1156[12]* 1595[3] 2058[13] 2548[4] 3424[9] 4223[8] 4714[7] 4998[12] **>59a 55f<**
Maraeinca **4** b f Inca Chief (USA)-Countess Mariga (Amboise) 638[12] 964[11]
Marahill Lad **2** b c Mazilier (USA)-Harmonious Sound (Auction Ring (USA)) 2147[6] 2409[6] 2926[8] 4229[8] **>47f<**
Maralinga (IRE) **5** ch g Simply Great (FR)-Bellinzona (Northfields (USA)) **1996:** *5204[7]* **1997:** (1659) 2656[2] 3051[9] 3634[6] **>100a 101f<**
Mara River **3** b f Efisio-Island Mill (Mill Reef (USA)) (970) 1243[3] (1935) (2309) 2871[5] 3128[5] 3913[11] 4424[6] **>90f<**
Maraschino **4** ch f Lycius (USA)-Mystery Ship (Decoy Boy) **1996:** *5093[12]* **>29a 55f<**
Maratana (IRE) **3** b f Don't Forget Me-Zenga (Try My Best (USA)) 3508a[4] **>88f<**
Marathon (USA) **3** b c Diesis-Most Precious (USA) (Nureyev (USA)) (3729a) (3996a) 4662a[3] 5059a[2] **>115f<**
Marathon Maid **3** gr f Kalaglow-El Rabab (USA) (Roberto (USA)) 1146[13] 2133[11] 3648[4] 3989[6] 4234[6] **>79f<**
Maraud **3** ch g Midyan (USA)-Peak Squaw (USA) (Icecapade (USA)) 2062[15] 2645[10] 3696[12] 4847[19] **>34f<**
March Crusader **3** b c Green Desert (USA)-Layaali (USA) (Diesis) 586[9] 1088[4] 1423[4] 1691[2] (1967) 2326[18] 2590[5] 2925[2] 3145[7] 3614[8] (3923) 4155[5] 4756[U] **>92f<**
March Fourteenth (USA) **2** b f Tricky Creek (USA)-Ruby Tuesday (USA) (T V Lark) 3574[14] 3743[5] 4007[6] **>67f<**
March Groom (USA) **3** ro c Runaway Groom (CAN)-Marfa's Alibi (USA) (Marfa (USA)) (3998a) (4650a) **>121f<**
Marchman **12** b g Daring March-Saltation (Sallust) 1642[2] **>59f<**
March Star (IRE) **3** b f Mac's Imp (USA)-Grade a Star (IRE) (Alzao (USA)) 988[2] 3747[8] (4226) **>93f<**
Mardi Gras (IRE) **3** b c Danehill (USA)-Gracieuse Majeste (FR) (Saint Cyrien (FR)) 502[5] 605[2] 1434[5] 2297[7] **>78f<**
Mardrew **3** b c Rambo Dancer (CAN)-Having Fun (Hard Fought) *(90) 175[3] 298[6] 414[3]* 644[3] 840[7] 886[3] 1096[3] 1248[4] 1632[2] 1694[4] 2182[2] 2667[6] 2885[2] 3200[11] 3633[4] 3813[4] 4310[5] 4477[5] **>75a 71f<**
Mareeba **2** b f Last Tycoon-Albufeira (IRE) (Be My Guest (USA)) 3282[4] 3920[4] 4567[3] 4849[5] **>67f<**
Maremma **3** b f Robellino (USA)-Maiden Way (Shareef Dancer (USA)) *425[7]* 534[3] *581[10]* 793[5] 1094[9] 1299[11] 1469[12] 1863[5] 2387[4] 2662[4] 2908[8] (3068) 3478[6] 3781[7] 4160[10] 4336[9] 4509[9] **>11a 53f<**
Marengo **3** b c Never so Bold-Born to Dance (Dancing Brave (USA)) 1012[2] 1374[13] 1989[3] 2220[2] 2393[6] 2964[11] 3473[5] 3800[7] 3984[9] 4333[16] 4738[7] **>50f<**
Marethea (FR) **3** gr f Bering-Maralinga (FR) (Nureyev (USA)) **1996:** 5153a[3] **>91f<**
Margaretrose Anna **5** b m Handsome Sailor-Be Bold (Bustino) **1996:** *5109[4]* **1997:** *288[5] 326[4] 385[6] 421[12]* 585[17] *1047[12] 1289[9]* **>25a 37f<**
Margaret's Dancer **2** b c Rambo Dancer (CAN)-Cateryne (Ballymoss) 447[14] *1136[7]* 1461[4] *1758[7]* 2493[14] 2587[8] *3586[11]* 4058[10] **>31a 52f<**
Margone (USA) **2** b br f Dayjur (USA)-Whispered Secret (CAN) (Secretariat (USA)) 4904[14] **>58f<**
Mariana **2** ch f Anshan-Maria Cappuccini (Siberian Express (USA)) 1797[W] 2042[3] 2545[8] 3629[5] 4042[9] 4327[13] 4566[7] **>58f<**
Marie Dora (FR) **3** gr f Kendor (FR)-Marie de Vez (FR) (Crystal Palace (FR)) 727[8] (1409) 1740[7] 2133[5] 2561[5] 3575[4] 3803[9] 4242[14] **>83f<**
Marie J (USA) **2** f *5060a[4]*
Mari-Ela (IRE) **2** ch f River Falls-Best Swinger

(IRE) (Ela-Mana-Mou) 836^{4} 1593^{6} 1806^{5} 2565^{4} 2719^{8} 4068^{8} (4753) 4898^{5} **>72f<**
Marie Loup (FR) 2 ch f Wolfhound (USA)-Marie de Fontenoy (FR) (Lightning (FR)) 4227^{3} 4425^{4} **>78+f<**
Marigliano (USA) 4 b g Riverman (USA)-Mount Holyoke (Golden Fleece (USA)) 4577^{7} **>93?f<**
Marigot Bay (IRE) 2 b f Fairy King (USA)-Prawn Cocktail (USA) 1531a^{4} 4090a^{3} 4391a^{8} **>94f<**
Marilaya (IRE) 3 b f Shernazar-Mariyada (USA) (Diesis) 2583^{2} (2888) 3128^{12} (4306) 4669^{10} **>94f<**
Marilia (IRE) 2 ch f River Falls-Bronze Celtic 2987a^{6} 3961a^{23} **>77f<**
Marimbo (IRE) 2 b br g Elbio-Nikara (FR) (Emerson) 2579^{8} 3692^{9} **>22f<**
Marino Street 4 b f Totem (USA)-Demerger (Dominion) **1996:** *5144^{9} 5163^{13}* **1997:** 1613^{15} *1790^{3}* 1865^{2} 2203^{10} *2305^{6}* 2536^{7} *2674^{4}* 3143^{14} 3756^{10} 4016^{14} **>38a 53f<**
Marion's Pet 2 ch f Tina's Pet-Fay Eden (IRE) (Fayruz) 3324^{11} 3782^{11} 4167^{17} **>26f<**
Marisa's Pet 3 gr f Petong-Always on a Sunday (Star Appeal) 1316^{16}
Marjaana (IRE) 4 b f Shaadi (USA)-Funun (USA) (Fappiano (USA)) 848^{2} (1422) 1599^{2} (1663) 2430^{6} 3048^{6} (3476) 3771^{8} 3982^{2} 4276^{2} 4561^{7} **>84f<**
Marjorie Rose (IRE) 4 b f Magical Strike (USA)-Arrapata (Thatching) **1996:** *(5234) 5264^{2}* **1997:** *35^{6} 275^{5} 318^{4} 386^{9}* 2382^{4} *2674^{3}* 2899^{8} *3399^{2} 3582^{6}* **>64a 60f<**
Markapen (IRE) 3 b f Classic Music (USA)-Dahsala (Top Ville) 732^{4} **>51?f<**
Markham (AUS) 4 b/br g Salieri (USA)-Fetoon (Persian Bold) 5055a^{3} **>117f<**
Mark of Prophet (IRE) 2 b c Scenic-Sure Flyer (IRE) (Sure Blade (USA)) 4174^{8} 4603^{5} 4852^{10} **>73f<**
Marksman (IRE) 2 b c Marju (IRE)-Warg (Dancing Brave (USA)) (2123) **>77+f<**
Marl 4 ch f Lycius (USA)-Pamela Peach (Habitat) 540^{5} 1317^{5} 1772^{10} 2833^{15} **>87f<**
Marlin (USA) 4 b c Sword Dancer (USA)-Syrian Summer (USA) (Damascus (USA)) (3880a) **>129f<**
Maroulla (IRE) 3 ch f Caerleon (USA)-Mamaluna (USA) (Roberto (USA)) (1591) 1875^{9} **>84f<**
Maroussie (FR) 4 br f Saumarez-Madiyma (FR) (Top Ville) **1996:** (5154a) **1997:** 1199a^{2} 3370a^{6} **>116f<**
Marozia (USA) 3 ch f Storm Bird (CAN)-Make Change (USA) (Roberto (USA)) 4848^{2} *5020^{3}* **>60a 82f<**
Marran (IRE) 2 b c Caerleon (USA)-Tanouma (USA) (Miswaki (USA)) 2524^{3} 2898^{2} 4157^{4} (4447) **>79f<**
Marsad (IRE) 3 ch c Fayruz-Broad Haven (IRE) (Be My Guest (USA)) 694^{9} 1141^{6} 2711^{7} **>75f<**
Marsayas (IRE) 4 ch g Classic Music (USA)-Babiana (CAN) (Sharpen Up) 1585^{3} 2000^{11} 2825^{3} 3284^{2} **>42a 66f<**
Marsh Marigold 3 br f Tina's Pet-Pulga (Blakeney) *7^{6} 130^{4}* 749^{13} 1024^{5} 1129^{10} 1268^{6} (1802) 1999^{4} 2158^{2} 2362^{3} 2468^{4} 2757^{5} 2907^{7} **>37a 68f<**
Marsh's Law 10 br g Kala Shikari-My Music (Sole Mio (USA)) 950^{12}
Marske Machine 2 ch f Prince Daniel (USA)-Ciboure (Norwick (USA)) 500^{6} 897^{6} 1228^{4} 1616^{5} 2222^{4} 2714^{4} 3067^{7} (3451) 3692^{4} (3911) 4427^{4} 4767^{6} 4806^{2} 4994^{4} **>65f<**
Marsul (USA) 3 b br c Cozzene (USA)-Beside (USA) (Sportin' Life (USA)) 2532^{4} 2924^{3} 3188^{3} (3419) 4101^{14} (4409) **>95f<**
Martindale (IRE) 4 b g Fairy King (USA)-Whist Awhile (Caerleon (USA)) 795^{8} 1315^{11} 1655^{8} 2177^{9} 2938^{4} **>40f<**
Martine 3 ch f Clantime-Marcroft (Crofthall) 2141^{6} 2567^{11} 3088^{7} 3470^{14} 4164^{8} **>55f<**
Martiniquais (IRE) 4 ch c Simply Great (FR)-Majolique (Irish River (FR)) 4530a^{4} **>114f<**
Marton Moss (SWE) 2 b g Polish Patriot (USA)-Arrastra (Bustino) 1267^{14} 1492^{8} (2361) 2685^{5} (3270) 3811^{4} 4737^{10} **>85f<**
Marx Mistress 3 b f Batshoof-No Jazz (Jaazeiro (USA)) 1144^{13} **>40f<**
Mary Cornwallis 3 ch f Primo Dominie-Infanta Real (Formidable (USA)) 2838^{4} 3425^{2} 3863^{4} 4182^{3} **>92df<**
Mary Culi 3 gr f Liboi (USA)-Copper Trader (Faustus (USA)) 1423^{5} 1826^{13} 2848^{6} 3227^{11} 4179^{9} 4503^{8} 4883^{3} **>58f<**
Mary Jane 2 b f Tina's Pet-Fair Attempt (IRE) (Try My Best (USA)) 4211^{9} *4479^{3}* (4921) **>54a 68f<**
Maryjo (IRE) 8 b m Tale Quale-Down The Aisle (Godswalk (USA)) *4590^{12}* 4821^{14} **>18f<**
Marylebone (IRE) 3 ch g River Falls-Pasadena Lady (Captain James) 469^{2} 636^{2} 792^{6} 2157^{4} 4047^{8} 4290^{6} 4738^{11} **>66f<**
Mary Lou (IRE) 2 b f Tirol-Kilcsem Eile (IRE) (Commanche Run) 1997^{8} 2222^{5} 3788^{6} 3967^{8} 4058^{12} 4334^{13} *4592^{7}* 4698^{5} *4984^{4}* **>37a 53f<**
Mary Magdalene 3 b f Night Shift (USA)-Indian Jubilee (Indian King (USA)) (2496) 2841^{3} 3145^{2} 3709^{8} 4307^{7} 4733^{16} **>74f<**
Marys Path 3 b f Rock Hopper-Jasmin Path (Warpath) 773^{10} 862^{10} 1095^{10} 2874^{10} 3129^{6} **>25f<**
Marytavy 3 b f Lycius (USA)-Rose Parade (Thatching) 2722^{2} 2909^{2} 3225^{6} *(4053)* **>72a 68f<**
Marzocco 9 ch g Formidable (USA)-Top Heights (High Top) 950^{13} 1862^{6} 2237^{3} 2854^{4} **>32f<**
Masamadas 2 ch c Elmaamul (USA)-Beau's Delight (USA) (Lypheor) 5040^{7} **>60f<**
Mashab 2 b c Pursuit of Love-Kukri (Kris) 3687^{9} 4708^{5} **>69f<**
Masha-Il (IRE) 2 b c Danehill (USA)-Valley Lights (IRE) (Dance of Life (USA)) 4145^{7} 4640^{3} (5042) **>79f<**
Masharik (IRE) 3 b f Caerleon (USA)-Rosia Bay (High Top) 2379^{2} (2731) 3727^{5} **>93f<**
Mashhaer (USA) 3 b br c Nureyev (USA)-Life's Magic (USA) (Cox's Ridge (USA)) 3220^{2} 3713^{3} 4141^{7} **>95f<**
Mashkorah (USA) 3 ch f Miswaki (USA)-Tom's Lassie (USA) (Tom Rolfe) 1322^{7} 1567^{7} 1987^{7} **>55f<**
Mashmoum 4 ch f Lycius (USA)-Flaming Rose (USA) (Upper Nile (USA)) **1996:** *5106^{7}* **>78a 93f<**
Masrrah (IRE) 3 b c Old Vic-Masarrah (Formidable (USA)) *373^{10} 491^{4} 658^{3}* 1140^{8} 1387^{7} **>63a 55f<**
Masruf (IRE) 5 b g Taufan (USA)-Queen's Share (Main Reef) *224^{7} 278^{9}* **>33a 52f<**
Massyar Seventeen 3 b g Chilibang-Westminster Waltz (Dance In Time (CAN)) 1409^{4} 2492^{8} 3140^{5} 3453^{4} 4714^{11} 4919^{5} **>65f<**
Master Beveled 7 b g Beveled (USA)-Miss Anniversary (Tachypous) **1996:** *5274^{5}* **1997:** *92^{3}* 538^{4} 647^{4} 1262^{2} 1559^{5} 1775^{12} 1979^{5} 2136^{7} 4410^{9} 4635^{2} 4757^{5} 4788^{5} 4882^{5} *5022^{3}* **>72a 79f<**
Master Bobby 3 b g Touch of Grey-Young Lady (Young Generation) **1996:** *5187^{8}* **1997:** *395^{9} 455^{4}* 2750^{8} 2956^{9} **>29da 33f<**
Master Boots 4 br c Warning-Arpero (Persian Bold) 1160^{11} *1578^{7}* 2598^{8} *(3075)* 3423^{13} 4787^{16} **>99a 97f<**
Master Caster (IRE) 2 b c Night Shift (USA)-Honourable Sheba (USA) (Roberto (USA)) 4575^{10} 4710^{13} **>65f<**
Master Charter 5 ch g Master Willie-Irene's Charter (Persian Bold) 892^{18} 2290^{3} **>88f<**
Master Foley 3 ch c Cigar-Sultans Gift (Homing) **1996:** *5107^{4} 5176^{5} (5239)* **1997:** *17^{4} 180^{6} 193^{2} 258^{5} 372^{2}* 466^{5} 532^{2} 649^{3} *2605^{6} 3040^{2} 3398^{10}* 3812^{10} **>64a 62f<**
Master Foodbroker (IRE) 9 br g Simply Great (FR)-Silver Mantle (Bustino) *5^{3} 167^{2} 232^{2} (272)* 442^{3} **>64a 57f<**
Masterkind (IRE) 3 b g Masterclass (USA)-Sententious (Kautokeino (FR)) 4260a^{3} **>102f<**
Master Mac (USA) 2 br c Exbourne (USA)-Kentucky Blonde (USA) (General Assembly (USA)) 1480^{4} 1933^{8} (2349) (2689) 3113^{8} 3794^{2} 4271^{12} 4778^{25} **>81f<**
Master M-E-N (IRE) 5 ch g My Generation-Secret Lightning (USA) (Secretariat (USA)) 560^{4} 791^{3} 1111^{5} 1442^{11} 1680^{7} 3980^{16} **>36a 65df<**
Master Millfield (IRE) 5 b g Prince Rupert (FR)-Calash (Indian King (USA)) **1996:** *5119^{2}* **1997:** 763^{15} 1001^{9} 1111^{10} 1273^{14} 3227^{10} 3297^{5} (4404) *4572^{4}* **>72a 60f<**
Master of Passion 8 b g Primo Dominie-Crime of Passion (Dragonara Palace (USA)) **1996:** *5131^{4} (5220)* **1997:** *53^{6} 357^{8}* 1223^{9} 2321^{5} 2769^{7} *3077^{4}* 3417^{9} 4791^{6} **>74a 68f<**
Masterpiece 3 br c Primo Dominie-Swift Return (Double Form) 475^{2} 693^{5} 991^{7} 1249^{9} 3138^{10} 3930^{11} 4546^{13} **>62f<**
Master Planner 8 b g Night Shift (USA)-Shaky Puddin (Ragstone) 942^{27} 1317^{16} **>85?f<**
Master Showman (IRE) 6 b g Alzao (USA)-Arctic Winter (CAN) (Briartic (CAN)) *869^{10}*
Masterstroke 3 b g Timeless Times (USA)-Fauve (Dominion) **1996:** *5083^{8} 5092^{3} 5212^{5}* **1997:** *44^{4} (94)* 1989^{7} *2319^{9}* 2921^{13} 3454^{5} 4043^{16} **>74a 39f<**
Mastro Cantore (IRE) 3 b c Marju (IRE)-Wish of Luck (USA) (Diesis) **1996:** (5193a)
Matata (IRE) 2 b f In The Wings-Ville Sainte (FR) (Saint Estephe (FR)) 2336^{2} 2840^{4} 3638^{2} 3990^{9} **>76f<**
Mateyev (USA) 3 ch c Woodman (USA)-Angelina Ballerina (USA) (Nureyev (USA)) 2457a^{3} **>96f<**
Matoaka 3 b f Be My Chief (USA)-Echoing (Formidable (USA)) 1423^{8} 1688^{2} 1929^{4} 2228^{5} 4008^{2} 4319^{6} (4505) *4913^{7}* **>58a 77f<**
Mattawan 4 ch c Nashwan (USA)-Sweet Mover (USA) (Nijinsky (CAN)) 2709^{7} **>91f<**
Matter Of Trust (IRE) 2 bb c Distinctly North (USA)-Cabin Brooke 5002a^{7} **>99f<**
Matthias Mystique 4 gr f Sharrood (USA)-Sheznice (IRE) (Try My Best (USA)) **1996:** *5084^{3} (5185) 5213^{3} 5277^{6}* **1997:** *133^{6} (262) 351^{3} 381^{6}* 1665^{2} 1953^{2} 2592^{F} **>67a 66f< (DEAD)**
Mattimeo (IRE) 4 b g Prince Rupert (FR)-Herila (FR) (Bold Lad (USA)) 1459^{6} 2122^{9} (2293) 2866^{10} (3184) 3722^{15} 4151^{7} 4477^{2} 4672^{3} 5053^{14} **>52a 89f<**
Maurangi 6 b g Warning-Spin Dry (High Top) 1128^{5} 1560^{9} *1944^{10}* 2109^{4} 2488^{4} 2564^{5} 2854^{7} 4923^{8} 5024^{11} **>3a 31f<**
Ma Vielle Pouque (IRE) 3 ch f Fayruz-Aussie Aisle (IRE) (Godswalk (USA)) *198^{4} 221^{3} 282^{3} 345^{5} 379^{7} (427) 546^{3} 4049^{4}* 4221^{15} **>65a 63?f<**
Mawared (IRE) 4 ch c Nashwan (USA)-Harmless Albatross (Pas de Seul) 1459^{10} 1763^{4} (2949) (3137) (3579) (3748) 4783^{3} 4969^{2} **>102f<**
Mawingo (IRE) 4 b c Taufan (USA)-Tappen Zee (Sandhurst Prince) 1397^{3} 2026^{12} 2666^{2} 3150^{7} 3810^{3} 4637^{2} **>69a 93f<**
Mawsoof 2 b c Alzao (USA)-Guilty Secret (IRE)

(Kris) 4309^{2} 4454^{2} >80f<

Max's Magic (USA) 4 b g Chief's Crown (USA)-Pattyville (USA) (Crozier) 2687^{6} 3463^{15} 3775^{10} >41f<

Maxzene (USA) 4 gr f Cozzene (USA)-Jacky Max (USA) (Sexton Blake) **1996:** (5156a) **1997:** 3879a^{2} 4651a^{2} >126f<

Maybank (IRE) 5 gr g Contract Law (USA)-Katysue (King's Leap) **1996:** *5115^{15}* >53a 31f<

Maydoro 4 b f Dominion Royale-Bamdoro (Cavo Doro) 636^{8} 698^{7} 760^{11} 1650^{8} 2019^{13} 2197^{9} 2540^{5} 2891^{9} 3241^{5} >43f<

Mayfair 3 b f Green Desert (USA)-Emaline (FR) (Empery (USA)) 968^{11} 1262^{15} 3772^{11} >72df<

Mayflower 3 b f Midyan (USA)-Chesnut Tree (USA) (Shadeed (USA)) 723^{11} 1000^{13} 1589^{13} 3931^{9} 4324^{11} 4695^{3} >55f<

May King Mayhem 4 ch g Great Commotion (USA)-Queen Ranavalona (Sure Blade (USA)) *410^{9}* 481^{5} *542^{8}* 689^{10} 1010^{6} 1222^{8} 1445^{3} 1779^{21} 2246^{2} 2398^{5} (2503) 2702^{3} 2843^{6} 3267^{5} >39a 54f<

Maylan (IRE) 2 br f Lashkari-Miysam (Supreme Sovereign) 4668^{7} 4892^{13} >19tf<

Maylane 3 b g Mtoto-Possessive Dancer (Shareef Dancer (USA)) 723^{U} 958^{5} (1869) 2585^{2} (3125) (4005) 4420^{U} >118f<

Maypole (IRE) 3 ch g Mujtahid (USA)-Dance Festival (Nureyev (USA)) 4408^{3} >75f<

May Queen Megan 4 gr f Petorius-Siva (FR) (Bellypha) 1003^{12} 1666^{12} 2665^{10} 2788^{11} 3056^{6} 3269^{4} 3573^{4} 3854^{2} 4228^{6} 4455^{3} 4606^{2} 4951^{19} >51f<

Maysimp (IRE) 4 ch f Mac's Imp (USA)-Splendid Yankee (Yankee Gold) *4^{8} 71^{15} 127^{13} 332^{9} 391^{12}* 585^{21} 3240^{14} 3378^{8} 3756^{16} >19a 25f<

Maytong 2 gr f Petong-Bit O' May (Mummy's Pet) 3033^{6} 3619^{6} 4428^{7} >63f<

Mazamet (USA) 4 b g Elmaamul (USA)-Miss Mazepah (USA) (Nijinsky (CAN)) 1027^{11} >75f<

Mazara (IRE) 3 b f High Estate-Shy Jinks (Shy Groom (USA)) 539^{5} 725^{13} 1094^{8} 1565^{4} >53f< **(DEAD)**

Mazboon (USA) 2 ch c Diesis-Secretaire (USA) (Secretariat (USA)) (1872) (2429) >93f<

Mazeed (IRE) 4 ch g Lycius (USA)-Maraatib (IRE) (Green Desert (USA)) 3900^{9} 4451^{10} 4738^{15} 4951^{12} 5023^{5} >60f<

Mazilla 5 b m Mazilier (USA)-Mo Ceri (Kampala) 887^{11} 1384^{10} 1803^{3} 2174^{5} *2668^{5}* 2876^{6} 3886^{7} >46a 53f<

Mazirah 6 b g Mazilier (USA)-Barbary Court (Grundy) 2118^{10} 2279^{4} >44a 44f<

Mazurek 4 b c Sadler's Wells (USA)-Maria Waleska (Filiberto (USA)) **1996:** *5085^{2} (5152)* **1997:** *330^{7} 358^{13} 410^{8}* (1010) (1169) 2028^{4} 2514^{9} 2767^{7} >76a 84f<

Mazzarello (IRE) 7 ch g Hatim (USA)-Royal Demon (Tarboosh (USA)) 1620^{19} 2148^{9} >9a 26df<

Mbulwa 11 ch g Be My Guest (USA)-Bundu (FR) (Habitat) 1266^{7} 1979^{15} 2290^{10} 2760^{13} 2857^{8} 3456^{2} 3605^{2} 3798^{4} 4063^{10} 4210^{2} 4371^{5} >43a 64f<

Mcgillycuddy Reeks (IRE) 6 b m Kefaah (USA)-Kilvarnet (Furry Glen) **1996:** *5143^{4}* **1997:** 796^{6} 898^{4} 1116^{5} 1390^{6} 1683^{2} 1818^{3} 2145^{12} (2569) (2907) (3104) (3315) 3570^{2} 3906^{2} 4151^{10} 4386^{7} (4635) 4788^{8} 4891^{6} 5044^{4} >37a 77f<

Meadgate's Dreamer (IRE) 2 br f Petardia-Avidal Park (Horage) 1386^{5} 1645^{9} 1933^{14} *2363^{7}* >15a 49f<

Meadow Blue 4 b f Northern State (USA)-Cornflower (USA) (Damascus (USA)) 2568^{11} 2825^{12} 3134^{11} *3612^{6}* 3855^{10} >7a 35f<

Means Business (IRE) 2 ch c Imp Society (USA)-Fantasise (FR) (General Assembly (USA)) 583^{7} 1274^{4} 2784^{2} (3055) 3288^{5} 3546^{3} 3892^{11} 4755^{15} >62f<

Meatball (FR) 2 ch c Nashamaa-Northern Bank (FR) 4387a^{4} >90f<

Mecca Princess 2 ch f Weldnaas (USA)-Parfait Amour (Clantime) 2752^{11}

Mechilie 3 b f Belmez (USA)-Tundra Goose (Habitat) **1996:** *5135^{12}* **1997:** 582^{7} 862^{9} 1853^{10} 3781^{5} 4170^{3} 4438^{5} >17a 53f<

Medaaly 3 gr c Highest Honor (FR)-Dance of Leaves (Sadler's Wells (USA)) 1159^{8} >117f<

Medaille Militaire 5 gr h Highest Honor (FR)-Lovely Noor (USA) (Fappiano (USA)) 1323^{3} 1960^{5} 3191^{7} 4732^{3} >111f<

Media Express 5 b g Sayf El Arab (USA)-Far Claim (USA) (Far North (CAN)) *76^{4} 93^{5} 143^{5} 338^{7}* >55a 37df<

Media Star (USA) 4 b c Lear Fan (USA)-Media Luna (Star Appeal) 841^{11} 1230^{6} (2131) (2381) (2589) (3110) 3705^{2} 4376^{2} 4783^{26} >104f<

Mediate (IRE) 5 b g Thatching-Unheard Melody (Lomond (USA)) **1996:** *5211^{4} 5254^{2}* **1997:** *61^{5} 197^{3} 290^{6} 340^{9}* 2121^{10} 3276^{8} 4373^{21} >57a 35f<

Medieval Lady 4 ch f Efisio-Ritsurin (Mount Hagen (FR)) 738^{6} 934^{3} 1261^{7} 1852^{7} >90df<

Medina Miss 2 b f Rudimentary (USA)-Podrida (Persepolis (FR)) *1124^{4} 1290^{2} 1789^{W}* 1984^{2} *2163^{3}* 2923^{4} 3078^{6} *4054^{15}* 4401^{9} >44a 52f<

Medland (IRE) 7 ch g Imperial Frontier (USA)-Miami Dancer (Miami Springs) **1996:** *5079^{9} 5129^{4} 5175^{15} 5242^{8}* **1997:** *105^{9} 1134^{4} 1576^{8} 1943^{5} 4484^{6}* >38a 36f<

Megan Carew 3 ch f Gunner B-Molly Carew (Jimmy Reppin) 3486^{11} 3858^{7} >38f<

Mega Tid 5 b g Old Vic-Dunoof (Shirley Heights) **1996:** *5247^{12}* **1997:** *13^{12}* 770^{8} 1779^{10} 2146^{10} >30a 31f<

Meglio Che Posso (IRE) 6 b m Try My Best (USA)-Knapping (Busted) 2267a^{7} 2441a^{7} >84f<

Megred 2 b f Soviet Star (USA)-Dancing Meg (USA) (Marshua's Dancer (USA)) 4514^{2} >68f<

Meg's Memory (IRE) 4 b f Superlative-Meanz Beanz (High Top) 2650^{5} 2843^{9} 3256^{3} >29a 61f<

Meilleur (IRE) 3 b g Nordico (USA)-Lucy Limelight (Hot Spark) 1851^{5} 2591^{7} 3095^{7} 3491^{15} 4045^{3} 4562^{6} 4821^{4} >67f<

Melbourne Princess 3 ch f Primo Dominie-Lurking (Formidable (USA)) **1996:** *5176^{7} 5245^{2}* **1997:** 783^{9} 2235^{4} 2354^{8} 2883^{4} 3271^{11} 3698^{4} 4563^{9} 4586^{8} >60a 54f<

Meliksah (IRE) 3 ch c Thatching-Lady of Shalott (Kings Lake (USA)) 968^{4} 1254^{3} 1608^{5} 2872^{7} 3065^{8} 4183^{12} >93f<

Mellors (IRE) 4 b c Common Grounds-Simply Beautiful (IRE) (Simply Great (FR)) *27^{5} (107) 172^{2} 241^{6} 349^{5} 404^{2} 512^{10}* 638^{7} 1089^{16} 2698^{14} 2852^{10} 3082^{13} 4248^{10} 4518^{10} *4985^{10}* >65a 38f<

Mellwood (IRE) 3 b g Maledetto (IRE)-Traminer (Status Seeker) 1094^{6} 1469^{10} >8a 41f<

Melodian 2 b c Grey Desire-Mere Melody (Dunphy) 3753^{12} 4211^{14} >13f<

Melodica 3 b f Machiavellian (USA)-Melodist (USA) (The Minstrel (CAN)) 1420^{2} 1922^{2} (2692) 2963^{5} 3412^{8} >87f<

Melodic Drive 7 b or br g Sizzling Melody-Gleneagle (Swing Easy (USA)) 1225^{13} 1501^{11} >44da 43f< **(DEAD)**

Melodic Squaw 3 b f Merdon Melody-Young Whip (Bold Owl) *191^{8} 314^{8} 373^{9}* 4336^{18} >20a 16f<

Melomania (USA) 5 b h Shadeed (USA)-Medley of Song (USA) (Secretariat (USA)) *544^{13}* >16a 60f<

Melos 4 b f Emarati (USA)-Double Stretch (Double-U-Jay) 2777^{5} 3394^{8} >12a f<

Mels Baby (IRE) 4 br g Contract Law (USA)-Launch The Raft (Home Guard (USA)) **1996:** *5200^{6}* **1997:** *327^{4}* 435^{2} 608^{3} (1117) 1268^{5} 1979^{11} 2155^{8} >48a 84f<

Meltemison 4 b g Charmer-Salchow (Niniski (USA)) 598^{13} >66a 73?f<

Members Welcome (IRE) 4 b g Eve's Error-Manuale Del Utente (Montekin) *367^{11} 404^{7}* >13a 45f<

Memorable 6 b g Don't Forget Me-Jhansi Ki Rani (USA) (Far North (CAN)) 2498^{2} 4171^{15} >29f<

Memorial (IRE) 2 b c Imperial Frontier (USA)-Alitos Choice (Baptism) 985^{4} 1251^{9} 3686^{20} 4152^{11} 4545^{13} *4796^{5}* >57a 55f<

Memories Of Silver (USA) 4 b f Silver Hawk (USA)-All My Memories (USA) (Little Current (USA)) (3879a) 4651a^{3} 5039a^{3} >126f<

Memorise (USA) 3 b c Lyphard (USA)-Shirley Valentine (Shirley Heights) 740^{4} 1014^{4} (1331) 2058^{4} (2585) 3125^{D} 4134^{2} 4549^{2} >117f<

Memory's Music 5 b g Dance of Life (USA)-Sheer Luck (Shergar) *22^{10} 76^{9}* 4371^{14} 4858^{13} >46a 33f<

Mempari (IRE) 2 b f Fairy King (USA)-Sharaya (USA) (Youth (USA)) 4093a^{5} >102f<

Memphis Dancer 2 b f Shareef Dancer (USA)-Wollow Maid (Wollow) 2943^{7} 3985^{7} >49f<

Mendoza 3 b g Rambo Dancer (CAN)-Red Poppy (IRE) (Coquelin (USA)) *50^{7} (162) 174^{4} 240^{2} 366^{4} 456^{2}* 642^{4} 2733^{13} 3452^{8} >70a 62f<

Mengaab (USA) 3 b c Silver Hawk (USA)-Cherie's Hope (USA) (Flying Paster (USA)) 1130^{4} 2126^{5} 2379^{3} 2731^{4} 3120^{6} (3739) 3915^{14} >90?f<

Meniatarra (USA) 2 ch f Zilzal (USA)-Snow Bride (USA) (Blushing Groom (FR)) 4973^{7} >63f<

Men Of Wickenby 3 b c Shirley Heights-Radiant Bride (USA) (Blushing Groom (FR)) 550^{8} *658^{6}* 825^{5} 1129^{12} >52f<

Men's Exclusive (USA) 4 *5061a^{6}* >120a f<

Mentalasanythin 8 b g Ballacashtal (CAN)-Lafrowda (Crimson Beau) *857^{7}* (1118) 1232^{3} 3221^{2} 3722^{7} 3921^{4} 4235^{15} 4279^{11} 4466^{7} >79?a 71f<

Meranti 4 b g Puissance-Sorrowful (Moorestyle) 473^{9} (585) 702^{4} (734) 1089^{14} 1225^{6} 1957^{7} 2002^{2} (2698) 2788^{9} 2933^{7} 3208^{14} 3565^{16} 4228^{19} >22a 46f<

Merch Rhyd-Y-Grug 2 b f Sabrehill (USA)-Al Washl (USA) (The Minstrel (CAN)) 4216^{13} 4332^{14} *4479^{12}* >38f<

Merciless 2 gr f Last Tycoon-Galava (CAN) (Graustark) (4873) >88f<

Merciless Cop 3 ch g Efisio-Naturally Bold (Bold Lad (IRE)) **1996:** *5113^{4} 5224^{5}* **1997:** 1422^{15} 1748^{6} (1929) *(2052)* 2245^{6} 2374^{10} (2877) 3236^{10} 3741^{6} 3897^{3} >76a 65f<

Merci Monsieur 4 ch g Cadeaux Genereux-Night Encounter (Right Tack) 3790^{4} 4072^{10} 4292^{5} >49f<

Mercury (IRE) 4 b g Contract Law (USA)-Monrovia (FR) (Dancers Image (USA)) 529^{16} *663^{4} 860^{10}* 1117^{5} *1291^{5}* 1463^{6} *2071^{4}* 2843^{10} 3200^{9} 3570^{6} >59da 36f<

Mercury Falling 2 ch f Magic Ring (IRE)-Try the Duchess (Try My Best (USA)) 1821^{11} 2959^{4} 3471^{9} 4566^{13} 4819^{15} *5017^{7}* >23a 58f<

Merit (IRE) 5 b h Rainbow Quest (USA)-Fur Hat (Habitat) 4639^{5} 4783^{13} 5052^{6} >78+a 84f<

Merlin's Ring 2 br c Magic Ring (IRE)-Dramatic Mood (Jalmood (USA)) 2181^{2} (2706) (3215) 3644^{5} 4106^{3} (4647a) (4861a) >101f<

Merrily 4 gr f Sharrood (USA)-Babycham Sparkle (So Blessed) 469^{3} 779^{6} 3241^{6} 3431^{21} >46f<

Merryhill Mariner 3 ch g Superlative-Merryhill Maid (IRE) (M Double M (USA)) *234^{5}* >8a 36f<

Mersey Beat 3 ch c Rock Hopper-Handy Dancer (Green God) **1996:** *(5147)* **1997:** *365*^{2} 741^{8} 2585^{3} 3125^{13} 3773^{W} **>93a 94f<**

Meshhed (USA) 3 ch f Gulch (USA)-Umniyatee (Green Desert (USA)) 1318^{4} (1621) 2023^{19} 2774^{4} 3594^{7} 4181^{2} 4666a^{15} (4902) **>108f<**

Messina (IRE) 3 b f Sadler's Wells (USA)-Magic of Life (USA) (Seattle Slew (USA)) 4177^{3} 4736^{4} **>81f<**

Metastasio 5 b g Petoski-Top of the League (High Top) 4620a^{7} **>90f<**

Meteor Strike (USA) 3 ch g Lomond (USA)-Meteoric (High Line) (2532) 3444^{2} 4102^{10} 4409^{9} **>90f<**

Methmoon (IRE) 2 b c Darshaan-Truly Special (Caerleon (USA)) 4318^{8} **>63+f<**

Mezzoramio 5 ch g Cadeaux Genereux-Hopeful Search (USA) (Vaguely Noble) 587^{12} 763^{8} 1128^{2} 1501^{2} 2121^{7} (2922) 3421^{2} 3718^{5} 4228^{3} 4249^{2} 4510^{8} 4629^{12} 4951^{9} **>50a 59f<**

Miami Moon 3 ch f Keen-Two Moons (Bold Lad (IRE)) **1996:** *5111*^{7} *5201*^{3} **1997:** 1221^{10} *1757*^{6} 2021^{6} 2386^{2} 2662^{5} 4713^{13} 4986^{13} **>53a 45f<**

Michael's Choice (USA) 5 b g Theatrical-Fairway Flag (USA) (Fairway Phantom (USA)) **1996:** 5218a^{3} **>117f<**

Michael Venture 3 b c Shirley Heights-Ski Michaela (USA) (Devil's Bag (USA)) 700^{8} 1103^{5} 1679^{4} 2187^{8} 2570^{6} *(3054)* 3442^{5} **>73a 57f<**

Michelee 2 b f Merdon Melody-Hsian (Shantung) 1614^{7} *(1789) (2163)* 2489^{3} **>70+a 39f<**

Mick's Tycoon (IRE) 9 b g Last Tycoon-Ladytown (English Prince) 1779^{15} 2207^{8} **>23f<**

Midas Man 6 ch g Gold Claim-Golden Starfish (Porto Bello) 1604^{7} 1835^{16} 2032^{6} 2221^{4} 2470^{5} **>11f<**

Midday Cowboy (USA) 4 b g Houston (USA)-Perfect Isn't Easy (USA) (Saratoga Six (USA)) 734^{15} 866^{11} 1248^{11} 1495^{12} 2152^{8} 2564^{14} 2828^{11} **>40df<**

Middle East 4 b g Beveled (USA)-Godara (Bustino) 949^{13} 1225^{18} 3034^{10} 3625^{12} 3761^{8} 3856^{9} 4016^{3} 4249^{5} (4333) 4580^{4} (4738) **>72f<**

Middle Temple 2 b c Midyan (USA)-Temple Fortune (USA) (Ziggy's Boy (USA)) 1744^{5} 2176^{5} 2768^{4} 4849^{2} **>79f<**

Midnight Cookie 4 b c Midyan (USA)-Midnight's Reward (Night Shift (USA)) **1996:** *5097*^{10} **>33a 27f<**

Midnight Escape 4 b g Aragon-Executive Lady (Night Shift (USA)) 726^{9} 941^{10} 3023^{5} 3410^{2} (4203a) 4239^{9} 4964a^{3} **>114f<**

Midnight Line (USA) 2 ch f Kris S (USA)-Midnight Air (USA) (Green Dancer (USA)) 2597^{5} (3151) (3740) (4119) 4442^{5} **>105f<**

Midnight Romance 3 b f Inca Chief (USA)-Run Amber Run (Run The Gantlet (USA)) 790^{6} 889^{10} 2158^{8} *2602*^{15} **>41f<**

Midnight Shift (IRE) 3 b f Night Shift (USA)-Old Domesday Book (High Top) 685^{10} 1141^{17} 1496^{3} 1687^{4} (2157) 2665^{8} 2921^{10} 3691^{2} 4059^{7} 4375^{9} (4905) 4995^{7} **>70f<**

Midnight Sting 2 gr f Inchinor-Halvoya (Bay Express) 3278^{6} 3926^{9} 4701^{8} **>64+f<**

Midnight Times 3 b f Timeless Times (USA)-Midnight Lass (Today and Tomorrow) 1479^{7} *3040*^{3} *3398*^{13} **>47a 38f<**

Midnight Watch (USA) 3 b c Capote (USA)-Midnight Air (USA) (Green Dancer (USA)) 2566^{6} 3977^{4} 4360^{6} 4920^{3} **>82f<**

Midsummer Night (IRE) 2 b f Fairy King (USA)-Villota (Top Ville) 1847^{3} 1970^{2} 4103^{12} 4522^{4} 4970^{5} **>77f<**

Midsummer Romance (IRE) 2 b f Fairy King (USA)-Jealous One (USA) (Raise A Native) 4892^{10} **>59f<**

Midyan Blue (IRE) 7 ch g Midyan (USA)-Jarretiere (Star Appeal) 430^{13} 499^{3} 762^{11} 1162^{3} 1478^{7} 2014^{20} 2767^{4} 3137^{5} 3974^{4} 4794^{5} 4896^{5} **>63a 68f<**

Midyan Call 3 b c Midyan (USA)-Early Call (Kind of Hush) 503^{7} 693^{2} 957^{5} (3425) 4282^{29} 4554^{2} 4787^{23} **>98f<**

Midyan Queen 3 b f Midyan (USA)-Queen of Aragon (Aragon) 1030^{7} 1650^{4} 2313^{17} (2705) 3119^{8} 3855^{4} 3987^{15} **>60f<**

Might And Power (NZ) 4 b g Zabeel (AUS)-Benediction (Day Is Done) (5055a) **>125f<**

Mighty Flow 3 b f Nicholas (USA)-Mighty Flash (Rolfe (USA)) 725^{8} 967^{7} 1239^{13} 2730^{13} 2921^{W} **>51f< (DEAD)**

Mighty Magic 2 b f Magic Ring (IRE)-Mighty Flash (Rolfe (USA)) 965^{3} 1564^{4} 2138^{5} 2728^{9} 4042^{11} 4271^{9} **>76f<**

Mighty Phantom (USA) 4 b f Lear Fan (USA)-Migiyas (Kings Lake (USA)) 881^{8} 1278^{6} 1871^{3} 2694^{2} 2949^{8} 3279^{5} 3719^{3} **>74a 70f<**

Mighty Sure (IRE) 2 b f Treasure Kay-Mighty Special (IRE) (Head for Heights) (1019) 2031^{3} 2565^{6} 3226^{2} 3480^{4} 3823^{4} (4419) 4522^{6} **>67f<**

Migrate (USA) 2 ch f Storm Bird (CAN)-Home Leave (USA) (Alydar (USA)) 1783^{5} 2312^{4} 4567^{5} **>72f<**

Migwar 4 b g Unfuwain (USA)-Pick of the Pops (High Top) 4294^{9} **>101df<**

Mihnah (IRE) 2 br f Lahib (USA)-Nafhaat (USA) (Roberto (USA)) 2680^{4} 3602^{2} (4640) 4892^{11} **>85+f<**

Mihriz (IRE) 5 b g Machiavellian (USA)-Ghzaalh (USA) (Northern Dancer) 1166^{3} 2678^{13} (3392) 4141^{15} 4558^{16} 4680^{6} **>79f<**

Mijana (IRE) 2 b c Tenby-Fabled Lifestyle (Kings Lake (USA)) (722) 3233^{2} (3464) 3811^{3} (4106) 4293^{4} 4790^{2} **>102f<**

Mijas 4 ch f Risk Me (FR)-Out of Harmony (Song) **1996:** *5097*^{6} *5150*^{11} *(5225)* *5246*^{12} **1997:** *95*^{D} *170*^{7} *348*^{7} *406*^{4} *488*^{2} 786^{10} 1083^{6} 1419^{10} 1814^{7} *2050*^{9} *5021*^{14} **>77a 54f<**

Mike's Double (IRE) 3 br g Cyrano de Bergerac-Glass Minnow (IRE) (Alzao (USA)) 532^{3} 649^{5} 1925^{3} 2231^{2} 2510^{8} *(3043)* *3397*^{4} 3749^{5} *4574*^{2} 4738^{4} 4816^{3} **>73a 67f<**

Mile High 3 b g Puissance-Jobiska (Dunbeath (USA)) 453^{2} (531) 968^{6} 3410^{16} **>92f<**

Miletrian City 4 gr g Petong-Blueit (FR) (Bold Lad (IRE)) *297*^{6} 467^{11} 526^{5} 896^{11} 1389^{7} 1993^{4} 2109^{2} 2237^{9} 2716^{9} 2880^{2} 3264^{7} 3487^{10} 3627^{8} 4472^{10} 4510^{9} **>41a 44f<**

Miletrian Refurb (IRE) 4 b br g Anita's Prince-Lady of Man (So Blessed) **1996:** *5268*^{12} **1997:** *20*^{10} *332*^{11} 473^{4} 4770^{16} **>30a 60f<**

Milford Track (IRE) 4 4530a^{3} **>101f<**

Miliardaire (IRE) 3 ch c Night Shift (USA)-Measuring (Moorestyle) 917a^{12} **>88f<**

Military (USA) 3 b c Danzig (USA)-Wavering Girl (USA) (Wavering Monarch (USA)) 829^{4} 1023^{3} (2315) 2839^{4} 3238^{2} **>97f<**

Milky Way 3 b f Statoblest-Evening Star (Red Sunset) 4848^{12} *4980*^{11} **>14a 32f<**

Mill Dancer (IRE) 5 b m Broken Hearted-Theatral (Orchestra) **1996:** *5115*^{12} **1997:** *2160*^{7} *2322*^{7} **>5a 36f<**

Mill End Boy 3 ch g Clantime-Annaceramic (Horage) 995^{10} 1604^{9} 1687^{5} 1864^{3} 2169^{8} 2891^{7} 3088^{9} 4601^{21} **>38f<**

Mill End Quest 2 b f King's Signet (USA)-Milva (Jellaby) 460^{5} *1941*^{7} (2538) 2942^{6} 3707^{6} 3932^{15} 4152^{13} 4419^{5} 4922^{14} **>30a 66f<**

Millesime (IRE) 5 ch g Glow (USA)-Persian Myth (Persian Bold) 779^{2} 956^{5} 1089^{10} 1734^{8} 1816^{6} **>54f<**

Milligan (FR) 2 b c Exit To Nowhere (USA)-Madigan Mill (Mill Reef (USA)) 3874a^{2} 4657a^{6} **>82f<**

Milling (IRE) 2 b f In The Wings-Princess Pati (Top Ville) 4973^{14} **>47f<**

Millitrix 2 br f Doyoun-Galatrix (Be My Guest (USA)) 3979^{2} 4273^{4} **>77f<**

Mill King (GER) 4 b c Dashing Blade-Marcasita (GER) (Mille Balles (FR)) 2821a^{8} **>112f<**

Mill Orchid 3 b f Henbit (USA)-Milinetta (Milford) 2045^{9} 2846^{10} 4469^{8} **>41f<**

Millpet 3 br f Petong-Pattis Pet (Mummy's Pet) 935^{7} 1237^{9} 1401^{2} 1681^{5} 2125^{6} 2353^{3} 3299^{7} *4809*^{9} **>35a 47f<**

Millroy (USA) 3 ch g Carnivalay (USA)-Royal Millinery (USA) (Regal And Royal (USA)) **1996:** *5121*^{2} *(5214)* *5238*^{3} *5272*^{2} **1997:** *(84)* *138*^{2} *227*^{2} *281*^{6} *331*^{2} *388*^{3} 449^{8} 597^{7} 958^{12} 1737^{13} **>92a 87f<**

Milly of The Vally 3 b f Caerleon (USA)-Mill on the Floss (Mill Reef (USA)) 725^{12} (1258) 2284^{2} 3218^{7} 3805^{2} **>96f<**

Milos 6 b g Efisio-Elkie Brooks (Relkino) **1996:** *5249*^{12} **1997:** *(59)* *105*^{2} *224*^{2} *248*^{5} **>70a 66f<**

Mils Mij 12 br g Slim Jim-Katie Grey (Pongee) 3401^{3} 3623^{8} **>33f<**

Milton Abbot 4 b g Full Extent (USA)-Auto Connection (Blushing Scribe (USA)) 2492^{17} 4872^{22} *5019*^{12}

Miltonfield 8 ch g Little Wolf-Kingsfold Flash (Warpath) 1698a^{5} 2014^{10} **>93f<**

Mimosa 4 ch f Midyan (USA)-Figini (Glint of Gold) **1996:** *5079*^{6} *5118*^{4} *5210*^{10} **1997:** *305*^{4} *380*^{3} 476^{12} 554^{2} 895^{6} *1086*^{4} 1926^{7} 2285^{6} 3787^{6} 4114^{7} 4373^{3} **>60a 59f<**

Minarello (USA) 3 b c Blushing John (USA)-Inuvik (ITY) (Herat (USA)) 1068a^{3} **>77f<**

Mind Games 5 b h Puissance-Aryaf (CAN) (Vice Regent (CAN)) 3724^{7} **>120?f<**

Mindrace 4 b g Tina's Pet-High Velocity (Frimley Park) 443^{13} 541^{9} 834^{17} 1083^{8} 1627^{11} 1814^{2} 1957^{8} 2732^{4} (2950) 3126^{13} 3500^{10} 4048^{6} 4249^{11} 4329^{9} 4580^{7} **>15a 65f<**

Minersville (USA) 3 b g Forty Niner (USA)-Angel Fever (USA) (Danzig (USA)) (524) 741^{6} 2113^{6} 2594^{6} 3824^{8} **>87df<**

Minetta 2 ch f Mujtahid (USA)-Minwah (USA) (Diesis) *1136*^{3} (1510) 2103^{8} 3237^{9} 3750^{4} 4778^{27} **>54a 80f<**

Mingling Glances (USA) 3 b f Woodman (USA)-Last Glance (USA) 1896a^{3} **>94f<**

Ministerial Model (IRE) 3 b f Shalford (IRE)-Swift Reply (He Loves Me) 2447a^{5} 2816a^{5} 3510a^{4} **>96f<**

Minister's Melody (USA) 3 f *5062a*^{5} **>93a f<**

Minivet 2 b c Midyan (USA)-Bronzewing (Beldale Flutter (USA)) 4526^{3} **>81f<**

Minjara 2 b c Beveled (USA)-Honey Mill (Milford) 2693^{13} 4917^{13} **>48f<**

Minster Moorgate 2 ch f Minster Son-Find The Sun (Galivanter) 5029^{8}

Minster Star 3 ch f Minster Son-Star of the Sea (Absalom) 2492^{12} 2783^{3} 3133^{8} 4060^{9} *4800*^{9} 4918^{8} **>53a 67f<**

Miquelon 2 b c Primo Dominie-Miquette (FR) (Fabulous Dancer (USA)) 432^{7} (460) 696^{3} 893^{4} 2658^{3} 3270^{2} 3961a^{11} 4690^{4} 4849^{4} **>88f<**

Miracle Kid (USA) 3 b c Red Ransom (USA)-Fan Mail (USA) (Zen (USA)) **1996:** *(5087)* **1997:** (431) 4141^{13} 4558^{34} 4788^{15} **>75a 87f<**

Mirror Four Life (IRE) 3 b f Treasure Kay-

Gazettalong (Taufan (USA)) 1238^{14} 2542^{7} 2954^{14} **>51df<**

Mirror Four Sport **3** ch f Risk Me (FR)-Madison Girl (Last Fandango) **1996:** *5164^{9}* **1997:** *8^{6} 110^{3} 132^{2} (168) 234^{4} 314^{6} 377^{5} (414) 454^{3} 513^{5}* 582^{10} *(662) 873^{5}* 1229^{2} 1513^{7} *(2364) 3074^{7}* 3210^{7} **>58a 50f<**

Misalliance **2** ch f Elmaamul (USA)-Cabaret Artiste (Shareef Dancer (USA)) 3818^{7} 4209^{4} (4514) 4767^{8} **>71+f<**

Misbah (USA) **2** b c Gilded Time (USA)-For Dixie (USA) (Dixieland Band (USA)) 4237^{4} 4581^{2} (4853) **>91f<**

Mischievous Time **3** ch g Clantime-Mischievous Tyke (Flying Tyke) 1764^{5} 2496^{6} 2734^{4} 3086^{7} 4600^{5} 4916^{9} **>39f<**

Misconduct **3** gr f Risk Me (FR)-Grey Cree (Creetown) 1876^{7} *2300^{10}* 2491^{8} *4913^{15}* **>53a 50f<**

Misellina (FR) **3** b f Polish Precedent (USA)-Misallah (IRE) (Shirley Heights) 1207^{13} 1420^{7} 1623^{8} 2487^{12} 4465^{R} **>38f<**

Mishraak (IRE) **2** ch c Mujtahid (USA)-Dora da Caserta (IRE) (Caerleon (USA)) 583^{6} 1692^{2} 2123^{4} (2578) 2942^{4} 3152^{6} (3556) 3925^{3} **>92f<**

Misinterrex **6** 2997a^{2} **>14f<**

Miskin Heights (IRE) **3** ch f Sharp Victor (USA)-Nurse Jo (USA) (J O Tobin (USA)) **1996:** *5135^{15}* **1997:** 3897^{10} 4607^{4} 4858^{11} **>27f<**

Misky Bay **4** b g Shareef Dancer (USA)-Rain Date (Rainbow Quest (USA)) **1996:** *5209^{12}* **1997:** *144^{6} 200^{2} 322^{R} 416^{6}* **>49da 69df<**

Mislead (IRE) **2** b f Distinctly North (USA)-Chez Nous (Habitat) 1635^{9} (2003) 2243^{13} 2578^{2} (2942) (3152) 3480^{7} **>76f<**

Mislemani (IRE) **7** b g Kris-Meis El-Reem (Auction Ring (USA)) *91^{6} 194^{8}* (2310) 2533^{7} 4112^{10} 4448^{8} 4629^{16} **>52a 47f<**

Mismewmew **2** b f Weldnaas (USA)-Joan's Gift (Doulab (USA)) 3743^{7} 3927^{10} **>56f<**

Miss Alice **3** b f Komaite (USA)-Needle Sharp (Kris) 2152^{6} 2522^{8} 2908^{13} 3129^{4} **>31a 43f<**

Miss All Alone **2** ch f Crofthall-Uninvited (Be My Guest (USA)) 583^{9}

Miss Aragon **9** b m Aragon-Lavenham Blue (Streetfighter) **1996:** *5109^{6} 5144^{3} 5183^{5} 5220^{3}* **1997:** 2788^{18} *2915^{13}* 3146^{7} 3431^{14} 3746^{6} 4430^{5} **>39a 49f<**

Miss Bananas **2** b f Risk Me (FR)-Astrid Gilberto (Runnett) *2604^{5} 3072^{8}* 3808^{8} *4054^{2}* **>54a 22f<**

Miss Barcelona (IRE) **3** b f Mac's Imp (USA)-National Ballet (Shareef Dancer (USA)) *265^{4} 378^{8}* 582^{5} 641^{4} 700^{6} 878^{12} 1469^{9} 1642^{5} 1780^{4} 1988^{6} 2332^{3} 2392^{4} 2733^{7} 2836^{8} 3421^{10} **>39a 34f<**

Miss Beveled **2** b f Beveled (USA)-Reach Forward (Reach) 631^{8} 1019^{3} 1298^{3} *1432^{6}* 1600^{6} 1829^{10} 3544^{4} 4162^{10} *4483^{12} 4812^{13}* **>17a 46f<**

Miss Bussell **2** ch f Sabrehill (USA)-Reel Foyle (USA) (Irish River (FR)) 4973^{8} **>61f<**

Miss Carolina (IRE) **3** f 815a^{11} **>77f<**

Miss Carottene **4** b f Siberian Express (USA)-Silk St James (Pas de Seul) **1996:** *5112^{14}* **1997:** 585^{22} **>52a 36f<**

Miss Charlie **7** ch m Pharly (FR)-Close to You (Nebbiolo) **1996:** *5236^{9}* **1997:** *54^{4} 71^{12} 134^{10} 143^{7} 342^{5}* **>36a 60f<**

Miss Chief Maker **2** ch f Be My Chief (USA)-Waitingformargaret (Kris) 1240^{14} 3638^{12} 3985^{15} 4446^{8} **>28f<**

Miss Dangerous **2** b f Komaite (USA)-Khadine (Astec) 1407^{2} 1616^{8} 1821^{9} 4411^{6} *4593^{4}* **>39a 74f<**

Miss Darling **3** b f Clantime-Slipperose (Persepolis (FR)) **1996:** *5080^{9} 5107^{8}* **>31a 48f<**

Miss Dilletante **2** b f Primo Dominie-Misguided (Homing) 3687^{10} 3985^{12} 4298^{15} **>45f<**

Missed Domino **2** ch f Ron's Victory (USA)-Far Claim (USA) (Far North (CAN)) 3306^{11} 4209^{11} 4508^{7} **>54f<**

Missed May **3** br f Petong-Altara (GER) (Tarim) *215^{6} 230^{11} 292^{5}* 539^{6} 665^{6} 862^{12} 1095^{9} **>26a 38f<**

Missed the Boat (IRE) **7** b g Cyrano de Bergerac-Lady Portobello (Porto Bello) *315^{10}* **>24a 44f<**

Missed The Cut (IRE) **2** b f Classic Secret (USA)-Missish (Mummy's Pet) 4402^{2} 4542^{2} **>72f<**

Miss Eliminator **2** b f Komaite (USA)-Northern Line (Camden Town) 2545^{13} 2736^{3} 2904^{6} (3106) 3258^{7} 3823^{12} **>62f<**

Miss Equal **2** ch f Presidium-Dissolution (Henbit (USA)) 1109^{10} 1444^{R} *1789^{8}*

Missfortuna **3** b f Priolo (USA)-Lucky Round (Auction Ring (USA)) (2879) 2928^{2} 3311^{4} 4109^{8} 4323^{3} 4516^{11} **>72f<**

Miss Fugit Penance **3** br f Puissance-Figment (Posse (USA)) 760^{9} *903^{9}* **>35f<**

Miss Golden Sands **3** ch f Kris-Miss Kuta Beach (Bold Lad (IRE)) 507^{5} **>83f<**

Miss Hit **2** b f Efisio-Jennies' Gem (Sayf El Arab (USA)) 828^{10} **>43f<**

Missile Toe (IRE) **4** b g Exactly Sharp (USA)-Debach Dust (Indian King (USA)) 895^{16} 1972^{6} 2187^{2} 4998^{16} **>59a 65f<**

Miss Imp (IRE) **3** b f Mac's Imp (USA)-Be Nimble (Wattlefield) 727^{19} 989^{13} 1088^{12} 4607^{18} **>6f<**

Missing Link (FR) **4** b c Saumarez-Mistreat (Gay Mecene (USA)) 4863a^{5} **>106f<**

Miss Kalaglow **3** b f Kalaglow-Dame du Moulin (Shiny Tenth) 3230^{2} 3813^{8} *4053^{13}* **>62f<**

Miss Kemble **3** b f Warning-Sarah Siddons (FR) (Le Levanstell) 2532^{8} **>52f<**

Miss Kypros (GER) **3** f 1202a^{8} **>73f<**

Miss Lady Lydia **2** ch f Tina's Pet-Kinfauns Dancer (Celtic Cone) 3055^{7} 3228^{10}

Miss Main Street (IRE) **2** b f Shalford (IRE)-Bonvin (Taufan (USA)) 1253^{11} 1997^{5} 2935^{4} (3307) 3545^{4} 3990^{7} 4382^{10} **>61f<**

Miss Mezzanine **3** b f Norton Challenger-Forest Fawn (FR) (Top Ville) 1168^{16} 1591^{8} 1951^{12} 3129^{8} 3467^{11} **>22f<**

Miss Mighty **4** b f Bigivor-Fancy Blue (Fine Blue) *3041^{11}*

Miss Money Spider (IRE) **2** b f Statoblest-Dream of Jenny (Caerleon (USA)) 4668^{5} **>72a 70tf<**

Miss Muffett (IRE) **2** b f Hero's Honor (USA)-Grain de Folie (FR) (Top Ville) 1240^{11} 1440^{11} 3799^{6} 4185^{6} 4545^{4} 4856^{16} **>51f<**

Miss Offset **4** ch f Timeless Times (USA)-Farinara (Dragonara Palace (USA)) **1996:** *5124^{6}* **1997:** *81^{8}* **>75da 37f<**

Miss Peregrine **3** b f Polar Falcon (USA)-Good Thinking (USA) (Raja Baba (USA)) 882^{4} 1167^{8} 1401^{5} 2313^{3} **>51f<**

Miss Pickpocket (IRE) **4** b f Petorius-Fingers (Lord Gayle (USA)) **1996:** *5188^{W}* **1997:** *11^{6} 117^{3}* **>56a 74f<**

Miss Pigalle **6** b m Good Times (ITY)-Panayr (Faraway Times (USA)) (1285) 1603^{9} 2144^{8} 2355^{4} 2937^{2} 3443^{9} 3565^{5} 4471^{9} **>42f<**

Miss Pravda **4** ch f Soviet Star (USA)-Miss Paige (AUS) (Luskin Star (AUS)) **1996:** *5139^{12}* **1997:** 753^{7} 1278^{7} **>52a 49df<**

Miss Prism **4** b f Niniski (USA)-Reflected Glory (SWE) (Relko) **1996:** *5139^{2} 5185^{2}* **1997:** *86^{16} 163^{6}* **>61a 61f<**

Miss Puci **2** b f Puissance-Kind of Shy (Kind of Hush) 1126^{3} *2066^{6}* 2473^{3} 3106^{3} 3602^{4} (3857) 4166^{14} **>29a 62f<**

Miss Pugh **2** b f Puissance-Crymlyn (Welsh Pageant) 2324^{10} 3306^{18} **>25f<**

Miss Riviera **4** b f Kris-Miss Beaulieu (Northfields (USA)) 839^{6} 1326^{3} 3147^{3} 3577^{9} 4120^{3} 4393a^{4} **>108f<**

Miss Riviera Rose **3** ch f Niniski (USA)-Miss Beaulieu (Northfields (USA)) 773^{4} 1144^{9} 1563^{2} 2059^{5} 2507^{6} 2772^{10} 3320^{4} *3583^{9}* 3854^{3} 4243^{10} 4886^{11} **>18a 55f<**

Miss Salsa Dancer **2** ch f Salse (USA)-Thakhayr (Sadler's Wells (USA)) 2856^{5} 3060^{3} 3629^{4} 4265^{6} 4767^{10} **>73f<**

Miss Sancerre **3** b f Last Tycoon-Miss Bergerac (Bold Lad (IRE)) 672^{4} **>106f<**

Miss Scooter **2** ch f Beveled (USA)-Donosa (Posse (USA)) 536^{7} 767^{2} *2367^{6}* 2746^{5} **>22a 59f<**

Miss Skye (IRE) **2** b f Common Grounds-Swift Chorus (Music Boy) 472^{8} 2388^{9} 2893^{6} 3818^{5} 4068^{9} 4819^{16} **>65df<**

Miss Slender **2** br f Inchinor-Tulapet (Mansingh (USA)) 4103^{13} 4458^{11} 4581^{8} **>50f<**

Miss St Kitts **3** ch f Risk Me (FR)-So Beguiling (USA) (Woodman (USA)) 1995^{10} 2169^{9} 2354^{9} 2899^{14} **>24f<**

Miss The Beat **5** b m Music Boy-Bad Start (USA) (Bold Bidder) *99^{10}* **>11a f<**

Miss Vita (USA) **3** b f Alleged (USA)-Torrid Tango (USA) (Green Dancer (USA)) 3775^{5} 3903^{4} 4177^{9} 4400^{3} 4971^{21} **>65f<**

Miss Vivien **2** b f Puissance-Madam Bold (Never so Bold) 2713^{6} 3306^{4} 4231^{4} (4588) 4702^{7} **>75f<**

Miss Waterline **4** br f Rock City-Final Shot (Dalsaan) 4431^{2} **>62f<**

Miss Zafonic (FR) **2** b f Zafonic (USA)-Miss Silca Key (Welsh Saint) (2728) 3049^{2} 3723^{4} 4475^{8} **>87f<**

Mister Aspecto (IRE) **4** b g Caerleon (USA)-Gironde (USA) (Raise A Native) *402^{3}* 470^{12} 613^{14} 865^{15} *1156^{2}* 1562^{7} *1940^{3} 2048^{3} 2365^{2}* 3108^{2} *(3231) (3415)* 3626^{5} 3867^{3} *4572^{2}* 4794^{12} 4956^{15} **>85a 63f<**

Mister Bankes **2** ch c Risk Me (FR)-Eternal Triangle (USA) (Barachois (CAN)) 432^{2} (548) 750^{5} 965^{6} 1391^{4} 1829^{6} 1952^{4} 2370^{8} **>85f<**

Mister Benjamin (IRE) **2** b c Polish Patriot (USA)-Frau Ahuyentante (ARG) (Frari (ARG)) 3687^{6} *(4052)* 4778^{26} **>69+a 65f<**

Mister Bunch **2** b g Efisio-Mellow Gold (Meldrum) 3479^{12} 3806^{15} 4165^{11} **>43f<**

Mister Copper **3** b g Sharpo-Nineteenth of May (Homing) **1996:** 5193a^{2}

Mister Damask **2** b c Damister (USA)-Smelter (Prominer) 1657^{9} **>22f<**

Mister Glum **3** ch g Ron's Victory (USA)-Australia Fair (AUS) (Without Fear (FR)) 768^{10} **>42f<**

Mister Jay **3** b g Batshoof-Portvasco (Sharpo) 642^{7} 900^{14} 2182^{8} *2607^{8}* 3601^{13} **>40df<**

Mister Jolson **8** br g Latest Model-Impromptu (My Swanee) 835^{3} 1107^{5} (1410) 1594^{6} 1824^{7} 2232^{5} 2377^{7} 2950^{3} 3326^{3} 3765^{13} 4280^{16} 4820^{2} **>83f<**

Mister Pink **3** ch gr g Absalom-Blush Rambler (IRE) (Blushing Groom (FR)) (502) 690^{12} 788^{3} 1025^{5} 2058^{16} 2589^{8} 4476^{10} 4639^{3} 4774^{7} **>86f<**

Mister Raider **5** ch g Ballacashtal (CAN)-Martian Melody (Enchantment) **1996:** *5097^{7} 5173^{8} (5280)* **1997:** *24^{6} 95^{8}* 541^{5} 601^{7} 756^{2} 1236^{8} (1620) 2115^{10} *2663^{3}* 3083^{11} 3637^{4} 4249^{6} 4518^{9} **>65a 51f<**

Mister Rambo **2** b g Rambo Dancer (CAN)-Ozra (Red Alert) (4884) **>87f<**

Mister Sean (IRE) **4** b g Mac's Imp (USA)-Maid of Mourne (Fairy King (USA)) 473^{12} 760^{10} 879^{12}

1639[14] 1676[8] 2536[15] 3271[8] 3922[18] **>28f<**

Misterton **3** ch g Mystiko (USA)-South Shore (Caerleon (USA)) 645[10] 793[8] 1115[12] 1689[7] 2171[6] 2357[8] 3601[6] (4608) 4847[10] **>37f<**

Mister Tricky **2** ch c Magic Ring (IRE)-Splintering (Sharpo) 4908[7] **>46f<**

Mister Valentin (FR) **3** b g Iron Duke (FR)-Lady Eglantine (FR) (Lightning (FR)) (268a) **>80?f<**

Mister Westsound **5** b g Cyrano de Bergerac-Captivate (Mansingh (USA)) 610[10] 827[11] 951[7] 1315[17] 1560[12] 1835[4] (2033) (2144) 2472[2] 2711[10] 2857[9] 3484[3] 4927[10] **>51f<**

Mister Woodstick (IRE) **4** b g Distinctly North (USA)-Crannog (Habitat) 3921[14] **>58f<**

Mistra (IRE) **4** b f Rainbow Quest (USA)-Mackla (Caerleon (USA)) **1996:** (5157a) **>104f<**

Mistral Lord (IRE) **3** br g Fairy King (USA)-Walkyria (Lord Gayle (USA)) 740[14] 1167[10] 3632[11] **>49f<**

Misty Cay (IRE) **3** b f Mujadil (USA)-Quai des Brumes (USA) (Little Current (USA)) **1996:** *5092[4]* **1997:** *(8) (44) 96[5] 237[3] 362[4] 2319[3]* 2645[11] 2772[7] 2957[2] (3966) **>58a 66f<**

Misty Moor **2** b f Wolfhound (USA)-Corley Moor (Habitat) 3619[2] 3799[8] **>71+f<**

Misty Point **3** ch f Sharpo-Clouded Vision (So Blessed) 1415[4] 1823[8] 2506[8] 3202[3] 3690[5] 3982[5] 4431[2] 4695[12] **>69df<**

Misty Rain **3** br f Polar Falcon (USA)-Ballerine (USA) (Lyphard's Wish (FR)) 681[7] *1121[4]* 1568[9] 2178[3] 2593[5] 3478[4] 3813[3] 3968[8] 4596[9] 4858[7] **>59a 57f<**

Mitch Passi (IRE) **2** ch g Exit To Nowhere (USA)-Stormed (USA) (Storm Bird (CAN)) 4575[7] 4752[2] **>79a 86f<**

Mithak (USA) **3** b c Silver Hawk (USA)-Kapalua Butterfly (USA) (Stage Door Johnny) (445) 782[3] 2676[5] 2963[4] 3333[6] 3648[2] 3974[15] 4774[2] **>93f<**

Mithali **4** b c Unfuwain (USA)-Al Bahathri (USA) (Blushing Groom (FR)) (2172) 2830[7] 3824[5] (4102) (4577) 4893[7] **>101f<**

Mizog **2** b f Selkirk (USA)-Embroideress (Stanford) 4439[7] **>17f<**

Mizyan (IRE) **9** b g Melyno-Maid of Erin (USA) (Irish River (FR)) *3046[6]* 3283[8] **>59a 49f<**

Mo-Addab (IRE) **7** b g Waajib-Tissue Paper (Touch Paper) (1436) 1845[3] 2340[3] 2557[8] 3622[9] 4297[16] 4441[8] 4781[20] 4920[8] **>64f<**

Mockery **2** b f Nashwan (USA)-Laughsome (Be My Guest (USA)) 4973[12] **>48f<**

Mock Trial (IRE) **4** b g Old Vic-Test Case (Busted) 838[14] 994[6] **>71f<**

Modesto (USA) **9** b g Al Nasr (FR)-Modena (USA) (Roberto (USA)) *2911[7]* **>5?a f<**

Modigliani (GER) **3** 3555a[6] **>100f<**

Moet (IRE) **2** b f Mac's Imp (USA)-Comfrey Glen (Glenstal (USA)) 3757[6] **>60f<**

Mogin **4** ch f Komaite (USA)-Misdevious (USA) (Alleged (USA)) **1996:** *5152[12] 5211[2]* **1997:** *47[7] 305[10]* 1009[9] 1373[8] **>45da 46f<**

Mogul **3** b g Formidable (USA)-Madiyla (Darshaan) **1996:** *5214[5]* **1997:** *26[2] 239[2]* 431[9] 764[7] 1387[9] *2159[6] 3054[8]* **>72da 66f<**

Mohaajir (USA) **6** b h Sadler's Wells (USA)-Very Charming (USA) (Vaguely Noble) 3511a[4] 3842a[5] 4191a[3] **>114f<**

Mohawk (IRE) **2** b c Indian Ridge-Dazzling Fire (IRE) (Bluebird (USA)) 1418[3] 1760[4] *2363[5]* 3215[11] 4545[3] 4897[11] **>43a 72f<**

Mohawk River (IRE) **4** b c Polish Precedent (USA)-High Hawk (Shirley Heights) (3238) 3705[5] 3902[10] **>107f<**

Moi Canard **4** ch c Bold Owl-Royal Scots Greys (Blazing Saddles (AUS)) 1320[16] 1968[10] 2150[11] 3083[4] 3195[6] 3561[11] *3860[16] 4301[9]* **>33a 45f<**

Mojito (GER) **3** c 2097a[5] 2642a[13] **>104f<**

Mole Creek **2** gr f Unfuwain (USA)-Nicholas Grey (Track Spare) 5041[7] **>62f<**

Molly Music **3** b f Music Boy-Carlton Glory (Blakeney) **1996:** *5162[4] 5176[8]* **1997:** 466[6] *1433[3] 1580[2] (1757)* 1843[10] *2303[5] 2672[6]* 4043[17] *4591[3] 4798[3]* **>63a 64df<**

Momentarily (USA) **2** b f Gilded Time (USA)-Saratoga Dame (USA) (Saratoga Six (USA)) 2875[5] **>55f<**

Monaassib **6** ch g Cadeaux Genereux-Pluvial (Habat) (519) (671) (1309) (1720a) 2056[4] (3001a) 3554a[2] 4011[7] 4421[2] **>120f<**

Monacle **3** b g Saddlers' Hall (IRE)-Endless Joy (Law Society (USA)) 2873[13] 3320[6] 4072[5] 4521[12] 4743[10] 4850[8] 4946[5] **>51f<**

Monaco (IRE) **3** b g Classic Music (USA)-Larosterna (Busted) 1870[4] 2059[4] 2323[3] 3236[4] 3696[11] 4748[11] 4842[19] 5023[13] **>67f<**

Monaco Gold (IRE) **5** b g Durgam (USA)-Monaco Ville (Rheingold) 2034[7] (2225) (2386) 3223[2] 3626[9] **>55f<**

Monarch's Pursuit **3** b g Pursuit of Love-Last Detail (Dara Monarch) 524[8] 1129[6] 1469[3] 2064[5] 3272[6] (3870) 4509[5] **>64f<**

Mon Bruce **3** ch c Beveled (USA)-Pendona (Blue Cashmere) **1996:** *5083[2] 5121[5]* **1997:** *(588)* 845[14] 1141[24] 1573[5] 1931[4] 2780[3] 2964[7] 3473[9] *(4049)* (4385) 4512[2] 4636[19] 4844[3] 5047[21] **>72a 71f<**

Mon Domino **8** ch h Dominion-Arderelle (FR) (Pharly (FR)) 267a[3] (3734a) **>109f<**

Mondschein **2** b f Rainbow Quest (USA)-River Spey (Mill Reef (USA)) 4526[10] 4789[2] **>85f<**

Moneghetti **6** ch g Faustus (USA)-The Victor Girls (Crofthall) 864[4] *1048[13]* 1389[9] 1622[5] 2039[9] 2488[2] 2646[11] *3041[6]* 3330[7] **>45a 45f<**

Mongol Warrior (USA) **4** b c Deputy Minister (CAN)-Surely Georgie's (USA) (Alleged (USA)) 736[11] 1073a[3] 1365a[7] 2104[8] 2459a[3] 3182a[5] 4420[6] 4863a[6] 4963a[2] **>119f<**

Monis (IRE) **6** ch g Waajib-Gratify (Grundy) **1996:** *5178[3] 5241[2] 5262[5]* **1997:** *152[15] 203[11] 243[10] 429[10]* 687[4] 1118[7] 1796[5] 2000[12] 2896[8] 3315[5] 3627[4] 3853[4] (4846) **>31a 47f<**

Monitor **3** ch c Machiavellian (USA)-Instant Desire (USA) (Northern Dancer) 676[3] 847[5] 2126[3] 2846[2] (3275) **>92f<**

Monkey Face **6** gr m Clantime-Charming View (Workboy) 1127[12] **>39f<**

Mono Lady (IRE) **4** b f Polish Patriot (USA)-Phylella (Persian Bold) **1996:** *5082[4] 5235[6]* **1997:** *(34) (125) 169[3] 346[2] 410[7]* 538[3] 838[5] *(1086)* 1668[3] 2582[2] 2782[7] 3245[2] (3970) **>77a 74f<**

Monongahela (IRE) **3** b c Caerleon (USA)-Monoglow (Kalaglow) 2967a[7] 4191a[10] **>96f<**

Monopolize (AUS) **7** b g Rubiton-Gay Rosalind **1996:** (5218a) **>121f<**

Monopoly (IRE) **2** ch c Sharp Victor (USA)-Faye (Monsanto (FR)) 836[10] *1286[5]* 2018[11] *4984[11]* **>57a 59f<**

Mons **4** b c Deploy-Morina (USA) (Lyphard (USA)) 932[3] 1172[2] (4549) 4866a[3] **>123f<**

Monsajem (USA) **2** ch c Woodman (USA)-Fairy Dancer (USA) (Nijinsky (CAN)) 1174[4] 1933[4] (3789) 4116[5] 4778[5] **>78f<**

Montano (USA) **2** b c Manila (USA)-Leery Baba (USA) (Well Decorated (USA)) 1961[3] 2314[5] 4061[15] 4362[2] *4589[4]* 4856[3] **>78a 72f<**

Monte Cavo **6** b g Bustino-Dance Festival (Nureyev (USA)) *544[2]* 598[5] *1291[2]* 1315[15] *1754[5]* (2121) *(2368)* 2660[3] 2845[3] 3105[8] (3200) 3466[3] 3542[3] 3976[16] 4210[9] 4757[25] **>54a 66f<**

Montecristo **4** br g Warning-Sutosky (Great Nephew) *52[4] 182[10] 389[5] 419[6]* 1371[5] 1694[8] 2909[4] (3631) (4275) *(4810)* (4986) **>57+a 80f<**

Monte Lemos (IRE) **2** b c Mukaddamah (USA)-Crimbourne (Mummy's Pet) 1952[3] (3094) (3546) 4296[3] (4560) 4890[6] **>91f<**

Montendre **10** b g Longleat (USA)-La Lutine (My Swallow) 519[8] 980[5] 1317[17] 1676[2] 1937[2] 2575[3] 2780[2] 3251[2] 3580[3] (4048) 4321[8] 4733[12] **>84f<**

Montfort (USA) **3** b c Manila (USA)-Sable Coated (Caerleon (USA)) 1014[3] (1372) (1949) (2241) **>112+f<**

Montone (IRE) **7** b g Pennine Walk-Aztec Princess (Indian King (USA)) **1996:** *(5151) 5210[2]* **1997:** *15[4] 116[5] (210) 294[11]* 607[9] *870[2]* 1422[12] 1677[11] *1944[8]* 2146[11] 3421[8] 3476[13] *4050[8]* 4335[12] *5022[11]* **>48a 51f<**

Montrestar **4** ch g Mon Tresor-Wing of Freedom (Troy) 3590[2] 3771[4] 3922[6] **>35a 69f<**

Monument **5** ch g Cadeaux Genereux-In Perpetuity (Great Nephew) 1414[4] 1923[3] 2373[9] (3134) 3466[6] 4109[3] 4516[15] **>71f<**

Monza (USA) **3** b c Woodman (USA)-Star Pastures (Northfields (USA)) 692[8] 1159[5] 2135[2] 2515[5] **>107f<**

Moonax (IRE) **6** ch h Caerleon (USA)-Moonsilk (Solinus) 1033[3] 2055[9] **>126df<**

Moon Blast **3** gr g Reprimand-Castle Moon (Kalamoun) (754) 990[5] 1427[4] (1813) 1928[2] 2877[8] 3115[14] 4002[4] 4320[2] **>97f<**

Moonclaret **2** b f Beveled (USA)-Miss Monte Carlo (Reform) 4401[11]

Moon Colony **4** b g Top Ville-Honeymooning (USA) (Blushing Groom (FR)) 944[7] 1277[6] 1477[18] 2592[2] 3291[2] 4046[2] (4743) 4874[6] 5052[3] **>87f<**

Moon Fairy **3** ch f Interrex (CAN)-Zamoon (Zambrano) 1858[2] 2756[2] (3313) 3691[12] **>70f<**

Moon Flower (IRE) **3** b f Sadler's Wells (USA)-Mill Princess (Mill Reef (USA)) 809a[8] 2267a[10] **>85f<**

Moon Gorge **2** b f Pursuit of Love-Highland Light (Home Guard (USA)) 4884[5] **>64f<**

Moonlightandroses **2** b f Aragon-Lively (IRE) (Digamist (USA)) 3450[20] 4332[18] **>5f<**

Moonlight Calypso **6** ch m Jupiter Island-Moonlight Bay (Palm Track) **1996:** *5116[8]* **>36a 51f< (DEAD)**

Moonlight Flit **2** b f Presidium-Moonwalker (Night Shift (USA)) 3427[5] 3808[5] 4014[7] (4208) 4382[5] **>63f<**

Moonlight Invader (IRE) **3** br c Darshaan-Mashmoon (USA) (Habitat) 1105[10] 1844[7] 2474[4] **>63f<**

Moonlight Paradise (USA) **3** b f Irish River (FR)-Ottomwa (USA) (Strawberry Road (AUS)) 960[10] 2025[6] 4226[5] **>102f<**

Moonraking **4** gr g Rusticaro (FR)-Lunaire (Try My Best (USA)) *328[3] (410)* 552[3] 762[5] 955[3] 1452[9] 3867[6] *4055[15]* 5024[3] **>62a 47f<**

Moonshadow (IRE) **2** b f Be My Guest (USA)-Ballet Shoes (IRE) (Ela-Mana-Mou) 4604[5]

Moonshift **3** b g Cadeaux Genereux-Thewaari (USA) (Eskimo (USA)) 740[15] 1106[12] 4331[5] **>43f<**

Moonshine Girl (USA) **3** ch f Shadeed (USA)-Fly to the Moon (USA) (Blushing Groom (FR)) 1770[3] 2056[21] 2690[7] **>93f<**

Moonshiner (USA) **3** b c Irish River (FR)-Marling (IRE) (Lomond (USA)) 479[5] 674[6] 1029[13] 2925[10] 3921[9] (4408) 4583[10] **>87f<**

Moon Song **3** b f Presidium-Martian Melody (Enchantment) 474[3] 1485[4] 1690[4] 2836[10] 3206[6] 3454[6] 3756[11] 4586[6] **>59f<**

Moonspell **3** b f Batshoof-Shimmer (Bustino)

1140[6] 1435[7] **>69f<**

Moonstone (IRE) 2 b f Statoblest-Opening Day (Day Is Done) 2840[6] 3151[6] 3961a[18] 4332[7] 4588[2] 4897[B] 5050[15] **>72f<**

Moon Strike (FR) 7 b or br g Strike Gold (USA)-Lady Lamia (USA) (Secreto (USA)) 1468[2] (2289) 3011[3] (3410) 3914[4] 4239[8] 4444[10] **>85a 105f<**

Moontabeh 2 b c Mujtahid (USA)-Desert Girl (Green Desert (USA)) 1791[2] 2320[3] (2720) (3446) 3708[5] 4315[8] 4670[12] **>85f<**

Moontalk 3 b f Emarati (USA)-Pearl Pet (Mummy's Pet) 2392[7] 3230[6] **>32f<**

Moonvoor (IRE) 6 gr g Duca Di Busted-Reprieved Run 1005a[P]

Moorbird (IRE) 3 b g Law Society (USA)-Heather Lark (Red Alert) *544[11] 658[5]* 1094[15] 1502[4] *1785[5]* 2207[14] **>43a 47f<**

Moor Hall Princess 3 gr f Chilibang-Forgiving (Jellaby) *2159[7]* 2780[8] *3043[5]* **>20a 34f<**

Moothyeb (USA) 2 b br c Dayjur (USA)-Orca (ARG) (Southern Halo (USA)) 1692[3] 2176[10] 3331[3] 3924[11] 4778[22] **>63f<**

Moran 3 b c Bustino-Ower (IRE) (Lomond (USA)) 2731[7] 3014[7] 3977[8] 4319[17] **>77df<**

Moratorium (USA) 2 b c El Gran Senor (USA)-Substance (USA) (Diesis) 4952[7] **>66f<**

More Bills (IRE) 5 b g Gallic League-Lady Portobello (Porto Bello) *1125[7]* **>23a 43f<**

Moredun (IRE) 3 b g Waajib-Izba (Thatching) 1921[7] 2947[13] 3206[9] **>37f<**

More Risk (IRE) 4 b f Fayruz-La Mortola (Bold Lad (IRE)) 2447a[6] **>73f<**

More Than You Know (IRE) 4 ch f Kefaah (USA)-Foston Bridge (Relkino) **1996:** *5091[3] 5137[10] 5277[3]* **1997:** *163[3] 187[3]* 3286[2] *3585[6]* 3796[8] **>72a 55f<**

Morigi 6 b h Rousillon (USA)-Ibtidaar (USA) (Danzig (USA)) 1728a[3] 4660a[6] **>115f<**

Morning Sir 4 b g Southern Music-Morning Miss (Golden Dipper) 598[11] **>56df<**

Morning Star 3 b f Statoblest-Moushka (Song) 685[13] 1227[9] *1942[11]* 2354[11] 2755[8] 3240[9] **>6a 36f<**

Morning Surprise 4 b br f Tragic Role (USA)-Fleur de Foret (USA) (Green Forest (USA)) **1996:** *5215[4] 5262[7]* **>46a 52f<**

Morocco (IRE) 8 b g Cyrano de Bergerac-Lightning Laser (Monseigneur (USA)) 1395[4] 1849[3] 2109[6] 2282[2] 2546[10] 2835[9] 3018[6] **>66f<**

Mosconi (IRE) 3 b c Last Tycoon-Volnost (USA) 713a[3] 1195a[7] 1541a[7] 2078a[5] 4834a[8] **>102f<**

Moscow Mist (IRE) 6 b g Soviet Star (USA)-Ivory Dawn (USA) (Sir Ivor) 3712[6] 3901[16] 4283[19] 4924[9] **>38a 81df<**

Moss Side Monkey 2 b g Presidium-Lady of Leisure (Record Run) 664[2] *1136[6]* 1330[10] 1581[4] 1815[5] 2383[5] 4208[15] **>27a 60f<**

Most Respectful 4 ch g Respect-Active Movement (Music Boy) 528[7] 599[9] 823[5] 1079[7] 1285[11] **>58f<**

Most Wanted (IRE) 4 ch f Priolo (USA)-Dewan's Niece (USA) (Dewan (USA)) 4438[14] 4846[8] **>32f<**

Most Welcome News 5 b g Most Welcome-In the Papers (Aragon) 4450[6] **>47a 22f<**

Motcombs Club 3 ch c Deploy-Unique Treasure (Young Generation) **1996:** *5100[6] 5212[10]* **1997:** 1474[7] 1938[12] 2397[4] 3057[4] **>51a 47f<**

Motet 3 b c Mtoto-Guest Artiste (Be My Guest (USA)) *(491)* 1852[3] 2230[4] 2850[3] 3383[2] (3805) (4246) 4783[20] **>72+a 96f<**

Mothers Help 2 b f Relief Pitcher-Laundry Maid (Forzando) 4907[8] **>53f<**

Mouche 3 b br f Warning-Case for the Crown (USA) (Bates Motel (USA)) (584) 1021[5] 1495[P] 2325[9] 2708[11] 3092[8] 3460[5] 3812[5] (4168) 4456[10] 4565[4] 4842[2] 4995[10] **>77f<**

Moultazim (USA) 7 b g Diesis-Maysoon (Shergar) 2375[7] 2848[7] **>29f<**

Mountaineer (IRE) 3 b c Tirol-Icecapped (Caerleon (USA)) *373[5]* 495[2] *658[4]* 1094[3] 1565[5] 4562[10] 4748[4] 4896[W] **>56a 67f<**

Mountain Magic 2 b f Magic Ring (IRE)-Nevis (Connaught) 2520[5] 3247[5] 3927[4] 4166[8] 4545[6] 4819[9] **>59f<**

Mountain Song 2 b c Tirol-Persian Song (Persian Bold) 1819[3] (2022) (2243) 4357a[3] 4889[8] **>105f<**

Mountgate 5 b g Merdon Melody-Young Whip (Bold Owl) 1219[2] 1471[4] 1655[6] 2124[7] 3243[2] 3428[9] 3810[8] 4147[9] 4410[16] 4792[W] 4927[14] 4988[12] **>46f<**

Mount Genius (USA) 4 b br g Beau Genius (CAN)-Mount Jackie (USA) (Mount Hagen (FR)) 841[14] 1630[5] 5043[7] **>36f<**

Mount Holly (USA) 3 b c Woodman (USA)-Mount Helena (Danzig (USA)) 1409[2] 4277[3] 4757[16] (4848) 5049[3] **>87f<**

Mount Row 4 b f Alzao (USA)-Temple Row (Ardross) 1698a[8] 2267a[11] **>99f<**

Mousehole 5 b g Statoblest-Alo Ez (Alzao (USA)) 863[16] 1225[12] 1666[4] 2061[2] 2321[7] 2581[2] (2895) 3107[2] 3280[3] (3473) 3771[10] **>78f<**

Mousse Glacee (FR) 3 b f Mtoto-Madame Est Sortie (FR) (Longleat (USA)) 818a[2] 1203a[6] 1916a[2] 4256a[4] 4869a[2] **>119f<**

Move Smartly (IRE) 7 b h Smarten (USA)-Key Maneuver (USA) (Key To Content (USA)) 896[4] 1089[17] 2239[6] 2542[3] 2723[9] 4114[11] 4184[15] **>47a 53f<**

Move The Clouds 3 gr f Environment Friend-Che Gambe (USA) (Lyphard (USA)) **1996:** *5168[3]* **1997:** *83[5] 124[16]* 462[4] 575[9] 757[9] 995[19] *4053[14]* **>61da 53f<**

Move With Edes 5 b g Tragic Role (USA)-Good Time Girl (Good Times (ITY)) 791[W] 1085[6] 1471[7] 2501[4] 3276[16] *4570[10]* **>70a 61f<**

Moving Arrow 6 ch g Indian Ridge-Another Move (Farm Walk) *1123[9]* 1450[12] 1775[6] 2341[6] 2678[7] 3243[10] 4147[5] 4283[15] **>63a 89f<**

Moving Out 9 b g Slip Anchor-New Generation (Young Generation) 4171[6] 4609[6] **>54f<**

Moving Princess 2 b f Prince Sabo-Another Move (Farm Walk) 3602[3] 3825[3] 4211[5] 4286[7] **>64+f<**

Moving Up (IRE) 4 ch f Don't Forget Me-Our Pet (Mummy's Pet) **1996:** *5148[16]* **1997:** 2536[4] 3083[6] 3227[9] **>3a 40f<**

Mowbray (USA) 2 b br c Opening Verse (USA)-Peppy Raja (USA) (Raja Baba (USA)) 2680[2] (3282) (3688) 4357a[4] 4865a[2] **>104f<**

Mowelga 3 ch c Most Welcome-Galactic Miss (Damister (USA)) 740[9] 4407[3] (4883) **>71f<**

Mowjood (USA) 3 b c Mr Prospector (USA)-Bineyah (IRE) (Sadler's Wells (USA)) 1087[5] 2487[3] 3315[2] 3478[3] 3849[7] **>76f<**

Mowlaie 6 ch g Nashwan (USA)-Durrah (USA) (Nijinsky (CAN)) 928[4] *1138[8]* 1422[16] (1748) 2063[8] *2911[6]* 3272[3] 3919[12] 4161[11] 4235[14] 4453[14] **>31a 36f<**

Moy (IRE) 2 ch f Beveled (USA)-Exceptional Beauty (Sallust) 971[6] 1447[11] 2519[5] 2739[5] 3905[14] 4801[5] **>55f<**

Mozambique (IRE) 3 b c Fayruz-Lightning Laser (Monseigneur (USA)) 4316[3] 4563[5] *4809[2]* **>64a 78f<**

Mr Bean 7 b g Salse (USA)-Goody Blake (Blakeney) **1996:** *5143[6] 5177[9]* **1997:** *43[6]* 3919[13] **>50a 16f<**

Mr Bergerac (IRE) 6 b g Cyrano de Bergerac-Makalu (Godswalk (USA)) **1996:** *5203[7]* **1997:** 726[7] 834[13] 942[16] (1446) 2105[28] 2326[8] 2649[3] 3130[5] 3198[2] (3385) 3649[7] 3888[5] 4121[14] 4280[5] 4550[11] *4797[10]* 4902[4] *4983[10]* 4995[9] **>78a 95f<**

Mr Bombastique (IRE) 3 b c Classic Music (USA)-Duende (High Top) 502[2] 1146[7] 1487[3] **>86df<**

Mr Browning (USA) 6 br g Al Nasr (FR)-Crinoline (Blakeney) 1169[11] (1641) 2218[8] 2749[4] 3739[6] 4108[20] **>47a 64f<**

Mr Cahill (USA) 2 b c Cahill Road (USA)-Sympathetic Miss (USA) (Proudest Roman (USA)) (3322) 3644[8] **>83+f<**

Mr Cube (IRE) 7 ch h Tate Gallery (USA)-Truly Thankful (CAN) (Graustark) **1996:** *5089[11]* **1997:** 733[17] 1005[3] 1422[2] 1506[4] 1639[8] 2019[2] 2204[2] (2573) 2745[9] 3442[2] 3930[16] 4448[6] 4741[6] **>35a 64f<**

Mr Finch (USA) 3 1544a[10] **>96f<**

Mr Fortywinks (IRE) 3 ch g Fools Holme (USA)-Dream on (Absalom) 2203[7] 2847[6] (3487) 3933[2] 4235[2] 4584[2] 4972[4] **>57f<**

Mr Frosty 5 b g Absalom-Chadenshe (Taufan (USA)) **1996:** *(5174) (5230) (5236)* **1997:** *89[6] 201[5] 253[7] 357[7]* 1107[3] 1324[15] **>76a 68f<**

Mr Fund Switch 2 ch g Chilibang-Purple Fan (Dalsaan) 447[13] 611[6] 948[7] 1255[10] 2752[7] 3270[6] *4054[5]* 4419[6] 4588[4] *4808[9]* **>35a 43f<**

Mr Hacker 4 b g Shannon Cottage (USA)-Aosta (Shack (USA)) *171[8]* **>15a 51f<**

Mr Keating (FR) 7 gr g King Cyrus (FR)-Guichardiere (FR) (Guiche (FR)) (190a) **>66f<**

Mr Lightfoot (IRE) 3 b c Dancing Dissident (USA)-Lundylux (Grundy) 1198a[4] 4356a[2] **>105f<**

Mr Lowry 5 b g Rambo Dancer (CAN)-Be Royal (Royal Palm) *516[11]* **>38?a 39f<**

Mr Majica 3 b c Rudimentary (USA)-Pellinora (USA) (King Pellinore (USA)) 517[2] 983[6] 4047[3] (4182) 4787[18] **>86f<**

Mr Miyagi 2 b g Full Extent (USA)-All the Girls (IRE) (Alzao (USA)) 3818[10] 4017[6] 4236[13] 4266[6] 4753[17] **>66f<**

Mr Montague (IRE) 5 b g Pennine Walk-Ballyewry (Prince Tenderfoot (USA)) 686[6] 842[15] 1221[8] 2065[6] 3248[15] **>55f<**

Mr Moriarty (IRE) 6 ch g Tate Gallery (USA)-Bernica (FR) (Caro) *151[3] 360[7]* **>39a 40f<**

Mr Music 3 ch g La Grange Music-Golden (Don) *1121[6] 1756[16]* 1956[8] **>52a 27f<**

Mr Nevermind (IRE) 7 b g The Noble Player (USA)-Salacia (Seaepic (USA)) **1996:** *(5211)* **1997:** *(120) (201) 238[3] (316)* 1849[12] **>91a 73f<**

Mr Oscar 5 b g Belfort (FR)-Moushka (Song) 596[18] 953[10] 1561[10] **>89df<**

Mr Paradise (IRE) 3 b g Salt Dome (USA)-Glowlamp (IRE) (Glow (USA)) **1996:** 5190a[2] **1997:** *576[2] 868[3]* 1272[3] 1443[2] (1651) 1741[9] (2149) *2303[7]* 3798[10] 4176[2] 4297[6] 4578[7] 4781[18] **>61a 75f<**

Mr Peillon (USA) 6 ch h Irish River (FR)-Mlle Lyphard (USA) (Lyphard (USA)) 270a[2] **>76f<**

Mr Rough 6 b g Fayruz-Rheinbloom (Rheingold) **1996:** *5186[5] 5221[6]* **1997:** 1024[11] 1320[11] (1689) 1878[5] 2408[7] 2868[7] 3573[16] *4069[10]* 4224[6] 4371[8] 4711[14] **>53a 55f<**

Mrs Drummond (IRE) 4 br f Dromod Hill-Dear France (USA) (Affirmed (USA)) *1125[8] 1417[5]* 3317[6] *3587[3]* **>40a 43f<**

Mrs Keen 4 b f Beveled (USA)-Haiti Mill (Free State) *2070[13]* **>41f<**

Mrs Malaprop 2 b f Night Shift (USA)-Lightning Legacy (USA) (Super Concorde (USA)) 4103[17] 4311[2] (4428) 4675[13] 4948[8] **>82f<**

Mrs McBadger 4 ch f Weldnaas (USA)-Scottish Lady (Dunbeath (USA)) *51[12]* **>43a 56f<**

Mrs Middle 2 b f Puissance-Ibadiyya (Tap On

Wood) 1440[6] 1664[4] 2740[6] 3556[4] (3817) 3924[13] 4185[10] **>66f<**
Mrs Miniver (USA) 3 b f Septieme Ciel (USA)-Becomes A Rose (CAN) (Deputy Minister (CAN)) 959[5] 3727[4] 4177[6] 4557[5] **>108?f<**
Mr Speaker (IRE) 4 ch g Statoblest-Casting Vote (USA) (Monteverdi) 977[2] 1225[21] 1977[22] 2698[8] 3690[2] 4112[7] 4580[15] 4741[9] 4951[6] **>37a 61f<**
Mr Speculator 4 ch g Kefaah (USA)-Humanity (Ahonoora) **1996:** *5136[3] (5233)* **1997:** *30[2] 66[3] (219) 315[9] 516[3]* 2843[15] 3915[13] *4304[3]* 4562[17] 4821[16] **>59a 20f<**
Mrs Pickles 2 gr f Northern Park (USA)-Able Mabel (Absalom) 2917[20] 3985[14] *4569[10]* **>34a 12f<**
Mrs Pollock 4 b f Precocious-Power and Red (Skyliner) *3041[10]*
Mr Sponge (USA) 3 ch c Summer Squall (USA)-Dinner Surprise (USA) (Lyphard (USA)) 1587[3] (1851) 2229[3] 3594[5] 3901[3] 4297[9] 4550[3] *4983[9]* **>71a 94f<**
Mr Teigh 5 b g Komaite (USA)-Khadino (Relkino) 1117[7] 1268[15] 1422[5] (1683) 1831[5] 2340[4] 2760[5] (3254) 3604[7] 3649[6] 4121[3] 4280[18] 4561[6] **>82a 81f<**
Mr Titch 4 b g Totem (USA)-Empress Nicki (Nicholas Bill) *313[7]* **>8a 36f<**
Mr Wild (USA) 4 b g Wild Again (USA)-Minstress (USA) (The Minstrel (CAN)) (986) 1325[5] **>86f<**
M T Vessel 3 b g Risk Me (FR)-Brown Taw (Whistlefield) 1781[11] 2298[6] 2481[8] 2883[11] 3557[5] **>12f<**
Muara Bay 3 gr c Absalom-Inca Girl (Tribal Chief) 474[11] 606[5] *1151[7] 1756[2] 1944[3]* 3299[3] (3849) 4504[2] 4845[5] **>40a 57f<**
Mu-Arrik 9 b or br h Aragon-Maravilla (Mandrake Major) **1996:** *5114[11] 5165[6] 5174[9]* **1997:** *192[9] 243[11]* 956[11] 1220[9] 1315[8] 1395[9] 1620[5] 1865[9] 2384[7] 2938[5] 3240[10] 3431[4] **>32a 34f<**
Mubariz (IRE) 5 b g Royal Academy (USA)-Ringtail (Auction Ring (USA)) 484[4] 687[15] 896[10] 1388[13] 1689[10] 2342[10] 2724[10] 3134[12] **>42f<**
Mubrik (IRE) 2 b c Lahib (USA)-Bequeath (USA) (Lyphard (USA)) 3862[4] 4237[3] **>80f<**
Much Commended 3 b f Most Welcome-Glowing With Pride (Ile de Bourbon (USA)) 815a[3] 1202a[3] **>99f<**
Muchea 3 ch c Shalford (IRE)-Bargouzine (Hotfoot) 737[3] 940[10] 4011[6] 4240[8] 4421[6] 4782[3] **>116f<**
Mudalal (USA) 2 b c Dixieland Band (USA)-Barakat (Bustino) 4710[4] 4901[3] **>83f<**
Mudeer 2 b c Warning-Colorvista (Shirley Heights) (4061) (4439) 4889[2] **>113f<**
Mudflap 3 b f Slip Anchor-River's Rising (FR) (Mendez (FR)) 1314[5] **>76a 87f<**
Mudlark 5 b g Salse (USA)-Mortal Sin (USA) (Green Forest (USA)) 1100[10] **>34a 51df<**
Muftuffenuf 2 ch f Elmaamul (USA)-Tower Glades (Tower Walk) 1386[2] 1664[3] 2147[4] 2893[7] 3468[3] 3635[3] 4065[9] **>72f<**
Mugello 2 b f Emarati (USA)-Fleur de Foret (USA) (Green Forest (USA)) 536[2] (1806) 2024[10] (2648) 2863[2] 3192[2] 3595[8] 4150[6] **>94f<**
Muhaba (USA) 2 ch f Mr Prospector (USA)-Salsabil (Sadler's Wells (USA)) 4067[5] (4437) 4961a[4] **>100f<**
Muhandam (IRE) 4 b g Common Grounds-Unbidden Melody (USA) (Chieftain II) (2313) 3024[8] *3584[16]* 4742[4] 4872[11] **>35a 72f<**
Muhandis 4 b c Persian Bold-Night At Sea (Night Shift (USA)) 3930[14] 4859[8] **>24a 80?f<**
Muhassil (IRE) 4 ch g Persian Bold-Nouvelle Star (AUS) (Luskin Star (AUS)) 518[7] 4060[10] 4386[5] 4714[8] **>72f<**
Muhawwil 3 b c Green Desert (USA)-Ardassine (Ahonoora) 586[7] **>61f< (DEAD)**
Muhib (USA) 2 b c Red Ransom (USA)-Sensorious (CAN) (Vice Regent (CAN)) 3862[3] 4715[4] **>79+f<**
Muhtadi (IRE) 4 br g Marju (IRE)-Moon Parade (Welsh Pageant) 2063[11] **>63?f<**
Muhtafel 3 b c Nashwan (USA)-The Perfect Life (IRE) (Try My Best (USA)) 1499[2] (2156) 2877[2] 3391[5] **>92f<**
Muhtathir 2 ch c Elmaamul (USA)-Majmu (USA) (Al Nasr (FR)) 1607[6] (1933) (2482) 4255a[2] 4440[8] **>105+f<**
Muja's Magic (IRE) 2 b f Mujadil (USA)-Grave Error (Northern Treat (USA)) 1812[19] 1954[4] 2138[9] 2578[5] 2786[9] 2923[6] 3228[3] 3384[9] *4054[9]* 4366[8] 4627[12] **>30a 59f<**
Muji 2 b f Safawan-Tame Duchess (Saritamer (USA)) 4042[12] 4236[6] 4966[12] **>63f<**
Mujova (IRE) 3 b c Mujadil (USA)-Kirsova (Absalom) 448[8] 560[3] 635[4] 688[9] *3397[9]* 3888[6] (4175) 4436[6] 4511[4] 4792[7] 4902[5] **>36a 93f<**
Mujtahida (IRE) 4 b f Mujtahid (USA)-Domino's Nurse (Dom Racine (FR)) **1996:** *5088[4] (5222)* **>57+a 51f<**
Mukaddar (USA) 3 ch c Elmaamul (USA)-Both Sides Now (USA) (Topsider (USA)) 679[9] 1212[7] 1462[6] 2525[3] 3051[10] 4148[9] 4637[8] **>100f<**
Mukdar (USA) 3 b br c Gulch (USA)-Give Thanks (Relko) 2008[16] 2315[10] **>61f<**
Mukhatab 5 b h Soviet Star (USA)-Azyaa (Kris) 3605[10] 3937[9] 4596[3] 4741[W] **>71f<**
Mukhlles (USA) 4 b c Diesis-Serenely (USA) (Alydar (USA)) 559[4] 680[17] 1268[11] 1631[4] 2922[11] 3470[3] 4139[12] 4404[3] 4773[8] **>74df<**
Mulahen 2 b c Robellino (USA)-Moon Watch (Night Shift (USA)) 1933[3] 2524[4] 4709[3] 4914[3] **>86f<**
Mullagh Hill Lad (IRE) 4 b g Cyrano de Bergerac-Fantasise (FR) (General Assembly (USA)) *1942[4]* 2308[3] 2703[P] **>66?a 65?f<**
Mull House 10 b g Local Suitor (USA)-Foudre (Petingo) **1996:** *5084[9] 5185[5]* **>41a 46f<**
Mullitover 7 ch g Interrex (CAN)-Atlantic Air (Air Trooper) 1214[6] 1935[9] 4121[19] 4561[9] 4787[12] **>65a 81f<**
Multan 5 b g Indian Ridge-Patchinia (Patch) *57[5]* **>47a 54f<**
Multicoloured (IRE) 4 b c Rainbow Quest (USA)-Greektown (Ela-Mana-Mou) 852[2] 4134[4] **>116f<**
Multi Franchise 4 ch g Gabitat-Gabibti (IRE) (Dara Monarch) *61[9] 105[7] 210[8]* 1506[9] 1972[8] 2552[4] 2745[4] 3227[15] 3465[3] 3767[10] 4371[7] 4448[4] 4858[5] **>43a 52f<**
Mumaris (USA) 3 b br c Capote (USA)-Barakat (Bustino) 586[5] 842[2] 1130[2] (2046) 2348[4] **>95f<**
Mumkin 3 b c Reprimand-Soon to Be (Hot Spark) 2649[8] 3130[14] 3812[14] 4586[7] 4872[12] **>61f<**
Mumtaaz 2 b c Warning-Jameelaty (USA) (Nureyev (USA)) 1607[5] 2680[8] **>76+f<**
Munaaji (USA) 6 b h Storm Cat (USA)-Growth Rate (USA) (Blushing Groom (FR)) 816a[2] 4124a[9] **>116f<**
Munasib (IRE) 2 br c Treasure Kay-Pipe Opener (Prince Sabo) 2439a[5] **>72f<**
Mungo Park 3 b g Selkirk (USA)-River Dove (USA) (Riverman (USA)) 448[9] 575[8] 886[15] 1096[13] (1514) 2017[3] 2504[3] 2759[9] 4385[8] 4583[9] (4844) 5047[3] **>68f<**
Municipal Girl (IRE) 3 b f Mac's Imp (USA)-Morning Welcome (IRE) (Be My Guest (USA)) **1996:** *5107[9] 5166[5]* **1997:** (758) 882[8] 1236[7] 1573[2] 1661[4] 2177[14] 2883[7] 3249[5] 3851[6] 4328[9] 4586[10] **>32a 44f<**
Munif (IRE) 5 ch h Caerleon (USA)-Forest Lair (Habitat) 2967a[2] **>97f<**
Murchan Tyne (IRE) 4 ch f Good Thyne (USA)-Ardnamurchan (Ardross) 2315[13] 2656[6] 2940[5] 3858[4] 4046[5] **>62f<**
Murmoon 2 b c Danehill (USA)-Reflection (Mill Reef (USA)) 2688[3] 3103[6] 3986[6] **>75f<**
Murphy's Gold (IRE) 6 ch g Salt Dome (USA)-Winter Harvest (Grundy) 1128[4] 1422[3] (1652) 2205[13] 2237[12] 3476[11] 4510[5] 4628[8] 4792[14] **>27a 57f<**
Murray Grey 3 gr f Be My Chief (USA)-Couleur de Rose (Kalaglow) 549[4] 667[2] (925) **>61f<**
Murray's Mazda (IRE) 8 ch g M Double M (USA)-Lamya (Hittite Glory) **1996:** *(5264)* **1997:** *113[14]* **>52a 52f<**
Murron Wallace 3 gr f Reprimand-Fair Eleanor (Saritamer (USA)) 551[5] 667[5] 1838[5] 2903[3] 3249[2] (3488) (4043) 4471[14] **>56f<**
Musafi (USA) 3 b c Dayjur (USA)-Ra'a (USA) (Diesis) 1237[3] **>79f<**
Musalsal (IRE) 3 b c Sadler's Wells (USA)-Ozone Friendly (USA) (Green Forest (USA)) (449) 1159[3] 1769[8] 4133[3] 4396a[8] 4776[4] **>111f<**
Musalse 2 b g Salse (USA)-Musical Sally (USA) (The Minstrel (CAN)) 5040[15] **>10f<**
Muscadel 3 f 4655a[5] **>111f<**
Muscatana 3 b f Distant Relative-Sauhatz (GER) (Alpenkonig (GER)) (785) *873[9]* 1663[4] 2214[2] 2415[9] 3930[13] 4220[5] 4601[6] 4773[6] **>27a 62f<**
Musharak 3 b c Mujtahid (USA)-Mahasin (USA) (Danzig (USA)) 503[2] 1087[8] (4316) 4689[5] **>92f<**
Mushraaf 2 b br c Zafonic (USA)-Vice Vixen (CAN) (Vice Regent (CAN)) 2295[4] (3204) 4096[5] **>93f<**
Musical Dancer (USA) 3 ch c Dixieland Band (USA)-Parrish Empress (USA) (His Majesty (USA)) 931[3] 1553a[D] 2107[3] 2515[2] **>110f< (DEAD)**
Musical Myth (USA) 2 b f Crafty Prospector (USA)-Think Music (USA) (Stop The Music (USA)) 2987a[7] 3506a[5] **>63f<**
Musical Pet (IRE) 2 ch f Petardia-Musical Gem (USA) (The Minstrel (CAN)) 1569[13] 2493[10] 3212[9] **>23f<**
Musical Pursuit 3 b c Pursuit of Love-Gay Music (FR) (Gay Mecene (USA)) 940[16] 1541a[10] 3728[7] 4292[3] **>109f<**
Musical Twist (USA) 2 ch f Woodman (USA)-Musicale (USA) (The Minstrel (CAN)) 3574[2] **>85+f<**
Music Express (IRE) 3 b f Classic Music (USA)-Hetty Green (Bay Express) **1996:** *5111[8]* **1997:** 667[3] 925[12] 1333[5] **>41a 50f<**
Music Gold (IRE) 4 b br g Taufan (USA)-Nonnita (Welsh Saint) 2529[3] 2872[5] 3649[20] 4062[8] **>96f<**
Musick House (IRE) 4 b c Sadler's Wells (USA)-Hot Princess (Hot Spark) 981[3] 1160[6] 2136[10] 3725[11] 4121[20] 4680[7] 4787[25] **>78f<**
Musk Lime (USA) 2 ch f Private Account (USA)-Foreign Aid (USA) 5002a[2] **>100f<**
Mustang 4 ch g Thatching-Lassoo (Caerleon (USA)) *16[5] 86[4] 115[4] 202[4] 284[8] 312[7] (367) 386[6] 429[4] 1944[2]* 2177[6] *2368[4]* **>39a 45f<**
Mustang Scally 3 b f Makbul-Another Scally (Scallywag) **1996:** *5135[14]* **>23f<**
Mustard 4 ch f Keen-Tommys Dream (Le Bavard (FR)) 1631[14] 1798[12] 2128[7] **>24f<**
Mustique Dream 2 b f Don't Forget Me-Jamaican Punch (IRE) (Shareef Dancer (USA)) 2781[2] *3072[2]* 3450[2] **>79a 79f<**
Mustn't Grumble (IRE) 7 b g Orchestra-Gentle Heiress (Prince Tenderfoot (USA)) **1996:** *5129[6]*

5206^{5} 5270^{11} **>57a 70f<**

Mutabari (USA) 3 ch c Seeking the Gold (USA)-Cagey Exuberance (USA) (Exuberant (USA)) 700^{3} 837^{8} 4378^{9} 4631^{4} 4757^{15} 4848^{5} 4958^{4} **>54a 75f<**

Mutabassir (IRE) 3 ch c Soviet Star (USA)-Anghaam (USA) (Diesis) 3820^{5} **>42f<**

Mutadarra (IRE) 4 ch g Mujtahid (USA)-Silver Echo (Caerleon (USA)) *131^{8}* 1139^{10} 1588^{5} 2118^{8} 2839^{2} (3026) 3689^{4} 4108^{9} 4477^{7} 4882^{11} **>39a 77f<**

Mu-Tadil 5 ch g Be My Chief (USA)-Inveraven (Alias Smith (USA)) 4519^{8} **>36f<**

Mutafarij (USA) 2 ch c Diesis-Madame Secretary (USA) (Secretariat (USA)) 4111^{5} 4739^{7} **>76f<**

Mutahadeth 3 ch g Rudimentary (USA)-Music in My Life (IRE) (Law Society (USA)) *84^{5} (235) 277^{2} 388^{5} 513^{2}* 575^{11} 1800^{12} *2071^{3}* 2522^{5} 3038^{3} 3321^{10} 3421^{3} 3696^{10} *4050^{9}* **>70a 55f<**

Mutamam 2 b c Darshaan-Petal Girl (Caerleon (USA)) (3861) (4364) 4889^{3} **>111+f<**

Mutasawwar 3 ch g Clantime-Keen Melody (USA) (Sharpen Up) 964^{4} 1275^{2} 1792^{4} 3898^{10} 4791^{9} *5020^{6}* **>45a 67f<**

Mutawwaj (IRE) 2 b c Caerleon (USA)-Himmah (USA) (Habitat) 3047^{3} 3644^{2} 4132^{3} (4367) **>102f<**

Muyassir (IRE) 2 b c Brief Truce (USA)-Twine (Thatching) 2829^{10} 4298^{18} 4544^{4} 4755^{16} **>63f<**

My Abbey 8 b m Hadeer-Rose Barton (Pas de Seul) 2480^{4} 3761^{W} 3856^{15} **>54f<**

My Achates 4 b f Prince Sabo-Persian Air (Persian Bold) 896^{24}

Myasha (USA) 8 b g Imp Society (USA)-Mauna Loa (USA) (Hawaii) 604^{6} **>54a 47f<**

My Beloved (IRE) 3 b f Polish Patriot (USA)-Arbour (USA) (Graustark) 654^{11} 895^{17} 1167^{2} 1633^{18} 1929^{3} 2294^{4} 2836^{2} 3557^{2} 4139^{11} **>65df<**

My Best Valentine 7 b h Try My Best (USA)-Pas de Calais (Pas de Seul) 540^{4} 786^{4} 1035^{17} 1324^{5} 1596^{2} 1772^{5} (2529) 3217^{2} 3604^{17} 4100^{3} 4421^{12} (4777) (4881) 5054^{2} **>50a 119f<**

My Bet 2 b f Noble Patriarch-Estefan (Taufan (USA)) 500^{7} 631^{4} 743^{3} *(872)* 1091^{5} *1137^{4}* 1330^{6} 1626^{6} 3067^{6} 3438^{8} 3751^{5} 4208^{5} **>55a 60f<**

My Betsy 3 gr f Absalom-Formidable Task (Formidable (USA)) *1044^{13}* **>55f<**

Mybotye 4 br g Rambo Dancer (CAN)-Sigh (Highland Melody) 435^{19} 571^{9} 763^{14} 2036^{12} 2395^{13} 3285^{D} 3561^{2} 3987^{3} (4112) 4738^{6} 4951^{3} 5049^{5} **>70f<**

My Branch 4 b f Distant Relative-Pay the Bank (High Top) 713a^{4} 1776^{3} 2334^{4} 2830^{3} 3147^{5} **>109f<**

My Brother 3 b g Lugana Beach-Lucky Love (Mummy's Pet) 4316^{13} **>41f<**

My Cadeaux 5 ch m Cadeaux Genereux-Jubilee Song (Song) **1996:** 5155a^{10} **1997:** 816a^{6} **>94f<**

My Cherrywell 7 br m Kirchner-Cherrywood Blessin (Good Times (ITY)) **1996:** *5109^{8}* **>56a 56f<**

My Emma 4 b f Marju (IRE)-Pato (High Top) 3006a^{3} (3704) 4665a^{11} **>123f<**

My Firebird 3 b f Rudimentary (USA)-Miss Rossi (Artaius (USA)) 983^{11} 1497^{12} **>32f<**

My Floosie 2 b f Unfuwain (USA)-My Chiara (Ardross) 4873^{18}

Myfontaine 10 b h Persepolis (FR)-Mortefontaine (FR) (Polic) **1996:** *5123^{4} 5222^{11}* **1997:** *195^{3} 274^{8} 369^{7}* 1142^{8} **>54a 74f<**

My Girl 3 b f Mon Tresor-Lady of Itatiba (BEL) (King Of Macedon) *102^{3} 259^{9} 399^{8}* **>43a 42f<**

My Girl Lucy 3 b f Picea-English Mint (Jalmood (USA)) 1087^{11} 1823^{7} 2427^{4} 2705^{9} 3119^{10} *3396^{9} 3609^{7}* **>17a 59f<**

My Godson 7 br g Valiyar-Blessit (So Blessed) 2906^{9} 3285^{15} 3456^{16} *4051^{13} 4570^{12}* 4711^{15} 4843^{12} **>39a 30f<**

My Handsome Prince 5 b g Handsome Sailor-My Serenade (USA) (Sensitive Prince (USA)) **1996:** *5140^{4}* **1997:** 1077^{6} 1266^{4} 1441^{13} *1576^{10}* 2488^{3} 2651^{W} 2887^{2} 3269^{8} 3469^{8} **>49a 55f<**

My Hero (IRE) 3 b f Bluebird (USA)-Risacca (ITY) (Sir Gaylord) 4104^{14} **>73?f<**

My Jess 3 b f Jester-Miss Levantine (Levanter) 1110^{9} 1563^{6} 2506^{10} **>46f<**

My Learned Friend 6 b or br g Broken Hearted-Circe (Main Reef) 962^{6} 1325^{8} 2122^{2} 2514^{2} 2865^{4} 3498^{6} 3722^{9} 4136^{10} 4409^{7} **>83f<**

My Legal Eagle (IRE) 3 b g Law Society (USA)-Majestic Nurse (On Your Mark) *26^{4}* **>62a 63f<**

My Lewicia (IRE) 4 b f Taufan (USA)-Christine Daae (Sadler's Wells (USA)) 1490^{5} 1793^{4} 2242^{4} 2766^{11} 3263^{2} 3722^{10} 4151^{13} **>100f<**

My Lost Love 2 b c Green Desert (USA)-Love of Silver (USA) (Arctic Tern (USA)) 1839^{6} 4381^{7} 4747^{4} **>58f<**

My Melody Parkes 4 b f Teenoso (USA)-Summerhill Spruce (Windjammer (USA)) 671^{7} 2211^{7} 3252^{2} 3447^{2} 3747^{4} (3863) 4282^{16} 4457^{4} **>108f<**

My Millie 4 ch f Midyan (USA)-Madam Millie (Milford) 733^{12} 796^{7} 898^{2} 2128^{2} 2544^{5} (2753) 3085^{4} 3826^{8} 4432^{6} 4584^{17} **>47f<**

Myosotis 3 ch g Don't Forget Me-Ella Mon Amour (Ela-Mana-Mou) **1996:** *5121^{12}* **1997:** 1164^{16} 1633^{12} 1677^{6} 2246^{13} 3896^{7} **>34a 56f<**

My Pledge (IRE) 2 b c Waajib-Pollys Glow (IRE) (Glow (USA)) 4515^{9} **>58f<**

Myrmidon 3 b g Midyan (USA)-Moorish Idol (Aragon) 501^{2} 854^{8} 1254^{5} 1403^{6} 2134^{9} 2377^{10} **>88f<**

My Roland (IRE) 3 ch c Topanoora-Value Voucher (IRE) (Kings Lake (USA)) 2287^{6} 2731^{10} 4322^{10} 4821^{9} **>54f<**

My Rossini 8 b g Ardross-My Tootsie (Tap On Wood) 2035^{9} **>53a 56?f<**

Myrtlebank 3 ch f Salse (USA)-Magical Veil (Majestic Light (USA)) 2594^{3} 3689^{5} 4002^{11} **>87f<**

Myrtle Quest 5 b g Rainbow Quest (USA)-Wryneck (Niniski (USA)) 499^{6} 735^{11} (4319) 4680^{8} 4978^{26} **>86f<**

My Saltarello (IRE) 3 b g Salt Dome (USA)-Daidis (Welsh Pageant) 609^{8} 1129^{13} 1604^{4} 2032^{5} 3088^{12} **>47f<**

Mystagogue 2 ch c Mystiko (USA)-Malibasta (Auction Ring (USA)) 2509^{8} 2893^{5} 3711^{11} 3859^{6} 4806^{9} 4875^{6} 4974^{6} **>45a 65f<**

Mysterious Ecology 2 gr f Mystiko (USA)-Ecologically Kind (Alleged (USA)) 2840^{8} 4318^{4} **>64f<**

Mysterium 3 gr c Mystiko (USA)-Way to Go (Troy) *(296) 368^{5}* 864^{14} 1958^{7} *2364^{2} 2670^{3}* **>61a 43f<**

Mystery 3 b f Mystiko (USA)-Dismiss (Daring March) **1996:** *5083^{9} 5121^{10} 5251^{4}* **1997:** *(77)* **>57+a 59f<**

Mystery Guest (IRE) 2 b c Alzao (USA)-Lora's Guest (Be My Guest (USA)) 2320^{11} 2388^{5} 2740^{2} 3226^{8} **>57f<**

Mystery Hill (USA) 3 b f Danehill (USA)-Tendermark (Prince Tenderfoot (USA)) 727^{11} 1030^{9} 1823^{5} 2183^{6} 2695^{6} 3800^{6} **>73df<**

Mystery Man 2 gr g Mystiko (USA)-Baileys by Name (Nomination) 1797^{11} 2904^{14} **>27f<**

Mystery Matthias 4 b f Nicholas (USA)-Devils Dirge (Song) **1996:** *5093^{4} 5188^{2}* **1997:** *24^{4} 57^{3} 97^{2} 128^{6} 339^{2}* **>52a 56f<**

Mystical 3 b f Mystiko (USA)-Midnight Imperial (Night Shift (USA)) 882^{2} 1119^{10} 1566^{5} 1667^{3} 1828^{10} 2167^{4} (2354) 3327^{2} 3637^{8} (3851) 4115^{9} 4328^{2} 4820^{9} *5018^{7}* **>51a 70f<**

Mystical Island 3 b f Deploy-Do Run Run (Commanche Run) 605^{8} *2067^{7}* **>10a 49f<**

Mystical Rodge 2 b g Mystiko (USA)-Deux Etoiles (Bay Express) 3753^{11} 4921^{12} **>40f<**

Mystical Song 2 ch f Mystiko (USA)-Jubilee Song (Song) 4818^{8} **>62+f<**

Mystic Flight (USA) 2 b f Silver Hawk (USA)-Wand (IRE) (Reference Point) 5041^{10} **>57f<**

Mysticism 2 ch f Mystiko (USA)-Abuzz (Absalom) 971^{4} 1213^{5} 2356^{2} 2712^{2} 2862^{5} 3192^{8} 3711^{4} 4042^{6} 4790^{22} **>81f<**

Mystic Legend (IRE) 5 gr g Standaan (FR)-Mandy Girl (Manado) **1996:** *5095^{10} 5145^{11}* **>34a 43f<**

Mystic Maid (IRE) 4 b f Mujtahid (USA)-Dandizette (Danzig (USA)) 1266^{11} 1467^{20} **>66?f<**

Mystic Quest (IRE) 3 b g Arcane (USA)-Tales of Wisdom (Rousillon (USA)) 537^{3} 976^{2} 1465^{2} 2035^{10} 4562^{8} *(4912) 5022^{10}* **>83a 73f<**

Mystic Ridge 3 ch g Mystiko (USA)-Vallauris (Faustus (USA)) 742^{3} 1239^{9} 1637^{2} 2005^{3} 4996^{15} **>83f<**

Mystic Strand 4 b f Lugana Beach-Tantra (Song) 754^{2} 1276^{10} 1986^{6} 2399^{9} *(2673) 3074^{3} 4981^{10}* **>49a 64?f<**

Mystic Times 4 b f Timeless Times (USA)-Chikala (Pitskelly) 925^{10} 1229^{16} 2170^{8} 2502^{10} 2543^{4} 2716^{4} 3264^{13} 3487^{4} 3627^{15} **>35f<**

Mystique Air (IRE) 3 b f Mujadil (USA)-Romany Pageant (Welsh Pageant) 1030^{5} 1582^{3} 2113^{5} 2234^{2} (2756) 3855^{5} 3987^{9} 4436^{10} 4601^{11} 4773^{10} **>65f<**

Mystique Smile 4 ch f Music Boy-Jay Gee Ell (Vaigly Great) 2540^{13} 3431^{7} 3756^{9} 3922^{17} 4169^{10} **>35f<**

Mythical 3 gr f Mystiko (USA)-Geryea (USA) (Desert Wine (USA)) (936) *1121^{2}* 1385^{14} *2671^{2} (2912) 3044^{6} (4050)* **>73a 47+f<**

Mythical Creek (USA) 3 b f Pleasant Tap (USA)-Martha Queen (USA) (Nijinsky (CAN)) **1996:** (5197a)

Myttons Mistake 4 b g Rambo Dancer (CAN)-Hi-Hunsley (Swing Easy (USA)) **1996:** *5163^{9} 5266^{3}* **1997:** *81^{6} 165^{2} 208^{2} 303^{4} 371^{3}* 1511^{9} 1658^{7} 2144^{4} (2651) 2900^{4} 3254^{4} 3285^{4} 3565^{2} (3759) 3901^{8} 3987^{11} (4219) 4270^{8} 4561^{10} (4899) 4988^{6} **>69a 84?f<**

My Tyson (IRE) 2 b c Don't Forget Me-Shuckran Habibi (Thatching) 4379^{9} 4526^{13} 4779^{15} 4901^{10} 4966^{8} **>66a 66f<**

My Valentina 3 b f Royal Academy (USA)-Imperial Jade (Lochnager) 1264^{5} 2478^{8} 2866^{8} 3891^{2} 4242^{6} 4435^{7} 4552^{8} **>78f<**

My Way (FR) 2 b c Shining Steel-Tourova (FR) (Tourangeau (FR)) 3995a^{3} **>76f<**

N

Naayel (IRE) 2 b c Brief Truce (USA)-Diamond Lake (Kings Lake (USA)) 1744^{10} 2926^{5} 3489^{10} 4545^{12} **>59f<**

Nabhaan (IRE) 4 b c In The Wings-Miss Gris (USA) (Hail the Pirates (USA)) (761) 962^{2} 1241^{6} 1597^{2} 2028^{2} 2514^{4} 2837^{4} 4005^{4} 4412^{3} **>111f<**

Nabjelsedr 7 b g Never so Bold-Klewraye (Lord Gayle (USA)) 1689^{3} 1926^{9} 2646^{R} **>46df<**

Naburn Loch 7 b m Lochnager-Balgownie (Prince Tenderfoot (USA)) 1567^{8} 1951^{6} 2200^{8} **>13a 41f<**

Nadwah (USA) 2 b f Shadeed (USA)-Tadwin (Never so Bold) (1211) 1475^{3} (2024) 3723^{3} 4475^{6} **>98f<**

Nagnagnag (IRE) 5 b m Red Sunset-Rubina Park (Ashmore (FR)) 4625a^{9} **>97f<**

Nagobelia 9 b or br g Enchantment-Lost Valley (Perdu) *3073^{8}* 3617^{5} **>8a 25f<**

Na Huibheachu (IRE) 6 ch g Nostrum (USA)-Royal Slip (Royal Match) 3081^{4} 3560^{6} **>37tf<**

Nails Tails 4 b g Efisio-Northern Dynasty (Breeders Dream) *9^{6} 108^{4} 216^{6} 294^{5}* 607^{3} 770^{5} 2146^{5} 2318^{4} 2344^{5} **>46a 47?f<**

Naissant 4 b f Shaadi (USA)-Nophe (USA) (Super Concorde (USA)) **1996:** *5105^{10}* **1997:** *386^{10}* 610^{12} 824^{12} 953^{2} 1079^{9} 1227^{8} 3910^{15} 4169^{5} 4291^{12} 4707^{14} **>46a 57f<**

Naivasha 3 gr f Petong-Nevis (Connaught) *871^{11} 904^{4} 1044^{2} 1580^{8} 1756^{13}* (2029) 2543^{3} 2715^{6} 2903^{5} **>55a 61f<**

Najjar (USA) 2 gr c El Prado (IRE)-With Strawberries (USA) (Maudlin (USA)) 3047^{6} 3760^{3} 4165^{10} **>74f<**

Najm Mubeen (IRE) 4 b c Last Tycoon-Ah Ya Zein (Artaius (USA)) 939^{3} 1450^{7} 2026^{10} 2710^{2} 3112^{9} 3703^{9} **>102f<**

Nakama (IRE) 7 b m General Holme (USA)-Whampoa (FR) (Wittgenstein (USA)) 3181a^{3} **>86f<**

Nakami 5 b g Dashing Blade-Dara's Bird (Dara Monarch) 541^{13} **>63f<**

Nakayama Express (IRE) 4 b g Warning-Bluebook (USA) (Secretariat (USA)) (2815a) 3508a^{7} **>87f<**

Naked Oat 2 b g Imp Society (USA)-Bajina (Dancing Brave (USA)) 1978^{6} 2349^{5} 2699^{11} 4044^{6} 4334^{10} 4605^{5} 4806^{17} **>71f<**

Nakhal 4 b g Puissance-Rambadale (Vaigly Great) *9^{2} 61^{8} 108^{2} 141^{2} 188^{5} 228^{2} 266^{4}* **>65a 59f<**

Nambucca 3 b f Shirley Heights-Cephira (FR) (Abdos) 445^{2} **>72f<**

Name of Love (IRE) 2 b f Petardia-National Ballet (Shareef Dancer (USA)) 3070^{2} (4007) (4555) (4786) **>104f<**

Name of Our Father (USA) 4 b g Northern Baby (CAN)-Ten Hail Marys (USA) (Halo (USA)) *83^{9}* 3896^{9} **>45a 75f<**

Nampara Bay 3 b f Emarati (USA)-Dewberry (Bay Express) 474^{9} 751^{3} 924^{8} *1151^{2}* 1375^{9} *1942^{9}* 3693^{14} 4168^{14} **>53a 26f<**

Nancys Gem 3 b f Most Welcome-Nancy Chere (USA) (Gallant Man) 4400^{6} **>16f<**

Nancy's Glitter (USA) 2 f *5060a^{12}*

Naninja (USA) 4 Alysheba (USA)-Nijinsky's Lover (USA) (Nijinsky (CAN)) 5063a^{12} **>112f<**

Nanouche 3 b f Dayjur (USA)-Habibti (Habitat) 727^{15} **>32f<**

Nanoushka (IRE) 2 b f Taufan (USA)-West Chazy (USA) (Gone West (USA)) (3187) 3981^{3} 4555^{4} **>91f<**

Nantgarw 4 b f Teamster-Dikay (IRE) (Anita's Prince) *111^{10} 208^{7}* **>12f<**

Nanton Point (USA) 5 b g Darshaan-Migiyas (Kings Lake (USA)) 728^{10} 1778^{2} 1871^{5} 2014^{8} 2530^{4} 2834^{4} 4156^{4} 4879^{5} **>79f<**

Nant Y Gamer (FR) 3 b c Warning-Norfolk Lily (Blakeney) 555^{5} 1029^{5} 1175^{8} 1583^{2} *2303^{6}* 2691^{8} (3268) 3749^{6} (4586) (4872) **>78a 80f<**

Naphtali 4 b f Nicholas Bill-My Concordia (Belfort (FR)) **1996:** *5182^{9}* **1997:** *9^{11}*

Napier Star 4 b f Inca Chief (USA)-America Star (Norwick (USA)) **1996:** *5097^{2} (5173) 5184^{3} 5225^{2}* **1997:** *4^{9} 95^{2} 137^{3} 301^{13} 663^{9} 1046^{2} (1428) 1942^{6} 2050^{3} 2162^{3}* 2732^{8} *2913^{2} 3077^{6}* 3323^{7} *3860^{13}* 4168^{16} *4301^{3} 5018^{6}* **>72a 47df<**

Napoleonic 3 b c Suave Dancer (USA)-Noble Lily (USA) (Vaguely Noble) **1996:** 5190a^{3} **>65f<**

Napoleon's Return 4 gr g Daring March-Miss Colenca (Petong) **1996:** *5110^{4} 5130^{5}* **1997:** *15^{8}* 526^{10} 668^{10} 1127^{11} 2854^{8} (2937) 3227^{12} **>60a 44f<**

Napoleon Star (IRE) 6 ch g Mulhollande (USA)-Lady Portobello (Porto Bello) *113^{13} 152^{9} 203^{10} 235^{4} 318^{7} (326) 423^{5}* (541) 759^{5} 1020^{6} 1250^{8} 1620^{3} (1734) 2002^{5} 2372^{7} 2497^{4} 2738^{14} 2788^{8} 3143^{8} 3431^{11} **>49a 48f<**

Napoli Express (FR) 3 629a^{6} **>95f<**

Narbonne 6 b m Rousillon (USA)-Historical Fact (Reform) 4858^{19} **>14a 27f<**

Narrabeth (IRE) 4 bl c Shaadi (USA)-Nocturna (IRE) (Diu Star) 1073a^{8} 1724a^{4} 3376a^{4} 4127a^{4} 4537a^{5} **>121f<**

Narrogin (USA) 2 ch c Strike The Gold (USA)-Best Regalia (Sharpen Up) 965^{4} 1263^{6} 1735^{7} 2681^{5} 3307^{6} 3750^{3} 4116^{21} 4334^{3} 4576^{2} 4806^{4} 4953^{5} **>73f<**

Nashaat (USA) 9 b g El Gran Senor (USA)-Absentia (USA) (Raise A Cup (USA)) *82^{8} 143^{2} 171^{6} 192^{4} 254^{W}* **>69a 83f<**

Nashalong (IRE) 4 ch g Nashamaa-Rousalong (Rousillon (USA)) *164^{11}* **>54f<**

Nashcash (IRE) 4 ch c Nashamaa-Six Penny Express (Bay Express) (3375a) **>112f<**

Naskhi 2 b f Nashwan (USA)-Calpella (Ajdal (USA)) 3433^{4} 3753^{3} 4061^{5} (4382) 4690^{8} **>79+f<**

Natalia Bay (IRE) 3 b f Dancing Dissident (USA)-Bayazida (Bustino) 1412^{6} 1621^{2} 2219^{2} 3017^{6} **>102f<**

Natalie's Pet 2 b f Merdon Melody-Tripolitaine (FR) (Nonoalco (USA)) 2959^{7} 3638^{14} **>44f<**

Natalis (IRE) 2 b c Selkirk (USA)-Dawnsio (IRE) (Tate Gallery (USA)) 3962a^{3} 4357a^{7} 5002a^{4} **>103f<**

Natal Ridge 4 b g Indian Ridge-Song Grove (Song) *243^{13} 288^{4} 367^{8} 411^{9}* **>49a 57f<**

Natayig 2 b f Fairy King (USA)-Cunning (Bustino) 4973^{16} **>38f<**

National Academy (GER) 2 b c Royal Academy (USA)-Narola (GER) (Nebos (GER)) 3368a^{2} 3997a^{2} **>89f<**

Nationalore (USA) 2 c *5064a^{3}*

National Wish (USA) 2 ch c Forty Niner (USA)-Regent's Walk (CAN) (Vice Regent (CAN)) 4309^{5} **>57f<**

Native Princess (IRE) 3 ch f Shalford (IRE)-Jealous One (USA) (Raise A Native) 431^{13} 534^{7} 1301^{5} 1642^{4} 2040^{7} 2171^{15} **>59f<**

Native Rhythm (IRE) 3 ch f Lycius (USA)-Perfect Time (IRE) (Dance of Life (USA)) 2143^{3} 2506^{6} *3058^{4}* 4112^{9} **>20a 65f<**

Native Thatch (IRE) 3 b br f Thatching-Native Guile (Lomond (USA)) *50^{6} 145^{6} 265^{5}* 475^{9} 549^{2} 685^{6} **>38a 49f<**

Nattie 3 b g Almoojid-Defy Me (Bustino) *96^{7} 124^{15}* 4371^{19} **>49?f<**

Natural Eight (IRE) 3 b c In The Wings-Fenny Rough (Home Guard (USA)) 676^{5} 875^{2} 1277^{3} 4882^{18} **>83f<**

Natural Key 4 ch f Safawan-No Sharps Or Flats (USA) (Sharpen Up) 567^{5} 1410^{4} 1835^{2} 2033^{2} 2711^{21} 2900^{9} 3224^{3} (3484) 3922^{12} 4467^{6} 4733^{17} **>79f<**

Nature Dancer 3 ch f Environment Friend-Preobrajenska (Double Form) 3275^{2} 3809^{6} **>63tf<**

Naughty Blue (USA) 2 b c Danehill (USA)-Blue Note (FR) (Habitat) 3726^{7} (4229) 4880^{4} **>99f<**

Naughty Pistol (USA) 5 ch m Big Pistol (USA)-Naughty Nile (USA) (Upper Nile (USA)) **1996:** *(5138)* **1997:** *166^{3} 201^{2} 254^{5} 357^{10}* 468^{7} 734^{3} 827^{16} 1285^{9} *1754^{6}* 2021^{3} 2502^{4} *2671^{5}* 3039^{8} 3315^{9} 3573^{8} **>57a 57f<**

Nautical Jewel 5 b g Handsome Sailor-Kopjes (Bay Express) **1996:** *5179^{9} 5240^{10}* **1997:** *16^{15}* **>28a 48f<**

Nautical Star 2 b c Slip Anchor-Comic Talent (Pharly (FR)) 2524^{5} (3402) 4778^{17} **>80+f<**

Nautical Warning 2 b c Warning-Night At Sea (Night Shift (USA)) 3770^{6} 4231^{9} 4779^{16} 4989^{9} **>68f<**

Nautiker (GER) 6 h 2640a^{3} 4124a^{11} 5037a^{3} **>112f<**

Navajo 11 ch h Adonijah-Speed Baby (USA) (Diplomat Way) 2096a^{3} **>47f<**

Naval Games 4 b g Slip Anchor-Plaything (High Top) 3277^{5} 4521^{4} 4713^{2} **>65f<**

Naviasky (IRE) 2 b br g Scenic-Black Molly (IRE) (High Top) 2361^{6} 2706^{6} (3459) 3802^{6} 4116^{8} 4265^{15} 4885^{5} 5050^{12} **>79f<**

Nawaji (USA) 4 b f Trempolino (USA)-Nobile Decretum (USA) (Noble Decree (USA)) **1996:** *5223^{9}* **1997:** *9^{5} 73^{2} 147^{4} 232^{5} 283^{3}* 1010^{5} *1156^{5}* 1445^{6} 2154^{P} **>52a 46f<**

Nawasib (IRE) 3 b f Warning-Tanouma (USA) (Miswaki (USA)) 958^{9} (2287) **>105f<**

Nazmi (IRE) 5 b g Doyoun-Nawazish (Run The Gantlet (USA)) 2108^{13} **>64f<**

Nebl 2 ch f Persian Bold-Maraatib (IRE) (Green Desert (USA)) 3985^{3} (4217) 4778^{28} **>67f<**

Nebuchadnezzar 2 gr g Absalom-Golden Decoy (Decoy Boy) 2473^{8} 4278^{11} 4470^{7} **>48f<**

Nec Plus Ultra (FR) 6 b h Kendor (FR)-Quintefolle (FR) (Luthier) 1067a^{7} **>124f<**

Ned's Bonanza 8 b g Green Ruby (USA)-Miss Display (Touch Paper) 702^{13} 863^{11} 1098^{10} 1514^{3} 1848^{7} 1957^{3} 2563^{7} 2738^{5} 2844^{11} 3625^{16} 4385^{13} 4629^{15} 4844^{17} **>47f<**

Needle Gun (IRE) 7 b or br h Sure Blade (USA)-Lucayan Princess (High Line) **1996:** 5219a^{7} **1997:** *627a^{2}* 852^{6} 1200a^{2} 1724a^{3} 2100a^{6} 3376a^{6} **>122a 119f<**

Needle Knot (IRE) 4 b g Don't Forget Me-Needlewoman (Moorestyle) *1940^{P}* 3261^{8} **>56df<**

Needle Match 4 ch c Royal Academy (USA)-Miss Tatting (USA) (Miswaki (USA)) *(318) 391^{3} (423)* 610^{6} 827^{8} 956^{8} 1079^{8} 2203^{2} 2384^{8} 2828^{3} 3285^{3} 3573^{2} 3759^{3} (3855) 3976^{22} 4510^{6} 4628^{5} 4924^{12} 5030^{6} **>67a 64f<**

Needwood Epic 4 b f Midyan (USA)-Epure (Bellypha) 2035^{2} 2882^{8} 3317^{4} *3587^{2}* 3758^{3} *4055^{3} 4590^{5} (4811)* **>64a 51f<**

Needwood Legend 4 b br c Rolfe (USA)-Enchanting Kate (Enchantment) 686^{7} 842^{12} 4918^{9} 4988^{5} **>50f<**

Needwood Nutkin 4 b f Rolfe (USA)-Needwood Nut (Royben) *164^{8} 230^{10} 313^{8}* 796^{4} 1229^{5} 1686^{3} *2049^{3}* 2503^{7} **>30a 50df<**

Needwood Poppy 9 b m Rolfe (USA)-Needwood Nap (Some Hand) 1232^{6} *1755^{4}* **>53a 31f<**

Needwood Spirit 2 b c Rolfe (USA)-Needwood Nymph (Bold Owl) 4740^{5} 4915^{4} **>76f<**

Needwood Spitfire 2 b f Rolfe (USA)-Lime Brook (Rapid River) 4904^{20} 5040^{19} **>36f<**

Nefertiti 3 b f Superpower-Vico Equense (Absalom) *427^{9} 1046^{11}* 1572^{10} **>13a 1f<**

Negative 3 gr f Deploy-Rashah (Blakeney) 2532^{10} 4045^{11} **>17f<**

Nellie North 4 b f Northern State (USA)-Kimble Princess (Kala Shikari) 601^{10} 887^{13} 1089^{2} 2177^{12} 2384^{6} 2732^{3} 2852^{2} 3092^{13} 3393^{4} 3590^{7} 4168^{17} **>49f<**

Nenna (IRE) 5 4535a^{3} **>96f<**

Neon Deion (IRE) 3 b g Alzao (USA)-Sharnazad (IRE) (Track Barron (USA)) **1996:** *5212^{9}* **1997:** *124^{3} 168^{5} 277^{5} 347^{3}* **>47a 48f<**

Neronian (IRE) 3 ch c Mujtahid (USA)-Nimieza (USA) (Nijinsky (CAN)) 517^{6} 795^{7} 1004^{4} 1651^{2} (1833) 2113^{3} **>78f<**

Nero Zilzal (USA) 4 b c Zilzal (USA)-Golden Bowl (USA) (Vaguely Noble) (439a) 625a^{2} 1067a^{6}

1554a^{5} 3731a^{3} **>117f<**
Nervous Rex 3 b g Reprimand-Spinner (Blue Cashmere) 475^{4} 642^{5} 751^{4} *1289^{14}* 1638^{4} 1864^{2} (2203) 2554^{4} 2921^{8} 3251^{4} 4016^{7} 4328^{3} 4877^{12} **>32a 61f<**
Nesala 2 gr f Neshad (USA)-Waadi Hatta (USA) (Upper Nile (USA)) 3783^{10} **>42f<**
Nesbet 3 b c Nicholas (USA)-Brera (IRE) (Tate Gallery (USA)) *2300^{5} 2669^{6} 3043^{4}* **>36a f<**
Neuilly (USA) 3 ch c Trempolino (USA)-Haleallah (FR) (Hawaii) (2820a) 3733a^{3} 4129a^{6} **>120f<**
Neuwest (USA) 5 b h Gone West (USA)-White Mischief (Dance In Time (CAN)) 450^{19} 752^{2} 892^{19} (1874) 2598^{18} (3423) 4240^{6} 4423^{24} **>84a 111f<**
Never Cease 2 ch c Nomadic Way (USA)-Cease To Be (Sharpo) 4017^{16}
Neverold (IRE) 7 br g Never so Bold-Fraulein Tobin (USA) (J O Tobin (USA)) 3491^{13} 3792^{11} **>32f<**
Never Think Twice 4 b g Never so Bold-Hope and Glory (USA) (Well Decorated (USA)) **1996:** *5124^{8} 5150^{7} 5183^{2} 5249^{2}* **1997:** *21^{2}* 2006^{5} 2179^{2} 2372^{2} 2424^{4} 2833^{16} 3227^{7} *3582^{10}* 3642^{5} 4016^{4} 4221^{9} 4328^{4} **>71a 57f<**
Neville The Devil 3 gr g Thethingaboutitis (USA)-Sovereign Love (He Loves Me) *658^{7}*
Newala 2 b f Royal Academy (USA)-African Dance (USA) (El Gran Senor (USA)) 4542^{6} 4630^{10} **>56a 52f<**
Newbridge Boy 4 b g Bustino-Martyrdom (USA) (Exceller (USA)) 461^{18} 2342^{8} *4571^{8}* 4751^{7} 4998^{4} **>38a 56f<**
Newbury Coat 7 b g Chilibang-Deanta in Eirinn (Red Sunset) 2997a^{3} **>51a 60f<**
New Century (USA) 5 gr g Manila (USA)-Casessa (USA) (Caro) *(344) 398^{2}* 450^{12} *661^{2}* 677^{10} 1160^{7} **>104a 100?f<**
New Frontier (IRE) 3 b c Sadler's Wells (USA)-Diamond Field (USA) (Mr Prospector (USA)) 819a^{4} 1070a^{7} (2996a) 3179a^{3} 4257a^{4} 4658a^{7} **>112f<**
Newgate Noblesse 2 b f Noble Patriarch-Mummys Colleen (Mummy's Pet) 948^{9} 1815^{9} 2935^{12} **>8f<**
Newhargen (IRE) 2 b g Astronef-Brandywell (Skyliner) 861^{8} 948^{5} 1026^{5} 1253^{4} 1600^{2} 2016^{5} 2425^{5} 3055^{4} 3257^{8} **>61f<**
Newington Butts (IRE) 7 br m Dowsing (USA)-Cloud Nine (Skymaster) *152^{16} 303^{2} 2069^{10}* 3561^{13} **>42a 25f<**
New Inn 6 b g Petoski-Pitroyal (Pitskelly) 4363^{6} 4562^{9} 4667^{2} 4804^{8} **>50a 57f<**
Newlands Corner 4 b f Forzando-Nice Lady (Connaught) 520^{13} 1166^{6} 1439^{2} 1680^{5} 1963^{4} 2216^{4} 3207^{4} *(3582)* 4168^{5} 4905^{16} **>64a 60f<**
Newport Knight 6 ch g Bairn (USA)-Clara Barton (Youth (USA)) 789^{12} *1156^{13}* 1427^{10} 1811^{7} 2373^{10} 2928^{4} 3279^{3} 3864^{4} 4548^{4} 4860^{8} **>33a 65f<**
New Regime (IRE) 4 b f Glenstal (USA)-Gay Refrain (Furry Glen) *195^{8}* 480^{11} **>11f<**
New Technique (FR) 4 br f Formidable (USA)-Dolly Bea Sweet (USA) (Super Concorde (USA)) *9^{7}* **>25a 42f<**
Newtons Corner (IRE) 3 ch g Masterclass (USA)-Princess Galicia (Welsh Pageant) 2734^{6} 2938^{6} 3037^{9} **>39f<**
Next Going (IRE) 5 b m Doulab (USA)-Regal Promise (Pitskelly) 4262a^{2} **>84f<**
Next Round (IRE) 2 b f Common Grounds-Debbie's Next (USA) (Arctic Tern (USA)) 2138^{4} (2394) 2962^{5} 3904^{9} 4473^{12} **>84f<**
Ngaere Princess 2 br f Terimon-Zippy Zoe (Rousillon (USA)) 822^{7} 938^{8} 1126^{9} 1328^{9} 1839^{8} 1990^{5} 2538^{8} 2823^{6} 3483^{3} 3866^{5} *4054^{13}* 4163^{8} 4470^{3} 4750^{12} 5026^{8} **>18a 51f<**
Nichol Fifty 3 b g Old Vic-Jawaher (IRE) (Dancing Brave (USA)) 676^{10} 841^{7} 2117^{5} 2570^{2} (2652) 3915^{5} 4234^{4} (4919) 5027^{3} **>82f<**
Nicker 3 b g Nicholas (USA)-Glimmer (Hot Spark) 1237^{8} 1688^{3} 2125^{8} 2747^{2} 2922^{15} 3590^{10} 3969^{5} **>48f<**
Nick of Time 3 b f Mtoto-Nikitina (Nijinsky (CAN)) 842^{7} 1465^{7} 2397^{2} 3028^{4} 3896^{4} 4609^{4} 4879^{8} **>70f<**
Nicola's Princess 4 b f Handsome Sailor-Barachois Princess (USA) (Barachois (CAN)) *428^{9} 857^{3}* 1093^{4} 1623^{6} 1796^{7} *2049^{2}* 2209^{2} 2652^{7} *2911^{2}* 3286^{4} *3585^{3}* 3886^{4} 4179^{18} **>56a 52f<**
Nicole Pharly 3 b f Pharly (FR)-Debbie Harry (USA) (Alleged (USA)) (815a) (1368a) **>104f<**
Niederhoff (FR) 3 b c Epervier Bleu-El Quahirah (FR) (Cadoudal (FR)) 4251a^{2} **>116f<**
Nifty Norman 3 b g Rock City-Nifty Fifty (IRE) (Runnett) (1119) 1673^{7} (2141) 2655^{8} 3460^{6} 4137^{21} **>79f<**
Nigels Choice 5 gr g Teenoso (USA)-Warm Winter (Kalaglow) 1276^{8} 1434^{13} **>41f<**
Nigel's Lad (IRE) 5 b g Dominion Royale-Back To Earth (FR) (Vayrann) 647^{8} 955^{4} (1494) (1585) (1648) 2014^{25} 4288^{5} *4481^{6}* 4783^{24} **>59a 83f<**
Night Auction (IRE) 2 b f Night Shift (USA)-Maria Stuarda (Royal And Regal (USA)) 3471^{8} 4167^{9} 4332^{5} 4566^{12} 4953^{7} **>68f<**
Nightbird (IRE) 3 b f Night Shift (USA)-Pippas Song (Reference Point) 1203a^{5} (1610) 2023^{5} 2677^{4} **>122df<**
Night Chorus 3 b c Most Welcome-Choral Sundown (Night Shift (USA)) (886) 1249^{3} 1392^{7} 1775^{8} 2495^{4} 2877^{4} 3225^{2} 4308^{6} 4583^{4} 4924^{19} **>13a 76f<**
Night City 6 b g Kris-Night Secret (Nijinsky (CAN)) 1261^{W} 1456^{17} 3797^{4} 4003^{8} 4264^{4} 4281^{8} *4572^{11}* 4768^{2} 4920^{14} *(5019)* **>74a 79tf<**
Night Dance 5 ch h Weldnaas (USA)-Shift Over (USA) (Night Shift (USA)) 444^{6} (635) 832^{11} 4225^{13} 4561^{16} 4878^{8} **>59a 84df<**
Night Express 3 ch g Night Shift (USA)-New Edition (Great Nephew) 795^{6} 1087^{3} 1394^{4} *1787^{2}* 2149^{4} 2510^{5} 2703^{8} 3037^{8} 3241^{3} 3425^{5} 3606^{3} *4049^{6}* 4385^{17} **>80da 65df<**
Night Flight 3 gr g Night Shift (USA)-Ancestry (Persepolis (FR)) (863) 1029^{9} 1170^{14} 1673^{3} 2141^{3} 2326^{14} 3812^{9} 4270^{14} 4280^{26} **>63f<**
Night Flyer 2 b c Midyan (USA)-Scandalette (Niniski (USA)) 1744^{3} 2534^{7} 2720^{5} 3113^{6} (3794) 4116^{7} 4447^{2} **>77f<**
Night Harmony (IRE) 4 ch c Digamist (USA)-Quaver (Song) **1996:** *5105^{5} 5134^{3} 5163^{4}* **1997:** *301^{10} 421^{7}* 541^{6} 1250^{5} (1279) 1488^{7} 3327^{6} 3936^{17} 4805^{5} 4954^{12} **>64a 55f<**
Nightingale Song 3 b f Tina's Pet-Songlines (Night Shift (USA)) *25^{5} 258^{3} 320^{6} 569^{11}* 2964^{10} 3816^{5} 4048^{7} 4233^{25} 4696^{13} **>71a 64f<**
Nightlark (IRE) 3 b f Night Shift (USA)-Overcall (Bustino) 944^{2} 1258^{3} 1868^{2} 2568^{2} 3188^{2} (3903) 4242^{13} 4704^{4} **>88f<**
Night Mirage (USA) 3 b f Silver Hawk (USA)-Colony Club (USA) (Tom Rolfe) 558^{2} 826^{2} 1278^{3} 1773^{5} 2155^{7} 2521^{2} (2884) (3225) 3311^{2} 3381^{2} 4015^{4} 4147^{21} 4876^{3} 4996^{2} **>83f<**
Night of Glass 4 b g Mazilier (USA)-Donna Elvira (Chief Singer) 633^{3} 866^{6} 1422^{11} 2465^{2} 2906^{5} 3105^{3} 3759^{13} 3976^{2} 4410^{3} (4773) 4979^{11} 5049^{10} **>21a 71f<**
Night Owl 2 b f Night Shift (USA)-Sarah Georgina (Persian Bold) 2829^{3} 3187^{6} 4103^{5} 4474^{12} **>76+f<**
Night People 2 ch c Night Shift (USA)-Front Line Romance (Caerleon (USA)) 1255^{7} 2320^{8} 3031^{4} 3774^{9} **>62+f<**
Night Petticoat (GER) 4 b f Petoski-Nightrockette (GER) (Rocket) 1724a^{6} 3737a^{5} 4127a^{7} **>112f<**
Night Player (IRE) 3 b c Night Shift (USA)-Racquette (Ballymore) (2457a) 3180a^{4} **>107?f<**
Night Rule 2 b f Shirley Heights-Hafwah (Gorytus (USA)) 4330^{3} 4977^{2} **>83f<**
Night Sceptre (IRE) 3 b f Night Shift (USA)-Spire (Shirley Heights) **1996:** *5243^{2}* **>69a 69f<**
Night Shot 2 br c Night Shift (USA)-Optaria (Song) 2699^{2} 3193^{5} 3799^{2} 4152^{3} **>87f<**
Night Time 5 b g Night Shift (USA)-Gathering Place (USA) (Hawaii) 2998a^{3} **>62a 66f<**
Night Vigil (IRE) 2 b c Night Shift (USA)-Game Plan (Darshaan) 1263^{10} 1933^{9} *2363^{4}* 4898^{14} **>55a 65f<**
Night Watch (USA) 4 b g Night Shift (USA)-Christchurch (FR) (So Blessed) 1659^{2} 2528^{3} 3051^{11} **>101f<**
Night Wink (USA) 5 ch g Rahy (USA)-Lady in White (Shareef Dancer (USA)) **1996:** *5120^{2} 5186^{2}* **1997:** *291^{4} 365^{5}* 444^{8} 832^{12} 947^{15} 1739^{14} 1955^{4} 2576^{6} 2743^{6} 2929^{5} (3081) 3435^{B} 3616^{5} 3848^{2} (3969) **>85a 84+f<**
Nigrasine 3 b c Mon Tresor-Early Gales (Precocious) 679^{7} 1412^{5} 2013^{12} (2517) 3217^{15} 4100^{8} 4282^{15} 4888^{3} **>105f<**
Nijmegen 9 b g Niniski (USA)-Petty Purse (Petingo) *88^{9}* **>55?a 67f<**
Nijo 6 b g Top Ville-Nibabu (FR) (Nishapour (FR)) **1996:** *5204^{8}* **>91a 113f<**
Niki (IRE) 2 b f Fairy King (USA)-Nicola Wynn (Nicholas Bill) 4212^{2} 4425^{6} 4873^{4} **>77f<**
Nikita's Star (IRE) 4 ch g Soviet Lad (USA)-Sally Chase (Sallust) **1996:** *(5171)* **1997:** *23^{5} 100^{4} 182^{2} 299^{2} 389^{7} 426^{6}* 1169^{9} 2696^{13} 2787^{6} 4213^{9} *4981^{5}* **>70a 60f<**
Nikki Star 3 b f Presidium-Nikki Noo Noo (Precocious) 1921^{8} 2780^{11} 2946^{5} **>4f<**
Nil (IRE) 4 b c Danehill (USA)-Padula (ITY) (Artaius (USA)) 1201a^{3} 4765a^{3} **>104f<**
Nile Valley (IRE) 3 b f Royal Academy (USA)-Sphinx (GER) (Alpenkonig (GER)) 537^{5} 746^{5} 1565^{2} 1808^{2} 2397^{9} 3020^{4} *4481^{8}* **>50a 71df<**
Nilo of Time (ITY) 3 f 815a^{10} **>82f<**
Nineacres 6 b g Sayf El Arab (USA)-Mayor (Laxton) *663^{3}* 980^{4} 1089^{7} 3984^{3} 4733^{8} *4985^{6}* **>57a 69f<**
Ninth Chord 3 gr c Alzao (USA)-Jazz (Sharrood (USA)) 2687^{4} **>89df<**
Ninth Symphony 3 ch g Midyan (USA)-Good as Gold (IRE) (Glint of Gold) **1996:** *5113^{6} 5238^{6}* **1997:** 1256^{15} 1493^{4} 1837^{8} 2224^{5} **>54a 70df<**
Nirvana (USA) 3 f 1202a^{13}
Nirvana Prince 8 ch g Celestial Storm (USA)-Princess Sunshine (Busted) 435^{18} **>72a 64?f<**
Nisaba (IRE) 2 b f Belmez (USA)-Nibabu (FR) (Nishapour (FR)) 3070^{5} 4007^{7} 4330^{7} 4605^{6} **>66f<**
Nishamira (IRE) 5 gr m Lashkari-Nishila (USA) (Green Dancer (USA)) *(37)* 612^{4} **>64+a 65f<**
Nite Bites 3 b g Thatching-Buraida (Balidar) *1155^{13}*
Nite Owler 3 b g Saddlers' Hall (IRE)-Lorne Lady (Local Suitor (USA)) 945^{8} 4290^{8} 4331^{7} **>43f<**
Niteowl Raider (IRE) 4 ch g Standaan (FR)-Havana Moon (Ela-Mana-Mou) **1996:** *5138^{10}* **1997:** *326^{9} 421^{13}* 4328^{21} **>26a 14f<**
Nite Wonder 3 br g Magical Wonder (USA)-Black Fighter (USA) (Secretariat (USA)) 1423^{12} 1643^{5} **>44f<**
Nkapen Rocks (SPA) 4 b g Risk Me (FR)-Debutina Park (Averof) **1996:** *5130^{11} 5174^{10}* **1997:**

1020^{4} 1285^{7} 2144^{6} 2418^{5} 2546^{2} 2828^{10} 4629^{5} 4991^{14} 5030^{3} **>47a 57f<**

Nobady Els (IRE) 3 b c Topanoora-Zazu (Cure The Blues (USA)) 1911a^{3}

Nobalino 3 ch c Sharpo-Zipperti Do (Precocious) *3043^{2}* 4047^{6} 4214^{4} 4563^{2} *4809^{4}* 4997^{2} **>65a 78f<**

Nobby Barnes 8 b g Nordance (USA)-Loving Doll (Godswalk (USA)) *424^{9}* 461^{7} 689^{7} 951^{3} 1231^{2} 1472^{2} 1615^{4} 1979^{10} 2385^{4} 2546^{5} 2660^{2} 3029^{8} 3262^{4} 3605^{7} 3630^{5} 3972^{3} 4471^{12} **>37a 48f<**

Nobby Beach 3 ch g Sharpo-Sunshine Coast (Posse (USA)) *1939^{9}* 2591^{13} 3715^{12} **>6a 31f<**

Nobel Lad 3 b c Highest Honor (FR)-Aldbourne (Alzao (USA)) 586^{11} 795^{3} 1271^{5} 1747^{9} 2885^{6} 4406^{3} 4918^{15} **>67f<**

Nobility (IRE) 3 ch c Diesis-Royal Touch (Tap On Wood) 3674a^{5} 4344a^{8} **>106f<**

Noble Canonire 5 b m Gunner B-Lucky Candy (Lucky Wednesday) *39^{10} 88^{13} 410^{10} 516^{7} 578^{4}* 796^{10} 2041^{13} *2302^{8} 2368^{10}* **>44a 34f<**

Noble Dane (IRE) 3 b f Danehill (USA)-Noble Dust (USA) (Dust Commander (USA)) 723^{4} 1146^{9} 1442^{9} 1878^{7} 2340^{6} 3153^{10} 3445^{2} 3694^{3} 4002^{10} 4242^{8} 4632^{16} **>71f<**

Noble Demand (USA) 2 b c Red Ransom (USA)-Noble Nordic (USA) (Vaguely Noble) 3094^{8} 3331^{4} 3602^{7} (3990) 4778^{2} **>80f<**

Nobledil (IRE) 2 b c Dilum (USA)-Noble Kara (FR) (Noblequest (FR)) 4868a^{3} **>89f<**

Noble Hero 3 b c Houston (USA)-Noble Devorcee (USA) (Vaguely Noble) **1996:** *5100^{2} 5147^{3}* **1997:** *307^{4} 366^{7}* 537^{9} 1011^{8} 1247^{4} 1507^{5} **>73a 57f<**

Noble Investment 3 b g Shirley Heights-Noble Destiny (Dancing Brave (USA)) 700^{7} 1104^{5} *1155^{4}* 2192^{9} **>49a 71df<**

Noble Lord 4 ch g Lord Bud-Chasers' Bar (Oats) 1215^{5} **>62f<**

Noble Patriot 2 b c Polish Patriot (USA)-Noble Form (Double Form) 4064^{15} 4543^{10} *4796^{9}* **>51a 58f<**

Noble Saja 2 b g Noble Patriarch-Saja (USA) (Ferdinand (USA)) 447^{12} **>15f<**

Noble Story 3 br f Last Tycoon-Certain Story (Known Fact (USA)) 2838^{8} **>66f<**

Nocatchim 8 b g Shardari-Solar (Hotfoot) 4713^{12} **>32f<**

No Class 3 ch f Keen-Plie (Superlative) 1484^{12} **>26a 66df<**

No Cliches 4 ch g Risk Me (FR)-Always on a Sunday (Star Appeal) 468^{19} 610^{14} 1097^{16} 2043^{9} 2845^{2} 3026^{2} 3120^{7} 3798^{9} 4147^{24} 4596^{13} 4802^{19} **>53f<**

Nocturne (IRE) 2 b f Tenby-Phylella (Persian Bold) 3979^{11} **>33f<**

Noemie (FR) 2 f 4663a^{10} **>82f<**

Noeprob (USA) 7 b m Majestic Shore (USA)-Heat Haze (USA) (Jungle Savage (USA)) 1273^{2} 1632^{18} 1955^{8} 2004^{6} 2310^{4} 2552^{12} 3276^{6} 3469^{3} 3787^{8} 4114^{9} **>30a 58f<**

Noetic 3 ch f Nomadic Way (USA)-Pretty Soon (Tina's Pet) **1996:** *5180^{10}* **1997:** *41^{9}*

No Extras (IRE) 7 b g Efisio-Parkland Rose (Sweet Candy (VEN)) 766^{8} 1324^{4} 1935^{7} (2346) 2508^{2} (3115) 3217^{7} 3765^{2} 4155^{2} 4423^{15} 4881^{14} **>95f<**

No Grousing (IRE) 3 b g Robellino (USA)-Amenaide (Known Fact (USA)) 701^{2} 1041^{2} 2045^{2} 4792^{15} **>83f<**

Noirie 3 br c Warning-Callipoli (USA) (Green Dancer (USA)) 463^{4} 600^{9} 764^{10} 995^{13} 1096^{16} 2130^{9} 2548^{5} 2908^{14} **>50?f<**

Noisette 3 ch f Nashwan (USA)-Nadma (USA) (Northern Dancer) (890) 1147^{8} (2561) 3147^{7} 4120^{7} 4424^{3} 5056a^{4} **>111f<**

Nombre Premier 3 gr c Kendor (FR)-Sabiola (FR) (The Wonder (FR)) 717a^{2} (1719a) 3001a^{3} 3554a^{8} **>120f<**

Nominator Lad 3 b c Nomination-Ankara's Princess (USA) (Ankara (USA)) 2214^{4} 2877^{5} (3030) *3584^{5}* 3987^{7} 4176^{7} (4436) 4578^{9} **>56a 77f<**

No Monkey Nuts 4 ch g Clantime-Portvally (Import) **1996:** *5089^{13}* **>68a 84f< (DEAD)**

No More Hassle (IRE) 4 ch g Magical Wonder (USA)-Friendly Ann (Artaius (USA)) **1996:** *5116^{4}* **>43a 49f<**

Nomore Mr Niceguy 3 b c Rambo Dancer (CAN)-Lariston Gale (Pas de Seul) **1996:** *5113^{3} 5229^{3} (5238)* **1997:** *103^{4} 138^{3} 180^{2}* 448^{3} *(514)* 794^{2} 1017^{5} 1170^{3} 1658^{2} 2013^{6} 2871^{4} 3150^{11} 3888^{9} 4121^{15} 4307^{4} 4787^{11} **>94a 87f<**

No More Pressure (IRE) 3 ch g Thatching-High Pressure (Kings Lake (USA)) **1996:** *(5228)* **1997:** 635^{2} 853^{3} 1017^{9} 1670^{8} 4757^{7} 4920^{12} 5049^{17} **>84a 78f<**

Nomothetis (IRE) 3 b f Law Society (USA)-Tamassos (Dance In Time (CAN)) 3463^{17}

Nononito (FR) 6 b h Nikos-Feuille D'Automne (FR) (Crystal Palace (FR)) 1365a^{6} 2055^{11} **>124f<**

Non Vintage (IRE) 6 ch g Shy Groom (USA)-Great Alexandra (Runnett) 1779^{4} 3931^{7} **>63a 46f<**

Nopalea 3 b f Warrshan (USA)-Nophe (USA) (Super Concorde (USA)) *45^{4} 282^{4} 339^{4}* 876^{2} 1375^{3} 1566^{2} (1681) 1995^{3} 2481^{3} 4820^{12} **>53a 72f<**

No Pattern 5 ch g Rock City-Sunfleet (Red Sunset) **1996:** *5189^{4} 5274^{4}* **1997:** *131^{7}* **>68a 68f<**

No Problem Jac 4 b f Safawan-Out on a Flyer (Comedy Star (USA)) 2501^{7} 2902^{5} 3089^{5} **>39?f<**

Norbello (GER) 2 br c Greinton-Noble Girl (Esclavo (FR)) 1723a^{2}

Norcroft Joy 2 b f Rock Hopper-Greenhills Joy (Radetzky) 4739^{13} 4853^{8} 4957^{8} **>50f<**

Nordansk 8 ch g Nordance (USA)-Free on Board (Free State) 1459^{2} 1811^{10} 2118^{11} 2949^{4} 3689^{8} 4374^{9} **>60f<**

Nordic Breeze (IRE) 5 b or br g Nordico (USA)-Baby Clair (Gulf Pearl) *72^{2}* 2375^{4} **>75a 71f<**

Nordic Crest (IRE) 3 b c Danehill (USA)-Feather Glen (Glenstal (USA)) 686^{4} 1649^{3} 2230^{9} 2927^{3} 3466^{5} 3864^{12} **>73f<**

Nordic Gift (DEN) 4 ch g Bold Arrangement-Nordic Rose (DEN) (Drumhead) 495^{7} 951^{16} **>18f<**

Nordic Hero (IRE) 4 b g Nordico (USA)-Postscript (Final Straw) **1996:** *5259^{5}* **>54a 8f<**

Nordico Melody (IRE) 3 b g Nordico (USA)-Musical Essence (Song) 2020^{6} *2603^{14}* 3038^{11} 3601^{11} 3933^{7} **>18a 34f<**

Nordic Pirjo 2 b f Nordico (USA)-Victoria Mill (Free State) 3753^{W} 4209^{12} 4459^{8} 4801^{7} **>50f<**

Nordic Project (IRE) 3 b c Project Manager-Nordic Relation 2081a^{5} **>85+f<**

Nordinex (IRE) 5 b g Nordico (USA)-Debbie's Next (USA) (Arctic Tern (USA)) *294^{9} 403^{6}* 4175^{9} 4878^{16} **>61a 67f<**

Nordisk Legend 5 b g Colmore Row-Nordic Rose (DEN) (Drumhead) 493^{15} 950^{11} **>10f<**

Nord Lys (IRE) 6 b g Nordico (USA)-Beach Light (Bustino) *66^{10}* **>25f<**

Nor-Do-I 3 ch g Primo Dominie-True Nora (Ahonoora) **1996:** *(5162)* **1997:** 1243^{10} 1608^{8} 2298^{5} 2547^{8} *3075^{5} (3397) 3584^{15}* 4436^{3} 4792^{16} **>87a 76f<**

Noreastern (IRE) 2 ch c Zafonic (USA)-Hayati (Hotfoot) 3687^{W} 4113^{7} **>49f<**

Norfolk Glory 5 ch g Weldnaas (USA)-Caviar Blini (What A Guest) **1996:** *5082^{10}* **>49da 52df<**

Norling (IRE) 7 ch g Nashamaa-Now Then (Sandford Lad) *20^{4} 117^{4} 172^{5} 224^{8} 404^{4} 1047^{4}* 1676^{6} *1790^{7}* 2006^{20} **>50a 38f<**

Norman Conquest (USA) 3 ch c Miswaki (USA)-Grand Luxe (USA) (Sir Ivor) 797^{5} 1877^{6} 2315^{15} 2929^{6} 4158^{6} 4371^{16} **>64f<**

Nornax Lad (USA) 9 b g Northern Baby (CAN)-Naxos (USA) (Big Spruce (USA)) 898^{8} 1169^{5} 1445^{9} 1618^{2} 1825^{17} 2307^{3} 2531^{4} 3245^{6} *3415^{3}* 3472^{4} 3758^{4} 4170^{10} 4519^{7} 4804^{5} **>50a 36f<**

Norski Lad 2 b c Niniski (USA)-Lady Norcliffe (USA) (Norcliffe (CAN)) 4581^{9} 4793^{11} 4871^{8} 4994^{8} **>58f<**

Norsong 5 b g Northern State (USA)-Winsong Melody (Music Maestro) 650^{6} 888^{15} 1424^{9} 1779^{22} (1825) (3640) 4275^{21} **>54f<**

North Ardar 7 b g Ardar-Langwaite (Seaepic (USA)) **1996:** *5175^{6} 5240^{7}* **1997:** *67^{6} 295^{15} 390^{6}* **>18a 57?f<**

North Bear 5 b g North Briton-Sarah Bear (Mansingh (USA)) 763^{13} 1093^{12} **>59df<**

Northern Accord 3 b g Akarad (FR)-Sioux City (Simply Great (FR)) 4417^{9} 4587^{11} *4980^{5}* **>42a 41f<**

Northern Afleet (USA) 4 *5061a^{7}* **>115a f<**

Northern Angel (IRE) 3 b c Waajib-Angel Divine (Ahonoora) 1297^{8} 2591^{2} 3095^{4} 3281^{3} (3715) 4071^{11} *5021^{3}* **>66a 83f<**

Northern Blessing 3 b f Waajib-Last Blessing (Final Straw) (4331) 4669^{5} **>94f<**

Northern Charmer 5 b g Charmer-Trading (Forlorn River) *410^{6}* **>39a 51f<**

Northern Chief 7 b g Chief Singer-Pacific Gull (USA) (Storm Bird (CAN)) **1996:** *5132^{9} 5250^{6} 5271^{14}* **>14a 48f<**

Northern Clan 4 b g Clantime-Northern Line (Camden Town) 2997a^{7} 3276^{18} 3469^{17} **>24df<**

Northern Diamond (IRE) 4 b g Distinctly North (USA)-Mitsubishi Diamond (Tender King) *28^{10}* **>14a 41f<**

Northern Drums 4 b g Sadler's Wells (USA)-Repercutionist (USA) (Beaudelaire (USA)) 451^{4} 888^{10} 2535^{6} 3462^{3} 4046^{9} **>61f<**

Northern Fan (IRE) 5 b g Lear Fan (USA)-Easy Romance (USA) (Northern Jove (CAN)) *179^{8} 220^{9} 243^{5} 273^{3} (359) 390^{2} 415^{5} 424^{8}* 480^{2} *579^{5}* 843^{5} 925^{5} 1016^{3} 1231^{9} 1660^{8} 4918^{14} **>63a 49f<**

Northern Flash 3 b g Rambo Dancer (CAN)-Spinster (Grundy) 1497^{6} 2059^{3} 2330^{2} 3071^{6} 4015^{16} 4692^{6} **>47f<**

Northern Fleet 4 b c Slip Anchor-Kamkova (USA) (Northern Dancer) 831^{4} 1413^{7} 2014^{12} 2589^{11} **>77f<**

Northern Grey 5 gr g Puissance-Sharp Anne (Belfort (FR)) **1996:** *5256^{9}* **1997:** 1441^{6} 4607^{17} **>50da 48f<**

Northern Judge 4 ch g Highest Honor (FR)-Nordica (Northfields (USA)) 1003^{7} 1511^{15} *1754^{16}* 2282^{4} 2418^{9} 2892^{10} 3573^{13} **>34a 25f<**

Northern Lass (IRE) 2 br f Rainbows For Life (CAN)-Intrepid (Rousillon (USA)) 4067^{14} 4526^{19} 4853^{12} **>47f<**

Northern Maestro 3 ch g Rock Hopper-Thimbalina (Salmon Leap (USA)) 1130^{11} 1405^{5} 1950^{4} 2226^{6} 3488^{9} **>23f<**

Northern Motto 4 b g Mtoto-Soulful (FR) (Zino) **1996:** *5171^{4}* **1997:** *(260) 315^{7}* 470^{9} 613^{4} 1232^{4} 1605^{3} (1763) 2014^{9} 2291^{6} 2682^{8} 5027^{13} **>63a 51f<**

Northern Saga (IRE) 4 b g Distinctly North (USA)-Saga's Humour (Bustino) 1951^{4} 2646^{8} 2916^{13} 4608^{12} **>36a 48f<**

Northern Sal **3** ch f Aragon-Sister Sal (Bairn (USA)) 549[5] 1571[2] 1730[5] 1995[8] 2883[10] 3224[9] 3756[12] 3922[16] **>23f<**

Northern Spark **9** b g Trojan Fen-Heavenly Spark (Habitat) **1996:** *5114[12]* **>53a 57f<**

Northern Spruce (IRE) **5** ch g Astronef-Perle's Fashion (Sallust) **1996:** *5269[9]* **1997:** *122[7]* **>43f<**

Northern Sun **3** b g Charmer-Princess Dancer (Alzao (USA)) (509) 789[9] 966[4] 2230[7] 2574[8] **>90f<**

Northern Touch **3** b f Warrshan (USA)-Shirley's Touch (Touching Wood (USA)) 641[6] 1144[4] 2005[7] 2521[11] 2770[3] 3102[2] **>60f<**

North Ofthe Border **2** b c Primo Dominie-Valika (Valiyar) 4706[3] 4901[4] 5041[4] **>83f<**

North Reef (IRE) **6** b h Danehill (USA)-Loreef (Main Reef) **1996:** *5106[6]* *5231[2]* **1997:** (1427) 1588[W] 2187[D] 3184[3] 3739[8] 4108[12] 4406[4] 4714[3] 4918[11] **>83a 69f<**

North White Plains **3** b c Shareef Dancer (USA)-Clare Court (Glint of Gold) 812a[5] 875[R] 1106[9] 1612[7] **>27f<**

Norwegian Blue (IRE) **4** b g Mac's Imp (USA)-Opening Day (Day Is Done) (3508a) **>73f<**

Nosey Native **4** b g Cyrano de Bergerac-Native Flair (Be My Native (USA)) 430[21] 657[8] 866[8] 1427[3] 1981[12] (2063) 2469[8] 2696[11] 3015[8] 3197[4] 3401[6] 3719[4] *4590[7]* **>41a 65f<**

No Shame **2** b f Formidable (USA)-Jalopy (Jalmood (USA)) 1240[12] 1760[17] 1997[6] 2943[5] 4044[13] 4245[7] 4382[11] 4849[8] **>57f<**

No Slouch (IRE) **3** b c Royal Academy (USA)-Hastening (Shirley Heights) 3362a[7] 4204a[6] 4356a[6] **>95f<**

No Speeches (IRE) **6** b g Last Tycoon-Wood Violet (USA) (Riverman (USA)) *23[4]* 148a[6] 190a[8] 270a[12] *457[2]* **>71a 63f<**

No Submission (USA) **11** b h Melyno-Creeping Kate (USA) (Stop The Music (USA)) **1996:** *5086[8]* *5110[7]* *5143[10]* *5260[7]* **1997:** *284[6]* *360[12]* 553[12] *580[7]* **>48a 23f<**

Not A Lot **3** ch g Emarati (USA)-Spanish Chestnut (Philip of Spain) 600[10] 997[12] 1127[6] **>44f<**

Notary **3** b g Mtoto-Nadina (Shirley Heights) 1497[11] 2046[16] **>38f<**

Notation (IRE) **3** b c Arazi (USA)-Grace Note (FR) (Top Ville) 3909[7] 4326[8] 4417[11] *4811[8]* 5028[8] **>36a 54f<**

Not Forgotten (USA) **3** b g St Jovite (USA)-Past Remembered (USA) (Solford (USA)) **1996:** 5193a[5] 5196a[10] **1997:** *350[6]* 670[4] 825[4] 975[4] 1218[4] 2430[10] 2879[8] 3317[10] *3587[6]* 3896[14] 4170[6] **>40a 55f<**

Nothing Doing (IRE) **8** b g Sarab-Spoons (Orchestra) **1996:** *5222[3]* *5255[4]* **1997:** *43[2]* *115[6]* 1636[2] 2279[3] 2398[7] (2916) 3279[7] **>41a 55f<**

Nothin' Leica Dane (AUS) **5** b h Danehill (USA)-Leica Pretender 4258a[2] 4665a[17] 4965a[7] **>121f<**

Not Out Lad **3** b c Governor General-Sorcha (IRE) (Shernazar) *379[8]* 1167[13] 4916[16] **>16a 37f<**

Noufari (FR) **6** b g Kahyasi-Noufiyla (Top Ville) **1996:** *5205[5]* **1997:** *55[3]* *101[2]* *419[2]* 442[2] *858[3]* 982[8] *1122[2]* 1252[5] 1672[2] 2327[12] (2718) 3412[3] 3805[9] 4279[10] *4594[3]* 4874[10] **>79a 77f<**

Novize (GER) **6** dk b h Zampano (GER)-Nombreuse (Nebos (GER)) 3375a[3] **>105f<**

Nubile **3** b f Pursuit of Love-Trojan Lady (USA) (Irish River (FR)) 992[3] 1567[4] 2380[6] (2727) *4800[11]* 4971[18] **>23a 56f<**

Nuclear Debate (USA) **2** b g Geiger Counter (USA)-I'm An Issue (USA) (Cox's Ridge (USA)) 2467[6] 3094[2] 3331[2] 3774[3] 4522[7] 4755[5] **>86f<**

Nuit d'Or (IRE) **2** ch c Night Shift (USA)-Sister Golden Hair (IRE) (Glint of Gold) *4052[6]* 4433[7] *4592[6]* *4808[8]* **>51a 66f<**

Nukud (USA) **5** b g Topsider (USA)-Summer Silence (USA) (Stop The Music (USA)) *126[6]* *150[5]* *312[2]* 668[14] 900[13] 1312[3] 2041[10] 2502[15] 2909[6] 3442[6] 3762[4] **>38a 28f<**

Numbered Account **6** b h Forzando-Societe Secrete (FR) (Luthier) 308a[2] **>102f<**

Nunthorpe **2** ch f Mystiko (USA)-Enchanting Melody (Chief Singer) 3070[6] 4381[2] 4638[13] **>76f<**

Nuvellino **2** b c Robellino (USA)-Furry Dance (USA) (Nureyev (USA)) 3859[13] **>33a 33f<**

Nwaamis (USA) **5** b h Dayjur (USA)-Lady Cutlass (USA) (Cutlass (USA)) (894) (1598) 2009[4] 4117[5] 4377[3] **>117?f<**

O

Oakbrook Rose **3** b f Forzando-Oakbrook Tern (USA) (Arctic Tern (USA)) 885[11] 2921[17] 3897[12] **>29f<**

Oakbury (IRE) **5** ch g Common Grounds-Doon Belle (Ardoon) 4453[10] 4768[9] **>37a 30f<**

Oaken Wood (IRE) **3** ch c Lycius (USA)-Little Red Rose (Precocious) **1996:** *5087[8]* *5251[6]* **>39a 44f<**

Oare Kite **2** b f Batshoof-Portvasco (Sharpo) 2473[6] 4332[6] 4604[3] **>66f<**

Oatey **4** ch f Master Willie-Oatfield (Great Nephew) 901[7] 1223[B] 1765[3] 1828[11] 2001[7] **>38a 63f<**

Obelos (USA) **6** ch g Diesis-Fair Sousanne (Busted) **1996:** *5140[3]* *5205[6]* *5233[6]* *5269[2]* **1997:** *72[9]* *299[7]* *422[8]* (482) 633[6] 3380[6] 3620[4] 4063[7] 4172[16] 4386[6] **>33a 67df<**

Oberons Boy (IRE) **4** b g Fairy King (USA)-Bold Starlet (Precocious) **1996:** *5209[6]* **1997:** *47[2]* *120[6]* 477[13] *1082[9]* 1244[14] 1427[2] 1641[6] 1985[3] 2218[5] 2475[4] 2824[8] 4109[14] **>66a 60f<**

Oberon's Dart (IRE) **4** b g Fairy King (USA)-Key Maneuver (USA) (Key To Content (USA)) 1035[18] 1320[13] *2162[10]* 2424[5] *3075[12]* *(3581)* 3987[19] *4570[3]* 4872[15] **>73a 57f<**

Oberon's Mistral **2** b f Fairy King (USA)-La Venta (USA) (Drone) 3151[7] 3769[2] 4057[3] **>78f<**

Obsessed **2** b f Storm Bird (CAN)-Secret Obsession (USA) (Secretariat (USA)) 2597[7] 2962[4] 3770[3] (4752) **>81f<**

Obvious Appeal (IRE) **2** b f Danehill (USA)-Croglin Water (Monsanto (FR)) 4619a[10] **>83f<**

Occam (IRE) **3** ch c Sharp Victor (USA)-Monterana (Sallust) 586[12] 1443[4] 4331[4] 4629[14] **>70f<**

Occhi Verdi (IRE) **2** ch f Mujtahid (USA)-Mali (USA) (Storm Bird (CAN)) (697) 893[6] 1328[2] 2439a[4] 2862[16] 3802[8] 4097[4] 4473[5] 4790[11] **>78f<**

Occupandiste (IRE) **4** b f Kaldoun (FR)-Only Seule (2273a) 3001a[5] (3554a) (4864a) **>128f<**

Ocean Breeze **3** ch g Most Welcome-Sea Power (Welsh Pageant) 1115[7] 1469[8] 2207[5] 2357[3] 2908[10] 3284[3] 3858[6] **>43f<**

Ocean Light **3** ch f Anshan-Waveguide (Double Form) *341[6]* **>53a 37f<**

Ocean Line (IRE) **2** b c Kefaah (USA)-Tropic Sea (IRE) (Sure Blade (USA)) 2948[7] 3193[10] 4113[8] 4994[3] **>56f<**

Ocean Park **6** b g Dominion-Chiming Melody (Cure The Blues (USA)) *4051[10]* 657[6] 1142[4] 1481[4] 2843[4] 3466[2] 3929[2] **>90a 74f<**

Ocean Ridge (USA) **3** b f Storm Bird (CAN)-Polar Bird (Thatching) 960[5] 2025[2] 2586[2] 3371a[6] **>119f<**

Ocean Sea (USA) **4** ch c Bering- 440a[2] 1073a[10] **>104f<**

Ocean Stream (IRE) **4** b g Waajib-Kilboy Concorde (African Sky) *177[9]* *383[8]* 3937[16] 4248[13] 4751[8] **>35a 50f<**

Ochos Rios (IRE) **6** br g Horage-Morgiana (Godswalk (USA)) 1020[3] 1248[10] 2019[11] 2567[5] 3310[3] 3573[15] 4210[10] 4628[10] 4711[10] 4979[25] **>62a 53f<**

Ocker (IRE) **3** br g Astronef-Violet Somers (Will Somers) 768[5] 1090[6] 2143[4] 3100[8] 3691[5] 3969[4] 4249[9] 4711[4] **>64f<**

Octagonal (NZ) **5** br h Zabeel (AUS)-Eight Carat (AUS) (Pieces of Eight) (437a) **>115f<**

Octavia Hill **4** ch f Prince Sabo-Clara Barton (Youth (USA)) *579[13]* 1395[2] 1843[4] 2745[3] 3207[3] 3470[6] (4008) **>2a 63f<**

Odette **2** b f Pursuit of Love-On Tiptoes (Shareef Dancer (USA)) 3031[2] 4211[3] 4630[3] 4769[2] **>70+f<**

Off And Running **2** gr g Paris House-I Don't Mind (Swing Easy (USA)) *872[4]* *2606[5]* **>38a f<**

Office Hours **5** b g Danehill (USA)-Charmina (FR) (Nonoalco (USA)) 668[12] **>49a 30f<**

Off The Rails **3** b f Saddlers' Hall (IRE)-Sliprail (USA) (Our Native (USA)) 1420[3] 1866[9] 2782[8] 3452[9] 4406[5] **>61f<**

Oggi **6** gr g Efisio-Dolly Bevan (Another Realm) (835) 942[10] (1317) 2105[4] 2711[4] 3217[5] 3765[3] 4282[9] **>100f<**

Oh Dearie Me **5** b m Puissance-Tyrian Princess (Comedy Star (USA)) 4464[4] **>21f<**

Oh Hebe (IRE) **2** b f Night Shift (USA)-Why so Silent (Mill Reef (USA)) 3187[4] 3471[3] **>74f<**

O' Higgins (IRE) **2** b g Magical Wonder (USA)-Lightning Laser (Monseigneur (USA)) 447[3] 557[10] 884[10] 2786[6] 3545[5] 4460[4] 4793[3] **>74f<**

Ohio Royale **3** ch g Shalford (IRE)-Jupiter's Message (Jupiter Island) 1582[5] 1864[12] 4586[16] **>48f<**

Oh Nellie (USA) **3** b f Tilt The Stars (CAN)-Miss Enjoleur (USA) (L'Enjoleur (CAN)) 519[2] 672[2] 960[2] 1533a[5] 3147[6] 4377[5] 4759[7] **>105df<**

Oh Never Again (IRE) **2** br c Ballad Rock-Play The Queen (IRE) (King of Clubs) 822[3] 993[2] *(1577)* 2689[6] 2936[6] **>70a 72f<**

Ohnonotagain **5** b m Kind of Hush-Dear Glenda (Gold Song) 526[13] 774[5] *903[7]* 1332[8] 1514[13] 1586[2] 1828[16] 2416[7] 2788[12] 2891[6] 2939[3] 3240[20] *3583[11]* 4417[6] 4430[4] 4791[12] **>15a 46f<**

Oh So Easy **2** ch c Forzando-Hat Hill (Roan Rocket) 3094[18] 3497[6] 3686[4] 4216[4] 4315[3] 4753[4] 4856[18] **>68f<**

Oh So Misty **4** b f Teenoso (USA)-Miss Bali Beach (Nonoalco (USA)) 1106[10] 1247[5] 1622[6] **>34f<**

Oh Whataknight **4** b f Primo Dominie-Carolside (Music Maestro) 1627[12] 1828[15] *3582[14]* 3910[19] **>30f<**

Oisin (IRE) **2** b c Maledetto (IRE)-Morgiana (Godswalk (USA)) 850[9] 1163[7] 1812[8] 2196[9] 2697[4] 3961a[17] 4044[9] 4745[8] 4875[12] **>76f<**

Okay Baby (IRE) **5** b m Treasure Kay-Miss Tuko (Good Times (ITY)) 587[17] 896[8] 1484[8] 1639[2] 2041[12] 2724[4] 2954[6] 3240[7] 3565[10] 4169[6] **>19a 38f<**

Ok Babe **2** b f Bold Arrangement-Celtic Bird (Celtic Cone) 4602[5] 4818[6] **>67f<**

O'Kelly (DEN) **2** b f Last Tycoon-Laser Show (IRE) (Wassl) 2176[7] 3201[7] (3887) 4653a[3] **>79f<**

Ok John (IRE) **2** b c Mac's Imp (USA)-Ching A Ling (Pampapaul) 2571[8] 3055[2] 3324[4] *3586[2]* 3965[3] 4403[3] **>62a 59f<**

Okra **3** ch f Chilibang-Mollified (Lombard (GER)) 2496[9] 3335[4] 4408[5] **>55f<**

Old Colony **3** b f Pleasant Colony (USA)-Annoconnor (USA) (Nureyev (USA)) **1996:** *5087[4]* **1997:** 1565[3] **>48a 66f<**

Old Hook (IRE) **6** b or br h Digamist (USA)-Day Dress (Ashmore (FR)) 1483[7] **>78a 46f<**

Old Hush Wing (IRE) 4 b g Tirol-Saneena (Kris) *13[8] 22[6] 86[14] 262[2]* 2207[6] (2662) **>53a 50f<**
Old Queen (GER) 3 f 1918a[8] **>80f<**
Old Red (IRE) 7 ch g Ela-Mana-Mou-Sea Port (Averof) 3805[10] 3974[14] **>68a 81?f<**
Old Roma (IRE) 4 b f Old Vic-Romantic Past (USA) (Miswaki (USA)) 3469[10] 3933[12] 4184[16] **>32f<**
Old Rouvel (USA) 6 b g Riverman (USA)-Marie de Russy (FR) (Sassafras (FR)) 498[2] 1027[5] 2108[2] 2327[17] (3935) 4118[5] 4559[7] **>67a 101f<**
Olifantsfontein 9 b g Thatching-Taplow (Tap On Wood) 1816[9] 2463[13] **>49a 20f<**
Oliver (IRE) 3 b c Priolo (USA)-Daniella Drive (USA) (Shelter Half (USA)) **1996:** *5087[7]* **1997:** 478[4] 534[8] **>39a 51f<**
Olive The Twist (USA) 2 ch f Theatrical-Lady of the Light (USA) (The Minstrel (CAN)) 5041[5] **>74+f<**
Oliviero (FR) 4 dk b c Vaguely Pleasant (FR)-My Green Eyes (USA) (Big Spruce (USA)) 3883a[6] **>118f<**
Olivo (IRE) 3 ch g Priolo (USA)-Honourable Sheba (USA) (Roberto (USA)) 1477[17] 1870[3] 2695[10] (2957) 3591[2] 3741[8] 4176[17] 4372[8] **>78df<**
Ollie's Chuckle (IRE) 2 b c Mac's Imp (USA)-Chenya (Beldale Flutter (USA)) 2762[4] 3459[6] **>80f<**
Olympic Majesty (FR) 3 b c Law Society (USA)-Bella Senora (USA) (Northern Dancer) 1896a[2] **>106f<**
Omaha City (IRE) 3 b g Night Shift (USA)-Be Discreet (Junius (USA)) 679[11] 1212[5] 2023[9] 2526[7] 2861[6] 3189[3] 3214[6] (3764) 4003[6] 4240[10] 4423[14] 4777[14] **>97f<**
Omar's Odyssey (IRE) 2 ch c Sharifabad (IRE)-Tales Of Homer (Home Guard (USA)) 4603[13] 4910[7] **>46f<**
Ombra di Nube (FR) 2 gr ro f Bakharoff (USA)-Shamsha (FR) (Bold Lad (USA)) 3711[12] 4066[13] 4815[8] **>59f<**
On Call 2 gr f Alleged (USA)-Doctor Bid (USA) (Spectacular Bid (USA)) 4330[11] 4567[11] 4789[10] **>40f<**
Once More for Luck (IRE) 6 b g Petorius-Mrs Lucky (Royal Match) *(285)* 4521[11] (4692) 4896[4] **>68a 68f<**
One Dinar (FR) 2 b c Generous (IRE)-Lypharitissima (FR) (Lightning (FR)) 3598[14] 4157[13] **>42f<**
One Dream 4 b g Weldnaas (USA)-Superb Lady (Marcus Superbus) **1996:** *5273[4]* **1997:** *28[7]* **>34a 58f<**
One For Baileys 3 b c Unfuwain (USA)-Three Stars (Star Appeal) 445[4] (1230) 2596[7] 3974[11] 4704[5] **>80f<**
Oneforthe ditch (USA) 4 gr f With Approval (CAN)-Wee Dram (USA) (Nostrum (USA)) *(28) (140)* 1117[9] 4172[14] (4568) 4854[10] **>76a 74?f<**
Onefourseven 4 b g Jumbo Hirt (USA)-Dominance (Dominion) **1996:** *(5116)* **1997:** *400[4]* (442) 777[3] (1224) 2327[3] 3122[8] 4101[13] *(4481)* 4783[23] **>70a 86f<**
One In The Eye 4 br c Arrasas (USA)-Mingalles (Prince de Galles) **1996:** *5094[7]* **1997:** *22[7] 105[11]* 476[9] 587[6] 1632[11] 1779[11] 1968[13] 2246[3] 3329[3] 3496[9] 3971[8] 4465[3] 4899[13] **>39a 42f<**
Oneknight With You 3 gr f Rudimentary (USA)-Inshirah (USA) (Caro) 685[11] 1000[11] 1826[12] 3930[9] 4059[11] 4711[13] **>57f<**
One Life To Live (IRE) 4 gr c Classic Music (USA)-Fine Flame (Le Prince) 1231[4] 1838[W] 2030[2] 2342[5] 2660[9] *2910[9]* **>37a 58f<**
One Man Band (IRE) 6 ch g Chief Singer-Star Attention (Northfields (USA)) (353a) 354a[3] **>64f<**
Onemoretime 3 b f Timeless Times (USA)-Dear Glenda (Gold Song) 1451[6] 2313[18] 3038[9] 3266[10] 4455[12] **>19f<**
One Off the Rail (USA) 7 b h Rampage (USA)-Catty Queen (USA) (Tom Cat) *402[6] 486[2] 580[3] 908[2] 1152[2]* **>73a 46f<**
Oneoftheoldones 5 b g Deploy-Waveguide (Double Form) *72[10] 91[5] 206[5] 235[10] 284[10] 578[16]* 1024[8] 1395[6] 1800[7] 2340[10] 2876[10] **>52a 44f<**
One Singer 2 ch c Anshan-Moushka (Song) *(902)* (1126) 1310[2] 2103[6] 2762[3] 3222[2] 4173[7] 4468[5] *4589[2]* 4790[23] **>86a 92f<**
One So Wonderful 3 b f Nashwan (USA)-Someone Special (Habitat) (3913) (4557) **>122f<**
One To Go (IRE) 2 b g Petorius-Caroline's Mark (On Your Mark) 3060[8] 3819[6] 4209[9] 4508[11] 4922[4] 5029[2] **>63f<**
On Fair Stage (IRE) 4 b f Sadler's Wells (USA)-Fair Salinia (Petingo) 2989a[4] 3362a[3] **>101f<**
Only For Gold 2 b c Presidium-Calvanne Miss (Martinmas) (1026) (1684) *3610[4]* **>67a 84f<**
Only In Dreams 2 b f Polar Falcon (USA)-Dream Baby (Master Willie) 4332[9] 4564[3] (4694) **>79f<**
Only Josh (IRE) 3 gr g Waajib-Carlyle Suite (USA) (Icecapade (USA)) *230[4] 341[9] 387[3]* 535[18] 785[10] 995[11] 1467[21] *2368[13]* **>60a 38f<**
On Merit 3 b g Terimon-Onika (Great Nephew) 3319[6] 4331[W] **>3f<**
On The Green 4 br f Pharly (FR)-Regal Wonder (Stupendous) *173[6]* 686[10] 1501[12] 1965[5] 2317[4] 2730[12] 3100[2] 3448[3] 3718[8] 4228[17] (4843) **>49f<**
On The Mat 2 b c Reprimand-Secret Freedom (USA) (Secreto (USA)) 1396[12] 2022[6] 2477[10] 2752[2] 3307[10] 3869[9] **>63f<**
On The Piste 4 gr f Shirley Heights-Snowing (USA) (Icecapade (USA)) *173[5]* **>31a 76f<**
On The Right Side 2 b c Pursuit of Love-La Masse (High Top) 4739[8] 4914[4] **>85f<**
On The Wildside 4 ch f Charmer-No Control (Bustino) 481[8] 796[9] 881[7] 1001[11] 1229[9] 1809[12] **>41f<**
Oops Pettie 4 ch f Machiavellian (USA)-Miquette (FR) (Fabulous Dancer (USA)) 2028[11] 3492[7] 3722[4] 4151[16] 4891[4] (5044) **>99f<**
Oozlem (IRE) 8 b g Burslem-Fingers (Lord Gayle (USA)) **1996:** *5145[8] 5271[4]* **1997:** *104[3] 183[12] 236[4]* 2947[11] 3276[3] 3767[3] 4608[3] *5019[W]* **>48a 42f<**
Opalette 4 b f Sharrood (USA)-Height of Folly (Shirley Heights) 735[21] 1001[13] (1390) (1668) (2043) 2907[2] 3128[6] 4449[11] **>77f<**
Opaque 5 b g Shirley Heights-Opale (Busted) 465[8] 994[2] 1162[2] 1672[5] 2327[8] 3242[8] 3974[3] 4269[2] 4744[6] (5052) **>81f<**
Open Affair 4 ch f Bold Arrangement-Key to Enchantment (Key To Content (USA)) *205[7]* 435[17] 595[4] 1507[7] 1779[6] **>19a 55f<**
Open Air (GER) 3 b f Nebos (GER)-Oakville (GER) (Alpenkonig (GER)) 3005a[3] (5035a) **>104f<**
Open Credit 3 ch f Magical Wonder (USA)-Forest Treasure (USA) (Green Forest (USA)) 672[9] 3790[2] 4120[8] 4467[2] 4881[8] **>103f<**
Opening Meet 2 ch f Wolfhound (USA)-Carnival Spirit (Kris) 4227[2] **>78f<**
Opening Night 2 b g Theatrical Charmer-First Time Over (Derrylin) 4753[12] 4917[12] **>53f<**
Opening Range 6 b m Nordico (USA)-Waveguide (Double Form) *1433[11] 1790[5] 2305[2] (2674)* (3637) 3910[4] 4248[4] **>41a 48f<**
Opera Buff (IRE) 6 br g Rousillon (USA)-Obertura (USA) (Roberto (USA)) **1996:** *5091[5] 5120[9] 5205[3]* **1997:** *(100)* 430[10] *591[10] 858[8]* 1169[13] (1371) 1481[6] 2015[8] 2650[3] 3183[4] (3559) 3796[7] 4275[6] (4406) *4572[5]* 4860[3] **>84a 80f<**
Opera Fan (IRE) 5 b g Taufan (USA)-Shannon Lady (Monsanto (FR)) 1574[10] 2039[5] 2701[8] **>59?a 46f<**
Opera King (USA) 2 ch c Storm Bird (CAN)-Jewel In My Crown (CAN) (Secretariat (USA)) 2562[2] (3117) **>85f<**
Operatic 2 b f Goofalik (USA)-Choir Mistress (Chief Singer) 2840[11] *(3045)* 3212[2] **>54a 58f<**
Operatic Dancer 6 b g Germont-Indian Dancer (Streak) 1838[9] 2662[7] 2825[15] **>16f<**
Opopmil (IRE) 2 b f Pips Pride-Limpopo (Green Desert (USA)) *2066[3]* 2467[2] 3541[5] **>57+a 58f<**
Opportune (GER) 2 br c Shirley Heights-On The Tiles (Thatch (USA)) 2948[9] 3598[11] 3789[7] 4157[10] 4366[5] 4576[12] 4974[9] **>63f<**
Opposition Leader 2 b g Be My Chief (USA)-Seek the Pearl (Rainbow Quest (USA)) 695[4] 1251[3] (2196) 2688[9] 3904[5] 4605[2] 4875[7] **>78f<**
Ops Smile (USA) 5 5065a[7] **>117f<**
Optimistic 2 b f Reprimand-Arminda (Blakeney) 2597[11] (3099) (3650) 4119[7] **>81+f<**
Options Open 5 b h Then Again-Zahiah (So Blessed) (4260a) **>105f<**
Opulent 6 b g Robellino (USA)-One Half Silver (CAN) (Plugged Nickle (USA)) 955[7] 1313[5] 2293[2] (2465) 3066[6] **>85df<**
Orange And Blue 4 br f Prince Sabo-Mazarine Blue (Bellypha) *209[7] 233[9] 326[12]* **>32a 33f<**
Orange Bush (IRE) 2 ch g Pips Pride-Kew Gift (Faraway Son (USA)) 4747[5] **>56f<**
Orange Grouse (IRE) 4 b f Taufan (USA)-Winter Tern (USA) (Arctic Tern (USA)) 1062a[4] 2079a[5] 2447a[4] 4625a[2] 4834a[3] **>117f<**
Orange Jasmine (IRE) 3 b f Masterclass (USA)-La Mortola (Bold Lad (IRE)) 815a[2] 1368a[5] **>100f<**
Orange Order (IRE) 4 ch g Generous (IRE)-Fleur D'Oranger (Northfields (USA)) 1139[17] **>76df<**
Orange Place (IRE) 6 ch g Nordance (USA)-Little Red Hut (Habitat) 786[9] 1035[3] 1320[2] 1739[18] 2117[8] 3712[2] *4050[10]* 4219[3] 4410[17] *4913[13]* **>61a 82f<**
Orchestra Stall 5 b g Old Vic-Blue Brocade (Reform) 498[3] (891) 1454[7] (2456a) 3883a[2] (4130a) **>122+f<**
Ordained 4 b f Mtoto-In the Habit (USA) (Lyphard (USA)) 1313[3] 1623[2] 2763[3] 2889[6] 3035[4] 3412[4] 3694[4] 4063[9] 4435[4] 4598[2] 4886[2] (4971) 5051[9] **>51a 66f<**
Orfijar (FR) 7 dk b h In Fijar (USA)- 2821a[9] **>116f<**
Orford Ness (FR) 3 b f Selkirk (USA)-Nesaah (USA) (Topsider (USA)) (1727a) **>104f<**
Oriane 4 ch f Nashwan (USA)-Rappa Tap Tap (FR) (Tap On Wood) 4094a[7] **>107f<**
Oriel Girl 2 b f Beveled (USA)-St Helena (Monsanto (FR)) 447[5] 548[4] 1280[2] 1569[8] *1941[5]* 1990[3] 2165[3] (2412) (2823) 3209[5] 3483[2] 3571[4] (3699) 3866[2] 4178[10] 4500[6] **>38a 71df<**
Oriel Lad 4 b g Colmore Row-Consistent Queen (Queen's Hussar) **1996:** *5132[7]* **1997:** 896[13] 1127[12] *1291[14]* 1448[9] 1655[3] 1830[6] 2204[7] 2463[6] 2906[6] 3487[2] 3627[6] 3822[10] **>45a 46f<**
Oriole 4 b g Mazilier (USA)-Odilese (Mummy's Pet) *579[11]* 864[16] 1020[12] (1128) 1560[11] 1761[9] 3064[2] 3143[3] (3443) 3777[3] 4059[19] 4792[3] 4924[13] **>18a 56f<**
Orleans (IRE) 2 b g Scenic-Guest House (What A Guest) 3117[15] 4017[13] 4309[9] **>45f<**
Ornamental 2 b f Saddlers' Hall (IRE)-Hope and Glory (USA) (Well Decorated (USA)) 5048[17] **>30f<**
Orontes (USA) 3 b g Lomond (USA)-Chateau Princess (USA) (Majestic Prince (USA)) 1104[6] 1458[10] 2508[5] 3897[8] 4742[7] **>70f<**
Orsay 5 b h Royal Academy (USA)-Bellifontaine (FR) (Bellypha) 1308[3] 1606[2] (1934) 2528[4] 2710[17]

3424[3] 3773[11] 4141[16] **>87f<**

Orsetto (GER) 3 4531a[4] **>105f<**

Orsino 2 b g Theatrical Charmer-Sonoco (Song) 3490[5] 4145[5] 4379[5] **>81f<**

Orsuno (GER) 3 1544a[8] **>96f<**

Ortelius 3 b g Rudimentary (USA)-Third Movement (Music Boy) 853[9] 1320[14] 1811[13] 2005[10] 3591[3] 3798[12] 4179[16] 4505[3] 4568[14] **>75?f<**

Oscar (IRE) 3 b c Sadler's Wells (USA)-Snow Day (FR) (Reliance II) 1070a[2] 1726a[2] **>119f<**

Oscar Rose 4 b g Aragon-Mossy Rose (King of Spain) 1001[10] 1636[12] 1825[11] 2307[10] 2535[3] 3203[9] **>34f<**

Oscar Schindler (IRE) 5 ch h Royal Academy (USA)-Saraday (Northfields (USA)) 1542a[2] 1736[5] 3675a[3] (4346a) 4665a[4] 4965a[3] **>132f<**

Oscilights Gift 5 b m Chauve Souris-Oscilight (Swing Easy (USA)) **1996:** *5280[U]* **1997:** *65[6] 135[7]* **>13a 36f<**

Osomental 3 gr g Petong-Proper Madam (Mummy's Pet) 1410[12] 1946[8] 2347[9] 2708[16] 3923[5] **>67f<**

Oso Rich 2 b g Teenoso (USA)-Weareagrandmother (Prince Tenderfoot (USA)) 3789[9] 4014[13] **>36f<**

Otaiti (IRE) 5 b m Sadler's Wells (USA)-Ode (USA) (Lord Avie (USA)) 3370a[2] **>109f<**

Otto E Mezzo 5 bl g Persian Bold-Carolside (Music Maestro) 728[3] **>81f<**

Ouaisne 2 b c Warning-Noirmant (Dominion) (2127) 2639a[4] 3192[9] 3872a[4] **>97f<**

Our Dad's Lad 2 ch g Inchinor-Depeche (FR) (Kings Lake (USA)) 2587[13] **>44f<**

Our Drowsy Maggie 3 b f Puissance-Loadplan Lass (Nicholas Bill) *662[8]* 876[10] 4916[18] **>33f<**

Our Eddie 8 ch g Gabitat-Ragusa Girl (Morston (FR)) **1996:** *5094[6] 5145[4]* **1997:** *10[7] 76[5] 160[4] 213[5]* **>51a 21f<**

Our Emma 8 b m Precocious-Miller's Daughter (Mill Reef (USA)) *490[12]*

Our Future (IRE) 3 b g Imp Society (USA)-Petite Realm (Realm) *662[7] 1939[7]* 2888[5] **>14a 64f<**

Our Kevin 3 gr g Chilibang-Anse Chastanet (Cavo Doro) **1996:** *5113[8]* **1997:** *130[2] 168[4] 325[6] 362[5]* 477[16] *579[12]* 771[12] **>54da 41f<**

Our Kris 5 b g Kris-Our Reverie (USA) (J O Tobin (USA)) 632[7] **>73?f<**

Our Main Man 7 ch g Superlative-Ophrys (Nonoalco (USA)) **1996:** *5102[3] 5136[2] 5167[2] 5222[6]* **1997:** 2154[13] *(2365)* 2843[13] 3272[5] *4304[8]* **>63+a 35f<**

Our Molly Malone 2 ch f Deploy-Lady Clementine (He Loves Me) 3862[7] 4332[16] 4694[10] 4901[11] **>62f<**

Our People 3 ch g Indian Ridge-Fair and Wise (High Line) 1104[4] 1242[7] 1647[6] 3243[8] *3584[4]* 3937[13] 4436[11] **>65a 82f<**

Our Robert 5 b g Faustus (USA)-Duck Soup (Decoy Boy) *112[5]* **>60?a 68f<**

Our Shadee (USA) 7 b g Shadeed (USA)-Nuppence (Reform) **1996:** *5124[9] 5149[3] 5208[5] 5249[11]* **1997:** *20[7] 57[6] 105[3] 197[2] 238[5] 321[5] 349[8]* **>54a 58f<**

Our Tom 5 br g Petong-Boa (Mandrake Major) *91[10]* 1128[17] 1441[18] 2041[15] **>24a 22f<**

Our Way 3 ch f Forzando-Hanglands (Bustino) 723[14] 1131[7] (1500) 1973[4] 2331[7] 2772[6] 3128[10] **>77f<**

Out Like Magic 2 ch f Magic Ring (IRE)-Thevetia (Mummy's Pet) 432[4] (594) 730[2] 861[2] 1161[2] 1391[2] 2012[15] 2359[4] 2681[2] 2905[4] 3904[6] 5050[20] **>80f<**

Out Line 5 gr m Beveled (USA)-Free Range (Birdbrook) 518[6] 1012[9] 1166[9] (1453) 2119[4] (2665) 2833[5] 3615[9] 3982[12] 4518[2] 4820[8] **>74f<**

Out of Sight (IRE) 3 ch c Salse (USA)-Starr Danias (USA) (Sensitive Prince (USA)) 741[10] 847[4] (1175) 1404[4] **>85f<**

Out on a Promise (IRE) 5 b g Night Shift (USA)-Lovers' Parlour (Beldale Flutter (USA)) *23[8] 100[7]* 2030[7] 2503[3] **>44a 66f<**

Out On The Street (USA) 2 br c Known Fact (USA)-Fat To Fit (USA) (Fit To Fight (USA)) 4454[12] **>10f<**

Outset (IRE) 7 ch g Persian Bold-It's Now Or Never (High Line) (4794) (5027) **>74f<**

Outsourcing (USA) 2 ch c Alwuhush (USA)-Nice Dancing (USA) (Bering) 1607[7] 1839[2] 2562[4] 2768[2] 2953[2] (3750) **>85f<**

Outstayed Welcome 5 b g Be My Guest (USA)-Between Time (Elegant Air) *116[8] 381[2]* 789[14] **>56a 60f<**

Out West (USA) 3 br f Gone West (USA)-Chellingoua (USA) (Sharpen Up) (1326) 1740[3] 2338[4] **>107df<**

Over The Moon 3 ch f Beveled (USA)-Beyond the Moon (IRE) (Ballad Rock) **1996:** *5121[6]* **1997:** 1167[9] 1851[7] 2921[14] 3230[7] 3470[15] **>50a 46f<**

Over To You (USA) 3 ch c Rubiano (USA)-Overnight (USA) (Mr Leader (USA)) 688[7] 933[4] 1175[3] 2013[15] 2585[11] 3408[7] 4308[11] **>82f<**

Overture (IRE) 2 gr c Fairy King (USA)-Everything Nice (Sovereign Path) (1932) 2215[3] 2829[7] 3556[2] **>86f<**

Owdy 3 ch g Country Classic-Miami Pride (Miami Springs) 558[6] *1044[10]* 1247[8] 1807[12] **>29f<**

Oxalagu (GER) 5 gr h Lagunas-Oxalis (GER) (Ashmore (FR)) (719a) (1724a) (2459a) (3376a) **>122f<**

Oxbane 3 b f Soviet Star (USA)-Oxslip (Owen Dudley) 889[6] 1265[5] 2510[7] 2745[12] 3029[6] 3454[3] 4008[13] 4248[2] 4371[9] 4695[6] 4877[6] 4979[7] **>52f<**

P

Paarl Rock 2 ch c Common Grounds-Markievicz (IRE) (Doyoun) 3235[8] 3770[8] 4454[7] **>59+f<**

Pabella Bluebird (IRE) 2 b f Mac's Imp (USA)-Blue Diana (IRE) (Bluebird (USA)) 4159[11] 4428[8] 4630[13] 4921[16] **>42f<**

Pacajas (GER) 5 1073a[9] **>102f<**

Pacifica 2 b f Robellino (USA)-Pooh Wee (Music Boy) 500[2] (682) 1211[2] 2024[13] 3934[4] 4097[16] 4473[7] 4790[15] **>79f<**

Padauk 3 b c Warrshan (USA)-Free on Board (Free State) 676[17] 990[7] 1296[9] 1742[3] 1938[3] 2486[3] 3057[3] 3549[8] 4405[2] **>67a 73f<**

Paddy Deux 2 b c Perpendicular-Plie (Superlative) 4735[11] 4908[10] **>31f<**

Paddy Hurry 3 b g Silver Kite (USA)-Little Preston (IRE) (Pennine Walk) 771[13] 1487[7] 1689[13] *2319[5] 3054[4] 3413[11]* 4547[4] **>49a 69f<**

Paddy Lad (IRE) 3 b br c Anita's Prince-Lady of Man (So Blessed) 854[6] 968[5] 1609[10] 2185[3] 2691[10] 2939[4] **>26a 88df<**

Paddy McGoon (USA) 2 ch c Irish River (FR)-Flame McGoon (USA) (Staff Writer (USA)) 3047[7] 3862[11] **>60tf<**

Paddy's Rice 6 ch g Hadeer-Requiem (Song) 759[12] 1273[11] (1506) 1640[7] 2552[8] 2929[4] **>58f<**

Paetro (GER) 7 b h Acatenango (GER)-Palmas (GER) (Neckar) 3734a[3] **>89f<**

Pageboy 8 b g Tina's Pet-Edwin's Princess (Owen Dudley) *(48) 253[6] 2162[9]* 2563[11] 3130[8] 3484[8] 3761[16] 4249[8] *4482[11]* **>81a 58f<**

Paint It Black 4 ch g Double Schwartz-Tableaux (FR) (Welsh Pageant) *3[4] 40[8] 166[4] 233[5]* 468[17] (733) 848[16] 946[5] 1631[6] 1800[10] 1979[12] 2723[10] 2880[12] **>56a 49f<**

Pair of Jacks (IRE) 7 ch g Music Boy-Lobbino (Bustino) *13[3]* **>31a 31f<**

Pairumani Star (IRE) 2 ch c Caerleon (USA)-Dawn Star (High Line) 3861[9] 4165[6] 4413[6] **>68f<**

Palacegate Chief 4 b g Inca Chief (USA)-Sports Post Lady (IRE) (M Double M (USA)) *135[8]* **>16a 25f<**

Palacegate Jack (IRE) 6 gr g Neshad (USA)-Pasadena Lady (Captain James) **1996:** *5131[2] 5236[6]* **1997:** *58[4] 178[5] 545[6] 856[3]* 972[4] 1311[7] 1602[6] (1671) (2032) 2657[9] (2826) *3077[3]* 3816[9] *(4051)* 4365[13] 4791[4] *5018[2]* **>80a 73f<**

Palacegate Jo (IRE) 6 b m Drumalis-Welsh Rhyme (Welsh Term) *125[6] 169[7] 206[9] 245[7] 3074[8]* **>12a 20f<**

Palacegate Touch 7 gr g Petong-Dancing Chimes (London Bells (CAN)) 596[8] 698[3] 823[6] (972) 1158[10] (1572) 1937[3] 2339[5] (2472) 2711[19] 2939[2] 3195[3] (3378) 3566[6] 3900[8] 4221[8] 4414[7] 4770[5] *5021[2]* **>73a 79f<**

Palace River (IRE) 9 b m Dragon Palace (USA)-Rosebrook (Brother Birdbrook) 1838[7] 2207[P] **>35f<**

Palacoona (GER) 3 b f Last Tycoon-Palavera (Bikala) 921a[3] **>100f<**

Palaemon 3 b g Slip Anchor-Palace Street (USA) (Secreto (USA)) 1164[12] 1474[6] 1877[5] 3390[2] 3864[3] 4374[3] 4633[3] **>67f<**

Palamon (USA) 4 ch c Sanglamore (USA)-Gantlette (Run The Gantlet (USA)) 655[6] 789[11] 1092[6] 2139[10] 2373[2] 3559[4] **>81f<**

Palatial Style 10 b g Kampala-Stylish Princess (Prince Tenderfoot (USA)) 4102[8] 4294[7] 4558[11] 4854[6] **>85f<**

Paldost 3 b c Efisio-Fishki (Niniski (USA)) 1041[4] 1392[9] 2017[10] 2169[5] (2659) 2903[7] 3240[17] 3484[13] **>55df< (DEAD)**

Palio Sky 3 b c Niniski (USA)-Live Ammo (Home Guard (USA)) (505) (788) 2107[2] 3109[6] 3763[2] (4251a) 4661a[4] **>119+f<**

Palisade (USA) 3 b f Gone West (USA)-Peplum (USA) (Nijinsky (CAN)) 4226[4] 4669[7] **>85f<**

Palisander (IRE) 3 ch g Conquering Hero (USA)-Classic Choice (Patch) **1996:** *5090[7]* **1997:** 268a[9] 4009[7] *4913[11] 5022[4]* **>66a 56f<**

Pallium (IRE) 9 b g Try My Best (USA)-Jungle Gardenia (Nonoalco (USA)) 1602[4] 1613[3] 1835[6] 2033[7] 2111[6] 2382[2] 2540[2] (2657) 2826[4] 2900[7] 3484[11] 3856[13] 3871[2] 3922[5] 4233[16] 4707[5] 4770[6] 5047[11] **>51a 55f<**

Palme D'Or (IRE) 3 b f Sadler's Wells (USA)-Pampa Bella (FR) (Armos (FR)) 1916a[10] (5031a) **>116f<**

Palmetto Bay (IRE) 2 b c Royal Academy (USA)-Surmise (USA) (Alleged (USA)) 3022[4] 3780[3] 4502[3] 4747[6] **>79f<**

Palo Blanco 6 b m Precocious-Linpac Mapleleaf (Dominion) 977[5] 1127[2] 1439[7] 1662[2] 2119[2] 2280[3] *2603[6]* 2918[8] *3584[13]* 3982[8] (4221) 4456[14] 4636[5] 5047[2] **>54a 76f<**

Pamela's Boy 3 ch c Clantime-Allez-Oops (Moulin) *6[10] 41[6] 90[12]* **>15a f<**

Pampasa (FR) 3 br f Pampabird-Dounasa (FR) (Kaldoun (FR)) 2228[11] **>55f<**

Panama City (USA) 3 b c El Gran Senor (USA)-Obeah (Cure The Blues (USA)) 691[2] (1015) 1553a[3] 2107[4] 3596[2] 4149[6] **>118f<**

Panama House 2 ch c Rudimentary (USA)-Lustrous (Golden Act (USA)) 1801[2] 2202[2] 2842[2] 3060[2] (3458) 3802[13] 4116[16] (4875) **>81f<**

Panooras Lord (IRE) 3 b c Topanoora-Ladyship (Windjammer (USA)) **1996:** *5098[8]* **>30a 43f<**

Panorama 3 b f Shirley Heights-Lycia (USA) (Lyphard (USA)) 3419[9] 3720[5] 4378[10] **>58f<**

Pantar (IRE) 2 b c Shirley Heights-Spring Daffodil (Pharly (FR)) 4237^{13} 4474^{7} **>80f<**

Panther (IRE) 7 ch g Primo Dominie-High Profile (High Top) *134^{8} 159^{8}* 2480^{8} 2651^{W} 2788^{14} 3034^{7} 3287^{7} 3378^{3} 3702^{4} 3936^{7} 4016^{6} 4385^{14} 4844^{15} **>50da 53f<**

Panthere (GER) 3 f 1918a^{6} **>90f<**

Panto Queen 6 b m Lepanto (GER)-Tyqueen (Tycoon II) *369^{12}* **>34a 55df<**

Papering (IRE) 4 b f Shaadi (USA)-Wrapping (Kris) (1157) 2099a^{2} 3216^{3} 3704^{5} (4131a) (4535a) **>121+f<**

Paperwork Pete (IRE) 5 b g Kahyasi-Palitana (Nonoalco (USA)) 1570^{9} 1798^{9} 2128^{6} 2531^{10} 2880^{10} **>24f<**

Papita (IRE) 3 b f Law Society (USA)-Fantasise (FR) (General Assembly (USA)) 506^{6} 694^{8} 1141^{21} 2220^{8} 2390^{7} 2730^{6} 2907^{3} 3080^{7} **>66df<**

Pappa Reale 4 ch f Indian Ridge-Daffodil Fields (Try My Best (USA)) (2102a) **>99f<**

Papua 3 ch g Green Dancer (USA)-Fairy Tern (Mill Reef (USA)) 508^{3} 788^{2} 1103^{4} 1769^{13} 2765^{3} 3190^{16} 3648^{9} 4476^{6} 4754^{5} **>95f<**

Paradise Navy 8 b g Slip Anchor-Ivory Waltz (USA) (Sir Ivor) **1996:** *5167^{4}* **1997:** *419^{4}* (769) 1114^{6} 1424^{3} 1654^{3} 1953^{3} 2198^{8} 2702^{6} 3010^{10} (3141) *3415^{5}* (3719) 3915^{10} 3974^{13} *4302^{6} 4590^{4}* 4713^{4} (4946) **>75a 80?f<**

Paradise Soul (USA) 2 b f Dynaformer (USA)-River Valley (FR) (Riverman (USA)) 3979^{13} 4413^{3} 4582^{3} **>77f<**

Pardan 3 b g Pharly (FR)-Silent Pool (Relkino) 1144^{10} 1477^{8} 1804^{5} 2722^{8} 3285^{8} *3581^{8}* 4043^{10} 4431^{3} *4809^{12}* **>28a 54f<**

Parellie 4 b f Inca Chief (USA)-Parklands Belle (Stanford) **1996:** *5140^{8}* **1997:** *3^{11}* 1925^{14} **>14a f<**

Parfait Glace (FR) 5 b h Pampabird-Star System 3996a^{2} 4660a^{8} 5059a^{3} **>111f<**

Parijazz (IRE) 3 b f Astronef-Brandywell (Skyliner) 649^{17} *871^{13}* 1167^{7} 2192^{6} 3249^{11} 3637^{10} **>28a 43df<**

Pariofige (USA) 3 1553a^{14} **>88f<**

Paris Babe 5 b m Teenoso (USA)-Kala's Image (Kala Shikari) 1634^{4} 2105^{29} (2575) **>83+f<**

Parish Walk (IRE) 6 ch g Pennine Walk-Baby Caroline (Martin John) 3467^{9} **>5a 49?f<**

Parisian Lady (IRE) 2 b f Paris House-Mia Gigi (Hard Fought) (1821) (2697) 3422^{4} 3934^{2} 4555^{8} **>93+f<**

Parklife (IRE) 5 ch g Double Schwartz-Silk Trade (Auction Ring (USA)) *(16) 101^{6} 167^{6} 272^{5}* **>45a 49f<**

Parlez Moi d'Amour (IRE) 2 gr f Precocious-Normanby Lass (Bustino) 1997^{11} *3072^{5}* **>39a 39f<**

Paronomasia 5 b g Precocious-The Crying Game (Manor Farm Boy) **1996:** *5094^{2} 5123^{2} 5175^{13} 5247^{10}* **1997:** *226^{9} 352^{5} 566^{2}* 1503^{9} **>50a 32f<**

Parrot's Hill (IRE) 4 b g Nashamaa-Cryptic Gold (Glint of Gold) 430^{6} 4794^{7} **>47f<**

Parsa (USA) 4 b f Risen Star (USA)-Pallanza (USA) (Lyphard (USA)) 864^{8} 1116^{10} *3609^{5}* 3980^{12} 4741^{7} 4991^{7} **>29a 45f<**

Particular Friend 2 ch f Cadeaux Genereux-Pamela Peach (Habitat) 2840^{2} 3422^{5} **>82f<**

Party Romance (USA) 3 gr c Black Tie Affair-Tia Juanita (USA) (My Gallant (USA)) 676^{12} 1017^{15} (1558) 1747^{2} 2058^{7} 2585^{13} (3061) 3575^{8} 4102^{4} **>96f<**

Pas de Memoires (IRE) 2 b c Don't Forget Me-Bally Pourri (IRE) (Law Society (USA)) 4236^{9} 4638^{14} 4814^{6} 4994^{2} **>72f<**

Pas De Reponse (USA) 3 b f Danzig (USA)-Soundings (USA) (Mr Prospector (USA)) (718a) 960^{4} (4001a) 4664a^{2} *5061a^{11}* **>81a 122f<**

Pasolini 6 b h Cagliostro-Passeggiata (USA) (Elocutionist (USA)) (4123a) **>114f<**

Passage Creeping (IRE) 4 b f Persian Bold-Tiptoe (Dance In Time (CAN)) **1996:** *5122^{2} 5253^{2}* **1997:** *108^{3} 173^{2} 305^{8}* 1373^{3} 1668^{2} 1968^{12} 3081^{3} 3432^{11} 4858^{17} **>57a 48f<**

Passi d'Orlando (IRE) 3 ch c Persian Bold-When Lit (Northfields (USA)) 1399^{5} 2101a^{2} 2462a^{5} **>104f<**

Passiflora 3 ch f Night Shift (USA)-Pineapple (Superlative) 675^{18} 958^{14} 1458^{11} 1928^{4} **>63f<**

Passing Strangers (USA) 4 b g Lyphard (USA)-The Way We Were (USA) (Avatar (USA)) 553^{6} 1393^{6} 2199^{2} (2843) 3183^{2} 3475^{8} 4409^{5} 4568^{2} 4802^{5} **>73f<**

Passion 3 ch f Risk Me (FR)-Gotcher (Jalmood (USA)) 3850^{5} *4795^{11} 4906^{7}* **>37a 58?f<**

Passionatti 3 b f Emarati (USA)-Ration of Passion (Camden Town) 3606^{10} *4051^{10}* 4214^{6} (4431) 4527^{3} 4770^{3} *5018^{5}* **>53a 70f<**

Passionelle 3 b f Nashwan (USA)-Height of Passion (Shirley Heights) 2360^{4} 2568^{6} **>61f<**

Passion For Life 4 br g Charmer-Party Game (Red Alert) 452^{6} 811a^{7} 1721a^{8} 2289^{11} 3011^{10} 4062^{4} 4282^{23} 4457^{5} **>97f<**

Pass The Rest (IRE) 2 b c Shalford (IRE)-Brown Foam (Horage) 4735^{2} 4925^{3} 5040^{4} **>80f<**

Pasternak 4 b c Soviet Star (USA)-Princess Pati (Top Ville) (2710) (4558) **>106+f<**

Pastiche 3 b f Kylian (USA)-Titian Beauty (Auction Ring (USA)) **1996:** *5243^{4}* **1997:** *(185) 264^{4}* 1139^{5} 1464^{8} 4448^{11} **>61a 53f<**

Past Master (USA) 9 b g Chief's Crown (USA)-Passing Look (USA) (Buckpasser) *231^{8}*

Pater Noster (USA) 8 b h Stately Don (USA)-Sainera (USA) (Stop The Music (USA)) *82^{6} 179^{3} 220^{4} 344^{2} 396^{3}* 450^{24} 832^{8} 974^{4} 1300^{9} 1473^{6} **>93a 90df<**

Pathaze 4 b f Totem (USA)-Stilvella (Camden Town) 901^{8} *1046^{9}* 1332^{9} 1734^{7} 1828^{2} 3285^{12} 3406^{10} 3625^{11} 3761^{6} 3922^{10} 4168^{2} 4707^{15} **>34a 43f<**

Patiala (IRE) 4 b f Nashwan (USA)-Catherine Parr (USA) (Riverman (USA)) **1996:** *5091^{9} 5139^{6}* **1997:** *13^{11}* **>29a 28f<**

Patina 3 ch f Rudimentary (USA)-Appledorn (Doulab (USA)) **1996:** *5103^{3} 5207^{3}* **1997:** *19^{2} 60^{7} 420^{3} 547^{5} 590^{4} 1580^{5}* 1963^{6} 2317^{14} 2554^{7} 3268^{3} 3454^{9} 4846^{4} **>56a 58f<**

Patricia Olive (IRE) 2 ch f Case Law-My Special Guest (IRE) (Be My Guest (USA)) 999^{5} 1447^{4} 1821^{6} 2031^{2} 2587^{12} 2786^{7} 3289^{3} 3692^{3} 4058^{5} 4753^{18} 4856^{5} **>58f<**

Patricius 2 b f Noble Patriarch-Bad Payer (Tanfirion) 1466^{11} **>16f< (DEAD)**

Patrick 3 b g Backchat (USA)-Girton Degree (Balliol) *90^{9} 230^{9} 425^{9}* 480^{6} 582^{9} 644^{4} 4043^{8} 4180^{7} **>21a 57df<**

Patriot Games (IRE) 3 b c Polish Patriot (USA)-It's Now Or Never (High Line) 683^{6} 991^{6} (1234) 2528^{2} 3190^{11} 3916^{3} 4320^{4} 4639^{6} **>92f<**

Patrita Park 3 br f Flying Tyke-Bellinote (FR) (Noir Et Or) **1996:** *5113^{11} 5202^{5}* **1997:** 882^{9} 1115^{8} 3240^{21} 3971^{11} 4548^{8} **>44a 44f<**

Pat Said No (IRE) 3 b f Last Tycoon-Fiddle-Faddle (Silly Season) 693^{10} 1859^{10} 2945^{13} **>43f<**

Pat's Splendour 6 b m Primitive Rising (USA)-Northern Venture **1996:** *5148^{12}* **>37a 53f<**

Patsy Culsyth 2 b f Tragic Role (USA)-Regal Salute (Dara Monarch) 828^{6} 979^{6} *1137^{5}* 1569^{2} 1860^{2} 2736^{5} 3062^{2} 3247^{4} (3544) 3804^{3} 4014^{8} 4230^{2} **>16a 69f<**

Patsy Grimes 7 b m Beveled (USA)-Blue Angel (Lord Gayle (USA)) 452^{4} 519^{6} 1160^{10} 2105^{16} 2447a^{8} 3185^{6} 3580^{5} 3771^{2} 3914^{2} 4100^{11} 4239^{12} (4434) 4553^{8} 4677^{3} 4881^{7} 4954^{10} **>70a 94f<**

Payaso 3 b g Midyan (USA)-Sugar Plum Fairy (Sadler's Wells (USA)) 3632^{12} 3848^{11}

Pay Homage 9 ch g Primo Dominie-Embraceable Slew (USA) (Seattle Slew (USA)) 430^{15} 657^{3} 735^{10} 1001^{5} 1244^{18} 1588^{6} 1805^{2} 2464^{3} 2696^{6} (2928) 3245^{5} 3475^{4} 4109^{12} 4516^{12} **>75f<**

Pay Me Back (IRE) 7 ch h Master Willie-Princess Reema (USA) (Affirmed (USA)) 1549a^{4} 4131a^{3} **>118f<**

Pay On Red (USA) 2 br c Red Ransom (USA)-Mo Jo Kate (USA) (Mr Leader (USA)) 2336^{7} 2680^{5} 3613^{3} 3802^{5} 4670^{3} **>78f<**

Pc's Cruiser (IRE) 5 b g Homo Sapien-Ivy Holme (Silly Season) **1996:** *5179^{10}* **1997:** *123^{11} 870^{5}* 1024^{15} *1287^{4} 1576^{5} 1944^{11} 2070^{4} 2603^{5} 3041^{7}* 3276^{4} **>47a 41f<**

Peace And Quiet 3 ch f Niniski (USA)-Quiet Harbour (Mill Reef (USA)) 2555^{5} **>54f<**

Peacefull Reply (USA) 7 b h Hold Your Peace (USA)-Drone Answer (USA) (Drone) **1996:** *5110^{10} 5234^{6} 5258^{5}* **1997:** *297^{8}* 2938^{7} 3269^{10} **>45da 33f<**

Peaceful Reign 2 ch g King's Signet (USA)-Consistent Queen (Queen's Hussar) 2288^{12} **>28f<**

Peaceful Sarah 2 b f Sharpo-Red Gloves (Red God) 4544^{12} 4752^{4} 4966^{7} **>61f<**

Peak Path (IRE) 2 b c Polish Precedent (USA)-Road To The Top (Shirley Heights) 4174^{3} **>78+f<**

Pearl Dawn (IRE) 7 b m Jareer (USA)-Spy Girl (Tanfirion) 638^{5} 755^{10} 1009^{8} *1086^{12}* 1236^{2} 1373^{10} 1479^{5} 1814^{8} 1965^{6} 2724^{3} 2745^{6} 2954^{5} 3082^{12} 3561^{3} 3848^{3} **>41?a 58f<**

Pearl Silk 4 br f Cigar-Purrlea Atoll (Gulf Pearl) 2783^{9} 3335^{5} *3611^{7}* **>28a 15f<**

Pearl Venture 5 b m Salse (USA)-Our Shirley (Shirley Heights) 746^{4} **>78f<**

Pearly Queen 2 ch f Superlative-Miss Kimmy (Tower Walk) 3613^{14}

Peartree House (IRE) 3 b c Simply Majestic (USA)-Fashion Front (Habitat) 723^{2} (973) 1541a^{9} 2023^{6} 2761^{5} 3150^{20} 3766^{3} 4292^{4} **>103f<**

Peatsville (IRE) 5 b g Ela-Mana-Mou-Windy Cheyenne (USA) (Tumble Wind (USA)) **1996:** *5185^{12}* **>7a 46f<**

Pecan Princess (IRE) 4 b f Prince Rupert (FR)-Route Royale (Roi Soleil) 896^{21}

Peckinpah's Soul (FR) 5 b h Zino-Nashra (Brustolon) **1996:** 5126a^{2} **1997:** (267a) (310a) **>118f<**

Pedaltothemetal (IRE) 5 b m Nordico (USA)-Full Choke (Shirley Heights) *78^{2} 167^{12}* **>56a 55df<**

Pedro (IRE) 2 b c Brief Truce (USA)-Mrs Fisher (IRE) (Salmon Leap (USA)) 4061^{9} *(4299) 4589^{5}* **>78a 68f<**

Peep O Day 6 b m Domynsky-Betrothed (Aglojo) **1996:** *5136^{11}* **1997:** 3108^{9} 3919^{8} 4768^{6} 5028^{5} **>32f<**

Peetsie (IRE) 5 b m Fairy King (USA)-Burning Ambition (Troy) **1996:** *5186^{7} 5233^{8}* **>54a 60f<**

Pegasus Bay 6 b g Tina's Pet-Mossberry Fair (Mossberry) 3469^{2} 3814^{3} 4114^{5} (4224) 4453^{2} *(4913) 5022^{5}* **>70a 63f<**

Peggy Lane (FR) 3 f 3998b^{3} **>87f<**

Pegnitz (USA) 2 b c Lear Fan (USA)-Likely Split (USA) (Little Current (USA)) 4439^{2} 4784^{5} **>100?f<**

Peintre Celebre (USA) 3 ch c Nureyev (USA)-Peinture Bleue (USA) (Alydar (USA)) (819a) (1726a) (2274a) 4257a^{2} (4665a) **>141f<**

Pekay 4 b g Puissance-K-Sera (Lord Gayle (USA)) *1123^{7}* 1248^{3} 1459^{5} (1615) 1652^{3} 1862^{2} 2660^{6}

3453^{2} 3630^{2} 3921^{10} 4210^{17} 4635^{4} (4691) 4788^{4} 4891^{3} **>44a 78f<**

Pelagius (IRE) 2 gr g Kenmare (FR)-Pallas's Blue (Pitskelly) 3672a^{5} 3961a^{15} **>80f<**

Pelagos (FR) 2 gr c Exit To Nowhere (USA)-Southern Maid (USA) (Northern Dancer) 4237^{6} 4715^{6} **>71f<**

Pelham (IRE) 3 b c Archway (IRE)-Yavarro (Raga Navarro (ITY)) 449^{6} (508) 692^{6} **>106f<**

Pemberley (IRE) 3 b g Taufan (USA)-Miss Darcy (IRE) (Glow (USA)) 2059^{6} 2392^{6} 2591^{10} 3234^{14} 3601^{15} **>45f<**

Penalty (GER) 3 2642a^{7} 4661a^{7} **>106f<**

Pendolino (IRE) 6 b g Thatching-Pendulina (Prince Tenderfoot (USA)) 461^{3} (595) (689) 838^{17} **>54f<**

Pen Friend 3 b g Robellino (USA)-Nibbs Point (IRE) (Sure Blade (USA)) 479^{6} 586^{15} *1939^{6}* 2667^{4} (2908) 3096^{3} (3461) 3826^{4} 4509^{2} **>15a 60f<**

Pengamon 5 b h Efisio-Dolly Bevan (Another Realm) *316^{10} 661^{7}* 677^{9} *(1082) 1154^{3}* 1935^{8} 2124^{8} 2390^{6} 2922^{9} **>84a 76df<**

Penlop 3 b g Mac's Imp (USA)-Marton Maid (Silly Season) 473^{8} 532^{7} 752^{5} *903^{3} (1044)* 1217^{4} 4139^{10} *4485^{8}* 4696^{4} **>60a 64f<**

Penniless (IRE) 2 b f Common Grounds-Tizzy (Formidable (USA)) 594^{4} (730) 1013^{7} 1253^{3} (1829) 2712^{6} 2904^{5} 4885^{14} 4989^{13} **>74f<**

Penny Peppermint 5 b br m Move Off-Cheeky Pigeon (Brave Invader (USA)) 898^{6} 1585^{6} 1996^{8} 2207^{3} 3461^{6} 3567^{4} 3858^{2} 3935^{4} **>35f<**

Pennys From Heaven 3 gr c Generous (IRE)-Heavenly Cause (USA) (Grey Dawn II) 523^{4} 1296^{4} 1868^{3} 2379^{5} 2897^{3} 3137^{7} (3475) 4144^{2} 4372^{6} 4699^{10} **>86f<**

Penny's Wishing 5 b m Clantime-Lady Pennington (Blue Cashmere) **1996:** *5112^{13}* **>9a 19f<**

Pennywell 3 b f Nicholas (USA)-Fee (Mandamus) *255^{2} (341)* 431^{12} 535^{2} 886^{6} *(1969) 2303^{3}* **>71a 71f<**

Penny Whistle 2 b f Clantime-Penny Hasset (Lochnager) 3239^{8} 4012^{21} 4230^{10} **>61f<**

Penrose (IRE) 2 ch f Wolfhound (USA)-Mill Path (Mill Reef (USA)) 4066^{5} **>77+f<**

Pension Fund 3 b g Emperor Fountain-Navarino Bay (Averof) 699^{9} 840^{18} 1117^{8} 1256^{8} 1472^{14} 2130^{2} 2238^{2} 2340^{7} 2715^{8} 3441^{2} (3478) 3722^{2} **>87f<**

Pentad (USA) 3 b c Quest for Fame-Nifty Fifty (USA) (Honey Jay (USA)) 725^{4} (2311) 2837^{2} (3763) 4658a^{6} 4894^{5} **>120f<**

Pentire 5 b h Be My Guest (USA)-Gull Nook (Mill Reef (USA)) **1996:** 5159a^{8} **>122a 132+f<**

Penygarn Guv'nor 4 b g Governor General-Alumia (Great Nephew) 3213^{10} **>45a 39?f<**

People Direct 4 ch f Ron's Victory (USA)-Ayr Classic (Local Suitor (USA)) *589^{11} 857^{10} 1135^{8} 1786^{10} (2160) 2368^{2} (2672) 2913^{10}* 3254^{9} *3608^{10}* **>57a 43f<**

Peppers (IRE) 4 b f Bluebird (USA)-Pepilin (Coquelin (USA)) 647^{3} 887^{2} 1244^{4} 1811^{6} 2195^{5} 2421^{2} 2928^{3} 3291^{4} 3855^{7} 4268^{5} **>49a 67f<**

Peppiatt 3 ch c Efisio-Fleur du Val (Valiyar) (768) 2229^{2} (2691) **>85f<**

Perang Polly 5 br m Green Ruby (USA)-Perang Peggy (Bay Express) **1996:** *5182^{P}* **1997:** *215^{2} 306^{3}* 864^{7} 1388^{8} **>51a 47f<**

Perchance To Dream (IRE) 3 b f Bluebird (USA)-Foliage (Thatching) 1279^{17} 1848^{12} 2231^{7} 2555^{7} 2730^{7} 3095^{6} **>54f<**

Percutant 6 br h Perrault-Estada (FR) (Luthier) 3880a^{3} **>126f<**

Percy 2 ch g Precocious-Manna Green (Bustino) 1819^{7} 2467^{7} 2706^{10} *3076^{3} 3395^{7}* 4595^{6} *4812^{2}* **>62a 48f< (DEAD)**

Percy Isle (IRE) 3 br c Doyoun-Percy's Girl (IRE) (Blakeney) 732^{2} (967) 1242^{3} 2142^{2} 2767^{5} 3333^{3} 3498^{5} **>90f<**

Percy-P 2 ch c Superpower-Song's Best (Never so Bold) 500^{5} 1163^{3} **>76f<**

Perecapa (IRE) 2 b f Archway (IRE)-Cupid Miss (Anita's Prince) *3072^{6}* 3450^{15} **>21a 35f<**

Perfect Angel (IRE) 3 b f Maledetto (IRE)-Blue Infanta (Chief Singer) *1138^{12}* 1390^{13} 1503^{11} **>9a 23f<**

Perfect Bear 3 b g Wing Park-Sarah Bear (Mansingh (USA)) 2420^{9} 3037^{10} 3601^{12} **>39f<**

Perfect Bertie (IRE) 5 b g Cyrano de Bergerac-Perfect Chance (Petorius) 2531^{12} 3015^{5} 3929^{8} **>44f<**

Perfect Brave 6 b g Indian Ridge-Perfect Timing (Comedy Star (USA)) **1996:** *5131^{17}* **1997:** *515^{5} 659^{2} 856^{8} 905^{5} 1942^{7} 2366^{9}* 2480^{5} *3077^{10}* **>57a 57f<**

Perfect Harmony (IRE) 2 b f Pips Pride-Harmer (IRE) (Alzao (USA)) 2227^{2} 2356^{3} 4042^{13} 4702^{9} 4897^{B} **>78f<**

Perfect Lady 2 gr f Petong-Petit Peu (IRE) (Kings Lake (USA)) 4332^{17} 4567^{12} **>21f<**

Perfect Pal (IRE) 6 ch g Mulhollande (USA)-Gone (Whistling Wind) *73^{10}* 1088^{2} 1237^{4} 1489^{14} 3138^{5} 3437^{5} **>24a 76f<**

Perfect Paradigm (IRE) 3 b c Alzao (USA)-Brilleaux (Manado) (528) (1025) 1726a^{13} **>107f<**

Perfect Peach 2 b f Lycius (USA)-Perfect Timing (Comedy Star (USA)) 2356^{6} 2762^{2} (3239) (3480) 3823^{5} **>78f<**

Perfect Poppy 3 b f Shareef Dancer (USA)-Benazir (High Top) *387^{6}* 749^{7} 1009^{6} 1219^{3} 1680^{8} 2317^{13} 3591^{5} 4008^{6} 4404^{11} **>42a 61f<**

Perfect Vintage 7 b h Shirley Heights-Fair Salinia (Petingo) 4530a^{2} **>104f<**

Perfect Way 2 b c Norton Challenger-Russet Way (Blushing Scribe (USA)) 4064^{17} 4627^{16} **>29f<**

Periannath (GER) 4 c 4661a^{P}

Pericles 3 b g Primo Dominie-Egalite (FR) (Luthier) 835^{11} 1170^{18} (1958) 2149^{2} *(2303)* 2708^{13} *3075^{16}* 3443^{4} 3777^{2} 3801^{13} 3987^{8} 4270^{3} *4482^{5} (4570)* 4757^{9} *4983^{11}* **>91a 82f<**

Peridot 2 b f Green Desert (USA)-Alinova (USA) (Alleged (USA)) 4909^{10} **>45f<**

Perilous Plight 6 ch g Siberian Express (USA)-Loveskate (USA) (Overskate (CAN)) **1996:** *5089^{6} 5215^{12}* **1997:** *146^{6} 201^{4} 383^{3}* 477^{8} 571^{7} 823^{9} 1603^{11} 1830^{13} 3691^{9} *4069^{12}* **>62da 35f<**

Perim (FR) 4 b c Apeldoorn (FR)-Pear of Dawn (FR) (Noir Et Or) (1914a) **>115f<**

Perla Nera (IRE) 3 f 815a^{16} **>48f<**

Perlethorpe 3 b f Anshan-Naturally Fresh (Thatching) 4854 681^{10} 1237^{11} 2521^{9} 2725^{4} *3074^{2}* 3210^{4} 3643^{2} 3858^{3} 4519^{9} **>60a 59f<**

Perpetual Light 4 b f Petoski-Butosky (Busted) *72^{6} 244^{4}* 3316^{8} 4235^{17} *(4571)* 4695^{7} 4991^{6} **>69a 43f<**

Perryston View 5 b h Primo Dominie-Eastern Ember (Indian King (USA)) (942) 2105^{20} 3273^{10} 3649^{8} (4280) 4887^{2} **>98f<**

Persephone 4 ch f Lycius (USA)-Elarrih (USA) (Sharpen Up) 1020^{15} 1116^{13} 1501^{9} 1796^{9} 2121^{9} 2785^{7} 3321^{8} 3565^{13} 4184^{14} 4850^{7} **>31f<**

Persevere 3 b f Pursuit of Love-Seastream (USA) (Alleged (USA)) 1110^{3} *1787^{4}* 4047^{4} 4700^{9} 4958^{15} **>57a 68df<**

Pershex (IRE) 5 ch m Persian Heights-Hexton (IRE) (Be My Guest (USA)) 4763a^{3} **>94f<**

Persian Blue 3 b f Persian Bold-Swift Pursuit (Posse (USA)) 885^{7} 1168^{7} 1465^{3} 1938^{10} 3234^{8} 3495^{3} 3970^{7} 4821^{13} **>69f<**

Persian Bud (IRE) 9 b or br g Persian Bold-Awakening Rose (Le Levanstell) *43^{4} 78^{5} 139^{7} 262^{5}* **>37a 43?f<**

Persian Butterfly 5 b m Dancing Dissident (USA)-Butterfly Kiss (Beldale Flutter (USA)) *340^{7}* 1809^{7} 2199^{6} **>17a 50f<**

Persian Conquest (IRE) 5 b g Don't Forget Me-Alaroos (IRE) (Persian Bold) **1996:** *5091^{6} (5149) 5222^{9} 5276^{3}* **1997:** *(93) (129) 219^{2} (302)* **>69a 55f<**

Persian Dawn 4 br f Anshan-Visible Form (Formidable (USA)) 1441^{15} *2070^{11}* 2228^{3} 2646^{17} 2947^{9} **>4a 51df<**

Persian Fantasia 2 b f Alzao (USA)-Persian Fantasy (Persian Bold) 1927^{8} **>33f<**

Persian Fayre 5 b g Persian Heights-Dominion Fayre (Dominion) *398^{13}* 529^{15} 892^{12} 1397^{2} 1874^{4} 2325^{7} 2708^{W} 2857^{2} 3403^{2} 4282^{18} 4787^{17} 4978^{6} **>93f<**

Persian Fortune 2 b f Forzando-Persian Air (Persian Bold) 999^{8} *(1137)* 1504^{4} 1952^{5} 2378^{2} 2741^{3} *3076^{2} 3395^{10}* 3924^{3} 4044^{14} **>59a 55f<**

Persiano 2 ch c Efisio-Persiandale (Persian Bold) 3986^{5} 4167^{10} 4564^{4} 4755^{4} **>74f<**

Persian Punch (IRE) 4 ch g Persian Heights-Rum Cay (USA) (Our Native (USA)) 932^{7} (1241) (1454) 2055^{12} 3149^{5} 3883a^{5} 4118^{2} 4346a^{2} 4654a^{3} **>128f<**

Persian Sabre 2 b f Sabrehill (USA)-Wassl's Sister (Troy) 1593^{5} 2862^{20} 3636^{6} 3926^{6} 4815^{7} **>61f<**

Persian Sunset (IRE) 5 b m Persian Mews-Fifth Gear (Red Sunset) *424^{10}* 463^{6} *511^{6}* 1246^{4} 1445^{14} 1683^{14} 1798^{6} *2602^{13}* 2887^{8} 3116^{4} **>35a 42f<**

Persian Venture 2 b c Midyan (USA)-Scharade (Lombard (GER)) 1812^{16} 2196^{6} 2741^{4} 3215^{10} 3911^{2} 4068^{12} **>67f<**

Persica 4 b f Persian Bold-Nadina (Shirley Heights) 2557^{19} **>61f<**

Personal Best (IRE) 3 ch f Kris-Penultimate (USA) (Roberto (USA)) 4962a^{2} **>97f<**

Persuasion 4 b f Batshoof-Primetta (Precocious) **1996:** *(5101)* **1997:** *(163) 283^{4}* **>80+a 55f<**

Pertemps Mission 3 b c Safawan-Heresheis (Free State) 670^{8} 1299^{10} 2908^{15} **>53f<**

Petaling (IRE) 2 b f Petardia-Lyphards Goddess (IRE) (Lyphard's Special (USA)) 1163^{8} 1827^{7} 2489^{2} 2943^{6} 3468^{7} 3859^{3} 4819^{7} **>51a 56f<**

Petane (IRE) 2 b c Petardia-Senane (Vitiges (FR)) 2509^{9} 2893^{W} 3278^{8} 3686^{14} 4778^{10} **>63f<**

Petara (IRE) 2 ch c Petardia-Romangoddess (IRE) (Rhoman Rule (USA)) 1076^{6} 1267^{4} 1760^{13} 2018^{3} 2499^{7} 2936^{5} 3212^{3} 3545^{10} (4285) 4588^{3} 4767^{5} 4994^{10} **>66f<**

Petarga 2 b f Petong-One Half Silver (CAN) (Plugged Nickle (USA)) 1213^{4} 1564^{2} (1954) 2862^{7} 3774^{8} **>78f<**

Petaz 3 b br f Petong-Tasmim (Be My Guest (USA)) 1671^{7} 2045^{10} 2156^{10} **>36f<**

Peter Perfect 3 gr g Chilibang-Misdevious (USA) (Alleged (USA)) **1996:** *5083^{3}* **1997:** 1012^{14} 1485^{7} 1666^{2} 1931^{6} 2575^{2} 3139^{2} 3864^{15} 4210^{19} **>49a 63df<**

Peter's Imp (IRE) 2 b g Imp Society (USA)-Catherine Clare (Sallust) 979^{3} 1557^{3} *1941^{4}* (3258) 3755^{8} 4411^{3} 4790^{24} **>48a 81f<**

Pet Express 3 b g Petoski-Hush it Up (Tina's Pet) **1996:** *5207^{8} 5239^{10}* **1997:** *(19) (110) (193) 225^{3} 247^{2} 372^{6}* 1256^{7} 1958^{2} 2130^{5} 2546^{18} **>62a 66f<**

Petite Danseuse 3 b f Aragon-Let Her Dance (USA) (Sovereign Dancer (USA)) **1996:** *5133^{8}* **1997:**

62^3 1780^8 2050^8 2734^5 3206^5 (3454) 3749^2 3968^2 4184^4 (4328) 4601^9 **>77a 67f<**

Petite Heritiere 4 b f Last Tycoon-Arianna Aldini (Habitat) **1996:** 5115^5 **>48a 42f<**

Petite Lady 2 b f Noble Patriarch-Rough Guess (IRE) (Believe It (USA)) 844^4 897^7 **>44f<**

Petite Risk 3 ch f Risk Me (FR)-Technology (FR) (Top Ville) 945^6 1078^3 1115^2 1249^5 2495^5 2733^9 2906^{11} 3266^9 (3477) **>62f<**

Petite Tache 2 b f Minster Son-Perioscope (Legend of France (USA)) 2500^{10} 2827^{10} 3563^{11} 4470^9 **>34f<**

Petit Flora 5 b m Lord Bud-Pretty Soon (Tina's Pet) 574^3 1390^{12} 2502^{11} 2753^6 3627^{12} **>34f<**

Petoskin 5 b g Petoski-Farcical (Pharly (FR)) **1996:** 5115^7 (5169) (5232) **1997:** 139^3 205^{11} (256) 324^2 400^6 430^{11} 493^8 595^3 (753) (1152) 1570^6 (2048) (2777) 3096^6 **>77a 61f<**

Petraco (IRE) 9 b g Petorius-Merrie Moira (Bold Lad (IRE)) 541^4 759^{10} 1003^4 1080^5 1446^9 1620^6 2177^{11} 2852^W 3240^{12} 3625^6 4016^{15} **>64a 38f<**

Petrico 5 b g Petong-Balearica (Bustino) 3308^7 3627^{14} 4510^{10} **>4a 34f<**

Petronilla (USA) 2 b f Lyphard (USA)-Central City (Midyan (USA)) 3873a^2 **>89f<**

Petros Pride 4 b f Safawan-Hala (Persian Bold) 2951^6 **>50f<**

Petruchio (IRE) 2 b c Petardia-Rising Lady (Alzao (USA)) 2524^8 4007^{10} 4174^{12} 4739^9 **>64f<**

Petsong 3 b br c Petong-Petriece (Mummy's Pet) 2183^{15} 2704^{11} 2891^{17} **>12f<**

Petula Boy 3 gr g Nicholas (USA)-Tulapet (Mansingh (USA)) 289^5 373^8 600^5 1756^{10} 1998^9 2159^3 2364^4 2521^{12} 3213^6 3583^8 3762^{17} **>41a 37df<**

Petuntse 3 b g Phountzi (USA)-Alipampa (IRE) (Glenstal (USA)) 1121^8 2941^6 3196^3 3601^{16} 4586^8 **>2a 53f<**

Pfizer Ascot (DEN) 2 ch g Prince Mab (FR)-No Call (DEN) (Cawston's Clown) 4653a^2

Phanan 11 ch g Pharly (FR)-L'Ecossaise (Dancers Image (USA)) **1996:** 5189^9 5244^{10} **1997:** 66^5 151^8 1748^9 2063^9 3015^{13} **>37a 19f<**

Phantom Ring 2 ch f Magic Ring (IRE)-Follow the Stars (Sparkler) 2212^4 2516^8 4597^7 4948^6 **>61a 55f<**

Phantom Waters 2 b f Pharly (FR)-Idle Waters (Mill Reef (USA)) 1564^8 1927^6 2699^{10} 2953^7 3757^5 4245^6 **>66f<**

Pharaoh's Joy 4 b f Robellino (USA)-Joyce's Best (Tolomeo) 601^{14} 901^6 1419^3 1828^4 2665^5 3032^3 3323^2 4248^9 4452^3 4985^7 **>52a 63f<**

Pharly Dancer 8 b g Pharly (FR)-Martin-Lavell Mail (Dominion) **1996:** 5169^3 (5177) **1997:** 196^6 580^2 869^4 1133^{12} 1570^4 1755^6 **>71a 53f<**

Pharly Reef 5 b g Pharly (FR)-Hay Reef (Mill Reef (USA)) **1996:** 5270^5 **1997:** 88^{12} **>36a 63f<**

Pharly Star 3 ch g Pharly (FR)-Norapa (Ahonoora) 1271^6 1787^9 2420^{13} **>56f<**

Philanthrop (FR) 5 dk b h Machiavellian (USA)-Schezerade (USA) (Tom Rolfe) (148a) 310a^2 923a^2 1365a^3 (2269a) (2819a) **>119f<**

Philgem 4 b f Precocious-Andalucia (Rheingold) 570^9 843^6 1116^4 (1229) 1601^4 1943^6 2145^3 2386^3 2541^4 3221^5 3477^5 3919^7 **>11a 33f<**

Philistar 4 ch c Bairn (USA)-Philgwyn (Milford) **1996:** 5088^3 5171^6 5281^4 **1997:** 633^2 781^6 1142^6 1292^3 1473^2 (1674) (1739) (1837) (1985) 2528^7 2866^{12} 3150^9 3423^2 4283^5 4423^{11} 4558^{23} 4978^{24} **>73a 81df<**

Philmist 5 b m Hard Fought-Andalucia (Rheingold) **1996:** 5222^5 **1997:** 30^4 115^7 256^3 553^3 613^{13} 721^{14} 950^4 1039^6 2034^4 (2469) (3221) 3485^2 3631^5 (4235) 4691^4 5027^{14} **>59a 56f<**

Philosophic 3 b g Be My Chief (USA)-Metaphysique (FR) (Law Society (USA)) 771^3 1043^2 2908^2 4633^7 4749^6 **>55a 62f<**

Phoenix Princess 3 b f Nomination-Princess Poquito (Hard Fought) 889^{12} 1044^4 1429^4 1757^3 2040^3 2332^6 (2602) 2912^3 3608^7 4798^2 **>62a 52f<**

Phone Alex (IRE) 2 b f Tirol-Parkeen Princess (He Loves Me) 739^{11} 828^2 1827^2 (2147) 2862^9 3237^6 (3416) 4097^{13} 4473^{13} **>72f<**

Phonetic 4 b g Shavian-So True (So Blessed) 895^{24} (1262) 1979^9 2508^4 3976^{11} 4680^{12} 4920^{11} **>60f<**

Photogenic 2 b f Midyan (USA)-Colorsnap (Shirley Heights) 3672a^3 (3839a) 4474^6 **>92f<**

Phylida 3 b f Mazilier (USA)-May the Fourteenth (Thatching) **1996:** 5142^6 5261^3 **1997:** 1807^6 (2836) (3695) 4696^{12} **>44a 60f<**

Physicien (FR) 3 ch c Sillery (USA)-Philycia (FR) (Lydian (FR)) 3732a^2 **>69f<**

Pianist (IRE) 2 ch c Balla Cove-Hit For Six (Tap On Wood) 1418^8 2007^5 2571^6 3639^2 3911^5 4334^5 4698^2 **>70f<**

Pibarnon (FR) 7 h 267a^2 **>105f<**

Picard (IRE) 4 b g Durgam (USA)-Miner's Society (Miner's Lamp) 373^6 461^{13} 495^4 595^{19} **>52a 50f<**

Piccadilly 2 ch f Belmez (USA)-Polly's Pear (USA) (Sassafras (FR)) 3757^4 4209^6 4739^6 **>69f<**

Piccolo Cativo 2 b f Komaite (USA)-Malcesine (IRE) (Auction Ring (USA)) (1045) 2516^6 **>68a 47f<**

Pichon Baron (USA) 2 ch c Zilzal (USA)-Flora Lady (USA) (Track Barron (USA)) 4140^5 4218^4 4517^6 **>62f<**

Pickens (USA) 5 b g Theatrical-Alchi (USA) (Alleged (USA)) **1996:** 5116^7 **1997:** 4161^{10} 4415^5 4802^{14} 4886^8 (4923) 4998^{13} **>38a 57f<**

Pierpoint (IRE) 2 ch g Archway (IRE)-Lavinia (Habitat) (1614) 1959^2 (2658) 2858^3 3707^4 4178^2 4468^3 4634^4 **>78f<**

Pietro Bembo (IRE) 3 b g Midyan (USA)-Cut No Ice (Great Nephew) 3234^3 4108^{16} 4406^8 4751^2 **>73f<**

Pigeon 2 b f Casteddu-Wigeon (Divine Gift) (1581) 2500^8 3270^3 3564^2 **>67?f<**

Pike Creek (USA) 4 b f Alwasmi (USA)-Regal Heights (USA) (Forli (ARG)) 789^4 881^2 1162^{15} 1841^2 2867^6 4108^{11} 4426^7 **>83f<**

Pilsudski (IRE) 5 b h Polish Precedent (USA)-Cocotte (Troy) 922a^3 2104^2 (2527) 3050^2 (4204a) 4665a^2 (4785) **>140f<**

Pinchincha (FR) 3 b g Priolo (USA)-Western Heights (Shirley Heights) **1996:** (5160) **1997:** 7^2 281^2 298^3 509^6 (771) (976) 1242^4 (1647) 2341^3 3012^4 3444^4 4136^{11} 4383^2 4891^9 5053^{19} **>72a 91f<**

Pine Ridge Lad (IRE) 7 gr g Taufan (USA)-Rosserk (Roan Rocket) 1761^{13} 3264^9 3622^{10} (4472) 4842^{16} 4924^{17} 5030^4 **>85a 65f<**

Pinfloron (USA) 5 5063a^{11} **>113f<**

Pink Ticket 2 b f Emarati (USA)-Foreign Mistress (Darshaan) 441^3 530^3 592^4 767^6 859^3 3751^3 3967^4 4303^2 4576^{11} (4799) 4984^7 **>62a 55f<**

Pinmix (FR) 2 gr c Linamix (FR)-Pinaflore (FR) (Formidable (USA)) (4528a) **>92f<**

Pinochet (USA) 2 ch f Storm Cat (USA)-Pink Turtle (USA) (Blushing Groom (FR)) 4311^6 **>57+f<**

Pinsharp (IRE) 2 b c Sharp Victor (USA)-Binnissima (USA) (Tilt Up (USA)) 4478^8 4871^{12} 5041^{17} **>36f<**

Pinup 2 gr f Risk Me (FR)-Princess Tara (Prince Sabo) 2728^{13} 3416^5 4052^{11} 4401^5 4543^4 **>34a 54f<**

Piped Aboard (IRE) 2 b c Pips Pride-Last Gunboat (Dominion) 2286^5 4955^6 5040^6 **>62f<**

Pipe Music (IRE) 2 b g Mujadil (USA)-Sunset Cafe (IRE) (Red Sunset) 4840^8 5042^{11} **>53f<**

Piperi (IRE) 3 b c Machiavellian (USA)-Gwydion (USA) (Raise A Cup (USA)) 3733a^6 4129a^9 **>69f<**

Pippas Pride (IRE) 2 ch c Pips Pride-Al Shany (Burslem) 2553^{12} 2917^{11} 3278^{15} **>39f<**

Pip's Addition (IRE) 2 ch f Pips Pride-Mint Addition (Tate Gallery (USA)) 2784^{10} 3106^8 3324^3 **>54f<**

Pips Song (IRE) 2 ch g Pips Pride-Friendly Song (Song) 2829^6 **>77f<**

Piquant 10 b or br g Sharpo-Asnoura (MOR) (Asandre (FR)) 224^4 352^4 1395^{12} 1588^3 2668^7 3134^7 3491^8 3768^8 4139^{14} 4858^4 **>63a 60f<**

Pirongia 3 b f Wing Park-Gangawayhame (Lochnager) 1500^{10} 1681^7 **>26f<**

Pistol (IRE) 7 ch g Glenstal (USA)-First Wind (Windjammer (USA)) 735^{20} 986^5 1414^6 2866^9 3184^5 3491^4 4108^4 4406^2 **>75f<**

Pistole Bliss (FR) 3 ch c Pistolet Bleu (IRE)-Embraze Moi (FR) (Vacarme (USA)) 4648a^2 **>63f<**

Pistols At Dawn (USA) 7 b g Al Nasr (FR)-Cannon Run (USA) (Cannonade (USA)) 39^9 99^7 151^7 **>41a 57f<**

Pisum Sativum 3 ch f Ron's Victory (USA)-Trojan Desert (Troy) 1690^7 2756^7

Pitchmark (IRE) 2 ch f Mac's Imp (USA)-Sassalin (Sassafras (FR)) 1797^{14} 4278^{12} **>12f<**

Pixielated (IRE) 2 b f Fairy King (USA)-Last Embrace (IRE) (Shernazar) 4066^7 4694^8 4884^{23} **>73f<**

Pizzicato 3 b f Statoblest-Musianica (Music Boy) (2300) (2751) 3121^4 3709^5 3871^9 **>58a 65f<**

Plaisir d'Amour (IRE) 3 b f Danehill (USA)-Mira Adonde (USA) (Sharpen Up) (483) (560) 694^4 1453^8 1609^4 2134^3 (2393) 2561^2 (3649) 4282^{22} 4553^2 4777^{16} **>99f<**

Plan-B 2 b c Polish Precedent (USA)-Draft Board (Rainbow Quest (USA)) 4105^5 4244^2 **>82f<**

Plan For Profit (IRE) 3 b g Polish Patriot (USA)-Wild Sable (IRE) (Kris) 138^5 217^2 307^2 413^4 675^{12} (1458) 1737^{10} 2062^3 2290^{11} 2478^9 3153^4 3403^6 3605^5 4680^{13} 4872^4 4983^6 **>85a 88f<**

Plasir Des Yeux (FR) 2 ch f Funambule (USA)-My Darling (Arctic Slave) 4663a^3 **>94f<**

Plastered In Paris (IRE) 2 b c Paris House-Sarah-Clare (Reach) 3686^8 3927^7 4318^{17} **>45f<**

Platin Queen (IRE) 3 ch f Common Grounds-Sallywell (Manado) 1551a^2 **>96f<**

Platinum Plus 5 ch h Hadeer-Verchinina (Star Appeal) **1996:** 5084^5 **>53a 62f< (DEAD)**

Playgroup 2 ch f Rudimentary (USA)-Miss Paige (AUS) (Luskin Star (AUS)) 4973^{10} **>55f<**

Playmaker 4 b g Primo Dominie-Salacious (Sallust) 152^{13} 222^6 772^7 949^{14} 1098^{13} 1315^{12} **>42a 41f<**

Play Safe 2 b c Sanglamore (USA)-Livry (USA) (Lyphard (USA)) 4901^6 **>63f<**

Play The Tune 4 b g Music Boy-Stepping Gaily (Gay Fandango (USA)) 2313^{13} 4844^{20} 4918^{19} **>30f<**

Plaza De Toros (USA) 3 b c El Gran Senor (USA)-Wool Princess (FR) (Direct Flight) 807a^3 1195a^4 1896a^4 2456a^6 **>95f<**

Pleading 4 b g Never so Bold-Ask Mama (Mummy's Pet) 1397^6 2478^7 2775^8 3423^{11} 4071^4 4456^7 4787^8 5047^{17} **>81f<**

Pleasant Dreams 2 ch f Sabrehill (USA)-Tafila (Adonijah) 1557^5 2713^8 4278^6 **>51f<**

Pleaselookatmenow (USA) 4 ch f Irish River (USA)-Pointed Path (Kris) **1996:** 5192a^3 **>97f<**

Pleasure **2** ch f Most Welcome-Peak Squaw (USA) (Icecapade (USA)) 4973^{17} **>36f<**

Pleasure Boat **3** ch c Suave Dancer (USA)-Pilot (Kris) 1239^{15} 4322^{9} 4631^{7} **>52f<**

Pleasuredancer (USA) **2** gr g Thorn Dance (USA)-Istiara (FR) (Crystal Palace (FR)) 4575^{3} **>81f<**

Pleasureland (IRE) **4** ch g Don't Forget Me-Elminya (IRE) (Sure Blade (USA)) 1665^{6} 2014^{6} 2511^{8} **>61a 71df<**

Pleasure Shared (IRE) **9** ch g Kemal (FR)-Love-in-a-Mist (Paddy's Stream) 2108^{7}

Pleasure Time **4** ch g Clantime-First Experience (Le Johnstan) (1250) *1759^{13}* 2754^{3} 2934^{11} 3693^{2} 4137^{22} 4329^{5} 4636^{3} 4770^{7} **>27a 65f<**

Pleasure Trick (USA) **6** br g Clever Trick (USA)-Pleasure Garden (USA) (Foolish Pleasure (USA)) **1996:** *5114^{7} (5161) 5256^{7}* **1997:** *(40) 113^{3} 153^{6} 209^{2} 235^{7} (330) 358^{5} 578^{15}* 946^{9} 1389^{11} 1511^{8} 1631^{3} 1800^{2} 2144^{11} *2368^{8}* (2845) 3105^{6} 3382^{7} 3937^{10} 4927^{12} 4991^{10} **>62a 41f<**

Plenty of Sunshine **4** ch f Pharly (FR)-Zipperti Do (Precocious) *173^{8} 296^{8}* **>33a f<**

Plumbird **3** b c Statoblest-Plum Bold (Be My Guest (USA)) $1201a^{2}$ **>104f<**

Plum First **7** b g Nomination-Plum Bold (Be My Guest (USA)) **1996:** *5138^{12} 5174^{3}* **1997:** *40^{2} 109^{7}* 3625^{8} 3910^{9} 3936^{2} 4228^{8} 4414^{10} 4844^{5} 4927^{6} 4997^{8} **>51a 52f<**

Poddington **6** b g Crofthall-Bold Gift (Persian Bold) 1762^{6} **>90f<**

Poetry In Motion (IRE) **2** gr f Ballad Rock-Nasseem (FR) (Zeddaan) 3411^{8} 4267^{13} 4597^{5} **>59+f<**

Poetto **2** ch c Casteddu-Steamy Windows (Dominion) 985^{3} 1255^{4} 1328^{8} 3113^{7} 3474^{6} 3742^{2} 4065^{10} *4573^{2}* **>68a 75df<**

Pointe Fine (FR) **3** b f Homme de Loi (IRE)-Pointe Argentee (Pas de Seul) 765^{2} *1121^{3}* 1624^{12} 2132^{2} 2908^{4} 3298^{2} *3612^{3} 4302^{9}* 4438^{9} **>63a 65f<**

Pointelle **3** b f Sharpo-Clymene (Vitiges (FR)) 1587^{10} 2184^{7} 2554^{13} 4972^{7} **>22a 57f<**

Pointer **5** b g Reference Point-Greenhill Lass (Upper Case (USA)) 520^{5} 585^{4} 834^{5} 1395^{8} 1849^{6} 2232^{2} 2698^{7} 4048^{8} 4115^{3} 4333^{15} 4518^{5} 4636^{8} 4805^{13} **>41a 62f<**

Poker-B (IRE) **3** ch c Shalford (IRE)-Far From Home (Habitat) $3508a^{5}$ $4203a^{4}$ $4625a^{6}$ $4834a^{5}$ **>112f<**

Poker Princess **3** br f Waajib-Mory Kante (USA) (Icecapade (USA)) 535^{8} *873^{2} 1048^{5}* 1500^{3} 1694^{6} 1859^{3} *2159^{4}* 2332^{2} 2522^{3} 2836^{7} 3762^{6} 4243^{16} **>55a 61f<**

Poker School (IRE) **3** b c Night Shift (USA)-Mosaique Bleue (Shirley Heights) 2601^{12} 2961^{16} 3423^{16} 3916^{11} **>70f<**

Polar Champ **4** b g Polar Falcon (USA)-Ceramic (USA) (Raja Baba (USA)) **1996:** *5091^{2}* **1997:** 633^{11} (974) 1414^{10} 2187^{3} 2594^{4} 2930^{5} 3380^{3} 4108^{18} *(4572)* **>91a 80f<**

Polar Eclipse **4** ch g Polar Falcon (USA)-Princess Zepoli (Persepolis (FR)) *661^{5}* 1016^{15} 4680^{10} 4757^{18} 4979^{15} **>53a 60f<**

Polar Flight **3** br c Polar Falcon (USA)-Fine Honey (USA) (Drone) 449^{9} 690^{13} $918a^{3}$ (1072a) 1146^{6} 4893^{5} **>101f<**

Polarize **3** ch g Polar Falcon (USA)-Cornhail (USA) (Nodouble (USA)) *377^{4}* (497) 1129^{7} 1284^{3} 2158^{5} *2368^{7}* (3038) 3205^{P} **>51a 63f<**

Polar Prince (IRE) **4** b c Distinctly North (USA)-Staff Approved (Teenoso (USA)) 839^{2} (1552a) (1767) $2453a^{3}$ $2820a^{3}$ 3766^{2} 4003^{5} **>119f<**

Polar Prospect **4** b g Polar Falcon (USA)-Littlemisstrouble (USA) (My Gallant (USA)) 3420^{9} 3690^{8} 3921^{2} 4210^{4} 4477^{3} (4596) **>66f<**

Polar Refrain **4** ch f Polar Falcon (USA)-Cut No Ice (Great Nephew) **1996:** *5112^{6} 5179^{6} 5215^{6}* **1997:** 733^{14} 887^{9} 1116^{8} 1441^{16} 2041^{9} **>36a 43f<**

Poleaxe **3** b f Selkirk (USA)-Sarmatia (USA) (Danzig (USA)) 2183^{9} 2420^{5} **>48f<**

Polenista **3** b f Polish Precedent (USA)-Princess Genista (Ile de Bourbon (USA)) 1866^{5} 2583^{10} 3277^{7} 3931^{3} 4794^{13} **>66f<**

Polenka (IRE) **3** ch f Polish Precedent (USA)-Amana River (USA) (Raise A Cup (USA)) 1682^{3} 2859^{3} 3909^{9} 4291^{6} 4601^{7} **>55f<**

Polgwynne **3** ch f Forzando-Trelissick (Electric) *161^{6} (361)* 1089^{12} 1966^{5} 3251^{8} 3561^{8} 4168^{8} 4328^{5} *4913^{16}* **>55a 48f<**

Polished Steel (IRE) **3** ch c Polish Precedent (USA)-Galava (CAN) (Graustark) 742^{14} 991^{14} 1409^{12} **>40f<**

Polish Pilot (IRE) **2** b c Polish Patriot (USA)-Va Toujours (Alzao (USA)) 3686^{19} 4311^{11} 4752^{3} **>48a 67f<**

Polish Rhythm (IRE) **4** b f Polish Patriot (USA)-Clanjingle (Tumble Wind (USA)) 887^{12} (2408) 2569^{4} 3913^{7} 4319^{2} 4523^{3} 4680^{5} 4978^{15} **>80f<**

Polish Romance (USA) **3** b f Danzig (USA)-Some Romance (USA) (Fappiano (USA)) 1394^{3} 1764^{2} 2838^{3} 3244^{2} 3437^{2} (3800) 4071^{12} **>80f<**

Polish Swinger (IRE) **4** b g Polish Patriot (USA)-Girl On A Swing (High Top) 754^{4} **>51?f<**

Polish Warrior (IRE) **3** ch g Polish Patriot (USA)-Opuntia (Rousillon (USA)) 1254^{6} 1609^{5} 2134^{4} 2339^{3} 2655^{2} 3709^{12} **>89f<**

Polly Golightly **4** ch f Weldnaas (USA)-Polly's Teahouse (Shack (USA)) 541^{7} 604^{5} *860^{12}* 1083^{3} 1250^{2} (1419) (1743) 1814^{5} 2148^{2} 2339^{12} 3126^{14} 3323^{4} 3600^{7} 3795^{9} 4137^{17} 4365^{5} 4636^{2} (4770) 5047^{4} **>32a 67f<**

Polly In Paris (IRE) **2** b f Paris House-Persian Tapestry (Tap On Wood) 880^{11} 3055^{5} 4230^{11} **>28f<**

Polly Peculiar **6** b m Squill (USA)-Pretty Pollyanna (General Assembly (USA)) **1996:** *5151^{4}* **1997:** 763^{18} 1422^{14} **>52a 73f<**

Pollyteknick **2** gr f Terimon-Flute Royale (Horage) 2022^{11} *2606^{6}* 2904^{15} **>21a f<**

Polonaise Prince (USA) **4** b g Alleged (USA)-La Polonaise (USA) (Danzig (USA)) 4045^{7} *4304^{10}* 4568^{13} **>38a 52f<**

Polo Venture **2** ch c Polar Falcon (USA)-Ceramic (USA) (Raja Baba (USA)) 3717^{8} 3770^{5} *4056^{3}* 4380^{8} 4806^{3} **>72a 72f<**

Polska Modelle (FR) **2** ch c Polish Precedent (USA)-Model Village (Habitat) 4735^{7} **>41f<**

Polska Princess (GER) **3** br f Polish Precedent (USA)-Pikante (GER) (Surumu (GER)) 992^{7} 1591^{7} 2379^{4} $3998b^{4}$ 4883^{7} **>75f<**

Poltarf (USA) **6** b h Alleged (USA)-La Polonaise (USA) (Danzig (USA)) **1996:** $5199a^{8}$ **1997:** $2269a^{3}$ 2709^{W} 4412^{2} 4732^{5} 4969^{4} **>112df<**

Poly Blue (IRE) **2** ch f Thatching-Mazarine Blue (USA) (Chief's Crown (USA)) 3979^{8} (4298) 4425^{8} 4897^{10} **>80f<**

Polyphony (USA) **3** b c Cox's Ridge (USA)-Populi (USA) (Star Envoy (USA)) *658^{2}* (825) 1387^{4} 1841^{3} **>68a 78f<**

Pomona **4** b f Puissance-Plum Bold (Be My Guest (USA)) 832^{7} 1264^{3} 1775^{3} 2026^{18} 2678^{5} (3786) 4148^{5} 4424^{4} 4978^{8} **>95f<**

Pontoon **2** br f Zafonic (USA)-Dockage (CAN) (Riverman (USA)) (4973) **>84f<**

Pool Music **2** ch c Forzando-Sunfleet (Red Sunset) (1163) (1475) 2054^{5} 2584^{3} $3534a^{9}$ 4293^{3} 4790^{7} **>96f<**

Poppy My Love **4** ch f Clantime-Yankeedoodledancer (Mashhor Dancer (USA)) 1236^{19} 1479^{9} **>37a 37f<**

Portend **5** b g Komaite (USA)-Token of Truth (Record Token) **1996:** *5105^{4} (5131)* **>85a 96f<**

Porthilly Buoy **2** ch c Keen-Hissma (Midyan (USA)) 2768^{15} 3686^{21} 4603^{11} **>52f<**

Portite Sophie **6** b m Doulab (USA)-Impropriety (Law Society (USA)) 570^{3} 608^{4} 796^{2} 881^{4} 1116^{6} 1229^{4} 1390^{16} 2541^{2} *(2911) 3074^{4}* 3256^{4} 3570^{4} 3758^{2} 3886^{5} 4213^{8} *4484^{2} 4800^{2}* 4847^{7} **>54a 49f<**

Port-Lao (BEL) **6** Bacalao (USA)-Princess of Import (Import) (4649a) **>69f<**

Porto Foricos (USA) **2** b c Mr Prospector (USA)-Gallanta (FR) (Nureyev (USA)) 3127^{6} 3726^{4} **>67f<**

Portuguese Lil **4** ch f Master Willie-Sabonis (USA) (The Minstrel (CAN)) 1682^{5} **>75f<**

Posative **3** ch f Charmer-Suprette (Superlative) 1876^{9} **>49f<**

Poseidon **3** b c Polar Falcon (USA)-Nastassia (FR) (Noble Decree (USA)) 449^{5} $917a^{7}$ (1762) 2135^{4} $2641a^{2}$ 3109^{2} 4149^{8} 4420^{5} $4963a^{5}$ **>118f<**

Posidonas **5** b h Slip Anchor-Tamassos (Dance In Time (CAN)) 1476^{5} 4005^{3} (4238) $4665a^{9}$ **>126f<**

Positive Air **2** b f Puissance-Breezy Day (Day Is Done) 730^{5} 836^{14} 1091^{2} 2312^{6} 2565^{10} 4012^{3} 4166^{2} 4362^{8} 4750^{6} 4904^{2} **>78f<**

Positive Result (IRE) **5** ch m Doulab (USA)-Second Service (Red Regent) *1046^{13}* 1279^{18} **>2a 10f<**

Poteen (USA) **3** b c Irish River (FR)-Chaleur (CAN) (Rouge Sang (USA)) (673) 940^{3} 2011^{5} 3728^{2} 4117^{4} **>123f<**

Pot of Tea **3** b f Tina's Pet-Ebony Park (Local Suitor (USA)) 1443^{9} **>19f< (DEAD)**

Power Flame (GER) **4** ch g Dashing Blade-Pikante (GER) (Surumu (GER)) (3369a) (4531a) **>122f<**

Powerful Spirit **5** b g Presidium-Spiritofaffection (Raga Navarro (ITY)) 2940^{10} **>7f<**

Power Game **4** b g Puissance-Play the Game (Mummy's Game) 571^{4} 653^{5} 864^{5} 1266^{3} (1283) (1603) 1800^{15} 2036^{9} 2239^{5} 2471^{3} 2845^{10} **>22a 59f<**

Pow Wow **3** b c Efisio-Mill Hill (USA) (Riva Ridge (USA)) 1426^{7} 4114^{20} **>37f<**

Pradesh **3** ch f Generous (IRE)-Bareilly (USA) (Lyphard (USA)) 2583^{8} 4177^{8} 4378^{5} 4748^{5} 4996^{4} **>68f<**

Praeditus **3** b c Cadeaux Genereux-Round Midnight (Star Appeal) 740^{5} (1088) 1238^{3} 2013^{25} 2691^{9} 3976^{15} 4176^{16} 4632^{9} 4876^{6} **>64f<**

Praetorian Gold **2** ch c Presidium-Chinese Princess (Sunny Way) 1954^{9} 3598^{6} 3862^{8} 4116^{13} (4459) 4856^{8} 4953^{3} **>75f<**

Praia Grande (GER) **3** f $1202a^{10}$ **>71f<**

Prairie Falcon (IRE) **3** b c Alzao (USA)-Sea Harrier (Grundy) 523^{2} 670^{5} (1434) 2058^{5} 3125^{9} 3705^{9} 4882^{16} **>95f<**

Prairie Flame (IRE) **3** b f Marju (IRE)-Prairie Venus (GER) (Surumu (GER)) $1193a^{5}$ **>87f<**

Prairie Minstrel (USA) **3** b g Regal Intention (CAN)-Prairie Sky (USA) (Gone West (USA)) 1956^{7} 2521^{8} 3470^{5} 3696^{9} **>57f<**

Pre Catelan **2** ch f Polar Falcon (USA)-Anneli Rose (Superlative) 2597^{10} 3094^{12} 4211^{16} **>59f<**

Precedency **5** b g Polish Precedent (USA)-Allegedly Blue (USA) (Alleged (USA)) *867^{5} 1133^{11}* 1809^{13} 2039^{8} 2200^{6} **>57a 47f<**

Precious Girl **4** ch f Precious Metal-Oh My Oh My (Ballacashtal (CAN)) 610^{11} **>70f<**

Precious Island 4 b f Jupiter Island-Burmese Ruby (Good Times (ITY)) 865^{13} **>58f<**

Precious Ring (USA) 4 b c Bering-Most Precious (USA) (Nureyev (USA)) 716a^{2} **>115f<**

Precisely (IRE) 2 b g Petorius-Indigent (IRE) (Superlative) *4479*^{13} *4593*^{13} **>1a f<**

Precision Finish 2 ch f Safawan-Tricky Tracey (Formidable (USA)) 4694^{14} **>25f<**

Predappio 4 b c Polish Precedent (USA)-Khalafiya (Darshaan) 1476^{2} (2104) 3050^{7} 4127a^{3} 4665a^{5} **>132f<**

Premier 3 b g Rainbow Quest (USA)-Formosanta (USA) (Believe It (USA)) **1996:** *5090*^{2} *(5168)* **1997:** *337*^{3} 2015^{11} 4578^{10} 4741^{13} **>73a 68f<**

Premier Bay 3 b c Primo Dominie-Lydia Maria (Dancing Brave (USA)) 646^{W} 973^{4} 1257^{3} 1762^{4} (1982) 2656^{3} 3051^{7} 3575^{7} 4148^{8} 4383^{4} 4678^{6} **>100f<**

Premier Dance 10 ch g Bairn (USA)-Gigiolina (King Emperor (USA)) **1996:** *5205*^{10} **1997:** *39*^{11} *70*^{5} *182*^{4} *219*^{3} *315*^{4} *(400)* *516*^{2} *858*^{6} *(908)* *1431*^{4} 2279^{6} **>74a 53f<**

Premier Eclipse 3 b c Primo Dominie-Remany (Bellypha) 599^{8} 740^{12} 991^{12} **>59f<**

Premier Generation (IRE) 4 b g Cadeaux Genereux-Bristle (Thatch (USA)) *589*^{4} 838^{2} 1117^{2} (1244) 1559^{3} 1923^{5} 2483^{2} 2776^{5} 4672^{7} 4882^{9} **>55a 77f<**

Premier Jet 2 br f Dilum (USA)-Lady Shikari (Kala Shikari) 2720^{14} **>14f<**

Premier League (IRE) 7 gr g Don't Forget Me-Kilmara (USA) (Caro) **1996:** *5081*^{6} *5221*^{8} *5247*^{5} **1997:** *13*^{2} *93*^{4} *295*^{7} *543*^{8} **>42a 72f<**

Premier Night 4 b f Old Vic-Warm Welcome (General Assembly (USA)) (605) 984^{4} (1491) 2108^{9} 2834^{2} 3110^{8} 3705^{13} 4101^{4} 4241^{6} **>89f<**

Premier Project (IRE) 5 b g Project Manager-Lady Beck (FR) 2456a^{7} **>89f<**

Premier Star 7 ch g Precocious-Grove Star (Upper Case (USA)) **1996:** *5242*^{13} **1997:** 1779^{26} **>27da 6f<**

Premium Gift 5 ch m Most Welcome-Emerald Eagle (Sandy Creek) 1828^{5} 2339^{11} **>59f<**

Premium Princess 2 b f Distant Relative-Solemn Occasion (USA) (Secreto (USA)) 2545^{12} 2739^{8} 3407^{2} 3821^{7} 4166^{6} 4458^{2} 4807^{2} 4922^{3} **>66f<**

Premium Pursuit 2 b g Pursuit of Love-Music in My Life (IRE) (Law Society (USA)) 500^{9} 1328^{5} (1760) 2140^{2} 2758^{3} 4152^{12} 4284^{2} 4755^{13} **>84f<**

Premium Quest 2 b g Forzando-Sabonis (USA) (The Minstrel (CAN)) 3103^{12} 4209^{15} 4508^{3} (4806) 4994^{21} **>70f<**

Premium Rate (USA) 2 ch c Phone Trick (USA)-Excitable Gal (USA) (Secretariat (USA)) 1396^{3} **>72f<**

Prends Ca (IRE) 4 b f Reprimand-Cri de Coeur (USA) (Lyphard (USA)) 677^{18} 1101^{5} 2476^{6} 3220^{7} 3436^{2} 3765^{10} 4013^{2} (4307) 4553^{4} 4777^{4} 4881^{3} 5054^{5} **>101f<**

Prenonamoss 9 b g Precocious-Nonabella (Nonoalco (USA)) 3980^{4} 4319^{10} 4680^{9} **>55a 60f<**

Prerogative 7 ch g Dominion-Nettle (Kris) 2592^{12} 3080^{9} **>35f<**

Present Arms (USA) 4 b c Affirmed (USA)-Au Printemps (USA) (Dancing Champ (USA)) (2341) 2676^{7} (3051) 3703^{10} 4004^{6} 4754^{8} **>106f<**

Present Chance 3 ch c Cadeaux Genereux-Chance All (FR) (Glenstal (USA)) 1394^{2} 1650^{2} 1983^{2} *2303*^{8} 2496^{5} 2708^{3} 3052^{7} 3211^{3} 3991^{4} 4290^{3} 4408^{4} 4578^{14} **>58a 63f<**

Present Generation 4 ch c Cadeaux Genereux-Penny Mint (Mummy's Game) 2124^{10} 2346^{8} 2557^{18} 2922^{2} 3087^{2} 3290^{2} (3437) 3649^{14} 4071^{16} 4423^{19} **>83f<**

Presentiment 3 b g Puissance-Octavia (Sallust) 667^{6} 1864^{8} 2313^{5} 2510^{4} 2891^{3} 3088^{5} 3213^{7} *4980*^{4} **>50a 52f<**

Present 'n Correct 4 ch g Cadeaux Genereux-Emerald Eagle (Sandy Creek) **1996:** *5236*^{12} **1997:** 464^{5} 956^{7} 1223^{U} 2738^{20} **>31a 51f<**

Present Situation 6 ch g Cadeaux Genereux-Storm Warning (Tumble Wind (USA)) **1996:** *5152*^{8} **1997:** *(238)* 3115^{12} 3435^{4} (3798) 4141^{6} 4297^{20} 4441^{10} 4781^{15} **>76a 75?f<**

Press Again 5 ch m Then Again-Silver Empress (Octavo (USA)) **1996:** *5188*^{11} *5221*^{12} **1997:** 2179^{7} 2892^{5} 3227^{16} 4008^{7} **>14a 41f<**

Press Ahead 2 b c Precocious-By Line (High Line) *1577*^{5} 2842^{13} 4061^{18} *4569*^{7} **>67a 48f<**

Press On Nicky 4 b f Nicholas (USA)-Northern Empress (Northfields (USA)) 766^{7} 1111^{4} 1588^{7} 2346^{12} 2835^{18} 4441^{18} **>67f<**

Pressurise 2 ch g Sanglamore (USA)-Employ Force (USA) (Alleged (USA)) 4515^{13} 4603^{15} 4710^{11} **>45f<**

Prestige Lass 4 ch f Weldnaas (USA)-Monalda (FR) (Claude) 3091^{18} **>31f<**

Presuming Ed (IRE) 4 b g Nordico (USA)-Top Knot (High Top) *285*^{5} **>36a f<**

Pretty In Pink (USA) 3 ch f Elmaamul (USA)-La Plus Belle (USA) (Robellino (USA)) (3732a) **>80f<**

Pretty Sally (IRE) 3 b f Polish Patriot (USA)-Sally Chase (Sallust) *181*^{2} *259*^{3} *317*^{7} *399*^{9} **>58a 24f<**

Pretty Sharp 3 ch f Interrex (CAN)-To The Point (Sharpen Up) 485^{5} 887^{14} **>62f<**

Priceless 2 b g Rock City-Good as Gold (IRE) (Glint of Gold) (3331) 3688^{5} 4140^{4} 4368^{6} **>91f<**

Priddy Green 2 b f Formidable (USA)-No Can Tell (USA) (Clev Er Tell (USA)) 4564^{12} 4750^{8} **>49f<**

Pride of Brixton 4 b g Dominion-Caviar Blini (What A Guest) 1034^{7} 1946^{11} 4233^{24} *4482*^{7} 4770^{12} 5047^{16} **>68a 52f<**

Pride of Bryn 2 br f Efisio-Alpine Sunset (Auction Ring (USA)) *2606*^{7} 2823^{4} 3062^{4} 3265^{9} 3628^{5} 4230^{8} 4595^{2} **>9a 51f<**

Pride of Fashion 2 gr g Triune-Fashion Princess (Van Der Linden (FR)) 4366^{12} 4627^{15}

Pride of Hayling (IRE) 6 ch m Bold Arrangement-Malham Tarn (Riverman (USA)) 1509^{10} 2006^{6} 2698^{13} 3473^{3} 3642^{3} 4048^{14} 4370^{F} **>17a 63f<** **(DEAD)**

Pride of My Heart 2 b f Lion Cavern (USA)-Hearten (Hittite Glory) 2919^{4} 3547^{6} 4066^{6} **>83f<**

Pride of Narvik 3 b c Pharly (FR)-Ulla Laing (Mummy's Pet) 4277^{11} 4587^{7} 4700^{10} **>46f<**

Pride of Pendle 8 ro m Grey Desire-Pendle's Secret (Le Johnstan) 1131^{9} 1472^{8} 1739^{10} 2205^{7} (2340) 2557^{9} 2678^{3} 3064^{4} 3150^{3} (3311) 3605^{8} 3810^{2} 3976^{10} 4147^{17} 4283^{12} 4441^{14} 4558^{26} 4781^{13} **>71f<**

Pride of Place (IRE) 2 b f Caerleon (USA)-Pro Patria (Petingo) 4067^{3} 4502^{6} **>80f<**

Pridewood Picker 10 b g Joshua-Guinea Feather (Over The River (FR)) *83*^{11}

Priena (IRE) 3 ch f Priolo (USA)-Isabena (Star Appeal) 1318^{2} 1875^{2} 2585^{10} 3190^{9} 4110^{4} 4424^{2} 4669^{9} 4712^{3} **>100f<**

Prilora (IRE) 2 ch f Priolo (USA)-Karine (Habitat) 1538a^{9} **>48f<**

Priluki 3 b f Lycius (USA)-Pripet (USA) (Alleged (USA)) 3775^{6} 4060^{11} 4400^{2} (4771) 4971^{15} **>68f<**

Prima Facie 2 b f Primo Dominie-Soluce (Junius (USA)) 5042^{8} **>60f<**

Primaly (CAN) 2 f *5060a*^{3}

Primary Colours 2 b f Saddlers' Hall (IRE)-Go For Red (IRE) (Thatching) 4753^{10} 4974^{3} **>58f<**

Prima Silk 6 b m Primo Dominie-Silk St James (Pas de Seul) **1996:** *(5105)* *5150*^{8} *5246*^{5} **1997:** *89*^{8} *(166)* *257*^{8} *357*^{4} 1857^{2} 1963^{2} *2162*^{11} 2567^{10} 2711^{8} 2922^{7} *3075*^{2} 3565^{15} **>82a 68f<**

Primaticcio (IRE) 2 b c Priolo (USA)-Martinova (Martinmas) 4544^{13} **>41f<**

Primavera 2 b f Anshan-Fair Maid of Kent (USA) (Diesis) 1240^{10} 2524^{9} 2893^{2} **>68f<**

Prima Verde 4 b f Leading Counsel (USA)-Bold Green (FR) (Green Dancer (USA)) (1834) (2331) 2772^{3} **>84+f<**

Prime Hand 2 ch f Primo Dominie-Rechanit (IRE) (Local Suitor (USA)) 2545^{2} **>79+f<**

Prime Light 4 ch g Primo Dominie-Flopsy (Welsh Pageant) *1082*^{5} 1837^{5} 2408^{9} 2845^{4} 4071^{9} 4606^{4} **>66a 76f<**

Primelta 4 b f Primo Dominie-Pounelta (Tachypous) *855*^{11} 2115^{8} 2665^{7} (3292) 3787^{16} 4404^{13} 4695^{15} **>10a 54f<**

Prime Minister 3 ch c Be My Chief (USA)-Classic Design (Busted) 1936^{6} **>64f<**

Prime Partner 4 b g Formidable (USA)-Baileys by Name (Nomination) 1220^{8} 1388^{6} 1683^{8} (2041) 2237^{4} 2418^{3} 2463^{3} 2845^{5} 2880^{3} 3039^{9} 3456^{11} 3573^{7} 4373^{9} *4484*^{4} **>45a 36f<**

Primero (IRE) 3 b g Lycius (USA)-Pipitina (Bustino) 3014^{8} 4903^{5}

Prime Time Girl 2 b f Primo Dominie-Timely Raise (USA) (Raise A Man (USA)) 4103^{9} **>57f<**

Primeval 3 b g Primo Dominie-Class Adorns (Sadler's Wells (USA)) 3632^{5} 3909^{3} **>69f<**

Primfaheights 2 b f Reprimand-Hafhafah (Shirley Heights) 767^{5} 1370^{7} 3782^{14} **>38f<**

Primo Lara 5 ch h Primo Dominie-Clara Barton (Youth (USA)) 4276^{5} 4561^{3} 4787^{9} (4995) **>49a 93f<**

Primordial (FR) 2 b g Lesotho (USA)-Prilly (FR) (Saint Cyrien (FR)) 4884^{14} **>50f<**

Primrose Place (USA) 3 b f Dayjur (USA)-Fitzwilliam Place (Thatching) 4960a^{2} **>108f<**

Primula Bairn 7 b m Bairn (USA)-Miss Primula (Dominion) **1996:** *5131*^{8} *5178*^{2} *5234*^{4} **1997:** *32*^{6} *137*^{13} **>66da 50f<**

Prince Alex (IRE) 3 b c Night Shift (USA)-Finalist (Star Appeal) 1023^{W} 1846^{8} 2315^{8} 2731^{12} (3234) 4372^{3} **>77f<**

Prince Ashleigh 2 b g Anshan-Fen Princess (IRE) (Trojan Fen) 1492^{6} 3306^{6} 4361^{4} 4690^{2} 4767^{2} 4875^{8} **>79f<**

Prince Babar 6 b g Fairy King (USA)-Bell Toll (High Line) 678^{9} 1160^{2} 2105^{11} 2598^{6} **>108f<**

Prince Baltasar 8 ch g Claude Monet (USA)-Farababy (FR) (Faraway Son (USA)) 3620^{5}

Prince Batshoof 2 b c Batshoof-Sipsi Fach (Prince Sabo) 2336^{9} 4564^{8} 4815^{3} **>66f<**

Prince Danzig (IRE) 6 ch g Roi Danzig (USA)-Veldt (High Top) **1996:** *(5205)* **1997:** *100*^{5} *299*^{5} *365*^{3} *405*^{2} 481^{3} 680^{5} 1010^{2} 1641^{5} 2694^{5} 3559^{6} **>90a 56f<**

Prince de Loir 3 b c Be My Chief (USA)-Princesse Vali (FR) (Val de L'Orne (FR)) 2332^{W} 2583^{9} 2836^{4} 3551^{2} **>79f<**

Prince Dome (IRE) 3 ch g Salt Dome (USA)-Blazing Glory (IRE) (Glow (USA)) (636) 1254^{10} (1673) 1980^{6} (2134) 2560^{10} 3011^{5} 3709^{3} 3975^{3} 4100^{18} **>93f<**

Prince Emar 3 b g Emarati (USA)-Selaginella (Pharly (FR)) *164*^{10} *259*^{7} *317*^{8} **>23a f< (DEAD)**

Prince Foley 2 ch c Greensmith-Jadebelle (Beldale Flutter (USA)) (557) 637^{2} 884^{3} (1084) (1328) 1684^{4} (2007) (2758) 3098^{2} **>92f<**

Prince Jordan 3 ch g Keen-Diami (Swing Easy (USA)) *4300*^{4} **>28a 43f<**

Prince Kinsky 4 ch c Master Willie-Princess Lieven (Royal Palace) **1996:** *5091^{4}* **1997:** (789) 1325^{9} 1592^{3} 4101^{12} **>76a 86f<**

Princely Affair 4 b g Prince Sabo-Shillay (Lomond (USA)) *34^{5} 88^{7} 401^{7}* 538^{13} 3315^{17} 3570^{9} 3919^{11} **>42a 32f<**

Princely Heir (IRE) 2 b c Fairy King (USA)-Meis El-Reem (Auction Ring (USA)) (1492) (2466) 2811a^{3} (3534a) **>104f<**

Princely Sound 4 b g Prince Sabo-Sound of the Sea (Windjammer (USA)) *(253) 323^{7} 488^{7}* 756^{6} 1020^{16} 3746^{3} 4137^{19} 4365^{12} 4580^{18} **>82a 66f<**

Prince Minata (IRE) 2 b c Machiavellian (USA)-Aminata (Glenstal (USA)) 1538a^{7} **>63f<**

Prince Moshar 3 b g Primitive Rising (USA)-Mostimus (Doulab (USA)) 2046^{W}

Prince Nicholas 2 ch c Midyan (USA)-Its My Turn (Palm Track) 432^{12} 594^{10} 2499^{6} 2881^{11} **>44f<**

Prince of Andros (USA) 7 b h Al Nasr (FR)-Her Radiance (USA) (Halo (USA)) **1996:** *(5204)* **1997:** 943^{4} 1323^{4} **>111a 115f<**

Prince of Bhutan (IRE) 3 ch c Night Shift (USA)-Lassalia (Sallust) 683^{16} 1207^{14} 4886^{12} 4987^{7} **>66f<**

Prince of Denial 3 b c Soviet Star (USA)-Gleaming Water (Kalaglow) (990) 1595^{8} 3575^{3} (4297) 4558^{27} 4781^{6} (4893) 4978^{12} **>100f<**

Prince of Fortune 3 b g Prince Sabo-Beautiful Orchid (Hays) *1044^{9}* 1167^{4} 1568^{8} 1921^{3} 2171^{4} 2723^{4} 2954^{8} 3206^{8} **>1a 51f<**

Prince of India 5 b g Night Shift (USA)-Indian Queen (Electric) 2525^{P} 4550^{13} 4888^{4} 4978^{25} **>96f<**

Prince of My Heart 4 ch c Prince Daniel (USA)-Blue Room (Gorytus (USA)) 439a^{7} 522^{5} (1261) 1767^{7} 2710^{9} 3112^{5} 3409^{7} 3703^{6} **>111f<**

Prince of Parkes 3 b g Full Extent (USA)-Summerhill Spruce (Windjammer (USA)) 729^{3} 1451^{3} 1650^{5} 2017^{7} 2167^{2} 2417^{6} 3606^{8} **>59f<**

Prince of Salsa 2 b g Emarati (USA)-Salinas (Bay Express) 4910^{8} **>35f<**

Prince Oxley 2 ch c King's Signet (USA)-Precious Air (IRE) (Precocious) 3497^{7} 4753^{24} 4884^{20} **>44f<**

Prince Rudolf (IRE) 5 b g Cyrano de Bergerac-Princess Raisa (Indian King (USA)) **1996:** *5247^{14}* **1997:** *224^{9}* **>37da 52f<**

Princess Belfort 4 b f Belfort (FR)-Domino Rose (Dominion) 3116^{6} **>14a 26f<**

Princess Danielle 5 b m Prince Daniel (USA)-Bells of St Martin (Martinmas) 1244^{3} (1463) (1811) 2550^{3} 2920^{D} 3279^{6} 3824^{3} 4063^{12} 4635^{6} **>73f<**

Princess Deya 2 b f Be My Guest (USA)-Sumoto (Mtoto) 2728^{21} 3493^{13} **>2f<**

Princess Efisio 4 b f Efisio-Cutlass Princess (USA) (Cutlass (USA)) *589^{8} 860^{5} (1754)* 2036^{3} **>66a 67f<**

Princesse Lyphard 4 gr f Keen-Bercheba (Bellypha) **1996:** *5274^{9}* **1997:** *35^{5}* **>12a 46f<**

Princess Londis 2 ch f Interrex (CAN)-Princess Lucianne (Stanford) 739^{4} 965^{5} 1240^{6} **>67f<**

Princess Mona (GER) 2 b f Mondrian (GER)-Princess Taufan (Taufan (USA)) (2637a)

Princess Natalie 2 b f Rudimentary (USA)-X-Data (On Your Mark) (2314) 3192^{11} 4411^{11} 4560^{7} 4767^{13} 4885^{11} 4994^{14} **>79f<**

Princess of Hearts 3 b f Prince Sabo-Constant Delight (Never so Bold) (644) 886^{18} 1464^{2} 1633^{3} 1859^{5} 1985^{5} 4455^{11} 4629^{11} **>75a 63f<**

Princess Olivia 2 b f Prince Sabo-Les Amis (Alzao (USA)) 2771^{4} 2926^{7} **>44f<**

Princess Renata (IRE) 4 ch f Maelstrom Lake-Sajanjal (Dance In Time (CAN)) 2724^{11} 3716^{4} 4168^{18} 4248^{7} **>40f<**

Princess Sarara (USA) 3 ch f Trempolino (USA)-Name And Fame (USA) (Arts And Letters) **1996:** *5168^{8} 5243^{8}* **1997:** *145^{8}* **>27a f<**

Princess Senorita 2 gr f Timeless Times (USA)-Misty Rocket (Roan Rocket) 1827^{10} **>7f<**

Princess Topaz 3 b f Midyan (USA)-Diamond Princess (Horage) 690^{7} 887^{10} 1641^{8} 1859^{7} 2722^{3} 2961^{3} (3197) (3549) 3763^{5} 4426^{2} 4774^{9} **>88f<**

Prince Zando 3 b g Forzando-Paradise Forum (Prince Sabo) 474^{5} 768^{3} 1087^{6} 1931^{3} 2231^{6} **>64f<**

Prince Zizim 4 b g Shareef Dancer (USA)-Possessive Lady (Dara Monarch) *236^{9} 284^{11}* 2395^{5} 3029^{10} 4373^{19} 4404^{12} 4899^{11} **>42f<**

Principal Boy (IRE) 4 br g Cyrano de Bergerac-Shenley Lass (Prince Tenderfoot (USA)) **1996:** *5114^{4} 5161^{11} 5262^{4}* **1997:** *72^{8} 127^{10} 152^{12}* (1231) 1615^{2} 1837^{2} (2030) 2223^{3} 2385^{5} 2660^{11} 4471^{6} 5030^{7} **>49a 53f<**

Prinia 3 b f Priolo (USA)-Calandra (USA) (Sir Ivor) 727^{18} 1415^{10} 4883^{W} **>33f<**

Printers Quill 5 b g Squill (USA)-On Impulse (Jellaby) 1233^{7} 1803^{6} 3229^{7} **>50f<**

Priolette (IRE) 2 b f Priolo (USA)-Celestial Path (Godswalk (USA)) 2881^{10} 3541^{6} 3986^{4} 4215^{4} 4994^{25} **>54f<**

Priolo Prima 4 b c Priolo (USA)-Jungle Rose (Shirley Heights) *(98) 194^{11}* 2868^{3} 3029^{5} 4386^{10} 4596^{2} (4714) **>60+a 78f<**

Priors Moor 2 br c Petong-Jaziyah (IRE) (Lead on Time (USA)) 3490^{7} 4157^{7} 4502^{7} 4898^{8} **>62f<**

Priory Gardens (IRE) 3 b g Broken Hearted-Rosy O'Leary (Majetta) 1467^{4} 1925^{4} (2017) 2206^{6} 2721^{6} 3251^{9} 4249^{14} **>38f<**

Private Fixture (IRE) 6 ch g The Noble Player (USA)-Pennyala (Skyliner) **1996:** *5082^{7}* **1997:** *27^{6} 47^{4} 92^{6} 203^{3} 278^{6} 327^{2} 407^{9} 870^{11}* 1507^{3} *(2067)* 2531^{2} *(3073)* 3896^{3} **>78a 56f<**

Private Peace (IRE) 7 gr g Roselier (FR)-Private Affair (Julio Mariner) (1005a)

Private Seal 2 b g King's Signet (USA)-Slender (Aragon) 1984^{3} 2320^{6} 2741^{2} 3113^{11} 3556^{5} (4500) 4772^{6} **>70f<**

Privilege (IRE) 6 b g Last Tycoon-Spire (Shirley Heights) **1996:** 5217a^{3} **1997:** 720a^{2} **>120f<**

Priwings (IRE) 2 b c In The Wings-Primisca (Double Form) (5033a)

Prix de Clermont (IRE) 3 b g Petorius-Sandra's Choice (Sandy Creek) **1996:** *5162^{10}* **1997:** *489^{5}* 4518^{18} **>26a 65df<**

Prix Star 2 ch c Superpower-Celestine (Skyliner) 822^{2} 1076^{2} 1328^{4} 2110^{2} (2473) 3152^{4} 3602^{6} **>76f<**

Prizefighter 6 b g Rambo Dancer (CAN)-Jaisalmer (Castle Keep) *380^{8}* **>68?a 70f<**

Prodigal Son (IRE) 2 b c Waajib-Nouveau Lady (IRE) (Taufan (USA)) 2768^{13} 3201^{8} *3607^{5}* 4245^{9} **>59a 57f<**

Projectvision (IRE) 3 b c Roi Danzig (USA)-Avidal Park (Horage) *(154)* **>75a f<**

Prolix 2 ch c Kris-Ajuga (USA) (The Minstrel (CAN)) 3598^{2} 4132^{2} 4440^{2} **>106f<**

Prominent 3 b c Primo Dominie-Mary Bankes (USA) (Northern Baby (CAN)) 453^{7} 462^{3} 701^{6} 1471^{6} 2177^{15} 2417^{4} 2735^{8} 3034^{14} 3241^{10} 3697^{5} **>57?f<**

Prompt Delivery (USA) 2 b c Zilzal (USA)-Bold 'n Determined (USA) (Bold And Brave) 2870^{4} 3260^{2} *3607^{3} 4052^{W}* (4381) 4634^{13} **>79a 82f<**

Proof Positive 2 b c Pursuit of Love-Pravolo 1192a^{3} **>66f<**

Propellant 3 b g Formidable (USA)-Kirsheda (Busted) *581^{11}* 1299^{9} *1785^{8}* 2166^{7} **>48f<**

Proper Blue (USA) 4 b c Proper Reality (USA)-Blinking (USA) (Tom Rolfe) 522^{3} 736^{6} 1323^{6} 4272^{4} 4369^{2} 4776^{3} 4968^{3} **>110f<**

Prophets Honour 5 ch g Deploy-Cat's Claw (USA) (Sharpen Up) *2^{5} 83^{2} 100^{9}* **>60a 83f<**

Prophits Pride (IRE) 5 ch g Carmelite House (USA)-Asinara (Julio Mariner) 4466^{16} 4692^{13}

Prose (IRE) 2 b c Priolo (USA)-Nicea (IRE) (Dominion) 697^{3} 850^{3} 1267^{2} *(2363)* 2707^{2} **>82a 82f<**

Prospectheus (USA) 2 c 4528a^{4} **>80f<**

Prospector's Cove 4 b g Dowsing (USA)-Pearl Cove (Town And Country) 499^{9} 1145^{9} 1482^{7} 1597^{3} 1831^{6} 2187^{5} 2550^{7} 2776^{8} 2867^{7} 3317^{3} **>65f<**

Prospectress (USA) 2 ch f Mining (USA)-Seductive Smile (USA) (Silver Hawk (USA)) 4581^{3} **>64f<**

Prospectus (IRE) 2 b c Petorius-So Stylish (Great Nephew) 2439a^{3} **>80f<**

Prospering 3 b f Prince Sabo-Flourishing (IRE) (Trojan Fen) 1090^{9} (1921) 2705^{12} 3092^{14} **>54df<**

Prospero 4 b g Petong-Pennies to Pounds (Ile de Bourbon (USA)) 1169^{10} 3475^{7} 3864^{2} 4002^{12} 4275^{5} 4461^{2} 4879^{6} **>80f<**

Protaras Bay 3 b c Superpower-Vivid Impression (Cure The Blues (USA)) 3465^{15} 3762^{7} 4010^{2} 4972^{3} 5024^{5} **>47f<**

Protektor (GER) 8 b h Acatenango (GER)-Prioritat (FR) (Frontal) 1073a^{5} 2459a^{4} 3182a^{3} 3737a^{4} 4537a^{3} 4963a^{3} **>123f<**

Protocol (IRE) 3 ch c Taufan (USA)-Ukraine's Affair (USA) (The Minstrel (CAN)) **1996:** *5087^{2}* **1997:** *568^{2}* 878^{4} (1474) 1868^{4} 2230^{8} 3218^{13} 3633^{5} 4896^{2} 4919^{4} **>74a 77f<**

Proud Brigadier (IRE) 9 b g Auction Ring (USA)-Naughty One Gerard (Brigadier Gerard) 476^{5} 721^{6} 1273^{6} 1383^{12} 1748^{11} 1926^{8} 2375^{5} 2577^{13} 2916^{11} **>42f<**

Proud Fillie (FR) 3 gr f Linamix (FR)-Proud Poppy (FR) (Proud Appeal (USA)) 3000a^{2} **>107f<**

Proud Image 5 b g Zalazl (USA)-Fleur de Foret (USA) (Green Forest (USA)) **1996:** *5143^{8}* **>68a 71f<**

Proud Monk 4 gr g Aragon-Silent Sister (Kind of Hush) 444^{18} 791^{10} 2117^{4} 2374^{9} 4878^{9} **>40a 60f<**

Proud Native (IRE) 3 b c Imp Society (USA)-Karamana (Habitat) 679^{8} 2526^{4} 2861^{11} 3111^{5} (3447) 3747^{7} 4282^{17} **>107f<**

Provence 10 ch g Rousillon (USA)-Premier Rose (Sharp Edge) *3046^{10}* **>23a 86f<**

Prove The Point (IRE) 4 b f Maelstrom Lake-In Review (Ela-Mana-Mou) 653^{10} 1445^{W} 1825^{18} 2200^{9} **>14f<**

Prudent Pet 5 b m Distant Relative-Philgwyn (Milford) **1996:** *5175^{12}* **>67da 48f<**

Prudent Princess 5 b m Puissance-Princess Story (Prince de Galles) **1996:** *5163^{8}* **1997:** *855^{4} 1289^{11} 1944^{9}* 2428^{8} **>50a 53f<**

Prussian Blue (USA) 5 b h Polish Navy (USA)-Lit'l Rose (USA) (Mr Prospector (USA)) 630a^{2} 916a^{2} 1365a^{4} **>113f<**

Psicossis 4 b c Slip Anchor-Precious Jade (Northfields (USA)) 944^{4} 1434^{4} 1974^{5} **>82f<**

Psylla (FR) 3 b f Fabulous Dancer (USA)-Silicon Lady (FR) (Milles Balles (FR)) 718a^{3}

Public Purse (USA) 3 b c Private Account (USA)-Prodigious (FR) (Pharly (FR)) 2027^{5} **>103f<**

Publisher (USA) 2 b c Kris S (USA)-Andover Way (USA) (His Majesty (USA)) (4950) **>88++f<**

Puce 4 b f Darshaan-Souk (IRE) (Ahonoora) 1934^{5} 2749^{2} 3110^{2} 3705^{3} 4099^{3} (4445) 5035a^{2} **>110f<**

Puiwee 2 b f Puissance-Glow Again (The

Brianstan) 5040[18] **>2f<**
Pulsar (FR) 2 b c Tropular-Banderille (FR) (Moulin) 3995a[2] **>82f<**
Punishment 6 b h Midyan (USA)-In the Shade (Bustino) **1996:** *5204[4]* **>109a 102f<**
Punkah (USA) 4 b g Lear Fan (USA)-Gentle Persuasion (Bustino) *82[3] 220[8] (291) 405[12]* 647[10] 735[4] 895[21] 4275[7] 4714[9] **>82a 74f<**
Pupil Master (IRE) 3 b g Masterclass (USA)-Lamya (Hittite Glory) 471[5] 826[7] **>26a 48f<**
Purchasing Power (IRE) 3 b c Danehill (USA)-Purchasepaperchase (Young Generation) **1996:** *5090[6]* **1997:** (609) 791[2] 933[11] (1219) 1458[5] 1782[4] (2216) 2337[3] **>55a 78f<**
Pure Coincidence 2 b c Lugana Beach-Esilam (Frimley Park) 1306[5] *(1941)* 2212[3] 2862[2] 3192[6] (3776) 4305[2] 4675[7] **>77+a 97f<**
Pure Nobility (IRE) 2 br c Darshaan-Ma Pavlova (USA) (Irish River (FR)) 4061[17] (4361) 4900[3] **>85f<**
Purist 3 b c Polish Precedent (USA)-Mill Line (Mill Reef (USA)) 676[2] 1625[2] (2410) 3705[17] **>89f<**
Purple Fling 6 ch g Music Boy-Divine Fling (Imperial Fling (USA)) **1996:** *5150[4]* **1997:** *403[4] 569[6]* 1317[9] (1824) (3066) 3649[16] 3910[3] 4137[11] 4280[13] **>69a 82f<**
Purple Maize 3 b c Mazilier (USA)-Hen Night (Mummy's Game) 606[6] 841[16] *1044[5]* 1416[6] *1756[7]* 2372[11] **>41a 34f<**
Purple Splash 7 b g Ahonoora-Quay Line (High Line) *858[9]* 1162[7] (1947) 3805[6] 4156[6] **>53a 101f<**
Pursuit Venture 2 b f Pursuit of Love-Our Shirley (Shirley Heights) 4701[3] 4909[2] **>76f<**
Pusey Street Girl 4 ch f Gildoran-Pusey Street (Native Bazaar) 450[19] 677[16] 835[9] **>87f<**
Push A Venture 3 b f Shirley Heights-Push a Button (Bold Lad (IRE)) *581[9]* 886[11] 1388[7] 1843[3] *2151[8]* 2922[12] **>32a 57f<**
Puteri Wentworth 3 b f Sadler's Wells (USA)-Sweeping (Indian King (USA)) 1168[15] 1434[8] 1866[8] 3390[4] 4743[7] (5028) **>74f<**
Putra (USA) 3 ch c Dixie Brass (USA)-Olatha (USA) (Miswaki (USA)) 940[15] **>118?f<**
Putuna 2 b f Generous (IRE)-Ivoronica (Targowice (USA)) 4474[3] 4873[3] **>82f<**
Puzzlement 3 gr g Mystiko (USA)-Abuzz (Absalom) *225[5] (264) (298) 331[5]* 509[2] 654[8] 840[8] 3772[10] 4172[6] **>70a 60f<**
Pwllglas 3 br g Puissance-Glas Y Dorlan (Sexton Blake) *3611[9]*
Pyrrhic Dance 7 b g Sovereign Dancer (USA)-Cherubim (USA) (Stevward) *2161[0] 252[7] 302[5]* **>41a f<**

Q

Q Factor 5 br m Tragic Role (USA)-Dominiana (Dominion) 895[18] 1262[7] 1442[8] 1775[7] 2201[3] (2280) 2478[10] 2835[6] (3207) 3408[4] 3888[3] 4121[12] 4680[2] **>71a 94f<**
Qilin (IRE) 2 b f Second Set (IRE)-Usance (GER) (Kronenkranich (GER)) 4103[11] (4556) 4786[9] **>91f<**
Qismat 2 b f Selkirk (USA)-Plaything (High Top) 4853[10] **>30f<**
Quaint Desire 4 br g Grey Desire-Aquainted (Known Fact (USA)) 1834[5] 2046[17] 2156[5] 2890[12] **>45f<**
Quakeress (IRE) 2 b f Brief Truce (USA)-Deer Emily (Alzao (USA)) 1954[3] 2886[2] 3776[3] **>66f<**
Qualitair Beauty 4 b f Damister (USA)-Mac's Princess (USA) (Sovereign Dancer (USA)) 2544[13] 2787[7] 3027[6] *3611[2]* 3933[13] **>50a 30f<**
Qualitair Pride 5 b m Siberian Express (USA)-Qualitairess (Kampala) *115[2] (157) 196[5] 261[8] 375[11]* 553[11] *3585[7]* **>38a 41?f<**
Qualitair Silver 3 gr f Absalom-Irish Limerick (Try My Best (USA)) *296[3] 377[6] 399[3]* 532[15] *590[7] 2305[3] 2366[8] 2602[7] 2913[8]* **>24a 29f<**
Quarterstaff 3 b g Charmer-Quaranta (Hotfoot) 784[9] *1155[8]* 2004[9] 3390[5] 4224[3] **>35a 60f<**
Que Belle (USA) 3 b f Seattle Dancer (USA)-Qui Bid (GER) (Spectacular Bid (USA)) (1202a) (1918a) 3737a[3] 4665a[8] **>125f<**
Queenfisher 5 b or br m Scottish Reel-Mavahra (Mummy's Pet) **1996:** *5150[12]* **1997:** *120[9]* **>58a 87f<**
Queen Maud (IRE) 3 b f Akarad (FR)-Modiyna (Nishapour (FR)) (921a) 1916a[9] 3007a[3] (4256a) 4665a[15] **>117f<**
Queen of All Birds (IRE) 6 b m Bluebird (USA)-Blue Bouquet (Cure The Blues (USA)) **1996:** *(5186)* **1997:** *52[5] 238[7]* **>80a 77df<**
Queen of Shannon (IRE) 9 b m Nordico (USA)-Raj Kumari (Vitiges (FR)) 1292[4] (2488) 3276[13] 3465[14] 4112[5] 4711[7] 4843[5] 4991[16] **>24a 61f<**
Queen Of Silk (IRE) 2 b f Brief Truce (USA)-Danzig Lass (USA) 5002a[6] **>96f<**
Queen of Tides (IRE) 2 b f Soviet Star (USA)-Tidesong (Top Ville) 4067[7] 4437[6] **>72f<**
Queen Salote 2 b f Mujtahid (USA)-Island Ruler (Ile de Bourbon (USA)) 2870[7] 3151[9] 3770[4] 4097[8] **>69f<**
Queens Check 4 b f Komaite (USA)-Ski Baby (Petoski) **1996:** *5109[2] 5230[10]* **1997:** 494[5] *545[10]* **>67a 45f<**
Queens Consul (IRE) 7 gr m Kalaglow-Queens Connection (Bay Express) 468[12] *589[5]* 947[12] 1097[13] 1818[2] 2884[2] 3039[12] (3105) 3311[3] (3408) 3622[7] (3901) 4147[2] 4424[8] 4637[5] 4781[24] 4978[27] **>49a 86f<**
Queens Fancy 4 ch f Infantry-Sagareina (Sagaro) **1996:** *5223[10] 5277[7]* **>34a 36f<**
Queen's Hat 2 b f Cadeaux Genereux-Greenlet (IRE) (Green Desert (USA)) 2597[13] **>53f<**
Queen Sigi (IRE) 2 b f Fairy King (USA)-Quinsigimond (Formidable (USA)) 1228[9] **>15f<**
Queen's Insignia (USA) 4 b f Gold Crest (USA)-Years (USA) (Secretariat (USA)) **1996:** *5082[5] 5123[8]* **1997:** 1005[5] 1506[2] 1668[4] 1987[3] (2369) 2730[5] 3115[13] 3465[2] 3787[4] 4695[8] **>51a 64f<**
Queen's Pageant 3 ch f Risk Me (FR)-Mistral's Dancer (Shareef Dancer (USA)) 2334[7] 2677[8] 5054[10] **>95f<**
Queens Stroller (IRE) 6 b m Pennine Walk-Mount Isa (Miami Springs) **1996:** *5210[6]* **1997:** *169[2] 235[5] 305[3] 428[2]* 587[4] *(1135)* 1660[4] 2150[8] 2507[5] 3248[9] **>44a 36f<**
Quel Senor (FR) 2 g 4657a[5]
Quest Express 3 ch c Rudimentary (USA)-Swordlestown Miss (USA) (Apalachee (USA)) **1996:** 5128a[7] **>102f<**
Quest For Best (USA) 3 b br f Quest for Fame-Chic Monique (USA) (Halo (USA)) 833[8] 1234[6] 1470[4] 2132[3] 2414[2] **>64f<**
Questing Star 4 ch f Rainbow Quest (USA)-Guest Artiste (Be My Guest (USA)) **1996:** *5122[3]* **>57a 62f<**
Quezon City 3 ch c Keen-Calachuchi (Martinmas) 599[10] *868[6]* 1129[8] 1449[2] (1617) 2387[3] 2885[5] **>44a 67df<**
Quibbling 3 b f Salse (USA)-Great Exception (Grundy) 2506[2] 3236[7] 3453[5] 4139[16] 4319[16] 4631[3] 4971[17] **>60f<**
Quiet Arch (IRE) 4 b g Archway (IRE)-My Natalie (Rheingold) **1996:** *5260[5]* **1997:** *(10) 92[2] (131) 226[3] 291[3] 405[8] 457[4]* 1414[2] 1660[2] 1934[8] 2961[12] 3453[6] **>73a 74f<**
Quiet Assurance (USA) 2 ch c St Jovite (USA)-Silent Turn (USA) (Silent Cal (USA)) 3013[3] 3576[2] 4274[2] (4526) 4889[5] **>98f<**
Quiet Venture 3 b c Rainbow Quest (USA)-Jameelaty (USA) (Nureyev (USA)) 3909[8] 4060[4] 4378[3] 4699[14] **>83f<**
Quilling 5 ch g Thatching-Quillotern (USA) (Arctic Tern (USA)) 824[2] 1097[9] 1471[2] 2205[6] **>83f<**
Quillwork (USA) 5 b m Val de L'Orne (FR)-Quaff (USA) (Raise A Cup (USA)) **1996:** *5084[13] 5177[6]* **>20a 48f<**
Quintus (USA) 2 ch c Sky Classic (CAN)-Superbe Dawn (USA) (Grey Dawn II) 2860[4] 3117[2] 3494[8] **>83f<**
Quinzii Martin 9 b g Song-Quaranta (Hotfoot) **1996:** *(5241) 5264[8]* **1997:** *150[7] 235[6] 243[9] 342[4] 403[8] 424[5] 1291[13]* 3276[14] *3581[4]* 3966[7] **>42a 39f<**
Quirinale (IRE) 3 b c Slip Anchor-Newquay (Great Nephew) 1911a[9]
Quite Happy (IRE) 2 b f Statoblest-Four-Legged Friend (Aragon) 4630[14] 4921[2] **>66f<**
Quiver Tree 2 b f Lion Cavern (USA)-Quaver (USA) (The Minstrel (CAN)) 2870[5] 3117[10] 3744[9] **>56+f<**
Quiz Master 2 ch c Superpower-Ask Away (Midyan (USA)) 594[3] 836[2] 1120[2] 1510[6] 2110[5] 2467[4] 2736[4] 2904[2] 3265[6] 4211[10] 4411[7] 4737[3] 4921[3] **>67f<**
Quiz Show 2 b f Primo Dominie-Aryaf (CAN) (Vice Regent (CAN)) 2103[11] 2831[4] 3979[5] 4166[4] 4327[11] **>76f<**
Quws 3 b c Robellino (USA)-Fleeting Rainbow (Rainbow Quest (USA)) 2441a[5] (4356a) (4837a) **>109+f<**

R

Raaha 3 b f Polar Falcon (USA)-Ostora (USA) (Blushing Groom (FR)) (1302) 1958[8] (2772) 3236[5] (3615) 4121[18] 4561[18] **>90f<**
Raased 5 b g Unfuwain (USA)-Sajjaya (USA) (Blushing Groom (FR)) 4161[13] 4415[12] 4768[12] 4923[6] 5024[9] **>31f<**
Raazi 2 ch f My Generation-Botvyle Flame (IRE) (Reprimand) *1124[6]* 1635[10] 1873[5] **>15a 34f<**
Rabah 2 b c Nashwan (USA)-The Perfect Life (IRE) (Try My Best (USA)) 2680[7] 3201[2] (3780) 4116[2] 4674[3] (4967) **>94f<**
Rabea (USA) 2 b f Devil's Bag (USA)-Racing Blue (Reference Point) 4567[9] 4873[14] **>50f<**
Rabi (IRE) 2 b c Alzao (USA)-Sharakawa (IRE) (Darshaan) (3386) (4325) **>96+f<**
Rachaels North (IRE) 2 gr c Night Shift (USA)-Anne de Beaujeu (Ahonoora) 5042[6] **>69f<**
Rachel's Rock 4 b f Rock City-Rachel's Dancer (IRE) (Lomond (USA)) *105[6] 200[5]* **>30a f<**
Racing Brenda 6 b m Faustus (USA)-Icecapped (Caerleon (USA)) **1996:** *5231[12]* **1997:** *2071[11]* 2502[16] **>25a 53f<**
Racing Carr 3 ch f Anshan-Bamian (USA) (Topsider (USA)) **1996:** *5135[7] 5180[4]* **1997:** *8[9] 277[7]* **>25a 40f<**
Racing Hawk (USA) 5 ch g Silver Hawk (USA)-Lorn Lady (Lorenzaccio) *61[13]* 1005[12] 1383[17] 1825[13] 1951[3] 2039[7] 2307[7] **>31a 48f<**
Racing Heart 3 b f Pursuit of Love-Hearten (Hittite Glory) 1164[7] 1500[4] *1756[12]* (2878) 3205[2] 3452[6] 4695[10] **>7a 64f<**
Racing Surveyor 2 b f Mazilier (USA)-Ruthenia (IRE) (Taufan (USA)) 441[9] 631[10]
Racing Telegraph 7 b g Claude Monet (USA)-Near Enough (English Prince) **1996:** *5086[5] 5110[12] 5276[7]* **1997:** 3966[5] 4228[7] 4373[11] 4713[14] **>40a 40f<**
Radar (IRE) 2 b c Petardia-Soignee (Night Shift

(USA)) 2336^{5} 2768^{12} 4318^{12} 4856^{2} (4953) **>79+f<**

Radar O'Reilly 3 b g Almoojid-Travel Bye (Miller's Mate) 1780^{7} *1939^{3}* 2323^{2} (2742) *3058^{3}* **>54a 74+f<**

Radiancy (IRE) 3 ch f Mujtahid (USA)-Bright Landing (Sun Prince) 1030^{2} 1983^{4} **>72f<**

Radu Cool (USA) 5 m *$5062a^{4}$* **>106a f<**

Raed 4 b c Nashwan (USA)-Awayed (USA) (Sir Ivor) 899^{3} 1472^{13} 1833^{5} 2205^{11} 2937^{5} 3143^{7} 3987^{21} 4846^{6} **>65f<**

Rae Un Soleil 3 b f Rushmere-Double Shuffle (Tachypous) *2319^{11}* 3557^{W} **>5a f<**

Raffaello (IRE) 2 b c Fairy King (USA)-Silver Dollar (Shirley Heights) 4949^{4} **>66f<**

Raffles Rooster 5 ch g Galetto (FR)-Singapore Girl (FR) (Lyphard (USA)) *16^{2}* *(86)* *(123)* 430^{2} *542^{2}* *(591)* 1036^{2} 1162^{5} (1981) 2514^{3} 3255^{2} 3705^{11} 4241^{8} **>79a 86f<**

Rafter-J 6 b or br g Petoski-Coming Out (Fair Season) 480^{5} 587^{16} 687^{5} 864^{18} **>33a 43f<**

Ragazzo (IRE) 7 b g Runnett-Redecorate (USA) (Hatchet Man (USA)) **1996:** *5099^{4}* **1997:** *59^{9}* *126^{5}* *209^{6}* *332^{10}* 1127^{9} 1861^{7} 2938^{8} 3477^{10} **>44a 40df<**

Ragford (IRE) 2 b g Shalford (IRE)-Raggy (Smoggy) 971^{W} 1267^{12} *2047^{10}*

Ragtime Cowgirl 4 ch f Aragon-Echo Chamber (Music Boy) 668^{11} 951^{14} 1037^{3} 1613^{16} 1838^{11} 2109^{12} (2221) 2541^{5} 2659^{11} 3224^{8} 3487^{11} **>42a 33f<**

Raheen (USA) 4 b c Danzig (USA)-Belle de Jour (USA) (Speak John) **1996:** *(5267)* **1997:** *52^{6}* 433^{5} 946^{3} 1598^{4} 2830^{8} **>87a 97f<**

Rainbow Dancer (FR) 6 b h Rainbow Quest (USA)-Ramanouche (FR) **1996:** (5126a) **>116f<**

Rainbow Frontier (IRE) 3 b g Law Society (USA)-Tatchers Mate $4620a^{14}$ **>91f<**

Rainbow High 2 b c Rainbow Quest (USA)-Imaginary (IRE) (Dancing Brave (USA)) 2556^{4} 3013^{4} 4735^{4} **>76f<**

Rainbow Rain (USA) 3 b c Capote (USA)-Grana (USA) (Miswaki (USA)) 448^{13} 1119^{6} 1781^{4} (2205) 2557^{10} 2735^{5} 4978^{21} **>81f<**

Rainbow Ways 2 b c Rainbow Quest (USA)-Siwaayib (Green Desert (USA)) 4575^{2} 4758^{4} **>88+f<**

Raindancing (IRE) 3 b f Tirol-Persian Song (Persian Bold) 507^{3} 741^{7} 959^{9} 3128^{11} 3575^{11} **>70f<**

Raindeer Quest 5 ch m Hadeer-Rainbow Ring (Rainbow Quest (USA)) **1996:** *5114^{5}* *5210^{4}* *(5260)* **1997:** *67^{2}* *157^{2}* *260^{6}* *360^{8}* (3854) 3992^{16} 4415^{4} 4471^{4} 4802^{6} 4847^{5} 4998^{9} **>55a 57f<**

Rainmaker 2 b c Last Tycoon-Starr Danias (USA) (Sensitive Prince (USA)) 4237^{14} 4715^{8} 4914^{10} **>54f<**

Rainwatch 3 b c Rainbow Quest (USA)-Third Watch (Slip Anchor) 742^{2} 1173^{5} (1877) (2230) 2596^{8} 3902^{6} 4295^{5} (4732) **>115?f<**

Rainy Day Song 4 br f Persian Bold-Sawaki (Song) **1996:** *5123^{10}* *5188^{10}* **>24a 64f<**

Raise A King 2 b g Ardkinglass-Bias (Royal Prerogative) 3094^{3} (3497) (4247) 4560^{2} **>94f<**

Raise A Prince (FR) 4 b g Machiavellian (USA)-Enfant D'Amour (USA) (Lyphard (USA)) 933^{10} *1430^{3}* 2122^{10} (2521) (4896) **>72a 87+f<**

Raivue 3 ch g Beveled (USA)-Halka (Daring March) 1512^{2} (2059) 2855^{3} 4102^{6} 4583^{13} 4788^{10} **>90df<**

Raiyoun (IRE) 4 b c Doyoun-Raymouna $713a^{6}$ $1058a^{2}$ $2079a^{4}$ **>113f<**

Rajah 4 b br g Be My Chief (USA)-Pretty Thing (Star Appeal) *369^{6}* **>52a 52f<**

Rajati (USA) 2 b c Chief's Crown (USA)-Charming Life (NZ) (Sir Tristram) 4758^{22}

Rajpoute (FR) 3 b c Double Bed (FR)-Gai Lizza (FR) (Gairloch) $3002a^{2}$ (3730a) (4257a) $5065a^{6}$ **>119f<**

Rakis (IRE) 7 b or br g Alzao (USA)-Bristle (Thatch (USA)) **1996:** *5203^{4}* **1997:** *(257)* *363^{5}* *514^{7}* 567^{3} 832^{6} 946^{2} 1264^{2} 1489^{11} 1935^{2} 2124^{4} 2666^{3} 3548^{10} 3764^{10} 4175^{12} **>93a 72f<**

Ralitsa (IRE) 5 b g Nordico (USA)-Bold-E-Be (Persian Bold) 2824^{10} 3116^{7} 4160^{14} **>48df<**

Rambling Bear 4 ch c Sharrood (USA)-Supreme Rose (Frimley Park) 671^{6} 941^{6} 1590^{3} 2106^{7} 2329^{3} 2599^{7} 3111^{9} 4062^{3} 4239^{5} 4421^{7} 4599^{2} **>113f<**

Rambling Rose 2 ch f Cadeaux Genereux-Blush Rambler (IRE) (Blushing Groom (FR)) 3386^{3} 4057^{2} (4330) 4803^{2} **>93f<**

Ramblin Rose (GER) 3 f $1202a^{6}$ **>87f<**

Rambold 6 b m Rambo Dancer (CAN)-Boldie (Bold Lad (IRE)) 1385^{10} 1857^{5} 2852^{9} 3092^{12} **>61a 59f<**

Rambo Rally 2 b c Rambo Dancer (CAN)-Petiller (Monsanto (FR)) $2098a^{2}$

Rambo's Rumtime 5 b m Rambo Dancer (CAN)-Errol Emerald (Dom Racine (FR)) 1266^{12} **>24f<**

Rambo Tango 3 b g Rambo Dancer (CAN)-Jumra (Thatch (USA)) 1807^{11} 2173^{5} 2733^{10} 4324^{16} 4607^{8} **>13a 44f<**

Rambo Waltzer 5 b g Rambo Dancer (CAN)-Vindictive Lady (USA) (Foolish Pleasure (USA)) **1996:** *5269^{12}* **1997:** *1^{5}* *(111)* *150^{2}* *(192)* *243^{2}* *273^{2}* *330^{2}* *(358)* *(398)* 468^{3} 571^{2} (608) 734^{5} 776^{6} 1389^{5} *1576^{3}* *1788^{5}* **>84da 77df<**

Ramike (IRE) 3 b g Caerleon (USA)-Marie Noelle (FR) (Brigadier Gerard) *(266)* (534) (975) 2530^{2} 2682^{5} 3069^{4} 3218^{14} 4461^{4} **>59+a 87df<**

Ramooz (USA) 4 b c Rambo Dancer (CAN)-My Shafy (Rousillon (USA)) 839^{3} 981^{2} 2026^{7} (2334) (2816a) 3063^{4} 3728^{6} $4252a^{2}$ 4523^{4} $5037a^{4}$ **>115f<**

Ramsey Hope 4 b c Timeless Times (USA)-Marfen (Lochnager) **1996:** *5096^{2}* **1997:** *53^{3}* *137^{4}* *301^{12}* *(348)* *394^{8}* 702^{7} 827^{15} 1269^{10} *1578^{10}* (1865) 2111^{8} 2754^{8} 2937^{14} 3481^{14} 3856^{5} 3922^{11} *4482^{9}* 4905^{15} **>62a 58f<**

Random Kindness 4 b g Alzao (USA)-Lady Tippins (USA) (Star de Naskra (USA)) *73^{5}* *133^{2}* *202^{2}* *266^{2}* *(419)* 510^{10} *(858)* *1122^{4}* 4295^{12} (4548) 4860^{2} 4956^{11} **>83a 72f<**

Rangatira (IRE) 2 ch c Royal Academy (USA)-Chief's Quest (USA) (Chief's Crown (USA)) 4706^{W}

Ranger Sloane 5 ch g Gunner B-Lucky Amy (Lucky Wednesday) 4287^{2} (4432) 4585^{5} **>3a 49f<**

Ranna 2 b f Warning-Jasoorah (IRE) (Sadler's Wells (USA)) 4789^{3} **>76f<**

Rapid Liner 4 b g Skyliner-Stellaris (Star Appeal) *210^{6}* 1825^{14} 2307^{8} **>16a 28f<**

Rapid Mover 10 ch g Final Straw-Larive (Blakeney) 493^{10} 552^{5} 955^{11} 1231^{8} 1615^{5} 1837^{7} 2145^{13} 2385^{7} 2469^{10} 2660^{12} 3221^{3} 3484^{4} 3631^{4} **>34f<**

Rapid Reliance 2 b f Emarati (USA)-Chiquitita (Reliance II) 2917^{5} 3114^{12} 4042^{14} (4178) 4403^{6} *5017^{5}* **>55a 72f<**

Rapier 3 b c Sharpo-Sahara Breeze (Ela-Mana-Mou) 688^{2} 853^{5} 1595^{11} 2013^{3} 2601^{8} 3391^{2} 4554^{4} 4893^{13} **>95f<**

Rapier Point (IRE) 6 gr g Cyrano de Bergerac-Renzola (Dragonara Palace (USA)) **1996:** *5134^{13}* **1997:** *11^{9}* *40^{9}* *105^{10}* **>18a 45?f<**

Rapture 2 b f Primo Dominie-Hello Cuddles (He Loves Me) 3411^{13} **>4f<**

Ra Ra Rasputin 2 b c Petong-Ra Ra Girl (Shack (USA)) 1492^{10} 1791^{6} *2047^{6}* 3131^{7} *(3610)* 3904^{8} 4152^{8} **>82a 71f<**

Rare Indigo 2 b f Timeless Times (USA)-Miss Ritz (Robellino (USA)) 2545^{5} 3407^{7} 4159^{4} *(4573)* (4772) 4911^{2} 5045^{5} **>76a 86f<**

Rare Talent 3 b c Mtoto-Bold As Love (Lomond (USA)) 445^{6} 605^{3} 825^{2} 1230^{4} 2224^{4} 2667^{5} 3234^{9} (3601) 3813^{7} 4015^{17} (4326) 4632^{7} 4802^{7} 4876^{15} **>66f<**

Rasayel (USA) 7 b m Bering-Reham (Mill Reef (USA)) **1996:** *5139^{3}* *5181^{4}* *5210^{8}* *(5240)* *5270^{6}* *(5277)* **1997:** *63^{2}* *116^{2}* *163^{5}* (763) 887^{6} 1036^{3} 1278^{2} 1660^{7} 1981^{11} *2049^{7}* 2210^{3} 2533^{3} 2653^{6} 3255^{7} (3886) 3992^{13} 4435^{10} 4667^{10} *4800^{7}* 4986^{3} **>60a 62f<**

Rash Gift 4 ch f Cadeaux Genereux-Nettle (Kris) *322^{5}* 2121^{W} 2195^{2} **>18a 62f<**

Rashik 3 ch c Cadeaux Genereux-Ghzaalh (USA) (Northern Dancer) (740) **>103f<**

Rasin (IRE) 3 b c Lahib (USA)-Yaqatha $809a^{5}$ $2967a^{4}$ **>92f<**

Raspberry Sauce 3 b f Niniski (USA)-Sobranie (High Top) 3437^{6} **>35f<**

Ratb 3 ch g Be My Guest (USA)-Al Shaqrah (USA) (Sir Ivor) 683^{19} 842^{P} **>30f< (DEAD)**

Rate Cut (USA) 3 b c Lyphard (USA)-Sylph (USA) (Alleged (USA)) **1996:** $5191a^{3}$ **1997:** $819a^{5}$ **>100f<**

Ratiyya (IRE) 2 ch f Mujtahid (USA)-Sharayif (IRE) (Green Desert (USA)) 1457^{5} 3033^{5} 3638^{3} 4185^{4} 4567^{6} **>72f<**

Rattle 4 b g Mazilier (USA)-Snake Song (Mansingh (USA)) 496^{8} 608^{15} 668^{8} 1040^{7} 1285^{8} 1511^{14} 2114^{7} 2470^{3} 2660^{10} **>43a 39?f<**

Rave-on-Hadley (IRE) 7 b g Commanche Run-Fleet Fact (Known Fact (USA)) 4585^{9} 4804^{13} **>46?a 14f<**

Ravier (ITY) 6 gr h Highest Honor (FR)-Revarola (ITY) (Marracci) $1728a^{6}$ (2643a) **>117f<**

Raw Deal 4 ch f Domynsky-Close the Deal (Nicholas Bill) *2673^{4}* **>4a f<**

Rawi 4 ch g Forzando-Finally (Final Straw) **1996:** *5093^{3}* *(5273)* **1997:** *47^{5}* *(128)* *197^{5}* *383^{4}* *458^{7}* 1484^{10} 1639^{11} *1969^{8}* (2724) 2954^{3} 3261^{3} *3860^{12}* 4373^{2} 4872^{8} **>57da 56f<**

Rayik 2 br c Marju (IRE)-Matila (IRE) (Persian Bold) 4871^{5} **>81+f<**

Ray of Sunshine (IRE) 2 ch g Rainbows For Life (CAN)-Maura's Guest (IRE) (Be My Guest (USA)) 3239^{10} 3458^{2} 4564^{11} (4767) 5050^{19} **>73f<**

Rayouni (IRE) 3 b c Zayyani-Raymouna $3675a^{2}$ $4204a^{4}$ $4837a^{5}$ **>119+f<**

Ray River 5 b g Waki River (FR)-Mrs Feathers (Pyjama Hunt) *384^{10}* **>18a f<**

Ray's Folly (IRE) 2 b c Scenic-Avec L'Amour (Realm) 2524^{2} 3084^{7} 4007^{9} **>84f<**

Razor 2 b c Warning-Smarten Up (Sharpen Up) 4474^{8} **>79f<**

Reach For A Star 2 b g Midyan (USA)-Hard Task (Formidable (USA)) 1492^{14} 2324^{7} 3060^{6} 4265^{11} 4698^{10} **>55f<**

Ready Fontaine 2 b c Dilum (USA)-Prepare (IRE) (Millfontaine) 1293^{7} 2181^{22} 2571^{9} **>38f<**

Ready Teddy (IRE) 4 b f Fayruz-Racey Naskra (USA) (Star de Naskra (USA)) 924^{3} 1037^{8} 1311^{4} 1602^{7} 2540^{12} 2899^{5} 3698^{7} **>36?f<**

Reaganesque (USA) 5 b g Nijinsky (CAN)-Basoof (USA) (Believe It (USA)) 481^{4} 762^{6} 1022^{6} 1491^{3} 1805^{3} 2592^{3} 2949^{9} 3245^{4} **>57f<**

Real Estate 3 b c High Estate-Haitienne (FR) (Green Dancer (USA)) 1499^{6} 2005^{2} (2182) (2548) 3125^{3} **>89f<**

Real Fire (IRE) 3 b g Astronef-Golden Arum (Home Guard (USA)) **1996:** *5141^{9}* **1997:** 2200^{7}

2357[5] **>27a 37f<**
Really Done It Now (IRE) 2 b f Distinctly North (USA)-Judy Loe (Red Alert) 985[7] 1457[4] 1806[3] 2942[5] 3152[10] 3635[9] 4014[14] 4634[11] *4808[7]* **>28a 65f<**
Real Madrid 6 b g Dreams to Reality (USA)-Spanish Princess (King of Spain) *216[9] 295[6] 340[5]* **>44a 34f<**
Realms of Glory (IRE) 4 b c Reprimand-Wasaif (IRE) (Lomond (USA)) *340[10]* **>51a 12f<**
Realt Dhun Eibhir 4 ch f Indian Ridge-Deux Etoiles (Bay Express) (2447a) **>81f<**
Reams of Verse (USA) 3 ch f Nureyev (USA)-Modena (USA) (Roberto (USA)) 960[6] (1147) (1738) 3704[4] 4557[3] **>122f<**
Reap Rewards 2 gr c Barrys Gamble-Bo' Babbity (Strong Gale) 1120[4] (1557) 1684[3] **>76f<**
Rear Window 3 b c Night Shift (USA)-Last Clear Chance (USA) (Alleged (USA)) 725[17] 1239[5] 2568[8] *3865[3]* 4633[10] **>60a 47f<**
Reasilvia (IRE) 7 br m Supreme Leader-Quiteamazing (Flair Path) 4620a[16] **>84f<**
Rebalza (IRE) 2 b c Alzao (USA)-Rebecca's Song (Artaius (USA)) 1418[9] 1692[4] 2057[9] 3307[2] 4044[8] 4245[2] **>68f<**
Rebecca Sharp 3 b f Machiavellian (USA)-Nuryana (Nureyev (USA)) (681) 960[13] (2025) 2586[6] 3371a[2] 4129a[7] 4422[2] 4782[2] **>125f<**
Rebel County (IRE) 4 b f Maelstrom Lake-Haven Bridge (Connaught) **1996:** *5204[11]* **1997:** *56[8]* 1979[13] 2346[13] 3254[12] 3403[7] 3824[6] 3921[12] 4151[15] 4268[2] 4283[4] 4441[11] 5049[20] **>66a 78f<**
Rebuke 3 b g Reprimand-Lyra (Blakeney) **1996:** *(5098)* **>57a 49f<**
Recessions Over 6 b g Komaite (USA)-Lucky Councillor (Lucky Wednesday) *192[8] 312[4] 367[2] 1944[14]* **>38a f<**
Rechullin 3 ch f Niniski (USA)-Rechanit (IRE) (Local Suitor (USA)) **1996:** *(5142)* **1997:** 688[5] 1017[10] (1583) *2303[4]* 2561[4] **>84a 90f<**
Reckless 3 gr f Mystiko (USA)-Swift and Sure (USA) (Valdez (USA)) 586[18]
Recluse 6 b g Last Tycoon-Nomadic Pleasure (Habitat) 928[3] 1081[9] 1605[4] 1996[6] 2350[6] **>32f<**
Recognition 2 b c Rock City-Star Face (African Sky) 2181[16] 3711[8] 3927[2] 4458[4] 4807[3] **>65f<**
Recondite (IRE) 3 b c Polish Patriot (USA)-Recherchee (Rainbow Quest (USA)) 691[7] **>103df<**
Record Lover (IRE) 7 b g Alzao (USA)-Spun Gold (Thatch (USA)) *5[2] 68[7] 167[9] 375[9]* **>40a 50f<**
Recourse (USA) 3 b c Alleged (USA)-Queens Only (USA) (Marshua's Dancer (USA)) 676[7] 837[2] (4579) **>91f<**
Red Admiral 7 ch g Formidable (USA)-Dancing Meg (USA) (Marshua's Dancer (USA)) 2922[14] 3642[14] *3860[14]* **>40a 37f<**
Red Affair (IRE) 3 b f Generous (IRE)-Red Comes Up (USA) (Blushing Groom (FR)) 2267a[8] 4191a[7] **>106f<**
Redbridge (USA) 3 b c Alleged (USA)-Red Slippers (USA) (Nureyev (USA)) 725[3] **>93f<**
Red Brook Lad 2 ch g Nomadic Way (USA)-Silently Yours (USA) (Silent Screen (USA)) 4318[15] 4740[12] **>40f<**
Red Camellia 3 b f Polar Falcon (USA)-Cerise Bouquet (Mummy's Pet) 1203a[3] 4377[4] **>113?f<**
Red Cascade (IRE) 2 b f Danehill (USA)-Fair Flutter (Beldale Flutter (USA)) 2680[9] **>37f<**
Red Embers 3 gr f Saddlers' Hall (IRE)-Kala Rosa (Kalaglow) *237[4] 377[3] 513[3] 581[5]* 690[W] 793[6] 3285[16] 3601[14] 4010[7] *4798[12]* 4971[22] **>57a 24f<**
Red Guard 3 ch g Soviet Star (USA)-Zinzara (USA) (Stage Door Johnny) 508[7] 686[3] 2591[5] 2873[3] 3424[6] 3807[2] **>85f<**
Red Head And Dotty 2 ch f Risk Me (FR)-Sharper Still (Sharpen Up) 2181[25]
Red Leggings 2 b f Shareef Dancer (USA)-Anchorage (IRE) (Slip Anchor) 4317[5] (4604) 4892[5] **>75f<**
Red Light 5 b g Reprimand-Trull (Lomond (USA)) *867[10]* **>66df<**
Red Maple (USA) 2 br c With Approval (CAN)-Sheer Gold (USA) (Cutlass (USA)) 1263[5] 1480[7] 1961[4] 2681[7] 3215[9] 3924[5] 4068[14] 4334[4] 4698[3] **>67f<**
Redoubtable (USA) 6 b h Grey Dawn II-Seattle Rockette (USA) (Seattle Slew (USA)) 3566[9] 4270[18] **>41f<**
Red Pepper (IRE) 2 br g Chilibang-Magic Flame (Sayf El Arab (USA)) *1941[6]* 2176[8] 2870[8] 3136[5] 3589[5] 4311[8] 4402[3] 4602[9] *5017[8]* **>42a 73f<**
Red Phantom (IRE) 5 ch g Kefaah (USA)-Highland Culture (Lomond (USA)) **1996:** *5104[3]* **1997:** *30[9] 55[8] (3611) 4055[13] 4304[9]* **>58a 24f<**
Red Rabbit 2 b f Suave Dancer (USA)-Turban (Glint of Gold) 3985[2] 4217[5] 4907[2] **>77f<**
Red Raja 4 b g Persian Heights-Jenny Splendid (John Splendid) *30[8]* 3928[2] 4374[6] **>38a 69f<**
Red Risk 2 ch c Risk Me (FR)-Red Sails (Town And Country) 648[12] *1577[10]* 2022[10] 2509[12] **>5a 36f<**
Red Robbo (CAN) 4 b c Red Ransom (USA)-Aunt Jobiska (USA) (What Luck (USA)) 1176[12] (2026) 2766[17] 3725[12] 4314[8] **>102df<**
Red Romance 3 b g Prince Daniel (USA)-Rio Piedras (Kala Shikari) 494[9] 783[10] 1080[10] 1864[4] 2167[7] 2235[6] **>57df<**
Red Rusty (USA) 4 ch g The Carpenter (USA)-Super Sisters (AUS) (Call Report (USA)) **1996:** *5271[9]* **1997:** *47[12]* **>40a 53f<**
Red Shift (IRE) 2 b c Night Shift (USA)-Histoire Douce (USA) (Chief's Crown (USA)) 4910[9]
Redskin Lady 4 ch f Indian Ridge-Meritsu (IRE) (Lyphard's Special (USA)) **1996:** *5109[10]* **>26a 68df<**
Red Sky Charlie 2 b c Warning-Shameem (USA) (Nureyev (USA)) 3825[5] 4237[7] **>69f<**
Redspet 3 ch f Tina's Pet-Manabel (Manado) *577[8] 1044[8]* 1496[16] 2523[7] *2602[16] 3399[4] 4049[13]* 4601[20] *4795[8]* **>32a 30f<**
Redswan 2 ch g Risk Me (FR)-Bocas Rose (Jalmood (USA)) 4167[7] 4921[9] **>63f<**
Red Tel (IRE) 5 b g Alzao (USA)-Arbour (USA) (Graustark) *3073[6]* **>30a f<**
Red Tie Affair (USA) 4 b c Miswaki (USA)-Quiet Rendezvous (USA) (Nureyev (USA)) *29[6] 86[7]* **>35a 55f<**
Red Time 4 br g Timeless Times (USA)-Crimson Dawn (Manado) *57[10]* 1003[9] 1620[11] 1848[11] *2070[10]* **>30a 50f<**
Red Whirlwind 7 b g Shadeed (USA)-Red Red Rose (USA) (Blushing Groom (FR)) *1152[5]* 1413[10] *1940[8] 3073[5]* **>42a 56?f<**
Redwing 3 b g Reprimand-Bronzewing (Beldale Flutter (USA)) 675[7] 2013[13] 2691[6] 3185[3] 3801[8] **>91f<**
Reeds 3 b g Thatching-Bayadere (USA) (Green Dancer (USA)) *50[5] 164[5]* 2773[4] 3236[13] 3696[7] 3897[7] 4224[5] 4850[9] **>51a 51f<**
Reem Fever (IRE) 4 b f Fairy King (USA)-Jungle Jezebel (Thatching) **1996:** *5130[7] 5247[13]* **>36a 52f<**
Referendum (IRE) 3 b c Common Grounds-Final Decision (Tap On Wood) 679[6] 1212[2] 1596[7] **>108f<**
Refined (IRE) 2 b f Statoblest-Annsfield Lady (Red Sunset) 1961[7] (4311) (4746) **>93+f<**
Refuse To Lose 3 ch c Emarati (USA)-Petrol (Troy) 506[4] 694[2] 2925[7] 4175[2] 4375[6] 4757[8] **>83f<**
Regait 3 b c In The Wings-Rowa (Great Nephew) (732) 2589[7] 3412[7] **>86f<**
Regal Arrow 2 br g Superlative-A Little Hot (Petong) 4917[16] 5042[21] **>44f<**
Regal Dynasty (IRE) 3 b f Royal Academy (USA)-Reality (Known Fact (USA)) 815a[9] **>85f<**
Regal Eagle 4 b g Shirley Heights-On The Tiles (Thatch (USA)) 632[5] 1654[7] 2291[7] **>72df<**
Regal Equity 3 b c Keen-Nazmiah (Free State) *868[13]* 1388[16] **>66f<**
Regal Fanfare (IRE) 5 b m Taufan (USA)-Tender Time (Tender King) **1996:** *5095[11]* **>19a 62f<**
Regalo 2 b c Nalchik (USA)-Stardrop (Starch Reduced) 1109[9] 1425[7] 1954[8] 2781[4] 3314[8] 4517[7] 4737[5] 4911[3] **>83?f<**
Regal Patriarch (IRE) 2 br c Marju (IRE)-Early Rising (USA) (Grey Dawn II) 4526[20] 4758[8] 4957[5] **>67f<**
Regal Patrol 3 b g Red Ransom (USA)-River Patrol (Rousillon (USA)) 517[5] (797) 1104[3] 1595[2] 3441[4] **>87f<**
Regal Reprimand 3 b c Reprimand-Queen Caroline (USA) (Chief's Crown (USA)) 475[11] 797[3] 1129[2] 1296[2] 1747[3] 2004[7] (2722) (2909) 3184[4] 4109[4] **>74f<**
Regal Revolution 2 br f Hamas (IRE)-True Queen (USA) (Silver Hawk (USA)) 2306[2] (2579) (2858) (3468) 3740[4] (3981) (4267) **>97f<**
Regal Splendour (CAN) 4 ch g Vice Regent (CAN)-Seattle Princess (USA) (Seattle Slew (USA)) *108[5] (211) 294[8]* 752[6] 1320[9] **>68a 66f<**
Regal Thunder (USA) 3 b c Chief's Crown (USA)-Summertime Showers (USA) (Raise A Native) 674[9] 1088[3] 2585[9] 3012[8] 3937[5] 4270[9] 4283[13] 4848[3] **>77f<**
Reggie Buck (USA) 3 b br c Alleged (USA)-Hello Memphis (USA) (Super Concorde (USA)) 683[2] 4736[3] 4883[6] **>89f<**
Rehaab 4 b f Mtoto-Top Treat (USA) (Topsider (USA)) *74[5] 123[12] 380[6] 487[5]* 647[9] 1383[6] 1623[5] 1779[17] 2577[14] 3026[10] 3321[2] 3491[2] 3848[5] 4179[13] 4275[14] *4912[2]* **>58a 55f<**
Rehearsal (IRE) 3 b g Royal Academy (USA)-Yashville (Top Ville) 597[P] **>84f<**
Reimei 8 b g Top Ville-Brilliant Reay (Ribero) 680[12] 3015[9] 3714[7] 4179[8] 4821[7] **>59f<**
Reine Wells (IRE) 4 b f Sadler's Wells (USA)-Rivoltade (USA) (Sir Ivor) 1199a[3] 2099a[4] 3370a[5] 4676[4] **>104f<**
Reinhardt (IRE) 4 b g Bluebird (USA)-Rhein Bridge (Rheingold) (1687) 1830[3] 2129[8] 2543[6] 2651[6] 2759[6] 3240[8] 3431[9] 3627[7] 3759[4] 3992[9] **>46f<**
Rejected 2 b c Puissance-Dalby Dancer (Bustiki) 557[4] (1774) 2054[6] 2862[22] 3379[4] 3817[3] 4790[25] **>86+f<**
Relate 2 b f Distant Relative-Pulga (Blakeney) 2147[5] 2862[12] 3247[2] 3407[5] 4236[4] 4567[2] 4701[7] **>71f<**
Remaadi Sun 5 gr g Cadeaux Genereux-Catch The Sun (Kalaglow) 521[8] 680[7] 974[2] 1145[2] 1450[10] 2136[11] 2514[13] 2676[2] 2865[3] 3053[5] 3333[5] 3722[3] 4002[6] 4136[6] 4443[11] **>51a 91f<**
Remarkable Style (USA) 2 b f Danzig (USA)-Ophidian (USA) 4093a[8] **>99f<**
Remember Frimley 2 b f Presidium-Frimley Dancer (Northern Tempest (USA)) *2304[6]* 4402[10] *4573[8]* **>15a 33f<**
Renata's Prince (IRE) 4 b g Prince Rupert (FR)-Maria Renata (Jaazeiro (USA)) **1996:** *5094[8] 5200[13]* **1997:** 1384[7] 1632[5] 1796[2] 2150[3] (2485) 2576[2]

3153^{17} **>48a 63f<**

Rennyholme 6 ch g Rich Charlie-Jacqui Joy (Music Boy) **1996:** *5130^{13} 5225^{8} 5268^{8}* **1997:** *137^{7} 222^{7} 304^{5} 371^{5} 394^{9} 515^{4} 659^{8}* 949^{5} 1514^{6} 1671^{6} 2540^{10} 2738^{2} 2934^{7} 3431^{13} 3625^{13} **>40a 56?f<**

Reno's Treasure (USA) 4 ch f Beau Genius (CAN)-Ligia M (USA) (Noholme Jr (USA)) *218^{5}* **>7a 46f<**

Renown 5 b g Soviet Star (USA)-Starlet (Teenoso (USA)) **1996:** *5205^{12}* **1997:** *226^{2} 405^{5}* 521^{10} 1371^{3} **>79a 76f<**

Renzo (IRE) 4 b g Alzao (USA)-Watership (USA) (Foolish Pleasure (USA)) 986^{9} 1478^{5} 1974^{4} 3110^{12} 4108^{2} (4313) 4426^{3} **>95f<**

Repertory 4 b g Anshan-Susie's Baby (Balidar) (726) 877^{4} 1158^{12} 1766^{11} 2105^{27} 2377^{9} 3914^{3} 4100^{14} 4677^{4} 4756^{6} 4887^{4} **>92f<**

Repose (IRE) 2 gr f Posen (USA)-Dream Trader (Auction Ring (USA)) 3306^{16} 3973^{16} **>34f<**

Repton 2 ch g Rock City-Hasty Key (USA) (Key To The Mint (USA)) 4231^{11} 4752^{6} 4921^{14} **>36f<**

Requested 10 b g Rainbow Quest (USA)-Melody Hour (Sing Sing) 650^{12} 2139^{12} **>57f<**

Requestor 2 br c Distinctly North (USA)-Bebe Altesse (GER) (Alpenkonig (GER)) 2467^{3} 2706^{2} 3569^{2} 3825^{2} 4231^{3} 4790^{10} **>83f<**

Reservation Rock (IRE) 6 ch g Ballad Rock-Crazyfoot (Luthier) 430^{24} **>48?f<**

Resist the Force (USA) 7 br g Shadeed (USA)-Countess Tully (Hotfoot) *1082^{4} (1154)* 1324^{7} 1606^{4} *1969^{4}* 2721^{2} (2958) (3082) 3198^{3} 3580^{4} 3765^{15} **>68a 74f<**

Resounder (USA) 4 b g Explodent (USA)-Rub Al Khali (USA) (Mr Prospector (USA)) 892^{8} 1160^{14} 3713^{4} **>88f<**

Respectable Jones 11 ch g Tina's Pet-Jonesee (Dublin Taxi) *134^{11} 303^{7}* 774^{9} **>35a 29f<**

Respond 2 b f Reprimand-Kina (USA) (Bering) 1240^{9} 1970^{7} 2349^{3} *2595^{3}* 3186^{8} 4767^{14} 4898^{6} **>68a 78f<**

Restiv Star (FR) 5 b m Soviet Star (USA)-Restiver **1996:** 5154a^{3} **>113f<**

Restless Spirit (USA) 3 b c Sheikh Albadou-Wayward Lass (USA) (Hail the Pirates (USA)) 1243^{9} 1737^{4} 1980^{11} 2325^{8} 2517^{2} **>95f<**

Restructure (IRE) 5 b h Danehill (USA)-Twine (Thatching) 678^{8} 852^{7} 2009^{9} 2679^{3} 2830^{2} 3764^{4} 4148^{7} 4377^{2} (4599) **>115f<**

Resurrection (IRE) 2 b f Midyan (USA)-Tolstoya (Northfields (USA)) 3493^{7} 4066^{14} 4178^{13} 4753^{26} **>61f<**

Retention (IRE) 2 b c Statoblest-Olean (Sadler's Wells (USA)) 2439a^{6} 2811a^{4} **>75f<**

Ret Frem (IRE) 4 b g Posen (USA)-New Light (Reform) 3921^{15} **>76df<**

Retoto 3 ch f Totem (USA)-Responder (Vitiges (FR)) *5021^{15}* **>58f<**

Return of Amin 3 ch c Salse (USA)-Ghassanah (Pas de Seul) **1996:** *(5164)* **1997:** 483^{4} 610^{2} 845^{4} 1017^{6} 1737^{5} (1980) 2326^{2} 2560^{6} 3975^{2} 4280^{21} 4423^{7} 4787^{2} **>82a 92f<**

Return To Brighton 5 b m Then Again-Regency Brighton (Royal Palace) **1996:** *5118^{9}* **1997:** *407^{7}* 526^{6} 587^{3} 848^{10} 1128^{7} 1383^{9} 1689^{12} 2310^{8} **>25a 42df<**

Reunion (IRE) 3 br f Be My Guest (USA)-Phylella (Persian Bold) (672) 960^{15} **>119df<**

Reve Indien 3 ro c Indian Ridge-Thames Glow (Kalaglow) 821a^{3}

Revenge Is Sweet 2 b c Absalom-Welsh Secret (Welsh Captain) *1941^{11}* 3031^{8} **>31a 41f<**

Reverse Charge 0 G Teenoso (USA)-Ebb And Flo (Forlorn River) *235^{14}* **>36f<**

Revoque (IRE) 3 b c Fairy King (USA)-La Bella Fontana (Lafontaine (USA)) 737^{2} 940^{2} 1541a^{6} (4138) 4422^{8} 4785^{5} **>126f<**

Reward 3 gr c Highest Honor (FR)-Intimate Guest (Be My Guest (USA)) 1409^{3} 1637^{7} 1870^{6} **>75f<**

Rewardia (IRE) 2 b f Petardia-Riwaya (IRE) (Nishapour (FR)) 2516^{5} 3253^{3} 3426^{4} 3887^{5} 4361^{3} *4569^{12}* **>25a 75f<**

Rex Mundi 5 b g Gunner B-Rose Standish (Gulf Pearl) **1996:** *5148^{3}* **1997:** 1748^{8} 2236^{3} 2464^{2} (2682) 2944^{2} 3333^{7} 3890^{W} 4235^{6} 4363^{9} *(4594)* 4771^{10} *4981^{4}* **>72a 67f<**

Rhapsody In Blue (IRE) 2 b c Magical Strike (USA)-Palace Blue (IRE) (Dara Monarch) 3686^{9} 4515^{17} 4917^{15} **>38f<**

Rhapsody In White (IRE) 3 b g Contract Law (USA)-Lux Aeterna (Sandhurst Prince) 1006^{3} (1508) 1928^{3} 2391^{6} 3616^{11} 4108^{14} 4386^{11} 4742^{9} **>30a 49f<**

Rheinbold 3 br g Never so Bold-Rheinbloom (Rheingold) *868^{2}* (1282) 1649^{7} 3242^{2} 4774^{8} 4996^{8} **>64a 81f<**

Rhein Hill (IRE) 2 b c Danehill (USA)-Rhein Bridge (Rheingold) 4113^{9} 4603^{4} **>73f<**

Rhein Lady 3 b f Gildoran-Houston Belle (Milford) 4400^{4} **>47f<**

Rhinefield Beauty (IRE) 2 ch f Shalford (IRE)-Humble Mission (Shack (USA)) 897^{4} 2140^{5} 2545^{6} 2862^{18} 4162^{8} 4419^{4} 4702^{5} **>58f<**

Ribble Assembly 2 ch g Presidium-Spring Sparkle (Lord Gayle (USA)) 2383^{2} 2935^{2} 3212^{8} 4588^{15} 4994^{9} **>61f<**

Ribblesdale 2 b f Northern Park (USA)-Tarib (Habitat) 4779^{11} 4917^{6} 5048^{4} **>68f<**

Ribbonletta 3 b f Goldsmiths' Hall-Ribbon Lady (Kinglet) 2470^{4} 2661^{6} 2716^{W} **>18tf<**

Ribelle Umbro (ITY) 3 b c Sikeston (USA)-Rebel Computer (ITY) (Anfield) **1996:** (5196a)

Ribot's Pearl 3 b f Indian Ridge-Lovers Light (Grundy) 821a^{2} 1367a^{7}

Ricardo 3 b g Sanglamore (USA)-Nurica (USA) (Nureyev (USA)) 2583^{3} 3738^{2} 4705^{2} 4883^{2} **>89?f<**

Riccarton 4 b g Nomination-Legendary Dancer (Shareef Dancer (USA)) 733^{3} 1024^{3} 1384^{4} 1994^{5} 3382^{6} (3762) 4335^{2} 4751^{4} **>59f<**

Richard House Lad 4 b c Warrshan (USA)-Sirenivo (USA) (Sir Ivor) **1996:** *5079^{8} 5137^{8}* **1997:** 587^{5} 1005^{13} 1689^{14} 3456^{17} **>32a 44df<**

Rich Choice 2 gr f Presidium-Gratclo (Belfort (FR)) 1669^{4} 2361^{3} 2886^{4} 4097^{7} 4922^{2} **>68f<**

Rich Glow 6 b g Rich Charlie-Mayglow (Sparkling Boy) 596^{16} 702^{16} 949^{15} 1098^{14} (1311) 1594^{8} 1865^{10} 2111^{3} 2480^{2} 2563^{8} 2717^{3} 2844^{6} *3077^{9}* 3208^{5} 3334^{6} 3621^{8} 4233^{10} 4329^{12} 4385^{15} 4707^{7} 4844^{16} **>44a 43f<**

Rich Ground 3 gr c Common Grounds-Gratclo (Belfort (FR)) 679^{3} 1060a^{2} **>104f<**

Rich In Love (IRE) 3 b f Alzao (USA)-Chief's Quest (USA) (Chief's Crown (USA)) 853^{11} 959^{8} 1595^{6} 1869^{5} 2551^{4} 3026^{11} (3448) 3718^{11} 3772^{7} 4121^{21} **>81f<**

Richmond Hill 2 b c Sabrehill (USA)-Mrs Warren (USA) (Hail To Reason) 4526^{16} **>57f<**

Richter Scale (USA) 3 *5061a^{13}* **>72a f<**

Rickenbacker (IRE) 3 b c Bluebird (USA)-Sodium's Niece (Northfields (USA)) (983) 1836^{3} 3388^{4} 3891^{8} **>103?f<**

Ricky Ticky Tavie (USA) 3 b c Dixieland Band (USA)-Save The Doe (USA) (Spend A Buck (USA)) (4417) 4689^{3} **>97f<**

Rico Suave (IRE) 2 b g Persian Bold-Ballet Review (IRE) (Sadler's Wells (USA)) 2176^{4} *2363^{2}* (2898) 4044^{10} (4380) **>66a 88f<**

Ridaiyma (IRE) 3 b f Kahyasi-Riyda (Be My Guest (USA)) 1234^{3} (1922) (3689) 4256a^{6} (4443) 5053^{9} **>106f<**

Ridgeway (IRE) 2 b c Indian Ridge-Regal Promise (Pitskelly) 4064^{7} 4474^{11} **>71f<**

Ridiyara (IRE) 3 b f Persian Bold-Ridiya (IRE) 3362a^{4} 4094a^{8} **>94f<**

Rififi 4 ch g Aragon-Bundled Up (USA) (Sharpen Up) *(282) (304) 364^{5}* 834^{14} 1083^{5} 1166^{11} 1488^{3} (2006) 2179^{12} 2573^{W} (3198) (3765) 4155^{11} 4456^{5} 4777^{10} 4954^{7} **>72a 100f<**

Right Cross Jonny (USA) 2 ch c Regal Classic (CAN)-Bounteous (USA) (Master Derby (USA)) 3760^{8} 4367^{8} **>31f<**

Right Man 3 gr c Robellino (USA)-High Matinee (Shirley Heights) 537^{6} 771^{4} (1140) (1387) 2139^{2} (2530) 3218^{6} **>91+f<**

Right Tune 3 b f Green Desert (USA)-Triste Oeil (USA) (Raise A Cup (USA)) 699^{11} 1314^{3} 1845^{11} 2021^{2} 2508^{6} (2593) (3119) **>91f<**

Right Wing (IRE) 3 b c In The Wings-Nekhbet (Artaius (USA)) 725^{7} 963^{3} (2137) 2766^{7} 4463^{3} (4689) 4893^{9} **>104+f<**

Righty Ho 3 b g Reprimand-Challanging (Mill Reef (USA)) 791^{8} 1009^{5} 1392^{4} 1633^{6} (2245) 2854^{3} 3248^{6} (3432) 3971^{2} 4235^{13} 4449^{7} **>77f<**

Riley 2 b c Komaite (USA)-Miss Calculate (Mummy's Game) 2509^{13} 2953^{3} 3479^{7} 4044^{15} 4447^{4} **>72f<**

Rimouski 9 b h Sure Blade (USA)-Rimosa's Pet (Petingo) *67^{11}* **>30a 34f<**

Ring Dancer 2 b c Polar Falcon (USA)-Ring Cycle (Auction Ring (USA)) (3905) 4955^{2} **>93+f<**

Ringleader 2 b g Magic Ring (IRE)-Kinlet Vision (IRE) (Vision (USA)) *1577^{4}* 1842^{5} 2181^{8} 3186^{3} 3597^{10} 3926^{7} 4380^{5} 4753^{15} (4974) **>53a 70f<**

Ring the Chief 5 b g Chief Singer-Lomond Ring (Lomond (USA)) *151^{3} 85^{9} 177^{5} 235^{3} 313^{3} (327) 385^{3} 423^{4}* 1315^{9} 1632^{6} 1926^{6} *(2070) 2305^{7}* 3091^{3} (3394) 3465^{5} 4179^{4} 4373^{4} **>45a 46f<**

Ring The Rafters 2 b f Batshoof-Soprano (Kris) 739^{5} **>51f<**

Rinus Magic 4 ch g Timeless Times (USA)-Callace (Royal Palace) *387^{9} 417^{5}* 689^{12} 1128^{8} **>22a 32f<**

Rio (IRE) 2 b g Superpower-Apocalypse (Auction Ring (USA)) 2739^{6} 3265^{3} *3610^{13}* 4236^{10} *4592^{8}* 4801^{10} **>7a 69f<**

Rioja 2 ch c Anshan-Executive Flare (Executive Man) 2022^{2} 2881^{3} 3270^{4} 3932^{9} 5050^{5} **>69f<**

Rio Napo (IRE) 3 b c Law Society (USA)-My Southern love (ITY) (Southern Arrow (USA)) 1553a^{8} **>97f<**

Riot 2 b c Fairy King (USA)-Lucia Tarditi (FR) (Crystal Glitters (USA)) 4884^{8} **>64f<**

Risada (IRE) 2 b f Lahib (USA)-Sparkish (IRE) (Persian Bold) 2728^{18} 3638^{15} 3861^{3} 4185^{8} 4806^{19} **>77f<**

Riscatto (USA) 3 b c Red Ransom (USA)-Ultima Cena (USA) (Leonardo da Vinci (FR)) *300^{3}* (582) 771^{9} 2531^{11} 2727^{7} *3413^{9}* 4584^{15} **>61a 47f<**

Rise Above (IRE) 3 b f Simply Great (FR)-La Tanque (USA) (Last Raise (USA)) 2172^{7} **>45f<**

Rise 'n Shine 3 ch f Night Shift (USA)-Clunk Click (Star Appeal) 1107^{9} 1644^{5} 1931^{8} 2536^{11} 2751^{5} 3083^{7} 3771^{13} 4248^{8} **>36f<**

Rise Up Singing 9 ch g Noalto-Incarnadine (Hot Spark) 2785^{17} 3100^{11} 3420^{7} 4561^{22} **>41f<**

Risiat (IRE) 3 b c Waajib-Ratafia (Rousillon (USA)) 917a^{2} 1553a^{5} (4760a) **>114f<**

Rising Dough (IRE) 5 br g Dowsing (USA)-

Shortning Bread (Blakeney) 435^{10} 1010^{4} *1153^{6}* 2318^{2} (2574) 2749^{5} **>28a 76f< (DEAD)**
Rising Mane 2 b c Reprimand-Petastra (Petoski) 4910^{6} **>43f<**
Rising of The Moon (IRE) 2 gr f Warning-Dazzlingly Radiant (Try My Best (USA)) (447) (651) 2558^{11} **>83f<**
Rising Spray 6 ch g Waajib-Rose Bouquet (General Assembly (USA)) (770) (969) 1491^{7} 2696^{3} 3475^{3} 4156^{8} 4313^{4} **>77f<**
Risking 4 b f Risk Me (FR)-Dark Kristal (IRE) (Gorytus (USA)) **1996:** *5124^{7}* **1997:** 1373^{14} 4043^{18} 4608^{18} **>43a 9f<**
Risk Me Too 3 b c Risk Me (FR)-Mandrake Madam (Mandrake Major) *412^{5}* **>22a f<**
Risknowt Getnowt 2 b g Ron's Victory (USA)-Scottish Tina (Scottish Reel) *1286^{11} 2163^{6}* 3253^{9} 3818^{13} 4058^{13} 4459^{10} **>22f<**
Risky Flight 3 ch g Risk Me (FR)-Stairway to Heaven (IRE) (Godswalk (USA)) 779^{12} 2883^{9} 3088^{8} 3271^{15} 3601^{10} 4326^{10} **>37f<**
Risky Girl 2 ro f Risk Me (FR)-Jove's Voodoo (USA) (Northern Jove (CAN)) (1997) 2500^{9} **>66f<**
Risky Lover 4 b f Risk Me (FR)-Dawn Love (He Loves Me) *424^{12}* 469^{7} *577^{5} 855^{10}* **>29a 31tf<**
Risky Missile 3 b f Risk Me (FR)-Veuve Perrin (Legend of France (USA)) 4872^{18} **>64f<**
Risky Rose 5 b m Risk Me (FR)-Moharabuiee (Pas de Seul) 570^{4} 1570^{2} 2200^{B} 2753^{3} 2896^{7} **>40a 51f<**
Risky Tu 6 ch m Risk Me (FR)-Sarah Gillian (USA) (Zen (USA)) **1996:** *5260^{3}* **1997:** *123^{4}* **>46a 47f<**
Risky Whisky 2 b g Risk Me (FR)-Desert Gem (Green Desert (USA)) (500) 611^{2} 696^{6} 1310^{6} *1758^{9} (2051)* (2233) 2658^{5} *3042^{5}* 3699^{4} 4737^{12} *(5017)* **>64a 64f<**
Risque 2 ch g Risk Me (FR)-Sweet And Sour (Sharpen Up) 2579^{9} 3278^{21} 3818^{12} 4058^{15} **>21f<**
Risque Lady 2 ch f Kenmare (FR)-Christine Daae (Sadler's Wells (USA)) (3636) 4106^{7} (4305) 4560^{6} **>96f<**
Rissaga 3 ch f Meqdaam (USA)-Crosby Place (Crooner) **1996:** *5103^{8}* **>20a f<**
Rita's Rock Ape 2 b f Mon Tresor-Failand (Kala Shikari) 2875^{17} 3782^{8} 4178^{4} 4566^{2} 5045^{2} **>72f<**
Rithab 4 b f Shaadi (USA)-Lawahed (USA) 2079a^{3} **>97f<**
Ritual 2 ch g Selkirk (USA)-Pure Formality (Forzando) 4708^{6} **>63f<**
Rival Bid (USA) 9 b g Cannonade (USA)-Love Triangle (USA) (Nodouble (USA)) *226^{8} 369^{4} 422^{9}* 1001^{15} 3315^{16} 4063^{15} 4172^{17} 4562^{16} 4607^{12} *4810^{8}* **>59a 45f<**
River Ball (FR) 2 ro c Balleroy (USA)-Split River (FR) (Riverman (USA)) 3872a^{2}
River Bay (USA) 4 ch c Irish River (FR)-Buckeye Gal (USA) (Good Counsel (USA)) (625a) 922a^{4} **>120+f<**
River Beat (IRE) 2 b c River Falls-Aughamore Beauty (IRE) (Dara Monarch) 2556^{8} 3201^{12} 3687^{11} **>50f<**
River Captain (USA) 4 ch g Riverman (USA)-Katsura (USA) (Northern Dancer) *73^{4} (373) 516^{12} 2164^{11}* **>68a 54f<**
River Ensign 4 br f River God (USA)-Ensigns Kit (Saucy Kit) 480^{9} 653^{13} *907^{4}* 1236^{9} *1428^{3} 1790^{4} 2674^{5}* (3241) 3431^{19} 4328^{7} **>31a 47f<**
River Flare (USA) 2 ch f Riverman (USA)-Proflare (USA) (Mr Prospector (USA)) 4387a^{3} **>90f<**
River Foyle (USA) 3 ch c Irish River (FR)-Katsura (USA) (Northern Dancer) 2641a^{3} **>106f<**
River Frontier (IRE) 2 b f Imperial Frontier (USA)-River Low (IRE) (Lafontaine (USA)) 2283^{4} 2917^{17} 3324^{10} *3586^{8}* 3911^{7} 4178^{8} *4593^{7}* **>40a 50f<**
River Keen (IRE) 5 ch h Keen-Immediate Impact (Caerleon (USA)) *(426)* 499^{8} **>110+a 88f<**
Riverlution 2 gr c Absolution-River Fire (IRE) (Petong) 3692^{W}
River North (IRE) 7 ch g Lomond (USA)-Petillante (USA) (Riverman (USA)) 1490^{4} 1960^{2} 2333^{4} (3365a) 4123a^{4} **>116f<**
River of Fortune (IRE) 3 b f Lahib (USA)-Debach Delight (Great Nephew) 1000^{10} 1500^{8} 2178^{4} 2468^{5} 3320^{2} 3695^{3} 3870^{3} **>59f<**
River Pilot 3 b c Unfuwain (USA)-Cut Ahead (Kalaglow) 740^{10} (1277) 1962^{5} 2585^{14} **>96f<**
River Run (IRE) 5 b h Nordico (USA)-Irish Call (USA) (Irish River (FR)) **1996:** *5181^{12} 5200^{11}* **1997:** *369^{9} 457^{10}* 1247^{3} 1383^{14} 1441^{5} 1798^{4} 2039^{15} **>39a 54f<**
River Seine (FR) 5 b m Shining Steel-River Sans Retour (FR) (Vacarme (USA)) **1996:** *5183^{3} 5253^{4} (5282)* **1997:** *65^{9} 134^{3} 186^{7} 278^{2} 349^{4} 490^{7}* 601^{8} 2395^{7} 2848^{9} 3394^{3} **>50a 48f<**
Riverside Girl (IRE) 3 b f River Falls-Ballywhat (IRE) (Be My Native (USA)) 2941^{5} 3276^{7} 3762^{12} **>46f<**
Rivers Magic 4 b g Dominion-Rivers Maid (Rarity) 1634^{8} *2160^{6}* 2228^{4} 2390^{10} 2727^{6} **>42a 64f<**
River's Source (USA) 3 b c Irish River (FR)-Singing (USA) (The Minstrel (CAN)) 436^{2} (690) 1741^{10} 2341^{8} 2729^{8} 3120^{3} **>83f<**
River Tern 4 b g Puissance-Millaine (Formidable (USA)) 702^{2} 879^{9} (1127) 1385^{4} 1599^{7} 2001^{3} (2703) 2847^{5} 3016^{6} 3280^{4} (3566) 3795^{6} 3922^{9} 4329^{7} **>44a 68f<**
River Tweed 3 ch f Selkirk (USA)-Twixt (Kings Lake (USA)) 1499^{9} 2045^{3} 2506^{9} 3241^{15} 3716^{6} **>42f<**
River Usk 3 b c Caerleon (USA)-Shining Water (Kalaglow) 4004^{3} 4281^{7} **>102f<**
Riyadian 5 ch h Polish Precedent (USA)-Knight's Baroness (Rainbow Quest (USA)) (1836) 2460a^{3} **>125f<**
Road Racer (IRE) 4 br g Scenic-Rally (Relko) *284^{5} (375)* 465^{4} 650^{2} 762^{7} (866) 1022^{7} (1393) 1660^{3} 1832^{2} 2293^{8} 2843^{8} 3104^{4} **>64a 70f<**
Roar on Tour 8 b g Dunbeath (USA)-Tickled Trout (Red Alert) **1996:** *5179^{15}* **1997:** *358^{9} 870^{13}* 1040^{3} **>35a 29f<**
Robanna 2 b f Robellino (USA)-Pounelta (Tachypous) 3638^{11} 4317^{9} 4694^{7} **>64f<**
Robban Hendi (USA) 3 b br c A P Indy (USA)-Real Jenny (USA) (Valid Appeal (USA)) 1271^{8} 1646^{2} 2583^{12} **>80f<**
Robbo 3 b g Robellino (USA)-Basha (USA) (Chief's Crown (USA)) *425^{5} 1121^{5} 1430^{6} 1756^{8}* 2029^{2} 2238^{3} 2521^{5} *(3587) 3865^{10} 4055^{6} (4302) (4590)* 4749^{3} **>76a 67f<**
Robec Girl (IRE) 3 ch f Masterclass (USA)-Resiusa (ITY) (Niniski (USA)) 883^{9} 1666^{5} 1810^{9} **>66a 56f<**
Robeena 2 b f Robellino (USA)-Raheena (USA) (Lyphard (USA)) 2516^{3} 2697^{3} 2962^{6} 3278^{4} 4006^{8} 4362^{7} **>78f<**
Robellion 6 b g Robellino (USA)-Tickled Trout (Red Alert) *120^{2} 131^{9} 211^{2} 238^{2} 294^{3} 382^{3} 405^{6} 457^{8}* 1824^{8} 2232^{8} 2698^{6} 2852^{6} 3016^{4} 3290^{7} 4115^{8} 4221^{5} (4518) 4580^{12} 4805^{3} **>72a 59f<**
Robereva (IRE) 4 b f Red Sunset-Gay Reign (Lord Gayle (USA)) 2099a^{6} **>101f<**
Robert's Daughter 2 b f Robellino (USA)-Cache (Bustino) *1045^{11}* 4595^{13} *4796^{12}* **>23a f<**
Robert The Bruce 2 ch g Distinct Native-Kawarau Queen (Taufan (USA)) 3427^{9} 3751^{11} **>34f<**
Roberty Bob (IRE) 2 ch c Bob Back (USA)-Inesdela (Wolver Hollow) 3686^{13} 4017^{10} 4454^{9} **>51f<**
Robin Goodfellow 2 b c Fairy King (USA)-La Tuerta (Hot Spark) 4298^{14} (4747) 4897^{13} **>83f<**
Robin Island 5 b g Robellino (USA)-Irish Isle (Realm) **1996:** *5118^{11} 5149^{12}* **>61df<**
Robin Lane 2 b f Tenby-Hiawatha's Song (USA) (Chief's Crown (USA)) 1847^{6} 2312^{5} 3471^{11} 4097^{5} 4750^{10} **>68f<**
Robins (IRE) 5 b h Scenic-Roman Walk (Petorius) 1552a^{3} (5037a) **>114f<**
Robo Magic (USA) 5 b g Tejano (USA)-Bubble Magic (USA) (Clever Trick (USA)) **1996:** *5246^{14}* **1997:** *117^{6} (184) 253^{2} 323^{6} 397^{3} 406^{5} 569^{2}* 759^{4} *(905) 1578^{3} 2162^{5}* 2732^{11} *3075^{13} 4482^{10} 4797^{11}* **>82da 37f<**
Roborant 2 b c Robellino (USA)-Sunny Davis (USA) (Alydar (USA)) 1812^{10} 2181^{19} 2943^{3} 3750^{6} 4778^{12} **>78f<**
Robsart (IRE) 2 b f Robellino (USA)-Sharp Girl (FR) (Sharpman) 2728^{5} 3753^{2} **>72+f<**
Rochea 3 br f Rock City-Pervenche (Latest Model) *96^{3} 154^{4} 246^{3} 378^{7} 414^{5}* 535^{10} 582^{3} 862^{5} 1095^{5} 1246^{3} 1383^{18} 1622^{2} 2040^{5} 2733^{12} 2941^{2} 3316^{10} 3454^{8} 4043^{15} 4916^{3} **>55a 55f<**
Rockaroundtheclock 3 b g Rock City-Times (Junius (USA)) 532^{10} *588^{6}* 757^{3} 882^{5} 1586^{3} 1864^{5} 3470^{8} 4016^{19} 4465^{16} **>35a 56f<**
Rockcracker (IRE) 5 ch g Ballad Rock-Forest Blaze (USA) (Green Forest (USA)) 541^{10} 835^{6} 1279^{6} (1666) 2006^{13} 2698^{8} 3082^{11} 3290^{6} 4248^{11} 4580^{3} 4905^{17} **>55da 59f<**
Rockette 2 ch f Rock Hopper-Primulette (Mummy's Pet) 2752^{9} 3103^{8} 3479^{10} 3990^{8} 4208^{14} **>58f<**
Rock Falcon (IRE) 4 ch g Polar Falcon (USA)-Rockfest (USA) (Stage Door Johnny) (1087) 1598^{5} 2117^{R} 2390^{R} (4114) 4511^{5} (4680) **>97f<**
Rock Fantasy 3 b f Keen-Runelia (Runnett) *124^{7} 168^{8} 191^{4} 314^{9}* 556^{11} *1044^{12}* **>44a 55f<**
Rockforce 5 ch g Rock City-Sleepline Princess (Royal Palace) 450^{22} (735) 1016^{4} 1768^{9} 2028^{16} 2341^{2} 2514^{15} **>98f<**
Rock From The Sun 2 b f Rock City-Amathus Glory (Mummy's Pet) 664^{3} *1045^{7} 1432^{4} (2304) 2914^{3}* 3451^{6} *4303^{5} 4573^{4} 4593^{6} 4799^{7}* **>56a 51f<**
Rockie The Jester 3 b g Rock Hopper-Magic Steps (Nomination) 2173^{8} 2492^{9} 2846^{11} *3587^{9}* **>37f<**
Rock Island Line (IRE) 3 b g New Express-Gail's Crystal (Crofter (USA)) (551) (997) 1333^{2} 2130^{3} 2214^{3} 2517^{7} 3254^{11} 4114^{10} *4570^{2}* 4742^{14} **>61a 71df<**
Rock It Rosie 3 ch f Rock Hopper-Rockin' Rosie (Song) 641^{7} 862^{7} 1095^{3} **>46f<**
Rock River 3 ch f Rock Hopper-Emmer Green (Music Boy) 2960^{9} **>47f<**
Rock Scene (IRE) 5 b g Scenic-Rockeater (Roan Rocket) 4063^{18} **>68a f<**
Rock Sounds 2 br g Rock City-Shernborne (Kalaglow) 4229^{9} 4526^{21} 4753^{22} **>39f<**
Rockswain (IRE) 2 ch g Ballad Rock-Uninvited Guest (Be My Guest (USA)) 2288^{13} **>24f<**
Rock Symphony 7 ch g Ballad Rock-Shamasiya (FR) (Vayrann) 2006^{17} 2220^{7} 2892^{8} 3691^{6} 3910^{13} **>63f<**
Rock The Barney (IRE) 8 b h Coquelin (USA)-Lady Loire (Wolverlife) **1996:** *5102^{4} 5148^{7}* **1997:** 1441^{7} 1636^{6} 1825^{3} 2483^{4} 2949^{10} 3183^{7} 3491^{7} 3758^{5} (4179) 4453^{8} 4584^{16} 4918^{2} **>44a 55f<**
Rock The Casbah 3 ch g Rock City-Romantic

Saga (Prince Tenderfoot (USA)) **1996:** *5164^{10} 5212^{6}* **1997:** 2885^{4} 3102^{5} **>33a 41f<**

Rock To The Top (IRE) 3 b c Rudimentary (USA)-Well Bought (IRE) (Auction Ring (USA)) **1996:** *5080^{4} 5146^{7} 5278^{2}* **1997:** *107^{3}* **>72a 71f<**

Rocky Dance (FR) 3 b f Rock Hopper-Open Date (IRE) (Thatching) 833^{W} 1322^{2} 2389^{7} 2731^{9} (3205) 3452^{2} 3696^{5} **>76f<**

Rocky Oasis (USA) 4 b c Gulch (USA)-Knoosh (USA) (Storm Bird (CAN)) 678^{10} (842) 1176^{11} 1476^{4} 1771^{8} 4759^{5} **>112f<**

Rocky's Profiles (IRE) 4 b g Roi Danzig (USA)-Viceroy Princess (Godswalk (USA)) 3929^{10} **>25f<**

Rocky Waters (USA) 8 b or br g Rocky Marriage (USA)-Running Melody (Rheingold) *490^{6}* 755^{8} 1009^{4} *2070^{7}* 2369^{11} 3276^{2} 3849^{4} 4504^{7} **>54a 40f<**

Rodinia (USA) 2 ch c Diesis-Rangoon Ruby (Sallust) 1163^{4} 1933^{11} **>71f<**

Roffey Spinney (IRE) 3 ch c Masterclass (USA)-Crossed Line (Thatching) **1996:** *5248^{7}* **1997:** *145^{3} (251) (320) 459^{3} 871^{7}* 3418^{8} 4565^{5} 4820^{3} 4905^{10} *5021^{11}* **>79a 75f<**

Roger de Berksted (USA) 9 b h Topsider (USA)-Liberty Spirit (USA) (Graustark) 919a^{3} 3735a^{2} **>97f<**

Roi Brisbane 2 b c Roi Danzig (USA)-Crystal Cup (USA) (Nijinsky (CAN)) 4513^{3} 4884^{17} *(4982)* **>79a 79+f<**

Roi de Danse 2 ch c Komaite (USA)-Princess Lucy (Local Suitor (USA)) 2306^{11} 2706^{8} 3278^{5} (3686) 4143^{7} 4790^{17} **>72f<**

Roi du Nord (FR) 5 b g Top Ville-Ridja (FR) (Djakao (FR)) 3824^{7} 4172^{10} **>54f<**

Roi Gironde (IRE) 2 c Chief III- 3178a^{4} 3882a^{6} 4861a^{2} (5057a) **>101f<**

Roi Hoi (FR) 6 br m Holst (USA)-Reine Ka (FR) (Kaldoun (FR)) (149a) **>68f<**

Roisin Clover 6 ch m Faustus (USA)-Valiyen (Valiyar) (1592) 2391^{7} **>74f<**

Roisin Splendour (IRE) 2 ch f Inchinor-Oriental Splendour (Runnett) 2579^{3} 2875^{10} **>56f<**

Rokeby Bowl 5 b g Salse (USA)-Rose Bowl (USA) (Habitat) 775^{3} 962^{3} 1319^{6} 2028^{8} 2514^{6} (2764) (3599) 4443^{8} 4754^{16} **>102f<**

Rolling High (IRE) 2 ch c Roi Danzig (USA)-Sally Chase (Sallust) 4715^{17}

Rolling Stone 3 b c Northern Amethyst-First Sapphire (Simply Great (FR)) 1936^{3} **>77f<**

Romalito 7 b g Robellino (USA)-Princess Zita (Manado) 465^{5} 632^{3} 1100^{4} 1424^{2} 1654^{2} 1808^{3} 2198^{9} 2702^{10} 3623^{5} **>47a 48f<**

Romanov (IRE) 3 b c Nureyev (USA)-Morning Devotion (USA) (Affirmed (USA)) (503) (829) 1541a^{3} 1769^{3} 3002a^{3} (3409) 4420^{2} 4870a^{3} **>123f<**

Roman Reel (USA) 6 ch g Sword Dance-Our Mimi (USA) (Believe It (USA)) *321^{10} (401) 457^{6}* 607^{6} 753^{3} *870^{6}* 1011^{3} 1422^{10} (1642) 2150^{9} 2195^{7} 3588^{5} (3971) 4449^{4} 4504^{3} *5022^{7}* **>56a 61f<**

Romantic Secret 2 ch f Executive Man-Tria Romantica (Another Realm) *1789^{9}* 2784^{9} **>25f<**

Romantic Warrior 4 b g Welsh Captain-Romantic Melody (Battle Hymn) *373^{13}* 481^{9} **>49f<**

Roman Winner 3 b c Tisserand-Roman Walk (Petorius) **1996:** 5196a^{3}

Romios (IRE) 5 ch h Common Grounds-Domino's Nurse (Dom Racine (FR)) (521) 939^{4} 1450^{4} 1771^{5} 2136^{4} 2348^{2} **>95f<**

Ronquista d'Or 3 b c Ron's Victory (USA)-Gild the Lily (Ile de Bourbon (USA)) 539^{3} *1043^{11}* 1426^{2} 1825^{7} *2301^{5}* 2511^{6} 3714^{W} 4289^{2} 4519^{13} **>54a 58f<**

Ron's Pet 2 ch c Ron's Victory (USA)-Penny Mint (Mummy's Game) 850^{2} 979^{2} 1235^{3} 2571^{7} 3113^{2} (3295) 3750^{2} 4778^{15} **>86f<**

Ron's Round 3 ch c Ron's Victory (USA)-Magical Spirit (Top Ville) *296^{7} 341^{8}* 2554^{20} *3044^{4} 3413^{3}* 4043^{5} 4326^{2} 4465^{2} 4817^{4} **>43a 66f<**

Rood Music 6 ro g Sharrood (USA)-Rose Music (Luthier) **1996:** *5231^{7}* **1997:** *55^{2} 101^{8}* **>77da 51f<**

Rooftop Flyer (IRE) 6 b h Nordico (USA)-Audenhove (GER) (Marduk (GER)) 353a^{3} **>48f<**

Rosabella 3 f 4655a^{8} **>102f<**

Rosalee Royale 5 ch m Out of Hand-Miss Ark Royal (Broadsword (USA)) *336^{5} 486^{6}* 2200^{U} 2748^{5} 3196^{6} 3293^{8} **>38f<**

Rosa Royale 3 b f Arazi (USA)-Gussy Marlowe (Final Straw) 2846^{6} 3389^{6} 3632^{8} 4324^{6} **>54f<**

Roseate Lodge 11 b g Habitat-Elegant Tern (USA) (Sea Bird II) *209^{14} 327^{8}* 496^{10} 1603^{6} 1631^{7} 1830^{8} (2237) 2573^{3} 2937^{3} (3039) 3240^{5} 3476^{8} 3565^{6} **>6a 46f<**

Roseate Wood (FR) 4 ch f Kaldoun (FR)-Touch of Pink (SWI) (Pink) 354a^{2} (816a) 1720a^{2} 3372a^{6} 4124a^{6} **>112f<**

Rose Bourbon (USA) 4 b f Woodman (USA)-River Rose (FR) (Riverman (USA)) **1996:** 5155a^{3} **>104f<**

Rose Burton 3 b f Lucky Wednesday-Holly Burton (King Emperor (USA)) *49^{7} 135^{5} (246) 366^{6}* **>60a f<**

Rose Carnival 3 b f Salse (USA)-Jungle Rose (Shirley Heights) 4015^{12} **>74f<**

Rose Flyer (IRE) 7 b m Nordico (USA)-String of Straw (Thatching) 3716^{5} 3910^{23} 4249^{16} **>19f<**

Rosenkavalier (IRE) 3 b g Classic Music (USA)-Top Bloom (Thatch (USA)) 1000^{8} 1680^{9} 2004^{16} 2646^{16} **>55df<**

Rose of Glenn 6 b m Crofthall-May Kells (Artaius (USA)) **1996:** *5108^{2} 5139^{8} 5232^{5}* **1997:** *43^{5}* 1114^{10} (1570) 2035^{5} 2175^{3} 2531^{9} 2874^{4} 3203^{W} 3283^{11} 3623^{2} 3928^{6} 4170^{12} 4432^{11} 4519^{6} 4946^{4} **>45a 48f<**

Rose Tint (IRE) 4 b f Salse (USA)-Sally Rose (Sallust) **1996:** *5081^{4} 5137^{5}* **>43a 51f<**

Rosewood Lady (IRE) 2 b f Maledetto (IRE)-Thrill Seeker (IRE) (Treasure Kay) *592^{2} 902^{10}* 2003^{4} 2191^{2} 2283^{2} (3782) 4068^{17} *4483^{4} 4799^{8}* **>51a 64f<**

Rossel (USA) 4 b g Blushing John (USA)-Northern Aspen (USA) (Northern Dancer) 553^{8} 613^{8} 950^{3} 1039^{7} **>63f<**

Rossi Osvaldo (ITY) 3 b c Big Reef-Roll on (Nabirpour (USA)) (812a) **>77?f<**

Rossmore Girl (IRE) 4 b f Scenic-Rosa Van Fleet (Sallust) 2267a^{6} 4191a^{6} **>102f<**

Rosy Outlook (USA) 3 b br f Trempolino (USA)-Rosyphard (USA) (Lyphard (USA)) (778) 968^{7} 1781^{3} 2547^{5} **>83f<**

Rotherfield Park (IRE) 5 b m High Estate-Alriyaah (Shareef Dancer (USA)) 883^{18} 1828^{13} 2938^{3} 3107^{6} 3378^{7} **>43a 42tf<**

Rotor Man (IRE) 3 b g River Falls-Need For Cash (USA) (Raise A Native) 518^{5} 699^{10} 1458^{3} 2019^{6} 2313^{7} 2951^{6} 4164^{9} **>54f<**

Roufontaine 6 gr m Rousillon (USA)-Bellifontaine (FR) (Bellypha) 881^{6} (1142) 1435^{2} 1923^{2} 2210^{5} 2839^{3} 3246^{3} 4109^{7} **>70a 86f<**

Round Robin (IRE) 3 ch c Royal Academy (USA)-Flying Fantasy (Habitat) 983^{4} 1302^{3} 1834^{6} 3274^{5} 3404^{2} **>74df<**

Rousitto 9 ch g Rousillon (USA)-Helenetta (Troy) **1996:** *5108^{7} 5143^{5}* **>69a 50f<**

Roussi (USA) 5 b g Nureyev (USA)-Iva Reputation (USA) (Sir Ivor) *29^{4} (153) 194^{2}* 435^{11} 461^{15} **>50a 37f<**

Roving Minstrel 6 ch h Cree Song-Klairove (Averof) 450^{8} **>62a 101f<**

Rowlandsons Charm (IRE) 4 b f Fayruz-Magic Gold (Sallust) **1996:** *5088^{2} 5148^{5} 5222^{8}* **>63a 43f<**

Rowlandsons Stud (IRE) 4 b br g Distinctly North (USA)-Be My Million (Taufan (USA)) **1996:** *5138^{11}* **1997:** 2780^{5} 3083^{3} *3398^{9}* 3816^{10} 3852^{8} 4248^{U} **>63da 49f<**

Roy 2 ch c Keen-Billante (USA) (Graustark) 4318^{13} **>45f<**

Royal Acclaim 12 ch g Tender King-Glimmer (Hot Spark) *15^{5} 42^{2} (66) 188^{9} 205^{12} 333^{4} 360^{6} 411^{8}* 2696^{15} 2848^{4} 3048^{8} 3196^{4} 3248^{10} 3588^{4} 3814^{7} 3971^{5} 4548^{6} **>42a 53f<**

Royal Action 4 b g Royal Academy (USA)-Ivor's Honey (Sir Ivor) **1996:** *(5117)* **1997:** *(52) (220) (365) 398^{9}* 787^{12} **>96a 74f<**

Royal Affinity (IRE) 3 ch c Royal Academy (USA)-Tuyenu 2815a^{7} 4834a^{6} **>101f<**

Royal Amaretto (IRE) 3 b c Fairy King (USA)-Melbourne Miss (Chaparral (FR)) (741) 1541a^{11} 2274a^{5} 2864^{3} **>116f<**

Royal Applause 4 b c Waajib-Flying Melody (Auction Ring (USA)) (452) (1171) (2056) 2599^{2} (4011) 4664a^{3} *5061a^{14}* **>60a 125f<**

Royal Aty (IRE) 3 b c Royal Academy (USA)-Atyaaf (USA) (Irish River (FR)) *(60)* 508^{6} 917a^{10} 1216^{2} 1462^{3} 2105^{22} **>87a 104f<**

Royal Axminster 2 b c Alzao (USA)-Number One Spot (Reference Point) 1263^{11} **>23f<**

Royal Blackbird 3 br f Most Welcome-Thulium (Mansingh (USA)) 675^{19} 1385^{12} 2406^{W} 2554^{21} **>67f<**

Royal Blue 2 ch c Ron's Victory (USA)-Angels Are Blue (Stanford) 4311^{12} 4630^{5} 4818^{10} **>62f<**

Royal Bounty (IRE) 2 b f Generous (IRE)-Queen Helen (Troy) 1933^{6} 2693^{2} (3757) 4116^{10} **>84f<**

Royal Carlton (IRE) 5 b g Mulhollande (USA)-Saintly Angel (So Blessed) **1996:** *5221^{3} (5253)* **1997:** *(21) 121^{4} (186) 257^{5} 358^{6} 382^{2}* 477^{11} **>76a 46f<**

Royal Cascade (IRE) 3 b g River Falls-Relative Stranger (Cragador) **1996:** *5239^{6} 5265^{2}* **1997:** *(259)* 845^{9} 1691^{6} 2206^{5} *3040^{7} 3582^{5}* **>57a 49f<**

Royal Castle (IRE) 3 b c Caerleon (USA)-Sun Princess (English Prince) 725^{14} 1277^{5} (1649) 3915^{7} 4372^{4} (4598) 4774^{3} **>86f<**

Royal Ceilidh (IRE) 4 b f Prince Rupert (FR)-Isa (Dance In Time (CAN)) 947^{4} 1300^{6} 1583^{5} 2325^{10} 2857^{5} 3061^{4} 3243^{4} 3622^{5} 4283^{18} 4596^{12} **>74f<**

Royal Circus 8 b g Kris-Circus Ring (High Top) *147^{11} 202^{3}* (2531) 2702^{5} 2932^{5} 3283^{13} **>47a 48f<**

Royal Citizen (IRE) 8 b g Caerleon (USA)-Taking Steps (Gay Fandango (USA)) *80^{2}* 465^{16} *660^{7} 858^{7}* **>66a 51f<**

Royal Court (IRE) 4 b c Sadler's Wells (USA)-Rose of Jericho (USA) (Alleged (USA)) (1033) 1917a^{5} 2104^{4} 3182a^{4} **>119f<**

Royal Crown (IRE) 3 b c Sadler's Wells (USA)-Rose of Jericho (USA) (Alleged (USA)) 1165^{4} 2311^{2} 2568^{3} 4234^{2} 4743^{2} 4879^{4} **>95f<**

Royal Crusade (USA) 3 b c Diesis-Sainte Croix (USA) (Nijinsky (CAN)) 931^{6} 3499^{5} 4151^{19} 4639^{10} 4792^{18} **>86df<**

Royal Diversion (IRE) 4 b f Marju (IRE)-Royal Recreation (USA) (His Majesty (USA)) 4521^{3} 4672^{9} **>80df<**

Royal Dome (IRE) 5 b g Salt Dome (USA)-Brook's Dilemma (Known Fact (USA)) 744^{13} 1468^{11} 1602^{8} (2001) 2563^{5} 2717^{5} 2844^{5} (3107) 3146^{2} 3410^{14} 3649^{21} 3761^{11} 4183^{8} 4385^{11} 4636^{17} 4791^{2} 4905^{7} 4995^{19} **>18a 75f<**

Royal Dream 2 b f Ardkinglass-Faraway Grey (Absalom) *1045^{5}* (1298) (2060) 2516^{9} 3257^{3} 3438^{6} 4014^{11} **>54a 73f<**

Royale (IRE) 3 b f Royal Academy (USA)-Societe Royale (Milford) 1533a^{10} 4834a^{7} **>102f<**

Royale Figurine (IRE) 6 ch m Dominion Royale-Cree's Figurine (Creetown) (1112) 1455^{4} 2056^{6} 2106^{17} 2426^{3} **>108f<**

Royale Finale (IRE) 3 ch c Royal Academy (USA)-Final Farewell (USA) (Proud Truth (USA)) 742^{5} 963^{12} **>69f<**

Royal Emblem 3 gr f Presidium-Lily of France (Monsanto (FR)) **1996:** *5083^{11}* **1997:** 652^{6} *873^{12}* 1089^{11} 1810^{11} 2244^{11} 2747^{7} 3592^{8} **>27a 32f<**

Royale Rose (FR) 3 ch f Bering-Rose Blanche (USA) (Nureyev (USA)) 3211^{5} 3463^{9} (3775) 4015^{14} 4220^{2} 4308^{8} 4583^{11} **>77f<**

Royal Expression 5 b g Sylvan Express-Edwin's Princess (Owen Dudley) 470^{8} 777^{4} 1224^{2} 1648^{3} (1817) 2225^{2} 2530^{5} **>60a 73f<**

Royal Groom (FR) 3 b c Al Nasr (FR)-Fight Right (FR) (Crystal Glitters (USA)) 268a^{3} **>73f<**

Royal Ground (IRE) 2 b c Common Grounds-Miss Goodbody (Castle Keep) 3687^{7} 3887^{6} 4157^{6} 4366^{3} 4627^{2} 4698^{8} 4875^{9} **>70f<**

Royal Interview (IRE) 2 b g Mukaddamah (USA)-Empress Wu (High Line) 504^{6} 722^{6} 4542^{5} 4767^{16} 4856^{14} **>61f<**

Royal Intrusion 4 ch g Roman Warrior-Image of War (Warpath) 1925^{15} **>45f<**

Royal Legend 5 b g Fairy King (USA)-Legend of Arabia (Great Nephew) **1996:** *5259^{2}* **1997:** *236^{8} (1287) 1579^{6} 1943^{3} 2067^{5}* **>57a 62f<**

Royal Mark (IRE) 4 b g Fairy King (USA)-Take Your Mark (USA) (Round Table) 946^{6} 1948^{5} 2326^{W} 2708^{10} (3310) 3423^{17} 3888^{4} **>95f<**

Royal Orchid (IRE) 3 ch f Shalford (IRE)-Indigo Blue (IRE) (Bluebird (USA)) **1996:** *5251^{7}* **1997:** 2481^{10} 2742^{P} **>76?f<**

Royal Philosopher 5 b h Faustus (USA)-Princess Lucy (Local Suitor (USA)) **1996:** *5204^{3}* **1997:** 830^{8} 1261^{9} 4312^{4} 4671^{4} **>113a 80f<**

Royal Result (USA) 4 b br g Gone West (USA)-Norette (Northfields (USA)) 444^{16} 521^{11} 824^{6} 947^{8} 1097^{6} 3777^{5} 3987^{16} 4270^{4} (4561) 4927^{5} **>78f<**

Royal Rights 2 ch c Lion Cavern (USA)-Noble Destiny (Dancing Brave (USA)) 2771^{3} 3127^{5} 4706^{5} **>70f<**

Royal Roulette 3 ch f Risk Me (FR)-Princess Lily (Blakeney) **1996:** *5135^{5} 5180^{2} 5226^{7}* **1997:** *(6) 1429^{3} 2052^{3} 4304^{2} 4594^{7}* 4713^{7} 4817^{3} **>62a 57f<**

Royal Scimitar (USA) 5 ch h Diesis-Princess of Man (Green God) 962^{9} 1319^{8} **>105df<**

Royal Seaton 8 b g Blakeney-Aldbury Girl (Galivanter) 521^{9} 735^{6} 969^{6} 1208^{4} 2483^{7} 4002^{8} 4673^{7} 4874^{11} **>74f<**

Royal Shock (IRE) 2 b c Brief Truce (USA)-Rince Deas (IRE) (Alzao (USA)) 4064^{6} *4299^{6}* 4507^{3} **>63a 73f<**

Royal Shyness 2 b f Royal Academy (USA)-Miss Demure (Shy Groom (USA)) 3009^{3} 3636^{2} (4103) 4475^{3} **>96f<**

Royal Snack (AUS) 9 b g Lunchtime-Queen Gipsy **1996:** 5217a^{2} **>125f<**

Royal South (IRE) 4 b c Common Grounds-Arkadina's Million (King of Clubs) 540^{6} 635^{7} 946^{7} 1225^{16} 2036^{18} 2201^{9} 2546^{11} 3029^{12} 3759^{10} **>54df<**

Royal Square (CAN) 11 ch g Gregorian (USA)-Dance Crazy (USA) (Foolish Pleasure (USA)) *3073^{2}* **>71a f<**

Royal Star (GER) 2 f 4126a^{6} **>32f<**

Royal Velvet 2 b f Perpendicular-Stellaris (Star Appeal) 3270^{5} 3479^{9} 3806^{16} **>50f<**

Roy Boy 5 b g Emarati (USA)-Starky's Pet (Mummy's Pet) 1599^{10} 1965^{3} **>62f<**

Royrace 5 b g Wace (USA)-Royal Tycoon (Tycoon II) *360^{9}* **>18a 45f<**

Rozel Bay 4 ch f Beveled (USA)-Salinas (Bay Express) **1996:** *5175^{14} 5240^{12}*

Rub Al Khali 6 br g Green Ruby (USA)-Nullah (Riverman (USA)) **1996:** *5179^{14}* **>17a 19?f<**

Rubamma 2 b c Kris-Idle Gossip (USA) (Lyphard (USA)) 3219^{9} 3789^{10} 4502^{4} 4767^{3} **>78f<**

Ruby Angel 4 ch f Superlative-Queen Angel (Anfield) **1996:** *5129^{3}* **1997:** *14^{8}* 1244^{21} **>46a 56f<**

Ruby Bear 2 gr f Thethingaboutitis (USA)-Hitravelscene (Mansingh (USA)) 2700^{9} *3072^{7} 4799^{6}* **>21a 33f<**

Rude Awakening 3 b g Rudimentary (USA)-Final Call (Town Crier) 448^{12} 694^{11} 845^{16} 1096^{4} 1256^{9} 1513^{4} 1800^{9} 3565^{8} 3868^{7} 4210^{15} 4333^{18} **>60f<**

Rude Shock 2 gr c Rudimentary (USA)-Frighten The Life (Kings Lake (USA)) 2943^{12} 3745^{6} 4165^{12} 4849^{12} **>55f<**

Rudi Knight 2 ch g Rudimentary (USA)-Fleeting Affair (Hotfoot) 4914^{W}

Rudimental 3 b g Rudimentary (USA)-Full Orchestra (Shirley Heights) (1973) 2120^{2} 2601^{7} 3012^{2} 4102^{3} 4558^{2} **>70a 98f<**

Rudi's Pet (IRE) 3 ch c Don't Forget Me-Pink Fondant (Northfields (USA)) 501^{3} 1018^{12} 1305^{7} 1737^{16} 2134^{6} 2347^{2} 2529^{11} 3194^{5} (3914) 4280^{9} 4677^{7} (4887) **>103f<**

Rudolphine (IRE) 6 ch g Persian Bold-Ruffling Point (Gorytus (USA)) *200^{4}* **>41a f<**

Rufalda (IRE) 3 b f Sadler's Wells (USA)-Smageta (High Top) 1556a^{7} 1784^{7} 2008^{14} 2568^{5} 3694^{7} 3970^{4} 4438^{3} **>77f<**

Rumbustious 3 b f Rambo Dancer (CAN)-Persian Alexandra (Persian Bold) 791^{9} 1245^{9} 1373^{7} (1780) 2040^{8} 2310^{8} 3292^{4} 3452^{4} 4695^{16} **>57f<**

Rum Lad 3 gr g Efisio-She's Smart (Absalom) 448^{10} 575^{10} 785^{5} 998^{7} 1225^{4} 1496^{4} (1586) 1673^{5} 2017^{4} (2235) (2417) 2711^{18} 3936^{11} 4565^{8} 4733^{11} **>67f<**

Rumpelstiltskin 5 ch g Sharpo-Ouija (Silly Season) **1996:** *5134^{12}* **1997:** *66^{7} 144^{8}* **>25a 56f<**

Rumuz (IRE) 3 b br f Marju (IRE)-Balqis (USA) (Advocator) 2687^{2} 2952^{4} 3917^{9} **>75f<**

Runadrum 2 b g Prince Daniel (USA)-Runabay (Run The Gantlet (USA)) 4752^{9} 4993^{13} **>34f<**

Runaround 2 b f Northern Park (USA)-Party Game (Red Alert) 2728^{12} 3114^{11} 3416^{6} **>53f<**

Runic Symbol 6 b g Warning-Pagan Deity (Brigadier Gerard) 1384^{5} 1588^{8} 1683^{11} 2200^{3} 2399^{6} 2701^{3} 3297^{2} 3469^{6} 3848^{4} 4114^{6} 4224^{7} 4608^{9} **>26a 53f<**

Run Lucy Run 3 b f Risk Me (FR)-Pat Or Else (Alzao (USA)) **1996:** *5272^{5}* **1997:** *77^{5}* **>54a 57f<**

Running Bear 3 ch g Sylvan Express-Royal Girl (Kafu) 1451^{9} 2234^{4} 2939^{8} **>27tf<**

Running Free (IRE) 3 b g Waajib-Selchis (Main Reef) 878^{8} 1296^{5} 1938^{13} 2487^{11} 2727^{3} 2916^{5} 2955^{3} (3129) (3390) 3593^{4} 4667^{5} **>54a 61f<**

Running Green 6 b g Green Desert (USA)-Smeralda (GER) (Dschingis Khan) **1996:** *5132^{4} (5179) 5241^{10}* **1997:** *153^{8}* 496^{2} 608^{7} 925^{4} 1315^{5} 1560^{2} (2109) 3264^{3} 3573^{9} 3921^{5} 4283^{11} 4596^{15} 4924^{11} 5023^{7} **>65a 63f<**

Running Stag (USA) 3 b c Cozzene (USA)-Fruhlingstag (FR) (Orsini) *(350)* 505^{2} 692^{5} 1307^{2} 2011^{7} 3214^{4} 4125a^{4} 4389a^{2} 4369^{4} **>65++a 109f<**

Run Or Bust (IRE) 4 b f Commanche Run-Busteds Fancy (Busted) 1004^{7} **>54f<**

Runs in the Family 5 b m Distant Relative-Stoneydale (Tickled Pink) *404^{6} 545^{12}* 883^{2} *1046^{5}* (1083) 1250^{6} 1279^{2} 1479^{3} 1814^{3} (2197) 2377^{2} 2590^{7} 3126^{11} 3473^{8} 3898^{8} 4115^{7} **>52a 59f<**

Rupert Manners 4 b g Mazilier (USA)-Entourage (Posse (USA)) *28^{13}* **(DEAD)**

Rushcutter Bay 4 br g Mon Tresor-Llwy Bren (Lidhame) 1946^{10} 2105^{24} 3011^{4} 3410^{18} 3600^{13} 4183^{13} 4456^{4} **>41a 84f<**

Rushen Raider 5 br g Reprimand-Travel Storm (Lord Gayle (USA)) 982^{6} 1100^{14} 1224^{8} 2737^{10} **>71f<**

Rush Me Not (IRE) 4 b g Treasure Kay-Elegant Act (USA) (Shecky Greene (USA)) 1389^{8} 1686^{8} 1834^{8} **>38f<**

Rush Off 2 b c Robellino (USA)-Arusha (IRE) (Dance of Life (USA)) 4779^{9} **>67f<**

Rusk 4 b g Pharly (FR)-Springwell (Miami Springs) 2297^{2} 2653^{5} (3010) 3805^{8} 4874^{12} **>81f<**

Russian About (IRE) 2 b f Polish Patriot (USA)-Molly Carter (IRE) (Dr Carter (USA)) 1486^{8} 3106^{7} 3289^{2} 3635^{8} 3819^{8} *4054^{7}* 4327^{12} **>49a 64f<**

Russian Aspect 3 br g Al Nasr (FR)-Bourbon Topsy (Ile de Bourbon (USA)) 2059^{9} 2415^{11} **>56df<**

Russian Delight (IRE) 2 b f Soviet Lad (USA)-Geraldville (Lord Gayle (USA)) 4668^{6} 4815^{5} **>53f<**

Russian Music 4 b g Forzando-Sunfleet (Red Sunset) 450^{18} (540) 678^{11} 839^{4} 1160^{5} 1598^{3} 2056^{22} 2690^{4} 3051^{3} 3725^{3} (4148) 4423^{4} 4558^{22} **>111f<**

Russian Olive 3 b f Primo Dominie-Cottonwood (Teenoso (USA)) 2183^{8} 2569^{6} 2928^{7} **>62f<**

Russian Party (IRE) 2 ch c Lycius (USA)-Sherkova (USA) (State Dinner (USA)) 4710^{3} 4952^{8} **>78f<**

Russian Revival (USA) 4 ch c Nureyev (USA)-Memories (USA) (Hail the Pirates (USA)) 1596^{3} (4240) 4421^{4} 4864a^{6} **>123f<**

Russian Romeo (IRE) 2 b c Soviet Lad (USA)-Aotearoa (IRE) (Flash of Steel) *902^{7} 1045^{6}* 1510^{11} 1797^{10} 2306^{14} 2520^{4} *2606^{4}* 3282^{5} 3563^{8} (3692) 3932^{14} *4573^{5} (4796)* **>74a 74f<**

Russian Rose (IRE) 4 b f Soviet Lad (USA)-Thornbeam (Beldale Flutter (USA)) 1169^{4} 1481^{2} (1953) 2589^{2} 2834^{5} 4295^{6} **>82f<**

Russian Ruler (IRE) 3 b c Bering-Whitecairn (Sure Blade (USA)) 1936^{2} 2566^{9} 3012^{9} 3319^{4} **>80f<**

Rustic Song (IRE) 4 b f Fayruz-Red Note (Rusticaro (FR)) 1467^{24} *1757^{10} 2070^{15}* **>27a 19f<**

Rusty Babe (IRE) 2 ch g Red Sunset-Derring Dee (Derrylin) 557^{7} (884) 1126^{2} (1391) 1684^{2} 2012^{10} **>84f<**

Ruths Gem (IRE) 2 ch f Imperial Frontier (USA)-Hossvend (Malinowski (USA)) *902^{13} 2066^{11}* 2425^{10} **>8a f<**

Rutland Chantry (USA) 3 b c Dixieland Band (USA)-Christchurch (FR) (So Blessed) 3095^{5} *3396^{2}* 3809^{4} *4485^{2}* (4802) **>68a 72f<**

Ruzen (IRE) 2 b c Fayruz-Stifen (Burslem) (836) 1161^{4} 1959^{3} 2851^{2} **>84f<**

Ryafan (USA) 3 b f Lear Fan (USA)-Carya (USA) (Northern Dancer) 1533a^{4} 1916a^{4} (2586) (3216) (4652a) (5039a) **>123f<**

Ryefield 2 b c Petong-Octavia (Sallust) 4236^{2} 4640^{W} 4840^{2} **>81f<**

Ryefield Star 2 b c Marju (IRE)-Awayed (USA) (Sir Ivor) 4231^{14} 4706^{W} 4993^{12} **>43f<**

Rymer's Rascal 5 b g Rymer-City Sound (On Your Mark) *429^{12}* 610^{17} *663^{5}* 733^{7} 929^{2} 1079^{3} 1285^{3} 1511^{3} 1830^{12} 2204^{6} (2906) 3264^{6} (3565) (3987) 4270^{6} 4561^{4} 4773^{15} **>42a 71f<**

S

Saafeya (IRE) 3 b f Sadler's Wells (USA)-Safa (Shirley Heights) 2583[5] 3014[3] (3624) 4102[2] (4435) 4676[3] (4968) **>107+f<**

Sabadilla (USA) 3 b c Sadler's Wells (USA)-Jasmina (USA) (Forli (ARG)) 3632[4] 3977[5] 4322[2] (4736) (5053) **>100+f<**

Sabhaan 2 b c Green Desert (USA)-Al Theraab (USA) (Roberto (USA)) 2829[2] 3127[3] 4145[3] **>85f<**

Sabina 3 b f Prince Sabo-High Savannah (Rousillon (USA)) 854[2] 1018[4] 2134[14] 2779[4] 3194[7] 3795[7] 4048[13] **>78f<**

Sable Cloak 2 b f Prince Sabo-Edge of Darkness (Vaigly Great) 4769[11]

Sabo's Joy 2 b f Prince Sabo-Port Na Blath (On Your Mark) 4216[7] **>43f<**

Sabot 4 b c Polar Falcon (USA)-Power Take Off (Aragon) *82[2]* *220[2]* *396[2]* 450[10] 1214[2] **>98a 97f<**

Sabre Butt 2 gr c Sabrehill (USA)-Butsova (Formidable (USA)) 1607[12] 4715[16] 4957[10] **>49f<**

Sabre Dancer 3 b g Rambo Dancer (CAN)-My Candy (Lorenzaccio) 3089[3] **>57f<**

Sabre Girl 2 b f Sabrehill (USA)-Yasmeen Valley (USA) (Danzig Connection (USA)) 3136[10] 3450[13] 3927[11] 4178[9] **>55f<**

Sabre Mountain (USA) 2 ch c Zilzal (USA)-Seminole Gold (USA) 4836a[7] **>91f<**

Sabu 5 gr g Jumbo Hirt (USA)-Shankhouse Girl (General Ironside) 1512[5] 2046[9] 2156[9] 2503[11] 2854[11] **>64f<**

Sacchetti (IRE) 2 b c Alzao (USA)-Merriment (USA) (Go Marching (USA)) 564[5] 4012[W] 4145[9] 4542[3] 4746[7] **>74f<**

Sacho (IRE) 4 b c Sadler's Wells (USA)-Oh So Sharp (Kris) (4060) 4281[6] 5043[W] **>100f<**

Sacrament 6 b h Shirley Heights-Blessed Event (Kings Lake (USA)) **1996:** 5217a[8] **1997:** 736[7] 932[10] 1172[8] **>112f<**

Sacred Spirit 5 b g Totem (USA)-Dream Again (Blue Cashmere) 1220[11] 1937[6] **>58f<**

Sada 2 b br f Mujtahid (USA)-Peace Girl (Dominion) 1457[3] 1653[8] 2371[3] 2728[4] 3152[5] 3474[3] 3965[9] 4597[4] **>78a 78f<**

Saddlehome (USA) 8 b g Aragon-Kesarini (USA) (Singh (USA)) **1996:** *5105[11]* *5131[5]* **>80a 75f<**

Saddler's Cove (FR) 2 c b Saddlers' Hall (IRE)-Lyme Bay (USA) (Pharly (FR)) 5033a[3]

Saddlers' Hope 3 b f Saddlers' Hall (IRE)-Hope and Glory (USA) (Well Decorated (USA)) 1004[2] 1301[4] 2015[7] (2782) 3026[3] (3445) 3803[5] **>85f<**

Saddlers' Roe (IRE) 2 b c Saddlers' Hall (IRE)-Ladyfish (Pampapaul) 1396[5] 2243[6] 3479[W] 3686[3] 4116[12] **>66f<**

Sadeebah 2 b c Prince Sabo-Adeebah (USA) (Damascus (USA)) *4056[9]* 4216[9] 4458[9] **>37a 43f<**

Sadian 2 b c Shirley Heights-Rafha (Kris) (3862) **>83+f<**

Sadir 2 ch c Zafonic (USA)-Ghanimah (Caerleon (USA)) 1872[14] 3117[9] 4061[13] **>62f<**

Sadler's Blaze (IRE) 3 b c Alzao (USA)-Christine Daae (Sadler's Wells (USA)) 841[8] 1277[9] 1636[13] 1999[3] 2398[8] **>56df<**

Sadlers Home (IRE) 3 b f Sadler's Wells (USA)-Ivory Home (FR) (Home Guard (USA)) 1698a[3] 2446a[6] 3511a[3] **>100f<**

Sadler's Walk 6 b g Sadler's Wells (USA)-Widows Walk (Habitat) **1996:** *5120[10]* **>34a 80f< (DEAD)**

Sad Mad Bad (USA) 3 b g Sunny's Halo (CAN)-Quite Attractive (USA) (Well Decorated (USA)) 533[7] 700[5] 975[2] 1387[10] 2198[11] 2718[3] 3440[6] 3623[9] *3865[7]* 4749[2] 4804[4] **>46a 63f<**

Saeedah 2 ch f Bustino-Galaxie Dust (USA) (Blushing Groom (FR)) 2768[3] 3450[3] **>79f<**

Saeko-Beauty 3 b f Warrshan (USA)-Jalopy (Jalmood (USA)) **1996:** *5142[9]* *5214[6]* **>48a f<**

Safabee 2 ch f Safawan-Bewails (IRE) (Caerleon (USA)) 2728[19] 3547[10] 3862[10] 4178[7] *4796[11]* *4984[10]* **>27a 74f<**

Safa Dancer 4 b f Safawan-Dalby Dancer (Bustiki) 843[8] *1138[14]* *1430[7]* 1689[15] *2067[6]* 2310[6] 2488[14] **>48a 32f<**

Safari Sam (IRE) 2 b g Cyrano de Bergerac-Light Hand (Star Appeal) 3707[14] 3859[12] 3927[12] **>34a 36f<**

Safecracker 4 ch g Sayf El Arab (USA)-My Polished Corner (IRE) (Tate Gallery (USA)) *4594[4]* 4858[18] *5019[5]* **>56a 50df<**

Safety (USA) 10 b g Topsider (USA)-Flare Pass (USA) (Buckpasser) **1996:** *5210[9]* **>32a 58f<**

Safey Ana (USA) 6 b g Dixieland Band (USA)-Whatsoraire (USA) (Mr Prospector (USA)) 560[6] (755) 895[7] 1219[12] (1501) 2868[8] (3056) 3254[5] 3712[4] (4071) 4225[5] **>77f<**

Saffron Lane (IRE) 2 b f Hamas (IRE)-Saffron (FR) (Fabulous Dancer (USA)) 1213[3] (1386) 1945[4] (3597) 4218[2] 4473[15] **>85f<**

Saffron Rose 3 b f Polar Falcon (USA)-Tweedling (USA) (Sir Ivor) 886[4] 1164[8] 1747[6] (2040) (2523) 3132[5] 3328[8] 3894[7] **>76f<**

Safio 4 ch g Efisio-Marcroft (Crofthall) *316[8]* *394[6]* 443[2] 610[7] 835[5] 863[8] 2422[4] (3087) (3406) (3801) (4121) 4283[3] 4423[20] 4787[5] 4979[3] **>55+a 86f<**

Sage 2 ch c Greensmith-Bluebell Copse (Formidable (USA)) *(592)* **>58a f<**

Sagebrush Roller 9 br g Sharpo-Sunita (Owen Dudley) **1996:** *5134[7]* **1997:** 529[5] 1020[10] 1315[7] 2342[3] 2854[5] 3104[3] 3627[11] 3886[3] 4235[10] **>53a 55f<**

Saguaro 3 b g Green Desert (USA)-Badawi (USA) (Diesis) 4700[2] **>80f<**

Sahara 2 b f Green Desert (USA)-Marie D'Argonne (FR) (Jefferson) 3985[5] 4217[2] 4873[9] **>69f<**

Sahara River (USA) 3 b f Riverman (USA)-Sahara Forest (Green Desert (USA)) 1587[14] 2492[4] 4015[10] **>67f<**

Saibhreas (IRE) 3 b f Last Tycoon-Angor 809a[6] **>83f<**

Saifan 8 ch g Beveled (USA)-Superfrost (Tickled Pink) 738[3] 1214[4] 1782[9] 2026[32] 2766[18] 3052[10] (3428) 4297[4] 4781[29] 4978[28] **>91df<**

Sailormaite 6 ch g Komaite (USA)-Marina Plata (Julio Mariner) **1996:** *5203[6]* **1997:** *357[R]* 835[R] 3273[14] *3584[7]* 3801[14] 4905[21] *4983[7]* **>74a 43f<**

Saint Albert 2 ch c Keen-Thimbalina (Salmon Leap (USA)) 2500[11] 2893[12] 3701[4] 4068[7] **>54f<**

Saint Amigo 5 gr g Presidium-Little Token (Shack (USA)) **1996:** *5099[8]* **1997:** 2937[11] 3116[5] 3477[11] *3609[6]* **>34a 40f<**

Saint Ann (USA) 2 b f Geiger Counter (USA)-Swan Princess (So Blessed) 1619[4] 2477[6] 2886[6] 3226[7] **>68df<**

Saint Ciel (USA) 9 b h Skywalker (USA)-Holy Tobin (USA) (J O Tobin (USA)) 4275[3] **>46f<**

Sainte Marine (IRE) 2 b f Kenmare (FR)-Pont Aven (Try My Best (USA)) (3873a) 3999a[2] 4391a[6] **>97+f<**

Saintes 2 b g Be My Chief (USA)-Latakia (Morston (FR)) 3260[5] 3973[17] 4231[7] 4514[10] **>45f<**

Saint Express 7 ch g Clantime-Redgrave Design (Nebbiolo) 2129[2] 2289[5] 2711[12] 3481[5] 3856[3] 4048[5] 4307[3] 4414[2] 4512[15] 4842[13] (4927) **>89f<**

Saint Keyne 7 b h Sadler's Wells (USA)-Sancta (So Blessed) *543[6]* **>20a 104f<**

Saintly Manner (USA) 3 b f St Jovite (USA)-Azzurrina (Knightly Manner (USA)) 978[4] **>41f<**

Saint Malo (USA) 2 b br c Nureyev (USA)-Jeany's Halo (CAN) (Sunny's Halo (CAN)) 1480[5] 3806[12] **>66f<**

Saints Be Praised (USA) 2 ch c St Jovite (USA)-Cincinnati Pops (USA) (Dixieland Band (USA)) 2057[5] 2562[5] **>78f<**

Sakbah (USA) 8 b m Al Nasr (FR)-Delray Dancer (USA) (Chateaugay) *68[12]*

Sakharov 8 b g Bay Express-Supreme Kingdom (Take A Reef) 2004[15] *2368[6]* *2603[8]* *3041[8]* 3276[10] 3469[13] **>40a 37f<**

Salamah 3 b c Sadler's Wells (USA)-Ala Mahlik (Ahonoora) 670[2] (1105) 1399[7] 2058[15] **>93f<**

Salamanca 2 gr f Paris House-Amber Mill (Doulab (USA)) (492) 651[2] 1013[4] 2862[11] 3152[3] (3414) 3908[8] **>86f<**

Saleela (USA) 2 b f Nureyev (USA)-Allegretta (Lombard (GER)) 4575[6] **>69f<**

Salford 2 ch c Salse (USA)-Bustellina (Busted) 3745[8] 4318[10] 4715[9] **>51f<**

Salford Lad 3 b c Don't Forget Me-Adjusting (IRE) (Busted) 4587[9] **>39f<**

Saligo (IRE) 2 b f Elbio-Doppio Filo (Vision (USA)) 1847[7] 2306[13] 2943[8] 3493[3] 4014[4] 4166[5] **>66f<**

Salinger 9 b g Rousillon (USA)-Scholastika (GER) (Alpenkonig (GER)) 4751[13] 4986[11] **>36?a 39?f<**

Sally Armstrong 4 b f Batshoof-Salinity (NZ) (Standaan (FR)) **1996:** *5234[7]* **1997:** *1[8]* *28[5]* *305[9]* *385[10]* **>53a f<**

Sally Green (IRE) 3 b f Common Grounds-Redwood Hut (Habitat) **1996:** *(5111)* *5164[5]* **1997:** *904[5]* 1141[3] 1810[2] (2481) 2964[3] 4527[7] 4805[15] **>66a 82f<**

Sally Slade 5 b m Dowsing (USA)-Single Gal (Mansingh (USA)) **1996:** *5220[2]* **1997:** *48[6]* *(95)* *(170)* *348[6]* *406[2]* *488[6]* 1410[10] 1743[5] 2197[4] 2277[3] 2526[9] 2581[5] 3126[12] 3323[6] 3716[2] 3913[5] **>76a 85?f<**

Sally's Twins 4 b f Dowsing (USA)-Bird of Love (Ela-Mana-Mou) *660[11]* **>49a 57f<**

Salmon Ladder (USA) 5 b h Bering-Ballerina Princess (USA) (Mr Prospector (USA)) 736[4] 1033[7] (3634) 4131a[2] 4420[7] 4894[10] **>120df<**

Salsee Lad 3 b g Salse (USA)-Jamarj (Tymavos) 1936[4] 2315[16] 2879[4] 3549[5] 3928[9] *4302[3]* 4633[16] **>56a 64f<**

Salsette 2 b f Salse (USA)-Amber Fizz (USA) (Effervescing (USA)) 2771[5] 3114[5] 3889[3] 4473[11] **>75f<**

Salska 6 b m Salse (USA)-Anzeige (GER) (Soderini) 1408[7] 1763[9] (1795) 2198[5] 2702[7] (2882) 3010[5] 3141[5] 4562[5] 4783[28] 4956[2] 5027[12] **>41a 69f<**

Saltando (IRE) 6 b g Salt Dome (USA)-Ange de Feu (Double Form) 567[6] 1093[17] 1219[5] 1606[8] 1845[7] 2174[13] 2868[11] 3767[11] 3972[5] 4114[16] 4224[9] 4324[5] 4606[11] 4742[16] 4987[17] **>66?a 57?f<**

Saltimbanco 3 ch c Green Forest (USA)-Tea and Scandals (USA) (Key to the Kingdom (USA)) 694[15] 1012[13] 1458[15] 1988[9] 2667[7] 3390[6] 3617[3] 4519[11] **>35f<**

Salty Behaviour (IRE) 3 ch c Salt Dome (USA)-Good Behaviour (Artaius (USA)) 968[9] (3206) 4586[2] 4872[6] **>76f<**

Salty Girl (IRE) 4 b f Scenic-Sodium's Niece (Northfields (USA)) 510[8] **>71f<**

Salty Jack (IRE) 3 b c Salt Dome (USA)-Play The Queen (IRE) (King of Clubs) 4375[8] 4787[19] 4975[5] **>70f<**

Saltz (IRE) 5 b g Salt Dome (USA)-Heather Hut (Shack (USA)) 4991[W] **>52a 72f<**

Samapour (IRE) 3 b c Kahyasi-Samneeza (FR) (Storm Bird (CAN)) 819a[6] **>108f<**

Samara (IRE) 4 ch f Polish Patriot (USA)-Smeralda (GER) (Dschingis Khan) 832[14] 1456[3]

(1740) 4117^{3} 4666a^{5} (4976) **>116f<**
Samara Song 4 ch g Savahra Sound-Hosting (Thatching) *860^{7}* 1677^{2} 2004^{2} 2848^{3} 2929^{2} 3293^{4} 3470^{2} 3849^{3} (4059) 4112^{2} 4324^{3} **>60a 70f<**
Samarinka (FR) 3 b f General Holme (USA)-Self Made (FR) (Persepolis (FR)) 4648a^{2} **>70f<**
Samata One (IRE) 2 b c River Falls-Abadila (IRE) (Shernazar) 4807^{10} 4917^{19} **>37f<**
Sambac (USA) 3 b f Mr Prospector (USA)-Kingscote (Kings Lake (USA)) 957^{6} 1101^{6} **>100df<**
Sambakonig (GER) 4 c 3993a^{3} 4396a^{6} 4762a^{3} **>114f<**
Samim (USA) 4 b c Nureyev (USA)-Histoire (FR) (Riverman (USA)) 1162^{14} 1463^{14} 3108^{10} **>51f<**
Samorelle 4 ch f High Kicker (USA)-Lemelasor (Town Crier) **1996:** *5175^{16}* **>56f<**
Sam Peeb 3 b g Keen-Lutine Royal (Formidable (USA)) *581^{4}* 665^{3} *(1043)* 1299^{5} *1785^{3}* 2564^{10} **>48a 44f<**
Sampower Lady 2 ch f Rock City-Travel On (Tachypous) 2553^{5} 3094^{15} *3610^{5}* 4315^{6} 4898^{13} **>51a 55f<**
Samraan (USA) 4 br c Green Dancer (USA)-Sedra (Nebbiolo) 736^{10} 932^{6} 1172^{4} 2055^{5} 3149^{6} 3645^{2} 3983^{2} 4346a^{6} (4659a) **>121f<**
Sam Rockett 4 b g Petong-Art Deco (Artaius (USA)) **1996:** *5185^{11} 5276^{2}* **1997:** *63^{8} 260^{8}* 1022^{4} 1393^{3} 1678^{3} 1968^{2} 2199^{7} *3054^{5}* 3792^{5} **>32a 64f<**
Samsolom 9 b g Absalom-Norfolk Serenade (Blakeney) **1996:** *5099^{6} 5188^{4} 5209^{8}* **1997:** *24^{8} 1047^{7} 1132^{5}* 1584^{11} **>42a 53f< (DEAD)**
Samspet 3 ch g Pharly (FR)-Almond Blossom (Grundy) *124^{5}* 1078^{5} 1284^{2} 1603^{13} *2368^{15}* 2463^{2} 2733^{6} 3336^{7} 4472^{13} 4846^{15} **>36a 52f<**
Samstotry 7 b g Starch Reduced-Karousa Girl (Rouser) 550^{12} 599^{15} 823^{12} **>21f<**
Samsung Spirit 3 b f Statoblest-Sarong (Taj Dewan) 1029^{3} 1243^{6} 2062^{9} 3119^{12} (3812) 3923^{6} 4733^{21} **>78f<**
Sam's Yer Man 3 b g Full Extent (USA)-Falls of Lora (Scottish Rifle) 3695^{8} **>41f<**
Samuel Scott 4 b g Shareef Dancer (USA)-Revisit (Busted) 762^{2} 1260^{3} (1778) 2139^{P} **>87f< (DEAD)**
Samwar 5 b g Warning-Samaza (USA) (Arctic Tern (USA)) 726^{12} 892^{13} 1148^{13} 3580^{11} 3900^{5} 4155^{27} 4280^{27} 4636^{10} 4733^{14} **>76a 70f<**
Sandabar 4 b g Green Desert (USA)-Children's Corner (FR) (Top Ville) 942^{20} 1324^{10} 1739^{16} 2124^{9} **>77f<**
Sandar 2 ch f Sanglamore (USA)-Darnelle (Shirley Heights) 3547^{9} 4212^{3} **>75f<**
Sandbaggedagain 3 b g Prince Daniel (USA)-Paircullis (Tower Walk) 448^{5} 575^{3} (1950) 2015^{10} 2328^{11} 3542^{5} 3976^{7} **>75f<**
Sandblaster 4 ch f Most Welcome-Honeychurch (USA) (Bering) 574^{9} 776^{5} 1116^{3} *1580^{10}* 1830^{5} (2355) 2502^{12} 3456^{14} **>24a 52f<**
Sand Cay (USA) 3 ch c Geiger Counter (USA)-Lily Lily Rose (USA) (Lypheor) 1140^{19} 1568^{6} 1826^{2} 2231^{5} 2695^{5} 3980^{15} **>64f<**
Sandicliffe (USA) 4 b f Imp Society (USA)-Sad Song (USA) (Roberto (USA)) *1086^{7}* (1483) 2918^{5} (3421) 4228^{4} 4561^{13} **>27a 66f<**
Sandmoor Chambray 6 ch g Most Welcome-Valadon (High Line) 444^{4} 947^{13} 1775^{9} 1979^{3} 2155^{4} 2341^{4} 2678^{6} (2890) (3263) 3703^{2} 3824^{2} (4004) 4281^{2} 4558^{5} 4759^{3} 4968^{2} **>110f<**
Sandmoor Denim 10 b g Red Sunset-Holernzaye (Sallust) **1996:** *5110^{3} 5181^{10}* **1997:** *111^{3} 153^{3} 192^{3} 235^{2} 359^{4} 411^{6}* 526^{2} *579^{9} 870^{15}* 1266^{2} 1463^{2} 1802^{7} 2039^{14} *2368^{5}* 2488^{9} *3608^{2}* 3992^{14} **>45a 39f<**
Sandmoor Tartan 2 b c Komaite (USA)-Sky Fighter (Hard Fought) 948^{4} 1126^{8} 1760^{18} (3257) 3564^{3} 3823^{7} 3932^{6} 4767^{4} 4885^{7} **>58f<**
Sandown Sue 3 b f Norton Challenger-Tino Reppin (Neltino) *1943^{9}*
Sandpit (BRA) 8 ch h Baynoun-Sand Dancer (FR) (Green Dancer (USA)) 393a^{2} *628a^{3}* 3880a^{2} **>128a 128f<**
Sandside 2 b g Mazaad-Deverells Walk (IRE) (Godswalk (USA)) 993^{4} (1280) (1447) 1675^{2} 2212^{2} 2466^{4} 2858^{4} 3222^{3} (3483) 3707^{7} 4014^{5} 4230^{5} **>70df<**
Sand Star 5 b m Lugana Beach-Overseas (Sea Hawk II) *1082^{12} 1754^{7}* 2036^{13} 2788^{19} 3018^{10} **>75da 39f<**
Sandstone (IRE) 3 b c Green Desert (USA)-Rose De Thai (USA) (Lear Fan (USA)) 646^{3} (931) 2643a^{2} 3409^{4} (4252a) 4369^{3} **>111f<**
Sandweld 3 b c Weldnaas (USA)-Scottish Lady (Dunbeath (USA)) 1587^{15} 1780^{5} 2313^{19} 2724^{13} *2915^{16}* **>43a 48df< (DEAD)**
Sandy Floss (IRE) 4 b g Green Desert (USA)-Mill on the Floss (Mill Reef (USA)) 1111^{9} 1678^{4} 2139^{11} 2381^{6} 2865^{6} 3093^{2} 4046^{10} 4374^{5} **>71f<**
Sandy Saddler 3 ch g Most Welcome-Beryl's Jewel (Siliconn) 1967^{8} 3437^{4} 3715^{5} **>65f<**
Sandy Shore 2 b f Lugana Beach-City Link Lass (Double Jump) 530^{4} 1444^{3} 1829^{2} 2176^{2} 3468^{4} 3545^{7} 4166^{13} **>72f<**
Sandystones 3 b f Selkirk (USA)-Sharanella (Shareef Dancer (USA)) 989^{9} 1322^{4} 2132^{5} **>62f<**
San Francisco 3 b g Aragon-Sirene Bleu Marine (USA) (Secreto (USA)) 3991^{6} 4469^{6} 4705^{8} **>46f<**
Sang d'Antibes (FR) 3 ch f Sanglamore (USA)-Baratoga (USA) (Bering) 584^{5} 935^{9} 1780^{12} 2406^{2} 2747^{6} 3083^{8} 3454^{12} **>43f<**
San Glamore Melody (FR) 3 b g Sanglamore (USA)-Lypharitissima (FR) (Lightning (FR)) 1130^{10} 1405^{4} 1930^{3} 2131^{2} 2511^{9} *3865^{11}* **>14a 50f<**
Sans Pere 4 b g Shadow Minister (USA)-Creetown Sally (Creetown) 1951^{7} *2301^{9}* 3462^{5} **>14a 40f<**
Sans Rivale 2 ch f Elmaamul (USA)-Strawberry Song (Final Straw) 1498^{3} 1626^{2} 2037^{13} 2746^{4} (3866) 4162^{6} **>71f<**
San Suru (GER) 3 ch c Surumu (GER)-Sweet Virtue (GER) (Halo (USA)) 2097a^{2} 2642a^{16} **>107f<**
Santa Court 2 b g Be My Native (USA)-Christmas Show (Petorius) 1924^{5} 2509^{5} 3386^{10} 3932^{2} 4271^{16} **>65f<**
Santa Faye (IRE) 2 b f Fayruz-Florissa (FR) (Persepolis (FR)) 884^{4} (3247) 3932^{12} *4589^{3} (4808)* **>74a 74f<**
Santarene (IRE) 2 b f Scenic-Rising Spirits (Cure The Blues (USA)) 4367^{7} 4873^{11} **>55f<**
Santa Rosa (IRE) 3 b f Lahib (USA)-Bequeath (USA) (Lyphard (USA)) 886^{12} 2832^{10} **>64f<**
Santella Katie 4 ch f Anshan-Mary Bankes (USA) (Northern Baby (CAN)) *1^{10} 57^{8}* 748^{9} 1383^{13} **>30a 49f<**
Santella Twinkle (IRE) 3 b f Jareer (USA)-Hellicroft (High Line) **1996:** *5098^{6}* **>25a 32f<**
Santillana (USA) 4 ch c El Gran Senor (USA)-Galway (FR) (Irish River (FR)) (4759) **>118f<**
Santone (IRE) 2 b c Fairy King (USA)-Olivia Jane (IRE) (Ela-Mana-Mou) 1486^{9} 2693^{4} 3494^{5} **>76f<**
Sapphire Ring 2 b f Marju (IRE)-Mazarine Blue (Bellypha) (1440) (1945) 2335^{4} 4267^{2} 4474^{2} **>93f<**
Sapphire Son (IRE) 5 ch g Maelstrom Lake-Gluhwein (Ballymoss) **1996:** *5089^{12} 5151^{8} 5179^{11} 5242^{2}* **1997:** *13^{5} 63^{5} 104^{9} 147^{3} 183^{4}* 640^{3} 770^{4} 1636^{4} 2577^{7} 2916^{2} 2955^{2} (3229) 3559^{2} 4860^{5} **>48a 61f<**
Sarabi 3 b f Alzao (USA)-Sure Enough (IRE) (Diesis) 494^{12} 652^{9} 1131^{10} 1573^{10} 1828^{14} **>23f<**
Sarah Stokes (IRE) 2 b f Brief Truce (USA)-Almaaseh (IRE) (Dancing Brave (USA)) 3471^{4} 4012^{2} 4211^{2} 4955^{4} **>73f<**
Saralea (FR) 2 b f Sillery (USA)-Solidarite (USA) (Far North (CAN)) 2268a^{3} (3874a) 4663a^{8} **>85f<**
Saramah (USA) 3 ch f Forty Niner (USA)-Cheval Volant (USA) (Kris S (USA)) 3463^{10} 3909^{10} **>44f<**
Sara Moon Classic (IRE) 2 b c Fayruz-Irish Affaire (IRE) (Fairy King (USA)) 3127^{4} 3569^{6} 4146^{6} 4755^{14} *4982^{6}* **>58a 72f<**
Sarasi 5 ch g Midyan (USA)-Early Call (Kind of Hush) **1996:** *5206^{10}* **1997:** *(18) (273) 359^{7} 390^{7} 411^{7}* **>62da 61f<**
Sarasota Ryde 4 gr f Komaite (USA)-Freedom Line (Absalom) **1996:** *5163^{16}* **>42f<**
Sarasota Storm 5 b g Petoski-Challanging (Mill Reef (USA)) 2166^{4} 2702^{8} 3826^{7} 4160^{7} **>52f<**
Saratoga Red (USA) 3 ch c Saratoga Six (USA)-Wajibird (USA) (Storm Bird (CAN)) *412^{8}* 675^{17} *1291^{15}* 1384^{12} *2368^{3}* 2645^{2} 2868^{9} 4696^{10} 4916^{2} *(5020)* **>71a 76f<**
Saratoga Springs (CAN) 2 ch c El Gran Senor (USA)-Population (General Assembly (USA)) (3644) 4135^{3} (4836a) (4889) **>113+f<**
Sarawat 9 b g Slip Anchor-Eljazzi (Artaius (USA)) *88^{8} 195^{2} 231^{5}* **>56a 75f<**
Sarayir (USA) 3 b f Mr Prospector (USA)-Height of Fashion (FR) (Bustino) 960^{9} 2053^{9} 3017^{4} 3388^{2} (3803) 4557^{8} **>106f<**
Sarbaron (IRE) 3 b c Danehill (USA)-Salette (Sallust) 842^{6} 1106^{7} 1625^{6} *2068^{4}* 2374^{4} 2776^{4} 3234^{7} *3612^{5}* **>71da 65f<**
Sarmatian (USA) 6 br g Northern Flagship (USA)-Tracy L (USA) (Bold Favorite (USA)) 2385^{3} 2660^{7} **>78f<**
Sarum 11 b g Tina's Pet-Contessa (HUN) (Peleid) **1996:** *5145^{7} 5182^{6} 5211^{7}* **1997:** *116^{9} 210^{4} 1575^{9}* 1663^{6} 2375^{10} 2785^{13} *3041^{9}* 3971^{12} **>14a 36f<**
Saseedo (USA) 7 ch g Afleet (CAN)-Barbara's Moment (USA) (Super Moment (USA)) 677^{12} 1799^{10} 2598^{17} 4561^{24} **>80a 85f<**
Sassiver (USA) 7 b g Riverman (USA)-Sassabunda (Sassafras (FR)) *63^{3} 106^{5}* **>41a 42f<**
Sassy (IRE) 2 b f Imp Society (USA)-Merrie Moment (IRE) (Taufan (USA)) 1321^{6} 2728^{17} 2875^{7} (3090) 3446^{2} 3635^{4} 3924^{6} 4185^{5} 4856^{15} **>65f<**
Sassy Lady (IRE) 2 b f Brief Truce (USA)-Taken By Force (Persian Bold) 3717^{4} 4556^{7} 4758^{20} **>64f<**
Sassy Street (IRE) 4 b g Danehill (USA)-Sassy Lane (Sassafras (FR)) 842^{10} 1276^{12} 2785^{9} 3015^{7} 3928^{16} **>44a 45f<**
Sasuru 4 b c Most Welcome-Sassalya (Sassafras (FR)) (852) (1554a) 2527^{5} **>125f<**
Satin Stone (USA) 3 b c Mr Prospector (USA)-Satin Flower (USA) (Shadeed (USA)) 674^{12} 1587^{2} 2023^{20} **>85f<**
Satis (IRE) 2 b f Last Tycoon-Nazwa (Tarboosh (USA)) 447^{10} 2378^{4} 3228^{6} 3892^{7} *4483^{2} 4573^{9}* 5026^{2} **>49a 53f<**
Satisfied Prince 5 b h Full Extent (USA)-Princess Lucianne (Stanford) 353a^{2} **>74df<**
Saturiba (USA) 4 b g Fighting Fit (USA)-My Popsicle (USA) (Raja Baba (USA)) 687^{18} 1020^{17} 1467^{22} **(DEAD)**
Saudi 2 b c Green Desert (USA)-Emaline (FR) (Empery (USA)) 3806^{5} 4061^{10} 4708^{9} **>64f<**
Saugerties (USA) 3 ch c Trempolino (USA)-Stalwart Moment (USA) (Stalwart (USA)) 2097a^{3} 2642a^{18} (4963a) **>118f<**
Saunders Wren 3 b f Handsome Sailor-Saunders Lass (Hillandale) 1098^{17} **>64df<**

Sausalito Bay 3 b c Salse (USA)-Cantico (Green Dancer (USA)) 690^4 1647^3 2027^8 2647^2 3218^{11} (3648) (4101) $4658a^4$ **>111f<**

Savinio (USA) 7 ch g The Minstrel (CAN)-Fabulous Native (USA) (Le Fabuleux) *$5066a^5$* **>99a 117f<**

Savona (IRE) 3 b f Cyrano de Bergerac-Shannon Lady (Monsanto (FR)) 1141^9 2491^3 3393^{10} **>60f<**

Savoury 2 b f Salse (USA)-Metaphysique (FR) (Law Society (USA)) 3979^4 4317^{12} 4604^8 **>67f<**

Savu Sea (IRE) 3 b f Slip Anchor-Soemba (General Assembly (USA)) 847^6 1258^8 3021^4 3495^{11} 4748^7 **>63f<**

Sawlajan (USA) 6 ch h Woodman (USA)-Crafty Satin (USA) (Crimson Satan) 4878^{22} **>101df<**

Saxon Bay 5 ch g Cadeaux Genereux-Princess Athena (Ahonoora) **1996:** *5129^5* **1997:** 790^4 *1048^{16}* 1292^6 1925^6 2115^6 2852^{13} *2915^{15}* 3849^9 *4051^{11}* 4465^{11} 4608^{16} **>58a 36f<**

Saxonbury 3 b g Shirley Heights-Dancing Vaguely (USA) (Vaguely Noble) *249^4* *347^6* **>51?a 29f<**

Saxon Victory (USA) 2 b g Nicholas (USA)-Saxon Shore (USA) (Halo (USA)) 3136^7 3857^7 4286^9 4576^3 **>51f<**

Sayyaramix (FR) 4 gr c Linamix (FR)-Sayyara (Kris) 519^9 **>80f<**

Scapestrata (USA) 2 b f Distinctive Pro (USA)-Southern Tradition (USA) (Family Doctor (USA)) 4604^{12}

Scaraben 9 b g Dunbeath (USA)-Varushka (Sharpen Up) 1389^4 1622^3 1837^4 (2223) 2470^2 4264^5 4742^2 4924^W **>80df<**

Scarlet Crescent 3 b f Midyan (USA)-Scarlet Veil (Tyrnavos) 639^4 887^3 *1153^4* (1794) 2331^8 2778^3 3787^{13} 4578^{13} 4854^{12} **>56a 72f<**

Scarrots 3 b c Mazilier (USA)-Bath (Runnett) *513^6* 771^6 1129^4 (1465) (1863) 2064^6 3234^6 3441^3 3781^{10} 4213^2 4699^{12} **>55a 76f<**

Scathebury 4 b g Aragon-Lady Bequick (Sharpen Up) **1996:** *5089^{10}* *5130^8* *5174^6* **1997:** 477^3 601^2 (668) (1139) 1482^8 1878^{13} 1993^2 2369^{12} 3290^5 3930^7 4112^{14} 4373^8 (4711) 4899^3 5023^3 **>41a 60f<**

Scattergun 3 ch c Rainbow Quest (USA)-Cattermole (USA) (Roberto (USA)) 1239^2 **>89f<**

Scboo 8 b g Full Extent (USA)-Maygo (Maystreak) *215^8* **>42a 6f<**

Scene (IRE) 2 b f Scenic-Avebury Ring (Auction Ring (USA)) 880^4 1013^8 1616^6 1760^{11} 2781^8 3228^9 4602^3 4753^6 4801^3 (5050) **>70f<**

Scenery (IRE) 2 b c Lycius (USA)-La Vue (USA) (Reviewer (USA)) (2268a)

Scenic Point (USA) 4 b f Unbridled (USA)-Bankok (USA) (Riverman (USA)) *$5038a^3$* **>114f<**

Scenicris (IRE) 4 b f Scenic-Princesse Smile (Balidar) **1996:** *5175^4* **1997:** *91^4* *125^7* *346^6* 482^7 571^5 689^{13} *1291^{12}* 1660^6 2036^{11} 2546^{13} 3027^2 3316^2 3937^4 4471^{13} 4628^4 4847^8 4991^2 **>42a 53f<**

Scent of Success (USA) 2 b f Quiet American (USA)-Mousquet (USA) (Shadeed (USA)) 3426^3 3757^2 (4215) 4670^4 **>83?f<**

Sceptre Lady (IRE) 3 ch f Common Grounds-The Saltings (FR) (Morston (FR)) 727^4 1030^3 1316^{12} 2654^3 3030^5 (3917) **>73f<**

Scharnhorst 5 b g Tacheron-Stardyn (Star Appeal) 4013^9 4280^{28} 4467^7 4773^{17} **>55a 65f<**

Scherma 4 b f Green Desert (USA)-Escrime (USA) (Sharpen Up) **1996:** *5117^4* *5235^{12}* **>47a 70f<**

Schisandra 3 b f Petong-Volcalmeh (Lidhame) 1139^{11} 2040^{10} **>39f<**

Schnozzle (IRE) 6 b g Cyrano de Bergerac-Sun Gift (Guillaume Tell (USA)) 1445^4 (2199) 2702^4 **>58f<**

School Boy 4 b c Aragon-Grovehurst (Homing) **1996:** *5093^2* *5132^{11}* **>58a 64f<**

School of Science 7 b g Then Again-Girl's Brigade (Brigadier Gerard) 2661^5 2854^9 3223^5 3486^4 3627^5 3697^3 **>43f<**

Schwarz Fairy 3 b f High Estate-Salesca (ITY) (Kronzeuge) (1367a) $4535a^5$ **>92f<**

Scissor Ridge 5 ch g Indian Ridge-Golden Scissors (Kalaglow) **1996:** *5096^7* *(5150) (5184)* *5246^4* **1997:** *48^2* *146^4* *170^3* *253^4* *323^5* 1743^{11} 2006^{19} 2529^{10} 2698^{10} 2833^{10} 3056^3 3195^5 3580^2 3765^6 4155^7 4370^{14} 4518^4 4878^4 4979^{12} **>78a 67f<**

Scolding 2 b f Reprimand-Tinkerbird (Music Boy) 1091^6 1569^U 2037^9 2739^7 3905^{18} **>52f<**

Sconced (USA) 2 ch c Affirmed (USA)-Quaff (USA) (Raise A Cup (USA)) 3770^{10} 4229^4 4852^5 **>72f<**

Scorned (GER) 2 b c Selkirk (USA)-Spurned (USA) (Robellino (USA)) 4758^{16} (5040) **>88f<**

Scoss 3 b c Batshoof-Misguided (Homing) $1068a^6$ 1144^2 (1563) 1852^2 2296^7 3424^8 (4541a) **>96f<**

Scotch Time 2 ch g Timeless Times (USA)-Scotch Imp (Imperial Fling (USA)) 1255^9 1616^4 1797^{13} 3483^4 **>61f<**

Scotland Bay 2 b f Then Again-Down the Valley (Kampala) 4904^{21} **>35f<**

Scottish Bambi 9 ch g Scottish Reel-Bambolona (Bustino) 4063^6 **>65f<**

Scottish Hero 4 b c North Briton-Tartan Pimpernel (Blakeney) 476^{13} 1388^U 1622^8 **>45f<**

Scottish Park 8 ch m Scottish Reel-Moss Agate (Alias Smith (USA)) *1576^7* 1951^{10} 2228^8 2488^{16} 2896^4 **>49a 36f<**

Scottish Wedding 7 b m Scottish Reel-Pearl Wedding (Gulf Pearl) *55^7* **>19a 58f< (DEAD)**

Scott's Risk 7 b g Risk Me (FR)-Madam de Seul (Pas de Seul) *342^6* **>19f<**

Screen Idol (IRE) 2 b f Sadler's Wells (USA)-Spring to Light (USA) $4619a^9$ **>81+f<**

Scurrilous 2 ch f Sharpo-Tea and Scandals (USA) (Key to the Kingdom (USA)) 4630^{15} 4769^{10} **>25f<**

Sea Buck 11 b g Simply Great (FR)-Heatherside (Hethersett) 4171^9 **>44f<**

Sea Dane 4 b c Danehill (USA)-Shimmering Sea (Slip Anchor) 519^7 745^8 1148^{15} 2861^{14} **>93f<**

Sea Danzig 4 ch g Roi Danzig (USA)-Tosara (Main Reef) **1996:** *5227^4* *5241^3* **1997:** *27^8* *48^3* *(109)* *121^2* *186^4* 1107^7 1488^4 1743^6 1972^5 2282^3 2573^2 2835^8 3138^9 3227^8 3793^6 4109^5 4324^{13} 4516^2 4821^5 *(5022)* **>75a 60f<**

Sea-Deer 8 ch g Hadeer-Hi-Tech Girl (Homeboy) 443^3 520^2 726^5 942^5 1317^3 1948^2 2105^{15} (2185) 2675^{14} 3217^{24} 4887^{12} 4995^{11} **>83a 93df<**

Sea Devil 11 gr g Absalom-Miss Poinciana (Averof) *1^3* *71^3* *87^4* *165^3* *(243)* *297^4* *326^2* *424^7* **>61a 51f<**

Sea Dreams (IRE) 6 b g Midyan (USA)-Davill (Record Token) *903^5* 1292^{16} *1786^9* **>39a f<**

Sea Fig 2 gr f Robellino (USA)-Aimee Jane (USA) (Our Native (USA)) 3753^7 **>36f<**

Sea Freedom 6 b h Slip Anchor-Rostova (Blakeney) 510^5 (613) (888) 1215^2 1413^4 1778^3 (2014) 2696^7 2867^5 3122^{10} **>77f<**

Sea God 6 ch g Rainbow Quest (USA)-Sea Pageant (Welsh Pageant) *39^5* *66^2* *115^9* *151^2* *196^3* *205^6* *244^5* *285^6* *374^P* **>59a 50f<**

Sea Imp (IRE) 2 b f Mac's Imp (USA)-Sea Glen (IRE) (Glenstal (USA)) 557^3 648^3 767^7 2412^7 **>67f<**

Sealed By Fate (IRE) 2 b c Mac's Imp (USA)-Fairy Don (Don) 979^9 1251^6 1684^6 1819^8 2060^6 3384^8 **>63f<**

Sea Magic (IRE) 2 b br f Distinctly North (USA)-Danger Ahead (Mill Reef (USA)) (1407) 1945^3 2516^4 2858^2 3186^4 3597^3 4885^4 **>86f<**

Sea Mist (IRE) 3 ch f **1996:** *5141^7* **1997:** 1826^{17} **>21a 63f<**

Seamus 3 ch c Almoojid-Royal Celerity (USA) (Riverman (USA)) 556^{10} 757^8 1272^{14} 2171^9 2748^6 3082^{10} 3299^8 3592^9 **>32f<**

Seanchai (IRE) 4 b g Treasure Kay-Blue Infanta (Chief Singer) **1996:** *5163^{14}* *5236^{11}* **1997:** *3^{10}* *177^8* *423^7* 2496^{12} 3241^{13} **>34da f<**

Seascay (NZ) 7 ch h Maizcay (HK)-Kurdasea (HK) (Beaufort Sea (USA)) **1996:** $5219a^2$ **>125f<**

Season Of Love (FR) 2 c $4657a^7$

Sea Spouse 6 ch g Jalmood (USA)-Bambolona (Bustino) **1996:** *5161^5* *5237^4* **1997:** *153^2* *(194)* *274^4* *330^3* *376^6* *870^{14}* *1048^{10}* 1878^9 2004^{10} 2395^2 3285^{10} *3584^6* *4485^4* **>56a 44f<**

Seattle Alley (USA) 4 b g Seattle Dancer (USA)-Alyanaabi (USA) (Roberto (USA)) *74^3* *291^5* 763^6 1233^4 4516^5 **>71a 73f<**

Seattle Art (USA) 3 b c Seattle Slew (USA)-Artiste (Artaius (USA)) 1846^2 2188^2 2692^3 3549^7 **>79f<**

Seattle Swing 3 b f Saddlers' Hall (IRE)-Sweet Slew (USA) (Seattle Slew (USA)) 523^5 790^3 (2178) 2380^4 2920^6 (3466) 3768^7 4109^{13} 4372^2 **>86f<**

Sea Victor 5 b g Slip Anchor-Victoriana (USA) (Storm Bird (CAN)) **1996:** *5205^2* **1997:** *39^4* 3890^6 4101^5 4246^5 4313^2 4426^6 4673^9 4783^{18} 5027^{11} **>87a 80f<**

Sea Wave (IRE) 2 b c Sadler's Wells (USA)-Three Tails (Blakeney) 4957^4 **>76f<**

Sea Ya Maite 3 b g Komaite (USA)-Marina Plata (Julio Mariner) *868^{12}* 1090^{10} *1759^4* *1942^3* 2313^8 *(2605)* *2915^3* *3077^7* *3397^3* 3696^2 *(4798)* 4877^{11} 4958^{18} **>71a 57f<**

Sebastian Duke (FR) 5 br g Iron Duke (FR)-Abimaba (Vayrann) *164^7* *218^7* **>34a f<**

Seborga (GER) 2 br c Dashing Blade-Standpauke (GER) (Zank) $3997a^3$ **>82f<**

Second Chorus (IRE) 2 b f Scenic-Never so Fair (Never so Bold) 3574^{10} **>53f<**

Second Colours (USA) 7 b or br g Timeless Moment (USA)-Ruffled Silk (USA) (Our Hero (USA)) *(56)* *105^8* *179^2* *299^3* *344^5* *389^6* **>90a 70f<**

Second Empire (IRE) 2 b c Fairy King (USA)-Welsh Love (4255a) (4766a) **>116f<**

Seconds Away 6 b g Hard Fought-Keep Mum (Mummy's Pet) *313^5* 526^3 929^8 1285^5 1613^4 2109^5 (2828) 2899^3 3240^{13} 3456^3 3627^2 4472^2 4707^{11} 4843^{16} **>17a 43f<**

Second Sun 2 ch c Clantime-Sun Follower (Relkino) 2534^{12} 2917^{15} 3414^4 3791^6 4145^{12} **>38f<**

Second Term (IRE) 2 b f Second Set (IRE)-Trinida (Jaazeiro (USA)) 4841^{10} 4925^4 4993^{16} **>40f<**

Second Wind 2 ch c Kris-Rimosa's Pet (Petingo) (696) **>79f<**

Secrecy 2 b c Polish Precedent (USA)-Blonde Prospect (USA) (Mr Prospector (USA)) 4715^{10} 4914^8 **>70f<**

Secret Aly (CAN) 7 b g Secreto (USA)-Bouffant (USA) (Alydar (USA)) *291^2* *344^6* *(405)* 521^2 738^{14} 2296^8 2710^5 3112^6 3444^5 3773^9 4223^4 4558^{25} **>88a 85f<**

Secret Archive 2 b c Salse (USA)-Lycia (USA) (Lyphard (USA)) 3193^3 (3687) **>79f<**

Secret Ballot (IRE) 3 b c Taufan (USA)-Ballet Society (FR) (Sadler's Wells (USA)) 2121^6 2337^2

(2522) 2722^{4} 4063^{3} 4172^{8} 4568^{6} (4632) (4699) 4876^{2} 4903^{3} 5051^{10} **>91f<**
Secret Bourne (USA) 2 b f Exbourne (USA)-Secret Angel (Halo (USA)) 4909^{8} **>52f<**
Secret Combe (IRE) 3 b f Mujadil (USA)-Crimbourne (Mummy's Pet) **1996:** *5133^{5}* **1997:** 1589^{5} 1958^{14} 2705^{2} 3092^{10} 3454^{4} **>69a 83f<**
Secret Miss 5 ch m Beveled (USA)-Zamindara (Crofter (USA)) 541^{12} 760^{5} *1046^{8}* 1236^{12} 2321^{8} **>29a 42f<**
Secret Service (IRE) 5 b g Classic Secret (USA)-Mystery Bid (Auction Ring (USA)) *419^{3}* 1408^{4} 2142^{4} 2718^{4} 3568^{3} **>78a 68f<**
Secret Spring (FR) 5 b g Dowsing (USA)-Nordica (Northfields (USA)) 4314^{3} 4558^{6} (4859) **>89a 91f<**
Secret Strength 3 ch g Formidable (USA)-Lovers Tryst (Castle Keep) 1088^{11} 1415^{8} 2278^{7} 2852^{8} 3592^{5} 4164^{6} **>50f<**
Secret Tango 2 ch f Interrex (CAN)-Seymour Ann (Krayyan) 836^{15} 2728^{20} 3289^{6} 3847^{5} **>34f<**
Sedbergh (USA) 4 b g Northern Flagship (USA)-Crumbaugh Pike (USA) (Within Hail (USA)) *(542) 591^{2} 858^{10}* 1224^{5} 1452^{4} *(1755) 1940^{2}* 2175^{6} **>79a 77df< (DEAD)**
Seebe (USA) 3 b f Danzig (USA)-Annie Edge (Nebbiolo) 724^{2} 1203a^{2} 1533a^{6} **>115f<**
See You Soon 3 b g Distant Relative-Our Resolution (Caerleon (USA)) *377^{7}* 550^{7} 1284^{7} **>34a 28f<**
Sefton Blake 3 b g Roscoe Blake-Rainbow Lady (Jaazeiro (USA)) 2046^{8} 2566^{11} 2846^{8} 4015^{8} 4771^{7} 4996^{5} **>60f<**
Sejaal (IRE) 5 b g Persian Heights-Cremets (Mummy's Pet) 895^{22} 1506^{15} 3849^{15} 3966^{2} **>57f<**
Sekari 3 b c Polish Precedent (USA)-Secret Seeker (USA) (Mr Prospector (USA)) (646) 917a^{W} **>104f<**
Selberry 3 b g Selkirk (USA)-Choke Cherry (Connaught) **1996:** *5168^{2}* **1997:** *49^{2} (138)* 431^{4} 4788^{13} **>84a 87f<**
Select Choice (IRE) 3 b g Waajib-Stella Ann (Ahonoora) 586^{8} 784^{2} 1980^{13} 2580^{5} 2773^{5} **>59f<**
Select Star (IRE) 3 b g Arcane (USA)-Chevrefeuille (Ile de Bourbon (USA)) 1140^{20} 1694^{10} 2521^{3} 2650^{7} 3028^{8} *3400^{5}* 3814^{4} 4858^{15} **>5a 56f<**
Selfish 3 ch f Bluebird (USA)-Sariza (Posse (USA)) 727^{3} 992^{2} 1304^{2} 2133^{8} 2591^{3} **>97df<**
Selhurstpark Flyer (IRE) 6 b g Northiam (USA)-Wisdom to Know (Bay Express) 786^{2} 1034^{2} 1772^{3} (2105) 2211^{5} 3217^{28} 4282^{21} **>111df<**
Selkirk Rose (IRE) 2 b f Pips Pride-Red Note (Rusticaro (FR)) 1310^{4} 2713^{2} (3265) 3823^{10} 4267^{11} 4702^{4} **>80f<**
Sellette (IRE) 3 ch f Selkirk (USA)-Near the End (Shirley Heights) 889^{2} 1110^{2} 1773^{3} (2183) 2832^{6} 3891^{6} 4015^{2} 4242^{16} **>87f<**
Selmeston (IRE) 5 b g Double Schwartz-Baracuda (FR) (Zeddaan) (2307) 2539^{6} (3540) (4269) 4744^{5} 5027^{17} **>52da 55f<**
Semi Circle 2 b f Noble Patriarch-True Ring (High Top) 2018^{6} 2500^{13} (2935) 3307^{11} 4285^{13} **>60f<**
Senador (IRE) 5 b g Alzao (USA)-Congress Lady (General Assembly (USA)) (3373a) **>95f<**
Senate Swings 3 gr c Timeless Times (USA)-Heaven-Liegh-Grey (Grey Desire) **1996:** *5166^{2} 5202^{3} 5261^{5}* **1997:** *33^{3} 124^{4} 168^{9}* **>56a 61f<**
Sendoro (IRE) 3 b c Shahrastani (USA)-Sendana (FR) (Darshaan) **1996:** 5191a^{2} **1997:** 629a^{2} 1070a^{5} 3006a^{5} 4251a^{3} **>117f<**
Senor Hurst 2 b c Young Senor (USA)-Broadhurst (Workboy) 2923^{10}
Senorita Matilda (USA) 3 b f El Senor (USA)-Copperama (AUS) (Comeram (FR)) 1316^{10} 1963^{9} 2665^{2} (2747) 4321^{10} **>78f<**
Sensation 4 b f Soviet Star (USA)-Outstandingly (USA) (Exclusive Native (USA)) 1728a^{8} 4666a^{12} **>94f<**
Sense of Priority 8 ch g Primo Dominie-Sense of Pride (Welsh Pageant) *40^{7} (71) (126) (165) 208^{3} (288) (342)* 443^{17} 467^{6} *1786^{4}* 1861^{2} 2540^{8} 2755^{6} 2939^{6} 3625^{15} **>65a 46f<**
Sense of Wonder 2 br f Inchinor-Downshire (IRE) (Darshaan) 4103^{8} (4597) 4885^{9} 4989^{6} **>80f<**
Sensitivity (USA) 3 ch f Blushing John (USA)-Andora (USA) (Conquistador Cielo (USA)) 3007a^{2} **>112f<**
Sensory 2 b c Selkirk (USA)-Illusory (Kings Lake (USA)) 3687^{5} (4064) 4880^{2} **>104f<**
Sentinella Key (IRE) 2 b f Statoblest-Key Tothe Minstrel (USA) (The Minstrel (CAN)) 1619^{8} **>40f<**
Sentosa Star (IRE) 6 b g Reasonable (FR)-Khazna (229a) 311a^{3} **>100f<**
Sequoia Prince (CAN) 3 ch g Woodman (USA)-Loren's Baby (USA) (Czaravich (USA)) 683^{18} 1006^{9} 1237^{13} 2182^{11} 3336^{12} **>24f<**
Seralia (FR) 2 ch f Royal Academy (USA)-Serafica (FR) (No Pass No Sale) 3999a^{3} **>76f<**
Serape 4 b f Primo Dominie-Absaloute Service (Absalom) *65^{10} 336^{4}* 571^{15} 748^{2} 925^{8} 1220^{7} 1448^{10} 1733^{2} 2353^{5} 2724^{12} **>14a 44f<**
Serenade (IRE) 3 gr g Classic Music (USA)-Friendly Thoughts (USA) (Al Hattab (USA)) **1996:** *5090^{4} 5147^{9}* **1997:** *8^{2} 60^{5} 119^{4}* **>62da 65f<**
Serendipity (FR) 4 b g Mtoto-Bint Damascus (USA) (Damascus (USA)) 521^{19} 735^{13} 933^{16} 2508^{7} 3115^{17} 3548^{8} 3980^{3} 4297^{15} 4516^{3} 4802^{4} **>69f<**
Serengetti 2 ch f Lion Cavern (USA)-Melanoura (Imperial Fling (USA)) 4167^{8} **>56f<**
Serenity 3 b f Selkirk (USA)-Mystery Ship (Decoy Boy) 1216^{6} 2774^{2} 4550^{6} **>103f<**
Seretse's Nephew 3 b g Chilibang-Bunnyloch (Lochnager) **1996:** *(5083) 5146^{3} 5224^{11}* **1997:** *75^{3} 132^{9} 181^{12} 345^{4} 378^{5}* 2575^{6} 2938^{2} 3417^{2} 3625^{17} 3868^{5} 4249^{18} **>45a 50f<**
Sergeant Imp (IRE) 2 b c Mac's Imp (USA)-Genzyme Gene (Riboboy (USA)) 985^{6} 1084^{9} 1635^{7} 3489^{9} 3924^{10} 4143^{8} 4402^{4} 4543^{9} 4856^{10} **>70f<**
Sergeyev (IRE) 5 ch h Mulhollande (USA)-Escape Path (Wolver Hollow) 839^{7} **>103f<**
Serious Account (USA) 4 b c Danzig (USA)-Topicount (USA) (Private Account (USA)) 2549^{3} 2940^{11} 4164^{12} **>54df<**
Serious Hurry 9 ch g Forzando-Lady Bequick (Sharpen Up) 1835^{14} 2934^{16} **>54a 34f<**
Serious Trust 4 b c Alzao (USA)-Mill Line (Mill Reef (USA)) 1169^{2} 1478^{11} 1805^{7} 2279^{8} 2592^{8} 3203^{5} 3640^{7} (3714) 3896^{11} **>41a 59f<**
Serpentara 3 ch f Kris-Sardegna (Pharly (FR)) 3021^{7} 3501^{3} 4060^{3} 4883^{W} 4996^{17} **>81f<**
Setmatt 3 b c Rudimentary (USA)-Persian Air (Persian Bold) 1069a^{3} **>81f<**
Setteen 2 b c Robellino (USA)-Agama (USA) (Nureyev (USA)) 2295^{3} (3013) (4218) **>101f<**
Set the Fashion 8 br g Green Desert (USA)-Prelude (Troy) **1996:** *5233^{12}* **1997:** *23^{7} 81^{5}* **>67a 65f<**
Set Trail (IRE) 2 b f Second Set (IRE)-Trail (Thatch (USA)) 3411^{10} 3753^{10} 4231^{2} (4706) **>81f<**
Seven 2 ch c Weldnaas (USA)-Polly's Teahouse (Shack (USA)) 4145^{10} 4564^{15} 5042^{7} **>68f<**
Seventh Edition 4 b g Classic Music (USA)-Funny-Do (Derring-Do) *140^{5} 284^{13}* 1636^{17} 1825^{19} **>36a 67f<**
Seventh Heaven 2 ch g Clantime-Portvally (Import) 557^{9} 1076^{4} 1267^{6} 1614^{6} 3209^{8} 3427^{6} 3866^{6} 4208^{17} **>68f<**
Severity 3 b c Reprimand-Neenah (Bold Lad (IRE)) 2580^{7} 2773^{3} 3030^{3} **>77f<**
Severn Mill 6 ch g Librate-Staryllis Girl (Star Moss) 538^{10} 900^{12} 1467^{8} 1849^{11} 1925^{5} 2721^{8} 3018^{8} 3213^{8} **>33f<**
Shaanxi Romance (IRE) 2 b c Darshaan-Easy Romance (USA) (Northern Jove (CAN)) 3201^{5} 3920^{3} **>64f<**
Shabanaz 12 b g Imperial Fling (USA)-Claironcita (Don Carlos) 1247^{2} 1642^{8} 1809^{4} 2479^{3} 2777^{2} 2916^{9} 3308^{5} 3792^{6} **>67a 50f<**
Shaddad (USA) 3 b c Shadeed (USA)-Desirable (Lord Gayle (USA)) 991^{8} 2120^{4} **>75df<**
Shaded (IRE) 3 b g Night Shift (USA)-Sarsaparilla (FR) (Shirley Heights) 535^{5} 797^{6} *1043^{3}* 1284^{5} *1756^{5}* 3491^{14} 3864^{13} 4243^{17} *4906^{8}* **>59a 50f<**
Shades of Love 3 b c Pursuit of Love-Shadiliya (Red Alert) 1851^{6} 2173^{4} 2847^{2} 3710^{4} 4059^{12} 4333^{14} **>65f<**
Shadiann (IRE) 3 b c Darshaan-Shakanda (IRE) (Shernazar) 676^{15} 2311^{3} 3977^{2} 4736^{2} 4883^{4} **>87f<**
Shadirwan (IRE) 6 b h Kahyasi-Shademah (Thatch (USA)) 831^{6} 1260^{8} 2014^{22} 2932^{2} 3122^{2} 3896^{13} 4783^{7} 5052^{9} **>81f<**
Shadoof 3 b c Green Desert (USA)-Bermuda Classic (Double Form) 693^{3} 945^{3} 1265^{3} 1458^{6} (1773) 3263^{6} 3575^{6} 4151^{4} 4310^{8} **>84f<**
Shadow Jury 7 ch g Doulab (USA)-Texita (Young Generation) **1996:** *5131^{9} 5246^{6}* **1997:** *53^{4} 89^{9} 233^{3} 391^{9} 397^{7}* 666^{3} 924^{6} (1003) 1080^{4} (1602) *1759^{2} 2050^{5}* 2497^{7} *3077^{5}* 3334^{13} 3856^{7} 4137^{7} *4301^{11}* 4414^{8} 4636^{14} 4844^{10} *4985^{8}* **>64a 57f<**
Shadow of Doubt (IRE) 2 b c Pips Pride-Sarah Siddons (Reform) (1321) 2012^{6} **>80f<**
Shaffishayes 5 ch g Clantime-Mischievous Miss (Niniski (USA)) **1996:** *5104^{2} 5181^{13}* **1997:** *589^{3}* 866^{2} 1022^{3} (1329) 1981^{2} (2297) 3722^{6} 4279^{5} 4691^{2} 4998^{11} **>72a 79f<**
Shaft of Light 5 gr g Sharrood (USA)-Reflection (Mill Reef (USA)) 735^{14} 2139^{3} 2676^{3} (3255) (3796) 4101^{3} 4241^{5} 5053^{3} **>75a 103f<**
Shahboor (USA) 3 b c Zilzal (USA)-Iva Reputation (USA) (Sir Ivor) 963^{15} 2190^{4} 2961^{9} 3318^{2} 4313^{8} **>81f<**
Shaheen (USA) 3 b c Danzig (USA)-Hidden Light (USA) (Majestic Light (USA)) 586^{3} 991^{2} 1207^{2} (1587) 2023^{15} 3189^{8} **>95f<**
Shahik (USA) 7 b g Spectacular Bid (USA)-Sham Street (USA) (Sham (USA)) **1996:** *5206^{11} 5231^{4} 5270^{4}* **1997:** *39^{6} 123^{10}* 2920^{2} 3382^{5} 3864^{9} *5022^{12}* **>68da 74f<**
Shahrur (USA) 4 b br g Riverman (USA)-Give Thanks (Relko) 4426^{14} **>83f<**
Shahtoush (IRE) 2 b f Alzao (USA)-Formulate (Reform) 4093a^{3} 4619a^{4} **>104+f<**
Shailendra (IRE) 3 ch f Persian Bold-Good Policy (IRE) (Thatching) 2731^{13} 2952^{6} 3720^{7} 4172^{18} **>52f<**
Shaji (IRE) 2 ch c Mukaddamah (USA)-Alkariyh (USA) (Alydar (USA)) 5042^{4} **>72f<**
Shaka 3 b c Exit To Nowhere (USA)-Serafica (FR) (No Pass No Sale) 629a^{3} (1070a) 1726a^{6} 2274a^{3} **>117f<**
Shakiyr (FR) 6 gr g Lashkari-Shakamiyn (Nishapour (FR)) **1996:** *5116^{6}* **1997:** *68^{3} (139) 256^{5} 400^{2}* 465^{12} *543^{3} 660^{10} 4481^{10}* 4794^{8} **>67a 55f<**
Shalaal (USA) 3 b g Sheikh Albadou-One Fine Day (USA) (Quadratic (USA)) 675^{20} 4182^{4} 4587^{10} (4700) 4877^{7} **>84f<**
Shalabella (IRE) 2 br f Shalford (IRE)-Perfect Swinger (Shernazar) 828^{15} 2699^{13} 3294^{3} 4366^{9} **>58f<**

Shalad'or **2** b f Golden Heights-Shalati (FR) (High Line) 999^{7} 1827^{5} 2700^{6} (2943) 3468^{2} 4044^{2} **>80f<**
Shalateeno **4** b f Teenoso (USA)-Shalati (FR) (High Line) 482^{2} 657^{4} 1001^{4} 1435^{3} (1822) 2507^{2} 4002^{2} 4295^{3} **>79f<**
Shalford's Honour (IRE) **2** ch c Shalford (IRE)-Petite Epaulette (Night Shift (USA)) 1486^{3} 4305^{4} (4630) 4790^{19} **>89f<**
Shalstayholy (IRE) **3** ch f Shalford (IRE)-Saintly Guest (What A Guest) *(265) 904^{2}* 1245^{4} 1589^{3} (1781) 1966^{4} 2192^{3} 2841^{4} (2964) 3709^{2} 4137^{2} 4527^{4} 4677^{13} **>68a 88f<**
Shalverton (IRE) **3** b f Shalford (IRE)-Kilfenora (Tribal Chief) 2555^{9} 3095^{11} 3550^{4} **>51f<**
Shalyah (IRE) **2** ch f Shalford (IRE)-Baheejah (Northfields (USA)) 1466^{9} 1839^{5} 2713^{4} 3209^{2} 3387^{3} 3750^{8} 4097^{12} **>70+f<**
Shamanic **5** b g Fairy King (USA)-Annie Albright (USA) (Verbatim (USA)) 2185^{2} 2649^{6} 3024^{5} 3198^{8} 4219^{9} 4511^{2} 4859^{6} **>87f<**
Shambles **2** ch f Elmaamul (USA)-Rambadale (Vaigly Great) 4701^{13} 4917^{9} **>40f<**
Shamikh **3** b c Unfuwain (USA)-Narjis (USA) (Blushing Groom (FR)) 940^{14} **>100?f<**
Shamokin **5** b g Green Desert (USA)-Shajan (Kris) 461^{5} 689^{9} 955^{8} 2145^{8} 2716^{6} 3442^{3} 3627^{13} **>17a 53f<**
Shamwari Song **2** b c Sizzling Melody-Spark Out (Sparkler) 1774^{4} 2356^{8} 3031^{5} 3438^{5} 4285^{5} (4508) 4900^{8} **>63f<**
Shanghai Lil **5** b m Petong-Toccata (USA) (Mr Leader (USA)) **1996:** *(5221) 5247^{3}* **1997:** *(47) 186^{2} 305^{2} 566^{3} 857^{11} 1086^{8}* 2228^{10} 2310^{7} 2488^{11} **>63a 30f<**
Shanillo **2** gr c Anshan-Sea Fret (Habat) 4237^{8} **>67f<**
Shannon (IRE) **2** b f Mujadil (USA)-Eimkar (Junius (USA)) 472^{7} 750^{7} 1569^{9} 2579^{2} 2923^{8} (3289) 3635^{7} 3967^{6} 4166^{16} 4401^{4} *4796^{6}* **>43a 64f<**
Shannon's Secret (IRE) **2** b c Shalford (IRE)-Shenley Lass (Prince Tenderfoot (USA)) 1872^{18} 2181^{10} 2768^{5} 3103^{9} 4152^{15} 4362^{10} 4898^{11} **>65f<**
Shanons Shinanigan (IRE) **3** ch g Salt Dome (USA)-Insight (Ballad Rock) 4579^{12} **>34f<**
Shanoora (IRE) **4** gr f Don't Forget Me-Shalara (Dancers Image (USA)) *85^{4} 114^{7} 169^{10} 203^{12}* **>38a 57f<**
Shantarskie (IRE) **3** b c Mujadil (USA)-Bay Supreme (Martinmas) 3715^{7} 4214^{5} **>70f<**
Shanthi **2** b f Reprimand-Scarlett Holly (Red Sunset) 1867^{3} 2283^{3} 2746^{3} 3090^{3} 3294^{2} 3967^{12} *4483^{6} 4812^{11}* **>26a 62f<**
Shantou (USA) **4** b c Alleged (USA)-Shaima (USA) (Shareef Dancer (USA)) (2100a) (2559) 3050^{5} 3596^{3} **>129f<**
Shantung (IRE) **2** ch f Anshan-Bamian (USA) (Topsider (USA)) 4132^{7} 4909^{4} 5042^{13} **>71f<**
Shape Shifter (IRE) **2** ch c Night Shift (USA)-Zabeta (Diesis) 3386^{7} **>70f<**
Sharaf (IRE) **4** b c Sadler's Wells (USA)-Marie de Flandre (FR) (Crystal Palace (FR)) 612^{5} 831^{7} 982^{5} *1125^{5}* 1974^{8} **>45a 62f<**
Sharaf Kabeer **4** ch c Machiavellian (USA)-Sheroog (USA) (Shareef Dancer (USA)) 1960^{3} **>114f<**
Sharazan (IRE) **4** b g Akarad (FR)-Sharaniya (USA) (Alleged (USA)) 1058a^{6} **>115f<**
Sharbadarid (IRE) **3** b g Night Shift (USA)-Sharenara (USA) (Vaguely Noble) 1207^{8} 1512^{3} 1983^{3} 3026^{5} 3813^{2} 3992^{19} **>79+f<**
Share Delight (IRE) **3** b c Common Grounds-Dorado Llave (USA) (Well Decorated (USA)) **1996:** *5187^{2} 5257^{6}* **1997:** (448) 675^{13} 958^{11} 1175^{6} 2290^{5} 2855^{5} 3408^{9} **>54+a 85f<**
Shareef Allah **3** f **1996:** 5263a^{5} 5283a^{2} **1997:** 64a^{9}
Sharemono (USA) **3** br c Woodman (USA)-Perfect Circle (Caerleon (USA)) 807a^{5} 1060a^{6} 1541a^{12} **>98f<**
Sharera (IRE) **2** b f Kahyasi-Sharenara (USA) (Vaguely Noble) 4907^{4} **>73f<**
Shark (IRE) **4** b g Tirol-Gay Appeal (Star Appeal) *1430^{10}* 2203^{12} 2887^{3} 3321^{3} (4243) 4711^{16} **>5a 55f<**
Sharkhan **5** b h Siberian Express (USA)-Rhein Jewel (Sandhurst Prince) 190a^{2} **>64f<**
Sharkiyah (IRE) **3** ch f Polish Precedent (USA)-Peace Girl (Dominion) 681^{4} 885^{8} 3775^{4} 4070^{10} 4731^{13} **>61f<**
Sharp Cat (USA) **3** f *5062a^{2}* **>114a f<**
Sharp Command **4** ch g Sharpo-Bluish (USA) (Alleged (USA)) **1996:** *(5108) 5185^{10}* **1997:** *5^{P} 101^{5} 157^{6}* 613^{18} **>43a 52f<**
Sharp Consul (IRE) **5** br g Exactly Sharp (USA)-Alicia Markova (Habat) 933^{2} 1208^{2} 2710^{18} 3053^{3} 3246^{5} (4294) 4882^{3} **>93f<**
Sharp Cracker (IRE) **2** b f Hamas (IRE)-Ascensiontide (Ela-Mana-Mou) 897^{2} 1038^{3} 1466^{3} 1774^{2} 2700^{4} 3106^{4} 3307^{3} 4468^{7} 4750^{2} (4801) **>77f<**
Sharp Deed (IRE) **3** ch g Sharp Victor (USA)-Fabulous Deed (USA) (Shadeed (USA)) 1087^{9} 1624^{5} 2733^{2} 3134^{4} 3470^{16} 4465^{10} 4607^{7} 4850^{4} 4986^{10} **>54f<**
Sharp Domino **2** ch c Sharpo-Prompting (Primo Dominie) 4126a^{2} **>96f<**
Sharp Fellow **2** ch g Keen-Clarandal (Young Generation) 2959^{6} *4982^{10}* **>51a 52f<**
Sharp Gazelle **7** ch m Beveled (USA)-Shadha (Shirley Heights) *276^{3}* **>60a 48f<**
Sharp Hat **3** ch c Shavian-Madam Trilby (Grundy) 675^{5} 942^{4} (1243) 1609^{3} 1980^{4} 3217^{19} 3594^{6} 4100^{2} 4282^{12} 4444^{7} **>101f<**
Sharp Holly (IRE) **5** b m Exactly Sharp (USA)-Children's Hour (Mummy's Pet) *577^{3} 855^{6} 907^{7}* 1639^{10} 1925^{9} **>32a 43?f<**
Sharp Imp **7** b g Sharpo-Implore (Ile de Bourbon (USA)) **1996:** *5246^{3}* **1997:** *11^{2} (24) 107^{7} 325^{W} 364^{4} 459^{5} 569^{5}* 643^{4} 1374^{2} 1509^{2} 1849^{2} 2745^{5} 2958^{2} 3082^{2} (3642) *3860^{10}* 4071^{14} **>65a 69f<**
Sharp Label **2** ch f Sharpo-Labelon Lady (Touching Wood (USA)) 4017^{15} 4454^{10} **>29f<**
Sharp Monkey **2** b c Man Among Men (IRE)-Sharp Thistle (Sharpo) *4303^{4}* 4627^{6} 4745^{11} *4984^{6}* **>52a 58f<**
Sharp Move **5** ch m Night Shift (USA)-Judeah (Great Nephew) **1996:** *5161^{12}* **>51f<**
Sharp 'n' Shady **4** b f Sharpo-Shadiliya (Red Alert) 883^{7} 1439^{4} (1843) 2317^{3} (2416) 2730^{10} **>23a 66f<**
Sharp 'n Smart **5** ch g Weldnaas (USA)-Scottish Lady (Dunbeath (USA)) **1996:** *5099^{3}* **1997:** *109^{6} 171^{5} 241^{10}* (477) 766^{6} 1324^{11} 1599^{9} 2698^{15} 4820^{15} **>66a 58df<**
Sharpo Wassl **3** ch g Sharpo-Wasslaweyeh (USA) (Damascus (USA)) *296^{2}* (475) 634^{6} 3100^{3} (3591) 4436^{9} 4601^{10} **>64a 78f<**
Sharp Pearl **4** ch g Sharpo-Silent Pearl (USA) (Silent Screen (USA)) **1996:** *5097^{3} 5150^{14}* **1997:** *95^{7} 214^{4}* 638^{4} (756) 1113^{7} 1634^{6} 2220^{4} 2844^{8} 2933^{2} 3296^{3} 3600^{2} (3771) 4155^{21} 4365^{4} 4512^{W} **>72da 87f<**
Sharp Pet **2** b f Petong-Harmony Park (Music Boy) 844^{8} *1124^{8}* 2412^{11} **>2a f<**
Sharp Play **2** b c Robellino (USA)-Child's Play (USA) (Sharpen Up) (2680) 3672a^{2} 3895^{4} 4440^{7} **>101f<**
Sharp Rebuff **6** b h Reprimand-Kukri (Kris) 1166^{12} 1489^{3} (2201) 2525^{6} 4637^{3} 4978^{23} **>4a 88f<**
Sharp Return **3** b c Sharpo-Langtry Lady (Pas de Seul) **1996:** *5164^{3} 5224^{4}* **1997:** *17^{5} 110^{6}* 995^{15} 1107^{6} 1141^{20} 1620^{20} 2424^{9} *2915^{14}* 4628^{7} 4711^{17} 4816^{4} **>39a 57f<**
Sharp Shooter (IRE) **2** b g Sabrehill (USA)-Kermesse (IRE) (Reference Point) 1492^{7} 1839^{7} 2706^{11} 4588^{5} 4806^{18} **>57f<**
Sharp Shuffle (IRE) **4** ch g Exactly Sharp (USA)-Style (Homing) 444^{3} (639) 787^{6} 1308^{2} 1436^{3} (1745) 3153^{5} 3408^{3} 3901^{18} 4297^{10} 4558^{33} 4781^{21} *5022^{8}* **>72a 71f<**
Sharp Steel **2** ch g Beveled (USA)-Shift Over (USA) (Night Shift (USA)) 3136^{6} 3686^{17} 3859^{14} **>26a 45f<**
Sharp Stock **4** b g Tina's Pet-Mrewa (Runnymede) 879^{13} 1327^{4} 1743^{12} 1848^{10} 2148^{6} 2703^{3} 3016^{5} 3126^{10} 3500^{12} 3984^{13} 4580^{20} **>46f<**
Sharp Temper **3** ch c Sharpo-Kerali (High Line) 475^{3} (784) 973^{5} 1737^{3} 2013^{16} 4308^{7} 4558^{35} **>84f<**
Sharp Thrill **6** ch g Squill (USA)-Brightelmstone (Prince Regent (FR)) *183^{5} 236^{3}* **>40a 47f<**
Sharp to Oblige **10** ch g Dublin Taxi-Please Oblige (Le Levanstell) 1100^{20}
Sharpwitted **3** b f Sadler's Wells (USA)-Oh So Sharp (Kris) 1858^{4} 2184^{6} 4009^{6} **>67f<**
Shart (IRE) **2** b c Last Tycoon-Simaat (USA) (Mr Prospector (USA)) 4064^{2} 4309^{3} 4779^{3} **>90f<**
Shashi (IRE) **5** br m Shaadi (USA)-Homely Touch (Touching Wood (USA)) **1996:** *(5112) 5163^{6} 5234^{2}* **1997:** *4^{W} 20^{6} 48^{5} 127^{7} 166^{6} 209^{5} 286^{4} 326^{7}* 1965^{8} 2177^{3} 2244^{9} (2723) 3292^{5} 3448^{5} 3590^{3} 3642^{8} 3855^{8} 4184^{3} 4333^{6} 4711^{9} **>57a 58f<**
Shaska **3** ch f Kris-Dance Machine (Green Dancer (USA)) 2583^{6} (3893) 4242^{2} **>91f<**
Shaveling **2** ch c Sharpo-Sancta (So Blessed) 4993^{6} **>73+f<**
Shavinsky **4** b c Shavian-Alteza Real (Mansingh (USA)) 1083^{7} 1385^{9} 1666^{13} 2424^{7} *3398^{7} 3582^{13}* **>37a 35f<**
Shawaf (USA) **3** b c Mr Prospector (USA)-Shadayid (USA) (Shadeed (USA)) (674) 1216^{5} 1793^{3} **>98f<**
Shawdon **2** b c Inchinor-Play With Me (IRE) (Alzao (USA)) 1120^{7} (1251) (1854) (2042) 2644a^{6} 3215^{5} (4006) 4247^{2} 4522^{2} 4890^{9} **>97f<**
Shawm **3** b c Alzao (USA)-Flute (USA) (Woodman (USA)) 586^{2} 1302^{4} 1737^{6} 1976^{2} (2549) 2871^{11} (3894) (4308) 4637^{11} **>102f<**
Shaya **3** ch c Nashwan (USA)-Gharam (USA) (Green Dancer (USA)) 1173^{2} 1477^{2} 3014^{2} (3501) 4149^{7} 4549^{4} **>115f<**
Shaynes Domain **6** b g Dominion-Glen Na Smole (Ballymore) *109^{8} 134^{6} 319^{11}* 755^{14} **>26a 46f<**
Sheath Kefaah **4** ch c Kefaah (USA)-Wasslaweyeh (USA) (Damascus (USA)) 3463^{13} **>63?f<**
Shebar (USA) **6** b g Alysheba (USA)-Exotic Source (USA) (The Minstrel (CAN)) 3004a^{2} 4396a^{5} **>109f<**
She Bat **3** f 815a^{6} (4867a) **>110f<**
Shecando (IRE) **2** ch f Second Set (IRE)-Carado (Manado) 1812^{7} 2306^{8} 3278^{16} 4068^{15} 4401^{6} **>57f<**
Shedansar (IRE) **5** b g In The Wings-Evening Kiss (Kris) **1996:** *5115^{14} 5129^{13} 5262^{9}* **1997:** *157^{8}* **>14a 19f<**
Sheemore (IRE) **4** b g Don't Forget Me-Curie Abu (Crofter (USA)) *86^{5} 167^{11}* 613^{16} 866^{12} **>42a 22f<**

Sheep Stealer 9 gr g Absalom-Kilroe's Calin (Be Friendly) 1434[9] *1940[5]* 3277[6] 4275[18] 4548[5] *5022[9]* **>47a 63f<**

Sheer Danzig (IRE) 5 b h Roi Danzig (USA)-Sheer Audacity (Troy) (451) 630a[4] 761[2] 4968[5] 5053[24] **>73a 108f<**

Sheer Face 3 b c Midyan (USA)-Rock Face (Ballad Rock) 690[16] 853[8] 1104[2] 1595[9] 3012[10] 3274[3] 3616[4] 3752[2] 4151[9] 4176[3] 4410[5] 4578[12] **>85f<**

Sheer Folly (USA) 3 ch c Woodman (USA)-Why So Much (USA) (Northern Baby (CAN)) 1962[6] 2309[8] 3786[9] **>71f<**

Shegardi 2 b c Primo Dominie-Party Doll (Be My Guest (USA)) 1306[2] 1669[2] 2103[9] **>90a 84f<**

Sheila-B 2 ch f Formidable (USA)-Good Woman (Good Times (ITY)) 4884[9] **>57f<**

Sheilas Dream 4 b f Inca Chief (USA)-Windlass (Persian Bold) 1233[14] 1796[6] *2602[14]* 2727[5] 2916[6] *3413[6]* **>23a 51f<**

Shell Ginger (IRE) 3 ch f Woodman (USA)-Truly Bound (USA) (In Reality) 806a[4] 1540a[4] 2814a[10] **>112df<**

Shelteez (USA) 3 b br f St Jovite (USA)-Dictina (FR) (Dictus (FR)) 1784[8] 2008[23] 2172[10] 3028[2] 3461[2] 3623[3] **>57f<**

Sheltering Sky (IRE) 3 b c Selkirk (USA)-Shimmering Sea (Slip Anchor) 1611[6] (2420) 2835[2] 4270[5] 4787[3] **>92f<**

Shepherds Rest (IRE) 5 b g Accordion-Mandy's Last (Krayyan) *16[3]* **>35a 53f<**

Sheraton Girl 3 b f Mon Tresor-Sara Sprint (Formidable (USA)) *513[7]* *662[6]* *(873)* 1096[15] *1429[5]* 3249[9] 3558[8] **>48a 22f<**

Sheraz (IRE) 5 b g Persian Bold-Miss Siddons (Cure The Blues (USA)) **1996:** *5130[6] 5179[8] 5223[4] 5244[4] 5260[6]* **1997:** *61[4] 144[2] 188[2] 260[5] 340[4]* 526[4] 687[10] 848[5] 997[4] 1266[6] 1603[10] 4872[14] **>55a 53f<**

Sherganzar 2 b c Shernazar-Victory Kingdom (CAN) (Viceregal (CAN)) 3789[3] 4439[6] 4758[5] 4917[5] 5048[6] **>74f<**

Sheriff 6 b g Midyan (USA)-Daisy Warwick (USA) (Ribot) 888[13] 2035[7] 3472[5] **>62a 53f<**

Shermood 4 b f Shere Khan-Jalebird Blues (Jalmood (USA)) **1996:** *5188[9] 5211[5] 5282[7]* **1997:** *59[10] 57[7][6]* 1009[16] 1292[11] 1374[6] 1483[12] 2395[8] 2724[5] 2922[10] 3321[11] *3581[10]* **>21a 37df<**

Sherpa (IRE) 2 ch g Shernazar-Ezana (Ela-Mana-Mou) 3494[10] **>58f<**

Sherqy (IRE) 5 br g Persian Bold-Turkish Treasure (USA) (Sir Ivor) *330[9] 405[11]* 461[9] 598[2] 781[4] 1562[4] 1840[2] 1981[8] (2208) 2503[5] 2824[3] 3104[5] (3308) **>34a 65f<**

Sherzetto 3 b f Classic Music (USA)-Lake Isle (IRE) (Caerleon (USA)) **1996:** *5133[15]* **1997:** *155[8] 181[10]* 1248[15] 1509[11] **>21a 49f<**

She's A Cracker 3 b f Deploy-Red Secret (IRE) (Valiyar) 2172[4] 2555[8] *3044[12]* **>59f<**

She's A Gem 2 b f Robellino (USA)-Rose Gem (IRE) (Taufan (USA)) 5048[12] **>49f<**

She Said No 5 ch m Beveled (USA)-She Said Yes (Local Suitor (USA)) **1996:** *5223[12] 5271[11]* **>41a 51f<**

She's a Madam 6 b m Kabour-Mrs Buzby (Abwah) **1996:** *5144[12] 5220[7]* **1997:** *51[9] 69[10]* **>21a 18f<**

She's A Winner (IRE) 4 ch f Classic Music (USA)-Eyre Square (IRE) (Flash of Steel) 1283[3] 1601[10] 1996[12] 2225[W] **>42f<**

She's Dawan (IRE) 3 b f Taufan (USA)-Bellinzona (Northfields (USA)) *118[3] 265[2]* 475[14] **>59a 63f<**

She's Electric 3 ch f Superlative-What A Looker (USA) (Raise A Native) **1996:** *5092[7] 5187[11] 5214[8] 5279[6]* **1997:** *265[6]* 2956[10] 3230[10] 3641[8] **>22a 24f<**

She's Simply Great (IRE) 4 b f Simply Great (FR)-Petrine (IRE) (Petorius) 843[9] 1798[5] 2502[9] 2845[11] 3456[7] *3611[6]* **>28a 34f<**

Shfoug (USA) 2 b f Sheikh Albadou-Pure Misk (Rainbow Quest (USA)) 4425[3] (4750) **>82+f<**

Shift Again (IRE) 5 b m Siberian Express (USA)-Pushkinia (FR) (Pharly (FR)) 4562[7] 4744[11] **>65?f<**

Shifting 2 ch f Night Shift (USA)-Preening (Persian Bold) 2343[3] 2713[5] 3547[11] **>73f<**

Shifting Moon 5 b g Night Shift (USA)-Moonscape (Ribero) 2930[6] **>62f<**

Shifting Time 3 b f Night Shift (USA)-Timely Raise (USA) (Raise A Man (USA)) 1141[23] 1479[4] 1810[7] 2197[12] 2745[13] **>60df<**

Shifty Mouse 2 b f Night Shift (USA)-Top Mouse (High Top) 3331[7] 3692[7] **>40f<**

Shii-Take 3 b c Deploy-Super Sally (Superlative) 692[7] 940[7] 1307[3] 2027[10] **>108f<**

Shilling (IRE) 3 b f Bob Back (USA)-Quiche (Formidable (USA)) 773[8] 1986[3] 2783[4] 3210[2] 3781[11] 4213[4] *4800[8]* **>60a 66f<**

Shimaal 2 b f Sadler's Wells (USA)-Grace Note (FR) (Top Ville) 3744[2] 4330[4] **>90f<**

Shindium 2 b f Presidium-Shining Wood (Touching Wood (USA)) 631[5] 4753[23] **>52f<**

Shinerolla 5 b g Thatching-Primrolla (Relko) *398[5]* 444[2] 1097[11] 3921[11] 4147[8] 4781[7] **>87a 80f<**

Shining Cloud 4 ch f Indian Ridge-Hardiheroine (Sandhurst Prince) 942[7] 1225[15] 2006[22] 2406[3] 3746[5] 4333[5] 4951[10] **>60f<**

Shining Dancer 5 b m Rainbow Quest (USA)-Strike Home (Be My Guest (USA)) 510[3] 789[10] (1413) 2014[5] 2767[3] 3010[8] 3122[7] 3498[8] 4426[5] 4874[14] **>38a 72f<**

Shining Example 5 ch g Hadeer-Kick the Habit (Habitat) 735[8] 1244[8] 1463[5] (1926) 2375[8] 3135[7] 3768[2] 4714[18] **>74f<**

Shipley Glen 2 b c Green Desert (USA)-Lady Shipley (Shirley Heights) 4747[7] 4884[22] 5042[20] **>44f<**

Ship's Dancer 4 b f Shareef Dancer (USA)-Sunderland (Dancers Image (USA)) *232[7] 356[8]* 465[9] 570[7] 595[13] 1452[10] 1654[8] 1817[5] 2207[9] 2737[7] 2874[3] 3284[4] 3461[4] 3540[3] **>36f<**

Shirazan (IRE) 3 b c Doyoun-Sharaniya (USA) (Alleged (USA)) 1637[12] 2008[18] **>41f<**

Shirlaty 4 b f Shirley Heights-Jameelaty (USA) (Nureyev (USA)) 1840[7] *3074[11]* **>24f<**

Shirleys Girl (IRE) 2 br f Contract Law (USA)-Maiden's Dance (Hotfoot) 2288[14] 2412[12] 2545[15] 3062[9] 3866[7] **>23f<**

Shirley Sue 4 b f Shirley Heights-Dame Ashfield (Grundy) 632[2] 777[2] 982[9] 1400[6] 2014[2] 3122[3] 3383[4] 3805[5] 4269[6] 4783[14] 5052[8] **>75a 82f<**

Shirley Venture 4 b f Be My Chief (USA)-Our Shirley (Shirley Heights) 769[2] **>59a 80f<**

Shirty 3 b g Shirley Heights-Sassy Lassy (IRE) (Taufan (USA)) 3319[5] **>33f<**

Shmoose (IRE) 2 b f Caerleon (USA)-Kerrera (Diesis) (3574) 4475[7] **>89+f<**

Shmoozy 8 b m Nomination-Myricagale (Wollow) 550[11] 698[9]

Shocker (IRE) 2 b f Sabrehill (USA)-Fenjaan (Trojan Fen) 4769[8] *4982[8]* **>47a 17f<**

Shock Value (IRE) 3 b c Danehill (USA)-Rince Deas (IRE) (Alzao (USA)) 691[6] 2426[4] 2775[6] 4881[17] **>100f<**

Shohra Wa Jaah 2 b g Mtoto-Pipina (USA) (Sir Gaylord) 4244[8] 4957[6] **>66f<**

Shoja 4 ch g Persian Bold-Dancing Berry (Sadler's Wells (USA)) *14[11]* **>2a 22f<**

Shonara's Way 6 b m Slip Anchor-Favorable Exchange (USA) (Exceller (USA)) 5027[16] **>40f<**

Shontaine 4 b g Pharly (FR)-Hinari Televideo (Caerleon (USA)) **1996:** *5089[3] (5130) 5227[6] 5249[6]* **1997:** *57[4] 121[7] 136[7] (404) 421[10]* 484[6] 587[18] 827[10] 929[4] *1048[2]* (1511) 1830[9] 2033[6] 2109[3] *2366[6]* 2463[11] 2659[4] 3406[5] (3456) 3910[8] 4016[8] 4184[2] (4471) *4813[6]* 4924[10] 5030[5] **>52a 65f<**

Shooting Light (IRE) 4 b g Shernazar-Church Light (Caerleon (USA)) (3915) **>83f<**

Shooting Star (IRE) 3 b c Polish Precedent (USA)-Outstandingly (USA) (Exclusive Native (USA)) 3738[5] 3909[4] 4158[9] *4594[8]* **>68f<**

Shoreleave 3 ch c Superlative-Lunagraphe (USA) (Time For A Change (USA)) 1502[6]

Short Romance (IRE) 2 b f Brief Truce (USA)-Lady's Turn (Rymer) 3019[4] 3458[3] 3819[7] 4068[3] 4380[4] **>65f<**

Shoshaloza (USA) 3 ch f Diesis-Martha Sophia (USA) (Drone) 2020[4] 2506[4] 2704[5] 3119[9] 4220[6] 4958[13] **>56f<**

Shoshone 4 ch f Be My Chief (USA)-Bridestones (Jan Ekels) **1996:** *5139[4]* **>46a 52f<**

Shotley Marie (IRE) 2 b f Scenic-Hana Marie (Formidable (USA)) 4332[15] 4750[11] 4840[11] **>34f<**

Shotley Princess 3 ch f Risk Me (FR)-Miss Camellia (Sonnen Gold) *1939[11]* 2387[6] 2468[7] 2569[13] **>18a 7f<**

Shouk 3 b f Shirley Heights-Souk (IRE) (Ahonoora) 833[U] (978) **>83+f<**

Shouldbegrey 4 ch g Siberian Express (USA)-Miss Magnetism (Baptism) 587[8] 848[17] 1273[5] 1506[8] 2369[4] 2552[7] 2646[10] **>41a 42f<**

Shoumatara (USA) 3 ch c Seeking the Gold (USA)-Crown Quest (USA) (Chief's Crown (USA)) 723[17] 1268[16] (1643) **>73f<**

Showboat 3 b c Warning-Boathouse (Habitat) 957[3] 1412[7] (3713) 4153[6] **>99f<**

Showcase 3 b f Shareef Dancer (USA)-Perfolia (USA) (Nodouble (USA)) *1155[10]* 1574[9] 2178[9] 2535[5] 2879[10] **>17a 37f<**

Show Faith (IRE) 7 ch g Exhibitioner-Keep the Faith (Furry Glen) **1996:** *5082[9]* **1997:** 3115[16] 3465[7] (3768) **>46a 65f<**

Showgirl 3 ch f Handsome Sailor-Early Doors (Ballad Rock) **1996:** *5135[6] (5172)* **1997:** *873[6]* 2847[10] 3812[13] 4291[17] **>63a 33f<**

Showstopper 3 b g Today and Tomorrow-Alexzena (Upper Case (USA)) 1798[10] 2059[12] *3581[9]* 4429[5] 4692[12] **>16f<**

Shturm (RUS) 4 ch c Raut-Askanija (RUS) 229a[2] 311a[2] 3884a[2] **>93f<**

Shudder 2 b c Distant Relative-Oublier L'Ennui (FR) (Bellman (FR)) (3743) 4387a[2] 4790[3] 4975[3] **>97f<**

Shuhrah (USA) 2 b br f Danzig (USA)-Sajjaya (USA) (Blushing Groom (FR)) (3009) 3723[9] 4555[3] **>98f<**

Shuttlecock 6 ch g Pharly (FR)-Upper Sister (Upper Case (USA)) *68[4] 139[6] 231[2] 276[2] 284[4] 908[8] 1287[5] 2365[8]* **>41a 39f<**

Shy Paddy (IRE) 5 b g Shy Groom (USA)-Griqualand (Connaught) 1825[8] 2381[4] *2607[2] 2910[2]* **>46a 41f<**

Siberian Mystic 4 gr f Siberian Express (USA)-Mystic Crystal (IRE) (Caerleon (USA)) 3495[2] 3970[8] 4275[10] (4584) 4971[16] **>49f<**

Sibor Star 3 b g Man Among Men (IRE)-My Ratbag (Main Reef) *425[8]* 479[7] *906[4]* **>45a 46f<**

Sick As A Parrot 2 ch c Casteddu-Sianiski (Niniski (USA)) (1856) 2587[2] 3025[3] 3387[2] 3650[12] (4245) (4849) **>79f<**

Side Bar 7 b g Mummy's Game-Joli's Girl (Mansingh (USA)) *1417[2]* 2874[12] **>39a 22f<**

Sideman (IRE) 2 b c Brief Truce (USA)-Millie Musique (Miller's Mate) (1192a) 2057^{8} 3962a^{8} 4357a^{8} 4616a^{3} **>106f<**

Sidney The Kidney 3 b f Mystiko (USA)-Martin-Lavell Mail (Dominion) **1996:** *5142^{7} 5226^{4}* **1997:** 582^{2} 1441^{19} 2407^{7} 4817^{13} 4987^{9} **>40a 36f<**

Siege Perilous (IRE) 4 b g Taufan (USA)-Carado (Manado) 510^{2} 846^{3} 1162^{4} (1974) 2327^{4} 3498^{2} (3896) 4783^{6} 5052^{15} **>58a 83f<**

Siena (GER) 2 ch f Platini (GER)-Smeralda (GER) (Nebos (GER)) 1927^{7} 2394^{9} 4057^{7} (4366) 4849^{11} **>61f<**

Sifwa 3 ch f Safawan-Wigeon (Divine Gift) *1155^{7}* 1485^{5} 2742^{2} 3091^{16} **>34a 56f<**

Siggiewi 3 ro f Mystiko (USA)-Shadiyama (Nishapour (FR)) 3572^{4} 4045^{14} **>45f<**

Sighisoara (ITY) 2 b f Imperial Frontier (USA)-Walkyria (Lord Gayle (USA)) 4128a^{3} **>72f<**

Signatory 2 ch c King's Signet (USA)-Pearl Pet (Mummy's Pet) 1675^{4} 2196^{2} *2595^{5}* 3025^{6} 3818^{3} 4065^{4} 4670^{10} (4855) **>45a 75+f<**

Signed And Sealed (USA) 3 b g Rahy (USA)-Heaven's Mine (USA) (Graustark) 1866^{12} 3021^{8} 3419^{10} *4055^{4} 4302^{8} 4811^{7}* **>51a 57f<**

Signs And Wonders 3 b f Danehill (USA)-Front Line Romance (Caerleon (USA)) 694^{16} *1151^{3}* 1294^{5} 1458^{2} 1651^{3} 1966^{6} 2601^{5} 2957^{4} *3058^{2} 3232^{2}* 3423^{15} *3860^{4}* **>67a 75f<**

Sihafi (USA) 4 ch g Elmaamul (USA)-Kit's Double (USA) (Spring Double) **1996:** *5124^{12} (5183) 5280^{2}* **1997:** *95^{5} (263)* 468^{14} 610^{9} 827^{13} 1225^{5} 1655^{7} 2788^{20} 3271^{10} 3431^{8} **>63a 45f<**

Sikesting 2 b c Sikeston (USA)-Lasting Lass (IRE) (Last Tycoon) 4533a^{2}

Silankka 3 b f Slip Anchor-Mary Sunley (Known Fact (USA)) 833^{10} 2537^{4} **>69f<**

Silca Key Service 2 b f Bering-Aquaglow (Caerleon (USA)) 3219^{5} 3638^{9} **>71tf<**

Silca Key Silca 3 ch f Polar Falcon (USA)-Night Transaction (Tina's Pet) 1958^{6} (2192) 2347^{7} 2560^{5} 2925^{4} 3649^{11} 3982^{4} 4280^{22} *4591^{2}* **>86a 87f<**

Silence in Court (IRE) 6 b g Law Society (USA)-Fair Flutter (Beldale Flutter (USA)) 4874^{2} 5052^{W} **>110f<**

Silence Reigns 3 b g Saddlers' Hall (IRE)-Rensaler (USA) (Stop The Music (USA)) 2008^{2} (2360) 2765^{2} 3109^{4} **>115f<**

Silently 5 b g Slip Anchor-Land of Ivory (USA) (The Minstrel (CAN)) 1592^{4} 2198^{2} 2767^{2} 2949^{2} **>90f<**

Silent Miracle (IRE) 3 b f Night Shift (USA)-Curie Point (USA) (Sharpen Up) 453^{3} 584^{3} 778^{2} *(904)* 1170^{6} 1980^{9} 2141^{3} 2563^{6} 2964^{8} 3460^{3} 3771^{5} 3984^{5} 4321^{5} 4636^{15} **>81+a 70f<**

Silent Pride (IRE) 2 ch f Pips Pride-Suppression (Kind of Hush) 828^{3} 1109^{8} 1295^{4} 1675^{8} 1867^{4} *2051^{6} 2304^{2} 3045^{6}* 3451^{11} 3546^{4} 3782^{2} 3892^{6} 4327^{8} 4545^{10} 4819^{8} **>45a 52f<**

Silent Symphony 5 ch m Music Boy-City Link Rose (Lochnager) *117^{9} 215^{9}* 2491^{12} 3016^{10} 3394^{5} **>28a 6f<**

Silent System (IRE) 4 gr g Petong-Light Thatch (Thatch (USA)) *3261^{0}* 526^{17} 827^{14} 1467^{11} 1631^{10} 2109^{9} 2226^{4} 2362^{5} 2502^{6} 2564^{13} 3762^{8} 3919^{9} **>12a 21f<**

Silent Tribute (IRE) 2 b f Lion Cavern (USA)-Tribal Rite (Be My Native (USA)) (1213) 2335^{3} 2600^{2} 3422^{3} (4259a) 4663a^{6} **>93f<**

Silent Valley 3 b f Forzando-Tremmin (Horage) **1996:** *5092^{2} 5180^{6}* **1997:** *84^{3} 124^{10} 168^{10}* 1998^{3} 2569^{7} 2733^{8} 2878^{4} (3133) 3336^{3} 3605^{11} 4102^{11} 4386^{13} 4847^{12} **>53a 56f<**

Silent Warning 2 b c Ela-Mana-Mou-Buzzbomb (Bustino) 4708^{12} 4853^{11} **>44f<**

Silent Weapon 3 ch g Primo Dominie-On Request (IRE) (Be My Guest (USA)) *19^{4} 97^{3} 132^{8}* **>49a 58f<**

Silent Wells 3 b f Saddlers' Hall (IRE)-Silent Plea (Star Appeal) *906^{5}* **>43f<**

Silic (FR) 2 c 4657a^{4}

Silk Cottage 5 b g Superpower-Flute Royale (Horage) **1996:** *5096^{8} 5131^{14} 5225^{7}* **1997:** *(515) 593^{2}* 702^{10} *856^{6}* 956^{6} *1289^{2} 1759^{7} 2050^{4} 2366^{4}* 2755^{4} 2826^{3} *2915^{8} 3398^{8} 4049^{3} 4985^{4}* **>66a 56f<**

Silken Dalliance 2 b f Rambo Dancer (CAN)-A Sharp (Sharpo) 4332^{10} *4569^{2}* 4917^{4} **>77a 65f<**

Silk St John 3 b g Damister (USA)-Silk St James (Pas de Seul) 2408^{3} (3236) 3418^{3} 3894^{4} 4314^{2} 4558^{12} 4757^{22} 4978^{13} **>87f<**

Silly Imp (IRE) 3 b f Imperial Frontier (USA)-Silly Song (Silly Season) 3508a^{6} **>92f<**

Silvazine 2 gr f Silver Kite (USA)-Dorazine (Kalaglow) 1564^{14} 2276^{4}

Silverani (IRE) 3 b c High Estate-Rose Society (Caerleon (USA)) (701) 1146^{2} 4552^{2} 4759^{6} (4947) **>108f<**

Silver Button 3 b g Silver Kite (USA)-Klairover (Smackover) 497^{5} 600^{8} 1731^{3} *3400^{4} 3611^{8}* **>32a 50f<**

Silver Charm (USA) 3 ro c Silver Buck (USA)-Bonnie's Poker (USA) (Poker (USA)) (1071a) *(1364a) 1912a^{2}* **>125a 124f<**

Silver Fun (FR) 3 b f Saumarez-Riviere d'Argent (FR) (Nijinsky (CAN)) 1360a^{2} (2275a) 4256a^{9} 4965a^{4} **>115f<**

Silver Groom (IRE) 7 gr g Shy Groom (USA)-Rustic Lawn (Rusticaro (FR)) 521^{6} 787^{5} 3424^{2} 3773^{15} 4294^{15} **>86f<**

Silver Harrow 4 ch g Belmez (USA)-Dancing Diana (Raga Navarro (ITY)) **1996:** *5235^{5} 5262^{6}* **1997:** *92^{5} 578^{13}* 1642^{6} 1965^{2} 2651^{2} 3254^{10} *3608^{W}* 4043^{2} 4228^{18} 4899^{2} **>46a 66f<**

Silver Hope (IRE) 2 ch c Silver Kite (USA)-Cloven Dancer (USA) (Hurok (USA)) 1819^{9} 3212^{6} 4061^{16} 4384^{13} 4698^{11} **>54f<**

Silver Hunter (USA) 6 b g Silver Hawk (USA)-Martha Queen (USA) (Nijinsky (CAN)) **1996:** *5102^{8}* **>58a 56f<**

Silvering (FR) 5 b h Polish Precedent (USA)-Silvermine (FR) (Bellypha) 3728^{9} **>111?f<**

Silver Joy 2 b f Silver Kite (USA)-Oh My Joy (Grundy) 2320^{10} 2752^{7} **>38f<**

Silver Jubilee 3 b f Sylvan Express-Addison's Jubilee (Sparkler) 586^{14} 889^{11} 1963^{14} 2376^{7} **>35f<**

Silver Kristal 3 gr f Kris-Reine D'Beaute (Caerleon (USA)) 2591^{4} 3189^{5} 3800^{2} 4316^{2} 4563^{4} **>76f<**

Silver Lining 3 b g Beveled (USA)-Seymour Ann (Krayyan) 758^{4} 876^{3} 1141^{16} 1566^{9} (1849) 2552^{14} (2785) 3138^{4} **>70f<**

Silver Marble (IRE) 3 b f Silver Kite (USA)-Friendly Song (Song) 3850^{6} 4506^{4} **>32f<**

Silver Moon 3 gr f Environment Friend-High and Bright (Shirley Heights) 795^{10} *1135^{15}* 1620^{17} **>35a 24f<**

Silver Patriarch (IRE) 3 gr c Saddlers' Hall (IRE)-Early Rising (USA) (Grey Dawn II) 851^{3} (1103) 1769^{2} 2454a^{5} 3647^{2} (4149) **>127f<**

Silver Pearl 6 gr g Insan (USA)-Vanishing Trick (Silly Season) (950) 1840^{6} 2145^{14} 2503^{12} 4692^{14} **>1f<**

Silver Purse 3 ch f Interrex (CAN)-Money Supply (Brigadier Gerard) 863^{15} 1141^{19} 1275^{3} 1439^{6} 1781^{7} 1955^{9} 2665^{11} 2788^{7} 2958^{5} 3561^{9} **>59f<**

Silver Rhapsody (USA) 2 b f Silver Hawk (USA)-Sister Chrys (USA) (Fit To Fight (USA)) 4873^{2} **>85f<**

Silver Sea (USA) 2 gr ro f Java Gold (USA)-Gray And Red (USA) (Wolf Power (SAF)) 3247^{9} **>45f<**

Silver Secret 3 ro c Absalom-Secret Dance (Sadler's Wells (USA)) 1670^{7} 2369^{7} 2645^{4} 3452^{7} (3641) 4059^{15} 4333^{8} **>66f<**

Silversmith (FR) 2 b c Always Fair (USA)-Phargette (FR) (Lyphard (USA)) 3219^{7} 3613^{2} 4855^{2} **>70f<**

Silver Strand (IRE) 2 b f Waajib-Jendeal (Troy) 1872^{7} (2519) 2697^{2} **>74f<**

Silver Sun 2 gr f Green Desert (USA)-Catch The Sun (Kalaglow) 4758^{9} **>60f<**

Silvertown 2 b c Danehill (USA)-Docklands (USA) (Theatrical) 2948^{2} 3598^{13} **>79+f<**

Silver Whirl (USA) 3 b f Silver Hawk (USA)-With a Twist (USA) (Fappiano (USA)) 1168^{3} 1625^{5} 3140^{4} 4242^{4} 4429^{3} 4971^{24} **>73f<**

Silver Wonder (USA) 3 ch c Silver Hawk (USA)-Upper Class Lady (USA) (Upper Nile (USA)) 1218^{2} 1612^{6} **>84f<**

Silvery 3 gr f Petong-Petit Peu (IRE) (Kings Lake (USA)) 1110^{8} 1637^{10} 2008^{17} 2522^{2} 2897^{4} (4158) 4731^{11} **>75f<**

Silvretta (IRE) 4 br f Tirol-Lepoushka (Salmon Leap (USA)) 3279^{9} 3694^{8} 3928^{11} 4744^{7} 4971^{R} **>56df<**

Simafar (IRE) 6 b g Kahyasi-Sidama (FR) (Top Ville) 493^{13} **>52a 32f<**

Simlet 2 b c Forzando-Besito (Wassl) 2176^{6} 2768^{6} 2953^{10} 3924^{2} 4068^{2} **>70f<**

Simon du Desert (FR) 4 b c Kaldoun (FR)-Canaletto (USA) (Iron Duke (FR)) (716a) 1067a^{2} 1554a^{3} 2820a^{2} **>122f<**

Simple Logic 3 ch f Aragon-Dancing Chimes (London Bells (CAN)) 988^{7} 1238^{7} 3418^{5} 3690^{14} **>71f<**

Simply Gifted 2 b c Simply Great (FR)-Souveniers (Relko) 2022^{3} (3084) 3650^{4} 3990^{3} **>74f<**

Simply Super 2 ch f Superlative-Real Princess (Aragon) (3847) 4107^{6} **>81f<**

Simply Times (USA) 3 b f Dodge (USA)-Nesian's Burn (USA) (Big Burn (USA)) **1996:** *5111^{10}* **>23a f<**

Sinan (USA) 2 ch c Mr Prospector (USA)-Gmaasha (IRE) (Kris) 4526^{9} 4915^{9} **>67f<**

Sinch 2 ch f Inchinor-Swinging Gold (Swing Easy (USA)) 3331^{9} 3780^{4} **>43f<**

Sing And Dance 4 b f Rambo Dancer (CAN)-Musical Princess (Cavo Doro) 461^{2} 552^{7} 721^{10} 900^{3} 1313^{6} 2043^{4} 2293^{3} 2502^{5} 2907^{6} (3430) 3906^{4} 4161^{4} 4471^{8} 4691^{7} 4845^{10} **>50f<**

Sing For Me (IRE) 2 b br f Songlines (FR)-Running For You (FR) (Pampabird) 1569^{7} 1997^{10} 2700^{3} 3131^{4} 3545^{8} 3819^{4} 4362^{5} 4922^{6} 4989^{7} **>70f<**

Singforyoursupper 3 ch f Superlative-Suzannah's Song (Song) 1500^{7} *2071^{10}* 2481^{2} 2738^{17} 3083^{13} **>39a 46f<**

Single Empire (IRE) 3 ch c Kris-Captive Island (Northfields (USA)) (523) 741^{5} (937) (1553a) 1769^{11} **>107f<**

Single Man (IRE) 4 b g Mansooj-Sniggy (Belfort (FR)) 2479^{4} 2753^{8} 4360^{8} 4986^{12} **>48f<**

Singspiel (IRE) 5 b h In The Wings-Glorious Song (CAN) (Halo (USA)) **1996:** (5159a) **1997:** *(628a)* (1736) 3050^{4} (3646) **>132a 135f<**

Sing With the Band 6 b m Chief Singer-Ra Ra Girl (Shack (USA)) *301^{3} 394^{5}* 541^{8} 585^{9} 702^{15} 883^{13} *905^{9}* 1080^{7} 1402^{9} 1514^{7} 2002^{6} 2317^{8} 2788^{2} 3285^{2} 3565^{7} 4169^{9} **>80a 52f<**

Sinon (IRE) 2 ch c Ela-Mana-Mou-Come In (Be My Guest (USA)) (4413) 4977^{6} **>86f<**

Sinyar 5 b or br h 3369a^{3} **>121f<**

Sioux 3 ch f Kris-Lassoo (Caerleon (USA)) 524^{5} 2328^{5} 4310^{7} 4466^{10} 4704^{8} **>69f<**

Siouxrouge 3 b g Indian Ridge-Scarlett Holly (Red Sunset) **1996:** *5133^{3}* **1997:** *17^{2} 50^{3} (135) 180^{5} 258^{6}* 1008^{3} 1661^{9} **>84da 71f<**

Siphon (BRA) 6 b h Itajara (USA)-Ebrea (USA) (Kublai Khan (USA)) (393a) *628a^{2}* **>130a 126f<**

Sipowitz 3 b g Warrshan (USA)-Springs Welcome (Blakeney) 790^{8} 967^{8} *(1785) 2068^{5}* 2397^{7} (3057) 3325^{3} *3415^{4} (3865)* 4171^{5} 4336^{2} (4585) (4804) **>56a 70f<**

Sipping Soda 2 b f Silver Kite (USA)-Red Magic (Red God) 441^{7} *872^{6}* 3384^{7} 3639^{5} 3782^{13} **>17a 23f<**

Sir Alidaf 3 b g Broadsword (USA)-Bolton Flyer (Aragon) *255^{9} 355^{6} 544^{12}* **>18a f<**

Sir Arthur Hobbs 10 b g Lyphard's Special (USA)-Song Grove (Song) 1220^{5} 1631^{2} **>63f<**

Sirinndi (IRE) 3 b c Shahrastani (USA)-Sinntara 4620a^{3} **>109f<**

Sir Joey (USA) 8 ch g Honest Pleasure (USA)-Sougoli (Realm) 443^{14} 520^{10} 726^{8} 942^{2} 1317^{2} 1824^{3} 2347^{4} 2833^{2} 3217^{16} 3765^{9} 4013^{4} *4797^{4} 4983^{2}* **>86a 89f<**

Sir Pageant 8 b g Pharly (FR)-National Dress (Welsh Pageant) 4633^{12}

Sir Ricky (USA) 3 b g Woodman (USA)-Opera Queen (IRE) (Sadler's Wells (USA)) 2311^{4} 3021^{2} 3419^{2} 4045^{2} **>89f<**

Sir Silver Sox (USA) 5 gr g Corwyn Bay-Sox In The Box (USA) (Cresta Rider (USA)) 467^{5} 596^{17} **>84df< (DEAD)**

Sir Talbot 3 b c Ardross-Bermuda Lily (Dunbeath (USA)) (479) 690^{14} 1973^{2} (2729) 3190^{17} 3998a^{8} **>95f<**

Sir Tasker 9 b h Lidhame-Susie's Baby (Balidar) **1996:** *5131^{11} 5144^{13} 5236^{5}* **1997:** *69^{4} 79^{5} (199) 263^{9} 318^{2} 348^{3} 569^{9}* 601^{5} 759^{16} *1047^{9}* 1620^{7} 2755^{2} 3261^{5} 4184^{8} 4249^{7} **>50a 54f<**

Sir Warren (IRE) 4 b c Warning-Sistadari (Shardari) 2459a^{6} **>113f<**

Si Seductor (USA) 4 b c Diesis-Miss Evans (FR) (Nijinsky (CAN)) 916a^{3} 2270a^{2} 3731a^{2} **>116f<**

Si Senorita 2 b f Young Senor (USA)-Raunchy Rita (Brigadier Gerard) 2856^{6} **>43f<**

Sis Garden 4 b f Damister (USA)-Miss Nanna (Vayrann) **1996:** *5152^{9} 5170^{3} 5266^{8}* **1997:** 477^{5} *860^{2} 1135^{6}* (1373) 1640^{3} 2119^{7} 2730^{11} (3248) 3316^{5} 3787^{2} 3980^{6} 4319^{4} 4628^{9} 5049^{22} **>66a 66f<**

Sispre (ITY) 4 b f Master Willie-Sweet Snow (USA) (Lyphard (USA)) 1369a^{2}

Six Clerks (IRE) 4 b g Shadeed (USA)-Skidmore Girl (USA) (Vaguely Noble) 1042^{3} 1574^{2} 2843^{14} 3134^{8} **>64a 58f<**

Six for Luck 5 b g Handsome Sailor-Fire Sprite (Mummy's Game) 610^{18} 2384^{10} 2540^{4} 2657^{5} 2826^{5} 2900^{13} 3484^{14} 3922^{8} 4233^{18} 4707^{12} 5023^{14} **>42f<**

Sixpence 2 b f Saddlers' Hall (IRE)-Half a Dozen (USA) (Saratoga Six (USA)) 4103^{14} 4556^{5} 4904^{15} **>68f<**

Six Shooter 3 b f Damister (USA)-Ten to Six (Night Shift (USA)) 4290^{13} 4631^{9} **>37f<**

Sixth Avenue (IRE) 2 b f Common Grounds-Tarativa (USA) (Sensitive Prince (USA)) 1019^{6} 1253^{7} 2016^{17} *2914^{4} 3395^{9}* 4413^{10} *4812^{16}* **>17a 36df<**

Sixties Melody 3 b g Merdon Melody-Balidilemma (Balidar) *239^{3}* 1637^{11} 2189^{8} 3325^{2} *3865^{P}* 4171^{7} **>34a 56f<**

Six Zero (FR) 3 gr c Linamix (FR)-Six Love (FR) (Mr Prospector (USA)) 1362a^{2} **>108f<**

Siyadah (USA) 3 ch f Mr Prospector (USA)-Roseate Tern (Blakeney) (959) 1738^{11} 2053^{7} **>101df<**

Sizzling 5 b g Sizzling Melody-Oriental Splendour (Runnett) (638) 1009^{10} 1509^{5} 2179^{3} 2698^{12} 3082^{6} 3417^{6} 4248^{14} **>53f<**

Skelton Countess (IRE) 4 ch f Imperial Frontier (USA)-Running Brook (Run The Gantlet (USA)) **1996:** *5170^{12}* **1997:** 774^{11} 1005^{17} 2738^{16} 3241^{4} 4214^{7} 4899^{7} **>4a 43f<**

Skelton Sovereign (IRE) 3 b c Contract Law (USA)-Mrs Lucky (Royal Match) **1996:** *5141^{5}* **1997:** *7^{3} 33^{4} 84^{4} 277^{3} 314^{3} 368^{3} 456^{3}* 537^{4} *581^{8}* 862^{4} *906^{3}* 1095^{2} 1299^{8} *(1579)* 1863^{4} *2301^{2}* 2423^{4} 3129^{5} 4289^{4} 4509^{7} **>66a 57f<**

Skiddaw Samba 8 b m Viking (USA)-Gavea (African Sky) 1686^{6} 3919^{15} **>37f<**

Skip Away (USA) 4 gr c Skip Trial (USA)-Ingot Way (USA) (Diplomat Way) *(5066a)* **>134a 121f<**

Skippool Creek (IRE) 2 b br f Petardia-Tambora (Darshaan) 572^{8} 743^{5} 1330^{8} 1581^{5} **>42f<**

Skippy Was A Kiwi (IRE) 3 b f River Falls-Hit For Six (Tap On Wood) *513^{10}* 779^{9} 1167^{16} 1484^{14} **>25a 42f<**

Skram 4 b g Rambo Dancer (CAN)-Skarberg (FR) (Noir Et Or) *375^{10}* **>21a 58f<**

Sky Commander (USA) 3 b br c Storm Bird (CAN)-Fairy Footsteps (Mill Reef (USA)) 983^{2} *(1155)* 1404^{5} (2296) 2839^{5} 4306^{4} **>81+a 96f<**

Sky Dome (IRE) 4 ch c Bluebird (USA)-God Speed Her (Pas de Seul) 450^{7} 738^{5} 2026^{24} 2775^{9} 4757^{12} **>81f<**

Skyers A Kite 2 b f Deploy-Milady Jade (IRE) (Drumalis) 4212^{9} **>33f<**

Skyers Flyer (IRE) 3 b br f Magical Wonder (USA)-Siwana (IRE) (Dom Racine (FR)) 462^{2} 757^{7} (882) 995^{8} 1080^{3} 1493^{2} 1734^{2} 1861^{6} 2734^{3} (3261) **>25a 76?f<**

Skyers Tryer 3 b f Lugana Beach-Saltina (Bustino) 3855^{11} 4586^{12} **>40a 70df<**

Sky Mountain (IRE) 2 b c Danehill (USA)-Molvina (ITY) (Final Straw) 1418^{10} 1932^{7} 2320^{12} 2740^{3} **>58f<**

Sky Red 2 gr f Night Shift (USA)-Noble Haven (Indian King (USA)) 1031^{4} 4556^{8} 4904^{11} **>61f<**

Sky Rocket 2 ch c Storm Cat (USA)-Oriental Mystique (Kris) 4146^{2} (4564) **>99+f<**

Skywasser (IRE) 2 ch c Suave Dancer (USA)-Kaweah Maid (General Assembly (USA)) 4532a^{2}

Slaney Squire (IRE) 2 b c Scenic-Surreale (ITY) (New Model (FR)) (2098a) 2644a^{3}

Slapy Dam 5 b g Deploy-Key to the River (USA) (Irish River (FR)) 595^{7} 955^{10} 1779^{16} 1844^{4} 2490^{5} 3758^{10} **>60da 56f<**

Slasher Jack (IRE) 6 b g Alzao (USA)-Sherkraine (Shergar) 430^{23} 598^{8} 746^{7} 4466^{11} 4714^{5} 5024^{2} **>70f<**

Sledmere (IRE) 2 ch g Shalford (IRE)-Jazirah (Main Reef) 4384^{12} 4507^{8} 4753^{27} **>37f<**

Sleepless 3 b f Night Shift (USA)-Late Evening (USA) (Riverman (USA)) 675^{4} (1245) 1737^{11} 2331^{3} 3119^{7} 3982^{10} **>91f<**

Sleeptite (FR) 7 gr g Double Bed (FR)-Rajan Grey (Absalom) **1996:** *5084^{12}* **>71a 10f<**

Sleepytime (IRE) 3 b f Royal Academy (USA)-Alidiva (Chief Singer) 724^{4} (960) 2025^{3} **>125f<**

Slew Magic (IRE) 2 b f Don't Forget Me-Sound Pet (Runnett) 2823^{3} *3045^{8}* (3294) 3563^{7} 3751^{12} **>3a 61f<**

Sliema Creek 3 gr g Beveled (USA)-Sea Farer Lake (Gairloch) **1996:** *5257^{5}* **1997:** *50^{2} 154^{2} 230^{3} 868^{10}* **>72da f<**

Slieu Whallian 3 b f In The Wings-Ladyfish (Pampapaul) 3917^{10} 4587^{5} 4883^{5} 4996^{13} **>52f<**

Slievenamon 4 br g Warning-Twice A Fool (USA) (Foolish Pleasure (USA)) **1996:** *(5262)* **1997:** *2071^{12}* 3321^{13} *4069^{6} 4480^{10}* **>58a 27f<**

Slightly Oliver (IRE) 3 b g Silver Kite (USA)-Red Note (Rusticaro (FR)) **1996:** *5098^{3} 5166^{8}* **>43a 50f<**

Slightly Special (IRE) 5 ch g Digamist (USA)-Tunguska (Busted) *1579^{5}* 2521^{10} *3587^{7}* **>44da 34f<**

Slim Prior 2 gr c Norton Challenger-Hopeful Katie (Full of Hope) 1019^{12} *1124^{7}* 2191^{5} 2419^{5} 4543^{7} *4812^{4}* **>59a 52f<**

Slip Jig (IRE) 4 b c Marju (IRE)-Taking Steps (Gay Fandango (USA)) **1996:** *5208^{3} 5250^{2} 5274^{2}* **1997:** *(22) 176^{2} 260^{7}* 1036^{4} 1325^{7} 2155^{6} 2652^{2} 2889^{5} 3110^{7} *3231^{4}* **>71a 75f<**

Slipper 2 b f Suave Dancer (USA)-Horseshoe Reef (Mill Reef (USA)) 4212^{5} 4873^{6} **>75f<**

Slippery Fin 5 b m Slip Anchor-Finyska (FR) (Niniski (USA)) *73^{11}* **>59da f<**

Slippery Slope (IRE) 2 b f Imperial Frontier (USA)-Cartagena Lady 3961a^{8} **>83f<**

Slipping 3 1368a^{9}

Slipstream 3 b c Slip Anchor-Butosky (Busted) 676^{9} 963^{14} **>77f<**

Slipstream Star 3 b f Slip Anchor-Alsiba (Northfields (USA)) 1105^{8} 2555^{2} 3079^{3} 3463^{3} 4176^{18} 4469^{2} 4988^{11} **>69f<**

Slip Venture 2 b c Slip Anchor-Sherkraine (Shergar) 4740^{8} 4950^{8} 5048^{9} **>63f<**

Small Risk 3 b f Risk Me (FR)-Small Double (IRE) (Double Schwartz) 1780^{10} 2244^{12} **>25a 7f<**

Smart Beau (USA) 2 ch c Beau Genius (CAN)-Brittney Erin (USA) (Restless Restless (USA)) 1961^{5} 2849^{4} 3117^{12} 3635^{6} 3924^{14} **>61f<**

Smart Boy (IRE) 3 ch c Polish Patriot (USA)-Bouffant (High Top) 675^{16} 840^{11} *(1153) (1421)* 4996^{14} **>75a 56f<**

Smart Dominion 3 b c Sharpo-Anodyne (Dominion) 1265^{7} **>75f<**

Smarter Charter 4 br c Master Willie-Irene's Charter (Persian Bold) 444^{7} 529^{7} 635^{3} 824^{3} 1097^{10} 1300^{7} 3153^{7} 3477^{7} 3848^{7} 3966^{4} 4324^{2} **>34a 61f<**

Smart Guest 5 ch g Be My Guest (USA)-Konbola (Superlative) *512^{11} 545^{14}* 759^{17} 972^{9} *1433^{6} 1754^{12} 2302^{9}* 2463^{5} 2785^{5} 3100^{5} **>58a 52f<**

Smart Kid (IRE) 3 b c Lahib (USA)-Diamond Lake (Kings Lake (USA)) 740^{7} (964) 4307^{12} *4591^{10}* **>67a 76f<**

Smart Play (USA) 4 gr c Sovereign Dancer (USA)-Casessa (USA) (Caro) 2241^{3} 2764^{4} 3137^{8} **>92f<**

Smart Prince 2 b g Prince Sabo-She's Smart (Absalom) 2127^{6} 2467^{10} 2762^{5} 3239^{5} 3753^{6} **>71f<**

Smart Prospect 3 b g Superpower-Bustilly (Busted) 862^{14} **>27a 23f<**

Smarts Castle (IRE) 5 m Mansooj-Miss Lillian (FR) 4620a^{18} **>86f<**

Smart Spirit (IRE) 3 b f Persian Bold-Sharp Ego (USA) (Sharpen Up) 998^{2} 1175^{16} 1845^{4} 2570^{4} 2884^{3} 4568^{12} 4695^{9} 4972^{5} **>62f<**

Smart Squall (USA) 2 b c Summer Squall (USA)-Greek Wedding (USA) (Blushing Groom (FR)) 3094^{11} (4113) (4670) 4880^{5} **>99f<**

Smart Venture 2 b c Sabrehill (USA)-Water Well (Sadler's Wells (USA)) 1026^{6} *3607^{12}* **>31a 30f<**

Smile Forever (USA) 4 b f Sunshine Forever (USA)-Awenita (Rarity) **1996:** *5086^{4} 5119^{7}* **1997:** 595^{16} **>42a 55f<**

Smiling Bess 4 b f Salse (USA)-Wanda (Taufan

(USA)) 1509^{8} 2310^{15} 2723^{8} 4168^{10} 4370^{17} **>13a 37f<**

Smiling Voter (IRE) 2 b c Balla Cove-Ravensdale Rose (IRE) (Henbit (USA)) 3711^{10} *4056*^{7} 4165^{4} 4582^{4} 4745^{6} **>54a 78f<**

Smilin N Wishin (USA) 4 b f Lyphard's Wish (FR)-Smilin Michele (USA) (Sharpen Up) **1996:** *5091*^{7} **>61a 86f<**

Smithereens 4 ch f Primo Dominie-Splintering (Sharpo) **1996:** *(5089) 5124*^{2} **>77a 70f<**

Smoke'n'jo (IRE) 3 ch c Masterclass (USA)-Alpine Dance (USA) (Apalachee (USA)) 3762^{10} *4053*^{11} **>61f<**

Smokey From Caplaw 3 b g Sizzling Melody-Mary From Dunlow (Nicholas Bill) 610^{15} 785^{8} (995) (1225) 1561^{6} 2857^{6} 3208^{6} 3621^{4} 3801^{7} 4308^{P} 4410^{15} (4601) 4773^{13} 4924^{8} **>75f<**

Smooth Princess (IRE) 2 gr f Roi Danzig (USA)-Sashi Woo (Rusticaro (FR)) 2706^{12} 3821^{10} 4209^{7} 4427^{8} *(4812)* **>78+a 39f<**

Smooth Sailing 2 gr g Beveled (USA)-Sea Farer Lake (Gairloch) 557^{5} (850) 1084^{2} 1411^{2} 1735^{5} 3990^{11} 4218^{3} 4679^{4} 4897^{16} 5045^{6} **>80f<**

Smuggler's Point (USA) 7 b g Lyphard (USA)-Smuggly (USA) (Caro) **1996:** *5240*^{11} **>32a 56?f<**

Snap Crackle Pop (IRE) 3 b f Statoblest-Spinelle (Great Nephew) 854^{7} 988^{3} 1609^{8} 2185^{4} 2561^{10} **>85f<**

Snappy Times 2 ch g Timeless Times (USA)-Hill of Fare (Brigadier Gerard) 664^{5} 1447^{9} 1616^{10} 1797^{3} 2565^{12} 2736^{11} 3062^{3} 3427^{4} 3563^{2} 3751^{4} *4054*^{3} *(4593)* **>57a 57f<**

Snowballs 2 gr c Chilibang-Golden Panda (Music Boy) 3857^{3} 4236^{12} 4840^{5} **>72f<**

Snowcap (IRE) 3 b f Snow Chief (USA)-Very Subtle (USA) (Hoist The Silver (USA)) 3021^{10} 3419^{8} 3893^{5} **>50f<**

Snow Carnival 4 ch g Belmez (USA)-Winter Queen (Welsh Pageant) 1682^{7} 2008^{22} 2116^{4} 3640^{12} 4210^{14} **>53f<**

Snow Cloud 3 b f Today and Tomorrow-Fancy Pages (Touch Paper) *4809*^{14}

Snow Domino (IRE) 4 ch g Habyom-Magic Picture (Deep Diver) 1601^{9} **>44a 15f<**

Snow Eagle (IRE) 3 b f Polar Falcon (USA)-Icefern (Moorestyle) **1996:** *5080*^{6} *5201*^{4} *5228*^{6} **>52a 51f<**

Snow Kid 3 b c Indian Ridge-Sarcita (Primo Dominie) *(1787)* (2229) (2426) 2820a^{7} 4344a^{2} 4777^{3} (5054) **>91+a 117f<**

Snow Partridge (USA) 3 ch c Arctic Tern (USA)-Lady Sharp (FR) (Sharpman) 1207^{6} 2647^{3} 3218^{5} 3632^{2} 4072^{3} 4372^{7} **>83df<**

Snow Princess (IRE) 5 b m Ela-Mana-Mou-Karelia (USA) (Sir Ivor) **1996:** 5125a^{4} **1997:** 1027^{9} 1319^{4} 2709^{5} 4099^{4} 4676^{2} 4965a^{2} **>116f<**

Snowy Mantle 4 b f Siberian Express (USA)-Mollified (Lombard (GER)) 574^{16} 1116^{2} 1463^{4} 2145^{7} 2502^{3} (3029) 3200^{3} 3777^{8} 4695^{20} 4992^{17} **>27a 48f<**

Soaked 4 b g Dowsing (USA)-Water Well (Sadler's Wells (USA)) *71*^{6} *112*^{2} *177*^{11} *327*^{5} *423*^{6} 1514^{12} *2305*^{4} 2738^{18} 3334^{11} 3625^{3} 3761^{9} 4707^{6} **>37a 36f<**

Soaking 7 b g Dowsing (USA)-Moaning Low (Burglar) **1996:** *5095*^{2} *(5227)* **1997:** *(105) 171*^{3} *403*^{5} *1082*^{7} 1606^{11} 1972^{4} 3184^{8} 3496^{11} 4371^{17} 4628^{11} **>65a 32f<**

So Amazing 5 b m Hallgate-Jussoli (Don) **1996:** *5106*^{13} *5266*^{5} **1997:** *72*^{F} **>84a 61f< (DEAD)**

Soap Stone 2 b f Gunner B-Tzarina (USA) (Gallant Romeo (USA)) 3819^{10} **>42f<**

Social Charter (USA) 2 b c Nureyev (USA)-Aunt Pearl (USA) (Seattle Slew (USA)) 3047^{2} (3489) 3706^{6} 4517^{5} (4709) **>94f<**

Society Fair (FR) 4 ch f Always Fair (USA)-Society Bride (USA) 3510a^{6} **>72f<**

Society King (IRE) 2 b c Fairy King (USA)-Volga (USA) (Riverman (USA)) 4779^{17} **>35f<**

Society Rose 3 b f Saddlers' Hall (IRE)-Ruthless Rose (USA) (Conquistador Cielo (USA)) 1147^{5} **>88f<**

Society Times (USA) 4 b g Imp Society (USA)-Mauna Loa (USA) (Hawaii) 996^{6} 1230^{8} 1512^{6} **>50f<**

Socket Set 2 b f Tragic Role (USA)-Elsocko (Swing Easy (USA)) *(2066)* 2335^{7} (2712) 3049^{4} 3595^{3} (3889) **>73+a 85f<**

Soda 3 gr g Belfort (FR)-Bella Seville (King of Spain) **1996:** *5083*^{4} *5176*^{12} **1997:** *378*^{3} 466^{2} 532^{14} 783^{4} 997^{6} 1925^{8} *2366*^{10} 2510^{9} 2536^{14} **>58a 27f<**

Soda Pop (IRE) 3 b c River Falls-Riviere Salee (FR) (Luthier) *1155*^{12} 1624^{2} 1938^{11} 2428^{4} 2770^{2} (2955) 3229^{9} 3588^{7} 3929^{6} 4858^{16} **>10a 65f<**

Sodelk 3 ch f Interrex (CAN)-Summoned by Bells (Stanford) *204*^{8} *317*^{9} **>7a 43f<**

Soden (IRE) 3 b f Mujadil (USA)-Elminya (IRE) (Sure Blade (USA)) 990^{12} 1416^{3} 1999^{9} *(3232)* 3721^{5} 4172^{9} *4485*^{3} *4906*^{5} **>74a 55f<**

Soeur Ti (FR) 2 b f Kaldoun (FR)-Habigael (FR) (Habitat) (4529a) 5058a^{2} **>84f<**

Soft Touch (IRE) 2 b f Petorius-Fingers (Lord Gayle (USA)) 637^{3} 750^{2} 1480^{8} 2439a^{2} 3019^{2} 4067^{4} *4569*^{8} **>54a 80f<**

Sofyaan (USA) 4 b g Silver Hawk (USA)-Tanwi (Vision (USA)) 521^{20} 962^{10} 1414^{5} 2122^{3} 2483^{W} 2653^{4} 2961^{11} **>87f<**

So Intrepid (IRE) 7 ch h Never so Bold-Double River (USA) (Irish River (FR)) *394*^{7} 443^{4} 520^{11} 786^{8} 942^{8} (1259) 1410^{7} 1594^{3} 1799^{3} 1977^{9} 2347^{3} (2377) (3195) (3273) 3604^{8} 3765^{19} 4280^{11} **>64a 88f< (DEAD)**

So Keen 4 ch g Keen-Diana's Bow (Great Nephew) 1408^{9} 1654^{9} 2208^{6} 2487^{6} *4053*^{12} 4946^{9} **>37f<**

Solar Dawn 3 ch f Soviet Star (USA)-Haebeh (USA) (Alydar (USA)) *296*^{9} *350*^{3} *395*^{6} *456*^{7} *1043*^{16} **>46a f<**

Solar Storm 3 ch c Polar Falcon (USA)-Sister Sophie (USA) (Effervescing (USA)) 479^{8} 674^{4} (3991) (4283) (4637) **>101f<**

Soldier Cove (USA) 7 ch g Manila (USA)-Secret Form (Formidable (USA)) **1996:** *5145*^{2} **1997:** *22*^{2} *80*^{6} *114*^{4} *172*^{6} *(319) (390) (411)* (496) 607^{4} *870*^{9} 3793^{8} **>62a 56f<**

Soldier Mak 4 ch g Infantry-Truly Blest (So Blessed) *374*^{3} 2944^{6} 3453^{7} **>45a 54f<**

Soldiers Bay 7 b h Robellino (USA)-Yankee Special (Bold Lad (IRE)) 190a^{3} **>64f<**

Soleil Trompeur (IRE) 3 4660a^{7} **>81f<**

Solfegietto 3 b f Music Boy-Maria Isabella (FR) (Young Generation) 958^{15} 1794^{4} 3066^{5} **>75f<**

Solitario Wells 3 1553a^{15}

Solo Mio (IRE) 3 b c Sadler's Wells (USA)-Marie de Flandre (FR) (Crystal Palace (FR)) 1014^{2} (1276) 2107^{5} 3109^{9} 3648^{8} 4136^{8} (4476) 4754^{3} **>108f<**

Solo Song 2 ch f Executive Man-Aosta (Shack (USA)) 954^{8} 1310^{5} 2856^{7} **>51f<**

Solo Spirit 2 b f Northern Park (USA)-Brown Taw (Whistlefield) 1321^{W} 1783^{4} 3744^{10} 4103^{4} 4522^{9} (4904) **>81f<**

Solway Lass (IRE) 2 b f Anita's Prince-Northern Amber (Shack (USA)) 472^{4} 611^{5} 880^{10} 1084^{7} *2595*^{7} **>53f<**

Somayda (IRE) 2 b c Last Tycoon-Flame of Tara (Artaius (USA)) 3013^{5} 3598^{5} **>69f<**

Some Horse (IRE) 4 ch g Astronef-Daniela Lepida (ITY) (El-Muleta) 2065^{7} **>21a 60f<**

Somerton Boy (IRE) 7 b h Thatching-Bonnie Bess (Ardoon) 529^{9} 734^{13} 1020^{2} (1560) 2290^{12} 2760^{3} 3822^{6} 4283^{2} 4792^{17} 4924^{18} **>43a 77f<**

Somerton Reef 3 br c Mystiko (USA)-Lady Reef (Mill Reef (USA)) 807a^{6} **>98f<**

Somethingbeautiful (USA) 2 b f Lil E.Tee (USA)-Bubali (ARG) 4090a^{5} **>70f<**

Sommersby (IRE) 6 b g Vision (USA)-Echoing (Formidable (USA)) **1996:** *5108*^{8} **1997:** *2164*^{5} *2365*^{7} *2668*^{9} *2910*^{12} 3091^{12} **>35a 35f<**

Somosierra (IRE) 2 b g Paris House-Island Heather (IRE) (Salmon Leap (USA)) 432^{13} 697^{5} 2685^{4} 3113^{10} 3474^{12} 4162^{12} **>76f<**

So Natural (IRE) 5 ch m Sharpo-Sympathy (Precocious) *192*^{7} *243*^{8} *286*^{6} **>37a 1f<**

Sonderise 8 br g Mummy's Game-Demderise (Vaigly Great) 863^{10} 1098^{16} 1734^{6} **>49f<**

Song For Jess (IRE) 4 b f Accordion-Ritual Girl (Ballad Rock) *276*^{5} **>46f<**

Song Mist (IRE) 3 gr f Kenmare (FR)-Farewell Song (USA) (The Minstrel (CAN)) 685^{2} 1029^{4} 1243^{5} 1691^{3} 1958^{4} 2705^{8} 3296^{6} 3852^{6} 4451^{5} **>64f<**

Song of Freedom 3 ch c Arazi (USA)-Glorious Song (CAN) (Halo (USA)) 1866^{2} (2566) 3012^{5} (3575) 3916^{13} 4151^{5} 4443^{6} **>96f<**

Song of Skye 3 b f Warning-Song of Hope (Chief Singer) 968^{8} 1453^{5} 1737^{12} 2119^{3} 2951^{2} 3138^{8} 3185^{4} 3615^{7} **>86f<**

Song Of The Sword 4 b g Kris-Melodist (USA) (The Minstrel (CAN)) 499^{5} 680^{13} 4754^{19} **>78f<**

Songsheet 4 b f Dominion-Songstead (Song) *391*^{11} 604^{2} 756^{5} 1385^{8} (1479) (1814) 2148^{5} 2308^{7} (2406) 2563^{10} 3016^{3} 3126^{7} 3326^{5} 3693^{6} 3898^{7} 3984^{2} 4115^{2} 4370^{4} 4636^{6} 4791^{5} *5018*^{4} **>51a 73f<**

Son of Good Times 2 ch g Good Times (ITY)-Pullandese (Kinglet) 4113^{13} 4462^{4} 4698^{13} **>33f<**

Son of Skelton 2 ch g Minster Son-Skelton (Derrylin) 2016^{10} 2493^{2} **>64f<**

Sonya Marie 4 b f Green Ruby (USA)-Susie Hall (Gold Rod) *87*^{8} *111*^{6} *183*^{14} **>10a 45f< (DEAD)**

Soojama (IRE) 7 b g Mansooj-Pyjama Game (Cavo Doro) *116*^{3} *147*^{7} *(295) 334*^{2} *(351)* 603^{2} 831^{3} (1215) 1424^{8} 2550^{R} *3415*^{9} **>59a 66f<**

Sooty Tern 10 br h Wassl-High Tern (High Line) **1996:** *5079*^{4} *5151*^{2} *5227*^{5} *5266*^{2} **1997:** *31*^{2} *47*^{3} *120*^{3} *186*^{3} 791^{4} 1035^{11} *1433*^{4} (1640) 1955^{3} 2201^{7} (2576) (2743) 2929^{3} 3428^{5} *3608*^{6} 3798^{13} 3921^{13} 4225^{14} **>60a 79df<**

Sophie Lockett 4 b f Mon Tresor-Silverdale Rose (Nomination) 2498^{6} *2607*^{9} 4171^{16} **>13f<**

Sophomore 3 b c Sanglamore (USA)-Livry (USA) (Lyphard (USA)) 741^{9} 1173^{4} 1869^{4} 4882^{6} **>90f<**

Sopran Bistop (ITY) 3 64a^{3} **>54f<**

Sopran Dandy (IRE) 2 b f Doyoun-Danzica (Rusticaro (FR)) 4259a^{3} **>85f<**

Sopran Londa (IRE) 2 b f Danehill (USA)-Longobarda (FR) (Crystal Palace (FR)) (4397a) 4764a^{2} **>91f<**

Sopran Mariduff 3 dk f Persian Bold-Marina Duff (Caerleon (USA)) 815a^{4} 1075a^{2} 1368a^{3} 2099a^{3} **>106f<**

Sopran Newar 3 br f Warning-La Neva (FR) (Arctic Tern (USA)) 1556a^{2}

Sopran Tycoon (ITY) 3 b f Last Tycoon-Samadhi (Runnett) 1556a^{3}

Sorridar 2 b f Puissance-Sorrowful (Moorestyle) 4012^{8} 4159^{5} 4381^{4} 4737^{7} **>60f<**

Sostenuto 4 b f Northern State (USA)-Pride of Ayr (Recoil) 3903^{5} 4360^{7} 4736^{9} **>7f<**

Sotonian (HOL) 4 br g Statoblest-Visage (Vision

(USA)) **1996:** *5225^{9} 5268^{3}* **1997:** *(53) (79) 137^{10} 222^{9} 301^{7} 391^{5}* 541^{2} *593^{5}* 949^{10} 1250^{3} 1627^{4} *1759^{3} 1942^{5}* 2563^{9} 2703^{4} 3287^{5} 3910^{11} 4329^{11} **>44a 43f<**

Sottvus (IRE) 2 b c Royal Academy (USA)-Lorne Lady (Local Suitor (USA)) (4533a)

Soul Sister 4 b f Distant Relative-Lappet (Kampala) **1996:** *5114^{14}* **>16a 23f<**

Sound Appeal 3 b f Robellino (USA)-Son Et Lumiere (Rainbow Quest (USA)) 723^{7} 1245^{7} 1826^{7} 2246^{4} 2750^{6} 4324^{14} **>64f<**

Sounds Legal 4 b f Rich Charlie-Legal Sound (Legal Eagle) **1996:** *5267^{5}* **1997:** *28^{8} 336^{3} 417^{4}* 496^{6} 896^{9} **>36a 35f<**

Sound the Trumpet (IRE) 5 b g Fayruz-Red Note (Rusticaro (FR)) **1996:** *5258^{6}* **1997:** *65^{8} 152^{10} 241^{9} 321^{6}* 477^{4} 585^{6} 1098^{5} 1620^{4} 1667^{6} 3280^{2} 3693^{10} 4016^{18} 4844^{12} **>35a 57df<**

Souperficial 6 gr g Petong-Duck Soup (Decoy Boy) **1996:** *5178^{4} 5230^{9} 5237^{8}* **1997:** 759^{6} 863^{9} 1098^{7} 1225^{11} 1816^{8} 2177^{4} (2384) 2567^{6} 2788^{4} 3208^{11} 3693^{7} 3759^{14} 4333^{11} 4580^{13} **>50a 46f<**

Soura (USA) 3 ch f Beau Genius (CAN)-First Division (CHI) (Domineau (USA)) **1996:** *5248^{6} 5252^{3}* **1997:** 681^{12} *903^{4}* 1217^{2} 1464^{3} 1807^{3} **>53a 58f<**

Souris Grise (USA) 3 b f Conquistador Cielo (USA)-No Choice (AUS) (Navajo (USA)) (4388a) **>109f<**

South China Sea 3 b f Robellino (USA)-Danzig Harbour (USA) (Private Account (USA)) 3463^{8} 3749^{7} 3972^{4} 4371^{11} **>62f<**

Southdown Cyrano (IRE) 2 b c Cyrano de Bergerac-Value Voucher (IRE) (Kings Lake (USA)) 3278^{22} 3497^{8} 4174^{13} **>41f<**

South Eastern Fred 6 b h Primo Dominie-Soheir (Track Spare) **1996:** *5120^{3} (5231)* **1997:** *52^{3} (176) 220^{3} 344^{7} 405^{7}* 476^{3} 838^{8} *1123^{8}* **>97+a 56f<**

Southerly Wind 3 b c Slip Anchor-Karavina (Karabas) (1392) 1647^{2} 2058^{9} 2710^{6} 3190^{12} 3622^{4} 4558^{21} **>94f<**

Southern-Be-George 2 b c Be My Chief (USA)-Southern Sky (Comedy Star (USA)) 4384^{9} **>47f<**

Southern Dominion 5 ch g Dominion-Southern Sky (Comedy Star (USA)) *152^{11} 199^{3} 263^{10} 386^{5} 593^{7}* 760^{7} (924) 956^{9} 1236^{10} 1572^{4} 2177^{5} 2540^{3} 2759^{2} 3287^{8} 3566^{7} 3871^{4} 4249^{4} 4580^{2} (4707) 4844^{4} (5047) **>39a 62f<**

Southern Memories (IRE) 7 b g Don't Forget Me-Our Pet (Mummy's Pet) 3420^{10} 4373^{16} 4843^{2} **>43f<**

Southern Rule 10 b g Law Society (USA)-Isobelline (USA) (Pronto) **1996:** *5138^{6} 5188^{6} 5234^{8}* **1997:** *29^{5} 42^{5}* 480^{7} 2382^{8} **>24a 22f<**

Souvenir Copy (USA) 2 c *5064a^{4}*

Sovereign 3 b f Interrex (CAN)-Shiny Penny (Glint of Gold) 656^{6} 1008^{7} 1292^{14} 1566^{13} **>36f<**

Sovereign Crest (IRE) 4 gr g Priolo (USA)-Abergwrle (Absalom) 1169^{6} 1506^{13} 1968^{3} 2150^{6} 2955^{4} (3080) 3559^{3} 3714^{4} 4222^{10} 4519^{12} **>53f<**

Sovereign Page (USA) 8 ch g Caro-Tashinsky (USA) (Nijinsky (CAN)) 1414^{8} 1678^{5} **>87f<**

Sovereigns Court 4 ch g Statoblest-Clare Celeste (Coquelin (USA)) 1166^{16} 1489^{13} 2006^{8} 2216^{6} 3115^{8} 3392^{7} 4139^{4} (4741) (4988) **>79+f<**

Soviet Bride (IRE) 5 b m Soviet Star (USA)-Nihad (Alleged (USA)) *131^{4}* 482^{6} 787^{7} **>64a 79f<**

Soviet Bureau (IRE) 2 ch c Soviet Lad (USA)-Redwood Hut (Habitat) (3494) **>86+f<**

Soviet Dreamer 4 ch g Soviet Star (USA)-Splendid Girl (USA) (Golden Eagle (FR)) 2441a^{12} **>75f<**

Soviet King (IRE) 4 b g Soviet Lad (USA)-Finessing (Indian King (USA)) *28^{6} 73^{3} (122) 147^{6} 260^{4} 351^{4}* **>56a 60f<**

Soviet Lady (IRE) 3 b f Soviet Lad (USA)-La Vosgienne (Ashmore (FR)) 467^{3} 685^{12} 896^{16} 1115^{4} *2070^{8}* 3561^{12} 3849^{5} 4451^{12} **>51a 36f<**

Soviet Leader 3 b g Soviet Star (USA)-Noirmant (Dominion) 693^{8} (1090) 1460^{3} 2044^{4} 2134^{18} 2560^{3} 3914^{6} 4155^{13} 4280^{10} **>84f<**

Soviet Line (IRE) 7 b g Soviet Star (USA)-Shore Line (High Line) 5063a^{7} **>128f<**

Soviet Lynk (IRE) 2 b f Soviet Lad (USA)-Arfjah (Taufan (USA)) 3008a^{3}

Soviet State (USA) 3 b c Nureyev (USA)-Absentia (USA) (Raise A Cup (USA)) **1996:** 5194a^{5} **1997:** (745) 2056^{13} 2861^{2} 3111^{12} 3447^{5} 4240^{5} 4954^{6} **>112f<**

Space Race 3 b g Rock Hopper-Melanoura (Imperial Fling (USA)) 673^{4} 963^{11} (1272) 2930^{2} 3548^{6} 3741^{5} **>86f<**

Space Trucker (IRE) 6 b g Kambalda-Seat of Learning (Balliol) 4620a^{10} **>94f<**

Spa Lane 4 ch g Presidium-Sleekit (Blakeney) *151^{9}* 1398^{7} 1685^{4} 2035^{8} 2316^{2} 2589^{14} 2882^{7} *4055^{14}* 4170^{7} 4633^{8} 4794^{6} **>24a 53f<**

Spaniards Close 9 b g King of Spain-Avon Belle (Balidar) 3327^{5} *4049^{2} 4482^{13}* 4733^{15} **>80a 75df<**

Spaniard's Mount 3 b c Distant Relative-Confection (Formidable (USA)) **1996:** *5113^{5}* **1997:** *119^{2} (225)* 2332^{10} (2428) **>72a 70f<**

Spanish Eyes 2 b f Belmez (USA)-Night Transaction (Tina's Pet) 4914^{11} **>41f<**

Spanish Fern (USA) 2 b br f El Gran Senor (USA)-Chain Fern (USA) (Blushing Groom (FR)) 4973^{3} **>84f<**

Spanish Knot (USA) 3 b f El Gran Senor (USA)-Ingenuity (Clever Trick (USA)) 1629^{2} 4316^{8} **>77f<**

Spanish Serenade 3 b f Nashwan (USA)-Fair Rosamunda (Try My Best (USA)) 3822^{9} **>36f<**

Spanish Stripper (USA) 6 b g El Gran Senor (USA)-Gourmet Dinner (USA) (Raise A Cup (USA)) **1996:** *5115^{11}* **1997:** *14^{10} 72^{5} 91^{3} 123^{8} 165^{4} 192^{6} 203^{4} 243^{7} 288^{8} 333^{6}* 772^{6} 896^{14} *1134^{7}* 1501^{14} 1689^{11} 1855^{4} *2070^{2}* 2428^{5} 2544^{4} 3100^{9} 3972^{8} 4224^{8} **>36a 49?f<**

Spanish Verdict 10 b g King of Spain-Counsel's Verdict (Firestreak) 461^{10} 733^{5} 824^{9} 1128^{6} 1472^{4} 1631^{8} 1862^{5} 2205^{12} 2546^{8} 2828^{2} 3039^{10} 3264^{12} 3573^{3} 3777^{10} 4210^{8} 4472^{3} 4792^{12} **>55f<**

Spanish Warrior 3 b g Warrshan (USA)-Spanish Heart (King of Spain) 645^{12} *868^{5}* 1388^{17} *2159^{8}* 2376^{6} **>46da 43df<**

Spare My Blushes 3 b f Puissance-Juris Prudence (IRE) (Law Society (USA)) 1512^{8} *1939^{8}* 2568^{10} 3027^{4} 3316^{11} **>4a 38f<**

Spargo Express 3 b c Mystiko (USA)-Noora's Rose (NZ) (Ahonoora) **1996:** *5265^{6}*

Sparkling Edge 3 b f Beveled (USA)-Sparkalot (USA) (Duel) **1996:** *(5107) 5176^{9}* **1997:** *132^{3} (142) 258^{4} 320^{4} 379^{3}* 1566^{7} *2305^{11}* **>61da 49f<**

Sparkling Harry 3 ch g Tina's Pet-Sparkling Hock (Hot Spark) 995^{16} 1119^{13} 1394^{6} 1496^{7} 1864^{6} 2313^{6} 3088^{6} 4586^{15} *4809^{8}* 4899^{9} **>45a 50f<**

Sparkling Secret 2 ch g Tina's Pet-Sparkling Hock (Hot Spark) 1856^{7} **>32f<**

Sparky 3 b g Warrshan (USA)-Pebble Creek (IRE) (Reference Point) 998^{6} 1256^{13} 1513^{3} *(1756)* 1820^{2} 1999^{6} *3044^{2}* 3264^{2} *3584^{2}* 3921^{3} 4015^{7} 4161^{7} 4596^{7} **>77a 77f<**

Spartan Girl (IRE) 3 ch f Ela-Mana-Mou-Well Head (IRE) (Sadler's Wells (USA)) (2389) 4962a^{12} **>86f<**

Spartan Heartbeat 4 b c Shareef Dancer (USA)-Helen's Dream (Troy) 4360^{2} 4547^{2} 4874^{9} 4956^{6} 5053^{17} **>82f<**

Spartan Royale 3 b c Shareef Dancer (USA)-Cormorant Creek (Gorytus (USA)) 841^{2} 931^{5} 1150^{4} 1877^{8} 4521^{14} **>72df<**

Spazaca (USA) 2 f 4534a^{5} (5036a)

Speaker's Chair 2 b c Shirley Heights-Lead Note (USA) (Nijinsky (CAN)) 3201^{3} 3576^{5} 4915^{2} **>87f<**

Special-K 5 br m Treasure Kay-Lissi Gori (FR) (Bolkonski) 1603^{12} 2041^{6} (2463) (2887) 3105^{4} 3264^{8} 3477^{4} 3822^{2} 4742^{12} 4843^{15} **>57f<**

Special Lad (ITY) 3 b c Lead on Time (USA)-Mary Lad (ITY) (Bold Lad (IRE)) (1068a) **>84f<**

Special Nash (IRE) 2 ch c Nashwan (USA)-Northshiel (Northfields (USA)) 2822a^{2} (4128a) 4865a^{5} **>99f<**

Special Quest (FR) 2 b c Rainbow Quest (USA)-Mona Stella (USA) Nureyev (USA)4657a^{2} (5034a) **>97f<**

Special Star 3 1996: 5128a^{5} **1997:** 1553a^{10} **>92f<**

Special Treat 2 b f Wolfhound (USA)-Just a Treat (IRE) (Glenstal (USA)) 3114^{8} 3985^{4} (4418) (4634) 4890^{2} **>92f<**

Spectacle Jim 8 b g Mummy's Game-Welsh Blossom (Welsh Saint) *197^{4} 210^{5} 321^{8} 401^{10}* 601^{6} 1599^{8} 1663^{5} 2146^{7} *2322^{6}* **>15a 41f<**

Speculative 3 b c Suave Dancer (USA)-Gull Nook (Mill Reef (USA)) 4692^{5} 4768^{7} 4923^{9} **>36f<**

Speculator (IRE) 3 b c Last Tycoon-Abbeydale (Huntercombe) 517^{7} 645^{3} (2492) 2871^{2} 3435^{2} 4441^{21} **>93f<**

Speedball (IRE) 3 b c Waajib-Lady Taufan (IRE) (Taufan (USA)) 646^{6} 930^{2} 1170^{4} 4153^{5} 4423^{8} 4637^{10} **>97f<**

Speedboat (USA) 3 ch c Diesis-Ocean Ballad (Grundy) 1130^{6} 1656^{4} 4417^{4} 4733^{20} 4926^{6} **>62f<**

Speedfit Too (IRE) 2 b c Scenic-Safka (USA) (Irish River (FR)) 1812^{3} 2012^{7} 3013^{6} (3278) 3464^{2} (3774) 4391a^{3} **>97f<**

Speedfriend (GER) 3 gr c Unfuwain (USA)-Batchelor's Button(FR)(Kenmare(FR))1726a^{14} **>99f<**

Speed On 4 b g Sharpo-Pretty Poppy (Song) 1034^{5} 1590^{7} 1766^{6} 2529^{12} 2872^{3} 4457^{3} **>99f<**

Speed to Lead (IRE) 5 b m Darshaan-Instant Desire (USA) (Northern Dancer) 2108^{10} **>93f<**

Speedy Classic (USA) 8 br g Storm Cat (USA)-Shadows Lengthen (Star Appeal) **1996:** *5089^{5} (5249)* **1997:** *121^{8} 201^{3} (364)* 1680^{4} 2006^{18} 3018^{2} 3251^{5} 3690^{12} 4112^{8} 4404^{5} (4951) **>86a 66f<**

Speedy Snaps Pride 5 gr g Hallgate-Pineapple's Pride (John de Coombe) *318^{13}* 1441^{14} **>33a 37f<**

Spencer's Revenge 8 ch g Bay Express-Armour of Light (Hot Spark) **1996:** *5132^{6} 5208^{4}* **1997:** *14^{2} 54^{10} 114^{9} 171^{2} 211^{7} 248^{4} (290) 363^{4} 403^{3} 458^{3}* 3227^{17} 3496^{14} **>66a 25f<**

Spencer Stallone 4 b g Rambo Dancer (CAN)-Armour of Light (Hot Spark) 4609^{U} **>46a 52f<**

Spender 8 b or br g Last Tycoon-Lady Hester (Native Prince) *488^{4}* (643) 786^{6} 1113^{8} 1468^{5} (1957) 3600^{11} 3765^{20} 3984^{12} (4183) 4452^{8} 4887^{13} **>93?a 88f<**

Spice Girl 2 ch f Alhijaz-Imagery (Vision (USA)) 1645^{8} 2477^{11} 3450^{17} **>52f<**

Spicetress 3 gr f Chilibang-Foreign Mistress (Darshaan) 4112^{13} **>62f<**

Spick And Span 3 b g Anshan-Pretty Thing (Star Appeal) 1497^{8} 1950^{3} 2315^{14} 3234^{5} 4235^{8} 4794^{4} **>61f<**

Spinning World (USA) 4 ch c Nureyev (USA)-Imperfect Circle (USA) (Riverman (USA)) (1067a) 1210^{4} (3733a) (4129a) (5063a) **>132f<**

Spiral Flyer (IRE) 4 b br f Contract Law (USA)-Souveniers (Relko) 1388^{9} 1445^{5} 2146^{9} 2307^{2} 2511^{3} *3046^{7}* 3714^{13} **>26a 38f<**

Spirit Lady 3 b f Salse (USA)-Wanda (Taufan (USA)) 2506^{7} 3389^{8} 3893^{4} 4323^{19} **>57f<**

Spirito **2** b c Mystiko (USA)-Classic Beam (Cut Above) 4745^{10} **>49f<**

Spirit of Love (USA) **2** ch c Trempolino (USA)-Dream Mary (USA) (Marfa (USA)) 4915^{11} **>45f<**

Spirit of Sport **4** b f Forzando-What's the Matter (High Top) 1473^{11} 2488^{F} 4465^{W} **>28a 14f<**

Spirit Of Tara (IRE) **3** b f Sadler's Wells (USA)-Flame of Tara (Artaius (USA)) $4837a^{2}$ **>104f<**

Spirit of The Nile (FR) **2** b f Generous (IRE)-Egyptale (Crystal Glitters (USA)) 3547^{7} 3788^{4} 3985^{10} **>82f<**

Spirito Libro (USA) **4** b f Lear Fan (USA)-Teeming Shore (USA) (L'Emigrant (USA)) 1157^{5} 1768^{10} **>94f<**

Spitfire Bridge (IRE) **5** b g Cyrano de Bergerac-Maria Renata (Jaazeiro (USA)) 66^{9} **>64a 60f<**

Splashed **3** gr f Absalom-Riverain (Bustino) **1996:** 5080^{3} **1997:** 372^{4} 416^{4} 469^{4} 845^{15} 995^{9} 1467^{12} **>57a 58f<**

Splendid (IRE) **2** ch f Mujtahid (USA)-Braneakins (Sallust) 4688^{3} 4841^{8} 5042^{17} **>46f<**

Splendid Isolation (USA) **2** b br c Hermitage (USA)-Hord (USA) (Private Account (USA)) 4779^{7} 4966^{3} **>88f<**

Splicing **4** ch f Sharpo-Soluce (Junius (USA)) 834^{15} 953^{12} **>89a 74f<**

Spondulicks (IRE) **3** b g Silver Kite (USA)-Greek Music (Tachypous) 537^{11} 582^{4} 662^{3} 906^{2} 1043^{6} 1094^{5} 1469^{7} 2213^{2} 2652^{8} **>57a 51f<**

Sporty Spice (IRE) **2** b f Indian Ridge-Intrinsic (Troy) 2875^{16} 3260^{7} 3788^{7} **>42f<**

Spotted Eagle **4** ch g Risk Me (FR)-Egnoussa (Swing Easy (USA)) 977^{10} 1127^{3} 1471^{5} 1799^{9} 2129^{10} (2755) 3208^{13} 3565^{11} 4049^{10} **>38a 52f<**

Spree Rose **2** ch f Dancing Spree (USA)-Pinkie Rose (FR) (Kenmare (FR)) 4103^{10} 4604^{2} 4901^{13} **>57f<**

Spring Campaign (IRE) **4** b g Sayaarr (USA)-March The Second (Millfontaine) 1244^{13} 1445^{7} 2039^{3} **>53f<**

Spring Fever **2** b c Indian Ridge-Tender Moment (IRE) (Caerleon (USA)) 3464^{6} 3825^{9} 4966^{6} **>76f<**

Spring Marathon (USA) **7** b g Topsider (USA)-April Run (Run The Gantlet (USA)) 1260^{7} 1665^{7} 2014^{15} 2381^{5} **>60f<**

Spy Knoll **3** b c Shirley Heights-Garden Pink (FR) (Bellypha) 586^{13} 966^{3} 1270^{3} 2230^{3} 2411^{2} 3010^{4} 3974^{12} (4360) **>89f<**

Squabble **2** b f Reprimand-Hability (Habitat) 4884^{7} **>59f<**

Squared Away **5** b h Blakeney-Maureen Mhor (Taj Dewan) 435^{9} 763^{3} 848^{7} 1422^{4} 1748^{7} 1926^{10} 2430^{2} 3048^{5} 3432^{6} 3476^{5} **>58f<**

Square Deal (FR) **6** b g Sharpo-River Dove (USA) (Riverman (USA)) **1996:** 5134^{9} 5181^{15} **1997:** (415) 578^{5} 589^{2} 860^{6} 1048^{15} 2369^{18} **>64a 31f<**

Square Mile Miss (IRE) **4** b f Last Tycoon-Call Me Miss (Hello Gorgeous (USA)) **1996:** 5282^{6} **1997:** 108^{6} 322^{4} 687^{2} 1388^{11} 1689^{8} 2593^{3} 3101^{W} 3588^{8} **>32a 45f<**

Squeak **3** ch f Selkirk (USA)-Santa Linda (USA) (Sir Ivor) (1875) (2513) 3704^{6} $4666a^{2}$ $5039a^{4}$ **>117f<**

Squire Corrie **5** b g Distant Relative-Fast Car (FR) (Carwhite) **1996:** 5131^{13} 5174^{12} 5280^{3} **1997:** 137^{8} (222) 253^{5} 263^{2} (323) 364^{2} 459^{10} 744^{4} 772^{4} 1098^{4} (1223) 1468^{6} (1835) (1946) (2111) 2339^{2} 2675^{5} 2717^{7} 3217^{12} 3410^{7} 3771^{3} 3900^{2} 4233^{23} 4365^{8} 4434^{3} 4512^{3} 4770^{2} 4887^{17} **>77a 89f<**

Squire's Occasion (CAN) **4** b g Black Tie Affair-Tayana (USA) (Wajima (USA)) 61^{10} (116) 334^{3} 3796^{12} 4104^{13} **>63a 30f<**

Stackattack (IRE) **4** b g Salt Dome (USA)-Must Hurry (Kampala) 1268^{9} 1511^{2} (1584) (1920) 2325^{15} (2708) 2857^{7} 3243^{7} 3476^{2} 4561^{5} **>69a 83f<**

Stage Affair (USA) **3** bb c Theatrical-Wooing $4346a^{5}$ **>117f<**

Stage Manner **4** b f In The Wings-Air Distingue (USA) (Sir Ivor) **1996:** $5198a^{2}$ **>109f<**

Stage Whisper **2** b c Alzao (USA)-Starlet (Teenoso (USA)) 4857^{4} **>67f<**

Stahr **3** b g Liboi (USA)-Celia Brady (Last Tycoon) 1277^{7} 1956^{3} (2398) (2725) 3915^{8} 4409^{6} **>77f<**

Stakis Casinos Boy (IRE) **3** ch g Magical Wonder (USA)-Hardiona (FR) (Hard To Beat) 773^{7} (996) 1649^{2} 2064^{4} 3267^{6} 4279^{12} 4891^{17} **>82f<**

Stakis Casinos Lad (IRE) **3** ch c Red Sunset-Stradey Lynn (Derrylin) 94^{4} 168^{7} **>57da 33f<**

Stalled (IRE) **7** b g Glenstal (USA)-Chauffeuse (Gay Fandango (USA)) **1996:** 5102^{5} 5167^{5} 5244^{2} **1997:** 78^{8} 205^{4} 324^{7} 384^{6} 1133^{3} 1424^{7} 2063^{3} 2469^{3} 3046^{2} 3401^{8} 4275^{8} 4481^{7} 4590^{10} **>52a 55f<**

Stalwart Legion (IRE) **2** b f Distinctly North (USA)-La Posada (Procida (USA)) 2893^{8} 3450^{10} 3818^{9} 4576^{18} **>58f<**

Stamp (IRE) **3** ch c Sharpo-Likeness (Young Generation) 4990^{10} **>67?f<**

Standown **4** b g Reprimand-Ashdown (Pharly (FR)) **1996:** 5099^{5} 5163^{10} 5234^{5} **1997:** 1^{7} (774) 1127^{5} (1676) **>56a 65f<**

Stand Tall **5** b g Unfuwain (USA)-Antilla (Averof) 323^{4} 376^{3} (1505) 2115^{3} 2282^{7} 2745^{2} (3290) 3690^{7} (3936) 4307^{2} (4456) **>80a 84f<**

Stanott (IRE) **2** b c Mukaddamah (USA)-Seme de Lys (USA) (Slew O' Gold (USA)) $3176a^{8}$

Stanton Harcourt (USA) **3** b c Sovereign Dancer (USA)-Island Style (USA) (Manila (USA)) (559) (775) $1553a^{9}$ 2585^{5} (2871) 4148^{10} 4558^{30} 4978^{10} **>104f<**

Star **2** b f Most Welcome-Marista (Mansingh (USA)) (1091) 4305^{3} 4790^{18} **>86f<**

Starborough **3** ch c Soviet Star (USA)-Flamenco Wave (USA) (Desert Wine (USA)) (747) 940^{4} (1725a) (2011) 3124^{2} $3733a^{4}$ **>128f<**

Star Crystal (IRE) **2** b f Brief Truce (USA)-Crystal Spray (Beldale Flutter (USA)) 4950^{2} **>82+f<**

Star Entry **3** b f In The Wings-Top Berry (High Top) **1996:** 5103^{4} 5180^{5} **1997:** 3793^{11} 4045^{4} 4222^{6} (4817) 4971^{7} **>48a 69f<**

Star Gambit (USA) **3** b f Defensive Play (USA)-Etoile Eternelle (USA) (Timeless Moment (USA)) 3917^{2} 4277^{5} **>72f<**

Star Invader **3** b c Nashwan (USA)-Sahara Star (Green Desert (USA)) 1304^{3} 4316^{5} 4700^{4} **>73f<**

Starkey **2** b c Risk Me (FR)-Veuve Perrin (Legend of France (USA)) (4387a) **>97f<**

Starlight Waltzer **4** b g Arzanni-Marchiness Drake (Marechal Drake) 4743^{12} **>33f<**

Starliner (IRE) **2** ch f Statoblest-Dancing Line (High Line) 1760^{3} 2545^{9} 2842^{14} 3307^{14} 4166^{12} 4508^{6} **>64f<**

Starmaker (IRE) **2** b c Fairy King (USA)-Miss Toshiba (USA) (Sir Ivor) 1872^{2} 2499^{2} **>89f<**

Star Manager (USA) **7** b g Lyphard (USA)-Angel Clare (FR) (Mill Reef (USA)) 832^{3} 987^{7} 1176^{6} 1768^{2} 2136^{6} 2710^{4} 3112^{12} 3434^{5} 4294^{4} 4882^{12} **>93f<**

Star of Gold **5** b g Night Shift (USA)-Sure Gold (Glint of Gold) 2340^{14} **>37a 81df<**

Star of Grosvenor (IRE) **2** b f Last Tycoon-Castilian Queen (USA) (Diesis) 3114^{9} (3638) 4097^{14} 4473^{9} **>77f<**

Star of Lugana **4** b f Lugana Beach-Cala Galera (Mummy's Pet) **1996:** 5143^{12} 5232^{9}

Star of Ring (IRE) **4** b g Taufan (USA)-Karine (Habitat) (748) 895^{20} 1219^{9} 1811^{8} 2533^{9} 4628^{14} **>56f<**

Star of The Course (USA) **2** b f Theatrical-Water Course (USA) (Irish River (FR)) 3769^{4} 3979^{14} **>39f<**

Star of The Road **3** b c Risk Me (FR)-Astrid Gilberto (Runnett) 636^{6} 792^{11} 1098^{12} 1496^{6} 1730^{6} 2235^{3} 2891^{14} 3812^{16} 4214^{17} **>48df<**

Star Performer (IRE) **6** b g Petorius-Whitstar (Whitstead) $2999a^{2}$ **>55a 54f<**

Star Precision **3** ch f Shavian-Accuracy (Gunner B) (887) (1278) (1435) 2058^{6} 2513^{4} 2869^{9} (4712) 5043^{6} **>106f<**

Star Profile (IRE) **3** b f Sadler's Wells (USA)-Sandhurst Goddess (Sandhurst Prince) $1203a^{7}$ 1621^{3} 2219^{3} **>105f<**

Star Rage (IRE) **7** b g Horage-Star Bound (Crowned Prince (USA)) 100^{2} 133^{3} 655^{7} 3242^{4} (3440) 3543^{8} 3748^{2} 4156^{3} 4241^{10} 4426^{4} 4783^{17} 4956^{7} **>87a 90f<**

Star Selection **6** b g Rainbow Quest (USA)-Selection Board (Welsh Pageant) 849^{2} 3902^{9} 4281^{5} 4732^{7} **>101f<**

Star Talent (USA) **6** b g Local Talent (USA)-Sedra (Nebbiolo) **1996:** 5209^{2} 5249^{5} **1997:** 82^{4} 109^{2} 146^{3} 175^{4} (653) (832) 987^{6} 1308^{4} 1739^{3} 2525^{4} 2690^{3} 3150^{12} 3888^{11} 4276^{8} **>70a 94df<**

Star Turn (IRE) **3** ch c Night Shift (USA)-Ringtail (Auction Ring (USA)) 2523^{3} 2733^{4} 3029^{2} 3236^{14} 3690^{4} 3860^{3} 4008^{5} 4696^{2} 4958^{5} **>67a 68f<**

Star Witness (IRE) **5** b g Contract Law (USA)-Star Heading (Upper Case (USA)) 4714^{10} 4918^{17} **>42a 27f<**

Statajack (IRE) **9** b g King of Clubs-Statira (Skymaster) 1016^{10} 1244^{10} 1473^{7} 1809^{2} 2218^{6} 2391^{3} 2696^{12} 2928^{5} 3093^{4} 3491^{3} 3767^{6} 3792^{2} (3929) 4521^{7} 4713^{3} (4987) 5019^{2} **>73a 68f<**

State Approval **4** b g Pharly (FR)-Tabeeba (Diesis) 74^{6} 100^{8} 419^{5} (516) 612^{6} 660^{6} 908^{5} 1636^{3} (2164) 4608^{5} 4981^{2} **>80a 67f<**

State Fair **3** b c Shirley Heights-Lobinda (Shareef Dancer (USA)) 1015^{3} $1553a^{11}$ 2027^{11} 2596^{4} 3149^{9} 3902^{7} 4101^{9} 4241^{7} 4732^{2} **>100f<**

State Gala (IRE) **2** b f High Estate-Our Galadrial (Salmon Leap (USA)) 1812^{20} **>25f<**

Stately Favour **2** ch f Statoblest-Dixie Favor (USA) (Dixieland Band (USA)) 3239^{9} 3541^{4} 3825^{10} 4989^{15} **>65f<**

Stately Princess **2** b f Robellino (USA)-Affair of State (IRE) (Tate Gallery (USA)) 432^{3} (525) 1475^{6} 3237^{7} $3961a^{22}$ **>71f<**

State of Caution **4** b g Reprimand-Hithermoor Lass (Red Alert) (164) 274^{3} (376) 398^{7} 514^{3} 4013^{5} 4155^{20} 4307^{10} (4482) (4797) (4983) **>102a 82f<**

State of Gold (IRE) **3** b g High Estate-Mawaal Habeebee (Northfields (USA)) **1996:** 5229^{6} **1997:** 6^{6} 41^{4} 84^{6} 124^{8} 191^{3} (277) (314) 347^{2} 366^{5} **>68a 60f<**

Statistician **5** b g Statoblest-Sharp Lady (Sharpen Up) **1996:** 5089^{2} 5134^{8} 5215^{11} **1997:** 57^{2} 134^{7} 241^{7} 280^{2} 321^{3} 383^{6} 407^{5} $624a^{2}$ **>61a 65f<**

Stato King **3** b c Statoblest-Sinking (Midyan (USA)) **1996:** $5195a^{3}$

Stato One **5** b h Statoblest-Million Heiress (Auction Ring (USA)) (3885a) **>98f<**

Statorhythm **2** b g Statoblest-Blue Rhythm (Blue Cashmere) 697^{8} 872^{5} **>13a 35f< (DEAD)**

Statoyork **4** b g Statoblest-Ultimate Dream (Kafu) 567^{4} 1324^{8} 1505^{2} 2144^{7} 2416^{5} 4905^{20} **>66f<**

Statua (IRE) **2** b f Statoblest-Amata (USA) (Nodouble (USA)) 2706^{5} 2959^{2} 3723^{5} 3926^{3} 4786^{3} **>97f<**

Stayingalive (USA) **2** ch f Gone West (USA)-Lady for Two (USA) (Storm Bird (CAN)) (1783) 2558^{7}

>85f<

St Blaine (CAN) 3 b f St Jovite (USA)-Blaine (USA) (Lyphard's Wish (FR)) (1512) 1935^{4} 2280^{4} 2561^{7} **>90df<**

St Clair Shores (USA) 2 b f Northern Flagship (USA)-Dom Chandon (USA) (Seattle Slew (USA)) 4107^{7} 4638^{8} 4793^{6} **>77df<**

Steal 'Em 4 b f Efisio-Eastern Ember (Indian King (USA)) **1996:** *5105^{6} 5170^{7}* **1997:** *385^{7}* 1765^{9} 2004^{13} 2209^{4} 2651^{8} *2915^{7}* **>57da 43f<**

Steam on 6 ch g Common Grounds-Oh My Joy (Grundy) 4547^{8} **>13f<**

Steamroller Stanly 4 b g Shirley Heights-Miss Demure (Shy Groom (USA)) **1996:** *(5091)* **1997:** *(23) 131^{2} (250)* 3739^{7} 4136^{4} 4416^{3} **>96a 82f<**

Stellar Line (USA) 4 ch g Zilzal (USA)-Stellaria (USA) (Roberto (USA)) *290^{2} 336^{2}* 639^{2} (1011) 1414^{15} 1495^{6} 1833^{4} 4757^{29} 4899^{15} **>72a 76f<**

St Enodoc (FR) 2 ch c Sanglamore (USA)-Exemina (USA) (Slip Anchor) 3386^{9} 4367^{6} 4914^{12} **>64f<**

Stephangeorge 2 b g La Grange Music-Telegraph Callgirl (Northern Tempest (USA)) 1669^{7} 1791^{7} 3459^{8} 4807^{8} 4922^{15} **>54f<**

Stephensons Rocket 6 ch g Music Boy-Martian Princess (Cure The Blues (USA)) *318^{12}* 464^{6} *593^{3}* 759^{2} 1079^{5} *1289^{10}* 1631^{11} 2144^{9} 2384^{2} 2657^{6} 3240^{4} 3431^{6} 3910^{10} 4414^{5} **>46a 55f<**

Step In To The Sun 2 ch f Primo Dominie-June Fayre (Sagaro) 1298^{4} 1626^{8} *1789^{7}* **>27a 27f<**

Step N Go (IRE) 3 b f Alzao (USA)-River Jet (USA) (Lear Fan (USA)) 609^{2} (1024) (1301) 1390^{5} 3722^{13} 4015^{18} 4268^{6} 4714^{6} **>58f<**

Step On Degas 4 b f Superpower-Vivid Impression (Cure The Blues (USA)) **1996:** *5163^{5} 5246^{2}* **1997:** *(27) 121^{9} 325^{3}* 520^{12} 2732^{13} 3082^{4} 3393^{5} (3561) 4139^{2} 4373^{7} *4913^{8}* **>69a 61f<**

Sterling Fellow 4 b c Pharly (FR)-Favorable Exchange (USA) (Exceller (USA)) *55^{4}* 777^{8} **>54a 71df< (DEAD)**

Sternsinger (USA) 2 b c Seeking the Gold (USA)-Song Maker (IRE) (Sadler's Wells (USA)) 4950^{7} **>71f<**

Stevie's Wonder (IRE) 7 ch g Don't Forget Me-Azurai (Dance In Time (CAN)) **1996:** *5143^{7}* **1997:** *67^{7} 157^{5} 231^{7} 256^{7}* **>41a 33f<**

Steward (FR) 4 b c Saumarez 625a^{4} (916a) (1917a) 4665a^{14} **>120f<**

St Helensfield 2 ch c Kris-On Credit (FR) (No Pass No Sale) (4460) 4697^{2} 4977^{3} **>87f<**

Stilett (IRE) 3 b c Tirol-Legal Steps (IRE) (Law Society (USA)) 1006^{10} 1221^{5} (1437) 2309^{3} (2601) 2871^{10} **>96+f<**

Still Here (IRE) 4 b g Astronef-Covey's Quick Step (Godswalk (USA)) **1996:** *5232^{3}* **1997:** *70^{6}* **>49da 48f<**

Still Waters 2 b c Rainbow Quest (USA)-Krill (Kris) 4914^{9} **>68f<**

Stingray (IRE) 2 b c Darshaan-Sovereign Dona (Sovereign Path) 4895^{4} 5046^{5} **>75f<**

Stingray City (USA) 8 b g Raft (USA)-Out of This World (High Top) 493^{14} 553^{9} **>22f<**

Sting Umbro (ITY) 2 b c Sikeston (USA)-Berlinga (GER) (Sassafras (FR)) 3367a^{3} **>69f<**

Stingy 3 3180a^{5} 4125a^{2} **>102f<**

Stitched Up (IRE) 8 ch h Ahonoora-Needlewoman (Moorestyle) 2096a^{2} **>72f<**

St Lawrence (CAN) 3 gr c With Approval (CAN)-Mingan Isle (USA) (Lord Avie (USA)) 3319^{2} 3974^{9} **>76f<**

St Lucia (IRE) 2 b f Common Grounds-Scarlet Slipper (Gay Mecene (USA)) 4103^{18} 4298^{5} 4630^{7} 4769^{3} **>65f<**

Stockbrook 4 b g Marju (IRE)-Burning Ambition (Troy) 1809^{8} 2410^{11} 3027^{5} **>38f<**

Stock Hill Dancer 3 ch f Interrex (CAN)-Stocktina (Tina's Pet) 1141^{12} 1375^{7} 1644^{6} 2921^{3} 3698^{5} 4016^{12} 4115^{16} 4586^{13} **>47f<**

Stolen Kiss (IRE) 5 b or br m Taufan (USA)-Sweet Goodbye (Petorius) 527^{9} 949^{9} 1037^{7} 1250^{10} 1327^{3} 1627^{14} 1765^{4} *1942^{2} 2069^{2}* 2221^{2} 2504^{5} 2738^{3} *3077^{8}* 3287^{17} *3582^{8}* **>67a 63f<**

Stolen Music (IRE) 4 b f Taufan (USA)-Causa Sua (Try My Best (USA)) 574^{11} 733^{16} 900^{7} 1467^{17} 1818^{8} 2063^{12} 2937^{9} 3213^{4} 3565^{9} 4768^{8} 4843^{11} **>25f<**

Stone Beck 2 b f Lapierre-Dovey (Welsh Pageant) 4212^{7} 4507^{4} 4735^{5} **>68f<**

Stone Cross (IRE) 5 b g Pennine Walk-Micro Mover (Artaius (USA)) 864^{10} 1222^{11} 3627^{18} **>49a 30f<**

Stonecutter 4 b br g Warning-South Shore (Caerleon (USA)) **1996:** *5267^{7}* **1997:** *22^{9} (80) 167^{8}* 603^{4} 865^{12} 1779^{7} *2164^{8}* 2696^{9} *3046^{8}* **>44a 51f<**

Stoned Imaculate (IRE) 3 ch f Durgam (USA)-Rose Deer (Whistling Deer) 1258^{7} 2131^{3} 2940^{8} (3858) (4170) (4336) **>75+f<**

Stone Flower (USA) 3 b f Storm Bird (CAN)-Lively Living (USA) (Key To The Mint (USA)) 507^{4} 675^{9} 1146^{8} 2113^{2} 3128^{9} 4102^{5} 4268^{11} **>85f<**

Stone of Destiny 2 ch c Ballad Rock-Shamasiya (FR) (Vayrann) 1932^{8} 2771^{2} 3022^{2} 3597^{4} 4007^{4} 4135^{5} (4814) **>93f<**

Stone Ridge (IRE) 5 b g Indian Ridge-Cut in Stone (USA) (Assert) 450^{13} 832^{5} 1016^{8} 2117^{6} 2346^{5} 2557^{16} **>79f<**

Stoney Valley 7 b g Caerleon (USA)-Startino (Bustino) *106^{9}* **>8a 84df<**

Stop Out 2 b f Rudimentary (USA)-Breakaway (Song) (1970) 2862^{10} 3422^{2} 3839a^{9} **>93f<**

Stoppes Brow 5 b g Primo Dominie-So Bold (Never so Bold) **1996:** *5203^{2}* **1997:** *357^{11} 905^{6} 1154^{6}* 1324^{6} 1489^{2} 1658^{4} 2216^{12} 4787^{20} *4983^{4}* **>87a 75f<**

Stopwatch (IRE) 2 b c Lead on Time (USA)-Rose Bonbon (FR) 4836a^{6} **>88f<**

Stories To Tell (USA) 3 ch c Shadeed (USA)-Million Stories (USA) (Exclusive Native (USA)) 4671^{5} 4848^{8} **>86df<**

Storm Command 3 b g Gildoran-Summer Sky (Skyliner) 4883^{9} **>27f<**

Storm Cry (USA) 2 b c Hermitage (USA)-Doonesbury Lady (USA) (Doonesbury (USA)) 2534^{9} 4910^{2} **>75f<**

Storm Fromthe East 2 b c Formidable (USA)-Callas Star (Chief Singer) 2829^{8} 3136^{2} 3497^{2} 3743^{2} 4315^{4} 4966^{4} **>84f<**

Stormless 6 b g Silly Prices-Phyl's Pet (Aberdeen) (951) 1231^{3} 1560^{4} 4471^{5} 4691^{6} 4847^{2} **>68f<**

Storm River (USA) 2 ch f Riverman (USA)-Storm Dove (USA) (Storm Bird (CAN)) 4107^{5} 4437^{2} **>87f<**

Storm Wind (IRE) 4 ch g Digamist (USA)-Hilton Gateway (Hello Gorgeous (USA)) *183^{8} 256^{6} 328^{6}* **>39a 34f<**

Stormy Blue (IRE) 2 b c Bluebird (USA)-Angel Divine (Ahonoora) 4710^{9} **>52f<**

Stormy Story (USA) 3 b c Storm Bird (CAN)-Silver Clover (USA) (Secretariat (USA)) 2566^{8} 2846^{5} 3277^{9} 3685^{6} **>70f<**

Story Line 4 ch f In The Wings-Known Line (Known Fact (USA)) 1176^{9} 1981^{14} 2528^{12} 2865^{9} 3915^{4} 4426^{10} 4673^{8} 4896^{3} **>85f<**

Storyteller (IRE) 3 b c Thatching-Please Believe Me (Try My Best (USA)) 765^{5} 1630^{6} 1834^{4} 2238^{5} 2715^{4} (3121) 3334^{3} 3812^{7} 4137^{13} 4414^{6} 4527^{9} **>61f<**

Stowaway 3 b c Slip Anchor-On Credit (FR) (No Pass No Sale) 1399^{2} (3109) (3647) 4785^{4} **>123f<**

St Petersburg (FR) 3 ch f Galetto (FR)-Shahmy (FR) (Lear Fan (USA)) 3732a^{3} **>64f<**

Strachin 3 b c Salse (USA)-Collage (Ela-Mana-Mou) 4760a^{2} 4848^{6} **>99?f<**

St Radegund 3 b f Green Desert (USA)-On The House (FR) (Be My Guest (USA)) 727^{10} (1316) **>72f<**

Straffan Gold (USA) 3 b c Lear Fan (USA)-Oro Bianco (USA) (Lyphard's Wish (FR)) 1646^{9} 2487^{18} *3400^{2}* 3858^{5} 4287^{14} 4509^{10} **>60a 51f<**

Strategic Air 2 ch c Anshan-Kimbolton Katie (Aragon) 4514^{6} 4793^{12} 4993^{11} **>59f<**

Strategic Choice (USA) 6 b h Alleged (USA)-Danlu (USA) (Danzig (USA)) **1996:** 5159a^{3} **1997:** 922a^{5} 2100a^{4} 3050^{6} 3596^{4} (4263a) 4870a^{4} **>128df<**

Strathmore Clear 3 b c Batshoof-Sunflower Seed (Mummy's Pet) (517) (654) 990^{2} 1741^{6} 2137^{8} 3150^{15} 4141^{14} **>78f<**

Strat's Legacy 10 b g Chukaroo-State Romance (Free State) **1996:** *5148^{10} 5213^{4}* **1997:** 1779^{12} 2146^{8} 2592^{6} 3317^{9} 3714^{2} 3928^{13} 4275^{16} 4519^{10} **>41a 43f<**

Strat's Quest 3 b f Nicholas (USA)-Eagle's Quest (Legal Eagle) **1996:** *5133^{11}* **1997:** 532^{17} (1141) 1439^{9} 1810^{10} 2062^{11} 2372^{12} *2913^{11}* 4276^{6} 4878^{15} **>26a 62f<**

Stravano 3 b f Handsome Sailor-La Stravaganza (Slip Anchor) 882^{10} 1115^{13} **>1a 26f<**

Stravsea 2 b f Handsome Sailor-La Stravaganza (Slip Anchor) *1577^{7}* 1997^{17} 2419^{2} 2786^{11} 3312^{8} **>15a 66f<**

Strawberry Roan (IRE) 3 b f Sadler's Wells (USA)-Doff the Derby (USA) (Master Derby (USA)) 809a^{4} (1193a) 1533a^{2} 2454a^{8} 2814a^{4} 3172a^{3} 3675a^{7} **>109f<**

Strazo (IRE) 4 b g Alzao (USA)-Ministra (USA) (Deputy Minister (CAN)) 2242^{6} 2528^{13} 2866^{2} 3150^{4} 3712^{7} (4554) 4893^{2} (4990) **>110f<**

Street General 3 b c Generous (IRE)-Hotel Street (USA) (Alleged (USA)) (670) 937^{3} **>88f<**

Street Rebel (CAN) 9 b m 919a^{2} **>106f<**

Street Singer 2 b c Efisio-Dream Chaser (Record Token) 1635^{12} **>32f<**

Strelitza (IRE) 3 b f Taufan (USA)-Strident Note (The Minstrel (CAN)) *873^{11}* 1078^{9} 1229^{12} 1493^{6} **>39a 38f<**

Strength of Vision 3 b g Unfuwain (USA)-Tootsiepop (USA) (Robellino (USA)) 2873^{9} 3095^{12} 3335^{2} 4335^{16} *4912^{11}* **>18a 41f<**

Stretarez (FR) 4 b c Saumarez-Street Opera (Sadler's Wells (USA)) (923a) (1365a) 3883a^{7} 4965a^{8} **>120f<**

Stretching (IRE) 4 br g Contract Law (USA)-Mrs Mutton (Dancers Image (USA)) **1996:** *5101^{7}* **1997:** *373^{2}* 495^{6} *1138^{13}* **>64a 14f<**

Strictly Hard 3 b f Reprimand-Formidable Dancer (Formidable (USA)) 3200^{16} 3455^{9} **>49f<**

Strictly Rhythm 2 b c Hamas (IRE)-Halimah (Be My Guest (USA)) 3905^{7} 4286^{5} 4381^{5} 4588^{11} **>65f<**

Striding King 2 ch c King's Signet (USA)-Stride Home (Absalom) 1163^{6} 1480^{3} 2509^{3} 2781^{6} **>68f<**

Strike-a-Pose 7 ch m Blushing Scribe (USA)-My Bushbaby (Hul A Hul) *68^{5} 151^{4} 1755^{5}* **>56a 33?f<**

Strillo 3 b g Safawan-Silvers Era (Balidar) 1023^{7} 1443^{7} **>63f<**

Struggler 5 b h Night Shift (USA)-Dreamawhile (Known Fact (USA)) 2106^{6} 2526^{2} 2683^{7} (3372a) 3724^{13} 4098^{7} **>112f<**

Studio Thirty 5 gr g Rock City-Chepstow Vale

(USA) (Key To The Mint (USA)) *182[3] 260[2] 295[10]* **>46a 43f<**
Stuffed 5 ch g Clantime-Puff Pastry (Reform) 744[6] 1158[11] 2675[7] **>86f<**
Sturgeon (IRE) 3 ch c Caerleon (USA)-Ridge The Times (USA) (Riva Ridge (USA)) 723[16] 1006[5] 3277[3] **>81f<**
Style Dancer (IRE) 3 b g Dancing Dissident (USA)-Showing Style (Pas de Seul) 506[3] 694[13] 1225[17] 1629[3] 1980[8] 2547[2] 2711[11] 3145[3] 3621[2] 3812[3] 4436[3] 4787[7] 4927[11] 4979[9] **>81f<**
Stylish Allure (USA) 4 b g Topsider (USA)-Excellent Fettle (USA) (State Dinner (USA)) 2441a[11] **>94f<**
Stylish Storm (USA) 2 b f Storm Bird (CAN)-Purify (USA) (Fappiano (USA)) 4317[14] **>48f<**
Stylish Ways (IRE) 5 b g Thatching-Style Of Life (USA) (The Minstrel (CAN)) 610[5] 942[25] 1219[7] 4636[12] 4773[3] 4979[16] **>61f<**
Sualtach (IRE) 4 b c Marju (IRE)-Astra Adastra (Mount Hagen (FR)) 776[4] 1035[7] 1658[8] 2201[4] 2708[8] 2760[2] 3018[3] 3976[20] 4410[4] 4757[27] (4924) **>87a 80f<**
Suave Tern (USA) 6 b h Arctic Tern (USA)-Suavite (USA) (Alleged (USA)) **1996:** 5125a[3] **>118f<**
Sublime Beauty (USA) 3 ch f Caerleon (USA)-Shakela (USA) (Alydar (USA)) 1540a[2] 2053[5] **>105f<**
Subtle Touch (IRE) 6 b g Lomond (USA)-Lobbino (Bustino) *660[13] 2668[12] 2910[6] 3587[5]* 3896[10] *4302[11]* **>33a 7f<**
Success And Glory (IRE) 2 b c Alzao (USA)-More Fizz (Morston (FR)) 1978[4] 2680[3] 4157[2] (4478) **>93f<**
Such Boldness 3 b c Persian Bold-Bone China (IRE) (Sadler's Wells (USA)) 1088[7] 2572[2] **>80f<**
Such Charisma (CAN) 3 ch c Zilzal (USA)-Starstruck Gal (FR) (Stage Door Johnny) **1996:** (5190a) **1997:** (4125a) **>110f<**
Such Presence 3 ch g Arzanni-Marchiness Drake (Marechal Drake) 2487[14] 2879[9] 4743[16] **>25f<**
Sudden Spin 7 b g Doulab (USA)-Lightning Legacy (USA) (Super Concorde (USA)) *(167) 205[5] 232[4]* 632[8] 865[16] 4171[13] **>73da 39f<**
Sudest (IRE) 3 b c Taufan (USA)-Frill (Henbit (USA)) 509[12] 771[7] (1002) 1140[4] (1565) (1956) 2139[4] 2963[3] 3472[2] **>85f<**
Suedoro 7 b m Hard Fought-Bamdoro (Cavo Doro) 1613[11] 1835[9] 2033[3] 2144[3] 2237[11] 2384[U] 2543[8] 2657[3] 3224[5] 3406[6] 3484[15] 3761[4] 3856[12] (3922) 4168[3] 4235[12] 4414[9] **>51f<**
Suellajoy 2 ch f Weldnaas (USA)-Jeethgaya (USA) (Critique (USA)) 2394[7] 3788[3] 4057[9] **>68f<**
Sue Me (IRE) 5 b or br g Contract Law (USA)-Pink Fondant (Northfields (USA)) **1996:** *5163[12]* **1997:** *32[5] 51[7]* 1098[3] 1227[3] 1269[5] 1395[10] 1613[13] 4844[2] 5047[8] **>55a 58f<**
Sue's Return 5 b m Beveled (USA)-Return to Tara (Homing) 1035[16] 1320[5] 1745[2] 2346[6] 2772[4] 3115[3] 3548[4] 4283[7] 4558[31] **>84f<**
Suez Tornado (IRE) 4 ch g Mujtahid (USA)-So Stylish (Great Nephew) *396[5]* 444[11] 552[11] 657[9] 895[23] 1097[4] 1489[4] 1761[4] (1845) 2290[4] 2557[3] 3066[4] 3262[8] 3976[19] 4147[15] 4410[6] 4781[25] 4920[7] 5049[13] **>82a 68f<**
Suga Hawk (IRE) 5 b g Pennine Walk-Ishtar Abu (St Chad) *34[3] 82[12] 150[4] 284[3] (369) 422[11]* 461[4] 552[4] 1763[3] 2236[5] 2503[2] 2652[4] 2824[6] (3603) 3890[3] 4802[9] 4918[4] **>66a 71f<**
Sugarfoot 3 ch c Thatching-Norpella (Northfields (USA)) 673[3] 957[4] 1146[11] 2137[2] 2871[8] **>94f<**
Sugarland Express (IRE) 6 br h Roi Danzig (USA)-Island Time (USA) (Bold Hour) 1549a[7] **>117f<**
Sugar Mill 7 b g Slip Anchor-Great Tom (Great Nephew) (499) **>91f<**
Sugar Plum 3 br f Primo Dominie-Ile de Danse (Ile de Bourbon (USA)) 935[8] 1110[10] 1439[13] **>46f<**
Sugar Reef 3 br g High Kicker (USA)-Miss Poll Flinders (Swing Easy (USA)) 4848[13] **>9f<**
Suggest 2 b c Midyan (USA)-Awham (USA) (Lear Fan (USA)) 432[10] 564[6] 2784[7] (3212) (3384) 3802[7] 4767[15] **>70f<**
Suile Mor 5 b m Satin Wood-Ra Ra (Lord Gayle (USA)) 2039[11] 2375[2] 2646[13] **>53?f<**
Suite Factors 3 b g Timeless Times (USA)-Uptown Girl (Caruso) **1996:** *5083[7] 5176[10]* **1997:** *79[9] 142[4] 223[7]* 473[10] 602[2] 652[2] 751[2] 1029[11] 1327[9] 1644[2] 1792[2] 1995[5] 2751[3] 3121[3] 3500[4] 3851[3] 4048[4] 4249[3] 4404[10] 4565[11] 4877[13] **>46a 61f<**
Suitor 4 b g Groom Dancer (USA)-Meliora (Crowned Prince (USA)) **1996:** *5148[8] 5185[4] 5222[10] 5281[2]* **1997:** *61[3] 141[4]* 1233[10] 1636[14] 1953[5] 4171[14] **>54a 44f<**
Suivez 7 b g Persian Bold-Butterfly Kiss (Beldale Flutter (USA)) 2512[6] 2776[9] 3315[14] **>64a 50f<**
Suivez La Trace 2 ch c Shalford (IRE)-Miss Petella (Dunphy) (2356) 3022[5] 3899[5] 4284[12] 4702[10] 4875[14] 5045[4] **>80+f<**
Sujud (IRE) 5 b br m Shaadi (USA)-Sit Elnaas (USA) (Sir Ivor) *375[8]* **>36a 54f<**
Sulb (USA) 5 b h El Gran Senor (USA)-Stricly (ARG) (Dancing Moss) *626a[3]* **>100a 101f<**
Suleika Dancer 4 b f Slip Anchor-Starr Danias (USA) (Sensitive Prince (USA)) **1996:** *5169[4] 5232[6]* **1997:** 605[7] 838[18] 1796[10] 1985[7] 2399[10] **>53a 22f<**
Sumbawa (IRE) 2 ch f Magic Ring (IRE)-Tittlemouse (Castle Keep) 3278[7] 3862[6] 4332[12] **>63f<**
Summer Dance 3 b f Sadler's Wells (USA)-Hyabella (Shirley Heights) (3807) 4242[10] **>97f<**
Summer Day Blues (IRE) 2 b f Petorius-Atmospheric Blues (IRE) (Double Schwartz) 682[8] 1091[4] 1457[7] 2578[7] **>58f<**
Summer Deal (USA) 2 b f Summer Squall (USA)-Dariela (USA) (Manila (USA)) 1211[W] 1295[3] 2007[2] 2371[6] 3025[2] 3387[6] 4185[3] 4382[2] 4841[3] **>78f<**
Summerhill Special (IRE) 6 b m Roi Danzig (USA)-Special Thanks (Kampala) 470[2] (598) 781[5] 955[2] 1162[9] 1393[2] (1562) 1763[6] 2063[D] 2316[6] 2652[5] (3562) 3907[5] 4235[5] 4466[5] 4751[15] **>70f<**
Summerosa (USA) 3 ch f Woodman (USA)-Rose Red (USA) (Northern Dancer) 1423[6] 2420[3] 3079[2] 3437[3] 3800[3] (4009) 4220[7] **>76f<**
Summer Princess 4 ch f Prince Sabo-Lafrowda (Crimson Beau) **1996:** *5109[13] 5134[16]* **1997:** 574[17] **>37f< (DEAD)**
Summer Queen 3 b f Robellino (USA)-Carolside (Music Maestro) (675) 930[6] 1238[13] 2133[7] 2945[12] 4175[11] 4878[20] **>62a 71f<**
Summer River (IRE) 2 b g River Falls-Rose of Summer (IRE) (Taufan (USA)) 880[9] 1267[11] *2047[9]* 2923[9] **>13a 45f<**
Summerseat 2 b f Thatching-Sudden Hope (FR) (Darshaan) 572[4] *902[6] (1124)* 3932[7] 4746[3] **>56a 42f<**
Summer Thyme 3 b f Henbit (USA)-Hasty Sarah (Gone Native) 2046[13] 2687[7] 3404[3] **>53f<**
Summer Villa 5 b m Nomination-Maravilla (Mandrake Major) *114[6]* **>47a 46f<**
Summerville Wood 3 b g Nomination-Four Love (Pas de Seul) *365[6]* 484[3] (601) 772[9] 2721[10] 3394[6] 3685[5] *4069[11]* 4335[10] 4453[7] **>46?a 55f<**
Sun Alert (USA) 3 b f Alysheba (USA)-Sunerta (USA) (Roberto (USA)) 937[4] 1218[3] 1612[3] 1949[3] (2188) 2589[5] 2963[9] 3122[11] 3643[4] 3796[5] 3928[4] 4242[15] 4323[11] 4771[12] 4971[19] **>42f<**
Sunbeam Dance (USA) 3 b c Gone West (USA)-Encorelle (FR) (Arctic Tern (USA)) 3144[5] 3741[7] 4238[4] 4558[27] **>114?f<**
Sun Dancer 2 b g Sizzling Melody-Petite Melusine (IRE) (Fairy King (USA)) 2781[13]
Sun Dancing (IRE) 2 ch f Magical Wonder (USA)-Lockwood Girl (Prince Tenderfoot (USA)) 4159[W] 4807[5] **>46f<**
Sunday Mail Too (IRE) 5 b m Fayruz-Slick Chick (Shiny Tenth) 666[6] 924[2] 1037[6] 1613[9] 1835[5] 2221[W] 2382[6] 2657[7] 3224[6] 3484[9] 3756[13] 3922[13] **>1a 22f<**
Sun Fairy 3 ch f Hatim (USA)-Petite Melusine (IRE) (Fairy King (USA)) 1448[5] 1780[3] 1998[2] 2522[4] 2941[4] 3456[8] 3762[3] **>52f<**
Sun In The Morning 2 gr f Petardia-Rich Lass (Broxted) 739[7] 828[5] (1444) 1614[3] 1867[2] *2051[7]* 3314[7] 3791[5] 4162[5] 4500[4] **>31a 68f<**
Sunley Seeker 2 b f Elmaamul (USA)-Sunley Sinner (Try My Best (USA)) 2728[11] *(3072)* 3802[11] (4271) **>81a 81f<**
Sun Lion (IRE) 2 b c Shalford (IRE)-Suzie Sunshine 2439a[12] **>75f<**
Sun Mark (IRE) 6 ch g Red Sunset-Vivungi (USA) (Exbury) 550[2] 612[3] (1042) 1281[10] 1674[4] 2225[4] (2544) (3223) **>67f<**
Sunny Isle 3 b f Cadeaux Genereux-Highsplasher (USA) (Bucksplasher (USA)) 3389[3] (4407) 4731[3] **>82f<**
Sunny Sample (IRE) 3 ch c Royal Academy (USA)-Sentimental Mood (ITY) (Dunbeath (USA)) 1069a[2] 2101a[3] **>99f<**
Sun of Spring 7 b g Green Desert (USA)-Unsuspected (Above Suspicion) 1601[3] (1686) 1825[9] 2154[2] (2351) 2469[4] 2696[4] 3141[4] 3562[4] **>63f<**
Sun O'Tirol (IRE) 3 b c Tirol-Nous (Le Johnstan) 840[5] 1164[17] 1568[4] 1826[18] 2369[13] 2552[13] 2921[15] 3558[5] **>43f<**
Sunset Harbour (IRE) 4 br f Prince Sabo-City Link Pet (Tina's Pet) 494[11] 702[13] 1332[5] 1602[3] (1828) 1865[6] 2197[3] 2540[6] 3871[14] 4707[17] **>63a 45f<**
Sunset Reigns (IRE) 4 b f Taufan (USA)-More Candy (Ballad Rock) 2815a[9] 3508a[8] **>95df<**
Sunshine Pet (IRE) 2 b f Petardia-Faapette (Runnett) 492[7] 780[7] 1019[8] 1600[4] 1815[6] 2016[16] 4230[12] **>44f<**
Sunstreak 2 ch c Primo Dominie-Florentynna Bay (Aragon) 4952[9] 5048[14] **>57f<**
Supacalifragilistk 2 b f Sabrehill (USA)-Lucky Thing (Green Desert (USA)) 1321[4] 1619[9] 2840[10] 4285[2] 4576[15] 4994[7] **>60f<**
Superapparos 3 b g Superpower-Ayodessa (Lochnager) *412[6] 576[7] 874[13]* 2523[12] 3241[11] 3693[12] *4051[8]* 4601[24] *4795[3]* **>59a 8f<**
Superbelle 3 b f Damister (USA)-Nell of The North (USA) (Canadian Gil (CAN)) **1996:** *5142[2] 5228[3]* **1997:** *(26) 281[4]* 431[15] 2961[15] 3695[2] 3970[10] 4180[5] **>79a 62f<**
Super Bely (FR) 4 b c Lesotho (USA)-Superstition (Touching Wood (USA)) 269a[2] **>84f<**
Super Benz 11 ch g Hello Gorgeous (USA)-Investiture (Welsh Pageant) 1220[3] (1448) **>76?a 82?f<**
Superbit 5 b g Superpower-On A Bit (Mummy's Pet) **1996:** *5138[3] 5173[5]* **1997:** 1734[4] (2177) 2480[3] 2759[3] 2844[7] 3130[13] 3481[4] 3693[13] 3984[11] 4333[3] 4580[17] 4905[4] **>49a 62f<**
Supercal 3 gr f Environment Friend-Sorayah (Persian Bold) (506) 724[5] 959[6] (1101) 1326[8] 2023[7] 2334[9] 2766[2] 3371a[3] 3674a[3] 4094a[2] 4666a[14] **>109f<**

Supercharmer 3 ch g Charmer-Surpassing (Superlative) 49^{5} 155^{4} 193^{3} 287^{6} 649^{11} 729^{4} 845^{6} 1119^{4} 1451^{5} 3814^{9} 4300^{13} **>68a 67f<**
Superchief 2 b g Precocious-Rome Express (Siberian Express (USA)) 4237^{9} **>65+f<**
Super Cub (USA) 3 c 2274a^{7} **>73f<**
Superfrills 4 b f Superpower-Pod's Daughter (IRE) (Tender King) 972^{6} 1250^{15} 1332^{4} 1604^{3} 1828^{17} 2167^{6} 2738^{4} 3086^{5} 3271^{W} 4791^{10} **>10a 41f<**
Super Geil 2 b f Superlative-Mild Deception (IRE) (Glow (USA)) 3097^{5} 3586^{5} 3859^{9} (4054) 4573^{3} 4796^{7} 4911^{7} **>57a 72?f<**
Supergold (IRE) 4 ch g Keen-Superflash (Superlative) 9^{8} 37^{4} **>30a f<**
Super High 5 b g Superlative-Nell of The North (USA) (Canadian Gil (CAN)) **1996:** 5106^{8} **1997:** 56^{2} 82^{9} (244) 299^{9} 858^{5} 1036^{10} 1384^{13} **>93a 56f<**
Superior Force 4 ch g Superlative-Gleeful (Sayf El Arab (USA)) 47^{11} 120^{4} 186^{6} 383^{5} 1320^{6} 1972^{10} 3768^{4} 4139^{21} **>66a 54f<**
Superior Premium 3 br c Forzando-Devils Dirge (Song) (501) 941^{8} 4282^{3} 4444^{6} 4777^{11} 5054^{4} **>108f<**
Superlao (BEL) 5 b m Bacalao (USA)-Princess of Import (Import) 24^{7} 58^{6} 107^{5} 159^{6} 199^{4} 263^{3} 304^{3} 473^{7} 1083^{11} 1236^{3} 1327^{5} 1419^{6} 1676^{3} 1965^{13} 2244^{3} (2321) 2581^{8} 2895^{6} 3092^{6} 3195^{4} 3642^{12} 4518^{14} **>38a 60f<**
Supermick 6 ch g Faustus (USA)-Lardana (Burglar) 2650^{2} 3015^{6} 3229^{2} 3568^{2} 4275^{17} **>49a 49f<**
Supermodel (GER) 2 ch f Czaravich (USA)-Superminis (GER) (Super Concorde (USA)) 1723a^{3} 2637a^{5}
Super Monarch 3 ch c Cadeaux Genereux-Miss Fancy That (USA) (The Minstrel (CAN)) 963^{4} 1423^{2} 1670^{5} **>81f<**
Super Park 5 b g Superpower-Everingham Park (Record Token) **1996:** 5140^{7} 5175^{11} **1997:** 1374^{8} 1965^{4} 3285^{11} 3476^{7} 4951^{16} **>21a 42f<**
Superpride 5 b g Superpower-Lindrake's Pride (Mandrake Major) 571^{17} 733^{15} 1315^{2} 2144^{12} 2239^{2} 2465^{3} 2906^{13} 3403^{5} 3976^{6} **>56f<**
Super Rascal 2 b c Superpower-Gild the Lily (Ile de Bourbon (USA)) 902^{9} 1797^{4} 2047^{3} 2324^{6} **>68a 52f<**
Super Rocky 8 b g Clantime-Starproof (Comedy Star (USA)) 371^{6} 760^{6} 972^{7} 2177^{16} 2738^{12} 4051^{9} 4844^{11} 4985^{9} **>48a 39f<**
Super Saint 3 b g Superpower-Martyrdom (USA) (Exceller (USA)) 602^{10} **>33a 61f<**
Super Scravels 3 ch f Superlative-Scravels Saran (IRE) (Indian King (USA)) 2723^{3} 3133^{7} 3230^{4} 3592^{4} 3968^{4} **>12a 53f<**
Super Serenade 8 b g Beldale Flutter (USA)-Super Melody (Song) 2375^{9} 3091^{8} (3276) 3467^{7} 3971^{9} **>62?f<**
Super Snip 2 ch c Superpower-Marcroft (Crofthall) 2212^{5} 4012^{10} **>57f<**
Supertop 9 b or br g High Top-Myth (Troy) (721) **>61?f<**
Suplizi (IRE) 6 b h Alzao (USA)-Sphinx (GER) (Alpenkonig (GER)) 4894^{9} 5051^{8} **>97?f<**
Supply And Demand 3 b g Belmez (USA)-Sipsi Fach (Prince Sabo) (790) 958^{2} (1104) 1741^{2} 2058^{8} 3190^{2} 3703^{14} **>104f<**
Supreme Angel 2 b f Beveled (USA)-Blue Angel (Lord Gayle (USA)) 536^{8} (739) 1386^{4} 3546^{2} 3892^{2} 4296^{6} (4737) **>81f<**
Supreme Commander (FR) 4 b c Saumarez-Autocratic (Tyrant) 1200a^{4} **>119f<**
Supreme Desire 9 gr m Grey Desire-Fire Mountain (Dragonara Palace (USA)) **1996:** 5114^{15} **>1a 34df<**
Supreme Illusion (AUS) 4 ch f Rory's Jester (AUS)-Counterfeit Coin (AUS) (Comeram (FR)) **1996:** 5183^{9} 5267^{10} **1997:** 36^{3} 91^{7} 128^{9} 209^{11} 312^{9} **>24a 31f< (DEAD)**
Supreme Maimoon 3 b c Jareer (USA)-Princess Zena (Habitat) **1996:** 5111^{W} (5226) **1997:** 227^{3} 1458^{14} 1691^{8} 1958^{9} 2281^{11} 2573^{7} **>79a 48f<**
Supreme Sound 3 b c Superlative-Sing Softly (Luthier) 690^{19} 986^{7} 1414^{13} 2064^{3} 2411^{8} 3315^{4} (3616) (4223) 4449^{3} 4635^{11} **>79f<**
Supreme Star (USA) 6 b g Gulch (USA)-Just A Game (Tarboosh (USA)) **1996:** 5185^{3} **1997:** (43) 106^{3} (183) 252^{P} **>75a 74f<**
Supreme Thought 5 b m Emarati (USA)-Who's That Girl (Skyliner) 2721^{5} (3393) 3984^{16} 4518^{15} 4738^{2} **>69f<**
Supremism 3 b c Be My Chief (USA)-Ever Welcome (Be My Guest (USA)) 1239^{12} 1611^{5} 2309^{7} **>79?f<**
Surako (GER) 4 bl c Konigsstuhl (GER)-Surata (GER) (Lagunas) 1073a^{2} 1724a^{7} 2459a^{2} **>117f<**
Sure Quest 2 b f Sure Blade (USA)-Eagle's Quest (Legal Eagle) 4701^{6} 4909^{5} **>63f<**
Sure To Dream (IRE) 4 b f Common Grounds-Hard to Stop (Hard Fought) 964^{6} 1139^{9} 1423^{11} 4711^{12} **>48f<**
Surf City 4 ch g Rock City-Waveguide (Double Form) **1996:** 5130^{2} 5161^{4} **1997:** 40^{6} 164^{4} 579^{10} 1584^{4} 1830^{10} 2501^{3} (3269) 3759^{8} 4059^{8} 4813^{8} **>52a 56f<**
Surgeon 4 ch c Sharrood (USA)-Suva (USA) (Northjet) (1359a) 1917a^{2} (3006a) **>121f<**
Surpresa Cara 2 ch f Risk Me (FR)-Yukosan (Absalom) 2138^{8} 3136^{8} 4515^{10} **>49f<**
Surprised 2 b g Superpower-Indigo (Primo Dominie) 4012^{11} 4211^{4} 4428^{2} **>71f<**
Surprise Event 3 b g Tragic Role (USA)-Eleckydo (Electric) 4505^{7} 4858^{8} **>46a 56f<**
Surprise Mission 5 ch g Clantime-Indigo (Primo Dominie) 464^{3} (527) (744) (1034) 1158^{4} 1766^{4} 2289^{3} 3011^{2} 4100^{20} 4677^{5} 4756^{11} 4887^{15} **>89f<**
Surprise Present (IRE) 2 ch c Indian Ridge-Lady Redford (Bold Lad (IRE)) 2556^{6} 4779^{10} **>66f<**
Surtsey 3 ch c Nashwan (USA)-Fire and Shade (USA) (Shadeed (USA)) 559^{2} 732^{3} 2046^{10} 2387^{5} 3567^{8} **>67df<**
Surveyor 2 ch c Lycius (USA)-Atacama (Green Desert (USA)) 3219^{4} (3613) 3899^{2} (4315) **>93f<**
Suselja (IRE) 6 b m Mon Tresor-Stifen (Burslem) 1605^{6} **>35a 43f<**
Sushi Bar (IRE) 6 gr g Petorius-Sashi Woo (Rusticaro (FR)) 888^{16} 1133^{13} 1232^{10} 1654^{4} 2000^{3} 2154^{11} (2539) 3317^{8} 3540^{5} (3758) 3919^{3} 4160^{3} 4584^{7} **>64?a 52f<**
Susie's Sonny 3 ch g Timeless Times (USA)-Pickwood Sue (Right Boy) 856^{9} **>16a f<**
Sussex Gorse 6 ch g Arrasas (USA)-Testarossa (Tower Walk) **1996:** 5149^{13} **1997:** 333^{10} 407^{10} 607^{13} 2146^{13} 3046^{12} **>16?f<**
Susun Kelapa (USA) 2 ch f St Jovite (USA)-Tiramisu (USA) (Roberto (USA)) 3839a^{5} 4619a^{5} **>93f<**
Suvalu (USA) 5 b g Woodman (USA)-Danlu (USA) (Danzig (USA)) 3568^{4} **>65a 54f<**
Swain (IRE) 5 b h Nashwan (USA)-Love Smitten (CAN) (Key To The Mint (USA)) 2559^{2} (3050) 4238^{3} 4665a^{7} **>135f<**
Swallow Breeze 3 b f Salse (USA)-Pica (Diesis) 837^{6} 1094^{13} **>75?f<**
Swallow Warrior (IRE) 2 b c Warrshan (USA)-Pica (Diesis) 4957^{12} **>8f<**
Swan At Whalley 5 b g Statoblest-My Precious Daisy (Sharpo) 494^{W} 1627^{5} 1946^{4} (2339) 2563^{13} 2754^{9} 3756^{14} 3900^{3} 4137^{16} (4365) 5047^{18} **>44a 70f<**
Swandale Flyer 5 ch g Weldnaas (USA)-Misfire (Gunner B) 16^{4} 86^{8} 122^{2} 167^{7} 218^{P} 1133^{8} **>37a 37f<**
Swan Hunter 4 b c Sharrood (USA)-Cache (Bustino) 426^{7} 591^{7} 908^{4} 1145^{6} 1408^{2} 1844^{8} 2175^{2} 2411^{7} 3284^{5} (4713) (4768) **>67a 68+f<**
Swan Island 3 ch f Hubbly Bubbly (USA)-Green's Cassatt (USA) (Apalachee (USA)) 535^{11} 764^{5} 871^{2} 1048^{3} 1568^{7} 1958^{W} 3697^{4} 4112^{20} 4465^{6} **>70a 61f<**
Swan Lane (USA) 3 b f Theatrical-Fortunate Facts (USA) (Sir Ivor) 1499^{7} 3140^{6} **>62f<**
Swanmore Lady (IRE) 2 b f Forzando-Steffi (Precocious) 472^{9} 767^{3} 1293^{10} 2578^{3} 3226^{5} 4054^{10} (4327) 4419^{2} 4755^{11} 4948^{9} 5017^{2} **>60a 58f<**
Swaybus 2 ch f Pursuit of Love-Gong (Bustino) 2898^{4} 3757^{8} 4592^{9} **>6a 52f<**
Sweet Amoret 4 b f Forzando-Primrose Way (Young Generation) **1996:** 5081^{2} 5145^{6} 5271^{6} **1997:** 43^{8} 92^{7} 319^{10} 338^{6} **>19a 55f<**
Sweet Bettsie 3 b f Presidium-Sweet and Sure (Known Fact (USA)) 988^{10} 1243^{13} **>75df<**
Sweetchildofmine 3 gr f Mon Tresor-Sincerely Yours (Kind of Hush) 868^{11} 1144^{6} 1637^{8} 2178^{7} **>26a 65f<**
Sweet Ciseaux (IRE) 4 b g Be My Guest (USA)-Wild Abandon (USA) (Graustark) 235^{15} 538^{5} 755^{15} 1384^{9} 1632^{21} 2144^{10} 3015^{14} **>26f<**
Sweet Contralto 3 b f Danehill (USA)-Sweet Soprano (High Line) (1406) 2137^{7} 2672^{8} 3119^{2} 3274^{2} (3741) 4268^{7} 5044^{3} **>19a 94f<**
Sweet Dreams 2 b f Selkirk (USA)-Ahohoney (Ahonoora) 3547^{12} 3985^{8} 4330^{5} **>71f<**
Sweet Emmaline 3 b f Emarati (USA)-Chapelfell (Pennine Walk) **1996:** 5172^{4} **>43a 62f<**
Sweet Fortune (USA) 3 b br c Lear Fan (USA)-Sweet Delilah (USA) (Super Concorde (USA)) 2156^{3} (2704) 3185^{9} (3752) 4314^{7} **>90f<**
Sweet Glow (FR) 10 b g Crystal Glitters (USA)-Very Sweet (Bellypha) 650^{7} **>85?f<**
Sweetheart (USA) 3 b f Mr Prospector (USA)-Gorgeous (USA) (Slew O' Gold (USA)) **1996:** 5194a^{3} **>86f< (DEAD)**
Sweet Magic 6 ch g Sweet Monday-Charm Bird (Daring March) 464^{7} 731^{8} 834^{11} 1743^{9} 2148^{8} 3126^{3} (3898) 4370^{6} 4636^{21} 5047^{20} **>69f<**
Sweet Mate 5 ch g Komaite (USA)-Be My Sweet (Galivanter) **1996:** 5152^{7} **1997:** 3^{3} 111^{11} 233^{6} 332^{4} 429^{3} 760^{4} (1089) (1289) 1754^{11} 1944^{7} 2177^{10} 2603^{12} **>35a 48f<**
Sweet Mazarine (IRE) 3 b f Dancing Dissident (USA)-Idara (Top Ville) 2815a^{2} **>105f<**
Sweetness Herself 4 ch f Unfuwain (USA)-No Sugar Baby (FR) (Crystal Glitters (USA)) (498) 1033^{4} 1241^{3} 1548a^{2} 2327^{2} 4099^{5} 4783^{22} 4969^{3} (5043) **>111f<**
Sweet Note (IRE) 3 ch f La Grange Music-Screenable (USA) (Silent Screen (USA)) 551^{6} 784^{10} 952^{3} 1284^{10} 1615^{6} 1838^{6} 2029^{5} 2226^{11} 3221^{7} 3488^{7} 3919^{4} 4469^{4} 4692^{7} **>36f<**
Sweet Patoopie 3 b f Indian Ridge-Patriotic (Hotfoot) 778^{5} 1030^{6} **>59f<**
Sweet Reward 2 ch c Beveled (USA)-Sweet Revival (Claude Monet (USA)) 884^{6} 1120^{3} (1961) 2359^{5} **>72f<**
Sweet Rosie (IRE) 2 b f Petardia-White's Pet (Mummy's Pet) 902^{3} 1569^{10} 2147^{2} 2545^{16} **>45a 64f<**

Sweet Senorita 2 b f Young Senor (USA)-Sweet N' Twenty (High Top) 1984^{6} 2664^{8} 3078^{5} **>34f<**
Sweet Seventeen 4 gr f Touch of Grey-Westminster Waltz (Dance In Time (CAN)) 296^{10} 1116^{9} 1483^{10} 2488^{5} 2916^{15} 3321^{4} 3848^{9} **>18a 29f<**
Sweet Sondra (USA) 4 ch f Wolf Power (IRE)-Seattle Paige (USA) (Seattle Song (USA)) $5038a^{2}$ **>113f<**
Sweet Sorrow (IRE) 2 b f Lahib (USA)-So Long Boys (FR) (Beldale Flutter (USA)) 3574^{5} 4066^{4} **>78f<**
Sweet Supposin (IRE) 6 b h Posen (USA)-Go Honey Go (General Assembly (USA)) **1996:** 5151^{5} 5189^{7} 5200^{10} **1997:** 131^{3} (226) 291^{7} 380^{5} 422^{4} (457) 566^{5} 1082^{3} 1421^{6} 1969^{3} 2668^{3} 3064^{6} 4813^{5} **>70a 36f<**
Sweet Wilhelmina 4 b f Indian Ridge-Henpot (IRE) (Alzao (USA)) **1996:** 5124^{10} **1997:** (248) (325) 1262^{8} (1442) 1739^{2} 2346^{4} 3982^{14} 4297^{2} 4441^{3} 4781^{30} **>78a 79f<**
Sweetzie (USA) 5 ch m Zie World (USA)-Sweet Miranda (USA) (Persian Bold) (5038a) **>118?f<**
Swift 3 ch g Sharpo-Three Terns (USA) (Arctic Tern (USA)) 264^{2} 307^{3} (368) 535^{9} 845^{3} 871^{3} 1243^{7} (1496) 2002^{13} (2130) 2372^{5} 2557^{6} 3100^{6} 3236^{2} 3772^{9} 3798^{6} 4591^{5} 4741^{4} 4913^{6} 4979^{13} **>67a 73f<**
Swift Alliance 2 b c Belong To Me (USA)-One Quick Bid (USA) (Commemorate (USA)) 1263^{9} (1480) 2012^{8} 2584^{6} **>78+f<**
Swift Gulliver (IRE) 3 ch c Gulch (USA)-Aminata (Glenstal (USA)) $3362a^{5}$ (3674a) $4204a^{7}$ 4421^{8} 4782^{10} **>112f<**
Swift Sovereign 3 gr g Petong-Flitteriss Park (Beldale Flutter (USA)) 1406^{5} 1870^{W} 3715^{10} **>60?f<**
Swift Time 2 b f Timeless Times (USA)-Bustling Around (Bustino) 536^{9} 884^{7} 1019^{2} 1444^{5} 3247^{10} 3324^{6} 3742^{7} **>67f<**
Swiftway 3 ch g Anshan-Solemn Occasion (USA) (Secreto (USA)) 445^{5} 533^{9} 1624^{6} 1832^{5} 2548^{2} 2889^{9} 2908^{3} 3309^{11} 3543^{3} **>66f<**
Swifty Nifty (IRE) 4 b f Runnett-Swift Verdict (My Swallow) **1996:** 5109^{9} **>15a 31f<**
Swing Along 2 ch f Alhijaz-So it Goes (Free State) 4779^{2} **>86f<**
Swing And Brave (IRE) 3 b f Ela-Mana-Mou-Sweet Snow (USA) (Lyphard (USA)) **1996:** $5197a^{6}$ **1997:** (814a) $1369a^{6}$
Swinging Sixties (IRE) 6 b g Fairy King (USA)-La Bella Fontana (Lafontaine (USA)) 384^{8} **>46a 73f<**
Swinging The Blues (IRE) 3 b c Bluebird (USA)-Winsong Melody (Music Maestro) 3281^{4} 3916^{14} 4139^{7} 4741^{5} 4918^{13} **>63f<**
Swing Sister 2 b f Rock City-Santa Magdalena (Hard Fought) (4458) 4709^{2} 4892^{6} 5046^{4} **>85f<**
Swingtime 2 ch f Beveled (USA)-Superfina (USA) (Fluorescent Light (USA)) 4694^{11} 4907^{9} **>56f<**
Swing West (USA) 3 b c Gone West (USA)-Danlu (USA) (Danzig (USA)) 1415^{6} 1787^{5} 2152^{5} 2487^{2} 2667^{3} 3234^{13} **>48a 69f<**
Swino 3 b g Forzando-St Helena (Monsanto (FR)) 434^{4} 501^{4} 744^{14} 1018^{6} 1254^{2} 1799^{12} 2134^{12} 2211^{9} 2655^{3} 3194^{9} 3900^{6} 4233^{13} 4365^{6} 4565^{6} 4733^{4} (4791) 4820^{10} 5047^{5} **>73f<**
Swiss Coast (IRE) 3 b g Mujadil (USA)-Rose A Village (River Beauty) 395^{8} 551^{4} 748^{6} 1115^{6} 1467^{9} 1620^{8} 4326^{11} **>20a 47f<**
Swiss Law 3 b c Machiavellian (USA)-Seductress (Known Fact (USA)) (957) 1412^{4} 2013^{14} 3764^{2} 4523^{2} 4888^{2} **>110f<**
Switch To Senate 3 b c Sharpo-La Reine de France (Queen's Hussar) 1292^{10} 2008^{21} 2294^{3} 2577^{15} **>51df<**
Swith Water (IRE) 3 b f Classic Music (USA)-Snow Storm (ITY) (Ercolano (USA)) **1996:** $5197a^{2}$
Swoosh 2 gr g Absalom-Valldemosa (Music Boy) 850^{6} 979^{4} 1330^{2} 1438^{3} 1616^{7} **>72f<**
Sword Arm 3 b g Be My Guest (USA)-Gai Bulga (Kris) (387) 431^{11} 509^{3} 723^{3} (2695) (2778) 3190^{14} 3712^{3} 4276^{9} 4375^{7} 4859^{3} **>68+a 97f<**
Swordking (IRE) 8 ch g Kris-Reine Mathilde (USA) (Vaguely Noble) 2607^{6} 3046^{9} 4302^{W} **>39a 46f<**
Swynford Charmer 3 ch g Charmer-Qualitairess (Kampala) **1996:** 5202^{8} **1997:** 155^{7} 3813^{12} 4751^{18} **>21a 44f<**
Swynford Dream 4 b g Statoblest-Qualitair Dream (Dreams to Reality (USA)) 744^{15} 1034^{6} 1158^{6} 1468^{13} 1946^{6} 2289^{12} 2872^{8} 3410^{19} 4233^{3} 4434^{7} 4636^{W} 4844^{14} 5047^{19} **>73df<**
Swynford Supreme 4 ch g Statoblest-Comtec Princess (Gulf Pearl) 272^{9} **>36a 60f<**
Sycamore Boy (USA) 3 ch g Woodman (USA)-Kafiyah (USA) (Shadeed (USA)) 3281^{5} 3775^{2} 4308^{4} 4680^{4} 4882^{19} **>79f<**
Sycamore Lodge (IRE) 6 ch g Thatching-Bell Tower (Lyphard's Wish (FR)) 3910^{14} 4410^{10} 5049^{14} **>61a 61f<**
Sylphide 2 b f Ballet Royal (USA)-Shafayif (Ela-Mana-Mou) 3493^{14}
Sylvan Cloud 2 ch f Sylvan Express-Kept Waiting (Tanfirion) 844^{7} 993^{8} 1432^{3} 1789^{5} 2153^{9} 2419^{6} 2904^{12} **>36a 34f<**
Sylvan Dancer (IRE) 3 b br f Dancing Dissident (USA)-Unspoiled (Tina's Pet) 783^{5} 1294^{8} 3032^{4} 3393^{3} 3716^{10} 4565^{9} 4738^{8} **>62f<**
Sylvania Lights 3 b f Emarati (USA)-Harmony Park (Music Boy) 1132^{8} **>15a 24f<**
Sylvan Jubilacion 3 b g Sylvan Express-This Sensation (Balidar) 1936^{7} 2667^{9} 3291^{7} **>59df<**
Sylvan Princess 4 b f Sylvan Express-Ela-Yianni-Mou (Anfield) (554) 749^{11} 895^{5} 1111^{2} 1219^{8} 1739^{8} 1987^{2} 2557^{17} 2668^{11} **>47a 75f<**
Sylva Paradise (IRE) 4 b c Dancing Dissident (USA)-Brentsville (USA) (Arctic Tern (USA)) 671^{3} 941^{7} $1201a^{6}$ 1455^{6} 2106^{18} 2526^{12} 3217^{27} 4100^{19} 4239^{10} 4444^{9} **>101f<**
Symboli Kildare (IRE) 4 b c Kaldoun (FR)-Quiche (Formidable (USA)) $1532a^{4}$ $1881a^{7}$ $2815a^{4}$ $3508a^{11}$ **>98f<**
Symonds Inn 3 ch c In The Wings-Shining Eyes (USA) (Mr Prospector (USA)) (1173) 1769^{7} **>109f<**
Szarlatan (POL) 5 $4127a^{8}$ **>86f<**

T

Taalluf (USA) 2 b f Hansel (USA)-Tatwij (USA) (Topsider (USA)) 1306^{3} 2875^{2} 4462^{2} 4873^{5} **>78f<**
Ta Aruf (USA) 2 ch f A P Indy (USA)-Mashaarif (USA) (Mr Prospector (USA)) 4715^{2} 4952^{4} **>79+f<**
Tabasco (IRE) 2 b f Salse (USA)-El Taranda (Ela-Mana-Mou) 4425^{7} 4789^{5} **>70f<**
Tabasco Jazz 3 b f Salse (USA)-Melody Park (Music Boy) 485^{3} 784^{5} 945^{2} 1245^{8} 1458^{12} 1810^{8} 2554^{18} 2705^{4} 2945^{6} 3299^{10} 3558^{3} 4243^{4} 4504^{16} 4632^{6} 4817^{8} **>54f<**
Taberann (IRE) 3 b c Doyoun-Tabessa (USA) (Shahrastani (USA)) (4705) **>85+f<**
Tablets of Stone (IRE) 4 b g Contract Law (USA)-Remember Mulvilla (Ballad Rock) **1996:** 5136^{8} **>46a 54f<**
Taborite (USA) 3 gr g Gulch (USA)-Ziska (USA) (Danzig (USA)) 3977^{9} 4407^{5} 4736^{7} **>70f<**
Tachycardia 5 ch m Weldnaas (USA)-Gold Ducat (Young Generation) **1996:** 5096^{4} 5188^{7} **1997:** 11^{8} 24^{9} 107^{4} (159) (172) 263^{8} 339^{3} 569^{12} 756^{7} 1009^{12} 1509^{7} 2115^{5} 2321^{4} 2665^{4} 3292^{2} 3637^{5} 4248^{12} **>47a 45f<**
Tadeo 4 ch g Primo Dominie-Royal Passion (Ahonoora) 1034^{9} 1303^{2} $1910a^{5}$ 2211^{12} 2675^{12} (2872) 3065^{3} 3217^{8} 3410^{4} (3604) 3975^{13} 4100^{7} 4282^{24} (4457) 4756^{10} 4887^{11} **>101f<**
Tadwiga 2 b f Fairy King (USA)-Euromill (Shirley Heights) 1240^{3} 1783^{2} (2439a) 4106^{2} 4267^{9} 4786^{2} **>97f<**
Tael of Silver 5 b m Today and Tomorrow-Schula (Kala Shikari) **1996:** 5165^{2} 5175^{10} **1997:** 3105^{12} 3465^{16} 3854^{8} 4291^{5} 4448^{2} 4480^{12} 4695^{5} 4951^{11} 4992^{2} **>40a 54f<**
Taffs Well 4 b g Dowsing (USA)-Zahiah (So Blessed) 970^{7} 2580^{2} 3202^{4} 4219^{2} 4561^{14} 4878^{3} **>82f<**
Tagatay 4 b g Nomination-Salala (Connaught) **1996:** 5136^{7} **1997:** 493^{9} 595^{17} 898^{9} **>26a 47f<**
Tagula (IRE) 4 b c Taufan (USA)-Twin Island (IRE) (Standaan (FR)) **1996:** $5218a^{4}$ **>120f<**
Tahara (IRE) 3 ch f Caerleon (USA)-Tarwiya (IRE) (Dominion) 2838^{7} 3550^{5} **>51f<**
Taiki Blizzard (USA) 6 b h Seattle Slew (USA)-Tree of Knowledge (Sassafras (FR)) $5066a^{6}$ **>96a 125f<**
Taiki Fortune (USA) 4 **1996:** $5159a^{6}$ **>128f<**
Tailwind 3 ch c Clantime-Casbar Lady (Native Bazaar) 1141^{13} (1451) 1691^{7} 2206^{3} 2605^{3} 2833^{14} **>63a 61f<**
Taipan (IRE) 5 b h Last Tycoon-Alidiva (Chief Singer) $1542a^{3}$ $2100a^{3}$ 2559^{3} (4000a) (4537a) $4866a^{4}$ **>126?f<**
Tajar (USA) 5 b g Slew O' Gold (USA)-Mashaarif (USA) (Mr Prospector (USA)) 40^{12} 496^{5} 526^{14} 843^{7} (3015) 3267^{2} 3907^{7} 4179^{3} 4335^{4} 4584^{11} 4874^{17} **>51f<**
Tajasur (IRE) 2 ch c Imperial Frontier (USA)-Safiya (USA) (Riverman (USA)) (2343) **>79+f<**
Tajawall (USA) 5 b h Dixieland Band (USA)-Conjinx $1550a^{3}$ $4531a^{8}$ **>110f<**
Tajawuz 2 ch f Kris-Na-Ayim (IRE) (Shirley Heights) 4567^{4} 4841^{4} **>75f<**
Taj Mahal (IRE) 2 b c High Estate-Verthumna (Indian King (USA)) 4840^{12} **>38f<**
Tajmil (IRE) 2 ch f Wolfhound (USA)-Nouvelle Star (AUS) (Luskin Star (AUS)) 1564^{3} 1927^{4} 4103^{7} 4694^{4} 4898^{10} **>72f<**
Tajrebah (USA) 3 b f Dayjur (USA)-Petrava (NZ) (Imposing (AUS)) 584^{4} 778^{3} 1245^{12} 1439^{5} (1966) 2149^{5} 3448^{7} **>74f<**
Takarian (IRE) 2 b c Doyoun-Takarouna (USA) (Green Dancer (USA)) $4357a^{6}$ $5002a^{3}$ **>103f<**
Take (ITY) 3 f **1996:** $5263a^{2}$
Take A Risk 2 ch f Risk Me (FR)-Hinari Televideo (Caerleon (USA)) 3857^{5} 4012^{17} (4159) 4566^{8} 4737^{4} **>61f<**
Take A Turn 2 br c Forzando-Honeychurch (USA) (Bering) 1932^{3} $2439a^{8}$ 2473^{2} 2684^{2} 2862^{19} 3113^{5} 3474^{5} (3904) 4265^{10} 4670^{15} 4849^{9} **>79f<**
Take Notice 4 b c Warning-Metair (Laser Light) 435^{20} 608^{14} 827^{19} 924^{10} 953^{13} 1128^{16} 1603^{8} **>40f<**
Takhlid (USA) 6 b h Nureyev (USA)-Savonnerie (USA) (Irish River (FR)) 208^{4} 318^{8} (386) 429^{7} (870) 1048^{4} 1495^{8} 1663^{2} 1837^{3} 1979^{5} 2302^{6} 2708^{7} 3476^{9} 3584^{8} 3810^{6} (4301) 4482^{12} 4842^{18} 5049^{8} **>79a 67f<**
Takkatamm (USA) 5 ch h Forty Niner (USA)-Relasure (USA) (Relaunch (USA)) $308a^{5}$ **>108f<**
Taklif (IRE) 5 b g Sadler's Wells (USA)-Porphyrine (FR) (Habitat) $4620a^{20}$ **>79f<**
Talaheart 2 b f Alnasr Alwasheek-Spring In Rome (USA) (Forli (ARG)) 750^{6} 1213^{6} 2304^{5} 3076^{6}

>42f<
Talented Ting (IRE) **8** ch g Hatim (USA)-An Tig Gaelige (Thatch (USA)) 1472[16] 2205[14] 2854[10] 3223[F] **>50da 31f<**
Tales of Bounty (IRE) **2** b g Ela-Mana-Mou-Tales of Wisdom (Rousillon (USA)) 4318[9] **>60f<**
Tales Of Hearsay (GER) **7** gr g Celestial Storm (USA)-Trying Girl (Try My Best (USA)) 763[17] **>26f<**
Talib (USA) **3** b c Silver Hawk (USA)-Dance For Lucy (USA) (Dance Bid (USA)) 3211[4] 3478[8] 4243[9] **>65f<**
Talisman (IRE) **3** b g Silver Kite (USA)-Sports Post Lady (IRE) (M Double M (USA)) *145[5] 225[8] 292[3] 361[3] 456[4]* 642[9] 3592[11] **>60a 36f<**
Talk Back (IRE) **5** br g Bob Back (USA)-Summit Talk (Head for Heights) 538[12] 769[9] 3091[17] **>53f<**
Tallulah Belle **4** b f Crowning Honors (CAN)-Fine a Leau (USA) (Youth (USA)) *28[3] (83) 141[3] 176[8] (305) 369[5] 405[3] 457[3] 566[6]* 689[5] (796) 887[8] *2672[7]* 3153[13] *3609[4]* 3793[10] 3970[5] 4108[3] (4323) 4449[2] 4635[8] (4926) **>72a 74f<**
Tal-Y-Llyn (IRE) **3** ch c Common Grounds-Welsh Fantasy (Welsh Pageant) 930[10] (1264) 1973[6] 2325[16] 2645[9] 4059[17] 4741[14] **>45f<**
Tamandu **7** b m Petoski-Gohar (USA) (Barachois (CAN)) *93[3] 183[10]* **>38a 18f<**
Tamarisk (IRE) **2** b c Green Desert (USA)-Sine Labe (USA) (Vaguely Noble) (3219) (4105) (4474) 4784[2] **>111f<**
Tamarpour (USA) **10** b g Sir Ivor-Tarsila (High Top) 2014[4] **>73f<**
Tamayaz (CAN) **5** b h Gone West (USA)-Minstrelsy (USA) (The Minstrel (CAN)) *408a[2] (627a)* 1554a[6] 3409[6] **>124a 124f<**
Tamburello (IRE) **2** b f Roi Danzig (USA)-Peach Melba (So Blessed) *2604[7]* 3306[19] 4418[4] **>31a 44f<**
Tamerin Bay **2** b c Lugana Beach-Quenlyn (Welsh Pageant) 1251[2] (1797) 2243[9] 2697[9] 2942[8] 3288[4] **>69f<**
Tamhid (USA) **4** b c Gulch (USA)-Futuh (USA) (Diesis) *438a[2] 627a[9]* **>110a 107f<**
Tam O'Shanter **3** gr g Persian Bold-No More Rosies (Warpath) 983[10] 1230[9] 2046[14] 2474[2] *2910[10]* **>23a 64f<**
Tamure (IRE) **5** b h Sadler's Wells (USA)-Three Tails (Blakeney) 852[4] 1359a[3] 2270a[5] 4258a[5] 4863a[2] 5051[2] **>119f<**
Tanaasa (IRE) **3** b c Sadler's Wells (USA)-Mesmerize (Mill Reef (USA)) (841) 1103[2] **>98f<**
Tancred Mischief **6** b m Northern State (USA)-Mischievous Miss (Niniski (USA)) 493[3] (669) 865[6] 1605[5] (2000) 2350[4] 2413[2] 2737[8] **>48f<**
Tancred Times **2** ch f Clantime-Mischievous Miss (Niniski (USA)) 1829[11] (2016) 2288[W] (2936) 3932[3] 4097[18] 4285[8] 4427[5] **>68f<**
Tangerine Flyer **2** ch g Presidium-Factuelle (Known Fact (USA)) *1577[2]* 1797[2] 2037[6] 2538[7] 3821[6] *4479[7]* **>68a 72f<**
Tango King **3** b c Suave Dancer (USA)-Be My Queen (Be My Guest (USA)) 537[2] (1094) 1649[4] 2963[8] 3549[10] **>79f<**
Tango Man (IRE) **5** ch g King Luthier-Amour Libre (He Loves Me) *83[8] 98[6] 139[9]* **>31a f<**
Tangshan (CAN) **3** ch f Zilzal (USA)-Manzanares (USA) (Sir Ivor) 1168[5] 1567[2] 2645[6] (2897) 3445[4] 4788[14] **>81f<**
Tanimbar (IRE) **2** b g Persian Bold-Try My Rosie (Try My Best (USA)) 4884[16] 5042[16] **>49f<**
Taniyar (FR) **5** b g Glenstal (USA)-Taeesha (Mill Reef (USA)) **1996:** *5102[2] 5242[7] 5259[6]* **1997:** *2[3] 37[6] 202[9] 312[5]* 461[11] 4287[13] 4360[5] **>42da 47f<**
Tankersley **2** ch c Timeless Times (USA)-Busted Love (Busted) 5040[8] **>54f<**
Taoiste **4** ch c Kris-Tenue de Soiree (USA) (Lyphard (USA)) 540[8] 839[8] 1303[4] 1608[10] 2211[11] 2769[3] 3198[7] 3914[9] **>84f<**
Taome (IRE) **3** b f Roi Danzig (USA)-Blue Bell Lady (Dunphy) *62[6] 94[3] 130[3] 240[5] 300[6]* **>37a 66f<**
Tappeto **5** b g Liboi (USA)-Persian Carpet (FR) (Kalamoun) 1022[2] 1169[8] (2391) 2944[3] 3498[3] 3815[6] 4108[6] 4751[11] **>80df<**
Taragona **4** b f Handsome Sailor-Queen of Aragon (Aragon) 1834[3] 2209[5] 3378[4] 3822[12] *4300[12] 4480[11]* **>22a 46f<**
Tarascon (IRE) **2** b f Tirol-Breyani (Commanche Run) 3534a[5] (4093a) **>106f<**
Tarashaan **2** b g Darshaan-Tarasova (USA) (Green Forest (USA)) 2688[7] 2881[5] 3117[6] 4116[19] (4334) **>74f<**
Tarator (USA) **4** ch c Green Dancer (USA)-Happy Gal (FR) (Habitat) 923a[4] **>122f<**
Tarian (USA) **5** b g Lyphard (USA)-Chain Fern (USA) (Blushing Groom (FR)) 2228[W] **>56f<**
Tarictic (GER) **3** 1544a[13] **>89f<**
Tarradale **3** br g Interrex (CAN)-Encore L'Amour (USA) (Monteverdi) 1023[6] 1221[7] 1496[10] 2130[7] 2313[16] 3813[6] 4164[5] 4472[5] 4847[14] **>43f<**
Tarry **4** b f Salse (USA)-Waitingformargaret (Kris) (3792) 4222[12] (4519) 4971[2] 5027[6] **>64f<**
Tarski **3** ch c Polish Precedent (USA)-Illusory (Kings Lake (USA)) 3713[2] 3988[5] **>99f<**
Tart (FR) **4** br f Warning-Sharp Girl (FR) (Sharpman) **1996:** *5171[2]* **1997:** *23[6] 182[9] 346[4]* 1606[9] 1845[10] 2331[9] 2582[3] 3134[9] 3495[5] 3767[8] 3970[6] (4415) 4584[4] *4800[3]* 4971[23] **>67a 52f<**
Tart and a Half **5** b m Distant Relative-Vaigrant Wind (Vaigly Great) **1996:** *5105[12] 5150[13]* **1997:** 1468[12] 1828[7] 2061[3] 2497[6] 2895[4] 3334[4] 3625[14] 3771[7] 4370[11] 4518[11] **>28a 61f<**
Tartan Lass **2** b f Selkirk (USA)-Gwiffina (Welsh Saint) 4758[12] 4973[9] **>61f<**
Tartan Party **3** gr c Environment Friend-Northern Scene (Habitat) 878[11] 1140[13] 1272[13] 1636[18] **>41a 49f<**
Tarxien **3** b g Kendor (FR)-Tanz (IRE) (Sadler's Wells (USA)) 1477[10] 1866[11] 2420[6] 2879[2] 3467[2] (3568) (3931) 3974[6] 4234[3] 4699[4] 4919[2] **>75f<**
Tashannah **4** b f Sizzling Melody-Liu Liu San (IRE) (Bairn (USA)) 1967[11] 2575[7] **>15f<**
Tashiriya (IRE) **3** gr f Kenmare (FR)-Tashtiya (Shergar) 921a[2] 1918a[5] **>101f<**
Tashkent **5** b g Thowra (FR)-Royal Bat (Crowned Prince (USA)) 4070[6] 4221[17] 4606[12] **>61f<**
Tasik Chini (USA) **3** b br g St Jovite (USA)-Ten Hail Marys (USA) (Halo (USA)) (478) 837[7] 1387[6] 1805[5] 2182[9] 3080[6] 3714[11] 4275[11] 4336[6] **>59f<**
Tassili (IRE) **4** b g Old Vic-Topsy (Habitat) 1682[4] 2117[7] 2906[15] **>71f<**
Taste of Success **2** b c Thatching-Tastiera (USA) (Diesis) 2181[13] 2720[4] **>65f<**
Taswib (USA) **4** gr g Housebuster (USA)-Umbrella Rig (USA) (Jig Time (USA)) 559[6] 944[11] **>65f<**
Tatika **7** ch g Tate Gallery (USA)-Independentia (Home Guard (USA)) **1996:** *(5182)* **1997:** *(363)* 468[15] *661[8]* 1878[6] **>90a 76f<**
Tattinger **2** b f Prince Sabo-Tight (Lochnager) 3686[7] 4103[3] **>84f<**
Taufan Boy **4** b c Taufan (USA)-Lydia Maria (Dancing Brave (USA)) 1592[5] 1974[7] 2316[8] 4104[4] 4562[4] 4771[3] **>80a 73df<**
Taufan's Melody **6** b g Taufan (USA)-Glorious Fate (Northfields (USA)) 1108[2] (1597) 2271a[2] 3705[15] 3902[4] 4443[2] 4894[4] (5051) **>120f<**
Taunt **3** b c Robellino (USA)-Minute Waltz (Sadler's Wells (USA)) 773[6] 1130[3] 1497[2] 2058[2] (2572) 4443[7] (4672) 5053[2] **>103+f<**
Taurean **2** b c Dilum (USA)-Herora (IRE) (Heraldiste (USA)) 3094[17] *3607[11]* 4167[16] **>31a 24f<**
Tauten (IRE) **7** br m Taufan (USA)-Pitaka (Pitskelly) *98[4] 147[14]* 1441[10] 1632[20] 4607[P] **>30a 32f<**
Taverner Society (IRE) **2** b c Imp Society (USA)-Straw Boater (Thatch (USA)) 3201[6] 3687[2] 4061[4] (4318) **>81f<**
Tawafek (USA) **4** br c Silver Hawk (USA)-Tippy Tippy Toe (USA) (Nureyev (USA)) *(9) 226[4]* 435[12] 680[6] 986[3] 1795[2] 2139[8] 2490[3] (2694) 2949[5] 3137[3] 3318[5] 4426[8] 4804[14] **>67a 73f<**
Tawafij (USA) **8** ch g Diesis-Dancing Brownie (USA) (Nijinsky (CAN)) 1761[16] **>75f<**
Tawny Artist **3** b f Pontevecchio Notte-Artistic Peace (Prince of Peace) 4579[13] **>16f<**
Taxi de Nuit (USA) **5** dk h Runaway Groom (CAN)-Mot d'Amour 1200a[3] 4660a[4] **>119f<**
Taylor's Pride **2** b f Nordico (USA)-Jendor (Condorcet (FR)) 1819[11] 3426[6] 4212[8] **>40f<**
Tayovullin (IRE) **3** ch f Shalford (IRE)-Fifth Quarter (Cure The Blues (USA)) *395[4] (547) 590[3]* 1373[2] 1505[7] 2369[14] 2945[4] 3393[8] *4591[12]* **>69a 68f<**
Tayseer (USA) **3** ch c Sheikh Albadou-Millfit (USA) (Blushing Groom (FR)) (1170) 2023[8] 2334[5] 2598[4] **>106f<**
Tazibari **3** b f Barrys Gamble-Jersey Maid (On Your Mark) 1995[11] 2415[13] 2715[5] 2903[8] **>51f<**
Tazkiya **2** ch f King's Signet (USA)-Irene's Charter (Persian Bold) 4067[12] **>56f<**
Te Amo (IRE) **5** b h Waajib-Avebury Ring (Auction Ring (USA)) *76[10]* **>44a 68f<**
Tea Party (USA) **4** b f Night Shift (USA)-Meringue Pie (USA) (Silent Screen (USA)) **1996:** 5192a[10] **1997:** *52[8] 179[7] 305[5] 358[11]* 554[5] 892[14] 1166[7] 1439[8] *(1580)* (2119) 2390[3] 3982[15] 4155[25] *4570[7]* **>70a 68f<**
Teapot Row (IRE) **2** b c Generous (IRE)-Secrage (USA) (Secreto (USA)) (3235) 3644[4] (4096) (4440) **>107f<**
Tearaway **2** gr c Efisio-Hoosie (Niniski (USA)) 2324[3] 2898[3] 3282[3] 3802[9] 4265[2] 4690[6] **>74f<**
Tear White (IRE) **3** b g Mac's Imp (USA)-Exemplary (Sovereign Lord) **1996:** *5224[10]* **1997:** *25[3] 142[2] 221[4]* 783[6] 876[5] *1151[8]* 1509[3] (1644) 1989[2] 2220[9] 2581[4] 2964[4] 3082[7] (3194) 4137[9] 4370[12] 4452[6] **>68a 75f<**
Technical Move (IRE) **6** br m Move Off-Technical Merit (Gala Performance (USA)) 4045[13]
Technician (IRE) **2** ch g Archway (IRE)-How It Works (Commanche Run) 2181[12] 2467[8] 2917[16] **>52f<**
Technicolour (IRE) **3** b f Rainbow Quest (USA)-Grecian Urn (Ela-Mana-Mou) 2764[5] **>81f<**
Tedburrow **5** b g Dowsing (USA)-Gwiffina (Welsh Saint) (1402) (1948) 2056[10] 2526[6] (2683) 3747[6] 4011[5] 4282[13] (4444) 4677[10] **>118f<**
Teddy's Bow (IRE) **3** b br f Archway (IRE)-Gale Force Seven (Strong Gale) 4214[15] **>51f<**
Tedross **6** b br h Ardross-Town Fair (Town Crier) 1809[15] 2008[20] 2116[5] **>36f<**
Tee-Emm **7** b g Lidhame-Tower Glades (Tower Walk) 879[4] 1236[4] 1667[5] **>55a 42f<**
Teejay'n'aitch (IRE) **5** b g Maelstrom Lake-Middle Verde (USA) (Sham (USA)) 608[9] 1281[4] 2564[11] 4160[11] **>35f<**
Teepee (IRE) **2** b f Indian Ridge-Princess of Zurich (IRE) (Law Society (USA)) 2409[4] 3411[9] 3859[8] **>40a 56f<**
Tee Tee Too (IRE) **5** ch g Hatim (USA)-Scottish Welcome (Be My Guest (USA)) *5[6]* **>61?a 31f<**

Teishebaini (IRE) **2** ch c Hamas (IRE)-Tea House (Sassafras (FR)) 4253a[2] **>96?f<**
Telalanjon **2** b c Tirol-Akkazao (IRE) (Alzao (USA)) 4914[6] 5048[7] **>79f<**
Telemania (IRE) **3** b f Mujtahid (USA)-African Dance (USA) (El Gran Senor (USA)) 688[6] 2331[5] 2877[7] 3115[5] 3548[2] 3894[6] 4375[3] **>89f<**
Telephus **8** b g Efisio-Mrs Bizz (Status Seeker) 3560[5] 4224[14] **>22a 17f<**
Tellion **3** b g Mystiko (USA)-Salchow (Niniski (USA)) 1090[4] *1430[4]* 1646[6] *2052[5]* 2521[4] 2725[3] *4811[10]* **>71a 73f<**
Telloff **3** b f Reprimand-La Primavera (Northfields (USA)) 3030[6] 3299[9] **>58f<**
Temeraire (USA) **2** b c Dayjur (USA)-Key Dancer (USA) (Nijinsky (CAN)) 5041[9] **>65f<**
Teme Valley **3** br c Polish Precedent (USA)-Sudeley (Dancing Brave (USA)) 3909[2] 4072[2] 4322[3] **>79f<**
Temper Lad (USA) **2** b c Riverman (USA)-Dokki (USA) (Northern Dancer) 1933[13] **>47f<**
Tempting Prospect **3** b f Shirley Heights-Trying for Gold (USA) (Northern Baby (CAN)) 1209[2] 2053[6] 4445[5] 5035a[3] **>103f<**
Temptress **4** br f Kalaglow-Circe (Main Reef) 762[12] 962[4] 1145[3] 1157[4] 1398[5] 1981[3] 2122[8] 2483[8] 4063[11] 4751[17] 4971[12] **>66f<**
Tempus Fugit **2** ch f Timeless Times (USA)-Kabella (Kabour) 1564[12] (2037) 2370[2] 2648[2] 2931[3] 4737[6] 4897[14] **>84f<**
Temujin **2** ch c Presidium-Too Familiar (Oats) 1480[11] **>10f<**
Ten Bob (IRE) **2** br c Bob Back (USA)-Tiempo (King of Spain) 4852[6] (5025) **>91+f<**
Tenbyssimo (IRE) **2** b c Tenby-Wish You Were Here (USA) (Secretariat (USA)) 4255a[3] **>95f<**
Tender Doll (IRE) **2** b f Don't Forget Me-Mistress Vyne (Prince Tenderfoot (USA)) 2425[4] 2664[4] *3045[5]* 3451[13] **>21a 50f<**
Tennessee (SWI) **2** b c Homme de Loi (IRE)-Tocaima (SWI) (Nebos (GER)) 4538a[3] **>73f<**
Tennyson Bay **5** b g Allazzaz-Richards Folly (Hotfoot) *43[12]* **>27f<**
Ten Past Six **5** ch g Kris-Tashinsky (USA) (Nijinsky (CAN)) 550[6] 635[5] (843) 955[9] 1266[9] **>65f<**
Tensile (IRE) **2** b c Tenby-Bonnie Isle (Pitcairn) 2562[7] 3386[4] 3789[2] 4116[15] 4778[13] **>75f<**
Tenuous **3** b f Generous (IRE)-Atropa (USA) (Vaguely Noble) 2275a[2] (3552a) 4666a[9] **>108f<**
Teofilio (IRE) **3** ch c Night Shift (USA)-Rivoltade (USA) (Sir Ivor) (795) 1032[3] 1658[11] 2013[7] **>99f<**
Teraab **3** b g Primo Dominie-Valika (Valiyar) 518[9] **>37f<**
Terdad (USA) **4** ch g Lomond (USA)-Istiska (FR) (Irish River (FR)) *373[3]* 463[2] 633[10] 866[13] 1097[17] 1388[4] 1631[5] 2019[3] 2152[2] (2353) 2416[4] 4926[5] **>63a 70f<**
Tereyna **2** gr f Terimon-Lareyna (Welsh Pageant) 4914[7] **>70f<**
Termon **4** b f Puissance-Alipura (Anfield) 496[7] 929[9] 1315[4] 1613[7] 2144[5] 2385[6] 2543[9] 3487[6] 3854[5] 4510[14] 4843[13] **>34f<**
Teroom **2** br c Mtoto-Ballad Opera (Sadler's Wells (USA)) 4853[5] **>67+f<**
Territory (IRE) **2** b c Common Grounds-Chouette (Try My Best (USA)) 4446[3] 4630[2] 4772[3] **>83f<**
Terry's Rose **3** br f Nomination-Moharabuiee (Pas de Seul) **1996:** *5239[2]* **1997:** *181[5]* *246[4]* *317[5]* 556[2] 757[2] 882[3] *1428[9]* 1998[10] 2203[9] 2941[7] 3266[8] 4168[12] 4431[6] **>43a 29f<**
Tertium (IRE) **5** b g Nordico (USA)-Nouniya (Vayrann) 824[8] 947[6] 1097[8] 1450[6] 1652[2] 1768[7] 2026[13] 2325[2] 2708[6] 3052[2] 3150[8] 3408[2] 3752[4] 4121[9] 4283[17] 4561[12] 4792[11] **>87f<**
Tessajoe **5** ch g Clantime-Busted Love (Busted) 781[3] 1036[6] (1628) (2015) 2514[8] (2889) 3333[2] 3722[11] (4288) 4891[12] **>94f<**
Test The Water (IRE) **3** ch c Maelstrom Lake-Baliana (CAN) (Riverman (USA)) 723[6] 1017[11] 2332[5] 3894[3] 4283[14] 4680[11] **>85f<**
Tetris (IRE) **3** b f Nordico (USA)-Firefly Night (Salmon Leap (USA)) 1110[11] 1297[6] 2040[11] **>54f<**
Teulada (USA) **3** b br f Riverman (USA)-Triple Tipple (USA) (Raise A Cup (USA)) 2330[5] 2555[4] 3095[13] **>57f<**
Texas Cowgirl (IRE) **7** ch m Salt Dome (USA)-Cloven Dancer (USA) (Hurok (USA)) 1666[3] 2277[4] **>35a 58f<**
Texas Scramble **8** b g Norwick (USA)-Orange Parade (Dara Monarch) 4986[15] **>13f<**
Tezaab **3** gr g Petong-Very Nice (FR) (Green Dancer (USA)) 945[5] *1155[5]* *1430[9]* 2522[6] 2750[10] 2941[3] 3293[3] 3421[9] 3592[3] 4243[8] 4415[15] **>46a 57f<**
Thahabyah (USA) **3** b f Sheikh Albadou-Golden Cap (USA) (Hagley (USA)) 1256[12] **>75f<**
Thahib **3** b c Polish Precedent (USA)-Hamama (USA) (Majestic Light (USA)) 2940[7] 3317[12] **>53f<**
Thai Morning **4** gr c Petong-Bath (Runnett) **1996:** *(5079) (5120) 5204[5]* **1997:** *398[3]* 521[18] **>109a 59f<**
Thaleros **7** b g Green Desert (USA)-Graecia Magna (USA) (Private Account (USA)) 3937[11] 4161[14] *4571[9]* 4998[17] **>35a 46f<**
Thaljanah (IRE) **5** ch g In The Wings-Dawn is Breaking (Import) 442[10] 655[4] 1027[3] 1260[2] 1947[3] 2327[10] 2834[3] 3579[4] 4956[12] 5052[7] **>88df<**
Thames (FR) **6** b h Fabulous Dancer (USA)-Three Terns (USA) (Arctic Tern (USA)) 439a[3] 625a[5] **>117f<**
Thanksgiving (IRE) **2** ch f Indian Ridge-Thank One's Stars (Alzao (USA)) 2831[3] 3574[3] (3925) 4267[3] 4675[5] **>89f<**
Thanks Keith **2** ch g Risk Me (FR)-Nannie Annie (Persian Bold) 822[4] *1045[3]* *1577[8]* 4362[14] **>65a 62f<**
Thatcham Island **4** ch f Jupiter Island-Floreal (Formidable (USA)) 4060[16] *4300[6]* **>26a 39f<**
Thatched (IRE) **7** b g Thatching-Shadia (USA) (Naskra (USA)) 571[14] (824) 1495[9] 1862[7] 1994[4] 2205[4] 2465[8] 2760[9] 2906[4] 3105[5] 3264[4] 3622[12] 3759[7] 4510[11] 4847[9] 4924[4] 5023[8] **>51f<**
Thatchmaster (IRE) **6** b g Thatching-Key Maneuver (USA) (Key To Content (USA)) 1745[4] 1972[3] 2533[10] (3767) 4172[4] 4516[8] **>73f<**
That Man Again **5** ch g Prince Sabo-Milne's Way (The Noble Player (USA)) 726[4] 1034[4] 1766[12] 2111[2] 2529[2] 2675[6] 3410[17] 4183[3] 4365[11] 4512[5] **>73a 90df<**
That Old Feeling (IRE) **5** b g Waajib-Swift Reply (He Loves Me) 1448[6] *1576[4]* 1798[8] 2385[9] 3456[13] 3758[12] 4415[14] *4484[9]* **>46a 30f<**
That's The Way **2** b f Hamas (IRE)-That'll Be the Day (IRE) (Thatching) 2644a[2]
Theano (IRE) **4** b f Thatching-Akamantis (Kris) 1198a[3] 2079a[2] 2056[20] 2586[3] 3535a[6] 4344a[4] 4625a[7] **>109f<**
The Artful Dodger **2** b g Alhijaz-Madam Millie (Milford) 4167[12] 4458[8] **>53f<**
Theatre Magic **4** b g Sayf El Arab (USA)-Miss Orient (Damister (USA)) **1996:** *5165[3]* *5230[4]* **1997:** *589[6]* *(860)* 951[15] 1225[7] *(1433)* 2061[13] *2161[7]* 2418[6] *2603[4]* *3075[11]* 3143[15] **>74a 40f<**
Theatre of Dreams **2** b f Tragic Role (USA)-Impala Lass (Kampala) 460[3] 536[4] 648[2] (927) **>75f<**
Theatreworld (IRE) **5** b g Sadler's Wells (USA)-Chamonis (USA) (Affirmed (USA)) 4191a[4] 4620a[4] **>115f<**
The Barnsley Belle (IRE) **4** b f Distinctly North (USA)-La Tanque (USA) (Last Raise (USA)) **1996:** *5134[2]* *(5165)* *5215[7]* *5256[5]* **1997:** *85[3]* *(579)* *870[8]* 946[8] 2019[12] 2317[2] 2543[5] 2892[2] 3143[12] 5023[6] **>69a 48f<**
The Beat Rolls On (IRE) **2** b f Roi Danzig (USA)-Miss Pennine (IRE) (Pennine Walk) 536[12] (631) **>64f<**
The Black Dubh (IRE) **4** b g Classic Secret (USA)-Coral Cave (Ashmore (FR)) 570[12] 900[16] **>24f<**
The Blues Academy (IRE) **2** b c Royal Academy (USA)-She's the Tops (Shernazar) 4309[6] 4433[8] 4840[4] **>76f<**
The Boozing Brief (USA) **4** b g Turkoman (USA)-Evening Silk (USA) (Damascus (USA)) 721[17] 950[7] **>33a 63f<**
The Bower (IRE) **8** br g Don't Forget Me-Nyama (USA) (Pretense (USA)) 2441a[2] **>108f<**
The Boy John (USA) **2** b c Groovy (USA)-La Chaux (Welsh Saint) 684[2] 965[2] 1143[4] 3433[2] 3799[4] 3965[W] 4296[7] 4446[2] 4814[2] 4897[B] **>81f<**
The Butterwick Kid **4** ch g Interrex (CAN)-Ville Air (Town Crier) (762) 888[2] (1036) (1281) 1515[2] 1992[6] 4279[9] 4956[8] 5027[4] **>66f<**
The Cannie Rover **2** ch c Beveled (USA)-Sister Rosarii (USA) (Properantes (USA)) 1120[5] 1510[10] 2022[4] 2904[13] 3307[15] 3990[13] 4285[16] 4588[8] **>49f<**
Thecomebackking **2** ch c Mystiko (USA)-Nitouche (Scottish Reel) 648[9] 3707[16] 3927[8] 4208[6] 4576[4] 4806[12] *4984[5]* **>35a 55f<**
The Deejay (IRE) **3** ch g Desse Zenny (USA)-White Jasmin (Jalmood (USA)) 431[3] 764[8] 3714[10] **>73f<**
The Dilettanti (USA) **4** br c Red Ransom (USA)-Rich Thought (USA) (Rich Cream (USA)) 787[4] (939) 1768[12] 2729[3] 4558[17] 4754[14] **>98f<**
The Downtown Fox **2** br c Primo Dominie-Sara Sprint (Formidable (USA)) 3219[6] 3726[3] 4458[5] 4755[2] 4955[3] **>79f<**
The Druidess (IRE) **2** b f Distinctly North (USA)-Moody Lover (Jalmood (USA)) 1593[9] 4216[10] 4459[7] 4753[29] *5017[6]* **>24a 47f<**
The Dubious Goose **3** b g Yaheeb (USA)-Dunnington (Risk Me (FR)) 3336[11] 3868[4] 4164[11] **>47f<**
The Executor **7** ch g Vaigly Great-Fee (Mandamus) 1622[4] 2117[3] 2374[2] 2722[5] *3041[3]* (3469) 3767[5] 4114[2] **>61a 68f<**
The Faraway Tree **3** b f Suave Dancer (USA)-Sassalya (Sassafras (FR)) 1875[7] 3017[5] 3492[3] 3727[2] 4099[2] (4412) 4559[5] **>111f<**
The Fed **7** ch g Clantime-Hyde Princess (Touch Paper) 3871[7] 4249[12] **>22a 36f<**
The Fly **3** gr c Pharly (FR)-Nelly Do Da (Derring-Do) (1146) 1769[5] 2454a[9] 4149[3] 4549[3] **>123f<**
The Flying Phantom **6** gr g Sharrood (USA)-Miss Flossa (FR) (Big John (FR)) 1027[7] 3318[4] 4783[31] **>77f<**
The Four Isles **3** b g Never so Bold-Far Claim (USA) (Far North (CAN)) 3248[18] **>39f<**
The Frisky Farmer **4** b g Emarati (USA)-Farceuse (Comedy Star (USA)) **1996:** *5163[15]* *5209[4]* **1997:** *59[3]* *109[5]* *117[7]* *184[3]* *263[11]* 774[4] 1220[4] 1509[4] 1620[13] 1965[9] 2575[4] 2939[5] (3590) 4328[6] **>56a 64f<**
The Fuelologist **2** b g Skyliner-Munequita (Marching On) 3239[12] *3586[13]* 4211[15] **>5a 57f<**
The Fugative **4** b f Nicholas (USA)-Miss Runaway (Runnett) **1996:** *5122[7]* *5242[14]* **1997:** *31[7]* 1237[7] 1479[2] 1848[8] (2220) (2277) (2581) 2703[5] 2841[5]

3280^{7} 3580^{8} 4370^{15} 4452^{7} *4913^{12}* **>56a 68f<**
The Fullbangladesh **4** ch f Hubbly Bubbly (USA)-Oakhurst (Mandrake Major) *284^{12}* **>37a 40f<**
The Gay Fox **3** b gr c Never so Bold-School Concert (Music Boy) 453^{6} 636^{4} (1000) 1170^{11} 1609^{9} 1977^{4} (2298) 2560^{8} (2655) 3217^{21} 3649^{12} 3975^{4} 4280^{15} 4756^{2} **>93f<**
The Gene Genie **2** b c Syrtos-Sally Maxwell (Roscoe Blake) 3386^{2} 4433^{2} 4803^{4} 4977^{4} **>87f<**
The Glow-Worm (IRE) **2** b c Doyoun-Shakanda (IRE) (Shernazar) (2336) 2707^{3} 3688^{6} 4116^{3} (4778) **>89f<**
The Great Flood **4** ch g Risk Me (FR)-Yukosan (Absalom) *(30) 133^{5}* **>65a 49?f<**
The Green Grey **3** gr g Environment Friend-Pea Green (Try My Best (USA)) 641^{5} 840^{17} 1474^{8} *2668^{13}* 2879^{7} 3850^{2} (4465) 4629^{8} **>41a 57f<**
The Grey Weaver **4** gr c Touch of Grey-Foggy Dew (Smoggy) **1996:** *5145^{P}* **>3f< (DEAD)**
The Groveller **2** b c Prince Sabo-Estonia (Kings Lake (USA)) 1749^{4} 2037^{4} 2477^{4} 2786^{3} 2943^{10} *(3607)* 3899^{3} 3932^{11} **>81a 81f<**
The Happy Fox (IRE) **5** ch g Ballad Rock-Amanzi (African Sky) **1996:** *5236^{3}* **1997:** *(301) (397)* 596^{5} 731^{6} *1578^{4}* 1662^{7} *(2162)* 2567^{4} 3024^{4} 3208^{7} 3273^{8} 3566^{2} 3761^{17} 4137^{4} 4456^{16} *4797^{6}* **>90a 70f<**
The Hobby Lobby (IRE) **2** b g Shalford (IRE)-Chepstow House (USA) (Northern Baby (CAN)) 530^{6} *592^{7}* 1370^{4} 1856^{5} 3090^{5} 3324^{7} 3782^{4} 3967^{10} **>37a 68f<**
The Honorable Lady **2** b f Mystiko (USA)-Mrs Thatcher (Law Society (USA)) 1293^{9} 1461^{2} 1812^{12} 2153^{3} (2923) 3186^{10} 4285^{9} 4427^{3} 4605^{7} 4856^{12} **>67f<**
The Imposter (IRE) **2** ch c Imp Society (USA)-Phoenix Dancer (IRE) (Gorytus (USA)) 2378^{6} 2664^{3} 2784^{4} **>56f<**
The In-Laws (IRE) **3** ch f Be My Guest (USA)-Amboselli (Raga Navarro (ITY)) 2894^{6} 3119^{5} 4141^{3} 4383^{10} 4788^{3} **>88f<**
The Institute Boy **7** b g Fairy King (USA)-To Oneiro (Absalom) *95^{4} 107^{2} 159^{3} 170^{5} 214^{8}* **>70a 53f<**
The King Of Cloyne (USA) **2** b c Chief's Crown (USA)-Seattle Kaper (USA) (Seattle Slew (USA)) 3962a^{4} 4616a^{4} **>101f<**
The Lambton Worm **3** b c Superpower-Springwell (Miami Springs) 596^{9} 1021^{2} 1561^{5} 2044^{9} 2326^{4} 2472^{4} 3034^{15} 3987^{14} 4270^{15} **>71f<**
The Limping Cat (IRE) **2** b c Emarati (USA)-Little Madam (Habat) 2037^{5} (3031) 3708^{3} **>84f<**
Thelonius (IRE) **2** ch c Statoblest-Little Sega (FR) (Bellypha) 2959^{5} 3278^{18} 3818^{2} 3973^{5} 4315^{5} **>71f<**
The Magistrate (IRE) **2** br c Case Law-Bel Ria (Gay Fandango (USA)) 3783^{6} 4113^{5} 4361^{5} 4814^{4} **>77f<**
Theme Arena **4** b f Tragic Role (USA)-Sea Siesta (Vaigly Great) *86^{6}* (4609) (4744) 4879^{7} 5027^{8} **>48a 61f<**
Theme Tune **2** b f Dilum (USA)-Souadah (USA) (General Holme (USA)) 2700^{10} 3099^{2} 3985^{13} **>67f<**
The Munro's **3** b c Safawan-Some Cherry (Some Hand) 4290^{12} 4469^{7} 4705^{5} **>50f<**
The Negotiator **3** ch g Nebos (GER)-Baie des Anges (Pas de Seul) 518^{2} 790^{5} 1207^{12} 2036^{16} 2523^{4} 3029^{11} 3466^{4} 4988^{10} **>68df<**
The Noble Oak (IRE) **9** ch g The Noble Player (USA)-Sea Palace (Huntercombe) 1279^{15} **>45a 21f<**
Thenorthernplayboy (IRE) **4** gr g Distinctly North (USA)-Monetary Wish (Wishing Star) 2209^{6} **>35a 22f< (DEAD)**
The Oddfellow **4** b g Efisio-Agnes Jane (Sweet Monday) *2^{8} 91^{9}* **>12a 22f< (DEAD)**
The Orraman (IRE) **3** b g Taufan (USA)-Miss Pennine (IRE) (Pennine Walk) 2360^{6} 3401^{9} 3919^{18} **>15f<**
The Other Risk **2** b g Risk Me (FR)-First Fastnet (Ahonoora) 432^{14} 4470^{10} 4769^{13} **>20f<**
The Prince **3** b c Machiavellian (USA)-Mohican Girl (Dancing Brave (USA)) 683^{4} 963^{2} (1611) 1982^{5} 3725^{4} 4314^{6} **>93f<**
The Prussian Queen **2** b f Dilum (USA)-Dewberry (Bay Express) 1653^{10}
The Puzzler (IRE) **6** b or br g Sharpo-Enigma (Ahonoora) 980^{7} 2861^{13} 3975^{10} 4100^{15} (4756) 4881^{12} 5054^{9} **>105f<**
The Real McCoy **3** b g Deploy-Mukhayyalah (Dancing Brave (USA)) 3029^{14} **>17f<**
There Be Demons (USA) **2** b c Devil's Bag (USA)-Krisalya (Kris) 4950^{6} **>75f<**
Therhea (IRE) **4** b g Pennine Walk-Arab Art (Artaius (USA)) 444^{12} 832^{13} 1111^{7} 1244^{7} 1442^{6} 1878^{2} (2036) 2346^{2} 2485^{2} 2678^{2} 3496^{4} (3976) 4297^{7} 4441^{4} 4781^{16} **>87f<**
The Rich Man (IRE) **2** b c Last Tycoon-Diavolina (USA) (Lear Fan (USA)) 1274^{3} 1924^{3} 2176^{3} (2359) (2714) 3215^{7} **>86+f<**
The Robe **2** b f Robellino (USA)-Outward's Gal (Ashmore (FR)) 4604^{W} 4974^{4} 5048^{10} **>58f<**
The Roundsills **3** ch g Handsome Sailor-Eye Sight (Roscoe Blake) **1996:** *5087^{5}* **1997:** 1384^{15} 1804^{3} (2757) 3028^{9} 4275^{4} 4562^{13} **>41a 59f<**
The Stager (IRE) **5** b g Danehill (USA)-Wedgewood Blue (USA) (Sir Ivor) 4319^{13} 4606^{6} **>75f<**
The Thruster **2** b g Elmaamul (USA)-Moon Spin (Night Shift (USA)) 1396^{7} *2047^{6}* 3861^{8} 4380^{2} **>47a 62f<**
The Tig **3** b g Tigani-The Ranee (Royal Palace) 701^{7} 925^{13} **>52?f<**
The Vale (IRE) **5** b g Satco (FR)-Lady Kasbah (Lord Gayle (USA)) 2501^{8} 2902^{4} 3211^{10} 3631^{7} **>45?f<**
The Wad **4** b g Emarati (USA)-Fair Melys (FR) (Welsh Pageant) 698^{8} 823^{10} 977^{11} 1662^{3} 1977^{21} 2759^{8} 2899^{2} (2938) 3126^{U} 3481^{11} 3566^{3} 3816^{3} 4137^{12} 4233^{17} **>49a 64f<**
The West (USA) **3** ch c Gone West (USA)-Lady for Two (USA) (Storm Bird (CAN)) 737^{5} **>115f<**
The Wild Widow **3** gr f Saddlers' Hall (IRE)-No Cards (No Mercy) 4689^{2} **>86f<**
The Woodcock **2** b g Handsome Sailor-Game Germaine (Mummy's Game) 4564^{13} **>48f<**
Thewrightone (IRE) **3** b f Fayruz-Vote Barolo (Nebbiolo) **1996:** *5135^{11}* **1997:** *588^{9}* 1467^{16} 1864^{9} 2756^{6} **>22a 28f<**
The Wyandotte Inn **3** ch c Ballacashtal (CAN)-Carolynchristensen (Sweet Revenge) **1996:** *5162^{2} 5176^{3} 5224^{2} 5251^{2} (5275)* **1997:** *62^{4} 155^{2} (180) (307) 413^{2}* 483^{5} 634^{2} 794^{7} 1000^{14} 1807^{9} 2192^{4} *2303^{2} 3075^{10} 3397^{6}* **>85a 48f<**
Thick as Thieves **5** b g Shavian-Vivienda (Known Fact (USA)) *24^{2} 65^{2} 199^{8} 223^{3} 263^{7} 391^{4} 659^{6}* 779^{8} 1098^{8} 1236^{5} 1865^{4} 2934^{10} 3856^{14} **>50a 40f<**
Thief Of Hearts (IRE) **2** b c In The Wings-Love Smitten (CAN) (Key To The Mint (USA)) (4657a)
Think Again (IRE) **3** b g Long Pond-Either Or (Boreen (FR)) 495^{5} 773^{9} 825^{7} 1820^{8} 2017^{11} **>48f<**
Third Cousin (IRE) **2** b c Distant Relative-Queen Caroline (USA) (Chief's Crown (USA)) 3783^{13} *4569^{3}* (4818) 4989^{4} **>81a 82f<**
Third Party **3** gr f Terimon-Party Game (Red Alert) 768^{6} 1083^{13} (1638) 1989^{4} 2244^{13} 3417^{11} 3590^{6} 4168^{4} 4333^{4} **>57f<**
Thisonesforalice **9** b g Lochnager-Bamdoro (Cavo Doro) 2145^{5} 2342^{6} 2716^{3} 3221^{4} 3401^{2} 3700^{3} **>45f<**
Thistle Park **2** ch g Selkirk (USA)-Kimberley Park (Try My Best (USA)) 3239^{3} 3905^{3} 4236^{8} **>73f<**
Thomas O'Malley **2** ch c Wing Park-Martini Time (Ardoon) 2781^{10} 4145^{11} 4379^{8} *4593^{8}* **>29a 56f<**
Thordis **4** b g Mazilier (USA)-Doppio (Dublin Taxi) **1996:** *5249^{10}* **1997:** *1786^{7} 2366^{2} 2915^{6} 3583^{2} (4574)* **>73a 82f<**
Thornby Park **3** b f Unfuwain (USA)-Wantage Park (Pas de Seul) 841^{4} 1270^{2} (2284) 2423^{2} 3218^{4} 3763^{4} 4426^{9} 4673^{5} 4774^{6} **>91f<**
Thorniwama **6** b m Hadeer-Hidden Asset (Hello Gorgeous (USA)) *116^{11} 160^{9}* **>21a 20f<**
Thorntoun Belle (IRE) **2** b f Rainbows For Life (CAN)-Manzala (USA) (Irish River (FR)) 2110^{6} **>51f<**
Thorntoun Estate (IRE) **4** b g Durgam (USA)-Furry Friend (USA) (Bold Bidder) *99^{5} 139^{2}* 493^{6} 613^{11} 865^{4} **>64a 38f<**
Thorntoun House (IRE) **4** b g Durgam (USA)-Commanche Song (Commanche Run) *256^{10}* 493^{7} **>35f<**
Thorntoun Jewel (IRE) **4** b f Durgam (USA)-Blue Bouquet (Cure The Blues (USA)) 2828^{14} 2937^{10} 3269^{7} **>32f<**
Thor's Phantom **4** ch g Weldnaas (USA)-La Carlotta (Ela-Mana-Mou) 1825^{20} **>38f<**
Thrashing **2** b c Kahyasi-White-Wash (Final Straw) 2562^{9} **>66f<**
Three Angels (IRE) **2** b c Houmayoun (FR)-Mullaghroe (Tarboosh (USA)) 2688^{6} 4815^{2} 5029^{3} **>66f<**
Three Arch Bridge **5** ch m Sayf El Arab (USA)-Alanood (Northfields (USA)) **1996:** *5165^{13} 5200^{8} 5241^{6} 5256^{4}* **1997:** *72^{4} 125^{2} (169) 194^{5} (245) 316^{9} 344^{4} 376^{7}* 468^{6} (529) 571^{11} 749^{9} 895^{8} 951^{10} (1116) (1495) 1606^{7} 1652^{4} **>76a 83f<**
Three Cheers (IRE) **3** b br g Slip Anchor-Three Tails (Blakeney) 558^{3} (1612) 2027^{2} (2596) (4658a) **>116f<**
Three For A Pound **3** b g Risk Me (FR)-Lompoa (Lomond (USA)) (469) 977^{9} 1496^{12} 1781^{6} *2069^{7}* (2415) 2735^{3} 3143^{6} 3573^{6} 4210^{5} 4308^{12} **>45a 71f<**
Threeplay (IRE) **3** b c Mac's Imp (USA)-Houwara (IRE) (Darshaan) **1996:** *5146^{5} 5176^{2} 5224^{6} 5245^{3}* **1997:** *221^{2} 379^{5} 427^{6}* 3898^{9} 4115^{15} **>64a 63f<**
Threesocks **4** ch f Weldnaas (USA)-Jeethgaya (USA) (Critique (USA)) *18^{3} 80^{4} 122^{4}* **>46da 62?f< (DEAD)**
Three Star Rated (IRE) **2** b f Pips Pride-Preponderance (IRE) (Cyrano de Bergerac) 664^{4} 3265^{2} 3821^{13} (4162) **>90+f<**
Three Tenners **2** b f Distinctly North (USA)-Hollia (Touch Boy) 1492^{9} 1860^{8} (2419) 2587^{4} 2936^{7} 3212^{4} 4152^{9} 4285^{6} **>68f<**
Three Weeks **4** ch g Formidable (USA)-Zilda (FR) (Zino) **1996:** *5110^{2} (5175) (5235)* **1997:** *34^{2} 82^{5} 140^{10} 369^{10}* 444^{22} 3328^{10} 3793^{12} *4050^{6}* 4371^{15} *4480^{7}* **>50a 29f<**
Thrilling Day **4** b f Groom Dancer (USA)-Pushoff (USA) (Sauce Boat (USA)) **1996:** 5156a^{9} **>112f<**
Thrower **6** b g Thowra (FR)-Atlantic Line (Capricorn Line) 553^{4} **>48a 50?f<**
Thumbellina **2** b f Robellino (USA)-Welwyn (Welsh Saint) 3288^{6} **>41f<**
Thunderheart **6** b g Celestial Storm (USA)-Lorelene (FR) (Lorenzaccio) 1840^{4} 2166^{5} (2825) 3309^{9} 3485^{6} 4160^{8} 4269^{12} **>54f<**
Thundering Papoose **2** b f Be My Chief (USA)-

Thunder Bug (USA) (Secreto (USA)) 1645[11] 3426[9] 4113[14] **>36f<**

Thwaab 5 b g Dominion-Velvet Habit (Habitat) 942[24] 1259[6] 1594[2] 1977[3] 2711[20] 3208[10] 3428[3] 3801[12] 4414[3] 4456[13] 4792[9] **>49a 73f<**

Thwing 2 b f Presidium-Swinging Baby (Swing Easy (USA)) *3586[7]* **>41a f<**

Tiaphena 6 b m Derrylin-Velda (Thatch (USA)) *660[4]* *1133[14]* **>52a 51f<**

Tiara 2 b f Risk Me (FR)-Dona Krista (King of Spain) 2781[5] 3136[9] 3686[22] **>47f<**

Tibbi Blues 10 b m Cure The Blues (USA)-Tiberty (FR) (Lyphard (USA)) 721[13] 951[6] 1037[5] 1315[3] 1560[5]

Ticka Ticka Timing 4 b g Timeless Times (USA)-Belltina (Belfort (FR)) *327[10]* 734[16] 1620[12] *2366[5]* 2934[13] *3399[3]* 3756[15] **>66a 21f<**

Tickntima 3 ch g Precocious-Stolon Time (Good Times (ITY)) 1761[14] 5028[12] **>62f<**

Tidewater 3 b f Shirley Heights-Widows Walk (Habitat) 4158[7] **>54f<**

Tie Break (IRE) 2 ch g Second Set (IRE)-Karayasha (Posse (USA)) 4801[9] **>54f<**

Tierra Del Fuego 3 b f Chilibang-Dolly Bevan (Another Realm) *5020[8]* **>27a f<**

Tiger Lake 4 ch g Nashwan (USA)-Tiger Flower (Sadler's Wells (USA)) 4672[8] **>79f<**

Tiggy Silvano 2 b f Tigani-Infanta Maria (King of Spain) 2781[11] **>27f<**

Tightrope 2 b c Alzao (USA)-Circus Act (Shirley Heights) 2534[10] 2720[9] 2926[4] *3395[4]* 4065[2] (4576) 4670[6] **>59a 79+f<**

Tigi 2 ch f Tigani-Molly Brazen (Risk Me (FR)) 3426[7] 3821[12] 4159[9] 4595[10] **>37f<**

Tigrello 3 ch c Efisio-Prejudice (Young Generation) 524[2] 723[5] (1004) 1175[14] 2013[4] 2290[6] 2871[9] **>93f<**

Tigullio (IRE) 2 b c Rainbows For Life (CAN)-L'Americaine (USA) (Verbatim (USA)) 4949[6] 5048[21] **>55f<**

Tikopia 3 b g Saddlers' Hall (IRE)-Shesadelight (Shirley Heights) 967[3] 1434[2] 1850[4] 2287[2] 3246[6] 3739[5] (4045) 4310[3] **>84f<**

Tilaal (USA) 5 ch h Gulch (USA)-Eye Drop (USA) (Irish River (FR)) 974[8] 2884[5] 4596[14] **>55f<**

Tilburg 2 b f High Kicker (USA)-Touch My Heart (Steel Heart) *2066[10]* 2520[7] 3106[9] 3619[9] 3819[9] 4058[9] 4208[8] 4698[16] **>25a 58f<**

Tiler (IRE) 5 br g Ballad Rock-Fair Siobahn (Petingo) **1996:** *5105[7]* **1997:** 443[22] 596[6] 786[3] 892[23] 953[11] 1259[5] (2900) 3034[4] 3273[5] 3604[3] 3649[2] 3765[4] 3856[2] 4280[7] 4456[9] 4787[15] 4842[15] 4927[3] 4995[16] **>77a 86f<**

Tiller Girl (IRE) 2 ch f Mujtahid (USA)-Till You (USA) (Exclusive Native (USA)) 4789[12] 4957[11] **>26f<**

Timbervati (USA) 2 br f Woodman (USA)-Never Scheme (USA) (Never Bend) 4852[2] **>79f<**

Time Allowed 4 b f Sadler's Wells (USA)-Time Charter (Saritamer (USA)) (932) **>119f< (DEAD)**

Time Can Tell 3 ch g Sylvan Express-Stellaris (Star Appeal) *138[4]* *162[3]* *174[2]* *281[5]* *298[4]* *331[4]* 431[5] 533[2] 700[4] 878[3] 976[5] 1474[5] 1826[11] 2125[3] 3696[3] 4015[15] 4210[16] **>70a 72f<**

Time Clash 4 b f Timeless Times (USA)-Ash Amour (Hotfoot) **1996:** *5130[9]* **1997:** *4[6]* *85[8]* **>30a 59df<**

Time for Action (IRE) 5 b g Alzao (USA)-Beyond Words (Ballad Rock) *626a[5]* 787[13] 3773[12] 4136[12] 4477[6] 4788[9] (4886) **>83a 87f<**

Time for a Run 10 b g Deep Run-Hourly Rate (Menelek) 4620a[6] **>93f<**

Time For Tea (IRE) 4 ch f Imperial Frontier (USA)-Glowing Embers (Nebbiolo) **1996:** *5093[5]* *5151[12]* *5221[11]* **1997:** 520[7] 601[12] 883[8] 1003[6] 1373[5] 1639[3] **>30a 58f<**

Timekeeper (USA) 2 b br c Exbourne (USA)-Falabella (Steel Heart) 695[2] (822) 1411[7] 2243[3] 2429[5] (2822a) (3367a) 4128a[2] 4836a[3] **>83f<**

Time Lapse 8 ch m The Noble Player (USA)-Low Line (High Line) 2999a[3] **>63df<**

Time Limit (USA) 2 c *5064a[7]*

Timely Example (USA) 6 ch g Timeless Moment (USA)-Dearest Mongo (USA) (Mongo) 1246[9] **>33a 13f<**

Time of Night (USA) 4 gr ro f Night Shift (USA)-Tihama (USA) (Sassafras (FR)) 560[8] 734[14] 1248[14] 1388[3] 1503[6] 1506[12] 1991[4] 4184[17] *4484[11]* **>5a 57f<**

Times of Times (IRE) 4 b f Distinctly North (USA)-Lady Fandet (Gay Fandango (USA)) 3292[9] 3852[9] 4168[19] **>53a 38f<**

Time To Fly 4 b g Timeless Times (USA)-Dauntless Flight (Golden Mallard) *87[7]* *178[6]* *326[5]* *(593)* 949[11] *1759[5]* *(2366)* *2915[2]* *3398[3]* 3761[12] **>57a 42f<**

Time To Hunt 2 gr c Timeless Times (USA)-Hunting Gold (Sonnen Gold) 3459[7] 4286[8] **>56f<**

Time To Tango 4 b f Timeless Times (USA)-Tangalooma (Hotfoot) 596[7] 901[3] 1225[8] 1561[8] 1828[8] 2061[9] 3287[14] **>53f<**

Time To Time 2 ch f Timeless Times (USA)-Supergreen (Superlative) 2684[4] 2886[9] 3544[3] 3905[9] *4054[6]* **>49a 55f<**

Timissa (IRE) 3 b f Kahyasi-Timissara (USA) (Shahrastani (USA)) 1023[2] (1420) 1822[4] **>79f<**

Timothy George (IRE) 3 b g Don't Forget Me-Ward of Court (IRE) (Law Society (USA)) 4516[17] 4918[18] **>26f<**

Tina Knows (IRE) 2 b f Cyrano de Bergerac-Nec Precario (Krayyan) 1797[12] 2736[10] **>17f< (DEAD)**

Tindaya 2 b g Polar Falcon (USA)-Flitcham (Elegant Air) 822[5] 1510[12] 1749[6] 2419[7] **>61f<**

Tinker Amelia 5 b m Damister (USA)-Miss Primula (Dominion) 3508a[9] 4834a[4] **>49a 109f<**

Tinkerbell 3 ch f Sharpo-Chasing Moonbeams (Final Straw) *388[6]* *(420)* 448[17] **>69a 79f<**

Tinker Osmaston 6 br m Dunbeath (USA)-Miss Primula (Dominion) 879[5] 1113[4] 1279[14] 1439[14] 2244[4] (2372) 2590[4] 3092[4] 3251[3] 3473[6] 3898[2] 4048[15] 4321[13] 4905[14] **>72f<**

Tinker's Surprise (IRE) 3 b g Cyrano de Bergerac-Lils Fairy (Fairy King (USA)) **1996:** *5107[5]* **1997:** 783[3] 1571[3] 1730[2] 1995[4] 2738[11] 3121[5] 3460[7] 3871[10] 4527[12] **>54a 52f<**

Tinklers Folly 5 ch g Bairn (USA)-Lucky Straw (Tumble Wind (USA)) 571[16] 733[9] 947[16] 1631[13] 1802[3] 2845[8] 3134[6] 3315[8] 3456[4] 3627[10] *4813[9]* **>30a 55f<**

Tinos Island (IRE) 2 b f Alzao (USA)-Lady Windley (Baillamont (USA)) 682[9] 767[9] 1856[4] **>42f<**

Tip it In 8 gr g Le Solaret (FR)-Alidante (Sahib) *1133[15]* **>2a f<**

Tipperary Sunset (IRE) 3 gr g Red Sunset-Chapter And Verse (Dancers Image (USA)) 1041[3] 2045[11] 2733[5] *3044[9]* (3336) (3813) 4472[7] 4632[2] 4802[3] (4972) (5049) **>24a 70f<**

Tippitt Boy 2 b c Prince Sabo-Space Travel (Dancing Dissident (USA)) 504[3] 583[8] 1447[5] (1675) (2054) 2584[5] 3192[5] 4150[2] 4675[8] **>100f<**

Tipsy Creek (USA) 3 b c Dayjur (USA)-Copper Creek (Habitat) 4239[7] 4525[3] 4777[15] **>113f<**

Tirmizi (USA) 6 b g Shahrastani (USA)-Tikarna (FR) (Targowice (USA)) *68[2]* *4055[8]* **>52a f<**

Tirol's Treasure (IRE) 3 b f Tirol-Lisa's Favourite (Gorytus (USA)) **1996:** *5243[10]* **1997:** *26[12]* **>13a 12f<**

Tisima (FR) 3 ch f Selkirk (USA)-Georgia Stephens (USA) (The Minstrel (CAN)) 765[3] 1004[U] **>62f<**

Tissue of Lies (USA) 4 b br g Ascot Knight (CAN)-Choral Group (CAN) (Lord Durham (CAN)) **1996:** *(5122)* *5171[3]* *5206[13]* *5221[2]* **1997:** 1414[14] 1693[3] 2034[3] 2316[9] 2828[7] 3573[10] 4516[9] **>75a 58f<**

Titan 2 b c Lion Cavern (USA)-Sutosky (Great Nephew) 2243[7] 2719[2] 3711[15] (4143) 4368[2] 4670[5] **>76f<**

Titanic (IRE) 2 b c Nashwan (USA)-White Star Line (USA) (Northern Dancer) (2762) (3098) 3708[6] 4150[3] 4911[4] **>94f<**

Tithcar 3 b f Cadeaux Genereux-Miznah (IRE) (Sadler's Wells (USA)) 1643[2] 1858[3] 3086[2] 3698[2] 4047[2] 4563[3] 4820[14] **>72f<**

Title Bid (USA) 2 b c Danzig (USA)-Triple Tiara (USA) (Majestic Light (USA)) 4145[2] (4286) 4851[4] **>90f<**

Titta Ruffo 3 b c Reprimand-Hithermoor Lass (Red Alert) 446[2] 479[2] 1207[4] 1637[3] (1928) 3891[4] 4294[6] 4552[4] **>86f<**

Tittle Tattle (IRE) 2 b f Soviet Lad (USA)-Saint Cynthia (Welsh Saint) 3672a[4] 3839a[3] **>90f<**

Titus Livius (FR) 4 ch c Machiavellian (USA)-Party Doll (Be My Guest (USA)) 811a[3] 1206a[2] (1721a) 2106[2] 3554a[3] 4124a[5] 4664a[6] **>122f<**

Tiye 2 b f Salse (USA)-Kiya (USA) (Dominion) 3985[9] 4273[5] **>68f<**

T'Niel 6 ch m Librate-Classy Colleen (St Paddy) 1247[R]

T-N-T Express 3 b c Sizzling Melody-Lady Minstrel (Tudor Music) **1996:** *5202[7]* **1997:** *90[11]* *124[11]* *191[6]* **>45a 48f<**

Toba (IRE) 8 h 4654a[7]

Toblersong 2 b c Tirol-Winsong Melody (Music Maestro) (2388) 4106[6] 4517[2] (4851) 4890[5] **>93f<**

Tocco Jewel 7 br m Reesh-Blackpool Belle (The Brianstan) 1246[7] 1445[8] 2701[9] *2911[8]* *3073[9]* 3933[6] **>27f<**

Toffolux 2 b f Sharpo-Coca (Levmoss) 4779[20] 4873[17] **>10f<**

Toi Toi (IRE) 3 b f In The Wings-Walliser (Niniski (USA)) 436[5] 2210[4] 2380[2] 2944[4] 3197[5] 3815[2] 3974[8] 4234[9] 4743[3] 4919[3] **>73f<**

Tokay 2 b f Kylian (USA)-Tokyo (Mtoto) 4745[5] **>61f<**

Token Gesture (IRE) 3 b f Alzao (USA)-Temporary Lull (USA) (Super Concorde (USA)) 806a[5] 1540a[3] (2267a) 2454a[10] **>113f<**

Tolepa (IRE) 4 b f Contract Law (USA)-Our Investment (Crofter (USA)) 796[8] 929[10] 1116[7] **>30a 29f<**

Toll's Times 2 ch g Clantime-Petroc Concert (Tina's Pet) 743[8] 993[7] *1136[12]* 1298[8] 1815[7] 2016[6] 2233[6] **>9a 56f<**

To Love With Love 2 ch f Cadeaux Genereux-Miss Loving (Northfields (USA)) 2227[6] 2831[12] (3589) 3965[4] **>81f<**

Tom 2 gr c Petong-Wanton (Kris) 2553[8] 2917[12] 3686[11] 4208[3] 4690[15] 5025[5] **>54f<**

Tomal 5 b g King Among Kings-Jacinda (Thatching) *290[8]* 476[8] 866[5] 1005[6] **>30a 46f<**

Tomashenko 8 ch g Efisio-Stockingful (Santa Claus) 1384[16] 1677[12] **>57?f<**

Tomba 3 ch c Efisio-Indian Love Song (Be My Guest (USA)) **1996:** (5194a) **1997:** 519[5] 717a[4] (980) (1212) (1403) 1770[4] (2329) 3375a[2] (3553a) 4011[2] 4864a[3] 5054[3] **>121f<**

Tom Dooly (SWI) 4 b g Aguarico (GER)-Tocaima

(SWI) (Nebos (GER)) 4540a^{3} **>89f<**

Tom Dougal 2 b c Ron's Victory (USA)-Fabulous Rina (FR) (Fabulous Dancer (USA)) 1120^{10} 1492^{5} 2361^{5} *3610^{6}* 3905^{4} 4285^{10} 4753^{2} **>56a 66f<**

Tom Mi Dah 3 b g Superlative-Queensbury Star (Wishing Star) 2547^{9} 2891^{16} 3105^{11} 3488^{6} **>40f<**

Tom Morgan 6 b g Faustus (USA)-Pirate Maid (Auction Ring (USA)) **1996:** *5249^{13}* **1997:** *56^{7} 146^{8}* 4878^{18} **>51a 52?f<**

Tommy Cooper 6 br h Macmillion-My Charade (Cawston's Clown) 3203^{7} 3714^{8} **>41f<**

Tommy Tempest 8 ch g Northern Tempest (USA)-Silently Yours (USA) (Silent Screen (USA)) 2536^{3} (2732) 3280^{12} 3637^{11} *4049^{9}* 4518^{17} **>32a 48f<**

Tommy Tortoise 3 b c Rock Hopper-Wish You Well (Sadler's Wells (USA)) 1140^{10} 1296^{7} (1986) 2189^{3} 4313^{9} (4509) 4783^{29} **>78f<**

Tom Pladdey 3 ch c Clantime-Croft Original (Crofthall) 644^{12} 785^{16} 2017^{12} 2354^{6} 2891^{13} 3405^{3} 4846^{16} **>21a 29f<**

Tom Tailor (GER) 3 b g Beldale Flutter (USA)-Thoughtful (Northfields (USA)) 967^{4} (1144) 1679^{2} 2230^{6} 2574^{7} 4699^{8} **>82f<**

Tonight's Prize (IRE) 3 b g Night Shift (USA)-Bestow (Shirley Heights) 847^{7} 2873^{5} 3140^{2} 3463^{2} 4060^{2} 4177^{2} (4587) **>90f<**

Tonka 5 b g Mazilier (USA)-Royal Meeting (Dara Monarch) **1996:** *5260^{8}* **1997:** 838^{9} (1093) 1491^{6} 1803^{4} 2174^{7} 2398^{9} **>40a 69f<**

Tonnerre 5 b g Unfuwain (USA)-Supper Time (Shantung) 430^{22} 728^{6} 888^{9} 1081^{4} 1693^{4} (2174) 2686^{6} 3134^{3} 3315^{15} *3609^{9}* 3992^{2} 4172^{15} **>7a 68f<**

Too Logical 3 b g Broken Hearted-Logical Lady (Tina's Pet) 4045^{10} **>38f<**

Top 3 gr f Shirley Heights-Whirl (Bellypha) 1023^{W} 1420^{6} 2008^{7} 2360^{2} 2763^{6} (3210) 3907^{2} 4363^{10} **>77f<**

Topaglow (IRE) 4 ch g Topanoora-River Glow (River Knight (FR)) 2702^{9} **>43f<**

Topatori (IRE) 3 ch f Topanoora-Partygoer (General Assembly (USA)) 675^{15} 1234^{4} (1858) 2205^{3} 2691^{7} 3548^{11} 3937^{6} 4268^{3} (4731) **>81f<**

Topaz 2 b c Alhijaz-Daisy Topper (Top Ville) 4520^{12} **>44f<**

Top Banana 6 ch g Pharly (FR)-Oxslip (Owen Dudley) 942^{15} 1309^{4} 3423^{12} 3764^{12} 4121^{8} 4456^{12} 4787^{6} 4954^{11} **>90f<**

Top Cees 7 b g Shirley Heights-Sing Softly (Luthier) 728^{2} (1027) 2327^{5} 3110^{5} 3705^{6} (4279) 4783^{2} **>105f<**

Top Floor (IRE) 2 ch c Waajib-Keen Note (Sharpo) 1120^{8} 1396^{6} 1760^{5} 3306^{8} 3707^{15} 3905^{19} **>68f<**

Top Gear (IRE) 2 ch c Case Law-Fleur-de-Luce (Tumble Wind (USA)) 4526^{22} 4966^{11} **>59f<**

Top Jem 3 b f Damister (USA)-Sharp Top (Sharpo) 586^{10} 885^{5} 1443^{6} (1859) 2178^{2} (2328) 2507^{3} 4731^{2} 4854^{7} 4882^{2} **>86f<**

Top Maite 2 ch c Komaite (USA)-Top Yard (Teekay) 1872^{11} 2509^{6} 3193^{9} **>69f<**

Top of The Form (IRE) 3 ch f Masterclass (USA)-Haraabah (USA) (Topsider (USA)) 1468^{9} (2939) (3332) 3709^{9} 4365^{9} 4586^{3} 4805^{16} 4995^{23} **>73f<**

Top of The Green (IRE) 3 b c Common Grounds-Grayfoot (Grundy) 991^{11} 1870^{5} **>55f<**

Top Prize 9 b g High Top-Raffle (Balidar) *167^{10}* 465^{7} *543^{2}* 632^{10} 865^{8} 1100^{13} *2607^{4}* 2737^{11} **>20a 27f<**

Top Shelf 3 b f Warning-Troy Moon (Troy) *(337)* 690^{18} 976^{3} *1153^{5}* 1474^{3} 1859^{4} 2398^{11} 3813^{11} **>76a 66f<**

Top Titfer 3 ch f Cap Diamant (USA)-Top Yard (Teekay) 582^{12} **>32f<**

Topton (IRE) 3 b g Royal Academy (USA)-Circo (High Top) 1265^{4} 1777^{3} 3037^{4} 3250^{2} 3800^{4} 4059^{2} 4290^{2} (4820) **>80f<**

Topup 4 b g Weldnaas (USA)-Daisy Topper (Top Ville) **1996:** *5254^{8}* **1997:** *129^{6}* **>12a 62f<**

Torch Vert (IRE) 5 b g Law Society (USA)-Arctic Winter (CAN) (Briartic (CAN)) 4461^{3} **>84?f<**

Torianna (USA) 2 b f Hermitage (USA)-The High Dancer (High Line) 1997^{13} 3776^{2} **>78f<**

Tormount (USA) 4 b c Local Talent (USA)-Virginia Hills (USA) (Tom Rolfe) **1996:** *5094^{5} 5140^{5} 5206^{4}* **>57a 64f<**

Tornado Prince (IRE) 2 ch c Caerleon (USA)-Welsh Flame (Welsh Pageant) 3726^{5} 4278^{10} 4852^{9} **>64f<**

Torn Silk 3 b g Top Ville-Cut Velvet (USA) (Northern Dancer) 4620a^{2} **>101f<**

Toronto 3 b c Puissance-Impala Lass (Kampala) *855^{12}* 1080^{6} (1604) 1995^{9} 2235^{5} 2354^{U} 2540^{14} 2883^{6} 3271^{W} 3871^{5} 4016^{21} 4328^{10} **>8a 50f<**

Torrent 2 ch c Prince Sabo-Maiden Pool (Sharpen Up) 3743^{6} 3986^{3} 4379^{4} 4603^{10} **>79f<**

Torrismondo (USA) 6 b or br h Tasso (USA)-Miss Cabell Co (USA) (Junction (USA)) **1996:** 5158a^{3} **>103f<**

Torso 2 b c Rudimentary (USA)-Tosara (Main Reef) 3117^{11} 3479^{8} 4278^{7} **>61f<**

Toshiba Talk (IRE) 5 ch g Horage-Court Ballet (Barrons Court) 3603^{4} **>47f<**

Toss And Tumble 3 b f Syrtos-Breakfast in Bed (Tickled Pink) 3244^{4} 3807^{3} *4049^{11}* 4601^{14} *4795^{6}* **>36a 45f<**

Totally Yours (IRE) 4 b f Classic Music (USA)-Dominia (Derring-Do) 595^{2} **>53f<**

Total Rach (IRE) 5 b m Nordico (USA)-Miss Kelly (Pitskelly) *88^{11} 194^{9} 305^{6}* **>33a 57f<**

Total Tropix 2 b f Saddlers' Hall (IRE)-Ivana (IRE) (Taufan (USA)) 4381^{14} 4502^{8} 4627^{8} *4799^{5}* **>36a 54f<**

Totem Dancer 4 b f Mtoto-Ballad Opera (Sadler's Wells (USA)) 680^{16} 1162^{6} 2014^{23} *3231^{5}* (4466) 4783^{16} **>57a 85f<**

To the Roof (IRE) 5 b g Thatching-Christine Daae (Sadler's Wells (USA)) 726^{2} 941^{5} 1171^{6} 1590^{4} 2105^{6} 2526^{5} 3217^{20} **>65a 113f<**

To The Skies (USA) 2 gr f Sky Classic (CAN)-Dawn's Flame (USA) 2439a^{11} **>74f<**

Toto le Moko (IRE) 4 b c Marju (IRE)-Shyoushka (Shy Groom (USA)) 1549a^{2} 2100a^{5} 4399a^{2} **>121f<**

Totom 2 b f Mtoto-A Lyph (USA) (Lypheor) 5036a^{2}

Touchanova 2 gr f Touch of Grey-Mazurkanova (Song) *2367^{4}* 2875^{11} 4779^{13} 4948^{7} 5045^{9} **>52a 54f<**

Touch Gold (USA) 3 b c Deputy Minister (CAN)-Passing Mood (USA) (Buckpasser) *(1912a) 5066a^{9}* **>126a f<**

Touch'n'go 3 b c Rainbow Quest (USA)-Mary Martin (Be My Guest (USA)) **1996:** *5168^{7}* **1997:** *83^{4} (289) (366) 581^{2}* 1094^{7} 1820^{3} **>76a 65f<**

Touch of Colour 2 b c Weldnaas (USA)-Fauve (Dominion) 3131^{11} 3701^{5} 3905^{13} 4208^{12} **>50f<**

Tough Act 3 b g Be My Chief (USA)-Forelino (USA) (Trempolino (USA)) 4158^{2} 4378^{2} 4506^{2} **>80f<**

Tough Leader 3 b c Lead on Time (USA)-Al Guswa (Shernazar) 794^{5} 1589^{12} **>85f<**

Tough Nell (IRE) 2 ch f Archway (IRE)-Mousseux (IRE) (Jareer (USA)) 3638^{13} 4818^{9} 4904^{9} **>64f<**

Toujours Riviera 7 ch g Rainbow Quest (USA)-Miss Beaulieu (Northfields (USA)) 1471^{3} 1739^{11} 2065^{4} 2557^{4} 2868^{2} 3115^{4} 3328^{6} (3630) 4225^{3} (4448) 4859^{5} **>83a 91f<**

Toulston Lady (IRE) 5 b m Handsome Sailor-Rainbow Lady (Jaazeiro (USA)) **1996:** *5115^{9} 5139^{11}* **1997:** *86^{3} 122^{3}* 4171^{11} **>41a 51?f<**

Tout A Coup (IRE) 4 b f Ela-Mana-Mou-Coupe D'Hebe (Ile de Bourbon (USA)) 1058a^{3} (2079a) 2446a^{5} (3362a) 4094a^{6} **>103f<**

Tovarich 6 b g Soviet Star (USA)-Pretty Lucky (Shirley Heights) *1943^{7} 2301^{7} 2911^{3} 3073^{7}* **>49a 60?f<**

Townville Cee Cee 2 b f Anshan-Holy Day (Sallust) 1120^{9} 1645^{4} 1997^{14} 3973^{18} 4166^{11} 4508^{8} 4841^{6} **>59f<**

Toy (IRE) 2 b f Shalford (IRE)-Advantageous (Top Ville) 1812^{22} **>22f<**

Traceability 4 b g Puissance-Miss Petella (Dunphy) 680^{10} 986^{4} 1427^{6} 1763^{5} 2296^{3} 2574^{3} (2961) 3135^{2} 3542^{6} 3773^{7} **>85f<**

Track Gal (USA) 6 Track Barron (USA)-Golden Galaxy (USA) *5061a^{10}* **>85a f<**

Tracking 2 ch c Machiavellian (USA)-Black Fighter (USA) (Secretariat (USA)) (2038) (2707) 3142^{2} 3895^{2} 4551^{4} **>101f<**

Tracks of My Tears 3 gr f Damister (USA)-Carose (Caro) *355^{4} 454^{2}* **>52a 53f<**

Trading Aces 3 b f Be My Chief (USA)-Corn Futures (Nomination) 483^{8} *(590)* 1000^{3} 1131^{4} 1245^{2} 2340^{8} 2945^{9} 3976^{18} 4757^{11} **>77a 75f<**

Trafalgar Lady (USA) 4 b f Fairy King (USA)-Tremulous (USA) (Gregorian (USA)) 468^{16} **>84f<**

Trafalger (USA) 3 *5061a^{8}* **>90a f<**

Trailblazer 3 b g Efisio-Flicker Toa Flame (USA) (Empery (USA)) **1996:** *5229^{4}* **1997:** 1874^{6} 2326^{15} 2678^{14} 3987^{20} **>81a 56f<**

Trait De Genie (FR) 5 ch g Diamond Prospect (USA)-Garmeritte (FR) (Garde Royale) 2271a^{3} 3365a^{3} (4539a) **>115f<**

Tramline 4 b c Shirley Heights-Trampship (High Line) 841^{10} 1023^{5} 1276^{5} (1841) 2284^{4} 2589^{10} 3915^{11} **>85f<**

Transcript (USA) 8 ch h Secretariat (USA)-Devon Ditty (919a) **>113f<**

Trans Island 2 b c Selkirk (USA)-Khubza (Green Desert (USA)) 1607^{2} (1873) (2860) (3995a) 4528a^{2} **>91+f<**

Transom (USA) 6 b or br g Private Account (USA)-Trestle (USA) (Tom Rolfe) 1325^{4} (1871) 2327^{18} 3122^{5} 4783^{9} **>94f<**

Transylvania 2 b f Wolfhound (USA)-Slava (USA) (Diesis) 3574^{7} **>66f<**

Trapped (IRE) 3 ch f River Falls-Surprise Move 2447a^{12} **>84f<**

Trapper Norman 5 b g Mazilier (USA)-Free Skip (Free State) **1996:** *5084^{11} 5148^{15}* **1997:** *108^{9}* **>30a 23f<**

Trauma (IRE) 5 b m Broken Hearted-Remoosh (Glint of Gold) **1996:** *5177^{15}* **>32da 29f<**

Travelling Clock 2 ch c Deploy-Travel Mystery (Godswalk (USA)) 4739^{12} **>39f<**

Travelmate 3 b g Persian Bold-Ustka (Lomond (USA)) 645^{7} 991^{10} (1384) 1877^{2} (2122) **>85f<**

Treasure Chest (IRE) 2 b c Last Tycoon-Sought Out (IRE) (Rainbow Quest (USA)) 3760^{6} 4157^{5} 4460^{3} **>83f<**

Treasure Hill (IRE) 3 ch g Roi Danzig (USA)-Grass Court (Thatch (USA)) 774^{8} 1000^{12} 1256^{6} 1333^{11} 2415^{12} **>34f<**

Treasure Island 2 b f Rainbow Quest (USA)-Cockatoo Island (High Top) 4604^{10} 5041^{15} **>39f<**

Treasure Touch (IRE) 3 b g Treasure Kay-Bally Pourri (IRE) (Law Society (USA)) **1996:** *5164^{6}* **1997:** *38^{3} 110^{2} (204)* (532) (649) (694) 854^{5} (1254)

1980[14] 3332[3] 3709[10] 4270[12] 4770[17] 4995[18] **>75a 86df<**
Treaty (USA) 3 b c Trempolino (USA)-Zonda (Fabulous Dancer (USA)) 3425[8] 4009[R] **>43?f<**
Treble Term 2 ch f Lion Cavern (USA)-Treble Hook (IRE) (Ballad Rock) 4012[7] 4904[7] **>65f<**
Tregaron (USA) 6 b h Lyphard (USA)-Klarifi (Habitat) 677[2] (892) 2026[28] 2690[2] 3728[8] 4423[5] **>109f<**
Tremendisto 7 b g Petoski-Misty Halo (High Top) *30[5]* 4335[14] **>45a 32f<**
Tremonnow 2 b f Reprimand-Tree Mallow (Malicious) 999[6] 1438[4] 2016[3] 2509[11] 2700[5] 3564[5] 4327[7] **>59f<**
Tremplin (USA) 5 b g Trempolino (USA)-Stresa (Mill Reef (USA)) 1320[8] 1739[9] 1923[4] 2512[5] **>78f<**
Tres Heureux (GER) 7 b h Konigsstuhl (GER)-Tres Magnifique 4762a[6] **>115f<**
Trevor Mitchell 3 b f Backchat (USA)-Versaillesprincess (Legend of France (USA)) **1996:** *5080[10] 5187[9] 5248[9]* **1997:** 3715[11] 4008[15] 4373[18] 4465[7] *4906[11]* **>18a 48f<**
Trianna 4 b f General Holme (USA)-Triemma (IRE) (M Double M (USA)) *42[8]* **>39a 45f<**
Tribal Mischief 3 br f Be My Chief (USA)-Lammastide (Martinmas) 1037[11] 2130[10] 2544[6] 2757[10] 3336[5] 4472[14] **>47f<**
Tribal Moon (IRE) 4 b g Ela-Mana-Mou-Silk Blend (Busted) 2008[8] 2487[5] 2726[4] **>64f<**
Tribal Peace (IRE) 5 ch g Red Sunset-Mirabiliary (USA) (Crow (FR)) **1996:** *5088[5]* **1997:** *(61) 1123[6] 1421[7]* 1926[3] 2285[4] 2550[5] 2866[3] (3153) 3616[8] 3768[3] 4141[4] 4449[9] **>76a 67f<**
Trible Pet 4 b f Petong-Fire Sprite (Mummy's Game) *57[7] 143[6] 188[10]* **>35a 50f<**
Trickery (IRE) 3 b f Cyrano de Bergerac-Beguiled 1186a[4] 2447a[9] **>90f<**
Trident (USA) 2 b c Red Ransom (USA)-Lady di Pomadora (USA) (Danzig Connection (USA)) 2562[3] (2948) **>85+f<**
Trienta Mil 3 b g Prince Sabo-Burmese Ruby (Good Times (ITY)) 4060[15] **>52f<**
Trigger Happy (IRE) 2 ch f Ela-Mana-Mou-Happy Tidings (Hello Gorgeous (USA)) 4873[7] (4977) **>85f<**
Trilby 4 b f In The Wings-Fur Hat (Habitat) 613[9] 1081[7] 1585[4] 1840[3] 2034[2] (2166) 2350[2] 2682[4] 3309[10] 3890[4] 4160[6] **>50a 58f<**
Trinity Reef 2 b f Bustino-Triple Reef (Mill Reef (USA)) 3450[11] 3862[5] 4330[8] **>64f<**
Triple Challenge 3 gr f Norton Challenger-Trois Filles (French Mamy) *255[8]* 2008[24] **>21a f<**
Triple Hay 3 ch c Safawan-Davinia (Gold Form) 930[5] 1170[7] (1634) 1980[18] 3217[9] 3975[12] 4550[4] **>104f<**
Triple Leap 4 b c Sadler's Wells (USA)-Three Tails (Blakeney) 4306[2] **>93f<**
Triple Term 3 br g Terimon-Triple Reef (Mill Reef (USA)) 2695[11] *3044[11]* **>22a 74f<**
Tristan's Comet 10 br g Sayf El Arab (USA)-Gleneagle (Swing Easy (USA)) *68[14]* **>32a 34f<**
Troia (IRE) 3 b f Last Tycoon-Dubai Lady (Kris) **1996:** *5248[5]* **1997:** *60[6]* 1822[6] 2199[12] **>56a 54df<**
Trojan Hero (SAF) 6 ch g Raise A Man (USA)-Helleness (SAF) (Northfields (USA)) (1622) 2428[2] 3310[5] 3621[9] 3855[3] 4414[15] 4843[6] 5030[11] **>63f<**
Trojan Risk 4 ch g Risk Me (FR)-Troyes (Troy) *591[9]* 787[11] 1092[5] 1768[11] 2118[4] (2528) 2961[14] 4923[2] **>66a 82f<**
Trojan Sea (USA) 6 b h Bering-Trojan Miss (Troy) 716a[3] 922a[8] 1914a[3] 2818a[2] 3996a[3] **>114f<**
Trojan Wolf 2 ch c Wolfhound (USA)-Trojan Lady (USA) (Irish River (FR)) 4993[9] **>52f<**
Troon 7 gr h Beveled (USA)-Cestrefeld (Capistrano) 1910a[3] 4124a[7] 4260a[2] **>104f<**
Trooper 3 b g Rock Hopper-Silica (USA) (Mr Prospector (USA)) 990[13] 1592[11] 2725[2] 3057[2] 4046[13] 4336[8] *4811[2]* **>73a 78f<**
Trophy Wife (FR) 2 b/f Double Bed (FR)-Hornblower Girl (Faraway Times (USA)) 3994a[3] **>71f<**
Tropical Beach 4 b g Lugana Beach-Hitravelscene (Mansingh (USA)) 494[3] 610[3] 702[6] 924[4] 1037[2] 1613[8] 1835[15] 2001[5] 2382[3] (2504) 2738[15] 3334[8] 3484[7] 3936[12] 4385[12] 5047[15] **>41a 54f<**
Tropicool (USA) 4 b c Carr de Naskra (USA)-Mended Heart (UAE) (Le Febuleux (UAE)) *(408a) 627a[7]* **>125a f<**
Troubadour Song 5 b g King of Clubs-Silver Singing (USA) (Topsider (USA)) **1996:** *5205[9]* **>80a 60f<**
True Ballad 5 ch g Ballad Rock-Ajuga (USA) (The Minstrel (CAN)) 668[7] 929[7] 956[13] 2659[8] **>36f<**
True Glory (IRE) 3 b f In The Wings-Truly Special (Caerleon (USA)) 2008[3] 2315[2] 3125[11] (3441) **>89f<**
True Perspective 3 b c Presidium-Madam Muffin (Sparkler) **1996:** *5176[14]* **>50f<**
Truly Bay 4 b g Reprimand-Daymer Bay (Lomond (USA)) **1996:** *5130[4] 5179[7]* **1997:** *(112) 153[4] 203[2] 333[2]* **>57a 36f< (DEAD)**
Trulyfan (IRE) 3 b br f Taufan (USA)-Whateveryousay (USA) (Verbatim (USA)) *873[13]* **>59f<**
Truly Generous (IRE) 4 ch f Generous (IRE)-Arctique Royale (Royal And Regal (USA)) **1996:** (5198a) **>108f<**
Truly Parched (USA) 3 b g Known Fact (USA)-Drought (IRE) (Rainbow Quest (USA)) 729[5] 1017[13] 1436[5] 4741[8] **>65f<**
Trump 8 b g Last Tycoon-Fleeting Affair (Hotfoot) 4160[5] **>57?a 42f<**
Trust Deed (USA) 9 ch g Shadeed (USA)-Karelia (USA) (Sir Ivor) 2511[5] **>11f<**
Truth Teller 2 ch c Statoblest-Dreams Are Free (IRE) (Caerleon (USA)) 1143[7] (1504) 1735[8] 3589[7] 3859[4] 4044[17] (4501) 4897[9] **>66a 66f<**
Try Again (GER) 6 b h Konigsstuhl (GER)-Try My Luck (GER) (Try My Best (USA)) 440a[3] 719a[2] 1073a[4] 3737a[6] **>115f<**
Trying Times (IRE) 4 b g Sadler's Wells (USA)-Ozone Friendly (USA) (Green Forest (USA)) 996[7] 1230[16] 1838[2] (2226) 2386[7] 2716[2] 2845[7] 3487[8] 3627[3] 3966[8] 4264[9] **>53f<**
Try Omnipotent 5 b g Nomination-Try G's (Hotfoot) 898[11] **>44?f<**
Try Prospect (USA) 5 b h Allen's Prospect (USA)-Golden Triad *(392a)* **>106a f<**
Tsarnista 4 b f Soviet Star (USA)-Princess Genista (Ile de Bourbon (USA)) 934[2] 1326[6] 1919a[5] 2690[8] 4424[11] **>96f<**
Ttyfran 7 b g Petong-So it Goes (Free State) 570[10] 669[5] **>29a 25f<**
Tudor Island 8 b g Jupiter Island-Catherine Howard (Tower Walk) 1974[2] 2767[8] 2949[7] 3748[4] 4104[7] **>77f<**
Tugela (USA) 2 br f Riverman (USA)-Rambushka (USA) (Roberto (USA)) 4215[5] 4873[12] **>57f<**
Tui 2 b f Tina's Pet-Curious Feeling (Nishapour (FR)) 2509[10] 2781[7] 3247[6] *3586[10]* **>32a 56f<**
Tuigamala 6 b g Welsh Captain-Nelliellamay (Super Splash (USA)) *278[7] 352[3] 383[2] 566[10] 857[8] 1154[8]* 2550[10] 2955[6] **>62a 37f<**
Tulipa (USA) 4 b f Alleged (USA)-Black Tulip (FR) (Fabulous Dancer (USA)) 932[9] (2099a) 2513[2] (4655a) *5038a[4]* **>117f<**
Tullich Refrain 2 b f Petardia-Norfolk Serenade (Blakeney) 2917[3] 4042[7] 4216[8] 4473[10] *4808[10]* 4897[4] **>13a 64f<**
Tulsa (IRE) 3 b g Priolo (USA)-Lagrion (USA) (Diesis) 1106[11] 1416[4] 1929[2] 2281[10] 2552[17] 2785[14] 3227[14] 3557[3] 3897[5] 4002[13] 4335[11] 4696[3] 4916[6] **>64f<**
Tumbleweed Hero 2 b c Alzao (USA)-Julip (Track Spare) 1873[2] 3489[6] 4113[2] **>79f<**
Tumbleweed Pearl 3 b f Aragon-Billie Blue (Ballad Rock) (988) 1216[4] 2023[13] **>96f<**
Tumbleweed Ridge 4 ch c Indian Ridge-Billie Blue (Ballad Rock) 450[3] *514[6]* 892[10] 1148[2] 1598[2] 2105[13] (2598) 2775[3] 3577[8] 3764[13] 4153[4] 4423[25] **>80a 106f<**
Tumblweed Prospect 2 ch c Lion Cavern (USA)-Ring of Pearl (Auction Ring (USA)) 2829[4] 3494[11] 3717[2] 4298[2] **>83f<**
Tundra (IRE) 2 b f Common Grounds-Miss Krispy (FR) (Bellypha) 828[11] 3471[16] 3967[15] **>42f<**
Tuning 2 ch f Rainbow Quest (USA)-Discomatic (USA) (Roberto (USA)) 4330[2] **>82+f<**
Turbo Drive 3 2459a[7] 3004a[3] **>101f<**
Turf Moor (IRE) 2 b f Mac's Imp (USA)-Tuft Hill (Grundy) 948[2] 1280[5] 2886[8] 3751[6] 3904[3] 4166[19] *4483[13]* **>56f<**
Turgenev (IRE) 8 b g Sadler's Wells (USA)-Tilia (ITY) (Dschingis Khan) 465[10] 613[10] (982) 1162[8] 1408[5] 2035[6] 2316[5] (2475) (3498) 3705[8] 3974[2] 4620a[8] 4744[9] 5052[12] **>87f<**
Turia 4 b f Slip Anchor-Tura (Northfields (USA)) *73[9]* **>24a 75f<**
Turkappeal (USA) 4 b f Turkoman (USA)-Chief Appeal (USA) (Valid Appeal (USA)) **1996:** 5156a[3] **>112f<**
Turners Way 3 b c Precocious-Murmuring (Kind of Hush) 2580[4] 3202[7] 3641[3] **>59f<**
Turning Wheel (USA) 4 b f Seeking the Gold (USA)-Misinskie (USA) (Nijinsky (CAN)) (3878a) (4530a) **>111f<**
Turnpole (IRE) 6 br g Satco (FR)-Mountain Chase (Mount Hagen (FR)) (612) 846[2] (1162) 1400[2] 4101[7] 4363[2] (4783) **>91f<**
Turn To Stone (IRE) 3 b g West China-Marronzina (IRE) (Burslem) 2650[10] **>36f<**
Turrill House 5 b m Charmer-Megabucks (Buckskin (FR)) *16[11] 106[7] 2322[3]* 2511[4] **>29a 24?f<**
Tuscan Dawn 7 ch g Clantime-Excavator Lady (Most Secret) *488[5]* 744[12] 1946[5] 2590[2] 2895[2] 3126[5] 3473[2] 3795[2] 3900[4] 4137[14] **>64a 73f<**
Tussle 2 b c Salse (USA)-Crime Ofthecentury (Pharly (FR)) 4668[2] (4966) **>95+f<**
Tutankhamun 2 b c Lion Cavern (USA)-Menhaad (IRE) (Sadler's Wells (USA)) 4915[8] **>65f<**
Tutu Sixtysix 6 br m Petong-Odilese (Mummy's Pet) *208[5] 233[11] 332[3] 423[12] 545[9]* 2061[10] *2366[3]* 2497[9] 2844[14] 3271[3] 3334[7] 3484[2] 3716[8] **>32a 38f<**
Twentytwo Black 2 b f Ron's Victory (USA)-Fall About (Comedy Star (USA)) 1293[11] 1504[3] **>23f< (DEAD)**
Twice as Sharp 5 ch h Sharpo-Shadiliya (Red Alert) 744[5] (1158) 1608[2] 2675[3] 3011[7] 3600[3] 4100[12] 4444[8] 4756[7] 4887[7] **>91f<**
Twilight Sleep (USA) 5 b g Shadeed (USA)-Sleeping Beauty (Mill Reef (USA)) 310a[13] *(2301)* 2653[2] 2944[7] **>77a 86df<**
Twin Creeks 6 b g Alzao (USA)-Double River (USA) (Irish River (FR)) **1996:** *(5124)* **1997:** *15[15] 121[5] (146) 201[8]* 734[6] 863[5] 1009[3] 1584[8] (1680) 2002[3] 2216[2] 2573[6] 3930[3] 4219[5] *4482[4] (5021)* **>84a 71f<**

Twin Time 3 b f Syrtos-Carramba (CZE) (Tumble Wind (USA)) 161^{3} 1272^{2} 1443^{5} 2602^{8} 3030^{2} 3316^{4} 4972^{6} **>42a 73f<**
Two Bills 3 b g Totem (USA)-Chess Mistress (USA) (Run The Gantlet (USA)) 2878^{9} **>46f<**
Twoforten 2 b c Robellino (USA)-Grown At Rowan (Gabitat) 3613^{6} 4379^{6} 4520^{13} **>64f<**
Two On The Bridge 3 b g Chilibang-Constant Companion (Pas de Seul) 524^{6} 729^{2} 977^{3} 1254^{9} 1673^{6} 2017^{2} 2157^{3} 2417^{5} 3088^{4} 3241^{2} 3621^{7} 3812^{12} 4164^{2} 4601^{8} **>68f<**
Two Socks 4 ch g Phountzi (USA)-Mrs Feathers (Pyjama Hunt) 1825^{5} 2490^{4} 2787^{2} 3475^{2} 3864^{6} 4275^{2} **>56a 72f<**
Two To Tango (IRE) 4 ch f Anshan-Marie de Sologne (Lashkari) **1996:** 5120^{7} **>70a f<**
Two Williams 2 b g Polar Falcon (USA)-Long View (Persian Bold) 2202^{7} 2361^{2} (2467) 2905^{7} 3036^{3} 3908^{7} 4014^{16} 4634^{14} 4737^{9} 4922^{12} 5050^{22} **>82?f<**
Tycooness (IRE) 3 b f Last Tycoon-Smash (Busted) 1850^{2} 2853^{2} (3809) 4288^{4} 4704^{6} 4874^{15} 4956^{5} **>82f<**
Tycoon Girl (IRE) 3 b f Last Tycoon-Forest Berries (IRE) (Thatching) 483^{10} 1000^{5} 1249^{6} 1679^{3} 2005^{11} 2645^{7} 2945^{5} 3205^{7} **>74f<**
Tycoon Ted 4 b g Starch Reduced-Royal Tycoon (Tycoon II) 2479^{5} **>20f<**
Tycoon Tina 3 b f Tina's Pet-Royal Tycoon (Tycoon II) 551^{2} 609^{4} 926^{2} 1078^{6} (1284) 1465^{5} 4693^{5} 4817^{7} 5028^{2} **>23a 57f<**
Tycoon Todd (USA) 3 gr c Cozzene (USA)-Thirty Below (USA) (It's Freezing (USA)) 940^{11} 1770^{6} 3594^{9} 3891^{5} **>87f<**
Tykeyvor (IRE) 7 b g Last Tycoon-Ivoronica (Targowice (USA)) 1414^{7} 1685^{2} 2028^{5} 2528^{11} (3053) 3599^{2} 4101^{8} 4443^{13} **>100f<**
Tymeera 4 b f Timeless Times (USA)-Dear Glenda (Gold Song) **1996:** 5178^{10} **1997:** 109^{11} 759^{9} 1003^{2} 1279^{9} 1620^{10} 1963^{7} 2197^{7} 2721^{4} 3287^{16} **>50a 47f<**
Typhoon Eight (IRE) 5 b h High Estate-Dance Date (IRE) (Sadler's Wells (USA)) 1459^{3} 2483^{3} 2961^{4} 3689^{7} 3916^{4} **>76f<**
Tyrolean Dancer (IRE) 3 b f Tirol-Waffling (Lomond (USA)) 2428^{6} 2955^{8} **>52df<**
Tyrolean Dream (IRE) 3 b c Tirol-Heavenly Hope (Glenstal (USA)) 4060^{12} (4469) 4699^{6} 4891^{13} **>76f<**

U

U K Magic (IRE) 2 b g Alzao (USA)-Lightino (Bustino) 4758^{21} 4957^{7} **>61f<**
Ukraine Venture 3 b f Slip Anchor-Sherkraine (Shergar) (833) 1102^{3} 1738^{12} 4181^{4} 4557^{6} 4968^{6} **>102f<**
Ultimate Smoothie 5 b g Highest Honor (FR)-Baino Charm (USA) (Diesis) 2692^{5} (2853) 3412^{5} 3915^{9} 4461^{5} **>78f<**
Ultra Beet 5 b g Puissance-Cassiar (Connaught) **1996:** 5234^{3} **1997:** (11) (51) 184^{2} 224^{5} 512^{7} 610^{16} 1676^{4} 2203^{3} 2504^{7} 2738^{10} **>78a 56f<**
Ultra Boy 3 b g Music Boy-Golden Award (Last Tycoon) 12^{5} 103^{2} 155^{5} 448^{18} 1115^{3} (1493) (2125) 2735^{4} 3225^{4} 3397^{7} **>78a 82f<**
Unchanged 5 b m Unfuwain (USA)-Favorable Exchange (USA) (Exceller (USA)) 510^{7} 831^{8} 3890^{5} 4246^{4} (4405) **>73f<**
Uncle Doug 6 b g Common Grounds-Taqa (Blakeney) 4287^{8} 4771^{2} **>67f<**
Uncle Errol 3 b g Common Grounds-Saint Navarro (Raga Navarro (ITY)) 3089^{6} 3822^{15} 4417^{12} **>4f<**

Unconditional Love (IRE) 4 b f Polish Patriot (USA)-Thatcherite (Final Straw) 1148^{14} 1739^{7} 1836^{2} 3147^{2} 3577^{3} 3913^{12} 4120^{10} 4424^{9} $4867a^{7}$ 4947^{2} 4990^{5} 5044^{2} **>99f<**
Undawaterscubadiva 5 ch g Keen-Northern Scene (Habitat) **1996:** 5129^{11} **1997:** 18^{4} (67) 206^{4} 242^{5} 284^{7} 356^{2} 542^{5} **>44a 40f<**
Undercover Agent (IRE) 3 b f Fairy King (USA)-Audenhove (GER) (Marduk (GER)) 1000^{2} 1589^{2} 2331^{4} 3128^{7} 4561^{23} 4859^{2} 4979^{17} **>88f<**
Understudy 3 b f In The Wings-Pipina (USA) (Sir Gaylord) 2360^{3} 2566^{12} 2846^{7} 3089^{2} 4731^{10} **>57f<**
Unforgetable Charm (IRE) 3 b f Don't Forget Me-Polynesian Charm (USA) (What A Pleasure (USA)) 2773^{9} 3133^{10} 3313^{6}
Ungaro (GER) 3 b c Goofalik (USA)-Ustina (GER) (Star Appeal) (920a) $1553a^{2}$ $3555a^{5}$ $4127a^{6}$ (4661a) **>118f<**
Uniform 2 ch f Unfuwain (USA)-Trachelium (Formidable (USA)) 3602^{8} 3806^{11} 4215^{7} **>55f<**
Uninhibited (IRE) 2 b f Lahib (USA)-Etiquette (Law Society (USA)) $3366a^{3}$ $4647a^{2}$ **>91f<**
Union Town (IRE) 3 b c Generous (IRE)-Exclusive Life (USA) (Exclusive Native (USA)) (966) 1982^{2} 2345^{3} **>105f<**
Unitus (IRE) 4 b c Soviet Star (USA)-Unite (Kris) 738^{9} 1261^{11} **>84f<**
Universal Lady 2 b f Beveled (USA)-Lady of Itatiba (BEL) (King Of Macedon) 828^{8} 1425^{5} 1847^{2} 2306^{3} 2700^{2} 3113^{9} 3819^{2} 4065^{6} 4271^{11} **>74f<**
Unknown Quest 2 b c Rainbow Quest (USA)-Annoconnor (USA) (Nureyev (USA)) 3789^{8} **>39f<**
Unknown Territory (IRE) 3 ch g Imperial Frontier (USA)-Lilac Lass (Virginia Boy) 377^{9} 546^{6} **>69f<**
Un Melodie 2 b f Caerleon (USA)-Vaguar (USA) (Vaguely Noble) 4950^{3} **>80+f<**
U-No-Harry (IRE) 4 b c Mansooj-Lady Roberta (USA) (Roberto (USA)) 1223^{8} 1402^{7} 1662^{5} 1977^{10} 2711^{15} 2847^{3} 3481^{13} 3761^{7} 3856^{10} 4365^{7} 4512^{12} 4738^{14} 4842^{8} 4905^{12} **>61a 50f<**
Uno Sobotica (GER) 3 c $2097a^{11}$ **>72f<**
Unshaken 3 b c Environment Friend-Reel Foyle (USA) (Irish River (FR)) 1243^{11} 1410^{14} 2124^{5} 2408^{6} 3457^{7} 3900^{12} 4436^{15} 4877^{20} **>67df<**
Unspoken Prayer 4 br f Inca Chief (USA)-Dancing Doll (USA) (Buckfinder (USA)) **1996:** 5258^{4} **1997:** 27^{7} 112^{3} **>39a 47f<**
Uoni 4 ch f Minster Son-Maid of Essex (Bustino) **1996:** 5254^{5} **1997:** 171^{7} 216^{3} 261^{7} 295^{11} 381^{8} 4912^{12} **>34a 56f<**
Up At The Top (IRE) 2 b f Waajib-Down The Line (Brigadier Gerard) 2706^{3} (3927) 4185^{9} **>65+f<**
Up in Flames (IRE) 6 br g Nashamaa-Bella Lucia (Camden Town) 207^{8} 315^{6} 1097^{12} 1384^{6} 1495^{11} 2036^{8} 2340^{9} 2546^{14} 4628^{3} 4847^{13} (4991) **>53a 52f<**
Uplifting 2 b f Magic Ring (IRE)-Strapless (Bustino) 3114^{10} 4379^{2} 4884^{3} **>77f<**
Upper Class (GER) 4 b c Konigsstuhl (GER)-Ustina (GER) (Star Appeal) $4659a^{2}$ **>115f<**
Upper Mount Clair 7 b m Ela-Mana-Mou-Sun Street (Ile de Bourbon (USA)) 442^{4} 655^{5} 865^{7} 1027^{8} 3122^{12} 3928^{14} **>68a 63f<**
Up The Clarets (IRE) 2 b g Petardia-Madeira Lady (On Your Mark) 822^{6} 1557^{6} 2233^{5} 2383^{8} 3563^{5} 4058^{4} 4595^{3} 4994^{13} **>61f<**
Up The Wall 2 b c Aragon-Ridalia (Ridan (USA)) 1854^{3} 2191^{7} 3278^{12} 3905^{W} 4318^{7} 4545^{2} 4715^{14} 4856^{9} 4974^{8} **>61f<**
Urgent Reply (USA) 4 b g Green Dancer (USA)-Bowl of Honey (USA) (Lyphard (USA)) 605^{4} 842^{8} 1106^{5} 1408^{8} 1641^{7} 2164^{9} 2369^{15} (2661) (3286) 3482^{2} 3867^{2} 4104^{9} 4160^{9} 4466^{14} **>21a 67f<**

Urgent Swift 4 ch g Beveled (USA)-Good Natured (Troy) 430^{3} 538^{9} 789^{2} 2776^{7} 3318^{3} 3739^{2} 4279^{13} **>88f<**
Ursa Major 3 b c Warning-Double Entendre (Dominion) **1996:** (5187) **1997:** 3024^{7} 3423^{14} 3604^{18} 4153^{7} 4423^{22} 4756^{17} **>70?a 90df<**
Utah (IRE) 3 b c High Estate-Easy Romance (USA) (Northern Jove (CAN)) 1105^{6} 1207^{15} **>58f<**
Uther Pendragon (IRE) 2 b c Petardia-Mountain Stage (IRE) (Pennine Walk) 3686^{23} 4303^{10} **>11a 12f<**
Utmost Zeal (USA) 4 b c Cozzene (USA)-Zealous Lady (USA) (Highland Blade (USA)) **1996:** 5124^{3} 5151^{9} **1997:** 477^{12} 587^{7} 838^{10} 1273^{7} 1694^{7} **>65a 64f<**

V

Vagabond Chanteuse 3 ch f Sanglamore (USA)-Eclipsing (IRE) (Baillamont (USA)) 688^{4} 959^{3} 1147^{2} $1722a^{3}$ 2869^{6} 3492^{8} 3902^{11} **>100df<**
Vain Tempest 3 b c Warning-North Wind (IRE) (Lomond (USA)) 1611^{4} (2045) 2601^{9} 3012^{7} 4310^{4} 4996^{7} **>86+f<**
Valagalore 3 b f Generous (IRE)-Victoria Cross (USA) (Spectacular Bid (USA)) 944^{3} 1474^{4} (2940) (3412) 4101^{15} 4783^{11} **>91f<**
Valedictory 4 b c Slip Anchor-Khandjar (Kris) (962) 1325^{2} **>108f<**
Vales Ales 4 b g Dominion Royale-Keep Mum (Mummy's Pet) 3240^{24} **>14f<**
Valet De Coeur (USA) 3 b c Chief's Crown (USA)-Color Of Love (FR) (Conquistador Cielo (USA)) $268a^{2}$ **>75f<**
Valiant Dash 11 b g Valiyar-Dame Ashfield (Grundy) 1996^{7} 2207^{13} 2539^{2} 2825^{7} 3623^{4} **>38f<**
Valise 4 b f Salse (USA)-Secret Valentine (Wollow) 1139^{8} 1503^{10} 1689^{19} **>38f<**
Valslastchance 2 b g Clantime-Panay (Arch Sculptor) 441^{8} 1298^{9} **>8f<**
Val's Prince (USA) 5 ch g Eternal Prince (USA)-Key Buy (USA) (Valid Appeal (USA)) $4395a^{2}$ $5065a^{8}$ **>128f<**
Vanadium Ore 4 b g Precious Metal-Rockefillee (Tycoon II) **1996:** 5235^{7} **1997:** (4845) 4998^{5} **>33a 59f<**
Vanborough Lad 8 b g Precocious-Lustrous (Golden Act (USA)) **1996:** 5123^{9} 5208^{6} **1997:** (1273) 1955^{5} 2004^{3} 2310^{3} 2369^{3} 3328^{2} 3465^{4} 4472^{8} **>42a 50f<**
Van Chino 3 b c Suave Dancer (USA)-Atlantic Flyer (USA) (Storm Bird (CAN)) 945^{4} 1777^{5} 2711^{14} 3121^{12} 3691^{8} 3977^{10} 4210^{11} 4480^{2} 4700^{5} **>53a 60f<**
Van Gurp 4 ch c Generous (IRE)-Atlantic Flyer (USA) (Storm Bird (CAN)) 661^{10} 775^{5} 1176^{10} 1658^{3} 3243^{9} 3901^{9} 4558^{36} **>13a 87f<**
Vanishing Trick (USA) 3 ch f Gone West (USA)-Wand (IRE) (Reference Point) 1268^{14} 1794^{2} 2062^{14} 2832^{7} 3128^{3} 3445^{3} 4859^{4} 5044^{5} **>86f<**
Vaporize 5 ch g Handsome Sailor-Belle Appeal (Teenoso (USA)) 2780^{9} 3048^{9} 3249^{12} **>2f<**
Varnishing Day (IRE) 5 b g Royal Academy (USA)-Red Letter Day (Crepello) 540^{7} 1317^{19} 2026^{31} 3420^{4} **>15a 68f<**
Varxi (FR) 3 gr c Kaldoun (FR)-Girl Of France $1361a^{3}$ $3180a^{6}$ **>107f<**
Vasari (IRE) 3 ch c Imperial Frontier (USA)-Why Not Glow (IRE) (Glow (USA)) 501^{5} 854^{9} 1018^{7} **>97f<**
Vassia (USA) 3 b/f Machiavellian (USA)-Domludge (USA) (Lyphard (USA)) (4648a) **>76f<**
Vax New Way 4 gr g Siberian Express (USA)-Misty Arch (Starch Reduced) 601^{16} **>73a 65f<**

Vax Rapide 2 ch f Sharpo-Vax Lady (Millfontaine) (536) 893^{7} **>82f<**

Vax Star 3 gr f Petong-Vax Lady (Millfontaine) 877^{9} 1980^{19} 2683^{9} 3065^{4} 3273^{15} 3709^{13} **>88f<**

Veesey 4 b f Rock City-Travel On (Tachypous) *199^{9} 286^{8} 328^{8}* 608^{16} **>24f<**

Veiled Threat (IRE) 3 f 1727a^{3} 4666a^{8} **>109f<**

Velour 3 b f Mtoto-Silk Braid (USA) (Danzig (USA)) 4094a^{9} **>105f<**

Velvet Appeal (IRE) 3 b f Petorius-Sugarbird (Star Appeal) 806a^{7} 1062a^{5} 2447a^{11} **>81f<**

Velvet Jones 4 b gr g Sharrood (USA)-Cradle of Love (USA) (Roberto (USA)) 601^{4} 1009^{7} 1639^{5} 1972^{14} 2580^{6} 3561^{10} 3710^{7} 4008^{8} 4373^{10} 4608^{11} **>52a 52f<**

Velvet Story 2 ch c Aragon-Lucy Manette (Final Straw) 1492^{16} 1797^{6} 2233^{2} 3564^{7} **>55f<**

Vendimia 4 b f Dominion-Villasanta (Corvaro (USA)) *37^{8}*

Venetian Scene 3 ch f Night Shift (USA)-Revisit (Busted) (837) **>75f<**

Venice Beach 5 b g Shirley Heights-Bold and Beautiful (Bold Lad (IRE)) *387^{4} 422^{6} 511^{3}* 753^{6} **>63a 64df<**

Veni Vidi Vici (IRE) 4 b c Fayruz-Divine Apsara (Godswalk (USA)) 1878^{8} 2201^{2} 2408^{2} 2760^{8} 3328^{4} 3987^{10} 4219^{6} 4319^{3} 4878^{10} **>21a 73f<**

Venture Capitalist 8 ch g Never so Bold-Brave Advance (USA) (Bold Laddie (USA)) 452^{5} 745^{3} 1855^{2} 1975^{6} 3023^{4} 3118^{2} 3604^{20} 3649^{9} 4100^{10} 4221^{4} 4467^{3} 4599^{4} **>97f<**

Venture Connect 3 ch g Interrex (CAN)-Tricata (Electric) *255^{3} 341^{10}* 1844^{13} **>71da f<**

Vera's First (IRE) 4 b f Exodal (USA)-Shades of Vera (Precocious) *278^{10}* **>32a 72f<**

Verasica 3 b f Handsome Sailor-Vera Musica (USA) (Stop The Music (USA)) 778^{8} *1787^{11}*

Verdant Express 2 b f Greensmith-Ballynora (Ballacashtal (CAN)) *2367^{8}* 2396^{2} 3055^{W} 3324^{8} *4054^{12}* 4500^{5} **>22a 58f<**

Verdi (IRE) 3 b c Green Desert (USA)-Flying Bid (Auction Ring (USA)) 964^{5} 1851^{4} 3632^{7} 4046^{15} 4802^{13} **>63f<**

Vereva (IRE) 3 b f Kahyasi-Vearia (Mill Reef (USA)) (1916a) 3877a^{2} **>121+f<**

Verglas (IRE) 3 gr c Highest Honor (FR)-Rahaam (USA) (Secreto (USA)) 1060a^{4} 1541a^{2} 2454a^{6} 3674a^{6} **>118df<**

Veridian 4 b g Green Desert (USA)-Alik (FR) (Targowice (USA)) 552^{10} 789^{15} 982^{7} (1398) 1981^{5} (2653) 3053^{2} 3434^{4} 4672^{6} 4891^{2} **>91f<**

Verinder's Gift 3 ch g Chilibang-A Nymph Too Far (IRE) (Precocious) *8^{7} 96^{4} 225^{7}* 4243^{18} 4972^{11} **>45a 28f<**

Veri's Game (IRE) 4 f 4535a^{4} **>91f<**

Verity 3 ch f Pharly (FR)-Persian Victory (IRE) (Persian Bold) *4795^{12}*

Vernoy (USA) 3 ch c Forty Niner (USA)-Marble Maiden (Lead on Time (USA)) 2273a^{2} **>115f<**

Verocity (FR) 2 b c Groom Dancer (USA)-Villella (Sadler's Wells (USA)) 4949^{8} **>16f<**

Veronica Franco 4 b f Darshaan-Maiden Eileen (Stradavinsky) **1996:** *5085^{4} 5145^{9}* **1997:** 1478^{6} 1665^{11} 2139^{9} 2916^{3} (3291) 3640^{6} (4222) 4562^{3} 4821^{2} 4971^{4} **>44a 61f<**

Verro (USA) 10 ch g Irish River (FR)-Royal Rafale (USA) (Reneged) *903^{8} 1134^{9}* 3469^{16} **>20a 16f<**

Versatility 4 b f Teenoso (USA)-Gay Criselle (Decoy Boy) 2687^{3} 3277^{11} 3501^{6} 3992^{20} 4998^{14} **>64f<**

Vertical Speed (FR) 3 ch c Bering-Victoire Bleue (Legend of France (USA)) (1913a) (3179a) 4149^{2} **>124f<**

Vert Val (USA) 3 b f Septieme Ciel (USA)-Valthea (FR) (Antheus (USA)) (4393a) **>112f<**

Verulam (IRE) 4 b br g Marju (IRE)-Hot Curry (USA) (Sharpen Up) 3767^{12} **>50?f<**

Very Simple (IRE) 2 ch f Shalford (IRE)-Whist Up (Artaius (USA)) 3636^{14} **>8f<**

Vet's Deceit (IRE) 2 ch c Statoblest-Maniusha (Sallust) 594^{13} 780^{5} **>32f<**

Veuve Clicquot 3 b f Saddlers' Hall (IRE)-False Lift (Grundy) 2126^{9} 2486^{5} 3188^{6} *4053^{15}* **>64f<**

Via Del Quatro (IRE) 5 b m Posen (USA)-Gulistan (Sharpen Up) 4374^{12} **>41f<**

Via Splendida (IRE) 2 b f Project Manager-Closette (FR) (Fabulous Dancer (USA)) 1880a^{4} **>79f<**

Via Verbano (IRE) 3 b f Caerleon (USA)-Closette (FR) (Fabulous Dancer (USA)) 1533a^{8} 2023^{12} 2814a^{7} 3510a^{3} 3675a^{5} 4094a^{4} 4356a^{3} **>105f<**

Viburnum 3 b f Old Vic-Burning Desire (Kalaglow) 2116^{2} 2568^{9} 3133^{5} 4743^{4} 4821^{11} **>71?f<**

Vice Presidential 2 ch g Presidium-Steelock (Lochnager) (1038) 1310^{3} 2103^{12} 3908^{6} 4143^{4} 4284^{5} 4468^{11} **>93f<**

Vicious Circle 3 b c Lahib (USA)-Tight Spin (High Top) 1646^{3} **>77f<**

Vicki Romara 3 ch f Old Vic-Romara (Bold Lad (IRE)) 1258^{2} 1612^{5} 1950^{2} 3579^{2} (3890) 4749^{4} **>86f<**

Vicky Jazz 2 ch f Alhijaz-Kinkajoo (Precocious) 2943^{15} 4753^{20} 4974^{13} **>37f<**

Victor Blum (USA) 4 b g Dr Blum (USA)-Victoria Elena (USA) (Gold Stage (USA)) 605^{9} 790^{9} 1105^{11} 1636^{16} 2199^{13} 2916^{4} 3091^{15} 3291^{3} 4405^{5} **>44f<**

Victoria House (IRE) 3 b f River Falls-Double Grange (IRE) (Double Schwartz) 485^{6} *874^{10}* 1423^{14} 4601^{23} **>30f<**

Victoria Sioux 4 ch f Ron's Victory (USA)-Blues Indigo (Music Boy) *79^{10} 126^{8}* **>33a 40f<**

Victory At Hart 3 ch g Ron's Victory (USA)-Ceramic (USA) (Raja Baba (USA)) 963^{16} 1464^{6} 1798^{11} 2200^{5} **>41f<**

Victory Note (USA) 2 b c Fairy King (USA)-Three Piece (Jaazeiro (USA)) 2556^{2} (2863) 4524^{5} 4880^{3} **>103f<**

Victory Team (IRE) 5 b g Danehill (USA)-Hogan's Sister (USA) (Speak John) 477^{2} 560^{5} (766) 946^{4} 1489^{7} 2006^{12} 2216^{7} 2743^{2} 2933^{8} (3930) 4071^{3} (4878) 4979^{24} **>78a 87f<**

Viennese Dancer 4 b f Prince Sabo-Harmony Park (Music Boy) *20^{8} 404^{8}* **>10a 25f<**

Vignette (USA) 2 b f Diesis-Be Exclusive (Be My Guest (USA)) 3151^{5} (3569) **>82+f<**

Viking Dream (IRE) 5 b m Vision (USA)-Nordic Pride (Horage) 969^{3} 1822^{7} **>62f<**

Village Native (FR) 4 ch g Village Star (FR)-Zedative (FR) (Zeddaan) 604^{4} 1327^{6} 1419^{8} 2096a^{12} 2372^{4} 2581^{9} *(3398)* 3852^{2} 3984^{4} 4649a^{7} *4574^{5} 4985^{5}* **>65a 65f<**

Village Pub (FR) 3 ch c Village Star (FR)-Sloe Berry (Sharpo) **1996:** *5133^{10} 5207^{5}* **1997:** 602^{8} 1141^{11} 1633^{16} 2148^{3} *2300^{4} 2605^{5}* 4648a^{9} 4817^{9} *4980^{6}* **>41a 50f<**

Villarica (IRE) 3 b f Fairy King (USA)-Bolivia (GER) (Windwurf (GER)) 2654^{2} 3037^{5} 3389^{2} 3820^{2} 4015^{11} 4176^{15} *(4980)* **>63+a 68f<**

Vincent 2 b c Anshan-Top-Anna (IRE) (Ela-Mana-Mou) 3260^{4} 3920^{6} **>50f<**

Vintage Escape (IRE) 4 b f Cyrano de Bergerac-Overstay 2447a^{2} **>75f<**

Vintage Red 7 b g Sulaafah (USA)-Armonit (Town Crier) 3487^{5} **>32a 37f<**

Vintage Taittinger (IRE) 5 b g Nordico (USA)-Kalonji (Red Alert) 1232^{9} 2145^{6} (2350) 2825^{6} 3401^{4} **>50a 38f<**

Viola Royale (IRE) 2 b f Royal Academy (USA)-Wood Violet (USA) (Riverman (USA)) 3839a^{2} 4619a^{6} **>91f<**

Violette Sabo 3 b f Prince Sabo-Kajetana (FR) (Caro) 4214^{16} 4431^{5} **>32f<**

V I P Charlie 3 b c Risk Me (FR)-Important Guest (Be My Guest (USA)) *(247) (293) 413^{3}* 1141^{10} 1294^{6} 2006^{7} 2554^{11} 2691^{11} **>80a 69f<**

Virtual Reality 6 b g Diamond Shoal-Warning Bell (Bustino) 735^{2} 933^{7} 1482^{2} 1739^{4} 2866^{7} 3435^{F} 4225^{12} **>78f<**

Virtuous 2 b f Exit To Nowhere (USA)-Exclusive Virtue (USA) (Shadeed (USA)) 3744^{3} 4119^{4} (4567) 4786^{7} **>89f<**

Viscoumtess Brave (IRE) 3 b or br f Law Society (USA)-Vadrouille (USA) (Foolish Pleasure (USA)) **1996:** (5195a) **1997:** 1075a^{3} 1875^{4} 3005a^{2} (4763a) **>100f<**

Vishnu (USA) 7 b g Storm Bird (CAN)-Vachti (FR) (Crystal Palace (FR)) *375^{5}* **>47a 53f<**

Visimotion (USA) 7 ch g Imp Society (USA)-Ditdad (USA) (Tudor Grey) *71^{8}* **>33a 72f<**

Visionary (FR) 3 b c Linamix (FR)-Visor (FR) 1204a^{3} 1725a^{4} 4656a^{3} 5032a^{3} **>115f<**

Vision Of Spirit (USA) 3 ch c Chief's Crown (USA)-Viendra (USA) (Raise A Native) 1544a^{12} **>91f<**

Vista Alegre 2 b g Petong-Duxyana (IRE) (Cyrano de Bergerac) 1932^{9} 2917^{18} 4012^{13} 4311^{9} **>90a 50f<**

Viva Verdi (IRE) 3 b f Green Desert (USA)-Vaison la Romaine (Arctic Tern (USA)) 645^{9} 886^{10} (1248) 1966^{3} 3316^{3} 4695^{14} **>70f<**

Vivid Angel (USA) 2 f *5060a^{6}*

Vivo (IRE) 4 b g Shaadi (USA)-Gay Nocturne (2441a) 4191a^{2} 4837a^{3} **>109f<**

Vocation (IRE) 2 ch f Royal Academy (USA)-Petite Liqueurelle (IRE) (Shernazar) (4067) 4325^{3} **>81f<**

Vogue Imperial (IRE) 2 b g Imperial Frontier (USA)-Classic Choice (Patch) 2042^{7} 2736^{9} *2914^{5} 3076^{5}* **>34a 26f<**

Voila Premiere (IRE) 5 b g Roi Danzig (USA)-Salustrina (Sallust) 1208^{3} 1398^{3} 3246^{4} 3916^{6} 3992^{12} **>71f<**

Vola Via (USA) 4 b br g Known Fact (USA)-Pinking Shears (USA) (Sharpen Up) 538^{2} 657^{2} 735^{12} 1268^{4} (1588) 1811^{3} (2120) 2574^{4} 3238^{5} **>91f<**

Volley (IRE) 4 b f Al Hareb (USA)-Highdrive (Ballymore) **1996:** 5192a^{11} **1997:** 1308^{11} 1874^{3} 2894^{2} 3220^{4} 3423^{3} 3982^{3} 4121^{5} 4423^{18} **>91f<**

Volontiers (FR) 2 b c Common Grounds-Senlis (USA) (Sensitive Prince (USA)) 5041^{2} **>87f<**

Voodoo Saint (USA) 2 ch c St Jovite (USA)-Voo Doo Dance (USA) (Stage Door Johnny) 3598^{3} 4096^{6} **>85f<**

Voyagers Quest (USA) 3 b br c Dynaformer (USA)-Orange Sickle (USA) (Rich Cream (USA)) **1996:** (5191a) **1997:** (851) 1726a^{7} **>125df<**

Vrennan 3 ch f Suave Dancer (USA)-Advie Bridge (High Line) 1405^{2} 2046^{5} 2486^{2} 3867^{7} *4481^{3}* **>72a 77f<**

W

Waasef 4 b g Warning-Thubut (USA) (Tank's Prospect (USA)) 1023^{9} 1297^{10} 2960^{7} 3605^{12} 3793^{16} **>46f<**

Wadada 6 b or br g Adbass (USA)-No Rejection (Mummy's Pet) *99^{6} 139^{4}* **>49a 52f<**

Waders Dream (IRE) 8 b g Doulab (USA)-Sea Mistress (Habitat) 1666^{8} 1857^{6} 2721^{7} 3290^{8}

3642^{13} 3855^{9} 4184^{6} 4228^{9} 4451^{11} **>39a 51f<**

Wadi 2 b c Green Desert (USA)-Eternal (Kris) 4165^{3} 4739^{3} **>81f<**

Wafa (IRE) 3 ch f Kefaah (USA)-Shomoose (Habitat) *511^{5}* **>50a f<**

Waff's Folly 2 b f Handsome Sailor-Shirl (Shirley Heights) 4298^{7} 4884^{12} **>56f<**

Wafir (IRE) 5 b h Scenic-Taniokey (Grundy) 933^{9} 1450^{2} (1559) 2136^{F} 2710^{13} 3263^{4} 3773^{8} 4151^{3} 4383^{5} 5053^{10} **>89f<**

Waft (USA) 4 ch f Topsider (USA)-Gliding By (USA) (Tom Rolfe) **1996:** *5151^{7}* **>50a 71f<**

Wagga Moon (IRE) 3 b g Mac's Imp (USA)-Faapette (Runnett) 634^{3} 845^{13} 998^{8} 2157^{6} 2415^{10} 2505^{3} 2715^{7} 3266^{12} 3431^{18} 3762^{9} **>60f<**

Wahab 4 b g Unfuwain (USA)-Mileeha (USA) (Blushing Groom (FR)) **1996:** *5177^{8}* **1997:** *424^{14}* 4184^{18} **>6a 3f<**

Wahiba Sands 4 b g Pharly (FR)-Lovely Noor (USA) (Fappiano (USA)) 1176^{5} 2028^{19} 2710^{7} 3051^{5} 4136^{9} 4416^{2} (4704) (4903) 5043^{3} **>105f<**

Waikiki Beach (USA) 6 ch g Fighting Fit (USA)-Running Melody (Rheingold) **1996:** *5208^{2} (5254)* **1997:** *105^{5} 176^{7} 1575^{2}* 1878^{12} 2285^{5} 3248^{2} 4757^{30} 5049^{23} **>81a 72f<**

Wait For Rosie 3 b f Reprimand-Turbo Rose (Taufan (USA)) 2925^{9} 3185^{10} **>83?f<**

Waiting Game (IRE) 3 b c Reprimand-Walesiana (GER) (Star Appeal) 597^{4} 2341^{9} **>82+a 96df<**

Wait'n'see 2 b g Komaite (USA)-Kakisa (Forlorn River) 743^{10} 1396^{9} (1860) 3932^{16} 4746^{10} 4922^{13} 5050^{21} **>77f<**

Wakeel (USA) 5 b g Gulch (USA)-Raahia (CAN) (Vice Regent (CAN)) 832^{10} 987^{16} 1262^{3} 1442^{7} 1979^{8} 2242^{3} 2391^{5} (2749) 2944^{5} 3434^{2} 4295^{11} **>92f<**

Waky Nao 4 b c Alzao (USA)-Waky Na (GER) (Ahonoora) 811a^{2} (4122a) 4762a^{5} **>121f<**

Wala (GER) 3 ch f Acatenango (GER)-Wanateluthspilgrim (GER) (Pilgrim (USA)) 2458a^{3} **>101f<**

Wales 2 ch c Caerleon (USA)-Knight's Baroness (Rainbow Quest (USA)) 1174^{3} 2057^{3} (4157) 5034a^{6} **>87f<**

Wali (USA) 7 b g Lomond (USA)-Magic Slipper (Habitat) *203^{14} 326^{11}* **>7a 33f<**

Walkabout 3 ch c Generous (IRE)-Nomadic Pleasure (Habitat) 740^{11} 1014^{8} 1612^{4} 1956^{6} 2414^{4} **>67f<**

Walk On By 3 gr c Terimon-Try G's (Hotfoot) 725^{9} 1592^{6} 1986^{4} 2323^{4} 2879^{3} **>73f<**

Walk the Beat 7 b g Interrex (CAN)-Plaits (Thatching) *79^{8} (127) 364^{6} (424) (512)* 1035^{8} 1395^{5} 1488^{5} 1743^{4} 2179^{11} (3417) 4321^{9} 4518^{6} 4979^{18} **>74a 69f<**

Wallflower 2 b f Polar Falcon (USA)-Stufida (Bustino) 2553^{10} **>39f<**

Walpole 2 b c High Estate-Walesiana (GER) (Star Appeal) 3235^{13} **>23f<**

Walton Grey (IRE) 2 gr g Paris House-Green Bonnet (FR) (Green Dancer (USA)) 3753^{5} 4231^{12} 4384^{11} **>43f<**

Walworth Wizard 2 b g Presidium-Mrs Magic (Magic Mirror) 2127^{9} 2538^{6} 3306^{12} **>48f<**

Wandering Thoughts (IRE) 8 ch g Boyne Valley-Moves Well (Green God) 1198a^{6} **>86f<**

Wandering Wolf 2 ch c Wolfhound (USA)-Circle of Chalk (FR) (Kris) 2103^{13} 4311^{4} 4526^{7} **>69f<**

Warbler 3 b f Warning-Bold and Beautiful (Bold Lad (IRE)) 3000a^{3} 4658a^{3} **>110f<**

Wardara 5 ch m Sharpo-Ward One (Mr Fluorocarbon) 1206a^{3} 1721a^{2} 3001a^{6} 3554a^{7} **>66a 110f<**

War Declaration (IRE) 3 (4398a) 4866a^{8} **>109f<**

Warhurst (IRE) 6 b g Nordance (USA)-Pourboire (Star Appeal) *3^{9} 36^{7} 273^{11} 401^{6}* **>33a 62f<**

Warm Hearted (USA) 5 ch g Known Fact (USA)-Lovin' Lass (USA) (Cutlass (USA)) *32^{W}* **>59a f<**

Warm Spell 7 b g Northern State (USA)-Warm Wind (Tumble Wind (USA)) 2344^{2} 2564^{6} *3231^{6}* **>49a 65f<**

Warning Express 3 b f Warning-Ivoronica (Targowice (USA)) 2873^{4} 3550^{2} 4290^{4} 4820^{11} **>59f<**

Warningford 3 b c Warning-Barford Lady (Stanford) 683^{5} 991^{4} (1976) 2525^{9} 3144^{6} **>96f<**

Warning Reef 4 b g Warning-Horseshoe Reef (Mill Reef (USA)) *73^{12}* 777^{6} 1027^{6} 1491^{9} 2236^{6} 2682^{11} 3015^{10} 3567^{9} **>57f<**

Warning Time 4 b c Warning-Ballad Island (Ballad Rock) 452^{7} 726^{13} 942^{21} 1317^{4} *1578^{11}* 1634^{3} (1772) 2105^{5} **>46a 110f<**

Warp Drive (IRE) 3 ch c Bluebird (USA)-Red Roman (Solinus) **1996:** *5201^{7} 5243^{6}* **1997:** *234^{2} 296^{5} 414^{7} 547^{4}* **>52a f<**

Warren Knight 4 b g Weldnaas (USA)-Trigamy (Tribal Chief) 1320^{17} 1926^{5} 2848^{13} 3392^{8} **>54f<**

Warring 3 b g Warrshan (USA)-Emerald Ring (Auction Ring (USA)) 1000^{4} 1272^{7} 1568^{2} 1826^{6} *2151^{12}* 2695^{8} 3968^{9} 4877^{21} **>15a 64f<**

Warrior King (IRE) 3 b g Fairy King (USA)-It's All Academic (IRE) (Mazaad) 478^{5} 640^{8} 1094^{12} 1426^{4} 1951^{5} 2245^{7} 2376^{2} 2727^{4} 3205^{3} 3336^{2} 3592^{2} (3868) 4228^{10} 4472^{9} 4696^{9} 4877^{15} **>59f<**

Warrlin 3 b c Warrshan (USA)-Lahin (Rainbow Quest (USA)) *373^{7} 425^{4}* 534^{5} *1043^{7} 1785^{4}* 1996^{4} 2207^{7} 2423^{5} **>36a 64f<**

War Shanty 4 b f Warrshan (USA)-Daring Ditty (Daring March) 1168^{13} 2782^{9} **>60f<**

Warspite 7 b g Slip Anchor-Valkyrie (Bold Lad (IRE)) **1996:** *5271^{5}* **1997:** *67^{5} 104^{6}* **>43a 46f<**

Washm (USA) 2 b f Diesis-Jathibiyah (USA) (Nureyev (USA)) 2875^{9} 3757^{7} **>59f<**

Wasp Ranger (USA) 3 b c Red Ransom (USA)-Lady Climber (USA) (Mount Hagen (FR)) 674^{8} (1304) 1770^{2} 2013^{21} 2871^{6} 3189^{4} 3725^{8} 4383^{6} **>97f<**

Watchman 2 b g Mazaad-High Heather (Shirley Heights) 2202^{6} 2499^{3} 2905^{8} 3307^{8} 4208^{13} **>50f<**

Watch Me (IRE) 4 b f Green Desert (USA)-Fenny Rough (Home Guard (USA)) 519^{10} 745^{4} 877^{8} **>90f<**

Watch Me Go (IRE) 8 b g On Your Mark-Nighty Night (Sassafras (FR)) 595^{8} **>47a 47f<**

Watch My Lips 5 b g Vin St Benet-Manor Farm Toots (Royalty) 3933^{5} **>45?f<**

Watch The Fire 4 b f Statoblest-Thulium (Mansingh (USA)) 786^{7} 1219^{11} 1501^{15} (2358) (2505) 2841^{7} 3198^{11} 4169^{3} *4301^{13}* 4561^{21} 4905^{19} **>26a 70f<**

Watercolour (IRE) 3 b f Groom Dancer (USA)-River Nomad (Gorytus (USA)) 431^{16} **>35f<**

Water Flower 3 b f Environment Friend-Flower Girl (Pharly (FR)) 683^{12} 2583^{7} 2952^{3} 3318^{7} 4108^{8} (4521) **>74f<**

Water Force 2 b c River Falls-Quelle Chemise (Night Shift (USA)) 1486^{10} 2306^{9} 2509^{4} 3186^{5} 4143^{6} 4271^{6} 4670^{9} **>68f<**

Water Garden 3 ch c Most Welcome-On Show (Welsh Pageant) *(576) (1048) 2161^{4}* 3418^{9} **>80a 50f<**

Water Hazard (IRE) 5 b g Maelstrom Lake-Simply Inch (Simply Great (FR)) *213^{6}* **>45a 59f<**

Water's Edge 2 b f Saddlers' Hall (IRE)-Irish Impulse (USA) (Irish River (FR)) 4227^{7} 4694^{5} **>69f<**

Waterspout (USA) 3 b c Theatrical-Water Angel (USA) (Halo (USA)) 2873^{11} 4579^{2} 4788^{11} **>79f<**

Waterville Boy (IRE) 3 ch c Don't Forget Me-East River (FR) (Arctic Tern (USA)) **1996:** *5098^{5}* **>51a 59f<**

Waterwave (USA) 4 ch c Irish River (FR)-Wajna (USA) (Nureyev (USA)) 4060^{8} 4331^{3} 4705^{3} **>80f<**

Wathbat Lion 2 ch c Lion Cavern (USA)-Alwathba (USA) (Lyphard (USA)) 1267^{5} 2215^{4} 3103^{7} 3597^{5} **>72f<**

Wathbat Nashwan 3 ch c Nashwan (USA)-Alwathba (USA) (Lyphard (USA)) 1239^{8} 1811^{4} 2062^{6} (2512) 2890^{3} 3238^{8} **>88f<**

Wathik (USA) 7 ch h Ogygian (USA)-Copper Creek (Habitat) *309a^{3}* **>94a f<**

Watkins 2 ch c King's Signet (USA)-Windbound Lass (Crofter (USA)) 2022^{5} 2881^{4} 3260^{6} 3973^{9} 4111^{8} **>70f<**

Waverley Star 12 br g Pitskelly-Quelle Blague (Red God) *208^{6}* **>17?a 18f<**

Wave Rock 2 br g Tragic Role (USA)-Moonscape (Ribero) 3598^{17} 4064^{8} 4454^{4} (4745) **>82f<**

Wayne Lukas 2 b c Don't Forget Me-Modern Dance (USA) (Nureyev (USA)) 4526^{12} **>65f<**

Way Out Yonder 2 b c Shirley Heights-Patsy Western (Precocious) 1607^{3} 4478^{2} **>83+f<**

Waypoint 4 b f Cadeaux Genereux-Princess Athena (Ahonoora) **1996:** *5215^{5}* **1997:** *(459) 663^{2}* 892^{3} (1397) 2280^{2} (2835) 3217^{10} 3982^{9} 4423^{12} *4797^{5}* **>78a 95f<**

Waytogomo 2 b f Midyan (USA)-Running Glimpse (IRE) (Runnett) 3055^{6} 3228^{7} 3493^{8} **>50f< (DEAD)**

Wedding Band 2 b f Saddlers' Hall (IRE)-Priceless Bond (USA) (Blushing Groom (FR)) 2706^{14} 2875^{14} 3078^{2} 4953^{8} **>45f<**

Wedding Music 3 b f Music Boy-Diamond Wedding (USA) (Diamond Shoal) **1996:** *5172^{6}* **1997:** *77^{4}* **>32a 54f<**

Wee Christy (IRE) 2 gr c Contract Law (USA)-Eternal Optimist (Relko) 993^{14} 1267^{13} 2288^{8} 2827^{6} 3563^{9} 4508^{10} 4807^{9} 4994^{18} **>48f<**

Wee Dram 3 ch f Most Welcome-Scottish Legend (Legend of France (USA)) (474) 675^{8} 2945^{10} **>79f<**

Weet A Bit (IRE) 3 b c Archway (IRE)-Aridje (Mummy's Pet) **1996:** *5265^{5}* **1997:** *204^{6}* 2549^{2} *3396^{7}* 4326^{6} 4415^{8} 4607^{16} **>17a 44f<**

Weet-A-Minute (IRE) 4 ro c Nabeel Dancer (USA)-Ludovica (Bustino) **1996:** *5120^{4}* **1997:** 2679^{2} 3144^{4} 3728^{4} 3988^{2} 4281^{4} 4523^{5} 4671^{3} 4776^{6} **>77a 80f<**

Weet And See 3 b g Lochnager-Simply Style (Bairn (USA)) *49^{6} 164^{3} 255^{6} 395^{2} (513)* 764^{6} 1249^{4} 1513^{6} *2052^{7} 3044^{10} 4571^{12}* **>22a 68f<**

Weet Ees Girl (IRE) 3 ro f Common Grounds-Kastiliya (Kalamoun) 434^{12} 731^{4} 783^{8} 1029^{8} 1661^{8} *2050^{10}* 3332^{6} *3581^{12}* **>64f<**

Weetman's Weigh (IRE) 4 b c Archway (IRE)-Indian Sand (Indian King (USA)) 443^{18} *514^{5}* 835^{4} (946) (1471) (1629) 2325^{5} 2478^{4} 3087^{3} 3310^{2} 3801^{9} 4270^{2} 4561^{14} 4927^{7} **>80a 88f<**

Welcome Heights 3 b g Most Welcome-Mount Ida (USA) (Conquistador Cielo (USA)) 842^{11} 1633^{17} *2151^{2}* 2245^{3} (2510) 2785^{3} (3143) 4112^{4} 4741^{2} 4958^{7} **>63a 66f<**

Welcome Home 3 b f Most Welcome-Miss Cindy (Mansingh (USA)) 599^{13} 983^{3} 2040^{6} 2231^{4} 2523^{5} 3696^{8} 3906^{8} 3992^{5} 4213^{6} 4633^{15} *(4800)* 5028^{9} **>56a 50f<**

Welcome Lu 4 ch f Most Welcome-Odile (Green Dancer (USA)) 1390^{17} 1631^{12} 2204^{8} 2937^{12} 4170^{8} 4432^{3} 4609^{5} 4768^{10} *4811^{9}* **>25a 34f<**

Welcome Sunset 2 b c Most Welcome-Deanta in

Eirinn (Red Sunset) 1492^{12} (2520) 3131^{3} 4271^{17} 4885^{10} **>84f<**
Wellaki (USA) 3 ch c Miswaki (USA)-Wellomond (FR) (Lomond (USA)) 4635^{5} 4788^{12} **>83f<**
Well Appointed (IRE) 8 b g Petorius-So Stylish (Great Nephew) 1081^{3} **>59f<**
Well Armed (IRE) 6 b g Moscow Society (USA)-Sales Centre (Deep Run) 996^{4} 1230^{10} 1497^{5} 2475^{6} 2825^{14} 3858^{8} **>59f<**
Wellcome Inn 3 ch c Most Welcome-Mimining (Tower Walk) 558^{5} 1230^{12} 2351^{2} 2414^{3} 2825^{9} (3482) 3781^{9} 3937^{19} 4213^{7} **>65f<**
Well Drawn 4 b g Dowsing (USA)-Classic Design (Busted) 1427^{8} 2550^{9} 3018^{5} 3980^{10} **>70a 54f<**
Wellesiena (GER) 3 f 1918a^{7} **>90f<**
Well Set (IRE) 2 br f Second Set (IRE)-Wolkenlos (GER) (Lagunas) 2637a^{3}
Wellspring (IRE) 3 b f Caerleon (USA)-Marwell (Habitat) (1394) 1975^{3} 2299^{2} 2677^{7} 4553^{9} **>96f<**
Well Warned 3 b f Warning-Well Beyond (IRE) (Don't Forget Me) 724^{3} 1621^{4} 3003a^{8} 4120^{6} 4599^{3} **>98f<**
Welsh Melody 4 b f Merdon Melody-Young Whip (Bold Owl) **1996:** *5134^{15}* **1997:** *54^{9}* **>50da 31f<**
Welsh Mill (IRE) 8 b g Caerleon (USA)-Gay Milly (FR) (Mill Reef (USA)) 470^{10} 982^{2} 1215^{6} (2479) 2787^{3} 3867^{8} **>74f<**
Welsh Mountain 4 b g Welsh Captain-Miss Nelski (Most Secret) 759^{14} 1384^{11} 1796^{8} 2552^{9} 3143^{9} (3321) 4992^{14} **>49f<**
Welsh Poppy 2 ch f 5036a^{3}
Welsh Queen (IRE) 3 b f Caerleon (USA)-Stellar Empress (USA) 806a^{6} 1193a^{2} 3510a^{5} **>85f<**
Welton Arsenal 5 b g Statoblest-Miller's Gait (Mill Reef (USA)) 987^{4} (1214) 1456^{15} 2124^{6} 2598^{14} 4893^{11} 4978^{17} **>86f<**
Welville 4 b g Most Welcome-Miss Top Ville (FR) (Top Ville) 981^{4} **>100?f<**
Wenda (IRE) 2 ch f Priolo (USA)-Pennine Drive (IRE) (Pennine Walk) 4012^{6} (4425) 4786^{12} **>86f<**
Wentbridge Lad (IRE) 7 b g Coquelin (USA)-Cathryn's Song (Prince Tenderfoot (USA)) 1016^{11} 1035^{9} 1422^{7} *1575^{6}* 1677^{7} *2302^{7}* 3382^{4} (3570) (3588) 3767^{9} 3886^{2} 3901^{6} *4304^{5}* 4449^{8} 4802^{8} 4845^{11} **>56a 67f<**
Were Not Stoppin 2 b c Mystiko (USA)-Power Take Off (Aragon) 4745^{W}
Wesley's Lad (IRE) 3 b br g Classic Secret (USA)-Galouga (FR) (Lou Piguet (FR)) *1043^{14}* 1296^{8} 2035^{4} 2307^{6} 2518^{3} *4590^{8}* **>56a 60f<**
Westcourt Magic 4 b g Emarati (USA)-Magic Milly (Simply Great (FR)) 573^{4} 745^{6} 1148^{16} 1303^{5} 1948^{7} 2211^{2} 2377^{8} 2900^{8} 3273^{9} (3900) 4100^{13} 4280^{23} 4887^{14} 4995^{22} **>84f<**
Westcourt Ruby 2 b f Petong-Red Rosein (Red Sunset) 4211^{11} 4428^{9} 4769^{12} **>42f<**
Western Chief (IRE) 3 b c Caerleon (USA)-Go Honey Go (General Assembly (USA)) 4191a^{11} **>100f<**
Western General 6 ch g Cadeaux Genereux-Patsy Western (Precocious) 2223^{2} 2385^{2} 2660^{15} **>81f<**
Western Hour (USA) 3 b f Gone West (USA)-Out On The Town (USA) (Spend A Buck (USA)) (1168) 1875^{3} 3000a^{7} 3492^{6} **>95f<**
Western Lord 2 b g Noble Patriarch-Sophia Western (Steel Heart) 2359^{6} 2752^{10} 3103^{11} 3973^{12} 4208^{9} 4470^{5} 4582^{9} **>44f<**
Western Playboy 5 b g Law Society (USA)-Reine D'Beaute (Caerleon (USA)) *216^{12}* 969^{7} 2311^{9} 2694^{6} 2928^{8} **>21a 49f<**
Western Sonata (IRE) 4 b f Alzao (USA)-Musique Classique (USA) (Exclusive Native (USA)) *491^{2}* 1023^{4} *1421^{2}* **>67a 73f<**
Western Venture (IRE) 4 ch g Two Timing (USA)-Star Gazing (IRE) (Caerleon (USA)) **1996:** *5104^{5}* **1997:** 496^{12} 668^{5} 721^{11} 951^{8} 1040^{8} 1229^{13} 1615^{3} 2880^{8} (3627) **>44a 37f<**
West Humble 4 ch f Pharly (FR)-Humble Pie (Known Fact (USA)) 1101^{4} 1948^{10} 2211^{10} 3786^{8} **>95df<**
Westminster (IRE) 5 ch g Nashamaa-Our Galadrial (Salmon Leap (USA)) 1233^{9} 1748^{5} 1992^{2} (2145) 2236^{8} 2650^{6} 3091^{5} 3200^{5} 4235^{20} 4751^{14} 4926^{3} 5028^{10} **>67f<**
Wey River Mist 4 b f General Wade-Donroya (Don) **1996:** *5085^{7}*
Whacker-Do (IRE) 2 ch c Archway (IRE)-Denowski (Malinowski (USA)) 979^{7} 1510^{7} 2361^{4} 2786^{8} *3042^{8}* 3306^{9} 3961a^{25} 4602^{8} **>45a 59f<**
What A Fuss 4 b g Great Commotion (USA)-Hafwah (Gorytus (USA)) *(177) 330^{5}* 1093^{5} 1844^{9} 2150^{2} 2399^{2} (2776) **>73a 67f<**
Whatever's Right (IRE) 8 b g Doulab (USA)-Souveniers (Relko) *143^{3} 248^{6} 352^{7}* 1262^{12} (2552) 2892^{6} 3091^{6} 3328^{7} *3860^{6}* 4139^{20} **>64a 70f<**
What Happened Was 3 b f Deploy-Berberana (Never so Bold) 1017^{14} 1301^{8} 1955^{7} 2309^{2} 2557^{11} 2645^{5} 2918^{7} 3218^{10} 3377^{4} 4268^{9} **>72f<**
What Jim Wants (IRE) 4 b g Magical Strike (USA)-Sally Gone (IRE) (Last Tycoon) *5^{5}* 4438^{13} 4804^{11} **>31a 25f<**
What's That Amy 3 b f Sizzling Melody-Lady Pennington (Blue Cashmere) *329^{5} 427^{7} 577^{7}* **>36a f<**
Wheildon 3 ch g Keen-Arabian Rose (USA) (Lyphard (USA)) 765^{10} 1464^{4} 1780^{9} 2039^{17} 2357^{10} **>53df<**
Whenby (USA) 4 ch f Bering-Nether Poppleton (USA) (Deputy Minister (CAN)) **1996:** 5192a^{2} **1997:** 2273a^{3} 3371a^{8} **>107f<**
Whimoweh 2 b f Son of Shaka-Hollie Dancing (Frimley Park) 4543^{12} **>9f<**
Whippers Delight (IRE) 9 ch g King Persian-Crashing Juno (Crash Course) **1996:** *5276^{4}* **1997:** *63^{9}* 1142^{9} **>23a 51f<**
Whirlawhile (USA) 3 b g Silver Hawk (USA)-My Turbulent Beau (USA) (Beau's Eagle (USA)) 1106^{6} 1277^{4} 1841^{5} 2297^{4} **>73df<**
Whiskey Wisdom (CAN) 4 *5066a^{4}* **>118a f<**
Whisky Mack (IRE) 2 b g Mac's Imp (USA)-Merville (Fairy King (USA)) 880^{3} 1084^{3} 2370^{4} (2786) 3237^{15} 4772^{5} **>85df<**
Whispered Melody 4 b f Primo Dominie-Sing Softly (Luthier) 538^{11} 755^{4} 1373^{4} (1987) 2369^{8} 2576^{3} 3138^{13} 4448^{12} **>66a 58f<**
Whispering Dawn 4 b f Then Again-Summer Sky (Skyliner) *220^{7} 369^{2}* 2374^{8} 2552^{15} 2782^{4} 3153^{14} 3491^{6} **>68a 65f<**
Whisper Low (IRE) 3 ch f Shalford (IRE)-Idle Gossip (Runnett) **1996:** *5146^{10} 5245^{5} 5257^{9}* **1997:** *221^{6} 345^{7}* 2197^{14} 3030^{8} 3332^{4} 3698^{3} **>25a 46f<**
Whitechapel (USA) 9 br g Arctic Tern (USA)-Christchurch (FR) (So Blessed) **1996:** 5126a^{4} **1997:** 267a^{7} 310a^{7} (1208) 2514^{11} 4426^{11} 4667^{3} (4879) **>88f<**
White Emir 4 b g Emarati (USA)-White African (Carwhite) 726^{17} 942^{11} 1158^{8} 1410^{5} 1488^{2} 1772^{8} (1937) (2232) 2529^{8} 2769^{11} 3217^{26} 3600^{9} 3816^{2} 4137^{20} 4321^{12} 4636^{11} 4770^{9} **>66f<**
Whitegate's Son 3 ch g Minster Son-Whitegates Lady (Le Coq d'Or) 4847^{17} **>43f<**
White Gulch 3 b c Gulch (USA)-White Wisteria (Ahonoora) **1996:** 5128a^{6} **>87f<**
White Hare 4 b f Indian Ridge-Pomade (Luthier) 1818^{7} 2569^{12} **>38f<**
Whitelock Quest 9 b g Rainbow Quest (USA)-Sagar (Habitat) *36^{6} 150^{6} 589^{7}* **>50a 20f<**
White Plains (IRE) 4 b g Nordico (USA)-Flying Diva (Chief Singer) (647) 789^{7} 1208^{6} 1592^{8} 1951^{2} (2470) 2890^{11} 3112^{17} 3496^{8} 3768^{5} 3972^{7} *4981^{8}* **>57a 75f<**
White Scissors (USA) 2 b c St Jovite (USA)-Scissors (USA) (Blade (USA)) 4526^{6} **>71f<**
White Settler 4 b g Polish Patriot (USA)-Oasis (Valiyar) 895^{26} 1166^{4} 1446^{6} 1849^{5} 2282^{5} 2508^{W} 2698^{3} 3018^{9} 3710^{11} 4333^{9} **>50f<**
Whitewater Affair 4 ch f Machiavellian (USA)-Much Too Risky (Bustino) (736) 1172^{3} 2104^{3} (3370a) 3704^{2} 4346a^{3} **>122f<**
White Willow 8 br g Touching Wood (USA)-Dimant Blanche (USA) (Gummo (USA)) *5^{4} 68^{11}* **>56a 76f<**
Whitley Grange Boy 4 b g Hubbly Bubbly (USA)-Choir (High Top) *248^{8} 416^{5}* 461^{6} 598^{6} 3762^{16} *4053^{5}* 4438^{8} (4751) **>41a 61f<**
Whittle Rock 4 b f Rock City-Lurking (Formidable (USA)) 450^{16} 1085^{5} 1389^{2} 1782^{7} 2209^{3} 2569^{11} 3064^{7} 3443^{6} 3484^{16} **>59f<**
Whizz Kid 3 b f Puissance-Panienka (POL) (Dom Racine (FR)) *158^{4} 212^{4} 320^{8}* 602^{5} 751^{6} 876^{4} 1236^{11} 1566^{3} 1814^{4} 2321^{6} 2481^{7} 2732^{9} 2921^{9} 3206^{7} 3637^{3} 4328^{14} 4546^{6} 4816^{11} **>43a 47f<**
Who Dealt 3 ch f Nalchik (USA)-Lana's Secret (Most Secret) 2360^{7} *3396^{6}* 4290^{11} *4795^{7} 4980^{13}* **>26a 30f<**
Who Nose (IRE) 2 b g Cyrano de Bergerac-Epoch (Wolver Hollow) 441^{5} 530^{2} *592^{3}* 631^{6} (1370) (1461) 2240^{3} 2697^{5} 2786^{2} 2942^{2} 3152^{7} 4006^{4} 4143^{3} 4551^{8} 4670^{11} 4897^{2} **>56a 76f<**
Who's That Man 3 gr c Mystiko (USA)-Milne's Way (The Noble Player (USA)) *296^{6}* 475^{8} 636^{7} 925^{3} 1296^{6} (1820) 2005^{5} (2750) 2956^{5} 3478^{9} 4176^{14} 4632^{14} 4876^{10} **>42a 62f<**
Whothehellisharry 4 ch g Rich Charlie-Ballagarrow Girl (North Stoke) *273^{3} 580^{9}* 900^{8} 1222^{4} 1424^{10} 1802^{8} 2039^{6} 2228^{15} 2701^{4} 2896^{5} **>58a 44f<**
Why O Six 3 b g Efisio-Scotch Imp (Imperial Fling (USA)) 549^{6} 667^{4} 1333^{7} *1756^{9}* 4601^{17} 4877^{19} **>34a 50f<**
Wicklow Boy (IRE) 6 b g Roi Danzig (USA)-Pickety Place (Prince Tenderfoot (USA)) *487^{6}* 1114^{R} *1417^{R}* **>30?a 21?f<**
Widar 3 b c Soviet Star (USA)-Waseela (IRE) (Ahonoora) 2097a^{4} 2642a^{8} **>106f<**
Wideyedbushytailed 2 b f Elmaamul (USA)-Run for Love (Runnett) *1290^{6} 2367^{9}* 2664^{10}
Wigging 2 b f Warning-Pushy (Sharpen Up) 3187^{7} 4332^{3} **>75f<**
Wijara (IRE) 5 b h Waajib-Nawara (Welsh Pageant) 1261^{2} 2180^{5} 3784^{3} **>103f<**
Wilawander 4 ch c Nashwan (USA)-Wilayif (USA) (Danzig (USA)) 451^{2} 891^{2} 1172^{7} **>115f<**
Wilcuma 6 b g Most Welcome-Miss Top Ville (FR) (Top Ville) **1996:** (5216a) **1997:** 943^{3} 1261^{8} 2136^{9} 3051^{6} 3703^{13} 4312^{3} 4678^{5} 4893^{15} **>106f<**
Wildcat (IRE) 2 b g Lion Cavern (USA)-Kentucky Starlet (USA) (Cox's Ridge (USA)) 2688^{4} 3193^{8} (3493) 4068^{16} *(4303)* **>72+a 73+f<**
Wild City (USA) 3 b br c Wild Again (USA)-Garvin's Gal (USA) (Seattle Slew (USA)) 586^{16} **>28f<**
Wild Event (USA) 4 5063a^{9} **>114f<**
Wildfire (SWI) 6 br g Beldale Flutter (USA)-Little White Star (Mill Reef (USA)) **1996:** *5181^{5} 5240^{4}* **1997:** *88^{3} 123^{9} (206) 410^{16} 857^{2} 2164^{2}* 2279^{7} *3609^{3} 4304^{4}* **>57a 40f<**
Wild Lilly 2 b f Elmaamul (USA)-Chrisanthy (So

Blessed) 1619^{7} 1812^{6} 2147^{7} 4566^{10} 4819^{14} **>51f<**

Wildmoor 3 ch g Common Grounds-Impropriety (Law Society (USA)) 471^{7} 793^{4} 1094^{10} 1299^{4} 1863^{2} (2387) 2757^{6} 3485^{8} 4213^{12} *4810^{3}* **>43a 62df<**

Wild Nettle 3 ch f Beveled (USA)-Pink Pumpkin (Tickled Pink) 652^{10} 1141^{7} 1439^{15} 1620^{15} 4878^{23} *5020^{10}* **>1a 36f<**

Wild Palm 5 b g Darshaan-Tarasova (USA) (Green Forest (USA)) 1324^{9} 1606^{6} 2201^{6} 2424^{3} *2671^{4}* 2922^{6} 3385^{6} 3718^{6} 3936^{9} **>65a 68f<**

Wild Prospect 9 b g Homing-Cappuccilli (Lorenzaccio) **1996:** *5114^{13}* **1997:** 896^{23} 2203^{15} **>23f<**

Wild Rice 5 b g Green Desert (USA)-On Show (Welsh Pageant) 677^{13} 1634^{7} **>82a 98df<**

Wild Rita 5 ch m Risk Me (FR)-Ma Pierrette (Cawston's Clown) 789^{5} 2028^{9} 2514^{12} (2944) 3259^{2} 3748^{3} 4672^{5} **>89f<**

Wild Sky (IRE) 3 br c Warning-Erwinna (USA) (Lyphard (USA)) **1996:** *5121^{4}* **1997:** 453^{4} 654^{5} 840^{2} 1256^{5} 1782^{2} 2695^{4} 4578^{8} 4700^{3} (4979) **>68a 82f<**

Wildwood Flower 4 b f Distant Relative-Tolstoya (Northfields (USA)) 671^{8} 1171^{8} 1532a^{W} 1610^{3} 2105^{8} 2299^{3} 3217^{14} 3764^{6} 3975^{8} (4155) (4282) 4553^{5} 4777^{9} **>108f<**

Wilfred Sherman (IRE) 2 b g Silver Kite (USA)-Algonquin Park (High Line) 530^{7} *592^{5} (859) 1124^{5}* 2412^{8} 3062^{10} *4054^{8}* **>57a 33f<**

Wilkins 8 b g Master Willie-Segos (Runnymede) 4374^{2} 4519^{2} **>61f<**

Willa Wooster 2 b f Sure Blade (USA)-Bertrade (Homeboy) 4901^{5} **>63f<**

Will Do 4 br g Weldnaas (USA)-Philogyny (Philip of Spain) **1996:** *5184^{5}* **1997:** *11^{5} 215^{3} 416^{3} 459^{9}* 585^{7} 766^{9} 1020^{13} 1166^{17} **>66a 65df<**

William's Well 3 ch g Superpower-Catherines Well (Junius (USA)) 466^{7} 649^{9} 845^{8} 995^{5} (1730) (1995) 2235^{2} 2417^{2} 2547^{6} 3121^{6} 3287^{4} 3460^{2} 3756^{6} 3922^{3} 4233^{11} 4636^{16} 4805^{14} **>65df<**

William Wallace 3 b g Rudimentary (USA)-Irish Impulse (USA) (Irish River (FR)) 565^{5} 1117^{6} 1256^{4} 1427^{12} 1837^{10} 2226^{7} **>55f<**

Willie Conquer 5 ch g Master Willie-Maryland Cookie (USA) (Bold Hour) 1771^{7} 2028^{3} 2709^{2} 3705^{19} 4443^{5} 4754^{17} 5053^{7} **>102f<**

Willie Miles 4 b g Dancing Dissident (USA)-Madam Bold (Never so Bold) 529^{17} 687^{14} 925^{14} 1467^{23} **>13a 26f<**

Willie Rushton 4 ch f Master Willie-Amberush (No Rush) *1156^{9} 2049^{6} 3232^{5} 3415^{6}* 3970^{9} **>46a 42f<**

Willow Dale (IRE) 4 b f Danehill (USA)-Miss Willow Bend (USA) (Willow Hour (USA)) 643^{5} 786^{5} 1083^{2} 1327^{2} 1410^{2} 1666^{7} 1743^{3} 2006^{3} (2179) 2393^{3} 2563^{4} 2769^{2} 2950^{6} 3217^{22} (3600) 3765^{14} 3914^{8} **>87f<**

Willskip (USA) 3 b g Minshaanshu Amad (USA)-Eighty Lady (USA) (Flying Lark (USA)) 537^{12} 609^{7} 793^{9} 952^{5} **>40f<**

Will To Win 3 b f Mazilier (USA)-Adana (FR) (Green Dancer (USA)) **1996:** *5142^{12} 5239^{3}* **1997:** *51^{10} (221) 259^{4} 345^{2} (399)* 1141^{4} 1279^{4} 1810^{3} 2244^{8} 2554^{3} 2921^{11} 3393^{9} 4115^{4} *4574^{9} 4985^{12}* **>64a 60f<**

Will You Dance 3 b f Shareef Dancer (USA)-Padelia (Thatching) (773) 1242^{10} 3377^{5} **>75f<**

Wilton 2 ch c Sharpo-Poyle Amber (Sharrood (USA)) 2361^{7} 2736^{6} **>47f<**

Windborn 3 b f Superpower-Chablisse (Radetzky) **1996:** *5214^{4} 5275^{3}* **1997:** *44^{3} 77^{3} 124^{6} 247^{3} 293^{3} 361^{4} 417^{3}* 2407^{3} 2724^{9} 2836^{9} *3054^{9}* **>52a 42f<**

Wind Cheetah (USA) 3 b br c Storm Cat (USA)-Won't She Tell (USA) (Banner Sport (USA)) 2023^{11} 2334^{3} 3063^{5} **>113f<**

Wind In The Park 2 ch f Clantime-She's a Breeze (Crofthall) 1827^{8} 2276^{3} 3324^{12} **>37f<**

Windrush Boy 7 br g Dowsing (USA)-Bridge Street Lady (Decoy Boy) **1996:** *5131^{15} 5184^{8} 5220^{5} 5280^{5}* **1997:** *58^{5}* 1572^{6} 2703^{6} 2895^{3} 3287^{15} 4115^{10} 4221^{7} 4370^{16} 4791^{11} **>35a 51f<**

Windrush Holly 4 br f Gildoran-Bridge Street Lady (Decoy Boy) **1996:** *5235^{13}* **1997:** 1006^{7} 1168^{12} 1632^{8} **>17a 65f<**

Windsor Castle 3 b c Generous (IRE)-One Way Street (Habitat) 937^{5} 1150^{2} (2027) (2327) 3645^{3} 4149^{5} **>122f<**

Windspeed 2 ch g Sheerwind-Speed Baby (USA) (Diplomat Way) 4454^{14} 4627^{14} *4812^{15}* **>12f<**

Windswept (IRE) 4 b f Taufan (USA)-Sutica (Don) 3465^{13} 3787^{5} 4043^{11} *4484^{8}* 4607^{9} 4899^{6} **>33a 51f<**

Windy Day (IRE) 3 b f Waajib-Money Spinner (USA) (Teenoso (USA)) 4763a^{2} **>94f<**

Windyedge (USA) 4 ch g Woodman (USA)-Abeesh (USA) (Nijinsky (CAN)) 595^{20} *857^{12}* **>4a 60f<**

Windy Treat (USA) 3 b br g Shadeed (USA)-Widaad (USA) (Mr Prospector (USA)) 2173^{3} 2549^{9} 3196^{2} (3420) **>75f<**

Winged Hussar 4 b g In The Wings-Akila (4620a) **>103+f<**

Wingnut (IRE) 4 ch f Digamist (USA)-Royal Cloak (Hardicanute) **1996:** *5079^{10} 5118^{10}* **1997:** *321^{9} 486^{5}* **>38da 53f<**

Wing of A Prayer 3 b c Statoblest-Queen Angel (Anfield) 606^{3} *1151^{13}* 1484^{11} 2332^{4} **>16a 55f<**

Winnebago 4 b f Kris-Siouan (So Blessed) 553^{13} 1390^{11} 1795^{3} 2114^{2} 2825^{13} 3283^{14} (3485) 3626^{4} **>59f<**

Winning Smile (FR) 7 br h Never so Bold-Funny Reef (FR) (Mill Reef (USA)) 1721a^{5} 3554a^{6} **>108f<**

Winona (IRE) 2 b f Alzao (USA)-My Potters (USA) 4093a^{10} 4619a^{2} 5002a^{5} **>98f<**

Winsa (USA) 2 b f Riverman (USA)-Wasnah (USA) (Nijinsky (CAN)) 3117^{4} 4066^{2} 4437^{3} 4875^{3} **>83f<**

Winsome George 2 b c Marju (IRE)-June Moon (IRE) (Sadler's Wells (USA)) 697^{6} 954^{6} 1267^{3} 1510^{2} (2112) 2707^{4} 2905^{3} 3545^{6} 4690^{9} 4875^{10} **>77f<**

Winsome Wooster 6 ch m Primo Dominie-Bertrade (Homeboy) (1489) 1680^{2} 2835^{7} (3138) **>74f<**

Winston 4 b g Safawan-Lady Leman (Pitskelly) *578^{14}* 895^{15} 1097^{7} 1384^{8} 2290^{7} 2465^{5} 3428^{7} 3573^{5} 3759^{11} 4471^{3} 4629^{3} 4924^{14} 5030^{8} **>46a 57f<**

Wintered Out 3 b f Digamist (USA)-Record Song (Indian King (USA)) 1316^{14} 1780^{11} **>59f<**

Winter Garden 3 ch c Old Vic-Winter Queen (Welsh Pageant) 773^{5} (944) 1242^{2} (1850) 2027^{4} 2596^{2} 3109^{7} **>104f<**

Winter Romance 4 ch c Cadeaux Genereux-Island Wedding (USA) (Blushing Groom (FR)) 894^{4} 1160^{4} (2136) 3797^{2} (3988) 4281^{3} 4678^{7} **>113f<**

Winter Scout (USA) 9 ch g It's Freezing (USA)-His Squaw (USA) (Tom Rolfe) 827^{3} 1225^{10} 1613^{5} (1861) (2204) 2501^{2} 2708^{12} 3702^{6} 4059^{14} **>18+a 67f<**

Wintertime 2 b c Robellino (USA)-Naturally Fresh (Thatching) 3494^{9} 4061^{11} 4857^{D} **>71f<**

Wira (IRE) 3 ch c Lahib (USA)-Mother Courage (Busted) 518^{8} **>58f<**

Wiscalina (GER) 2 b f Linamix (FR)-Wiscaria (GER) (Ashmore (FR)) 2637a^{2}

Wishbone Alley (IRE) 2 b c Common Grounds-Dul Dul (USA) (Shadeed (USA)) 2881^{6} 3260^{3} 3479^{11} 3869^{8} 4566^{5} 4702^{11} **>61f<**

Wishing Stone (USA) 3 b f Dayjur (USA)-Worood (USA) (Vaguely Noble) 2020^{3} (2555) (2918) 3128^{2} 3786^{2} 4242^{6} **>88f<**

Wiston Cheese (USA) 2 b c Cryptoclearance (USA)-Happy Gal (FR) (Habitat) (4668) **>94tf<**

Witchfinder (USA) 5 b g Diesis-Colonial Witch (USA) (Pleasant Colony (USA)) 3909^{5} 4139^{19} 4696^{7} **>58f<**

Witching Hour (IRE) 3 b f Alzao (USA)-Itching (IRE) (Thatching) 890^{4} **>84f<**

With A Will 3 b g Rambo Dancer (CAN)-Henceforth (Full of Hope) 1005^{11} 1958^{3} 2395^{4} (2645) 3248^{12} 4210^{18} 4958^{9} **>72df<**

With Fire (USA) 3 b c Gulch (USA)-Fran's Valentine (Saros (FR)) 1362a^{3} **>107f<**

Without Friends (IRE) 3 b g Thatching-Soha (USA) (Dancing Brave (USA)) (462) 556^{4} 643^{3} 1008^{6} 1141^{14} 1509^{12} *2319^{4}* 2748^{2} 2947^{6} 3969^{6} 4371^{6} 4504^{4} 4858^{3} **>61a 55f<**

With The Tempo (IRE) 4 b f Last Tycoon-Starlust (Sallust) 554^{6} *855^{8}* 1012^{10} *4300^{7}* **>18a 41f<**

Witney-La-Roche 3 ch g Superlative-Ever Reckless (Crever) 882^{12} **>51f<**

Wixim (USA) 4 ch c Diesis-River Lullaby (USA) (Riverman (USA)) 678^{2} (830) 1554a^{2} 2009^{5} 2453a^{4} 4660a^{3} **>125f<**

Wizard King 6 b h Shaadi (USA)-Broomstick Cottage (Habitat) (839) 1198a^{2} 1719a^{3} (2078a) (3063) (4344a) (4625a) **>127f<**

Wolfhunt 2 b c Wolfhound (USA)-Vayavaig (Damister (USA)) 2370^{7} 3986^{2} 4640^{5} 4897^{12} **>68f<**

Wolf Mountain 3 ch c Selkirk (USA)-Cubby Hole (Town And Country) (1460) 3124^{8} 3447^{3} **>106f<**

Wollstonecraft (IRE) 4 b f Danehill (USA)-Ivory Thread (USA) (Sir Ivor) **1996:** *5131^{12}* **>50a 80f<**

Wonderboy (IRE) 3 ch c Arazi (USA)-Alsaaybah (USA) (Diesis) 693^{12} 2183^{10} 2592^{7} 3549^{9} **>60f<**

Wontcostalotbut 3 b f Nicholas Bill-Brave Maiden (Three Legs) 841^{9} 1006^{8} 1409^{9} *2365^{5}* 2582^{8} **>46a 56f<**

Won't Forget Me (IRE) 2 br g Don't Forget Me-Lucky Realm (Realm) 1251^{10} 1812^{21} 2579^{4} 3384^{2} (3639) (3967) 4068^{10} *4589^{9}* **>35a 71f<**

Woodbeck 3 b br f Terimon-Arminda (Blakeney) 889^{4} 1302^{2} (1582) (2214) 2601^{4} 3119^{3} 3803^{8} **>89f<**

Woodbury Lad (USA) 4 ch c Woodman (USA)-Habibti (Habitat) **1996:** *5085^{3}* **1997:** *98^{5}* **>61a 81f<**

Wooderine (USA) 3 ch f Woodman (USA)-Exuberine (FR) (Be My Guest (USA)) 815a^{12} **>76f<**

Woodetto (IRE) 3 b g Maledetto (IRE)-Wood Kay (IRE) (Treasure Kay) 4431^{8} 4600^{4} *4809^{13}* **>24a 48f<**

Woodland Dove 3 ch f Weldnaas (USA)-Jove's Voodoo (USA) (Northern Jove (CAN)) **1996:** *5160^{9}* **>7a 18f<**

Woodland Melody (USA) 2 b f Woodman (USA)-Eloquent Minister (USA) (Deputy Minister (CAN)) (2516) (2962) (3999a) **>94f<**

Woodland Nymph 3 gr f Norton Challenger-Royal Meeting (Dara Monarch) *255^{5} 355^{3}* 534^{2} *1043^{12} 1785^{7} 2049^{5}* 2199^{10} **>49da 60f<**

Woodlands Energy 6 b m Risk Me (FR)-Hallowed (Wolver Hollow) 2200^{10} **>25f<**

Woodlands Lad Too 5 b g Risk Me (FR)-Hallowed (Wolver Hollow) 1463^{17} **>11?f<**

Woodlands Pride (IRE) 2 ch f Petardia-Valediction (Town Crier) 2545^{17} 3099^{5} 4694^{13}

>33f<
Woodren (USA) 4 ch f Woodman (USA)-Whitethroat (Artaius (USA)) 440a[7] 934[5] 2513[7] 2869[8] 3017[7] 3498[7] **>98f<**
Woodrising 5 b m Nomination-Bodham (Bustino) 2920[7] *3232[6]* 3467[6] **>37?a 39f<**
Woods of Cisterna (IRE) 3 **1996:** 5128a[4] **1997:** 917a[9] **>98f<**
Woody's Boy (IRE) 3 gr g Roi Danzig (USA)-Smashing Gale (Lord Gayle (USA)) 1276[7] 2532[6] 2783[5] 3279[4] 3633[2] 4046[3] 4336[12] 4744[8] **>74f<**
Woopi Gold (IRE) 3 b f Last Tycoon-Borough Counsel (Law Society (USA)) 1919a[3] **>96f<**
World Express (IRE) 7 b g Jareer (USA)-Eight Mile Rock (Dominion) 4667[8] **>6a 62f<**
World of Joy 2 b f Selkirk (USA)-Realisatrice (USA) (Raja Baba (USA)) 3979[9] 4332[11] **>57f<**
World Premier 4 b c Shareef Dancer (USA)-Abuzz (Absalom) *398[11]* 519[3] 892[2] 1148[3] 2105[21] 2334[8] 2598[7] 3011[5] 3649[4] 4240[9] **>43a 103f<**
Worldwide Elsie (USA) 4 b f Java Gold (USA)-Tender Camilla (Prince Tenderfoot (USA)) **1996:** *5231[11]* **1997:** *175[5]* *382[7]* 796[5] 1001[19] *1086[3]* 1373[12] **>57a 52f<**
World Without End (USA) 8 ch g World Appeal (USA)-Mardie's Bid (USA) (Raise A Bid (USA)) *272[6]* *356[3]* *375[6]* *543[5]* *580[4]* **>61a f<**
Worms (IRE) 2 c 4766a[5] **>96f<**
Worth The Effort 2 b f Beveled (USA)-Haiti Mill (Free State) 4556[10] **>32f<**
Wosaita 2 b f Generous (IRE)-Eljazzi (Artaius (USA)) 4433[6] **>63f<**
Wot No Fax 4 ch g Sharrood (USA)-Priors Dean (Monsanto (FR)) 789[18] 1016[13] 1459[16] **>68f<**
Wottashambles 6 b or br g Arrasas (USA)-Manawa (Mandamus) **1996:** *(5213) (5255)* **1997:** *106[2]* *(202)* *252[3]* *402[5]* 2592[9] **>73a 43f<**
Woven Silk (USA) 3 b f Danzig (USA)-Ribbon (USA) (His Majesty (USA)) (4960a) **>109f<**
Wray (IRE) 5 ch h Sharp Victor (USA)-Faye (Monsanto (FR)) 1058a[5] 2441a[8] **>100f<**
Wrekin Pilot 2 b g Ron's Victory (USA)-Lunaire (Try My Best (USA)) 432[6] (504) 722[4] 2860[2] 3204[2] 3688[7] 3934[3] 4247[4] **>87f<**
Wren (IRE) 2 ch f Bob Back (USA)-In the Rigging (USA) (Topsider (USA)) (3008a) (3872a) (4764a) **>100+f<**
Wrn Princess 3 ch f Handsome Sailor-Sovereign Rose (Sharpen Up) 1966[12] 2179[9] 2705[11] **>32f<**
Wrought Iron (USA) 2 b br f Dayjur (USA)-Pris de Fer (USA) (Sir Ivor) 2875[12] 4694[9] **>62f<**
Wurftaube (GER) 4 ch f Acatenango (GER)-Wurfbahn (GER) (Frontal) (1073a) 1724a[2] 3182a[2] **>122f<**
Wuxi Venture 2 b c Wolfhound (USA)-Push a Button (Bold Lad (IRE)) 2409[3] 3745[3] 4061[6] *4299[3]* 4551[5] 5025[2] **>74a 95?f<**
Wychwood Sandy 6 b g Mansingh (USA)-Do-Run-Do (Palm Track) 4370[22] 4580[19] **>7f<**
Wynbury Flyer 2 ch g Risk Me (FR)-Woolcana (Some Hand) 1829[9] 2935[8] 3563[4] 3751[7] 4595[6] **>55f<**

X

Xaar 2 b c Zafonic (USA)-Monroe (USA) (Sir Ivor) (3366a) 3882a[2] (4391a) (4784) **>127+f<**
Xenophon of Cunaxa (IRE) 4 b g Cyrano de Bergerac-Annais Nin (Dominion) **1996:** *5099[9]* *5161[6]* **1997:** *159[2]* *263[13]* 1489[12] 1935[5] 2337[4] 2835[19] 4328[13] 4518[16] 4738[13] **>60a 34f<**
X-Ray (IRE) 4 gr g Actinium (FR)-Charter Lights (Kalaglow) *184[5]*
Xwife (IRE) 2 b f Alzao (USA)-Dawning Beauty (USA) (Well Decorated (USA)) 4474[13] **>22f<**
Xylem (USA) 6 ch h Woodman (USA)-Careful (USA) (Tampa Trouble (USA)) 3937[18] 4225[7] (4510) 4667[12] 4920[4] 5049[7] **>78f<**

Y

Yaakum 8 b g Glint of Gold-Nawadder (Kris) 3401[10] 3623[11] **>54?a 34?f<**
Yabint El Sultan 3 ch f Safawan-Dalby Dancer (Bustiki) 778[4] 1030[4] 1423[3] 1582[2] 2172[2] 2495[3] (2654) 3048[3] (3891) 4015[5] 4242[3] 4435[5] **>91f<**
Yacht 5 ch g Warning-Bireme (Grundy) *5019[4]* **>42a 51f<**
Yajtahed (IRE) 2 ch c Mujtahid (USA)-Rainstone (Rainbow Quest (USA)) 1607[10] **>56f<**
Yak Alfaraj 3 b c Sadler's Wells (USA)-Clara Bow (USA) (Coastal (USA)) 1105[5] 1434[6] 2410[7] 3020[2] 3440[3] 3815[4] **>78f<**
Yalaietanee 3 b c Sadler's Wells (USA)-Vaigly Star (Star Appeal) (737) 1204a[4] 1541a[4] 4240[11] **>123df<**
Yalta (IRE) 4 b g Soviet Star (USA)-Gay Hellene (Ela-Mana-Mou) 738[8] 1262[9] 2026[23] 2729[6] (2947) 3392[2] 3786[6] (4314) 4637[W] 4757[17] **>88f<**
Ya Malak 6 b g Fairy King (USA)-La Tuerta (Hot Spark) 573[5] (1303) 1455[5] (1766) 2106[10] (2526) 2683[4] 3111[11] (3724) **>121f<**
Ya Marhaba 4 b g Efisio-Ichnusa (Bay Express) **1996:** *5114[3]* *5179[2]* **>57a 36f< (DEAD)**
Yanabi (USA) 2 b f Silver Hawk (USA)-Halholah (USA) (Secreto (USA)) 3114[3] 3979[6] 4317[3] 4701[2] **>80f<**
Yanavanavano (IRE) 3 b g Maledetto (IRE)-Dublin Millennium (Dalsaan) *1155[9]* 2004[18] 2392[F] **>29a 37f<**
Yangtze (IRE) 3 b g River Falls-Sister Dympna (Grundy) 534[6] 1465[11] 2245[5] **>45f<**
Yanomami (USA) 2 ch f Slew O' Gold (USA)-Sunerta (USA) (Roberto (USA)) 3769[3] 4418[2] **>71f<**
Yanshan 2 b c Anshan-Joy of Freedom (Damister (USA)) 3818[8] 3973[8] 4244[5] **>66f<**
Yarob (IRE) 4 ch c Unfuwain (USA)-Azyaa (Kris) 4004[4] 4754[13] **>86f<**
Yashmak (USA) 3 b f Danzig (USA)-Slightly Dangerous (USA) (Roberto (USA)) 960[14] (1209) 1738[4] (2053) 2814a[2] (4651a) **>123f<**
Yaverland (IRE) 5 b h Astronef-Lautreamont (Auction Ring (USA)) 4568[11] 4802[16] 4992[16] **>56a 43f<**
Yavlensky (IRE) 3 b c Caerleon (USA)-Schwanensee (USA) (Mr Leader (USA)) **1996:** 5128a[2] **1997:** 851[4] 1099[2] 1553a[12] 2462a[3] 4133[4] 4398a[12] **>101df<**
Yazaly (USA) 8 ch h Blushing Groom (FR)-Capricorn Belle (Nonoalco (USA)) *392a[2]* **>104a f<**
Yeast 5 b g Salse (USA)-Orient (Bay Express) 433[2] 892[25] 4148[11] **>102f<**
Yeath (IRE) 5 ch g Exhibitioner-Grain of Sand (Sandford Lad) 640[9] **>49f<**
Yellow Dragon (IRE) 4 b g Kefaah (USA)-Veldt (High Top) *302[6]* **>39a 34f<**
Yeoman Oliver 4 b g Precocious-Impala Lass (Kampala) **1996:** *5137[2]* *5206[7]* *5235[3]* *5269[7]* **1997:** *(150)* *207[2]* *257[3]* *514[8]* *4813[4]* 4992[5] **>70a 66f<**
Yet Again 5 ch g Weldnaas (USA)-Brightelmstone (Prince Regent (FR)) **1996:** *(5276)* **1997:** *(13) (63)* 538[6] (640) 1641[4] 1844[2] 2170[2] 2208[5] 3093[5] (3245) 3603[3] **>59+a 62f<**
Yokohama (USA) 6 gr h Theatrical-Griddle (Off Shore Gamble (FR)) 1359a[2] 2269a[2] 2819a[2] (4258a) 4665a[18] **>122f<**
Yo-Mate 6 b g Komaite (USA)-Silent Sun (Blakeney) 1809[W] 2175[8] **>38a 19f<**
Yorkie George 3 b c Efisio-Petonica (IRE) (Petoski) 694[12] 1148[12] 1634[2] 1980[5] 2325[3] (2775) 3217[17] 4148[4] **>103f< (DEAD)**
Yorkies Boy 2 ro c Clantime-Slipperose (Persepolis (FR)) 432[8] 500[4] 684[7] 1425[2] (1657) 2314[4] 2862[4] 3209[7] 3708[2] 3908[4] 4296[5] 4890[4] **>94f<**
Yorkshire (IRE) 3 ch c Generous (IRE)-Ausherra (USA) (Diesis) 1159[7] 1762[2] 1962[3] 2642a[10] 3048[4] 3578[2] **>112f<**
Youdontsay 5 ch m Most Welcome-Fabulous Luba (Luthier) (1107) 1772[6] 2105[26] 2649[5] 3795[8] 3914[5] 4155[29] 4979[22] **>82f<**
Young Annabel (USA) 4 ch f Cahill Road (USA)-Only for Eve (USA) (Barachois (CAN)) *578[2]* *1082[8]* *1132[3]* **>77da 66f<**
Young Ben (IRE) 5 ch g Fayruz-Jive (Ahonoora) *326[8]* *429[11]* 972[8] 1687[3] 2540[9] (2738) 2934[2] 3208[12] 3625[9] 3856[W] *4051[12]* 4329[3] 4707[9] 4844[13] **>46a 52f<**
Young Benson 5 b g Zalazl (USA)-Impala Lass (Kampala) **1996:** *5269[6]* **1997:** 4324[17] **>35a 22f<**
Young Bigwig (IRE) 3 b g Anita's Prince-Humble Mission (Shack (USA)) 745[5] 1403[5] 1609[7] 3410[8] 3649[13] 3975[11] 4307[8] 4511[3] 4995[24] **>69a 82f<**
Young Butt 4 ch g Bold Owl-Cymbal (Ribero) *4304[12]* 4757[19] **>27a 69?f<**
Young Dalesman 4 br g Teenoso (USA)-Fabulous Molly (Whitstead) 2036[10] 2521[14] **>56?f<**
Young Duke (IRE) 9 gr g Double Schwartz-Princess Pamela (Dragonara Palace (USA)) 2228[2] **>72a 80f<**
Young Frederick (IRE) 4 ch g Polish Patriot (USA)-Notre Histoire (Habitat) *160[6]* *280[5]* *312[10]* *367[7]* 2777[4] 3276[9] **>35a 45?f<**
Young Ibnr (IRE) 2 b g Imperial Frontier (USA)-Zalatia (Music Boy) 500[8] (684) 884[2] 1013[5] 1255[6] 1729[4] **>82f<**
Young Josh 2 b c Warning-Title Roll (IRE) (Tate Gallery (USA)) 4167[6] (4379) 4790[16] **>83f<**
Young Marcius (USA) 3 ch g Green Dancer (USA)-Manhatten Miss (Artaius (USA)) 2008[12] **>61f<**
Young Precedent 3 b c Polish Precedent (USA)-Guyum (Rousillon (USA)) (945) 1495[2] 1739[6] (3594) 4423[17] 4757[13] **>88f<**
Young Tess 7 b m Teenoso (USA)-Bundu (FR) (Habitat) *68[9]* **>4a 57f<**
Your Most Welcome 6 b m Most Welcome-Blues Player (Jaazeiro (USA)) **1996:** *5119[4]* *5210[12]* **1997:** 2150[5] 2550[2] 2782[3] 3091[2] (3491) 3916[10] 4108[5] **>65a 69f<**
Yours In Sport 3 b g Slip Anchor-Birthdays' Child (Caerleon (USA)) 599[5] 1646[7] 2846[9] 3455[7] 4234[10] **>60f<**
Yulara (IRE) 2 b f Night Shift (USA)-Fifth Quarter (Cure The Blues (USA)) 1538a[6] **>65f<**
Yuppy Girl (IRE) 4 ch f Salt Dome (USA)-Sloane Ranger (Sharpen Up) **1996:** *5115[6]* **1997:** *428[10]* 687[6] 843[3] 2174[10] 2487[13] 3486[10] 3762[15] **>41a 30f<**
Yvecrique (FR) 3 f 2275a[6] **>73f<**
Yxenery (IRE) 3 b f Sillery (USA)-Polyxena (FR) (Pretendre) **1996:** (5153a) **1997:** 815a[8] 1366a[6] **>98f<**

Z

Zaahir (IRE) 3 b g Marju (IRE)-Abhaaj (Kris) 446[6] 1006[4] 1221[4] 2045[7] 4691[10] **>74f<**
Zaaleff (USA) 5 ch h Zilzal (USA)-Continual (USA) (Damascus (USA)) 4568[7] 4696[19] **>57a 56f<**
Zabriskie 3 b c Polish Precedent (USA)-Somfas (USA) (What A Pleasure (USA)) *1787[7]* 2020[2] 2183[4] 3250[4] 3614[10] **>42a 67df<**

Zacaroon **6** b m Last Tycoon-Samaza (USA) (Arctic Tern (USA)) *76^{3} (104) 346^{3} 402^{F}* **>56a 57f<**

Zada **2** b c Distant Relative-Handy Dancer (Green God) 2768^{14} 4857^{U} 4908^{8} 5048^{22} **>42f<**

Zafarabad (IRE) **3** gr c Shernazar-Zarafa (Blushing Groom (FR)) 809a^{2} 2081a^{2} 2456a^{2} 2642a^{5} **>110f<**

Zafarelli **3** gr g Nishapour (FR)-Voltigeuse (USA) (Filiberto (USA)) *377^{W}* 1502^{2} 1986^{5} (2397) 3057^{6} 3896^{12} **>63f<**

Zaforum **4** b c Deploy-Beau's Delight (USA) (Lypheor) 728^{9} **>105f<**

Zagros (IRE) **3** b g Persian Heights-Hana Marie (Formidable (USA)) 599^{12} 1777^{6} 3937^{17} **>52f<**

Zahaalie (USA) **5** ch g Zilzal (USA)-Bambee T T (USA) (Better Bee) *3611^{5}* 4324^{20} **>45a 11f<**

Zahid (USA) **6** ch g Storm Cat (USA)-Time An' Care (USA) (Twin Time (USA)) **1996:** *5118^{8} 5223^{3} 5244^{3} 5274^{6}* **1997:** *99^{3} 129^{3} 338^{2}* **>60a 65df<**

Zahir (USA) **3** b c Riverman (USA)-Manwah (USA) (Lyphard (USA)) 936^{2} **>36f<**

Zahran (IRE) **6** b h Groom Dancer (USA)-Welsh Berry (USA) (Sir Ivor) **1996:** *(5082) 5123^{11} 5152^{3} 5221^{9}* **1997:** *35^{2} 47^{10} 85^{5}* 1005^{4} 1484^{3} 1677^{4} 1694^{2} 2174^{11} 2646^{4} 2880^{4} 3091^{9} 3276^{14} *3413^{4}* **>42a 39f<**

Za-Im **3** b c Green Desert (USA)-Al Bahathri (USA) (Blushing Groom (FR)) 673^{2} 940^{12} 1462^{2} (2476) 2861^{7} 3975^{15} 4777^{8} **>110f<**

Zaima (IRE) **3** b f Green Desert (USA)-Usaylah (Siberian Express (USA)) 483^{3} 654^{4} 1305^{2} 1737^{17} 2390^{9} **>98f<**

Zain Dancer **5** ch g Nabeel Dancer (USA)-Trojan Lady (USA) (Irish River (FR)) 494^{13} 585^{20} 827^{12} *1289^{7} 1754^{4}* 2567^{14} *(2915)* 3143^{10} 3406^{7} 3910^{24} **>52a 44f<**

Zalaiyka (FR) **2** b f Royal Academy (USA)-Zanadiyka (FR) (Akarad (FR)) (4961a) **>109f<**

Zalitzine (USA) **3** b f Zilzal (USA)-Bitooh (Seattle Slew (USA)) (989) 2594^{2} 3797^{3} 4110^{3} 4893^{3} **>99f<**

Zalotto (IRE) **3** b g Polish Patriot (USA)-Honest Penny (USA) (Honest Pleasure (USA)) 729^{7} 1119^{5} 1315^{18} 2510^{14} *2605^{2} 3044^{8} 3582^{2} 4050^{2}* 4164^{14} *4813^{3}* **>68a 43df<**

Zamalek (USA) **5** b g Northern Baby (CAN)-Chellingoua (USA) (Sharpen Up) *21^{6} 47^{8} (92) 188^{3}* 1233^{13} (1968) 2150^{4} 2399^{5} 3026^{8} (3135) 3496^{2} 3640^{2} 4063^{4} 4179^{10} 4374^{13} **>52a 56f<**

Zamarra **2** ch f Clantime-Poshteen (Royal Smoke) 3471^{10} 3711^{14} 4042^{8} 4545^{14} **>63f<**

Zambezi (USA) **2** b br f Rahy (USA)-Zonda (Fabulous Dancer (USA)) 2875^{4} 3282^{2} **>68f<**

Zamhareer (USA) **6** b g Lear Fan (USA)-Awenita (Rarity) 1494^{7} 1732^{4} 1996^{9} 2166^{3} 2413^{4} 2539^{5} **>47f<**

Zamindar (USA) **3** b c Gone West (USA)-Zaizafon (USA) (The Minstrel (CAN)) 940^{5} 3001a^{2} 3733a^{5} **>121+f<**

Zanabay **3** b f Unfuwain (USA)-Chrisanthy (So Blessed) *94^{5}* 1731^{4} 2170^{9} 2757^{7} **>6a 41f<**

Zankle (USA) **4** b g Opening Verse (USA)-Capre (USA) (Seattle Slew (USA)) 4558^{8} **>96f<**

Zany Lady **2** gr f Arzanni-Lady Antonia (Owen Anthony) 4604^{4}

Zaralaska **6** ch g Shernazar-Eskimo Spring (USA) (Riverman (USA)) 1145^{5} (2028) (2514) 3112^{4} **>120+f<**

Zaretski **3** b g Pursuit of Love-Tolstoya (Northfields (USA)) (446) 508^{4} 942^{18} 1770^{5} 1980^{17} 2775^{10} 4561^{11} **>79f<**

Zatopek **5** b or br g Reprimand-Executive Lady (Night Shift (USA)) **1996:** *5175^{7}* **1997:** *2^{6} 123^{5} 218^{2} 285^{4} 328^{2} 410^{11} 544^{4}* 721^{15} *1287^{2}* 1636^{8} *2067^{4}* 2279^{10} 3792^{9} **>56a 36f<**

Zaya **2** ch c Zafonic (USA)-Ayah (USA) (Secreto (USA)) (4871) **>89++f<**

Zelah (IRE) **2** b f Alzao (USA)-Marie Noelle (FR) (Brigadier Gerard) 3636^{4} **>64f<**

Zelanda (IRE) **2** gr f Night Shift (USA)-Zafadola (IRE) (Darshaan) 2597^{3} 2919^{2} (3411) 3723^{6} **>85+f<**

Zelaya (IRE) **4** b f Shaadi (USA)-Zizania (Ahonoora) **1996:** *5211^{3} 5273^{2}* **1997:** *177^{7} 306^{2} 404^{5}* 484^{8} **>55a 68?f<**

Zelda Zonk **5** b m Law Society (USA)-Massive Powder (Caerleon (USA)) 892^{17} 1131^{3} 1453^{7} 1935^{3} 2708^{15} 2835^{12} 4071^{6} 4175^{4} 4561^{8} 4878^{19} 4927^{4} **>77f<**

Zelding (IRE) **2** b f Warning-Zelda (USA) (Caerleon (USA)) 2268a^{2} (2639a) 3178a^{3} 3882a^{7} 4664a^{9} **>109?f<**

Zeliba **5** br m Doyoun-Zia (USA) (Shareef Dancer (USA)) **1996:** *5232^{7} 5255^{9}* **1997:** 3096^{5} **>24?a 48f<**

Zena **2** ch f Highest Honor (FR)-Lady Lamia (USA) (Secreto (USA)) 2519^{3} (3131) 3468^{5} 4427^{6} 4778^{24} **>84+f<**

Zenith Rose (FR) **3** gr c Zayyani-Miss Pluvignon (FR) (Air du Nord (USA)) 1205a^{2} 2274a^{6} 3002a^{4} **>111f<**

Zeppo (IRE) **2** ch c Fayruz-Chase Paperchase (Malinowski (USA)) 1932^{5} 2181^{9} 4298^{19} **>62f<**

Zeptepi (IRE) **2** b f Astronef-Tangle Thorn (Thatching) 3636^{15} 4067^{16} 5025^{8} **>14f<**

Zermatt (IRE) **7** b h Sadler's Wells (USA)-Chamonis (USA) (Affirmed (USA)) 521^{13} 838^{15} 987^{12} 1459^{9} 1972^{16} 2340^{11} (2508) 2866^{5} 3138^{12} 3248^{17} 3793^{13} 3980^{2} 4112^{19} 4297^{18} *4571^{3}* 4696^{11} **>64a 65f<**

Zero Problemo (IRE) **4** b c Priolo (USA)-Zivania (IRE) (Shernazar) 719a^{3} 1728a^{2} 2272a^{3} 3364a^{3} 3993a^{2} **>116f<**

Zero Three Fifteen (IRE) **2** b c Archway (IRE)-Sales Talk (Auction Ring (USA)) *3607^{9}* 3818^{4} 4544^{10} 4814^{7} **>45a 67f<**

Zerpour (IRE) **3** b c Darshaan-Zerzaya (Beldale Flutter (USA)) 1846^{7} 2566^{4} (3021) 3648^{7} 4577^{2} 4891^{5} **>100f<**

Zest (USA) **3** gr ro f Zilzal (USA)-Toveris (Homing) 935^{6} *1155^{11}* 1929^{6} **>6a 54f<**

Zibak (USA) **3** b br c Capote (USA)-Minifah (USA) (Nureyev (USA)) 524^{7} 1682^{6} **>68df<**

Zibeth **3** b f Rainbow Quest (USA)-Tiger Flower (Sadler's Wells (USA)) 992^{9} 1405^{3} (4372) 4774^{10} **>65f<**

Zidac **5** b or br g Statoblest-Sule Skerry (Scottish Rifle) 482^{5} 647^{14} 1142^{2} 1459^{11} 1968^{4} 2485^{5} 2961^{8} 3491^{12} 4172^{3} 4742^{5} 4886^{10} **>63a 74f<**

Zielana Gora **2** b f Polish Precedent (USA)-La Lutine (My Swallow) 651^{7} 4174^{11} **>40f<**

Ziggy's Dancer (USA) **6** b h Ziggy's Boy (USA)-My Shy Dancer (USA) (Northjet) **1996:** *5105^{9}* **1997:** 529^{18} 744^{2} *905^{2}* 1034^{8} 1269^{11} (1662) 1799^{4} 2211^{4} 2289^{6} 2529^{6} 2683^{3} 3252^{3} 3604^{15} 4062^{7} 4282^{7} 4467^{4} *4797^{7}* 4887^{19} **>92a 93f<**

Ziggy Stardust (IRE) **2** b g Roi Danzig (USA)-Si Princess (Coquelin (USA)) 4064^{18} *4592^{10}* **>4a 24f<**

Ziggy's Viola (IRE) **3** b f Roi Danzig (USA)-Olivia Jane (IRE) (Ela-Mana-Mou) **1996:** *5141^{8}* **1997:** 975^{6} 1469^{5} 1863^{6} 2908^{6} 3567^{5} 3781^{13} (4289) 4768^{3} **>57a 58f<**

Zig Zag (IRE) **2** b f Bob Back (USA)-Bebe Auction (IRE) (Auction Ring (USA)) 836^{9} 1461^{3} 1498^{5} 3911^{8} **>55f<**

Zillion (IRE) **2** b g Priolo (USA)-Arab Scimetar (IRE) (Sure Blade (USA)) 3613^{13} *4052^{9}* 4514^{8} 4900^{11} **>41a 51f<**

Zimiri **3** ch c Keen-Annabrianna (Night Shift (USA)) **1996:** *(5243)* **1997:** 1869^{6} 2309^{9} 3591^{7} 4139^{22} **>74a 57f<**

Zimzie **2** gr c Aragon-Zimzizizim (Most Welcome) 2720^{12} 3687^{W} 3783^{11} 4007^{8} 4157^{12} 4401^{7} 4753^{21} **>70f<**

Zine Lane **5** ch g Minster Son-Pine (Supreme Sovereign) *218^{3} 328^{4}* **>54a 69f<**

Zingaro (IRE) **3** b c Mujtahid (USA)-Zia (USA) (Shareef Dancer (USA)) 1876^{8} **>63f<**

Zingibar **5** b g Caerleon (USA)-Duende (High Top) 689^{11} **>71f<**

Zinzari (FR) **3** ch c Arctic Tern (USA)-Model Girl (FR) (Lyphard (USA)) 773^{2} 1150^{3} 1647^{5} 2058^{14} 2749^{7} 2940^{4} 4072^{6} **>80df<**

Zizi (IRE) **2** b f Imp Society (USA)-Timinala (Mansingh (USA)) 1821^{3} 2545^{3} (2886) 3113^{3} 3650^{11} 4097^{3} **>80f<**

Zobaida (IRE) **2** b f Green Desert (USA)-Charmante (USA) (Alydar (USA)) 4526^{8} 4789^{6} **>63+f<**

Zomaradah **2** b f Deploy-Jawaher (IRE) (Dancing Brave (USA)) 5048^{5} **>64+f<**

Zoom Up (IRE) **3** ch g Bluebird (USA)-Senane (Vitiges (FR)) 701^{3} (1006) 1314^{4} 2601^{2} 3408^{6} 3894^{9} 4141^{10} 4477^{4} 4876^{4} **>86f<**

Zorba **3** b g Shareef Dancer (USA)-Zabelina (USA) (Diesis) **1996:** *5141^{4}* **1997:** *164^{2} 217^{4} 300^{2} 417^{2} 544^{9}* (1838) (2128) 2328^{8} 2678^{11} 3071^{3} 3225^{3} 3478^{5} 3813^{9} 4264^{3} *4485^{6}* (4693) 4876^{5} 5030^{9} **>68a 70f<**

Zorro **3** gr c Touch of Grey-Snow Huntress (Shirley Heights) **1996:** *5121^{9}* **1997:** 771^{5} 1105^{9} (1694) 1938^{6} 2667^{13} 3183^{3} 3685^{3} **>53a 57f<**

Zugudi **3** b c Night Shift (USA)-Overdrive (Shirley Heights) (1691) 2835^{17} 3423^{4} 3615^{5} 3772^{8} 4121^{13} 4175^{7} 4441^{17} 4565^{10} 4759^{2} 4854^{3} 4968^{8} 5051^{3} **>100f<**

Zuhair **4** ch g Mujtahid (USA)-Ghzaalh (USA) (Northern Dancer) *661^{9} (903)* 1148^{7} 1410^{3} *1578^{6}* 2476^{5} 2711^{3} 2900^{10} 3508a^{2} 3649^{15} 3888^{13} 4282^{26} *4797^{2}* 4954^{2} 5054^{8} **>82a 105?f<**

Zuno Flyer (USA) **5** br g Lyphard (USA)-Triple Tipple (USA) (Raise A Cup (USA)) **1996:** *(5244) 5276^{5}* **1997:** *78^{9} 183^{13}* **>51a 66f<**

Zurs (IRE) **4** b g Tirol-Needy (High Top) *(200) 396^{4}* 444^{14} 677^{8} 895^{25} 1166^{10} 1489^{9} 1935^{11} 2216^{9} 2947^{5} 3091^{4} 3297^{3} 4139^{6} (4324) (4404) 4680^{3} 4878^{2} 4979^{19} **>82a 71f<**

Zuryaf (IRE) **2** b c Fayruz-The Way She Moves (North Stoke) 2693^{8} 2893^{11} 3862^{9} 4900^{2} 5050^{8} **>65f<**

Zydeco (IRE) **2** b c Darshaan-Cajun Melody (Cajun) 3386^{6} 3862^{2} 4603^{2} **>82f<**

Zygo (USA) **5** b g Diesis-La Papagena (Habitat) 4680^{15} 4882^{17} **>73f<**

WINNING OWNERS

(Win and place prizemoney in Britain from 20th March to 8th November)

		Races Won	Stakes £
1.	Sheikh Mohammed	87	1,480,859
2.	Mr Hamdan Al Maktoum	85	1,343,877
3.	Mr K. Abdulla	48	1,180,853
4.	Godolphin	40	1,161,199
5.	Maktoum Al Maktoum	55	911,425
6.	Mr Landon Knight	2	743,842
7.	Mr M Tabor & Mrs John Magnier	19	690,138
8.	Lord Weinstock	13	654,208
9.	Mr R. E. Sangster	28	630,871
10.	Mr Peter Winfield	5	494,649
11.	H R H Prince Fahd Salman	27	396,961
12.	Mr A. E. Oppenheimer	19	381,853
13.	Greenbay Stables Ltd	4	293,555
14.	Cheveley Park Stud	32	286,524
15.	Sheikh Ahmed Al Maktoum	24	256,845
16.	Highclere Thoroughbred Racing Ltd	16	248,793
17.	Mr Mohamed Obaida	2	246,337
18.	Lucayan Stud	19	233,510
19.	Mr Wafic Said	10	217,317
20.	H H Aga Khan	14	213,815
21.	Duke of Devonshire	6	201,962
22.	Mr Christopher Spence	4	192,283
23.	Mr P. D. Savill	24	187,903
24.	Mr J. C. Smith	12	179,306
25.	Mr Daniel Wildenstein	0	153,810
26.	Lord Howard de Walden	7	153,327
27.	The Queen	10	146,372
28.	Mr Robert Smith	4	134,322
29.	Fittocks Stud	5	130,501
30.	Mollers Racing	7	125,694
31.	Mr Cyril Humphris	8	117,956
32.	Mr George Strawbridge	7	116,421
33.	Mr Graham Rock	2	113,383
34.	Sheikh Marwan Al Maktoum	3	110,596
35.	Mr R. M. Cyzer	14	110,129
36.	Matthews Breeding and Racing	3	109,606
37.	Cliveden Stud	5	108,774
38.	Mr J. R. Good	8	108,670
39.	Sunpak Potatoes	2	106,071
40.	Mr Chris Hardy	9	105,770
41.	Mr M. Calvert	2	102,973
42.	Miss B. Swire	13	98,326
43.	Mr P. R. C. Morrison	2	92,546
44.	Al Muallim Partnership	9	89,816
45.	Mr D. J. Deer	4	89,052
46.	Mrs J. M. Corbett	5	88,803
47.	C H Newton Jnr Ltd	5	87,679
48.	The Bibby Halliday Partnership	4	87,165

WINNING TRAINERS

(Win and place prizemoney in Britain from 20th March to 8th November)

		Races Won	Stakes £
1.	M. R. Stoute	84	2,140,949
2.	J. H. M. Gosden	91	1,812,411
3.	H. R. A. Cecil	78	1,622,721
4.	J. L. Dunlop	97	1,441,331
5.	S bin Suroor	41	1,175,283
6.	B. W. Hills	78	1,022,465
7.	L. M. Cumani	66	1,013,308
8.	M. Johnston	92	809,506
9.	D. R. Loder	55	774,316
10.	P. F. I. Cole	58	757,472
11.	R. Hannon	85	710,643
12.	P. W. Chapple-Hyam	37	674,005
13.	I. A. Balding	52	611,944
14.	G. Wragg	26	540,684
15.	J. Berry	80	476,194
16.	Sir Mark Prescott	43	453,558
17.	D. Morley	24	443,854
18.	Mrs J. R. Ramsden	44	441,992
19.	B. J. Meehan	54	436,623
20.	C. E. Brittain	19	411,678
21.	T. D. Easterby	33	397,624
22.	R. Charlton	38	385,360
23.	J. L. Eyre	39	340,499
24.	E. A. L. Dunlop	27	335,008
25.	Lady Herries	32	311,143
26.	R. Akehurst	24	307,766
27.	P. W. Harris	34	295,213
28.	A. P. O'Brien,Ireland	3	285,874
29.	M. W. Easterby	46	283,925
30.	Mrs M. Reveley	38	282,013
31.	A. Fabre,France	1	275,444
32.	J. A. R. Toller	14	257,581
33.	W. R. Muir	30	255,795
34.	M. R. Channon	36	254,906
35.	E. J. Alston	21	245,707
36.	Lord Huntingdon	20	240,801
37.	B. Hanbury	26	240,025
38.	Miss Gay Kelleway	41	240,006
39.	D. Nicholls	29	232,697
40.	P. T. Walwyn	31	231,424
41.	M. Bell	30	227,268
42.	N. A. Callaghan	17	225,907
43.	B. A. McMahon	26	210,183
44.	G. L. Moore	34	207,861
45.	G. Lewis	25	202,029
46.	D. R. C. Elsworth	23	200,282
47.	T. D. Barron	25	196,847
48.	R. Guest	23	195,642
49.	Mrs J. Cecil	11	192,867
50.	A. C. Stewart	18	190,972

LEADING FLAT JOCKEYS

(Wins in Britain from 20th March to 8th November)

	Win £	1st	2nd	3rd	Unpl	Total Mts	Per cent		£1 Level stake
K. Fallon	1,845,353	196	137	116	460	909	21.6	+	**118.23**
L. Dettori	1,892,853	173	113	93	388	767	22.6	-	29.07
K. Darley	719,789	128	107	96	509	840	15.2	-	64.18
Pat Eddery	1,288,172	116	87	65	363	631	18.4	-	151.44
J. Reid	1,137,912	110	105	97	511	823	13.4	-	151.28
R. Hills	655,488	85	73	86	281	525	16.2	-	48.08
S. Sanders	613,597	84	98	91	502	775	10.8	-	129.03
M. Hills	852,183	83	64	72	342	561	14.8	-	21.82
J. Weaver	358,769	80	72	62	359	573	14.0	-	91.67
J. Fortune	413,545	78	75	79	443	675	11.6	-	170.27
D. Holland	399,001	77	71	66	390	604	12.8	-	143.18
T. Sprake	325,479	75	65	75	445	660	11.4	-	27.95
R. Ffrench	320,841	73	61	58	403	595	12.3	-	14.57
G. Duffield	422,810	71	68	56	406	601	11.8	-	178.68
T. Quinn	586,304	71	72	86	435	664	10.7	-	215.66
J. F. Egan	215,672	61	63	62	402	588	10.4	-	12.46
Dane O'Neill	273,375	55	63	77	516	711	7.7	-	318.64
Martin Dwyer	194,964	51	60	45	369	525	9.7	-	90.75
A. Culhane	186,247	50	63	37	444	594	8.4	-	224.86
R. Cochrane	383,883	50	64	65	391	570	8.8	-	148.26
G. Carter	265,863	49	53	52	387	541	9.1	-	234.64
W. Ryan	838,630	48	62	64	323	497	9.7	-	247.34
M. Roberts	343,784	48	50	40	342	480	10.0	-	102.42
J. Quinn	225,143	48	60	73	571	752	6.4	-	325.18
C. Lowther	233,839	47	32	36	286	401	11.7	+	**22.40**
J. Carroll	179,201	46	65	71	485	667	6.9	-	294.75
L. Charnock	257,163	43	51	52	416	562	7.7	-	179.12
S. Drowne	172,877	41	40	42	499	622	6.6	-	250.63
Paul Eddery	180,144	40	36	37	383	496	8.1	-	307.58
D. Harrison	166,884	39	39	29	240	347	11.2	-	47.11
P. Fessey	141,606	37	45	33	342	457	8.1	-	230.56
Dean McKeown	189,829	36	29	40	389	494	7.3	-	76.01
A. Clark	129,600	35	50	35	368	488	7.2	-	112.66
M. Fenton	133,657	32	24	37	284	377	8.5	-	122.71
B. Doyle	194,225	31	39	33	188	291	10.7	-	24.66
D. Sweeney	101,579	31	16	24	181	252	12.3	-	22.83
R. Hughes	137,406	30	33	37	157	257	11.7	-	50.46
O. Peslier	872,994	29	11	14	98	152	19.1	+	**98.39**
G. Hind	182,966	29	34	35	223	321	9.0	-	120.76
C. Rutter	156,403	26	37	30	321	414	6.3	-	115.53
S. Whitworth	97,113	26	29	30	247	332	7.8	-	76.25
F. Lynch	94,163	26	33	38	270	367	7.1	-	201.75
A. McGlone	157,790	24	24	20	232	300	8.0	-	161.28
M. J. Kinane	863,052	23	16	22	99	160	14.4	-	46.80
M. Henry	121,973	23	25	24	247	319	7.2	-	96.19
R. Mullen	74,029	23	24	29	228	304	7.6	-	141.21
T. Williams	174,437	22	21	38	294	375	5.9	-	130.00
P. P. Murphy	66,189	21	17	17	146	201	10.5	-	34.80
R. Winston	72,525	21	23	25	165	234	9.0	-	67.00
G. Parkin	70,983	20	27	22	160	229	8.7	-	53.20

REVIEW OF THE SEASON
by Richard Onslow

Among the features of the Flat racing season was the dramatic surge in the fortunes of Henry Cecil and Kieren Fallon, from the crests of the waves to the troughs, as the tide of their first year of their association rolled along.
The form of the principal events of the York Spring meeting worked out amazingly well. As usual the Godolphin operation, spearheaded by Sheikh Mohammed, was well to the fore, albeit after a surprisingly slow start. James Toller, who has fewer than 30 horses in his yard at Whitsbury, Hampshire, played David to the Goliath of the fashionable establishments on more than one occasion, and 45-year-old Pat Eddery reached a notable landmark in his 30th season just before being forced onto the sidelines temporarily. For her part Alex Greaves also contributed a paragraph to the history of British racing.

The association between Cecil and his new stable jockey began on a less than propitious note when Sleepytime was demoted from favouritism for the 1,000 Guineas following her defeat in the Fred Darling Stakes at Newbury in the middle of April. Ridden with restraint in the early stages, Sleepytime had no room for manoeuvre when Fallon asked her to improve a quarter of a mile out, and although she ran on after securing clearance entering the final furlong, she failed to accelerate with that impressive authority that she had asserted at Sandown the previous September.
The long faces left on the connections of Sleepytime at Newbury were replaced by the broadest of smiles after the 1,000 Guineas. Undeterred by his disappointment of a fortnight earlier, Fallon held up the bay filly again and, riding with the most admirable confidence, sent her to the front inside the final furlong and let her stride well clear.
After coughing in the early spring, and then finding the mile of the 1,000 Guineas somewhat sharp, as Henry Cecil suspected would be the case, Reams of Verse returned to peak form by winning York's Musidora Stakes by eleven lengths, the greatest margin of success in the thirty-seven-year history of the race. On the strength of that performance Reams of Verse was installed as odds-on favourite for the Oaks.

Bosra Sham, champion three-year-old filly of 1996, was ridden in public by Fallon for the first time in the Brigadier Gerard Stakes at Sandown Park. Without being spectacular, Bosra Sham raised hopes that her career was no longer threatened by the deficiency in a wall of a hoof, as she did all that Fallon asked of her in beating Godolphin's Predappio by half a length without being extended and pulled up sound.
Fallon's triumphal progress on fillies trained by Cecil was now threatened by a check, which, though temporary, would be extremely expensive to him. While riding in the Italian Derby he had incurred a ten-day ban, running from 3rd to 12th of June, costing him the mount on Reams of Verse in the Oaks and his rides on all four days at Royal Ascot. On a day trip to Rome early in June, Fallon persuaded the Italian authorities to defer the starting point of the sentence until the 22nd.
With less than two furlongs to run in the Oaks, the ban might as well have stood as Fallon

was in an even more parlous position than ever he had been on Sleepytime at Newbury, as Reams of Verse was hopelessly shut in behind the French outsider Gazelle Royale. As Jimmy Fortune on Gazelle Royale changed his whip hand a furlong out his mount veered towards the rails, and Fallon settled the issue instantly by shooting Reams of Verse through the resultant gap.
A fortnight later Bosra Sham put up a breathtaking performance at Royal Ascot. After she had won the Prince of Wales's Stakes by eight lengths the trainer of the winners of nineteen classics was moved to acclaim her as absolutely the best horse he had ever had through his hands.

Cecil and Fallon also shared the successes of Yashmak and Canon Can at the Royal meeting, though on the debit side of the ledger appeared the failure of Sleepytime in the Coronation Stakes. Yashmak enhanced the collective prestige of the Warren Place fillies by winning the Ribblesdale Stakes, and Canon Can overcame recent problems when outstaying the field for the Queen Alexandra Stakes. After two nails had pierced his feet when he spread a plate on the Tuesday, the condition of Canon Can had been maintained by swimming him the next couple of mornings.
According to the script Sleepytime was to have run the opposition ragged in the Coronation Stakes. Unfortunately she was a long way from being in her element on the fast ground, and by the time she began to come into contention the verdict was otherwise settled.

Pilsudski was the consummate professional

Whereas Bosra Sham had caused a sensation at Royal Ascot, she played a most unenviable leading role in the high drama that constituted the Eclipse Stakes. After a slow early pace, Fallon sent her through what he perceived would be a gap on the rails three furlongs out. On the gap failing to materialise, Fallon switched Bosra Sham to the outside, thereby forfeiting the ground that enabled Pilsudski to beat her into third place. A bitterly disappointed Henry Cecil made no secret of his opinion that defeat had been snatched out of the jaws of victory. Such is the resilience of Kieren Fallon that he was to regain the favour of his employers and the racing public within the week. On the second day of the Newmarket July meeting he won the July Stakes on Bold Fact and three other races for Henry Cecil, who announced that he would be first jockey to the Warren Place stable again in 1998. By the end of the month the partnership was further cemented by another Group One success when Ali-Royal won the Sussex Stakes at Goodwood.

Henry Cecil derived anything but his customary enjoyment from the Ebor meeting at York in August. With Pat Eddery replacing Fallon and a bar-shoe protecting her bruised near-fore foot, Bosra Sham was fully expected to obtain compensation for her defeat in the Eclipse Stakes by winning the Juddmonte International Stakes. Yet to the horror of her supporters she was seen to be under pressure on the turn into the straight, and it subsequently transpired that she had already lost the shoe that afforded the vital protection to the near-fore, so that her finishing last of four became readily understandable.
The following day Reams of Verse seemed all but sure to stage a successful return to the Knavesmire in the Yorkshire Oaks, only to be beaten before entering the final furlong. Ruefully Henry Cecil admitted that Reams of Verse did not stay a mile and a half, attributing her success in the Oaks to the lack of a true gallop at Epsom. Later in the afternoon Cecil and his jockey endured a third blow when Bold Fact failed to follow up his success in the July Stakes by winning the Gimcrack Stakes, being caught close home by Carrowkeel.

Another reversal for Fallon followed quickly. At the outset of the week after York he lost his lead in the Jockeys' Championship to Frankie Dettori, who rode three winners at Chepstow including, most appropriately, Bin Rosie in the Frankie Dettori Ton-Up Stakes. After Fallon had completed the nap hand for the first time in his career at Lingfield on the day before the start of the St Leger meeting, he and Cecil avenged the reverses suffered at the Ebor fixture by staging a successful return to Yorkshire at Doncaster. Canon Can confirmed that he had completed the transition from the status of handicapper to top-class stayer by beating Persian Punch in the Doncaster Cup. Daggers Drawn reasserted his claims to be amongst the best of the two-year-olds by winning the Champagne Stakes and Midnight Line provided Cecil with a remarkable eleventh success in the May Hill Stakes, a race founded as recently as 1976.

Soon afterwards came the announcement that Bosra Sham would be retired to Stud. The trouble with her foot that had been the bane of the career of Wafic Said's brilliant filly had recurred. By that time Fallon had regained the lead from Frankie Dettori in the jockeys' table. He had ridden his 150th winner of the turf season on Clan Ben, trained by Cecil, at Newbury in the middle of July then consolidated his claims to the title by riding three winners at Redcar and bringing off a four timer at Hamilton Park a few days later.

Not only did Reams of Verse win the Musidora Stakes at the York Spring meeting as a prelude to success in the Oaks, but Royal Applause showed that he would be a big factor in the season's top sprints by landing the Duke of York Stakes and Celeric made plain that he had come on a long way since success in a handicap at the fixture in 1996 by landing the Yorkshire Cup, while Benny The Dip became the sixth colt to win the Dante Stakes on his way to triumph in the Derby.

After Benny The Dip, ridden by Olivier Peslier, had beaten Desert Story convincingly in the Dante his trainer John Gosden was sceptical about his chances of beating the 2,000 Guineas winner Entrepreneur at Epsom. All the same the bookmakers' reaction was to slash the price from 25/1 to 7/1.

Before the matter could be put to the test, though, Gosden was faced with the dilemma of finding a rider for Benny The Dip, as Peslier was claimed for Cloudings and Frankie Dettori, who rides for the Stanley House trainer regularly, would be wearing the Godolphin jacket on Bold Demand. It was only on the Tuesday before the race that Gosden solved his problem by engaging Willie Ryan, who has been a thoroughly reliable second jockey to Henry Cecil for several years.

Benny The Dip inched out Silver Patriarch in a memorable Derby

Ryan rode Benny The Dip in a couple of canters up Newmarket's Warren Hill on the

Thursday without being unduly impressed. By way of complete contrast to the lack of enthusiasm with which he had worked, Benny The Dip continually answered the calls that were made on him at Epsom, though Ryan must have feared that the fast-finishing Silver Patriarch had caught him on the post.
Benny The Dip carries the colours of his 72-year-old breeder Landon Knight, of Ohio, who maintains an old association with Gosden, having been one of the first owners to send him horses when the Englishman embarked upon his career in the United States in 1979. Landon Knight is confined to a wheelchair as a result of contracting polio when he was nine, and unlike so many Americans who race in England he breeds on a very small scale.
Romanov, third in the Derby, was unraced as a two-year-old in 1996 as he fractured a pastern the day before he was to run at York in August.

After spending the winter in the sunshine of Dubai, twenty-six of the Goldolphin string returned to the care of Saeed bin Suroor in the Moulton Paddocks yard at Newmarket on 28th April in readiness for the Guineas meeting a few days later.
Ominously, perhaps, the stable's first runner Haltarra was beaten a head at the first stage of the fixture. Later in the day Tulipa could finish only ninth of ten in the Jockey Club Stakes, then Zahir failed to justify favouritism in a two-horse race for The Whip. The following day Shamikh finished well down the field in the 2,000 Guineas, for which he had been a leading public fancy at one time, but on the third day things took a turn for the better when Swiss Law won the opener prior to the success of Siyadah in the listed Pretty Polly Stakes.
That rather belated double at Newmarket proved no harbinger of the wholescale recovery of the Godolphin fortunes. At York, Classic Cliche ran well below expectations when bidding to win the Yorkshire Cup for the second season in succession. An hour later the highly regarded two-year-old Monsajem was only fourth. Simon Crisford, the Godolphin racing manager, announced there were unlikely to be any runners over the weekend, and activity could well be suspended for even longer.
By 16th May Godolphin had managed only three winners from twenty-one runners. Stowaway was withdrawn from the Predominate Stakes at Goodwood and Happy Valentine declared a doubtful runner for the Derby. Theories about the loss of form of the stable were widespread and varied from viral infection to failure to re-acclimatise. Meanwhile intensive work by the operation's veterinary surgeon Dr Michael Hauser failed to diagnose the source of the trouble.
Soon Simon Crisford was able to announce that though the cause of the failures of so many of the spring runners remained unsolved, exhaustive tests were continually proving negative. The first sign of recovery of the Godolphin fortunes came when Bold Demand, Saeed bin Suroor's first runner for three weeks, won Sandown Park's evening fixture in late May.

Godolphin was right back on song in time for Royal Ascot, where Allied Forces added to his international reputation by winning the opening event, the Queen Anne Stakes. During a spell with Kieran McLaughlin in the United States Allied Forces had won a Grade One race and three other events.

There was also a strong American flavour to the success of Predappio in the Hardwicke Stakes. The colt was the first winner at the Royal Meeting for the top-class American jockey Gary Stevens. Among more than 4,000 races that he has won in his own country have been three Kentucky Derbies. While trained for Sheikh Mohammed by John Oxx in Ireland in 1996, Predappio won a listed race at Galway. The third Godolphin success of the meeting materialised when Asfurah became the stable's first two-year-old winner of the season by accounting for Cortachy Castle in the Windsor Castle Stakes.

Godolphin also occupied centre stage at the Ascot July meeting when the strength and tenacity of Swain enabled him to overcome underfoot conditions in the King George VI and Queen Elizabeth Diamond Stakes. As a result of heavy rainfall immediately before racing, the ground put a premium on endurance, and not surprisingly the time was 8.4 seconds slower than that of Pentire twelve months previously. Swain, placed in each of his fourteen previous races, had been recruited to Godolphin from Andre Fabre's Chantilly yard.
Stowaway laid strong claims to the St Leger by winning the Gordon Stakes at Goodwood and then taking the measure of Derby runner-up Silver Patriarch in the Great Voltigeur Stakes at York. Unfortunately he was not able to renew rivalry with Silver Patriarch at Doncaster, being found to be lame on the morning of the race as he had injured a hock.
In early October Godolphin gave notice of its intention to be still more formidable in 1998 by recruiting three highly-regarded performers from Michael Stoute, another three from John Gosden, two from David Loder and one apiece from Michael Jarvis, who had Stowaway as a two-year-old, Alec Stewart, Luca Cumani and Andre Fabre. All twelve will spend the winter in Dubai before joining Saeed bin Suroor's string in the spring. The same programme will be followed by the four choice youngsters bought from Robert Sangster.

While Saeed bin Suroor, Henry Cecil, John Dunlop and others were going their usual rounds, James Toller edged into the limelight by landing races of the quality that generally fall to their lot. In midsummer he obtained his first Group One success when the Duke of Devonshire's Compton Place won the July Cup at Newmarket. As well as winning at Bath and Salisbury in 1996, Compton Place was only beaten half a length in the Gimcrack Stakes and was also runner-up in the Flying Childers Stakes. He was coughing in the spring and would almost certainly not have figured amongst the rank outsiders for the July Cup had he not totally failed to do justice to himself on soft ground in the King's Stand Stakes at Royal Ascot.

In September Toller obtained successes with two-year-olds who also carried the all-straw colours of the Duke. At Newbury Duck Row won the Haynes, Hanson and Clark Stakes, thereby emulating the Derby winners Shergar and Shahrastani. A week after Duck Row had won, Teapot Row followed in the hoofprints of other Derby winners by landing the Royal Lodge Stakes at Ascot. Both Teapot Row and Duck Row are named after cottages on the Chatsworth Estate.
Pat Eddery displayed all the qualities that have taken him to eleven championships when winning the Gold Cup on Celeric, who makes heavy demands on the patience and self-

confidence of his rider by having to be held up for a very late run indeed. After being last for a great deal of the way, Eddery refused to be tempted into making precipitate action as the 1995 St Leger winner Classic Cliche tried to settle the issue by taking the lead shortly after turning into the straight. Only inside the last 200 yards of the twenty furlongs did Eddery begin to weave his way through the field in the manner of the highly-polished race rider that he is and, finally going through a gap between Samraan and Double Trigger, he collared Classic Cliche and secured a verdict of three-parts of a length.

Celeric struck Gold at Ascot

Celeric is owned in partnership by his breeder Christopher Spence, Chairman of United Racecourses and former High Sheriff of Berkshire, and Jake Morley, brother of the gelding's trainer David Morley. Needless to say Christopher Spence was the first to pay a well-deserved compliment to David Morley for improving Celeric from a smart handicapper to a Group One stayer, as well as to Eddery for riding with such superb judgement.

Eddery completed the century for the twenty-fourth time when Risque took the measure of the mount of his brother Paul at Windsor in August. Within a month he passed a far more important landmark in his career in singularly appropriate circumstances as it was in no less an event than the St Leger that he rode his 4,000th winner under Jockey Club Rules by driving Silver Patriarch three lengths clear of Vertical Speed.

The only jockeys to have ridden more winners in Britain are Sir Gordon Richards (4,870) and Lester Piggott (4,493). As Eddery is only 45 he has very realistic prospects of surpassing Piggott's record.

The week after the St Leger Pat Eddery was obliged to retire for the remainder of the season and enter the Chilton Hospital in Buckinghamshire for an operation on his back. His achievements of the summer and early autumn had been all the more remarkable as he had been in intermittent pain, sometimes of considerable severity, as a result of wrenching his back while pulling up Dancing Cavalier after winning at Nottingham in April.

Alex Greaves achieved the distinction of becoming the first woman to ride the winner of a Group One race in Britain when she had the mount on Ya Malak, who shared the honours with Coastal Bluff, Kevin Darley up, after a dramatic race for the Nunthorpe Stakes at York in August. Just after the start Coastal Bluff's bit broke, yet even deprived of steering Darley enabled the massive grey gelding to use his speed to such good effect that he was upsides Ya Malak as they flashed past the post.

Coastal Bluff and Ya Malak shared an historic Nunthorpe

The judge Jane Stickels took 15 minutes examining the photograph, and after calling for a second print announced the dead-heat.

Coastal Bluff is trained by David Barron and Ya Malak by David Nicholls in stableyards within ten miles of each other on opposite sides of the picturesque town of Thirsk in North Yorkshire. The proximity of the quarters of the participants was by no means the only irony of that wonderful finish. Alex Greaves is married to David Nicholls, formerly stable jockey to David Barron, and served her apprenticeship with Barron, to whom her mother Val has been assistant for many years.

Few, if any, more lightly-raced horses have won the Lincoln than Kuala Lipis, trained by Paul Cole for Sultan Ahmed Shah, ruler of the Malaysian state of Pahang. Having been unraced as a two-year-old Kuala Lipis was beset by sinus trouble in 1996, and had had only five races when he went to the post for the Lincoln.

Early in April a cat was put amongst the classic pigeons. Bahhare, who had been winter

favourite for the 2,000 Guineas, bruised a foot in late March, and shortly afterwards John Dunlop announced that the unbeaten colt had developed a problem with his pelvis, and as he would need several weeks' rest he would miss the Guineas.
At that time there had been few enquiries for Entrepreneur, a 25/1 chance at the end of 1996, as it was widely assumed that Michael Stoute would train him for the Derby. However Entrepreneur was working increasingly impressively in the middle of April, and when it was known that the Guineas had become his immediate objective his price was cut from 7/1 to 7/2 favouritism in anticipation of his providing Walter Swinburn with yet another classic success. As it happened Swinburn became unavailable to take the mount on him as the 35-year-old found himself obliged to withdraw from race-riding on account of serious problems with his weight, though he was not retiring and would resume his career in due course.
With Michael Kinane standing in for Swinburn, Entrepreneur ran on impressively to beat Revoque in a manner that suggested that he would have no difficulty in coping with another four furlongs, and became a strong favourite for the Derby. Entrepreneur is owned jointly by Michael Tabor, the former bookmaker, and Sue Magnier, and at 600,000 guineas was the joint highest-priced yearling sold by Tattersalls in 1995. The enhanced status of Entrepreneur was reflected by his being insured for £10 million after the Guineas. He finished only fourth at Epsom, however, and ran just once more.

With his close affinity with the North-West, Robert Sangster has always enjoyed winning at Chester, and at the Spring meeting on the Roodeye brought off a notable treble. The Chester Cup he won with Top Cees, whom he bought shortly after the horse had landed that race in controversial circumstances in 1995. He also won the Chester Vase with Panama City and the Ormonde Stakes with Royal Court, who defied going that was testing in the extreme.
The other feature of the York Spring Meeting, over and above the successes of the four horses who were to enhance their reputation so greatly later in the season, was Michael Hills riding his 1,000th winner under Jockey Club Rules. Fittingly that feat was achieved on The Fly, trained by his father Barry, in the Shepherd Trophy Rated Stakes. Michael Hills had ridden his first winner on Sky Thief at Nottingham in 1979.
Toby Balding was rewarded with his first winner at Royal Ascot after training for forty years when Sea Freedom emerged successful in the Ascot Stakes. Sea Freedom cost 400,000 guineas as a yearling and is a full-brother to User Friendly, winner of the Oaks and St Leger in 1992. He had injured a knee at Newmarket as a three-year-old and only regained his form slowly.

Irish trainer Aidan O'Brien obtained his first success on the Flat in England when Harbour Master came out best in the Coventry Stakes. Although only 27 years of age, the trainer is maintaining the fame of the Ballydoyle Stable in County Tipperary made world-famous by Vincent O'Brien, to whom he is unrelated. Peter Savill, who had a quarter-share in Polish Patriot, a winner at Royal Ascot in 1991, saw his own colours carried successfully at the meeting for the first time when Fly To The Stars landed the Britannia Handicap.
Royal Applause followed up his success in the Duke of York by winning the Cork and

Orrery Stakes. After being the unbeaten winner of the Coventry Stakes over the same course and distance and his other three races as a two-year-old in 1995, Royal Applause failed to stay the mile of the 2,000 Guineas and thereafter seemed to lose the edge to his speed, winning only one small event. The relaxation afforded by a ten-week holiday at the Dalham Hall Stud had the desired result of bringing him back to his best.

There was a surprise result to the Coronation Stakes, in which Rebecca Sharp reversed 1,000 Guineas running by beating Sleepytime into third place. It transpired that Rebecca Sharp had failed to do herself justice in the Guineas as she blew for forty-five minutes afterwards. Paul Cole, whose two-year-olds have a big following at the meeting, saddled both Central Park and Wales for the Chesham Stakes. Stable jockey Richard Quinn elected to ride Wales, and had to be content with third place behind the other. Cole's former assistant Kevin McAuliffe was another to break his duck during the four days. The rank outsider Tippitt Boy gave him his first success at the fixture in only his fourth season with a licence by landing the Windsor Castle Stakes.

Guy Henrot, who has a stable near Le Mans, earned the distinction of winning with his first runner in England when Don't Worry Me beat her compatriot Titus Livius in the King's Stand Stakes. Don't Worry Me was formerly in the Wilmslow, Cheshire, stable of Francis Lee, who had rated her no more than a fast handicapper when consigning her to Tattersalls Sales.

Despite an unfavourable draw Michael Tabor backed Danetime, on whom Gary Stevens wore his colours in the Wokingham Stakes, to win a substantial amount of money. The 11/1 at which the three-year-old opened on the course was steadily reduced as the public followed the owner's lead, so that he started favourite. Stevens tacked over to the favoured stands' rails and, after looking in danger of being denied an opening two furlongs out, found the gap he needed and brought Danetime through with a powerful run that only just failed to collar Selhurstpark Flyer. Had the post come a single stride later, the gamble would have been landed.

Heavy ground, rather than an unpropitious draw, was regarded as likely to prevent Windsor Castle from improving the uninspiring record of three-year-olds in the Northumberland Plate, Orpheus in 1989 having been the only winner of the Pitmen's Derby of that age since Joe Chamberlain in 1909. Showing a nice indifference to the going, Windsor Castle duly defied his penalty.

Tumbleweed Ridge, who had not quite seen out the mile of the Lincoln and been slowly away in the Wokingham, made his contribution to the fine season enjoyed by Brian Meehan when coming good in the Bunbury Cup, the principal handicap of the Newmarket July meeting. Tumbleweed Ridge had won the Group Three Horris Hill Stakes at Newbury in 1995, but lost his confidence after developing a temporary wind problem as a three-year-old.

Lord Kintyre won the biggest prize ever landed by a Flat horse trained in Devon when he beat Pure Coincidence in the Weatherbys Super Sprint at Newbury in the middle of July. Trained near Cullompton by Rod Millman, who began his career as an apprentice with Reg Akehurst, Lord Kintyre cost only 9,200 guineas, and is the only horse running on the Flat

sired by Makbul, many of whose mares have been point-to-pointers.
Michael Tabor recovered the heavy losses incurred over the desperately unlucky defeat of Danetime in the Wokingham Stakes when the three-year-old justified favouritism by scraping home from My Best Valentine in the Stewards' Cup at Goodwood. The owner was reckoned to have taken a sum in the region of £200,000 out of the ring.
Double Trigger showed that he was no light of other days when repeating his success of 1995 in the Goodwood Cup by beating Classic Cliche. Trainer Mark Johnston had never lost faith in Double Trigger even though the horse had been beset by a series of minor problems over the past twelve months such as pus in a foot and the consequences of the recurrent loss of shoes. The winner's full brother Double Eclipse did extraordinarily well to finish third. Although Double Eclipse possessed a great deal of ability his legs were a cause of constant concern, and he had had only one serious gallop in more than a year.

Les Eyre achieved the ambition of every Yorkshireman when he won the Ebor Handicap, with Far Ahead. The son of a Barnsley miner, Eyre has a string of seventy horses in the famous Hambleton House Stable, near Thirsk, having sold his kitchen equipment business ten years ago to embark upon his new career with a permit. The owner of Far Ahead is the trainer's longstanding friend Tony Yates, whose Sunpak Potatoes business is the sponsor of the stables.
My Emma became the first Group One winner in England for the hard-working Newmarket trainer Rae Guest when she came from last to first in the Yorkshire Oaks. Owned and bred by Ian Matthews, My Emma is half-sister to Classic Cliche, who was sold as a foal.
Cape Verdi was lucky to beat Embassy by a short-head in the Lowther Stakes as the runner-up propped almost on the line, as a result of stumbling on a piece of soft ground. Luca Cumani continued his domination of the Galtres Stakes, of which Kaliana was his seventh winner in the last eight years.
At Epsom's August Bank Holiday meeting the Queen won the Moet & Chandon Silver Magnum for the second year running when Shaft of Light became the first winner Andrew Balding had ridden in the royal colours by beating Brandon Magic, trained by his father, decisively. The top Spanish amateur Luis Urbano, who had won the race on the Queen's Arabian Story in 1996, was to have had the mount on Shaft of Light until meeting with an injury, and Ian Balding agreed to release his son to ride Shaft of Light for Lord Huntingdon, Andrew's uncle, providing he could find a suitable replacement to partner Brandon Magic.
The remarkable Further Flight won for a twenty-third time when having the sixty-first race of his career in the listed Chester Rated Stakes on the Roodeye in late August. Further Flight, five-times winner of the Jockey Club Cup between 1991 and 1995, belongs to Simon Wingfield Digby, the 87-year-old Dorset landowner.
In early September, Richard Quinn, who had declined a lucrative offer from Hong Kong in April, made a successful return to the saddle on Generosity at Hamilton Park. He had been out of action since fracturing his left wrist at Brighton in the middle of July. Two other riders in the news in early September were Martin Dwyer and Jason Weaver. At Salisbury, Dwyer lost his allowance by winning the Winterbourne Handicap on Dulcinea, trained by

Ian Balding, to whom he was apprenticed. Weaver terminated his retainer from Mark Johnston by declining to ride Fly To The Stars in a Group Two race in Turkey.
Royal Applause confirmed he is one of the outstanding sprinters of his generation by winning the Haydock Park Sprint Cup. In doing so he became the 1,900th winner to be saddled by Barry Hills.
At Doncaster Dashing Blue won the Portland Handicap, which he contested in preference to the five-furlong Scarbrough Stakes as Ian Balding considered he would be suited by the extra yardage. By defying 9st 12lb Dashing Blue laid claims to class as it was the highest weight to be carried to win the race since the legendary Irish Elegance shouldered 10st 2lb in 1919.
Charles Cyzer had his first Group winner when Book At Bedtime came out best in the Park Hill Stakes. As she struck buyers at the yearling sales as having the size and scope to make a chaser, Book At Bedtime was largely ignored, with the result that she was recruited to Cyzer's West Sussex yard for a mere 4,200 guineas.
Wildwood Flower enjoyed a more advantageous draw, 24, in the Ayr Gold Cup than she had in 1996 when leading those on the far side into fifth place behind Coastal Bluff, and avenged that defeat. That was well-deserved compensation for Richard Hannon, who had gone close in Scotland's showpiece with Echo-Logical, second to Lochsong in 1992, and Venture Capitalist, third to Hard to Figure in 1993.
Linda Perratt, who has the Cree Lodge stable at Ayr, won the richest race ever staged at Hamilton Park when Jacmar landed the final heat of the Lord Hamilton of Dalziel Nursery. At the same time she clinched the £10,000 bonus for being leading trainer on the course for the season.

Clive Brittain reaped rich rewards with Air Express (second right)

Clive Brittain did not win a Group One event on the home front in 1997 until Air Express prevailed in the Queen Elizabeth II Stakes at Ascot's Festival of Racing in September. Air Express had earned a reputation on the continent by winning the Italian 2,000 Guineas and the German equivalent of that classic. Immediately before the Festival he had run disappointingly in the Sussex Stakes at Goodwood, where he was not at home on the camber and not balanced in time to enter into contention. Back at Ascot, where he had been a good second in the St James's Palace Stakes at the Royal Meeting, Air Express had no such problems in keeping on an even keel.

Tim Easterby, in his second season at the Habton Grange Stable near Malton, collected his richest prize to date when Jo Mell won the £50,000 Tote Festival Handicap. Jo Mell was ridden by Olivier Peslier instead of his regular partner Lindsay Charnock, who had seven booked rides at Catterick whereas he might have had none at all at Ascot if Jo Mell had been withdrawn because of firm ground. At Catterick Charnock rode his forty-ninth winner of his best season on Kingdom Pearl.
A week later Sir Mark Prescott was responsible for the ring having to pay out some £5 million by winning the Cambridgeshire with the heavily-backed Pasternak, carrying the colours of Graham Rock, racing correspondent of *The Observer* and BBC TV betting pundit. For good measure Sir Mark also saddled the runner-up Rudimental. Although Pasternak had landed another gamble in the Magnet Cup on ground too firm for his liking at York in July, the trainer did not decide to run him until the stable's runners at the meeting earlier in the week returned with no ill-effects.

The progressive Pasternak twice rocked the bookmakers

The somewhat unseasonably-fast ground was certainly appreciated by Grey Shot who shattered the existing record for the two miles of the Jockey Club Cup by 2.4 seconds. The dual representation of Roger Charlton's Beckhampton Stable in the Tattersalls Houghton Sales Stakes paid rich dividends as Tamarisk won from Sapphire Ring. As well as first prize Tamarisk earned a bonus of £100,000 while Sapphire Ring earned £30,000 for the first filly home on top of second money. Tamarisk is owned by Highclere Thoroughbred

Racing and cost 78,000 guineas as a yearling. Tim Sprake, the rider of Tamarisk, equalled his best tally of sixty-three winners on the turf in a season.
Embassy removed any doubts about her having been unlucky to have lost out to Cape Verdi in the Lowther Stakes by beating the other soundly in the Cheveley Park Stakes. As was all-but-inevitable Embassy then joined the Godolphin operation and is amongst the select party to spend the winter in Dubai.

Newmarket's Champions Day, with the Dewhurst transferred from the Friday to make its card the second most valuable in the season after Derby Day, was a really outstanding success, apart from a false start to the Rockfel Stakes. The attendance was an increase of 36% on 1996 and the weather perfect.
As was widely expected the Andre Fabre-trained Xaar advertised the likelihood of his return to the course to land the 2,000 Guineas by the overwhelming authority with which he won the Dewhurst Stakes. Pilsudski assured a fifth trainers' championship for Michael Stoute by the admixture of sheer class and resilience that won him the Champion Stakes, bringing his earnings to £1,931,913. Less than a fortnight earlier Pilsudski had been runner-up in the Arc to the brilliant Peintre Celebre, trained by Fabre.

Turnpole was a ready winner of the Cesarewitch

Turnpole gave Mary Reveley and Lindsay Charnock a second Cesarewitch within three years, following Old Red in 1995. Doubtless Turnpole derived much advantage from a break on the Lincolnshire farm of his owners John and Marilyn Williams during the summer.
Having already established the reputations of Second Empire and King of Kings, Aidan O'Brien confirmed that he is likely to field the strongest opposition to Xaar in the 2,000 Guineas of 1998 when he sent out Saratoga Springs to win the Racing Post Trophy at Doncaster. Given the choice of Michael Tabor's runners, Michael Kinane opted for Saratoga Springs in preference to Kilimanjaro, and his powerful finish produced success by

a short-head. The narrow verdict hardly flattered a colt of classic aspirations, but connections were quite undismayed. Saratoga Springs is endowed with a singularly lethargic disposition, which never allows him to do more than the minimum required, hence his recent race at the Curragh to ensure that he was at the peak of condition. O'Brien had won the first three Irish classics of the season, with Desert King carrying Tabor's colours to victory in the 2,000 Guineas and Derby, and Classic Park landing the 1,000 Guineas.

Singspiel, the equine superstar who has been so successful on his trips abroad, gained his first Group One victory in Britain in the Coronation Cup, and later added the Juddmonte International. However, his career came to a sad end when he fractured a bone in a foreleg while preparing for his second attempt at a Breeders' Cup Turf in November. At the time of writing he was recovering from a successful operation, and will ultimately pursue a stud career. There were just three British runners at the Breeders' Cup, with Decorated Hero's third in the Mile the best placing.

Kieren Fallon, whose conduct throughout the season was exemplary, fully deserved his first Jockeys' Championship. His victory on Filial at Wolverhampton in November was his 200th of the year, although six on the All-Weather early in the year did not count towards the title. With the apprentices' Championship already in the bag, Royston Ffrench obtained his first success in a Group race when bringing Kaliana home in the St Simon Stakes at Newbury. Ffrench, who had ridden his fiftieth winner of the season at Epsom in August, is the third winner of the apprentices' title to emanate from Luca Cumani's tuition following Frankie Dettori and Jason Weaver.

The achievements of two racing personalities were recognised by their being awarded honours during 1997. Lord Hartington, whose tact and foresight were largely responsible for the creation of the British Horseracing Board, received the CBE in the New Year's Honours List. Great pleasure was also taken in the Knighthood conferred upon Sir Peter O'Sullevan in the Queen's Birthday Honours. For fifty years Sir Peter's masterful commentaries on TV and incisive writing have added incalculably to the enjoyment that millions have derived from racing.

After holding a trainer's licence for forty years Major Dick Hern brought one of the greatest careers in the whole history of British racing to a close at the end of the season. As well as being champion four times he won the Derby three times, with Troy in 1979, Henbit in 1980 and Nashwan in 1989. Other trainers to retire included Reg Akehurst, who specialised in winning big handicaps, Bill Watts, responsible for the success of Waterloo in the 1,000 Guineas in 1972, Ron Boss, and Paul Kelleway, from whose lance windmills were not always immune.

Willie Carson, who had been badly kicked at Newbury in September 1996, announced that he would not be returning to the saddle in March. Five times champion jockey, Carson rode all three of Major Hern's Derby winners and also won the race on Erhaab in 1994. His other

classics included the St Leger on Minster Son, whom he bred, in 1988. Top Northern jockey Mark Birch retired at the age of forty-seven in May after winning 1,329 races including the Chester Cup on Sea Pigeon in 1977 and 1978.
John Stubbs, who joined *The Sporting Life* in 1949, also retired in May after being a starting price reporter for many years.

Ron Smyth, the former doyen of the Epsom trainers, died at the age of 81 in July. Prior to opening his stable he had been an outstanding steeplechase jockey. Frank Carr, who trained the 1969 Royal Hunt Cup winner Kamundu and other useful horses at Malton, died at the age of 69 in March. Joe Hartigan, a member of a famous Anglo-Irish racing family and former Middleham trainer, was seventy-eight when he died in June.

George Bridgland, who won the Derby on Pearl Diver in 1947, died in July aged 82. Henry Zeisel, owner of Rheingold, narrowly beaten in the Derby in 1972 and winner of the Prix de l'Arc de Triomphe, died in August.
John Rickman known as the "politest man on television" and renowned for his trilby-doffing greeting also passed away. He was for many years the front-man for the ITV Seven, he originally started as a columnist for the Daily Sketch.

FLAT RECORD TIMES

ASCOT

Distance	Time	Age	Weight	Going	Horse	Date	
5f	59.1 secs	3	8-8	Firm	Orient	Jun 21,	1986
5f	59.72 secs	2	8-8	Firm	Lyric Fantasy (IRE)	Jun 17,	1992
6f	1m 12.53	4	9-4	Firm	Shalford (IRE)	Jun 17,	1992
6f	1m 13.63	2	8-8	Firm	Minstrella (USA)	Jun 19,	1986
7f	1m 25.94	3	9-1	Firm	Prince Ferdinand	Jun 17,	1992
7f	1m 27.25	2	8-11	Fast	Celtic Swing	Oct 8,	1994
1m(Rnd)	1m 38.58	3	9-0	Good to firm	Ridgewood Pearl	Jun 21,	1995
1m(Rnd)	1m 40.92	2	8-7	Fast	Untold	Spt 26,	1985
1m(St)	1m 38.07	4	7-8	Firm	Colour Sergeant	Jun 17,	1992
1m 2f	2m 2.76	4	9-3	Good to firm	First Island (IRE)	Jun 18,	1996
1m 4f	2m 26.95	5	8-9	Firm	Stanerra	Jun 17,	1983
2m 45y	3m 25.29	3	9-3	Firm	Landowner (IRE)	Jun 17,	1992
2m 4f	4m 15.67	5	9-0	Firm	Royal Gait (disq)	Jun 16,	1988
2m 6f 34y	4m 51.32	4	8-8	Firm	Otabari	Jun 20,	1986

AYR

Distance	Time	Age	Weight	Going	Horse	Date	
5f	57.2 secs	4	9-5	Fast	Sir Joey (USA)	Spt 16,	1993
5f	57.62 secs	2	8-6	Good to firm	Conspiracy	Spt 19,	1996
6f	68.98 secs	7	8-8	Fast	Sobering Thoughts	Spt 10,	1993
6f	69.73 secs	2	7-10	Good	Sir Bert	Spt 17,	1969
7f	1m 24.97	5	7-11	Firm	Sir Arthur Hobbs	Jun 19,	1992
7f	1m 25.71	2	9-0	Fast	Jazeel (USA)	Spt 16,	1993
1m	1m 36.0	4	7-13	Firm	Sufi	Spt 16,	1959
1m	1m 39.21	2	9-0	Firm	Kribensis	Spt 17,	1986
1m 1f	1m 53.46	3	11-2	Good to firm	Epic Stand	Jly 19,	1997
1m 2f	2m 5.2	8	10-0	Fast	Knock Knock	Spt 18,	1993
1m 2f 192y	2m 13.31	4	9-0	Good	Azzaam (USA)	Spt 18,	1991
1m 5f 13y	2m 45.81	4	9-7	Fast	Eden's Close	Spt 18,	1993
1m 7f	3m 13.16	3	9-4	Good	Romany Rye	Spt 19,	1991
2m 1f 105y	3m 45.0	4	6-13	Good	Curry	Spt 16,	1955

BATH

Distance	Time	Age	Weight	Going	Horse	Date	
5f 11y	60.1 secs	4	9-9	Good to firm	To The Roof (IRE)	May 11,	1996
5f 11y	60.8 secs	2	8-11	Fast	Cheyenne Spirit	Aug 9,	1994
5f 161y	68.1 secs	6	9-0	Firm	Madraco	May 22,	1989
5f 161y	1m 10.0	2	8-13	Fast	Morocco (IRE)	Jly 22,	1991
1m 5y	1m 38.2	4	9-9	Firm	Air Commodore (IRE)	Jly 1,	1995
1m 5y	1m 40.3	2	8-12	Good to firm	Khassah	Spt 9,	1996
1m 2f 46y	2m 6.5	4	9-4	Firm	Farmost	Jly 23,	1997
1m 3f 144y	2m 25.9	4	9-2	Firm	Alriffa	May 13,	1995
1m 5f 22y	2m 47.3	4	10-0	Firm	Flown	Aug 13,	1991
2m 1f 34y	3m 43.9	6	7-9	Fast	Patroclus	Jly 10,	1991

BEVERLEY

Distance	Time	Age	Weight	Going	Horse	Date	
5f	60.3 secs	4	9-11	Firm	Eager Deva	Apr 25,	1991
5f	61.3 secs	2	9-0	Good to firm	Jhazi	Spt 18,	1996
7f 100y	1m 29.4	3	7-8	Firm	Who's Tef (IRE)	Jly 30,	1991
7f 100y	1m 30.9	2	9-0	Firm	Majal (IRE)	Jly 30,	1991
1m 100y	1m 42.3	3	8-4	Firm	Legal Case	Jun 14,	1989
1m 100y	1m 43.3	2	9-0	Firm	Arden	Spt 24,	1986
1m 1f 207y	2m 0.65	4	11-7	Good to firm	Ooh Ah Cantona	Jly 8,	1995
1m 3f 216y	2m 30.6	3	8-1	Hard	Coinage	Jun 18,	1986
2m 35y	3m 29.3	4	9-2	Good to firm	Rushen Raider	Aug 14,	1996

BRIGHTON

Distance	Time	Age	Weight	Going	Horse	Date	
5f 59y	59.4 secs	3	8-9	Firm	Play Hever Golf	May 27,	1993
5f 59y	60.1 secs	2	9-0	Firm	Bid For Blue	May 6 ,	1993
5f 213y	67.3 secs	3	8-9	Firm	Third Party	Jun 3 ,	1997
5f 213y	68.1 secs	2	8-9	Firm	Song Mist (IRE)	Jly 16,	1996
6f 209y	1m 19.4	4	9-3	Firm	Sawaki	Spt 4 ,	1991
6f 209y	1m 19.9	2	8-11	Hard	Rain Burst	Spt 15,	1988
7f 214y	1m 30.9	5	8-12	Hard	Chase The Door	Jly 26,	1990
7f 214y	1m 32.8	2	9-7	Firm	Asian Pete	Oct 3 ,	1989
1m 1f 209y	1m 57.2	3	9-0	Firm	Get The Message	Apr 30,	1984
1m 3f 196y	2m 25.8	4	8-2	Firm	New Zealand	Jly 4 ,	1985

CARLISLE

Distance	Time	Age	Weight	Going	Horse	Date	
5f	59.4 secs	7	8-8	Hard	Serious Hurry	Aug 21,	1995
5f	60.2 secs	2	8-9	Hard	Metal Boys	Jun 1 ,	1989
5f 207y	1m 11.8	6	8-13	Firm	Night Patrol	Aug 27,	1970
5f 207y	1m 12.9	2	8-9	Hard	Parfait Amour	Spt 10,	1991
6f 206y	1m 25.4	4	9-1	Firm	Move With Edes	Jly 6 ,	1996
6f 206y	1m 26.6	2	9-4	Hard	Sense Of Priority	Spt 10,	1991
7f 214y	1m 37.3	5	7-12	Hard	Thatched (IRE)	Aug 21,	1995
7f 214y	1m 44.6	2	8-8	Firm	Blue Garter	Spt 9 ,	1980
1m 4f	2m 28.8	3	8-5	Firm	Desert Frolic (IRE)	Jun 27,	1996
1m 6f 32y	3m 2.2	6	8-10	Firm	Explosive Speed (USA)	May 26,	1994

CATTERICK

Distance	Time	Age	Weight	Going	Horse	Date	
5f	57.1 secs	4	8-7	Fast	Kabcast	Jly 7 ,	1989
5f	57.7 secs	2	9-0	Fast	Verde Alitalia (IRE)	Spt 21,	1991
5f 212y	1m 10.4	3	8-8	Firm	Triad Treble	May 31,	1984
5f 212y	1m 11.4	2	9-4	Firm	Captain Nick	Jly 11,	1978
7f	1m 23.0	4	7-12	Firm	Royal Ziska	Jun 9 ,	1973
7f	1m 24.1	2	8-11	Firm	Lindas Fantasy	Spt 18,	1982
1m 3f 214y	2m 34.1	5	9-10	Good to firm	Keep Your Distance	Oct 13,	1995
1m 5f 175y	2m 54.8	3	8-5	Firm	Geryon	May 31,	1984
1m 7f 177y	3m 20.8	4	7-11	Firm	Bean Boy	Jly 8 ,	1982

CHEPSTOW

Distance	Time	Age	Weight	Going	Horse	Date	
5f 16y	56.8 secs	3	8-4	Firm	Torbay Express	Spt 15,	1979
5f 16y	57.6 secs	2	8-11	Firm	Micro Love	Jly 8 ,	1986
6f 16y	68.8 secs	4	8-6	Fast	African Rex (FR)	May 12,	1987
6f 16y	69.4 secs	2	9-0	Fast	Royal Fi Fi (USA)	Spt 9 ,	1989
7f 16y	1m 19.9	3	9-10	Firm	Prince Titian	Aug 29,	1978
7f 16y	1m 20.8	2	9-0	Good to firm	Royal Amaretto	Spt 12,	1996
1m 14y	1m 31.8	6	9-6	Firm	Traditional Miss	Jun 27,	1981
1m 14y	1m 33.1	2	8-11	Good to firm	Ski Academy (IRE)	Aug 28,	1995
1m 2f 36y	2m 4.1	5	8-9	Hard	Leonidas (USA)	Jly 5 ,	1983
1m 4f 23y	2m 31.0	7	9-6	Hard	Maintop	Aug 27,	1984
2m 49y	3m 27.7	4	9-0	Fast	Wizzard Artist	Jly 1 ,	1989
2m 2f	4m 0.2	8	9-1	Good to firm	Tamarpour (USA)	Jly 4 ,	1995

CHESTER

Distance	Time	Age	Weight	Going	Horse	Date	
5f 16y	59.2 secs	3	10-0	Firm	Althrey Don	Jly 10,	1964
5f 16y	60.4 secs	2	8-11	Firm	Cynara	May 3 ,	1960
6f 18y	1m 12.78	6	9-2	Good	Stack Rock	Jun 23,	1993
6f 18y	1m 13.4	2	9-3	Good	Stung	Jly 27,	1968
7f 2y	1m 25.27	3	9-3	Fast	Mizaaya	May 7 ,	1992
7f 2y	1m 26.28	2	8-4	Fast	By Hand	Aug 31,	1991
7f 122y	1m 32.0	6	8-5	Firm	Cee-Jay-Ay	May 6 ,	1993

7f 122y	1m 35.0	2	9-0	Firm	Double Value	Spt 1,	1972
1m 2f 75y	2m 7.98	3	8-10	Firm	Beneficial	May 10,	1993
1m 3f 79y	2m 23.71	3	8-11	Fast	Braiswick	May 10,	1989
1m 4f 66y	2m 34.21	3	8-11	Fast	Old Vic	May 9,	1989
1m 5f 89y	2m 45.43	5	8-11	Firm	Rakaposhi King	May 7,	1987
1m 7f 195y	3m 24.53	7	7-11	Good to firm	Moonlight Quest	Jly 30,	1995
2m 2f 147y	4m 3.35	5	8-8	Good to firm	Top Cees	May 10,	1995

DONCASTER

Distance	Time	Age	Weight	Going	Horse	Date	
5f	58.05 secs	4	9-2	Good to firm	Bollin Joanne	Spt 10,	1997
5f	58.4 secs	2	9-5	Firm	Sing Sing	Spt 11,	1959
5f 140y	66.2 secs	3	9-2	Good	Welsh Abbot	Spt 12,	1958
5f 140y	68.0 secs	2	8-10	Good	Crown Flatts	Oct 25,	1947
6f	69.74 secs	3	8-9	Good to firm	Iltimas (USA)	Jly 26,	1995
6f	1m 11.2	2	8-11	Firm	Paddy's Sister	Spt 9,	1959
7f	1m 22.6	3	9-4	Hard	Pinolli	Jun 3,	1963
7f	1m 23.21	2	8-10	Good to firm	Bahhare (USA)	Spt 13,	1996
1m(St)	1m 36.71	3	8-10	Good to firm	Mushahid (USA)	Jly 17,	1996
1m(St)	1m 37.52	2	9-5	Good to firm	Lend A Hand	Spt 11,	1997
1m(Rnd)	1m 35.34	3	9-0	Fast	Gneiss (USA)	May 2,	1994
1m(Rnd)	1m 37.49	2	9-0	Good to firm	Midnight Line (USA)	Spt 11,	1997
1m 2f 60y	2m 5.48	3	8-8	Good to firm	Carlito Brigante	Jly 26,	1995
1m 2f 60y	2m 13.47	2	8-8	Good	Yard Bird	Nov 6,	1981
1m 4f	2m 29.72	3	8-6	Good to firm	Busy Flight	Spt 13,	1996
1m 6f 132y	3m 2.22	3	8-3	Firm	Brier Creek (USA)	Spt 10,	1992
2m 110y	3m 34.44	4	9-12	Fast	Farsi	Jun 12,	1992
2m 2f	3m 52.17	4	9-0	Good to firm	Canon Can (USA)	Spt 11,	1997

EPSOM

Distance	Time	Age	Weight	Going	Horse	Date	
5f	53.6 secs	4	9-5	Firm	Indigenous	Jun 2,	1960
5f	55.02 secs	2	8-9	Good	Prince Aslia	Jun 9,	1995
6f	67.91 secs	5	7-7	Firm	Moor Lane	Jun 7,	1973
6f	67.85 secs	2	8-11	Fast	Showbrook (IRE)	Jun 5,	1991
7f	1m 20.15	4	8-7	Firm	Capistrano	Jun 7,	1972
7f	1m 22.17	2	8-9	Fast	Shamrock Fair (IRE)	Aug 30,	1994
1m 114y	1m 40.75	3	8-6	Fast	Sylva Honda	Jun 5,	1991
1m 114y	1m 42.8	2	8-5	Fast	Nightstalker	Aug 30,	1988
1m 2f 18y	2m 3.5	5	7-13	Good	Crossbow (unofficial)	Jun 7,	1967
1m 4f 10y	2m 32.31	3	9-0	Firm	Lammtarra (USA)	Jun 10,	1995

FOLKESTONE

Distance	Time	Age	Weight	Going	Horse	Date	
5f	58.7 secs	6	10-0	Firm	Friendly Brave (USA)	Jun 28,	1996
5f	58.5 secs	2	9-2	Good to firm	Pivotal	Nov 6,	1995
6f	1m 10.4	3	8-9	Firm	Spotted Eagle	Apr 23,	1996
6f	1m 11.0	2	7-13	Hard	Fashion Model	Aug 31,	1970
6f 189y	1m 21.3	3	8-9	Firm	Cielamour (USA)	Aug 9,	1988
6f 189y	1m 23.7	2	8-11	Good to firm	Hen Harrier	Jly 3,	1996
1m 1f 149y	1m 57.8	4	8-11	Firm	Lord Raffles	Jun 2,	1980
1m 4f	2m 33.3	4	8-8	Hard	Snow Blizzard	Jun 30,	1992
1m 7f 92y	3m 23.1	3	9-11	Firm	Mata Askari	Spt 12,	1991
2m 93y	3m 32.5	6	7-13	Firm	North West	Jly 21,	1981

GOODWOOD

Distance	Time	Age	Weight	Going	Horse	Date	
5f	56.25 secs	4	9-5	Good to firm	Hever Golf Rose	Jly 25,	1995
5f	57.53 secs	2	8-12	Fast	Poets Cove	Aug 3,	1990
6f	69.58 secs	4	8-3	Firm	For the Present	Jly 30,	1994
6f	1m 10.08	2	9-7	Good to firm	April The Eighth	Jly 25,	1995
7f	1m 23.88	3	8-7	Good to firm	Brief Glimpse (IRE)	Jly 25,	1995
7f	1m 25.97	2	8-11	Fast	Maroof (USA)	Jly 30,	1992

1m	1m 35.71	3	8-13	Firm	Distant View (USA)	Jly 27, 1994
1m	1m 38.94	2	9-0	Good to firm	Mutawwaj (IRE)	Spt 24, 1997
1m 1f	1m 52.81	3	9-6	Firm	Vena (IRE)	Jly 27, 1995
1m 2f	2m 4.96	3	8-6	Firm	Kartajana	Aug 4, 1990
1m 4f	2m 31.57	3	8-10	Firm	Presenting	Jly 25, 1995
1m 6f	2m 58.8	3	8-10	Firm	Secret Waters	Aug 2, 1990
2m	3m 23.57	4	9-5	Firm	Tioman Island	Jly 28, 1994
2m 4f	4m 11.75	3	7-10	Firm	Lucky Moon	Aug 2, 1990

HAMILTON

Distance	Time	Age	Weight	Going	Horse	Date
5f 4y	58.0 secs	5	8-6	Firm	Golden Sleigh	Spt 6, 1972
5f 4y	58.0 secs	2	7-8	Firm	Fair Dandy	Spt 25, 1972
6f 5y	69.3 secs	4	8-7	Firm	Marcus Game	Jly 11, 1974
6f 5y	1m 10.1	2	7-5	Hard	Yoohoo	Spt 8, 1976
1m 65y	1m 42.7	6	7-7	Firm	Cranley	Spt 25, 1972
1m 65y	1m 45.8	2	8-11	Firm	Hopeful Subject	Spt 24, 1973
1m 1f 36y	1m 54.2	3	8-2	Hard	Fairman	Aug 20, 1976
1m 3f 16y	2m 20.5	3	9-3	Firm	Wang Feihoong	Jly 21, 1983
1m 4f 17y	2m 32.0	4	7-4	Firm	Fine Point	Aug 24, 1981
1m 5f 9y	2m 45.2	6	9-6	Firm	Mentalasanythin	Jun 14, 1995

HAYDOCK

Distance	Time	Age	Weight	Going	Horse	Date
5f	58.9 secs	3	7-5	Firm	Fish and Chips	Jun 6, 1970
5f	59.2 secs	2	9-4	Firm	Money For Nothing	Aug 12, 1964
6f	69.92 secs	4	9-0	Good to firm	Iktamal (USA)	Spt 7, 1996
6f	1m 11.63	2	8-11	Good to firm	Tamnia	Jly 8, 1995
7f 30y	1m 27.21	4	9-4	Firm	Indian King	Jun 5, 1982
7f 30y	1m 29.4	2	9-0	Good to firm	Apprehension	Spt 7, 1996
1m 30y	1m 40.2	4	8-10	Good to firm	Moving Arrow	Aug 5, 1995
1m 30y	1m 40.69	2	8-12	Good to firm	Besiege	Spt 7, 1996
1m 2f 120y	2m 8.53	3	8-7	Good to firm	Fahal (USA)	Aug 5, 1995
1m 3f 200y	2m 26.4	5	8-2	Firm	New Member	Jly 4, 1970
1m 6f	2m 59.9	4	9-10	Good	Soloman's Dancer	Aug 6, 1994
2m 45y	3m 27.09	4	8-13	Firm	Prince of Peace	May 26, 1984

KEMPTON

Distance	Time	Age	Weight	Going	Horse	Date
5f	57.42 secs	4	9-3	Good to firm	Almaty (IRE)	May 31, 1997
5f	58.3 secs	2	9-7	Firm	Schweppeshire Lad	Jun 3, 1978
6f	1m 10.04	7	7-10	Firm	Jokist	Apr 6, 1990
6f	1m 10.8	2	8-10	Good	Zabara	Spt 22, 1951
7f(Rnd)	1m 23.59	3	9-2	Good to firm	Wild Rice	Aug 2, 1995
7f(Rnd)	1m 27.52	2	8-6	Good	Duke of Ragusa	Spt 1, 1972
7f (Jub)	1m 23.63	3	9-0	Good to firm	Shaheen (USA)	May 31, 1997
7f (Jub)	1m 24.78	2	9-0	Good to firm	Canons Park	Jun 28, 1995
1m(Jub)	1m 35.39	3	8-12	Good to firm	Private Line (USA)	Jun 28, 1995
1m(Jub)	1m 38.78	2	9-0	Good to firm	Taverner Society (IRE)	Spt 22, 1997
1m(Rnd)	1m 35.81	4	9-1	Firm	County Broker	May 23, 1984
1m(Rnd)	1m 43.4	2	7-0	Good	Fascinating	Nov 3, 1956
1m 1f	1m 50.56	3	8-12	Fast	Sky Conqueror (USA)	Jun 29, 1988
1m 2f	1m 59.53	4	9-6	Firm	Batshoof	Apr 6, 1990
1m 3f 30y	2m 16.2	4	9-2	Firm	Shernazar	Spt 6, 1985
1m 4f	2m 30.18	6	8-5	Firm	Going Going	Spt 7, 1985
1m 6f 92y	3m 6.59	4	9-8	Good	Renzo	Spt 21, 1997
2m	3m 26.53	4	9-10	Good to firm	Latahaab (USA)	May 27, 1995

LEICESTER

Distance	Time	Age	Weight	Going	Horse	Date
5f 2y	58.2 secs	4	9-5	Fast	Lucky Parkes	Spt 6, 1994
5f 2y	58.4 secs	2	9-0	Firm	Cutting Blade	Jun 9, 1986
5f 218y	69.4 secs	3	8-12	Fast	Lakeland Beauty	May 29, 1990

5f 218y	1m 10.1	2	9-0	Firm	Thordis	Oct 24,	1995
7f 9y	1m 20.8	3	8-7	Firm	Flower Bowl	Jun 9,	1986
7f 9y	1m 22.9	2	9-2	Good to firm	Rabi (IRE)	Spt 22,	1997
1m 8y	1m 33.8	3	9-0	Good to firm	Clifton Fox	May 29,	1995
1m 8y	1m 34.6	2	8-9	Firm	Lady Carla	Oct 24,	1995
1m 1f 218y	2m 2.4	3	8-11	Firm	Effigy	Nov 4,	1985
1m 1f 218y	2m 5.3	2	9-1	Good to firm	Windsor Castle	Oct 14,	1996
1m 3f 183y	2m 27.9	3	8-12	Firm	Al Widyan (IRE)	Oct 23,	1995

LINGFIELD (Turf)

Distance	Time	Age	Weight	Going	Horse	Date	
5f	56.24 secs	3	9-1	Fast	Eveningperformance	Jly 25,	1994
5f	57.25 secs	2	8-9	Fast	Quiz Time	Aug 6,	1994
6f	68.2 secs	6	9-10	Firm	Al Amead	Jly 2,	1986
6f	68.6 secs	2	9-3	Firm	The Ritz	Jun 11,	1965
7f	1m 20.2	8	7-10	Hard	Polar Jest	Aug 19,	1955
7f	1m 21.34	2	7-6	Firm	Mandav	Oct 3,	1980
7f 140y	1m 26.73	3	8-6	Fast	Hiaam (USA)	Jly 11,	1987
7f 140y	1m 29.93	2	8-12	Firm	Rather Warm	Nov 7,	1978
1m 1f	1m 52.4	4	9-2	Good to firm	Quandary (USA)	Jly 15,	1995
1m 2f	2m 5.79	3	9-3	Firm	Aromatic	Jly 14,	1990
1m 3f 106y	2m 23.95	3	8-5	Firm	Night-Shirt	Jly 14,	1990
1m 6f	3m 2.7	4	9-3	Good to firm	Ballynakelly	Jly 13,	1996
2m	3m 28.96	3	9-0	Firm	Lothian	Spt 20,	1990

LINGFIELD (AWT)

Distance	Time	Age	Weight	Going	Horse	Date	
5f	58.01 secs	4	8-5	Standard	Little Saboteur	Feb 20,	1993
5f	59.11 secs	2	9-2	Standard	Fruitana (IRE)	Nov 7,	1996
6f	1m 10.58	4	9-4	Standard	J Cheever Loophole	Nov 23,	1989
6f	1m 11.65	2	9-7	Standard	Time's Arrow (IRE)	Jly 10,	1992
7f	1m 22.99	3	9-3	Standard	Confronter	Jly 18,	1992
7f	1m 24.0	2	8-12	Standard	Scottish Castle	Nov 2,	1990
1m	1m 36.32	5	9-5	Standard	Vanroy	Nov 30,	1989
1m	1m 36.5	2	9-5	Standard	San Pier Niceto	Nov 30,	1989
1m 2f	2m 2.93	4	9-3	Standard	Rapporteur	Nov 2,	1990
1m 2f	2m 7.5	2	8-11	Standard	Star Fighter	Nov 26,	1994
1m 4f	2m 29.3	4	8-6	Standard	Puff Puff	Nov 8,	1990
1m 5f	2m 43.82	3	8-9	Standard	Ela Man Howa	Nov 26,	1994
2m	3m 20.09	3	9-0	Standard	Yenoora (IRE)	Aug 8,	1992

MUSSELBURGH

Distance	Time	Age	Weight	Going	Horse	Date	
5f	57.4 secs	4	7-2	Firm	Palm Court Joe	Jly 4,	1977
5f	57.5 secs	2	8-2	Firm	Arasong	May 16,	1994
7f 15y	1m 26.0	6	9-0	Firm	Show of Hands	Apr 19,	1982
7f 15y	1m 27.5	2	9-1	Fast	Mubdi (USA)	Oct 6,	1986
1m 16y	1m 38.3	4	8-13	Firm	Churchillian	Jly 11,	1977
1m 16y	1m 40.9	2	8-11	Fast	Trompe d'Oeil	Oct 6,	1986
1m 3f 32y	2m 19.7	3	8-10	Firm	Old Court	Jly 4,	1977
1m 4f 31y	2m 32.2	5	7-9	Good	Glengrigor	Apr 15,	1946
1m 7f 16y	3m 10.4	3	8-0	Good	Cunningham	Spt 21,	1953

NEWBURY

Distance	Time	Age	Weight	Going	Horse	Date	
5f 34y	59.77 secs	4	9-4	Good to firm	Struggler	Spt 20,	1996
5f 34y	60.52 secs	2	8-7	Good to firm	Lord Kintyre	Jly 19,	1997
6f 8y	1m 10.71	5	9-3	Good to firm	Jayannpee	Jly 20,	1996
6f 8y	1m 11.49	2	8-6	Good to firm	Crystal Crossing (IRE)	Jly 20,	1996
7f	1m 23.84	5	9-3	Good to firm	Celestial Key (USA)	Jun 15,	1995
7f	1m 24.13	2	8-13	Good to firm	Imperial President	Jly 20,	1996
7f 64y(Rnd)	1m 26.13	4	9-12	Good to firm	Green Perfume (USA)	Jly 19,	1996
7f 64y(Rnd)	1m 28.81	2	8-10	Fast	Duty Time	Aug 14,	1993

1m	1m 35.76	4	9-0	Fast	Emperor Jones (USA)	May 13, 1994
1m	1m 38.96	2	8-10	Good to firm	King Sound	Spt 20, 1996
1m 7y(Rnd)	1m 34.91	3	8-9	Fast	Philidor	May 16, 1992
1m 7y(Rnd)	1m 37.29	2	8-11	Firm	Master Willie	Oct 1, 1979
1m 1f	1m 49.65	3	8-0	Good to firm	Holtye (IRE)	May 21, 1995
1m 2f 6y	2m 1.29	3	8-7	Fast	Wall Street (USA)	Jly 20, 1996
1m 3f 5y	2m 17.51	4	9-0	Fast	Hateel	May 19, 1990
1m 4f 5y	2m 29.2	4	8-9	Hard	Vidi Vici	Jun 21, 1951
1m 5f 61y	2m 44.9	5	10-0	Good to firm	Mystic Hill	Jly 20, 1996
2m	3m 25.42	8	9-12	Good to firm	Moonlight Quest	Jly 19, 1996

NEWCASTLE

Distance	Time	Age	Weight	Going	Horse	Date
5f	58.0 secs	4	9-2	Fast	Princess Oberon (IRE)	Jly 23, 1994
5f	58.83 secs	2	9-0	Firm	Atlantic Viking (IRE)	Jun 4, 1997
6f	1m 11.21	3	9-2	Good	Tadwin	Jun 30, 1990
6f	1m 12.67	2	9-0	Firm	Sundance Kid (USA)	Oct 3, 1989
7f	1m 23.53	3	8-5	Firm	Beaudelaire (USA)	Jly 23, 1983
7f	1m 25.1	2	9-0	Good to firm	Multitone	Aug 4, 1996
1m(Rnd)	1m 38.96	3	8-12	Firm	Jacamar	Jly 27, 1989
1m(Rnd)	1m 39.97	2	9-0	Firm	Laxey Bay	Oct 3, 1989
1m 3y(St)	1m 39.9	3	9-0	Good	Epic Stand	May 22, 1997
1m 3y(St)	1m 38.8	2	8-6	Good	The Fly	Aug 26, 1996
1m 1f 9y	1m 52.3	3	6-3	Good	Ferniehurst	Jun 23, 1936
1m 2f 32y	2m 6.59	3	8-11	Fast	Missionary Ridge	Jun 29, 1990
1m 4f 93y	2m 37.3	5	8-12	Firm	Retender (USA)	Jun 25, 1994
2m 19y	3m 22.0	4	7-12	Good	Nectar II	Jun 23, 1937

NEWMARKET (Rowley)

Distance	Time	Age	Weight	Going	Horse	Date
5f	56.81 secs	6	9-2	Fast	Lochsong	Apr 30, 1994
5f	58.78 secs	2	8-13	Good	Clifton Charlie	Oct 4, 1990
6f	1m 10.25	4	9-8	Good to firm	Lake Coniston (IRE)	Apr 18, 1995
6f	1m 10.14	2	9-0	Good	Lycius (USA)	Oct 4, 1990
7f	1m 22.24	4	9-5	Fast	Perfolia (USA)	Oct 18, 1991
7f	1m 23.45	2	9-0	Fast	Dr Devious (IRE)	Oct 18, 1991
1m	1m 35.08	3	9-0	Fast	Mister Baileys	Apr 30, 1994
1m	1m 36.74	2	9-0	Fast	Bold Pursuit (IRE)	Oct 18, 1991
1m 1f	1m 47.45	3	8-3	Firm	Sin Timon	Oct 1, 1977
1m 2f	2m 1.04	3	8-10	Good	Palace Music (USA)	Oct 20, 1984
1m 2f	2m 4.65	2	9-4	Good	Highland Chieftain	Nov 2, 1985
1m 4f	2m 27.67	3	8-5	Fast	Kiveton Kabooz	Oct 17, 1991
1m 6f	2m 54.34	5	8-6	Fast	Tudor Island	Spt 30, 1994
2m	3m 19.51	5	9-5	Good to firm	Grey Shot	Oct 4, 1997

NEWMARKET (July)

Distance	Time	Age	Weight	Going	Horse	Date
5f	58.12 secs	4	8-11	Firm	Sweet Magic	Jly 22, 1995
5f	58.52 secs	2	8-10	Good	Seductress	Jly 10, 1990
6f	69.82 secs	4	9-6	Good	Cadeaux Genereux	Jly 13, 1989
6f	1m 10.61	2	8-10	Fast	Mujtahid (USA)	Jly 11, 1990
7f	1m 23.56	3	8-12	Good	Inchinor	Jun 26, 1993
7f	1m 24.46	2	8-11	Good to firm	Ruznama (USA)	Aug 25, 1995
1m	1m 36.8	4	9-7	Hard	Pink Flower	Jun 6, 1944
1m	1m 39.01	2	8-11	Good to firm	Traceability	Aug 25, 1995
1m 2f	2m 2.31	4	9-1	Fast	Vallance	Aug 1, 1992
1m 4f	2m 26.7	3	8-1	Fast	Desert Team (USA)	Jly 6, 1993
1m 6f 175y	3m 6.07	3	8-10	Fast	Spring to Action	Jly 8, 1993
2m 24y	3m 24.32	5	10-0	Fast	Jack Button	Aug 5, 1994

NOTTINGHAM

Distance	Time	Age	Weight	Going	Horse	Date
5f 13y	58.4 secs	6	8-8	Good	Minstrel King	Mar 29, 1960

5f 13y	57.9 secs	2	8-9	Firm	Hoh Magic	May 13,	1994
6f 15y	1m 10.0	4	9-2	Firm	Ajanac	Aug 8 ,	1988
6f 15y	1m 11.4	2	8-11	Firm	Jameelapi (USA)	Aug 8 ,	1983
1m 54y	1m 39.6	4	8-2	Fast	Blake's Treasure	Spt 2 ,	1991
1m 54y	1m 40.8	2	9-0	Fast	King's Loch (IRE)	Spt 3 ,	1991
1m 1f 213y	2m 2.3	3	8-8	Firm	Ayaabi	Jly 21,	1984
1m 1f 213y	2m 5.6	2	9-0	Firm	Al Salite	Oct 28,	1985
1m 6f 15y	2m 57.8	3	8-10	Firm	Buster Jo	Oct 1 ,	1985
2m 9y	3m 24.0	5	7-7	Firm	Fet	Oct 5 ,	1936

PONTEFRACT

Distance	Time	Age	Weight	Going	Horse	Date	
5f	61.1 secs	5	7-7	Hard	Regal Bingo	Spt 29,	1971
5f	61.4 secs	2	8-9	Fast	Breakaway	Aug 6 ,	1987
6f	1m 12.6	3	7-13	Firm	Merry One	Aug 29,	1970
6f	1m 14.0	2	9-3	Firm	Fawzi	Spt 6 ,	1983
1m 4y	1m 41.4	5	8-12	Firm	Nevison's Lad	May 14,	1965
1m 4y	1m 42.8	2	9-13	Firm	Star Spray	Spt 6 ,	1983
1m 2f 6y	2m 6.2	4	7-8	Hard	Happy Hector	Jly 9 ,	1979
1m 2f 6y	2m 13.0	2	9-0	Good to firm	Warbrook	Oct 2 ,	1995
1m 4f 8y	2m 34.3	4	8-9	Hard	Ezra	Jun 23,	1975
2m 1f 22y	3m 42.1	3	9-2	Firm	Night Eye (USA)	Spt 6 ,	1983
2m 1f 216y	3m 51.1	3	8-8	Firm	Kudz (USA)	Spt 9 ,	1986
2m 5f 122y	4m 47.8	4	8-4	Firm	Physical (USA)	May 14,	1984

REDCAR

Distance	Time	Age	Weight	Going	Horse	Date	
5f	56.5 secs	3	9-7	Firm	Nazela	Aug 10,	1990
5f	56.9 secs	2	9-0	Firm	Mister Joel	Oct 24,	1995
6f	68.6 secs	3	9-2	Fast	Sizzling Saga (IRE)	Jun 21,	1991
6f	69.5 secs	2	9-7	Firm	Times of Times	Oct 24,	1995
7f	1m 21.0	3	9-1	Firm	Empty Quarter	Oct 3 ,	1995
7f	1m 21.9	2	8-11	Firm	Nagwa	Spt 27,	1975
1m	1m 33.1	3	9-5	Firm	Night Wink (USA)	Oct 24,	1995
1m	1m 36.7	2	8-8	Fast	Carbonate	Spt 15,	1987
1m 1f	1m 48.5	5	8-12	Firm	Mellottie	Jly 25,	1990
1m 1f	1m 53.8	2	9-0	Good	Double Trigger (IRE)	Spt 25,	1993
1m 2f	2m 1.5	5	9-3	Firm	Inaad	May 29,	1989
1m 3f	2m 17.0	3	8-9	Firm	Photo Call	Aug 7 ,	1990
1m 5f 135y	2m 54.6	6	9-10	Firm	Brodessa	Jun 20,	1992
1m 6f 19y	2m 59.9	3	8-6	Firm	Trainglot	Jly 25,	1990
2m 4y	3m 24.9	3	9-3	Fast	Subsonic (IRE)	Oct 8 ,	1991

RIPON

Distance	Time	Age	Weight	Going	Horse	Date	
5f	57.6 secs	5	8-10	Good	Broadstairs Beauty (IRE)	May 21,	1995
5f	57.8 secs	2	8-8	Firm	Super Rocky	Aug 5 ,	1991
6f	69.8 secs	5	7-0	Firm	Quoit	Jly 23,	1966
6f	1m 10.9	2	8-11	Good	Kahir Almaydan (IRE)	Aug 28,	1995
1m	1m 37.0	4	7-10	Firm	Crown Witness	Aug 25,	1980
1m	1m 41.2	2	7-2	Good	Roanstreak	Spt 5 ,	1970
1m 1f	1m 50.5	3	9-2	Good to firm	Bold Words (CAN)	Apr 9 ,	1997
1m 2f	2m 2.7	3	9-4	Firm	Swift Sword	Jly 20,	1991
1m 4f 60y	2m 32.2	6	8-7	Firm	Cholo	Spt 27,	1941
2m	3m 26.2	5	9-6	Good to firm	Nigels Lad (IRE)	May 28,	1997

SALISBURY

Distance	Time	Age	Weight	Going	Horse	Date	
5f	59.4 secs	3	8-11	Firm	Bellsabanging	May 5 ,	1993
5f	59.8 secs	2	8-5	Good to firm	Tarf (USA)	Aug 17,	1995
6f	1m 11.54	4	8-7	Fast	Prince Sky	Jun 25,	1986
6f	1m 12.41	2	9-1	Fast	Basma (USA)	Spt 6 ,	1991
6f 212y	1m 24.98	3	9-7	Firm	High Summer	Spt 5 ,	1996

6f 212y	1m 25.97	2	9-0	Firm	More Royal (USA)	Jun 29, 1995
1m	1m 38.94	5	8-10	Firm	Weaver Bird	Jun 29, 1995
1m	1m 43.86	2	9-3	Firm	Carocrest	Spt 1, 1983
1m 1f 209y	2m 4.46	4	7-7	Fast	Kala Nashan	Jun 25, 1986
1m 4f	2m 32.08	3	8-9	Good	Chief Contender (IRE)	May 5, 1996
1m 6f	2m 58.01	4	10-0	Fast	Dancing Affair	Aug 16, 1984

SANDOWN

Distance	Time	Age	Weight	Going	Horse	Date
5f 6y	58.82 secs	6	8-9	Good to firm	Palacegate Touch	Spt 17, 1996
5f 6y	59.48 secs	2	9-3	Firm	Times Time	Jly 22, 1982
7f 16y	1m 26.36	3	9-0	Firm	Mawsuff	Jun 14, 1986
7f 16y	1m 27.87	2	8-12	Good to firm	Red Camellia	Jly 25, 1996
1m 14y	1m 39.08	3	8-8	Firm	Linda's Fantasy	Aug 19, 1983
1m 14y	1m 41.14	2	8-11	Fast	Reference Point	Spt 23, 1986
1m 1f	1m 54.01	3	9-7	Firm	Al Shafa	Jun 15, 1996
1m 1f	1m 57.62	2	9-0	Good to firm	Night Watch (USA)	Aug 30, 1995
1m 2f 7y	2m 2.14	4	8-11	Firm	Kalaglow	May 31, 1982
1m 3f 91y	2m 21.61	4	8-3	Fast	Aylesfield	Jly 7, 1984
1m 6f	2m 58.85	3	9-2	Fast	Sun of Spring	Aug 11, 1993
2m 78y	3m 29.93	6	9-2	Firm	Sadeem (USA)	May 29, 1989

SOUTHWELL

Distance	Time	Age	Weight	Going	Horse	Date
5f	57.7 secs	3	9-6	Standard	Case Law	Aug 15, 1990
5f	58.9 secs	2	8-9	Standard	Nor-Do-I	Nov 29, 1996
6f	1m 13.3	3	9-2	Standard	Rambo Express	Dec 18, 1990
6f	1m 13.9	2	9-0	Standard	Superstrike	Jly 31, 1991
7f	1m 26.8	5	8-4	Standard	Amenable	Dec 13, 1990
7f	1m 27.0	2	8-4	Standard	Rejoice (IRE)	Nov 30, 1990
1m	1m 17.0	4	9-12	Standard	Bella Parkes	Mar 3, 1995
1m	1m 38.0	2	8-9	Standard	Alpha Rascal	Nov 13, 1990
1m 3f	2m 21.5	4	9-7	Standard	Tempering	Dec 5, 1990
1m 4f	2m 34.1	4	9-12	Standard	Fast Chick	Nov 8, 1989
1m 6f	3m 1.6	3	7-7	Standard	Qualitair Aviator	Dec 1, 1989
2m	3m 37.8	4	9-12	Standard	Megan's Flight	Dec 6, 1989

THIRSK

Distance	Time	Age	Weight	Going	Horse	Date
5f	56.9 secs	4	8-6	Firm	Singing Star	Aug 3, 1990
5f	57.4 secs	2	9-1	Firm	Nifty Fifty (IRE)	Jly 19, 1991
6f	69.4 secs	4	10-0	Firm	Tiler (IRE)	Jly 26, 1996
6f	69.2 secs	2	9-6	Good to firm	Westcourt Magic	Aug 25, 1995
7f	1m 22.6	5	6-11	Firm	Tuanwun	May 29, 1970
7f	1m 24.6	2	8-12	Firm	Man of Harlech	Aug 2, 1975
1m	1m 34.8	4	8-13	Firm	Yearsley	May 5, 1990
1m	1m 38.5	2	8-9	Good to firm	Ivan Luis (FR)	Spt 7, 1996
1m 4f	2m 30.0	4	8-2	Firm	Casting Vote	Aug 1, 1964
2m	3m 22.3	3	8-11	Firm	Tomaschek (USA)	Jly 17, 1981

WARWICK

Distance	Time	Age	Weight	Going	Horse	Date
5f	57.8 secs	5	9-4	Fast	Another Episode (IRE)	Aug 29, 1994
5f	58.6 secs	2	8-11	Firm	Olympic Spirit	Jun 10, 1996
6f	1m 11.8	4	9-5	Firm	Pride of Kilmallock	Jly 1, 1960
6f	1m 12.1	2	7-7	Firm	Sum Mede	Jly 14, 1989
7f	1m 23.5	4	9-2	Good to firm	Russian Music	Mar 31, 1997
7f	1m 24.8	2	9-4	Firm	Nocino	Jly 28, 1979
1m	1m 36.0	3	9-0	Firm	Academic World (USA)	Aug 25, 1975
1m	1m 37.5	2	9-3	Firm	Perfect Stranger	Oct 14, 1986
1m 2f 169y	2m 13.2	3	8-8	Firm	Classic Tale	Jly 7, 1987
1m 4f 115y	2m 37.2	5	8-12	Hard	Noirmont Buoy	Jun 19, 1967
1m 6f 194y	3m 8.9	4	9-1	Firm	Chucklestone	Jly 7, 1987

2m 20y	3m 25.8	4	9-7	Fast	Sanamar (disq)	Aug 29,	1988

WINDSOR

Distance	Time	Age	Weight	Going	Horse	Date	
5f 10y	59.2 secs	3	9-7	Fast	La Tuerta	Jly 15,	1985
5f 10y	58.9 secs	2	9-0	Firm	Strictly Private	Jly 22,	1974
5f 217y	1m 10.1	3	8-4	Firm	Sweet Relief	Spt 11,	1978
5f 217y	69.0 secs	2	8-7	Fast	Options Open	Jly 25,	1994
1m 67y	1m 41.5	4	7-2	Firm	Blowing Bubbles	Jly 16,	1984
1m 2f 7y	2m 3.0	3	9-1	Firm	Moomba Masquerade	May 19,	1980
1m 3f 135y	2m 21.5	3	9-2	Firm	Double Florin (USA)	May 19,	1980

WOLVERHAMPTON

Distance	Time	Age	Weight	Going	Horse	Date	
5f	60.5 secs	7	8-7	Standard	Sir Tasker	Jan 4 ,	1995
5f	62.3 secs	2	8-10	Standard	Imperial Garden (IRE)	Aug 31,	1996
6f	1m 13.2	7	9-8	Standard	Sea-Deer	Aug 31,	1996
6f	1m 14.4	2	9-0	Standard	Trailblazer	Nov 2 ,	1996
7f	1m 27.3	4	10-0	Standard	Rocketeer	Jan 4 ,	1995
7f	1m 28.5	2	8-9	Standard	Mudflap	Aug 17,	1996
1m	2m 38.4	5	8-13	Standard	Johns Act (USA)	Mar 8 ,	1995
1m 100y	1m 48.6	3	9-0	Standard	Contrafire (IRE)	Jan 4 ,	1995
1m 100y	1m 50.6	2	9-0	Standard	Upper Grosvenor	Dec 27,	1993
1m 1f 79y	1m 59.3	12	9-6	Standard	Aitch N'Bee	Jan 4 ,	1995
1m 4f	2m 38.4	3	8-2	Standard	New Inn	Nov 26,	1994
1m 6f 166y	3m 11.3	4	8-11	Standard	Noufari (FR)	Jan 4 ,	1995
2m 46y	3m 39.3	4	9-6	Standard	Secret Serenade	Jan 18,	1995

YARMOUTH

Distance	Time	Age	Weight	Going	Horse	Date	
5f 43y	60.2 secs	3	8-11	Fast	Charm Bird	Spt 15,	1988
5f 43y	60.9 secs	2	8-8	Firm	Aberbevine	Jun 14,	1967
6f 3y	1m 10.1	3	8-10	Good to firm	Proud Native	Aug 10,	1997
6f 3y	1m 10.4	2	9-0	Fast	Lanchester	Aug 15,	1988
7f 3y	1m 22.2	3	8-7	Fast	Cielamour (USA)	Spt 15,	1988
7f 3y	1m 22.2	2	9-0	Fast	Warrshan (USA)	Spt 14,	1988
1m 3y	1m 34.6	3	8-11	Firm	Bonne Etoile	Jun 27,	1995
1m 3y	1m 34.4	2	8-11	Fast	Alderney	Spt 14,	1988
1m 2f 21y	2m 3.5	3	8-7	Firm	Supreme Sound	Spt 17,	1997
1m 3f 101y	2m 23.0	3	8-9	Firm	Rahil (IRE)	Jly 1 ,	1993
1m 6f 17y	2m 57.8	3	8-2	Fast	Barakat	Jly 24,	1990
2m	3m 28.9	3	8-13	Firm	Dawn Summit	May 28,	1997
2m 2f 51y	3m 57.2	3	9-8	Firm	Motet	Spt 18,	1997

YORK

Distance	Time	Age	Weight	Going	Horse	Date	
5f	56.16 secs	3	9-3	Fast	Dayjur (USA)	Aug 23,	1990
5f	57.39 secs	2	7-8	Firm	Lyric Fantasy (USA)	Aug 20,	1992
6f	68.82 secs	4	9-4	Fast	Shalford (IRE)	May 14,	1992
6f	69.59 secs	2	9-0	Good	Indiscreet (CAN)	Aug 22,	1996
6f 214y	1m 21.77	3	8-4	Good	Ruznama (USA)	Aug 22,	1996
6f 214y	1m 22.98	2	8-10	Fast	Options Open	Aug 16,	1994
7f 202y	1m 34.81	4	8-10	Good	Concer Un	Aug 22,	1996
7f 202y	1m 37.43	2	9-0	Good	Prince of My Heart	Oct 4 ,	1995
1m 205y	1m 48.89	6	8-4	Fast	No Comebacks	Jun 10,	1994
1m 205y	1m 52.43	2	8-1	Firm	Oral Evidence	Oct 6 ,	1988
1m 2f 85y	2m 6.18	3	9-0	Firm	Erhaab (USA)	May 11,	1994
1m 3f 195y	2m 25.79	3	9-0	Fast	Diminuendo (USA)	Aug 16,	1988
1m 5f 194y	2m 52.77	4	9-0	Good to firm	Classic Cliche (IRE)	May 16,	1996
1m 7f 195y	3m 18.49	3	8-0	Fast	Dam Busters (USA)	Aug 16,	1988

RACEFORM STANDARD TIMES 1997

ASCOT

5f 1m 00.2
6f 1m 14.0
7f 1m 27.2
1m (Rnd) 1m 40.8
1m (Str) 1m 40.0
1m 2f 2m 05.5
1m 4f 2m 30.0
2m 45y 3m 27.2
2m 4f 4m 20.0
2m 6f 34y 4m 50.0

AYR

5f ....57.0 secs
6f 1m 09.8
7f 1m 24.4
1m 1m 37.4
1m 1f 1m 50.5
1m 2f 2m 05.8
1m 2f 192y 2m 15.9
1m 5f 13y 2m 44.8
1m 7f 3m 10.7
2m 1f 105y 3m 42.5

BATH

5f 11y 1m 00.5
5f 161y 1m 09.5
1m 5y 1m 38.2
1m 2f 46y 2m 06.5
1m 3f 144y 2m 26.7
1m 5f 22y 2m 45.7
2m 1f 34y 3m 41.4

BEVERLEY

5f 1m 01.8
7f 100y 1m 32.0
1m 100y 1m 44.0
1m 1f 207y 2m 03.1
1m 3f 216y 2m 33.0
2m 35y 3m 30.5

BRIGHTON

5f 59y 1m 00.0
5f 213y 1m 07.2
6f 209y 1m 20.0
7f 214y 1m 31.3
1m 1f 209y 1m 58.3
1m 3f 196y 2m 27.6

CARLISLE

5f 1m 00.2
5f 207y 1m 11.8
6f 206y 1m 25.7
7f 214y 1m 37.0
1m 4f 2m 29.0
1m 6f 32y 3m 01.0
2m 1f 52y 3m 37.0

CATTERICK

5f ....57.7 secs
5f 212y 1m 10.9
7f 1m 23.6
1m 3f 214y 2m 31.4
1m 4f 44y 2m 34.0
1m 5f 175y 2m 56.0
1m 7f 177y 3m 22.0

CHEPSTOW

5f 16y ....57.0 secs
6f 16y 1m 09.2
7f 16y 1m 19.3
1m 14y 1m 31.2
1m 2f 36y 2m 05.3
1m 4f 23y 2m 32.4
2m 49y 3m 28.0
2m 2f 3m 50.0
2m 2f 33y 3m 52.0

CHESTER

5f 16y 1m 00.2
6f 18y 1m 13.3
7f 2y 1m 25.2
7f 122y 1m 32.0
1m 2f 75y 2m 08.7
1m 3f 79y 2m 23.6
1m 4f 66y 2m 36.2
1m 5f 89y 2m 50.0
1m 7f 195y 3m 22.9
2m 2f 147y 4m 02.5

DONCASTER

5f ....58.4 secs
5f 140y 1m 07.0
6f 1m 11.0
7f 1m 24.5
1m (Str) 1m 37.2
1m (Rnd) 1m 38.4
1m 2f 60y 2m 07.8
1m 4f 2m 30.0
1m 6f 132y 3m 03.6
2m 110y 3m 30.0
2m 2f 3m 52.0

EPSOM

5f ....54.5 secs
6f 1m 08.0
7f 1m 20.3
1m 114y 1m 42.0
1m 2f 18y 2m 04.0
1m 4f 10y 2m 34.5

FOLKESTONE

5f ....57.6 secs
6f 1m 10.2
6f 189y 1m 21.4
1m 1f 149y 1m 57.7
1m 4f 2m 31.2
1m 7f 92y 3m 18.0
2m 93y 3m 30.0

GOODWOOD

5f ....56.7 secs
6f 1m 09.8
7f 1m 24.8
1m 1m 37.2
1m 1f 1m 53.0
1m 2f 2m 06.6
1m 4f 2m 33.2
1m 6f 2m 59.0
2m 3m 24.0
2m 4f 4m 15.0

HAMILTON

5f 4y ....58.3 secs
6f 5y 1m 10.0
1m 65y 1m 44.1
1m 1f 36y 1m 54.3
1m 3f 16y 2m 19.4
1m 4f 17y 2m 32.0
1m 5f 9y 2m 45.7

HAYDOCK

5f ....59.5 secs
6f 1m 11.7
7f 30y 1m 28.0
1m 30y 1m 40.6
1m 2f 120y 2m 11.5
1m 3f 200y 2m 29.4
1m 6f 2m 58.2
2m 45y 3m 27.2

KEMPTON

5f ....58.2 secs
6f 1m 11.2
7f (Rnd) 1m 24.0
7f (Jub) 1m 24.5
1m (Jub) 1m 37.7
1m (Rnd) 1m 37.2
1m 1f (Rnd) 1m 50.6
1m 2f (Jub) 2m 03.5
1m 3f 30y 2m 18.8
1m 4f 2m 30.0
1m 6f 92y 3m 03.0
2m 3m 24.6

LEICESTER

5f 2y ....58.5 secs
5f 218y 1m 10.0
7f 9y 1m 22.6
1m 8y 1m 35.0
1m 1f 218y 2m 03.7
1m 3f 183y 2m 28.5

LINGFIELD (TURF)

5f ....57.0 secs
6f 1m 09.0
7f 1m 21.2
7f 140y 1m 29.0
1m 1f 1m 50.5
1m 2f 2m 04.7
1m 3f 106y 2m 24.7
1m 6f 2m 58.3
2m 3m 24.0

LINGFIELD (AWT)

5f ....58.2 secs
6f 1m 11.1
7f 1m 24.4
1m 1m 37.4
1m 2f 2m04.3
1m 4f 2m 30.0
1m 5f 2m 42.0
2m 3m 21.0

MUSSELBURGH

5f ....57.7 secs
7f 30y 1m 26.0
1m 16y 1m 39.0
1m 3f 32y 2m 19.7
1m 4f 31y 2m 33.5
1m 7f 16y 3m 12.0

NEWBURY

5f 34y 1m 00.2
6f 8y 1m 11.8
7f (Str) 1m 24.1
7f 64y (Rnd)....................1m 28.1
1m (Str) 1m 38.0
1m 7y (Rnd) 1m 36.0
1m 1f 1m 50.3
1m 2f 6y 2m 04.0
1m 3f 5y 2m 17.2
1m 4f 5y 2m 30.0
1m 5f 61y 2m 46.5
2m 3m 24.2

NEWCASTLE

5f ....58.4 secs
6f 1m 11.5
7f 1m 24.5
1m (Rnd) 1m 39.0
1m 3y (Str)....................1m 38.6
1m 1f 9y 1m 52.3
1m 2f 32y 2m 06.7
1m 4f 93y 2m 37.5
2m 19y 3m 25.5

NEWMARKET (ROWLEY MILE COURSE)

5f ....58.7 secs
6f 1m 11.8
7f 1m 24.5
1m 1m 37.3
1m 1f 1m 50.5
1m 2f 2m 04.7
1m 4f 2m 30.5
1m 6f 2m 56.0
2m 3m 23.3
2m 2f 3m 50.4

(JULY COURSE)

5f ....58.5 secs
6f 1m 12.0
7f 1m 25.0
1m 1m 38.0
1m 1f 1m 50.5
1m 2f 2m 03.6
1m 4f 2m 29.0

1m 6f 175y 3m 08.5
2m 24y 3m 23.0

NOTTINGHAM

5f 13y ....58.9 secs
6f 15y 1m 11.5
1m 54y 1m 41.3
1m 1f 213y 2m 02.5
1m 6f 15y 2m 58.5
2m 9y 3m 23.0
2m 1f 188y 3m 49.5

PONTEFRACT

5f 1m 01.7
6f 1m 15.0
1m 4y 1m 42.4
1m 2f 6y 2m 09.6
1m 4f 8y 2m 34.3
2m 1f 22y 3m 39.5
2m 1f 216y 3m 52.0
2m 5f 122y 4m 42.5

REDCAR

5f ....57.5 secs
6f 1m 10.2
7f 1m 23.0
1m 1m 35.0
1m 1f 1m 50.7
1m 2f 2m 03.6
1m 3f 2m 17.0
1m 5f 135y 2m 52.0
1m 6f 19y 2m 59.3
2m 4y 3m 25.0

RIPON

5f ....57.8 secs
6f 1m 10.5
1m 1m 38.2
1m 1f 1m 51.0
1m 2f 2m 03.5
1m 4f 60y 2m 33.5
2m 3m 25.0

SALISBURY

5f 1m 00.0
6f 1m 13.0
6f 212y 1m 26.0
1m 1m 40.0
1m 1f 209y 2m 05.3
1m 4f 2m 31.0
1m 6f 2m 58.7

SANDOWN

5f 6y ....59.8 secs
7f 16y 1m 28.6
1m 14y 1m 41.2
1m 1f 1m 53.1
1m 2f 7y 2m 06.7
1m 3f 91y 2m 23.4
1m 6f 2m 58.9
2m 78y 3m 32.0

SOUTHWELL (AWT)

5f ....57.0 secs
6f 1m 13.5
7f 1m 26.5
1m 1m 39.0
1m 3f 2m 20.0
1m 4f 2m 33.0
1m 6f 2m 58.0
2m 3m 26.0

THIRSK

5f ....57.6 secs
6f 1m 09.7
7f 1m 24.9
1m 1m 36.5
1m 4f 2m 30.7
2m 3m 23.0

WARWICK

5f ....58.0 secs
6f 1m 12.0
7f 1m 24.6
1m 1m 36.4
1m 2f 169y 2m 14.0
1m 4f 115y 2m 38.5
1m 6f 194y 3m 10.0
2m 20y 3m 25.5

WINDSOR

5f 10y ....59.7 secs
5f 217y 1m 10.5
1m 67y 1m 42.2
1m 2f 7y 2m 04.9
1m 3f 135y 2m 26.0

WOLVERHAMPTON (AWT)

5f ....58.0 secs
6f 1m 11.2
7f 1m 24.7
1m 100y 1m 45.0
1m 1f 79y 1m 56.0
1m 4f 2m 32.5
1m 6f 166y 3m 07.4
2m 46y 3m 27.0

YARMOUTH

5f 43y 1m 01.0
6f 3y 1m 10.9
7f 3y 1m 24.2
1m 3y 1m 36.0
1m 2f 21y 2m 03.8
1m 3f 101y 2m 21.8
1m 6f 17y 2m 58.0
2m 3m 23.5
2m 2f 51y 3m 54.6

YORK

5f ....57.7 secs
6f 1m 10.5
6f 214y 1m 23.0
7f 202y 1m 37.0
1m 205y 1m 49.0
1m 2f 85y 2m 09.0
1m 3f 195y 2m 27.8
1m 5f 194y 2m 53.6
1m 7f 195y 3m 20.0

1997 SPEED FIGURES

Turf

Aardwolf 38 (22f,Asc,S,Jun 20)
Abajany 60 (8f,San,GF,Spt 16)
Able Player (USA) 31 (12f,Crl,G,Jun 25)
Able Sheriff 49 (5f,Pon,GF,Apr 22)
Aboo Hom 39 (13½f,Chs,G,Spt 24)
Abou Zouz (USA) 45 (7f,Nwm,S,Jun 28)
A Breeze 41 (7f,Don,GF,Mar 22)
Absolute Liberty (USA) 38 (10f,Lin,G,Jun 24)
Absolutely Fayre 32 (8f,Pon,GF,Jun 9)
Absolutelystunning 36 (10f,Not,GF,Apr 11)
Absolute Utopia (USA) 50 (10f,Sal,G,Oct 1)
Abtaal 38 (8f,War,G,May 5)
Academy House (IRE) 37 (20f,Asc,G,Jun 17)
Academy Star 44 (10f,Goo,G,Spt 13)
Acharne 80 (8f,San,GF,Apr 25)
Action Jackson 48 (10f,Bri,F,Aug 16)
Admirals Flame (IRE) 49 (8f,Nwm,G,Jun 7)
Admirals Secret (USA) 40 (12f,Fol,S,Jun 27)
Advance East 30 (12½f,War,G,Jun 24)
Aerleon Pete (IRE) 53 (12f,Hay,G,Spt 26)
Afaan (IRE) 68 (5f,Red,G,Nov 4)
Aficionado (IRE) 38 (8f,Not,GF,Apr 11)
Afon Alwen 54 (12f,Bri,F,Jly 28)
African-Pard (IRE) 57 (10f,Chp,G,Aug 25)
Agent Mulder 31 (8f,Sal,GF,May 15)
Agony Aunt 45 (10f,Rip,G,Aug 30)
Ailleacht (USA) 46 (5f,Cur,G,Jly 13)
Air Express (IRE) 94 (8f,Asc,G,Jun 17)
Air Quest 60 (14f,Goo,GS,May 21)
Ajayib (USA) 51 (11f,Ayr,S,Oct 13)
Ajcombe (IRE) 49 (16f,Goo,GF,Spt 25)
Akalim 51 (7f,Chp,G,Spt 11)
Akdariya (IRE) 53 (12f,Asc,G,Jun 19)
Al Abraq (IRE) 54 (8f,San,GF,May 27)
Alaflak (IRE) 45 (10f,Bat,F,Jly 23)
Alakdar (CAN) 37 (10f,Don,GS,Jun 28)
Alamein (USA) 66 (7f,Yar,G,Jly 16)
Alamode 30 (5f,Don,G,May 24)
Alarico (FR) 33 (14f,San,GF,Jly 30)
Alarme Belle 35 (6f,Cur,S,Oct 18)
Alarmist 54 (10f,Goo,GF,Jun 12)
Al Azhar 75 (12f,Don,S,Nov 8)
Albaha (USA) 62 (12f,Thi,G,Aug 2)
Albert The Bear 69 (7f,Lin,GF,Aug 17)
Alcalali (USA) 53 (12f,Yor,G,Aug 20)
Alekos (USA) 41 (10f,Lon,,Jun 22)
Alezal 57 (8f,Asc,G,Jun 17)
Alfahaal (IRE) 56 (8f,Lei,S,Oct 13)
Alfredo Alfredo (USA) 38 (10f,Not,GF,Apr 11)
Alhaarth (IRE) 96 (10f,Lon,G,Oct 4)
Alhawa (USA) 68 (8f,San,GF,Apr 25)
Alhosaam 54 (16f,Chs,G,Spt 24)
Alifandango (IRE) 44 (9f,Goo,GF,Jly 30)
Alikhlas 47 (7f,San,GF,Spt 16)
Ali-Royal (IRE) 86 (9f,Nwm,G,Apr 16)
Aliya (IRE) 59 (15f,Lon,G,Oct 4)
Allied Forces (USA) 90 (8f,Asc,G,Spt 27)
Allinson's Mate (IRE) 55 (7f,Don,G,Jun 7)
All Is Fair 51 (7f,Nwm,GF,Oct 3)
All On 41 (16f,Nwc,G,Aug 6)
Allstars Express 36 (10f,Fol,F,Apr 10)
Almasi (IRE) 79 (6f,Ayr,G,Spt 20)
Al Masroor (USA) 60 (7f,San,GF,Jly 30)
Almaty (IRE) 76 (5f,Don,GF,Spt 10)
Almond Rock 77 (7½f,Chs,S,Aug 30)
Almost Skint (IRE) 38 (7f,Leo,G,Apr 19)
Al Muallim (USA) 66 (6f,Lin,GF,Aug 17)
Almuhimm (USA) 56 (7f,Asc,G,Aug 1)
Almuhtaram 43 (12f,Bri,F,Jun 3)
Almushtarak (IRE) 94 (8½f,Eps,G,Jun 7)
Alphabet 60 (8f,Wnd,G,Aug 23)
Alpine Hideaway (IRE) 63 (8f,Nwm,GF,May 31)
Alpine Panther (IRE) 52 (11f,Ayr,GS,Spt 18)
Alpine Time (IRE) 58 (7f,San,G,May 26)
Al Reet (IRE) 41 (7f,Don,GS,Jun 28)
Alsahib (USA) 52 (8f,Nwb,S,May 18)
Al's Alibi 57 (12f,Hay,S,Mar 29)
Alumisiyah (USA) 70 (6f,Hay,S,Oct 15)
Always Alight 64 (6f,Ayr,G,Spt 20)
Always Earnest (USA) 93 (20f,Lon,G,Oct 4)
Always Grace 34 (6f,Fol,GF,Jun 4)
Always Happy 39 (8f,Bri,F,May 23)
Always Loyal (USA) 94 (9f,Lon,GF,Oct 5)
Always On My Mind 66 (6f,Nwm,GF,Nov 1)
Amadour (IRE) 40 (11½f,Wnd,GF,Jun 2)
Amazing Bay 52 (5f,Nwm,G,May 3)
Amber Fort 67 (8f,Nwb,G,Jun 12)
Ambidextrous (IRE) 47 (10½f,Hay,G,Jly 5)
American Whisper 48 (10f,Don,G,Oct 24)
Amiarge 37 (16f,Rip,GF,May 28)
Amid Albadu (USA) 83 (8½f,Eps,G,Jun 7)
Among Men (USA) 89 (7f,Asc,GF,Jun 18)
Amrak Ajeeb (IRE) 82 (9f,Nwm,G,Apr 16)
Amron 52 (6f,Crl,G,Apr 25)
Amyas (IRE) 88 (10½f,Yor,G,Aug 20)
Anak-Ku 63 (10f,Chp,GF,Aug 3)
Anchored In Love 34 (7f,Goo,GS,May 21)
Anchorena 36 (16f,Rip,GF,May 28)
Anchor Venture 45 (10f,Pon,GF,Jun 9)
Ancient Quest 59 (11½f,Wnd,GS,Jun 30)
Andreyev (IRE) 65 (7f,Nwm,G,Apr 16)
Anetta 32 (7f,Cat,GF,Spt 20)
Aneysar (IRE) 67 (9f,Lon,S,May 15)
Angel Chimes 55 (9f,Nwm,GF,Oct 4)
Angel Face (USA) 56 (11f,War,GF,Apr 12)
Angus-G 73 (12f,Nwm,G,Apr 16)
Anjou 43 (14f,Yar,F,Oct 29)
Annaba (IRE) 53 (12½f,Lon,G,Oct 4)
Anna Thea (IRE) 83 (10½f,Cha,S,Jun 8)
Anno Luce 62 (14½f,Don,GF,Spt 10)
Annus Mirabilis (FR) 91 (10f,Wnd,G,Aug 23)
Anokato 50 (5f,Goo,G,Spt 24)
Anonym (IRE) 44 (7f,Yor,G,Jly 12)
Anotheranniversary 75 (5f,Nwm,G,Jly 19)
Another Batchworth 44 (5f,Red,GF,Oct 18)
Another Episode (IRE) 40 (5f,Ayr,S,Oct 14)
Another Night (IRE) 62 (10f,Don,GF,Spt 10)
Another Nightmare (IRE) 35 (5f,Ham,S,Jly 1)
Another Time 75 (9f,Nwb,GF,Jly 19)
Ansellman 75 (5f,Asc,Hy,Oct 11)
Antarctic Storm 55 (8f,Nwm,G,Oct 18)
Antithesis (IRE) 32 (5f,Rip,GF,Apr 17)
Antonia's Choice 34 (6f,Lin,GF,Aug 17)
Antonias Melody 49 (6f,Nwm,G,May 3)
Anyar Reem 60 (10f,Don,GS,Jun 29)
Apache Star 65 (8f,Nwm,G,Oct 18)
Apollo Red 66 (7f,Lin,GF,May 31)
Apprehension 74 (10f,Don,G,May 24)
Aquatic Queen 38 (6f,Fol,GF,Aug 5)
Aquavita 39 (12f,Bri,F,May 29)
Arabian King 48 (12f,Cha,G,Jun 1)
Arabian Story 96 (10f,Nwb,GF,Jly 19)
Araboybill 39 (12f,Chp,G,Aug 25)
Arcady 48 (20f,Asc,G,Jun 17)
Arcatura 31 (10f,Not,G,May 9)
Archello (IRE) 46 (5f,Bev,GF,Jun 5)
Arco Colora 45 (10f,Goo,G,Spt 13)
Arctic Fancy (USA) 60 (14f,Yor,GS,Jun 13)
Arctic Owl 63 (12f,Asc,GF,Spt 28)
Arctiid (USA) 52 (10f,Kem,G,May 24)
Ardarroch Prince 41 (10f,Ayr,GF,May 30)
Ardent 42 (8f,Lei,S,Oct 13)
Arethusa 61 (6f,Bat,Hy,May 11)
Arian Spirit (IRE) 34 (15f,Ayr,GF,Aug 9)
Arif (IRE) 38 (14f,Not,S,Jly 5)
Arletty 34 (11f,Kem,GF,Spt 22)
Arnie (IRE) 30 (6f,Goo,S,Jun 20)
Arriving 53 (10f,Nwb,GF,Spt 18)
Arruhan (IRE) 65 (7f,Nwc,GF,Oct 1)
Arterxerxes 69 (7f,Yar,GF,Aug 21)
Artful Dane (IRE) 67 (8f,Goo,GS,Jun 20)
Artic Courier 72 (12f,Eps,G,Spt 5)
Arzani (USA) 48 (12½f,War,GF,Jly 19)
Asas 46 (10f,Lin,GF,May 31)
Asef Alhind 65 (7f,San,GF,Jly 23)
Ashby Hill (IRE) 63 (10f,Nwm,G,May 2)
Ashkernazy (IRE) 36 (5f,Wnd,GF,Jly 14)
Ashley Park (IRE) 55 (10f,Cur,GS,Aug 16)
As-Is 32 (12f,Lei,GF,May 27)
Askern 47 (10½f,Hay,GF,Aug 8)
Assailable 51 (8f,Nwm,G,May 4)
Assured Gamble 58 (16f,Asc,GF,Jun 18)
Astarabad (USA) 80 (10f,Lon,G,Oct 4)
Astrac (IRE) 63 (6f,Hay,S,May 5)
Astral Invader (IRE) 45 (7f,Lei,GF,Mar 27)
Atlantic Desire (IRE) 68 (10f,Goo,GF,Aug 1)
Atlantic Mist 38 (12f,Kem,G,May 5)
At Large (IRE) 62 (6f,Not,GF,Oct 4)
At Liberty (IRE) 50 (12f,Bri,F,May 23)
Atnab (USA) 39 (7f,Kem,GF,May 31)
Attarikh (IRE) 35 (8f,Bat,G,Spt 8)
Attitre (FR) 67 (10f,Nwm,G,May 4)
Attitude 58 (8f,Lei,GF,Oct 5)
Augustan 54 (10f,Pon,GF,Aug 7)
Aunty Jane 78 (8f,Asc,S,Jly 26)
Aurelian 32 (14f,Red,F,Aug 23)
Autumn Cover 61 (8f,Kem,G,May 5)
Autumn Time (IRE) 32 (12f,Nwm,G,Apr 15)
Averring (USA) 55 (7f,Cur,G,Oct 4)
Averti (IRE) 99 (6f,Asc,GF,Spt 27)
Awad (USA) 78 (12f,Hpk,F,Nov 8)
Awassi (IRE) 38 (6f,Don,G,Jly 31)
Awesome Wells (IRE) 59 (11½f,Lin,G,Spt 9)
Azizzi 73 (6f,Ayr,G,Spt 20)
Azores 54 (9f,San,GS,Aug 29)
Azra (IRE) 46 (7f,Cur,S,Spt 20)
Aztec Flyer (USA) 40 (16f,Not,GF,Aug 6)

Baba Au Rhum (IRE) 54 (8f,Goo,GF,Jly 29)
Babsy Babe 49 (6f,Rip,GF,Aug 4)
Baby Jane 36 (11f,Ham,S,Jun 25)
Bacchus 63 (6f,Nwm,GS,Jly 18)
Bachelors Pad 46 (7f,Nwm,GF,Oct 3)
Backhander (IRE) 37 (7f,Lei,GF,Mar 27)
Back Row 48 (12f,Nwm,GF,Oct 31)
Badenoch (IRE) 41 (12f,Chp,G,May 26)
Badge of Fame (IRE) 52 (14f,Yor,S,Spt 3)
Badlesmere (USA) 55 (8f,Kem,G,May 5)
Bahamian Beauty (USA) 51 (5f,Yor,G,Aug 20)
Bahamian Bounty 51 (6f,Nwm,G,Jly 10)
Bahamian Knight (CAN) 66 (12f,Don,GF,Spt 12)
Bahamian Sunshine (USA) 69 (12f,Goo,GF,Aug 1)
Bahhare (USA) 88 (8f,Asc,G,Spt 27)
Bajan Rose 57 (5f,Sal,GS,Jun 25)
Baked Alaska 55 (7f,Nwm,G,Apr 15)
Bakers Daughter 51 (10f,Wnd,GF,Jly 28)
Balalaika 97 (9f,Lon,GF,Oct 5)
Balance of Power 31 (7f,Eps,GS,Jly 9)
Bali Paradise (USA) 69 (10f,Nwb,GS,Spt 20)
Bali-Pet 31 (7f,Cat,GF,May 31)
Ballard Lady (IRE) 32 (7f,Hay,GS,Jly 3)
Ball Gown 66 (10½f,Yor,G,May 14)
Ballpoint 50 (12f,Cat,G,Apr 23)
Ballymote 62 (5f,Cat,G,Apr 23)
Bally Souza (IRE) 61 (12f,Hay,GF,Aug 8)
Banbury (USA) 52 (7f,Hay,S,Mar 29)
Band on the Run 70 (8f,Yor,G,Jly 11)
Banzhaf (USA) 60 (7f,Bri,F,Spt 28)
Barba Papa (IRE) 70 (10f,Goo,GF,Aug 1)
Barbason 62 (7f,Bri,F,Spt 28)
Bardon Hill Boy (IRE) 63 (10f,San,GF,Jly 24)
Barings (FR) 66 (11f,Lon,G,Apr 6)
Baritone 48 (8f,Rip,GF,Apr 17)
Barnburgh Boy 57 (8f,Pon,GF,Oct 6)
Barnum Sands 69 (10f,Kem,G,Spt 21)
Baron Ferdinand 58 (10f,Nwm,GF,Oct 31)

Barrack Yard 44 (7f,Don,G,May 6)
Barranak (IRE) 51 (5f,Lin,S,Jun 28)
Barrel of Hope 35 (8f,Don,GF,Mar 21)
Barresbo 40 (8f,Edi,GF,May 31)
Barrier Ridge 54 (8f,Thi,F,Jun 2)
Bartex (FR) 69 (8f,Cha,S,May 12)
Bashful Brave 35 (5f,Rip,GF,Aug 4)
Basman (IRE) 63 (12f,Eps,G,Spt 5)
Basse Besogne (IRE) 70 (8f,Dea,G,Aug 3)
Batabanoo 40 (16f,Not,GF,Spt 15)
Bataleur 43 (6f,Crl,G,Apr 25)
Bathe In Light (USA) 45 (12f,Bri,GF,Spt 3)
Batoutoftheblue 31 (16f,Nwc,G,Aug 6)
Batsman 34 (6f,Wnd,G,Jly 7)
Battleship Bruce 31 (8f,Wnd,GS,Jun 30)
Baubigny (USA) 37 (8f,Not,G,Apr 29)
Bayford Thrust 48 (6f,Lin,G,Jun 24)
Bayin (USA) 53 (6f,Nwb,GF,May 28)
Bay of Islands 69 (10f,Nwm,G,May 2)
Beach Buoy (IRE) 38 (9f,Rip,GF,Jly 19)
Beacon Silver 40 (10f,San,GF,Spt 16)
Beano Script 45 (8f,Edi,G,Jun 16)
Bear Hug 46 (10f,Lin,S,May 10)
Bea's Ruby (IRE) 56 (7f,Chs,S,May 7)
Beauchamp Jade 70 (13f,Nwb,GS,Spt 20)
Beauchamp King 72 (8f,Asc,G,Jun 17)
Beauchamp Lion 34 (14f,Red,F,Aug 23)
Beaumont (IRE) 63 (14f,Not,G,Oct 30)
Beautiful Fire (IRE) 33 (8f,Leo,G,Apr 19)
Beau Venture (USA) 58 (5f,Goo,G,Spt 24)
Bedazzle 35 (8f,Rip,G,Jun 18)
Bedouin Honda 45 (10f,Nwm,G,Apr 15)
Bedouin Prince (USA) 42 (12f,Bri,F,Apr 21)
Bee Health Boy 55 (6f,Red,G,Jun 20)
Begorrat (IRE) 46 (11f,Ayr,S,Oct 14)
Behaviour 80 (9f,Nwm,G,Apr 16)
Behind The Scenes 39 (9f,Goo,G,May 22)
Bel Canto (IRE) 36 (10f,San,GF,Spt 16)
Bellagrana 32 (12f,Bri,F,Oct 1)
Bellara 40 (14f,Hay,S,May 5)
Bellas Gate Boy 43 (7f,Lin,GF,May 31)
Belle Bijou 32 (13f,Ham,G,Aug 13)
Bello (ARG) 62 (10f,Lon,G,Oct 4)
Belmarita (IRE) 58 (12f,Nwm,GF,Oct 2)
Benatom (USA) 77 (14f,Goo,GF,Jly 29)
Bend Wavy (IRE) 41 (8f,Don,GS,Nov 8)
Ben Gunn 65 (8f,Nwm,G,Jly 8)
Benjamins Law 43 (10f,Pon,G,Jly 8)
Benny The Dip (USA) 91 (12f,Eps,G,Jun 7)
Bentico 35 (8f,Wnd,GS,Jun 30)
Benzoe (IRE) 62 (6f,Yor,G,Aug 19)
Bequeath 75 (10f,Don,GF,Jun 7)
Berlin Blue 53 (14½f,Don,GF,Spt 10)
Beryllium 45 (9f,San,GS,Aug 29)
Besiege 43 (12f,Lei,G,Oct 27)
Best Before Dawn (IRE) 75 (6f,Asc,GS,Jun 20)
Best of All (IRE) 63 (8f,Edi,GS,Jun 30)
Be True 37 (12f,Bri,GF,Oct 23)
Better Offer (IRE) 73 (12f,Asc,GF,Spt 28)
Bevier 32 (8f,Lei,GF,Oct 5)
Be Warned 44 (7f,Nwc,GF,Mar 31)
Bewitching Lady 32 (11½f,Yar,GF,Spt 16)
Beyond Calculation (USA) 51 (7f,Thi,G,Jly 25)
Bianca Nera 43 (8f,Nwm,G,May 4)
Big Ander (SPA) 40 (15f,Lon,G,Oct 4)
Big Ben 35 (7f,Nwm,GF,Aug 9)
Big Sky Chester (USA) 87 (12f,Hpk,F,Nov 8)
Big Target (IRE) 38 (10f,Bat,GS,May 19)
Bijou d'Inde 91 (8f,Asc,G,Spt 27)
Bilko 38 (6f,Kem,G,Mar 29)
Billy Bushwacker 69 (10f,Don,GF,Spt 10)
Billy Nomaite 36 (8f,Thi,F,Jun 2)
Bimsey (IRE) 70 (14f,San,GF,Jly 16)
Bina Gardens 54 (10f,Chp,G,Spt 11)
Bin Rosie 81 (8f,Nwb,GS,Spt 20)
Bint Albaadiya (USA) 75 (6f,Nwm,S,Jun 27)
Bintang Timor (USA) 41 (6f,Nwm,GF,Apr 17)
Bint Baladee 63 (12f,Eps,G,Jun 6)
Bint Shihama (USA) 51 (7f,Yar,G,Jly 16)
Birchwood Sun 42 (7f,Lei,GS,Oct 14)
Bishops Court 82 (5f,Asc,S,Jun 21)
Bit on the Side (IRE) 66 (12f,Eps,G,Aug 10)
Blane Water (USA) 46 (7f,Nwm,G,Jly 8)
Blatant Outburst 30 (14f,Not,GF,Apr 21)
Blaze of Song 36 (10f,Lei,G,Oct 28)
Blazer's Baby 30 (7f,Kem,GF,May 31)
Blazing Imp (USA) 45 (5f,Edi,GS,Jun 23)
Blenheim Terrace 43 (12f,Edi,GF,Spt 15)
Blessed Spirit 68 (8f,Nwm,G,Jly 19)
Blessingindisguise 81 (6f,Yor,G,Aug 19)
Blewbury Hill (IRE) 61 (7f,Kem,GF,May 31)
Blockade (USA) 43 (10f,Not,GF,Jun 9)
Blood Orange 31 (6f,Nwm,GF,Apr 17)
Blooming Amazing 49 (10f,Red,GF,Oct 18)
Blot 39 (8f,San,GF,Jly 24)
Blowing Away (IRE) 38 (7f,Yar,F,Spt 17)
Bluebell Miss 38 (10f,Yar,G,Jly 16)
Blue Duster (USA) 69 (6f,Asc,G,Jun 19)
Blue Flyer (IRE) 56 (7f,Yar,GF,Aug 21)
Blue Goblin (USA) 71 (6f,Asc,G,Jun 19)
Blue Imperial (FR) 46 (8f,Bat,F,Jly 23)
Blue Iris 67 (6f,Bat,Hy,May 11)
Blue Lamp (USA) 33 (5f,Rip,GF,Aug 16)
Blue Ridge 54 (5f,Lin,GS,Aug 28)
Blue River (IRE) 69 (10½f,Yor,G,May 13)
Blues Queen 47 (6f,Hay,G,Jly 5)
Blueygreen 51 (7f,Yar,G,Jly 16)
Blurred (IRE) 40 (10f,Nwm,G,May 2)
Boater 52 (8f,Thi,GS,May 17)
Bold Becky 33 (8f,Bat,GF,May 30)
Bold Brief 38 (5f,Crl,G,Jly 5)
Bold Buster 66 (11f,Ayr,GS,Spt 18)
Bold Demand 58 (12f,Eps,G,Jun 7)
Bold Effort (FR) 77 (5f,Dea,G,Aug 3)
Bold Elect 40 (20f,Goo,GF,Jly 30)
Bold Faith 41 (8f,Not,G,Nov 3)
Bold Gayle 30 (5f,Not,GF,Mar 31)
Bold Oriental (IRE) 60 (10f,Nwm,GF,Jly 9)
Bold Spring (IRE) 42 (6f,Nwm,G,Jun 7)
Bold Tina (IRE) 44 (7f,Bri,GF,Spt 3)
Bold Top 45 (10f,Pon,GF,Jun 9)
Bold Tycoon (IRE) 36 (7f,Cur,GS,Jun 28)
Bold Words (CAN) 83 (8f,San,GF,May 26)
Bolino Star (IRE) 34 (16f,Cur,GS,Oct 4)
Bolivar (IRE) 59 (16f,Asc,S,Jun 21)
Bollero (IRE) 39 (7½f,Bev,GF,Jly 15)
Bollin Dorothy 42 (7f,Cat,GF,Aug 15)
Bollin Frank 49 (8f,Rip,GF,Aug 25)
Bollin Harry 56 (6f,Red,G,Jun 20)
Bollin Joanne 92 (6f,Asc,GS,Jun 20)
Bollin Terry 51 (8f,Nwc,F,Jun 4)
Bolshoi (IRE) 85 (5f,Asc,GS,Jun 20)
Bombazine (IRE) 54 (12f,Asc,Hy,Oct 11)
Bonanza Peak (USA) 61 (10f,Pon,GS,Oct 20)
Bonapartiste (FR) 78 (15f,Lon,G,Oct 4)
Bon Guest (IRE) 31 (8f,Not,GF,Jly 19)
Bon Luck (IRE) 46 (7f,Fol,GF,Apr 22)
Bonnie Lassie 35 (9f,Ayr,S,Oct 13)
Boojum 48 (8f,Nwm,GF,Nov 1)
Book At Bedtime (IRE) 64 (14½f,Don,GF,Spt 10)
Bookcase 37 (11f,War,GF,Apr 12)
Border Falcon 30 (8f,Nwb,GF,Apr 19)
Borgia (GER) 87 (12f,Hpk,F,Nov 8)
Bosra Sham (USA) 95 (10f,Asc,G,Jun 17)
Boss Lady (IRE) 45 (10½f,Hay,S,Oct 15)
Bowcliffe 52 (8f,Red,GF,Oct 28)
Bowcliffe Court (IRE) 63 (16½f,San,GS,Jly 5)
Bowcliffe Grange (IRE) 44 (5f,Thi,GF,Aug 22)
Bowden Rose 71 (6f,Not,GF,Jly 30)
Bowled Over 54 (12f,Nwm,G,Apr 16)
Bowlers Boy 59 (6f,Rip,G,Aug 30)
Bramble Bear 45 (6f,Kem,GF,Spt 22)
Brambles Way 41 (10f,Nwc,GF,Oct 22)
Brand New Dance 52 (14f,San,GF,Aug 14)
Brandon Jack 41 (10f,San,GF,Jly 24)
Brandon Magic 73 (14f,Yor,GS,Jun 13)
Brandonville 52 (7f,Hay,GS,Jly 3)
Brave Edge 85 (5f,Dea,G,Aug 3)
Brave Envoy 43 (8f,Lei,S,Oct 13)
Braveheart (IRE) 55 (7f,Nwm,GF,Nov 1)
Brave Kris (IRE) 56 (8f,Asc,S,Jun 21)
Brave Montgomerie 48 (9f,Ayr,G,Jun 20)
Break the Rules 73 (10f,Don,GF,Mar 20)
Brecon 36 (13f,Bat,G,Spt 8)
Brecongill Lad 53 (6f,Cat,G,Jun 6)
Breezed Well 35 (8f,Chp,G,Aug 3)
Bridie's Pride 38 (18f,Chp,GS,Jly 5)
Brigand (IRE) 65 (8f,Nwb,S,Spt 19)
Brighstone 54 (10f,Eps,GS,Jly 9)
Brighter Byfaah (IRE) 38 (17f,Bat,F,Jly 23)
Bright Fountain (IRE) 30 (9f,San,GS,Aug 29)
Bright Heritage (IRE) 60 (8f,Wnd,G,Aug 23)
Bright Water 77 (12f,Goo,GF,Aug 1)
Brilliance (FR) 88 (10½f,Cha,S,Jun 8)
Brilliant Red 81 (8f,Goo,GS,Jun 29)
Briska (IRE) 30 (8f,Kem,GF,Spt 22)
Broad River (USA) 46 (7f,Goo,G,May 20)
Broadstairs Beauty (IRE) 59 (6f,Lei,G,Oct 27)
Broctune Gold 65 (7f,Crl,G,Apr 25)
Brodessa 45 (14f,Not,GF,Jly 19)
Broken Rites (IRE) 31 (16f,Cur,GS,Oct 4)
Broughtons Error 36 (7f,Nwm,G,May 16)
Broughton's Pride (IRE) 42 (8f,Ham,S,May 4)
Broughtons Turmoil 65 (8f,Asc,GF,Apr 30)
Brutal Fantasy (IRE) 65 (5f,Cat,G,Apr 23)
Brynkir 31 (8f,Not,G,Apr 29)
Bubble Wings (FR) 59 (10f,Chp,G,Spt 11)
Bubbly 59 (7f,Bri,F,Spt 28)
Buck's Boy (USA) 88 (12f,Hpk,F,Nov 8)
Buddy Marvel (IRE) 45 (10f,Leo,YS,May 11)
Bulington (FR) 69 (10½f,Lon,S,Apr 27)
Bulsara 31 (10f,Bev,GF,Jun 5)
Burden Of Proof (IRE) 57 (6f,Asc,G,Jun 19)
Burning (USA) 61 (11½f,Yar,G,Jly 16)
Burning Truth (USA) 52 (8f,San,GS,Apr 26)
Burn Out 51 (20f,Asc,G,Jun 17)
Burnt Offering 43 (14f,San,GF,May 27)
Burundi (IRE) 39 (10½f,Hay,G,Jly 5)
Bushwhacker 41 (7f,Hay,GS,Jly 3)
Busy Flight 91 (12f,Lon,GF,Oct 5)
Butrinto 49 (6f,Nwm,GS,Jly 18)
Byzantium 56 (8f,Kem,G,May 24)

Cadeaux Cher 54 (6f,Red,G,Nov 4)
Cadeaux Tryst 82 (8f,Asc,GF,Jun 18)
Ca'd'oro 57 (8f,Don,GS,Nov 8)
Caerfilly Dancer 55 (5f,Asc,S,Jun 21)
Caiseal Ros (IRE) 47 (10f,Leo,G,Apr 19)
Calamander (IRE) 44 (8f,Wnd,GF,Jly 14)
Calder King 41 (9f,Ham,S,Apr 2)
Calendula 56 (10f,Lei,G,Oct 28)
Calypso Grant (IRE) 71 (10f,Goo,GF,Aug 1)
Calypso Lady (IRE) 36 (8f,War,GF,Oct 7)
Cambridge Ball (IRE) 30 (10f,Yar,F,Jun 11)
Camionneur (IRE) 51 (5f,Thi,GF,Aug 22)
Campaign 36 (14f,Not,G,Nov 3)
Campaspe 52 (12f,Rip,GF,Aug 4)
Camp David (GER) 47 (20f,Asc,G,Jun 19)
Camporese (IRE) 65 (12f,Hay,G,Jly 5)
Canadian Fantasy 38 (9f,Ham,S,Jly 1)
Can Can Lady 60 (8f,Nwc,G,May 5)
Candereli (IRE) 42 (10f,Leo,YS,May 11)
Canon Can (USA) 82 (18f,Nwm,G,Oct 18)
Canovas Heart 75 (5f,Yor,G,Oct 8)
Cantina 38 (7f,Cat,GF,Spt 20)
Canton Venture 50 (12f,Thi,G,Jun 17)
Canyon Creek (IRE) 42 (8f,Don,GF,Mar 20)
Cape Cross (IRE) 80 (8f,Goo,GF,Aug 2)
Cape Pigeon (USA) 36 (8f,Sal,GS,Jun 25)
Capilano Princess 72 (10f,Don,G,Jly 30)

Cap Juluca (IRE) 97 (8½f,Eps,G,Jun 7)
Capsoff (IRE) 42 (11½f,Yar,GS,Jly 2)
Captain Carat 45 (5f,Cat,GF,May 30)
Captain Carparts 32 (7f,Cat,G,Apr 23)
Captain Collins (IRE) 78 (7f,Asc,GF,Jun 18)
Captain Horatius (IRE) 64 (10f,Goo,G,May 22)
Captain Jack 61 (18f,Nwm,G,Oct 18)
Captain Scott (IRE) 56 (8f,Yor,G,May 15)
Captain's Guest (IRE) 67 (15f,Nwm,G,Jly 19)
Captain Sinbad 35 (5f,War,GF,Apr 12)
Carati 33 (6f,Yar,GF,Jly 22)
Carburton 55 (10f,Wnd,GF,Jun 9)
Caribbean Star 60 (7f,San,GF,Spt 17)
Carisbrooke 48 (12f,Rip,GF,Aug 25)
Carlisle Bay (IRE) 37 (9f,Cur,S,Spt 21)
Carlton (IRE) 48 (8f,Nwc,G,May 22)
Carlys Quest 40 (8f,Sal,GF,May 15)
Carmine Lake (IRE) 67 (5f,Don,GF,Spt 10)
Carnelly (IRE) 48 (12f,Leo,G,Jly 19)
Carol's Dream (USA) 34 (11f,War,GF,Apr 12)
Carranita (IRE) 91 (6f,Nwm,G,Apr 15)
Carreamia 33 (6f,Don,GS,Jun 28)
Casey Tibbs (IRE) 58 (10f,Leo,G,Apr 19)
Cashmere Lady 67 (8f,Red,F,Aug 23)
Cashmirie 35 (10f,Bev,G,Jly 29)
Castel Rosselo 53 (7f,Thi,G,Jun 17)
Castle Courageous 56 (16f,Goo,G,Jun 12)
Casual Water (IRE) 52 (12½f,War,GF,Jun 9)
Catchable 61 (12f,Don,GF,Spt 12)
Catchment 34 (10f,Goo,G,Spt 13)
Catch The Blues (IRE) 79 (6f,Asc,G,Jun 19)
Cathedral (IRE) 74 (5f,Lin,GS,Aug 28)
Catienus (USA) 80 (10f,Cur,GS,Aug 16)
Cats Bottom 36 (8f,Bat,G,Jun 28)
Cauda Equina 48 (6f,Nwb,GF,Jly 18)
Caudillo (IRE) 49 (6f,Sal,S,Jun 26)
Caution 53 (6f,Not,GF,Oct 4)
Caviar Royale (IRE) 59 (10½f,Yor,G,May 13)
Cayman Kai (IRE) 92 (6f,Nwm,G,Apr 15)
Cedez le Passage (FR) 54 (12f,Eps,G,Apr 23)
Cee-Jay-Ay 42 (8f,War,F,Jun 4)
Cee-N-K (IRE) 52 (8f,Red,GF,Oct 18)
Celandine 45 (7f,Cat,GF,Spt 20)
Celebrant 30 (10f,Lei,GF,Spt 9)
Celebration Cake (IRE) 48 (8f,Ayr,G,Spt 20)
Celeric 95 (20f,Lon,G,Oct 4)
Celestial Choir 75 (12f,Don,GF,Spt 12)
Celestial Key (USA) 60 (8f,Asc,GF,Jun 18)
Censor 47 (12f,Thi,G,Aug 2)
Centre Stalls (IRE) 94 (8f,Yor,G,May 14)
Chabrol (CAN) 49 (14f,Not,GF,Apr 11)
Chadwell Hall 47 (6f,Not,GF,Apr 8)
Chairmans Choice 42 (9f,Goo,GF,Jly 31)
Chairmans Daughter 36 (16½f,Fol,GF,Aug 19)
Chai-Yo 62 (8f,Asc,Hy,Oct 10)
Champagne Prince 80 (10f,Nwm,G,May 2)
Champagne Warrior (IRE) 31 (12f,Rip,GF,Apr 9)
Change For A Buck (USA) 45 (7f,Nwm,G,Apr 16)
Chania (IRE) 57 (9f,Cur,S,Spt 21)
Charity Crusader 32 (12f,Bev,GF,Apr 5)
Charlie Sillett 66 (6f,Chs,S,Jun 25)
Charlotte Corday 80 (10½f,Yor,G,May 14)
Charlton Imp (USA) 32 (8f,Chp,GF,Jly 11)
Charming Admiral (IRE) 44 (14f,Not,G,Nov 3)
Charnwood Jack (USA) 48 (10f,Lei,F,Apr 3)
C-Harry (IRE) 52 (6f,Chs,GF,Jun 4)
Charter 52 (16f,Rip,GF,May 28)
Chasetown Flyer (USA) 42 (8f,Wnd,GF,Jun 16)
Chateauherault (IRE) 32 (13f,Ham,G,Aug 13)
Chatham Island 40 (15f,Nwm,GS,Jun 11)
Chauncy Lane (IRE) 37 (10f,Cur,GS,May 25)
Check The Band (USA) 70 (5f,Asc,GS,Jun 20)
Cheek To Cheek 41 (12f,Bri,F,Jly 28)
Chemcast 52 (5f,Rip,G,Jun 19)
Cherokee Flight 46 (10f,Lei,GF,Spt 9)
Cherry Blossom (IRE) 35 (6f,Nwm,GF,Apr 17)
Chewit 62 (8f,Nwm,GF,Nov 1)
Chickawicka (IRE) 68 (7f,Nwm,G,Apr 16)
Chief Bearhart (CAN) 95 (12f,Hpk,F,Nov 8)
Chief Contender (IRE) 95 (20f,Lon,G,Oct 4)
Chief Monarch 55 (10f,Don,GF,Spt 13)
Chief's Song 32 (16f,Goo,GF,Spt 25)
Children's Choice (IRE) 45 (14f,Not,GF,Oct 4)
Chili Concerto 54 (5f,Wnd,S,May 19)
Chinaberry 43 (7f,Goo,GS,May 21)
China Girl (IRE) 44 (6f,Eps,G,Aug 10)
China Red (USA) 52 (8f,Not,GF,Apr 11)
Chinour (IRE) 35 (8f,War,GF,Apr 12)
Chris's Lad 57 (12f,Nwm,G,Jun 7)
Churchill's Shadow (IRE) 32 (6f,Bat,G,Spt 8)
Cim Bom Bom (IRE) 62 (5f,Pon,GF,Jly 18)
Cinema Paradiso 57 (8½f,Eps,G,Jun 6)
Circle of Magic 32 (8f,Lei,G,Jly 23)
Cirino (USA) 72 (9f,Cha,G,Jun 1)
Ciro's Pearl (IRE) 57 (12f,Asc,G,Jun 19)
Ciste (IRE) 32 (8f,Leo,YS,May 11)
Cittern 42 (16f,Nwc,G,Aug 6)
City Gambler 55 (8f,Lei,G,Aug 11)
City Hall (IRE) 57 (16f,Not,S,Oct 15)
Civil Liberty 51 (12f,Asc,Hy,Oct 10)
Clan Ben (IRE) 75 (10f,Nwm,G,May 3)
Clan Chief 69 (6f,Eps,G,Jun 7)
Classical Dance (IRE) 31 (11f,Ham,G,Aug 13)
Classic Ballet (FR) 50 (12f,Edi,GF,Spt 15)
Classic Beauty (IRE) 49 (10f,Bev,GF,Apr 24)
Classic Cliche (IRE) 89 (16f,Goo,GF,Jly 31)
Classic Colours (USA) 39 (10f,Pon,GS,Oct 20)
Classic Dame (FR) 43 (12f,Fol,GF,Aug 19)
Classic Fan (USA) 32 (10f,Wnd,G,Aug 4)
Classic Find (USA) 59 (12f,Nwm,G,Apr 16)
Classic Flyer (IRE) 55 (12f,Edi,GF,Spt 15)
Classic Jenny (IRE) 41 (10f,Wnd,GF,Jun 16)
Classic Leader 52 (6f,Chp,GF,Jun 13)
Classic Line 44 (14f,Not,G,Oct 30)
Classic Parisian (IRE) 40 (10f,Bat,GF,Jly 17)
Classic Park 63 (8f,Asc,GF,Jun 18)
Classy Chief 31 (10f,Fol,F,Apr 10)
Clerio 39 (8f,Cur,S,Spt 7)
Clerkenwell (USA) 66 (11f,Nwb,GF,Spt 18)
Clever Caption (IRE) 61 (5f,Nwm,G,May 3)
Cliburnel News (IRE) 40 (16f,Not,GF,Spt 15)
Clinking 32 (14f,Yar,F,Oct 29)
Clodora (FR) 97 (9f,Lon,GF,Oct 5)
Cloudings (IRE) 59 (10½f,Lon,S,May 11)
Cloud Inspector (IRE) 64 (20f,Goo,GF,Jly 30)
Clouds Hill (FR) 45 (8f,Goo,GF,Jly 29)
Clued Up 46 (8f,Chp,GS,Jly 1)
Clytha Hill Lad 42 (8f,Hay,GF,Aug 15)
Coastal Bluff 83 (6f,Goo,GF,Aug 2)
Coastguards Hero 30 (7f,San,GF,Jly 30)
Coble 39 (8f,Nwm,G,May 4)
Coh Sho No 46 (15½f,Fol,F,Apr 10)
Cointosser (IRE) 34 (8f,Sal,F,Jly 18)
Cois Na Farraige (IRE) 30 (13f,Ham,GS,Apr 10)
Cold Steel 40 (8f,Nwm,GS,Jly 18)
College Night (IRE) 32 (6f,Bri,GF,May 6)
College Princess 30 (5f,Red,GF,Jly 19)
Collier Bay 45 (16f,Hay,S,Mar 29)
Colour Code 73 (10f,Ayr,GF,May 30)
Colour Counsellor 31 (10f,Bri,F,Aug 16)
Colway Ritz 57 (7f,Red,F,Aug 10)
Comanche Companion 52 (8f,Nwm,GS,Oct 16)
Come Together 38 (10f,Nwb,GF,Spt 18)
Compass Pointer 39 (14f,Hay,GS,May 24)
Compatibility (IRE) 53 (6f,Hay,G,Jly 5)
Compromise (IRE) 42 (7f,War,GF,May 24)
Compton Place 72 (5f,Asc,GS,Jun 20)
Concer Un 73 (7f,Nwm,G,Apr 16)
Confronter 48 (8f,Goo,GF,Jly 29)
Connemara (IRE) 65 (6f,Nwm,GF,May 31)
Conon Falls (IRE) 53 (10f,Goo,G,May 20)
Consort 72 (8f,Nwm,GS,Oct 16)
Conspicuous (IRE) 66 (10f,Eps,G,Jun 7)
Conspiracy 53 (7f,Nwm,G,Jly 8)
Contentment (IRE) 45 (10f,Wnd,GF,Jun 16)
Contrarie 35 (16f,Not,S,Oct 15)
Cool Edge (IRE) 64 (7f,Cur,G,Apr 12)
Copper Shell 32 (10f,Bat,GF,Apr 29)
Cordate (IRE) 41 (8f,Kem,G,May 24)
Coretta (IRE) 48 (12f,Asc,GF,Spt 28)
Corniche Quest (IRE) 56 (6f,Not,G,May 23)
Corradini 62 (16½f,San,GF,May 26)
Cosmic Prince (IRE) 59 (8f,War,GF,Apr 12)
Cottage Prince (IRE) 36 (12f,Cat,G,Jun 6)
Count Tony 41 (10f,Yar,GF,Aug 21)
Courageous Knight 31 (14f,Sal,GF,Aug 1)
Courbaril 42 (14f,Sal,GF,Aug 1)
Court Express 47 (6f,Crl,GF,Jun 25)
Court House 31 (6f,Pon,GF,Oct 6)
Courtship 56 (8f,Pon,GF,Apr 22)
Craigary 39 (12f,Ham,G,Aug 2)
Craigievar 72 (7f,Hay,S,May 5)
Crazy Chief 44 (9f,Nwb,GS,Oct 25)
Credit Squeeze 35 (12f,Bat,G,Aug 12)
Cretan Gift 90 (6f,Asc,GF,Spt 27)
Crimson Tide (IRE) 76 (9f,Nwm,GF,Apr 17)
Crissem (IRE) 44 (7f,Cat,GF,Spt 20)
Croeso Cynnes 39 (6f,Chp,GS,Aug 3)
Crofters Ceilidh 76 (5f,Yor,GS,Jun 13)
Croft Pool 84 (5f,Asc,GS,Jun 20)
Cross The Border 66 (5f,Thi,GF,Aug 22)
Crowded Avenue 71 (5f,Asc,GF,Spt 28)
Crown Court (USA) 73 (8f,Asc,GF,Jun 18)
Crown of Light 76 (12f,Eps,G,Jun 6)
Crown of Thorns (USA) 44 (8f,San,GF,Jly 24)
Crumpton Hill (IRE) 87 (7f,Asc,GF,Spt 27)
Cryhavoc 57 (6f,Goo,GS,Spt 13)
Crystal Crossing (IRE) 36 (6f,Nwm,GF,May 31)
Crystal Falls (IRE) 48 (12f,Thi,G,Jun 17)
Crystal Gold 66 (10½f,Hay,GF,Jun 7)
Crystal Hearted 63 (8f,Not,GF,Apr 11)
Crystal Heights (FR) 47 (7f,Bri,F,Jly 15)
Cuban Nights (USA) 40 (15½f,Fol,GF,Apr 22)
Cuban Reef 43 (10f,Pon,GF,Aug 7)
Cuesta Rey (USA) 35 (8½f,Eps,G,Spt 5)
Cuff Link (IRE) 60 (16f,Nwb,GF,Spt 18)
Cugina 53 (10f,San,S,Aug 30)
Curzon Street 49 (12f,Bri,GF,Spt 3)
Cybertechnology 65 (8f,Nwm,GS,Oct 16)
Cyrano's Lad (IRE) 86 (6f,Yor,G,May 13)
Cyrian (IRE) 54 (14f,Yor,G,Aug 19)
Czarna (IRE) 39 (8f,Bri,F,Apr 21)

Daawe (USA) 70 (6f,Red,G,Jun 20)
Dahiyah (USA) 41 (7f,Lei,GF,Mar 27)
Daira 45 (12½f,Nwc,G,Jly 28)
Dalliance (IRE) 62 (9f,San,GF,Jun 14)
Dalwhinnie 40 (12f,Nwm,GS,Jun 11)
Damancher 57 (10f,Cur,GS,May 25)
Dame Kiri (FR) 58 (12½f,Lon,G,Oct 4)
Dame Laura (IRE) 80 (6f,Asc,GF,Spt 27)
Dance Design (IRE) 75 (10f,Cur,GS,May 25)
Dance Parade (USA) 52 (7f,Nwb,GF,Apr 18)
Dance So Suite 86 (12f,Eps,G,Spt 5)
Dances With Dreams 82 (8f,Lon,S,May 11)
Dances With Hooves 35 (10f,San,GF,Jly 30)
Dancethenightaway 81 (5f,Asc,Hy,Oct 11)
Dancing Cavalier 59 (14f,Not,GF,Apr 11)
Dancing Cormorant 30 (11f,Ham,S,Jly 1)
Dancing Drop 70 (7f,San,G,May 26)
Dancing Feather 31 (12f,Chp,GF,Jun 13)
Dancing Image 77 (7f,Goo,GS,May 22)

Dancing Lawyer 39 (7f,Lin,GF,May 31)
Dancing Mystery 38 (6f,Bat,G,Spt 8)
Dancing Queen (IRE) 30 (10f,Yar,GF,Jly 28)
Dande Flyer 51 (5f,Fol,G,Mar 26)
Danegold (IRE) 41 (10f,Chp,G,Spt 11)
Danehill Dancer (IRE) 68 (6f,Yor,G,May 15)
Daneskaya 85 (8f,Dea,G,Aug 3)
Danesman (IRE) 32 (13f,Nwb,GS,Spt 20)
Danetime (IRE) 82 (6f,Goo,GF,Aug 2)
Dangerous Diva (IRE) 56 (7f,Nwm,G,Oct 18)
Danish Rhapsody (IRE) 72 (9f,Goo,G,Spt 12)
Dannistar 32 (11f,War,F,May 5)
Dantesque (IRE) 79 (12f,Don,GF,Spt 12)
Danzas 47 (10f,Bat,F,Jly 23)
Darapour (IRE) 54 (13f,Nwb,GS,Spt 20)
Darashandeh (IRE) 80 (10½f,Cha,S,Jun 8)
Daraydan (IRE) 41 (22f,Asc,S,Jun 20)
Darazari (IRE) 68 (12f,Cha,S,Jun 8)
Darb Alola (USA) 51 (5f,Asc,S,Jun 21)
Darcy 49 (9f,Rip,GS,May 18)
Darien 38 (13f,Bat,G,Spt 8)
Daring Destiny 61 (6f,Nwm,G,May 4)
Dark Age (IRE) 46 (11½f,Wnd,GF,Jun 9)
Dark Green (USA) 52 (12f,Goo,G,Jun 13)
Dark Menace 36 (7f,Bri,F,Jun 3)
Dark Mile (USA) 64 (6f,Hay,S,Oct 15)
Darnaway 49 (7f,Lin,G,Spt 9)
Dashing Blue 86 (6f,Goo,GF,Aug 2)
Dashing Dancer (IRE) 37 (6f,Pon,GF,Apr 22)
Dauphin (IRE) 43 (12f,Nwm,GF,Oct 2)
Davids Revenge 36 (6f,Wnd,G,Jly 7)
Davis Rock 44 (6f,Lin,GF,Jly 11)
Davoski 56 (10½f,Hay,GF,Aug 15)
Dawam Allail (IRE) 50 (8f,War,S,Jly 4)
Daylami (IRE) 86 (8f,Asc,G,Jun 17)
Daylight Dreams 37 (8f,Lin,GF,Jly 26)
Dayville (USA) 49 (7f,War,GF,Jly 19)
Dazzle 91 (6f,Asc,GF,Spt 27)
Dead Aim (IRE) 50 (10½f,Hay,GS,Spt 5)
Deadline Time (IRE) 31 (11f,Ayr,S,Oct 14)
Deadly Dudley (IRE) 58 (7f,Nwm,G,Oct 18)
Debutante Days 59 (12½f,Nwc,G,Jly 28)
Decorated Hero 93 (8f,Hpk,F,Nov 8)
Dee Pee Tee Cee (IRE) 55 (8f,Red,F,Aug 23)
Deep Finesse 73 (5f,Asc,GS,Jun 20)
Deeply Vale (IRE) 48 (7f,Yor,S,Spt 4)
Deep Water (USA) 55 (10f,Nwm,GF,Oct 3)
Deerly 32 (6f,Chp,G,May 26)
Defined Feature (IRE) 58 (7f,Yar,GF,Aug 21)
Degree 44 (8f,Edi,G,Jun 16)
Delight of Dawn 46 (7f,Cat,GF,Spt 20)
Delilah (IRE) 65 (12f,Asc,Hy,Oct 11)
Dellua (IRE) 53 (9f,Ayr,S,Oct 13)
Delta Soleil (USA) 67 (6f,Red,G,Jun 20)
Democrat 30 (7f,Lei,S,Oct 13)
Denbrae (IRE) 49 (6f,Wnd,GS,Jun 30)
Densben 35 (7f,Crl,F,May 29)
Denton Lad 45 (6f,Rip,G,Apr 26)
Depreciate 53 (6f,Pon,GS,Spt 2)
Desert Beauty (IRE) 64 (8f,Nwm,GF,Nov 1)
Desert Cat (IRE) 39 (7f,Crl,G,Apr 25)
Desert Dunes 51 (15f,Nwm,GS,Jun 11)
Desert Fighter 58 (10f,Don,GF,Mar 20)
Desert Horizon 74 (10f,Goo,GF,Aug 1)
Desert King (IRE) 85 (8f,Asc,G,Jun 17)
Desert Lynx (IRE) 49 (6f,Not,GF,Jly 30)
Desert Mountain (IRE) 43 (12f,Don,GF,Mar 22)
Desert Story (IRE) 78 (10f,Lon,G,Oct 4)
Desert Time 46 (8f,San,GF,Jun 14)
Desert Track 74 (8f,Red,GF,Oct 18)
Devilish Charm (USA) 45 (14f,Red,GF,Oct 18)
Diamond Crown (IRE) 38 (10f,Pon,GF,Jun 9)
Dick Turpin (USA) 54 (10f,Goo,G,Spt 13)
Dictation (USA) 60 (7f,Thi,G,May 16)
Diego 54 (16f,Asc,S,Jun 21)
Diffident (FR) 70 (6f,Yor,G,May 15)
Diminutive (USA) 39 (10f,Yar,F,Spt 17)
Dirab 50 (16f,Nwc,G,Aug 6)
Disallowed (IRE) 34 (10f,Not,GF,Spt 23)
Dispol Diamond 44 (7f,Red,F,May 1)
Dispol Gem 62 (8f,Rip,G,Jly 7)
Distinctive Dream (IRE) 67 (6f,Not,GF,Oct 4)
Divide And Rule 41 (5f,Chs,S,May 6)
Divina Luna 66 (7f,War,GF,Jly 19)
Divine Miss-P 47 (5f,War,GS,Aug 25)
Divinity 30 (10f,San,GF,Apr 25)
Dizzy Tilly 48 (12f,Nwm,GF,Oct 31)
Docklands Carriage (IRE) 38 (6f,Cat,GF,May 30)
Docklands Limo 56 (14f,Yor,G,Aug 20)
Doc Ryan's 49 (12f,Edi,GS,Nov 6)
Doctor Bravious (IRE) 54 (8f,Asc,GF,Apr 30)
Dokos (USA) 59 (8f,Don,GS,May 5)
Domappel 57 (14f,Red,GF,May 26)
Dominant Air 70 (6f,Kem,GF,Spt 22)
Dominant Duchess 50 (14f,Goo,GF,Aug 2)
Dominelle 32 (5f,Crl,F,May 29)
Domino Flyer 60 (10f,Nwc,G,Mar 25)
Dona Filipa 32 (5f,Red,G,Nov 4)
Don Pepe 52 (6f,Yar,F,Jun 11)
Don Sebastian 39 (8½f,Eps,S,Jly 2)
Don't Care (IRE) 60 (7f,Nwc,GF,Mar 31)
Don't Worry Me (IRE) 94 (5f,Asc,GS,Jun 20)
Don't Worry Mike 30 (7f,Crl,GF,Aug 4)
Dormy Three 30 (10f,Lei,GS,Apr 26)
Double Action 75 (6f,Ayr,G,Spt 20)
Double Alleged (USA) 59 (12f,Nwm,GS,Oct 16)
Double Bounce 69 (6f,Not,G,Spt 28)
Double Eclipse (IRE) 89 (16f,Nwm,GF,Oct 4)
Double Eight (IRE) 41 (12f,Cat,GF,Spt 20)
Double Espresso (IRE) 53 (12f,Eps,G,Spt 5)
Double Flight 40 (9f,Ham,GS,Jun 18)
Double Gold 33 (10f,Nwb,GF,May 28)
Double-J (IRE) 52 (6f,Nwc,F,Jun 4)
Double March 32 (6f,Lei,G,Oct 27)
Double Matt (IRE) 38 (6f,Lei,G,Jly 17)
Double Oscar (IRE) 67 (5f,Crl,F,Aug 27)
Double Splendour (IRE) 78 (6f,Yor,G,May 13)
Double Trigger (IRE) 92 (20f,Lon,G,Oct 4)
Dovebrace 44 (6f,Hay,S,Oct 15)
Dovedon Star 61 (12f,Lei,S,Oct 13)
Doyella (IRE) 52 (10f,Chp,GS,Jly 1)
Dragonada (USA) 74 (8f,Goo,GF,Aug 2)
Dramatic Moment 39 (10f,Goo,GS,Jun 20)
Dream of Nurmi 52 (12f,Goo,GF,Jly 30)
Dreams End 77 (9f,Nwm,G,Apr 16)
Drift 42 (12f,Bri,F,Oct 1)
Drive Assured 31 (12f,Lei,GS,Apr 26)
Dr Johnson (USA) 69 (10f,Cur,GS,May 25)
Dr Martens (IRE) 43 (8f,Nwm,G,Jly 19)
Dr Massini (IRE) 49 (10f,Kem,GF,Mar 31)
Duello 60 (8f,Nwb,S,May 18)
Duke Valentino 47 (7½f,Bev,S,Jun 11)
Dukhan (USA) 42 (10f,Lei,GF,Spt 9)
Dulcinea 41 (7f,Kem,GF,May 31)
Dummer Golf Time 51 (7f,Yor,S,Spt 4)
Dunabrattin 33 (14f,Not,G,Nov 3)
Duncombe Hall 30 (15½f,Fol,F,Spt 26)
Dundel (IRE) 53 (9f,Goo,GF,Aug 22)
Duraid (IRE) 57 (8f,Hay,G,Spt 26)
Durgams First (IRE) 53 (12f,Nwm,GF,Oct 2)
Durham 59 (16f,Goo,GF,Spt 25)
Dushyantor (USA) 83 (12f,Eps,G,Spt 5)
Dust Dancer 48 (10f,Sal,GF,Aug 13)
Dyhim Diamond (IRE) 82 (5f,Dea,G,Aug 3)

Eager To Please 37 (7f,War,GF,Jun 9)
Eagle Canyon (IRE) 44 (12½f,Nwc,G,May 22)
Eagle Dancer 59 (10f,Lin,S,May 10)
Eastern Prophets 66 (5f,San,GF,Apr 25)
Easycall 81 (5f,Asc,GS,Jun 20)
Easy Dollar 96 (6f,Nwm,G,Apr 15)
Easy Song (USA) 45 (10f,Yar,F,Spt 17)
Ebadiyla (IRE) 76 (12f,Lon,GF,Oct 5)
Edan Heights 65 (10f,Nwm,G,May 2)
Eden Rock (GER) 76 (8f,Lon,GF,Oct 5)
Edipo Re 45 (12f,Lei,G,Oct 27)
Ed's Folly (IRE) 44 (7f,Lei,GS,Oct 14)
Effectual 67 (10f,Kem,G,May 24)
Effervescence 36 (7f,San,GF,Spt 17)
Egoli (USA) 60 (8f,Lei,GF,Oct 5)
Eider Hill 31 (8f,Nwb,S,Spt 19)
Ela-Aristokrati (IRE) 77 (12f,Asc,G,Jun 20)
El Angelo (USA) 83 (8f,Hpk,F,Nov 8)
Ela-Yie-Mou (IRE) 35 (14½f,Kem,G,Spt 10)
Elbaaha 67 (12f,Don,GF,Spt 12)
Election Day (IRE) 81 (16f,Goo,GF,Jly 31)
Elegant Dance 30 (8f,Kem,G,May 5)
Elegant Warning (IRE) 68 (7f,Nwm,G,Apr 15)
Eleos 47 (10½f,Lon,S,May 11)
Elfland (IRE) 73 (7f,Nwm,GS,Jun 20)
Elite Hope (USA) 30 (7f,San,G,May 26)
Ella Lamees 32 (6f,Wnd,GF,Jly 21)
Ellens Lad (IRE) 54 (5f,Wnd,S,May 19)
Ellway Lady (IRE) 37 (12f,Bri,F,Oct 1)
Elly Fleetfoot (IRE) 43 (12f,Chp,G,May 26)
Elnadim (USA) 105 (6f,Asc,GF,Spt 27)
El Opera (IRE) 47 (6f,Nwm,GF,May 31)
Embroidered 30 (6f,Bat,G,Aug 7)
Embryonic (IRE) 51 (17f,Pon,GF,Apr 22)
Emerging Market 77 (7f,Nwm,G,Apr 16)
Energy Man 34 (8f,Edi,GF,May 2)
English Invader 40 (12f,Nwm,G,Apr 16)
Enlisted (IRE) 32 (10f,Red,GS,Jly 26)
Entice (FR) 92 (9f,Lon,GF,Oct 5)
Entrepreneur 92 (8f,Nwm,G,May 3)
Epic Stand 63 (8f,Nwm,G,Oct 18)
Eponine 39 (14f,Yar,F,Jun 11)
Epworth 49 (10f,Nwc,Hy,Jun 28)
Erlking (IRE) 45 (12f,Chp,G,Aug 25)
Ertlon 64 (7f,Yar,GF,May 28)
Erupt 43 (6f,Sal,GF,Jly 12)
Es Go 33 (12f,Bri,F,Oct 1)
Eshtiaal (USA) 71 (10f,Pon,GF,Spt 25)
Eskimo Nel (IRE) 60 (12f,Hay,S,Mar 29)
Esperto 33 (10f,Fol,G,Jly 9)
Essayeffsee 45 (12f,Edi,GF,Jly 18)
Eternal Joy 39 (8f,Cur,G,Jly 13)
Eternity 35 (12f,Nwm,GF,Oct 31)
Ethbaat (USA) 35 (8f,War,GF,Apr 12)
Etoile (FR) 75 (12f,Eps,G,Jun 6)
Etterby Park (USA) 62 (16f,Chs,G,Spt 24)
Eurobox Boy 60 (8f,San,G,Aug 13)
Eurolink Profile 49 (7f,Lin,GF,Jly 12)
Euro Sceptic (IRE) 38 (8½f,Bev,GF,Spt 17)
Eva Luna (USA) 65 (12f,Lei,G,Jun 14)
Eveningperformance 77 (5f,Nwb,GF,Spt 18)
Even Top (IRE) 77 (10f,Wnd,G,Aug 23)
Everglades (IRE) 60 (6f,Goo,G,May 20)
Evezio Rufo 30 (11f,War,F,May 5)
Evidently (IRE) 30 (8f,Nwb,S,Spt 19)
Exactly (IRE) 46 (16f,Cat,GF,Spt 20)
Executive Design 52 (14f,Hay,S,May 5)
Expialiodoocius 34 (11f,War,GF,Jun 9)
Express Gift 43 (14f,Hay,GS,May 24)
Express Girl 37 (5f,Rip,GS,May 18)

Fabled Light (IRE) 40 (10½f,Chs,S,May 6)
Fabulous Mtoto 40 (14f,Sal,GF,Aug 1)
Fahris (IRE) 83 (9f,Nwm,GF,Apr 17)
Fahs (USA) 66 (10f,Don,GF,Spt 13)
Fairhonor (FR) 75 (15½f,Lon,S,May 18)
Fairly Sure (IRE) 37 (7f,Bri,F,Spt 28)
Fairy Knight 49 (10f,Wnd,GF,Jun 2)
Fairy Prince (IRE) 53 (6f,Don,G,Jly 31)
Faith Alone 60 (6f,Yar,GS,Jly 3)
Faithful Son (USA) 88 (8f,Asc,G,Spt 27)
Falak (USA) 82 (10f,Don,G,May 24)
Falls O'Moness (IRE) 43 (9f,Ayr,GS,Spt 19)
Fame Again 52 (7f,Don,G,May 6)
Family Man 66 (8f,Nwm,GF,May 31)
Family Tradition (IRE) 49 (14f,Cur,S,Spt 20)

Fancy A Fortune (IRE) 46 (7f,Thi,G,Aug 1)
Fancy Design (IRE) 32 (8f,San,G,Aug 13)
Fantail 65 (10f,Nwm,GF,Oct 3)
Fantastic Fellow (USA) 77 (8f,Hpk,F,Nov 8)
Fantastic Flame (IRE) 50 (10f,Ayr,GS,Spt 19)
Far Ahead 66 (14f,Hay,GF,Aug 9)
Farasan (IRE) 77 (9f,Nwm,G,Apr 16)
Faraway Lass 66 (6f,Goo,GF,Aug 2)
Farewell My Love (IRE) 39 (6f,Wnd,S,May 12)
Farfields Prince 41 (11f,Ayr,GS,Spt 18)
Farhan (USA) 31 (10f,Pon,GF,Jun 3)
Farhana 70 (6f,Yor,G,May 15)
Faringdon Future 47 (8f,San,GF,Spt 16)
Farley Green 37 (6f,Wnd,GF,Jly 28)
Farley Mount 42 (8f,Lei,G,May 26)
Farmost 65 (10f,Bat,F,Jly 23)
Farringdon Hill 56 (11½f,Wnd,GF,Aug 11)
Fatal Baraari 33 (8f,San,GF,Jly 24)
Fatefully (USA) 76 (10f,Nwm,GF,Oct 4)
Father Dan (IRE) 54 (10f,Bri,F,Aug 16)
Father Sky 65 (16f,Goo,GF,Spt 25)
Fayik 44 (6f,Nwm,GF,Aug 9)
Faym (IRE) 37 (8f,Lei,G,Aug 11)
Featherstone Lane 47 (5f,Nwc,F,Jun 4)
Feel A Line 47 (7f,Yar,GS,Jly 2)
Fern's Governor 53 (10f,Nwm,G,May 2)
Ferny Hill (IRE) 65 (12f,Don,GF,Spt 12)
Fiametta 49 (8f,Asc,Hy,Oct 10)
Field of Vision (IRE) 30 (14f,Cat,G,Mar 26)
Fieldridge 51 (17f,Bat,Hy,May 11)
Fier Danseur (FR) 53 (12f,Cha,G,Jun 1)
Fife Major (USA) 40 (12f,Bri,F,Oct 1)
Fighting Times 43 (10f,Nwc,GF,Oct 22)
Fiji 45 (10f,Chp,GF,Jly 25)
Filial (IRE) 51 (10f,Red,F,Spt 26)
Filmore West 41 (12f,Don,G,Oct 25)
Final Stab (IRE) 52 (8f,San,G,Aug 13)
Final Stage (IRE) 35 (10f,Nwm,G,Apr 15)
Final Warning 30 (8f,Not,GF,Apr 8)
Finarts Bay 32 (7f,Kem,G,Spt 21)
Fine Fellow (IRE) 58 (8f,Lon,G,Apr 20)
Finisterre (IRE) 35 (6f,Pon,GF,Apr 22)
Finsbury Flyer (IRE) 44 (8f,San,GF,May 27)
Fionn de Cool (IRE) 47 (8f,San,GS,Jly 4)
First Chance (IRE) 47 (8f,San,GF,Spt 16)
First Gold 40 (7f,Crl,GS,May 9)
First Island (IRE) 88 (8f,San,GF,Apr 25)
First Maite 63 (6f,Hay,S,Oct 15)
First Principle 51 (6f,Bat,G,Spt 8)
Fisiostar 41 (6f,Nwc,GF,Aug 3)
Flag Down (CAN) 93 (12f,Hpk,F,Nov 8)
Flag Fen (USA) 53 (8f,Rip,GS,May 18)
Flagship 49 (10f,San,GF,Spt 16)
Flamboyance (USA) 64 (7f,Asc,GF,Spt 27)
Flashtalkin' Flood 44 (8f,Not,S,Jun 23)
Fleeting Glimpse 66 (10f,Lon,S,May 18)
Fleet River (USA) 38 (8½f,Eps,G,Spt 5)
Fletcher 65 (15f,Nwm,GF,Jly 10)
Flint Knapper 72 (10f,Nwm,GF,Spt 30)
Flirting Around (USA) 62 (16f,Asc,GF,Jun 18)
Floating Charge 35 (7f,Lin,G,Spt 9)
Florentino (IRE) 55 (12f,Bri,F,May 23)
Flowing Fortune 46 (10f,Goo,GF,Jun 12)
Flying Colours (IRE) 32 (7f,Goo,GS,May 21)
Flying Harold 37 (5f,Goo,GF,Jun 6)
Flying North (IRE) 72 (10f,Bev,S,Jun 11)
Flying Pennant (IRE) 50 (7f,Lin,GF,May 31)
Fly To The Stars 83 (8f,Asc,G,Jun 17)
Flyway (FR) 67 (12f,Cha,S,Jun 8)
Foist 48 (7f,Thi,GF,Apr 18)
Fond Embrace 55 (5f,Chp,GS,Jly 1)
Fonteyn 35 (6f,Fol,G,Jly 9)
Fooled You (USA) 31 (8f,Rip,GF,Apr 9)
Foot Battalion (IRE) 58 (10½f,Hay,GF,Jun 7)
Forcing Bid 31 (6f,Fol,G,Oct 21)
Foreign Rule (IRE) 37 (12½f,War,GF,Jun 9)
Forest Buck (USA) 65 (10f,Nwm,G,May 3)
Forest Fantasy 44 (8f,Not,GF,Aug 6)
Forest Robin 49 (10f,Don,GF,Mar 20)
Forgie (IRE) 63 (16f,Chs,G,Spt 24)
Forgotten Times (USA) 46 (6f,Wnd,G,Jly 7)
For the Present 63 (6f,Red,G,Jun 20)
Fort Knox (IRE) 34 (7f,Bri,F,Jun 3)
Fortunes Course (IRE) 40 (17f,Bat,Hy,May 11)
For Your Eyes Only 71 (8f,Nwm,G,Oct 18)
Forza Figlio 75 (10f,Nwm,G,May 3)
Forzair 40 (12f,Edi,GF,Jly 18)
Foundry Lane 65 (14f,Yor,S,Spt 3)
Fourdaned (IRE) 48 (10f,Don,GF,Mar 20)
Foxes Tail 32 (8f,Rip,GF,Apr 17)
Fragrant Mix (FR) 75 (11f,Lon,G,Apr 6)
Frederick James 42 (7f,Red,G,Jun 20)
Fredrik The Fierce (IRE) 35 (5f,Chs,S,May 6)
Free As A Bird 37 (7f,Yar,F,Jun 5)
Freedom Chance (IRE) 51 (12f,Bri,F,Jly 28)
Freequent 75 (10½f,Yor,G,Aug 20)
Free To Speak (IRE) 44 (10f,Cur,GS,May 25)
French Ballerina (IRE) 56 (14f,Leo,G,May 28)
French Ginger 31 (8f,Rip,GF,Aug 26)
French Grit (IRE) 54 (6f,Pon,GF,Jun 9)
French Ivy (USA) 54 (16f,Rip,GF,May 28)
French Mist 39 (14f,Yar,G,Jun 23)
Fresh Fruit Daily 53 (10f,Not,GF,Apr 21)
Friendly Brave (USA) 45 (5f,Wnd,G,Aug 4)
Frozen Sea (USA) 46 (12f,Eps,G,Apr 23)
Fuenji (FR) 64 (8f,Dea,G,Aug 3)
Fullopep 34 (12f,Cat,GF,Jly 16)
Fun Galore (USA) 56 (7f,Goo,GF,Aug 1)
Furnish 40 (5f,Ayr,G,Jun 21)
Further Flight 79 (16f,Nwm,GF,Oct 4)
Further Outlook (USA) 57 (8f,Asc,G,Jun 17)
Fur Will Fly 44 (6f,Sal,GF,May 4)
Future Perfect 71 (10f,Goo,GF,Aug 1)

Gadge 60 (7f,Goo,GS,May 22)
Gadroon 35 (9f,Ayr,S,Oct 13)
Gaelic Storm 66 (5f,Eps,G,Aug 25)
Gain Line (USA) 45 (7f,Yar,GF,May 28)
Galapino 55 (16f,Asc,G,Spt 27)
Galine 60 (6f,Nwm,G,May 3)
Game Ploy (POL) 89 (10½f,Yor,G,Aug 20)
Ganga (IRE) 69 (10f,Red,GF,Oct 18)
Garnock Valley 65 (6f,Thi,GS,May 17)
Garolo (FR) 59 (16f,Asc,GF,Apr 30)
Garuda (IRE) 52 (10f,Nwm,G,Apr 15)
Gates (USA) 38 (8f,Asc,GF,Jun 18)
Gay Breeze 37 (6f,Yar,F,Spt 18)
Gazelle Royale (FR) 77 (12f,Eps,G,Jun 6)
Gee Bee Boy 34 (10f,Red,GF,Oct 28)
Gee Bee Dream 56 (7f,Nwc,Hy,Jun 28)
Geimhriuil (IRE) 61 (7f,Hay,GS,May 24)
General Academy (IRE) 75 (8f,San,GF,May 26)
General Assembly (IRE) 76 (12f,Nwm,G,May 4)
General Glow 32 (12f,Edi,GF,Jly 18)
General Haven 57 (11f,War,F,May 5)
General Monty 42 (8f,Thi,F,Jun 2)
General Mouktar 47 (14f,Hay,GS,May 24)
General Sir Peter (IRE) 39 (5f,Chp,G,Spt 11)
Generosa 33 (16f,Cur,GS,Oct 4)
Generous Gift 69 (10f,Goo,GF,Aug 1)
Generous Libra 70 (8f,Nwb,GS,May 16)
Genevra (IRE) 86 (9f,Lon,GF,Oct 5)
Gentilesse 40 (10f,Lin,S,May 10)
Genuine John (IRE) 55 (7½f,Bev,GF,Apr 5)
Georgia Venture 59 (14½f,Don,GF,Spt 10)
Geri (USA) 94 (8f,Hpk,F,Nov 8)
Germano 99 (10f,Nwb,GF,Jly 19)
Get A Life 36 (12f,Edi,G,Jly 7)
Get The Point 47 (8f,Rip,GF,Apr 17)
Ghalib (IRE) 68 (8f,Asc,Hy,Oct 10)
Gharib (USA) 48 (5f,Bev,GF,Spt 17)
Ghataas 70 (11f,Ayr,G,Spt 20)
Ghillies Ball 47 (12f,Asc,G,Aug 1)
Gift Token 64 (10f,Nwb,GF,Spt 18)
Giko 41 (7f,Kem,GF,May 31)
Gi La High 54 (6f,Not,GF,Spt 15)
Gilling Dancer (IRE) 32 (8f,Rip,GF,May 28)
Ginger Rogers 38 (16f,Not,GF,Spt 15)
Ginzbourg 60 (10f,Don,G,Jly 30)
Gipsy Princess 40 (7f,Cat,GF,Spt 20)
Give Me A Ring (IRE) 79 (8f,San,GF,Apr 25)
Gladys Althorpe (IRE) 36 (8f,Thi,G,Jly 25)
Glen Ogil 33 (9f,Nwm,GF,Oct 31)
Glen Parker (IRE) 67 (8f,Wnd,G,Aug 23)
Globe Runner 39 (12f,Ham,GF,Aug 18)
Glow Forum 52 (12f,Nwm,GF,Oct 31)
Go Britannia 73 (20f,Goo,GF,Jly 30)
Godmersham Park 48 (8f,Not,G,May 17)
Go For Salt (USA) 47 (10f,Bat,G,Jly 7)
Go Hence 42 (12f,Bev,G,Jly 29)
Going For Broke 35 (10f,Bev,GF,Apr 24)
Gold Blade 59 (9f,Ayr,GF,Jly 19)
Gold Desire 54 (10½f,Yor,S,Spt 4)
Gold Edge 44 (5f,Ayr,S,Oct 14)
Golden Ace (IRE) 51 (10½f,Yor,S,Spt 4)
Golden Arches (FR) 85 (10½f,Cha,S,Jun 8)
Golden Hadeer 38 (15f,War,G,Jun 24)
Golden Hello 35 (12f,Don,GF,Spt 12)
Golden Melody 30 (16f,Not,S,Oct 8)
Golden Pound (USA) 63 (6f,Eps,S,Jly 2)
Golden Saddle (USA) 32 (10f,Bri,F,Jly 16)
Golden Thunderbolt (FR) 47 (12f,Bev,GF,Jun 5)
Golden Touch (USA) 43 (11f,War,F,May 5)
Gold Lance (USA) 48 (8f,Goo,G,Spt 12)
Gold Millenium (IRE) 36 (8f,Kem,G,May 24)
Gold Spats (USA) 81 (8f,Goo,G,May 20)
Gone for a Burton (IRE) 52 (10f,Don,G,Oct 25)
Gone Savage 67 (5f,San,GF,Apr 25)
Goodbye Gatemen (IRE) 45 (6f,Bri,F,Jun 3)
Good Reputation 35 (9f,Goo,G,May 22)
Good To Talk 38 (5f,Edi,GS,Jun 23)
Gordi (USA) 64 (12f,Leo,G,Jly 19)
Goretski (IRE) 61 (5f,Bev,GS,Aug 13)
Gothenberg (IRE) 85 (8f,San,GF,Apr 25)
Graceful Lass 60 (12f,Chp,GF,Jly 11)
Gracie Lady (IRE) 57 (10f,Lon,S,May 18)
Grand Chapeau (IRE) 54 (6f,Pon,GS,Spt 2)
Grand Cru 39 (16½f,San,GS,Jly 5)
Grand Lad (IRE) 56 (6f,Lei,F,Apr 3)
Grand Musica 62 (8f,Nwm,GS,Oct 16)
Grand Ovation (IRE) 31 (8f,Kem,G,May 24)
Grand Splendour 58 (10f,Bev,GF,Jun 5)
Granny's Pet 67 (6f,Hay,G,Jly 5)
Grapeshot (USA) 72 (8f,Nwm,GF,Apr 17)
Grapevine (IRE) 41 (11½f,Chs,S,May 7)
Grate Times 46 (7f,Thi,F,Jun 2)
Great Child 62 (8f,Nwm,GF,Oct 3)
Great Easeby (IRE) 39 (18f,Nwm,G,Oct 18)
Greatest 40 (7f,Lei,GS,Oct 14)
Great Oration (IRE) 37 (17f,Pon,GF,Aug 17)
Greek Palace (IRE) 49 (8f,Nwb,GF,Apr 19)
Greenaway Bay (USA) 56 (10f,Don,G,May 24)
Green Card (USA) 74 (8f,Kem,G,May 24)
Green Jewel 57 (9f,Goo,G,Jun 12)
Green Lady (IRE) 73 (8f,Dea,G,Aug 3)
Green Power 58 (8f,Rip,G,Jun 19)
Greenstead (USA) 48 (12f,Don,G,Oct 25)
Gresatre 38 (7f,Nwm,G,Aug 22)
Gretel 44 (8f,Goo,G,May 22)
Grey Again 33 (7f,Cat,GF,Spt 20)
Grey Kingdom 58 (7f,Yor,S,Spt 4)
Grey Shot 93 (16f,Nwm,GF,Oct 4)
Grey Way (USA) 78 (10f,Goo,GF,Aug 2)
Grief (IRE) 71 (10f,San,S,Aug 30)
Grooms Gold (IRE) 39 (8f,Not,G,Nov 3)
Groom's Gordon (FR) 65 (7f,Asc,GF,Jun 18)
Groucho (USA) 40 (10f,Nwm,G,Apr 15)
Ground Game 56 (12f,Asc,GF,Jun 18)
Grovefair Venture 30 (8f,Nwm,G,Jly 19)
Guesstimation (USA) 49 (10f,Bri,GF,Aug 27)
Guest Alliance (IRE) 32 (15½f,Fol,GF,Apr

22)
Gulf Harbour (IRE) 36 (10½f,Chs,S,May 6)
Gulf Shaadi 79 (8f,Nwm,G,Oct 18)
Gulliver 59 (8f,Thi,F,Jun 2)
Gumair (USA) 37 (14f,Not,GF,Jun 9)
Gunners Glory 39 (7f,Nwm,G,Aug 22)
Gwespyr 42 (7f,Bri,F,May 29)
Gymcrak Flyer 51 (7f,Red,G,May 12)
Gymcrak Premiere 54 (8f,Red,GF,Oct 28)
Gymcrak Tiger (IRE) 33 (14f,Not,GF,Apr 21)

Hachiyah (IRE) 57 (10f,Eps,GS,Jly 9)
Hadawah (USA) 36 (8f,Sal,GF,May 15)
Hadidi 34 (12f,Cat,GF,Jly 16)
Hajr (IRE) 58 (8f,Goo,GF,Jly 29)
Half Tone 49 (5f,Goo,G,Spt 24)
Hal Hoo Yaroom 39 (12f,Eps,G,Spt 5)
Halmanerror 39 (7f,Lei,GS,Oct 14)
Halowing (USA) 57 (7f,Cat,S,Oct 17)
Hal's Pal 77 (8f,Asc,GF,Jun 18)
Haltarra (USA) 73 (10f,Kem,G,Spt 21)
Hanan (USA) 31 (6f,Nwm,GF,Aug 9)
Hanbitooh (USA) 34 (15½f,Fol,F,Apr 10)
Handaza (IRE) 49 (9f,Cur,S,Spt 21)
Handsome Ridge 77 (8f,Asc,G,Jun 17)
Hannah's Usher 31 (7f,Lin,GF,Jun 14)
Hannalou (FR) 32 (8f,Bri,F,May 29)
Happy Go Lucky 55 (10f,Nwb,GF,Spt 18)
Happy Minstral (USA) 45 (12f,Goo,GF,Jly 30)
Harbour Dues 92 (12f,Eps,G,Jun 7)
Hard to Figure 77 (6f,Ayr,G,Spt 20)
Hardy Dancer 64 (10f,Kem,GF,Mar 31)
Harlequin Walk (IRE) 36 (10f,Bri,F,Oct 1)
Harmony Hall 42 (14f,Sal,GF,Aug 21)
Haroldon (IRE) 54 (10f,Wnd,G,Jly 7)
Harry's Treat 33 (8f,Edi,S,Mar 27)
Harry Wolton 89 (10½f,Yor,G,Aug 20)
Harvey White (IRE) 38 (11f,War,GF,Oct 7)
Hasta la Vista 39 (16f,Thi,GF,Aug 11)
Hattaafeh (IRE) 40 (16f,Kem,G,Mar 29)
Hattab (IRE) 79 (6f,Nwb,GF,Jly 19)
Havago 43 (7f,San,G,May 26)
Hawait (IRE) 67 (8f,Don,GF,Spt 13)
Hawker Hunter (USA) 68 (12f,Don,GF,Jun 7)
Hawkish (USA) 34 (10f,Bev,GF,Jun 5)
Hawksbill Henry (USA) 34 (6f,Nwm,GF,Aug 9)
Hawksley Hill (IRE) 83 (8f,Yor,G,Aug 21)
Hayes Way (IRE) 56 (8f,Nwm,G,Jly 19)
Hazard a Guess (IRE) 74 (10f,Kem,GF,Mar 31)
Heart Full of Soul 39 (10f,Lei,GF,Spt 22)
Heart of Armor 59 (12f,Hay,GF,Aug 8)
Heart of Gold (IRE) 61 (12½f,Nwc,G,Jun 27)
Heathyards Rock 52 (12f,Nwm,G,Jun 7)
Heavenly Calm (USA) 72 (15f,Lon,G,Oct 4)
Heavenly Miss (IRE) 43 (6f,Wnd,S,May 12)
Heavenly Ray (USA) 59 (8f,Nwm,GF,Nov 1)
Heaven's Command 74 (8f,Dea,G,Aug 3)
Heighth of Fame 38 (12f,Crl,G,Jun 25)
Height of Heights (IRE) 61 (14f,Sal,GF,Aug 1)
Helicon (IRE) 55 (10f,San,GF,Jly 16)
Helios 49 (8f,Chp,GS,Jly 1)
Helissio (FR) 99 (10½f,Lon,S,Apr 27)
Hello Mister 79 (6f,Nwb,GF,Jly 19)
Helmsman (USA) 80 (8f,Hpk,F,Nov 8)
Hen Harrier 62 (8f,Rip,GF,Apr 17)
Henley (USA) 60 (10f,Don,G,Jly 30)
Henry's Mother 44 (8f,Kem,G,May 5)
Henry The Fifth 51 (10f,Nwm,G,May 3)
Herbshan Dancer 31 (11½f,Wnd,S,Jun 23)
Here Comes a Star 41 (5f,Nwc,F,Jun 4)
Here Comes Herbie 42 (16f,Nwm,GF,Aug 8)
Here's To Howie (USA) 33 (8f,Not,GS,Oct 8)
Heritage 71 (12f,Nwm,GS,Oct 16)
Heron Island (IRE) 72 (20f,Asc,G,Jun 19)
Herr Trigger 55 (12f,Goo,GF,Aug 22)
He's Got Wings (IRE) 40 (13f,Ham,GS,Apr 10)
Hever Golf Charmer 34 (8f,Edi,G,Jun 16)
Hever Golf Glory 66 (8f,Cha,S,May 12)
Hever Golf Magic (IRE) 34 (6f,Fol,GF,Apr 22)
Hever Golf Mover 38 (6f,Not,GF,Spt 15)
Hever Golf Rocket 49 (6f,Lin,GF,Aug 17)
Hever Golf Rose 90 (5f,Asc,GS,Jun 20)
Hever Golf Star 42 (5f,Fol,GF,Apr 10)
Hidden Meadow 90 (7f,Yor,G,Aug 21)
Highborn (IRE) 78 (7f,Nwm,GS,Jun 20)
High Domain (IRE) 46 (5f,Sal,GF,Jun 11)
Highfield Fizz 34 (18f,Pon,GS,Oct 20)
High Five (IRE) 35 (17f,Bat,Hy,May 11)
Highflying 48 (16f,Rip,GF,May 28)
High Intrigue (IRE) 43 (14f,San,GF,Jly 24)
High Low (USA) 37 (11f,Ham,GS,Jly 4)
Highly Prized 41 (12f,Sal,GF,May 4)
Highly Respected (IRE) 31 (7½f,Chs,S,May 6)
High On Life 41 (12f,Bev,G,Jly 29)
High Premium 74 (9f,Yor,GS,Jun 14)
High Spirits (IRE) 54 (8f,Nwm,G,Oct 18)
Hill Farm Blues 46 (10f,Bat,G,Jly 7)
Hill Farm Dancer 34 (12f,Bat,GF,Apr 29)
Hillswick 37 (16f,Goo,GF,Spt 25)
Hiltons Executive (IRE) 32 (5f,Rip,GF,Aug 16)
Hi Mujtahid (IRE) 31 (7f,Crl,GF,Aug 4)
Hi Nod 68 (8f,Asc,S,Jly 26)
Hirasah (IRE) 54 (8f,San,G,Aug 13)
Hisar (IRE) 52 (10f,Pon,GF,Spt 25)
Hoh Express 69 (14f,Goo,GF,Jly 29)
Hoh Flyer (USA) 34 (11f,Red,GF,May 26)
Hoh Returns (IRE) 54 (5f,Nwb,GF,Apr 18)
Holloway Melody 30 (8f,Lei,G,Oct 27)
Homestead 35 (8f,Not,G,Nov 3)
Honourable 62 (12f,Yor,S,Spt 4)
Hoofprints (IRE) 36 (12f,Fol,GF,Aug 19)
Hopesay 37 (6f,Red,F,Spt 26)
Hornbeam 79 (7f,Asc,GF,Jun 18)
House of Dreams 33 (9f,Red,GF,Oct 7)
Howaida (IRE) 51 (7f,San,GF,Spt 16)
How Long 76 (7f,Nwm,G,Apr 16)
Hulal 43 (7f,Cat,S,Jly 3)
Hullbank 43 (16f,Bev,GF,Jun 4)
Humourless 66 (12f,Asc,GF,Jun 18)
Hunters of Brora (IRE) 73 (9f,Nwm,GF,Oct 4)
Hurricane State (USA) 56 (8½f,Eps,G,Jun 7)
Hurtleberry (IRE) 66 (8f,Goo,GS,May 21)
Husun (USA) 37 (6f,Lin,GF,Jun 14)
Hype Energy 36 (5f,War,GS,Aug 25)
Hype Superior (IRE) 30 (5f,Bev,Hy,Jly 5)

Iamus 76 (8f,Nwc,G,Jly 26)
Ibin St James 46 (10f,Rip,GF,Apr 9)
Iblis (IRE) 71 (8f,Lei,G,May 26)
I Can't Remember 52 (7½f,Chs,S,May 6)
Ice Age 47 (5f,Lei,G,Aug 20)
Icy Guest (USA) 36 (7f,Nwb,S,May 18)
Idrica 62 (12f,Hay,GF,Aug 8)
Iechyd-Da (IRE) 52 (10½f,Hay,S,Mar 29)
Ihtiyati (USA) 79 (10f,Don,GF,Spt 13)
Ijtinab 46 (7f,San,GF,Jly 23)
Ikatania 51 (12f,Goo,G,Jun 12)
Ikhtisar (USA) 35 (12f,Chp,GF,Jun 13)
Ile de Librate 31 (10f,Goo,G,Spt 13)
Ile Distinct (IRE) 50 (10f,Not,GF,Spt 15)
Illusion 64 (10½f,Yor,G,Aug 20)
Il Principe (IRE) 41 (16f,Cat,GF,Spt 20)
Impala 42 (8½f,Eps,S,Jly 2)
Imperial Scholar (IRE) 61 (7f,Nwm,G,Apr 15)
Imp Express (IRE) 34 (5f,Thi,GF,Aug 22)
Impish (IRE) 31 (5f,Ham,S,May 8)
Imposing Time 37 (5f,War,GF,Jly 19)
Impulsif (USA) 48 (7f,Lin,GF,Jly 12)
Impulsive Air (IRE) 56 (8f,Rip,G,Jly 7)
Imroz (USA) 70 (7f,Yor,G,Aug 21)
I'm Still Here 36 (6f,Ham,S,Apr 2)
Inchacooley (IRE) 38 (8f,Leo,GS,Aug 4)
Inchcailloch (IRE) 61 (20f,Asc,G,Jun 17)
Inclination 44 (8f,Lei,G,Aug 11)
In Command (IRE) 71 (8f,Asc,G,Jun 17)
Indian Relative 52 (6f,Lin,GF,May 31)
Indian Rocket 74 (6f,Asc,G,Jun 19)
Indian Spark 63 (6f,Sal,GF,May 4)
Indigo Dawn 34 (16f,Nwc,G,Aug 6)
Indiscreet (CAN) 45 (7f,Asc,GF,Jun 18)
Indium 45 (10f,Bat,GF,Apr 29)
Infatuation 74 (10f,Red,GF,Oct 18)
Influence Pedler 33 (14f,Not,G,Oct 30)
In Good Nick 39 (7½f,Bev,G,May 10)
Inimitable 38 (12f,Don,G,Jly 16)
In Question 43 (11f,War,GF,Jun 9)
Insatiable (IRE) 89 (8f,San,GF,May 26)
Insider Trader 45 (5f,Ham,G,Jun 11)
Interdream 47 (9f,Kem,G,Aug 20)
In The Genes 41 (10f,Lei,G,Oct 28)
In the Money (IRE) 31 (12f,Lei,GF,Mar 27)
Intiaash (IRE) 62 (5f,Bat,GF,Apr 29)
Intikhab (USA) 73 (8f,Thi,GS,May 17)
Intisab 70 (7f,San,G,May 26)
Invermark 66 (12f,Don,S,Nov 8)
Invest Wisely 38 (18f,Don,GF,Mar 21)
Invocation 30 (6f,Goo,S,Jun 20)
Irish Accord (USA) 62 (7f,Yor,G,Jly 12)
Irish Light (USA) 53 (8f,Nwm,GF,Nov 1)
Irsal 46 (14f,San,GF,Aug 14)
Irtifa 35 (7f,Kem,GF,May 31)
Isitoff 62 (11½f,Wnd,G,Aug 4)
Island Lore (IRE) 53 (7f,Nwb,GF,Apr 18)
Island Sanctuary (IRE) 49 (12f,Hay,G,Spt 21)
Isle of Man (USA) 63 (10f,Don,G,May 24)
Ismaros 54 (10f,San,GF,Jly 16)
Italian Symphony (IRE) 30 (7f,Fol,G,Oct 21)
Ithaki (IRE) 61 (12f,Cha,G,Jun 1)
Ivan Luis (FR) 68 (12f,Goo,GF,Jly 29)
Ivor's Deed 41 (6f,Cat,G,Apr 23)
Ivor's Flutter 52 (18f,Nwm,G,Oct 18)
Ivory Dawn 52 (5f,Nwm,S,Jun 27)
Ivory's Grab Hire 49 (7f,Yar,GF,Jly 22)

Jack Doyle (IRE) 36 (10f,Ayr,GF,May 30)
Jack Flush (IRE) 40 (8f,Thi,GS,May 17)
Jack The Lad (IRE) 46 (10½f,Yor,GS,Jun 14)
Jafn 56 (8f,Asc,Hy,Oct 10)
Jalb (IRE) 47 (8f,Nwc,G,May 5)
Jamaican Flight (USA) 55 (16f,Rip,GF,Aug 26)
Jameel Asmar 61 (9f,Yor,GS,Jun 14)
Jamrat Jumairah (IRE) 57 (8f,Don,G,Jly 31)
Jaseur (USA) 70 (16f,Asc,G,Spt 27)
Jaunty Jack 64 (10f,Eps,G,Jun 6)
Java Red (IRE) 39 (10f,Red,G,Nov 4)
Java Shrine (USA) 44 (8f,Chp,GF,Jly 11)
Jawah (IRE) 60 (14f,Not,G,Oct 30)
Jawhari 56 (8f,Lin,GF,Jly 10)
Jayannpee 96 (6f,Goo,G,May 20)
Jay-Owe-Two (IRE) 64 (8f,Nwm,GS,Oct 16)
Jazz King 67 (14f,Goo,GF,Jly 29)
Jazz Track (IRE) 48 (12f,Rip,GF,Aug 25)
J B Quick 33 (10f,Pon,G,Jly 8)
Jean Pierre 45 (10f,Pon,GF,Apr 16)
Jedi Knight 60 (8f,Red,GF,Oct 28)
Jeffrey Anotherred 68 (7½f,Chs,S,May 6)
Jennelle 60 (6f,Nwm,S,Jun 27)
Jibereen 50 (8f,Nwm,G,Jly 19)
Jilly Woo 31 (8½f,Eps,G,Spt 5)
Jiyush 78 (16f,Nwm,GF,Oct 4)
Johan Cruyff 61 (10f,Cur,GS,Jun 6)
Johayro 48 (7f,Red,GF,Oct 28)
John Emms (IRE) 49 (6f,Fol,GF,Apr 22)
Johnny Staccato 49 (6f,Nwb,GF,Jly 19)
John O'Dreams 33 (5f,Bat,GF,Apr 29)
Joli's Son 36 (10f,Lin,S,May 10)
Jo Maximus 49 (7f,Don,G,Jun 7)
Jo Mell 92 (7f,Asc,GF,Spt 27)
Jona Holley 44 (8f,San,GF,May 27)

Jorrocks (USA) 60 (7f,Goo,GF,Aug 1)
Jubilee Scholar (IRE) 30 (7f,Fol,GF,Jly 14)
Jucea 37 (6f,Lei,GF,Oct 5)
Jude 30 (12f,Chp,GF,Jun 13)
Judicial Supremacy 56 (8f,Goo,GS,May 21)
Juggler 41 (10f,Don,G,Oct 25)
Jukebox Jive 30 (10f,Pon,G,Jly 8)
Junikay (IRE) 38 (12f,Fol,G,Oct 21)
Jupiter (IRE) 46 (6f,Not,GF,Apr 11)
Just Alex (IRE) 32 (10f,Asc,G,Jly 25)
Just Bob 61 (5f,Nwc,GF,Oct 1)
Just Dissident (IRE) 46 (5f,Pon,GF,Jly 18)
Just Grand (IRE) 48 (12f,Chp,GF,Jly 11)
Justinianus (IRE) 46 (7f,Bri,F,Spt 28)
Just Loui 55 (6f,Lin,S,May 10)
Just Nick 61 (8f,Asc,G,Jun 17)
Just Visiting 47 (6f,Hay,G,Jly 5)
Juvenilia (IRE) 30 (7f,Yar,F,Jun 5)
Juwwi 52 (7f,Nwm,G,Apr 16)

Kadeena 41 (8f,Nwc,F,Jun 4)
Kafaf (USA) 50 (7f,Yar,G,Jly 16)
Kafil (USA) 40 (8f,War,S,Jly 4)
Kahal 85 (7f,Asc,GF,Jun 18)
Kailey Goddess (USA) 37 (7f,San,GF,Jly 30)
Kailey Senor (USA) 61 (8f,San,GS,Jly 4)
Kaiser Kache (IRE) 46 (7f,Kem,GF,May 31)
Kala Sunrise 67 (8f,Nwm,G,Oct 18)
Kaldou Star 80 (8f,Lon,GF,Oct 5)
Kaliana (IRE) 77 (12f,Yor,G,Aug 21)
Kalimat 46 (7f,Crl,F,Aug 27)
Kalimisik (FR) 54 (10½f,Lon,S,May 11)
Kalinini (USA) 38 (8f,Yar,GS,Jly 2)
Kalinka (IRE) 64 (9f,Goo,GF,Jly 30)
Kamanev (IRE) 40 (10f,Wnd,GF,Jly 14)
Kamin (USA) 54 (8f,San,GF,Spt 16)
Kammtarra (USA) 83 (8½f,Eps,G,Jun 7)
Karakia (IRE) 34 (8f,Wnd,GF,Jly 28)
Karawan 40 (7f,Sal,GF,Aug 1)
Karinska 48 (7f,Yar,GF,Aug 10)
Karisma (IRE) 44 (13f,Ham,GS,Apr 10)
Kashwan (SPA) 63 (10½f,Lon,G,Apr 20)
Kass Alhawa 52 (8f,Not,G,Oct 8)
Kassana (IRE) 57 (12½f,Lon,G,Oct 4)
Kathryn's Pet 48 (10f,Pon,GF,Apr 16)
Katie Komaite 36 (8f,Not,G,Nov 3)
Kawa-Ib (IRE) 40 (7f,Hay,G,Spt 26)
Kayf Tara 51 (10f,Asc,G,Jly 25)
Kayvee 79 (7f,Asc,GF,Spt 27)
Kaziranga (USA) 42 (10f,Rip,G,Aug 30)
Kedwick (IRE) 38 (10f,Goo,GS,Jun 20)
Keen Dancer 40 (8f,Bat,G,May 19)
Keep Battling 33 (12f,Edi,G,Jun 16)
Keepsake (IRE) 31 (16f,Not,S,Oct 8)
Kemo Sabo 60 (7f,Crl,G,Apr 25)
Kenmist 77 (8f,Asc,GF,Spt 27)
Kennemara Star (IRE) 68 (8f,Nwm,G,Jly 8)
Kentucky Fall (FR) 56 (6f,Yar,GF,Aug 21)
Kernof (IRE) 51 (12f,Edi,GF,Jly 18)
Keroub (FR) 69 (11f,Lon,G,Apr 6)
Keston Pond (IRE) 49 (7f,Nwc,GF,Mar 31)
Kewarra 70 (10f,Nwm,GF,Oct 3)
Keyboogie (USA) 44 (8f,San,G,Aug 13)
Key to My Heart (IRE) 70 (10½f,Yor,G,Jly 12)
Khafaaq 61 (7f,Hay,GS,Jly 3)
Khalik (IRE) 47 (7f,Goo,G,Jun 12)
Khassah 62 (8f,Asc,GF,Jun 18)
Khawafi 56 (10f,Goo,GF,Jun 12)
Khayali (IRE) 60 (10f,Nwm,G,Aug 2)
Khazinat El Dar (USA) 37 (8f,San,S,Aug 30)
Kid Ory 34 (7f,Thi,GF,Apr 18)
Kilcullen Lad (IRE) 55 (5f,Yar,GF,Spt 16)
Kildee Lad 52 (6f,Eps,GS,Jun 25)
Kilernan 37 (12f,Thi,G,Aug 2)
Kilma (USA) 64 (14f,Nwm,GS,Oct 17)
Kilnamartyra Girl 30 (12f,Edi,G,Jly 7)
Kilshanny 37 (10f,Goo,G,Jun 13)
Kilvine 43 (7f,San,GF,Jly 30)
Kind of Light 51 (6f,Goo,GS,Spt 13)
King Alex 89 (10f,Cur,GS,Aug 16)
King Athelstan (USA) 47 (8f,War,G,May 5)
Kingchip Boy 54 (8½f,Eps,G,Apr 23)
Kingdom Pearl 33 (12f,Edi,GS,Nov 6)
Kingfisher Mill (USA) 81 (12f,Asc,G,Spt 27)
King Kato 50 (12f,Asc,S,Jly 26)
King of Peru 78 (6f,Asc,GS,Jun 20)
King of Tunes (FR) 67 (8f,Asc,GF,Apr 30)
King Parrot (IRE) 31 (8f,Sal,F,Jly 18)
Kings Assembly 51 (10f,Chp,G,Spt 11)
Kings Harmony (IRE) 50 (7f,Bri,F,Apr 21)
King Sound 74 (12f,Asc,G,Spt 27)
King Uno 36 (7f,Red,GF,Oct 7)
Kinnescash (IRE) 54 (10½f,Hay,G,Jly 5)
Kintavi 43 (12f,Lei,G,May 26)
Kira 75 (6f,Eps,G,Jun 7)
Kirkwall 76 (9f,Cha,G,Jun 1)
Kirov Protege (IRE) 34 (12f,Bri,F,Spt 28)
Kissel 37 (7f,Cat,S,Jly 3)
Kistena (FR) 53 (5f,Lon,GF,Oct 5)
Klondike Charger (USA) 35 (10f,Red,GF,May 27)
Knave 32 (8f,Edi,S,Mar 27)
Knave's Ash (USA) 50 (7f,Nwc,G,Aug 25)
Knobbleeneeze 66 (7f,Goo,GS,May 22)
Knotty Hill 55 (6f,Lei,GS,Apr 26)
Koathary (USA) 58 (8f,Nwb,S,May 18)
Komi 74 (8f,Asc,G,Jun 17)
Komlucky 55 (7f,Thi,G,May 16)
Kool Kat Katie (IRE) 82 (10f,Nwm,GF,Oct 4)
Koraloona (IRE) 48 (11½f,Wnd,G,Aug 4)
Kota 47 (12f,Lei,F,Apr 3)
Kram 37 (5f,Yor,G,Oct 8)
Kristal Breeze 41 (12f,Fol,G,Jly 9)
Kristal Bridge 30 (10f,Wnd,GF,Jly 14)
Krosno 45 (11½f,Lin,GF,Aug 2)
Krystal Max (IRE) 31 (6f,Kem,G,May 24)
Kuala Lipis (USA) 80 (10½f,Yor,G,Aug 20)
Kulepopsie (IRE) 32 (12½f,Nwc,GF,Aug 6)
Kumait (USA) 54 (8f,Don,G,Jly 31)
Kutta 67 (12f,Nwm,G,May 2)
Kyle Rhea 56 (11½f,Chs,S,May 7)

Labeq (IRE) 49 (10f,Nwm,GF,Aug 23)
La Blue (GER) 98 (9f,Lon,GF,Oct 5)
La Brief 37 (16f,Nwc,G,Mar 25)
Lachesis 30 (6f,Rip,G,Aug 30)
La Curamalal (IRE) 37 (10f,San,GF,Apr 25)
La Dolce Vita 50 (7f,Red,F,Aug 10)
Lady Arpel (IRE) 31 (14f,Leo,G,May 28)
Lady Assassin (IRE) 30 (5f,Leo,G,Spt 13)
Lady Carla 57 (12f,Asc,G,Jun 20)
Lady Caroline Lamb (IRE) 48 (5f,Cat,GF,Aug 5)
Lady Diesis (USA) 54 (6f,Pon,S,Jun 30)
Lady of The Lake 48 (16f,Bev,GS,Aug 14)
Lady Sheriff 68 (5f,Eps,G,Aug 25)
Lago Di Varano 66 (5f,Yor,G,May 14)
Laguna Bay (IRE) 40 (10f,Goo,GF,Aug 23)
Lalindi (IRE) 44 (10f,Fol,F,Apr 10)
Lallans (IRE) 69 (14f,Goo,GF,Jly 29)
Lamarita 58 (5f,Nwm,S,Jun 27)
La Modiste 72 (8f,Nwb,GS,Spt 20)
Lamorna 43 (7f,Cat,GF,Spt 20)
La Nana (FR) 87 (10½f,Cha,S,Jun 8)
Lancashire Legend 35 (6f,Bri,F,May 23)
Landlord 33 (15f,War,GF,May 24)
La Petite Fusee 67 (6f,Lin,S,May 10)
Lapu-Lapu 45 (10f,Nwc,GF,Oct 22)
Largesse 53 (12f,Hay,G,Spt 21)
Last Chance 31 (7f,Yar,GF,Jly 28)
Last Laugh (IRE) 48 (12f,Bat,GF,Apr 29)
Last Second (IRE) 72 (10f,Goo,GF,Aug 2)
Latalomne (USA) 61 (8f,Not,GF,Apr 8)
Latvian 45 (12f,Edi,GS,Jun 23)
Laurel Delight 48 (5f,Eps,G,Jun 7)
Laurel Seeker (USA) 37 (11½f,Lin,F,Oct 3)
Lavender Della (IRE) 49 (12½f,War,G,Jun 24)
La Volta 41 (6f,Not,GF,Spt 15)
Lawahik 71 (10f,Don,G,May 24)
Law Commission 76 (8f,Goo,G,May 20)
Law Dancer (IRE) 42 (10f,San,GF,Spt 16)
Lawz (IRE) 41 (8½f,Eps,G,Spt 5)
Lay The Blame 54 (8f,Rip,GF,May 28)
Leading Note (USA) 48 (11½f,Yar,G,Jly 16)
Leading Princess (IRE) 40 (5f,Ham,S,May 4)
Lear Jet (USA) 50 (12f,Fol,GF,Aug 19)
Le Destin (FR) 85 (10½f,Lon,S,Apr 27)
Ledgendry Line 63 (12f,Don,G,May 24)
Legal Issue (IRE) 48 (7½f,Bev,GF,Jun 4)
Legendary Lover (IRE) 43 (10½f,Hay,GS,Spt 5)
Legend Maker (IRE) 40 (13½f,Dea,G,Aug 3)
Le Grand Gousier (USA) 36 (11½f,Yar,GF,Spt 16)
Leif the Lucky (USA) 48 (10f,Don,GS,Jun 29)
Lennox Lewis 31 (5f,Cat,GF,Jly 23)
Leonard Quercus (FR) 87 (20f,Lon,G,Oct 4)
Levelled 58 (6f,Kem,GF,Spt 22)
Leviticus (IRE) 41 (10f,Bev,Hy,Jly 5)
Liathach 31 (14f,Not,S,Jly 5)
Lidanna 37 (5f,Leo,G,Jun 2)
Life of Riley 53 (12f,Nwm,GS,Jun 20)
Liffre (IRE) 58 (14f,Yor,G,Aug 19)
Light Programme 60 (10f,Nwm,GF,Jly 9)
Light Reflections 40 (12f,Bat,G,May 11)
Lila Pedigo (IRE) 33 (10f,Bev,GF,Apr 5)
Lillibella 32 (5f,Pon,GF,Spt 25)
Lilli Claire 65 (8f,Goo,G,May 22)
Lil's Boy (USA) 45 (7f,Cur,G,May 3)
Lime Street Blues (IRE) 39 (8f,War,GF,May 24)
Limni (USA) 48 (8f,Nwb,S,Spt 19)
Lindrick Lady (IRE) 46 (10f,Bev,Hy,Jly 4)
Linoise (FR) 81 (5f,Dea,G,Aug 3)
Lionize (USA) 55 (8f,Lei,G,Oct 28)
Liquid Gold (IRE) 51 (8f,Don,G,Jly 16)
Listed Account (USA) 56 (6f,Nwm,GS,Jly 18)
Literary 57 (8f,Lei,S,Oct 13)
Literary Society (USA) 61 (5f,Yar,GF,Spt 16)
Little Acorn 49 (14f,San,GF,Jly 24)
Little Pilgrim 37 (7f,Fol,GF,Jly 14)
Littlestone Rocket 34 (5f,Fol,G,Jly 9)
Livius (IRE) 40 (10f,Bat,G,Jly 7)
Lochangel 85 (6f,Asc,GF,Spt 27)
Loch-Hurn Lady 34 (5f,Cat,G,Mar 26)
Loch Patrick 65 (7f,Nwb,GF,Aug 16)
Loch Style 33 (7f,Cat,G,Mar 26)
Lomberto 65 (10f,Nwb,GS,Spt 20)
London Lights 49 (11f,Kem,GF,Mar 31)
London News (SAF) 77 (10f,Asc,G,Jun 17)
London's Heart (USA) 30 (10f,Lei,F,Apr 3)
Lonely Heart 60 (10f,Goo,GF,Aug 22)
Lonely Leader (IRE) 85 (8f,Kem,G,May 5)
Longwick Lad 47 (5f,Thi,GF,May 3)
Lookingforarainbow (IRE) 54 (10f,Kem,GF,Mar 31)
Lookout 36 (10f,Don,GS,Jun 28)
Look Who's Calling (IRE) 54 (7f,Hay,GS,May 24)
Lord Advocate 45 (13f,Ham,G,Jun 11)
Lord Cromby (IRE) 85 (10f,Lon,G,Oct 4)
Lord Discord 40 (10f,Rip,GF,Aug 25)
Lord Eurolink (IRE) 65 (8f,Asc,S,Jun 21)
Lord Hastie (USA) 39 (13f,Ham,GS,Apr 10)
Lord High Admiral (CAN) 73 (5f,Sal,GS,Spt 4)
Lord Jim (IRE) 59 (16f,Asc,GF,Apr 30)
Lord Oberon (IRE) 32 (8f,Goo,G,Spt 24)
Lord of Men 71 (10f,San,GF,Jly 16)
Lord Olivier (IRE) 68 (6f,Eps,G,Apr 23)
Lord Sky 43 (5f,Ham,S,May 4)
Lorins Gold 31 (8f,War,F,Jun 4)
Lough Erne 30 (6f,Red,G,Nov 4)
Loup Sauvage (USA) 76 (10f,Nwm,G,Oct 18)
Love Has No Pride (USA) 49 (9f,Kem,G,May 5)

Love Me Do (USA) 41 (11f,Ham,GS,Jly 4)
Love Venture 32 (8f,Not,GF,Jly 30)
Loveyoumillions (IRE) 45 (10f,Don,GF,Mar 20)
Loving And Giving 49 (6f,Nwb,GF,Jly 18)
Lucayan Beach 36 (6f,Nwb,G,Oct 24)
Lucayan Prince (USA) 70 (6f,Asc,G,Jun 19)
Lucky Archer 45 (8f,War,GF,Oct 7)
Lucky Begonia (IRE) 37 (8f,Not,G,Jun 18)
Lucky Coin (USA) 93 (8f,Hpk,F,Nov 8)
Lucky Dip 42 (5f,Bat,GF,May 30)
Ludo 38 (12f,Bat,GF,Jun 14)
Lunar Mist 51 (6f,Lei,G,May 26)
Lunch Party 30 (7f,Yar,F,Spt 17)
Luso 73 (12f,Nwm,G,May 2)
Lycility (IRE) 46 (10f,Pon,GF,Spt 25)
Lynton Lad 55 (8f,Not,G,Jun 18)
Lysandros (IRE) 40 (10f,San,GF,Spt 16)

Macaribo 35 (8f,Pon,GF,Oct 6)
Macgillycuddy (IRE) 37 (5f,Sal,GS,Jun 25)
Machiavelli 38 (12f,Nwb,GF,Aug 16)
Mac Oates 32 (8f,Goo,G,Spt 24)
Madame Chinnery 50 (11½f,San,GF,May 27)
Madison Mist 31 (8f,Not,GF,Apr 11)
Madison Welcome (IRE) 46 (11f,Ham,GS,Jly 4)
Madly Sharp 68 (7f,Nwm,G,Apr 16)
Mad Militant (IRE) 51 (11½f,Wnd,GF,Aug 11)
Maftool 60 (8f,Asc,S,Jun 21)
Maftun (USA) 35 (12f,Rip,GF,Apr 9)
Magellan (USA) 83 (8f,Hpk,F,Nov 8)
Magellano (USA) 60 (12f,Lon,S,May 15)
Magical Cliche (USA) 39 (8f,Leo,YS,May 11)
Magic Combination (IRE) 50 (11½f,San,GS,Jly 4)
Magic Lahr (GER) 43 (8f,Bat,G,Aug 12)
Magic Lake 34 (6f,Not,GF,Spt 15)
Magic Mill (IRE) 63 (8f,Red,GF,Oct 28)
Maiden Castle 43 (10½f,Yor,G,May 15)
Maid of Camelot 61 (10f,Nwc,G,Aug 25)
Maiteamia 37 (5f,Nwc,GF,Mar 31)
Majal (IRE) 37 (12f,Cat,G,Jun 6)
Majesty (IRE) 52 (10f,Goo,GF,Aug 22)
Major Change 77 (10f,Eps,G,Jun 7)
Majorien 73 (12f,Hpk,F,Nov 8)
Make Ready 40 (5f,Lei,G,Aug 20)
Malabi (USA) 43 (6f,Lin,GF,Jun 14)
Maladerie (IRE) 46 (7f,Red,GF,Oct 7)
Male-Ana-Mou (IRE) 77 (12f,Eps,G,Spt 5)
Malibu Man 57 (5f,Lin,GF,Jly 10)
Mallia 60 (6f,Nwm,G,May 3)
Mamalik (USA) 76 (9f,Cha,G,Jun 1)
Manaloj (USA) 32 (10f,Nwm,G,May 3)
Manazil (IRE) 58 (10f,Nwm,GF,Jly 9)
Mandilak (USA) 58 (12f,Goo,GF,Jly 30)
Manful 63 (12f,Edi,G,Jun 16)
Mangus (IRE) 52 (5f,Chs,S,May 6)
Man Howa (IRE) 59 (6f,Hay,S,May 5)
Manikato (USA) 36 (7f,Fol,GF,Apr 22)
Manileno 40 (12f,Bri,F,May 29)
Mannenberg (IRE) 73 (10f,Lon,G,Oct 4)
Manolo (FR) 52 (5f,Pon,GF,Apr 22)
Mantles Prince 59 (12f,Asc,Hy,Oct 10)
Manuetti (IRE) 35 (10f,Eps,S,Jly 2)
Mapengo 33 (12f,Chp,G,Aug 25)
Maple Bay (IRE) 39 (8f,Nwc,GF,Oct 1)
Maradata (IRE) 38 (10½f,Hay,GF,Aug 15)
Maradi (IRE) 42 (10f,Lin,GF,May 31)
Maralinga (IRE) 60 (10½f,Chs,GF,Jly 11)
Mara River 62 (9f,Goo,GF,Jly 30)
Marathon (USA) 79 (8f,Lon,GF,Oct 5)
Marathon Maid 49 (14f,Yor,G,Aug 19)
March Crusader 66 (6f,Goo,GS,Spt 13)
Marchman 36 (10f,Bri,F,Jun 3)
March Star (IRE) 45 (6f,Yar,F,Spt 17)
Mardi Gras (IRE) 40 (10½f,Hay,S,Mar 29)
Mardrew 49 (10f,Nwm,GF,Spt 30)
Marengo 51 (6f,Eps,GS,Jun 25)
Marie Dora (FR) 49 (8f,Kem,G,May 24)
Marilaya (IRE) 55 (10f,Nwm,GF,Jly 9)
Marino Street 46 (5f,Crl,F,Jun 12)
Marjaana (IRE) 66 (7½f,Bev,GS,Aug 13)
Marjorie Rose (IRE) 40 (5f,Ham,S,Jly 1)
Marl 57 (6f,Goo,GS,May 21)
Maroulla (IRE) 32 (9f,Kem,GF,May 31)
Maroussie (FR) 46 (13½f,Dea,G,Aug 3)
Marozia (USA) 38 (8f,Yar,G,Oct 22)
Marsad (IRE) 41 (6f,Wnd,S,May 12)
Marsayas (IRE) 38 (16f,Cat,GF,May 31)
Marsh Marigold 36 (12f,Cat,GF,Jly 16)
Marsul (USA) 50 (12f,Hay,G,Spt 26)
Mary Cornwallis 55 (6f,Nwm,GF,Aug 9)
Marylebone (IRE) 46 (5f,Bev,GF,Apr 11)
Mary Magdalene 55 (6f,Hay,G,Spt 21)
Masharik (IRE) 55 (12f,Yor,G,Aug 21)
Mashhaer (USA) 48 (7f,Goo,GF,Aug 2)
Massyar Seventeen 37 (8f,San,GF,Jly 30)
Master Beveled 65 (8f,Nwb,S,May 18)
Master Boots 64 (7f,Nwm,GF,Jly 10)
Master Charter 50 (8f,Nwc,G,Jun 27)
Master Foley 33 (6f,Not,GF,Apr 11)
Master M-E-N (IRE) 50 (8½f,Eps,G,Apr 23)
Master Millfield (IRE) 38 (11f,War,F,May 5)
Master of Passion 50 (5f,Lin,S,Jun 28)
Masterpiece 40 (6f,Nwm,GF,Apr 17)
Master Planner 53 (6f,Nwm,G,May 3)
Matoaka 43 (7f,Eps,G,Spt 5)
Matthias Mystique 37 (16½f,Fol,GF,Jun 4)
Mattimeo (IRE) 78 (10f,Nwm,GF,Spt 30)
Mawared (IRE) 68 (18f,Nwm,G,Oct 18)
Mawingo (IRE) 63 (8f,Rip,GF,Aug 25)
Mayflower 32 (8f,Lei,S,Oct 13)
May King Mayhem 35 (15f,War,GF,Jly 12)
Maylane 75 (10f,Nwm,GF,Jly 9)
Maypole (IRE) 43 (7f,Hay,G,Spt 26)
May Queen Megan 48 (8f,War,GF,Oct 7)
Mazeed (IRE) 37 (7f,Bri,F,Spt 28)
Mazilla 32 (11f,War,GF,Jun 9)
Mazurek 55 (14f,San,GF,Jly 16)
Mbulwa 41 (8f,Thi,GF,Aug 11)
Mcgillycuddy Reeks (IRE) 57 (10f,Rip,G,Aug 30)
Medaaly 52 (10½f,Yor,G,May 14)
Medaille Militaire 71 (10f,Goo,G,May 22)
Media Star (USA) 70 (14f,Goo,GF,Jly 29)
Medieval Lady 51 (9f,Nwm,G,May 2)
Meg's Memory (IRE) 37 (12f,Chp,GF,Jly 11)
Meilleur (IRE) 42 (12f,Bat,G,Spt 8)
Meliksah (IRE) 67 (5f,Nwm,G,Jly 19)
Mellors (IRE) 30 (6f,Bri,F,Apr 11)
Melodica 43 (14f,San,GF,Jly 24)
Mels Baby (IRE) 65 (10f,Don,GF,Mar 20)
Memorise (USA) 68 (12f,Don,GF,Spt 12)
Mengaab (USA) 62 (12f,Goo,GF,Aug 22)
Mentalasanythin 57 (11f,Ham,,Aug 2)
Meranti 46 (6f,Not,GF,Apr 8)
Merciless Cop 48 (9f,San,GS,Aug 29)
Merit (IRE) 53 (16½f,Don,S,Nov 8)
Merrily 34 (6f,Cat,G,Apr 23)
Mersey Beat 65 (10f,Nwm,GF,Jly 9)
Meshhed (USA) 69 (7f,Nwb,GF,Aug 16)
Messina (IRE) 43 (10f,San,GF,Spt 16)
Meteor Strike (USA) 52 (10f,Don,GF,Spt 10)
Mezzoramio 42 (7f,Yar,F,Spt 17)
Middle East 49 (6f,Not,S,Oct 15)
Midnight Escape 79 (5f,Hay,GF,Aug 9)
Midnight Shift (IRE) 54 (6f,Lei,G,Oct 27)
Midnight Watch (USA) 44 (8f,Lei,G,Oct 28)
Midyan Blue (IRE) 57 (12f,Hay,S,Mar 29)
Midyan Call 70 (8f,Nwm,GF,Oct 3)
Midyan Queen 41 (7f,Crl,F,Aug 27)
Mighty Phantom (USA) 51 (11½f,Wnd,G,Aug 4)
Migwar 47 (10f,Nwb,GS,Spt 20)
Mihriz (IRE) 44 (9f,Nwm,GF,Oct 4)
Mijas 37 (5f,Lin,G,May 9)
Mike's Double (IRE) 47 (7f,Nwm,G,Aug 22)
Mile High 63 (5f,Not,GF,Mar 31)
Miletrian Refurb (IRE) 36 (5f,Fol,G,Mar 26)
Military (USA) 60 (10f,Nwm,G,Aug 2)
Mill End Boy 34 (5f,Bev,GF,Jun 5)
Millesime (IRE) 42 (6f,Cat,G,Apr 23)
Millroy (USA) 39 (8f,Don,GF,Mar 22)
Milly of The Vally 54 (14f,Goo,GF,Aug 2)
Miltonfield 68 (20f,Asc,G,Jun 17)
Mimosa 47 (8f,Asc,GF,Apr 30)
Mind Games 68 (5f,Yor,G,Aug 21)
Mindrace 51 (5f,Wnd,GF,Jly 14)
Minersville (USA) 34 (9f,Ayr,G,Jun 20)
Mingling Glances (USA) 42 (10f,Cur,GS,Jun 6)
Ministerial Model (IRE) 40 (7f,Cur,GS,Jun 28)
Miracle Kid (USA) 43 (10f,Don,GF,Mar 20)
Mislemani (IRE) 41 (8f,Bat,G,Jun 28)
Missfortuna 43 (11f,Kem,GF,Spt 22)
Missile Toe (IRE) 32 (8f,San,GF,Jun 14)
Miss Riviera 63 (8f,Goo,G,May 22)
Miss Riviera Rose 36 (10f,Pon,GF,Apr 22)
Miss Sancerre 61 (7f,Nwm,G,Apr 15)
Mister Aspecto (IRE) 45 (12f,Bev,G,Jly 29)
Mister Jolson 66 (6f,Fol,G,Oct 21)
Mister Pink 54 (10f,Nwm,GF,Apr 17)
Mister Raider 33 (5f,Wnd,GF,Aug 18)
Mister Westsound 34 (6f,Ham,G,Aug 13)
Misty Point 42 (8f,Kem,G,May 24)
Misty Rain 43 (10f,Rip,GF,Aug 25)
Mithak (USA) 66 (14f,Nwm,GS,Oct 17)
Mithali 80 (10f,Don,GF,Spt 10)
Mo-Addab (IRE) 63 (8f,Don,GS,Jun 29)
Mohaajir (USA) 57 (14f,Leo,GS,Aug 4)
Mohawk River (IRE) 75 (10f,Nwm,G,Aug 2)
Monaassib 99 (6f,Asc,GF,Spt 27)
Monaco (IRE) 45 (7f,Goo,G,Jun 12)
Monaco Gold (IRE) 51 (12f,Ham,S,Jun 25)
Monarch's Pursuit 30 (12f,Edi,G,Aug 28)
Mon Bruce 51 (5f,Nwc,GF,Oct 22)
Mongol Warrior (USA) 74 (15½f,Lon,S,May 18)
Monis (IRE) 30 (10f,Not,GF,Jun 9)
Monitor 54 (10f,Rip,GF,Aug 4)
Mono Lady (IRE) 61 (12f,Bri,GF,Spt 3)
Mons 73 (12f,Nwm,G,May 2)
Monte Cavo 46 (10f,Nwm,G,Aug 1)
Montecristo 61 (14f,Not,G,Nov 3)
Montendre 64 (6f,Bat,G,Spt 8)
Montfort (USA) 65 (12f,Yor,GS,Jun 13)
Montone (IRE) 36 (8f,War,GF,May 24)
Montrestar 42 (5f,Nwm,GF,Aug 23)
Monument 50 (10f,Chp,G,Spt 11)
Monza (USA) 73 (10½f,Yor,G,May 14)
Moonax (IRE) 55 (20f,Asc,G,Jun 19)
Moon Blast 65 (12f,Eps,G,Spt 5)
Moon Colony 59 (14f,Not,S,Oct 15)
Moon Fairy 37 (7f,Yar,F,Jun 11)
Moonlight Paradise (USA) 54 (8f,Asc,GF,Jun 18)
Moonshine Girl (USA) 59 (7f,Eps,G,Jun 7)
Moonshiner (USA) 58 (7f,Hay,G,Spt 26)
Moon Song 30 (7f,Yar,F,Jun 5)
Moon Strike (FR) 74 (5f,Hay,GF,Aug 9)
Moran 32 (10f,Wnd,GF,Jly 14)
Morocco (IRE) 48 (7f,Sal,GF,Jun 11)
Mosconi (IRE) 32 (7f,Cur,G,Apr 12)
Moscow Mist (IRE) 60 (8f,Red,GF,Oct 28)
Most Respectful 32 (7f,Crl,G,Apr 25)
Motet 57 (18f,Yar,F,Spt 18)
Mouche 55 (6f,Nwc,GF,Oct 22)
Mountaineer (IRE) 32 (14f,Not,GF,Oct 4)
Mountgate 55 (7f,Nwm,G,May 16)
Mount Genius (USA) 36 (8f,Thi,F,Jun 2)
Mount Holly (USA) 64 (8f,Don,GS,Nov 8)
Mousehole 59 (5f,Rip,G,Jun 19)
Mousse Glacee (FR) 91 (10½f,Cha,S,Jun 8)
Move Smartly (IRE) 40 (7f,Red,F,May 1)
Move With Edes 37 (7f,Crl,G,Jly 5)

Moving Arrow 66 (8f,Hay,GF,Jun 7)
Moving Out 36 (16f,Not,GF,Spt 15)
Mowelga 32 (10f,Nwb,G,Oct 24)
Mowjood (USA) 36 (10f,Not,GF,Aug 6)
Mowlaie 42 (10½f,Hay,GF,Jun 6)
Mozambique (IRE) 43 (7f,Kem,G,Spt 21)
Mr Bergerac (IRE) 76 (6f,Ayr,G,Spt 20)
Mr Bombastique (IRE) 51 (10½f,Yor,G,May 13)
Mr Browning (USA) 56 (12f,Bri,F,Jun 3)
Mr Cube (IRE) 42 (8f,War,GF,May 24)
Mr Fortywinks (IRE) 39 (11f,Ayr,GS,Spt 18)
Mr Frosty 51 (6f,Lin,S,May 10)
Mr Lightfoot (IRE) 64 (9f,Cur,S,Spt 21)
Mr Majica 46 (6f,Bat,G,Spt 8)
Mr Paradise (IRE) 55 (8f,San,GF,Spt 16)
Mr Rough 43 (8f,Nwb,G,Jun 12)
Mrs Miniver (USA) 68 (10f,Nwm,GF,Oct 4)
Mr Speaker (IRE) 42 (7f,Chp,G,Spt 11)
Mr Sponge (USA) 62 (8f,Nwb,GS,Spt 20)
Mr Teigh 55 (7f,Nwm,GF,Oct 4)
Mr Wild (USA) 59 (12f,Kem,G,May 5)
Muara Bay 34 (10f,Bri,F,Oct 1)
Mubariz (IRE) 36 (7f,Lei,GF,Mar 27)
Muchea 93 (6f,Asc,GF,Spt 27)
Muhandam (IRE) 51 (6f,Don,GS,Jun 28)
Muhassil (IRE) 42 (10f,Pon,GF,Spt 25)
Muhtafel 49 (8f,Not,GF,Jly 19)
Mujova (IRE) 57 (7f,Hay,G,Spt 27)
Mukaddar (USA) 60 (8f,San,GS,Jly 5)
Mukhatab 46 (9f,Red,GF,Oct 7)
Mukhlles (USA) 57 (8f,Bat,G,Aug 12)
Mullagh Hill Lad (IRE) 42 (6f,Bat,G,Jun 28)
Mullitover 53 (7f,Nwm,G,May 16)
Multicoloured (IRE) 64 (12f,Don,GF,Spt 12)
Multi Franchise 34 (7f,Bri,F,Jly 15)
Mumaris (USA) 37 (8f,Not,GF,Apr 8)
Mungo Park 56 (5f,Nwc,GF,Oct 22)
Municipal Girl (IRE) 30 (6f,Cat,GF,May 30)
Murchan Tyne (IRE) 32 (13f,Bat,G,Spt 8)
Murphy's Gold (IRE) 43 (8f,War,GF,May 24)
Murron Wallace 33 (8f,Bat,G,Spt 8)
Musalsal (IRE) 77 (10½f,Yor,G,May 14)
Muscadel 53 (12½f,Lon,G,Oct 4)
Muscatana 35 (7f,Red,GF,Oct 7)
Musharak 57 (7f,Kem,G,Spt 21)
Musical Dancer (USA) 56 (10f,Nwm,G,May 2)
Musical Pursuit 62 (8f,Nwb,GS,Spt 20)
Music Gold (IRE) 73 (5f,Nwm,G,Jly 19)
Musick House (IRE) 65 (8f,Yor,G,May 14)
Mutabari (USA) 40 (8f,Not,G,Oct 30)
Mutadarra (IRE) 59 (10f,Nwm,GF,Spt 30)
Mutahadeth 30 (8f,Nwm,GF,Aug 9)
Mutasawwar 44 (6f,Sal,GF,May 4)
My Abbey 40 (5f,Hay,G,Jly 4)
My Beloved (IRE) 38 (8f,Nwm,GS,Jly 18)
My Best Valentine 85 (6f,Asc,GF,Spt 27)
Mybotye 53 (7f,Chp,G,Spt 11)
My Branch 61 (7f,Nwm,S,Jun 28)
My Emma 85 (12f,Lon,GF,Oct 5)
My Godson 37 (7½f,Bev,GF,Jly 21)
My Handsome Prince 41 (8f,Rip,GF,Jly 19)
My Learned Friend 61 (13f,Nwb,GF,Jly 19)
My Lewicia (IRE) 66 (10f,Nwc,GF,Aug 3)
My Melody Parkes 72 (6f,Nwm,G,Apr 15)
Myrmidon 51 (5f,Asc,S,Jun 21)
Myrtlebank 54 (12f,Eps,G,Spt 5)
Myrtle Quest 66 (8f,Kem,GF,Spt 22)
Mystical 48 (6f,Lei,GF,Spt 22)
Mystic Quest (IRE) 35 (12f,Lei,GF,May 27)
Mystic Ridge 41 (8f,Nwb,GF,Apr 19)
Mystique Air (IRE) 40 (7f,Yor,S,Spt 4)
Myttons Mistake 66 (8f,Lei,G,Oct 27)
My Valentina 54 (10f,Nwb,GF,Spt 18)

Nabhaan (IRE) 85 (12f,Nwm,G,May 4)
Naissant 44 (6f,Not,GF,Spt 15)
Naivasha 33 (8f,Edi,G,Jly 7)
Najm Mubeen (IRE) 80 (10f,Nwm,G,May 3)
Nambucca 41 (10f,Don,GF,Mar 21)
Naninja (USA) 78 (8f,Hpk,F,Nov 8)
Nanton Point (USA) 62 (20f,Asc,G,Jun 17)
Nant Y Gamer (FR) 46 (7f,Nwm,G,Aug 22)
Napier Star 30 (5f,Wnd,GF,Jly 14)
Napoleon Star (IRE) 38 (6f,Cat,G,Jun 6)
Napoli Express (FR) 58 (11f,Lon,G,Apr 6)
Natalia Bay (IRE) 61 (8f,Kem,G,May 24)
Native Rhythm (IRE) 31 (7f,Chp,G,Spt 11)
Natural Eight (IRE) 49 (10f,Nwm,G,Apr 15)
Natural Key 60 (7f,Lin,F,Apr 4)
Nature Dancer 36 (10f,Rip,GF,Aug 4)
Naughty Pistol (USA) 46 (7f,Thi,GF,Apr 18)
Naval Games 50 (12f,Nwm,GF,Oct 2)
Nawasib (IRE) 38 (10f,Goo,GS,Jun 27)
Ned's Bonanza 36 (5f,Crl,F,May 29)
Needle Gun (IRE) 55 (10f,San,GS,Apr 26)
Needle Match 58 (7f,Crl,F,Aug 27)
Needwood Epic 33 (12f,Bev,G,Aug 23)
Nellie North 38 (5f,Wnd,GF,Jly 14)
Neronian (IRE) 40 (9f,Ayr,G,Jun 20)
Nervous Rex 39 (6f,Lei,GF,Spt 22)
Neuwest (USA) 70 (7f,Nwm,GF,Aug 9)
Never Think Twice 52 (6f,Wnd,GS,Jun 30)
Newbridge Boy 35 (10f,Red,G,Nov 4)
New Century (USA) 62 (7f,Nwm,G,Apr 16)
New Frontier (IRE) 68 (15f,Lon,G,Oct 4)
New Inn 36 (12f,Asc,Hy,Oct 10)
Newlands Corner 50 (6f,Lei,G,Jun 14)
Newport Knight 54 (12f,Eps,G,Apr 23)
Nichol Fifty 44 (12f,Chs,GF,Jly 11)
Nicker 33 (6f,Bri,F,Jly 16)
Nick of Time 37 (15½f,Fol,S,Jly 2)
Nicola's Princess 35 (12f,Chs,GF,Jly 11)
Nifty Norman 62 (5f,Bev,Hy,May 11)
Nigel's Lad (IRE) 73 (16f,Rip,GF,May 28)
Nightbird (IRE) 76 (7f,Asc,GF,Jun 18)
Night Chorus 50 (8f,Not,G,Apr 29)
Night City 61 (11f,Ayr,G,Spt 20)
Night Dance 67 (7½f,Bev,GF,Apr 11)
Night Express 40 (5f,Rip,GF,Aug 16)
Night Flight 49 (6f,Nwc,F,Jun 4)
Night Harmony (IRE) 42 (6f,Bat,GS,May 19)
Nightingale Song 42 (6f,Bat,G,Spt 8)
Nightlark (IRE) 53 (10f,Nwb,GF,Spt 18)
Night Mirage (USA) 48 (10½f,Hay,GS,Spt 5)
Night of Glass 53 (7f,Cat,S,Oct 17)
Night Watch (USA) 64 (10f,San,GS,Jly 5)
Night Wink (USA) 51 (10f,Bri,GF,Aug 27)
Nigrasine 75 (6f,Hay,G,Jly 5)
Nile Valley (IRE) 33 (17f,Bat,GF,May 30)
Nineacres 58 (6f,Hay,S,May 5)
Ninth Symphony 35 (8f,Rip,GF,May 28)
Nkapen Rocks (SPA) 48 (8f,Rip,G,Jly 7)
Nobalino 52 (5f,Red,G,Nov 4)
Nobby Barnes 34 (9f,Yor,S,Spt 3)
Nobel Lad 40 (8½f,Bev,GF,Apr 24)
Nobility (IRE) 45 (8f,Cur,GS,Aug 16)
Noble Dane (IRE) 47 (10f,Nwb,GF,Spt 18)
Noble Hero 31 (12f,Bri,F,May 29)
No Cliches 59 (8f,Pon,GF,Jly 18)
Noeprob (USA) 48 (8f,Bat,G,May 19)
No Extras (IRE) 71 (6f,Goo,GS,Spt 13)
No Grousing (IRE) 37 (8f,Rip,G,Jun 18)
Noisette 78 (8f,Asc,GF,Spt 27)
Nominator Lad 49 (7f,Hay,G,Spt 27)
Nomore Mr Niceguy 69 (8f,Asc,G,Jun 17)
No More Pressure (IRE) 55 (8f,Nwm,GS,Oct 16)
Nononito (FR) 78 (15½f,Lon,S,May 18)
Non Vintage (IRE) 32 (12f,Nwm,G,Jun 7)
Nopalea 47 (5f,Edi,G,Jun 16)
Nordansk 44 (16f,Goo,GF,Spt 25)
Nordic Breeze (IRE) 54 (8f,Chp,GS,Jly 1)
Nordic Crest (IRE) 45 (12f,Pon,GF,Jun 3)
Nordinex (IRE) 39 (7f,San,GF,Spt 16)
Nor-Do-I 48 (7f,Hay,G,Spt 27)
Norman Conquest (USA) 39 (10f,Goo,G,Spt 13)
Nornax Lad (USA) 30 (13f,Bat,G,Jly 7)
Northern Angel (IRE) 53 (8f,Lin,GF,Jly 10)
Northern Blessing 52 (8f,Not,GF,Spt 23)
Northern Drums 60 (12f,Don,GF,Mar 22)
Northern Fan (IRE) 42 (7f,Lei,GF,Mar 27)
Northern Flash 40 (8f,Nwc,Hy,Jun 28)
Northern Fleet 53 (20f,Asc,G,Jun 17)
Northern Judge 34 (6f,War,F,May 5)
Northern Motto 43 (12f,Don,GF,Jun 7)
Northern Sun 54 (9f,Kem,G,Mar 29)
Northern Touch 32 (12f,Bev,G,Jly 29)
North Reef (IRE) 49 (10f,Lei,GS,Oct 14)
Nosey Native 49 (11f,Ham,GS,Jly 4)
No Slouch (IRE) 50 (9f,Cur,S,Spt 21)
Not Forgotten (USA) 45 (12f,Nwm,G,Apr 15)
Nothing Doing (IRE) 36 (11½f,Wnd,GF,Jly 21)
Nothin' Leica Dane (AUS) 74 (12f,Lon,GF,Oct 5)
Noufari (FR) 51 (14f,Hay,GF,Aug 9)
Nwaamis (USA) 78 (8f,Asc,G,Jun 17)

Oatey 40 (6f,Don,G,Jun 7)
Obelos (USA) 46 (10f,Lei,GF,Spt 9)
Oberons Boy (IRE) 37 (12f,Edi,GF,Jly 18)
Oberon's Dart (IRE) 39 (6f,Yar,GS,Jly 3)
Occam (IRE) 37 (8f,Not,GF,Spt 23)
Occupandiste (IRE) 96 (7f,Lon,,Jun 22)
Ocean Park 48 (11f,War,GF,Apr 12)
Ocean Ridge (USA) 73 (8f,Dea,G,Aug 3)
Ochos Rios (IRE) 49 (7f,Don,G,May 6)
Ocker (IRE) 42 (7f,Lei,GS,Oct 14)
Octavia Hill 43 (7f,Bri,F,Jly 15)
Off The Rails 33 (12f,Fol,F,Spt 26)
Oggi 76 (6f,Asc,GS,Jun 20)
Oh Nellie (USA) 72 (7f,Nwm,G,Apr 15)
Ohnonotagain 35 (6f,Cat,GF,May 31)
Old Rouvel (USA) 64 (16f,Nwm,GF,Oct 4)
Olivo (IRE) 45 (7f,Goo,G,Jun 12)
Olympic Majesty (FR) 55 (10f,Cur,GS,Jun 6)
Omaha City (IRE) 77 (7f,Asc,GF,Spt 27)
Once More for Luck (IRE) 40 (12f,Nwm,GF,Oct 2)
One For Baileys 51 (15f,Nwm,GF,Jly 10)
Onefourseven 58 (20f,Goo,GF,Jly 30)
Oneknight With You 32 (7f,War,F,May 5)
One Life To Live (IRE) 43 (9f,Ham,GS,Jun 18)
One So Wonderful 82 (10f,Nwm,GF,Oct 4)
On Fair Stage (IRE) 50 (12f,Leo,G,Jly 19)
On The Green 31 (7f,Yar,GF,Jly 28)
Oops Pettie 72 (10f,Don,G,Nov 7)
Opalette 56 (10f,Pon,G,May 23)
Opaque 60 (14f,Yor,S,Spt 3)
Open Affair 48 (12f,Bri,F,May 29)
Open Credit 48 (6f,Ham,G,Spt 29)
Opening Range 31 (6f,Yar,F,Spt 18)
Opera Buff (IRE) 62 (12f,Bri,GF,Oct 23)
Ops Smile (USA) 83 (12f,Hpk,F,Nov 8)
Opulent 43 (10f,Nwc,G,Jun 27)
Orange Grouse (IRE) 47 (7f,Cur,GS,Jun 28)
Orange Place (IRE) 70 (8f,Goo,GS,May 21)
Orchestra Stall 70 (16f,Asc,GF,Apr 30)
Ordained 51 (12f,Nwm,GF,Oct 31)
Orford Ness (FR) 60 (8f,Cha,G,Jun 1)
Oriane 30 (8f,Cur,S,Spt 7)
Oriel Lad 31 (7½f,Bev,GF,Jun 4)
Oriole 43 (7f,Red,F,Aug 10)
Orontes (USA) 47 (7f,San,G,May 26)
Orsay 64 (8f,Nwm,GF,May 31)
Ortelius 33 (8f,Goo,GS,May 21)
Oscar (IRE) 73 (12f,Cha,G,Jun 1)
Oscar Schindler (IRE) 98 (12f,Lon,GF,Oct 5)
Osomental 40 (5f,Yor,GS,Jun 13)
Otaiti (IRE) 52 (13½f,Dea,G,Aug 3)
Our People 53 (9f,Lin,S,May 10)
Our Way 40 (9f,San,GF,Jun 14)
Out Line 50 (6f,Lin,GF,Jly 11)
Out of Sight (IRE) 54 (8f,Yor,G,May 15)
Out on a Promise (IRE) 46 (12f,Crl,G,Jly 5)
Outset (IRE) 47 (14f,Red,GF,Oct 18)

Out West (USA) 54 (8f,Goo,G,May 22)
Over To You (USA) 61 (10f,Nwm,G,May 2)
Oxbane 39 (6f,Yar,F,Spt 18)

Padauk 42 (15½f,Fol,F,Spt 26)
Paddy Lad (IRE) 50 (6f,Sal,GF,May 4)
Paddy's Rice 42 (8f,Bri,F,May 29)
Pageboy 37 (6f,Not,GF,Jly 30)
Paint It Black 38 (8f,Thi,F,Jun 2)
Palacegate Jack (IRE) 56 (5f,Edi,GF,Jly 18)
Palacegate Touch 58 (5f,Cat,S,Oct 17)
Palacoona (GER) 45 (9f,Lon,S,Apr 27)
Palaemon 42 (16f,Goo,GF,Spt 25)
Palamon (USA) 61 (12f,Eps,G,Apr 23)
Palatial Style 68 (10f,Don,GF,Spt 10)
Paldost 30 (6f,Ham,GF,Jly 11)
Palio Sky 57 (12f,Goo,GF,Jly 29)
Palisade (USA) 36 (6f,Yar,F,Spt 17)
Pallium (IRE) 37 (5f,Ayr,S,Oct 14)
Palme D'Or (IRE) 81 (10½f,Cha,S,Jun 8)
Palo Blanco 56 (7f,Goo,GS,Jun 20)
Panama City (USA) 78 (9f,Nwm,GF,Apr 17)
Panther (IRE) 47 (5f,Hay,G,Jly 4)
Papering (IRE) 84 (10½f,Yor,G,May 14)
Papita (IRE) 35 (6f,Nwm,GF,Apr 17)
Papua 65 (12f,Nwm,GS,Oct 16)
Paradise Navy 61 (14f,Yar,GF,Aug 21)
Pardan 34 (6f,Cat,G,Spt 27)
Paris Babe 47 (6f,Eps,GS,Jly 9)
Party Romance (USA) 72 (10f,Don,GF,Spt 10)
Pas De Reponse (USA) 63 (8f,Nwm,G,May 4)
Passage Creeping (IRE) 42 (10f,Lin,GF,Jun 14)
Passi d'Orlando (IRE) 72 (10f,Don,G,May 24)
Passiflora 37 (7f,San,G,May 26)
Passing Strangers (USA) 52 (10f,Pon,GS,Oct 20)
Passionatti 50 (5f,Cat,S,Oct 17)
Passion For Life 53 (6f,Don,GF,Mar 22)
Pasternak 79 (9f,Nwm,GF,Oct 4)
Pater Noster (USA) 66 (8f,San,GF,Apr 25)
Patina 31 (6f,Lei,G,Jun 14)
Patriot Games (IRE) 53 (10f,San,S,Aug 30)
Patsy Grimes 77 (5f,Hay,G,Spt 27)
Pay Homage 55 (12f,Chp,GF,Aug 3)
Pearl Dawn (IRE) 39 (5f,Lin,G,May 17)
Peartree House (IRE) 75 (7f,Asc,GF,Jun 18)
Pegasus Bay 39 (8f,Bat,G,Aug 12)
Peintre Celebre (USA) 100 (12f,Lon,GF,Oct 5)
Pekay 56 (10f,Red,GF,Oct 18)
Pelham (IRE) 66 (8f,Nwm,GF,Apr 17)
Pendolino (IRE) 36 (10f,Pon,GF,Apr 16)
Pengamon 54 (7f,Nwm,G,Apr 16)
Penlop 48 (8f,Lei,S,Oct 13)
Pennys From Heaven 51 (11½f,Wnd,S,May 19)
Pennywell 42 (8f,Not,G,Apr 29)
Pension Fund 47 (12f,Yor,G,Aug 21)
Pentad (USA) 70 (15f,Lon,G,Oct 4)
Peppers (IRE) 51 (12f,Bat,F,Jly 23)
Peppiatt 60 (7f,Lin,GF,Jly 12)
Percy Isle (IRE) 58 (14f,San,GF,Jly 16)
Perfect Brave 43 (5f,Hay,G,Jly 4)
Perfect Pal (IRE) 58 (7f,San,GF,Jly 30)
Perfect Paradigm (IRE) 54 (12f,Chs,S,May 7)
Perfect Poppy 41 (7f,Nwm,G,May 16)
Pericles 59 (8f,Red,F,Aug 23)
Perilous Plight 43 (7f,Fol,G,Mar 26)
Perryston View 81 (6f,Ayr,G,Spt 20)
Persevere 39 (6f,Bat,G,Spt 8)
Persian Blue 40 (12f,Sal,GF,Aug 13)
Persian Butterfly 33 (11½f,Wnd,GF,Jun 9)
Persian Fayre 63 (8f,Nwm,GF,Nov 1)
Persian Punch (IRE) 94 (20f,Lon,G,Oct 4)
Peter Perfect 30 (7f,San,GF,Jly 30)
Petite Danseuse 45 (6f,Lei,GF,Spt 22)
Petoskin 46 (12f,Bri,F,Apr 21)
Petraco (IRE) 45 (5f,War,GF,Mar 31)
Pharaoh's Joy 45 (5f,Lin,GF,May 24)
Philanthrop (FR) 77 (15½f,Lon,S,May 18)
Philistar 66 (8½f,Eps,G,Jun 6)
Philmist 49 (11f,Ayr,GS,Spt 18)
Phonetic 66 (8f,Nwb,S,May 18)
Phylida 33 (8f,Nwm,GS,Jly 18)
Pickens (USA) 39 (10f,Don,G,Oct 25)
Pietro Bembo (IRE) 49 (12f,Nwm,G,Aug 2)
Pike Creek (USA) 65 (15f,Nwm,GS,Jun 11)
Pilsudski (IRE) 101 (12f,Lon,GF,Oct 5)
Pinchincha (FR) 57 (10f,Pon,GF,Spt 25)
Pine Ridge Lad (IRE) 36 (8f,Ham,G,Spt 29)
Pinfloron (USA) 79 (8f,Hpk,F,Nov 8)
Piquant 36 (7f,Don,G,May 24)
Pistol (IRE) 54 (12f,Fol,F,Spt 26)
Pizzicato 43 (5f,Bri,F,Jly 16)
Plaisir d'Amour (IRE) 70 (6f,Yor,G,Aug 19)
Plan For Profit (IRE) 58 (9f,Goo,GF,Jly 31)
Plaza De Toros (USA) 47 (10f,Leo,YS,May 11)
Pleading 57 (7f,Lin,G,Spt 9)
Pleasureland (IRE) 47 (20f,Asc,G,Jun 17)
Pleasure Time 56 (5f,Lei,G,Aug 20)
Pleasure Trick (USA) 35 (8f,Pon,GF,Jly 18)
Plum First 43 (6f,Pon,GS,Spt 2)
Poddington 46 (10f,Don,GF,Jun 7)
Pointelle 36 (7f,Kem,GF,May 31)
Pointer 48 (5f,Chp,G,Spt 11)
Poker-B (IRE) 38 (5f,Leo,G,Spt 13)
Poker School (IRE) 33 (10f,San,S,Aug 30)
Polar Champ 58 (10½f,Hay,GF,Aug 8)
Polar Eclipse 39 (7f,Nwm,GF,Nov 1)
Polar Flight 59 (10½f,Yor,G,May 13)
Polarize 30 (8f,Thi,G,Jly 25)
Polar Prince (IRE) 101 (8½f,Eps,G,Jun 7)
Polar Prospect 53 (10f,Nwm,GF,Spt 30)
Polenista 43 (10f,Goo,GF,Jun 12)
Polenka (IRE) 39 (7f,Cat,GF,Spt 20)
Polish Rhythm (IRE) 57 (8f,Kem,GF,Spt 22)
Polish Romance (USA) 55 (6f,Nwm,GS,Jly 18)
Polish Warrior (IRE) 55 (5f,Asc,S,Jun 21)
Polly Golightly 54 (5f,Cat,S,Oct 17)
Polly Peculiar 36 (8f,War,GF,May 24)
Polonaise Prince (USA) 36 (12f,Bat,G,Spt 8)
Polska Princess (GER) 34 (10f,Chp,GS,Jly 1)
Poltarf (USA) 40 (14f,Hay,G,Spt 26)
Polyphony (USA) 40 (15f,Nwm,GS,Jun 11)
Pomona 71 (8f,Wnd,G,Aug 23)
Portite Sophie 37 (10f,Bev,GF,Apr 24)
Portuguese Lil 43 (8½f,Bev,GF,Jun 5)
Poseidon 69 (12f,Goo,GF,Jly 29)
Posidonas 92 (12f,Lon,GF,Oct 5)
Poteen (USA) 88 (8f,Nwm,G,May 3)
Power Game 47 (8f,Edi,GF,May 31)
Pradesh 39 (10f,Nwm,GF,Jly 9)
Praeditus 39 (7f,Lin,GF,Jly 12)
Prairie Falcon (IRE) 60 (12f,Asc,G,Jun 19)
Prairie Minstrel (USA) 32 (8f,Bat,G,Aug 12)
Predappio 98 (12f,Lon,GF,Oct 5)
Premier 34 (8f,Lei,GF,Oct 5)
Premier Bay 71 (10½f,Yor,GS,Jun 14)
Premier Dance 35 (12f,Fol,S,Jun 27)
Premier Generation (IRE) 53 (10f,Lei,GS,Apr 26)
Premier Night 66 (14½f,Don,GF,Spt 10)
Premium Gift 33 (5f,Bev,G,Jun 11)
Prends Ca (IRE) 77 (6f,Hay,G,Spt 21)
Present Arms (USA) 70 (10½f,Yor,G,Aug 20)
Present Chance 51 (7f,Yor,G,Jly 12)
Present Generation 65 (6f,Fol,GF,Aug 5)
Present Situation 48 (8½f,Eps,GS,Aug 25)
Press On Nicky 38 (8f,Bat,GS,May 11)
Pride of Brixton 40 (5f,Cat,S,Oct 17)
Pride of Hayling (IRE) 37 (6f,Fol,GF,Aug 19)
Pride of Pendle 59 (8f,Yor,G,Jly 11)
Priena (IRE) 66 (8f,Asc,GF,Spt 27)
Prima Silk 66 (6f,Lei,G,Jun 14)
Prima Verde 50 (7½f,Bev,S,Jun 11)
Prime Light 58 (8f,Pon,GF,Jly 18)
Prime Partner 34 (8f,Rip,G,Jun 18)
Primo Lara 66 (7f,Nwm,GF,Oct 4)
Prince Alex (IRE) 45 (12f,Nwm,G,Aug 2)
Prince Babar 81 (6f,Asc,GS,Jun 20)
Prince Danzig (IRE) 46 (12f,Nwm,G,Apr 16)
Prince de Loir 51 (8f,Nwm,GS,Jly 18)
Prince Dome (IRE) 65 (5f,Asc,S,Jun 21)
Prince Kinsky 62 (12f,Eps,G,Apr 23)
Princely Sound 37 (6f,Nwm,G,Aug 22)
Prince of Andros (USA) 71 (10f,Goo,G,May 22)
Prince of Denial 74 (8f,Nwb,GS,Spt 20)
Prince of India 56 (7f,Don,G,Oct 25)
Prince of My Heart 90 (10½f,Yor,G,Aug 20)
Prince of Parkes 39 (5f,Edi,GS,Jun 23)
Princess Danielle 53 (11½f,Wnd,G,Aug 4)
Princess Efisio 48 (8f,Not,G,Jun 18)
Princess of Hearts 36 (8f,Not,GF,Apr 11)
Princess Topaz 58 (16f,Asc,G,Spt 27)
Prince Zando 39 (6f,Fol,GF,Apr 22)
Principal Boy (IRE) 39 (9f,Ham,GS,Jun 18)
Priolo Prima 58 (10f,Lei,GS,Oct 14)
Private Fixture (IRE) 45 (12f,Bri,F,May 29)
Proper Blue (USA) 68 (10f,Goo,G,May 22)
Prospector's Cove 49 (10f,Wnd,G,Jly 7)
Prospero 58 (17f,Bat,GF,Spt 29)
Protocol (IRE) 46 (11½f,San,GF,May 27)
Proud Monk 42 (8f,Goo,GS,Jun 20)
Proud Native (IRE) 64 (6f,Ayr,G,Spt 20)
Prussian Blue (USA) 75 (15½f,Lon,S,May 18)
Psicossis 56 (12f,Chp,G,May 26)
Public Purse (USA) 65 (16f,Asc,GF,Jun 18)
Puce 75 (14½f,Don,GF,Spt 10)
Punkah (USA) 45 (10f,Not,GF,Apr 11)
Purchasing Power (IRE) 52 (7f,Nwm,G,May 16)
Purist 55 (10f,Nwm,G,Apr 15)
Purple Fling 64 (6f,Rip,G,Aug 30)
Purple Splash 79 (14f,Yor,GS,Jun 13)
Pusey Street Girl 31 (6f,Lei,GS,Apr 26)
Puteri Wentworth 46 (12f,Edi,GS,Nov 6)
Putra (USA) 34 (8f,Nwm,G,May 3)
Puzzlement 36 (9f,Kem,G,Mar 29)

Q Factor 63 (8f,Nwb,S,May 18)
Que Belle (USA) 84 (12f,Lon,GF,Oct 5)
Queen Maud (IRE) 81 (10½f,Cha,S,Jun 8)
Queen of Shannon (IRE) 44 (7f,Chp,G,Spt 11)
Queens Consul (IRE) 69 (7½f,Chs,S,Aug 30)
Queen's Insignia (USA) 46 (8f,Wnd,GS,Jun 30)
Queen's Pageant 38 (7f,Nwm,S,Jun 28)
Quest For Best (USA) 35 (10f,San,GF,Apr 25)
Quezon City 31 (11f,Red,GF,May 26)
Quibbling 37 (8f,Nwm,G,Aug 2)
Quiet Arch (IRE) 49 (10f,Kem,G,May 24)
Quiet Venture 43 (10f,Lei,GF,Spt 9)
Quilling 47 (8f,Crl,F,Jun 25)
Quws 68 (9f,Cur,S,Spt 21)

Raaha 58 (7f,Lin,GF,Aug 17)
Racing Heart 34 (8f,Lei,G,Aug 11)
Radiancy (IRE) 55 (7f,Chs,S,May 7)
Raed 44 (7f,Don,G,Jly 31)
Raffles Rooster 57 (12f,Yor,GS,Jun 14)
Raheen (USA) 69 (7f,Thi,GF,May 3)
Rainbow Rain (USA) 52 (6f,Nwm,G,Jun 7)
Raindancing (IRE) 41 (9f,Goo,GF,Jly 30)
Raindeer Quest 39 (10f,Nwc,GF,Oct 22)
Rainwatch 65 (12f,Hay,S,Oct 15)
Raise A Prince (FR) 56 (10f,Nwm,G,May 2)
Raivue 66 (10f,Don,GF,Spt 10)

Raiyoun (IRE) 46 (10f,Cur,G,May 3)
Rajpoute (FR) 79 (12f,Hpk,F,Nov 8)
Rakis (IRE) 71 (7f,Lin,F,Apr 4)
Ralitsa (IRE) 30 (12f,Edi,GF,Jly 18)
Rambling Bear 93 (6f,Nwm,G,Apr 15)
Rambold 40 (6f,Yar,F,Jun 11)
Rambo Waltzer 59 (7f,Thi,GF,Apr 18)
Ramike (IRE) 47 (16½f,San,GS,Jly 5)
Ramooz (USA) 83 (8f,Asc,GF,Jun 18)
Ramsey Hope 52 (5f,Crl,F,Jun 12)
Random Kindness 54 (12f,Bri,GF,Oct 23)
Rapier 64 (8f,Asc,G,Jun 17)
Rare Talent 40 (10f,Rip,GF,Aug 16)
Rasayel (USA) 60 (10f,Not,GF,Apr 21)
Rash Gift 38 (10f,Lin,G,Jun 24)
Rashik 57 (8f,Nwb,GF,Apr 19)
Rasin (IRE) 41 (10f,Leo,G,Apr 19)
Rate Cut (USA) 57 (10½f,Lon,G,Apr 20)
Rawi 39 (6f,Nwc,GF,Aug 3)
Rayouni (IRE) 81 (10f,Cur,GS,Aug 16)
Reaganesque (USA) 36 (12f,Chp,GF,Aug 3)
Real Estate 48 (11½f,Wnd,S,Jun 23)
Realt Dhun Eibhir 35 (7f,Cur,GS,Jun 28)
Reams of Verse (USA) 82 (10f,Nwm,GF,Oct 4)
Rebecca Sharp 89 (8f,Asc,G,Spt 27)
Rebel County (IRE) 54 (9f,Yor,GS,Jun 14)
Rechullin 51 (7f,Nwm,G,Jly 8)
Recourse (USA) 45 (10f,Nwm,G,Apr 15)
Redbridge (USA) 39 (11f,Nwb,GF,Apr 18)
Red Camellia 82 (8f,Lon,S,May 11)
Red Guard 52 (8f,Lin,GF,Jly 10)
Red Raja 53 (16f,Goo,GF,Spt 25)
Red Robbo (CAN) 73 (8f,Asc,GF,Jun 18)
Redwing 61 (8f,Asc,G,Jun 17)
Referendum (IRE) 65 (7f,Nwm,G,Apr 16)
Refuse To Lose 52 (7f,San,GF,Spt 16)
Regait 42 (16f,Nwm,GF,Jly 9)
Regal Eagle 31 (16f,Bev,GF,Jun 4)
Regal Patrol 50 (9f,Lin,S,May 10)
Regal Reprimand 48 (10f,Chp,G,Spt 11)
Regal Splendour (CAN) 36 (8f,Goo,GS,May 21)
Regal Thunder (USA) 45 (10f,Nwm,GF,Jly 9)
Reggie Buck (USA) 44 (8f,Nwm,G,Apr 16)
Rehaab 40 (8f,Yar,GF,Aug 6)
Reimei 40 (14f,Sal,GF,Aug 21)
Reine Wells (IRE) 63 (12f,Asc,Hy,Oct 11)
Reinhardt (IRE) 32 (5f,Bev,GF,Jun 5)
Remaadi Sun 75 (12f,Eps,G,Spt 5)
Renata's Prince (IRE) 48 (8f,San,GS,Jly 4)
Rennyholme 39 (5f,Bev,GF,Jly 15)
Renown 55 (12f,Bri,F,May 23)
Renzo (IRE) 77 (16f,Asc,G,Spt 27)
Repertory 66 (5f,Asc,Hy,Oct 11)
Resist the Force (USA) 50 (6f,Nwm,G,Aug 1)
Resounder (USA) 51 (7f,Asc,GF,Apr 30)
Restless Spirit (USA) 61 (6f,Hay,G,Jly 5)
Restructure (IRE) 78 (7f,Nwb,GF,Jly 18)
Return of Amin 63 (7f,Nwm,G,Oct 18)
Reunion (IRE) 74 (7f,Nwm,G,Apr 15)
Revoque (IRE) 91 (8f,Nwm,G,May 3)
Reward 42 (8f,Kem,G,May 24)
Rex Mundi 60 (11f,Ayr,GS,Spt 18)
Rhapsody In White (IRE) 51 (10f,Goo,G,Jun 13)
Rheinbold 54 (12f,Thi,G,Aug 2)
Ricardo 57 (10f,Goo,GF,Aug 22)
Riccarton 38 (10f,Not,GF,Spt 23)
Rich Glow 46 (5f,Hay,G,Jly 4)
Rich Ground 65 (7f,Nwm,G,Apr 16)
Rich In Love (IRE) 62 (7f,Yar,GF,Aug 10)
Rickenbacker (IRE) 49 (9f,Ham,G,Jun 11)
Ricky Ticky Tavie (USA) 55 (7f,Red,F,Spt 26)
Ridaiyma (IRE) 64 (12f,Asc,GF,Spt 28)
Rififi 62 (6f,Nwm,GS,Oct 17)
Right Man 51 (16½f,San,GS,Jly 5)
Right Tune 59 (8f,Don,G,Jly 30)
Right Wing (IRE) 67 (8f,Asc,S,Jun 21)
Righty Ho 47 (10f,Bri,GF,Spt 3)
Ring the Chief 31 (10f,Wnd,GF,Jly 28)
Rising Dough (IRE) 46 (10f,Eps,GS,Jly 9)
Rising Spray 55 (12f,Bat,G,Aug 12)
Risky Rose 34 (14f,Cat,GF,May 30)
River Bay (USA) 80 (10½f,Lon,S,Apr 27)
River North (IRE) 52 (12f,Lei,G,Jun 14)
River of Fortune (IRE) 30 (7f,War,F,May 5)
River Pilot 50 (10f,Nwm,GF,Jly 9)
River Run (IRE) 37 (10f,Pon,GF,Jun 9)
Rivers Magic 32 (11½f,Wnd,GF,Jly 14)
River's Source (USA) 55 (10f,Don,G,Jly 30)
River Tern 51 (5f,Wnd,G,Aug 4)
River Usk 55 (11f,Ayr,G,Spt 20)
Riyadian 70 (9f,Ham,G,Jun 11)
Road Racer (IRE) 44 (10f,Bev,G,Jly 29)
Robban Hendi (USA) 45 (10f,Pon,GF,Jun 3)
Robellion 37 (5f,San,GF,Spt 17)
Rochea 31 (8f,Lei,G,Jly 23)
Rockcracker (IRE) 40 (6f,Fol,GF,Jun 4)
Rock Falcon (IRE) 56 (7f,Nwc,GF,Oct 1)
Rockforce 66 (10½f,Chs,S,May 6)
Rock Island Line (IRE) 62 (8f,Nwc,G,May 22)
Rock Symphony 47 (7f,War,GF,Jly 19)
Rock The Barney (IRE) 37 (10f,San,GF,Spt 16)
Rocky Dance (FR) 52 (8f,Lei,G,Aug 11)
Rocky Oasis (USA) 69 (10f,Nwm,GS,Oct 16)
Roffey Spinney (IRE) 57 (6f,Fol,G,Oct 21)
Roi du Nord (FR) 36 (10f,Not,GF,Spt 15)
Roisin Clover 39 (12f,Kem,GF,May 31)
Rokeby Bowl 76 (12f,Nwm,G,May 4)
Romanov (IRE) 84 (12f,Eps,G,Jun 7)
Roman Reel (USA) 44 (12f,Bri,F,Apr 21)
Romios (IRE) 80 (10f,Kem,GF,Mar 31)
Ron's Round 39 (10f,Lei,GF,Spt 22)
Rosabella 44 (12½f,Lon,G,Oct 4)
Rosa Royale 30 (8f,Lei,GF,Spt 22)
Roseate Lodge 30 (7f,Crl,G,Jun 26)
Roseate Wood (FR) 87 (5f,Dea,G,Aug 3)
Rose Carnival 31 (10½f,Hay,GS,Spt 5)
Rose of Glenn 37 (14f,Not,GF,Jly 19)
Rossel (USA) 42 (13f,Ham,S,May 4)
Rosy Outlook (USA) 57 (6f,Nwm,G,Jun 7)
Rotor Man (IRE) 43 (7f,San,G,May 26)
Roufontaine 72 (12f,Chp,G,May 26)
Round Robin (IRE) 46 (7½f,Bev,GS,May 20)
Roving Minstrel 62 (8f,Don,GF,Mar 22)
Royal Acclaim 32 (11½f,Lin,F,Oct 3)
Royal Affinity (IRE) 32 (5f,Cur,G,Jly 13)
Royal Amaretto (IRE) 78 (10f,Nwb,GF,Jly 19)
Royal Applause 86 (6f,Asc,G,Jun 19)
Royal Aty (IRE) 54 (6f,Asc,GS,Jun 20)
Royal Castle (IRE) 58 (14f,Nwm,GS,Oct 17)
Royal Ceilidh (IRE) 54 (8f,Thi,GF,May 3)
Royal Circus 30 (13f,Bat,G,Jly 7)
Royal Court (IRE) 78 (12f,Asc,G,Jun 20)
Royal Crown (IRE) 58 (12f,Bat,G,Jun 28)
Royal Crusade (USA) 37 (8f,San,G,Aug 13)
Royal Diversion (IRE) 56 (12f,Nwm,GF,Oct 2)
Royal Dome (IRE) 57 (6f,Lei,G,Oct 27)
Royale Figurine (IRE) 77 (6f,Bat,Hy,May 11)
Royale Finale (IRE) 38 (8f,Nwb,GF,Apr 19)
Royale Rose (FR) 33 (8f,San,GF,Spt 17)
Royal Expression 55 (12f,Ham,S,Jun 25)
Royal Mark (IRE) 67 (7f,Nwc,G,Aug 6)
Royal Philosopher 51 (8f,San,GF,Apr 25)
Royal Result (USA) 55 (7f,Nwm,GF,Oct 4)
Royal Roulette 30 (10f,Fol,G,Oct 21)
Royal Scimitar (USA) 66 (12f,Nwm,G,May 4)
Royal Seaton 62 (10f,Kem,GF,Mar 31)
Royal South (IRE) 44 (7f,Thi,GF,May 3)
Roy Boy 44 (7f,Lin,GF,Jun 14)
Rude Awakening 42 (7f,Don,GF,Mar 22)
Rudimental 72 (10f,Don,GF,Spt 10)
Rudi's Pet (IRE) 69 (6f,Ayr,G,Spt 20)
Rufalda (IRE) 50 (12f,Bri,GF,Spt 3)
Rumbustious 33 (8f,Lei,G,Aug 11)
Rum Lad 46 (6f,Not,GF,Oct 4)
Runic Symbol 33 (10f,Bri,GF,Aug 27)
Running Free (IRE) 31 (12f,Bri,F,Jly 24)
Running Green 54 (8f,Edi,S,Mar 27)
Running Stag (USA) 74 (8f,Goo,GF,Aug 2)
Runs in the Family 48 (5f,War,G,Jun 24)
Rushcutter Bay 61 (6f,Not,G,Spt 28)
Rusk 50 (12f,Nwm,S,Jun 27)
Russian Music 90 (7f,Asc,GF,Spt 27)
Russian Revival (USA) 98 (6f,Asc,GF,Spt 27)
Russian Rose (IRE) 56 (16f,Nwm,GF,Jly 9)
Rutland Chantry (USA) 54 (10f,Pon,GS,Oct 20)
Ryafan (USA) 87 (10½f,Cha,S,Jun 8)
Rymer's Rascal 49 (7f,Yor,S,Spt 4)

Saafeya (IRE) 70 (10f,Don,GF,Spt 10)
Sabadilla (USA) 76 (12f,Don,S,Nov 8)
Sabina 54 (5f,San,G,Apr 26)
Sabot 60 (7f,Nwm,G,May 16)
Sacho (IRE) 64 (11f,Ayr,G,Spt 20)
Sacrament 52 (14f,Yor,G,May 15)
Saddlers' Hope 53 (10f,Bat,GF,Jly 17)
Sadlers Home (IRE) 43 (14f,Leo,GS,Aug 4)
Safey Ana (USA) 58 (7f,Yar,GF,May 28)
Saffron Rose 46 (8f,Not,G,Apr 29)
Safio 65 (7f,Nwm,GF,Nov 1)
Sagebrush Roller 45 (10f,Don,GS,Jun 29)
Saguaro 59 (7f,Lei,S,Oct 13)
Saibhreas (IRE) 34 (10f,Leo,G,Apr 19)
Saifan 74 (8f,Nwb,GS,Spt 20)
Saint Express 70 (6f,Red,G,Jun 20)
Salamah 58 (10f,Don,G,May 24)
Sally Green (IRE) 44 (5f,Nwm,G,Oct 2)
Sally Slade 50 (5f,War,G,Jun 24)
Salmon Ladder (USA) 55 (10f,Wnd,GF,Aug 18)
Salsee Lad 33 (14f,San,GF,Aug 14)
Salska 51 (14f,Not,G,Oct 30)
Saltando (IRE) 47 (7f,Nwm,G,May 16)
Salty Behaviour (IRE) 42 (6f,Pon,GF,Oct 6)
Salty Jack (IRE) 43 (6f,Nwm,GF,Nov 1)
Samapour (IRE) 48 (10½f,Lon,G,Apr 20)
Samara (IRE) 96 (9f,Lon,GF,Oct 5)
Samara Song 53 (7f,Chp,G,Spt 11)
Sambac (USA) 39 (7f,Nwm,G,May 4)
Samraan (USA) 76 (16f,Goo,GF,Jly 31)
Sam Rockett 52 (12f,Chp,G,Aug 25)
Samsung Spirit 47 (6f,Rip,GF,Aug 25)
Samuel Scott 45 (14f,Not,GF,Apr 21)
Samwar 55 (5f,Chs,S,Aug 30)
Sandabar 59 (7f,Goo,GS,May 22)
Sandbaggedagain 43 (12f,Yor,GS,Jun 13)
Sandblaster 34 (8f,Edi,GS,Jun 30)
Sand Cay (USA) 34 (7f,Sal,GS,Jun 25)
Sandicliffe (USA) 48 (7f,Yar,F,Spt 17)
Sandmoor Chambray 86 (10½f,Yor,G,Aug 20)
Sandmoor Denim 45 (8f,Rip,GS,May 18)
Sandstone (IRE) 61 (8f,Not,GF,Apr 11)
Sandy Floss (IRE) 59 (16f,Goo,GF,Spt 25)
Sandystones 30 (9f,Goo,G,May 22)
Santillana (USA) 70 (10f,Nwm,GS,Oct 16)
Sapphire Son (IRE) 41 (12f,Bri,F,Jly 24)
Sarasota Storm 33 (15f,War,GF,Jly 12)
Saratoga Red (USA) 34 (8f,Lei,S,Oct 13)
Sarayir (USA) 62 (10f,Nwc,G,Aug 25)
Sarbaron (IRE) 34 (12f,Nwm,G,Aug 2)
Sarmatian (USA) 47 (9f,Ham,GF,Jly 11)
Saseedo (USA) 55 (7f,Nwm,G,Apr 16)
Sasuru 66 (10f,San,GS,Apr 26)
Satin Stone (USA) 64 (7f,Kem,GF,May 31)
Sausalito Bay 75 (15f,Lon,G,Oct 4)
Savona (IRE) 34 (6f,Wnd,S,May 12)
Saxon Bay 39 (6f,Chp,GF,Jun 13)
Sayyaramix (FR) 42 (6f,Kem,GF,Mar 31)
Scaraben 52 (8f,Lei,GF,Jun 2)
Scarlet Crescent 37 (8f,Bat,GF,Jly 17)
Scarrots 49 (12f,Nwm,G,Aug 2)
Scathebury 48 (8f,Edi,GF,Apr 14)

Scattergun 46 (10f,Nwb,S,May 17)
Scenicris (IRE) 46 (7½f,Bev,GF,Apr 5)
Sceptre Lady (IRE) 44 (7f,Nwb,GF,Apr 18)
Schnozzle (IRE) 40 (12½f,War,G,Jun 24)
Scissor Ridge 43 (6f,Nwb,GF,Aug 15)
Scoss 39 (10f,Nwm,S,Jun 27)
Scottish Bambi 41 (10f,Lei,GF,Spt 9)
Sea Dane 55 (6f,Kem,GF,Mar 31)
Sea Danzig 51 (6f,Nwb,GF,May 28)
Sea-Deer 70 (6f,Nwm,G,May 3)
Sea Freedom 56 (14f,Nwm,G,May 16)
Seattle Alley (USA) 52 (10f,Sal,G,Oct 1)
Seattle Art (USA) 36 (12f,Nwm,GS,Jun 11)
Seattle Swing 46 (10f,Chp,G,Spt 11)
Sea Victor 62 (16f,Asc,G,Spt 27)
Secret Aly (CAN) 76 (10f,Kem,GF,Mar 31)
Secret Ballot (IRE) 52 (12f,Lei,S,Oct 13)
Secret Combe (IRE) 41 (7f,Kem,GF,May 31)
Secret Service (IRE) 60 (14f,Hay,GS,May 24)
Secret Spring (FR) 63 (9f,Nwm,GF,Oct 4)
Sedbergh (USA) 54 (14f,Red,GF,May 26)
Seebe (USA) 84 (8f,Lon,S,May 11)
Sekari 64 (8f,Not,GF,Apr 11)
Selberry 43 (10f,Don,GF,Mar 20)
Select Choice (IRE) 37 (7f,Cat,G,Apr 23)
Selfish 53 (8f,Kem,G,May 5)
Selhurstpark Flyer (IRE) 88 (6f,Asc,GS,Jun 20)
Sellette (IRE) 58 (10½f,Hay,GF,Jun 7)
Selmeston (IRE) 33 (16f,Not,S,Oct 15)
Sendoro (IRE) 71 (11f,Lon,G,Apr 6)
Senorita Matilda (USA) 45 (6f,Lin,GF,Jly 11)
Sense of Priority 33 (7f,Cat,G,Mar 26)
Serape 43 (7f,Thi,GF,Apr 19)
Serendipity (FR) 51 (10f,Sal,G,Oct 1)
Serenity 59 (7f,Nwm,GF,Oct 3)
Sergeyev (IRE) 46 (7f,Lei,GS,Apr 26)
Serious Trust 40 (14f,Sal,GF,Aug 21)
Serpentara 41 (10f,Lei,GF,Spt 9)
Severity 47 (7f,Yar,G,Jly 16)
Shabanaz 36 (11½f,Wnd,GF,Jun 9)
Shades of Love 41 (6f,Pon,GF,Jly 18)
Shadiann (IRE) 56 (12f,Bat,G,Jun 28)
Shadirwan (IRE) 59 (17f,Bat,F,Jly 23)
Shadoof 60 (10f,Don,GF,Spt 13)
Shadow Jury 51 (6f,War,F,May 5)
Shaffishayes 53 (12f,Yor,GS,Jun 14)
Shaft of Light 85 (12f,Eps,GS,Aug 25)
Shahboor (USA) 35 (14f,Yar,GF,Aug 6)
Shaheen (USA) 73 (8f,Nwb,GS,May 16)
Shahik (USA) 43 (10f,Wnd,GF,Jly 21)
Shaka 70 (11f,Lon,G,Apr 6)
Shalaal (USA) 63 (7f,Lei,S,Oct 13)
Shalateeno 63 (12f,Eps,G,Spt 5)
Shalstayholy (IRE) 57 (5f,Don,GF,Spt 12)
Shamanic 63 (7f,Nwc,GF,Oct 1)
Shamikh 34 (8f,Nwm,G,May 3)
Shantarskie (IRE) 41 (5f,Bev,GF,Spt 17)
Shantou (USA) 71 (12f,Asc,S,Jly 26)
Sharaf Kabeer 55 (12f,Lei,G,Jun 14)
Sharbadarid (IRE) 60 (10f,Rip,GF,Aug 25)
Share Delight (IRE) 54 (8f,Yor,G,May 15)
Sharemono (USA) 30 (8f,Leo,G,Apr 19)
Shark (IRE) 36 (8f,Rip,GF,Jly 19)
Sharkiyah (IRE) 41 (7f,Nwm,G,Apr 16)
Sharp Consul (IRE) 75 (10f,Nwm,G,May 2)
Sharp Deed (IRE) 38 (8½f,Bev,GF,Jly 15)
Sharp Hat 64 (6f,Yor,GS,Jun 14)
Sharp Imp 49 (7f,Sal,GF,Jun 11)
Sharp 'n' Shady 47 (7f,Don,GS,Jun 28)
Sharp 'n Smart 58 (7f,Fol,G,Mar 26)
Sharpo Wassl 52 (7f,Yar,GF,Jly 28)
Sharp Pearl 68 (5f,Nwm,GF,Aug 23)
Sharp Rebuff 67 (7f,Nwb,GF,May 28)
Sharp Return 33 (7f,Fol,G,Oct 21)
Sharp Shuffle (IRE) 66 (9f,Goo,GF,Jly 31)
Sharp Stock 45 (5f,Goo,GS,May 22)
Sharp Temper 51 (8f,Asc,G,Jun 17)
Sharpwitted 34 (7f,Yar,F,Jun 11)
Shashi (IRE) 41 (7f,Lin,GF,Jun 14)
Shaska 67 (10f,Nwb,GF,Spt 18)
Shavinsky 33 (6f,Not,G,May 23)
Shawaf (USA) 52 (7f,Nwm,G,Apr 15)
Shawm 67 (8f,Hay,G,Spt 21)
Shaya 46 (10f,Asc,G,Jly 25)
Sheep Stealer 47 (10f,Wnd,G,Aug 4)
Sheer Danzig (IRE) 76 (12f,Don,GF,Mar 22)
Sheer Face 62 (8f,San,GF,Spt 16)
Sheilas Dream 33 (11½f,Wnd,GF,Jly 14)
Shell Ginger (IRE) 43 (10f,Cur,GS,May 25)
Sheltering Sky (IRE) 65 (7f,Nwb,GF,Jly 18)
Sheraz (IRE) 33 (7f,Nwc,G,May 5)
Sherqy (IRE) 47 (12½f,Nwc,GF,Aug 6)
Shift Again (IRE) 37 (14f,Not,GF,Oct 4)
Shifting Moon 43 (10f,Bat,F,Jly 23)
Shii-Take 73 (8f,Nwm,G,May 3)
Shinerolla 61 (8f,Nwm,G,Oct 18)
Shining Cloud 51 (6f,Nwm,G,May 3)
Shining Dancer 54 (14f,San,GF,Jly 16)
Shining Example 57 (9f,Goo,G,Jun 13)
Shirley Sue 58 (20f,Goo,GF,Jly 30)
Shirley Venture 55 (15½f,Fol,GF,Apr 22)
Shock Value (IRE) 65 (7f,Yar,G,Jly 16)
Shontaine 46 (8f,Ham,G,Spt 29)
Shooting Light (IRE) 56 (14f,San,S,Aug 30)
Shooting Star (IRE) 34 (10f,Goo,G,Spt 13)
Shouk 48 (10½f,Hay,S,May 5)
Shoumatara (USA) 41 (7f,Bri,F,Jun 3)
Showboat 52 (7f,Nwm,G,May 4)
Show Faith (IRE) 42 (9f,Goo,GF,Aug 23)
Siberian Mystic 31 (12f,Sal,GF,Aug 13)
Siege Perilous (IRE) 52 (16½f,San,GS,Aug 29)
Signs And Wonders 44 (7f,San,G,May 26)
Sihafi (USA) 35 (7½f,Bev,GF,Jun 4)
Silankka 36 (10f,Bat,G,Jly 7)
Silca Key Silca 66 (6f,Lin,G,Jun 24)
Silence in Court (IRE) 55 (14½f,Don,G,Oct 24)
Silence Reigns 66 (12f,Goo,GF,Jly 29)
Silently 72 (14f,San,GF,Jly 16)
Silent Miracle (IRE) 53 (5f,Nwm,GF,Aug 23)
Silent Valley 32 (10f,Don,GF,Spt 10)
Silk Cottage 39 (5f,Edi,GF,Jly 18)
Silk St John 65 (8f,Kem,G,Spt 21)
Silverani (IRE) 85 (10f,Nwm,GF,Oct 3)
Silver Groom (IRE) 66 (10f,Kem,GF,Mar 31)
Silver Harrow 48 (8f,Bat,G,Spt 8)
Silvering (FR) 41 (7f,Yor,G,Aug 21)
Silver Kristal 48 (7f,Goo,GF,Aug 1)
Silver Lining 45 (7f,Lei,G,Jly 17)
Silver Patriarch (IRE) 91 (12f,Eps,G,Jun 7)
Silver Purse 38 (6f,Nwm,G,Jun 7)
Silver Secret 39 (8f,Lei,G,Aug 11)
Silver Whirl (USA) 49 (10f,Nwb,GF,Spt 18)
Silver Wonder (USA) 35 (12f,Nwm,G,May 16)
Silvery 50 (10f,Goo,G,Spt 13)
Silvretta (IRE) 40 (11½f,Wnd,G,Aug 4)
Simple Logic 35 (7f,Lin,G,Aug 9)
Sing And Dance 32 (10f,Nwc,G,Mar 25)
Single Empire (IRE) 57 (12f,Nwm,G,May 3)
Singspiel (IRE) 90 (10½f,Yor,G,Aug 19)
Sing With the Band 32 (6f,Not,GF,Apr 8)
Sioux 39 (12f,Hay,G,Spt 21)
Siouxrouge 30 (7f,Bri,GF,May 6)
Sipowitz 37 (18f,Pon,GS,Oct 20)
Sir Arthur Hobbs 43 (8f,Thi,F,Jun 2)
Sirinndi (IRE) 36 (16f,Cur,GS,Oct 4)
Sir Joey (USA) 68 (6f,Nwm,G,May 3)
Sir Ricky (USA) 51 (12f,Bat,G,Spt 8)
Sir Talbot 56 (9f,San,GF,Jun 14)
Sir Tasker 35 (6f,Cat,GF,Jly 16)
Sis Garden 48 (8f,Wnd,G,Aug 23)
Six Clerks (IRE) 34 (12f,Cat,GF,May 30)
Six Zero (FR) 58 (12f,Lon,S,May 15)
Siyadah (USA) 68 (10f,Nwm,G,May 4)
Sizzling 40 (6f,Bri,F,Apr 11)
Sky Commander (USA) 56 (10f,Nwm,S,Jun 27)
Sky Dome (IRE) 58 (8f,Don,GF,Mar 22)
Skyers Flyer (IRE) 48 (6f,Cat,G,Jun 6)
Slasher Jack (IRE) 52 (12f,Edi,GS,Nov 6)
Sleepless 48 (7f,Nwb,S,May 17)
Sleepytime (IRE) 73 (8f,Nwm,G,May 4)
Slip Jig (IRE) 57 (12f,Chs,GF,Jly 11)
Slipstream 43 (10f,Nwm,G,Apr 15)
Slipstream Star 30 (9f,Ham,G,Spt 29)
Smarter Charter 66 (7½f,Bev,GF,Apr 11)
Smart Guest 33 (7f,Lei,G,Jly 17)
Smart Kid (IRE) 54 (6f,Sal,GF,May 4)
Smart Play (USA) 56 (11½f,San,GF,Jly 16)
Smart Spirit (IRE) 54 (8f,Nwc,G,May 5)
Smokey From Caplaw 55 (8f,Red,GF,Oct 28)
Snap Crackle Pop (IRE) 38 (5f,San,G,Apr 26)
Snow Kid 74 (6f,Don,S,Nov 8)
Snow Partridge (USA) 53 (12f,Chp,GF,Jly 11)
Snow Princess (IRE) 71 (14½f,Don,GF,Spt 10)
Snowy Mantle 30 (10f,Nwm,G,Aug 1)
Society Rose 42 (10½f,Yor,G,May 13)
Soda Pop (IRE) 48 (12f,Bri,F,Jly 24)
Soden (IRE) 30 (10f,Not,GF,Spt 15)
Sofyaan (USA) 62 (12f,Nwm,GS,Jun 20)
So Intrepid (IRE) 69 (6f,Ayr,G,Spt 20)
Solar Storm 68 (8f,Ayr,G,Spt 20)
Soldier Cove (USA) 45 (8f,Edi,S,Mar 27)
Solfegietto 43 (7f,Red,GS,Jly 26)
Solo Mio (IRE) 78 (12f,Nwm,GS,Oct 16)
Somerton Boy (IRE) 59 (8f,Don,G,Jly 16)
Song Mist (IRE) 49 (7f,Bri,F,Spt 28)
Song of Freedom 72 (10f,Don,GF,Spt 13)
Song of Skye 62 (7f,San,GF,Jly 23)
Song Of The Sword 58 (12f,Hay,S,Mar 29)
Songsheet 58 (5f,Chp,G,Spt 11)
Soojama (IRE) 48 (14f,Nwm,G,May 16)
Sooty Tern 55 (8f,Bat,F,Jly 23)
Sophomore 46 (9f,Goo,G,Jun 12)
Sotonian (HOL) 33 (5f,Not,G,May 17)
Sound Appeal 32 (10f,Sal,S,Jun 26)
Sound the Trumpet (IRE) 39 (7f,Fol,G,Mar 26)
Souperficial 34 (6f,Ham,S,Jly 1)
South China Sea 42 (7f,Nwm,G,Aug 22)
Southerly Wind 57 (8f,Pon,GF,Aug 17)
Southern Dominion 42 (5f,Ayr,S,Oct 14)
Sovereign Crest (IRE) 42 (12f,Bri,F,Jly 24)
Sovereign Page (USA) 44 (11f,War,F,Jun 4)
Sovereigns Court 53 (8f,Not,S,Oct 15)
Soviet Leader 65 (6f,Ayr,G,Spt 20)
Soviet Line (IRE) 81 (8f,Hpk,F,Nov 8)
Soviet State (USA) 76 (6f,Nwb,GF,Jly 19)
Space Race 57 (10f,Bat,F,Jly 23)
Spaniards Close 42 (6f,Bat,G,Aug 7)
Spaniard's Mount 32 (8f,Yar,GS,Jly 3)
Spanish Knot (USA) 49 (7f,Thi,F,Jun 2)
Spanish Verdict 41 (8f,Red,G,May 12)
Sparky 46 (12f,Edi,GF,Spt 15)
Spartan Girl (IRE) 38 (10f,Eps,S,Jly 2)
Spartan Heartbeat 64 (14f,Not,G,Oct 30)
Special-K 42 (8f,Rip,GF,Jly 19)
Speculator (IRE) 60 (8½f,Eps,G,Aug 10)
Speedball (IRE) 73 (7f,Asc,GF,Spt 27)
Speedboat (USA) 37 (7f,Red,F,Spt 26)
Speedfriend (GER) 36 (12f,Cha,G,Jun 1)
Speed On 75 (5f,Nwm,G,Jly 19)
Speedy Classic (USA) 51 (7f,Chp,GF,Jly 25)
Spender 60 (6f,Bat,GF,Jun 14)
Spick And Span 38 (11f,Ayr,GS,Spt 18)
Spinning World (USA) 98 (8f,Hpk,F,Nov 8)
Spirito Libro (USA) 61 (10½f,Yor,G,May 14)
Spotted Eagle 53 (6f,Red,G,May 12)
Spring Marathon (USA) 35 (20f,Asc,G,Jun 17)
Spy Knoll 50 (13½f,Chs,G,Spt 24)
Squared Away 36 (8f,War,GF,May 24)
Square Mile Miss (IRE) 30 (8f,Pon,GF,Apr

16)
Squeak 95 (9f,Lon,GF,Oct 5)
Squire Corrie 77 (5f,Cat,S,Oct 17)
Stackattack (IRE) 65 (7½f,Bev,GS,Aug 13)
Stage Affair (USA) 51 (14f,Cur,S,Spt 20)
Stahr 35 (12f,Fol,GF,Jly 14)
Stakis Casinos Boy (IRE) 50 (12f,Pon,GF,Jun 3)
Stalled (IRE) 44 (11f,Ham,GS,Jly 4)
Standown 42 (6f,Red,G,May 12)
Stand Tall 63 (6f,Hay,G,Spt 21)
Stanton Harcourt (USA) 71 (8f,Nwm,GF,Nov 1)
Starborough 96 (8f,Asc,G,Jun 17)
Star Entry 42 (10f,Fol,G,Oct 21)
Star Gambit (USA) 38 (8f,Nwb,S,Spt 19)
Star Invader 43 (7f,Lei,S,Oct 13)
Star Manager (USA) 77 (8f,San,GF,Apr 25)
Star of Ring (IRE) 54 (7f,Thi,GF,Apr 19)
Star Precision 67 (12f,Chp,G,May 26)
Star Profile (IRE) 68 (8f,Lon,S,May 11)
Star Rage (IRE) 72 (16f,Asc,G,Spt 27)
Star Selection 65 (11f,Ayr,G,Spt 20)
Star Talent (USA) 78 (8½f,Eps,G,Jun 6)
Star Turn (IRE) 51 (8f,Lei,S,Oct 13)
Statajack (IRE) 56 (12f,Chp,G,Aug 25)
State Approval 47 (11½f,Wnd,GF,Jun 2)
State Fair 71 (15f,Nwm,GF,Jly 10)
State of Caution 55 (6f,Hay,G,Spt 21)
Statoyork 56 (7f,Lin,F,Apr 4)
St Blaine (CAN) 50 (7f,Fol,S,Jun 27)
Steamroller Stanly 64 (12f,Don,GF,Spt 12)
Stellar Line (USA) 51 (8f,Rip,GF,May 28)
Stephensons Rocket 41 (6f,Not,GF,Apr 21)
Step N Go (IRE) 45 (10f,Pon,G,May 23)
Step On Degas 43 (8f,Goo,G,Spt 12)
Steward (FR) 80 (12f,Lon,GF,Oct 5)
Stilett (IRE) 46 (8f,Nwm,GF,Jly 10)
St Lawrence (CAN) 39 (14f,Yor,S,Spt 3)
Stolen Kiss (IRE) 46 (5f,Bev,GF,Jly 15)
Stonecutter 39 (15½f,Fol,F,Apr 10)
Stoned Imaculate (IRE) 38 (16f,Not,GF,Spt 23)
Stone Flower (USA) 61 (10f,Don,GF,Spt 10)
Stone Ridge (IRE) 74 (8f,San,GF,Apr 25)
Stoppes Brow 66 (7f,Nwb,GF,May 28)
Stormless 50 (10f,Nwc,GF,Oct 22)
Stormy Story (USA) 34 (10f,Wnd,G,Aug 4)
Story Line 67 (16f,Asc,G,Spt 27)
Storyteller (IRE) 32 (6f,Red,F,Spt 26)
Stowaway 79 (10f,Don,G,May 24)
St Radegund 52 (7f,Goo,GS,May 21)
Strategic Choice (USA) 75 (10½f,Lon,S,Apr 27)
Strathmore Clear 56 (8f,War,GF,Apr 12)
Strat's Quest 43 (6f,Wnd,S,May 12)
Strawberry Roan (IRE) 50 (8f,Leo,YS,May 11)
Strazo (IRE) 78 (9f,Nwb,GF,Jly 19)
Street General 57 (12f,Nwm,G,Apr 15)
Stretarez (FR) 78 (15½f,Lon,S,May 18)
Struggler 88 (5f,Dea,G,Aug 3)
Stuffed 48 (5f,Yor,G,May 14)
Sturgeon (IRE) 48 (10f,Wnd,G,Aug 4)
Style Dancer (IRE) 53 (7f,Hay,G,Spt 27)
Stylish Ways (IRE) 43 (7f,Cat,S,Oct 17)
Sualtach (IRE) 63 (8f,Red,GF,Oct 28)
Sublime Beauty (USA) 63 (10f,Cur,GS,May 25)
Such Boldness 33 (12f,Eps,GS,Jly 9)
Sudest (IRE) 45 (12f,Bat,GF,Jun 14)
Suedoro 32 (5f,Ham,GF,Jly 11)
Sue Me (IRE) 48 (5f,Nwc,GF,Oct 22)
Sue's Return 69 (8f,Goo,GF,Jly 29)
Suez Tornado (IRE) 67 (8f,Nwm,G,Jly 8)
Suga Hawk (IRE) 54 (12f,Chs,GF,Jly 11)
Sugarfoot 66 (8f,Asc,S,Jun 21)
Sugar Mill 73 (12f,Hay,S,Mar 29)
Suile Mor 36 (8f,Chp,GS,Jly 1)
Suite Factors 41 (6f,Bat,G,Spt 8)
Suivez 32 (10½f,Hay,G,Jly 5)
Summer Dance 63 (10f,Nwb,GF,Spt 18)
Summerhill Special (IRE) 62 (11f,Ayr,GS,Spt 18)
Summerosa (USA) 49 (7f,Hay,GS,Jly 3)
Summer Queen 43 (7f,Nwm,G,Apr 15)
Sun Alert (USA) 40 (12f,Yor,GS,Jun 13)
Sunbeam Dance (USA) 68 (11f,Nwb,GF,Spt 18)
Sun Mark (IRE) 49 (12f,Ham,S,Jun 25)
Sunny Isle 45 (10½f,Hay,S,Oct 15)
Sun of Spring 52 (11f,Ham,GS,Jly 4)
Sunset Reigns (IRE) 38 (5f,Cur,G,Jly 13)
Superbelle 30 (11½f,Yar,GF,Spt 16)
Super Benz 48 (7f,Thi,G,May 16)
Superbit 58 (5f,Hay,G,Jly 4)
Supercal 76 (8f,Dea,G,Aug 3)
Superior Force 41 (8f,Goo,GS,May 21)
Superior Premium 77 (6f,Ayr,G,Spt 20)
Superlao (BEL) 34 (5f,War,GF,Jly 19)
Super Monarch 52 (8f,Nwm,G,May 4)
Superpride 45 (7f,Ayr,S,May 21)
Super Scravels 35 (7f,Fol,GF,Jly 14)
Super Serenade 30 (10f,Bri,GF,Spt 3)
Supply And Demand 78 (10f,Goo,GF,Aug 1)
Supreme Sound 46 (10f,Bri,F,Spt 28)
Supreme Thought 50 (6f,Sal,GS,Aug 8)
Supremism 38 (8f,Nwm,GF,May 31)
Surf City 48 (7f,Cat,GF,May 31)
Surgeon 65 (12f,Cha,S,Jun 8)
Surprise Mission 70 (5f,Asc,Hy,Oct 11)
Surtsey 36 (10f,Lei,F,Apr 3)
Sushi Bar (IRE) 31 (12f,Ham,G,Spt 1)
Swain (IRE) 97 (12f,Lon,GF,Oct 5)
Swan At Whalley 51 (5f,Chs,S,Aug 30)
Swan Hunter 58 (14f,Hay,GS,May 24)
Swan Island 37 (8f,Bat,GF,Spt 29)
Sweet Contralto 61 (9f,Goo,GF,Aug 22)
Sweet Fortune (USA) 47 (8f,Kem,G,Spt 21)
Sweet Glow (FR) 33 (14f,Not,GF,Apr 11)
Sweet Magic 51 (5f,Goo,G,Spt 24)
Sweet Mate 37 (6f,Not,G,May 9)
Sweetness Herself 73 (16f,Nwc,Hy,Jun 28)
Sweet Wilhelmina 62 (8f,Nwb,GS,Spt 20)
Swift 48 (8f,Nwm,G,Aug 2)
Swift Gulliver (IRE) 89 (6f,Asc,GF,Spt 27)
Swift Sovereign 34 (7f,Hay,GS,May 24)
Swiftway 38 (10f,Don,GF,Mar 21)
Swinging The Blues (IRE) 40 (8f,Goo,G,Spt 12)
Swing West (USA) 40 (8f,Kem,G,May 24)
Swino 54 (5f,Red,GF,Oct 18)
Swiss Law 73 (8f,Asc,G,Jun 17)
Sword Arm 60 (8f,Bat,GF,Jly 17)
Swynford Dream 56 (5f,Yor,G,May 14)
Sycamore Boy (USA) 33 (8f,Hay,G,Spt 21)
Sycamore Lodge (IRE) 43 (6f,Rip,G,Aug 30)
Sylvan Dancer (IRE) 44 (6f,Sal,GS,Aug 8)
Sylvan Princess 59 (8f,Asc,GF,Apr 30)
Sylva Paradise (IRE) 92 (6f,Nwm,G,Apr 15)
Symboli Kildare (IRE) 41 (5f,Cur,G,Jly 13)
Symonds Inn 69 (12f,Eps,G,Jun 7)

Tabasco Jazz 36 (7f,Thi,GF,May 3)
Taberann (IRE) 51 (10f,Ayr,S,Oct 14)
Tadeo 81 (5f,Nwm,G,Jly 19)
Tael of Silver 35 (7f,Cat,GF,Spt 20)
Taffs Well 61 (7f,San,GF,Spt 17)
Tailwind 34 (6f,Crl,GF,Jun 25)
Taipan (IRE) 62 (10f,Cur,GS,May 25)
Tajar (USA) 33 (10f,San,GF,Spt 16)
Tajrebah (USA) 46 (7f,Lin,GF,Jun 14)
Takhlid (USA) 62 (7f,Fol,GF,Jun 4)
Talib (USA) 32 (8f,Yar,F,Spt 18)
Tallulah Belle 57 (10f,Bev,GF,Apr 24)
Tal-Y-Llyn (IRE) 44 (7f,Nwb,S,May 18)
Tamarpour (USA) 50 (20f,Asc,G,Jun 17)
Tamayaz (CAN) 68 (10½f,Hay,GF,Aug 9)
Tamure (IRE) 62 (12f,Don,S,Nov 8)
Tanaasa (IRE) 62 (11½f,Lin,S,May 10)
Tango King 42 (12f,Pon,GF,Jun 3)
Tangshan (CAN) 35 (8f,Bat,GF,May 30)
Taoiste 54 (5f,San,GF,Jly 16)
Tappeto 50 (14f,San,G,Aug 13)
Taragona 32 (7½f,Bev,S,Jun 11)
Tarator (USA) 79 (15½f,Lon,S,Apr 27)
Tarry 49 (12f,Nwm,GF,Oct 31)
Tarski 39 (9f,Yor,S,Spt 4)
Tart (FR) 44 (12f,Fol,G,Jly 9)
Tart and a Half 59 (5f,Rip,G,Jun 19)
Tarxien 49 (12f,Lei,S,Oct 13)
Tashiriya (IRE) 46 (9f,Lon,S,Apr 27)
Tasik Chini (USA) 35 (12½f,War,GF,Jun 9)
Tassili (IRE) 50 (8½f,Bev,GF,Jun 5)
Taswib (USA) 47 (10f,Lei,F,Apr 3)
Tatika 55 (8f,Nwb,G,Jun 12)
Taufan Boy 51 (14f,Not,GF,Oct 4)
Taufan's Melody 85 (12f,Asc,GF,Spt 28)
Taunt 80 (12f,Don,S,Nov 8)
Tawafek (USA) 55 (16f,Asc,G,Spt 27)
Tayovullin (IRE) 31 (7f,Lei,G,Jly 23)
Tayseer (USA) 68 (7f,Asc,GF,Jun 18)
Tea Party (USA) 40 (7f,Goo,GS,Jun 20)
Tear White (IRE) 49 (5f,Goo,G,Spt 24)
Technicolour (IRE) 31 (11½f,San,GF,Jly 16)
Tedburrow 87 (5f,Asc,GF,Spt 28)
Telemania (IRE) 64 (8f,Goo,GF,Jly 29)
Tellion 34 (12f,Fol,GF,Jly 14)
Teme Valley 54 (11½f,Lin,G,Spt 9)
Tempting Prospect 47 (12f,Asc,GF,Spt 28)
Temptress 61 (10½f,Yor,G,May 14)
Ten Past Six 46 (10f,Rip,G,Apr 26)
Tenuous 88 (9f,Lon,GF,Oct 5)
Teofilio (IRE) 71 (8f,Asc,G,Jun 17)
Terdad (USA) 51 (8f,Red,G,Jun 21)
Tertium (IRE) 66 (7f,Nwc,Hy,Jun 28)
Tessajoe 65 (12f,Cat,GF,Spt 20)
Test The Water (IRE) 43 (7½f,Chs,S,May 6)
Texas Cowgirl (IRE) 41 (6f,Fol,GF,Jun 4)
Tezaab 33 (8f,Lei,G,Jly 23)
Thaljanah (IRE) 67 (14f,Yor,GS,Jun 13)
Thatched (IRE) 42 (7½f,Bev,GF,Jly 21)
Thatchmaster (IRE) 59 (10f,Goo,GF,Aug 23)
That Man Again 67 (5f,Nwc,GF,Oct 1)
Theano (IRE) 58 (8f,Nwm,GF,Jly 9)
Theatreworld (IRE) 53 (16f,Cur,GS,Oct 4)
The Barnsley Belle (IRE) 30 (7f,Don,GS,Jun 28)
The Bower (IRE) 35 (8f,Cur,GS,Jun 27)
The Butterwick Kid 45 (12f,Edi,G,Jun 16)
The Dilettanti (USA) 83 (10f,Nwm,G,May 3)
The Executor 53 (10f,Goo,GF,Aug 23)
The Faraway Tree 73 (12f,Yor,G,Aug 21)
The Fly 76 (12f,Eps,G,Jun 7)
The Flying Phantom 44 (14f,Yar,GF,Aug 6)
The Frisky Farmer 44 (7f,Thi,G,May 16)
The Fugative 52 (5f,Fol,G,Jly 9)
The Gay Fox 62 (6f,Ayr,G,Spt 20)
The Green Grey 38 (8f,Bat,GF,Spt 29)
The Happy Fox (IRE) 47 (6f,Pon,G,Jly 8)
The In-Laws (IRE) 65 (10f,Red,GF,Oct 18)
The Lambton Worm 46 (6f,Nwc,Hy,Jun 28)
Theme Arena 42 (16f,Not,S,Oct 15)
The Negotiator 30 (7f,Kem,GF,Mar 31)
The Prince 66 (8f,Kem,G,Spt 21)
The Puzzler (IRE) 65 (5f,Nwm,GS,Oct 16)
Therhea (IRE) 68 (8f,Asc,GF,Spt 28)
The Roundsills 31 (12f,Cat,GF,Jly 16)
The Stager (IRE) 42 (8f,War,GF,Oct 7)
The Wad 46 (5f,War,GS,Aug 25)
The West (USA) 42 (7f,Nwb,GF,Apr 19)
The Wyandotte Inn 37 (7½f,Bev,GF,Apr 24)
Thick as Thieves 33 (6f,Cat,G,Apr 23)
Third Party 41 (6f,Bri,F,Jun 3)
Thisonesforalice 35 (11f,Ayr,GF,Jly 14)
Thornby Park 61 (16f,Asc,G,Spt 27)
Three Arch Bridge 58 (8f,Rip,GF,May 28)
Three Cheers (IRE) 80 (15f,Lon,G,Oct 4)
Three For A Pound 46 (7f,Cat,S,Jly 3)
Thunderheart 38 (13f,Ham,G,Jun 11)

Thwaab 51 (6f,Lin,GF,May 31)
Tiger Lake 41 (12f,Asc,Hy,Oct 10)
Tigrello 65 (8f,Asc,G,Jun 17)
Tikopia 56 (12f,Goo,GF,Aug 22)
Tiler (IRE) 68 (6f,Ayr,G,Spt 20)
Time Allowed 72 (12f,Nwm,G,May 2)
Time Can Tell 39 (8f,Lei,G,Aug 20)
Time for Action (IRE) 69 (10f,Don,G,Oct 25)
Time For Tea (IRE) 32 (6f,War,F,May 5)
Time of Night (USA) 43 (8f,Not,G,May 23)
Time To Tango 42 (5f,Red,F,May 1)
Tinker Amelia 36 (6f,Cur,S,Oct 18)
Tinker Osmaston 54 (5f,San,GS,Aug 29)
Tinklers Folly 38 (10f,Pon,GF,Jun 9)
Tipperary Sunset (IRE) 50 (8f,Don,GS,Nov 8)
Tipsy Creek (USA) 67 (5f,Nwb,GF,Spt 18)
Tissue of Lies (USA) 46 (13f,Ham,GS,Jun 18)
Tithcar 46 (5f,Edi,GF,Aug 20)
Titta Ruffo 64 (10f,Nwm,GF,Oct 3)
Titus Livius (FR) 96 (5f,Asc,GS,Jun 20)
Toi Toi (IRE) 49 (10f,Chp,GS,Jly 1)
Token Gesture (IRE) 65 (10f,Cur,GS,May 25)
Tomba 78 (6f,Nwc,Hy,Jun 28)
Tommy Tempest 30 (5f,Wnd,GF,Jly 14)
Tommy Tortoise 41 (14f,Yar,G,Jun 23)
Tom Tailor (GER) 44 (12f,Lei,S,Oct 13)
Tonight's Prize (IRE) 51 (10f,San,GF,Spt 16)
Tonka 51 (10f,Not,G,May 9)
Tonnerre 54 (10½f,Yor,S,Spt 4)
Top 32 (12f,Thi,G,Aug 1)
Topatori (IRE) 45 (10f,Ayr,GS,Spt 19)
Top Banana 67 (6f,Nwm,G,May 3)
Top Cees 72 (14f,Goo,GF,Jly 29)
Top Jem 49 (10f,Nwc,Hy,Jun 28)
Top of The Form (IRE) 49 (5f,Chs,G,Spt 24)
Top Shelf 36 (10f,Yar,F,Jun 11)
Topton (IRE) 62 (6f,Fol,G,Oct 21)
Torch Vert (IRE) 53 (17f,Bat,GF,Spt 29)
Toronto 32 (5f,Edi,GF,May 31)
Totem Dancer 59 (12f,Ham,G,Spt 29)
To the Roof (IRE) 90 (6f,Asc,GS,Jun 20)
Tough Act 55 (10f,Goo,G,Spt 13)
Tough Leader 51 (7½f,Bev,GF,Apr 24)
Toujours Riviera 64 (8f,Nwm,G,Jly 8)
Tout A Coup (IRE) 48 (10f,Cur,GS,Jun 28)
Traceability 59 (10f,San,GF,Jly 30)
Trading Aces 46 (7f,War,F,May 5)
Tramline 70 (15f,Nwm,GS,Jun 11)
Transom (USA) 70 (20f,Goo,GF,Jly 30)
Travelmate 44 (12f,Nwm,GS,Jun 20)
Treasure Touch (IRE) 57 (6f,Not,GF,Apr 11)
Tregaron (USA) 84 (7f,Asc,GF,Spt 27)
Tremplin (USA) 55 (10½f,Hay,G,Jly 5)
Tribal Moon (IRE) 36 (10f,Wnd,GF,Jun 16)
Tribal Peace (IRE) 49 (9f,Goo,GF,Jly 31)
Trilby 47 (13f,Ham,GS,Jun 18)
Triple Hay 69 (6f,Goo,GF,Aug 2)
Triple Leap 34 (10½f,Hay,G,Spt 21)
Trojan Hero (SAF) 58 (8f,Lei,GF,Jun 2)
Trojan Risk 49 (10f,Goo,GS,Jun 20)
Trojan Sea (USA) 43 (10½f,Lon,S,Apr 27)
Trooper 33 (12f,Fol,GF,Jly 14)
Tropical Beach 51 (5f,Crl,G,Jly 5)
True Glory (IRE) 51 (10f,Don,GS,Jun 28)
Trying Times (IRE) 42 (11f,Ayr,GF,Jly 14)
Tsarnista 57 (8f,Goo,G,May 22)
Tudor Island 48 (14f,San,GF,Jly 16)
Tulipa (USA) 70 (12f,Hay,G,Jly 5)
Tulsa (IRE) 48 (8f,Lei,S,Oct 13)
Tumbleweed Pearl 49 (7f,Asc,GF,Jun 18)
Tumbleweed Ridge 78 (7f,Yar,G,Jly 16)
Turgenev (IRE) 68 (14f,Yor,S,Spt 3)
Turnpole (IRE) 66 (16f,Chs,G,Spt 24)
Tuscan Dawn 59 (5f,Lin,GF,Jly 10)
Twice as Sharp 70 (5f,Nwb,GF,Aug 16)
Twilight Sleep (USA) 52 (12f,Chs,GF,Jly 11)
Twin Creeks 50 (7f,San,GF,Spt 17)
Twin Time 43 (8f,Not,GF,Aug 6)
Two On The Bridge 34 (6f,Thi,G,Jun 17)
Two Socks 49 (12f,Bat,G,Aug 12)
Tycooness (IRE) 54 (14f,Not,G,Oct 30)
Tycoon Girl (IRE) 54 (7f,War,F,May 5)
Tycoon Tina 31 (9f,Ayr,S,Oct 13)
Tycoon Todd (USA) 60 (8f,Nwm,G,May 3)
Tykeyvor (IRE) 69 (14½f,Don,GF,Spt 10)
Tymeera 47 (6f,War,F,May 5)
Typhoon Eight (IRE) 56 (10f,San,GF,May 26)
Tyrolean Dream (IRE) 52 (12f,Lei,S,Oct 13)

Ukraine Venture 57 (10f,San,GF,Apr 25)
Ultimate Smoothie 52 (14f,Hay,GF,Aug 9)
Ultra Beet 37 (5f,Crl,G,Jly 5)
Ultra Boy 54 (8f,Rip,GF,May 28)
Unchanged 55 (15½f,Fol,F,Spt 26)
Uncle Doug 35 (16f,Cat,GF,Spt 20)
Unconditional Love (IRE) 77 (8½f,Eps,G,Jun 6)
Undercover Agent (IRE) 59 (7f,War,F,May 5)
Union Town (IRE) 73 (10½f,Yor,GS,Jun 14)
U-No-Harry (IRE) 42 (5f,Chs,GF,Jun 4)
Unshaken 32 (7f,Nwm,GS,Jun 20)
Up in Flames (IRE) 35 (8f,Not,G,Jun 18)
Upper Mount Clair 41 (15f,War,GF,Apr 12)
Urgent Reply (USA) 42 (10f,Lin,S,May 10)
Urgent Swift 70 (12f,Goo,GF,Aug 22)
Ursa Major 38 (7f,Goo,GS,Spt 13)
Utmost Zeal (USA) 41 (8f,Bat,G,May 19)

Vagabond Chanteuse 67 (10f,Nwm,G,May 4)
Vain Tempest 51 (12f,Hay,G,Spt 21)
Valagalore 52 (14f,Hay,GF,Aug 9)
Valedictory 80 (12f,Nwm,G,May 4)
Val's Prince (USA) 78 (12f,Hpk,F,Nov 8)
Vanadium Ore 38 (10f,Red,G,Nov 4)
Vanborough Lad 31 (8f,Wnd,GS,Jun 30)
Van Chino 39 (7f,Lei,S,Oct 13)
Van Gurp 63 (7f,Chs,GF,Jun 4)
Vanishing Trick (USA) 56 (9f,Goo,GF,Jly 30)
Varnishing Day (IRE) 36 (7f,Nwm,GF,Aug 9)
Varxi (FR) 65 (9f,Lon,S,May 15)
Vasari (IRE) 50 (5f,Chs,S,May 6)
Vax Star 30 (5f,Nwc,G,Jly 26)
Veiled Threat (IRE) 89 (9f,Lon,GF,Oct 5)
Veni Vidi Vici (IRE) 53 (8f,Kem,GF,Spt 22)
Venture Capitalist 68 (6f,Yor,G,Aug 19)
Verdi (IRE) 39 (6f,Sal,GF,May 4)
Vereva (IRE) 93 (10½f,Cha,S,Jun 8)
Verglas (IRE) 52 (12f,Cur,GS,Jun 29)
Veridian 66 (12f,Don,G,May 24)
Vernoy (USA) 89 (7f,Lon,,Jun 22)
Veronica Franco 46 (12f,Nwm,GF,Oct 31)
Versatility 30 (10f,Red,G,Nov 4)
Vertical Speed (FR) 51 (14½f,Don,GF,Spt 13)
Via Verbano (IRE) 67 (10f,Cur,GS,Aug 16)
Viburnum 34 (14f,Not,S,Oct 15)
Vicious Circle 42 (10f,Pon,GF,Jun 3)
Vicki Romara 44 (12f,Thi,GS,May 17)
Victory Team (IRE) 59 (7f,Nwb,G,Oct 24)
Village Native (FR) 42 (5f,Goo,GS,May 22)
Villarica (IRE) 37 (7½f,Chs,GF,Jly 11)
Vintage Escape (IRE) 32 (7f,Cur,GS,Jun 28)
V I P Charlie 35 (6f,Wnd,G,Jly 7)
Virtual Reality 69 (10f,Nwm,G,May 2)
Viscoumtess Brave (IRE) 32 (10f,Nwb,G,Jun 12)
Visionary (FR) 81 (10f,Lon,G,Oct 4)
Viva Verdi (IRE) 43 (8f,Not,GF,Aug 6)
Vivo (IRE) 34 (8f,Cur,GS,Jun 27)
Voila Premiere (IRE) 54 (12f,Don,G,May 24)
Vola Via (USA) 64 (11f,War,GF,Apr 12)
Volley (IRE) 64 (7f,War,GF,Jly 19)
Voyagers Quest (USA) 67 (10f,San,GS,Apr 26)
Vrennan 32 (10½f,Hay,GS,May 24)

Waders Dream (IRE) 32 (7f,Crl,F,Aug 27)
Wafir (IRE) 72 (10f,Don,GF,Spt 13)
Wahiba Sands 75 (12f,Don,GF,Spt 12)
Waikiki Beach (USA) 54 (8f,Chp,G,Aug 3)
Waiting Game (IRE) 51 (9f,Rip,GF,Apr 9)
Wakeel (USA) 70 (12f,Eps,G,Aug 10)
Walkabout 36 (14f,Nwm,GF,May 31)
Walk the Beat 52 (7f,Don,G,May 24)
Warbler 74 (15f,Lon,G,Oct 4)
Wardara 38 (5f,Lon,S,May 11)
Warm Spell 46 (10f,Pon,G,Jly 8)
Warning Express 35 (6f,Fol,G,Oct 21)
Warningford 50 (8f,Don,G,Jly 31)
Warning Reef 48 (17f,Pon,GF,Apr 22)
Warning Time 87 (6f,Asc,GS,Jun 20)
Warren Knight 36 (9f,Goo,G,Jun 13)
Warring 33 (7f,War,F,May 5)
Warrior King (IRE) 41 (8f,Lei,S,Oct 13)
Wasp Ranger (USA) 70 (7f,Eps,G,Jun 7)
Watch Me (IRE) 31 (5f,Bat,GF,Apr 29)
Watch The Fire 57 (6f,Not,GF,Spt 15)
Water Flower 46 (12f,Nwm,GF,Oct 2)
Waterspout (USA) 30 (10f,Red,GF,Oct 18)
Waterwave (USA) 51 (10f,Ayr,S,Oct 14)
Wathbat Nashwan 53 (10½f,Hay,G,Jly 5)
Waypoint 77 (7f,Nwb,GF,Jly 18)
Wee Dram 35 (7f,Nwm,G,Apr 15)
Weet-A-Minute (IRE) 77 (7f,Yor,G,Aug 21)
Weet Ees Girl (IRE) 31 (5f,Cat,G,Apr 23)
Weetman's Weigh (IRE) 69 (7f,Thi,F,Jun 2)
Welcome Heights 45 (7f,Chp,G,Spt 11)
Welcome Home 32 (7f,Sal,GS,Jun 25)
Wellaki (USA) 48 (10½f,Yor,G,Oct 8)
Well Armed (IRE) 34 (10f,Nwc,GF,May 5)
Wellcome Inn 31 (14f,Red,F,Aug 23)
Well Drawn 37 (7f,Chp,GF,Jly 25)
Wellspring (IRE) 64 (6f,Nwm,S,Jun 27)
Well Warned 50 (7f,Red,GF,Oct 7)
Welsh Mill (IRE) 65 (14f,Hay,S,May 5)
Welsh Mountain 34 (8f,Yar,GF,Aug 6)
Welsh Queen (IRE) 40 (8f,Leo,YS,May 11)
Welton Arsenal 70 (8f,Kem,G,May 5)
Welville 38 (7f,Hay,S,May 5)
Wentbridge Lad (IRE) 48 (10f,Bri,F,Aug 16)
Wesley's Lad (IRE) 34 (14f,Not,S,Jly 5)
Westcourt Magic 77 (5f,Chs,S,Aug 30)
Western General 47 (9f,Ham,S,Jly 1)
Western Hour (USA) 34 (10f,Nwb,G,Jun 12)
Western Sonata (IRE) 34 (8f,Don,G,May 6)
West Humble 51 (7f,Lin,G,May 10)
Westminster (IRE) 52 (10f,Wnd,GF,Jly 28)
What A Fuss 44 (11½f,Yar,G,Jly 16)
Whatever's Right (IRE) 52 (10f,Wnd,GF,Jly 28)
What Happened Was 41 (8f,Nwm,G,Jly 8)
Whenby (USA) 90 (7f,Lon,,Jun 22)
Whirlawhile (USA) 35 (10f,Bat,GS,May 19)
Whispering Dawn 47 (10f,Bat,GF,Jly 17)
Whitechapel (USA) 69 (12f,Asc,Hy,Oct 10)
White Emir 71 (6f,Nwb,GF,May 28)
White Plains (IRE) 62 (12f,Eps,G,Apr 23)
White Settler 52 (7f,Sal,GF,Jun 11)
Whitewater Affair 82 (12f,Yor,G,Aug 20)
Whitley Grange Boy 42 (10f,Nwc,G,Mar 25)
Whittle Rock 47 (8f,Pon,G,May 23)
Whizz Kid 32 (5f,Bat,GF,Apr 29)
Who's That Man 34 (10f,Bri,F,Jly 16)
Wijara (IRE) 61 (11½f,Wnd,G,Aug 23)
Wilawander 66 (12f,Don,GF,Mar 22)
Wilcuma 72 (10f,Kem,G,Spt 21)
Wild Event (USA) 80 (8f,Hpk,F,Nov 8)
Wild Palm 51 (7f,Goo,GS,May 22)
Wild Rice 53 (7f,Nwm,G,Apr 16)
Wild Rita 66 (12f,Eps,G,Apr 23)
Wild Sky (IRE) 60 (7f,Nwm,GF,Nov 1)
Wildwood Flower 79 (6f,Ayr,G,Spt 20)
Wilkins 48 (16f,Goo,GF,Spt 25)
Will Do 48 (6f,Not,GF,Apr 8)
William's Well 43 (5f,Crl,G,Jun 26)

Willie Conquer 71 (12f,Don,S,Nov 8)
Willow Dale (IRE) 61 (6f,Eps,S,Jly 2)
Will To Win 36 (5f,Chp,G,Spt 11)
Will You Dance 40 (12f,Hay,GF,Aug 8)
Wind Cheetah (USA) 63 (7f,Asc,GF,Jun 18)
Windrush Boy 42 (5f,War,GF,Jly 19)
Windrush Holly 33 (10f,Wnd,GF,Jun 2)
Windsor Castle 69 (16f,Asc,GF,Jun 18)
Windswept (IRE) 33 (8f,Wnd,G,Aug 23)
Windy Treat (USA) 42 (7f,Nwm,GF,Aug 9)
Winged Hussar 41 (16f,Cur,GS,Oct 4)
Winnebago 40 (13f,Ham,G,Aug 13)
Winsome Wooster 56 (7f,San,GF,Jly 30)
Winston 38 (8f,Ham,G,Spt 29)
Winter Garden 74 (15f,Nwm,GF,Jly 10)
Winter Romance 75 (8f,Yor,G,May 14)
Winter Scout (USA) 43 (7f,Crl,G,Jly 5)
Wishing Stone (USA) 64 (10f,Nwb,GF,Spt 18)
Witchfinder (USA) 45 (8f,Lei,S,Oct 13)
Witching Hour (IRE) 49 (8f,Asc,GF,Apr 30)
With A Will 30 (8f,Chp,G,Aug 3)
With Fire (USA) 57 (12f,Lon,S,May 15)
Without Friends (IRE) 32 (6f,Bri,F,Apr 11)
Wixim (USA) 82 (8f,San,GF,Apr 25)
Wizard King 90 (7f,Nwc,G,Jly 26)
Wolf Mountain 53 (6f,Yar,GF,Aug 10)
Woodbeck 57 (8f,Don,G,Jly 30)
Woodren (USA) 57 (12f,Hay,G,Jly 5)
Woody's Boy (IRE) 40 (11½f,Wnd,G,Aug 4)
World Premier 83 (6f,Yor,G,May 13)
Worldwide Elsie (USA) 47 (10f,Bev,GF,Apr 24)
Wot No Fax 44 (12f,Eps,G,Apr 23)
Wray (IRE) 30 (10f,Cur,G,May 3)

Xenophon of Cunaxa (IRE) 40 (7f,Nwm,S,Jun 28)
Xylem (USA) 58 (8f,Nwc,GF,Oct 1)

Yabint El Sultan 67 (10f,Nwb,GF,Spt 18)
Yak Alfaraj 36 (12f,Chp,G,May 26)
Yalaietanee 64 (7f,Nwb,GF,Apr 19)
Yalta (IRE) 70 (8f,Kem,G,Spt 21)
Ya Malak 88 (5f,Eps,G,Jun 7)
Yarob (IRE) 45 (10f,Eps,G,Spt 5)
Yashmak (USA) 75 (12f,Eps,G,Jun 6)
Yavlensky (IRE) 43 (10f,San,GS,Apr 26)
Yeast 37 (8f,Don,GF,Mar 20)
Yeoman Oliver 46 (8f,Not,G,Nov 3)
Yet Again 42 (12f,Chp,GF,Aug 3)
Yokohama (USA) 72 (12f,Lon,GF,Oct 5)
Yorkie George 74 (7f,Yar,G,Jly 16)
Yorkshire (IRE) 64 (10½f,Yor,G,May 14)
Youdontsay 70 (6f,Lin,S,May 10)
Young Ben (IRE) 30 (5f,Cat,GF,Jly 23)
Young Bigwig (IRE) 63 (6f,Hay,G,Spt 21)
Young Duke (IRE) 31 (8f,Sal,GS,Jun 25)
Young Precedent 57 (7f,Nwb,GF,Aug 16)
Your Most Welcome 51 (10f,Wnd,GF,Jly 28)
Yours In Sport 30 (8f,Rip,GF,Apr 9)
Yxenery (IRE) 56 (10f,Lon,S,May 18)

Zaahir (IRE) 32 (7f,Don,GF,Mar 21)
Zafarabad (IRE) 56 (10f,Leo,G,Apr 19)
Zafarelli 33 (15½f,Fol,S,Jly 2)
Zahran (IRE) 30 (7f,Fol,GF,May 28)
Za-Im 64 (6f,Nwb,GF,Jly 19)
Zaima (IRE) 66 (7f,Goo,G,May 20)
Zalitzine (USA) 54 (9f,Nwb,GS,Oct 25)
Zamalek (USA) 39 (8f,San,G,Aug 13)
Zamindar (USA) 86 (8f,Nwm,G,May 3)
Zankle (USA) 66 (9f,Nwm,GF,Oct 4)
Zaralaska 89 (10f,Goo,GF,Jly 29)
Zaretski 47 (7f,Nwm,GF,Oct 4)
Zelda Zonk 65 (7f,Red,G,May 12)
Zenith Rose (FR) 59 (10½f,Lon,S,May 11)
Zermatt (IRE) 43 (9f,Nwb,GF,Jly 19)
Zerpour (IRE) 60 (12f,Don,G,Oct 25)
Zidac 55 (10f,Lin,GF,Jun 14)
Ziggy's Dancer (USA) 64 (6f,Ayr,G,Spt 20)
Zinzari (FR) 49 (10f,Pon,GF,Jun 3)
Zoom Up (IRE) 69 (10f,Nwm,GF,Spt 30)
Zorba 54 (9f,Ayr,S,Oct 13)
Zorro 30 (10f,Yar,F,Jun 5)
Zugudi 64 (10f,Nwm,GS,Oct 16)
Zuhair 72 (6f,Kem,G,May 24)
Zurs (IRE) 55 (7f,Nwm,G,Apr 16)

THREE YEAR-OLDS AND UPWARDS - Sand

Absolute Liberty (USA) 51 (8½f,Wol,Std,Aug 8)
Advance Repro 37 (6f,Sou,Std,Apr 1)
Afaan (IRE) 48 (6f,Sou,Std,Mar 17)
African-Pard (IRE) 34 (11f,Sou,Std,Feb 17)
Agent 32 (7f,Lin,Std,Feb 20)
Ajina (USA) 86 (9f,Hpk,Fst,Nov 8)
Alarico (FR) 48 (10f,Lin,Std,Jan 28)
Albaha (USA) 49 (12f,Wol,Std,Mar 5)
Al Helal 35 (12f,Lin,Std,Jan 23)
Aljaz 36 (5f,Wol,Std,Aug 8)
All In Leather 34 (9½f,Wol,Std,Aug 8)
All On 54 (12f,Wol,Std,May 11)
Alpine Hideaway (IRE) 52 (7f,Sou,Std,Jly 10)
Al Reet (IRE) 42 (6f,Sou,Std,Jun 19)
Alsahib (USA) 57 (9½f,Wol,Std,Jun 7)
Always Happy 36 (12f,Lin,Std,Jan 30)
Amadour (IRE) 51 (12f,Lin,Std,Feb 25)
Ambidextrous (IRE) 32 (12f,Wol,Std,Feb 12)
Amico 33 (10f,Lin,Std,Mar 1)
Amington Lass 31 (5f,Wol,Slw,Jan 4)
Amy Leigh (IRE) 38 (5f,Wol,Slw,Jan 4)
Anak-Ku 52 (10f,Lin,Std,Apr 4)
Anchor Venture 42 (10f,Lin,Std,May 14)
Angel Face (USA) 57 (9½f,Wol,Std,Mar 15)
Anita's Contessa (IRE) 40 (6f,Sou,Std,Jan 10)
Anokato 43 (5f,Lin,Std,Nov 6)
Anonym (IRE) 54 (8½f,Wol,Std,May 30)
Another Batchworth 37 (5f,Lin,Std,Nov 6)
Another Nightmare (IRE) 30 (6f,Wol,Std,Mar 5)
Ansellman 46 (5f,Wol,Std,Mar 8)
Antonias Melody 63 (6f,Sou,Std,Feb 14)
Anyar Reem 56 (11f,Sou,Std,Jun 19)
Apollo Red 51 (6f,Lin,Std,Apr 4)
Arcatura 30 (10f,Lin,Std,Jan 11)
Arian Spirit (IRE) 32 (16f,Wol,Std,Jly 25)
Around Fore Alliss 44 (8f,Lin,Std,Jun 21)
Arzani (USA) 40 (10f,Lin,Std,Jan 2)
Ashgore 30 (6f,Sou,Std,Jan 13)
As-Is 30 (12f,Lin,Std,Feb 27)
Aspecto Lad (IRE) 34 (8f,Sou,Std,Jan 13)
Assume (USA) 32 (8f,Lin,Std,Mar 24)
Astrac (IRE) 57 (7f,Wol,Std,Nov 1)
At Liberty (IRE) 51 (12f,Lin,Std,Mar 27)
Awesome Power 38 (10f,Lin,Std,Jan 2)
Awesome Venture 56 (6f,Sou,Std,Jan 13)

Baaheth (USA) 34 (8f,Lin,Std,Jan 14)
Baby Jane 30 (8½f,Wol,Std,Mar 8)
Backview 30 (12f,Wol,Std,Feb 21)
Bagshot 46 (8f,Lin,Std,Feb 27)
Bailieborough Boy (IRE) 33 (8½f,Wol,Std,Feb 19)
Bakers Daughter 30 (10f,Lin,Std,Feb 25)
Ballard Lady (IRE) 34 (7f,Sou,Std,Feb 3)
Banzhaf (USA) 70 (8f,Lin,Std,May 9)
Bapsford 35 (8½f,Wol,Std,Spt 30)
Barbara's Jewel 45 (12f,Wol,Std,May 11)
Barbason 51 (8f,Lin,Std,Mar 27)
Bardon Hill Boy (IRE) 48 (9½f,Wol,Std,Jan 29)
Barrack Yard 39 (6f,Wol,Std,Apr 12)
Barrel of Hope 51 (7f,Lin,Std,Jan 28)
Bashful Brave 45 (5f,Sou,Std,Spt 8)
Batabanoo 31 (12f,Sou,Std,Apr 28)
Batoutoftheblue 38 (15f,Wol,Std,Spt 30)
Beauman 31 (9½f,Wol,Slw,Jan 4)
Beaumont (IRE) 37 (15f,Wol,Std,Jan 8)
Bedouin Prince (USA) 33 (13f,Lin,Std,Jun 28)
Behrens (USA) 56 (10f,Hpk,Fst,Nov 8)
Ben Gunn 34 (10f,Lin,Std,Jan 2)
Benjamins Law 47 (8f,Sou,Std,Apr 28)
Bentico 61 (8f,Lin,Std,Jun 24)
Bernard Seven (IRE) 43 (8f,Lin,Std,Feb 18)
Besweetome 36 (8f,Lin,Std,Feb 22)
Bet On Sunshine (USA) 97 (6f,Hpk,Fst,Nov 8)
Be Warned 38 (8½f,Wol,Std,Oct 18)
Beyond Calculation (USA) 31 (6f,Wol,Std,Spt 20)
Big Bang 32 (8½f,Wol,Std,Feb 26)
Big Ben 50 (7f,Lin,Std,Jun 28)
Biya (IRE) 35 (10f,Lin,Std,Jan 30)
Blue Flyer (IRE) 64 (7f,Lin,Std,Jan 18)
Blues Magic (IRE) 31 (5f,Lin,Std,Feb 22)
Blues Queen 32 (5f,Sou,Std,Spt 8)
Blushing Desert 39 (7f,Lin,Std,Nov 6)
Blushing Grenadier (IRE) 33 (8f,Lin,Std,Feb 22)
Boffy (IRE) 39 (5f,Wol,Slw,Jan 4)
Bogan (IRE) 39 (7f,Lin,Std,Aug 28)
Bogart 31 (7f,Wol,Std,Feb 19)
Bold Aristocrat (IRE) 55 (6f,Sou,Std,Jun 19)
Bold Effort (FR) 73 (5f,Wol,Std,Mar 8)
Bold Frontier 60 (5f,Wol,Std,Mar 8)
Bold Street (IRE) 32 (6f,Sou,Std,Jly 21)
Bon Guest (IRE) 35 (9½f,Wol,Std,Jly 11)
Bonne Ville 32 (12f,Wol,Std,Nov 1)
Bon Secret (IRE) 47 (8½f,Wol,Std,Jan 8)
Bowled Over 30 (12f,Lin,Std,May 14)
Brand New Dance 37 (12f,Wol,Std,Apr 12)
Brilliant Red 57 (10f,Lin,Std,Feb 11)
Broadstairs Beauty (IRE) 60 (6f,Sou,Std,Jan 27)
Broughtons Formula 44 (16f,Lin,Std,Feb 11)
Broughton's Pride (IRE) 40 (7f,Sou,Std,Feb 24)
Broughtons Turmoil 40 (8½f,Wol,Std,Jun 21)
Brutal Fantasy (IRE) 46 (6f,Sou,Std,Jan 3)

Calendula 41 (10f,Lin,Std,May 9)
Canadian Fantasy 39 (9½f,Wol,Std,Jun 18)
Canary Falcon 31 (15f,Wol,Slw,Jan 4)
Can Can Charlie 33 (10f,Lin,Std,Jan 9)
Canton Venture 66 (12f,Lin,Std,May 14)
Captain Carat 35 (6f,Sou,Std,Jan 20)
Captain Scott (IRE) 35 (8f,Sou,Std,Mar 17)
Captain's Day 43 (10f,Lin,Std,Feb 25)
Carmine Lake (IRE) 56 (6f,Hpk,Fst,Nov 8)
Carol Again 34 (11f,Sou,Std,Feb 17)
Carol's Dream (USA) 33 (12f,Sou,Std,Apr 28)
Cartouche 33 (8f,Sou,Std,Apr 28)
Cashmere Lady 62 (8½f,Wol,Std,Jun 21)
Castle Ashby Jack 34 (6f,Lin,Std,May 14)
Castles Burning (USA) 49 (8f,Lin,Std,Mar 24)
Castle Secret 40 (16f,Wol,Std,Jly 25)
Caudillo (IRE) 38 (8½f,Wol,Std,Mar 8)
Ceanothus (IRE) 32 (12f,Wol,Std,Aug 16)
Cedez le Passage (FR) 31 (9½f,Wol,Std,Jan 8)
Celestial Choir 47 (9½f,Wol,Std,Jan 8)
Certain Magic 32 (15f,Wol,Std,Oct 6)
Chadleigh Lane (USA) 51 (9½f,Wol,Std,Mar 15)
Chadwell Hall 62 (5f,Sou,Std,Apr 1)
Champagne Warrior (IRE) 43 (11f,Sou,Std,Jun 19)

Chemcast 43 (5f,Wol,Std,Jan 22)
Cherokee Flight 45 (9½f,Wol,Std,Aug 16)
Chewit 69 (8f,Lin,Std,Mar 1)
Chilling 33 (5f,Wol,Std,Feb 26)
China Castle 67 (12f,Wol,Std,Feb 19)
Cim Bom Bom (IRE) 64 (7f,Wol,Std,Feb 12)
Circled (USA) 41 (12f,Sou,Std,Jan 10)
Classic Ballet (FR) 49 (12f,Wol,Std,Oct 18)
Classy Chief 30 (13f,Lin,Std,Feb 13)
Clear Mandate (USA) 57 (9f,Hpk,Fst,Nov 8)
Coleridge 38 (16f,Lin,Std,Mar 4)
Colins Choice 37 (8½f,Wol,Std,Aug 16)
Colosse 30 (13f,Lin,Std,Feb 8)
Concer Arall 39 (8½f,Wol,Std,Nov 1)
Concer Un 48 (8½f,Wol,Std,Jun 21)
Confide (USA) 87 (6f,Hpk,Fst,Nov 8)
Corinchili 34 (5f,Sou,Std,May 8)
Cotteir Chief (IRE) 63 (12f,Wol,Std,Apr 8)
Count Tony 38 (10f,Lin,Std,Jly 11)
Crafty Friend (USA) 51 (6f,Hpk,Fst,Nov 8)
Cretan Gift 86 (6f,Sou,Std,Feb 28)
Crystal Gold 38 (9½f,Wol,Std,May 11)
Cyrian (IRE) 43 (8½f,Wol,Std,Mar 8)
Czarna (IRE) 31 (12f,Lin,Std,Feb 18)

Daawe (USA) 65 (5f,Sou,Std,Apr 1)
Dahiyah (USA) 34 (7f,Sou,Std,Jan 13)
Daintree (IRE) 30 (6f,Sou,Std,Oct 20)
Dalliance (IRE) 67 (9½f,Wol,Std,Jun 7)
Dances With Hooves 39 (10f,Lin,Std,Jan 16)
Dancing-Alone 32 (12f,Sou,Std,Feb 10)
Dancing Mystery 44 (6f,Sou,Std,Oct 20)
Dancing Sioux 44 (8½f,Wol,Std,May 30)
Dande Flyer 41 (5f,Wol,Std,Jan 8)
Daring Flight (USA) 30 (8½f,Wol,Std,Feb 26)
Dark Waters (IRE) 33 (16f,Lin,Std,Aug 2)
Daryabad (IRE) 36 (7f,Lin,Std,Jan 4)
Davis Rock 36 (7f,Wol,Std,Oct 6)
Davoski 40 (10f,Lin,Std,Apr 4)
Dawalib (USA) 45 (7f,Lin,Std,Feb 8)
Dawam Allail (IRE) 42 (9½f,Wol,Std,May 24)
Deeply Vale (IRE) 44 (7f,Sou,Std,Aug 15)
Defined Feature (IRE) 41 (7f,Wol,Std,Feb 26)
Delrob 37 (6f,Sou,Std,Feb 14)
Deputy Commander (USA) 86 (10f,Hpk,Fst,Nov 8)
Desert Calm (IRE) 30 (8f,Lin,Std,Feb 18)
Desert Invader (IRE) 49 (7f,Sou,Std,Jan 6)
Dictation (USA) 32 (6f,Sou,Std,Feb 24)
Digpast (IRE) 50 (10f,Lin,Std,Mar 4)
Dirab 38 (12f,Sou,Std,Mar 14)
Dominant Air 39 (6f,Wol,Std,Jan 29)
Domino Flyer 36 (8f,Sou,Std,Jan 10)
Don Sebastian 47 (9½f,Wol,Std,Feb 12)
Don't Worry Mike 46 (8½f,Wol,Std,Nov 1)
Double Espresso (IRE) 30 (10f,Lin,Std,Jan 7)
Double March 31 (10f,Lin,Std,Jan 9)
Double-O 47 (6f,Sou,Std,Mar 14)
Double Oscar (IRE) 48 (6f,Wol,Std,Oct 18)
Double Rush (IRE) 41 (10f,Lin,Std,May 24)
Dowty (USA) 89 (10f,Hpk,Fst,Nov 8)
Dragonjoy 45 (8½f,Wol,Std,Apr 8)
Dream Carrier (IRE) 37 (7f,Sou,Std,Feb 24)
Dr Edgar 41 (12f,Wol,Std,Mar 15)
Duello 31 (8½f,Wol,Std,Apr 12)
Duke Valentino 62 (7f,Lin,Std,Jan 23)

Eager To Please 34 (7f,Lin,Std,Jan 2)
Eagle Dancer 49 (9½f,Wol,Std,May 24)
Eastleigh 37 (8f,Lin,Std,Mar 13)
Effectual 53 (8½f,Wol,Std,Apr 12)
Effervescence 52 (7f,Lin,Std,Jan 2)
Ela Man Howa 39 (12f,Lin,Std,Jan 18)
Elite Hope (USA) 59 (7f,Wol,Slw,Jan 4)
Elmhurst (USA) 99 (6f,Hpk,Fst,Nov 8)
El Nido 35 (12f,Sou,Std,Jan 24)
Elton Ledger (IRE) 57 (6f,Sou,Std,Jan 13)
Enchanting Eve 35 (6f,Sou,Std,Jan 3)
English Invader 51 (13f,Lin,Std,Mar 4)
Ertlon 59 (8f,Lin,Std,May 14)
Escena (USA) 79 (9f,Hpk,Fst,Nov 8)
Ethbaat (USA) 51 (9½f,Wol,Std,Mar 15)
Etterby Park (USA) 36 (12f,Wol,Std,Apr 8)
Eurobox Boy 32 (8½f,Wol,Std,Jly 11)
Euro Forum 36 (15f,Wol,Std,Oct 6)
Eurolink the Lad 32 (9½f,Wol,Std,Apr 26)
Everset (FR) 47 (8½f,Wol,Std,May 30)
Exotic Wood (USA) 91 (6f,Hpk,Fst,Nov 8)
Explosive Power 41 (9½f,Wol,Slw,Jan 4)

Failed To Hit 46 (8½f,Wol,Std,Jly 25)
Fairy Knight 42 (10f,Lin,Std,Mar 4)
Farley Mount 35 (10f,Lin,Std,Apr 4)
Farmost 72 (9½f,Wol,Std,Spt 30)
Father Dan (IRE) 45 (8f,Lin,Std,Feb 11)
Faym (IRE) 37 (7f,Wol,Std,Apr 8)
Featherstone Lane 49 (5f,Sou,Std,Spt 8)
Fife Major (USA) 41 (7f,Wol,Std,Jly 11)
Filial (IRE) 58 (12f,Wol,Std,Nov 1)
First Maite 52 (5f,Wol,Std,Apr 26)
Flag Fen (USA) 31 (8f,Sou,Std,Feb 28)
Flagstaff (USA) 31 (8½f,Wol,Std,Feb 21)
Foot Battalion (IRE) 48 (8½f,Wol,Std,Mar 5)
Forcing Bid 52 (6f,Wol,Std,Spt 30)
Forest Boy 40 (9½f,Wol,Std,Jan 4)
Forgotten Times (USA) 43 (6f,Lin,Std,Feb 25)
Fort Knox (IRE) 40 (7f,Lin,Std,Jan 4)
Fresh Fruit Daily 42 (12f,Wol,Std,May 11)
Friendly Brave (USA) 37 (6f,Lin,Std,Apr 4)

Gadge 43 (6f,Wol,Std,Oct 4)
Gad Yakoun 32 (7f,Wol,Slw,Jan 4)
Galapino 48 (8½f,Wol,Std,Jan 8)
General Haven 56 (12f,Lin,Std,May 14)
General Sir Peter (IRE) 42 (5f,Wol,Std,Apr 12)
Genuine John (IRE) 44 (8f,Sou,Std,Jan 24)
Gi La High 49 (5f,Wol,Std,Mar 5)
Globetrotter (IRE) 60 (9½f,Wol,Std,Feb 19)
Glow Forum 53 (12f,Wol,Std,Oct 4)
Going For Broke 33 (8½f,Wol,Std,May 24)
Gold Blade 47 (13f,Lin,Std,Mar 4)
Golden Hadeer 46 (15f,Wol,Std,Jan 8)
Golden Pound (USA) 35 (6f,Wol,Std,Oct 18)
Golden Touch (USA) 34 (9½f,Wol,Std,Jan 8)
Goodbye Gatemen (IRE) 50 (7f,Lin,Std,May 14)
Goodwood Lass (IRE) 32 (12f,Wol,Std,Jun 18)
Goretski (IRE) 50 (5f,Sou,Std,Jun 6)
Grand Cru 31 (12f,Sou,Std,Apr 28)
Grand Hotel (IRE) 32 (9½f,Wol,Std,Aug 16)
Greatest 55 (7f,Lin,Std,Feb 25)
Greenspan (IRE) 55 (12f,Wol,Std,Nov 1)
Gresatre 49 (6f,Sou,Std,Mar 3)
Ground Game 51 (12f,Wol,Std,May 24)
Guest Alliance (IRE) 47 (16f,Lin,Std,Feb 11)
Gulf Shaadi 55 (8f,Sou,Std,Jan 13)

Hal's Pal 77 (8½f,Wol,Std,Apr 12)
Hannah's Usher 51 (6f,Wol,Std,Nov 1)
Happy Medium (IRE) 30 (11f,Sou,Std,Mar 3)
Harmony In Red 31 (7f,Lin,Std,Feb 6)
Haroldon (IRE) 30 (10f,Lin,Std,Spt 9)
Hattaafeh (IRE) 52 (16f,Lin,Std,Feb 22)
Hatta Sunshine (USA) 36 (8f,Lin,Std,Jan 23)
Hawaii Storm (FR) 42 (7f,Lin,Std,Jan 21)
Hayes Way (IRE) 36 (8f,Lin,Std,Feb 6)
Hazel 37 (9½f,Wol,Std,Jan 11)
Heathyards Lady (USA) 34 (8½f,Wol,Std,Oct 18)
Heighth of Fame 58 (13f,Lin,Std,Mar 4)
Henry the Hawk 39 (5f,Sou,Std,Spt 8)
Hesabull (USA) 98 (6f,Hpk,Fst,Nov 8)
Hever Golf Charger (IRE) 34 (7f,Lin,Std,Feb 15)
Hever Golf Eagle 34 (10f,Lin,Std,Feb 25)
Hidden Lake (USA) 50 (9f,Hpk,Fst,Nov 8)
Hill Farm Dancer 52 (9½f,Wol,Std,Feb 26)
Hoh Majestic (IRE) 40 (6f,Sou,Std,May 19)
Holders Hill (IRE) 36 (8f,Sou,Std,Jun 19)
Honor Glide (USA) 37 (10f,Hpk,Fst,Nov 8)
Hurtleberry (IRE) 54 (7f,Lin,Std,Jan 28)

Iamus 50 (7f,Sou,Std,Mar 3)
Iblis (IRE) 67 (7f,Sou,Std,Mar 3)
Icy Guest (USA) 43 (7f,Sou,Std,Jly 21)
Illuminate 31 (12f,Lin,Std,Feb 6)
Il Trastevere (FR) 31 (12f,Lin,Std,Jan 4)
Imperial Garden (IRE) 33 (5f,Lin,Std,Jan 23)
Indigo Dawn 43 (12f,Wol,Std,Oct 6)
Infamous (USA) 31 (9½f,Wol,Std,Jan 29)
In Good Faith 39 (8f,Sou,Std,Jan 6)
In the Money (IRE) 45 (12f,Lin,Std,Feb 18)
Intiaash (IRE) 44 (7f,Sou,Std,Jly 10)
Invocation 52 (8f,Lin,Std,Feb 18)
Island Sanctuary (IRE) 34 (8f,Sou,Std,Apr 28)
Italian Symphony (IRE) 50 (6f,Wol,Std,Nov 1)
Itsinthepost 52 (7f,Wol,Std,Jly 11)
Ivory's Grab Hire 34 (5f,Lin,Std,Feb 20)

Jewel Princess (USA) 30 (9f,Hpk,Fst,Nov 8)
Jibereen 63 (7f,Sou,Std,Jan 13)
Jigsaw Boy 36 (7f,Sou,Std,May 12)
Johnnie the Joker 58 (8½f,Wol,Std,Jun 27)
Jolly Jackson 34 (8½f,Wol,Std,Feb 26)
Jo Maximus 42 (7f,Lin,Std,Jan 4)
Jona Holley 40 (8f,Sou,Std,Oct 20)
Joseph's Wine (IRE) 36 (9½f,Wol,Std,Jan 29)
Juggler 37 (7f,Lin,Std,May 14)
Justinianus (IRE) 37 (6f,Lin,Std,Feb 20)
Just Loui 41 (7f,Lin,Std,Jun 28)

Kafil (USA) 42 (10f,Lin,Std,Oct 27)
Kalamata 39 (12f,Sou,Std,Feb 10)
Kalar 52 (5f,Wol,Std,Mar 8)
Kalimat 45 (8f,Sou,Std,Jly 10)
Keen Companion 30 (10f,Lin,Std,Jly 26)
Ki Chi Saga (USA) 47 (8f,Lin,Std,Mar 27)
Kildee Lad 35 (6f,Lin,Std,Apr 4)
Kilnamartyra Girl 30 (12f,Sou,Std,Jan 24)
Kingchip Boy 48 (8f,Sou,Std,Feb 14)
Kira 52 (5f,Wol,Std,Mar 8)
Klipspinger 43 (6f,Sou,Std,Jan 1)
Knotty Hill 67 (7f,Sou,Std,Mar 3)
Komasta 35 (8½f,Wol,Slw,Jan 4)
Kriscliffe 42 (10f,Lin,Std,Mar 24)
Kristopher 33 (8f,Lin,Std,Jun 21)
Krystal Max (IRE) 46 (6f,Wol,Std,Jan 8)
Kuala Lipis (USA) 67 (8½f,Wol,Std,Mar 8)

Labudd (USA) 39 (12f,Lin,Std,Jan 16)
La Dolce Vita 43 (7f,Sou,Std,Mar 3)
Lady Sheriff 52 (5f,Sou,Std,May 8)
Lady Silk 35 (7f,Sou,Std,Feb 3)
La Modiste 47 (10f,Lin,Std,Jly 11)
Lancashire Legend 57 (7f,Lin,Std,Jan 16)
Law Dancer (IRE) 43 (8f,Lin,Std,Jun 24)
Lawn Lothario 41 (12f,Wol,Std,Mar 1)
Leading Spirit (IRE) 66 (12f,Wol,Std,Feb 19)
Legal Issue (IRE) 43 (8½f,Wol,Std,Aug 16)
Leigh Crofter 50 (6f,Sou,Std,Jan 10)
Lennox Lewis 36 (5f,Sou,Std,Spt 8)
Le Sport 48 (8f,Sou,Std,Jan 31)
Lift Boy (USA) 42 (7f,Lin,Std,Feb 15)
Liquid Gold (IRE) 53 (8f,Sou,Std,Aug 15)
Little Ibnr 53 (6f,Sou,Std,Jan 13)
Live Project (IRE) 45 (8f,Lin,Std,Mar 4)
Loch Style 52 (8½f,Wol,Std,Jan 8)
Lord Sky 45 (5f,Lin,Std,Mar 27)
Lucky Revenge 34 (6f,Sou,Std,Jan 27)
Lucy of Arabia (IRE) 37 (6f,Sou,Std,Mar 3)

Madrina 43 (5f,Wol,Std,Feb 19)
Maftun (USA) 38 (12f,Sou,Std,Feb 28)
Magazine Gap 30 (8f,Lin,Std,Jun 24)
Magic Fizz 30 (6f,Wol,Std,Apr 26)
Magic Mill (IRE) 62 (10f,Lin,Std,Nov 6)
Major Change 58 (12f,Wol,Std,Mar 5)
Malibu Man 55 (6f,Wol,Std,Spt 30)
Manful 30 (11f,Sou,Std,Jan 13)
Mangus (IRE) 38 (5f,Wol,Std,Feb 12)
Manikato (USA) 33 (7f,Lin,Std,Nov 6)
Mansab (USA) 65 (6f,Sou,Std,Feb 7)
Maradata (IRE) 39 (9½f,Wol,Std,Jan 22)
Mardrew 37 (8f,Sou,Std,Jan 13)
Marjorie Rose (IRE) 36 (6f,Sou,Std,Feb 14)
Marozia (USA) 35 (7f,Lin,Std,Nov 6)
Master Beveled 53 (10f,Lin,Std,Jan 14)
Master Boots 61 (7f,Sou,Std,Jly 26)
Master Foley 32 (5f,Wol,Std,Jly 25)
Master Millfield (IRE) 34 (12f,Wol,Std,Oct 4)
Master of Passion 39 (5f,Wol,Std,Jan 8)
Matthias Mystique 39 (16f,Lin,Std,Feb 13)
Ma Vielle Pouque (IRE) 46 (5f,Sou,Std,Spt 8)
Mellors (IRE) 40 (7f,Lin,Std,Feb 8)
Mels Baby (IRE) 38 (7f,Sou,Std,Feb 24)
Mendoza 35 (8f,Lin,Std,Mar 24)
Men's Exclusive (USA) 89 (6f,Hpk,Fst,Nov 8)
Mentalasanythin 37 (9½f,Wol,Std,Apr 26)
Merciless Cop 35 (9½f,Wol,Std,Jun 18)
Mersey Beat 30 (10f,Lin,Std,Mar 1)
Michael Venture 38 (10f,Lin,Std,Jly 26)
Mijas 54 (5f,Lin,Std,Jan 14)
Mike's Double (IRE) 54 (6f,Wol,Std,Oct 4)
Millroy (USA) 53 (8½f,Wol,Std,Jan 22)
Milos 41 (7f,Lin,Std,Jan 9)
Mimosa 36 (10f,Lin,Std,Mar 4)
Minister's Melody (USA) 61 (9f,Hpk,Fst,Nov 8)
Mister Aspecto (IRE) 55 (12f,Wol,Std,Oct 4)
Mizyan (IRE) 42 (16f,Wol,Std,Jly 25)
Molly Music 45 (8½f,Wol,Std,Oct 18)
Mon Bruce 54 (5f,Sou,Std,Spt 8)
Mono Lady (IRE) 57 (10f,Lin,Std,May 9)
Montecristo 31 (12f,Sou,Std,Oct 20)
Montone (IRE) 50 (12f,Lin,Std,Jan 18)
Moonraking 30 (12f,Sou,Std,Feb 24)
More Than You Know (IRE) 33 (12f,Lin,Std,Jan 25)
Mozambique (IRE) 39 (6f,Sou,Std,Oct 20)
Mr Bergerac (IRE) 47 (6f,Wol,Std,Oct 18)
Mr Frosty 44 (7f,Lin,Std,Feb 1)
Mr Nevermind (IRE) 58 (8f,Lin,Std,Feb 8)
Mr Sponge (USA) 35 (7f,Wol,Std,Nov 1)
Mullagh Hill Lad (IRE) 36 (5f,Sou,Std,Jun 13)
Mutahadeth 36 (8f,Sou,Std,Jun 19)
Mystery Matthias 30 (6f,Lin,Std,Feb 25)
Mystic Quest (IRE) 36 (12f,Lin,Std,Oct 27)
Mystic Strand 30 (12f,Sou,Std,Jly 26)
Mythical 50 (8f,Sou,Std,Spt 8)
Myttons Mistake 41 (6f,Sou,Std,Jan 27)

Nakhal 38 (10f,Lin,Std,Jan 2)
Napier Star 50 (5f,Wol,Std,May 24)
Napoleon Star (IRE) 31 (6f,Sou,Std,Feb 24)
Nashaat (USA) 37 (8f,Lin,Std,Jan 23)
Naughty Pistol (USA) 46 (6f,Sou,Std,Jan 27)
Needle Match 53 (6f,Sou,Std,Mar 17)
Needwood Epic 34 (15f,Wol,Std,Oct 6)
Never Think Twice 46 (7f,Lin,Std,Jan 4)
New Century (USA) 80 (8½f,Wol,Std,Mar 8)
Newlands Corner 44 (6f,Sou,Std,Aug 15)
Night City 63 (12f,Lin,Std,Nov 6)
Night Express 42 (7f,Wol,Std,Jun 7)
Nightingale Song 38 (5f,Wol,Std,Feb 12)
Night Wink (USA) 47 (10f,Lin,Std,Feb 18)
Nikita's Star (IRE) 59 (12f,Wol,Std,Feb 19)
Nineacres 38 (6f,Wol,Std,Nov 1)
Nobalino 33 (6f,Sou,Std,Oct 20)
Nomore Mr Niceguy 45 (8½f,Wol,Std,Jan 22)
Nordic Breeze (IRE) 42 (8f,Sou,Std,Jan 10)
Nordinex (IRE) 34 (8f,Lin,Std,Feb 18)
Nor-Do-I 59 (8½f,Wol,Std,Aug 8)
Northern Accord 31 (8½f,Wol,Std,Nov 1)
Northern Afleet (USA) 74 (6f,Hpk,Fst,Nov 8)
Northern Angel (IRE) 48 (7f,Lin,Std,Nov 6)
Northern Fan (IRE) 37 (9½f,Wol,Std,Mar 5)
Northern Motto 42 (12f,Wol,Std,Feb 12)
No Speeches (IRE) 37 (10f,Lin,Std,Mar 24)
No Submission (USA) 33 (11f,Sou,Std,Feb 17)
Noufari (FR) 49 (15f,Wol,Std,Jan 8)

Oberons Boy (IRE) 44 (8f,Lin,Std,Jan 7)
Oberon's Dart (IRE) 55 (7f,Sou,Std,Aug 15)
Once More for Luck (IRE) 43 (12f,Sou,Std,Feb 17)
Onefortheditch (USA) 43 (9½f,Wol,Std,Jan 22)
Onefourseven 35 (15f,Wol,Std,Spt 30)
One Off the Rail (USA) 38 (12f,Lin,Std,Mar 27)
Oneoftheoldones 34 (8f,Sou,Std,Jan 13)
Opera Buff (IRE) 54 (12f,Wol,Std,Oct 4)
Orange Place (IRE) 33 (8f,Sou,Std,Spt 8)
Our Eddie 30 (10f,Lin,Std,Jan 2)
Our People 30 (8f,Sou,Std,Aug 15)
Our Shadee (USA) 32 (8f,Lin,Std,Jan 16)
Outstayed Welcome 30 (16f,Lin,Std,Mar 4)

Pageboy 37 (6f,Lin,Std,Feb 11)
Paint It Black 32 (6f,Sou,Std,Jan 27)
Palacegate Jack (IRE) 62 (5f,Sou,Std,Spt 8)
Palacegate Touch 56 (7f,Lin,Std,Nov 6)
Palisander (IRE) 43 (10f,Lin,Std,Nov 6)
Palo Blanco 34 (7f,Sou,Std,Jly 10)
Paradise Navy 40 (15f,Wol,Std,Oct 6)
Pas De Reponse (USA) 50 (6f,Hpk,Fst,Nov 8)
Passionatti 33 (5f,Sou,Std,Spt 8)
Pater Noster (USA) 61 (9½f,Wol,Std,Feb 26)
Pegasus Bay 45 (10f,Lin,Std,Nov 6)
Pengamon 66 (8f,Lin,Std,May 9)
Pennywell 42 (8f,Lin,Std,Jun 14)
People Direct 35 (8½f,Wol,Std,Jun 21)
Perfect Brave 32 (5f,Wol,Std,Apr 12)
Pericles 61 (7f,Wol,Std,Oct 4)
Perilous Plight 39 (8f,Lin,Std,Mar 4)
Perpetual Light 43 (9½f,Wol,Std,Oct 4)
Persian Conquest (IRE) 37 (12f,Lin,Std,Jan 21)
Persuasion 41 (12f,Lin,Std,Jan 25)
Petoskin 54 (16f,Lin,Std,Feb 22)
Pharaoh's Joy 34 (6f,Wol,Std,Nov 1)
Pharly Dancer 32 (12f,Sou,Std,Apr 28)
Phoenix Princess 47 (8½f,Wol,Std,Oct 18)
Pinchincha (FR) 42 (9½f,Wol,Std,Feb 19)
Piquant 39 (8f,Lin,Std,Feb 27)
Plan For Profit (IRE) 43 (7f,Wol,Std,Nov 1)
Pleasure Trick (USA) 34 (7f,Sou,Std,Jan 6)
Plum First 32 (7f,Sou,Std,Jan 6)
Pointe Fine (FR) 33 (12f,Wol,Std,Aug 16)
Polar Champ 55 (12f,Wol,Std,Oct 4)
Polyphony (USA) 34 (12f,Wol,Std,Apr 12)
Premier Dance 45 (12f,Wol,Std,Mar 29)
Premier Generation (IRE) 37 (8½f,Wol,Std,Apr 8)
Presentiment 39 (8½f,Wol,Std,Nov 1)
Present Situation 46 (8f,Lin,Std,Feb 8)
Pride of Brixton 39 (6f,Wol,Std,Spt 30)
Prima Silk 61 (6f,Sou,Std,Jan 27)
Prime Light 48 (8f,Lin,Std,May 9)
Prince Danzig (IRE) 65 (12f,Wol,Std,Feb 19)
Princely Sound 57 (6f,Lin,Std,Feb 11)
Princess Efisio 43 (7f,Sou,Std,Jun 6)
Private Fixture (IRE) 55 (11f,Sou,Std,Jun 19)
Prophets Honour 45 (9½f,Wol,Std,Jan 11)
Protocol (IRE) 37 (10f,Lin,Std,Apr 4)
Punkah (USA) 44 (10f,Lin,Std,Feb 18)
Purple Fling 35 (7f,Lin,Std,Mar 13)
Puzzlement 43 (9½f,Wol,Std,Feb 19)

Qualitair Pride 34 (12f,Sou,Std,Jan 24)
Queenfisher 30 (8f,Lin,Std,Jan 18)
Queen of All Birds (IRE) 41 (8f,Lin,Std,Feb 8)
Queens Consul (IRE) 31 (8½f,Wol,Std,Apr 8)
Quiet Arch (IRE) 45 (10f,Lin,Std,Jan 14)

Radu Cool (USA) 77 (9f,Hpk,Fst,Nov 8)
Raffles Rooster 39 (12f,Wol,Std,Apr 8)
Raindeer Quest 33 (12f,Sou,Std,Jan 24)
Raise A Prince (FR) 54 (9½f,Wol,Std,May 24)
Rakis (IRE) 62 (7f,Wol,Std,Feb 12)
Rambo Waltzer 63 (8½f,Wol,Std,Mar 8)
Ramsey Hope 53 (5f,Lin,Std,Feb 27)
Random Kindness 47 (13f,Lin,Std,Feb 1)
Rasayel (USA) 46 (12f,Lin,Std,Jan 18)
Rawi 35 (7f,Lin,Std,Jan 21)
Regal Splendour (CAN) 50 (8f,Lin,Std,Feb 4)
Renown 40 (10f,Lin,Std,Feb 6)
Resist the Force (USA) 50 (8f,Lin,Std,Jun 14)
Rex Mundi 52 (12f,Wol,Std,Oct 6)
Richter Scale (USA) 41 (6f,Hpk,Fst,Nov 8)
Rififi 56 (5f,Lin,Std,Feb 20)
Ring the Chief 30 (7f,Sou,Std,Feb 24)
River Captain (USA) 42 (11f,Sou,Std,Mar 3)
River Keen (IRE) 62 (12f,Sou,Std,Mar 17)
River Seine (FR) 31 (7f,Lin,Std,Jan 21)
Road Racer (IRE) 37 (11f,Sou,Std,Feb 17)
Robbo 42 (15f,Wol,Std,Oct 6)
Robellion 57 (8f,Lin,Std,Feb 18)
Robo Magic (USA) 56 (6f,Lin,Std,Feb 11)
Rock Island Line (IRE) 31 (7f,Wol,Std,Oct 4)
Roffey Spinney (IRE) 43 (5f,Lin,Std,Feb 22)
Roman Reel (USA) 56 (8f,Lin,Std,Mar 13)
Rood Music 54 (15f,Wol,Std,Jan 8)
Royal Action 53 (10f,Lin,Std,Mar 1)
Royal Aty (IRE) 43 (8f,Lin,Std,Jan 9)
Royal Carlton (IRE) 58 (8f,Lin,Std,Mar 4)
Royal Cascade (IRE) 31 (6f,Wol,Std,Feb 12)
Royal Legend 30 (11f,Sou,Std,May 19)
Running Stag (USA) 37 (10f,Lin,Std,Feb 27)
Rutland Chantry (USA) 45 (9½f,Wol,Std,Spt 30)

Sabot 62 (8½f,Wol,Std,Mar 8)
Safa Dancer 30 (9½f,Wol,Std,May 24)
Safecracker 36 (12f,Wol,Std,Oct 6)
Safio 36 (5f,Wol,Std,Mar 8)
Sailormaite 43 (8f,Sou,Std,Aug 15)
Sally Slade 45 (5f,Lin,Std,Jan 14)
Sapphire Son (IRE) 31 (12f,Lin,Std,Jan 23)
Saratoga Red (USA) 46 (7f,Lin,Std,Nov 6)
Savinio (USA) 65 (10f,Hpk,Fst,Nov 8)
Scissor Ridge 52 (7f,Lin,Std,Jan 23)
Sea Danzig 56 (10f,Lin,Std,Nov 6)
Sea Devil 43 (6f,Sou,Std,Feb 24)
Sea God 38 (12f,Sou,Std,Jan 24)
Sea Spouse 45 (8f,Sou,Std,Jan 31)
Sea Victor 37 (11f,Sou,Std,Jan 6)
Sea Ya Maite 56 (8½f,Wol,Std,Oct 18)
Second Colours (USA) 70 (12f,Wol,Std,Feb 19)
Secret Aly (CAN) 50 (10f,Lin,Std,Feb 18)
Sedbergh (USA) 37 (14f,Sou,Std,Apr 1)
Selberry 45 (8½f,Wol,Std,Jan 22)
Sense of Priority 49 (6f,Sou,Std,Jan 20)
Shadow Jury 47 (6f,Sou,Std,Feb 7)
Shaffishayes 43 (8½f,Wol,Std,Apr 8)
Shalstayholy (IRE) 32 (7f,Lin,Std,Feb 13)
Shanghai Lil 35 (10f,Lin,Std,Apr 4)
Sharp Cat (USA) 82 (9f,Hpk,Fst,Nov 8)
Sharp Imp 38 (6f,Lin,Std,Jan 4)
Sharp 'n Smart 40 (7f,Lin,Std,Jan 16)

Sharp Shuffle (IRE) 53 (10f,Lin,Std,Nov 6)
Shashi (IRE) 34 (6f,Sou,Std,Jan 27)
Sheraz (IRE) 36 (10f,Lin,Std,Jan 30)
Shinerolla 66 (8½f,Wol,Std,Mar 8)
Shontaine 36 (7f,Lin,Std,Jan 9)
Shuttlecock 32 (11f,Sou,Std,Feb 17)
Signs And Wonders 40 (10f,Lin,Std,Aug 2)
Sihafi (USA) 45 (6f,Lin,Std,Feb 13)
Silca Key Silca 49 (7f,Wol,Std,Oct 6)
Silk Cottage 49 (5f,Sou,Std,Spt 8)
Sing With the Band 52 (5f,Wol,Std,Feb 19)
Siouxrouge 50 (6f,Wol,Std,Jan 22)
Sir Joey (USA) 51 (7f,Wol,Std,Nov 1)
Sis Garden 48 (7f,Wol,Std,Apr 26)
Skip Away (USA) 100 (10f,Hpk,Fst,Nov 8)
Sky Commander (USA) 55 (7f,Lin,Std,May 14)
Slip Jig (IRE) 48 (12f,Lin,Std,Jan 4)
Smart Boy (IRE) 40 (10f,Lin,Std,May 14)
Smart Guest 31 (7f,Wol,Std,May 24)
Smart Kid (IRE) 30 (7f,Wol,Std,Oct 6)
Snow Kid 53 (7f,Wol,Std,Jun 7)
Soaking 52 (8f,Lin,Std,Jan 16)
Soda 39 (6f,Sou,Std,Mar 3)
Soden (IRE) 47 (10f,Lin,Std,Aug 2)
Soldier Cove (USA) 41 (9½f,Wol,Std,Mar 5)
Soojama (IRE) 35 (12f,Lin,Std,Feb 18)
Sooty Tern 38 (8f,Lin,Std,Jan 7)
South Eastern Fred 58 (9½f,Wol,Std,Jan 29)
Soviet King (IRE) 32 (12f,Wol,Std,Feb 12)
Spaniards Close 63 (5f,Sou,Std,Spt 8)
Spaniard's Mount 39 (7f,Lin,Std,Feb 6)
Sparkling Edge 30 (5f,Lin,Std,Jan 23)
Sparky 48 (9½f,Wol,Std,Jly 25)
Speedy Classic (USA) 55 (6f,Lin,Std,Mar 1)
Spencer's Revenge 41 (8f,Lin,Std,Feb 11)
Spender 58 (5f,Lin,Std,Mar 27)
Square Deal (FR) 46 (8½f,Wol,Std,Apr 8)
Squire Corrie 52 (6f,Lin,Std,Feb 13)
Squire's Occasion (CAN) 52 (12f,Lin,Std,Jan 18)
Stalled (IRE) 35 (16f,Wol,Std,Jly 25)
Stand Tall 62 (7f,Sou,Std,Mar 3)
Star Rage (IRE) 38 (12f,Wol,Std,Jan 15)
Star Talent (USA) 62 (7f,Lin,Std,Jan 16)
Star Turn (IRE) 37 (7f,Lin,Std,Aug 28)
Statajack (IRE) 60 (12f,Lin,Std,Nov 6)
State Approval 62 (12f,Wol,Std,Jun 21)
State of Caution 69 (7f,Sou,Std,Mar 3)
Statistician 39 (7f,Lin,Std,Jan 9)
Steal 'Em 39 (6f,Wol,Std,Mar 5)
Steamroller Stanly 66 (10f,Lin,Std,Feb 11)
Stellar Line (USA) 37 (10f,Lin,Std,Feb 25)
Step On Degas 45 (7f,Lin,Std,Jan 4)
Stolen Kiss (IRE) 48 (6f,Sou,Std,Jun 19)
Stoppes Brow 58 (8f,Lin,Std,May 14)
Stretching (IRE) 38 (11f,Sou,Std,Mar 3)
Suez Tornado (IRE) 46 (8½f,Wol,Std,Mar 8)
Suga Hawk (IRE) 46 (11f,Sou,Std,Feb 17)
Superapparos 30 (5f,Sou,Std,Spt 8)
Superbelle 36 (10f,Lin,Std,Feb 15)
Super High 69 (9½f,Wol,Std,Jan 8)
Superior Force 38 (8f,Lin,Std,Jan 18)
Super Rocky 30 (5f,Sou,Std,Spt 8)
Supreme Star (USA) 40 (13f,Lin,Std,Jan 30)
Surf City 31 (7f,Sou,Std,Jan 27)
Swan Island 33 (6f,Sou,Std,Apr 28)
Sweet Mate 35 (6f,Sou,Std,May 19)
Sweet Supposin (IRE) 54 (8f,Lin,Std,May 9)
Sweet Wilhelmina 47 (7f,Lin,Std,Feb 22)
Swift 31 (8½f,Wol,Std,Mar 1)
Swinging Sixties (IRE) 32 (13f,Lin,Std,Mar 4)
Sword Arm 31 (8½f,Wol,Std,Mar 5)

Taiki Blizzard (USA) 62 (10f,Hpk,Fst,Nov 8)
Tailwind 34 (6f,Sou,Std,Jly 10)
Takhlid (USA) 49 (8f,Sou,Std,Apr 28)
Tallulah Belle 46 (9½f,Wol,Std,Jan 11)
Tart (FR) 39 (12f,Wol,Std,Oct 18)
Tatika 60 (8f,Lin,Std,Mar 1)
Tawafek (USA) 41 (10f,Lin,Std,Jan 2)
Tayovullin (IRE) 34 (7f,Sou,Std,Apr 1)
Tear White (IRE) 35 (5f,Lin,Std,Jan 23)
Tellion 40 (9½f,Wol,Std,May 24)
Terdad (USA) 37 (11f,Sou,Std,Mar 3)
Thai Morning 81 (8½f,Wol,Std,Mar 8)
Theatre Magic 54 (7f,Wol,Std,Apr 26)
The Barnsley Belle (IRE) 33 (8f,Sou,Std,Jan 13)
The Executor 42 (8½f,Wol,Std,Jly 25)
The Frisky Farmer 34 (7f,Lin,Std,Jan 9)
The Happy Fox (IRE) 55 (6f,Wol,Std,Oct 18)
The Institute Boy 38 (6f,Lin,Std,Jan 25)
The Wyandotte Inn 42 (6f,Sou,Std,Mar 14)
Thick as Thieves 32 (5f,Lin,Std,Feb 6)
Thordis 53 (6f,Wol,Std,Oct 4)
Three Arch Bridge 48 (8f,Sou,Std,Feb 10)
Three Weeks 38 (9½f,Wol,Slw,Jan 4)
Time Can Tell 44 (9½f,Wol,Std,Feb 19)
Time To Fly 39 (6f,Sou,Std,Jly 21)
Touch Gold (USA) 37 (10f,Hpk,Fst,Nov 8)
Touch'n'go 36 (10f,Lin,Std,Mar 1)
Track Gal (USA) 54 (6f,Hpk,Fst,Nov 8)
Trading Aces 42 (7f,Wol,Std,Apr 8)
Trafalger (USA) 59 (6f,Hpk,Fst,Nov 8)
Treasure Touch (IRE) 45 (6f,Sou,Std,Feb 3)
Tribal Peace (IRE) 46 (10f,Lin,Std,Jan 9)
Truly Bay 38 (7f,Sou,Std,Feb 24)
Tuigamala 39 (8f,Lin,Std,Mar 4)
Tumbleweed Ridge 37 (7f,Wol,Std,Mar 29)
Tuscan Dawn 38 (5f,Lin,Std,Mar 27)
Twilight Sleep (USA) 36 (12f,Wol,Std,Jun 27)
Twin Creeks 66 (7f,Lin,Std,Nov 6)

Ultra Beet 53 (6f,Wol,Std,Jan 8)

Venice Beach 38 (8½f,Wol,Std,Mar 5)
Venture Connect 40 (9½f,Wol,Std,Feb 12)
Village Native (FR) 48 (5f,Wol,Std,Aug 8)
Villarica (IRE) 52 (8½f,Wol,Std,Nov 1)
V I P Charlie 42 (6f,Sou,Std,Feb 10)

Waikiki Beach (USA) 55 (8½f,Wol,Std,May 30)
Walk the Beat 46 (6f,Sou,Std,Jan 20)
Waypoint 47 (6f,Wol,Std,Oct 18)
Weet And See 37 (8½f,Wol,Std,Mar 8)
Weetman's Weigh (IRE) 31 (7f,Wol,Std,Mar 29)
Wentbridge Lad (IRE) 30 (8½f,Wol,Std,May 30)
Western Sonata (IRE) 41 (10f,Lin,Std,May 24)
What A Fuss 36 (7f,Wol,Std,Jan 29)
Whatever's Right (IRE) 36 (8f,Lin,Std,Jan 23)
Whiskey Wisdom (CAN) 84 (10f,Hpk,Fst,Nov 8)
Whispering Dawn 36 (9½f,Wol,Std,Mar 1)
Whitelock Quest 32 (8½f,Wol,Std,Apr 8)
White Plains (IRE) 37 (12f,Wol,Std,Nov 1)
Wildfire (SWI) 39 (9½f,Wol,Std,Aug 16)
Wild Palm 41 (7f,Wol,Std,Jly 11)
Will Do 37 (6f,Lin,Std,Jan 2)
Will To Win 32 (6f,Wol,Std,Mar 8)
Without Friends (IRE) 31 (7f,Lin,Std,Jun 28)
Worldwide Elsie (USA) 37 (10f,Lin,Std,May 9)
Wottashambles 50 (16f,Lin,Std,Feb 11)

Xenophon of Cunaxa (IRE) 30 (6f,Lin,Std,Jan 25)

Yacht 31 (12f,Lin,Std,Nov 6)
Yeoman Oliver 50 (8f,Sou,Std,Jan 24)
Yet Again 45 (12f,Lin,Std,Jan 2)
Young Annabel (USA) 34 (7f,Sou,Std,May 12)

Zacaroon 32 (12f,Lin,Std,Jan 16)
Zahid (USA) 33 (10f,Lin,Std,Feb 25)
Zain Dancer 34 (6f,Sou,Std,Jly 21)
Zalotto (IRE) 45 (8f,Sou,Std,Spt 8)
Zamalek (USA) 33 (10f,Lin,Std,Jan 30)
Zatopek 36 (12f,Sou,Std,Feb 24)
Zermatt (IRE) 38 (9½f,Wol,Std,Oct 4)
Ziggy's Dancer (USA) 52 (6f,Wol,Std,Oct 18)
Zorba 35 (9½f,Wol,Std,Spt 30)
Zuhair 54 (6f,Wol,Std,May 1)
Zurs (IRE) 46 (8½f,Wol,Std,Mar 8)

TWO YEAR-OLDS - Turf

Aberkeen 32 (6f,Nwc,GF,Aug 3)
Abreeze (USA) 53 (7f,San,GF,Spt 16)
Absalom's Lad 31 (7f,Bri,GF,Oct 23)
Absolutly Sparklin 44 (7f,Lei,GS,Oct 14)
Abuhail (USA) 40 (8f,San,S,Aug 30)
Abusamrah (USA) 36 (6f,Nwm,GF,Oct 31)
Acebo Lyons (IRE) 41 (7f,Nwb,GS,Oct 25)
Achilles 46 (8f,Yor,S,Oct 8)
Acid Test 32 (7f,Nwb,GF,Aug 16)
Adjutant 34 (6f,Hay,GF,Aug 15)
Admire 32 (8f,Chp,GS,Aug 25)
After Eight 32 (6f,Red,GF,Oct 28)
After The Rain 44 (8f,Nwc,G,Aug 25)
Aganon 35 (6f,Nwb,GS,Spt 20)
Air Attache (USA) 38 (7f,Nwm,G,Aug 22)
Aix En Provence (USA) 56 (7f,Nwm,GF,Oct 3)
Ajig Dancer 40 (6f,Nwb,S,May 17)
Akarita (IRE) 31 (7f,Hay,Hy,Oct 15)
Albarahin (USA) 53 (8f,Nwm,GF,Oct 31)
Alboostan 56 (8f,Goo,G,Spt 12)
Alborada 48 (7f,Cur,GS,Oct 4)
Alcayde 38 (7f,Hay,G,Spt 27)
Alconleigh 58 (6f,Rip,GS,May 18)
Al-Fateh (IRE) 40 (7f,Don,G,Nov 7)
Alfiglia 47 (5f,Asc,G,Jun 20)
Alharir (USA) 49 (8f,Don,GF,Spt 11)
Alignment (IRE) 30 (7f,San,GF,Aug 14)
Al Mabrook (IRE) 39 (6f,Nwm,G,Aug 2)
Almandab (IRE) 50 (8f,Not,G,Oct 30)
Almutawakel 69 (8f,Asc,GF,Spt 28)
Alpen Wolf (IRE) 32 (5f,Wnd,S,May 12)
Al's Fella (IRE) 31 (5f,Wnd,S,May 19)
Altibr (USA) 57 (7f,Lei,G,Oct 27)
Always Lucky 30 (5f,Fol,F,Spt 26)
Amabel (USA) 51 (7f,Nwb,GS,Oct 25)
Ambitious 35 (6f,Fol,G,Spt 2)
Anemos (IRE) 39 (7f,Don,G,Nov 7)
Angel Hill 44 (6f,Don,GF,Spt 13)
Angelina 37 (6f,Fol,G,Spt 2)
Angstrom (IRE) 41 (8f,Don,G,Nov 7)
Anita At Dawn (IRE) 33 (6f,Not,S,Jun 23)
Anna Palariva (IRE) 47 (8f,Lon,GF,Oct 5)
Another Fantasy (IRE) 50 (6f,Asc,S,Jly 26)
Anstand 39 (5f,Red,GF,Oct 28)
Anvil (USA) 43 (7f,Asc,G,Jun 19)
Apache Red (IRE) 40 (7f,Nwm,GF,Spt 30)
Arawak Cay (IRE) 46 (5f,Asc,G,Jun 19)
Arbenig (IRE) 33 (6f,Red,GF,Oct 28)
Arctic Star 37 (7f,Nwb,GS,Oct 25)
Arian Da 55 (5f,Fol,F,Spt 26)
Ariant (USA) 32 (6f,Nwb,GF,Jly 18)
Arjan (IRE) 45 (5f,Cat,S,Oct 17)
Arkadian Hero (USA) 69 (6f,Rip,GF,Aug 25)
Arm And A Leg (IRE) 36 (7f,Nwm,GS,Oct 16)
Arpeggio 32 (6f,Nwm,GF,May 31)
Asad 38 (7f,Yar,F,Oct 29)
Asakir 43 (10f,Lei,S,Oct 13)
Ascot Cyclone (USA) 53 (6½f,Don,GF,Spt

10)
Asfurah (USA) 57 (6f,Nwm,G,Jly 8)
Ashraakat (USA) 57 (8f,Lon,GF,Oct 5)
Astrapi 57 (6f,Asc,GF,Spt 27)
Astrologer 48 (6f,Nwb,GS,Spt 20)
Asyaad (USA) 30 (6f,Cat,GF,Spt 20)
Atlanta 42 (6f,Nwb,GS,Spt 20)
Atlantic Viking (IRE) 52 (5f,Nwm,GF,Oct 31)
Attractive Crown (USA) 31 (7f,Cur,GS,Oct 4)
Atuf (USA) 65 (6f,Asc,GF,Spt 27)
Aurigny 51 (5f,Asc,G,Jun 20)

Baajil 47 (6f,Nwm,GF,Oct 31)
Baby Grand (IRE) 46 (5f,Ayr,GS,Spt 18)
Bahamian Melody (USA) 42 (6f,Lin,G,Spt 9)
Bahr 57 (7f,Nwb,GF,Aug 15)
Balaclava (IRE) 34 (7f,Kem,G,Aug 20)
Balaitini (IRE) 30 (7f,Lin,G,Spt 9)
Balanita (IRE) 40 (7f,Bri,GF,Oct 23)
Baltic State (USA) 52 (6f,Yar,F,Jun 5)
Bandbox (IRE) 49 (6f,Lei,G,Oct 28)
Banningham Blade 49 (5f,San,GF,May 27)
Barrelbio (IRE) 32 (5f,Edi,GS,Nov 6)
Batswing 42 (7f,Asc,Hy,Oct 11)
Bawsian 37 (8f,Red,G,Nov 4)
Bayleaf 41 (5f,Don,GF,Spt 13)
Bay Prince (IRE) 50 (5f,Yor,G,Aug 20)
Bedevilled 43 (6f,Lei,G,Oct 28)
Behold 36 (7f,Yar,GS,Jly 3)
Belladera (IRE) 45 (6f,Nwm,G,Jly 8)
Belle de Nuit (IRE) 50 (7f,Nwm,GF,Spt 30)
Bellow (IRE) 36 (7f,Nwm,GF,Jly 9)
Bemsha Swing (IRE) 52 (6f,Nwm,GF,Aug 23)
Be My Wish 38 (5f,Nwb,GF,Jly 19)
Beneventus 36 (7f,San,GF,Spt 16)
Benin (USA) 42 (7f,Lei,GF,Oct 5)
Ben Rinnes 42 (6f,Wnd,S,Jun 23)
Bergen (IRE) 32 (6f,Pon,GF,Jly 18)
Bering Gifts (IRE) 45 (8f,Nwm,GS,Oct 16)
Bermuda Boy 54 (6f,Sal,GF,Aug 21)
Bernardo Bellotto (IRE) 40 (6f,Eps,G,Aug 10)
Best of Our Days 40 (5f,Red,GF,Oct 28)
Bettron 53 (7f,Nwb,GS,Oct 25)
Beware 44 (6f,Nwm,G,Jly 19)
Bintang (IRE) 73 (6f,Yor,G,Aug 21)
Blakeset 59 (6f,Nwm,GF,Oct 4)
Bliss (IRE) 39 (5f,Nwm,G,Oct 2)
Blue Desert 44 (8f,Not,G,Oct 8)
Blue Gentian (USA) 44 (7f,Nwb,S,Spt 19)
Blue Kite 49 (6f,Don,GF,Spt 13)
Blueprint (IRE) 33 (8f,Nwb,S,Spt 19)
Blueridge Dancer (IRE) 47 (6f,Nwm,G,Jly 9)
Blue Shadow 32 (6f,Wnd,G,Aug 23)
Bluewain Lady 30 (7f,San,GF,Aug 14)
Blue Zola (IRE) 33 (8f,Nwm,GF,Nov 1)
Blundell Lane (IRE) 60 (6f,Red,GF,Oct 28)
Bobbydazzle 38 (8f,Nwc,G,Aug 25)
Bodfaridistinction (IRE) 55 (5f,Chs,Hy,May 8)
Bodyguard 43 (5f,Asc,G,Jun 19)
Bold Edge 61 (6f,Nwb,GF,Jly 19)
Bold Fact (USA) 66 (6f,Asc,G,Jun 17)
Bold King 30 (6f,Chp,GS,Jly 5)
Bolero Kid 44 (7½f,Bev,GS,Aug 14)
Borani 54 (8f,Goo,G,Spt 13)
Border Arrow 58 (8f,Nwm,GS,Oct 16)
Bound To Please 38 (5f,Wnd,GF,Jly 21)
Braganza (USA) 30 (5f,Lin,F,Oct 3)
Branston Berry (IRE) 60 (6f,Hay,G,Spt 26)
Brave Reward (USA) 54 (7f,Lei,GS,Oct 14)
Brimming 39 (7f,Yar,F,Spt 17)
Brimstone (IRE) 35 (6f,Bat,G,Aug 12)
Bristol Channel 39 (7f,Nwb,GS,Oct 25)
Broughtons Mill 32 (6f,Nwm,G,Jly 19)
Browning 31 (6f,Nwb,GS,Spt 20)
Bullion 40 (7f,Nwb,GS,Spt 19)
Burnt Yates (IRE) 49 (7f,Chs,G,Spt 24)
Buzz 30 (5f,Rip,G,Aug 30)

Caernarfon Bay (IRE) 31 (6f,Nwb,G,Oct 24)
Calchas (IRE) 58 (7½f,Bev,GF,Jly 21)
Call To Order 49 (5f,San,GF,Spt 17)
Campari (IRE) 30 (8f,Pon,GF,Spt 25)
Canadian Puzzler (USA) 45 (8f,Nwm,GS,Oct 17)
Cape Verdi (IRE) 72 (6f,Yor,G,Aug 21)
Capital Prince (FR) 40 (7f,Yar,G,Oct 22)
Capri 32 (8f,Not,G,Oct 30)
Captain Logan (IRE) 38 (7f,Yar,G,Oct 22)
Captain Tim 44 (7f,Yar,G,Oct 22)
Carambo 30 (5f,Thi,G,May 17)
Carbon 37 (7f,Yor,G,Aug 19)
Carinthia (IRE) 36 (6f,Wnd,G,Aug 23)
Carol Singer (USA) 36 (5f,Ayr,GS,Spt 18)
Carrowkeel (IRE) 63 (7f,Don,GF,Spt 12)
Carry The Flag 43 (8f,War,GF,Oct 7)
Casino King (IRE) 54 (7f,Asc,GF,Spt 28)
Catch The Rainbow 33 (7f,San,S,Aug 30)
Caversfield 40 (7f,Lei,G,Oct 27)
Cease Fire (IRE) 42 (6f,Sal,GF,Aug 21)
Celtic Cavalier (IRE) 45 (7f,San,GS,Aug 29)
Celtic Cross 42 (6f,Nwb,GF,Aug 15)
Celtic Pageant 51 (7f,Lei,GS,Oct 14)
Central Committee (IRE) 41 (7½f,Bev,GF,Spt 17)
Central Park (IRE) 70 (7f,Asc,G,Jun 19)
Centre Court 35 (5f,Wnd,G,Jly 7)
Cerisette (IRE) 36 (7f,Lin,GF,Jly 12)
Chattan 53 (7f,Yar,G,Oct 22)
Chester House (USA) 61 (7f,Yor,G,Aug 19)
Chieftain (IRE) 38 (5f,Lin,G,Aug 9)
Chief Whip (USA) 38 (6f,Goo,G,Spt 25)
Child Prodigy (IRE) 40 (5f,Asc,GF,Jun 18)
Chim Chiminey 42 (8f,Yor,S,Oct 8)
Chinaider (IRE) 43 (6f,Yor,G,Aug 20)
Chips (IRE) 54 (5f,Wnd,S,May 12)
Chist (USA) 41 (7f,Red,G,Nov 4)
Chocolate (IRE) 44 (7f,Yar,GF,Spt 16)
Chrysalis 35 (5f,Bri,GF,May 6)
Circus 37 (7f,Nwm,GF,Spt 30)
City Honours (USA) 69 (8f,Asc,GF,Spt 28)
Clapham Common (IRE) 43 (8f,Pon,GS,Oct 20)
Classic Manoeuvre (USA) 54 (7f,Asc,G,Jun 19)
Classy Cleo (IRE) 47 (5f,Hay,Hy,Oct 15)
Clef of Silver 46 (6f,Nwm,G,Aug 2)
Cloak of Darkness (IRE) 32 (7f,San,GF,Spt 16)
Close Shave 39 (7f,Yar,G,Oct 22)
Close Up (IRE) 41 (8f,Hay,S,Oct 15)
Cloudberry 48 (6f,Ayr,GS,Spt 19)
Cloud Castle 30 (7f,Nwm,GS,Oct 17)
Colleville 38 (7f,Lei,G,Aug 11)
Commander Charlie 38 (7f,San,GF,Jly 16)
Composition 32 (6f,Goo,G,Jun 13)
Compradore 44 (5f,Nwb,GF,May 28)
Conectis (IRE) 49 (6f,Nwm,G,Jly 8)
Confirmation 39 (7f,Ayr,GS,Spt 19)
Connoisseur Bay (USA) 50 (7f,Nwm,G,Oct 2)
Contrary Mary 47 (5f,Lin,GF,May 31)
Cool Prospect 33 (5f,Rip,GF,Aug 26)
Cool Secret 50 (6f,Hay,G,Spt 26)
Corniche (IRE) 46 (8f,Ayr,G,Spt 20)
Cortachy Castle (IRE) 62 (5f,Asc,G,Jun 20)
Cosmic Countess (IRE) 30 (6f,Bri,F,Spt 28)
Country Garden 37 (8f,Nwc,G,Aug 25)
Courageous (IRE) 45 (6f,Asc,Hy,Oct 10)
Court Lane (USA) 52 (6f,Nwm,GF,Oct 4)
Craigsteel 68 (8f,Asc,GF,Spt 28)
Crazee Mental 58 (6f,Nwm,GF,Spt 30)
Critical Air 32 (6f,Fol,G,Oct 21)
Cruinn A Bhord 46 (7f,Nwm,GF,Nov 1)
Cumbrian Cadet 43 (6f,Yor,G,Aug 20)
Cumbrian Caruso 51 (6f,Pon,S,Jun 30)
Czar Wars 32 (7f,War,GS,Aug 25)

Da Boss 39 (7f,San,GS,Jly 5)
Daggers Drawn (USA) 75 (7f,Don,GF,Spt 12)
Dance Trick (USA) 54 (6f,Eps,G,Jun 6)
Dancing Icon (IRE) 35 (5f,Hay,GF,Aug 9)
Dancing Phantom 36 (8f,Lin,GS,Aug 28)
Danyross (IRE) 50 (6f,Nwm,G,Jly 8)
Daring Derek (USA) 37 (6f,Lin,F,Oct 3)
Dark Moondancer 42 (7f,Hay,Hy,Oct 15)
Dashing Chief (IRE) 63 (10f,Nwm,GF,Nov 1)
Daunting Lady (IRE) 64 (5f,Chs,S,May 6)
Daymarti (IRE) 74 (15f,Lon,G,Oct 4)
Days of Grace 31 (5f,Nwm,G,Apr 16)
Dazilyn Lady (USA) 55 (6f,Yor,G,Aug 21)
Decisive Action (USA) 46 (8f,Not,S,Oct 15)
Deep Space (IRE) 33 (6f,Asc,S,Jly 26)
Defiance 37 (6f,Eps,G,Aug 10)
Dekelsmary 32 (6f,Lei,GF,Spt 22)
Deki (USA) 45 (7½f,Bev,GS,Aug 14)
Delciana (IRE) 30 (6f,Lei,GF,Spt 22)
Demolition Jo 54 (6f,Nwm,GS,Oct 16)
Dernier Croise (FR) 34 (5f,Fol,G,Spt 2)
Derryquin 44 (8f,Don,G,Nov 7)
Desert Drama (IRE) 57 (8f,Lon,GF,Oct 5)
Desert Lady (IRE) 37 (5f,Don,GS,Jun 28)
Desert Prince (IRE) 67 (6f,Asc,G,Jun 17)
Designer (USA) 58 (6f,Nwm,G,Oct 2)
Deterrent 46 (6f,Don,G,Oct 25)
Deva Lady 35 (6f,Yor,G,Aug 20)
Diamond White 48 (6f,Nwm,G,Aug 2)
Dil 33 (5f,Hay,GS,Spt 5)
Diligence (IRE) 66 (5f,Goo,GS,May 20)
Dilkusha (IRE) 33 (6f,Nwm,GS,Oct 17)
Dim Ots 39 (5f,Bat,GS,May 19)
Distant Mirage (IRE) 54 (8f,Nwb,GS,Oct 25)
Dixie Dynamo (USA) 37 (6f,Cur,GS,Jun 29)
D'Marti 37 (6f,Red,GS,Jly 26)
Docksider (USA) 70 (7f,Don,GF,Spt 12)
Dodo (IRE) 40 (6f,Asc,G,Aug 1)
Dog Watch 44 (7f,Red,G,Nov 4)
Doomna (IRE) 35 (7f,Goo,GF,Jly 31)
Doraid (IRE) 45 (7f,Hay,G,Spt 27)
Double Brandy 48 (6f,Lei,G,Oct 28)
Double Edged 42 (8f,Don,GS,Nov 8)
Dover Soul 30 (6f,Sal,GF,Aug 21)
Dower House 37 (8f,Yar,F,Spt 18)
Dr Fong (USA) 60 (8f,Asc,S,Oct 11)
Duck Row (USA) 53 (8f,Nwb,S,Spt 19)
Due South 53 (8f,Nwc,G,Aug 25)
Dutch Lad 35 (8f,Nwm,GS,Oct 17)

Eagle's Cross (USA) 31 (8f,Nwm,GS,Oct 16)
Eastern Lyric 42 (5f,Nwb,GS,Spt 20)
Eastern Purple (IRE) 51 (5f,Ayr,GS,Spt 18)
Easter Ogil (IRE) 38 (6f,Cat,S,Oct 16)
Eco Friendly 43 (8f,Don,GS,Nov 8)
Edwardian 30 (8f,Not,S,Oct 15)
Elakik 44 (8f,Yar,G,Oct 22)
Elanaaka 33 (7½f,Bev,GF,Spt 17)
Eleonora d'Arborea 45 (6f,Red,GS,Jly 26)
Eleventh Duke (IRE) 50 (5f,Fol,G,Spt 2)
Elhabub 53 (6f,Nwc,GF,Oct 1)
Eljjanah (USA) 30 (7f,Red,GF,Jly 19)
Ella (IRE) 50 (5f,Asc,Hy,Oct 11)
Ellenbrook (IRE) 32 (5f,Red,F,Spt 26)
Eloquent 51 (7f,San,GF,Jly 24)
Elshamms 55 (7f,Nwm,G,Oct 18)
Elsurur (USA) 39 (7f,Nwm,G,Oct 18)
Embassy 77 (6f,Asc,S,Jly 26)
Emmajoun 32 (6f,Fol,G,Spt 2)
Emperor Naheem (IRE) 42 (5f,Nwb,GS,Spt 20)
Empirical (USA) 32 (6f,Lei,G,Oct 27)
Enchant 36 (6f,Nwm,GF,Oct 4)
Epsom Cyclone (USA) 33 (6f,Nwb,GS,Spt 20)
Equity Princess 54 (8f,Asc,S,Oct 11)
Erro Codigo 33 (6f,Red,GF,Aug 9)
Escudo (IRE) 46 (5f,Fol,F,Spt 26)
Euro Venture 34 (5f,Don,G,May 5)
Evander (IRE) 51 (8f,Nwb,GS,Oct 25)
Evening World (FR) 43 (8f,Nwb,S,Spt 19)

Exbourne's Wish (USA) 45 (6f,Nwm,GF,Oct 4)
Exclusive 59 (8f,Asc,GF,Spt 28)
Exit To Somewhere (IRE) 37 (7½f,Bev,G,Jly 29)
Expect To Shine 51 (7f,Nwm,G,Oct 18)

Face-Off 30 (7f,Lin,F,Oct 3)
Facile Tigre 32 (5f,Nwb,GS,Spt 20)
Fa-Eq (IRE) 48 (6f,Nwb,G,Oct 24)
Fairy Flight (IRE) 34 (6f,Cur,S,Spt 7)
Fairy Rock (IRE) 30 (6f,Lei,G,Oct 27)
Fakhr (USA) 34 (7f,Sal,GF,Jly 12)
Fantasy Island (IRE) 46 (7f,Nwm,G,Aug 22)
Far Removed (IRE) 47 (6f,Don,GF,Spt 13)
Fast Franc (IRE) 33 (5f,Fol,S,Jun 27)
Fast Tempo (IRE) 36 (5f,Wnd,GS,Jun 30)
Fayrana (IRE) 42 (7f,Goo,GF,Aug 2)
Festival Song (USA) 33 (6f,Cur,GS,Jun 29)
Ffestiniog (IRE) 50 (7f,Nwb,GS,Oct 25)
Fiamma (IRE) 48 (7f,Nwm,G,Oct 18)
Fields of Omagh (USA) 30 (7f,Don,G,Nov 7)
Filey Brigg 71 (6f,Asc,S,Jly 26)
Filfilah 57 (6f,Asc,S,Jly 26)
Final Tango 52 (7f,Red,GF,Oct 18)
Fire Goddess 32 (6f,Asc,S,Jun 21)
First Village (IRE) 40 (5f,Hay,G,Spt 21)
Fiveo'clock Shadow (IRE) 40 (5f,Bri,GF,May 6)
Five of Spades (IRE) 51 (6f,Not,G,Nov 3)
Fizzed 48 (6f,Ayr,GS,Spt 19)
Flame Tower (IRE) 37 (6f,Fol,G,Oct 21)
Flame Violet (IRE) 45 (7f,Cur,S,Spt 7)
Flaming Ember (IRE) 49 (6f,Eps,G,Jun 6)
Flawless 61 (7f,Nwm,GF,Oct 4)
Fleetwood (IRE) 53 (7f,Hay,G,Spt 21)
Flight 34 (6f,Yar,GF,Aug 21)
Florazi 56 (7f,Don,G,Oct 25)
Flow By 32 (7f,Nwm,GF,Aug 8)
Flower O'Cannie (IRE) 46 (7½f,Bev,Hy,Jly 5)
Flying Bold (IRE) 37 (7f,Nwb,GS,Oct 25)
Folklore 54 (5f,Rip,GF,Aug 26)
Forest Treasure (IRE) 57 (6f,Asc,S,Jly 26)
Former Love (USA) 37 (7f,Lei,G,Oct 27)
Forum 47 (6f,Nwm,G,Jly 8)
Free As The Wind (IRE) 33 (8f,Not,G,Oct 30)
Freedom Quest (IRE) 33 (7f,Chs,G,Spt 24)
Free Option (IRE) 44 (7f,Red,G,Nov 4)
Friar Tuck 57 (6f,Ham,G,Spt 29)
Friendly Warning (FR) 47 (6f,Nwm,G,Aug 2)
Frond 54 (7f,Nwc,GF,Oct 22)
Fruits of Love (USA) 57 (7f,Nwb,GF,Aug 15)
Fundance 36 (6f,Not,G,Spt 28)

Gandoura (USA) 34 (6f,Nwb,GF,Aug 15)
General Monck 32 (8f,Not,G,Oct 30)
Generosity 35 (7f,Goo,GF,Aug 1)
Generous Embrace 32 (6f,Lin,Std,Aug 28)
Genoa 37 (7f,Nwm,GF,Nov 1)
Ghali (USA) 46 (7f,Asc,GF,Spt 28)
Gipsy Moth 55 (5f,Hay,GF,Aug 15)
Giveaway 41 (8f,Hay,S,Oct 15)
Glass River 40 (5f,Red,GF,Oct 28)
Glorosia (FR) 64 (8f,Asc,GF,Spt 28)
Glory of Grosvenor (IRE) 41 (8f,Nwb,S,Spt 19)
Going Places 39 (5f,Nwm,G,Apr 16)
Golden Dice (USA) 55 (7f,Don,GF,Spt 10)
Golden Fortune 43 (7f,Nwm,GF,Spt 30)
Golden Hawk (USA) 41 (8f,Kem,GF,Spt 22)
Golden Mirage (IRE) 47 (5f,Wnd,S,May 12)
Golden Reprimand (IRE) 40 (6f,Nwm,GS,Oct 17)
Golden Strategy (IRE) 38 (5f,Wnd,GF,Jly 21)
Goodwood Cavalier 32 (7f,Lei,GS,Oct 14)
Grace Browning 30 (6f,War,GF,Oct 7)
Grand Slam (IRE) 36 (7f,Nwb,GF,Spt 18)
Grazia 58 (6f,Nwm,GF,Oct 4)
Great Dane (IRE) 35 (7f,Yar,F,Oct 29)
Greek Dance (IRE) 36 (7f,Kem,G,Spt 10)
Greenbrook 39 (7f,San,S,Aug 30)
Guaranteed 40 (7f,Chs,GS,Aug 29)
Guildhall 34 (8f,Yor,S,Oct 8)
Gulland 59 (8f,Pon,GS,Oct 20)
Gurkha 41 (6f,Yor,S,Spt 4)
Gypsy Passion (IRE) 49 (7f,Red,G,Nov 4)

Haami (USA) 63 (7f,Nwm,GF,Oct 3)
Hadayik 48 (8f,Don,GF,Spt 11)
Hadid (USA) 47 (5f,Nwb,GF,May 28)
Hadith 31 (8f,Bri,GF,Oct 23)
Hakeem (IRE) 54 (6f,Nwm,GF,Oct 4)
Half-Hitch (USA) 30 (6f,Thi,G,Jly 25)
Halmahera (IRE) 84 (5f,Asc,Hy,Oct 11)
Hanzanar (IRE) 35 (8f,Cur,S,Oct 18)
Happy Days 39 (6f,Yor,G,May 15)
Happy Days Again (IRE) 46 (6f,Nwm,G,Aug 2)
Happy Wanderer 31 (5f,Red,GF,Oct 28)
Harbour Master (FR) 71 (6f,Asc,G,Jun 17)
Harmonic Way 43 (7f,Lei,GS,Oct 14)
Hayil (USA) 61 (6f,Nwm,G,Oct 2)
Headhunter (IRE) 46 (7f,Nwm,GF,Spt 30)
Heavenly Abstone 50 (6f,Chs,GF,Aug 3)
Heed My Warning (IRE) 50 (7f,Cur,S,Spt 7)
Heeremandi (IRE) 51 (6f,Nwm,GF,Spt 30)
Herminius (IRE) 41 (8f,Red,GF,Oct 18)
Hickory (IRE) 37 (6f,Asc,G,Jun 17)
High And Low 43 (7f,Don,G,Nov 7)
High Carry 47 (5f,Nwm,G,Oct 2)
High-Rise (IRE) 43 (7f,Don,G,Nov 7)
High Sheriff (IRE) 48 (7f,War,GF,Jly 19)
Highwayman (IRE) 35 (7f,Yar,F,Spt 17)
Hill Magic 45 (6f,Nwb,GF,Jly 19)
Himself (USA) 33 (8f,Lei,G,Oct 28)
Hirst Bridge (IRE) 39 (5f,Thi,G,May 17)
Hoh Chi Min 59 (6f,Ayr,GS,Spt 19)
Hoh Justice 37 (5f,San,GF,Spt 17)
Ho Leng (IRE) 45 (6f,Red,GF,Oct 18)
Hollow Haze (USA) 45 (7f,Nwb,S,Spt 19)
Holy Wine (USA) 35 (8f,Lin,G,Spt 9)
Honest Borderer 34 (7f,Nwm,G,Oct 2)
Honey Storm (IRE) 34 (7f,Lin,G,Spt 9)
Hopping Higgins (IRE) 50 (6f,Leo,GS,Aug 10)
Housekeeper (IRE) 37 (7f,Lin,G,Oct 27)
Howies Choice (IRE) 30 (5f,Cat,G,Spt 27)
Hujoom (IRE) 52 (6f,Ayr,G,Spt 20)
Huntswood 35 (5f,Fol,GF,Aug 5)

Iceband (USA) 55 (6f,Nwm,G,Jly 19)
I Cried For You (IRE) 33 (5f,Not,GF,Oct 4)
Ikhteyaar (USA) 51 (6f,Kem,G,Spt 10)
Impressionist (IRE) 62 (7f,Nwm,G,Oct 18)
Impulsive Decision (IRE) 41 (6f,Fol,G,Oct 21)
Inchalong 44 (6f,Not,G,Nov 3)
Inchtina 33 (7f,Kem,GF,Spt 22)
Indian Missile 48 (7f,Asc,Hy,Oct 10)
Indimaaj 32 (7½f,Bev,G,Jly 29)
Iris May 36 (6f,Ham,S,Jun 25)
Iron Mountain (IRE) 30 (10f,Not,GF,Spt 23)
Islamabad 43 (5f,Wnd,GF,Jun 2)
Isle De France (USA) 59 (8f,Lon,GF,Oct 5)
Its All Relative 51 (5f,Ayr,GS,Spt 18)
Ivory's Joy 40 (5f,Nwb,GS,Spt 20)

Jaazim (USA) 38 (8f,Not,S,Oct 15)
Jackerin (IRE) 43 (5f,Hay,GF,Aug 15)
Jacmar (IRE) 60 (6f,Ham,G,Spt 29)
Jay Gee (IRE) 56 (6f,Nwm,G,Aug 2)
Jazz Club (USA) 45 (7f,Yor,G,Aug 19)
Jewel (IRE) 31 (5f,Nwm,G,Apr 16)
Jibe (USA) 63 (8f,Asc,GF,Spt 28)
Jila (IRE) 43 (7f,Yar,G,Oct 22)
Jilted (IRE) 39 (6f,Nwm,GF,Oct 4)
Jimmy Too 57 (6f,Nwb,GS,Spt 20)
Jocasta 30 (6f,Nwm,GS,Oct 17)
Joint Regent (USA) 34 (7f,Nwm,G,Oct 2)
Julies Jewel (IRE) 34 (6f,Not,G,Spt 28)
Jungle Story (IRE) 31 (7f,Cat,G,Spt 27)
Junior Muffin (IRE) 37 (5f,San,G,Spt 16)
Just Another Time 39 (6f,Fol,F,Spt 26)
Just In Time 46 (7f,Goo,GF,Aug 1)

Kahtan 35 (8f,Don,GF,Spt 12)
Kameez (IRE) 38 (7f,Nwc,GF,Oct 22)
Karakorum (IRE) 38 (7f,Cur,S,Spt 7)
Kathies Pet 40 (6f,Fol,G,Oct 21)
Kawafil (IRE) 44 (8f,Bat,G,Spt 8)
Kennet 47 (6f,Kem,G,Spt 21)
Kettlesing (IRE) 41 (5f,Not,GF,Oct 4)
Khalas 36 (7f,Nwc,G,Aug 25)
Kheyrah (USA) 66 (6f,Hay,G,Spt 26)
Khumba Mela (IRE) 57 (8f,Lon,GF,Oct 5)
Kilcora (IRE) 39 (5f,Chs,S,May 6)
Kilimanjaro 69 (8f,Asc,GF,Spt 28)
Kim's Brave 60 (10f,Nwm,GF,Nov 1)
King Darius (IRE) 41 (7f,Goo,GF,Aug 2)
King Of Kings (IRE) 60 (7f,Cur,GS,Aug 16)
Kings Arrow (IRE) 38 (7f,Lei,GS,Oct 14)
Kitza (IRE) 40 (6f,Cur,S,Spt 7)
Komistar 57 (8f,Nwb,GS,Oct 25)
Krisamba 47 (7f,Lei,GS,Oct 14)
Krispy Knight 45 (6f,Nwm,GF,Jly 25)

Lady Alexander (IRE) 44 (7f,Cur,S,Spt 7)
Lady Charlotte 32 (6f,Bat,GF,Spt 29)
Lady In Waiting 63 (6f,Yor,GS,Jun 13)
Lady Moll 40 (5f,Rip,G,Apr 26)
La-Faah (IRE) 49 (7f,Asc,Hy,Oct 11)
Lakeland Pride (IRE) 32 (6f,Yor,G,May 15)
Land of Dreams 57 (6f,Rip,GF,Aug 25)
La Nuit Rose (FR) 38 (7f,Lei,S,Oct 13)
Last Christmas 49 (7f,Hay,G,Spt 27)
Late Night Out 53 (6f,Not,G,Oct 30)
La Tiziana 31 (7f,Cat,S,Oct 16)
Law Library (IRE) 48 (6f,Cur,S,Spt 7)
Lea Grande 53 (7f,Nwm,GF,Nov 1)
Lear Spear (USA) 35 (7f,Kem,G,Spt 10)
Legal Lark (IRE) 41 (6f,Fol,F,Spt 26)
Legend of Love 34 (6f,Hay,GF,Aug 15)
Leggera (IRE) 48 (7f,Nwb,GS,Oct 25)
Legs Be Frendly (IRE) 51 (5f,Lin,G,Oct 27)
Lend A Hand 58 (8f,Don,GF,Spt 11)
Leofric 35 (6f,Lin,G,Spt 9)
Lets Be Fair 40 (5f,Ham,G,Aug 2)
Lido (IRE) 50 (7f,Don,G,Oct 25)
Lift The Offer (IRE) 33 (7f,Lei,G,Jly 23)
Light Step (USA) 35 (7f,Don,GS,Jun 28)
Likely Story (IRE) 56 (6f,Ayr,GS,Spt 19)
Lincolnshire (USA) 33 (5f,Sal,GF,May 15)
Linden Heights 56 (6f,Nwm,G,Jly 9)
Little Indian 61 (7f,San,GS,Aug 29)
Little Miss Huff (IRE) 34 (7f,War,GS,Aug 25)
Lobuche (IRE) 31 (5f,Bri,GF,May 6)
Loch Laird 39 (5f,Lin,F,Apr 4)
Lone Piper 36 (7f,Yar,GS,Jly 3)
Lonesome Dude (CAN) 53 (7f,Lei,G,Oct 27)
Long Bond (IRE) 34 (7½f,Bev,GF,Spt 17)
Long Siege (IRE) 32 (6f,Nwm,G,Jly 9)
Lord Kintyre 71 (5f,Asc,Hy,Oct 11)
Lord Lieutenant 38 (5f,Bev,GF,Spt 17)
Lord Smith 53 (7f,Nwm,GF,Jly 25)
Lord Warford 34 (7f,Hay,G,Spt 27)
Love Academy 40 (6f,Nwc,GF,Oct 22)
Love Kiss (IRE) 31 (8f,Don,G,Nov 7)
Lovers Knot 53 (7f,Nwm,GF,Nov 1)
Loving Claim (USA) 62 (8f,Lon,GF,Oct 5)
Lucayan Indian (IRE) 58 (6f,Nwc,GF,Oct 1)
Lucky Double 32 (7f,Sal,G,Oct 1)
Lucky Myst 31 (7f,War,GF,Jly 19)

Madjamila (IRE) 40 (7f,Lin,G,Oct 27)
Magical 41 (6f,Rip,GF,Aug 25)
Magical Minty (IRE) 34 (7f,Cur,GS,Aug 30)
Magic of Aloha (IRE) 40 (7f,Nwm,GF,Spt 30)

Mahboob (IRE) 58 (7f,Don,GF,Spt 10)
Main Street 33 (6f,Wnd,G,Aug 23)
Majaari 43 (6f,Kem,G,Spt 10)
Mantles Pride 55 (5f,Fol,F,Spt 26)
Mantles Star 54 (7f,Goo,GF,Aug 2)
Mantusis (IRE) 45 (8f,Kem,GF,Spt 22)
Marie Loup (FR) 57 (6f,Asc,GF,Spt 27)
Marigot Bay (IRE) 32 (6f,Cur,S,Spt 7)
Mark of Prophet (IRE) 31 (7f,War,GF,Oct 7)
Marksman (IRE) 53 (6f,Nwm,GS,Jun 20)
Marran (IRE) 47 (7f,Bri,F,Spt 28)
Marske Machine 33 (7f,San,S,Aug 30)
Marton Moss (SWE) 45 (6f,Rip,GF,Aug 25)
Mary Jane 42 (5f,Red,GF,Oct 28)
Mashab 36 (7f,Lei,GS,Oct 14)
Masha-Il (IRE) 32 (6f,Don,G,Nov 7)
Master Mac (USA) 36 (6f,Lin,GF,Jly 12)
Mawsoof 41 (8f,Not,G,Spt 28)
Mazboon (USA) 44 (7f,Yar,GS,Jly 3)
Means Business (IRE) 35 (5f,Lin,GF,Jly 26)
Mempari (IRE) 47 (7f,Cur,S,Spt 7)
Meniatarra (USA) 32 (7f,Nwm,GF,Nov 1)
Merciless 38 (8f,Don,G,Oct 24)
Merlin's Ring 57 (7f,Goo,GF,Aug 2)
Middle Temple 40 (8f,Yar,G,Oct 22)
Midnight Line (USA) 67 (8f,Don,GF,Spt 11)
Midsummer Night (IRE) 36 (5f,Nwm,G,Oct 2)
Mighty Sure (IRE) 39 (5f,Red,F,Spt 26)
Mihnah (IRE) 42 (6f,Yor,S,Oct 8)
Mijana (IRE) 61 (6f,Rip,GF,Aug 25)
Milligan (FR) 56 (9f,Lon,G,Oct 4)
Millitrix 37 (7f,Nwb,S,Spt 19)
Minivet 38 (7f,Nwm,G,Oct 2)
Miquelon 38 (8f,Yar,G,Oct 22)
Misalliance 32 (7f,Nwc,GF,Oct 1)
Misbah (USA) 56 (7f,Yar,G,Oct 22)
Mishraak (IRE) 48 (5f,Fol,G,Spt 2)
Miss Bussell 30 (7f,Nwm,GF,Nov 1)
Missed The Cut (IRE) 30 (5f,Fol,F,Spt 26)
Miss Money Spider (IRE) 31 (6f,Asc,Hy,Oct 10)
Miss Zafonic (FR) 72 (6f,Asc,S,Jly 26)
Mister Bankes 30 (5f,Wnd,GS,Jun 30)
Mister Rambo 49 (6f,Nwb,G,Oct 24)
Mitch Passi (IRE) 37 (6f,Cat,S,Oct 16)
Mohawk (IRE) 37 (7f,Lin,F,Oct 3)
Mondschein 51 (7f,Red,GF,Oct 18)
Monsajem (USA) 39 (8f,Nwm,GS,Oct 17)
Montano (USA) 45 (7f,Bri,GF,Oct 23)
Monte Lemos (IRE) 67 (6f,Nwm,GF,Oct 4)
Moonlight Flit 34 (7½f,Bev,GF,Spt 17)
Moontabeh 34 (5f,Lin,S,Jun 28)
Moothyeb (USA) 35 (6f,Yar,F,Jun 5)
Mountain Song 34 (8f,Cur,S,Spt 21)
Mowbray (USA) 36 (7f,Kem,G,Aug 20)
Mr Cahill (USA) 39 (7f,Yar,GF,Aug 6)
Mrs Malaprop 47 (5f,Cat,G,Spt 27)
Mubrik (IRE) 44 (7f,Nwb,GF,Spt 18)
Mudalal (USA) 39 (7f,Lei,G,Oct 27)
Mudeer 73 (8f,Don,G,Oct 25)
Mugello 57 (6f,Nwb,GF,Jly 19)
Muhaba (USA) 49 (8f,Hay,G,Spt 27)
Muhtathir 65 (7f,San,GS,Jly 4)
Mulahen 44 (7f,Lei,GS,Oct 14)
Mushraaf 50 (7f,Don,GF,Spt 10)
Musical Twist (USA) 53 (6f,Nwb,GF,Aug 15)
Mustique Dream 32 (6f,Bat,GF,Jly 17)
Mutamam 71 (8f,Don,G,Oct 25)
Mutawwaj (IRE) 57 (7f,Yor,G,Aug 19)
Mystagogue 30 (7f,War,GF,Jly 19)
Mysterious Ecology 32 (8f,Kem,GF,Spt 22)
Mysticism 41 (5f,Nwb,GF,Jly 19)

Nadwah (USA) 71 (6f,Yor,G,Aug 21)
Name of Love (IRE) 66 (7f,Nwm,GF,Oct 4)
Nanoushka (IRE) 53 (7f,Nwm,GF,Oct 4)
Narrogin (USA) 37 (8f,Lei,GF,Oct 5)
Naskhi 42 (8f,Pon,GF,Spt 25)
Natalis (IRE) 42 (7f,Cur,GS,Aug 30)
Naughty Blue (USA) 50 (7f,Yar,F,Spt 17)
Nautical Star 41 (7f,San,GS,Jly 5)
Naviasky (IRE) 35 (7f,Don,G,Oct 25)
Next Round (IRE) 41 (7f,San,GF,Jly 24)
Night Flyer 45 (7f,Bri,F,Spt 28)
Night Owl 32 (6f,Kem,G,Spt 10)
Night Rule 58 (10f,Nwm,GF,Nov 1)
Night Shot 55 (6f,Don,GF,Spt 13)
Niki (IRE) 56 (6f,Asc,GF,Spt 27)
Noble Demand (USA) 48 (8f,Nwm,GS,Oct 17)
Noemie (FR) 46 (8f,Lon,GF,Oct 5)
North Ofthe Border 37 (7f,Lei,G,Oct 27)
Nuclear Debate (USA) 59 (6f,Nwm,GS,Oct 16)
Nuit d'Or (IRE) 32 (7f,Hay,G,Spt 27)
Nunthorpe 38 (6f,Pon,GF,Spt 25)

Oberon's Mistral 31 (8f,Lei,GF,Spt 9)
Obsessed 38 (7f,San,GF,Jly 24)
Occhi Verdi (IRE) 37 (7f,Nwm,GF,Spt 30)
Odette 37 (5f,Cat,S,Oct 17)
Oh Hebe (IRE) 30 (5f,Bat,G,Aug 12)
O' Higgins (IRE) 35 (8f,Red,GF,Oct 18)
Oh So Easy 38 (5f,San,GF,Spt 17)
O'Kelly (DEN) 39 (7f,Chs,GS,Aug 29)
Ok John (IRE) 31 (5f,Fol,F,Spt 26)
Olive The Twist (USA) 30 (7f,Don,G,Nov 7)
One Singer 51 (5f,Red,G,May 12)
One To Go (IRE) 32 (6f,Red,GF,Oct 28)
Only For Gold 44 (5f,Bev,GF,Jun 5)
Only In Dreams 30 (7f,Lei,S,Oct 13)
Opera King (USA) 33 (7f,Don,G,Jly 30)
Opposition Leader 40 (7f,War,G,Jun 24)
Optimistic 43 (8f,Don,GF,Spt 11)
Oriel Girl 32 (5f,Edi,GF,Aug 20)
Ouaisne 44 (5f,Red,G,Jun 20)
Out Like Magic 34 (6f,Pon,S,Jun 30)
Outsourcing (USA) 35 (7f,San,GF,Jly 16)

Pacifica 47 (5f,Nwm,G,Apr 16)
Panama House 37 (7f,Thi,GF,Aug 11)
Pantar (IRE) 43 (7f,Nwm,GF,Spt 30)
Parisian Lady (IRE) 41 (6f,Sal,GF,Jly 12)
Particular Friend 32 (7f,Nwm,GS,Jly 18)
Pas de Memoires (IRE) 37 (8f,Red,G,Nov 4)
Pass The Rest (IRE) 39 (7f,Hay,Hy,Oct 15)
Patsy Culsyth 42 (5f,Ayr,GS,Spt 18)
Pay On Red (USA) 37 (7f,Asc,Hy,Oct 10)
Peak Path (IRE) 37 (7f,San,GF,Spt 16)
Pegnitz (USA) 59 (7f,Asc,GF,Spt 28)
Pelagos (FR) 35 (7f,Nwb,GF,Spt 18)
Percy-P 39 (5f,Sal,GF,May 15)
Perfect Peach 40 (5f,Bev,GS,Aug 13)
Persiano 47 (6f,Nwm,GS,Oct 16)
Persian Venture 39 (7f,San,S,Aug 30)
Petara (IRE) 33 (6f,Rip,GS,May 18)
Petarga 38 (5f,Nwb,GF,Jly 19)
Peter's Imp (IRE) 54 (6f,Hay,G,Spt 26)
Phone Alex (IRE) 38 (5f,San,GF,Apr 25)
Photogenic 38 (7f,Nwm,GF,Spt 30)
Pierpoint (IRE) 39 (6f,Ham,G,Spt 29)
Plan-B 35 (8f,Yar,F,Spt 18)
Plasir Des Yeux (FR) 58 (8f,Lon,GF,Oct 5)
Pleasuredancer (USA) 34 (7f,Lei,GF,Oct 5)
Poetto 32 (6f,Goo,GF,Aug 22)
Polo Venture 32 (8f,Pon,GS,Oct 20)
Poly Blue (IRE) 53 (6f,Nwb,GS,Spt 20)
Pontoon 53 (7f,Nwm,GF,Nov 1)
Pool Music 56 (5f,San,GF,May 27)
Positive Air 36 (6f,Not,GF,Spt 15)
Praetorian Gold 36 (6f,Not,G,Spt 28)
Premium Princess 50 (6f,Red,GF,Oct 28)
Premium Pursuit 45 (6f,Ayr,G,Spt 20)
Premium Quest 33 (8f,Pon,GS,Oct 20)
Priceless 31 (8f,Goo,G,Spt 12)
Pride of Place (IRE) 34 (7f,Lin,G,Spt 9)
Primavera 32 (7f,War,GF,Jly 19)
Prime Hand 32 (5f,Rip,G,Jly 7)
Prince Ashleigh 31 (7f,Cat,S,Oct 17)
Prince Foley 40 (5f,Bev,GF,Jun 5)
Princely Heir (IRE) 59 (6f,Leo,GS,Aug 10)
Princess Natalie 38 (6f,Nwm,GF,Oct 4)
Priors Moor 34 (8f,Goo,G,Spt 13)
Prix Star 30 (5f,Crl,GS,May 9)
Prolix 70 (8f,Asc,GF,Spt 28)
Prompt Delivery (USA) 44 (6f,Pon,GF,Spt 25)
Prose (IRE) 57 (6f,Rip,GS,May 18)
Publisher (USA) 32 (8f,Yar,F,Oct 29)
Pure Coincidence 66 (5f,Hay,G,Spt 21)
Pure Nobility (IRE) 46 (7f,Lei,G,Oct 27)
Pursuit Venture 32 (7f,Lin,G,Oct 27)
Putuna 45 (7f,Nwm,GF,Spt 30)

Qilin (IRE) 61 (6f,Nwm,GF,Oct 4)
Quel Senor (FR) 63 (9f,Lon,G,Oct 4)
Quiet Assurance (USA) 58 (8f,Don,G,Oct 25)
Quintus (USA) 40 (7f,Nwb,GF,Jly 19)
Quite Happy (IRE) 40 (5f,Red,GF,Oct 28)
Quiver Tree 30 (6f,Nwm,G,Jly 19)
Quiz Master 41 (5f,Red,GF,Oct 28)
Quiz Show 34 (6f,Not,GF,Spt 15)

Rabah 56 (8f,Nwm,GF,Oct 31)
Rabi (IRE) 66 (7f,Lei,GF,Spt 22)
Radar (IRE) 43 (7f,Bri,GF,Oct 23)
Rainbow High 32 (7f,Hay,Hy,Oct 15)
Rainbow Ways 44 (8f,Nwm,GS,Oct 16)
Raise A King 70 (6f,Nwm,GF,Oct 4)
Rambling Rose 53 (8f,Not,GF,Spt 23)
Ranna 42 (7f,Red,GF,Oct 18)
Rapid Reliance 32 (5f,San,G,Spt 16)
Ra Ra Rasputin 32 (6f,Don,GF,Spt 13)
Rare Indigo 48 (5f,Lin,G,Oct 27)
Ratiyya (IRE) 35 (7f,Yar,GF,Spt 16)
Ray of Sunshine (IRE) 33 (7f,Thi,GF,Aug 11)
Ray's Folly (IRE) 48 (7f,San,GS,Jly 5)
Razor 42 (7f,Nwm,GF,Spt 30)
Really Done It Now (IRE) 31 (5f,War,GF,Jun 9)
Reap Rewards 36 (5f,Bev,GF,Jun 5)
Rebalza (IRE) 33 (7f,Nwc,GF,Aug 6)
Recognition 44 (6f,Fol,G,Spt 2)
Red Leggings 38 (7f,War,GF,Oct 7)
Red Pepper (IRE) 31 (5f,Fol,F,Spt 26)
Red Sky Charlie 33 (7f,Nwb,GF,Spt 18)
Refined (IRE) 52 (5f,Cat,S,Oct 16)
Regalo 45 (5f,Lin,G,Oct 27)
Regal Patriarch (IRE) 30 (8f,Nwm,GS,Oct 16)
Regal Revolution 75 (6f,Ayr,GS,Spt 19)
Rejected 40 (5f,Hay,GF,Jun 7)
Remarkable Style (USA) 38 (7f,Cur,S,Spt 7)
Requestor 37 (6f,Rip,GF,Aug 26)
Respond 34 (7f,Nwb,GS,Oct 25)
Rhein Hill (IRE) 31 (7f,War,GF,Oct 7)
Rich Choice 52 (6f,Red,GF,Oct 28)
Rico Suave (IRE) 37 (8f,Goo,G,Spt 25)
Ridgeway (IRE) 34 (7f,Nwm,GF,Spt 30)
Riley 31 (7f,Bri,F,Spt 28)
Ring Dancer 55 (6f,Not,G,Oct 30)
Ringleader 38 (8f,Nwm,GF,Nov 1)
Risada (IRE) 30 (8f,Lin,GS,Aug 28)
Risque Lady 65 (5f,Hay,G,Spt 21)
Rita's Rock Ape 36 (5f,Not,GF,Oct 4)
Ritual 30 (7f,Lei,GS,Oct 14)
Robeena 39 (6f,Hay,G,Jly 5)
Robin Goodfellow 45 (6f,Cat,S,Oct 16)
Roborant 34 (7f,Lei,G,Jly 23)
Rodinia (USA) 34 (5f,Sal,GF,May 15)
Roi Brisbane 49 (6f,Nwc,GF,Oct 1)
Roi de Danse 32 (6f,Kem,G,Aug 20)
Ron's Pet 31 (5f,Hay,S,May 5)
Rosewood Lady (IRE) 30 (6f,Wnd,G,Aug 23)
Royal Bounty (IRE) 39 (7½f,Bev,G,Aug 23)
Royal Dream 43 (6f,Chs,GF,Aug 3)
Royal Ground (IRE) 44 (8f,Goo,G,Spt 13)
Royal Rights 34 (6f,Yar,G,Jly 16)
Royal Shyness 55 (6f,Nwm,GF,Spt 30)
Rubamma 33 (7f,Cat,S,Oct 17)
Rusty Babe (IRE) 44 (5f,Bev,GF,Jun 5)

Ruzen (IRE) 32 (5f,Lei,GS,Apr 26)
Ryefield 35 (6f,Nwc,GF,Oct 22)

Sabhaan 31 (6f,Goo,G,Spt 12)
Sacchetti (IRE) 30 (5f,Lin,F,Oct 3)
Sada 33 (6f,Red,GF,Oct 7)
Sadian 30 (8f,Lin,GS,Aug 28)
Saeedah 31 (7f,Lei,G,Aug 11)
Saffron Lane (IRE) 46 (7f,Nwb,GF,Aug 16)
Saints Be Praised (USA) 51 (7f,Asc,G,Jun 19)
Salamanca 49 (5f,Lin,G,Aug 9)
Salsette 30 (6f,Chs,GS,Aug 29)
Sandside 41 (5f,Chs,S,Jun 25)
Sandy Shore 32 (6f,Not,S,Jun 23)
Sans Rivale 31 (5f,Edi,G,Aug 28)
Sapphire Ring 69 (6f,Ayr,GS,Spt 19)
Sarah Stokes (IRE) 38 (6f,Not,G,Oct 30)
Saralea (FR) 49 (8f,Lon,GF,Oct 5)
Saratoga Springs (CAN) 73 (8f,Don,G,Oct 25)
Sassy Lady (IRE) 32 (6f,Nwm,GF,Oct 4)
Scent of Success (USA) 40 (7f,Asc,Hy,Oct 10)
Sconced (USA) 31 (7f,Yar,G,Oct 22)
Scorned (GER) 54 (7f,Don,G,Nov 7)
Sea Magic (IRE) 51 (7f,Don,G,Oct 25)
Season Of Love (FR) 45 (9f,Lon,G,Oct 4)
Second Empire (IRE) 69 (8f,Lon,G,Spt 14)
Secret Archive 45 (7f,Goo,GF,Aug 1)
Selkirk Rose (IRE) 42 (6f,Ayr,GS,Spt 19)
Sense of Wonder 43 (6f,Not,G,Nov 3)
Sensory 44 (7f,Nwb,G,Oct 24)
Setteen 56 (7f,Asc,G,Jly 25)
Shadow of Doubt (IRE) 54 (6f,Asc,G,Jun 17)
Shahtoush (IRE) 49 (7f,Cur,S,Spt 7)
Shalford's Honour (IRE) 58 (5f,Hay,G,Spt 21)
Shanillo 31 (7f,Nwb,GF,Spt 18)
Sharp Cracker (IRE) 45 (7f,Nwc,GF,Aug 6)
Sharp Play 65 (8f,Asc,GF,Spt 28)
Shart (IRE) 44 (6f,Nwm,GS,Oct 17)
Shaveling 37 (7f,Red,G,Nov 4)
Shawdon 62 (5f,Nwm,G,Oct 2)
Shegardi 64 (5f,Goo,GS,May 20)
Sherganzar 38 (6f,Lei,G,Oct 28)
Shfoug (USA) 61 (6f,Asc,GF,Spt 27)
Shimaal 52 (7f,Nwm,G,Aug 22)
Shmoose (IRE) 57 (6f,Nwb,GF,Aug 15)
Shudder 48 (6f,Nwm,GF,Nov 1)
Shuhrah (USA) 60 (7f,Nwm,GF,Oct 4)
Sick As A Parrot 40 (8f,Yar,G,Oct 22)
Sideman (IRE) 37 (5f,Leo,YS,May 11)
Signatory 46 (7f,Bri,GF,Oct 23)
Silca Key Service 37 (6f,Goo,GF,Aug 2)
Silent Pride (IRE) 30 (5f,San,GF,Apr 25)
Silent Tribute (IRE) 57 (8f,Lon,GF,Oct 5)
Silic (FR) 74 (9f,Lon,G,Oct 4)
Silken Dalliance 36 (6f,Lei,G,Oct 28)
Silver Rhapsody (USA) 35 (8f,Don,G,Oct 24)
Silversmith (FR) 37 (6f,Lin,GF,Aug 17)
Silvertown 37 (7f,San,GF,Jly 23)
Sinon (IRE) 62 (10f,Nwm,GF,Nov 1)
Sixpence 38 (6f,Nwm,GF,Oct 4)
Sky Red 31 (6f,Nwm,GF,Oct 4)
Sky Rocket 47 (6f,Don,GF,Spt 13)
Smart Squall (USA) 54 (7f,Asc,Hy,Oct 10)
Smooth Sailing 47 (6f,Kem,G,May 24)
Social Charter (USA) 52 (7f,Lei,GS,Oct 14)
Socket Set 67 (6f,Asc,S,Jly 26)
Soft Touch (IRE) 34 (7f,Lin,G,Spt 9)
Solo Spirit 38 (6f,Lei,G,Oct 27)
Somayda (IRE) 34 (7f,Nwb,GF,Aug 16)
Son of Skelton 33 (7½f,Bev,Hy,Jly 5)
Soviet Bureau (IRE) 42 (7f,Sal,GF,Aug 13)
Spanish Fern (USA) 53 (7f,Nwm,GF,Nov 1)
Speaker's Chair 33 (7f,Nwb,GF,Aug 15)
Special Quest (FR) 74 (9f,Lon,G,Oct 4)
Special Treat 53 (6f,Yor,G,Oct 8)
Speedfit Too (IRE) 56 (6f,Nwm,GF,Aug 23)
Splendid Isolation (USA) 45 (6f,Nwm,GF,Oct 31)
Spree Rose 31 (7f,War,GF,Oct 7)
Spring Fever 33 (6f,Nwm,GF,Oct 31)
Star 55 (5f,Hay,G,Spt 21)
Starmaker (IRE) 42 (7½f,Bev,Hy,Jly 5)
Star of Grosvenor (IRE) 37 (7f,Nwm,GF,Spt 30)
Stately Princess 31 (6f,Nwm,G,Aug 2)
Statua (IRE) 59 (6f,Yor,G,Aug 21)
Stayingalive (USA) 46 (6f,Nwm,G,Jly 8)
St Helensfield 63 (10f,Nwm,GF,Nov 1)
St Lucia (IRE) 38 (6f,Nwb,GS,Spt 20)
Stone of Destiny 54 (7f,Nwb,GF,Aug 16)
Stop Out 39 (7f,Nwm,GF,Aug 9)
Storm Fromthe East 43 (6f,Kem,G,Spt 21)
Storm River (USA) 37 (8f,Hay,G,Spt 27)
Striding King 31 (5f,Sal,GF,May 15)
Success And Glory (IRE) 58 (8f,Goo,G,Spt 13)
Suivez La Trace 40 (5f,Pon,S,Jun 30)
Summer Deal (USA) 48 (7f,Nwc,GF,Oct 22)
Sunley Seeker 39 (7f,Nwb,GS,Spt 19)
Super Geil 34 (5f,Lin,G,Oct 27)
Supreme Angel 50 (5f,Hay,Hy,Oct 15)
Surprised 36 (5f,Cat,G,Spt 27)
Surveyor 66 (6f,Kem,G,Spt 21)
Susun Kelapa (USA) 40 (7f,Cur,GS,Oct 4)
Swanmore Lady (IRE) 37 (5f,Red,F,Spt 26)
Sweet Reward 38 (6f,Pon,S,Jun 30)
Sweet Sorrow (IRE) 36 (6f,Nwb,GF,Aug 15)
Swift Alliance 48 (6f,Asc,G,Jun 17)
Swing Along 40 (6f,Nwm,GS,Oct 17)
Swing Sister 43 (7f,Lei,GS,Oct 14)

Taalluf (USA) 39 (6f,Not,GF,Jly 19)
Tabasco (IRE) 49 (6f,Asc,GF,Spt 27)
Tadwiga 57 (7f,Nwm,G,Oct 18)
Tajasur (IRE) 40 (6f,Don,GS,Jun 29)
Tajawuz 45 (7f,Nwc,GF,Oct 22)
Tajmil (IRE) 32 (6f,Goo,G,Jun 13)
Takarian (IRE) 31 (7f,Leo,GS,Oct 27)
Tamarisk (IRE) 69 (7f,Nwm,GF,Spt 30)
Tarascon (IRE) 50 (7f,Cur,S,Spt 7)
Tarashaan 34 (10f,Not,GF,Spt 23)
Tartan Lass 30 (7f,Nwm,GF,Nov 1)
Tattinger 40 (6f,Kem,G,Spt 10)
Taverner Society (IRE) 49 (8f,Kem,GF,Spt 22)
Teapot Row (IRE) 71 (8f,Asc,GF,Spt 28)
Tempus Fugit 49 (5f,Wnd,GS,Jun 30)
Ten Bob (IRE) 34 (8f,Edi,GS,Nov 6)
Tenbyssimo (IRE) 54 (8f,Lon,G,Spt 14)
Tensile (IRE) 32 (8f,Chp,G,Aug 25)
Teroom 32 (7f,Yar,G,Oct 22)
Territory (IRE) 45 (5f,Not,S,Oct 8)
Thanksgiving (IRE) 67 (6f,Ayr,GS,Spt 19)
The Blues Academy (IRE) 30 (6f,Nwc,GF,Oct 22)
The Boy John (USA) 39 (5f,Nwb,GS,Spt 20)
The Downtown Fox 52 (6f,Nwm,GS,Oct 16)
The Gene Genie 63 (10f,Nwm,GF,Nov 1)
The Glow-Worm (IRE) 57 (8f,Nwm,GS,Oct 17)
The Groveller 38 (6f,Chs,S,Aug 30)
The Hobby Lobby (IRE) 34 (6f,Wnd,G,Aug 23)
The King Of Cloyne (USA) 40 (7f,Cur,GS,Aug 30)
The Limping Cat (IRE) 32 (5f,Yor,G,Aug 20)
Thelonius (IRE) 34 (7f,War,GS,Aug 25)
The Rich Man (IRE) 46 (6f,Pon,S,Jun 30)
Thief Of Hearts (IRE) 76 (9f,Lon,G,Oct 4)
Third Cousin (IRE) 43 (6f,Not,G,Nov 3)
Three Star Rated (IRE) 45 (5f,Edi,GF,Spt 15)
Tightrope 43 (8f,Lei,GF,Oct 5)
Timbervati (USA) 38 (7f,Yar,G,Oct 22)
Timekeeper (USA) 38 (7f,Yar,GS,Jly 3)
Tippitt Boy 54 (5f,Don,GF,Spt 13)
Titan 33 (7f,Asc,Hy,Oct 10)
Titanic (IRE) 54 (5f,Lin,G,Oct 27)
Title Bid (USA) 43 (6f,Cat,GF,Spt 20)
Toblersong 45 (6f,Eps,S,Jly 2)
Tom Dougal 31 (7f,Nwm,GS,Oct 16)
Torianna (USA) 31 (5f,Red,F,Aug 23)
Torrent 35 (6f,Goo,G,Spt 25)
Tracking 62 (7f,Don,G,Jly 31)
Trans Island 60 (7f,Nwb,GF,Jly 19)
Transylvania 34 (6f,Nwb,GF,Aug 15)
Treasure Chest (IRE) 44 (8f,Goo,G,Spt 13)
Trident (USA) 43 (7f,San,GF,Jly 23)
Trigger Happy (IRE) 61 (10f,Nwm,GF,Nov 1)
Tullich Refrain 30 (5f,Wnd,GF,Jly 21)
Tumblweed Prospect 56 (6f,Nwb,GS,Spt 20)
Tuning 52 (8f,Not,GF,Spt 23)
Tussle 54 (6f,Asc,Hy,Oct 10)
Two Williams 41 (5f,Bev,Hy,Jly 4)

Up At The Top (IRE) 43 (6f,Fol,G,Spt 2)
Uplifting 39 (6f,Nwb,G,Oct 24)

Vice Presidential 40 (6f,Ayr,G,Spt 20)
Victory Note (USA) 66 (6f,Nwb,GF,Jly 19)
Vignette (USA) 43 (6f,Hay,GF,Aug 15)
Viola Royale (IRE) 38 (7f,Cur,GS,Oct 4)
Virtuous 51 (8f,Don,GF,Spt 11)
Vocation (IRE) 35 (7f,Lin,G,Spt 9)
Volontiers (FR) 43 (7f,Don,G,Nov 7)
Voodoo Saint (USA) 42 (7f,Don,GF,Spt 10)

Wadi 31 (8f,Not,S,Oct 15)
Wait'n'see 44 (5f,Crl,F,Jun 12)
Wales 61 (8f,Goo,G,Spt 13)
Wathbat Lion 32 (7f,Nwb,GF,Aug 16)
Wave Rock 31 (8f,Not,G,Spt 28)
Way Out Yonder 36 (6f,Nwm,GF,May 31)
Wenda (IRE) 65 (6f,Asc,GF,Spt 27)
Whisky Mack (IRE) 36 (6f,Lei,G,Jly 17)
Who Nose (IRE) 37 (7f,Nwm,GF,Oct 3)
Wigging 32 (6f,Not,GF,Spt 23)
Winona (IRE) 43 (7f,Cur,GS,Oct 4)
Winsa (USA) 34 (8f,Don,G,Oct 24)
Winsome George 51 (6f,Rip,GS,May 18)
Wiston Cheese (USA) 55 (6f,Asc,Hy,Oct 10)
Wolfhunt 33 (5f,Wnd,GS,Jun 30)
Woodland Melody (USA) 51 (7f,San,GF,Jly 24)
Wrekin Pilot 56 (7f,Nwb,GF,Jly 19)
Wuxi Venture 48 (7f,Nwm,GF,Oct 3)

Xaar 84 (7f,Nwm,G,Oct 18)

Yanabi (USA) 33 (6f,Goo,GF,Jly 29)
Yorkies Boy 61 (5f,Nwb,GS,Spt 20)
Young Ibnr (IRE) 38 (5f,Chs,S,May 6)
Young Josh 39 (6f,Goo,G,Spt 25)

Zaya 32 (7f,Don,G,Oct 24)
Zelanda (IRE) 58 (6f,Yor,G,Aug 21)
Zero Three Fifteen (IRE) 30 (7f,War,GS,Aug 25)
Zizi (IRE) 41 (6½f,Don,GF,Spt 10)
Zydeco (IRE) 40 (7f,War,GF,Oct 7)

TWO YEAR-OLDS - Sand

Arbenig (IRE) 40 (6f,Wol,Std,Oct 4)

Beautiful Pleasure (USA) 34 (8½f,Hpk,Fst,Nov 8)
Beechwood Quest (IRE) 30 (5f,Sou,Std,Jly 10)
Blue Kite 45 (5f,Wol,Std,Spt 30)
Bound To Please 41 (6f,Wol,Std,Oct 4)

Calchas (IRE) 39 (6f,Wol,Std,Jun 18)
Carambo 50 (7f,Wol,Std,Oct 6)
Career Collection (USA) 57 (8½f,Hpk,Fst,Nov 8)
Carrielle (USA) 37 (8½f,Hpk,Fst,Nov 8)
Confirmation 48 (7f,Sou,Std,Spt 8)
Countess Diana (USA) 73 (8½f,Hpk,Fst,Nov 8)
Critical Air 35 (6f,Wol,Std,Oct 4)

Dawson's Legacy (USA) 72 (8½f,Hpk,Fst,Nov 8)
Diamond On The Run (USA) 38 (8½f,Hpk,Fst,Nov 8)
Double Honor (USA) 64 (8½f,Hpk,Fst,Nov 8)

Emperor's Gold 31 (8½f,Wol,Std,Nov 1)

Favorite Trick (USA) 82 (8½f,Hpk,Fst,Nov 8)

Guaranteed 31 (7f,Wol,Std,Aug 16)

Happy Days Again (IRE) 30 (5f,Sou,Std,Jun 19)
Happy Wanderer 35 (6f,Wol,Std,Oct 4)

Johnbill (USA) 70 (8½f,Hpk,Fst,Nov 8)

Kirby's Song (CAN) 45 (8½f,Hpk,Fst,Nov 8)

Long Island 30 (6f,Wol,Std,Nov 1)
Love Again 39 (5f,Wol,Std,Spt 30)
Love Lock (USA) 34 (8½f,Hpk,Fst,Nov 8)

Main Street 31 (6f,Wol,Std,Nov 1)
Marie J (USA) 46 (8½f,Hpk,Fst,Nov 8)
Montano (USA) 31 (7f,Wol,Std,Oct 6)

Nationalore (USA) 71 (8½f,Hpk,Fst,Nov 8)

One Singer 50 (7f,Wol,Std,Oct 6)

Pedro (IRE) 42 (7f,Wol,Std,Oct 6)
Poetto 30 (5f,Wol,Std,Oct 4)
Press Ahead 30 (6f,Wol,Std,Oct 4)
Primaly (CAN) 50 (8½f,Hpk,Fst,Nov 8)
Prompt Delivery (USA) 30 (7f,Wol,Std,Aug 16)

Ra Ra Rasputin 37 (6f,Wol,Std,Aug 16)
Rare Indigo 38 (5f,Wol,Std,Oct 4)
Roi Brisbane 42 (6f,Wol,Std,Nov 1)

Santa Faye (IRE) 42 (6f,Sou,Std,Oct 20)
Silken Dalliance 40 (6f,Wol,Std,Oct 4)
Snappy Times 31 (5f,Sou,Std,Spt 8)
Socket Set 35 (5f,Sou,Std,Jun 19)
Souvenir Copy (USA) 70 (8½f,Hpk,Fst,Nov 8)

Super Geil 31 (5f,Sou,Std,Spt 8)

The Groveller 32 (7f,Wol,Std,Aug 16)
Third Cousin (IRE) 44 (6f,Wol,Std,Oct 4)
Time Limit (USA) 60 (8½f,Hpk,Fst,Nov 8)

Vivid Angel (USA) 43 (8½f,Hpk,Fst,Nov 8)

Name	Suspended/Injured & Race No.	Date(s)	Offence/Injury
BARDWELL Gary	suspended (1859)	20-21/6/97	careless riding
BASTIMAN Harvey	suspended (3285)	14-23/8/97 *& 25-30/8/97*	reckless riding *excessive/incorrect use of whip*
BOSLEY James	injured (2536)	returned (4179)	broken ankle
BOYLE Finbarr	injured (1223)	returned (2177)	leg, knee and back injuries
CARROLL John	suspended (2024)	27-28/6/97	careless riding
CARTER Gary	suspended (660)	21-25/4/97	failure to ensure best placing
CHARNOCK Lindsay	injured (1223) *suspended (3990)*	returned (1447) *13 & 15/9/97*	bruised ribs *careless riding*
CHIN Stanley	suspended (3122)	8-11/8/97	excessive use of whip
CLARK Tony	suspended (825) *suspended (4897)*	5-6/5/97 *3-4, 6-8/11/97*	failure to ensure best placing *careless riding*
COCHRANE Ray	injured 23/6/97	returned (2483)	neck problem
CULHANE Tony	suspended (3269) *suspended (4365)*	13-14/8/97 *6-7/10/97*	excessive use of whip *improper use of whip*
DALY Alan	suspended (2182) *suspended (3580)*	2-3/7/97 *25-30/8/97*	excessive use of whip *incorrect/improper use of whip*
DARLEY Kevin	suspended (666) *suspended (1872)* suspended (3186)	23-26 & 28-29/4/97 *21 & 23-24/6/97* 10-11/8/97	irresponsible riding *careless riding* careless riding
DAY Nigel	suspended (3428)	18 & 22/8/97	improper use of whip
DEERING Vic	suspended (3038)	3-11/8/97	improper/excessive use of whip
DETTORI Frankie	injured (791) *suspended (724)* suspended (1740) *injured (2230)* suspended (2872) *suspended (3766)* suspended (4144) *referred to Portman Sq.*	24-25/4/97 *28-29/4/97* 16 & 20/6/97 *26/6/97* 28-30/7/97 *1-5/9/97* 21-26/9/97 *31/10/97*	concussion *careless riding* careless riding *concussion* careless riding *irresponsible riding* irresponsible riding *careless riding*
DOE Paul	suspended (1166)	24 & 26-29/5/97	irresponsible riding
DROWNE Steven	suspended (1465)	5 & 9/6/97	careless riding
DUFFIELD George	suspended (1249) *suspended (2745)* suspended (4482)	26-27/5/97 *24-26 & 28/7/97* 9-11/10/97	excessive use of whip *careless riding* careless riding
DURCAN Ted	suspended (1603)	9-10/6/97	excessive use of whip
DWYER Martin	suspended (2920) *suspended (2961)*	30-31/7/97 *2-3/8/97*	failure to weigh in *careless riding*

EDDERY Alan	suspended (4385)	4-5/10/97	careless riding
EDDERY Pat	suspended (1113) *suspended (1172)* suspended (3635) *suspended (3809)* last ride (4222)	20-24/5/97 *26-27/5/97* 27-29/8/97 *3-6 & 8-9/9/97* returning next season	careless riding *improper use of whip* careless riding *failure to ensure best placing* chronic back problem
EDDERY Paul	suspended (4857)	1 & 3/11/97	failure to weigh-in
EDMUNDS Jason	suspended (4327)	1-2/10/97	careless riding
EGAN John	suspended (863) *suspended (1255)* suspended (1991) *suspended (2724)*	7-8/5/97 *26-31/5/97* 25-26/6/97 *23-26/7/97*	careless riding *irresponsible riding* excessive use of whip *careless riding*
FALLON Kieren	suspended (1397) *suspended (1553a)* suspended (2552) *suspended (3125)*	2-5/6/97 *22/6-2/7/97* 16-17/7/97 *8-12/8/97*	failure to ensure best placing *dangerous riding* excessive use of whip *irresponsible riding*
FAULKNER Gavin	suspended (4248)	27-30/9/97	irresponsible riding
FENTON Michael	suspended (778)	1-4/5/97	excessive use of whip
FFRENCH Royston	suspended (1145) *suspended (1642)* suspended (3325)	22-24 & 26/5/97 *12-14 & 16-18/6/97* 16-17/8/97	schooling in public *irresponsible riding* excessive use of whip
FORTUNE Jimmy	injured (1223) *suspended (1738)* suspended (4148) *suspended (4269)*	returned (1447) *16 & 20/6/97* 22-23/9/97 *28/9-1/10/97*	bruised back *careless riding* careless riding *excessive use of whip*
GIBSON Dale	suspended (3034)	3-12/8/97	failure to ensure best placing
GRIFFITHS David	suspended (506)	7-8/4/97	careless riding
HANNON Gabriel	suspended (4897)	3-4, 6-8, 13-15/11/97	careless riding
HAVLIN Robert	suspended (4895)	3-4, 6-8, 10 & 13/11/97	excessive use of whip
HAYES David	suspended (480)	5 & 7/4/97	improper/incorrect use of whip
HILLS Michael	suspended (1322)	31/5 & 2-4/6/97	irresponsible riding
HILLS Richard	suspended (1725a) *suspended (4968)*	10-13/6/97 *10-11 & 13-15/11/97*	dangerous riding *failure to ensure best placing*
HIND Gary	suspended (3293)	12-14/8/97	failure to obtain best placing
HOLLAND Darryll	suspended (576) *suspended (738)* suspended (4733)	16-17/4/97 *29/4/97 - 6/5/97* 24-25 & 27-28/10/97	improper use of whip *carelessriding* excessive use of whip
HUGHES Richard	suspended (886) *suspended (2958)*	8-12/5/97 *2-3/8/97*	excessive/improper use of whip *careless riding*
JARNET Thierry	injured 7/7/97	returned (3731a)	perforated spleen in a fall at Chantilly
KINANE Michael	suspended (4011)	15-16/9/97	careless riding
LAPPIN Roddy	suspended (760) *suspended (2655)*	30/4/97 - 6/5/97 *21-26/7/97*	schooling in public *failure to ensure best placing*

LOWTHER Carl	suspended (3855) *suspended (4767)*	5/9/97 *27-28/10/97*	careless riding *careless riding*
LYNCH Fergal	suspended (1333) *suspended (3782)*	2-5/6/97 *6, 8-13 & 15-17/9/97*	irresponsible riding *improper, incorrect & excessive use of whip*
MACKAY Allan	suspended (3488) *suspended (4300)*	22-23 & 25/8/97 29/9-2/10/97	excessive/improper use of whip schooling in public
McAULEY John	suspended (2111) *suspended (2715)*	29/6/97 *23-24/7/97*	careless riding *improper use of whip*
McCABE Pat	suspended (1371)	2-7 & 9-12/6/97	reckless riding
McGAFFIN Derek	suspended (637) *suspended (1448)*	21-24/4/97 *4-5/6/97*	excessive/improper use of whip *incorrect use of whip*
McKEOWN Dean	suspended (1232)	26-28/5/97	excessive use of whip
MOFFATT Darren	suspended (2130)	29-30/6/97	improper use of whip
MULLEN Richie	suspended (2282) *suspended (3076)*	7/797 *4-5/8/97*	careless riding *excessive use of whip*
MURPHY Peter	suspended (2779)	26/7 & 28/7-2/8/97	irresponsible riding
NEWTON Lee	suspended (3134) *suspended (4453)*	8-10/8/97 *7/10/97*	careless riding *improper use of whip*
NICHOLLS Adrian	suspended (3334)	16-17/8/97	careless riding
O'CONNOR Warren	suspended (1594) *suspended (3791)* injured (4897)	9-11/6/97 *3-6/9/97* returning November	careless riding *irresponsible riding* bruised face & neck
O'DONOHOE Daragh	suspended (1260)	27-29/5/97	careless riding
O'NEILL Dane	suspended (1370)	2-3/6/97	careless riding
O'SHEA Declan	injured (1858)	returned (4438)	broken wrist
PAINTER Richard	suspended (3563)	25-26/8/97	incorrect use of whip
PARKIN Gyles	suspended (1089) *suspended (3545)*	18-22/5/97 *23 &25-29/8/97*	careless riding *excessive use of whip*
PEARCE Lydia	suspended (5022)	15, 17-18 & 21/11/97	riding an ill-judged race
PEARS Oliver	suspended (4290)	29/9 & 1/10/97	incorrect use of whip
PERHAM Richard	injured (2917)	returned (4070)	broken ankle
POLLI Antonio	suspended (3910) *suspended (4097)*	8-9/9/97 *19/9/97*	incorrect use of whip *careless riding*
PRICE Russell	suspended (2380) *suspended (3916)*	10-12/7/97 *8-10/9/97*	careless riding *excessive use of whip*
QUINN Richard	injured (2745)	returned (3920)	broken wrist
RAMSDEN Emma	suspended (2063)	28/6-2/7/97	irresponsible riding
REID John	suspended (1643) *injured (2860)* suspended (3109)	12-13/6/97 *returned (2947)* 7-11/8/97	excessive use of whip *jarred right ankle* irresponsible riding

RIGHTON Shashi	suspended (1796)	20-21/6/97	careless riding
RIMMER Mark	injured (2200)	returned (2766)	concussion and severe bruising
ROBERTS Michael	suspended (604) *suspended (1112)* injured (2915)	19 & 21/4/97 *20-24/5/97* returned (3049)	incorrect use of whip *failure to ensure best placing* aggravated rib injury
RUTTER Chris	suspended (1094) *suspended (3814)* injured (4897)	18-19/5/97 *3-6/9/97* returning January	careless riding *careless riding* broken wrist
SANDERS Seb	suspended (1509) *suspended (4703)* suspended (4786)	9-10/6/97 *23-24/10/97* 27-29/10/97	careless riding *excessive use of whip* excessive use of whip
SHANAHAN Pat	suspended (2811a)	22-24/7/97	excessive use of whip
SPRAKE Tim	suspended (549)	11-12/4/97	excessive use of whip
STACK John	suspended (4290)	14-22/10/97	schooling in public
STEVENS Gary	suspended (2105)	29/6 & 6/7/97	excessive use of whip
STREET Robert	injured 30/4/97	returned (1488)	concussion from fall on gallops
STUDHOLME Ross	suspended (4112)	20-21/9/97	careless riding
SWINBURN Walter	sabbatical	return date unknown	weight problems
TATE Jason	suspended (495)	5 & 7/4/97	excessive use of whip
TEBBUTT Michael	injured 10/4/97	returned (1873)	cracked vertebrae on gallops
URBINA Oscar	injured 5/6/97	returning next season	broken ankle
VARLEY Neil	suspended (645)	21-26/4/97	schooling in public
WEAVER Jason	suspended (807a) *suspended (1458)* suspended (3534a) *suspended (3541)*	28-29/4/97 *3-4/6/97* 19-22/8/97 *23 & 25-27/8/97*	excessive use of whip *careless riding* excessive use of whip *excessive use of whip*
WEBB Charles	injured 31/5/97	return date unknown	broken thumb, collarbone & ribs
WHELAN Tony	suspended (1989) *suspended (2071)* suspended (2161) *suspended (3408)* suspended (5021)	25-29/6/97 *30/6-3/7/97* 4-5 & 7-8/7/97 *18 & 22/8/97* 15 & 17/11/97	careless riding *careless riding* excessive use of whip *careless riding* failure to ensure best placing
WHITWORTH Simon	injured (3687)	returned (4172)	injured hand
WIGHAM Michael	suspended (2187) *suspended (2749)*	2-5, 10-12 & 14-15/7/97 *25-26 & 28/7/97*	intentional interference *improper use of whip*
WILKINSON Jason	suspended (4450)	7-8/10/97	excessive use of whip
WILLIAMS Darren	suspended (3205) *suspended (3868)*	10-13/8/97 *8/9/97*	careless riding *careless riding*
WILLIAMS Tyrone	suspended (3224)	11-14/8/97	improper use of whip
WINSTON Robert	suspended (3264)	13-14/8/97	careless riding
WINTLE Adrian	suspended (3467)	22-23/8/97	improper use of whip

N.B. For ease of reading, some information is in *Italics*.